Mandell, Douglas, and Bennett's

Principles and Practice of Infectious Diseases

Mandell, Douglas, and Bennett's
Principles and Practice of Infectious Diseases

SIXTH EDITION

Gerald L. Mandell, MD, MACP

Professor of Medicine
Owen R. Cheatham Professor of the Sciences
Division of Infectious Diseases
University of Virginia School of Medicine
Charlottesville, Virginia

John E. Bennett, MD, MACP

Adjunct Professor of Medicine
Uniformed Services University of the Health Sciences
Head, Clinical Mycology Section
Laboratory of Clinical Infectious Diseases
National Institute of Allergy and Infectious Diseases
National Institutes of Health
Bethesda, Maryland

Raphael Dolin, MD

Maxwell Finland Professor of Medicine (Microbiology and Molecular Genetics)
Dean for Academic and Clinical Programs
Harvard Medical School
Boston, Massachusetts

With illustrations by George V. Kelvin

ELSEVIER
CHURCHILL
LIVINGSTONE

ELSEVIER
CHURCHILL
LIVINGSTONE

The Curtis Center
170 S Independence Mall W 300E
Philadelphia, Pennsylvania 19106

NOTICE

Pharmacology is an ever-changing field. Standard safety precautions must be followed, but as new research and clinical experience broaden our knowledge, changes in treatment and drug therapy may become necessary or appropriate. Readers are advised to check the most current product information provided by the maufacturer of each drug to be administered to verify the recommended dose, the method and duration of administration, and contraindications. It is the responsibility of the licensed prescriber, relying on experience and knowledge of the patient, to determine dosages and the best treatment for each individual patient. Neither the publisher nor the author assumes any liability for any injury and/or damage to persons or property arising from this publication.

Previous editions copyrighted 2000, 1995, 1990, 1985, 1979 by Elsevier Inc.

Library of Congress Cataloging-in-Publication Data

Mandell, Douglas, and Bennett's principles and practice of infectious diseases / [edited by]
   Gerald L. Mandell, John E. Bennett, Raphael Dolin.—6th ed.
      p . ; cm.
   Includes bibliographical references and index.
   ISBN 0-443-06643-4
   1. Communicable diseases. I. Title:Principles and practice of infectious diseases. II.
Mandell, Gerald L. III. Douglas, R. Gordon (Robert Gordon) IV. Bennett, John E.
(John Eugene) V. Dolin, Raphael.
   [DNLM: 1. Communicable Diseases. WC 100 M2713 2005]
RC111.M224.2005
616.9—dc22   2004050158

Acquisitions Editor: Tom Hartman
Developmental Editor: Melissa Dudlick
Publishing Services Manager: Frank Polizzano
Design Coordinator: Karen O'Keefe Owens

Printed in the United States of America

Last digit is print number: 9   8   7   6   5   4   3   2   1

CONTRIBUTORS

N. Franklin Adkinson, Jr., MD
Professor of Medicine, Johns Hopkins University School
of Medicine; Johns Hopkins Asthma and Allergy Center,
Baltimore, Maryland
β-Lactam Allergy

David M. Allen, MD, FAMS
Infectious Diseases Consultant, Medical City Dallas Hospital;
Partner, ID Specialists, P.A., Dallas, Texas
Acinetobacter Species

Ban M. Allos, MD
Assistant Professor, Departments of Medicine and Preventive
Medicine, Vanderbilt University School of Medicine,
Nashville, Tennessee
Campylobacter jejuni and Related Species

Harvey J. Alter, MD
Chief, Infectious Diseases Section and Associate Director for
Research, Department of Transfusion Medicine, National Institutes
of Health, Bethesda, Maryland; Clinical Professor of Medicine,
Department of Medicine, Georgetown University Medical School,
Washington, District of Columbia
Hepatitis G Virus and TT Virus

Guy W. Amsden, PharmD, FCP
Adjunct Assistant Professor, Department of Pharmacology, College
of Physicians and Surgeons of Columbia University, New York;
Attending Pharmacologist in Medicine and Research Scientist,
Department of Adult and Pediatric Medicine and Clinical
Pharmacology Research Center, Bassett Healthcare,
Cooperstown, New York
Pharmacokinetics and Pharmacodynamics of Anti-infective
Agents; Tables of Antimicrobial Agent Pharmacology

David A. Anderson, BSc(Hons), PhD
Deputy Director, Macfarlane Burnet Institute for Medical Research
and Public Health, Melbourne, Victoria, Australia
Hepatitis A Virus

Larry J. Anderson, MD
Chief, Respiratory and Enteric Viruses Branch, Division of Viral
and Rickettsial Diseases, National Center for Infectious Diseases,
Centers for Disease Control and Prevention, Atlanta, Georgia
Coronaviruses, Including Severe Acute Respiratory Syndrome
(SARS)—Associated Coronaviruses

David R. Andes, MD
Assistant Professor, Medicine and Microbiology/Immunology,
University of Wisconsin School of Medicine, Madison, Wisconsin
Cephalosporins

Michael A. Apicella, MD
Professor and Chair, Department of Microbiology, University
of Iowa Roy J. and Lucille A. Carver College of Medicine; Staff
Physician, University of Iowa Hospital and Clinics, Iowa City, Iowa
Neisseria meningitidis

Gordon L. Archer, MD
Professor, Department of Medicine and Microbiology/Immunology,
Virginia Commonwealth University Medical Center,
Richmond, Virginia
Staphylococcus epidermidis and Other Coagulase-Negative
Staphylococci

Michael H. Augenbraun, MD
Associate Professor of Medicine and of Preventive Medicine
and Community Health, State University of New York–Downstate
Medical Center, Brooklyn, New York
Genital Skin and Mucous Membrane Lesions

Dimitri T. Azar, MD
Professor, Department of Ophthalmology, Harvard Medical School;
Director, Department of Corneal, External Disease, and Refractive
Surgery Services, Massachusetts Eye and Ear Infirmary; Senior
Scientist, Department of Ophthalmology, Schepens Eye Research
Institute, Boston, Massachusetts
Microbial Conjunctivitis; Microbial Keratitis

Larry M. Baddour, MD
Professor of Medicine, Division of Infectious Diseases, Mayo Clinic
College of Medicine; Consultant, Division of Infectious Diseases,
Mayo Clinic, Rochester, Minnesota
Infections of Prosthetic Valves and Other Cardiovascular Devices

Lindsey R. Baden, MD
Assistant Professor of Medicine, Harvard Medical School; Clinical
Research Director, Division of Infectious Diseases, Brigham and
Women's Hospital, Boston, Massachusetts
Vaccines for Human Immunodeficiency Virus-1 Infection

Carol J. Baker, MD
Professor of Pediatrics, Molecular Virology, and Microbiology,
Department of Pediatrics, Section of Infectious Diseases, Baylor
College of Medicine; Attending Physician, Texas Children's
Hospital, Houston, Texas
Streptococcus agalactiae (Group B Streptococcus)

Ronald C. Ballard, MD
Associate Professor, Department of Clinical Microbiology
and Infectious Diseases, School of Pathology, University of the
Witwatersrand and South African Institute for Medical Research,
Johannesburg, South Africa; Centers for Disease Control
and Prevention, Atlanta, Georgia
Calymmatobacterium granulomatis (Donovanosis,
Granuloma Inguinale)

Charles H. Ballow, PharmD, FCCP
Director, Buffalo Clinical Research Center, Buffalo, New York
Pharmacokinetics and Pharmacodynamics of Anti-infective Agents

Scott D. Barnes, MD
Clinical Fellow in Ophthalmology, Department of Ophthalmology,
Massachusetts Eye and Ear Infirmary, Harvard Medical School,
Boston, Massachusetts
Microbial Conjunctivitis; Microbial Keratitis

Miriam J. Baron, MD
Instructor, Department of Medicine, Harvard Medical School;
Associate Physician, Department of Medicine, Brigham
and Women's Hospital, Boston, Massachusetts
    Pancreatic Infections

Dan H. Barouch, MD
Instructor in Medicine, Harvard Medical School; Division of Viral
Pathogenesis, Department of Medicine, Beth Israel Deaconess
Medical Center; Division of Infectious Diseases, Department of
Medicine, Brigham and Women's Hospital, Boston, Massachusetts
    Vaccines for Human Immunodeficiency Virus-1 Infection

Kenneth J. Bart, MD, MPH, MSHPM
Director and Professor of Epidemiology and Biostatistics,
Graduate School of Public Health, San Diego State University,
San Diego, California
    Immunization

Byron E. Batteiger, MD
Professor, Department of Medicine and Microbiology
and Immunology, Indiana University School of Medicine,
Indianapolis, Indiana
    Introduction to Chlamydial Diseases; *Chlamydia trachomatis*
    (Trachoma, Perinatal Infections, Lymphogranuloma Venereum,
    and Other Genital Infections)

Gregory J. Bauer, MD
Assistant Professor of Surgery, Department of Surgery, Division of
Burn Surgery, Weill Medical College of Cornell University, New
York, New York
    Burns

Stephen G. Baum, MD
Professor, Department of Medicine, Microbiology and Immunology,
Albert Einstein College of Medicine of Yeshiva University, Bronx,
New York; Chairman, Department of Medicine, Beth Israel Medical
Center, New York, New York
    Adenovirus; Mumps Virus; Introduction to *Mycoplasma* Diseases;
    Mycoplasma pneumoniae and Atypical Pneumonia

Arnold S. Bayer, MD, FACP, FCCP, FIDSA
Professor of Medicine, Department of Internal Medicine, David
Geffen School of Medicine at UCLA, Los Angeles; Associate Chief,
Adult Infectious Diseases, Department of Internal Medicine,
Harbor–UCLA Medical Center; Senior Investigator, St. John's
Cardiovascular Research Center, LA Biomedical Research Institute,
Torrance, California
    Endocarditis and Intravascular Infections

Susan E. Beekmann, RN, MPH
Nurse Epidemiologist, Department of Pathology, University of Iowa
Roy J. and Lucille A. Carver College of Medicine, Iowa City, Iowa
    Infections Caused by Percutaneous Intravascular Devices

Irmgard Behlau, MD
Assistant Professor and Program Director, Infectious Diseases,
Department of Medicine, New Jersey Medical School, University of
Medicine and Dentistry of New Jersey, Newark, New Jersey
    Chronic Meningitis

Beth P. Bell, MD, MPH
Chief, Epidemiology Branch, Division of Viral Hepatitis, National
Center for Infectious Diseases, Centers for Disease Control
and Prevention, Atlanta, Georgia
    Hepatitis A Virus

John E. Bennett, MD, MACP
Adjunct Professor of Medicine, Uniformed Services University of the
Health Sciences; Head, Clinical Mycology Section, Laboratory of
Clinical Infectious Diseases, National Institute of Allergy and
Infectious Diseases, National Institutes of Health, Bethesda, Maryland
    Introduction to Mycoses

Elie F. Berbari, MD
Assistant Professor, Department of Internal Medicine, Division
of Infectious Diseases, Mayo Clinic, Rochester, Minnesota
    Osteomyelitis

Jonathan D. Berman, MD, PhD
Director, Office of Clinical and Regulatory Affairs, National Center
for Complementary and Alternative Medicine, National Institutes
of Health, Bethesda, Maryland
    Complementary and Alternative Medicines for Infectious Diseases

Joseph S. Bertino, Jr., PharmD
Associate Professor of Clinical Pharmacology (in Medicine), College
of Physicians and Surgeons, Columbia University, New York;
Section Chief, Clinical Pharmacology, Department of Medicine,
Bassett Healthcare, Cooperstown, New York
    Pharmacokinetics and Pharmacodynamics of Anti-infective Agents

Holly H. Birdsall, MD, PhD
Associate Professor, Department of Otolaryngology and
Immunology, Baylor College of Medicine; Associate Chief of Staff
for Research, Michael E. DeBakey Veterans Affairs Medical Center,
Houston, Texas
    Antibodies

Alan L. Bisno, MD
Professor, Department of Medicine, University of Miami School of
Medicine; Staff Physician, Miami Veterans Affairs Medical Center,
Miami, Florida
    Pharyngitis; Classification of Streptococci; *Streptococcus
    pyogenes*; Nonsuppurative Poststreptococcal Sequelae:
    Rheumatic Fever and Glomerulonephritis

Martin J. Blaser, MD
Frederick H. King Professor and Chair, Department of Medicine,
New York University School of Medicine; Chief, Medical Services,
Bellevue Hospital Center; Chief, Medical Services, Tisch New York
University Hospital; Staff Physician, Department of Medical
Services, New York Harbor Veterans Affairs Medical Center,
New York, New York
    Introduction to Bacteria and Bacterial Diseases; *Campylobacter
    jejuni* and Related Species; *Helicobacter pylori* and Other Gastric
    Helicobacter Species

William Blattner, MD
Associate Professor and Director of Epidemiology and Prevention
Division, Institute of Human Virology, University of Maryland,
Baltimore, Maryland
    Human T-Cell Lymphotropic Virus Types I and II

Thomas P. Bleck, MD
Louise Nerancy Eminent Scholar in Neurology and Professor of
Neurology, Neurological Surgery, and Internal Medicine, University
of Virginia School of Medicine, Charlottesville, Virginia
    Rhabdoviruses; *Clostridium tetani* (Tetanus); *Clostridium botulinum*
    (Botulism); Botulinum Toxin as a Biological Weapon

David A. Bobak, MD
Associate Professor, Division of Infectious Diseases, Department
of Medicine, Case Western Reserve University School of Medicine;
Director, Traveler's Healthcare Center, and Staff Physician,
University Hospitals of Cleveland/Case Medical Center; Staff
Physician, Department of Hepatitis C Clinic, Louis Stokes Cleveland
Veterans Affairs Medical Center, Cleveland, Ohio
    Nausea, Vomiting, and Noninflammatory Diarrhea

William Bonnez, MD
Associate Professor, Department of Medicine, University
of Rochester School of Medicine and Dentistry; Attending Physician,
Department of Medicine, Strong Memorial Hospital,
Rochester, New York
Papillomaviruses

Luciana L. Borio, MD
Assistant Professor of Medicine, Division of Infectious Diseases,
University of Pittsburgh, Pittsburgh, Pennsylvania; Assistant
Professor of Medicine, Division of Infectious Diseases, Johns
Hopkins Hospital, Baltimore, Maryland
Bioterrorism: An Overview; Plague as an Agent of Bioterrorism

Richard C. Boucher, MD
William Rand Kenan Professor of Medicine, University of North
Carolina at Chapel Hill School of Medicine; Director, Cystic
Fibrosis Center, Chapel Hill, North Carolina
Cystic Fibrosis

Christopher R. Braden, MD
Medical Epidemiologist, Foodborne and Diarrheal Disease Branch,
Division of Bacterial and Mycotic Diseases, National Center for
Infectious Diseases, Centers for Disease Control and Prevention,
Atlanta, Georgia
Foodborne Disease

Barry D. Brause, MD
Clinical Professor of Medicine, Weill Medical College of Cornell
University; Attending Physician, New York Weill Cornell Medical
Center at New York–Presbyterian, Hospital, New York, New York
Infections with Prostheses in Bones and Joints

Kevin E. Brown, MD
Senior Investigator, Hematology Branch, National Heart, Lung, and
Blood Institute, National Institutes of Health, Bethesda, Maryland
Parvovirus

Patricia D. Brown, MD
Associate Professor of Medicine, Division of Infectious Diseases,
Department of Internal Medicine, Wayne State University School
of Medicine, Detroit, Michigan
Infections in Injection Drug Users

Barbara A. Brown-Elliott, MS, MT(ASCP)SM
Senior Research Scientist, Supervisor, Mycobacteria/Nocardia
Laboratory, Department of Microbiology–Biomedical Research,
The University of Texas Health Science Center, Tyler, Texas
Infections Due to Nontuberculous Mycobacteria

Sandra K. Burchett, MD
Assistant Professor, Department of Pediatrics, Harvard Medical
School; Division of Infectious Diseases, Children's Hospital,
Boston, Massachusetts
Pediatric Human Immunodeficiency Virus Infection

James E. Burns, MD, MBA
Clinical Assistant Professor, Department of Pediatrics, University
of Virginia School of Medicine, Charlottesville; Deputy
Commissioner for Public Health Programs, Virginia Department
of Health, Richmond, Virginia
Epiglottitis

Larry M. Bush, MD, FACP
Chief, Infectious Diseases, Department of Medicine, John F.
Kennedy Medical Center; Medical Director, South Florida Clinical
Research, Atlantis Medicine Center, West Palm Beach, Florida
Peritonitis and Intraperitoneal Abscesses

Thomas Butler, MD
Lubbock, Texas
Yersinia Species, Including Plague

David P. Calfee, MD, MS
Assistant Professor, Department of Medicine, Mount Sinai School
of Medicine; Assistant Attending, Mount Sinai Hospital,
New York, New York
Rifamycins

Ellis S. Caplan, MD
Associate Professor of Medicine, University of Maryland School
of Medicine; Section Chief, Infectious Disease, Division of Trauma
Infectious Disease, Shock Trauma Center, University of Maryland
Medical System, Baltimore, Maryland
Hyperbaric Oxygen

Charles C. J. Carpenter, MD, MACP
Professor of Medicine, Department of Medicine, Brown Medical
School; Director, Lifespan/Tufts/Brown Center for AIDS Research,
Providence, Rhode Island
Other Pathogenic Vibrios

Mary T. Caserta, MD
Associate Professor, Department of Pediatrics, University of
Rochester School of Medicine and Dentistry; Attending Physician,
Department of Pediatrics, Golisano Children's Hospital at Strong,
Rochester, New York
Acute Laryngitis

Elio Castagnola, MD
Section for Infections in the Immunocompromised Cancer Patient,
Infectious Diseases Unit, Department of Hematology and Oncology,
G. Gaslini Children's Teaching Hospital, Genoa, Italy
Prophylaxis and Empirical Therapy for Infection
in Cancer Patients

Richard E. Chaisson, MD
Professor of Medicine, Epidemiology, and International Health,
Johns Hopkins University School of Medicine, Baltimore, Maryland
General Clinical Manifestations of Human Immunodeficiency Virus
Infection (Including the Acute Retroviral Syndrome and Oral,
Cutaneous, Renal, Ocular, and Cardiac Diseases); Gastrointestinal
and Hepatobiliary Manifestations of Human Immunodeficiency
Virus Infection

Henry F. Chambers, MD
Professor, Department of Medicine, University of California,
San Francisco, School of Medicine; Chief, Infectious Diseases,
Department of Medicine, San Francisco General Hospital,
San Francisco, California
Penicillins; Other β-Lactam Antibiotics

Stanley W. Chapman, MD
Professor of Medicine and Associate Professor of Microbiology,
University of Mississippi School of Medicine; Division of Infectious
Diseases, University of Mississippi Medical Center, Jackson,
Mississippi
Blastomyces dermatitidis

Manhattan Charurat
Assistant Professor, Institute of Human Virology, University of
Maryland, Baltimore, Maryland
Human T-Cell Lymphotropic Virus Types I and II

Sanjiv Chopra, MD
Faculty Dean for Continuing Education and Professor of Medicine,
Harvard Medical School; Director, Clinical Hepatology, Department
of Medicine, Division of Gastroenterology, Beth Israel Deaconess
Medical Center, Boston, Massachusetts
Acute Viral Hepatitis

Anthony W. Chow, MD, FRCPC, FACP
Professor of Medicine and Director, MD/PhD Program, University of British Columbia Faculty of Medicine; Vancouver Hospital Health Science Center, Vancouver, British Columbia, Canada
  Infections of the Oral Cavity, Neck, and Head

Nicholas P. Cianciotto, PhD
Professor, Department of Microbiology-Immunology, Northwestern University Medical School, Chicago, Illinois
  Legionella

Rebecca A. Clark, MD, PhD
Medicine Department, Louisiana State University Health Sciences Center; HIV Outpatient Program, Medical Center of Louisiana at New Orleans, New Orleans, Louisiana
  Human Immunodeficiency Virus Infection in Women

Robert A. Clark, MD
Professor and Chair, Department of Medicine, University of Texas Health Science Center at San Antonio Medical School; Staff Physician and Chief, Department of Medicine, University Health System; Staff Physician, Medical Service, South Texas Veterans Health Care System, San Antonio, Texas
  Granulocytic Phagocytes

Farley R. Cleghorn, MD, MPH
Adjunct Professor of Medicine, Institute of Human Virology, University of Maryland, Baltimore, Maryland; Director, Center for HIV/AIDS, The Futures Group International, Washington, District of Columbia
  Human Immunodeficiency Viruses

Michael W. Climo, MD
Associate Professor of Medicine and Microbiology/Immunology, Virginia Commonwealth University Medical Center; Hospital Epidemiologist, Infectious Disease Division; Medical Director, HIV/AIDS Program, Hunter Holmes McGuire Veteran Affairs Medical Center, Richmond, Virginia
  Staphylococcus epidermidis and Other Coagulase-Negative Staphylococci

Myron S. Cohen, MD
J. Herbert Bate Distinguished Professor of Medicine, Microbiology, Immunology, and Public Health, University of North Carolina at Chapel Hill School of Medicine, Chapel Hill, North Carolina
  The Acutely Ill Patient with Fever and Rash

Susan E. Cohn, MD, MPH
Associate Professor of Medicine, Department of Medicine, University of Rochester Medical Center, Rochester, New York
  Human Immunodeficiency Virus Infection in Women

Mark Connors, MD
Senior Clinical Investigator, Laboratory of Immunoregulation, National Institutes of Health, Bethesda, Maryland
  The Immunology of Human Immunodeficiency Virus Infection

Joanne Cono, MD, ScM
Senior Medical Officer, Bioterrorism Preparedness and Response Program, National Center for Infectious Diseases, Centers for Disease Control and Prevention, Atlanta, Georgia
  Smallpox and Bioterrorism

Lawrence Corey, MD
Head, Program in Infectious Diseases; Head, Virology Division; and Professor of Laboratory Medicine and Medicine, University of Washington School of Medicine, Seattle, Washington
  Herpes Simplex Virus

William A. Craig, MD
Professor of Medicine and Pharmaceutics, and Consultant, Department of Medicine, University of Wisconsin School of Medicine; Investigator, Department of Research Service, William S. Middleton Memorial Veterans Hospital, Madison, Wisconsin
  Cephalosporins

Kent B. Crossley, MD
Professor, Department of Medicine, University of Minnesota School of Medicine; Veterans Affairs Medical Center, Minneapolis, Minnesota
  Infections in the Elderly

Clyde S. Crumpacker, MD
Professor of Medicine, Harvard Medical School; Physician, Division of Infectious Diseases, Beth Israel Deaconess Medical Center, Boston, Massachusetts
  Cytomegalovirus

James W. Curran, MD, MPH
Dean and Professor, Department of Epidemiology, and Director, Emory Center for AIDS, Rollins School of Public Health, Emory University, Atlanta, Georgia
  Epidemiology and Prevention of Acquired Immunodeficiency Syndrome and Human Immunodeficiency Virus Infection

Bart J. Currie, FRACP, DTM&H
Professor in Medicine, Northern Territory Clinical School, Menzies School of Health Research and Flinders University; Infectious Diseases Physician, Royal Darwin Hospital, Darwin, Northern Territory, Australia
  Burkholderia pseudomallei and *Burkholderia mallei*: Melioidosis and Glanders

Michael P. Curry, MD
Instructor, Department of Medicine, Harvard Medical School; Medical Director, Liver Transplantation, Department of Medicine, Beth Israel Deaconess Medical Center, Boston, Massachusetts
  Acute Viral Hepatitis

Inger Damon, MD, PhD
Chief, Poxvirus Program, Division of Viral and Rickettsial Diseases, National Center for Infectious Diseases, Centers for Disease Control and Prevention, Atlanta, Georgia
  Orthopoxviruses: Vaccinia (Smallpox Vaccine), Variola (Smallpox), Monkeypox, and Cowpox; Other Poxviruses That Infect Humans: Parapoxviruses, Molluscum Contagiosum, and Tanapox; Smallpox and Bioterrorism

Rabih O. Darouiche, MD
Professor, Departments of Medicine and Physical Medicine and Rehabilitation, Infectious Disease Section, Baylor College of Medicine; Director, Center for Prostheses Infection; Staff Physician, Department of Medical (Infectious Disease Section) and Spinal Cord Injury Care Lines, Michael E. Debakey Veterans Affairs Medical Center, Houston, Texas
  Infections in Patients with Spinal Cord Injury

George S. Deepe, Jr., MD
Professor, Department of Internal Medicine, University of Cincinnati College of Medicine; Chief, Division of Infectious Diseases, University Hospital, Cincinnati, Ohio
  Histoplasma capsulatum

Carlos Del Rio, MD
Professor of Medicine (Infectious Diseases), Department of Medicine, Emory University School of Medicine; Chief of Medical Services, Department of Medicine, Grady Memorial Hospital, Atlanta, Georgia
Epidemiology and Prevention of Acquired Immunodeficiency Syndrome and Human Immunodeficiency Virus Infection; Other Gram-Negative and Gram-Variable Bacill

Lisa M. Demeter, MD
Associate Professor, Infectious Diseases Unit, Department of Medicine, University of Rochester School of Medicine and Dentistry, Rochester, New York
JC, BK, and Other Polyomaviruses; Progressive Multifocal Leukoencephalopathy

David T. Dennis, MD, MPH
Faculty Affiliate, Department of Microbiology, Immunology, and Pathology, Colorado State University College of Veterinary Medicine and Biomedical Sciences; Guest Researcher, Division of Vector-Borne Infectious Diseases, Centers for Disease Control and Prevention, Fort Collins, Colorado
Yersinia Species, Including Plague

Peter Densen, MD
Professor, Division of Infectious Diseases, Department of Internal Medicine, University of Iowa Roy J. and Lucille A. Carver College of Medicine, Iowa City, Iowa
Complement

Ben E. De Pauw, MD, PhD
Professor of Medicine, Bloodtransfusion and Transplant Immunology, University Medical Center St. Radboud, Nijmegen, The Netherlands
Infections in the Immunocompromised Host: General Principles; Infections in Patients with Hematologic Malignancies

Terence S. Dermody, MD
Professor, Departments of Pediatrics and Microbiology and Immunology, Vanderbilt University School of Medicine; Director, Elizabeth B. Lamb Center for Pediatric Research; Attending Physician, Pediatric Infectious Diseases, Vanderbilt Children's Hospital, Nashville, Tennessee
Introduction to Viruses and Viral Diseases

Carl W. Dieffenbach, PhD
Director, Basic Science Program, Division of AIDS, National Institute of Allergy and Infectious Diseases, National Institutes of Health, Bethesda, Maryland
Innate (General or Nonspecific) Host Defense Mechanisms

Jules L. Dienstag, MD
Professor of Medicine and Associate Dean for Academic and Clinical Programs, Harvard Medical School; Physician, Gastrointestinal Unit (Medical Services), Massachusetts General Hospital, Boston, Massachusetts
Chronic Viral Hepatitis

William E. Dismukes, MD
Professor of Medicine and Director, Division of Infectious Diseases; Vice-Chairman, Department of Medicine, University of Alabama School of Medicine at Birmingham; Attending Physician, Department of Internal Medicine, University Hospital, UAB Medical Center, Birmingham, Alabama
Chronic Pneumonia

Raphael Dolin, MD
Maxwell Finland Professor of Medicine (Microbiology and Molecular Genetics) and Dean for Academic and Clinical Programs, Harvard Medical School, Boston, Massachusetts
Vaccines for Human Immunodeficiency Virus-1 Infection; Zoonotic Paramyxoviruses: Hendra, Nipah, and Menangle Viruses; Noroviruses and Other Caliciviruses; Astroviruses and Picobirnaviruses

J. Peter Donnelly, PhD
Coordinator, Studies in Supportive Care, Department of Hematology, University Medical Center St. Radboud, Nijmegen University Center for Infectious Diseases, Nijmegen, The Netherlands
Infections in the Immunocompromised Host: General Principles

Michael S. Donnenberg, MD
Professor of Medicine and Professor of Microbiology and Immunology; Head, Division of Infectious Diseases, Department of Medicine, University of Maryland School of Medicine, Baltimore, Maryland
Enterobacteriaceae

Gerald R. Donowitz, MD
Professor of Medicine and Infectious Diseases, Department of Internal Medicine, University of Virginia Health Systems, Charlottesville, Virginia
Oxazolidinones; Acute Pneumonia

Philip R. Dormitzer, MD, PhD
Assistant Professor, Department of Pediatrics, Harvard Medical School; Scientific Associate, Laboratory of Molecular Medicine, Children's Hospital, Boston, Massachusetts
Rotaviruses

J. Stephen Dumler, MD
Professor of Pathology, Division of Medical Microbiology, and Professor, Cellular and Molecular Medicine Program, Johns Hopkins University School of Medicine; Associate Director, Division of Medical Microbiology, Department of Pathology, Johns Hopkins Hospital; Professor, Department of Molecular Microbiology and Immunology, Johns Hopkins University Bloomberg School of Public Health, Baltimore, Maryland
Rickettsia typhi (Murine Typhus); *Ehrlichia chaffeensis* (Human Monocytotropic Ehrlichiosis), *Anaplasma phagocytophilum* (Human Granulocytotropic Anaplasmosis), and Other Ehrlichieae

J. Stephen Dummer, MD
Professor of Medicine, Vanderbilt University School of Medicine; Director, Transplant Infectious Diseases, Vanderbilt Transplant Center, Nashville, Tennessee
Risk Factors and Approaches to Infections in Transplant Recipients; Infections in Solid Organ Transplant Recipients

Herbert L. DuPont, MD
Director, Center for Infectious Diseases, and Professor of Epidemiology, Mary W. Kelsey Chair of Medical Sciences, Department of Medicine, University of Texas-Houston School of Public Health; Chief, Internal Medicine, St. Luke's Episcopal Hospital; H. Irving Schweppe, Jr., MD, Chair in Internal Medicine and Vice Chairman, Department of Medicine, and Clinical Professor, Department of Microbiology and Immunology, Baylor College of Medicine, Houston, Texas
Shigella Species (Bacillary Dysentery)

David T. Durack, MB, PhD
Consulting Professor of Medicine, Duke University School of Medicine, Durham; Becton Dickinson & Co., Research Triangle Park, North Carolina
Fever of Unknown Origin; Prophylaxis of Infective Endocarditis

Marlene L. Durand, MD
Assistant Professor, Department of Medicine, Harvard Medical School; Director, Infectious Disease Service, Massachusetts Eye and Ear Infirmary; Associate Physician, Infectious Disease Unit, Massachusetts General Hospital, Boston, Massachusetts
   Endophthalmitis; Infectious Causes of Uveitis; Periocular Infections

Mark Dybul, MD
Deputy Chief Medical Officer, Office of the U.S. Global AIDS Coordinator, Washington, D.C.
   The Immunology of Human Immunodeficiency Virus Infection

Paul H. Edelstein, MD
Professor, Department of Pathology and Laboratory Medicine, University of Pennsylvania School of Medicine; Director of Clinical Microbiology, Department of Pathology and Laboratory Medicine, University of Pennsylvania Medical System; Attending Physician, Division of Infectious Diseases, University of Pennsylvania Medical Center, Philadelphia, Pennsylvania
   Legionella

Michael B. Edmond, MD, MPH, MPA
Professor and Associate Chair for Education, Department of Internal Medicine, Virginia Commonwealth University School of Medicine; Hospital Epidemiologist and Medical Director of Performance Improvement, Virginia Commonwealth University Medical Center, Richmond, Virginia
   Organization for Infection Control; Isolation

John E. Edwards, Jr., MD
Professor of Medicine, David Geffen School of Medicine at UCLA, Los Angeles; Chief, Division of Infectious Diseases, Harbor/UCLA Medical Center, Torrance, California
   Candida Species

Morven S. Edwards, MD
Professor of Pediatrics, Section of Infectious Diseases, Baylor College of Medicine; Attending Physician, Texas Children's Hospital, Houston, Texas
   Streptococcus agalactiae (Group B Streptococcus)

George M. Eliopoulos, MD
Professor of Medicine, Harvard Medical School; Division of Infectious Diseases, Department of Medicine, Beth Israel Deaconess Medical Center, Boston, Massachusetts
   Principles of Anti-infective Therapy

Jerrold J. Ellner, MD
Professor and Chair, Department of Medicine, New Jersey Medical School, University of Medicine and Dentistry of New Jersey, Newark, New Jersey
   Chronic Meningitis

Suzanne U. Emerson, PhD
Head, Molecular Hepatitis Section, Laboratory of Infectious Diseases, National Institutes of Health, Bethesda, Maryland
   Hepatitis E Virus

N. Cary Engleberg, MD
Professor and Chief, Division of Infectious Diseases, Departments of Internal Medicine and Microbiology and Immunology, University of Michigan Medical School, Ann Arbor, Michigan
   Chronic Fatigue Syndrome

Joel D. Ernst, MD
Director, Division of Infectious Diseases, and Jeffrey Bergstein Professor of Medicine, and Professor of Microbiology, Departments of Medicine and Microbiology, New York University School of Medicine; Attending Physician, Department of Medicine, Bellevue Hospital Center; Attending Physician, Department of Medicine, Tisch Hospital of New York University Medical Center, New York, New York
   Mycobacterium leprae (Leprosy, Hansen's Disease)

Rick M. Fairhurst, MD, PhD
Staff Clinician, Laboratory of Malaria and Vector Research, National Institute of Allergy and Infectious Diseases, National Institutes of Health, Bethesda, Maryland
   Plasmodium Species (Malaria)

Stanley Falkow, PhD
Robert W. and Vivian K. Cahill Professor of Microbiology and Immunology and Professor of Medicine, Departments of Microbiology and Immunology and Medicine, Stanford University School of Medicine, Stanford, California
   A Molecular Perspective of Microbial Pathogenicity

Ann R. Falsey, MD
Associate Professor of Medicine, Department of Medicine, University of Rochester School of Medicine and Dentistry; Attending Physician, Infectious Disease Unit, Rochester General Hospital, Rochester, New York
   Human Metapneumovirus

W. Edmund Farrar, MD
Professor Emeritus of Medicine, Medical University of South Carolina College of Medicine, Charleston, South Carolina
   Erysipelothrix rhusiopathiae

Anthony S. Fauci, MD
Professor, Department of Medicine, University of Maryland School of Medicine, Baltimore; Director, National Institute of Allergy and Infectious Diseases, National Institutes of Health, Bethesda, Maryland
   The Immunology of Human Immunodeficiency Virus Infection

Daniel P. Fedorko, PhD
Staff Scientist, Department of Laboratory Medicine, Warren G. Magnuson Clinical Center, National Institutes of Health, Bethesda, Maryland
   The Clinician and the Microbiology Laboratory

Stephen M. Feinstone, MD
Chief, Laboratory of Hepatitis Viruses, U.S. Food and Drug Administration, Center for Biologics Evaluation and Research, Bethesda, Maryland
   Hepatitis A Virus

Thomas Fekete, MD
Professor of Medicine, Section of Infectious Diseases, Temple University School of Medicine; Professor, Department of Internal Medicine, Temple University Hospital, Philadelphia, Pennsylvania
   Bacillus Species and Related Genera Other than *Bacillus anthracis*

Steven M. Fine, MD, PhD
Assistant Professor of Medicine, Infectious Diseases Unit, University of Rochester School of Medicine and Dentistry; University of Rochester Medical Center, Rochester, New York
   Vesicular Stomatitis Virus and Related Viruses

Neil O. Fishman, MD
Assistant Professor of Medicine, Division of Infectious Diseases,
University of Pennsylvania School of Medicine; Director,
Department of Healthcare Epidemiology and Infection Control,
Department of Antimicrobial Management Program, University
of Pennsylvania Health System, Philadelphia, Pennsylvania
  Antimicrobial Management: Cost and Resistance

Tamara L. Fisk, MD
Assistant Professor, Division of Infectious Diseases, Emory
University School of Medicine; Assistant Professor, Department
of Infectious Diseases, Emory Crawford Long Hospital, Atlanta,
Georgia; Visiting Scientist, International Emerging Infections
Program, Thailand Centers for Disease Control and Prevention,
Nonthaburi, Thailand
  Cyclospora cayetanensis, Isospora belli, Sarcocystis Species,
  Balantidium coli, and *Blastocystis hominis*

Daniel Fitzgerald, MD
Assistant Professor of Medicine, Division of International Medicine
and Infectious Diseases, Department of Medicine, Weill Medical
College of Cornell University, New York, New York
  Mycobacterium tuberculosis

Vance G. Fowler, Jr., MD, MHS
Assistant Professor, Department of Medicine, Duke University
School of Medicine, Durham, North Carolina
  Endocarditis and Intravascular Infections

David O. Freedman, MD
Professor of Medicine and Epidemiology/International Health,
Division of Geographic Medicine, University of Alabama at
Birmingham; Director, UAB Travelers Health Clinic, The Kirklin
Clinic, University of Alabama Hospital, Birmingham, Alabama;
Co-Director, The Gorgas Course in Clinical Tropical Medicine,
Tropical Medicine Institute, Cayetano Heredia University,
Lima, Peru
  Protection of Travelers; Infections in Returning Travelers

Alicia M. Fry, MD, MPH
Medical Epidemiologist, Foodborne and Diarrhea Diseases Branch,
National Center for Infectious Diseases, Centers for Disease Control
and Prevention, Atlanta, Georgia
  Foodborne Disease

John Galgiani, MD
Director, Valley Fever Center for Excellence; Professor, Department
of Medicine, University of Arizona College of Medicine; Program
Director, Department of Infectious Diseases, Southern Arizona
Veterans Affairs Health Care System, Tucson, Arizona
  Coccidioides Species

John I. Gallin, MD
Director, Warren G. Magnuson Clinical Center, National Institutes
of Health, Bethesda, Maryland
  Evaluation of the Patient with Suspected Immunodeficiency

Robert C. Gallo, MD
Director, Institute of Human Virology and Division of Basic Science,
University of Maryland Biotechnology Institute, University of
Maryland, Baltimore, Maryland
  Human Immunodeficiency Viruses

Amy Gates, MD
Assistant Clinical Professor in Hematology/Oncology, Positive
Health Program, University of California, San Francisco, School
of Medicine, San Francisco, California
  Malignancies in Human Immunodeficiency Virus Infection

Jeffrey A. Gelfand, MD
Visiting Professor of Medicine, Harvard Medical School; Professor
of Medicine, Tufts University School of Medicine; Physician,
Infectious Diseases Division, Department of Medicine,
Massachusetts General Hospital; Associate Staff, Department
of Medicine, New England Medical Center, Boston, Massachusetts
  Babesia Species

Julie L. Gerberding, MD, MPH
Director, Centers for Disease Control and Prevention; Administrator,
Agency for Toxic Substances and Disease Registry, Atlanta, Georgia
  Human Immunodeficiency Virus in Health Care Settings

Anne A. Gershon, MD
Professor, Department of Pediatrics, Columbia University College
of Physicians and Surgeons, New York, New York
  Rubella Virus (German Measles); Measles Virus (Rubeola)

David N. Gilbert, MD
Professor of Medicine, Department of Internal Medicine, Oregon
Health and Science University School of Medicine; Director of
Medical Education and Earle A. Chiles Research Department
of Medical Education, Providence Portland Medical Center,
Portland, Oregon
  Aminoglycosides

Vee J. Gill, PhD
Microbiology Consultant, Microbiology Laboratory,
Department of Pathology, Suburban Hospital Healthcare System,
Bethesda, Maryland
  The Clinician and the Microbiology Laboratory; *Capnocytophaga*

Peter II. Gilligan, PhD, D(ABMM), FAAM
Professor, Department of Microbiology-Immunology and
Pathology-Laboratory Medicine, University of North Carolina at
Chapel Hill School of Medicine; Director, Clinical Microbiology-
Immunology Laboratories, University of North Carolina Hospitals,
Chapel Hill, North Carolina
  Cystic Fibrosis

Michel P. Glauser, MD
Professor, University of Lausanne; Chief of Service, Service of
Infectious Diseases, Department of Medicine, Centre Hospitalier
Universitaire Vaudois, Lausanne, Switzerland
  Staphylococcus aureus (Including Staphylococcal Toxic Shock)

Michael S. Glickman, MD
Assistant Professor, Department of Medicine and Immunology, Weill
Medical College of Cornell University; Attending Physician,
Infectious Diseases Service, Memorial Hospital for Cancer and
Allied Diseases; Department Head, Laboratory of Microbial
Pathogenesis Immunology Program, Sloan-Kettering Institute, New
York, New York
  Cell-Mediated Defense against Infection

Ulf B. Göbel, MD, PhD
Director, Institute for Microbiology and Hygiene, Charité University
Hospital, Berlin, Germany
  Stenotrophomonas maltophilia and *Burkholderia cepacia*

Ellie J. C. Goldstein, MD
Clinical Professor, Department of Medicine, David Geffen School
of Medicine at UCLA; Chair, Department of Infectious Diseases,
Kindred–LA Hospital, Los Angeles; Director, R. M. Alden Research
Laboratory, Santa Monica, California
  Bites

Fred M. Gordin, MD
Professor of Medicine, Department of Medicine, George Washington
University School of Medicine; Chief, Infectious Diseases,
Department of Infectious Diseases, Veterans Affairs Medical Center,
Washington, District of Columbia
Mycobacterium avium Complex

Eduardo Gotuzzo, MD, FACP
Professor, Department of Medicine, Cayetano Heredia University;
Director, Alexander von Humboldt Tropical Medicine Institute;
Head, Department of Infectious Diseases and Tropical Medicine,
Hospital Nacional Cayetano Heredia, Lima, Peru
Vibrio cholerae

Paul S. Graman, MD
Professor of Medicine, University of Rochester School of Medicine
and Dentistry; Attending Physician and Clinical Director, Infectious
Diseases Unit, Strong Memorial Hospital, Rochester, New York
Esophagitis

Diane E. Griffin, MD, PhD
Professor and Chair, W. Henry Feinstone Department of Molecular
Microbiology and Immunology, Johns Hopkins University
Bloomberg School of Public Health, Baltimore, Maryland
Encephalitis, Myelitis, and Neuritis

Patricia M. Griffin, MD
Chief, Foodborne Diseases Epidemiology Section, Division
of Bacterial and Mycotic Diseases, National Center for Infectious
Diseases, Centers for Disease Control and Prevention, Atlanta,
Georgia
Foodborne Disease

David E. Griffith, MD
Professor of Medicine, Specialty Care Medicine, University of Texas
Health Center at Tyler, Tyler, Texas
Antimycobacterial Agents

David I. Grove, MD, DSc
Clinical Professor of Infectious Diseases, Department of Medicine,
University of Adelaide Faculty of Medicine; Director, Department of
Clinical Microbiology and Infectious Diseases, Institute of Medical
and Veterinary Science, The Queen Elizabeth Hospital, Adelaide,
South Australia, Australia
Tissue Nematodes, Including Trichinosis, Dracunculiasis,
and the Filariases

Richard L. Guerrant, MD
Thomas H. Hunter Professor of International Medicine; Director,
Center for Global Health, Division of Infectious Diseases and
International Health, University of Virginia School of Medicine,
Charlottesville, Virginia
Principles and Syndromes of Enteric Infection; Nausea, Vomiting,
and Noninflammatory Diarrhea; Inflammatory Enteritides; Enteric
Fever and Other Causes of Abdominal Symptoms with Fever

Jack M. Gwaltney, Jr., MD
Professor Emeritus, Department of Internal Medicine, University
of Virginia School of Medicine; University of Virginia Health
System, Charlottesville, Virginia
The Common Cold; Sinusitis; Acute Bronchitis; Rhinovirus

David W. Haas, MD
Associate Professor, Departments of Medicine, Microbiology,
and Immunology, Vanderbilt University School of Medicine,
Nashville, Tennessee
Mycobacterium tuberculosis

Caroline Breese Hall, MD
Professor of Pediatrics and Medicine, Department of Infectious
Diseases, University of Rochester School of Medicine and Dentistry,
Rochester, New York
Acute Laryngotracheobronchitis (Croup); Bronchiolitis; Respiratory
Syncytial Virus

H. Hunter Handsfield, MD
Professor, Department of Medicine, University of Washington;
Director, STD Control Program, Public Health–Seattle and King
County, Seattle, Washington
Neisseria gonorrhoeae

George J. Hanna, MD
Antiviral Global Project Head, Abbott Laboratories, Abbott Park,
Illinois
Antiretroviral Therapy for Human Immunodeficiency Virus Infection

Barry J. Hartman, MD
Clinical Professor of Medicine, Division of Internal Medicine and
Infectious Diseases, Weill Medical College of Cornell University;
Attending Physician, New York–Presbyterian Hospital–Cornell
Campus, New York, New York
Acinetobacter Species

Roderick J. Hay, MD
Dean and Professor of Dermatology, Faculty of Medicine and Health
Sciences, Queens University Belfast; Attending Physician,
Department of Dermatology, Belfast City Hospital, Belfast, Northern
Ireland, United Kingdom
Dermatophytosis and Other Superficial Mycoses

Frederick G. Hayden, MD
Stuart S. Richardson Professor of Clinical Virology and Professor
of Internal Medicine and Pathology, University of Virginia School
of Medicine, Charlottesville, Virginia
Antiviral Drugs (Other Than Antiretrovirals)

Craig W. Hedberg
Associate Professor, Division of Environmental Health Sciences,
University of Minnesota School of Public Health, Minneapolis,
Minnesota
Epidemiologic Principles

David K. Henderson, MD
Deputy Director for Clinical Care, National Institutes of Health,
Bethesda, Maryland
Hospital Preparedness for Emerging and Highly Contagious
Infectious Diseases: Getting Ready for SARS or Whatever Comes
Next; Infections Caused by Percutaneous Intravascular Devices;
Human Immunodeficiency Virus in Health Care Settings;
Nosocomial Herpesvirus Infections

Donald A. Henderson, MD, MPH
Dean Emeritus, Johns Hopkins University School of Hygiene and
Public Health, Baltimore, Maryland; Professor of Medicine and
Public Health, University of Pittsburgh School of Medicine; Staff,
University of Pittsburgh Center for Biosecurity, Pittsburgh,
Pennsylvania
Bioterrorism: An Overview

J. Owen Hendley, MD
Professor of Pediatrics, University of Virginia School of Medicine;
Attending Physician, Division of Pediatric Infectious Diseases,
University of Virginia Health System, Charlottesville, Virginia
Epiglottitis

Erik L. Hewlett, MD
Professor, Departments of Medicine and Pharmacology,
University of Virginia School of Medicine; Attending Physician,
Department of Internal Medicine, University of Virginia Hospital,
Charlottesville, Virginia
Toxins; *Bordetella* Species

Kevin P. High, MD
Associate Professor of Medicine, Sections of Infectious Diseases
and Hematology/Oncology, Wake Forest University School of
Medicine, Winston-Salem, North Carolina
Nutrition, Immunity, and Infection

Adrian V. S. Hill, MD
Professor of Human Genetics, Wellcome Trust Centre for Human
Genetics, University of Oxford, Oxford, United Kingdom
Human Genetics and Infection

David R. Hill, MD, DTM&H
Honorary Professor, Department of Infectious and Tropical Diseases,
London School of Hygiene and Tropical Medicine; Director,
National Travel Heath Network and Centre, London, United
Kingdom
Giardia lamblia

Alan R. Hinman, MD, MPH
Adjunct Professor, Department of Epidemiology and International
Health, Rollins School of Public Health, Emory University, Atlanta;
Senior Public Health Scientist, Task Force for Child Survival and
Development, Decatur, Georgia
Immunization

Martin S. Hirsch, MD
Professor, Department of Medicine, Harvard Medical School;
Physician, Department of Medicine, Massachusetts General Hospital;
Professor, Infectious Diseases and Immunology, Harvard School
of Public Health, Boston, Massachusetts
Antiretroviral Therapy for Human Immunodeficiency Virus Infection

Steven M. Holland, MD
Chief, Immunopathogenesis Section, Laboratory of Host Defenses,
National Institute of Allergy and Infectious Diseases, National
Institutes of Health, Bethesda, Maryland
Evaluation of the Patient with Suspected Immunodeficiency

Edward W. Hook III, MD
Professor of Medicine and Epidemiology, University of Alabama
School of Medicine, University of Alabama at Birmingham;
Director, STD Control Program for Jefferson County Department of
Health, Birmingham, Alabama
Endemic Treponematoses

David C. Hooper, MD
Chief, Infection Control Unit, Division of Infectious Diseases,
Massachusetts General Hospital, Boston, Massachusetts
Quinolones; Urinary Tract Agents: Nitrofurantoin and Methenamine

C. Robert Horsburgh, Jr., MD, MUS
Professor of Epidemiology, Biostatistics, and Medicine; Chair,
Department of Epidemiology, Boston University School of Public
Health, Boston, Massachusetts
Mycobacterium avium Complex

Duane R. Hospenthal, MD, PhD
Associate Professor of Medicine, F. Edward Hébert School of
Medicine, Uniformed Services University of the Health Sciences,
Bethesda, Maryland; Chief, Infectious Disease Service, Brooke
Army Medical Center, Fort Sam Houston, Texas
Agents of Chromoblastomycosis; Agents of Mycetoma;
Uncommon Fungi

James M. Hughes, MD
Director, National Center for Infectious Diseases, Centers
for Disease Control and Prevention, Atlanta, Georgia
Emerging and Reemerging Infectious Disease Threats;
Foodborne Disease

Molly A. Hughes, MD, PhD
Assistant Professor, Department of Medicine, University of Virginia
School of Medicine; Attending Physician, Department of Internal
Medicine, University of Virginia Hospital, Charlottesville, Virginia
Toxins

Christopher D. Huston, MD
Assistant Professor, Department of Medicine, University of Vermont
College of Medicine; Attending Physician, Department of Medicine,
Division of Infectious Diseases, Fletcher Allen Health Care,
Burlington, Vermont
Microbial Adherence

Jonathon R. Iredell, MD, PhD, FRACP, FRCPA
Senior Lecturer, Department of Medicine, University of Sydney;
Senior Staff Specialist, Centre for Infectious Diseases and
Microbiology, Westmead Hospital, Sydney, New South Wales,
Australia
Nocardia Species

Lisa A. Jackson, MD, MPH
Associate Professor, Department of Epidemiology, School of Public
Health and Community Medicine, University of Washington;
Associate Investigator, Center for Health Studies, Group Health
Cooperative, Seattle, Washington
Chlamydophila (Chlamydia) pneumoniae

Selma M. B. Jeronimo, MD, PhD
Professor, Department of Biochemistry, Federal University of Rio
Grande do Norte, Natal, RN, Brazil
Leishmania Species: Visceral (Kala-Azar), Cutaneous,
and Mucocutaneous Leishmaniasis

Eric C. Johannsen, MD
Instructor, Department of Medicine, Harvard Medical School;
Associate Physician, Division of Infectious Diseases, Brigham
and Women's Hospital, Boston, Massachusetts
Infections of the Liver and Biliary System; Epstein-Barr Virus
(Infectious Mononucleosis)

Caroline C. Johnson, MD
Adjunct Associate Professor, School of Public Health, Drexel
University; Director, Division of Disease Control, Philadelphia
Department of Public Health, Philadelphia, Pennsylvania
Viridans Streptococci, Groups C and G Streptococci,
and *Gemella morbillorum*

Warren D. Johnson, Jr., MD
B.H. Kean Professor of Tropical Medicine; Chief, Division of
International Medicine and Infectious Diseases; Director,
International Health Care Service, Weill Medical College of Cornell
University, New York, New York
Borrelia *Species (Relapsing Fever)*

Robert B. Jones, MD, PhD
Executive Associate Dean for Strategic Planning, Analysis, and
Operations, Indiana University School of Medicine, Indianapolis,
Indiana
Introduction to Chlamydial Diseases; *Chlamydia trachomatis*
(Trachoma, Perinatal Infections, Lymphogranuloma Venereum,
and Other Genital Infections)

Allen B. Kaiser, MD
Chief of Staff, Vanderbilt University Hospital; Vice Chairman
for Clinical Affairs, Department of Medicine, Vanderbilt University
Medical Center, Nashville, Tennessee
  Postoperative Infections and Antimicrobial Prophylaxis

Angela D. M. Kashuba, PharmD, DABCP
University of North Carolina at Chapel Hill, Chapel Hill,
North Carolina
  Pharmacokinetics and Pharmacodynamics of Anti-infective Agents

Dennis L. Kasper, MD
William Ellery Channing Professor of Medicine; Professor of
Microbiology and Molecular Genetics, Harvard Medical School;
Director, Channing Laboratory, Department of Medicine, Brigham
and Women's Hospital, Boston, Massachusetts
  Anaerobic Infections: General Concepts

Bruce A. Kaufman, MD
Professor of Neurosurgery, Medical College of Wisconsin; Chief,
Division of Pediatric Neurosurgery Froedtert Hospital,
Neurosciences Center, Milwaukee, Wisconsin
  Cerebrospinal Fluid Shunt Infections

Donald Kaye, MD, MACP
Professor of Medicine, Drexel University College of Medicine;
Medical Staff, Department of Medicine, Hospital of the Medical
College of Pennsylvania, Philadelphia, Pennsylvania
  Polymyxins (Polymyxin B and Colistin); Urinary Tract Infections

Keith S. Kaye, MD, MPH
Assistant Professor of Medicine, Division of Infectious Diseases
and International Health, Duke University Medical Center,
Durham, North Carolina
  Polymyxins (Polymyxin B and Colistin)

Kenneth M. Kaye, MD
Assistant Professor, Department of Medicine, Harvard Medical
School; Staff Physician, Division of Infectious Diseases, Department
of Medicine, Brigham and Women's Hospital,
Boston, Massachusetts
  Epstein-Barr Virus (Infectious Mononucleosis); Kaposi's
  Sarcoma-Associated Herpesvirus (Human Herpesvirus Type 8)

George E. Kenny, PhD
Professor Emeritus, Department of Pathobiology, University
of Washington School of Medicine, Seattle, Washington
  Genital Mycoplasmas: *Mycoplasma genitalium, Mycoplasma
  hominis,* and *Ureaplasma* Species

Jay S. Keystone, MD, FRCPC, MSc
Centre for Travel and Tropical Medicine, University of Toronto
Faculty of Medicine; Toronto General Hospital, Toronto, Ontario,
Canada
  Cyclospora cayetanensis, Isospora belli, Sarcocystis Species,
  Balantidium coli, and *Blastocystis hominis*

Charles H. King, MD
Associate Professor of International Health, Center for Global Health
and Diseases, Case Western Reserve University, Cleveland, Ohio
  Cestodes (Tapeworms)

Louis V. Kirchhoff, MD, MPH
Professor, Departments of Internal Medicine and Epidemiology,
University of Iowa Roy J. and Lucille A. Carver College of
Medicine; Staff Physician, Medical Service, Department of Veterans
Affairs Medical Center, Iowa City, Iowa
  Trypanosoma Species (American Trypanosomiasis, Chagas'
  Disease): Biology of Trypanosomes; Agents of African
  Trypanosomiasis (Sleeping Sickness)

Jerome O. Klein, MD
Professor, Department of Pediatrics, Boston University School
of Medicine and Boston Medical Center, Boston, Massachusetts
  Otitis Externa, Otitis Media, and Mastoiditis

Michael R. Knowles, MD
Professor of Medicine, University of North Carolina at Chapel Hill
School of Medicine; Pulmonary/Critical Care Medicine and
CF/Pulmonary Research and Treatment Center, Chapel Hill, North
Carolina
  Cystic Fibrosis

Igor J. Koralnik, MD
Assistant Professor of Neurology, Harvard Medical School; Director,
HIV/Neurology Center, Department of Neurology and Medicine,
Beth Israel Deaconess Medical Center, Boston, Massachusetts
  Neurologic Diseases Caused by Human Immunodeficiency
  Virus-1 and Opportunistic Infections

Joseph A. Kovacs, MD
Head, AIDS Section, Critical Care Medicine Department, Warren G.
Magnuson Clinical Center, National Institutes of Health, Bethesda,
Maryland
  Toxoplasma gondii

Phyllis Kozarsky, MD
Professor of Medicine, Division of Infectious Diseases, Emory
University School of Medicine, Atlanta, Georgia
  Cyclospora cayetanensis, Isospora belli, Sarcocystis Species,
  Balantidium coli, and *Blastocystis hominis*

Margaret James Koziel, MD
Assistant Professor of Medicine, Harvard Medical School, Harvard
Institutes of Medicine, Beth Israel Deaconess Medical Center,
Boston, Massachusetts
  Hepatitis B Virus and Hepatitis Delta Virus

John N. Krieger, MD
Professor of Urology, University of Washington School of Medicine;
Chief of Urology, Veterans Affairs Puget Sound Health Care System;
Attending Urologist, Harbor Medical Center and Children's Hospital
and Medical Center, Seattle, Washington
  Prostatitis, Epididymitis, and Orchitis

James W. LeDuc, PhD
Director, Division of Viral and Rickettsial Diseases, National Center
for Infectious Diseases, Centers for Disease Control and Prevention,
Atlanta, Georgia
  Emerging and Reemerging Infectious Disease Threats

Stanley M. Lemon, MD
Dean of Medicine, University of Texas Medical Branch, University
of Texas Medical School at Galveston, Galveston, Texas
  Hepatitis C

Paul N. Levett, PhD
Director, WHO Collaborating Center on Leptospirosis, Centers
for Disease Control and Prevention, Atlanta, Georgia
  Leptospirosis

Donald P. Levine, MD
Professor of Medicine and Chief, Division of General Internal
Medicine,Wayne State University; Vice-Chief of Medicine,
Detroit Receiving Hospital, Detroit, Michigan
  Infections in Injection Drug Users

William R. Levis, MD
Attending Physician, Department of Dermatology, New York University School of Medicine; Hansen's Disease Clinic, Bellevue Hospital, New York, New York
  Mycobacterium leprae (Leprosy, Hansen's Disease)

Matthew E. Levison, MD
Professor of Medicine and Public Health, Department of Medicine, Drexel University College of Medicine; Attending Staff, Department of Medicine/Infectious Diseases, Medical College of Pennsylvania Hospital, Philadelphia, Pennsylvania
  Peritonitis and Intraperitoneal Abscesses

W. Conrad Liles, MD, PhD
Associate Professor of Medicine, Division of Infectious Diseases, and Adjunct Associate Professor, Department of Pathology, University of Washington School of Medicine; Attending Physician, Department of Medicine, University of Washington Medical Center; Attending Physician, Department of Medicine, Harborview Medical Center, Seattle, Washington
  Immunomodulators

Aldo A. M. Lima, MD, PhD
Federal University of Ceara, Fortaleza, Brazil
  Inflammatory Enteritides

Nathan Litman, MD
Professor, Department of Pediatrics, Albert Einstein College of Medicine of Yeshiva University; Department of Pediatrics, Montefiore Medical Center, Bronx, New York
  Mumps Virus

Bennett Lorber, MD, DSc(Hon)
Thomas M. Durant Professor of Medicine and Professor of Microbiology and Immunology, Temple University School of Medicine; Chief, Section of Infectious Diseases, Temple University Hospital, Philadelphia, Pennsylvania
  Lung Abscess; *Listeria monocytogenes;* Gas Gangrene and Other *Clostridium*-Associated Diseases; *Bacteroides, Prevotella, Porphyromonas,* and *Fusobacterium* Species (and Other Medically Important Anaerobic Gram-Negative Bacilli)

Daniel Lucey, MD
Professor of Medicine, Uniformed Services University of the Health Sciences, Bethesda, Maryland; Adjunct Professor of Microbiology and Immunology, Georgetown University School of Medicine; Director, Center for Biologic Counterterrorism and Emerging Diseases, Washington Hospital Center, Washington, DC
  Bacillus anthracis (Anthrax); Anthrax

Larry I. Lutwick, MD
Professor of Medicine, Division of Infectious Diseases, State University of New York–Downstate School of Medicine; Director, Infectious Diseases, Veterans Affairs New York Harbor Health Care System, Brooklyn Campus, Brooklyn, New York; Bacterial Diseases Moderator, Program for Monitoring Emerging Diseases (ProMED-mail), International Society for Infectious Diseases, New York, New York
  Infections in Asplenic Patients

Rob Roy MacGregor, MD
Professor, Department of Medicine, University of Pennsylvania School of Medicine; Attending Physician, Department of Medicine/Infectious Diseases, Hospital of the University of Pennsylvania; Attending Physician, Department of Medicine/Infectious Diseases, Philadelphia Veterans Affairs Medical Center, Philadelphia, Pennsylvania
  Corynebacterium diphtheriae

Philip A. Mackowiak, MD, MBA
Professor and Vice Chairman, Department of Medicine, University of Maryland School of Medicine; Chief, Medical Care Clinical Center, Veterans Affairs Maryland Health Care System, Baltimore, Maryland
  Temperature Regulation and the Pathogenesis of Fever; Fever of Unknown Origin

Lawrence C. Madoff, MD
Assistant Professor, Department of Medicine, Harvard Medical School; Associate Physician, Department of Medicine, Division of Infectious Diseases and Channing Laboratory, Brigham and Women's Hospital, Boston, Massachusetts
  Infections of the Liver and Biliary System; Pancreatic Infections; Splenic Abscess; Appendicitis; Diverticulitis and Typhlitis

James H. Maguire, MD
Chief, Parasitic Diseases Branch, National Center for Infectious Diseases, Centers for Disease Control and Prevention, Atlanta, Georgia
  Introduction to Helminth Infections; Intestinal Nematodes (Roundworms); Trematodes (Schistosomes and Other Flukes)

Frank Maldarelli, MD, PhD
Staff Clinician, HIV Drug Resistance Program, National Cancer Institute; Warren G. Magnuson Clinical Center, National Institutes of Health, Bethesda, Maryland
  Diagnosis of Human Immunodeficiency Virus Infection

Gerald L. Mandell, MD, MACP
Professor of Medicine, Owen R. Cheatham Professor of the Sciences, Division of Infectious Diseases, University of Virginia School of Medicine, Charlottesville, Virginia
  Acute Pneumonia

Lionel A. Mandell, MD, FRCPC, FRCP[Lond]
Professor of Medicine and Chief, Division of Infectious Diseases, McMaster University, Henderson Site, Division of Infectious Diseases, Hamilton, Ontario, Canada
  Fusidic Acid

Barbara J. Mann, PhD
Associate Professor, Department of Internal Medicine and Microbiology, University of Virginia School of Medicine, Charlottesville, Virginia
  Microbial Adherence

Lewis Markoff, MD
Chief, Laboratory of Vector-Borne Virus Diseases, Division of Viral Products, Center for Biologics Research and Review, U.S. Food and Drug Administration, Bethesda, Maryland
  Alphaviruses

Thomas J. Marrie, MD
Professor and Chair, Department of Medicine, University of Alberta Faculty of Medicine; Site Chief for Medicine, University of Alberta Hospital, Edmonton, Alberta, Canada
  Coxiella burnetii (Q Fever)

Thomas Marth, Priv.-Doz. DrMed
Chefarzt der Abteilung Innere Medizin mit Schwerpunkten, Gastroenterologie, Onkologie, Diabetologie, und Ernahrungsmedizin, St. Josef-Krankenhaus Zell, Zell/Mosel, Germany
  Whipple's Disease

David H. Martin, MD
Harry E. Dascomb, MD, Professor of Medicine and Professor of Microbiology, Immunology, and Parasitology, Louisiana State University School of Medicine; Chief, Section of Infectious Diseases, Department of Medicine, Louisiana State University Health Sciences Center, New Orleans, Louisiana
  Trichomonas vaginalis

Georg Maschmeyer, MD
Professor of Internal Medicine, Department of Hematology
and Oncology, Charite University Hospital, Berlin, Germany
  Stenotrophomonas maltophilia and *Burkholderia cepacia*

Ellen M. Mascini
Eijkman-Winkler Institute for Microbiology, Infection, and
Inflammation, Utrecht University, Utrecht, The Netherlands
  Anaerobic Cocci; Anaerobic Gram-Positive Nonsporulating Bacilli

Henry Masur, MD
Chief, Critical Care Medicine Department, Warren G. Magnuson
Clinical Center, National Institutes of Health, Bethesda, Maryland
  Management of Opportunistic Infections Associated with Human
  Immunodeficiency Virus Infection

Michael Eric Mathieu, MD
Instructor in Clinical Dermatology, Department of Dermatology,
University of Virginia School of Medicine, Charlottesville; Medical
Staff, Department of Medicine, Winchester Medical Center,
Winchester, Virginia; Medical Staff, Department of Medicine, City
Hospital, Martinsburg, West Virginia
  Introduction to Ectoparasitic Diseases; Lice (Pediculosis); Scabies;
  Myiasis and Tungiasis; Mites (Including Chiggers); Ticks (Including
  Tick Paralysis)

Kenneth H. Mayer, MD
Professor of Medicine and Community Health, Brown Medical
School; Department of Medicine/Infectious Diseases, Miriam
Hospital, Providence, Rhode Island; Director of Medical Research,
Fenway Community Health, Boston, Massachusetts
  Sulfonamides and Trimethoprim

John T. McBride, MD
Professor, Department of Pediatrics, Northeast Ohio Universities
College of Medicine, Rootstown; Vice Chair, Department
of Pediatrics, Akron Children's Hospital, Akron, Ohio
  Acute Laryngotracheobronchitis (Croup); Bronchiolitis

Carol A. McCarthy, MD
Associate Professor, Department of Pediatrics, University of Vermont
College of Medicine, Burlington, Vermont; Director, Pediatric
Infectious Diseases, Department of Pediatrics, Maine Medical
Center, Portland, Maine
  Respiratory Syncytial Virus

William M. McCormack, MD
Chief, Infectious Diseases Division, Department of Medicine,
State University of New York–Downstate Medical Center,
Brooklyn, New York
  Urethritis; Vulvovaginitis and Cervicitis

Joseph E. McDade, PhD
Orise Fellow, National Center for Infectious Diseases, Centers
for Disease Control and Prevention, Atlanta, Georgia
  Emerging and Reemerging Infectious Disease Threats

Kenneth McIntosh, MD
Professor, Department of Pediatrics, Harvard Medical School; Senior
Associate in Medicine, Division of Infectious Diseases, Children's
Hospital; Professor, Department of Immunology and Infectious
Diseases, Harvard School of Public Health, Boston, Massachusetts
  Coronaviruses, Including Severe Acute Respiratory Syndrome
  (SARS)–Associated Coronaviruses

Philip B. Mead, MD
Professor and Chair Emeritus, Department of Obstetrics and
Gynecology, University of Vermont College of Medicine; Emeritus
Staff, Department of Obstetrics and Gynecology, Fletcher Allen
Health Care, Burlington, Vermont
  Infections of the Female Pelvis

Antone A. Medeiros, MD
Professor, Department of Medicine, Brown Medical School,
Providence, Rhode Island
  Molecular Mechanisms of Antibiotic Resistance in Bacteria

Michael H. Merson, MD
Anna M. R. Lauder Professor of Public Health, Dean of Public
Health, and Director, Center for Interdisciplinary Research on AIDS,
Department of Epidemiology and Public Health, Yale University
School of Medicine, New Haven, Connecticut
  Global Perspectives on Human Immunodeficiency Virus
  Infection and Acquired Immunodeficiency Syndrome

Daniel K. Meyer, MD
Assistant Professor of Medicine, Division of Infectious Diseases,
University of Medicine and Dentistry of New Jersey Robert Wood
Johnson Medical School at Camden; Program Director, Fellowship
Training Program, Division of Infectious Diseases, Cooper
University Hospital, Camden, New Jersey
  Other Coryneform Bacteria and *Rhodococcus*

Burt Meyers, MD
Clinical Professor of Medicine, Mount Sinai Hospital, New York,
New York
  Tetracyclines and Chloramphenicol; Metronidazole

Samuel I. Miller, MD
Professor, Department of Medicine, Microbiology, and Genome
Sciences, and Professor, Department of Medicine, University
of Washington School of Medicine, Seattle, Washington
  Salmonella Species, Including *Salmonella typhi*

Yazdan Mirzanejad, MD, FRCPC, FACP
Clinical Instructor, Division of Infectious Diseases,
Department of Medicine, University of British Columbia Faculty
of Medicine; Clinical Associate, Oak Tree HIV Clinic, Children and
Women Hospital, Vancouver; Consultant, Department of Infectious
Diseases, Surrey Memorial Hospital, Surrey; Consultant, Infectious
Diseases, Department of Infectious Diseases, Royal Columbian
Hospital, New Westminster, British Columbia, Canada
  Streptococcus anginosus Group

Candace L. Mitchell, MD
Assistant Professor of Medicine, Section of Infectious Diseases,
Louisiana State University School of Medicine in Shreveport,
Shreveport, Louisiana
  Francisella tularensis (Tularemia) as an Agent of Bioterrorism

David H. Mitchell, MBBS, MMedSci (Epi)
Clinical Lecturer, Department of Infectious Diseases, University of
Sydney Faculty of Medicine; Senior Staff Specialist, Centre for
Infectious Diseases and Microbiology, Westmead Hospital,
Westmead, New South Wales, Australia
  Nocardia Species

John F. Modlin, MD
Professor and Chair, Department of Pediatrics, Dartmouth Medical
School; Children's Hospital at Dartmouth, Dartmouth-Hitchcock
Medical Center, Lebanon, New Hampshire
  Introduction to the Enteroviruses; Poliovirus; Coxsackieviruses,
  Echoviruses, and Newer Enteroviruses

Robert C. Moellering, Jr., MD
Herrman L. Blumgart Professor of Medicine, Harvard Medical
School; Physician-in-Chief and Chairman, Department of Medicine,
Beth Israel Deaconess Medical Center, Boston, Massachusetts
  Principles of Anti-infective Therapy; *Enterococcus* Species,
  Streptococcus bovis, and *Leuconostoc Species*

Jose G. Montoya, MD
Associate Professor, Department of Medicine, Division of Infectious Diseases and Geographic Medicine, Stanford University School of Medicine; Attending Physician, Stanford University Medical Center, Stanford; Associate Staff Scientist, Department of Immunology and Infectious Diseases, Research Institute, Palo Alto Medical Foundation, Palo Alto, California
Toxoplasma gondii

Philippe Moreillon, MD
Division of Infectious Diseases, Department of Medicine, University Hospital CHUV, Lausanne, Switzerland
Staphylococcus aureus (Including Staphylococcal Toxic Shock)

J. Glenn Morris, Jr., MD, MPH
Professor and Chairman, Department of Epidemiology and Preventive Medicine, Professor of Medicine (Infectious Diseases), and Professor of Microbiology and Immunology, University of Maryland School of Medicine, Baltimore, Maryland
Human Illness Associated with Harmful Algal Blooms

Caryn Gee Morse, MD
Staff Clinician and Research Fellow, Critical Care Medicine, Warren G. Magnuson Clinical Center, National Institutes of Health, Bethesda, Maryland
Nutrition, Immunity, and Infection

Robert R. Muder, MD
Professor, Department of Medicine, University of Pittsburgh School of Medicine; Hospital Epidemiologist, Infectious Disease Section, Veterans Affairs Pittsburgh Healthcare System, Pittsburgh, Pennsylvania
Other *Legionella* Species

Jean Marie Mulinde, MD
Lead Medical Officer, U.S. Food and Drug Administration, Rockville, Maryland
Hyperbaric Oxygen

Robert S. Munford, MD
Jan and Henri Bromberg Chair in Internal Medicine and Professor, Department of Internal Medicine and Microbiology, University of Texas–Southwestern Medical Center; Parkland Memorial Hospital and Zale-Lipshy University Hospital, Dallas, Texas
Sepsis, Severe Sepsis, and Septic Shock

Timothy F. Murphy, MD
Professor of Medicine and Microbiology, State University of New York at Buffalo School of Medicine and Biomedical Sciences; Chief, Division of Infectious Diseases, Department of Medicine, Veterans Affairs Medical Center, Buffalo, New York
Moraxella (Branhamella) catarrhalis and Other Gram-Negative Cocci; *Haemophilus* Infections

Barbara E. Murray, MD
Professor and Director, Division of Infectious Diseases, Department of Internal Medicine, University of Texas–Houston Medical School; Co-Director, Center for Emerging and Re-emerging Pathogens, University of Texas Health Science Center, Houston, Texas
Glycopeptides (Vancomycin and Teicoplanin), Streptogramins (Quinupristin-Dalfopristin), and Lipopeptides (Daptomycin)

Daniel M. Musher, MD
Professor of Medicine and Microbiology and Immunology, Baylor College of Medicine; Chief, Infectious Diseases Section, Veterans Affairs Medical Center, Houston, Texas
Streptococcus pneumoniae

Esteban C. Nannini, MD
Attending Physician, Department of Infectious Diseases, Sanatorio Parque, Rosario, Santa Fe, Argentina
Glycopeptides (Vancomycin and Teicoplanin), Streptogramins (Quinupristin-Dalfopristin), and Lipopeptides (Daptomycin)

Theodore E. Nash, MD
Head, Gastrointestinal Parasites Section, Laboratory of Parasitic Diseases, National Institute of Allergy and Infectious Disease, National Institutes of Health, Bethesda, Maryland
Visceral Larva Migrans and Other Unusual Helminth Infections

William M. Nauseef, MD
Professor, Inflammation Program and Department of Medicine, University of Iowa Roy J. and Lucille A. Carver College of Medicine; Department of Veterans Affairs, Iowa City, Iowa
Granulocytic Phagocytes

Marguerite A. Neill, MD
Associate Professor, Department of Medicine, Brown Medical School, Providence; Attending Physician, Division of Infectious Disease, Memorial Hospital of Rhode Island, Pawtucket, Rhode Island
Other Pathogenic Vibrios

Judith A. O'Donnell, MD
Associate Professor of Medicine and Public Health, Division of Infectious Disease, Drexel University College of Medicine; Attending Physician and Hospital Epidemiologist, Department of Medicine, Medical College of Pennsylvania Hospital, Philadelphia, Pennsylvania
Topical Antibacterials

Christopher A. Ohl, MD
Associate Professor of Medicine, Section of Infectious Diseases, Wake Forest University School of Medicine; Medical Director, Center for Antimicrobial Utilization, Stewardship, and Epidemiology, North Carolina Baptist Hospital, Winston-Salem, North Carolina
Infectious Arthritis of Native Joints

Michael E. Ohl, MD
Postdoctoral Research Fellow and Clinical Instructor, Departments of Internal Medicine and Family and Community Medicine, University of Missouri School of Medicine, Columbia, Missouri
Salmonella Species, Including *Salmonella typhi*

Pablo C. Okhuysen, MD, FACP
Professor, Department of Medicine, Division of Infectious Diseases, University of Texas–Houston Medical School; Associate Professor, Center for Infectious Diseases, University of Texas Health Science Center–Houston School of Public Health; UTHSC–Houston Director, Memorial Hermann Hospital Clinical Research Center; Staff Physician, Department of Infectious Diseases, Lyndon B. Johnson General Hospital, Houston, Texas
Sporothrix schenckii

Steven M. Opal, MD
Professor, Department of Medicine/Division of Infectious Diseases, Brown Medical School, Providence; Chief, Infectious Disease Division, Department of Medicine/Division of Infectious Diseases, Memorial Hospital of Rhode Island, Pawtucket, Rhode Island
Molecular Mechanisms of Antibiotic Resistance in Bacteria

Walter A. Orenstein, MD
Director, Emory Program for Vaccine Policy and Development, and Associate Director, Emory Vaccine Center, Emory University School of Medicine, Atlanta, Georgia
Immunization

Douglas R. Osmon, MD, MPH
Associate Professor of Medicine, Mayo Clinic College of Medicine
and Mayo Clinic, Rochester, Minnesota
Osteomyelitis

Michael T. Osterholm, PhD, MPH
Director, Center for Infectious Disease Research and Policy,
and Professor, University of Minnesota School of Public Health,
Minneapolis, Minnesota
Epidemiologic Principles

Stephen M. Ostroff, MD
Deputy Director, National Center for Infectious Diseases, Centers
for Disease Control and Prevention, Atlanta, Georgia
Emerging and Reemerging Infectious Disease Threats

Michael N. Oxman, MD
Professor of Medicine and Pathology, University of California,
San Diego, School of Medicine; Veterans Affairs San Diego,
San Diego, California
Myocarditis and Pericarditis

Eric G. Pamer, MD
Chief, Infectious Diseases Service, Department of Medicine,
Memorial Sloan-Kettering Cancer Center; Head, Laboratory of
Antimicrobial Immunity, Immunology Program, Sloan-Kettering
Institute, New York, New York
Cell-Mediated Defense against Infection

Peter G. Pappas, MD
Professor, Department of Medicine, University of Alabama School
of Medicine, Birmingham, Alabama
Chronic Pneumonia

Mark S. Pasternack, MD
Associate Professor of Pediatrics, Harvard Medical School; Chief,
Pediatric Infectious Disease Unit, Massachusets General Hospital
for Children, Massachusetts General Hospital, Boston,
Massachusetts
Cellulitis and Subcutaneous Tissue Infections; Myositis;
Lymphadenitis and Lymphangitis

Thomas F. Patterson, MD
Professor, Department of Medicine, Division of Infectious Diseases,
University of Texas Health Science Center at San Antonio, San
Antonio, Texas
Aspergillus Species

Deborah Pavan-Langston, MD, FACS
Associate Professor, Department of Ophthalmology, Harvard
Medical School; Surgeon, Director of Clinical Virology, Department
of Corneal and External Disease, Massachusetts Eye and Ear
Infirmary, Boston, Massachusetts
Microbial Conjunctivitis; Microbial Keratitis

Richard D. Pearson, MD
Professor, Departments of Internal Medicine and Pathology,
University of Virginia School of Medicine; Attending Physician,
Department of Internal Medicine, University of Virginia Health
System, Charlottesville, Virginia
Agents Active against Parasites and Pneumocystis;
Leishmania Species: Visceral (Kala-Azar), Cutaneous,
and Mucocutaneous Leishmaniasis

David A. Pegues, MD
Professor of Clinical Medicine, Department of Medicine, David
Geffen School of Medicine at UCLA; Hospital Epidemiologist and
Attending Physician, Division of Infectious Diseases, University
of California, Los Angeles, Medical Center, Los Angeles, California
Salmonella Species, Including *Salmonella typhi*

Robert L. Penn, MD
Professor of Medicine and Chief, Section of Infectious Diseases,
Louisiana State University School of Medicine in Shreveport; Chief,
Infectious Diseases Section, Louisiana State University Health
Sciences Center, University Hospital, Shreveport, Louisiana
Francisella tularensis (Tularemia); *Francisella tularensis* (Tularemia)
as an Agent of Bioterrorism

John R. Perfect, MD
Professor, Department of Medicine, Duke University Medical Center,
Durham, North Carolina
Cryptococcus neoformans

C. J. Peters, MD
John Sealy Distinguished University Chair in Tropical and Emerging
Virology, Department of Pathology and Microbiology/Immunology,
University of Texas Medical Branch, University of Texas Medical
School at Galveston, Galveston, Texas
Marburg and Ebola Virus Hemorrhagic Fevers; California
Encephalitis, Hantavirus Pulmonary Syndrome, and Bunyavirid
Hemorrhagic Fevers; Lymphocytic Choriomeningitis Virus, Lassa
Virus, and the South American Hemorrhagic Fevers; Bioterrorism:
Viral Hemorrhagic Fevers

Phillip K. Peterson, MD
Professor of Medicine, Department of Internal Medicine, University
of Minnesota Medical School-Minneapolis; Director, Infectious
Diseases and International Medicine, Department of Internal
Medicine, Fairview University Medical Center; Director, Infectious
Diseases and International Medicine, Department of Internal
Medicine, Hennepin County Medical Center,
Minneapolis, Minnesota
Infections in the Elderly

William A. Petri, Jr., MD, PhD
Wade Hampton Frost Professor of Epidemiology and Professor
of Medicine, Microbiology, and Pathology, University of Virginia
School of Medicine; Chief, Division of Infectious Diseases and
International Health, University of Virginia Health System,
Charlottesville, Virginia
Microbial Adherence

Gerald B. Pier, PhD
Professor of Medicine, Microbiology, and Molecular Genetics,
Harvard Medical School; Microbiologist, Department of Medicine,
Brigham and Women's Hospital, Boston, Massachusetts
Pseudomonas aeruginosa

Peter Piot, MD, PhD
Executive Director, Joint United Nations Programme on HIV/AIDS
(UNAIDS); Under Secretary-General, United Nations, Geneva,
Switzerland
Global Perspectives on Human Immunodeficiency Virus Infection
and Acquired Immunodeficiency Syndrome

Ronald E. Polk, PharmD
Professor and Chairman, Department of Pharmacy, School
of Pharmacy, Virginia Commonwealth University School of
Medicine, Richmond, Virginia
Antimicrobial Management: Cost and Resistance

Mikulas Popovic, MD, PhD
Professor, Institute of Human Virology, University of Maryland
Biotechnology Institute, Baltimore, Maryland
Human Immunodeficiency Viruses

John H. Powers, MD, FACP
Infectious Diseases Attending, National Institute of Allergy and Infectious Diseases, National Institutes of Health, Bethesda, Maryland; Clinical Assistant Professor, Department of Medicine, George Washington University School of Medicine, Washington, District of Columbia; Clinical Assistant Professor, Department of Medicine/Infectious Diseases, University of Maryland School of Medicine, Baltimore; Lead Medical Officer, Antimicrobial Drug Development and Resistance Initiatives, Center for Drug Evaluation and Research, U.S. Food and Drug Administration, Rockville, Maryland
　Interpreting the Results of Clinical Trials on Antimicrobial Agents

Robert H. Purcell, MD
Co-Chief, Laboratory of Infectious Diseases, and Head, Hepatitis Viruses Section, National Institute of Allergy and Infectious Diseases, National Institutes of Health, Bethesda, Maryland
　Hepatitis E Virus

Yok-Ai Que, MD, PhD
Centre Hospitalier Universitaire Vaudois, Medical Critical Care Division, Department of Internal Medicine, Lausanne, Switzerland
　Staphylococcus aureus (Including Staphylococcal Toxic Shock)

Anastácio de Queiroz Sousa, MD
Associate Professor of Medicine, Department of Internal Medicine; Director, Nucleo de Medicina Tropical, Federal University of Ceara; Physician and Head, Epidemiology Surveillance Service, Hospital Sao Jose for Infectious Diseases, Fortaleza, Ceara, Brazil
　Leishmania Species: Visceral (Kala-Azar), Cutaneous, and Mucocutaneous Leishmaniasis

Ronald Rabinowitz, MD
Assistant Professor of Medicine, Division of Trauma Infectious Disease, University of Maryland School of Medicine; Shock Trauma Center, University of Maryland Health System, Baltimore, Maryland
　Hyperbaric Oxygen

Reuben Ramphal, MD
Professor, Department of Medicine, University of Florida College of Medicine, Gainesville, Florida
　Pseudomonas aeruginosa

Didier Raoult, MD, PhD
Faculté de Médecine de Marseille, Unité des Rickettsies, Marseille, France
　Introduction to Rickettsioses and Ehrlichioses; *Rickettsia rickettsii* and Other Spotted Fever Group Rickettsiae (Rocky Mountain Spotted Fever and Other Spotted Fevers); *Rickettsia akari* (Rickettsialpox); *Coxiella burnetii* (Q Fever); *Rickettsia prowazekii* (Epidemic or Louse-Borne Typhus); Scrub Typhus

Jonathan I. Ravdin, MD
Nesbitt Professor and Chairman, Department of Medicine, University of Minnesota Medical School–Minneapolis; Minneapolis Veterans Affairs Medical Center, Fairview-University Medical Center, Minneapolis, Minnesota
　Introduction to Protozoal Diseases; *Entamoeba histolytica* (Amebiasis)

Stuart C. Ray, MD
Associate Professor of Medicine, Division of Infectious Diseases, Department of Medicine, Johns Hopkins University School of Medicine; Active Staff, Department of Medicine, Johns Hopkins Hospital, Baltimore, Maryland
　Hepatitis C

Annette C. Reboli, MD
Professor, Department of Medicine, Division of Infectious Diseases, University of Medicine and Dentistry of New Jersey Robert Wood Johnson Medical School, New Brunswick; Hospital Epidemiologist and Head, Infectious Diseases Division, Cooper University Hospital, Camden, New Jersey
　Other Coryneform Bacteria and *Rhodococcus*; *Erysipelothrix rhusiopathiae*

Richard C. Reichman, MD
Professor of Medicine, Microbiology, and Immunology, University of Rochester School of Medicine; Head, Infectious Diseases Unit, University of Rochester Medical Center, Rochester, New York
　Papillomaviruses

Michael F. Rein, MD
Professor of Medicine, Department of Infectious Diseases and International Health, University of Virginia School of Medicine; Attending Physician, Department of Internal Medicine, University of Virginia Hospital; Medical Director, Sexually Transmitted Disease Clinic, Thomas Jefferson District Health Department, Charlottesville, Virginia
　Urethritis; *Trichomonas vaginalis*

Marvin S. Reitz, Jr., PhD
Professor, Institute of Human Virology; Member, Greenebaum Cancer Center, University of Maryland, Baltimore, Maryland
　Human Immunodeficiency Viruses

David A. Relman, MD
Associate Professor, Department of Microbiology and Immunology, Stanford University School of Medicine, Stanford; Chief, Infectious Diseases, Veterans Affairs Palo Alto Health Care System, Palo Alto, California
　A Molecular Perspective of Microbial Pathogenicity

Jack S. Remington, MD
Professor, Division of Infectious Diseases, Department of Medicine, Stanford University School of Medicine; Attending Physician, Stanford University Medical Center and Lucille Packard Medical Center, Stanford; Marcus A. Krupp Research Chair and Chairman, Department of Immunology and Infectious Diseases, Research Institute, Palo Alto Medical Foundation, Palo Alto, California
　Toxoplasma gondii

Angela Restrepo, MD
Scientific Advisor, Medical and Experimental Mycology Group, Corporación para Investigaciones Biológicas (CIB), Medellin, Antioquia, Colombia, South America
　Paracoccidioides brasiliensis

John H. Rex, MD, FACP
Adjunct Professor of Medicine, Department of Internal Medicine, University of Texas–Houston Medical School, Houston, Texas; Vice President and Medical Director for Infection, Astra Zeneca Pharmaceuticals, Macclesfield, Cheshire, United Kingdom
　Systemic Antifungal Agents; *Sporothrix schenckii*

Herbert Y. Reynolds, MD
Emeritus Professor of Medicine, Pennsylvania State University College of Medicine; Milton S. Hershey Medical Center, Hershey, Pennsylvania; Medical Officer, Division of Lung Diseases, National Heart, Lung, and Blood Institute, National Institutes of Health, Bethesda, Maryland
　Chronic Obstructive Pulmonary Disease, Chronic Bronchitis, and Acute Exacerbations

Kyu Y. Rhee, MD, PhD
Clinical Fellow, Division of International Medicine and Infectious Diseases, Weill Medical College of Cornell University and New York–Presbyterian Hospital–Weill Cornell Medical Center, New York, New York
Borrelia Species (Relapsing Fever)

Lisa D. Rotz, MD
Acting Director, Bioterrorism Preparedness and Response Program, National Center for Infectious Diseases, Centers for Disease Control and Prevention, Atlanta, Georgia
Smallpox and Bioterrorism

Kathryn L. Ruoff, PhD
Department of Pathology, Dartmouth Hitchcock Medical Center, Lebanon, New Hampshire
Classification of Streptococci

Mark E. Rupp, MD
Professor, Department of Internal Medicine, University of Nebraska College of Medicine; Medical Director, Department of Healthcare Epidemiology, Nebraska Medical Center, Omaha, Nebraska
Mediastinitis

Charles E. Rupprecht, VMD, PhD
Chief, Rabies Section, Viral and Rickettsial Zoonoses Branch, Division of Viral and Rickettsial Diseases, Centers for Disease Control and Prevention, Atlanta, Georgia
Rhabdoviruses

Thomas A. Russo, MD, CM
Associate Professor, Department of Medicine, Division of Infectious Diseases, State University of New York at Buffalo School of Medicine and Biomedical Sciences; Staff Physician, Department of Medicine, Division of Infectious Diseases, Veterans Affairs Medical Center; Staff Physician, Department of Medicine, Division of Infectious Diseases, Erie County Medical Center, Buffalo, New York
Agents of Actinomycosis

William A. Rutala, PhD, MPH
Professor, Department of Medicine, University of North Carolina at Chapel Hill School of Medicine; Director, Statewide Program for Infection Control and Epidemiology, and Director, Hospital Epidemiology, Occupational Health, and Safety, University of North Carolina Health Care System, Chapel Hill, North Carolina
The Acutely Ill Patient with Fever and Rash; Disinfection, Sterilization, and Control of Hospital Waste

Mirella Salvatore, MD
Associate, Clinical Fellow, Department of Infectious Diseases, Mount Sinai Medical Center, New York, New York
Tetracyclines and Chloramphenicol; Metronidazole

Frank T. Saulsbury, MD
Professor, Department of Pediatrics, University of Virginia School of Medicine; Head, Division of Immunology and Rheumatology, Department of Pediatrics, University of Virginia Health System, Charlottesville, Virginia
Kawasaki Syndrome

Maria C. Savoia, MD
Vice Dean for Medical Education and Professor, Department of Medicine/Infectious Diseases, University of California, San Diego, School of Medicine; Attending Physician, Department of Medicine/Infectious Diseases, University of California, San Diego, Medical Center, San Diego Veterans Affairs Medical Center, San Diego, California
Myocarditis and Pericarditis

Paul E. Sax, MD
Assistant Professor of Medicine, Harvard Medical School; Clinical Director, Division of Infectious Diseases and HIV Program, Brigham and Women's Hospital, Boston, Massachusetts
Pulmonary Manifestations of Human Immunodeficiency Virus Infection

W. Michael Scheld, MD
Wyeth Professor of Infectious Diseases, Professor of Internal Medicine, and Clinical Professor of Neurosurgery, Department of Internal Medicine, University of Virginia School of Medicine; University of Virginia Health System, Charlottesville, Virginia
Endocarditis and Intravascular Infections; Acute Meningitis

David Schlossberg, MD, FACP
Professor, Department of Medicine, Temple University School of Medicine; Adjunct Professor, Department of Medicine, Jefferson Medical College of Thomas Jefferson University, Philadelphia; Director, Medical Services, Merck & Company, Inc., North Wales, Pennsylvania
Chlamydophila (Chlamydia) psittaci (Psittacosis)

Robert T. Schooley, MD
Tim Gill Professor and Head, Division of Infectious Diseases, University of Colorado Health Sciences Center, Denver; Physician, Department of Medicine, University of Colorado Hospital, Aurora; Physician, Department of Veterans Affairs Medical Center and Denver Department of Health and Hospitals, Denver, Colorado
Epstein-Barr Virus (Infectious Mononucleosis)

Carlos Seas, MD
Associate Professor, Department of Medicine, and Associate Investigator, Alexander von Humboldt Tropical Medicine Institute, Cayetano Heredia University; Attending Physician, Department of Infectious, Tropical, and Dermatological Diseases, Cayetano Heredia National Hospital, Lima, Peru
Vibrio cholerae

Kent A. Sepkowitz, MD
Professor, Department of Medicine, Weill Medical College of Cornell University; Director, Infection Control, Department of Medicine, Memorial Sloan-Kettering Cancer Center, New York, New York
Nosocomial Hepatitis and Other Infections Transmitted by Blood and Blood Products

Edward Septimus, MD
Clinical Professor of Medicine, Department of Infectious Diseases, University of Texas–Houston Medical School; Medical Director, Department of Infectious Diseases and Occupational Health, Memorial Hermann Healthcare System, Houston, Texas
Pleural Effusion and Empyema

Aleem Siddiqui, PhD
Professor, Department of Microbiology, Program in Molecular Biology, University of Colorado Health Sciences Center, Denver, Colorado
Hepatitis B Virus and Hepatitis Delta Virus

Costi D. Sifri, MD
Instructor, Department of Medicine, Harvard Medical School; Clinical Associate, Division of Infectious Diseases, Massachusetts General Hospital, Boston, Massachusetts
Appendicitis; Diverticulitis and Typhlitis

Upinder Singh, MD
Assistant Professor, Departments of Internal Medicine and Microbiology and Immunology, Stanford University School of Medicine, Stanford, California
Free-Living Amebas

Sumathi Sivapalasingam
Instructor, Division of Infectious Diseases, Department of Medicine,
New York University School of Medicine, New York, New York
Macrolides, Clindamycin, and Ketolides

Leonard N. Slater, MD
Professor, Department of Medicine, Infectious Disease Section,
University of Oklahoma College of Medicine; Staff Physician and
Chairman, Infection Control Committee, Department of Medicine,
Oklahoma University Medical Center; Staff Physician and Chairman,
Infection Control, Medical Service, Veterans Affairs Medical Center,
Oklahoma City, Oklahoma
Bartonella, Including Cat-Scratch Disease

A. George Smulian, MBBCh
Associate Professor of Medicine, Division of Infectious Diseases,
University of Cincinnati College of Medicine; Chief, Infectious
Disease Section, Medical Service, Cincinnati Veterans Affairs
Medical Center, Cincinnati, Ohio
Pneumocystis Species

Jack D. Sobel, MD
Professor of Medicine, Division of Infectious Diseases, Wayne State
University School of Medicine; Chief, Division of Infectious
Diseases, Department of Internal Medicine, Detroit Medical Center,
Detroit, Michigan
Urinary Tract Infections

Tom Solomon, MD, PhD
Lecturer in Neurology, Department of Neurological Science, Clinical
Lecturer in Medical Microbiology, University of Liverpool,
Liverpool, United Kingdom
Flaviviruses (Yellow Fever, Dengue, Dengue Hemorrhagic Fever,
Japanese Encephalitis, West Nile Encephalitis, St. Louis
Encephalitis, Tick-Borne Encephalitis)

David E. Soper, MD
Professor and Vice-Chairman, Department of Obstetrics and
Gynecology, Medical University of South Carolina College
of Medicine, Charleston, South Carolina
Infections of the Female Pelvis

Tania C. Sorrell, MB, BS, MD, FRACP
Professor of Clinical Infectious Diseases, Department of Medicine,
University of Sydney Faculty of Medicine, Sydney; Director,
Department of Infectious Diseases, Westmead Hospital, Westmead,
New South Wales, Australia
Nocardia Species

P. Frederick Sparling, MD
J. Herbert Bate Professor Emeritus, Departments of Medicine and
Microbiology and Immunology, University of North Carolina at
Chapel Hill School of Medicine; University of North Carolina
Hospitals, Chapel Hill, North Carolina
Neisseria gonorrhoeae

Walter E. Stamm, MD
Professor of Medicine and Head, Division of Allergy and Infectious
Diseases, University of Washington School of Medicine, Seattle,
Washington
Introduction to Chlamydial Diseases; *Chlamydia trachomatis*
(Trachoma, Perinatal infections, Lymphogranuloma Venereum,
and Other Genital Infections)

William M. Stauffer, MD, MSPH, DTM&H
Instructor of Medicine, Department of Internal Medicine, Division
of Infectious Disease and International Medicine, University of
Minnesota Medical School–Minneapolis, Minneapolis; Clinical
Faculty, Center for International Health and International Travel
Clinic, Regions Hospital/HealthPartners, St. Paul, Minnesota
Introduction to Protozoal Diseases; *Entamoeba histolytica*
(Amebiasis)

James M. Steckelberg, MD
Professor of Medicine and Chair, Division of Infectious Diseases,
Mayo Clinic College of Medicine, Rochester, Minnesota
Osteomyelitis

Allen C. Steere, MD
Professor, Department of Medicine, Harvard Medical School;
Director of Rheumatology, Department of Medicine, Massachusetts
General Hospital, Boston, Massachusetts
Borrelia burgdorferi (Lyme Disease, Lyme Borreliosis)

Neal H. Steigbigel, MD
Professor, Department of Medicine, Division of Infectious Disease
and Immunology, New York University School of Medicine; Staff
Physician, Medical Service, New York Veterans Affairs Medical
Center; Attending Physician, Department of Medicine, Bellevue
Hospital Center and New York University Medical Center,
New York, New York
Macrolides, Clindamycin, and Ketolides

James P. Steinberg, MD
Associate Professor of Medicine, Division of Infectious Diseases,
Emory University School of Medicine; Hospital Epidemiologist,
Chief of Infectious Diseases, and Associate Chief of Medicine,
Emory Crawford Long Hospital, Atlanta, Georgia
Other Gram-Negative and Gram-Variable Bacilli

Theodore S. Steiner, MD
Assistant Professor, Department of Medicine, University of British
Columbia Faculty of Medicine; Attending Physician, Vancouver
Hospital and Health Sciences Centre, Vancouver, British Columbia,
Canada
Principles and Syndromes of Enteric Infection

Timothy R. Sterling, MD
Associate Professor, Department of Medicine, Division of Infectious
Diseases, Vanderbilt University School of Medicine, Nashville,
Tennessee
General Clinical Manifestations of Human Immunodeficiency Virus
Infection (Including the Acute Retroviral Syndrome and Oral,
Cutaneous, Renal, Ocular, and Cardiac Diseases)

David A. Stevens, MD, FACP
Professor, Department of Medicine, Stanford University School of
Medicine, Stanford; Chief, Division of Infectious Diseases, Hospital
Epidemiologist, and Co-Director, Clinical Microbiology Laboratory,
Santa Clara Valley Medical Center; President, California Institute for
Medical Research, San Jose, California
Systemic Antifungal Agents

Dennis L. Stevens, PhD, MD
Professor, Department of Medicine, University of Washington
School of Medicine, Seattle, Washington; Chief, Infectious Diseases,
Department of Medicine, Veterans Affairs Medical Center,
Boise, Idaho
Streptococcus pyogenes

Charles W. Stratton, MD
Associate Professor, Departments of Medicine and Pathology,
Vanderbilt University School of Medicine; Director, Clinical
Microbiology Laboratory, Department of Pathology, Vanderbilt
University Medical Center, Nashville, Tennessee
Streptococcus anginosus Group

Stephen E. Straus, MD
Senior Investigator, Laboratory of Clinical Infectious Diseases,
National Institute of Allergy and Infectious Diseases; Director,
National Center for Complementary and Alternative Medicine,
National Institutes of Health, Bethesda, Maryland
Complementary and Alternative Medicines for Infectious Diseases;
Introduction to Herpesviridae; Human Herpesvirus Types 6 and 7;
Herpes B Virus

Larry J. Strausbaugh, MD
Professor, Department of Medicine, Oregon Health and Science University School of Medicine; Hospital Epidemiologist and Staff Physician, Division of Hospital and Specialty Medicine, Portland Veterans Affairs Medical Center, Portland, Oregon
Nosocomial Respiratory Infections

Alan M. Sugar, MD
Professor, Department of Medicine, Boston University School of Medicine, Boston; Director, HIV/AIDS Program and Hepatitis C Virus Program, Director, Infectious Diseases Clinical Services, and Attending Physician, Department of Medicine, Cape Cod Hospital, Hyannis; Attending Physician, Department of Medicine, Boston Medical Center, Boston, Massachusetts
Agents of Mucormycosis and Related Species

Mark S. Sulkowski, MD
Associate Professor, Department of Medicine, Division of Infectious Diseases, Johns Hopkins University School of Medicine; Johns Hopkins Hospital, Baltimore, Maryland
Gastrointestinal and Hepatobiliary Manifestations of Human Immunodeficiency Virus Infection

Morton N. Swartz, MD
Professor, Department of Medicine, Harvard Medical School; Chief, James Jackson Firm, Department of Medicine, Massachusetts General Hospital, Boston, Massachusetts
Cellulitis and Subcutaneous Tissue Infections; Myositis; Lymphadenitis and Lymphangitis

Thomas R. Talbot, MD, MPH
Assistant Professor, Departments of Medicine and Preventive Medicine, Vanderbilt University School of Medicine; Associate Hospital Epidemiologist, Vanderbilt University Medical Center, Nashville, Tennessee
Postoperative Infections and Antimicrobial Prophylaxis

Nathan M. Thielman, MD, MPH
Assistant Professor, Department of Medicine, Division of Infectious Diseases and International Health, Duke University School of Medicine, Durham, North Carolina
Antibiotic-Associated Colitis; Enteric Fever and Other Causes of Abdominal Symptoms with Fever

David L. Thomas, MD
Professor, Johns Hopkins University School of Medicine and Johns Hopkins Hospital, Baltimore, Maryland
Hepatitis C

Anna R. Thorner, MD
Research Fellow, Department of Pathology, Harvard Medical School; Clinical and Research Fellow, Infectious Disease Division, Massachusetts General Hospital and Brigham and Women's Hospital, Boston, Massachusetts
Zoonotic Paramyxoviruses: Hendra, Nipah, and Menangle Viruses

Alan D. Tice, MD, FACP
Associate Professor, Infectious Diseases and Public Health Sciences, University of Hawaii at Mānoa John A. Burns School of Medicine; Active Medical Staff, Department of Internal Medicine, Queen's Medical Center, Honolulu, Hawaii
Outpatient Parenteral Antimicrobial Therapy

Angela María Tobón, MD
Scientific Advisor, Medical and Experimental Mycology Group, Corporación para Investigaciones Biólogicas (CIB); Department of Internal Medicine, Hospital La Maria, Medellin, Colombia
Paracoccidioides brasiliensis

Gregory C. Townsend, MD
Associate Professor, Department of Internal Medicine, University of Virginia School of Medicine, Charlottesville, Virginia
The Infectious Diseases Physician and Digital Resources

Edmund C. Tramont, MD
Director, Division of AIDS, National Institute of Allergy and Infectious Diseases, National Institutes of Health, Bethesda, Maryland
Innate (General or Nonspecific) Host Defense Mechanisms; *Treponema pallidum* (Syphilis)

John J. Treanor, MD
Professor of Medicine, Infectious Diseases Unit, University of Rochester School of Medicine and Dentistry; Attending Physician, Department of Medicine, Strong Memorial Hospital, Rochester, New York
Influenza Virus; Noroviruses and Other Caliciviruses; Astroviruses and Picobirnaviruses

Phoebe R. Trubowitz, MD
Oncologist, Department of Hematology/Oncology, Kaiser Permanente Northwest, Portland, Oregon
Malignancies in Human Immunodeficiency Virus Infection

Theodore F. Tsai, MD, MPH
Senior Director, Department of Vaccines, Global Medical Affairs, Wyeth, Collegeville, Pennsylvania
Orthoreoviruses and Orbiviruses; Coltiviruses and Seadornaviruses (Colorado Tick Fever); Flaviviruses (Yellow Fever, Dengue, Dengue Hemorrhagic Fever, Japanese Encephalitis, West Nile Encephalitis, St. Louis Encephalitis, Tick-Borne Encephalitis)

Allan R. Tunkel, MD, PhD
Professor of Medicine and Associate Dean for Admissions, Drexel University College of Medicine, Philadelphia, Pennsylvania
Topical Antibacterials; Approach to the Patient with Central Nervous System Infection; Acute Meningitis; Cerebrospinal Fluid Shunt Infections; Brain Abscess; Subdural Empyema, Epidural Abscess, and Suppurative Intracranial Thrombophlebitis; Viridans Streptococci, Groups C and G Streptococci, and *Gemella morbillorum*

Kenneth L. Tyler, MD
Reuler-Lewin Family Professor of Neurology and Professor of Medicine, Microbiology, and Immunology, University of Colorado School of Medicine; Chief, Neurology Service, Department of Neurology, Denver Veterans Affairs Medical Center, Denver, Colorado
Introduction to Viruses and Viral Diseases; Prions and Prion Diseases of the Central Nervous System (Transmissible Neurodegenerative Diseases)

Arthur O. Tzianabos, PhD
Associate Professor of Medicine, Harvard Medical School; Channing Laboratory, Department of Medicine, Brigham and Women's Hospital, Boston, Massachusetts
Anaerobic Infections: General Concepts

Jo-Anne Van Burik, MD, FACP
Associate Professor, Department of Medicine, University of Minnesota Medical School–Minneapolis, Minneapolis, Minnesota
Infections in Recipients of Hematopoietic Stem Cell Transplantation

Edouard Vannier, PhD
Assistant Professor, Department of Medicine, Tufts University School of Medicine; Attending Physician, Division of Geographic Medicine and Infectious Diseases, Tufts–New England Medical Center, Boston, Massachusetts
Babesia Species

David W. Vaughn, MD, MPH
Director, Military Infectious Diseases Research Program, U.S. Army Medical Research and Materiel Command, Fort Detrick, Maryland
Flaviviruses (Yellow Fever, Dengue, Dengue Hemorrhagic Fever, Japanese Encephalitis, West Nile Encephalitis, St. Louis Encephalitis, Tick-Borne Encephalitis)

Jan Verhoef, MD, PhD
Professor of Clinical Microbiology, Medical Microbiology, Utrecht University; Eijkman-Winkler Institute, University Medical Center, Utrecht, The Netherlands
Anaerobic Cocci; Anaerobic Gram-Positive Nonsporulating Bacilli

Paul E. Verweij, MD, PhD
Professor of Medicine (Medical Microbiology), Department of Medical Microbiology, University Medical Center St. Radboud, Nijmegen, The Netherlands
Infections in Patients with Hematologic Malignancies

Claudio Viscoli, MD
Professor, University of Genoa, Infectious Disease Unit, National Institute of Cancer Research, Genoa, Italy
Prophylaxis and Empirical Therapy for Infection in Cancer Patients

Paul A. Volberding, MD
Professor and Vice Chair, Department of Medicine, and Co-Director, UCSF-GIVI Center for AIDS Research, University of California, San Francisco, School of Medicine; Chief, Medical Service, San Francisco Veterans Affairs Medical Center, San Francisco, California
Malignancies in Human Immunodeficiency Virus Infection

Sanjivini Wadhwa, MD
Fellow in Infectious Disease, Department of Medicine, Harvard Medical School and Beth Israel Deaconess Medical Center, Boston, Massachusetts
Cytomegalovirus

David H. Walker, MD
Professor and Chairman, Department of Pathology; Executive Director, Center for Biodefense and Emerging Infectious Diseases, University of Texas Medical Branch, University of Texas Medical School at Galveston, Galveston, Texas
Rickettsia rickettsii and Other Spotted Fever Group Rickettsiae (Rocky Mountain Spotted Fever and Other Spotted Fevers); *Rickettsia prowazekii* (Epidemic or Louse-Borne Typhus); *Rickettsia typhi* (Murine Typhus); *Ehrlichia chaffeensis* (Human Monocytotropic Ehrlichiosis), *Anaplasma phagocytophilum* (Human Granulocytotropic Anaplasmosis), and Other Ehrlichieae

Richard J. Wallace, Jr., MD
Chairman, Department of Microbiology, University of Texas Health Center at Tyler, Tyler, Texas
Antimycobacterial Agents; Infections Due to Nontuberculous Mycobacteria

Peter D. Walzer, MD
Professor and Associate Chair for Research, Department of Internal Medicine, University of Cincinnati College of Medicine; Associate Chief of Staff, Department of Research Service, Veterans Affairs Medical Center, Cincinnati, Ohio
Pneumocystis Species

Christine A. Wanke, MD
Associate Professor, Department of Medicine, Tufts University School of Medicine; Director of Clinical HIV Research, Department of Medicine, Tufts–New England Medical Center, Boston, Massachusetts
Tropical Sprue/Enteropathy

John W. Warren, MD
Professor, Department of Medicine, Division of Infectious Diseases, University of Maryland School of Medicine, Baltimore, Maryland
Nosocomial Urinary Tract Infections

Ronald G. Washburn, MD
Professor, Department of Internal Medicine/Infectious Diseases, Louisiana State University School of Medicine in Shreveport; Chief, Department of Infectious Diseases, Shreveport Veterans Affairs Medical Center, Shreveport, Louisiana
Streptobacillus moniliformis (Rat-Bite Fever); *Spirillum minus* (Rat-Bite Fever)

David J. Weber, MD, MPH
Department of Medicine, Division of Infectious Diseases, University of North Carolina at Chapel Hill School of Medicine, Chapel Hill, North Carolina
The Acutely Ill Patient with Fever and Rash; Disinfection, Sterilization, and Control of Hospital Waste

Arnold N. Weinberg, MD
Professor of Medicine, Harvard Medical School; Physician and Associate Firm Chief, Department of Medicine and Infectious Disease, Massachusetts General Hospital, Boston, Massachusetts
Zoonoses

Geoffrey A. Weinberg, MD
Associate Professor, Department of Pediatrics, University of Rochester School of Medicine and Dentistry; Director, Pediatric HIV Program, Golisano Children's Hospital at Strong and Strong Memorial Hospital, Rochester, New York
Pediatric Human Immunodeficiency Virus Infection

Daniel Weisdorf, MD, FACP
Professor of Medicine and Director, Adult Blood and Marrow Transplant Program, Division of Hematology, Oncology, and Transplantation, Department of Medicine, University of Minnesota, Minneapolis, Minnesota
Infections in Recipients of Hematopoietic Stem Cell Transplantation

Louis M. Weiss, MD, MPH
Professor, Departments of Medicine (Division of Infectious Diseases) and Pathology (Division of Parasitology and Tropical Medicine), Albert Einstein College of Medicine of Yeshiva University; Attending Physician, Department of Medicine, Jack D. Weiler Hospital of the Albert Einstein College of Medicine—Montefiore Medical Center; Attending Physician, Department of Medicine, Jacobi Medical Center, Bronx, New York
Microsporidiosis

Michael E. Weiss, MD
Northwest Asthma and Allergy, Redmond, Washington
β-Lactam Allergy

David F. Welch, PhD
Associate Clinical Professor of Pathology, University of Texas Southwestern Medical Center at Dallas; Medical Microbiologist, Laboratory Corporation of America, Dallas, Texas
Bartonella, Including Cat-Scratch Disease

Thomas E. Wellems, MD, PhD
Head, Malaria Genetics Section, and Acting Chief, Laboratory of Malaria and Vector Research, National Institutes of Allergy and Infectious Diseases, National Institutes of Health, Bethesda, Maryland
Plasmodium Species (Malaria)

Richard P. Wenzel, MD, MSc
Professor and Chairman, Department of Internal Medicine, Virginia
Commonwealth University School of Medicine, Richmond, Virginia
 Organization for Infection Control; Isolation

Melinda Wharton, MD, MPH
Acting Deputy Director, National Immunization Program, Centers
for Disease Control and Prevention, Atlanta, Georgia
 Immunization

A. Clinton White, Jr., MD
Professor, Infectious Diseases Section, Department of Medicine,
Baylor College of Medicine; Chief, Infectious Diseases Section,
Department of Medicine, Ben Taub General Hospital, Houston,
Texas
 Cryptosporidiosis (*Cryptosporidium hominis, Cryptosporidium
 parvum*, and Other Species)

Richard J. Whitley, MD
Professor of Pediatrics, Microbiology, and Medicine; Loeb Scholar
in Pediatrics; Director, Division of Pediatric Infectious Diseases;
Vice-Chair, Department of Pediatrics; Senior Scientist, Department
of Gene Therapy; Senior Scientist, Cancer Research and Training
Center; Associate Director for Clinical Studies, Center for AIDS
Research; Director, Center for Biodefense and Emerging Infection,
University of Alabama School of Medicine, University of Alabama at
Birmingham, Birmingham, Alabama
 Varicella-Zoster Virus

Barbara Braunstein Wilson, MD
Associate Professor, Department of Dermatology, University
of Virginia School of Medicine, Charlottesville, Virginia
 Introduction to Ectoparasitic Diseases; Lice (Pediculosis); Scabies;
 Myiasis and Tungiasis; Mites (Including Chiggers); Ticks (Including
 Tick Paralysis)

Kenneth H. Wilson, MD
Professor, Department of Medicine, Duke University School of
Medicine; Chief, Infectious Diseases Section, Veterans Affairs
Medical Center, Durham, North Carolina
 Antibiotic-Associated Colitis

Walter R. Wilson, MD
Professor of Medicine, Division of Infectious Diseases, Mayo Clinic
College of Medicine; Consultant, Mayo Clinic, Rochester, Minnesota
 Infections of Prosthetic Valves and Other Cardiovascular Devices

Frank G. Witebsky, MD
Assistant Chief, Microbiology Service, Department of Laboratory
Medicine, Warren G. Magnuson Clinical Center, National Institutes
of Health, Bethesda, Maryland
 The Clinician and the Microbiology Laboratory

Peter F. Wright, MD
Professor of Pediatrics, Pathology, Microbiology, and Immunology,
and Head, Pediatric Infectious Diseases, Vanderbilt University
School of Medicine, Nashville, Tennessee
 Parainfluenza Viruses

Edward J. Young, MD
Professor, Department of Medicine and Molecular Virology and
Microbiology, Baylor College of Medicine; Staff Physician, Section
of Infectious Diseases, Veterans Affairs Medical Center,
Houston, Texas
 Brucella Species

Roger W. Yurt, MD
Johnson & Johnson Distinguished Professor and Vice Chairman,
Department of Surgery, Weill Medical College of Cornell University;
Director, William Randolph Hearst Burn Center, Department of
Surgery, New York–Presbyterian–Weill Cornell Medical Center, New
York, New York
 Burns

Stephen H. Zinner, MD
Charles S. Davidson Professor of Medicine, Harvard Medical
School, Boston; Chair of Medicine, Mount Auburn Hospital,
Cambridge, Massachusetts
 Sulfonamides and Trimethoprim

John J. Zurlo, MD
Professor, Department of Medicine, Division of Infectious Diseases
and Epidemiology, Pennsylvania State University, School of
Medicine, Hershey, Pennsylvania
 Pasteurella Species

PREFACE TO THE FIRST EDITION

Infectious diseases traverse the usual boundaries established by medical specialists. All organ systems may be involved, and all physicians caring for patients may have to deal with infected patients. The format of this book was chosen with the intent that it would contain the necessary information to aid the practitioner in the understanding, diagnosis, and treatment of infectious diseases. Thus, internists, family or general practitioners, pediatricians, surgeons, obstetrician-gynecologists, urologists, residents and fellows in training, medical students, hospital infection control personnel, and clinical microbiologists should find the book a valuable reference.

In planning this book the editors considered several different patterns of organization. The system adopted allows the reader to approach an infected patient three different ways: (a) by major clinical syndrome, (b) by specific etiologic organisms, and (c) by host characteristics for patients who are compromised.

Principles and Practice of Infectious Diseases consists of four major parts. The book may be perused as whole, or individual chapters may be examined when the reader is concerned with a specific problem. Part I covers the basic principles necessary for a clear understanding of the concepts of diagnosis and management of infectious disease. Chapters dealing with microbial virulence factors, host defense mechanisms, the epidemiology of infectious diseases, and the clinician and microbiology laboratory are included. In addition, there is a comprehensive discussion of anti-infective chemotherapy.

Part II considers major clinical syndromes. The syndromes are described, followed by a discussion of the potential etiologic agents, evaluation of differential diagnostic possibilities, and an outline of presumptive therapy. All major infectious diseases are discussed in this part of the book.

Part III describes all important pathogenic microbes for man and the diseases they cause. The pathogen is classified and described, the epidemiology is discussed, clinical manifestations are listed, and specific information on therapy and prevention is presented. The most comprehensive discussion of a disease entity can be found by reading about both the etiologic agent and the clinical syndrome. Thus, a comprehensive treatment of pneumococcal pneumonia could be found in reading the appropriate sections of the chapters on acute pneumonia and *Streptococcus pneumoniae.* We attempted to make the chapters dealing with etiologic agents and those dealing with syndromes complete. Therefore some repetition was unavoidable.

The final section, Part IV, covers special problems in infectious diseases including nosocomial infections, infections in impaired hosts, immunizations, and protection of travelers.

The editors are grateful to our expert contributors. These physicians are the world's leaders in their fields, and they diligently prepared carefully written, well-referenced "state of the art" chapters. Our secretaries were skillful and meticulous in their attention to the complexities of assembling *Principles and Practice of Infectious Diseases.* John de Carville, executive editor of John Wiley & Sons, encouraged, cajoled, and advised us from the formative steps all the way through to completion. Lastly, and perhaps most important, we are grateful to our wives and children for putting up with interminable editorial work and meetings.

GERALD L. MANDELL, M.D.
R. GORDON DOUGLAS, JR., M.D.
JOHN E. BENNETT, M.D.

PREFACE TO THE SIXTH EDITION

Knowledge about infectious diseases has undergone an extraordinary expansion during the years between publication of the fifth edition of this book, and this, the sixth one. During that time, previously unrecognized infections have emerged, and awareness of the role of microbes as potential agents of terrorism has been heightened. The population of patients whose host defenses are compromised by underlying diseases or by medical treatments continues to increase, and this has resulted in increasingly complex and challenging infections. In those years, important new advancements were made in the development of highly sensitive and specific diagnostic techniques, in antimicrobial therapy, in vaccines, and in appreciation of public health control measures against the spread of infectious diseases.

This new edition has attempted to capture this explosion of new knowledge in an authoritative, complete, yet readable and readily accessible text. Every chapter has been revised, and many new chapters have been added since the last edition. Examples of the latter include chapters on SARS, metapneumovirus, Nipah and Hendra viruses, uncommon fungi, bioterrorism agents, and hospital preparedness for emerging and highly contagious infections. New color figures and revised tables have been added throughout, which will facilitate use of the book.

The continually changing names of microorganisms remains a vexing challenge for infectious disease practitioners and book editors alike. For the sixth edition, we have generally adhered to the names of organisms given in the eighth edition of the *Manual of Clinical Microbiology,* ASM Press, 2003.

As always, a work of this magnitude is impossible without the contributions of our many authors, who brought extraordinary knowledge, experience, and perspective to each of their chapters. Their dedication to the goals of our book is a source of continued inspiration to us, for which we express a most heartfelt gratitude. We also want to express our appreciation for the superb assistance that has been provided by Janet Morgan and Stacy McGrath.

Finally, none of this would have been possible without the encouragement, understanding, and sometimes forbearance of Judy, Shirley, and Kelly, who once again saw their husbands through the process of bringing this book to fruition.

GERALD L. MANDELL, M.D.
JOHN E. BENNETT, M.D.
RAPHAEL DOLIN, M.D.

CONTENTS

PART II
MAJOR CLINICAL SYNDROMES

SECTION A

Fever, 703

SECTION B

Upper Respiratory Tract Infections, 747

SECTION C

Pleuropulmonary and Bronchial Infections, 803

SECTION D

Urinary Tract Infection, 875

SECTION E

Sepsis, 906

SECTION F

Intra-abdominal Infection, 927

VOLUME 2

PART III

INFECTIOUS DISEASES

AND THEIR ETIOLOGIC

AGENTS

CHAPTER **128**

Introduction to Viruses and Viral Diseases

TERENCE S. DERMODY

KENNETH L. TYLER

HISTORY

Viruses are enormously important human pathogens, accounting for considerable morbidity and mortality worldwide. Viral diseases in humans were first noted in ancient times and have played a major role in our history. Scientific approaches to the study of viruses and viral diseases began in the 19th century and led to the identification of specific disease entities of viral etiology. Careful clinical observations enabled the identification of many viral illnesses and allowed several viral diseases to be differentiated (e.g., smallpox versus chickenpox and measles versus rubella). Enhancements in pathologic techniques, exemplified by the work of Virchow, allowed the pathology of many viral diseases to be defined. Finally, the work of Pasteur led to the systematic use of laboratory animals for studies of the pathogenesis of infectious diseases, including those caused by viruses.

The first viruses were identified as the 19th century ended. Ivanovsky and Beijerinck identified tobacco mosaic virus, and Loeffler and Frosch discovered foot-and-mouth disease virus. These observations were quickly followed by the discovery of yellow fever virus and the seminal research on the pathogenesis of yellow fever by Walter Reed and the U. S. Army Yellow Fever Commission.[1] By the end of the 1930s, tumor viruses, bacteriophages, influenza virus, mumps virus, and many arthropod-borne viruses had been identified. This process of discovery has continued unabated to the present, with the human metapneumoviruses[2,3] (Chapter 156) and the severe acute respiratory syndrome (SARS) coronavirus[4-6] (Chapter 152) being the most recent additions to the catalog of human disease-causing viruses.

In the 1940s, Delbruck, Luria, and others used bacteriophages as models to establish many basic principles of microbial genetics and molecular biology and identified key steps in viral replication.[7,8] The pioneering experiments of Avery and associates on the transformation of pneumococci established that DNA is the genetic material[9] and set the stage for the experiments by Hershey and Chase[10] showing that the genetic material of bacteriophage T2 is also DNA. In the late 1940s, Enders and colleagues cultivated poliovirus in tissue culture.[11] This accomplishment led to the development of both formalin-inactivated (Salk)[12] and live-attenuated (Sabin)[13] vaccines for polio and ushered in the modern era of virology.

X-ray crystallography has allowed structures of viruses to be defined at an atomic level of resolution. Nucleotide sequences of entire genomes of most human viruses are known, and functional domains of many viral structural and enzymatic proteins have been defined. This information is being applied to the development of new strategies to diagnose viral illnesses and design effective antiviral therapies. Modern techniques to detect viral genomes, such as the polymerase chain reaction (PCR), have proved superior to conventional serologic assays and culture techniques for the diagnosis of many viral diseases. PCR-based strategies are now used routinely in the diagnosis of infections caused by enteroviruses, hepatitis C virus (HCV), herpesviruses, and human immunodeficiency virus (HIV).

Perhaps an even more exciting development is the means to introduce new genetic material into viral genomes. Strategies now exist in which specific mutations or even entire genes can be inserted into the genomes of many viruses. Such approaches can be exploited in the rational design of vaccines and the development of viral vectors for use in gene delivery. Among the challenges for the future will be the application of these powerful new techniques to expand an understanding of how viruses interact with target cells to alter their physiology, how the interactions of viruses and cells produce disease, and how events in the infected host result in transmission of disease and maintenance of infectious virus in the environment. Improved understanding of these aspects of viral infection should facilitate new approaches to the diagnosis, prevention, and treatment of viral diseases.

VIRUS STRUCTURE AND CLASSIFICATION

The first classification of viruses as a group distinct from other microorganisms was based on their capacity to pass through filters of a small pore size ("filterable agents"). Initial subclassifications were based primarily on pathologic properties such as specific organ tropism (e.g., hepatitis viruses) or common epidemiologic features such as transmission by arthropod vectors (e.g., arboviruses). Current classification systems are based on (1) the type and structure of the viral nucleic acid and the strategy used in its replication, (2) the type of symmetry of the virus capsid (helical versus icosahedral), and (3) the presence or absence of a lipid envelope (Table 128-1).

Virus particles or *virions* can be schematically represented as a delivery system that surrounds a payload (Fig. 128-1).[14] The delivery system consists of structural components used by the virus to survive in the environment and bind to host cells. The payload contains the viral genome and often includes enzymes required for the initial steps in viral replication. In virtually all cases, the delivery system must be removed from the virion to allow viral replication to commence.

In addition to facilitating attachment to target cells, the delivery system plays a crucial role in determining the mode of transmission between hosts. Viruses containing lipid envelopes are sensitive to desiccation in the environment and for the most part are transmitted by the respiratory, parenteral, and sexual routes. Nonenveloped viruses are stable to harsh environmental conditions and often are transmitted by the fecal-oral route.

Structural details of many viruses have now been defined at an atomic level of resolution (Fig. 128-2). General features of virus structure can be gained from examination of electron micrographs of negatively stained virions and thin-section electron micrographs of virus-infected tissues and cultured cells. These techniques allow rapid identification of viral size, shape, symmetry, and surface features; the presence or absence of an envelope; and the intracellular site of viral assembly. Cryo-electron microscopy and computer image-processing techniques have been used as powerful tools to determine the three-dimensional structures of spherical viruses at a level of resolution superior to that of negatively stained electron micrographs. A major advantage of cryo-electron microscopy is that it allows structural studies of viruses to be performed using conditions that do not alter native virion structure. High-resolution x-ray crystallographic techniques provide views of virus structure at an atomic level of resolution. In addition to providing information about virus structure, both image reconstructions of cryo-electron micrographs and x-ray crystallography can be used to investigate structural aspects of various virus functions, including binding to receptors[15-17] and interaction with antibodies.[18,19] Identification of key structural motifs, such as receptor binding sites or immunodominant domains, provides the framework for understanding the structural basis of virus-cell interactions.

Viral genomes exist in a variety of forms and sizes and are composed of either RNA or DNA (see Table 128-1). Viral genomes range in size from 3 kilobases in small viruses such as the Hepadnaviridae to more than 300 kilobases in large viruses such as the Poxviridae. The genomes of the smallest viruses encode only three or four proteins,

TABLE 128-1 Classification of Viruses

Family	Example	Type of Nucleic Acid	Genome Size (Kilobases or Kilobase Pairs)	Envelope	Capsid Symmetry
RNA-Containing Viruses					
Picornaviridae	Poliovirus	SS (+) RNA	7-8	No	I
Astroviridae	Astrovirus	SS (+) RNA	7-8	No	I
Caliciviridae	Norwalk virus	SS (+) RNA	8	No	I
Togaviridae	Rubella virus	SS (+) RNA	10-12	Yes	I
Flaviviridae	Yellow fever virus	SS (+) RNA	10-12	Yes	P
Coronaviridae	Coronavirus	SS (+) RNA	20-33	Yes	H
Rhabdoviridae	Rabies virus	SS (−) RNA	13-16	Yes	H
Paramyxoviridae	Measles virus	SS (−) RNA	15-16	Yes	H
Filoviridae	Ebola virus	SS (−) RNA	19	Yes	H
Arenaviridae	Lymphocytic choriomeningitis virus	2 circular SS (ambisense) RNA segments	5-7	Yes	H
Bunyaviridae	California encephalitis virus	3 circular SS (ambisense) RNA segments	10-23	Yes	H
Orthomyxoviridae	Influenza virus	8 SS (−) RNA segments*	12-15	Yes	H
Reoviridae	Rotavirus	10-12 DS RNA† segments	18-30	No	I
Retroviridae	HIV-1	2 identical SS (+) RNA segments	7-11	Yes	I—capsid H—nucleo-capsid
DNA-Containing Viruses					
Hepadnaviridae	Hepatitis B virus	Circular DS DNA with SS portions	3	Yes	I
Parvoviridae	Human parvovirus B19	SS (+) or (−) DNA	5	No	I
Polyomaviridae	JC virus	Circular DS DNA	5	No	I
Papillomaviridae	Human papillomavirus	Circular DS DNA	8	No	I
Adenoviridae	Adenovirus	Linear DS DNA	30-42	No	I
Herpesviridae	Herpes simplex virus	Linear DS DNA	120-220	Yes	I
Poxviridae	Vaccinia virus	Linear DS DNA with covalently closed ends	130-375	Yes	Complex

*Influenza C virus: seven segments.

†Reovirus and orbivirus, 10 segments; rotavirus, 11 segments; Colorado tick fever virus, 12 segments.

HIV, human immunodeficiency virus; DS, double stranded; SS, single stranded; (+), message sense; (−), complement of message sense; I, icosahedral; H, helical; P, polyhedral.

Information from Condit RC. Principles of virology. In: Knipe DM, Howley PM, eds. Fields Virology, 4th ed. Philadelphia: Lippincott-Raven; 2001:19-51.

whereas those of the largest viruses can encode several hundred. Viral genomes are either single or double stranded and are either circular or linear. RNA genomes are composed of either a single molecule of nucleic acid or multiple discrete segments. The number of RNA segments can vary from as few as 2 in the Arenaviridae to as many as 12 in some members of the Reoviridae. Viral nucleic acid is packaged in a protein coat, or *capsid*, that consists of multiple protein subunits. The combination of the viral nucleic acid and the surrounding protein capsid is referred to as the nucleocapsid (Fig. 128-3).

A number of general principles have emerged from studies of virus structure.[20] In almost all cases the capsid is composed of a repeating series of structurally similar subunits, each of which in turn is composed of only a few different proteins. The parsimonious use of structural proteins in a repetitive motif minimizes the amount of genetic information that must be committed to encode the capsid components. The repetition of subunits also leads to structural arrangements of virus capsids with symmetrical features. All but the most complex viruses exhibit either helical or icosahedral symmetry (see Table 128-1). Viruses with helical symmetry contain repeating protein subunits that are bound at regular intervals along a helical spiral formed by the viral nucleic acid. Interestingly, all animal viruses that show this type of symmetry have RNA genomes. Viruses with icosahedral symmetry usually have a spherical shape, with twofold, threefold, and fivefold axes of rotational symmetry. The nucleic acid is packed inside the spherical core and is intimately associated with specific viral capsid proteins.

The use of repeating subunits with symmetrical protein-protein interactions facilitates the assembly of the viral capsid. In most cases, viral assembly appears to be a spontaneous process that occurs under the appropriate physiologic conditions and often can be reproduced when recombinant viral proteins are expressed in the absence of viral replication.[21,22] For many viruses, assembly of the capsid proceeds through a series of intermediates or subassemblies, each of which nucleates the addition of subsequent components in the assembly sequence.

One of the most poorly understood aspects of viral assembly is the process that ensures that the viral nucleic acid is correctly packaged into the capsid. In the case of viruses with helical symmetry, there may be an initiation site on the nucleic acid to which the initial capsid protein subunit binds, triggering the addition of subsequent subunits. In preparations of many icosahedral viruses, empty capsids (i.e., capsids lacking nucleic acid) are frequently observed, indicating that assembly may proceed to completion without a requirement for the presence of the viral genome.

In some viruses, the nucleocapsid is surrounded by a lipid envelope acquired as the virus particle buds from the host cell cytoplasmic, nuclear, or endoplasmic reticular membrane (see Fig. 128-3). Inserted

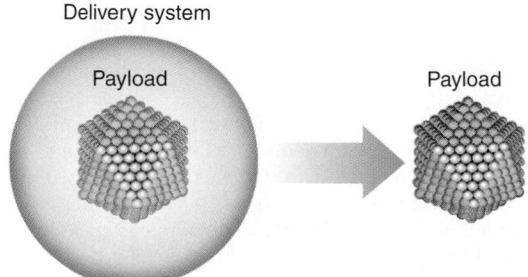

Delivery system

Payload → Payload

FIGURE 128-1. Schematic diagram of a virus particle. Viruses are simple structures consisting of a delivery system and a payload. The delivery system of a virus protects it against degradation in the environment and contains structures used to bind target cells in the host. The payload of a virus contains the genome and enzymes necessary to initiate the first steps in viral replication. *(Figure prepared by Dr. Mehmet Goral, Vanderbilt University.)*

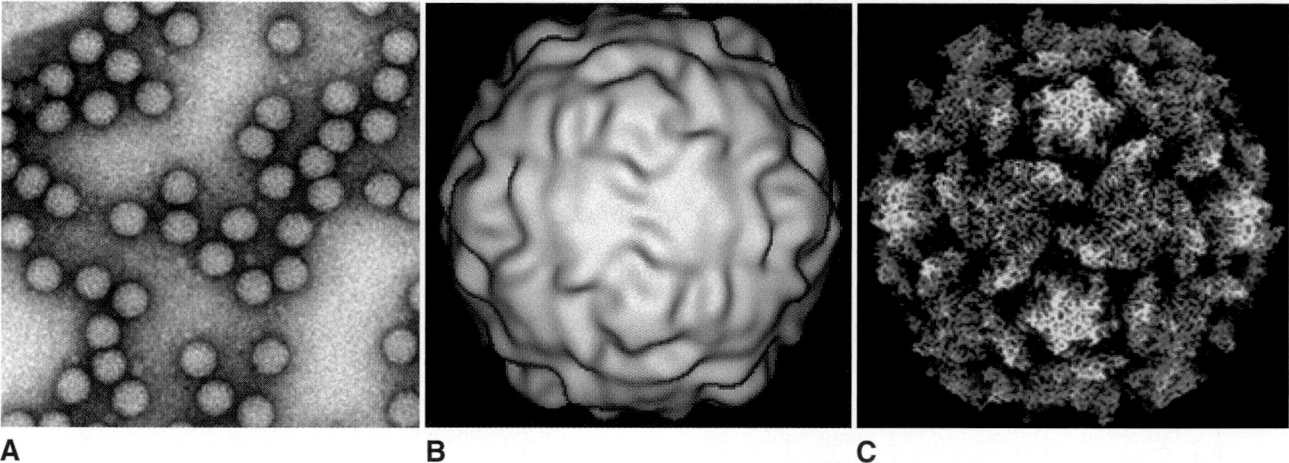

FIGURE 128-2. Structural studies of poliovirus. **A,** Negative-stained electron micrograph. **B,** Three-dimensional image reconstruction of multiple cryo-electron micrographs. **C,** Structure determined by x-ray crystallography. *(Figure prepared by Dr. James Hogle, Harvard University.)*

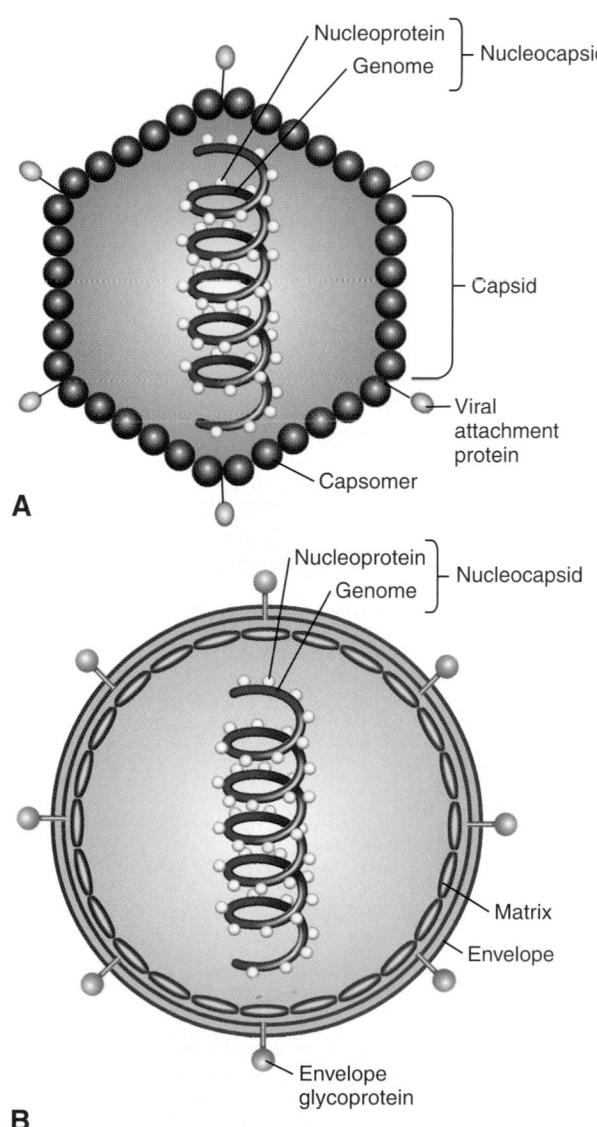

FIGURE 128-3. Schematic diagrams of the structure of (**A**) a nonenveloped icosahedral virus and (**B**) an enveloped helical virus. *(Figure prepared by Denise Wetzel, Vanderbilt University.)*

into this lipid bilayer are virus-encoded proteins (e.g., the hemagglutinin [HA] and neuraminidase proteins of influenza virus), which are exposed on the surface of the virus particle. These viral proteins typically contain a glycosylated hydrophilic external portion and internal hydrophobic domains that span the lipid membrane and serve to anchor the protein into the viral envelope. In some cases another viral protein, often termed a matrix protein, associates with the internal (cytoplasmic) surface of the lipid envelope, where it can interact with the cytoplasmic domains of the envelope glycoproteins. Matrix proteins may play roles in stabilizing the interaction between viral glycoproteins and the lipid envelope, in directing the viral genome to intracellular sites of viral assembly, or in facilitating viral budding. Matrix proteins can also influence a diverse set of cellular functions, such as inhibition of host cell transcription.[23,24]

VIRUS-CELL INTERACTIONS

Viruses require an intact cell to replicate and can direct the synthesis of hundreds to thousands of progeny viruses during a single cycle of infection. In contrast to other microorganisms, viruses do not replicate by binary fission. Instead, viruses must disassemble the infecting particle in order to direct synthesis of viral progeny.

Attachment

Viral replication occurs through an ordered series of steps (Table 128-2). The interaction between a virus and its target cell begins with attachment of the virus particle to specific receptors on the cell surface. Viral proteins that mediate the attachment function (viral attachment proteins) include single capsid components that extend from the virion surface, such as the attachment proteins of adenovirus,[25] reovirus,[26] and rotavirus[27,28]; surface glycoproteins of enveloped viruses, such as influenza virus (Fig. 128-4)[29,30] and HIV[31,32]; viral capsid proteins that form binding pockets that engage cellular receptors, such as the canyon formed by the capsid proteins of poliovirus[33] and rhinovirus[34]; or viral capsid proteins that contain extended loops capable of binding receptors, such as foot-and-mouth disease virus.[35] Until recently, a rather simple mechanism of viral attachment was envisaged in which the virus makes stable contact with the cell through a monophasic binding event involving one type of cellular receptor and a single structure on the virus. However, studies of the attachment of several diverse virus groups, including adenoviruses, coronaviruses, herpesviruses, lentiviruses, and reoviruses, are establishing a unifying mechanistic theme in which multiple interactions between virus and cell occur during the attachment step. These observations are reshaping thought on viral attachment so that the process is increasingly regarded as a sequential series of binding events between virus and cell that optimizes specificity and contributes significant stability to the association.[36]

One of the most dynamic areas of current research in virology concerns the identification of virus receptors on host cells. This interest stems in part from the critical importance of the attachment step as a determinant of target cell selection by many viruses. Many virus receptors have now been identified (Table 128-3), and three important principles have emerged from studies of these receptors. First, viruses have adapted to utilize cell surface molecules designed to facilitate a variety of normal cellular functions. Virus receptors may be either highly specialized proteins with limited tissue distribution such as complement receptors, growth factor receptors, or neurotransmitter receptors or more ubiquitous components of cellular membranes such as integrins and other intercellular adhesion molecules, phospholipids, or sialic acid–containing oligosaccharides. Second, many viruses use more than a single receptor to mediate multistep attachment and internalization. For example, adenovirus binds coxsackievirus and adenovirus receptor (CAR)[37] and the integrins $\alpha_V\beta_3$ or $\alpha_V\beta_5$[38]; herpes simplex virus (HSV) binds heparan sulfate[39-41] and herpesvirus entry mediator A (HVEM/HveA),[42] nectin 1 (PRR1/HveC),[43] or nectin 2 (PRR2/HveB)[44]; and HIV binds CD4[45,46] and chemokine receptors CXCR4[47,48] or CCR5.[49-51] Third, in many cases, receptor expression is not the sole determinant of viral tropism for particular cells and tissues in the host. Therefore, although receptor binding is the first step in the interaction between virus and cell, subsequent events in the viral replication cycle must also be supported for productive viral infection to occur.

TABLE 128-2 Stages in Virus-Cell Interaction

1. Attachment	5. Translation
2. Penetration	6. Replication
3. Disassembly	7. Assembly
4. Transcription	8. Release

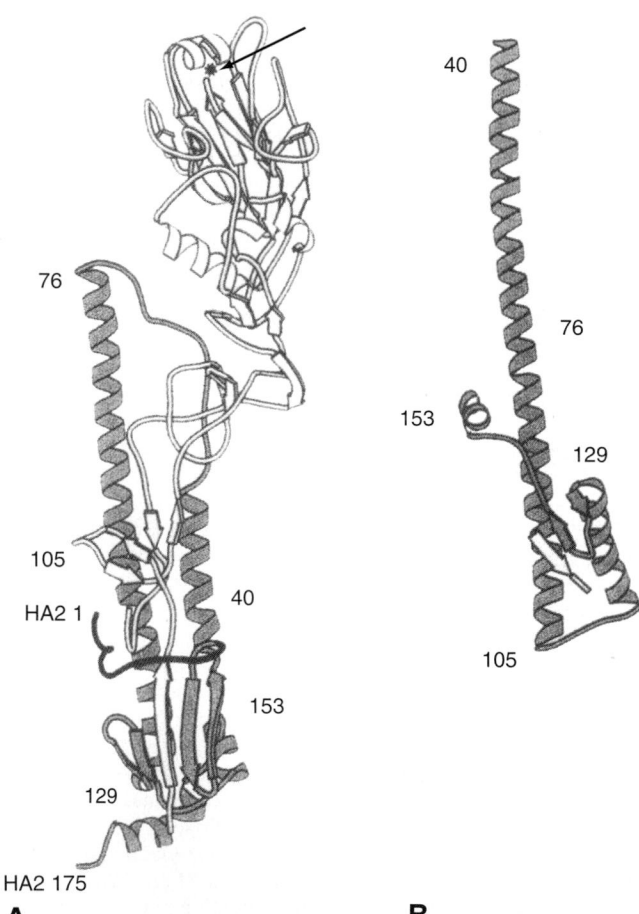

A

B

FIGURE 128-4. The folded structure of the influenza virus hemagglutinin (HA) and its rearrangement when exposed to low pH. **A,** The HA monomer. HA1 is light, HA2 is dark, and the fusion peptide at the amino terminus of HA2 is black. The receptor-binding pocket in the virion-distal domain of HA is indicated with an *arrow* and an *asterisk*. The viral membrane would be at the bottom of this figure. **B,** Conformational change in HA2 induced by exposure to low pH. Note the dramatic structural rearrangement in which amino acid residues 40 to 105 become a continuous α helix. Numbers indicate amino acid residues in HA2. *(From Harrison S, Wiley DC, Skehel JJ. Virus structure. In: Fields BN, ed. Fields Virology. 3rd ed. Philadelphia: Lippincott-Williams & Wilkins; 1995:59-99. Figure prepared by Drs. Donald Wiley and Frederick Hughson, Harvard University.)*

TABLE 128-3 Receptors for Selected Viruses

Virus	Receptor	Reference
Adenovirus	Coxsackievirus and adenovirus receptor (CAR)	37, 211
	CD46	212, 213
	Integrins $\alpha_V\beta_3$, $\alpha_V\beta_5$	38
Coronavirus	Carcinoembryonic antigen glycoprotein family	214-216
	Aminopeptidase N	217, 218
	Angiotensin-converting enzyme 2	219
	9-*O*-acetylated sialic acid–containing oligosaccharides	220
Coxsackievirus	Decay-accelerating factor (CD55)	221,222
	Integrin $\alpha_V\beta_3$	223
	Coxsackievirus and adenovirus receptor (CAR)	37
Cytomegalovirus	Heparan sulfate	224, 225
	Epidermal growth factor receptor	226
Echovirus	Integrin $\alpha_2\beta_1$	227
	Decay-accelerating factor (CD55)	228, 229
Epstein-Barr virus	Complement receptor 2 (CD21)	230, 231
Herpes simplex virus	Heparan sulfate	39-41
	Herpesvirus entry mediator (HVEM/HveA)	42
	Nectin 1 (PRR1/HveC)	43
	Nectin 2 (PRR2/HveB)	44
Human immunodeficiency virus	CD4	45, 46
	Chemokine receptor CXCR4	47, 48
	Chemokine receptor CCR5	49-51
Human T cell leukemia virus	Glucose transporter GLUT-1	232
Influenza virus	Sialic acid–containing oligosaccharides	30, 233
Lassa fever virus	α-Dystroglycan	234
Lymphocytic choriomeningitis virus	α-Dystroglycan	234
Measles virus	CD46	235, 236
	Signaling lymphocyte-activation molecule (SLAM)	237
Parvovirus (human)	Erythrocyte P antigen (globoside)	238
Parvovirus (canine and feline)	Transferrin receptor	239
Poliovirus	Poliovirus receptor (PVR)	144
Rabies virus	Acetylcholine receptor	147, 148
	Neural cell adhesion molecule	240
	Nerve growth factor receptor	241
	Gangliosides	242
Reovirus	Sialic acid–containing oligosaccharides	243-245
	Junctional adhesion molecule 1 (JAM1)	53, 246
Rhinovirus	Intercellular adhesion molecule 1 (ICAM-1)	247-249
Rotavirus	Sialic acid–containing oligosaccharides	250-253
Vesicular stomatitis virus	Phosphatidylserine	254

Several viruses bind receptors expressed at regions of cell-cell contact.[52] Junctional adhesion molecule 1, which serves as a receptor for reovirus,[53] and CAR, which serves as a receptor for some coxsackieviruses and adenoviruses,[37] are expressed at tight junctions.[54,55] Nectins, which serve as receptors for HSV,[43,44] are expressed at adherens junctions.[56,57] Interestingly, each of these viruses is capable of infecting both epithelial surfaces and neurons in some types of host organisms. Junctional regions are sites of enhanced membrane recycling, endocytic uptake, and intracellular signaling.[58] Therefore, it is possible that viruses have selected junction-associated proteins as receptors to usurp the physiologic functions of these molecules.

A detailed description of physical interactions between viruses and their receptors is beginning to emerge through high-resolution analyses performed with complexes of receptor and attachment protein. Structures of viral proteins or whole viral particles in complex with sialic acid have been determined for some viruses, including the influenza virus HA (see Fig. 128-4),[30,59] polyomavirus,[60,61] and foot-and-mouth disease virus.[62] Sialic acid binding in each of these cases occurs in a shallow groove at the surface of the viral protein; however, the architectures of the binding sites differ. In a few cases, the structures of complexes of viral proteins or viral particles and cell surface protein receptors have been determined. These include HIV gp120 and CD4,[32] adenovirus fiber knob and CAR,[63] HSV glycoprotein D and HVEM/HveA,[64] Epstein-Barr virus (EBV) gp42 and major histocompatibility complex (MHC) class II protein,[65] and rhinovirus bound to ICAM-1.[66] Although these studies have permitted examination of virus-receptor interactions at atomic resolution, they do not address the potential for more complex receptor engagement mechanisms that may represent the "functional" events leading to viral entry.

Penetration and Disassembly

Once attachment has occurred, the virus must penetrate the cell membrane and the capsid must undergo a series of disassembly steps (uncoating) that prepare the virus for the next steps in viral replication. Enveloped viruses such as the paramyxoviruses and retroviruses enter cells by fusion of the viral envelope with the cell membrane (Fig. 128-5).[67] The attachment of these viruses to the cell surface induces changes in viral envelope proteins required for membrane fusion. For example, the binding of CD4 and certain chemokine receptors by HIV envelope glycoprotein gp120 induces a series of conformational changes in gp120 that lead to exposure of transmembrane protein gp41.[68,69] Fusion of viral and cellular membranes proceeds through subsequent interactions of the hydrophobic gp41 fusion peptide with the cell membrane.[70-72] Paramyxoviruses enter cells by a mechanism analogous to that used by HIV. After receptor binding by the paramyxovirus G protein, a hydrophobic domain within the viral F protein mediates fusion of viral and cellular membranes.[73]

Other viruses enter cells by receptor-mediated endocytosis (see Fig. 128-5).[67] After receptor binding, virus-receptor complexes induce formation of clathrin-coated pits that invaginate from the cell membrane to form coated vesicles. These vesicles are rapidly uncoated and fuse with early endosomes, which sort internalized proteins for recycling to the cell surface or other cellular compartments, such as late endosomes or lysosomes.[74] Acidification of endosomes and lysosomes is mediated by vacuolar proton adenosine triphosphatases, and pH in the endocytic compartment varies from approximately 5.5 to 6.5 (early endosomes) to 5.0 to 5.5 (late endosomes and lysosomes).[75] For enveloped viruses such as influenza virus,[76,77] Semliki Forest virus,[78,79] and tick-borne encephalitis virus,[80] acid-dependent conformational changes involving envelope glycoproteins are required for fusion of the viral envelope with the endocytic membrane. High-resolution structures at acidic pH of the influenza virus HA demonstrate the dramatic alterations in the conformation of viral attachment proteins required for membrane fusion (see Fig. 128-4).[77]

Less is known about internalization and disassembly of nonenveloped viruses, which must traverse cell membranes without a fusion mechanism involving a viral envelope. Endocytic uptake and acidification are required for entry of some nonenveloped viruses, such as adenovirus,[81,82] astrovirus,[83] parvovirus,[84] reovirus,[85,86] and rhinovirus.[87] Moreover, proteolysis of certain capsid components by endosomal proteases also appears to be required for entry of some of these viruses.[88] However, other nonenveloped viruses, such as poliovirus[89-91] and rotavirus,[92-95] do not require endocytic uptake for cell entry and may enter host cells by direct penetration.

Genome Replication

Once a virus has entered a target cell, it must replicate its genome and proteins. Replication strategies used by single-stranded RNA-containing viruses depend on whether the genome can be used as messenger RNA (mRNA).[96] Translation-competent genomes, which include those of the coronaviruses, flaviviruses, picornaviruses, and togaviruses, are termed plus (+) sense and are translated by cellular ribosomes immediately after entry of the genome into the cytoplasm. For most viruses containing (+) sense RNA genomes, translation results in the synthesis of a large polyprotein that is cleaved into several smaller proteins through the action of viral proteases. One of these proteins is an RNA-dependent RNA polymerase, which replicates the viral RNA. Genome replication of (+) sense RNA-containing viruses requires synthesis of a minus (−) sense RNA intermediate, which serves as template for production of (+) sense genomic RNA.

A different strategy is used by viruses containing (−) sense RNA genomes. The genomes of these viruses, which include the filoviruses, orthomyxoviruses, paramyxoviruses, and rhabdoviruses, cannot serve directly as mRNA. The virions of these viruses must contain a preformed RNA-dependent RNA polymerase to transcribe (+) sense mRNAs using the (−) sense genomic RNA as template. Genome replication of (−) sense RNA-containing viruses requires synthesis of a (+) sense RNA intermediate, which serves as template for production of (−) sense genomic RNA. Mechanisms that regulate whether the (+) sense RNAs transcribed from (−) sense genomic RNA are used as templates for translation or genome replication are not well understood.

RNA-containing viruses belonging to the family Reoviridae have segmented double-stranded RNA genomes. The innermost protein shell of these viruses (termed a single-shelled particle or core) contains an RNA-dependent RNA polymerase that catalyzes the synthesis of (+) sense mRNA using as template the (−) sense strand of each double-stranded RNA segment. The mRNAs of these viruses are capped at their 5′-termini by virus-encoded enzymes and then extruded into the cytoplasm through channels in the single-shelled particle.[97]

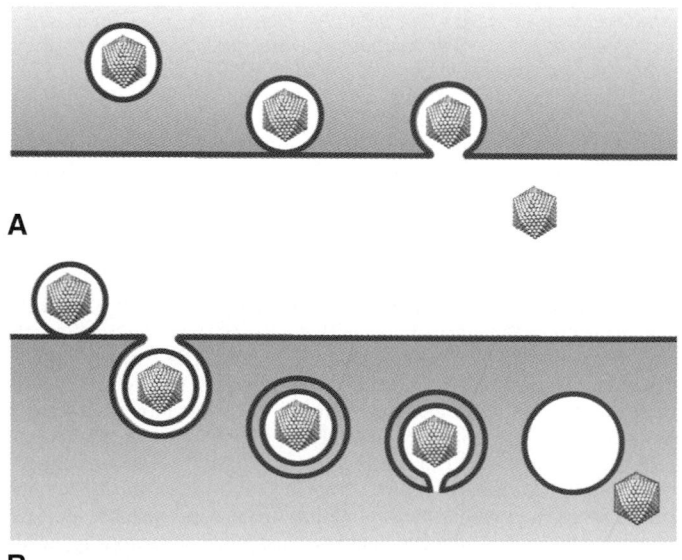

FIGURE 128-5. Mechanisms of viral entry into cells. **(A)** Viral penetration at the cell surface. **(B)** Viral internalization by receptor-mediated endocytosis. *(Figure prepared by Denise Wetzel, Vanderbilt University.)*

The (+) sense mRNAs also serve as template for replication of double-stranded RNA gene segments.

The retroviruses are RNA-containing viruses that replicate using a DNA intermediate.[98] The viral genomic RNA is (+) sense and single stranded; however, it does not serve as mRNA after viral entry. Instead, the retrovirus RNA genome is the template for synthesis of a double-stranded DNA copy, termed the provirus. Synthesis of the provirus is mediated by a virus-encoded RNA-dependent DNA polymerase or "reverse transcriptase," so named because of the reversal of genetic information from RNA to DNA. The provirus is translocated to the nucleus and is integrated into host DNA. Transcription of this integrated DNA is regulated for the most part by cellular transcriptional machinery. However, the human retroviruses HIV and human T-cell leukemia virus (HTLV) encode proteins that augment transcription of viral genes. It is also apparent that intracellular signaling pathways are capable of activating retroviral gene expression and play important roles in inducing high levels of viral replication in response to certain stimuli.[99] Transcription of the provirus yields mRNAs that encode viral proteins and genome-length RNAs that are packaged into progeny virions. Such a replication strategy results in persistent infection in the host because the viral genome is maintained in the host cell and replicated with each cell division.

With the exception of the poxviruses, viruses containing DNA genomes replicate in the nucleus and for the most part use cellular enzymes for transcription and replication of their genomes.[100] Transcription of most DNA-containing viruses is tightly regulated and results in synthesis of early and late mRNA transcripts. The early transcripts encode regulatory proteins and proteins important for DNA replication, and the late transcripts encode structural proteins. Several DNA-containing viruses, such as adenovirus and human papillomavirus (HPV), induce cells to express host proteins required for viral DNA replication by stimulating cell-cycle progression. For example, the HPV E7 protein binds the retinoblastoma gene product pRB and liberates transcription factor E2F, which induces the cell cycle.[101,102] To prevent programmed cell death in response to E7-mediated unscheduled cell-cycle progression, the HPV E6 protein mediates the ubiquitination and degradation of tumor suppressor protein p53.[103-105] An additional degree of complexity is added by the fact that some DNA-containing viruses, such as the herpesviruses, can establish latent infections in the host.[106] Unlike those of the retroviruses, genomes of the herpesviruses do not integrate into host chromosomes but instead exist as plasmid-like episomes. Mechanisms that govern latency establishment and reactivation are not well understood (see Chapter 131).

Cell Killing

Viral infection can compromise numerous cellular processes, such as nucleic acid and protein synthesis, maintenance of cytoskeletal architecture, and preservation of membrane integrity.[107] Many viruses are also capable of inducing the genetically programmed mechanism of cell death that leads to apoptosis of host cells.[108,109] Apoptotic cell death is characterized by cell shrinkage, membrane blebbing, condensation of nuclear chromatin, and activation of an endogenous endonuclease, which results in cleavage of cellular DNA into oligonucleosome-length DNA fragments.[110] These changes occur according to predetermined developmental programs or in response to certain environmental stimuli. In some cases, apoptosis may serve as an antiviral defense mechanism to limit viral replication by either destruction of virus-infected cells or reduction of potentially harmful inflammatory responses elicited by viral infection.[111] In other cases, apoptosis may result from viral induction of cellular factors required for efficient viral replication.[108,109] In a general sense, RNA-containing viruses, including influenza virus, measles virus, poliovirus, reovirus, and Sindbis virus, induce apoptosis of their host cells, whereas DNA-containing viruses, including adenovirus, cytomegalovirus (CMV), EBV, HPV, and the poxviruses, encode proteins that block apoptosis. For some viruses, the duration of the viral infectious cycle may determine whether apoptosis is induced or inhibited. Viruses capable of

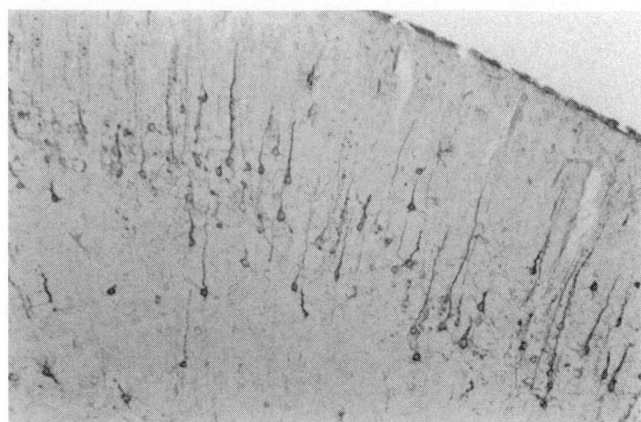

A

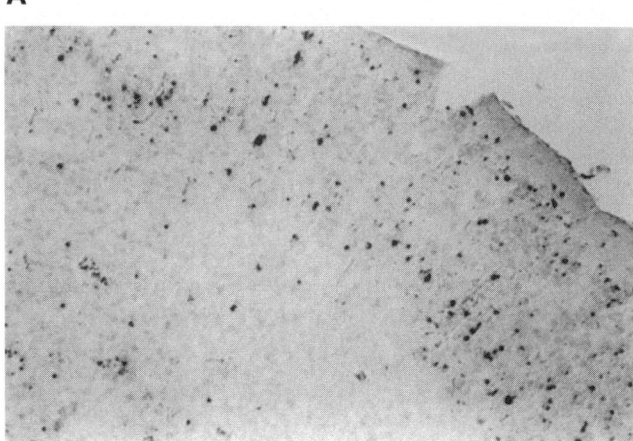

B

FIGURE 128-6. Reovirus induces apoptosis in the murine central nervous system. Cells staining positive for (**A**) reovirus antigen and (**B**) fragmented DNA using terminal deoxy-UTP nick-end labeling (TUNEL) in consecutive sections of cerebral cortex obtained from a newborn mouse 6 days after intracranial inoculation with reovirus strain type 3 Dearing. Reovirus antigen-positive cells contain a dark precipitate in the cytoplasm, including neuronal processes. TUNEL-positive cells contain a dark precipitate in the nucleus. Original magnification, ×25. *(Modified from Oberhaus SM, Smith RL, Clayton GH, et al. Reovirus infection and tissue injury in the mouse central nervous system are associated with apoptosis. J Virol. 1997;71:2100-2106.)*

completing an infectious cycle before induction of apoptosis would not require a means to inhibit this cellular response to viral infection. Interestingly, several viruses that cause encephalitis are capable of inducing apoptosis of infected neurons (Fig. 128-6).[112-114]

Antiviral Drugs

Knowledge of viral replication strategies has provided insights into critical steps in the viral life cycle that can serve as potential targets for antiviral therapy[115] (see Chapters 38 and 124). For example, drugs can be designed to interfere with virus binding to target cells or prevent penetration and disassembly once receptor engagement has occurred. Two currently available antiviral agents, amantadine and rimantadine, which are effective in prophylaxis and treatment of influenza A virus infection,[116] act by inhibiting viral disassembly.[117] Steps involved in the replication of the viral genome are also obvious targets for antiviral therapy. A number of currently available antiviral agents inhibit viral polymerases, including those active against herpesviruses (e.g., acyclovir) and HIV (e.g., zidovudine). Drugs that inhibit viral proteases have also been developed, and several are now used to treat HIV infection. These drugs block the processing of the Gag and Gag-Pol polyproteins and serve as potent inhibitors of HIV replication.[118] The use of these drugs in combination with agents that inhibit HIV reverse transcriptase has resulted in dramatic improvements in the survival of persons infected with HIV.[119] Other viral enzymes also serve as targets for antiviral therapy. The influenza virus neuraminidase is required for the release of progeny influenza virus particles from infected cells.[120] Oseltamivir and zanamivir bind the neuraminidase catalytic site and are potent inhibitors of the enzyme.[121] These drugs have been used in the prophylaxis and treatment of influenza virus infection.[116]

In the future, a better understanding of viral replication strategies and mechanisms of virus-induced cell killing will undoubtedly pave the way for the rational design of novel antiviral agents. One of the most exciting approaches to the development of antiviral agents is the use of high-resolution x-ray crystallography to optimize interactions between viral proteins and antiviral drugs. Such structure-based drug design has led to the development of new HIV antiviral therapeutics that inhibit viral entry by blocking gp41-mediated membrane fusion.[122]

VIRUS-HOST INTERACTION

One of the most fundamental challenges in virology is to apply knowledge gained from studies of virus-cell interactions in tissue culture systems to an understanding of how viruses interact with living hosts to produce disease. Virus-host interactions are often described in terms of pathogenesis and virulence. *Pathogenesis* is the process by which a virus interacts with its host in a discrete series of stages to produce disease (Table 128-4). *Virulence* is the capacity of a virus to produce disease in a susceptible host. Virulence is often measured in terms of the quantity of virus required to produce illness or death in 50% of a cohort of experimental animals infected with the virus. Virulence is dependent on both viral and host factors and must be measured using carefully defined conditions (e.g., virus strain, dose, and route of inoculation and host species, age, and immune status). In many cases, it has been possible to identify roles played by individual viral proteins at specific stages in viral pathogenesis and to define the importance of these proteins in viral virulence.

Entry into the Host

The first step in the process of virus-host interaction is the exposure of a susceptible host to viable virus under conditions that promote infection (Fig. 128-7).[123] Infectious virus may be present in respiratory droplets or aerosols, in fecally contaminated food or water, or in a body fluid or tissue (e.g., blood, saliva, urine, semen, or a transplanted organ) to which the susceptible host is exposed. In some cases, the virus is inoculated directly into the host through the bite of an animal vector or through the use of a contaminated needle.

Infection can also be transmitted from mother to infant through virus that has infected the placenta or birth canal or by virus in breast milk. In some cases, acute viral infections result from the reactivation of endogenous latent virus (e.g., reactivation of HSV giving rise to herpes labialis) rather than de novo exposure to exogenous virus.

Exposure of respiratory mucosa to virus by direct inoculation or inhalation is an important route of viral entry into the host. A simple cough can generate up to 10,000 small, potentially infectious aerosol particles, and a sneeze can produce nearly 2 million! The distribution of these particles depends on a variety of environmental factors, the most important of which are temperature, humidity, and air currents.

TABLE 128-4 Stages in Virus-Host Interaction
1. Entry into the host
2. Primary replication
3. Spread
4. Cell and tissue tropism
5. Secondary replication
6. Cell injury or persistence
7. Host immune response

In addition to these factors, particle size is an important determinant of particle distribution. In general, smaller particles remain airborne longer than larger ones. Particle size also contributes to particle fate after inhalation. Larger particles (>6 μm) are generally trapped in the nasal turbinates, whereas smaller particles may ultimately travel to the alveolar spaces of the lower respiratory tract.

Fecal-oral spread represents an additional important route of viral entry into the host. Food, water, or hands contaminated by infected fecal material can facilitate the entry of a virus through the mouth into the gastrointestinal tract. When a virus has reached the gastrointestinal tract, it faces formidable physicochemical challenges. Gastric contents are extremely acidic, at times approaching pH 2.0. Bile and proteolytic enzymes are secreted from the gallbladder and pancreas into the duodenum. Intestinal epithelial cells are covered by a carpet of mucus se-

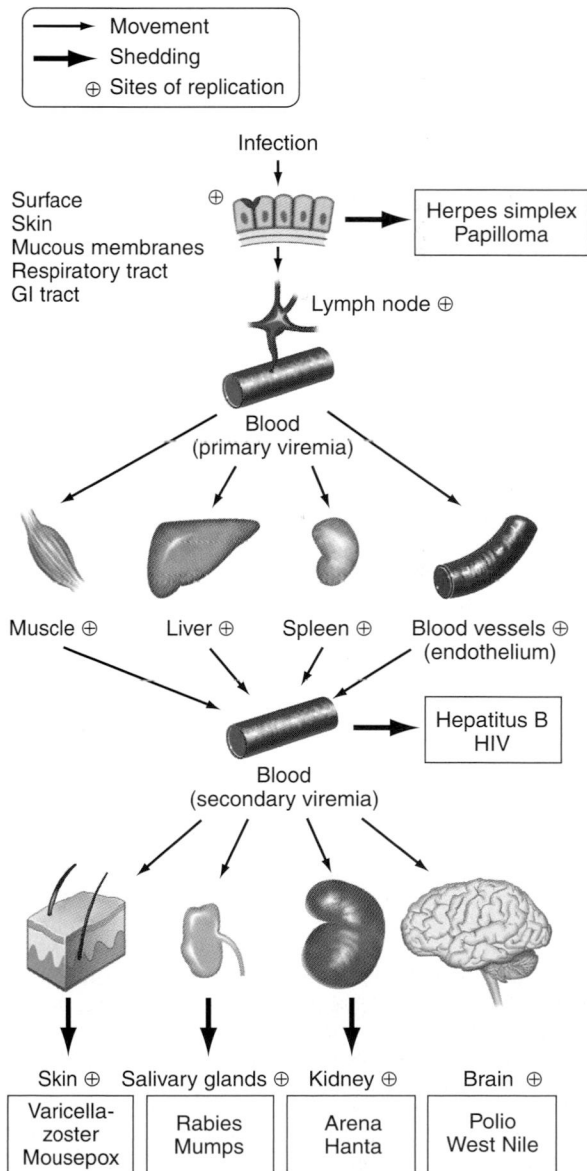

FIGURE 128-7. Entry and spread of viruses in human hosts. This scheme illustrates entry, primary replication, primary viremia, secondary replication, secondary viremia, and invasion of target organs. A few illustrative examples are shown. This scheme does not illustrate neural spread. GI, gastrointestinal; HIV, human immunodeficiency virus. *(Modified from Nathanson N, Tyler KL. Entry, dissemination, shedding, and transmission of viruses. In: Nathanson N, ed. Viral Pathogenesis. Philadelphia: Lippincott-Raven; 1997:13-33.)*

creted by adjacent goblet cells. Secretory immunoglobulin A as well as nonimmunoglobulin inhibitory substances are also present.

The environment of the gastrointestinal tract requires viruses that infect by this route to have certain physical properties. Viruses capable of enteric transmission must be acid stable and resistant to bile salts. Because conditions in the stomach and intestine are destructive to lipids contained in viral envelopes, most viruses spread by the fecal-oral route are nonenveloped. Interestingly, many viruses that enter the host through the gastrointestinal tract require proteolysis of certain capsid components to infect intestinal cells productively. Treatment of mice with inhibitors of intestinal proteases blocks infection by reovirus[124] and rotavirus,[125] which demonstrates the critical importance of proteolysis in the initiation of enteric infection by these viruses.

To produce systemic disease, a virus must cross the mucosal barrier that separates the luminal compartments of the respiratory, gastrointestinal, and genitourinary tracts from the host's parenchymal tissues. Studies with reovirus illustrate one strategy used by viruses to cross mucosal surfaces to invade the host after entry into the gastrointestinal tract.[126,127] After oral inoculation of mice, reovirus adheres to the surface of intestinal microfold cells (M cells) that overlie collections of intestinal lymphoid tissue (Peyer's patches). In electron micrographs, reovirus virions can be followed sequentially as they are transported within vesicles from the luminal to the subluminal surface of M cells. Virions subsequently appear within Peyer's patches and then spread to regional lymph nodes and extraintestinal lymphoid organs such as the spleen. A similar pathway of spread has been described for poliovirus[128] and HIV,[129] suggesting that M cells represent an important portal for viral invasion of the host after entry into the gastrointestinal tract.

Spread within the Host

Once a virus has entered the host, it can replicate locally or spread from the site of entry to distant organs to produce systemic disease (see Fig. 128-7). Examples of localized infections in which viral entry and replication occur at the same anatomic site include the respiratory infections caused by influenza virus, respiratory syncytial virus, and rhinovirus; the enteric infections produced by astrovirus, calicivirus, and rotavirus; and the dermatologic infections caused by HPV (warts) and paravaccinia virus (milker's nodules). Other viruses spread to distant sites in the host after primary replication at sites of entry. For example, poliovirus spreads from the gastrointestinal tract to the central nervous system (CNS) to produce meningitis, encephalitis, or poliomyelitis. Measles virus and varicella-zoster virus (VZV) enter the host through the respiratory tract and then spread to lymph nodes, skin, and viscera.

Release of some viruses occurs preferentially from either the apical or basolateral surface of polarized cells, such as epithelial cells.[130] In the case of enveloped viruses, polarized release is frequently determined by preferential sorting of envelope glycoproteins to sites of viral budding. Specific amino acid sequences in these viral proteins direct their transport to a particular cell surface.[131,132] Mechanisms responsible for polarized release of most nonenveloped viruses are not understood. Polarized release of virus at apical surfaces may facilitate local spread of infection, whereas release at basolateral surfaces may facilitate systematic invasion by providing virus access to subepithelial lymphoid, neural, or vascular tissues.

Many viruses use the blood stream to spread in the host from sites of primary replication to distant target tissues (see Fig. 128-7). In some cases, viruses may enter the blood stream directly, such as during a blood transfusion or an arthropod bite. More commonly, viruses enter the blood stream after replication at some primary site. Important sites of primary replication preceding hematogenous spread of viruses include Peyer's patches and mesenteric lymph nodes for enteric viruses, epithelial and alveolar cells for respiratory viruses, and subcutaneous tissue and skeletal muscle for alphaviruses and flaviviruses.

Classic studies by Fenner with mousepox (ectromelia) virus suggest that an initial low-titer viremia ("primary viremia") serves to seed

virus to a variety of organs where a period of further replication leads to a high-titer viremia ("secondary viremia") that disseminates virus to target organs (Fig. 128-8).[133] It is often difficult to identify primary and secondary viremias in naturally occurring viral infections. However, replication of many viruses in reticuloendothelial organs (liver, spleen, lymph nodes, and bone marrow), muscle, fat, and even vascular endothelial cells can play an important role in maintaining viremia.

Viruses that reach the blood stream may travel either free in plasma (e.g., enteroviruses and togaviruses) or in association with specific blood cells.[123] A number of viruses are spread hematogenously by macrophages (e.g., CMV, HIV, and measles virus) or lymphocytes (e.g., CMV, EBV, HIV, HTLV, and measles virus). Although many viruses have the capacity to agglutinate erythrocytes in vitro (a process called hemagglutination), only in exceptional cases (e.g., Colorado tick fever virus) have erythrocytes been shown to transport virus in the blood stream.

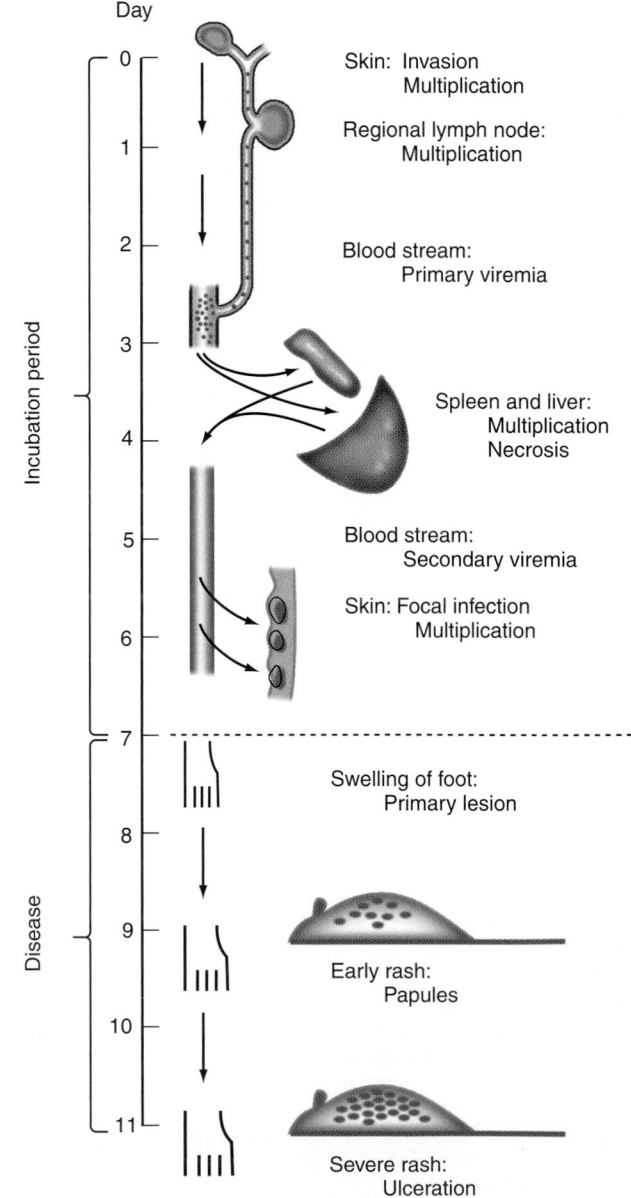

FIGURE 128-8. The pathogenesis of mousepox (ectromelia) virus infection. Successive waves of viremia are shown to seed the spleen and liver and then skin. *(From Fenner F. Mousepox [infectious ectromelia of mice]: A review. J Immunol. 1949;63:341-373. Copyright 1949, The American Association of Immunologists.)*

The maintenance of viremia depends on the interplay between factors that promote virus production and those that favor viral clearance. A number of variables have been identified that can affect the efficiency of virus removal from plasma. In general, the larger the viral particle, the more efficiently it is cleared. Viruses that induce high titers of neutralizing antibodies are more efficiently cleared than those that do not induce strong humoral immune responses. Finally, phagocytosis of virus by cells in the host reticuloendothelial system can contribute to viral clearance.

A major pathway used by viruses to spread from sites of primary replication to the nervous system is through nerves. A large number of diverse viruses, including Borna disease virus, coronavirus, HSV, poliovirus, rabies virus, reovirus, and Venezuelan equine encephalitis virus (VEE), are capable of neural spread. Several of these viruses, including rabies virus, have been shown to accumulate at the neuromuscular junction after inoculation and replication in skeletal muscle.[134,135] HSV also appears to enter nerve cells through receptors that are located primarily at synaptic endings rather than on the nerve cell body.[136] Spread to the CNS of both rabies virus[134,135] and HSV[137] can be inhibited by interruption of the appropriate nerves or by chemical agents that inhibit axonal transport. Neural spread of some of these viruses occurs by the microtubule-based system of fast axonal transport.[138]

Viruses are not limited to a single route of spread. VZV, for example, enters the host by the respiratory route and then spreads from respiratory epithelium to the reticuloendothelial system and skin through the blood stream. Infection of the skin produces the characteristic exanthem of chickenpox. The virus subsequently enters distal terminals of sensory neurons and travels to dorsal root ganglia, where it establishes latent infection. Reactivation of VZV from latency results in transport of the virus in sensory nerves to skin, where it gives rise to vesicular lesions in a dermatomal distribution characteristic of zoster or shingles.

Poliovirus is also capable of spreading by both hematogenous and neural routes. Poliovirus is generally thought to spread from the gastrointestinal tract to the CNS through the blood stream, although it has been suggested that the virus may spread through autonomic nerves in the intestine to the brain stem and spinal cord.[139,140] This hypothesis is supported by experiments using transgenic mice expressing the human poliovirus receptor.[141] When these mice are inoculated with poliovirus intramuscularly in the hind limb, virus does not reach the CNS if the sciatic nerve ipsilateral to the site of inoculation is sectioned.[142] When poliovirus reaches the CNS, axonal transport is the major route of viral dissemination. Similar mechanisms of spread may be used by other enteroviruses.

Tropism

The capacity of a virus to infect a distinct group of cells in the host is referred to as *tropism*. For many viruses, tropism is determined by the availability of virus receptors on the surface of a host cell. This concept was first appreciated in studies of poliovirus when it was recognized that the capacity of the virus to infect specific tissues paralleled its capacity to bind homogenates of the susceptible tissues in vitro.[143] The importance of receptor expression as a determinant of poliovirus tropism was conclusively demonstrated by showing that cells not permissive for poliovirus replication could be made permissive by recombinant expression of the poliovirus receptor.[144] In addition to poliovirus, the availability of virus receptors is a critical determinant of the tropism of many other viruses, including coronavirus,[145,146] HIV,[46] rabies virus,[147,148] and reovirus.[149,150]

However, attachment of a virus to its receptor is only the first in a series of events that lead to productive virus infection. In addition to the availability of virus receptors, tropism can be determined by postattachment steps in viral replication, such as the regulation of viral gene expression. For example, some viruses contain genetic elements, termed enhancers, that act to stimulate transcription of viral genes.[151,152] Some enhancers are active in virtually all types of cells, whereas others show exquisite tissue specificity. The promoter-enhancer region of the JC polyomavirus is active in cultured human glial cells but not in HeLa cervical epithelial cells.[153] This tissue-specific expression of the JC virus genome correlates well with the capacity of this virus in immunocompromised persons to produce progressive multifocal leukoencephalopathy, a disease in which JC virus infection is limited to oligodendroglia in the CNS.

Specific steps in virus-host interaction, such as the route of entry and pathway of spread, can also strongly influence viral tropism.[123] For example, encephalitis viruses such as VEE are transmitted to humans by insect bites. These viruses undergo primary replication and then spread to the CNS by both hematogenous and neural routes.[154] After oral inoculation, VEE is incapable of primary replication and spread to the CNS, illustrating that tropism can be determined by the site of entry into the host. Influenza virus buds exclusively from the apical surface of respiratory epithelial cells,[130] which may limit its capacity to spread within the host and infect cells at distant sites.

In addition to the route of entry and pathway of spread, a wide variety of host factors can influence viral tropism. These include age, nutritional status, and immune responsiveness as well as certain genetic polymorphisms that affect susceptibility to viral infection. Age-related susceptibility to infection is observed for many viruses, including reovirus,[155,156] respiratory syncytial virus,[157-159] and rotavirus.[160,161] The increased susceptibility of young children to infections by these viruses may in part be due to immaturity of the host immune response but also may be related to intrinsic age-specific factors that enhance host susceptibility to viral infection. Nutritional status is a critical determinant of the tropism and virulence of many viruses. For example, persons with vitamin A deficiency have enhanced susceptibility to measles virus infection.[162,163] Similarly, the outcome of most viral infections is strongly linked to the immune competence of the host.

The basis for genetic determinants of host susceptibility to viral infections is complex. Studies with inbred strains of mice indicate that genetic variations can alter susceptibility to viral disease by a variety of mechanisms.[164] These can involve differences in immune responses, variability in the capacity to induce antiviral mediators such as interferon, and the differential expression of functional virus receptors. Polymorphisms in the expression of chemokine receptor CCR5, which serves as a co-receptor for HIV,[49 51] are associated with alterations in susceptibility to HIV infection in humans.[165,166]

Persistent Infections

Many viruses are capable of establishing persistent infections, of which two types are recognized: chronic and latent.[123] *Chronic viral infections* are characterized by continuous shedding of virus for prolonged periods of time. Congenital infections with rubella virus and CMV and chronic infections with hepatitis B virus (HBV) and HCV are examples of chronic viral infections. Disease associated with chronic viral infections may be caused by progressive injury to host tissues as a consequence of viral infection or by immune-mediated destruction of virus-infected cells. *Latent viral infections* are characterized by maintenance of the viral genome in host cells in the absence of viral replication. Herpesviruses and retroviruses can establish latent infections. Disease produced by latent viral infections is usually associated with reactivation of productive viral infection with subsequent cytopathicity or alteration of cell-cycle control mechanisms leading to neoplasia. The distinction between chronic and latent infections is not readily apparent for some viruses, such as HIV, which can establish both chronic and latent infections in the host.[167-169]

Viruses capable of establishing persistent infections must have a means of evading the host immune response and a mechanism of attenuating their virulence.[123] Viruses use several strategies to evade immune-mediated clearance. Lentiviruses, such as equine infectious anemia virus[170] and HIV,[171-173] are capable of extensive antigenic variation resulting in escape from neutralizing-antibody responses of the host. Several viruses encode proteins that directly attenuate the host immune response. The adenovirus E3/19K protein blocks cell surface expression of MHC class I proteins, resulting in diminished presentation of viral antigens to cytotoxic T lymphocytes.[174] Similarly, the CMV US11 gene product downregulates MHC class I protein expression by targeting those molecules to proteasomes for degradation.[175] The poxviruses encode a variety of immunomodulatory molecules including CrmA, which is capable of blocking T-cell–mediated apoptosis of virus-infected cells.[176] Viruses capable of establishing latent infections can evade both humoral and cell-mediated immune responses by decreasing expression of viral proteins.

Many viruses that cause persistent infections can regulate their lytic potential. Some viruses, such as lymphocytic choriomeningitis virus (LCMV), which establishes persistent infections in rodents,[177] replicate without producing cell lysis or alterations in cell growth.[178] Cells infected with LCMV survive, and persistent infections are established. Other viruses must restrict viral gene expression or become less cytopathic (e.g., by selection of viral mutants that interfere with replication of wild-type virus) to establish persistent infections. For example, latent HSV infections of neurons are not associated with synthesis of viral proteins.[179]

A number of tissues within the host are preferred sites for establishment of persistent viral infections. Several viruses, including HSV, measles virus, poliovirus, JC virus, and VZV, establish persistent infections in the nervous system. HBV and HCV establish persistent infections in the liver, and CMV, EBV, HIV, and HTLV establish persistent infections in either lymphocytes or monocytes. In some cases (e.g., the CNS), preferential sites for persistent viral infections are not readily accessible to the immune system,[180] which may favor establishment of persistent infection.

Viruses and Cancer

Several viruses produce disease by promoting malignant transformation of host cells.[181] Work by Peyton Rous with an avian retrovirus was the first to demonstrate that viral infections can cause cancer.[182] Rous sarcoma virus encodes an oncogene, *v-src*, that is a homologue of a cellular proto-oncogene, *c-src*.[183,184] Cells infected with Rous sarcoma virus become transformed[185,186] and give rise to tumors as a consequence of perturbations of cell-cycle control mediated by the *v-src* gene product.[187-189] Several viruses are associated with malignancies in humans. EBV is associated with many neoplasms, including Burkitt's lymphoma, Hodgkin's disease, large B-cell lymphoma, leiomyosarcoma, and nasopharyngeal carcinoma. HBV and HCV are associated with hepatocellular carcinoma. HPV is associated with cervical cancer and a variety of anogenital neoplasms. Human herpesvirus 8 is associated with Kaposi's sarcoma and primary effusion lymphoma in persons with HIV infection.

In many cases, the linkage of a virus to a particular neoplasm can be attributed to transforming properties of the virus itself. For example, EBV encodes several latency-associated proteins that are responsible for immortalization of B cells; these proteins probably play crucial roles in the pathogenesis of EBV-associated malignancies.[190] Similarly, HPV encodes proteins that induce cell-cycle progression[101,102] and block apoptosis.[103-105] It is hypothesized that unregulated expression of these proteins induced by the aberrant integration of the HPV genome into host DNA is responsible for malignant transformation.[191]

In other cases, mechanisms of malignancy triggered by viral infection are less clear. HCV is an RNA-containing virus that lacks reverse transcriptase and a means of viral genome integration. However, chronic infection with HCV is strongly associated with hepatocellular cancer.[192] It is possible that increased cell turnover and inflammatory mediators elicited by chronic HCV infection increase the risk of genetic damage, which results in malignant transformation. Some HCV proteins may also play a contributory role in neoplasia. For example, the HCV core protein can protect cells against apoptosis induced by a variety of stimuli, including tumor necrosis factor-α.[193]

Viral Virulence Determinants

One of the most important areas of recent research in viral pathogenesis has been the identification of specific determinants of viral virulence. Although the nature of these "virulence determinants" varies for each virus group, a common theme is that virulence determinants are often viral surface proteins involved in attachment and entry. For example, polymorphisms in the attachment proteins of influenza virus,[194,195] polyomavirus,[196] reovirus,[197] rotavirus,[198] and VEE[199] are strongly linked to the virulence of these viruses. Polymorphisms in viral attachment proteins can influence virulence by altering the affinity of virus-receptor interactions or modulating the kinetics of viral disassembly. Sequences in viral genomes that do not encode protein can also influence viral virulence. Mutations that contribute to the attenuated virulence of the Sabin strains of poliovirus are located in the 5′ nontranslated region of the viral genome.[200] These mutations attenuate poliovirus virulence by altering the efficiency of viral protein synthesis.

A number of viruses encode proteins that enhance virulence by modulation of host immune responses.[123] In many cases, these proteins are dispensable for viral replication in cultured cells but are required for viral pathogenicity. In this way, immunomodulatory viral virulence determinants resemble classic bacterial virulence factors such as various types of secreted toxins. Viral virulence can also be altered by the introduction of immune modulators. A striking example of such an alteration was the construction of a mousepox virus variant capable of expressing interleukin-4.[201] The virulence of this virus was substantially enhanced in comparison with that of wild-type mousepox virus. Moreover, infection of previously immunized mice with the interleukin-4–expressing variant produced significant mortality. Concerns have been expressed about the exploitation of technologies that enhance viral virulence for use in bioterrorism.[202]

VIRUS-ENVIRONMENT INTERACTIONS

For a virus to survive in nature, the outcome of virus-host interaction must be the shedding of infectious virus into the environment in a manner that results in its spread to susceptible hosts. Viruses can be shed from infected hosts by a variety of mechanisms. Virus in respiratory secretions can be expelled in aerosols generated by coughing or sneezing. Virus in saliva can be transmitted through biting or intimate personal contact. Virus in feces can contaminate food or water. Virus in semen or genital secretions can be transmitted during sexual intercourse. Virus in blood can be transmitted by animal vectors. Each of these modes of transmission requires that the virus be stable (i.e., remain infectious) under defined environmental conditions. Because of the public health implications of viral stability in the environment, the effects of temperature, pH, and a variety of chemical and physical agents on the infectivity of a number of viruses have been defined.

In some cases, it is possible to correlate susceptibility of viruses to specific inactivating agents with particular aspects of virus structure. In the case of poliovirus, many conditions that result in viral inactivation (e.g., basic pH, heat, and ultraviolet irradiation) are associated with the loss or alteration of structural protein VP4.[203-205] Absence of functional VP4 promotes escape of viral RNA from the poliovirus capsid, which renders the virus noninfectious. Studies of the effects of chemical and physical inactivating agents on the infectivity of reovirus indicate that viral surface proteins play critical roles in determining viral susceptibility to inactivation.[206,207]

The effects of physical and chemical treatments on viral infectivity can be used to predict survival of viruses in the environment and facilitate development of rational inactivation strategies. Future directions for research on transmission of viruses between hosts will focus in part on defining how specific viral structural components determine the stability of viral particles in defined physicochemical settings. In addition to improving an understanding of factors that affect survival of viruses in the environment, this work is applicable to the development of viral vaccines with enhanced stability.

REFERENCES

1. Reed W. Recent researches concerning the etiology, propagation and prevention of yellow fever by the United States Army Commission. J Hyg. 1902;2:101-109.
2. van den Hoogen BG, de Jong JC, Groen J, et al. A newly discovered human pneumovirus isolated from young children with respiratory tract disease. Nat Med. 2001;7:719-724.

3. Boivin G, Abed Y, Pelletier G, et al. Virological features and clinical manifestations associated with human metapneumovirus: A new paramyxovirus responsible for acute respiratory-tract infections in all age groups. J Infect Dis. 2002;186:1330-1334.
4. Ksiazek TG, Erdman D, Goldsmith CS, et al. A novel coronavirus associated with severe acute respiratory syndrome. N Engl J Med. 2003;348:1953-1966.
5. Poutanen SM, Low DE, Henry B, et al. Identification of severe acute respiratory syndrome in Canada. N Engl J Med. 2003;348:1995-2005.
6. Drosten C, Gunther S, Preiser W, et al. Identification of a novel coronavirus in patients with severe acute respiratory syndrome. N Engl J Med. 2003;348:1967-1976.
7. Delbruck M. The growth of bacteriophage and lysis of the host. J Gen Physiol. 1940;23:643-660.
8. Luria SE. Bacteriophage: An essay on virus reproduction. Science. 1950;111: 507-511.
9. Avery OT, MacLeod CM, McCarty M. Studies on the chemical nature of the substance inducing transformation of pneumococcal types. Induction of transformation by a desoxyribonucleic acid fraction isolated from pneumococcus type III. J Exp Med 1944;79:137-158.
10. Hershey AD, Chase M. Independent functions of viral protein and nucleic acid in the growth of bacteriophage. J Gen Physiol. 1952;36:39-56.
11. Enders JF, Weller TH, Robbins FC. Cultivation of the Lansing strain of poliomyelitis virus in cultures of various human embryonic tissues. Science. 1949;109:85-87.
12. Salk JE. Studies in human subjects on active immunization against poliomyelitis. I. A preliminary report of experiments in progress. JAMA. 1953;151:1081-1098.
13. Sabin AB, Boulger LR. History of Sabin attenuated poliovirus oral live vaccine strains. J Biol Stand. 1973;1:115-118.
14. Nibert ML, Furlong DB, Fields BN. Mechanisms of viral pathogenesis: Distinct forms of reoviruses and their roles during replication in cells and host. J Clin Invest. 1991;88:727-734.
15. Chiu CY, Mathias P, Nemerow GR, Stewart PL. Structure of adenovirus complexed with its internalization receptor, αvβ5 integrin. J Virol. 1999;73:6759-6768.
16. He Y, Bowman VD, Mueller S, et al. Interaction of the poliovirus receptor with poliovirus. Proc Natl Acad Sci USA. 2000;97:79-84.
17. Xiao C, Bator CM, Bowman VD, et al. Interaction of coxsackievirus A21 with its cellular receptor, ICAM-1. J Virol. 2001;75:2444-2451.
18. Che Z, Olson NH, Leippe D, et al. Antibody-mediated neutralization of human rhinovirus 14 explored by means of cryoelectron microscopy and X-ray crystallography of virus-Fab complexes. J Virol. 1998;72:4610-4622.
19. Nason E, Wetzel J, Mukherjee S, et al. A monoclonal antibody specific for reovirus outer-capsid protein σ3 inhibits σ1-mediated hemagglutination by steric hindrance. J Virol. 2001;75:6625 6634.
20. Harrison S. Principles of virus structure. In: Knipe DM, Howley PM, eds. Fields Virology. 4th ed. Philadelphia: Lippincott-Raven; 2001:53-85.
21. Bertolotti-Ciarlet A, White LJ, Chen R, et al. Structural requirements for the assembly of Norwalk virus-like particles. J Virol. 2002;76:4044-4055.
22. Biemelt S, Sonnewald U, Galmbacher P, et al. Production of human papillomavirus type 16 virus like particles in transgenic plants. J Virol. 2003;77:9211-9220.
23. Ahmed M, Lyles DS. Effect of vesicular stomatitis virus matrix protein on transcription directed by host RNA polymerases I, II, and III. J Virol. 1998;72:8413-8419.
24. Ahmed M, McKenzie MO, Puckett S, et al. Ability of the matrix protein of vesicular stomatitis virus to suppress beta interferon gene expression is genetically correlated with the inhibition of host RNA and protein synthesis. J Virol. 2003;77:4646-4657.
25. van Raaij MJ, Mitraki A, Lavigne G, Cusack S. A triple β-spiral in the adenovirus fibre shaft reveals a new structural motif for a fibrous protein. Nature. 1999;401: 935-938.
26. Chappell JD, Prota A, Dermody TS, Stehle T. Crystal structure of reovirus attachment protein σ1 reveals evolutionary relationship to adenovirus fiber. EMBO J. 2002;21:1-11.
27. Shaw AL, Rothnagel R, Chen D, et al. Three-dimensional visualization of the rotavirus hemagglutinin structure. Cell. 1993;74:693-701.
28. Dormitzer PR, Sun ZY, Wagner G, Harrison SC. The rhesus rotavirus VP4 sialic acid binding domain has a galectin fold with a novel carbohydrate binding site. EMBO J. 2002;21:885-897.
29. Wilson IA, Skehel JJ, Wiley DC. Structure of the hemagglutinin membrane glycoprotein of influenza virus at 3 angstrom resolution. Nature. 1981;289:366-373.
30. Weis W, Brown JH, Cusack S, et al. Structure of the influenza virus haemagglutinin complexed with its receptor, sialic acid. Nature. 1988;333:426-431.
31. Lasky LA, Nakamura G, Smith DH, et al. Delineation of a region of the human immunodeficiency virus type 1 gp120 glycoprotein critical for interaction with the CD4 receptor. Cell. 1987;50:975-985.
32. Kwong PD, Wyatt R, Robinson J, et al. Structure of an HIV gp120 envelope glycoprotein in complex with the CD4 receptor and a neutralizing antibody. Nature. 1998;393:648-659.
33. Hogle JM, Chow M, Filman DJ. Three dimensional structure of poliovirus at 2.9 angstrom resolution. Science. 1985;229:1358-1365.
34. Rossmann MG, Arnold E, Erickson JW, et al. Structure of a human common cold virus and functional relationship to other picornaviruses. Nature. 1985;317:145-153.
35. Acharya R, Fry E, Stuart D, et al. The three dimensional structure of foot-and-mouth disease virus at 2.9 angstrom resolution. Nature. 1989;327:709-716.
36. Haywood AM. Virus receptors: Binding, adhesion strengthening, and changes in viral structure. J Virol. 1994;68:1-5.
37. Bergelson JM, Cunningham JA, Droguett G, et al. Isolation of a common receptor for Coxsackie B viruses and adenoviruses 2 and 5. Science. 1997;275:1320-1323.
38. Wickman TJ, Mathias P, Cheresh DA, Nemerow GR. Integrins alpha v beta 3 and alpha v beta 5 promote adenovirus internalization but not virus attachment. Cell. 1993;73:309-319.
39. WuDunn D, Spear PG. Initial interaction of herpes simplex virus with cells is binding to heparan sulfate. J Virol. 1989;63:52-58.
40. Lycke E, Johansson M, Svennerholm B, Lindahl U. Binding of herpes simplex virus to cellular heparan sulphate; an initial step in the adsorption process. J Gen Virol. 1991;72:1131-1137.
41. Shieh MT, WuDunn D, Montgomery RI, et al. Cell surface receptors for herpes simplex virus are heparan sulfate proteoglycans. J Cell Biol. 1992;116:1273-1281.
42. Montgomery RI, Warner MS, Lum BJ, Spear PG. Herpes simplex virus-1 entry into cells mediated by a novel member of the TNF/NGF receptor family. Cell. 1996;87:427-436.
43. Geraghty RJ, Krummenacher C, Cohen GH, et al. Entry of alphaherpesviruses mediated by poliovirus receptor-related protein 1 and poliovirus receptor. Science. 1998;280:1618-1620.
44. Warner MS, Geraghty RJ, Martinez WM, et al. A cell surface protein with herpesvirus entry activity (HveB) confers susceptibility to infection by mutants of herpes simplex virus type 1, herpes simplex virus type 2, and pseudorabies virus. Virology. 1998;246:179-189.
45. Dalgleish AG, Beverley PCL, Clapham PR, et al. The CD4 (T4) antigen is an essential component of the receptor for the AIDS retrovirus. Nature. 1984;312:763-767.
46. Maddon PJ, Dalgleish AG, McDougal JS, et al. The T4 gene encodes the AIDS virus receptor and is expressed in the immune system and the brain. Cell. 1986;47:333-348.
47. Feng Y, Broder CC, Kennedy PE, Berger EA. HIV-1 entry cofactor: Functional cDNA cloning of a seven-transmembrane, G protein-coupled receptor. Science. 1996; 272:872-877.
48. Oberlin E, Amara A, Bachelerie F, et al. The CXC chemokine SDF-1 is the ligand for LESTR/fusin and prevents infection by T-cell-line-adapted HIV-1. Nature. 1996;382:833-835.
49. Deng H, Liu R, Ellmeier W, et al. Identification of a major co-receptor for primary isolates of HIV-1. Nature. 1996;381:661-666.
50. Dragic T, Litwin V, Allaway GP, et al. HIV-1 entry into CD4⁺ cells is mediated by the chemokine receptor CC-CKR-5. Nature. 1996;381:667-673.
51. Alkhatib G, Combadiere C, Broder CC, et al. CC CKR5: A RANTES, MIP-1alpha, MIP-1beta receptor as a fusion cofactor for macrophage-tropic HIV-1. Science. 1996;272:1955-1958.
52. Spear PG. Viral interactions with receptors in cell junctions and effects on junctional stability. Dev Cell. 2002;3:462-464.
53. Barton ES, Forrest JC, Connolly JL, et al. Junction adhesion molecule is a receptor for reovirus. Cell. 2001;104:441-451.
54. Martin-Padura I, Lostaglio S, Schneemann M, et al. Junctional adhesion molecule, a novel member of the immunoglobulin superfamily that distributes at intercellular junctions and modulates monocyte transmigration. J Cell Biol. 1998;142:117-127.
55. Cohen CJ, Shieh JT, Pickles RJ, et al. The coxsackievirus and adenovirus receptor is a transmembrane component of the tight junction. Proc Natl Acad Sci USA. 2001;98:15191-15196.
56. Takahashi K, Nakanishi H, Miyahara M, et al. Nectin/PRR: An immunoglobulin-like cell adhesion molecule recruited to cadherin-based adherens junctions through interaction with Afadin, a PDZ domain-containing protein. J Cell Biol. 1999;145:539-549.
57. Yoon M, Spear PG. Disruption of adherens junctions liberates nectin-1 to serve as receptor for herpes simplex virus and pseudorabies virus entry. J Virol. 2002;76:7203-7208.
58. Zahraoui A, Louvard D, Galli T. Tight junction, a platform for trafficking and signaling protein complexes. J Cell Biol. 2000;151:F31-36.
59. Eisen MB, Sabesan S, Skehel JJ, Wiley DC. Binding of the influenza A virus to cell-surface receptors: Structures of five hemagglutinin-sialyloligosaccharide complexes determined by X-ray crystallography. Virology. 1997;232:19-31.
60. Stehle T, Yan Y, Benjamin TL, Harrison SC. Structure of murine polyomavirus complexed with an oligosaccharide receptor fragment. Nature. 1994;369:160-163.
61. Stehle T, Harrison SC. High-resolution structure of a polyomavirus VP1-oligosaccharide complex: Implications for assembly and receptor binding. EMBO J. 1997;16:5139-5148.
62. Fry EE, Lea SM, Jackson T, et al. The structure and function of a foot-and-mouth disease virus-oligosaccharide receptor complex. EMBO J. 1999;18:543-554.
63. Bewley MC, Springer K, Zhang YB, et al. Structural analysis of the mechanism of adenovirus binding to its human cellular receptor, CAR. Science. 1999;286:1579-1583.
64. Carfi A, Willis SH, Whitbeck JC, et al. Herpes simplex virus glycoprotein D bound to the human receptor HveA. Mol Cell. 2001;8:169-179.
65. Mullen MM, Haan KM, Longnecker R, Jardetzky TS. Structure of the Epstein-Barr virus gp42 protein bound to the MHC class II receptor HLA-DR1. Mol Cell. 2002;9:375-385.
66. Kolatkar PR, Bella J, Olson NH, et al. Structural studies of two rhinovirus serotypes complexed with fragments of their cellular receptor. EMBO J. 1999;18:6249-6259.
67. Young JAT. Virus entry and uncoating. In: Knipe DM, Howley PM, eds. Fields Virology. 4th ed. Philadelphia: Lippincott-Raven; 2001:87-103.
68. Doranz BJ, Berson JF, Rucker J, Doms RW. Chemokine receptors as fusion cofactors for human immunodeficiency virus type 1 (HIV-1). Immunol Res. 1997;16:15-28.
69. Moore JP, Trkola A, Dragic T. Co-receptors for HIV-1 entry. Curr Opin Immunol. 1997;9:551-562.
70. Kowalski M, Potz J, Basiripour L, et al. Functional regions of the envelope glycoprotein of human immunodeficiency virus type 1. Science. 1988;237:1351-1355.
71. Sattentau QJ. CD4 activation of HIV fusion. Int J Cell Clon. 1992;10:323-332.
72. Weissenhorn W, Dessen A, Harrison SC, et al. Atomic structure of the ectodomain from HIV-1 gp41. Nature. 1997;387:426-430.
73. Dutch RE, Jardetzky TS, Lamb RA. Virus membrane fusion proteins: Biological machines that undergo a metamorphosis. Biosci Rep. 2000;20:597-612.
74. Trowbridge IS, Collawn JE, Hopkins CR. Signal-dependent membrane protein trafficking in the endocytic pathway. Annu Rev Cell Biol. 1993;9:129-161.

75. Mellman I, Fuchs R, Helenius A. Acidification of the endocytic and exocytic pathways. Annu Rev Biochem. 1986;55:663-700.

76. Stegmann T, White JM, Helenius A. Intermediates in influenza induced membrane fusion. EMBO J. 1990;9:4231-4241.

77. Bullough PA, Hughson FM, Skehel JJ, Wiley DC. Structure of influenza haemagglutinin at the pH of membrane fusion. Nature. 1994;371:37-43.

78. Kielian MC, Helenius A. pH-induced alterations in the fusogenic spike protein of Semliki Forest virus. J Cell Biol. 1985;101:2284-2291.

79. Wahlberg JM, Bron R, Wischut J, Garoff H. Membrane fusion of Semliki Forest virus involves homotrimers of the fusion protein. J Virol. 1992;66:7309-7318.

80. Allison SL, Schalich J, Stiansy K, et al. Oligomeric rearrangement of tick-borne encephalitis virus envelope proteins induced by an acidic pH. J Virol. 1995;69:695-700.

81. Varga MJ, Weibull C, Everitt E. Infectious entry pathway of adenovirus type 2. J Virol. 1991;65:6061-6070.

82. Greber UF, Willetts M, Webster P, Helenius A. Stepwise dismantling of adenovirus 2 during entry into cells. Cell. 1993;75:477-486.

83. Donelli G, Superti F, Tinari A, Marziano ML. Mechanism of astrovirus entry into Graham 293 cells. J Med Virol. 1992;38:271-277.

84. Basak S, Turner H. Infectious entry pathway for canine parvovirus. Virology. 1992;186:368-376.

85. Maratos-Flier E, Goodman MJ, Murray AH, Kahn CR. Ammonium inhibits processing and cytotoxicity of reovirus, a nonenveloped virus. J Clin Invest. 1986;78:617-625.

86. Sturzenbecker LJ, Nibert ML, Furlong DB, Fields BN. Intracellular digestion of reovirus particles requires a low pH and is an essential step in the viral infectious cycle. J Virol. 1987;61:2351-2361.

87. Prchla E, Kuechler E, Blaas D, Fuchs R. Uncoating of human rhinovirus serotype 2 from late endosomes. J Virol. 1994;68:3713-3723.

88. Ebert DH, Deussing J, Peters C, Dermody TS. Cathepsin L and cathepsin B mediate reovirus disassembly in murine fibroblast cells. J Biol Chem. 2002;277:24609-24617.

89. Kaplan G, Freistadt MS, Racaniello VR. Neutralization of poliovirus by cell receptors expressed in insect cells. J Virol. 1990;64:4697-4702.

90. Curry S, Chow M, Hogle JM. The poliovirus 135S particle is infectious. J Virol. 1996;70:7125-7131.

91. Tosteson MT, Chow M. Characterization of the ion channels formed by poliovirus in planar lipid membranes. J Virol. 1997;71:507-511.

92. Kaijot J-KT, Shaw RD, Rubin DH, Greenberg HB. Infectious rotavirus enters cells by direct cell membrane penetration, not by endocytosis. J Virol. 1988;62:1136-1144.

93. Nandi P, Charpilienne A, Cohen J. Interaction of rotavirus particles with liposomes. J Virol. 1992;66:3363-3367.

94. Ruiz MC, Alonso-Torre SR, Charpilienne A, et al. Rotavirus interaction with isolated membrane vesicles. J Virol. 1994;68:4009-4016.

95. Falconer MM, Gilbert JM, Roper AM, et al. Rotavirus-induced fusion from without in tissue culture cells. J Virol. 1995;69:5582-5591.

96. Ball LA. Replication strategies of RNA viruses. In: Knipe DM, Howley PM, eds. Fields Virology. 4th ed. Philadelphia: Lippincott-Raven; 2001:105-118.

97. Lawton JA, Estes MK, Prasad BVV. Three-dimensional visualization of mRNA release from actively transcribing rotavirus particles. Nat Struct Biol. 1997;4:118-121.

98. Goff SP. Retroviridae: The retroviruses and their replication. In: Knipe DM, Howley PM, eds. Fields Virology. 4th ed. Philadelphia: Lippincott-Raven; 2001:1871-1939.

99. Nabel GJ. The role of cellular transcription factors in the regulation of human immunodeficiency virus gene expression. In: Cullen BR, ed. Human Retroviruses. Oxford: IRL Press; 1993:49-73.

100. DiMaio D, Coen DM. Replication strategies of DNA viruses. In: Knipe DM, Howley PM, eds. Fields Virology. 4th ed. Philadelphia: Lippincott-Raven; 2001:119-132.

101. Dyson N, Howley PM, Munger K, Harlow E. The human papilloma virus-16 E7 oncoprotein is able to bind to the retinoblastoma gene product. Science. 1989;243:934-937.

102. Dyson N, Guida P, Munger K, Harlow E. Homologous sequences in adenovirus E1A and human papillomavirus E7 proteins mediate interaction with the same set of cellular proteins. J Virol. 1992;66:6893-6902.

103. Scheffner M, Werness BA, Huibregtse JM, et al. The E6 oncoprotein encoded by human papillomavirus types 16 and 18 promotes the degradation of p53. Cell. 1990; 63:1129-1136.

104. Werness BA, Levine AJ, Howley PM. Association of human papillomavirus types 16 and 18 E6 proteins with p53. Science. 1990;248:76-79.

105. Scheffner M, Huibregtse JM, Vierstra RD, Howley PM. The HPV-16 E6 and E6-AP complex functions as a ubiquitin-protein ligase in the ubiquitination of p53. Cell. 1993;75:495-505.

106. Roizman B, Pellett PE. The family Herpesviridae: A brief introduction. In: Knipe DM, Howley PM, eds. Fields Virology. 4th ed. Philadelphia: Lippincott-Raven; 2001:2381-2397.

107. Wagner RR. Cytopathic effects of viruses: A general survey. In: Fraenkel-Conrat H, Wagner RR, eds. Comprehensive Virology. New York: Plenum Press; 1984:1-63.

108. O'Brien V. Viruses and apoptosis. J Gen Virol. 1998;79:1833-1845.

109. Roulston A, Marcellus RC, Branton PE. Viruses and apoptosis. Annu Rev Microbiol. 1999;53:577-628.

110. Wyllie AH, Kerr JFR, Currie AR. Cell death: the significance of apoptosis. Int Rev Cytol. 1980;68:251-306.

111. Everett H, McFadden G. Apoptosis: an innate immune response to virus infection. Trends Microbiol. 1999;7:160-165.

112. Lewis J, Wesselingh SL, Griffin DE, Hardwick JM. Alphavirus-induced apoptosis in mouse brains correlates with neurovirulence. J Virol. 1996;70:1828-1835.

113. Jackson AC, Rossiter JP. Apoptosis plays an important role in experimental rabies virus infection. J Virol. 1997;71:5603-5607.

114. Oberhaus SM, Smith RL, Clayton GH, et al. Reovirus infection and tissue injury in the mouse central nervous system are associated with apoptosis. J Virol. 1997;71:2100-2106.

115. Crumpacker C. Antiviral therapy. In: Knipe DM, Howley PM, eds. Fields Virology. 4th ed. Philadelphia: Lippincott-Raven; 2001:393-433.

116. Stiver G. The treatment of influenza with antiviral drugs. CMAJ. 2003;168:49-56.

117. Wang C, Takeuchi K, Pinto L, Lamb R. Ion channel activity of influenza A virus M2 protein: Characterization of the amantadine block. J Virol. 1993;67:5585-5594.

118. McQuade TK, Tomasselli AG, Liu L, et al. HIV-1 protease inhibitor with antiviral activity arrests HIV-like particle maturation. Science. 1990;247:454-456.

119. Palella F, Delaney KM, Moorman AC, et al. Declining morbidity and mortality among patients with advanced human immunodeficiency virus infection. N Engl J Med. 1998;338:853-860.

120. Lamb RA, Krug RM. Orthomyxoviridae: The viruses and their replication. In: Knipe DM, Howley PM, eds. Fields Virology. 4th ed. Philadelphia: Lippincott-Raven; 2001:1487-1531.

121. Woods JM, Bethell RC, Coates JA, et al. 4-Guanidino-2,4-dideoxy-2,3-dehydro-N-acetylneuraminic acid is a highly effective inhibitor both of the sialidase (neuraminidase) and of growth of a wide range of influenza A and B viruses in vitro. Antimicrob Agents Chemother. 1993;37:1473-1479.

122. Kilby JM, Eron JJ. Novel therapies based on mechanisms of HIV-1 cell entry. N Engl J Med. 2003;348:2228-2238.

123. Tyler KL, Nathanson N. Pathogenesis of viral infections. In: Knipe DM, Howley PM, eds. Fields Virology. 4th ed. Philadelphia: Lippincott-Raven; 2001:199-243.

124. Bass DM, Bodkin D, Dambrauskas R, et al. Intraluminal proteolytic activation plays an important role in replication of type 1 reovirus in the intestines of neonatal mice. J Virol. 1990;64:1830-1833.

125. Vonderfecht SL, Miskuff RL, Wee S, et al. Protease inhibitors suppress the in vitro and in vivo replication of rotaviruses. J Clin Invest. 1988;82:2011-2016.

126. Wolf JL, Rubin DH, Finberg R, et al. Intestinal M cells: A pathway of entry of reovirus into the host. Science. 1981;212:471-472.

127. Wolf JL, Kauffman RS, Finberg R, et al. Determinants of reovirus interaction with the intestinal M cells and absorptive cells of murine intestine. Gastroenterology. 1983;85:291-300.

128. Sicinski P, Rowinski J, Warchol JB, et al. Poliovirus type 1 enters the human host through intestinal M cells. Gastroenterology. 1990;98:56-58.

129. Amerongen HM, Weltzin R, Farnet CM, et al. Transepithelial transport of HIV-1 by intestinal M cells: A mechanism for transmission of AIDS. J AIDS. 1991;4:760-765.

130. Tucker SP, Compans RW. Virus infection of polarized epithelial cells. Adv Virus Res. 1993;42:187-247.

131. Ball JM, Mulligan MJ, Compans RW. Basolateral sorting of the HIV type 2 and SIV envelope glycoproteins in polarized epithelial cells: Role of the cytoplasmic domain. AIDS Res Hum Retroviruses. 1997;13:665-675.

132. Huang XF, Compans RW, Chen S, et al. Polarized apical targeting directed by the signal/anchor region of simian virus 5 hemagglutinin-neuraminidase. J Biol Chem. 1997;272:27598-27604.

133. Fenner F. The pathogenesis of acute exanthems. Lancet. 1948;2:915.

134. Tsiang H. Evidence for intraaxonal transport of fixed and street rabies virus. J Neuropathol Exp Neurol. 1979;38:286-297.

135. Lycke E, Tsiang H. Rabies virus infection of cultured rat sensory neurons. J Virol. 1987;61:2733-2741.

136. Ziegler RJ, Herman RE. Peripheral infection in culture of rat sensory neurons by herpes simplex virus. Infect Immun. 1980;28:620-623.

137. Kristensson K, Lycke E, Sjostrand J. Spread of herpes simplex virus in peripheral nerves. Acta Neuropathol (Berl). 1971;17:44-53.

138. Smith GA, Gross SP, Enquist LW. Herpesviruses use bidirectional fast-axonal transport to spread in sensory neurons. Proc Natl Acad Sci USA. 2001;98:3466-3470.

139. Bodian D. Poliomyelitis: Pathogenesis and histopathology. In: Rivers TM, Horsfall FL, eds. Viral and Rickettsial Infections of Man. 3rd ed. Philadelphia: Lippincott; 1959:479-518.

140. Sabin AB. Paralytic poliomyelitis: Old dogmas and new perspectives. Rev Infect Dis. 1981;3:543-564.

141. Ren R, Costantini FC, Gorgacz EJ, et al. Transgenic mice expressing a human poliovirus receptor: A new model for poliomyelitis. Cell. 1990;63:353-362.

142. Ren R, Racaniello VR. Poliovirus spreads from muscle to central nervous system by neural pathways. J Infect Dis. 1992;166:747-752.

143. Holland JJ. Receptor affinities as major determinants of enterovirus tissue tropisms in humans. Virology. 1961;15:312-326.

144. Mendelsohn CL, Wimmer E, Racaniello VR. Cellular receptor for poliovirus: Molecular cloning, nucleotide sequence, and expression of a new member of the immunoglobulin superfamily. Cell. 1989;56:855-865.

145. Baric RS, Sullivan E, Hensley L, et al. Persistent infection promotes cross-species transmissibility of mouse hepatitis virus. J Virol. 1999;73:638-649.

146. Blau DM, Turbide C, Tremblay M, et al. Targeted disruption of the Ceacam1 (MHVR) gene leads to reduced susceptibility of mice to mouse hepatitis virus infection. J Virol. 2001;75:8173-8186.

147. Lentz TL, Burrage TG, Smith AL, et al. Is the acetylcholine receptor a rabies virus receptor? Science. 1982;215:182-184.

148. Hanham CA, Zhao F, Tignor GH. Evidence from the anti-idiotypic network that the acetylcholine receptor is a rabies virus receptor. J Virol. 1993;67:530-542.

149. Weiner HL, Powers ML, Fields BN. Absolute linkage of virulence and central nervous system tropism of reoviruses to viral hemagglutinin. J Infect Dis. 1980;141:609-616.

150. Barton ES, Youree BE, Ebert DH, et al. Utilization of sialic acid as a coreceptor is required for reovirus-induced biliary disease. J Clin Invest. 2003;111:1823-1833.

151. McKnight S, Tijan R. Transcriptional selectivity of viral genes in mammalian cells. Cell. 1986;46:795-805.
152. Maniatis T, Goodbourn S, Fischer JA. Regulation of inducible and tissue-specific gene expression. Science. 1987;236:1237-1245.
153. Kenney S, Natarajan V, Strike D, et al. JC virus enhancer-promoter active in human brain cells. Science. 1984;226:1337-1339.
154. Davis NL, Grieder FB, Smith JF, et al. A molecular genetic approach to the study of Venezuelan equine encephalitis virus pathogenesis. Arch Virol Suppl. 1994;9:99-109.
155. Tardieu M, Powers ML, Weiner HL. Age-dependent susceptibility to reovirus type 3 encephalitis: Role of viral and host factors. Ann Neurol. 1983;13:602-607.
156. Mann MA, Knipe DM, Fischbach GD, Fields BN. Type 3 reovirus neuroinvasion after intramuscular inoculation: Direct invasion of nerve terminals and age-dependent pathogenesis. Virology. 2002;303:222-231.
157. Hall CB, Hall WJ, Speers DM. Clinical and physiologic manifestations of bronchiolitis and pneumonia: Outcome of respiratory syncytial virus. Am J Dis Child. 1979;133:798-802.
158. Henderson FW, Collier AM, Clyde WA, Denny FW. Respiratory-syncytial-virus infections: Reinfections and immunity: A prospective, longitudinal study in young children. N Engl J Med. 1979;300:530-534.
159. Glezen WP, Taber LH, Frank AL, Kasel JA. Risk of primary infection and reinfection with respiratory syncytial virus. Am J Dis Child. 1986;140:543-546.
160. Rodriguez WJ, Kim HW, Brandt CD, et al. Rotavirus gastroenteritis in the Washington, D.C. area. Incidence of cases resulting in admission to the hospital. Am J Dis Child. 1980;134:777-779.
161. Bishop RF. Natural history of human rotavirus infections. In: Kapikian AZ, ed. Viral Infections of the Gastrointestinal Tract. New York: Marcel Dekker; 1994:131-168.
162. Barclay AJG, Foster A, Sommer A. Vitamin A supplements and mortality related to measles: A randomised clinical trial. Br Med J. 1987;294:294-296.
163. Hussey GD, Klein M. Routine high-dose vitamin A therapy for children hospitalized with measles. J Trop Pediatr. 1993;39:342-345.
164. Rosenstreich DL, Weinblatt AC, O'Brien AD. Genetic control of resistance to infection in mice. CRC Crit Rev Immunol. 1982;3:263-300.
165. Dean M, Carrington M, Winkler C, et al. Genetic restriction of HIV-1 infection and progression to AIDS by a deletion allele of the CKR5 structural gene. Hemophilia Growth and Development Study, Multicenter AIDS Cohort Study, Multicenter Hemophilia Cohort Study, San Francisco City Cohort, ALIVE Study. Science. 1996;273:1856-1862.
166. Hoffman TL, MacGregor RR, Burger H, et al. CCR5 genotypes in sexually active couples discordant for human immunodeficiency virus type 1 infection status. J Infect Dis. 1997;176:1093-1096.
167. Ho DD, Neumann AU, Perelson AS, et al. Rapid turnover of plasma virions and CD4 lymphocytes in HIV-1 infection. Nature. 1995;373:123-126.
168. Wong JK, Hezareh M, Gunthard HF, et al. Recovery of replication-competent HIV despite prolonged suppression of plasma viremia. Science. 1997;278:1291-1295.
169. Finzi D, Hermankova M, Pierson T, et al. Identification of a reservoir for HIV-1 in patients on highly active antiretroviral therapy. Science. 1997;278:1295-1300.
170. Montelaro RC, Parekh B, Orrego A, Issel CJ. Antigenic variation during persistent infection by equine infectious anemia virus, a retrovirus. J Biol Chem. 1984;259:10539-10544.
171. Robert-Guroff M, Brown M, Gallo RC. HTLV-III-neutralizing antibodies in patients with AIDS and AIDS-related complex. Nature. 1985;316:72-74.
172. Weiss RA, Clapham PR, Cheingsong-Popou R, et al. Neutralization of human T lymphotropic virus type III by sera of AIDS and AIDS-risk patients. Nature. 1985;316:69-72.
173. Fauci A. Immunopathogenesis of HIV infection. AIDS. 1993;6:655-662.
174. Burgert H, Maryanski J, Kvist S. "E3/19K" protein of adenovirus type 2 inhibits lysis of cytolytic T lymphocytes by blocking cell-surface expression of histocompatibility class I antigens. Proc Natl Acad Sci USA. 1987;84:1356-1360.
175. Wiertz E, Jones T, Sun L, et al. The human cytomegalovirus US11 gene product dislocates MHC class I heavy chains from the endoplasmic reticulum to the cytosol. Cell. 1996;84:769-779.
176. Tewari M, Telford WG, Miller RA, Dixit VM. CrmA, a poxvirus-encoded serpin, inhibits cytotoxic T-lymphocyte-mediated apoptosis. J Biol Chem. 1995;270:22705-22708.
177. Lehmann-Grube F. Portraits of viruses: Arenaviruses. Intervirology. 1984;22:121-145.
178. Buchmeier MJ, Welsh RM, Dutko FJ, Oldstone MBA. The virology and immunobiology of lymphocytic choriomeningitis virus infection. Adv Immunol. 1980;30:275-331.
179. Fraser NW, Block TB, Spivack JG. The latency-associated transcripts of herpes simplex virus: RNA in search of function. Virology. 1992;191:1-8.
180. Stevenson PG, Hawke S, Sloan DJ, Bangham CR. The immunogenicity of intracerebral virus infection depends on anatomical site. J Virol. 1997;71:145-151.
181. Nevins JR. Cell transformation by viruses. In: Knipe DM, Howley PM, eds. Fields Virology. 4th ed. Philadelphia: Lippincott-Raven; 2001:245-283.
182. Rous P. A transmissible avian neoplasm: Sarcoma of the common fowl. J Exp Med. 1910;12:696-705.
183. Stehelin D, Varmus HE, Bishop JM, Vogt PK. DNA related to the transforming gene(s) of avian sarcoma viruses is present in normal avian DNA. Nature. 1976;260:170-173.
184. Takeya T, Hanafusa H. Nucleotide sequences of c-src. Cell. 1983;32:881-890.
185. Manaker RA, Groupe V. Discrete foci of altered chicken embryo cells associated with Rous sarcoma virus in tissue culture. Virology. 1956;2:838-840.
186. Temin HM, Rubin H. Characteristics of an assay for Rous sarcoma virus and Rous sarcoma cells in tissue culture. Virology. 1958;6:669-688.

187. Toyoshima K, Vogt PK. Temperature sensitive mutants of an avian sarcoma virus. Virology. 1969;39:930-931.
188. Martin GS. Rous sarcoma virus: A function required for the maintenance of the transformed state. Nature. 1970;227:1021-1023.
189. Cooper JA, Howell B. The when and how of Src regulation. Cell. 1993;73:1051-1054.
190. Dolcetti R, Masucci MG. Epstein-Barr virus: Induction and control of cell transformation. J Cell Physiol. 2003;196:207-218.
191. Wentzensen N, Ridder R, Klaes R, et al. Characterization of viral-cellular fusion transcripts in a large series of HPV16 and 18 positive anogenital lesions. Oncogene. 2002;21:419-426.
192. Tsukuma H, Hiyana T, Tanka S, et al. Risk factors for hepatocellular carcinoma among patients with chronic liver disease. N Engl J Med. 1993;328:1797-1801.
193. Marusawa H, Hijikata M, Chiba T, Shimotohno K. Hepatitis C virus core protein inhibits Fas- and tumor necrosis factor alpha-mediated apoptosis via NF-kappaB activation. J Virol. 1999;73:4713-4720.
194. Nestorowicz A, Kawaoka Y, Bean WJ, Webster RG. Molecular analysis of the hemagglutinin genes of Australian H7N7 influenza viruses: Role of passerine birds in maintenance or transmission? Virology. 1987;11:400-418.
195. Horimoto T, Kawaoka Y. Reverse genetics provides direct evidence for a correlation of hemagglutinin cleavability and virulence of an avian influenza A virus. J Virol. 1994;68:3120-3128.
196. Chen MH, Benjamin T. Roles of N-glycans with alpha2,6 as well as alpha2,3 linked sialic acid in infection by polyoma virus. Virology. 1997;233:440-442.
197. Bassel-Duby R, Spriggs DR, Tyler KL, Fields BN. Identification of attenuating mutations on the reovirus type 3 S1 double-stranded RNA segment with a rapid sequencing technique. J Virol. 1986;60:64-67.
198. Offit PA, Blavat G, Greenberg HB, Clark HF. Molecular basis of rotavirus virulence: Role of gene segment 4. J Virol. 1986;57:46-49.
199. Grieder FB, Davis NL, Aronson JF, et al. Specific restrictions in the progression of Venezuelan equine encephalitis virus-induced disease resulting from single amino acid changes in the glycoproteins. Virology. 1995;206:994-1006.
200. Brown F, Lewis BP. Poliovirus attenuation: Molecular mechanisms and practical aspects. Dev Biol Stand. 1993;78:1-187.
201. Jackson RJ, Ramsay AJ, Christensen CD, et al. Expression of mouse interleukin-4 by a recombinant ectromelia virus suppresses cytolytic lymphocyte responses and overcomes genetic resistance to mousepox. J Virol. 2001;75:1205-1210.
202. Finkel E. Australia. Engineered mouse virus spurs bioweapon fears. Science. 2001;291:585.
203. De Sena J, Jarvis DL. Modification of the poliovirus capsid by ultraviolet light. Can J Microbiol. 1981,27.1185-1193.
204. Grimmel M, Zibirre R, Koch G. Fluorescence spectrophotometric study of structural alterations in the capsid of poliovirus. Arch Virol. 1983;78:191-201.
205. Wetz K, Kucinski T. Influence of different ionic and pH environments on structural alterations of poliovirus and their possible relation to virus uncoating. J Gen Virol. 1991;72:2541-2544.
206. Drayna D, Fields BN. Genetic studies on the mechanism of chemical and physical inactivation of reovirus. J Gen Virol. 1982;63:149-160.
207. Wessner DR, Fields BN. Isolation and genetic characterization of ethanol-resistant reovirus mutants. J Virol. 1993;67:2442-2447.
208. Nathanson N, Tyler KL. Entry, dissemination, shedding, and transmission of viruses. In: Nathanson N, ed. Viral Pathogenesis. Philadelphia: Lippincott-Raven; 1997:13-33.
209. Fenner F. Mousepox (infectious ectromelia of mice): A review. J Immunol. 1949;63:341-373.
210. Condit RC. Principles of virology. In: Knipe DM, Howley PM, eds. Fields Virology. 4th ed. Philadelphia: Lippincott-Raven; 2001:19-51.
211. Tomko RP, Xu R, Philipson L. HCAR and MCAR: The human and mouse cellular receptors for subgroup C adenoviruses and group B coxsackieviruses. Proc Natl Acad Sci. 1997;94:3352-3356.
212. Segerman A, Atkinson JP, Marttila M, et al. Adenovirus type 11 uses CD46 as a cellular receptor. J Virol. 2003;77:9183-9191.
213. Gaggar A, Shayakhmetov DM, Lieber A. CD46 is a cellular receptor for group B adenoviruses. Nat Med. 2003;9:1408-1412.
214. Williams RK, Jiang GS, Holmes KV. Receptor for mouse hepatitis virus is a member of the carcinoembryonic antigen family of glycoproteins. Proc Natl Acad Sci USA. 1991;88:5533-5536.
215. Yokomori K, Lai MM. Mouse hepatitis virus utilizes two carcinoembryonic antigens as alternative receptors. J Virol. 1992;66:6194-6199.
216. Dveksler GS, Diffenbach CW, Cardellichio CB, et al. Several members of the mouse carcinoembryonic antigen-related glycoprotein family are functional receptors for the coronavirus mouse hepatitis virus-A59. J Virol. 1993;67:1-8.
217. Delmas B, Gelfi J, L'Haridon R, et al. Aminopeptidase N is a major receptor for the entero-pathogenic coronavirus TGEV. Nature. 1992;357:417-420.
218. Yeager CL, Ashmun RA, Williams RK, et al. Human aminopeptidase N is a receptor for human coronavirus 229E. Nature. 1992;357:420-422.
219. Li W, Moore MJ, Vasilieva N, et al. Angiotensin-converting enzyme 2 is a functional receptor for the SARS coronavirus. Nature. 2003;426:450-454.
220. Vlasak R, Luytjes W, Spaan W, Palese P. Human and bovine coronaviruses recognize sialic acid-containing receptors similar to those of influenza C viruses. Proc Natl Acad Sci USA. 1988;85:4526-4529.
221. Bergelson JM, Mohoanty JG, Crowell RL, et al. Coxsackievirus B3 adapted to growth in RD cells binds to decay-accelerating factor (CD55). J Virol. 1995;69:1903-1906.
222. Shafren DR, Bates RC, Agrez MV, et al. Coxsackieviruses B1, B3, and B5 use decay accelerating factor as a receptor for cell attachment. J Virol. 1995;69:3873-3877.

223. Roivainen M, Piirainen L, Hovi T, et al. Entry of coxsackievirus A9 into host cells: Specific interactions with αvβ3 integrin, the vitronectin receptor. Virology. 1994;203:357-365.
224. Neyts J, Snoeck R, Schols D, et al. Sulfated polymers inhibit the interaction of human cytomegalovirus with cell surface heparan sulfate. Virology. 1992;189:48-58.
225. Compton T, Nowlin DM, Cooper NR. Initiation of human cytomegalovirus infection requires initial interaction with cell surface heparan sulfate. Virology. 1993;193: 834-841.
226. Wang X, Huong SM, Chiu ML, et al. Epidermal growth factor receptor is a cellular receptor for human cytomegalovirus. Nature. 2003;424:456-461.
227. Bergelson JM, Shepley MP, Chan BM, et al. Identification of the integrin VLA-2 as a receptor for echovirus 1. Science. 1992;255:1718-1720.
228. Bergelson JM, Chan M, Solomon KR, et al. Decay-accelerating factor (CD55), a glycosylphosphatidylinositol-anchored complement regulatory protein, is a receptor for several echoviruses. Proc Natl Acad Sci USA. 1994;91:6245-6249.
229. Ward T, Pipkin PA, Clarkson NA, et al. Decay-accelerating factor CD55 is identified as the receptor for echovirus 7 using CELICS, a rapid immuno-focal cloning method. EMBO J. 1994;13:5070-5074.
230. Fingeroth JD, Weis JJ, Tedder TF, et al. Epstein-Barr virus receptor of human B lymphocytes is the C3d receptor CR2. Proc Natl Acad Sci USA. 1984;81:4510-4514.
231. Frade R, Barel M, Ehlin-Henriksson B, Klein G. gp140, the C3d receptor of human B lymphocytes, is also the Epstein-Barr virus receptor. Proc Natl Acad Sci USA. 1985;82:1490-1493.
232. Manel N, Kim FJ, Kinet S, et al. The ubiquitous glucose transporter GLUT-1 is a receptor for HTLV. Cell. 2003;115:449-459.
233. Higa HH, Rogers GN, Paulson JC. Influenza virus hemagglutinins differentiate between receptor determinants bearing N-acetyl-, N-glycolyl-, and N,O-diacetylneuraminic acid groups. Virology. 1985;144:279-282.
234. Cao W, Henry MD, Borrow P, et al. Identification of alpha-dystroglycan as a receptor for lymphocytic choriomeningitis virus and Lassa fever virus. Science. 1998;282:2079-2081.
235. Dörig RE, Marcil A, Chopra A, Richardson CD. The human CD46 molecule is a receptor for measles virus (Edmonston strain). Cell. 1993;75:295-305.
236. Naniche D, Varior-Krishnan G, Cervoni F, et al. Human membrane cofactor protein (CD46) acts as a cellular receptor for measles virus. J Virol. 1993;67:6025-6032.
237. Tatsuo H, Ono N, Tanaka K, Yanagi Y. SLAM (CDw150) is a cellular receptor for measles virus. Nature. 2000;406:893-897.
238. Brown KE, Anderson SM, Young NS. Erythrocyte P antigen: cellular receptor for B19 parvovirus. Science. 1993;262:114-117.
239. Parker JS, Murphy WJ, Wang D, et al. Canine and feline parvoviruses can use human or feline transferrin receptors to bind, enter, and infect cells. J Virol. 2001;75: 3896-3902.
240. Thoulouze MI, Lafage M, Schachner M, et al. The neural cell adhesion molecule is a receptor for rabies virus. J Virol. 1998;72:7181-7190.
241. Tuffereau C, Benejean J, Blondel D, et al. Low-affinity nerve-growth factor receptor (P75NTR) can serve as a receptor for rabies virus. EMBO J. 1998;17:7250-7259.
242. Superti F, Hauttecoeur B, Morelec MJ, et al. Involvement of gangliosides in rabies virus infection. J Gen Virol. 1986;67:47-56.
243. Gentsch JR, Pacitti AF. Effect of neuraminidase treatment of cells and effect of soluble glycoproteins on type 3 reovirus attachment to murine L cells. J Virol. 1985; 56:356-364.
244. Paul RW, Choi AH, Lee PWK. The α-anomeric form of sialic acid is the minimal receptor determinant recognized by reovirus. Virology. 1989;172:382-385.
245. Chappell JD, Gunn VL, Wetzel JD, et al. Mutations in type 3 reovirus that determine binding to sialic acid are contained in the fibrous tail domain of viral attachment protein σ1. J Virol. 1997;71:1834-1841.
246. Prota AE, Campbell JA, Schelling P, et al. Crystal structure of human junctional adhesion molecule 1: implications for reovirus binding. Proc Natl Acad Sci USA. 2003;100:5366-5371.
247. Greve JM, Davis G, Meyer AM, et al. The major human rhinovirus receptor is ICAM-1. Cell. 1989;56:839-847.
248. Staunton DE, Merluzzi VJ, Rothlein R, et al. A cell adhesion molecule, ICAM-1, is the major surface receptor for rhinoviruses. Cell. 1989;56:849-853.
249. Tomassini JE, Graham D, DeWitt CM, et al. cDNA cloning reveals that the major group rhinovirus receptor on HeLa cells is intercellular adhesion molecule 1. Proc Natl Acad Sci USA. 1989;86:4907-4911.
250. Fukudome K, Yoshie O, Konno T. Comparison of human, simian, and bovine rotaviruses for requirement of sialic acid in hemagglutination and cell adsorption. Virology. 1989;172:196-205.
251. Willoughby RE, Yolken RH, Schnaar RL. Rotaviruses specifically bind to the neutral glycosphingolipid asialo-GM1. J Virol. 1990;64:4830-4835.
252. Superti F, Donelli G. Gangliosides as binding sites in SA-11 rotavirus infection of LLCC-MK2 cells. J Gen Virol. 1991;72:2467-2474.
253. Rolsma MD, Gelberg HB, Kuhlenschmidt MS. Assay for evaluation of rotavirus-cell interactions: Identification of an enterocyte ganglioside fraction that mediates group A porcine rotavirus recognition. J Virol. 1994;68:258-268.
254. Schlegel R, Tralka S, Willingham MC, Pastan I. Inhibition of VSV binding and infectivity by phosphatidylserine. Is phosphatidylserine a VSV binding site? Cell. 1983;32:639-646.

CHAPTER 129

Orthopoxviruses: Vaccinia (Smallpox Vaccine), Variola (Smallpox), Monkeypox, and Cowpox

INGER DAMON

BACKGROUND

The genus *Orthopoxvirus* belongs to the family of Poxviridae, a group of large, complex double-stranded DNA viruses that replicate in the cytoplasm of their host cell and are defined by their genomic, structural, and antigenic similarities.[1,2] Humans can be infected by members of multiple poxvirus genera, but they are usually accidental hosts. Most human infections are zoonotic, and animal exposure and geographic location give clues to the etiologic agent. The orthopoxvirus, variola, however, is a selective human pathogen. Variola is the causative agent of smallpox, which in 1980 was declared by the World Health Organization (WHO) to be eradicated worldwide. Other orthopoxviruses known to infect humans are cowpox, vaccinia, and monkeypox. Species of poxvirus genera that infect humans, other than within the Orthopoxvirus genus, are discussed in Chapter 130. Recent comprehensive reviews of poxvirus virology have been published.[3,4]

The ability of sera raised against one orthopoxvirus species to cross-neutralize another species is one of the fundamental reasons for cross-protection provided by vaccination. Vaccinia virus is the orthopoxvirus species now characterized as the constituent of smallpox vaccine. In part because of the concern that variola could be used as an agent of bioterror or as a bioweapon (see Chapter 323), there has been both increased interest and research on orthopoxviruses and poxviruses. There has been significant new research on vaccinia, targeting both fundamental viral properties and use of the virus as a (vaccina) vector. The emergence in 2003 of human clinical illness caused by monkeypox in the United States has also increased the need for knowledge of these viral pathogens.

MORPHOLOGY AND CHEMICAL STRUCTURE

Poxviruses described in these chapters belong to the family Poxviridae, subfamily Chordopoxviridae.[1] There are eight genera of vertebrate poxviruses: *Orthopoxvirus, Parapoxvirus, Avipoxvirus, Capripoxvirus, Leporipoxvirus, Suipoxvirus, Molluscipoxvirus,* and *Yatapoxvirus.* Only species of *Orthopoxvirus, Parapoxvirus, Molluscipoxvirus,* and *Yatapoxvirus* are known to infect humans. The last three are discussed in Chapter 130. Orthopoxvirus virions are large and brick shaped (as are the virions of yatapoxvirus and molluscipoxvirus). Poxvirus virions range in length from 220 to 450 nm and in width and depth from 140 to 260 nm.[5,6] The electron microscopic appearance of virions varies somewhat with sample preparation.[3] On cryoelectron microscopy of unstained, unfixed vitrified specimens, vaccinia and other orthopoxviruses appear as smooth rounded rectangles; a uniform core is surrounded by a 30-nm membrane. In conventional negatively stained thin sections, the core appears dumbbell shaped and is surrounded by a complex series of membranes. The majority of virions have short surface tubules 10 nm in diameter and are referred to as M (mulberry) forms; a minority, slightly larger and electron dense, appear to have a thick (20 to 25 nm) membrane or capsule (C form) (Fig. 129-1). Poxvirus particles contain about half of the approximately 200 potential virus-encoded proteins; virions include structural proteins and enzymes, including a virtually complete RNA

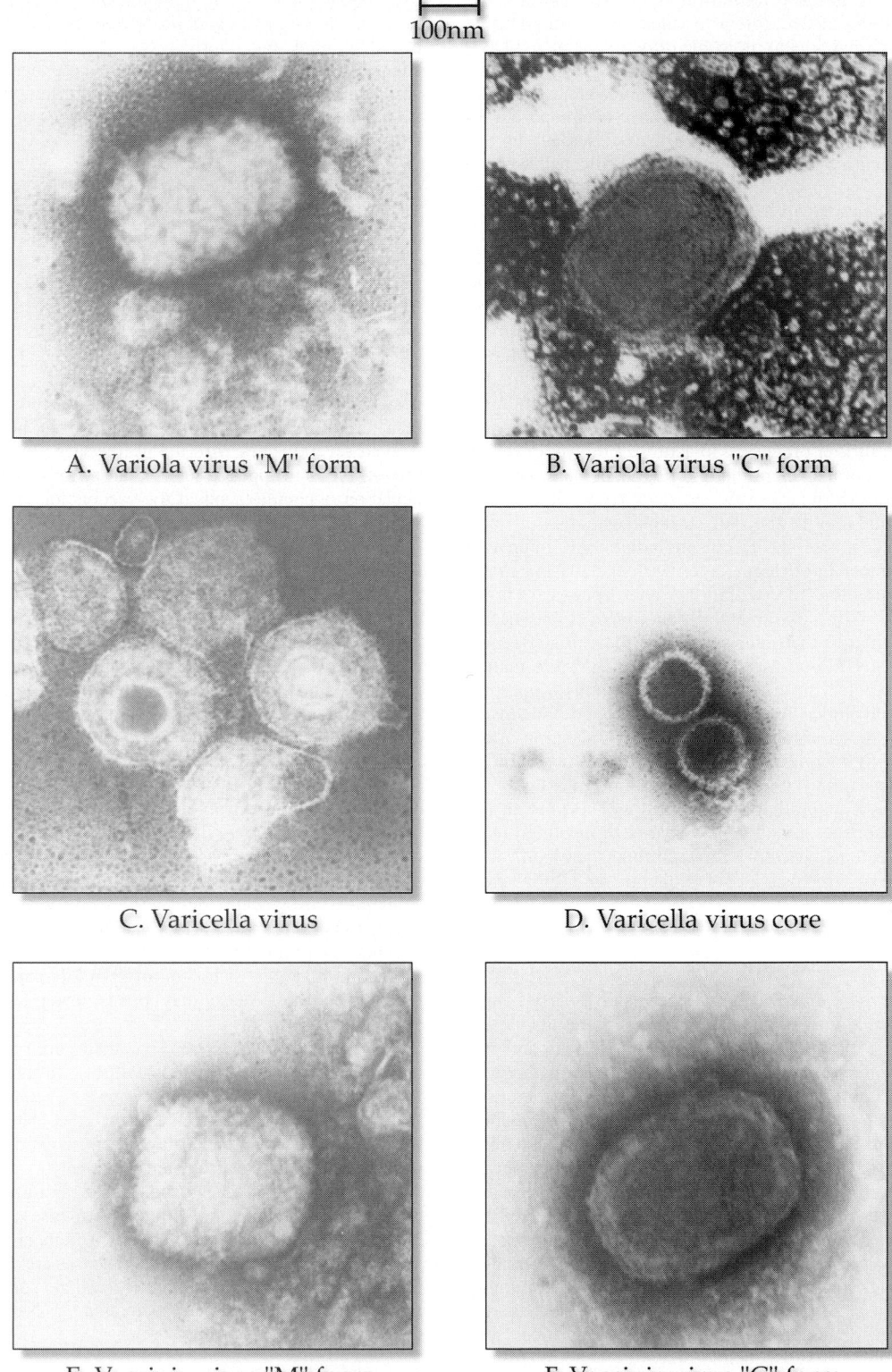

100nm

A. Variola virus "M" form

B. Variola virus "C" form

C. Varicella virus

D. Varicella virus core

E. Vaccinia virus "M" form

F. Vaccinia virus "C" form

Electron micrographs of Variola, Varicella,
and Vaccinia Viruses.

FIGURE 129-1. Electron micrographs of variola, varicella, and vaccinia virions. *(From the U.S. Centers for Disease Control and Prevention [CDC] Public Health Information Library [PHIL] at http://phil.cdc.gov/phil/default.asp. Image ID 5 2426. Electron micrograph taken in 1975 by Dr. James Nakano, CDC. This image is in the public domain and thus free of any copyright restrictions.)*

polymerase system for primary transcription of viral genes.[3] The genome, which is within a nucleoprotein complex (nucleosome) inside the core, consists of a single linear molecule of double-stranded DNA composed, depending on the strain, of about 130 to 375 kilobase pairs of DNA that is covalently closed at each end; the ends are hairpin-like telomeres. Complete genome DNA sequences have been reported for several different species of the orthopoxviruses described in this chapter; GenBank entries are compiled at a dedicated website (www.poxvirus.org).

During virus replication,[3,7] virion morphogenesis begins in the cytoplasm. Thin-section electron microscopic observations of cells early after infection show crescent-shaped membrane structures that progress to circular structures, called immature virions, which enclose a dense nucleoprotein complex. Primary transcription precedes the production of the crescents (cup shaped in three dimensions) and the immature virions. The bilayer surface membrane of the immature virion differentiates, with one layer becoming the outer membrane and the other becoming the core membrane, thereby forming an intracellular mature virion (IMV). A small portion of IMVs may be further processed to acquire a bilayer envelope of Golgi intermediate compartment membrane that contains specific viral proteins. The intracellular enveloped IMV (IEV) then moves along cellular microtubules to the cell surface, where actin polymerizes behind IEV. IEVs exit the cell through distinctive microvilli by fusing the outermost lipoprotein layer with the plasma membrane, thereby releasing the IMV within the inner lipoprotein layer. The released particle is the extracellular enveloped virion (EEV); EEVs that stay attached to the outer surface of the cell are termed cell-associated EEVs (CEVs). IMVs, EEVs, and CEVs are mature infectious particles, each with distinct surface antigenic properties. Enveloped and nonenveloped forms have different mechanisms of cell entry; however, the common result of entry is uncoating of the particle, release of viral contents into the cell, and initiation of virus-controlled transcription of early-class proteins.[8]

The dissemination of naturally released virions (EEVs) is an important aspect of pathogenesis, and genes have been identified (e.g., *B5R*) that code for proteins necessary for the proper development of EEVs and expression of virulence. Host cell factors are also involved in EEV dissemination.[7,9]

PATHOGENESIS

Poxvirus infections evolve either as a localized (skin), fairly benign infection or as a systemic infection. Systemic infection results in viral dissemination, with the formation of generalized skin lesions, and usually involves some degree of morbidity and mortality. The pathogenesis of human systemic orthopoxvirus infections is largely extrapolated and modeled from studies of the pathogenesis of the related orthopoxvirus infections in animals: mousepox (ectromelia) in mice, rabbitpox in rabbits, and monkeypox in nonhuman primates.[10-14] In addition, there is an extensive literature on animal models used to examine the role of virally encoded proteins predicted to be involved in viral pathogenesis or used to examine the effect of therapeutic modalities, or both.[15-17] The general paradigm for systemic orthopoxvirus pathogenesis is that virus enters the host, by a respiratory route, through a mucosal surface, or through a break in the skin, and replicates locally. Virus then spreads through local lymphatics, causing a primary viremia, and subsequently spreads to the reticuloendothelial system. Replication in these organs results in the secondary viremia, usually associated with fever. Virus then ultimately seeds skin, causing a characteristic "pock" rash.

The host immune response probably involves all arms of the immune system. Complement, interferon, natural killer cells, and inflammatory cells are implicated in the early innate response; pox-specific antibodies (including neutralizing antibodies) are subsequent components of the humoral response, and pox-specific cytotoxic lymphocytes are involved in cellular clearance of infection.[18-23] Within their large genomes, poxviruses encode a number of proteins predicted

to modulate the host's immune response, which affect both viral survival and disease pathogenesis. Various pox-encoded proteins are predicted to bind and interfere with the function of host cytokines, chemokines, interferon, and complement. Other pox-encoded proteins may interfere with apoptosis. Articles on immunomodulatory properties of poxviruses review specific properties of these virally encoded gene products.[24-26]

VACCINIA—VACCINE AND VACCINE ADVERSE EVENTS

Vaccinia is an orthopoxvirus and is the most studied of all poxviruses. At some point, it replaced cowpox as the smallpox "vaccine." The origin of vaccinia virus is uncertain.[27] A single strain of the virus, the New York City Board of Health (NYCBOH) strain, is used for smallpox vaccine in the United States. Other strains have been used outside the United States.

Smallpox vaccine is administered with a special bifurcated needle designed to hold a small, standardized inoculum of a live virus suspension between its prongs. The skin over the deltoid or triceps is pierced several times with the needle using enough vigor to allow a trace of blood to appear after several seconds. Within 2 to 5 days of inoculation, a papule forms at the vaccination site. This evolves into a vesicle and then a pustule, reaching its maximum size (about 1 cm in diameter) by 8 to 10 days after vaccination, after which it dries to a scab, which usually separates by day 14 to 21.[28,29] An areola may encircle the site as the lesion evolves. Low-grade fever is sometimes observed in children but rarely in adults. Regional lymphadenopathy may also occur. A scar at the inoculation site often provides lifelong evidence of successful vaccination, although a scar's presence may not guarantee a history of successful smallpox vaccination because it may have resulted from bacterial superinfection or vaccination with Calmette-Guérin bacillus.

Immunity Resulting from Vaccination

Vaccinia immunization is cross-protective against other orthopoxvirus infections, including variola. Preexposure vaccine efficacy is estimated to be as high as 100% for 1 to 3 years after vaccination,[30] and reports from the smallpox eradication efforts noted that "smallpox rarely occurs during the 4 or 5 years following successful vaccination in infancy."[31] Complete protection against smallpox after vaccination is not lifelong, although data suggest that substantial protection may persist for up to 15 to 20 years.[31] Protection against death from the disease may persist even longer than protection against disease.[32,33]

Vaccinia is also effective as postexposure prophylaxis when given to contacts of patients with smallpox. Vaccination should be performed as soon as possible after exposure; interpretation of data from the eradication program suggests that vaccination may not be as effective if given more than 3 days after the exposure.[34-37] Effectiveness was greater for those vaccinated previously.

Despite recent advances, the correlates of immunity against smallpox are poorly understood. Humoral responses, including neutralizing antibody, correlate with protection in both animal[38] and human[39-41] studies. Cell-mediated and T-cell responses are also believed to be critical for successful vaccination.[42] T-cell responses have been documented up to 35 years after vaccination.[43-45] Neutralizing antibody responses are also long lived.[44,46,47]

Complications Resulting from Vaccination

Of all vaccines used today, the smallpox vaccine has one of the highest rates of adverse events (http://www.cdc.gov/mmwr/preview/ mmwrhtml/ rr5204a1.htm).[28,48-52] Major complications include progressive vaccinia, eczema vaccinatum, generalized vaccinia, accidental infection, postvaccinial encephalitis, and carditis.

Progressive vaccinia, previously called vaccinia necrosum or vaccinia gangrenosum, is a rare and often fatal vaccine complication in persons with severe deficiencies of cellular immunity.[48] In 1 year (1968) in the United States, there were 5 cases among 6 million primary vaccinees and 6 cases among 8.6 million persons revaccinated.[50] Four of these 11 patients died. Progressive vaccinia is characterized by progressive, often painless growth and spread of the vaccine virus beyond the inoculation site, often leading to necrosis, sometimes with metastases to other body sites.[53] This diagnosis should be considered if the vaccination site lesion continues to progress and expand without apparent healing more than 15 days after vaccination.[54] Initially, limited or no inflammation is present at the site, and histopathologic examination shows an absence of inflammatory cells.[55] Management of progressive vaccinia has historically included aggressive therapy with vaccinia immune globulin (VIG), methisazone, débridement, and whole blood transfusions from previously vaccinated individuals. The last procedure, designed to bolster cell-mediated immunity, often resulted in a graft-versus-host reaction.[53] Methisazone is now regarded as ineffective therapy. Supportive measures and attention to prevention of secondary bacterial infections would be beneficial, and newer therapeutic agents such as cidofovir may also have a role, although its efficacy is unproven.[28,48] VIG is available from the Centers for Disease Control and Prevention (CDC) as an intravenous formulation.

Eczema vaccinatum can occur in people with a history of atopic dermatitis (eczema) irrespective of disease severity or activity. This complication is the clinical result of local spread or dissemination from the primary vaccination site in such persons or the result of inadvertent contact of another's unscabbed vaccination site with a susceptible atopic individual's skin.[56,57] A localized or generalized papular, vesicular, or pustular rash anywhere on the body or localized to previous eczematous lesions is the clinical presentation. Systemic illness with fever, malaise, and lymphadenopathy may occur. In the 1968 national survey there were 66 cases (no deaths) among 14.5 million vaccinees (4.6 cases per million) and 60 cases (one death) among their several million contacts. Treatment of eczema vaccinatum includes the administration of VIG (0.6 mL/kg per 24 hours, repeated until no further lesions arise),[30] hemodynamic support with fluid replacement and electrolyte monitoring, and skin care.[28] In one study, early VIG administration reduced the mortality from 30% to 40% to 7%.[58]

Generalized vaccinia is a nonspecific term that is used to describe a vesicular rash that develops after vaccination. Excluding dissemination associated with eczema vaccinatum and progressive vaccinia, it has been extremely rare to document virus in these vesicular rash lesions[59]; true generalized vaccinia is believed to represent the end product of viremic spread of virus. No predisposing factors have been identified. Treatment is generally not required as the generalized rash is self-limited. The lesions evolve and resolve more quickly than the primary vaccination site, presumably because of a developing immune response to the virus. This complication is estimated to occur in about 242 of every 1 million primary vaccinations (http://www.bt.cdc.gov/agent/smallpox/vaccination/reactions-vacc-clinic.asp). In general, this complication of vaccination does not require the administration of VIG unless it is severe and the patient is systemically ill or the patient has an underlying immunocompromising condition. Treatment with nonsteroidal anti-inflammatory agents or oral antipruritics may provide symptomatic relief.[28]

Postvaccination encephalomyelitis (PVEM) is a rare but serious complication that usually occurs only in primary vaccinees. The frequency of its occurrence differed widely from country to country and with the strain of vaccinia virus utilized in the vaccine. In the survey conducted in the United State in 1968, the frequency was 2.9 to 12.3 per million first-time vaccinees.[28] The incidence of PVEM was lower with the NYCBOH vaccinia virus strain than with the strain utilized in other countries.[60] No predisposing factors are known, although host factors are believed to be important; the pathophysiology is not well understood. Cases have variably displayed clinical and diagnostic features suggestive of a postimmunization demyelinating encephalomyelitis or direct viral invasion of the nervous system. This postvaccination reaction typically occurs 11 to 15 days after vaccination. Symptoms of PVEM include fever,

headache, vomiting, confusion, delirium, disorientation, restlessness, drowsiness or lethargy, seizures, and coma. The cerebrospinal fluid can demonstrate an elevated pressure but generally has a normal cell count and chemistry profile.[61-63]

Infants younger than 2 years can also develop a rare postvaccination encephalopathy (PVE) similar to PVEM. Acute onset of PVE occurs earlier in the postvaccination period (6 to 10 days after vaccination), involves the same symptoms as PVEM, and may also include hemiplegia and aphasia.[4,28]

The diagnosis of PVE or PVEM is one of exclusion as there are no specific tests to confirm the diagnosis of this complication, and many other infectious and toxic etiologies can result in a similar clinical picture. Because this complication is not known to be the result of viral proliferation, the role of modern antiviral medications is unclear; the use of VIG has not shown clear benefit.

Accidental infection occurs when virus from the vaccination site is transferred to another site or to another person through intimate skin contact. It usually occurs in primary vaccinees rather than revaccinees. Accidental self-inoculation, which most commonly occurs on the face, mouth, lips, or genitalia, is usually not serious and requires no specific treatment. Inoculation of the conjunctiva, cornea, or eyelid is more serious and can be sight threatening if not evaluated and treated appropriately. In the 5 years between 1963 and 1968, ocular vaccinia was observed in 348 persons; 259 were vaccinees and 66 contacts. Of these, 22 had evidence of corneal involvement and 11 had permanent defects.[64] No controlled trials of therapeutics exist; current topical optic antivirals (trifluorothymidine, vidarabine)[65] have in vitro activity against vaccinia and their off-label use for this purpose has been recommended by some ophthalmologists.[28]

Cardiac adverse events are rare and had not been reported before 2003 in any person vaccinated with the NYCBOH strain. Myocarditis had been reported after vaccination with the more virulent strain used in Europe and Australia,[66,67] and in the U.S. military population myopericarditis was documented in 18 of 230,734 primary vaccinees immunized with the NYCBOH strain between 2002 and 2003.[68] Arrhythmias and myocardial ischemia have also been described, but the association with vaccination is not as clear.[69-73]

Vaccination programs designed to help civilian public health preparedness and military preparedness for the possible use of smallpox as a weapon of bioterror, implemented in 2002 through 2003, have documented lower adverse event rates than previously seen, in part because of stringent criteria and education programs to screen out persons at risk for complications[69,74,75] (http://www.bt.cdc.gov/agent/smallpox/vaccination/index.asp). Nonetheless, instances of generalized rash, which may arise 10 to 14 days after vaccination, continue to be reported. On a clinical basis alone, it is often difficult to distinguish among generalized vaccinia, which represents virus presumably spread hematogenously; a form of erythema multiforme; or erythematous urticaria eruptions that may be immunologically mediated. Laboratory identification of virus within the disseminated rash may differentiate these conditions. Studies of recent vaccination efforts have also identified focal and generalized folliculitis associated with vaccination.[76]

The 2001 recommendations of the Advisory Committee on Immunization Practices (ACIP) on vaccinia vaccination are available at http://www.cdc.gov/mmwr/preview/mmwrhtml/rr5010a1.htm. The ACIP recommends vaccination as a safeguard for laboratory and health care workers who are at high risk for orthopoxvirus infection. In the United States, the CDC Drug Service provides the vaccine after CDC approval of a formal request for this purpose by the administering physician. Vaccinia immunoglobulin is available to treat possible postvaccination complications, which can be severe. Supplemental recommendations of the ACIP were published in 2003 and constitute advice on vaccination of persons designated by public health authorities to conduct investigation and follow-up of initial smallpox cases that might necessitate direct contact with the patient. These recommendations are available at http://www.cdc. gov/mmwr/preview/mmwrhtml/rr5207a1.htm.[77]

Vaccinia Virus as a Zoonosis

Vaccinia virus infections are not generally regarded as naturally occurring, although vaccinee-to-cattle and cattle-to-human transmissions occurred on farms during the smallpox eradication campaign. Sporadic outbreaks of infection caused by the vaccinia virus subspecies buffalopox virus that involve transmission between milking buffalo, cattle, and people have been reported, mainly in India but also in Egypt, Bangladesh, Pakistan, and Indonesia. Vaccinia-like lesions have been observed on the animals' teats and the milkers' hands. Biologic data and limited DNA analyses of isolates from an outbreak in India in 1985 suggest that buffalopox virus may be derived from vaccinia virus strains transmitted from humans to livestock during the smallpox vaccination era.[78,79] A vaccinia virus possibly related to the vaccine strain used during smallpox eradication in Brazil was found in cattle and their farm worker handlers in rural Rio de Janeiro.[80,81] In addition, there is at least one instance of human infection with a vaccinia-vector recombinant rabies virus vaccine in a bait dispersed to control rabies in wildlife; the bait was carried home by the family dog.[82]

VARIOLA

In 1980, the WHO General Assembly declared that smallpox had been eradicated; destruction of the remaining virus stocks, scheduled for 1999 and then 2002, has been delayed in an effort to permit research for improved preparedness in the event smallpox recurs as the result of the malevolent use of variola virus. The virus has a strict human host range and no animal reservoir. Variola major strains produced a disease with a severe prodrome, fever, and prostration. The virus was most often transmitted between humans by large-droplet respiratory particles inhaled by susceptible persons who had prolonged, close, face-to-face contact with an infectious person; it was spread less commonly by aerosol or direct contact with the rash lesion or sloughed crust material from the scab.[83] A "toxemia" or other form of systemic shock led to case-fatality rates of up to 30%. Secondary attack rates among unvaccinated contacts within households ranged from 30% to 80%. Variola minor strains (alastrim, amass, or Kaffir viruses) produced less severe infection and case-fatality rates of less than 1%, although secondary attack rates among unvaccinated contacts within households also ranged from 30% to 80%. The last naturally occurring smallpox case occurred in Somalia in October 1977, although a fatal laboratory-associated infection with variola major virus occurred at the University of Birmingham, England, in August 1978.[83]

Naturally acquired variola virus infection caused a systemic febrile rash illness. For ordinary smallpox, the most common clinical presentation, after an asymptomatic incubation period of 10 to 14 days (range 7 to 17 days), was fever, with the temperature quickly rising to about 103° F, sometimes with dermal petechiae. Associated constitutional symptoms included backache, headache, vomiting, and prostration. Within a day or two after incubation, a systemic rash appeared that was characteristically centrifugally distributed (i.e., lesions were present in greater numbers on the oral mucosa, face, and extremities than on the trunk). Lesions were commonly manifest on the palms and soles (Figs. 129-2 and 129-3). Initially, the rash lesions appeared macular, then papular, enlarging and progressing to a vesicle by day 4 to 5 and a pustule by day 7; lesions were encrusted and scabby by day 14 and sloughed off (Fig. 129-4). Skin lesions were deep seated and in the same stage of development in any one area of the body. Milder and more severe forms of the rash were also documented. Less severe manifestations (modified smallpox or variola sine eruptione) occurred in some vaccinated individuals, whereas hemorrhagic or flat-pox types of smallpox are thought to have developed as a result of impaired immune response of patients.

Variola major smallpox was differentiated into four main clinical types.

1. Ordinary smallpox (90% of cases) produced viremia, fever, prostration, and rash; mortality rates were generally proportionate to the extent of rash. Using the WHO classification, mortality ranged from less than 10% for "ordinary discrete" smallpox to 50% to 75% for the rarer "ordinary confluent" presentation.
2. (Vaccine)-modified smallpox (5% of cases) produced a mild prodrome with few skin lesions in previously vaccinated people and a mortality rate well under 10%.
3. Flat smallpox (5% of cases) produced slowly developing focal lesions with generalized infection and an approximately 50% fatality rate.
4. Hemorrhagic smallpox (<1% of cases) induced bleeding into the skin and the mucous membranes and was invariably fatal within a week of onset.

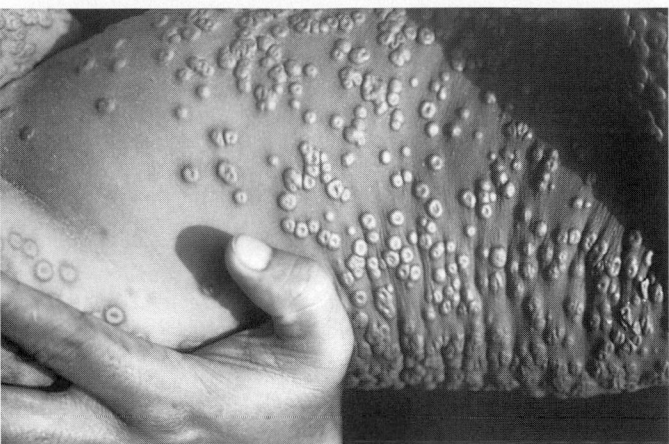

FIGURE 129-2. Smallpox lesions on skin of trunk. *(From the U.S. Centers for Disease Control and Prevention [CDC] Public Health Information Library [PHIL] at http://phil.cdc.gov/phil/default.asp. Image ID 5 284. Photograph taken in 1973 by James Hicks, CDC. This image is in the public domain and thus free of any copyright restrictions.)*

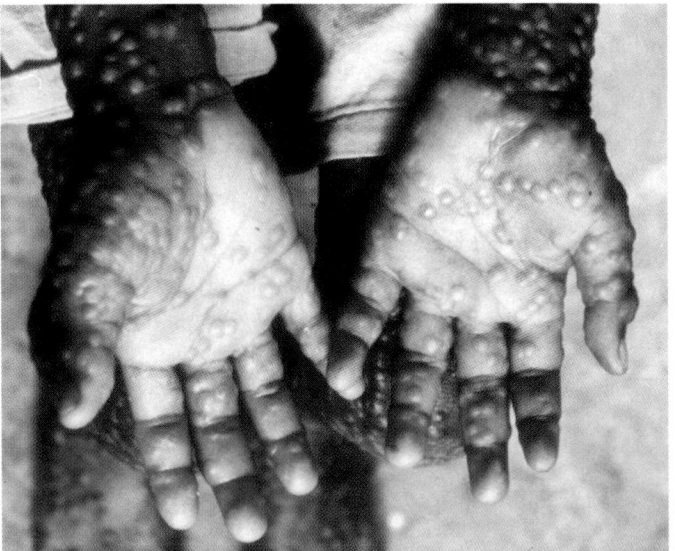

FIGURE 129-3. This child was infected with the smallpox virus and on day 8 of the rash shows the typical lesions on his palms. *(From the U.S. Centers for Disease Control and Prevention [CDC] Public Health Information Library [PHIL] at http://phil.cdc.gov/phil/default.asp. Image ID 5 3303. Photograph taken in 1972 by Dr. Paul B. Dean, CDC. This image is in the public domain and thus free of any copyright restrictions.)*

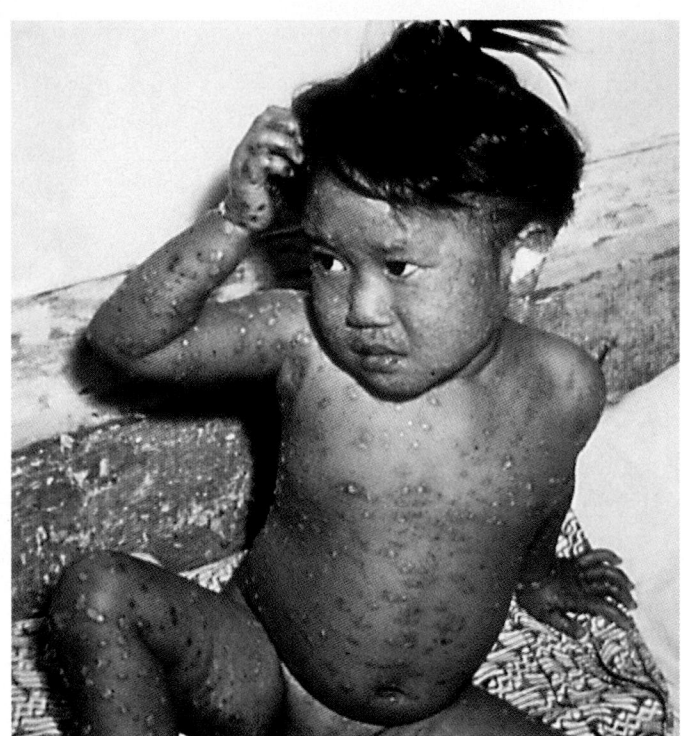

FIGURE 129-4. Smallpox lesions at day 17 of rash on a 5-year-old convalescing Indonesian child. *(From the U.S. Centers for Disease Control and Prevention [CDC] Public Health Information Library [PHIL] at http://phil.cdc.gov/phil/default.asp. Image ID 5 2041. Photograph taken in 1963 by J. D. Millar, CDC. This image is in the public domain and thus free of any copyright restrictions.)*

TABLE 129-1   Differential Diagnosis of Febrile Vesicular Pustular Rash Illnesses That May Be Confused with Smallpox

Disease	Clues
Varicella	Most common in children younger than 10; children do not usually have a viral prodrome
Disseminated herpes zoster	Immunocompromised or elderly persons; rash looks like varicella, usually begins or erupts in dermatomal pattern
Impetigo (*Streptococcus pyogenes, Staphylococcus aureus*)	Honey-colored crusted plaques with bullae are classic but may begin as vesicles
Drug eruptions	Exposure to medications
Erythema multiforme minor	Target or "bull's-eye" lesions, often follows systemic viral infections such as herpes simplex; may include palms and soles
Erythema multiforme (including Stevens-Johnson)	Involves conjunctivae and mucous membranes
Enteroviral infections (especially hand, foot, and mouth disease)	Seasonal—summer and fall
Disseminated herpes simplex	Similar to varicella
Scabies and insect bites	Pruritus, patient not febrile
Molluscum contagiosum	May disseminate in immunosuppressed individuals
Generalized vaccinia	History of vaccination with smallpox vaccine or contact with vaccinated individual
Monkeypox	Travel to endemic area; animal exposure

Adapted from Evaluating Patients for Smallpox: Acute Generalized Vesicular or Pustular Rash Illness Protocol, at http://www.bt.cdc.gov/agent/smallpox/diagnosis/pdf/spox-poster-full.pdf

http://www.bt.cdc.gov/agent/smallpox/diagnosis/evalposter.asp and at http://www.bt.cdc.gov/agent/smallpox/diagnosis/rashtestingprotocol.asp

The differential diagnosis of febrile vesicular pustular rash illnesses is presented in Table 129-1.

A discrete type of the ordinary form, with a typical febrile prodrome and rash, resulted from alastrim variola minor infection.[83] The WHO established a classification system for smallpox case types based on disease presentation and rash burden. The hemorrhagic and flat types have already been briefly described. The ordinary type was subgrouped into three categories on the basis of the extent of rash on the face and the body. In the ordinary confluent category, no area of skin was visible between vesiculopustular rash lesions on the trunk or the face. Patches of normal skin were visible between rash lesions on the trunk in ordinary semiconfluent disease as well as on the face in ordinary discrete disease. (Vaccine)-modified disease arose with sparse numbers of lesions. Infection conferred lifelong immunity.[83,84]

Before its eradication, smallpox as a clinical entity was relatively easy to recognize, but other exanthematous illnesses were mistaken for this disease.[83-85] For example, the rash of severe chickenpox, caused by varicella-zoster virus, was often misdiagnosed as that of smallpox. However, chickenpox produces a centripetally distributed rash and rarely appears on the palms and soles. In addition, in the case of chickenpox, prodromal fever and systemic manifestations are mild, if manifest at all; the lesions are superficial in nature; and lesions in different developmental stages may be present in the same area of the body. Other diseases confused with vesicular-stage smallpox included monkeypox, generalized vaccinia, disseminated herpes zoster, disseminated herpes simplex virus infection, drug reactions (eruptions), erythema multiforme, enteroviral infections, scabies, insect bites, impetigo, and molluscum contagiosum. Diseases confused with hemorrhagic smallpox included acute leukemia, meningococcemia, and idiopathic thrombocytopenic purpura. The CDC, in collaboration with numerous professional organizations, has developed an algorithm for evaluating patients for smallpox. The algorithm assists in differential diagnoses of the vesiculopustular stage of rash. The algorithm and additional laboratory testing information are available at

MONKEYPOX

Monkeypox virus was so named because it was first detected in captive Asiatic monkeys; however, the virus has been found naturally only in Africa (although it emerged in the United States as a result of global commerce) and evidence points to rodents as important reservoir hosts. Reviews of human monkeypox infection are available.[86,87]

Monkeypox was first recognized by Von Magnus in Copenhagen in 1958 as an exanthem of primates in captivity. Later, the disease was seen in other captive animals, including primates in zoos and animal import centers. Particular attention was focused on it in 1970 when smallpox surveillance activities in Africa revealed cases of human monkeypox, clinically indistinguishable from smallpox, particularly in Zaire (now Democratic Republic of Congo [DRC]). Serosurveys and virologic investigations in the 1980s in the DRC by the WHO indicated that monkeys are sporadically infected, as are humans; that three fourths of cases, mainly in children younger than 15 years, resulted from animal contact; that vaccinia vaccination has about 85% protective efficacy; that monkeypox virus probably has a broad host range, including squirrels (*Funisciurus* spp. and *Heliosciurus* spp.); and that human monkeypox has a secondary attack rate of 9% among unvaccinated contacts within households (i.e., it is much less transmissible than smallpox). Since 1970, the disease has been seen in the DRC, Liberia, Ivory Coast, Sierra Leone, Nigeria, Benin, Cameroon, and Gabon; most cases have been in the DRC, which in 1980 had a population of about 30 million (338 cases were discovered prospectively during WHO-intensified monkeypox surveillance in Zaire from 1981 to 1986). Human monkeypox has recently been reported from the DRC, mainly in children younger than 15. On the basis of reported monkeypox onset dates in a largely retrospective study complicated by a concurrent outbreak of chickenpox, about 250 serosubstantiated cases of monkeypox occurred among 0.5 million people in 78 villages from February 1996 to October 1997. About three fourths of the cases appeared to result from human-to-human transmission; however, the secondary attack rate of 8% among unvaccinated contacts within households appeared to be about the same as in the 1981 to 1986 surveillance.[86,88]

Sporadic outbreaks continue to occur and cause concern,[86,89] but the most detailed clinical, epidemiologic, and ecologic information about virological laboratory–confirmed disease in Africa was obtained before 1988. Initial animal surveys in Zaire detected monkeypox-specific antibodies in 85 of 347 (25%) squirrels sampled but from none of 233 terrestrial rodents. Monkeypox-specific antibody has been detected in very few monkeys, which, like humans, are probably only occasional hosts.[90] Subsequent work[88] in the DRC found evidence of orthopoxvirus seroreactivity in some terrestrial rodents tested, including Gambian rats (*Cricetomys emini*) and elephant shrews (*Petrodromus tetradactylus*). Studies in the 1980s, using direct virus sampling of trapped animals, revealed virus in only one *Funisciurus* species.

In 2003, monkeypox infection of humans was identified in the United States as a result of exposure to ill prairie dogs, probably infected after exposure to infected West African small mammals imported as exotic pets.[91] From that work, a Gambian rat (*Cricetomys gambianus*), rope squirrel (*Funisciurus* sp.), and dormouse (*Graphiurus* sp.) from the affected African shipment of exotic species, originating in Ghana and implicated in the U.S. monkeypox outbreak, were found to be infected with monkeypox by viral isolation and nucleic acid detection (polymerase chain reaction).[91]

Pathogenesis

The pathogenesis of human monkeypox is essentially the same as that of smallpox, an acute febrile exanthem with an incubation period of about 12 days. During the incubation period, virus is distributed initially to internal organs and then to the skin.[83,87] The main differences are a greater degree of lymphadenopathy and a lower capacity for human case-to-case spread. The major concerns are the source of infection and the mode of transmission.

Clinical Features

In general, the clinical features of disease as seen in central Africa are those of a classic or modified case of smallpox. The most obvious difference is the pronounced lymphadenopathy, which involves the submandibular, cervical, and sublingual regions.

Most cases occur in unvaccinated children. In Zaire during 1981 to 1986, 291 cases (86%) occurred in children younger than 10 years and only 12 (4%) of them had vaccination scars. The illness lasts 2 to 4 weeks. Of 292 unvaccinated patients, 22 (7.5%) had a mild illness with less than 25 skin lesions and were not incapacitated; 55 (19%) had 25 to 99 lesions, were incapable of most physical activity, and required nursing; and 218 (75%) had more than 100 lesions, were totally incapacitated, and required intensive nursing. Complications occurred in about 40% of patients; the most common were bacterial skin infections (16%), respiratory (12%) and gastrointestinal (5%) disorders, and keratitis (3.8%). The overall mortality was approximately 10%; however, all the deaths occurred in unvaccinated children, in whom group mortality is about 15%.[87] In the United States, disease in the 2003 outbreak appears to have been milder, and only 3 of the 37 laboratory-confirmed cases had complications or serious disease: keratitis, encephalopathy,[91] and upper respiratory tract lymphadenitis with dysphagia and airway compromise.[92] No deaths were observed. Although routes of exposure and host factors may have been significantly different in the African and U.S. outbreaks, evidence of differences between DRC and U.S. viral strains is also evident.[93] The skin lesions of monkeypox are illustrated in Figure 129-5.

Diagnosis

Until 2003, human monkeypox had not been detected outside Africa. Clinical diagnosis may present a problem because fewer physicians

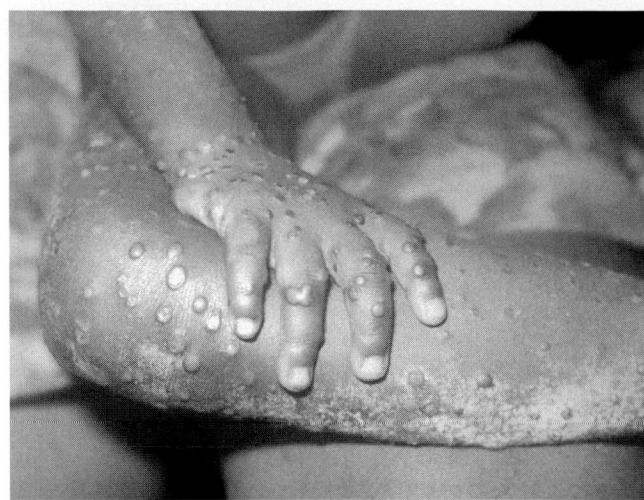

FIGURE 129-5. Monkeypox skin lesions.

now have experience with smallpox, which human monkeypox closely resembles. In vaccinated individuals, the rash may be more pleomorphic and not in a uniform stage of development.[87] Access to a virus diagnostic laboratory should permit detection of virus by electron microscopy and molecular methods, and this provides a diagnosis. In some circumstances, it may be important to distinguish between monkeypox and tanapox. In the past it was essential to differentiate between monkeypox and variola, which could be done by examination of the pock appearance (hemorrhagic or not) and presence of pocks produced on chorioallantoic membrane at 39° C, a temperature that inhibits smallpox. Currently, an array of nucleic acid diagnostic techniques permit the speciation of these viruses.[94-98]

The close serologic relationships among orthopoxviruses make detection of monkeypox-specific antigens difficult, but methods are available and being refined that may be of value, particularly for epidemiologic studies of monkeypox virus in its natural reservoirs.[5,90]

Epidemiology and Control

Management of individual cases has been supportive, with case-to-case spread reduced by isolation and, if available, the use of smallpox vaccine for contacts. Potential use of newer therapeutics is discussed at the end of this chapter. Human cases in Africa occur in villages in the rain forests, where a variety of animals are captured for food. Infection of children might be explained by their playing or working with carcasses. The results of the comprehensive surveys carried out in the 1980s indicated that those infected were principally unvaccinated children and that case-to-case spread was unusual. Control measures are based on interposing a buffer zone of cleared land between the arboreal reservoir and cultivated land, the development of animal husbandry as a source of meat, and education in the handling of wildlife, with emphasis on any trapping done by those previously vaccinated; continued vaccination was not thought necessary.[87,90]

Only occasional human cases were reported from central Africa after cessation of routine surveillance activities after smallpox eradication, but there was a resurgence in 1996 to 1997 that has not yet been fully explained. Increased political unrest leads to population displacement and breakdown of routine control measures, and the levels of vaccine-induced immunity decline with time. A potentially serious finding that requires clarification is the observation that case-to-case transmission appears to have occurred more frequently during 1996 to 1997 than earlier.[89] Monkeypox continues to be sporadically reported.[99] Comparison of the genomes of smallpox virus and monkeypox virus strains isolated up to 1986 suggested that they have evolved separately,[100] and the results of complete genome analysis[101] confirm this observation. Laboratory workers studying monkeypox virus should be vaccinated with vaccinia and handle the virus in certified biosafety cabinets. Biosafety level 2 (BSL-2) containment, according to the *Biosafety in Microbiological and Biomedical Laboratories* definition, should be the minimum containment used. BSL-3 laboratory practices provide additional biosafety protection.

COWPOX

Cowpox Virus

Cowpox sometimes occurs as a rare occupational infection of humans and can be acquired by contact with infected cows; more often, other animals (e.g., infected rats, pet cats, and zoo and circus elephants) have been sources of the disease. Cowpox virus is a rather diverse species and is geographically restricted; it has been isolated from humans and a variety of animals in Europe and adjoining regions of Asia.[102-104] A serosurvey of wild animals in Great Britain found orthopoxvirus antibodies in a portion of bank and field voles and wood mice that were collected, which is consistent with small rodents being reservoir hosts for cowpox virus.[105]

Clinical

Most information is available from a detailed analysis of 54 human cases investigated during 1969 to 1993.[103] Lesions are generally restricted to the hands and face, and most patients (72%) have only one lesion. Multiple lesions may be caused by multiple primary inoculations, autoinoculation, and very occasionally by lymphatic or viremic spread. Lesions in humans occur mainly on the fingers, with reddening and swelling; autoinoculation of other parts of the body may occur, and systemic severe infections have been reported, often in individuals with immunosuppressing conditions.[106] Skin lesions are initially likened to those of a primary vaccinia virus vaccination; the site becomes papular, and in 4 to 5 days a vesicle develops. The lesion passes through macular, papular, vesicular, and pustular stages before forming a hard black crust. The lesion is usually very painful, and erythema and edema are common at the late vesicular and pustular stages. There is usually lymphadenitis, fever, and general malaise, often referred to as influenza-like. These features are usually severe in children; 16 of 54 patients (30%) were hospitalized. Most cases take 6 to 8 weeks to recover; in some cases it may take more than 12 weeks. Scarring is usually permanent.

Laboratory

Electron microscopy of vesicle fluid or extracts of crusts is particularly valuable because it distinguishes between parapox, herpes simplex, and presumptive cowpox infections. Of 24 cases of cowpox in which adequate material was available, electron microscopy was successful in 23. Molecular diagnostics[95-97] may also be used to identify cowpox.

Virus may be isolated on the chorioallantoic membrane, where the production of characteristic hemorrhagic pocks is diagnostic. A cytopathic effect occurs in many cell lines (Vero, MRC-5, RK13) and detection of A-type inclusions is usually diagnostic, as it would be if found in biopsy material. Not all strains of cowpox are identical, and genome analysis may show differences of epidemiologic value.

THERAPY—ORTHOPOXVIRUSES

An active area of research involves the development and evaluation of therapeutics for orthopoxvirus infections. Currently, there are no antiviral drugs licensed for use in the treatment of orthopox or other poxviral illnesses. Comprehensive reviews of the history and latest developments in poxvirus antivirals have been published.[65,107] In addition, such compounds are being tested on experimental models of variola-infected nonhuman primates[108] as well as other animal models of orthopoxvirus infections.[16,17,109] Cidofovir, an antiviral in use for treatment of cytomegalovirus infections in immunosuppressed patients, appears to show promise as an antiviral for treatment of some poxvirus infections. The use of VIG is best described for treatment of certain complications of vaccinia (smallpox) vaccine administration,[28] but it may have utility in treatment of certain other orthopoxvirus infections. No clear benefit has been shown for this product alone in treatment of smallpox.[83]

The earliest drug compounds shown to have activity against orthopoxviruses, including vaccinia, were thiosemicarbazone derivatives. Initial case studies and case series suggested that they were effective in prophylaxis of smallpox and in treatment of progressive vaccinia and eczema vaccinatum.[110,111] However, subsequent double-blind controlled trials of smallpox prophylaxis revealed no benefit.[112]

A number of different classes of antivirals have been tested for potential systemic or topical use against orthopoxviruses. These include compounds predicted to interfere with specific viral enzymes as well as cellular targets.[113] In vitro studies have usually focused on compounds currently licensed or under phase I or II study, although some novel compounds have also been studied. Promising candidates have then been studied in small animal models (mouse, rabbit, and others) and in nonhuman primates. Because monkeypox and smallpox both cause human illness, with mortality ranging from 10% to 40% in nonvaccinated individuals, models have been designed to evaluate drug efficacy in systemic, lethal disease created by intranasal, aerosol, or (historically) intracerebral virus challenge. Intravenous challenges classically have been designed to evaluate the effect of drug on rash development, although higher challenge doses of virus have been used for a lethal model.[114] The primary animal models currently used involve a challenge of aerosolized or intranasal virus, resulting in pulmonary disease and lethality. Models of localized rash lesions have involved scarification of animal skin. Treatment models of keratitis involve scarification of corneal tissue. Work evaluating the potential use of antivirals for treatment of systemic complications of vaccination (progressive vaccinia and eczema vaccinatum) has used immunodeficient mouse populations.

The most studied compounds are inhibitors of DNA polymerase. Some nucleoside analogue compounds with activity against herpesviruses, most notably acyclovir and its derivatives, do not have activity against poxviruses. Other compounds with antiherpesvirus activity do show in vitro and in vivo activity against poxviruses, specifically 5-iodo-2′-deoxyuridine, adenine arabinoside, and trifluorothymidine.[115-118] Because of their systemic toxicity, these compounds have also been used topically for treatment of orthopoxvirus (and herpes) ocular infections. Of the three compounds, trifluorothymidine appears to be most widely available. Many phosphonate-nucleoside analogues, for example, cidofovir, have antiorthopoxviral activity. In vitro, cidofovir has been shown to be active against the orthopoxviruses cowpox, vaccinia, monkeypox, and variola.[17,119,120] In in vivo studies, cidofovir has successfully protected challenged animals when given prophylactically or early in the evolution of disease, often before the onset of overt symptoms. Cidofovir has known renal toxicity and is administered with hydration and probenecid. It has a long intracellular half-life but is not orally bioavailable; the alkoxyalkyl ester analogue of cidofovir, 1-*O*-hexadecyloxypropyl cidofovir (HDP-CDV), is orally bioavailable, and a preliminary report of the protective effect of HDP-CDV in mice challenged with aerosolized cowpox has been noted.[120] Other nucleoside analogues are under study.[121,122]

Other antivirals tested against orthopoxviruses have predicted cellular targets. Ribavirin, an inosine monophosphate dehydrogenase inhibitor, shows in vitro activity against a number of orthopoxviruses[123] and has shown antiorthopoxviral activity in animal models of vaccinia-induced keratitis[124] and mouse tail pock lesions.[125] There are case reports of the use of ribavirin and VIG in the treatment of progressive vaccinia.[126] Initial therapy with ribavirin alone was ineffective at stemming new lesions; however, with the addition of VIG, new lesion development was stopped. More comprehensive summaries of antiorthopox therapeutic development are available[113,114,127]; anticipate ongoing updates as this is an emerging research area.

REFERENCES

1. Moyer RW, Arif BM Black DN, et al. Poxviridae. In: van Regenmortel MHV, Fauquet CM, Bishop DHL, et al, eds. Virus Taxonomy: Seventh Report of the International Committee on Taxonomy of Viruses. San Diego: Academic Press; 2000:137-157.
2. Fenner F, Wittek R, Dumbell KR. The Orthopoxviruses. Boston: Academic Press; 1989:6.
3. Moss B. Poxviridae: The viruses and their replication. In: Fields BN, Knipe DM, Howley PM, Griffin DE, eds. Fields' Virology. 4th ed. Philadelphia: Lippincott Williams & Wilkins; 2001:2849-2883.
4. Esposito JJ, Fenner F. Poxviruses. In: Fields BN, Knipe DM, Howley PM, Griffin DE, eds. Fields' Virology. 4th ed. Philadelphia: Lippincott Williams & Wilkins; 2001:2885-2923.
5. Damon IK, Esposito JJ. Poxviruses that infect humans. In: Murray PR, Baron EJ, Jorgensen JH, et al, eds. Manual of Clinical Microbiology. Washington, DC: ASM Press; 2003:1583-1592.
6. Nakano JH. Poxviruses. In: Lennette EH, Schmidt NJ, eds. Diagnostic Procedures for Viral, Rickettsial, and Chlamydial Infections. 5th ed. Washington, DC: American Public Health Association; 1979:257-308.
7. Smith GL, Vanderplasschen A, Law M. The formation and function of extracellular enveloped vaccinia virus. J Gen Virol. 2002;83:2915-2931.
8. Vanderplasschen A, Smith GL. A novel binding assay using confocal microscopy: Demonstration that the intracellular vaccinia virions bind to different cellular receptors. J Virol. 1997;71:4032-4041.
9. Payne LG. Significance of extracellular enveloped virus in the in vitro and in vivo dissemination of vaccinia virus. J Gen Virol. 1980;50:89-100.
10. Fenner F, Wittek R, Dumbell KR. The Pathogenesis, Pathology, and Immunology of Orthopoxvirus Infections. The Orthopoxviruses. Boston: Academic Press; 1989: 85-141.
11. Roberts JA. Histopathogenesis of mousepox. I. Respiratory infection. Br J Exp Pathol. 1962;43:451-461.
12. Bedson HS, Duckworth MJ. Rabbitpox: An experimental study of the pathways of infection in rabbits. J Pathol Bacteriol. 1963;85:1-20.
13. Buller RM, Palumbo GJ. Poxvirus pathogenesis. Microbiol Rev. 1991;55:80-122.
14. Zaucha GM, Jahrling PB, Geisbert TW, et al. The pathology of experimental aerosolized monkeypox virus infection in cynomolgus monkeys (Macaca fascicularis). Lab Invest. 2001;81:1581-1600.
15. Smith S, Kotwal GJ. Immune response to poxvirus infections in various animals. Crit Rev Microbiol. 2002;28:149-185.
16. Martinez MJ, Bray M, Huggins JW. A mouse model of aerosol-transmitted orthopoxviral disease. Arch Pathol Lab Med. 2000;124:362-377.
17. Bray M, Martinez M, Smee DF, et al. Cidofovir protects mice against lethal aerosol or intranasal cowpox virus challenge. J Infect Dis. 2000;181:10-19.
18. Karupiah G, Fredrickson TN, Holmes KL, et al. Importance of interferons in recovery from mousepox. J Virol. 1993;63:4214-4226.
19. Wakamiya N, Okada N, Wang YL, et al. Tumor cells treated with vaccinia virus can activate the alternate pathway of mouse complement. Jpn J Cancer Res. 1989;80: 765-770.
20. West BC, Eschete ML, Cox ME, et al. Neutrophil uptake of vaccinia virus in vitro. J Infect Dis. 1987;156:597-606.
21. Jones JF. Interactions between human neutrophils and vaccinia virus: Induction of oxidative metabolism and virus inactivation. Pediatr Res. 1982;16:525-529.
22. Doherty PC, Korngold R. Characteristics of poxvirus-induced meningitis: Virus specific and non-specific cytotoxic effectors in the inflammatory exudates. Scand J Immunol. 1983;18:1-7.
23. Blanden RV, Gardner ID. The cell-mediated response to ectromelia virus infection. I. Kinetics and characteristics of the primary effector T cell response in vivo. Cell Immunol. 1976;22:271-282.
24. Seet BT, Johnston JB, Brunetti CR, et al. Poxviruses and immune evasion. Annu Rev Immunol. 2003;21:377-423.
25. Smith GL, Symons JA, Khanna A, et al. Vaccinia virus immune evasion. Immunol Rev. 1997;159:137-154.
26. Johnston JB, MacFadden G. Poxvirus immunomodulatory strategies: Current perspectives. J Virol. 2003;77:6093-6100.
27. Baxby D. Jenner's Smallpox Vaccine: The Riddle of Vaccinia Virus and Its Origin. London: Heinemann Educational; 1981:1-214.
28. Cono J, Casey CG, Bell D. Smallpox vaccination and adverse reactions: Guidance for clinicians. MMWR Recomm Rep. 2003;52(RR-4):1-28.
29. Arenstein AW, Rubins K, Relman DA. Smallpox vaccination. N Engl J Med. 2003;348:1925.
30. Neff JM. Vaccinia virus (cowpox). In: Mandell GL, Bennett JE, Dolin R, eds. Principles and Practice of Infectious Diseases. New York: Churchill Livingstone; 2000:1553-1555.
31. World Health Organization Expert Committee on Smallpox Eradication: Second report. WHO Tech Rep Ser. 1972;493:35.
32. Mack TM. Smallpox in Europe, 1950-1971. J Infect Dis. 1972;125:161-169.
33. Hanna W, Baxby B. Studies in small-pox and vaccination. 1913. Rev Med Virol 2002;12:201-209.
34. Massoudi MS, Barker L, Schwartz B. Effectiveness of postexposure vaccination for the prevention of smallpox: Results of a Delphi analysis. J Infect Dis. 2003;188: 973-976.
35. Rao AR, Jacob ES, Kamalakshi S, et al. Epidemiological studies in smallpox: A study of intrafamilial transmission in a series of 254 infected families. Indian J Med Res. 1968;56:1826-1854.
36. Heiner GG, Fatima N, McCrumb FR. A study of intrafamilial transmission of smallpox. Am J Epidemiol. 1974;99:316-326.
37. Sommer A. The 1972 smallpox outbreak in Khulna Municipality, Bangladesh. II. Effectiveness of surveillance and containment in urban epidemic control. Am J Epidemiol. 1974;99:303-313.
38. Fenner F. Studies in mousepox: Infectious ectromelia of mice. IV. Quantitative investigations on the spread of virus through the host in actively and passively immunized animals. Aust J Exp Biol Med. 1947;27:1-18.
39. Mack TM, Noble J Jr, Thomas DB. A prospective study of serum antibody and protection against smallpox Am J Trop Med Hyg. 1972;21:214-218.
40. Sarkar JK, Mitra AC, Mukherjee MK. The minimum protective levels of antibodies in smallpox. Bull World Health Organ. 1975;52:307-311.
41. McClain DJ, Harrison S, Yeager CL, et al. Immunologic responses to vaccinia vaccines administered by different parenteral routes. J Infect Dis. 1997;175:756-763.
42. Ennis FA, Cruz J, Demkowicz WE Jr, et al. Primary induction of human CD8+ cytotoxic T lymphocytes and interferon-γ–producing T cells after smallpox vaccination. J Infect Dis. 2002;185:1657-1659.
43. Demkowicz WE Jr, Littaua RA, Wang J, Ennis FA. Human cytotoxic T-cell memory: Long lived responses to vaccinia virus. J Virol. 1996;70: 2627-2631.
44. Hammersland E, Lewis MW, Hansen SG, et al. Duration of antiviral immunity after smallpox vaccination. Nat Med. 2003;9:1131-1137.
45. Hsieh SM, Pan SC, Chen SY, et al. Age distribution for T cell reactivity to vaccinia virus in a healthy population. Clin Infect Dis. 2003;38:86-89.
46. Baruch E, Roth Y, Winder A, et al. The persistence of neutralizing antibodies after revaccination against smallpox. J Infect Dis. 1990;161:446-448.
47. Frey SE, Newman FK, Yan L, Belshe RB. Response to smallpox vaccine in persons immunized in the distant past. JAMA. 2003;289:3295-3296.
48. Bray M, Wright M. Progressive vaccinia. Clin Infect Dis. 2003;36:766-774.
49. Neff JM, Lane MM, Pert J, et al. Complications of smallpox vaccination. I. National survey in the United States, 1963. N Engl J Med. 1967;276:125-132.
50. Lane JM, Ruben FL, Beff JM, Millar JD. Complications of smallpox vaccination, 1968: National surveillance in the United States. N Engl J Med 1969;281:1201-1208.
51. Lane JM, Ruben F, Neff JM, Millar JD. Complications of smallpox vaccination, 1968: Results of ten statewide surveys. J Infect Dis. 1970;122:303-309.
52. Feery BJ. Adverse reactions after smallpox vaccination. Med J Aust. 1977;2:41-42.
53. Fulginetti V, Kempe C, Hathaway W, et al. Progressive vaccinia in immunologically deficient individuals. Birth Defects Orig Artic Ser. 1968;4:129-145.
54. Goldstein J, Neff J, Lane J, Koplan J. Smallpox vaccination reactions, prophylaxis and therapy of complications. Pediatrics. 1975;55:342-347.
55. Keidan SE, McCarthy K, Haworth JC. Fatal generalized vaccinia with failure of antibody production and absence of serum gamma globulin. Arch Dis Child. 1953;28:110-116.
56. Copeman PWM, Wallace HJ. Eczema vaccinatum. Br Med J. 1964;5414:906-908.
57. Rachelefsky GS, Opelz G, Mickey R. Defective T cell function in atopic dermatitis. J Allergy Clin Immunol. 1976;57:569-576.
58. Kempe CH. Studies on smallpox and complications of smallpox vaccination. Pediatrics. 1960;26:176-189.
59. Miller JR, Cirino NM, Philbin EF. Generalized vaccinia 2 days after smallpox revaccination. Emerg Infect Dis. 2003;12:1649-1650.
60. Fenner F, Henderson DA, Arita I, Jezek Z. Smallpox and Its Eradication. Geneva: World Health Organization; 1988:307.
61. De Vries E. Postvaccinial Perivenous Encephalitis. Amsterdam: Elsevier; 1960.
62. Tenembaum S, Nestor C, Fejerman N. Acute disseminated encephalomyelitis: A long term follow-up study of 84 pediatric patients. Neurology. 2002;59:1224-1231.
63. Guvich E, Viseova I. Vaccinia virus in postvaccinial encephalitis. Acta Virol. 1983;27:154-159.
64. Ruben FL, Lane JM. Ocular vaccinia: An epidemiologic analysis of 348 cases. Arch Ophthalmol. 1970;84:45-48.
65. Kern E. In vitro activity of potential anti-poxvirus agents. Antivir Res. 2003;57:35-40.
66. Karjalainen J, Heikkila J, Nieminen MS, et al. Etiology of mild acute infectious myocarditis. Acta Med Scand. 1983;213:65-73.
67. Helle EJ, Koskenvuo K, Heikkila J, et al. Myocardial complications of immunisations. Ann Clin Res. 1978;10:280-287.
68. Halsell JS, Riddle JR, Atwood JE, et al. Myopericarditis following smallpox vaccination among vaccinia-naïve US military personnel. JAMA. 2003; 289:3283-3289.
69. Grabenstein JD, Winkenwerder W. US military smallpox vaccination program experience. JAMA. 2003;289:3278-3282.
70. Supplemental recommendations on adverse events following smallpox vaccine in the pre-event vaccination program: Recommendations of the Advisory Committee on Immunization Practices. MMWR Morb Mortal Wkly Rep. 2003;52:282-284. http://www.cdc.gov/mmwr/preview/mmwrhtml/mm5213a5.htm
71. Cardiac adverse events following smallpox vaccination—United States, 2003. MMWR Morb Mortal Wkly Rep. 2003;52:248-250.
72. Macadam DB, Whitaker W. Cardiac complication after vaccination for smallpox. Br Med J. 1962;5312:1099-1100.
73. Ahlborg B, Linroth K, Nordgren B. ECG—changes without subjective symptoms after smallpox vaccination of military personnel. Acta Med Scand. 1966;S464:127-134.
74. Update: Adverse events following civilian smallpox vaccination—United States, 2003. MMWR Morb Mortal Wkly Rep. 2003;52:819-820.
75. Update on cardiac and other adverse events following civilian smallpox vaccination—United States, 2003. MMWR Morb Mortal Wkly Rep. 2003;52:639-642.
76. Talbot TR, Bredenberg HK, Smith M, et al. Focal and generalized folliculitis following smallpox vaccination among vaccinia-naïve recipients. JAMA. 2003;289: 3290-3294.

77. Wharton M, Strikas RA, Harpaz R, et al. Recommendations for using smallpox vaccine in a pre-event vaccination program. MMWR Recomm Rep. 2003;52(RR-7): 1-16.

78. Dumbell KR, Richardson M. Virological investigations of specimens from buffaloes affected by buffalopox in Maharashtra State, India between 1985 and 1987. Arch Virol. 1993;128:257-267.

79. Mathew T. Advances in Medical and Veterinary Virology, Immunology and Epidemiology: Cultivation and Immunological Studies on Pox Groups of Viruses with Special Reference to Buffalo Pox Virus. New Delhi, India: Thajema Publishers; 1987.

80. Damaso CRA, Esposito JJ, Condit RC, Moussatche N. An emergent poxvirus from humans and cattle in Rio de Janeiro state: Cantagalo virus may derive from Brazilian smallpox vaccine. Virology. 2000;277:439-449.

81. Schatzmayr HG, Sampaio de Lemos ER, Mazur C, et al. Detection of poxvirus in cattle associated with human cases in the state of Rio de Janeiro: Preliminary report. Mem Inst Oswaldo Cruz. 2000;95:625-627.

82. Rupprecht CE, Blass L, Smith K, et al. Human infection due to recombinant vaccinia-rabies glycoprotein virus N Engl J Med. 2001;345:582-586.

83. Fenner F, Henderson DA, Arita I, et al. Smallpox and Its Eradication. Geneva: World Health Organization; 1988.

84. Breman JA, Henderson DA. Diagnosis and management of smallpox. N Engl J Med 2002;346:1300-1308.

85. Dixon CW. Differential Diagnosis Laboratory Diagnosis Post-mortem Appearance in Smallpox. London: Churchill; 1962:67-91.

86. Bremen JG. Monkeypox: An emerging infection for humans? In: Scheld WM, Craig WA, Hughes JM, eds. Emerging Infections 4. Washington, DC: ASM Press; 2000: 45-67.

87. Jezek Z, Fenner F. Human monkeypox. Monogr Virol. 1988;17:1-140.

88. Hutin YJF, Williams RJ, Malfait P, et al. Outbreak of human monkeypox in the Democratic Republic of Congo, 1996-1997. Emerg Infect Dis. 2000;7:434-438.

89. Heymann DL, Szczeniowski M, Esteves K. Re-emergence of monkeypox in Africa: A review of the past six years. Br Med Bull. 1998;54:693-702.

90. Khodacevich L, Jezek Z, Messinger D. Monkeypox virus: Ecology and public health significance. Bull World Health Organ. 1988;66:747-752.

91. Update: Multistate outbreak of monkeypox—Illinois, Indiana, Kansas, Missouri, Ohio, and Wisconsin, 2003. MMWR Morb Mortal Wkly Rep. 2003;52:642-646.

92. Anderson M, Frenkel LD, Homann S, Guffey JA. A case of severe monkeypox virus disease in an American child: Emerging infections and changing professional values. Pediatr Infect Dis J. 2003;22:1093-1096.

93. Reed KD, Melski JW, Graham MB, et al. The detection of monkeypox in humans in the western hemisphere. N Engl J Med 2004;350:342-350.

94. Ibrahim MS, Kulesh D, Saleh SS, et al. Real-time PCR assay to detect smallpox virus. J Clin Microbiol. 2003;41:3385-3389.

95. Meyer H, Ropp SL, Esposito JJ. Gene for A-type inclusion body protein is useful for a polymerase chain reaction assay to differentiate orthopoxviruses. J Virol Methods. 1997;64:217-222.

96. Meyer H, Ropp SL, Esposito JJ. Poxviruses. In: Warnes A, Stephenson J, eds. Methods in Molecular Biology: Diagnostic Virology Protocols, 1998. Totowa, NJ: Humana Press; 1998:199-211.

97. Ropp SL, Jin Q, Knight JC, et al. PCR strategy for identification and differentiation of smallpox and other orthopoxviruses. J Clin Microbiol. 1995;33:2069-2076.

98. Loparev VN, Massung RF, Esposito JJ, Meyer H. Detection and differentiation of Old World orthopoxviruses: Restriction length polymorphism of the crmB gene region. J Clin Microbiol. 2001;39:94-100.

99. Meyer H, Perrichot M, Stemmler P, et al. Outbreaks of disease suspected of being due to human monkeypox virus infection in the Democratic Republic of Congo in 2001. J Clin Microbiol. 2002;40:2919-2921.

100. Douglas NJ, Dumbell KR. Independent evolution of monkeypox and variola viruses. J Virol. 1992;66:7565-7567.

101. Shchelkunov SN, Totmenin AV, Safronov PF, et al. Analysis of the monkeypox genome. Virology. 2002;297:172-194.

102. Baxby D. Poxvirus infections in domestic animals. In: Darai G, ed. Virus Diseases in Laboratory and Captive Animals. Boston: Nijhoff; 1988:17-35.

103. Baxby D, Bennett M, Getty B. Human cowpox 1969-93: A review based on 54 cases. Br J Dermatol. 1994;131:598-607.

104. Bennett M, Gaskell CJ, Baxby D, et al. Feline cowpox infection. J Small Anim Pract. 1990;31:167-173.

105. Bennett M, Crouch AJ, Begon M, et al. Cowpox in British voles and mice. J Comp Pathol. 1997;116:35-44.

106. Pelkonen PM, Tarvainen K, Hynninen A, et al. Cowpox with severe generalized eruption, Finland. Emerg Infect Dis. 2003;9:1458-1461.

107. Neyts J, De Clerq E. Therapy and short term prophylaxis of poxvirus infections: Historical background and perspectives. Antiviral Res. 2003;57:25-33.

108. LeDuc J, Damon I, Meegan J, et al. Smallpox research activities: U.S. interagency collaboration. Emerg Infect Dis. 2002;8:742-745.

109. Keith KA, Hitchcock MJ, Lee WA, et al. Evaluation of nucleoside phosphonates and their analogs and prodrugs for inhibition of orthopoxvirus replication. Antimicrob Agents Chemother. 2003;47:2193-2198.

110. Bauer DJ. The antiviral and synergistic actions of isatin thiosemicarbazone and certain phenoxypyrimidines in vaccinia infection in mice. Br J Exp Pathol. 1955;36: 105-114.

111. Rao M, McFadzean J, Squires S. The laboratory and clinical assessment of an isothiazole thiosemicarbazone (M&B 7714) against pox viruses. Ann NY Acad Sci. 1965;130:118-127.

112. Heiner GG, Fatima N, Russell PK, et al. Field trials of methisazone as a prophylactic agent against smallpox. Am J Epidemiol. 1971;94:435-449.

113. Neyts J, De Clerq ED. Therapy and short term prophylaxis of poxvirus infections: Historical background and perspectives. Antiviral Res. 2003;57:25-33.

114. Smee DF, Sidwell RW. A review of compounds exhibiting anti-orthopoxvirus activity in animal models. Antiviral Res. 2003;57:41-52.

115. Neyts J, Verbeken E, De Clerq E. Effect of 5-iodo-2'-deoxyuridine on vaccinia virus (orthopoxvirus) infections in mice. Antimicrob Agents Chemother. 2002;46: 2842-2847.

116. Hyndiuk R, Seideman S, Leibsohn JM. Treatment of vaccinial dermatitis with trifluorothymidine. Arch Ophthalmol. 1976;94:1785-1786.

117. Hyndiuk R, Okumoto M, Damiano R, et al. Treatment of vaccinial keratitis with vidarabine. Arch Ophthalmol. 1976;94:1363-1364.

118. Kaufman H, Nesburn A, Maloney E. Cure of vaccinia infection by 5-iodo-2-deoxyuridine. Virology. 1962;18:567-569.

119. Quenelle DC, Collins DJ, Kern ER. Efficacy of multiple or single dose cidofovir against vaccinia and cowpox virus infections in mice. Antimicrob Agents Chemother. 2003;47:3275-3280.

120. Winegarden KL, Ciesla SL, Aldern KA, et al. Oral pharmacokinetics and preliminary toxicology of 1-O-hexadecyloxypropyl-cidofovir in mice. Abstracts of the 15th International Conference on Antiviral Research, Prague, Czech Republic, March 17-21, 2002. Antiviral Res. 2002;53:A67.

121. Smee D, Bailey K, Sidwell R. Treatment of lethal cowpox virus respiratory infections in mice with 2-amino-7-[(1,3-dihydroxy-2-propoxy)methyl]purine and its orally active diacetate ester prodrug. Antiviral Res. 2002;54:113-120.

122. Neyts J, De Clerq E. Efficacy of 2-amino-7-(1,3-dihydroxy-2-propoxymethyl)purine for treatment of vaccinia virus (orthopoxvirus) infections in mice. Antimicrob Agents Chemother. 2002;45:84-87.

123. Baker RO, Bray M, Huggins JW. Potential antiviral therapeutics for smallpox, monkeypox and other orthopoxvirus infections. Antiviral Res. 2003;57:13-23.

124. Sidwell R, Allen L, Khare G, et al. Effect of 1-beta-D-ribofuranosyl-1,2,4-triazole-3-carboxamide (Virazole, ICN 1229) on herpes and vaccinia keratitis and encephalitis in laboratory animals. Antimicrob Agents Chemother. 1973;3:242-246.

125. De Clerq E, Luczak M, Shugar D, et al. Effect of cytosine arabinoside, iododeoxyuridine, ethyldeoxyuridine, thiocyanatodeoxyuridine, and ribavirin on tail lesion formation in mice infected with vaccinia virus. Proc Soc Exp Biol Med. 1976;151:487-490.

126. Kesson A, Ferguson J, Rawlinson W, Cunningham A. Progressive vaccinia treated with ribavirin and vaccinia immune globulin. Clin Infect Dis. 1997;25:911-914.

127. Bray M. Pathogenesis and potential antiviral therapy of complications of smallpox vaccination. Antiviral Res. 2003;58:101-114.

Other Poxviruses That Infect Humans: Parapoxviruses, Molluscum Contagiosum, and Tanapox

INGER DAMON

PARAPOXVIRUSES

Parapoxviruses, which are found worldwide, are common pathogens of sheep, goats, and cattle. Human infection, characterized by localized epithelial lesions, is an occupational hazard for those who handle infected animals. Parapoxvirus infection in sheep and goats is usually referred to as *contagious pustular dermatitis/ecthyma* or *orf*, and the corresponding human infection as *orf*. Parapoxvirus infection of dairy cattle is usually referred to as *paravaccinia, pseudocowpox*, or *ring sores*, and the human equivalent as *paravaccinia, pseudocowpox*, or *milker's nodes*. Parapoxviruses of beef cattle are referred to as *bovine papular stomatitis virus*. Other zoonotic parapoxviruses demonstrated to infect humans are derived from camel exposure (contagious ecthyma) or, less often, from seals (sealpox).[1] Lesions in animals are found on the skin, in the oropharyngeal mucosa, and on external surfaces. Detailed reviews are available.[2-4]

Morphology and Composition of the Agent

The parapoxviruses have a unique appearance among poxviruses, as revealed by negative-stain transmission electron microscopy. Most poxvirus virions are brick-shaped, but parapoxvirus particles are oblong, rounded, or ovoid. In addition, members of the Parapoxvirus genus have a characteristic M form that can be observed by negative-stain electron microscopy: one long spicule wraps the particle, giving a crisscross effect.[5] The stability of the virus in scabs is correlated with possible transmission of the virus through fomites.

The parapoxvirus genome consists of a linear, double-stranded DNA of about 135 kbp with covalently closed terminal hairpins; the genome is relatively high in G+C content and is smaller than other poxvirus genomes. Complete genome sequences of orf virus and bovine stomatitis virus have recently been reported.[6] Several proteins described to have potential roles in viral pathogenesis include a chemokine-binding protein,[7] an interleukin (IL)-10 homologue,[8] a vascular endothelial growth factor homologue,[9] an interferon resistance gene,[10] and a cytokine-binding protein.[11]

Pathogenesis and Immune Response

Infection, which occurs via cuts and scratches, usually remains localized. Human lesions of orf are produced by hypertrophy and proliferation of epidermal cells, which is often marked and perhaps related to the endothelial growth factor homologue encoded by the virus and to leukocyte infiltration. Histologic examination of human lesions demonstrates many small multilocular vesicles within the dermis; true macrovesicles rarely occur.[12,13] Generalized symptoms of lymphadenopathy, malaise, and disseminated lesions are uncommon, and the immune response is not protective against disease recurrence on a lifelong basis.[13,14] Second attacks occur in 8% to 12% of individuals.[13,15]

Clinical Features

Detailed descriptions of human disease progression are available,[12-14] as are illustrations.[16,17] In brief, infection manifests as localized lesions

at the site of inoculation by a diseased animal. The portal of entry is usually a break in the skin. After a brief incubation period of 3 to 5 days, lesions begin as (pruritic) erythematous macules, then raise to form papules, often with a target appearance. Lesions become nodular or vesicular, and orf lesions often ulcerate after 2 to 3 weeks. Complete healing can take up to 4 to 6 weeks.[13] Very large granulomatous lesions occur, and these may need surgical removal.[18] Milker's node lesions may have a more nodular appearance, without ulceration.

Diagnosis

Polymerase chain reaction diagnostic tests generic for parapoxvirus[19] and orf[20] have been reported; however, the infection is usually clinically diagnosed on the basis of exposure history and the presence of a characteristic lesion(s). Negative-stain transmission microscopy of lesional material examined by a skilled observer can be diagnostic if the characteristic structure is observed. Virus isolation in tissue culture usually requires primary ovine or bovine cells and may be difficult to attain.[21] The development of immunologic sera specific for parapoxviruses is another source for diagnostic reagents.[22]

Epidemiology

Infection with parapoxvirus is an occupational hazard of farm workers, abattoir workers, veterinarians, students, and others with frequent exposure to sheep, cattle, or goats. Human orf infection is most common in the spring, a time when the bottle-feeding of lambs may predispose humans to exposure risks, and in the fall, when slaughtering and shearing occur.[13] Of 191 cases of orf or milker's nodule with a known source surveyed from 1978 to 1995, 84% had an ovine source and 16% were transmitted by cattle. An additional 32 cases occurred in abattoir workers.[23] Most workers at risk get infected at some point in their career, and reinfection is not uncommon. Infected individuals should take care not to further infect themselves by autoinoculation or to spread infection to contacts, including animals. The vaccine used to control orf in sheep is fully virulent and has caused human infection.

Treatment

In most cases, the disease is self-limited. Anecdotal reports of the use of 3% cidofovir topical cream[24,25] have described apparent beneficial effects; however, no controlled trials are available.

MOLLUSCUM CONTAGIOSUM

Molluscum contagiosum, a disease causing a benign, self-limited skin "tumor" or papular eruption, occurs worldwide and is regarded as a specific human infection.[26] Although there is no evidence of disease transmission between humans and other animals, lesions resembling molluscum and containing pox virions have been detected in species other than humans (e.g., horses and chimpanzees).

Description of the Agent

Four subtypes, characterized by restriction endonuclease digests, have been described.[27] Disease presentation by all subtypes appears to be similar. The genome of molluscum contagiosum virus (MCV) subtype I has been sequenced.[28] This genome encodes several novel gene products involved in its pathogenesis and in evasion of the immune system, including an IL-18–binding protein[29] and apoptosis inhibitors,[30] among others.

Pathogenesis and Pathology

Molluscum contagiosum lesions have long been known to have a distinctive pathology. In 1841, the first description of characteristic molluscum bodies—Henderson-Paterson bodies—was provided by Henderson and Paterson. Onset of infection occurs when the virus begins replication in the lower layers of the epidermis,[31] extending upward. The incubation period is quite variable and can be lengthy (2 to 7 weeks; as long as 6 months has been suggested). The epidermis hypertrophies and extends down into the underlying dermal strata.

Characteristic inclusions (Henderson-Paterson bodies, or molluscum bodies) are formed in the prickle cell layer and gradually enlarge as cells age and migrate to the surface. These cells are replaced by hyperplasia of the basal cell layer. The structure of the basement membrane remains intact; the hypertrophied epidermal cells, with their cytoplasm occupied by a large acidophilic granular mass (the molluscum body), project above the skin to appear as a tumor.[32] Little to no inflammatory infiltrate is seen until late in disease, just before natural resolution of the lesion occurs.[33]

Clinical Features

Infection occurs after breakage of the skin. The characteristic lesion begins as a small papule and, when mature, is a discrete, 2- to 5-mm-diameter, smooth, dome-shaped, pearly or flesh-colored nodule that is often umbilicated (Fig. 130-1). A cheesy off-white, sometimes yellowish, material is easily expressed from lesions. Usually, 1 to 20 lesions occur, but occasionally, there may be hundreds. Because of multiple simultaneous infections, or mechanical spread, these lesions may become confluent along the line of a scratch, and satellite lesions are occasionally seen.

In children, lesions occur mainly on the trunk and proximal extremities. In adults, they tend to occur on the trunk, pubic area, and thighs, but in all cases, infection may be transmitted to other parts by autoinoculation.[33] In human immunodeficiency virus (HIV), infections appear to occur along the beard line in males; with facial involvement, there have been reports of ocular involvement such as lesions on the bulbar conjunctiva.[34] Individual lesions last for about 2 months, but the disease usually persists for 6 to 9 months.[35] Severe and prolonged infection tends to occur in individuals with impaired cell-mediated immunity, including persons with HIV infection.[26,36]

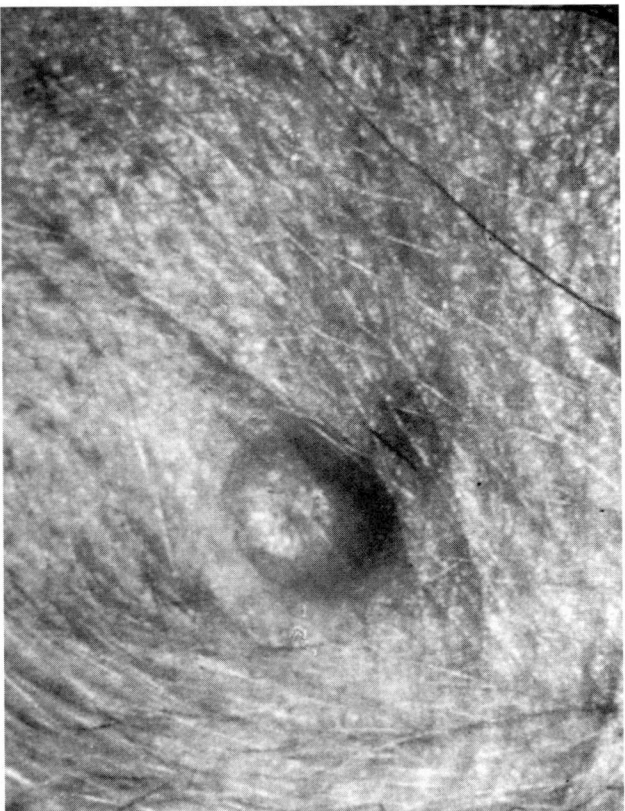

FIGURE 130-1. Molluscum contagiosum. *(Reprinted by permission from Wood MJ. Skin and soft tissue infection. In: Farrar WE, Wood MJ, Innes JA, et al, eds. Infectious Diseases Text and Color Atlas. Hong Kong: Gower Medical Publishing; 1992:11.17, Fig. 11.69. By permission of Mosby International Ltd.)*

Diagnosis

The clinical appearance of lesions is generally sufficiently characteristic to permit clinical diagnosis. Brick-shaped virions can usually be seen in large numbers if the cheesy material expressed from the lesion is examined by transmission negative-stain electron microscopy. The virus has not been cultured in standard tissue culture systems. The characteristic histopathology of these lesions is diagnostic; PCR methods have been described.[37,38] On occasion, similar-appearing umbilicated lesions have been seen in acquired immunodeficiency syndrome (AIDS) patients with disseminated cryptococcosis.

Epidemiology and Control

The virus occurs worldwide, and reports of increasing disease have paralleled reports of AIDS. Traditional modes of transmission are associated with mild skin trauma and in some cases fomites (shared towels); however, evidence is increasing that the disease is sexually transmitted and that genital lesions are common.[26] This disease presents a significant concern for individuals whose children are in day care or school situations, where concerns about potential transmission to other children may exist. Covering of lesions and hand hygiene after contact with lesions should prevent transmission in these situations.

Therapeutics

Infection is benign and recovery is usually spontaneous, but treatment may be sought for cosmetic reasons, particularly for facial or multiple lesions. Various treatments have been tried.[26] Cryotherapy,[39] mechanical curettage,[39,40] and chemical treatments include podophyllin/podofilox, cantharidin, iodine, and tretinoin.[40-42] Irritation has been an adverse effect of many of the chemical methods of treatment. Topical application of an antiviral 3% cidofovir cream or suspension[43,44] has been reported to be beneficial, as has potentially immune-modulating cimetidine[45] or topical imiquimod therapy.[46] The absence of well-controlled trials makes it difficult for the clinician to assess the efficacy of various therapeutic regimens. For individuals with AIDS and molluscum, the use of highly active antiretroviral therapy, with improved CD4 counts, appears to be efficacious.

YATAPOXVIRUSES

Tanapox

Human infection with tanapox virus, which was first recognized in the Lake Tana area of Kenya in 1957, was best characterized during post-smallpox eradication surveillance efforts. An account of 264 laboratory-confirmed cases from Zaire (Democratic Republic of Congo), with color illustrations, is available,[47] as is information on the virus itself.[48] The genome of the virus has been sequenced.[49] Yaba-like disease virus of monkeys is the virus that causes tanapox in humans.[50] Recent anecdotal reports of human disease outside Africa have been published and illustrate the need to consider poxvirus causes of illness in travelers returning from and emigrants from areas where the virus is endemic.[51-53]

Pathophysiology and Clinical Features

Tanapox infection begins with a short febrile illness of 2 to 4 days with temperatures of 38° C to 39° C, that is sometimes accompanied by headache, backache, or prostration. The eruption of a lesion is often heralded by pruritus at the site. The lesion appears as a hyperpigmented macule, often with central elevation. The macule then evolves to a papule, with palpable induration. Fever and systemic symptoms wane as the lesion manifests. The papule then becomes more "pocklike" but contains no fluid; umbilication or the formation of a pseudocrust has been reported at this stage. Typically, the papule evolves into a firm, deep-seated, elevated nodule. At the end of the first week, the lesion is surrounded by erythema and by indurated skin. Regional adenopathy is common at this stage. After this stage, lesions either ulcerate or became larger nodules—up to 2 cm in diameter. In the African series, maximum size was usually reached within 2 weeks, then the local inflammatory response began to wane and the lesion began to granulate. Resolution of lesions occurred within 6 weeks.[47]

Most cases (78% in one series[47]) involve a solitary nodule; however, as many as 10 lesions on one individual have been described. The most common location (72%) for lesions is the lower extremities, and the least common locations are the face and parts of the body that are normally covered by clothing.[47] Infection appears to confer lifelong immunity.

Diagnosis

For diagnosis of tanapox, the limited geographic distribution should be considered, as well as travel history. Unique clinical features that allow the differentiation of tanapox from other orthopoxvirus infections include the nodular nature of the rash lesion, local adenopathy, the paucity of lesions, the benign disease course, and the protracted course of rash resolution. As well, the solid nodular/ulcerated lesions are larger and develop more slowly than those of monkeypox, but they are smaller and develop more rapidly than do tropical ulcers.

Tanapox virus can be detected by electron microscopy, and the virions usually appear enveloped,[54] but this finding would not exclude the possibility of infection with other morphologically similar brick-shaped poxviruses; nucleic acid testing[51,52] on lesion extract could be used for that purpose. Tanapox virus grows in a number of cell lines (e.g., owl monkey kidney, Vero, MRC-5, BSC-1) but not on CAM.

Epidemiology and Control

Tanapox virus is restricted to Africa, principally to Kenya and the Democratic Republic of the Congo, and likely has a simian reservoir.[50] Cases of direct primate-to-human transmission, via a break in skin, have been described in animal handlers, although such cases appear to be extremely rare.[55,56] Several factors have led to speculation that an insect or arthropod intermediary may be involved in transmission of tanapox virus to humans: persons confirmed to have tanapox infection have denied contact with non-human primates but have reported arthropod and culcine mosquito bites prior to infection, and in patients who developed multiple lesions, there was no evidence that the virus had been spread mechanically.[47] Furthermore, the seasonal variation of human tanapox infections follows the activity of local arthropod populations. No human-to-human transmission has been reported. With the exception of vaccination, measures for the prevention of monkeypox would be applicable to tanapox.

REFERENCES

1. Becher P, Konig M, Muller G, Siebert U, Thiel HJ. Characterization of sealpox, a separate member of the parapoxviruses. Arch Virol. 2002;147:113-114.
2. Haig DM, Mercer AA. Ovine diseases: Orf. Vet Res. 1998;29:311-326.
3. Mercer A, Fleming S, Robinson A, Nettleton P, Reid H. Molecular genetic analyses of parapoxviruses pathogenic for humans. Arch Virol Suppl. 1997;13:25-34.
4. Robinson AJ, Lyttle DJ. Parapoxviruses: Their biology and potential as recombinant vaccines. In: Binns MM, Smith GL, eds. Recombinant Poxviruses. Boca Raton: CRC Press; 1992:285-327.
5. Nakano JH. Poxviruses. In: Lennette EH, Schmidt NJ, eds. Diagnostic Procedures for Viral, Rickettsial, and Chlamydial Infections. 5th ed. Washington, DC: American Public Health Association, Inc; 1979:257-308.
6. Delhon G, Tulman ER, Alfonso CL. Genomes of parapoxviruses, orf virus, and bovine papular stomatitis virus. J Virol. 2004;78:168-177.
7. Seet BT, McCaughan CA, Handel TM, et al. Analysis of an orf virus chemokine-binding protein: Shifting ligand specificities among a family of poxvirus viroceptors. PNAS. 2003;100:15137-15142.
8. Fleming SB, Haig DM, Nettleton P, et al. Sequence and functional analysis of a homolog of interleukin-10 encoded by the parapoxvirus orf virus. Virus Genes. 2000;21:85-95.
9. Savory LJ, Stacker SA, Fleming SB, Niven BE, Mercer AA. Viral vascular endothelial growth factor plays a critical role in orf virus infection. J Virol. 2000;74:10699-10706.
10. Haig DM, McInnes CJ, Thompson J, Wood A, Bunyan K, Mercer AA. The orf virus OV20.0L gene product is involved in interferon resistance and inhibits an interferon-inducible, double-stranded RNA-dependent kinase. Immunology. 1998;93:335-340.
11. Deane D, McInnes CJ, Percival A, et al. Orf virus encodes a novel secreted protein inhibitor of granulocyte-macrophage colony-stimulating factor and interleukin-2. J Virol. 2000;74:1313-1320.
12. Johanneson JV, Krogh HK, Solberg I, et al. Human orf. J Cutan Pathol. 1975;2:265-283.
13. Yirrell DL, Vestey JP. Human orf infections. J Eur Acad Dermatol Venereol. 1994;3:451-459.
14. Leavell UW, McNamara MJ, Muelling R, et al. Orf: Report of 19 human cases with clinical and pathological observations. JAMA. 1968;204:657-664.
15. Robinson AJ, Peterson GV. Orf virus infection of workers in the meat industry. N Z Med J. 1983;96:81-85.
16. Baxby D, Bennett M, Getty B. Human cowpox 1969-93: A review based on 54 cases. Br J Dermatol. 1994;131:598-607.
17. Diven DG. An overview of poxviruses. J Am Acad Dermatol. 2001;44:1-16.
18. Pether JVS, Guerrier CJW, Jones SM, et al. Giant orf in a normal individual. Br J Dermatol. 1986;115:497-499.
19. Inoshima Y, Morooka A, Sentsui H. Detection and diagnosis of parapoxvirus by the polymerase chain reaction. J Virol Methods. 2000;84:201-208.
20. Torafson EG, Gunadottir S. Polymerase chain reaction for laboratory diagnosis of orf cirus infections. J Clin Virol. 2002;24:79-84.
21. Fenner F, Nakano JH. Poxviridae: The poxviruses. In: Lennette EH, Halonen P, Murpy FA, eds. The Laboratory Diagnoses of Infectious Diseases: Principles and Practices, v II. Viral, Rickettsial, and Chlamydial Diseases. New York: Springer Verlag; 1988:177-210.
22. Czerny CP, Waldmann R, Scheubeck T. Identification of three distinct antigenic sites in parapoxviruses. Arch Virol. 1997;142:807-821.
23. Baxby D, Bennett M. Poxvirus zoonoses. J Med Microbiol. 1997;46:17-20.
24. Geerinck K, Lukito G, Snoeck G, et al. A case of human orf in an immunocompromised patient treated successfully with cidofovir cream. J Med Virol. 2001;75:1205-1210.
25. McCabe D, Weston B, Storch G. Treatment of orf poxvirus lesion with cidofovir cream. Pediatr Infect Dis J. 2003;22:1027-1028.
26. Birthistle K, Carrington D. Molluscum contagiosum virus. J Infect. 1997;34:21-28.
27. Nakamura J, Muraki Y, Yamada M, et al. Analysis of molluscum contagiosum genomes isolated in Japan. J Med Virol. 1995;46:339-348.
28. Senkevich TG, Bugert JJ, Sisler JJ, Koonin EV, Darai G, Moss B. Genome sequence of a human tumorigenic poxvirus: Prediction of specific host response evasion genes. Science. 1996;273:813-816.
29. Xiang Y, Moss B. IL-18 binding and inhibition of interferon gamma induction by human interferon-encoding proteins. Proc Natl Acad Sci USA. 1999;96:11537-11542.
30. Bertin J, Armstrong RC, Ottilie S, et al. Death effector domain-containing herpesvirus and poxvirus proteins inhibit both Fas- and TNFR1-induced apoptosis. Proc Natl Acad Sci USA. 1997;94:1172-1176.
31. Pierard-Franchimont C, Legrain A, Pierard GE. Growth and regression of molluscum contagiosum. J Am Acad Dermatol. 1983;9:669-672.
32. Shelly WB, Burmeister V. Demonstration of a unique viral structure: The molluscum viral colony sac. Dr J Dermatol. 1986;115:557-562.
33. Brown S, Nalley JF, Kraus SJ. Molluscum contagiosum. Sex Transm Dis. 1981;8:227-234.
34. Pepose JS, Esposito JJ. Molluscum contagiosum, orf and vaccinia ocular infections in humans. In: Pepose JS, Holland GN, Wilhelmus KR, eds. Ocular Infection and Immunity. St Louis: Mosby; 1996:846-856.
35. Steffen C, Markman J. Spontaneous disappearance of molluscum contagiosum. Arch Dermatol. 1989;116:923-924.
36. Gottlieb SL, Myskowski PL. Molluscum contagiosum. Int J Dermatol. 1994;33:453-461.
37. Nunez A, Funes JM, Agromayor M, et al. Detection and typing of molluscum contagiosum virus in skin lesions using a simple lysis method and polymerase chain reaction. J Med Virol. 1996;50:342-349.
38. Thompson CH. Identification and typing of molluscum contagiosum virus in clinical specimens by polymerase chain reaction. J Med Virol. 1997;53:205-211.
39. Janniger CK, Schwartz RA. Molluscum contagiosum in children. Cutis. 1993;52:194-196.
40. Valentine CL, Diven DG. Treatment modalities for molluscum contagiosum. Dermatol Ther. 2000;13:285-289.
41. Silverburg NB, Sidbury R, Mancini AJ. Childhood molluscum contagiosum: Experience with cantharidin therapy in 300 patients. J Am Acad Dermatol. 2000;43:503-507.
42. Ohkuma M. Molluscum contagiosum treated with iodine solution and salicylic plaster. Int J Dermatol. 1990;29:443-445.
43. Calista D. Topical cidofovir for severe cutaneous human papillomavirus and molluscum contagiosum infection in patient with HIV/AIDS. A pilot study. J Eur Acad Dermatol Venereol. 2000;14:484.
44. Zabawaski EJ Jr, Cockerell CJ. Topical cidofovir for molluscum contagiosum in children. Pediatr Dermatol. 1999;16:414-415.
45. Dohil M, Prendiville JS. Treatment of molluscum contagiosum with oral cimetidine: Clinical experience on 13 patients. Pediatr Dermatol. 1996;13:310-312.
46. Hengge UR, Esser S, Schultewolter T, et al. Self administered topical 5% imiquod for the treatment of common warts and molluscum contagiosum. Br J Dermatol. 2000;143:1026-1031.
47. Jezek Z, Arita I, Szczeniowski M, Paluku KM, Ruti K, Nakano J. Human tanapox in Zaire: Clinical and epidemiological observations on cases confirmed by laboratory studies. Bull World Health Organ. 1985;63:1027-1035.
48. Knight JC, Novembre FJ, Brown DR, et al. Studies on tanapox virus. Virology. 1989;172:116-124.
49. Lee HJ, Essani K, Smith GL. The genome sequence of Yaba-like disease virus, a yatapoxvirus. Virology. 2001;281:170-192.
50. Downie A, Espana C. Comparison of tanapox and yaba-like viruses causing epidemic diseases in monkeys. J Hyg Camb. 1972;70:23-33.
51. Croitoru AG, Birge MB, Rudikoff D, Tan MH, Phelps RG. Tanapox virus infection. Skin Med. 2002;1:56.

52. Stich A, Meyer H, Kohler B, Fleischer K. Tanapox: First report in a European traveller and identification by PCR. Trans R Soc Trop Med Hyg. 2002;96:178-179.
53. Dhar AD, Werchniak AE, Li Y, et al. Tanapox infection in a college student. N Engl J Med. 2004;350:361-366.
54. Fenner F, Nakano JH: Poxviridae: The poxviruses. In: Lennette EH, Halonen P, Murphy FA, eds. The Laboratory Diagnosis of Infectious Diseases: Principles and Practice, v II. Viral, Rickettsial, and Chlamydial Diseases. New York: Springer Verlag; 1988:177-210.
55. McNulty WPJ, Lobitz WCJ, Hu F, et al. A pox disease in monkeys transmitted to man: Clinical and histological features. Arch Dermatol. 1968;97:286-293.
56. Hall AS, McNulty WP Jr. A contagious pox disease in monkeys. J Am Vet Med Assoc. 1967;151:833-838.

CHAPTER **131**

Introduction to Herpesviridae

STEPHEN E. STRAUS

The members of the Herpesviridae family are large, DNA-containing, enveloped viruses. Nearly 100 known herpesviruses infect species ranging across a broad spectrum of the animal kingdom. Eight human viruses are recognized (Table 131-1). Several other herpesviruses infect New or Old World monkeys, one of which, the herpes B virus (see Chapter 138), is a rare cause of disease in humans. Among other herpesviruses that do not infect humans are several economically important viruses of horses, pigs, and cattle.[1]

CLASSIFICATION AND STRUCTURE

The herpesviruses are classified into three subfamilies according to genome organization and homology, virus host range, and other biologic properties (see Table 131-1).[2] All herpesviruses are large particles (150 to 250 nm) that are composed of four structural elements (Fig. 131-1): an outer envelope, the tegument, the nucleocapsid, and an internal core consisting of proteins and the viral genome.

All material in this chapter is in the public domain, with the exception of any borrowed figures or tables.

The envelope derives from portions of the host cellular membranes that are pinched off by incipient particles as they traverse the nucleus into the cytoplasm and eventually exit the cell. In the process, viral glycoproteins that had been inserted into cellular membranes are captured, with the result that they project outward from the virion envelope, which permits some of them to bind to cell surface receptors (listed in Table 131-1) and initiate infection.[3-7] Homologues of glycoproteins B and D in many of the herpesviruses serve this role.[8,9] Activities of several other herpesvirus glycoproteins have been described. For example, herpes simplex virus glycoprotein E is an Fc receptor, glycoprotein C has complement component C3b–binding activity,[10,11] and glycoprotein H is required for spread from infected to contiguous uninfected cells. Many herpesvirus envelope glycoproteins elicit antibodies that neutralize virus infectivity and cellular immune responses that limit the duration and severity of infections.[9,12]

The virion tegument is a seemingly amorphous assemblage of virus-encoded proteins, some of which help initiate the replicative cycle within susceptible cells, whereas others tether the envelope to the nucleocapsid.

Herpesvirus nucleocapsids are approximately 100 nm in diameter and consist of 162 discrete protein capsomeres in an icosapentahedral array. Each nucleocapsid contains a dense core of nucleoproteins entwined about the virion's linear, double-stranded DNA genome.

The organization of human herpesvirus genomes represents variations of five structural patterns depending on the number, size, and position of repeated DNA sequences relative to unique sequences. For example, herpes simplex viruses 1 and 2 possess pairs of longer and shorter stretches of unique DNA sequences that are each flanked by repeated sequences (Fig. 131-2).[13] For some herpesviruses, the unique sequences can be inverted, one relative to the other, during the course of replication, which yields two or four different isomeric forms of the genome. All isomers of herpesvirus DNAs are infectious.

Although many herpesvirus DNAs are similarly organized, most individual virus types share little nucleic acid sequence identity. The two herpes simplex virus types, however, share more than 50% sequence identity. The individual subtypes A and B of Epstein-Barr virus are nearly identical except for sequences in a few genes. The same is true for variants A and B of herpesvirus type 6. Across the eight human herpesvirus types, there are scattered regions of DNA homology sufficient for all to possess at least weak (<5%) overall sequence identity. The relatedness among herpesviruses is best appreciated by com-

TABLE 131-1 Classification and Structure of Herpesviridae That Infect Humans

Common Name	Other Designation	Subfamily	Genome Size (Kbp × 10⁶)	Genome Isomers (No.)	Genome Type	Receptor(s)
Human Virus						
Herpes simplex virus type 1	Human herpesvirus 1	α	152	4	1	TNFRSF14; nectin 1; nectin 2; 3-O-S-heparin sulfate
Herpes simplex virus type 2	Human herpesvirus 2	α	152	4	1	TNFRSF14; nectin 1; nectin 2; 3-O-S-heparin sulfate
Varicella-zoster virus	Human herpesvirus 3	α	125	2	2	?
Epstein-Barr virus	Human herpesvirus 4	γ	172	1	3	CD21; MHC class II (co-receptor)
Cytomegalovirus	Human herpesvirus 5	β	229	1	1	?
Human herpesvirus 6	—	β	165	1	4	CD46
Human herpesvirus 7	—	β	145	1	4	CD4
Human herpesvirus 8	Kaposi's sarcoma herpesvirus	γ	165	1	5	Integrin α₃β₁
Simian Virus						
Herpes B virus	Herpesvirus simiac; cercopithecine herpesvirus 1	α	150	4	1	?

Kbp, kilobase pairs; MHC, major histocompatibility complex; TNFRSF14, tumor necrosis factor receptor superfamily, member 14; ?, not known.

FIGURE 131-1. Electron micrographs of varicella-zoster virus negatively stained with phosphotungstic acid (×40,000). **A,** The complete enveloped virion. **B,** A purified viral nucleocapsid. *(From Straus SE, Ostrove JM, Inchauspe G, et al. Varicella-zoster virus infections—biology, natural history, treatment, and prevention. Ann Intern Med. 1988;108:221-237, with permission.)*

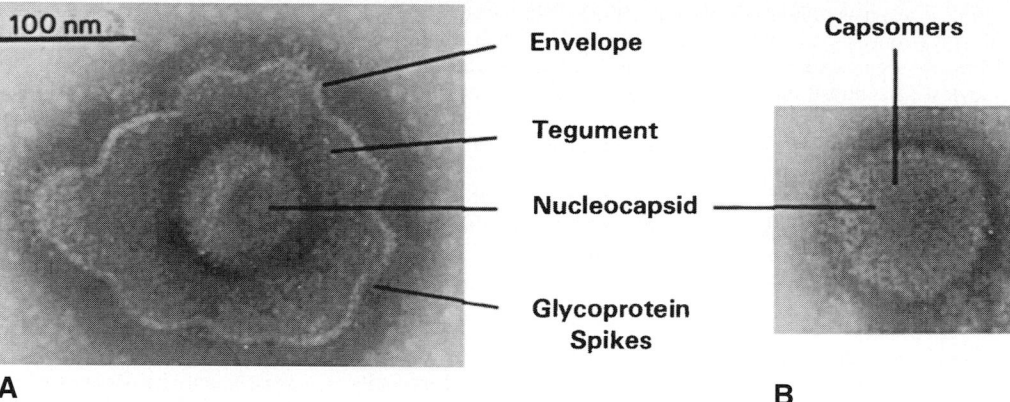

paring the amino acid sequences of domains of selected viral proteins and the clustering of related genes. For example, all of the herpesvirus DNA polymerase genes have similar functional domains, and the genes neighboring them are also similar to each other.

As herpesviruses spread through the community, minor mutations that do not appreciably alter virulence gradually accrue in their DNA sequences. These minor changes, such as the ones that distinguish the wild-type and vaccine strains of varicella-zoster virus, can be identified by restriction endonuclease cleavage analysis or DNA sequencing. The virus strain identified in person A is indistinguishable from the strain in person B from whom the infection was acquired. Viruses from individuals who have not been in contact usually differ. The relative stability of these genomes, in contrast to those of many RNA viruses, permits molecular epidemiologic analyses that have contributed to our understanding of herpesvirus spread and reactivation.[14]

Herpesvirus genomes each encode 70 to over 150 distinct proteins. The viral RNAs for these proteins are transcribed efficiently from both strands of the genome, with relatively small noncoding regions between the genes.

VIRUS REPLICATION

Herpesvirus replication is a well-regulated, multistep process.[15] Within hours after infection, virion tegument protein signals the transcription of one or a few "immediate-early" genes. These encode proteins that regulate their own synthesis and stimulate the synthesis of a second, larger wave of proteins from the "early" set of viral genes. Herpesvirus

early proteins, such as the viral thymidine kinases and DNA polymerases, support viral genome replication.

All herpesvirus DNAs contain short terminal repeat sequences that permit their circularization as a prelude to genome replication. Progeny DNA molecules appear to be generated continuously from circular parental molecules by a rolling circle mechanism.[16] Newly synthesized multimers of the genome are cleaved at specific terminal region sequences into "unit length" genomes that are packaged into newly assembled nucleocapsids.

Most herpesvirus genes are expressed after DNA replication. These "late" gene products are incorporated into or aid in the assembly of progeny virions. New particles bud from their host cells and infect contiguous susceptible cells. The predominant means by which herpesviruses spread through the body is from cell to cell. Cell-free virions usually do not circulate.

TROPISM

Herpesviruses vary widely in their abilities to infect different types of cells, which is a feature that is used in the classification of viruses into subfamilies (see Table 131-1). For example, herpes simplex viruses grow readily in epithelial cells and fibroblasts of humans, monkeys, rabbits, mice, and many other animals. Varicella-zoster virus grows best in human epithelial cells and fibroblasts in vitro. In cell culture, cytomegalovirus grows well only in human fibroblasts. Epstein-Barr virus can be cultivated only in B lymphocytes, whereas herpesvirus type 7 replicates only in CD4+ T lymphocytes.[17] Herpesvirus type 8 has yet to be grown efficiently in the laboratory.

The relative breadth of a herpesvirus's host range, however, has more than taxonomic importance; it is predictive of the tissues that it clinically infects. Thus, the lymphotropic herpesviruses predominantly cause lymphoproliferative diseases. In contrast, the herpesviruses that replicate readily in tissues of epithelial origin are primarily associated with mucocutaneous infections.

LATENCY

All herpesviruses induce lifelong latent infection in their natural hosts. The mechanisms of virus latency are still incompletely understood, but some key questions regarding them have been resolved. For each herpesvirus, latency occurs only within small numbers of specific types of cells (Table 131-2). Latent herpes simplex viruses, varicella-zoster virus, Epstein-Barr virus genomes, and possibly all herpesviruses are carried extrachromosomally.[18,19] In transformed lymphoblastoid cell lines, one or more copies of Epstein-Barr virus DNA are integrated into the cellular genome.[20]

Although latent herpesvirus genomes were long postulated to be totally quiescent, compelling data now show that latency is characterized by expression of a limited repertoire of viral genes. Up to nine Epstein-Barr virus latency genes are expressed in virus-immortalized

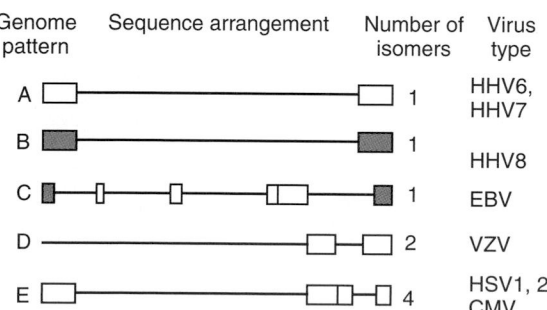

FIGURE 131-2. Organization of five genome types of human herpesviruses. The *large boxes* denote major repeat elements, between or adjacent to which are unique sequences. Some major repeats contain multiple copies of the same sequences, as indicated by *vertically divided boxes*. (Based on Roizman B, Pellett PE. Herpesviridae: A brief introduction. In: Knipe DM, Howley RM, Griffin DE, et al, eds. Field's Virology. 4th ed. Philadelphia: Lippincott-Williams & Wilkins; 2001:2381-2397, with permission.)

cell lines: seven as proteins displayed on the cell surface or within nuclei, and two as small RNAs that do not encode proteins.[21] Only two of these genes are expressed in latently infected peripheral blood lymphocytes. In contrast, the members of only a single family of herpes simplex virus transcripts accumulate in latently infected neurons, and these have not been proven to encode proteins.[22] Analyses of herpesvirus latency genes suggest that some prevent host immune recognition of virus-infected cells. Others may serve to prevent the programmed death (apoptosis) of host cells, to maintain the virus in its latent state, or to keep it poised for reactivation.

PATHOGENESIS

Herpesviruses induce disease by direct destruction of tissues, by provoking immunopathologic ("friendly fire") responses, and by facilitating neoplastic transformation. Some herpesviruses are also immunosuppressive, which increases the risk not only of virus dissemination but also of concomitant opportunistic infections.

Mucocutaneous herpes simplex virus, varicella-zoster virus, and herpesvirus simiae lesions represent the direct consequences of tissue destruction by replicating virus. Visceral infections, such as encephalitis, pneumonitis, and hepatitis, with these viruses or with cytomegalovirus also reflect virus-induced cytopathogenicity.

Certain complications of herpesvirus infections, however, such as erythema multiforme, hemolytic anemia, and thrombocytopenia, are mediated immunopathologically.[23,24] Whether the neurologic complications of varicella and zoster are also mediated immunopathologically has been widely debated. Because encephalitis, transverse myelitis, and cranial nerve palsies, which develop in association with varicella-zoster infection, typically develop after the cutaneous lesions have begun to resolve, they are often considered to be immune mediated.[25] However, isolated instances in which the virus or its DNA has been detected in the involved central nervous system tissues suggest that the virus itself can also contribute directly to neurologic disease.[26]

Most manifestations of Epstein-Barr virus infection, including the hematologic and neurologic complications, are immunopathologically mediated. During acute infection, only a fraction of B lymphocytes that infiltrate the lymph nodes, liver, and spleen are actually infected with the virus. Most of the infiltrating cells are reactive T cells.[27] For this reason, corticosteroids have a role in the management of some complications of Epstein-Barr virus infection and, conversely, antiviral drugs are not useful in the treatment of acute infectious mononucleosis.[28,29]

Herpesviruses persist in humans and can induce recurrent disease because they have captured and altered, or otherwise interfered with the functions of, an array of host cell genes to permit latency, inhibit apoptosis, and avoid immune detection and clearance.[12,27,30-32] Latency is sustained by virus sequestration in immunologically privileged sites, such as the neuron in the case of herpes simplex viruses,[22] and by lack of expression of proteins that could be detected by the immune system, as in some B cells infected with Epstein-Barr virus.[33] In the course of infection, *when* (or *whether*) the host cell dies is of critical importance to the success of a virus in replication, spread, and latency. Several herpesviruses express proteins that alter the efficiency of receptor-mediated or mitochondrial pathways for apoptosis.[32]

TABLE 131-2 Features of the Usual Productive, Latent, and Transforming Infections Caused by Herpesviruses in Humans

Virus	Infection in Healthy Humans		Infection in the Compromised Host	Site of Latency	Association with Human
	Primary Infections	Recurrent Infections			
Herpes simplex virus 1	Gingivostomatitis Keratoconjunctivitis Cutaneous herpes Genital herpes	Herpes labialis Keratoconjunctivitis Cutaneous herpes	Gingivostomatitis Keratoconjunctivitis Cutaneous herpes Visceral infections	Sensory neurons	None
Herpes simplex virus 2	Genital herpes Cutaneous herpes Gingivostomatitis Aseptic meningitis Neonatal herpes	Genital herpes Cutaneous herpes Aseptic meningitis	Genital herpes Cutaneous herpes Disseminated infection	Sensory neurons	None
Varicella-zoster virus	Varicella	Dermatomal zoster	Disseminated infection	Sensory neurons	None
Cytomegalovirus	Mononucleosis Hepatitis Congenital cytomegalic inclusion disease	?	Hepatitis Retinitis Other visceral infections	Monocytes? Neutrophils?	None
Epstein-Barr virus	Mononucleosis Hepatitis Encephalitis	?	Polyclonal and monoclonal lymphoproliferative syndromes Oral hairy leukoplakia	B lymphocytes	African-type Burkitt's lymphoma, CNS lymphoma, Hodgkin's disease, and other lymphomas Nasopharyngeal carcinoma Leiomyosarcoma
Human herpesvirus 6	Roseola infantum Fever and otitis media Encephalitis	?	Fever Pneumonitis Encephalitis Bone marrow suppression	CD4 lymphocytes?	Rare B cell lymphomas?
Human herpesvirus 7	Roseola infantum	?	?	CD4 lymphocytes?	None
Human herpesvirus 8	Mononucleosis? Febrile exanthem?	?	Fever Bone marrow aplasia?	?	Kaposi's sarcoma Multicentric Castleman's disease Primary effusion lymphoma
Simian herpes B virus	Mucocutaneous lesions Encephalitis	?	?	Sensory neurons in monkeys	None

?, Inadequate data.

IMMUNE AVOIDANCE

Dozens of herpesvirus gene products "cloak" infected cells from immune surveillance and destruction.[12,27,30,31] In binding the Fc portion of immunoglobulin molecules or C3b, herpes simplex virus envelope glycoproteins E and C, respectively, inhibit neutralization by antibody and complement.[11] Herpes simplex virus–infected cell protein 47 blocks transport of viral peptides into the Golgi so that they will not be presented in the context of major histocompatibility complex (MHC) class I.[34] Epstein-Barr virus–associated nuclear antigen 1 (EBNA-1) is the only protein expressed in some forms of B-cell latency. It contains glycine-arginine repeats that prevent peptide presentation by MHC class I.[33] Cytomegalovirus encodes four gene products that downregulate class I presentation and two gene products that downregulate class II production.[30] This leaves infected cells vulnerable to natural killer (NK) cells, which destroy only targets that display no MHC proteins. To solve this problem, cytomegalovirus evolved to encode an MHC homologue. As if these strategies were not sufficient, some herpesviruses encode proteins that are decoys for or inhibit interferon pathways, cytokines, chemokines, or their receptors. For example, Epstein-Barr virus and cytomegalovirus synthesize their own versions of interleukin (IL)-10 that, like their human counterpart, induce B-cell growth and suppress T-cell responses.[35]

Human herpesvirus type 8 literally bristles with defenses against host clearance.[31] One gene product represses transcriptional activation induced by interferon. Three proteins are homologous to macrophage inhibitory protein-1, a chemokine. Overexpression of one protein that mimics the receptor for IL-8 induces angioproliferative lesions in mice. Human herpesvirus type 8 also encodes homologues of the cellular complement control proteins and a protein that downregulates expression of intercellular adhesion molecule (ICAM)-1 and B7-2 protein, and thereby inhibits NK cell–mediated cytotoxicity.

VIRUS-VIRUS INTERACTIONS

Immune compromise permits infection of people with many viruses simultaneously—herpesviruses, hepatitis viruses, and the human immunodeficiency virus (HIV)—and the interactions among them can be complex. Immune impairment may be exacerbated, as during cytomegalovirus or herpesvirus type 6 infections, thereby increasing risks of activation of other, coinfecting agents.[36] The best-studied interactions are between HIV and herpes simplex viruses.[37] Genital herpes ulcers increase transmission of HIV, and HIV-induced immunosuppression promotes herpes simplex virus reactivation and spread.

ONCOGENESIS

Many herpesviruses can transform cells in vitro. Some of the viruses transform only cells of animals different from their natural hosts, whereas others transform their hosts' cells as well. However, there is no clinical relevance to transformation that arises only in laboratory-derived model systems, as is seen with herpes simplex virus type 1 or 2, herpesvirus type 6, cytomegalovirus, or parts of their genomes.[38] The lymphotropic herpesviruses, however, are tumorigenic, both in animals and humans. Epstein-Barr virus is associated primarily with B- and T-cell lymphomas, but also with nasopharyngeal carcinoma, especially in African and Asian peoples, and with leiomyosarcomas in patients with acquired immunodeficiency syndrome (AIDS). Human herpesvirus type 8 causes a disseminated polyclonal tumor—Kaposi's sarcoma—as well as multicentric Castleman's disease and primary effusion lymphoma, which is a monoclonal malignancy.[39,40]

EPIDEMIOLOGY AND TRANSMISSION

As enveloped particles, herpesviruses are fragile and do not survive for prolonged periods in the environment. Thus, transmission generally requires the inoculation of a fresh, virus-containing body fluid of an infected person directly onto the susceptible tissues of a previously uninfected person. Susceptible sites include oral, ocular, genital, and anal mucosa; the respiratory tract; and the blood stream. Herpesviruses do not penetrate keratinized skin efficiently.

Thus, most herpesviruses are spread by intimate contact (Table 131-3). Direct contact with infected lesions and body fluids transfers herpes simplex, varicella-zoster, and herpesvirus simiae (B virus). Sexual intercourse and oral-genital contact clearly transmit herpes simplex viruses and cytomegalovirus. The major vehicle for transmission of Epstein-Barr virus is probably infected saliva, although the virus has been detected in exfoliated cervical cells.[41] Herpesvirus types 6 and 7 are very common early in childhood; their presence in saliva of healthy adults suggests a simple and efficient means of transmission.[42,43] Herpesvirus type 8 has been detected in the saliva and semen of patients with Kaposi's sarcoma,[44,45] which is thought to account for transmission to infants and between sexual partners.

Given the prolonged intimate contact between mother and baby during pregnancy and delivery, it is not surprising that several human herpesviruses cause congenital and neonatal infections; those associated with cytomegalovirus are the most prevalent.[46] Only one herpesvirus is known to be transmitted without person-to-person contact: varicella is spread by infectious aerosols.[47]

TABLE 131-3   **Transmission and Seroepidemiology of Herpesviruses That Infect Humans**

Virus	Modes of Transmission to Humans				Seroprevalence (%)			Groups or Activities with Higher Risk of Infection
					Healthy Children	Healthy Adults		
	Perinatal	Transfusion, Transplantation	Direct Contact*	Aerosol		United States	Developing World	
Herpes simplex virus 1	+	−	+	−	20-40	50-70	50-90	Frequent intimate contact
Herpes simplex virus 2	+	−	+	−	0-5	20-50	20-60	Frequent intimate contact
Varicella-zoster virus	+	−	+	+	50-75	85-95	50-80	Children in daycare
Cytomegalovirus	+	+	+	−	10-30	40-70	40-80	Children in daycare Promiscuous gay men Transplant or blood recipients
Epstein-Barr virus	+	+	+	−	10-30	80-95	90-100	Frequent intimate contact
Human herpesvirus 6	?	?	+	?	80-100	60-100	60-100	Cellular immune deficiency states
Human herpesvirus 7	?	?	+	?	40-80	60-100	40-100	?
Human herpesvirus 8	?	+	+	?	<3	<3	10-60	Cellular immune deficiency states
Simian herpes B virus	−	−	+	+	0	<<1	<<1	Monkey handlers

*Includes saliva, semen, breast milk, and other body fluids.
+, well-recognized or probable association; −, rare or no association; ?, inadequate data.

TABLE 131-4 Spectrum of Clinical Syndromes Associated with Herpesviruses

Syndrome	Herpes Simplex Virus 1	Herpes Simplex Virus 2	Varicella-Zoster Virus	Cytomegalovirus	Epstein-Barr Virus	Human Herpes-virus 6	Human Herpes-virus 7	Human Herpes-virus 8	Herpes-virus Simiae
Gingivostomatitis	+	+	−	−	−	−	−	−	−
Genital lesions	+	+	+	−	−	−	−	−	−
Cutaneous lesions	+	+	+	−	−	−	−	+	+
Neonatal infection	+	+	+	+	−	−	−	−	−
Keratoconjunctivitis	+	+	+	−	−	−	−	−	+
Retinitis	+	+	+	+	−	−	−	−	−
Esophagitis	+	+	+	+	−	−	−	−	−
Pneumonitis	+	+	+	+	+	+	−	−	−
Hepatitis	+	+	+	+	+	+	−	−	−
Myopericarditis	−	−	+	+	+	−	−	−	−
Meningitis	−	+	+	−	−	+	−	−	−
Encephalitis	+	+	+	+	+	+	−	−	+
Myelitis	+	+	+	+	+	−	−	−	+
Erythema multiforme	+	+	+	−	−	−	−	−	−
Other rashes	−	−	−	+	+	+	+	−	−
Arthritis	−	−	+	−	+	−	−	−	−
Hemolytic anemia	−	−	+	+	+	−	−	−	−
Leukopenia	−	−	+	+	+	+	−	−	−
Thrombocytopenia	−	−	+	+	+	+	−	−	−
Mononucleosis	−	−	−	+	+	+	+	+	−
Lymphoma	−	−	−	−	+	−	−	+	−
Kaposi's sarcoma	−	−	−	−	−	−	−	+	−
Other malignancies	−	−	−	−	+	−	−	+	−

Cytomegalovirus and Epstein-Barr virus are transmitted by blood transfusion and organ transplantation,[48,49] and transmission of herpesvirus type 8 by transplanted kidneys has been reported in two cases.[50]

Herpesviruses are transmitted by individuals in whom active virus replication occurs either during the course of their own primary infections or during reactivation infections. Most people who transmit herpesviruses, however, are asymptomatic. For all herpesviruses except varicella-zoster virus, episodes of asymptomatic shedding exceed those of symptomatic shedding, and thus there are more opportunities to transmit herpesviruses asymptomatically than symptomatically.

With herpes simplex viruses, asymptomatic reactivation and shedding of infectious virus occurs on about 1% to 3% of days; viral DNA can be detected on genital swabs even more frequently.[51,52] Epstein-Barr virus and herpesvirus type 7 shedding rates are much higher, exceeding 15% and 80% of the days in normal seropositive individuals, respectively. This indicates that infections caused by those viruses are truly more persistent than latent.[43,53]

The likelihood of transmission depends on the quantity of virus shed. The titer of recoverable virus or the quantity of viral DNA detected during symptomatic infections greatly exceeds that of asymptomatic infec-

TABLE 131-5 Means Available to Prevent or Treat Herpesvirus Infections in Humans

Virus	Host	Indication	Prevention	Treatment/Suppression
Herpes simplex virus 1	Any	Primary mucocutaneous infection	Avoid contact	PO ACV, FAM, VAL
	Healthy	Recurrent mucocutaneous infection	None	None or PO ACV, VAL, FAM, topical PCV
	Immunocompromised	Any syndrome	None	IV ACV or PO ACV, FAM, VAL
	Any	Visceral infection	None	IV ACV
Herpes simplex virus 2	Any	Primary mucocutaneous infection	Avoid contact	PO VAL, FAM, ACV or IV ACV
	Healthy	Recurrent mucocutaneous infection	None	PO ACV, VAL, FAM
	Neonate	Visceral infection	Cesarean section	IV ACV
	Immune compromised	Any syndrome	None	IV ACV
Varicella-zoster virus	Healthy	Varicella	Live, attenuated vaccine	None or PO ACV
	Immunocompromised	Varicella	Varicella-zoster immuno-globulin, vaccine	IV ACV or PO VAL
	Healthy	Zoster	None	None or PO FAM, VAL, ACV
				PO VAL, FAM, ACV or IV ACV
	Immunocompromised	Zoster	None	
Cytomegalovirus	Healthy	Any syndrome	None	None
	Immunocompromised	Visceral or retinal infection	Seronegative donor tissues & blood; specific immuno-globulin, ACV, VAL, GCV, VGCV	GCV, FOS, CDV, VGCV
Epstein-Barr virus	Healthy	Infectious mononucleosis	None	None, steroids in selected cases
	Immunocompromised	Any infection	None	None or ACV? GCV?; cytotoxic T cells
Human herpes-virus 6	Healthy	Any infection	?	None
	Immunocompromised	Any infection	?	GCV?
Human herpes-virus 7	Any	Any infection	?	?
Human herpes-virus 8	Immunocompromised	Kaposi's sarcoma	None	Radiation, cytotoxic drugs, IFN-α
Herpesvirus simiae	Any	Any infection	Avoid infected monkeys	IV ACV, GCV, or PO VAL

ACV, acyclovir; CDV, cidofovir; FAM, famciclovir; FOS, foscarnet; GCV, ganciclovir; IFN-α, alpha interferon; PCV, penciclovir; VAL, valacyclovir; VGCV, val-ganciclovir.

tions.[52] The net result of all factors is that both symptomatic and asymptomatic infections contribute substantially to rates of herpesvirus transmission. Between one half and three fourths of herpes simplex infections are acquired from asymptomatic sexual partners.[54] It is likely that nearly all infections with Epstein-Barr virus, cytomegalovirus, and herpesviruses 6, 7, and 8 are acquired from asymptomatic host sources. In contrast, essentially all cases of varicella are acquired from people with clinically apparent varicella or zoster infections.

DIAGNOSIS

Many herpesvirus infections can be diagnosed clinically, but there are situations in which specific tests are needed, and such tests are now increasingly rapid, available, and helpful. Laboratory confirmation of a herpesvirus infection excludes similar illnesses,[55] may allay anxiety, guides counseling and treatment, and can detect drug-resistant viruses.

Serologic tests are used for diagnosing recent infections or confirming past infections. Serial serologic tests are of little value for chronic or recurrent infections. The diagnosis of a herpesvirus infection can be confirmed by isolation of virus from or detection of antigens or nucleic acids in clinical specimens.[56] However, because these viruses are ubiquitous, their detection in some settings does not prove that they are the cause of the clinical symptoms or signs in question.

On the basis of their successful use in monitoring HIV and hepatitis virus infections, quantitative polymerase chain reaction (PCR) assays are used increasingly to measure the "viral load" of cytomegalovirus and other herpesviruses, to help predict clinical disease in transplant recipients, and to monitor antiviral therapy. These same assays help to elucidate interactions among the various herpesviruses and HIV in multiply infected immunocompromised patients.[36]

CLINICAL SYNDROMES

Herpesviruses are associated with a wide spectrum of clinical diseases (Table 131-4, and see Table 131-2). These can be grouped into mucocutaneous, visceral, central nervous system, malignant, and reactive syndromes. The specific infections are covered in detail in Chapters 132 to 138.

PREVENTION AND TREATMENT

Formidable progress has been made in the prevention and treatment of herpesvirus infections (Table 131-5). A live varicella vaccine is approved for universal use in children and is recommended for susceptible adults and selected immunocompromised patients.[57] Mild cases of varicella are now being documented in children exposed several years after vaccination, suggesting that protective immunity wanes with time.[58] Varicella-zoster immunoglobulin modifies acute disease if administered within 4 days of exposure.[59] Cytomegalovirus-specific immunoglobulin may prevent serious infection in selected transplant recipients, and candidate vaccines may do so, as well.[60,61] Infusions of Epstein-Barr virus–specific and cytomegalovirus-specific cytotoxic T cells have shown encouraging activity in clearing post-transplantation lymphoproliferative disorders[62] and might be effective for cytomegalovirus infections in transplant recipients,[63] respectively.

Acyclovir and its congeners, valacyclovir, penciclovir, and famciclovir, are indicated for the treatment of several forms of herpes simplex infections, varicella, and zoster.[64-67] Ganciclovir and its oral prodrug, valganciclovir, treat and suppress sight- and life-threatening cytomegalovirus infections in immunocompromised patients.[68] Cidofovir is an effective but toxic alternative for long-term management of cytomegalovirus retinitis.[69] Foscarnet treats severe cytomegalovirus infections as well as acyclovir-resistant infections with herpes simplex viruses and varicella-zoster virus.[62,67] Acyclovir suppresses Epstein-Barr virus–associated oral hairy leukoplakia in AIDS patients; otherwise, antiviral drugs are of no proven value for treatment of any other form of infection with this virus or with herpesviruses 6, 7, or 8.

Drug Resistance

Immunologically normal people rarely experience herpesvirus infections that are truly resistant to the current antiviral drugs, but resistant infections challenge upward of 6% of transplant recipients and AIDS patients. Reduction of immune suppression and adherence to highly active antiretroviral drug cocktails are the best strategies for restoring the needed competence to resolve these infections. Otherwise, the benefits afforded by switching from nucleoside analogues to cidofovir or foscarnet may be only transient.[67,70]

REFERENCES

1. Roizman B, Pellett PE. Herpesviridae: A brief introduction. In: Knipe DM, Howley PM, Griffin DE, et al, eds. Field's Virology. 4th ed. Philadelphia: Lippincott-Williams & Wilkins; 2001:2381-2397.
2. Roizman B, desRosiers RC, Fleckenstein B, et al. The family Herpesviridae: An update. Arch Virol. 1992;123:425-449.
3. Frade R, Barel M, Ehlin-Henriksson B, et al. gp140, the C3d receptor of human B lymphocytes, is also the Epstein-Barr virus receptor. Proc Natl Acad Sci U S A. 1985;82:1490-1493.
4. Montgomery RI, Warner MS, Lum BJ, Spear PG. Herpes simplex virus-1 entry into cells mediated by a novel member of the TNF/NGF receptor family. Cell. 1996;87:427-436.
5. Shukla D, Liu J, Blaiklock P, et al. A novel role for 3-O-sulfated heparan sulfate in herpes simplex virus 1 entry. Cell. 1999;99:13-22.
6. Santoro F, Kennedy PE, Locatelli G, et al. CD46 is a cellular receptor for human herpesvirus 6. Cell. 1999;99:817-827.
7. Akula SM, Pramod NP, Wang FZ, Chandran B. Integrin a2β1 (CD 49c/29) is a cellular receptor for Kaposi's sarcoma-associated herpesvirus (KSHV/HHV-8) entry into the target cells. Cell. 2002;108:407-419.
8. Shukla D, Spear PG. Herpesviruses and heparan sulfate: An intimate relationship in aid of viral entry. J Clin Invest. 2001;108:503-510.
9. Highlander SL, Sutherland SL, Gage PJ, et al. Neutralizing monoclonal antibodies specific for herpes simplex virus glycoprotein D inhibit virus penetration. J Virol. 1987;61:3356-3364.
10. Baucke RB, Spear PG. Membrane proteins specified by herpes simplex virus: V. Identification of an Fc-binding glycoprotein. J Virol. 1979;32:779-789.
11. Friedman HM, Cohen GH, Eisenberg RJ, et al. Glycoprotein C of HSV-1 functions as a C3b receptor on infected endothelial cells. Nature. 1984;309:633-635.
12. Koelle DM, Corey L. Recent progress in herpes simplex virus immunobiology and vaccine research. Clin Microbiol Rev. 2003;16:96-113.
13. Roizman B. The structure and isomerization of herpes simplex virus genomes. Cell. 1979;16:481-494.
14. Roizman B, Tognon M. Restriction endonuclease patterns of herpes simplex virus DNA: Applications to diagnosis and molecular epidemiology. Curr Top Microbiol Immunol. 1983;104:273-286.
15. Jones PC, Roizman B. Regulation of herpesvirus macromolecular synthesis: VII. The transcription program consists of three phases during which transcription and accumulation of RNA in the cytoplasm are regulated. J Virol. 1979;31:299-314.
16. Ben-Porat T, Tokazewski S. Replication of herpesvirus DNA: II. Sedimentation characteristics of newly synthesized DNA. Virology. 1977;79:292-301.
17. Frenkel N, Schirmer EC, Wyatt LS, et al. Isolation of a new herpesvirus from CD4+ T cells. Proc Natl Acad Sci U S A. 1990;87:748-752.
18. Mellerick DM, Fraser NW. Physical state of the latent herpes simplex virus genome in a mouse model system: Evidence suggesting an episomal state. Virology. 1987;158:265-275.
19. Adams A, Lindahl T. Epstein-Barr virus genomes with properties of circular DNA molecules in carrier cells. Proc Natl Acad Sci U S A. 1975;72:1477-1481.
20. Adams A, Lindahl T, Klein G. Linear associations between cellular DNA and EBV DNA in a human lymphoblastoid cell line. Proc Natl Acad Sci U S A. 1973;70:2888-2892.
21. Kieff E, Rickinson AB. Epstein-Barr virus and its replication. In: Knipe DM, Howley PM, Griffin DE, et al, eds. Field's Virology. 4th ed. Philadelphia: Lippincott-Williams & Wilkins; 2001:2511-2573.
22. Stevens JG, Wagner EK, Devi-Rao GB, et al. RNA complementary to a herpes virus α gene mRNA is prominent in latently infected neurons. Science. 1987;235:1056-1059.
23. Orton PW, Huff JC, Tonnesen MG, Weston WL. Detection of a herpes simplex viral antigen in skin lesions of erythema multiforme. Ann Intern Med. 1984;101;48-50.
24. Yenicescu I, Yetgin S, Ozyurek E, Aslan D. Virus-associated immune thrombocytopenic purpura in childhood. Pediatr Hematol Oncol. 2002;19:433-437.
25. Jemsek J, Greenberg SB, Taber L, et al. Herpes zoster-associated encephalitis: Clinicopathologic report of 12 cases and review of the literature. Medicine. 1983;62:81-97.
26. Puchhammer-Stockl E, Popow-Kraupp T, Heinz FX, et al. Detection of varicella-zoster virus DNA by polymerase chain reaction in the cerebrospinal fluid of patients suffering from neurological complications associated with chicken pox or herpes zoster. J Clin Microbiol. 1991;29:1513-1516.
27. Levitsky V, Masucci MG. Manipulation of immune responses by Epstein-Barr virus. Virus Res. 2002;88:71-86.

28. Bender CE. The value of corticosteroids in the treatment of infectious mononucleosis. JAMA. 1967;199:529-531.

29. Andersson J, Britton S, Ernberg I, et al. Effect of acyclovir on infectious mononucleosis: A double-blind placebo-controlled study. J Infect Dis. 1986;153:283-290.

30. Mocarski ES Jr. Immunomodulation by cytomegaloviruses: Manipulative strategies beyond evasion. Trends Microbiol. 2002;10:332-339.

31. Means RE, Choi JK, Nakamura H, et al. Immune evasion strategies of Kaposi's sarcoma-associated herpesvirus. Curr Top Microbiol Immunol. 2002;269:187-201.

32. Derfuss T, Meinl E. Herpesviral proteins regulating apoptosis. Curr Top Microbiol Immunol. 2002;269:257-272.

33. Levitskaya J, Coram M, Levitsky V, et al. Inhibition of antigen processing by the internal repeat region of the Epstein-Barr virus nuclear antigen-1. Nature. 1995;375:685-688.

34. Hill A, Jugovic P, York I, et al. Herpes simplex virus turns off the TAP to evade host immunity. Nature. 1995;375:411-415.

35. Vieira P, deWaal-Malefyt T, Dang MN, et al. Isolation and expression of human cytokine synthesis inhibitory factor cDNA clones: Homology to Epstein-Barr virus open reading frame BCRFI. Proc Natl Acad Sci U S A. 1991;88:1172-1176.

36. Mendez JC, Dockrell DH, Espy MJ, et al. Human β-herpesvirus interactions in solid organ transplant recipients. J Infect Dis. 2001;183:179-184.

37. Wald A, Link K. Risk of human immunodeficiency virus infection in herpes simplex virus type 2-seropositive persons: A meta-analysis. J Infect Dis. 2002;185:45-52.

38. Tevethia MJ. Transforming potential of herpes simplex viruses and human cytomegalovirus. In: Roizman B, ed. The Herpesviruses, v. 3. New York: Plenum; 1982:257-314.

39. Chang Y, Cesarman E, Pessin MS, et al. Identification of herpesvirus-like DNA sequences in AIDS-associated Kaposi's sarcoma. Science. 1994;266:1865-1869.

40. Ablashi DV, Chatlynne LG, Whitman JE Jr, Cesarman E. Spectrum of Kaposi's sarcoma-associated herpesvirus, or human herpesvirus 8, diseases. Clin Microbiol Rev. 2002;15:439-464.

41. Sixbey JW, Lemon SM, Pagano JS. A second site for Epstein-Barr virus shedding: The uterine cervix. Lancet. 1986;2:1122-1124.

42. Dockrell CH. Human herpesvirus 6: Molecular biology and clinical features. J Med Microbiol. 2003;52:5-18.

43. Wyatt LS, Frenkel N. Human herpesvirus 7 is a constitutive inhabitant of adult human saliva. J Virol. 1992;66:3206-3209.

44. Viera J, Huang ML, Koelle DM, Corey L. Transmissible Kaposi's sarcoma-associated herpesvirus (human herpesvirus 8) in saliva of men with a history of Kaposi's sarcoma. J Virol. 1997;71:7083-7087.

45. Huang YQ, Li JJ, Poiesz BJ, et al. Detection of the herpesvirus-like DNA sequences in matched specimens of semen and blood from patients with AIDS-related Kaposi's sarcoma by polymerase chain reaction in situ hybridization. Am J Pathol. 1997;150:147-153.

46. Nelson CT, Demmler GJ. Cytomegalovirus infection in the pregnant mother, fetus, and newborn infant. Clin Perinatol. 1997;42:151-160.

47. Leclair JM, Zaia JA, Levin MJ, et al. Airborne transmission of chickenpox in a hospital. N Engl J Med. 1980;302:450-453.

48. Prince AM, Szmuness W, Millian SJ, David DS. A serologic study of cytomegalovirus infections associated with blood transfusions. N Engl J Med. 1971;284:1125-1131.

49. Gerber P, Walsh JH, Rosenblum EN, Purcell RH. Association of EB-virus infection with the post-perfusion syndrome. Lancet. 1969;2:593-595.

50. Luppi M, Barozzi P, Santagostino G, et al. Molecular evidence of organ-related transmission of Kaposi sarcoma-associated herpesvirus or human herpesvirus-8 in transplant patients. Blood. 2000;96:3279-3281.

51. Wald A, Zeh J, Barnum G, et al. Suppression of subclinical shedding of herpes simplex virus type 2 with acyclovir. Ann Intern Med. 1996;124:8-15.

52. Cone RW, Hobson AC, Brown Z, et al. Frequent detection of genital herpes simplex virus DNA by polymerase chain reaction among pregnant women. JAMA. 1994;272:792-796.

53. Chang RS, Lewis JP, Abildgaard CF. Prevalence of oropharyngeal excreters of leukocyte-transforming agents among a human population. N Engl J Med. 1973;289:1325-1329.

54. Mertz GJ, Schmidt O, Jourden JL, et al. Frequency of acquisition of first-episode genital infection with herpes simplex virus from symptomatic and asymptomatic source contacts. Sex Transm Dis. 1985;12:33-39.

55. Kalman CM, Laskin OL. Herpes zoster and zosteriform herpes simplex virus infections in immunocompetent adults. Am J Med. 1986;81:775-778.

56. Cohen PR. Tests for detecting herpes simplex virus and varicella-zoster virus infections. Dermatol Clin. 1994;12:51-68.

57. Weibel RE, Neff BJ, Kuter BJ, et al. Live attenuated varicella virus vaccine: Efficacy trial in healthy children. N Engl J Med. 1984;310:1409-1415.

58. Galil K, Lee B, Strine T, et al. Outbreak of varicella at a day-care center despite vaccination. N Engl J Med. 2002;347:1909-1915.

59. Centers for Disease Control and Prevention. Varicella-zoster immune globulin for the prevention of chickenpox: Recommendations of the Immunization Practices Advisory Committee. Ann Intern Med. 1984;100:859-865.

60. Condie RM, O'Reilly RJ. Prevention of cytomegalovirus infection by prophylaxis with an intravenous, hyperimmune, native, unmodified cytomegalovirus globulin: Randomized trial in bone marrow transplant recipients. Am J Med. 1984;76(Suppl 3A):134-141.

61. Pass RF, Burke RL. Development of cytomegalovirus vaccines: Prospects for prevention of congenital CMV infection. Semin Pediatr Infect Dis. 2002;13:196-204.

62. Rooney CM, Smith CA, Ng CY, et al. Use of gene-modified virus-specific T lymphocytes to control Epstein-Barr virus-related lymphoproliferation. Lancet. 1995;345:9-13.

63. Walter EA, Greenberg PD, Gilbert MJ, et al. Reconstitution of cellular immunity against cytomegalovirus in recipients of allogeneic bone marrow by transfer of T-cell clones from the donor. N Engl J Med. 1995;333:1038-1044.

64. Whitley RJ, Gnann JW Jr. Acyclovir: A decade later. N Engl J Med. 1992;327:782-789.

65. Beutner KR, Friedman DJ, Forszpaniak C, et al. Valacyclovir HCl compared with acyclovir for improved therapy for herpes zoster in immunocompetent adults. Antimicrob Agents Chemother. 1995;39:1546-1553.

66. Sacks SL, Aoki FY, Diaz-Mitoma F, et al. Patient-initiated, twice-daily oral famciclovir for early recurrent genital herpes: A randomized, double-blind, multicenter trial. JAMA. 1996;276:44-49.

67. Coen DM, Schaffer PA. Antiherpesvirus drugs: A promising spectrum of new drugs and drug targets. Nature. 2003;2:278-288.

68. Crumpacker CS. Ganciclovir. N Engl J Med. 1996;335:721-729.

69. Studies of Ocular Complications of AIDS Research Group in collaboration with the AIDS Clinical Trials Group. Parenteral cidofovir for cytomegalovirus retinitis in patients with AIDS: The HPMPC peripheral cytomegalovirus retinitis trial. A randomized, controlled trial. Ann Intern Med. 1997;126:264-274.

70. Weinberg A, Jabs DA, Chou S, et al. Mutations conferring foscarnet resistance in a cohort of patients with acquired immunodeficiency syndrome and cytomegalovirus retinitis. J Infect Dis. 2003;187:777-784.

71. Straus SE, Ostrove JM, Inchauspe G, et al. Varicella-zoster virus infections—biology, natural history, treatment, and prevention. Ann Intern Med. 1988;108:221-237.

CHAPTER **132**

Herpes Simplex Virus

LAWRENCE COREY

Herpes simplex viruses (HSV-1 and HSV-2) produce a wide variety of illnesses, including mucocutaneous infections, infections of the central nervous system, and an occasional infection of visceral organs; some of these conditions may be life threatening. The advent of effective chemotherapy for HSV infection has made their prompt recognition of clinical importance.

The word herpes (from the Greek, "to creep") has been used in medicine since antiquity. Cold sores (herpes febrilis) were described by the Roman physician Herodotus in 100 AD.[1] Genital herpes was first described by John Astruc, physician to the king of France, in 1736, and the first English translation appeared in his treatise on venereal disease in 1754.[2,3] Infection in oral-labial lesions was transmitted to other humans in the late 19th century. The disease was successfully transferred to rabbits in the early 20th century, and HSV was grown in vitro in 1925.[4,5]

DESCRIPTION OF THE AGENT

The eight known human herpesviruses (HHVs) are divided by genomic and biologic behavior into three groups: the α-herpesviruses (HSV-1, HSV-2, and varicella-zoster), the β-herpesviruses (cytomegalovirus, HHV-6, HHV-7), and the γ-herpesviruses (Epstein-Barr virus, Kaposi's sarcoma–associated herpesvirus [KSHV], or HHV-8) (see Chapter 131).[6] Herpesviruses are morphologically similar, possessing an internal core containing double-stranded DNA, an icosahedral capsid with 162 capsomers, an amorphous material surrounding the capsid called a tegument, and a lipid envelope containing viral glycoproteins on its surface. Their overall diameter is about 160 nm.[7] Despite this common morphologic feature, the biologic and epidemiologic features of each of the herpesviruses are distinct. Although HSV-1 and HSV-2 are the two most closely related herpesviruses, the two agents are serologically and genetically distinct.[8]

The genome of HSV is a linear, double-stranded DNA molecule (molecular weight about 100×10^6) that encodes about 90 transcriptional units, 84 of which appear to encode proteins. The genetic organization has sequences from both terminal ends of the genome repeated in an inverted fashion. This divides the genome into two unique components.[9] The overall sequence homology between HSV-1 and HSV-2 is about 50%.[7,10] The homologous sequences are distributed over the entire genome map, and most of the polypeptides specified by one viral type are antigenically related to polypeptides of the other viral type. Many type-specific regions unique to HSV-1 and HSV-2 proteins do exist, however, and many of these regions appear to be important in host immunity.

Restriction endonuclease or sequence analysis of viral DNA can be used to distinguish between the two subtypes and among strains of each subtype.[11-13] The variability of nucleotide sequences from clinical strains of HSV-1 and HSV-2 is such that HSV isolates obtained from two individuals can be differentiated by restriction enzyme patterns or direct genomic sequencing.[14] Isolates from epidemiologically related sources, such as sexual partners, mother-infant pairs, or victims of a common-source outbreak, are identical.[15-18]

Viral replication has both nuclear and cytoplasmic phases. The initial steps of replication include attachment and fusion between the viral envelope and the cell membrane to liberate the nucleocapsid into the cytoplasm of the cell. This de-enveloped tegument capsid structure is then transported to the nuclear pores, where viral DNA is released into the nucleus. Several cellular receptors required for viral attachment have been identified. The initial attachment involves the interactions of the viral glycoproteins C and B with cellular heparin sulfate.[19-21] Subsequently, the viral glycoprotein D binds to a cellular co-receptor. These viral co-receptors belong to the tumor necrosis factor family of proteins or the immunoglobulin superfamily (nectin family), or both.[22-24] The ubiquity of these receptors underscores the wide host range of both HSV-1 and HSV-2.[25]

Transcription of the viral genome, replication of viral DNA, and assembly of new capsids take place in the nucleus.[26] Replication of HSV is highly regulated. After fusion of the virion envelope with the host cell membrane, several viral proteins are released from the HSV virion and begin preparing the cell for viral production immediately. The virion host shutoff (VHS) protein shuts off synthesis (by increasing cellular RNA degradation), whereas others (e.g., VP16) "turn on" transcription of immediate early genes of HSV replication.[27] These immediate early gene products (designated α-genes), are required for synthesis of the subsequent polypeptide group, the β or early polypeptides, many of which are regulatory proteins and enzymes required for DNA replication. Most current antiviral drugs interfere with β-proteins, such as the viral DNA polymerase enzyme. The third (γ) or late class of HSV genes requires viral DNA replication for expression and constitutes most of the structural proteins specified by the virus. DNA replication takes place in a "rolling circle" pattern much like a roll of toilet paper. Specific viral genes "clip" the end of the viral DNA into the procapsid.

Nucleocapsids are assembled in the nucleus of the cell. Envelopment occurs as the nucleocapsids bud through the inner nuclear membrane into the perinuclear space. In some cells, viral replication in the nucleus forms two types of inclusion bodies: type A basophilic Feulgen-positive bodies that contain viral DNA and an eosinophilic inclusion body that is devoid of viral nucleic acid or protein and represents a "scar" of viral infection. Virions are then transported through the endoplasmic reticulum and the Golgi apparatus to the cell surface. The entire replication cycle takes 4 to 12 hours, depending on the cell type. HSV is cytopathic to cells that harbor the full cycle of HSV replication.[6]

HSV infection of some neuronal cells does not, however, result in cell death. Instead, viral genomes are maintained by the cell in a repressed state compatible with survival and normal activities of the cell, a condition called *latency*.[28-30] Latency is associated with transcription of only a limited number of virus-encoded proteins.[31-34] Subsequently, activation of the viral genome may occur, resulting in the normal pattern of regulated viral gene expression, replication, and release of HSV. The release of virus from the neuron and its subsequent entry into epithelial cells result in viral replication. This process is termed *reactivation*.[35-37] Although infectious virus can rarely be recovered

from sensory or autonomic nervous system ganglia dissected from cadavers, maintenance and growth of the neural cells in tissue culture result in production of infectious virions (*explantation*) and in subsequent permissive infection of susceptible cells (*cocultivation*).[38-40] The fact that HSV replication was first detected in neurons during reactivation in vitro suggested that the neuron harbors the latent virus in vivo.[31,41] Viral DNA and RNA have since been found in neural tissue at times when infectious virus cannot be isolated.[32,33,40,41] Three RNA "latency-associated" transcripts that overlap the immediate early (α) gene products, called ICP0, are in abundance in the nuclei of latently infected neurons. These latency-associated transcripts encode proteins in an antisense direction.[31,42-45] Deletion mutants of this region that can become latent have been made; however, the efficiency of their later reactivation is reduced. Thus, the antisense transcripts may play a role in maintaining, rather than in establishing, latency. At present, the molecular mechanisms of the latency of HSV-1 and HSV-2 are not well understood, and strategies to interrupt latency or to maintain molecular latency in neurons are not available.[46-48]

EPIDEMIOLOGY

Herpes simplex viruses have a worldwide distribution and are found even in the most remote human populations. There are no known animal vectors for HSV, and although experimental animals can easily be infected, humans appear to be the only natural reservoir.

Infection with HSV-1 is acquired more frequently and earlier than infection with HSV-2.[49] More than 90% of adults have antibodies to HSV-1 by the fifth decade of life. Prevalence of antibody to HSV increases with age and demonstrates an inverse correlation with socioeconomic status. In western populations in the post–World War II era, 80% to 100% of middle-aged adults of lower socioeconomic status had antibodies to HSV, compared with 30% to 50% of adults of higher socioeconomic groups.[49-52] Serosurveys have shown a decline in the age-specific prevalence rates for HSV-1 in both the United States and most of western Europe.[49,50] In the United States in the 1970s, HSV-1 antibodies were detected in about 50% of persons of high and 80% of persons of lower socioeconomic class by age 30 years.[49] This drop in HSV-1 acquisition in childhood appears to account for the increased frequency of sexually acquired HSV-1 infections in adolescent and young adults.[49-53]

Evaluation of the seroprevalence to HSV-1 and HSV-2 has been markedly enhanced by the development of type-specific serologic assays.[54-56] These assays allow the detection of HSV-2 in the presence of HSV-1 antibodies and vice versa. Most of these assays measure antibodies to purified HSV-1– or HSV-2–specific proteins such as glycoprotein gG1 and glycoprotein gG2, which are antigenically distinct between the two subtypes.[56,57] The gG1 and gG2 assays are quite accurate for defining persons with long-standing HSV infections. Another assay using an immunoblot format that identifies several type-specific antibodies, for example, gG2 and ICP-35 complex, has also been developed.[57] The Western blot assay has a sensitivity of greater than 98% and a specificity of greater than 98% for distinguishing HSV-1–specific and HSV-2–specific antibodies.[58-60] Assays that use whole viral extracts or antigens are inaccurate and should not be used for clinical diagnosis or seroepidemiologic studies.[61,62]

Antibodies to HSV-2 appear routinely in puberty and correlate with past sexual activity of either the individuals or their partners.[63,64] Several serosurveys have documented that a worldwide pandemic of HSV-2 infection has been ongoing in the last two decades (Table 132-1).[49] In the United States, two nationwide surveys have shown that the HSV-2 seroprevalence has increased from 16.4% to 21.7% of adults.[64,65] The cumulative lifetime incidence of HSV-2 reaches 25% in white women, 20% in white men, 80% in black women, and 60% in black men. Table 132-1 illustrates HSV-2 seroprevalence data from a variety of areas of the world.[49,63-67] Seroprevalence of HSV-2 in women in South Africa averages 40%. In Africa, seroprevalence rates of HSV-2 among men infected with the human immunodeficiency virus (HIV) average 50% to 60%. The frequency of HSV-2 antibody is higher among persons

TABLE 132-1 Herpes Simplex Virus Type 2 Seroprevalence in Selected Populations

Population	Frequency of HSV-2 Infection (%)
United States	
General population	22
Women	26
Men	18
Women's clinic, Albuquerque, NM	31
Women in STD clinic, Birmingham, AL	64
HIV-1–negative MSM, Seattle, WA	26
San Francisco neighborhood survey	
Women	41
Men	25
Europe	
Blood donors, Germany	13
STD clinic, France	55
STD clinic, Milan, Italy	25
MSM, Italy	55
OB GYN clinic, Italy	18
Blood donors, London, UK	8
General population, Helsinki, Finland	16
STD clinic, London, UK	
Women	25
Men	17
Randomly selected German population, 1996	13
STD clinic, Netherlands	32
STD clinic, Sweden	17
Obstetrical clinic, Sweden	33
Obstetrical clinic, Estonia	24
Africa	
Rural adults, Rakai, Uganda	
Women	74
Men	57
Urban adults, Kisumu, Kenya	
Women	68
Men	35
Urban adults, Cotonou, Benin	
Women	30
Men	12
Urban adults, Yaounde, Cameroon	
Women	51
Men	27
Urban adults, Kinshasa, Zaire	41
Male factory workers, Zimbabwe	45
STD clinics, South African male	60
Commercial sex workers, Zaire	90
Latin America/South America	
Women seeking HIV-1 testing, Mexico City	29
Household survey of women, Costa Rica	39
Pregnant women, Sao Paulo, Brazil	39
MSM, Peru	52
STD clinic, Peru	83
Women in Brazil	42
Asia	
Married women, Bangladesh	12
Pregnant women, Japan	7
Commercial sex workers, Thailand	76
Women, Philippines	9
Antenatal clinic, India	14
Antenatal clinic, Sri Lanka	21
Australia	
Pregnant women	15
STD clinic	
Women	55
Men	35
STD clinic, Auckland, New Zealand	26

HIV, human immunodeficiency virus; HSV, herpes simplex virus; MSM, men who have sex with men; OB GYN, obstetrics and gynecology; STD, sexually transmitted disease.

Adapted from Corey L, Wald A, Celum C, Quinn TC. The effects of HSV-2 on HIV-1 acquisition and transmission: A review of two overlapping epidemics. J Acquir Immune Defic Syndr. 2004;35:435-445.

recruited from sexually transmitted disease (STD) clinics and among homosexual men.[66-74] HSV-2 antibody levels are closely related to the lifetime number of sexual partners, age of sexual debut, and a history of other STDs.[75,76] Women have higher prevalence rates of HSV-2 than men as the efficiency of transmission is greater from men to women than vice versa.[77,78]

Incidence rates of HSV infection are difficult to estimate. In prospective studies of sexually active populations such as pregnant women and persons attending STD clinics, rates of HSV-1 seroconversion were between 1% and 4% per 100 person years; for HSV-2 they were 2% to 6% yearly.[77-80] Among HSV-seronegative women, 50% of the seroconversions were clinically symptomatic.[81] For men, these figures were 30% and 70%, respectively. It is unclear whether past HSV-1 infection reduces the risk of infection with HSV-2.[80] However, persons with prior HSV-1 are three times as likely to acquire HSV-2 subclinically.[81] Retrospective surveys indicate that only 20% to 25% of persons who have HSV-1 antibodies and 10% to 20% of persons with HSV-2 antibodies report oral-labial or genital lesions.[64-66] The differences in the prospective and retrospective studies suggest that many acquisitions are only mildly symptomatic and do not bring persons to regular medical attention. Many persons who acquire genital infection subclinically manifest symptomatic reactivation on follow-up.[81]

TRANSMISSION OF HERPES SIMPLEX VIRUS INFECTION

In 1921, Lipschutz inoculated material from genital herpetic lesions into the skin of humans, eliciting clinical infection within 48 to 72 hours in six persons and within 24 days in one case.[5] Transmission of HSV infections most frequently occurs through close contact with a person who is shedding (excreting) virus at a peripheral site, at a mucosal surface, or in genital or oral secretions.[79,82,83] Because HSV is readily inactivated at room temperature and by drying, aerosol and fomitic spread are unusual means of transmission.[84] Infection occurs by inoculation of virus onto susceptible mucosal surfaces (e.g., the oropharynx, cervix, conjunctivae) or through small cracks in the skin.[83-85] Subclinical or asymptomatic shedding of HSV in oral and genital secretions is common even in immunocompetent persons.[83,86,87] Transmission to any mucosal site by direct contact can occur. Transmission of HSV-1 from oral-genital contact is being increasingly recognized, perhaps because of the reduction in age-specific prevalence of HSV-1 at the time of sexual debut.[88] The acquisition rates of genital HSV-1 and oral-labial HSV-1 vary according to the age, sexual history, and serologic status of sexual partners.[89]

Spread of HSV-1 infection from oral secretions to other skin areas is a hazard of certain occupations (e.g., dentists, respiratory care unit personnel), and laboratory-acquired and nosocomial outbreaks in hospital personnel or in neonatal nurseries have been reported.[84,85] Similarly, outbreaks among wrestlers are well recognized.[90,91] Transmission of HSV can occur in infants born to mothers excreting HSV at delivery.[92] Anal and perianal infections with HSV-1 or HSV-2 are also common among sexually active male homosexual populations.[93,94]

PATHOGENESIS

Exposure to HSV at mucosal surfaces or abraded skin sites permits entry of the virus and initiation of its replication in cells of the epidermis and dermis.[95,96] Initial HSV infection is often subclinical—that is, without clinically apparent lesions. Both clinical acquisition and subclinical acquisition are associated with sufficient viral replication to permit infection of either sensory or autonomic nerve endings.[33,95-97] On entry into the neuronal cell, the virus or, more likely, the nucleocapsid is transported intra-axonally to the nerve cell bodies in ganglia.[98] For HSV-1 infection, trigeminal ganglia are most commonly infected, although extension to other areas (i.e., inferior and superior cervical ganglia) also occurs.[28-30,36] With genital infection, sacral nerve root ganglia (S2 to S5) are most commonly affected.[35] In humans, the interval from inoculation of virus in peripheral tissue to spread to the ganglia is unknown. During the initial phase of infection, viral replication occurs in ganglia and contiguous neural tissue.[95,97] Virus then spreads to other mucosal skin surfaces by centrifugal migration of infectious virions through peripheral sensory nerves. This mode of spread helps explain the large surface area involved, the high frequency of new lesions distant from the initial crop of vesicles that is characteristic in patients with primary genital or oral-labial HSV infection, and the recovery of virus from neural tissue distant from neurons innervating the inoculation site.[99] Contiguous spread of locally inoculated virus may also take place and allow further mucosal extension of disease. Histologically, herpetic lesions involve a thin-walled vesicle or ulceration in the basal region, multinucleated cells that may include intranuclear inclusion, necrosis, and an acute inflammatory infection.

After the resolution of primary disease, infectious HSV can no longer be recovered in the ganglia. However, viral DNA can be found in 10% to 25% of ganglion cells in the anatomic region of the initial infection.[92] Only about 1% of such cells express latency-associated transcripts of RNA detectable by current techniques.[47] The mechanisms by which various stimuli cause the reactivation of HSV infection are unknown. Ultraviolet light, immunosuppression, and trauma to the skin or ganglia are associated with reactivation.[37-39]

One of the intriguing differences in reactivation is related to the interaction between viral subtype and anatomic site of infection. Among immunocompetent persons who acquire HSV-1 both orally and genitally, HSV-1 is reactivated more frequently in the oral than in the genital region. Similarly, for HSV-2, reactivation in the genital region is 8 to 10 times more frequent than oral-labial reactivation of HSV-2.[100,101] In experimental animal systems, both sacral and trigeminal ganglia contain latent virus, but reactivation differs according to the anatomic site of injection.[102,103] When the region containing the latency-associated transcripts of HSV-2 is inserted into an HSV-1 virus, increasing reactivation in sacral nerve root ganglia has occurred, indicating that viral factors influence reactivation.[45]

Host factors clearly influence rates of reactivation. Immunocompromised patients have both more frequent and more severe reactivation.[104-110] Alterations in T-cell immunity are critical to viral containment.[111-113] Although agammaglobulinemic patients appear to handle HSV infection well, widespread local extension and dissemination are common in infants and immunocompromised patients such as organ transplant recipients and HIV-infected persons.[113] Viremic spread of virus to visceral organs can lead to life-threatening disease.[109,110] Experimental ablation of lymphocytes indicated that T cells play a major role in preventing lethal disseminated disease, although antibodies help reduce viral titer in neural tissue.[111-113] The surface viral glycoproteins have been shown to be antigens recognized by antibodies mediating neutralization and immune-mediated cytolysis (antibody-dependent cell-mediated cytotoxicity).[114,115] Monoclonal antibodies specific for each of the known viral glycoproteins have, in experimental infections, conferred protection against subsequent neurologic disease or ganglionic latency.[116,117] Multiple cell populations, including natural killer cells, macrophages, a variety of T lymphocytes, and lymphokines generated by these cells, play a role in host defenses against HSV infections.[113,118] In animals, passive transfer of primed lymphocytes confers protection against subsequent challenge.[119,120] Maximal protection usually requires the activation of multiple T-cell subpopulations, including cytotoxic T cells and T cells responsible for delayed hypersensitivity.[121-124] The latter cells may confer protection by the antigen-stimulated release of lymphokines (e.g., interferons), which may have a direct antiviral effect or may activate other nonspecific effector cells.[125-127] Innate immune defenses also appear to influence clinical expression of HSV. Individuals with defects in natural killer T cells have been reported to suffer from severe, even fatal HSV infections. Both HSV-1 and HSV-2 encode proteins that are directed at subverting host T-cell responses.[128-132] The HSV protein ICP47 (infected cell protein 47) interacts with the transporter activity protein to prevent the interaction between HSV-specific peptides and human leukocyte antigen (HLA) class I molecules.[131] This interaction downregulates certain HSV peptides with HLA class I antigen

on the cell surface and subverts the host CD8+ cytotoxic T-cell response to HSV.[132,133] Other proteins such as the VHS protein shut down host cell RNA and subsequent host defenses.[124] Other viral proteins, such as gJ, inhibit cellular mechanisms of apoptosis and hence increase viral replication, whereas others, such as ICP47, alter antigen presentation and class II expression.[134-136]

Biopsies of herpetic lesions have shown that the predominant infiltrating cell is the CD4+ lymphocyte.[137,138] These lesion-infiltrating cells show evidence of activation markers such as interleukin-2 receptor, DR+, and ICAM-1+ and also secrete large amounts of γ-interferons. Within 2 to 4 days, lesions are infiltrated with CD8+ T cells.[139,140] Clearance of HSV-2 from genital lesions is associated with the infiltration of HSV-specific CD8+ T cells.[140,141] Further evidence of the importance of the CD8+ T cells in HSV pathogenesis is the association between quantity of circulating CD8+ T cells to HSV and severity of infection among persons positive for HIV and HSV-2 s.[142]

Some aspects of HSV disease may be related to immunopathologic events. In experimental animals, stromal keratitis associated with HSV-1 infection is precipitated by HSV-specific T cells.[143-145] Molecular cross-reactivity between the HSV proteins and cellular proteins appears to play a role in this phenomenon.[146]

SPECTRUM OF DISEASES CAUSED BY HERPES SIMPLEX VIRUS

HSV has been isolated from nearly all visceral and mucocutaneous sites. The clinical manifestations and course of HSV infection depend on the anatomic site involved, the age and immune status of the host, and the antigenic type of the virus. First episodes of HSV disease, especially primary infections (i.e., first infections with either HSV-1 or HSV-2 in which the host lacks HSV antibodies in acute-phase serum), are frequently accompanied by systemic signs and symptoms, involve both mucosal and extramucosal sites, and have a longer duration of symptoms, a longer duration of virus isolation from lesions, and a higher rate of complications than recurrent episodes of disease.[147-149] Both viral subtypes can cause genital and oral-facial infections, and the infections caused by the two subtypes are clinically indistinguishable. However, the frequency of reactivation of infection is influenced by anatomic site and virus type.[150,151]

ORAL-FACIAL HERPES SIMPLEX VIRUS INFECTION

Gingivostomatitis and pharyngitis are the most frequent clinical manifestations of first-episode HSV-1 infection, whereas recurrent herpes labialis is the most frequent clinical manifestation of reactivation HSV infection.[152-154] HSV pharyngitis and gingivostomatitis usually result from primary infection and are most commonly seen in children and young adults.[155-157] Clinical symptoms and signs, which include fever, malaise, myalgias, inability to eat, irritability, and cervical adenopathy, may last from 3 to 14 days. Lesions may involve the hard and soft palate, gingiva, tongue, lip, and facial areas (Fig. 132-1). HSV-1 and HSV-2 infection of the pharynx usually results in exudative or ulcerative lesions of the posterior pharynx or tonsillar pillars, or both. Lesions of the tongue, buccal mucosa, or gingiva may occur later in the course in one third of cases. Fever lasting from 2 to 7 days and cervical adenopathy are common. It can be difficult to differentiate HSV pharyngitis clinically from bacterial pharyngitis, *Mycoplasma pneumoniae* infections, and pharyngeal ulcerations of noninfectious causes (e.g., Stevens-Johnson syndrome). No substantial evidence suggests that reactivation of oral-labial HSV infection is associated with symptomatic recurrent pharyngitis.[158]

Reactivation of HSV from the trigeminal ganglia may be associated with asymptomatic virus excretion in the saliva, development of intraoral mucosal ulcerations, or herpetic ulcerations on the vermilion border of the lip or external facial skin.[158] About 50% to 70% of seropositive patients undergoing trigeminal nerve root decompression and 10% to 15% of those undergoing dental extraction acquire oral-labial HSV infection a median of 3 days after these procedures.[159,160]

In immunosuppressed patients, infection may extend into mucosal and deep cutaneous layers. Friability, necrosis, bleeding, severe pain, and inability to eat or drink may result.[161,162] The lesions of HSV mucositis are clinically similar to mucosal lesions caused by cytotoxic drug therapy, trauma, or fungal or bacterial infection.[163,164] Persistent ulcerative HSV infections are among the most common infections in patients with acquired immunodeficiency syndrome.[165] HSV and *Candida* infections often occur concurrently. Systemic acyclovir therapy speeds the rate of healing and relieves the pain of mucosal HSV infections in immunosuppressed patients.[161-164] Patients with atopic eczema or burns may also acquire severe oral-facial HSV infections (eczema herpeticum), which may rapidly come to involve extensive areas of skin and occasionally disseminate to visceral organs.[166,167]

Extensive eczema herpeticum has resolved promptly with the administration of intravenous acyclovir.[168] Erythema multiforme may also be associated with HSV infections, and evidence suggests that HSV infection is the precipitating event in about 75% of cases of cutaneous erythema multiforme.[169,170] HSV antigen has been demonstrated both in circulatory immune complexes and in skin lesion biopsy samples from these patients.[171] Patients with severe HSV-associated erythema multiforme are candidates for chronic suppressive oral antiviral therapy.[172]

HSV-1 and varicella-zoster virus have, for several years, been implicated in the cause of Bell's palsy (facial paralysis of the mandibular portion of the facial nerve).[173,174] HSV DNA has been found in ganglionic fluid in a high percentage of persons undergoing decompressive surgery for this entity, suggesting recent viral reactivation as the cause of the disease.[175,176] These findings have been corroborated by studies that show faster and more frequent resolution of facial paralyses with the prompt use of antiviral therapy directed at HSV-1 or varicella-zoster virus.[177-179]

GENITAL INFECTION

First-episode primary genital herpes is characterized by fever, headache, malaise, and myalgias. Pain, itching, dysuria, vaginal and urethral discharge, and tender inguinal lymphadenopathy are the predominant local symptoms. Widely spaced bilateral lesions of the external genitalia are characteristic (Fig. 132-2). Lesions may be present in varying stages, including vesicles, pustules, or painful erythematous ulcers (Fig. 132-3).[148,149] The cervix and urethra are involved in more than 80% of women with first-episode infections (Fig. 132-4).[180-183] First episodes of genital herpes in patients who have had prior HSV-1 infection are associated with less frequent systemic symptoms and faster healing than primary genital herpes.[148,149] The clinical courses of acute first-episode genital herpes among patients with HSV-1 and HSV-2 infections are similar; however, the recurrence rates of genital disease differ with the viral subtype; the 12-month recurrence rates among patients with first-episode HSV-2 and HSV-1 infections are 90% and 55%, respectively.[111,151] HSV has been isolated from the urethra and urine of men and women without external genital lesions.[183] A clear mucoid discharge and dysuria are characteristics of HSV urethritis. HSV has been isolated from the urethra of 5% of women with the dysuria-frequency syndrome.[184,185] Occasionally, HSV genital tract disease is manifested by endometritis and salpingitis in women and by prostatitis in men.[186-88]

Both HSV-1 and HSV-2 can cause symptomatic or asymptomatic rectal and perianal infections.[189-192] HSV proctitis is usually associ-

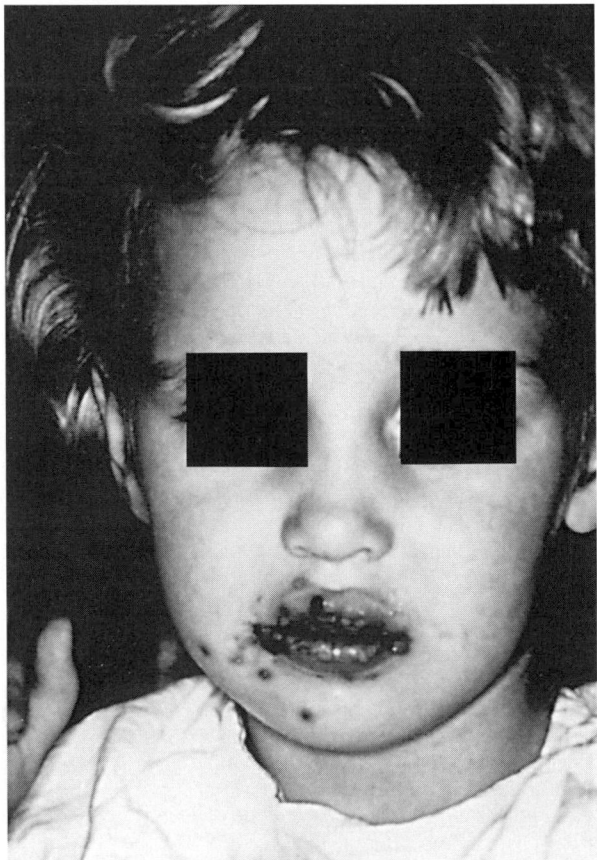

FIGURE 132-1. Primary herpes simplex virus gingivostomatitis in a child, extending to involve the cheek, chin, and periocular skin.

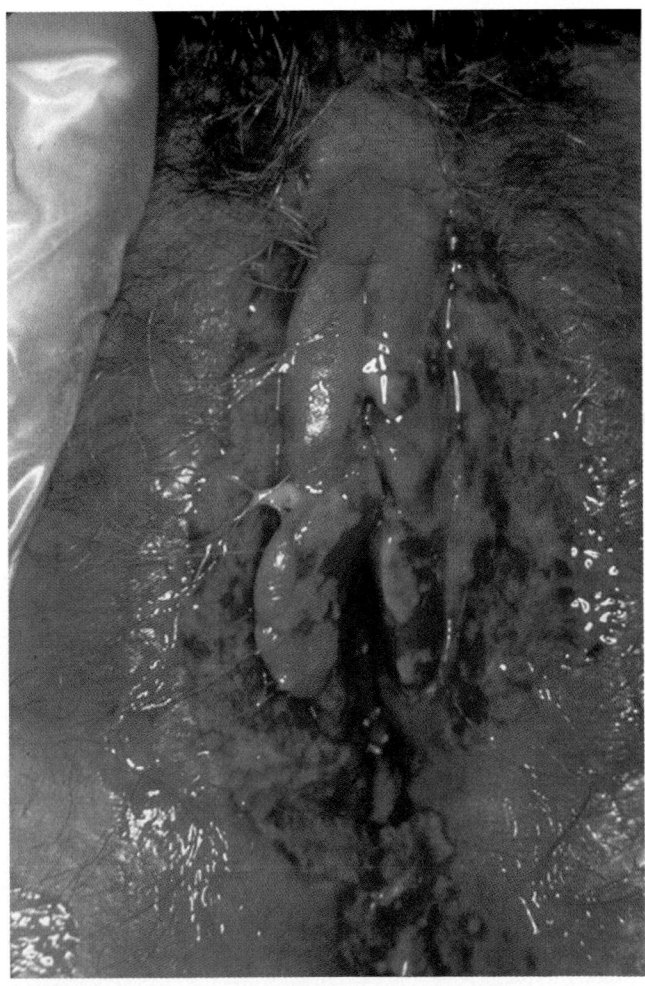

FIGURE 132-2. Primary genital herpes simplex virus type 2 infection of the vulva.

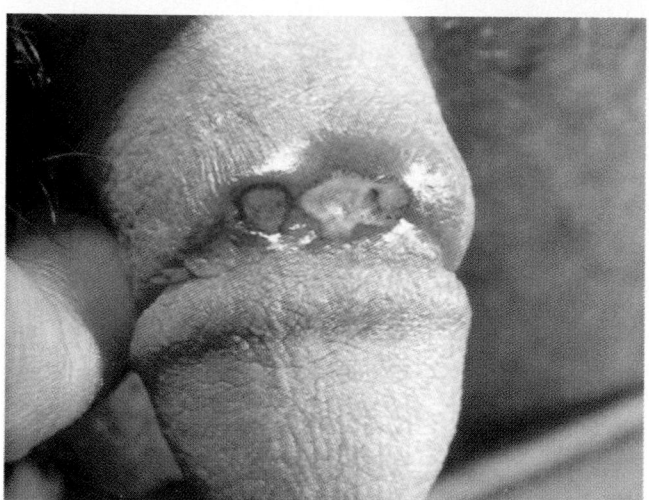

FIGURE 132-3. Chancroidal herpes simplex virus lesion on penis. *(From Corey L. Herpes simplex virus infections. In: Mandell GL, series ed. Atlas of Infectious Diseases, v. V, Sexually Transmitted Diseases. Rein MF, ed. Philadelphia: Churchill Livingstone/Current Medicine; 1996, Fig. 15-35. Courtesy of H. H. Handsfield, M.D.)*

ated with rectal intercourse. However, subclinical perianal shedding of HSV is detected both in heterosexual men and in women who report no rectal intercourse.[192-194] This phenomenon is due to the establishment of latency in the sacral dermatome from prior genital tract infection, with subsequent reactivation in epithelial cells in the perianal region. Such reactivations are often subclinical. Symptoms

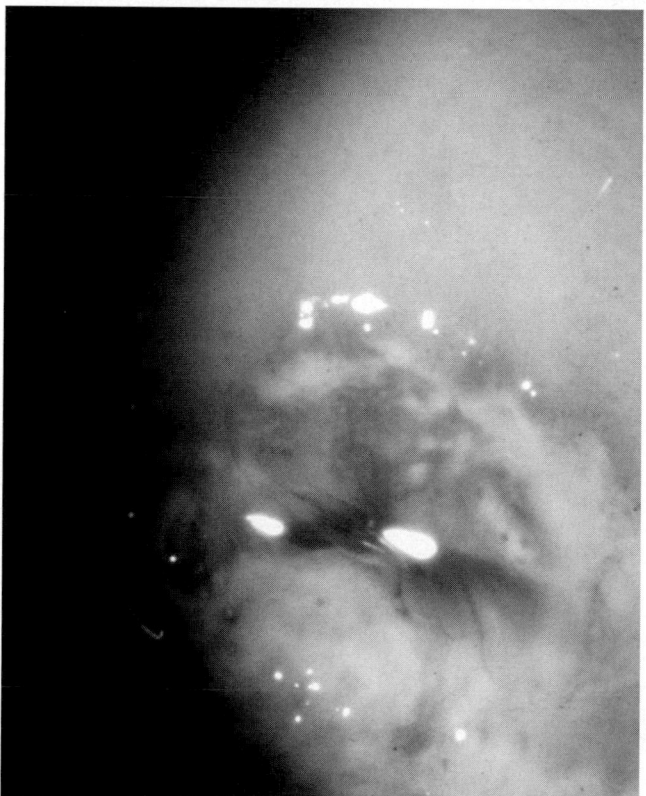

FIGURE 132-4. Herpes simplex virus cervicitis. *(From Corey L. Herpes simplex virus infections. In: Mandell GL, series ed. Atlas of Infectious Diseases, v. V, Sexually Transmitted Diseases. Rein MF, ed. Philadelphia: Churchill Livingstone/Current Medicine; 1996, Fig. 15-21B.)*

of HSV proctitis include anorectal pain, anorectal discharge, tenesmus, and constipation. Sigmoidoscopy reveals ulcerative lesions of the distal 10 cm of the rectal mucosa. Rectal biopsies show mucosal ulceration, necrosis, polymorphonuclear and lymphocytic infiltration of the lamina propria, and (in occasional cases) multinucleated intranuclear inclusion–bearing cells.[189] Antiviral therapy speeds healing.[191,192] Perianal herpetic lesions are also found in immunosuppressed patients receiving cytotoxic therapy. Extensive perianal herpetic lesions, HSV proctitis, or both are common among patients with HIV infection.[165]

COMPLICATIONS OF GENITAL HERPES

The complications of genital herpes are related to local extension or spread of virus to extragenital sites, or both.[81,195,196] Complications of primary genital herpes occur more frequently in women than in men.[148,149]

Aseptic Meningitis

Central nervous system (CNS) involvement may be manifested as aseptic meningitis, transverse myelitis, or sacral radiculopathy.[197-202] In one series, 36% of women and 13% of men with primary genital HSV-2 infection had stiff neck, headache, and photophobia on two consecutive examinations.[148] Hospitalization was necessary in 6.4% of women and 1.6% of men for aseptic meningitis in association with primary HSV-2 infections.[81,148] A high frequency of cerebrospinal fluid (CSF) pleocytosis in patients without overt clinical evidence of meningeal irritation was reported in a study of primary genital herpes in the early 1900s, suggesting that meningeal involvement may be a frequent occurrence with primary genital herpes.[203]

Both HSV-1 and HSV-2 have been isolated from CSF, although overt viral meningitis is much more common with HSV-2. Fever, headache, vomiting, photophobia, and nuchal rigidity are the predominant symptoms of HSV aseptic meningitis. Meningeal symptoms usually start 3 to 12 days after the onset of genital lesions. Use of systemic antiviral chemotherapy early in the course of primary genital herpes decreases the subsequent development of aseptic meningitis. Symptoms generally reach a maximum 2 to 4 days into the illness and gradually recede over 2 to 3 days. The CSF in HSV aseptic meningitis is usually clear, and the opening pressures may be somewhat elevated. White blood cell counts in the CSF may range from 10 to more than 1000 cells/mm^3. The pleocytosis is predominantly lymphocytic in adults, although early in the course of disease and in neonates, a predominantly polymorphonuclear response may be seen. The CSF glucose level is usually more than 50% of the blood glucose, although hypoglycorrhachia has been reported on occasion. The CSF protein is usually slightly elevated.[204] In cases of aseptic meningitis HSV may be isolated from the CSF, although HSV DNA polymerase chain reaction (PCR) assay is a more sensitive diagnostic test.[200] The differential diagnosis of HSV aseptic meningitis includes diseases that result in neurologic involvement and genital ulcerations: sacral herpes zoster, Behçet's syndrome, collagen vascular disease, inflammatory bowel disease, and porphyria.

Among immunocompetent persons, aseptic meningitis associated with genital herpes is usually a benign (albeit uncomfortable) disease and gradually resolves without sequelae. Controlled trials of intravenous acyclovir for established HSV meningitis have not been conducted. However, intravenous acyclovir 5 mg/kg every 8 hours is recommended for hospitalized symptomatic patients. Most series have reported a low frequency of neurologic sequelae.

Autonomic nervous system dysfunction as well as transverse myelitis can occur in association with genital HSV infection.[205-210] Autonomic nervous system dysfunction can be associated with hyperesthesia or anesthesia of the perineal, lower back, or sacral regions as well as urinary retention and constipation. This complication occurs more frequently among women with genital herpes and men with HSV proctitis. Physical examination reveals a large bladder, decreased sacral sensation, and poor rectal and perineal sphincter tone. Impotence and absent bulbocavernous reflexes have been noted in men. CSF pleocytosis may be present in some patients. Electromyography usually reveals slowed nerve conduction velocities and fibrillation potentials in the affected area, and urinary cystometric examination shows a large atonic bladder. Resolution occurs in most cases over 4 to 8 weeks.

Transverse myelitis has also been reported in association with primary genital HSV infection.[210-212] Decreased deep tendon reflexes and muscle strength in the lower extremities, as well as the previously described autonomic nervous system signs and symptoms, are present. Residual neurologic dysfunction may occur.[212] Whether autonomic nervous system dysfunction results from viral invasion of the CNS or an unusual immunologic response to infection is unknown. Mollaret's meningitis, a recurrent lymphocytic meningitis, appears to be caused in some cases by HSV.

Extragenital Lesions

Extragenital lesions commonly develop during the course of a first episode of primary genital herpes and are seen more commonly in women than in men.[213,214] Extragenital lesions are most frequently located in the buttock, groin, or thigh area, although the finger and eye can also be involved. Among patients with primary HSV-2, 9% acquire extragenital lesions, most commonly on the buttocks.[214] Among patients with primary HSV-1, 25% acquire extragenital lesions, most commonly in or around the mouth.[212] Typically, the extragenital lesions develop after the onset of genital lesions, usually during the second week of disease. The distribution of lesions on the extremities or areas near the genital lesions, or both, and their occurrence later in the course of disease suggest that the majority of extragenital lesions develop by autoinoculation of virus or by viral reactivation in another part of the affected dermatome rather than viremic spread.[148,211,212] However, the demonstration of plasma viremia during the course of severe HSV infection suggests that viremic spread may also be a factor.[215,216] Both HSV-1 and HSV-2 have been shown to be rare causes of pelvic inflammatory disease. Although this may represent dual infection with other sexually transmitted pathogens such as *Neisseria gonorrhoeae* and *Chlamydia trachomatis*, extension of HSV infection into the uterine cavity and laparoscopic evidence of vesicular lesions on the fallopian tube from which HSV has been isolated have been reported.[186,187]

Disseminated Infection

Blood-borne dissemination as manifested by multiple vesicles over widespread areas of the thorax and extremities occurs rarely in persons with primary mucocutaneous herpes.[217-219] Cutaneous dissemination usually occurs early in the disease and is often associated with aseptic meningitis, hepatitis, pneumonitis, or arthritis. Other complications of primary genital HSV-2 infection include monoarticular arthritis,[220,221] hepatitis,[222,223] thrombocytopenia,[224] and myoglobinuria.[225] Pregnancy may predispose to severe visceral dissemination of primary genital HSV disease.[226-232] Reactivation of genital HSV in immunosuppressed patients, especially those with impaired cellular immune responses, can be associated with interstitial pneumonia, hepatitis, and pneumonitis, similar to the manifestations of disseminated infection of the neonate.[218,230-232] Disseminated visceral infections in immunosuppressed and pregnant patients are associated with high mortality and should be treated with systemic antiviral chemotherapy.

Superinfection

Bacterial superinfection of genital herpes in immunocompetent patients is not a common complication. Rarely, pelvic cellulitis appearing as an advancing erythema and swelling of the perineal area can be seen, and systemic antimicrobial therapy should be administered to such patients. Fungal vaginitis is, however, frequently encountered during the course of initial genital herpes, and concurrent yeast infection was reported to occur more frequently in women with genital herpes.[148]

RECURRENT MUCOCUTANEOUS HERPES SIMPLEX VIRUS INFECTIONS

In contrast to findings in first episodes of genital infection, the symptoms, signs, and anatomic sites of infection of recurrent genital or oral-labial herpes are usually localized to a defined mucocutaneous site.[233-236] Local symptoms such as pain and itching are mild to moderate compared with first episodes of infection, and the duration of the episode is shorter. Lesions are usually confined to one side, and the area of involvement is usually one tenth that of primary infection.[148,237] Recurrent oral-labial HSV tends to be of shorter duration than genital HSV. Oral-labial lesions tend to pass through clinical stages of infection more rapidly, and the median time from onset of tingling to healing averages 5 days.[152,153] Both oral and genital HSV reactivations are frequently associated with "prodromal signs and symptoms."[235] Prodromal symptoms vary from a mild tingling sensation, occurring 0.5 to 48 hours before eruption, to shooting pains in the buttocks, legs, or hips 1 to 5 days before the episode. In many patients, the prodromal symptoms are the most bothersome part of the episode. HSV is present on mucosal surfaces more frequently during these prodrome-only episodes, suggesting that viral reactivation is associated with these symptoms.[236,237]

Increasingly, the diverse clinical spectrum of recurrent HSV ulcerations is being recognized. As described later, subclinical reactivation of virus on mucosal surfaces is common.[238] Some evidence suggests that such reactivation is associated with "microscopic" perineal lesions. In addition, studies of both oral-labial and genital ulcerative lesions have found a surprisingly high frequency of HSV isolated from "atypical" clinical syndromes, including lesions that are described as linear fissures or serpiginous ulcers without an erythematous base (see Fig. 132-3).[185] Studies have shown that even among experienced clinicians, false-positive and false-negative clinical diagnoses of genital herpes are common.[81,239] Therefore, I recommend that all ulcerative lesions on oral and genital mucosa be sampled for HSV.[240] A definitive etiologic diagnosis is best established by the demonstration of viral nucleic acid or isolation of virus from the affected area.[240,241] HSV DNA detection by PCR is three to four times more sensitive than viral detection for identifying HSV as a cause of genital ulcers.[241]

FREQUENCY OF REACTIVATION

The major morbidity of HSV reactivations, especially genital herpes, is a result of the frequency of reactivation.[242,243] Ninety percent of persons who present with symptomatic first-episode genital HSV-2 experience subsequent clinical reactivation of infection, and 98% experience subclinical HSV-2 shedding in genital mucosa.[244-248] The median recurrence rate is between four and five recurrences per year.[151] Studies of clinical reactivation of HSV-2 infection show a steady but gradual decrease in recurrence rates over time. In one study, clinical reactivations of genital herpes decreased from an average of five to an average of two recurrences per year over a 5- to 8-year period.[249] This decrease is gradual and appears to occur most frequently 3 to 5 years after acquisition. However, great variability is seen and up to 20% of patients report increasing reactivations over time.[249]

Subclinical or asymptomatic viral shedding is a critical concept for understanding the epidemiologic and transmission features of genital and oral-labial HSV infections.[250-257] Two thirds of the episodes of mucosal HSV-1 or HSV-2 reactivation are subclinical.[238,244,245] Episodes of sexual and maternal-fetal transmissions occur during such episodes of subclinical shedding.[252-258] HSV has been cultured from the lower genitourinary tract of women and men in the absence of genital ulcerations or other lesions. In women, the anatomic sites of asymptomatic shedding include the cervix, vulva, anus, and urethra.[238,244] In men, asymptomatic shedding occurs from the penile skin, urethra, anus, and occasionally semen.[245,246] Transmission of genital herpes can occur by sexual contact with a person who is shedding HSV without symptoms or lesions.[256-258] Similar patterns of subclinical reactivation and transmission occur in the oropharynx.

PCR assays for HSV DNA detect HSV on mucosal surfaces three to four times more frequently than viral isolation.[240-242] Studies of antiviral therapy have shown that chronic daily therapy reduces viral excretion by 70% to 95% (from 30% to 5% of days), indicating that HSV DNA as detected by PCR on mucosal surfaces represents potentially infectious virus.[240,242] Subclinical episodes of HSV may last more than 1 day, may involve more than one anatomic site, and follow a pattern similar to that of clinical recurrences (i.e., occur most frequently shortly after acquisition, then gradually decline to stable levels over a 2- to 3-year period). Counseling of patients with genital herpes needs to emphasize the potential for infectivity during episodes of subclinical shedding and provide appropriate strategies to decrease the risk to patients' sexual partners.[258] Antiviral therapy with 500 mg of valacyclovir per day has been shown to reduce transmission of genital herpes by 50% by suppression of such episodes of subclinical shedding.[257] Similarly, subclinical shedding usually appears to account for transmission of genital HSV-1 through oral-genital sexual activity.[192,259]

INTERACTIONS BETWEEN GENITAL HERPES SIMPLEX VIRUS INFECTION AND HUMAN IMMUNODEFICIENCY VIRUS INFECTION

Persistent HSV infections are one of the most common clinical presentations of HIV infection. Almost all homosexual men with HIV infection have antibodies to HSV: 80% to 90% with HSV-1 and 80% to 95% with HSV-2.[260] Moreover, HSV reactivation, especially perianal shedding in men and subclinical vulvar shedding in women, is more frequent in HIV-positive persons than HIV-negative control subjects and mucosal HSV-2 reactivation varies considerably in the HIV-positive persons.[192,260] HSV DNA can be detected on 30% to 80% of days in HIV-positive persons.[260,261] Low CD4 counts and high HIV viral loads are associated with an increased frequency of HSV reactivation.[262-264] Highly active antiretroviral therapy appears to reduce the frequency of genital lesions, but subclinical reactivation is still frequently detected.[262] Antiviral therapy has been advocated as a means of reducing frequent HSV shedding in HIV-infected persons.[265,266]

Perhaps more important are the effects of HSV infection on the global epidemiology of HIV. Case-control and cohort studies have shown that prior HSV-2 infection is associated with an increased risk of acquisition of HIV.[267,268-279] A review of these data indicated that the relative risk for HIV seroconversion among persons with genital herpes has varied from 1.2 to 8.5 but most studies found an increased relative risk of 2 to 3.[280] The elevated risk has been found in male-to-male, male-to-female, and female-to-male transmission. These epidemiologic data support the role of genital herpes and other ulcerative STDs in fueling the HIV epidemic in developed and developing countries.[279-281] The risk of HIV transmission attributable to genital ulcers may be especially great among heterosexuals, who are currently the fastest growing segment of the HIV-infected population.[280,281] Studies are under way to evaluate whether treating high-risk HSV-2–seropositive persons with daily oral acyclovir would reduce the acquisition of HIV.[282]

Laboratory studies have provided evidence that HSV may be an important cofactor in influencing the titer and frequency of mucosal HIV infection. The HSV regulatory proteins ICP0 and ICP4 can upregulate the rate of HIV replication in vitro.[283-285] Herpetic lesions are associated with an influx of activated CD4-bearing lymphocytes,[138,139] which may result in increased expression of HIV on mucosal surfaces. In vivo, HSV-1 and HIV coinfection of epithelial cells results in a higher copy number of HSV virions.[286] HIV virions can be detected in genital herpes lesions, and higher titers of HIV-1 RNA are found in genital secretions during episodes of subclinical HSV-2 reactivation.[287]

HERPETIC WHITLOW

Herpetic whitlow (HSV infection of the finger) may occur as a complication of primary oral or genital herpes by inoculation of virus through a break in the epidermal surface or by direct introduction of

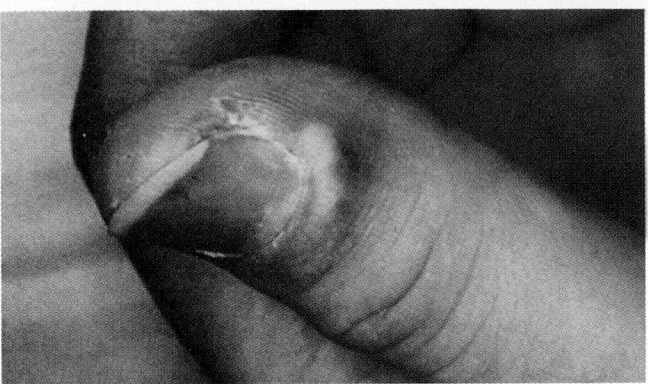

FIGURE 132-5. Herpetic whitlow (herpes simplex virus infection of the thumb). *(From Corey L. Herpes simplex virus infections. In: Mandell GL, series ed. Atlas of Infectious Diseases, v. V, Sexually Transmitted Diseases. Rein MF, ed. Philadelphia: Churchill Livingstone/Current Medicine; 1996, Fig. 15-25.)*

virus into the hand through occupational or some other type of exposure.[288,289] Before the increased use of gloves in health care settings, HSV-1 was most commonly isolated from herpetic infections of the hand.[85] However, one survey of herpetic infection of the hand found HSV-2 as the predominant causative agent.[213] Clinical signs and symptoms of herpetic whitlow include the abrupt onset of edema, erythema, and localized tenderness of the infected finger. Vesicular or pustular lesions of the fingertip that are difficult to distinguish from lesions of pyogenic bacterial infection are seen (Fig. 132-5). Fever, lymphadenitis, and epitrochlear and axillary lymphadenopathy are common. The infection may recur. Prompt diagnosis (to avoid unnecessary and potentially exacerbating surgical therapy or transmission, or both) is essential. Antiviral chemotherapy to speed the healing of the process is usually recommended.

HERPES GLADIATORUM

HSV may infect almost any area of skin. Mucocutaneous HSV infections of the thorax, ears, face, and hands have been described among wrestlers.[289,290] Transmission of these infections is facilitated by trauma to the skin sustained during wrestling. Prompt diagnosis and therapy are required to contain the spread of this infection.[291]

EYE INFECTIONS

HSV infection of the eye is the most frequent cause of corneal blindness in the United States.[291-293] HSV keratitis arises with an acute onset of pain, blurring of vision, chemosis, conjunctivitis, and characteristic dendritic lesions of the cornea (Fig. 132-6). Use of topical glucocorticoids may exacerbate symptoms and lead to involvement of deep structures of the eye. Débridement, topical antiviral treatment, interferon therapy, or a combination of these methods hastens healing. However, recurrences are common, and the deeper structures of the eye may sustain immunopathologic injury. Chorioretinitis, usually a manifestation of disseminated HSV infection, may occur in neonates or in patients with HIV infection. HSV and varicella-zoster virus can cause acute necrotizing retinitis.[293-296] This entity can be seen both in immunocompetent persons and in persons with HIV-1 infection. Retinal necrosis is rapid, and prompt systemic antiviral chemotherapy is required. Residual blindness is common.[297]

HERPES SIMPLEX VIRUS ENCEPHALITIS

HSV is the most commonly identified cause of acute, sporadic viral encephalitis in the United States, accounting for 10% to 20% of all cases.[297] The estimated incidence is about 2.3 cases per million persons

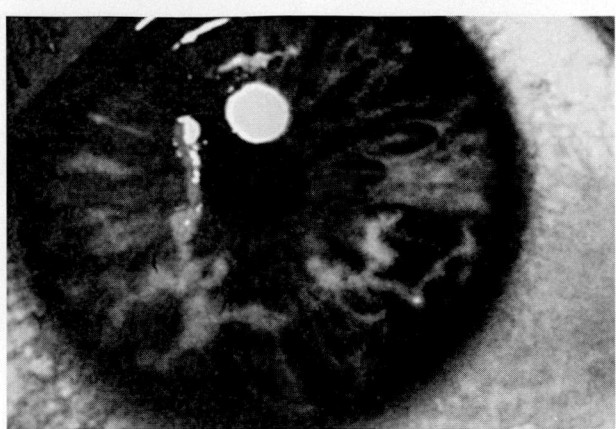

FIGURE 132-6. Herpes simplex virus type 1 dendritic keratitis. *(From Pavan-Langston D, ed. Ocular Viral Disease, v. 15. Boston: Little, Brown; 1975:19-36.)*

per year. Cases are distributed throughout the year, and the age distribution appears to be biphasic, with peaks at 5 to 30 and more than 50 years of age.[298] Subtype 1 virus causes more than 95% of cases of HSV encephalitis.[299-301]

The pathogenesis of HSV encephalitis varies. In children and young adults, primary HSV infection may result in encephalitis; presumably, exogenously acquired virus enters the CNS by neurotropic spread from the periphery through the olfactory bulb. However, most adults with HSV encephalitis have clinical or serologic evidence of mucocutaneous HSV-1 infection before the onset of the CNS symptoms.[301,302] In about 25% of the patients examined, the HSV-1 strains from the oropharynx and brain tissue of the same patient differ; thus, some cases may result from reinfection with another strain of HSV-1 that reaches the CNS.[300] The mechanism behind the development of actively replicating HSV in localized areas of the CNS in persons whose ganglionic and CNS isolates are similar is unclear. Reactivation of latent HSV-1 infection in trigeminal or autonomic nerve roots may be associated with extension of virus into the CNS through nerves innervating the middle cranial fossa. HSV DNA has been demonstrated by DNA hybridization in brain tissue obtained at autopsy, even from healthy adults.[302] Thus, reactivation of long-standing latent CNS infection may be another mechanism of the development of HSV encephalitis.

The clinical hallmark of HSV encephalitis has been the acute onset of fever and focal neurologic (especially temporal lobe) symptoms.[303] Differentiation of HSV encephalitis from other viral encephalitides, as well as from other focal infections and noninfectious processes, is difficult.[304] The most sensitive noninvasive method for early diagnosis of HSV encephalitis is the demonstration of HSV DNA in CSF by PCR, although uncommonly PCR may become positive a few days after onset. Although titers of CSF and serum antibodies to HSV increase in most cases of HSV encephalitis, they rarely do so earlier than 10 days into the illness and therefore, although useful retrospectively, are generally not helpful in establishing an early clinical diagnosis.[305-310] Magnetic resonance imaging is the neuroimaging technique of choice for detection of abnormalities associated with HSV encephalitis, and frequently gadolinium-enhanced lesions are seen in the temporal lobe. Brain biopsy was used extensively in the past to make the diagnosis of HSV encephalitis; demonstration of HSV antigen, HSV DNA, or HSV replication in brain tissue obtained by biopsy is highly sensitive and has a low complication rate. Brain biopsy is infrequently used now, but it provides the best opportunity to identify alternative, potentially treatable causes of encephalitis and may be considered when the clinical presentation is atypical or the diagnosis remains unclear.[304] All cases of HSV encephalitis should be treated with intravenous acyclovir at a dose of 30 mg/kg/day in three divided doses for 14 to 21 days.[311] Cases of clinical recurrence of en-

cephalitis have been reported after therapy has been stopped and have required a course of treatment. For this reason, some authorities prefer to treat initially for 21 days. Even with therapy, however, neurologic sequelae are frequent, especially in persons older than 35 years. Most authorities recommend the administration of intravenous acyclovir to patients with presumed HSV encephalitis until the diagnosis is confirmed or an alternative diagnosis is made.[301]

VISCERAL INFECTIONS

HSV infection of visceral organs usually results from viremia, and multiple-organ involvement is common. Occasionally, however, the clinical manifestations of HSV infection involve only the esophagus, lung, or liver. HSV esophagitis may result from direct extension of oral-pharyngeal HSV infection into the esophagus or may occur de novo by reactivation and spread of HSV to the esophageal mucosa through the vagus nerve.[312-314] The predominant symptoms of HSV esophagitis are odynophagia, dysphagia, substernal pain, and weight loss. The distal esophagus is most commonly involved with multiple oval ulcerations on an erythematous base, with or without a patchy white pseudomembrane. With extensive disease, diffuse friability may spread to the entire esophagus. Neither endoscopic nor barium examination can differentiate HSV esophagitis from *Candida* esophagitis or from esophageal ulcerations related to thermal injury, radiation, or corrosives. Endoscopically obtained secretions for cytologic examination and culture provide the most useful material for diagnosis. Systemic antiviral chemotherapy usually reduces symptoms and heals esophageal ulcerations.

HSV pneumonitis is uncommon except in severely immunosuppressed patients and may result from extension of herpetic tracheobronchitis into lung parenchyma.[110,315-318] Focal necrotizing pneumonitis usually ensues. Hematogenous dissemination of virus from sites of oral or genital mucocutaneous disease may also occur and produce bilateral interstitial pneumonitis. Bacterial, fungal, and parasitic pathogens are commonly present in HSV pneumonitis. The mortality rate from untreated HSV pneumonia in immunosuppressed patients is high (>80%).[110,317,318]

HSV has also been observed in association with the acute respiratory disease syndrome (ARDS).[319-321] Most authorities feel the presence of HSV in tracheal aspirates in such settings is due to reactivation of HSV in the tracheal region and localized tracheitis in persons with long-standing intubation. Such patients should be evaluated for potential HIV infection. Controlled trials evaluating the role antivirals for HSV play in ARDS morbidity and mortality have not been conducted.

HSV is an uncommon cause of hepatitis in immunocompetent patients. HSV infection of the liver is associated with fever, abrupt elevations of bilirubin and serum aminotransferase levels, and leukopenia (<4000 white blood cells/μL). Disseminated intravascular coagulation may also develop.[220,221]

HERPES SIMPLEX VIRUS INFECTIONS IN IMMUNOCOMPROMISED HOSTS OTHER THAN PATIENTS INFECTED WITH HUMAN IMMUNODEFICIENCY VIRUS

Organ transplant recipients, patients undergoing cancer chemotherapy, or those compromised by malnutrition or disorders of skin integrity such as burns or eczema are at greater risk for the development of severe HSV infections (Fig. 132-7).[322-326] Besides extensive mucocutaneous infections, HSV may disseminate to visceral organs such as adrenal glands, liver, bone marrow, and the gastrointestinal tract in such persons. Most kidney, liver, and bone marrow transplant recipients excrete HSV-1 in saliva during the first 2 to 3 weeks after grafting.[322,324] Although these reactivations are often asymptomatic, extensive mucocutaneous ulcerations may occur and, if persistent, may extend to the esophagus or lung. Because of the difficulty in distinguishing HSV from chemotherapy-related mucositis, most oncology centers use routine "prophylaxis" against HSV reactivation during the initial period af-

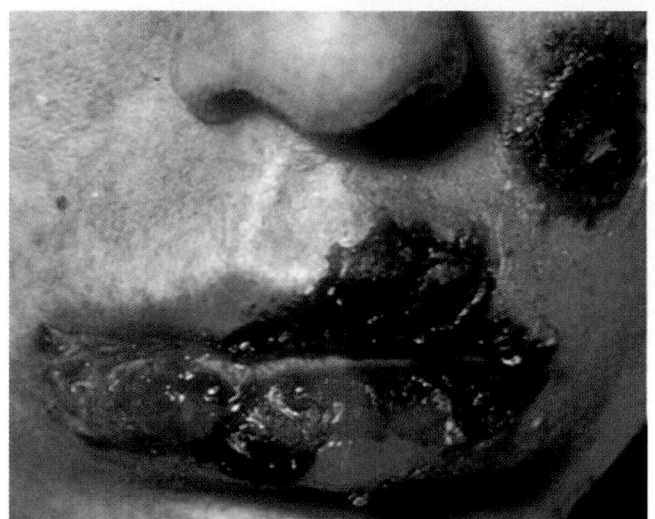

FIGURE 132-7. Severe mucocutaneous herpes simplex virus type 1 infection in a bone marrow transplant patient. *(From Corey L. Herpes simplex virus infections. In: Mandell GL, series ed. Atlas of Infectious Diseases, v. V, Sexually Transmitted Diseases. Rein MF, ed. Philadelphia: Churchill Livingstone/Current Medicine; 1996, Fig. 15-47B.)*

ter transplantation or initiation of chemotherapy.[322-325] Prophylaxis for HSV infection is routinely used in most organ and bone marrow transplantation settings.[327] The importance of adoptive T-cell immunity in controlling HSV resolution has been demonstrated. Persons who were HSV-1 seropositive and who received a bone marrow transplant from an HSV-seronegative donor were at higher risk for recurrence and were more likely to develop acyclovir-resistant strains of HSV than those who received marrow from HSV-1–positive donors.[328]

HERPES SIMPLEX VIRUS IN PREGNANCY

A major concern of patients with genital herpes is the effect the disease might have on pregnancy and the risk of transmission to the newborn, which is associated with high mortality and morbidity.[329-331] The prevalence of genital HSV infection during pregnancy as well as the relative incidence of neonatal HSV infection is influenced by the socioeconomic status, age, and past sexual activity of the population of patients being examined.[329-331] In the United States, serologic evidence of past HSV-2 infection is present in about 30% of middle-class women attending prenatal clinics; the percentage is 50% to 70% in nonwhite women of lower socioeconomic class who receive obstetric care.[331,333]

Studies have shown that the highest risk for transmitting HSV in the perinatal period occurs during the acquisition of HSV at or near the time of labor.[332-334] Table 132-2 depicts the frequency of neonatal infection in relation to maternal serologic states.

TABLE 132-2 Transmission Rates of Neonatal Herpes Simplex Virus (HSV) by Maternal HSV Serologic Status among Women Who Delivered at the University of Washington and Madigan Army Hospitals

Maternal HSV Serostatus	No./Total (%) of Infants with Neonatal HSV	Rate per 100,000 Live Births (95% Confidence Interval)
HSV seronegative	6/11,115 (0.054)	54 (19.8-118)
HSV-1 seropositive only	6/23,480 (0.026)	26 (9.3-56)
All HSV-2 seropositive	3/13,795 (0.022)	22 (4.4-64)
HSV-2 only	2/5761 (0.035)	35 (4.2-126)
HSV-1 and HSV-2	1/8034 (0.012)	12 (0.3-7.0)

Adapted from Brown ZA, Ashley RL, Selka S, et al. Effect of serologic status and cesarean delivery on transmission rates of herpes simplex virus from mother to infant. JAMA. 2003;289:203.

CLINICAL COURSE OF GENITAL HERPES IN PREGNANCY

In general, the clinical manifestations of recurrent genital herpes, including the frequency of subclinical versus clinical infection and the duration of lesions, pain, and constitutional symptoms, are similar in pregnant and nonpregnant women.[335-337] Recurrences appear to increase in frequency over the course of pregnancy.[334] Among women who are HSV-2 seropositive entering pregnancy, several clinical series and another study indicate that there is no effect of recurrent clinical infection on neonatal outcome, including birth weight and gestational age.[336,337] First-episode infections in pregnancy have more severe consequences for mother and infant.[330,337-341] Visceral dissemination during the third trimester occasionally occurs and prematurity or intrauterine growth retardation, or both, may be seen.[330-342] The acquisition of primary disease in pregnancy, whether related to HSV-1 or HSV-2, carries the risk of potential transplacental transmission of virus to the neonate.[339-341] Primary HSV infection in pregnancy can result in spontaneous abortion, although this appears to be relatively uncommon.[342,343]

Criteria for laboratory screening and surveillance, as well as delivery procedures for women with recurrent genital HSV infections, are the questions most frequently encountered by physicians caring for pregnant women with genital herpes.[344-347] The high prevalence rate of HSV-2 infection in pregnancy (antibody prevalence 30% to 60%) and the low incidence of neonatal disease (1 per 6000 to 1 per 20,000 live births) indicate that only a few infants are at risk for acquiring disease (see Table 132-2). Cesarean section is therefore not routinely warranted for all women with recurrent genital disease.[348] Because intrapartum transmission of infection accounts for the vast majority of cases, only women who shed HSV at the time of delivery need be considered for abdominal delivery.[331,347,348] Several studies have shown no correlation between recurrences of viral shedding before delivery and the presence of viral shedding at term.[347-350] Therefore, weekly cytologic and virologic monitoring is no longer recommended. A rapid, simple, and specific assay to detect HSV shedding at delivery would be a useful management tool for guiding the use of cesarean delivery.[331] Unfortunately, such an assay is not presently available.

The frequency of transmission of infection from mother to infant is markedly higher among women who acquire HSV near term (25% to 50%) than among those who have past HSV-2 and reactivated HSV at delivery (<1%).[331] Several studies have shown that about 2% of women who are HSV-2 seropositive have HSV-2 isolated from their cervical secretions at delivery; that is, their genital herpes is reactivated at delivery.[331,351] However, only about 1% of such exposed infants develop neonatal herpes, presumably because of the protective effects of maternally transferred antibodies.[330,331] Although the frequency of transmission of newborn HSV in this setting is low, the high prevalence rate of HSV-2 accounts for the fact that nearly one half of the infants diagnosed with neonatal HSV are born to mothers who are HSV-2 seropositive. Cesarean section appears to be an effective means of reducing maternal-fetal transmission.[331]

Patients with recurrent genital herpes should be encouraged to come to the delivery room early at the time of delivery. At this time, careful examination of the external genitalia and cervix should be performed. In addition, a swab of the cervix or vulvar area, or both, for viral isolation should be performed. Women who have no clinical evidence of lesions should have a vaginal delivery. The presence of active lesions of the cervix or external genitalia (i.e., clinical evidence of HSV infection of the lower genital tract) is an indication for abdominal delivery. This policy results in the exposure of some infants to episodes of cervical or vulvar shedding, or both. However, only a few infants exposed to maternal secretions containing HSV acquire neonatal herpes.[330,331] The identification of HSV-exposed infants provides important information to the attending pediatrician.[352] If first-episode exposure has occurred (e.g., if HSV serologies show that the mother is seropositive or if the mother is HSV-1 seropositive and the isolate at delivery is HSV-2), many authorities would initiate antiviral therapy of the infant with intravenous acyclovir.[352-354] At a minimum, most experts advise obtaining viral cultures from the throat, nasopharynx, eyes, and rectum of these infants immediately and then at 5- to 10-day intervals. accompanied by clinical follow-up. Any clinical evidence of lethargy, skin lesions, or other symptoms of neonatal HSV should be evaluated promptly. All infants from whom HSV is isolated 24 hours after delivery should be treated with intravenous acyclovir at recommended treatment doses (see later).

The relationship between the duration of ruptured membranes in the woman with clinically apparent lesions and transmission of HSV to the infant is not well defined. Delivery of infants by cesarean section, even in women with intact membranes, occasionally results in neonatal herpes.[348] Prolonged contact with infected secretions may increase the relative risk of acquisition of disease. Many authorities recommend that if membranes have been ruptured for more than 4 to 6 hours, cesarean section should no longer be considered for protection against HSV transmission. However, studies of neonatal HSV infection in Seattle have shown that transmission can occur from exposure to external genital lesions alone, that is, from women who are culture positive only on vulvar and not cervicovaginal swabs.[326] Thus, in women with recurrent genital herpes who have active external genital lesions at the time of labor, I still recommend abdominal delivery.

PREVENTION OF HERPES SIMPLEX VIRUS ACQUISITION IN PREGNANCY BY USE OF ANTIVIRALS

Controversy exists regarding the use of antiviral therapy during pregnancy.[351,352] A series of studies has shown that delaying antiviral therapy can reduce but not totally abrogate HSV-2 reactivation at delivery of women with recurrent genital herpes. A statistical analysis of several studies suggests that the frequency of cesarean delivery can also be reduced.[351,355]

Because the incidence of neonatal HSV-2 is low among women with recurrent genital herpes, the use of oral antiviral agents in late pregnancy to prevent neonatal HSV would not be cost effective; one would treat 99 to 100 women to prevent one case of neonatal HSV-2.

NEONATAL HERPES

Ninety percent of neonatal herpes is perinatally acquired, 5% to 8% is congenital, and a few cases are acquired postnatally[356]; the infant acquires infection at the time of delivery through contact with HSV-infected secretions. More than 70% of infants with neonatal HSV infection are born to mothers who lack symptoms or signs of HSV lesions at delivery.[357] The risk of transmission of neonatal herpes to the infant from a woman with primary HSV infection, whether it is due to HSV-1 or -2, is between 40% and 50%. The transmission rate for an infant from a mother who acquires HSV-2 infection but who is HSV-1 seropositive is 25%. The risk of neonatal transmission through vaginal delivery from a woman who is HSV-2 seropositive is less than 1%.[331]

Neonates (infants younger than 6 weeks) have the highest frequency of visceral or CNS infection, or both, of any HSV-infected population of patients. If not treated, neonatal herpes undergoes dissemination or develops into CNS infection in more than 70% of cases. Without therapy, the overall rate of death from neonatal herpes is 65%; less than 20% of neonates with CNS infection develop normally.[356,357] Although skin lesions are the most commonly recognized features of disease, many infants do not acquire visible lesions until well into the course of disease.[353] Of the 70% of neonatal HSV infections caused by HSV-2, almost all result from contact with infected genital secretions at the time of delivery. Although congenitally infected infants have been reported, as noted earlier, these infants almost invariably are born to mothers who have acquired primary HSV infection during pregnancy.[339,358] In most series, 30% of neonatal HSV infections are due to HSV-1.[257,321,357] Most of these cases are associated with the maternal acquisition of primary genital HSV-1 late in pregnancy and the consequent contact of the infant with infectious genital secretions at birth.[351] Neonatal HSV-1 infections may also be acquired through postnatal contact with health care workers or immediate family members who have symptomatic or asymptomatic oral-labial HSV-1 infection

through nosocomial transmission. CNS morbidity is less severe with HSV-1 than with HSV-2 infection.[359] High-dose (60 mg/kg/day) intravenous acyclovir divided in three daily doses for 21 days has reduced the mortality and morbidity, but long-term disabilities are still seen, especially in infants with HSV-2 infection involving the CNS.[360,361]

The key to prevention of neonatal HSV is prevention of the acquisition of genital HSV-1 or HSV-2 infection late in pregnancy. Several approaches are possible. One is to counsel abstinence for all women from 34 weeks of gestation. Alternatively, serologic screening for HSV near the third trimester can be done for all HSV-2–seronegative women, with counseling about the potential of acquiring HSV near term. All HSV-2–seronegative women should avoid unprotected sex from week 35 onward. If the woman is HSV-1 seronegative, avoidance of oral-genital contact is also recommended. As nearly 30% of neonatal HSV is due to HSV-1, attention to reducing HSV-1 acquisition through oral-genital sex in late pregnancy is needed.

Another approach is to screen the partner serologically and counsel the 20% of couples who have discordant HSV serologies. High risk exists in HSV-seronegative women with an HSV-1– or HSV-2–seropositive partner or HSV-1–seropositive women with an HSV-2–seropositive partner.[362] This requires testing the pregnant woman and counseling the HSV-2–seronegative woman to avoid unprotected sexual contact in late pregnancy. There are some who feel this is a difficult and expensive approach.

Infants born by cesarean section to women before the rupture of membranes or by vaginal delivery to women with no evidence of recent HSV infection are at minimal risk for the development of HSV infection, and most hospitals do not recommend segregating the infant from the rest of the newborn nursery. If a more cautious approach is desired, the infant can be put into an Isolette incubator to make hospital personnel aware of the necessity to use wound and skin precautions and proper hand-washing techniques.

Infants born to women at risk of transmitting disease to the neonate (i.e., women with active lesions) should be placed in isolation. Viral cultures, liver function studies, and CSF examinations should be obtained, and the infant should be observed closely for the first month of life. Any symptoms of neonatal disease (e.g., poor feeding, fever, hypothermia, skin lesions, or CNS symptoms such as seizures) should be investigated expeditiously for evidence of neonatal HSV infection. Management of contact between infant and mother should also be handled on an individual basis. In women who acquire primary genital herpes late in pregnancy, the high incidence of extragenital lesions and the potential for viremia suggest that separation of mother and infant is warranted until therapy has produced a clinical and virologic response. Because recurrent genital herpes is rarely associated with frequent dissemination of disease or the development of extragenital lesions in exposed extremities, protection of the infant from exposure to infected genital secretions is adequate. When handling the infant in the hospital, the mother should wear a gown and observe proper hand-washing techniques. Oral-labial herpes presents a greater risk of postnatal acquisition of HSV infections to the newborn than genital herpes.[17] Thus, nursery personnel and other adults with external labial lesions caused by HSV should also be excluded from intimate contact with the newborn infant.

DIAGNOSIS

Both clinical and laboratory criteria are useful for establishing the diagnosis of HSV infections. A clinical diagnosis can be made accurately when characteristic multiple vesicular lesions on an erythematous base are present. However, it is increasingly being recognized that herpetic ulcerations may clinically resemble skin ulcerations of other causes.[76,240] Mucosal HSV infection may also appear as urethritis or pharyngitis without cutaneous lesions. Thus, laboratory studies to confirm the diagnosis and to guide therapy are recommended.[81]

HSV infection is best confirmed in the laboratory either by isolation of virus in tissue culture or by demonstration of HSV DNA in scrapings or surplus from lesions.[240,241] HSV causes a discernible cytopathic effect in a variety of cell culture systems, and most specimens can be identified within 48 to 96 hours after inoculation. Spin-amplified culture with subsequent staining for HSV antigen has shortened the time needed to identify HSV to less than 24 hours. The sensitivity of viral isolation depends on the stage of lesions (with higher sensitivity in vesicular than in ulcerative lesions), on whether the patient has a first or a recurrent episode of the disease (with higher sensitivity in first than in recurrent episodes), and on whether the sample is from an immunosuppressed or an immunocompetent patient (with more antigen in immunosuppressed patients). HSV DNA detection has been shown to be three to four times more sensitive than viral isolation and is less affected by variation in specimen transport.[241] Laboratory confirmation permits subtyping of the virus; information on subtype may be useful epidemiologically and may help to predict the frequency of reactivation after first-episode oral-labial or genital HSV infection (see earlier).

Staining of scrapings from the base of the lesions with Wright, Giemsa (Tzanck preparation), or Papanicolaou stain demonstrates characteristic giant cells or intranuclear inclusions of HSV infection. These cytologic techniques are often useful as quick office procedures to confirm the diagnosis. Limitations of the cytologic method are that it does not differentiate between HSV and varicella-zoster virus infections, that it is relatively insensitive, and that the correct identification of giant cells requires experience.

Acute- and convalescent-phase serum can be useful in demonstrating seroconversion during primary HSV-1 or HSV-2 infection. However, only 5% of patients with recurrent mucocutaneous HSV infections have a fourfold or greater rise in titer of antibody to HSV in the interval between the collection of first and second samples. No commercially available accurate immunoglobulin M antibody assay is available. Serologic assays, especially type-specific assays, should be used to identify asymptomatic carriers of HSV-1 or HSV-2 infection. Commercial enzyme immunoassays using whole virus antigens should not be used to define serologically the presence of HSV-1, HSV-2, or clinical HSV-1 and HSV-2 infection.[363]

Several studies have shown that persons seropositive for HSV-2 to whom the clinical manifestations of HSV have been explained are able to identify symptomatic reactivations.[66,364] Individuals seropositive for HSV-2 should be told about the high frequency of subclinical reactivation in mucosal surfaces not visible to the eye (e.g., cervix, urethra, perianal skin) or in microscopic ulcerations that may not be clinically symptomatic. Transmission of infection during such episodes is well established.

TREATMENT

The advent of antiviral drugs for HSV-1 and HSV-2 infections has made clinical management of these infections a part of standard clinical practice (see Chapter 38). For mucocutaneous and visceral HSV infections, acyclovir and its related compounds famciclovir and valacyclovir have been the mainstay of therapy. Several antiviral agents are available for topical use in HSV eye infections: idoxuridine, trifluorothymidine, topical vidarabine, and cidofovir. For HSV encephalitis and neonatal herpes, intravenous acyclovir is the treatment of choice. Acyclovir-resistant virus can be encountered in immunocompromised hosts (see later).

Acyclovir was the first antiviral clearly demonstrated to be effective against HSV infections. It is an acyclic nucleoside analogue that is a substrate for HSV-specified thymidine kinase.[365-368] Acyclovir is selectively phosphorylated by HSV-infected cells to acyclovir monophosphate. Cellular enzymes then phosphorylate acyclovir monophosphate to acyclovir triphosphate, a competitive inhibitor of viral DNA polymerase.[366-369] Acyclovir triphosphate is incorporated into the growing DNA chain of the virus and causes chain termination. Acyclovir has potent in vitro activity against both HSV-1 and HSV-2.[370] Numerous trials of acyclovir in mucocutaneous HSV infections of the immunocompetent and immunosuppressed host have been conducted.[371-382] General recommendations are outlined in Table 132-3. Increasingly, shorter courses of therapy are being utilized for treatment of recurrent mucocutaneous HSV-1 or HSV-2 in immunocompetent patients.[382-384]

TABLE 132-3 Antiviral Chemotherapy for Herpes Simplex Virus Infection

Mucocutaneous HSV Infections
Infections in Immunosuppressed Patients
Acute symptomatic first or recurrent episodes: IV acyclovir (5 mg/kg q8h) and oral acyclovir (400 mg qid), famciclovir (500 mg PO tid), or valacyclovir (500 mg PO bid) for 7-10 days are effective. Treatment duration may vary from 7 to 14 days.
Suppression of reactivation disease: IV acyclovir (5 mg/kg q8h), valacyclovir (500 mg PO bid), or oral acyclovir (400-800 mg three to five times per day) prevents recurrences during the immediate 30-day posttransplantation period. Longer term suppression is often used for persons with continued immunosuppression. In bone marrow and renal transplant recipients, valacyclovir 2 g four times daily is also effective in preventing CMV infection. Valacyclovir 4 g four times daily has been associated with TTP after extended use in HIV-positive persons. In HIV-infected persons, oral famciclovir (500 mg bid) is effective in reducing clinical and subclinical reactivations of HSV-1 and -2.
Genital Herpes
First episodes: Oral acyclovir (200 mg five times per day or 400 mg tid), oral valacyclovir (1000 mg bid), or famciclovir (250 mg bid) for 10-14 days is effective. IV acyclovir 5 mg/kg q8h for 5 days is given for severe disease or neurologic complications such as aseptic meningitis.
Symptomatic recurrent genital herpes: Oral acyclovir (200 mg five times per day for 5 days, 800 mg PO tid for 2 days), valacyclovir (500 mg bid for 3 or 5 days), or famciclovir (125 mg bid for 5 days). All these therapies are effective in shortening lesion duration.
Suppression of recurrent genital herpes: Oral acyclovir (200-mg capsules bid or tid, 400 mg bid, or 800 mg qd), famciclovir (250 mg bid), or valacyclovir (500 mg or 1000 mg qd or 500 mg bid) prevents symptomatic reactivation. Persons with frequent reactivation (<9 episodes/year) can take 500 mg daily; those with >9 episodes/year should take 1000 mg/daily or 500 mg bid.

Oral-Labial HSV Infections
First episode: Oral acyclovir (200 mg) is given four or five times per day. Famciclovir (250 mg bid) or valacyclovir (1000 mg bid) has been used clinically.
Recurrent episodes: Valacyclovir 1000 mg bid for 1 day or 500 mg bid for 3 days is effective in reducing pain and speeding healing. Self-initiated therapy with six times daily topical 1% penciclovir cream is effective in speeding the healing of oral-labial HSV; topical acyclovir cream has also been shown to speed healing.
Suppression of reactivation of oral-labial HSV: Oral acyclovir (400 mg bid), if started before exposure and continued for the duration of exposure (usually 5-10 days), prevents reactivation of recurrent oral-labial HSV infection associated with severe sun exposure.
Herpetic Whitlow
Oral acyclovir (200 mg) five times daily for 7-10 days.
HSV Proctitis
Oral acyclovir (400 mg five times per day) is useful in shortening the course of infection. In immunosuppressed patients or in patients with severe infection, IV acyclovir (5 mg/kg q8h) may be useful.
Herpetic Eye Infections
In acute keratitis, topical trifluorothymidine, vidarabine, idoxuridine, acyclovir, penciclovir, and interferon are all beneficial. Débridement may be required; topical steroids may worsen disease (see Chapter 107).
CNS HSV Infections
HSV encephalitis: Intravenous acyclovir (10 mg/kg q8h; 30 mg/kg per day) for 14-21 days is preferred.
HSV aseptic meningitis: No studies of systemic antiviral chemotherapy exist. If therapy is to be given, IV acyclovir (15-30 mg/kg/day) should be used.
Autonomic radiculopathy: No studies are available.

CMV, cytomegalovirus; CNS, central nervous system; HIV, human immunodeficiency virus; HSV, herpes simplex virus; TTP, thrombotic thrombocytopenic purpura.

Table continued on following page

TABLE 132-3 Antiviral Chemotherapy for Herpes Simplex Virus Infection—Continued

Neonatal HSV infections: Acyclovir (60 mg/kg/day, divided into three doses) is given. The recommended duration of treatment is 21 days. Monitoring for relapse should be undertaken, and some authorities recommend continued suppression with oral acyclovir suspension for 3 to 4 months.

Visceral HSV Infections

HSV esophagitis: IV acyclovir (15 mg/kg per day). In some patients with milder forms of immunosuppression, oral therapy with valacyclovir or famciclovir is effective.

HSV pneumonitis: No controlled studies exist. IV acyclovir (15 mg/kg per day) should be considered.

Disseminated HSV infections: No controlled studies exist. Intravenous acyclovir (10 mg/kg q8h) nevertheless should be tried. No definite evidence indicates that therapy decreases the risk of death.

Erythema multiforme–associated HSV: Anecdotal observations suggest that oral acyclovir (400 mg bid or tid) or valacyclovir (500 mg bid) suppresses erythema multiforme.

Surgical prophylaxis: Several surgical procedures such as laser skin resurfacing, trigeminal nerve root decompression, and lumbar disk surgery have been associated with HSV reactivation. Intravenous acyclovir (3 mg/kg) and oral acyclovir 800 bid, valacyclovir 500 bid, or famciclovir 250 bid is effective in reducing reactivation. Therapy should be initiated 48 hours before surgery and continued for 3 to 7 days.

Infections with acyclovir-resistant HSV: Foscarnet (40 mg/kg IV q8h) should be given until lesions heal. The optimal duration of therapy and the usefulness of its continuation to suppress lesions are unclear. Some patients may benefit from cutaneous application of trifluorothymidine or 5% cidofovir gel.

CMV, cytomegalovirus; CNS, central nervous system; HIV, human immunodeficiency virus; HSV, herpes simplex virus; TTP, thrombotic thrombocytopenic purpura.

Famciclovir, the oral formulation of penciclovir, is also clinically effective in the treatment of a variety of HSV-1 and HSV-2 infections.[385-391] Valacyclovir is a valyl ester of acyclovir that has greater bioavailability than acyclovir.[392-397] The high blood levels of acyclovir achieved have made this useful for once-daily suppressive therapy and for short-course, 1-day or 2-day treatment of oral-genital HSV-1 infection.[382-384] Ganciclovir has activity against both HSV-1 and HSV-2; but because it is more toxic than acyclovir, valacyclovir, and famciclovir, it is generally not recommended for treatment of HSV infections.[398]

Table 132-3 outlines a variety of treatment options for the use of these compounds.

Intravenous acyclovir (30 mg/kg/day, given as a 10 mg/kg infusion over 1 hour at 8-hour intervals) is effective in reducing the morbidity and mortality associated with HSV encephalitis.[311] Early initiation of therapy is a critical factor in outcome. The major side effect associated with intravenous acyclovir is transient renal insufficiency, usually caused by crystallization of the compound in the renal parenchyma. This adverse reaction can be avoided if the medication is given slowly over 1 hour and the patient is well hydrated. Because CSF levels of acyclovir average only 30% to 50% of plasma levels, the dosage of acyclovir used for treatment of CNS infection (30 mg/kg/day) is double that used for the treatment of mucocutaneous or visceral disease (15 mg/kg/day). For neonatal HSV, high-dose intravenous therapy is recommended (60 mg/kg/day in three divided doses). Intravenous therapy for neonatal herpes should be given for 21 days.[360] In immunosuppressed patients, intravenous acyclovir or oral valacyclovir is utilized to prevent HSV reactivations during transplantation or chemotherapy; high doses of valacyclovir also prevent cytomegalovirus reactivations.[390,398]

Acyclovir-resistant strains of HSV are being identified with increasing frequency, especially in HIV-infected persons.[399-403] Almost all clinically significant acyclovir resistance has been seen in immunocompromised patients. Most acyclovir-resistant strains of HSV have a deficiency in thymidine kinase, the enzyme that phosphorylates acyclovir.[386,404-407] Thus, cross-resistance to famciclovir is usually found (see Chapter 38). Occasionally, an isolate with altered thymidine kinase specificity arises and is sensitive to famciclovir but not to acyclovir. In some patients infected with thymidine kinase–deficient virus, higher doses of acyclovir are associated with clearing of lesions.[408] In others, clinical disease progresses despite high-dose therapy.[409-411] Isolation of HSV from persisting lesions despite adequate dosages and blood levels of acyclovir should raise the suspicion of acyclovir resistance. Therapy with the antiviral drug foscarnet is useful.[411] Because of its toxicity and cost, this drug is usually reserved for patients with extensive mucocutaneous infections. Cidofovir is a nucleotide analogue and exists as a phosphonate or monophosphate form. Most thymidine kinase–deficient strains of HSV are sensitive to cidofovir.[412,413] Cidofovir ointment has been shown to speed healing of acyclovir-resistant lesions. Similarly, trifluorothymidine ointment has been reported to be of utility.[414,415]

REFERENCES

1. Wildy P. Herpes history and classification. In: As K, ed. The Herpes Viruses. New York: Academic Press; 1973:1.
2. Astruc J. De morbis venereis libri sex Paris. 1736.
3. Hutfield D. History of herpes genitalis. Br J Vener Dis. 1996;42:263.
4. Parker F, Nye R. Studies on filterable viruses: II. Cultivation of herpes virus. Am J Pathol. 1925;1:337.
5. Lipschutz B. Untersuchungen uber die Aetiologie der Krankheiten der Herpes Gruppe (herpes zoster, herpes genitalis, herpes febrillis). Arch Dermatol Symp (Berl). 1921;136:428.
6. Roizman B, Knipe D. Herpes simplex viruses and their replication. In: Fields BN, Knipe DM, Howley PM, eds. Field's Virology, v. 2. 4th ed. Philadelphia: Williams & Wilkins; 2001:2399.
7. Roizman B. The structure and isomerization of herpes simplex virus genomes. Cell. 1979;16:481.
8. Nahmias A, Dowdle W. Antigenic and biologic differences in herpesvirus hominis. Prog Med Virol. 1968;10:110.
9. Dolan A, Jamieson FE, Cunningham C, et al. The genome sequence of herpes simplex virus type 2. J Virol. 1998;72:2010.
10. Gentry GA, Lowe M, Alford G, Nevins R. Sequence analyses of herpesviral enzymes suggest an ancient origin for human sexual behavior. Proc Natl Acad Sci USA. 1988;85:2658.
11. Buchman TG, Roizman B, Adams G, et al. Restriction endonuclease finger-printing of herpes simplex virus DNA: A novel epidemiological tool applied to a nosocomial outbreak. J Infect Dis. 1978;138:488.
12. Schmidt OW, Fife KH, Corey L. Reinfection is an uncommon occurrence in patients with symptomatic recurrent genital herpes. J Infect Dis. 1984;149:645.
13. Umene K, Kawana T. Divergence of reiterated sequences in a series of genital isolates of herpes simplex virus type 1 from individual patients. J Gen Virol. 2003;84:917-923.
14. Buchman TG, Roizman B, Nahmias AJ. Demonstration of exogenous genital reinfection with herpes simplex virus type 2 by restriction endonuclease fingerprinting of viral DNA. J Infect Dis. 1979;140:259.
15. Hammer SM, Buchman TG, D'Angelo LJ, et al. Temporal cluster of herpes simplex encephalitis: Investigation by restriction endonuclease cleavage of viral DNA. J Infect Dis. 1980;141:436.
16. Lakeman AD, Nahmias AJ, Whitley RJ. Analysis of DNA from recurrent genital herpes simplex virus isolates by restriction endonuclease digestion. J Sex Trans Dis. 1986;13:61.
17. Douglas JM, Schmidt O, Corey L. Acquisition of neonatal HSV-1 infection from a paternal source contact. Pediatrics. 1983;103:908-910.
18. Warren KG, Koprowski H, Lonsdale DM, et al. The polypeptide and the DNA restriction enzyme profiles of spontaneous isolates of herpes simplex virus type 1 from explants of human trigeminal, superior cervical and vagus ganglia. J Gen Virol. 1979;43:151.
19. Spear PG, Longnecker R. Herpes virus entry: An update. J Virol. 2003;77:10179.
20. Menotti L, Lopez M, Dubreuil P, et al. The murine homolog of human nectin 1 delta serves as a species nonspecific mediator for entry of human and animal alpha herpesviruses in a pathway independent of a detectable binding to gD. Proc Natl Acad Sci USA. 2000;97:4867.
21. Shukla D, Liu J, Blaiklock P. et al. A novel role for 3-O-sulfated heparan sulfate in herpes simplex virus 1 entry. Cell. 1999;99:13.
22. Montgomery RI, Warner MS, Lum BJ, Spear PG. Herpes simplex virus-1 entry into cells mediated by a novel member of the TNF/NGF receptor family. Cell. 1996;87:427.
23. Krummenacher C, Nicola AV, Whitbeck JC, et al. Herpes simplex virus glycoprotein D can bind to poliovirus receptor-related protein 1 of herpesvirus entry mediator, two structurally unrelated mediators of virus entry. J Virol. 1998;72:6064.
24. Mauri DN, Ebner R, Montgomery RI, et al. LIGHT, a new member of the TNF superfamily, and lymphotoxin α are ligands for herpesvirus entry mediator. Immunity. 1998;8:21.

25. Struyf F, Posavad CM, Keyaerts E, et al. Search for polymorphisms in the genes for herpes simplex virus entry mediators, HVEM, nectin-1 and nectin-2, in seronegative and immune seronegative individuals. J Infect Dis. 2002;185:36.

26. Homa FL, Brown JC. Capsid assembly and DNA packaging in herpes simplex virus. Rev Med Virol. 1997;7:107.

27. Zelus BD, Stewart RS, Ross J. The virion host shutoff protein of herpes simplex virus type 1: Messenger ribonucleolytic activity in vitro. J Virol. 1996;70:2411.

28. Cushing H. Surgical aspects of major neuralgia of trigeminal nerve: Report of 20 cases of operation upon the gasserian ganglion with anatomic and physiologic notes on the consequences of its removal. JAMA. 1925;4:1002.

29. Stevens JG, Cook ML. Latent herpes simplex virus in spinal ganglia. Science. 1971;173:843.

30. Baringer JR, Pisani P. Herpes simplex virus genomes in human nervous system tissue analyzed by polymerase chain reaction. Ann Neurol. 1994;36:823.

31. Stevens JG, Haarr L, Porter DD, et al. Prominence of the herpes simplex virus latency-associated transcript in trigeminal ganglia from seropositive humans. J Infect Dis. 1988;158:117.

32. Rock DL, Fraser NW. Latent HSV type 1 DNA contains two copies of the DNA joint region. J Virol. 1985;55:849.

33. Burke R, Hartog K, Croen KD, Ostrove JMI. Detection and characterization of latent HSV RNA by in situ and northern blot hybridization in guinea pigs. Virology. 1991;181:793.

34. Mehta A, Maggioncalda J, Bagasra O, et al. In situ DNA PCR and RNA hybridization detection of herpes simplex virus sequences in trigeminal ganglia of latently infected mice. Virology. 1995;206:633.

35. Barringer J. Recovery of herpes simplex virus from human sacral ganglions. N Engl J Med. 1974;291:828.

36. Warren K, Brown SM, Wroblewska Z, et al. Isolation of latent herpes simplex virus from the superior cervical and vagus ganglions of human being. N Engl J Med. 1978;298:1068.

37. Sawtell NM, Thompson RL. Rapid in vivo reactivation of HSV in latently infected murine ganglionic nerves after transient hypothermia. J Virol. 1992;66:2150.

38. Blyth WA, Hill TJ, Field HJ, Harbour DA. Reactivation of HSV infection by ultraviolet light and possible involvement of prostaglandins. J Gen Virol. 1976;33:547.

39. Sawtell RD, Thompson RL. HSV type 1 latency associated transcription promotes anatomical site dependent establishment and reactivation from latency. J Virol. 1992;66:2157.

40. Sawtell NM. Quantitative analysis of herpes simplex virus reactivation in vivo demonstrates that reactivation in the nervous system is not inhibited at early times postinoculation. J Virol. 2003;77:4127.

41. Carlton CA, Kilbourne ED. Activation of latent herpes simplex by trigeminal sensory-root section. N Engl J Med. 1952;246:172.

42. Javier RT, Stevens JG, Dissette VB, Wagner EK. A herpes simplex virus transcript abundant in latently infected neurons is dispensable for establishment of the latent state. Virology. 1988;166:254.

43. Thompson RL, Sawtell NM. The herpes simplex virus type 1 latency-associated transcript gene regulates the establishment of latency. J Virol. 1997;71:5432.

44. Block TM, Deshmane S, Masonis J, et al. An HSV LAT null mutant reactivates slowly from latent infection and makes small plaques on CV-1 monolayers. Virology. 1993;192:618.

45. Yoshikawa T, Hill JM, Stanberry LR, et al. The characteristic site-specific reactivation phenotypes of HSV-1 and HSV-2 depend upon the latency-associated transcript region. J Exp Med. 1996;184:659.

46. Perng GC, Thompson RL, Sawtell NM, et al. An avirulent ICP34.5 deletion mutant of herpes simplex virus type 1 is capable of in vivo spontaneous reactivation. J Virol. 1995;69:3033.

47. Coen DM, Kosz-Vnenchak M, Jacobson JG, et al. Thymidine kinase-negative herpes simplex virus mutants establish latency in mouse trigeminal ganglia but do not reactivate. Proc Natl Acad Sci USA. 1989;86:4736.

48. Kang W, Mukerjee R, Fraser NW. Establishment and maintenance of HSV latent infection is mediated through correct splicing of the LAT primary transcript. Virology. 2003;312:233.

49. Corey L. Global epidemiology of genital herpes and the interaction of herpes simplex virus with HIV (Editorial). Herpes. 2004; April (Suppl 1A).

50. Cowan FM, Copas A, Johnson AM, et al. Herpes simplex virus type 1 infection: A sexually transmitted infection of adolescence? Sex Transm Infect. 2002;78:346-348.

51. Tunback P, Bergstrom T, Andersson AS, et al. Prevalence of herpes simplex virus antibodies in childhood and adolescence: A cross-sectional study. Scand J Infect Dis. 2003;35:498.

52. Malkin JE, Morand P, Malvy D, et al. Seroprevalence of HSV-1 and HSV-2 infection in the general French population. Sex Transm Infect. 2002;78:201.

53. Vyse A, Gay NJ, Slomka MJ, et al. The burden of infection with HSV-1 and HSV-2 in England and Wales: Implications for the changing epidemiology of genital herpes. Sex Transm Infect. 2000;76:183.

54. Lee F, Coleman RM, Pereira L, et al. Detection of herpes simplex virus type 2 specific antibody with glycoprotein G. J Clin Microbiol. 1985;22:642.

55. Ashley RL, Wu L, Pickering JW, et al. Premarket evaluation of a commercial glycoprotein-G based enzyme immunoassay for herpes simplex virus type-specific antibodies. J Clin Microbiol. 1998;36:294.

56. Cowan FM, French RS, Mayaud P, et al. Seroepidemiological study of herpes simplex virus types 1 and 2 in Brazil, Estonia, India, Morocco, and Sri Lanka. Sex Transm Infect. 2003;79:286-290.

57. Ashley RL, Militoni J, Lee F, et al. Comparison of Western blot (Immunoblot) and glycoprotein G-specific immunodot enzyme assay for detecting antibodies to herpes simplex virus types 1 and 2 in human sera. J Clin Microbiol. 1988;26:662.

58. Ashley RL, Wald A, Eagleton M. Premarket evaluation of the POCkitTM-HSV-2 type specific serologic test in culture-documented cases of genital herpes simplex virus type 2. Sex Transm Dis. 2000;27:266.

59. Martins TB, Woolstenholme RD, Jaskowski TD, et al. Comparison of 4 enzyme immunoassays with a western blot assay for determination of type specific antibodies to herpes simplex virus. Am J Clin Pathol. 2001;115:272.

60. Turner KR, Wong EH, Kent CK, Klausner JD. Serologic herpes testing in the real world. Validation of new type-specific serologic herpes simplex virus tests in a public health laboratory. Sex Transm Dis. 2002;29:422-425.

61. Ashley R, Cent A, Maggs V, et al. Inability of enzyme immunoassays to discriminate between infections with herpes simplex virus types 1 and 2. Ann Intern Med. 1991;115:520.

62. Morrow RA, Friedrich D. Inaccuracy of certain commercial enzyme immunoassays in diagnosing genital infections with herpes simplex virus types 1 or 2. Am J Clin Pathol. 2003;120:839.

63. Cowan F, Johnson AM, Ashley R, et al. Antibody to herpes simplex virus type 2 as serological marker of sexual lifestyle in populations. BMJ. 1994;9:1325.

64. Johnson R, Nahmias AJ, Magder LS, et al. A seroepidemiologic survey of the prevalence of herpes simplex virus type 2 infection in the United States. N Engl J Med. 1990;321:7.

65. Fleming DT, McQuillan GM, Johnson RE, et al. Herpes simplex virus type 2 in the United States, 1976 to 1994. N Engl J Med. 1997;337:1105-1111.

66. Oliver L, Wald A, Kim M, et al. Seroprevalence of herpes simplex virus infections in a family medicine clinic. Arch Fam Med. 1995;4:228.

67. Cusini M, Cusan M, Parolin C, et al. Seroprevalence of herpes simplex virus type 2 (HSV-2) infection among attendees of a sexually transmitted disease clinic in Italy. Sex Transm Dis. 2000;27:292.

68. Kapiga SH, Sam SE, Shao JF, et al. Herpes simplex virus type 2 infection among bar and hotel workers in northern Tanzania. Prevalence and risk factors. Sex Transm Dis. 2003;30:187-192.

69. Eis-Hubinger AM, Nyankiye E, Bitoungui DM, Ndjomou J. Prevalence of herpes simplex virus type 2 antibody in Cameroon. Sex Transm Dis. 2002;29:637-642.

70. Obasi A, Mosha E, Quigley M, et al. Antibody to herpes simplex virus type 2 as a marker of sexual risk behavior in rural Tanzania. J Infect Dis. 1999;179:16.

71. Chen CY, Ballard RC, Beck-Sague CM, et al. Human immunodeficiency virus and herpes simplex virus type 2 infection among male STD clinic patients in South Africa. Sex Transm Dis. 2000;27:21.

72. Cunningham A, Lee FK, Ho DW, et al. Herpes simplex virus type 2 antibody in patients attending antenatal or STD clinics. Med J Aust. 1993;158:525.

73. Gopal R, Gibbs T, Slomka MJ, et al. A monoclonal blocking EIA for herpes simplex virus type 2 antibody, validation for serological studies in Africa. J Virol Methods. 2000;87:71-80.

74. Gottlieb SL, Douglas JM Jr, Schmid DS, et al. Seroprevalence and correlates of herpes simplex virus type 2 infection in five sexually transmitted-disease clinics. J Infect Dis. 2002;186:1381.

75. Cherpes TL, Meyn LA, Krohn MA, Hillier SL. Risk factors for infection with herpes simplex virus type 2: Role of smoking, douching, uncircumcised males, and vaginal flora. Sex Transm Dis. 2003;30:405.

76. Koutsky LA, Ashley RL, Holmes KK, et al. The frequency of unrecognized type 2 herpes simplex virus infection among women: Implications for the control of genital herpes. Sex Trans Dis. 1990;17:90-94.

77. Stanberry LR, Spruance SL, Cunningham AL, et al. Glycoprotein-D-adjuvant vaccine to prevent genital herpes. N Engl J Med. 2002;347:1703.

78. Corey L, Langenberg AGM, Ashley R, et al. Recombinant glycoprotein vaccine for the prevention of genital HSV-2 infection: Two randomized, double-blind placebo-controlled trials. JAMA. 1999;282:331.

79. Wald A, Langenberg AGM, Link K, et al. Effect of condoms on reducing the transmission of herpes simplex virus type-2 from men to women. JAMA. 2001;285:3100-3106.

80. Brown Z, Selke S, Zeh J, et al. Acquisition of herpes simplex virus during pregnancy. N Engl J Med. 1997;337:509.

81. Langenberg AGM, Corey L, Ashley RL, et al. A prospective study of new infections with herpes simplex virus type 1 and herpes simplex virus type 2. N Engl J Med. 1999;341:1532.

82. Blank H, Haines HG. Experimental human reinfection with herpes simplex virus. J Invest Dermatol. 1973;61:223.

83. Wald A, Zeh J, Selke S, et al. Reactivation of genital herpes simplex type 2 infection in asymptomatic seropositive persons. N Engl J Med. 2000;342:844.

84. Perl T, Haugen TH, Pfaller MA, et al. Transmission of herpes simplex virus type 1 infection in an intensive care unit. Ann Intern Med. 1992;117:584.

85. Stern H, Elek SD, Millar DM, Anderson HF. Herpetic whitlow, a form of cross infection in hospitals. Lancet. 1959;2:871.

86. Cesario T, Poland JD, Wulff H, et al. Six years' experience with herpes simplex virus in a children's home. Am J Epidemiol. 1969;90:416.

87. Wald A, Corey L, Cone R, et al. Frequent genital herpes simplex virus 2 shedding in immunocompetent women: Effect of acyclovir treatment. J Clin Invest. 1997;99:1092.

88. Rosato FE, Rosato EF, Plotkin SA. Herpetic paronychia—An occupational hazard of medical personnel. N Engl J Med. 1970;283:804-805.

89. Woolley P, Kudesia G. Incidence of herpes simplex virus type-1 and type-2 from patients with primary (first attack) genital herpes in Sheffield. Int J STD AIDS. 1990;1:184.

90. Anderson BJ. The epidemiology and clinical analysis of several outbreaks of herpes gladiatorum. Med Sci Sports Exerc. 2003;35:1809.

91. Belognia EA, Goodman JL, Holland EJ, et al. An outbreak of herpes gladiatorum at a high-school wrestling camp. N Engl J Med. 1991;325:906.

92. Nahmias A, Dowdle WR, Josey WE, et al. Newborn infection with herpesvirus hominis types 1 and 2. J Pediatr. 1969;75:1194.

93. Quinn T, Corey L, Chaffee RG, et al. The etiology of anorectal infection in homosexual men. Am J Med. 1981;71:395-406.

94. Goldmeier D. Herpetic proctitis and sacral radiculomyelopathy in homosexual men. BMJ. 1979;2:549.

95. Stanberry LR, Kern ER, Richards JT, et al. Genital herpes in guinea pigs: Pathogenesis of primary infection and description of recurrent disease. J Infect Dis. 1983;146:397.

96. Stanberry LR, Kit S, Myers MG. Thymidine kinase–deficient herpes simplex virus type 2 genital infection in guinea pigs. J Virol. 1985;55:322.

97. Sawtell NM. Quantitative analysis of herpes simplex virus reactivation in vivo demonstrates that reactivation in the nervous system is not inhibited at early times postinoculation. J Virol. 2003;77:4127-4138.

98. Rock DL, Fraser NW. Detection of HSV-1 genome in central nervous system of latently infected mice. Nature. 1983;302:523.

99. Corey L, Spear PG. Infections with herpes simplex virus. N Engl J Med. Part 1: 1986;314:686, Part 2: 1986;314:749.

100. Lafferty WE, Coombs RW, Benedetti J, et al. Recurrences after oral and genital herpes simplex virus infection: Influence of anatomic site and viral type. N Engl J Med. 1987;316:1444-1449.

101. Engelberg R, Carrell D, Corey L, Wald A. Natural history of genital herpes simplex virus type 1 (HSV-1) Infection. Sex Transm Dis. 2003;30:174-177.

102. Landry ML, Zibello TA. Ability of herpes simplex virus (HSV) types 1 and 2 to induce clinical disease and establish latency following previous genital infection with the heterologous HSV type. J Infect Dis. 1988;158:1220.

103. Thomas E, Lycke E, Vahlne A. Retrieval of latent HSV type 1 genital infection by murine trigeminal ganglia by superinfection with heterotypic virus in vivo. J Gen Virol. 1985;66:1763.

104. Pass RF, Whitley RJ, Whelchel JD, et al. Identification of patients with increased risk of infection with herpes simplex virus after renal transplantation. J Infect Dis. 1979;140:487.

105. Meyers JD, Wade JC, Mitchell CD, et al. Multicenter collaborative trial of intravenous acyclovir for treatment of mucocutaneous herpes simplex virus infection in immunocompromised host. Am J Med. 1982;73:229.

106. Kusne S, Schwartz M, Breinig MK, et al. Herpes simplex virus hepatitis after solid organ transplantation in adults. J Infect Dis. 1991;163:1001.

107. Modiano P, Salloum E, Gillet-Terver MN, et al. Acyclovir-resistant chronic cutaneous herpes simplex in Wiskott-Aldrich syndrome. Br J Dermatol. 1995;133:475-478.

108. Johnson JR, Egaas S, Gleaves CA, et al. Hepatitis due to herpes simplex virus in marrow-transplant recipients. Clin Infect Dis. 1992;14:38.

109. Muller SA, Herrmann EC Jr, Winkelmann RD. Herpes simplex infections in hematologic malignancies. Am J Med. 1972;52:102.

110. Ramsey PG, Fife KH, Hackman RC, et al. Herpes simplex virus pneumonia: Clinical, virological, and pathologic features in 20 patients. Ann Intern Med. 1982;97:813.

111. Kapor AK, Nash AA, Wildy P, et al. Pathogenesis of herpes simplex virus in congenitally athymic mice: The relative roles of cell-mediated and humoral immunity. J Gen Virol. 1982;60:225.

112. Simmons A, Tschmuke D, Speck P. The role of immune mechanisms in the control of HSV infection of the peripheral reservoir system. Curr Top Microbiol Immunol. 1992;179:31.

113. Koelle DM, Corey L. Recent progress in herpes simplex virus immunobiology and vaccine research. Clin Microbiol Rev. 2003;16:96-113.

114. Dubin G, Fishman NO, Eisenberg RJ, et al. The role of herpes simplex virus glycoproteins in immune evasion. Curr Top Microbiol Immunol. 1992;179:111.

115. Norrild B, Shore SL, Cromeans TL, Nahmias AJ. Participation of three major glycoprotein antigens of herpes simplex virus type 1 early in the infectious cycle as determined by antibody-dependent cell-mediated cytotoxicity. Infect Immun. 1980;28:38.

116. Balachandran N, Bacchetti S, Rawls WE. Protection against lethal challenge of BALB/c mice by passive transfer of monoclonal antibodies to five glycoproteins of herpes simplex virus type-2. Infect Immun. 1982;37:1132.

117. Eisenberg R, Cerini CP, Heilman CJ, et al. Synthetic glycoprotein D-related peptides protect mice against herpes simplex virus challenge. J Virol. 1985;55:1014.

118. Nichols WG, Boeckh M, Carter RA, et al. Transferred herpes simplex virus immunity after stem-cell transplantation: Clinical implications. J Infect Dis. 2003;187:801-808.

119. Manickan E, Rouse BT. Role of different T cell subsets in control of herpes simplex virus infection determined by using T-cell-deficient mouse-models. J Virol. 1995;69:8178.

120. Niemialtowski MG, Rouse BT. Cytotoxic T lymphocyte response to herpes simplex virus type 1 is composed of both CD8+ and CD4+ T cell phenotypes in acute and memory states. Arch Immunol Ther Exp (Warsz). 1994;42:319-324.

121. Smith CM, Belz GT, Wilson NS, et al. Cutting edge: conventional CD8a+ dendritic cells are preferentially involved in CTL priming after footpad infection with herpes simplex virus-1. J Immun. 2003;170:4437-4440.

122. Khanna KM, Bonneau RH, Kinchington PR, Hendricks RL. Herpes simplex virus-specific memory CD8+ T cells are selectively activated and retained in latently infected sensory ganglia. Immunity. 2003;18:593-603.

123. Koelle DM, Liu Z, McClurkan CM, et al. Immunodominance amongst herpes-simplex virus-specific CD8 T-cells expressing a tissue-specific homing receptor. Proc Natl Acad Sci USA. 2003;100:12899-12904.

124. Murphy JA, Duerst RJ, Smith TJ, Morrison LA. Herpes simplex virus type 2 virion host shutoff protein regulates alpha/beta interferon but not adaptive immune responses during primary infection in vivo. J Virol. 2003;77:9337-9345.

125. Ashkar AA, Bauer S, Mitchell WJ, et al. Local delivery of CpG oligodeoxynucleotides induces rapid changes in the genital mucosa and inhibits replication, but not entry, of herpes simplex virus type 2. J Virol. 2003;77:8948-8956.

126. Kobelt D, Lechmann M, Stein-Kasserer A, et al. The interaction between dendritic cells and herpes simplex virus-1. Curr Top Microbiol Immunol. 2003;276:145-161.

127. Lund J, Sato A, Akira S, et al. Toll-like receptor 9–mediated recognition of herpes simplex virus-2 by plasmacytoid dendritic cells. J Exp Med. 2003;198:513-520.

128. Posavad CM, Wald A, Hosken N, et al. T cell immunity to herpes simplex viruses in seronegative subjects: Silent infection of acquired immunity? J Immunol. 2003;170:4380-4388.

129. Jerome KR, Fox R, Chen Z, et al. Inhibition of apoptosis by primary isolates of herpes simplex virus. Arch Virol. 2001;146:2219-2225.

130. Banks TA, Rouse BT. Herpesviruses: Immune escape artists? Clin Infect Dis. 1992;14:933.

131. York IA, Roop C, Andrews DW, et al. A cytosolic herpes simplex virus protein inhibits antigen presentation to CD8+ T lymphocytes. Cell. 1994;77:525.

132. Posavad CM, Koelle DM, Corey L. Tipping the scales of herpes simplex virus reactivation: The important responses are local. Nat Med. 1998;4:381-382.

133. Tigges M, Levy S, Johnson DC, et al. Human herpes simplex virus (HSV)–specific CD8+ CTL clones recognize HSV-2 infected fibroblasts after treatment with IFN-gamma or when virion host shutoff functions are disabled. J Immunol. 1996;156:3901.

134. Jerome KR, Tait JF, Koelle DM, Corey L. Herpes simplex virus type 1 renders infected cells resistant to cytotoxic T-lymphocyte–induced apoptosis. J Virol. 1998;72:436.

135. Jerome KR, Chen Z, Lang R, et al. HSV and glycoprotein J inhibit caspase activation and apoptosis induced by granzyme B or Fas1. J Immunol. 2001;167:3928-3935.

136. Barcy S, Corey L. Herpes simplex inhibits the capacity of lymphoblastoid B cell lines to stimulate CD4+ T cells. J Immunol. 2001;166:4242-4249.

137. Cunningham A, Turner RR, Miller AC, et al. Evolution of recurrent herpes simplex lesions. An immunohistologic study. J Clin Invest. 1985;75:226.

138. Koelle DM, Abbo H, Ziegwied K, et al. Direct recovery of HSV-specific T cell clones from human recurrent HSV-2 lesions. J Infect Dis. 1994;169:956.

139. Cunningham AL, Merigan TC. γ Interferon production appears to predict time of recurrence of herpes labialis. J Immunol. 1983;130:2397.

140. Koelle D, Posavad C, Barnum GR, et al. Clearance of HSV-2 from recurrent genital lesions correlates with infiltration of HSV-specific cytotoxic T lymphocytes. J Clin Invest. 1998;101:1500.

141. Koelle DM, Chen H, Gavin MA, et al. CD8 CTL from genital herpes simplex lesions: Recognition of viral tegument and immediate early proteins and lysis of infected cutaneous cells. J Immunol. 2001;166:4049-4058.

142. Posavad CM, Koelle DM, Shaughnessy MF, Corey L. Severe genital herpes infections in HIV-infected individuals with impaired HSV-specific CD8+ CTL responses. Proc Natl Acad Sci USA. 1997;94:10289-10294.

143. Doymaz MZ, Rouse BT. Herpetic stromal keratitis: An immunopathologic disease mediated by CD4+ T lymphocytes. Invest Ophthalmol Vis Sci. 1992;33:2165.

144. Meyers-Elliott RH, Pettit TH, Maxwell WA. Viral antigens in the immune ring of herpes simplex stromal keratitis. Arch Ophthalmol. 1980;90:897.

145. Thomas J, Rouse BT. Immunopathogenesis of herpetic ocular disease. Immunol Res. 1997;16:375.

146. Zhao Z, Granucci F, Yeh L, et al. Molecular mimicry by herpes simplex virus-type 1: Autoimmune disease after viral infection. Science. 1998;279:1344-1347.

147. Corey L, Holmes KK. Genital herpes simplex virus infection: Current concepts in diagnosis, therapy and prevention. Ann Intern Med. 1983;98:973-983.

148. Corey L, Adams HG, Brown ZA, Holmes KK. Genital herpes simplex virus infection: Clinical manifestations, course and complications. Ann Intern Med. 1983;98:958.

149. Reeves W, Corey L, Adams HG, et al. Risk of recurrence after first episodes of genital herpes: Relation to HSV type and antibody response. N Engl J Med. 1981; 305:315.

150. Benedetti J, Corey L, Ashley R. Recurrence rates of genital herpes after acquisition of symptomatic first episode infection. Ann Intern Med. 1994;121:847.

151. Spruance ST, Overall JC Jr, Kern ER. The natural history of recurrent herpes simplex labialis—Implications for antiviral therapy. N Engl J Med. 1977;297:69.

152. Bader C, Crumpacker CS, Schnipper LE, et al. The natural history of recurrent facial-oral infection with herpes simplex virus. J Infect Dis. 1978;138:897.

153. Young SK, Rowe NH, Buchanan RA. A clinical study for the control of facial mucocutaneous herpes virus infections. I. Characterization of natural history in a professional school population. Oral Surg Oral Med Oral Pathol. 1976;41:498.

154. Glezen WP, Fernald GW, Lohr JA. Acute respiratory disease of university students with special reference to the etiologic role of herpesvirus hominis. Am J Epidemiol. 1975;101:111.

155. Schmitt DL, Johnson DW, Henderson FW. Herpes simplex type 1 infections in a group day care. Pediatr Infect Dis J. 1991;10:729.

156. Amir J, Harel L, Smetana Z, Varsano I. Treatment of herpes simplex virus gingivostomatitis with acyclovir in children: A randomized double blind placebo controlled study. BMJ. 1997;314:1800-1803.

157. Kriesel JD, Pisani PL, McKeough MB, et al. Correlation between detection of herpes simplex virus in oral secretions by PCR and susceptibility to experimental UV radiation–induced herpes labialis. J Clin Microbiol. 1994;32:3088.

158. Openshaw H, Bennett HE. Recurrence of herpes simplex virus after dental extraction. J Infect Dis. 1982;146:707.

159. Pazin GJ, Armstrong JA, Lam MT, et al. Prevention of reactivated herpes simplex infection by human leukocyte interferon after operation on the trigeminal root. N Engl J Med. 1978;301:225.

160. Shepp DH, Newton BA, Dandliker PA, et al. Oral acyclovir therapy for mucocutaneous herpes simplex virus infections in immunocompromised marrow transplant recipients. Ann Intern Med. 1985;102:783.

161. Straus SE, Smith HA, Brickman C, et al. Acyclovir for chronic mucocutaneous herpes simplex virus infection in immunosuppressed patients. Ann Intern Med. 1982;96:270.

162. Eisen D, Essell J, Broun ER, et al. Post transplant complications. Clinical utility of oral valacyclovir compared with oral acyclovir for the prevention of herpes simplex virus mucositis following autologous bone marrow transplantation or stem cell rescue therapy. Bone Marrow Transplant. 2003;31:51-55.

163. Liesveld JL, Abboud CN, Ifthikharuddin JJ, et al. Oral valacyclovir versus intravenous acyclovir in preventing herpes simplex virus infections in autologous stem cell transplant recipients. Bio Blood Marrow Transplant. 2002;8:662-665.

164. Seigal FP, Lopez C, Hammer GS, et al. Severe acquired immunodeficiency in male homosexuals manifested by chronic perianal ulcerative herpes simplex lesions. N Engl J Med. 1981;305:1439.

165. Foley FD, Greenwald KA, Nash G, Pruitt BA Jr. Herpes virus infection in burned patients. N Engl J Med. 1970;282:652.

166. Garland SM, Hill PJ. Eczema herpeticum in pregnancy successfully treated with acyclovir. Aust NZ J Obstet Gynaecol. 1994;34:214.

167. Hazen PG, Bennett-Eppes R. Eczema herpeticum caused by herpesvirus type 2. A case in a patient with Darier disease. Arch Dermatol. 1977;113:1085.

168. Shelley WB. Herpes simplex virus as a cause of erythema multiforme. JAMA. 1967;201:153.

169. Britz M, Sibulkin D. Recurrent erythema multiforme and herpes genitalis (type 2). JAMA. 1975;233:812.

170. Orton PW, Huff JC, Tonnesen MG, et al. Detection of a herpes viral antigen in skin lesions of erythema multiforme. Ann Intern Med. 1984;101:48.

171. Green JA, Spruance SL, Wenerstrom G, Piepkorn MW. Post-herpetic erythema multiforme prevented with prophylactic oral acyclovir. Ann Intern Med. 1985;102:632.

172. Valne A, Edstrom S, Arstila P, et al. Bell's palsy and herpes simplex virus. Arch Otolaryngol. 1981;107:72.

173. Baringer JR. Herpes simplex virus and Bell palsy. Ann Intern Med. 1996;124:63.

174. Furuta Y, Fukuda S, Chida E, et al. Reactivation of herpes simplex virus type 1 in patients with Bell's palsy. J Med Virol. 1998;54:162.

175. Burgess RC, Michaels L, Bale JR Jr, Smith RJ. Polymerase chain reaction amplification of herpes simplex viral DNA from the geniculate ganglion of a patient with Bell's palsy. Ann Otol Rhinol Laryngol. 1994;103:775.

176. Bell's palsy. Early treatment with antiviral medications and corticosteroids may improve the chances for full recovery from this condition that suddenly paralyzes one side of the face. Harv Health Lett. 2003,28(6).5.

177. Axelsson S, Lindberg S, Stjernquist-Desatnik A. Outcome of treatment with valacyclovir and prednisone in patients with Bell's palsy. Ann Otol Rhinol Laryngol. 2003;112:197-201.

178. Shannon S, Meadows S, Horowit SH. Are drug therapies effective in treating Bell's palsy? J Fam Pract. 2003;52:156-159.

179. Adams H. Genital herpetic infection in men and women: Clinical course and effect of topical application of adenine arabinoside. J Infect Dis. 1976;133:A151.

180. Mertz GJ, Critchlow C, Benedetti J, et al. Double-blind placebo-controlled trial of oral acyclovir in first-episode genital herpes simplex virus infection. JAMA. 1984;252:1147.

181. Bryson YJ, Dillon M, Lovett M, et al. Treatment of first episodes of genital herpes simplex virus infection with oral acyclovir. N Engl J Med. 1983;308:916.

182. Corey L, Fife KH, Benedetti JK, et al. Intravenous acyclovir for the treatment of primary genital herpes. Ann Intern Med. 1983;98:914.

183. Stamm WE, Wagner KF, Amsel R, et al. Causes of the acute urethral syndrome in women. N Engl J Med. 1980;303:409.

184. Koutsky LA, Stevens CE, Holmes KK, et al. Underdiagnosis of genital herpes by current clinical and viral isolation procedures. N Engl J Med. 1992;326:1533-1539.

185. Lehtinen M, Rantala I, Teisala K, et al. Detection of herpes simplex virus in women with acute pelvic inflammatory disease. J Infect Dis. 1985;152:78.

186. Schneider V, Behm FG, Mumaw VR. Ascending herpetic endometritis. Obstet Gynecol. 1982;59:259.

187. Morrisseau PM, Phillips CA, Leadbetter GW. Viral prostatitis. J Urol. 1970;103:767.

188. Goodell S, Quinn TC, Mkrtichian E, et al. Herpes simplex virus proctitis in homosexual men: Clinical, sigmoidoscopic, and histopathological features. N Engl J Med. 1983;308:868.

189. Goldmeier D. Proctitis and herpes simplex virus in homosexual men. Br J Vener Dis. 1980;56:111.

190. Rompalo A, Mertz GJ, Davis LG, et al. Oral acyclovir for treatment of first-episode herpes simplex virus proctitis. JAMA. 1988;259:2879-2881.

191. Schacker T, Hu HL, Koelle DM, et al. Famciclovir for the suppression of symptomatic and asymptomatic herpes simplex virus reactivation in HIV-infected persons. Ann Intern Med. 1998;128:21-28.

192. Krone MR, Tabet SR, Paradise M, et al. Herpes simplex virus shedding among HIV-negative men who have sex with men (MSM): Site and frequency of herpes shedding. J Infect Dis. 1998;178:978.

193. Wald A, Zeh J, Selke S, et al. Virologic characteristics of subclinical and symptomatic genital herpes infections. N Engl J Med. 1995;333:770-775.

194. Whitley R. Mucocutaneous herpes simplex virus infections in immunocompromised patients. Am J Med. 1982;73:236.

195. McMillan JA, Weiner LB, Higgins AM, Lamparella VJ. Pharyngitis associated with herpes simplex virus in college students. Pediatr Infect Dis J. 1993;12:280.

196. Skoldenberg B, Jeansson S, Wolontis S. Herpes simplex virus 2 and acute aseptic meningitis. Scand J Infect Dis. 1975;7:227-232.

197. Ross C, Stevenson J. Herpes simplex meningoencephalitis. Lancet. 1961;2:682.

198. Klastensky J, Cappel R, Snoeck JM, et al. Ascending myelitis in association with herpes simplex virus. N Engl J Med. 1972;187:182.

199. Schlesinger Y, Tebas P, Gaudreault-Keener M, et al. Herpes simplex virus type 2 meningitis in the absence of genital lesions: Improved recognition with use of the polymerase chain reaction. Clin Infect Dis. 1995;20:842.

200. Tedder D, Ashley R, Tyler KL, et al. Herpes simplex virus infection as a cause of benign recurrent lymphocytic meningitis. Ann Intern Med. 1994;121:334-338.

201. Caplan L, Kleman FJ, Berg S. Urinary retention probably secondary to herpes genitalis. N Engl J Med. 1977;197:920.

202. Ravaut P, Darre M. Les réactions nerveuses au cours de herpes genitaux. Ann Dermatol Syphiligr. 1904;5:481.

203. Brenton D. Hypoglycorrhachia in herpes simplex type 2 meningitis. Arch Neurol. 1980;37:317.

204. Goldmeier D, Bateman JR, Rodin P, et al. Urinary retention and intestinal obstruction associated with anorectal herpes simplex virus infection. Br Med J. 1975;1:425.

205. Oates J, Greenhouse P. Retention of urine in anogenital herpetic infection. Lancet. 1978;1:691.

206. Jacobs S, Jacobs SC, Herbert LA, et al. Acute motor paralytic bladder in renal transplant patients with anogenital herpes infection. J Urol. 1980;123:426.

207. Riehle RA Jr, Williams JJ. Transient neuropathic bladder following herpes simplex genitalis. J Urol. 1979;122:263-264.

208. Jacome D, Yanez G. Herpes genitalis and neurogenic bladder and bowel. J Urol. 1980;124:752.

209. Samarasinghe P, Oates JK, MacLennan IP, et al. Herpetic proctitis and sacral radiomyelopathy: A hazard for homosexual men. Br Med J. 1979;2:365.

210. Shturman-Ellstein R, Borkowsky W, Fish I, et al. Myelitis associated with genital herpes in a child. J Pediatr. 1976;88:523.

211. Aurelius E, Forsgren M, Gille E, Skoldenberg B. Neurologic morbidity after herpes simplex virus type 2 meningitis: A retrospective study of 40 patients. Scand J Infect Dis. 2002;34:278-283.

212. Crane L, Lerner A. Herpetic whitlow: A manifestation of primary infection with herpes simplex virus type 1 and 2. J Infect Dis. 1978;137:855.

213. Benedetti J, Zeh J, Selke S, et al. Frequency and reactivation of nongenital lesions among patients with genital herpes simplex virus. Am J Med. 1995;98:237.

214. Diamond C, Mohan K, Hobson A, et al. High frequency of viremia in neonatal herpes simplex virus infections. Pediatr Infect Dis J. 1999;18:487-489.

215. Frederick DM, Bland D, Gollin Y. Fatal disseminated herpes simplex virus infection in a previously healthy pregnant woman. A case report. J Reprod Med. 2002;47:591-596.

216. Moedy JL, Lerman SJ, White RJ, et al. Fatal disseminated herpes simplex virus infection in a healthy child. Am J Dis Child. 1981;135:45.

217. Nahmias A. Disseminated herpes simplex virus infections. N Engl J Med. 1979;282:684.

218. Ruchman I, Dodd K. Recovery of herpes simplex virus from the blood of a patient with herpetic rhinitis. J Lab Clin Med. 1950;35:434.

219. Friedman HM, Pincus T, Gibilisco P, et al. Acute monarticular arthritis caused by herpes simplex virus and cytomegalovirus. Am J Med. 1980;69:241.

220. Shelley W. Herpetic arthritis associated with disseminated herpes simplex virus and cytomegalovirus. Am J Med. 1980;69:241.

221. Flewett T, Parker RG, Philip WM, et al. Acute hepatitis due to herpes simplex in an adult. J Clin Pathol. 1969;22:60.

222. Joseph T, Bogt P. Disseminated herpes with hepatoadrenal necrosis in an adult. Am J Med. 1974;56:735.

223. Whittaker J, Hardson M. Severe thrombocytopenia after generalized HSV-2 infection. South Med J. 1978;72:864.

224. Schlesinger J, Gandara D, Bensch KG, et al. Myoglobinuria associated with herpes group viral infections. Arch Intern Med. 1978;138:422.

225. Goyette R, Donowho EM Jr, Hieger LR, Plunkett GD. Fulminant hepatitis during pregnancy. Obstet Gynecol. 1974;43:191.

226. Young E, Killam AP, Greene JF Jr, et al. Disseminated herpesvirus infection associated with primary genital herpes in pregnancy. JAMA. 1976;235:2731.

227. Kobbermann T, Clark L, Griffin WT, et al. Maternal death secondary to disseminated herpesvirus hominis. Am J Obstet Gynecol. 1980;137:742.

228. Hillard P, Seeds J, Cefalo R. Disseminated herpes simplex in pregnancy: Two cases and a review. Obstet Gynecol Surv. 1982;37:449.

229. Sutton A, Smithwick EM, Seligman SJ, Kim DS. Fatal disseminated herpesvirus hominis type 2 infection in an adult with associated thymic dysplasia. Am J Med. 1974;56:545.

230. Keane J, Malkinson FD, Bryant J, Levin S. Herpesvirus hominis hepatitis and disseminated intravascular coagulation: Occurrence in an adult with pemphigus vulgaris. Arch Dermatol. 1976;93:1312.

231. Zahariadis G, Jerome KR, Corey L. Herpes simplex virus–associated sepsis in a previously infected immunocompetent adult. Ann Intern Med. 2003;139:153.

232. Frenkel LM, Garratty EM, Shen JP, et al. Clinical reactivation of herpes simplex virus type 2 infection in seropositive pregnant women with no history of genital herpes. Ann Intern Med. 1993;118:414.

233. Corey L, Nahmias AJ, Guinan ME, et al. A trial of topical acyclovir in genital herpes simplex virus infections. N Engl J Med. 1982;306:1313.

234. Corey L, Wald A. Genital herpes. In: Holmes KK, Sparling PF, Mardh PA, et al, eds. Sexually Transmitted Diseases. 3rd ed. New York: McGraw-Hill; 1999:285-312.

235. Sacks S. Frequency and duration of patient-observed recurrent genital herpes simplex virus infection: Characterization of the nonlesional prodrome. J Infect Dis. 1984;150:873.

236. Diaz-Mitoma F, Ruben M, Sacks S, et al. Detection of viral DNA to evaluate outcome of antiviral treatment of patients with recurrent genital herpes. J Clin Microbiol. 1996;34:657.

237. Wald A, Zeh J, Selke S, et al. Virologic characteristics of subclinical and symptomatic genital herpes infections. N Engl J Med. 1995;333:770-775.

238. Chapel T, Jeffries CD, Brown WJ. Simultaneous infection with *Treponema pallidum* and herpes simplex virus. Cutis. 1979;24:191.

239. Morse S, Trees DL, Htun Y, et al. Comparison of clinical diagnosis and standard laboratory and molecular methods for the diagnosis of genital ulcer disease in Lesotho: Association with human immunodeficiency virus infection. J Infect Dis. 1997;175:583.

240. Wald A, Huang ML, Carrell D, et al. Polymerase chain reaction for detection of herpes simplex virus (HSV) on mucosal surfaces: Comparison with HSV isolation in cell culture. J Infect Dis. 2003;188:1345.

241. Catotti D, Clarke P, Catoe KE. Herpes revisited: Still a cause of concern. Sex Transm Dis. 1993;20:77.

242. Rand K, Houn EF, Massey JK, Johnson JH. Daily stress and recurrence of genital herpes simplex. Arch Intern Med. 1990;150:1889.

243. Wald A, Corey L, Cone R, et al. Frequent genital herpes simplex virus 2 shedding in immunocompetent women: Effect of acyclovir treatment. J Clin Invest. 1997;99:1092-1097.

244. Wald A, Zeh J, Selke S, et al. Genital shedding of herpes simplex virus among men. J Infect Dis. 2002;186(Suppl 1):S34.

245. Krone MR, Tabet SR, Paradise M, et al. Herpes simplex virus shedding among HIV-negative men who have sex with men (MSM): Site and frequency of herpes shedding. J Infect Dis. 1998;178:978.

246. Cone RW, Hobson AC, Brown Z, et al. Frequent reactivation of genital herpes simplex viruses among pregnant women. JAMA. 1994;272:792.

247. Wald A, Zeh J, Barnum G, et al. Suppression of subclinical shedding of herpes simplex virus type 2 with acyclovir. Ann Intern Med. 1996;124:8-15.

248. Benedetti JK, Zeh J, Corey L. Clinical reactivation of HSV-2 decreases in frequency over time. Ann Intern Med. 1999;131:14-20.

249. Rattray MC, Corey L, Reeves WC, et al. Recurrent genital herpes among women: Symptomatic versus asymptomatic viral shedding. Br J Vener Dis. 1978;54:262.

250. Corey L. Challenges in genital herpes simplex virus management (Valtrex symposium). J Infect Dis 2002;186(Suppl 1):S29-S33.

251. Mertz G, Benedetti J, Ashley R, et al. Risk factors for the sexual transmission of genital herpes. Ann Intern Med. 1992;116:197.

252. Rooney J, Felser JM, Ostrove JM, Straus SE. Acquisition of genital herpes from an asymptomatic sexual partner. N Engl J Med. 1986;314:1561.

253. Bryson Y, Dillon M, Bernstein DI, et al. Risk of acquisition of genital herpes simplex virus type 2 in sex partners of persons with genital herpes: A prospective couple study. J Infect Dis. 1993;167:942.

254. Mertz G, Coombs RW, Ashley RL, et al. Transmission of genital herpes in couples with one symptomatic and one asymptomatic partner: A prospective study. J Infect Dis. 1988;157:1169-1177.

255. Mertz G, Schmidt O, Jourden JL, et al. Frequency of acquisition of first-episode genital infection with herpes simplex virus from symptomatic and asymptomatic source contacts. Sex Transm Dis. 1985;12:33.

256. Moore D, Ashley RL, Zarutskie PW, et al. Transmission of genital herpes by donor insemination. JAMA. 1989;261:3441.

257. Corey L, Wald A, Patel R, et al. Once-daily valacyclovir to reduce the transmission of genital herpes. N Engl J Med. 2004;350:11.

258. Ahmed HJ, Mbwana J, Gunnarsson E, et al. Etiology of genital ulcer disease and association with human immunodeficiency virus infection in two Tanzanian cities. Sex Transm Dis. 2003;30:114-119.

259. Greenblatt R, Lukehart SA, Plummer FA, et al. Genital ulceration as a risk factor for human immunodeficiency virus infection. AIDS. 1988;2:47.

260. Siegel D, Golden E, Washington AG, et al. Prevalence and correlates of herpes simplex infections: The population-based AIDS in multiethnic neighborhoods study. JAMA. 1992;268:1700.

261. Augenbraun M, Feldman J, Chirgwin K, et al. Increased genital shedding of herpes simplex virus type 2 in HIV-seropositive women. Ann Intern Med. 1995;123:845.

262. Schacker T, Zeh J, Hu H, et al. Changes in plasma HIV-1 RNA associated with HSV reactivation and suppression. J Infect Dis. 2002;186:1718-1725.

263. McClelland RS, Wang CC, Overbaugh J, et al. Association between cervical shedding of herpes simplex virus and HIV-1. AIDS. 2002;16:1-6.

264. Posavad CM, Wald A, Kuntz S, et al. Frequent reactivation of herpes simplex virus among HIV infected patients treated with highly active antiretroviral therapy. J Infect Dis. In press.

265. Schacker T, Hu H-L, Koelle DM, et al. Famciclovir for the suppression of symptomatic and asymptomatic herpes simplex virus reactivation in HIV-infected persons. Ann Intern Med. 1998;128:21.

266. Augenbraun M, Corey L, Reichelderfer P, et al. The effect of herpes simplex virus shedding on plasma HIV RNA levels in coinfected women. Clin Infect Dis. 2001;33:885-890.

267. Kriesel JD, Pisani PL, McKeough MB, et al. Correlation between detection of herpes simplex virus in oral secretions by PCR and susceptibility to experimental UV radiation–induced herpes labialis. J Clin Microbiol. 1994;31:3088.

268. Serwadda D, Gray RH, Sewankambo NK, et al. Human immunodeficiency virus acquisition associated with genital ulcer disease and herpes simplex virus type 2 infection: A nested case-control study in Rakai, Uganda. J Infect Dis. 2003;188:1492.

269. Stamm W, Handsfield HH, Rompalo AM, et al. Association between genital ulcer disease and acquisition of HIV infection in homosexual men. JAMA 1988;260:1429.

270. Hook EW 3rd, Cannon RO, Nahmias AJ, et al. Herpes simplex virus infection as a risk factor for human immunodeficiency virus infection in heterosexuals. J Infect Dis. 1992;165:251.

271. Holmberg SD, Stewart JA, Gerber AR, et al. Prior HSV type 2 infection as a risk factor for HIV infection. JAMA. 1988;259:1048.

272. Keet I, Lee FK, van Griensven GJ. Herpes simplex virus type 2 and other genital ulcerative infections as a risk factor for HIV-1 acquisition. Genitourin Med. 1990;66:330-333.

273. Telzak E, Chiasson MA, Bevier PJ, et al. HIV-1 seroconversion in patients with and without genital ulcer disease. Ann Intern Med. 1993;119:1181-1186.

274. Dickerson M, Johnston J, Delea TE, et al. The causal role for genital ulcer disease as a risk factor for transmission of human immunodeficiency virus: An application of the Bradford Hill criteria. Sex Transm Dis. 1996;23:429.

275. Reynolds SJ, Risbud AR, Shepherd ME, et al. Recent herpes simplex virus type 2 infection and the risk of human immunodeficiency virus type 1 acquisition in India. J Infect Dis. 2003;187:1513-1521.

276. Lai W, Chen CY, Morse SA, et al. Increasing relative prevalence of HSV-2 infection among men with genital ulcers from a mining community in South Africa. Sex Transm Infect. 2003;79:202-207.

277. de Vincenzi I. A longitudinal study of human immunodeficiency virus transmission by heterosexual partners. N Engl J Med. 1994;331:341.

278. O'Farrell N, Torer ST. High cumulative incidence of genital herpes among HIV-1 seropositive heterosexuals in South London. Int J STD AIDS. 1994;5:415.

279. Wald A, Link K. Risk of human immunodeficiency virus infection in herpes simplex virus type 2–seropositive persons: A meta-analysis. J Infect Dis. 2002;185:45.

280. Blower S. Ma L. Calculating the contribution of HSV-2 epidemics to increasing HIV incidence rates: Treatment implications. Clin Infect Dis. In press.

281. Corey L, Wald A, Celum C, Quinn TC. The effects of HSV-2 on HIV-1 acquisition and transmission: A review of two overlapping epidemics. J Acquir Immune Defic Syndr. 2004;35:435-445.

282. Crumpacker CS. Use of antiviral drugs to prevent herpesvirus transmission. N Engl J Med. 2004;350:67.

283. Albrecht M, DeLuca NA, Byrn RA, et al. The herpes simplex virus immediate-early protein, ICP4 is required to potentiate replication of human immunodeficiency virus in CD4+ lymphocytes. J Virol. 1989;63:1861.

284. Margolis DM, Rabson AB, Straus SE, Ostrove JM. Transactivation of the HIV-1 LTR by HSV-1 immediate early genes. Virology. 1992;186:788.

285. Kucera L, Leake E, Tyer N, et al. Human immunodeficiency virus type 1 (HIV-1) and herpes simplex virus type 2 (HSV-2) can coinfect and simultaneously replicate in the same human CD4+ cell: Effect of coinfection on infectious HSV-2 and HIV-1 replication. AIDS Res Hum Retroviruses. 1990;6:641-647.

286. Schacker T, Ryncarz AJ, Goddard J, et al. Frequent recovery of HIV-1 from genital herpes simplex virus lesions in HIV-1 infected men. JAMA. 1998;280:61.

287. Mbopi Keou FX, Gresenguet G, Mayaud P, et al. Interactions between herpes simplex virus type 2 and HIV infection in women in Africa: Opportunities for intervention. J Infect Dis. 2000;182:1090-1096.

288. Ioannidis JPA, Collier AC, Cooper DA, et al. Clinical efficacy of high dose acyclovir in human immunodeficiency virus infection: A meta-analysis of randomized individual patient data. J Infect Dis. 1998;178:349.

289. Gill MJ, Arlette J, Buchan K. Herpes simplex virus infections of the hand. A profile of 79 cases. Am J Med. 1988;84:89-93.

290. Becker TM. Herpes gladiatorum: A growing problem in sports medicine. Cutis. 1992;50:150.

291. Anderson BJ. The effectiveness of valacyclovir in preventing reactivation of herpes gladiatorum in wrestlers. Clin J Sport Med. 1999;9:86.

292. Liesengang TJ, Melton J III, Daly PJ, Ilstrup DM. Epidemiology of ocular herpes simplex. Incidence in Rochester, Minn, 1950 through 1982. Arch Ophthalmol. 1989;107:1155.

293. Dawson CR, Togni B. Herpes simplex eye infections: Clinical manifestations, pathogenesis and management. Surv Ophthalmol. 1976;21:121.

294. Pepose JS, Leib DA, Stuart PM, Easty DL. Herpes simplex virus diseases: Anterior segment of the eye. In: Pepose JS, Holland GN, Wilhelmus KR, eds. Ocular Infection and Immunity. St. Louis: CV Mosby; 1996:905.

295. Culbertson WW, Blumenkrantz MS, Haines H, et al. The acute retinal necrosis syndrome. Ophthalmology. 1982;89:1317.

296. Forster DJ, Dugel PU, Frangieh GT, et al. Rapidly progressive outer retinal necrosis in the acquired immunodeficiency syndrome. Am J Ophthalmol. 1990;110:341.

297. Holland GN. Acquired immunodeficiency syndrome and ophthalmology. The first decade. Am J Ophthalmol. 1992;114:86.

298. Olson L, Buescher EL, Artenstein MS, Parkman PD. Herpesvirus infections of the human central nervous system. N Engl J Med. 1967;172:1271.

299. Whitley RJ, Lakeman F. Herpes simplex virus infections of the central nervous system: Therapeutic and diagnostic considerations. Clin Infect Dis. 1995;20:414.

300. Whitley RJ, Soong S-J, Hirsch MS, et al. Herpes simplex encephalitis. Vidarabine therapy and diagnostic problems. N Engl J Med. 1981;304:313.

301. Whitley R, Lakeman AD, Nahmias A, et al. DNA restriction-enzyme analysis of a herpes simplex virus isolate obtained from patients with encephalitis. N Engl J Med. 1982;307:1060.

302. Fraser NW, Lawrence WC, Wroblewska A, et al. Herpes simplex type 1 DNA in human brain tissue. Proc Natl Acad Sci USA. 1981;78:6461.

303. Whitley RJ, Soong S-J, Linneman C Jr, et al. Herpes simplex encephalitis. Clinical assessment. JAMA. 1982;247:217.

304. Whitley RJ, Cobbs CG, Alford CA Jr, et al. Diseases that mimic herpes simplex encephalitis. Diagnosis, presentation, and outcome. JAMA. 1989;262:234.

305. Aurelius E, Johansson B, Skoldenberg B, et al. Rapid diagnosis of herpes simplex encephalitis by nested polymerase chain reaction assay of cerebrospinal fluid. Lancet. 1991;337:189.

306. Aurelius E, Johansson B, Skoldenberg B, Forsgren M. Encephalitis in immunocompetent patients due to herpes simplex virus type 1 or 2 as determined by type-specific polymerase chain reaction and antibody assays of cerebrospinal fluid. J Med Virol. 1993;39:179.

307. Rowley A, Lakeman F, Whitley R, Wolinsky S. Rapid detection of herpes simplex virus DNA in cerebrospinal fluid of patients with herpes simplex encephalitis. Lancet. 1990;335:440.

308. Lakeman FD, Whitley RJ. National Institute of Allergy and Infectious Disease CASG. Diagnosis of herpes simplex encephalitis: Application of polymerase chain reaction to cerebrospinal fluid from brain biopsied patients and correlation with disease. J Infect Dis. 1995;171:857.

309. Yamamoto LJ, Tedder DG, Ashley R, et al. Herpes simplex virus type 1 DNA in cerebrospinal fluid of a patient with Mollaret's meningitis. N Engl J Med. 1991;325:1082.

310. Lakeman FD, Whitley RJ. Diagnosis of herpes simplex encephalitis: Application of polymerase chain reaction to cerebrospinal fluid from brain-biopsied patients and correlation with disease. J Infect Dis. 1995;71:857.

311. Whitley RJ, Alford CA, Hirsch MS, et al. Vidarabine versus acyclovir therapy in herpes simplex encephalitis. N Engl J Med. 1986;314:144.

312. McDonald GB, Sharma P, Hackman RC, et al. Esophageal infections in immunosuppressed patients after marrow transplantation. Gastroenterology. 1985;88:1111.

313. McBane RD, Gross JB. Herpes esophagitis: Clinical syndrome, endoscopic appearance, and diagnosis in 23 patients. Gastrointest Endosc. 1991;37:600.

314. Buss DH, Scharyj M. Herpes virus infection of the esophagus and other visceral organs in adults: Incidence and clinical significance. Am J Med. 1979;66:457.

315. Graham BS, Snell JD. Herpes simplex virus infection of the adult lower respiratory tract. Medicine (Baltimore). 1983;62:384.

316. Tuxen DV, Cade JF, McDonald MI, et al. Herpes simplex virus from the lower respiratory tract in adult respiratory distress syndrome. Am Rev Respir Dis. 1982;126:416.

317. Cook CH, Yenchar JK, Kraner TO, et al. Occult herpes family viruses may increase mortality in critically ill surgical patients. Am J Surg. 1998;176:357.

318. Ulmar SH, Konth A. Disseminated cutaneous HSV1 with interstitial pneumonia as a first presentation of AIDS. J Natl Med Assoc. 1999;8:471.

319. Camps K, Jurens PG, Denney HE, et al. Clinical significance of HSV in the lower respiratory tract of critically ill patients. Eur J Clin Microbiol Infect Dis. 2002;10:758.

320. Byers RJ, Hasleton PS, Quigley A, et al. Pulmonary herpes simplex in burn patients. Eur Respir J. 1996;9:2313.

321. Prellner T, Flamhole L, Haidl S, et al. Herpes simplex virus—The most frequently isolated pathogen in the lungs of patients with severe respiratory distress. Scand J Infect Dis. 1992;24:283.

322. Wade JC, Newton B, McLaren C, et al. Intravenous acyclovir to treat mucocutaneous herpes simplex virus infection after marrow transplantation: A double-blind trial. Ann Intern Med. 1982;96:265.

323. Meyers J, Flournoy, Thomas ED, et al. Infection with herpes simplex virus and cell-mediated immunity after marrow transplant. J Infect Dis. 1980;142:338.

324. Saral R, Burns WH, Laskin OL, et al. Acyclovir prophylaxis of herpes simplex virus infections: A randomized double-blind controlled trial in bone-marrow-transplant recipients. N Engl J Med. 1981;305:63.

325. Straus SE, Seidlin M, Takiff H, et al. Oral acyclovir to suppress recurring herpes simplex virus infection in immunodeficient patients. Ann Intern Med. 1984;100:522.

326. Shepp DH, Newton BA, Dandliker PS, et al. Oral acyclovir therapy for mucocutaneous herpes simplex virus infections in immunocompromised marrow transplant recipients. Ann Intern Med. 1985;102:783.

327. Fiddian P, Sabin CA, Griffiths PD. Valacyclovir provides optimum acyclovir exposure for prevention of cytomegalovirus and related outcomes after organ transplantation. J Infect Dis. 2002;186(Suppl 1):S110-S115.

328. Nichols WG, Corey L, Gooley T, et al. High risk of death due to bacterial and fungal infection among cytomegalovirus (CMV)-seronegative recipients of stem cell transplants from seropositive donors: Evidence for "indirect" effects of primary CMV infection. J Infect Dis 2002;185:273-282.

329. Forsgren M. Prevalence of antibodies to herpes simplex virus in pregnant women in Stockholm in 1969, 1983 and 1989: Implications for STD epidemiology. Int J STD AIDS. 1994;5:113.

330. Brown Z, Benedetti J, Ashley R, et al. Neonatal herpes simplex virus infection in relation to asymptomatic maternal infection at the time of labor. N Engl J Med. 1991;324:1247.

331. Brown ZA, Ashley RL, Selke S, et al. Effect of serologic status and cesarean delivery on transmission rates of herpes simplex virus from mother to infant. JAMA. 2003;289:203.

332. Prober CG, Sullender WM, Yasukawa LL, et al. Low risk of herpes simplex virus infections in neonates exposed to the virus at the time of vaginal delivery to mothers with recurrent genital HSV infections. N Engl J Med. 1987;316:240.

333. Nahmias AJ, Lee FK, Beckman-Nahmias S. Sero-epidemiological and -sociological patterns of herpes simplex virus infection in the world. Scand J Infect Dis Suppl. 1990;69:19-36.

334. Vontver LA, Hickok DG, Brown Z, et al. Recurrent genital herpes simplex virus infection in pregnancy: Infant outcome and frequency as asymptomatic recurrences. Am J Obstet Gynecol. 1982;143:75.

335. Brown ZA, Vontver LA, Benedetti J, et al. Genital herpes in pregnancy: Risk factors associated with recurrences and asymptomatic shedding. Am J Obstet Gynecol. 1985;153:24.

336. Brown ZA, Benedetti JK, Selke S. Asymptomatic maternal shedding of herpes simplex virus at the onset of labor: Relationship to preterm labor. Obstet Gynecol. 1996;87:483.

337. Malm G, Berg U, Forsgren M. Neonatal herpes simplex: Clinical findings and outcome in relation to type of maternal infection. Acta Paediatr. 1995;84:256.

338. Hain J, Doshi N, Harger JH. Ascending transcervical herpes simplex infection with intact fetal membranes. Obstet Gynecol. 1980;56:106.

339. Florman A. Intrauterine infection with herpes simplex virus: Resultant congenital malformations. JAMA. 1973;225:129.

340. Hutto C, Arvin A, Jacobs R, et al. Intrauterine herpes simplex virus infections. J Pediatr. 1987;110:97.

341. Chalhub EG, Baenziger J, Feigen RD, et al. Congenital herpes simplex type II infection with extensive hepatic calcification, bone lesions and cataracts: Complete post-mortem examination. Dev Med Child Neurol. 1977;19:527.

342. Libman MD, Dascal A, Kramer MS. Strategies for the prevention of neonatal infection with herpes simplex virus: A decision analysis. Rev Infect Dis. 1991;13:1093.

343. Abrams CA. Isolation of herpes simplex from a mother and aborted fetus. Ghana Med J. 1966;5:41.

344. Prober CG, Corey L, Brown ZA, et al. The management of pregnancies complicated by genital infections with herpes simplex virus. Clin Infect Dis. 1992;15:1031.

345. Yeager AS, Arvin AM, Urbani LJ, Kemp JA 3rd. Relationship of antibody to outcome in neonatal herpes simplex virus infections. Infect Immun. 1980;19:532.

346. Kulhanjian JA, Soroush V, Au DS, et al. Identification of women at unsuspected risk of primary infection with herpes simplex virus type 2 during pregnancy. N Engl J Med. 1992;326:916.

347. Naib ZM, Nahmias AJ, Josey WE, Wheeler JH. Association of maternal genital herpetic infection with spontaneous abortion. Obstet Gynecol. 1970;35:260.

348. Gibbs RS, Mead PB. Preventing neonatal herpes—Current strategies. N Engl J Med. 1991;326:946.

349. Rouse DJ, Stringer JS. Cesarean delivery and risk of herpes simplex virus infection. JAMA. 2003;289:2208-2209.

350. Arvin A, Hensleigh PA, Prober CG, et al. Failure of antepartum maternal cultures to predict the infant's risk of exposure to herpes simplex virus at delivery. N Engl J Med. 1986;315:796.

351. Garland SM, Lee TN, Sacks S. Do antepartum herpes simplex virus cultures predict intrapartum shedding for pregnant women with recurrent disease? Infect Dis Obstet Gynecol. 1999;7:230.

352. Watts DH, Brown Z, Money D, et al. A double-blind, randomized, placebo-controlled trial of acyclovir in late pregnancy for reduction of herpes simplex virus shedding and cesarean delivery. Am J Obstet Gynecol. 2003;188:836-843.

353. Arvin AM, Yeager AS, Bruhn FW, Grossman M. Neonatal herpes simplex infection in the absence of mucocutaneous lesions. J Pediatr. 1982;100:715.

354. Frenkel LM, Drown ZA, Bryson YJ, et al. Pharmacokinetics of acyclovir in the term human pregnancy and neonate. Am J Obstet Gynecol. 1991;164:569.

355. Ratanajamit C, Vinther Skriver M, Jepsen P, et al. Adverse pregnancy outcome in women exposed to acyclovir during pregnancy: A population-based observational study. Scand J Infect Dis. 2003;35:255-259.

356. Whitley R, Nahmias AJ, Visintine AM, et al. The natural history of genital herpes simplex virus infection of mother and newborn. Pediatrics. 1980;66:489.

357. Whitley RJ, Arvin A, Prober C, et al. Predictors of morbidity and mortality in neonates with herpes simplex virus infections. N Engl J Med. 1991;324:450.

358. Kimura H, Futamura M, Kito H, et al. Detection of viral DNA in neonatal herpes simplex virus infections: Frequent and prolonged presence in serum and cerebrospinal fluid. J Infect Dis. 1991;164:289.

359. Corey L, Whitley RJ, Stone EF, Mohan K. Difference in neurologic outcome after antiviral therapy of neonatal central nervous system herpes simplex virus type I versus herpes simplex virus type 2 infection. Lancet. 1988;2:1.

360. Kimberlin DW, Lin CY, Jacobs RF, et al. Safety and efficacy of high-dose intravenous acyclovir in the management of neonatal herpes simplex virus infections. Pediatrics. 2001;108:230-238.

361. Kimberlin DW, Lin CY, Jacobs RF, et al. Natural history of neonatal herpes simplex virus infections in the acyclovir era. Pediatrics. 2001;108:223-229.

362. Morrow RA, Friedrich D. Inaccuracy of certain commercial enzyme immunoassays for diagnosing genital infections with herpes simplex virus types 1 or 2. Am J Clin Pathol. 2003;120:839.

363. Langenberg A, Benedetti J, Jenkins J, et al. Development of clinically recognizable genital lesions among women previously identified as having "asymptomatic" HSV-2 infection. Ann Intern Med. 1989;110: 882-887.

364. Fisman DN, Hook EW 3rd, Goldie SJ. Estimating the costs and benefits of screening monogamous, heterosexual couples for unrecognized infection with herpes simplex virus type 2. Sex Transm Infect. 2003;79:45-52.

365. Lipsitch M, Davis G, Corey L. Potential benefits of a serodiagnostic test for herpes simplex virus type 1 (HSV-1) to prevent neonatal HSV-1 infections. Sex Transm Dis. 2002;29:399-405.

366. Dorsky D, Crumpacker C. Acyclovir: Drugs 5 years later. Ann Intern Med. 1987; 207:859.

367. Elion G, Furman PA, Fyfe JA, et al. Selectivity of action of an antiherpetic agent, 9-(2-hydroxyethoxymethyl)guanine. Proc Natl Acad Sci USA. 1977;79:5716-5720.

368. Schaeffer H, Beauchamp L, deMiranda P, et al. 9-(2-Hydroxyethoxymethyl) guanine activity against viruses of herpes group. Nature. 1978;272:583.

369. Brigden D, Whitman P. The clinical pharmacology of acyclovir and its prodrug. Scand J Infect Dis. 1985;47(Suppl):33.

370. Coen D, Schaffer P. Two distinct loci confer resistance to acycloguanosine in herpes simplex virus type 1. Proc Natl Acad Sci USA. 1980;77:2265.

371. Crumpacker C, Schnipper LE, Zaia JA, Levin MJ. Growth inhibition by acy-cloguanosine of herpesviruses isolated from human infections. Antimicrob Agents Chemother. 1979;15:642.

372. Raborn GW, McGaw WT, Grace M, et al. Oral acyclovir and herpes labialis: A randomized, double-blind, placebo controlled study. J Am Dent Assoc. 1987;115:38.

373. Spruance SL, Stewart JCB, Rowe NM, et al. Treatment of recurrent herpes simplex labialis with oral acyclovir. J Infect Dis. 1990;161:185.

374. Rooney JF, Straus SE, Mannix ML, et al. Oral acyclovir to suppress frequently recurrent herpes labialis. A double-blind placebo-controlled trial. Ann Intern Med. 1993;118:268.

375. Reichman R, Badger GJ, Mertz GJ, et al. Treatment of recurrent genital herpes simplex infections with oral acyclovir: A controlled trial. JAMA. 1984;251:2103.

376. Douglas JM, Critchlow C, Benedetti J, et al. A double blind study of oral acyclovir for suppression of recurrences of genital herpes simplex virus infection. N Engl J Med. 1984;310:1551.

377. Straus S, Reinhold W, Smith HA, et al. Suppression of frequently recurring genital herpes: A placebo-controlled double blind trial of oral acyclovir. N Engl J Med. 1984;310:1545.

378. Mindel A, Faherty A, Carney O, et al. Dosage and safety of long term suppressive therapy for recurrent genital herpes. Lancet. 1988;1:926.

379. Kaplowitz L, Baker D, Gelb R, et al. Prolonged continuous acyclovir treatment of normal adults with frequently recurring genital herpes simplex virus infection. The Acyclovir Study Group. JAMA. 1991;265:747-751.

380. Goldberg LH, Kaufman R, Kurtz TO, et al. Long-term suppression of recurrent genital herpes with acyclovir. Arch Dermatol. 1993;129:582.

381. Wolf R, Wolf D, Orion E, Matz H. Long-term prophylactic antiviral therapy for recurrent herpes simplex: The controversy goes on. Clin Dermatol. 2003;21:164.

382. Spruance SL, Jones TM, Blatter MM, et al. High-dose, short-duration, early valacyclovir therapy in episodic treatment of cold sores: Results of two randomized, placebo-controlled, multicenter studies. Antimicrob Agents Chemother. 2003;47:1072-1080.

383. Wald A, Carrell D, Remington M, et al. Two-day regimen of acyclovir for treatment of recurrent genital herpes simplex virus type 2 infection. Clin Infect Dis. 2002;34:944-948.

384. Chosidow O, Drouault Y, Garraffo R, et al. Valaciclovir as a single dose during prodrome of herpes facialis: A pilot randomized double-blind clinical trial. Br J Dermatol. 2003;148:142-146.

385. Hodge R, Cheng Y. The mode of action of penciclovir. Antiviral Chem Chemother. 1993;4S1:13.

386. Bacon TH, Levin MJ, Leary JJ, et al. Herpes simplex virus resistance to acyclovir and penciclovir after two decades of antiviral therapy. Clin Microbiol Rev. 2003;16:114-128.

387. Romanowski B, Marina RB, Roberts JN; Valtrex HS 230017 Study Group. Patients' preference of valacyclovir once-daily suppressive therapy versus twice-daily episodic therapy for recurrent genital herpes: A randomized study. Sex Transm Dis. 2003;30:226-231.

388. Strand A, Patel R, Wulf HC, et al. Aborted genital herpes simplex virus lesions: Findings from a randomized controlled trial with valacyclovir. Sex Transm Infect. 2002;78:435-439.

389. Lin L, Chen XS, Cui PG, et al. Topical application of penciclovir cream for the treatment of herpes facialis/labialis: A randomized, double-blind, multicenter, acyclovir-controlled trial. J Dermatolog Treat. 2002;13:67-72.

390. Weinberg A, Bate BJ, Masters HB, et al. In vitro activities of penciclovir and acyclovir against herpes simplex virus types 1 and 2. Antimicrob Agents Chemother. 1992;36:2037.

391. Pue M, Benet L. Pharmacokinetics of famciclovir in man. Antiviral Chem Chemother. 1993;4(s):47.

392. Sacks SL, Aoki FY, Diaz-Mitoma F, et al. Patient-initiated, twice-daily oral famciclovir for early recurrent genital herpes. A randomized, double-blind multicenter trial. JAMA. 1996;276:44.

393. Mertz GJ, Loveless MO, Levin MJ, et al. Oral famciclovir for suppression of recurrent genital herpes simplex virus infection in women: A multicenter, double-blind, placebo-controlled trial. Arch Intern Med. 1997;157:343.

394. Griffiths PD. Tomorrow's challenges for herpesvirus management: Potential application of valacyclovir. J Infect Dis. 2002;186(Suppl 1):S131-S137.

395. Laiskonis A, Thune T, Neldam S, Hiltunen-Back E. Valacyclovir in the treatment of facial herpes simplex virus infection. J Infect Dis. 2002;186(Suppl 1):S66-S70.

396. Beeson WH, Rachel JD. Valacyclovir prophylaxis for herpes simplex virus infection or infection recurrence following laser skin resurfacing. Dermatol Surg. 2002;28:331-336.

397. Soul-Lawton J, Seaber E, On N, et al. Absolute bioavailability and metabolic disposition of valaciclovir, the L-Val ester of acyclovir, following oral administration to humans. Antimicrob Agents Chemother. 1995;36:2759.

398. Reitano M, Tyring S, Levy W, et al. Valaciclovir for the suppression of recurrent genital HSV infection, a large scale dose range finding study. J Infect Dis. 1998;176:603.

399. Burns LJ, Miller W, Kandaswamy C, et al. Randomized clinical trial of ganciclovir vs acyclovir for prevention of cytomegalovirus antigenemia after allogeneic transplantation. Bone Marrow Transplant. 2002;30:945-951.

400. Erlich K, Mills J, Chatis P, et al. Acyclovir-resistant herpes simplex virus infections in patients with the acquired immunodeficiency syndrome. N Engl J Med. 1989;320:293.

401. Englund JA, Zimmerman ME, Swierkoz EM, et al. Herpes simplex resistant to acyclovir. A study in a tertiary care center. Ann Intern Med. 1990;112:416.

402. Birch CJ, Tachedjian G, Doherty RR, et al. Altered sensitivity to antiviral drugs of herpes simplex isolates from a patient with acquired immunodeficiency syndrome. J Infect Dis. 1990;162:731.

403. Sacks SL, Wanklin RJ, Reece DE, et al. Progressive esophagitis from acyclovir-resistant herpes simplex. Clinical roles for DNA polymerase mutants and viral heterogeneity. Ann Intern Med. 1989;111:893-899.

404. Saijo M, Yasuda Y, Yabe H, et al. Bone marrow transplantation in a child with Wiskott-Aldrich syndrome latently infected with acyclovir-resistant (ACVʳ) herpes simplex virus type 1: Emergence of foscarnet-resistant virus originating from the ACVʳ virus. J Med Virol. 2002;68:99-104.

405. Kost R, Hill EL, Tigges M, Straus SE. Brief report: Recurrent acyclovir-resistant genital herpes in an immunocompetent patient. N Engl J Med. 1993;329:1777.

406. Chibo D, Mijch A, Doherty R, Birch C. Novel mutations in the thymidine kinase and DNA polymerase genes of acyclovir and foscarnet resistant herpes simplex viruses infecting an immunocompromised patient. J Clin Virol. 2002;25:165-170.

407. Reyes M, Shaik NS, Graber JM, et al. Acyclovir-resistant genital herpes among persons attending sexually transmitted disease and human immunodeficiency virus clinics. Arch Intern Med. 2003;163:76.

408. McLaren C, Corey L, Dekket C, Barry DW. In vitro sensitivity to acyclovir in genital herpes simplex viruses from acyclovir treated patients. J Infect Dis. 1983;148:868.

409. Lehrman SN, Douglas JM, Corey L, Barry DW. Recurrent genital herpes and suppressive oral acyclovir therapy: Relationship between clinical outcome and in vitro drug sensitivity. Ann Intern Med. 1986;204:786-790.

410. Safrin S, Elbeik T, Phan L, et al. Correlation between response to acyclovir and foscarnet therapy and in vitro susceptibility result for isolates of herpes simplex virus from human immunodeficiency virus–infected patients. Antimicrob Agents Chemother. 1994;38:1246.

411. Safrin S, Kemmerly S, Plotkin B, et al. Foscarnet-resistant herpes simplex virus infection in patients with AIDS. J Infect Dis. 1994;169:193.

412. Safrin S, Crumpacker C, Chatis P, et al. A controlled trial comparing foscarnet with vidarabine for acyclovir-resistant mucocutaneous herpes simplex in the acquired immunodeficiency syndrome. N Engl J Med. 1991;325:551.

413. Mendel DB, Barkhimer D, Chen MS, et al. Biochemical basis for increased susceptibility to cidofovir of herpes simplex viruses with altered or deficient thymidine kinase activity. Antimicrob Agents Chemother. 1995;39:2120.

414. Lalezari JP, Drew WL, Blutzer E, et al. Treatment with intravenous (S)-1[3-Hydroxy-2(phosphonylmethoxy) propyl]-cytosine of acyclovir resistant mucocutaneous infection with herpes simplex virus in a patient with AIDS. J Infect Dis. 1994;170:570.

415. Kessler HA, Hurwitz S, Farthing C, et al. Pilot study of topical trifluridine for the treatment of acyclovir-resistant mucocutaneous herpes simplex disease in patients with AIDS (ACTG 172). J Acquir Immune Defic Syndr Hum Retrovirol. 1996;12:147.

CHAPTER **133**

Varicella-Zoster Virus

RICHARD J. WHITLEY

Varicella-zoster virus (VZV) causes two distinct clinical diseases. Varicella, more commonly called chickenpox, is the primary infection and results from exposure of a person susceptible to the virus. Chickenpox is ubiquitous and extremely contagious, but for the most part, it is a benign illness characterized by a generalized exanthematous rash. It occurs seasonally and in epidemics. Recurrence of infection results in the more localized phenomenon known as *herpes zoster*, often referred to as *shingles*, a common infection among the elderly. A live, attenuated vaccine for the prevention of chickenpox is available in the United States and vaccination is recommended for use in healthy children and in susceptible adults (see Chapter 319). The incidence of chickenpox has approached the annual birth rate: 3 to 4 × 10⁶ cases yearly, although this is being reduced as use of the vaccine becomes more widespread. Surveillance for varicella in three counties in California, Texas, and Pennsylvania from 1995 to 2000 showed reductions in cases of varicella from 71% to 84% by years 1999 and 2000.[1] It is estimated that there are approximately 500,000 cases of herpes zoster yearly in the United States, which result in over 1.5 million physician visits per year. Likely, this approximation is a gross underestimation of disease occurrence. Many of these individuals require long-term follow-up medical care for postherpetic neuralgia.

HISTORICAL OVERVIEW

Shingles has been recognized since ancient times as a unique clinical entity because of the dermatomal vesicular rash; however, chickenpox was often confused with smallpox.[2] In 1875, Steiner successfully transmitted VZV by inoculation of the vesicular fluid from a person suffering from chickenpox to "volunteers."[3] The infectious nature of VZV was further defined by von Bokay,[4,5] who observed chickenpox in persons who had close contact with others suffering from herpes zoster. He correctly described the mean incubation period for the development of chickenpox in susceptible patients as well as the average range in days. Kundratitz in 1925[6] showed that the inoculation of vesicular fluid from patients with herpes zoster into susceptible persons resulted in chickenpox. Similar observations were reported by Brunsgaard[7] and others,[8] and in 1943 Garland[9] suggested that herpes zoster was the consequence of the reactivation of latent VZV.

Since early in the 20th century, similarities in the histopathologic features of skin lesions and in epidemiologic and immunologic studies indicated that varicella and herpes zoster were caused by the same agent.[10,11] Tyzzer[12] described the histopathologic features of skin lesions resulting from VZV infections and noted the appearance of intranuclear inclusions and multinucleated giant cells. These descriptions came from histologic studies performed on serial skin biopsy specimens that were obtained during the first week of illness. The histopathologic descriptions were amplified by Lipschutz in 1921[13] for herpes zoster.

Isolation of VZV in 1958 permitted a definition of the biology of this virus.[11] Viral isolates from patients with either chickenpox or herpes zoster demonstrated similar changes in tissue culture, specifically the appearance of eosinophilic intranuclear inclusions and multinucleated giant cells. These findings are virtually identical to those present on clinically available biopsy material. Taken together, these data provided a universal acceptance that both diseases were caused by VZV. By 1958, Weller and colleagues[11,14-16] had been able to establish that there were neither biologic nor immunologic differences between the viral agents isolated from patients with these two clinical entities. Later studies provided their identity by rigorous biochemical methods.[17] Viral DNA from a patient with chickenpox who subsequently developed herpes zoster was examined by restriction endonuclease analysis, and the molecular identity of these two viruses was verified.[18,19]

THE PATHOGEN AND ITS REPLICATION

VZV is a member of the Herpesviridae family and shares structural characteristics with other members of the family. The virus has icosapentahedral symmetry and contains centrally located double-stranded DNA with a surrounding envelope. The size of the virus is approximately 150 to 200 nm, and it has a lipid-containing envelope with glycoprotein spikes.[18] The naked capsid has a diameter of approximately 90 to 95 nm.[20-22] The DNA contains 125,000 base pairs, or approximately 80 megadaltons, and encodes about 75 proteins. The organization of the viral genome is similar to that of other herpesviruses. There are unique long (105-kb) and unique short (5.2-kb) regions of the viral genome. Each unique sequence contains terminal repeat sequences. With replication, the unique short (U_s) region can invert upon itself and result in two isomeric forms.[23-25]

Five families of VZV glycoproteins (gp) have been identified: gpI, gpII, gpIII, gpIV, and gpV. The herpes simplex virus (HSV) homologues are gE, gB, gH, U_s7, and gC, respectively. Viral infectivity can be neutralized by monoclonal antibodies directed against gp I, gp II, and gp III. These glycoproteins have been the subject of intense investigative interest because they represent the primary markers for both humoral and cell-mediated immune responses.

Only enveloped virions are infectious; this may account for the lability of VZV. Furthermore, the envelope is sensitive to detergent, ether, and air drying. VZV is highly cell associated and spreads from cell to cell by direct contact. Virus can be isolated in a variety of continuous and discontinuous cell culture systems of human and simian origin. Approximately 8 to 10 hours after infection, virus-specific immunofluorescence can be detected in the cells immediately adjacent to the initial focus of infection. This parallels the microscopic observation of the radial spread of the cytopathologic process.[26,27] Electron microscopic studies demonstrate the appearance of immature viral particles within 12 hours of the onset of infection. As with HSV, the naked capsids acquire their envelope at the nuclear membrane, being released into the perinuclear space where large vacuoles are formed.[20,28] Infectious virus is then spread to adjacent cells after fusion of plasma membranes.

EPIDEMIOLOGY OF VARICELLA-ZOSTER VIRUS INFECTIONS

Chickenpox

Humans are the only known reservoir for VZV. Chickenpox follows exposure of the susceptible or seronegative person to VZV and represents the primary form of infection. Although it is assumed that the virus is spread by the respiratory route and replicates in the nasopharynx or upper respiratory tract, retrieval of virus from persons incubating VZV has been uncommon. However, the application of polymerase chain reaction (PCR) techniques to nasopharyngeal secretions of exposed and susceptible persons has detected VZV DNA and supports this hypothesis. Chickenpox is a common infection of childhood and affects both genders equally and people of all races. To a certain extent, the virus is endemic in the population at large; however, it becomes epidemic among susceptible persons during seasonal periods, namely, late winter and early spring.[29] Intimate contact appears to be the key determinant for transmission.

Overall, chickenpox is a disease of childhood, because 90% of cases occur in children younger than 13 years. Typically, the virus is introduced into the susceptible school-aged or preschool child. In a study by Wells and Holla,[30] 61 of 67 susceptible children in kindergarten through the fourth grade contracted chickenpox. Approximately 10% of persons older than 15 years are considered susceptible to VZV infection. The incubation period of chickenpox (i.e., the time interval between exposure of a susceptible person to the time the vesicular rash develops in an index case) is generally regarded to be 14 to 15 days, but disease can appear within a range of 10 to 20 days.[31,32] Secondary attack rates among susceptible siblings within a household are between 70% and 90%.[33] Patients are infectious for a period of approximately 48 hours before the period of vesicle formation and generally for 4 to 5 days thereafter until all vesicles are crusted.

Although chickenpox exists worldwide among children, it occurs more frequently in adults who reside in tropical regions than in those who reside in other geographic areas. Stokes noted a higher incidence of chickenpox among soldiers serving abroad during World War II, in whom the incidence was 1.41 to 2.27 per 1000 persons annually. These rates contrast with those in the United States, which were approximately half those reported among the soldiers.[34]

Herpes Zoster

The epidemiology of herpes zoster is somewhat different. VZV characteristically becomes latent after primary infection within the dorsal root ganglia. Reactivation leads to herpes zoster, a sporadic disease. Histopathologic examination of the nerve root after infection with VZV demonstrates characteristics indicative of VZV infection. In persons who die after recent herpes zoster infection, an examination of the dorsal root ganglia reveals satellitosis, lymphocytic infiltration in the nerve root, and degeneration of the ganglia cells.[35,36] Intranuclear inclusions can be found within the ganglia cells. Although it is possible to demonstrate the presence of VZV by electron microscopy, it has not been possible to isolate this virus in cultures, usually from explants of dorsal root ganglia, as has been done after HSV infection. The biologic mechanism by which VZV establishes latency remains unknown.

Herpes zoster is a disease that occurs at all ages, but it afflicts about 20% or more of the population overall, mainly the elderly.[37,38] Herpes zoster, known also as shingles, occurs in persons who are seropositive for VZV or, more specifically, in those who have had chickenpox. Reactivation appears to be dependent on a balance between virus and host factors. Most patients who develop herpes zoster have no history of exposure to other persons with VZV infection at the time of the appearance of lesions. The highest incidence of disease varies between 5 and 10 cases per 1000 for persons older than 60 years.[14] Approximately 4% of patients experience a second episode of herpes zoster; however, recurrences of dermatomal lesions are usually caused by HSV. In a 7-year study performed by McGregor,[39] the annualized rate of herpes zoster was 4.8 cases per 1000 patients and three fourths of those patients were older than 45 years. Persons who are immunocompromised have a higher incidence of both chickenpox and shingles.[40-43] Herpes zoster occurs within the first 2 years of life in children born to women who have had chickenpox during pregnancy. These cases probably reflect in utero chickenpox with reactivation early in life.

PATHOGENESIS

Chickenpox occurs in susceptible persons who are exposed to virus after close personal contact. Histopathologic findings in human VZV infections, whether chickenpox or herpes zoster, are virtually identical. The vesicles involve the corium and dermis. As viral replication progresses, the epithelial cells undergo degenerative changes characterized by ballooning, with the subsequent appearance of multinucleated giant cells and prominent eosinophilic intranuclear inclusions. Under unusual circumstances, necrosis and hemorrhage may appear in the upper portion of the dermis. As the vesicle evolves, the fluid becomes cloudy as a consequence of the appearance of polymorphonuclear leukocytes, degenerated cells, and fibrin. Ultimately, either the vesicles rupture and release infectious fluid, or the fluid gradually becomes reabsorbed.

Transmission is likely by the respiratory route, followed by localized replication at an undefined site, which leads to seeding of the reticuloendothelial system and, ultimately, viremia. The occurrence of viremia in patients with chickenpox is supported by the diffuse and scattered nature of the skin lesions and can be verified in selected cases by the recovery of virus from the blood.[44] The mechanism of VZV reactivation that results in herpes zoster is unknown.

CLINICAL MANIFESTATIONS

Chickenpox

The medical importance of chickenpox should be stressed. There have been approximately 250 deaths per year in the United States from this infection—even in the vaccine era. For the normal child, chickenpox-associated mortality is less than 2 per 100,000 cases. This risk increases by more than 15-fold for adults. The presenting manifestations of chickenpox are a rash, low-grade fever, and malaise. A prodrome of symptoms may occur 1 to 2 days before the onset of the exanthem in a few patients. For the most part, chickenpox in the immunocompetent child is a benign illness associated with lassitude and a temperature of 100° to 103° F of 3 to 5 days' duration. Subsequent constitutional symptoms include malaise, pruritus, anorexia, and listlessness; these symptoms gradually resolve as the illness abates. The skin manifestations, which are the hallmark of infection, consist of maculopapules, vesicles, and scabs in varying stages of evolution. The lesions initially contain clear vesicular fluid, but over a very short period of time they pustulate and scab. Most lesions are small, having an erythematous base with a diameter of 5 mm to as large as 12 to 13 mm. The lesions can be round or oval; central umbilication occurs as healing progresses. The lesions have often been referred to as "dewdrop-like" dur-

ing the early stages of formation. If they do not rupture within a few hours, the contents rapidly become purulent in appearance. The lesions appear on the trunk and face, and rapidly spread centrifugally to involve other areas of the body. Successive crops of lesions generally appear over a period of 2 to 4 days. Thus, early in the disease, the hallmark of the infection is the appearance of lesions at all stages, as noted previously. The lesions can also be found on the mucosa of the oropharynx and even the vagina; however, these sites are less commonly involved. The crusts completely fall off within 1 to 2 weeks after the onset of infection and leave a slightly depressed area of skin.

Immunocompromised children, particularly those with leukemia, have more numerous lesions, often with a hemorrhagic base. Healing takes nearly three times longer in this population.[40] These children are at greater risk for visceral complications, which occur in 30% to 50% of cases and can be fatal in as many as 15% of cases in the absence of therapy. A notable complication of cutaneous lesions is secondary bacterial infection, often in association with gram-positive organisms. Streptococcal toxic shock is a rare but potentially lethal complication of varicella. Infection in the neutropenic host can be systemic.

The most frequent noncutaneous site of involvement after chickenpox is the central nervous system (CNS); the neurologic abnormalities are manifested as acute cerebellar ataxia or encephalitis.[29,45-47] Cerebellar ataxia has been estimated to occur in 1 in 4000 cases among children younger than 15 years. Cerebellar ataxia can appear as late as 21 days after the onset of rash. It is more common, however, for acute cerebellar ataxia to present within 1 week of the onset of the exanthem. An extensive review by Underwood[47] of 120 cases demonstrated that ataxia, vomiting, altered speech, fever, vertigo, and tremor all were common on physical examination. Cerebrospinal fluid (CSF) from these patients often demonstrates lymphocytosis and elevated levels of protein. This is usually a benign complication in children, and resolution occurs within 2 to 4 weeks. PCR techniques can detect VZV DNA in the CSF.[48]

A more serious CNS complication is encephalitis, which can be life threatening in adults. Encephalitis is reported to occur in 0.1% to 0.2% of persons with the disease.[49] Underwood's[47] review reveals this illness to be characterized by depression in the level of consciousness with progressive headaches, vomiting, altered thought patterns, fever, and frequent seizures. The duration of disease in these patients is at least 2 weeks. Some patients experience progressive neurologic deterioration that leads to death. Mortality in patients who develop encephalitis has been estimated to range between 5% and 20%, and neurologic sequelae occur in as many as 15% of survivors.

A neurologic complication of note is the late appearance of cerebral angiitis after herpes zoster ophthalmicus. This problem has been noted in several patients and defined as being progressive, with a high mortality rate. Other nervous system manifestations of chickenpox include meningitis, transverse myelitis, and Reye's syndrome.

A serious and life-threatening complication is the appearance of varicella pneumonitis, a complication that occurs more commonly in adults and in immunocompromised persons.[29,45,50] Among adults, it is estimated to occur in 1 in 400 cases of infection and, not infrequently, in the absence of clinical symptoms, it appears 3 to 5 days into the course of illness and is associated with tachypnea, cough, dyspnea, and fever. Chest radiographs usually reveal nodular or interstitial pneumonitis. Varicella pneumonitis can be life threatening when it occurs in pregnant women during the second or third trimester.

In a prospective study of male military personnel, radiographic abnormalities were detected in nearly 16% of enlisted men who developed varicella, yet only one fourth of these persons had evidence of cough.[51] Only 10% of those with radiographic abnormalities developed evidence of tachypnea, indicating that asymptomatic pneumonitis may exist more commonly than was initially predicted. Other manifestations of noncutaneous and non-neurologic involvement include the appearance of myocarditis, nephritis, bleeding diatheses, and hepatitis.

Perinatal varicella is associated with a high death rate when maternal disease develops 5 days before delivery or up to 48 hours postpartum.[52,53] In large part, this is the consequence of the newborn failing to receive protective transplacental antibodies as well as the immaturity of the neonatal immune system. Under such circumstances, the mortality has been reported to be as high as 30%. Affected children have progressive disease involving visceral organs, especially the lung. The outcome in these children was summarized by Brunell.[54] Congenital varicella, while uncommon, is characterized by skin scarring, hypoplastic extremities, eye abnormalities, and evidence of CNS impairment.[55]

Varicella has been associated epidemiologically with the development of Reye's syndrome and coadministration of aspirin. Therefore, the administration of aspirin is contraindicated in persons with varicella.

Chickenpox in the Immunocompromised Patient

Chickenpox in the immunocompromised child or adult is a cause of significant morbidity and mortality. As noted previously, the duration of healing of cutaneous lesions can be extended by a minimum of threefold. However, a more important problem is the progressive involvement of visceral organs. Data from a variety of immunocompromised patient populations indicate a broad spectrum of disease in persons with lymphoproliferative malignancies and solid tumors versus bone marrow transplant recipients. Approximately one third of children develop progressive disease with involvement of multiple organs, including the lungs, liver, and CNS.[40] Most of these children developed pneumonitis within the first week after the onset of infection, as do 20% of all of those who acquire chickenpox. Mortality in this patient population has approximated 15% to 18%.[40,58,59] Patients with lymphoproliferative malignancies who require continuous chemotherapy appear to be at the greatest risk for visceral involvement.

In persons undergoing human stem cell transplantation, the incidence of VZV infections over the first year has been estimated to be 30% by 1 year after transplantation. Eighty percent of these infections occurred within the first 9 months after transplantation, and 45% of these patients had cutaneous or visceral dissemination (see Chapter 311). Overall, 23 deaths occurred in one prospective series.[60] Risk factors identified for the acquisition of VZV infection included an age between 10 and 29 years, a diagnosis other than chronic myelogenous leukemia, the post-transplant use of antithymocyte globulin, allogenic transplant, and acute or chronic graft-versus-host disease. Notably, graft-versus-host disease increases the probability of visceral dissemination significantly.

Herpes Zoster

Herpes zoster, or shingles, is characterized by a unilateral vesicular eruption with a dermatomal distribution. Thoracic and lumbar dermatomes are most commonly involved. Herpes zoster may involve the eyelids when the first or second branch of the fifth cranial nerve is affected, but herpes zoster ophthalmicus is a sight-threatening condition. Although lesions on the tip of the nose are said to presage corneal lesions, absence of such skin lesions does not guarantee corneal sparing. Keratitis may be followed by severe iridocyclitis, secondary glaucoma, or neuroparalytic keratitis. Ophthalmologic consultation should be requested for any patient with suspected herpes zoster ophthalmicus. Generally, the onset of disease is heralded by pain within the dermatome that precedes the lesions by 48 to 72 hours. Early in the disease course, erythematous, maculopapular lesions appear that rapidly evolve into a vesicular rash. Vesicles may coalesce to form bullous lesions. In the normal host, these lesions continue to form over a period of 3 to 5 days, with the total duration of disease being 10 to 15 days. However, it may take as long as 1 month before the skin returns to normal.

Unusual cutaneous manifestations of herpes zoster, in addition to herpes zoster ophthalmicus, include the involvement of the maxillary or mandibular branch of the trigeminal nerve, which results in intraoral involvement with lesions on the palate, tonsillar fossa, floor of the mouth, and tongue. When the geniculate ganglion is involved, the Ramsay Hunt syndrome may occur, with pain and vesicles in the external auditory meatus, loss of taste on the anterior two thirds of the tongue, and ipsilateral facial palsy.

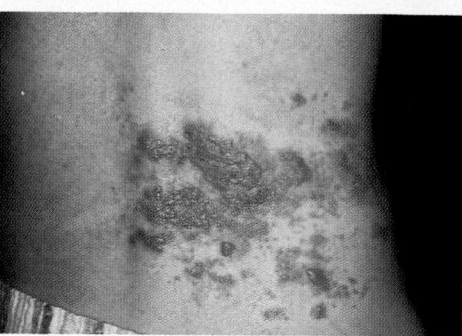

FIGURE 133-1. Herpes zoster involving the lumbar dermatome.

No known factors are responsible for the precipitation of the episodes of herpes zoster. If herpes zoster occurs in children, the course is generally benign and not associated with progressive pain or discomfort. In adults, systemic manifestations are mainly those associated with pain, as noted in the following paragraphs.

The most significant clinical manifestations of herpes zoster are the associated acute neuritis and, later, postherpetic neuralgia. Modeling of pain attributed to herpes zoster defines three phases of disease: acute, subacute, and chronic.[61] Historically, the latter two compose postherpetic neuralgia. As identified later, the impact of therapy on each phase can be defined. Postherpetic neuralgia, although uncommon in young people, may occur in as many as 25% to 50% of patients older than 50 years.[62-64] As many as 50% of persons older than 50 years have debilitating pain that persists for more than 1 month. Postherpetic neuralgia may cause constant pain in the involved dermatome or consist of intermittent stabbing pain. Pain may be worse at night or on exposure to temperature changes, and at its worst, the neuralgia can be incapacitating.[65]

Extracutaneous sites of involvement include the CNS, as manifested by meningoencephalitis or encephalitis. The clinical manifestations are similar to those of other viral infections of the brain. However, a rare manifestation of CNS involvement by herpes zoster is granulomatous cerebral angiitis, which usually follows zoster ophthalmicus. Involvement of the CNS with cutaneous herpes zoster probably is more common than recognized clinically. Frequently, patients who undergo CSF examination for other reasons during episodes of shingles are found to have evidence of pleocytosis without elevated protein levels. These patients are without signs of meningeal irritation and infrequently complain of headaches.

Classically, VZV infection involves dorsal root ganglia. Motor paralysis can occur as a consequence of the involvement of the anterior horn cells, in a manner similar to that encountered with polio. Patients with involvement of the anterior horn cells are particularly likely to have excruciating pain. Other neuromuscular disorders associated with herpes zoster include Guillain-Barré syndrome, transverse myelitis,[66] and myositis.[67,68]

Herpes zoster in the immunocompromised patient is more severe than in the normal person. Lesion formation continues for up to 2 weeks, and scabbing may not take place until 3 to 4 weeks into the disease course.[43] Patients with lymphoproliferative malignancies are at risk for cutaneous dissemination and visceral involvement, including varicella pneumonitis, hepatitis, and meningoencephalitis. However, even in the immunocompromised patient, disseminated herpes zoster is rarely fatal.

In recent years, herpes zoster has been recognized as a frequent infection in persons with human immunodeficiency virus (HIV) infection, occurring in 8% to 11% of patients. Although the occurrence of cutaneous dissemination is infrequent, complications such as VZV retinitis, acute retinal necrosis, and chronic progressive encephalitis have been reported.[69]

Chronic herpes zoster may also occur in immunocompromised patients, particularly those persons with a diagnosis of HIV infection.

Patients have experienced new lesion formation with an absence of healing of the existing lesions. These syndromes can be particularly debilitating and, of interest, have been associated with the isolation of VZV isolates resistant to acyclovir.

DIAGNOSIS

The diagnosis of both chickenpox and shingles is usually made by history and physical examination. In the latter part of the 20th century, the differential diagnosis of varicella and herpes zoster is less confusing than it was 20 to 30 years ago. Smallpox or disseminated vaccinia was confused with varicella because of the similar appearance of the cutaneous lesions and could again pose a problem in the era of bioterrorism. With the worldwide eradication of smallpox, these disease entities only serve to confound the diagnosis if used by a bioterrorist or as a complication of vaccination. The characteristic skin rash of chickenpox with lesions in all stages of development provides the basis for the clinical diagnosis of infection. The presence of pruritus, pain, and low-grade fever also helps to establish a diagnosis of chickenpox. The localization and distribution of a vesicular rash make the diagnosis of herpes zoster highly likely; however, other viral exanthemas can occasionally be confused with this disease.

Impetigo and varicella can also be confused clinically. Impetigo is usually caused by group A β-hemolytic streptococci, often follows an abrasion of the skin or inoculation of bacteria at the site of the skin break, and can be associated with the formation of small vesicles in the surrounding area. Systemic signs of disease may be present if progressive cellulitis or secondary bacteremia develops. Unroofing lesions and careful Gram staining of the scraping of the base of the lesion should reveal gram-positive cocci in chains, which is suggestive of streptococci, or gram-positive cocci in clusters, which is suggestive of staphylococci, another cause of vesicular skin lesions. Treatment for these latter infections is distinctly different from that for chickenpox and requires administration of an appropriate antibiotic.

In a smaller number of cases, disseminated vesicular lesions can be caused by HSV. In these cases, disseminated HSV infection is usually a consequence of an underlying skin disease such as atopic dermatitis or eczema. An unequivocal diagnosis can be made only by isolation of the virus in tissue culture.

More recently, disseminated enteroviral infections, particularly those caused by group A coxsackieviruses, have been reported to cause widespread distal vesicular lesions. These rashes are more commonly morbilliform in nature, with a hemorrhagic component rather than vesicular or vesiculopustular appearance. Generally, these infections occur during the enterovirus season in late summer and early fall and are associated with lesions of the oropharynx, palms, and soles. This latter finding is helpful in distinguishing enteroviral disease from chickenpox.

Unilateral vesicular lesions in the dermatomal pattern should immediately lead the clinician to suspect a diagnosis of shingles. HSV and coxsackievirus infections can also cause dermatomal vesicular lesions. In such situations, diagnostic viral cultures remain the best method of establishing the cause of infection. Confirmation of the diagnosis is possible through the isolation of VZV in susceptible tissue culture cell lines or by the demonstration of either seroconversion or serologic rises using standard antibody assays of acute and convalescent serum specimens. A Tzanck smear, performed by scraping the base of the lesion, can demonstrate multinucleated giant cells; however, the sensitivity of this test is no better than 60%. Commercially available reagents are useful for direct fluorescent antibody staining of smears obtained from scraping vesicular lesions. With atypical skin lesions, such smears have adequate sensitivity and specificity to guide early management decisions. In research laboratories, PCR is a useful diagnostic tool; however, its expense and lack of uniform performance standards preclude routine diagnostic use. Useful antibody assays include immune adherence hemagglutination assay, fluorescence antibody to membrane antigen (FAMA) assay, or enzyme-linked immunosorbent assay (ELISA).[70] The application of PCR to the CSF can be used to detect VZV DNA and, therefore, infections of the CNS.

THERAPY

The medical management of chickenpox and shingles in the normal host is directed toward reduction of complications. For chickenpox, hygiene is important, including bathing, astringent soaks, and closely cropped fingernails to avoid a source for secondary bacterial infection associated with scratching of the pruritic skin lesions. Pruritus can be decreased with topical dressing or the administration of antipruritic drugs. Aluminum acetate or soaks with Burow's solution in the management of herpes zoster can be both soothing and cleansing.[71] Acetaminophen should be used to reduce fever in patients with chickenpox because of the association between aspirin and Reye's syndrome.

Acyclovir is approved in the United States for the treatment of both chickenpox and herpes zoster in the normal host. Oral acyclovir therapy in normal children, adolescents, and adults shortens the duration of lesion formation by about 1 day, reduces the total number of new lesions by approximately 25%, and diminishes constitutional symptoms in one third of patients.[71-74] The American Academy of Pediatrics recommends therapy for adolescents and adults as well as for high-risk groups of patients (e.g., premature infants, children with bronchopulmonary dysplasia) within 24 hours of onset of disease. In children 2 to 16 years old, the oral dosage is 20 mg/kg 4 times daily for 5 days (maximum of 800 mg daily). Adolescents and adults can receive up to 800 mg 5 times a day. Oral therapy of herpes zoster in the normal host accelerates cutaneous healing and reduces acute neuritis.

Acyclovir has been evaluated in controlled studies for all herpesvirus infections. Acyclovir is a guanine derivative that has a high degree of selectivity for the inhibition of VZV replication because of its selected phosphorylation and activation by the virus-coded thymidine kinase and its subsequent selective inhibition of the viral DNA polymerase. It is estimated that the concentration of acyclovir required to inhibit VZV replication in vitro is between 2.1 and 6.3 μM, which is a concentration easily achieved after intravenous administration of acyclovir.[75] However, such concentrations are not easily achieved even after administration of high-dose oral acyclovir as summarized.[76] The recommended dosage for acyclovir is from 5 to 10 mg/kg administered intravenously every 8 hours or, as suggested by some, 500 mg/m² intravenously every 8 hours, especially for children.

The prodrugs of acyclovir and penciclovir, namely, valaciclovir and famciclovir, respectively, have been licensed for therapy of herpes zoster.[77,78] The use of valaciclovir results in enhanced oral bioavailability, approximately 60%, compared with acyclovir. Famciclovir's oral bioavailability is approximately 80%. Both drugs appear superior to acyclovir for acceleration of cutaneous healing and are at least equally, if not more, efficacious for resolution of pain. Valaciclovir is administered at 1 g 3 times daily for 7 to 10 days.[77] Famciclovir is given at 500 mg 3 times daily for 7 to 10 days.[77] Both medications are well tolerated. These medications primarily affect the acute and subacute phases of diseases, as cited in the model earlier.

The concomitant administration of corticosteroids and an antiviral remains controversial. In one study, such regimens failed to affect postherpetic neuralgia, although resolution of acute neuritis was accelerated.[79] This study was not placebo controlled. A placebo-controlled trial, using a 2 × 2 factorial design, demonstrated significant improvement in quality of life.[80] Patients older than 50 years who received acyclovir (800 mg 5 times daily for 3 weeks) and tapering doses of prednisone (60 mg daily for 7 days, 30 mg daily for 7 days, and 15 mg daily for 7 days) experienced resolution of acute neuritis, were able to sleep uninterrupted, and returned to their usual activity levels more promptly than controls and also had lower analgesic requirements. Complications were not encountered; however, patients at risk for complications of high-dose steroid therapy were excluded.

Management of varicella pneumonitis and other complications requires excellent supportive nursing care in addition to evaluation, on an individual basis, of the potential need for antiviral therapy. The management of acute neuritis and postherpetic neuralgia can be particularly problematic. It requires the judicious use of analgesics ranging from non-narcotic to narcotic derivatives and may include the deployment of such drugs as amitriptyline hydrochloride, fluphenazine hydrochloride, lidocaine patches, and gabapentin.[81-83] Further, intrathecal administration of narcotics has been reported to be of value.[84]

PREVENTION

In the normal host, prophylaxis of chickenpox is achieved via vaccination. The potential for transmission of VZV within the hospital to immunosuppressed patients, particularly children, is a serious problem, which is discussed in detail in Chapter 305. Patients who require hospitalization because of varicella are a source of nosocomial infection within the hospital environment. Because approximately 10% of adults are seronegative, the risks in the medical care environment can be high. Those most likely to become infected are nurses and other medical personnel providing care to infected persons. Airflow can be documented as a means of transmission of infection from one area to another in the hospital environment.

In the immunocompromised person who has not been previously exposed to chickenpox, the administration of varicella-zoster immune globulin (VZIG) and varicella-zoster immune plasma (ZIP) has been shown to be useful for both prevention and amelioration of symptomatic chickenpox in high-risk persons.[85-88] VZIG should be administered to the immunodeficient patient younger than 15 years who has a negative or unknown history of chickenpox, who has not been vaccinated against VZV, or who has had contact in the household with a playmate or in a shared hospital room for more than 1 hour. Recent guidelines also recommend administration of VZIG to a pregnant woman who is known to be seronegative and who has had a significant exposure. VZIG should also be administered to a newborn infant whose mother had onset of chickenpox less than 5 days before delivery or up to 48 hours postpartum. The use of VZIG for susceptible immunocompetent persons older than 15 years must be evaluated on an individual basis.

A vaccine is licensed for the prevention of chickenpox in immunocompetent persons.[89-93] Studies performed to date indicate protection after vaccination. The Oka strain of VZV was developed by Takahashi and colleagues in Japan and studied as a vaccine extensively in both healthy and leukemic children. In immunocompromised children, serologic evidence of host response after vaccination has been achieved in between 89% and 100% of vaccinated individuals. Vaccine-induced rash, however, is not uncommon and occurs in variable percentages of patients from approximately 6% to as high as 47%. The factor most predictive of the appearance of rash is the degree of immunosuppression. Specifically, for children with acute lymphoblastic leukemia, the likelihood of rash can be as high as 40% to 50%. The subsequent occurrence of natural varicella after community exposure is decreased in the larger control studies and averages 8% to 16%. Vaccination did not appear to increase the likelihood of subsequent herpes zoster during the period of follow-up.

Similar studies have been performed in healthy children and have led to the recommendation by ACIP of routine childhood vaccination.[23] In clinical trials, the development of antibody responses was higher than in the immunocompromised host and varied between 94% and 100%. Vaccine-induced rash was far less common in these individuals and occurred at a frequency of 0.5% to approximately 19% overall, with the rate for subsequent appearance of varicella after community exposure averaging between 1% and 5%. The impact of this vaccine is now being appreciated as documented in sentinel cities where the incidence of chickenpox has fallen dramatically.[96,97]

This vaccine might be useful for boosting immunity in older persons as a mechanism to prevent herpes zoster infection; this hypothesis is currently being tested. Notably, the risk of subsequent development of herpes zoster does not appear to be increased in vaccine recipients.[98] Further, the use of an inactivated OKA vaccine has proved to be successful in decreasing the incidence of herpes zoster after human stem cell transplantation.[99]

REFERENCES

1. Seward JF, Watson BM, Peterson CL, et al. Varicella disease after introduction of varicella vaccine in the United States, 1995-2000. JAMA. 2002;287;505-611.
2. Gordon JE, Meader FM. The period of infectivity and serum prevention of chickenpox. JAMA. 1929;93:2013.
3. Steiner P. Zur Inokulation der Varicellen. Wien Med Wochenschr. 1875;25:306.
4. von Bokay J. Das Auftreten der Schafblattern unter besonderen Umstanden. Unger Arch Med. 1892;1:159.
5. von Bokay J. Uber den atiologischen Zusammenhang der Varizellen mit Gewissen fallen von herpes zoster. Wien Klin Wochenschr. 1909;22:1323.
6. Kundratitz K. Experimentelle ubertragungen von herpes zoster auf menschen und die beziehungen von herpes zoster zu varicellen. Z Kinderheilkd. 1925;39:379.
7. Brunsgaard E. The mutual relation between zoster and varicella. Br J Dermatol Syph. 1932;44:1.
8. School Epidemics Committee of Great Britain. Epidemics in Schools. Medical Research Council. Special Report Series, No. 227. London: His Majesty's Stationery Office; 1938.
9. Garland J. Varicella following exposure to herpes zoster. N Engl J Med. 1943;228:336.
10. Seiler HE. A study of herpes zoster particularly in its relationship to chickenpox. J Hyg. 1949;47:253-262.
11. Weller TH, Witton HM. The etiologic agents of varicella and herpes zoster: Serologic studies with the viruses as propagated in vitro. J Exp Med. 1958;228:336-337.
12. Tyzzer EE. The histology of the skin lesions in varicella. Philippine J Sci. 1906;1:349.
13. Lipschutz B. Untersuchungen uber die Atiologies der Krankheiten der Herpesgruppe (Herpes Zoster, Herpes Genitalis, Herpes Febrilis). Arch Dermatol Syph. 1921;136:428.
14. Weller TH. Serial propagation in vitro of agents producing inclusion bodies derived from varicella and herpes zoster. Proc Soc Exp Biol Med. 1953;83:340-346.
15. Weller TH, Coons AH. Fluorescent antibody studies with agents of varicella and herpes zoster propagated in vitro. Proc Soc Exp Biol Med. 1954;86:789.
16. Weller TH, Stoddard MB. Intranuclear inclusion bodies in cultures of human tissue inoculated with varicella vesicle fluid. J Immunol. 1952;68:311.
17. Davison AJ, Scott JE. The complete DNA sequence of varicella-zoster virus. J Gen Virol. 1986;67:1759-1816.
18. Sawyer MH, Ostrove JM, Felser JM, et al. Mapping of the varicella-zoster virus deoxypyrimidine kinase gene and preliminary identification of its transcript. Virology. 1986;149:1-9.
19. Dumas AM, Geelen JL, Mares W, et al. Infectivity and molecular weight of varicella-zoster virus DNA. J Gen Virol. 1980;47:233-235.
20. Achong BC, Meurisse EV. Observations on the fine structure and replication of varicella virus in cultivated human amnion cells. J Gen Virol. 1968;3:305.
21. Almeida JD, Howatson AF, Williams MG. Morphology of varicella (chickenpox) virus. Virology. 1962;16:353.
22. Tournier P, Cathala F, Bernhard W. Ultrastructure et developement intracellulaire du virus de la varicelle. Observe ou microscope electronique. Presse Med. 1957;65:1229.
23. Straus SE, Ostrove JM, Inchauspe G. Varicella-zoster virus infections: Biology, natural history, treatment and prevention. Ann Intern Med. 1988;108:221-237.
24. Gelb L. Varicella-zoster virus. In: Fields B, Knipe DM, eds. Virology. New York: Raven Press; 1990:2011-2054.
25. Arvin AM. Varicella-zoster virus. In: Fields BN, Knipe DM, Howley PM, et al, eds. Fields Virology. 3rd ed. New York: Lippincott-Raven; 1996:2547.
26. Rapp F, Vanderslice D. Spread of zoster virus in human embryonic lung cells and the inhibitory effect of idoxyuridine. Virology. 1964;22:321.
27. Vaczi L, Geder L, Koller M, et al. Influence of temperature on the multiplication of varicella virus. Acta Microbiol Acad Sci Hung. 1963;10:109.
28. Grose C, Perrotta DM, Brunell PA, et al. Cell-free varicella-zoster virus in cultured human melanoma cells. J Gen Virol. 1979;43:15.
29. Preblud SR. Varicella: Complications and costs. Pediatrics. 1986;78:728-735.
30. Wells MW, Holla WA. Ventilation in the flow of measles and chickenpox through a community. JAMA. 1950;142:1337.
31. Preblud SR, Orenstein WA, Bart KJ. Varicella: Clinical manifestations, epidemiology, and health impact in children. Pediatr Infect Dis. 1984;3:505-509.
32. Hope-Simpson RE. Infectiousness of communicable diseases in the household (measles, chickenpox, and mumps). Lancet. 1952;2:549.
33. Ross AH. Modification of chickenpox in family contacts by administration of gamma globulin. N Engl J Med. 1962;267:369-376.
34. Stokes J Jr. Chickenpox. Communicable diseases transmitted chiefly through respiratory and alimentary tracts. In: Preventive Medicine in World War II. v. 4. Washington, DC: Department of the Army; 1958:55.
35. Bastian FO, Rabson AS, Yee CL, et al. Herpesvirus varicellae: Isolated from human dorsal root ganglia. Arch Pathol. 1974;97:331.
36. Esiri MM, Tomlinson AH. Herpes zoster: Demonstration of virus in trigeminal nerve and ganglion by immunofluorescence and electron microscopy. J Neurol Sci. 1972;15:35.
37. Ragozzino MW, Melton LJ III, Kurland LT, et al. Population-based study of herpes zoster and its sequelae. Medicine (Balt.) 1982;51:310-316.
38. Hope-Simpson RE. The nature of herpes zoster: A long-term study and a new hypothesis. Proc R Soc Med. 1965;58:9.
39. McGregor RM. Herpes zoster, chickenpox, and cancer in general practice. Br Med J. 1957;1:84.
40. Feldman S, Hughes WT, Daniel CB. Varicella in children with cancer: Seventy-seven cases. Pediatrics. 1975;56:388-397.

41. Arvin AM, Pollard RB, Rasmussen LE, et al. Cellular and humoral immunity in the pathogenesis of recurrent herpes viral infections in patients with lymphoma. J Clin Invest. 1980;68:869-878.

42. Locksley RM, Flournoy N, Sullivan KM, et al. Infection with varicella-zoster virus after marrow transplantation. J Infect Dis. 1985;152:1172-1181.

43. Whitley RJ. Varicella-zoster infections. In: Galasso G, Merigan T, Buchanan R, eds. Antiviral Agents and Viral Infections of Man. New York: Raven Press; 1984:517-541.

44. Asano Y, Itakura N, Hiroishi Y, et al. Viremia is present in incubation period in non-immunocompromised children with varicella. J Pediatr. 1985;106:69-71.

45. Fleisher G, Henry W, McSorley M, et al. Life-threatening complications of varicella. Am J Dis Child. 1981;135:896-899.

46. Johnson R, Milbourne PE. Central nervous system manifestations of chickenpox. Can Med Assoc J. 1970;102:831-834.

47. Underwood EA. The neurological complications of varicella: A clinical and epidemiological study. Br J Child Dis. 1935;32:83,177,241.

48. Burke DG, Kalayjian RC, Vann VR, et al. Polymerase chain reaction detection and clinical significance of varicella-zoster virus in cerebrospinal fluid from human immunodeficiency virus-infected patients. J Infect Dis. 1996;176:1080.

49. Johnson R, Milbourn PE. Central nervous system manifestations of chickenpox. Can Med J. 1970;102:831.

50. Triebwasser JH, Harrie RE, Bryant RE, et al. Varicella pneumonia in adults: Report of seven cases and a review of literature. Medicine (Balt..) 1967;46:409-423.

51. Weber DM, Pellechia JA. Varicella pneumonia. JAMA. 1965;192:572.

52. Brunell PA. Fetal and neonatal varicella zoster infections. Semin Perinatol. 1983;7:47-56.

53. Preblud SR, Bregman DJ, Vernon LL. Deaths from varicella in infants. Pediatr Infect Dis. 1985;4:503-507.

54. Brunell PA. Placental transfer of varicella-zoster antibody. Pediatrics. 1966;38:1034.

55. Paryani SG, Arvin AM. Intrauterine infection with varicella zoster virus after maternal varicella. N Engl J Med. 1986;314:1542-1546.

56. Linnemann CC, Shea L, Partin JC, et al. Reye's syndrome: Epidemiologic and viral studies. Am J Epidemiol. 1975;101:517.

57. Hilty M, Romshe CA, Delamater PV. Reye's syndrome and hyperaminoacidemia. J Pediatr. 1974;84:362.

58. Arvin AM, Kushner JH, Feldman S, et al. Human leukocyte interferon for treatment of varicella in children with cancer. N Engl J Med. 1982;306:761.

59. Whitley RJ, Soong SJ, Dolin R, et al. Early vidarabine therapy to control the complications of herpes in immunosuppressed patients. N Engl J Med. 1982;307:971.

60. Loxley RM, Flournoy N, Sullivan KM, et al. Infection with varicella-zoster virus after marrow transplantation. J Infect Dis. 1985;6:1172-1181.

61. Arani RB, Soong S-J, Weiss HL, et al. Phase specific analysis of herpes zoster associated pain data: A new statistical approach. Stat Med. 2001; 20:2429-2439.

62. deMoragas JM, Kierland RR. The outcome of patients with herpes zoster. Arch Dermatol. 1957;73:193-196.

63. Watson PN, Evans RJ. Postherpetic neuralgia: A review. Arch Neurol. 1986;43:836-840.

64. Esmann V, Kroon S, Petersblund NA, et al. Prednisolone does not prevent post-herpetic neuralgia. Lancet. 1987;2:126-129.

65. Kost RG, Straus SE. Drug therapy: Postherpetic neuralgia—pathogenesis, treatment, and prevention. N Engl J Med. 1996;335:32.

66. Hogan EL, Krigman MR. Herpes zoster myelitis. Arch Neurol. 1973;29:309.

67. Norris FH, Dramov B, Calder CD, et al. Virus-like particles in myositis accompanying herpes zoster. Arch Neurol. 1969;21:25.

68. Rubin D, Fusfeld RD. Muscle paralysis in herpes zoster. Calif Med. 1965;103:261.

69. Gnann JW, Whitley RJ. Natural history and treatment of varicella-zoster in high risk populations. J Hosp Infect. 1991;18:317-329.

70. Forghani B, Schmidt NJ, Dennis J. Antibody assays for varicella-zoster virus; comparison of enzyme immunoassay with neutralization, immune adherence hemagglutination and complement fixation. J Clin Microbiol. 1978;8:545-552.

71. Balfour HH, Kelly JM, Suarez, CS, et al. Acyclovir treatment of varicella in otherwise healthy children. J Pediatr. 1990;116:633-639.

72. Dunkle LM, Arvin LM, Whitley RJ, et al. A controlled trial of acyclovir for chickenpox in the normal host. N Engl J Med. 1991;325:1539-1544.

73. Balfour HH, Dunkle LM, Feder HM, et al. Acyclovir treatment in otherwise healthy adolescents. J Pediatr. 1992;120:627-633.

74. Wallace MR, Bowler WA, Murray NB, et al. Treatment of adult varicella with oral acyclovir. A randomized, placebo-controlled trial. Ann Intern Med. 1992;117:358-363.

75. Huff JC, Bean B, Balfour HH, et al. Therapy of herpes zoster with oral acyclovir. Am J Med. 1988;85(2A):84-89.

76. Whitley RJ, Gnann JW. Acyclovir: A decade later. N Engl J Med. 1992;327:782-789.

77. Beutner KR, Friedman DJ, Forszpaniak C, et al. Valaciclovir compared with acyclovir for improved therapy for herpes zoster in immunocompetent adults. Antimicrob Agents Chemother. 1995;39:1546.

78. Tyring S, Barbarash, RA, Nahlik JE, et al. Famciclovir for the treatment of acute herpes zoster: Effects on acute disease and postherpetic neuralgia. A randomized, double-blind, placebo-controlled trial. Collaborative Famciclovir Herpes Zoster Study Group. Ann Intern Med. 1995;123:89.

79. Wood MJ, Johnson RW, McKendrick MW, et al. A randomized trial of acyclovir for 7 days or 21 days with and without prednisolone for treatment of acute herpes zoster. N Engl J Med. 1994;330:896.

80. Whitley RJ, Weiss H, Gnann JW Jr, et al. Acyclovir with and without prednisone for the treatment of herpes zoster. A randomized placebo-controlled trial. The National Institute of Allergy and Infectious Diseases Collaborative Antiviral Study Group. Ann Intern Med. 1996;125:831.

81. Dworkin RH, Schmader KE. Treatment and prevention of postherpetic neuralgia. Clin Infect Dis. 2003;36:877-882.

82. Rowbotham M, Harden N, Stacey B, et al. Gabapentin for the treatment of postherpetic neuralgia. A randomized controlled trial. JAMA 1998; 280:1837-1842.

83. Galer BS, Jensen MP, Ma T, Davies PS, Rowbotham MC. The lidocaine patch 5% effectively treats all neuropathic pain qualities: results of a randomized, double-blind, vehicle-controlled, 3-week efficacy study with use of the neuropathic pain scale. Clin J Pain 2002; 18:297-301.

84. Gnann JW, Whitley RJ. Herpes zoster. N Engl J Med. 2002;347:340-346.

85. Brunell PA, Ross A, Miller LH, et al. Prevention of varicella by zoster immune globulin. N Engl J Med. 1969;280:1191-1194.

86. Gershon AA, Steinberg S, Brunell PA. Zoster immune globulin: A further assessment. N Engl J Med. 1974;290:243-245.

87. Zaia J, Levin MJ, Preblud SR, et al. Evaluation of varicella zoster immune globulin: Protection of immunosuppressed children after household exposure to varicella. J Infect Dis. 1983;147:737-743.

88. Centers for Disease Control and Prevention. Varicella zoster immune globulin for the prevention of chickenpox: Recommendations of the immunization practices advisory committee. Ann Intern Med. 1984;100:859-865.

89. Takahashi M, Otsuka T, Okuno Y, et al. Live vaccine used to prevent the spread of varicella in children in hospital. Lancet. 1974;2:1288-1290.

90. Gershon AA, Steinberg SP, Gelb L. Live attenuated varicella vaccine use in immunocompromised children and adults. Pediatrics. 1986;78:757-762.

91. Takahashi M. Clinical overview of varicella vaccine: Development and early studies. Pediatrics. 1986;78:736-741.

92. Yabuuchi H, Baba K, Tsuda N, et al. A live varicella vaccine in a pediatric community. Biken J. 1984;27:43-49.

93. Horiuchi K. Chickenpox vaccination of healthy children: Immunological and clinical responses and protective effect in 1978-1982. Biken J. 1984;27:37-38.

94. Weibel RE, Neff BJ, Kutter BJ, et al. Live attenuated varicella virus vaccine: Efficacy trial in healthy children. N Engl J Med. 1984;310:1409-1415.

95. Asano Y, Nagai T, Miyata T, et al. Long-term protective immunity of recipients of the OKA strain of live varicella vaccine. Pediatrics. 1985;75:667-671.

96. Seward JF, Watson BM, Peterson CL, et al. Varicella disease after introduction of varicella vaccine in the United States, 1995-2000. JAMA 2002; 287:606-611.

97. Anonymous. Prevention of varicella. Update recommendations of the Advisory Committee on Immunization Practices (ACIP). MMWR 1999;48 (RR-6):1-5.

98. Lawrence R, Gershon AA, Holzman R, et al. The risk of zoster after vaccination in children with leukemia. N Engl J Med. 1988;318:543-548.

99. Hata A, Asanuma H, Rinki M, et al. Use of an inactivated varicella vaccine in recipients of hematopoietic-cell transplants. N Engl J Med. 2002;347:26-34.

CHAPTER **134**

Cytomegalovirus

CLYDE S. CRUMPACKER

SANJIVINI WADHWA

Human cytomegalovirus (HCMV), a β herpes virus (see Chapter 131), is the largest virus to infect human beings. Its genome is sufficient to encode 230 proteins, many of which play a significant role in downregulation of the immune response. Infection is common in all human populations, reaching 60% to 70% in U.S. cities[1] and nearly 100% in some parts of Africa. Disease is varied in humans infected with CMV, ranging from no disease in normal hosts and congenital CMV syndrome in neonates (which is frequently fatal) to the infectious mononucleosis syndrome in young adults. In the immunocompromised patient, CMV produces its most significant and severe disease syndromes in lung, liver, kidney, and heart transplant recipients. CMV, the most common opportunistic pathogen detected, causes significant mortality and morbidity.[2] In bone marrow transplant recipients, CMV pneumonia is the most common life-threatening infectious complication after transplantation.[3] In patients with the acquired immunodeficiency syndrome (AIDS), CMV is the most common viral pathogen, and CMV retinitis is the most frequent sight-threatening infection even in the era of highly active antiretroviral therapy.[4] Fortunately, effective therapies for the treatment and prevention of serious CMV disease in immunocompromised patients are being established, and principles for the use of these therapies are becoming more clear.[5]

As with all herpesviruses, CMV has the ability to establish latent infection in the host after recovery from acute infection. The exact mechanisms that control latency are unclear, but polymorphonuclear cells, T lymphocytes, endothelial vascular tissue, renal epithelial cells, and salivary glands may all harbor the virus in a nonreplicating or slowly replicating form. Activation from this latent state can occur after immunosuppression, other illness, or the use of chemotherapeutic agents.[6]

Both primary and secondary infection with CMV can occur. Primary infection occurs in seronegative patients who have never been infected with CMV. Secondary infection represents activation of a latent infection or reinfection in a seropositive immune person. Both infants and adults can be infected with multiple strains. Several different strains of CMV have been found at the same time in the urine of patients with AIDS.[7] Clinical CMV disease can result from either primary or secondary infection; in primary infection, virus usually replicates to a higher level and disease is more severe. Congenital infection of the neonate within the mother's womb is almost always the result of primary infection of the mother during pregnancy.[8]

The emphasis in this chapter is on the clinical manifestations of CMV disease and the mechanisms of pathogenesis. Treatment and prevention with antiviral drugs have greatly changed the way CMV disease is managed in the immunocompromised patient; this development is highlighted. Limitations of antiviral therapy such as resistance to antiviral drugs are discussed.

DESCRIPTION OF THE PATHOGEN

The era of modern virology of CMV began with the isolation of murine CMV.[9] Shortly after this time, the isolation of human CMV was reported by three independent groups led by Smith, Weller, Rowe, and colleagues.[10-12] Human CMV was isolated from the human salivary gland, and the term *cytomegalovirus* was first used to replace the term *salivary gland virus* or *cytomegalic inclusion disease virus*.[13] The first description of recognizable CMV disease in a normal healthy adult was documented in 1965.[14] A syndrome of CMV mononucleosis was found to occur sporadically and after transfusion with blood[15] or leukocyte products.[16]

Human CMV is the largest member of the human herpesvirus group and in fact is the largest known virus to infect humans. The CMV genome is a linear, double-stranded DNA molecule (230 million Da) that has been completely sequenced[17] and has been shown to contain nonoverlapping open reading frames for 230 proteins. Not all of the proteins have been identified, and the functions of many of the proteins are not known. The laboratory strain AD169 has been the best studied and was the first strain to have its nucleotide sequence determined. AD169 has been shown to have a shorter genome than do many clinical isolates, and the Toledo strain of HCMV contains an additional 15 kb of DNA that is not present in strain AD169.[18] This large block of duplex DNA contains 19 genes that encode viral glycoproteins. The structure of the HCMV genome makes it a member of the β group of human herpesviruses because it contains terminal repeat sequences that are complementary to each other. The HCMV genome contains a single origin of replication, and, like all human herpesviruses, it encodes a DNA polymerase gene and a complete package of genes needed for its own DNA replication. Viral DNA polymerase is an important target for antiviral drugs, and all current therapies for CMV disease inhibit viral DNA polymerase as the final target.[5] CMV DNA polymerase is encoded by a CMV open reading frame designated UL54, and it has an important accessory protein, UL44, which enhances the processivity of DNA polymerase.[19] The UL54 and UL44 proteins form the functional complex of complete DNA polymerase in infected cells.

The CMV genome also encodes a protein phosphotransferase enzyme, the product of UL97, the role of which in CMV DNA replication is not well understood.[20] This UL97 protein is able to phosphorylate ganciclovir to form ganciclovir monophosphate; this activation step is needed for ganciclovir to become an effective inhibitor of CMV DNA replication.[5,21,22] The role of UL97 in CMV replication is still be-

ing defined, but recent work has shown that it is able to phosphorylate serine residues.[23] The UL97 protein may phosphorylate other proteins involved in DNA replication.

CMV also contains many genes that encode proteins directly involved in downregulating the host immune system as a way of evading immune control of the virus. One of the most important of these CMV proteins prevents cellular HLA-1 molecules from reaching the cell surface.[24] Thus, HLA-1 and CMV glycoproteins cannot form complexes on the cell surface to trigger recognition and destruction by CD8+ T lymphocytes. This enables the CMV genome to remain in infected cells and avoid immune destruction.

In the infectious virion, CMV double-stranded DNA is wrapped in a nucleoprotein core that is surrounded by matrix proteins and the pp65 antigen of CMV, which is important for diagnosis of CMV because it can be readily detected in the infected cells of patients by immunofluorescence, immunoperoxidase, and other antigen detection methods.[25] A lipid envelope that surrounds the matrix and inner core contains many viral glycoproteins that are involved in viral entry.

The cellular protein that serves as the specific receptor for CMV entry has not been identified, but CMV infects cells by a process of endocytosis. The CMV genome is uncoated within the cell, and the DNA protein core is transported to the nucleus of the cell. Following synthesis of viral DNA polymerase, CMV replication occurs in the nuclei of infected cells, and the large nuclear inclusions that are the hallmark of CMV infection in tissue culture and in infected cells represent aggregates of replicating CMV nucleoprotein cores. Recognition of these CMV nuclear inclusions is valuable in establishing a diagnosis of CMV infection.[26]

The ability of CMV to remain latent after infection contributes a great deal to serious CMV disease. Evidence for persistent CMV genomes and antigens exists in many tissues after initial infection, and CMV has been found in circulating mononuclear cells and in polymorphonuclear neutrophils.[27] CMV antigens have been detected in vascular endothelial cells; this site has been suggested as a cause of vascular inflammation and development of atherosclerosis. Detection of cells that contain CMV intranuclear inclusions in renal epithelial tissue and in pulmonary secretions provides evidence that CMV may persist in these tissues as well. The mechanisms that control latency are not known, but the ability of CMV to evade immune destruction of infected cells through downregulation of cell surface markers such as HLA-1 may contribute to the capacity of the virus to remain undetected.[24] When immune suppression occurs in patients by means of HIV infection or through immunosuppressive therapy, such as antilymphocyte antibody (OKT3) infusion,[28] CMV can reactivate and grow to high titers, producing end-organ disease.

Previous claims that CMV had oncogenic properties are now regarded with great skepticism. CMV is not associated with immortalization of cells in culture or with enhanced proliferation of cell DNA; rather, CMV infection may be associated with cellular arrest or decreased growth. CMV is not closely linked to any tumor in immunocompromised patients and is distinguished from the oncogenic association of viruses such as Epstein-Barr virus (see Chapter 135).

LABORATORY DIAGNOSIS

The laboratory diagnosis of CMV infection depends on the growth of the virus from urine or other body fluids or on the demonstration of virion components such as viral antigens or viral DNA. Diagnosis almost always depends on laboratory confirmation and cannot be made on clinical grounds alone. The first useful laboratory test relied on the detection of large, nuclear inclusion–bearing cells in the urine sediment.[26] This was particularly useful for the newborn period, and the associated disease was called *cytomegalic inclusion disease of infancy*. Growth of virus in human fibroblast cultures (MRC-5 cells) was laborious, and several weeks was required for cell cultures to grow the virus. The culture technique could be greatly speeded up by the use of "shell vials" of cultured cells in which immediate early antigens were detected through the use of monoclonal antibodies.[25,29]

The direct detection of antigens in neutrophils by means of a monoclonal antibody against the CMV matrix protein pp65 has proved particularly useful.[30] This test provides a direct measure of the presence of CMV and can detect CMV antigen in the spinal fluid of patients with CMV polyradiculopathy syndrome, as well as in the peripheral blood of immunocompromised patients. Other methods for detecting CMV DNA or RNA have employed labeled viral nucleic acid probes and nucleic acid hybridization in body fluids or tissue specimens.[1,31,32]

The polymerase chain reaction (PCR), which employs primers in the gene that encodes CMV immediate early antigen[33] or in the CMV DNA polymerase,[34] has provided a very sensitive technique by which CMV can be detected. PCR can detect small amounts of CMV DNA in many body fluids. It has been useful for the detection of CMV DNA in the cerebrospinal fluid of patients with CMV encephalitis or the CMV polyradiculopathy syndrome.[35,36]

Three important papers have described the use of PCR for detecting CMV DNA in the blood of AIDS patients; these findings reveal that the presence of CMV DNA could predict the development of CMV retinitis several months later.[37-39] Although all three studies employed different PCR techniques, they demonstrated remarkable agreement with a positive predictive value of approximately 60% in correlating the presence of CMV DNA with the subsequent development of clinical disease. Quantitative PCR has also been employed to show that a high quantitative number of CMV DNA copies per milliliter of plasma was correlated with CMV disease activity in patients with AIDS.[40] The PCR assay for CMV DNA is also revolutionizing the approach to the management of CMV disease in liver, kidney, and bone marrow transplant recipients (see farther on).[41] With the availability of effective antiviral therapy, one goal of management is to prevent CMV disease through the use of the PCR assay to detect CMV DNA in plasma before end-organ disease has developed. Antiviral therapy can then be used to lower CMV DNA levels and prevent the development of CMV end-organ disease. This approach has been labeled *preemptive therapy*.[42] CMV antigen detection in cerebrospinal fluid cells and cerebrospinal fluid DNA levels determined by PCR have provided comparable information on the course of antiviral therapy for CMV infection of the central nervous system (CNS).[43] Another study has suggested that prophylactic treatment with ganciclovir may be better than CMV antigen–guided preemptive therapy in preventing CMV pneumonia during the first 100 days after transplantation.[44] Additional comparative studies on the use of assays in plasma and in neutrophils are needed to assess their relative merits in different clinical conditions.

Clinical laboratories are rapidly adopting kit-based molecular technology to diagnose active CMV disease. Kits are based on PCR or on a solution hybridization capture assay.[45] Technology based on nucleic acid sequence–based amplification (NASBA), although promising,[16] is not widely employed at the present time.

A research kit–based assay that employs PCR technology is the COBAS Amplicor CMV Monitor (Roche Molecular Diagnostics, Pleasanton, CA). This assay uses plasma and is based on the coamplification of a 365–base pair sequence in the amino terminus of the CMV DNA polymerase gene, as well as on a quantitation standard of a known concentration. Although the specimen extraction is performed manually, amplification and detection steps are automated. The instrument displays the results in copies per milliliter, with a range of detection between 400 and 100,000 copies per milliliter. Several studies in a variety of populations susceptible to CMV infection have demonstrated high sensitivity and specificity of this assay in detecting the presence of CMV DNAemia.[46-49]

The Hybrid Capture CMV DNA Assay version 2.0 (Digene, Gaithersburg, MD) is a rapid signal–amplified solution hybridization assay that uses RNA probes for CMV DNA present in leukocytes and antibodies to capture the resulting RNA-DNA hybrids. Subsequently, a reaction with alkaline phosphatase–conjugated antibodies specific for RNA-DNA hybrids takes place, followed by a chemiluminescent reaction. The quantitative results are expressed as picograms per milliliter. For qualitative assessment, all specimens with a ratio of sample relative light units (RLUs) to positive-cutoff RLUs >0.75 are considered positive for CMV DNA. As with the Cobas Amplicor, several studies have demonstrated high sensitivity and specificity of this assay for detecting the presence of CMV DNAemia in a variety of patient groups.[50,51]

Although data are accumulating to support the usefulness of these assays for the early detection of CMV disease, it is still not clear whether these tests are equally effective in predicting disease or response to therapy.[52-57] Two studies that compared the properties of the Digene Hybrid Capture Assay (2.0) with those of the quantitative Cobas Amplicor in a cohort of renal transplant recipients noted a correlation between the results with each assay. However, 8% to 9% discordance between results was observed within each group independently. Both studies noted a lower detection limit by the Digene 2.0. Tong and associates observed that discordance was more likely to occur at the beginning or toward the end of infection. It was estimated that in this population, a CMV DNA cutoff of $>40,000$ copies/mL is specific for CMV disease. The sensitivity for this cutoff is only 29.4% (Cobas Amplicor) and 41.2% (Digene), but it may be increased to 76.5% and 82.4%, respectively, if the cutoff to predict disease is decreased to >1000 copies/mL. Because this cutoff was found to be associated with a low positive predictive value (46.2% [Cobas Amplicor] and 56% [Digene]), the authors suggest that this value should be used only to rule out CMV disease for this specific population.[58]

One study,[54] which prospectively analyzed the clinical use of weekly Cobas Amplicor assays and the pp65 antigenemia assay for predicting the development of active CMV disease in 97 consecutive liver transplant recipients, found that CMV viral loads were highly correlated with levels of CMV antigenemia. Twenty-one patients were found to have active CMV disease. It was determined that the optimal cutoff for CMV copy load to predict disease was in the range of 2000 to 5000 copies/mL; at >5000 copies/mL, 18 of 21 of cases of CMV would have been predicted. This cutoff was associated with a sensitivity of 85.7%, a specificity of 86.8%, a positive predictive value (PPV) of 64.3%, and a negative predictive value (NPV) of 95.7%. The optimal cutoff for antigenemia was determined to be in the range of four to six positive cells per slide (PPV: 50%–60.7%; NPV: 96.6%–94.2%). A second independent study observed that high peak viral loads ($>10,000$ copies/mL) were consistently associated with D+/R− patients after liver transplantation with active CMV infection.[55] Peak viral loads varied in symptomatic infections of D+/R+ and D–/R+ patients. Because peak viral loads of asymptomatic, nontreated D+/R+ patients did not exceed 5500 copies/mL, it was suggested that the optimal cutoff for this particular population should be 5000 copies/mL.

Additional comparative studies on the use of these assays in plasma and neutrophils are needed to assess their relative merits in different clinical conditions.[58-61] As new study findings become available, rapid laboratory diagnosis and its correlation with clinical conditions and outcomes will significantly change the clinical management of multiple aspects of CMV disease.

CULTIVATION OF CYTOMEGALOVIRUS

HCMV has been cultured in human cells only, and previous claims that CMV could be grown in other animal cells have not been substantiated.[62] Although CMV can be readily cultured in human fibroblast cells, growth is characteristically slow. One to 4 weeks of growth may be required for the development of typical cytopathic changes in tissue culture. CMV produces characteristic infected cells, which are large and rounded and contain "ground-glass"–appearing inclusions in the cytoplasm. These infected cells—the hallmark of CMV—indicate the presence of CMV in the sample.[26]

CMV can be readily isolated from urine, mouth swabs, buffy coat, cervical tissue, and tissues obtained by biopsy or at postmortem examination. Virus is demonstrable even in the presence of neutralizing antibody.

CMV is not usually cultured from normal adults and may be difficult to culture from blood, even in immunocompromised patients.

Virus may be cultured from the cervix in healthy women[63] and from semen in healthy homosexual men.[64]

The growth of CMV from throat, urine, or blood is an abnormal finding, but only culture from blood is highly suggestive of a pathogenic CMV infection because CMV in throat or urine is frequently associated with asymptomatic infection. Patients who recover from acute CMV mononucleosis may shed CMV in the urine and throat for several weeks. Immunosuppressed patients may also shed CMV in throat washings or bronchoalveolar lavage. In the latter cases, histologic changes, such as intranuclear inclusions, are needed for the establishment of a diagnosis of CMV pneumonitis.[26]

CYTOMEGALOVIRUS MONONUCLEOSIS

Primary infection with CMV in a young adult can produce an infectious mononucleosis syndrome with fever, lymphadenopathy, and relative lymphocytosis. It is estimated that 79% of infectious mononucleosis is caused by the Epstein-Barr virus (EBV) (see Chapter 135); the other 21% is caused by acute CMV infection.[65] The heterophil agglutinin test is negative in CMV mononucleosis and is usually positive in EBV mononucleosis. Another distinguishing feature of diseases caused by these two viruses is a sore throat with enlarged, exudate-covered tonsils (more common with EBV infection). CMV-induced infectious mononucleosis syndrome has been called *typhoidal* because symptoms may be systemic in nature, fever may predominate, and few signs of enlarged lymph nodes or splenomegaly may be noted.[65]

The hematologic hallmark of the infectious mononucleosis syndrome is a relative lymphocytosis, in which more than 50% of the peripheral white blood cell differential is composed of lymphocytes. Of these, 10% or more should comprise atypical lymphocytes that possess abnormal nuclei and exhibit rosetting around red blood cells.

The landmark study that defined the clinical features of infectious mononucleosis was an 8-year prospective study of 494 patients by investigators from Finland.[65] In that study, 79% of patients had a positive heterophil agglutinin and acute EBV infection; 73 patients older than 15 years of age had a negative heterophil response, and 33 of these patients (45%) had CMV infection. The first serum, which was taken 3 to 20 days after the onset of disease, showed that 11 of 19 patients were seronegative (titer ≤ 1:4) and experienced a rise in complement-fixing antibodies. The peak titer was reached 4 to 7 weeks after the onset of disease. The presence of CMV in the urine was documented in 10 of 12 patients tested. This analysis led to the conclusion that CMV mononucleosis represents a primary infection in previously seronegative persons. The age range of infected patients was 18 to 66 years, with a median age of 29 years (this was higher than in the group with EBV-induced mononucleosis). Fever was common in all patients and persisted for 9 to 35 days (mean, 19 days). Lymphocytosis in these patients ranged from 55% to 86%; 12% to 55% of total leukocytes were atypical lymphocytes. In the CMV-infected patients, pharyngitis and tonsillitis were rare. Enlargement of both lymph nodes and spleen was not a prominent feature of CMV mononucleosis, although this can occur. Low-level liver function abnormalities are regular features of CMV mononucleosis and can be an important clue to diagnosis. The occurrence of severe hepatitis or jaundice is rare.

CMV mononucleosis may occur without a clear source, but "kissing" and direct transfer of infected lymphocytes and polymorphonuclear cells is sometimes identified as a source. Other forms of intimate sexual contact are also important in the transmission of CMV.

The most clearly identified source for transmission of CMV and EBV is blood transfusion. CMV is also readily transmitted by transfusion of leukocytes alone.[66] The greater the number of units of transfused blood a patient receives, the greater is the risk of infection from this source. When large amounts of blood have been transfused, CMV should be considered as a potential cause of postoperative fever. The risk of transmission of CMV from blood has been greatly reduced by the screening of blood for the presence of antibodies and by elimination of units from seropositive donors.[63,67]

In both CMV- and EBV-induced mononucleosis, laboratory abnormalities or transient immunologic aberrations can occur. These abnormalities include cold agglutinins, rheumatoid factor, mixed cryoglobulinemia, antinuclear antibodies, and anticomplementary activity.[65]

A study of 124 patients used elevated CMV immunoglobulin (Ig)M levels (>300 U/mL) as a measure of acute CMV infection; patients presented with fever, malaise, jaundice, hepatitis, sweats, or a mononucleosis-like illness, and a detailed analysis of symptoms was provided. The specificity of the CMV IgM assay was confirmed in every case by the use of a CMV IgG avidity assay. The authors were careful to include patients who exhibited the absence of EBV infection, hepatitis A, antibody to hepatitis B core antigen, *Toxoplasma gondii*, IgM antibodies, and rheumatoid factor. The study examined samples obtained from 7630 patients in the United Kingdom from December of 1998 to June of 2001 and found 106 patients with CMV infection who were treated by general practitioners and 18 who were hospitalized. In this group, the most frequent symptoms were malaise (67%), fever (46%), and sweats (46%). The most frequent laboratory finding was abnormal liver function test results (69%). Relapsing illness was observed in 12% of patients; symptoms persisted for up to 32 weeks with a mean duration of symptoms of 7.8 weeks. No significant differences were seen between patients who were treated by general practitioners and those who were hospitalized, except that the same symptoms were more severe in those who were hospitalized. Four patients were pregnant at the time of acute CMV infection. Three delivered healthy children, but one child had severe intrauterine growth retardation and a severe hearing impairment. This study expands the range of clinical symptoms associated with laboratory-documented acute CMV infection.[68]

ASSOCIATED COMPLICATIONS

A series of associated findings can occur with CMV infection; these may be the initial manifestation of disease even in the normal host. The following sections describe these complications.

Interstitial Pneumonia

Interstitial pneumonia is the most severe complication of CMV disease in the bone marrow transplantation patient, and it may also occur uncommonly in CMV-induced mononucleosis in the normal host. In the large series from Finland,[65] CMV pneumonitis occurred in 2 of 33 patients. The main finding is one of interstitial infiltrates on chest radiography that eventually clear (Fig. 134-1). This is in sharp distinction to the finding of CMV pneumonitis in bone marrow transplant recipients, in whom CMV pneumonitis has a high mortality rate even with aggressive antiviral therapy. CMV pneumonitis that occurs with CMV mononucleosis is usually mild, and no treatment is required.

Hepatitis

Hepatitis is commonly associated with CMV mononucleosis, but it is usually mild and is rarely symptomatic in the immunocompetent patient. A 21-year-old immunocompetent patient has been described in whom infectious hepatitis was suspected and who had a large and tender liver but no atypical lymphocytes. CMV was isolated from the urine, and a significant rise in complement-fixing antibodies was observed; this confirmed the diagnosis of acute CMV infection.[69] Granulomatous hepatitis may also be an initial manifestation of CMV infection that accompanies mononucleosis.[70] In these patients, fever, vomiting, and a profound atypical lymphocytosis of nearly 50% have been noted. CMV was isolated from the throat, and a diagnostic rise in complement-fixing antibodies was seen. Liver biopsy in these patients revealed a resolving hepatitis with mononuclear cells infiltrating portal areas, along with microscopic granulomas with giant cells. In the setting of acute CMV infection, hepatitis usually resolves fully. When scattered microscopic granulomas are found on liver biopsy, CMV infection should be considered.

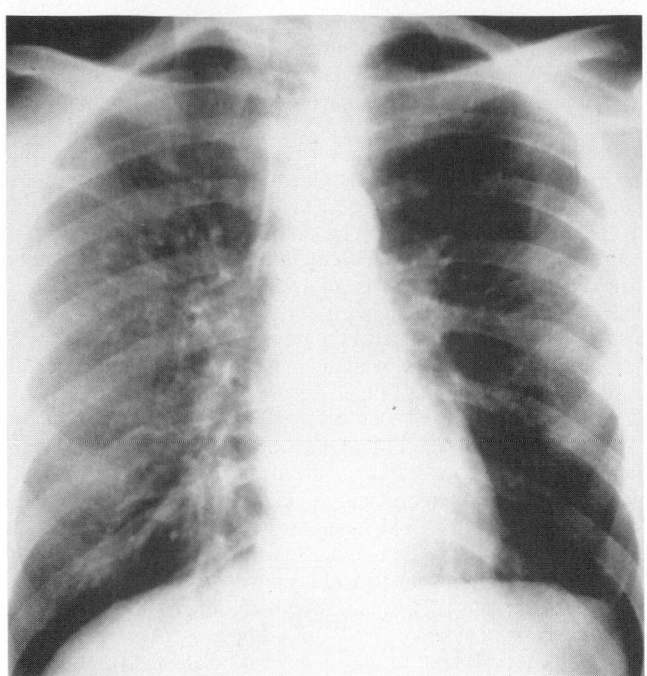

FIGURE 134-1. Bilateral interstitial pneumonitis caused by cytomegalovirus in a bone marrow transplant recipient.

Guillain-Barré Syndrome

The association of Guillain-Barré syndrome with CMV mononucleosis was initially described in 1971 when nine patients with acute CMV mononucleosis presented with polyneuritis that was characterized by sensory and motor weakness in the extremities. Cranial nerve involvement was also common, and four patients were treated in the respiratory unit.[71] Return of sensation was followed by motor improvement, and complete recovery required about 3 months for most patients.

In a large series of 94 cases of Guillian-Barré syndrome, acute CMV infection was documented in 10 patients.[72] In 9 of these patients, a high IgM immunofluorescent antibody titer was found on the initial specimen; this showed a decline that was diagnostic for acute CMV infection by the time of discharge. The complement fixation antibody titer was already elevated in these patients, and no further rises were observed. All patients had atypical lymphocytes in a blood smear, and all recovered.

The strongest evidence that CMV may be a direct cause of polyradiculopathy and myopathy has been observed in AIDS patients, in whom CMV inclusions have been demonstrated in the nuclei of Schwann cells in association with a syndrome of motor weakness that leads to loss of bowel and bladder control (see farther on).[73]

Meningoencephalitis

In association with CMV-induced infectious mononucleosis, meningoencephalitis has been infrequently reported in immunocompetent patients.[74] Such patients may also have motor and sensory weakness very similar to polyradiculopathy. Severe headache, photophobia, lethargy, and pyramidal tract findings are features that are more indicative of meningocephalitis. The spinal fluid usually shows a moderate number of lymphocytes. In both CMV meningoencephalitis and CMV polyradiculopathy, the presence of CMV DNA that is detected by PCR can be helpful to the clinician in establishing a diagnosis.[35,36]

Myocarditis

Complications of CMV-induced mononucleosis can include myocardial involvement. In three of eight cases, inversion of T waves was noted.[75] One patient was a 14-year-old boy who died with serologic evidence of acute CMV infection, hepatitis, myocarditis, and consumptive coagulopathy. Another report described a 43-year-old immunocompetent woman with acquired myocarditis, heart failure, encephalitis, hepatitis, and adrenal insufficiency.[76] At autopsy, CMV was cultured from the adrenals. In children with congenital CMV infection, myocardial involvement is rarely reported.

Thrombocytopenia and Hemolytic Anemia

Thrombocytopenia and hemolytic anemia occur regularly in children with congenital CMV disease and occasionally as a complication of CMV mononucleosis in healthy adults. A 33-year-old man with serologic evidence of acute CMV infection and viruria experienced a profound decrease in platelet count to 500/mm^3, a hemolytic anemia and hemoglobin of 3.6 g/dL, and a reticulocyte count of 12%.[77] The patient had generalized purpura and bleeding gums and recovered completely with prednisone treatment. In a 26-year-old man with acute CMV infection who presented with thrombocytopenia and purpura, decreased red cell survival and elevated reticulocyte count were demonstrated.[78]

Skin Eruptions

Maculopapular and rubelliform rashes may also occur in the setting of CMV mononucleosis. These rashes may develop after administration of ampicillin[79] and are thought to result from immunologic reactions to cellular antigens that are uncovered or expressed in association with the acute CMV infection. In an unusual report, a 40-year-old man with acute CMV viremia and viruria acquired epidermolysis 8 weeks after the onset of hepatitis.[80] Thus, the skin manifestations of acute CMV infection are usually mild but can occasionally be severe.

CYTOMEGALOVIRUS INFECTION IN PATIENTS WITH ACQUIRED IMMUNODEFICIENCY SYNDROME

The profound immunodeficiency caused by infection with human immunodeficiency virus-1 (HIV-1) results in defects in cellular immunity to many common infectious agents, including CMV. Coinfection with CMV has been noted in more than 90% of homosexual men with HIV-1 infection by serologic status.[81] A high percentage of homosexual men also have CMV that is detected in the urine, even in the absence of HIV-1 infection.[82] Patients who are infected with HIV-1 in whom CD4 cells are decreased to fewer than 100 cells/mm^3 have a significantly increased risk for the development of serious CMV disease.

CMV is the most common viral opportunistic infection in patients with AIDS; it has been estimated that 21% to 44% of patients with AIDS acquired CMV disease in the era before the availability of highly active antiretroviral therapy (HAART).[4] CMV retinitis, by far the most common form of CMV disease, usually occurs when the CD4 cell count falls to below 50 cells/mm^3.[83] Autopsy studies have shown that up to 81% of HIV-infected patients had clinical or pathologic evidence of CMV disease by the time they died, and 32% had CMV retinitis.[84] Retinal disease due to CMV occurs only rarely in patients with bone marrow or solid organ transplantation. CMV retinitis causes a complete-thickness infection through the retinal cells and results in progressive retinal destruction that leads to blindness within 4 to 6 months. Now that HAART is able to suppress HIV, the incidence of CMV end-organ disease has decreased by more than 80%.[85] This has greatly changed the management of CMV retinitis, which is discussed in detail in Chapter 125.[4] The most likely reason for the reduction in CMV disease that has occurred is the improvement in CMV-specific immune responses that results from HAART.[86]

CMV retinitis is diagnosed predominantly on the basis of its clinical appearance. The characteristic appearance is a white, fluffy retinal infiltrate that occurs with several areas of hemorrhage (Fig. 134-2). It can also appear as a granular white area without hemorrhage. This form must be distinguished from cotton wool spots, which are seen on the retinal tissue of patients with AIDS and are unrelated to CMV.

Initially, treatment of CMV retinitis included intravenous ganciclovir for 3 weeks at a dose of 7.5 to 15 mg/kg/day in three divided doses for 14 to 21 days, followed by a maintenance regimen of 5 to 6

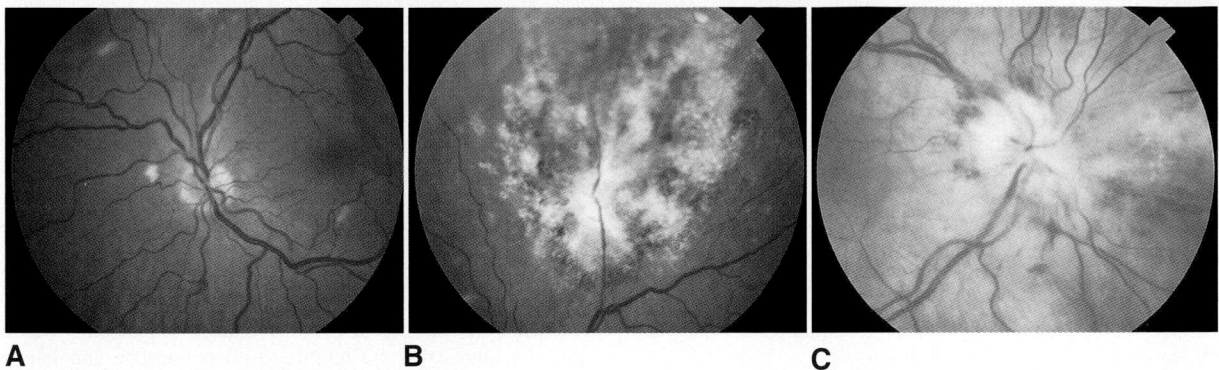

FIGURE 134-2. Cytomegalovirus (CMV) Retinitis. A, Early disease with retinal involvement along blood vessals. **B,** Extensive retinal damage and retinal hemorrhages. **C,** CMV retinitis with papillitis.

mg/kg/day for 5 to 7 days per week[87] to prevent a relapse. Oral ganciclovir, despite its low oral bioavailability (8%),[88] administered at a dose of 1000 mg taken three times a day, was found to be nearly equivalent to intravenous ganciclovir in preventing progression and preserving vision, particularly if the initial CMV retinitis was not sight-threatening.[89] Valganciclovir has supplanted oral ganciclovir for the treatment of CMV infection (see later).

A sustained-release ganciclovir implant device plus oral ganciclovir (4.5 g/day) to prevent infection in the other eye has significant advantages when used as therapy for CMV retinitis. This device is implanted surgically in the eye and does not interfere with vision. The implant releases a high intravitreal concentration of ganciclovir that maintains adequate levels of drug for 8 to 10 months.[89] New implants that can release ganciclovir for up to 2 years are now in use. The ganciclovir implant plus oral ganciclovir was able to prevent relapse of CMV retinitis for about 270 days in 25% of patients.[90] This outcome was far superior to that seen in patients on intravenous ganciclovir alone and compared favorably with that in patients who received implant and intravenous ganciclovir. The incidence of severe complications of ganciclovir toxicity, namely, marrow suppression leading to neutropenia and thrombocytopenia, was also decreased by approximately 40% in patients receiving oral ganciclovir.[89] However, in patients who received oral ganciclovir at a dose of 4.5 g/day, a higher rate of neutropenia was seen than in those who received either intravenous ganciclovir or placebo, limiting this effective dose for some patients.[91] Another important benefit among patients who received oral ganciclovir at a dose of 4.5 g/day along with the ganciclovir implant was a statistically significant decrease in the occurrence of Kaposi's sarcoma associated with AIDS.[91] Kaposi's sarcoma is closely linked with human herpesvirus 8 (see Chapter 137), and this virus is sensitive to ganciclovir in vitro.

Central Nervous System

In patients with AIDS, the most common CNS infection caused by CMV is polyradiculopathy.[73] This syndrome has a characteristic onset of ascending weakness in the lower extremities associated with a loss of deep tendon reflexes and ultimately loss of bowel and bladder control. The syndrome frequently begins as low back pain with a radicular or perianal radiation, followed in 1 to 6 weeks by a progressive flaccid paralysis. Marked pathologic changes are found in the cauda equina and the lumbosacral nerve roots with distinct mononuclear cell infiltrate destruction of axons, along with CMV inclusion in Schwann cells and epithelial cells.[73] Lumbar puncture reveals a characteristic picture of polymorphonuclear cells, mildly elevated protein, and modest lowering of cerebrospinal fluid sugar. The findings are frequently mistaken for those of bacterial meningitis, but bacterial cultures are negative. The diagnosis is usually made by detection of CMV DNA through PCR in the spinal fluid,[35,36] or by culture of CMV from the spinal fluid.

Treatment with ganciclovir has improved weakness and polyradiculopathy in a few patients who were treated with ganciclovir alone or with ganciclovir and foscarnet early in the disease,[92,93] but treatment with ganciclovir alone generally has been disappointing.[94] Some of the poor treatment results may be due to the fact that only about one third of the plasma concentration of intravenous ganciclovir is found in the cerebrospinal fluid; the CNS may represent a privileged site where only low concentrations of ganciclovir penetrate.[95]

The current favored treatment for CMV polyradiculopathy is early therapy with ganciclovir and foscarnet, even though no vigorous clinical trials to document benefit have been published. Anecdotal observations have been reported that suggest that CMV meningoencephalitis in patients with AIDS will respond to ganciclovir and foscarnet.[96]

Other CNS findings in patients with AIDS include mononeuritis multiplex and painful peripheral neuropathy, which have been attributed to CMV.[97] The benefits of antiviral therapy for these conditions are uncertain.

Gastrointestinal Tract

Infection of the gastrointestinal tract with CMV had been frequent in patients with AIDS before the era of HAART. CMV can cause ulcers in the esophagus, and patients present with pain and difficulty swallowing. Through endoscopic examination, shallow ulcers are seen. The diagnosis of CMV esophagitis is made by demonstration of intranuclear inclusions on biopsy specimens of the ulcers, or by culture of CMV from biopsy tissue.

Patients with AIDS may present with explosive watery diarrhea as a result of CMV colitis. Fever is common with CMV colitis, and occasionally, bloody diarrhea may be present. The diagnosis is made by sigmoidoscopy, which reveals plaquelike pseudomembranes, numerous erosions, and serpiginous ulcers.[98]

CMV colitis may present as a mass lesion that produces partial obstruction, or as lesions that resemble Kaposi's sarcoma.[99] CMV may be present in the colon with other pathogens such as *Mycobacterium avium* complex and *Cryptosporidium*. With severe CMV colitis, perforation and gangrene have been described, although CMV infection alone may not be the only condition found in association with these findings. Diagnosis of CMV colitis is made by biopsy, which demonstrates typical CMV inclusion bodies, or by culture of CMV from biopsy material. CMV inclusion bodies are usually seen in the mucosal epithelium[98] or in mucosal crypts.[99] The first report of successful treatment of CMV colitis described the use of ganciclovir in 1986[100]; this was followed by a placebo-controlled study with intravenous ganciclovir at a dose of 5 mg/kg for 14 days, in which a reduction was observed in the frequency of CMV-infected colonic and urinary cultures in the ganciclovir treatment group compared with the placebo group ($P = .03$ and $P < .001$, respectively). Colonoscopy scores improved more frequently in those who received ganciclovir (23% of patients) than in the placebo group (9%; $P = .03$).[101] However, diarrhea persisted at the end of treatment in both groups. These results suggest that treatment for 14 days may be inadequate for the colon to heal and diarrhea to resolve. In another study of bone marrow transplantation patients with CMV colitis who were treated with ganciclovir, cultures became negative with ganciclovir treatment, but gastrointestinal symptoms improved in both the ganciclovir- and placebo-treated groups, and ganciclovir had no apparent clinical benefit.[102] No evidence has been found that maintenance therapy with ganciclovir is useful in preventing a relapse of CMV colitis.

Other parts of the digestive system can be infected with CMV. Patients with AIDS may acquire acute CMV pancreatitis.[103] Cholecystitis has been associated with the presence of CMV in the bile duct, gallbladder, and biliary tree,[103] including acalculous cholecystitis, papillary stenosis, and sclerosing cholingitis.[104]

ANTIVIRAL THERAPY

Three antiviral drugs that act to inhibit the viral DNA polymerase have been shown to be effective in the treatment of CMV end-organ disease and have been approved for use in the United States—ganciclovir, foscarnet, and cidofovir (see Chapters 38 and 125). Another drug, valacyclovir, appears to delay the time to retinitis progression in patients with CMV retinitis.[105] An antisense inhibitor of CMV, fomivirsen, can be used for direct injection into intravitreal fluid for the treatment of CMV retinitis; it has also been recently approved.[106] These drugs have been used to treat many forms of CMV disease in patients with AIDS and in other immunocompromised patients, for example, recipients of bone marrow transplants or solid organ transplants. Individual drugs that have been useful in the treatment of CMV-associated disease are discussed in the following sections.

Ganciclovir

Ganciclovir, a nucleoside analogue of guanosine and a homologue of acyclovir, was the first antiviral drug demonstrated to be effective in the treatment of CMV disease in humans.[5,107-109] It inhibits all the herpesviruses and blocks transformation of normal cord blood lymphocytes by EBV.[110,111]

For antiviral activity, ganciclovir requires phosphorylation by a virus-specific enzyme, but CMV does not have a thymidine kinase enzyme homologue to the herpes simplex virus thymidine kinase. The phosphotransferase product of the UL97 gene of CMV converts ganciclovir to ganciclovir monophosphate. Monophosphate is then phosphorylated by cellular enzymes to triphosphate. Ganciclovir triphosphate, a potent inhibitor of the CMV DNA polymerase enzyme, is a competitive inhibitor of the incorporation of deoxyguanosine triphosphate into elongating viral DNA. After cleavage of the pyrophosphate, ganciclovir monophosphate is incorporated into the end of the growing chain of viral DNA, greatly slowing replication.[112] Ganciclovir is not an absolute chain terminator, and short fragments of CMV DNA continue to be synthesized.[113,114] All of the drug's antiviral effects are due to its ability to inhibit the synthesis of CMV DNA and CMV replication by slowing the elongation of viral DNA.[5]

The half-life of ganciclovir triphosphate in CMV-infected cells is 16.5 hours, compared with only 2.5 hours for acyclovir triphosphate.[115] Although ganciclovir triphosphate is not as effective an inhibitor of CMV DNA polymerase as is acyclovir triphosphate, this concentration of ganciclovir triphosphate in CMV-infected cells is 10 times the concentration of acyclovir triphosphate.[115] The high level of ganciclovir triphosphate and the prolonged intracellular half-life make ganciclovir a more effective inhibitor than acyclovir of CMV replication in vivo.

Valganciclovir

Valganciclovir is the valine ester of ganciclovir; it has a much greater oral bioavailability than does ganciclovir (about 68% is absorbed compared with 6% to 8% for oral ganciclovir). A valine esterase in the human intestinal mucosa cleaves the valine, and ganciclovir enters the blood stream. Two 450-mg tablets PO results in blood levels that are

equivalent to those attained with intravenous ganciclovir at a dose of 5 mg/kg/day. In a treatment study of CMV retinitis in HIV-infected patients, valganciclovir was found to be equivalent to intravenous ganciclovir for the treatment and maintenance of CMV retinitis in patients on HAART. The adverse effects of valganciclovir are similar to those of ganciclovir—mainly neutropenia and thrombocytopenia.[116] Data for the efficacy of valganciclovir are not yet available in clinical settings in which oral ganciclovir has been shown to be effective. Nonetheless, valganciclovir has largely supplanted oral ganciclovir because of its improved bioavailability and convenience.

Resistance to Ganciclovir

The major mechanism of CMV resistance to ganciclovir is the selection of mutants that are unable to phosphorylate ganciclovir. These viruses have mutations in two main regions of the UL97 protein. These are point mutations at codon 460 and point mutations or deletions around codons 590 to 596.[117,118] A mutation at codon 520 also confers an inability to phosphorylate ganciclovir.[119] Ganciclovir-resistant viruses that have mutations or deletions in regions of the UL97 protein that affect nucleotide binding and phosphate transfer have also been described.

CMV clinical isolates that were resistant to ganciclovir were first reported in 1989.[120] These isolates were taken from three immunocompromised patients with CMV disease who had disease progression and died despite therapy, and in whom all viral cultures remained positive. In a subsequent study of 72 patients with CMV retinitis who were receiving maintenance ganciclovir therapy, 80% became culture-negative after 3 months of treatment.[121] Among those who remained culture-positive, resistant CMV was isolated in 38% (with an overall incidence of 8%), and resistance was clearly associated with disease progression. Nine resistant strains of CMV were obtained from these 72 patients, and all failed to phosphorylate ganciclovir (Fig. 134-3).[122] All strains remained sensitive to foscarnet, a drug that acts directly on the viral DNA polymerase (see farther on).

Another mechanism of resistance to ganciclovir involves mutations that occur in the CMV DNA polymerase gene.[123] These have been identified in clinical isolates and are less common than mutations in the UL97 gene.[124] CMV strains with mutations in both the UL97 gene

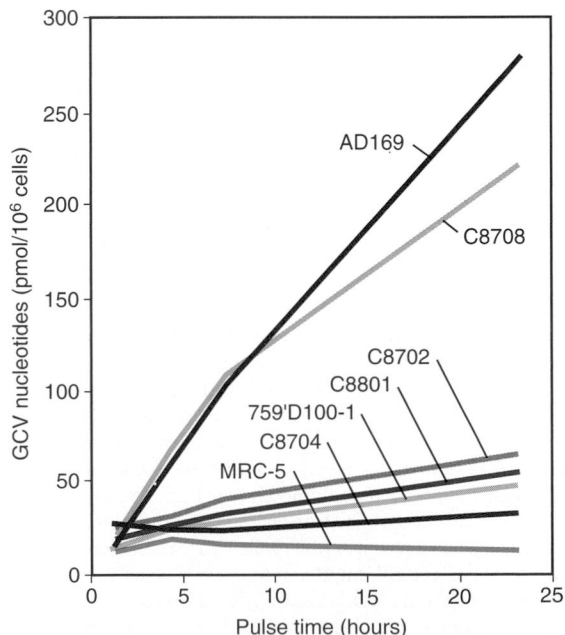

FIGURE 134-3. Intracellular Phosphorylation by Clinical Isolates. *(From Stanat SC, Reardon JE, Erice A, et al. Ganciclovir-resistant cytomegalovirus clinical isolates: Modes of resistance to ganciclovir. Antimicrob Agents Chemother. 1991;35:2191-2197.)*

and the CMV DNA polymerase gene have also been reported.[125] These exhibit a very high degree of resistance with an IC_{50} (50% inhibiting concentration) greater than 30 μM. The inhibitory concentration of CMV clinical isolates that are sensitive to ganciclovir is 6.0 μM or less.[125] Some clinical isolates reveal an intermediate sensitivity of between 6 and 12 μM. In a study undertaken to correlate mutations in either the UL97 gene or the DNA polymerase gene with resistance, the presence of a mutation in either gene was associated with an IC_{50} greater than 7 μM.[124] In an analysis of variability in the DNA polymerase gene of CMV, among 40 clinical isolates that were all sensitive to ganciclovir and foscarnet, less than 4% variability was found. No mutations were found in highly conserved regions of the viral DNA polymerase in wild-type isolates, indicating that mutations that occur in these highly conserved regions are more likely to be a result of selection by antiviral drugs.[126]

Of patients treated with ganciclovir for CMV retinitis over a prolonged period, 27% showed evidence of ganciclovir resistance after 9 months.[127] The detection of cytomegalovirus resistant to ganciclovir in the blood or urine of a patient with CMV retinitis was associated with an increased risk of adverse ocular outcomes.[128]

Foscarnet

Foscarnet, a pyrophosphate analogue that binds directly to the DNA polymerase of CMV and other herpesviruses (see Chapter 38), is a reversible competitive inhibitor that does not become incorporated into elongating viral DNA. Foscarnet must be present in high concentrations inside the cell to remain in contact with the DNA polymerase enzyme and inhibit DNA polymerase activity. When the intracellular concentration of foscarnet decreases, foscarnet no longer binds to the DNA polymerase, and viral DNA synthesis resumes.[129] Ganciclovir-resistant strains of CMV that have a mutation or a deletion in the UL97 protein kinase gene and are not able to phosphorylate ganciclovir remain sensitive to foscarnet.

Foscarnet has been used to treat patients with AIDS and CMV retinitis who have ganciclovir-resistant virus or who are intolerant of ganciclovir[130]; its use has resulted in stabilization of the retinitis and healing. Patients must be on long-term maintenance regimens with intravenous foscarnet to prevent the relapse or progression of CMV retinitis.

CMV strains that exhibit resistance to foscarnet have been reported, with mutations within the CMV DNA polymerase gene at codons 711 and 714[131] in the highly conserved region II of the polymerase. Additional mutations in the highly conserved regions VI and III of the polymerase have also been shown to confer resistance to foscarnet.[132] In patients with AIDS who were treated with foscarnet for CMV retinitis, the presence of foscarnet resistance was detected in 30 clinical isolates through sequencing of the CMV pol gene in these isolates. Nine isolates had foscarnet resistance mutations; seven of these were at codon V781L or V715M, which has previously been reported. Two new mutations were observed at V787L and E756Q, and these were confirmed by marker transfer experiments.[132] The clinical significance of CMV foscarnet resistance was also assessed in these patients with CMV retinitis and AIDS. The phenotypic plaque reduction assay (PRA) with IC_{50} >400 mM was found to correlate with genotypic resistance, whereas the DNA hybridization assay (DHA) for resistance showed that an IC_{50} >600 mM correlated with the presence of resistance mutations. Sixteen of 18 isolates showed a concordant plaque reduction assay and DNA hybridization assay phenotype. In 44 patients treated with foscarnet, resistance to foscarnet increased the risk of retinitis progression (odds ratio: 148; $P = .016$). The incidence of foscarnet resistance after 6 months was 13%; after 12 months of therapy, it was 37%.[133] To date, the resistance mutations in the CMV DNA polymerase that confer resistance to foscarnet do not occur in regions of the polymerase that confer resistance to ganciclovir.

Foscarnet 90 mg/kg/day given intravenously in two divided doses had been shown to be equivalent to ganciclovir for the initial treatment of CMV retinitis,[134] but mortality among patients with AIDS was improved in those who received foscarnet. In a subsequent study of CMV retinitis in patients with AIDS, the survival benefit was not confirmed,[135] but the combination of ganciclovir and foscarnet was superior for the treatment of retinitis.

Foscarnet is associated with significant nephrotoxicity and metabolic toxicity.[130] Renal failure, hypocalcemia, hypomagnesemia, and hypophosphatemia are serious consequences of foscarnet therapy that can be effectively managed through close monitoring of serum creatinine levels and replacement of magnesium, calcium, and phosphate losses by means of oral supplements.

Cidofovir

Cidofovir ((S)-1[3-hydroxy-2(phosphorylmethoxy) propyl] cytokine) is a nucleotide analogue of cytosine that has significant antiviral activity against CMV in vitro (see Chapter 38). The IC_{50} for cidofovir against CMV clinical isolates is 2.0 μM.[136] Cidofovir contains a phosphonate group and does not need to be phosphorylated by a viral enzyme. It is therefore active against thymidine kinase–deficient herpes simplex virus[137] and cytomegalovirus; mutations in the UL97 gene confer resistance to ganciclovir. Cidofovir is converted by cellular enzymes to cidofovir triphosphate, which is the active inhibitor of the viral DNA polymerase. Cidofovir triphosphate has a long intracellular half-life and needs to be given only once weekly. The maximal tolerated dose is 5 mg/kg weekly given intravenously.[138] This dose is given weekly for 2 weeks for induction and then is given once every 2 weeks. The drug has been approved for treatment only for CMV retinitis in patients with AIDS. Cidofovir must be administered with oral probenecid (2 g) before each intravenous dose. The major toxicity of cidofovir results from its uptake by the proximal convoluted renal tubular cells, which produces degeneration and necrosis of these cells that may be irreversible.[139] Patients who have experienced irreversible nephrotoxicity when cidofovir is given without probenecid have required dialysis. Probenecid prevents the uptake of cidofovir and spares the renal tubular cells from degenerative damage.

Cross-Resistance to Antiviral Drugs in Cytomegalovirus Clinical Isolates

All clinically approved systemic antiviral drugs act to inhibit the viral DNA polymerase as a final target. The possibility for cross-resistance among all drugs acting on the viral DNA polymerase exists, but at present, distinct patterns appear to be emerging. An early study showed that resistance to ganciclovir in the viral DNA polymerase of herpes simplex virus could be overcome by an analogue of foscarnet—phosphonoactive acid; this suggests that drugs that act on the viral polymerase could act synergistically[140] to overcome resistance to drugs that act on the DNA polymerase. Synergistic activity of ganciclovir and foscarnet against CMV has been shown in vitro.[141] If a clinical isolate of CMV is highly resistant to ganciclovir ($IC_{50} = 30$ μM) and contains mutations in both the UL97 and DNA polymerase genes, cross-resistance to cidofovir may also be observed.[142,143] These isolates still remain sensitive to foscarnet. Cross-resistance between ganciclovir and foscarnet has not been observed, which may reflect the fact that ganciclovir and foscarnet bind to different regions of the viral DNA polymerase. Resistance mutations to antiviral drugs against CMV appear to cluster in three distinct regions on the DNA polymerase; significant overlap has not been observed (Fig. 134-4).[143]

PREVENTION OF CYTOMEGALOVIRUS DISEASE

One of the most significant advances in the field was the demonstration that serious CMV disease could be prevented after bone marrow and solid organ transplantation with antiviral therapy. Prevention of life-threatening CMV pneumonia or other CMV-associated disease in recipients of bone marrow, heart, and liver transplants by administration of ganciclovir was clearly demonstrated in four independent studies from 1991 to 1995. In bone marrow transplantation patients in particular, the development of interstitial pneumonia up to 120 days after the transplantation procedure is most frequently caused by CMV and has a very high mortality. In one of the studies from 1991, a positive CMV culture from any site at any time after bone marrow transplantation was

FIGURE 134-4. Map of the Cytomegalovirus (CMV) DNA Polymerase. The CMV DNA polymerase showing functional domains and highly conserved regions of DNA nucleotide sequences (I–VII). Shaded areas are regions associated with drug-resistance phenotypes. Codons mapped to drug resistance in clinical isolates are shown as bars. CDV, cidofovir; GCV, ganciclovir; PFA, foscarnet. (*Adapted from Chou S, Lurain NS, Weinberg A, et al. Interstrain variation in the human cytomegalovirus DNA polymerase sequence and its effect on genotype diagnosis of antiviral drug resistance. Antimicrob Agents Chemother. 1999;43:1500-1502.*)

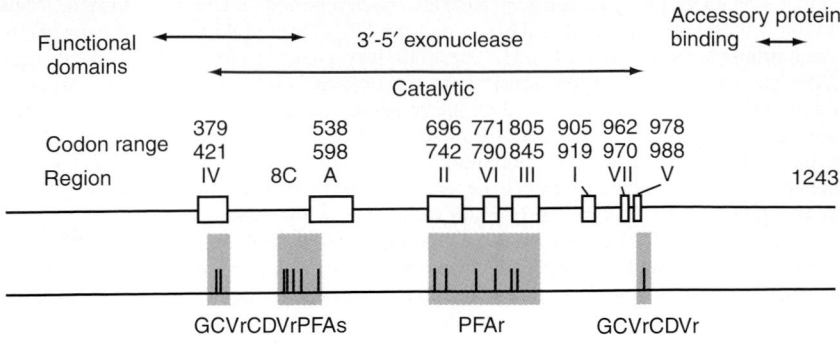

used as an indication of when intravenous ganciclovir therapy should be started.[144] This was found to be more effective in the prevention of CMV pneumonia or death (97% efficacy) than was screening for CMV by means of bronchoalveolar lavage at day 35 (75% efficacy)[145] and gave a reliable indication of when ganciclovir should be started. In a study in which CMV was detected by bronchoalveolar lavage in 20 patients who then received a full course of ganciclovir treatment, CMV pneumonia did not develop in any patient.[145] This strategy of preventing CMV pneumonia was quickly confirmed in heart transplant recipients who were seropositive for CMV and received ganciclovir or placebo for 28 days after transplantation.[146] Among patients who received ganciclovir, the incidence of CMV disease at 120 days after transplantation was reduced from 46% to 9%. The incidence of CMV infection at day 60 was 56% in the placebo group and only 19% in the ganciclovir group.[146] Among 250 patients who received ganciclovir or acyclovir intravenously after liver transplantation, ganciclovir almost completely prevented CMV disease during a follow-up period of 120 days, whereas CMV infection occurred in 38% of acyclovir recipients.[147]

Oral ganciclovir was first shown to be effective in preventing CMV disease in patients with AIDS who had fewer than 100 CD4 cells/mm³ of blood. In a study that compared oral ganciclovir at a dose of 1000 mg every 8 hours with placebo in 725 patients, only 14% of patients in the ganciclovir group acquired CMV disease compared with 26% of those in the placebo group.[148] A trend toward longer survival was noted in the ganciclovir group. Patients receiving ganciclovir also had significantly fewer positive urine cultures for CMV than did those receiving placebo, thus providing a virologic correlation with clinical benefit. Analysis of plasma CMV DNA in patients who acquired CMV disease showed that oral ganciclovir primarily benefitted those with very low plasma CMV DNA at baseline, and it was effective in preventing CMV retinitis among those with a low copy number of CMV DNA at baseline.[40] If a high copy number of CMV DNA was present at baseline, little evidence indicated that oral ganciclovir would prevent CMV disease.[149] Because oral ganciclovir has a low oral bioavailability (6% to 8%), the maximum serum concentration is 1.2 μg/mL.[88] This concentration is probably too low to be active against high copy numbers of actively replicating CMV.

Oral ganciclovir has also been shown to be effective in the prevention of CMV disease among liver transplant recipients and in the reduction of mortality due to CMV infection.[88,150] In kidney transplantation patients, oral ganciclovir has been effective in the prevention of CMV disease and in the reduction of CMV DNA levels in plasma. In patients who have received oral ganciclovir, the level of CMV DNA in plasma may be reduced to undetectable levels, but rejection of transplanted kidney still occurs. This suggests that CMV disease may not be the only reason for rejection of kidney transplants; rigorous control of CMV replication does not eliminate renal graft rejection.[151]

Although similar data are not yet available for the use of valganciclovir in the settings described earlier, most authorities prefer to use it rather than oral ganciclovir for the indications discussed here.

CYTOMEGALOVIRUS INFECTION IN TRANSPLANTATION PATIENTS

After bone marrow and solid organ transplantation, the severe immunosuppressive regimens that are employed to prevent rejection of the transplant make the recipient prone to severe CMV disease. In each form of transplantation, the occurrence of CMV disease is different. The severity of the end-organ disease caused by CMV is related to the degree of immune suppression. The more severe the immune suppression, such as that required after bone marrow transplantation, the more severe is the disease that occurs. Therefore, CMV pneumonia during the first 120 days after bone marrow transplantation is much more severe and life-threatening than it is in a patient after renal transplantation. All major transplantations (kidney, liver, heart, heart-lung, and bone marrow) are associated with an increased risk of CMV infection. In a summary of 16 studies of 1276 patients, it was found that the rate of infection after renal transplantation as measured by a serologic rise in antibody to CMV or isolation of virus from blood, urine, or throat ranged from 59% to 70%, with a median rate of 70%.[63] The infection rate was significantly higher among recipients who were seropositive before organ transplantation (84%), and it was lower in seronegative recipients (52%). Primary infections can occur in which a patient is infected from exposure to blood in a dialysis center or intensive care unit; however, this is uncommon now because of the use of filtered blood. Although CMV may be acquired from a transplanted organ, the vast majority of CMV-associated disease represents reactivation of virus in the recipient.[63]

Cytomegalovirus Infection Acquired from Donated Organs

Even though attempts to isolate infectious CMV from organs of normal hosts are usually unsuccessful, the presence of CMV antigen in major visceral organs has been reported. This makes it likely that CMV will be activated after transplantation. In the case of kidney transplant recipients, two studies have reported the development of primary infection in 83% of seronegative recipients who received kidneys from seropositive donors.[152,153] The development of CMV infection in those who received kidneys from seronegative donors was rare. CMV infection is also common among seronegative recipients who receive liver transplants from seropositive donors; in these cases, as many as 50% to 70% of recipients will acquire CMV disease. In a trial that compared oral ganciclovir at 3 g/day with placebo for the prevention of CMV disease, 44% of seronegative recipients who received a liver transplant from a seropositive donor acquired CMV disease.[150] Evidence that the donor organ is a source of CMV is provided by the demonstration that identical CMV strains were found in two organ recipients who acquired CMV disease and shared a common organ donor.[63]

Immunosuppressive Therapy

Immunosuppressive drugs play a major role in reactivation of CMV.[154] Cytologic drugs such as cyclophosphamide and azathioprine are sufficient in themselves to reactivate CMV.[155] Corticosteroids alone are not able to enhance CMV infection but act synergistically with other agents. The use of very high doses of corticosteroids plus azathioprine has been associated with a very high incidence of CMV reactivation.[156]

Cyclosporine has been widely used as a primary immunosuppressive agent, and its potency has contributed to the success of transplants. The use of cyclosporine by itself does not increase CMV disease. A controlled trial in kidney transplantation patients comparing azathioprine and prednisone with cyclosporine and prednisone showed that infection and severity of CMV disease were comparable in both groups of patients.[157] The other mainstay of immunosuppression, tacrolimus, does not enhance CMV infection, although CMV-associated disease is not eliminated by it.[158] Some novel immunosuppressive regimens, however, increase the frequency of severe CMV disease; the most notable of these is the OKT3 antiserum infusion that is used to treat rejection in liver transplantation patients.[28] The use of OKT3 is associated with an increase in CMV hepatitis and dissemination of CMV in such patients. The type of organ that is transplanted is an important determinant of the morbidity of CMV disease, as is discussed in the following sections.

Bone Marrow Transplantation

The most common life-threatening infectious complication of allogeneic bone marrow transplant is interstitial pneumonia due to CMV, which usually occurs within the first 120 days after transplantation. This pneumonitis usually shows an interstitial pattern rather than alveolar disease, but nodules may also be present on chest x-ray films. CMV pneumonia is usually rapid in onset with respiratory complaints of less than 2 weeks in duration. Fever, nonproductive cough, and dyspnea that progresses to hypoxia are common in severe cases. Hypoxia frequently requires assisted ventilation. In bone marrow transplantation patients, CMV pneumonia has a very high mortality (in one large series—84%).[3] It has been suggested that part of the severity of CMV pneumonia noted in bone marrow transplantation patients may be due to a graft-versus-host reaction in the lung. Graft-versus-host disease has been reported more commonly in those with CMV pneumonia (82%) than in those without CMV pneumonia (27%).[3]

In kidney transplant recipients, pneumonia due to CMV is less severe than that seen in bone marrow transplantation patients, and ganciclovir treatment has been lifesaving; however, in bone marrow transplant recipients, the severe interstitial pneumonia has been difficult to treat with any single therapy. Attempts to treat with ganciclovir, acyclovir, vidarabine, human leukocyte interferon, and lymphoblastoid interferon plus acyclovir have had only limited success.[100,159,160] Among 10 bone marrow transplant recipients treated with ganciclovir for CMV pneumonia, only one patient survived, even though CMV was promptly cleared from the urine and pulmonary secretions of all 10.[159] Among 20 bone marrow transplant recipients with CMV pneumonia, only 38% survived after treatment with ganciclovir. Four of these survivors also received high-titer CMV immune globulin.[160] In three uncontrolled trials, survival rates among bone marrow transplantation patients treated with intravenous ganciclovir and high-dose intravenous CMV immune globulin ranged from 52% to 69%.[161-163] Although these trials were uncontrolled, the combination of ganciclovir and high-titer CMV immune globulin is the currently recommended therapy for CMV pneumonia in bone marrow transplantation patients.

Results from European studies have not supported the favorable results observed in these three studies.[164] A retrospective study of 49 allogeneic bone marrow transplant recipients treated with ganciclovir and intravenous immune globulin showed that only 35% responded to treatment. At 1 month after diagnosis, the mortality of the combined treatment was 69%. It has been suggested that the American patients studied may not be comparable with the European patients who received this treatment because of differences in immunosuppressive regimens employed in the two locations.

Antiviral prophylaxis and preventive therapy are both effective in decreasing the incidence of CMV disease among transplant patients. Ganciclovir has been the most frequently used anti-CMV drug; it effectively prevents CMV disease during the first 3 months after allogeneic hematopoietic stem cell transplantation when administered during engraftment for pp65 antigenemia or detection of CMV DNA by PCR.[165-167] The use of ganciclovir also improves survival in selected high-risk patients.[167-169]

Another antiviral drug, valacyclovir, was compared with IV ganciclovir for prevention of CMV disease in 168 patients following allogeneic bone marrow transplant. Study patients received acyclovir following transplant, until the time of neutrophil engraftment; they then were randomly assigned to receive either oral valacyclovir or IV ganciclovir for 100 days. No significant difference was observed between the study arms for the incidence of CMV disease or the median time to onset of CMV disease. In this study, valacyclovir and ganciclovir were equivalent, and the authors concluded that oral valacyclovir may provide an alternative for patients who cannot tolerate ganciclovir because of neutropenia.[170]

The use of strategies to prevent CMV disease is resulting in a new syndrome called *late-onset CMV disease*, which in many cases involves infection with ganciclovir-resistant mutant viruses.[170,203a] Ganciclovir therapy and graft-versus-host disease and its treatment can delay recovery of CMV-specific T-cell immunity after marrow transplantation. This CMV-specific immunodeficiency can persist after ganciclovir therapy is stopped. The continued detection of CMV pp65 antigen or CMV DNA in plasma or peripheral blood leukocytes and lymphopenia noted after 3 months of ganciclovir preventive therapy are strong predictors of late CMV disease and death.[170] Late CMV disease developed at a median of 146 days after bone marrow transplantation in 18% of 146 patients with a mortality of 46%. Preventive measures against late CMV disease should be directed at patients in whom CMV became reactivated during the first 3 months after transplantation, as well as in patients with poor CMV-specific immunity and low CD4 cell counts.

Liver Transplantation

CMV remains the pathogen most commonly isolated after solid organ transplantation, including liver transplantation.[171,172] CMV hepatitis, an important problem that occurs after transplantation in adults, children, and infants, is more common after primary CMV infection. CMV disease, a leading cause of morbidity during the first 14 weeks after transplantation, increases costs and length of hospital stay.[173] The incidence of CMV hepatitis is greatest after transplantation from a CMV-seropositive donor. All cases of CMV hepatitis are characterized by prolonged fever, elevated bilirubinemia, and elevated liver enzyme concentrations. CMV hepatitis can also lead to liver failure that requires repeat transplantation. Management may be difficult because the signs of severe CMV hepatitis can be difficult to distinguish from graft rejection. Liver biopsy is the only reliable way to distinguish rejection from CMV hepatitis.[174] It is important that the clinician distinguish between these two possibilities because rejection is treated by an increase in immunosuppression, whereas CMV infection is treated by a decrease in immunosuppression and initiation of antiviral therapy. CMV predisposes to other opportunistic infections[175] and increases the risk for allograft rejection.[176] Attempts to prevent CMV disease in liver transplant recipients through administration of CMV immune globulin[177] or oral acyclovir[178,179] or a combination of the two[180] have had little effect on the incidence of CMV disease in seronegative recipients. The best results of prophylaxis for CMV disease in liver transplant recipients have been achieved with prolonged courses of intravenous ganciclovir.[146] Among 250 patients randomly assigned to receive ganciclovir or acyclovir intravenously after liver transplantation, ganciclovir recipients had an incidence of CMV disease of 0.8% during a follow-up period of 120 days, whereas CMV disease occurred in 38% of acyclovir recipients. Intravenous ganciclovir reduced the incidence of CMV infection in patients who were positive for CMV antigen and in those who were CMV antigen–negative. The striking decrease in CMV disease included decreases in pneumonia, gastrointestinal disease, hepatitis, retinitis, encephalitis, and CMV syndrome (see later).

A long course of oral ganciclovir 1000 mg three times/day was compared with matching placebo in liver transplant recipients.[150] The drug was begun no later than 10 days after transplantation and was continued until the 98th day after transplantation. Oral ganciclovir reduced the incidence of CMV disease in all subgroups when compared with placebo. The 6-month incidence of CMV disease was 18.9% in the placebo group and 4.8% (7 of 150) in the ganciclovir group ($P <$ .001). In the high-risk group of seronegative recipients of seropositive livers, the incidence of CMV disease was 44% in the placebo group and 14.8% in the ganciclovir group. A benefit was also seen among those who received antilymphocyte globulin in whom the frequency of CMV disease was 32.9% in the placebo group and 4.6% in the ganciclovir group. The study showed that oral ganciclovir prophylaxis was still effective despite the intense immunosuppression of antilymphocyte antibodies. Oral ganciclovir for prophylaxis was still not as effective as intravenous ganciclovir, which was associated with an incidence of 0.8% of CMV disease compared with 4.8% among oral ganciclovir recipients.[150]

The usual dose-limiting toxicity of ganciclovir is myelosuppression, which is less common in solid organ transplant recipients[146] than in bone marrow transplantation patients[144] or in patients with AIDS.[148] In the study of oral ganciclovir for liver transplant recipients, no associated significant myelotoxicity was observed. A trend toward a higher serum creatinine concentration was noted in ganciclovir recipients, which reflects the mild nephrotoxic effects of ganciclovir.[146] Valganciclovir has also supplanted the use of oral ganciclovir among these patients.

Kidney Transplantation

Morbidity due to CMV is lowest among kidney transplant recipients, but primary infection from a seropositive donor to a seronegative recipient can occur and is significantly more symptomatic than is secondary infection. Two studies[152,153] reported the clinical and laboratory findings from a total of 154 renal transplantation patients with CMV infection. In one of the series, 13 of 18 primary infections were associated with at least two of the following symptoms: fever, leukopenia, atypical lymphocytes, lymphocytosis, hepatosplenomegaly, myalgia, and arthralgia. This constellation of findings has been called the *CMV syndrome,* which is now defined as CMV infection accompanied by an otherwise unexplained fever of longer than 48 hours, malaise, and a fall in neutrophil count over 3 consecutive days.[150] This most common manifestation of CMV-associated illness in kidney transplant recipients contrasts with the appearance of secondary CMV infections, of which only 19% have been associated with fever.

Clinically significant CMV hepatitis is a rare occurrence among patients after renal transplantation,[181] but elevated hepatic enzymes (aspartate aminotransferase) were seen in 10 of 16 (63%) cases of primary CMV infection in kidney transplant recipients.[153] Five cases of CMV interstitial pneumonia were found in this group. Rejection of the transplanted kidney was also observed in 4 of 16 patients with primary infection. In this study, 24 seronegative patients who received kidneys from seronegative donors and remained seronegative did not undergo rejection. This is one of the very few studies that reached the conclusion that CMV infection may increase the likelihood of rejection of the transplanted organ.[153] In a large series of 126 kidney transplantation patients, hepatic dysfunction was observed in 22%.[182] Severe hepatitis was observed in seven, and CMV was isolated from the bodily fluids of all seven. At autopsy, five of these patients had evidence of CMV in the liver.

In a small series of kidney transplantation patients in whom CMV pneumonia developed, a mortality of 48% was noted.[183] This is much less than that observed among bone marrow transplantation patients in whom mortality as high as 84% has been reported.[3] In kidney transplant recipients who acquire CMV pneumonia, ganciclovir alone has been effective therapy for severe interstitial pneumonia, as has been noted earlier.[184]

Kidney transplant recipients have also been extensively studied in attempts to prevent CMV disease. In a study of CMV, hyperimmune globulin was administered to 24 seronegative kidney transplant recipients within 72 hours of transplantation and was continued for 16 weeks; the rate of CMV infection was 71% compared with 77% in 35

controls, but the rate of symptomatic disease decreased from 60% to 21%.[185] This study reported one death due to CMV in the treated group and five deaths in the control group; the higher rates of CMV disease and death may have been related to the widespread use of antithymocyte globulin. Prophylaxis with immunoglobulin was not shown to be effective in primary CMV disease following other solid organ transplants, such as liver transplants.[186] CMV antigen detection has been employed at the start of ganciclovir as preemptive therapy in CMV antibody–positive kidney transplantation patients and has met with success in the prevention of CMV disease.[187] Oral ganciclovir therapy has also been successful in lowering CMV DNA levels and in preventing CMV disease after renal transplantation; valganciclovir is now used for this indication.[151]

Resistance in Solid Organ Recipients

It is estimated that more than 67% of solid organ transplant recipients who are CMV-seronegative (R−) or who receive an organ from a seropositive donor (D+) have evidence of CMV infection. Only a small subgroup of these patients actually develops CMV end-organ disease. Primary infection with CMV that occurs in CMV-seronegative recipients of solid organ transplants from seropositive donors (D+/R−) is associated with the greatest increase in risk of disease. A long-term study of a large number of solid organ transplant recipients focused on the virologic characteristics related to drug resistance.[188] This study found that (D+/R−) serostatus was the only clear-cut predictor of drug resistance among patients in the Chicago and Cleveland cohorts. In the Cleveland cohort, high peak virus load was significantly associated with drug-resistant CMV. Ganciclovir was used for prophylaxis and treatment of all recipients; most of those who developed ganciclovir resistance received multiple courses of ganciclovir therapy. Two important host factors were strongly associated with the detection of ganciclovir-resistant CMV strains—lung transplantation and (D+/R−) CMV serostatus.[188] It was found that among all transplant groups, 28 of the 30 transplant recipients with resistant CMV strains were (D+/R−). This is similar to a finding by Limaye and colleagues.[189] Drug-resistant CMV was documented phenotypically and genotypically most frequently in lung transplant recipients in 2.2% of 228 Cleveland lung transplant recipients, and in 4.6% of 325 Chicago lung transplant recipients over a 7-year period from 1994 to 2001. When the (D+/R−) subgroup of recipients was examined, drug resistance in CMV isolates rose to 10.5% for the Cleveland cohort and 18.3% for the Chicago lung transplant recipients, respectively. This study also employed direct genotypic drug resistance assays, which use DNA extracts of clinical specimens as templates for direct PCR amplification and sequencing to detect known drug resistance mutations. This greatly shortens the time required to detect resistance, eliminates the need for cultures, and enables detection of all known mutations in either of the CMV genes UL97 and UL54, which indicate resistance of CMV to ganciclovir. This can make resistance testing available in 3 days and allows the clinician to use resistance assays when making patient management decisions. This study shows that drug resistance is an important aspect of CMV pathogenesis in solid organ transplant recipients. All patients with drug-resistant strains had CMV-related disease, and at least 50% died as a result of the infection.[188]

CONGENITAL CYTOMEGALOVIRUS INFECTION

Intrauterine CMV infections occur in 0.5% to 22% of all live births.[190] This mode of infection is less frequent than perinatal infection but is associated with the most serious CMV disease that occurs during the neonatal period. The diagnosis of congenital infection is best demonstrated by viruria within the first week of life. The presence of IgM antibodies against CMV in cord serum is suggestive of but not completely specific for congenital infection. Clinically significant congenital infection occurs most often in infants born to primiparous mothers with a primary infection during pregnancy.[63] Such infection is diagnosed in the mother through a change in antibody titer from negative to positive, or by detection of IgM antibody.

In a large group of 3712 pregnant women from upper and lower socioeconomic groups in Alabama, 21 primary infections were found in 1382 seronegative mothers.[191] Among this group of 21 mothers, 11 congenital infections occurred; three were symptomatic. This indicates that intrauterine infection of infants after primary CMV infection is high (55%). The rate of primary infection (0.52%) did not vary with socioeconomic status or immune status of the population. The rate of intrauterine CMV infection (24 in 8416 pregnancies) resulting from primary infection was 0.3%; 25% were symptomatic. These data indicate that primary infection at any stage of pregnancy presents a risk for intrauterine infection; the risk is highest during the first half of pregnancy.[192]

Congenital infection was observed in 20 babies from 2330 mothers (0.5%) who were seropositive.[191] This type of congenital infection occurs more frequently among mothers from lower socioeconomic groups with a high prevalence of past infection. None of the 20 babies had symptoms of congenital infection.[191] Other reports have claimed that symptomatic infection may rarely result from infection in an immune mother.[193] These results indicate that the neonate who acquires CMV disease generally acquires infection from a mother who is not immune. When mothers are immune, most infections among babies are asymptomatic. A small number of infections develop from transplacental infection. Perinatal infection occurs when CMV is carried in the cervix during late stages of pregnancy and when CMV is carried in breast milk.

Symptoms that occur in children who are infected congenitally from nonimmune mothers involve fulminant cytomegalic inclusion disease, which consists of jaundice, hepatosplenomegaly, petechial rash, and multiple organ involvement. CNS findings of microcephaly, motor disability, chorioretinitis, and cerebral calcifications are present.[194] At birth or shortly thereafter, onset of lethargy, respiratory distress, and seizures occurs. The child may die in days or a few weeks. Jaundice and hepatosplenomegaly may subside, but neurologic sequelae, microcephaly, and mental retardation persist. Many extraneural defects, including hearing disorders, have been associated with congenital infection, and most disease manifestations are the result of inflammation secondary to virus invasion.[194] Interference with organ development (such as occurs with rubella) is not seen with CMV infection.

Infections that occur in babies postnatally are very different from congenital infections; diffuse visceral and CNS diseases do not occur. The clinical picture may resemble CMV mononucleosis in some respects, although the full mononucleosis syndrome is usually absent. CMV mononucleosis may occur rarely in young children,[14] and much more severe CMV-associated disease can occur as the result of exchange transfusions.[195]

Although perinatal infections are completely asymptomatic and cause no obvious long-term abnormalities, subtle effects on hearing and intelligence have been reported. In a study of 8644 neonates from middle-class socioeconomic families, 53 were identified with IgM antibodies against CMV in cord blood (0.6%).[196] Forty-four of these children were evaluated at 3.5 to 7.0 years of age. The mean intelligence quotient (IQ) for the group was 103, which was lower than that of a matched control group. The school failure rate of this group was

2.7 times that of matched controls of the same socioeconomic status. Thirteen percent of these children (5 of 40) had severe bilateral hearing loss, and 3 had profound deafness. Inapparent CMV infection during the perinatal period is being invoked as a cause of the 1-in-1000 incidence of profound deafness in American children. Another report described the incidence of sensorineural hearing loss among those with neonatal CMV infection. In this study, 59 patients had congenital intrauterine infection, and 8 had symptoms at birth.[197] Twenty-one children had perinatal CMV infection, and none experienced hearing loss. Late-onset hearing loss developed in 17% of those with symptomatic congenital infection and in 14% of those with asymptomatic congenital CMV infection. In this study, pathology demonstrated virus in the cells of the organ of Corti and in neurons of the spira ganglia.[197] Rare typical nuclear inclusions were seen in cells of the cochlea. The problem of hearing loss associated with CMV cannot be predicted by severity of infection or IgM level at birth. This problem of hearing loss due to CMV has been cited as a major stimulus for the development of an effective vaccine for CMV and for research into other preventive measures.

CYTOMEGALOVIRUS INFECTION IN PREGNANT WOMEN

Possible sources of sexual transmission of CMV include virus in the uterine cervix and in semen. About 1% to 2% of women in the United States who undergo a routine medical examination in a private practice setting are found to carry the virus in the cervix.[63] In Taiwan, it was observed that 18% of a group with infrequent sexual relations had CMV isolated from the cervix.[198] A study of 134 women who attended a sexually transmitted diseases clinic in Seattle revealed that 34% of women older than 21 years of age had shed CMV in the cervix, and many of these women had evidence of shedding of multiple strains of CMV.[199] Frequency of colonization correlated with the number of sexual partners and age of first sexual intercourse, although no direct evidence has confirmed that CMV in the cervix comes from sexual intercourse or that it is transmitted by sexual intercourse. CMV is also found in high titers in the semen of both homosexual and heterosexual men.[64]

An increased rate of cervical infection occurs during the late stages of pregnancy. CMV in the uterine cervix is a source of infection transmitted to the neonate during passage through the birth canal. Three studies of 987 pregnant women showed an increasing prevalence of infection that progressed from first (0% to 2%), second (6% to 10%), and third trimesters (11% to 28%) (Table 134-1).[200-202] These three studies examined distinct populations. The study from Japan[200] included a nonpromiscuous middle-class population that was 85% CMV-seropositive. The study from Alabama in the United States included a young, sexually promiscuous group with a 10% rate of gonorrhea and a CMV-seropositive status of 89%.[201] The third study included 71 Native American Navajo and 125 middle-class white and black pregnant women.[202]

High cervical CMV excretion during the third trimester of pregnancy presents a risk of infection for the neonate during the birth process, but this risk may not be as important as that associated with transmission of perinatal infection from infected milk. In a study of 50 babies born to mothers who were nonsecretors, only 2 (4%) became

TABLE 134-1 Cervical Cytomegalovirus Infection during Pregnancy

| | Infection in Trimester | | | |
Source	First	Second	Third	Overall Infection
Numazaki et al.[169]	0/30 (0%)*	6/62 (9.7%)	17/61 (27.9%)	23/153 (15.0%)
Montgomery et al.[171]	1/43 (2%)	6/83 (7.2%)	6/49 (12.2%)	13/175 (7.4%)
Stagno et al.[170]	3/183 (1.6%)†	22/359 (6.1%)	42/371 (11.3%)	63/659 (9.6%)
Total infected/tested	4/256	34/504	65/481	99/987
Percentage infected	1.6	6.7	13.5	10.0

*Represents number of positive patients per number of patients tested.
†Number infected per number of specimens tested.
From Ho M. Cytomegalovirus. In: Mandell GL, Bennett JE, Dolin R, eds. Principles and Practice of Infectious Diseases, 4th ed. New York: Churchill Livingstone; 1995:1351.

infected, but 12.5% of babies born to mothers who secreted CMV from the cervix during the first or second trimester became infected, and 37% of babies born to mothers who secreted during the third trimester became infected. The infection rate of babies whose mothers shed virus postpartum and who were presumably shedding at birth rose to 57%.[203] During pregnancy, primary infection in the mother may manifest as a mild mononucleosis syndrome, but it is usually asymptomatic and is associated with CMV viruria for 4 to 7 days. Until recently, it was believed that recurrent infections during pregnancy were largely asymptomatic. Boppana and coworkers have demonstrated that reinfection with a different strain of CMV during pregnancy can lead to intrauterine transmission and symptomatic congenital infection.[204] This conclusion was based on the appearance of antibodies directed against new strain-specific epitopes of CMV glycoprotein H not present in maternal blood before the current pregnancy. To promote our understanding of the true frequency and clinical importance of congenital CMV infection caused by recurrent maternal infections, further investigation with larger, long-term prospective studies is required.[204]

REFERENCES

1. Zhang LJ, Hanpf P, Rutherford C, et al. Detection of cytomegalovirus, DNA, RNA, and antibody in normal donor blood. J Infect Dis. 1995;171:1002-1006.
2. Patel R, Surydman DR, Rubin RH, et al. Cytomegalovirus prophylaxis in solid organ transplant recipients. Transplantation. 1996;61:1279-1289.
3. Myers JD, Flournoy N, Thomas ED. Risk factors for cytomegalovirus infection after human marrow transplantation. J Infect Dis. 1986;153:478-488.
4. Masur H, Whitcup SM, Cartwright C, et al. Advances in the management of AIDS-related CMV retinitis. Ann Intern Med. 1996;125:126-136.
5. Crumpacker CS. Ganciclovir. N Engl J Med. 1996;335:721-729.
6. Ho M. Cytomegalovirus. In: Mandell GM, Bennett JE, Dolin R, eds. Principles and Practice of Infectious Diseases. 4th ed. New York: Churchill Livingstone; 1995.
7. Spector SA, Hirata KK, Neumann TR. Identification of multiple cytomegalovirus strains in homosexual men with acquired immunodeficiency syndrome. J Infect Dis. 1984;6:953-956.
8. Griffiths PD, Stagno S, Pass RF, et al. Infection with cytomegalovirus during pregnancy: Specific IgM antibodies as a marker of recent primary infection. J Infect Dis. 1982;145:647-653.
9. Smith MG. Propagation of salivary gland virus of the mouse in tissue cultures. Proc Soc Exp Biol Med. 1954;86:435-440.
10. Smith MG. Propagation in tissue cultures of a cytopathogenic virus from human salivary gland virus (SGV) disease. Proc Soc Exp Biol Med. 1956;92:424-430.
11. Weller TH, Macauley JC, Craig JM, et al. Isolation of intranuclear inclusion producing agents from infants with illnesses resembling cytomegalic inclusion disease. Proc Soc Exp Biol Med. 1957;94:4-12.
12. Rowe WP, Hartley JW, Waterman S, et al. Cytopathogenic agent resembling human salivary gland virus recovered from tissue cultures of human adenoids. Proc Soc Exp Biol Med. 1956;92:418-424.
13. Weller TH, Hanshaw JB, Scott DE. Serologic differentiation of viruses responsible for cytomegalic inclusion disease. Virology. 1960;12:130-132.
14. Klemola E, Kaarianen L. Cytomegalovirus as a possible cause of a disease resembling infectious mononucleosis. Br Med J. 1965;1099:102.
15. Kaarianen L, Klemola E, Paloheimo J. Rise of cytomegalovirus antibodies in an infectious-mononucleosis-like syndrome after transfusion. Br Med J. 1966;2:1270-1272.
16. Winston DJ, Ho WG, Howell CL, et al. Cytomegalovirus infections associated with leukocyte transfusions. Ann Intern Med. 1980;93:671-675.
17. Chee MS, Bankier AT, Becks S, et al. Analysis of the protein-coding content of the sequence of human cytomegalovirus strain—AD 169. Curr Top Microbiol Immunol. 1990;154:125-169.
18. Cha T, Tom S, Kemble GW, et al. Human cytomegalovirus clinical isolates carry at least 19 genes not found in laboratory strains. J Virol. 1996;70:78-83.
19. Rul PF, Powell KL. Physical and functional interaction of human cytomegalovirus DNA polymerase and its accessory protein (ZCP36) expressed in insect cells. J Virol. 1992;66:4126-4133.
20. Chee MS, Lawrence GL, Barell BG. Alpha-, beta- and gamma-herpesviruses encode a putative phosphotransferase. J Gen Virol. 1989;70:1151-1160.
21. Sullivan V, Talarico CL, Stanat SC, et al. A protein kinase homologue controls phosphorylation of ganciclovir in human cytomegalovirus infected cells. Nature. 1992;358:162-164. [Errata. Nature. 1992;359:85 and 1993;366:756.]
22. Littler E, Stuart AD, Chee MS. Human cytomegalovirus UL 97 open reading frame encodes a protein that phosphorylates the antiviral nucleoside analogue ganciclovir. Nature. 1992;358:160-162.
23. He Z, He YS, Kim Y, et al. The human cytomegalovirus UL97 protein is a protein kinase that autophosphorylates on serines and threonines. J Virol. 1997;71:405-411.
24. Beersma MF, Bizlemaker MJ, Ploegh HL. Human cytomegalovirus down regulates HLA class I expression by reducing the stability of class I H chains. J Immunol. 1993;151:4455-4464.
25. Schuster EA, Bencke JS, Tegtmeier GE, et al. Monoclonal antibody for rapid laboratory detection of cytomegalovirus infections: Characterization and diagnostic application. Mayo Clin Proc. 1985;60:577-585.
26. Fetterman GH. A new laboratory aid in the clinical diagnosis of inclusion disease of infancy. Am J Clin Pathol. 1952;22:424-425.
27. Rinaldo CR, Black PH, Hirsch MS. Interactions of cytomegalovirus with leukocytes from patients with mononucleosis due to cytomegalovirus. J Infect Dis. 1977;136:667-678.
28. Singh N, Dummer JS, Ho M, et al. Infections with cytomegalovirus and other herpesviruses in 121 liver transplant recipients: Transmission by donated organ and the effect of OKT3 antibodies. J Infect Dis. 1988;158:124-131.
29. Martin WJ, Smith TJ. Rapid detection of cytomegalovirus in bronchoalveolar lavage specimens by a monoclonal antibody method. J Clin Microbiol. 1986;23:1006-1008.
30. van der Bij W, Schirm J, Torensma R, et al. Comparison between viremia and antigenemia for detection of cytomegalovirus in blood. J Clin Microbiol. 1988;26:2531-2535.
31. Chou S, Merigan TC. Rapid detection and quantitation of human cytomegalovirus in urine through DNA hybridization. N Engl J Med. 1983;308:921-925.
32. Churchill MA, Zaia JA, Forman SJ, et al. Quantitation of human cytomegalovirus DNA in lungs from bone marrow transplant recipients with interstitial pneumonia. J Infect Dis. 1987;155:501-509.
33. Stanier P, Kitchen AD, Taylor DL, et al. Detection of human cytomegalovirus in peripheral mononuclear cells and urine samples using PCR. Mol Cell Probes. 1992;6:51-58.
34. Gerna G, Zipeto D, Parea M, et al. Monitoring of human cytomegalovirus infections and ganciclovir treatment in heart transplant recipients by determination of viremia, antigenemia, and DNAemia. J Infect Dis. 1991;164:488-498.
35. Wolf DG, Spector SA. Diagnosis of human cytomegalovirus central nervous system disease in AIDS patients by DNA amplification from cerebrospinal fluid. J Infect Dis. 1992;166:1412-1415.
36. Fox JD, Brink NS, Zuckerman MA, et al. Detection of herpesvirus DNA by nested polymerase chain reaction in cerebrospinal fluid of human immunodeficiency virus-infected persons with neurologic disease: A prospective evaluation. J Infect Dis. 1995;172:1087-1090.
37. Bowen F, Sabiwca, Wilson P, et al. Cytomegalovirus (CMV) viraemia detected by polymerase chain reaction identifiers. A group at high risk of CMV disease. AIDS. 1997;11:889-893.
38. Shinkai M, Boizette SA, Powderly W, et al. Utility of urine and leukocyte cultures and plasma DNA PCR for identification of AIDS patients at risk for developing human cytomegalovirus disease. J Infect Dis. 1997;175:302-332.
39. Dodt KK, Jacobsen PH, Hofman B, et al. Development of cytomegalovirus (CMV) disease can be predicted in HIV infected patients by CMV polymerase chain reaction and antigenemia test. AIDS. 1997;11F:21-28.
40. Spector SA, Wong R, Hiza K, et al. Plasma cytomegalovirus (CMV) DNA load predicts CMV disease and survival in AIDS patients. J Clin Invest. 1998;101:497-502.
41. Imbert-Marcille BM, Cantarovich D, Ferre-Aubineau V, et al. Usefulness of DNA viral load quantification for cytomegalovirus disease monitoring in renal and pancreas/renal transplant recipients. Transplantation. 1997;63:1476-1481.
42. Singh N, Yu VL, Mieles L, et al. High-dose acyclovir compared with short-course preemptive ganciclovir therapy to prevent cytomegalovirus disease in liver transplant recipients: A randomized trial. Ann Intern Med. 1994;120:375-381.
43. Flood J, Drew WL, Miner R, et al. Diagnosis of cytomegalovirus (CMV) polyradiculopathy and documentation of in vivo anti-CMV activity in cerebrospinal fluid by using branched DNA signal amplification and antigen assays. J Infect Dis. 1997;176:348-352.
44. Boeckl M, Gooley TA, Myerson D, et al. Cytomegalovirus pp65 antigenemia guided early treatment with ganciclovir marrow transplantation: A randomized double blind study. Blood. 1997;88:4063-4071.
45. Avery RK, Adal KA, Longworth DL, Bolwell BJ. A survey of allogeneic bone marrow transplant programs in the United States regarding cytomegalovirus prophylaxis and pre-emptive therapy. Bone Marrow Transplant. 2000;26:763-767.
46. Schulenburg A, Watkins-Riedel T, Greinix HT, et al. CMV monitoring after peripheral blood stem cell and bone marrow transplantation by pp65 antigen and quantitative PCR. Bone Marrow Transplant. 2001;28:765-768.
47. Boivin G, Belanger R, Delage R, et al. Quantitative analysis of cytomegalovirus (CMV) viremia using the pp65 antigenemia assay and the COBAS AMPLICOR CMV MONITOR PCR test after blood and marrow allogeneic transplantation. J Clin Microbiol. 2000;38:4356-4360.
48. Masaoka T, Hiraoka A, Ohta K, et al. Evaluation of the AMPLICOR CMV, COBAS AMPLICOR CMV monitor and antigenemia assay for cytomegalovirus disease. Jpn J Infect Dis. 2001;54:12-16.
49. Sia IG, Wilson JA, Smith TF, et al. Evaluation of the COBAS AMPLICOR CMV MONITOR test for detection of viral DNA in specimens taken from patients after liver transplantation. J Clin Microbiol. 2000;38:600-606.
50. Ho SK, Li FK, Lai KN, Chan TM. Comparison of the CMV brite turbo assay and the digene hybrid capture CMV DNA (Version 2.0) assay for quantitation of cytomegalovirus in renal transplant recipients. J Clin Microbiol. 2000;38:3743-3745.
51. Mazzulli T, Drew LW, Yen-Lieberman B, et al. Multicenter comparison of the digene hybrid capture CMV DNA assay (Version 2.0), the pp65 antigenemia assay, and cell culture for detection of cytomegalovirus viremia. J Clin Microbiol. 1999;37:958-963.
52. Tong CY, Cuevas LE, Williams H, Bakran A. Comparison of two commercial methods for measurement of cytomegalovirus load in blood samples after renal transplantation. J Clin Microbiol. 2000;38:1209-1213.

53. Siennicka J, Rechnio M, Durlik M, et al. Quantitative detection of CMV DNA by PCR and hybridization methods in renal transplant recipients. Acta Microbiol Pol. 2000;49:261-264.

54. Humar A, Gregson D, Caliendo AM, et al. Clinical utility of quantitative cytomegalovirus viral load determination for predicting cytomegalovirus disease in liver transplant recipients. Transplantation. 1999;68:1305-1311.

55. Piiparinen H, Hockerstedt K, Lappalainen M, et al. Monitoring of viral load by quantitative plasma PCR during active cytomegalovirus infection of individual liver transplant patients. J Clin Microbiol. 2002;40:2945-2952.

56. Flexman J, Kay I, Fonte R, et al. Differences between the quantitative antigenemia assay and the cobas amplicor monitor quantitative PCR assay for detecting CMV viraemia in bone marrow and solid organ transplant patients. J Med Virol. 2001;64 275-282.

57. Caliendo AM, St George K, Allega J, et al. Distinguishing cytomegalovirus (CMV) infection and disease with CMV nucleic acid assays. J Clin Microbiol. 2002;40: 1581-1586.

58. Erice A, Tierney C, Hirsch M, et al. Cytomegalovirus (CMV) and human immunodeficiency virus (HIV) burden, CMV end-organ disease, and survival in subjects with advanced HIV infection (AIDS Clinical Trials Group Protocol 360). Clin Infect Dis. 2003;37:567-578.

59. Razonable RR, Brown RA, Wilson J, et al. The clinical use of various blood compartments for cytomegalovirus (CMV) DNA quantitation in transplant recipients with CMV disease. Transplantation. 2002;73:968-973.

60. Gerna G, Baldanti F, Lilleri D, et al. Human cytomegalovirus pp67 mRNAemia versus pp65 antigenemia for guiding preemptive therapy in heart and lung transplant recipients: A prospective, randomized, controlled, open-label trial. Transplantation. 2003;75:1012-1019.

61. Weinberg A, Schissel D, Giller R. Molecular methods for cytomegalovirus surveillance in bone marrow transplant recipients. J Clin Microbiol. 2002;40:4203-4206.

62. Dunkel EC, Scheer DI, Zhu Q, et al. A rabbit model for human cytomegalovirus-induced chorioretinal disease (retraction). J Infect Dis. 1998;177:1778.

63. Ho M. Cytomegalovirus: Biology and Infection. 2nd ed. New York: Plenum; 1991:440.

64. Lang DJ, Kummer JF. Demonstration of cytomegalovirus in semen. N Engl J Med. 1972;287:756-758.

65. Klemola E, von Essen R, Henle G, et al. Infectious-mononucleosis-like disease with negative heterophil agglutination test. Clinical features in relation to Epstein-Barr virus and cytomegalovirus and antibodies. J Infect Dis. 1970;121:608-614.

66. Chou S, Kim DY, Norman DJ. Transmission of cytomegalovirus by pretransplant leukocyte transfusions in renal transplant candidates. J Infect Dis. 1987;155:565-567.

67. Bowden RA, Sayers M, Flourney N, et al. Cytomegalovirus immune globulin and seronegative blood products to prevent primary cytomegalovirus infection after marrow transplantation. N Engl J Med. 1986;314:1006-1010.

68. Wreghitt TG, Teare EL, Sule O, et al. Cytomegalovirus infection in immunocompetent patients. Clin Infect Dis. 2003;37:1603-1606.

69. Carter AR. Cytomegalovirus disease presenting as hepatitis. Br Med J. 1968;3:786.

70. Bonkowsky HL, Lee RV, Klatskin G. Acute granulomatous hepatitis: Occurrence in cytomegalovirus mononucleosis. JAMA. 1984;37:1284-1288.

71. Leonard JC, Tobin JOH. Polyneuritis associated with cytomegalovirus infections. Q J Med. 1971;40:435-442.

72. Schmitz H, Enders G. Cytomegalovirus as a frequent cause of Guillain-Barre syndrome. J Med Virol. 1977;1:21-27.

73. Eidelberg D, Sotrel A, Vogel H, et al. Progressive polyradiculopathy in acquired immune deficiency syndrome. Neurology. 1986;36:912-916.

74. Klemola E, Kaariainen L, von Essen R, et al. Further studies on cytomegalovirus mononucleosis in previously healthy individuals. Acta Med Scand. 1967;182: 311-322.

75. Tiula E, Leinikki P. Fatal cytomegalovirus infection in a previously healthy boy with myocarditis and consumption coagulopathy as presenting signs. Scand J Infect Dis. 1972;4:57-60.

76. Waris E, Rasanen P, Kreus KE, et al. Fatal cytomegalovirus disease in a previously healthy adult. Scand J Infect Dis. 1972;4:61-67.

77. Chanarin I, Walford DM. Thrombocytopenic purpura in cytomegalovirus mononucleosis. Lancet. 1973;1:238-239.

78. Harris AI, Meyer RJ, Brody EA. Cytomegalovirus-induced thrombocytopenia and hemolysis in an adult. Ann Intern Med. 1975;83:670-671.

79. Klemola E. Hypersensitivity reactions to ampicillin in cytomegalovirus mononucleosis. Scand J Infect Dis. 1970;2:29-31.

80. Muller-Stamou A, Senn HJ, Emody G. Epidermolysis in a case of severe cytomegalovirus infection. Br Med J. 1974;3:609-610.

81. Collier AC, Meyers JD, Corey L, et al. Cytomegalovirus infection in homosexual men. Am J Med. 1987;82:493-600.

82. Drew WL, Mills J, Levy J, et al. Cytomegalovirus infection and abnormal T-leukocyte subset ratios in homosexual men. Ann Intern Med. 1985;103:61-63.

83. Gallant JE, Moore RD, Richman DP, et al. Incidence and natural history of cytomegalovirus disease in patients with advanced human immunodeficiency virus disease treated with zidovudine. J Infect Dis. 1992;166:1223-1227.

84. McKenzie R, Travis WD, Dolan SA, et al. The causes of death in patients with human immunodeficiency virus infection: A clinical and pathologic study with emphasis on the role of pulmonary diseases. Medicine (Baltimore). 1991;70:326-343.

85. Hammer SM, Squires KE, Hughes MD, et al. A controlled trial of two nucleosides analogues plus indinavir in persons with immunodeficiency virus infection and CD4 cell counts of 200 per cubic millimeter or less. N Engl J Med. 1997;337:725-732.

86. Autran B, Carcelain G, Li TS, et al. Positive effects of combined antiretroviral therapy on CD4 T-cell homeostasis and function in advanced HIV disease. Science. 1997;277:112-116.

87. Mills J, Jacobsen MA, O'Donnell JJ, et al. Treatment of cytomegalovirus retinitis in patients with AIDS. Rev Infect Dis. 1988;3:S522-5531.

88. Anderson RD, Griffy KG, Jung D, et al. Ganciclovir absolute bioavailability and steady state pharmacokinetics after oral administration of two 3000-mg/d dosing regimens in human immunodeficiency virus- and cytomegalovirus-seropositive patients. Clin Ther. 1995;17:425-432.

89. Drew WI, Ives D, Lalezari JP, et al. Oral ganciclovir as maintenance treatment for cytomegalovirus retinitis in patients with AIDS. N Engl J Med. 1995;333:615-620.

90. Martin DF, Parks DJ, Mellow SD, et al. Treatment of cytomegalovirus retinitis with an intraocular sustained release ganciclovir implant: A randomized controlled clinical trial. Arch Ophthalmol. 1994;112:1531-1539.

91. Martin DF, Kuppermann BD, Wolitz RA, et al, for the Roche Ganciclovir Study Group. Oral ganciclovir for patients with cytomegalovirus retinitis treated with a ganciclovir implant. N Engl J Med. 1999;340:1063-1070.

92. Miller RG, Storcy JR, Greco CM. Ganciclovir in the treatment of progressive AIDS-related polyradiculopathy. Neurology. 1990;40:569-574.

93. Fuller GN, Gill SK, Guiloff RJ, et al. Ganciclovir for lumbosacral polyradiculopathy in AIDS. Lancet. 1990;335:48-49.

94. Jacobson MA, Mills J, Rush J, et al. Failure of antiviral therapy for acquired immunodeficiency syndrome-related cytomegalovirus myelitis. Arch Neurol. 1988;45:1090-1092.

95. Fletcher CV, Balfour HH. Evaluation of ganciclovir for cytomegalovirus disease. DICP. 1989;23:5-12.

96. Enting R, de Gans J, Reiss P, et al. Ganciclovir/foscarnet for cytomegalovirus meningoencephalitis in AIDS. Lancet. 1992;340:559-560.

97. Fuller GN. Cytomegalovirus and the peripheral nervous system in AIDS. J Acquir Immune Defic Syndr. 1992;5(Suppl 1):S33-S36.

98. Knapp AB, Horst DA, Eliopoulos G, et al. Widespread cytomegalovirus gastroenterocolitis in a patient with acquired immunodeficiency syndrome. Gastroenterology. 1983;85:1399-1402.

99. Meiselman MS, Cello JP, Margaretten W. Cytomegalovirus colitis. Report of the clinical, endoscopic, and pathologic findings in two patients with acquired immune deficiency syndrome. Gastroenterology. 1985;88:171-175.

100. Collaborative DHPG Treatment Study Group. Treatment of serious cytomegalovirus infections with 9-(1,3-dihydroxy-2-propoxymethyl)guanine in patients with AIDS and other immunodeficiencies. N Engl J Med. 1986;314:801-805.

101. Dieterich DT, Kotler DP, Busch DF, et al. Ganciclovir treatment of cytomegalovirus colitis in AIDS: A randomized, double-blind, placebo-controlled multicenter study. J Infect Dis. 1992;167:278-282.

102. Reed EC, Bowden RA, Dandliker PS, et al. Treatment of cytomegalovirus pneumonia with ganciclovir and intravenous cytomegalovirus immunoglobulin in patients with bone marrow transplants. Ann Intern Med. 1988;109:783-788.

103. Texidor HS, Honig CL, Norsoph E, et al. Cytomegalovirus infection of the alimentary canal: Radiologic findings with pathologic correlation. Radiology. 1987;163:317-323.

104. Blumberg RS, Kelsey P, Perrone T, et al. Cytomegalovirus- and cryptosporidium-associated acalculous gangrenous cholecystitis. Am J Med. 1984;76:1118-1123.

105. Feinberg JE, Hurwitz S, Cooper D, Satler FR. A randomized double-blind trial of valaciclovir prophylates for cytomegalovirus disease in patients with advanced human immunodeficiency virus infection. J Infect Dis. 1998;177:48-56.

106. Goudrield J, Khardori N. Cytomegalovirus: The taming of the beast? Lancet. 1997;350:1718-1719.

107. Martin JC, Dvorak CA, Smee DF, et al. 9-[(1,3-Dihydroxy-2-propoxy)methyl] guanine: A new potent and selective antiherpes agent. J Med Chem. 1983;26:759-761.

108. Ashton WT, Karkas JD, Field AK, Tolman RI. Activation by thymidine kinase and potent antiherpetic activity of 2'-nor-2'-deoxyguanosine (2'NDG). Biochem Biophys Res Commun. 1982;108:1716-1721.

109. Ogilvie UK, Cheriyan UD, Radatus OX, et al. Biologically active acyclonucleoside analogues. II. The synthesis of 9-(2-hydroxy-1-[hydroxymethyl, ethoxymethyl]guanine) BIOLF-62. Can J Chem. 1982;60:3005-3010.

110. Cheng YC, Huang ES, Lin JC, et al. Unique spectrum of activity of 9-[(1,3-dihydroxy-2-propoxy)methyl]-guanine against herpesviruses in vitro and its mode of action against herpes simplex virus type 1. Proc Natl Acad Sci USA. 1983;80: 2767-2770.

111. Field AK, Davies ME, DeWitt C, et al. 9[{2-Hydroxy-1-(hydroxymethyl) ethoxy}methyl]guanine: A selective inhibitor of herpes group virus replication. Proc Natl Acad Sci USA. 1983;80:4139-4143.

112. Cheng YC, Grill SP, Dutschman GE, et al. Metabolism of 9-(1,3-dihydroxy-2-propoxymethyl)guanine, a new anti-herpes virus compound, in herpes simplex virus-infected cells. J Biol Chem. 1983;258:12460-12464.

113. Hamzeh FM, Lietman PS. Intranuclear accumulation of subgenomic noninfectious human cytomegalovirus DNA in infected cells in the presence of ganciclovir. Antimicrob Agents Chemother. 1991;35:1818-1823.

114. Hamzeh FM, Lietman PS, Gibson W, Hayward GS. Identification of the lytic origin of DNA replication in human cytomegalovirus by a novel approach utilizing ganciclovir-induced chain termination. J Virol. 1990;64:6184-6195.

115. Biron KK, Stanat SC, Sorrell JB, et al. Metabolic activation of the nucleoside analog 9-[{hydroxy-1-(hydroxymethyl)ethoxy}methyl]guanine in human diploid fibroblasts infected with human cytomegalovirus. Proc Natl Acad Sci USA. 1985;82:2473-2477.

116. Martin DF, Sierra-Madero J, Walmsley S, et al. A controlled trial of valganciclovir as induction therapy for cytomegalovirus retinitis. N Engl J Med. 2002;346:1119-1126.

117. Chou S, Erice A, Jordan MC, et al. Analysis of the UL 97 phosphotransferase coding sequence in clinical cytomegalovirus isolates and identification of mutations conferring ganciclovir resistance. J Infect Dis. 1995;171:576-583.

118. Lurain NS, Spatford LE, Thompson KD. Mutation in the UL 97 open reading frame of human cytomegalovirus strains resistant to ganciclovir. J Virol. 1994;68:4427-4431.

119. Erice A, Gil-Roda C, Perez JL, et al. Antiviral susceptibilities and analysis of UL97 and DNA polymerase sequences of clinical cytomegalovirus isolates from immunocompromised patients. J Infect Dis. 1997;175:1087-1092.

120. Erice A, Chou S, Biron KK, et al. Progressive disease due to ganciclovir-resistant cytomegalovirus in immunocompromised patients. N Engl J Med. 1989;320:289-293.

121. Drew WL, Miner RC, Busch DF, et al. Prevalence of resistance in patients receiving ganciclovir for serious cytomegalovirus infection. J Infect Dis. 1991;163:716-719.

122. Stanat SC, Reardon JE, Erice A, et al. Ganciclovir resistant cytomegalovirus clinical isolates: Mode of resistance to ganciclovir. Antimicrob Agents Chemother. 1991;35:2191-2197.

123. Lurain NS, Thompson KD, Holmes EW, Read GS. Point mutations in the DNA polymerase gene of human cytomegalovirus that result in resistance to antiviral agents. J Virol. 1992;66:7146-7152.

124. Chou S, Guentzel S, Michels KR, et al. Frequency of UL 97 phosphotransferase mutations related to ganciclovir resistance in clinical cytomegalovirus isolates. J Infect Dis. 1995;172:239-242.

125. Sullivan V, Biron KK, Talarico C, et al. A point mutation in the human cytomegalovirus DNA polymerase gene confers resistance to ganciclovir and phosphonylmethoxyalkyl derivatives. Antimicrob Agents Chemother. 1993;37:19-25.

126. Chou S, Lurain NS, Weinberg A, et al. Interstrain variation in the human cytomegalovirus DNA polymerase sequence and its effect on genotype diagnosis of antiviral drug resistance. Antimicrob Agents Chemother. 1999;43:1500-1502.

127. Jabs DA, Enger C, Dunn JP, Forman M, for the CMV Retinitis and Viral Resistance Study Group. Cytomegalovirus retinitis and viral resistance: Ganciclovir resistance. J Infect Dis. 1998;177:770-773.

128. Jabs DA, Martin BK, Forman MS, et al. Cytomegalovirus resistance to ganciclovir and clinical outcomes of patients with cytomegalovirus retinitis. Am J Ophthalmol. 2003;135:26-34.

129. Crumpacker CS. Mechanism of action of foscarnet against viral polymerases. Am J Med. 1992;92(Suppl 2A):2A3S-2A7S.

130. Jacobson MA, Wulfsohn M, Feinberg JE, et al. Phase II dose-ranging trial of foscarnet salvage therapy for cytomegalovirus retinitis in AIDS patients intolerant of or resistant to ganciclovir (ACTG protocol 093). AIDS. 1994;8:451-459.

131. Baldanti F, Underwood MR, Stanat SC, et al. Single amino acid changes in the DNA polymerase confer foscarnet resistance and slow growth phenotype, while mutation in the UL 97 encoded phosphotransferase confers ganciclovir resistance in the double-resistant human cytomegalovirus strains removed from patients with AIDS. J Virol. 1996;70:1390-1395.

132. Chou S, Marousek G, Parenti DM, et al. Mutation in region III of the DNA polymerase gene conferring foscarnet resistance in cytomegalovirus isolates from 3 subjects receiving prolonged antiviral therapy. J Infect Dis. 1998;178:526-530.

133. Weinberg A, Jabs DA, Chou S, et al. Mutations conferring foscarnet resistance in a cohort of patients with acquired immunodeficiency syndrome and cytomegalovirus retinitis. J Infect Dis. 2003;187:777-784.

134. Studies of Ocular Complications of AIDS Research Group, AIDS Clinical Trials Group. Mortality in patients with the acquired immunodeficiency syndrome treated with either foscarnet or ganciclovir for cytomegalovirus retinitis. N Engl J Med. 1992;326:213-220. [Erratum, N Engl J Med. 1992;326:1172.]

135. Studies of Ocular Complications of AIDS Research Group, AIDS Clinical Trials Group. Combination foscarnet and ganciclovir therapy vs. monotherapy for the treatment of relapsed cytomegalovirus retinitis in patients with AIDS: The Cytomegalovirus Retreatment Trial. Arch Ophthalmol. 1996;114:23-33.

136. Ho HT, Woods KL, Bronson JJ, et al. Intercellular metabolism of the antiherpes agent (S)-1-{3-hydroxy-2-(phosphonylmethoxy)propyl}cytosine. Mol Pharmacol. 1992;41:197-202.

137. Lalezari JP, Jaffe HS, Stagg RG, et al. Randomized controlled study of the safety and efficacy of intravenous cidofovir for the treatment of relapsing cytomegalovirus retinitis in patients with AIDS. J AIDS. 1998;17:339-344.

138. Polis MA, Spooner KM, Baird BF, et al. Anticytomegaloviral activity and safety of ganciclovir in patients with human immunodeficiency virus infection and cytomegaloviruses. Antimicrob Agents Chemother. 1995;39:882-886.

139. Lalezari JP, Stagg RJ, Kupperman BD, et al. Intravenous ganciclovir for peripheral cytomegalovirus retinitis in patients with AIDS. Ann Intern Med. 1997;126:257-263.

140. Crumpacker CS, Kowalsky PN, Oliver SA, et al. Resistance of herpes simplex virus to 9-{[2-hydroxy-1-(hydroxymethyl)ethoxy]methyl}guanine: Physical mapping of drug synergism within the viral DNA polymerase locus. Proc Natl Acad Sci USA. 1984;81:1556-1560.

141. Manischevitz JF, Quinnan GV, Lane HC, Witter AE. Synergistic effect of ganciclovir and foscarnet on cytomegalovirus replication in vitro. Antimicrob Agents Chemother. 1990;34:373-375.

142. Cherrington JM, Fuller MD, Lamy PD, et al. In vitro antiviral susceptibilities of isolates from CMV retinitis patients receiving first or second line cidofovir therapy, relationship to clinical outcome. J Infect Dis. 1998;178:1821-1825.

143. Chilar T, Fuller MD, Cherrington JM. Characterization of drug resistance associated mutations in the human cytomegalovirus DNA polymerase gene by using recombinant mutant viruses generated from overlapping DNA fragments. J Virol. 1998;72:5927-5936.

144. Goodrich JM, Mori M, Gleaves CA, et al. Early treatment with ganciclovir to prevent cytomegalovirus disease after allogeneic bone marrow transplantation. N Engl J Med. 1991;325:1601-1607.

145. Schmidt GM, Horack DA, Niland JC, et al. A randomized, controlled trial of prophylactic ganciclovir for cytomegalovirus pulmonary infection in recipients of allogeneic bone marrow transplants. N Engl J Med. 1991;324:1005-1011.

146. Merigan TC, Renlund DG, Keay S, et al. A controlled trial of ganciclovir to prevent cytomegalovirus disease after heart transplantation. N Engl J Med. 1992;326:1182-1186.

147. Winston DJ, Wirin D, Shaked A, Busuttil RW. Randomized comparison of ganciclovir and high-dose acyclovir for long-term cytomegalovirus prophylaxis in liver-transplant recipients. Lancet. 1995;346:69-74.

148. Spector SA, McKinley GF, Lalezari JP, et al. Oral ganciclovir for the prevention of cytomegalovirus disease in persons wth AIDS. N Engl J Med. 1996;334:1491-1497.

149. Spector SA, Wong R, Hiza K, et al. Plasma cytomegalovirus (CMV) DNA load predicts CMV disease and survival in AIDS patients. J Clin Invest. 1998;101:497-502.

150. Gane E, Salida F, Valdecasas GJC, et al. Randomized trial of efficacy and safety of oral ganciclovir in the prevention of cytomegalovirus disease in liver transplant recipients. Lancet. 1997;350:1729-1733.

151. Brennan D, Garlick K, Singer G, et al. Prophylactic oral ganciclovir compared to deferred therapy for control of cytomegalovirus disease in renal transplant patients. Transplantation. 1997;64:1843-1846.

152. Ho M, Suwansirikul S, Dowling JN, et al. The transplanted kidney as a source of cytomegalovirus infection. N Engl J Med. 1975;293:1109-1112.

153. Betts RF, Freeman RB, Douglas RG Jr, et al. Transmission of cytomegalovirus infection with renal allograft. Kidney Int. 1975;8:387-394.

154. Ho M. Virus infections after transplantation in man. Arch Virol. 1977;55:1-24.

155. Dowling JN, Saslow AR, Ho M, et al. Cytomegalovirus infection in patients receiving immunosuppressive therapy for rheumatologic disorders. J Infect Dis. 1976;133:399-408.

156. Rubin RH. Infection in the renal transplant patient. In: Rubin RH, Young LS, eds. Clinical Approach to Infection in the Compromised Host. New York: Plenum; 1981:553-605.

157. Dummer JS, Hardy A, Poorsatter A, et al. Early infections in kidney, heart and liver transplant recipients on cyclosporine. Transplantation. 1983;36:259-267.

158. Thomason AW. FK-506—How much potential? Immunol Today. 1990;11:6-9.

159. Shepp DH, Dandliker PS, de Miranda P, et al. Activity of 9-[2-hydroxy-1-(hydroxymethyl)ethoxymethyl]guanine in the treatment of cytomegalovirus pneumonia. Ann Intern Med. 1985;103:368-373.

160. Crumpacker CS, Marlowe S, Zhang JL, et al. Ganciclovir Bone Marrow Transplant Treatment Group. Treatment of cytomegalovirus pneumonia. Rev Infect Dis. 1988;10(Suppl 3):S538-S546.

161. Emmanuel D, Cunningham I, Jules-Elysee K, et al. Cytomegalovirus pneumonia after bone marrow transplantation successfully treated with the combination of ganciclovir and high-dose intravenous immune globulin. Ann Intern Med. 1988;109:783-788.

162. Reed EC, Bowden RA, Dandliker PS, et al. Treatment of cytomegalovirus pneumonia with ganciclovir and intravenous cytomegalovirus immunoglobulin in patients with bone marrow transplants. Ann Intern Med. 1988;109:783-788.

163. Schmidt GM, Kovacs A, Zaia JA, et al. Ganciclovir/immunoglobulin combination therapy for the treatment of human cytomegalovirus-associated interstitial pneumonia in bone marrow allograft recipients. Transplantation. 1988;46:905-907.

164. Ljungman P, Engelhard D, Link H. Treatment of interstitial pneumonitis due to cytomegalovirus with ganciclovir and intravenous immune globulin: Experience of European bone marrow transplantation. Clin Infect Dis. 1992;14:831-835.

165. Winston DJ, Ho WG, Bartoni K, et al. Ganciclovir prophylaxis of cytomegalovirus infection and disease in allogeneic bone marrow transplant recipients. Results of a placebo-controlled, double-blind trial. Ann Intern Med. 1993;118:179-184.

166. Boeckh M, Gooley TA, Myerson D, et al. Cytomegalovirus pp65 antigenemia-guided early treatment with ganciclovir versus ganciclovir at engraftment after allogeneic marrow transplantation: A randomized double-blind study. Blood. 1996;88:4063-4071.

167. Einsele H, Ehninger G, Hebart H, et al. Polymerase chain reaction monitoring reduces the incidence of cytomegalovirus disease and the duration and side effects of antiviral therapy after bone marrow transplantation. Blood. 1995;86:2815-2820.

168. Ljungman P, Aschan J, Lewensohn-Fuchs I, et al. Results of different strategies for reducing cytomegalovirus-associated mortality in allogeneic stem cell transplant recipients. Transplantation. 1998;66:1330-1334.

169. Boeckh M, Leisenring W, Riddell SR, et al. Late cytomegalovirus disease and mortality in recipients of allogeneic hematopoietic stem cell transplants: Importance of viral load and T-cell immunity. Blood. 2003;101:407-414.

170. Winston DJ, Yeager AM, Chandrasekar PH, et al. Randomized comparison of oral valacyclovir and intravenous ganciclovir for prevention of cytomegalovirus disease after allogeneic bone marrow transplantation. Clin Infect Dis. 2003;36:749-758.

171. Patel R, Snydman DR, Rubin RH, et al. Cytomegalovirus prophylaxis in solid organ transplant recipients. Transplantation. 1996;61:1279-1289.

172. Stratta RJ, Shaeffer MS, Markin RS, et al. Clinical patterns of cytomegalovirus disease after liver transplantation. Arch Surg. 1989;124:1433-1450.

173. McCarthy JM, Karim MA, Keown PA. The cost impact of cytomegalovirus disease in renal transplant recipients. Transplantation. 1993;55:1277-1282.

174. Demetris AJ, Lasky S, Van Thiel DH, et al. Pathology of hepatic transplantation. Am J Pathol. 1985;116:151-161.

175. Paya CV, Weisner RH, Hermans PE, et al. Risk factors for cytomegalovirus and severe bacterial infections following liver transplantation: A prospective multivariate time-dependent analysis. J Hepatol. 1993;18:185-195.
176. O'Grady JG, Alexander GJ, Sutherland S, Williams R. CMV infection and donor/recipient HLA antigens: Interdependent co-factors in the pathogenesis of vanishing bile duct syndrome after liver transplantation. Lancet. 1988;2:302-305.
177. Snydman DR, Werner BG, Dougherty NN, et al, for the Boston Center for Liver Transplantation CMVIG Study Group. Cytomegalovirus immune globulin prophylaxis in liver transplantation. A randomized, double-blind, placebo-controlled trial. Ann Intern Med. 1993;119:984-991.
178. Singh N, Yu VL, Mieles L, et al. High-dose acyclovir compared with short-course preemptive ganciclovir therapy to prevent cytomegalovirus disease in liver transplant recipients. Ann Intern Med. 1994;120:375-381.
179. Martin M, Manez R, Linden P, et al. A prospective randomized trial comparing sequential ganciclovir-high dose acyclovir to high dose acyclovir for prevention of cytomegalovirus disease in adult liver transplant recipients. Transplantation. 1994;58:779-785.
180. Stratta RJ, Shaefer MS, Cushing KA, et al. A randomized prospective trial of acyclovir and immune globulin prophylaxis in liver transplant recipients receiving OKT3 therapy. Arch Surg. 1992;127:55-64.
181. Ho M. Cytomegalovirus. In: Mandell J, Bennett J, Dolin R, eds. Principles of Infectious Disease. Philadelphia: WB Saunders; 1996.
182. Aldrete JS, Sterling WA, Hathaway BM, et al. Gastrointestinal and hepatic complications affecting patients with renal allografts. Am J Surg. 1975;129:115-124.
183. Petersen PK, Balfour HH Jr, Marker SC, et al. Cytomegalovirus disease in renal allograft recipients: A prospective study of the clinical features, risk factors and impact on renal transplantation. Medicine (Baltimore). 1980;59:283-300.
184. Hecht DW, Snydman DR, Crumpacker CS, et al, for the Boston Renal Transplant CMV Study Group. Ganciclovir for treatment of renal transplant-associated primary cytomegalovirus pneumonia. J Infect Dis. 1988;157:187-190.
185. Snydman DR, Werner BG, Heinze-Lacey B, et al. Use of cytomegalovirus immune globulin to prevent cytomegalovirus disease in renal-transplant recipients. N Engl J Med. 1987;317:1049-1054.
186. Snydman DR, Werner BG, Dougherty NN, et al. Cytomegalovirus prophylaxis in liver transplantation. Ann Intern Med. 1993;119:984-991.
187. Hibberd PL, Tolkoff-Rubin NE, Conti D, et al. Preemptive ganciclovir therapy to prevent cytomegalovirus disease in cytomegalovirus antibody-positive renal transplant recipients: A randomized controlled trial. Ann Intern Med. 1995;123:18-26.
188. Lurain NS, Bhorade SM, Pursell KJ, et al. Analysis and characterization of antiviral drug-resistant cytomegalovirus isolates from solid organ transplant recipients. J Infect Dis. 2002;186:760-768.
189. Limaye AP, Raghu G, Koelle DM, et al. High incidence of ganciclovir-resistant cytomegalovirus infection among lung transplant recipients receiving preemptive therapy. J Infect Dis. 2002;185:20-27.
190. Stagno S, Pass RF, Dworsky ME, et al. Congenital and perinatal cytomegalovirus infections. Semin Perinatol. 1983;7:31-42.
191. Stagno S, Pass RF, Dworsky ME, et al. Congenital cytomegalovirus infection: The relative importance of primary and recurrent maternal infection. N Engl J Med. 1982;306:945-949.
192. Stagno S, Whitley RJ. Herpesvirus infections of pregnancy. Part I: Cytomegalovirus and Epstein-Barr virus infection. N Engl J Med. 1985;313:1270-1274.
193. Ahlfors K, Harris S, Ivarsson S, et al. Secondary maternal cytomegalovirus infection causing symptomatic congenital infection. N Engl J Med. 1981;305:284.
194. Hanshaw JB. Developmental abnormalities associated with congenital cytomegalovirus infection. In: Wollam DHM, ed. Advances in Teratology. v. 4. New York: Academic Press; 1970:64.
195. Yeager AS, Grumet FC, Hafleigh EB, et al. Prevention of transfusion-acquired cytomegalovirus infection in newborn infants. J Pediatr. 1981;98:281-287.
196. Hanshaw JB, Scheiner AP, Moxley AW, et al. School failure and deafness after "silent" congenital cytomegalovirus infection. N Engl J Med. 1976;295:468-470.
197. Stagno S, Reynolds DW, Amos CS, et al. Auditory and visual defects resulting from symptomatic and subclinical congenital cytomegaloviral and *Toxoplasma* infections. Pediatrics. 1977;59:669-678.
198. Alexander ER. Maternal and neonatal infection with cytomegalovirus in Taiwan (Abstract). Pediatr Res. 1967;1:210.
199. Chandler SH, Handsfield HH, McDougall JK. Isolation of multiple strains of cytomegalovirus from women attending a clinic for sexually transmitted diseases. J Infect Dis. 1987;155:655-660.
200. Numazaki Y, Yano N, Morizuka T, et al. Primary infection with human cytomegalovirus: Virus isolation from healthy infants and pregnant women. Am J Epidemiol. 1970;91:410-417.
201. Stagno S, Reynolds D, Tsiantos A, et al. Cervical cytomegalovirus excretion in pregnant and non-pregnant women: Suppressions in early gestation. J Infect Dis. 1975;131:522-527.
202. Montgomery RL, Youngblood LA, Medearis DN Jr. Recovery of cytomegalovirus from the cervix in pregnancy. Pediatrics. 1972;49:524-531.
203. Reynolds DW, Stagno S, Hosty TS, et al. Maternal cytomegalovirus excretion and perinatal infection. N Engl J Med. 1973;289:1-5.
203a. Krause H, Hebart H, Jahn G, et al. Screening for CMV-specific T cell proliferation to identify patients at risk of developing late onset CMV disease. Bone Marrow Transplant. 1997;19:1111-1116.
204. Boppana SB, Rivera LB, Fowler KB, et al. Intrauterine transmission of cytomegalovirus to infants of women with preconceptional immunity. N Engl J Med. 2001;344:1366-1371.

Epstein-Barr Virus (Infectious Mononucleosis)

ERIC C. JOHANNSEN
ROBERT T. SCHOOLEY
KENNETH M. KAYE

Epstein-Barr virus (EBV) is a ubiquitous human herpesvirus. Infection with EBV is common, worldwide in distribution, and largely subclinical in early childhood. EBV has been established as the causative agent of heterophile-positive infectious mononucleosis, which occurs most frequently in late adolescence or early adulthood. In addition, EBV is associated with the development of multiple malignancies, including Burkitt's lymphoma, lymphoproliferative disease, Hodgkin's lymphoma, primary central nervous system (CNS) lymphomas in acquired immunodeficiency syndrome (AIDS), and nasopharyngeal carcinoma based on seroepidemiologic data and the detection of EBV genomes in these tumors. Evidence supporting a causal role for EBV in the development of these malignancies continues to accumulate.

HISTORY

Historical accounts of infectious mononucleosis often attribute the initial description of the disease to Filatov or Pfeiffer, who nearly simultaneously at the end of the 19th century described an illness characterized by malaise, fever, hepatosplenomegaly, lymphadenopathy, and abdominal discomfort.[1,2] This illness came to be known as Drusenfieber (glandular fever) and occurred in family outbreaks. However, without specific techniques with which to establish the diagnosis, the concept of Drusenfieber as a clinical entity fell into disrepute. Between 1910 and 1920, a number of observers reported cases of apparent spontaneous remission of leukemia, with a clinical course that is consistent with the spontaneous resolution of infectious mononucleosis.[3,4] The establishment of infectious mononucleosis as a clinical entity is credited to Sprunt and Evans, who in 1920 described six cases of fever, lymphadenopathy, and prostration occurring in previously healthy young adults.[5] The authors pointed out the mononuclear lymphocytosis that developed in each of the patients and contrasted the "pathologic" appearance of these lymphocytes with the uniform lymphocyte morphologic characteristics observed in children with other infections. Two years later, Downey and McKinlay described additional cases of infectious mononucleosis and provided a more detailed morphologic description of the atypical lymphocyte.[6] The recognition of atypical lymphocytosis as a hematologic marker for the disease led to more accurate descriptions of the clinical manifestations of this illness.

A major advance occurred in 1932, when Paul and Bunnell, investigating immunologic mechanisms in serum sickness, unexpectedly encountered high titers of spontaneously occurring sheep red blood cell agglutinins in the sera of patients with infectious mononucleosis.[7] Davidsohn later enhanced the specificity of detection of this heterophile antibody by differential absorption of serum with guinea pig kidney and beef erythrocytes.[8]

During the 1940s and 1950s, substantial efforts were made to detect a causative agent for infectious mononucleosis. Attempts to culture etiologically related bacteria and viruses from patients with infectious mononucleosis proved unsuccessful. The disease could not be transmitted to animals. Interpretation of experimental attempts to transmit the disease to humans was hindered by the failure to appreciate the widespread occurrence of asymptomatic infection in preadolescents as well as the absence of a serologic marker of immunity.[9-11]

The identification of EBV followed the description by Burkitt in 1958 of an unusual lymphoma with a predilection for the head and neck.[12] The geographic distribution of this tumor paralleled that of certain mosquito-borne diseases in Africa, and a search for an etiologically related arbovirus was undertaken. Epstein and associates in 1964 described the presence of particles that resembled herpesviruses in tissue cultures of biopsy specimens from patients with Burkitt's lymphoma.[13] However, attempts to propagate the virus in conventional tissue cultures were unsuccessful. An indirect immunofluorescent antibody technique to this virus, now called *Epstein-Barr virus,* was developed by Werner and Gertrude Henle,[14] and high titers of this antibody were detected in patients with Burkitt's lymphoma. Additional studies revealed that 90% of American adults had demonstrable EBV antibodies as well.[14] The development of infectious mononucleosis in a technician in the Henles' laboratory on whom sequentially obtained sera were analyzed for EBV antibody suggested that acute EBV infection may be associated with this illness.[15] Large-scale epidemiologic studies[16-19] demonstrated that heterophile-positive infectious mononucleosis occurred in patients without preexisting EBV antibody and, conversely, heterophile-positive infectious mononucleosis was always accompanied by acquisition of EBV antibodies. These epidemiologic studies indicated that subclinical EBV infection also occurred. With specific antibody tests for EBV, it became apparent that 10% to 20% of the cases of mononucleosis, of which most are heterophile negative, were caused by other agents, of which the most frequent was cytomegalovirus (CMV). This chapter deals primarily with EBV-induced infectious mononucleosis.

DESCRIPTION OF EPSTEIN-BARR VIRUS

Physical Properties

EBV, or human herpesvirus 4, is a gamma-1 herpesvirus. Like the other members of the Herpesviridae family, EBV has a double-stranded DNA genome encased in an icosahedral protein nucleocapsid surrounded by a lipid envelope embedded with viral glycoproteins. Herpesviruses also have an amorphous protein layer, the tegument, which lies between the capsid and envelope. The B95-8 laboratory strain of EBV, the first herpesvirus genome sequenced, was found to have a 12-kb deletion, and we now know the wild-type EBV genome to be approximately 184 kb in size and to encode almost 100 proteins.[20,21]

Life Cycle

Primary infection with EBV results from exposure to the oral secretions of seropositive individuals through kissing, sharing of food, or other intimate contact. The long accepted concept that EBV infection spreads to B lymphocytes after initial productive (lytic) infection of oral epithelial cells[22,23] has been challenged. Tonsillar biopsies from patients with primary EBV infection did not reveal any infected epithelial cells but infected lymphocytes were readily demonstrated.[24,25] EBV undoubtedly has clinically significant tropism for epithelial cells as is seen in nasopharyngeal carcinoma and oral hairy leukoplakia. It remains possible that significant infection of oral epithelial cells occurs in nontonsillar sites or that an initial round of lytic replication precedes spread to the B-cell compartment and the onset of symptoms.[26,27] Infected B lymphocytes incite an intense cytotoxic T-cell response, and it is these T cells that constitute the atypical lymphocytosis characteristic of primary EBV infection.[28,29] In normal individuals, most infected B lymphocytes are cleared through immune surveillance, but between 1 and 50 B cells per million remain quiescently infected and serve as the reservoir for lifelong infection of the individual.[30,31] Thus, EBV shares the properties of lifelong latency and persistence with other members of the herpesvirus family. In contrast to that of alpha herpesviruses (herpes simplex virus and varicella-zoster virus), shedding of infectious EBV particles into the saliva from periodic reactivation of latently infected cells is entirely asymptomatic. This shedding occurs in otherwise healthy persons but is more frequent in immunosuppressed hosts (Table 135-1).

The host range of the virus is limited. In vitro cultivation of the virus has been described primarily in B lymphocytes and also in nasopharyngeal epithelial cells of humans and certain nonhuman primates.[32] EBV binds to its receptor, the CD21 molecule, through an interaction with its major envelope glycoprotein, gp350. CD21 is a 145-kD glycoprotein that is also the receptor for the d region of the third component of complement and is also termed the C3d receptor or CR2.[33,34] This receptor is demonstrable on B lymphocytes and nasopharyngeal epithelial cells of humans and certain nonhuman primates as well as a small proportion of complement receptor–bearing, non-B, non-T lymphocytes.[35-39] Another EBV glycoprotein, gp42, binds major histocompatibility complex (MHC) class II molecules, which serve as coreceptors for infection of B cells.[40-44]

Latent Infection and Growth Transformation

After infection by EBV, B lymphocytes enter the cell cycle and proliferate continuously in a process termed *transformation* or *immortalization*, and these cells can be propagated in vitro indefinitely.[45] This ability of EBV to convert peripheral blood B cells into immortalized cell lines is widely utilized in genomic studies as a means of preserving DNA samples from volunteer donors for future use.[46] In vivo, EBV-driven B-cell proliferation is observed during infectious mononucleosis, in which it probably serves to expand rapidly the pool of infected B lymphocytes. These B lymphocytes are usually rapidly cleared from the circulation.[47-50] However, in the absence of an intact immune response, EBV infection can result in life-threatening lymphoproliferative disease (LPD).[51,52] The growth-transforming properties of EBV can act in concert with genetic and environmental cofactors to cause malignancies in immunocompetent hosts as well.[53,54]

EBV infection of B lymphocytes is characterized by a state of viral latency, in which the genome circularizes in the nucleus and is replicated as an episome in concert with host chromosomes by cell enzymes. The infection is latent in the sense that viral particles are not being produced, but it is anything but quiescent. Limited viral gene expression persists, and these genes exert effects on the infected cell. In vitro, latent infection of B lymphocytes by EBV is characterized by the expression of latent infection membrane proteins 1 and 2 (LMP1 and LMP2), six EBV nuclear antigens (EBNAs), and two small, nuclear, noncoding RNAs (EBV-encoded RNAs [EBERs]) that are transcribed by RNA polymerase III (Table 135-2).[63] Additional EBV transcripts have been detected in latent infection and are termed complementary strand transcripts (CSTs) or BamH1 A rightward transcripts (BARTs). It is not clear that these transcripts are translated into proteins, and their role in EBV biology remains obscure.[64] Recombinant reverse genetic analysis has determined that of these EBV genes, only *LMP1, EBNA1, EBNA2, EBNA3A, EBNA3C,* and *EBNALP* are critical for B-cell growth transformation.[63] The mechanisms by which these EBV genes promote B-lymphocyte growth has been the subject of intense investigation.

After the virus gains entry to susceptible B lymphocytes, EBNA2 and EBNALP are the first proteins expressed. EBNA2 is an acidic transactivator that acts as the major switch to turn on latent virus gene expression as well as several B-cell gene products (including CD21,

TABLE 135-1 Frequency of Epstein-Barr Virus Shedding

Population Description	Oropharyngeal Shedding Rate (%) (Range)	Reference
EBV-seronegatives	0	55
Seropositive healthy adults	12-25	55-58
Solid tumor patients	27	57, 58
HIV-1–infected individuals	50	59
Renal transplant recipients	56-70	56, 58
Infectious mononucleosis patients	50-100	55, 60-62
Critically ill leukemia or lymphoma patients	74-92	57, 58

EBV, Epstein-Barr virus; HIV, human immunodeficiency virus.

CD23, and c-fgr). It has no intrinsic sequence-specific DNA binding capacity but rather is targeted to promoters by binding to a host DNA binding protein RBP-Jκ (also called CBF1 or CSL), a downstream component of the Notch signaling pathway.[65,66] By an incompletely understood mechanism, EBNALP cooperates with EBNA2 to activate expression of the remaining nuclear proteins and LMP1 and LMP2.[67] *LMP1* is the major EBV-encoded oncogene, and its expression in transgenic mice results in B-cell lymphomas.[68,69] It constitutively activates signaling pathways that mimic the growth and survival signals given to B cells by CD4+ T lymphocytes through the CD40 surface glycoprotein. LMP1 sends this signal through its cytoplasmic tail, which binds a set of second messenger proteins similar but not identical to those utilized by CD40.[70,71] Unlike CD40, LMP1 does not require the presence of ligand to form patches in the cell membrane but self-associates constitutively, approximating its cytoplasmic tails to activate signaling.[72] This results in the activation of nuclear factor κB (NF-κB), c-jun, up-regulation of adhesion molecules (intercellular adhesion molecule 1, LFA-1, and LFA-3), cytokine production, B-cell proliferation, and induction of an antiapoptotic state.[47,54] A second EBV latent membrane protein, LMP2, mimics another signal required for B-cell survival.[73] By interacting with signaling molecules of the B-cell receptor (BCR), LMP2 mimics BCR engagement by constitutive patching in the membrane in a manner analogous to LMP1. LMP2 probably also interferes with normal signaling through the BCR by antigenic stimulation to inhibit activation of lytic viral replication (discussed later). Interestingly, LMP2 is not required for EBV-mediated outgrowth of B cells in vitro but is probably a critical component of the viral strategy in vivo. The nuclear protein EBNA1 acts to promote the replication of the viral genome by the host machinery when the virus is in the latent, episomal state and ensure proper segregation of the EBV genome to both daughter cells. The EBNA3 proteins are of uncertain function but are known to interact with the same DNA binding protein as EBNA2, RBP-Jκ, and may modulate virus and cell gene expression. The function of the highly expressed, noncoding EBV RNAs (EBERs) is incompletely understood.

EBV-associated malignancies are exclusively associated with latent infection and latent gene expression. Three general patterns of expression of EBV-encoded proteins have been observed in association with latency (see Table 135-2).[47,48] Expression of all latent genes is seen in LPD in immunosuppressed hosts, in primary CNS lymphoma of AIDS patients, and during primary EBV infection (infectious mononucleosis), and this program of gene expression is often referred to as latency III.[53] EBV-associated nasopharyngeal carcinomas, Hodgkin's lymphoma, and T-cell lymphomas exhibit a more restricted pattern of EBV gene expression (latency II) that includes LMP1, LMP2, EBNA1, and the EBERs and EBNA1.[74-76] In Burkitt's lymphoma (latency I) only EBERs and EBNA1 are expressed.[53] The more restricted patterns of latent gene expression in some tumors are probably due in part to the intense immune response against viral proteins.

Lytic Infection

Latent infection can be activated to lytic infection by stimulation of host B cells by certain chemicals, calcium ionophores, or antibodies to surface immunoglobulin.[77] The physiologic signals that reactivate EBV lytic replication are unknown, but signaling through the B-cell receptor after antigenic stimulation is a possible scenario. After this inciting event, two EBV-encoded transcriptional activators are expressed: BZLF1 and BRLF1. Expression of these immediate early genes leads to a cascade of events culminating in the production of early EBV gene (early antigen [EA]) products responsible for viral replication (e.g., thymidine kinase and DNA polymerase) and late (structural) genes of the virus including viral capsid antigens (VCAs).[78] Lytic infection produces EBV virions and causes host cell death.

EPIDEMIOLOGY

Serum Antibody Prevalence

Antibodies to EBV have been found in all population groups studied, and most studies have shown no predilection for either sex. Antibodies are acquired earlier in life in developing than in industrialized countries, but by adulthood 90% to 95% of most populations have demonstrable EBV antibodies.[79,80] In the United States and in Great Britain, EBV seroconversion occurs before the age of 5 years in about 50% of the population.[80-82] A second wave of seroconversion occurs midway through the second decade of life. EBV seroconversion may occur at a younger average age in the southern United States than in other areas of that country.[83] Lower socioeconomic groups have a higher EBV antibody prevalence than more affluent age-matched control groups.

Two strains of EBV have been defined on the basis of viral gene sequences expressed during latency and their ability to transform B lymphocytes.[77] The strains (type 1 [A] or 2 [B]) are not distinguishable serologically, but they express unique epitopes that are identified by cytotoxic T lymphocytes (CTLs). Although it was initially thought that there were specific geographic distributions for these two strains of EBV, it is now clear that both are widely distributed and that individuals can be coinfected with both strains.

Incidence of Infection

Clinically apparent infectious mononucleosis occurs most frequently in populations in which primary EBV exposure is delayed until the second decade of life. The disease is diagnosed most frequently among adolescents of higher socioeconomic groups in industrialized countries.[84] The incidence of infectious mononucleosis in a large epidemiologic study in the United States was 45.2 cases per 100,000 per year.[85] The incidence was highest in the 15- to 24-year-old age group. The incidence was the same for women as for men, but the peak age-specific incidence occurred 2 years earlier in women. The incidence of infectious mononucleosis was 30 times higher in whites than in blacks. The infrequency of infectious mononucleosis among blacks,

TABLE 135-2 Patterns of Epstein-Barr Virus Latent Gene Expression

| | | Acute Infection | Healthy Carrier | EBV-Associated Malignancies | | | | |
| | | | | Latency III | | Latency II | | Latency I |
EBV Gene	*Function*	*IM*	*PBB*	*LPD*	*PCNSL*	*HL*	*NPC*	*BL*
EBNA1	EBV genome maintenance	+	?	+	+	+	+	+
EBNA2	Activate expression of EBV/host genes	+	−	+	+	−	−	−
*EBNA3s**	Unknown	+	−	+	+	−	−	−
EBNALP	Coactivate with EBNA2	+	−	+	+	−	−	−
LMP1	Mimics CD40 signaling	+	−	+	+	+	+	−
LMP2	Mimics BCR signaling	+	+	+	+	+	+	−
EBERs	Noncoding, highly expressed RNAs	+	+	+	+	+	+	+

*Includes *EBNA3A*, *EBNA3B*, and *EBNA3C*.
BCR, B-cell receptor; BL, Burkitt's lymphoma; EBV, Epstein-Barr virus; HL, Hodgkin's lymphoma; IM, infectious mononucleosis; LPD, lymphoproliferative disease; NPC, nasopharyngeal carcinoma; PBB, peripheral blood B cell; PCNSL, primary central nervous system lymphoma.

noted as early as 1940, is probably a reflection of earlier primary EBV infection and the higher frequency of subclinical infections in children.[86-88] No clear seasonal incidence has been noted.

Methods of Spread

Low titers of EBV are present in throat washings of those with infectious mononucleosis.[55,60,61] Susceptible roommates of students with infectious mononucleosis or with inapparent EBV infection experience EBV seroconversion no more frequently than the general susceptible college population.[18,83] Only 6% of those with infectious mononucleosis cite previous contact with another case of infectious mononucleosis.[85] The virus persists in the B-cell compartment for the life of the infected host and can be cultured from throat washings from 10% to 20% of normal healthy adults, from 50% of kidney transplant recipients, and from greater proportions of those critically ill with leukemia or lymphoma (see Table 135-1).[56-58] Approximately 50% of human immunodeficiency virus type 1 (HIV-1)–infected men who have sex with men shed EBV in oropharyngeal secretions.[59] EBV sequences or antigens, or both, have also been identified in parotid duct and uterine cervical epithelia, although the implications of this distribution are unclear with respect to viral transmission.[89,90]

EBV, like other herpesviruses, is relatively labile in the laboratory, and the virus has not been recovered from environmental sources, including fomites. These data suggest that EBV is a widespread agent that is not particularly contagious and that most cases of infectious mononucleosis are probably contracted by intimate contact between susceptible individuals and asymptomatic shedders of EBV. Among young adults, spread of the virus may be facilitated by the transfer of saliva with kissing.[91,92] Serologic evidence suggests that the virus may also be spread among susceptible individuals within families.[93,94] Infectious mononucleosis has also been spread by blood transfusion and after open heart surgery as the "postpump perfusion" syndrome.[95] Most postpump perfusion infectious mononucleosis is, however, attributable to CMV.

Although several apparent epidemics of infectious mononucleosis have been described, these reports have not been substantiated with EBV serologic data and have lacked rigorous epidemiologic, clinical, or laboratory support. Some of these have resulted from errors in the performance of Monospot tests.[96] On the basis of the previously discussed information, it is unlikely that true epidemics of infectious mononucleosis occur.

Public Health Impact

College and military populations experience the highest morbidity from infectious mononucleosis, although cases occur in other groups as well. Infectious mononucleosis accounted for 5% of all hospitalizations of University of Wisconsin students, with an incidence of 450 admissions per 100,000 students per year. Other American universities have reported similar incidences.[97,98] Approximately 12% of susceptible college students undergo EBV seroconversion yearly.[18,19] Many of these infections are subclinical (see later).[18,83] Although primary EBV infection may be clinically apparent in only about 10% of military cases, infectious mononucleosis ranked fourth as the cause of days lost because of illness in army personnel.[99,100] Detailed information about the impact of infectious mononucleosis on the general population is not available because infectious mononucleosis is not a reportable disease in most states. However, it is likely that morbidity from infectious mononucleosis is generally underestimated because a specific diagnosis may not be made and the nonspecific illness can be attributed to a variety of other causes.

PATHOGENESIS

Host Immune Response

EBV presents a formidable challenge to the immune system. At the height of acute infection, up to 20% of peripheral blood B lymphocytes may express EBNA, and 0.005% to 0.5% of circulating mononuclear cells are capable of forming continuous cell lines if cultured in vitro.[101,102] The immune response to EBV-infected transformed lymphocytes is complex and involves both humoral and cell-mediated immune mechanisms.[28] An intact immune response is critical to preventing the unchecked proliferation of these cells as seen in LPD but is also responsible for most of the symptoms of infectious mononucleosis. The increase in prevalence in symptomatic acute EBV infection with age of seroconversion is probably due to differences in the immune responses of different age groups.

The cellular immune response to EBV is complex, well integrated, and includes CD8+ and CD4+ CTLs as well as natural killer (NK) cells.[29,103-106] The massive atypical lymphocytosis of infectious mononucleosis is composed primarily of antigen-stimulated CD8+ cytotoxic T cells. In one study, 40% of circulating CD8+ T cells were reactive against a single EBV epitope.[107] These lymphocytes probably produce most of the signs and symptoms of infectious mononucleosis through the abundant production of cytokines, including tumor necrosis factor, interleukin-1 (IL-1), and IL-6.[108] During acute infection, CD8+ T cells specific for lytic antigens predominate, but with convalescence a shift occurs toward cells recognizing latent proteins, particularly the EBNA3 proteins.[28,107,109] T cells reactive against EBV latent proteins are sufficiently numerous that unselected mononuclear cells from EBV-immune adults suppress the outgrowth of autologous EBV-infected B lymphocytes in vitro.[106] An expansion of EBV-specific CD4+ lymphocytes has also been described in infectious mononucleosis but is small in magnitude and its significance in containing acute EBV infection is unclear.[110,111]

The humoral immune response to EBV has been extensively studied, primarily as a means to diagnose EBV infection (see "Laboratory Diagnosis" for detailed discussion). In general, specific antibodies directed against EBV lytic antigens (VCA and EA) are demonstrable in most patients with infectious mononucleosis. By contrast, antibody responses to the latency-associated EBV nuclear antigens (EBNA1, EBNA2, EBNA3s, and EBNALP) do not develop until convalescence.[28] The significance of any of these antibody responses to containing EBV infection is not established; however, antibodies to EBV surface glycoproteins have been demonstrated to prevent experimental EBV infection.[112-114]

For unclear reasons, acute EBV infection is associated with the synthesis of large amounts of antibodies reactive against antigens found on sheep, horse, and beef red cells. These so-called heterophile antibodies are a heterogeneous group of predominantly immunoglobulin M (IgM) antibodies that do not react with specific EBV proteins.[115] Detection of these antibodies in sera of patients with mononucleosis syndromes predicts acute EBV infection with high sensitivity and specificity and is discussed under "Laboratory Diagnosis." There is no good correlation between the heterophile titer and the severity of the illness, and there is no clearly defined role for heterophile antibodies in the pathogenesis of EBV disease or in immune clearance of the virus.

EBV has evolved multiple strategies to elude this aggressive immune response. The EBV BCRF1 protein shares 70% homology with the cytokine IL-10. This EBV protein is functional and is thought to mimic IL-10 inhibition of interferon-γ synthesis by mononuclear cells in the peripheral blood. Thus, BCRF1 expression during lytic infection would be expected to promote a shift toward Th2 differentiated CD4+ effectors that can provide B-cell help but do not promote the CD8+ responses needed to kill EBV-infected cells.[116,117] Another EBV protein, BARF1, can function as a soluble receptor for colony-stimulating factor 1 and may interfere with the ability of this cytokine to enhance expression of interferon-α from monocytes.[118] EBV also encodes a bcl2 homologue that is expressed during lytic replication and may act to prevent apoptosis of the host cell.[119] Finally, the virus has evolved a strategy for ensuring its persistence in the memory B-cell compartment. After acute infection resolves, strong immune pressure is exerted against the EBV protein expression. Consequently, there is strong selection against expression of the full repertoire of EBV proteins associated with B-cell proliferation. However, in any cycling cell, EBV must express EBNA1 in order to ensure that its genome is replicated. To circumvent this liability, the virus has evolved a strategy to prevent targeting of this key protein. EBNA1 contains a sequence of expanded glycine-alanine repeats, not required for its function in genome maintenance, capable of inhibiting proteasomal processing of the protein.[120] Without this processing, EBNA1 peptides cannot be presented on class I MHC molecules and cells expressing EBNA1 can elude immune surveillance.

Histopathologic Findings

Because biopsies are rarely obtained in patients with uncomplicated infectious mononucleosis, most data come from pathologic examination of tissues obtained from fatal cases or from cases with atypical features in which biopsy specimens were obtained for diagnostic evaluation. During the acute phase of the illness, lymph nodes throughout the body are moderately enlarged. Individual nodes reveal increased numbers of enlarged, moderately active lymphoid follicles. Germinal centers are also enlarged, with cores containing blast cells, histiocytes, and lymphocytes. Although the reticulin framework remains intact, invasion by the hyperplastic pulp makes its borders less distinct.[121] In studies of spleens obtained at autopsy or at surgery after rupture, the organ is usually two to three times its normal weight.[122] The splenic capsule and trabeculae are edematous, thinned, and invaded by lymphoid cells. Most of the increased splenic size is the result of hyperplasia of the red pulp. Throughout the red pulp, pleomorphic blast cells are evident. The spleen is often congested with focal, particularly subcapsular, hemorrhages. The white pulp is relatively normal. Tonsillar biopsy specimens obtained during the course of mononucleosis reveal intense proliferation with numerous mitoses.[123] Bone marrow aspirate and biopsy specimens are often strikingly normal when compared with the florid changes noted in peripheral blood. Biopsy specimens are usually normocellular to mildly hypercellular. Small granulomas may be present, but these are not specific for mononucleosis and have no prognostic significance.[124,125]

Changes in hepatic histologic features are usually mild. Hepatocytes demonstrate minimal swelling and vacuolization. Pleomorphic lymphocytic and monocytic portal infiltration is usually evident. Bile ducts may be minimally swollen, but frank biliary stasis is rare.[126,127] A number of histopathologic changes have been reported in the nervous system in fatal cases of infectious mononucleosis.[123,128,129] These changes include neuronal degeneration, perivascular cuffing, perivascular hemorrhage, and astrocytic hyperplasia. Little mononuclear infiltration may be present despite demonstrable degenerative changes in the neurons of the cortex, basal ganglia, cerebellum, or spinal cord.

CLINICAL MANIFESTATIONS

Infectious Mononucleosis (Primary Infection)

Spectrum of Illness

EBV induces a broad spectrum of illness in humans. Classic or typical infectious mononucleosis is an acute illness characterized clinically by sore throat, fever, and lymphadenopathy; serologically by the transient appearance of heterophile antibodies; and hematologically by a mononuclear leukocytosis that consists, in part, of atypical lymphocytes (Table 135-3). An individual case may have most but not necessarily all the aforementioned characteristics. Specific serologic tests for EBV infection indicate that infection results in a spectrum of clinical manifestations. Attempts to exclude cases that fail to meet the classic criteria for infectious mononucleosis result in artificial and often misleading distinctions.

The age of the patient has a profound influence on the clinical expression of EBV infection. In children, primary EBV infection is often asymptomatic. Young children may be more likely to exhibit rashes, neutropenia, or pneumonia than individuals undergoing primary EBV infection at an older age.[130] Clinically apparent infections in very young children are heterophile negative in about one half of the cases.[131] The ratios of clinically apparent to inapparent disease and of

TABLE 135-3   Manifestations of Epstein-Barr Virus–Induced Infectious Mononucleosis

Clinical
  Fever
  Sore throat
  Lymphadenopathy
Hematologic
  More than 50% mononuclear cells
  More than 10% atypical lymphocytes
Serologic
  Transient appearance of heterophile antibodies
  Permanent emergence of antibodies to EBV

EBV, Epstein-Barr virus.

EBV-induced heterophile-positive to heterophile-negative cases increase with age. By 4 years of age, 80% of children undergoing primary EBV infection are heterophile antibody positive.[132]

In patients of college age, the ratio of clinically apparent to inapparent EBV infection ranges from 1:3 to 3:1.[18,83] In military recruits, this ratio has been as low as 1:10.[100] Because of previously existing immunity, the disease is less common in older patients. When it does occur, however, clinical and serologic manifestations are similar to those found in adolescents.[133] During the course of the illness, 90% of the adolescents with clinically apparent infectious mononucleosis should be heterophile positive. Therefore, EBV infection is generally inapparent or is a self-limited illness lasting 2 or 3 weeks. In rare cases the disease can be devastating and can be accompanied by severe prostration, major complications, and even death,[134] as discussed further on.

Symptoms

In most cases, the clinical manifestation of infectious mononucleosis is that of the clinical triad of sore throat, fever, and lymphadenopathy (Table 135-4). Although a prior epidemiologically based study suggested that the incubation period of acute infectious mononucleosis is 30 to 50 days, this observation has not yet been confirmed using molecular epidemiologic techniques.[83,138] Thus, the incubation period of the illness is somewhat speculative. The onset may be abrupt, but often several days of prodromal symptoms can be elicited, including chills, sweats, feverish sensations, anorexia, and malaise. Loss of taste for cigarettes is common early in the illness but is not specific for infectious mononucleosis. Retro-orbital headaches, myalgias, and feelings of abdominal fullness are other common prodromal symptoms. The most frequent complaint is sore throat, which may be the most severe the patient has experienced.[135,136] Other patients seek medical attention because of prolonged fever or malaise and less frequently because of incidentally encountered lymphadenopathy. Rarely, the first manifestation of illness is one of the complications of infectious mononucleosis described later.

TABLE 135-4   Symptoms of Infectious Mononucleosis

Symptom	Rate	Percentage	Range (%)
Sore throat	409/502	82	70-88
Malaise	243/426	57	43-76
Headache	216/426	51	37-55
Anorexia	117/546	21	10-27
Myalgias	66/326	20	12-22
Chills	54/326	16	9-18
Nausea	18/156	12	2-17
Abdominal discomfort	37/426	9	2-14
Cough	3/56	5	5
Vomiting	3/56	5	5
Arthralgias	1/56	2	2

Data from references 97 and 135-137.

TABLE 135-5 Signs of Infectious Mononucleosis

Sign	Rate	Percentage	Range (%)
Lymphadenopathy	495/526	94	93-100
Pharyngitis	444/526	84	69-91
Fever	399/526	76	63-100
Splenomegaly	244/470	52	50-63
Hepatomegaly	34/370	12	6-14
Palatal enanthem	18/156	11	5-13
Jaundice	37/426	9	4-10
Rash	49/470	10	0-15

Data from references 135-137 and 139.

Signs

The signs of infectious mononucleosis are summarized in Table 135-5. Fever is present in more than 90% of the patients with infectious mononucleosis. The fever usually peaks in the afternoon with temperatures of 38° C to 39° C, although a temperature as high as 40° C is not uncommon. In most cases, fever resolves over a 10- to 14-day period. A rash, which may be macular, petechial, scarlatiniform, urticarial, or erythema multiforme–like, is present in about 5% of patients. The administration of ampicillin or amoxicillin produces a pruritic, maculopapular eruption in 90% to 100% of the patients (Fig. 135-1), and this rash may appear after cessation of treatment with the drug.[140,141] The ampicillin-related rash does not necessarily predict future intolerance to ampicillin or amoxicillin.[142,143] Periorbital edema has been reported in up to one third of cases in some series,[136] but it has been observed less frequently in others.[137] Tonsillar enlargement is usually present, occasionally with tonsils meeting at the midline. The pharynx is erythematous with an exudate in about one third of cases. Palatal petechiae may be seen in 25% to 60% of cases but are not diagnostic of infectious mononucleosis. The petechiae are usually multiple, 1 to 2 mm in diameter, occur in crops lasting 3 to 4 days, and are usually seen at the junction of the hard and soft palate.[144] Cervical adenopathy, usually symmetrical, is present in 80% to 90% of patients. Posterior adenopathy is most common, but submandibular and anterior adenopathies are quite frequent as well, and axillary and inguinal adenopathies also occur. Individual nodes are freely movable, are not spontaneously painful, and are only mildly tender to palpation. The results of examination of the lungs and heart are usually normal. Abdominal examination may detect hepatomegaly in 10% to 15% of cases, although mild tenderness to fist percussion over the liver is present somewhat more frequently.[135,137] Jaundice is present in approximately 5% of cases.[136] Splenomegaly is present in about one half of cases if sought carefully over the course of the illness. The splenomegaly is usually maximal at the beginning of the second week of illness and regresses over the next 7 to 10 days. The results of neurologic examination are generally normal, although occasional complications may occur (see later).

Complications

Most patients with infectious mononucleosis recover uneventfully. Complications that occasionally occur have been extensively reported in the literature, but even these complications have generally resolved fully, although there have been rare fatalities.

Hematologic. Autoimmune hemolytic anemia occurs in 0.5% to 3% of the patients with infectious mononucleosis.[145,146] Cold agglutinins, almost always of the IgM class, are present in 70% to 80% of cases.[147] Anti-i specificity has been reported in 20% to 70% of cases.[148,149] Most but not all cases of autoimmune hemolytic anemia in infectious mononucleosis are mediated by antibodies of this specificity.[150-153] The hemolysis usually becomes clinically apparent during the second or third week of illness and subsides over a 1- to 2-month period.[154] Corticosteroids may hasten recovery in some cases. Hemophagocytic syndrome has also been reported with both acute and chronic EBV infection.[155,156]

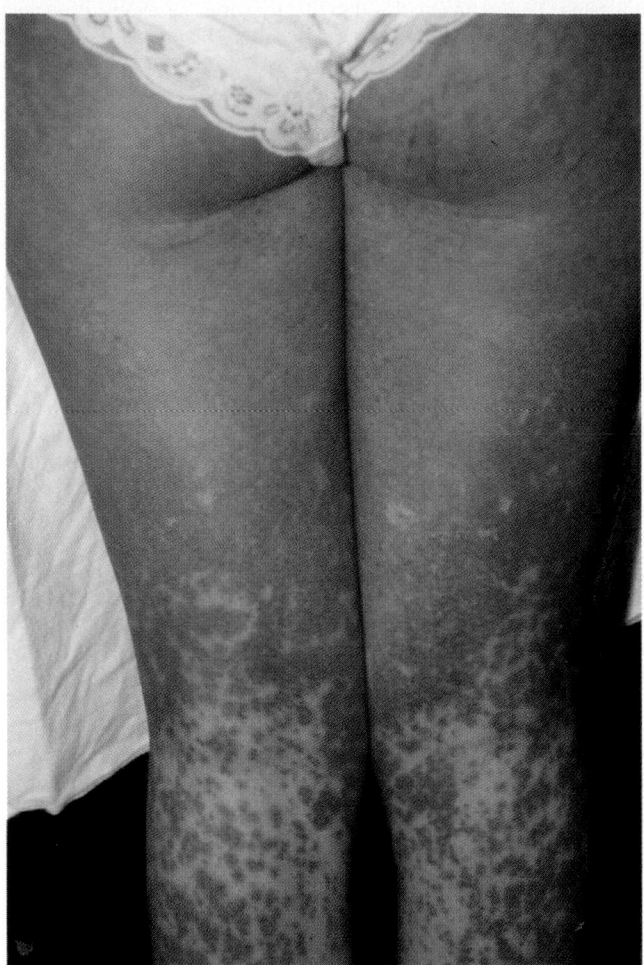

FIGURE 135-1. A patient with infectious mononucleosis and ampicillin-induced rash. A maculopapular rash extends over the trunk and extremities. The rash frequently has a violaceous hue and is often accompanied by pruritus. *(Courtesy of Dr. Stephen Gellis.)*

Mild thrombocytopenia is common in infectious mononucleosis. Platelet counts less than 140,000/mm³ were noted in 50% of patients with uncomplicated infectious mononucleosis in one series.[157] Profound thrombocytopenia with bleeding occurs rarely,[158] but platelet counts less than 1000/mm³ and deaths from intracerebral bleeding have been reported.[159,160] The mechanism for the thrombocytopenia is not known. The presence of normal or increased numbers of megakaryocytes in the marrow coupled with reports of antiplatelet antibodies suggests that peripheral destruction of platelets may be occurring, possibly on an autoimmune basis.[148,152,161] Corticosteroids have been reported to be beneficial for the thrombocytopenia in some but not all cases.[158-160,162] For refractory cases splenectomy may be indicated.[161] Neutropenia is seen rather frequently in uncomplicated infectious mononucleosis. The neutropenia is usually mild and self-limiting, although deaths associated with bacterial sepsis or pneumonia, or both, have been reported.[163-170] Anaerobic sepsis without associated granulocytopenia, presumably of pharyngeal origin, has also been reported.[171]

Splenic Rupture. Splenic rupture is a rare but dramatic complication of infectious mononucleosis. Lymphocytic infiltration of the capsule, trabeculae, and vascular walls coupled with rapid splenic enlargement predisposes the organ to rupture. The incidence of rupture is highest in the second or third week of illness but may be the first sign of infectious mononucleosis. Abdominal pain is uncommon in infectious mononucleosis,[172] and splenic rupture must be strongly considered whenever abdominal pain occurs. The onset of this pain may be insidious or abrupt. Pathologic examination of some of the ruptured spleens has revealed subcapsular hematomas that suggest that rupture may be preceded by intermittent subcapsular bleeding. The pain, usually in the left upper quadrant, may radiate to the left scapular area. Left upper quadrant tenderness to palpation, with or without rebound tenderness, is usually present along with peritoneal signs or shifting dullness. In rare cases, splenic rupture is unaccompanied by pain and is manifested as shock. Laboratory findings include a falling hematocrit and, in some cases, an elevated left hemidiaphragm. The abdominal catastrophe may reverse the usual differential count of infectious mononucleosis and evoke a neutrophilia. Confirmatory findings should not be awaited if splenic rupture is suspected. Prompt splenectomy is the treatment of choice, although nonoperative observation and splenorrhaphy have a role in the management of selected patients with subcapsular splenic hematoma.[173,174] Because a history of trauma may be elicited in about one half the cases of splenic rupture,[175] elimination of contact sports, attention to constipation, and caution in splenic palpation are prudent measures for at least the first month after diagnosis (see "Treatment").

Neurologic. Neurologic complications, which occur in less than 1% of the cases, can dominate the clinical presentation (Table 135-6).[176-191] On occasion, these neurologic signs can be the first or only manifestation of infectious mononucleosis. In many cases, the heterophile antibody determination is negative, atypical lymphocytes may be low in number or delayed in appearance, and the diagnosis must be made by changes in EBV-specific antibodies.[176,177,182] The encephalitis seen with infectious mononucleosis may be acute in onset and rapidly progressive and severe but is usually associated with complete recovery. The encephalitis is commonly manifested as a cerebellitis but may also be global.[178-180] The clinical presentation may also resemble that of aseptic meningitis. In both encephalitis and meningitis, changes in the spinal fluid are mild. The opening pressure is normal or slightly elevated. A predominantly mononuclear pleocytosis may be present, with most cell counts much less than 200/mm³. Atypical lymphocytes have been seen in the cerebrospinal fluid (CSF) in a number of cases. The protein level is usually normal to mildly elevated, and the glucose concentration is usually normal. Low titers of EBV VCA can be found in the CSF.[181] Cases of Guillain-Barré syndrome, Bell's palsy, and transverse myelitis have been reported in primary EBV infection.[182] Although neurologic complications are the most frequent cause of death in infectious mononucleosis, the benign outcome of most of these episodes should be emphasized.[192] Eighty-five percent of the patients with neurologic complications recover completely.[176]

Hepatic. Hepatic manifestations consist largely of self-limited elevations of hepatocellular enzyme levels, which are present in 80% to 90% of the cases of infectious mononucleosis.[193] Reported cases of infectious mononucleosis leading to cirrhosis or other chronic sequelae are poorly documented.

Renal. Abnormal urinary sediment is not uncommon in acute infectious mononucleosis.[194,195] Microscopic hematuria and proteinuria are the most frequently noted abnormalities.[196] Overt renal dysfunction is, however, extremely rare, although sporadic cases of acute renal failure in association with acute infectious mononucleosis have been reported.[197] It has been hypothesized that the renal manifestations of infectious mononucleosis are usually attributable to interstitial nephritis, which occurs as a manifestation of renal infiltration by activated T lymphocytes.[197] Renal dysfunction in association with EBV-associated rhabdomyolysis has also been reported, although not all cases of rhabdomyolysis are accompanied by renal dysfunction.[198]

Cardiac. Clinically significant cardiac disease is very uncommon. Electrocardiographic abnormalities, usually confined to ST-T wave abnormalities, were reported in 6% of the cases in one series.[199] Pericarditis and fatal myocarditis have also been observed.[200,201]

Pulmonary. Pulmonary manifestations of infectious mononucleosis are rare.[202-205] Early studies reported the presence of interstitial infiltrates in 3% to 5% of the cases. However, systematic examination for other causes of nonbacterial pneumonias, for example,

TABLE 135-6 Neurologic Complications of Infectious Mononucleosis

Neurologic Complication	Reference
Encephalitis	177-181
Meningitis	177
Myelitis	181
Guillain-Barré syndrome	181
Optic neuritis	183
Retrobulbar neuritis	184
Cranial nerve palsies	181
Mononeuritis multiplex	185
Brachial plexus neuropathy	186
Seizures	177, 181
? Subacute sclerosing panencephalitis	187
Transverse myelitis	188
Psychosis	189
Demyelination	190
Hemiplegia	191

Mycoplasma, was not carried out in these studies, and it is not clear that these infiltrates were related to EBV infection. Pneumonia has, however, been reported, and in at least one instance, EBERs have been demonstrated in pulmonary tissue.[206,207] The attribution of pulmonary lesions to EBV infection should be made only after other pathogens have been carefully excluded.

Death. Death from infectious mononucleosis is rare.[192,208] Death may occur either as a result of overwhelming EBV infection or from complications of the disease. Neurologic complications of the illness, splenic rupture, and upper airway obstruction are the most frequent causes of death from infectious mononucleosis in previously healthy persons. Deaths from complications associated with granulocytopenia, thrombocytopenia, hepatic failure, and myocarditis have also been reported.[153,168,192,201,209,210]

Clinical Course

Most cases of infectious mononucleosis resolve spontaneously over a 2- to 3-week period. The sore throat is usually maximal for 3 to 5 days and then gradually resolves over the course of a week to 10 days. Patients remain febrile for 10 to 14 days, but in the last 5 to 7 days, the fever is usually low grade and associated with little morbidity. The prostration associated with infectious mononucleosis is generally more gradual in its resolution. As the illness resolves, patients often have days of relative well-being that alternate with recrudescence of symptoms.

X-Linked Lymphoproliferative Disease

An X-linked syndrome has been described in which boys, without other evidence of immunodeficiency, develop overwhelming primary EBV infection with demonstrable virus in lymph nodes, spleen, thymus, and other organs.[211,212] This syndrome has been designated X-linked lymphoproliferative syndrome and is sometimes referred to as Purtilo's syndrome or Duncan's disease. Affected boys develop a large proliferation of polyclonal B and T cells in response to primary EBV infection that frequently results in fulminant hepatitis and hemophagocytic syndrome. Patients who survive primary EBV infection frequently develop progressive agammaglobulinemia, or lymphoma may develop over a several-year period after initial infection.[213-218] This disorder was linked to mutations in the signaling lymphocyte activation molecule (SLAM)–associated protein (SAP) gene in 1998.[219] SAP is thought to be an important mediator of signal transduction in T and NK cells; however, the reason why mutations in SAP confer a specific susceptibility to EBV infection remains to be explained.[220,221]

Chronic or Persistent Epstein-Barr Virus Infection

It has been suggested that persistent EBV infection is a frequent cause of fatigue and malaise in young and middle-aged adults.[222-225] This speculation has arisen from reports of a syndrome characterized by fatigue, sore throat, mild cognitive dysfunction, and myalgias initially noted in association with an apparent increase in antibody titers to the

EBV EA complex[222,223] (see "Laboratory Diagnosis"). These reports have included primarily young adults, usually with a female preponderance, who report a nonspecific symptom complex more reminiscent of the prodrome of infectious mononucleosis than of the syndrome itself (often known as "chronic mononucleosis syndrome" or "chronic fatigue syndrome"). These patients have been noted either sporadically[222,223,226] or in epidemic clusters.[225] The initial suggestion that the syndrome is attributable to EBV has become untenable on the basis of serologic and epidemiologic observations.[226,227] Investigation of the syndrome has been hampered by the vagueness of the symptoms and the absence of objective laboratory diagnostic criteria. A consensus case definition has emerged that focuses on fatigue rather than on EBV as the central feature of the syndrome.[228,229] The chronic fatigue syndrome is discussed in more detail in Chapter 127.

In contrast to patients with the nonspecific syndrome just noted, patients have rarely been identified in whom EBV appears to be playing a direct role in ongoing objective organ system dysfunction.[230-234] This syndrome of chronic active EBV (CAEBV) infection has been defined by the presence of three features.[224] First, patients have severe illness lasting more than 6 months that began as primary EBV infection and is associated with markedly elevated titers to EBV lytic antigens (VCA IgG = 5120 or EA IgG = 640). Second, histologic evidence of major organ involvement is present such as interstitial pneumonia, hemophagocytosis, uveitis, lymphadenitis, or persistent hepatitis. Third, elevated EBV DNA, RNA or proteins are found by in situ hybridization or immunohistochemical staining of the affected tissues. Patients with CAEBV usually also have extremely high serum EBV viral loads by polymerase chain reaction (PCR).[235,236] The majority of these patients have at the time of diagnosis, or go on to develop, a clonal expansion of EBV-infected CD4+, CD8+, or NK lymphocytes.[237,238] The prognosis for these patients is extremely poor with most succumbing to progressive pancytopenia and hypogammaglobulinemia or T-cell LPD within a few years, although survival for more than 10 years after diagnosis has been observed.[239] Antiviral therapy with acyclovir or ganciclovir is of no proven benefit, but there have been case reports of adoptive immunotherapy and bone marrow transplantation for patients with CAEBV.[240-244]

Oral Hairy Leukoplakia

As previously stated, reactivation of lytic EBV replication with viral shedding in the saliva is usually entirely asymptomatic. An important exception to this rule is seen in oral hairy leukoplakia (OHL), which arises as a corrugated or "hairy" white lesion on the lateral surface of the tongue that is not removed by gentle scraping. This nonmalignant lesion seen in AIDS and other states of immunosuppression is caused by unchecked lytic replication of EBV.[245,246] The diagnosis of OHL is generally based on the typical appearance of the lesions in the appropriate clinical setting. The differential includes oral candidiasis, which can be distinguished by its ease of removal from the tongue, a KOH wet mount, or an empirical trial of antifungal therapy. Biopsy for histology and in situ hybridization or immunofluorescence staining for EBV is rarely necessary but confirms the diagnosis. PCR detection of EBV in "oral scrapes" is neither sensitive nor specific for OHL.[247]

Epstein-Barr Virus–Associated Malignancies

EBV is an extremely well-adapted parasite, establishing lifelong latent infection without lasting adverse effects in about 95% of the human population. However, in immunosuppressed hosts the growth-transforming properties of EBV can result in malignancy. EBV in conjunction with environmental or genetic factors, or both, can rarely result in malignancy in immunocompetent hosts (Table 135-7).

Lymphoproliferative Disease

In the absence of effective immune surveillance, uncontrolled proliferation of EBV-infected B lymphocytes can occur. This disorder is referred to as lymphoproliferative disease and represents the in vivo equivalent of the immortalized B-cell lines seen with EBV infection in vitro. Proliferating B cells in LPD express all EBV latent proteins (latency III), including the EBNA3 proteins that are strong targets for CD8+ cytotoxic T cells (see Table 135-2).[28,63] Patients with LPD typically present with symptoms similar to those of infectious mononucleosis or with fever and lymphomatous infiltration of lymph nodes, spleen, liver, bone marrow, kidney, lung, CNS, or intestine (Fig. 135-2). The frequency of this disease in solid organ and bone marrow transplant recipients has led to the designation post-transplantation lymphoproliferative disease (PTLD), but it can be seen in any patient receiving high-dose immune suppression or in those with inherited disorders affecting T-cell immunity. Patients with more severe cellular immune impairment, such as those receiving T cell–depleted bone marrow transplants or antithymocyte globulin, are at increased risk for PTLD, as are those who experience primary EBV infection after transplantation.[51,52] EBV viral load elevations, reflecting an increase in circulating EBV-transformed B cells, may precede the onset of overt LPD.[248] A B-cell lymphoma seen in HIV infected patients, diffuse large cell lymphoma, bears a striking resemblance to PTLD. As with PTLD, it occurs in the setting of profound immunosuppression; those with the lowest CD4 counts for the longest time are at greatest risk. Presentation as primary CNS lymphoma is frequent and essentially all CNS lymphomas are EBV positive, whereas about two thirds of diffuse large cell lymphomas outside the CNS are EBV positive.[249]

Burkitt's Lymphoma

Burkitt's lymphoma is a high-grade lymphoma with characteristic small, noncleaved B cells and is endemic in equatorial Africa. Endemic Burkitt's lymphoma is geographically associated with *Plasmodium falciparum* malaria and usually arises as a tumor of the jaw. Despite the long-appreciated association of more than 90% of Burkitt's lymphomas with EBV, the role of the virus in its pathogenesis is unclear because most of the EBV transforming genes are not expressed. In fact, viral gene expression is restricted to EBNA1 and the EBERs (latency I) (see Table 135-2).[48,53,54] It is unlikely that EBV is merely a passenger, as terminal repeat analysis of EBV genomes has confirmed that the viral infection occurred before expansion of the tumor.[250] Also, persons in endemic regions with elevated titers to EBV structural proteins are at high risk for Burkitt's lymphoma.[251] In addition to EBV association, Burkitt's lymphomas virtually all contain a chromosomal translocation involving the c-*myc* oncogene and an im-

---

TABLE 135-7 Epstein-Barr Virus–Associated Malignancies

Malignancy	EBV Association	Population at Risk	Cofactors
Lymphoproliferative disease	~90%	Transplant patients	Immunosuppression
Primary CNS lymphoma	100%	AIDS with very low CD4+ count	Immunosuppression
Hodgkin's lymphoma	~50% depending on histologic subtype	Children (developing countries) Young adults (western countries)	Unknown
Nasopharyngeal carcinoma	100% undifferentiated 30%-100% squamous	Southern Chinese, Inuit	Genetic predisposition and ?dietary factors
Burkitt's lymphoma	> 95% endemic ~20% sporadic ~40% HIV associated	African children Independent of CD4+ count	c-*myc* translocations (all) ?Malaria (endemic only)

AIDS, acquired immunodeficiency syndrome; CNS, central nervous system; EBV, Epstein-Barr virus; HIV, human immunodeficiency virus.
Adapted from Kieff E, Rickinson AB. Epstein-Barr virus and its replication. In: Knipe D, Howley P, Griffin D, et al, eds. Fields' Virology. Philadelphia: Lippincott-Raven; 2001:2511-2574.

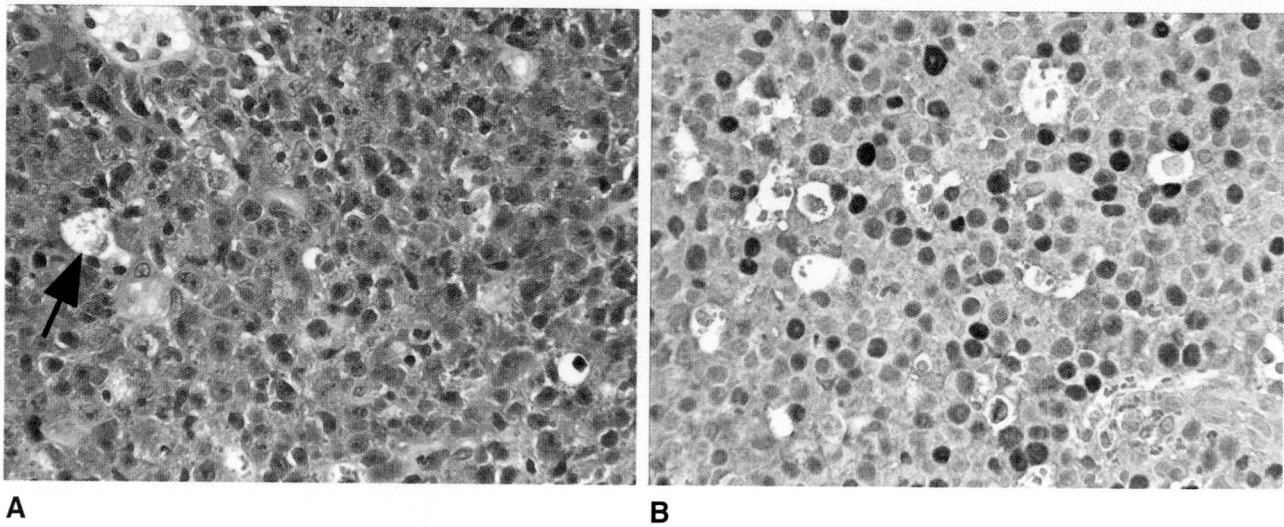

FIGURE 135-2. Post-transplantation lymphoproliferative disease involving the colon. **A,** The tumor is composed of large, atypical lymphoid cells (hematoxylin and eosin). Scattered macrophages (*arrow*) are seen, producing a "starry-sky" appearance. **B,** In situ hybridization for Epstein-Barr virus (EBV)–encoded RNA (EBER) (*brown*) shows variably intense nuclear staining in the majority of tumor cells, indicating EBV infection. (Original magnification ×400.) *(Courtesy of Dr. Jeffery Kutok.)*

munoglobulin heavy or light chain locus. The unregulated expression of this potent oncogene probably supplants the need for expression of many of the EBV transforming genes that otherwise would serve as targets for immune surveillance. In addition to the endemic form of the disease, sporadic Burkitt-like lymphomas are seen that typically arise as abdominal masses. These lymphomas also contain c-*myc* translocations but are less consistently associated with EBV (only about 25% of cases).[249] HIV-infected persons are at increased risk for Burkitt-like lymphoma, independent of degree of immunodeficiency.[252]

Hodgkin's Lymphoma

Hodgkin's lymphoma is an unusual malignancy in that the malignant Hodgkin and Reed-Sternberg (HRS) cells constitute as little as 1% of the tumor. The balance of the tumor mass is composed of an infiltrate of reactive mononuclear and stromal cells. An infectious etiology for Hodgkin's lymphoma was proposed as early as 1966 on the basis of the epidemiology of the disease, but definitive evidence was slow to

evolve because of technical difficulties presented by the scarcity of the HRS cells.[253-255] Subsequently, EBV DNA and protein expression were demonstrated in HRS cells from some forms of Hodgkin's lymphoma.[256,257] The strongest associations are with the mixed cellularity (Fig. 135-3) and lymphocyte-depleted histologic subtypes.[74] No association with the lymphocyte predominant subtype could be proved, and this is now considered a distinct, non–EBV-associated entity. Even in classic Hodgkin's lymphoma, there is considerable variation in the strength of the association with EBV, which depends on other factors such as age, sex, ethnicity, and country of residence. There is, however, general agreement that in EBV-associated Hodgkin's lymphoma, the malignant HRS cells represent postgerminal center B cells that express a latency II EBV gene pattern (LMP1, LMP2, EBNA1, and EBERs; see Table 135-2). EBV genomes, when present in HRS cells, are monoclonal by terminal repeat analysis, suggesting that EBV infection preceded the development of the malignancy.[257] Activation of NF-κB signaling is typical of HRS cells, suggesting activation of this

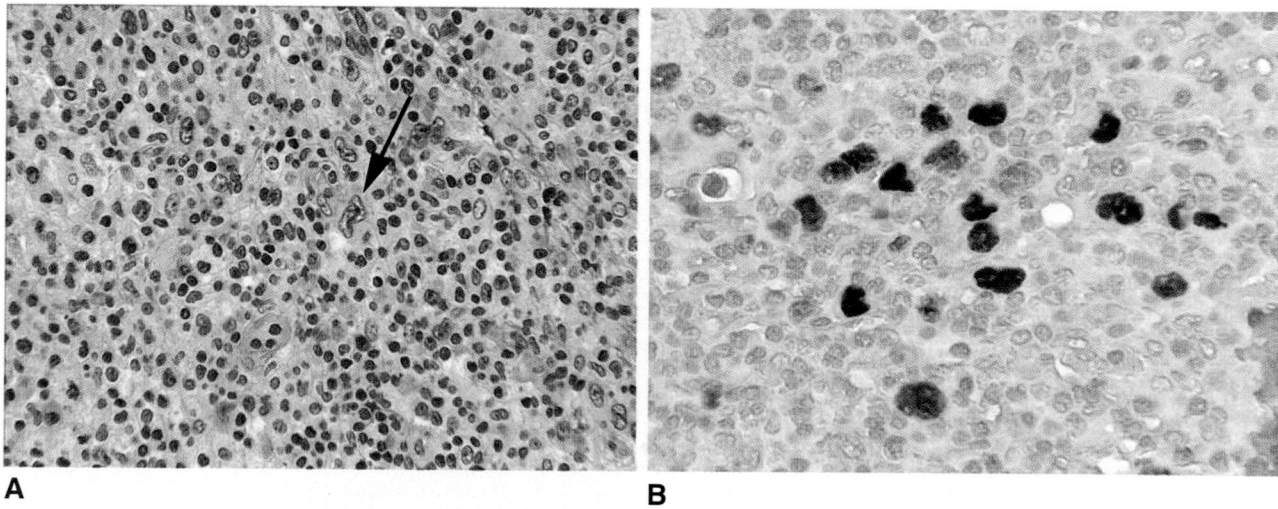

FIGURE 135-3. Mixed cellularity classic Hodgkin's lymphoma. **A,** Lymph node architecture is effaced by an infiltrate comprised of small lymphocytes, epithelioid histiocytes, plasma cells, eosinophils, and Hodgkin and Reed-Sternberg cells (*arrow*) (hematoxylin and eosin). **B,** In situ hybridization for Epstein-Barr virus (EBV)–encoded RNA (EBER) (*brown*) demonstrates EBV infection in the malignant Hodgkin and Reed-Sternberg cells. (Original magnification ×400.) *(Courtesy of Dr. Jeffery Kutok.)*

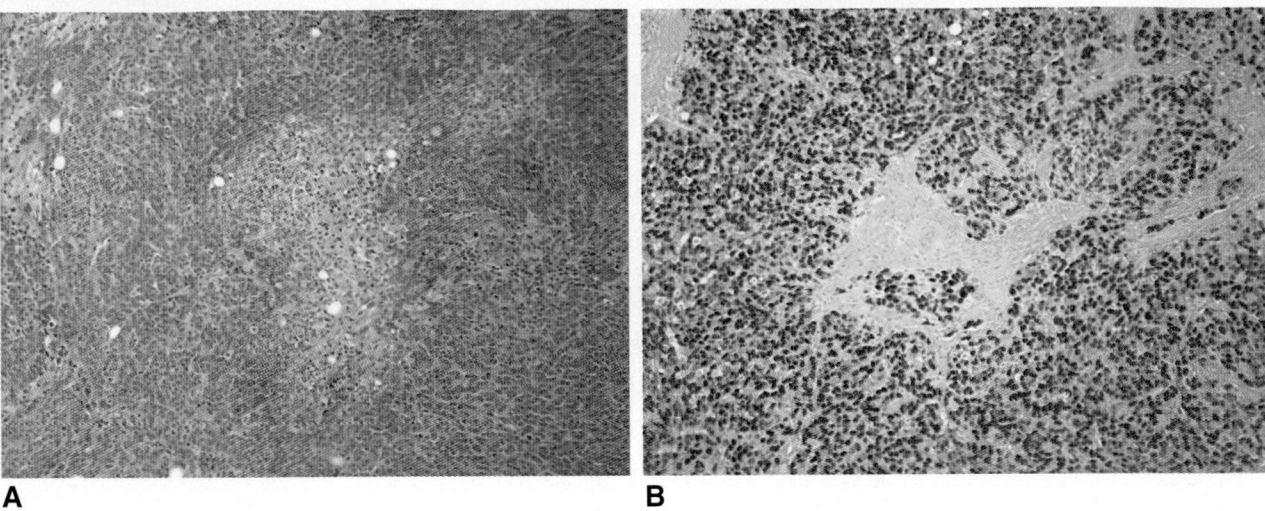

FIGURE 135-4. Nasopharyngeal carcinoma. **A,** Nests of metastatic undifferentiated nasopharyngeal carcinoma in a fibrous stroma in a lymph node (hematoxylin and eosin). Metastases often lack infiltrating lymphocytes. **B,** In situ hybridization for Epstein-Barr virus (EBV)–encoded RNA (EBER) (*brown*) demonstrates EBV infection in most cells in the same area of the tissue. (Magnification ×100.) *(Courtesy of Dr. Miguel Rivera.)*

pathway by LMP1.[258] In some EBV-negative HRS cells, IκBα gene mutations have been reported that could serve as an alternative means of constitutively activating the NF-κB pathway.[259] It is tempting to speculate that EBV gene expression can serve as one step in the malignant transformation of HRS cells that is circumvented by other mutational events in EBV-negative forms of the disease.

Nasopharyngeal Carcinoma

Nasopharyngeal carcinoma is a rare disease in most western countries, but its prevalence approaches 50 per 100,000 in southern China and among the Inuit in Alaska.[260] An association between EBV and nasopharyngeal carcinoma was first suggested by the observation that patients with this malignancy had elevated IgG and IgA titers to EBV lytic antigens (VCA and EA).[261] The undifferentiated form (Fig. 135-4) is EBV associated in nearly 100% of cases, whereas squamous nasopharyngeal carcinomas are inconsistently EBV associated, particularly outside endemic regions. The undifferentiated form bears some resemblance to Hodgkin's lymphoma in that the tumor consists of EBV-positive cells (of epithelial origin in this case) expressing a latency II gene pattern infiltrated with nonmalignant lymphoid cells.[75,262,263] Terminal repeat assays have confirmed that these epithelial cells contain monoclonal EBV genomes, placing EBV infection early in the genesis of the malignancy as seen in EBV-associated B-cell neoplasia.[264] In addition to EBV, there is evidence indicating that genetic and environmental factors may have roles in tumor development.[265-267]

Other Malignancies

T-cell lymphomas seen in patients with CAEBV frequently contain EBV genomes and have been reported to express a latency II gene pattern.[268] EBV is also consistently found in nasal T-cell/NK-cell lymphoma.[269] An EBV association has been reported in some gastric cancers, breast cancer, hepatocellular cancers, and smooth muscle tumors, but the association and the contribution of EBV to the pathogenesis of these malignancies remain to be established.[270-272]

In addition to the Burkitt-like lymphomas and diffuse large cell lymphomas, HIV-infected (or other immunosuppressed) persons are at increased risk for an unusual EBV-associated lymphoma, primary effusion lymphoma.[273,274] These human herpesvirus 8 (Kaposi's sarcoma–associated herpesvirus) related tumors are often coinfected with EBV. These aggressive tumors arise within potential body cavities such as the pleural, pericardial, or peritoneal spaces. In pediatric AIDS patients, EBV has been reported in leiomyosarcoma biopsy specimens as well.[275]

LABORATORY DIAGNOSIS

Infectious Mononucleosis

Hematologic Findings

The central hematologic manifestation of the illness is a circulating lymphocytosis. At presentation, a relative and absolute mononuclear lymphocytosis is found in about 70% of the cases. The lymphocytosis peaks during the second or third week of illness, and monocytes and lymphocytes account for 60% to 70% of the total white cell counts of 12,000 to 18,000/mm³. However, higher white cell counts are not uncommon, and occasional patients manifest 30,000 to 50,000 leukocytes/mm³. Atypical lymphocytes are the hematologic hallmark of infectious mononucleosis and account for about 30% of the differential count at their zenith.[136,137] The wide range in the atypical lymphocytosis is well recognized, and some cases show none or only a few atypical lymphocytes, whereas 90% or more of the circulating lymphocytes may be atypical in other cases. These atypical lymphocytes are composed largely of reactive CD8+ cytotoxic T cells and are not pathognomonic for infectious mononucleosis (Table 135-8). They are also noted in other syndromes, including CMV infection, primary HIV, viral hepatitis, toxoplasmosis, rubella, mumps, and roseola as well as in drug reactions.[276,277] The atypical lymphocyte is generally larger than the mature lymphocyte encountered in peripheral blood. The cytoplasm is often vacuolated and basophilic, and its edges have a rolled-up appearance. Nuclei are often lobulated and are eccentrically placed. Although the cells may appear quite immature, the heterogeneity of morphologic and tinctorial characteristics of such cells helps to distinguish atypical lymphocytes from the more uniform lymphoblasts of acute lymphocytic leukemia.[6,276]

TABLE 135-8 Differential Diagnosis of Atypical Lymphocytosis

Epstein-Barr virus primary infection (infectious mononucleosis)
Cytomegalovirus primary infection (heterophile-negative mono)*
Human herpesvirus 6 primary infection (roseola)
Primary HIV infection
Toxoplasmosis
Acute viral hepatitis
Rubella, mumps
Drug reactions (e.g., phenytoin, sulfa)

*CMV is the most common cause of heterophile-negative mononucleosis.

TABLE 135-9 Heterophile Antibodies: Effect of Absorption

Source of Serum	Unabsorbed	Guinea Pig Kidney	Beef Red Cells
		After Absorption with:	
Infectious mononucleosis	+ + + +	+ + +	0
Serum sickness	+ + +	0	0
Normal serum (Forssman's antibody)	+	0	+

A relative and absolute neutropenia is evident in 60% to 90% of the cases, and neutrophils that remain in circulation exhibit a mild left shift.[164,165] In most cases, the neutropenia is mild, with total granulocyte counts of 2000 to 3000/mm^3, although profound granulocytopenia has also been reported.[163,166-170,214,278] The neutropenia is usually self-limited, and counts rise gradually toward normal by a month after presentation.[164]

Thrombocytopenia is also common, and 50% of the patients in one series manifested platelet counts of less than 140,000/mm^3.[157] Although cases of profound thrombocytopenia with bleeding have been reported,[158-162] these are rare and contrast markedly with the generally benign course of the common, mild thrombocytopenia.

Heterophile Antibodies

Heterophile antibodies, originally described by Paul and Bunnell[7] as sheep erythrocyte agglutinins, are present in about 90% of the cases at some point during the illness. Beef erythrocyte hemolysins and agglutinating antibodies to horse, goat, and camel erythrocytes are also demonstrable in infectious mononucleosis. The classic heterophile antibody titer is reported as the highest serum dilution at which sheep erythrocytes are agglutinated after absorption of the test serum by guinea pig kidney (Table 135-9). The differential absorption permits a distinction between naturally occurring Forssman antibodies, the antibodies of serum sickness, and heterophile antibodies of infectious mononucleosis. Beef red cell hemolysins do not require differential absorption for interpretation. Although titers may vary depending on laboratory techniques, a titer of 40 or greater after guinea pig absorp-

tion along with a compatible clinical presentation is strong evidence for infectious mononucleosis.

Heterophile antibodies may be demonstrable at the onset of illness or may appear later in the course of the illness. A delayed appearance of heterophile antibodies may be associated with a more prolonged convalescence.[279] Horse red cell agglutination is more sensitive than tests for sheep red cell agglutination or beef red cell hemolysis. Horse red cell agglutinins persist for a year after diagnosis in 75% of the cases,[280] whereas sheep cell agglutinins fall to titers of less than 40 by a year in 70% of cases. False-positive titers greater than 40 of sheep and horse erythrocyte agglutinins have been found in 12% and 6.7% of sera, respectively.[281] Commercial spot kits are available and are generally specific and sensitive for the demonstration of heterophile antibodies. The correlation between the results obtained by the use of these kits and results of the classic tube heterophile method is quite good, although the sensitivity of the spot and slide tests is slightly greater than that of the classic tube heterophile test. Occasional false-positive Monospot test responses have been reported in patients with lymphoma or hepatitis, but the rarity of this event makes confirmation of a positive Monospot test result by classic sheep cell agglutination unnecessary.[282-284]

Epstein-Barr Virus–Specific Antibodies

In addition to the transient heterophile antibodies, infection with EBV results in the development of virus-specific antibodies. Antibodies are formed to structural proteins or VCAs, nonstructural proteins expressed early in the lytic cycle or EAs, and nuclear proteins expressed during latent infections or EBNAs. A determination of EBV-specific antibodies is rarely necessary for the diagnosis of infectious mononucleosis because 90% of the cases are heterophile positive and few false-positive results are obtained if the test is properly performed (see earlier). For heterophile-negative cases and for diagnosis in atypical cases, a determination of EBV antibodies may help to establish a cause (Table 135-10).[285]

Antibodies to VCA as measured by immunofluorescence arise early in the course of the illness and are demonstrable at presentation in most cases. IgG antibodies to VCA are usually present at titers of 80 or greater on the first visit to a physician. Because these initially detected levels are close to peak VCA titers, a fourfold rise in titer is demonstrable in only 10% to 20% of the cases. After recovery, detectable titers of VCA IgG antibody are maintained for life. Thus, IgG VCA antibody titers may be of little help in establishing the diagnosis

TABLE 135-10 Antibodies to Epstein-Barr Virus

Antibody Specificity	Time of Appearance in Infectious Mononucleosis	Percentage of Epstein-Barr Virus–Induced Mononucleosis Cases with Antibody	Persistence	Comments
Viral Capsid Antigens				
IgM VCA	At clinical presentation	100	4-8 wk	Highly sensitive and specific; major diagnostic utility
IgG VCA	At clinical presentation	100	Lifelong	High titer at presentation and lifelong persistence make IgG VCA more useful as an epidemiologic tool than as a diagnostic tool in individual cases
Early Antigens				
Anti-D	Peaks at 3-4 wk after onset	70	3-6 mo	Correlated with severe disease; also seen in nasopharyngeal carcinoma
Anti-R	2 wk to several months after onset	Low	2 mo to >3 yr	Occasionally seen with unusually severe or protracted illness; also seen in African Burkitt's lymphoma
Epstein-Barr nuclear antigen	3-4 wk after onset	100	Lifelong	Late appearance helpful in diagnosis of heterophile-negative cases
Soluble complement-fixing antigens (anti-S)	3-4 wk after onset	100	Lifelong	Late appearance helpful in diagnosis of heterophile-negative cases

IgM, immunoglobulin M; VCA, viral capsid antigen.

of infectious mononucleosis. Conversely, IgM antibodies to VCA are sensitive and specific for infectious mononucleosis. IgM antibody titers greater than 5 as measured by indirect immunofluorescence are demonstrable in 90% of cases early in the illness. Titers fall rapidly thereafter, and in only 10% of the cases are titers greater than 5 retained by 4 months after diagnosis.[280,286] IgM VCA antibodies are not demonstrable in the general population, and thus their presence is virtually diagnostic of acute EBV infection.

Serum antibodies to EAs are also demonstrable by indirect immunofluorescence, and two distinct patterns of fluorescence emerge.[285,286] Certain sera stain both nuclei and cytoplasm diffusely (anti-D), whereas the staining of other sera is restricted (anti-R) to cytoplasmic aggregates. Anti-D antibody is found in about 70% of patients with acute infectious mononucleosis (see Table 135-10). Anti-D titers arise later in the course of illness than those to VCA and disappear after recovery. Anti-D antibodies may be found in the sera of patients with advanced nasopharyngeal carcinoma but are absent from the general population. The appearance of anti-D antibodies in a patient with IgG VCA antibodies suggests recent EBV infection. Unfortunately, only 70% of EBV-induced cases manifest anti-D antibodies. The presence and titer of anti-D antibodies correlate with the duration and severity of clinical illness.[286] Anti-R antibodies are only occasionally seen in infectious mononucleosis (see Table 135-10). They are present more often in protracted or atypical cases, arise after the anti-D antibodies peak, and remain detectable for up to 2 years.[287] Anti-R antibodies are also present in higher titers in patients with African Burkitt's lymphoma and occasionally in healthy persons who also have high VCA titers.[288]

Antibodies to EBNA appear late in the course of all cases of infectious mononucleosis and persist for life.[289] The appearance of EBNA antibodies in a patient who was previously VCA positive and EBNA negative is strong evidence of recent EBV infection. These antibodies may be reactive against any of the six nuclear proteins expressed during latent infection. Neutralizing antibodies to EBV also appear late in the course of infectious mononucleosis and reach maximal levels 6 to 7 weeks after the onset of illness.[290] Neutralizing antibodies persist at stable titers (mean of 40) for life. The appearance or a rise in titer of neutralizing antibodies to EBV also indicates recent EBV infection. Neutralizing antibodies are, however, difficult to measure, and tests for them are not routinely available. Complement-fixing antibodies to soluble antigens (anti-S) appear in infectious mononucleosis in a time course similar to that of the appearance of EBNA antibodies.[291] A fourfold rise in titer of anti-S antibody suggests recent EBV infection. Anti-S antibody persists for life.

Detection of Epstein-Barr Virus

EBV may be cultured from oropharyngeal washings or from circulating lymphocytes of 80% to 90% of patients with infectious mononucleosis.[60-62,91,101] Cultivation of the virus is, however, not routinely available in most diagnostic virology laboratories. This, coupled with the ubiquity of virus shedding in both healthy persons and in those with unrelated illnesses, renders cultivation of the virus of little clinical use (see Table 135-1). Rapid diagnostic techniques based on DNA hybridization or monoclonal antibody techniques have also been developed but are not practical for diagnosis of mononucleosis.[292-294]

Other Laboratory Abnormalities

Liver function test results are abnormal in almost all cases of infectious mononucleosis.[193,295,296] The hepatocellular enzymes aspartate aminotransferase, alanine aminotransferase, and lactate dehydrogenase are most commonly elevated, and one of the three is abnormal in about 90% of the cases. Elevations are usually mild, with individual values in the range of two to three times the upper limit of normal. Elevation to more than 10 times the upper limit of normal requires a search for another diagnosis.[193] The alkaline phosphatase level is elevated in about 60% of the cases.[295,296] Mild elevation of the bilirubin level is noted in approximately 45% of cases, although frank jaundice occurs in only about 5%. Elevations are maximal in the second week of illness and decline gradually over a 3- to 4-week period.

Cryoproteins are present in modest amounts in 90% to 95% of patients.[149,297] The cryoproteins are generally mixed cryoglobulins of IgG and IgM classes. When the cryoglobulins are dissociated, antibody of anti-i or anti-I or both specificities is usually demonstrable.[297,298]

Differential Diagnosis

In most cases, the diagnosis of infectious mononucleosis is straightforward. The clinical manifestations of sore throat, fever, lymphadenopathy, and malaise coupled with atypical lymphocytosis and a positive heterophile test result establish the diagnosis of EBV-induced infectious mononucleosis. Difficulties arise, however, when the clinical manifestations are less striking, particularly when the heterophile test is negative.

Heterophile-negative infectious mononucleosis may be caused by several different agents. Attention to the clinical manifestations of the illness and proper use of the laboratory provide an etiologic diagnosis in 85% to 90% of all cases of infectious mononucleosis. The frequency with which heterophile-negative infectious mononucleosis is seen depends largely on three factors: (1) age of the population of patients—EBV-induced infectious mononucleosis tends to be a milder illness and is more often heterophile negative in pediatric populations than in young adults; (2) sensitivity of the heterophile test—heterophile antibodies are more often demonstrable by horse red cell agglutination than by beef red cell hemolysis or by sheep red cell agglutination; and (3) diligence with which heterophile antibodies are sought—typical cases of infectious mononucleosis may be heterophile negative on presentation but, if retested later in the course of the illness, may become heterophile positive.

The most frequent cause of heterophile-negative infectious mononucleosis in most populations is CMV.[299] Although differentiation of individual cases of EBV- versus CMV-induced infectious mononucleosis may be difficult, certain features are more common in CMV infections. CMV more frequently follows transfusion and is more frequently manifested as a typhoid-like syndrome without sore throat and lymphadenopathy. Splenomegaly may be slightly more prominent with CMV-induced disease, whereas the atypical lymphocytosis is usually less intense in CMV-induced infectious mononucleosis. In age-matched control subjects, the results of liver function tests are less elevated when the agent is CMV. Cryoglobulins are demonstrable in both EBV- and CMV-induced disease, but anti-i specificity is not seen in CMV-induced mononucleosis.[298] The illness may be attributed to CMV if there is serologic evidence of acute CMV infection and no evidence of acute EBV infection.

Heterophile-negative infectious mononucleosis may also be caused by EBV. As previously noted, this is not uncommon in the pediatric age group.[131,132] The diagnosis rests on the demonstration of appropriate changes in specific EBV serologic tests (see Table 135-10).

Viral hepatitis may result in fever, lymphadenopathy, malaise, and an atypical lymphocytosis. Generally, the atypical lymphocytosis is of lesser magnitude, and atypical lymphocytes account for less than 10% of the leukocytes. In viral hepatitis, hepatocellular enzyme levels are usually markedly elevated at the initial visit, whereas in infectious mononucleosis the results of liver function tests are only mildly elevated initially and rise gradually over a 1- to 2-week period. In addition, specific serologic tests are currently available for the detection of infection with hepatitis A, B, and C viruses.

Acute toxoplasmosis may also give rise to an infectious mononucleosis–like illness. Usually the degree of the lymphocytosis is mild, and a diagnosis can be made by serologic tests for *Toxoplasma*. Rubella may also occasionally be manifested by fever, lymphadenopathy, and a mild atypical lymphocytosis, but the appearance of the exanthem and the clinical course of the illness are generally not confused with those of infectious mononucleosis. A serologic diagnosis of recent rubella infection can be obtained if the diagnosis remains in doubt. Infectious lymphocytosis of childhood is a disease of uncertain cause that is characterized by fever, lymphadenopathy, occasionally diarrhea, and a lymphocytosis that consists almost exclusively of small mature lymphocytes. The disease is most common in the pediatric age group, may occur in epidemics, and is not associated with EBV infection.[300]

A streptococcal sore throat may also mimic infectious mononucleosis clinically. Adenopathy is generally submandibular and anterior cervical, and splenomegaly is absent in streptococcal sore throat. Culture of group A β-hemolytic streptococci from the throat is supportive but not conclusive evidence for this diagnosis because colonization with the organism is common in this population of patients. Serologic tests for recent infection with group A streptococci may help to establish the cause.

Primary HIV-1 infection may also arise with fever, lymphadenopathy, and pharyngitis.[301-303] Such patients may also exhibit a maculopapular rash and signs of aseptic meningitis. Patients with primary HIV-1 infection are not heterophile positive and are diagnosed by the detection of HIV-1 p24 antigen or HIV-1 RNA in serum or plasma or both (see Chapter 117). It is important to note that patients with primary HIV infection typically have negative or indeterminate HIV serology.

Nasopharyngeal Carcinoma

Nasopharyngeal carcinoma is difficult to diagnose in its early stages, and therefore patients typically present with advanced disease. The most common initial presenting complaint is a neck mass (Fig. 135-5). Diagnosis requires endoscopy to visualize the nasopharynx and histologic examination of biopsy tissue.[304] Radiologic studies are helpful in revealing the extent of disease (Fig. 135-6). Patients with nasopharyn-

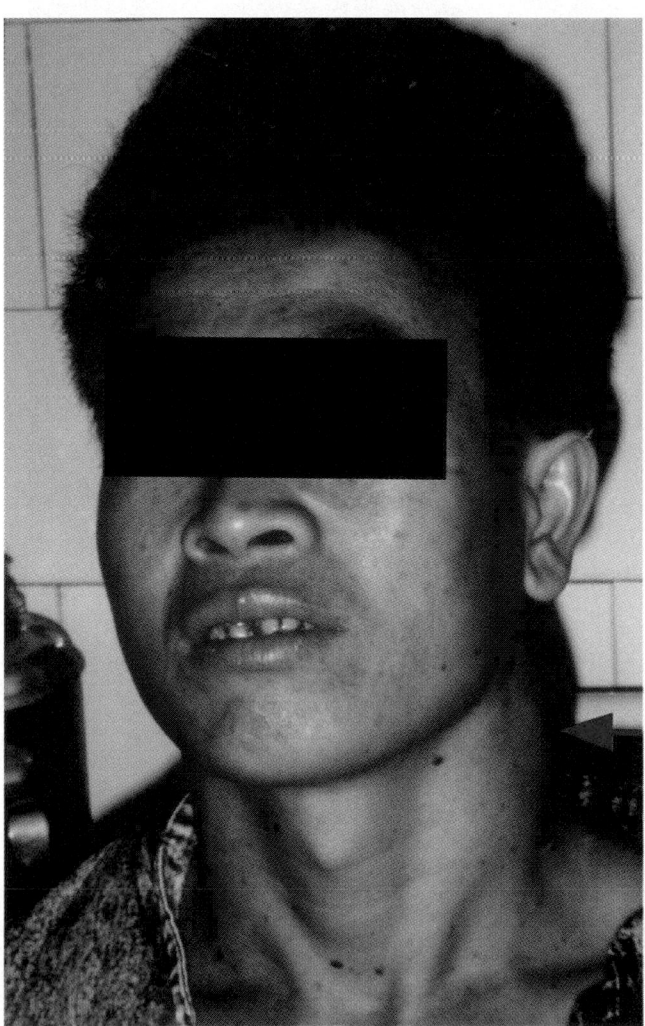

FIGURE 135-5. A patient with nasopharyngeal carcinoma and a neck mass (*arrow*).

geal carcinoma have elevated levels of serum IgA directed against EBV VCA and EA.[305-307] The elevation of the IgA antibodies may occur several years before the onset of nasopharyngeal carcinoma. In light of this finding, a program of screening individuals for elevated EBV IgA VCA and EA titers has been instituted in southern China, where nasopharyngeal carcinoma is one of the leading malignancies. Those with elevated IgA titers are then observed closely for the development of disease. This screening program enhanced the diagnosis of nasopharyngeal carcinoma in earlier as opposed to more advanced stages of disease.

Detection of EBV DNA in nasopharyngeal brush biopsies has also been proposed in one study as a possible screening mechanism in high-risk populations. This study detected EBV DNA in 19 of 21 brush biopsies from patients with recently diagnosed nasopharyngeal carcinoma but only in 1.3% of control subjects.[308]

Although EBV is typically cell associated, cell-free EBV DNA has been detected in patients with nasopharyngeal carcinoma.[304] It is postulated that cell-free EBV DNA is released into the circulation upon tumor cell death. In two studies by the same authors,[309,310] quantitative analysis of the concentration of DNA in plasma was useful in monitoring patients for recurrence of disease. Of note, cell-free DNA has also been found in other EBV-associated diseases including mononucleosis, Hodgkin's lymphoma, and LPD.[311]

Central Nervous System Lymphoma in Acquired Immunodeficiency Syndrome

PCR detection of EBV DNA in CSF has been useful in the diagnosis of CNS lymphoma in HIV-infected patients.[312-315] Nearly all primary CNS lymphomas in HIV disease are EBV associated, as discussed earlier. Whereas HIV-infected patients without CNS lymphoma rarely have detectable EBV DNA in CSF, EBV DNA is frequently detected when CNS lymphoma is present. Therefore, CSF PCR for EBV used in conjunction with radiologic studies may reduce the need for brain biopsy in certain instances. Quantification of EBV DNA in CSF may also be useful for monitoring the effects of CNS lymphoma therapy.[316]

TREATMENT

Infectious Mononucleosis

Supportive

Treatment of infectious mononucleosis is largely supportive because more than 95% of the patients recover uneventfully without specific therapy. The level of activity is generally tailored to what the individual patient can tolerate comfortably. To avoid trauma to the spleen, contact sports or heavy lifting should be avoided during the first month of illness and until any splenomegaly has resolved. Ultrasound examination can be used to monitor spleen size. If constipation is present, it should be treated with a gentle laxative. Acetaminophen or nonsteroidal anti-inflammatory agents can be helpful in relieving the sore throat and in suppressing the fever. Sore throat may be further alleviated by gargling with warm salt water.

Antiviral Agents

Phosphonoacetic acid, adenine arabinoside, acyclovir, desciclovir, and ganciclovir inhibit EBV replication in vitro.[317-329] However, these agents target the viral DNA polymerase, which is expressed only during lytic infection. Because EBV infection is predominantly latent, it is not surprising that these agents are ineffective in treatment of infectious mononucleosis. Further, the clinical symptoms and signs of infectious mononucleosis are largely due to the vigorous immune response directed against EBV. A meta-analysis of five randomized, controlled trials demonstrated no significant benefit of acyclovir in the treatment of infectious mononucleosis. These trials included patients with mild, moderate, and severe mononucleosis. As expected, viral shedding from the oropharynx, where lytic replication commonly occurs, was reduced, but inhibition of shedding was lost 3 weeks after withdrawal of the antiviral agent.[330-334]

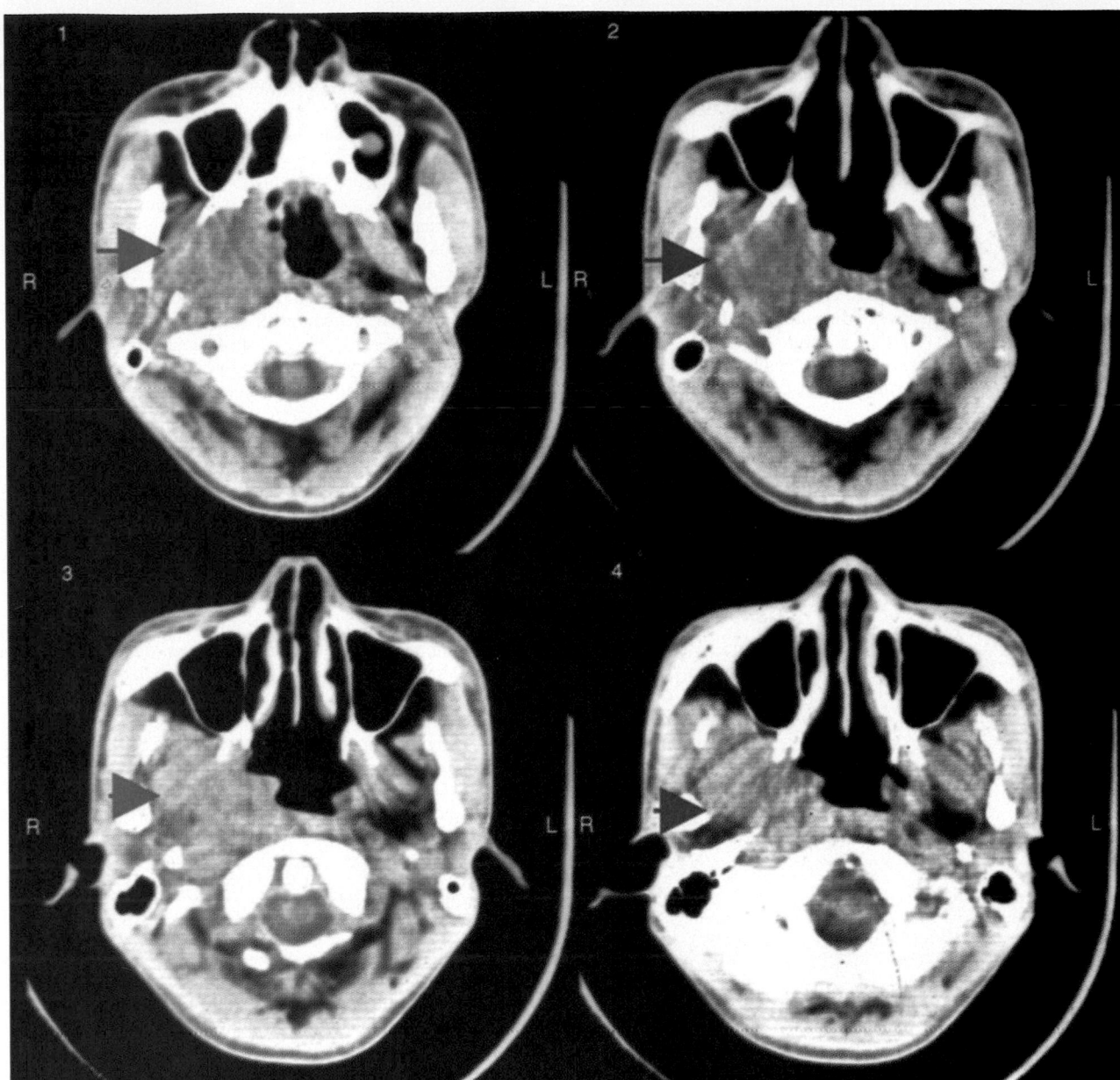

FIGURE 135-6. Computed tomographic images of a 25-year-old man with nasopharyngeal carcinoma (*arrows*). The tumor involves the right parapharyngeal space. *(Courtesy of Dr. Yi Zeng.)*

Corticosteroids

Corticosteroids should not generally be used in uncomplicated infectious mononucleosis. A double-blind, placebo-controlled trial demonstrated that the combination of acyclovir and prednisolone did not reduce the duration of symptoms or result in an earlier return to work.[333] Other studies with corticosteroids have indicated that corticosteroids decrease the period of febrility and hasten the resolution of tonsillopharyngeal symptoms but do not reproducibly affect lymphadenopathy or liver and spleen involvement.[335-339] One particular reason to avoid corticosteroids in uncomplicated disease is that they have rarely been linked with complications such as encephalitis and myocarditis.[47,339] In addition, there is a theoretical risk that corticosteroids may inhibit the host immune response, resulting in a larger reservoir of latently infected cells that could potentially put patients at risk for EBV-associated malignancy.

Corticosteroids may be helpful in cases of complicated infectious mononucleosis.[339-341] Tonsillar enlargement causing airway compromise may respond rapidly to corticosteroids, eliminating the need for tracheostomy. Corticosteroids may also be helpful in autoimmune hemolytic anemia, severe thrombocytopenia, and aplastic anemia. Some also advocate the use of corticosteroids for CNS involvement, myocarditis, or pericarditis. In selected cases of severe or prolonged prostration, corticosteroids may be of benefit. If corticosteroids are administered in these situations, treatment should be initiated in doses equivalent to 60 to 80 mg of prednisone per day given in a split daily regimen. The response is usually rapid, and the dosage can be tapered over a 1- to 2-week period.

Lymphoproliferative Disease

Multiple modalities are used in the treatment of LPD.[51,52,342] The mainstay of LPD therapy is reduction of immune suppression. This strategy is logical because LPD most likely results from ineffective immune surveillance of EBV-infected B cells. Reduction of immune suppression leads to regression of tumors in up to 50% of cases.

Complications of this approach include organ rejection or graft-versus-host disease (GVHD) in allogeneic stem cell recipients. Surgical resection and radiotherapy are often used in localized LPD and can be combined with reduction of immune suppression with good results. Interferon-α produces antiviral effects and boosts immune function and is used for LPD treatment. It is difficult to assess accurately the efficacy of interferon-α because it is usually combined with other treatment modalities.

Antiviral therapy with agents such as acyclovir or ganciclovir is commonly used to treat LPD, with or without immunoglobulin.[51,52,342] The vast majority of LPD cells are latently infected by EBV and therefore do not express the EBV DNA polymerase. Because acyclovir and ganciclovir are directed against the EBV DNA polymerase, the latently infected tumor cells should not be susceptible to these agents. It is possible that acyclovir or ganciclovir prevents expansion of the overall pool of EBV-infected B cells by preventing cell-to-cell spread through inhibition of lytic replication that otherwise would occur in a small percentage of cells. Immune globulin may possibly neutralize released EBV virus or exert antibody-dependent cell-mediated toxicity on tumor cells. One experimental approach has been to induce lytic infection (and therefore induce expression of the EBV DNA polymerase) in LPD cells by treatment with arginine butyrate followed by ganciclovir.[343] Initial results have been promising. Cytotoxic chemotherapy, usually with regimens used for non-Hodgkin's lymphoma, is often used after other initial approaches have failed.

Treatment of LPD with antibodies targeted against B cells is another approach.[51,52,342] Rituximab is a monoclonal antibody directed against the CD20 B-cell antigen. Binding of this antibody to B cells results in B-cell death through CTLs and activation of the complement cascade. Anti-CD20 antibodies can also be linked to radionuclides such as iodine-131 (tositumomab) or yttrium-90 (ibritumomab tiuxetan). Data on the efficacy of these approaches are currently accumulating.

Cellular immunotherapy is another approach to LPD treatment. This strategy is based on reconstituting a cellular immune response against EBV to treat the infected tumor cells. Allogeneic stem cell recipients with LPD have been treated with unselected, donor mononuclear cells.[344,345] This approach results in response rates of up to 90% but also results in a high rate of GVHD because of the presence of the infused alloreactive T cells. To avoid GVHD, another approach has been to infuse selected, donor-derived, EBV-specific CTLs.[346,347] Marking of transferred T cells has demonstrated that they persist up to 18 months. Cell immunotherapy has also been used with success as prophylaxis for LPD in stem cell transplant recipients. Of note, a patient died of PTLD despite receiving adoptive immunotherapy. Analysis of the patient's tumor demonstrated a deletion in EBNA 3B a gene that is not required for B-cell growth transformation. Because the infused CTLs were largely directed against EBNA 3B, they selected for the mutated EBV. This report raises concern about escape mutants with CTL therapy.[348] Cell immunotherapy can also be used in solid organ transplant recipients. The organ recipient's CTLs can be expanded in vitro and then infused back into the patient.[349]

Studies have indicated that measurement of the EBV DNA load in the blood of immunosuppressed individuals can be helpful for the early detection and management of LPD.[350-352] A decrease in the EBV DNA load often correlates with response to therapy. Of note, however, after treatment with rituximab, peripheral blood mononuclear cell EBV DNA levels can fall even in the setting of tumor progression.[353]

Oral Hairy Leukoplakia

OHL differs from most EBV-related diseases in that the EBV infection is predominantly lytic rather than latent. In this setting of active lytic infection, agents such as acyclovir, ganciclovir, and foscarnet are effective in therapy.[354-357] Topical therapy, such as with podophyllum resin, has also been shown to have efficacy against OHL.[358,359] In the setting of HIV-related OHL, oral lesions usually regress with the institution of effective antiretroviral therapy.

PREVENTION

Public Health Measures

Because the spread of virus requires intimate contact, isolation of patients with infectious mononucleosis is not necessary. Because viremia is demonstrable for several months after recovery, consideration should be given to postponement of blood donation by patients with infectious mononucleosis for at least 6 months after the onset of illness.

Vaccine

EBV vaccine development has been an elusive goal for many years. Because EBV infection does not cause severe disease in most instances, a vaccine must be particularly safe.[49] The only herpesvirus vaccine currently licensed by the Food and Drug Administration is a live attenuated varicella-zoster vaccine. Because of EBV's associations with malignancies, it is highly unlikely that a live attenuated vaccine will be acceptable. Two major approaches have been taken to EBV vaccine development. One approach is to induce EBV neutralizing antibody directed against the viral glycoprotein gp350, which binds to the EBV cellular receptor.[360] Immunization with gp350 protects against EBV-induced lymphomas in an animal model.[361] Interestingly, despite initial expectations, cell-mediated immunity appears to play an important role in the gp350 vaccination prevention of lymphoma in this model.[362] Some animals have developed lymphomas despite the presence of neutralizing antibody to gp350.[363] In addition, in other work, gp350 vaccine has protected animals from EBV-induced lymphoma even in the absence of neutralizing antibody.[364] Phase I trials have now been completed for a gp350 vaccine in a vaccinia vector in China and a gp350 plus adjuvant vaccine in the United States.[365]

The second approach has been to develop a vaccine using known EBV MHC class I restricted CTL epitopes.[365-367] Although such a vaccine would not necessarily be designed to prevent primary infection, it is expected to ameliorate the symptoms of mononucleosis.[365] Another important potential use of such a vaccine would be to boost the CTL response to avoid development of, or possibly treat, EBV-associated malignancies. A significant number of EBV epitopes recognized by CTLs have now been identified. A phase I trial has been completed in Australia using a single EBV epitope.[365] To generate a broad-based CTL response, a vaccine containing multiple EBV epitopes is necessary. In addition, because CTLs from individuals with different human leukocyte antigen alleles recognize different EBV epitopes, inclusion of relevant epitopes in a vaccine is important. Therefore, current efforts have fused multiple peptide epitopes together for use in vaccines. Such a vaccine is currently in development.[49,365]

REFERENCES

1. Filatov NF. Lektuse ob ostrikh infektsion Nikh Lolieznyak (Lectures on Acute Infectious Disease of children). Moscow: U. Deitel; 1885.
2. Pfeiffer E. Drusenfieber. Jahrb Kinderheilkd. 1889;29:257.
3. Türk W. Septische Erkrankungen bei Verkümmerung des Granulozytensystems. Wien Klin Wochenschr. 1907;20:157.
4. Hall AJ. A case resembling acute lymphatic leukaemia, ending in complete recovery. Proc R Soc Med. 1915;8:15-19.
5. Sprunt TP, Evans FA. Mononuclear leukocytosis in reaction to acute infections ("infectious mononucleosis"). Johns Hopkins Hosp Bull. 1920;31:410.
6. Downey H, McKinlay CA. Acute lymphadenosis compared with acute lymphatic leukemia. Arch Intern Med. 1923;32:82-112.
7. Paul JR, Bunnell W. The presence of heterophile antibodies in infectious mononucleosis. Am J Med Sci. 1932;183:90-104.
8. Davidsohn I. Serologic diagnosis of infectious mononucleosis. JAMA. 1937;108:289-295.
9. Evans AS. Experimental attempts to transmit infectious mononucleosis to man. Yale J Biol Med. 1947;20:19-26.
10. Evans AS. Further experimental attempts to transmit infectious mononucleosis to man. J Clin Invest. 1950;29:508-512.
11. Niederman JC, Scott RB. Studies on infectious mononucleosis: Attempts to transmit the disease to human volunteers. Yale J Biol Med. 1965;38:1-10.
12. Burkitt D. A sarcoma involving the jaws in African children. Br J Surg. 1958;46:218-223.

13. Epstein MA, Achong BA, Barr YM. Virus particles in cultured lymphoblasts from Burkitt's lymphoma. Lancet. 1964;1:702-703.

14. Henle G, Henle W. Immunofluorescence in cells derived from Burkitt lymphoma. J Bacteriol. 1966;91:1248-1256.

15. Henle G, Henle W, Diehl V. Relation of Burkitt's tumor associated herpes-type virus to infectious mononucleosis. Proc Natl Acad Sci USA. 1968;59:94-101.

16. Niederman JC, McCollum RW, Henle G, et al. Infectious mononucleosis: Clinical manifestations in relation to EB virus antibodies. JAMA. 1968;203:205-209.

17. Evans AS, Niederman JC, McCollum RW. Seroepidemiologic studies of infectious mononucleosis with EB virus. N Engl J Med. 1968;279:1121-1127.

18. Sawyer RN, Evans AS, Niederman JC, et al. Prospective studies of a group of Yale University freshmen. I. Occurrence of infectious mononucleosis. J Infect Dis. 1971;123:263-270.

19. University Health Physicians and PHLS Laboratories. A joint investigation of infectious mononucleosis and its relationship to EB virus antibody. Br Med J. 1971;4:643-646.

20. Baer R, Bankier AT, Biggin MD, et al. DNA sequence and expression of the B95-8 Epstein-Barr virus genome. Nature. 1984;310:207-211.

21. Parker BD, Bankier A, Satchwell S, et al. Sequence and transcription of Raji Epstein-Barr virus DNA spanning the B95-8 deletion region. Virology. 1990;179:339-346.

22. Allday MJ, Crawford DH. Role of epithelium in EBV persistence and pathogenesis of B-cell tumours. Lancet. 1988;1:855-857.

23. Sixbey JW, Nedrud JG, Raab-Traub N, et al. Epstein-Barr virus replication in oropharyngeal epithelial cells. N Engl J Med. 1984;310:1225-1230.

24. Anagnostopoulos I, Hummel M, Kreschel C, Stein H. Morphology, immunophenotype, and distribution of latently and/or productively Epstein-Barr virus–infected cells in acute infectious mononucleosis: Implications for the interindividual infection route of Epstein-Barr virus. Blood. 1995;85:744-750.

25. Niedobitek G, Agathanggelou A, Herbst H, et al. S. Epstein-Barr virus (EBV) infection in infectious mononucleosis: Virus latency, replication and phenotype of EBV-infected cells. J Pathol. 1997;182:151-159.

26. Borza CM, Hutt-Fletcher LM. Alternate replication in B cells and epithelial cells switches tropism of Epstein-Barr virus. Nat Med. 2002;8:594-599.

27. Farrell PJ. Cell-switching and kissing. Nat Med. 2002;8:559-560.

28. Moss DJ, Burrows SR, Silins SL, et al. The immunology of Epstein-Barr virus infection. Philos Trans R Soc Lond B Biol Sci. 2001;356:475-488.

29. Rickinson AB, Moss DJ. Human cytotoxic T lymphocyte responses to Epstein-Barr virus infection. Annu Rev Immunol. 1997;15:405-431.

30. Babcock GJ, Decker LL, Volk M, Thorley-Lawson DA. EBV persistence in memory B cells in vivo. Immunity. 1998;9:395-404.

31. Wagner HJ, Bein G, Bitsch A, Kirchner H. Detection and quantification of latently infected B lymphocytes in Epstein-Barr virus–seropositive, healthy individuals by polymerase chain reaction. J Clin Microbiol. 1992;30:2826-2829.

32. Sixbey JW, Vesterinen EH, Nedrud JG, et al. Replication of Epstein-Barr virus in human epithelial cells infected in vitro. Nature. 1983;306:480-483.

33. Fingeroth JD, Weiss JJ, Tedder TF, et al. Epstein-Barr virus receptor of human B lymphocytes is the C3d receptor CR2. Proc Natl Acad Sci USA. 1984;81:4510-4514.

34. Frade R, Barel M, Ehlin-Eriksson B, et al. gp140, the C3d receptor of human B lymphocytes, is also the Epstein-Barr virus receptor. Proc Natl Acad Sci USA. 1985;82:1490-1493.

35. Young LS, Sixbey JW, Clark D, et al. Epstein-Barr virus receptor on human pharyngeal epithelia. Lancet. 1986;1:240-242.

36. Sixbey JW, Davis DS, Young LS, et al. Human epithelial cell expression of an Epstein-Barr virus receptor. J Gen Virol. 1987;68:805-811.

37. Jondal M, Klein G. Surface markers on human B and T lymphocytes. II. Presence of Epstein-Barr virus receptors on B lymphocytes. J Exp Med. 1973;138:1365-1378.

38. Yefenof E, Bakacs T, Einhorn L, et al. Epstein-Barr virus receptors, complement receptors and EBV infectibility of different lymphocyte fractions of human peripheral blood. I. Complement receptor distribution and complement binding by separated lymphocyte subpopulations. Cell Immunol. 1978;35:34-42.

39. Einhorn L, Steinitz M, Yefenof E, et al. Epstein-Barr virus receptors, complement receptors and EBV infectibility of different lymphocyte fractions of human peripheral blood. II. Epstein-Barr virus studies. Cell Immunol. 1978;35:43-58.

40. Haan KM, Kwok WW, Longnecker R, Speck P. Epstein-Barr virus entry utilizing HLA-DP or HLA-DQ as a coreceptor. J Virol. 2000;74:2451-2454.

41. Li Q, Spriggs MK, Kovats S, et al. Epstein-Barr virus uses HLA class II as a cofactor for infection of B lymphocytes. J Virol. 1997;71:4657-4662.

42. McShane MP, Mullen MM, Haan KM, et al. Mutational analysis of the HLA class II interaction with Epstein-Barr virus glycoprotein 42. J Virol. 2003;77:7655-7662.

43. Mullen MM, Haan KM, Longnecker R, Jardetzky TS. Structure of the Epstein-Barr virus gp42 protein bound to the MHC class II receptor HLA-DR1. Mol Cell. 2002;9:375-385.

44. Wang X, Hutt-Fletcher LM. Epstein-Barr virus lacking glycoprotein gp42 can bind to B cells but is not able to infect. J Virol. 1998;72:158-163.

45. Pope JH, Horne MK, Scott W. Transformation of foetal human leukocytes in vitro by filtrates of a human leukaemic cell line containing herpes-like virus. Int J Cancer. 1968;3:857-866.

46. Steinberg K, Beck J, Nickerson D, et al. DNA banking for epidemiologic studies: A review of current practices. Epidemiology. 2002;13:246-254.

47. Cohen JI. Epstein-Barr virus infection. N Engl J Med. 2000;343:481-492.

48. Crawford DH. Biology and disease associations of Epstein-Barr virus. Philos Trans R Soc Lond B Biol Sci. 2001;356:461-473.

49. Macsween KF, Crawford DH. Epstein-Barr virus—Recent advances. Lancet Infect Dis. 2003;3:131-140.

50. Thorley-Lawson DA. Epstein-Barr virus: Exploiting the immune system. Nat Rev Immunol. 2001;1:75-82.

51. Andreone P, Gramenzi A, Lorenzini S, et al. Posttransplantation lymphoproliferative disorders. Arch Intern Med. 2003;163:1997-2004.

52. Loren AW, Porter DL, Stadtmauer EA, Tsai DE. Post-transplant lymphoproliferative disorder: A review. Bone Marrow Transplant. 2003;31:145-155.

53. Kuppers R. B cells under influence: Transformation of B cells by Epstein-Barr virus. Nat Rev Immunol. 2003;3:801-812.

54. Young LS, Murray PG. Epstein-Barr virus and oncogenesis: From latent genes to tumours. Oncogene. 2003;22:5108-5121.

55. Gerber P, Nonoyama M, Lucas S, et al. Oral excretion of Epstein Barr virus by healthy subjects and patients with infectious mononucleosis. Lancet. 1972;2:988-989.

56. Strauch B, Siegel N, Andrews LL, et al. Oropharyngeal excretion of Epstein Barr virus by renal transplant recipients and other patients treated with immunosuppressive drugs. Lancet. 1974;1:234-237.

57. Chang RS, Lewis JP, Abildgaard CF. Prevalence of oropharyngeal excreters of leukocyte transforming agents among a human population. N Engl J Med. 1973;289:1325-1329.

58. Chang RS, Lewis JS, Reynolds RD, et al. Oropharyngeal excretion of Epstein Barr virus by patients with lymphoproliferative disorders and by recipients of renal homografts. Ann Intern Med. 1978;88:34-40.

59. Ferbas J, Rahman MA, Kingsley LA, et al. Frequent oropharyngeal shedding of Epstein-Barr virus in homosexual men during early HIV infection. AIDS. 1992;6:1273-1278.

60. Chang RS, Golden HD. Transformation of human leukocytes from throat washings from infectious mononucleosis patients. Nature. 1971;234:359-360.

61. Niederman JC, Miller G, Pearson HA, et al. Infectious mononucleosis: Epstein Barr virus shedding in saliva and the oropharynx. N Engl J Med. 1976; 294:1355-1359.

62. Miller G, Niederman JC, Andrews LL. Prolonged oropharyngeal excretion of Epstein Barr virus after infectious mononucleosis. N Engl J Med. 1973;288:229-232.

63. Kieff E, Rickinson AB. Epstein-Barr virus and its replication. In: Knipe D, Howley P, Griffin D, et al, eds. Fields' Virology. Philadelphia: Lippincott-Raven; 2001:2511-2574.

64. Smith P. Epstein-Barr virus complementary strand transcripts (CSTs/BARTs) and cancer. Semin Cancer Biol. 2001;11:469-476.

65. Grossman SR, Johannsen E, Tong X, et al. The Epstein-Barr virus nuclear antigen 2 transactivator is directed to response elements by the J kappa recombination signal binding protein. Proc Natl Acad Sci USA. 1994;91:7568-7572.

66. Henkel T, Ling PD, Hayward SD, Peterson MG. Mediation of Epstein-Barr virus EBNA2 transactivation by recombination signal-binding protein J kappa. Science. 1994;265:92-95.

67. Harada S, Kieff E. Epstein-Barr virus nuclear protein LP stimulates EBNA-2 acidic domain–mediated transcriptional activation. J Virol. 1997;71:6611-6618.

68. Kulwichit W, Edwards RH, Davenport EM, et al. Expression of the Epstein-Barr virus latent membrane protein 1 induces B cell lymphoma in transgenic mice. Proc Natl Acad Sci USA. 1998;95:11963-11968.

69. Wang D, Liebowitz D, Kieff E. An EBV membrane protein expressed in immortalized lymphocytes transforms established rodent cells. Cell. 1985;43:831-840.

70. Mosialos G, Birkenbach M, Yalamanchili R, et al. The Epstein-Barr virus transforming protein LMP1 engages signaling proteins for the tumor necrosis factor receptor family. Cell. 1995;80:389-399.

71. Uchida J, Yasui T, Takaoka-Shichijo Y, et al. Mimicry of CD40 signals by Epstein-Barr virus LMP1 in B lymphocyte responses. Science. 1999;286:300-303.

72. Gires O, Zimber-Strobl U, Gonnella R, et al. Latent membrane protein 1 of Epstein-Barr virus mimics a constitutively active receptor molecule. EMBO J. 1997;16:6131-6140.

73. Merchant M, Swart R, Katzman RB, et al. The effects of the Epstein-Barr virus latent membrane protein 2A on B cell function. Int Rev Immunol. 2001;20:805-835.

74. Flavell KJ, Murray PG. Hodgkin's disease and the Epstein-Barr virus. Mol Pathol. 2000;53:262-269.

75. Raab-Traub N. Epstein-Barr virus in the pathogenesis of NPC. Semin Cancer Biol. 2002;12:431-441.

76. Su IJ. Epstein-Barr virus and T-cell lymphoma. EBV Rep. 1996;3:1-6.

77. Straus SE, Cohen JI, Tosato G, et al. Epstein-Barr virus infections: Biology, pathogenesis and management. Ann Intern Med. 1992;118:45-58.

78. Ragoczy T, Heston L, Miller G. The Epstein-Barr virus Rta protein activates lytic cycle genes and can disrupt latency in B lymphocytes. J Virol. 1998;72:7978-7984.

79. Henle G, Henle W, Clifford P, et al. Antibodies to Epstein-Barr virus in Burkitt's lymphoma and control groups. J Natl Cancer Inst. 1969;43:1147-1154.

80. Pereira MS, Blake JM, Macrae AD. EB virus antibody at different ages. Br Med J. 1969;4:526-527.

81. Porter DD, Wimberly I, Benyesh-Melnick M. Prevalence of antibodies to EB virus and other herpesviruses. JAMA. 1969;208:1675-1679.

82. Gerber P, Birch SM, Rosenblum EN. The incidence of complement fixing antibodies in sera of human and non-human primates to viral antigens derived from Burkitt's lymphocyte cells. Proc Natl Acad Sci USA. 1967;58:478-484.

83. Hallee TJ, Evans AS, Niederman JC, et al. Infectious mononucleosis at the United States Military Academy. A prospective study of a single class over 4 years. Yale J Biol Med. 1974;47:182-195.

84. Nye FJ. Social class and infectious mononucleosis. J Hyg (Lond). 1973;71:145-149.

85. Heath CW Jr, Brodsky AL, Potolsky AI. Infectious mononucleosis in a general population. Am J Epidemiol. 1972;95:46-52.

86. Bernstein A. Infectious mononucleosis. Medicine (Baltimore). 1940;19:85-159.

87. Henle G, Henle W. Observations on childhood infections with the Epstein-Barr virus. J Infect Dis. 1970;121:303-310.

88. Tamir D, Benderly A, Levy J, et al. Infectious mononucleosis and Epstein-Barr virus in childhood. Pediatrics. 1974;53:330-335.
89. Wolf H, Haus M, Wilmer E. Persistence of Epstein Barr virus in the parotid gland. J Virol. 1984;51:795-798.
90. Sixbey JW, Lemon SM, Pagano JS. A second site for Epstein-Barr virus shedding: The uterine cervix. Lancet 1986;2:122-124.
91. Lipman M, Andrews L, Niederman J, et al. Direct visualization of enveloped Epstein-Barr herpesvirus in throat washing with leukocyte transforming activity. J Infect Dis. 1975;132:520-523.
92. Hoagland RS. The transmission of infectious mononucleosis. Am J Med Sci. 1955;229:262-272.
93. Fleisher GR, Pasquariello PS, Warren WS, et al. Intrafamilial transmission of Epstein-Barr virus infections. J Pediatr. 1981;98:16-19.
94. Larsson BO, Linde A. Intrafamilial transmission of Epstein-Barr virus infection among six adult members of one adult family. Scand J Infect Dis. 1990;22:363-366.
95. Gerber P, Walsh JH, Rosenblum EN, et al. Association of EB virus infection with the post perfusion syndrome. Lancet. 1969;1:593-595.
96. Herbert JT, Feorino P, Caldwell GG. False-positive epidemic infectious mononucleosis. Am Fam Physician. 1977;115:119-121.
97. Evans AS. Infectious mononucleosis in University of Wisconsin students. Report of a 5 year investigation. Am J Hyg. 1960;71:342-362.
98. Evans AS. Epidemiology and pathogenesis of infectious mononucleosis. In: Proceedings of the International Infectious Mononucleosis Symposium. Evanston, Ill: American College Health Association; 1967:40.
99. Evans AS. Infectious mononucleosis in the Armed Forces. Mil Med. 1970;135:300-304.
100. Lehane DE. A seroepidemiologic study of infectious mononucleosis. The development of EB virus antibody in a military population. JAMA. 1970;212:2240-2242.
101. Rocchi G, DeFelici A, Ragona G, et al. Quantitative evaluation of Epstein-Barr virus infected mononuclear peripheral blood leukocytes in infectious mononucleosis. N Engl J Med. 1977;296:132-134.
102. Robinson JE, Smith D, Niederman J. Plasmacytic differentiation of circulating Epstein-Barr virus infected B-lymphocytes during acute infectious mononucleosis. J Exp Med. 1981;153:235-244.
103. Blazar B, Patarroyo M, Klein E, et al. Increased sensitivity of human lymphoid lines to natural killer cells after induction of the Epstein-Barr viral cycle by superinfection or sodium butyrate. J Exp Med. 1980;151:614-627.
104. Rickinson AB, Crawford D, Epstein MA. Inhibition of the in vitro outgrowth of Epstein-Barr virus transformed lymphocytes by thymus dependent lymphocytes from infectious mononucleosis patients. Clin Exp Immunol. 1977;28:72-79.
105. Thorley-Lawson DA, Chess L, Strominger JA. Suppression of in vitro Epstein Barr virus infection: A new role for the adult human T lymphocyte. J Exp Med. 1977;146:495-508.
106. Schooley RT, Haynes BF, Payling-Wright CR, et al. Development of suppressor T-lymphocytes for Epstein-Barr virus induced B-lymphocyte outgrowth: Assessment by two quantitative systems. Blood. 1981;57:510-517.
107. Callan MF, Tan L, Annels N, et al. Direct visualization of antigen-specific CD8+ T cells during the primary immune response to Epstein-Barr virus in vivo. J Exp Med. 1998;187:1395-1402.
108. Foss HD, Herbst H, Hummel M, et al. Patterns of cytokine gene expression in infectious mononucleosis. Blood. 1994;83:707-712.
109. Catalina MD, Sullivan JL, Bak KR, Luzuriaga K. Differential evolution and stability of epitope-specific CD8+ T cell responses in EBV infection. J Immunol. 2001;167:4450-4457.
110. Amyes E, Hatton C, Montamat-Sicotte D, et al. Characterization of the CD4+ T cell response to Epstein-Barr virus during primary and persistent infection. J Exp Med. 2003;198:903-911.
111. Precopio ML, Sullivan JL, Willard C, et al. Differential kinetics and specificity of EBV-specific CD4+ and CD8+ T cells during primary infection. J Immunol. 2003;170:2590-2598.
112. Hoffman GJ, Lazarowitz SG, Hayward SD. Monoclonal antibody against a 250,000-dalton glycoprotein of Epstein-Barr virus identifies a membrane antigen and a neutralizing antigen. Proc Natl Acad Sci USA. 1980;77:2979-2983.
113. Qualtiere LF, Chase R, Pearson GR. Purification and biologic characterization of a major Epstein Barr virus–induced membrane glycoprotein. J Immunol. 1982;129:814-818.
114. Thorley-Lawson DA, Geilinger K. Monoclonal antibodies against the major glycoprotein (gp350/220) of Epstein-Barr virus neutralize infectivity. Proc Natl Acad Sci USA.1980;77:5307-5311.
115. Henle W, Henle G, Hewetson J, et al. Failure to detect heterophile antigens in Epstein Barr virus infected cells and to demonstrate interaction of heterophile antibodies with Epstein Barr virus. Clin Exp Immunol. 1974;17:281-286.
116. Hsu DH, de Waal Malefyt R, Fiorentino DF, et al. Expression of interleukin-10 activity by Epstein-Barr virus protein BCRF1. Science. 1990;250:830-832.
117. Moore KW, Vieira P, Fiorentino DF, et al. Homology of cytokine synthesis inhibitory factor (IL-10) to the Epstein-Barr virus gene *BCRFI*. Science. 1990;248:1230-1234.
118. Cohen JI, Lekstrom K. Epstein-Barr virus BARF1 protein is dispensable for B-cell transformation and inhibits alpha interferon secretion from mononuclear cells. J Virol. 1999;73:7627-7632.
119. Henderson S, Huen D, Rowe M, et al. Epstein-Barr virus–coded BHRF1 protein, a viral homologue of Bcl-2, protects human B cells from programmed cell death. Proc Natl Acad Sci USA. 1993;90:8479-8483.
120. Levitskaya J, Coram M, Levitsky V, et al. Inhibition of antigen processing by the internal repeat region of the Epstein-Barr virus nuclear antigen-1. Nature. 1995;375:685-688.
121. Downey H, Stasney J. The pathology of the lymph nodes in infectious mononucleosis. Folia Haematol (Leipz). 1936;54:417-438.
122. Smith EB, Custer RP. Rupture of spleen in infectious mononucleosis: Clinicopathologic report of 7 cases. Blood. 1946;1:317-333.
123. Custer RP, Smith EB. The pathology of infectious mononucleosis. Blood. 1948;3:830-857.
124. Hovde RF, Sundberg RD. Granulomatous lesions in the bone marrow in infectious mononucleosis. Blood. 1950;5:209-232.
125. Pease GL. Granulomatous lesions in bone marrow. Blood. 1956;11:720-734.
126. Nelson RS, Darragh JH. Infectious mononucleosis hepatitis. A clinicopathologic study. Am J Med. 1956;21:26-33.
127. Sullivan BH, Irey NS, Pieggi VJ, et al. The liver in infectious mononucleosis. Am J Dig Dis. 1957;2:210-223.
128. Bergin JD. Fatal encephalopathy in glandular fever. J Neurol Neurosurg Psychiatry. 1960;23:69-73.
129. Ambler M, Stoll J, Tzamaloukas A, et al. Focal encephalomyelitis in infectious mononucleosis. A report with pathologic description. Ann Intern Med. 1971;75: 579-583.
130. Sumaya CV, Ench Y. Epstein-Barr virus infectious mononucleosis in children. I. Clinical and general laboratory findings. Pediatrics. 1985;75:1003-1010.
131. Schmitz H, Volz D, Krainick-Riechert CH, et al. Acute Epstein-Barr virus infections in children. Med Microbiol Immunol. 1972;158:58-63.
132. Sumaya CV, Ench Y. Epstein-Barr virus infectious mononucleosis in children. II. Heterophil antibody and viral-specific responses. Pediatrics. 1985;75:1011-1019.
133. Horwitz CA, Henle W, Henle G, et al. Clinical and laboratory evaluation of elderly patients with heterophile antibody positive infectious mononucleosis. Report of seven patients ages 40 to 78. Am J Med. 1976;61:333-339.
134. Britton S, Andersson-Anvret M, Gergely P, et al. Epstein Barr virus immunity and tissue distribution in a fatal case of infectious mononucleosis. N Engl J Med. 1978;298:89-92.
135. Cameron D, MacBear LM. A Clinical Study of Infectious Mononucleosis and Toxoplasmosis. Baltimore: Williams & Wilkins; 1973:8.
136. Hoagland RJ. Infectious mononucleosis. Am J Med. 1952;13:158-171.
137. Mason WR Jr, Adams EK. Infectious mononucleosis. An analysis of 100 cases with particular attention to diagnosis, liver function tests, and treatment of selected cases with prednisone. Am J Med Sci. 1958;236:447-459.
138. Hoagland RJ. The incubation period of infectious mononucleosis. Am J Public Health Nations Health. 1964;54:1699-1705.
139. Joncas J, Chaisson JP, Turcotte J, et al. Studies on infectious mononucleosis. III. Clinical data, serologic and epidemiologic findings. Can Med Assoc J. 1968;98:848-854.
140. Pullen H, Wright N, Murdock J McC. Hypersensitivity reactions to antibacterial drugs in infectious mononucleosis. Lancet. 1967;2:1176-1178.
141. Patel BM. Skin rash with infectious mononucleosis and ampicillin. Pediatrics. 1967;40:910-911.
142. Bierman CW, Pierson WE, Zeitz SJ, et al. Reactions associated with ampicillin therapy. JAMA. 1972;220:1098-1100.
143. Nazareth I, Mortimer P, McKendrick GD. Ampicillin sensitivity in infectious mononucleosis—Temporary or permanent? Scand J Infect Dis. 1972;4:229-230.
144. Caird FI, Holt PR. The enanthem of glandular fever. Br Med J. 1958;1:85-87.
145. Karzon DT. Infectious mononucleosis. Adv Pediatr. 1976;22:231-265.
146. Hoagland RJ. Infectious Mononucleosis. New York: Grune & Stratton; 1967:64.
147. Horwitz CA, Moulds J, Henle W, et al. Cold agglutinins in infectious mononucleosis and heterophile antibody negative mononucleosis like syndromes. Blood. 1977;50:195-202.
148. Jenkins WJ, Koster HG, Marsh WL, et al. Infectious mononucleosis: An unsuspected source of anti-i. Br J Haematol. 1965;11:480-483.
149. Capra JD, Dowling P, Cook S, et al. An incomplete cold reactive γ G antibody with i specificity in infectious mononucleosis. Vox Sang. 1969;16:10-17.
150. Bowman HS, Marsh WL, Schumacher HR, et al. Auto anti-N immunohemolytic anemia in infectious mononucleosis. Am J Clin Pathol. 1974;61:465-472.
151. Troxel DB, Innella F, Cohen RJ. Infectious mononucleosis complicated by hemolytic anemia due to anti-i. Am J Clin Pathol. 1966;46:625-631.
152. Wilkinson LS, Petz LD, Garraty G. Reappraisal of the role of anti-i in haemolytic anemia in infectious mononucleosis. Br J Haematol. 1973;25:715-722.
153. Rosenfield RE, Schmidt PJ, Calvo RC, et al. Anti-i, a frequent cold agglutinin in infectious mononucleosis. Vox Sang. 1965;10:631-634.
154. Worlledge SM, Dacie JV. Hemolytic and other anemias in infectious mononucleosis. In: Carter RL, Penman HG, eds. Infectious Mononucleosis. Oxford: Blackwell Scientific; 1969:82-120.
155. Ohshima K, Kikuchi M, Eguchi F, et al. Virus-associated haemophagocytic syndrome with Epstein-Barr virus syndrome. Virchows Arch Pathol Anat Histopathol. 1991;419;519-522.
156. Ross CW, Schnitzer B, Weston BW, et al. Chronic active Epstein-Barr virus infection and virus-associated hemophagocytic syndrome. Arch Pathol Lab Med. 1991;115:470-474.
157. Carter RL. Platelet levels in infectious mononucleosis. Blood. 1965;25:817-821.
158. Clark BF, Davies SH. Severe thrombocytopenia in infectious mononucleosis. Am J Med Sci. 1964;248:703-708.
159. Radel EG, Schorr JB. Thrombocytopenic purpura with infectious mononucleosis. J Pediatr. 1963;63:46-60.
160. Goldstein E, Porter DY. Fatal thrombocytopenia with cerebral hemorrhage in mononucleosis. Arch Neurol. 1969;20:533-535.

161. Ellman L, Carvalho A, Jacobson BM, et al. Platelet autoantibody in a case of infectious mononucleosis presenting as thrombocytopenic purpura. Am J Med. 1973;55:723-726.

162. Grossman LA, Wolff SM. Acute thrombocytopenic purpura in infectious mononucleosis. JAMA. 1959;171:2208-2210.

163. Schooley RT, Densen P, Harmon D, et al. Antineutrophil antibodies in infectious mononucleosis. Am J Med. 1984;76:85-90.

164. Carter RL. Granulocyte changes in infectious mononucleosis. J Clin Pathol. 1966;19:279-283.

165. Cantow EK, Kostinas JE. Studies on infectious mononucleosis. IV. Changes in the granulocytic series. Am J Clin Pathol. 1966;46:43-47.

166. Wulff HR. Acute agranulocytosis following infectious mononucleosis. Report of a case. Scand J Haematol. 1965;2:180-182.

167. Habib MA, Babka JC, Burningham RA. Case report. Profound granulocytopenia associated with infectious mononucleosis. Am J Med Sci. 1973;265:339-346.

168. Neel EU. Infectious mononucleosis. Death due to agranulocytosis and pneumonia. JAMA. 1976;236:1493-1494.

169. Eriksson KF, Holmberg L, Gustafbergstrand C. Infectious mononucleosis and agranulocytosis. Scand J Infect Dis. 1979; 11:307-309.

170. Hammond WP, Harlan JM, Steinberg SE. Severe neutropenia in infectious mononucleosis. West J Med. 1979;131:92-97.

171. Dagan R, Powell KR. Postanginal sepsis following infectious mononucleosis. Arch Intern Med. 1987;147:1581-1583.

172. Hoagland RJ, Henson HM. Splenic rupture in infectious mononucleosis. Ann Intern Med. 1957;46:1184-1191.

173. Peters RM, Gordon LA, Nonsurgical treatment or splenic hemorrhage in an adult with infectious mononucleosis. Am J Med. 1986;80:123-125.

174. McLean ER, Diehl W, Edoga JK, et al. Failure of conservative management of splenic rupture in a patient with infectious mononucleosis. J Pediatr Surg. 1987;22:1034-1035.

175. Smith EB. The anatomic pathology of infectious mononucleosis and its complications. In: Proceedings of the International Infectious Mononucleosis Symposium. Washington, DC: American College Health Association; 1967:109.

176. Bernstein TC, Wolff HG. Involvement of the nervous system in infectious mononucleosis. Ann Intern Med. 1950;33:1120-1138.

177. Silverstein A, Steinberg S, Nathanson M. Nervous system involvement in infectious mononucleosis. The heralding and/or major manifestation. Arch Neurol. 1972;26:353-358.

178. Bennett DR, Peters HA. Acute cerebellar syndrome secondary to infectious mononucleosis in a 52 year old man. Ann Intern Med. 1961;55:147-149.

179. Gilbert JW, Culebras A. Cerebellitis in infectious mononucleosis. JAMA. 1972;220:727.

180. Bejada S. Cerebellitis in glandular fever. Med J Aust. 1976;1:153-156.

181. Joncas JH, Chicoine L, Thivierge R, et al. Epstein-Barr virus antibodies in the cerebrospinal fluid. Am J Dis Child. 1974;127:282-285.

182. Grose C, Henle W, Henle G, et al. Primary Epstein Barr virus infections in acute neurologic diseases. N Engl J Med. 1975;292:392-395.

183. Tanner OR. Ocular manifestations of infectious mononucleosis. Arch Ophthalmol. 1954;51:229-241.

184. Shechter FR, Lipsius EI, Rasansky HN. Retrobulbar neuritis. Am J Dis Child. 1955;89:58-61.

185. Gautier-Smith PC. Neurological complications of glandular fever (infectious mononucleosis). Brain. 1965;88:323-324.

186. Watson P, Ashby P. Brachial plexus neuropathy associated with infectious mononucleosis. Can Med Assoc J. 1970;114:758-767.

187. Forino PM, Humphrey D, Hochberg F, et al. Mononucleosis associated subacute sclerosing panencephalitis. Lancet. 1975;2:530-532.

188. Cotton PB, Webb-Peploe MM. Acute transverse myelitis as a complication of glandular fever. Br Med J. 1966;654-655.

189. Raymond RW, Williams RL. Infectious mononucleosis with psychosis. Report of a case. N Engl J Med. 1948;239:542-544.

190. Bray PF, Culp KW, McFarlin DE, et al. Demyelinating disease after neurologically complicated primary Epstein-Barr virus infection. Neurology. 1992;42:278-282.

191. Adamson DJ, Gordon PM. Hemiplegia—A rare complication of acute Epstein-Barr virus (EBV) infection. Scand J Infect Dis. 1992;24:379-380.

192. Penman HG. Fatal infectious mononucleosis: A critical review. J Clin Pathol. 1970;23:765-771.

193. Finkel M, Parker GW, Fanselau HA. The hepatitis of infectious mononucleosis: Experience with 235 cases. Mil Med. 1964;129:533-538.

194. Hoagland RJ. The clinical manifestations of infectious mononucleosis: A report of two hundred cases. Am J Med Sci. 1960;240:21-29.

195. Stevens JE. Infectious mononucleosis: A clinical analysis of 210 sporadic cases. Va Med Mon. 1952;79:74-80.

196. Lee S, Kjellstrand CM. Renal disease in infectious mononucleosis. Clin Nephrol. 1978;9:236-240.

197. Mayer HB, Wanke CA, Williams M, et al. Epstein-Barr virus–induced infectious mononucleosis complicated by acute renal failure: Case report and review. Clin Infect Dis. 1996;22:1009-1018.

198. Osmah H, Finkelstein R, Brook JG. Rhabdomyolysis complicating acute Epstein-Barr virus infection. Infection. 1995;23:119-120.

199. Hoagland RJ. Mononucleosis and heart disease. Am J Med Sci. 1964;248:1-6.

200. Shapiro SC, Dimich I, Steier M. Pericarditis as the only manifestation of infectious mononucleosis. Am J Dis Child. 1973;126:662-663.

201. Frishman W, Kraus ME, Zabkar J, et al. Infectious mononucleosis and fatal myocarditis. Chest. 1977;72:535-538.

202. Mundy GR. Infectious mononucleosis with pulmonary parenchymal involvement. Br Med J. 1972;1:219-220.

203. Offit PA, Fleisher GR, Koven NI, et al. Severe Epstein-Barr virus pulmonary involvement. J Adolesc Health Care. 1981;2:121-125.

204. Andiman WA, McCarthy P, Markowitz RI, et al. Clinical, virologic, and serologic evidence of Epstein-Barr virus infection in association with childhood pneumonia. J Pediatr. 1981;99:880-886.

205. Barbera JA, Hayashi S, Hegele RG, et al. Detection of Epstein-Barr virus in lymphocytic interstitial pneumonia by in situ hybridization. Am Rev Respir Dis. 1992;145:940-946.

206. Sriskandan S, Labrecque LG, Schofield J. Diffuse pneumonia associated with infectious mononucleosis: Detection of Epstein-Barr virus in lung tissue by in situ hybridization. Clin Infect Dis. 1996;22:578-579.

207. Haller A, von Segesser L, Baumann PC, Krause M. Severe respiratory insufficiency complicating Epstein-Barr virus infection: Case report and review. Clin Infect Dis. 1995;21:206-209.

208. Lukes RJ, Cox FH. Clinical and morphologic findings in 30 fatal cases of infectious mononucleosis. Am J Pathol. 1958;34:586.

209. Allen UR, Bass BH. Fatal hepatic necrosis in glandular fever. J Clin Pathol. 1963;16:337-341.

210. Dorman JM, Glick TH, Shannon DC, et al. Complications of infectious mononucleosis: A fatal case in a 2-year-old child. Am J Dis Child. 1974;128:239-243.

211. Purtilo DT, Cassel CK, Yang JPS, et al. X-linked recessive progressive combined variable immunodeficiency (Duncan's disease). Lancet. 1975;1:935-940.

212. Purtilo DT, Cassel CK, Yang JPS. Fatal infectious mononucleosis in familial lymphohistiocytosis. N Engl J Med. 1974;291:736.

213. Purtilo DT, Bhawan J, Hutt LM, et al. Epstein-Barr virus infections in the X-linked recessive lymphoproliferative syndrome. Lancet. 1978;1:798-801.

214. Provisor AJ, Iacuone JJ, Chilcote RR, et al. Acquired agammaglobulinemia after a life-threatening illness with clinical and laboratory features of infectious mononucleosis in three related male children. N Engl J Med. 1975;293:62-65.

215. Purtilo DT, Yang JP, Cassel CK, et al. X-linked recessive progressive combined variable immunodeficiency. Lancet. 1975;1:935-940.

216. Hamilton JK, Paquin L, Sullivan J, et al. X-linked lymphoproliferative syndrome registry report. J Pediatr. 1980;96:669-673.

217. Purtilo DT, DeFloria D Jr, Hutt L, et al. Variable phenotypic expression of an X-linked expressive lymphoproliferative syndrome. N Engl J Med. 1977;297:1077-1080.

218. Sullivan JL, Byron KS, Brewster FE, et al. X-linked lymphoproliferative syndromes: Natural history of the immunodeficiency. J Clin Invest. 1983; 71:1765-1778.

219. Sayos J, Wu C, Morra M, et al. The X-linked lymphoproliferative-disease gene product SAP regulates signals induced through the co-receptor SLAM. Nature. 1998;395:462-469.

220. Engel P, Eck MJ, Terhorst C. The SAP and SLAM families in immune responses and X-linked lymphoproliferative disease. Nat Rev Immunol. 2003;3:813-821.

221. Latour S, Veillette A. Molecular and immunological basis of X-linked lymphoproliferative disease. Immunol Rev. 2003;192:212-224.

222. Jones JF, Ray CG, Minnich LL, et al. Evidence for active Epstein Barr virus infection in patients with persistent, unexplained illnesses: Elevated anti-early antigen antibodies. Ann Intern Med. 1985;102:1-7.

223. Straus SE, Tosato G, Armstrong G, et al. Persisting illness and fatigue in adults with evidence of Epstein-Barr virus infection. Ann Intern Med. 1985;102:7-16.

224. Straus SE. The chronic mononucleosis syndrome. J Infect Dis. 1988;157:405-412.

225. Holmes GP, Kaplan JE, Stewart JA, et al. A cluster of patients with a chronic mononucleosis-like syndrome. JAMA. 1987;257:2297-3302.

226. Buchwald D, Sullivan JL, Komaroff AL. Frequency of "chronic active Epstein-Barr virus infection" in a general medical practice. JAMA. 1987;257:2303-2307.

227. Horwitz CA, Henle W, Henle G, et al. Long-term serological follow-up of patients for Epstein-Barr virus after recovery from infectious mononucleosis. J Infect Dis. 1985;151:1150-1153.

228. Holmes GP, Kaplan JE, Gantz NM, et al. Chronic fatigue syndrome: A working case definition. Ann Intern Med. 1988;108:387-389.

229. Holmes GP. Defining the chronic fatigue syndrome. Rev Infect Dis. 1991;13:S54-S55.

230. Schooley RT, Carey RW, Miller G, et al. Chronic Epstein-Barr virus infection associated with fever and interstitial pneumonitis. Ann Intern Med. 1986;104:636-643.

231. Snydman DR, Rudders RA, Daquest P, et al. Infectious mononucleosis in an adult progressing to fatal immunoblastic lymphoma. Ann Intern Med. 1982;96:737-742.

232. Virelizier J-L, Lenoir G, Griscelli C. Persistent Epstein-Barr virus infection in a child with hypergammaglobulinaemia and immunoblastic proliferation associated with a selective defect in immune interferon secretion. Lancet. 1978;2:231-234.

233. Kuis W, Roord JJ, Zegers BJM, et al. Heterogeneity of immune defects in three children with a chronic active Epstein-Barr virus infection. J Clin Immunol. 1985;5:377-385.

234. Miller G, Grogan E, Rowe D, et al. Selective lack of antibody to a component of EB nuclear antigen in patients with chronic active Epstein-Barr virus infection. J Infect Dis. 1987;156:26-35.

235. Kimura H, Morita M, Yabuta Y, et al. Quantitative analysis of Epstein-Barr virus load by using a real-time PCR assay. J Clin Microbiol. 1999;37:132-136.

236. Maeda A, Wakiguchi H, Yokoyama W, et al. Persistently high Epstein-Barr virus (EBV) loads in peripheral blood lymphocytes from patients with chronic active EBV infection. J Infect Dis. 1999;179:1012-1015.

237. Jones JF, Shurin S, Abramowsky C, et al. T-cell lymphomas containing Epstein-Barr viral DNA in patients with chronic Epstein-Barr virus infections. N Engl J Med. 1988;318:733-741.

238. Quintanilla-Martinez L, Kumar S, Fend F, et al. Fulminant EBV+ T-cell lymphoproliferative disorder following acute/chronic EBV infection: A distinct clinicopathologic syndrome. Blood. 2000;96:443-451.
239. Kimura H, Hoshino Y, Kanegane H, et al. Clinical and virologic characteristics of chronic active Epstein-Barr virus infection. Blood. 2001;98:280-286.
240. Kawa K, Okamura T, Yasui M, et al. Allogeneic hematopoietic stem cell transplantation for Epstein-Barr virus–associated T/NK-cell lymphoproliferative disease. Crit Rev Oncol Hematol. 2002;44:251-257.
241. Kuzushima K, Yamamoto M, Kimura H, et al. Establishment of anti–Epstein-Barr virus (EBV) cellular immunity by adoptive transfer of virus-specific cytotoxic T lymphocytes from an HLA-matched sibling to a patient with severe chronic active EBV infection. Clin Exp Immunol. 1996;103:192-198.
242. Okamura T, Hatsukawa Y, Arai H, et al. Blood stem-cell transplantation for chronic active Epstein-Barr virus with lymphoproliferation. Lancet. 2000;356:223-224.
243. Okano M. Therapeutic approaches for severe Epstein-Barr virus infection. Pediatr Hematol Oncol. 1997;14:109-119.
244. Okano M, Matsumoto S, Osato T, et al. Severe chronic active Epstein-Barr virus infection syndrome. Clin Microbiol Rev. 1991;4:129-135.
245. Greenspan JS, Greenspan D, Lennette ET, et al. Replication of Epstein-Barr virus within the epithelial cells of oral "hairy" leukoplakia, an AIDS-associated lesion. N Engl J Med. 1985;313:1564-1571.
246. Triantos D, Porter SR, Scully C, Teo CG. Oral hairy leukoplakia: Clinicopathologic features, pathogenesis, diagnosis, and clinical significance. Clin Infect Dis. 1997;25:1392-1396.
247. Scully C, Porter SR, Di Alberti L, et al. Detection of Epstein-Barr virus in oral scrapes in HIV infection, in hairy leukoplakia, and in healthy non–HIV-infected people. J Oral Pathol Med. 1998;27:480-482.
248. Riddler SA, Breinig MC, McKnight JL. Increased levels of circulating Epstein-Barr virus (EBV)–infected lymphocytes and decreased EBV nuclear antigen antibody responses are associated with the development of posttransplant lymphoproliferative disease in solid-organ transplant recipients. Blood. 1994;84:972-984.
249. Hamilton-Dutoit SJ, Raphael M, Audouin J, et al. In situ demonstration of Epstein-Barr virus small RNAs (EBER 1) in acquired immunodeficiency syndrome–related lymphomas: Correlation with tumor morphology and primary site. Blood. 1993;82:619-624.
250. Neri A, Barriga F, Inghirami G, et al. Epstein-Barr virus infection precedes clonal expansion in Burkitt's and acquired immunodeficiency syndrome–associated lymphoma. Blood. 1991;77:1092-1095.
251. de-The G, Geser A, Day NE, et al. Epidemiological evidence for causal relationship between Epstein-Barr virus and Burkitt's lymphoma from Ugandan prospective study. Nature. 1978;274:756-761.
252. Levine AM. Acquired immunodeficiency syndrome–related lymphoma: Clinical aspects. Semin Oncol. 2000;27:442-453.
253. Gutensohn N, Cole P. Epidemiology of Hodgkin's disease. Semin Oncol. 1980;7:92-102.
254. MacMahon B. Epidemiology of Hodgkin's disease. Cancer Res. 1966;26:1189-1201.
255. Mueller N, Evans A, Harris NL, et al. Hodgkin's disease and Epstein-Barr virus. Altered antibody pattern before diagnosis. N Engl J Med. 1989;320:689-695.
256. Pallesen G, Hamilton-Dutoit SJ, Rowe M, Young LS. Expression of Epstein-Barr virus latent gene products in tumour cells of Hodgkin's disease. Lancet. 1991;337:320-322.
257. Weiss LM, Movahed LA, Warnke RA, Sklar J. Detection of Epstein-Barr viral genomes in Reed-Sternberg cells of Hodgkin's disease. N Engl J Med. 1989;320:502-506.
258. Bargou RC, Leng C, Krappmann D, et al. High-level nuclear NF-kappa B and Oct-2 is a common feature of cultured Hodgkin/Reed-Sternberg cells. Blood. 1996;87:4340-4347.
259. Jungnickel B, Staratschek-Jox A, Brauninger A, et al. Clonal deleterious mutations in the IkappaBalpha gene in the malignant cells in Hodgkin's lymphoma. J Exp Med. 2000;191:395-402.
260. Zeng Y, Zhang LG, Li HY, et al. Serological mass survey for early detection of nasopharyngeal carcinoma in Wuzhou City, China. Int J Cancer. 1982;29:139-141.
261. Henle G, Henle W. Epstein-Barr virus–specific IgA serum antibodies as an outstanding feature of nasopharyngeal carcinoma. Int J Cancer. 1976;17:1-7.
262. Chan AT, Teo PM, Johnson PJ. Nasopharyngeal carcinoma. Ann Oncol. 2002;13:1007-1015.
263. Niedobitek G. Epstein-Barr virus infection in the pathogenesis of nasopharyngeal carcinoma. Mol Pathol. 2000;53:248-254.
264. Raab-Traub N, Flynn K. The structure of the termini of the Epstein-Barr virus as a marker of clonal cellular proliferation. Cell. 1986;47:883-889.
265. Farrow DC, Vaughan TL, Berwick M, et al. Diet and nasopharyngeal cancer in a low-risk population. Int J Cancer. 1998;78:675-679.
266. Liebowitz D. Nasopharyngeal carcinoma: The Epstein-Barr virus association. Semin Oncol. 1994;21:376-381.
267. Yuan JM, Wang XL, Xiang YB, et al. Preserved foods in relation to risk of nasopharyngeal carcinoma in Shanghai, China. Int J Cancer. 2000;85:358-363.
268. Kanegane H, Nomura K, Miyawaki T, Tosato G. Biological aspects of Epstein-Barr virus (EBV)–infected lymphocytes in chronic active EBV infection and associated malignancies. Crit Rev Oncol Hematol. 2002;44:239-249.
269. Kawa K. Diagnosis and treatment of Epstein-Barr virus–associated natural killer cell lymphoproliferative disease. Int J Hematol. 2003;78:24-31.
270. Herrmann K, Niedobitek G. Epstein-Barr virus–associated carcinomas: Facts and fiction. J Pathol. 2003;199:140-145.
271. Lee ES, Locker J, Nalesnik M, et al. The association of Epstein-Barr virus with smooth-muscle tumors occurring after organ transplantation. N Engl J Med. 1995;332:19-25.
272. Takada K. Epstein-Barr virus and gastric carcinoma. Mol Pathol. 2000;53:255-261.
273. Cesarman E, Chang Y, Moore PS, et al. Kaposi's sarcoma–associated herpesvirus-like DNA sequences in AIDS-related body-cavity-based lymphomas. N Engl J Med. 1995;332:1186-1191.
274. Cesarman E, Nador RG, Aozasa K, et al. Kaposi's sarcoma–associated herpesvirus in non-AIDS related lymphomas occurring in body cavities. Am J Pathol. 1996;149:53-57.
275. McClain KL, Leach CT, Jenson HB, et al. Association of Epstein-Barr virus with leiomyosarcomas in children with AIDS. N Engl J Med. 1995;332:12-18.
276. Wood TA, Frenkel EP. The atypical lymphocyte. Am J Med. 1967;42:923-936.
277. Chin TDY. Diagnosis of infectious mononucleosis. South Med J. 1976;69:654-658.
278. Penman HG. Extreme neutropenia in glandular fever. J Clin Pathol. 1968;21:48-49.
279. Chretien JH, Esswein JG, Holland WG, et al. Predictors of the duration of infectious mononucleosis. South Med J. 1977;70:437-439.
280. Evans AS, Niederman JC, Cenabre LC, et al. A prospective evaluation of heterophile and Epstein Barr virus specific IgM antibody tests in clinical and subclinical infectious mononucleosis. Specificity and sensitivity of the tests and persistence of antibody. J Infect Dis. 1975;132:546-554.
281. Hochberg FG, Miller G, Schooley RT, et al. Central nervous system lymphoma related to Epstein-Barr virus. N Engl J Med. 1983;309:745-748.
282. Basson V, Sharp AA. Monospot: A differential slide test for infectious mononucleosis. J Clin Pathol. 1969;22:324-325.
283. Seitanidis B. A comparison of the Monospot with the Paul-Bunnell test in infectious mononucleosis and other diseases. J Clin Pathol. 1969;22:321-323.
284. Wolf P, Dorfman R, McClenahan J, et al. False-positive infectious mononucleosis spot test in lymphoma. Cancer. 1970;25:626-628.
285. Henle W, Henle G, Horwitz CA. Epstein-Barr virus specific diagnostic tests in infectious mononucleosis. Hum Pathol. 1974;5:551-565.
286. Henle W, Henle G, Niederman JC, et al. Antibodies to early antigens induced by Epstein Barr virus in infectious mononucleosis. J Infect Dis. 1971;124:58-67.
287. Horwitz CA, Henle W, Henel G, et al. Clinical evaluation of patients with infectious mononucleosis and development of antibodies to the R component of the Epstein-Barr virus induced early antigen complex. Am J Med. 1975;58:330-338.
288. Reedman BM, Klein G. Cellular localization of an Epstein Barr virus associated complement fixing antigen in producer and nonproducer lymphoblastoid cell lines. Int J Cancer. 1973;11:499-520.
289. Henle G, Henle W, Horwitz CA. Antibodies to Epstein Barr virus associated nuclear antigen in infectious mononucleosis. J Infect Dis. 1974;130:231-239.
290. Hewetson JF, Rocchi S, Henle W, et al. Neutralizing antibodies to Epstein Barr virus in healthy populations and patients with infectious mononucleosis. J Infect Dis. 1973;128:283-289.
291. Benyesh-Melnick M, Lewis RT, Wimberly I. Some properties of the soluble (S) antigen of cultured lymphoblastoid cell lines. Arch Ges Virusforsch. 1970;31:113-124.
292. Yamamoto M, Kimura H, Hironaka T, et al. Detection and quantification of virus DNA in plasma of patients with Epstein-Barr virus–associated diseases. J Clin Microbiol. 1995;33:1765-1768.
293. Jones JF, Shurin S, Abramowsky C, et al. T cell lymphomas containing Epstein-Barr viral DNA in patients with chronic Epstein-Barr virus infections. N Engl J Med. 1988;318:733-741.
294. Diaz-Mitoma F, Preiksaitis JK, Leung WC, et al. DNA-DNA dot hybridization to detect Epstein-Barr virus in throat washings. J Infect Dis. 1987;155:297-303.
295. Baron DN, Bell JL, Demmett WN. Biochemical studies on hepatic involvement in infectious mononucleosis. J Clin Pathol. 1965;18:209-211.
296. Rosalki SB, Jones TG, Verney AF. Transaminase and liver function studies in infectious mononucleosis. Br Med J. 1960;1:929-932.
297. Kaplan ME. Cryoglobulinemia in infectious mononucleosis: Quantitation and characterization of the cryoproteins. J Lab Clin Med. 1968;71:754-765.
298. Horwitz CA, Moulds J, Henle W, et al. Cold agglutinins in infectious mononucleosis and heterophil-antibody-negative mononucleosis-like syndromes. Blood. 1977;50:195-202.
299. Horwitz CA, Henle W, Henle G, et al. Heterophile negative infectious mononucleosis and mononucleosis-like illness. Laboratory confirmation of 43 cases. Am J Med. 1977;63:947-957.
300. Blacklow NR, Kapikian AZ. Serological studies with EB virus in infectious lymphocytosis. Nature. 1970;226:647.
301. Ho DD, Sarngadharan MG, Resnick L, et al. Primary human T-lymphotropic virus type III infection. Ann Intern Med. 1985;103:880-883.
302. Cooper DA, Gold J, MacLean P, et al. Acute AIDS retrovirus infection: Definition of a clinical illness associated with seroconversion. Lancet. 1985;1:537-540.
303. Goudsmit J, de Wolf F, Paul DA, et al. Expression of human immunodeficiency virus antigen (HIV-Ag) in serum and cerebrospinal fluid during acute and chronic infection. Lancet. 1986;2:177-180.
304. Chan KC, Lo YM. Circulating EBV DNA as a tumor marker for nasopharyngeal carcinoma. Semin Cancer Biol. 2002;12:489-496.
305. de The G, Zeng Y. Population screening for EBV markers: toward improvement of nasopharyngeal carcinoma control. In: Epstein MA, Achong BG, eds. The Epstein-Barr Virus: Recent Advances. New York: Wiley; 1986:237-249.
306. Zeng Y. Seroepidemiological studies on nasopharyngeal carcinoma in China. Adv Cancer Res. 1985;44:121-138.

307. Zeng Y, Deng H, Zhong J, et al. A 10 year prospective study on nasopharyngeal carcinoma in Wuzhou city and Zangwu county, Guangxi, China. In: Tursz T, Ablashi DV, de The G, et al, eds. The Epstein-Barr Virus and Associated Diseases. Paris: Colloque INSERM/John Libbey Eurotext; 1993:735-741.

308. Tune CE, Liavaag PG, Freeman JL, et al. Nasopharyngeal brush biopsies and detection of nasopharyngeal cancer in a high-risk population. J Natl Cancer Inst. 1999;91:796-800.

309. Lo YM, Chan LY, Chan AT, et al. Quantitative and temporal correlation between circulating cell-free Epstein-Barr virus DNA and tumor recurrence in nasopharyngeal carcinoma. Cancer Res. 1999;59:5452-5455.

310. Lo YM, Chan LY, Lo KW, et al. Quantitative analysis of cell-free Epstein-Barr virus DNA in plasma of patients with nasopharyngeal carcinoma. Cancer Res. 1999;59:1188-1191.

311. Berger C, Day P, Meier G, et al. Dynamics of Epstein-Barr virus DNA levels in serum during EBV-associated disease. J Med Virol. 2001;64:505-512.

312. Antinori A, Ammassari A, De Luca A, et al. Diagnosis of AIDS-related focal brain lesions: A decision-making analysis based on clinical and neuroradiologic characteristics combined with polymerase chain reaction assays in CSF. Neurology. 1997;48:687-694.

313. Arribas JR, Clifford DB, Fichtenbaum CJ, et al. Detection of Epstein-Barr virus DNA in cerebrospinal fluid for diagnosis of AIDS-related central nervous system lymphoma. J Clin Microbiol. 1995;33:1580-1583.

314. De Luca A, Antinori A, Cingolani A, et al. Evaluation of cerebrospinal fluid EBV-DNA and IL-10 as markers for in vivo diagnosis of AIDS-related primary central nervous system lymphoma. Br J Haematol. 1995;90:844-849.

315. Lechowicz MJ, Lin L, Ambinder RF. Epstein-Barr virus DNA in body fluids. Curr Opin Oncol. 2002;14:533-537.

316. Antinori A, Cingolani A, De Luca A, et al. Epstein-Barr virus in monitoring the response to therapy of acquired immunodeficiency syndrome–related primary central nervous system lymphoma. Ann Neurol. 1999;45:259-261.

317. Thorley-Lawson D, Strominger JL. Transformation of human lymphocytes by Epstein-Barr virus is inhibited by phosphonoacetic acid. Nature. 1976;263:332-334.

318. Nyormoi O, Thorley-Lawson DA, Elkington J, et al. Differential effect of phosphonoacetic acid on the expression of Epstein-Barr viral antigens and virus production. Proc Natl Acad Sci USA. 1976;73:1745-1748.

319. Summers WC, Klein G. Inhibition of Epstein-Barr virus DNA synthesis and late gene expression by phosphonoacetic acid. J Virol. 1976;18:151-155.

320. Rickinson AB, Epstein MA. Sensitivity of the transforming and replicative functions of Epstein-Barr virus to inhibition by phosphonoacetate. J Gen Virol. 1978;40:409-420.

321. Thorley-Lawson DA, Strominger JL. Reversible inhibition by phosphonoacetic acid of human B-lymphocyte transformation by Epstein-Barr virus. Virology. 1978;86:423-431.

322. Coker-Vann M, Dolin R. Effect of adenine arabinoside on Epstein Barr virus in vitro. J Infect Dis. 1977;135:447-453.

323. Colby BM, Shaw JE, Elion GB, et al. Effect of acyclovir [9-(2-hydroxyethoxymethyl)guanine] on Epstein-Barr virus DNA replication. J Virol. 1980;34:560-568.

324. Colby BM, Shaw JE, Datta AK, et al. Replication of Epstein-Barr virus DNA in lymphoblastoid cells treated for extended periods with acyclovir. Am J Med. 1982;73:77-81.

325. Pagano JS, Datta AK. Perspectives on interactions of acyclovir with Epstein-Barr and other herpes viruses. Am J Med. 1982;73:18-26.

326. Adams A, Strander H, Cantell K. Sensitivity of the Epstein-Barr virus transformed human lymphoid cell lines to interferon. J Gen Virol. 1975;28:207-217.

327. Thorley-Lawson DA. The transformation of adult but not newborn lymphocytes by Epstein-Barr virus and phytohemagglutinin is inhibited by interferon: The early suppression by T-cells of Epstein-Barr infection is mediated by interferon. J Immunol. 1981;126:829-833.

328. Garner JG, Hirsch MS, Schooley RT. Prevention of Epstein-Barr virus–induced β-cell outgrowth by interferon-alpha. Infect Immun. 1984;43:920-924.

329. Greenspan D, DeSouza YG, Conant MA, et al. Efficacy of desciclovir in the treatment of Epstein-Barr virus infection in oral hairy leukoplakia. J AIDS. 1990;3:571-578.

330. Andersson J, Skoldenberg B, Henle W, et al. Acyclovir treatment in infectious mononucleosis: A clinical and virological study. Infection. 1987;15:14-20.

331. Andersson J, Britton S, Ernberg I, et al. Effect of acyclovir on infectious mononucleosis: A double-blind, placebo-controlled study. J Infect Dis. 1986;153:283-290.

332. van der Horst C, Joncas J, Aronheim G, et al. Lack of effect of peroral acyclovir for the treatment of infectious mononucleosis. J Infect Dis. 1991;164:788-792.

333. Tynell E, Aurelius E, Brandell A, et al. Acyclovir and prednisolone treatment of acute infectious mononucleosis: A multicenter, double-blind, placebo-controlled study. J Infect Dis 1996;174:324-331.

334. Torre D, Tambini R. Acyclovir for treatment of infectious mononucleosis: A meta-analysis. Scand J Infect Dis. 1999;31:543-547.

335. Schumacher HR, Jacobson WA, Bemiller CR. Treatment of infectious mononucleosis. Ann Intern Med. 1963;58:217-228.

336. Bender CE. The value of corticosteroids in the treatment of infectious mononucleosis. JAMA. 1967;15:529-531.

337. Klein EM, Cochran JF, Buck RL. The effects of short-term corticosteroid therapy on the symptoms of infectious mononucleosis pharyngotonsillitis: A double blind study. J Am Coll Health Assoc. 1969;17:446-452.

338. Collins M, Fleischer G, Kreisberg J, Fager S. Role of steroids in the treatment of infectious mononucleosis in the ambulatory college student. J Am Coll Health Assoc. 1984;33:101-105.

339. Straus SE, Cohen JI, Tosato G, Meier J. NIH conference. Epstein-Barr virus infections: Biology, pathogenesis, and management. Ann Intern Med. 1993;118:45-58.

340. Papesch M, Watkins R. Epstein-Barr virus infectious mononucleosis. Clin Otolaryngol. 2001;26:3-8.

341. McGowan JE Jr, Chesney PJ, Crossley KB, LaForce FM. Guidelines for the use of systemic glucocorticosteroids in the management of selected infections. Working Group on Steroid Use, Antimicrobial Agents Committee, Infectious Diseases Society of America. J Infect Dis. 1992;165:1-13.

342. Preiksaitis JK, Keay S. Diagnosis and management of posttransplant lymphoproliferative disorder in solid-organ transplant recipients. Clin Infect Dis. 2001;33(Suppl 1):S38-S46.

343. Faller DV, Mentzer SJ, Perrine SP. Induction of the Epstein-Barr virus thymidine kinase gene with concomitant nucleoside antivirals as a therapeutic strategy for Epstein-Barr virus–associated malignancies. Curr Opin Oncol. 2001;13:360-367.

344. Papadopoulos EB, Ladanyi M, Emanuel D, et al. Infusions of donor leukocytes to treat Epstein-Barr virus–associated lymphoproliferative disorders after allogeneic bone marrow transplantation. N Engl J Med. 1994;330:1185-1191.

345. Porter DL, Orloff GJ, Antin JH. Donor mononuclear cell infusions as therapy for B-cell lymphoproliferative disorder following allogeneic bone marrow transplant. Transplant Sci. 1994;4:12-14; discussion 14-16.

346. Rooney CM, Smith CA, Ng CY, et al. Use of gene-modified virus-specific T lymphocytes to control Epstein-Barr-virus–related lymphoproliferation. Lancet. 1995;345:9-13.

347. Rooney CM, Smith CA, Ng CY, et al. Infusion of cytotoxic T cells for the prevention and treatment of Epstein-Barr virus–induced lymphoma in allogeneic transplant recipients. Blood. 1998;92:1549-1555.

348. Gottschalk S, Ng CY, Perez M, et al. An Epstein-Barr virus deletion mutant associated with fatal lymphoproliferative disease unresponsive to therapy with virus-specific CTLs. Blood. 2001;97:835-843.

349. Nalesnik MA, Rao AS, Zeevi A, et al. Autologous lymphokine-activated killer cell therapy of lymphoproliferative disorders arising in organ transplant recipients. Transplant Proc. 1997;29:1905-1906.

350. Baldanti F, Grossi P, Furione M, et al. High levels of Epstein-Barr virus DNA in blood of solid-organ transplant recipients and their value in predicting posttransplant lymphoproliferative disorders. J Clin Microbiol. 2000;38:613-619.

351. Hoshino Y, Kimura H, Tanaka N, et al. Prospective monitoring of the Epstein-Barr virus DNA by a real-time quantitative polymerase chain reaction after allogenic stem cell transplantation. Br J Haematol. 2001;115:105-111.

352. van Esser JW, Niesters HG, Thijsen SF, et al. Molecular quantification of viral load in plasma allows for fast and accurate prediction of response to therapy of Epstein-Barr virus–associated lymphoproliferative disease after allogeneic stem cell transplantation. Br J Haematol. 2001;113:814-821.

353. Yang J, Tao Q, Flinn IW, et al. Characterization of Epstein-Barr virus–infected B cells in patients with posttransplantation lymphoproliferative disease: Disappearance after rituximab therapy does not predict clinical response. Blood. 2000;96:4055-4063.

354. Albrecht H, Stellbrink HJ, Brewster D, Greten H. Resolution of oral hairy leukoplakia during treatment with foscarnet. AIDS. 1994;8:1014-1016.

355. Greenspan D, De Souza YG, Conant MA, et al. Efficacy of desciclovir in the treatment of Epstein-Barr virus infection in oral hairy leukoplakia. J Acquir Immune Defic Syndr. 1990;3:571-578.

356. Newman C, Polk BF. Resolution of oral hairy leukoplakia during therapy with 9-(1,3-dihydroxy-2-propoxymethyl)guanine (DHPG). Ann Intern Med. 1987;107:348-350.

357. Resnick L, Herbst JS, Ablashi DV, et al. Regression of oral hairy leukoplakia after orally administered acyclovir therapy. JAMA. 1988;259:384-388.

358. Gowdey G, Lee RK, Carpenter WM. Treatment of HIV-related hairy leukoplakia with podophyllum resin 25% solution. Oral Surg Oral Med Oral Pathol Oral Radiol Endod. 1995;79:64-67.

359. Lozada-Nur F, Costa C. Retrospective findings of the clinical benefits of podophyllum resin 25% sol on hairy leukoplakia. Clinical results in nine patients. Oral Surg Oral Med Oral Pathol. 1992;73:555-558.

360. Thorley-Lawson DA, Poodry CA. Identification and isolation of the main component (gp350-gp220) of Epstein-Barr virus responsible for generating neutralizing antibodies in vivo. J Virol. 1982;43:730-736.

361. Morgan AJ. Epstein-Barr virus vaccines. Vaccine. 1992;10:563-571.

362. Wilson AD, Lovgren-Bengtsson K, Villacres-Ericsson M, et al. The major Epstein-Barr virus (EBV) envelope glycoprotein gp340 when incorporated into Iscoms primes cytotoxic T-cell responses directed against EBV lymphoblastoid cell lines. Vaccine. 1999;17:1282-1290.

363. Epstein MA, Randle BJ, Finerty S, Kirkwood JK. Not all potently neutralizing vaccine-induced antibodies to Epstein-Barr virus ensure protection of susceptible experimental animals. Clin Exp Immunol. 1986;63:485-490.

364. Morgan AJ, Mackett M, Finerty S, et al. Recombinant vaccinia virus expressing Epstein-Barr virus glycoprotein gp340 protects cottontop tamarins against EB virus–induced malignant lymphomas. J Med Virol. 1988;25:189-195.

365. Bharadwaj M, Moss DJ. Epstein-Barr virus vaccine: A cytotoxic T-cell-based approach. Expert Rev Vaccines. 2002;1:467-476.

366. Khanna R, Sherritt M, Burrows SR. EBV structural antigens, gp350 and gp85, as targets for ex vivo virus-specific CTL during acute infectious mononucleosis: Potential use of gp350/gp85 CTL epitopes for vaccine design. J Immunol. 1999;162:3063-3069.

367. Moss DJ, Schmidt C, Elliott S, et al. Strategies involved in developing an effective vaccine for EBV-associated diseases. Adv Cancer Res. 1996;69:213-245.

Human Herpesvirus Types 6 and 7

STEPHEN E. STRAUS

Human herpesviruses (HHV) 6 and 7 are ubiquitous lymphotropic agents whose biologic features and clinical relevance are still being defined. Rapid progress has been made in developing diagnostic tests for these viruses, and approaches to therapy of selected cases are conceivable but not yet realized.

HISTORY

That no new human herpesviruses were discovered in more than two decades since Epstein and Barr reported their eponymous virus suggested that no additional ones remained to be discovered. Methods for cultivating human lymphocytes in the presence of trophic factors such as interleukin-2, however, fortuitously amplified and permitted the recognition not only of the human T-lymphotropic retroviruses but also novel herpesviruses such as HHV-6 and HHV-7. Additional human lymphotropic herpesviruses could await discovery.

HUMAN HERPESVIRUS TYPE 6

Biology

HHV-6 was originally called human B-cell lymphotropic virus (HBLV) when Salahuddin and colleagues described it in 1986.[1] Subsequent in vitro studies showed that it grows in cells of diverse origin including T cells, monocytes, macrophages, megakaryocytes, and human embryonic glial cells as well as in Epstein-Barr virus (EBV)–transformed B cells.[2] In vivo, most HHV-6-infected cells express the T-cell marker CD4. The range of cells in which HHV-6 can replicate in vivo is, however, quite broad, as is its potential clinical spectrum.[3] Despite the expression of CD4 on most cells infected by HHV-6 in vivo, both its variants A and B use CD46 as a receptor for cellular entry.[4]

As summarized in Chapter 131 (Introduction to Herpesviridae), HHV-6 is a typical herpesvirus in view of its structure, genome organization, and expression. As more strains of HHV-6 were isolated, it became apparent that they can be segregated into variants A and B, which differ with respect to epidemiology, growth, and antigenic composition.[5] HHV-6A and 6B genomes share 90% sequence identity.[6,7]

Epidemiology

HHV-6 infects nearly all humans by age 2 years. Several studies estimated HHV-6 seroprevalence at 64% to 83% by age 13 months and upward of 95% in older children with no clear differences according to gender, race, socioeconomic status, or country.[8-11] One study of blood from 2427 U.S. children found 10% and 66% of these to be polymerase chain reaction–positive for HHV-6 DNA at 1 month and 1 year, respectively, verifying high rates of infection during the first year and persistence of virus in peripheral blood (Fig. 136-1).[12]

Serologic tests do not readily distinguish between the HHV-6A and B variants, but molecular studies can. With these techniques, their distribution in various populations was determined. Nearly all isolates from otherwise healthy adults and children represent variant B,[13] whereas variant A is recovered commonly from spinal fluid and from immunocompromised patients.[14]

Several studies suggest that intrauterine or perinatal transmission of HHV-6 may occur,[15] and virus has been found in genital secretions, breast milk, and urine, but most infections probably arise from exchange of infected saliva during the first years of life. HHV-6 is commonly detected in saliva, although rates have varied widely in different studies, in part due to initial misidentification of the far more

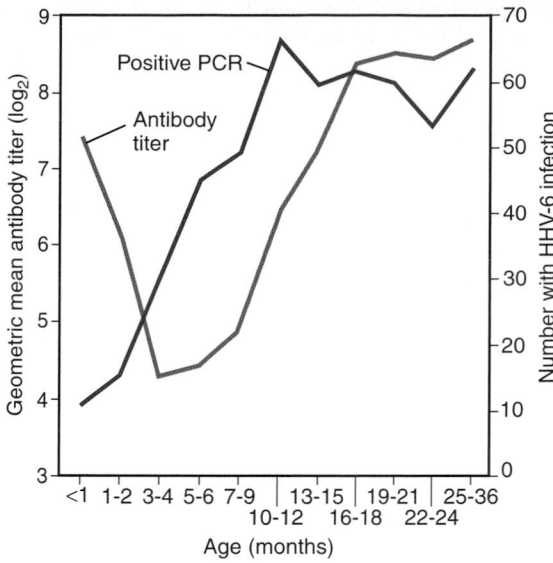

FIGURE 136-1. Antibody titers to HHV-6 and detection of HHV-6 DNA in peripheral blood by PCR in 2427 children, by age. *(From Hall CB, Long CE, Schnabel KC, et al. Human herpesvirus-6 infection in children: A prospective study of complications and reactivation. N Engl J Med. 1994;331:432-438, with permission.)*

prevalent HHV-7 isolates as HHV-6.[16,17] Viruses recovered from the blood of several acutely infected children were shown by molecular analysis to be identical to those in their mothers' saliva.[18] HHV-6 infections are usually sporadic, but outbreaks have been described in daycare centers.[19]

Pathogenesis

The existing data that implicate saliva as a potential vehicle for HHV-6, the known tropism of the virus for T cells, and analogies drawn to other herpesviruses suggest that primary infection may proceed from the oropharynx, through the regional lymphoid tissue, and then to mononuclear cell populations distributed throughout the body. Productive replication, persistence, and eventual virus reactivation in the setting of immune suppression could incite the known spectrum of HHV-6–associated clinical syndromes.

HHV-6 is found predominantly in circulating lymphocytes during primary infection, but it persists in monocytes-macrophages. As with the closely related betaherpesviruses, cytomegalovirus latency in monocytes-macrophages is characterized by expression only of selected immediate-early genes.[20] Chemical and cytokine activation of macrophages, or superinfection with HHV-7, induces lytic growth of HHV-6.[21]

Human immunodeficiency virus-1 (HIV-1) and HHV-6 enjoy a potentially important synergy. Both viruses infect and replicate in CD4+ lymphocytes in vitro and in SCID-hu mouse models.[22,23] HHV-6 infection induces CD4 expression in otherwise CD4- subpopulations of lymphocytes and natural killer cells, rendering them susceptible to HIV-1 entry.[24] HHV-6 accelerates HIV-1 transcription and replication.[22] In turn, HIV-1 upregulates HHV-6 replication, whereas immunodeficiency associated with progressive HIV disease permits the growth and spread of HHV-6.[25] Related observations made in vivo include higher levels of HIV deoxyribonucleic acid (DNA) in autopsy tissues coinfected with HHV-6[26] and more rapid progression of HIV disease following HHV-6 infection in infants.[27]

Immune Avoidance

The capacity of HHV-6 to persist and to be transmitted efficiently reflects its successful adaptation to its host by capturing human genes that deter immune surveillance. HHV-6 downregulates expression of CD3 and MHC class I molecules. HHV-6 open reading frames U12 and U51 encode G protein receptor homologues that bind and subvert the activity of the β-chemokines macrophage inflammatory protein (MIP)-1α, MIP-1β, and regulated upon activation and T-cell secretion (RANTES), whereas U83 encodes a potent chemokine, CCR2, that recruits lymphocytes and monocytes-macrophages to sites of infection, enhancing opportunities for the infection to spread.[28,29]

Clinical Manifestations

Exanthem Subitum (Roseola Infantum; Sixth Disease). Exanthem subitum, an illness of infants and young children, is heralded by 3 to 5 days of high but otherwise unremarkable fever, mild upper respiratory symptoms, and occasional cervical adenopathy.[30] As the fever abates a classic diffuse macular or maculopapular exanthem emerges (Fig. 136-2; Table 136-1) that is associated with a modest atypical lymphocytosis and relative neutropenia. The course is generally a benign one, but febrile seizures, meningitis, and encephalitis are well-recognized complications.

In 1950, exanthem subitum was successfully transmitted by inoculation of serum from ill infants to susceptible ones[31]; however, the identity of the pathogen was not determined until 1988, when Yamanishi reported acute infection and seroconversion to the recently described HHV-6.[32] Extensive subsequent studies verified that HHV-6 is the major cause of exanthem subitum, the other cause being HHV-7.[12,33,34] Most infants are infected subclinically; only 9% of subjects in one study[35] and 17% in another[12] developed exanthem subitum.

Infantile Fever. A more common manifestation of primary HHV-6 infection in infants than exanthem subitum is fever without rash.[36] In fact HHV-6 is a prominent cause of fevers in infants and young children. Of 1653 infants and young children in one hospital who were evaluated prospectively for acute febrile illnesses, nearly 10% were experiencing primary HHV-6 infection (Fig. 136-3).[12] These infections were commonly associated with irritability, otitis, respiratory symptoms, and/or diarrhea. Seizures accompanied 3% to 13% of febrile episodes.

TABLE 136-1 Signs and Symptoms in 34 Febrile Children with Acute HHV-6 Infection

Signs and Symptoms	Number (%) of Children
Malaise, irritability	28 (82)
Temperature ≥ 40° C	22 (65)
Inflamed tympanic membranes	21 (62)
Nasal congestion	19 (56)
Diarrhea	10 (29)
Cough	9 (27)
Rhonchi, wheezing, crackles	8 (24)
Vomiting	7 (21)
Rash	6 (18)
Seizure	1 (3)

Modified from Pruksananonda P, Hall CB, Insel RA, et al. Primary human herpesvirus 6 infection in young children. N Engl J Med. 1992; 326:1445-1450.

Febrile Seizures. HHV-6 is a major precipitant of seizures in infants, not merely because of the high fever that the infection provokes but also because HHV-6 replicates in the central nervous system.[12,37] Using PCR, HHV-6 DNA is commonly detected in the spinal fluid, not only during acute primary infection but for years afterward.[37,38]

Encephalitis and Other Neurologic Disorders. Reports of encephalitis as a complication of exanthem subitum and the appreciation that HHV-6 is highly neurotropic predicted that the virus might be associated with encephalitis in other settings as well. Detection of HHV-6 DNA in cerebrospinal fluid from patients with otherwise undiagnosed focal encephalitis supported this prediction, as has the direct demonstration of the virus in brain parenchyma.[39,40] The frequent presence of HHV-6 in the central nervous system, however, complicates its definitive attribution in individual cases of encephalitis as well as in other acute or chronic neurologic syndromes. This problem underlies an ongoing controversy regarding reports of HHV-6 DNA and antigens in the brain of patients with multiple sclerosis, especially in association with sclerotic plaques.[41-44]

Infectious Mononucleosis. Although Epstein-Barr virus is the most common cause of classic infectious mononucleosis and similar syndromes, other organisms can be as well (see Chapter 135, Epstein-

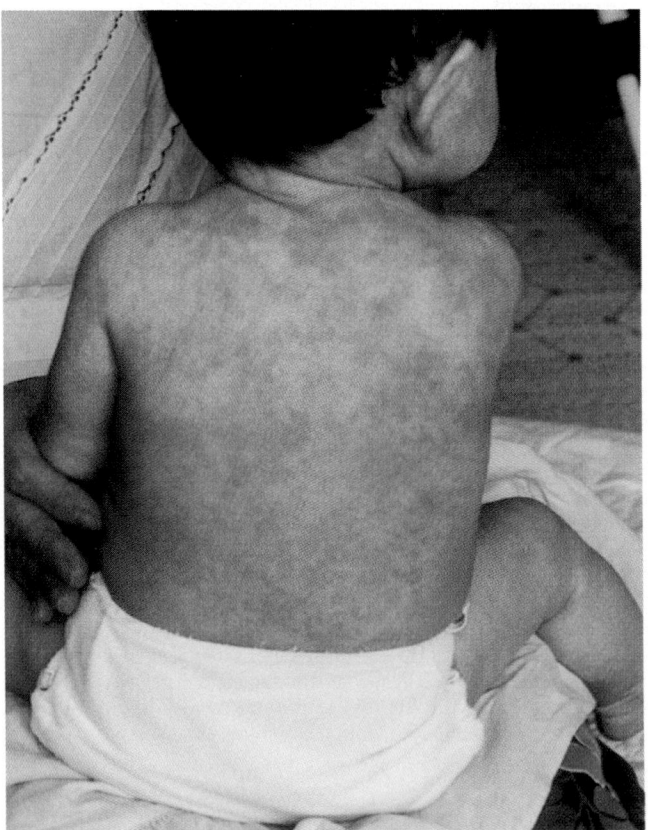

FIGURE 136-2. A child with roseola. *(Courtesy of Professor K. Yamanishi, Osaka University Medical School, Osaka, Japan.)*

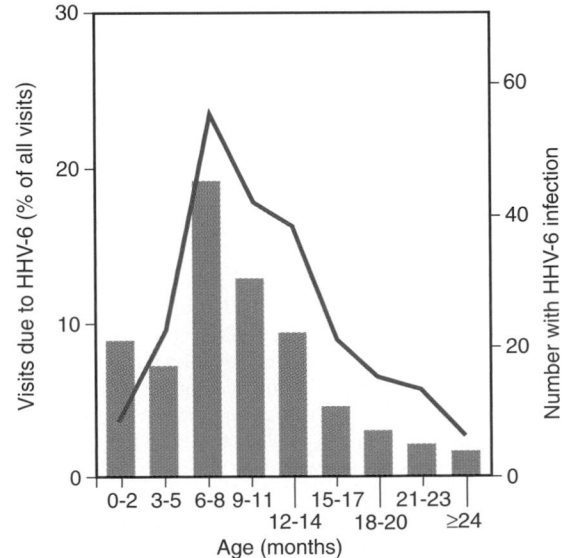

FIGURE 136-3. Percent of all emergency department visits for acute febrile illnesses that were associated with primary HHV-6 infections (curve) and the number of such cases by age. *(From Hall CB, Long CE, Schnabel KC, et al. Human herpesvirus-6 infection in children: A prospective study of complications and reactivation. N Engl J Med. 1994;331:432-438, with permission.)*

Barr Virus). It is not surprising then that the description of HHV-6, another human lymphotropic virus, would be followed with reports linking it to mononucleosis-like syndromes. These cases have been highly variable in age of presentation and severity, but most of them have been mild with a modest number of atypical lymphocytes, and heterophile antibody responses are not often seen.[45,46]

Hepatitis. Elevations in aminotransferases were not appreciated as a common feature of roseola in large case series,[12] but there are several reports of hepatitis in neonates and young children associated with primary HHV-6 infection, some of which have been fulminant.[47,48]

Skin Diseases. Given the prevalence of HHV-6 in human tissues and body fluids, it is not surprising that associations would be drawn between its presence and particular dermatologic conditions. HHV-6 is the major cause of roseola.[32,33,35] Moreover, it has been identified in 6% of children fully immunized against measles and rubella who develop morbilliform rashes.[49] Less well established are associations between HHV-6 and pityriasis rosea[50,51] or the Gianotti-Crosti syndrome, a papular acrodermatitis of childhood.[52]

Infection in the Immunocompromised Host. Although the only illnesses proven to be caused by HHV-6 are the typically benign primary infections such as roseola, a growing body of evidence strongly associates this virus with syndromes that complicate bone marrow and solid organ transplantation and other immunodeficiency states. The major difficulty in assigning greater credulity to these associations is that whereas HHV-6 is detected frequently in the setting of immune compromise, it often infects asymptomatically, and when symptoms are apparent, the severity of immune impairment tends to be greater and permits concomitant reactivation of cytomegalovirus, HHV-7, and other opportunistic pathogens.[53-57] In fact, the immediate post-transplantation period witnesses successive and overlapping waves of viruses whose individual contributions to transplant morbidity can be hard to define. Thus it is hard to determine whether HHV-6 reactivation is merely an epiphenomenon of immune compromise, exacerbates the immune compromise so as to promote symptomatic reactivation of cytomegalovirus and other pathogens, or contributes directly to disease symptoms and signs. Despite dozens of studies, then, the evidence still falls well short of defining optimal strategies for monitoring and managing HHV-6 in the compromised host.

Specifically, studies found that reactivation of HHV-6 in an average of one third of solid organ recipients and one half of bone marrow recipients by 4 weeks after transplantation was associated temporally with fever and rash, graft-versus-host disease, delayed bone marrow engraftment, interstitial pneumonitis, encephalitis, and prediction of invasive fungal infections.[58-61] Favoring an association between reactivation of HHV-6 and events such as delayed platelet engraftment, hepatitis, or encephalitis is the demonstration that complications arose more often in patients with significantly higher HHV-6 viral loads, as defined by quantitative PCR.[62] Moreover, ganciclovir prophylaxis reduced HHV-6 loads and attenuated cytomegalovirus disease in liver transplant recipients, but concomitant inhibition of cytomegalovirus and HHV-7 by ganciclovir complicates interpretation of the role played by HHV-6 in those patients.

As indicated above, the synergy that HHV-6 and HIV manifest in vitro encouraged attempts to correlate HHV-6 infection with progression of acquired immunodeficiency syndrome (AIDS). This remains an unsettled issue.[63,64] A recent case-control study showed no association between HHV-6 infection and the risk of HIV-related malignancies in children.[65]

HHV-6 has also been detected in and associated with various lymphoproliferative malignancies in non–HIV-infected people. Even these data could not be confirmed consistently.[66-70]

Chronic Fatigue Syndrome.[71] Several studies identified higher HHV-6 seroprevalence or rates of virus recovery from saliva or peripheral blood in patients with chronic fatigue syndrome than in controls, adding this virus to the many putative causes of the syndrome.[71] A more recent and careful case-control study, however, could not confirm an association between HHV-6 or HHV-7 and chronic fatigue syndrome.[72]

Diagnosis

Serodiagnosis. Commercial assays reliably detect HHV-6-specific immunoglobulin G (IgG) antibody responses, but they do not distinguish infection with variants A and B, and there is cross-reactivity with HHV-7.[73,74] Because nearly everyone older than age 2 is positive, a single HHV-6 serologic test result is generally meaningless; however, seroconversion from negative to positive or a fourfold or greater rise in titers in paired sera is good evidence of recent primary infection, especially in small children. IgM assays for HHV-6 are not always reliable indicators of acute, primary infection.[75]

Virus Detection. HHV-6 can be cultured from peripheral blood mononuclear cells. In the setting of an acute exanthem subitum–like illness, virus recovery may be truly diagnostic.[76] In healthy older children and adults, isolation of HHV-6 is uncommon. Higher rates of virus replication and recovery in immunocompromised patients, unrelated to clinical presentation, negate culture as a useful tool in that setting. Antigen-specific monoclonal antibodies permit definitive identification of HHV-6 in tissues, as does in situ hybridization, but it is always difficult to assign an etiologic role to the virus. Increasingly, HHV-6 is detected by PCR.[77,78] Amplification of HHV-6 sequences from serum or plasma seems more predictive of disease than PCR from whole blood, as are higher quantities of HHV-6 sequences.[61,62]

Treatment

Multiple HHV-6 isolates have been tested for their sensitivity to antiviral drugs. The in vitro virus sensitivity roughly parallels that of cytomegalovirus: acyclovir is inactive, ganciclovir responsiveness is variable, and cidofovir and foscarnet are inhibitory in pharmacologically meaningful concentrations.[79] Small case series suggest that ganciclovir or foscarnet is effective for prophylaxis or even treatment of HHV-6 infections in transplant recipients,[80,81] but controlled trials would be welcome. A placebo-controlled trial of valacyclovir in 70 patients with multiple sclerosis did not abate relapses.[82]

HUMAN HERPESVIRUS TYPE 7

Biology and Pathogenesis

In 1990 Frenkel and colleagues demonstrated a novel herpesvirus in the peripheral blood mononuclear cells of a healthy individual.[83] Since that time, the virus epidemiology and DNA sequence have been defined. Lacking is an understanding of what role HHV-7 plays in human disease and whether there is ever a need for treatment.[84]

HHV-7 infects activated cord blood or peripheral blood CD4+ lymphocytes.[83] In fact, CD4 is a component of the cellular receptor for HHV-7, allowing infection with HHV-7 to interfere with HIV-1 infection.[85] HHV-7 persists in circulating CD4+ cells and can be induced from latency by T-cell activation.[21] HHV-7 genes possess 21% to 76% nucleic acid homology to individual HHV-6 genes, resulting in sufficient antigenic relatedness to have complicated earlier serologic tests of these viruses.[86,87] As with HHV-6, HHV-7 encodes genes that can interfere with host immune responses to the virus.[88] One such interesting effect relates to the profound downregulation by HHV-7 of CD4 expression on T cells.[89] HHV-7 open reading frames N12 and N51 (situated in identical location to homologues in HHV-6) encode functional beta chemokine receptors.[90]

Epidemiology

HHV-7 infects nearly all humans by age 5 years, peaking later than the age of HHV-6 infections (Fig. 136-4). Among those infected, HHV-7 is virtually a commensal inhabitant of saliva.[17,91] This easy spread probably depends on these high rates of salivary excretion.

Diagnosis

HHV-7–specific serologic tests and antigen detection assays now exist, but most studies use qualitative or quantitative DNA PCR assays.

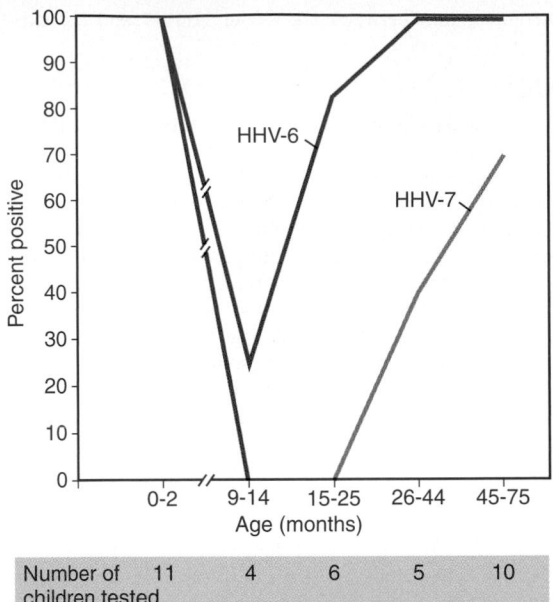

FIGURE 136-4. The percentage of children seropositive for HHV-6 and HHV-7, by age. *(From Wyatt LS, Frenkel J. Human herpesvirus 7 is a constitutive inhabitant of adult human saliva. J Virol. 1992;66:3206-3209, with permission.)*

All remain the province of research scientists, who labor to identify syndromes that may relate to its presence.[92,93]

Clinical Syndromes

The clear biologic and epidemiologic relatedness of HHV-6 and HHV-7 suggests that they should share similar clinical manifestations. The demonstration of acute HHV-7 seroconversion and virus shedding in association with second cases of exanthem subitum in HHV-6–positive Japanese infants supports HHV-7 as another cause for the syndrome.[34] Isolated reports of HHV-7 in encephalitis, hepatitis, and pityriasis rosea suggest that there may be a broader, still-undefined spectrum of illness provoked by this virus.[94-96] Its cellular tropism—more restricted than that of HHV-6 in vitro—may limit the extent of its clinical expression as well, whereas its ubiquitousness in patients and their specimens will confound efforts to establish causation. Although the quantity of circulating of HHV-6 correlates with disease in transplant recipients, the HHV-7 load does not.[61]

Treatment

HHV-7 replication in vitro is inhibited by achievable concentrations of ganciclovir and foscarnet, but there are as yet no settings in which treatment seems warranted.[97]

REFERENCES

1. Salahuddin SZ, Ablashi DV, Markham PD, et al. Isolation of a new virus, HBLV, in patients with lymphoproliferative disorders. Science. 1968;234:596-601.
2. Ablashi DV, Salahuddin SZ, Josephs SF, et al. HBLV (or HHV-6) in human cell lines. Nature. 1987;329:207.
3. Dockrell DH. Human herpesvirus 6: Molecular biology and clinical features. J Med Microbiol. 2003;52:5-18.
4. Santoro F, Kennedy PE, Locatelli G, et al. CD46 is a cellular receptor for human herpesvirus 6. Cell. 1999;99:817-827.
5. Schirmer EC, Wyatt LS, Yamanishi K, et al. Differentiation between two distinct classes of viruses now classified as human herpesvirus 6. Proc Natl Acad Sci U S A. 1991;88:5922-5926.
6. Gompels UA, Nicholas J, Lawrence G, et al. The DNA sequence of human herpesvirus-6: Structure, coding content, and genome evolution. Virology. 1995;209:29-51.
7. Dominguez G, Dambaugh TR, Stamey FR, et al. Human herpesvirus 6B genome sequence: Coding content and comparison with human herpesvirus 6A. J Virol. 1999;73:8040-8052.
8. Briggs M, Fox J, Tedder RS. Age prevalence of antibody to human herpesvirus 6. Lancet. 1988;i:1058-1059.
9. Huang LM, Lee CY, Chen JY, et al. Primary human herpesvirus 6 infections in children: A prospective serologic study. J Infect Dis. 1992;165:1163-1164.
10. Okuno T, Takahashi K, Balachandra K, et al. Seroepidemiology of human herpesvirus 6 infection in normal children and adults. J Clin Microbiol. 1989;27:651-653.
11. Yoshikawa T, Suga S, Asano Y, et al. Distribution of antibodies to a causative agent of exanthem subitum (human herpesvirus-6) in healthy individuals. Pediatrics. 1989;84:675-677.
12. Hall CB, Long CE, Schnabel KC, et al. Human herpesvirus-6 infection in children: A prospective study of complications and reactivation. N Engl J Med. 1994;331:432-438.
13. Dewhurst S, McIntyre K, Schnabel K, et al. Human herpesvirus 6 (HHV-6) variant B accounts for the majority of symptomatic primary HHV-6 infections in a population of U.S. infants. J Clin Microbiol. 1993;31:416-418.
14. Hall CB, Caserta MT, Schnabel KC, et al. Persistence of human herpesvirus 6 according to site and variant: Possible greater neurotropism of variant A. Clin Infect Dis. 1998;26:132-137.
15. Aubin JT, Poirel L, Agut H, et al. Intrauterine transmission of human herpesvirus 6. Lancet. 1992;340:482-483.
16. Levy JA, Ferro F, Greenspan D, et al. Frequent isolation of HHV-6 from saliva and high seroprevalence of the virus in the population. Lancet. 1990;335:1047-1050.
17. Wyatt LS, Frenkel J. Human herpesvirus 7 is a constitutive inhabitant of adult human saliva. J Virol. 1992;66:3206-3209.
18. Mukai T, Yamamoto T, Kondo T, et al. Molecular epidemiologic studies of human herpesvirus 6 in families. J Med Virol. 1994;42:224-227.
19. Freitas RB, Monteiro TA, Linhares AC. Outbreaks of human herpesvirus 6 (HHV-6) infection in day-care centers in Belem, Para, Brazil. Rev Inst Med Trop São Paulo. 2000;42:305-311.
20. Kondo K, Shimada K, Sashihara J, et al. Identification of human herpesvirus 6 latency-associated transcripts. J Virol. 2002;76:4145-4151.
21. Katsafanas GC, Schirmer EC, Wyatt LS, et al. In vitro activation of human herpesviruses 6 and 7 from latency. Proc Natl Acad Sci U S A. 1996;93:9788-9792.
22. Lusso P, Ensoli B, Markham PD, et al. Productive dual infection of human CD4+ T lymphocytes by HIV-1 and HHV-6. Nature. 1989;337:370-373.
23. Gobbi A, Stoddard CA, Locatelli G, et al. Coinfection of SCID-hu Thy/Liv mice with human herpesvirus 6 and human immunodeficiency virus type 1. J Virol. 2000;74:8726-8731.
24. Lusso P, Malnati MS, Garzino-Demo A, et al. Infection of natural killer cells by human herpesvirus 6. Nature. 1993;362:458-462.
25. Knox KK, Carrigan DR. Disseminated active HHV-6 infections in patients with AIDS. Lancet. 1994;343:577-578.
26. Emery VA, Atkins MC, Bowen EF, et al. Interactions between beta-herpesviruses and human immunodeficiency virus in vivo: Evidence for increased human immunodeficiency viral load in the presence of human herpesvirus 6. J Med Virol. 1999;57:278-282.
27. Kositanont U, Wasi C, Wanprapar N, et al. Primary infection with human herpesvirus 6 in children with vertical infection of human immunodeficiency virus type 1. J Infect Dis. 1999;180:50-55.
28. Zou P, Isegawa Y, Nakano K, et al. Human herpesvirus 6 open reading frame U83 encodes a functional chemokine. J Virol. 1999;73:5926-5933.
29. Lüttichau HR, Clark-Lewis I, Jensen P, et al. A highly selective CCR2 chemokine agonist encoded by human herpesvirus 6. J Biol Chem. 2003;278:10928-10933.
30. Asano Y, Yoshikawa T, Suga S, et al. Clinical features of infants with primary human herpesvirus-6 infection (exanthem subitum, roseola infantum). Pediatrics. 1994;93:104-108.
31. Kempe CH, Shaw EB, Jackson JR, et al. Studies on the etiology of exanthem subitum (roseola infantum). J Pediatr. 1950;37:561-568.
32. Yamanishi K, Okuno T, Shiraki K, et al. Identification of human herpesvirus-6 as a causal agent for exanthem subitum. Lancet. 1988;i:1065-1067.
33. Okada K, Ueda K, Kusuhara K, et al. Exanthem subitum and human herpesvirus-6 infection: Clinical observations in fifty-seven cases. Pediatr Infect Dis J. 1993;12:204-208.
34. Tanaka K, Kondo T, Torigoe S, et al. Human herpesvirus 7: Another causal agent for roseola (exanthem subitum). J Pediatr. 1994;125:1-5.
35. Pruksananonda P, Hall CB, Insel RA, et al. Primary human herpesvirus 6 infection in young children. N Engl J Med. 1992;326:1445-1450.
36. Suga S, Yoshikawa T, Asano Y, et al. Human herpesvirus-6 infection (exanthem subitum) without rash. Pediatrics. 1989;83:1003-1006.
37. Kondo K, Nagafuji H, Hata A, et al. Association of human herpesvirus 6 infection of the central nervous system with recurrence of febrile convulsions. J Infect Dis. 1993;167:1197-1200.
38. Caserta MT, Hall CB, Schnabel K, et al. Neuroinvasion and persistence of human herpesvirus 6 in children. J Infect Dis. 1994;170:1586-1589.
39. McCullers JA, Lakeman FD, Whitley RJ. Human herpesvirus 6 is associated with focal encephalitis. Clin Infect Dis. 1995;21:571-576.
40. Drobyski WR, Knox KK, Majewski D, et al. Fatal encephalitis due to variant B human herpesvirus-6 infection in a bone marrow-transplant recipient. N Engl J Med. 1994;330:1356-1360.
41. Challoner PB, Smith KT, Parker JD, et al. Plaque-associated expression of human herpesvirus 6 in multiple sclerosis. Proc Natl Acad Sci U S A. 1995;92:7440-7444.

42. Cermelli C, Berti R, Soldan SS, et al. High frequency of human herpesvirus 6 DNA in multiple sclerosis plaques isolated by laser microdissection. J Infect Dis. 2003;187:1377-1387.

43. Goodman AD, Mock DJ, Powers JM, et al. Human herpesvirus 6 genome and antigen in acute multiple sclerosis lesions. J Infect Dis. 2003;187:1365-1376.

44. Tyler KL. Human herpesvirus 6 and multiple sclerosis: The continuing conundrum (Editorial). J Infect Dis. 2003;187:1360-1364.

45. Niederman JC, Liu C-R, Kaplan MH, et al. Clinical and serological features of human herpesvirus-6 infection in three adults. Lancet. 1988;10:817-819.

46. Akashi K, Eizuru Y, Sumiyoshi Y, et al. Severe infectious mononucleosis-like syndrome and primary human herpesvirus 6 infection in an adult. N Engl J Med. 1993;328:168-171.

47. Asano Y, Yoshikawa T, Suga S, et al. Fatal fulminant hepatitis in an infant with human herpesvirus-6 infection. Lancet. 1990;335:862-863.

48. Harma M, Hockerstedt K, Lautenschlager I. Human herpesvirus-6 and acute liver failure. Transplantation. 2003;76:536-539.

49. Ramsay M, Reacher M, O'Flynn C, et al. Causes of morbilliform rash in a highly immunised English population. Arch Dis Child. 2002;87:202-206.

50. Watanabe T, Kawamura T, Jacob SE, et al. Pityriasis rosea is associated with systemic active infection with both human herpesvirus-7 and human herpesvirus-6. J Invest Dermatol. 2002;119:793-797.

51. Hall CB. In this issue: The human herpesviruses and pityriasis rosea: Curious covert companions? (Commentary). J Invest Dermatol. 2002;119:779-780.

52. Chuh AAT, Chab HHL, Chiu SSS, et al. A prospective case control study of the association of Gianotti-Crosti syndrome with human herpesvirus 6 and human herpesvirus 7 infections. Pediatr Dermatol. 2002;6:492-497.

53. Dockrell DH, Paya CV. Human herpesvirus-6 and -7 in transplantation. Rev Med Virol. 2001;11:23-36.

54. Mendez JC, Dockrell DH, Espy MJ, et al. Human beta-herpesvirus interactions in solid organ transplant recipients. J Infect Dis. 2001;183:179-184.

55. Clark DA, Griffiths PD. Human herpesvirus 6: Relevance of infection in the immunocompromised host. Br J Haematol. 2003;120:384-395.

56. Kidd IM, Clark DA, Sabin CA, et al. Prospective study of human betaherpesviruses after renal transplantation: Association of human herpesvirus 7 and cytomegalovirus co-infection with cytomegalovirus disease and increased rejection. Transplantation. 2000;69:2400-2404.

57. DesJardin JA, Cho E, Supran S, et al. Association of human herpesvirus 6 reactivation with severe cytomegalovirus-associated disease in orthotopic liver transplant recipients. Clin Infect Dis. 2001;33:1358-1362.

58. Carrigan DR, Drobyski WR, Russler SK, et al. Interstitial pneumonitis associated with human herpesvirus-6 infection after marrow transplantation. Lancet. 1991;338:147-149.

59. Carrigan DR, Knox KK. Human herpesvirus 6 (HHV-6) isolation from bone marrow: HHV-6-associated bone marrow suppression in bone marrow transplant patients. Blood. 1994;84:3307-3310.

60. Zerr DM, Gooley TA, Yeung L, et al. Human herpesvirus-6 reactivation and encephalitis in allogeneic bone marrow transplant recipients. Clin Infect Dis. 2001; 33:763-771.

61. Boutolleau D, Fernandez C, André E, et al. Human herpesvirus (HHV)-6 and HHV-7: Two closely related viruses with different infection profiles in stem cell transplantation recipients. J Infect Dis. 2003;187:179-186.

62. Ljungman P, Wang FZ, Clark DA, et al. High levels of human herpesvirus 6 DNA in peripheral blood leucocytes are correlated to platelet engraftment and disease in allogeneic stem cell transplant patients. Br J Haematol 2000;111:774-781.

63. Spira TJ, Bozeman LH, Sanderlin KC, et al. Lack of correlation between human herpesvirus-6 infection and the course of human immunodeficiency virus infection. J Infect Dis. 1990;161:567-570.

64. Fairfax MR, Schacker T, Cone RW, et al. Human herpesvirus 6 DNA in blood cells of human immunodeficiency virus-infected men: Correlation of high levels with high CD4 cell counts. J Infect Dis. 1994;169:1342-1345.

65. Pollock BH, Jenson HB, Leach CT, et al. Risk factors for pediatric human immunodeficiency virus-related malignancy. JAMA. 2003;289:2393-2399.

66. Di Luca D, Dolcetti R, Mirandola P, et al. Human herpesvirus 6: A survey of presence and variant distribution in normal peripheral lymphocytes and lymphoproliferative disorders. J Infect Dis. 1994;170:211-215.

67. Torelli G, Marasca R, Luppi M, et al. Human herpesvirus-6 in human lymphomas: Identification of specific sequences in Hodgkin's lymphomas by polymerase chain reaction. Blood. 1991;77:2251-2258.

68. Valente G, Secchiero P, Lusso P, et al. Human herpesvirus 6 and Epstein-Barr virus in Hodgkin's disease: A controlled study by polymerase chain reaction and in situ hybridization. Am J Pathol. 1996;149:1501-1510.

69. Luppi M, Barozzi P, Garber R, et al. Expression of human herpesvirus-6 antigens in benign and malignant lymphoproliferative diseases. Am J Pathol. 1998;153:815-823.

70. Shiramizu B, Chang CW, Cairo MS. Absence of human herpesvirus-6 genome by polymerase chain reaction in children with Hodgkin disease: A Children's Cancer Group lymphoma biology study. J Pediatr Hematol Oncol. 2001;23:282-285.

71. Buchwald D, Cheney PR, Peterson DL, et al. A chronic illness characterized by fatigue, neurologic and immunologic disorders, and active human herpesvirus type 6 infection. Ann Intern Med. 1992;116:103-113.

72. Reeves WC, Stamey FR, Black JB, et al. Human herpesviruses 6 and 7 in chronic fatigue syndrome: A case-control study. Clin Infect Dis. 2000;31:48-52.

73. Warn KN, Couto Parada X, Passas J, Thiruchelvam AD. Evaluation of the specificity and sensitivity of indirect immunofluorescence tests for IgG to human herpesviruses-6 and -7. J Virol Methods. 2002;106:107-113.

74. Black JB, Schwarz TF, Patton JL, et al. Evaluation of immunoassays for detection of antibodies to human herpesvirus 7. Clin Diagn Lab Immunol. 1996;3:79-83.

75. Suga S, Yoshikawa T, Asano Y, et al. IgM neutralizing antibody responses to human herpesvirus-6 in patients with exanthem subitum or organ transplantation. Microbiol Immunol. 1992;36:495-506.

76. Asano Y, Yoshikawa T, Suga S, et al. Viremia and neutralizing antibody response in infants with exanthem subitum. J Pediatr. 1989;114:535-539.

77. Cone RW, Huang ML, Ashley R. Human herpesvirus 6 DNA in peripheral blood cells and saliva from immunocompetent individuals. J Clin Microbiol. 1993;31:1262-1267.

78. Locatelli G, Santoro F, Veglia F, et al. Real-time quantitative PCR for human herpesvirus 6 DNA. J Clin Microbiol. 2000;38:4042-4048.

79. Yoshida M, Yamada M, Tsukazaki T, et al. Comparison of antiviral compounds against human herpesvirus 6 and 7. Antiviral Res. 1998;40:73-84.

80. Zerr DM, Gupta D, Huang ML, et al. Effect of antivirals on human herpesvirus 6 replication in hematopoietic stem cell transplant recipients. Clin Infect Dis. 2002;34:309-317.

81. Tokimasa S, Hara J, Osugi Y, et al. Ganciclovir is effective for prophylaxis and treatment of human herpesvirus-6 in allogeneic stem cell transplantation. Bone Marrow Transplant. 2002;29:595-598.

82. Bech E, Lycke J, Gadeberg P, et al. A randomized, double-blind, placebo-controlled MRI study of anti-herpesvirus therapy in MS. Neurology. 2002;58:31-36.

83. Frenkel N, Schirmer EC, Wyatt LS, et al. Isolation of a new herpesvirus from human CD4+ T cells. Proc Natl Acad Sci U S A. 1990;87:748-752.

84. Black JB, Pellett PE. Human herpesvirus 7. Rev Med Virol. 1999;9:245-262.

85. Lusso P, Secchiero P, Crowley RW, et al. CD4 is a critical component of the receptor for human herpesvirus 7: Interference with human immunodeficiency virus. Proc Natl Acad Sci U S A. 1994;91:3872-3876.

86. Berneman ZN, Ablashi DV, Li G, et al. Human herpesvirus 7 is a T-lymphotropic virus and is related to, but significantly different from, human herpesvirus 6 and human cytomegalovirus. Proc Natl Acad Sci U S A. 1992;89:10552-10556.

87. Foà-Tomasi L, Avitabile E, Ke L, et al. Polyvalent and monoclonal antibodies identify major immunogenic proteins specific for human herpesvirus 7-infected cells and have weak cross-reactivity with human herpesvirus 6. J Gen Virol. 1994;75:2719-2727.

88. Nicholas J. Determination and analysis of the complete nucleotide sequence of human herpesvirus 7. J Virol. 1996;70:5975-5989.

89. Secchiero P, Gibellini D, Flamand L, et al. Human herpesvirus 7 induces the downregulation of CD4 antigen in lymphoid T cells without affecting p56lck levels. J Immunol. 1997;159:3412-3423.

90. Nakano K, Tadagaki K, Isegawa Y, et al. Human herpesvirus 7 open ready frame U12 encodes a functional beta-chemokine receptor. J Virol. 2003;77:8108-8115.

91. Yoshikawa T, Asano Y, Kobayashi I. Seroepidemiology of human herpesvirus 7 in healthy children and adults in Japan. J Med Virol. 1993;41:319-323.

92. Kidd IM, Clark DA, Ait-Khaled M, et al. Measurement of human herpesvirus 7 load in peripheral blood and saliva of healthy subjects by quantitative polymerase chain reaction. J Infect Dis. 1996;174:396-401.

93. Hara S, Kimura H, Hoshino Y, et al. Detection of herpesvirus DNA in the serum of immunocompetent children. Microbiol Immunol. 2002;46:177-180.

94. Torigoe S, Koide W, Yamada M, et al. Human herpesvirus 7 infection associated with central nervous system manifestations. J Pediatr. 1996;129:301-305.

95. Hashida T, Komura E, Yoshida M, et al. Hepatitis in association with human herpesvirus-7 infection. Pediatrics. 1995;96:783-785.

96. Drago F, Malaguti F, Ranieri E, et al. Human herpesvirus-like particles in pityriasis rosea lesions: An electron microscopy study. J Cutan Pathol. 2002;29:359-361.

97. Zhang Y, Schols D, De Clercq E. Selective activity of various antiviral compounds against HHV-7 infection. Antiviral Res. 1999;43:23-35.

CHAPTER **137**

Kaposi's Sarcoma–Associated Herpesvirus (Human Herpesvirus Type 8)

KENNETH M. KAYE

Kaposi's sarcoma (KS)-associated human herpesvirus (KSHV, or HHV-8), the eighth and most recently discovered human herpesvirus, was discovered as a result of its link with KS; it is also linked with primary effusion lymphoma (PEL) and multicentric Castleman's disease. The role of KSHV in malignancy has generated much interest in this virus.

HISTORY

Kaposi's sarcoma was first described in 1872 by Moritz Kaposi, a prominent Hungarian dermatologist.[1] Kaposi described findings in five men of "idiopathic multiple pigmented sarcoma of the skin."[2] He noted aggressive disease and emphasized that the syndrome was incurable and rapidly lethal.[3] In fact, three of the men reported by Kaposi were dead within 16 months of presentation, and autopsy demonstrated disseminated disease. Despite the aggressive nature of the disease described by Kaposi, KS subsequently came to be regarded as an indolent disease in elderly men of Mediterranean and eastern European descent. It is not clear what accounted for the evolution in the defining features of KS from the aggressive, rapidly fatal disorder described by Kaposi to a relatively mild one. During the 1950s, KS was recognized as an important disease in parts of sub-Saharan Africa.[4] Then, in 1981, Alvin Friedman-Kein reported on 50 young men who had had sex with men with KS of the skin, lymph nodes, mucosa, and viscera.[5] This report heralded the acquired immunodeficiency syndrome (AIDS) epidemic. The similarity between the original syndrome described by Kaposi and that seen in human immunodeficiency virus (HIV) infection is striking and raises the question of whether AIDS-like immune suppression was present in the men initially described.[3]

KSHV was identified in 1994 in KS lesions by Chang and Moore and colleagues, who used a polymerase chain reaction (PCR)-based technique called *representational difference analysis*.[6] This technique searches for DNA, such as from a virus, that is present in diseased tissue and absent in normal tissue.[7] These investigations were based on epidemiologic observations that suggested that an infectious agent may have an etiologic role in KS. KS occurred at a 20-fold higher rate among men who have sex with men who have AIDS compared with those who contracted AIDS by other means, such as by a blood-borne route. Subsequent to this seminal discovery, work by many groups across the world has elucidated much about this virus.

CLASSIFICATION AND BIOLOGY

KSHV, the only known human rhadinovirus (gamma-2 herpesvirus), is related to other rhadinoviruses, including those that infect New (South American) and Old (African) World monkeys and rodents (murine gamma herpesvirus 68).[8-12] Two Old World monkey rhadinoviruses (RFHVMm and RFHVMn) are found in retroperitoneal fibromatosis. This entity has histologic similarities to KS. Herpesvirus saimiri (HVS), a New World virus, can cause T-cell lymphoma when it infects New World monkeys that are not its natural host.[13] Epstein-Barr virus, a gamma-1 herpesvirus, is the closest human relative of KSHV.

KSHV is an enveloped virus that measures 140 nm in diameter; its appearance by electron microscopy is indistinguishable from that of other herpesviruses.[14,15] KSHV attaches to cells before entry by binding to cell surface heparan sulfate and the integrin $\alpha_3\beta_1$.[16] The KSHV genome contains approximately 140 kb of unique sequence[8,17] that encodes nearly 100 open reading frames (ORFs). The nomenclature of the ORFs is based on that of HVS owing to (1) high sequence and positional homology with ORFs of HVS, and (2) the fact that HVS was the only fully sequenced gamma-2 herpesvirus before the discovery of KSHV. ORFs without homology to those in HVS are numbered sequentially with K prefixes. Many KSHV genes are homologues of human genes that were presumably "pirated" from mammalian cells during the evolution of the virus. The unique KSHV sequence is flanked by approximately 40 copies[18] of 0.8-kb guanine and cytosine–rich terminal repeat elements.

KSHV is capable of both latent and lytic infection.[9,19,20] Because of its capacity for latent infection, KSHV persistence in its human host is lifelong, similar to other herpesviruses. During lytic infection, many encapsidated viral progeny are produced in a cell and then released as the infected cell dies. Almost all of the nearly 100 KSHV genes are devoted to, and only expressed during, lytic infection. These genes encode proteins that are responsible for replication of the viral DNA and for packaging of the DNA into capsids. The viral genome is linear, with terminal repeats on each end when it is packaged in viral capsids. In addition to genes involved in virus replication, some genes expressed during lytic infection are involved in immune evasion, thereby preventing the host from properly responding to, and targeting, the infected cells.[21,22]

Latent KSHV infection sharply contrasts with lytic infection.[19,20,23] Latent infection predominates over lytic infection in KSHV-infected tumors and cell lines, with only a small fraction of infected cells undergoing lytic infection. In latently infected cells, the viral genome circularizes by fusing at its terminal repeat ends and persists as a multiple-copy (ranging in number from 10 to 50 copies) extrachromosomal episome (plasmid) within the nucleus. Only approximately 5 KSHV genes are expressed during latent infection. Rather than causing cell death, these genes encourage cell survival. Because promotion of cell survival is also a prominent feature of malignancy, it is not surprising that KSHV is associated with certain tumors.[24]

Genes expressed in latent infection have important roles in tumorigenesis.[19,20,23] To persist during latent infection in proliferating cells such as tumor cells, KSHV episomes must replicate and efficiently segregate to progeny nuclei. The viral latency-associated nuclear antigen 1 (LANA1 or ORF73) gene mediates KSHV DNA replication and then tethers episomes to chromosomes during mitosis to ensure efficient segregation to daughter cells. LANA1 also exerts effects on transcriptional regulation and cell growth. Viral cyclin D (ORF72), a homologue of cell cyclin D, stimulates the G1-to-S transition within the cell cycle. Viral cyclin D is resistant to the multiple inhibitors that normally inhibit cell cyclin D, resulting in unchecked cell growth. The KSHV viral FLICE-inhibitory protein (K13) inhibits apoptosis (or cell suicide), thereby preventing the cell from eliminating itself once it "knows" it is infected. Kaposin A (K12) exerts transforming effects, and latency-associated membrane protein (LAMP or K15) interacts with growth control proteins. LANA2 (K10.5) is expressed in B cells, not in KS tissue, and it inhibits apoptosis.

Although only a small percentage (~1%) of cells within tumors undergo lytic infection, these cells may have an important role in tumorigenesis. For instance, in lytic infection, a G protein–coupled receptor homologue (ORF74) is expressed that is constitutively active and has paracrine effects.[25] Therefore, even though the cell with lytic infection will die, it can produce factors that have growth effects on nearby cells. In fact, transgenic mice expressing this viral protein have KS-like lesions.[26,27]

Cell culture and transformation models of KSHV remain rather limited. Primary bone marrow endothelial cells can be infected and transformed, but only about 5% of the cells are infected, and paracrine effects stimulate growth in the other cells.[28] Owing to the lack of a cell line that is permissive for KSHV lytic replication, the mainstay of

KSHV production occurs in cell lines that are derived from KSHV primary effusion lymphomas. The vast majority of cells in these lines are latently infected, but lytic infection (and virions) can be induced by several methods such as by incubation with phorbol esters. However, this method produces relatively low titers of virus. The most tractable models so far used to study the effects of KSHV virus infection are in dermal microvascular cells.[20] KSHV induces phenotypic changes in these cells, such as spindle formation, but it does not immortalize or fully transform them.

PATHOGENESIS

KSHV has an etiologic role in KS, PEL, and multicentric Castleman's disease. Overall, KSHV is well adapted to its human host, and it usually does not cause disease. Such a situation is ideal from the point of view of the virus in that a commensal existence without harm to its host enhances its long-term survival. Suppression of the immune system appears to disturb the delicate balance between KSHV and its human host, and this can lead to KSHV-associated malignancy. However, other poorly understood factors also contribute to tumorigenesis. For instance, the cause of the more frequent occurrence of KS in men rather than women, despite a similar prevalence of KSHV infection, is not clear. Further, before the HIV epidemic, KS occurred relatively frequently in Uganda and Cameroon but not in Botswana and Gambia, despite the fact that KSHV infection was common to all these countries.[29] These findings argue for as yet unknown factors that interact with KSHV to induce KS.

EPIDEMIOLOGY

Assays to identify KSHV-infected individuals are still evolving.[9,20,30] Serologic assays for antibodies against specific KSHV antigens expressed during the latent or lytic phase of infection have been most commonly used. These assays differ in sensitivity and specificity, resulting in some that likely overestimate and others that underestimate seropositivity. With these limitations in mind, certain general conclusions regarding the prevalence of KSHV infection can be made. Detection of KSHV DNA by PCR of blood is less sensitive than are serologic assays, reflecting highly variable levels of viremia that occur in those with and without KSHV-induced disease.

KSHV differs from other herpesviruses in that it does not cause worldwide ubiquitous infection.[9,20,30] Instead, the prevalence of infection in the general population varies significantly in different areas of the world. Sub-Saharan Africa has the highest rate of infection with approximately 50% of the population infected. Seroprevalence is approximately 10% in the Mediterranean region, although in certain areas of Italy, it approaches 30%. Seroprevalence in the United States and Northern Europe is about 5%, but only 0.2% of individuals in Japan are positive. Despite the low prevalence of KSHV in the general population in the United States, approximately 15% to 20% of HIV-negative and approximately 40% of HIV-positive men who have sex with men are KSHV-seropositive.[31] In contrast to the general population, about 90% to 100% of individuals with KS are seropositive, consistent with the etiologic role of KSHV in this disease.

Several patterns of KSHV transmission have been observed. In the United States, KSHV is spread predominantly through sexual contact among men who have sex with men. Among men who have sex with men, KSHV seropositivity is associated with high numbers of sexual partners, a history of sexually transmitted diseases, and the use of amyl nitrates.[31,32] In parts of the world where KSHV infection is more prevalent, nonsexual transmission also occurs, and KSHV infection occurs among children before they are sexually active.[33,34] Intrafamilial clustering has also been documented as further evidence of nonsexual transmission.[35] Saliva is likely a unifying vehicle of both sexual and nonsexual KSHV transmission. Relatively high titers of KSHV DNA can be found in the saliva of infected individuals, whereas high levels of virus are not found in other sites. In one study of 50 KSHV-infected men who have sex with men without KS, 30% of oropharyngeal samples compared with 1% of anal and genital sam-

ples were positive for KSHV. KSHV from the oral cavity was 2.5 logs higher than the titer at other sites.[31] It is interesting to note that deep ("French") kissing was a risk factor for KSHV transmission among men who have sex with men.[31] Solid organ transplantation from a seropositive donor to a seronegative recipient has also been shown to transmit KSHV.[36] Vertical transmission from mother to infant can occur but appears to be rare.[37] The rate of transmission from blood products appears to be low but is still not known.

CLINICAL MANIFESTATIONS

Primary Infection

A primary infection syndrome for KSHV has not been clearly described; most infections are probably asymptomatic or unrecognized. In a prospective Egyptian study, 86 children 1 to 4 years of age who presented to the emergency department with fever of unclear origin were evaluated for KSHV infection. Six of the children had likely primary KSHV infection because they were seronegative but KSHV DNA was detected in saliva. In three of these subjects, follow-up serology was obtained, and all three had seroconverted to KSHV. All but one of the six had a maculopapular rash that began on the face and gradually spread downward over the trunk and extremities. Five of the six had associated upper respiratory tract symptoms. Fever persisted over a median of 10 days.[38] Primary KSHV infection was associated with mild symptoms of diarrhea, fatigue, localized rash (ankle and face), and lymphadenopathy (cervical and submental) in four of five HIV-negative men.[39] A 43-year-old HIV-infected man presented with fever, arthralgia, cervical lymphadenopathy, and splenomegaly 5 weeks after KSHV seroconversion; his illness spontaneously resolved within 10 weeks. Biopsy specimens revealed angiolymphoid hyperplasia and foci of KS. Neither lesions nor clinical symptoms had recurred after 8 years of follow-up (on highly active antiretroviral therapy [HAART]).[40] Four months after transplantation, primary KSHV infection developed in two renal allograft recipients who had received allografts from the same KSHV-positive donor. One recipient experienced disseminated KS, and the other, a syndrome of fever, splenomegaly, cytopenia, and marrow failure with plasmacytosis. KSHV infection of immature progenitor cells from aplastic bone marrow was noted in the patient with marrow failure.[41] Although these data are very limited, primary infection in immunocompetent hosts appears to be self-limited, whereas primary infection in immunosuppressed hosts can be severe and can have significant consequences.

Kaposi's Sarcoma

KS typically involves the skin and manifests as lesions that enlarge from patches to plaques to nodules.[42,43] These lesions often begin as violaceous and later evolve into a brown color owing to hemosiderin deposition (Fig. 137-1). KS lesions comprise vascular spaces, extravasated erythrocytes, and several different types of cells (Fig. 137-2). These include malignant spindle cells and infiltrating mononuclear cells, such as hemosiderin-laden macrophages. The highly vascular nature of KS gives it its purple color. In the nodular stage, nearly all spindle cells are KSHV-infected (see Fig. 137-2).

Four variants of KS occur that differ epidemiologically and clinically.[9,20,44,45] The occurrence of KS largely reflects the seroprevalence of the population, that is, KS is more common in areas with high KSHV seropositivity. Classic KS occurs in elderly men of Mediterranean or eastern European descent, predominantly involves the skin of the lower extremities, and is indolent. Endemic KS occurs in certain sub-Saharan African countries. At least two forms of endemic KS occurred before the HIV epidemic. In adults, cutaneous KS occurred in an approximately 20:1 ratio of men to women; it clinically resembled classic KS in adults. However, in children younger than age 10, KS manifested in an aggressive, multifocal, lymphadenopathic form, often without cutaneous lesions, that is frequently fatal.[42,43,46] Epidemic KS, which refers to KS in HIV-infected individuals, tends to be aggressive and commonly involves the skin, gastrointestinal tract, and respiratory tract. In contrast to classic KS, lesions commonly involve the face (often the nose), genitalia, and oral cavity (palatal and

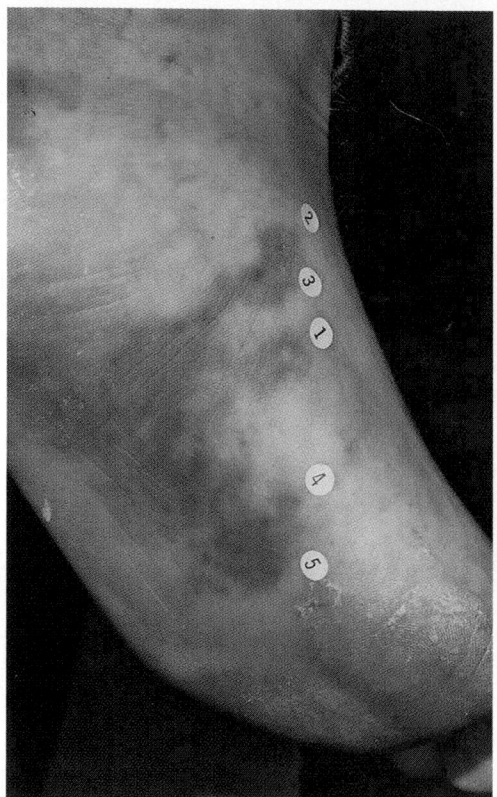
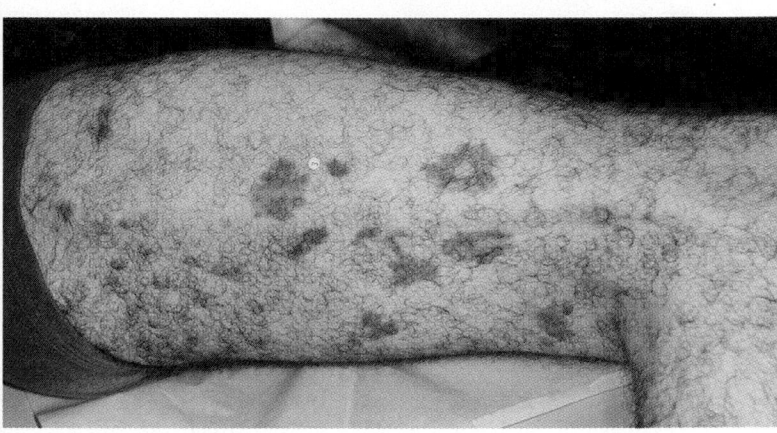

FIGURE 137-1. Kaposi's Sarcoma of the Foot (left) and Leg (right) in Two HIV-Positive Patients. Lesions are highly vascular and often occur on the lower extremities. Newer Kaposi's sarcoma lesions are typically violaceous (*foot*) and evolve to a brownish color (*leg*) over time owing to hemosiderin deposition. Labels are present as part of a clinical treatment trial. *(Courtesy of Bruce Dezube, MD.)*

gingival), in addition to the lower extremities.[47] This form is most common in the United States, where it predominantly affects men who have sex with men. However, KS largely occurs in heterosexual HIV-infected individuals in Africa. Since the start of the HIV epidemic in Africa, the ratio of men to women with KS has dropped 10-fold to approximately 2:1. The number of childhood cases of KS has also sig-

nificantly increased in Africa with the AIDS epidemic.[48,49] For instance, in Zambia in the early 1980s, KS accounted for 0% to 2% of childhood malignancies, but by 1992, it accounted for about 25% of childhood malignancies.[49-51] Iatrogenic KS occurs in individuals who are immunosuppressed as from organ transplantation, and it tends to be aggressive. Kidney allograft recipients appear to be at higher risk

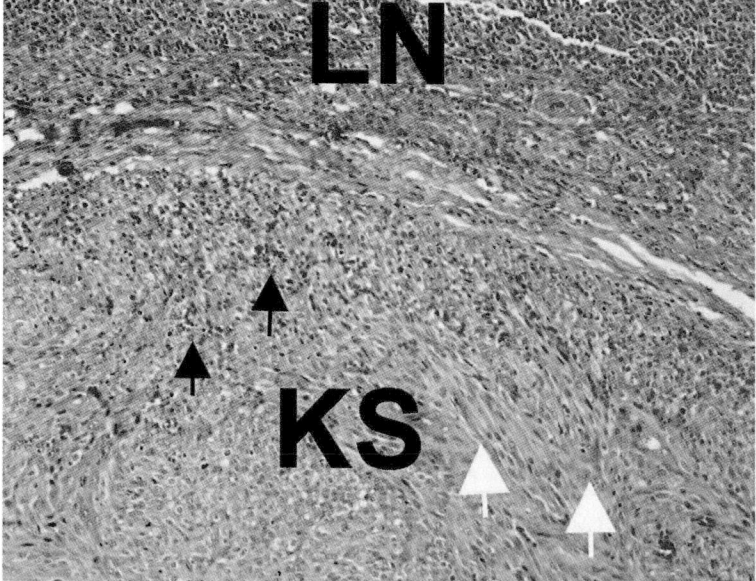
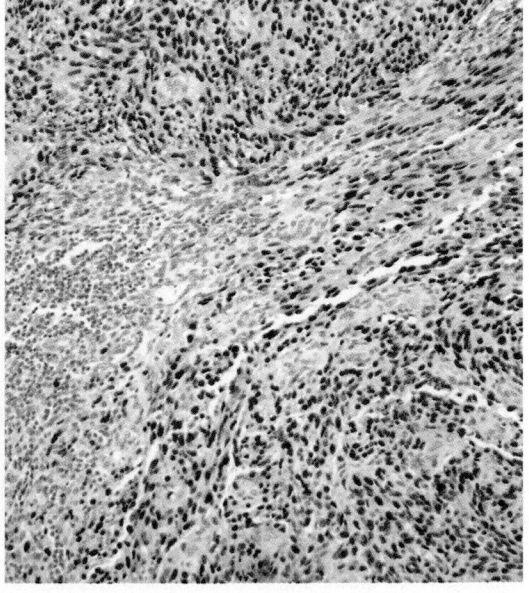

FIGURE 137-2. Kaposi's Sarcoma Involving a Lymph Node. Left panel, Spindle cell proliferation (*white arrows*) containing poorly formed vascular spaces with entrapped red blood cells (*black arrows*). Areas of uninvolved lymph node (LN) are seen at the top (H&E). **Right panel,** Immunohistochemical detection of Kaposi's sarcoma–associated human herpesvirus (KSHV) latency-associated nuclear antigen 1 (LANA1) (*brown*) in the nuclei of many spindle cells indicates KSHV infection (×200). *(Courtesy of Dan Jones, MD, PhD.)*

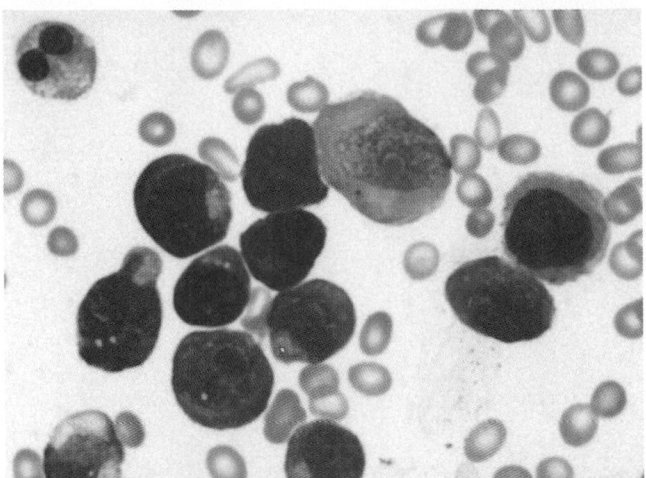

FIGURE 137-3. Kaposi's sarcoma–associated human herpesvirus (KSHV)-infected primary effusion lymphoma cells from this pleural effusion have plasmacytoid features and deeply basophilic cytoplasm. Red blood cells are interspersed among the lymphoma cells (Wright Giemsa, 1000×). *(Courtesy of Dan Jones, MD, PhD.)*

for developing KS than are other transplant recipients.[52] It is interesting to note that reduction in immunosuppression can lead to KS remission, highlighting the critical role of immune response in this infection. Similarly, epidemic KS often responds to boosting of the immune response with HAART (see Chapter 124).[43,53]

Although KS can often be recognized by a trained observer, the diagnosis is easily confirmed by biopsy.[43,47] Early stages of KS can be more difficult to recognize. The differential diagnosis of KS includes bacillary angiomatosis, which is caused by *Bartonella* species. Skin lesions of bacillary angiomatosis are very vascular and may mimic those of KS (see Chapter 232).[43]

Treatment of KS in HIV infection is palliative and not curative.[43,47,53] Depending on the severity of disease, treatment options may include observation, topical therapy, and systemic therapy (see

Chapter 121). Local therapy may include chemotherapeutic agents, laser treatment, cryotherapy, and radiation. Systemic therapy, which is reserved for more severe disease, includes liposomal anthracyclines, paclitaxel, vinorelbine, and interferon-alfa. Other treatment modalities, such as angiogenesis inhibitors, are currently being tested.

Primary Effusion Lymphoma

PEL was first described in 1989 in HIV-infected patients.[54] It occurs in potential body spaces of the pleural, pericardial, and peritoneal cavities.[9,55] Lymphoma cells (Fig. 137-3) grow in suspension with little or no contiguous solid mass component. Cells contain clonal immunoglobulin gene arrangements that indicate a B-cell origin, even though they lack most typical B-cell antigens. Malignant cells are infected with KSHV, and Epstein-Barr virus often coinfects the cells. PEL is rare, accounting for approximately 3% of AIDS-related lymphomas and only an estimated 0.4% of non–AIDS-associated large cell non-Hodgkin's lymphomas.[56] Prognosis is poor, and death often occurs within months of diagnosis.

Multicentric Castleman's Disease

Castleman's disease is a rare lymphoproliferative disorder first described in 1956[57] that occurs in two forms. Localized Castleman's disease (hyaline vascular variant) is not associated with KSHV and has an indolent clinical course. Multicentric Castleman's disease (plasma cell variant), first described in 1978,[58] is associated with KSHV and has an indolent much more aggressive clinical course, frequently resulting in death. Multicentric Castleman's disease is often associated with fever, hepatosplenomegaly, and generalized lymphadenopathy. Complications include infection (often a cause of death) and the development of either lymphoma or KS.[59] KSHV is almost always linked to multicentric Castleman's disease in HIV-infected individuals, and KSHV infection is linked to about 50% of cases in individuals without HIV infection.[60,61] Interleukin-6 (IL-6), which induces B-cell differentiation, is expressed at high levels in the germinal centers of affected lymph nodes and may be responsible for the high numbers of plasma cells present (Fig. 137-4A). It is interesting to note that KSHV encodes a homologue of IL-6 that is expressed in lytic infection and may have a role in disease.[62,63] KSHV-infected plasmablasts are typically seen in the mantle zone of affected lymph nodes (Fig. 137-4B).[64] Although optimal therapy for multicentric Castleman's disease has not been clearly defined, treatment modalities include steroids and chemotherapy.[59,65]

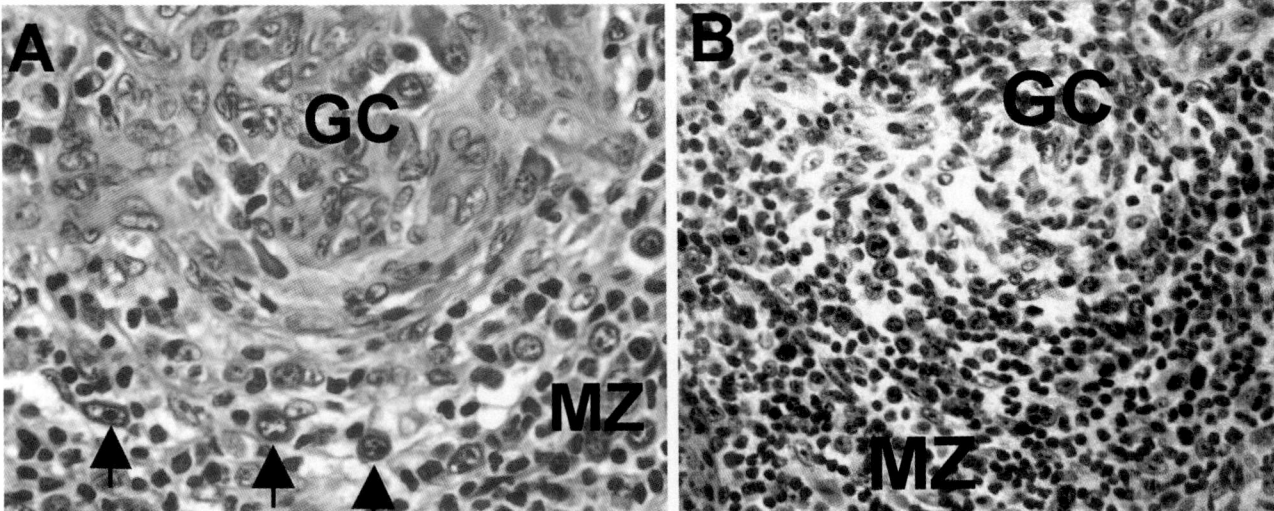

FIGURE 137-4. Multicentric Castleman's Disease in the Lymph Node of a Human Immunodeficiency Virus (HIV)-Negative Patient. **A,** Regressed germinal center (GC) has atypical plasmablasts *(arrows)* concentrated in the follicle mantle zone (MZ) (H&E, 600×). **B,** Immunohistochemical detection of Kaposi's sarcoma–associated human herpesvirus (KSHV) latency-associated nuclear antigen 1 (LANA1) *(brown)* in the nuclei of plasmablasts indicates KSHV-infected cells (×400). *(Courtesy of Dan Jones, MD, PhD.)*

Other Syndromes

Several syndromes that have been linked to KSHV infection either are disputed in the literature or have not yet been confirmed. These include pemphigus and bullous pemphigoid, sarcoid, Kikuchi's disease, multiple myeloma, hemophagocytic syndrome, and primary pulmonary hypertension.[9,66]

TREATMENT AND PREVENTION

Several agents have activity against KSHV lytic replication, but none has an established role in KSHV-associated disease. Ganciclovir, foscarnet, cidofovir, and adefovir, but not acyclovir, inhibit KSHV lytic replication.[67-70] A likely reason for the lack of efficacy of these agents in KSHV-associated disease is that they target lytic, rather than latent, replication of KSHV. A vast majority of KSHV-infected cells in these diseases are latently, not lytically, infected. Development of agents that target latent infection would therefore likely result in a major advance in the treatment of KSHV-associated disease.

REFERENCES

1. Kaposi M. Idiopathisches multiples Pigmentsarkom der Haut. Archiv fur Dermatologie und Syphilis. 1872;3:265-273.
2. Sternbach G, Varon J. Moritz Kaposi: Idiopathic pigmented sarcoma of the skin. J Emerg Med. 1995;13:671-674.
3. Breimer L. Original description of Kaposi's sarcoma. BMJ. 1994;308:1303-1304.
4. Antman K, Chang Y. Kaposi's sarcoma. N Engl J Med. 2000;342:1027-1038.
5. Kaposi's sarcoma and Pneumocystis pneumonia among homosexual men—New York City and California. MMWR Morb Mortal Wkly Rep. 1981;30:305-308.
6. Chang Y, Cesarman E, Pessin MS, et al. Identification of herpesvirus-like DNA sequences in AIDS-associated Kaposi's sarcoma. Science. 1994;266:1865-1869.
7. Lisitsyn N, Wigler M. Cloning the differences between two complex genomes. Science. 1993;259:946-951.
8. Russo JJ, Bohenzky RA, Chien M-C, et al. Nucleotide sequence of the Kaposi sarcoma-associated herpesvirus (HHV8). PNAS. 1996;93:14862-14867.
9. Ablashi DV, Chatlynne LG, Whitman JE Jr, Cesarman E. Spectrum of Kaposi's sarcoma-associated herpesvirus, or human herpesvirus 8, diseases. Clin Microbiol Rev. 2002;15:439-464.
10. Greensill J, Sheldon JA, Renwick NM, et al. Two distinct gamma-2 herpesviruses in African green monkeys: A second gamma-2 herpesvirus lineage among old world primates? J Virol. 2000;74:1572-1577.
11. Davison AJ. Evolution of the herpesviruses. Vet Microbiol. 2002;86:69-88.
12. Virgin HW, Latreille P, Wamsley P, et al. Complete sequence and genomic analysis of murine gammaherpesvirus 68. J Virol. 1997;71:5894-5904.
13. Jung JU, Trimble JJ, King NW, et al. Identification of transforming genes of subgroup A and C strains of Herpesvirus saimiri. Proc Natl Acad Sci U S A. 1991;88:7051-7055.
14. Wu L, Lo P, Yu X, et al. Three-dimensional structure of the human herpesvirus 8 capsid. J Virol. 2000;74:9646-9654.
15. Trus BL, Heymann JB, Nealon K, et al. Capsid structure of Kaposi's sarcoma-associated herpesvirus, a gammaherpesvirus, compared to those of an alphaherpesvirus, herpes simplex virus type 1, and a betaherpesvirus, cytomegalovirus. J Virol. 2001;75:2879-2890.
16. Akula SM, Pramod NP, Wang FZ, Chandran B. Integrin alpha3beta1 (CD 49c/29) is a cellular receptor for Kaposi's sarcoma-associated herpesvirus (KSHV/HHV-8) entry into the target cells. Cell. 2002;108:407-419.
17. Neipel F, Albrecht JC, Fleckenstein B. Cell-homologous genes in the Kaposi's sarcoma-associated rhadinovirus human herpesvirus 8: Determinants of its pathogenicity? J Virol. 1997;71:4187-4192.
18. Lagunoff M, Ganem D. The structure and coding organization of the genomic termini of Kaposi's sarcoma-associated herpesvirus (human herpesvirus 8). Virology. 1997;236:147-154.
19. Verma SC, Robertson ES. Molecular biology and pathogenesis of Kaposi sarcoma-associated herpesvirus. FEMS Microbiol Lett. 2003;222:155-163.
20. Dourmishev LA, Dourmishev AL, Palmeri D, et al. Molecular genetics of Kaposi's sarcoma-associated herpesvirus (human herpesvirus-8) epidemiology and pathogenesis. Microbiol Mol Biol Rev. 2003;67:175-212.
21. Moore PS, Chang Y. Kaposi's sarcoma-associated herpesvirus immunoevasion and tumorigenesis: Two sides of the same coin? Annu Rev Microbiol. 2003;57:609-639.
22. Means RE, Choi JK, Nakamura H, et al. Immune evasion strategies of Kaposi's sarcoma-associated herpesvirus. Curr Top Microbiol Immunol. 2002;269:187-201.
23. Schulz TF. Kaposi's sarcoma-associated herpesvirus (human herpesvirus-8). J Gen Virol. 1998;79:1573-1591.
24. Cesarman E. Kaposi's sarcoma-associated herpesvirus—the high cost of viral survival. N Engl J Med. 2003;349:1107-1109.
25. Bais C, Santomasso B, Coso O, et al. G-protein-coupled receptor of Kaposi's sarcoma-associated herpesvirus is a viral oncogene and angiogenesis activator. Nature. 1998;391:86-89.
26. Holst PJ, Rosenkilde MM, Manfra D, et al. Tumorigenesis induced by the HHV8-encoded chemokine receptor requires ligand modulation of high constitutive activity. J Clin Invest. 2001;108:1789-1796.
27. Yang TY, Chen SC, Leach MW, et al. Transgenic expression of the chemokine receptor encoded by human herpesvirus 8 induces an angioproliferative disease resembling Kaposi's sarcoma. J Exp Med. 2000;191:445-454.
28. Flore O, Rafii S, Ely S, et al. Transformation of primary human endothelial cells by Kaposi's sarcoma-associated herpesvirus. Nature. 1998;394:588-592.
29. Dedicoat M, Newton R. Review of the distribution of Kaposi's sarcoma-associated herpesvirus (KSHV) in Africa in relation to the incidence of Kaposi's sarcoma. Br J Cancer. 2003;88:1-3.
30. Chatlynne LG, Ablashi DV. Seroepidemiology of Kaposi's sarcoma-associated herpesvirus (KSHV). Semin Cancer Biol. 1999;9:175-185.
31. Pauk J, Huang ML, Brodie SJ, et al. Mucosal shedding of human herpesvirus 8 in men. N Engl J Med. 2000;343:1369-1377.
32. Martin JN, Ganem DE, Osmond DH, et al. Sexual transmission and the natural history of human herpesvirus 8 infection. N Engl J Med. 1998;338:948-954.
33. Gessain A, Mauclere P, van Beveren M, et al. Human herpesvirus 8 primary infection occurs during childhood in Cameroon, Central Africa. Int J Cancer. 1999;81:189-192.
34. Andreoni M, El-Sawaf G, Rezza G, et al. High seroprevalence of antibodies to human herpesvirus-8 in Egyptian children: Evidence of nonsexual transmission. J Natl Cancer Inst. 1999;91:465-469.
35. Angeloni A, Heston L, Uccini S, et al. High prevalence of antibodies to human herpesvirus 8 in relatives of patients with classic Kaposi's sarcoma from Sardinia [see comments]. J Infect Dis. 1998;177:1715-1718.
36. Munoz P, Alvarez P, de Ory F, et al. Incidence and clinical characteristics of Kaposi sarcoma after solid organ transplantation in Spain: Importance of seroconversion against HHV-8. Medicine (Baltimore). 2002;81:293-304.
37. Brayfield BP, Phiri S, Kankasa C, et al. Postnatal human herpesvirus 8 and human immunodeficiency virus type 1 infection in mothers and infants from Zambia. J Infect Dis. 2003;187:559-568.
38. Andreoni M, Sarmati L, Nicastri E, et al. Primary human herpesvirus 8 infection in immunocompetent children. JAMA. 2002;287:1295-1300.
39. Wang QJ, Jenkins FJ, Jacobson LP, et al. Primary human herpesvirus 8 infection generates a broadly specific CD8(+) T-cell response to viral lytic cycle proteins. Blood. 2001;97:2366-2373.
40. Oksenhendler E, Cazals-Hatem D, Schulz TF, et al. Transient angiolymphoid hyperplasia and Kaposi's sarcoma after primary infection with human herpesvirus 8 in a patient with human immunodeficiency virus infection. N Engl J Med. 1998;338:1585-1590.
41. Luppi M, Barozzi P, Schulz TF, et al. Bone marrow failure associated with human herpesvirus 8 infection after transplantation. N Engl J Med. 2000;343:1378-1385.
42. Habif TP. Clinical Dermatology: A Color Guide to Diagnosis and Therapy. St. Louis: Mosby-Year Book, Inc; 1996
43. Hengge UR, Ruzicka T, Tyring SK, et al. Update on Kaposi's sarcoma and other HHV8 associated diseases. Part 1: Epidemiology, environmental predispositions, clinical manifestations, and therapy. Lancet Infect Dis. 2002;2:281-292.
44. Friedman-Kien AE, Saltzman BR. Clinical manifestations of classical, endemic African, and epidemic AIDS-associated Kaposi's sarcoma. J Am Acad Dermatol. 1990;22:1237-1250.
45. Sarid R, Klepfish A, Schattner A. Virology, pathogenetic mechanisms, and associated diseases of Kaposi sarcoma-associated herpesvirus (human herpesvirus 8). Mayo Clin Proc. 2002;77:941-949.
46. Wabinga HR, Parkin DM, Wabwire-Mangen F, Nambooze S. Trends in cancer incidence in Kyadondo County, Uganda, 1960-1997. Br J Cancer. 2000;82:1585-1592.
47. Dezube BJ, Groopman JE. AIDS-related Kaposi's sarcoma: Clinical features and treatment. Available at www.uptodate.com. Version 11.3. Accessed Nov. 12, 2003.
48. Wabinga HR, Parkin DM, Wabwire-Mangen F, Mugerwa JW. Cancer in Kampala, Uganda, in 1989-91: Changes in incidence in the era of AIDS. Int J Cancer 1993;54:26-36.
49. Bayley AC. Occurrence, clinical behaviour and management of Kaposi's sarcoma in Zambia. Cancer Surv. 1991;10:53-71.
50. Patil PS, Elem B, Gwavava NJ, Urban MI. The pattern of paediatric malignancy in Zambia (1980-1989): A hospital-based histopathological study. J Trop Med Hyg. 1992;95:124-127.
51. Chintu C, Athale UH, Patil PS. Childhood cancers in Zambia before and after the HIV epidemic. Arch Dis Child. 1995;73:100-104; discussion 104-105.
52. Iscovich J, Boffetta P, Franceschi S, et al. Classic Kaposi sarcoma: Epidemiology and risk factors. Cancer. 2000;88:500-517.
53. Scadden DT. AIDS-related malignancies. Annu Rev Med. 2003;54:285-303.
54. Knowles DM, Inghirami G, Ubriaco A, Dalla-Favera R. Molecular genetic analysis of three AIDS-associated neoplasms of uncertain lineage demonstrates their B-cell derivation and the possible pathogenetic role of the Epstein-Barr virus. Blood. 1989;73:792-799.
55. Hengge UR, Ruzicka T, Tyring SK, et al. Update on Kaposi's sarcoma and other HHV8 associated diseases. Part 2: Pathogenesis, Castleman's disease, and pleural effusion lymphoma. Lancet Infect Dis. 2002;2:344-352.
56. Carbone A, Gloghini A, Vaccher E, et al. Kaposi's sarcoma-associated herpesvirus DNA sequences in AIDS-related and AIDS-unrelated lymphomatous effusions. Br J Haematol. 1996;94:533-543.
57. Castleman B, Iverson L, Menendez VP. Localized mediastinal lymph node hyperplasia resembling thymoma. Cancer. 1956;9:822-830.
58. Gaba AR, Stein RS, Sweet DL, Variakojis D. Multicentric giant lymph node hyperplasia. Am J Clin Pathol. 1978;69:86-90.
59. Herrada J, Cabanillas F, Rice L, et al. The clinical behavior of localized and multicentric Castleman disease. Ann Intern Med. 1998;128:657-662.
60. Soulier J, Grollet L, Oksenhendler E, et al. Kaposi's sarcoma-associated herpesvirus-like DNA sequences in multicentric Castleman's disease. Blood. 1995;86:1276-1280.

61. Gessain A, Sudaka A, Briere J, et al. Kaposi sarcoma-associated herpes-like virus (human herpesvirus type 8) DNA sequences in multicentric Castleman's disease: Is there any relevant association in non-human immunodeficiency virus-infected patients? Blood. 1996;87:414-416.
62. Moore PS, Boshoff C, Weiss RA, Chang Y. Molecular mimicry of human cytokine and cytokine response pathway genes by KSHV. Science. 1996;274:1739-1744.
63. Parravinci C, Corbellino M, Paulli M, et al. Expression of a virus-derived cytokine, KSHV vIL-6, in HIV-seronegative Castleman's disease. Am J Pathol. 1997;151:1517-1522.
64. Dupin N, Fisher C, Kellam P, et al. Distribution of human herpesvirus-8 latently infected cells in Kaposi's sarcoma, multicentric Castleman's disease, and primary effusion lymphoma. Proc Natl Acad Sci U S A. 1999;96:4546-4551.
65. Brown JR, Harris NL, Freedman AS. Castleman's disease. Available at www.uptodate.com. Version 11.3. Accessed Nov. 12, 2003.
66. Cool CD, Rai PR, Yeager ME, et al. Expression of human herpesvirus 8 in primary pulmonary hypertension. N Engl J Med. 2003;349:1113-1122.
67. Kedes DH, Ganem D. Sensitivity of Kaposi's sarcoma-associated herpesvirus replication to antiviral drugs. Implications for potential therapy. J Clin Invest. 1997;99:2082-2086.
68. Medvczky MM, Horvath E, Lund T, Medveczky PG. In vitro antiviral drug sensitivity of the Kaposi's sarcoma-associated herpesvirus. AIDS. 1997;11:1327-1332.
69. Neyts J, De Clercq E. Antiviral drug susceptibility of human herpesvirus 8. Antimicrob Agents Chemother. 1997;41:2754-2756.
70. Flore O, Gao SJ. Effect of DNA synthesis inhibitors on Kaposi's sarcoma-associated herpesvirus cyclin and major capsid protein gene expression. AIDS Res Hum Retroviruses. 1997;13:1229-1233.

CHAPTER **138**

Herpes B Virus

STEPHEN E. STRAUS

Herpes B virus is relatively benign and enzootic in some monkey species, but it can initiate dramatic illness upon experimental inoculation into small nonprimate animals or after inadvertent infection of humans. The occupational exposure of many thousands of individuals to captive monkeys and their tissues has, over the past 70 years, resulted in about 50 instances of herpes B virus infection. Most of these have been fatal but preventable.[1-3]

HISTORY

Herpes B virus was named by Sabin and Wright after the individual from whom it was recovered.[4] In 1932, Dr. W. B. was bitten on his left hand by a rhesus monkey during experimental studies of poliomyelitis. Lesions emerged at the wound site in 3 days and progressed to form a cluster of small vesicles. On day 10 after the bite, generalized abdominal cramps were experienced, followed by a progressive and ultimately fatal ascending myelitis.

Gay and Holden recovered a transmissible virus from autopsy tissues of W. B. but considered it a variant of herpes simplex virus (HSV).[5] In parallel studies, Sabin definitively established that the infection was caused by a novel herpesvirus that is distinct from yet antigenically related to HSV, and they proved that herpes B virus naturally infects monkeys and can do so asymptomatically.[6]

In the ensuing years, only a few dozen additional cases were recognized. Human herpes B virus infections have been most common during periods of intense use of monkeys for medical research: in the mid-1950s for poliovirus vaccine development and in the late 1980s for retrovirus studies.[1,2] The first instance of case clustering and person-to-person transmission of herpes B virus was documented among four individuals infected in Pensacola, Florida, in 1987.[7,8] Two monkey handlers succumbed to progressive encephalitis, and a supervisor at the same facility experienced cutaneous infection. One patient who later died inadvertently inoculated herpes B virus onto a patch of eczematous skin of his wife's finger while she attended to his lesions. In the last several years, additional cases have been identified that have led to new observations regarding herpes B virus biology, transmission, and treatment.[9-12]

CLASSIFICATION AND BIOLOGY

Herpes B virus is an alphaherpesvirus related to HSV. At times it has been called *Herpesvirus simiae,* which is a misleading term because there are numerous distinct herpesviruses of monkeys.[13] Now, the virus is formally named *Cercopithecine herpesvirus* 1.[2,14] It possesses the typical structural elements of all herpesviruses: a double-stranded viral genome in an icosahedral nucleocapsid, tegument proteins, and an envelope bearing virally encoded glycoproteins.[2] The genome of nearly 156,800 base pairs has been sequenced in its entirety.[15] Its organization closely resembles that of HSV. The 74 identified herpes B virus genes encode proteins that share 27% to 88% amino acid identity with HSV proteins.

Herpes B virus exhibits a broad host range in vitro and causes a productive cytocidal infection in the cells of virtually all types of human and nonhuman primates, small mammals, and many birds. Herpes B virus infection progresses rapidly in vitro and leads to infectious progeny in 12 to 16 hours. The limited knowledge of its replicative cycle suggests that it closely resembles HSV in terms of a coordinately regulated process that involves the successive synthesis of immediate-early (regulatory), early (replicative), and then late (structural) genes.[16]

The natural hosts of herpes B virus are diverse members of the *Macaca* genus of Asian monkeys, most notable of which are the rhesus (*Macaca mulatta*) and cynomolgus (*Macaca fascicularis*) species, which are frequently used for medical research; however, all species of macaques are susceptible. Many African and New World monkeys and humans suffer serious infections with herpes B virus, although its natural host species typically experiences relatively mild infection, which is largely analogous to that caused by HSV in humans.[17-22]

Herpes B virus is transmitted from monkey to monkey primarily by direct contact of mucous membranes or injured skin with virus-containing oral or genital secretions.[19,20] The prevalence of infection increases with age and conditions of crowding. Captive monkey colonies have an average seroprevalence rate of 30% to 100%.[22,23]

Most herpes B virus infections of *Macaca* monkeys are asymptomatic. The virus persists latently in trigeminal and sacral sensory nerve root ganglia, from which it may reactivate periodically.[18,22-24] Conditions of stress, such as shipping and crowding, and immunosuppression

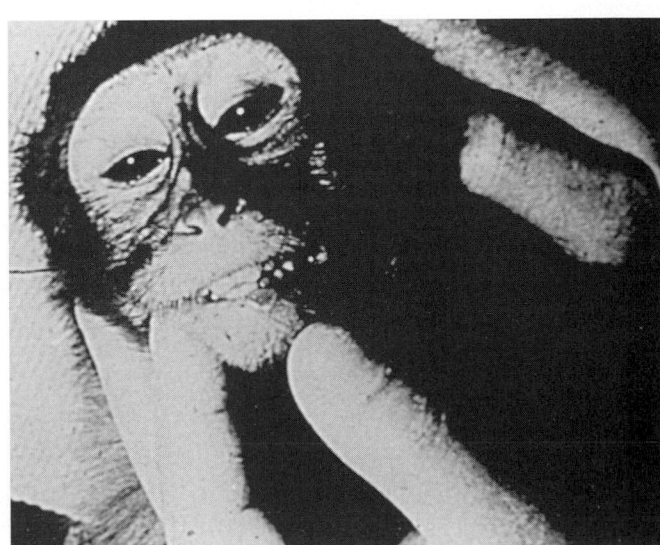

FIGURE 138-1. A lower lip ulceration in a rhesus monkey caused by herpes B virus infection.

stimulate virus reactivation.[25] One large series of virologic studies of stable monkey colonies showed that 2.3% of all *Macaca* genus monkeys were culture-positive from conjunctival, oral, or genital secretions.[17] Symptomatic primary or recurrent mucocutaneous lesions are seen occasionally and have features strikingly similar to those associated with HSV-1 or -2 infections in humans (Fig. 138-1).[21] Disseminated infections involving encephalitis, pneumonitis, hepatitis, and a diffuse exanthem have been reported in severely immunocompromised monkeys.[26]

HUMAN EPIDEMIOLOGY

Herpes B virus infection in humans is largely acquired from bites and scratches suffered while handling monkeys, or in the course of working directly with monkey tissues or primary cell cultures.[1,3] In isolated instances, the mode of transmission was unknown. Two cases involved needlestick injuries; one case is presumed to have arisen when a monkey handler was scratched with a jagged edge of a cage housing rhesus monkeys; in two cases, aerosol transmission was suspected; one case followed an eye splash; and, as reported from the Pensacola, Florida, outbreak, there is a single instance of person-to-person transmission.[7-10,12] Symptomatic herpes B virus infections have shown an incubation period of 2 to 21 days.[3,8] Asymptomatic human infection is unrecognized. A controlled seroprevalence study did not identify asymptomatic infections among 321 monkey handlers, many of whom had suffered numerous scratches and injuries by rhesus monkeys.[27]

CLINICAL MANIFESTATIONS

Most well-documented herpes B virus infections of humans were progressive and fatal, involving myelitis and hemorrhagic encephalitis with concomitant multiorgan involvement (Fig. 138-2). These progressive illnesses are variable in character but begin, typically, with either localized vesicular eruptions at inoculation sites or fever, malaise, diffuse pain, and headache. Regional lymphadenitis or frank lymphadenopathy is reported proximal to the site of inoculation. Abdominal pain and nausea may occur. These nonspecific symptoms gradually merge into a crescendoing neurologic syndrome with dysesthesia, ataxia, diplopia, seizures, and ascending flaccid paralysis, leading to death in days. Cerebrospinal fluid studies reveal a moderate lymphocytic pleocytosis and elevated protein, increased red cells, and rising titers of specific antibodies to herpes B virus. In short, the clinical findings indicate a multifocal, hemorrhagic myelitis or en-

cephalomyelitis. This is in contrast to herpes simplex encephalitis, in which focal involvement is typical.

Other clinical syndromes occur as well. Infections limited to the skin have been recognized, particularly in patients treated with acyclovir. Herpetic lesions were not common features of most earlier cases. One recent report involved an apparently self-limited aseptic meningitis.[9,11]

It is uncertain whether herpes B virus establishes latency and can reactivate in humans. An instance in which a patient's conjunctival and buccal cultures became positive again after discontinuing acute antiviral treatment is compatible with virus reactivation, but even in experimentally infected animals, resolution of primary infection is very slow with available drugs.[9,28,29] One controversial case report, however, suggests a zosteriform recurrence and subsequent encephalitis in a virologist several years after he discontinued active work with monkeys and their tissues.[30] Recent putative herpes B virus cases have been maintained on chronic acyclovir therapy and have thus not afforded an opportunity to learn whether asymptomatic or symptomatic reactivation and virus shedding can occur.

DIAGNOSIS

The potential severity of herpes B infection and the possible need for prolonged or even lifelong suppressive treatment make it imperative that efforts be undertaken to define promptly the exposure and to confirm a diagnosis rapidly.[3] If the monkey can be identified and safely evaluated, it should be cultured extensively and bled for antibody determinations.

All potential inoculation sites of the patient should be vigorously swabbed for culture. Serum should be held for later antibody determinations. Additional cultures should be taken from suspect lesions and from spinal fluid of symptomatic patients.

There are few facilities in the world suitable to undertake isolation and identification of herpes B virus. As a class 4 pathogen, herpes B virus handling requires special training and protective equipment. The B Virus Research and Resource Laboratory at Georgia State University in Atlanta is the major site for testing in the United States (contact, Dr. Julia K. Hilliard at 404-651-0808).

Because herpes B virus cross-reacts antigenically with HSV-1 and -2, serologic determination of recent or past infection of humans is difficult.[27,31,32] Current methods require absorption of serum to remove cross-reacting antibodies and parallel testing by immunoblot or competitive enzyme-linked immunosorbent assay (ELISA). Some patients with documented infection have shown slow or minimal virus-specific antibody rises, which confounds the problem of assessment and management of suspected cases.[8]

The development of polymerase chain reaction (PCR) technology has facilitated the study of herpes B virus biology and will permit faster and more sensitive detection of individuals who are actively shedding virus; however, a positive PCR on a specimen collected immediately after contact with a macaque only confirms that a high-risk exposure has occurred.[3,33]

TREATMENT

Prompt, vigorous, and exhaustive cleaning with strong soap, iodine, or bleach solutions is recommended to decontaminate monkey-inflicted wounds. Exposed ocular or mucous membranes should be irrigated. The advisability of immediate or delayed institution of antiviral therapy depends on the circumstances and severity of the wound, and authorities differ in their recommendations (Table 138-1).[3]

Some factors favor intervention. Acyclovir blocks herpes B virus replication in vitro with a minimal inhibitory concentration (MIC_{50}) of under 1 μg/mL, which is readily achieved with intravenous or high-dose oral administration.[28] Ganciclovir is about twice as potent in vitro.[29] Early treatment with acyclovir or ganciclovir has successfully arrested infection in some animal studies. In humans, however, the results of antiviral treatments have been mixed. Intravenous acyclovir

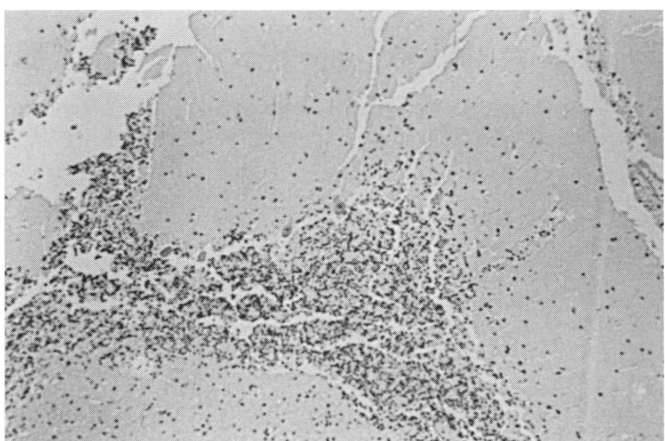

FIGURE 138-2. Herpes B virus encephalitis. Intense lymphocytic infiltration and isolated cells displaying eosinophilic intranuclear inclusions are seen in the cortical gray matter from a fatal human infection. *(Courtesy of J. Hilliard, PhD, B Virus Research and Resource Laboratory, Georgia State University, Atlanta.)*

TABLE 138-1 CDC Recommendations for Postexposure Prophylaxis of Persons Exposed to B Virus

Prophylaxis Recommended
Skin exposure* (with loss of skin integrity) or mucosal exposure (with or without injury) to a high-risk source (e.g., a macaque that is ill, immunocompromised, or known to be shedding virus, or one that has lesions compatible with B virus disease)
Inadequately cleaned skin or mucosal exposure
Laceration of the head, neck, or torso
Deep puncture bite
Needlestick associated with tissue or fluid from the nervous system, from lesions suspect for B virus, from eyelids, or from mucosa
Puncture or laceration after exposure to objects (1) contaminated either with fluid from monkey oral or genital lesions or with nervous system tissues, or (2) known to contain B virus
A postcleansing culture is positive for B virus

Prophylaxis Considered
Mucosal splash that was adequately cleaned
Laceration that was adequately cleaned
Needlestick involving blood from an ill or immunocompromised macaque
Puncture or laceration occurring after exposure to (1) objects contaminated with body fluid, or (2) potentially infected cell culture

Prophylaxis Not Recommended
Skin exposure in which the skin remains intact
Exposure associated with nonmacaque species of nonhuman primates

*Exposures include macaque bites or scratches; or contact with ocular, oral, or genital secretions, nervous system tissue, or cages or equipment contaminated by macaques.
Modified from Cohen JI, Davenport DS, Stewart JA, et al. Recommendations for prevention of and therapy for exposure to B virus (*Cercopithecine herpesvirus* 1). Clin Infect Dis. 2002;35:1191-1203, with permission.

and ganciclovir have not halted disease progression in all encephalitic patients. Nonetheless, prompt treatment has been associated with limited disease in a number of recent cases.[8-11]

Authorities advise the use of oral valacyclovir, 1 g three times daily for 14 days, for postexposure prophylaxis (Table 138-2).[3] Because virus shedding has been documented to resume after early discontinuation of treatment and because of the theoretical possibility of serious symptomatic recurrence and virus transmission, there has been a reluctance to discontinue antiviral drugs once treatment has been initiated[10,11]; however, it would seem appropriate to discontinue prophylaxis after 2 weeks and to observe the patient carefully, with repeated cultures and serology tests, in instances where infection has not been proved.

Individuals with proven B virus infection must be treated aggressively with high-dose intravenous acyclovir, or with ganciclovir if there are central nervous system symptoms, for 2 weeks or until the acute illness has resolved (see Table 138-2). Treatment with oral vala-

cyclovir should then continue for months or years, with observation for disease reactivation.

PREVENTION

Expert physicians and primate veterinarians working with the Centers for Disease Control and Prevention have recommended a series of practical guidelines to avoid herpes B virus infection (see website http://www.cdc.gov/ncidod/diseases/BVIRUS.pdf).[3,34] When feasible, animal studies should exclude *Macaca* species. All monkeys of the *Macaca* genus should be considered infected and should never be handled directly while awake or without extensive, full arm and facial protection. Efforts to create herpes B virus–free colonies of rhesus and cynomolgus monkeys have had mixed results.[35,36]

An inactivated herpes B virus candidate vaccine developed years ago is no longer available and its efficacy was never adequately assessed.[37] Candidate DNA and vaccinia vaccines expressing B virus glycoproteins are protective for animals but have not been tested in humans.[38,39]

REFERENCES

1. Weigler BJ. Biology of B virus in macaque and human hosts: A review. Clin Infect Dis. 1992;14:555-567.
2. Whitley RJ, Hilliard JK. Cercopithecine herpes virus 1 (B virus). In: Knipe DM, Howley PM, et al, eds. Field's Virology. 4th ed. Philadelphia: Lippincott Williams & Wilkins; 2001:2835-2848.
3. Cohen JI, Davenport DS, Stewart JA, et al. Recommendations for prevention of and therapy for exposure to B virus (*Cercopithecine herpesvirus* 1). Clin Infect Dis. 2002;35:1191-1203.
4. Sabin AB, Wright AM. Acute ascending myelitis following a monkey bite, with the isolation of a virus capable of reproducing the disease. J Exp Med. 1934;59:115-136.
5. Gay FP, Holden M. The herpes encephalitis problem. J Infect Dis. 1933;53:287-303.
6. Sabin AB. Studies on the B virus: III. The experimental disease in *Macaca rhesus* monkeys. Br J Exp Pathol. 1934;15:321-334.
7. Centers for Disease Control and Prevention. B-virus infection in humans—Pensacola, Florida. MMWR Morb Mortal Wkly Rep. 1987;36:289-296.
8. Holmes GP, Hilliard JK, Klontz KC, et al. B virus (*Herpesvirus simiae*) infection in humans: Epidemiologic investigation of a cluster. Ann Intern Med. 1990;112:833-839.
9. Centers for Disease Control and Prevention. B virus infection in humans—Michigan. MMWR Morb Mortal Wkly Rep. 1989;38:453-454.
10. Artenstein AW, Hicks CB, Goodwin BS, et al. Human infection with B virus following a needlestick injury. Rev Infect Dis. 1991;13:288-291.
11. Davenport DS, Johnson DR, Holmes GP, et al. Diagnosis and management of human B virus (*Herpesvirus simiae*) infections in Michigan. Clin Infect Dis. 1994;19:33-41.
12. Centers for Disease Control and Prevention. Fatal cercopithecine herpesvirus 1 (B virus) infection following mucocutaneous exposure and interim recommendations for worker protection. MMWR Morb Mortal Wkly Rep. 1998;47:1073-1076.
13. Eberle R, Hilliard J. The simian herpesviruses. Infect Agents Dis. 1995;4:55-70.
14. Roizman B, Carmichael LE, Deinhardt F, et al. Herpesviridae: Definition, provisional nomenclature and taxonomy. Intervirology. 1981;16:201-217.
15. Perelygina L, Zhu L, Zurkuhlen H, et al. Complete sequence and comparative analysis of the genome of herpes B virus (*Cercopithecine herpesvirus* 1) from a rhesus monkey. J Virol. 2993;77:6167-6177.
16. Roizman B, Sears A. Herpes simplex viruses and their replication. In: Fields BN, Knipe DM, Howley PM, et al, eds. Field's Virology. 3rd ed. New York: Lippincott-Raven; 1996;2231-2295.
17. Keeble SA. B virus infection in monkeys. Ann N Y Acad Sci. 1960;85:960-969.
18. Vizoso AD. Recovery of herpes simiae (B virus) from both primary and latent infections in rhesus monkeys. Br J Exp Pathol. 1975;56:485-488.
19. Zwartouw HT, Boulter EA. Excretion of B virus in monkeys and evidence of genital infection. Lab Anim. 1984;18:65-70.
20. Zwartouw HT, MacArthur JA, Boulter EA, et al. Transmission of B virus infection between monkeys especially in relation to breeding colonies. Lab Anim. 1984;18:125-130.
21. Anderson DC, Swenson RB, Orkin JL, et al. Primary *Herpesvirus simiae* (B-virus) infection in infant macaques. Lab Anim Sci. 1994;44:526-530.
22. Weigler BJ, Scinicariello F, Hilliard JK. Risk of venereal B virus (cercopithecine herpesvirus 1) transmission in rhesus monkeys using molecular epidemiology. J Infect Dis. 1995;171:1139-1143.
23. Weigler B, Roberts JA, Hird DW, et al. A cross-sectional survey for B virus antibody in a colony of group housed rhesus macaques. Lab Anim Sci. 1990;40:257-261.
24. Boulter EA. The isolation of monkey B virus (herpesvirus simiae) from the trigeminal ganglia of a healthy seropositive rhesus monkey. J Biol Stand. 1975;3:279-280.
25. Chellman GJ, Lukas VS, Eugui EM, et al. Activation of B virus (*Herpesvirus simiae*) in chronically immunosuppressed cynomolgus monkeys. Lab Anim Sci. 1992;42:146-151.
26. Carlson CS, O'Sullivan MG, Jayo MJ, et al. Fatal disseminated cercopithecine herpesvirus 1 (herpes B) infection in cynomolgus monkeys (*Macaca fascicularis*). Vet Pathol. 1997;34:405-414.

TABLE 138-2 Summary of CDC Recommendations for Prophylaxis and Treatment of B Virus Infection

Clinical Setting	Drug of Choice	Alternative Drug
Prophylaxis for exposure to B virus	Valacyclovir, 1 g PO q8h for 14 days	Acyclovir, 800 mg PO 5 times per day for 14 days
*Treatment of B virus disease**		
CNS symptoms are absent	Acyclovir, 12.5-15 mg/kg IV q8h	Ganciclovir, 5 mg/kg IV q12h
CNS symptoms are present	Ganciclovir, 5 mg/kg IV q12h	—

*To be given until symptoms resolve and the results of two cultures are negative for B virus.
CDC, Centers for Disease Control and Prevention; CNS, central nervous system.

27. Freifeld AG, Hilliard J, Southers J, et al. A controlled seroprevalence survey of primate handlers for evidence of asymptomatic herpes B virus infection. J Infect Dis. 1995;171:1031-1034.
28. Boulter EA, Thornton B, Bauer DJ, et al. Successful treatment of experimental B virus (Herpesvirus simiae) infection with acyclovir. Br Med J. 1980;280:681-683.
29. Zwartouw HT, Humphreys CR, Collins P. Oral chemotherapy of fatal B virus (Herpesvirus simiae) infection. Antiviral Res. 1989;11:275-284.
30. Fierer J, Bazeley P, Braude AI. Herpes B virus encephalomyelitis presenting as ophthalmic zoster: A possible latent infection reactivated. Ann Intern Med. 1973;79:225-228.
31. Eberle R, Black D, Hilliard JK. Relatedness of glycoproteins expressed on the surface of simian herpesvirus virions and infected cells to specific HSV glycoproteins. Arch Virol. 1989;109:233-252.
32. Blewett EL, Saliki JT, Eberle R. Development of a competitive ELISA for detection of primates infected with monkey B virus (Herpesvirus simiae). J Virol Methods. 1999;77:59-67.
33. Perelygina L, Patrusheva I, Manes N, et al. Quantitative real-time PCR for detection of monkey B virus (Cercopithecine herpesvirus 1) in clinical samples. J Virol Methods. 2003;109:245-251.
34. Wells DL, Lipper SL, Hilliard JK, et al. Herpesvirus simiae contamination of primary rhesus monkey kidney cell cultures: CDC recommendations to minimize risks to laboratory personnel. Diagn Microbiol Infect Dis. 1989;12:333-336.
35. Ward JA, Hilliard JK. B virus-specific pathogen-free (SPF) breeding colonies of macaques: Issues, surveillance, and results in 1992. Lab Anim Sci. 1994;44:222-228.
36. Ward JA, Hilliard JK. Herpes B virus-specific pathogen-free breeding colonies of macaques: Serologic test results and the B-virus status of the macaque. Contemp Top Lab Anim Sci. 2002;41:36-41.
37. Hull RN, Nash JC. Immunization against B virus infection: I. Preparation of an experimental vaccine. Am J Hyg. 1960;71:15-28.
38. Bennett AM, Slomka MJ, Brown DW, et al. Protection against herpes B virus infection in rabbits with a recombinant vaccinia virus expressing glycoprotein D. J Med Virol. 1999;57:47-56.
39. Hirano M, Nakamura S, Mitsunaga F, et al. Efficacy of a B virus gD DNA vaccine for induction of humoral and cellular immune responses in Japanese macaques. Vaccine. 2002;20:2523-2532.

CHAPTER **139**

Adenovirus

STEPHEN G. BAUM

Adenoviruses are most important clinically because of their capacity to cause acute infections of the respiratory system and conjunctivae. The current intense biologic interest in these viruses derives from their ability to cause tumors in animals and to oncogenically transform cells in tissue culture, their propensity for latent infection in several types of host cells, their ability to induce or inhibit apoptosis through suppression or expression of early viral proteins, and their use as vectors for introducing foreign genes into mammalian cells of diverse types. These varied capacities are exhibited by a virus with a relatively simple genetic composition, a fact that offers the promise of resolving the mechanisms of a number of important biologic phenomena.

The adenoviruses were discovered in 1953 by Rowe and colleagues,[1] who noted that adenoidal tissues removed at the time of surgery spontaneously underwent a characteristic degeneration when maintained in culture for several weeks. An agent was isolated from these degenerating tissues, and this agent, called *adenovirus* to denote its origin, could be serially passed in epithelial cells, leading to the typical cytopathic changes that have come to be attributed to the adenovirus group (Fig. 139-1). Over the next few years, several adenovirus serotypes were isolated from adenoidal tissues in which the virus appeared to cause a latent infection.[2] Other serotypes were isolated from pulmonary secretions of young adults with acute respiratory tract disease, and still other types were isolated from the eyes of patients with conjunctivitis. In the dozen years after the initial adenovirus isolation, 31 human serotypes were isolated and characterized; several new serotypes have since been described, bringing the total to at least 51.[3] Although many serotypes have been shown to cause specific syndromes, a role in human disease remains obscure for more than half of the known types. Adenovirus types 2, 5, 7, and 12 have been the subject of intensive physical and biochemical analyses. The genetic maps of these viruses have been constructed, and functions have been assigned to most of the regions of the DNA viral genome.[4]

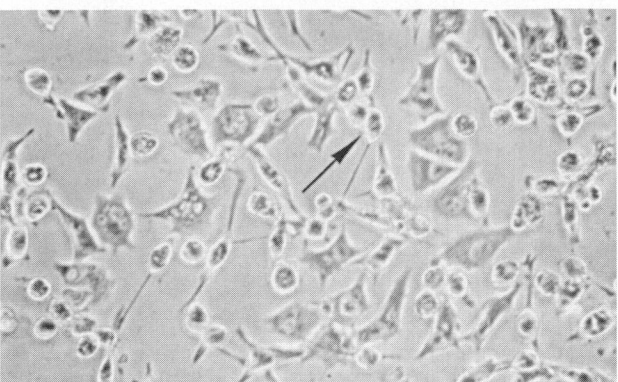

FIGURE 139-1. Typical cytopathogenic effect (CPE) seen in human epithelial cell tissue cultures 2 to 5 days after infection with adenovirus. Note the enlarged rounded cells *(arrow)* with strands connecting them to one another and to cells that have not yet begun to show CPE (phase contrast, original magnification ×400).

Viruses similar to human adenoviruses are found in many animal classes, including monkeys, bovine species, birds, and lower mammals. With the exception of avian adenoviruses, these agents share a cross-reacting group-specific antigen. All adenoviruses have similar morphology and nucleic acid composition and produce characteristic cytopathic changes in susceptible cells. The adenoviruses of lower animals play no known role in human disease.

DESCRIPTION OF THE PATHOGEN

Human adenoviruses have DNA as their genetic material. The outer covering of the virus is a protein coat, or *capsid,* which contains 252 subunits called *capsomeres.* These capsomeres are arranged in an icosahedral structure that has 20 sides and 12 vertices (Fig. 139-2). The capsid subunits are of three morphologic types. Hexons, which account for 240 of the capsomeres, have six nearest neighbors. The 12 vertices are occupied by pentons, which, as the name implies, have five nearest neighbors. Rodlike structures with knobs at the ends project from the penton base capsomeres; these rods are called *fibers.* The fiber is the attachment apparatus for viral adsorption to the cell. The cell receptor for all but the subgenus B adenovirus fibers is the same as that used by coxsackie B viruses; hence the name coxsackie-adenovirus receptor (CAR).[5] The hexons, pentons, and fibers differ from one another immunologically as well as morphologically. The hexon appears to have some antigenic sites that are common to all human adenoviruses and other sites that show type specificity. Fiber antigen seems to be primarily type specific with some group specificity, whereas the penton base antigen is common to the adenovirus family.[6] Neutralizing antibody is directed at the hexon type-specific antigen.

In addition to these surface structural proteins, there are at least 10 other proteins surrounding the DNA in the adenovirion. These proteins have been identified electrophoretically, and some play a role in maintaining the integrity of the DNA genome. Others have enzymatic activity.[6] Adenovirus DNA is double-stranded and linear and has a molecular weight of about 23×10^6. The DNA represents 10% to 15% of the mass of the virus, and the intact virion has a diameter of about 70 nm, which places it in the mid-range in size of animal viruses.[7]

In the decades since their discovery, adenoviruses have been classified variously depending on the viewpoint of the taxonomist and the state of knowledge in virology at the time. Some of these classifications and their interrelationships are given in Table 139-1. Of particular note

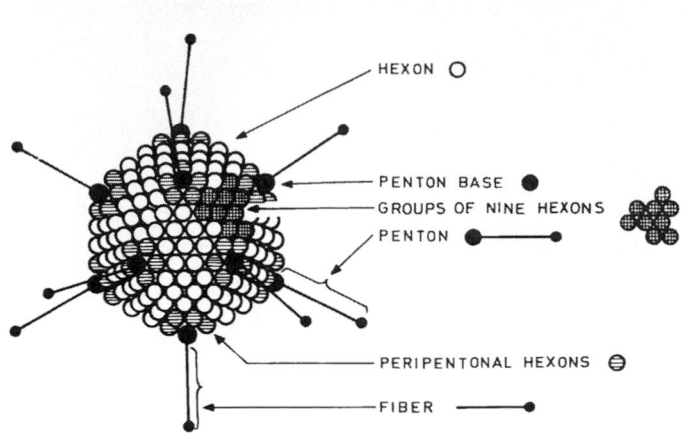

A

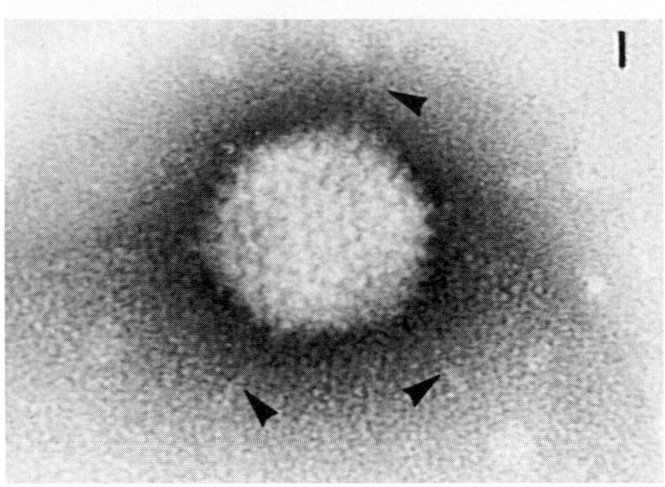

B

FIGURE 139-2. A, Adenovirion and its components. **B,** Electron micrograph of type 5 adenovirus negatively stained. (*Arrows* indicate fibers; *bar* represents 10 nm.) *(A from Philipson L, Pettersson U, Lindberg U. Molecular Biology of Adenoviruses. Virology Monographs 14. New York: Springer Publishing; 1975.)*

TABLE 139-1 Classification Schemes for Adenoviruses of Humans (Mastadenovirus h)

Subgenus[*]	Hemagglutination Groups[†]	Serotypes	Oncogenic Potential[‡]		Percentage of Guanine and Cytosine in DNA	Syndromes in Humans Associated With Some Members
			Tumors in Animals	Transformation in Tissue Culture		
A	IV (Little or no agglutination)	12, 18, 31	High	Moderate	48–49	Meningoencephalitis (T12)
B	I (Complete agglutination of monkey erythrocytes)	3, 7	Moderate	Moderate	50–52	Pharyngitis, tracheobronchitis, pneumonia, pharyngoconjunctival fever, meningoencephalitis
		11, 21				Hemorrhagic cystitis in children
		14, 16				Pneumonia, urinary tract
		34, 35[§]				and intestinal infection in
		50 (B1)[***]				immunocompromised patients
C	III (Partial agglutination of rat erythrocytes)	1, 2, 5, 6	Low or none	Low	57–59	Respiratory infection in children, intussusception
D	II (Complete agglutination of rat erythrocytes)	8, 9, 37[‖]	Low or none	Moderate	57–61	Epidemic keratoconjunctivitis
		9, 10, 13, 15, 17, 42[¶]				
		19, 20, 22–30				
		32, 33, 36[**]				
		38[††]				
		39[‡‡]				
		42[¶]				Opportunistic infection in patients
		43–47[§§]				with AIDS
		48, 49[‖‖]				
		51[***]				
E	III	4	Low or none	Low	57–59	Respiratory tract infection in children and closed populations
F		40, 41[¶]	Unknown			Enteritis and pneumonia in children

[*]According to Matthews.[8]
[†]According to Rosen.[9]
[‡]Derived from Freeman et al[10] and Ginsburg.[11]
[§]Stalder et al.[12]
[‖]Keenlyside et al.[13]
[¶]Wigand et al.[14]
[**]Wigand et al.[15]
[††]de Jong et al.[16]
[‡‡]Hierholzer et al.[17]
[§§]Hierholzer et al.[18]
[‖‖]Schnurr and Dondera.[19]
[¶]de Jong et al.[20]
[***]de Jong et al.[3]

is the association of a high oncogenic potential with a low guanine plus cytosine content in the virus DNA. The adenovirus family has now been divided into two genera: adenoviruses of mammals (mastadenoviruses) and those of birds (aviadenoviruses). Mastadenoviruses of humans have been further subdivided (see Table 139-1) on the basis of antigenicity into six subgenera (A through F) and 51 serotypes designated by the letter h (for human) and a type number (i.e., mastadenovirus h 7).[8]

The genomes of several adenovirus types have been elucidated in their entirety, and these viruses are being used extensively to analyze regulation of mammalian gene expression. The regions of the genome coding for the three capsid proteins have been identified, and the oncogenic potential of these viruses appears to reside in a small area constituting less than 10% of the genome near one end. The most intense area of research involves the use of modified adenoviruses as vectors for the insertion of genetic material into many different types of mammalian cells. Attempts at gene therapy using adenovirus vectors have been directed at regeneration of the central nervous system[21] and treatment of inherited cardiomyopathies,[22] hematopoietic malignancies,[23] cystic fibrosis,[24] and colon cancer,[25] among other entities. A complete discussion of adenovirus molecular biology is outside the scope of this chapter. Adenoviruses as vectors are the subject of several reviews,[26-28] and the molecular biology of adenoviruses is described in detail by Shenk,[4] Philipson,[29] and Horowitz.[30]

PATHOGENESIS

Adenoviruses are capable of at least three types of interaction with cells. The first is a lytic infection in which the virus goes through an entire replicative cycle.[4] Lytic infection occurs in human epithelial cells, results in cell death, and produces 10,000 to 1 million progeny viruses per cell, of which 1% to 5% are infectious.

The second interaction is a latent or chronic infection. This usually involves lymphoid cells, as in the tonsillar infection from which the virus was first isolated.[1,2] Studies have shown that monkey epithelial cells can also undergo latent infection with human adenoviruses.[30] During latent infection, only small numbers of viruses may be released, and cell death may be outstripped by cell multiplication, thereby resulting in inapparent infection. The mechanisms of latency are not clearly established.

The third type of virus–cell interaction that occurs with adenoviruses is that of oncogenic transformation.[32,33] In this situation, only the early steps in virus replication occur. The viral DNA is apparently integrated into and replicated with the cell's DNA, but no infectious virions are produced.

In all three types of infection, virus-specific proteins (T antigens) are synthesized.[31,34] These antigens indicate adenoviral presence, even in the absence of infectious virus. The T antigens are detected either by complement fixation or by immunofluorescence assays using serum from hamsters bearing tumors induced by adenovirus. The tumor cells contain large amounts of virus-specific T antigen to which the hamster makes antibody. Figure 139-3 shows the typical pattern of adenovirus T antigen as shown by immunofluorescence of human cells infected with adenoviruses.

EPIDEMIOLOGY

Human adenovirus infections are ubiquitous, although there are slight variations in the association of specific serotypes with various syndromes in different parts of the world. Primary infection with an adenovirus usually takes place in the first few years of life, and most of the population has experienced infection with one or more adenovirus serotypes by the end of the first decade.[35] The serotype of adenovirus that causes infection and the type of disease induced are closely related to the age of the patient.

Types 1, 2, 5, and 6 are frequently isolated from tonsils and adenoids of young children. Children may be asymptomatic or may have upper respiratory tract infection at the time of virus isolation, and it is clear from the work of Rowe and associates,[1] Schlesinger,[36] and others that the virus can remain latent in lymphoepithelial tissue in the nasopharynx and elsewhere. Types 3, 4, and 7 are most frequently isolated from young adults with acute upper and lower respiratory tract disease.[35] Military recruits seem particularly likely to be infected with these agents (see "Prevention"), as well as with mycoplasmal and meningococcal organisms. The reasons for these increased infection rates are probably related to crowding of a susceptible population. Infection in these cases seems to be spread by aerosols. Adenovirus types 8 and 19 have frequently been isolated from eye infections in adults,[37,38] and types 11 and 21 have been linked to infections of the lower urinary tract in children.[39,40]

Two major viral epidemiologic studies have been carried out in the United States in the past 35 years.[41,42] Both studies sought to establish the prevalence of various viruses in clinical and subclinical infections over an extended period in a large population. In each study, adenoviruses composed the largest number of isolates in children. Types 1, 2, 3, and 5 were most commonly isolated, and the stool rather than respiratory secretions was the most common source. It was estimated that 5% of all infectious illnesses in infants and 3% in children aged 2 to 4 years were caused by adenoviruses. When seroconversion rather than virus isolation was the criterion of infection, the proportion of illness caused by adenoviruses was even higher. A similar epidemiologic study using modern molecular and serologic diagnostic methods would be welcome.

CLINICAL SYNDROMES

Table 139-2 lists the syndromes caused by adenovirus serotypes.

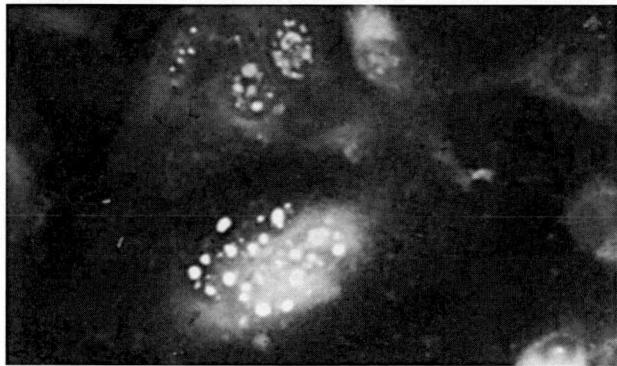

FIGURE 139-3 Adenovirus T antigen detected by immunofluorescence assay of human epithelial cells infected 24 hours earlier with adenovirus type 7 (original magnification ×500).

TABLE 139-2 Diseases Caused by Adenoviruses

Group Affected	Syndromes	Common Causal Adenovirus Serotypes
Neonates	Fatal disseminated infection	3, 7, 21, 30
Infants	Coryza, pharyngitis (most asymptomatic)	1, 2, 5
Children	Upper respiratory disease	1, 2, 4–6
	Pharyngoconjunctival fever	3, 7
	Hemorrhagic cystitis	7, 11, 21
	Diarrhea	2, 3, 5, 40, 41
	Intussusception	1, 2, 4, 5
	Meningoencephalitis	2, 6, 7, 12
Young adults	Acute respiratory disease and pneumonia	3, 4, 7
Adults	Epidemic keratoconjunctivitis	8, 19, 37
Immunocompromised patients	Pneumonia with dissemination, urinary tract infection	5, 31, 34, 35, 39
	Intestinal infection	42–51
	Central nervous system disease including encephalitis	7, 12, 32

RESPIRATORY INFECTION

In nonepidemic circumstances in the general population, at least half of the infections caused by adenovirus do not lead to clinically apparent illness.[35] On the other hand, serologic surveys have shown that about 10% of all respiratory diseases in children are caused by adenoviruses.[43] When respiratory disease in children results from infection with adenoviruses, illness usually takes the form of mild pharyngitis or tracheitis. In infants, adenovirus type 7 can cause fulminant bronchiolitis and pneumonia.[44] Some investigators have implicated adenovirus as the cause of whooping cough syndrome when *Bordetella pertussis* cannot be incriminated, and the virus has also been isolated in cases in which the bacterium was cultured.[45] Adenoviruses have been isolated more commonly than any other nonbacterial pathogen from patients with the whooping cough syndrome, although a causal relation has not been clearly established.

The first isolation of adenoviruses from patients with acute illness was in a study of military recruits in 1954.[46] The patients had a variety of influenza-like syndromes grouped under the term acute respiratory disease, and up to one fifth of these patients required hospitalization. Most of the recruits had tracheobronchitis. It was recognized that the isolates from these patients were similar to those first described by Rowe in 1953 and further characterized by Huebner and colleagues as adenoidal-pharyngeal-conjunctival viruses.[2] Serum specimens saved from patients having similar syndromes in World War II were later shown to contain antibodies against these viruses. Volunteer studies showed the incubation period to be 4 to 5 days.

Cough, fever, sore throat, and rhinorrhea are the most common signs and symptoms and usually last 3 to 5 days. Physical examination reveals pharyngitis, rales, and rhonchi commonly. Radiography of the chest in patients with pneumonia shows patchy ground-glass infiltrates primarily in the lower lung fields. The correlation between physical and radiographic findings in adenoviral pneumonia seems to be better than it is in *Mycoplasma*-induced pneumonia. In the latter condition, the extent of infiltrates on the roentgenogram is surprising because physical findings on chest examination are minimal.

Other infectious agents that cause a similar syndrome of "atypical" pneumonia are influenza and parainfluenza viruses, *Mycoplasma pneumoniae,* and the newly described variant of coronavirus causing the severe acute respiratory syndrome (SARS).[47] From cases of atypical pneumonia caused by adenoviruses, types 4 and 7 are the ones most often isolated. The disease usually is self-limited, and superinfection and death are rare.[35]

PHARYNGOCONJUNCTIVAL FEVER

In children, the best described syndrome attributed to adenoviruses is pharyngoconjunctival fever. This disease occurs in small outbreaks and is one of the most common illnesses seen by physicians at children's summer camps. It is characterized by conjunctivitis, pharyngitis, rhinitis, cervical adenitis, and temperatures to 38° C. The onset is acute, and fever and symptoms last 3 to 5 days. Bulbar and palpebral conjunctivitis may be the only finding, and the palpebral conjunctivae usually have a granular appearance. Although the onset is frequently monocular, the other eye usually becomes involved. There is little bacterial superinfection and no permanent damage to the eye.

Early reports of this syndrome in the 1950s mentioned meningismus as a prominent symptom in one sixth of the cases. At that time, this finding led to some diagnostic confusion with poliomyelitis. Today, other enteroviral infections and infectious mononucleosis should be considered in young patients with conjunctivitis and pharyngitis.

Respiratory involvement in this syndrome usually does not progress to bronchi or lungs, and bacterial superinfection is rare. Contaminated swimming pools and ponds have been implicated as sources of spread in this disease, and several studies of this syndrome have shown type 3 adenovirus to be the causative agent.[48]

EPIDEMIC KERATOCONJUNCTIVITIS

Keratoconjunctivitis occurring in epidemic form in adult populations was first ascribed to adenovirus infection by Jawetz and coworkers in 1955.[37] They showed that eyes of shipyard workers that had sustained minor trauma from paint and rust chips were frequently infected with adenovirus type 8. Other serotypes have caused sporadic cases, but the only other serotypes that have been involved in major epidemics are types 19 and 37.[13] An epidemic involving both types simultaneously has also been reported.[38] Infection in one epidemic was through the use of a roller towel for drying hands and faces.[49] Contaminated ophthalmic solutions have also provided a vector.[13]

The incubation period is 4 to 24 days, and conjunctivitis may last 1 to 4 weeks. The onset of conjunctivitis is insidious and frequently bilateral, and preauricular adenopathy is common. Keratitis begins as the conjunctivitis wanes, and the cornea may remain involved for several months and produce visual disturbance. There is secondary spread to household contacts in about 10% of the cases, with a higher incidence of secondary cases occurring with increased duration of the index case.[38] Virus can be isolated readily for at least 9 days after the onset of symptoms.[50]

HEMORRHAGIC CYSTITIS

A review of cases of hemorrhagic cystitis in Japanese and American children showed that 23% to 51% of these children had adenoviruria. Adenovirus types 11 and 21 were isolated more frequently than any other single bacterial or viral agent. Boys were affected 2 to 3 times more often than girls, whereas in bacterial hemorrhagic cystitis girls predominated. The average duration of gross hematuria was 3 days. Microscopic hematuria, dysuria, and urinary frequency persisted for several days longer.[39] Adenovirus type 7 also has been reported to cause this syndrome in children.[40] The duration and severity of the disease were increased in the Japanese compared with the American children. There was no seasonal preponderance. Serologic studies indicated a large proportion of subclinical infections with adenovirus type 11 in children.

No structural abnormalities were discovered in the sick children, and this fact, plus the predominance in boys, made it likely that the cystitis was not caused by retrograde spread from the urethra. However, no viremia was demonstrated. There have been increasing reports of hemorrhagic cystitis and tubulointerstitial nephritis in adults and children receiving renal and bone marrow transplants (BMTs). In this setting and in patients with human immunodeficiency virus (HIV) infection, subgenus B viruses (types 34 and 35) are relatively common etiologic agents[51,52,62] (see "Infections in Immunosuppressed Patients").

INFANTILE DIARRHEA

There has been much investigation of the viral cause of infantile diarrhea. Studies have shown that rotaviruses (see Chapter 146) and adenoviruses are the predominant pathogens in this disease.[53,54] Adenoviruses are readily seen in large numbers but are not culturable on standard human tissue culture cells. For in vitro culture, they require the use of tissue culture cells transformed by adenovirus[54] or Chang conjunctival cells.[53] These also have been called "enteric" or "uncultivatable" adenoviruses, but they have now been serotyped and are known as types 40 and 41 (see Table 139-1). In a 1993 study, adenovirus type 41 was the predominant serotype.[55]

Diarrhea is watery, is associated with fever, and may last for 1 to 2 weeks.

INTUSSUSCEPTION

Another intestinal syndrome in which adenoviruses have been etiologically implicated is intussusception in children. In one study, adenoviruses were the most commonly isolated agent, representing 41%

of all cases and 80% of all isolates. Serotypes 1, 2, 3, and 5 predominated, and many of the patients had a preceding or concurrent respiratory tract infection.[56] Viral isolations were, however, rarely accompanied by type-specific rises in antibody.

CENTRAL NERVOUS SYSTEM INFECTION

Encephalitis and meningoencephalitis cases occurring sporadically have been caused by adenoviruses. In addition, epidemics of central nervous system infection have occurred as complications of respiratory epidemics. Serotype 7 is most commonly found,[57] but serotypes 1, 6, and 12 are also found regularly. Pneumonia is a frequent finding in cases of adenovirus central nervous system disease. Spinal fluid findings are variable, and the values for cell count and protein and glucose levels are not helpful in establishing a diagnosis. Chronic meningoencephalitis with serotypes 7, 12, and 32 is well documented in patients with hypogammaglobulinemia.

INFECTIONS IN IMMUNOSUPPRESSED PATIENTS

Adenovirus infections have emerged as important pathogens in immunosuppressed patients, particularly in those undergoing bone marrow or solid organ transplantation.[58] Infection frequently involves the organ system transplanted (e.g., hepatitis in liver transplants, hemorrhagic cystitis in renal transplants), but disseminated disease involving the lung, colon, and central nervous system can also occur.[59-61] Disseminated disease occurs more frequently in children but also is seen in adults and is associated with a high mortality rate.[51,60] Allogeneic BMT recipients are twice as likely as autologous BMT recipients to develop hemorrhagic cystitis, and younger age, severe T-cell suppression, and isolation of adenovirus from multiple sites are the principal predictive risk factors.[58-61]

The most frequent clinical manifestations of adenovirus infection in immunocompromised patients involve the lungs, the liver, and the urinary tract. Pneumonia is most commonly interstitial and bilateral, but patchy localized infiltrates can also be seen. The reported clinical course of episodes of pneumonia is variable, ranging from fulminant hypoxic disease to a subacute illness. Hepatic involvement is also variable in severity, although in many cases, failure of hepatic function ensues, with a rapidly downhill course. In addition to hemorrhagic cystitis noted above, renal parenchymal involvement also occurs, although the contribution of adenovirus infection to renal dysfunction in individual cases is often unclear.

Adenoviruses are frequently detected in patients with acquired immunodeficiency syndrome (AIDS), most commonly in the urine or in the gastrointestinal tract. Serotypes from all subgenera have been isolated from AIDS patients, but particularly notable are types 34 and 35 (in urine) and types 42 through 50, which are highly unusual in immunocompetent patients.[17,51,60,61] The significance and spectrum of diseases associated with adenoviruses in these patients are unclear, because many patients are asymptomatic with respect to these adenoviral infections and others harbor multiple opportunistic pathogens. Diseases that have been attributed to adenovirus infections in AIDS patients include colitis,[64] parotitis,[65] and encephalitis.[66]

OTHER DISEASES INFREQUENTLY ATTRIBUTED TO ADENOVIRUSES

Fatal disseminated neonatal infections with adenovirus types 3, 7, 21, and 30 have been reported.[67]

Adenoviruses have at one time or another been implicated as a cause of pericarditis,[68] chronic interstitial fibrosis,[69] rubelliform illness,[70] and congenital anomalies.[71] Although adenovirus may be involved in these syndromes, it is unproved and unlikely that these viruses commonly play an etiologic role in any of these illnesses.

DIAGNOSIS

A diagnosis of adenoviral infection is frequently made in the proper setting on clinical criteria alone. A definitive diagnosis rests on visualization of the virus by electron microscopy,[72] isolation of the virus in tissue culture, or demonstration of adenovirus antigens in infected cells, adenoviral DNA in tissue samples or blood,[52,73] or a fourfold rise in serum antibodies to adenovirus during the course of the illness. Adenoviruses may be cultured from pharynx, sputum, stool, and conjunctival scrapings and from fresh urine in the appropriate syndromes. Viral culture is performed in monolayers of human epithelial cells, and typical cytopathogenic changes occur in 2 to 7 days, depending on the amount of virus in the inoculum. Isolated adenovirus can be grouped by hemagglutination (see Table 139-1) and then specifically serotyped. Virus can be isolated in 50% to 70% of serologically confirmed cases of respiratory disease or conjunctivitis.

Adenovirus antigens can be detected in sputum, nasopharyngeal washes, or throat swabs by immunofluorescence or enzyme-linked immunosorbent assay, which serves as a rapid diagnostic test. Adenovirus antigens also have been demonstrated in exfoliated cells in cases of epidemic keratoconjunctivitis, pharyngoconjunctival fever, and hemorrhagic cystitis. Indirect immunofluorescence correlates very well with virus isolation, is much quicker and cheaper than virus culture, and can be used to demonstrate both T antigens and capsid antigens in infected cells.[39,74]

Serologic diagnosis of adenovirus infection involves the demonstration of a fourfold rise in antibodies that fix complement, neutralize the virus, or prevent adenoviral hemagglutination or that can be detected in an enzyme-linked immunosorbent assay or by radioimmunoassay. Complement-fixing antibodies are group specific, whereas neutralizing and hemagglutination-inhibiting antibodies are type specific.

The rise in antibodies begins about 1 week after infection. As in other viral infections, complement-fixing antibodies are the earliest to fall and disappear by 1 year after infection. Neutralizing antibodies may persist for a decade or longer in relatively undiminished titer. Heterotypic reinfection may be responsible for repeated boosts of these long-lived antibodies.

Mufson and Belshe[39] reported that a single determination of neutralizing antibodies to adenovirus types 11 or 21 at a titer of greater than 1:32 in a patient with hemorrhagic cystitis may be taken as a confirmatory evidence of adenovirus-associated disease.

TREATMENT

Most adenoviral infections in immunocompetent patients are self-limited and require no or minimally supportive therapy. For severe cases, especially in immunosuppressed patients, specific antiviral therapy has been attempted with variable success. Retrospective case reports have suggested possible benefits after administration of ribavirin[75] and vidarabine.[76] Cidofovir showed promise in an animal model of ocular adenovirus disease[77] and has been used in stem cell[78] and solid organ transplant patients with adenovirus-associated disease. Although some anecdotal reports suggest benefit, the overall efficacy, if any, of cidofovir in adenovirus infections is unestablished. Nephrotoxicity has also been noted with the use of cidofovir in both normal and immunosuppressed patients. The use of human immune globulin alone, or in combination with antiviral agents, as treatment for adenovirus infection in an immunosuppressed patient has been described[79] but has not otherwise been studied.

PREVENTION

Because of the ubiquity and severity of adenovirus respiratory disease in certain populations, vaccines were developed to prevent the disease. Although these live and inactivated virus vaccines were reasonably effective, the findings that adenoviruses were oncogenic in animal models and that the adenoviruses could combine with simian virus 40 to produce an even more oncogenic hybrid virus curtailed the use of parenteral vaccines. Vaccines have also been produced by the use of capsid components free of DNA. These vaccines were effective in volunteer studies but are not currently available for general administration.[35]

Oral vaccines have been developed for use in military recruits. These vaccines contain live adenovirus types 4 and 7 in an enteric-coated capsule and are taken orally. These viruses are not attenuated but take advantage of the fact that infection of the gastrointestinal tract by these adenovirus types does not result in illness, in contrast to infection of the respiratory tract. Their efficacy and safety have been well established, and the problem of acute respiratory tract disease in recruits had been markedly diminished. However, lack of availability of this vaccine resulted in discontinuation of vaccination in 1999, and a recrudescence of epidemic adenovirus type 3, 4, and 7 infection in the military has occurred.[80,81]

ADENO-ASSOCIATED VIRUSES

Adenovirus preparations are often contaminated with a 22-nm icosahedral virus that has been called adeno-associated viruses (AAVs). These viruses have been classified as parvoviruses, and they are defective in that they require adenovirus coinfection of cells to replicate.[82] Herpesviruses and vaccinia can also provide a helper function for these viruses.[83] AAVs contain single-stranded DNA that is not homologous to adenovirus DNA and has a molecular weight of 1.4×10^6. AAVs are unique among DNA animal viruses in that complementary strands of viral DNA are made within the cell, and either strand may enter the virus particle to give rise to some virions with DNA of one polarity and others with the complementary strand. The presence of AAVs in an adenovirus preparation diminishes the infectivity of the adenovirus by an unknown mechanism.[84]

There are four serotypes of AAVs. Although they have not been implicated in any human disease, these viruses have been isolated from human pharyngeal secretions and stool, and most people have antibodies to one or another AAV serotype by 10 years of age.[85] Another parvovirus (B19) is the cause of erythema infectiosum (fifth disease) and hydrops fetalis, and causes a syndrome of arthralgias and anemia in otherwise healthy people. This may progress to aplastic crisis in patients with hemoglobinopathies[86,87] (see Chapter 143). AAVs are also under study as gene insertion vectors,[88,89] and infection with these agents has been shown to increase the sensitivity of some tumor cells to chemotherapy and radiation.[90]

REFERENCES

1. Rowe WP, Huebner RJ, Gillmore LK, et al. Isolation of a cytopathogenic agent from human adenoids undergoing spontaneous degeneration in tissue culture. Proc Soc Exp Biol Med. 1953;84:570.
2. Huebner RJ, Rowe WP, Ward TG, et al. Adenoidal-pharyngeal-conjunctival agents: A newly recognized group of common viruses of the respiratory system. N Engl J Med. 1954;251:1077.
3. De Jong JC, Wermenbol AG, Verweij-Uijterwaal MW, et al. Adenoviruses from immunodeficiency virus-infected individuals, including two strains that represent new candidate serotypes Ad50 and Ad51 of species B1 and D, respectively. J Clin Microbiol 1999;37:3940-3945.
4. Shenk T. Adenoviridae: The viruses and their replication. In: Knipe DM, Howley PM, eds. Field's Virology. 4th ed. Philadelphia: Lippincott Williams & Wilkins; 2001:2265-2300.
5. Carson SD. Receptor for the group B coxsackieviruses and adenoviruses: CAR. Rev Med Virol 2001;11:219-226.
6. Russel WC, Kemp GD. Role of adenovirus structural components in the regulation of adenovirus infection. Curr Top Microbiol Immunol. 1995;19:81-98.
7. Green M, Pina M, Kimes R, et al. Adenovirus DNA: I. Molecular weight and conformation. Proc Natl Acad Sci U S A. 1967;57:1302.
8. Matthews REF. The classification and nomenclature of viruses: Summary of results of meetings of the International Committee on Taxonomy of Viruses in Strasbourg, August 1981. Intervirology. 1981;16:53.
9. Rosen L. Hemagglutination by adenoviruses. Virology. 1958;5:574.
10. Freeman AE, Black PH, Vanderpool EA, et al. Transformation of primary rat embryo cells by adenovirus type 2. Proc Natl Acad Sci U S A. 1967;58:1205.
11. Ginsberg HS. Adenoviruses. In: Davis BD, Dulbecco R, Eisen HN, et al, eds. Microbiology. Hagerstown, Md: Harper & Row; 1980:1047.
12. Stalder H, Hierholzer JC, Oxman MN. New human adenovirus (candidate adenovirus type 35) causing fatal disseminated infection in a renal transplant recipient. J Clin Microbiol. 1977;6:257.
13. Keenlyside RA, Hierholzer JC, D'Angelo LJ. Keratoconjunctivitis associated with adenovirus type 37: An extended outbreak in an ophthalmologist's office. J Infect Dis. 1983;147:191.
14. Wigand R, Adrian T, Bricout F. A new human adenovirus of subgenus D: Candidate adenovirus type 42. Arch Virol. 1987;94:283-286.
15. Wigand R, Gelderblom H, Wadell G. New human adenovirus (candidate adenovirus 36): A novel member of subgroup D. Arch Virol. 1980;64:225.
16. de Jong JC, Wigand R, Adrian T, et al. Adenovirus 38: A new human adenovirus species of subgenus D. Intervirology. 1984;22:164-169.
17. Hierholzer JC, Kemp MC, Gary W Jr, et al. New human adenovirus associated with respiratory illness: Candidate adenovirus type 39. J Clin Microbiol. 1982;16:15-21.
18. Hierholzer JC, Wigand R, Anderson LJ, et al. Adenoviruses from patients with AIDS: A plethora of serotypes and a description of five new serotypes of subgenus D (types 43-47). J Infect Dis. 1988;158:804-813.
19. Schnurr D, Dondera ME. Two new candidate adenovirus serotypes. Intervirology. 1993;36:79-83.
20. de Jong JC, Wigand R, Kidd AH, et al. Candidate adenoviruses from human infant stool. J Med Virol. 1983;11:215.
21. Verhaagen J, Hermens WT, Dijkhuizen PA, et al. Use of viral vectors to promote neuroregeneration. Clin Neurosci. 1996;3:275-283.
22. Bowles NE, Wang Q, Towbin JA. Prospects for adenovirus-mediated gene therapy of inherited diseases of the myocardium. Cardiovasc Res. 1997;35:422-430.
23. Huang MR, Olsson M, Kallin A, et al. Efficient adenovirus-mediated gene transduction of normal and leukemic hematopoietic cells. Gene Ther. 1997;4:1093-1099.
24. Bellon G. Cystic fibrosis (CF) gene therapy. Pediatr Pulmonol. 1997;16:278-279.
25. Ogawa N, Fujiwara T, Kagawa S, et el. Novel combination therapy for human colon cancer with adenovirus-mediated wild-type p53 gene transfer and DNA-damaging chemotherapeutic agent. Int J Cancer. 1997;73:367-370.
26. Brody SL, Crystal RG. Adenovirus-mediated in vivo gene transfer. Ann N Y Acad Sci. 1994;716:90-101.
27. Miller N, Vile R. Targeted vectors for gene therapy. FASEB J. 1995;9:190-199.
28. Ilan Y, Droguett G, Chowdhury NR, et al. Insertion of a recombinant viral vector prevents antiviral humoral and cellular immune responses and permits long-term gene expression. Proc Natl Acad Sci U S A. 1997;94:2587-2592.
29. Philipson L. Adenovirus: An eternal archetype. Curr Top Microbial Immunol. 1995;99:1-24.
30. Horowitz MS. Adenoviruses. In: Knipe DM, Howley PM, eds. Field's Virology. 4th ed. Philadelphia: Lippincott Williams & Wilkins; 2001:2301-2326.
31. Baum SG. Persistent adenovirus infections of nonpermissive monkey cells. J Virol. 1977;23:412.
32. Huebner RJ, Rowe WP, Lane WT. Oncogenic effects in hamsters of human adenoviruses types 12 and 18. Proc Natl Acad Sci U S A. 1962;48:2051.
33. Trentin JJ, Yabe Y, Taylor G. The quest for human cancer viruses. Science. 1962;137:835.
34. Pope JH, Rowe WP. Immunofluorescent studies of adenovirus 12 tumors and of cells transformed or infected by adenovirus. J Exp Med. 1964;120:577.
35. Knight V, Kasel JA. Adenoviruses. In: Knight V, ed. Viral and Mycoplasmal Infections of the Respiratory Tract. Philadelphia: Lea & Febiger; 1973:65.
36. Schlesinger RW. Adenoviruses: The nature of the virion and controlling factors in productive or abortive infection and tumorigenesis. Adv Virus Res. 1969;14:1.
37. Jawetz E, Kimura S, Nicholas AN, et al. New type of APC virus from epidemic keratoconjunctivitis. Science. 1955;122:1190.
38. Guyer B, O'Day DM, Hierholzer JC, et al. Epidemic keratoconjunctivitis: A community outbreak of mixed adenovirus type 8 and type 19 infection. J Infect Dis. 1975;132:142.
39. Mufson MA, Belshe RB. A review of adenoviruses in the etiology of acute hemorrhagic cystitis. J Urol. 1976;115:191.
40. Lee H-J, Pyo J-W, Choi E-H, et al. Isolation of adenovirus type 7 from the urine of children with acute hemorrhagic cystitis. Pediatr Infect Dis J. 1996;7:633-634.
41. Fox JP, Brandt CD, Wasserman FE, et al. The Virus Watch Program: A continuing surveillance of viral infections in metropolitan New York families. Am J Epidemiol. 1969;89:25.
42. Fox JP, Hall CE, Cooney M. The Seattle virus watch: VII. Observations of adenovirus infections. Am J Epidemiol. 1977;105:362.
43. Brandt CD, Hyun WK, Vargosko AJ, et al. Infections in 18,000 infants and children in a controlled study of respiratory tract disease: I. Adenovirus pathogenicity in relation to serologic type and illness syndrome. Am J Epidemiol. 1969;90:484.
44. Angella JJ, Connor JD. Neonatal infection caused by adenovirus type 7. J Pediatr. 968;72:474.
45. Olson LC. Pertussis. Medicine (Baltimore). 1975;54:427.
46. Hilleman MR, Werner JH. Recovery of a new agent from patients with acute respiratory illness. Proc Exp Biol Med. 1954;85:183.
47. Drosten C, Gunther S, Preiser W, et al. Identification of a novel coronavirus in patients with severe acute respiratory syndrome. N Engl J Med 2003;348:1967-1976.
48. Sobel G, Aronson B, Aronson S, et al. Pharyngoconjunctival fever. Am J Dis Child. 1956;92:596.
49. Sprague JB, Hierholzer JC, Currier RW II, et al. Epidemic keratoconjunctivitis: A severe industrial outbreak due to adenovirus type 8. N Engl J Med. 1973;289:1341.
50. Koc J, Wigand R, Weil M. The efficacy of various laboratory methods for the diagnosis of adenovirus conjunctivitis. Zentralbl Bakteriol Mikrobiol Hyg [A]. 1987;263:607-615.
51. Kojaoghlanian T, Flomenberg P, Horwitz MS. The impact of adenovirus infection on the immunocompromised host. Rev Med Virol. 2003;13:1-17.

52. Akiyama H, Korosu T, Sakashita C, et al. Adenovirus is a key pathogen in hemorrhagic cystitis associated with bone marrow transplantation. Clin Infect Dis. 2001;32:1325-1330.

53. Kidd M, Cosgrove BP, Brown RA, et al. Faecal adenoviruses from Glasgow babies. J Hyg (Camb). 1982;88:463.

54. Yolken RH, Lawrence F, Leister F, et al. Gastroenteritis associated with enteric type adenovirus in hospitalized infants. J Pediatr. 1982;101:21.

55. deJong JC, Bijlsma K, Wermenbol AG, et al. Detection, typing and subtyping of enteric adenoviruses 40 and 41 from fecal samples and observation of changing incidences of infections with these types and subtypes. J Clin Microbiol. 1993;31:1562-1569.

56. Montgomery EA, Popek EJ. Intussusception, adenovirus and children: A brief reaffirmation. Hum Pathol. 1994;25:169-174.

57. Simila S, Jouppila R, Salmi A, et al. Encephalomeningitis in children associated with an adenovirus type 7 epidemic. Acta Pediatr Scand. 1970;59:310.

58. Howard DS, Phillips GL II, Reece DE, et al. Adenovirus infections in hematopoietic stem cell transplant recipients. Clin Infect Dis. 1999;29:1494-1501.

59. Whimbey E, Champlin RE, Couch RB. Community respiratory virus infections among hospitalized adult bone marrow transplant recipients. Clin Infect Dis. 1996;22:778-782.

60. Flomenberg P, Babbitt J, Drobyski WR. Increasing incidence of adenovirus disease in bone marrow transplant recipients. J Infect Dis. 1994;169:775-781.

61. Michael MG, Green M, Wald ER, et al. Adenovirus infection in pediatric liver transplant recipients. J Infect Dis. 1992;165:170-174.

62. Flomenberg PR, Chen M, Munk G, et al. Molecular epidemiology of adenovirus type 35 infections in immunocompromised hosts. J Infect Dis. 1987;155:1127-1134.

63. Khoo SH, Bailey AS, deJong JC. Adenovirus infections in human immunodeficiency virus-positive patients: Clinical features and molecular epidemiology. J Infect Dis. 1995;172:629-637.

64. Janoff EN, Orenstein JM, Manischewitz JF, et al. Adenovirus colitis in the acquired immunodeficiency syndrome. Gastroenterology. 1991;100:976-979.

65. Gelfand MS, Cleveland KO, Lancaster D, et al. Adenovirus parotitis in patients with AIDS. Clin Infect Dis. 1994;19:1045-1048.

66. Schnurr D, Bollen A, Crawford-Miksza L, et al. Adenovirus mixture isolated from the brain of an AIDS patient with encephalitis. J Med Virol. 1995;47:168-171.

67. Abzug MJ, Levine MJ. Neonatal adenovirus infection: Four patients and review of the literature. Pediatrics. 1991;87:890-896.

68. Rahal JJ, Millian SJ, Noriega ER. Coxsackie and adenovirus infection. Association with acute febrile and juvenile rheumatoid arthritis. JAMA. 1976;235:2496.

69. Kawai T, Fujiwara T, Aoyama Y, et al. Diffuse interstitial fibrosing pneumonitis and adenovirus infection. Chest. 1976;69:692.

70. Gutekunst RR, Heggie AD. Viremia and viruria in adenovirus infection: Detection in patients with rubella and rubelliform illness. N Engl J Med. 1961;264:374.

71. Evans TN, Brown GC. Congenital anomalies and virus infection. Am J Obstet Gynecol. 1963;87:749.

72. Madely CR, Cosgrove BP, Bell EJ, et al. Stool viruses in babies in Glasgow. J Hyg (Lond). 1977;78:261.

73. Kidd AH, Jonsson M, Garwicz D. Rapid subgenus identification of human adenovirus isolates by a general PCR. J Clin Microbiol. 1996;34:622-627.

74. Schwartz HS, Vastine DW, Yamashiroya H, et al. Immunofluorescent detection of adenovirus antigen in epidemic keratoconjunctivitis. Invest Ophthalmol. 1976;15:199.

75. Aebi C, Headrick CL, McCracken GH Jr, et al. Intravenous ribavirin therapy in a neonate with disseminated adenovirus infection undergoing extracorporeal membrane oxygenation: Pharmacokinetics and clearance by hemofiltration. J Pediatr. 1997;130:612-615.

76. Kitabayashi A, Hirokawa M, Kuroki J, et al. Successful vidarabine therapy for adenovirus type II-associated acute hemorrhagic cystitis after allogeneic bone marrow transplantation. Bone Marrow Transplant. 1994;14:853-854.

77. Gordon YJ, Romanowski E, Araullo-Cruz T, et al. Pretreatment with topical 0.2% (S)-1-(3-hydroxy-2-phosphonylmethoxypropyl) cytosine inhibits adenovirus type 5 replication in the New Zealand rabbit ocular model. Cornea. 1992;11:529-533.

78. Legrand F, Berrebi D, Houhou N, et al. Early diagnosis of adenovirus infection and treatment with cidofovir after bone marrow transplantation in children. Bone Marrow Transplant. 2001;27:621-626.

79. Dagan R, Schwartz RH, Insel RA, et al. Severe diffuse adenovirus 7a pneumonia in a child with combined immunodeficiency: Possible therapeutic effect of human immune serum globulin containing specific neutralizing antibody. Pediatr Infect Dis J. 1984;3:246.

80. Ryan MAK, Gray GC, Smith B, et al. Large epidemic of respiratory illness due to adenovirus types 7 and 3 in healthy young adults. Clin Infect Dis. 2002;34:577-582.

81. Kolavic-Gray SA, Binn LN, Sanchez JL, et al. Large epidemic of adenovirus type 4 infection among military trainees: Epidemiological, clinical and laboratory studies. Clin Infect Dis. 2002;35:808-818.

82. Ward P, Dean FB, O'Donnell ME. Role of the adenovirus DNA-binding protein in in vitro adeno-associated virus DNA replication. J Virol. 1998;72:420-427.

83. Schlehofer JR, Ehbar M, zur-Hausen H. Vaccinia virus, herpes simplex virus and carcinogens induce DNA amplification in a human cell line and support replication of helper virus dependent parvovirus. Virology. 1986;152:110-117.

84. Hoggan MD, Blacklow NR, Rowe WP. Studies of small DNA viruses found in various adenovirus preparations: Physical, biological and immunological characteristics. Proc Natl Acad Sci U S A. 1966;55:1467.

85. Parks WP, Boucher DW, Melnick JL, et al. Seroepidemiological and ecological studies of the adenovirus associated satellite viruses. Infect Immun. 1970;2:716-722.

86. Anderson MJ. Human parvovirus infections. J Virol Methods. 1987;17:175-181.

87. Conrad JR, Studdard H, Anderson LJ. Aplastic crisis in sickle cell disorders: Bone marrow necrosis and human parvovirus infection. Am J Med Sci. 1988;295:212-215.

88. Dunbar CE. Gene transfer to hematopoietic stem cells: Implications for gene therapy of human disease. Annu Rev Med. 1996;47:11-20.

89. Xiao X, Li J, Samulski RJ. Production of high-titer recombinant adeno-associated virus vectors in the absence of helper adenovirus. J Virol. 1998;72:2224-2232.

90. Hillenberg M, Schlehofer JR, Doeberitz M, et al. Enhanced sensitivity of small cell lung cancer cell lines to cisplatin and etoposide after infection with adeno-associated virus type 2. Eur J Cancer. 1999;35:106-110.

CHAPTER **140**

Papillomaviruses

WILLIAM BONNEZ

RICHARD C. REICHMAN

Papillomaviruses have been detected in a variety of vertebrates. Human papillomaviruses (HPVs) are widespread throughout the population, produce epithelial tumors of the skin and mucous membranes, and have been closely associated with genital tract malignancies. HPVs are highly species specific, and cross-species infections do not occur even under experimental conditions. The infectious nature of human warts was initially demonstrated in the late 19th century when human wart extracts were shown to produce warts when injected into humans. Ciuffo suggested that the infectious agent of warts was a virus after he was able to transmit the infection, through cell-free filtrates, in 1907.[1] Despite these early observations, HPVs have not been studied by standard virologic techniques because they have not been propagated successfully in tissue culture or in standard laboratory animals. For this reason, much of our knowledge of the biology of HPVs and the diseases with which they are associated has depended on the use of molecular biologic techniques. These techniques have led to an understanding of the genomic organization of these viruses, the functions of different viral genes, and the multiplicity of HPV types. Detailed reviews of these subjects are available.[2-9]

VIROLOGY

Papillomaviruses constitute the *Papillomavirus* genus of the Papillomaviridae. They are nonenveloped viruses that are 55 nm in diameter and have an icosahedral capsid composed of 72 capsomeres enclosing a double-stranded, circular DNA genome. Virion particles contain at least two capsid proteins. The major capsid protein constitutes 80% of the virion by weight and has a molecular weight of about 56,000. The minor capsid protein has a molecular weight of approximately 76,000.

The HPV genome consists of approximately 7900 base pairs. All putative coding sequences (open reading frames [ORFs]) are arranged on one DNA strand, and all papillomaviruses share the same genomic organization.[4] Specific protein products are derived from these ORFs. However, analyses of viral messenger RNA (mRNA) transcripts suggest that most viral proteins derive from splicing of more than one ORF-specific mRNA. The genome is divided functionally into three regions. A noncoding, upstream regulatory region contributes to the control of DNA replication and transcription of eight to nine ORFs that are divided into "early" (E1 to E7) and "late" (L1 and L2) regions.[4] E1 is involved in viral plasmid replication. The E2 product is an important modulator of viral transcription and also plays a role in viral replication. E4 proteins form filamentous cytoplasmic networks and share the same cellular distribution as cytokeratin intermediate filaments, with which they may interact. They appear to play a role in viral replication. The E5 protein is located in the cellular membrane and prevents the acidification of endosomes. This stimulates the transforming activity of the epidermal growth factor receptor and contributes to the oncogenicity of HPV.[7,8,10] The gene products of E6 and E7 of oncogenic HPV types have major transforming properties through the binding of various cellular factors and key tumor suppressor proteins.[7,8,10] The E6 protein binds to the p53 tumor suppressor gene product and abrogates its activity by accelerating its degradation. The E7 protein also binds to a tumor suppressor gene product, the retinoblastoma protein, and to related proteins, thus inhibiting their functions. The L1 and L2 ORFs encode the major and minor capsid proteins, respectively.

Although the genomes of several papillomaviruses can transform certain cell lines in tissue culture, the replicative cycle of HPV has not yet been completely reproduced in vitro. However, HPV virions can be recovered in vitro from naturally infected or experimentally transfected keratinocytes by induction of terminal differentiation of the cells.[11-14] In addition, HPV types 6, 11, 16, 40, and 59 have been propagated successfully in human skin grafted in the athymic (nude) mouse or the severe combined immunodeficiency mouse.[15,16] HPV-infected grafts recovered from these animals can maintain viral particle production in vitro.[17]

Virions of most HPV types cannot be purified from naturally occurring lesions in significant quantities, and well-characterized, type-specific antigens have not been available until recently.[18] Therefore, types are determined according to the degree of nucleic acid sequence homology rather than by serologic techniques. Distinct HPV types share less than 90% of their DNA sequences in the L1 ORF. At least 92 HPV types have now been characterized, and many others have been recognized. HPVs are host specific, and each type is, to a large extent, associated with a distinct histopathologic process (Table 140-1).

Broadly cross-reactive, genus-specific antigenic determinants, located in the middle of the major capsid protein,[19] can be prepared by denaturation of viral particles, typically from bovine papillomavirus, with detergents and reducing agents. Antisera prepared against this papillomavirus *common antigen* have been used in the immunocytochemical diagnosis of HPV infections (see "Diagnosis").[20] The antigenic characteristics of native viral particles can also be studied by the use of virus-like particles (VLPs). These are obtained by the expression in eukaryotic systems of the L1 or L1 and L2 ORFs (see "Prevention"). There appears to be a close correlation between genotype and serotype.[18]

EPIDEMIOLOGY

Incidence and Prevalence

Although clinical HPV infections are the most recognizable and most important for the patient and practitioner, subclinical and asymptomatic—latent—infections are probably most common, and past HPV infections represent an even larger group.[21-23] The study of these different types of infection poses different technical problems, and their respective interrelated epidemiologies are not equally well understood.

As Table 140-1 illustrates, HPV infections can also be divided according to their predominant anatomic location. Thus, one recognizes the "genital" or "mucosal" infections as distinct from the nongenital infections, which include the "cutaneous" infections.

Three types of cutaneous HPV infections are widespread throughout the general population.[24] Common warts, which represent up to 71% of all cutaneous warts, occur frequently among school-aged children, with prevalence rates of 4% to 20%.[25,26] Although less common (34% of cutaneous warts), plantar warts are observed frequently among adolescents and young adults. Juvenile or flat warts are the least common of the three types (4%) and occur predominantly in children. Other groups at high risk for the development of cutaneous warts include butchers, meat packers, and fish handlers.[27] Epidermodysplasia verruciformis is a rare, probably autosomal recessive condition characterized by the appearance early in life of disseminated cutaneous warts and frequent malignant transformation.[28,29]

TABLE 140-1 Human Papillomavirus Types and Their Disease Association

	Human Papillomavirus (HPV) Types*	
Disease	Frequent Association	Less Frequent Association
Plantar warts	1, 2	4, 63
Common warts	2, 1	4, 26,[†] 27, 29, 41,[‡] 57, 65, 77[‡]
Common warts of meat, poultry, and fish handlers	7, 2	1, 3, 4, 10, 28
Flat and intermediate warts	3, 10	26, 27,[†] 28, 38, 41,[‡] 49,[‡] 75, 76
Epidermodysplasia verruciformis	2, 3, 10, 5,[‡] 8,[‡] 9, 12, 14,[‡] 15, 17[‡]	19, 20,[‡§] 21, 22, 23, 24, 25, 36, 37, 38,[‡] 47,[‡] 50
Condylomata acuminata	6, 11	30,[‡] 42, 43, 44, 45,[‡] 51,[‡] 54, 55, 70[‡]
Intraepithelial neoplasia, unspecified		30,[‡] 34, 39,[‡] 40, 53, 54, 57, 59,[‡] 61, 62, 64, 66,[‡] 67,[‡] 68,[‡] 69, 71, 72, 82[‡]
Low grade	6, 11	16,[‡] 18,[‡] 31,[‡] 33,[‡] 35,[‡] 42, 43, 44, 45,[‡] 51,[‡] 52,[‡] 54, 61, 70, 72, 74,[†] 81, 83, 84, 86, 87, 89, 90, 91
High grade	16,[‡] 18[‡]	6, 11, 26,[‡] 31,[‡] 34, 33,[‡] 35,[‡] 39,[‡] 42, 44, 45,[‡] 51,[‡] 52,[‡] 53,[‡] 56,[‡] 58,[‡] 66[‡]
Cervical carcinoma	16,[‡] 18[‡]	26,[‡] 31,[‡] 33,[‡] 35,[‡] 39,[‡] 45,[‡] 51,[‡] 52,[‡] 53,[‡] 56,[‡] 58,[‡] 59,[‡] 68,[‡] 73,[‡] 82[‡]
Recurrent respiratory papillomatosis	6, 11	16,[‡] 18,[‡] 31,[‡] 33,[‡] 35,[‡] 39[‡]
Focal epithelial hyperplasia of Heck	13, 32	
Conjunctival papillomas and carcinomas	6, 11, 16[‡]	
Other cutaneous lesions[‖]		6, 11, 16,[‡¶] 30,[‡] 33,[‡] 36, 37, 38,[‡] 41,[‡] 48,[†‡] 60, 72,[†] 73[†]

*The distinction between frequent and less frequent association is arbitrary in many instances. Large descriptive statistics of HPV type distribution by disease are not available for the majority of HPV types. Moreover, many HPV types have been looked for or identified only once.

†Types first recovered from immunosuppressed patients.

‡Types with high malignant potential or isolated in only one or a few lesions that were malignant.

§HPV46 was found to be HPV20.

‖Includes epidermoid cysts, keratoacanthoma, laryngeal carcinoma, and malignant melanoma.

¶Kaposi's sarcoma and normal and neoplastic prostatic tissues.

The authors are grateful to Dr. Ethel-Michele de Villiers for sharing information. Further information on HPV DNA sequences and novel isolates is available on the World Wide Web at http://hpv-web.lanl.gov

Genital HPV infections have an estimated annual incidence of 5.5 million and, thus, are the most commonly acquired viral sexually transmitted disease (STD) in the United States.[30] At least three quarters of the population may have been infected in their lifetime.[21] The prevalence of condyloma acuminatum (pl., condylomata acuminata), or anogenital warts (venereal warts), in the general population is approximately 1%.[21] The incidence of the disease has risen. The annual number of initial visits to physicians' offices for genital warts rose eightfold between 1966 and 1988, then fell from 348,000 to 145,000 from 1988 to 1997, but increased up to 264,000 in 2002.[31] In an STD clinic setting in the United Kingdom, the rate of attendance for genital warts grew by 390% for men and 594% for women from 1971 to 1994.[32] This trend was maintained 4 years later.[33] Smaller studies in better-defined populations of patients have also shown dramatic increases in the prevalence of this disease.[34,35] It is estimated that approximately 500,000 persons each year acquire symptomatic genital warts.[36] HPV infection of the cervix gives rise to the most common cause of squamous cell abnormalities on Papanicolaou (Pap) smears.[37-39]

Prevalence data on recurrent respiratory papillomatosis, which is primarily a disease of the larynx, are not available, but the rate is estimated to be 11 per 100,000 for the juvenile-onset form of the disease and 4.5 per 100,000 for the adult-onset form.[40] Annual incidence rates are about 2.5-fold less.[40]

Transmission

Close personal contact is assumed to be important for the transmission of most cutaneous warts, although strong epidemiologic evidence for this assumption is lacking.[27,41] Minor trauma at the site of inoculation may also be important, as suggested by the high frequency of disease among meat handlers.[27]

Evidence that anogenital warts are sexually transmitted includes the observations that the age of onset is similar to that in other STDs and that the disease develops in approximately two thirds of sexual contacts of patients with anogenital warts.[42,43] In addition, patients with anogenital warts often have other concomitant STDs or a history of such infections. Also, as outlined in Table 140-1, particular HPV types are associated with these lesions. These types are rarely found at other sites. Finally, having a large number of sexual partners is associated with greater risk of condylomata acuminata or HPV infection of the cervix.[44-46] Despite these observations in adults, it appears that young children may acquire genital warts from hand contact with nongenital lesions.[47] Approximately one fifth of prepubertal children with condyloma acuminatum have HPV type 1 or 2 in their lesions.[48-50] Conversely, HPV6 DNA has been identified in cutaneous warts of family contacts of children with anogenital warts.[49]

Recurrent respiratory papillomatosis in young children is thought to be acquired by passage through an infected birth canal.[40] This hypothesis is based on the observations that similar HPV types are associated with both respiratory papillomatosis and anogenital warts and that a large percentage of the mothers of these children have a history of genital tract HPV disease.[40,51] In addition, neonates are more likely to harbor HPV DNA in their oral cavity if the cervix of the mother contains HPV DNA.[40] Many children with recurrent respiratory papillomatosis are first-born babies who were delivered vaginally to young (often teenaged) mothers. Although the median age of onset of recurrent respiratory papillomatosis is 3 years, cases have been documented at birth, even after cesarean section.[40] This observation suggests that the disease may be acquired in utero, probably by ascending infection from the mother's genital tract. The role of cesarean section, if any, in prevention of transmission is unknown, and the procedure is not recommended for that purpose.[40] Family members and others having close personal contact with these patients are not at risk for development of the disease. In the adult-onset form, recurrent respiratory papillomatosis is associated with a higher than expected number of lifetime sexual partners and with oral-genital contact.[40]

The role of fomites in the transmission of HPV infection is uncertain. However, nosocomial transmission appears possible because infectious virus can be recovered from the fumes released from lesions during treatment with carbon dioxide laser or electrocoagulation.[52] In addition, HPVs are resistant to heat, and use of an autoclave is probably necessary for sterilization of contaminated instruments.[53,54]

Association between Human Papillomavirus and Malignancies

The oncogenic potential of animal papillomaviruses was demonstrated many years ago.[55,56] Observations of patients with epidermodysplasia verruciformis provided the initial evidence suggesting that HPVs might also be carcinogenic. In these patients, characteristic skin lesions induced by specific HPV types frequently undergo malignant transformation, particularly when they occur in sun-exposed areas.[23] Most research investigating the oncogenic potential of HPVs has focused on genital tract malignancies.

A variety of clinical and epidemiologic observations suggest that a sexually transmissible agent is important in the pathogenesis of cancer of the uterine cervix. These observations include the low prevalence of cervical cancer among Catholic nuns,[57] the direct association of risk with number of sexual partners, and the increased risk of malignancy that is associated with having a male sexual partner whose previous consort had developed cervical cancer.[58-60] A history of condyloma acuminatum has also been linked prospectively with the development of cervical and other anogenital cancers.[61]

The causal role of HPV in cervical cancer is supported by several arguments[62]:

1. Virtually all cervical cancers contain HPV DNA, usually of type 16, 18, 31, or 45.[63-66]
2. The same HPV types are also found in the precursor lesions or cervical intraepithelial neoplasias (CINs).[63]
3. There is an increasing prevalence of high-risk HPV genotypes relative to low-risk ones with higher grades of CIN.[63]
4. HPV mRNA has been detected in cervical cancer tissues, indicating that the HPV genome is expressed in these lesions.[67,68]
5. The prevalence of antibodies to HPV16, HPV18, HPV31, HPV33, HPV39, HPV58, and HPV59 VLPs in the sera of patients with cervical cancer is higher than that in control sera.[69,70]
6. Infection by high-risk HPV types is not simply associated with progression of CIN but precedes it.[71,72] Two years after enrollment in a prospective cohort study of women with normal cervical cytology, the cumulative incidence of CIN was 28% among women with cervical HPV DNA compared with 3% among those without detectable HPV DNA.[71] Moreover, the risk of developing CIN was 11-fold greater among women with HPV type 16 or 18 than among women without HPV DNA.
7. It is persistent rather than transient exposure to HPV16 that is associated with a risk for cervical carcinoma in situ, indicating that disappearance of the causal agent reduces the risk of disease.[73,74]
8. No risk factor for incipient or invasive cervical cancer approaches the strength and consistency of HPV infections.[75]
9. Finally, immunization against HPV16 confers protection not only against HPV16 infection but also against HPV16–associated CIN.[76]

Similar lines of evidence, although not necessarily as strong, also implicate HPV as a major risk factor in the development of at least some vaginal, vulvar, anal, and penile squamous cell cancers.[77-82] The association of HPV with cancer is not limited to squamous cell carcinomas but also applies to at least a subset of cervical adenocarcinomas, especially with HPV18.[83-85] The association of HPV with squamous cell carcinomas is not limited to the anogenital area but also involves the aerodigestive tract (nose and paranasal sinuses, oropharynx, and esophagus), the conjunctiva, and the skin with respect to nonmelanoma skin cancers.[23,86-89]

Infection with a high-risk HPV appears to be necessary for the development of cervical cancer, but it is not necessarily a sufficient condition. Several cofactors are suspected to play an important role in the development of cervical cancer. They include multiparity, tobacco smoking, long-term usage of oral contraceptives, cervical inflammation (particularly when associated with *Chlamydia trachomatis* infection), antioxidant nutrients, and immunosuppression.[80,90-93] Immunogenetic factors are also implicated.[94] For example, an increased risk of cervical cancer has been associated with human leukocyte antigen (HLA) class II alleles DRB1*0401-DQB1*0301 and DRB1*1101-DQB1*0301, and a decreased risk has been identified with DRB1*0301-DQB1*02 and DRB1*13-DQB1*06.[95] The intriguing finding that having had common warts in childhood is associated with an increased risk of subsequent cervical cancer also suggests the existence of an innate susceptibility to HPV infection.[96]

PATHOGENESIS

The pathogenesis of HPV disease has been reviewed by several authors.[7,8,10] The incubation period was established experimentally by inoculation of human subjects with extracts of cutaneous warts.[1,97] Most

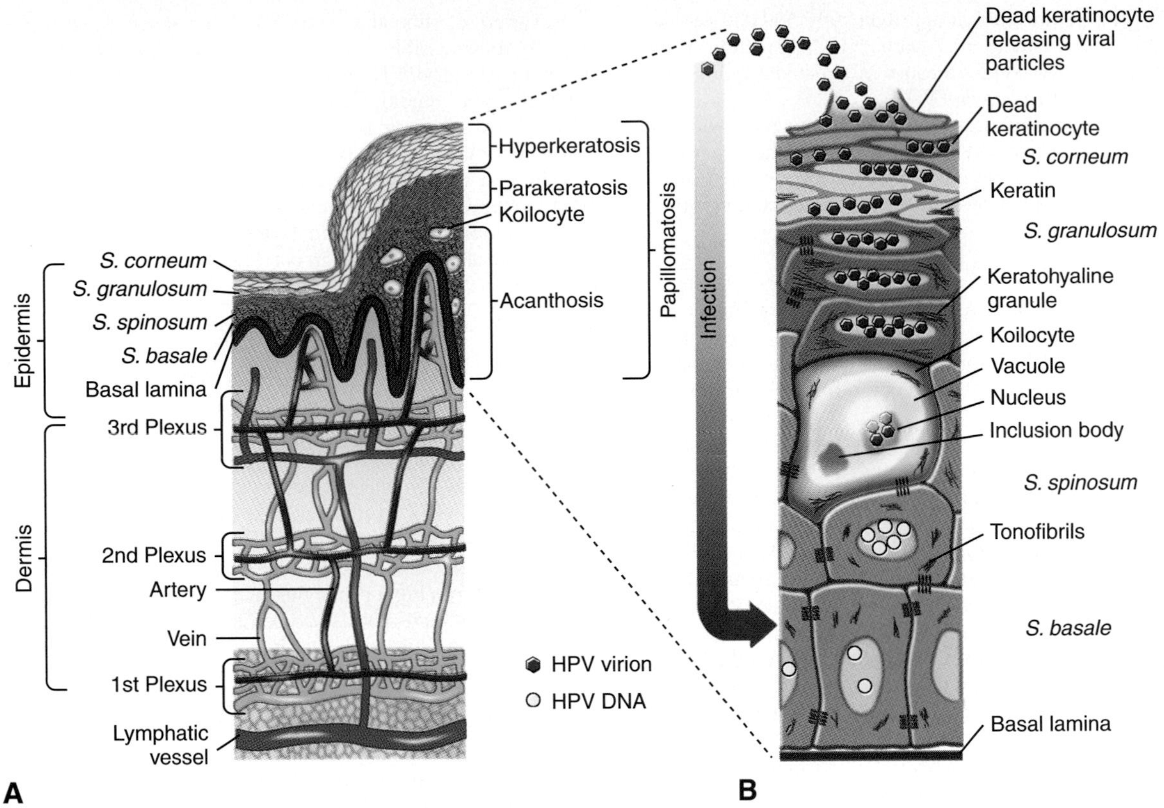

FIGURE 140-1. Exophytic cutaneous wart: human papillomavirus (HPV) pathogenesis. **A,** Histologic features. **B,** Cytologic features (see text for details). S., stratum.

often, warts developed within 3 to 4 months, although lesions occasionally grew as early as 6 weeks or as long as 2 years after inoculation. A similar incubation period was observed for genital warts among wives of American soldiers returning from the Korean War.[98] All types of squamous epithelium may be infected by HPV, but other tissues appear to be relatively resistant. Gross histologic appearances of individual lesions vary with the site of infection and the virus type. Figure 140-1 is a schematic diagram of a typical exophytic, cutaneous wart.

Although little is known about the first stage of HPV infection, it is assumed that the virus replicative cycle begins with the entry of particles into the stratum germinativum (basale) because viral DNA is detected in the nuclei of the basal cells.[67] As the basal cells differentiate and progress to the surface of the epithelium, HPV DNA replicates and is transcribed and viral particles are assembled in the nucleus. Ultimately, complete virions are released, probably still tightly associated with the remnants of the shed dead keratinocyte shell.[99] In a wart or condyloma, viral replication is associated with excessive proliferation of all of the epidermal layers except the basal layer. This process produces acanthosis, parakeratosis, and hyperkeratosis. There is also, where normally present, a deepening of the rete ridges, which produces the typical papillomatous cytoarchitecture. Some infected cells undergo the characteristic transformation of koilocytosis. By histology, koilocytes (from the Greek *koilos*, "cavity") are large, usually polygonal, squamous cells with a shrunken nucleus lodged inside a large cytoplasmic vacuole. Cytoplasmic keratohyalin inclusion bodies may also be observed. Excessive proliferation of the basal-like cells (basaloid proliferation) with a high nuclear/cytoplasmic ratio, accompanied by a high number of mitoses, some abnormal (dyskaryosis), is a feature of incipient and malignant HPV disease.

Normal-appearing epithelium may contain HPV DNA,[100,101] and the presence of residual DNA after the treatment of warts may lead to recurrent disease.

In benign lesions caused by HPV, viral DNA is located extrachromosomally in the nuclei of infected cells. However, when HPV DNA is detected in high-grade intraepithelial neoplasias and cancers, it is generally integrated.[3,7,8,10] Integration of HPV DNA may occur at preferential sites in host cell chromosomes,[3,102] and it specifically disrupts the E2 ORF. Interruption of E2 probably plays a role in the pathogenesis of malignancy because expression of this ORF normally leads to downregulation of E6 and E7, whose products interfere with the p53 and retinoblastoma tumor suppressor proteins (see "Virology").[3,7,8,10] Additional potential mechanisms of HPV oncogenicity include induction of chromosomal instability, cooperation with activated oncogenes, methylation of viral and cellular DNA sites, telomerase activation, and hormonal and immunogenetic factors.[3,7,8,10,94]

Host defense responses to HPV infection are poorly understood. Nevertheless, several clinical observations suggest that an effective immune system is important in the resolution of HPV infection. HPV diseases occur frequently and are often severe in patients with both primary and secondary immunodeficiencies (e.g., Wiskott-Aldrich syndrome, common variable immunodeficiency).[103] Severe, frequent HPV disease is also seen in patients with lymphoproliferative disorders and in those with human immunodeficiency virus (HIV) infections.[23,80,93,104-107] The range of HPV-related diseases in HIV infection includes anogenital warts, CIN in women, and anal intraepithelial neoplasia and cancer in homosexual men.[80,93,104] The prevalence of these conditions is greater with low counts of CD4+ T lymphocytes and high HIV-1 RNA levels. Compared with HIV-seronegative subjects, patients with the acquired immunodeficiency syndrome (AIDS) have an increased risk for the development of in situ or invasive squamous cell carcinomas of the cervix, vulva-vagina, anus (both sexes), and penis.[108] Contrary to the expectation that led to the inclusion of cervical cancer as an AIDS-defining illness, the progression to AIDS does not appear to augment the risk of cervical cancer.[108-110] It is unclear whether this reflects better appreciation among health care providers for disease in women and earlier detection of more easily treated lesions. Immunosuppressive therapy, notably in renal allograft recipients, has also been associated with high rates of extensive HPV infection.[106,107] Another indication of the role of the immune system comes from the observation that the regression of a wart may be promptly followed by the spontaneous regression of others.[111,112] Although the relative immunosuppression of pregnancy appears to be associated with an increased incidence and severity of HPV disease,[43,113] it is not clear that rates of HPV infection are substantially higher in this population than in nonpregnant women.[114-116]

Diverse nonspecific alterations of the immune system have been described among patients with HPV diseases. However, except for the decreased, local cell-mediated immunity observed in patients with epidermodysplasia verruciformis, most of these are of uncertain importance.[117]

Various cytokines, such as transforming growth factor-β, tumor necrosis factor-α, interleukin-1, and the interferons, appear to contribute to the control of HPV infections and diseases.[118] Delayed hypersensitivity reactions and lymphoproliferative and cytotoxic responses to HPV antigens, particularly E6 and E7, occur in infected patients but have been observed inconsistently.[118-121]

Histologic studies of HPV lesions have demonstrated alterations in the degree of immunologic activation of keratinocytes and natural killer cells and in the numbers of Langerhans and helper T cells.[122-124] In most patients, T cells infiltrating genital warts develop a proliferative response when exposed to E7 or L1 proteins of HPV6.[125] The presence of an epidermal lymphomonocytic infiltrate in resolving warts is consistent with a significant role of these T cells in curbing HPV infection.[126] These observations and others, along with the well-localized nature of HPV disease, suggest that lymphoid tissue associated with skin (or mucous membrane) may be more relevant to the pathogenesis and resolution of HPV infections than circulating peripheral blood mononuclear leukocytes.[117,125]

HPV infection may elicit a serologic response. In patients with cutaneous warts, condyloma acuminatum, or recurrent respiratory papillomatosis, antibodies directed against the viral capsid have been detected.[119,127,128] VLPs based on the L1 or L1 and L2 proteins offer the same antigenic properties as viral capsids.[129] They have been used extensively to show by enzyme-linked immunosorbent assay that about one half to almost 90% of patients with HPV infection have capsid antibodies.[70,130-133] In diseases associated with HPV16, including cervical carcinoma, antibodies develop to various antigens derived from the early ORFs, most notably E7.[134] Anti-HPV antibodies tend to disappear with disease resolution but can persist for several years in asymptomatic patients.[135-137] The significance of the serologic response to HPV is not well understood, but neutralizing antibodies are produced; they not only protect against infection but also are associated with lesion resolution.[76,138-141]

CLINICAL MANIFESTATIONS

Cutaneous Warts

Cutaneous warts include deep plantar warts, common warts, and plane or flat warts.[142,143]

Deep plantar warts (*verrucae plantaris*), also called *myrmecia* (from the Greek, meaning "ant hill"), affect mostly adolescents and young adults. The lesions characteristically look like raised bundles of soft keratotic fibers 2 mm to 1 cm in diameter, and shaving reveals punctate, bleeding blood vessels. These lesions are often painful and may also be located on the palms of the hands.

Common warts (*verrucae vulgaris*) appear as well-demarcated, exophytic, hyperkeratotic papules with a rough surface. They may occur on the dorsum of the hand, between the fingers, around the nails (periungual warts), on the palms or soles or, rarely, on mucous membranes. Warts may coalesce and reach a diameter of 1 cm. Morphologic variants of common warts include mosaic warts, which appear as cobblestone-like patches of aggregated warts several square centimeters in diameter and barely rising above an indurated base. Filiform warts on the head and vegetating, hyperproliferative warts on the hands of butchers, fish handlers, and meat packers also occur.[27]

Plane warts (*verrucae planae*) are commonly found on children and appear as multiple, slightly elevated papules with an irregular contour and distribution and a smooth surface. They occur on the face, neck, and hands. When more protuberant, these lesions are called *intermediate warts*.

Cutaneous warts are usually asymptomatic, although they may bleed and can be painful when located over weight-bearing surfaces or points of friction. Rarely, cutaneous warts may degenerate into verrucous carcinomas.[144] The natural history of cutaneous warts is poorly characterized. Spontaneous resolution appears to occur in 50% and 90% of children within 1 and 5 years, respectively.[24] In a given patient, two thirds of the warts that resolve spontaneously will do so within 2 months.[145]

Epidermodysplasia Verruciformis

Epidermodysplasia verruciformis is an autosomal recessive genodermatosis linked to gene loci on chromosome 17.[146] The lesions are associated with a large array of HPV types (see Table 140-1), most of which are specific for epidermodysplasia verruciformis.[28,147] These warts have several morphologic variants. They may resemble flat warts but more commonly resemble lesions of pityriasis versicolor, covering the torso and upper extremities. Over extensor surfaces these warts may become hypertrophic and coalescent. In most patients, warts appear in the first decade of life. Beginning in young adulthood, in about one third of patients, the lesions undergo malignant transformation into invasive squamous cell carcinomas, particularly in sun-exposed areas. Although these patients may have depressed cellular immunity,[117] they appear to have normal resistance to other pathogens. Epidermodysplasia verruciformis does not appear to be contagious to healthy contacts. It is of interest that lesions resembling epidermodysplasia verruciformis are observed in solid organ allograft recipients.[23,148] Furthermore, epidermodysplasia verruciformis–associated HPV types, in particular HPV5, have been identified in many psoriatic lesions.[149]

Anogenital Warts

Anogenital warts are flesh- to gray-colored, hyperkeratotic, exophytic papules, either sessile on the skin or, more frequently, attached by a short, broad peduncle (Fig. 140-2). Lesions range from smooth, pearly papules to more jagged, acuminate growths. They vary in size from less than a millimeter in diameter to several square centimeters when they merge into plaques. In uncircumcised men, the preputial cavity is involved in 85% to 90% of cases.[43,150] In the United States, where about 85% of the male population is circumcised, the penile shaft is the most common site of lesions.[34] The urethral meatus is also involved in 1% to 25% of patients.[151] Urethral warts are clearly visible by eversion of the meatus or with the use of a pediatric nasal speculum. They are mostly confined to the fossa navicularis or, less frequently, to the distal 3 cm of the urethra. Involvement of the bladder or proximal urethra is exceptional.[151] Involvement of the perianal area varies according to sexual practice, from very high among homosexual men to low among heterosexual men.[152,153] Lesions are only occasionally observed on the scrotum, perineum, groin, or pubic area.

In women, most lesions are distributed over the posterior introitus and, to a lesser degree, over the labia majora and minora and the clitoris (see Fig. 140-2). In order of decreasing frequency, the perineum, vagina, anus, cervix, and urethra each represent less than one quarter of the sites of involvement.[34,43]

The use of the colposcope and prior soaking of examined tissues with 3% to 5% acetic acid has expanded the clinical spectrum of anogenital warts, particularly those caused by HPV types 16 and 18, which can be small.[154] This technique was initially used to demonstrate the existence of flat condylomas on the uterine cervix. Typically, these lesions are shiny, white patches with poorly defined borders and an irregular surface containing characteristic capillary loops.[155,156] The presence of external genital warts may indicate the existence of cervical HPV squamous epithelial lesions, including CIN.[157,158] Morphologic differentiation among the grades of cervical squamous epithelial lesions is not sufficiently reliable, and biopsy is strongly recommended for diagnosis.[159,160]

In the vagina, in addition to flat condylomas, small white nodosities centered on a capillary loop, called *spiked condylomas*, have been

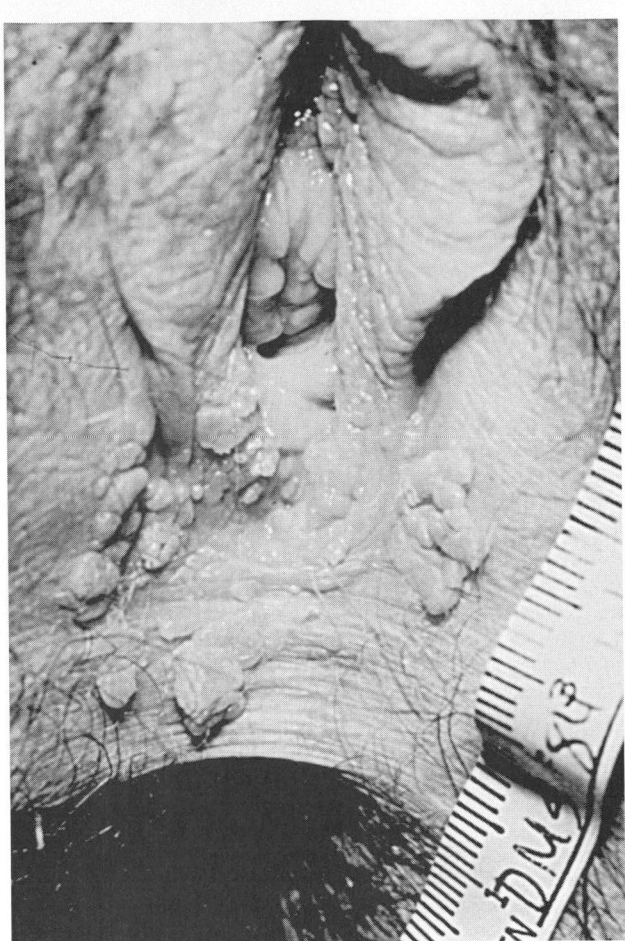

FIGURE 140-2. Vulvar condylomata acuminata.

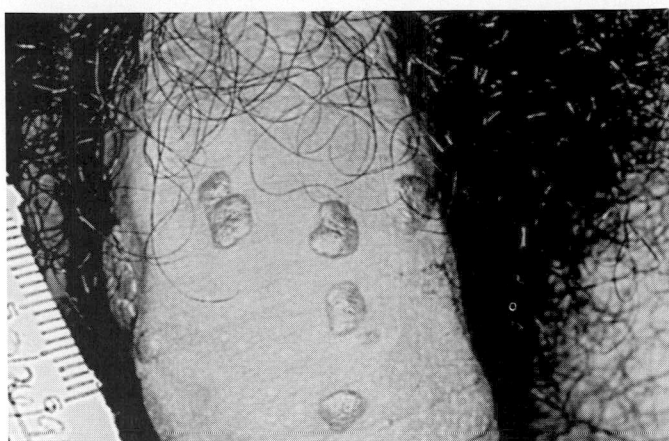

FIGURE 140-3. Pigmented penile warts mimicking bowenoid papulosis.

described.[161] The vulvar introitus may display prominent, sometimes painful, papillae whose relation to HPV infection is unlikely but controversial.[162,163] HPV infection of the vulva may also appear as white patches revealed or accentuated by the application of acetic acid, but acetowhitening lacks specificity.[164] A potential link between HPV infection and vulvar vestibulitis has been proposed.[165,166] This syndrome, which may be recognized in up to 15% of women, is characterized by severe pain on touching the vestibule, tenderness limited to the vestibule, and vestibular erythema, either focal or diffuse, of varying extent or intensity.

In men, acetic acid soaking or examination with a colposcope has shown HPV-infected papules and macules to be up to two times more common than exophytic condylomas, particularly on the prepuce and scrotum.[154,167] Ranging in size from minuscule to 1 cm in diameter, round, sessile papules with brown to slate blue pigmentation are encountered on both male and female external genitalia (Fig. 140-3). These lesions, as well as similarly colored macules, are important to recognize because they may represent either HPV6- or HPV11-infected benign condylomas,[168,169] seborrheic keratoses,[170] or intraepithelial neoplasias associated with HPV type 16 or 18 infection.[169-171]

About three quarters of patients with anogenital warts are asymptomatic.[34] However, itching and burning, pain, and tenderness are encountered frequently.[34] In addition, the disease can have serious psychological effects.[172] The natural history of genital warts, particularly of subclinical HPV disease, is poorly understood, but spontaneous remission may occur, as demonstrated by the results of randomized, placebo-controlled therapeutic trials that indicate up to 10% to 20% spontaneous remission rates in untreated lesions over a 3- to 4-month period.[173-177]

Exophytic genital warts may rarely transform into invasive squamous cell carcinomas, including verrucous carcinoma.[135] They may also reach considerable size, particularly during pregnancy or immunosuppression.[178] When large condylomas reveal histologic features of local destructive invasion without metastases, they may be called *Buschke-Löwenstein tumors*, a term that regroups verrucous carcinomas and giant condylomas.[179-181] A related lesion, condylomatous (warty) carcinoma, may metastasize.[181] Genital HPV infections may also belong to the spectrum of penile, vulvar, vaginal, and CINs.[182,183] Histologically, pigmented papules of the external genitalia may demonstrate condylomatous cytoarchitecture with evidence of intraepithelial neoplasia.[169] This clinicopathologic entity is called *bowenoid papulosis* (see Fig. 140-3).[184] *Bowenoid papulosis* can evolve to *Bowen's disease*, which manifests as a flat, red to brown plaque with well-demarcated borders and a scaly, irregular surface.[185] On the glans penis the lesion is known as *erythroplasia of Queyrat.* Histologically, carcinoma in situ is present. HPV16 and HPV18 have been recovered from both *bowenoid papulosis* and *Bowen's disease.*[186] The natural history of intraepithelial neoplasias is best understood in cervical lesions.[187] It is clear that the outcome (regression, no change, or progression) is highly variable and depends on the histologic grade of the tumor, the HPV type, and the method of diagnosis (conization, punch biopsy, or scraping). CIN grade 1 lesions have an approximate probability of 60% to regress, 30% to remain unchanged, 10% to progress to CIN 3, and 1% to progress to invasive cancer.[187] For CIN 2, the figures are 40%, 40%, 20%, and 5%, respectively. The risk of progression to cancer is the highest with CIN 3, 12%; only a third of these lesions disappear spontaneously.

Perianal warts are common among homosexual men, and up to two thirds of patients with external anal warts also have internal lesions.[188] Consequently, the presence of perianal warts or anal symptoms in association with a history of anal sexual play or intercourse should prompt an anoscopic evaluation. After the malignant transformation of anal condylomas was described,[189] the association between anorectal dysplasia or cancer and HPV infection was recognized in homosexual men.[190,191] Passive anal intercourse carries a risk of anal cancer in homosexual men, and heterosexual men and women with a history of anogenital warts have a 30-fold increased risk of disease compared with control populations.[192] In the general population, a history of anal warts increases by about 10 times the risk of anal cancer.[193] During pregnancy, HPV shedding may increase and condylomas may become so large as to impair normal delivery mechanically.[116,178,194] Anogenital warts in children should always raise the possibility of sexual abuse, but in very young children nongenital or possibly perinatal transmission may be the predominant mode of acquisition.[195-197]

Recurrent Respiratory Papillomatosis

Recurrent respiratory papillomatosis has been described by several authors.[40,198] Patients present with hoarseness or, in infants, with an altered cry. Sometimes these symptoms are accompanied by respiratory distress or stridor. The disease may spread to the trachea and lungs, leading to obstruction, infection, and respiratory failure. In young children, rapid growth of lesions often threatens the upper respiratory tract and frequently necessitates surgical excision to avoid asphyxiation. In adults, the course of the disease is usually less aggressive. Lesions may, however, undergo malignant transformation, particularly in patients who have received radiation therapy.[199]

Other Human Papillomavirus Infections

Oral squamous cell papillomas (or squamous papillomas) are the most common HPV-related oral lesions. A closely related entity, with slightly different histologic features, is oral condyloma acuminatum. Both types of lesions are caused by mucosal HPV (mostly HPV6, HPV11, and HPV16). Oral verrucae vulgaris are rarer and can be differentiated reliably only by histology. They are caused by cutaneous HPVs (HPV2, HPV4, HPV57).[200] Focal epithelial hyperplasia of the oral cavity (Heck's disease) is caused predominantly by HPV3 and HPV13 and tends to regress spontaneously.[201] Other HPV infections may also occur in the oral cavity.[201] In particular, HPV may coinfect Epstein-Barr virus–induced oral hairy leukoplakia lesions in HIV-infected patients.[202] Conjunctival HPV-related papillomas and carcinomas have been described.[88,203-205] HPV DNA has also been identified in epidermoid cysts,[206] seborrheic keratoses (especially vulvar),[207] skin squamous cell and basal carcinomas,[23,208,209] and aerodigestive carcinomas.[89,210] The prevalence of HPV in these different lesions varies, which makes it difficult to establish a causative link.

DIAGNOSIS

The diagnosis of warts is usually made clinically by physical examination. Exophytic warts have a characteristic appearance. Deep plantar warts may be confused with calluses, but paring usually reveals typical punctate, thrombosed capillaries. Nevi, seborrheic keratoses, acrochordons, acanthomas, molluscum contagiosum, lichen planus, syringomas, and dermofibromas may be confused with cutaneous warts. Lesions of epidermodysplasia verruciformis may be similar to those of flat warts or pityriasis versicolor, but the patient's history should clarify the diagnosis.

Condyloma acuminatum of the external anogenital tract should rarely be confused with other STDs such as condyloma latum of syphilis, nodular scabies, genital herpes, lymphogranuloma venereum, chancroid, or granuloma inguinale. Nevertheless, molluscum contagiosum, particularly in its more atypical presentations, may be difficult to distinguish from anogenital warts. In contrast to those of condyloma acuminatum, the lesions of molluscum contagiosum tend to predominate over the pubis and are rarely pedunculated but rather appear as very smooth, sessile domes, the color of the skin or lighter, with a depressed center, from which cheesy material can be expressed. In men, a normal anatomic variant of the corona, hirsutoid papillomatosis (pearly coronal papules, papillae corona glandis), can be difficult to differentiate from small warts. A similar anatomic presentation exists in the vulvar introitus, where lesions may appear identical to those of HPV-related vulvar papillomatosis. On the keratinized vulva, hidradenoma papilliferum may be confused with a large wart. On the scrotum, epidermoid cysts and angiokeratomas should be easy to identify. Small and flat HPV lesions may sometimes be difficult to distinguish from lichen planus, lichen sclerosus et atrophicus, lichen nitidus, or syringomas, even with the help of the colposcope and acetic acid application. Finally, pigmented HPV lesions may be confused with nevi or seborrheic keratoses (see Fig. 140-3).

Although initially designed for the evaluation of the female internal genital tract, the colposcope, with prior application for 3 to 5 minutes of a 3% to 5% acetic acid solution, has become an important di-

agnostic tool for other HPV infections as well.[211] In studies of male partners of women with either cervical condylomas or dysplasias, biopsy-proven genital condylomas were detected in 65% to 88% of the patients. More significantly, 43% to 73% of the lesions were seen only with a colposcope, whereas acetowhitening alone made the diagnosis in 22% of patients.[154,212,213] The same technique applied to the vulva revealed subclinical papillomavirus infection in 96% of women with vulvar warts and 80% of women who were partners of men with penile warts.[214] In the oral cavity, 83% of HPV lesions are seen only with the colposcope.[215] The clinical significance of lesions that are detectable by acetowhitening only is unknown, and acetowhitening lacks specificity for the diagnosis of HPV infection, particularly for external anogenital warts.[170,216,217]

Lesions of the external genitalia that are pigmented (see Fig. 140-3) appear as plaques, bleed, or are large should have biopsies to establish the diagnosis and rule out malignancy.[169] Biopsy is also indicated to confirm the diagnosis of epidermodysplasia verruciformis and to determine the cause of lesions of the oral cavity and upper airways.

Anoscopic examination should be considered in patients with perianal warts, anal symptoms, or a history of receptive anal intercourse. Most intra-anal lesions are below the pectinate line, and sigmoidoscopy is not routinely indicated.[218,219] The oral cavity should be examined in all patients with anogenital warts because they may have concomitant oral warts.[215]

Evaluation of the vagina and cervix, when appropriate, should include colposcopy and acetic acid application and should seek to rule out invasive cancer.[211] An international colposcopic terminology has now been developed, and this should improve diagnostic accuracy and reliability.[156] Women with a history of anogenital HPV disease, or whose sexual partners have had anogenital HPV disease, should have a cytologic examination of a cervical smear (Pap smear), at least as part of regular screening (see "Prevention"). Koilocytes on a cytologic smear are the hallmark of HPV infection.[220] More important, diagnoses of dysplasia and cancer can also be made from the smear.[9,221] Depending on the patient's age and the location and nature of the HPV infection, the sensitivity of the Pap smear in detecting HPV infection ranges from 30% to 90%.[222]

The use of the colposcope during the anoscopic examination ("high-resolution anoscopy") combined with anal cytology has been applied with success to the diagnosis of intra-anal HPV infections.[223] It can be a screening tool for anal intraepithelial neoplasias in homosexual or bisexual males or in the HIV-positive female.[224-226] Nevertheless, this approach has yet to be validated with randomized, "blinded," long-term studies of outcomes and costs.

A newer development in cervical cytology has been the introduction of a liquid-based collection technology that permits computer-aided diagnosis and rescreening (Auto Pap 300C, PapNet).[9,221,227] Now that HPV DNA testing is part of the screening strategy, this technology allows the performance of both cytology and HPV DNA testing on the same sample.[228,229]

Cervical cytology has benefited from the development of the Bethesda system, last revised in 2001 (http://www.bethesda2001. cancer.gov). This is an interpretation scheme that addresses the adequacy of the specimen, classifies its pathologic features, and provides guidelines for management and follow-up of the patient.[230,231] HPV-related squamous cell abnormalities are regrouped in four categories: (1) atypical squamous cells of (a) undetermined significance (ASC-US) or (b) for which a high-grade squamous intraepithelial lesion (ASC-H) cannot be excluded; (2) low-grade squamous intraepithelial lesion (LSIL), a diagnosis that regroups the previous cytologic and histologic diagnoses of koilocytic or condylomatous atypia, mild dysplasia, and CIN 1; (3) high-grade squamous intraepithelial lesion (HSIL), previously including moderate and severe dysplasia, CIN 2 and CIN 3, and carcinoma in situ (CIS); and (4) squamous cell carcinoma (SCC).

The general histopathologic features of HPV infection are usually characteristic (see "Pathogenesis"). Therefore, biopsy can be used to confirm most diagnoses. In addition, histologic examination can identify the presence of intraepithelial neoplasia or invasive cancer. Although histology is the "gold standard," like cytology, it suffers from lack of accuracy and reliability where disease grades are concerned.[221,232]

To enhance the sensitivity and specificity of cytohistopathology, several techniques are available, mostly in research settings.[9,233] They rely on demonstration of either papillomavirus antigens or nucleic acids in biopsy specimens. The papillomavirus common antigen is usually detected by peroxidase-antiperoxidase immunocytochemical staining. It is present in about half of HPV lesions, although less frequently with HPV16 or HPV18 infections.[20]

The detection of HPV DNA has become accessible to the clinician with the Hybrid Capture II assay (Digene Corporation), which was approved by the Food and Drug Administration (FDA) in 2000 for the triage of ASC-US Pap smears and since 2003 for the primary screening of cervical cancer in combination with cytology. This assay is based on a liquid hybridization reaction performed in a 96-well microplate. The sample DNA is reacted with RNA probes contained in two pools. The probes in pool A are directed at genital low-risk HPVs (types 6, 11, 42, 43, and 44), and, more relevant for screening, the probes in pool B are targeted to genital high-risk HPVs (types 16, 18, 31, 33, 35, 39, 45, 51, 52, 56, 58, 59, 68). This assay is rapid and, unlike the polymerase chain reaction (PCR)–based assays, not susceptible to cross-contamination. It is also only slightly less sensitive than PCR assays.

The PCR assays are not standardized and are not commercially available. They have the advantage of being highly sensitive and can be targeted to either specific HPV types or groups of HPV types by the use of consensus primers. HPV typing is nonetheless possible by the detection of the amplicons with type-specific oligonucleotide probes in a liquid phase or a solid support, as in the line probe assay.[9,233,234]

Virus cultivation and accurate serologic techniques are not available for the clinical diagnosis of HPV infections.

TREATMENT

Highly effective and safe treatments for HPV diseases are not yet available, and the current therapies are not designed to eradicate HPV infection. Rather, their purpose is to decrease or, if possible, eliminate clinical manifestations. The current therapeutic armamentarium has been largely developed empirically over decades and too often relies on the physical or chemical destruction of lesions. Newer approaches are directed at molecular viral targets and immunomodulation.[235,236]

Cutaneous Warts

The choice of treatments for cutaneous warts is complicated by the existence of weak and confusing evidence.[237] Nevertheless, it is clear that the most common approach, the topical application of preparations containing salicylic acid, a keratolytic agent, is effective for the treatment of common warts.[237] A meta-analysis of six placebo-controlled clinical trials revealed a complete response rate of 75% (144 of 191) in the cases compared with 48% (89 of 185) in the controls.[237] A widely available over-the-counter preparation for self-treatment is a salicylic acid and lactic acid paint (salicylic acid, lactic acid, collodion, 1:1:4; SAL; DuoFilm, Occlusal, Paplex) that is typically applied daily for up to 12 weeks. The cornified layer typically covering skin warts may need to be removed. This is done with a hot water soak, followed by abrasion with a pumice stone, sand paper, or an emery board. Occlusive bandages seem to increase treatment effectiveness. Mosaic warts tend to be more resistant to treatment than myrmecia.

Cryotherapy is a popular treatment, but it requires a health practitioner. It is typically accomplished with cotton wool buds dipped in liquid nitrogen and applied to the lesion or by spraying liquid nitrogen.[238] Randomized, placebo-controlled studies have been inconclusive on the efficacy of cryotherapy, but, when compared with salicylic acid preparations, cryotherapy appears to be equivalent.[237] Variations in technique may account for these confusing results. However, it is clear that aggressive cryotherapy, a 10-second sustained freeze, is more effective than briefer "traditional" cryotherapy despite a higher

incidence of pain and blisters.[239] More than one treatment is often needed. A 2-week interval offers the best balance between the occurrence of side effects and brevity of treatment.[240] Treatment beyond 3 months, or about four cryotherapies, presents little advantage.[241]

A randomized study with "blind" evaluation compared cryotherapy with duct tape application, an occlusive treatment that has long been in the medical lore, for the treatment of common warts.[242] Duct tape was left applied to the wart for 6 days. The wart was then soaked in water and débrided with a pumice stone or an emery board. The tape was reapplied the following morning for another cycle for up to 2 months or until the wart disappeared, whichever came first. Complete clearance of the warts occurred in 85% (22 of 26) of the patients receiving occlusive therapy but in only 60% (15 of 25) of the patients treated with cryotherapy.

Other treatment modalities, which are less often used, include glutaraldehyde, formaldehyde, podofilox, and cantharidin. Their use is empirical. Intralesional bleomycin has been better studied, but when it has been compared with placebo, the results have been inconclusive.[237] It is usually reserved for the treatment of periungual warts.

Allergic sensitization with dinitrochlorobenzene (DNCB) followed by direct application of DNCB on the lesions has been found to be twice as effective as placebo.[237,243] However, the use of DNCB is risky and other sensitizing agents, such as 2,3-diphenylcyclopropenone, squaric acid dibutyl ester, and 10% masoprocol cream (Actinex), appear to be safer and as effective.[243,244]

Imiquimod is an immunomodulator that is approved by the FDA for the topical treatment of genital warts (see next section). When used off label in an open study, imiquimod 5% cream applied once a day, 5 days per week, for up to 16 weeks on varied common warts resulted in a complete response.[245]

Cimetidine, an H_2 blocker that has immunomodulatory properties, has been widely publicized as an effective treatment for cutaneous warts on the basis of uncontrolled studies. Yet several placebo-controlled, double-blind studies have failed to confirm that claim.[243]

Electrosurgery and laser surgery are used, but they can be expensive and they have not been rigorously evaluated.[237,243,246-248] Electrosurgery is relatively contraindicated for the treatment of plantar warts because of the risk of permanent and painful scarring. Laser surgery is also not scar free, but it may be useful for the treatment of periungual and subungual warts.

Photodynamic therapy, which relies on laser light to activate locally the cytotoxicity of a compound administered systemically or applied topically, is superior to placebo for the treatment of cutaneous warts.[237] However, the technique is costly and not widely available.

Suggestion, hypnosis, homeopathy, and distant healing are among "alternative" approaches that have been proposed for the treatment of cutaneous warts.[249-253] More rigorous evaluations of these interventions showed little, if any, promise.

Particular treatment modalities have been proposed for some specific types of warts. For example, flat warts rarely need treatment, but when they do cryotherapy or electrosurgery (electrodesiccation) is used. Cryotherapy may also be used for the treatment of eyelid and periungual warts, and electrodesiccation is useful to remove flat or filiform warts.

Anogenital Warts

The treatment methods for condyloma acuminatum are numerous yet unsatisfactory, but guidelines that attempt to optimize the therapeutic approach have been published.[177,254-258] Because there is no or scant evidence that treatment directly affects eradication of HPV and transmission of infection or prevents the uncommon development of neoplasms, the rationale for treating is restricted.[100,259,260] It includes cosmesis, relief of local symptoms, alleviation of the adverse psychological impact caused by the presence of anogenital warts,[172] and restoration of normal physiologic function (e.g., debulking of lesions obstructing the birth canal). Before treatment is initiated, the goals of therapy, alternatives, costs, and potential side effects should be discussed with patients. It should also be remembered that within 3 to 4 months approximately 10% to 20% of patients have spontaneous resolution of their disease.[173-177] Independent of treatment, patient counseling is part of the management.[261]

None of the available treatment modalities is dramatically superior to the others, but each may have its particular advantages. As convenience is one of the greatest advantages, the availability over the past few years of patient-applied therapies, podofilox and imiquimod, has been of considerable interest.

Podofilox (podophyllotoxin) is a derivative of podophyllin, which was long the mainstay of genital wart treatment by practitioners. Podophyllin, a resin extract from the rhizome of *Podophyllum peltatum* (podophyllum resin, USP) or *Podophyllum emodi*, has been the principal mode of therapy for many years.[262,263] The active molecules are lignans, particularly podophyllotoxin. Although podophyllin is a mitotic poison, its mode of action in warts is unknown. The compound is usually applied as a 10% to 25% solution in benzoin, directly on the wart, once weekly. Washing of lesions within 12 hours is recommended to minimize local reactions. Lack of regression after four applications suggests the need for alternative therapy. Podophyllin has never been compared with a placebo. Its effectiveness has been evaluated in a series of randomized controlled trials against other treatment modalities; complete clearance rates ranged from 20% to 40% when the frequent recurrences were accounted for.[150,262] Side effects are both local and systemic.[262,263] Chemical burns are seen in one third to one half of the patients. Transient pseudoneoplastic histopathologic changes have also been reported. Neurologic, hematologic, and febrile complications, sometimes leading to death, and allergic sensitization have been associated with administration of topical podophyllin. Therefore, areas larger than 10 cm^2 should not be treated. The drug is contraindicated in pregnancy.

Podophyllotoxin is available in the United States under the generic name podofilox. It offers distinct advantages over podophyllin. It is chemically uniform and of standardized potency. Podofilox is also more efficacious and less toxic than podophyllin.[150,263-265] Finally, it does not need to be washed off. Randomized, controlled studies have shown that 0.5% podofilox solution applied twice daily for three consecutive days every week for up to 4 weeks results in rates of complete response ranging from 45% to 58%.[177,258,265-268] Side effects are mostly mild and similar in nature to those of podophyllin. As with podophyllin, relapses are common, occurring in 33% to 91% of patients.[177,258,265-268] Application of podofilox to prevent recurrences is effective and well tolerated, but the long-term outcome after cessation of treatment is unknown.[269] In addition to podofilox 0.5% (Condylox) solution, a 0.5% gel is now available. It yielded a 45% (81 of 181) complete clearance rate after 8 weeks in a large randomized controlled trial, as opposed to 4% (5 of 93) for the vehicle only.[270]

Imiquimod is an imidazoquinolineamine that induces the production of interferon-α and other cytokines. It appears to exert its unique antitumor and antiviral action by binding to the toll-like receptors 7 and possibly 8 of dendritic cells.[271] It is available as a 5% cream (Aldara) for the self-treatment of condyloma acuminatum.[272] This preparation was compared with vehicle alone in a randomized, double-blind trial and was given three times a week, on alternate days, for up to 8 weeks.[273] At the end of the treatment period, 108 patients were evaluable and the complete response rate was 37% in the imiquimod group compared with nil in the control group ($P < .001$). Nineteen percent of the patients had a recurrence during the 10 weeks of follow-up. In a similar study, the treatment duration was extended up to 16 weeks, and imiquimod 5% cream was compared with a 1% cream and with vehicle.[274] At the end of treatment the complete response rates were 50%, 21%, and 14% in the three respective groups. Imiquimod 5% cream was significantly superior to either of the two other preparations ($P < .001$). In the 5% imiquimod group, 72% of women had a complete response, compared with 33% of the men. During the 12 weeks of follow-up, recurrences were noted in 13%, 0%, and 10% of the subjects in the three groups, respectively. The adverse reactions were local and included itching and burning sensations, erythema, erosions, and swelling; they were well tolerated. The daily administration of imiquimod 5% cream

offers some enhancement of efficacy, mostly in men, but a substantially higher incidence of side effects.[275] Therefore, Aldara is approved for thrice-weekly use only. Additional clinical trials have complemented and supported the results of these pivotal studies.[257,276,277] Imiquimod also appears to be useful for the treatment of other possibly HPV-related conditions, such as actinic keratoses, basal cell carcinomas, and squamous cell carcinomas in situ.[245]

Various provider-applied therapies are available. They can be divided into nonsurgical and surgical treatments, which are as follows.

Podophyllin resin (see earlier) is still used widely, mostly because of low cost, even though podofilox 0.5% solution or gel is more effective and safer to use.[263]

Trichloracetic acid and, to a lesser extent, bichloracetic acid have been favored by gynecologists for the treatment of genital warts.[278] They can both be used during pregnancy. Trichloracetic acid in a 10% to 90% solution is used topically at weekly intervals. The application is painful and can cause ulcers. The unreacted acid should be removed with talcum powder or bicarbonate of soda. In one comparative trial, trichloracetic acid therapy appeared to be equivalent to cryotherapy, with complete response and relapse rates of 81% and 36%, respectively.[279] Another study was also unable to detect any differences, with complete response rates of 64% for cryotherapy and 70% for trichloracetic acid.[280] It has been shown that 50% trichloracetic acid does not add to the effects of podophyllin alone and is ineffective in the treatment of vaginal and cervical warts.[281,282]

Cryotherapy is administered with liquid nitrogen or cryoprobe. Lesions are frozen every 1 or 2 weeks. Cryotherapy is regarded as an effective treatment, with cure rates in the 50% to 100% range, and it is safe even during pregnancy.[279,283] One comparative study suggested that cryotherapy is more effective than podophyllin but probably less effective than electrosurgery.[284-286] Side effects are tolerable. They include burning, which resolves within a few hours, and ulceration, which heals in 7 to 10 days with little or no scarring.

Other surgical techniques are available for the treatment of anogenital warts.[256-258] Conventional surgery with scissors offers the advantage of providing immediate eradication of visible lesions. This technique has been reserved mainly for the treatment of perianal warts, but it can be advantageously applied to other genital warts if they are limited in number. Up to one third of patients have recurrences, and scarring, typically limited to some skin discoloration, is the most common complication.[287-290] Electrosurgical techniques have often been applied for the treatment of external genital warts, with results probably superior to those of cryotherapy, but scarring may occur.[285,286] Complete response rates of 80% to 90% have been reported with carbon dioxide laser therapy.[291-293] In a comparative assessment, however, laser therapy was not deemed to be superior to conventional surgery,[288] and subsequent, better designed studies indicated a long-term complete response rate of 19% to 39%.[294,295] Laser therapy is expensive, may require general anesthesia, and is frequently accompanied by pain and scarring.

The availability of lidocaine-prilocaine (EMLA) cream, which should be applied about 1 hour before the procedure, has facilitated local anesthesia before cryotherapy and laser surgery.[296-299]

Two treatments that are now rarely used but still deserve mention are 5-fluorouracil and intralesional interferon. 5-Fluorouracil, used topically as a 5% cream applied daily, has been reported to have cure rates of 30% to 95%; the best results have been obtained with intraurethral warts.[150,300,301] In a comparative trial in men, 5-fluorouracil appeared to be equivalent in efficacy to podophyllin.[302] In addition, prophylactic activity of 5-fluorouracil has been reported for vulvar warts.[303] This drug is not widely used because it often produces substantial pain, ulceration, and, if applied in the urethra, dysuria.[150] Like other antimetabolites, 5-fluorouracil is contraindicated during pregnancy.

Interferons have antiviral, immunomodulatory, and antiproliferative properties.[304,305] Encouraging in vitro and preliminary clinical studies were confirmed by four randomized, double-blind trials that demonstrated the efficacy of intralesionally administered interferon-α

and interferon-β compared with placebo.[111,306-308] Parenterally administered interferons have also been evaluated for treatment of condyloma acuminatum but have generally been ineffective.[173-175,309] Interferon, in the doses used, has been generally well tolerated. Side effects (influenza-like symptoms, neutropenia, and thrombocytopenia) are usually mild and are seen more frequently with higher doses. Imiquimod, an interferon-α inducer, is a more practical and cheaper substitute for interferon.

Cidofovir is an acyclic nucleotide that is a potent inhibitor of the DNA polymerase of cytomegalovirus and other herpesviruses and is licensed for the intravenous treatment of cytomegalovirus retinitis. Although HPV do not possess a DNA polymerase, this compound triggers the apoptosis of HPV-infected cells.[310] In a randomized, vehicle-controlled trial of a compounded 1% gel applied daily to genital warts for 5 consecutive days every other week, at 12 weeks the treated group had 47% (9 of 19) complete clearance compared with 0% (0 of 11) in the vehicle group ($P = .006$).[311] Pain, pruritus, rash, erosions, and ulcerations were frequently noted, but equally in both groups. The cost, the risk of carcinogenesis associated with cidofovir, and the absence of long-term data are reservations about this non–FDA-approved treatment.

Although guidelines are helpful, it is not always possible to make firm recommendations on the proper treatment strategy for condyloma acuminatum. The divergent results of several cost-benefit analyses reinforce this point.[312-314] Costs may vary widely for a given therapy, recurrences are common yet long-term outcomes are not well studied, and the significance of the antecedent genital wart history and treatment is poorly known. Furthermore, the importance of factors such as sex, wart location, size, or number is largely unknown with respect to each treatment. Nevertheless, it appears that the duration of lesions (>1 year), their number (>10), and their location on dry rather than moist skin are adverse predictors of treatment response.[257,315,316] Treatment response may improve with the discontinuation of oral contraceptive use, pubic hair shaving, and tobacco smoking.[317,318]

In practice, availability, convenience, adverse reactions, location of lesions, and characteristics of the patient are determinant in the treatment choice. Patient-applied therapies should receive preference. Warts of the urinary meatus can be treated by careful application of podophyllin, podofilox,[150] or cryotherapy.[319] 5-Fluorouracil cream may also be used.[150,320] Laser surgery and instillations of interferon-alfa can also be used with intraurethral warts.[167,321] Perianal and anal warts may be treated with scalpel removal,[287-289] cryotherapy,[322] laser surgery,[323] trichloracetic or bichloracetic acid,[256] or even, as adjunctive therapy, with imiquimod-soaked anal tampons.[324]

For vaginal warts, cryotherapy (sprays), trichloracetic acid, and podophyllin are simple options[325]; laser therapy[326,327] and cryotherapy[328] have the advantage of being relatively safe during pregnancy, and they may be used for treatment of cervical warts as well. Although intralesional interferon may be indicated for the treatment of single, very large warts, laser therapy seems to be better suited for large, extensive lesions.

The genital warts of immunocompromised patients, including those infected by HIV, seem relatively refractory to treatment.[329] Thus, podophyllin, podofilox, intralesional interferon, and imiquimod alone have been largely ineffective.[330-334] Combination therapy appears more successful, such as electrosurgery plus cold-blade excision[330,335] or plus intralesional interferon for anal warts.[336] Imiquimod may also be used as adjunctive therapy.[337] Nevertheless, single therapy, especially for small (<1 cm²) intra-anal lesions, may be effective, as shown with trichloracetic acid, liquid nitrogen, or the use of an infrared coagulator.[226] Lesion healing is generally not a problem after surgery.[338] The effects of highly active antiretroviral therapy (HAART) on HPV diseases are still debated. HAART appears to increase the incidence of genital and oral warts but may help the regression of CIN.[339-341]

Because internal genital warts are often associated with genital dysplasias and malignancies and because of the special skills and technical resources required for proper diagnosis and management, patients with internal lesions should be referred to a qualified specialist.

Other Warts

The lesions of epidermodysplasia verruciformis should be carefully observed, and any malignant changes should be treated by surgical techniques (cold blade or laser), cryotherapy, or 5-fluorouracil ointments.[28] Retinoids in combination with intralesional interferon or calciferol help with the management of the lesions of epidermodysplasia verruciformis.[28,342]

The management of recurrent respiratory papillomatosis is complex.[40,343,344] For the primary debulking of lesions, the vast majority of surgeons use the CO₂ laser. Mechanical devices such as a microresector are also used. Photodynamic laser therapy is gaining acceptance. The recurrent nature of the disease requires a careful balance between the risks and benefits of the surgery, which can be achieved only by experienced and skilled operators. Tracheostomy should be avoided because the papillomatosis could then extend to the tracheostomy site and further down the respiratory tree. Radiotherapy is contraindicated because of the known risk of malignant transformation. Different adjuvant therapies are available. Parenteral interferon-alfa may yield long-term complete responses in a quarter of patients. Over the past 5 years, the interest has moved to the intralesional injection of cidofovir.[345] The enthusiasm generated by the results of the early case series has precluded the completion of a properly designed study. Because of the small size of the case series, the long-term risks, including those of malignancy, are not well understood. Indole-3-carbinol (I3C) and its main active metabolite, diindolyl methane (DIM), are derivatives of cruciferous vegetables (e.g., broccoli, cabbage, cauliflower) that are widely used by patients with recurrent respiratory papillomatosis. By increasing the 2-hydroxylation of estradiol, these compounds favor the formation of 2-hydroxyestrone, a nonestrogenic, antiproliferative, anti-angiogenic, and apoptotic molecule, instead of 16α-hydroxyestrone. A randomized, placebo-controlled clinical trial has demonstrated the ability of I3C to induce regression of biopsy-proven CIN 2 or 3.[346] A similar trial has not been conducted for recurrent respiratory papillomatosis.

Oral warts (squamous papillomas, condylomata acuminata, and verruca vulgaris) can be treated by surgical excision, cryotherapy, laser surgery, or podophyllin application.[347] Because of its benign natural history, focal epithelial hyperplasia should not be treated.

PREVENTION

At present, no effective methods of prevention are available other than avoiding contact with infectious lesions. In the case of plantar warts, this is achieved effectively in swimming pools by wearing protective foot equipment ("verruca socks").[41]

It has been difficult to evaluate the effect of preventive measures against genital warts because recurrence of lesions is in part caused by disease relapse rather than new infection.[348,349] Nevertheless, the results of a meta-analysis indicate that condoms may protect against genital warts, CIN 2 or 3, and invasive cervical cancer.[350] Two randomized trials make a more dramatic argument in favor of condoms by showing that male condom use for at least 3 months promoted regression of CIN and clearance of HPV DNA in the female sexual partners as well as regression of HPV-associated penile lesions in the patient.[351,352] These results clearly underline the clinical importance of reinfection.

Although the U.S. Centers for Disease Control and Prevention state that the evaluation of partners is unnecessary for the management of genital warts, examining the partners provides an opportunity to educate, counsel, and screen for HPV disease and other STDs.[256,261]

The Pap smear is an essential tool for the screening and prevention of cervical cancer.[353] In 2002, the American Cancer Society, and in 2003, the U.S. Preventive Services Task Force and the American College of Obstetricians and Gynecologists released their latest guidelines for the screening of cervical cancer.[354-356] They are summarized in Table 140-2. Consensus guidelines for the management of the cytologic and histologic abnormalities have been issued by the American Society for Colposcopy and Cervical Pathology.[227,231] Additional

TABLE 140-2 Summary of Cervical Cancer Screening Guidelines

When to Begin Pap Test Screening

USPSTF and ACS	Approximately 3 years after a woman begins having sexual intercourse but no later than 21 years old

How Often?

USPSTF	Every 3 years (regardless of the cervical cytology technique used)
ACS	(1) Annually with conventional cytology *or* (2) At or after age 30, women who have had three consecutive, technically satisfactory normal-negative cytology results may be screened every 2 to 3 years UNLESS (a) they have a history of in utero diethylstilbestrol (DES) exposure (b) are HIV positive (c) are immunocompromised by organ transplantation, chemotherapy, or chronic corticosteroid treatment

When to Discontinue Screening

USPSTF	At age 65 in women who have had normal results previously and who are not otherwise at high risk for cervical cancer
ACS	At age 70 or older in women with an intact cervix and who have had three or more documented, consecutive, technically satisfactory, normal-negative cervical cytology tests, and no abnormal-positive cytology tests within the 10-year period before age 70 EXCEPTIONS: (a) women who have not been previously screened (b) women for whom information about previous screening is unavailable (c) women for whom past screening is unlikely (d) women with a history of (i) cervical cancer, (ii) in utero exposure to DES (e) women who are immunocompromised (e.g., because of organ transplantation, HIV infection, chemotherapy, or chronic corticosteroid treatment) (f) women who have tested positive for HPV DNA

Screening after Hysterectomy

USPSTF and ACS	Not necessary if (total) hysterectomy was for benign disease

Screening with HPV DNA Testing (Hybrid Capture II Test for High-Risk HPV)

USPSTF	Not recommended
ACS	It should be used, with cytology, only at age 30 or older and not more frequently than every 3 years

Additional Guidelines

ACOG	Yearly testing using cytology alone remains an acceptable screening plan
CDC	Women who have external genital warts do not need to have Pap tests more frequently than women who do not have warts, unless otherwise indicated

HIV, human immunodeficiency virus; HPV, human papillomavirus; Pap, Papanicolaou.

American Cancer Society (ACS),[354]—http://caonline.amcancersoc.org/cgi/content/short/52/6/342.

U.S. Preventive Services Task Force (USPSTF),[355] http://www.ahrq.gov/clinic/uspstf/uspscerv.htm.

American College of Obstetrics and Gynecology (ACOG),[356] Centers for Disease Control and Prevention (CDC),[232] http://www.cdc.gov/std/treatment/TOC2002TG.htm.

sources provide further guidance on the use of HPV DNA testing.[228,229] In the HIV-infected female, some experts suggest repeating the baseline Pap smear 6 months later if normal and then annually if it remains normal.[357] No clinically validated guidelines can be provided at the moment for the screening of anal cancer by anal cytology in the HIV-infected patient.

Cesarean section has probably only a limited role, if any, in the prevention of recurrent respiratory papillomatosis.[51]

Although vaccines against HPV disease are not currently available, this is likely to change within less than a decade in light of the promising results obtained with HPV VLP-based vaccines (see "Virology"). Early clinical work showed that immunization of healthy volunteers with either HPV11 or HPV16 L1 VLPs induced a strong binding and neutralizing antibody response.[358,359] The protective effectiveness of this type of vaccine was demonstrated in a randomized, placebo-controlled trial in which women, ages 16 to 23 years, free of HPV infection and abnormal cervical cytology were given an intramuscular HPV16 VLP vaccine at months 0, 2, and 6 or a placebo.[76] None of the women who received the vaccine developed HPV infection (0 of 768), whereas 5.4% (41 of 765) in the placebo group did ($P < .001$). As a secondary end point, none of the HPV16 vaccine recipients developed HPV16–associated CIN, but 9 of 41 (22%) HPV16–infected placebo recipients did. An equal number of subjects ($n = 22$) developed non–HPV16–associated CIN, indicating a lack of HPV type cross-protection. A similar trial has since validated these results for both HPV16 and HPV18.[359a] Phase III pivotal studies of a bivalent (HPV16, HPV18) or quadrivalent vaccine (HPV6, HPV11, HPV16, HPV18) are ongoing.

Several econometric studies have established the considerable impact such a vaccine could have on the prevention of cervical cancer and have delineated some of the conditions for its optimization.[360,361] If successful, this vaccine strategy could be extended to other HPV genotypes and against other diseases.

REFERENCES

1. Ciuffo G. Imnesto positivo con filtrato di verruca volgare. G Ital Mal Veneree. 1907;48:12-17.
2. Syrjänen SM, Syrjänen KJ. New concepts on the role of human papillomavirus in cell cycle regulation. Ann Med. 1999;31:175-187.
3. McGlennen RC. Human papillomavirus oncogenesis. Clin Lab Med. 2000;20:383-406.
4. Lowy DR, Howley PM. Papillomaviruses. In: Knipe DM, Howley PM, Griffin DE, et al, eds. Fields Virology. 4th ed. Philadelphia: Lippincott Williams & Wilkins; 2001:2231-2264.
5. McMurray HR, Nguyen D, Westbrook TF, et al. Biology of human papillomaviruses. Int J Exp Pathol. 2001;82:15-33.
6. Bonnez W. Papillomavirus. In: Richman RD, Whitley RJ, Hayden FG, eds. Clinical Virology. 2nd ed. Washington, DC: American Society for Microbiology; 2002: 557-596.
7. zur Hausen H. Papillomaviruses and cancer: From basic studies to clinical application. Nat Rev Cancer. 2002;2:342-350.
8. Fehrmann F, Laimins LA. Human papillomaviruses: Targeting differentiating epithelial cells for malignant transformation. Oncogene. 2003;22:5201-5207.
9. Burd EM. Human papillomavirus and cervical cancer. Clin Microbiol Rev. 2003;16:1-17.
10. Munger K, Howley PM. Human papillomavirus immortalization and transformation functions. Virus Res. 2002;89:213-228.
11. Chow LT, Broker TR. In vitro experimental systems for HPV: Epithelial raft cultures for investigations of viral reproduction and pathogenesis and for genetic analyses of viral proteins and regulatory sequences. Clin Dermatol. 1997;15:217-227.
12. Thomas JT, Oh ST, Terhune SS, et al. Cellular changes induced by low-risk human papillomavirus type 11 in keratinocytes that stably maintain viral episomes. J Virol. 2001;75:7564-7571.
13. Delvenne P, Hubert P, Jacobs N, et al. The organotypic culture of HPV-transformed keratinocytes: An effective in vitro model for the development of new immunotherapeutic approaches for mucosal (pre)neoplastic lesions. Vaccine. 2001;19:2557-2564.
14. Ozbun MA. Infectious human papillomavirus type 31b: Purification and infection of an immortalized human keratinocyte cell line. J Gen Virol. 2002;83:2753-2763.
15. Howett MK, Christensen ND, Kreider JW. Tissue xenografts as a model system for study of the pathogenesis of papillomaviruses. Clin Dermatol. 1997;15:229-236.
16. Bonnez W. Murine models of human papillomavirus-infected human xenografts. Papillomavirus Rep. 1998;9:27-38.
17. Dollard SC, Wilson JL, Demeter LM, et al. Production of human papillomavirus and modulation of the infectious program in epithelial raft cultures. Genes Dev. 1992;6:1131-1142.

18. Giroglou T, Sapp M, Lane C, et al. Immunological analyses of human papillomavirus capsids. Vaccine. 2001;19:1783-1793.

19. Strike DG, Bonnez W, Rose RC, et al. Expression in *Escherichia coli* of seven DNA segments comprising the complete L1 and L2 open reading frames of human papillomavirus type 6b and the location of the "common antigen." J Gen Virol. 1989;70:543-555.

20. Jenson AB, Kurman RJ, Lancaster WD. Detection of papillomavirus common antigens in lesions of skin and mucosa. Clin Dermatol. 1985;3:56-63.

21. Koutsky L. Epidemiology of genital human papillomavirus infection. Am J Med. 1997;102:3-8.

22. Antonsson A, Forslund O, Ekberg H, et al. The ubiquity and impressive genomic diversity of human skin papillomaviruses suggest a commensalic nature of these viruses. J Virol. 2000;74:11636-11641.

23. Pfister H. Chapter 8: Human papillomavirus and skin cancer. J Natl Cancer Inst Monogr. 2003;31:52-56.

24. Massing AM, Epstein WL. Natural history of warts. A two year study. Arch Dermatol. 1963;87:306-310.

25. Williams HC, Pottier A, Strachan D. The descriptive epidemiology of warts in British schoolchildren. Br J Dermatol. 1993;128:504-511.

26. Larsson PA, Liden S. Prevalence of skin diseases among adolescents 12-16 years of age. Acta Derm Venereol. 1980;60:415-423.

27. Bonnez W. A comment on "Butcher's warts: Dermatological heritage or testable misinformation?" Arch Dermatol. 2002;138:411.

28. Majewski S, Jablonska S. Epidermodysplasia verruciformis as a model of human papillomavirus-induced genetic cancer of the skin. Arch Dermatol. 1995;131: 1312-1318.

29. Lane JE, Bowman PH, Cohen DJ. Epidermodysplasia verruciformis. South Med J. 2003;96:613-615.

30. Cates W Jr. Estimates of the incidence and prevalence of sexually transmitted diseases in the United States. American Social Health Association Panel. Sex Transm Dis. 1999;26:S2-S7.

31. Centers for Disease Control and Prevention. Sexually Transmitted Disease Surveillance, 2002. Atlanta: Department of Health and Human Services, September 2003.

32. Simms I, Fairley CK. Epidemiology of genital warts in England and Wales: 1971 to 1994. Genitourin Med. 1997;73:365-367.

33. Sexually transmitted disease quarterly report: Anogenital warts and anogenital herpes simplex virus infection in England and Wales. CDR Wkly. 1999;9:388-390.

34. Chuang T-Y, Perry HO, Kurland LT, et al. Condyloma acuminatum in Rochester, Minn, 1950-1978—I. Epidemiology and clinical features. Arch Dermatol. 1984;120:469-475.

35. Becker TM. Genital human papillomavirus infection: An epidemiological perspective. In: Norrby SR, ed. New Antiviral Strategies. Edinburgh: Churchill Livingstone; 1988:44-49.

36. Stone KM. Epidemiologic aspects of genital HPV infection. Clin Obstet Gynecol. 1989;32:112-116.

37. de Villiers E-M, Schneider A, Miklaw H, et al. Human papillomavirus infections in women with and without abnormal cytology. Lancet. 1987;2:703-706.

38. Garrido JL. Pathological incidence study of human papilloma virus (HPV) carried out on 1,439 patients between 1982-1985 in Panama. Eur J Gynaecol Oncol. 1988;9: 144-148.

39. Rosenfeld WD, Vermund SH, Wentz SJ, et al. High prevalence rate of human papillomavirus infection and association with abnormal Papanicolaou smears in sexually active adolescents. Am J Dis Child. 1989;143:1443-1447.

40. Derkay CS. Recurrent respiratory papillomatosis. Laryngoscope. 2001;111:57-69.

41. Bunney MH. Prevention of plantar warts by the use of protective footwear in swimming pool. Commun Med. 1972;127:127-129.

42. Kashima HK, Shah K. Recurrent respiratory papillomatosis. Clinical overview and management principles. Obstet Gynecol Clin North Am. 1987;14:581-588.

43. Oriel JD. Natural history of genital warts. Br J Vener Dis. 1971;47:1-13.

44. Koutsky LA, Galloway DA, Holmes KK. Epidemiology of genital human papillomavirus infection. Epidemiol Rev. 1988;10:122-163.

45. Habel LA, van den Eeden SK, Sherman KJ, et al. Risk factors for incident and recurrent condylomata acuminata among women. A population-based study. Sex Transm Dis. 1998;25:285-292.

46. van den Eeden SK, Habel LA, Sherman KJ, et al. Risk factors for incident and recurrent condylomata acuminata among men. A population-based study. Sex Transm Dis. 1998;25:278-284.

47. Fairley CK, Gay NJ, Forbes A, et al. Hand-genital transmission of genital warts? An analysis of prevalence data. Epidemiol Infect. 1995;115:169-176.

48. Obalek S, Jablonska S, Favre M, et al. Condylomata acuminata in children: Frequent association with human papillomaviruses responsible for cutaneous warts. J Am Acad Dermatol. 1990;23:205-213.

49. Cohen BA, Honig P, Androphy E. Anogenital warts in children: Clinical and virologic evaluation for sexual abuse. Arch Dermatol. 1990;126:1575-1580.

50. Gutman LT, Herman-Giddens ME, Phelps WC. Transmission of human genital papillomavirus disease: Comparison of data from adults and children. Pediatrics. 1993;91:31-38.

51. Silverberg MJ, Thorsen P, Lindeberg H, et al. Condyloma in pregnancy is strongly predictive of juvenile-onset recurrent respiratory papillomatosis. Obstet Gynecol. 2003;101:645-652.

52. Sawchuk WS, Weber PJ, Lowy DR, et al. Infectious papillomavirus in the vapor of warts treated with carbon dioxide laser or electrocoagulation: Detection and protection. J Am Acad Dermatol. 1989;21:41-49.

53. Bonnez W, Rose RC, Borkhuis C, et al. Evaluation of the temperature sensitivity of human papillomavirus (HPV) type 11 using the human xenograft severe combined immunodeficiency (SCID) mouse model. J Clin Microbiol. 1994;32:1575-1577.

54. Roden RB, Lowy DR, Schiller JT. Papillomavirus is resistant to desiccation. J Infect Dis. 1997;176:1076-1079.

55. Lancaster WD, Olson C. Animal papillomaviruses. Microbiol Rev. 1982;46:191-207.

56. Campo MS. Animal models of papillomavirus pathogenesis. Virus Res. 2002;89: 249-261.

57. Fraumeni JF Jr, Lloyd JW, Smith EM, et al. Cancer mortality among nuns: Role of marital status in etiology of neoplastic disease in women. J Natl Cancer Inst. 1969;42:455-468.

58. Human papillomaviruses. IARC Monogr Eval Carcinog Risks Hum. 1995;94:1-379.

59. Morris M, Tortolero-Luna G, Malpica A, et al. Cervical intraepithelial neoplasia and cervical cancer. Obstet Gynecol Clin North Am. 1996;23:347-410.

60. Franco EL. Epidemiology of anogenital warts and cancer. Obstet Gynecol Clin North Am. 1996;23:597-623.

61. Friis S, Kjaer SK, Frisch M, et al. Cervical intraepithelial neoplasia, anogenital cancer, and other cancer types in women after hospitalization for condylomata acuminata. J Infect Dis. 1997;175:743-748.

62. Bosch FX, De Sanjose S. Chapter 1: Human papillomavirus and cervical cancer—Burden and assessment of causality. J Natl Cancer Inst Monogr. 2003;31:3-13.

63. Wheeler C. Human papillomavirus type-specific prevalence. In: Myers G, Halpern A, Baker C, et al, eds. Human Papillomaviruses 1996—A Compilation and Analysis of Nucleic Acid and Amino Acid Sequences. Los Alamos, NM: Los Alamos National Laboratory; 1996:III-112-III-124.

64. Walboomers JM, Jacobs MV, Manos MM, et al. Human papillomavirus is a necessary cause of invasive cervical cancer worldwide. J Pathol. 1999;189:12-19.

65. Munoz N, Bosch FX, de Sanjose S, et al. Epidemiologic classification of human papillomavirus types associated with cervical cancer. N Engl J Med. 2003;348:518-527.

66. Xi LF, Toure P, Critchlow CW, et al. Prevalence of specific types of human papillomavirus and cervical squamous intraepithelial lesions in consecutive, previously unscreened, West-African women over 35 years of age. Int J Cancer. 2003;103:803-809.

67. Stoler MH, Broker TR. In situ hybridization detection of human papillomavirus DNAs and messenger RNAs in genital condylomas and cervical carcinoma. Hum Pathol. 1986;17:1250-1258.

68. Lamarcq L, Deeds J, Ginzinge D, et al. Measurements of human papillomavirus transcripts by real time quantitative reverse transcription–polymerase chain reaction in samples collected for cervical cancer screening. J Mol Diagn. 2002;4:97-102.

69. Dillner J. The serological response to papillomaviruses. Semin Cancer Biol. 1999;9:423-430.

70. Combita AL, Bravo MM, Touze A, et al. Serologic response to human oncogenic papillomavirus types 16, 18, 31, 33, 39, 58 and 59 virus-like particles in Colombian women with invasive cervical cancer. Int J Cancer. 2002;97:796-803.

71. Koutsky LA, Holmes KK, Critchlow CW, et al. A cohort study of the risk of cervical intraepithelial neoplasia grade 2 or 3 in relation to papillomavirus infection. N Engl J Med. 1992;327:1272-1278.

72. Liaw KL, Glass AG, Manos MM, et al. Detection of human papillomavirus DNA in cytologically normal women and subsequent cervical squamous intraepithelial lesions. J Natl Cancer Inst. 1999;91:954-960.

73. Ylitalo N, Sorensen P, Josefsson AM, et al. Consistent high viral load of human papillomavirus 16 and risk of cervical carcinoma in situ: A nested case-control study. Lancet. 2000;355:2194-2198.

74. Wang SS, Hildesheim A. Chapter 5: Viral and host factors in human papillomavirus persistence and progression. J Natl Cancer Inst Monogr. 2003;31:35-40.

75. Bosch FX, Munoz N. The viral etiology of cervical cancer. Virus Res. 2002;89: 183-190.

76. Koutsky LA, Ault KA, Wheeler CM, et al. A controlled trial of a human papillomavirus type 16 vaccine. N Engl J Med. 2002;347:1645-1651.

77. Daling JR, Madeleine MM, Schwartz SM, et al. A population-based study of squamous cell vaginal cancer: HPV and cofactors. Gynecol Oncol. 2002;84:263-270.

78. Joura EA. Epidemiology, diagnosis and treatment of vulvar intraepithelial neoplasia. Curr Opin Obstet Gynecol. 2002;14:39-43.

79. Weiderpass E, Ye W, Tamimi R, et al. Alcoholism and risk for cancer of the cervix uteri, vagina, and vulva. Cancer Epidemiol Biomarkers Prev. 2001;10:899-901.

80. de Sanjose S, Palefsky J. Cervical and anal HPV infections in IIIV positive women and men. Virus Res. 2002;89:201-211.

81. Frisch M. On the etiology of anal squamous carcinoma. Dan Med Bull. 2002;49: 194-209.

82. Dillner J, von Krogh G, Horenblas S, et al. Etiology of squamous cell carcinoma of the penis. Scand J Urol Nephrol Suppl. 2000;205:189-193.

83. Andersson S, Larson B, Hjerpe A, et al. Adenocarcinoma of the uterine cervix: The presence of human papillomavirus and the method of detection. Acta Obstet Gynecol Scand. 2003;82:960-965.

84. Andersson S, Rylander E, Larson B, et al. Types of human papillomavirus revealed in cervical adenocarcinomas after DNA sequencing. Oncol Rep. 2003;10:175-179.

85. Andersson S, Rylander E, Larsson B, et al. The role of human papillomavirus in cervical adenocarcinoma carcinogenesis. Eur J Cancer. 2001;37:246-250.

86. Syrjänen KJ. HPV infections and lung cancer. J Clin Pathol. 2002;55:885-891.

87. Syrjänen KJ. HPV infections and oesophageal cancer. J Clin Pathol. 2002;55: 721-728.

88. Gillison ML, Shah KV. Chapter 9: Role of mucosal human papillomavirus in nongenital cancers. J Natl Cancer Inst Monogr. 2003;31:57-65.

89. Herrero R. Chapter 7: Human papillomavirus and cancer of the upper aerodigestive tract. J Natl Cancer Inst Monogr. 2003;2003:47-51.

90. Castle PE, Giuliano AR. Chapter 4: Genital tract infections, cervical inflammation, and antioxidant nutrients—Assessing their roles as human papillomavirus cofactors. J Natl Cancer Inst Monogr. 2003;31:29-34.

91. Castellsague X, Munoz N. Chapter 3: Cofactors in human papillomavirus carcinogenesis—Role of parity, oral contraceptives, and tobacco smoking. J Natl Cancer Inst Monogr. 2003;31:20-28.

92. Castellsague X, Bosch FX, Munoz N. Environmental co-factors in HPV carcinogenesis. Virus Res. 2002;89:191-199.

93. Palefsky JM, Holly EA. Chapter 6: Immunosuppression and co-infection with HIV. J Natl Cancer Inst Monogr. 2003;31:41-46.

94. Hildesheim A, Wang SS. Host and viral genetics and risk of cervical cancer: A review. Virus Res. 2002;89:229-240.

95. Madeleine MM, Brumback B, Cushing-Haugen KL, et al. Human leukocyte antigen class II and cervical cancer risk: A population-based study. J Infect Dis. 2002;186:1565-1574.

96. Montgomery SM, Ehlin AG, Sparen P, et al. Childhood indicators of susceptibility to subsequent cervical cancer. Br J Cancer. 2002;87:989-993.

97. Goldschmidt H, Klingman AM. Experimental inoculation of humans with ectodermotropic viruses. J Invest Dermatol. 1958;31:175-182.

98. Barrett TJ, Silbar JD, McGinley JP. Genital warts—A venereal disease. JAMA. 1954;154:333-334.

99. Lehr E, Jarnik M, Brown DR. Human papillomavirus type 11 alters the transcription and expression of loricrin, the major cell envelope protein. Virology. 2002;298:240-247.

100. Ferenczy A, Mitao M, Nagai N, et al. Latent papillomavirus and recurring warts. N Engl J Med. 1985;313:784-788.

101. Steinberg BM, Gallagher T, Stoler M, et al. Persistence and expression of human papillomavirus during interferon therapy. Arch Otolaryngol Head Neck Surg. 1988;114:27-32.

102. Thorland EC, Myers SL, Gostout BS, et al. Common fragile sites are preferential targets for HPV16 integrations in cervical tumors. Oncogene. 2003;22:1225-1237.

103. Kirchner H. Immunobiology of human papillomavirus infection. Prog Med Virol. 1986;33:1-41.

104. Garman ME, Tyring SK. The cutaneous manifestations of HIV infection. Dermatol Clin. 2002;20:193-208.

105. Peto J. Cancer epidemiology in the last century and the next decade. Nature. 2001;411:390-395.

106. Leigh IM, Buchanan JA, Harwood CA, et al. Role of human papillomaviruses in cutaneous and oral manifestations of immunosuppression. J Acquir Immune Defic Syndr. 1999;21:S49-S57.

107. Penn I. Cancers in renal transplant recipients. Adv Ren Replace Ther. 2000;7:147-156.

108. Frisch M, Biggar RJ, Goedert JJ. Human papillomavirus-associated cancers in patients with human immunodeficiency virus infection and acquired immunodeficiency syndrome. J Natl Cancer Inst. 2000;92:1500-1510.

109. 1993 revised classification system for HIV infection and expanded surveillance case definition for AIDS among adolescents and adults. MMWR Morb Mortal Wkly Rep. 1992;41:1-19.

110. Frisch M, Biggar RJ, Engels EA, et al. Association of cancer with AIDS-related immunosuppression in adults. JAMA. 2001;285:1736-1745.

111. Reichman RC, Oakes D, Bonnez W, et al. Treatment of condyloma acuminatum with three different interferons administered intralesionally: A double-blind, placebo-controlled trial. Ann Intern Med. 1988;108:675-679.

112. Tagami H. Regression phenomenon of numerous flat warts—An experiment on the nature of tumor immunity in man. Int J Dermatol. 1983;22:570-571.

113. Arena S, Marconi M, Ubertosi M, et al. HPV and pregnancy: Diagnostic methods, transmission and evolution. Minerva Ginecol. 2002;54:225-237.

114. Kemp EA, Hakenewerth AM, Laurent SL, et al. Human papillomavirus prevalence in pregnancy. Obstet Gynecol. 1992;79:649-656.

115. Morrison EA, Gammon MD, Goldberg GL, et al. Pregnancy and cervical infection with human papillomaviruses. Int J Gynaecol Obstet. 1996;54:125-130.

116. Nobbenhuis MA, Helmerhorst TJ, van den Brule AJ, et al. High-risk human papillomavirus clearance in pregnant women: Trends for lower clearance during pregnancy with a catch-up postpartum. Br J Cancer. 2002;87:75-80.

117. Majewski S, Jablonska S, Orth G. Epidermodysplasia verruciformis. Immunological and nonimmunological surveillance mechanisms: Role in tumor progression. Clin Dermatol. 1997;15:321-334.

118. Scott M, Nakagawa M, Moscicki AB. Cell-mediated immune response to human papillomavirus infection. Clin Diagn Lab Immunol. 2001;8:209-220.

119. Kienzler JL, Lemoine MT, Orth G, et al. Humoral and cell-mediated immunity to human papillomavirus type 1 (HPV-1) in human warts. Br J Dermatol. 1983;108:665-672.

120. Höpfl R, Sandblicher M, Sepp N, et al. Skin test for HPV-16 proteins in cervical intraepithelial neoplasia. Lancet. 1991;337:373-374.

121. Eiben GL, Velders MP, Kast WM. The cell-mediated immune response to human papillomavirus-induced cervical cancer: Implications for immunotherapy. Adv Cancer Res. 2002;86:113-148.

122. Charleson FC, Norval M, Benton EC, et al. Lymphoproliferative responses to human papillomavirus in patients with cutaneous warts. Br J Dermatol. 1992;127:551-559.

123. Malejczyk J, Malejczyk M, Majewski S, et al. NK-cell activity in patients with HPV 16–associated anogenital tumors: Defective recognition of HPV 16–harboring keratinocytes and restricted unresponsiveness to immunostimulatory cytokines. Int J Cancer. 1993;54:917-921.

124. Schneider A. Pathogenesis of genital HPV infection. Genitourin Med. 1993;69:165-173.

125. Hong K, Greer CE, Ketter N, et al. Isolation and characterization of human papillomavirus type 6–specific T cells infiltrating genital warts. J Virol. 1997;71:6427-6432.

126. Oguchi M, Komura J, Tagami H, et al. Ultrastructural studies of spontaneously regressing plane warts. Macrophages attack verruca-epidermal cells. Arch Dermatol Res. 1981;270:403-411.

127. Bonnez W, DaRin C, Rose RC, et al. Use of human papillomavirus type 11 virions in an ELISA to detect specific antibodies in humans with condylomata acuminata. J Gen Virol. 1991;72:1343-1347.

128. Bonnez W, Kashima HK, Leventhal B, et al. Antibody response to human papillomavirus (HPV) type 11 in children with juvenile-onset recurrent respiratory papillomatosis. Virology. 1992;188:384-387.

129. Rose RC, Reichman RC, Bonnez W. Human papillomavirus type 11 (HPV-11) recombinant virus-like particles (VLPs) induce the formation of neutralizing antibodies and detect HPV-specific antibodies in human sera. J Gen Virol. 1994;75:2075-2079.

130. Studentsov YY, Schiffman M, Strickler HD, et al. Enhanced enzyme-linked immunosorbent assay for detection of antibodies to virus-like particles of human papillomavirus. J Clin Microbiol. 2002;40:1755-1760.

131. Karem KL, Poon AC, Bierl C, et al. Optimization of a human papillomavirus-specific enzyme-linked immunosorbent assay. Clin Diagn Lab Immunol. 2002;9:577-582.

132. Marais DJ, Rose RC, Lane C, et al. Seroresponses to human papillomavirus types 16, 18, 31, 33, and 45 virus-like particles in South African women with cervical cancer and cervical intraepithelial neoplasia. J Med Virol. 2000;60:403-410.

133. Touze A, Dupuy C, Mahe D, et al. Production of recombinant virus-like particles from human papillomavirus types 6 and 11, and study of serological reactivities between HPV 6, 11, 16 and 45 by ELISA: Implications for papillomavirus prevention and detection. FEMS Microbiol Lett. 1998;160:111-118.

134. Meschede W, Zumbach K, Braspenning J, et al. Antibodies against early proteins of human papillomaviruses as diagnostic markers for invasive cervical cancer. J Clin Microbiol. 1998;36:475-480.

135. Bonnez W, DaRin C, Rose RC, et al. Evolution of the antibody response to human papillomavirus type 11 (HPV-11) in patients with condyloma acuminatum according to treatment response. J Med Virol. 1993;39:340-344.

136. Lehtinen M, Leminen A, Kuoppala T, et al. Pre- and posttreatment serum antibody responses to HPV 16 E2 and HSV 2 ICP8 proteins in women with cervical carcinoma. J Med Virol. 1992;37:180-186.

137. af Geijersstam V, Kibur M, Wang Z, et al. Stability over time of serum antibody levels to human papillomavirus type 16. J Infect Dis. 1998;177:1710-1714.

138. Bousarghin L, Combita-Rojas AL, Touze A, et al. Detection of neutralizing antibodies against human papillomaviruses (HPV) by inhibition of gene transfer mediated by HPV pseudovirions. J Clin Microbiol. 2002;40:926-932.

139. Kawana K, Yasugi T, Yoshikawa H, et al. Evidence for the presence of neutralizing antibodies against human papillomavirus type 6 in infants born to mothers with condyloma acuminata. Am J Perinatol. 2003;20:11-16.

140. Kawana K, Yasugi T, Kanda T, et al. Neutralizing antibodies against oncogenic human papillomavirus as a possible determinant of the fate of low-grade cervical intraepithelial neoplasia. Biochem Biophys Res Commun. 2002;296:102-105.

141. Ho GY, Studentsov Y, Hall CB, et al. Risk factors for subsequent cervicovaginal human papillomavirus (HPV) infection and the protective role of antibodies to HPV-16 virus-like particles. J Infect Dis. 2002;186:737-742.

142. Grussendorf-Conen E-I. Papillomavirus-induced tumors of the skin: Cutaneous warts and epidermodysplasia verruciformis. In: Syrjänen K, Gissmann L, Koss LG, eds. Papillomaviruses and Human Disease. New York: Springer Verlag; 1987:158-181.

143. Jablonska S, Orth G, Obalek S, et al. Cutaneous warts. Clinical, histologic, and virologic correlations. Clin Dermatol. 1985;3:71-82.

144. Schwartz RA. Verrucous carcinoma of the skin and mucosa. J Am Acad Dermatol. 1995;32:1-21.

145. Allington HV. Review of the psychotherapy of warts. AMA Arch Derm Syphilol. 1952;66:316-326.

146. Ramoz N, Rueda LA, Bouadjar B, et al. Mutations in two adjacent novel genes are associated with epidermodysplasia verruciformis. Nat Genet. 2002;32:579-581.

147. Orth G, Favre M, Majewski S, et al. Epidermodysplasia verruciformis defines a subset of cutaneous human papillomaviruses. J Virol. 2001;75:4952-4953.

148. Majewski S, Jablonska S. Human papillomavirus-associated tumors of the skin and mucosa. J Am Acad Dermatol. 1997;36:659-685.

149. Majewski S, Jablonska S. Do epidermodysplasia verruciformis human papillomaviruses contribute to malignant and benign epidermal proliferations? Arch Dermatol. 2002;138:649-654.

150. von Krogh G. Podophyllotoxin for condylomata acuminata eradication. Clinical and experimental comparative studies on Podophyllum lignans, colchicine and 5-fluorouracil. Acta Derm Venereol Suppl (Stockh). 1981;98:1-48.

151. Kaplinsky RS, Pranikoff K, Chasan S, et al. Indications for urethroscopy in male patients with penile condylomata. J Urol. 1995;153:1120-1121.

152. Goorney BP, Waugh MA, Clarke J. Anal warts in heterosexual men. Genitourin Med. 1987;63:216.

153. Oriel JD. Anal warts and anal coitus. Br J Vener Dis. 1971;47:373-376.

154. Barrasso R, De Brux J, Croissant O, et al. High prevalence of papillomavirus-associated penile intraepithelial neoplasia in sexual partners of women with cervical intraepithelial neoplasia. N Engl J Med. 1987;317:916-923.

155. Reid R, Laverty CR, Coppleson M, et al. Noncondylomatous cervical wart virus infection. Obstet Gynecol. 1980;55:476-483.

156. Walker P, Dexeus S, De Palo G, et al. International terminology of colposcopy: An updated report from the International Federation for Cervical Pathology and Colposcopy. Obstet Gynecol. 2003;101:175-177.

157. Walker PG, Colley NV, Grubb C, et al. Abnormalities of the uterine cervix in women with vulvar warts. Br J Vener Dis. 1983;59:120-123.

158. Schwebke JR, Zajackowski ME. Effect of concurrent lower genital tract infections on cervical cancer screening. Genitourin Med. 1997;73:383-386.

159. Väyrynen M, Syrjänen H, Castrén O, et al. Colposcopy in women with papillomavirus lesions of the uterine cervix. Obstet Gynecol. 1985;65:409-415.

160. Dexeus S, Cararach M, Dexeus D. The role of colposcopy in modern gynecology. Eur J Gynaecol Oncol. 2002;23:269-277.

161. Roy M, Meisels A, Fortier M, et al. Vaginal condylomata: A human papillomavirus infection. Clin Obstet Gynecol. 1981;24:461-483.

162. Strand A, Wilander E, Zehbe I, et al. Vulvar papillomatosis, aceto-white lesions, and normal-looking vulvar mucosa evaluated by microscopy and human papillomavirus analysis. Gynecol Obstet Invest. 1995;40:265-270.

163. Gentile G, Formelli G, Pelusi G, et al. Is vestibular micropapillomatosis associated with human papillomavirus infection? Eur J Gynaecol Oncol. 1997;18:523-525.

164. Strand A, Rylander E. Human papillomavirus. Subclinical and atypical manifestations. Dermatol Clin. 1998;16:817-822.

165. Boardman LA, Peipert JF. Vulvar vestibulitis: Is it a defined and treatable entity? Clin Obstet Gynecol. 1999;42:945-956.

166. Edwards L. New concepts in vulvodynia. Am J Obstet Gynecol. 2003;189(3 Suppl):S24-S30.

167. Rosemberg SK, Jacobs H, Fuller T. Some guidelines in the treatment of urethral condylomata with carbon dioxide laser. J Urol. 1982;127:906-908.

168. Campion MJ. Clinical manifestations and natural history of genital human papillomavirus infection. Obstet Gynecol Clin North Am. 1987;14:363-388.

169. Demeter LM, Stoler MH, Bonnez W, et al. Penile intraepithelial neoplasia: Clinical presentation and an analysis of the physical state of human papillomavirus DNA. J Infect Dis. 1993;168:38-46.

170. Gross G, Ikenberg H, Gissmann L, et al. Papillomavirus infection of the anogenital region: Correlation between histology, clinical picture, and virus type. Proposal of a new nomenclature. J Invest Dermatol. 1985;85:147-152.

171. Löwhagen G-B, Bolmstedt A, Ryd W, et al. The prevalence of "high-risk" HPV types in penile condyloma-like lesions: Correlation between HPV type and morphology. Genitourin Med. 1993;69:87-90.

172. Maw RD, Reitano M, Roy M. An international survey of patients with genital warts: Perceptions regarding treatment and impact on lifestyle. Int J STD AIDS. 1998;9:571-578.

173. Schonfeld A, Nitke S, Schattner A, et al. Intramuscular human interferon-β injections in treatment of condylomata acuminata. Lancet. 1984;1:1038-1042.

174. Reichman RC, Oakes D, Bonnez W, et al. Treatment of condyloma acuminatum with three different alpha interferon preparations administered parenterally: A double-blind, placebo-controlled trial. J Infect Dis. 1990;162:1270-1276.

175. Recurrent condylomata acuminata treated with recombinant interferon alfa-2a. A multicenter double-blind placebo-controlled clinical trial. Condylomata International Collaborative Study Group. JAMA. 1991;265:2684-2687.

176. Schiffman MH. Latest HPV findings: Some clinical implications. Contemp OB/GYN. 1993;38:27-40.

177. Beutner KR, Wiley DJ, Douglas JM, et al. Genital warts and their treatment. Clin Infect Dis. 1998;28:S37-S56.

178. Osborne NG, Adelson MD. Herpes simplex and human papillomavirus genital infections: Controversies around obstetric management. Clin Obstet Gynecol. 1990;33:801-811.

179. Becker FT, Walder HJ, Larson DM. Giant condylomata acuminata. Buschke-Lowenstein tumor. Arch Dermatol. 1969;100:184-186.

180. Kibrite A, Zeitouni NC, Cloutier R. Aggressive giant condyloma acuminatum associated with oncogenic human papilloma virus: A case report. Can J Surg. 1997;40:143-145.

181. Cubilla AL, Velazques EF, Reuter VE, et al. Warty (condylomatous) squamous cell carcinoma of the penis: A report of 11 cases and proposed classification of 'verruciform' penile tumors. Am J Surg Pathol. 2000;24:505-512.

182. Anderson MC, Brown CL, Buckley CH, et al. Current views on cervical intraepithelial neoplasia. J Clin Pathol. 1991;44:969-978.

183. Okagaki T. Impact of human papillomavirus research on the histopathologic concepts of genital neoplasms. Curr Top Pathol. 1992;85:273-307.

184. Wade TR, Kopf AW, Ackerman AB. Bowenoid papulosis of the penis. Cancer. 1978;42:1890-1903.

185. De Villez RL, Stevens CS. Bowenoid papules of the genitalia. A case progressing to Bowen's disease. J Am Acad Dermatol. 1980;3:149-152.

186. Ikenberg H, Gissmann L, Gross G, et al. Human papillomavirus type 16–related DNA in genital Bowen's disease and in bowenoid papulosis. Int J Cancer. 1983;32:563-565.

187. Östör AG. Natural history of cervical intraepithelial neoplasia: A critical review. Int J Gynecol Pathol. 1993;12:186-192.

188. Schlappner OLA, Schaffer EA. Anorectal condylomata acuminata: A missed part of the condyloma spectrum. Can Med Assoc J. 1978;118:172-173.

189. Prassad ML, Abcarian H. Malignant potential of perianal condyloma acuminatum. Dis Colon Rectum. 1980;23:191-197.

190. Metcalf AM, Dean T. Risk of dysplasia in anal condyloma. Surgery. 1995;118:724-726.

191. Koblin BA, Hessol NA, Zauber AG, et al. Increased incidence of cancer among homosexual men, New York City and San Francisco, 1978-1990. Am J Epidemiol. 1996;144:916-923.

192. Daling JR, Weiss NS, Hislop TG, et al. Sexual practices, sexually transmitted diseases, and the incidence of anal cancer. N Engl J Med. 1987;317:973-977.

193. Frisch M, Glimelius B, van den Brule AJ, et al. Sexually transmitted infection as a cause of anal cancer. N Engl J Med. 1997;337:1350-1358.

194. Ziegler A, Kastner C, Chang-Claude J. Analysis of pregnancy and other factors on detection of human papilloma virus (HPV) infection using weighted estimating equations for follow-up data. Stat Med. 2003;22:2217-2233.

195. Watts DH, Koutsky LA, Holmes KK, et al. Low risk of perinatal transmission of human papillomavirus: Results from a prospective cohort study. Am J Obstet Gynecol. 1998;178:365-373.

196. Armstrong DK, Handley JM. Anogenital warts in prepubertal children: Pathogenesis, HPV typing and management. Int J STD AIDS. 1997;8:78-81.

197. Hammerschlag MR. Sexually transmitted diseases in sexually abused children: Medical and legal implications. Sex Transm Dis. 1998;74:167-174.

198. Bauman NM, Smith RJ. Recurrent respiratory papillomatosis. Pediatr Clin North Am. 1996;43:1385-1401.

199. Lindeberg H, Elbrond O. Malignant tumours in patients with a history of multiple laryngeal papillomas: The significance of irradiation. Clin Otolaryngol. 1991;16:149-151.

200. Bonnez WA. Issues with HIV and oral human papillomavirus infections. AIDS Reader. 2002;12:174-176.

201. Syrjänen S. Human papillomavirus infections and oral tumors. Med Microbiol Immunol (Berl). 2003;192:123-128.

202. Adler-Storthz K, Ficarra G, Woods KV, et al. Prevalence of Epstein-Barr virus and human papillomavirus in oral mucosa of HIV-infected patients. J Oral Pathol Med. 1992;21:164-170.

203. Sjo NC, Heegaard S, Prause JU, et al. Human papillomavirus in conjunctival papilloma. Br J Ophthalmol. 2001;85:785-787.

204. Tabrizi SN, McCurrach FE, Drewe RH, et al. Human papillomavirus in corneal and conjunctival carcinoma. Aust NZ J Ophthalmol. 1997;25:211-215.

205. Karcioglu ZA, Issa TM. Human papilloma virus in neoplastic and non-neoplastic conditions of the external eye. Br J Ophthalmol. 1997;81:595-598.

206. Elston DM, Parker LU, Tuthill RJ. Epidermoid cyst of the scalp containing human papillomavirus. J Cutan Pathol. 1993;20:184-186.

207. Bai H, Cviko A, Granter S, et al. Immunophenotypic and viral (human papillomavirus) correlates of vulvar seborrheic keratosis. Hum Pathol. 2003;34:559-564.

208. Iftner A, Klug SJ, Garbe C, et al. The prevalence of human papillomavirus genotypes in nonmelanoma skin cancers of nonimmunosuppressed individuals identifies high-risk genital types as possible risk factors. Cancer Res. 2003;63:7515-7519.

209. Harwood CA, Surentheran T, McGregor JM, et al. Human papillomavirus infection and non-melanoma skin cancer in immunosuppressed and immunocompetent individuals. J Med Virol. 2000;61:289-297.

210. Syrjanen KJ. HPV infections in benign and malignant sinonasal lesions. J Clin Pathol. 2003;56:174-181.

211. Wright VC. Contemporary Colposcopy. Obstetrics and Gynecology Clinics. Philadelphia: WB Saunders; 1993.

212. Sedlacek TV, Cunnane M, Carpiniello V. Colposcopy in the diagnosis of penile condyloma. Am J Obstet Gynecol. 1986;154:494-496.

213. Krebs H-B, Schneider V. Human papillomavirus-associated lesions of the penis: Colposcopy, cytology, and histology. Obstet Gynecol. 1987;70:299-304.

214. Singer A, Campion MJ, Clarkson PK, et al. Recognition of subclinical human papillomavirus infection of the vulva. J Reprod Med. 1986;31:985-986.

215. Panici PB, Scambia G, Perrone L, et al. Oral condyloma lesions in patients with extensive genital human papillomavirus infection. Am J Obstet Gynecol. 1992;167:451-458.

216. Reid R, Greenberg M, Jenson AB, et al. Sexually transmitted papillomaviral infections: I. The anatomic distribution and pathologic grade of neoplastic lesions associated with different viral types. Am J Obstet Gynecol. 1987;156:212-222.

217. Jonsson M, Karlsson R, Evander M, et al. Acetowhitening of the cervix and vulva as a predictor of subclinical human papillomavirus infection: Sensitivity and specificity in a population-based study. Obstet Gynecol. 1997;90:744-747.

218. McMillan A. Sigmoidoscopy—A necessary procedure in the routine investigation of homosexual men? Genitourin Med. 1987;63:44-46.

219. Parker BJ, Cossart YE, Thompson H, et al. The clinical management and laboratory assessment of anal warts. Med J Aust. 1987;147:59-63.

220. Sidawy MK. Cytology in gynecological disorders. Curr Top Pathol. 1992;85:233-272.

221. Sherman ME. Chapter 11: Future directions in cervical pathology. J Natl Cancer Inst Monogr. 2003;31:72-79.

222. Nanda K, McCrory DC, Myers ER, et al. Accuracy of the Papanicolaou test in screening for and follow-up of cervical cytologic abnormalities: A systematic review. Ann Intern Med. 2000;132:810-819.

223. Palefsky JM, Holly EA, Hogeboom CJ, et al. Anal cytology as a screening tool for anal squamous intraepithelial lesions. J Acquir Immune Defic Syndr Hum Retrovirol. 1997;14:415-422.

224. Goldie SJ, Kuntz KM, Weinstein MC, et al. The clinical effectiveness and cost-effectiveness of screening for anal squamous intraepithelial lesions in homosexual and bisexual HIV-positive men. JAMA. 1999;281:1822-1829.

225. Palefsky JM, Holly EA, Ralston ML, et al. Anal squamous intraepithelial lesions in HIV-positive and HIV-negative homosexual and bisexual men: Prevalence and risk factors. J Acquir Immune Defic Syndr Hum Retrovirol. 1998;17:320-326.

226. Chin-Hong PV, Palefsky JM. Natural history and clinical management of anal human papillomavirus disease in men and women infected with human immunodeficiency virus. Clin Infect Dis. 2002;35:1127-1134.

227. Wright TC Jr, Cox JT, Massad LS, et al. 2001 consensus guidelines for the management of women with cervical intraepithelial neoplasia. Am J Obstet Gynecol. 2003;189:295-304.

228. Lorincz AT, Richart RM. Human papillomavirus DNA testing as an adjunct to cytology in cervical screening programs. Arch Pathol Lab Med. 2003;127:959-968.

229. Cuzick J, Szarewski A, Cubie H, et al. Management of women who test positive for high-risk types of human papillomavirus: The HART study. Lancet. 2003;362:1871-1876.

230. Solomon D, Davey D, Kurman R, et al. The 2001 Bethesda System: Terminology for reporting results of cervical cytology. JAMA. 2002;287:2114-2119.

231. Wright TC Jr, Cox JY, Massad LS, et al. 2001 consensus guidelines for the management of women with cervical cytological abnormalities. JAMA. 2002;287:2120-2129.

232. Stoler MH, Schiffman M. Interobserver reproducibility of cervical cytologic and histologic interpretations. Realistic estimates from the ASCUS-LSIL Triage Study. JAMA. 2001;285:1500-1505.

233. Iftner T, Villa LL. Chapter 12: Human papillomavirus technologies. J Natl Cancer Inst Monogr. 2003;31:80-88.

234. Kornegay JR, Roger M, Davies PO, et al. International proficiency study of a consensus L1 PCR assay for the detection and typing of human papillomavirus DNA: Evaluation of accuracy and intralaboratory and interlaboratory agreement. J Clin Microbiol. 2003;41:1080-1086.

235. Underwood MR, Shewchuk LM, Hassell AM, et al. Searching for antiviral drugs for human papillomaviruses. Antiviral Ther. 2000;5:229-242.

236. Stanley M. Chapter 17: Genital human papillomavirus infections—Current and prospective therapies. J Natl Cancer Inst Monogr. 2003;31:117-124.

237. Gibbs S, Harvey I, Sterling J, et al. Local treatments for cutaneous warts: Systematic review. BMJ. 2002;325:461.

238. Jackson AD. Cryosurgery: A guide for GPs. Practitioner. 1999;243:131-136.

239. Connolly M, Bazmi K, O'Connell M, et al. Cryotherapy of viral warts: A sustained 10-s freeze is more effective than the traditional method. Br J Dermatol. 2001;145:554-557.

240. Bourke JF, Berth-Jones J, Hutchinson PE. Cryotherapy of common viral warts at intervals of 1, 2 and 3 weeks. Br J Dermatol. 1995;132:433-436.

241. Berth-Jones J, Hutchinson PE. Modern treatment of warts: Cure rates at 3 and 6 months. Br J Dermatol. 1992;127:262-265.

242. Focht DR 3rd, Spicer C, Fairchok MP. The efficacy of duct tape vs cryotherapy in the treatment of verruca vulgaris (the common wart). Arch Pediatr Adolesc Med. 2002;156:971-974.

243. Torrelo A. What's new in the treatment of viral warts in children. Pediatr Dermatol. 2002;19:191-199.

244. Buckley DA, Du Vivier AW. The therapeutic use of topical contact sensitizers in benign dermatoses. Br J Dermatol. 2001;145:385-405.

245. Najarian DJ, English JC III. Imiquimod cream: A new multipurpose topical therapy for dermatology. P&T. 2003;28:122-126.

246. Benton EC. Therapy of cutaneous warts. Clin Dermatol. 1997;15:449-455.

247. Tanzi EL, Lupton JR, Alster TS. Lasers in dermatology: Four decades of progress. J Am Acad Dermatol. 2003;49:1-31; quiz 31-34.

248. Odell RC. Electrosurgery: Principles and safety issues. Clin Obstet Gynecol. 1995;38:610-620.

249. Shenefelt PD. Hypnosis in dermatology. Arch Dermatol. 2000;136:393-399.

250. Johnson RFQ, Barber TX. Hypnosis, suggestion, and warts: An experimental investigation implicating the importance of "believed-in efficacy." Am J Clin Hypn. 1978;20:165-174.

251. Spanos NP, Stenstrom RJ, Johnston JC. Hypnosis, placebo, and suggestion in the treatment of warts. Psychosom Med. 1988;50:245-260.

252. Smolle J, Prause G, Kerl H. A double-blind, controlled clinical trial of homeopathy and an analysis of lunar phases and postoperative outcome. Arch Dermatol. 1998;134:1368-1370.

253. Harkness EF, Abbot NC, Ernst E. A randomized trial of distant healing for skin warts. Am J Med. 2000;108:448-452.

254. Beutner KR, Reitano MV, Richwald GA, et al. External genital warts—Report of the American Medical Association Consensus Conference. Clin Infect Dis. 1998;27: 796-806.

255. von Krogh G. Management of anogenital warts (condylomata acuminata). Eur J Dermatol. 2001;11:598-603; quiz 604.

256. Sexually transmitted diseases treatment guidelines 2002. Centers for Disease Control and Prevention. MMWR Recomm Rep. 2002;51:1-78.

257. Wiley DJ, Douglas J, Beutner K, et al. External genital warts: Diagnosis, treatment, and prevention. Clin Infect Dis. 2002;35:S210-S224.

258. Wiley DJ. Genital warts. Clin Evid. 2002;1426-1436.

259. Krebs H-B, Helmkamp BF. Does the treatment of genital condylomata in men decrease the treatment failure rate of cervical dysplasia in the female sexual partner? Obstet Gynecol. 1990;76:660-663.

260. Sigurgeirsson B, Lindelöf B, Eklund G. Condylomata acuminata and risk of cancer: An epidemiological study. BMJ. 1991;303:341-344.

261. Gilbert LK, Alexander L, Grosshans JF, et al. Answering frequently asked questions about HPV. Sex Transm Dis. 2003;30:193-194.

262. Miller RA. Podophyllin. Int J Dermatol. 1985;24:491-498.

263. von Krogh G, Longstaff E. Podophyllin office therapy against condyloma should be abandoned. Sex Transm Infect. 2001;77:409-412.

264. Beutner KR. Podophyllotoxin in the treatment of genital human papillomavirus infection: A review. Semin Dermatol. 1987;6:10-18.

265. Lacey CJ, Goodall RL, Tennvall GR, et al. Randomised controlled trial and economic evaluation of podophyllotoxin solution, podophyllotoxin cream, and podophyllin in the treatment of genital warts. Sex Transm Infect. 2003;79:270-275.

266. Beutner KR, Friedman-Kien AE, Artman NN, et al. Patient-applied podofilox for treatment of genital warts. Lancet. 1989;1:831-834.

267. Kirby P, Dunne A, King DH, et al. Double-blind randomized clinical trial of self-administered podofilox solution versus vehicle in the treatment of genital warts. Am J Med. 1990;88:465-469.

268. Greenberg MD, Rutledge LH, Reid R, et al. A double-blind, randomized trial of 0.5% Podofilox and placebo for the treatment of genital warts in women. Obstet Gynecol. 1991;77:735-739.

269. Bonnez W, Elswick RK Jr, Bailey-Farchione A, et al. Efficacy and safety of 0.5% podofilox solution in the treatment and suppression of anogenital warts. Am J Med. 1994;96:420-425.

270. Tyring S, Edwards L, Cherry LK, et al. Safety and efficacy of 0.5-percent podofilox gel in the treatment of anogenital warts. Arch Dermatol. 1998;134:33-38.

271. Hurwitz DJ, Pincus L, Kupper TS. Imiquimod: A topically applied link between innate and acquired immunity. Arch Dermatol. 2003;139:1347-1350.

272. Slade HB, Owens ML, Tomai MA, et al. Imiquimod 5% cream (Aldara™). Exp Opin Invest Drugs. 1998;7:437-449.

273. Beutner KR, Spruance SL, Hougham AJ, et al. Treatment of genital warts with an immune-response modifier (imiquimod). J Am Acad Dermatol. 1998;38:230-239.

274. Edwards L, Ferenczy A, Eron L, et al. Self-administered topical 5% imiquimod cream for external anogenital warts. Arch Dermatol. 1998;134:25-30.

275. Beutner KR, Tyring SK, Trofatter KF Jr, et al. Imiquimod, a patient-applied immune-response modifier for treatment of external genital warts. Antimicrob Agents Chemother. 1998;42:789-794.

276. Moore RA, Edwards JE, Hopwood J, et al. Imiquimod for the treatment of genital warts: A quantitative systematic review. BMC Infect Dis. 2001;1:3.

277. Garland SM, Sellors JW, Wikstrom A, et al. Imiquimod 5% cream is a safe and effective self-applied treatment for anogenital warts—Results of an open-label, multicentre phase IIIB trial. Int J STD AIDS. 2001;12:722-729.

278. Richart RM, Kaufman RM, Woodruff JD. Advances in managing condylomas. Contemp OB/GYN. 1982;20:164-171, 175, 177, 180, 182, 187, 188, 190-192, 194.

279. Godley MJ, Bradbeer CS, Gellan M, et al. Cryotherapy compared with trichloracetic acid in treating genital warts. Genitourin Med. 1987;63:390-392.

280. Abdullah AN, Walzman M, Wade A. Treatment of external genital warts comparing cryotherapy (liquid nitrogen) and trichloracetic acid. Sex Transm Dis. 1993;20:344-345.

281. Gabriel G, Thin RNT. Treatment of anogenital warts: Comparison of trichloracetic acid and podophyllin versus podophyllin alone. Br J Vener Dis. 1983;59:124-126.

282. Boothby RA, Carlson JA, Rubin M, et al. Single application treatment of human papillomavirus infection of the cervix and vagina with trichloracetic acid: A randomized trial. Obstet Gynecol. 1990;76:278-280.

283. Stone KM. Human papillomavirus infection and genital warts: Update on epidemiology and treatment. Clin Infect Dis. 1995;20(Suppl 1):S91-S97.

284. Bashi SA. Cryotherapy versus podophyllin in the treatment of genital warts. Int J Dermatol. 1985;24:535-536.

285. Stone KM, Becker TM, Hadgu A, et al. Treatment of external genital warts: A randomised clinical trial comparing podophyllin, cryotherapy, and electrodesiccation. Genitourin Med. 1990;66:16-19.

286. Simmons PD, Langlet F, Thin RNT. Cryotherapy versus electrocautery in the treatment of genital warts. Br J Vener Dis. 1981;57:273-274.

287. Jensen SL. Comparison of podophyllin application with simple surgical excision in clearance and recurrence of perianal condylomata acuminata. Lancet. 1985;2: 1146-1148.

288. Duus BR, Philipsen T, Christensen JD, et al. Refractory condylomata acuminata: A controlled clinical trial of carbon dioxide laser versus conventional surgical treatment. Genitourin Med. 1985;61:59-61.

289. McMillan A, Scott GR. Outpatient treatment of perianal warts by scissor excision. Genitourin Med. 1987;63:114-115.

290. Bonnez W, Oakes D, Choi A, et al. Therapeutic efficacy and complications of excisional biopsy of condyloma acuminatum. Sex Transm Dis. 1996;23:273-276.

291. Baggish MS. Improved laser techniques for the elimination of genital and extragenital warts. Am J Obstet Gynecol. 1985;153:545-550.

292. Reid R. Physical and surgical principles governing expertise with the carbon dioxide laser. Obstet Gynecol Clin North Am. 1987;14:513-535.

293. Bar-Am A, Shilon M, Peyser MR, et al. Treatment of male genital condylomatous lesions by carbon dioxide laser after failure of previous nonlaser methods. J Am Acad Dermatol. 1991;24:87-89.

294. Petersen CS, Bjerring P, Larsen J, et al. Systemic interferon alpha-2b increases the cure rate in laser treated patients with multiple persistent genital warts: A placebo-controlled study. Genitourin Med. 1991;67:99-102.

295. Randomized placebo-controlled double-blind combined therapy with laser surgery and systemic interferon-alpha 2a in the treatment of anogenital condylomata acuminatum. Condylomata International Collaborative Study Group. J Infect Dis. 1993;167:824-829.

296. Lassus A, Kartamaa M, Happonen H-P. A comparative study of topical analgesia with a lidocaine/prilocaine cream (EMLA®) and infiltration anesthesia for laser surgery of genital warts in men. Sex Transm Dis. 1990;17:130-132.

297. Rylander E, Sjoberg I, Lillieborg S, et al. Local anesthesia of the genital mucosa with a lidocaine/prilocaine cream (EMLA) for laser treatment of condylomata acuminata: A placebo-controlled study. Obstet Gynecol. 1990;75:302-306.

298. Mansell-Gregory M, Romanowski B. Randomised double blind trial of EMLA for the control of pain related to cryotherapy in the treatment of genital HPV lesions. Sex Transm Infect. 1998;74:274-275.

299. Gupta AK, Koren G, Shear NH. A double-blind, randomized, placebo-controlled trial of eutectic lidocaine/prilocaine cream 5% (EMLA) for analgesia prior to cryotherapy of warts in children and adults. Pediatr Dermatol. 1998;15:129-133.

300. de Benedictis JT, Marmar JL, Praiss DE. Intraurethral condylomata acuminata: Management and a review of the literature. J Urol. 1977;118:767-769.

301. Dretler SP, Klein LA. The eradication of intraurethral condyloma acuminata with 5 per cent 5-fluorouracil cream. J Urol. 1975;113:195-198.

302. Wallin J. 5-Fluorouracil in the treatment of penile and urethral condyloma acuminata. Br J Vener Dis. 1977;53:240-243.

303. Krebs H-B. Prophylactic topical 5-fluorouracil following treatment of human papillomavirus-associated lesions of the vulva and vagina. Obstet Gynecol. 1986;68:837-841.

304. Edwards L. The interferons. Dermatol Clin. 2001;19:139-146, ix.
305. Parmar S, Platanias LC. Interferons: Mechanisms of action and clinical applications. Curr Opin Oncol. 2003;15:431-439.
306. Eron LJ, Judson F, Tucker S, et al. Interferon therapy for condylomata acuminata. N Engl J Med. 1986;315:1059-1064.
307. Friedman-Kien A, Eron LJ, Conant M, et al. Natural interferon alfa for treatment of condylomata acuminata. JAMA. 1988;259:533-538.
308. Vance JC, Bart BJ, Hansen RC, et al. Intralesional recombinant alpha-2 interferon for the treatment of patients with condyloma acuminatum or verruca plantaris. Arch Dermatol. 1986;122:272-277.
309. A comparison of interferon alfa-2a and podophyllin in the treatment of primary condyloma acuminata. The Condylomata International Collaborative Study Group. Genitourin Med. 1991;67:394-399.
310. Johnson JA, Gangemi JD. Selective inhibition of human papillomavirus-induced cell proliferation by (S)-1-[3-hydroxy-2-(phosphonylmethoxy)propyl]cytosine. Antimicrob Agents Chemother. 1999;43:1198-1205.
311. Snoeck R, Bossens M, Parent D, et al. Phase II double-blind, placebo-controlled study of the safety and efficacy of cidofovir topical gel for the treatment of patients with human papillomavirus infection. Clin Infect Dis. 2001;33:597-602.
312. Strauss MJ, Khanna V, Koenig JD, et al. The cost of treating genital warts. Int J Dermatol. 1996;35:340-348.
313. Langley PC, Tyring SK, Smith MH. The cost effectiveness of patient-applied versus provider-administered intervention strategies for the treatment of external genital warts. Am J Manag Care. 1999;5:69-77.
314. Alam M, Stiller M. Direct medical costs for surgical and medical treatment of condylomata acuminata. Arch Dermatol. 2001;137:337-341.
315. Bonnez W, Oakes D, Bailey-Farchione A, et al. A randomized, double-blind, placebo-controlled trial of systemically administered alpha-, beta-, or gamma-interferon in combination with cryotherapy for the treatment of condyloma acuminatum. J Infect Dis. 1995;171:1081-1089.
316. Wilson JD, Brown CB, Walker PP. Factors involved in clearance of genital warts. Int J STD AIDS. 2001;12:789-792.
317. Ross JD. Is oral contraceptive associated with genital warts? Genitourin Med. 1996;72:330-333.
318. Feldman JG, Chirgwin K, Dehovitz JA, et al. The association of smoking and risk of condyloma acuminatum in women. Obstet Gynecol. 1997;89:346-350.
319. Sand PK, Shen W, Bowen LW, et al. Cryotherapy for the treatment of proximal urethral condyloma acuminatum. J Urol. 1987;137:874-876.
320. Ng N, Vuignier BI, Hart LL. Fluorouracil in condyloma acuminatum. Drug Intel Clin Pharm. 1987;21:175-176.
321. Levine LA, Elterman L, Rukstalis DB. Treatment of subclinical intraurethral human papilloma virus infection with interferon alfa-2b. Urology. 1996;47:553-557.
322. Dodi G, Infantino A, Moretti R, et al. Cryotherapy of anorectal warts and condylomata. Cryosurgery. 1982;19:287-288.
323. Bullingham RP, Lewis RG. Laser versus electrical cautery in the treatment of condylomata acuminata of the anus. Surg Gynecol Obstet. 1982;155:865-867.
324. Kaspari M, Gutzmer R, Kaspari T, et al. Application of imiquimod by suppositories (anal tampons) efficiently prevents recurrences after ablation of anal canal condyloma. Br J Dermatol. 2002;147:757-759.
325. 1998 guidelines for the treatment of sexually transmitted diseases. MMWR Morb Mortal Wkly Rep. 1998;47:1-116.
326. Ferenczy A. Treating genital condyloma during pregnancy with the carbon dioxide laser. Am J Obstet Gynecol. 1984;148:9-12.
327. Wertheimer A. Indirect colposcopy and laser vaporization in the management of vaginal condylomata. J Reprod Med. 1986;31:39-42.
328. Matsunaga J, Bergman A, Bhatia NN. Genital condylomata acuminata in pregnancy: Effectiveness, safety and pregnancy outcome following cryotherapy. Br J Obstet Gynaecol. 1987;94:168-172.
329. Bonnez W. Sexually transmitted human papillomavirus infection. In: Dolin R, Masur H, Saag M, eds. AIDS Therapy. 2nd ed. Philadelphia: WB Saunders; 2002.
330. Beck DE, Jaso RG, Zajac RA. Surgical management of anal condylomata in the HIV-positive patient. Dis Colon Rectum. 1990;33:180-183.
331. Orkin BA, Smith LE. Perineal manifestations of HIV infection. Dis Colon Rectum. 1992;35:310-314.
332. Kilewo CD, Urassa WK, Pallangyo K, et al. Response to podophyllotoxin treatment of genital warts in relation to HIV-1 infection among patients in Dar es Salaam, Tanzania. Int J STD AIDS. 1995;6:114-116.
333. Douglas JM, Rogers M, Judson FN. The effect of asymptomatic infection with HTLV-III on the response of anogenital warts in intralesional treatment with recombinant alpha-2 interferon. J Infect Dis. 1986;154:331-334.
334. Gilson RJ, Shupack JL, Friedman-Kien AE, et al. A randomized, controlled, safety study using imiquimod for the topical treatment of anogenital warts in HIV-infected patients. Imiquimod Study Group. AIDS. 1999;13:2397-2404.
335. Miles AJG, Mellor CH, Gazzard B, et al. Surgical management of anorectal disease in HIV-positive homosexuals. Br J Surg. 1990;77:869-871.
336. Fleshner PR, Freilich MI. Adjuvant interferon for anal condyloma—A prospective, randomized trial. Dis Colon Rectum. 1994;37:1255-1259.
337. Conant MA. Immunomodulatory therapy in the management of viral infections in patients with HIV infection. J Am Acad Dermatol. 2000;43:S27-S30.
338. Lord RVN. Anorectal surgery in patients infected with human immunodeficiency virus—Factors associated with delayed wound healing. Ann Surg. 1997;226:92-99.
339. O'Brien ME, Clayton JL, Clark R, et al. Association between antiretroviral therapy and condyloma acuminatum. 39th Meeting of the Infectious Disease Society of America, San Francisco, 2001:659.
340. Greenspan D, Canchola AJ, MacPhail LA, et al. Effect of highly active antiretroviral therapy on frequency of oral warts. Lancet. 2001;357:1411-1412.
341. Heard I, Palefsky JM, Kazatchkine M. The impact of HIV antiviral therapy on human papillomavirus (HPV) infections and HPV-related diseases. Antivir Ther. 2004;9:13-22.
342. Majewski S, Skopinska M, Bollag W, et al. Combination of isotretinoin and calcitriol for precancerous and cancerous skin lesions. Lancet. 1994;344:1510-1511.
343. Auborn KJ. Therapy for recurrent respiratory papillomatosis. Antivir Ther. 2002;7:1-9.
344. Kimberlin DW. Pharmacotherapy of recurrent respiratory papillomatosis. Expert Opin Pharmacother. 2002;3:1091-1099.
345. Pransky SM, Albright JT, Magit AE. Long-term follow-up of pediatric recurrent respiratory papillomatosis managed with intralesional cidofovir. Laryngoscope. 2003;113:1583-1587.
346. Bell MC, Crowley-Nowick P, Bradlow HL, et al. Placebo-controlled trial of indole-3-carbinol in the treatment of CIN. Gynecol Oncol. 2000;78:123-129.
347. Dilley DC, Siegel MA, Budnick S. Diagnosing and treating common oral pathologies. Pediatr Clin North Am. 1991;38:1227-1264.
348. Ho L, Tay S-K, Chan S-Y, et al. Sequence variants of human papillomavirus type 16 from couples suggest sexual transmission with low infectivity and polyclonality in genital neoplasia. J Infect Dis. 1993;168:803-809.
349. Boxman ILA, Hogewoning A, Mulder LHC, et al. Detection of human papillomavirus types 6 and 11 in pubic and perianal hair from patients with genital warts. J Clin Microbiol. 1999;37:2270-2273.
350. Manhart LE, Koutsky LA. Do condoms prevent genital HPV infection, external genital warts, or cervical neoplasia? A meta-analysis. Sex Transm Dis. 2002;29:725-735.
351. Hogewoning CJ, Bleeker MC, van den Brule AJ, et al. Condom use promotes regression of cervical intraepithelial neoplasia and clearance of human papillomavirus: A randomized clinical trial. Int J Cancer. 2003;107:811-816.
352. Bleeker MC, Hogewoning CJ, Voorhorst FJ, et al. Condom use promotes regression of human papillomavirus-associated penile lesions in male sexual partners of women with cervical intraepithelial neoplasia. Int J Cancer. 2003;107:804-810.
353. Monsonego J, Bosch FX, Coursaget P, et al. Cervical cancer control, priorities and new directions. Int J Cancer. 2004;108:329-333.
354. Saslow D, Runowicz CD, Solomon D, et al. American Cancer Society guideline for the early detection of cervical neoplasia and cancer. CA Cancer J Clin. 2002;52:342-362.
355. U.S. Preventive Services Task Force. Screening for Cervical Cancer. AHRQ Publication No. 03-515A, January 2003. Rockville, Md: Agency for Healthcare Research and Quality, 2003.
356. ACOG Practice Bulletin. Cervical cytology screening. Number 45, August 2003. Int J Gynaecol Obstet. 2003;83:237-247.
357. Levine AM. Evaluation and management of HIV-infected women. Ann Intern Med. 2002;136:228-242.
358. Evans TG, Bonnez W, Rose RC, et al. A phase 1 study of a recombinant viruslike particle vaccine against human papillomavirus type 11 in healthy adult volunteers. J Infect Dis. 2001;183:1485-1493.
359. Harro CD, Pang Y-YS, Roden RBS, et al. Safety and immunogenicity trial in adult volunteers of a human papillomavirus 16 L1 virus-like particle vaccine. J Natl Cancer Inst. 2001;93:284-292.
359a. Dubin G, Glaxo Smith Kline HPV Vaccine Efficacy Study Group. A double-blind placebo controlled efficacy trial of an adjuvanted human papillomavirus (HPV) type 16/18 L1 virus like particle (VLP) vaccine. 21st International Papillomavirus Conference, Mexico City, Mexico. 2004;412.
360. Kulasingam SL, Myers ER. Potential health and economic impact of adding a human papillomavirus vaccine to screening programs. JAMA. 2003;290:781-789.
361. Goldie SJ, Grima D, Kohli M, et al. A comprehensive natural history model of HPV infection and cervical cancer to estimate the clinical impact of a prophylactic HPV-16/18 vaccine. Int J Cancer. 2003;106:896-904.

CHAPTER **141**

JC, BK, and Other Polyomaviruses; Progressive Multifocal Leukoencephalopathy

LISA M. DEMETER

JC virus (JCV) and BK virus (BKV) are human polyomaviruses. Infection with these viruses appears to be widespread but asymptomatic in most patients. JCV or BKV infection is acquired during childhood and persists in the kidney. JCV is the cause of progressive multifocal leukoencephalopathy (PML), a rare demyelinating disease of immunosuppressed patients. Nephropathy associated with BK virus infection has become an important cause of graft failure in renal allograft recipients. Polyomavirus viruria has been associated with ureteral stenosis in renal transplantation patients and with hemorrhagic cystitis in bone marrow transplantation patients. Asymptomatic shedding of JCV and BKV can be detected in the urine of pregnant women and of immunocompromised patients such as organ transplant recipients. This chapter summarizes characteristics of JCV and BKV infections and associated clinical manifestations, including PML.

DESCRIPTION OF THE PATHOGENS

Polyomaviruses are members of the Papovaviridae family, which comprises small, nonenveloped viruses with a covalently closed, circular, doubled-stranded DNA genome. The Papovaviridae capsid has icosahedral symmetry and consists of 72 capsomeres.[1] The Papovaviridae family is divided into the polyomavirus and papillomavirus genera. Polyomaviruses are distinguished from papillomaviruses by a smaller virion size (45 vs 55 nm in diameter) and a different genome size and organization.[1] Polyomaviruses are ubiquitous in nature and can be isolated from a number of different species, including humans (JCV, BKV), monkeys (simian virus 40 [SV40]), and mice (mouse polyomavirus, K virus).[1] Infection with polyomaviruses is relatively species specific, and natural infection with a given polyomavirus occurs in only one or a few related species.

JCV and BKV were first isolated in 1971. (J.C. and B.K. are the initials of the patients from whom the initial virus isolates were obtained.) JCV was first isolated from brain tissue obtained from a patient with PML.[2] BKV was initially isolated from urine specimens obtained from a renal transplantation patient who had developed ureteral stenosis postoperatively.[3] BKV and JCV share 75% homology at the level of nucleotide sequence, and each is 70% homologous with SV40.[4,5] JCV and BKV virions contain both species-specific and cross-reacting epitopes.[1,6] Polyomaviruses contain a genus-specific epitope that appears after denaturation of the virus capsid.[1,6] Intact JCV and BKV virions are not cross-reactive serologically,[7] and serologic tests for JCV and BKV antibodies in human sera are able to distinguish the two.[1] Viruses that are antigenically almost indistinguishable from SV40 (SV40-PML viruses) have been isolated from small numbers of patients with PML and may represent a third serologic type of human polyomavirus.[7-11]

The genomes of JCV and BKV are approximately 5000 base pairs long and can be divided into three regions: (1) the early region, which encodes the large and small T antigens that function in transformation, viral replication, and regulation of gene expression; (2) the late region, which codes for the three viral capsid proteins VP1, VP2, and VP3; and (3) a noncoding regulatory region that contains the replication origin, T antigen–binding sites, and transcriptional regulatory elements.[4,5,12] Transcription of the early region and that of the late region occur from different strands of the DNA genome.[4,5,12] Sequence variants of human polyomaviruses have been described that exhibit significant heterogeneity in regulatory regions. For example, variants of JCV or BKV may contain insertions, deletions, or duplications, or all three, in the regulatory region.[13-16] The functional significance of this marked variation is unknown, but it may play a role in the pathogenicity or tissue tropism of human polyomaviruses.

EPIDEMIOLOGY

Approximately 60% to 80% of adults in the United States and Europe have antibodies to JCV or BKV or both.[17-23] Antibodies are prevalent even in remote populations that have had no exposure to influenza or measles.[24] Comparison of the population distributions of JCV and BKV antibodies suggests that the two viruses circulate independently.[24] The seroprevalence of both JCV and BKV antibodies increases sharply during childhood.[17-21,23,25] Although the time of acquisition of antibodies to JCV and to BKV has not been examined comparatively in a single study, it appears that BKV infection is acquired in most children at an earlier age (3 to 4 years) than is JCV in-

fection (10 to 14 years).[17-20,25] No evidence indicates that an animal reservoir exists for JCV or BKV.[26]

Asymptomatic viruria with JCV or BKV occurs primarily in immunosuppressed patients and in pregnant women (see later on). The rising incidence of human immunodeficiency virus (HIV) infection has significantly altered the epidemiology of PML. In the pre-HIV era, PML was seen primarily in older patients with underlying hematologic malignancies.[27,28] PML was also sometimes seen in patients with other causes for depression of cell-mediated immunity, such as steroid use.[29] Rarely, patients have been described who developed PML in the absence of any identifiable immunodeficiency.[30-32] Reported deaths due to PML significantly increased with the rise in cases of acquired immunodeficiency syndrome (AIDS), from 1.5/10 million persons in 1974 to 6.1/10 million persons in 1987.[33] It is estimated that more than half of deaths due to PML are associated with HIV infection, and that approximately 1% to 4% of patients with HIV infection will develop PML.[33-35] PML, which is extremely rare among children with other immunodeficiencies, has been reported in some children with HIV infection.[36-38] PML has also been described as the initial manifestation of idiopathic CD4+ lymphopenia.[39]

PATHOGENESIS

Little is known about transmission of BKV and JCV or about events during primary infection. It is thought that transmission of JCV requires sustained close contact. Transmission of JCV to children from either parent occurs frequently, although approximately half of infections occur outside the family.[40,41] Detection of BKV and JCV in tonsillar tissue suggests that tonsils may serve as a site of initial infection, perhaps via inhalation or close contact.[42] The possibility of perinatal transmission of BKV in humans has been raised by studies that identified BKV immunoglobulin M (IgM) in newborns.[23,43] However, other studies have shown no evidence for viruria or acquisition of IgM in infants born to mothers with reactivation of BKV or JCV infection.[44-46] At present, no definitive evidence has been found that perinatal transmission of polyomavirus infection occurs in the setting of maternal JCV or BKV viruria. The question of whether polyomavirus transmission to the fetus can occur during primary maternal infection remains unresolved.

It is hypothesized that viremia during primary infection results in seeding of the kidney,[47] by which a clinically latent infection is established. JCV and BKV sequences can be detected in peripheral blood mononuclear cells obtained from patients with leukemia, HIV infection, or PML.[42,48] In addition, JCV DNA and capsid antigen can be demonstrated in mononuclear cells in bone marrow, central nervous system, and peripheral blood.[49] In one study, JCV DNA was detected more frequently in peripheral blood mononuclear cells from HIV-infected patients without PML than in those from healthy blood donors.[50] It is postulated that JCV infection of mononuclear cells may be important in the transport of virus to the central nervous system, although it does not appear that production of infectious JCV occurs in peripheral blood.[50]

The neuropathologic findings of PML are probably a result of direct infection of the oligodendrocytes with JCV, leading to decreased myelin production and demyelination. Electron microscopy and in situ hybridization techniques have been used to demonstrate the presence of polyomavirus in oligodendrocyte nuclei.[51-53] This hypothesis is further supported by the observation that transgenic mice with genomes that contain the JCV early region develop a demyelinating disease related to the expression of JCV T antigens in oligodendrocytes.[54,55] In addition, macaques that spontaneously develop a PML-like illness have evidence of SV40 infection in the white matter lesions.[56,57] Tropism of JCV for oligodendrocytes may be explained by an effect of cell-specific transcription factors on viral gene expression.[58] It is not known whether PML results from reactivation of latent JCV infection in the central nervous system established during primary infection, reactivation of latent infection in the kidney with subsequent viremia and seeding of the central nervous system, or primary infection in an immunocompromised host. JCV DNA can be detected by polymerase chain reaction (PCR) assay in brain tissue of patients with and without PML, suggesting that latent JCV infection does exist in the central nervous system.[59] The factors that determine whether PML develops in neural tissue infected with JCV are unknown.

Support for the hypothesis that a clinically latent viral infection exists in renal tissue is provided by the observation that approximately 30% to 50% of normal persons have detectable BKV or JCV sequences in renal tissue obtained at surgery or autopsy.[60-62] JCV DNA can also be detected in the kidneys of patients with PML,[63] although the frequency with which JCV exists in renal tissue in patients with PML is unknown. During periods of immunosuppression, such as after organ transplantation, it is postulated that viral infection is reactivated in the kidney, leading to viruria. Patients excrete the same JCV genotype in the urine for prolonged periods, suggesting that renal shedding of JCV reflects persistent infection rather than repeated reinfection.[64] In most patients, reactivation of JCV or BKV infection appears to be subclinical. Clinical manifestations reported to be associated with polyomavirus excretion (see later on) are thought to result from the direct effects of viral replication. Cofactors that are important in the genesis of these clinical syndromes presumably exist because specific syndromes occur only in a subset of patients at risk for reactivation of polyomavirus infection.

CLINICAL MANIFESTATIONS

Primary Infection

Most primary infections with BKV appear to be asymptomatic or minimally symptomatic.[21,65] A study of children in whom BKV seroconversion was demonstrated identified associated mild upper respiratory tract symptoms in approximately one third.[21] Another study of children with upper respiratory tract illnesses demonstrated BKV seroconversion in 8%; in addition, BKV viruria and seroconversion were reported in one child with tonsillitis.[65,66] Case reports have implicated polyomavirus infection as a cause of acute cystitis in three children.[67-70]

Progressive Multifocal Leukoencephalopathy

PML was first identified as a separate clinical entity by Aåström and coworkers[27] in 1958. Patients with PML characteristically present with rapidly progressive focal neurologic deficits without signs of increased intracranial pressure.[27,28,71] Neurologic abnormalities most commonly seen at the time of presentation include hemiparesis, visual field deficits, and cognitive impairment (Table 141-1).[27-34,71-75] Aphasia, ataxia, or cranial nerve deficits may also be noted. Late in the course of PML, patients can develop severe neurologic deficits, including cortical blindness, quadriparesis, profound dementia, and coma. Neurologic abnormalities are usually localized to cerebral white matter, although cerebellar and brain-stem involvement can also occur. Spinal cord involvement is rare in PML. Patients most commonly undergo rapid deterioration, and death usually occurs within 6 months of diagnosis.[27,28,34] However, a subset of patients experience spontaneous fluctuations in the clinical course over a period of 2 to 3 years after the onset of symptoms and signs.[34,74-77] The clinical presentation of PML in patients with HIV infection is similar to that in patients with other

TABLE 141-1 Neurologic Presentation of Progressive Multifocal Leukoencephalopathy

Neurologic Manifestation	Frequency (% of patients)
Aphasia	17
Ataxia	21
Cognitive disturbance	36
Cranial nerve deficits	13
Hemiparesis	42
Sensory deficits	9
Visual field deficits	32

Data from references 28, 34, and 71 to 75.

underlying immunodeficiencies.[34,72,73,78] PML is an AIDS-defining disease according to the Centers for Disease Control and Prevention (CDC) surveillance case definition[79] and may be the initial presentation of HIV infection.[34,72,73,78]

BK Nephropathy

Nephropathy associated with BKV infection in renal transplant recipients was first reported in 1995.[80] BK nephropathy is now recognized as a significant cause of graft failure in this patient population, occurring in 1% to 5% of renal transplant recipients.[81,82] BK nephropathy is asymptomatic and manifests as a subacute rise in serum creatinine concentrations, usually occurring over the course of several weeks. Diagnosis has classically been made by pathologic examination of a renal biopsy, which should be done to distinguish this entity from renal allograft rejection. A recent report found that patients with BK nephropathy had higher levels of BK plasma viremia, as measured by a real-time PCR assay.[83] Risk factors for BK nephropathy include treatment of graft rejection with pulse corticosteroid therapy and a high number of HLA mismatches between the allograft donor and recipient.[83] Approximately half of patients with BK nephropathy experience significant loss of allograft function.[81,82]

Other Manifestations of BK Virus Infection

BKV viruria has been associated with localized ureteral ulceration and subsequent ureteral stenosis in a small number of renal transplantation patients.[3,84-88] Nuclear inclusions and viral particles can be detected in epithelial cells that line the involved ureters.[3,88] On the basis of these observations, ureteral stenosis associated with human polyomavirus infection is postulated to result from direct cytopathic effects of reactivated virus present in the epithelium of the donor ureter during periods of immunosuppression.[3,88] The frequency with which postoperative ureteral stenosis in renal transplant recipients is associated with polyomavirus excretion is not known. Different studies have found conflicting results as to whether polyomavirus excretion after transplantation influences other clinical outcomes such as graft survival or risk of rejection.[89,90]

BKV viruria has been associated with tubulointerstitial nephritis in a child with hyper-IgM immunodeficiency[91] and with renal failure in a child with Hodgkin's disease and cartilage-hair hypoplasia.[92] A causal effect of BKV infection in both cases was supported by the presence of intranuclear inclusions and BKV DNA in renal tubular epithelium.[91,92] BK virus infection has also been implicated in a systemic vasculopathy in a renal transplant recipient who developed progressive muscular weakness, anasarca, and a fatal myocardial infarction.[93] Autopsy demonstrated vascular endothelial nuclear inclusions, primarily in small vessels of the myocardium and skeletal muscle, and viral particles compatible with BKV identified on electron microscopy.[93]

Asymptomatic BK Virus and JC Virus Viruria

BKV and JCV viruria, detected by cytologic examination, culture, or electron microscopy, is rare in humans with intact immune function. However, PCR assay can detect viral sequences in the urine of patients with no evidence of immunocompromise. Shedding of JCV DNA appears to increase with age, with a significant increase in prevalence occurring during young adulthood.[40]

Pregnant Women

Asymptomatic JCV or BKV viruria can be detected by cytologic examination in approximately 3% of pregnant women.[94] Virus shedding occurs primarily during the third trimester of pregnancy[94,95] and usually ceases in the immediate postpartum period.[94] The high seroprevalence of JCV and of BKV antibodies and the absence of seroconversion in the women studied suggest that polyomavirus excretion in pregnant women usually represents reactivation of previously acquired infection.[94] Both JCV and BKV shedding can occur, although JCV viruria is more common.[94]

Pregnant women appear to have more severe manifestations of infections in which cell-mediated immunity is important, although no consensus has been reached on the nature of the immune defects associated with pregnancy.[96] One study reported that monocytosis and lymphopenia were associated with reactivation of polyomavirus infection in pregnant women, which is consistent with the hypothesis that alterations in the immune system predispose these patients to polyomavirus reactivation.[95]

Renal Transplant Recipients

Urinary excretion of human polyomaviruses can be demonstrated by cytologic examination, culture, or electron microscopy in approximately 10% to 45% of patients after renal transplantation.[84-86,89] Serologic studies suggest that most JCV and BKV infections in renal transplant recipients represent reactivation, although primary infection has also been documented.[87,89] Both primary and reactivation infections are more common among patients who have received a kidney from a seropositive donor, suggesting that reactivation of latent virus in the donated tissue plays a role in viruria.[90] Most JCV and BKV infections occur within the first 3 months after transplantation, although infections occurring later than 2 years after transplantation have been reported.[87]

Bone Marrow Transplant Recipients

BKV viruria occurs in approximately 50% of patients after bone marrow transplantation,[97-99] usually within the first 2 months after the procedure.[99] Published reports have described virus shedding only in patients who were seropositive before transplantation, suggesting that viruria is secondary to reactivation of latent infection.[98,99] Late-onset prolonged hemorrhagic cystitis, which is thought to be unrelated to cyclophosphamide therapy, was present in 64% of patients with BKV viruria and was significantly more common in patients with BKV viruria than in those without detectable virus shedding.[98] BKV viruria frequently preceded the onset of clinical symptoms, suggesting that viral shedding was not a result of the cystitis.[97,98] Excretion of JCV has been detected in small numbers of bone marrow transplantation patients.[97-99] No consistent association of JCV viruria with clinical manifestations has been found among bone marrow transplantation patients.

Other Patients

Polyomavirus excretion can also be detected in the urine of approximately 10% of patients with malignancies, particularly in those patients with lymphoma.[100] Viruria detected with the use of cytologic techniques appears to be rare in nonimmunosuppressed patients, occurring in less than 1% of samples tested.[101]

Summary of Asymptomatic BK Virus and JC Virus Viruria

In summary, BKV and JCV viruria can be seen in patients with a variety of immunodeficiencies but appears to be most frequent among renal and bone marrow transplant recipients. In addition, pregnant women may excrete JCV or BKV in the third trimester, perhaps as a result of defects in cell-mediated immunity observed during pregnancy.[96] Most immunosuppressed patients who excrete BKV and JCV are asymptomatic. However, polyomavirus viruria has been found in renal transplantation patients with nephropathy and ureteral stenosis and in bone marrow transplantation patients with late-onset hemorrhagic cystitis. The prevalence and associated clinical manifestations of JCV and BKV viruria are summarized in Table 141-2.

Association of BK Virus and JC Virus Infections with Malignancy

BKV and JCV can induce tumors in mice and hamsters after intracerebral, intraperitoneal, subcutaneous, or intravenous injection.[102-105] The early region of the BKV genome can transform cells in culture, either alone or in cooperation with an activated *ras* oncogene.[106-109] A number of reports have been documented of human polyomavirus isolation or detection of polyomavirus sequences in human tumors,[16,110-112] particularly brain tumors.[16,93,110,113,114] Despite these suggestive reports, a causal relationship between polyomavirus infection and the development of tumors in humans has not been established.

DIAGNOSIS

Viral Culture

Routine use of virus isolation for the detection of JCV and BKV infections is hampered by the relatively slow growth of these viruses in tissue culture and the lack of readily available susceptible cells. Initial isolation of JCV or BKV from clinical specimens often requires weeks to months.[47] BKV-susceptible cells include human embryonic kidney, human diploid lung fibroblasts, infant urothelial cells, and human fetal brain cells.[1] JCV is more limited in its host range in cell culture and grows best in primary human fetal glial cells or in transformed cell lines derived from these.[1,115]

Detection of Viruria

Cytologic examination of urinary epithelial cells is the most widely used method for detecting JCV or BKV viruria. The most characteristic abnormality of infected cells is an enlarged nucleus with a single large basophilic intranuclear inclusion.[84,101] Cytoplasmic inclusions are not seen in association with JCV or BKV infection, in contrast to cytomegalovirus infection.[84,101] Advantages of this technique include its accuracy and its usefulness in analysis of large numbers of clinical specimens. However, cytologic examination of the urine does have limitations in the diagnosis of polyomavirus infection. Although strongly suggestive of polyomavirus infection, the cytopathologic changes induced by polyomaviruses can be confused with those due to malignancy or to other viral infections, such as those caused by cytomegalovirus and adenovirus.[116] In addition, JCV and BKV infections cannot be distinguished from each other on the basis of cytologic findings.[47,84] Finally, JCV or BKV viruria can occur in the absence of detectable cytologic abnormalities.[47,85] JCV or BKV viruria can also be discerned with the use of electron microscopic examination of urinary sediment for viral particles,[3,86] detection of viral nucleic acids by hybridization methods or PCR assay,[117,118] and detection of viral antigens by immunofluorescence assay[119] or enzyme-linked immunosorbent assay (ELISA).[118]

TABLE 141-2 Prevalence and Associated Clinical Manifestations of JC Virus and BK Virus Viruria*

Risk Group	Frequency (%)	Usual Time of Onset of Viruria	Associated Clinical Manifestations	Type of Infection	Reference(s)
Pregnant women	3	Third trimester	None	Reactivation	94
Renal transplant recipients	10–45	First 3 mo after transplantation	Nephropathy Ureteral stenosis May be asymptomatic	Reactivation or primary infection	84–86,89
Bone marrow transplant recipients	50	First 2 mo after transplantation	Late-onset hemorrhagic cystitis May be asymptomatic	Reactivation	97–99
Oncology patients	10	No correlation with chemotherapy	None	Reactivation	100
Non-immunosuppressed patients	0.3	Not known	None	Not known	101

*Cases of polyomavirus excretion detected by cytopathologic study, electron microscopy, or culture are included.

PCR testing can detect JCV and BKV sequences in the urine of a significant proportion of HIV-infected patients,[117,120] apparently normal control populations,[117] and elderly patients without evidence of overt immunosuppression.[121] Whether PCR positivity can be correlated with a positive result on urine culture or cytologic studies is not known, and the clinical significance of excretion of polyomavirus nucleic acids has not been established.

Brain Biopsy

A definitive diagnosis of PML requires identification of the characteristic pathologic changes on brain biopsy; these changes are illustrated in Figure 141-1. Multiple asymmetrical foci of demyelination at various stages of evolution can be seen in the cerebral white matter.[27,28,122] The oligodendrocytes, which are the myelin-producing cells of the central nervous system, demonstrate characteristic cytopathic effects that include nuclear enlargement, loss of normal chromatin pattern, and intranuclear accumulation of deeply basophilic homogeneous staining material (see Fig. 141-1A).[28,122] A significant proportion of lesions contain astrocytes that have undergone marked enlargement and that often have intensely hyperchromatic and irregularly shaped nuclei (see Fig. 141-1B).[27,28,122] Although PML lesions typically demonstrate minimal inflammatory changes, a subset of patients may have lesions with a marked inflammatory response.[27,74] Electron microscopy can be used to demonstrate polyomavirus particles in enlarged oligodendrocyte nuclei.[51,53] Techniques of fluorescent antibody staining, electron microscopic agglutination, immunocytochemistry, and in situ hybridization have demonstrated JCV infection in almost all PML lesions studied,[52,74,123,124] although a small number of cases have been linked with the SV40 PML group of viruses.[9-11,123] BKV infection has not been detected in PML. Although PML lesions in patients with AIDS may demonstrate increased numbers of JCV-infected cells and more extensive necrosis, no pathologic characteristics can reliably distinguish PML in patients with AIDS from PML in patients with other immunodeficiencies.[125,126]

Head Computed Tomography and Magnetic Resonance Imaging

Computed tomography (CT) scans in patients with PML characteristically reveal hypodense, nonenhancing lesions of the cerebral white matter.[34,75,127] The severity of clinical findings is often greater than is suggested by the extent of involvement seen on CT scan. This dissociation of clinical and CT findings in a patient with a compatible clinical picture should raise the possibility of PML.[75,128] Magnetic resonance imaging (MRI) appears to be more sensitive than CT in detecting PML lesions.[34,128,129] PML lesions typically appear as areas of increased signal intensity on proton density– and T2-weighted MRI scans (Fig. 141-2).[128,130] Stereotactic brain biopsy along with computer-assisted imaging techniques such as CT and MRI has been used successfully to diagnose PML in HIV-infected patients.[131-133]

Polymerase Chain Reaction Testing of Cerebrospinal Fluid and Plasma

PCR testing has been used to amplify JCV DNA in cerebrospinal fluid (CSF) samples from patients with PML.[134-143] Methods used in these studies differ with regard to specimen preparation, region of the genome amplified, amplification conditions, and methods for detection. Reported sensitivities range from 60% to 100%, reflecting differ-

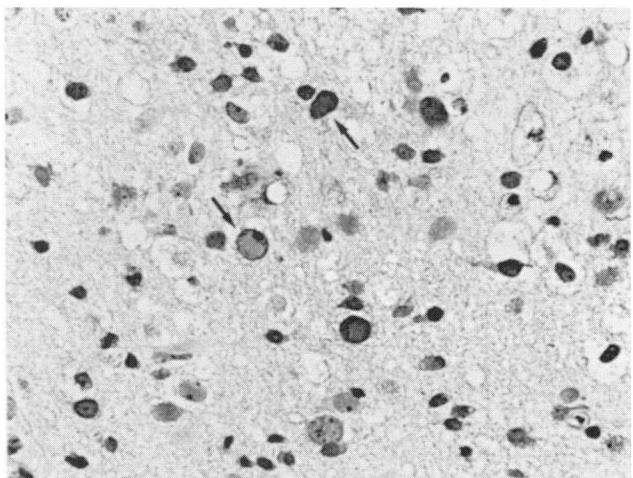

A

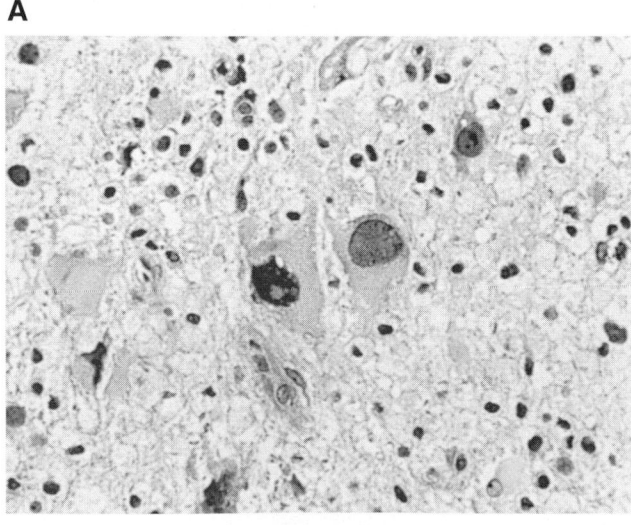

B

FIGURE 141-1. Progressive multifocal leukoencephalopathy. A, Arrows point to oligodendrocytes, each of which contains a homogeneous basophilic nuclear inclusion. **B,** Markedly enlarged astrocytes with hyperchromatic, irregularly shaped nuclei are apparent (H&E, ×500). *(Courtesy of Dr. Joshua Sickel, Department of Pathology, University of Rochester.)*

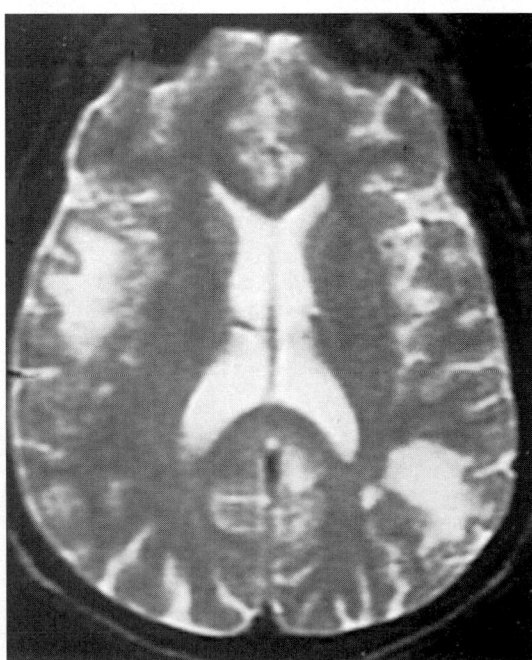

FIGURE 141-2. Axial T2-weighted magnetic resonance imaging scan of biopsy-proven progressive multifocal leukoencephalopathy. High signal lesions are seen in the right parietal and left parieto-occipital white matter. *(From Keetonen L, Tuite MJ. Brain imaging in the human immunodeficiency virus infection. Semin Neurol. 1992;12:57-69.)*

ences in the case definition of PML, the patient population studied, and the PCR methodology used. JCV DNA can be detected in the CSF of some immunosuppressed patients with no clinical evidence of PML, although the frequency of JCV DNA in the CSF of these patients is significantly lower than that noted in those with biopsy- or autopsy-proven PML. PCR testing for JCV DNA in the CSF should not be used to diagnose PML in the absence of compatible clinical and radiographic findings. The detection of JCV DNA in the CSF of a patient with a compatible clinical picture supports the diagnosis of PML,[143] but the absence of detectable JCV DNA cannot be used to rule out the diagnosis. Preliminary studies suggest that quantitation of JCV DNA in CSF may correlate with prognosis,[144] although another longitudinal study has demonstrated significant variability of JCV DNA concentrations in the CSF, suggesting fluctuations in the degree of viral shedding.[145] Studies also suggest that quantitation of BKV DNA in plasma may prove useful in the diagnosis and monitoring of BK nephropathy, although additional studies are needed to better define the sensitivity and specificity of this test.[83,146,147]

Other Diagnostic Tests

Other diagnostic tests may increase the clinician's index of suspicion for PML, but these are not helpful in establishing the diagnosis. Serum antibodies to JCV are common in the general population and are not helpful in predicting which patients are at risk for PML.[73] CSF cell count and chemistries are usually normal. Electroencephalography may reveal focal slowing or may be normal early in the course of PML.[148]

PREVENTION AND TREATMENT

Most patients with BKV or JCV infection are asymptomatic and do not require treatment. Case reports of patients with PML who have received cytosine arabinoside (cytarabine, or Ara-C) have provided conflicting data on the efficacy of this drug. The AIDS Clinical Trials Group (ACTG) of the National Institute of Allergy and Infectious Diseases conducted a randomized multicenter study to compare the efficacy of intravenous or intrathecal cytarabine added to dual nucleoside antiretroviral therapy with that of antiretroviral therapy alone in HIV-infected patients with biopsy-proven PML (ACTG 243).[149] No clinical benefit for either mode of administration of cytosine arabinoside was seen in this trial, and anemia and thrombocytopenia were more frequent among those patients who received intravenous cytarabine.[149] Thus, no evidence supports the use of this drug in HIV-infected patients with PML.

Other drugs reported to improve the clinical course of PML include interferon,[150,151] idoxuridine (IUDR),[152] and interleukin-2.[153] All reported studies were uncontrolled, and no firm recommendations can be made regarding the use of these agents for the treatment of JCV infection in PML.

Cidofovir, a nucleoside analogue that is active against mouse and primate polyomaviruses,[154] has been reported to provide benefit in some HIV-infected patients with PML.[155-157] However, results from ACTG 363, an open-label study of cidofovir in 24 HIV-infected patients with PML, have been disappointing.[158]

Some reports have described marked clinical and radiographic improvement in HIV-infected patients with PML after initiation of potent combination antiretroviral regimens.[159-162] If tolerated, aggressive antiretroviral treatment of underlying HIV infection appears to be the most reasonable therapeutic approach to the management of PML in HIV-infected patients. Neurologic deterioration has been reported soon after initiation of combination antiretroviral therapy, presumably resulting from immune reconstitution syndrome; therefore, caution should be exercised when an antiretroviral regimen is initiated.[163]

Interferon has demonstrated some activity against BKV in vitro but no effect on BKV viruria in renal transplantation patients.[164] Treatment of immunosuppressed patients with BKV-associated syndromes is largely supportive and is directed toward control of symptoms and reduction of immunosuppression, if appropriate.[165]

REFERENCES

1. Shah KV. Polyomaviruses. In: Fields BN, Knipe DM, Howley PM, et al, eds. Fields Virology. 3rd ed. Philadelphia: Lippincott-Raven; 1996:2027-2043.
2. Padgett BL, Walker DL, ZuRhein GM, et al. Cultivation of papova-like virus from human brain with progressive multifocal leukoencephalopathy. Lancet. 1971;1: 1257-1260.
3. Gardner SD, Field AM, Coleman DV, et al. New human papovavirus (B.K.) isolated from urine after renal transplantation. Lancet. 1971;1:1253-1257.
4. Yang RCA, Wu R. BK virus DNA: Complete nucleotide sequence of a human tumor virus. Science. 1979;206:456-462.
5. Frisque RJ, Bream GL, Cannella MT. Human polyomavirus JC virus genome. J Virol. 1984;51:458-469.
6. Shah KV, Ozer HL, Ghazey HN, et al. Common structural antigen of papovaviruses of the simian virus 40-polyoma subgroup. J Virol. 1977;21:179-186.
7. Penney JB Jr, Narayan O. Studies of the antigenic relationships of the new human papovaviruses by electron microscopy agglutination. Infect Immun. 1973;8:299-300.
8. Weiner LP, Herndon RM, Narayan O, et al. Isolation of virus related to SV40 from patients with progressive multifocal leukoencephalopathy. N Engl J Med. 1972;286:385-390.
9. Scherneck S, Geissler E, Jänisch W, et al. Isolation of an SV40-like virus from a patient with progressive multifocal leukoencephalopathy. Acta Virol. 1981;25:191-198.
10. Weiner LP, Herndon RM, Narayan O, et al. Further studies of a simian virus 40-like virus isolated from human brain. J Virol. 1972;10:147-149.
11. Weiner LP, Narayan O. Virologic studies of progressive multifocal leukoencephalopathy. Prog Med Virol. 1974;18:229-240.
12. Seif I, Khoury G, Dhar R. The genome of human papovavirus BKV. Cell. 1979;18:963-977.
13. Grinnell BW, Padgett BL, Walker DL. Comparison of infectious JC virus DNAs cloned from human brain. J Virol. 1983;45:299-308.
14. Martin JD, Foster GC. Multiple JC virus genomes from one patient. J Gen Virol. 1984;65:1405-1411.
15. Martin JD, King DM, Slauch JM, et al. Differences in regulatory sequences of naturally occurring JC virus variants. J Virol. 1985;53:306-311.
16. Negrini M, Rimessi P, Mantovani C, et al. Characterization of BK virus variants rescued from human tumors and tumor cell lines. J Gen Virol. 1990;71:2731-2736.
17. Flaegstad T, Rönne K, Filipe AR, et al. Prevalence of anti BK virus antibody in Portugal and Norway. Scand J Infect Dis. 1989;21:145-147.
18. Padgett BL, Walker DL. Prevalence of antibodies in human sera against JC virus, an isolate from a case of progressive multifocal leukoencephalopathy. J Infect Dis. 1973;127:467-470.
19. Shah KV, Daniel RW, Warszawski RM. High prevalence of antibodies to BK virus, an SV 40-related papovavirus, in residents of Maryland. J Infect Dis. 1973;128: 784-787.
20. Gardner SD. Prevalence in England of antibody to human polyomavirus (B.K.). Br Med J. 1973;1:77-78.
21. Mäntyjärvi RA, Meurman OH, Vihma L, et al. A human papovavirus (B.K.): Biological properties and seroepidemiology. Ann Clin Res. 1973;5:283-287.
22. Portolani M, Marzocchi A, Barbanti-Brodano G, et al. Prevalence in Italy of antibodies to a new human papovavirus (BK virus). J Med Microbiol. 1974;7:543-546.
23. Rziha HJ, Bornkamm GW, zur Hausen H. BK virus: Seroepidemiologic studies and serologic response to viral infection. Med Microbiol Immunol. 1978;165:73-81.
24. Brown P, Tsai T, Gajdusek DC. Seroepidemiology of human papovaviruses: Discovery of virgin populations and some unusual patterns of antibody prevalence among remote peoples of the world. Am J Epidemiol. 1975;102:331-340.
25. Dei R, Marmo F, Corte D, et al. Age-related changes in the prevalence of precipitating antibodies to BK virus in infants and children. J Med Microbiol. 1982;15: 285-291.
26. Hogan TF, Padgett BL, Walker DL. Human polyomaviruses. In: Belshse RB, ed. Textbook of Human Virology. 2nd ed. St. Louis: Mosby-Year Book; 1991:970-1000.
27. Aåström K-E, Mancall EL, Richardson EP Jr. Progressive multifocal leukoencephalopathy: A hitherto unrecognized complication of chronic lymphatic leukemia and Hodgkin's disease. Brain. 1958;81:93-110.
28. Richardson EP Jr. Progressive multifocal leukoencephalopathy. N Engl J Med. 1961;265:815-823.
29. Newton P, Aldridge RD, Lessells AM, et al. Progressive multifocal leukoencephalopathy complicating systemic lupus erythematosus. Arthritis Rheum. 1986;29:337-343.
30. Rockwell D, Ruben FL, Winkelstein A, et al. Absence of immune deficiencies in a case of progressive multifocal leukoencephalopathy. Am J Med. 1976;61:433-436.
31. Bolton CF, Rozdilsky B. Primary progressive multifocal leukoencephalopathy: A case report. Neurology. 1971;21:72-77.
32. Fermaglich J, Hardman JM, Earle KM. Spontaneous progressive multifocal leukoencephalopathy. Neurology. 1970;20:479-484.
33. Holman RC, Janssen RS, Buehler JW, et al. Epidemiology of progressive multifocal leukoencephalopathy in the United States: Analysis of national mortality and AIDS surveillance data. Neurology. 1991;41:1733-1736.
34. Berger JR, Kaszovitz B, Post JD, et al. Progressive multifocal leukoencephalopathy associated with human immunodeficiency virus infection: A review of the literature with a report of sixteen cases. Ann Intern Med. 1987;107:78-87.
35. Levy RM, Bredesen DE, Rosenblum ML. Neurological manifestations of the acquired immunodeficiency syndrome (AIDS): Experience at UCSF and review of the literature. J Neurosurg. 1985;62:475-495.
36. Berger JR, Scott G, Albrecht J, et al. Progressive multifocal leukoencephalopathy in HIV-1-infected children. AIDS. 1992;6:837-841.

37. Vandersteenhoven JJ, Dbaibo G, Boyko OB, et al. Progressive multifocal leukoencephalopathy in pediatric acquired immunodeficiency syndrome. Pediatr Infect Dis J. 1992;11:232-237.

38. Morriss MC, Rutstein RM, Rudy B, et al. Progressive multifocal leukoencephalopathy in an HIV-infected child. Neuroradiology. 1997;39:142-144.

39. Chikezie PU, Greenberg AL. Idiopathic CD4+ T lymphopenia presenting as progressive multifocal leukoencephalopathy: Case report. Clin Infect Dis. 1997;24:526-527.

40. Kitamura T, Kunitake T, Guo J, et al. Transmission of human polyomavirus JC virus occurs both within the family and outside the family. J Clin Microbiol. 1994;32:2359-2363.

41. Kunitake T, Kitamura T, Guo J, et al. Parent-to-child transmission is relatively common in the spread of human polyomavirus JC virus. J Clin Microbiol. 1995;33:1448-1451.

42. Sabath BF, Major EO. Traffic of JC virus from sites of initial infection to the brain: The path to progressive multifocal leukoencephalopathy. J Infect Dis. 2002;186:S180-S186.

43. Taguchi F, Nagaki D, Saito M. Transplacental transmission of BK virus in humans. Jpn J Microbiol. 1975;19:395-398.

44. Gibson PE, Field AM, Gardner SD, et al. Occurrence of IgM antibodies against BK and JC polyomaviruses during pregnancy. J Clin Pathol. 1981;34:674-679.

45. Daniel R, Shah K, Madden D, Stagno S. Serological investigation of the possibility of congenital transmission of papovavirus JC. Infect Immun. 1981;33:319-321.

46. Shah K, Daniel R, Madden D, et al. Serological investigation of BK papovavirus infection in pregnant women and their offspring. Infect Immun. 1980;30:29-35.

47. Arthur RR, Shah KV. Occurrence and significance of papovaviruses BK and JC in the urine. Prog Med Virol. 1989;36:42-61.

48. Schneider EM, Dörries K. High frequency of polyomavirus infection in lymphoid cell preparations after allogeneic bone marrow transplantation. Transplant Proc. 1993;25:1271-1273.

49. Gallia GL, Houff SA, Major EO, Khalili K. Review: JC virus infection of lymphocytes—revisited. J Infect Dis. 1997;176:1603-1609.

50. DuBois V, Dutronc H, Lafon M-E, et al. Latency and reactivation of JC virus in peripheral blood of human immunodeficiency virus type 1-infected patients. J Clin Microbiol. 1997;35:2288-2292.

51. Silverman L, Rubinstein LJ. Electron microscopic observations on a case of progressive multifocal leukoencephalopathy. Acta Neuropathol. 1965;5:215-224.

52. Dörries K, Johnson RT, ter Meulen V. Detection of polyoma virus DNA in PML-brain tissue by in situ hybridization. J Gen Virol. 1979;42:49-57.

53. ZuRhein GM, Chou S-M. Particles resembling papova viruses in human cerebral demyelinating disease. Science. 1965;148:1477-1479.

54. Trapp BD, Small JA, Pulley M, et al. Dysmyelination in transgenic mice containing JC virus early region. Ann Neurol. 1988;23:38-48.

55. Small JA, Scangos GA, Cork L, et al. The early region of human papovavirus JC induces dysmyelination in transgenic mice. Cell. 1986;46:13-18.

56. Holmberg CA, Gribble DH, Takemoto KK, et al. Isolation of simian virus 40 from rhesus monkeys (Macaca mulatta) with spontaneous progressive multifocal leukoencephalopathy. J Infect Dis. 1977;136:593-596.

57. Gribble DH, Haden CC, Schwartz LW, et al. Spontaneous progressive multifocal leukoencephalopathy in macaques. Nature. 1975;254:602-604.

58. Wegner M, Drolet DW, Rosenfeld MG. Regulation of JC virus by the POU-domain transcription factor Tst-1: Implications for progressive multifocal leukoencephalopathy. Proc Natl Acad Sci U S A. 1993;90:4743-4747.

59. White FA III, Ishaq M, Stoner GL, et al. JC virus DNA is present in many human brain samples from patients without progressive multifocal leukoencephalopathy. J Virol. 1992;66:5726-5734.

60. Chesters PM, Heritage J, McCance DJ. Persistence of DNA sequences of BK virus and JC virus in normal human tissues and in diseased tissues. J Infect Dis. 1983;147:676-684.

61. Tominaga T, Yogo Y, Kitamura T, et al. Persistence of archetypal JC virus DNA in normal renal tissue derived from tumor-bearing patients. Virology. 1992;186:736-741.

62. Heritage J, Chesters PM, McCance DJ. The persistence of papovavirus BK DNA sequences in normal renal tissue. J Med Virol. 1981;8:143-150.

63. Dörries K, ter Meulen V. Progressive multifocal leukoencephalopathy: Detection of papovavirus JC in kidney tissue. J Med Virol. 1983;11:307-317.

64. Kitamura T, Sugimoto C, Kato A, et al. Persistent JC virus (JCV) infection is demonstrated by continuous shedding of the same JCV strains. J Clin Microbiol. 1997;35:1255-1257.

65. Goudsmit J, Wertheim-van Dillen P, van Strien A, et al. The role of BK virus in acute respiratory tract disease and the presence of BKV DNA in tonsils. J Med Virol. 1982;10:91-99.

66. Goudsmit J, Baak ML, Slaterus KW, et al. Human papovavirus isolated from urine of a child with acute tonsillitis. Br Med J. 1981;283:1363-1364.

67. Padgett BL, Walker DL, Desquitado MM, et al. BK virus and non-hemorrhagic cystitis in a child. Lancet. 1983;1:770.

68. Hashida Y, Gaffney PC, Yunis EJ. Acute hemorrhagic cystitis of childhood and papovavirus-like particles. J Pediatr. 1976;89:85-87.

69. Mininberg DT, Watson C, Desquitado M. Viral cystitis with transient secondary vesicoureteral reflux. J Urol. 1982;127:983-985.

70. Saitoh K, Sugae N, Koike N, et al. Diagnosis of childhood BK virus cystitis by electron microscopy and PCR. J Clin Pathol. 1993;46:773-775.

71. Brooks BR, Walker DL. Progressive multifocal leukoencephalopathy. Neurol Clin North Am. 1984;2:299-313.

72. Gillespie SM, Chang Y, Lemp G, et al. Progressive multifocal leukoencephalopathy in persons infected with human immunodeficiency virus, San Francisco, 1981-1989. Ann Neurol. 1991;30:597-604.

73. von Einsiedel RW, Fife TD, Aksamit AJ, et al. Progressive multifocal leukoencephalopathy in AIDS: A clinicopathologic study and review of the literature. J Neurol. 1993;240:391-406.

74. Hair LS, Nuovo G, Powers JM, et al. Progressive multifocal leukoencephalopathy in patients with human immunodeficiency virus. Hum Pathol. 1992;23:663-667.

75. Krupp LB, Lipton RB, Swerdlow ML, et al. Progressive multifocal leukoencephalopathy: Clinical and radiographic features. Ann Neurol. 1985;17:344-349.

76. Price RW, Neilsen S, Horten B, et al. Progressive multifocal leukoencephalopathy: A burnt-out case. Ann Neurol. 1983;13:485-490.

77. Berger JR, Mucke L. Prolonged survival and partial recovery in AIDS-associated progressive multifocal leukoencephalopathy. Neurology. 1988;38:1060-1065.

78. Fong IW, Toma E, Canadian PML Study Group. The natural history of progressive multifocal leukoencephalopathy in patients with AIDS. Clin Infect Dis. 1995;20:1305-1310.

79. Centers for Disease Control and Prevention. 1993 revised classification system for HIV infection and expanded surveillance case definition for AIDS among adolescents and adults. MMWR Morb Mortal Wkly Rep. 1992;41:1-20.

80. Purighalla R, Shapiro R, MacCauley J, Randhawa P. BK virus infection in a kidney diagnosed by needle biopsy. Am J Kidney Dis 1995;26:671-673.

81. Hirsch HH. Polyomavirus BK nephropathy: A (re-)emerging complication in renal transplantation. Am J Transplant. 2002;2:25-30.

82. Randhawa PS, Demetrius AJ. Nephropathy due to polyomavirus type BK. N Engl J Med. 2000;342:1361-1363.

83. Hirsch HH, Knowles W, Dickenmann M, et al. Prospective study of polyomavirus type BK replication and nephropathy in renal transplant recipients. N Engl J Med. 2002;347:488.

84. Traystman MD, Gupta PK, Shah KV, et al. Identification of viruses in the urine of renal transplant recipients by cytomorphology. Acta Cytol. 1980;24:501-510.

85. Coleman DV, Gardner SD, Field AM. Human polyomavirus infection in renal allograft recipients. Br Med J. 1973;3:371-375.

86. Lecatsas G, Prozesky OW, Van Wyk J, et al. Papova virus in urine after renal transplantation. Nature. 1973;241:343-344.

87. Gardner SD, MacKenzie EFD, Smith C, et al. Prospective study of the human polyomaviruses BK and JC and cytomegalovirus in renal transplant recipients. J Clin Pathol. 1984;37:578-586.

88. Coleman DV, MacKenzie EFD, Gardner SD, et al. Human polyomavirus (BK) infection and ureteric stenosis in renal allograft recipients. J Clin Pathol. 1978;31:338-347.

89. Hogan TF, Borden EC, McBain JA, et al. Human polyomavirus infections with JC virus and BK virus in renal transplant patients. Ann Intern Med. 1980;92:373-378.

90. Andrews CA, Shah KV, Daniel RW, et al. A serological investigation of BK virus and JC virus infections in recipients of renal allografts. J Infect Dis. 1988;158:176-181.

91. Rosen S, Harmon W, Krensky AM, et al. Tubulo-interstitial nephritis associated with polyomavirus (BK type) infection. N Engl J Med. 1983;308:1192-1196.

92. de Silva LM, Bale P, de Courcy J, et al. Renal failure due to BK virus infection in an immunodeficient child. J Med Virol. 1995;45:192-196.

93. Petrogiannis-Haliotis T, Sakoulas G, Kirby J, et al. BK-related polyomavirus vasculopathy in a renal transplant recipient. N Engl J Med. 2001;345:1250-1255.

94. Coleman DV, Wolfendale MR, Daniel RA, et al. A prospective study of human polyomavirus infection in pregnancy. J Infect Dis. 1980;142:1-8.

95. Coleman DV, Gardner SD, Mulholland C, et al. Human polyomavirus in pregnancy: A model for the study of defense mechanisms to virus reactivation. Clin Exp Immunol. 1983;53:289-296.

96. Weinberg ED. Pregnancy-associated depression of cell-mediated immunity. Rev Infect Dis. 1984;6:814-831.

97. Apperley JF, Rice SJ, Bishop JA, et al. Late onset hemorrhagic cystitis associated with urinary excretion of polyomaviruses after bone marrow transplantation. Transplantation. 1987;43:108-112.

98. Arthur RR, Shah KV, Baust SJ, et al. Association of BK viruria with hemorrhagic cystitis in recipients of bone marrow transplants. N Engl J Med. 1986;315:230-234.

99. Arthur RR, Shah KV, Charache P, et al. BK and JC virus infections in recipients of bone marrow transplants. J Infect Dis. 1988;158:563-569.

100. Hogan TF, Padgett BL, Walker DL, et al. Survey of human polyomavirus (JCV, BKV) infections in 139 patients with lung cancer, breast cancer, melanoma, or lymphoma. Prog Clin Biol Res. 1983;105:311-324.

101. Kahan AV, Coleman DV, Koss LG. Activation of human polyomavirus infection—detection by cytologic techniques. Am J Clin Pathol. 1980;74:326-332.

102. Greenlee JE, Narayan O, Johnson RT, et al. Induction of brain tumors in hamsters with BK virus, a human papovavirus. Lab Invest. 1977;36:636-641.

103. Corallini A, Barbanti-Brodano G, Bortoloni W, et al. High incidence of ependymomas induced by BK virus, a human papovavirus: Brief communications. J Natl Cancer Inst. 1977;59:1561-1563.

104. Varakis J, ZuRhein GM, Padgett BL, et al. Induction of peripheral neuroblastomas in Syrian hamsters after injection as neonates with JC virus, a human polyomavirus. Cancer Res. 1978;38:1718-1722.

105. Walker DL, Padgett BL, ZuRhein GM, et al. Human papovavirus (JC): Induction of brain tumors in hamsters. Science. 1973;181:674-676.

106. Corallini A, Pagnani M, Viadana P, et al. Induction of malignant subcutaneous sarcomas in hamsters by a recombinant DNA containing BK virus early region and the activated human c-Harvey-ras oncogene. Cancer Res. 1987;47:6671-6677.

107. Corallini A, Pagnani M, Caputo A, et al. Cooperation in oncogenesis between BK virus early region gene and the activated human c-Harvey-ras oncogene. J Gen Virol. 1988;69:2671-2679.

108. Pagnani M, Corallini A, Caputo A, et al. Cooperation in cell transformation between BK virus and the human c-Harvey *ras* oncogene. Int J Cancer. 1988;42:405-413.

109. Grossi MP, Caputo A, Meneguzzi G, et al. Transformation of human embryonic fibroblasts by BK virus, BK virus DNA and a subgenomic BK virus DNA fragment. J Gen Virol. 1982;63:393-403.

110. Corallini A, Pagnani M, Viadana P, et al. Association of BK virus with human brain tumors and tumors of pancreatic islets. Int J Cancer. 1987;39:60-67.

111. Caputo A, Corallini A, Grossi MP, et al. Episomal DNA of a BK virus variant in a human insulinoma. J Med Virol. 1983;12:37-49.

112. Fiori M, Di Mayorca G. Occurrence of BK virus DNA in DNA obtained from certain human tumors. Proc Natl Acad Sci U S A. 1976;73:4662-4666.

113. Bergsagel DJ, Finegold MJ, Butel JS, et al. DNA sequences similar to those of simian virus 40 in ependymomas and choroid plexus tumors of childhood. N Engl J Med. 1992;326:988-993.

114. Dörries K, Loeber G, Meixensberger J. Association of polyomaviruses JC, SV40, and BK with human brain tumors. Virology. 1987;160:268-270.

115. Beckmann AM, Shah KV, Padgett BL. Propagation and primary isolation of papovavirus JC in epithelial cells derived from human urine. Infect Immun. 1982;38:774-777.

116. Coleman DV. The cytodiagnosis of human polyomavirus infection. Acta Cytol. 1975;19:93-96.

117. Markowitz RB, Thompson HC, Mueller JF, et al. Incidence of BK virus and JC virus viruria in human immunodeficiency virus-infected and -uninfected subjects. J Infect Dis. 1993;167:13-20.

118. Arthur RR, Beckmann AM, Li CC, et al. Direct detection of the human papovavirus BK in urine of bone marrow transplant recipients: Comparison of DNA hybridization with ELISA. J Med Virol. 1985;16:29-36.

119. Hogan TF, Padgett BL, Walker DL, et al. Rapid detection and identification of JC virus and BK virus in human urine by using immunofluorescence microscopy. J Clin Microbiol. 1980;11:178-183.

120. Shah KV, Daniel RW, Strickler HD, Goedert JJ. Investigation of human urine for genomic sequences of the primate polyomaviruses simian virus 40, BK virus and JC virus. J Infect Dis. 1997;176:1618-1621.

121. Kitamura T, Aso Y, Kuniyoshi N, et al. High incidence of urinary JC virus excretion in nonimmunosuppressed older patients. J Infect Dis. 1990;161:1128-1133.

122. Richardson EP Jr, Webster HDF. Progressive multifocal leukoencephalopathy: Its pathological features. Prog Clin Biol Res. 1983;105:191-203.

123. Narayan O, Penney JB Jr, Johnson RT, et al. Etiology of progressive multifocal leukoencephalopathy: Identification of papovavirus. N Engl J Med. 1973;289:1278-1282.

124. Itoyama Y, Webster HDF, Sternberger NH, et al. Distribution of papovavirus, myelin-associated glycoprotein, and myelin basic protein in progressive multifocal leukoencephalopathy lesions. Ann Neurol. 1982;11:396-407.

125. Aksamit AJ, Gendelman HE, Orenstein JM, Pezeshkpour GH. AIDS-associated progressive multifocal leukoencephalopathy (PML): Comparison to non-AIDS PML with in situ hybridization and immunohistochemistry. Neurology. 1990;40:1073-1078.

126. Kuchelmeister K, Gullotta F, Bergmann M, et al. Progressive multifocal leukoencephalopathy (PML) in the acquired immunodeficiency syndrome (AIDS): A neuropathological autopsy study of 21 cases. Pathol Res Pract. 1993;189:163-173.

127. Heinz ER, Drayer BP, Haenggeli CA, et al. Computed tomography in white-matter disease. Radiology. 1979;130:371-378.

128. Whiteman MLH, Post MJD, Berger JR, et al. Progressive multifocal leukoencephalopathy in 47 HIV-seropositive patients: Neuroimaging with clinical and pathologic correlation. Radiology. 1993;187:233-240.

129. Ciricillo SF, Rosenblum ML. Use of CT and MR imaging to distinguish intracranial lesions and to define the need for biopsy in AIDS patients. J Neurosurg. 1990;73:720-724.

130. Mark AS, Atlas SW. Progressive multifocal leukoencephalopathy in patients with AIDS: Appearance on MR images. Radiology. 1989;173:517-520.

131. Zimmer C, Märzheuser S, Patt S, et al. Stereotactic brain biopsy in AIDS. J Neurol. 1992;239:394-400.

132. Chappell ET, Guthrie BL, Orenstein J. The role of stereotactic biopsy in the management of HIV-related focal brain lesions. Neurosurgery. 1992;30:825-829.

133. Levy RM, Russell E, Yungbluth M, et al. The efficacy of image-guided stereotactic brain biopsy in neurologically symptomatic acquired immunodeficiency syndrome patients. Neurosurgery. 1992;30:186-190.

134. Gibson PE, Knowles WA, Hand JF, et al. Detection of JC virus DNA in the cerebrospinal fluid of patients with progressive multifocal leukoencephalopathy. J Med Virol. 1993;39:278-281.

135. Henson J, Rosenblum M, Armstrong D, et al. Amplification of JC virus DNA from brain and cerebrospinal fluid of patients with progressive multifocal leukoencephalopathy. Neurology. 1991;41:1967-1971.

136. Ferrante P, Caldarelli-Stefano R, Omodeo-Zorini E, et al. Comprehensive investigation of the presence of JC virus in AIDS patients with and without progressive multifocal leukoencephalopathy. J Med Virol. 1997;52:235-242.

137. Vago L, Cinque P, Sala E, et al. JCV-DNA and BKV-DNA in the CNS tissue and CSF of AIDS patients and normal subjects. Study of 41 cases and review of the literature. J Acquir Immune Defic Syndr Hum Retrovirol. 1996;12:139-146.

138. McGuire D, Barhite S, Hollander H, Miles M. JC virus DNA in cerebrospinal fluid of human immunodeficiency virus-infected patients: Predictive value for progressive multifocal leukoencephalopathy. Ann Neurol. 1995;37:395-399.

139. Weber T, Turner RW, Frye S, et al. Specific diagnosis of progressive multifocal leukoencephalopathy by polymerase chain reaction. J Infect Dis. 1994;169:1138-1141.

140. Hammarin A-L, Bogdanovic G, Svedhem V, et al. Analysis of PCR as a tool for detection of JC virus DNA in cerebrospinal fluid for diagnosis of progressive multifocal leukoencephalopathy. J Clin Microbiol. 1996;34:2929-2932.

141. Fong IW, Britton CB, Luinstra KE, et al. Diagnostic value of detecting JC virus DNA in cerebrospinal fluid of patients with progressive multifocal leukoencephalopathy. J Clin Microbiol. 1995;33:484-486.

142. De Luca A, Cingolani A, Linzalone A, et al. Improved detection of JC virus DNA in cerebrospinal fluid for diagnosis of AIDS-related progressive multifocal leukoencephalopathy. J Clin Microbiol. 1996;34:1343-1346.

143. Antinori A, Ammassari A, De Luca A, et al. Diagnosis of AIDS-related focal brain lesions: A decision-making analysis based on clinical and neuroradiologic characteristics combined with polymerase chain reaction assays in CSF. Neurology. 1997;48:687-694.

144. De Luca A, Giancola ML, Ammassari A, et al. The effect of potent antiretroviral therapy and JC virus load in cerebrospinal fluid on clinical outcome of patients with AIDS-associated progressive multifocal leukoencephalopathy. J Infect Dis. 2000;182:1077-1083.

145. Eggers C, Stellbrink H-J, Buhk T, Dörries K. Quantification of JC virus DNA in the cerebrospinal fluid of patients with human immunodeficiency virus-associated progressive multifocal leukoencephalopathy—a longitudinal study. J Infect Dis. 1999;180:1690-1694.

146. Nickeleit V, Klimkait T, Binet I, et al. Testing for polyomavirus type BK DNA in plasma to identify renal-allograft recipients with viral nephropathy. N Engl J Med. 2000;342:1309-1315.

147. Limaye AP, Jerome KR, Kuhr CS, et al. Quantitation of BK virus load in serum for the diagnosis of BK virus-associated nephropathy in renal transplant recipients. J Infect Dis. 2001;183:1669-1672.

148. Farrell DF. The EEG in progressive multifocal leukoencephalopathy. Electroencephalogr Clin Neurophys. 1969;26:200-205.

149. Hall CD, Dafni U, Simpson D, et al. Failure of cytarabine in progressive multifocal leukoencephalopathy associated with human immunodeficiency virus infection. N Engl J Med. 1998;338:1345-1351.

150. Steiger MJ, Tarnesby G, Gabe S, et al. Successful outcome of progressive multifocal leukoencephalopathy with cytarabine and interferon. Ann Neurol. 1993;33:407-411.

151. Tashiro K, Doi S, Moriwaka F, et al. Progressive multifocal leucoencephalopathy with magnetic resonance imaging verification in therapeutic trials of infection. J Neurol. 1987;234:427-429.

152. Tarsy D, Holden EM, Segarra JM, et al. 5-Iodo-2(-deoxyuridine (IUDR; NSC-39661) given intraventricularly in the treatment of progressive multifocal leukoencephalopathy. Cancer Chemother Rep. 1973;57:73-78.

153. Przepiorka D, Jaecle KA, Birdwell RR, et al. Successful treatment of progressive multifocal leukoencephalopathy with low-dose interleukin-2. Bone Marrow Transplant. 1997;20:983-987.

154. Andrei G, Snoeck R, Vandeputte M, et al. Activity of various compounds against murine and human polyomaviruses. Antimicrob Agents Chemother. 1997;41:587.

155. DeLuca A, Giancola ML, Ammassari A, et al. Cidofovir added to HAART improves virological and clinical outcome in AIDS-associated progressive multifocal leukoencephalopathy. AIDS. 2000;14:F117-F121.

156. DeLuca A, Giancola ML, Ammassari A, et al. Potent antiretroviral therapy with or without cidofovir for AIDS-associated progressive multifocal leukoencephalopathy: Extended follow-up of an observational study. J Neurovirol. 2001;7:364-368.

157. Razonable RR, Aksamit AJ, Wright AJ, Wilson JW. Cidofovir treatment of progressive multifocal leukoencephalopathy in a patient receiving highly active antiretroviral therapy. Mayo Clin Proc. 2001;76:1171-1175.

158. Marra CM, Rajicic N, Barker BA, et al. A pilot study of cidofovir for progressive multifocal leukoencephalopathy in AIDS. AIDS. 2002;16:1791-1797.

159. Elliot B, Aromin I, Gold R, et al. 2.5-Year remission of AIDS-associated progressive multifocal leukoencephalopathy with combined antiretroviral therapy. Lancet. 1997;349:850.

160. Domingo P, Guardiola JM, Iranzo A, Margall N. Remission of progressive multifocal leucoencephalopathy after antiretroviral therapy. Lancet. 1997;349:1554-1555.

161. Baqi M, Kucharczyk W, Walmsley SL. Regression of progressive multifocal encephalopathy with highly active antiretroviral therapy. AIDS. 1997;11:1526-1527.

162. Clifford DB, Yiannoutsos C, Glicksman M, et al. HAART improves prognosis in HIV-associated progressive multifocal leukoencephalopathy. Neurology. 1999;52:623-625.

163. DeSimone JA, Pomerantz RJ, Babinchak TJ. Inflammatory reactions in HIV-1-infected persons after initiation of highly active antiretroviral therapy. Ann Intern Med. 2000;133:447-454.

164. Cheeseman SH, Black PH, Rubin RH, et al. Interferon and BK papovavirus—clinical and laboratory studies. J Infect Dis. 1980;141:157-161.

165. Randhawa PS, Demetrius AJ. Nephropathy due to polyomavirus type BK. N Engl J Med. 2000;342:1361-1363.

CHAPTER **142**

Hepatitis B Virus and Hepatitis Delta Virus

MARGARET JAMES KOZIEL

ALEEM SIDDIQUI

HEPATITIS B VIRUS

Hepatitis B virus (HBV) infects more than 500 million people worldwide. It is a leading cause of chronic hepatitis, cirrhosis, and hepatocellular carcinoma (HCC), and these sequelae of chronic infection account for more than 1 million deaths annually. The outcome of infection and spectrum of illness vary widely. During the acute phase, infections range from asymptomatic hepatitis to icteric hepatitis, including fulminant hepatitis. When chronic infection is established, the spectrum of illness ranges from the healthy carrier state to all of the sequelae of chronic hepatitis, including cirrhosis and HCC. Although HBV cannot be cultured, molecular studies have led to the design of specific antivirals to control viral replication in patients. Moreover, the identification of the correlates of protective immunity has facilitated the widespread use of a highly effective vaccine, which, by preventing chronic carriage of the virus and the subsequent development of HCC, represents the first true vaccine to prevent cancer.

Historical Background and Classification

Hippocrates recognized the spread of jaundice by infectious agents as early as 400 BC. The early cases of HBV infection were linked to the use of conventional viral vaccines, which were prepared from or contained human serum. In 1885, Lurman described the appearance of jaundice in 15% of 1289 shipyard workers who received smallpox vaccine prepared from human lymph.[1] Epidemics of hepatitis were also recorded after the administration of yellow fever vaccine, which was stabilized with human serum.[2] In the early part of the 20th century, the increasing use of contaminated syringes and needles by diabetics taking insulin and by patients treated for syphilis at venereal disease clinics elevated the importance of serum hepatitis.[3,4] This led to the association of hepatitis B with blood and blood products and to its distinction from infectious hepatitis, caused by hepatitis A virus, a member of the Picornaviridae family.[5] The first hint of viral etiology came from the studies of Blumberg and colleagues, who reported the discovery of a human antigen in Australian Aborigines termed Australian (Au) antigen.[6] Subsequently, the Au antigen came to be known as hepatitis B surface antigen (HBsAg) and its association with acute hepatitis was established. For this discovery, Dr. Baruch Blumberg received the Nobel Prize in Physiology and Medicine in 1976. In 1971, Dane, an

electron microscopist, and associates visualized the presence of 22-nm HBsAg subviral particles along with the 42-nm complete virus particles in the blood of patients with hepatitis B (Fig. 142-1).[7]

Because of their unique biologic and molecular characteristics and their liver tropism, HBV and HBV-like animal viruses were given the status of a new family designated Hepadnaviridae (*hepa*totropic *DNA viru*ses).[8] HBV, the human pathogen, and other mammalian hepatitis viruses with sequence homology and similar genome organization are grouped in the genus Orthohepadnavirus. The genus Avihepadnavirus includes viruses that infect ducks, geese, and heron. The Hepadnavirus animal models, which include duck hepatitis B virus,[9] woodchuck hepatitis virus (WHV),[10] and ground squirrel hepatitis virus,[11] have been extensively studied and have contributed to the current knowledge of the molecular biology of HBV infection and replication. However, these viral genomes are considerably divergent from human HBV, and there are limited tools to study the immune reaction to the virus in these animals. The primary host for HBV is human, but other primates such as chimpanzees, gibbons, orangutans, African green monkeys, and squirrel monkeys have been found positive for HBsAg. However, the use of these animals for the study of pathogenesis is both difficult and expensive. Thus, a convenient animal model or an efficient tissue culture system for HBV still remains unavailable. HBV was molecularly cloned from patients' sera in 1979 and its complete DNA sequences determined.[12-14] These advances led to a surge of investigations on the molecular aspects of HBV molecular biology, chief among which are the regulatory schemes of gene expression and replication.

Biology

HBV is a small DNA virus, whose 3200-kb partially double-stranded DNA genome is maintained in a circular conformation.[15] Partially duplex DNA molecules represent incomplete synthesis of the viral DNA during morphogenesis (Fig. 142-2).[16] One of the unique features of HBV infection is the production of large quantities of subviral spherical and filamentous HBsAg particles in addition to complete virus particles. Under electron microscopy, these are distinguished by a diameter of 42 nm for complete virus (Dane) particles and 22-nm spherical and filamentous structures for subviral particles (see Fig. 142-1).[7] HBsAg is expressed on the exterior of all these particles. HBsAg subviral particles reach a titer of 10^{13}/mL, whereas viral particles range in titer from 10^4 to 10^9/mL. All of these particles circulate in blood and permit convenient diagnosis of viral antigen by enzyme-linked immunosorbent assay or radioimmunoassay.[17] HBsAg forms the viral component of the lipoprotein envelope, which encloses a core shell containing the viral DNA genome and the virus-encoded polymerase protein. The nucleocapsid or core is composed of a 21-kD basic phosphoprotein commonly known as hepatitis B core antigen (HB$_c$Ag).[18] A cell-derived kinase activity has been shown to be associated with the virion particles,[19] but the functional significance of this enzyme is not understood.

The 20-nm HBsAg particles and filaments are composed of three forms of surface antigen polypeptides and lipids derived from hepato-

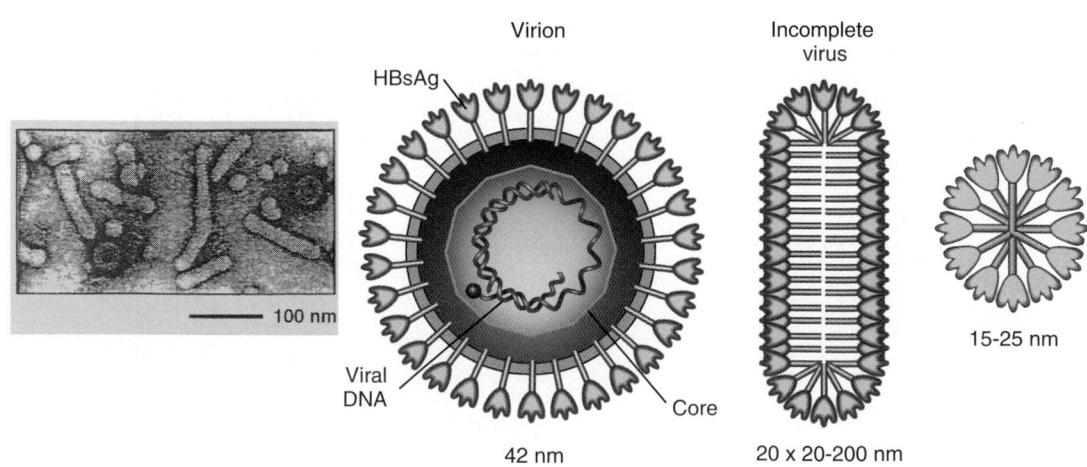

FIGURE 142-1. Structure of hepatitis B virus (HBV) and hepatitis B surface antigen (HBsAg) particles. **A,** Electron micrograph of negatively stained HBV. **B,** Diagram of 42-nm HBV showing partially duplex DNA genome with a covalently linked protein at the 5′ end of the complete minus strand. **C,** Diagram of 22-nm HBsAg filament. (*Adapted and modified from Flint SJ, Enquist LW, Racaniello VR, et al. Principles of Virology, 2nd ed. Washington, DC: ASM Press; 2004:808, with permission.*)

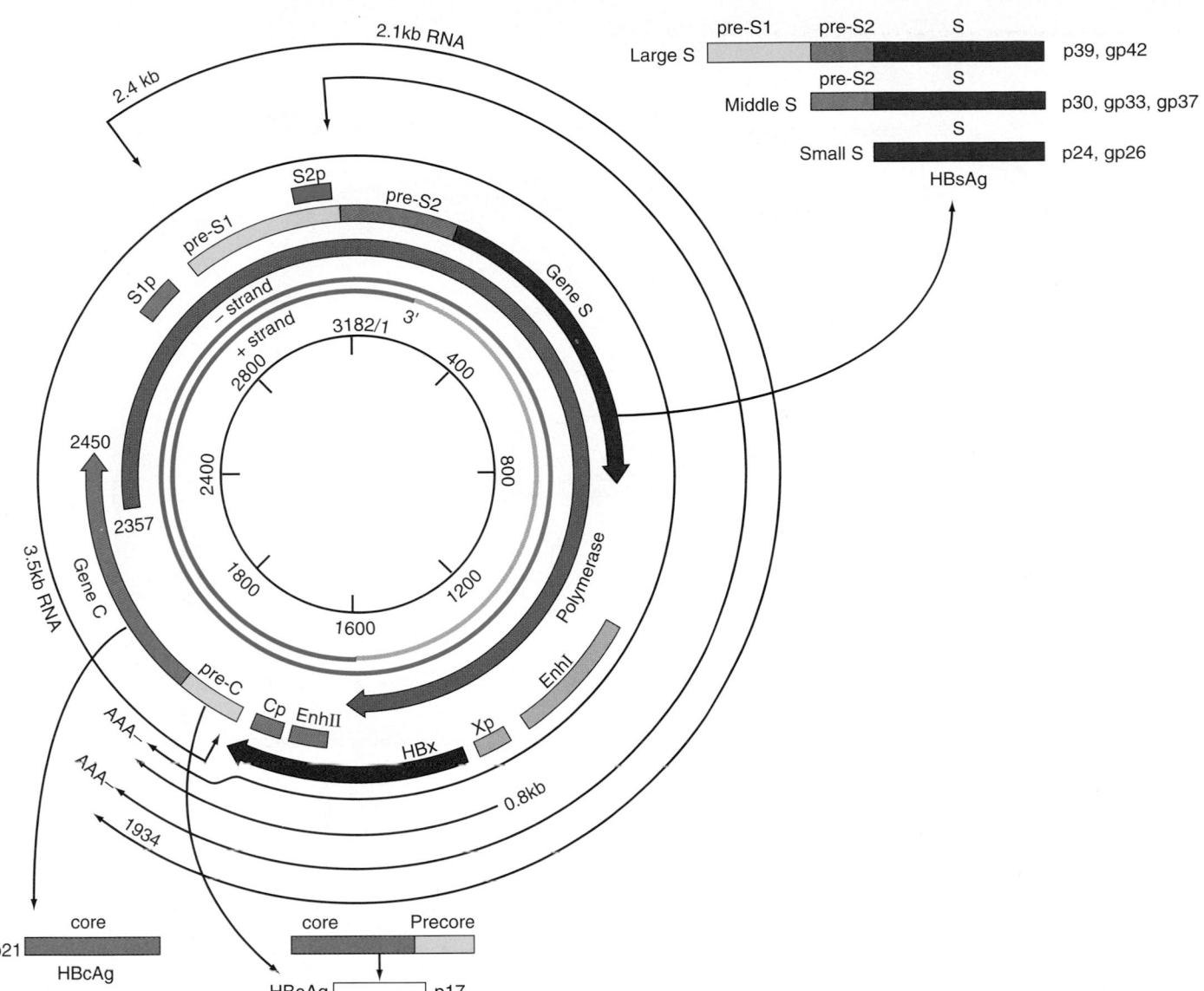

FIGURE 142-2. Hepatitis B virus (HBV) genome organization, map of viral transcripts, and proteins. The partially double-stranded 3.2-kb viral DNA is shown in the inner circle. The single-stranded (ss) region is indicated in yellow-orange. The extent of the ss region varies from molecule to molecule. HBV-encoded overlapping genes are indicated in the outer circles in various colors. Four promoter regions preceding a corresponding gene are indicated as S1p, S2p, Cp, and Xp. Two enhancer elements (I and II) are also shown. Viral transcripts are indicated in the outermost circles (thin lines). The three forms of HBsAg, HB$_c$Ag, and HB$_e$Ag (surface, core, and early antigen) polypeptides are also shown. (*Adapted and modified from Hepatitis viruses. In: Murray PA, Rosenthal KS, Kobayashi GS, et al, eds. Medical Microbiology, 4th ed. St. Louis, Mosby; 2002:591-605, with permission.*)

cyte membranes. The lipid content is approximately 30% by weight and includes phospholipids, cholesterol, cholesterol esters, and triglycerides.[20,21] These particles are devoid of HBV DNA genome and hence are noninfectious. Because of their high immunogenicity, purified HBsAg particles can be used as an HBV vaccine. HBsAg elicits neutralizing antibodies, which offer protection from reinfection.[22,23] The high titers of HBsAg in patients during natural infection can potentially serve to adsorb neutralizing antibody and thus protect the virus from host defenses.

Attachment, Entry, and Hepatotropism

HBV primarily infects hepatocytes. HBV makes its entry into hepatocytes through a liver cell–specific receptor, consistent with the strict hepatotropism exhibited by this and other members of Hepadnaviridae. The attempts to identify a strictly liver-specific receptor molecule have been largely unsuccessful. Several candidates have been identified as possible receptor molecules. These include endonexin, carboxypeptidase, and serum apolipoproteins, but none appears to fulfill the criteria for a liver cell–specific receptor that confers hepatotropism to HBV and

other related hepatitis viruses.[17] Bound virions deliver core particles into the cytoplasm, which make their way into the nucleus. In the nucleus, the virion DNA, which is partially duplex, is matured into a covalently closed circular (CCC) DNA form (Fig. 142-3).[24] Liver specificity is also displayed at the level of viral gene expression, which is controlled largely by the promoters and enhancers (see Fig. 142-2).[25]

The liver appears to be the major, but not the only, site of viral infection. The presence of HBV DNA in other cell types, especially lymphocytes, has been described.[26] Clear and coherent evidence for viral DNA replication, transcription, and translation in all of these cells has not been clearly demonstrated. However, infectious WHV can be found in lymphocytes after mitogenic stimulation, implicating lymphocytes as a second reservoir for HBV.[27,28]

Viral Genome

HBV employs unique transcriptional and translational strategies to maximize the limited coding capacity of its genome. The HBV DNA genome is a partially double-stranded molecule within the virions (see Fig. 142-1).[29] The complete (negative) strand contains a protein covalently linked to its

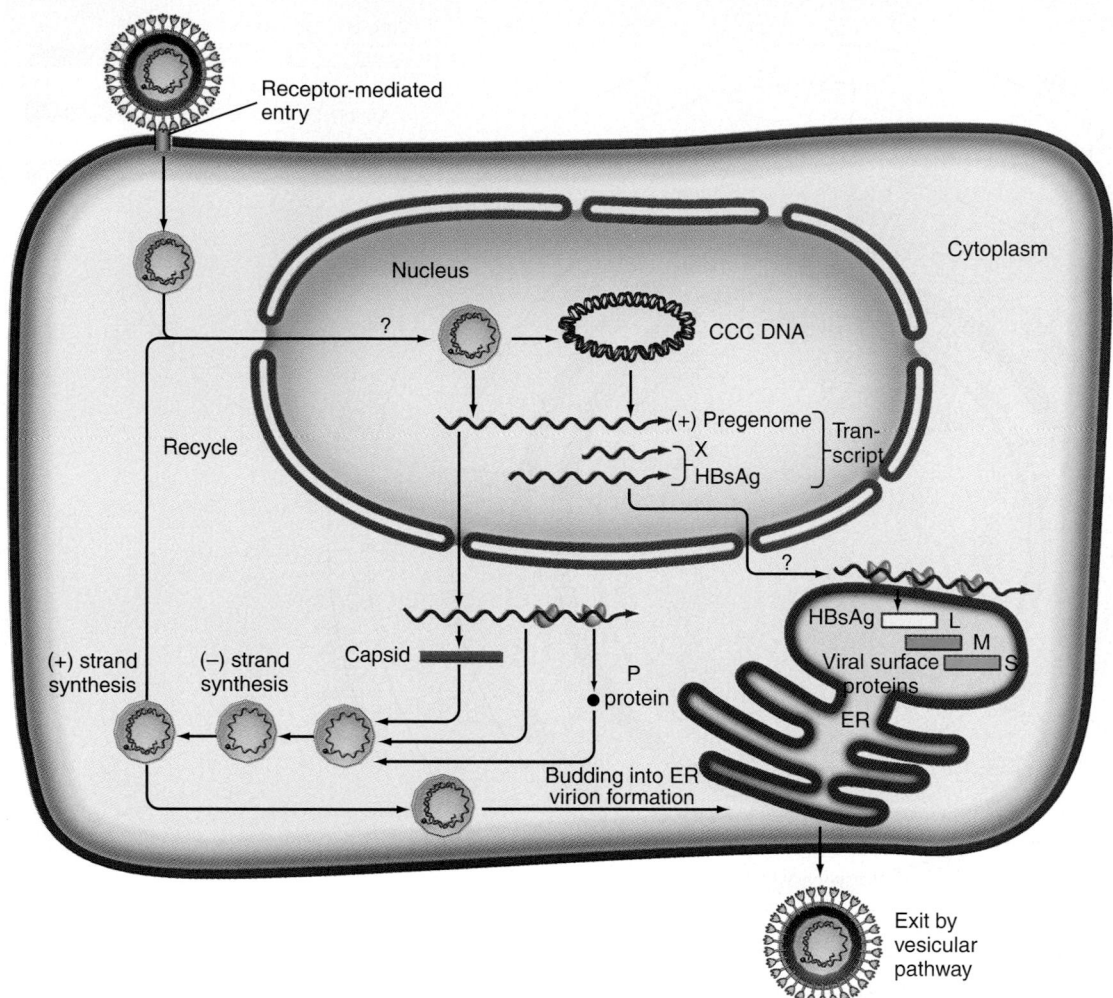

FIGURE 142-3. Hepatitis B virus (HBV) life cycle. The virion attaches to a susceptible hepatocyte through recognition of a cell surface receptor that has yet to be identified. The mechanism of virus uptake is unknown, and repair of the gapped (+) DNA strand is accomplished by as yet unidentified enzymes. The DNA is translocated to the nucleus, where it is found in a covalently closed circular form called CCC DNA. The (−) strand of such CCC DNA is the template for transcription by cellular RNA polymerase II of a longer-than-genome-length RNA called the pregenome and shorter, subgenomic transcripts. Viral messenger RNAs (mRNAs) are transported from the nucleus. The hepatitis B surface antigens encoding viral mRNAs are translated by ribosomes bound to the endoplasmic reticulum (ER), and the proteins enter the secretory pathway. The pregenome RNA is translated at low efficiency to produce a 90-kD polymerase protein, P, which possesses reverse transcriptase activity. This protein then binds to a specific site at the 5′ end of its own transcript, where viral DNA synthesis is eventually initiated. The pregenomic RNA also serves as mRNA for the capsid protein. Concurrently with capsid formation, the RNA-P protein complex is packaged and reverse transcription begins with synthesis of (−) strand DNA followed by (+) strand DNA synthesis. Before the completion of +-strand synthesis, core particles mature and these structures acquire envelopes by budding into the ER, where viral morphogenesis is completed. Progeny-enveloped virions are released from the cell by exocytosis or are recycled to the nucleus, where the process is repeated. *(Adapted and modified from Flint SJ, Enquist LW, Racaniello VR, et al. Principles of Virology, 2nd ed. Washington, DC: ASM Press; 2004:809, with permission.)*

5′ terminus.[30] The incomplete (plus) strand displays variable length and bears a 5′ capped oligoribonucleotide at its 5′ end (see Fig. 142-1).[31] The asymmetry of the DNA strands reflects the incomplete synthesis of DNA during maturation of viral particles. HBV DNA codes for four overlapping open reading frames: S, for the surface antigen or envelope gene (HBsAg); C, for the nucleocapsid (core) and e antigen gene (HB$_c$Ag, HB$_e$Ag); P, for the polymerase gene; and X, for the HBx gene (see Fig. 142-2). The surface antigen open reading frame contains three in-frame initiator codons from which small or major (S), middle (M), and large kD (L) HBsAg polypeptides are synthesized, respectively. These polypeptides are variably glycosylated to yield several species: S, p24/gp26; M, p30/gp33/gp37; and L p39/gp42 kD HBsAg polypeptides, respectively. L HBsAg and M HBsAg contain characteristic pre-S1 and pre-S2 domains and hence these proteins are also referred to as pre-S1 and pre-S2 proteins, respectively. The 22-nm subviral particles are composed of mostly S and lesser amounts of

M polypeptides and few or no L polypeptides. The 42-nm Dane particles, which represent the complete virus, contain all three HBsAg forms. The L polypeptide is believed to carry the receptor recognition domain.[32] Thus, the meager amounts or absence of L protein in the 22-nm particles prevents these abundant forms from competing with virions for cell surface receptors.

On the basis of the antibody response to HBsAg, four major subtypes of HBsAg have been recognized and designated *adw*, *ayw*, *adr*, and *ayr*. All HBsAg shares a group-specific determinant *a*, whereas two pairs of mutually exclusive subtype determinants *d* or *y* and *w* or *r* exist to give the combination described previously.[8] There is a correlation of each genotype with geographic distribution. For instance, *adw* is common in the United States, whereas *adr* is found predominantly in Southeast Asia and China. The *a* is a common determinant and can elicit protective immunity against any subtype,[22] but the antibody against subtype determinants is subtype specific.

The C region or the core open reading frame contains two in-frame initiator codons with the first ATG responsible for e antigen polypeptide synthesis (HB$_e$Ag) (see Fig. 142-2). The second ATG serves as an initiation codon for the core antigen (HB$_c$Ag) polypeptide. HB$_e$Ag is secreted from cells and accumulates in serum as an immunologically distinct soluble antigen and serves as a marker of ongoing viral replication.[33] Both gene products (core and e polypeptides) are made from the same reading frame. The P and X open reading frames encode the polymerase and the HBx proteins, respectively.

Transcription

The HBV genome displays a remarkable strategy to maximize the use of the limited capacity of its genomic size by utilizing multiple overlapping reading frames and multiple initiation codons to generate antigenically different proteins. The CCC viral DNA in the nucleus serves as the substrate for viral transcription and employs host polymerase II in the synthesis of viral transcripts (see Fig. 142-3). The DNA sequence analysis of the viral genome led to the identification of four different genes designated C, S, P, and X, which encode HB$_{c/e}$Ag, HBsAg, polymerase, and HBx proteins, respectively.[17] The expression of these genes is regulated by four promoter elements (S1p, S2p, Cp, and Xp) and two enhancer elements (enhancer I and II) (see Fig. 142-2).[17,25] These transcriptional regulatory elements direct the synthesis of multiple viral transcripts that are approximately 3.5, 2.4/2.1, and 0.8 kb in length, respectively. All viral transcripts are unspliced, capped, and polyadenylated. All the transcripts are encoded on one strand of the DNA and coterminate at an identical polyadenylation site.[34] This polyadenylation site, which is differentially utilized during the viral transcription process, is composed of a variant (UAUAAA) of the canonical eukaryotic polyadenylation site.[35]

The pre-S1 (S1p) promoter directs the synthesis of the 2.4-kb transcripts, which code for the large envelope (L HBsAg) polypeptide. This promoter contains binding sites for two liver-enriched transcription factors, HNF-3 and HNF-1, which are primarily responsible for the liver-specific activity of this promoter.[36] The pre-S2 or S (S2p) promoter directs the transcription of multiple species of messenger RNAs (mRNAs) coding for pre-S2/M and S HBsAg polypeptides. Collectively, these RNA species are approximately 2.1 kb in length with 5′ heterogeneous ends. The mRNAs, which initiate downstream of the pre-S2 initiator ATG, code for the S or the major polypeptide. The S2p promoter also displays liver specificity and is controlled by the enhancer II element located about 2000 bp away (see Fig. 142-2).[37] The S2p promoter is stronger than the S1p promoter, which results in the synthesis of an excess of the major S over the L (pre-S1) and M (pre-S2) forms of the HBsAg. This regulation is especially critical for synthesizing the appropriate levels of the three forms of surface protein within the cell. The basis for the differential regulation of these promoters is governed by mechanisms that involve both positive and negative *cis*-acting elements and the *trans*-acting transcriptional factors.[17,38]

The core/pregenomic promoter (Cp) governs the expression of two longer than genome-length transcripts (3.5 kb) designated precore (pre-C) and core (C) RNAs. The slightly longer pre-C RNA directs the translation of HB$_e$Ag polypeptide. The shorter C RNA is used for the translation of core and polymerase proteins. The ATG for the polymerase (reverse transcriptase) is located several hundred nucleotides from the 5′ end (see Fig. 142-2). The core RNA, after its translation into core polypeptides, packages its own RNA, which then functions as a pregenome RNA (pregenomic RNA). The Cp promoter contains binding sites for several liver-enriched and ubiquitous transcription factors.[39] Immediately juxtaposed to this lies enhancer II, which in concert with enhancer I plays a regulatory role in the overall HBV gene expression. A complex scheme of transcriptional regulation appears to operate within these control elements.[40]

The X promoter (Xp) is located immediately downstream of enhancer I and regulates the synthesis of the low-abundance 0.8-kb X transcripts, which correlates with similar levels of HBx protein synthesis in infected cells.[41,42] Both ubiquitous and liver-enriched factors binding to enhancer I regulate the biosynthesis of X transcripts.

Translation

As noted previously, HBV also employs unique translational strategies to maximize the limited coding capacity of its genome. HBV encodes three major viral transcripts (2.4/2.1, 3.5, 0.8 kb) (see Fig. 142-2). The S region contains three in-frame translational start codons from which the synthesis of three distinct surface antigen polypeptides is regulated (L/pre-S1, M/pre-S2, and S). These proteins exhibit distinct amino termini and differ with respect to the extent to which they are post-translationally modified by glycosylation.[43] The S protein is referred to as the major surface antigen because it represents approximately 85% of the HBsAg that is produced by the virus. The pre-S1 (L) and pre-S2 (M) proteins are present at an abundance of approximately 15% and 1% to 2%, respectively. This differential production of surface antigen proteins correlates with the differential regulation of the two surface antigen promoter elements, which direct their transcription (see "Transcription")

The pre-C and C mRNAs are translated into e and core polypeptides (HB$_{c/e}$Ag) respectively. The pre-C protein contains a signal peptide sequence encoding 19 amino acid residues, which targets this protein to the secretory pathway in the endoplasmic reticulum (ER).[44] Further processing of the protein includes cleavage of the signal peptide and several amino acid residues at the carboxyl terminus leading to the production of a 17-kD e antigen polypeptide (HB$_e$Ag) (see Fig. 142-2). HB$_e$Ag is secreted and is found in the serum of patients and serves as a marker of active replication in chronic hepatitis. The function of HB$_e$Ag is not clearly understood. It is dispensable for replication, as nonsense or frameshift mutations in the pre-C are found in nature. In HBV carriers, mutant viruses with defects in the pre-C region arise spontaneously and are both infectious and pathogenic.[45,46] The C-RNA initiates downstream of the precore ATG and translates into core antigen polypeptide (HB$_c$Ag) and less frequently into polymerase. Because polymerase ATG is located several hundred nucleotides downstream of the 5′ end (see Fig. 142-2), the ribosomes must reach this initiator codon by a mechanism different from ribosome scanning. As this process is inefficient, one polymerase protein is translated for every 200 to 300 molecules of core polypeptides.

HBV polymerase protein consists of 832 amino acids and is composed of four domains: terminal protein (TP), spacer, reverse transcriptase (RT), and ribonuclease H (RNaseH) (Fig. 142-4).[17] The TP domain represents the portion of the polymerase protein that is covalently bound to minus-strand DNA. The spacer domain or tether region connects the TP domain to the RT. The RT domain contains the characteristic YMDD consensus sequence, the catalytic site for RT. YMDD is a signature motif found in retroviral RTs and is a major focus of current drug development in HBV (see Fig. 142-4) (see also "Management of Hepatitis B"). The RT domain is followed by an RNaseH domain.[47,48] The function of RNaseH is to hydrolyze the pregenomic RNA template after reverse transcription within the nucleocapsid.[49]

Replication

Although HBV is a DNA-containing virus, the replication occurs through an RNA intermediate, a characteristic that places hepadnaviruses close to retroviruses. Much of our understanding of HBV replication strategy comes from the classic experiments of Mason and Summers,[24] which demonstrated that HBV amplifies by reverse transcription of an RNA intermediate and that these events occur within the subviral core particles in the cytoplasm. The complex mechanism by which pregenomic RNA is converted to partially double-stranded virion DNA has been studied in considerable detail (Fig. 142-5).[17,49] HBV replication begins with the encapsidation of pregenomic RNA by the core polypeptide along with the polymerase. The pregenomic RNA contains terminally redundant 200-nucleotide sequences, which include an epsilon (ε) stem-loop structure and a short sequence of 11 or 12 nucleotides termed DR1 (see Fig. 142-5).[50] The HBV polymerase binds pregenomic RNA preferentially at the 5′ copy of the ε stem-loop structure on its own molecule.[51] The interaction between the ε signal of the pregenomic RNA and the polymerase and the core leads to the formation of a ribonucleoprotein complex. The HBV capsid or core assembles into

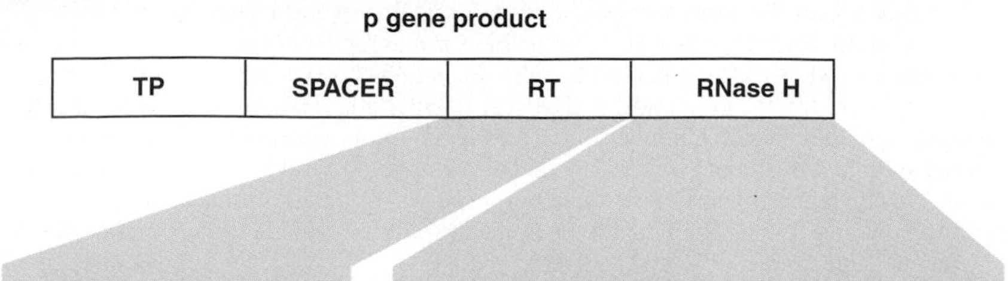

FIGURE 142-4. Domain structure of the hepadnaviral polymerase protein. **Top,** Schematic depiction of the functional domains of P protein. TP, terminal protein; RT, reverse transcriptase; RNaseH, ribonuclease H. **Bottom,** Amino acid sequence alignments with other RNA-dependent DNA polymerases; these homologies form the basis of the assignment of the RT and RNaseH domains. *(Adapted from Ganem DE, Schneider RI. Hepadnaviridae: The viruses and their replication. In: Knipe D, Howley P, eds. Fundamental Virology, 4th ed. Philadelphia: Lippincott Williams & Wilkins; 2001:1285-1331, with permission.)*

p gene product

TP	SPACER	RT	RNase H

	Conserved RT		Conserved RNaseH		
E. coli	LLPQGA--SP	YADDL	TDGS	MELMAAIVAL	TDSQYV	NERCD
Tyl	APPPHL--ND	FVDDM				
Copia	ALPQGI--NS	YVDDV				
RSV	VLPQGM--SP	YNDDL	TDAS	LEARAVAMAL	TDSAFV	NDVAD
MoMLV	RLPQGF--SP	YVDDL	TDGS	AELIALTQAL	TDSRYA	NRMAD
BLV	VLPQGF--SP	YNDDI	SDGA	GELAGLLAGL	VDSKYL	NNYVD
HIV	VLPQGW--SP	YMDDL	VDGA	TELQAIYLAL	TDSQYA	NEQVD
CaMV	VVPFGL--AP	YVDDI	TDAS	KETLAVINTI	TDNTHF	NHFAD
HBV	KIPMGV--SP	YNDDV	ADT	AELLAACFAR	TDNSVV	NP AD
DHVB	KAPMGV--SP	YMDDF	TDAT	QELIMSCLAK	SDSTFV	NP AD

a replication-competent particle.[17] The sequence of events and the mechanism of assembly remain to be characterized.

The TP domain of the polymerase protein functions as a protein primer for the initiation of reverse transcription in a process called nucleotide priming or protein-primed reverse transcription (see Fig. 142-4).[52] The positive strand is extended to variable lengths to yield mature HBV DNA replication. The cessation of the positive-strand synthesis at various stages coincides with the maturation of the core particles and their entry into the ER leading to the packaging of partially duplex genomic DNA found in HB virions (see Fig. 142-3).[53] This entry prevents access to cytoplasmic deoxynucleotide pools needed for completion of DNA synthesis. Matured core particles face two options at this stage: either they enter the ER, undergo virion packaging with HB$_s$Ag polypeptides, and bud from the membrane as 42-nm Dane particles or they enter the nucleus, deliver the partially duplex DNA, and repeat the cycle of replication (see Fig. 142-3). In the nucleus, virion DNA is repaired to produce CCC DNA molecules.[24] About 5 to 50 copies of CCC DNA accumulate in the nucleus of an infected hepatocyte. CCC DNA serves as a substrate of viral mRNA synthesis. In summary, the salient features of HBV replication are the use of viral RNA as a template for reverse transcription, protein priming in which both the TP and the RT domains of the viral polymerase participate, and incomplete plus-strand synthesis that results in a partially duplex DNA genome found within the HB virion particles.

HBx

HBx is a regulatory protein that is required for the viral life cycle.[54] However, the exact mechanism by which it affects the viral life cycle is not clearly understood. This protein acts as a regulator of both viral and cellular gene expression. It does not directly bind DNA but appears to interact with host factors that bind DNA,[55] including transcription factors and components of basal transcriptional machinery.[17] The cellular targets are numerous, and the list of the cellular functions HBx has been shown to modulate continues to grow.[17] HBx is widely acknowledged to be a transcriptional activator. As a transactivator of gene expression, HBx was shown to interact physically with transcription factors including components of basal transcriptional machinery. Within the cytoplasm, it also localizes to the mitochondria and induces oxidative stress by calcium signaling.[56,57] These activities may mediate mitochondria-mediated liver injury. HBx has also been shown to modulate cellular signal transduction pathways.[58,59] It was shown to activate Src kinase and stimulate the Ras-Raf-MAP kinase signal transduction pathway.[60] Studies show that HBx influences the HBV life cycle by calcium signaling possibly through mitochondria.[61]

Compared with other viral transactivators of gene expression, HBx modestly stimulates transcription of a wide variety of promoter elements, including its own enhancer, in the context of the whole viral genome.[17] Nuclear factor κB (NF-κB) was one of the first HBx-responsive elements identified.[62] Because the NF-κB site does not exist within the HBV genome, it is believed that the transactivating potential of HBx extends to cellular target genes involved in inflammation. Other HBx-responsive transcription factors include ATF-2/CREB, AP-1, STAT-3, and NF-AT.[63,64] Among the components of basal transcriptional machinery, TFIIH, TBP, TFIIB, and RBP5 have been shown to interact with HBx.[65-68] HBx's other partners include p53, UVDDB, and the components of proteasome machinery.[69-71] The evidence for these functions and those described subsequently is based largely on studies utilizing tissue culture transfections and in vitro techniques, and therefore the physiologic significance of any of these observations remains to be established in the context of human infections.

HBx has the potential both to stimulate and to inhibit apoptosis.[72,73] These contrasting properties are consistent with a role in initiating events leading to hepatocellular carcinoma. The HBx-induced elevation of reactive oxygen species (ROS) is correlated with the activation of NF-κB, NF-AT, and STAT-3.[64] When activated by phosphorylation, these factors translocate to the nucleus and stimulate target genes. In that role, its actions are largely antiapoptotic. One possible scenario is that ROS can directly cause oxidative damage to DNA. If the damaged DNA is not appropriately repaired, it can lead to accumulation of mutations and cause genomic instability and thus pave the way for liver oncogenesis. Because of the unavailability of an infectious system, none of the attributed functions of HBx outlined earlier has been confirmed in natural infection. HBx is not directly oncogenic, but on the basis of its role in altering various cellular functions already discussed, it is considered a potential contributor to the processes of liver oncogenesis.[17]

Morphogenesis and Assembly

Envelopment of the nucleocapsid occurs in the ER or ER-Golgi intermediate compartments.[17] All three forms of the surface proteins are synthesized in the ER as integral transmembrane proteins and are involved in the virion morphogenesis.[74] The overall ratio of these proteins is approximately 1000:10:1. Viral assembly begins with the translation of C RNA into core and polymerase proteins. After its translation, the polymerase protein apparently binds to the ε signal on the same molecule, which now functions as a pregenome, forming a preassembly complex that triggers core protein association. Core protein monomers rapidly dimerize and provide a pool of assembly intermediates. Virion formation begins by specific interactions between core particles, and, after budding, the virions are secreted by vesicular transport through the remaining compart-

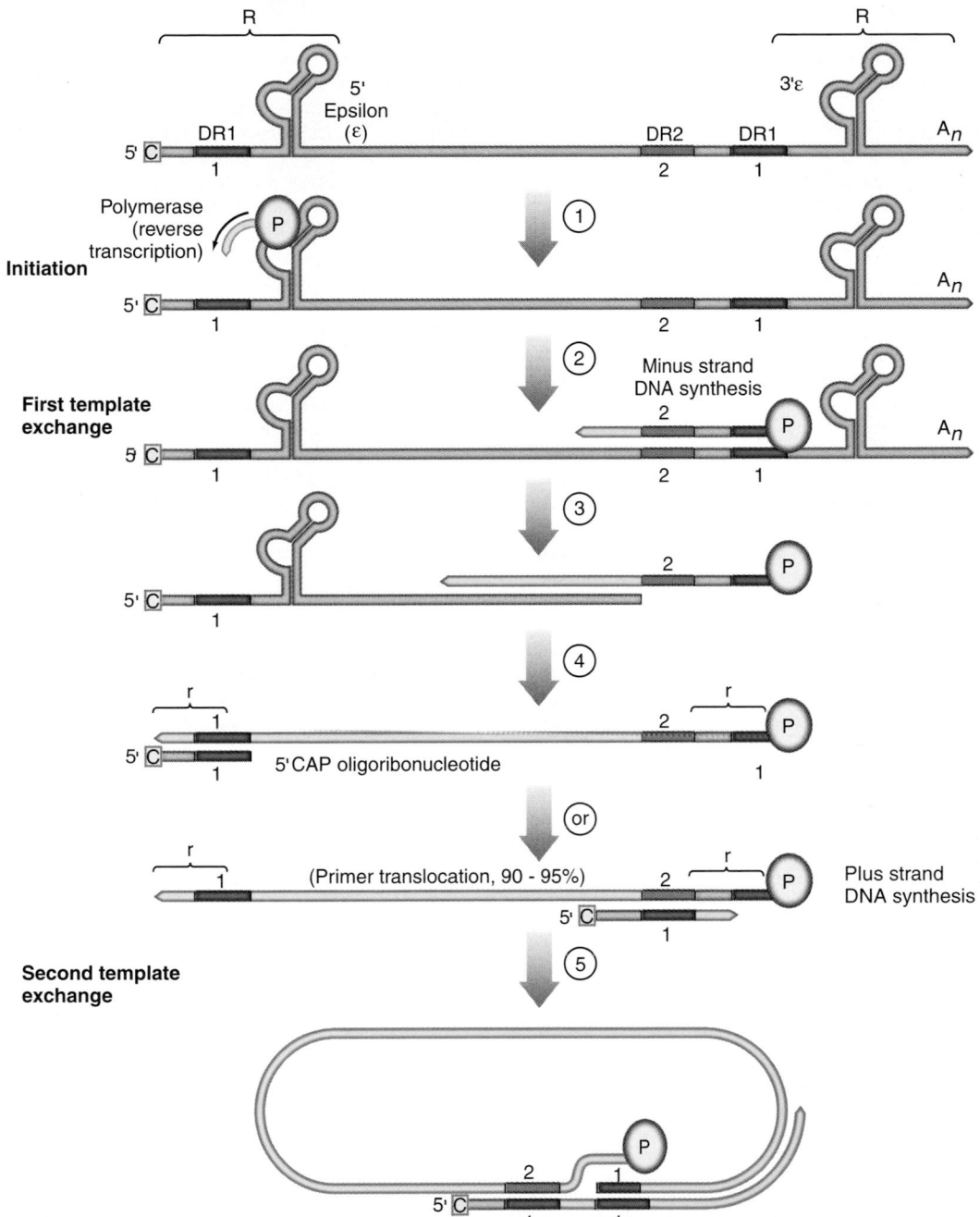

FIGURE 142-5. Hepatitis B virus (HBV) replication pathway. The terminally redundant pregenomic RNA (top line) is capped and polyadenylated. Boxes 1 and 2 represent DR1 and DR2, respectively. The horizontal bracket labeled R represents the terminally redundant region of the RNA. The epsilon (ε) stem-loops are indicated at the termini. Pregenome RNA packaging into cores is initiated by the interaction of polymerase (P) protein with the 5′ copy of ε. Minus-strand DNA synthesis is initiated at the 5′ε (epsilon) of the RNA and is primed by P protein. After the first template exchange (step 2), DNA synthesis continues, using the 3′ copy of DR1 as the template (step 3). As synthesis proceeds, the newly copied RNA template is degraded by the associated ribonuclease H activity of the polymerase (step 4). Elongation of (−) strand DNA is finished on complete copying of the pregenomic RNA template. The product is a terminally redundant complete (−) strand DNA species. The redundancies (8 to 10) nucleotides) are labeled r. At this time, the primer for (+) strand synthesis is generated from the 5′-terminal 15 to 18 nucleotides of the pregenomic RNA. The primer is capped and includes the sequence to the 3′ end of DR1. Elongation of the (+) strand results in a duplex linear genome. In the majority of cases, the primer is translocated to base pair with the DR2 sequence near the 5′ end of (−) strand DNA (step 5). The (+) strand synthesis is initiated, and then elongation begins. On reaching the 5′ end of (−) strand DNA, an intramolecular template exchange occurs, resulting in a circular DNA genome (step 5). This exchange is facilitated by the short terminal redundancy in (−) strand DNA. The (+) strand DNA synthesis then continues for a variable distance, resulting in the relaxed circular partially duplex form of the genome found in mature virions. *(Adapted and modified from Tavis JE. Viral hepatitis Rev. 1996;205-218, with permission.)*

ments of the secretory pathways and are eventually released into the blood stream. M protein is not important for morphogenesis but is required for infectivity. L protein is required for virion morphogenesis,[75] and its retention in an early compartment of the secretory pathway leads to the efficiency of the assembly process. During chronic hepatitis, accumulation of the L surface protein–containing particles has been associated with the pathologic phenotype of "ground glass" hepatocytes.[17]

HEPATITIS DELTA VIRUS

Delta agent was identified by Mario Rizzetto in 1977 as a nuclear antigen distinct from HBsAg, Hb$_c$Ag, and HB$_e$Ag in hepatocytes of some HBsAg carriers in Italy.[76,78] It soon became clear that this passenger virus, termed hepatitis D virus (HDV), accompanied HBV infection. This unique RNA genome resembles plant pathogens including viroids and virusoids.[76] HDV is the only member of the genus Deltavirus.[77] In nature, HDV is found only in patients who are also infected with HBV. The regions of highest prevalence include the Mediterranean basin, North Africa, and South America.[78] In the United States, the prevalence is low in the general population but high in drug users. Globally, about 10% of HBV-infected individuals are coinfected with HDV. HDV infection of chronic carriers is frequently associated with severe sequelae of chronic hepatitis and accounts for cases of fulminant hepatitis. There are three known genotypes (I, II, III).[79,80] Genotype I is the most common worldwide and associated with severe pathogenicity. Genotype II is found in Asia, and hepatitis D associated with this genotype is of milder forms. Genotype III is distributed in South America and is associated with the most severe form of hepatitis D.[81]

HDV is an enveloped virus of 36 nm that is distinct from 22-nm HB$_s$Ag or 42-nm HBV particles.[82] The HDV genome is a small single-stranded, circular RNA genome that is enclosed by hepatitis delta antigen (HDAg), which functions as a nucleocapsid for the viral genome (Fig. 142-6).[79,83] The viral envelope consists of the three forms (L, M,

S) of HBsAg. Because the HBsAg envelope is derived from the HBV-infected cells, HDV cannot be propagated without HBV.

Hepatitis Delta Antigen

The nucleocapsid or the HD antigen consists of two species: small S-HDAg (24 kD) and large L-HDAg (27 kD) (Fig. 142-6). Both are initiated from the same ATG codon and have similar N-terminal sequences but differ in the use of termination codons.[84] Each is translated from a distinct species of RNA. The L-HDAg transcript is produced by a unique RNA editing event, which results in the addition of 19 amino acid residues at its N-terminus.[85] Both L- and S-HDAgs are phosphorylated, contain a nuclear localization signal, and are localized to the nucleus.[86,87] They multimerize with each other through antiparallel coiled coils.[88] L-HDAg is required for assembly of new particles and acts as a dominant negative inhibitor of replication. S-HDAg is involved in the initiation of RNA replication and is believed to have RNA chaperone activity.[89]

Hepatitis D Virus RNA Genome and Replication

The HDV RNA genome contains an open reading frame, which codes for HDAg and contains a sequence of approximately 85 nucleotides with an intrinsic ribozyme activity[90,91] (Fig. 142-7). The HDV ribozyme activity is absolutely required for RNA replication[92] (Fig. 142-7). It is estimated that about 100,000 copies of genomic RNAs can be found in an infected hepatocyte. S-HDAg is believed to be involved in RNA replication and may serve as an RNA chaperone. Because HDV does not encode a polymerase and there is no known RNA-dependent RNA polymerase in mammalian cells, it is believed that host RNA polymerase II is recruited for this activity.[89,93] The mechanism by which cellular RNA polymerase is redirected to perform this reaction is not understood. HDAg was shown to have homology to a subunit of a negative elongation factor and can interact with polymerase II in vitro.[94] HDV envelopment follows a scheme of virion assembly similar to that of HBV. However, the production of a

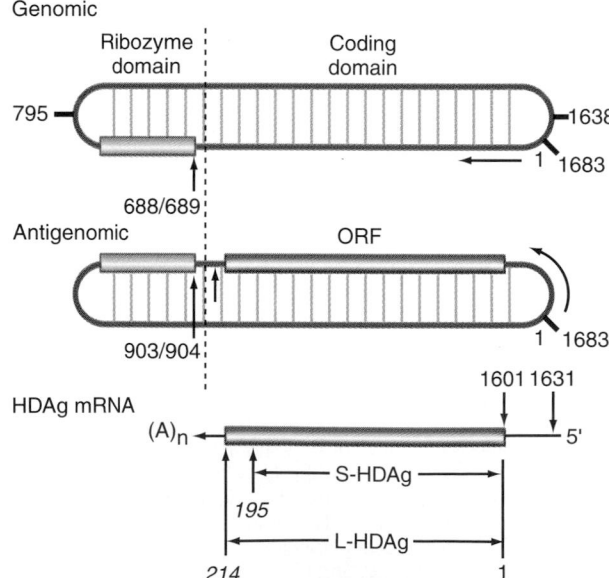

FIGURE 142-6. Schematic structures of hepatitis D virus genomic and antigenomic RNA and hepatitis D antigen (HDAg)-encoding messenger RNA (mRNA). The minimum ribozymes are indicated by light boxes. The italicized numbers for HDAg are amino acid residues. All other numbers are nucleotide positions on the genomic-sense RNA. ORF, open reading frame. *(Adapted from Macnaughton TB, Lai MC. The molecular biology of hepatitis delta virus. In: Ou JE, ed. Hepatitis Viruses. Norwell, Mass: Kluwer Academic Publishers; 2002:109-128 with permission.)*

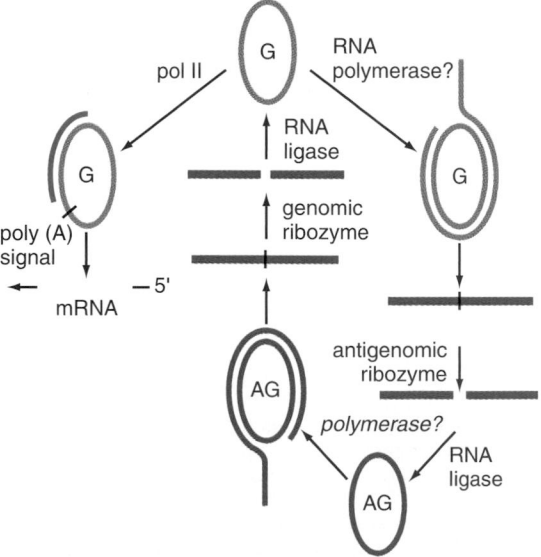

FIGURE 142-7. Proposed model of hepatitis D virus RNA replication. The hepatitis D antigen–encoding messenger RNA is synthesized by polymerase II (pol II) from the genomic RNA template independently of RNA replication. The enzymes for genomic and antigenomic RNA replication are not yet known. AG, antigenomic strand; G, genomic strand. *(Adapted from Macnaughton TB, Lai MC. The molecular biology of hepatitis delta virus. In: Ou JE, ed. Hepatitis Viruses. Norwell, Mass: Kluwer Academic Publishers; 2002:109-128, with permission.)*

large abundance (about 90%) of noninfectious HDV virions is explained by the fact that HDV assembly can also occur in an L protein–independent fashion.[95] These particles are noninfectious because of the absence of pre-S1 domain, which is required for infectivity.

HDV infects only hepatocytes with no evidence of extrahepatic sites of its replication. The mechanism of HDV entry is similar to that of HBV, as its outer envelope consists of HBsAg derived from an HBV infection. Entry of HDV is through a liver cell–specific receptor, which remains to be identified. As with HBV, there is no culture system for HDV. The host range of HDV is limited to species that can support the replication of hepadnaviruses and supply in *trans* the HBsAg envelope. For instance, HDV can infect woodchucks and can be packaged with HBsAg derived from WHV.[96] Chimpanzees are susceptible to HDV infection, and the infection is similar to that in humans.[78] Chimpanzees, therefore, have served as an experimental model and contributed to the current understanding of viral infection. In chimpanzees the HDV infection is confined to liver.

PATHOGENESIS OF DISEASE

The exact mechanisms by which chronic liver injury occurs in HBV infection are not known, although most studies suggest that the hepatitis virus is not directly cytopathic to the hepatocyte.[97] There is no robust tissue culture system, but the existence of asymptomatic hepatitis B carriers with normal liver histology and function suggests that the virus is not directly cytopathic. Extensive human and animal studies have now shown that the liver injury mediated by HBV is initiated by a viral-specific cellular immune response. In more than 95% of immunocompetent adults, the immune response is vigorous, polyclonal, and multispecific and results in acute self-limited hepatitis with reduction of viral load and the development of long-lasting humoral and cellular immunity. Persistent infection is associated with necroinflammatory activity, which eventually leads to cirrhosis. The mechanism for this viral persistence and immune-mediated liver injury is not known.

Acute Hepatitis B

Natural recovery from acute HBV probably depends upon multiple components of cellular immune responses, including natural killer (NK) cells, natural killer T (NK T) cells, and virus-specific CD4+ T cells and CD8+ cytotoxic T lymphocytes (CTLs). Both NK and NK T cells contribute to clearance through production of interferon (IFN)-α/β

which mediates noncytopathic control of viral replication.[98] Acute HBV infection is also accompanied by a strong and transient expansion of CD4+ T cells directed against multiple epitopes within the HBV. HB$_c$ is the dominant antigen recognized by CD4+ T cells in most cases of acute resolving HBV infection.[99] These HB$_c$-specific CD4+ cells provide help for the production of antibody to HBsAg and are also associated with the development of a vigorous and polyclonal cytotoxic CTL capable of recognizing different epitopes within HBV genome.[100] Individuals who clear HBV infection, either spontaneously or after IFN therapy, maintain these broad and strong peripheral CTL responses.[101] CD4+ and CTL memory in the presence of low levels of persisting HBV DNA has been shown to persist up to 23 years after infection despite markers of serologic recovery. Both virus-specific CD4+ and CTL contribute to control of HBV replication through direct cytolysis of infected cells and, more important, through production of cytokines that control viral replication.[102] Analysis of the NK, CTL, and CD4+ T-cell responses in the incubation phase has demonstrated that the CTL response increases in parallel with alanine aminotransferase (ALT), consistent with the idea that CTL activity is responsible for liver injury, and peaks about the time that the HBV DNA titers begin to fall.[103]

HB$_c$Ag is extremely immunogenic during HBV infection and after immunization. Immunoglobulin M (IgM) anti-HB$_c$ is the first antibody to be detected, usually appearing within 1 month of the appearance of HBsAg and 1 to 2 weeks before the rise in ALT (Fig. 142-8). During convalescence, the titer of IgM anti-HB$_c$ declines while the titer of IgG anti-HB$_c$ increases. Although IgM anti-HB$_c$ is frequently considered to be associated with acute infection, it can persist for up to 2 years in 20% of individuals and chronically infected individuals may have low titers, which rise during acute flares in HBV.

The development of surface antibody (anti-HBs) follows the disappearance of surface antigen and marks recovery from HBV infection. Anti-HBs is sufficient for protection against HBV infection, as demonstrated by the success of the current HBV vaccines, even if it is not the sole operative mechanism clearing acute infection. The *a* determinant is the predominant B-cell epitope common to all six HBV serotypes. Antibodies against this epitope confer immunity to all HBV subtypes. Coexistence of HBsAg and anti-HBs is reported in up to 24% of chronically infected individuals, in which case the anti-HBs is directed against one of the subtype determinants and is therefore not able to neutralize the virus. Other surface antigens that stimulate antibody responses include the pre-S1 and pre-S2 antigens.

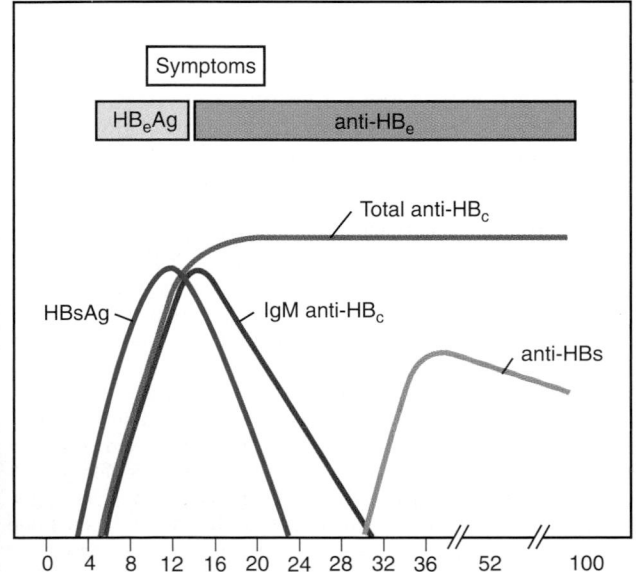

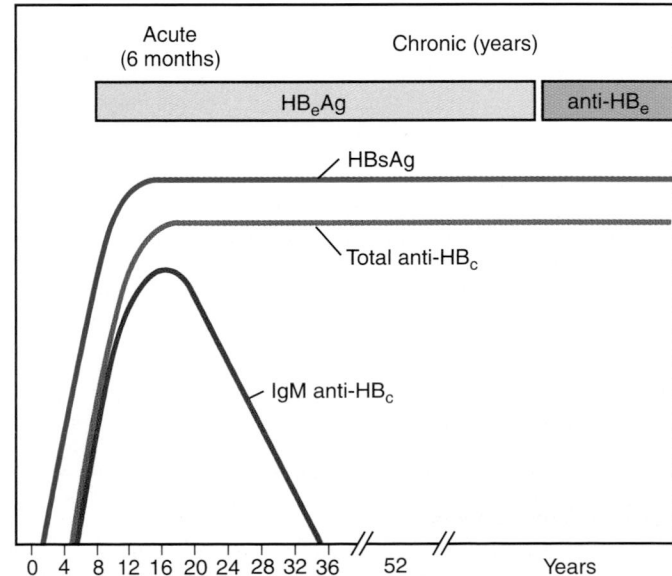

FIGURE 142-8. Typical course of hepatitis B. **Left,** Typical course of acute hepatitis B. **Right,** Chronic hepatitis B. HB$_c$, hepatitis B core; Hb$_e$, hepatitis B early; HBsAg, hepatitis B surface antigen; IgM, immunoglobulin M.

Antibody to these develops during recovery and can be detected before anti-HBs, but routine serologic assays are not readily available. Mutation in the S gene usually occurs in the a determinant, which allows the virus to escape antibody neutralization. This may occur after the use of hepatitis B immunoglobulin for passive immunization of newborns and transplant recipients.

Chronic Hepatitis B

Persistent HBV infection may result because of the failure of initial innate and adaptive immune responses. Among infants who become infected at birth, both viral and host factors play a role in the development of chronic infection. The presence of HBeAg and the viral titer in the mother are both directly related to the likelihood of infant infection. In addition, T-cell tolerance for the viral proteins HBeAg and HBcAg contributes to viral persistence. In animal models HBeAg may be tolerogenic,[104] and because HBeAg and HBcAg are cross-reactive at the T-cell level, deletion of the CD4+ HBc-specific T-cell responses results in ineffective CTL responses to HBcAg.

Immunocompetent adults who do not successfully clear acute HBV infection also have less vigorous CD4+ T-cell and CTL responses. In contrast to those in acute resolving infection, peripheral CD4+ T-cell and CTL responses in the individuals who develop chronic infection are weak and more narrowly focused.[105] The mechanisms by which HBV evades the immune response and results in chronic infection in these adults remain obscure. In part, this is determined by host genetic factors, as persons with certain human leukocyte antigen (HLA) alleles appear to be more susceptible to chronic infection.[106] It has also been suggested that the size of initial viral inoculum and viral kinetics may be such that the immune system is overwhelmed by the virus and becomes "exhausted."[107] Despite the weak and narrowly focused response of the peripheral blood CTLs, HBV-specific CD4+ and CD8+ T cells can be isolated from the livers of patients with chronic HBV that are capable of ex vivo class I–restricted cytolytic activity in response to envelope and core peptides. The cytotoxicity mediated by these cells appears to be strong enough to cause liver injury but not strong enough to eradicate virus from all hepatocytes.[108,109] In addition to the virus-specific cells, the inflamed liver contains other cells that may participate in hepatocyte damage.[110]

Hepatitis D Virus

HDAg is the only viral protein known to be expressed during HDV infection. Detection of antibody is the usual method for diagnosis of acute infection. During HDV infection, IgM and IgG antibodies can be detected in the serum of infected individuals. A high titer of IgM anti-HDV is strongly associated with elevated hepatitis D viremia and severity of liver injury, whereas a more favorable course of HDV infection is found in individuals with IgG anti-HDV. Although these antibody responses are present during acute and chronic infection, there is no convincing evidence of a protective role of anti-HDV antibodies.[111] Woodchucks immunized with recombinant HDAg are only partially protected from subsequent challenge with HDV, which suggests that other mechanisms are responsible for immunity.[112]

The mechanisms of liver damage in HDV infection are unclear. In contrast to the findings in HBV, the hepatocyte injury resulting from HDV infection may be caused by a direct viral cytopathic effect rather than immune-mediated damage.[113] The presence of HDV-specific T-cell responses correlates with lower ALT levels, suggesting that immune control of viral replication leads to lesser degrees of liver injury.[110,111] However, histologic assessment demonstrates that the degree of cellular infiltration in the portal tracts and lobules correlates with the degree of staining for HDAg in the liver, suggesting that the immune response contributes to hepatocellular injury.[114]

Hepatocellular Carcinoma

Although epidemiologic evidence supports the role of HBV as a causal agent of liver cancer (see "Epidemiology of Hepatitis B"),[115] the molecular mechanisms addressing the link between the viral infection and the development of HCC are highly debated. Despite a large body of work

on this subject, a clear view of how HBV infection triggers events that lead to liver oncogenesis remains elusive. Development of HCC, like that of other cancers, proceeds in multiple steps that correlate with specific lesions associated with livers of patients with HCC. These include altered hepatic foci, dysplastic (neoplastic) nodules, and low- and high-grade HCCs. These lesions are characterized as exhibiting different levels of cell differentiation. As with other well-characterized human cancers, HCC progresses through these individual stages. The molecular switches associated with each step of HCC development remain to be identified. Although the WHV model has been valuable in the study of hepadnavirus pathogenesis, there are important differences. Compared with HBV, the WHV is a more potent hepatocarcinogen. Nearly 100% of woodchucks infected with WHV develop HCC at about 18 to 24 months of age.[116] Similarly, in humans HCC is mostly associated with cirrhosis but in woodchucks this association is uncommon.

HBV-related HCCs are derived from the clonal expansion of a single transformed or cancerous cell.[117] Although 80% of HBV-associated HCC tumors contain integrated viral DNA, most of the HBV genes are either truncated or transcriptionally inactivated.[17] As opposed to retroviral replication, HBV DNA integration is not an obligatory part of the viral life cycle but may instead serve as an insertional mutagen.[118] After integration into the host chromosomes, the HBV DNA control elements such as enhancers or promoters can act in cis to activate a cellular oncogene. HBV integrates randomly at multiple sites in the host chromosomes, and molecular analyses of the HBV integration junction sites have not revealed specific integration adjacent to or neighboring cellular oncogenes. In the case of WHV, however, integration next to the cellular N-myc2 gene was observed in 40% to 50% of woodchuck HCC tumors.[119] Efforts to document a similar case for insertional activation by HBV have been largely unsuccessful. Integration of viral DNA, on the other hand, could have far-reaching consequences rather than merely activating or repressing neighboring genes. Unstable integration events might frequently lead to genomic instability by causing chromosomal aberrations such as amplifications, translocations, and deletions, all of which have the potential for initiating events that lead to liver neoplasia. Indeed, in HBV-associated liver tumors, the HBV DNA integrants are highly rearranged with deletions, inversions, and sequence reiterations.[119]

The pleiotropic functions of HBx in HCC have been implicated in the processes of liver oncogenesis and have been the subject of intense investigations.[120] Prominent among these are the ability of HBx to activate transcription factors by direct physical interaction or to modulate cellular signal transduction pathways, thereby modifying the host gene expression profile. Other functions include its effects on DNA repair processes and potential to cause direct oxidative damage to host DNA by elevating the intracellular levels of ROS in cells.[17,64] These and other properties of HBx have been implicated in contributing to the genesis of HCC. Because most of the HBV genes are extinguished in advanced tumors, the viral role in the development of HCC is most likely to be at the stage of initiation and promotion of hepatocarcinogenesis. This would preclude the presence of HBx in maintaining the transformed phenotype.

Finally, HBV-associated HCC may be due to the repeated cellular division associated with the inflammatory response.[17,49] HCC associated with HBV nearly always arises in the context of cirrhosis, although a few cases of HCC without cirrhosis have been reported.[121] Cirrhosis is the result of years of inflammation and associated repair processes, during which there is considerable cell killing and repeated hepatocyte regeneration. In all types of liver damage, there is evidence of enhanced production of free radicals or significant decrease of antioxidant defense.[122] Oxidative stress over a long period of time may give rise to high mutation rates in infected hepatocytes. Mutations, which confer in a cell a proliferative advantage and provide opportunities for achieving a transformed phenotype, are perpetuated. According to this model, the role of HBV, if any, is merely to induce liver injury and the subsequent events are all secondary to the host immune response.

Environmental carcinogens, including aflatoxins and ethanol, may be cofactors in hepatocarcinogenesis, as they are known to increase

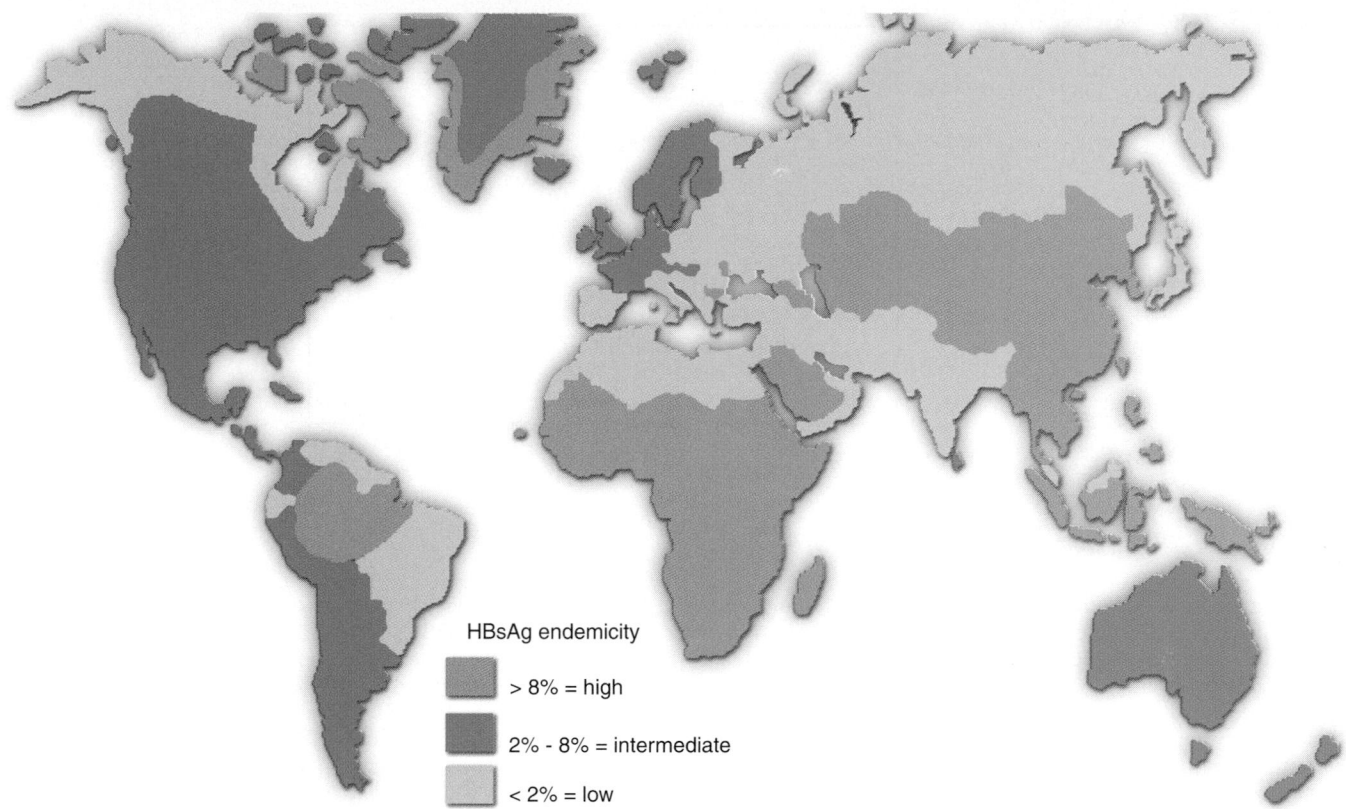

FIGURE 142-9. Global prevalence of hepatitis B surface antigenemia. *(From World Health Organization. Introduction of Hepatitis B Vaccine into Childhood Immunization Services. Geneva: WHO; 2001. WHO/V and B/01.31. Accessible online at http://www.who.int/emc-documents/hepatitis/docs.)*

the risk for developing HCC in HBV chronic carriers.[123,124] Epidemiologic studies support the view that populations exposed to high levels of dietary aflatoxin run a greater risk of developing HCC.[125,126] In Africa and Southeast Asia, a strong correlation between the contamination of food by aflatoxin and the risk of HCC has been reported.[127] Aflatoxin is a potent carcinogen produced by *Aspergillus flavus*, which contaminates food. Aflatoxin covalently binds to DNA, forms adducts, and functions as a mutagen.[128]

EPIDEMIOLOGY OF HEPATITIS B

The prevalence of HBV carriage varies widely and is inversely proportional to the age of acquisition of infection. The prevalence rates range from the low-prevalence areas with 0.1% to 2% (United States, Canada, western Europe, Australia, and New Zealand) to areas with intermediate risk (Japan, central Asia, Middle East, Central America, and South America) to areas of 10% to 20% seroprevalence (Southeast Asia, China, and sub-Saharan Africa) (Fig. 142-9 and Table 142-1). In areas of high seroprevalence, HBV is more likely to be acquired perinatally, with an attendant high risk of chronic infection of 90%. For infections acquired in later childhood, between the ages of 1 and 5 years, the risk of chronic infection is between 10% and 20%, and for infec-

tions acquired by immunocompetent adults the risk is less than 5%. This leads to a vicious circle whereby the infected infant is likely to acquire HBV and in turn pass it on to playmates, future sexual partners, and, in the case of infected women, infants.

The epidemiology of HBV is changing with the advent of universal vaccination programs adopted by many countries. For example, in the United States the estimated number of new infections per year was more than 275,000 in the mid-1980s, whereas after the adoption of universal vaccination for infants and "catch up" vaccination for older children in 1991 there were estimated to be 78,000 new cases in 2001 (Fig. 142-10).[129] However, there are still estimated to be between 750,000 and 1 million HBV carriers in the United States, of whom 20% to 40% will develop serious sequelae during their lifetime and 5000 will die annually from complications of chronic liver disease including HCC. Worldwide, the number of chronic carriers is estimated to be more than 400 million.

Despite an increasing incidence of HCC associated with hepatitis C virus (HCV) infection in Japan and the Western Hemisphere, chronic HBV infection remains the most important cause of HCC worldwide.[128] The classic epidemiologic studies conducted in Taiwan among HBV carriers established the absolute link between HBV infection and HCC.[91,103] These studies suggest that the interval between

TABLE 142-1	Global Seroprevalence Rates and Modes of Transmission of Hepatitis B		
Characteristic	*High*	*Intermediate*	*Low*
Carrier rate (%)	5-20	3-5	0.1-2
Distribution	Southeast Asia, China, Alaskan Eskimos, sub-Saharan Africa	Eastern Europe, Mediterranean, central Asia, Latin and South America, Middle East	United States, Canada, western Europe, Australia, New Zealand
Age at infection	Perinatal and early childhood	Childhood	Adult
Mode of transmission	Maternal and perinatal	Percutaneous	Sexual, percutaneous

FIGURE 142-10. Number of new cases of hepatitis B. Shown are the reported number of acute cases, estimated number of acute cases, and estimated number of new infections. Arrow indicates period when universal vaccination of infants began. *(Adapted from Summary of notifiable diseases—United States, 2000. MMWR Morb Mortal Wkly Rep. 2002;49[53]:i-xxii, 1-100.)*

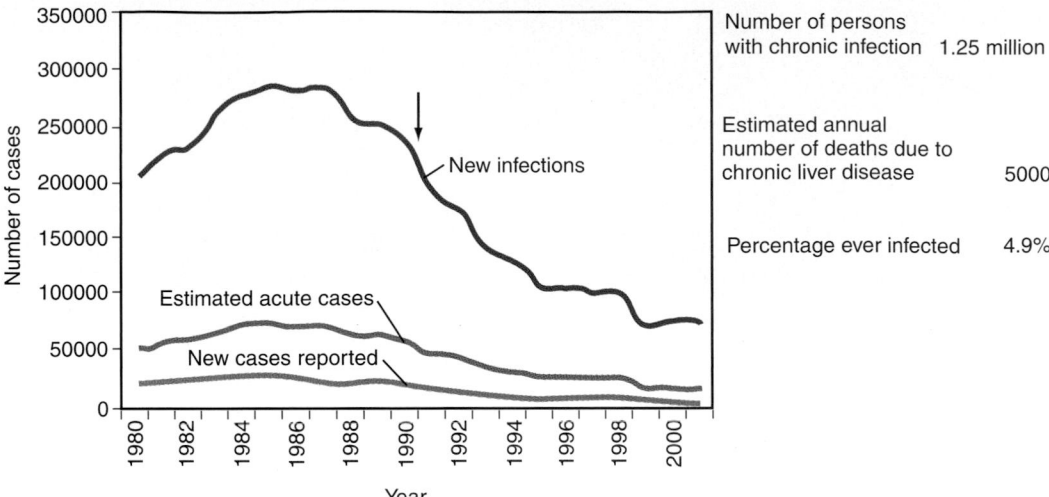

Number of persons with chronic infection 1.25 million

Estimated annual number of deaths due to chronic liver disease 5000

Percentage ever infected 4.9%

acquisition of infection and development of HCC spans several decades (average 30 years). HCC is the fifth most common cancer worldwide with an estimated half a million new cases diagnosed annually.[130] The lifetime risk for HBV chronic carriers is currently estimated to be about 20% to 40%.[128] The incidence of HCC varies geographically and among different ethnic groups. It occurs commonly in HBV-endemic areas, which include sub-Saharan Africa and Southeast Asia. In parts of sub-Saharan Africa and Asia, HBV-related HCC is one of the leading causes of cancer and HBV carriers have a 100-fold relative risk of HCC compared with noncarriers.[131] In western Europe and North America, HCC is rare and reflects a 0.1% to 0.5% rate of chronic hepatitis. A report from Taiwan indicates a dramatic reduction of the incidence of HCC in the population coinciding with mass vaccination against HBV (see "Active Immunization").[132]

Epidemiology of Delta Hepatitis

Infection with HDV has a worldwide distribution, although there are considerable geographic differences that do not entirely mirror the prevalence of HBV infection. In northern Europe and in the United States, where HDV is not endemic, the infection is mainly confined to intravenous drug users,[133] whereas it has virtually disappeared in multiply transfused subjects and hemophiliacs as a result of universal blood screening for HBsAg and HBV vaccination campaigns.[134] In areas where HDV is endemic in the general population, such as the Mediterranean basin, most cases of HDV transmission are due to inapparent parenteral exposure.[135]

ROUTES OF TRANSMISSION

Hepatitis B replicates to high titers in the blood (10^8 to 10^{10} virions per milliliter), especially during the acute phase of illness. Any parenteral or mucosal exposure to infected blood thus represents a potential risk for acquisition of hepatitis B and accounts for the much more efficient transmission of HBV than human immunodeficiency virus (HIV) after needlestick exposure.[136] HBV is also found in other body fluids to a variable degree, including semen, saliva, cervical secretions, and leukocytes, and can survive for long periods on environmental surfaces. Thus, exposure to even minute amounts of blood or contaminated secretions may transmit virus, and infection can occur in settings of prolonged close personal contact, such as occurs between children, or among residents of institutions for the developmentally disabled, probably because of inapparent contact of infected secretions with nonintact skin.

The typical mode of transmission of HBV varies in part with the prevalence of infection (see Table 142-1). Perinatal infection is the predominant mode of transmission in high-prevalence areas, whereas hor-

izontal transmission, particularly in early childhood, accounts for most cases of chronic HBV infection in intermediate-prevalence areas. Unprotected sexual intercourse and intravenous drug use in adults are the major routes of spread in low-prevalence areas. Persons at increased risk for acquiring HBV infection include members of the following groups: (1) parenteral drug users, (2) heterosexual men and women and homosexual men with multiple partners, (3) household contacts and sexual partners of HBV carriers, (4) infants born to HBV-infected mothers, (5) patients and staff in custodial institutions for the developmentally disabled, (6) recipients of certain plasma-derived products (including patients with congenital coagulation defects), (7) hemodialysis patients, (8) health and public-safety workers who have contact with blood, and (9) persons born in areas of high HBV endemicity and their children (Table 142-2). Persons at risk for exposure to HBV should be screened for markers of HBV infection and receive hepatitis B vaccine if seronegative (see section on vaccination).

CLINICAL MANIFESTATIONS AND PROGNOSIS

The spectrum of clinical manifestations of HBV infection varies in both acute and chronic infection. During the acute phase, manifestations range from subclinical or anicteric hepatitis to icteric hepatitis and, in some cases, fulminant hepatitis. During the chronic phase, manifestations range from an asymptomatic carrier state to the signs

TABLE 142-2 Prevalence of Hepatitis B in Selected Populations

Population	HBV Marker (%)	
	Prevalence HBsAg+	Any Marker
Residents in endemic areas	10-20	70-85
Alaskan natives	5-15	40-70
Residents of institutions for mentally disabled	10-20	35-38
Parenteral drug users	5-10	60-80
Men who have sex with men	4-8	35-80
Household contacts of HBsAg+	3-6	30-60
Hemodialysis patients	3-10	20-80
Prison inmates	1-8	10-80
Heterosexuals with multiple sex partners	0.5	5-20
Health care workers	0.5	3-10
General U.S. population	0.2	4.8
Blacks	0.85	13
Whites	0.19	3

HBsAg, hepatitis B surface antigen; HBV, hepatitis B virus.

and symptoms of cirrhosis and HCC. Extrahepatic manifestations can also occur with both acute and chronic infection.

Acute Hepatitis B

After exposure to HBV, there is an incubation period of 1 to 4 months.[137] Acute hepatitis B is a clinical syndrome indistinguishable from other acute hepatitides and often consists of an influenza-like syndrome with malaise, fatigue, anorexia, nausea, vomiting, and right upper quadrant discomfort. Serum sickness–like manifestations may be present before the onset of jaundice. Physical signs include jaundice and tender hepatomegaly. The likelihood of developing icteric illness is inversely proportional to age. Symptomatic hepatitis develops rarely in children younger than 1 year, in 10% of children younger than 5 years, and in 30% to 80% of adults.[138] Most reported cases of HBV are the result of icteric illness, but it is thought that a far larger number of infections result in subclinical illness or illness diagnosed only in retrospect. The acute illness may be more severe in the setting of other coinfections, such as simultaneous acquisition of hepatitis D, or with underlying conditions such as alcoholic liver disease. The symptoms and jaundice generally disappear after 1 to 3 months, but some patients have prolonged fatigue even after resolution of the elevated serum aminotransferases. Figure 142-8 shows a typical clinical and laboratory course of acute hepatitis B compared with that of chronic hepatitis B.

Laboratory Findings

Laboratory testing during the acute phase reveals elevations in the concentration of ALT and aspartate aminotransferase (AST); values up to 1000 to 2000 IU/L are typically seen during the acute phase with ALT being higher than AST. The serum bilirubin concentration may be normal in patients with anicteric hepatitis. The prothrombin time (PT) is the best indicator of prognosis, with a high PT indicative of fulminant liver failure.[139] Among patients who recover, normalization of serum aminotransferases usually occurs within 1 to 4 months. Persistent elevation of serum ALT for more than 6 months indicates progression to chronic hepatitis. During the acute phase, there is development of IgM against the core antigen, followed by the development of IgG anti-HB$_c$ (see also "Making a Viral Diagnosis"). Markers of viral replication, such as HBs antigenemia and HBV DNA in the serum, are present at the same time as anti-HB$_c$.

Most immunocompetent adult patients clear the infection, but chronic hepatitis (defined by persistent elevation in serum aminotransferases for more than 6 months or HBsAg in serum) develops in less than 5% of adults, 10% to 25% of young children, and 80% to 90% of infants.[138] Rates are similar whether or not there is symptomatic acute disease. Loss of HBV DNA, HB$_e$Ag, HBsAg, and IgM anti-HBc and the development of anti-HB$_e$ and anti-HBs characterize immunity. An individual who has acquired natural immunity through infection develops both anti-HBs and anti-HB$_c$. Patients who recover from acute hepatitis B are probably not truly cured of infection, as a significant number of patients have HBV DNA detectable by polymerase chain reaction (PCR) many years after clinical recovery.[140] They generally have lifelong protection from disease unless there is significant immunosuppression with loss of protective immune responses, such as in the setting of HIV or bone marrow transplantation.[141,142]

Fulminant Hepatitis

Fulminant hepatitis B is rare, occurring in only 0.1% to 0.5% of patients, and causes less than 10% of fulminant liver failures in the United States.[143] Patients typically present with rapidly progressive acute hepatitis, with less than 28 days from the time of symptom onset, accompanied by signs of liver failure such as coagulopathy, encephalopathy, and cerebral edema. Poor prognostic factors for transplant-free survival include a lower mean arterial pressure on admission and low platelet count.[143] Laboratory testing may not reveal HBsAg because of early clearance but shows IgM anti-HB$_c$ and a positive HBV DNA.

The pathogenesis of fulminant hepatic failure is not clear, but it may be related to massive immune responses against the virus. Staining of the liver in fulminant HBV often reveals few copies of HBV, suggesting that it is the exuberant immune response that is primarily responsible for the pathogenesis.[144] Fulminant hepatitis is also more common in the setting of coinfection with hepatitis D[145] and withdrawal of immunosuppressant therapy, such as may occur after transplantation.[146] In addition to host factors related to immune status, several variants of HBV have been implicated in several outbreaks of fulminant HBV.[147] At least some of the variants lead to premature termination of e antigen (the precore mutants), and there is detection of core antigen in the blood without detection of e antigen. Because HB$_e$Ag may serve as a tolerogen,[148] the postulated mechanism is that there is enhancement of the immune response. However, careful epidemiologic studies have raised questions about whether these mutants and other mutations within the core are truly more common in fulminant disease,[149,150] and the relatively low levels of virus and robust immune response may be due to other, as yet undefined, viral and host factors.

Chronic Hepatitis B

Chronic hepatitis is defined by at least 6 months of persistent HBV disease. In many patients, chronic hepatitis B is diagnosed not as a result of follow-up after a case of icteric illness or specific symptoms but rather as a result of incidental elevations in serum aminotransferases or membership in a specific risk category. Symptoms, if present, can be as nonspecific as fatigue unless cirrhosis or HCC is present. Other less common symptoms include nausea, right upper quadrant tenderness, anorexia, myalgias, and arthralgias. Symptoms often do not correlate with severity of disease, levels of serum aminotransferases, or hepatic injury on liver biopsy. The physical examination may be normal, or there may be an enlarged liver. The presence of jaundice, splenomegaly, ascites, encephalopathy, or pedal edema suggests cirrhosis.

Laboratory Testing in Chronic Hepatitis B

Laboratory findings in chronic hepatitis B are as variable as the clinical manifestations. Serum aminotransferases may be normal, although most patients with chronic active hepatitis have at least mild to moderate elevations. Patients have markers of viral replication including HBsAg and often HB$_e$Ag or HBV DNA as well. During flares of disease activity or just before seroconversion to anti-HB$_e$ status, there may be marked elevations in the serum aminotransferases to more than 20 times normal. Flares of disease activity may be due to changes in the level of baseline HBV replication, followed by an immune response against the virus. In some patients, this results in repopulation of the viral species with a new variant.[151] Patients with flares of disease activity should be observed for the development of anti-HB$_e$, which signals control of viral replication.[152] The spontaneous rate of seroconversion varies by age but in otherwise healthy adults is estimated as 10% to 20% per year.[153] Cirrhosis should be suspected if there is evidence of hypersplenism, manifesting as decreased platelet count, or impaired hepatic synthetic function, indicated by hypoalbuminemia, hyperbilirubinemia, or decreased albumin. As with the range of findings observed in other laboratory tests, findings on liver biopsy range from minimal inflammation to cirrhosis.

There are no characteristic findings that can distinguish hepatitis B from other forms of viral hepatitis, although liver biopsy specimens can be stained for the presence of HBsAg and HB$_e$Ag. The most characteristic feature of chronic HBV is the ground glass hepatocyte, which is thought to be due to accumulation of HBsAg within the ER.[154] Differentiation from alcoholic liver disease can be made by characteristic patterns of steatosis, Mallory bodies, and micronodular cirrhosis, whereas chronic HCV is marked by steatosis and characteristic lymphoid follicles within portal tracts. Immunosuppressed hosts may have a variant of HBV known as fibrosing cholestatic hepatitis, which reveals periportal fibrosis, hepatocyte ballooning, bile stasis, and mild or absent inflammation.[155]

Natural History of Chronic Hepatitis B

The natural history of hepatitis B can be viewed as three phases that are the result of the interplay between the virus and the host. Viral factors include the level of replication, and host factors include gender, alcohol consumption, infection with other hepatitis viruses such as hepatitis C, and the extent of immunosuppression. The first phase is the "immunotolerant" phase, in which there is circulating HBsAg, HB$_e$Ag, and high levels of HBV DNA. There is very little immune response against the virus, and so there are minimal elevations of serum aminotransferases and minimal inflammation in the liver. In cases of perinatal infection, this phase may last for decades during which there are very low rates of spontaneous seroconversion to anti-HB$_e$. The cumulative rate of spontaneous HB$_e$Ag clearance is estimated to be approximately 2% during the first 3 years of life and only 15% after 20 years of infection in cases of perinatal infection.[156,157] In contrast, among immunocompetent adults this phase is typically present only during the incubation period.

During the second phase of the infection, there is a reduction in HBV DNA levels and an increase in immunity, accompanied by increased aminotransferases and inflammation in the liver. This is thought to be the period in which there is augmentation of both innate and acquired HBV immunity, leading to cytolytic destruction of hepatocytes, as the peak of the immune response coincides with the aminotransferase elevations.[158] In adults this is usually the period of symptomatic acute hepatitis B, although this phase of infection can last for decades if the immune reaction is not sufficiently vigorous to lead to viral clearance.

The third phase heralds the conversion from HB$_e$ antigenemia to anti-HB$_e$, usually followed by a decrease in viral replication and reduction in aminotransferases. Viral replication is usually negative by hybridization assays, although more sensitive PCR-based assays still detect viremia. This seroconversion event is often, but not always, accompanied by an increase in aminotransferases above baseline, suggesting that there is immune clearance of the virus.[152] Seroconversion may be clinically silent or accompanied by dramatic elevations in aminotransferases, suggesting fulminant hepatitis. Because IgM anti-HB$_c$ may increase during these flares, an erroneous diagnosis of acute hepatitis may be made.[159] Not every acute exacerbation leads to anti-HB$_e$ seroconversion, and in fact repeated episodes of these flares are a risk factor for HCC.

In perinatally acquired infection this period usually occurs in the second to third decade of life, and seroconversion rates may approach 10% to 20% per year.[156,160] Similar rates are observed in adults with chronic infection. In a study of 1536 Alaskan natives who acquired HBV as adults, more than 70% of subjects cleared HB$_e$Ag during the first 10 years of follow-up.[161] The likelihood of seroconversion is inversely related to the serum aminotransferase. In children with normal ALT, the seroconversion rate is less than 2% during the first 3 years of life and 4% to 5% in older children. Spontaneous seroconversion occurs in 50% of those with serum aminotransferases greater than five times the upper limit of normal compared with less than 10% in those with lower aminotransferases.[162] Thus, spontaneous seroconversion is presumed to be an immune-mediated event, but the precise factors that lead up to this event are unknown and cannot be linked to specific viral mutants, as was previously believed.[163] Males and older individuals are also more likely to have spontaneous seroconversion, and viral genotype may play a role.[164] Trials of anti-HBV therapy should account for this rate of spontaneous seroconversion, as a therapeutic agent may not offer rates of HB$_e$ seroconversion above the rate observed in a given cohort.

After the development of anti-HB$_e$, patients are in the nonreplicative phase of illness. Termination of virus replication is associated in most patients with biochemical and histologic regression of inflammatory activity.[165] Some individuals also clear HBsAg, although this is unusual, occurring in less than 1% of adult patients per year and 0.05% to 0.8% of those with infection acquired in infancy or childhood.[161,166] Other individuals still have HBsAg but have negative HBV DNA by hybridization assays and normal aminotransferases and are considered healthy carriers. In the absence of cirrhosis, the prognosis for healthy carriers is generally good, although these patients can have reactivation of replication if immunosuppressed.[167]

Precore or HB$_e$-Negative Mutants

Early reports described patients in whom HB$_e$Ag was absent although HBV DNA continued to be present at high level, typically in association with severe liver disease.[168-171] This finding is due to the development of HBV mutants that cannot produce HB$_e$Ag because of mutations in the precore or core promoter (see the section on translation of hepatitis B).[172] The most frequent precore mutation is a G-to-A change at nucleotide 1986, which creates a premature stop codon in the precore region and abolishes production of HB$_e$Ag.[173] However, other variants are reported in both the precore and core promoter region. All these mutations abrogate HB$_e$Ag synthesis without affecting the replication of the virus. In fact, most of these precore mutations exhibit enhanced levels of HBV replication.[174] Other mutations, for example, in the signal peptide, lead to diminished levels of HB$_e$Ag expression.[175] Precore HBV mutants often become dominant viral quasispecies in the viral populations within an individual.

Originally, this was thought to be predominately a geographic phenomenon, as HB$_e$Ag-negative hepatitis is more prevalent in certain parts of the world, especially Asia and the Mediterranean. However, later studies suggest that the likelihood of HB$_e$Ag-negative chronic HBV is related to duration of infection, as suggested by the older age at presentation,[176] which would make it appear to be of higher prevalence in areas where perinatal transmission predominates. A prospective study demonstrated that HB$_e$Ag-negative chronic hepatitis accumulates over time, with a cumulative incidence of 25% at 16 years of follow-up.[177] Patients with HB$_e$Ag-negative but HBV DNA–positive hepatitis tend to have more severe inflammation and a higher likelihood of cirrhosis, with 29% to 38% cirrhotic at the time of initial presentation.[176,178] These patients have very low rates of spontaneous seroconversion of less than 0.5% per year[177] and are more difficult to treat.[169] An important but unresolved clinical issue is the association of precore mutations with severity of acute infection, as some reports have described outbreaks of fulminant hepatitis in association with precore mutants.[179,180]

Prognosis of Chronic Hepatitis B

The likelihood of morbidity and mortality in chronic hepatitis B is directly related to the development of cirrhosis. For persons who clear HBsAg, the prognosis is good although perhaps surprisingly is not entirely benign. In one study of 189 patients who were noncirrhotic at the time of HBsAg clearance, 3 (1.6%) developed cirrhosis, 2 (1.1%) developed HCC, and 1 died of HCC. These complications all developed in patients with concurrent HCV or HDV infection, however.[181] In the absence of cirrhosis, the long-term prognosis even for HBsAg-positive patients is good. In a 16-year follow-up study of 317 HBsAg-positive blood donors from Montreal, for example, only 3 died from HBV-related cirrhosis and none developed HCC.[182] Higher rates of mortality are reported in other cohorts and may be related to disease duration. In one study in England and Wales, during a mean 22 years of follow-up, 17.4% of deaths in a cohort of HBsAg-positive subjects were due to HCC or liver disease.[183] The risk of developing cirrhosis in chronic HBsAg-positive patients ranges from 1 to 5.4 per 100 person-years, with a 5-year cumulative probability of progression ranging from 8% to 20%.[176,184,185]

There are multiple variables that account for the wide estimates of risk. The rate of progression to cirrhosis may be higher in patients with HB$_e$Ag-negative hepatitis than in those with HB$_e$Ag,[169] although these findings may be confounded by a longer duration of disease in HB$_e$Ag-negative patients. Patients with more severe inflammation and fibrosis at the time of presentation are also more likely to progress to cirrhosis. Fattovich and colleagues found that 30% of patients with moderate chronic active hepatitis developed cirrhosis on histology after 6 years, whereas 50% of patients with severe chronic active hepatitis (bridging necrosis) developed cirrhosis on histology after 4 years.[162] Similarly, in one study the likelihood of cirrhosis was 0%, 6%, and

17% for individuals with no, mild, and moderate degrees of fibrosis present on the initial biopsy.[186] Consumption of alcohol also increases the risk of both cirrhosis and HCC.[187] Infection with hepatitis C, when accompanied by active replication of both viruses, also increases the rate of progression to cirrhosis,[188,189] as does hepatitis D.[190]

For patients with compensated cirrhosis, survival is 84% at 5 years and 68% at 10 years.[191] When cirrhosis develops, the risk of decompensation is 20% to 25% per year.[162,192] The prognosis is very poor after the development of decompensation, with estimated survival rates of only 55% to 70% at 1 year and 14% to 35% at 5 years.[184,193] In one study of European patients with biopsy-proven cirrhosis, during a 6-year period of follow-up HCC developed in 32 (9%) of the 349 patients and decompensation was observed in 88 (28%) of 317 tumor-free patients. After the first episode of decompensation, the probability of survival was only 35% at 5 years.[184]

Another major cause of mortality in chronic HBV is HCC, which, unless caught in a small surgically resectable stage, has a poor prognosis. The risk of HCC in persons with cirrhosis is estimated to be 6% to 15%.[178,184,194] For example, in one study the likelihood of developing HCC over a 5-year time period was 9% in persons with Child's A cirrhosis with an incidence per 100 person-years of 2.2.[191] The risk of HCC is much higher in patients who are HB$_e$Ag positive than those who are HBsAg positive only. In one study of more than 11,000 men the incidence rate of HCC was 1169 cases per 100,000 person-years among men who were positive for both HBsAg and HB$_e$Ag, 324 per 100,000 person-years for those who were positive for HBsAg only, and 39 per 100,000 person-years for those who were negative for both.[195] The relative risk of HCC was 9.6 (95% confidence interval, 6.0 to 15.2) among men who were positive for HBsAg alone and 60.2 (95% confidence interval, 35.5 to 102.1) among those who were positive for both HBsAg and HB$_e$Ag compared with men who were negative for both.[195] In one case-control study, the relative risk of HCC was 4.5 for alcohol use alone, 12.6 for HBsAg alone, and 53.9 for patients with both viral hepatitis and alcohol use.[196] Men are between two and four times more likely than women to develop HCC,[127] which may be due to the presence of other cofactors, such as alcohol, or a direct effect of testosterone on HBV replication.[197]

Hepatitis D

Like HBV, HDV is spread by blood, blood products, and bodily secretions.[198] After exposure, there is a short incubation period of 3 to 7 weeks. Because HDV requires helper function from HBV, disease may occur as an acute coinfection with HBV or as a superinfection of a chronic HBV infection. As with hepatitis B, the clinical presentation and natural history are highly variable. The incubation period during coinfection may display a biphasic pattern of ALT levels because of different titers of the virus, as the incubation period is inversely proportional to dose of the virus. Usually the first episode is due to hepatitis B replication and the immune response followed by that of hepatitis D. Superinfection of chronic carriers with HDV generally results in severe hepatitis with a relatively short incubation period followed by chronic hepatitis D in most of the cases. Superinfection with HDV is also associated with fulminant hepatitis and chronic active hepatitis with cirrhosis. Fulminant hepatitis, a severe form of acute hepatitis, is 10 times more common in coinfection. The diagnosis of HDV may be established using PCR, which is more sensitive than hybridization assays,[199] as well as both IgM and IgG anti-HDAg.

Most simultaneous acute infections in adults are cleared along with hepatitis B. One percent to 3% of acute coinfections become chronic, and 70% to 80% of superinfections develop into chronic hepatitis D. When chronic infection is established, the clinical course of hepatitis is accelerated. Cirrhosis occurs in 60% to 80% of patients with chronic hepatitis D and the risk of HCC increases about three-fold.[200] Superinfection progresses to chronicity in more than 90% of cases. These patients have more severe liver disease, with a 60% to 80% chance of cirrhosis and an increased risk of HCC.[201-203] In one study in which the seroprevalence rate for hepatitis D was 6%, the relative risk of cirrhosis and HCC was 2.58 and 2.87 in patients with both

infections compared with those with HBV alone.[201] The high risk of HCC may reflect the higher rate of cirrhosis.

Extrahepatic Manifestations of Hepatitis B

Extrahepatic manifestations, which are thought to be mediated by circulating immune complexes, can be seen in both acute and chronic HBV. Acute hepatitis may be manifest in 10% to 20% of patients as a serum sickness–like illness with fever, skin rash, arthralgias, and polyarthritis, typically occurring just before the onset and subsiding with the development of jaundice. The skin rash can be of virtually any type, including erythematous, macular, maculopapular, urticarial, or petechial. Polyarteritis nodosa is a rare complication of HBV. It is a vasculitis of small to medium-size arteries and typically arises with fever, rash, hypertension, eosinophilia, abdominal pain, renal disease, and polyarthritis. A variable proportion of patients with polyarteritis nodosa are HBV positive, and of those who are some may benefit from antiviral treatment.[204] Steroids may improve the manifestations but may worsen the hepatitis B. Both nucleosides and IFN-alfa have been used.[205,206] There is also a rare but distinctive manifestation in children, papular acrodermatitis (Gianotti-Crosti syndrome), which consists of 2- to 3-mm, flat erythematous and papular eruptions localized to the face and extremities, along with generalized lymphadenopathy in the setting of acute hepatitis B.[207-209]

Glomerular disease also occurs as a manifestation of HBV infection. Nephrotic syndrome secondary to membranous or membranoproliferative glomerulonephritis is a rare complication of HBV infection occurring predominantly in children with active viral replication. The typical presentation is with nephrotic range proteinuria. Approximately 30% to 60% of children with HBV-related membranous nephropathy undergo spontaneous remission, usually in association with seroconversion of HB$_e$Ag to anti-HB$_e$.[210] Progression to renal failure can occur, particularly in adults. The prognosis is variable, but in adults it may lead to progressive renal insufficiency.[211] It can be successfully treated with IFN-alfa.[212]

CLINICAL MANIFESTATIONS AND NATURAL HISTORY IN SPECIAL HOSTS

Individuals with Human Immunodeficiency Virus Infection

Because of common parenteral routes of transmission, HBV and HIV are frequently seen in concert. In a study of 16,248 HIV-infected patients receiving care, the incidence of acute HBV was 12.2 cases per 1000 person-years; it was lower in those taking either antiretroviral therapy with lamivudine, antiretroviral therapy without lamivudine, or one or more doses of HBV vaccine (14% of subjects).[213] Current estimates are that 65% of individuals who are HIV seropositive in the United States are positive for some marker of past HBV infection, and 7.1% are HBsAg positive.[214] Patients with HIV and the acquired immunodeficiency syndrome often have increased amounts of viral replication, HB$_e$Ag, and viral counts.[215] Despite lower serum aminotransferases, patients with HIV-HBV coinfection are more likely to have cirrhosis on biopsy.[216] This translates into higher observed mortality for patients with coinfection than those with either virus alone.[217] In coinfected individuals, the liver-related mortality rate was highest with lower nadir CD4$^+$ cell counts and was twice as high after 1996, when highly active antiretroviral therapy (ART) was introduced, which may be confounded by the longer duration of HBV infection in those surviving into the ART era. Loss of CD4$^+$ T cells in persons with HIV can be accompanied by reactivation of disease in previously healthy carriers[218] and rapidly progressive fibrosing cholestatic hepatitis in others.[219]

Hepatitis B after Liver Transplantation

In the absence of specific therapy, most patients with hepatitis B have reinfection of the allograft. In some patients, rapidly progressive liver failure develops, marked by a histologic variant known as fibrosing cholestatic hepatitis.[155] Hepatitis B immune globulin (HBIG) can prevent reinfection of the allograft, but it is expensive and must be continued indefinitely to prevent reinfection.

Lamivudine may also be used to treat and prevent recurrent HBV infection, although its long-term effectiveness is limited by lamivudine resistance (see "Management of Hepatitis B").[220] The long-term survival after liver transplantation for hepatitis B is generally very good when HBIG and antivirals are combined. In one large study conducted between 1988 and 2002, the 1-, 5-, and 10-year survival rates were 91%, 81%, and 73%,[221] comparable to those in other conditions leading to transplantation.

Hepatitis B after Other Types of Transplantation

Because of the frequent need for blood products in some groups of patients, these patients are also at risk for HBV infection, followed by progressive hepatitis during the period of immunosuppression. In the past, large numbers of patients receiving chronic hemodialysis became infected through contaminated dialysis equipment and blood transfusions because of chronic anemia. With better appreciation of appropriate infection control measures and vaccination of patients, the incidence of hepatitis B among patients with chronic renal disease has decreased. Renal transplantation is associated with reduced survival in HBsAg-positive hemodialysis patients, compared with improved survival in HCV-seropositive patients.[222] Similarly, recipients of bone marrow transplants are also at risk for recurrent hepatitis B, which may arise as a severe flare at the time of withdrawal of immunosuppression[223] or as progressive chronic liver disease.[224] T-cell–depleted recipients appear to be at particular risk.[225] Interestingly, however, there have also been case reports of cure of hepatitis B after bone marrow transplantation because of the transfer of HBV-specific immune cells in the graft.[226,227]

Coinfection with Hepatitis C Virus

Coinfection with HCV and active replication of both viruses are unusual, although 10% to 20% of patients with evidence of HBV may carry some marker of both infections.[162,228] Coinfection with hepatitis C often seems to result in suppression of HBV replication, and these patients are often negative for HB$_e$Ag.[229,230] However, when both viruses are replicating, the liver disease is usually more severe than in patients infected by HBV alone.[203,231] Patients with dual HBV and HCV infection may also have a higher rate of HCC than patients infected by either virus alone.[232] Patients with occult hepatitis B (HBV DNA by PCR only) may have a reduced response rate to IFN-alfa monotherapy of hepatitis C,[233] but the response rate to combined IFN and ribavirin appears equal to that of patients with HCV alone.[234]

MAKING A VIRAL DIAGNOSIS

Infection with HBV is associated with characteristic patterns of hepatitis B antigens and antibodies. New molecular tests may be useful to better define the status of viral replication. In addition to confirming the stage of HBV infection, proper interpretation of the available tests will aid in the monitoring of patients and selection for antiviral therapy.

Acute Hepatitis

The diagnosis of acute hepatitis B is based upon the detection of HBsAg and IgM anti-HB$_c$ (Table 142-3; see Fig. 142-8). During the replicative phase of infection HB$_e$Ag and HBV DNA are also present. Recovery is accompanied by the disappearance of markers of HBV replication and the appearance of antibodies to these proteins.

HBsAg is the serologic hallmark of HBV infection. It can be detected by radioimmunoassays or enzyme immunoassays. HBsAg appears in serum 1 to 10 weeks after an acute exposure to HBV, before the onset of symptoms or elevation of serum ALT. In patients who subsequently recover, HBsAg usually becomes undetectable after 4 to 6 months. Persistence of HBsAg for more than 6 months generally defines chronic infection, although in rare cases HBsAg may persist for as long as 1 year.[138] HB$_e$Ag is a secretory protein that is processed from the precore protein and is a marker of HBV replication and infectivity.[33] During recovery from acute infection, anti-HB$_e$ appears first followed by anti-HBs. In most patients who recover, anti-HBs persists for life, conferring long-term immunity.

HB$_c$Ag is an intracellular antigen that is not detectable in serum. Anti-HB$_c$ can be detected throughout the course of HBV infection and its presence signifies natural infection. During acute infection, anti-HB$_c$ is predominantly IgM class and can be the sole marker of HBV infection during the window period between the disappearance of HBsAg and the appearance of anti-HBs. The detection of IgM anti-HB$_c$ is usually regarded as an indication of acute HBV infection. However, IgM anti-HB$_c$ may remain detectable up to 2 years after the acute infection. IgG anti-HB$_c$ persists even in individuals with HBs antigenemia, indicating that the presence of this antibody does not confer protection against viral replication.

Past Hepatitis B Virus Infection

Previous HBV infection is characterized by the presence of anti-HBs and IgG anti-HB$_c$. Immunity to HBV infection after vaccination is indicated by the presence of anti-HBs only.

Chronic Hepatitis B Virus Infection

The diagnosis of chronic HBV infection is based upon the persistence of HBsAg for more than 6 months. Additional tests for HBV replication—HB$_e$Ag and serum HBV DNA—should be performed. HB$_e$Ag appears to enhance viral replication, although it is not strictly required in the viral life cycle. The presence of HB$_e$ antigenemia does signify increased infectivity, as demonstrated by higher rates of vertical and nosocomial transmission.[33] In adults, if HB$_e$Ag is negative and serum aminotransferases are normal, the patient is probably a healthy carrier and does not need further evaluation, although most experts recommend periodic (every 6 to 12 months) evaluation of aminotransferases to detect the rare instances of reactivation. Patients with perinatal HBV infection, in particular, may have normal or minimally elevated serum aminotransferases because of immune tolerance.[235] HB$_e$Ag-negative patients with elevated serum ALT concentrations should be tested for serum HBV DNA as well as other conditions such as hepatitis C.

	Acute Hepatitis B	Immunity through Infection*	Immunity through Vaccination	Chronic Hepatitis B	Chronic Infection with Precore Mutant	Healthy Carrier
TABLE 142-3 Interpretation of Serologic Tests in Hepatitis B						
Test						
HBsAg	+	−	+	+	+	+
Anti-HBs	−	+	−	−	−	−
HB$_e$Ag	+	−	−	+	−	−
Anti-HB$_e$	−	+/−	−	−	+	+
Anti-HB$_c$	+	+	−	+	+	+
IgM anti-HB$_c$	+	−	−	−	−	−
HBV DNA†	+	−	−	+/−	+	−
ALT	Elevated	Normal	Normal	Elevated	Elevated	Normal

*Occasionally individuals with past infection have isolated anti-HB$_c$ only. The presence of an isolated IgG anti-HB$_c$ may indicate a window period during acute infection or remote prior infection with loss of HBsAg or anti-HBs. In such cases, an HBV DNA test may prove useful.
†Presence of HBV DNA depends upon the sensitivity of the test used.
ALT, alanine aminotransferase; HB$_c$, hepatitis B core; HB$_e$, hepatitis B early; HBsAg, hepatitis B surface antigen; HBV, hepatitis B virus; IgM, immunoglobulin M.

Development of anti-HB$_e$ can occur at any point during chronic HBV infection. It is often accompanied by an increase in serum aminotransferases, followed by disappearance of HB$_e$Ag and HBV DNA from the serum and improvement in liver inflammation. However, some patients continue to have active liver disease and detectable HBV DNA in serum after HB$_e$Ag seroconversion.[236] These patients have a stop codon mutation in the precore region that prevents the production of Hb$_e$Ag[168] (see "Precore or HB$_e$-Negative Mutants").

Measures of Hepatitis B Virus Replication

New molecular techniques, particularly PCR, are also useful in the detection of HBV replication. The sensitivity of each test is dependent on the method used (Table 142-4), with PCR-based assays having significantly greater sensitivity than older hybridization assays. There are several circumstances in which HBV DNA is useful. The first is distinguishing the window period of acute infection from chronic infection in the patients who are IgG anti-HB$_c$ only. HBV DNA is also useful in cases of fulminant hepatitis, in which there may be undetectable levels of HBsAg upon presentation. HBV DNA testing is also indicated in patients with biochemical or histologic evidence of viral replication but negative HB$_e$Ag testing. These individuals are likely to have precore mutants. The major role of HBV DNA assays, however, is in patients with chronic HBV in order to assess both candidacy for and response to antiviral therapy. Patients with high pretreatment levels of HBV DNA are less likely to respond to IFN, although response to nucleoside agents appears not to be affected by the level of pretreatment HBV DNA.[237-239] Clearance of serum HBV DNA may be used as one of the end points in assessing response to antiviral treatment.

The enhanced sensitivity of the newer tests, especially PCR-based methods, has also raised questions about the significance of low-level viremia. Recovery from acute infection was formerly thought to be accompanied by complete clearance of HBV from serum. However, use of PCR-based methods has demonstrated that some individuals may have very low level replication in the absence of any biochemical or histologic markers of liver injury.[240] On the other hand, some studies have suggested that such "occult" hepatitis B is associated with progressive liver disease. The threshold level that is associated with a risk of progression of chronic liver disease is not known. An arbitrary value of greater than 10^5 copies/mL has been suggested as a diagnostic criterion for chronic hepatitis,[240] but lower levels may be seen in patients with ongoing liver injury, especially in HB$_e$Ag-negative patients. Because levels of HBV DNA may fluctuate over time in a given individual and the results of such tests are not currently standardized, the use of HBV DNA testing as a sole determination of future prognosis is not recommended.[241]

Isolated Anti-HB$_c$

Isolated anti-HB$_c$ is not uncommon, being present in 0.4% to 1.7% of blood donors in low-prevalence areas[242] and in 10% to 20% of the population in endemic countries.[243] Anti-HB$_c$ can be found in patients during the window period of acute hepatitis, many years after resolution of acute hepatitis, with decline of anti-HB$_s$ to undetectable titers; or rarely after years of chronic infection with decline of HBsAg to titers

below the limit of detection. Individuals with anti-HB$_c$ alone should have repeated testing to exclude false-positive results, IgM anti-HBc to exclude acute hepatitis, and HBV DNA testing. The clinical significance of isolated anti-HB$_c$ and a low-level positive HBV DNA test is not clear, but such patients should be considered potentially infectious, as transmission of HBV from blood and organ donors with anti-HB$_c$ alone has been reported.[244,245]

MANAGEMENT OF HEPATITIS B

Acute Hepatitis B

Treatment in acute hepatitis B is generally supportive. Medication lists should be reviewed, and patients should be reminded to avoid medications metabolized by the liver if possible or limit the doses. This is particularly true for agents such as acetaminophen, which patients may be taking to minimize discomfort and fever. Treatment of fulminant hepatitis is also supportive, including liver transplantation for patients who do not appear to have spontaneous recovery. Treatment with antiviral agents is not indicated for acute hepatitis B.

Chronic Hepatitis B

The goals of antiviral therapy in hepatitis B are suppression of viral replication and prevention of further liver injury. A variety of end points have been used to define response to treatment, including normalization of serum aminotransferases (biochemical response), improvement in liver histology (histologic response), undetectable serum HBV DNA by unamplified assay, and loss of HB$_e$Ag with or without anti-HB$_e$ (virologic response).[241] Elimination of HBsAg is rare but important, as the risk of liver cancer continues to be elevated above baseline among patients with persistent HB$_s$ antigenemia. Currently there are three licensed therapies for hepatitis B, which have different efficacy rates and side effects.

Selection of Patients for Treatment

The currently available treatments all have limited short- and long-term efficacy as well as substantial costs in terms of both side effects (in the case of IFN) and financial considerations. Thus, not all patients warrant treatment. Current recommendations are to treat patients with evidence of viral replication (either HB$_e$Ag positive or with a nonamplified HBV DNA of $>10^5$ copies/mL) and serum aminotransferases more than two times the upper limit of normal or with evidence of moderate to severe necroinflammation on biopsy (Table 142-5).[246] Although any approved therapy may be selected for initial use, except

---

TABLE 142-4 Sensitivity of Different Tests for the Detection of Hepatitis B Virus DNA in Serum

Assay	Sensitivity	
	Pg/mL	**Copies/mL***
Branched DNA	2.1	7×10^5
Hybrid capture†	0.5	1.4×10^5
Liquid hybridization	1.6	4.5×10^5
Polymerase chain reaction	−.001	4×10^2

*1 pg/mL = 283,000 copies.
†Sensitivity is dependent on sample volume.
Adapted from Lok AS, McMahon BJ. Chronic hepatitis B. Hepatology 2001;34:1225-1241.

TABLE 142-5 Selection of Patients for Treatment in Chronic Hepatitis B

HBeAg	HBV DNA*	ALT†	Treatment Strategy
+	+	<2 × ULN	Observe patient, consider treatment if ALT elevated
+	+	>2 × ULN	Treatment with IFN or LAM
−	+	>2 × ULN	Long-term treatment If receiving LAM: change to ADV
−	−	<2 × ULN	No treatment
+/−	+	Cirrhosis	Compensated: IFN or LAM Decompensated: LAM; consider liver transplantation
+/−	−	Cirrhosis	Compensated: observe Decompensated: consider liver transplantation

*Typically arbitrarily defined as $>10^5$ copies/mL but may be lower in hepatitis B early antigen positive and cirrhosis.
†May also use moderate to severe necroinflammation on liver biopsy as guide.
ADV, adefovir dipivoxil; ALT, alanine aminotransferase; HB$_e$Ag, hepatitis B early antigen; HBV, hepatitis B virus; IFN, interferon-alfa; LAM, lamivudine; ULN, upper limit of normal.
Adapted from AASLD Practice Guidelines (Lok AS, McMahon BJ. Chronic hepatitis B. Hepatology. 2001;34:1225-1241).

in the case of decompensated cirrhosis, in practice most specialists begin with lamivudine, with IFN as a less popular second choice because of its toxicities. Adefovir is generally reserved for treatment of lamivudine-resistant HBV in the absence of data regarding the long-term development of resistance to this agent and current higher cost. For decompensated cirrhosis, either lamivudine or adefovir is appropriate.

Interferon

IFN-α is the recombinant version of one or more proteins that are naturally produced by the body in response to viral infection. These proteins have antiviral, antiproliferative, immunomodulatory, and antifibrotic effects. The mechanism by which it is effective has not been established, although IFN-α has been used in the treatment of hepatitis B for more than 25 years.[238] Its substantial toxicity and limited efficacy in leading to anti-HB$_e$ seroconversion have limited its use. IFN-α is administered as subcutaneous injections. The recommended dose for adults is 5 MU daily or 10 MU three times a week and for children 6 MU/m^2 three times a week with a maximum of 10 MU. The recommended duration of treatment for patients with HB$_e$Ag-positive chronic hepatitis B is 16 to 24 weeks. Patients with HB$_e$Ag-negative chronic hepatitis B should be treated for at least 12 months, but it is not clear whether longer duration of treatment increases the rate of sustained response.[247] Pegylated IFN-α therapy has been used in small numbers of patients[248] and is likely to replace standard IFN-α because of its once-a-week dosing and improved tolerability. The efficacy, dose, and duration of pegylated IFN-α treatment are at present unknown, and it is not yet approved for use in the United States for the treatment of HB.

Efficacy

The efficacy of IFN-α depends on the patient.[249,250] In HB$_e$Ag-positive HB with elevations in aminotransferases, a meta-analysis of 837 patients in 15 trials showed that a higher percentage of treated patients had higher rates of anti-HB$_e$ seroconversion than untreated control subjects (7.8% compared with 1.8%, respectively) as well as loss of viral replication (33% versus 12% for loss of HB$_e$Ag).[251] Factors predictive of a high response are low HBV DNA, high aminotransferases, high hepatic activity index grade on biopsy, and infection as an adult. Prednisone priming, which was formerly used, does not appear to improve response.[252] Although Asian patients were previously believed to have a lower rate of response, this was probably due to the inclusion of HB$_e$Ag-negative patients, as HB$_e$Ag-positive patients with elevated aminotransferases have response rates similar to those of white patients.[253] Treatment of patients with normal ALT, whether adults or children, results in response rates of less than 10%,[254] suggesting the importance of the immune response in IFN-based therapy.

The durability of HB$_e$Ag clearance is good, with 80% to 90% of patients remaining HB$_e$Ag negative after a 4- to 8-year period of follow-up.[255-257] However, HBV DNA remained detectable in the serum of most of these patients when tested by PCR assays.[258] HBsAg clearance occurs less commonly than HB$_e$Ag seroconversion, and 12% to 65% of patients lose HBsAg over time.[259-262] Sustained virologic response is usually accompanied by a decrease in necroinflammation of the liver, but residual hepatic injury may be present.[178] The histologic improvement may be accompanied by an improvement in the rate of progression to decompensated cirrhosis and HCC,[259-262] although long-term studies are difficult because of the lack of control patients and slow natural history of progression.[263] In one study of 101 Chinese males, cumulative survival and incidence of HCC were significantly higher in untreated than in treated patients,[261] although other studies have failed to demonstrate a reduction in HCC, possibly because of the short follow-up period.[255,264]

In HB$_e$Ag-negative patients, the end point of therapy is usually normalization of ALT and loss of serum HBV DNA. Response rates at 12 months have ranged from 10% to 47% (average 24%) among the treated patients and 0% in the controls.[265-267] Longer courses of treatment (12 to 24 months) may be necessary to clear HBV DNA.[250] A major problem with IFN-α treatment of HB$_e$Ag-negative chronic

hepatitis B is relapse, as approximately half of the responders have relapses when therapy is discontinued, and relapses can occur up to 5 years after therapy.[268] Nevertheless, sustained response can be achieved in 15% to 25% of patients, and long-term follow-up showed that 15% to 30% of sustained responders cleared HBsAg.[250] Data on long-term outcome of patients treated for HB$_e$Ag-negative chronic hepatitis B are very limited. It has been estimated that up to 20% of long-term responders cleared HBsAg after 5 years of follow-up. In addition, long-term responders appear to have reduced risks of HCC and liver-related deaths.

IFN-α is contraindicated in decompensated cirrhosis as it may precipitate flares of disease activity with subsequent decompensation.[269,270] However, IFN-α is safe and may be effective in patients with compensated cirrhosis. In clinical trials involving patients with HB$_e$Ag-positive chronic hepatitis, up to 60% of patients included had histologic cirrhosis, and less than 1% of patients who received standard doses of IFN-α developed hepatic decompensation.[270]

Adverse Effects

IFN-α therapy causes many side effects, including influenza-like illness, fever, myalgias, headache, and fatigue. Many of these acute side effects improve after the first days to weeks of dosing, although they can linger in individual patients for the full duration of therapy. Other side effects seen after prolonged dosing include leukopenia and thrombocytopenia, hair loss, and changes in mood including irritability, sleep disorders, and depression, which can be severe. IFN therapy can also lead to the development of autoantibodies, such as antithyroid antibodies, and worsening of other autoimmune disorders.[271] An analysis of nine randomized controlled trials with 552 patients showed that 35% of the patients treated with IFN-α required dose reduction and 5% required premature cessation of treatment.[173]

Nucleoside Therapies

Recognition that HBV, like HIV, has an RT step in its life cycle led to the testing of many nucleoside agents. Because these agents are better tolerated than IFN-α, this has led to long-term use of these agents for the purpose of both viral eradication and improvement in histologic disease.

Lamivudine

Lamivudine is the negative enantiomer of 2′,3′-dideoxy-3′-thiacytidine. It is phosphorylated by host enzymes, and it is the incorporation of the triphosphate form into DNA that results in premature chain termination. Lamivudine is administered at 100 mg/day and, unlike IFN-α, is well tolerated, with side effects no different from those with placebo in most series. The recommended dose for children is 3 mg/kg/day with a maximum dose of 100 mg/day. Dose reduction is necessary for patients with renal insufficiency (creatinine clearance < 50 mL/min).

Efficacy. Several large randomized clinical trials in patients with HB$_e$Ag-positive HBV and elevated aminotransferases have demonstrated HB$_e$Ag seroconversion rates of 16% to 18% compared with 4% to 6% of control subjects.[272,273] In addition to virologic improvement, histologic improvement (defined as a reduction in necroinflammatory score greater than 2 points) was observed in 49% to 56% of treated patients and in 23% to 25% of control subjects. These benefits increased over time. A multinational study of Asian patients showed that seroconversion rates increased over time from 17% to 27% at 2 years, 40% at 3 years, 47% at 4 years, and 50% by 5 years.[274,275] An important predictor of response is the pretreatment aminotransferase level. At 1 year, HB$_e$Ag seroconversion was seen in 5% of patients with ALT less than two times the upper limit of normal, 26% of those with ALT two to five times the upper limit of normal, and 64% of those with ALT greater than five times the upper limit of normal.[276] Conversely, those with normal aminotransferases have less than a 10% chance of seroconversion.[239] Patients with HB$_e$Ag-negative hepatitis appear to have similar response rates,[256,277,278] as do patients who have previously not responded to IFN-α therapy.[279] Unlike IFN-α, lamivudine can be given in both compensated and decompensated cirrhosis, although the likelihood of HB$_e$Ag seroconversion is small in these groups.[280,281]

One of the major issues with lamivudine treatment is the duration and the durability of response. Lamivudine can suppress HBV replication but cannot eliminate CCC DNA, which leads to prompt relapse of viremia when therapy is discontinued in the majority of patients who do not achieve HB$_e$Ag seroconversion. For patients with HB$_e$Ag-positive hepatitis B who do have HB$_e$Ag seroconversion, current recommendations are to treat for 1 year and then discontinue therapy.[246] Therapy should not be discontinued before 1 year even if seroconversion occurs rapidly because of the risk of relapse. If patients do not have HB$_e$Ag seroconversion but have suppressed HBV DNA replication, therapy may be continued as there is evidence of progressive enhancement of the HB$_e$Ag seroconversion rate with longer duration of treatment and patients may continue to derive histologic benefit.[282] However, there is a risk of resistance, which accumulates over time (see later). If there is no evidence of biochemical or virologic response, lamivudine should be discontinued as the development of resistance mutations may preclude future therapy with other nucleoside agents.[283] When HB$_e$Ag seroconversion has occurred, the rate of durable response ranges from 30% to 80%.[284] The duration of additional lamivudine therapy after HB$_e$Ag seroconversion and pretreatment serum HBV DNA levels are independent predictors of posttreatment relapse.[279]

Patients should be observed after discontinuation of lamivudine for acute exacerbation of hepatitis, even after HB$_e$Ag seroconversion. This may occur months after cessation of treatment. If an acute exacerbation does develop, it can usually be managed with reinstitution of lamivudine therapy.[256]

Lamivudine Resistance. The major problem with long-term administration of lamivudine is the selection of resistant mutants. Mutations in the DNA polymerase develop that can discriminate between the natural substrate, dCTP, and lamivudine. The most common mutation affects the YMDD motif of the HBV DNA polymerase, which is essential for polymerase activity, and leads to substitution of isoleucine (I) or valine (V) for methionine at position 204 of the DNA polymerase (M204I/V).[275,285] Because of variations within genotypes, previous numbering systems have noted this amino acid as position 552, 550, 539, or 549.[286] HBV mutants with the YMDD appear to have reduced replication capacity in vitro and in vivo compared with wild-type HBV.[287] However, the YMDD variant is frequently accompanied by a leucine-to-methionine substitution in an upstream region (L180M; previously 528, 526, 515, or 525). The combined M204I/V/L180M double mutation restores replication capacity, at least in vitro.[287] Another novel mutation (Met → Ser change at rt204; M204S), which confers lamivudine resistance in vivo and in vitro, leading to virologic breakthrough and ALT increases, has been described.[288]

Genotypic resistance develops rapidly, with 14% to 32% of patients having evidence of mutations after 1 year of treatment.[272,273] Cumulative resistance increases over time, with one study demonstrating cumulative rates of 15%, 38%, 55%, 67%, and 69%, at 1, 2, 3, 4, and 5 years, respectively.[275] Assays for genotypic or phenotypic resistance are not yet commercially available, but lamivudine resistance is clinically manifested as reappearance of HBV DNA in serum using an unamplified assay during lamivudine therapy. Serum aminotransferases may or may not become elevated, and there are rare instances of acute exacerbations and hepatic decompensation.[289] However, most patients appear to have somewhat lower aminotransferases and HBV DNA than before treatment. The impact of this emergence on disease activity is unpredictable. Whereas continued disease suppression, or even HB$_e$Ag seroconversion, occurs in some patients, in others hepatitis may relapse and liver failure has been reported despite continuation of lamivudine. The rates of lamivudine resistance in patients treated for HB$_e$Ag-negative chronic hepatitis B appear to be more variable (0% to 27% at 1 year and 10% to 56% at 2 years).[278,290] Even in the presence of documented YMDD mutants, however, continuation of lamivudine appears to results in improvement in histologic injury.[282]

Thus, whether or not to continue lamivudine therapy in the presence of resistance is controversial.

Adefovir

Adefovir dipivoxil is the oral prodrug of adefovir, a phosphonate nucleotide analogue of adenosine monophosphate (AMP). It inhibits HBV DNA polymerase at much lower doses than those that inhibit human DNA polymerase. Phase I and II clinical trials showed that adefovir decreased serum HBV DNA levels by 2 to 4 logs.[291] Two large multicenter trials have demonstrated the efficacy of adefovir in chronic hepatitis B and have led to its approval in the United States. In a study of 515 patients with HB$_e$Ag-positive hepatitis B, 21% of patients treated with adefovir at 10 mg/day had suppression of HBV DNA to undetectable levels compared with 0% of control subjects, and 53% of treated patients had improvement in histology compared with 25% of control subjects.[292] Twelve percent of the adefovir group had HB$_e$Ag seroconversion compared with 6% of the control group. Similarly, in HB$_e$Ag-negative chronic hepatitis B, after 48 weeks of adefovir 10 mg/day, 51% of treated patients had suppression of HBV compared with 0% of untreated controls, and 64% had histologic improvement compared with 33% of controls.[293] Initially, it was believed that resistance did not develop, at least in up to 60 weeks of treatment,[294] although one report describes the development of a novel asparagine-to-threonine mutation at residue rt236 in domain D of the HBV polymerase, with increased serum HBV DNA and reduced susceptibility to adefovir in vitro.[295] The long-term efficacy and optimal duration of treatment of adefovir are not yet known, however.

In clinical trials, headache and abdominal pain are the most common side effects. Although adefovir at higher doses (120 mg/day) as used previously for HIV leads to substantial degrees of Fanconi-like renal toxicity, adefovir at the low doses used to treat HBV does not appear to lead to such renal toxicity.[293] In vitro and preliminary clinical data showed that adefovir is effective in suppressing the replication of lamivudine-resistant HBV mutants,[291,296] and so adefovir may prove particularly promising for treatment of individuals already resistant to lamivudine.

Other Agents

Given the limited long-term success of the current therapies, a number of new approaches are being tried. One approach is a combination of existing therapies based on the model of antiretroviral treatment. Combination of IFN-α and lamivudine has had mixed success in improving the rate of HB$_e$Ag seroconversion.[297,298] Although combination therapy appears to prevent emergence of lamivudine resistance, overall response rates are not significantly different from those for either therapy alone.[299] Tenofovir, a nucleotide agent, is not approved for use against HBV but has been shown to result in suppression of HBV, including lamivudine-resistant HBV, in individuals receiving this therapy for treatment of HIV.[300,301] Other nucleoside agents such as emtricitabine (FTC), entecavir, telbivudine (LdT), famciclovir, and clevudine (L-FMAU) as well as therapeutic vaccines are all in various phase I-II clinical trials.[302-304] Some of these agents have shown promise against lamivudine-resistant isolates,[305] although there is concern about cross-resistance limiting monotherapy with any one agent.[287]

MANAGEMENT IN SPECIAL POPULATIONS

Liver Transplantation

Historically, because rates of recurrence of HBV were high (90%) and the consequences of reinfection were devastating, HBV was considered a relative contraindication to liver transplantation. Treatment of HBV-related liver disease in transplant patients is difficult for several reasons including the high levels of HBV replication and the ongoing immunosuppressive treatment. HBIG was introduced in the early 1980s and nucleosides in the early 1990s, with progressive reduction in likelihood of recurrence with each intervention. U.S. transplantation centers typically use a fixed-dose schedule of HBIG, with monthly infusions of 10,000 IU, whereas European centers typically vary the dose of HBIG to maintain the trough anti-HBs at greater than 100 IU/mL. Using HBIG alone, recurrence rates are 20% to 25%, depending on the schedule and trough anti-HBs titer. Mutations in the HBs a determinant are associated with recurrence of hepatitis B.[306] Some data from studies involving further efforts to reduce expense suggest that HBIG can be stopped in patients who were HB$_e$Ag negative before transplantation,[307] although this needs to be confirmed in larger trials. Because of the significant expense of HBIG, lamivudine monotherapy was also attempted, with recurrence rates of 10% to 32% at 1 year and 40% to 50% at 3 years.[308]

Thus, the current standard of care typically uses lamivudine plus HBIG, with rates of reinfection as low as 10%.[309] A summary of a single clinical center's experience supports the excellent outcomes of patients undergoing liver transplantation for HBV-related liver disease.[221] From 1988 to 2000, 228 liver transplantations were performed in 206 hepatitis B patients. All patients received long-term immunoprophylaxis (anti-HBs > 100 U/L). The 1-, 5-, and 10-year survival rates of patients were 91%, 81%, and 73%, although they were lower in patients with HCC (60% 5-year survival, $P < .01$) or HBV reinfection (69% 5-year survival, $P < .01$). Patients with preoperative HB$_e$Ag had worse survival than patients negative for HB$_e$Ag ($P < .05$). Two-year survival increased from 85% in 1988 to 1993, before the availability of antivirals, to 94% since 1997, in which period patients received a combination of HBIG and lamivudine ($P < .05$). The 2-year recurrence rates in these two periods were 42% and 8% ($P < .05$). In summary, with currently available combination therapy, survival is excellent in patients undergoing liver transplantation for HBV disease, even in those with active pretransplantation viral replication.

Lamivudine is the most widely used nucleoside analogue,[310] although famciclovir has been used in Europe. Used before transplantation, lamivudine does not appear to increase the rate of pre- or post-transplantation survival, although a subset of patients with less advanced liver failure may derive clinical benefit from lamivudine therapy, delaying the need for transplantation.[311] In most studies, liver transplant recipients with documented HBV recurrence (elevated serum ALT levels and detectable HBsAg and HBV DNA) have been treated with lamivudine 100 mg daily (adjusted for renal function) with good tolerance and rapid loss of HBV DNA in serum. Good biochemical and virologic responses have been achieved not only in patients with chronic hepatitis B after transplantation but also in patients with acute hepatitis B of the graft and even in the most severe cases of fibrosing cholestatic hepatitis.[312] Histologic improvements in the inflammatory grade are also achieved with therapy. In a multicenter study based on 52 patients with detectable DNA after liver transplantation, lamivudine for 1 year resulted in 60% loss of HBV DNA in serum and 31% HB$_e$Ag seroconversion.[313] Other studies have confirmed these results, showing loss of HBV DNA in 68% to 100% of patients treated for periods of 12 to 36 months.[312,314,315] The downside of this agent is the need for continuous treatment because relapse is the rule when the drug is discontinued.

Monotherapy with both lamivudine and famciclovir has resulted in the emergence of HBV variants that are resistant to these compounds as discussed earlier. Molecular analysis of these mutations has shown changes in the gene for the viral DNA polymerase. Because of the overlapping nature of the HBV open reading frames, nucleotide changes in the polymerase may result in amino acid changes not only in the polymerase protein but also in the surface protein, which could in turn theoretically alter binding of HBIG.[316] Lamivudine resistance after transplantation has on occasion been associated with severe and even fatal post-transplantation disease in patients receiving combination therapy with lamivudine plus HBIG.[317] However, this is not universal and patients may derive continued benefit from maintaining lamivudine.[220,318]

Fortunately, the availability of new hepatitis B antivirals such as adefovir has resulted in viral suppression of lamivudine-resistant variants[291] and even resolution of graft failure in patients with lamivudine-resistant variants.[319] It is not yet known whether patients who are treated for lamivudine resistance with adefovir after transplantation need to continue on lamivudine.

Human Immunodeficiency Virus

Treatment of individuals with HIV is complicated by the need to consider resistance developing in HIV isolates. IFN-α has even lower efficacy rates, in terms of both HB$_e$Ag seroconversion and histologic responses, among individuals with HIV seropositivity than in immunocompetent hosts.[320] In addition, an injectable medication with multiple side effects, including leukopenia, is often a relative contraindication. If HIV patients are treated with IFN-α, patients should be warned that absolute CD4 counts decrease although the percentage of CD4$^+$ T cells remains unchanged. If patients are treated with lamivudine, they should be given 150 mg twice a day in addition to other active retroviral therapies. A patient whose HIV isolate exhibits lamivudine resistance can be given 100 mg lamivudine once a day in addition to the antiretroviral regimen. Use of adefovir at the approved 10 mg/day dose does not appear to lead to HIV resistance,[321] although clinicians should proceed with caution until further data are available. Small clinical series have reported success with tenofovir, used as part of an existing antiretroviral regimen, in controlling both wild-type and lamivudine-resistant HIV, but this agent is not approved for use in the therapy of hepatitis B.[300,301,322]

Hepatitis D Coinfection

Because lamivudine is ineffective at controlling HDV replication,[323] IFN-α is the only approved option for treatment. However, the efficacy of IFN-α in the treatment of hepatitis D is limited unless high doses (9 MU three times a week) are used.[324] Of note, IFN-α appears to affect the biochemical and histologic improvement but does not affect HDV DNA levels.[325] If HDV replication is controlled and there is normalization of serum aminotransferases, the effect appears to be very durable with improvement in liver histology maintained 10 years after treatment among patients who received high-dose IFN-α.[325]

OTHER MANAGEMENT ISSUES IN CHRONIC HEPATITIS B

Patients with chronic hepatitis B should be counseled about disease-modifying factors as well as means to prevent spread of HBV to other persons. For example, patients should be counseled about the means of spread of delta hepatitis and hepatitis C to avoid superinfection with these viruses. Patients should also be counseled to consume minimal if any alcohol in the absence of data regarding safe levels of consumption of alcohol, as consumption of large amounts of alcohol is clearly a risk factor for more rapid progression to cirrhosis. Other major issues in the management of patients with chronic hepatitis B include prevention of hepatitis A, prevention of spread of HBV, and surveillance for HCC.

Hepatitis A Vaccination

The official recommendation of the Advisory Committee for Immunization Practices (ACIP) in the United States is that all persons with chronic liver disease be vaccinated against hepatitis A.[326] The data supporting this recommendation are not strong,[327] as at least one study revealed that the risk of fulminant hepatitis A is significantly increased only in patients with underlying hepatitis C and not in those with hepatitis B.[328] However, the guidelines of the American Association for the Study of Liver Disease call for immunization against hepatitis A of all patients with chronic hepatitis B.[246]

Screening and Vaccination of Contacts

Sexual and household contacts of persons with hepatitis B are at increased risk for infection. All sexual partners and household contacts should be tested for hepatitis B and vaccinated if seronegative. Until the immunization series is complete, sexual partners should use barrier methods. Both patients and contacts should be counseled regarding the modes of transmission and advised on methods to prevent household transmission, including avoiding sharing of items that might be contaminated with small amounts of blood, such as toothbrushes, and the need to cover open wounds. Pregnant women or women who wish to become pregnant and who have hepatitis B should also be counseled on the risk of transmission to the newborn and the method of preventing such transmission, as the combination of HBIG and concurrent hepatitis B vaccine has been shown to be 95% efficacious in the prevention of perinatal transmission of hepatitis B.[129]

Recommendations for the infected health care worker who carries hepatitis B vary from country to country. Although there is general agreement that individuals with HB$_e$Ag or hepatitis B DNA greater than 5×10^4 copies/mL pose the greatest risk of transmission,[329] there have been documented cases of transmission from health care workers in the absence of HB$_e$Ag and during "low-risk" procedures.[330,331] In the United States, the Centers for Disease Control and Prevention (CDC) recommend that invasive procedures not be performed without expert guidance and review of procedures to be performed by the health care worker.[332,333] In other countries, HBsAg-positive carriers are specifically forbidden from performing invasive procedures in which there is risk of inadvertent exposure of the patient to the provider's blood (for example, deep surgical procedures in which there is limited visibility into the surgical wound).[334,335]

Surveillance for Hepatocellular Carcinoma

In multiple longitudinal studies, carriers of HBsAg have been shown to be at increased risk for developing HCC.[195] The goal of HCC screening is to detect small, surgically resectable tumors because the prognosis for more advanced lesions is poor. Current recommendations are for periodic screening in HBsAg-positive persons at high risk for HCC, such as men older than 45 years, patients with cirrhosis, and patients with a positive family history. In general, the longer the duration of disease in HBsAg-positive patients, the greater the risk for HCC. The combination of serum α-fetoprotein and ultrasonography repeated every 6 months appears to offer the best sensitivity and specificity, although lower risk individuals may be screened with α-fetoprotein alone.[246]

PREVENTION OF HEPATITIS B INFECTION

Successful vaccination not only is effective in preventing hepatitis B infection but also prevents the sequelae of chronic hepatitis B infection, and this is the first example that cancer can be prevented by vaccination.[132] The development of hepatitis B vaccines is considered one of the major achievements of modern medicine.[336] The impact of effective vaccination programs is seen in the rate of HCC in regions of high endemicity in which universal vaccine programs were adopted early. For example, in Taiwan the average annual incidence of HCC in children 6 to 14 years of age declined from 0.70 per 100,000 children between 1981 and 1986, before widespread vaccination, to 0.57 between 1986 and 1990 and to 0.36 between 1990 and 1994 ($P < .01$). The corresponding rates of mortality from HCC also decreased. The incidence of HCC in children 6 to 9 years of age declined from 0.52 for those born between 1974 and 1984 to 0.13 for those born between 1984 and 1986.[132] Currently available vaccines are both safe and effective, with seroconversion rates of more than 90% in healthy adults and children. The major obstacles to true universal vaccination have been cost in developing nations and failure to convince recipients in developed nations that vaccines are necessary outside traditional high-risk groups.

Postexposure Immunoprophylaxis

Postexposure prophylaxis with HBIG and vaccine is recommended for all nonimmune individuals who have percutaneous, sexual contact, ocular, or mucous membrane exposure to blood, including human bites that penetrate the skin. The first dose of 0.06 mL/kg (or 5 mL for adults) should be administered as soon as possible, preferably within 12 hours, although there is a window period of up to 24 hours.[337] The first vaccine dose should be given at the same time although in a different site, followed by the remainder of the series. For individuals who are vaccinated but who do not have documentation of adequate titers of anti-HBs, usual recommendations are to administer both HBIG and vaccine pending documentation of adequate anti-HBs.

Individuals who have failed to respond to a vaccine series require two doses of HBIG 1 month part.[129]

Active Immunization

Both plasma-derived and recombinant forms of vaccine are available. Both are comparable in terms of efficacy and durability. Plasma-derived vaccine was developed first and is no longer available in North America and Europe but is still widely used in parts of Asia and India. More than 200 million doses of plasma-derived vaccines have been distributed globally, and they are both safe and effective. They are cheaper to produce than recombinant preparations, especially in areas of high seroprevalence of HBs antigenemia. However, concerns about the use of any plasma-derived product have led to the widespread adoption of recombinant vaccines in developed countries. Because anti-HBs alone is sufficient to confer protective immunity, most recombinant vaccines have expressed HBsAg only. Two thimerosal-free vaccines that express HBsAg (Engerix-B and Recombivax HB) are widely available. These vaccines are approved for use in all age groups. A combination vaccine (Twinrix), which expresses both HBsAg and hepatitis A virus, is also available and is approved for use in adults in the United States and Europe. This vaccine is typically used for convenience when protection against both viruses is needed.

Indications for Vaccination

All persons at high risk for acquiring hepatitis B (see "Routes of Transmission") should be offered vaccination if nonimmune. The need for prevaccination testing for prior hepatitis B infection is dependent upon the likelihood of that individual having had past exposure. A cost-benefit analysis suggested that preimmunization testing is indicated only when the prevalence of infection in that population exceeds 30%.[338] Thus, in areas such as the United States and Europe, only patients at high risk for past exposure to hepatitis B should be screened, such as intravenous drug users, and that screening should consist of anti-HBs. In endemic areas, the most cost-effective approach is controversial. Some countries screen for anti-HB$_c$ only; however, individuals with isolated anti-HB$_c$ can respond to vaccination with measurable anti-HBs,[243] suggesting that both anti-HB$_c$ and anti-HBs should be included in prevaccination screening.

Targeting of high-risk groups alone, however, failed to attain acceptable rates of immunization and declines in the incidence of acute hepatitis B. Therefore, many countries have now moved to universal vaccination of all infants and incorporation of hepatitis B vaccines into routine childhood immunization programs. Universal vaccination of all neonates with catch-up vaccination of older children began in 1991 in the United States. Countries that adopted universal vaccination programs in the 1980s have already begun to see declines in the rate of chronic HCV infection and subsequent HCC.

Dose Regimen

Two recombinant hepatitis B vaccines have been licensed in the United States: Engerix-B and Recombivax HB. Engerix-B is formulated to contain 20 μg HBsAg/mL, and Recombivax HB contains 10 μg HBsAg/mL (Table 142-6). The recommendation for adults is to administer Engerix-B 20 μg or Recombivax HB 10 μg in three doses at months 0, 1 to 2, and then between months 6 to 12. In infants, three doses of 0.5 mL of vaccine are required to complete the course; the timing depends upon the clinical setting (see later).[129] For adolescents (11 to 19 years old), three doses of 0.5 mL of Recombivax HB or 1.0 mL of Engerix-B are recommended. Either vaccine can be interchanged during the series of injections. An optional two-dose regimen of Recombivax HB has also been approved for adolescents aged 11 to 15 (1.0 mL containing 10 μg of HBsAg with a second dose given 4 to 6 months after the first dose).[339]

Vaccines should be administered intramuscularly because deposition of the vaccine into adipose tissue results in a lower seroconversion rate.[340] The deltoid is the preferred site in adults, and the vastus lateralis is preferred in infants. Longer needles should be used in overweight individuals. Adverse reactions are uncommon, and most

TABLE 142-6 Doses and Schedules of Licensed Hepatitis B Vaccine*

Hepatitis B Vaccines	Age	Dose	Volume	Schedule
Engerix-B	<20 yr	10 μg	10 μg/0.5 mL	Infants†: birth, 1-4, 6-18 mo Older children: 0, 1-2, 4 mo
	>20 yr	20 μg	20 μg/1.0 mL	0, 1, 6 mo
	Dialysis	40 μg	2-20 μg/1.0 mL doses	0, 1, 2, 6 mo
Recombivax HB	<20 yr	5 μg	5 μg/0.5 mL	Infants†: birth, 1-4, 6-18 mo Older children: 0, 1-2, 4 mo
	11-15 yr	10 μg	10 μg/1.0 mL	0, 4-6 mo
	>20 yr	10 μg	10 μg/1.0 mL	0, 1, 6 mo
	Dialysis	40 μg‡	40 μg/1.0 mL	0, 1, 6 mo

Combination Vaccines	Age§	Antigen	Volume	Schedule
Comvax	6 wk-4 yr	PedvaxHIB‖ and Recombivax	0.5 mL	2, 4, 12-15 mo
Pediarix	6 wk-6 yr	Engerix B, Infarix (DTaP), and IPV	0.5 mL	2, 4, 6 mo
Twinrix	>18 yr	Havrix (HAV) and Engerix B (20 μg)	1.0 mL	0, 1, 6 mo

*All vaccines should be administered intramuscularly in the deltoid.
†Infants born to hepatitis B surface antigen (HBsAg)-positive mothers should have hepatitis B immune globulin (HBIG) within 12 hours of delivery, along with vaccine at a separate site. If mother's HBsAg status is unknown, administer vaccine within 12 hours and test mother. If mother is HBsAg positive, administer HBIG within 1 week.
‡Special formulation.
§Birth dose should be monovalent vaccine only; subsequent doses can be combination.
‖PedvaxHIB, licensed *Haemophilus influenzae* type B vaccine; Infarix, licensed diphtheria, tetanus, and acellular pertussis vaccine (DTaP); Havrix, licensed hepatitis A virus (HAV) vaccine.

consist of soreness at the injection site. Low-grade fever, malaise, headache, and myalgias are seen in less than 1% of vaccinees. The vaccine can be administered during pregnancy. There were case reports of neurologic sequelae after vaccination, including demyelinating disease,[341] raising concerns that hepatitis B immunization was linked to multiple sclerosis. However, numerous studies failed to confirm an association of multiple sclerosis with vaccination.[342,343]

Prevention of Perinatal Transmission

The risk of maternal-infant transmission is related to the HBV replicative status of the mother. It is 85% to 90% in infants born to HBeAg-positive mothers and 32% in infants born to HBeAg-negative mothers.[344,345] Maternal serum HBV DNA levels also correlate with the risk of transmission.[346] Maternal-infant transmission may occur in utero, at the time of birth, or after birth. The high protective efficacy (95%) of neonatal vaccination suggests that infection occurs predominantly at or after birth. There is no evidence that cesarean section prevents maternal-infant transmission, and thus routine cesarean section is not recommended. Neither breast-feeding nor amniocentesis appears to increase the risk of transmission.[347]

The current recommendation is to provide passive-active immunization to newborns of carrier mothers. Infants should receive both HBIG (0.06 mL/kg) and vaccine, and the first dose of vaccine should be given within 12 hours of birth and the second and third doses at 1 and 6 to 12 months, respectively. This regimen has a protective efficacy of 95%.[344,345]

Efficacy

A protective level of immune response after vaccination is defined as a titer of anti-HBs of greater than 10 IU/L. Although this was somewhat arbitrary, clinical studies suggest that a decrease in titer below this level is associated with a risk of infection. In one 5-year follow-up study of 773 homosexual men vaccinated in 1980, the acute infection rate increased seven times when the anti-HBs titer decreased below the level of 10 IU/L.[348]

Using the definition of greater than 10 IU/L anti-HBs as a positive response, the overall seroconversion rate is about 95% in healthy adults. Factors that may reduce the immunogenicity of the vaccine include age older than 40 years, weight, genetics, smoking, HIV or any form of immunosuppression, improper administration (e.g., administration into the buttock or subcutaneous injection), and freezing of the vaccine. In patients receiving chronic hemodialysis, the response rate to recombinant vaccines is 50% to 60%.[349] In patients with HIV response rates are 40% to 70% and are not necessarily tightly correlated

with CD4 count.[350,351] Because the response rate in otherwise healthy individuals is so high, routine postvaccination testing is not recommended except for health care workers and others who are at high risk for repeated exposure to HBV, such as intravenous drug users and homosexual men. Testing should be performed 1 to 2 months after the vaccine series, except in infants born to HBsAg-positive mothers, in whom testing should be performed at age 9 to 15 months.

In individuals with hemodialysis or chronic renal failure, several approaches have been used to increase vaccine efficacy. One approach was intradermal injection, which, although successful, was technically difficult.[352] Most individuals now receive an increased dose, which should be administered before the onset of dialysis if possible (refer to Table 142-6). For individuals with HIV, transient increases in the CD4 T-cell count through administration of interleukin-2 did not increase postvaccination titers.[353] It is not clear whether individuals who were vaccinated before a decline in CD4+ T-cell count retain immunity or whether vaccinations above a threshold CD4 count are more likely to result in protective immunity. Finally, there are other individuals for whom nonresponse is genetically determined by the presence of extended HLA haplotypes.[354]

The current recommendation for otherwise healthy individuals who have no or an inadequate anti-HBs titer after a primary series is to administer one or more doses of vaccine. After one or two doses, up to 25% of previous nonresponders or hyporesponders may have adequate titers, and with three doses up to 50% may have adequate titers.[129] Individuals who still have inadequate titers are not protected from HBV infection and should receive HBIG upon exposure.

Vaccine Strategies under Development

Although highly efficacious in most individuals, the current vaccines are limited by the need for multiple injections and costs. For individuals who do not respond to the current vaccines, a number of strategies are being tested. A vaccine containing pre-S1, pre-S2, and S antigens (Hepacare, Medeva Pharma Plc, Speke, UK) is in development. A controlled trial suggested that it was associated with an enhanced immunologic response compared with Engerix-B in a three-dose regimen and was equally effective in a two-dose regimen.[355] Novel adjuvants are being tested to increase immunogenicity.[356,357] Novel technologies are also in development to reduce production costs or decrease the need to maintain the cold chain. Examples include expression of HBsAg in transgenic plants, which would substantially reduce the costs of vaccine development.[358,359] Another strategy, which has entered clinical trials, is the use of DNA to transduce skeletal muscle directly.[360,361]

Durability of Response

There is excellent durability of response after a successful primary series. Fifty percent to 85% of infants and young children who have received hepatitis B vaccine continue to have protective titers of anti-HBsAg 9 to 15 years after immunization. In addition, even if titers of anti-HBs fall to less than the commonly defined protective level (10 IU), most of these infants and young children continue to be protected against HBV 9 to 15 years after immunization.[362-365] In a 5-year follow-up of 773 homosexual men vaccinated in 1980, the HBV infection rate was significantly lower in the vaccinated group (2.9% versus 21%) despite the observation that at 5 years, 15% of the vaccinees had undetectable anti-HBs and another 27% had anti-HBs titers below 10 IU/L.[348] The risk of late infection with HBV in those with an initially adequate vaccine response increased markedly when antibody levels decreased below 10 IU, but only 1 of 34 late infections resulted in viremia and liver inflammation.[348] Thus, the CDC does not currently recommend that otherwise healthy individuals who were vaccinated as adults or children have routine booster doses of vaccine. The only group in whom routine boosters are recommended are patients receiving hemodialysis, in whom antibody levels should be checked yearly and a booster dose of vaccine given if the anti-HBs is below 10 IU/mL.[366]

Hepatitis B Surface Antigen Escape Mutants

HBs mutants have been described in infants infected with HBV after passive-active vaccination[367] as well as in liver transplant recipients who have received prolonged courses of HBIG to prevent recurrence in the allograft.[306,368] The most common mutation is a glycine-to-arginine substitution at codon 145 (G145R) in the a determinant of HBsAg. This mutation decreases binding of HBsAg to anti-HBs and may explain why these infants develop "escape" infection. The G145R mutation has also been observed in liver transplant recipients who developed recurrent HBV infection despite HBIG prophylaxis. Other mutations in the a determinant have also been described but are of unclear significance. The prevalence of these escape mutants is increasing over time,[369,370] but the clinical and epidemiologic importance and the impact on current vaccination strategies are unclear. However, in a chimpanzee model of infection the current vaccines appear to protect against the spread of HBs mutants.[371]

REFERENCES

1. Lurman A. Eine icterus Epidemic. Berl Klin Wochenschr. 1885;22:20-23.
2. Findlay G, MacCallum F. Note on acute hepatitis and yellow fever immunization. Trans Soc Trop Med Hyg. 1937;31:297.
3. Bigger J, Dubi S. Jaundice in syphilitics under treatment. Lancet. 1943;1:457.
4. Flaum A, Malmros H, Persson E. Eine nosocomiale icterus Epidemic. Acta Med Scand Suppl 1926;16:544.
5. Feinstone S, Kapikian A, Purcell R, et al. Transfusion associated hepatitis not due to viral hepatitis type A or B. N Engl J Med. 1975;282:767.
6. Blumberg B, Alter H, Visnich S. A "new" antigen in leukemia sera. JAMA. 1965;191:541-546.
7. Dane DS, Cameron CH, Briggs M. Virus-like particles in serum of patients with Australia antigen associated hepatitis. Lancet. 1970;2:695-698.
8. Robinson W, Marion P, Feitelson M, et al. The hepadnavirus group: Hepatitis B and related viruses. In: Szmuness W, Alter HJ, Maynard JE, eds. Viral Hepatitis: 1981 International Symposium. Philadelphia: Franklin Institute Press; 1982.
9. Mason WS, Seal G, Summers J. Virus of Pekin ducks with structural and biological relatedness to human hepatitis B virus. J Virol. 1980;36:829-836.
10. Summers J, Smolec JM, Snyder R. A virus similar to human hepatitis B virus associated with hepatitis and hepatoma in woodchucks. Proc Natl Acad Sci USA. 1978;75:4533-4537.
11. Marion PL, Oshiro LS, Regnery DC, et al. A virus in Beechey ground squirrels that is related to hepatitis B virus of humans. Proc Natl Acad Sci USA. 1980;77:2941-2945.
12. Sninsky JJ, Siddiqui A, Robinson WS, Cohen SN. Cloning and endonuclease mapping of the hepatitis B viral genome. Nature. 1979;279:346-348.
13. Galibert F, Mandart E, Fitoussi F, et al. Nucleotide sequence of the hepatitis B virus genome (subtype ayw) cloned in E. coli. Nature. 1979;281:646-650.
14. Valenzuela P, Gray P, Quiroga M, et al. Nucleotide sequence of the gene coding for the major protein of hepatitis B virus surface antigen. Nature. 1979;280:815-819.
15. Landers TA, Greenberg HB, Robinson WS. Structure of hepatitis B Dane particle DNA and nature of the endogenous DNA polymerase reaction. J Virol. 1977;23:368-376.
16. Robinson WS, Clayton DA, Greenman RL. DNA of a human hepatitis B virus candidate. J Virol 1974;14:384-391.
17. Ganem D, Schneider RJ. Hepadnaviridae: The viruses and their replication. In: Knipe D, Howley P, eds. Fundamental Virology. Philadelphia: Lippincott Williams & Wilkins; 2001:1285-1331.
18. Roossinck MJ, Siddiqui A. In vivo phosphorylation and protein analysis of hepatitis B virus core antigen. J Virol. 1987;61:955-961.
19. Albin C, Robinson WS. Protein kinase activity in hepatitis B virus. J Virol. 1980;34:297-302.
20. Gavilanes F, Gonzalez-Ros JM, Peterson DL. Structure of hepatitis B surface antigen. Characterization of the lipid components and their association with the viral proteins. J Biol Chem. 1982;257:7770-7777.
21. Peterson DL. Isolation and characterization of the major protein and glycoprotein of hepatitis B surface antigen. J Biol Chem. 1981;256:6975-6983.
22. Gerin JL, Alexander H, Shih JW, et al. Chemically synthesized peptides of hepatitis B surface antigen duplicate the d/y specificities and induce subtype-specific antibodies in chimpanzees. Proc Natl Acad Sci USA. 1983;80:2365-2369.
23. Milich D, Hughes JC, McLachlan A, et al. Hepatitis B synthetic immunogen composed of nucleocapsid T cell response sites and an envelope B cell epitope. Proc Natl Acad Sci USA. 1988;85:1610-1614.
24. Summers J, Mason WS. Replication of the genome of a hepatitis B–like virus by reverse transcriptase of an RNA intermediate. Cell. 1982;29:403-415.
25. Kosovsky M, Qadri I, Siddiqui A. The regulation of hepatitis B virus gene expression: An overview of the cis- and trans-acting components. In: Koshy R, Caselmann WH, eds. Hepatitis B Virus: Molecular Mechanisms in Disease and Novel Strategies for Therapy. London: Imperial College Press; 1998.
26. Romet-Lemonne JL, McLane MF, Elfassi E, et al. Hepatitis B virus infection in cultured human lymphoblastoid cells. Science. 1983;221:667-669.
27. Korba BE, Cote PJ, Shapiro M, et al. In vitro production of infectious woodchuck hepatitis virus by lipopolysaccharide-stimulated peripheral blood lymphocytes. J Infect Dis. 1989;160:572-576.
28. Michalak TI, Pardoe IU, Coffin CS, et al. Occult lifelong persistence of infectious hepadnavirus and residual liver inflammation in woodchucks convalescent from acute viral hepatitis. Hepatology. 1999;29:928-938.
29. Hruska JF, Clayton DA, Rubenstein JL, Robinson WS. Structure of hepatitis B Dane particle DNA before and after the Dane particle DNA polymerase reaction. J Virol. 1977;21:666-672.
30. Gerlich WH, Robinson WS. Hepatitis B virus contains protein attached to the 5' terminus of its complete DNA strand. Cell. 1980;21:801-809.
31. Lien JM, Aldrich CE, Mason WS. Evidence that a capped oligoribonucleotide is the primer for duck hepatitis B virus plus-strand DNA synthesis. J Virol. 1986;57:229-236.
32. Neurath AR, Kent SB, Strick N, Parker K. Identification and chemical synthesis of a host cell receptor binding site on hepatitis B virus. Cell. 1986;46:429-436.
33. Baraldini M, Facchini A, Miglio F, et al. Radioimmunoassay for hepatitis B 'e' antigen and antibody: Correlations with viral replication and prognostic value. Vox Sang. 1981;41:139-145.
34. Russnak R, Ganem D. Sequences 5' to the polyadenylation signal mediate differential poly(A) site use in hepatitis B viruses. Genes Dev. 1990;4:764-776.
35. Cherrington J, Ganem D. Regulation of polyadenylation in human immunodeficiency virus (HIV): Contributions of promoter proximity and upstream sequences. EMBO J. 1992;11:1513-1524.
36. Raney AK, Milich DR, McLachlan A. Characterization of hepatitis B virus major surface antigen gene transcriptional regulatory elements in differentiated hepatoma cell lines. J Virol. 1989;63:3919-3925.
37. Zhou DX, Yen TS. Differential regulation of the hepatitis B virus surface gene promoters by a second viral enhancer. J Biol Chem. 1990;265:20731-20734.
38. Bulla GA, Siddiqui A. The hepatitis B virus enhancer modulates transcription of the hepatitis B virus surface antigen gene from an internal location. J Virol. 1988;62:1437-1441.
39. Lopez-Cabrera M, Letovsky J, Hu KQ, Siddiqui A. Multiple liver-specific factors bind to the hepatitis B virus core/pregenomic promoter: Trans-activation and repression by CCAAT/enhancer binding protein. Proc Natl Acad Sci USA. 1990;87:5069-5073.
40. Guo W, Chen M, Yen TS, Ou JH. Hepatocyte-specific expression of the hepatitis B virus core promoter depends on both positive and negative regulation. Mol Cell Biol. 1993;13:443-448.
41. Siddiqui A, Jameel S, Mapoles J. Expression of hepatitis B virus X gene in mammalian cells. Proc Natl Acad Sci USA. 1987;84:2513-2517.
42. Treinin M, Laub O. Identification of a promoter element located upstream from the hepatitis B virus X gene. Mol Cell Biol. 1987;7:545-548.
43. Heerman KH, Gerlich WH. Surface proteins of hepatitis B viruses. In: McLachlan A, ed. Molecular Biology of the Hepatitis B Virus. Boca Raton, Fla: CRC Press; 1991:109-144.
44. Ou JH, Laub O, Rutter WJ. Hepatitis B virus gene function: The precore region targets the core antigen to cellular membranes and causes the secretion of the e antigen. Proc Natl Acad Sci USA. 1986;83:1578-1582.
45. Brunetto MR, Giarin MM, Oliveri F, et al. Wild-type and e antigen-minus hepatitis B viruses and course of chronic infection. Proc Natl Acad Sci USA. 1991;88:4186-4190.
46. Gunther S, Meisel H, Reip A, et al. Frequent and rapid emergence of mutated pre-C sequences in HBV from e-antigen positive carriers who seroconvert to anti-HBe during interferon treatment. Virology. 1992;187:271-279.
47. Schodel F, Weimer T, Will H, Sprengel R. Amino acid sequence similarity between retroviral and E. coli RNase H and hepadnaviral gene products. AIDS Res Hum Retroviruses. 1988;4:ix-xi.
48. Radziwill G, Tucker W, Schaller H. Mutational analysis of the hepatitis B virus P gene product: Domain structure and RNase H activity. J Virol. 1990;64:613-620.
49. Seeger C, Mason WS. Hepatitis B virus biology. Microbiol Mol Biol Rev. 2000;64:51-68.

50. Pollack JR, Ganem D. An RNA stem-loop structure directs hepatitis B virus genomic RNA encapsidation. J Virol. 1993;67:3254-3263.
51. Wang GH, Zoulim F, Leber EH, et al. Role of RNA in enzymatic activity of the reverse transcriptase of hepatitis B viruses. J Virol. 1994;68:8437-8442.
52. Wang GH, Seeger C. The reverse transcriptase of hepatitis B virus acts as a protein primer for viral DNA synthesis. Cell. 1992;71:663-670.
53. Lutwick LI, Robinson WS. DNA synthesized in the hepatitis B Dane particle DNA polymerase reaction. J Virol. 1977;21:96-104.
54. Zoulim F, Saputelli J, Seeger C. Woodchuck hepatitis virus X protein is required for viral infection in vivo. J Virol. 1994;68:2026-2030.
55. Maguire HF, Hoeffler JP, Siddiqui A. HBV X protein alters the DNA binding specificity of CREB and ATF-2 by protein-protein interactions. Science. 1991;252:842-844.
56. Rahmani Z, Huh KW, Lasher R, Siddiqui A. Hepatitis B virus X protein colocalizes to mitochondria with a human voltage-dependent anion channel, HVDAC3, and alters its transmembrane potential. J Virol. 2000;74:2840-2846.
57. Shirakata Y, Koike K. Hepatitis B virus X protein induces cell death by causing loss of mitochondrial membrane potential. J Biol Chem. 2003;278:22071-22078.
58. Cross JC, Wen P, Rutter WJ. Transactivation by hepatitis B virus X protein is promiscuous and dependent on mitogen-activated cellular serine/threonine kinases. Proc Natl Acad Sci USA. 1993;90:8078-8082.
59. Kekule AS, Lauer U, Weiss L, et al. Hepatitis B virus transactivator HBx uses a tumour promoter signalling pathway. Nature. 1993;361:742-745.
60. Benn J, Schneider RJ. Hepatitis B virus HBx protein activates Ras-GTP complex formation and establishes a Ras, Raf, MAP kinase signaling cascade. Proc Natl Acad Sci USA. 1994;91:10350-10354.
61. Bouchard MJ, Wang LH, Schneider RJ. Calcium signaling by HBx protein in hepatitis B virus DNA replication. Science. 2001;294:2376-2378.
62. Siddiqui A, Gaynor R, Srivivasan A, et al. Trans-activation of viral enhancers including long terminal repeat of the human immunodeficiency virus by the hepatitis B virus X protein. Virology. 1989;169:479-484.
63. Benn J, Su F, Doria M, Schneider RJ. Hepatitis B virus HBx protein induces transcription factor AP-1 by activation of extracellular signal-regulated and c-Jun N-terminal mitogen-activated protein kinases. J Virol. 1996;70:4978-4985.
64. Waris G, Huh, K-W, Siddiqui A. Mitochondrially associated hepatitis B virus X protein constitutively activates transcription factors STAT-3 and NF-kappa B via oxidative stress. Mol Cell Biol. 2001;21:7721-7730.
65. Cheong J-H, Yi M-K, Lin Y, Murakami S. Human RPB5, a subunit shared by eukaryotic nuclear polymerases, binds human hepatitis B virus X protein and may play a role in X transactivation. EMBO J. 1995;14:143-150.
66. Haviv I, Shamay M, Doitsh G, Shaul Y. Hepatitis B virus pX targets TFIIB in transcription coactivation. Mol Cell Biol. 1998;18:1562-1569.
67. Qadri I, Conaway JW, Conaway RC, et al. Hepatitis B virus transactivator protein, HBx, associates with the components of TFIIH and stimulates the DNA helicase activity of TFIIH. Proc Natl Acad Sci USA. 1996;93:10578-10583.
68. Qadri I, Maguire HF, Siddiqui A. Hepatitis B virus transactivator protein X interacts with the TATA-binding protein. Proc Natl Acad Sci USA. 1995;92:1003-1007.
69. Becker SA, Lee TH, Butel JS, Slagle BL. Hepatitis B virus X protein interferes with cellular DNA repair. J Virol. 1998;72:266-272.
70. Hu Z, Zhang Z, Doo E, et al. Hepatitis B virus X protein is both a substrate and a potential inhibitor of the proteasome complex. J Virol. 1999;73:7231-7240.
71. Wang XW, Forrester K, Yeh H, et al. Hepatitis B virus X protein inhibits p53 sequence-specific DNA binding, transcriptional activity, and association with transcription factor ERCC3. Proc Natl Acad Sci USA. 1994;91:2230-2234.
72. Chirillo P, Pagano S, Natoli G, et al. The hepatitis B virus X gene induces p53-mediated programmed cell death. Proc Natl Acad Sci USA. 1997;94:8162-8167.
73. Elmore LW, Hancock AR, Chang SF, et al. Hepatitis B virus X protein and p53 tumor suppressor interactions in the modulation of apoptosis. Proc Natl Acad Sci USA. 1997;94:14707-14712.
74. Huovila AP, Eder AM, Fuller SD. Hepatitis B surface antigen assembles in a post-ER, pre-Golgi compartment. J Cell Biol. 1992;118:1305-1320.
75. Bruss V, Ganem D. The role of envelope proteins in hepatitis B virus assembly. Proc Natl Acad Sci USA. 1991;88:1059-1063.
76. Gerin JL. Animal models of hepatitis delta virus infection and disease. ILAR J. 2001;42:103-106.
77. van Regenmortel M, Fauquet C, Bishop D, et al. Virus taxonomy: The classification and nomenclature of viruses. In: The Seventh Report of the International Committee on Taxonomy of Viruses. San Diego: Academic Press; 2000.
78. Rizzetto M, Canese MG, Gerin JL, et al. Transmission of the hepatitis B virus–associated delta antigen to chimpanzees. J Infect Dis. 1980;141:590-602.
79. Gerin JC, Casey JL, Purcell RH. Hepatitis delta virus. In: Knipe D, Howley P, eds. Fields' Virology, v. 2. Philadelphia: Lippincott Williams & Wilkins; 2001:3037-3050.
80. Wu HN, Choo KB, Chen CM, et al. Genotyping of hepatitis D virus by restriction-fragment length polymorphism and relation to outcome of hepatitis D. Lancet. 1995;346:939-941.
81. Casey JL, Brown TL, Colan EJ, et al. A genotype of hepatitis D virus that occurs in northern South America. Proc Natl Acad Sci USA. 1993;90:9016-9020.
82. Rizzetto M, Purcell RH, Gerin JL. Epidemiology of HBV-associated delta agent: Geographical distribution of anti-delta and prevalence in polytransfused HBsAg carriers. Lancet.1980;1:1215-1218.
83. MacNaughton TB, Lai MM. Genomic but not antigenomic hepatitis delta virus RNA is preferentially exported from the nucleus immediately after synthesis and processing. J Virol. 2002;76:3928-3935.
84. Weiner AJ, Choo QL, Wang KS, et al. A single antigenomic open reading frame of the hepatitis delta virus encodes the epitope(s) of both hepatitis delta antigen polypeptides p24 delta and p27 delta. J Virol. 1988;62:594-599.
85. Luo GX, Chao M, Hsieh SY, et al. A specific base transition occurs on replicating hepatitis delta virus RNA. J Virol. 1990;64:1021-1027.
86. Chang MF, Chang SC, Chang CI, et al. Nuclear localization signals, but not putative leucine zipper motifs, are essential for nuclear transport of hepatitis delta antigen. J Virol. 1992;66:6019-6027.
87. Xia YP, Lai MM. Oligomerization of hepatitis delta antigen is required for both the trans-activating and trans-dominant inhibitory activities of the delta antigen. J Virol. 1992;66:6641-6648.
88. Wang JG, Lemon SM. Hepatitis delta virus antigen forms dimers and multimeric complexes in vivo. J Virol. 1993;67:446-454.
89. Lai MM. The molecular biology of hepatitis delta virus. Annu Rev Biochem. 1995;64:259-286.
90. Sharmeen L, Kuo MY, Dinter-Gottlieb G, Taylor J. Antigenomic RNA of human hepatitis delta virus can undergo self-cleavage. J Virol. 1988;62:2674-2679.
91. Wu HN, Lin YJ, Lin FP, et al. Human hepatitis delta virus RNA subfragments contain an autocleavage activity. Proc Natl Acad Sci USA. 1989;86:1831-1835.
92. Macnaughton TB, Wang YJ, Lai MM. Replication of hepatitis delta virus RNA: Effect of mutations of the autocatalytic cleavage sites. J Virol. 1993;67:2228-2234.
93. Taylor J. Replication of human hepatitis delta virus: Recent developments. Trends Microbiol. 2003;11:185-190.
94. Yamaguchi K, Ogata Y, Akagi Y, et al. Cronkhite-Canada syndrome associated with advanced rectal cancer treated by a subtotal colectomy: Report of a case. Surg Today. 2001;31:521-526.
95. Nassal M. Hepatitis B virus morphogenesis. Curr Top Microbiol Immunol. 1996;214:297-337.
96. Ponzetto A, Cote PJ, Popper H, et al. Transmission of the hepatitis B virus–associated delta agent to the eastern woodchuck. Proc Natl Acad Sci USA. 1984;81:2208-2212.
97. Koziel MJ. Hepatitis B immunopathogenesis. In: Thomas HC, ed. Therapies for Viral Hepatitis. London: International Medical Press; 1998:53-64.
98. Baron JL, Gardiner L, Nishimura S, et al. Activation of a nonclassical NKT cell subset in a transgenic mouse model of hepatitis B virus infection. Immunity. 2002;16:583-594.
99. Ferrari C, Bertoletti A, Penna A, et al. Identification of immunodominant T cell epitopes of the hepatitis B virus nucleocapsid antigen. J Clin Invest. 1991;88:214-222.
100. Penna A, Chisari FV, Bertoletti A, et al. Cytotoxic T lymphocytes recognize an HLA-A2–restricted epitope within the hepatitis B virus nucleocapsid antigen. J Exp Med. 1991;174:1565-1570.
101. Penna A, Artini M, Cavalli A, et al. Long-lasting memory T cell responses following self-limited acute hepatitis B. J Clin Invest. 1996;98:1185-1194.
102. Guidotti LG, Chisari FV. Noncytolytic control of viral infections by the innate and adaptive immune response. Annu Rev Immunol. 2001;19:65-91.
103. Guidotti LG, Chisari FV. Cytokine-induced viral purging—Role in viral pathogenesis. Curr Opin Microbiol. 1999;2:388-391.
104. Milich DR, Schodel F, Peterson DL, et al. Characterization of self-reactive T cells that evade tolerance in hepatitis B e antigen transgenic mice. Eur J Immunol. 1995;25:1663-1672.
105. Bertoletti A, Sette A, Chisari FV, et al. Natural variants of cytotoxic epitopes are T-cell receptor antagonists for antiviral cytotoxic T cells. Nature. 1994;369:407-410.
106. Thursz MR, Kwiatkowski D, Allsopp CE, et al. Association between an MHC class II allele and clearance of hepatitis B virus in the Gambia. N Engl J Med. 1995;332:1065-1069.
107. Chisari FV. Rous-Whipple Award Lecture. Viruses, immunity, and cancer: Lessons from hepatitis B. Am J Pathol. 2000;156:1117-1132.
108. Barnaba V, Franco A, Alberti A, et al. Recognition of hepatitis B virus envelope proteins by liver-infiltrating lymphocytes in chronic HBV infection. J Immunol. 1989;143:2650-2655.
109. Barnaba V, Franco A, Alberti A, et al. Selective killing of hepatitis B envelope antigen-specific B cells by class I–restricted, exogenous antigen-specific T lymphocytes. Nature. 1990;345:258-260.
110. Maini MK, Boni C, Lee CK, et al. The role of virus-specific CD8+ cells in liver damage and viral control during persistent hepatitis B virus infection. J Exp Med. 2000;191:1269-1280.
111. Nisini R, Paroli M, Accapezzato D, et al. Human CD4+ T-cell response to hepatitis delta virus: Identification of multiple epitopes and characterization of T-helper cytokine profiles. J Virol. 1997;71:2241-2251.
112. Karayiannis P, Saldanha J, Jackson AM, et al. Partial control of hepatitis delta virus superinfection by immunisation of woodchucks (Marmota monax) with hepatitis delta antigen expressed by a recombinant vaccinia or baculovirus. J Med Virol. 1993;41:210-214.
113. Cole SM, Gowans EJ, Macnaughton TB, et al. Direct evidence for cytotoxicity associated with expression of hepatitis delta virus antigen. Hepatology. 1991;13:845-851.
114. Negro F, Rizzetto M. Pathobiology of hepatitis delta virus. J Hepatol. 1993;17(Suppl 3):S149-S153.
115. Beasley RP, Hwang LY, Lin CC, Chien CS. Hepatocellular carcinoma and hepatitis B virus. A prospective study of 22,707 men in Taiwan. Lancet. 1981;2:1129-1133.
116. Popper H, Roth L, Purcell RH, et al. Hepatocarcinogenicity of the woodchuck hepatitis virus. Proc Natl Acad Sci USA. 1987;84:866-870.
117. Brechot C, Pourcel C, Louise A, et al. Presence of integrated hepatitis B virus DNA sequences in cellular DNA of human hepatocellular carcinoma. Nature. 1980;286:533-535.
118. Koike K, Kobayashi M, Gondo M, et al. Hepatitis B virus DNA is frequently found in liver biopsy samples from hepatitis C virus–infected chronic hepatitis patients. J Med Virol. 1998;54:249-255.
119. Buendia MA. Hepatitis B viruses and cancerogenesis. Biomed Pharmacother. 1998;52:34-43.

120. Caselmann W, Koshy R. Transactivators of HBV, signal transduction and tumorigenesis. In: Koshy R, Caselmann WH, eds. Hepatitis B Virus: Molecular Mechanisms in Disease and Novel Strategies for Therapy. London: Imperial College Press; 1998:161-181.
121. Yu MW, Hsu FC, Sheen IS, et al. Prospective study of hepatocellular carcinoma and liver cirrhosis in asymptomatic chronic hepatitis B virus carriers. Am J Epidemiol. 1997;145:1039-1047.
122. Hussain S, Hofseth L, Harris C. Radical causes of cancer. Nat Rev. 2003;3:276-285.
123. Chen J-H, Chen DS. Interaction of hepatitis B virus, chemical carcinogen, and genetic susceptibility: Multistage hepatocarcinogenesis with multifactorial etiology. Hepatology. 2002;36:1046-1049.
124. Hassan MM, Hwang LY, Hatten CJ, et al. Risk factors for hepatocellular carcinoma: Synergism of alcohol with viral hepatitis and diabetes mellitus. Hepatology. 2002;36:1206-1313.
125. Kew M, Rossouw E, Hodkinson J, et al. Hepatitis B virus status of southern African Blacks with hepatocellular carcinoma: Comparison between rural and urban patients. Hepatology. 1983;3:65-68.
126. Ming L, Thorgeirsson SS, Gail MH, et al. Dominant role of hepatitis B virus and cofactor role of aflatoxin in hepatocarcinogenesis in Qidong, China. Hepatology. 2002;36:1214-1220.
127. Chen CJ, Yu MW, Liaw YF. Epidemiological characteristics and risk factors of hepatocellular carcinoma. J Gastroenterol Hepatol. 1997;12:S294-S308.
128. Chen CJ, Chen DS. Interaction of hepatitis B virus, chemical carcinogen, and genetic susceptibility: Multistage hepatocarcinogenesis with multifactorial etiology. Hepatology. 2002;36:1046-1049.
129. Hepatitis B virus: A comprehensive strategy for eliminating transmission in the United States through universal childhood vaccination. Recommendations of the Immunization Practices Advisory Committee (ACIP). MMWR Recomm Rep. 1991;40:1-25.
130. Pisani P, Parkin DM, Bray F, Ferlay J. Estimates of the worldwide mortality from 25 cancers in 1990. Int J Cancer. 1999;83:18-29.
131. Beasley RP. Hepatitis B virus. The major etiology of hepatocellular carcinoma. Cancer. 1988;61:1942-1956.
132. Chang MH, Chen CJ, Lai MS, et al. Universal hepatitis B vaccination in Taiwan and the incidence of hepatocellular carcinoma in children. Taiwan Childhood Hepatoma Study Group. N Engl J Med. 1997;336:1855-1859.
133. Novick DM, Farci P, Croxson TS, et al. Hepatitis D virus and human immunodeficiency virus antibodies in parenteral drug abusers who are hepatitis B surface antigen positive. J Infect Dis. 1988;158:795-803.
134. Rosina F, Saracco G, Rizzetto M. Risk of post-transfusion infection with the hepatitis delta virus: A multicenter study. N Engl J Med. 1985;321:1488-1491.
135. Liaw YF, Chiu KW, Chu CM, et al. Heterosexual transmission of hepatitis delta virus in the general population of an area endemic for hepatitis B virus infection: A prospective study. J Infect Dis. 1990;162:1170-1172.
136. Gerberding JL. Incidence and prevalence of human immunodeficiency virus, hepatitis B virus, hepatitis C virus, and cytomegalovirus among health care personnel at risk for blood exposure: Final report from a longitudinal study. J Infect Dis. 1994;170:1410-1417.
137. Hoofnagle JH. Type B hepatitis: Virology, serology and clinical course. Semin Liver Dis. 1981;1:7-14.
138. McMahon BJ, Alward WL, Hall DB, et al. Acute hepatitis B virus infection: Relation of age to the clinical expression of disease and subsequent development of the carrier state. J Infect Dis. 1985;151:599-603.
139. Lee WM. Medical progress: Hepatitis B virus infection. N Engl J Med. 1997;337:1733-1745.
140. Rehermann B, Ferrari C, Pasquinelli C, Chisari FV. The hepatitis B virus persists for decades after patients' recovery from acute viral hepatitis despite active maintenance of a cytotoxic T lymphocyte response. Nat Med. 1996;2:1104-1108.
141. Al-Taie OH, Mork H, Gassel AM, et al. Prevention of hepatitis flare-up during chemotherapy using lamivudine: Case report and review of the literature. Ann Hematol. 1999;78:247-249.
142. Bessesen M, Ives D, Condreay L, et al. Chronic active hepatitis B exacerbations in human immunodeficiency virus–infected patients following development of resistance to or withdrawal of lamivudine. Clin Infect Dis. 1999;28:1032-1035.
143. Schiodt FV, Atillasoy E, Shakil AO, et al. Etiology and outcome for 295 patients with acute liver failure in the United States. Liver Transpl Surg. 1999;5:29-34.
144. Wright TL, Mamish D, Combs C, et al. Hepatitis B virus and apparent fulminant non-A, non-B hepatitis. Lancet. 1992;339:952-925.
145. Wu JC, Chen CL, Hou MC, et al. Multiple viral infection as the most common cause of fulminant and subfulminant viral hepatitis in an area endemic for hepatitis B: Application and limitations of the polymerase chain reaction. Hepatology. 1994;19:836-840.
146. Vento S, Cainelli F, Mirandola F, et al. Fulminant hepatitis on withdrawal of chemotherapy in carriers of hepatitis C virus. Lancet. 1996;347:92-93.
147. Liang TJ, Hasegawa K, Munoz SJ, et al. Hepatitis B virus precore mutation and fulminant hepatitis in the United States. A polymerase chain reaction–based assay for the detection of specific mutation. J Clin Invest. 1994;93:550-555.
148. Milich DR, Jones JE, Hughes JL, et al. Is a function of the secreted hepatitis B e antigen to induce immunologic tolerance in utero? Proc Natl Acad Sci USA. 1990;87:6599-6603.
149. Sterneck M, Kalinina T, Gunther S, et al. Functional analysis of HBV genomes from patients with fulminant hepatitis. Hepatology. 1998;28:1390-1397.
150. Bartholomeusz A, Locarnini S. Hepatitis B virus mutants and fulminant hepatitis B: Fitness plus phenotype. Hepatology. 2001;34:432-435.
151. Liu CJ, Chen PJ, Lai MY, et al. A prospective study characterizing full-length hepatitis B virus genomes during acute exacerbation. Gastroenterology. 2003;124:80-90.

152. Perrillo RP. Acute flares in chronic hepatitis B: The natural and unnatural history of an immunologically mediated liver disease. Gastroenterology. 2001;120:1009-1022.
153. Wong JB, Koff RS, Tine F, Pauker SG. Cost-effectiveness of interferon-alpha 2b treatment for hepatitis B e antigen–positive chronic hepatitis B. Ann Intern Med. 1995;122:664-675.
154. Gerber MA, Hadziyannis S, Vissoulis C, et al. Electron microscopy and immuno-electronmicroscopy of cytoplasmic hepatitis B antigen in hepatocytes. Am J Pathol. 1974;75:489-502.
155. Harrison RF, Davies MH, Goldin RD, Hubscher SG. Recurrent hepatitis B in liver allografts: A distinctive form of rapidly developing cirrhosis. Histopathology. 1993;23:21-28.
156. Lok AS, Lai CL, Wu PC, et al. Spontaneous hepatitis B e antigen to antibody seroconversion and reversion in Chinese patients with chronic hepatitis B virus infection. Gastroenterology. 1987;92:1839-1843.
157. Chang MH, Hsu HY, Hsu HC, et al. The significance of spontaneous hepatitis B e antigen seroconversion in childhood: With special emphasis on the clearance of hepatitis B e antigen before 3 years of age. Hepatology. 1995;22:1387-1392.
158. Yang PL, Althage A, Chung J, Chisari FV. Hydrodynamic injection of viral DNA: A mouse model of acute hepatitis B virus infection. Proc Natl Acad Sci USA. 2002;99:13825-13830.
159. Liaw YF, Chu CM, Huang MJ, et al. Determinants for hepatitis B e antigen clearance in chronic type B hepatitis. Liver. 1984;4:301-306.
160. Liaw YF, Chu CM, Lin DY, et al. Age-specific prevalence and significance of hepatitis B e antigen and antibody in chronic hepatitis B virus infection in Taiwan: A comparison among asymptomatic carriers, chronic hepatitis, liver cirrhosis, and hepatocellular carcinoma. J Med Virol. 1984;13:385-391.
161. McMahon BJ, Holck P, Bulkow L, Snowball M. Serologic and clinical outcomes of 1536 Alaska Natives chronically infected with hepatitis B virus. Ann Intern Med. 2001;135:759-768.
162. Fattovich G, Brollo L, Giustina G, et al. Natural history and prognostic factors for chronic hepatitis type B. Gut. 1991;32:294-298.
163. Schulte-Frohlinde E, Foster GR. Spontaneous seroconversion in chronic hepatitis B: Role of mutations in the precore/core gene. Dig Dis Sci. 1998;43:1714-1718.
164. Chu CJ, Hussain M, Lok AS. Hepatitis B virus genotype B is associated with earlier HBeAg seroconversion compared with hepatitis B virus genotype C. Gastroenterology. 2002;122:1756-1762.
165. Fattovich G, Rugge M, Brollo L, et al. Clinical, virologic and histologic outcome following seroconversion from HBeAg to anti-HBe in chronic hepatitis type B. Hepatology. 1986;6:167-172.
166. Liaw YF, Lin SM, Sheen IS, Chu CM. Acute hepatitis C virus superinfection followed by spontaneous HBeAg seroconversion and HBsAg elimination. Infection. 1991;19:250-251.
167. Kawatani T, Suou T, Tajima F, et al. Incidence of hepatitis virus infection and severe liver dysfunction in patients receiving chemotherapy for hematologic malignancies. Eur J Haematol. 2001;67:45-50.
168. Carman WF, Jacyna MR, Hadziyannis S, et al. Mutation preventing formation of hepatitis B e antigen in patients with chronic hepatitis B infection. Lancet. 1989;2:588-591.
169. Fattovich G, Brollo L, Alberti A, et al. Long-term follow-up of anti-HBe-positive chronic active hepatitis B. Hepatology. 1988;8:1651-1654.
170. Gunther S, Sommer G, Von Breunig F, et al. Amplification of full-length hepatitis B virus genomes from samples from patients with low levels of viremia: Frequency and functional consequences of PCR-introduced mutations. J Clin Microbiol. 1998;36:531-538.
171. Hawkins AE, Gilson RJ, Bickerton EA, et al. Conservation of precore and core sequences of hepatitis B virus in chronic viral carriers. J Med Virol. 1994;43:5-12.
172. Tong SP, Li JS, Vitvitski L, et al. Evidence for a base-paired region of hepatitis B virus pregenome encapsidation signal which influences the patterns of precore mutations abolishing HBe protein expression. J Virol. 1993;67:5651-5655.
173. Hadziyannis SJ, Vassilopoulos D. Immunopathogenesis of hepatitis B e antigen negative chronic hepatitis B infection. Antiviral Res. 2001;52:91-98.
174. Tong SP, Li JS, Vitvitski L, Trepo C. Active hepatitis B virus replication in the presence of anti-HBe is associated with viral variants containing an inactive pre-C region. Virology. 1990;176:596-603
175. Lok AS, Akarca U, Greene S. Mutations in the pre-core region of hepatitis B virus serve to enhance the stability of the secondary structure of the pre-genome encapsidation signal. Proc Natl Acad Sci USA. 1994;91:4077-4081.
176. Zarski JP, Marcellin P, Cohard M, et al. Comparison of anti-HBe–positive and HBe-antigen–positive chronic hepatitis B in France. French Multicentre Group. J Hepatol. 1994;20:636-640.
177. Hsu YS, Chien RN, Yeh CT, et al. Long-term outcome after spontaneous HBeAg seroconversion in patients with chronic hepatitis B. Hepatology. 2002;35:1522-1527.
178. Di Marco V, Lo Iacono O, Camma C, et al. The long-term course of chronic hepatitis B. Hepatology. 1999;30:257-264.
179. Fagan EA, Smith PM, Davison F, Williams R. Fulminant hepatitis B in successive female sexual partners of two anti-Hbe–positive males. Lancet. 1986;2:538-540.
180. Liang TJ, Hasegawa K, Rimon N, et al. A hepatitis B virus mutant associated with an epidemic of fulminant hepatitis. N Engl J Med. 1991;324:1705-1709.
181. Chen YC, Sheen IS, Chu CM, Liaw YF. Prognosis following spontaneous HBsAg seroclearance in chronic hepatitis B patients with or without concurrent infection. Gastroenterology. 2002;123:1084-1089.
182. Villeneuve JP, Desrochers M, Infante-Rivard C, et al. A long-term follow-up study of asymptomatic hepatitis B surface antigen–positive carriers in Montreal. Gastroenterology. 1994;106:1000-1005.
183. Crook PD, Jones ME, Hall AJ. Mortality of hepatitis B surface antigen–positive blood donors in England and Wales. Int J Epidemiol. 2003;32:118-124.

184. Fattovich G, Giustina G, Schalm SW, et al. Occurrence of hepatocellular carcinoma and decompensation in western European patients with cirrhosis type B. The EURO-HEP Study Group on Hepatitis B Virus and Cirrhosis. Hepatology. 1995;21:77-82.

185. Moreno-Otero R, Garcia-Monzon C, Garcia-Sanchez A, et al. Development of cirrhosis after chronic type B hepatitis: A clinicopathologic and follow-up study of 46 HBeAg-positive asymptomatic patients. Am J Gastroenterol. 1991;86:560-564.

186. Ikeda K, Saitoh S, Suzuki Y, et al. Disease progression and hepatocellular carcinogenesis in patients with chronic viral hepatitis: A prospective observation of 2215 patients. J Hepatol. 1998;28:930-938.

187. Donato F, Tagger A, Gelatti U, et al. Alcohol and hepatocellular carcinoma: The effect of lifetime intake and hepatitis virus infections in men and women. Am J Epidemiol. 2002;155:323-331.

188. Liaw YF. Hepatitis C virus superinfection in patients with chronic hepatitis B virus infection. J Gastroenterol. 2002;37:65-68.

189. Crespo J, Lozano JL, de la Cruz F, et al. Prevalence and significance of hepatitis C viremia in chronic active hepatitis B. Am J Gastroenterol. 1994;89:1147-1151.

190. Fattovich G, Boscaro S, Noventa F, et al. Influence of hepatitis delta virus infection on progression to cirrhosis in chronic hepatitis type B. J Infect Dis. 1987;155:931-935.

191. Realdi G, Fattovich G, Hadziyannis S, et al. Survival and prognostic factors in 366 patients with compensated cirrhosis type B: A multicenter study. The Investigators of the European Concerted Action on Viral Hepatitis (EUROHEP). J Hepatol. 1994;21:656-666.

192. Liaw YF, Lin DY, Chen TJ, Chu CM. Natural course after the development of cirrhosis in patients with chronic type B hepatitis: A prospective study. Liver. 1989;9:235-241.

193. de Jongh FE, Janssen HL, de Man RA, et al. Survival and prognostic indicators in hepatitis B surface antigen-positive cirrhosis of the liver. Gastroenterology. 1992;103:1630-1635.

194. Fattovich G. Progression of hepatitis B and C to hepatocellular carcinoma in Western countries. Hepatogastroenterology. 1998;45:1206-1213.

195. Yang HI, Lu SN, Liaw YF, et al. Hepatitis B e antigen and the risk of hepatocellular carcinoma. N Engl J Med. 2002;347:168-174.

196. Hassan MM, Hwang LY, Hatten CJ, et al. Risk factors for hepatocellular carcinoma: Synergism of alcohol with viral hepatitis and diabetes mellitus. Hepatology. 2002;36:1206-1213.

197. Farza H, Salmon AM, Hadchouel M, et al. Hepatitis B surface antigen gene expression is regulated by sex steroids and glucocorticoids in transgenic mice. Proc Natl Acad Sci USA. 1987;84:1187-1191.

198. Ponzetto A, Forzani B, Parravicini PP, et al. Epidemiology of hepatitis delta virus (HDV) infection. Eur J Epidemiol. 1985;1:257-263.

199. Jardi R, Buti M, Cotrina M, et al. Determination of hepatitis delta virus RNA by polymerase chain reaction in acute and chronic delta infection. Hepatology. 1995;21:25-29.

200. Beral V, Blum H, Ma B. Hepatitis D virus. IARC Monogr Eval Carcinog Risks Hum. 1994;59:223-253.

201. Tamura I, Kurimura O, Koda T, et al. Risk of liver cirrhosis and hepatocellular carcinoma in subjects with hepatitis B and delta virus infection: A study from Kure. Jpn J Gastroenterol Hepatology. 1993;8:433-436.

202. Lozano JL, Crespo J, de la Cruz F, et al. Correlation between hepatitis B viremia and the clinical and histological activity of chronic delta hepatitis. Med Microbiol Immunol (Berl). 1994;183:159-167.

203. Weltman MD, Brotodihardjo A, Crewe EB, et al. Coinfection with hepatitis B and C or B, C and delta viruses results in severe chronic liver disease and responds poorly to interferon-alpha treatment. J Viral Hepat. 1995;2:39-45.

204. Guillevin L, Lhote F, Cohen P, et al. Polyarteritis nodosa related to hepatitis B virus. A prospective study with long-term observation of 41 patients. Medicine (Baltimore). 1995;74:238-253.

205. Avsar E, Savas B, Tozun N, et al. Successful treatment of polyarteritis nodosa related to hepatitis B virus with interferon alpha as first-line therapy. J Hepatol. 1998;28:525-526.

206. Simsek H, Telatar H. Successful treatment of hepatitis B virus-associated polyarteritis nodosa by interferon alpha alone. J Clin Gastroenterol. 1995;20:263-265.

207. Boeck K, Mempel M, Schmidt T, Abeck D. Gianotti-Crosti syndrome: Clinical, serologic, and therapeutic data from nine children. Cutis. 1998;62:271-274; quiz 286.

208. De Gaspari G, Bardare M, Costantino D. AU antigen in Crosti-Gianotti acrodermatitis. Lancet. 1970;1:1116-1117.

209. Fergin P. Gianotti-Crosti syndrome. Non-parenterally acquired hepatitis B with a distinctive exanthem. Med J Aust. 1983;1:175-176.

210. Gilbert RD, Wiggelinkhuizen J. The clinical course of hepatitis B virus-associated nephropathy. Pediatr Nephrol. 1994;8:11-14.

211. Lhotta K. Beyond hepatorenal syndrome: Glomerulonephritis in patients with liver disease. Semin Nephrol. 2002;22:302-308.

212. Conjeevaram HS, Hoofnagle JH, Austin HA, et al. Long-term outcome of hepatitis B virus-related glomerulonephritis after therapy with interferon alfa. Gastroenterology. 1995;109:540-546.

213. Kellerman SE, Hanson DL, McNaghten AD, Fleming PL. Prevalence of chronic hepatitis B and incidence of acute hepatitis B infection in human immunodeficiency virus-infected subjects. J Infect Dis. 2003;188:571-577.

214. Sherman KE, Shire N, Rouster S, Rajicic N. Prevalence of occult hepatitis B infections in HIV patients: Analysis of a geographically distributed ACTG cohort. Presented at the 10th Conference on Retroviruses and Opportunistic Infections, Boston, 2003.

215. Gilson RJ, Hawkins AE, Beecham MR, et al. Interactions between HIV and hepatitis B virus in homosexual men: Effects on the natural history of infection. AIDS. 1997;11:597-606.

216. Colin JF, Cazals-Hatem D, Loriot MA, et al. Influence of human immunodeficiency virus infection on chronic hepatitis B in homosexual men. Hepatology. 1999;29:1306-1310.

217. Thio CL, Seaberg EC, Skolasky R Jr, et al. HIV-1, hepatitis B virus, and risk of liver-related mortality in the Multicenter Cohort Study (MACS). Lancet. 2002;360:1921-1926.

218. Altfeld M, Rockstroh JK, Addo M, et al. Reactivation of hepatitis B in a long-term anti-HBs-positive patient with AIDS following lamivudine withdrawal. J Hepatol. 1998;29:306-309.

219. Fang JW, Tung FY, Davis GL, et al. Fibrosing cholestatic hepatitis in a transplant recipient with hepatitis B virus precore mutant. Gastroenterology. 1993;105:901-904.

220. Terrault NA. Treatment of recurrent hepatitis B infection in liver transplant recipients. Liver Transpl. 2002;8:S74-S81.

221. Steinmuller T, Seehofer D, Rayes N, et al. Increasing applicability of liver transplantation for patients with hepatitis B-related liver disease. Hepatology. 2002;35:1528-1535.

222. Gane E, Pilmore H. Management of chronic viral hepatitis before and after renal transplantation. Transplantation. 2002;74:427-437.

223. Bird GL, Smith H, Portmann B, et al. Acute liver decompensation on withdrawal of cytotoxic chemotherapy and immunosuppressive therapy in hepatitis B carriers. Q J Med. 1989;73:895-902.

224. Locasciulli A, Alberti A, Bandini G, et al. Allogeneic bone marrow transplantation from HBsAg+ donors: A multicenter study from the Gruppo Italiano Trapianto di Midollo Osseo (GITMO). Blood. 1995;86:3236-3240.

225. Mertens T, Kock J, Hampl W, et al. Reactivated fulminant hepatitis B virus replication after bone marrow transplantation: Clinical course and possible treatment with ganciclovir. J Hepatol. 1996;25:968-971.

226. Ilan Y, Nagler A, Adler R, et al. Ablation of persistent hepatitis B by bone marrow transplantation from a hepatitis B-immune donor. Gastroenterology. 1993;104:1818-1821.

227. Lau GK, Suri D, Liang R, et al. Resolution of chronic hepatitis B and anti-HBs seroconversion in humans by adoptive transfer of immunity to hepatitis B core antigen. Gastroenterology. 2002;122:614-624.

228. Fong TL, Di Bisceglie AM, Waggoner JG, et al. The significance of antibody to hepatitis C virus in patients with chronic hepatitis B. Hepatology. 1991;14:64-67.

229. Shih CM, Lo SJ, Miyamura T, et al. Suppression of hepatitis B virus expression and replication by hepatitis C virus core protein in HuH-7 cells. J Virol. 1993;67:5823-5832.

230. Sagnelli E, Coppola N, Scolastico C, et al. Virologic and clinical expressions of reciprocal inhibitory effect of hepatitis B, C, and delta viruses in patients with chronic hepatitis. Hepatology. 2000;32:1106-1110.

231. Zarski JP, Bohn B, Bastie A, et al. Characteristics of patients with dual infection by hepatitis B and C viruses. J Hepatol. 1998;28:27-33.

232. Sun CA, Farzadegan H, You SL, et al. Mutual confounding and interactive effects between hepatitis C and hepatitis B viral infections in hepatocellular carcinogenesis: A population-based case-control study in Taiwan. Cancer Epidemiol Biomarkers Prev. 1996;5:173-178.

233. Zignego AL, Fontana R, Puliti S, et al. Impaired response to alpha interferon in patients with an inapparent hepatitis B and hepatitis C virus coinfection. Arch Virol. 1997;142:535-544.

234. Liu CJ, Chen PJ, Lai MY, et al. Ribavirin and interferon is effective for hepatitis C virus clearance in hepatitis B and C dually infected patients. Hepatology. 2003;37:568-576.

235. Bortolotti F. Chronic viral hepatitis in childhood. Baillieres Clin Gastroenterol. 1996;10:185-206.

236. Bonino F, Rosina F, Rizzetto M, et al. Chronic hepatitis in HBsAg carriers with serum HBV-DNA and anti-HBe. Gastroenterology. 1986;90:1268-1273.

237. Yuen MF, Sablon E, Hui CK, et al. Factors associated with hepatitis B virus DNA breakthrough in patients receiving prolonged lamivudine therapy. Hepatology. 2001;34:785-791.

238. Manns MP. Current state of interferon therapy in the treatment of chronic hepatitis B. Semin Liver Dis. 2002;22:7-13.

239. Perrillo RP, Lai CL, Liaw YF, et al. Predictors of HBeAg loss after lamivudine treatment for chronic hepatitis B. Hepatology. 2002;36:186-194.

240. Pawlotsky JM. Molecular diagnosis of viral hepatitis. Gastroenterology. 2002;122:1554-1568.

241. Lok AS, Heathcote EJ, Hoofnagle JH. Management of hepatitis B: 2000—Summary of a workshop. Gastroenterology. 2001;120:1828-1853.

242. Hadler SC, Murphy BL, Schable CA, et al. Epidemiological analysis of the significance of low-positive test results for antibody to hepatitis B surface and core antigens. J Clin Microbiol. 1984;19:521-525.

243. Lok AS, Lai CL, Wu PC. Prevalence of isolated antibody to hepatitis B core antigen in an area endemic for hepatitis B virus infection: Implications in hepatitis B vaccination programs. Hepatology. 1988;8:766-770.

244. Hoofnagle JH, Seefe LB, Bales ZB, Zimmerman HJ. Type B hepatitis after transfusion with blood containing antibody to hepatitis B core antigen. N Engl J Med. 1978;298:1379-1383.

245. Dickson RC, Everhart JE, Lake JR, et al. Transmission of hepatitis B by transplantation of livers from donors positive for antibody to hepatitis B core antigen. The National Institute of Diabetes and Digestive and Kidney Diseases Liver Transplantation Database. Gastroenterology. 1997;113:1668-1674.

246. Lok AS, McMahon BJ. Chronic hepatitis B. Hepatology. 2001;34:1225-1241.

247. Lampertico P, Del Ninno E, Vigano M, et al. Long-term suppression of hepatitis B e antigen-negative chronic hepatitis B by 24-month interferon therapy. Hepatology. 2003;37:756-763.

248. Cooksley WG, Piratvisuth T, Lee SD, et al. Peginterferon alpha-2a (40 kDa): An advance in the treatment of hepatitis B e antigen-positive chronic hepatitis B. J Viral Hepat. 2003;10:298-305.

249. Heathcote J. Treatment of HBe antigen–positive chronic hepatitis B. Semin Liver Dis. 2003;23:69-80.

250. Hadziyannis SJ, Papatheodoridis GV, Vassilopoulos D. Treatment of HBeAg-negative chronic hepatitis B. Semin Liver Dis. 2003;23:81-88.

251. Wong DK, Cheung AM, O'Rourke K, et al. Effect of alpha-interferon treatment in patients with hepatitis B e antigen–positive chronic hepatitis B. A meta-analysis. Ann Intern Med. 1993;119:312-323.

252. Cohard M, Poynard T, Mathurin P, Zarski JP. Prednisone-interferon combination in the treatment of chronic hepatitis B: Direct and indirect metanalysis. Hepatology. 1994;20:1390-1398.

253. Lok AS, Wu PC, Lai CL, et al. A controlled trial of interferon with or without prednisone priming for chronic hepatitis B. Gastroenterology. 1992;102:2091-2097.

254. Torre D, Tambini R. Interferon-alpha therapy for chronic hepatitis B in children: A meta-analysis. Clin Infect Dis. 1996;23:131-137.

255. Krogsgaard K. The long-term effect of treatment with interferon-alpha 2a in chronic hepatitis B. The Long-Term Follow-up Investigator Group. The European Study Group on Viral Hepatitis (EUROHEP). Executive Team on Anti-Viral Treatment. J Viral Hepat. 1998;5:389-397.

256. Lau DT, Khokhar MF, Doo E, et al. Long-term therapy of chronic hepatitis B with lamivudine. Hepatology. 2000;32:828-834.

257. Lok AS, Chung HT, Liu VW, Ma OC. Long-term follow-up of chronic hepatitis B patients treated with interferon alfa. Gastroenterology. 1993;105:1833-1838.

258. Fong TL, Di Bisceglie AM, Gerber MA, et al. Persistence of hepatitis B virus DNA in the liver after loss of HBsAg in chronic hepatitis B. Hepatology. 1993;18:1313-1318.

259. Fattovich G, Giustina G, Realdi G, et al. Long-term outcome of hepatitis B e antigen–positive patients with compensated cirrhosis treated with interferon alfa. European Concerted Action on Viral Hepatitis (EUROHEP). Hepatology. 1997;26:1338-1342.

260. Lau DT, Everhart J, Kleiner DE, et al. Long-term follow-up of patients with chronic hepatitis B treated with interferon alfa. Gastroenterology. 1997;113:1660-1667.

261. Lin SM, Sheen IS, Chien RN, et al. Long-term beneficial effect of interferon therapy in patients with chronic hepatitis B virus infection. Hepatology. 1999;29:971-975.

262. Niederau C, Heintges T, Lange S, et al. Long-term follow-up of HBeAg-positive patients treated with interferon alfa for chronic hepatitis B. N Engl J Med. 1996;334:1422-1427.

263. Tabor E. Interferon for preventing and treating hepatocellular carcinoma associated with the hepatitis B and C viruses. Dig Liver Dis. 2003;35:297-305.

264. Yuen MF, Hui CK, Cheng CC, et al. Long-term follow-up of interferon alfa treatment in Chinese patients with chronic hepatitis B infection: The effect on hepatitis B e antigen seroconversion and the development of cirrhosis-related complications. Hepatology. 2001;34:139-145.

265. Fattovich G, Farci P, Rugge M, et al. A randomized controlled trial of lymphoblastoid interferon-alpha in patients with chronic hepatitis B lacking HBeAg. Hepatology. 1992;15:584-589.

266. Lampertico P, Del Ninno E, Manzin A, et al. A randomized, controlled trial of a 24-month course of interferon alfa 2b in patients with chronic hepatitis B who had hepatitis B virus DNA without hepatitis B e antigen in serum. Hepatology. 1997;26:1621-1625.

267. Hadziyannis S, Bramou T, Makris A, et al. Interferon alfa-2b treatment of HBeAg negative/serum HBV DNA positive chronic active hepatitis type B. J Hepatol. 1990;11:S133-S136.

268. Papatheodoridis GV, Manesis E, Hadziyannis SJ. The long-term outcome of interferon-alpha treated and untreated patients with HBeAg-negative chronic hepatitis B. J Hepatol. 2001;34:306-313.

269. Hoofnagle JH, Di Bisceglie AM, Waggoner JG, Park Y. Interferon alfa for patients with clinically apparent cirrhosis due to chronic hepatitis B. Gastroenterology. 1993;104:1116-1121.

270. Perillo R, Schiff E, Davis G, et al. A randomized, controlled trial of interferon alfa-2b alone and after prednisone withdrawal for the treatment of chronic hepatitis B. N Engl J Med. 1990;323:295-301.

271. Deutsch M, Dourakis S, Manesis EK, et al. Thyroid abnormalities in chronic viral hepatitis and their relationship to interferon alfa therapy. Hepatology. 1997;26:206-210.

272. Dienstag JL, Schiff ER, Wright TL, et al. Lamivudine as initial treatment for chronic hepatitis B in the United States. N Engl J Med. 1999;341:1256-1263.

273. Lai C-L, Chien R-N, Leung NWY, et al. A one-year trial of lamivudine for chronic hepatitis B. N Engl J Med. 1998;339:61-68.

274. Leung NW, Lai CL, Chang TT, et al. Extended lamivudine treatment in patients with chronic hepatitis B enhances hepatitis B e antigen seroconversion rates: Results after 3 years of therapy. Hepatology. 2001;33:1527-1532.

275. Liaw YF, Leung NW, Chang TT, et al. Effects of extended lamivudine therapy in Asian patients with chronic hepatitis B. Asia Hepatitis Lamivudine Study Group. Gastroenterology. 2000;119:172-180.

276. Chien RN, Liaw YF, Atkins M. Pretherapy alanine transaminase level as a determinant for hepatitis B e antigen seroconversion during lamivudine therapy in patients with chronic hepatitis B. Asian Hepatitis Lamivudine Trial Group. Hepatology. 1999;30:770-774.

277. Hadziyannis SJ, Papatheodoridis GV, Dimou E, et al. Efficacy of long-term lamivudine monotherapy in patients with hepatitis B e antigen–negative chronic hepatitis B. Hepatology. 2000;32:847-851.

278. Tassopoulos NC, Volpes R, Pastore G, et al. Efficacy of lamivudine in patients with hepatitis B e antigen–negative/hepatitis B virus DNA-positive (precore mutant) chronic hepatitis B. Lamivudine Precore Mutant Study Group. Hepatology. 1999;29:889-896.

279. Schiff ER. Lamivudine for hepatitis B in clinical practice. J Med Virol. 2000;61:386-391.

280. Villeneuve JP, Condreay LD, Willems B, et al. Lamivudine treatment for decompensated cirrhosis resulting from chronic hepatitis B. Hepatology. 2000;31:207-210.

281. Yao FY, Bass NM. Lamivudine treatment in patients with severely decompensated cirrhosis due to replicating hepatitis B infection. J Hepatol. 2000;33:301-307.

282. Dienstag JL, Goldin RD, Heathcote EJ, et al. Histological outcome during long-term lamivudine therapy. Gastroenterology. 2003;124:105-117.

283. Ono-Nita SK, Kato N, Shiratori Y, et al. YMDD motif in hepatitis B virus DNA polymerase influences on replication and lamivudine resistance: A study by in vitro full-length viral DNA transfection. Hepatology. 1999;29:939-945.

284. Lee KM, Cho SW, Kim SW, et al. Effect of virological response on post-treatment durability of lamivudine-induced HBeAg seroconversion. J Viral Hepat. 2002;9:208-212.

285. Das K, Xiong X, Yang H, et al. Molecular modeling and biochemical characterization reveal the mechanism of hepatitis B virus polymerase resistance to lamivudine (3TC) and emtricitabine (FTC). J Virol. 2001;75:4771-4779.

286. Stuyver LJ, Locarnini SA, Lok A, et al. Nomenclature for antiviral-resistant human hepatitis B virus mutations in the polymerase region. Hepatology. 2001;33:751-757.

287. Ono SK, Kato N, Shiratori Y, et al. The polymerase L528M mutation cooperates with nucleotide binding-site mutations, increasing hepatitis B virus replication and drug resistance. J Clin Invest. 2001;107:449-455.

288. Bozdayi AM, Uzunalimoglu O, Turkyilmaz AR, et al. YSDD: A novel mutation in HBV DNA polymerase confers clinical resistance to lamivudine. J Viral Hepat. 2003;10:256-265.

289. Liaw YF. Acute exacerbation and superinfection in patients with chronic viral hepatitis. J Formos Med Assoc. 1995;94:521-528.

290. Lok AS, Hussain M, Cursano C, et al. Evolution of hepatitis B virus polymerase gene mutations in hepatitis B e antigen–negative patients receiving lamivudine therapy. Hepatology. 2000;32:1145-1153.

291. Perrillo R, Schiff E, Yoshida E, et al. Adefovir dipivoxil for the treatment of lamivudine-resistant hepatitis B mutants. Hepatology. 2000;32:129-134.

292. Marcellin P, Chang TT, Lim SG, et al. Adefovir dipivoxil for the treatment of hepatitis B e antigen–positive chronic hepatitis B. N Engl J Med. 2003;348:808-816.

293. Hadziyannis SJ, Tassopoulos NC, Heathcote EJ, et al. Adefovir dipivoxil for the treatment of hepatitis B e antigen–negative chronic hepatitis B. N Engl J Med. 2003;348:800-807.

294. Yang H, Westland CE, Delaney WE, et al. Resistance surveillance in chronic hepatitis B patients treated with adefovir dipivoxil for up to 60 weeks. Hepatology. 2002;36:464-473.

295. Angus P, Vaughan R, Xiong S, et al. Resistance to adefovir dipivoxil therapy associated with the selection of a novel mutation in the HBV polymerase. Gastroenterology. 2003;125:292-297.

296. Xiong X, Flores C, Yang H, et al. Mutations in hepatitis B DNA polymerase associated with resistance to lamivudine do not confer resistance to adefovir in vitro. Hepatology. 1998;28:1669-1673.

297. Barbaro G, Zechini F, Pellicelli AM, et al. Long-term efficacy of interferon alpha-2b and lamivudine in combination compared to lamivudine monotherapy in patients with chronic hepatitis B. An Italian multicenter, randomized trial. J Hepatol. 2001;35:406-411.

298. Schalm SW, Heathcote J, Cianciara J, et al. Lamivudine and alpha interferon combination treatment of patients with chronic hepatitis B infection: A randomised trial. Gut. 2000;46:562-568.

299. Tatulli I, Francavilla R, Rizzo GL, et al. Lamivudine and alpha-interferon in combination long term for precore mutant chronic hepatitis B. J Hepatol. 2001;35:805-810.

300. Nunez M, Perez-Olmeda M, Diaz B, et al. Activity of tenofovir on hepatitis B virus replication in HIV–co-infected patients failing or partially responding to lamivudine. AIDS. 2002;16:2352-2354.

301. Benhamou Y, Tubiana R, Thibault V. Tenofovir disoproxil fumarate in patients with HIV and lamivudine-resistant hepatitis B virus. N Engl J Med. 2003;348:177-178.

302. Lai CL, Rosmawati M, Lao J, et al. Entecavir is superior to lamivudine in reducing hepatitis B virus DNA in patients with chronic hepatitis B infection. Gastroenterology. 2002;123:1831-1838.

303. Gish RG, Leung NW, Wright TL, et al. Dose range study of pharmacokinetics, safety, and preliminary antiviral activity of emtricitabine in adults with hepatitis B virus infection. Antimicrob Agents Chemother. 2002;46:1734-1740.

304. Standring DN, Bridges EG, Placidi L, et al. Antiviral beta-L-nucleosides specific for hepatitis B virus infection. Antiviral Chem Chemother. 2001;12:119-129.

305. Levine S, Hernandez D, Yamanaka G, et al. Efficacies of entecavir against lamivudine-resistant hepatitis B virus replication and recombinant polymerases in vitro. Antimicrob Agents Chemother. 2002;46:2525-2532.

306. Ghany MG, Ayola B, Villamil FG, et al. Hepatitis B virus S mutants in liver transplant recipients who were reinfected despite hepatitis B immune globulin prophylaxis. Hepatology. 1998;27:213-222.

307. Naoumov NV, Lopes AR, Burra P, et al. Randomized trial of lamivudine versus hepatitis B immunoglobulin for long-term prophylaxis of hepatitis B recurrence after liver transplantation. J Hepatol. 2001;34:888-894.

308. Perrillo RP, Wright T, Rakela J, et al. A multicenter United States–Canadian trial to assess lamivudine monotherapy before and after liver transplantation for chronic hepatitis B. Hepatology. 2001;33:424-432.

309. Lok AS. Prevention of recurrent hepatitis B post-liver transplantation. Liver Transpl. 2002;8:S67-S73.

310. Fontana RJ, Hann HW, Wright T, et al. A multicenter study of lamivudine treatment in 33 patients with hepatitis B after liver transplantation. Liver Transpl. 2001;7:504-510.

311. Fontana RJ, Keeffe EB, Carey W, et al. Effect of lamivudine treatment on survival of 309 North American patients awaiting liver transplantation for chronic hepatitis B. Liver Transpl. 2002;8:433-439.

312. Al Faraidy K, Yoshida EM, Davis JE, et al. Alteration of the dismal natural history of fibrosing cholestatic hepatitis secondary to hepatitis B virus with the use of lamivudine. Transplantation. 1997;64:926-928.

313. Perrillo R, Rakela J, Dienstag J, et al. Multicenter study of lamivudine therapy for hepatitis B after liver transplantation. Lamivudine Transplant Group. Hepatology. 1999;29:1581-1586.

314. Ben-Ari Z, Mor E, Shapira Z, Tur-Kaspa R. Long-term experience with lamivudine therapy for hepatitis B virus infection after liver transplantation. Liver Transpl. 2001;7:113-117.

315. Malkan G, Cattral MS, Humar A, et al. Lamivudine for hepatitis B in liver transplantation: A single-center experience. Transplantation. 2000;69:1403-1407.

316. Locarnini S, McMillan J, Bartholomeusz A. The hepatitis B virus and common mutants. Semin Liver Dis. 2003;23:5-20.

317. Bock CT, Tillmann HL, Torresi J, et al. Selection of hepatitis B virus polymerase mutants with enhanced replication by lamivudine treatment after liver transplantation. Gastroenterology. 2002;122:264-273.

318. Seehofer D, Rayes N, Steinmuller T, et al. Occurrence and clinical outcome of lamivudine-resistant hepatitis B infection after liver transplantation. Liver Transpl. 2001;7:976-982.

319. Mutimer D, Feraz-Neto BH, Harrison R, et al. Acute liver graft failure due to emergence of lamivudine resistant hepatitis B virus: Rapid resolution during treatment with adefovir. Gut. 2001;49:860-863.

320. Wong DK, Yim C, Naylor CD, et al. Interferon alfa treatment of chronic hepatitis B: Randomized trial in a predominantly homosexual male population. Gastroenterology. 1995;108:165-171.

321. Delaugerre C, Marcelin AG, Thibault V, et al. Human immunodeficiency virus (HIV) type 1 reverse transcriptase resistance mutations in hepatitis B virus (HBV)-HIV-coinfected patients treated for HBV chronic infection once daily with 10 milligrams of adefovir dipivoxil combined with lamivudine. Antimicrob Agents Chemother. 2002;46:1586-1588.

322. Nelson M, Portsmouth S, Stebbing J, et al. An open-label study of tenofovir in HIV-1 and hepatitis B virus co-infected individuals. AIDS. 2003;17:F7-F10.

323. Lau DT, Doo E, Park Y, et al. Lamivudine for chronic delta hepatitis. Hepatology. 1999;30:546-549.

324. Villa E, Grottola A, Buttafoco P, et al. High doses of alpha-interferon are required in chronic hepatitis due to coinfection with hepatitis B virus and hepatitis C virus: Long term results of a prospective randomized trial. Am J Gastroenterol. 2001;96:2973-2977.

325. Farci P, Mandas A, Coiana A, et al. Treatment of chronic hepatitis D with interferon alfa-2a. N Engl J Med. 1994;330:88-94.

326. Prevention of hepatitis A through active or passive immunization: Recommendations of the Advisory Committee on Immunization Practices (ACIP). MMWR Recomm Rep. 1996;45:1-30.

327. Keeffe EB. Is hepatitis A more severe in patients with chronic hepatitis B and other chronic liver diseases? Am J Gastroenterol. 1995;90:201-205.

328. Vento S, Garofano T, Renzini C, et al. Fulminant hepatitis associated with hepatitis A virus superinfection in patients with chronic hepatitis C. N Engl J Med. 1998;338:286-290.

329. Corden S, Ballard AL, Ijaz S, et al. HBV DNA levels and transmission of hepatitis B by health care workers. J Clin Virol. 2003;27:52-58.

330. Transmission of hepatitis B to patients from four infected surgeons without hepatitis B e antigen. The Incident Investigation Teams and others. N Engl J Med. 1997;336:178-184.

331. Spijkerman IJ, van Doorn LJ, Janssen MH, et al. Transmission of hepatitis B virus from a surgeon to his patients during high-risk and low-risk surgical procedures during 4 years. Infect Control Hosp Epidemiol. 2002;23:306-312.

332. Leads from the MMWR. Update: Universal precautions for prevention of transmission of human immunodeficiency virus, hepatitis B virus, and other bloodborne pathogens in health-care settings. JAMA. 1988;260:462-465.

333. Management of healthcare workers infected with hepatitis B virus, hepatitis C virus, human immunodeficiency virus, or other bloodborne pathogens. AIDS/TB Committee of the Society for Healthcare Epidemiology of America. Infect Control Hosp Epidemiol. 1997;18:349-363.

334. Proceedings of the Consensus Conference on Infected Health Care Worker Risk for transmission of bloodborne pathogens. Can Commun Dis Rep. 1998;24:1-28.

335. Mele A, Ippolito G, Craxi A, et al. Risk management of HBsAg or anti-HCV positive healthcare workers in hospital. Dig Liver Dis. 2001;33:795-802.

336. Lemon SM, Thomas DL. Vaccines to prevent viral hepatitis. N Engl J Med. 1997;336:196-204.

337. Recommendation of the Immunization Practices Advisory Committee (ACIP) on post-exposure prophylaxis of hepatitis B. MMWR Morb Mortal Wkly Rep. 1984;33:285-290.

338. Dienstag JL, Silverstein MD, Mulley AG. The cost-effectiveness of hepatitis B vaccine. J Infect. 1983;7:81-84.

339. Alternate two dose hepatitis B vaccination schedule for adolescents aged 11 to 15 years. MMWR Morb Mortal Wkly Rep. 2000;49:261.

340. Lindsay KL, Herbert DA, Gitnick GL. Hepatitis B vaccine: Low postvaccination immunity in hospital personnel given gluteal injections. Hepatology. 1985;5:1088-1090.

341. Herroelen L, de Keyser J, Ebinger G. Central-nervous-system demyelination after immunisation with recombinant hepatitis B vaccine. Lancet. 1991;338:1174-1175.

342. Ascherio A, Zhang SM, Hernan MA, et al. Hepatitis B vaccination and the risk of multiple sclerosis. N Engl J Med. 2001;344:327-332.

343. DeStefano F, Verstraeten T, Jackson LA, et al. Vaccinations and risk of central nervous system demyelinating diseases in adults. Arch Neurol. 2003;60:504-509.

344. Stevens CE, Taylor PE, Tong MJ, et al. Yeast-recombinant hepatitis B vaccine. Efficacy with hepatitis B immune globulin in prevention of perinatal hepatitis B virus transmission. JAMA. 1987;257:2612-2616.

345. Stevens CE, Toy PT, Tong MJ, et al. Perinatal hepatitis B virus transmission in the United States. Prevention by passive-active immunization. JAMA. 1985;253:1740-1745.

346. Wong VC, Ip HM, Reesink HW, et al. Prevention of the HBsAg carrier state in newborn infants of mothers who are chronic carriers of HBsAg and HBeAg by administration of hepatitis-B vaccine and hepatitis-B immunoglobulin. Double-blind randomised placebo-controlled study. Lancet. 1984;1:921-926.

347. Beasley RP, Stevens CE, Shiao IS, Meng HC. Evidence against breast-feeding as a mechanism for vertical transmission of hepatitis B. Lancet. 1975;2:740-741.

348. Hadler SC, Francis DP, Maynard JE, et al. Long-term immunogenicity and efficacy of hepatitis B vaccine in homosexual men. N Engl J Med. 1986;315:209-214.

349. Propst T, Propst A, Lhotta K, et al. Reinforced intradermal hepatitis B vaccination in hemodialysis patients is superior in antibody response to intramuscular or subcutaneous vaccination. Am J Kidney Dis. 1998;32:1041-1045.

350. Wong EK, Bodsworth NJ, Slade MA, et al. Response to hepatitis B vaccination in a primary care setting: Influence of HIV infection, CD4+ lymphocyte count and vaccination schedule. Int J STD AIDS. 1996;7:490-494.

351. Collier AC, Corey L, Murphy VL, Handsfield HH. Antibody to human immunodeficiency virus (HIV) and suboptimal response to hepatitis B vaccination. Ann Intern Med. 1988;109:101-105.

352. Waite NM, Thomson LG, Goldstein MB. Successful vaccination with intradermal hepatitis B vaccine in hemodialysis patients previously nonresponsive to intramuscular hepatitis B vaccine. J Am Soc Nephrol. 1995;5:1930-1934.

353. Valdez H, Mitsuyasu R, Landay A, et al. Interleukin-2 Increases CD4+ lymphocyte numbers but does not enhance responses to immunization: Results of A5046s. J Infect Dis. 2003;187:320-325.

354. Alper CA, Kruskall MS, Marcus-Bagley D, et al. Genetic prediction of nonresponse to hepatitis B vaccine. N Engl J Med. 1989;321:708-712.

355. Zuckerman JN. Hepatitis B third-generation vaccines: Improved response and conventional vaccine non-response—Third generation pre-S/S vaccines overcome non-response. J Viral Hepat. 1998;5:13-15.

356. Thoelen S, Van Damme P, Mathei C, et al. Safety and immunogenicity of a hepatitis B vaccine formulated with a novel adjuvant system. Vaccine. 1998;16:708-714.

357. Traquina P, Morandi M, Contorni M, Van Nest G. MF59 adjuvant enhances the antibody response to recombinant hepatitis B surface antigen vaccine in primates. J Infect Dis. 1996;174:1168-1175.

358. Richter LJ, Thanavala Y, Arntzen CJ, Mason HS. Production of hepatitis B surface antigen in transgenic plants for oral immunization. Nat Biotechnol. 2000;18:1167-1171.

359. Thanavala Y, Yang YF, Lyons P, et al. Immunogenicity of transgenic plant-derived hepatitis B surface antigen. Proc Natl Acad Sci USA. 1995;92:3358-3361.

360. Davis HL, Michel ML, Mancini M, et al. Direct gene transfer in skeletal muscle: Plasmid DNA-based immunization against the hepatitis B virus surface antigen. Vaccine. 1994;12:1503-1509.

361. Swain WE, Heydenburg Fuller D, Wu MS, et al. Tolerability and immune responses in humans to a PowderJect DNA vaccine for hepatitis B. Dev Biol (Basel). 2000;104:115-119.

362. Ding L, Zhang M, Wang Y, et al. A 9-year follow-up study of the immunogenicity and long-term efficacy of plasma-derived hepatitis B vaccine in high-risk Chinese neonates. Clin Infect Dis. 1993;17:475-479.

363. Da Villa G, Peluso F, Picciotto L, et al. Persistence of anti-HBs in children vaccinated against viral hepatitis B in the first year of life: Follow-up at 5 and 10 years. Vaccine. 1996;14:1503-1505.

364. Wu JS, Hwang LY, Goodman KJ, Beasley RP. Hepatitis B vaccination in high-risk infants: 10-year follow-up. J Infect Dis. 1999;179:1319-1325.

365. Williams IT, Goldstein ST, Tufa J, et al. Long term antibody response to hepatitis B vaccination beginning at birth and to subsequent booster vaccination. Pediatr Infect Dis J. 2003;22:157-163.

366. Saab S, Weston SR, Ly D, et al. Comparison of the cost and effectiveness of two strategies for maintaining hepatitis B immunity in hemodialysis patients. Vaccine. 2002;20:3230-3235.

367. Carman WF, Zanetti AR, Karayiannis P, et al. Vaccine-induced escape mutant of hepatitis B virus. Lancet. 1990;336:325-329.

368. Carman WF, Trautwein C, van Deursen FJ, et al. Hepatitis B virus envelope variation after transplantation with and without hepatitis B immune globulin prophylaxis. Hepatology. 1996;24:489-493

369. Hsu HY, Chang MH, Liaw SH, et al. Changes of hepatitis B surface antigen variants in carrier children before and after universal vaccination in Taiwan. Hepatology. 1999;30:1312-1317.

370. He C, Nomura F, Itoga S, et al. Prevalence of vaccine-induced escape mutants of hepatitis B virus in the adult population in China: A prospective study in 176 restaurant employees. J Gastroenterol Hepatol. 2001;16:1373-1377.

371. Ogata N, Cote PJ, Zanetti AR, et al. Licensed recombinant hepatitis B vaccines protect chimpanzees against infection with the prototype surface gene mutant of hepatitis B virus. Hepatology. 1999;30:779-78

Parvovirus B19

KEVIN E. BROWN

Parvovirus B19, the only known human pathogenic parvovirus, was discovered in 1974 during evaluations of assays for hepatitis B surface antigen using panels of serum samples.[1] Sample 19 in panel B (hence B19) gave an anomalous result, a "false positive" in the relatively insensitive counterimmunoelectrophoresis assay, and when the precipitin line was excised, electron microscopy showed the presence of 23-nm particles resembling parvovirus. Although originally labeled serum parvovirus-like particle or human parvovirus, in 1985 the virus was officially recognized as a member of the Parvoviridae, and the International Committee on Taxonomy of Viruses recommended the name B19 to prevent confusion with other viruses.

An association of B19 with significant clinical disease was not made until 1981, but it is now known that B19 infection has a wide variety of disease manifestations dependent on the immunologic and hematologic status of the host (Table 143-1). In normal immunocompetent children B19 is the cause of erythema infectiosum (EI), also called fifth disease or "slapped cheek" disease, which is an innocuous rash illness. Occasionally, especially in women, fifth disease leads to an acute symmetrical polyarthropathy, which can mimic rheumatoid arthritis. In persons with underlying hemolytic disorders or increased erythropoiesis, or both, infection leads to a temporary failure of red blood cell production and transient aplastic crisis (TAC). In the immunocompromised host, persistent B19 viremia manifests as pure red cell aplasia (PRCA) and chronic anemia, and in the fetus, in which the immune response is immature, infection may lead to fetal death in utero, hydrops fetalis, or rarely the development of congenital anemia.

THE VIRUS

Parvum is Latin for small, and Parvoviridae are among the smallest known DNA-containing viruses that infect mammalian cells. The virions are nonenveloped particles about 22 nm in diameter with icosahedral symmetry. The Parvoviridae are divided into two subfamilies, Parvovirinae and Densovirinae, on the basis of their ability to infect vertebrate or invertebrate cells, respectively. The Parvovirinae are further subdivided into three genera on the basis of their transcription maps and the ability to replicate either autonomously (genus *Parvovirus*), with helper virus (genus *Dependovirus*), or in erythroid progenitor cells (genus *Erythrovirus*). Parvovirus B19 replication occurs only in human erythrocyte precursors, and B19 is therefore classified as a member of the *Erythrovirus* genus, of which it is the type species.[2]

TABLE 143-1 Disease Manifestations and Persistence of Parvovirus B19 Infection in Different Host Populations

Disease	Acute or Chronic	Host
Fifth disease	Acute	Normal children
Polyarthropathy syndrome	Acute or chronic	Normal adults
Transient aplastic crisis	Acute	Patients with increased erythropoiesis
Hydrops fetalis or congenital anemia	Acute or chronic	Fetus (<20 wk)
Persistent anemia	Chronic	Immunodeficient or immunocompromised patients

By electron microscopy, B19 particles have the typical parvovirus morphology (Fig. 143-1). Mature infectious particles have a molecular weight of 5.6×10^6 and a buoyant density in cesium chloride gradients of 1.41 g/mL. As a consequence of the lack of envelope and limited DNA content, B19 is resistant to physical inactivation. Although the virus can be inactivated by heat in low concentrations of protein,[3] the virus resists inactivation at 56° C for more than 60 minutes, and at high viral concentrations, it resists 80° C for 72 hours in clotting factor concentrates.[4] B19 is stable in lipid solvents such as ether and chloroform but can be inactivated by formalin, β-propiolactone, oxidizing agents, and γ-irradiation.

The B19 genome size is limited, consisting of a single strand of DNA of approximately 5600 nucleotides, with identical inverted, 365-nucleotide-long terminal repeat sequences at each end. The transcription map of B19 distinguishes it from other Parvovirinae. There is a single strong promoter at the far left side of the genome and unusual polyadenylation signals in the middle of the genome.[5] The three major viral proteins, one nonstructural protein and two capsid proteins, are produced by alternative splicing from the promoter and its accompanying leader sequence. The relative quantities of the major and minor capsid proteins are in part regulated by the presence of multiple upstream AUG codons situated before the authentic transcription initiation codon.[6] In addition, there are transcripts for several smaller peptides of 7.5 and 11 kD of unknown function.

The only unspliced transcript encodes the nonstructural protein, a 78-kD phosphoprotein.[7] Consistent with its role in viral propagation, the protein has DNA-binding properties and adenosine and guanosine triphosphatase activity.[8] Expression of the nonstructural protein causes host cell death through induction of apoptosis.[9]

The B19 virion is an icosahedron consisting of 60 copies of the capsid proteins. Most of the capsid is VP2, a 58-kD protein, with 5% or less of the larger 84-kD, VP1 protein. VP1 protein differs from VP2 by an additional 227 amino acids at the amino terminus. Using genetic engineering techniques, the capsid proteins can be expressed in a variety of both mammalian[10,11] and insect[12,13] cell lines. Capsid proteins self-assemble in the absence of B19 DNA, and in these systems protein expression leads to formation of recombinant empty capsids; VP1 is not required for capsid formation.

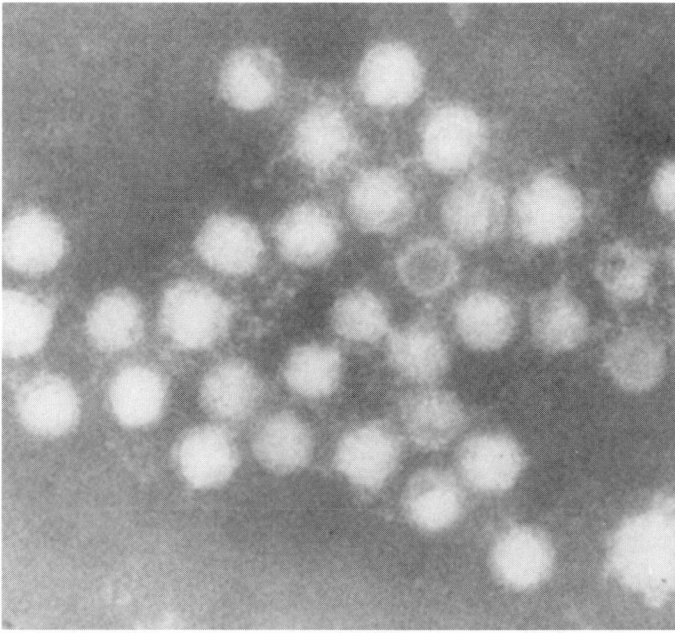

FIGURE 143-1. Electron micrograph of parvovirus B19 particles showing icosahedral symmetry. (*Electron micrograph courtesy of Dr. Anne Field.*)

The atomic structure of B19 VP2 empty capsids has been resolved to 0.8 nm,[14] and the virus has also been visualized by cryoelectron microscopy.[15] The virion surface has a major depression encompassing the fivefold axis, similar to the canyon structure found in RNA-containing icosahedral viruses. In B19 capsids, there is also a hollow cylindrical structure around the fivefold axes that appears to penetrate to the inside of the virion. The structural distribution of VP1 in the B19 capsid structure cannot be inferred from the crystallographic structures, but on the basis of antibody-binding studies, the VP1 unique region might extend through the fivefold axis cylinder of native capsids to the outside of the virion.[16] It has been shown that the VP1 unique region of all parvoviruses, including B19, has a phospholipase A$_2$ motif.[17] Infection studies with other parvoviruses show that this motif is required for viral infectivity,[17,18] but these studies have not been performed for B19.

No antigenic variation in B19 has been demonstrated. Small changes of nucleotide sequence have been detected by several investigators using restriction enzyme analysis or direct sequence analysis. Although isolates could be divided into groups (genome types) with particular enzyme digestion patterns, there is no correlation to specific disease presentation. Sequence divergence is generally less than 2%, with evidence for less variation in regions where antigenic epitopes are coded.[19]

Two groups of variants of B19 have been described with 10% variability at the DNA level from the majority of published B19 sequences and each other.[20-22] These sequences have been found in blood, bone marrow, skin,[23] and liver tissue.[24] However, the true prevalence of these viruses is currently unknown, with no variant B19 sequences detected in plasma pools from more than 120,000 Danish blood donors.[25] In addition, despite the differences in the DNA sequences, the capsid protein sequence is conserved, and V9 capsids show serologic cross-reactivity with B19 capsids.[26]

PATHOGENESIS

Parvovirus B19, like the other autonomous parvoviruses, is dependent on mitotically active cells for replication. However, B19 has a very narrow target cell range and can be propagated only in human (or primate) erythroid progenitor cells. The virus cannot be easily cultivated in the laboratory. Humans are the only known host of parvovirus B19; all primates tested are resistant to B19 infection, although primates have their own related erythroviruses.[27]

In human erythroid cells derived from bone marrow, susceptibility to parvovirus B19 increases with differentiation; the pluripotent stem cell appears to be spared, and the main target cells are erythroid progenitors (cells capable of giving rise to erythroid colonies in vitro) and erythroblasts.[28] Infection with parvovirus B19 is cytotoxic[29] because of

expression of the nonstructural protein in infected cells.[29] Infected cultures are characterized by the presence of giant pronormoblasts, 25 to 32 μm in diameter, with cytoplasmic vacuolization, immature chromatin, and large eosinophilic nuclear inclusion bodies (Fig. 143-2). By electron microscopy, virus particles are seen in the nucleus and cytoplasmic membrane lining, and infected cells show marginated chromatin, pseudopod formation, and cytoplasmic vacuolation,[30] all of which are typical of cells undergoing apoptosis.

Erythroid specificity of parvovirus B19 is due to the tissue distribution of the virus' cellular receptor globoside, also known as blood group P antigen.[31] P antigen is found on erythroid progenitors, erythroblasts, and megakaryocytes. It is also present on endothelial cells, which may be targets of viral infection involved in the pathogenesis of transplacental transmission, possibly vasculitis, and the rash of fifth disease and on fetal myocardial cells.[32] Rare individuals who genetically lack P antigen on erythrocytes are resistant to B19 infection, and their bone marrow cannot be infected with B19 in vitro.[33] However, erythroid specificity may also be modulated by specific erythroid cell transcription factors.[34]

Studies in healthy volunteers showed that B19 infection led to an acute but self-limited (4 to 8 days) cessation of red cell production and a corresponding decline in hemoglobin level.[35] In patients with normal erythroid turnover, this short interruption of red cell production does not lead to anemia, but in patients with high red cell turnover related to hemolysis, blood loss, or other causes, the temporary failure of erythropoiesis can precipitate an aplastic crisis. The anemia improves as

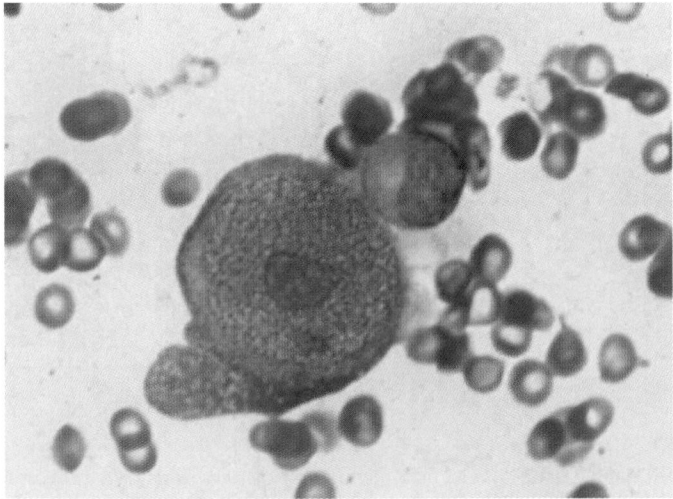

FIGURE 143-2. Giant pronormoblast in patient with B19 infection.

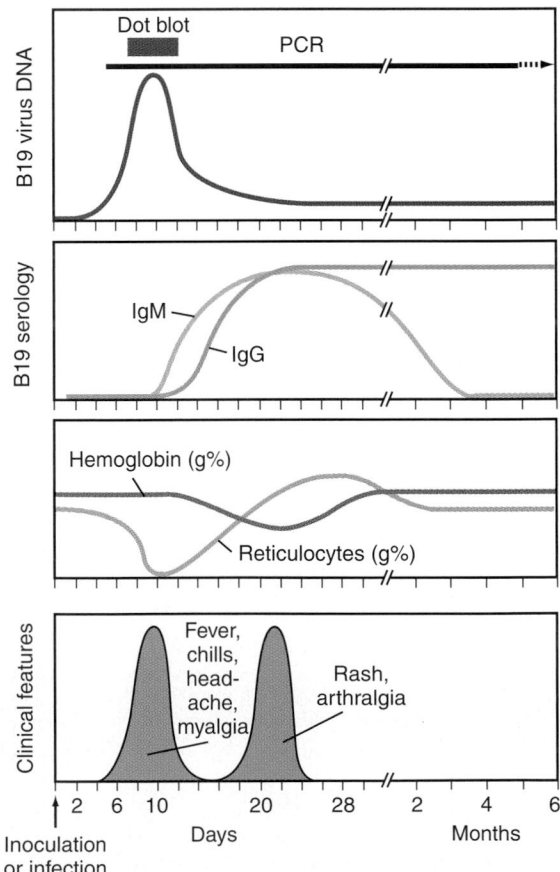

FIGURE 143-3. Virologic, immunologic, and clinical courses after acute B19 infection in a healthy individual. IgG, immunoglobulin G; PCR, polymerase chain reaction. (Data from Anderson MJ, Higgins PG, Davis LR, et al. Experimental parvoviral infection in humans. J Infect Dis. 1985;152:257-265; and Patou G, Pillay D, Myint S, Pattison J. Characterization of a nested polymerase chain reaction assay for detection of parvovirus B19. J Clin Microbiol. 1993;31:540-546.)

the immune response develops. In patients who are immunocompromised, infection may persist and produce chronic PRCA.

The infected fetus may suffer severe effects because red blood cell turnover is high and the immune response deficient. During the second trimester there is a great increase in red cell mass. Parvovirus particles can be detected by electron microscopy within the hematopoietic tissues of the liver and thymus.[36] B19 DNA and capsid antigen have been detected in the myocardium of infected fetuses,[37] and there is evidence that the fetus may develop myocarditis,[38,39] compounding the severe anemia and secondary cardiac failure. By the third trimester, a more effective fetal immune response to the virus probably accounts for the decrease in fetal loss at this stage of pregnancy.

The pathogenesis of the rash in EI and polyarthropathy is almost certainly immune complex mediated (Fig. 143-3). In volunteer studies, these appeared when high-titer viremia was no longer detectable and coincident with a detectable immune response.[35] Similar findings have been reported in chronically infected individuals who received immunoglobulin therapy.[40] However, in vitro studies have shown that the B19 nonstructural protein, as well as inducing apoptosis in host cells, also induces activation of interleukin-6,[41] which could contribute in vivo to the B19-induced arthropathy or autoimmune antibody production or both.

EPIDEMIOLOGY

Prevalence and Incidence

Parvovirus B19 infection is common in childhood, and by age 15 years approximately 50% of children have detectable immunoglobulin G (IgG). Infection also occurs in adult life, and more than 90% of elderly people have detectable antibody.[42] Women of childbearing age in the United States have an annual seroconversion rate of 1.5%.[43] Studies in different countries (United States, France, Germany, Japan) show similar patterns, with a slightly higher prevalence in children from countries such as Africa and Brazil. Some isolated tribal populations have a much lower prevalence: 2% on Rodriguez Island, Africa[44] and 4% to 10% among the tribes around Belem, Brazil.[45]

Although antibody is prevalent in the general population, high-titer viremia ($>10^6$ genome copies/mL) is rare. Among blood donors, approximately 1 per 20,000 to 1 per 40,000 units of blood during epidemic seasons contains high titers of B19.[46] Screening of pooled samples from blood donors showed that 1 per 3000 units contained detectable B19 DNA by the more sensitive polymerase chain reaction (PCR) technique.[47] In one study in an outbreak setting, more than 1 in 150 samples had B19 DNA detected by PCR.[48]

Mechanism and Routes of Transmission

Parvovirus B19 infections in temperate climates are more common in the late winter, spring, and early summer months.[49] Rates of infection may also increase every 3 to 4 years, as reflected by corresponding increases in the major clinical manifestations of B19 infection, transient aplastic crises and EI.[50]

B19 DNA has been found in the respiratory secretions of patients at the time of viremia,[51] suggesting that infection is generally spread by a respiratory route of transmission. The virus can be readily transmitted by close contact, and the secondary attack rate has been calculated in various settings; in one study, the rate of secondary attack from symptomatic TAC or EI patients to susceptible (IgG-negative) household contacts was approximately 50%.[51] For school outbreaks, serologic studies are generally not available, but 10% to 60% of students may develop a rash disease consistent with B19 infection.[52,53] The highest secondary attack rates and annual seroconversion rates, even in the absence of known community outbreaks, are for workers in close contact with affected children, such as daycare providers and school personnel.[54] Nosocomial transmission in hospital situations has been described[55] but is probably infrequent, especially from patients with chronic infection. Nevertheless, patients with TAC or persistent disease should be considered infectious and appropriate precautions taken to limit interaction with other patients and susceptible staff.

The virus can be found in serum, and infection can be transmitted by blood and blood products[56] including albumin and plasma.[57,58] As described previously, parvoviruses, including B19, are very heat resistant, and they can withstand the usual thermal treatment aimed at infectious agents in blood products. In addition, solvent-detergent methods, which inactivate only lipid-enveloped viruses, are ineffective. B19 infection has been transmitted by steam-treated, dry-heated, and solvent-detergent–treated factors, although hemophiliacs who received heat-treated factor VIII alone had a lower prevalence of B19 antibody and lower rates of seroconversion than those receiving non–heat-treated factor.[59]

CLINICAL MANIFESTATIONS

Erythema Infectiosum

Manifestations of parvovirus B19 infection vary, even in the normal host, from asymptomatic or subclinical infection (most people with B19 specific antibody have no recollection of any specific symptoms) to a biphasic illness with symptoms during the viremic and immune complex–mediated stages of the disease, but EI is the major manifestation. EI was well characterized clinically before the discovery of B19.[60] This exanthematous rash illness of childhood was probably first described by Robert Willan in 1799 and illustrated in his 1808 textbook. The disease was rediscovered in Germany, where in 1899 Sticker gave it the name erythema infectiosum, and 6 years later Cheinisse classified it as the "fifth rash disease" of the six classic exanthems of childhood.[61] Often the epidemiologic data suggested "a common-source exposure to a highly effective transmitter," and an atypical rubella virus or echovirus was thought to be responsible. However, neither virus could be reproducibly isolated from patients with fifth disease. In 1983, after an outbreak of EI in London, all 31 affected children or adolescents had anti-B19–specific IgM[62]; similar results were obtained in other epidemics of fifth disease, and parvovirus B19 is now recognized as the etiologic agent.

Clinical symptoms begin with a nonspecific prodromal illness, which often goes unrecognized; there may be symptoms of fever, coryza, headache, and mild gastrointestinal distress, including nausea and diarrhea. Two to 5 days later, the classic slapped-cheek rash appears, a fiery red eruption on the cheek, accompanied by relative circumoral pallor (Fig. 143-4). There may be a second-stage rash within a few days, an erythematous maculopapular exanthem on the trunk and limbs; as this eruption fades, it produces a typical lacy appearance. There is great variation in the dermatologic symptoms: the classic slapped cheek is much more common in children than adults; the second-stage eruption may vary from a very faint, barely perceptible

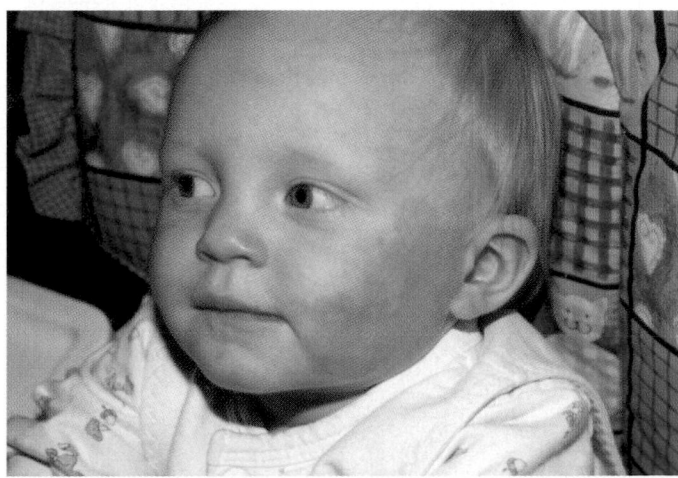

FIGURE 143-4. Slapped-cheek appearance of a child with fifth disease.

erythema to a florid exanthem; and the rash may be transient or recurrent for weeks. Rarely, other dermatologic presentations are seen: vesicopustular rash,[63] papular-purpuric glove and sock syndrome,[64] other purpuric rashes with or without Koplik spots,[65,66] and erythema multiforme.[67] Pruritus, especially on the soles of the feet, can be the dominant symptom.[68]

Arthropathy

Although B19 infection in children is usually mild and of short duration, a large proportion of adults, especially women, suffer arthralgia or frank arthritis, with painful joints often accompanied by swelling and stiffness.[53] The arthralgia is usually symmetrical, with mainly the small joints of hands and feet involved, and generally lasts for 1 to 3 weeks, although it may persist or recur for months or even years. In the absence of a history of rash, the symptoms may be mistaken for those of acute rheumatoid arthritis, especially because prolonged symptoms do not correlate with serologic studies, such as the duration of B19 IgM response, or persistent viremia. In addition, B19 infection can be associated with transient rheumatoid factor production.[69] In one large study of patients attending an "early synovitis" clinic in England, 12% had evidence of recent infection with B19.[70] Three patients would have fulfilled the American Rheumatism Association's diagnostic criteria for definite rheumatoid arthritis. B19 infection should be considered as part of the differential diagnosis in any patient presenting with acute arthritis.

It has been postulated that B19 is involved in the initiation and perpetuation of rheumatoid arthritis leading to joint lesions,[71] but these results have not been reproducible by other groups. In contrast, parvoviral B19 DNA is frequently found in synovial tissue of patients with rheumatoid arthritis, chronic arthropathy, and control subjects. In one carefully performed controlled study, although B19 DNA was indeed detected in synovial tissue of 28% of individuals with chronic arthritis, it was also found in 48% of nonarthropathy controls,[72] indicating that PCR-detectable DNA may persist in synovial tissues for months or years. In addition, in one study with long-term follow-up, none of the 54 patients with B19-associated arthralgia reported persistence of joint swelling or restricted motion, and no evidence of inflammatory joint disease was found.[73] Therefore, it seems unlikely that B19 plays a role in classic erosive rheumatoid arthritis, but understanding the pathogenesis of B19 arthropathy may provide insight into the mechanisms by which rheumatoid arthritis develops.

Transient Aplastic Crisis

TAC, the abrupt cessation of erythropoiesis characterized by reticulocytopenia, absent erythroid precursors in the bone marrow, and precipitous worsening of anemia, was the first clinical illness associated with B19 infection. When stored sera from children admitted to a London hospital were examined for B19 virus, samples from six Jamaican immigrants with sickle cell disease presenting with aplastic crisis showed evidence of recent infection with B19 (either antigenemia or seroconversion).[74] Retrospective studies of sera from Jamaican patients with sickle cell disease showed that 86% of transient aplastic crises were associated with recent parvovirus infection.[75]

TAC caused by B19 has now been described in a wide range of patients with underlying hemolytic disorders, including hereditary spherocytosis, thalassemia, red cell enzymopathies such as pyruvate kinase deficiency, and autoimmune hemolytic anemia.[76] TAC can also occur under conditions of erythroid "stress," such as hemorrhage, iron deficiency anemia, and kidney or bone marrow transplantation. Acute anemia has been described in hematologically normal persons,[77] and a drop in red cell count (within the normal range) and reticulocytes was seen in healthy volunteers.[35]

Although suffering from an ultimately self-limiting disease, patients with aplastic crisis can be severely ill. Symptoms may include dyspnea, lassitude, and even confusion related to the worsening anemia. Congestive heart failure and severe bone marrow necrosis may develop,[78] and the illness has been fatal.[50] Aplastic crisis can be the

first presentation of an underlying hemolytic disease in a well-compensated patient.

Community-acquired aplastic crisis is almost always due to parvovirus B19,[79] and B19 infection should be the presumptive diagnosis in any patient with anemia related to abrupt cessation of erythropoiesis as documented by reduced reticulocytes and bone marrow appearance. In contrast to patients with EI, patients with TAC are often viremic at the time of presentation, with concentrations of virus as high as 10^{14} genome copies/mL; thus, the diagnosis is readily made by detection of B19 DNA in the serum. As B19 DNA levels fall in serum, B19-specific IgM becomes detectable. TAC is easily treated by blood transfusion. After acute infection, immunity is lifelong.

TAC and B19 infection in hematologically normal patients are often associated with changes in other blood lineages, varying degrees of neutropenia,[80] and thrombocytopenia.[81] Some cases of idiopathic thrombocytopenic purpura[82] and Henoch-Schönlein purpura[83] have been reported to follow parvovirus B19 infection. Transient pancytopenia after parvovirus infection is rare.[84] Although some cases of chronic neutropenia of childhood have also been ascribed to parvovirus B19 infection,[85] other studies have not confirmed an association.[86] A case of recurrent agranulocytosis ascribed to persistent parvovirus B19 has also been published.[87]

Parvovirus B19 does not appear to be the cause of true (chronic) aplastic anemia[88] or transient erythroblastopenia of childhood (TEC),[89] the temporary failure of red cell production in normal children. Sporadic cases of TEC with thrombocytopenia with evidence of recent B19 infection have been described, whereas "classic" TEC is associated with *high* platelet counts.

Pure Red Cell Aplasia

Persistent B19 infection that results in PRCA has been reported in a wide variety of immunosuppressed patients, including patients with congenital immunodeficiency, acquired immunodeficiency syndrome (AIDS), and lymphoproliferative disorders and transplant recipients.[90] The stereotypical presentation is with persistent anemia rather than immune-mediated symptoms of rash or arthropathy. Patients have absent or low levels of B19-specific antibody and persistent or recurrent parvoviremia as detected by B19 DNA in the serum. Bone marrow examination generally reveals the presence of scattered giant pronormoblasts. Administration of immunoglobulin can be beneficial and ameliorative, if not curative.[91]

The prevalence of B19-induced anemia in human immunodeficiency virus (HIV)–seropositive patients is probably higher than that recognized. In one early study of 50 patients with AIDS, no patients with B19 viremia were identified. In a larger cohort study, B19 DNA was found in only 1 of 191 (0.5%) HIV-seropositive homosexuals. However, B19 DNA was found in 5 of 30 (17%) transfusion-dependent HIV-seropositive homosexuals, and when a hematocrit of less than 20 was used as a criterion, 4 of 13 (31%) were positive.[92] In contrast to the earlier studies, the marrow morphology need not be suggestive of PRCA, and giant pronormoblasts may not be present.

In less severely immunosuppressed patients (e.g., patients with systemic lupus erythematosus receiving steroid therapy), prolonged anemia after B19 infection has also been described.[93] However, in these patients there was a spontaneous, albeit delayed, development of antibodies, and viremia resolved without therapy. Presumably such patients represent one end of the spectrum of disease manifestations of B19 in patients with a compromised immune system.

Virus-Associated Hemophagocytic Syndrome

Virus-associated hemophagocytic syndrome (VAHS) is characterized by histiocytic hyperplasia, marked hemophagocytosis, and cytopenia in association with a systemic viral illness.[94] In contrast to malignant histiocytosis, VAHS is usually a benign, self-limiting illness in which histiocytic proliferation is reversible. Hemophagocytosis is not uncommon and occurs in the setting of a wide range of infections, not only viral but also bacterial, rickettsial, fungal, and parasitic.[95] However, in many patients there is underlying immunosuppression, usually iatrogenic, so that the role of the incriminated pathogen as an etiologic agent or coincidental opportunistic infection remains unclear.

Parvovirus B19 infection has been detected in 15 cases of hemophagocytosis syndrome among children and adults.[96] The majority of patients were previously healthy, but four patients were immunosuppressed by drug therapies. In all but one case there was a favorable outcome (one immunosuppressed patient died of fulminant aspergillosis). Further studies are required to determine whether parvovirus B19 is a major cause of VAHS as well as the rate of VAHS in otherwise uncomplicated parvovirus B19 infection.

Fetal Infection (Hydrops Fetalis and Miscarriage)

Parvovirus B19 probably causes 10% to 15% of all cases of nonimmune hydrops fetalis. Nonimmune hydrops fetalis is rare (1 per 3000 births), and in approximately 50% of cases the etiology is unknown.[97] In a study of 50 cases, the majority were due to cardiovascular or chromosomal abnormalities, but parvovirus B19 DNA was detected by in situ hybridization in the lungs of four fetuses.[98] When pathologic studies have been undertaken, B19-infected fetuses showed evidence of leukoerythroblastic reaction in the liver and large pale cells with eosinophilic inclusion bodies and peripheral condensation or margination of the nuclear chromatin. Parvovirus B19 DNA could be detected by DNA dot-blot or in situ hybridization and viral particles by electron microscopy.

Nevertheless, an adverse fetal outcome is not typical after maternal B19 infection. In a prospective British study of more than 400 women with serologically confirmed B19 during pregnancy, the excess rate of fetal loss was confined to the first 20 weeks of pregnancy and averaged only 9%.[99] No abnormalities were found at birth in the surviving infants, even when there was evidence of intrauterine infection by the presence of B19 IgM in the umbilical cord blood, and there were no long-term sequelae in the 129 children observed for more than 7 years.

No systematic studies have shown evidence for congenital abnormalities after B19 infection,[99,100] although there are case reports of congenital ocular[101] and neurologic abnormalities[102] and congenital anemia after a history of maternal B19 exposure.[103] In the congenital anemia cases, the virus load was low and localized; B19 DNA could be detected in bone marrow samples by PCR but not in concurrent serum samples. All three cases were treated with immunoglobulin therapy, and although there was a fatal outcome in one patient, in the other two cases B19 DNA could no longer be detected in bone marrow (by PCR) but the children remained severely anemic. B19 infection may mimic Diamond-Blackfan anemia,[104] and the role of in utero B19 infection inducing constitutional bone marrow failure such as that in Diamond-Blackfan anemia is still under investigation.

Other Disease Manifestations

B19 infection has been associated with a range of other disease manifestations including neurologic disease, myocarditis, kidney disease, hepatitis, and vasculitis. However, most of these are case reports or limited PCR-based studies with poorly documented controls. Determining the role of B19 in these diseases is often difficult; the diseases are rare, and B19 may not be the only cause. In addition, with sensitive PCR-based assays, B19 DNA can be detected in many tissues including bone marrow,[105] synovial tissues,[72] and other tissues[106] from healthy individuals. If the disease is rare, large multicenter trials may be required to substantiate or disprove the causal relationship.

Encephalitis and more often aseptic meningitis have been described in serologically confirmed B19 infection[107,108] with detection of B19 DNA in cerebrospinal fluid. In all these cases there have been no long-term neurologic sequelae. Brachial plexus neuropathy with weakness and sensory loss has also been described in patients with B19 infection,[109,110] and in one study, 50% of patients with classic fifth disease (confirmed serologically) experienced neurologic symptoms (tingling and numbness in the fingers or toes).[111]

There have been case reports of myocarditis associated with B19 infection in both children[112,113] and adults.[114-116] The role of B19 in the pathogenesis of myocarditis warrants further investigation, particu-

larly because P antigen is found on fetal myocardial cells and B19 appears to cause myocarditis in the fetus.[38,117]

Similarly, a number of case reports have described an association of parvovirus B19 infection and glomerulonephritis in both children and adults.[118-120]

The role of parvovirus B19 in both hepatitis and vasculitis remains unclear. Although transient elevation of liver transaminases is not uncommon in B19 infection, frank hepatitis associated with B19 infection has rarely been reported.[121] Parvovirus B19 has been suggested as a possible causative agent of fulminant liver failure and associated aplastic anemia on the basis of PCR studies.[122] However, the detection of B19 DNA in control liver tissue is not uncommon, and with appropriate controls we have been unable to confirm this putative relationship.[24]

Several case reports have described positive B19 serology in patients with vasculitis or polyarteritis nodosum,[123-126] systemic necrotizing vasculitis,[127] and Kawasaki disease, a multisystem vasculitis of early childhood. However, other studies have failed to confirm a relationship between B19 and vasculitis[128] or Kawasaki disease.[129,130]

IMMUNE RESPONSE

Both virus-specific IgM and IgG antibodies are made after experimental[35] and natural B19 parvovirus infection (see Fig. 143-3). After intranasal inoculation of volunteers, virus can be detected first at days 5 to 6, and levels peak at days 8 to 9. IgM antibody to virus appears about 10 to 12 days after experimental inoculation, and IgG antibody appears at about 2 weeks (see Fig. 143-3). The time course is similar in natural infections. In patients with TAC, 10^8 to 10^{14} genome copies/mL of viral DNA may circulate. IgM antibody may be present in patients with TAC at the time of reticulocyte nadir and during the subsequent 10 days; IgG usually appears during the period of hematopoietic recovery. Viremia is not detectable in patients with clinical fifth disease (the manifestations are secondary to immune complex formation).

IgM antibody may be found in serum samples for several months after exposure.[131] IgG presumably persists for life, and levels rise with reexposure.[35] Measurable IgA antibodies specific to B19 parvovirus may play a role in protection against infection by the nasopharyngeal route.[132]

In immunocompetent individuals, the early antibody response is to the major capsid protein VP2, but as the immune response matures reactivity to the minor capsid protein VP1 dominates. Sera from patients with persistent B19 infection typically contain antibody to VP2 but not to VP1.[133] The importance of an immune response to VP1 for protective immunity has been confirmed in animal experiments using recombinant capsids. Rabbits immunized with capsids containing only VP2 produced a strong antibody response, as measured by enzyme-linked immunosorbent assay (ELISA), but the sera had low neutralization titers. In contrast, rabbits immunized with capsids containing VP1 produced antibody with neutralizing titers comparable to those produced in humans after acute B19 infection.[134] The role of the cellular immune response in limiting parvovirus B19 infection is uncertain. Using recombinant capsids, but not native virions, a lymphocyte proliferative response to B19 capsid proteins has been produced in seropositive individuals.[135] The importance of the humoral arm of the immune response is shown by recovery from infection with the appearance of circulating specific antivirus antibody, and administration of commercial immunoglobulins can cure or ameliorate persistent parvovirus infection in immunodeficient patients (see later).

Persistent B19 parvovirus infection is the result of failure to produce effective neutralizing antibodies by the immunocompromised host. Perhaps because of the limited numbers of epitopes presented to the immune system by B19 parvovirus, the congenital immunodeficiency states associated with persistent infection may be clinically subtle, with susceptibility largely restricted to parvovirus, although multiple immune system defects are apparent when direct testing of T- and B-cell function is performed.

DIAGNOSIS

There is no suitable method for virus isolation from clinical specimens, and the detection of virus relies on DNA hybridization techniques. B19 DNA can be detected in serum at the time of TAC using dot-blot hybridization (sensitivity level $>10^6$ genome copies/mL), and in situ hybridization has been used to identify B19 DNA in bone marrow and other cells. In immunocompetent individuals B19 DNA is detectable for only 2 to 4 days by dot-blot hybridization (see Fig. 143-3), and the diagnosis of acute B19 infection is therefore based on IgM assays, ideally performed by the capture technique.[136] In an enzyme-linked format (ELISA), antibody can be detected in more than 90% of cases by the third day of TAC or at the time of rash in EI. IgM antibody remains detectable for 2 to 3 months after infection.

B19 IgG can be detected by capture assay or indirect assay. IgG is usually present by the seventh day of illness and is probably present for life thereafter. As more than 50% of the population has IgG antibody to B19 infection, this test is not helpful for the diagnosis of acute infection. Immunocompromised or immunodeficient patients with chronic infection typically do not mount an immune response to the virus, and testing for B19 antigens or more usually for viral DNA is necessary to document recent infection.

The sensitivity level of detection of B19 has greatly increased with the use of PCR but at the risk of possible contamination and false-positive results, confusing interpretation. Even in immunocompetent persons, low levels of B19 DNA may be detectable by PCR for more than 4 months in serum after acute infection[137,138] and for years in bone marrow,[105] synovial tissue,[72] liver,[24] and other tissues,[106] so detection of B19 in tissues does not prove that the disease is due to B19 infection. In general, the diagnosis of acute or chronic infection can be made on the basis of standard DNA hybridization or quantitative (real-time) PCR in combination with serologic assays for B19-specific IgG or IgM, or both.

Investigation of B19 fetal or congenital infection should be accompanied by serologic studies of the maternal serum. At the time of fetal infection, the mother should have evidence of recent B19 infection with detectable IgG and possibly IgM. If the IgM titer is low or absent, recent infection can be documented using IgG avidity studies. Fetal infection can be confirmed by amniotic fluid sampling, by fetal blood sampling, or from postmortem tissue.

TREATMENT

In the overwhelming majority of children and adults, B19 infection is a benign and self-limiting infection that results in lifelong immunity and requires no treatment other than symptomatic relief. Patients with arthralgia and arthritis usually respond to nonsteroidal anti-inflammatory drugs, although in some patients symptoms can persist for months and even years.[70] In patients with hematologic disease or persistent infection, specific treatment may be necessary.

Immunocompetent patients with TAC have a self-limiting illness, and typical TAC is readily treated by blood transfusion and supportive therapy alone. In one study of sickle cell patients with aplastic crisis, 87% required blood transfusions and 61% required hospitalization for their symptoms. One death occurred before transfusion could be given,[139] which underscores the importance of prompt medical intervention.

In immunosuppressed patients with documented, persistent B19 infection, temporary cessation of immunosuppression may be sufficient to allow the host to mount an immune response and resolve the B19 infection, and no additional treatment is required.[140] In cases in which cessation of immunosuppression is not feasible or is ineffective, administration of immunoglobulin can be beneficial[40,91]; the usual regimen is intravenous IgG at a dose of 0.4 g/kg for 5 days. Patients often respond with a marked reduction in the level of B19 viremia, reticulocytosis, and resolution of the anemia within 1 to 2 weeks of treatment. However, monitoring for relapse is important, by observation of the reticulocyte counts and assays for B19 viremia when indi-

cated. If relapse occurs less than 6 months after the initial treatment, especially in HIV-positive patients, an empirical maintenance treatment with a single-day infusion of 0.4 g/kg IgG every 4 weeks may control the B19 viremia.

The role of intrauterine blood transfusions in the treatment of hydrops fetalis related to maternal parvovirus B19 infection remains controversial. Intrauterine blood transfusions have risks, and B19-associated hydrops is known to resolve spontaneously and the fetus can be normal at delivery. However, several case reports have suggested that treatment with intrauterine blood transfusions leads to increased survival of B19-infected fetuses,[141] but there remains a risk that treatment may be confounded by an increased incidence of antibody-enhanced infection and damage especially to myocardial cells and the immune system.[103]

PREVENTION AND VACCINATION

The only measures currently available to prevent B19 infection are those designed to interrupt virus transmission. However, because patients are viremic and infectious before the symptoms of erythema infectiosum, isolation of patients with fifth disease is not rational. Patients with TAC and PRCA are both viremic and infectious and should be appropriately separated from high-risk contacts. The Centers for Disease Control and Prevention recommend that patients with TAC have droplet isolation precautions for 7 days, and for patients with chronic infection, isolation should be continued for the duration of their hospitalization.[142]

The humoral immune response plays the major role in the normal immune response to parvovirus. Although antibodies appear protective in both passive and active immunizations, insufficient data are available to assess the efficacy of immunoprophylaxis.[143,144]

Prospects for vaccination are good, with a B19 empty capsid vaccine currently under development. The presence of VP1 protein in the capsid immunogen appears critical for the production of antibodies that neutralize virus activity in vitro, and capsids with supranormal VP1 content are even more efficient in inducing neutralizing activity in immunized animals.[145] Phase I trials of a VP1-enhanced baculovirus-produced B19 vaccine look promising, and phase II trials are planned. However, the target populations for such a vaccine remain to be determined. Should only those at high risk for severe or life-threatening disease, such as sickle cell patients, be protected? Or, in view of the wide variety of disease manifestations affecting all strata of the population, should a universal vaccine policy be pursued?

REFERENCES

1. Cossart YE, Field AM, Cant B, Widdows D. Parvovirus-like particles in human sera. Lancet. 1975;1:72-73.
2. Berns KI, Bergoin M, Bloom M, et al. Family Parvoviridae. In: Murphy FA, Fauquet CM, Bishop DHL, et al, eds. Virus Taxonomy: Classification and Nomenclature of Viruses. New York: Springer-Verlag; 1995:169-178.
3. Yunoki M, Tsujikawa M, Urayama T, et al. Heat sensitivity of human parvovirus B19. Vox Sang. 2003;85:67-68.
4. Bartolomei Corsi O, Azzi A, Morfini M, et al. Human parvovirus infection in haemophiliacs first infused with treated clotting factor concentrates. J Med Virol. 1988;25:165-170.
5. Ozawa K, Ayub J, Hao YS, et al. Novel transcription map for the B19 (human) pathogenic parvovirus. J Virol. 1987;61:2395-2406.
6. Ozawa K, Ayub J, Young N. Translational regulation of B19 parvovirus capsid protein production by multiple upstream AUG triplets. J Biol Chem. 1988;263:10922-10926.
7. Ozawa K, Young N. Characterization of capsid and noncapsid proteins of B19 parvovirus propagated in human erythroid bone marrow cell cultures. J Virol. 1987;61:2627-2630.
8. Momoeda M, Wong S, Kawase M, et al. A putative nucleoside triphosphate-binding domain in the nonstructural protein of B19 parvovirus is required for cytotoxicity. J Virol. 1994;68:8443-8446.
9. Moffatt S, Yaegashi N, Tada K, et al. Human parvovirus B19 nonstructural (NS1) protein induces apoptosis in erythroid lineage cells. J Virol. 1998;72:3018-3028.
10. Kajigaya S, Shimada T, Fujita S, Young NS. A genetically engineered cell line that produces empty capsids of B19 (human) parvovirus. Proc Natl Acad Sci USA. 1989;86:7601-7605.

11. Beard C, St Amand J, Astell CR. Transient expression of B19 parvovirus gene products in COS-7 cells transfected with B19-SV40 hybrid vectors. Virology. 1989;172:659-664.

12. Kajigaya S, Fujii H, Field A, et al. Self-assembled B19 parvovirus capsids, produced in a baculovirus system, are antigenically and immunogenically similar to native virions. Proc Natl Acad Sci USA. 1991;88:4646-4650.

13. Brown CS, Van Lent JW, Vlak JM, Spaan WJ. Assembly of empty capsids by using baculovirus recombinants expressing human parvovirus B19 structural proteins. J Virol. 1991;65:2702-2706.

14. Agbandje M, Kajigaya S, McKenna R, et al. The structure of human parvovirus B19 at 8 Å resolution. Virology. 1994;203:106-115.

15. Chipman PR, Agbandje-McKenna M, Kajigaya S, et al. Cryo-electron microscopy studies of empty capsids of human parvovirus B19 complexed with its cellular receptor. Proc Natl Acad Sci USA. 1996;93:7502-7506.

16. Rosenfeld SJ, Yoshimoto K, Kajigaya S, et al. Unique region of the minor capsid protein of human parvovirus B19 is exposed on the virion surface. J Clin Invest. 1992;89:2023-2029.

17. Zadori Z, Szelei J, Lacoste MC, et al. A viral phospholipase A2 is required for parvovirus infectivity. Dev Cell. 2001;1:291-302.

18. Girod A, Wobus CE, Zadori Z, et al. The VP1 capsid protein of adeno-associated virus type 2 is carrying a phospholipase A2 domain required for virus infectivity. J Gen Virol. 2002;83(Pt 5):973-978.

19. Umene K, Nunoue T. Genetic diversity of human parvovirus B19 determined using a set of restriction endonucleases recognizing four or five base pairs and partial nucleotide sequencing: Use of sequence variability in virus classification. J Gen Virol. 1991;72:1997-2001.

20. Nguyen QT, Sifer C, Schneider V, et al. Novel human erythrovirus associated with transient aplastic anemia. J Clin Microbiol. 1999;37:2483-2487.

21. Stenner S, Enders G, Klee A, et al. [Diagnosis and therapy of a severe fetal parvovirus B19 infection with persistence of viral DNA in the mother's blood but inconspicuous serological tests. Case report]. Z Geburtshilfe Neonatol. 2002;206:102-106.

22. Servant A, Laperche S, Lallemand F, et al. Genetic diversity within human erythroviruses: Identification of three genotypes. J Virol. 2002;76:9124-9134.

23. Hokynar K, Soderlund-Venermo M, Pesonen M, et al. A new parvovirus genotype persistent in human skin. Virology. 2002;302:224-228.

24. Wong S, Young NS, Brown KE. Prevalence of parvovirus B19 in liver tissue: No association with fulminant hepatitis or hepatitis-associated aplastic anemia. J Infect Dis. 2003;187:1581-1586.

25. Nguyen QT, Wong S, Heegaard ED, Brown KE. Identification and characterization of a second novel human erythrovirus variant, A6. Virology. 2002;301:374-380.

26. Heegaard ED, Qvortrup K, Christensen J. Baculovirus expression of erythrovirus V9 capsids and screening by ELISA: Serologic cross-reactivity with erythrovirus B19. J Med Virol. 2002;66:246-252.

27. Brown KE, Young NS. The simian parvoviruses. Rev Med Virol. 1997;7:211-218.

28. Takahashi T, Ozawa K, Takahashi K, et al. Susceptibility of human erythropoietic cells to B19 parvovirus in vitro increases with differentiation. Blood. 1990;75:603-610.

29. Yaegashi N, Niinuma T, Chisaka H, et al. Parvovirus B19 infection induces apoptosis of erythroid cells in vitro and in vivo. J Infect. 1999;39:68-76.

30. Morey AL, Ferguson DJ, Fleming KA. Ultrastructural features of fetal erythroid precursors infected with parvovirus B19 in vitro: Evidence of cell death by apoptosis. J Pathol. 1993;169:213-220.

31. Brown KE, Anderson SM, Young NS. Erythrocyte P antigen: Cellular receptor for B19 parvovirus. Science. 1993;262:114-117.

32. Rouger P, Gane P, Salmon C. Tissue distribution of H, Lewis and P antigens as shown by a panel of 18 monoclonal antibodies. Rev Fr Transfus Immunohematol. 1987;30:699-708.

33. Brown KE, Hibbs JR, Gallinella G, et al. Resistance to parvovirus B19 infection due to lack of virus receptor (erythrocyte P antigen). N Engl J Med. 1994;330:1192-1196.

34. Liu JM, Green SW, Shimada T, Young NS. A block in full-length transcript maturation in cells nonpermissive for B19 parvovirus. J Virol. 1992;66:4686-4692.

35. Anderson MJ, Higgins PG, Davis LR, et al. Experimental parvoviral infection in humans. J Infect Dis. 1985;152:257-265.

36. Field AM, Cohen BJ, Brown KE, et al. Detection of B19 parvovirus in human fetal tissues by electron microscopy. J Med Virol. 1991;35:85-95.

37. Porter HJ, Heryet A, Quantrill AM, Fleming KA. Combined non-isotopic in situ hybridisation and immunohistochemistry on routine paraffin wax embedded tissue: Identification of cell type infected by human parvovirus and demonstration of cytomegalovirus DNA and antigen in renal infection. J Clin Pathol. 1990;43:129-132.

38. Naides SJ, Weiner CP. Antenatal diagnosis and palliative treatment of non-immune hydrops fetalis secondary to fetal parvovirus B19 infection. Prenatal Diagn. 1989;9:105-114.

39. Respondek M, Bratosiewicz J, Pertynski T, Liberski PP. Parvovirus particles in a fetal heart with myocarditis: Ultrastructural and immunohistochemical study. Arch Immunol Ther Exp (Warsz). 1997;45:465-470.

40. Frickhofen N, Abkowitz JL, Safford M, et al. Persistent B19 parvovirus infection in patients infected with human immunodeficiency virus type 1 (HIV-1): A treatable cause of anemia in AIDS. Ann Intern Med. 1990;113:926-933.

41. Moffatt S, Tanaka N, Tada K, et al. A cytotoxic nonstructural protein, NS1, of human parvovirus B19 induces activation of interleukin-6 gene expression. J Virol. 1996;70:8485-8491.

42. Cohen BJ, Buckley MM. The prevalence of antibody to human parvovirus B19 in England and Wales. J Med Microbiol. 1988;25:151-153.

43. Koch WC, Adler SP. Human parvovirus B19 infections in women of childbearing age and within families. Pediatr Infect Dis J. 1989;8:83-87.

44. Schwarz TF, Gürtler LG, Zoulek G, et al. Seroprevalence of human parvovirus B19 infection in Sao Tomé and Principe, Malawi and Mascarene Islands. Int J Med Microbiol. 1989;271:231-236.

45. de Freitas RB, Wong D, Boswell F, et al. Prevalence of human parvovirus (B19) and rubella virus infections in urban and remote rural areas in northern Brazil. J Med Virol. 1990;32:203-208.

46. Cohen BJ, Field AM, Gudnadottir S, et al. Blood donor screening for parvovirus B19. J Virol Methods. 1990;30:233-238.

47. McOmish F, Yap PL, Jordan A, et al. Detection of parvovirus B19 in donated blood: A model system for screening by polymerase chain reaction. J Clin Microbiol. 1993;31:323-328.

48. Yoto Y, Kudoh T, Haseyama K, et al. Incidence of human parvovirus B19 DNA detection in blood donors. Br J Haematol. 1995;91:1017-1018.

49. Anderson MJ, Cohen BJ. Human parvovirus B19 infections in United Kingdom 1984-86 (Letter). Lancet. 1987;1:738-739.

50. Serjeant GR, Serjeant BE, Thomas PE, et al. Human parvovirus infection in homozygous sickle cell disease. Lancet. 1993;341:1237-1240.

51. Chorba T, Coccia P, Holman RC, et al. The role of parvovirus B19 in aplastic crisis and erythema infectiosum (fifth disease). J Infect Dis. 1986;154:383-393.

52. Gillespie SM, Cartter ML, Asch S, et al. Occupational risk of human parvovirus B19 infection for school and day-care personnel during an outbreak of erythema infectiosum. JAMA. 1990;263:2061-2065.

53. Woolf AD, Campion GV, Chishick A, et al. Clinical manifestations of human parvovirus B19 in adults. Arch Intern Med. 1989;149:1153-1156.

54. Adler SP, Manganello AM, Koch WC, et al. Risk of human parvovirus B19 infections among school and hospital employees during endemic periods. J Infect Dis. 1993;168:361-368.

55. Koziol DE, Kurtzman G, Ayub J, et al. Nosocomial human parvovirus B19 infection: Lack of transmission from a chronically infected patient to hospital staff. Infect Control Hosp Epidemiol. 1992;13:343-348.

56. Azzi A, Morfini M, Mannucci PM. The transfusion-associated transmission of parvovirus B19. Transfus Med Rev. 1999;13:194-204.

57. Brown KE, Young NS, Alving BM, Barbosa LH. Parvovirus B19: Implications for transfusion medicine. Summary of a workshop. Transfusion. 2001;41:130-135.

58. Koenigbauer UF, Eastlund T, Day JW. Clinical illness due to parvovirus B19 infection after infusion of solvent/detergent treated pooled plasma. Transfusion 2000;40:1203-1206.

59. Williams MD, Cohen BJ, Beddall AC, et al. Transmission of human parvovirus B19 by coagulation factor concentrates. Vox Sang. 1990;58:177-181.

60. Balfour HH. Erythema infectiosum (fifth disease). Clinical review and description of 91 cases seen in an epidemic. Clin Pediatr. 1969;8:721-727.

61. Cheinisse L. Une cinquième maladie éruptive: Le mégal-érythème épidémique. Sem Med. 1905;25:205-207.

62. Anderson MJ, Jones SE, Fisher-Hoch SP, et al. Human parvovirus: The cause of erythema infectiosum (fifth disease)? (Letter). Lancet. 1983;1:1378.

63. Naides SJ, Piette W, Veach LA, Argenyi Z. Human parvovirus B19–induced vesiculopustular skin eruption. Am J Med. 1988;84:968-972.

64. Smith PT, Landry ML, Carey H, et al. Papular-purpuric gloves and socks syndrome associated with acute parvovirus B19 infection: Case report and review. Clin Infect Dis. 1998;27:164-168.

65. Shiraishi H, Umetsu K, Yamamoto H, et al. Human parvovirus (HPV/B19) infection with purpura. Microbiol Immunol. 1989;33:369-372.

66. Evans LM, Grossman ME, Gregory N. Koplik spots and a purpuric eruption associated with parvovirus B19 infection. J Am Acad Dermatol. 1992;27:466-467.

67. Lobkowicz F, Ring J, Schwarz TF, Roggendorf M. Erythema multiforme in a patient with acute human parvovirus B19 infection. J Am Acad Dermatol. 1989;20:849-850.

68. Jacks TA. Pruritus in parvovirus infection. J R Coll Gen Pract. 1987;37:210-211.

69. Luzzi GA, Kurtz JB, Chapel H. Human parvovirus arthropathy and rheumatoid factor (Letter). Lancet. 1985;1:1218.

70. White DG, Woolf AD, Mortimer PP, et al. Human parvovirus arthropathy. Lancet. 1985;1:419-421.

71. Takahashi Y, Murai C, Shibata S, et al. Human parvovirus B19 as a causative agent for rheumatoid arthritis. Proc Natl Acad Sci USA. 1998;95:8227-8232.

72. Soderlund M, von Essen R, Haapasaari J, et al. Persistence of parvovirus B19 DNA in synovial membranes of young patients with and without chronic arthropathy. Lancet. 1997;349:1063-1065.

73. Speyer I, Breedveld FC, Dijkmans BA. Human parvovirus B19 infection is not followed by inflammatory joint disease during long term follow-up. A retrospective study of 54 patients. Clin Exp Rheumatol. 1998;16:576-578.

74. Pattison JR, Jones SE, Hodgson J, et al. Parvovirus infections and hypoplastic crisis in sickle-cell anaemia. Lancet. 1981;1:664-665.

75. Serjeant GR, Topley JM, Mason K, et al. Outbreak of aplastic crisis in sickle cell anaemia associated with parvovirus-like agent. Lancet. 1981;2:595-597.

76. Young N. Hematologic and hematopoietic consequences of B19 parvovirus infection. Semin Hematol. 1988;25:159-172.

77. Hamon MD, Newland AC, Anderson MJ. Severe aplastic anaemia after parvovirus infection in the absence of underlying haemolytic anaemia (Letter). J Clin Pathol. 1988;41:1242.

78. Conrad ME, Studdard H, Anderson LJ. Aplastic crisis in sickle cell disorders: bone marrow necrosis and human parvovirus infection. Am J Med Sci. 1988;295:212-215.

79. Anderson MJ, Davis LR, Hodgson J, et al. Occurrence of infection with a parvovirus-like agent in children with sickle cell anaemia during a two-year period. J Clin Pathol. 1982;35:744-749.

80. Saunders PW, Reid MM, Cohen BJ. Human parvovirus induced cytopenias: A report of five cases (Letter). Br J Haematol. 1986;63:407-410.

81. Inoue S, Kinra NK, Mukkamala SR, Gordon R. Parvovirus B-19 infection: Aplastic crisis, erythema infectiosum and idiopathic thrombocytopenic purpura. Pediatr Infect Dis J. 1991;10:251-253.

82. Foreman NK, Oakhill A, Caul EO. Parvovirus-associated thrombocytopenic purpura (Letter). Lancet. 1988;2:1426-1427.

83. Lefrère JJ, Courouécé AM, Muller JY, et al. Human parvovirus and purpura (Letter). Lancet. 1985;2:730.

84. Frickhofen N, Raghavachar A, Heit W, et al. Human parvovirus infection (Letter). N Engl J Med. 1986;314:646.

85. McClain K, Estrov Z, Chen H, Mahoney DH Jr. Chronic neutropenia of childhood: Frequent association with parvovirus infection and correlations with bone marrow culture studies. Br J Haematol. 1993;85:57-62.

86. Hartman KR, Brown KE, Green SW, Young NS. Lack of evidence for parvovirus B19 viraemia in children with chronic neutropenia (Letter). Br J Haematol. 1994;84:895-896.

87. Pont J, Puchhammer-Stöckl E, Chott A, et al. Recurrent granulocytic aplasia as clinical presentation of a persistent parvovirus B19 infection. Br J Haematol. 1992;80:160-165.

88. Hsu HC, Lee YM, Su WJ, et al. Bone marrow samples from patients with aplastic anemia are not infected with parvovirus B19 and *Mycobacterium tuberculosis*. Am J Clin Pathol. 2002;117:36-40.

89. Skeppner G, Kreuger A, Elinder G. Transient erythroblastopenia of childhood: Prospective study of 10 patients with special reference to viral infections. J Pediatr Hematol Oncol. 2002;24:294-298.

90. Frickhofen N, Young NS. Persistent parvovirus B19 infections in humans. Microb Pathog. 1989;7:319-327.

91. Kurtzman GJ, Cohen B, Meyers P, et al. Persistent B19 parvovirus infection as a cause of severe chronic anaemia in children with acute lymphocytic leukaemia. Lancet. 1988;2:1159-1162.

92. Abkowitz JL, Brown KE, Wood RW, et al. Clinical relevance of parvovirus B19 as a cause of anemia in patients with human immunodeficiency virus infection. J Infect Dis. 1997;176:269-273.

93. Koch WC, Massey G, Russell CE, Adler SP. Manifestations and treatment of human parvovirus B19 infection in immunocompromised patients. J Pediatr. 1990;116:355-359.

94. Risdall RJ, McKenna RW, Nesbit ME, et al. Virus-associated hemophagocytic syndrome. Cancer. 1979;44:993-1002.

95. Reiner AP, Spivak JL. Hematophagic histiocytosis: A report of 23 new patients and a review of the literature. Medicine (Baltimore). 1988;67:369-388.

96. Shirono K, Tsuda H. Parvovirus B19–associated haemophagocytic syndrome in healthy adults. Br J Haematol. 1995;89:923-926.

97. Warsof SL, Nicolaides KH, Rodeck C. Immune and non-immune hydrops. Clin Obstet Gynecol. 1986;29:533-542.

98. Porter HJ, Khong TY, Evans MF, et al. Parvovirus as a cause of hydrops fetalis: Detection by in situ DNA hybridisation. J Clin Pathol. 1988;41:381-383.

99. Miller E, Fairley CK, Cohen BJ, Seng C. Immediate and long term outcome of human parvovirus B19 infection in pregnancy. Br J Obstet Gynaecol. 1998;105:174-178.

100. Rodis JF, Rodner C, Hansen AA, et al. Long-term outcome of children following maternal human parvovirus B19 infection. Obstet Gynecol. 1998;91:125-128.

101. Weiland HT, Vermey-Keers C, Salimans MM, et al. Parvovirus B19 associated with fetal abnormality (Letter). Lancet. 1987;1:682-683.

102. Katz VL, McCoy MC, Kuller JA, Hansen WF. An association between fetal parvovirus B19 infection and fetal anomalies: A report of two cases. Am J Perinatol. 1996;13:43-45.

103. Brown KE, Green SW, Antunez de Mayolo J, et al. Congenital anaemia after transplacental B19 parvovirus infection. Lancet. 1994;343:895-896.

104. Heegaard ED, Hasle H, Clausen N, et al. Parvovirus B19 infection and Diamond-Blackfan anaemia. Acta Paediatr. 1996;85:299-302.

105. Cassinotti P, Burtonboy G, Fopp M, Siegl G. Evidence for persistence of human parvovirus B19 DNA in bone marrow. J Med Virol. 1997;53:229-232.

106. Soderlund-Venermo M, Hokynar K, Nieminen J, et al. Persistence of human parvovirus B19 in human tissues. Pathol Biol (Paris). 2002;50:307-316.

107. Watanabe T, Satoh M, Oda Y. Human parvovirus B19 encephalopathy (Letter). Arch Dis Child. 1994;70:71.

108. Tabak F, Mert A, Ozturk R, et al. Prolonged fever caused by parvovirus B19-induced meningitis: Case report and review. Clin Infect Dis. 1999;29:446-447.

109. Denning DW, Amos A, Rudge P, Cohen BJ. Neuralgic amyotrophy due to parvovirus infection (Letter). J Neurol Neurosurg Psychiatry. 1987;50:641-642.

110. Walsh KJ, Armstrong RD, Turner AM. Brachial plexus neuropathy associated with human parvovirus infection. Br Med J (Clin Res Ed). 1988;296:896.

111. Faden H, Gary GW Jr, Korman M. Numbness and tingling of fingers associated with parvovirus B19 infection (Letter). J Infect Dis. 1990;161:354-355.

112. Saint-Martin J, Choulot JJ, Bonnaud E, Morinet F. Myocarditis caused by parvovirus (Letter). J Pediatr. 1990;116:1007-1008.

113. Enders G, Dotsch J, Bauer J, et al. Life-threatening parvovirus B19–associated myocarditis and cardiac transplantation as possible therapy: Two case reports. Clin Infect Dis. 1998;26:355-358.

114. Chia JK, Jackson B. Myopericarditis due to parvovirus B19 in an adult. Clin Infect Dis. 1996;23:200-201.

115. Orth T, Herr W, Spahn T, et al. Human parvovirus B19 infection associated with severe acute perimyocarditis in a 34-year-old man (Letter). Eur Heart J. 1997;18:524-525.

116. Lamparter S, Schoppet M, Pankuweit S, Maisch B. Acute parvovirus B19 infection associated with myocarditis in an immunocompetent adult. Hum Pathol. 2003;34:725-728.

117. Morey AL, Keeling JW, Porter HJ, Fleming KA. Clinical and histopathological features of parvovirus B19 infection in the human fetus. Br J Obstet Gynaecol. 1992;99:566-574.

118. Nakazawa T, Tomosugi N, Sakamoto K, et al. Acute glomerulonephritis after human parvovirus B19 infection. Am J Kidney Dis. 2000;35:E31.

119. Iwafuchi Y, Morita T, Kamimura A, et al. Acute endocapillary proliferative glomerulonephritis associated with human parvovirus B19 infection. Clin Nephrol. 2002;57:246-250.

120. Mori Y, Yamashita H, Umeda Y, et al. Association of parvovirus B19 infection with acute glomerulonephritis in healthy adults: Case report and review of the literature. Clin Nephrol. 2002;57:69-73.

121. Yoto Y, Kudoh T, Haseyama K, et al. Human parvovirus B19 infection associated with acute hepatitis. Lancet. 1996;347:868-869.

122. Langnas AN, Markin RS, Cattral MS, Naides SJ. Parvovirus B19 as a possible causative agent of fulminant liver failure and associated aplastic anemia. Hepatology. 1995;22:1661-1665.

123. Schwarz TF, Bruns R, Schröder C, et al. Human parvovirus B19 infection associated with vascular purpura and vasculitis (Letter). Infection. 1989;17:170-171.

124. Li Loong TC, Coyle PV, Anderson MJ, et al. Human serum parvovirus associated vasculitis. Postgrad Med J. 1986;62:493-494.

125. Corman LC, Dolson DJ. Polyarteritis nodosa and parvovirus B19 infection (Letter). Lancet. 1992;339:491.

126. Leruez-Ville M, Lauge A, Morinet F, et al. Polyarteritis nodosa and parvovirus B19 (Letter). Lancet. 1994;344:263-264.

127. Finkel TH, Torok TJ, Ferguson PJ, et al. Chronic parvovirus B19 infection and systemic necrotising vasculitis: Opportunistic infection or aetiological agent? Lancet. 1994;343:1255-1258.

128. Eden A, Mahr A, Servant A, et al. Lack of association between B19 or V9 erythrovirus infection and ANCA-positive vasculitides: A case-control study. Rheumatology (Oxford). 2003;42:660-664.

129. Yoto Y, Kudoh T, Haseyama K, et al. Human parvovirus B19 infection in Kawasaki disease (Letter). Lancet. 1994;344:58-59.

130. Cohen BJ. Human parvovirus B19 infection in Kawasaki disease (Letter). Lancet. 1994;344:59.

131. Anderson LJ, Tsou C, Parker RA, et al. Detection of antibodies and antigens of human parvovirus B19 by enzyme-linked immunosorbent assay. J Clin Microbiol. 1986;24:522-526.

132. Erdman DD, Usher MJ, Tsou C, et al. Human parvovirus B19 specific IgG, IgA, and IgM antibodies and DNA in serum specimens from persons with erythema infectiosum. J Med Virol. 1991;35:110-115.

133. Kurtzman GJ, Cohen BJ, Field AM, et al. Immune response to B19 parvovirus and an antibody defect in persistent viral infection. J Clin Invest. 1989;84:1114-1123.

134. Rosenfeld SJ, Young NS, Alling D, et al. Subunit interaction in B19 parvovirus empty capsids. Arch Virol. 1994;136:9-18.

135. von Poblotzki A, Gerdes C, Reischl U, et al. Lymphoproliferative responses after infection with human parvovirus B19. J Virol. 1996;70:7327-7330.

136. Cohen BJ, Mortimer PP, Pereira MS. Diagnostic assays with monoclonal antibodies for the human serum parvovirus-like virus (SPLV). J Hyg (Lond). 1983;91:113-130.

137. Patou G, Pillay D, Myint S, Pattison J. Characterization of a nested polymerase chain reaction assay for detection of parvovirus B19. J Clin Microbiol. 1993;31:540-546.

138. Musiani M, Zerbini M, Gentilomi G, et al. Parvovirus B19 clearance from peripheral blood after acute infection. J Infect Dis. 1995;172:1360-1363.

139. Goldstein AR, Anderson MJ, Serjeant GR. Parvovirus associated aplastic crisis in homozygous sickle cell disease. Arch Dis Child. 1987;62:585-588.

140. Smith MA, Shah NR, Lobel JS, et al. Severe anemia caused by human parvovirus in a leukemia patient on maintenance chemotherapy. Clin Pediatr. 1988;27:383-386.

141. Fairley CK, Smoleniec JS, Caul OE, Miller E. Observational study of effect of intrauterine transfusions on outcome of fetal hydrops after parvovirus B19 infection. Lancet. 1995;346:1335-1337.

142. Garner JS. Guideline for isolation precautions in hospitals. The Hospital Infection Control Practices Advisory Committee. Infect Control Hosp Epidemiol. 1996;17:53-80.

143. Pillay D, Patou G, Hurt S, et al. Parvovirus B19 outbreak in a children's ward. Lancet. 1992;339:107-109.

144. Torok TJ, Pavia AT, Anderson LJ. Efficacy of immune globulin for prevention of human parvovirus B19 infection (Abstract). VIth Parvovirus Workshop, Montpellier, France, P6 #8, 1995.

145. Bansal GP, Hatfield J, Dunn FE, et al. Immunogenicity studies of recombinant human parvovirus B19 proteins. In: Brown F, Chanock RM, Ginsberg HS, Lerner RA, eds. Vaccines 92. Cold Spring Harbor, NY: Cold Spring Harbor Laboratory Press; 1992:315-319.

Orthoreoviruses and Orbiviruses

THEODORE F. TSAI

The family Reoviridae comprises viruses of plants, fish, insects, and other terrestrial animals in nine genera; among them, some orthoreoviruses, rotaviruses, orbiviruses, and coltiviruses infect humans.[1] The rotaviruses (see Chapter 146) and Colorado tick fever virus (see Chapter 145), after which the last genus is named, are discussed separately; the others are described here.

Virions are 60 to 80 nm in diameter and icosahedral but may appear spherical. The inner core, containing 10 to 12 segments of linear double-stranded RNA in equimolar proportions, is surrounded by two or more protein layers but no lipid envelope. Individual genomic segments encode RNA polymerase and other nonstructural proteins and structural inner or outer capsid proteins that serve in cell attachment and, for some viruses, hemagglutination and that define group- and type-specific antigens. Antigenic relationships between viruses in different genera have not been observed.

ORTHOREOVIRUSES

Reoviruses 1 through 3 are ubiquitous and infect a broad range of mammals including humans, although their role in human disease has been considered unclear.[2] Infections are cosmopolitan and occur at an early age such that antibody prevalence rises from approximately 30% in the second year of life to more than 80% by the age of 60 years.[3] Most infections are probably inapparent or result in mild respiratory or gastrointestinal symptoms. The viruses, which are stable over a broad pH range and in aerosols, are often recovered from sewage and environmental sources and presumably are transmitted to humans by fecal-oral and airborne routes. Because infections are so widespread, the causal connection between a clinical syndrome and infection has often been difficult to establish, as underscored by the virus name, an acronym for *respiratory, enteric, orphan virus*.[2]

Mild respiratory illness with low-grade fever, malaise, rhinorrhea, and pharyngitis with mild diarrhea has been described in children in outbreaks and has been produced in experimental infections of adult volunteers, but in a 20-year study of children with diarrhea, reoviruses were implicated in only 0.1% of cases, and those occurred mainly in infants younger than 1 year.[2,4-8] A maculopapular or vesicular exanthem frequently has accompanied illnesses in children, and in one case a measles-like illness with conjunctivitis, photophobia, lymphadenopathy, and a confluent morbilliform rash was reported.[6,9-11] More serious cases of interstitial or confluent pneumonia, myocarditis, aseptic meningitis, and encephalomyelitis—three with concurrent hepatitis—have been described; some systemic illness have been fatal.[6,9-14]

A role for reovirus type 3 in the etiology of biliary atresia has been suggested by a mouse model of the disease, but results of serologic and histologic studies in patients with extrahepatic biliary atresia or choledochal cysts have been inconclusive.[2,15] A sporadic case of congenital biliary, anorectal, and esophageal atresia with an early switch of fetal to adult hemoglobin production has also been attributed to reovirus 3 infection.[16] The similarity of reovirus serotype 3 core lambda 1 protein with an autoantigen expressed on inner ear sensory cells and endothelial cells has suggested a potential role of the virus and molecular mimicry in the pathogenesis of Cogan's syndrome, a multisystemic disorder that includes vestibuloauditory dysfunction and vasculitis.[17]

Reoviruses are among several viruses being explored as oncolytic virotherapy, particularly for tumors expressing the Ras pathway.

ORBIVIRUSES

Virions of 80 nm constitute outer and inner capsid layers surrounding a core and genome of 10 RNA segments.[1,18] Outer capsid VP2 and core surface VP7 proteins define type-specific and group-specific antigens, respectively. The more than 100 cataloged orbiviruses are principally vector borne (transmitted by ticks, mosquitoes, midges, and gnats), and many cause important diseases of livestock animals (e.g., bluetongue, epizootic hemorrhagic fever of deer, and African horse sickness viruses) in which hematopoietic infection may occur. Several cause severe congenital anomalies, such as aqueductal stenosis, hydrocephalus, and arthrogryposis in animals, and have been proposed for models of these human disorders.

A trio of tick-borne orbiviruses transmitted in central Europe and Russia and all members of the Kemerovo antigenic complex have been implicated, with varying strength of evidence, in cases of neurologic infection.[19-22] Kemerovo virus was isolated from cerebrospinal fluid or implicated serologically in 12 encephalitis cases, in which Russian spring-summer encephalitis was excluded, in the Kemerovo region of Russia. For Lipovnik virus, serologic evidence of infection with that virus alone or with concurrent tick-borne encephalitis virus was shown in meningoencephalitis patients in the former Czechoslovakia. Serologic evidence of infection with Lipovnik or Tribec virus was also demonstrated in patients with polyradiculitis from the same geographic region. All three viruses have been isolated from *Ixodes* ticks that also transmit agents of tick-borne encephalitis, ehrlichiosis, and Lyme disease in overlapping areas of Europe, and their respective roles in the etiology of acute and subacute neurologic disease in these locations should be interpreted cautiously. Acute infection can be diagnosed serologically, preferably by demonstrating viral-specific immunoglobulin M in cerebrospinal fluid.[22]

In the southwestern United States, infection with a virus antigenically related to Kemerovo-group orbiviruses is suspected to cause an acute febrile illness with myalgia, vomiting, and abdominal pain, accompanied by leukopenia, thrombocytopenia, and anemia.[23] The observation comes from a study of patients in Oklahoma and Texas with tick exposure in whom Rocky Mountain spotted fever was ruled out and who demonstrated antibody seroconversions to Lipovnik and Six Gun City (another orbivirus) viruses, suggesting infection with a related agent. No virus was recovered from acute blood specimens, and the relationship of the infection to clinical illness is undetermined. A Kemerovo-related orbivirus of rabbits and large animals has also been reported in the Midwest, but its pathogenic potential for humans is unknown.[24]

Two orbiviruses in Africa and one in South America have been associated with nonspecific febrile illnesses.[25-27] Orungo virus has been isolated in East, central, and West Africa and has been implicated in sporadic cases and outbreaks of acute illness with myalgias and headache. However, infections, probably transmitted between humans by anopheline mosquitoes, are highly prevalent, and their role in these clinical illnesses is unclear. Lebombo virus was isolated from blood of a Nigerian child and also from mosquitoes and rodents, and Changuinola virus was isolated from a mosquito catcher in Panama.

REFERENCES

1. Van Regenmortel MHV, Fauquet CM, Bishop DHL, et al, eds. Virus Taxonomy. The Classification and Nomenclature of Viruses. The Seventh Report of the International Committee on Taxonomy of Viruses. San Diego: Academic Press; 2000.
2. Cherry JD. Reoviruses. In: Feigin RD, Cherry JD, Demmler GJ, Kaplan SL, eds. Textbook of Pediatric Infectious Diseases. 5th ed. Philadelphia: WB Saunders; 2003:2102-2106.
3. Selb B, Weber B. A study of human reovirus IgG and IgA antibodies by ELISA and Western blot. J Virol Methods. 1994;47:15-26.
4. Hilleman MR, Hamparian VV, Ketler A, et al. Acute respiratory illnesses among children and adults. JAMA. 1962;180:445-453.
5. Rosen L, Hovis JF, Mastrota FM, et al. An outbreak of infection with a type 1 reovirus among children in an institution. Am J Hyg. 1960;71:266-274.
6. Lerner AM, Cherry JD, Klein JO, et al. Infections with reoviruses. N Engl J Med. 1962;267:947-952.

7. Rosen L, Evans HE, Spickard A. Reovirus infections in human volunteers. Am J Hyg. 1963;77:29-37.

8. Giodano MO, Martinez LC, Isa MB, et al. Twenty year study of the occurrence of reovirus infection in hospitalized children with acute gastroenteritis in Argentina. Pediatr Infect Dis J. 2002;21:880-882.

9. El-Rai FM, Evans AS. Reovirus infections in children and young adults. Arch Environ Health. 1963;7:700-704.

10. Joske RA, Keall DD, Leak PJ, et al. Hepatitis-encephalitis in humans with reovirus infection. Arch Intern Med. 1964;113:811-816.

11. Tillotson JR, Lerner AM. Reovirus type 3 associated with fatal pneumonia. N Engl J Med. 1967;276:1060-1063.

12. Hugo Johansson PJ, Sveger T, Ahlfors K, et al. Reovirus type 1 associated with meningitis. Scand J Infect Dis. 1996;28:117-120.

13. Krainer L, Aronson BE. Disseminated encephalomyelitis in humans with recovery of hepatoencephalitis virus (HEV). J Neuropathol Exp Neurol. 1969;18:339-342.

14. Terheggen F, Benedikz E, Frissen PHJ, Brinkman K. Myocarditis associated with reovirus infection. Eur J Clin Microbiol Infect Dis. 2003;22:197-198.

15. Sokol RJ, Mack C. Etiopathogenesis of biliary atresia. Semin Liver Dis. 2001;21:517-524.

16. Dessanti A, Massarelli G, Piga MT, et al. Biliary, anorectal and esophageal atresia: A new entity? Tohoku J Exp Med. 1997;181:49-55.

17. Lunardi C, Bason C, Leandri M, et al. Autoantibodies to inner ear and endothelial antigens in Cogan's syndrome. Lancet. 2002;260:915-921.

18. Gould AR, Hyatt AD. The orbivirus genus. Diversity, structure, replication and phylogenetic relationships. Comp Immunol Microbiol Infect Dis. 1994;17:163-188.

19. Chumakov MP, Karpovich LG, Sarmanova ES, et al. Report on the isolation from *Ixodes persulcatus* ticks and from patients in western Siberia of a virus differing from the agent of tick-borne encephalitis. Acta Virol. 1963;7:82-83.

20. Libikova H, Heinz F, Ujhazyova D, Stunzner D. Orbiviruses of the Kemerovo complex and neurological disease. Med Microbiol Immunol. 1978;116:255-263.

21. Malkova D, Holubova J, Kolman JM, et al. Antibodies against some arboviruses in persons with various neuropathies. Acta Virol. 1980;24:298.

22. Lotric-Furlan S, Petrovec M, Avsic-Zupanc T, et al. Prospective assessment of the etiology of acute febrile illness after a tick bite in Slovenia. Clin Infect Dis. 2001;33:503-510.

23. Tsai TF. Arboviral infections in the United States. Infect Dis Clin North Am. 1991;5:73-102.

24. Theil KW, McCloskey CM, Scott DP. Serologic evidence for rabbit syncytium virus in eastern cottontail rabbits (*Sylvilagus floridanus*) in Ohio. J Wildl Dis. 1993;29:470-474.

25. Tomori O, Fabiyi A. Orungo virus: A new agent from mosquitoes and man in Uganda and Nigeria. Nigerian Med J. 1966;7:5-8.

26. Familusi JB, Moore DL, Fomufod AK, Causey OR. Virus isolates from children with febrile convulsions in Nigeria. A correlation study of clinical and laboratory observations. Clin Pediatr. 1972;11:272-276.

27. Karabatsos N, ed. International Catalogue of Arboviruses 1985, Including Certain Other Viruses of Vertebrates. 3rd ed. San Antonio, Tex: American Society of Tropical Medicine and Hygiene; 1987:198.

Banna virus, a tick-associated orbivirus, was first isolated from cerebrospinal fluid of 2 encephalitis patients and from serum of 25 patients with nonspecific febrile illness in Yunnan province in southern China and was subsequently isolated from 8 patients with febrile illness in Xinjiang province in far western China.[3,4] Beijing virus, which is antigenically distinct and exhibits a different RNA electrophoretic pattern, was isolated in 1991 from serum or cerebrospinal fluid, or both, of 33 patients with viral encephalitis hospitalized at the Beijing Children's Hospital and subsequently from mosquitoes captured near the city.[5] Another antigenically and electrophoretically distinct coltivirus, isolated from *Culex tritaeniorhychnus* mosquitoes in Gansu province, has been linked serologically to encephalitis cases occurring in Henan and Jiangsu provinces. However, a small serosurvey suggested a high level of endemic transmission, and the role of the infection in these cases is uncertain. Neutralization and enzyme-linked immunosorbent assays have been employed in antigenic characterization of the isolates and in serologic studies. A coltivirus, antigenically similar to a strain previously recovered from mosquitoes in Indonesia, was also isolated from an encephalitis patient in the 1997 EV71 outbreak in Malaysia, but its role in the patient's illness is still unclear. Other antigenically related viruses with unknown clinical significance have been isolated from mosquitoes in China. In conclusion, several distinct vector-borne seadornaviruses appear to cause neurologic infection in Asia, but clinical features of the infections, their epidemiology, and their transmission patterns are ill defined.

COLORADO TICK FEVER

CTF is an acute, self-limited febrile illness with the unusual feature that marrow erythrocytic precursors are infected, leading to prolonged viremia lasting the life span of infected red cells. The virus is transmitted in the western United States and Canada by the wood tick *Dermacentor andersoni*, which is distributed in mountainous terrain from 4000- to 10,000-foot elevations.[7] This area also corresponds to the virus's distribution, principally in the U.S. and Canadian Rocky Mountains, Wasatch and Sierra Nevada ranges, and Black Hills, and nearly all patients give a history of exposure to these locations, usually while hiking, fishing, or camping (Fig. 145-1). Patients presenting with the illness in other states have been diagnosed by astute clinicians

---

Coltiviruses and Seadornaviruses (Colorado Tick Fever)

THEODORE F. TSAI

GENERAL

Coltiviruses are morphologically and structurally similar to the orbiviruses (Chapter 144) but contain 12 RNA segments. The viruses all appear to be tick or mosquito borne. Coltiviruses include Colorado tick fever (CTF), the type species, and other U.S. and European isolates; Salmon River virus, isolated from a patient with a CTF-like illness in Idaho; Eyach virus, isolated in Germany and France; and isolate S6-14-03, recovered from a hare in California, and are either proved or suspected to cause self-limited febrile illness (see next section). Viruses from Asia that were previously assigned to an antigenic group of coltiviruses, including Banna virus, have now been reassigned to a distinct genus of *Seadornavirus* (Southeast Asia dodeca RNA virus), and some have been implicated in neurologic infection.[1-6]

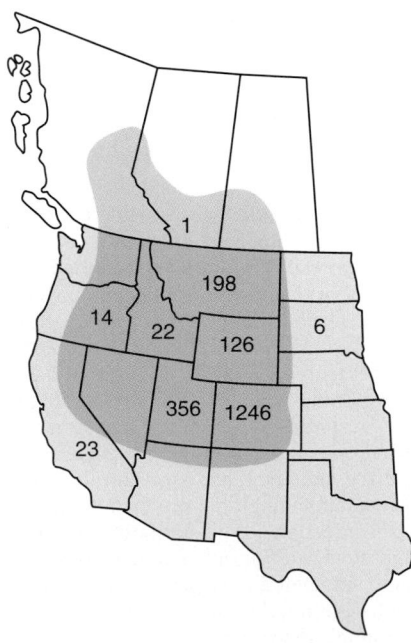

FIGURE 145-1. Geographic distribution of *Dermacentor andersoni* (wood ticks) and reported cases of Colorado tick fever, 1990 to 1996, United States and Canada.

who have elicited a travel and tick exposure history. In addition, several cases have occurred in persons who did not travel to an enzootic location but were infected by ticks carried on clothing, on equipment, or in the automobile of a returned household member-traveler.[8] One transfusion-acquired case has also been reported.[9] Transmission is seasonal, from March to September, with the peak period of risk in Colorado occurring between April and June.[9]

The virus is transmitted transtadially (between stages) in the tick, from its larval, nymphal, and adult forms, and horizontally, between the infected ticks and their mammalian hosts—rodents and other small mammals in the case of the immature forms and larger mammals, including deer and humans, in the case of the adult.[7] The virus is not transmitted transovarially in the tick, however. Most human infections are acquired from adult ticks. South-facing dry and rock-covered slopes, supporting open stands of ponderosa pine and juniper and sagebrush underbrush, favor the viral transmission cycle by providing sufficient humidity for the tick and cover and burrows for ground squirrels, chipmunks, marmots, and other small mammals that are the principal tick and virus-amplifying hosts.[10]

Sporadic cases of serologically diagnosed CTF have been reported from areas of California outside the range of *D. andersoni* (e.g., Contra Costa county). *Dermacentor variabilis* is suspected to be the vector, and a CTF-related virus (S1-14-03) isolated from a ground squirrel and hare in California may be the etiologic agent in these cases.[2] A second antigenically distinct virus, recovered from blood of a patient who acquired a CTF-like illness while rafting on the middle fork of the Salmon River, Idaho, appears to be responsible for the majority of CTF cases in Montana and Idaho (T. F. Tsai and N. Karabatsos, unpublished observations). Successive infections with this or another unrecognized related coltivirus could account for sporadic cases of repeated CTF-like illnesses. In Europe, yet another antigenically related virus, Eyach virus, isolated from *Ixodes ricinus* and *Ixodes ventalloi* ticks in Germany and France, has been implicated in cases of neurologic illness in the former Czechoslovakia.[1]

A discrete history of tick bite or exposure in 90% of cases has allowed estimation of a mean incubation period of 3 to 4 days (range 0 to 14 days).[11] The onset is usually abrupt, with fever, chills, intense headache, severe generalized myalgias, and hyperesthetic skin, leading to profound weakness and prostration.[11-13] Nausea, vomiting, and abdominal symptoms are not prominent, and compared with those in other febrile illnesses occurring in the same season, upper respiratory symptoms are significantly less common. Profound malaise may confine patients to bed, and in previous years as many as 14% of patients were hospitalized. There are few specific physical findings. The conjunctivae may be injected, and examination of the oral cavity may disclose an erythematous pharynx and palatal enanthem; lymphadenopathy and a slightly enlarged tender spleen may be present. A maculopapular or petechial rash may be seen in 15% of patients, and this can suggest Rocky Mountain spotted fever.

Acute symptoms generally resolve within a week, but their remission is followed in half of the cases by recurrent symptoms 2 to 3 days later, giving rise to a diphasic or saddleback fever curve. A third recrudescence may rarely occur. Although the acute toxic phase of the illness may be brief, extreme weakness, lassitude, and asthenia persist for weeks and even months. The duration of convalescence is age dependent, with continued fatigue after 3 weeks in 70% of patients older than 30 years and full recovery in 1 week or less in patients younger than 20 years.[11]

In children, illness is complicated by aseptic meningitis or encephalitis in 5% to 10% of cases, and fatal cases with generalized hemorrhage and shock have rarely been reported.[12-14] However, the unrecognized contribution of dual *Rickettsia rickettsii* infection could not be discounted in some cases. Epididymoorchitis, pneumonia, hepatitis, and myocarditis have also been reported to complicate cases in adults.[15,16] The possibility of vertically transmitted fetal infection has been suggested by cases of spontaneous abortion, occurring 2 weeks after infection in a pregnant woman, and of perinatal illness with leukopenia in a 3-day-old infant whose mother had developed CTF 6 days before delivery.

Leukopenia is characteristic, reaching a mean nadir count of 3900/mm^3 5 to 6 days after the onset of illness, often with the initial remission of symptoms.[17] The decline reflects an absolute decline in circulating neutrophils, often accompanied by a left shift, atypical lymphocytes, and a relative lymphocytosis. A moderate decrease in the platelet count is also usual. Examination of the bone marrow reveals a maturational arrest of granulocytic cells with a reduction in mature cells and increased numbers of metamyelocytes and myelocytes and also a reduction in megakaryocytes. The virus infects erythroblasts and primitive CD34$^+$ stem cells, but although cells remain infected as they pass through their maturational stages and are released into the peripheral circulation, persistent infection in marrow cells has not been demonstrated.[18] The duration of viremia parallels the survival of infected red cells and persists for 4 weeks after the onset of illness in approximately one half of the cases.

The virus can be recovered easily from the peripheral blood or from stored refrigerated clots, up to 6 weeks after the onset, in Vero or BHK-21 cells or in suckling mice, but a laboratory diagnosis is accessible by identifying infected red cells in a peripheral smear by indirect immunofluorescence.[19] Viral genomic products in acute blood have been identified by polymerase chain reaction, but serologic diagnosis by immunoglobulin M capture enzyme-linked immunosorbent assay, neutralization, or complement fixation is the usual method of laboratory confirmation.[20,21]

No specific therapy is available, although the sensitivity of most coltiviruses and orbiviruses to ribavirin suggests the potential utility of that drug. Bed rest, fluids, and antipyretics—avoiding aspirin, which could exacerbate the hemorrhagic diathesis associated with thrombocytopenia—are recommended as symptomatic therapy. Patients should not donate blood until at least 6 months after recovery.

Tick avoidance measures may be effective in preventing the disease. Walking over open spaces, avoiding grassy, vegetated areas; wearing long pants with overlapping socks, preferably of a light color to facilitate the discovery of adherent ticks; conducting periodic tick checks; spraying clothing and gear with permethrin (a repellent and acaricide); and applying diethyltoluamide-containing repellent on uncovered skin are recommended to reduce tick exposure and bites. A secular decline in CTF cases in Colorado in the last 2 decades at the same time that populations and park visitations have increased has suggested that increased public awareness of tick-avoidance measures may have had some effect on reducing the incidence of the disease.

REFERENCES

1. Attoui H, Billoir F, Biagini P, et al. Complete sequence determination and genetic analysis of Banna virus and Kadipiro virus: Proposal for assignment to a new genus (*Seadornavirus*) within the family Reoviridae. J Gen Virol. 2000;81:1507-1515.
2. Attoui H, Mohad Jaafar F, Biagini P, et al. Genus Coltivirus (family Reoviridae): Genomic and morphologic characterization of Old World and New World viruses. Arch Virol. 2002;147:533-561.
3. Chen BQ, Tao SJ. Arbovirus survey in China in recent ten years. Chin Med J (Engl). 1996;109:13-15.
4. Li QP. First isolation of 8 strains of new orbivirus (Banna) from patients with innominate fever in Xinjiang. Endemic Dis Bull. 1992;7:77-81.
5. Zhao ZJ, Huang YJ, Zhou YT, et al. Isolation and identification of a kind of new virus from patients with viral encephalitis in Beijing. Chin J Virol. 1994;8:297-299.
6. Brown SE, Gorman BM, Tesh RB, Knudson DL. Coltiviruses isolated from mosquitoes collected in Indonesia. Virology. 1993;196:363-367.
7. Burgdorfer W. Tick-borne disease in the United States: Rocky Mountain spotted fever and Colorado tick fever. Acta Trop. 1977;34:103-126.
8. Midoneck SR, Richard J, Murray HW. Colorado tick fever in a resident of New York City. Arch Fam Med. 1994;3:731-732.
9. Centers for Disease Control. Transmission of Colorado tick fever virus by blood transfusion—Montana. MMWR Morb Mortal Wkly Rep. 1975;24:422-427.
10. McLean RG, Shriner RB, Polorny KS, et al. The ecology of Colorado tick fever in Rocky Mountain National Park in 1974. III. Habitats supporting the virus. Am J Trop Med Hyg. 1989;40:86-93.
11. Goodpasture HC, Poland JD, Francy DB, et al. Colorado tick fever: Clinical, epidemiologic, and laboratory aspects of 228 cases in Colorado in 1973-1974. Ann Intern Med. 1978;88:303-310.
12. Spruance SL, Bailey A. Colorado tick fever. Arch Intern Med. 1973;131:288-293.
13. Silver HK, Meiklejohn G, Kempe CH. Colorado tick fever. Am J Dis Child. 1961;101:56-62.
14. Fraser CH, Schiff DW. Colorado tick fever encephalitis. Pediatrics. 1962;29:187-190.

15. Loge RV. Acute hepatitis associated with Colorado tick fever. West J Med. 1985;142:91-92.
16. Emmons RW, Schade HI. Colorado tick fever simulating acute myocardial infarction. JAMA. 1972;222:87-88.
17. Andersen RD, Entringe MA, Roginson WA. Virus-induced leukopenia: Colorado tick fever as a human model. J Infect Dis. 1985;151:449-453.
18. Phillip CS, Callaway C, Chu MC, et al. Replication of Colorado tick fever virus within human hematopoietic progenitor cells. J Virol. 1993;67:2389-2395.
19. Emmons RW, Lennette EH. Immunofluorescent staining in the laboratory diagnosis of Colorado tick fever. J Lab Clin Med. 1966;68:923-929.
20. Jaffar FM, Attoui H, Gallian P. Recombinant VP-7-based enzyme-linked immunosorbent assay for detection of immunoglobulin G antibodies to Colorado tick fever virus. J Clin Microbiol. 2003;41:2102-2105.
21. Johnson AJ, Karabatsos N, Lanciotti RS. Detection of Colorado tick fever virus by using reverse transcriptase PCR and application of the technique in laboratory diagnosis. J Clin Microbiol. 1997;35:1203-1208.

CHAPTER **146**

Rotaviruses

PHILIP R. DORMITZER

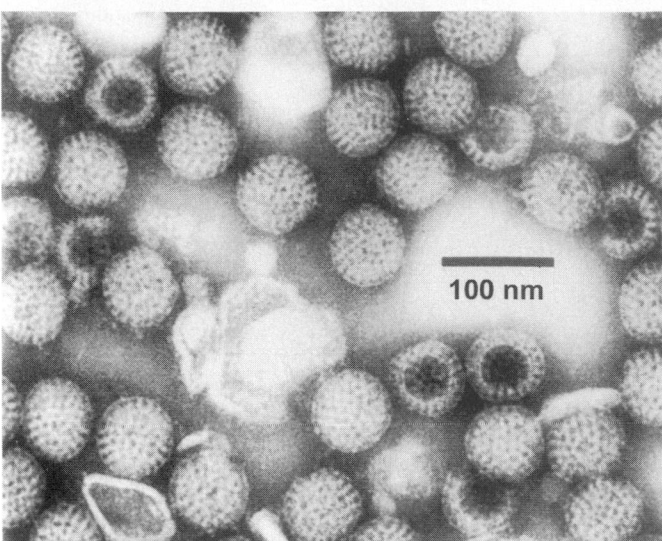

FIGURE 146-1. Electron micrograph of negatively stained rotavirus virions in a stool filtrate from a child with gastroenteritis. The outer capsid appears as a thin rim surrounding stubby protrusions made up of VP6 trimers. "Empty" particles with dark centers lack genomic RNA. *(From Kapikian AZ, Kim HW, Wyatt RG, et al. Reoviruslike agent in stools: Association with infantile diarrhea and development of serologic tests. Science. 1974;185:1049-1053.)*

HISTORY AND OVERVIEW

Rotaviruses constitute a genus within the Reoviridae, a family of non-enveloped, icosahedral animal viruses with double-stranded, segmented RNA genomes. The family Reoviridae also includes the reoviruses, which infect humans but have not been established as a cause of human disease, and the orbiviruses, which include the agents of bluetongue in sheep and Colorado tick fever in humans. Rotavirus is the most important cause of severe, dehydrating gastroenteritis in children younger than 5 years in all socioeconomic groups and in all regions of the world.[1-3] It is responsible for approximately 6% of all deaths of children younger than 5 years, with these deaths occurring primarily in the developing world.[2] In temperate climates, rotavirus causes the annual peak in pediatric hospitalizations for dehydration related to gastroenteritis during the cooler months of the year.[4,5]

Before the association of rotaviruses with human disease, an etiologic agent could be identified in only 15% to 20% of children with gastroenteritis.[6] In 1973, electron microscopic examination of duodenal biopsy specimens from six of nine children with acute gastroenteritis revealed similar viral particles, which were approximately 70 nm in diameter.[7] Morphologically, these particles were indistinguishable from viruses previously identified in specimens from mice and cows with diarrhea,[8,9] designated rotaviruses[10] because of their appearance in electron micrographs as wheels with spokes (Fig. 146-1). The antigenic similarity between the human and bovine agents was confirmed when an exchange of matched liquid stool and convalescent-phase sera between a veterinary and a medical laboratory showed that antibodies in the sera of children and calves agglutinated the rotavirus particles in the stools of both species.[10] The human sera also neutralized the infectivity of the bovine agent, which had been adapted to growth in cell culture.[10]

Understanding of rotavirus replication, the pathogenesis of rotavirus diarrhea, and the mechanisms of immunity has relied on the study of many rotavirus strains that grow well in cell culture and on the development of large and small animal models for rotavirus gastroenteritis. Because rotavirus strains can be "mated" by coinfecting cells to achieve reassortment of the 11 genome segments, classic genetic studies have been possible. However, the inability to package recombinant genes into infectious rotavirus particles has prevented genetic engineering of the virus. This difficulty has slowed basic research and hindered the development of vaccines. All immunization strategies tested in humans, to date, use animal or relatively attenuated human strains of the virus manipulated only by passage in cell culture or genetic reassortment through coinfection of cells, or both.

In contrast to the advances in basic research, routine clinical treatment of rotavirus gastroenteritis, which consists primarily of rehydration and supportive care, has changed relatively little since the adoption and promotion of oral rehydration therapy by international public health agencies in the 1970s.[11] Advances in the understanding of rotavirus pathogenesis, particularly related to the finding that the enteric nervous system is a mediator of intestinal secretion during infection,[12] are leading to new approaches to treatment,[13] which may supplement rehydration therapy in the future. Clinical research on rotavirus has focused primarily on the development of vaccines to prevent severely dehydrating rotavirus gastroenteritis. These efforts led to the development of a live, oral vaccine against rotavirus (RotaShield) that was licensed in the United States in 1998.[14] However, in a major setback for vaccine development, the recommendation for use of the RotaShield vaccine was withdrawn in 1999 because of a temporal association between immunization and intestinal intussusception.[15] Thus, rotavirus gastroenteritis remains a prime target for prevention by a safe and effective vaccine.

VIRAL STRUCTURE

The rotavirus virion is a nonenveloped icosahedral particle, which is approximately 770 Å in diameter, excluding the VP4 spikes (Fig. 146-2).[16,17] It consists of three concentric protein shells, which encapsidate 11 segments of tightly packed, double-stranded RNA. Each genome segment contains one or, in the case of genome segment 11, two open reading frames. These segments encode six structural proteins (VP1 to VP4, VP6, and VP7) and six nonstructural proteins (NSP1 to NSP6).

The innermost protein shell consists of 120 copies of VP2, which are arranged in a $T = 1$ icosahedral lattice, with two VP2 molecules making up each icosahedral asymmetric unit.[18] This VP2 shell contains the genomic RNA and 11 or 12 complexes consisting of VP1 (polymerase) and VP3 (guanyltransferase), distributed at the icosahedral fivefold vertices. The middle shell consists of an icosahedral $T = 13$ *levo* lattice of 780 copies of VP6, which forms thick trimeric pil-

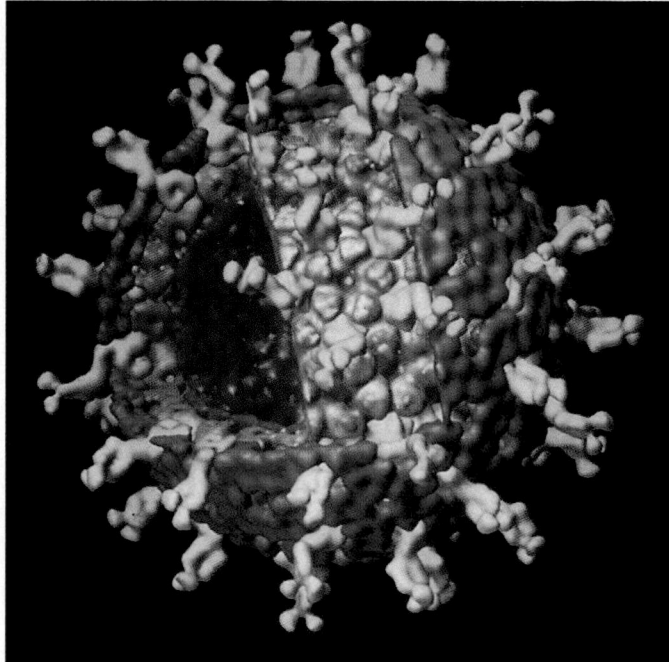

FIGURE 146-2. Reconstruction at 26 Å resolution of the rhesus rotavirus triple-layered particle, based on images from electron cryomicroscopy.[19] VP2, which makes up the innermost icosahedral capsid, is depicted in red. VP6, which makes up the middle icosahedral capsid, is depicted in purple. VP7, which makes up the outermost icosahedral shell, is depicted in blue. VP4, which forms the spikes that protrude from the virion, is depicted in yellow. The virions used to create this reconstruction were activated with trypsin, so that VP4 has been cleaved into VP5* and VP8*. *(From Yeager M, Berriman JA, Baker TS, et al. Three-dimensional structure of the rotavirus haemagglutinin VP4 by cryo-electron microscopy and difference map analysis. EMBO J. 1994;13:1011-1018 by permission of Oxford University Press.)*

lars[16] and is the target of the most abundant antibodies elicited by rotavirus infection. The genome, VP1, VP3, and the inner two protein capsids make up the transcriptionally active, double-layered subviral particle (DLP).

The thin outermost capsid consists of 780 copies of a coat glycoprotein, VP7, and 60 VP4 spikes, which protrude from the virion.[16,19] One hundred and thirty-two aqueous holes perforate the outer and middle capsid layers.[16,17] VP4 and VP7 translocate the DLP across a host membrane and into the cytoplasm. Both outer capsid proteins are neutralization antigens[20] and targets of protective active[21] and passive (maternally transferred)[22] immunity. VP4 is the major cell attachment protein[23] as well as a determinant of virulence[24] and of growth restriction in cell culture.[25] VP7 forms the T = 13 *levo* icosahedral lattice of the outermost capsid, which is in register with the VP6 lattice of the middle capsid. The outer capsid is shed from the virion during entry. In vitro, chelation of calcium from the virion causes trimers of VP7 to dissociate,[26] leading to virus uncoating and activation of the viral polymerase.[27]

The rotavirus particle is physically hardy and resists inactivation by treatment with fluorocarbons, ether, and concentrations of chlorine typically used to treat sewage effluent and drinking water.[28,29] The particle is inactivated by some antiseptic agents that contain relatively high concentrations of alcohols (>40%), free chlorine (>20,000 ppm), or iodophores (>10,000 ppm iodine)[30] and by calcium chelators. A commercial disinfectant spray (Lysol) that contains 79% ethanol and 0.1% *o*-phenylphenol has been demonstrated to prevent the experimental transmission of rotavirus from fomites to human volunteers.[31] Rotavirus survival in the environment is significantly decreased at high relative humidity.[29]

VIRAL REPLICATION

Efficient rotavirus infectivity requires cleavage of the spike protein VP4 by intestinal trypsin into an amino-terminal fragment VP8*, which contains a hemagglutination domain, and a carboxyl-terminal fragment, VP5*, which contains a membrane interaction domain.[32,33] It is probable that most virions are cleaved before being shed in stool. Trypsin cleavage triggers a rearrangement in VP4 that increases the rigidity of the spikes, which are not visible on electron microscopy reconstructions of uncleaved particles.[34] The hemagglutination domain constitutes the "heads" of the cleaved spikes, and the membrane interaction domain makes up the "body" (see Fig. 146-2).[35,36]

The complicated cell entry pathway of rotavirus particles involves interactions with cell surface proteins, lipids, and (in many cases) carbohydrates. Sialic acid–dependent strains of rotavirus initiate their attack on the host cell by binding sialosides on cell membrane glycoproteins or glycolipids through the VP8* fragment of VP4. Most strains of rotavirus that cause human disease do not require cell surface sialic acid for efficient infectivity.[37] Rather, these strains primarily bind an alternative receptor through the VP5* fragment of VP4.[38] A growing body of evidence suggests that one or more integrins can serve as the primary receptor for sialic acid–independent rotavirus strains and as a secondary receptor for sialic acid–dependent strains.[39] The VP5* fragment of VP4 contains a motif that is very similar to the fusion peptides of Semliki Forest virus and Sindbis virus and is thought to be involved in the actual attack on host cell membrane lipid bilayers.[40] This finding suggests common elements between the mechanisms of membrane fusion by enveloped viruses and the less well-understood process of membrane penetration by the nonenveloped rotavirus.

Because naked rotavirus RNA is noninfectious, the entire transcriptionally active 710-Å DLP must be translocated into the cytoplasm to initiate infection. The pathway of rotavirus entry into cells remains controversial. Treatment of target cells with inhibitors of energy metabolism and endosome acidification has little effect on rotavirus infectivity, which suggests that rotavirus does not need to be endocytosed for productive entry but rather may be able to penetrate the plasma membrane directly.[41] On the other hand, in vitro calcium chelation triggers uncoating of the triple-layered particle (TLP), which mimics the loss of the outer capsid during entry.[27] Maintaining a high endosomal calcium concentration with calcium ethylene glycol tetraacetic acid (CaEGTA) blocks viral entry, which suggests that falling calcium concentrations in endosomes may be required to mediate membrane penetration by endocytosed particles.[42]

Once in the cytoplasm, the rotavirus DLP functions as a self-contained transcriptase, extruding capped, nonpolyadenylated messenger RNA (mRNA) through channels at the fivefold icosahedral vertices.[43,44] The genome remains encapsidated throughout transcription. The translation of viral mRNAs is enhanced by circularization, mediated by the specific binding of the rotavirus nonstructural protein NSP3 to the 3′ end of viral mRNA and to the cellular cap-binding protein eIF4G.[45,46] Thus, NSP3 substitutes for a cellular polyadenylic acid binding protein to favor the translation of the nonpolyadenylated viral mRNAs over polyadenylated host mRNAs.

It is believed that the assembly of progeny DLPs in the cytoplasm requires the specific packaging of one copy of each of the 11 genome segments. The mechanism of this selection remains obscure and is of fundamental importance to efforts to engineer the virus genome. No method has yet been devised to incorporate a recombinantly produced rotavirus gene segment into an infectious rotavirus virion, possibly because of the rigorous packaging requirements and partitioning of the components of nascent DLPs in viroplasmic inclusions.

Negative-strand synthesis, which forms double-stranded genomic RNA from positive-stranded mRNA, takes place simultaneously with genome packaging into precursor "core replication intermediates" so that the newly synthesized double-stranded RNA is never free in the cytoplasm.[47] Negative strand synthesis is primed by guanosine dinucleotides, which are probably synthesized by the viral polymerase in a template-independent fashion and which bind to the CC sequence at the 3′ end of all viral mRNAs.[48] Several viral nonstructural proteins are involved in genome replication and the assembly of precursor particles.[49] One of these, NSP2, forms an octomeric doughnut-shaped structure with nucleoside triphosphatase and helix-destabilizing activities.[50] NSP2 may act as a molecular motor, which drives replicating mRNA into the nascent particles.[51] With the addition of VP6, the core replication intermediate is converted into a DLP, which can transcribe more mRNA, amplifying virus yield.[49]

The outer capsid is assembled through an unusual maturation process, in which the DLP buds through the endoplasmic reticulum (ER) membrane, transiently acquiring an envelope. A viral nonstructural protein, NSP4, is resident in the ER membrane, binds the DLP (and possibly VP4 and VP7),[52] and mediates budding.[53] The transient envelope is lost as VP4 and VP7 are added. Thus, rotavirus penetrates membranes twice: once during entry and once during assembly. There are key similarities between these processes: during entry, membrane penetration is associated with outer capsid disassembly and a transition from the high-calcium extracellular environment to the low-calcium intracytoplasmic environment; during maturation, membrane penetration is associated with outer capsid assembly and a transition from the low-calcium intracytoplasmic environment to the high-calcium ER luminal environment. There are also important differences in membrane penetration during entry and maturation: VP4 is cleaved only during entry; NSP4 is involved only in maturation. Thus, rotavirus uses two distinct but related mechanisms of membrane penetration at different stages of its replication cycle.

Rotavirus egress from infected enterocytes is accomplished by release from the apical surface after vesicular transport from the ER by a pathway that bypasses the Golgi apparatus.[54] Interaction of the spike protein VP4 with raft lipid microdomains may provide a basis for this targeting.[55] Release of rotavirus by vesicular transport allows the virus to exit the ER and cross the plasma membrane without physically penetrating two more membranes or reentering the chemical environment of the cytoplasm.

CLINICAL FEATURES

Infants and young children with diarrhea caused by rotavirus are more likely to have severe symptoms and become dehydrated than patients with diarrhea related to other common enteric pathogens.[1,56,57] The clinical features of rotavirus gastroenteritis in humans have been studied in experimental infections in adults. In one such study, 4 of 18 adult volunteers developed vomiting 1 to 3 days after oral administration of a virulent rotavirus strain.[58] This was followed by diarrhea lasting 1 to 4 days and associated with anorexia, crampy abdominal pain, and low-grade fever. Viral shedding in stool was detected for 6 to 10 or more days. Two thirds of the adult volunteers developed serologic evidence of infection without disease. Similarly, most natural rotavirus infections of adults are asymptomatic, manifested only by a rise in antibody titer.[59] However, natural rotavirus infection of adults can also cause severe and even fatal disease.[60]

Observational studies on children in North America hospitalized with rotavirus gastroenteritis reveal a similar, although more severe, pattern of disease.[56,57,61] Rotavirus gastroenteritis in children generally begins with vomiting and fever, which lasts 2 to 3 days, and progresses to profuse watery diarrhea, which continues for 4 to 5 days. Vomiting is more common and prolonged with rotavirus gastroenteritis than with pediatric gastroenteritis caused by other agents,[57] which complicates oral rehydration.

Laboratory findings in children hospitalized with rotavirus gastroenteritis reflect isotonic dehydration and include a high urine specific gravity and metabolic acidosis.[56,61] Rotavirus gastroenteritis is not generally associated with leukocytosis but is sometimes accompanied by a mild elevation in transaminases and uric acid levels.[56,61] Liquid stools from children with rotavirus diarrhea usually do not contain blood or fecal leukocytes,[56,61] although fecal leukocytes can occasionally be encountered.[57] Typically, virus is detected in stools of children by antigenic assays for 4 to 10 days after the onset of symptoms;[56]

however, when a sensitive reverse transcriptase–polymerase chain reaction (RT-PCR) assay is used, shedding of viral RNA can be detected for up to 57 days from immunocompetent children, although this does not necessarily indicate shedding of infectious particles.[62]

Dehydration and severe electrolyte abnormalities leading to cardiac arrest are the most common proximate causes of mortality from rotavirus gastroenteritis.[63] Seizures and aspiration of vomitus may also lead to death.[63] In a case series from Toronto, parents of 16 of 21 infants and young children who died from rotavirus gastroenteritis had made contact with a physician during the course of the illness. Nevertheless, after a median 2 days of illness, 20 of the 21 ultimately presented to the hospital either dead or moribund. In a number of cases, communication barriers between physician and parent related to language or culture may have contributed to the fatal outcomes.[63]

The spectrum of illness after rotavirus infection of infants and children also includes mild gastroenteritis and asymptomatic infection. In some newborn nurseries, difficult-to-eradicate endemic rotavirus strains asymptomatically infect neonates year round.[64-67] A common VP4 type (P type) and genetic stability over time suggest that these nursery strains may be less virulent than most circulating strains,[64-66] although maternally transmitted immunity or maturational resistance may also protect the neonates from disease. Because outbreaks of rotavirus diarrhea in neonatal nurseries also occur, any component of maturational resistance cannot be absolute.[68]

In immunocompromised children, rotavirus infection has been associated with chronic diarrhea and extraintestinal infection. Conditions associated with chronic rotavirus infection include severe combined immunodeficiency (SCID), X-linked agammaglobulinemia, cartilage hair hypoplasia, acquired immunodeficiency syndrome (AIDS), and DiGeorge syndrome.[69-72] Rotavirus shed from chronically infected children often has altered genome segments.[70,72] Immunohistochemical staining for rotavirus structural and nonstructural proteins in autopsy specimens has demonstrated rotavirus replication in the hepatocytes and renal tubular cells of immunodeficient children with chronic rotavirus infection at the time of death.[69] Relatively severe rotavirus gastroenteritis has been noted in adult inpatients with immunosuppression related to bone marrow or renal transplantation.[73,74] Thus far, rotavirus has not been found to be a major cause of diarrhea in adults with AIDS.[75]

Rotavirus has been detected in association with a number of syndromes other than gastroenteritis, including respiratory infections,[76] necrotizing enterocolitis (in infants),[77] pneumatosis intestinalis,[78] hepatic abscess,[79] biliary atresia (group C rotavirus),[80] pancreatitis,[81] myositis,[82] Kawasaki syndrome,[83] sudden infant death syndrome,[84] seizures,[85,86] and meningoencephalitis.[85] As rotavirus infection is universal, these associations may be coincidental rather than causative, and an etiologic association has not been established. The occurrence of hepatitis in immunodeficient (SCID) and normal (BALB/c) mice experimentally infected with simian (but not murine or bovine) rotavirus and of extrahepatic biliary obstruction with fibrosis in BALB/c mice infected with simian or human rotavirus [87,88] supports the possibility that rotavirus can cause hepatobiliary disease in humans. A possible association between rotavirus infection and intestinal intussusception is discussed later.

PATHOGENESIS

The pathogenesis of rotavirus diarrhea is complex and incompletely understood, with potential roles for a viral enterotoxin, malabsorption related to mucosal damage and depression of disaccharidases, and secretion mediated by the enteric nervous system (ENS). Postmortem examination of the gastrointestinal tract of gnotobiotic pigs with diarrhea after experimental infection with a virulent human rotavirus strain demonstrated that viral replication is primarily restricted to the villous epithelium of the small intestine.[89] This pattern is consistent with the patchy villous epithelial distribution of rotavirus antigen noted after immunofluorescent staining of duodenal biopsy specimens from children with severe gastroenteritis.[90] Light microscopic examination of such duodenal biopsy specimens reveals shortened and blunted villi with a cuboidal epithelium, crypt hypertrophy, and mononuclear cell infiltration of the lamina propria.[7,91]

The severity of diarrhea in children with rotavirus gastroenteritis correlates with the degree of mucosal damage, which suggests that malabsorption related to loss of absorptive cells may contribute to rotavirus diarrhea late in infection.[91] However, in experimentally infected gnotobiotic pigs, diarrhea preceded villous atrophy.[89] Similarly, small intestinal biopsies from children with relatively mild rotavirus gastroenteritis do not consistently display histologic changes, which probably reflects patchy epithelial injury.[92] These observations indicate that potentially absorptive villous epithelial cells remain despite net fluid losses and that factors other than destruction of the intestinal epithelium are also important in the pathogenesis of rotavirus gastroenteritis.

In several animal models, rotavirus infection induces a net secretion of fluid, sodium, and chloride from intestinal segments.[93] Glucose cotransport of electrolytes is inhibited, although the degree of inhibition in humans does not prevent the use of oral rehydration solutions.[94,95] Furthermore, decreased disaccharidase activity makes less glucose available for cotransport.[7,94] Changes in the molecular weight distribution of absorbed polyethylene glycol in children with rotavirus gastroenteritis indicate an increase in paracellular permeability, probably caused by disruption of tight junctions.[96] In contrast to cholera-like toxins, rotavirus infection does not increase intracellular cyclic adenosine monophosphate concentrations.[94]

The rotavirus nonstructural glycoprotein NSP4 appears to play a role in the pathogenesis of diarrhea. NSP4 (solubilized from membranes with detergent) or a peptide corresponding to residues 114 to 135 of NSP4 induces age-dependent diarrhea when injected intraperitoneally or introduced into the ileum of infant mice.[97] A variety of cellular effects have been attributed to NSP4. Addition of solubilized NSP4 to the medium of cultured human intestinal epithelial cells (HT29 cells) leads to calcium influx and release from stores mediated by phospholipase 3 activation and inositol 1,4,5-trisphosphate production.[98] The resulting increase in intracellular calcium leads to a secretory state by activation of an anion channel that is distinct from the cystic fibrosis transmembrane regulator.[99] In addition, NSP4 is reported to increase paracellular permeability of MDCK cell monolayers,[100] and the 114 to 135 peptide inhibits glucose-coupled sodium transport in intestinal brush border membrane vesicles from rabbits.[95] Two findings support the surprising hypothesis that NSP4, an integral ER membrane protein, acts as an extracellular toxin: first, a 7-kD fragment of NSP4 (residues 112 to 175) is secreted into the medium of rotavirus-infected cells in culture and can reproduce many of the activities attributed to NSP4[101]; second, oral administration of antibody against NSP4 can reduce the diarrhea caused by a simian rotavirus infection of mouse pups.[97] It is not clear, at present, to what degree the enterotoxin activity of NSP4 and its peptides observed in animal and cell culture models explains rotavirus diarrhea in children.

The ENS has a role in the pathogenesis of rotavirus gastroenteritis. Tetrodotoxin (a sodium channel blocker), lidocaine (a local anesthetic), and hexamethonium (a nicotinic receptor blocker), when applied to the serosal surface of simian rotavirus–infected, isolated mouse pup intestines, eliminated the net fluid secretion associated with rotavirus infection.[12] Furthermore, intraperitoneal injection of lidocaine in rotavirus-infected mice significantly decreased the incidence of diarrhea.[12] As diarrhea induced by bacterial toxins can be ameliorated by inhibition of the ENS, roles for an enterotoxin and the ENS in the pathogenesis of rotavirus diarrhea are not mutually exclusive. Activation of ENS-mediated fluid secretion by intestinal inflammation or other cellular interactions provides a potential explanation for the observation that genetically inactivated (psoralen-treated), nonreplicating simian rotavirus particles, when fed in high doses to infant mice, could induce diarrhea.[102] Most important, a clinical trial of an enkephalinase inhibitor in children with gastroenteritis indicated that ENS-mediated secretion is important in the pathogenesis of diarrhea in humans and is a target for therapeutic intervention (see "Treatment").[13]

SEROLOGIC CLASSIFICATION

Rotavirus strains have a complex serology and are classified by serogroup, subgroup, G serotype, and P serotype as well as by the genetic groupings of G genotype, P genotype, and electropherotype.

The broadest serologic grouping of rotaviruses is the serogroup, defined by the cross-recognition of particles by serum antibody obtained from parenterally hyperimmunized animals.[103] Genetic exchange has not been observed between members of different rotavirus serogroups, indicating that the serogroups have become genetically isolated from each other. The determinants that define serogroups A to G are predominantly located on VP2 and VP6, which make up the innermost and middle icosahedral layers of the rotavirus virion. Groups A, B, and C cause disease in humans and other animals, whereas groups D to G have been described only in nonhuman animals. Serogroup A is the most important clinically, as group A viruses cause the endemic gastroenteritis of children; groups B and C have been associated with epidemics of gastroenteritis affecting all ages. Group B contains the strain ADRV (adult diarrhea rotavirus), which has been associated with large outbreaks of severe diarrhea in adults in China[104]; group C viruses have been associated with less severe gastroenteritis in both children and adults.[105,106] For epidemiologic purposes, serogroup A has been subdivided into subgroups I, II, I+II, and non-I non-II on the basis of monoclonal antibody recognition of antigenic determinants on VP6.[25] There is no known absolute functional correlate for the subgroup classification.

Within group A, rotavirus serotypes are defined on the basis of reciprocal cross-neutralization by antibody. Initially, rotavirus serotypes were designated by a unitary system, but this system did not fully explain cross-neutralization patterns.[107-110] Group A rotaviruses are now classified into serotypes with a binomial nomenclature, in which neutralization by antibodies against VP4 defines "P" serotype (for protease-sensitive antigen) and neutralization by antibodies against VP7 defines "G" serotype (for glycoprotein antigen). Further complicating the serology, VP4 and VP7 both contain serotype-specific and heterotypic neutralizing epitopes.[40,111] In the case of VP4, the serotype-specific epitopes are predominantly found on the variable VP8* hemagglutination domain, located at the tips of the spikes, and the heterotypic epitopes are predominantly found on the more conserved membrane interaction domain, which constitutes the body of the spikes.[36,40]

To date, 14 G serotypes (G1 to G14) have been identified, of which 10 are known to infect humans.[112] The sequence of the genome segment encoding VP7 accurately predicts G serotype,[113] so genotyping provides a practical surrogate for G serotype determination. Serotype G2 viruses predominate in outbreaks of group A rotavirus gastroenteritis among adults, which suggests that heterotypic immunity after natural infection may protect less effectively against G2 viruses or that G2 viruses may be particularly virulent in adults.[114]

To date, 13 P serotypes (with serotypes 1, 2, and 5 each divided into subtypes A and B) have been identified.[103,112] Immunologic reagents for determining P serotype are limited,[115] and P serotyping is complicated by cross-reactivity between P serotypes. Therefore, P genotyping is more commonly used for classification. Twenty-two P genotypes (P1 to P22) have been identified thus far.[103,103a] Unlike G serotypes, which have a one-to-one correspondence with G genotypes, some P serotypes include more than one P genotype. In strain descriptions, the genotype is enclosed in brackets after the serotype designation. Thus, G2P1B[4] refers to a virus of G serotype 2, P serotype 1B, and P genotype 4. The P types known to infect humans include P1A[8], P1B[4], P2A[6], P3[9], P4[10], P5A[3], P7[5], P8[11], P11[14], and P12[19].[103] Reflecting the importance of VP4 as a determinant of virulence and host range, P type is correlated with virulence in humans. Thus, asymptomatic nursery strains of rotavirus are of P type P2A[6] and P8[11],[116,117] although some virulent strains are also P[6].[118]

Fortunately for vaccine development efforts, a limited number of serotypic combinations cause the majority of symptomatic infections. Four such combinations (G1P1A[8], G2P1B[4], G3P1A[8], and G4P1A[8]) constitute more than 90% of strains causing human disease in temperate climates.[119] However, a greater diversity of virus strains circulates in some tropical areas.[120] Less common G and P types provide a reservoir of variation that may allow "escape" from the protection offered by a vaccine. For example, P[6] strains have become prevalent among children with diarrhea in India and Africa;[117] G9 rotaviruses, first identified in 1983, have increased in prevalence in many regions of the world and have become the predominant G type in some African counties and the third most common G type in the United States.[117,121,122] Reassortment between human rotavirus strains, antigenic drift, and the occasional introduction of animal rotaviruses or their genome segments into the pool of viruses circulating among humans provide a continuous introduction of genetic diversity and will necessitate ongoing surveillance to maintain the efficacy of any future rotavirus vaccines.[123]

Before the widespread use of RT-PCR for genetic classification, rotavirus strains were commonly compared on the basis of RNA electropherotype. Group A rotaviruses are grouped into "long," "short," and "supershort" strains on the basis of the electrophoretic mobility of genome segments 10 and 11. In short and supershort strains, genome segment 11 migrates more slowly than genome segment 10 because of insertions and duplications in its 3′ untranslated region.[124] In general, subgroup I rotaviruses have a short electropherotype, and subgroup II rotaviruses have a long electropherotype.[112] Within these major categories of electropherotype, strains can be distinguished on the basis of more subtle differences in genome segment electrophoretic mobility. Because electrophoretic mobility is strongly influenced by RNA secondary structure, a single point mutation can perceptibly alter the electropherotype.[125]

EPIDEMIOLOGY

Rotavirus infection is universal, and almost all children acquire serum antibody against the virus in the first 2 or 3 years of life.[126] Severe gastroenteritis caused by rotavirus most commonly affects infants and children between 6 months and 2 years of age,[103] although in poorer populations the peak of illness may be somewhat earlier.[5,127,128] The age of greatest susceptibility to severe disease may be bracketed by the waning of maternally transferred passive immunity and the maturation of the gastrointestinal tract at about 6 months, and by the acquisition of active immunity related to natural infection later in childhood.

Rotavirus is the most common cause of severe dehydrating diarrhea leading to the hospitalization of infants and children in both the developed and developing world (reviewed in reference 103). An analysis of published studies indicates that rotavirus causes approximately 139 million cases of gastroenteritis, 25 million clinic visits, 2 million hospitalizations, and 440,000 childhood deaths each year worldwide.[3] Whereas the incidence of rotavirus gastroenteritis is similar in developed and developing countries, mortality is concentrated in poorer nations (Fig. 146-3).[3] The causes of higher mortality from rotavirus in the developing world may include the greater prevalence of malnutrition,[127] less access to treatment, larger inoculum size, and synergy with other intestinal flora or pathogens. In mice, malnutrition leads to more severe diarrhea upon rotavirus challenge.[129]

Despite the lack of a safe and effective vaccine against rotavirus, a widely used specific therapy for rotavirus gastroenteritis, or a substantial decrease in the overall incidence of rotavirus gastroenteritis, global mortality caused by rotavirus is thought to have fallen by approximately 50% since 1985.[3] Improved access to treatment, particularly increased use of oral rehydration solutions, probably plays a role in decreasing mortality, although better nutrition and a lower incidence of comorbidities may also contribute. Given the relative resistance of rotavirus to hygienic improvements, it is likely that overall mortality caused by gastroenteritis will continue to decline, but the proportion of diarrheal illness and deaths caused by rotavirus will increase. Indeed, the proportion of hospitalized children with diarrhea who shed rotavirus increases with rising income.[3] The physical hardiness of the rotavirus particle, the high particle concentration in stool (up to 10^{11} particles/mL),[130] and the small minimum infectious dose ($ID_{50} = 10$ focus-forming units)[131] account for the weak association between the incidence of rotavirus gastroenteritis and the level of economic development or hygiene.

In developed countries, rotavirus is a major cause of morbidity and health care costs. Although about 80% of children in the United States experience rotavirus gastroenteritis in the first 5 years of life, only about 20 to 40 die each year as a result.[132] In the United States, ro-

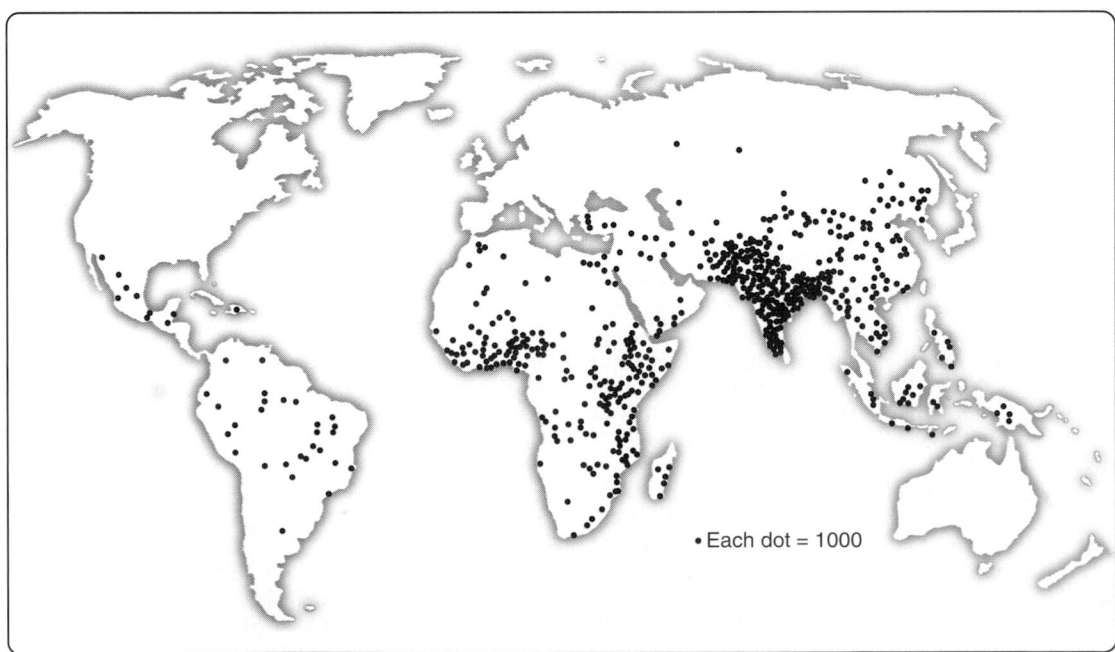

FIGURE 146-3. Estimated global distribution of deaths from rotavirus gastroenteritis. *(Based on data from Committee on Issues and Priorities for New Vaccine Development. New Vaccine Development. Establishing Priorities, v. II. Diseases of Importance in Developing Countries. Appendix D-13. The prospects for immunizing against rotavirus. Washington, DC: National Academy Press; 1986:308-318; adapted with permission from Glass RI, Bresee JS, Parashar U, et al. Rotavirus vaccines at the threshold. Nat Med. 1997;3:1324-1325.)*

tavirus gastroenteritis is responsible for 570,000 physician visits and 55,000 hospitalizations annually,[132,133] costing approximately $264 million in direct health care costs and $1 billion in total costs, including the cost of time missed from work by caregivers.[133]

Rotavirus gastroenteritis has a marked seasonality in temperate climates, with a peak of cases in the cooler months each year.[4,5] In North America, the annual rotavirus epidemic begins in the fall in the Southwest, spreads north and east, reaches the eastern seaboard by late winter, and tapers off in the spring (Fig. 146-4).[134] In the tropics, rotavirus causes disease throughout the year.[4] Although the cause of the seasonality of rotavirus circulation in temperate regions has not been definitively explained, its annual reemergence may be due to enhanced spread from more equatorial regions when environmental factors are most favorable. As the rotavirus particle is inactivated more quickly in conditions of relatively high humidity, dry weather during the winter months may promote transmission.[29] During a rotavirus season, multiple strains, representing several P and G types, usually circulate. In a single region, the dominant strains differ from year to year; in the same year, the dominant strains differ regionally.[119]

The best documented mode of rotavirus transmission is fecal-oral.[131] However, winter seasonality and universal infection early in life are more typical of pathogens with respiratory spread. Experiments on the transmission of rotavirus gastroenteritis (epizootic diarrhea of infant mice) between cages of mice support the possibility of airborne spread.[135] Although rotaviruses do not spread primarily through contaminated water or food, transmission by these vehicles can occur. A large outbreak of group B rotavirus gastroenteritis in China and an outbreak of group A rotavirus gastroenteritis in Colorado were associated with fecal contamination of water supplies.[104,136] A group A rotavirus gastroenteritis outbreak among university students in Washington, DC, was traced to contaminated dining hall food.[114]

Rotavirus has been associated with gastroenteritis outbreaks in daycare centers and playgroups, can spread in families, and may cause gastroenteritis in the adult caregivers for small children.[137,138] It is likely that the large viral inoculum ingested by these caregivers is, in part, responsible for illness despite some level of acquired immunity. Rotavirus outbreaks have occurred in nursing home populations and sometimes have resulted in fatalities.[60,114] Rotavirus is an important cause of nosocomial infection; in addition to the asymptomatic infections associated with rotavirus endemics in newborn nurseries, rotavirus causes symptomatic hospital-acquired outbreaks associated with circulation of rotavirus in the community.[139] Rotavirus also can cause traveler's diarrhea.[140]

Rotavirus is a major veterinary pathogen, causing disease in infant cattle, sheep, swine, and camels as well as in adult chickens and turkeys and in domestic pets such as cats and dogs. The genes of some strains that circulate and cause disease in humans are more closely related to those of animal rotavirus strains than to those of other human rotavirus strains.[141] This observation suggests that rotaviruses, on occasion, can be transmitted from nonhuman animals to humans.[141] In addition, some human rotaviruses have individual genome segments that are closely related to those of animal rotaviruses, suggesting reassortment between viruses with different primary hosts.[141,142] Nevertheless, in general, rotaviruses are attenuated in non-native hosts and are transmitted efficiently only in populations of their native hosts. No major outbreaks of disease have been directly linked to contact with infected animals.

IMMUNITY

Asymptomatic infection of neonates with nursery strains of rotavirus protects against subsequent severe rotavirus gastroenteritis but not against asymptomatic reinfection or mild to moderate disease.[143] Thus, rotavirus infections can provide partial protection from challenge without causing significant primary disease. Further encouragement for a live, oral vaccination strategy is provided by a prospective observational study in which 200 Mexican infants were monitored for rotavirus infection from birth to 2 years of age. This surveillance showed that protection from subsequent moderate or severe rotavirus diarrhea was 87% after one natural infection of any severity and 100% after two natural infections.[126]

Experimental mice can be infected by rotavirus at any age, but rotavirus infections cause gastroenteritis only in mouse pups younger than 2 weeks.[135,144] Resistance to disease in immunologically naïve older mice suggests that maturational events, such as the development of gastric acid and pepsin secretion, limit the severity of rotavirus infections.[145] In humans, however, the duration of immunity is limited, with repeated symptomatic rotavirus infections occurring (generally with decreasing severity) in both children and adults.[114,126,146] In isolated human communities with limited prior exposure to rotaviruses, explosive epidemics of rotavirus diarrhea with high attack rates in adults are seen.[60,147] These observations suggest that maturational resistance is less significant in humans and does not fully account for the lower incidence of severe disease in older children and adults. Rather, repeated asymptomatic or mildly symptomatic episodes of rotavirus gastroenteritis throughout life appear to be important for maintaining immunity.[59,148]

In experimental studies of passively transferred immunity to rotavirus in mice, circulating neutralizing antibody does not protect against disease; however, the presence of sufficient levels of neutralizing monoclonal or colostrum-derived antibody in the gut does protect.[149,150]

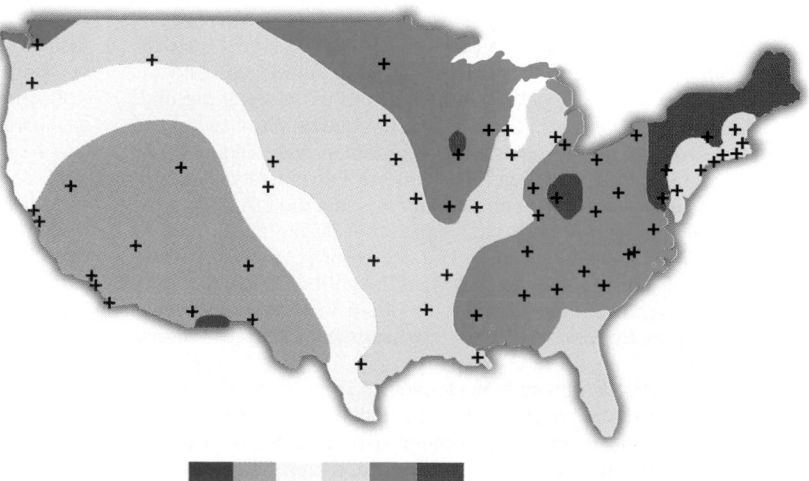

FIGURE 146-4. Average time of peak rotavirus activity in the United States, July 1991 to June 1997. Crosses indicate laboratories participating in the surveillance system upon which this map was based. *(Adapted from Parashar UD, Bresee JS, Gentsch JR, et al. Rotavirus. Emerg Infect Dis. 1998;4:561-570.)*

Nov Dec Jan Feb Mar Apr

In immunized mice, the appearance of immunoglobulin A (IgA) in the gut correlates with clearance of infection.[144] These experimental results corroborate the observation that, in children, fecal rotavirus-specific IgA levels, which reflect duodenal IgA levels, are associated with protection from symptomatic infection.[137,148] In humans, the presence of virus-specific serum antibody has a weaker correlation with protection from disease and appears to be a marker of previous infection rather than a primary effector of immunity.[128,151]

The evidence that breast-feeding protects human infants from rotavirus diarrhea is mixed. In Bangladesh, hospitalized children with rotavirus diarrhea are more likely to be breastfed than patients with diarrhea from other causes, which suggests that breast-feeding prevents rotavirus gastroenteritis less effectively than it prevents gastroenteritis caused by other agents.[152] Nevertheless, in some clinical studies of rotavirus gastroenteritis, breast-feeding is associated with reduced frequency of vomiting and less severe dehydration.[153,154] This modest protective effect of breast-feeding is consistent with the results of experimental studies in mice. Mouse pups suckled on dams that have been naturally infected with murine rotavirus are not protected from a virulent murine rotavirus challenge;[155] however, mouse pups suckled on dams that have been orally or parenterally hyperimmunized with simian rotavirus are protected from a relatively attenuated simian rotavirus challenge.[149]

Serotype influences but does not determine the degree of protection from challenge. Protection after natural infection or immunization appears to be somewhat more reliable against viruses of the same serotype (G type) as the immunizing strain.[126,146,156,157] On the other hand, cross-protection between serotypes clearly also occurs, particularly after multiple infections.[126,156] This finding correlates with the primarily homotypic neutralizing antibody response to primary infection and the increasingly heterotypic responses to reinfection with the same or other serotypes.[158,159]

The mechanisms of rotavirus neutralization by antibodies have been examined in detail. Neutralizing monoclonal antibodies that recognize the VP8* fragment of VP4 block the attachment of sialic acid–dependent rotaviruses to cells or trigger virus uncoating;[160,161] antibodies that recognize the VP5* fragment of VP4 block a postbinding entry event;[160] and antibodies against the VP7 coat protein block virion uncoating.[162] Although VP8*, which has high sequence variability, contains predominantly P-type specific neutralization epitopes, VP5*, which is relatively conserved, contains heterotypic neutralizing epitopes.[40,163] Most monoclonal antibodies that recognize VP4 and neutralize human strains of rotavirus bind the VP5* fragment,[163] possibly reflecting the role of this region in cell attachment for strains (including most that infect humans) that do not bind cell surface sialosides.[37,38] VP7 contains both G-type specific and heterotypic neutralizing epitopes.[164] Therefore, antibodies that recognize VP5* and VP7 probably make important contributions to heterotypic protection against rotavirus.

Surprisingly, non-neutralizing antibodies against the middle capsid protein, VP6, also mediate protection in some animal models. Specifically, VP6-specific monoclonal IgA, when secreted into the serum of mice by "backpack" hybridoma tumors, protects the mice from rotavirus challenge.[165] In addition, immunization of wild-type, but not J chain–deficient, mice with recombinant virus-like particles (VLPs) containing only VP2 and VP6 can mediate heterotypic protection.[166] This requirement for J chains suggests that the IgA protects by intracellular interference with viral replication during its transcytosis across the intestinal epithelium.[166] The degree of protection provided by preparations that do not elicit neutralizing antibodies appears to be limited, however, as immunization with VP2/6 VLPs does not protect gnotobiotic pigs from diarrhea upon challenge with a virulent human rotavirus strain.[167]

The role of cellular immunity in clearing and preventing rotavirus infection has been studied in an adult mouse model of rotavirus infection that does not result in diarrhea. Although some rotavirus-inoculated SCID mice persistently shed virus, 40% of SCID mice on a C57BL/6 background do clear the infection.[168] This observation suggests that mechanisms other than acquired immunity can resolve rotavirus infections but are unreliable. Mice that are T-cell deficient on the basis of an $\alpha\beta/\gamma\delta$ T-cell receptor knockout clear primary infection shortly after immunocompetent mice, mount a modest IgA antibody response (primarily against VP6), and are resistant to reinfection upon challenge.[168] Most B cell–deficient mice (J_HD knockouts) with intact CD8+ T cells also clear primary rotavirus infections but can be reinfected.[169] Thus, although cell-mediated or humoral immunity effectively clears primary infection, humoral immunity is essential for protection from challenge in mice.

DIAGNOSIS

Rotavirus gastroenteritis is not clearly distinguished from other causes of acute gastroenteritis on clinical grounds alone. However, rotavirus is shed in the stools of approximately two thirds of children younger than 5 years with diarrhea severe enough to warrant hospitalization during the peak of the rotavirus season in North America.[5] As the standard treatment for rotavirus gastroenteritis is rehydration and supportive care, a specific microbiologic diagnosis is not required in most cases. However, with prolonged diarrhea, in complicated cases, in immunocompromised hosts, when alternative diagnoses are considered, or when epidemiologic or infection control data are needed, it may be desirable to establish rotavirus as the etiologic agent. Definitively diagnosing rotavirus gastroenteritis may also prevent unnecessary and potentially harmful use of antibiotics.

Rotavirus can be detected by numerous techniques, including a variety of commercial antigenic assays, RT-PCR, electron microscopy, immune electron microscopy, polyacrylamide gel electrophoresis (PAGE) for viral genomic RNA, and viral culture. Detection of viral antigen in stool or rectal swabs, most commonly using enzyme-linked immunosorbent assay (ELISA) or latex agglutination formats, forms the basis for practical, commercially available, and widely used diagnostic kits.[170] Latex agglutination is particularly suitable for use in areas with limited resources, although a confirmatory technique is desirable to evaluate indeterminate results because of the limited sensitivity of the test.[170,171] Commercial antigenic assays primarily detect the VP2 and VP6 proteins of the subviral double-layered particle and detect only group A rotaviruses. Serotype-specific ELISAs, based on recognition of VP7 or VP4, allow determination of serotype without the need to perform neutralization assays.[109,115] Although there are various techniques for measuring serum, fecal, and salivary antibodies against rotavirus, the acute and generally self-limited nature of rotavirus infections limits the usefulness of these techniques for clinical decision making.

RT-PCR has become a major diagnostic technique used in epidemiologic studies. RT-PCR allows determination of P and G types and permits finer definition of strain differences.[172,173] Although this technique is very sensitive, it is also subject to inhibition by contaminants in fecal specimens, requiring careful sample preparation.[173]

Both electron microscopy and PAGE can detect unusual strains of rotavirus (such as non–group A rotaviruses) that might be missed by standard antigenic or nucleic acid–based assays. Electron microscopy of stool specimens negatively stained with phosphotungstic acid is rapid and, despite only moderate sensitivity, has high specificity because of the distinctive appearance of rotavirus particles (see Fig. 146-1).[174] Electrophoresis of simply prepared stool suspensions on polyacrylamide gels followed by silver staining for the pattern of 11 segments of genomic double-stranded RNA allows both diagnosis and tracking of rotavirus strains in molecular epidemiologic investigations.[175] Rotavirus can be detected, although with relatively low sensitivity, by growth in cell culture. Human rotavirus strains have proved more difficult to culture routinely than most animal rotavirus strains but in many cases can be propagated on MA104 cells or primary green monkey kidney cells grown in roller tubes with the addition of trypsin to the cell culture medium.[130,176]

TREATMENT

Recommendations for treatment are summarized in a practice guideline from the American Academy of Pediatrics.[177] As rotavirus gastroenteritis is generally self-limited and dehydration is the primary cause of morbidity and mortality, rehydration and restoration of electrolyte balance are the primary therapies. Oral rehydration solutions (ORSs) are effective in treating dehydration related to rotavirus gastroenteritis, even in the presence of moderate vomiting, and are preferred over intravenous rehydration in cases of mild or moderate dehydration.[177,178] The principle on which these solutions are based is the solute-coupled cotransport of sodium by enterocytes, which continues to operate even in the damaged gut.[179] Effective solutes include glucose, amino acids, and short oligopeptides.

The standard oral rehydration formulation recommended by the World Health Organization is 90 mM Na^+, 20 mM K^+, 80 mM Cl^-, 10 mM citrate, and 111 mM glucose. Although this formula is clearly effective in dehydration caused by rotavirus and is safe, the osmolarity of the solution is based on the higher sodium content of stool resulting from cholera infection than from rotavirus infection.[6] Equally or more effective hypo-osmolar formulations have a lower sodium content (50 to 60 mM) and decrease the osmotic load of the carbohydrate component by using either 90 mM glucose or complex carbohydrates to promote sodium cotransport.[11,180]

In cases in which oral hydration cannot be maintained because of severe vomiting, a depressed level of consciousness, or intestinal ileus and in cases of severe dehydration (with loss of more than 10% of body weight), intravenous hydration is recommended.[177] However, when the patient has been resuscitated and is able to take oral fluids, oral rehydration should be instituted. Despite the depressed disaccharidase levels associated with rotavirus gastroenteritis, it is recommended that nursing infants continue to breastfeed during rehydration and that children resume a diet as soon as they can tolerate feeding. The early reinstitution of an age-appropriate diet, avoiding fatty foods and foods high in simple sugars, has nutritional benefits and shortens the duration of diarrhea by about half a day.[177,181]

Racecadotril, of which no commercial preparations are currently available in the United States, is an enkephalinase inhibitor that inhibits intestinal hypersecretion rather than motility and has been evaluated as an adjunct to ORS in a placebo-controlled trial in Peru. Racecadotril combined with ORS cut total stool output and the duration of diarrhea by about half compared with the use of ORS alone for treatment of rotavirus gastroenteritis.[13] This trial provides a clinical correlate to basic studies in mice, which show a role for the ENS in the pathogenesis of rotavirus diarrhea.[12] Although these results are promising, the clinical role of racecadotril is not yet clearly established.

Passive immunotherapy with orally administered immunoglobulins has been considered for the treatment and prevention of rotavirus gastroenteritis. In case reports, feeding human serum immune globulin to children with chronic rotavirus diarrhea has been followed by resolution of diarrhea and viral shedding.[182] In double-blind, placebo-controlled studies, oral human immune globulin decreased the duration of diarrhea and hospitalization in inpatients with acute, community-acquired rotavirus gastroenteritis in Italy,[183] and oral administration of colostrum from hyperimmunized cows decreased the stool output, ORS intake, and duration of diarrhea in children hospitalized with rotavirus gastroenteritis in Bangladesh.[184] When given prophylactically to low-birth-weight infants, oral gamma globulin reduced the severity of diarrhea associated with neonatal rotavirus infections.[185] In a small trial in an orphanage, prophylactic feeding with hyperimmune bovine colostrum during the rotavirus season provided partial protection from rotavirus gastroenteritis.[186] Thus, although oral administration of immunoglobulins is not indicated for routine use, it may have a role in treating chronic rotavirus diarrhea and may merit further evaluation as a preventive agent, albeit an expensive one, in certain high-risk settings.

Because of complications including ileus and respiratory depression, antimotility agents such as loperamide have no role in the treatment of childhood gastroenteritis.[177] Bismuth subsalicylate (Pepto-Bismol) has been shown to decrease the duration of diarrhea and the intake of ORS in children with gastroenteritis,[187] but the modest benefits observed and a theoretical possibility of Reye's syndrome related to salicylate absorption argue against routine use of this agent.[177] Although its mechanism of action is unclear, "probiotic" treatment of childhood gastroenteritis, including rotavirus gastroenteritis, by oral administration of lactobacilli appears to shorten the duration of diarrhea by about 0.7 days, based on a meta-analysis of randomized, blinded, controlled trials.[188]

PREVENTION

Because lack of access to treatment is one of the major causes of childhood mortality from rotavirus, prevention by immunization is a critical approach to decreasing the impact of this infection. The most important goal of immunizing against rotavirus is to prevent severe dehydrating illness. Thus, an effective vaccine need not completely protect against all rotavirus infection or even against mild rotavirus gastroenteritis. As natural asymptomatic infections with wild-type virus protect against subsequent moderate or severe disease,[126,143] protection by immunization is a technically achievable goal.

Live attenuated vaccines have reached the furthest stage of development. This approach received a major setback with the withdrawal of RotaShield (Wyeth Lederle Vaccines). This quadrivalent, reassortant vaccine was based on a modified "jennerian" approach, using a live animal virus to immunize humans. To broaden the serotype specificity of the immune response to the vaccine,[157] VP7 molecules from each of the G types 1 to 4 were presented on the genetic background of a simian rotavirus strain (RRV) that is attenuated for humans on the basis of host range restriction and, presumably, passage in cell culture. In phase III trials, RotaShield proved highly effective against moderate to severe diarrhea in both developed (United States and Finland) and developing (Venezuela) economic settings.[156,189,190] Fever with accompanying irritability and decreased appetite after the first and second doses was the only significantly associated adverse reaction that was noted in multiple studies.[14,190,191] Some mild diarrhea after the first dose was also observed in a Finnish study.[191]

RotaShield was licensed by the U.S. Food and Drug Administration in 1998 and was recommended by the Advisory Committee on Immunization Practices (ACIP).[14] Over the course of 9 months, approximately 1 million doses were administered. During this time, 15 cases of intestinal intussusception were reported to the Vaccine Adverse Event Reporting System, a passive registry of potential vaccine-associated complications; 11 of these cases occurred within 1 week of receiving the first dose of the vaccine.[192] A case-control study revealed a significantly increased incidence of intestinal intussusception in vaccinees clustered in the 3 to 14 days after administration of the first dose of RotaShield (odds ratio = 21.7) and less of an increase after the second dose (odds ratio = 3.3).[193] In response to the association between immunization and intussusception, the ACIP withdrew its recommendation for immunization,[15] and the manufacturer voluntarily stopped vaccine production. Although the recommendations applied only to the United States, these events greatly diminished enthusiasm for potential use of the vaccine in the developing world, where mortality from rotavirus gastroenteritis is much higher.

The nature and magnitude of the association between immunization with RotaShield and intestinal intussusception remain controversial.[194,195] For example, an ecologic study of hospital discharges in 10 states during the period of RotaShield immunization revealed an overall increase of only 1% to 4% in intussusception admissions for infants 45 to 210 days of age during the period of RotaShield distribution, using a baseline that was adjusted for a trend of decreasing admissions since 1993.[196] Furthermore, a reanalysis of the case-control study database suggested that a compensatory decrease in intussusception may have followed the 3-week period of increased risk immediately after immunization, yielding no overall increased risk in vaccinees.[194] Such a decrease could result if natural rotavirus infection also causes intussusception or if immunization simply altered the timing of intussusception in predisposed individuals. A possible association between natural rotavirus infection and intestinal intussusception had been reported previously in a small case series.[197] However, the lack of a seasonal peak in intestinal intussusception (which is uncommon relative to rotavirus gastroenteritis) during the seasonal peak in rotavirus infection[198] suggests that any association with natural rotavirus infection must be weak. Proposed mechanisms of a possible association include altered intestinal motility or a "knuckle" of hypertrophied intestinal lymphoid tissue forming the leading edge of an intussusception. Although estimates of the risk of intussusception attributable to immunization with RotaShield clearly vary, a consensus based on a workshop held by the National Vaccine Advisory Committee and the National Vaccine Program Office is that immunization was associated with an attributable risk of intussusception of approximately 1 in 10,000 children immunized.[199]

The implications of the withdrawal of RotaShield for public health policy and future vaccine development are complex. A greater burden of adverse effects may be tolerable in countries with much higher rates of childhood mortality related to rotavirus gastroenteritis. On the other hand, intestinal intussusception is no longer commonly fatal in developed countries but may have a case-fatality rate of up to 50% in some developing nations.[198] In addition, many are uncomfortable with the assessment that a vaccine can have an acceptable safety profile for use in developing but not in developed countries.

Although intestinal intussusception was observed in several vaccine recipients after the second or third dose during extensive preclinical testing of RotaShield, the association between immunization and intussusception was not statistically significant in these studies.[14] Therefore, the difficulty of demonstrating the safety of other live, oral rotavirus vaccines before licensure is increased. It remains to be determined whether an association with intestinal intussusception is specific to RotaShield or will be a more general problem for live, orally administered rotavirus vaccines. Nevertheless, two other live oral vaccines against rotavirus are in phase III trials in the United States: a pentavalent reassortant vaccine, in which VP7 or VP4 molecules from human strains are presented in the context of a bovine rotavirus (strain WC3) background, is being developed by Merck,[200] and a monovalent vaccine based on a human rotavirus isolate (strain 89-12), attenuated by serial passage in cell culture, is being developed by Glaxo SmithKline.[201]

The failure of RotaShield has rekindled interest in alternative approaches to immunization against rotavirus. These alternatives include immunization with recombinant, noninfectious virus-like particles[202]; immunization with inactivated rotavirus particles[203]; immunization with DNA encoding specific rotavirus antigens, such as VP4, VP6, and VP7[204]; and parenteral immunization with individual rotavirus proteins.

Acknowledgments

I thank Roger I. Glass, Harry B. Greenberg, and Jacqueline M. Dormitzer for careful review of the manuscript and Albert Z. Kapikian for providing electron micrographs of rotavirus particles.

REFERENCES

1. de Zoysa I, Feachem RG. Interventions for the control of diarrhoeal diseases among young children: Rotavirus and cholera immunization. Bull World Health Organ. 1985;63:569-583.
2. Rotavirus vaccines. Wkly Epidemiol Rec. 1999;74:33-38.
3. Parashar UD, Hummelman EG, Bresee JS, et al. Global illness and deaths caused by rotavirus disease in children. Emerg Infect Dis. 2003;9:565-572.
4. Cook SM, Glass RI, LeBaron CW, et al. Global seasonality of rotavirus infections. Bull World Health Organ. 1990;68:171-177.
5. Brandt CD, Kim HW, Rodriguez WJ, et al. Pediatric viral gastroenteritis during eight years of study. J Clin Microbiol. 1983;18:71-78.
6. Duggan C, Santosham M, Glass RI. The management of acute diarrhea in children: Oral rehydration, maintenance, and nutritional therapy. MMWR Recomm Rep. 1992;41:1-20.
7. Bishop RF, Davidson GP, Holmes IH, et al. Virus particles in epithelial cells of duodenal mucosa from children with acute non-bacterial gastroenteritis. Lancet. 1973;2:1281-1283.
8. Adams WR, Kraft LM. Epizootic diarrhea of infant mice: Identification of the etiologic agent. Science. 1963;141:359-360.
9. Mebus CA, Underdahl NR, Rhodes MB, et al. Calf diarrhea (scours): Reproduced with a virus from a field outbreak. Univ Nebr Res Bull. 1969;233.
10. Flewett TH, Bryden AS, Davies H, et al. Relation between viruses from acute gastroenteritis of children and newborn calves. Lancet. 1974;2:61-63.
11. Farthing MJ. Treatment of gastrointestinal viruses. Novartis Found Symp. 2001;238:289-300.
12. Lundgren O, Peregrin AT, Persson K, et al. Role of the enteric nervous system in the fluid and electrolyte secretion of rotavirus diarrhea. Science. 2000;287:491-495.
13. Salazar-Lindo E, Santisteban-Ponce J, Chea-Woo E, et al. Racecadotril in the treatment of acute watery diarrhea in children. N Engl J Med. 2000;343:463-467.
14. Rotavirus vaccine for the prevention of rotavirus gastroenteritis among children. Recommendations of the Advisory Committee on Immunization Practices (ACIP). MMWR Recomm Rep. 1999;48:1-20.
15. Withdrawal of rotavirus vaccine recommendation. MMWR Morb Mortal Wkly Rep. 1999;48:1007.
16. Prasad BV, Wang GJ, Clerx JP, et al. Three-dimensional structure of rotavirus. J Mol Biol. 1988;199:269-275.
17. Yeager M, Dryden KA, Olson NH, et al. Three-dimensional structure of rhesus rotavirus by cryoelectron microscopy and image reconstruction. J Cell Biol. 1990;110:2133-2144.
18. Lawton JA, Zeng CQ, Mukherjee SK, et al. Three-dimensional structural analysis of recombinant rotavirus-like particles with intact and amino-terminal-deleted VP2: Implications for the architecture of the VP2 capsid layer. J Virol. 1997;71:7353-7360.
19. Yeager M, Berriman JA, Baker TS, et al. Three-dimensional structure of the rotavirus haemagglutinin VP4 by cryo-electron microscopy and difference map analysis. EMBO J. 1994;13:1011-1018.
20. Greenberg HB, Valdesuso J, van Wyke K, et al. Production and preliminary characterization of monoclonal antibodies directed at two surface proteins of rhesus rotavirus. J Virol. 1983;47:267-275.
21. Hoshino Y, Saif LJ, Sereno MM, et al. Infection immunity of piglets to either VP3 or VP7 outer capsid protein confers resistance to challenge with a virulent rotavirus bearing the corresponding antigen. J Virol. 1988;62:744-748.
22. Offit PA, Clark HF, Blavat G, et al. Reassortant rotaviruses containing structural proteins vp3 and vp7 from different parents induce antibodies protective against each parental serotype. J Virol. 1986;60:491-496.
23. Ludert JE, Feng N, Yu JH, et al. Genetic mapping indicates that VP4 is the rotavirus cell attachment protein in vitro and in vivo. J Virol. 1996;70:487-493.
24. Offit PA, Blavat G, Greenberg HB, et al. Molecular basis of rotavirus virulence: Role of gene segment 4. J Virol. 1986;57:46-49.
25. Greenberg HB, Flores J, Kalica AR, et al. Gene coding assignments for growth restriction, neutralization and subgroup specificities of the W and DS-1 strains of human rotavirus. J Gen Virol. 1983;64:313-320.
26. Dormitzer PR, Greenberg HB, Harrison SC. Purified recombinant rotavirus VP7 forms soluble, calcium-dependent trimers. Virology. 2000;277:420-428.
27. Cohen J, Laporte J, Charpilienne A, et al. Activation of rotavirus RNA polymerase by calcium chelation. Arch Virol. 1979;60:177-186.
28. Estes MK, Graham DY, Smith EM, et al. Rotavirus stability and inactivation. J Gen Virol. 1979;43:403-409.
29. Ansari SA, Springthorpe VS, Sattar SA. Survival and vehicular spread of human rotaviruses: Possible relation to seasonality of outbreaks. Rev Infect Dis. 1991;13:448-461.
30. Lloyd-Evans N, Springthorpe VS, Sattar SA. Chemical disinfection of human rotavirus–contaminated inanimate surfaces. J Hyg (Lond). 1986;97:163-173.
31. Ward RL, Bernstein DI, Knowlton DR, et al. Prevention of surface-to-human transmission of rotaviruses by treatment with disinfectant spray. J Clin Microbiol. 1991;29:1991-1996.
32. Denisova E, Dowling W, LaMonica R, et al. Rotavirus capsid protein VP5* permeabilizes membranes. J Virol. 1999;73:3147-3153.
33. Fiore L, Greenberg HB, Mackow ER. The VP8 fragment of VP4 is the rhesus rotavirus hemagglutinin. Virology. 1991;181:553-563.
34. Crawford SE, Mukherjee SK, Estes MK, et al. Trypsin cleavage stabilizes the rotavirus VP4 spike. J Virol. 2001;75:6052-6061.
35. Dormitzer PR, Greenberg HB, Harrison SC. Proteolysis of monomeric recombinant rotavirus VP4 yields an oligomeric VP5* core. J Virol. 2001;75:7339-7350.
36. Dormitzer PR, Sun ZY, Wagner G, et al. The rhesus rotavirus VP4 sialic acid binding domain has a galectin fold with a novel carbohydrate binding site. EMBO J. 2002;21:885-897.
37. Ciarlet M, Estes MK. Human and most animal rotavirus strains do not require the presence of sialic acid on the cell surface for efficient infectivity. J Gen Virol. 1999;80:943-948.
38. Zarate S, Espinosa R, Romero P, et al. The VP5 domain of VP4 can mediate attachment of rotaviruses to cells. J Virol. 2000;74:593-599.
39. Hewish MJ, Takada Y, Coulson BS. Integrins α2β1 and α4β1 can mediate SA11 rotavirus attachment and entry into cells. J Virol. 2000;74:228-236.

40. Mackow ER, Shaw RD, Matsui SM, et al. The rhesus rotavirus gene encoding protein VP3: Location of amino acids involved in homologous and heterologous rotavirus neutralization and identification of a putative fusion region. Proc Natl Acad Sci USA. 1988;85:645-649.

41. Kaljot KT, Shaw RD, Rubin DH, et al. Infectious rotavirus enters cells by direct cell membrane penetration, not by endocytosis. J Virol. 1988;62:1136-1144.

42. Chemello ME, Aristimuno OC, Michelangeli F, et al. Requirement for vacuolar H$^+$-ATPase activity and Ca^{2+} gradient during entry of rotavirus into MA104 cells. J Virol. 2002;76:13083-13087.

43. Lawton JA, Estes MK, Prasad BV. Three-dimensional visualization of mRNA release from actively transcribing rotavirus particles. Nat Struct Biol. 1997;4:118-121.

44. Imai M, Akatani K, Ikegami N, et al. Capped and conserved terminal structures in human rotavirus genome double-stranded RNA segments. J Virol. 1983;47:125-136.

45. Groft CM, Burley SK. Recognition of eIF4G by rotavirus NSP3 reveals a basis for mRNA circularization. Mol Cell. 2002;9:1273-1283.

46. Vende P, Piron M, Castagne N, et al. Efficient translation of rotavirus mRNA requires simultaneous interaction of NSP3 with the eukaryotic translation initiation factor eIF4G and the mRNA 3′ end. J Virol. 2000;74:7064-7071.

47. Patton JT, Gallegos CO. Rotavirus RNA replication: single-stranded RNA extends from the replicase particle. J Gen Virol. 1990;71:1087-1094.

48. Chen D, Patton JT. De novo synthesis of minus strand RNA by the rotavirus RNA polymerase in a cell-free system involves a novel mechanism of initiation. RNA. 2000;6:1455-1467.

49. Gallegos CO, Patton JT. Characterization of rotavirus replication intermediates: A model for the assembly of single-shelled particles. Virology. 1989;172:616-627.

50. Jayaram H, Taraporewala Z, Patton JT, et al. Rotavirus protein involved in genome replication and packaging exhibits a HIT-like fold. Nature. 2002;417:311-315.

51. Schuck P, Taraporewala Z, McPhie P, et al. Rotavirus nonstructural protein NSP2 self-assembles into octamers that undergo ligand-induced conformational changes. J Biol Chem. 2001;276:9679-9687.

52. Poruchynsky MS, Maass DR, Atkinson PH. Calcium depletion blocks the maturation of rotavirus by altering the oligomerization of virus-encoded proteins in the ER. J Cell Biol. 1991;114:651-656.

53. O'Brien JA, Taylor JA, Bellamy AR. Probing the structure of rotavirus NSP4: A short sequence at the extreme C terminus mediates binding to the inner capsid particle. J Virol. 2000;74:5388-5394.

54. Jourdan N, Maurice M, Delautier D, et al. Rotavirus is released from the apical surface of cultured human intestinal cells through nonconventional vesicular transport that bypasses the Golgi apparatus. J Virol. 1997;71:8268-8278.

55. Sapin C, Colard O, Delmas O, et al. Rafts promote assembly and atypical targeting of a nonenveloped virus, rotavirus, in CaCo-2 cells. J Virol. 2002;76:4591-4602.

56. Kovacs A, Chan L, Hotrakitya C, et al. Rotavirus gastroenteritis. Clinical and laboratory features and use of the Rotazyme test. Am J Dis Child. 1987;141:161-166.

57. Rodriguez WJ, Kim HW, Arrobio JO, et al. Clinical features of acute gastroenteritis associated with human reovirus–like agent in infants and young children. J Pediatr. 1977;91:188-193.

58. Kapikian AZ, Wyatt RG, Levine MM, et al. Oral administration of human rotavirus to volunteers: Induction of illness and correlates of resistance. J Infect Dis. 1983;147:95-106.

59. Kim HW, Brandt CD, Kapikian AZ, et al. Human reovirus-like agent infection. Occurrence in adult contacts of pediatric patients with gastroenteritis. JAMA. 1977;238:404-407.

60. Hrdy DB. Epidemiology of rotaviral infection in adults. Rev Infect Dis. 1987;9:461-469.

61. Tallett S, MacKenzie C, Middleton P, et al. Clinical, laboratory, and epidemiologic features of a viral gastroenteritis in infants and children. Pediatrics. 1977;60:217-222.

62. Richardson S, Grimwood K, Gorrell R, et al. Extended excretion of rotavirus after severe diarrhoea in young children. Lancet. 1998;351:1844-1848.

63. Carlson JA, Middleton PJ, Szymanski MT, et al. Fatal rotavirus gastroenteritis: An analysis of 21 cases. Am J Dis Child. 1978;132:477-479.

64. Steele AD, van Niekerk MC, Geyer A, et al. Further characterisation of human rotaviruses isolated from asymptomatically infected neonates in South Africa. J Med Virol. 1992;38:22-26.

65. Rodger SM, Bishop RF, Birch C, et al. Molecular epidemiology of human rotaviruses in Melbourne, Australia, from 1973 to 1979, as determined by electrophoresis of genome ribonucleic acid. J Clin Microbiol. 1981;13:272-278.

66. Gorziglia M, Green K, Nishikawa K, et al. Sequence of the fourth gene of human rotaviruses recovered from asymptomatic or symptomatic infections. J Virol. 1988;62:2978-2984.

67. Flewett TH. Rotavirus in the home and hospital nursery. Br Med J (Clin Res Ed). 1983;287:568-569.

68. Widdowson MA, van Doornum GJ, van der Poel WH, et al. An outbreak of diarrhea in a neonatal medium care unit caused by a novel strain of rotavirus: Investigation using both epidemiologic and microbiological methods. Infect Control Hosp Epidemiol. 2002;23:665-670.

69. Gilger MA, Matson DO, Conner ME, et al. Extraintestinal rotavirus infections in children with immunodeficiency. J Pediatr. 1992;120:912-917.

70. Wood DJ, David TJ, Chrystie IL, et al. Chronic enteric virus infection in two T-cell immunodeficient children. J Med Virol. 1988;24:435-444.

71. Saulsbury FT, Winkelstein JA, Yolken RH. Chronic rotavirus infection in immunodeficiency. J Pediatr. 1980;97:61-65.

72. Oishi I, Kimura T, Murakami T, et al. Serial observations of chronic rotavirus infection in an immunodeficient child. Microbiol Immunol. 1991;35:953-961.

73. Yolken RH, Bishop CA, Townsend TR, et al. Infectious gastroenteritis in bone-marrow-transplant recipients. N Engl J Med. 1982;306:1010-1012.

74. Peigue-Lafeuille H, Henquell C, Chambon M, et al. Nosocomial rotavirus infections in adult renal transplant recipients. J Hosp Infect. 1991;18:67-70.

75. Grohmann GS, Glass RI, Pereira HG, et al. Enteric viruses and diarrhea in HIV-infected patients. Enteric Opportunistic Infections Working Group. N Engl J Med. 1993;329:14-20.

76. Zheng BJ, Chang RX, Ma GZ, et al. Rotavirus infection of the oropharynx and respiratory tract in young children. J Med Virol. 1991;34:29-37.

77. Rotbart HA, Nelson WL, Glode MP, et al. Neonatal rotavirus-associated necrotizing enterocolitis: Case control study and prospective surveillance during an outbreak. J Pediatr. 1988;112:87-93.

78. Capitanio MA, Greenberg SB. Pneumatosis intestinalis in two infants with rotavirus gastroenteritis. Pediatr Radiol. 1991;21:361-362.

79. Grunow JE, Dunton SF, Waner JL. Human rotavirus–like particles in a hepatic abscess. J Pediatr. 1985;106:73-76.

80. Riepenhoff-Talty M, Gouvea V, Evans MJ, et al. Detection of group C rotavirus in infants with extrahepatic biliary atresia. J Infect Dis. 1996;174:8-15.

81. Nigro G. Pancreatitis with hypoglycemia-associated convulsions following rotavirus gastroenteritis. J Pediatr Gastroenterol Nutr. 1991;12:280-282.

82. Hattori H, Torii S, Nagafuji H, et al. Benign acute myositis associated with rotavirus gastroenteritis. J Pediatr. 1992;121:748-749.

83. Matsuno S, Utagawa E, Sugiura A. Association of rotavirus infection with Kawasaki syndrome. J Infect Dis. 1983;148:177.

84. Yolken R, Murphy M. Sudden infant death syndrome associated with rotavirus infection. J Med Virol. 1982;10:291-296.

85. Lynch M, Lee B, Azimi P, et al. Rotavirus and central nervous system symptoms: Cause or contaminant? Case reports and review. Clin Infect Dis. 2001;33:932-938.

86. Nishimura S, Ushijima H, Shiraishi H, et al. Detection of rotavirus in cerebrospinal fluid and blood of patients with convulsions and gastroenteritis by means of the reverse transcription polymerase chain reaction. Brain Dev. 1993;15:457-459.

87. Uhnoo I, Riepenhoff-Talty M, Dharakul T, et al. Extramucosal spread and development of hepatitis in immunodeficient and normal mice infected with rhesus rotavirus. J Virol. 1990;64:361-368.

88. Riepenhoff-Talty M, Schaekel K, Clark HF, et al. Group A rotaviruses produce extrahepatic biliary obstruction in orally inoculated newborn mice. Pediatr Res. 1993;33:394-399.

89. Ward LA, Rosen BI, Yuan L, et al. Pathogenesis of an attenuated and a virulent strain of group A human rotavirus in neonatal gnotobiotic pigs. J Gen Virol. 1996;77:1431-1441.

90. Davidson GP, Goller I, Bishop RF, et al. Immunofluorescence in duodenal mucosa of children with acute enteritis due to a new virus. J Clin Pathol. 1975;28:263-266.

91. Davidson GP, Barnes GL. Structural and functional abnormalities of the small intestine in infants and young children with rotavirus enteritis. Acta Paediatr Scand. 1979;68:181-186.

92. Kohler T, Erben U, Wiedersberg H, et al. [Histological findings of the small intestinal mucosa in rotavirus infections in infants and young children]. Kinderarztl Prax. 1990;58:323 327.

93. Lundgren O, Svensson L. Pathogenesis of rotavirus diarrhea. Microbes Infect. 2001;3:1145-1156.

94. Davidson GP, Gall DG, Petric M, et al. Human rotavirus enteritis induced in conventional piglets. Intestinal structure and transport. J Clin Invest. 1977;60:1402-1409.

95. Halaihel N, Lievin V, Ball JM, et al. Direct inhibitory effect of rotavirus NSP4(114-135) peptide on the Na$^+$-D-glucose symporter of rabbit intestinal brush border membrane. J Virol. 2000;74:9464-9470.

96. Stintzing G, Johansen K, Magnusson KE, et al. Intestinal permeability in small children during and after rotavirus diarrhoea assessed with different-size polyethyleneglycols (PEG 400 and PEG 1000). Acta Paediatr Scand. 1986;75:1005-1009.

97. Ball JM, Tian P, Zeng CQ, et al. Age-dependent diarrhea induced by a rotaviral nonstructural glycoprotein. Science. 1996;272:101-104.

98. Dong Y, Zeng CQ, Ball JM, et al. The rotavirus enterotoxin NSP4 mobilizes intracellular calcium in human intestinal cells by stimulating phospholipase C–mediated inositol 1,4,5- trisphosphate production. Proc Natl Acad Sci USA. 1997;94:3960-3965.

99. Morris AP, Scott JK, Ball JM, et al. NSP4 elicits age-dependent diarrhea and Ca^{2+} mediated I$^-$ influx into intestinal crypts of CF mice. Am J Physiol. 1999;277:G431-G444.

100. Tafazoli F, Zeng CQ, Estes MK, et al. NSP4 enterotoxin of rotavirus induces paracellular leakage in polarized epithelial cells. J Virol. 2001;75:1540-1546.

101. Zhang M, Zeng CQ, Morris AP, et al. A functional NSP4 enterotoxin peptide secreted from rotavirus-infected cells. J Virol. 2000;74:11663-11670.

102. Shaw RD, Hempson SJ. Replication as a determinant of the intestinal response to rotavirus. J Infect Dis. 1996;174:1328-1331.

103. Kapikian AZ, Hoshino Y, Chanock RM. Rotaviruses. In: Knipe DM, Howley PM, Griffin DE, eds. Fields' Virology. Philadelphia: Lippincott Williams & Wilkins; 2001:1787-1833.

103a. Martella V, Ciarlet M, Camarda A, et al. Molecular characterization of the VP4, VP6, VP7, and NSP4 genes of lapine rotaviruses identified in Italy: Emergence of a novel VP4 genotype. Virology. 2003;314:358-370.

104. Hung T, Chen GM, Wang CG, et al. Waterborne outbreak of rotavirus diarrhoea in adults in China caused by a novel rotavirus. Lancet. 1984;1:1139-1142.

105. Nilsson M, Svenungsson B, Hedlund KO, et al. Incidence and genetic diversity of group C rotavirus among adults. J Infect Dis. 2000;182:678-684.

106. Jiang B, Dennehy PH, Spangenberger S, et al. First detection of group C rotavirus in fecal specimens of children with diarrhea in the United States. J Infect Dis. 1995;172:45-50.

107. Hoshino Y, Wyatt RG, Greenberg HB, et al. Serotypic similarity and diversity of rotaviruses of mammalian and avian origin as studied by plaque-reduction neutralization. J Infect Dis. 1984;149:694-702.

108. Hoshino Y, Sereno MM, Midthun K, et al. Independent segregation of two antigenic specificities (VP3 and VP7) involved in neutralization of rotavirus infectivity. Proc Natl Acad Sci USA. 1985;82:8701-8704.

109. Coulson BS, Unicomb LE, Pitson GA, et al. Simple and specific enzyme immunoassay using monoclonal antibodies for serotyping human rotaviruses. J Clin Microbiol. 1987;25:509-515.

110. Ward RL, McNeal MM, Sander DS, et al. Immunodominance of the VP4 neutralization protein of rotavirus in protective natural infections of young children. J Virol. 1993;67:464-468.

111. Hoshino Y, Nishikawa K, Benfield DA, et al. Mapping of antigenic sites involved in serotype-cross-reactive neutralization on group A rotavirus outer capsid glycoprotein VP7. Virology. 1994;199:233-237.

112. Hoshino Y, Kapikian AZ. Classification of rotavirus VP4 and VP7 serotypes. Arch Virol Suppl. 1996;12:99-111.

113. Green KY, Sears JF, Taniguchi K, et al. Prediction of human rotavirus serotype by nucleotide sequence analysis of the VP7 protein gene. J Virol. 1988;62:1819-1823.

114. Griffin DD, Fletcher M, Levy ME, et al. Outbreaks of adult gastroenteritis traced to a single genotype of rotavirus. J Infect Dis. 2002;185:1502-1505.

115. Coulson BS. VP4 and VP7 typing using monoclonal antibodies. Arch Virol Suppl. 1996;12:113-118.

116. Flores J, Midthun K, Hoshino Y, et al. Conservation of the fourth gene among rotaviruses recovered from asymptomatic newborn infants and its possible role in attenuation. J Virol. 1986;60:972-979.

117. Gentsch JR, Woods PA, Ramachandran M, et al. Review of G and P typing results from a global collection of rotavirus strains: Implications for vaccine development. J Infect Dis. 1996;174(Suppl 1):S30-S36.

118. Santos N, Gouvea V, Timenetsky MC, et al. Comparative analysis of VP8* sequences from rotaviruses possessing M37-like VP4 recovered from children with and without diarrhoea. J Gen Virol. 1994;75:1775-1780.

119. Desselberger U, Iturriza-Gomara M, Gray JJ. Rotavirus epidemiology and surveillance. Novartis Found Symp. 2001;238:125-147.

120. Unicomb LE, Podder G, Gentsch JR, et al. Evidence of high-frequency genomic reassortment of group A rotavirus strains in Bangladesh: Emergence of type G9 in 1995. J Clin Microbiol. 1999;37:1885-1891.

121. Steele AD, Ivanoff B. Rotavirus strains circulating in Africa during 1996-1999: Emergence of G9 strains and P[6] strains. Vaccine. 2003;21:361-367.

122. Griffin DD, Kirkwood CD, Parashar UD, et al. Surveillance of rotavirus strains in the United States: Identification of unusual strains. The National Rotavirus Strain Surveillance System collaborating laboratories. J Clin Microbiol. 2000;38: 2784-2787.

123. Cunliffe NA, Bresee JS, Gentsch JR, et al. The expanding diversity of rotaviruses. Lancet. 2002;359:640-642.

124. Matsui SM, Mackow ER, Matsuno S, et al. Sequence analysis of gene 11 equivalents from "short" and "super short" strains of rotavirus. J Virol. 1990;64:120-124.

125. Dunn SJ, Ward RL, McNeal MM, et al. Identification of a new neutralization epitope on VP7 of human serotype 2 rotavirus and evidence for electropherotype differences caused by single nucleotide substitutions. Virology. 1993;197:397-404.

126. Velazquez FR, Matson DO, Calva JJ, et al. Rotavirus infections in infants as protection against subsequent infections. N Engl J Med. 1996;335:1022-1028.

127. Dagan R, Bar-David Y, Sarov B, et al. Rotavirus diarrhea in Jewish and Bedouin children in the Negev region of Israel: Epidemiology, clinical aspects and possible role of malnutrition in severity of illness. Pediatr Infect Dis J. 1990;9:314-321.

128. Velazquez FR, Matson DO, Guerrero ML, et al. Serum antibody as a marker of protection against natural rotavirus infection and disease. J Infect Dis. 2000;182: 1602-1609.

129. Uhnoo IS, Freihorst J, Riepenhoff-Talty M, et al. Effect of rotavirus infection and malnutrition on uptake of a dietary antigen in the intestine. Pediatr Res. 1990;27: 153-160.

130. Ward RL, Knowlton DR, Pierce MJ. Efficiency of human rotavirus propagation in cell culture. J Clin Microbiol. 1984;19:748-753.

131. Ward RL, Bernstein DI, Young EC, et al. Human rotavirus studies in volunteers: Determination of infectious dose and serological response to infection. J Infect Dis. 1986;154:871-880.

132. Glass RI, Kilgore PE, Holman RC, et al. The epidemiology of rotavirus diarrhea in the United States: Surveillance and estimates of disease burden. J Infect Dis. 1996;174(Suppl 1):S5-S11.

133. Tucker AW, Haddix AC, Bresee JS, et al. Cost-effectiveness analysis of a rotavirus immunization program for the United States. JAMA. 1998;279:1371-1376.

134. Laboratory-based surveillance for rotavirus—United States, July 1996–June 1997. MMWR Morb Mortal Wkly Rep. 1997;46:1092-1094.

135. Kraft LM. Studies on the etiology and transmission of epidemic diarrhea of infant mice. J Exp Med. 1957;106:743-755.

136. Hopkins RS, Gaspard GB, Williams FP Jr, et al. A community waterborne gastroenteritis outbreak: Evidence for rotavirus as the agent. Am J Public Health. 1984;74:263-265.

137. Matson DO, O'Ryan ML, Herrera I, et al. Fecal antibody responses to symptomatic and asymptomatic rotavirus infections. J Infect Dis. 1993;167:577-583.

138. Rodriguez WJ, Kim HW, Brandt CD, et al. Common exposure outbreak of gastroenteritis due to type 2 rotavirus with high secondary attack rate within families. J Infect Dis. 1979;140:353-357.

139. Ryder RW, McGowan JE, Hatch MH, et al. Reovirus-like agent as a cause of nosocomial diarrhea in infants. J Pediatr. 1977;90:698-702.

140. Black RE. Epidemiology of travelers' diarrhea and relative importance of various pathogens. Rev Infect Dis. 1990;12(Suppl 1):S73-S79.

141. Nakagomi O, Nakagomi T. Interspecies transmission of rotaviruses studied from the perspective of genogroup. Microbiol Immunol. 1993;37:337-348.

142. Browning GF, Snodgrass DR, Nakagomi O, et al. Human and bovine serotype G8 rotaviruses may be derived by reassortment. Arch Virol. 1992;125:121-128.

143. Bishop RF, Barnes GL, Cipriani E, et al. Clinical immunity after neonatal rotavirus infection. A prospective longitudinal study in young children. N Engl J Med. 1983;309:72-76.

144. Burns JW, Krishnaney AA, Vo PT, et al. Analyses of homologous rotavirus infection in the mouse model. Virology. 1995;207:143-153.

145. Bass DM, Baylor M, Broome R, et al. Molecular basis of age-dependent gastric inactivation of rhesus rotavirus in the mouse. J Clin Invest. 1992;89:1741-1745.

146. Chiba S, Yokoyama T, Nakata S, et al. Protective effect of naturally acquired homotypic and heterotypic rotavirus antibodies. Lancet. 1986;2:417-421.

147. Linhares AC, Pinheiro FP, Freitas RB, et al. An outbreak of rotavirus diarrhea among a nonimmune, isolated South American Indian community. Am J Epidemiol. 1981;113:703-710.

148. Coulson BS, Grimwood K, Hudson IL, et al. Role of coproantibody in clinical protection of children during reinfection with rotavirus. J Clin Microbiol. 1992;30: 1678-1684.

149. Offit PA, Clark HF. Protection against rotavirus-induced gastroenteritis in a murine model by passively acquired gastrointestinal but not circulating antibodies. J Virol. 1985;54:58-64.

150. Offit PA, Shaw RD, Greenberg HB. Passive protection against rotavirus-induced diarrhea by monoclonal antibodies to surface proteins vp3 and vp7. J Virol. 1986;58:700-703.

151. Ward RL, Clemens JD, Knowlton DR, et al. Evidence that protection against rotavirus diarrhea after natural infection is not dependent on serotype-specific neutralizing antibody. J Infect Dis. 1992;166:1251-1257.

152. Glass RI, Stoll BJ, Wyatt RG, et al. Observations questioning a protective role for breast-feeding in severe rotavirus diarrhea. Acta Paediatr Scand. 1986;75:713-718.

153. Weinberg RJ, Tipton G, Klish WJ, et al. Effect of breast-feeding on morbidity in rotavirus gastroenteritis. Pediatrics. 1984;74:250-253.

154. Duffy LC, Byers TE, Riepenhoff-Talty M, et al. The effects of infant feeding on rotavirus-induced gastroenteritis: A prospective study. Am J Public Health. 1986;76:259-263.

155. Little LM, Shadduck JA. Pathogenesis of rotavirus infection in mice. Infect Immun. 1982;38:755-763.

156. Rennels MB, Glass RI, Dennehy PH, et al. Safety and efficacy of high-dose rhesus-human reassortant rotavirus vaccines—Report of the National Multicenter Trial. United States Rotavirus Vaccine Efficacy Group. Pediatrics. 1996;97:7-13.

157. Bernstein DI, Glass RI, Rodgers G, et al. Evaluation of rhesus rotavirus monovalent and tetravalent reassortant vaccines in US children. US Rotavirus Vaccine Efficacy Group. JAMA. 1995;273:1191-1196.

158. Ward RL, Sander DS, Schiff GM, et al. Effect of vaccination on serotype-specific antibody responses in infants administered WC3 bovine rotavirus before or after a natural rotavirus infection. J Infect Dis. 1990;162:1298-1303.

159. Green KY, Taniguchi K, Mackow ER, et al. Homotypic and heterotypic epitope-specific antibody responses in adult and infant rotavirus vaccinees: Implications for vaccine development. J Infect Dis. 1990;161:667-679.

160. Ruggeri FM, Greenberg HB. Antibodies to the trypsin cleavage peptide VP8 neutralize rotavirus by inhibiting binding of virions to target cells in culture. J Virol. 1991;65:2211-2219.

161. Zhou YJ, Burns JW, Morita Y, et al. Localization of rotavirus VP4 neutralization epitopes involved in antibody-induced conformational changes of virus structure. J Virol. 1994;68:3955-3964.

162. Ludert JE, Ruiz MC, Hidalgo C, et al. Antibodies to rotavirus outer capsid glycoprotein VP7 neutralize infectivity by inhibiting virion decapsidation. J Virol. 2002;76:6643-6651.

163. Kobayashi N, Taniguchi K, Urasawa S. Identification of operationally overlapping and independent cross-reactive neutralization regions on human rotavirus VP4. J Gen Virol. 1990;71:2615-2623.

164. Mackow ER, Shaw RD, Matsui SM, et al. Characterization of homotypic and heterotypic VP7 neutralization sites of rhesus rotavirus. Virology. 1988;165:511-517.

165. Burns JW, Siadat-Pajouh M, Krishnaney AA, et al. Protective effect of rotavirus VP6-specific IgA monoclonal antibodies that lack neutralizing activity. Science. 1996;272:104-107.

166. Schwartz-Cornil I, Benureau Y, Greenberg H, et al. Heterologous protection induced by the inner capsid proteins of rotavirus requires transcytosis of mucosal immunoglobulins. J Virol. 2002;76:8110-8117.

167. Yuan L, Geyer A, Hodgins DC, et al. Intranasal administration of 2/6-rotavirus-like particles with mutant Escherichia coli heat-labile toxin (LT-R192G) induces antibody-secreting cell responses but not protective immunity in gnotobiotic pigs. J Virol. 2000;74:8843-8853.

168. Franco MA, Greenberg HB. Immunity to rotavirus in T cell deficient mice. Virology. 1997;238:169-179.

169. Franco MA, Greenberg HB. Role of B cells and cytotoxic T lymphocytes in clearance of and immunity to rotavirus infection in mice. J Virol. 1995;69:7800-7806.

170. Doern GV, Herrmann JE, Henderson P, et al. Detection of rotavirus with a new polyclonal antibody enzyme immunoassay (Rotazyme II) and a commercial latex agglutination test (Rotalex): Comparison with a monoclonal antibody enzyme immunoassay. J Clin Microbiol. 1986;23:226-229.

171. Raboni SM, Nogueira MB, Hakim VM, et al. Comparison of latex agglutination with enzyme immunoassay for detection of rotavirus in fecal specimens. Am J Clin Pathol. 2002;117:392-394.

172. Gouvea V, Glass RI, Woods P, et al. Polymerase chain reaction amplification and typing of rotavirus nucleic acid from stool specimens. J Clin Microbiol. 1990;28:276-282.

173. Gentsch JR, Glass RI, Woods P, et al. Identification of group A rotavirus gene 4 types by polymerase chain reaction. J Clin Microbiol. 1992;30:1365-1373.

174. Brandt CD, Kim HW, Rodriguez WJ, et al. Comparison of direct electron microscopy, immune electron microscopy, and rotavirus enzyme-linked immunosorbent assay for detection of gastroenteritis viruses in children. J Clin Microbiol. 1981;13:976-981.

175. Dolan KT, Twist EM, Horton-Slight P, et al. Epidemiology of rotavirus electropherotypes determined by a simplified diagnostic technique with RNA analysis. J Clin Microbiol. 1985;21:753-758.

176. Sato K, Inaba Y, Shinozaki T, et al. Isolation of human rotavirus in cell cultures: Brief report. Arch Virol. 1981;69:155-160.

177. Practice parameter: The management of acute gastroenteritis in young children. American Academy of Pediatrics, Provisional Committee on Quality Improvement, Subcommittee on Acute Gastroenteritis. Pediatrics. 1996;97:424-435.

178. Santosham M, Daum RS, Dillman L, et al. Oral rehydration therapy of infantile diarrhea: A controlled study of well-nourished children hospitalized in the United States and Panama. N Engl J Med. 1982;306:1070-1076.

179. Schedl HP, Clifton JA. Solute and water absorption by human small intestine. Nature. 1963;199:1264-1267.

180. Thillainayagam AV, Hunt JB, Farthing MJ. Enhancing clinical efficacy of oral rehydration therapy: Is low osmolality the key? Gastroenterology. 1998;114:197-210.

181. Brown KH, Gastanaduy AS, Saavedra JM, et al. Effect of continued oral feeding on clinical and nutritional outcomes of acute diarrhea in children. J Pediatr. 1988;112:191-200.

182. Guarino A, Guandalini S, Albano F, et al. Enteral immunoglobulins for treatment of protracted rotaviral diarrhea. Pediatr Infect Dis J. 1991;10:612-614.

183. Guarino A, Canani RB, Russo S, et al. Oral immunoglobulins for treatment of acute rotaviral gastroenteritis. Pediatrics. 1994;93:12-16.

184. Sarker SA, Casswall TH, Mahalanabis D, et al. Successful treatment of rotavirus diarrhea in children with immunoglobulin from immunized bovine colostrum. Pediatr Infect Dis J. 1998;17:1149-1154.

185. Barnes GL, Doyle LW, Hewson PH, et al. A randomised trial of oral gammaglobulin in low-birth-weight infants infected with rotavirus. Lancet. 1982;1:1371-1373.

186. Ebina T, Sato A, Umezu K, et al. Prevention of rotavirus infection by oral administration of cow colostrum containing antihuman rotavirus antibody. Med Microbiol Immunol. 1985;174:177-185.

187. Figueroa-Quintanilla D, Salazar-Lindo E, Sack RB, et al. A controlled trial of bismuth subsalicylate in infants with acute watery diarrheal disease. N Engl J Med. 1993;328:1653-1658.

188. Van Niel CW, Feudtner C, Garrison MM, et al. Lactobacillus therapy for acute infectious diarrhea in children: A meta-analysis. Pediatrics. 2002;109:678-684.

189. Joensuu J, Koskenniemi E, Vesikari T. Prolonged efficacy of rhesus-human reassortant rotavirus vaccine. Pediatr Infect Dis J. 1998;17:427-429.

190. Perez-Schael I, Guntinas MJ, Perez M, et al. Efficacy of the rhesus rotavirus based quadrivalent vaccine in infants and young children in Venezuela. N Engl J Med. 1997;337:1181-1187.

191. Joensuu J, Koskenniemi E, Vesikari T. Symptoms associated with rhesus-human reassortant rotavirus vaccine in infants. Pediatr Infect Dis J. 1998;17:334-340.

192. Intussusception among recipients of rotavirus vaccine—United States, 1998-1999. MMWR Morb Mortal Wkly Rep. 1999;48:577-581.

193. Murphy TV, Gargiullo PM, Massoudi MS, et al. Intussusception among infants given an oral rotavirus vaccine. N Engl J Med. 2001;344:564-572.

194. Murphy BR, Morens DM, Simonsen L, et al. Reappraisal of the association of intussusception with the licensed live rotavirus vaccine challenges initial conclusions. J Infect Dis. 2003;187:1301-1308.

195. Murphy TV, Smith PJ, Gargiullo PM, et al. The first rotavirus vaccine and intussusception: Epidemiological studies and policy decisions. J Infect Dis. 2003;187:1309-1313.

196. Simonsen L, Morens D, Elixhauser A, et al. Effect of rotavirus vaccination programme on trends in admission of infants to hospital for intussusception. Lancet. 2001;358:1224-1229.

197. Konno T, Suzuki H, Kutsuzawa T, et al. Human rotavirus infection in infants and young children with intussusception. J Med Virol. 1978;2:265-269.

198. Bines JE, Ivanoff B. Acute Intussusception in Infants and Children. Incidence, Clinical Presentation, and Management: A Global Perspective. Steering Committee on Diarrhoeal Disease Vaccines, Vaccine Development, Vaccines and Biologicals, World Health Organization. Geneva: World Health Organization; 2002:1-98.

199. Peter G, Myers MG. Intussusception, rotavirus, and oral vaccines: Summary of a workshop. Pediatrics. 2002;110:e67.

200. Clark HF, Offit PA, Ellis RW, et al. The development of multivalent bovine rotavirus (strain WC3) reassortant vaccine for infants. J Infect Dis. 1996;174(Suppl 1):S73-S80.

201. Bernstein DI, Sack DA, Reisinger K, et al. Second-year follow-up evaluation of live, attenuated human rotavirus vaccine 89-12 in healthy infants. J Infect Dis. 2002;186:1487-1489.

202. Crawford SE, Estes MK, Ciarlet M, et al. Heterotypic protection and induction of a broad heterotypic neutralization response by rotavirus-like particles. J Virol. 1999;73:4813-4822.

203. Johansen K, Schroder U, Svensson L. Immunogenicity and protective efficacy of a formalin-inactivated rotavirus vaccine combined with lipid adjuvants. Vaccine. 2003;21:368-375.

204. Herrmann JE, Chen SC, Fynan EF, et al. Protection against rotavirus infections by DNA vaccination. J Infect Dis. 1996;174(Suppl 1):S93-S97.

Alphaviruses

LEWIS MARKOFF

All of the medically important alphaviruses are arthropod vector borne. Most have hosts in nature other than humans and vectors that are crucial to the virus life cycle. Three mosquito-borne alphaviruses currently cause human disease in the United States: eastern equine encephalitis (EEE), western equine encephalitis (WEE), and Venezuelan equine encephalitis (VEE) viruses. These are among the "New World" alphaviruses, defined by their antigenic and nucleotide sequence relatedness as well as by their occurrence in North America or South America. "Old World" alphavirus species of major importance include chikungunya (in Africa and Asia), O'nyong-nyong (Africa), Mayaro (South America), Ross River (Australia, Oceania), Sindbis (Africa, Scandinavia, the countries of the former Soviet Union, Asia), and Barmah Forest virus (Australia). The Old World alphaviruses primarily cause fever, rash, and arthropathy. Properties of medically important alphaviruses and some related species are presented in Table 147-1.

HISTORY

WEE and EEE viruses were initially recovered from the brains of horses with encephalitis in California (1930) and New Jersey (1933), respectively. By 1938 both of these agents had been established as causes of encephalitis in humans.[1] Similarly, VEE virus was first isolated from the brains of horses in Venezuela during an epidemic of encephalitis in 1938.[2] The first reports of VEE infection of humans were from laboratories where equine isolates were being studied in 1943. Apparently, this outbreak was due to the aerosol spread of infectious virus to laboratory workers. Naturally acquired human illness related to VEE was first reported from Columbia in 1952 in association with an epizootic disease in equines.[3] The first reports of VEE virus infection of humans in the United States were published in 1968.[4] Retrospective analysis of historical accounts suggests that chikungunya virus caused epidemics of fever, rash, and arthralgia in Indonesia (1779), East Africa (1823, 1870), India (1824, 1871, 1901, 1923), the Far East (1901), West Africa (1925), and possibly the southeastern United States (1827). The virus was first isolated during an epidemic in Tanzania in 1952 and 1953.[5]

PATHOGENS

The alphaviruses constitute a genus in the family Togaviridae.[6] Formerly, alphaviruses were known as group A arboviruses (arthropod-borne viruses).[7] The alphavirus genus contains at least 24 distinct species.[8] These are lipid-enveloped virions with a diameter of 50 to 60 nm. The alphavirus genome is an 11- to 12-kilobase positive-strand (or message sense) RNA. In virus particles, genomic RNA is complexed with the virus-coded core protein in an icosahedral nucleocapsid structure. Two glycoproteins, E1 and E2, are inserted in the lipid membrane surrounding the nucleocapsid and project outward from the membrane. E1 and E2 appear to form both hetero- and homodimers, which are responsible for the structural stability of the virus particle.[9] An additional small viral structural protein, the 6K protein, is also associated with membranes and is heavily acylated.[10] E2 appears primarily responsible for attachment of virus to the cell surface. E2 antibodies, but not generally E1 antibodies, can neutralize virus infectivity. E1 has hemagglutinin activity and contains alphavirus cross-reactive epitopes.

Alphaviruses enter cells by receptor-mediated endocytosis. After the E2 envelope protein binds to the cellular receptor, the virus particle is engulfed in an endocytic vesicle, and a low-pH–dependent fusion reaction mediated by the E1 envelope protein results in the release of virus particle contents into the cytoplasm. Four viral

TABLE 147-1 Medically Important Alphaviruses and Some Related Alphavirus Species

Antigenic Complex	Virus*	Geographic Distribution†	Animal Reservoir	Human Vector‡	Human Disease (Animals Affected)
EEE	EEE	N.A., S.A., Caribbean	Birds	Aedes	Encephalitis (horses, birds)
WEE	WEE	N.A., S.A.	Birds, horses	Culex tarsalis	Fever, encephalitis (horses, birds [especially emus])
	Aura	S.A.	Birds		
	Fort Morgan	Colorado	Birds		
	Highlands J	Eastern U.S.	Birds	Culex, Aedes	(Encephalitis in turkeys, pheasants, partridges, ducks, emus, horses)
	Kyzylagach	Azerbaijan	Birds		
	Sindbis	AUS, AFR, EUR, Asia Minor	Birds	Aedes	Fever, arthritis, rash
	Whataroa	AUS, NZ	Birds		
VEE	VEE	N.A., S.A.	Horses, and others	Psorophora, Aedes	Fever, encephalitis (horses)
	Cabassou	S.A.			
	Everglades	Florida	Mammals	Ochlerotatus	Encephalitis
	Pixuna	Brazil	Mammals		
SF	Semliki Forest	AFR	Mammals	Aedes	Fever, arthritis, rash? (rare)
	Bebaru	Asia			
	Chikungunya	AFR, Southeast Asia, Philippines	Primates	Culex, Aedes	Fever, arthritis, rash
	Getah	Asia	Mammals	Culex, Aedes	Fever? (horses)
	Mayaro	S.A.		Haemagogus, Aedes	Fever, arthritis, rash
	O'nyong-nyong	AFR		Anopheles	Fever, arthritis, rash
	Ross River	AUS, South Pacific	Mammals	Aedes, Culex	Fever, arthritis, rash
BF	Barmah Forest	Australia	Birds	Aedes	Fever, arthritis, rash

*EEE, eastern equine encephalitis; WEE, western equine encephalitis; VEE, Venezuelan equine encephalitis.

†N.A., North America; S.A., South America; U.S., United States; AUS, Australia; AFR, Africa; EUR, Europe; NZ, New Zealand.

‡The mosquito vector genus or species required for epizootic transmission of infection is shown. No epizootic vector is listed for viruses that rarely cause disease or for which there are no reports of disease.

nonstructural proteins (NSPs) are then derived by translation of the 5'-terminal two thirds of genomic RNA. Viral structural proteins are encoded by a subgenomic (26S) messenger RNA colinear with the 3'-terminal third of the genome. Initial products of translation of the 26S messenger RNA include a 62-kD E2 precursor polypeptide, PE2 or "p62"; E1; and the hydrophobic 6K protein. PE2 and E1 form a stable heterodimer in the endoplasmic reticulum that is transported to the plasma membrane through the secretory pathway. PE2 is cleaved by cellular enzymes in acidic transport vesicles to produce E2, and the E2/E1 heterodimer is acquired on nascent particles by budding at the plasma membrane. The cleavage of PE2 destabilizes the heterodimer with E1 such that it is more readily dissociated by low pH, which activates the fusion process for mature virions.[11,12] The 6K protein is required for the specific interaction between E2, E1, and the nucleocapsid.[13]

Complement fixation (CF), hemagglutination-inhibition (HI), and the plaque reduction-neutralization test (PRNT) define seven distinct alphavirus antigenic complexes and distinguish among virus species within a complex. EEE, VEE, and WEE are prototype viruses for each of three antigenic complexes.[14] The WEE genome, and those of "WEE-like" viruses except for Aura virus (see later), is an intragenic recombinant: the nonstructural and core protein genes are derived from an EEE-like ancestral genome, whereas the structural glycoproteins E1 and E2 are derived from the genome of a Sindbis-like virus.[15,16] Because the results of CF, HI, and PRNT assays are largely dependent on antigenicity of E2, this explains why some of the Old World alphaviruses, Sindbis virus and Sindbis-like viruses, group with WEE and related New World viruses. Chikungunya, O'nyong-nyong, Mayaro, and Ross River viruses are grouped with Semliki Forest virus in a fourth complex. Middelburg, Nduma, and Barmah Forest virus, respectively, constitute the single species in each of the three additional alphavirus serogroups.

Partial or complete nucleotide sequencing of alphavirus genomes has permitted the phylogenetic subgrouping of the alphaviruses. When 3'-terminal sequences for more than two dozen different alphaviruses were compared, genetically distinct clades appeared to coincide with each of the seven complexes as defined by antigenic distinctions, with only minor discrepancies between the two methods.[8] Within each clade or complex there are viruses that exist in regions of the world that are geographically distant from one another, yet the member viruses share medically important characteristics in addition to their genetic and antigenic relatedness. For example, despite their nonoverlapping geographic distribution, members of the EEE and VEE complexes share encephalitic potential in equines and humans, and the Semliki Forest virus complex viruses Mayaro (limited to Latin America) and O'nyong-nyong (limited to Africa) produce identical fever-rash-arthralgia syndromes. The WEE complex includes viruses that produce either arthralgic (Sindbis virus–like subgroup) or encephalitic (WEE and Highlands J virus subgroup) syndromes, regardless of their respective geographic distributions. The encephalitic potential of the latter viruses probably reflects the genetic contribution of the EEE-like ancestral virus core and nonstructural genes rather than that of the Sindbis-like E1 and E2 genes.

Within the EEE antigenic complex, there are North American and South American subtypes based on HI testing. A phylogenetic analysis suggested that the North American subtypes constitute a single lineage and that there are three distinct lineages among South American subtypes. Each of the four lineages appeared to be antigenically distinct according to results of PRNTs.[17] This finding has significance in relation to EEE virus vaccine development. As mentioned, the WEE antigenic complex includes the New World viruses WEE, Buggy Creek, Highlands J, Fort Morgan, and Aura and the Old World viruses Sindbis and the Sindbis subtypes Babanki (Africa), Ockelbo (Northern Europe), Kyzylagach (Azerbaijan, China), and Whataroa (New Zealand). Five subtypes of VEE are recognized. Subtype I occurs in tropical America and is medically most important. Five geographic variants of subtype I are distinguishable. Variants IAB and IC were associated with equine epizootics and human epidemics that occurred between the 1920s and the early 1970s. Variants ID and IE and subtype II (Everglades virus) are less virulent and are associated with enzootic disease.

Mechanisms for epizootic spread of alphaviruses may involve either a mutation that adapts the virus to replication in large animals or a bridging vector (Fig. 147-1).

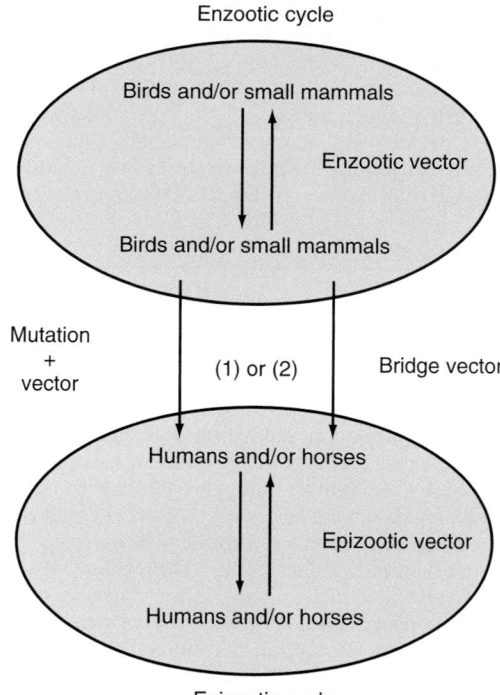

Enzootic cycle

Epizootic cycle

FIGURE 147-1. Two different mechanisms leading to epizootic spread of alphavirus infections are depicted. The normal enzootic life cycle depends upon the habits of mosquito vectors that are adapted to feed on the required small-animal hosts, including birds and rodents. Virus infection spreads to horses or humans, or both, when either (1) a mutation occurs in the viral genome adapting it to replication in large animals and in vector mosquitoes that are adapted to feed on them, or (2) a "bridging" vector transmits virus directly from animals involved in the enzootic cycle to humans or horses. Once the epizootic cycle is initiated, virus is spread by a different vector or set of vectors adapted to the large animal host. Venezuelan equine encephalitis virus is an example of an alphavirus that requires a mutation in order to initiate epizootic spread (mechanism 1). Eastern equine encephalitis virus is an example of an alphavirus that can spread to humans and horses by the action of a bridging vector mosquito (mechanism 2).

EPIDEMIOLOGY

Encephalitis-Causing Alphaviruses

Alphaviruses are all limited in their geographic spread by the range of their respective arthropod vectors. EEE virus infection occurs focally along the eastern and Gulf coasts of the United States, and documented cases have occurred as far north as southern Canada and as far south as northern areas of South America and the Caribbean.[18] EEE is a summertime disease, occurring most frequently in children and elderly people.[18] A few human cases occur each year. Although relatively rare, an outbreak is usually noteworthy because of the high case-fatality rate (50% to 70%). The incidence of equine cases greatly exceeds that in humans, and outbreaks resulting in the deaths of hundreds of horses have been reported in the northeastern United States and in Florida.[18] In horses, the infection may involve multiple organ systems, including the heart, spleen, urinary tract, and gastrointestinal tract as well as the entirety of the central nervous system (CNS).[19]

In North America, the principal enzootic vector for EEE is the mosquito *Culiseta melanura*, which breeds in freshwater swamps and feeds on passerine birds. Infection of avian species may result in death in some cases and may be without apparent consequence in others. In either case, it results in viremia of sufficient magnitude and frequency to maintain a reservoir of infected mosquitoes.[20] In the United States, EEE has caused major epidemics of hemorrhagic enterocolitis in emus,

which are bred for meat and other byproducts, thus providing a reservoir of infected birds in close contact with humans. Infected birds develop very high titer viremia, which facilitates spread of the virus to mosquito populations. Transmission from birds to horses and humans is mediated by mosquitoes other than *C. melanura*, which is highly ornithophilic. Possible vectors include *Aedes* and *Coquillettidia* spp.[21] Infection of horses and humans results in low or undetectable levels of viremia. Therefore, these hosts do not serve as reservoirs for further spread of virus. In summary, conditions for EEE epizootics include the presence of *C. melanura* and susceptible bird populations coincident with vector mosquitoes capable of feeding on both birds and the horses or humans in the vicinity. In temperate climates, maintenance of epizootics is further interdicted by winter, which is not suitable for survival of the vector population. This may account for the relative rarity of these epidemics. It is therefore surprising that virus can be isolated from the same endemic foci in successive years. Despite extensive investigation, the mechanism of virus persistence or "overwintering" is not understood.

The WEE viruses are distributed primarily in the Americas. A subtype of WEE, isolated in Argentina, is presumed to be representative of endemic strains in South America.[22] In North America, WEE is a summertime disease of horses and humans in states west of the Mississippi and in corresponding Canadian provinces. The vector is *Culex tarsalis*. Risk factors for infection include rural residence, outdoor employment in farming (because the vector favors irrigated areas), and male sex. Since 1955, the annual incidence of disease has varied from 0 to 200. Peaks occur in years of epizootic or epidemic activity. The most extensive epidemic ever recorded occurred on the western plains of the United States and Canada in 1941, resulting in 300,000 cases of encephalitis in horses and mules and 3336 cases of encephalitis in humans.[23] For WEE, during an epidemic a very high percentage of the adult population seroconverts, but the case/infection ratio ranges from less than 1:1000 in older adults to nearly 1:1 in infants. Thus, encephalitis is most frequent in infants younger than 1 year. However, encephalitis is most severe in older adults. Case-fatality rates are 3% to 4%. In contrast, EEE infection rates are low in an epidemic, but the case/infection ratio is higher than that for WEE and is highest in the young. As previously mentioned, a high proportion of cases of full-blown encephalitis caused by EEE are fatal.[24]

There were 640 total cases of WEE and 182 total cases of EEE reported to the Centers for Disease Control and Prevention (CDC) between 1964 and 2000. WEE occurred most commonly in Colorado (173 cases), Texas (94 cases), North Dakota (78 cases), and California (53 cases), with additional significant numbers of cases in Missouri, South Dakota, and Kansas. EEE occurred most commonly in Florida (53 cases), Georgia (22 cases), and Massachusetts (21 cases) as well as in New Jersey, North Carolina, and Louisiana. Between 1996 and 2000, there were no reported cases of WEE and 31 reported cases of EEE in the United States, suggesting that control efforts and other natural variables have had a dramatic negative effect on the incidence of the former disease.[25] For comparison, La Crosse virus, a member of the California serogroup of bunyaviruses, accounted for 250 cases of arboviral encephalitis during 1996 and 1997 alone.[26]

VEE infections in South America and Central America, caused primarily by the epizootic strains (subtypes IAB and IC), have been associated with tens of thousands of both equine and human cases.[27] For epizootic viruses, equines play an important role in maintenance because they become viremic. At least 10 species, including species of *Culex*, *Aedes*, *Mansonia*, *Psorophora*, and *Deinocerites*, have been identified as probable epidemic vectors.[28] Epizootics have been documented in Venezuela, Colombia, Ecuador, and Peru at intervals of 10 years or less since the 1930s. Typically, epizootics begin in areas of tropical forest during the rainy season. In the center of an epizootic, transmission usually continues until all horses are dead or immune. Spread may be to contiguous areas or may be sporadic. In Venezuela, in 1962 through 1964, 32,000 human cases were reported, with a fatality rate of 0.6%. In 1971, the spread of epidemic VEE into Texas resulted in the deaths of more than 10,000 horses. Increased incidence of human disease typically follows that of equine disease by 1 to 2 weeks. Severe human disease with encephalitis is most common in children. Like horses, humans also develop a viremia of sufficient magnitude to infect mosquitoes. However, humans have never been implicated in epidemic transmission. Similarly, although VEE can be isolated from throat washings, person-to-person transmission has not been documented.[29]

Molecular studies comparing epizootic strains with commonly isolated enzootic ones originally suggested that these sets of VEE subtypes were highly unrelated. In fact, the common vector for enzootic strains of VEE, *Culex taeniopus*, is refractory to oral infection with epizootic virus.[30] However, comparisons of the nucleotide sequences of newly emerging (1C-like) epizootic viruses in South America suggest that they evolved from a group of 1D-like viruses by a spontaneous mutation or mutations within the E2 gene sequence that increase the positive charge of the E2 ectodomain.[31,32]

Horses are not amplifying hosts for enzootic strains of VEE (subtypes ID, IE, and II). These viruses are principally maintained by their mosquito vector and rodents that thrive in tropical and subtropical swamps and forests. Humans living in these areas manifest a high prevalence of antibody. These viruses cause encephalitis sporadically in Central America (subtypes ID and IE) and Florida (subtype II).

Alphaviruses Causing Fever, Rash, and Polyarthritis

"Chikungunya" means "that which bends up," in reference to the crippling manifestations of the disease. *Aedes* mosquitoes of the subgenus *Stegomyia* are the principal vectors in Africa, and the virus seems to be maintained by transmission to nonhuman primates. Humans in appropriate concentrations may also provide a reservoir for the infection of mosquitoes. *Aedes aegypti* is implicated as a vector in urban epidemics in Africa and Asia. Serologic survey of native populations using the HI assay suggests that epidemics occur periodically when the youngest group of inhabitants of an endemic area are susceptible. Otherwise, disease occurrence is sporadic. From 20% to more than 90% of the population of tropical and subtropical Africa show serologic evidence of infection. Because *Aedes* mosquitoes are increasingly prevalent in North America and South America, where the population would be uniformly susceptible to infection, the possibility for epidemics is evident.[5]

O'nyong-nyong virus is antigenically related to chikungunya virus. It initially appeared in Uganda in the form of an epidemic that involved 2 million people in its final extent by the middle to late 1960s. Risk factors included residence in rural villages where the vector *Anopheles* mosquitoes congregate. A nonhuman primate reservoir of infection has not been identified.

Sindbis virus is transmitted among birds by *Culex* mosquitoes. Studies in South Africa show that extensive human disease occurs in parallel with years of abundant rainfall in association with flooding of usually arid regions. Thus, infected mosquitoes and susceptible humans are presumably brought into proximity. Infection rates may approach 15% during a major transmission season. Sindbis virus and the flavivirus West Nile virus (WNV) share the avian-*Culex* mosquito hosts (see Chapter 149). In South Africa, the Nile Valley of Egypt, and Israel, individuals with antibodies to Sindbis virus frequently also have antibodies to WNV. In Europe, symptomatic disease is recognized in the region between 60 and 65 degrees north latitude in Sweden, Finland, and the Commonwealth of Independent States. It is a disease of adults who work or vacation in forested areas. The virus has been isolated from *Culiseta*, *Aedes*, and *Culex* mosquitoes. Little is known about alternative natural hosts that might provide a reservoir for virus in this region.[33]

Ross River virus is a cause of epidemic polyarthritis in Australia in areas of heavy rainfall. Joint symptoms are especially intense and may be prolonged for up to 3 years after fever and rash have abated.[34] Spread to the Pacific Islands has been documented. The facts that this virus has been isolated from mosquitoes and that human disease is seasonal are clues to its dependence on vector transmission.

Mayaro virus was first isolated in the Caribbean in the 1950s in association with an epidemic of febrile illness with rash and occasional arthropathy. It has since been documented to have caused epidemics in Brazil and Bolivia. The virus has been isolated from *Haemagogus* mosquitoes and from marmosets as well as other nonhuman primates.[35] These may provide a reservoir for virus in the natural setting.

A long list of alphaviruses, including Bebaru, Cabassou, Getah, Kyzylagach, Middelburg, Nduma, Pixuna, Sagiyama, Semliki Forest, Una, and Whataroa viruses, either are not known to cause human disease or disease is of the fever-arthropathy type and is rare.

PATHOGENESIS

The locus of virus replication in the mosquito is the midgut epithelium, which is targeted after the mosquito has taken a blood meal from a viremic host. The infection is generally thought to be a lifelong, persistent, productive one, although there may be associated necrotic changes in the midgut.[36] Alphavirus infections of humans are initiated by the bite of an infected mosquito, which results in the deposition of virus in subcutaneous and possibly cutaneous tissues. VEE is also highly infectious for humans through contact with aerosol, as evidenced by outbreaks among laboratory workers. The initial phase of infection is marked by viremia and a febrile response, signaling the replication of virus in non-neural tissues. The earliest measurable VEE immune response is antibody directed against a virion surface component that is non-neutralizing but mediates viral clearance. This is followed by the advent of neutralizing antibodies with E2 specificity. Before CNS invasion in experimental animals, VEE replicates in lymphoid tissues, resulting in necrotic changes, and in bone marrow, resulting in lymphopenia. Lymphoid infection in mice is followed by high-titer viremia, during which the peripheral CNS is seeded, mainly through the olfactory system.[37] VEE also replicates in the pancreas and salivary glands of experimental animals but does not appear to have a diabetogenic effect in humans who have survived encephalitis. Infection of neurons by VEE in animals leads to an acute encephalitis with necrosis, mild to moderate neutrophilic infiltrate, gliosis, and perivascular cuffing with involvement of Purkinje cells.[38] Susceptibility of mice to VEE encephalitis and death is enhanced in mice lacking interferon (IFN) regulatory factors (IRF-1 and IRF-2), interferon receptors, or type I IFN itself.[39,40] In addition, inducible nitric oxide synthase gene function is associated with recovery from VEE encephalitis in mice. VEE-induced neuronal cell death is by apoptosis.[41]

EEE causes lesions throughout the brain and spinal cord, most severely involving the cerebral cortex and basal ganglia. WEE causes focal necrosis in the striatum, globus pallidus, cerebral cortex, thalamus, pons, and meninges. Transplacental spread of VEE and WEE may affect the fetus, resulting in massive cerebral necrosis.[27,42]

Although it does not commonly invade the human CNS, Sindbis virus causes a fatal encephalitis in mice that serves as a model for study of alphavirus encephalitis in humans. Neurovirulence is directly related to previous mouse brain adaptation of the virus, route of administration, and genetic differences among mouse strains. It is inversely related to age.[43] The initial event appears to be infection of capillary endothelial cells, allowing virus to reach neuronal cells through the microvasculature or through transport across vessel walls into the brain parenchyma.[44] Once infected, mature neurons are more resistant to the predominantly apoptotic cell death caused by Sindbis virus than immature neurons. Apoptosis is triggered by the fusion event that occurs during virus entry. Fusion-associated conformational changes in sphingomyelin activate the enzyme sphingomyelinase, resulting in an increase in ceramide, a proapoptotic substance.[45] The outcome of infection at the cellular level seems related to the neuronal response to produce mediators of apoptosis versus antagonists of apoptosis (e.g., BCL-2). The normally proapoptotic substance BAX acts in conjunction with BCL-2 to protect neonatal mice from a lethal outcome and cultured hippocampal neurons from apoptotic cell death. In contrast, BAX promotes apoptosis in cultured murine dorsal root ganglia.[46]

Sindbis-infected and neighboring uninfected neurons die by the necrotic pathway and secondary to inflammation, respectively, as well as by apoptosis.[47] Murine cortical neurons in culture were protected specifically from necrotic and inflammatory cell death by antagonists of a subclass of glutamate receptors, suggesting that necrotic death of both infected and uninfected cells may involve the excitatory pathway.[48] Also, mice were not protected from hind limb paralysis by inhibitors of apoptosis, apparently because virus-infected lower motor neurons die predominantly by the necrotic pathway.[49] Nevertheless, gross resistance of mice to Sindbis neurovirulence appears to involve primarily increased endogenous production of inhibitors of apoptosis, and this capacity increases with age.[50]

The humoral immune response is primarily responsible for clearance of virus from the CNS, not only by direct neutralization of virus infectivity but also by antibody-dependent, complement-mediated cytolysis of infected cells.[51] In addition, certain Sindbis-specific monoclonal antibodies can induce virus clearance from the CNS by restricting viral gene expression in neurons. Despite this effect of extracellular antibody, viral RNA could be shown to persist in infected neurons for several months. Removal of antibody resulted in recru-

descence of infection.[52] This phenomenon was completely independent of a cell-mediated immune response and suggested a mechanism for persistence of alphavirus infections in the CNS. Although neurologic symptoms may be among the sequelae of infection with the neurotropic flaviviruses, and arthritis of several years' duration may follow Ross River virus infection, persistence of infectious alphaviruses in humans has not been documented.

T cells appear to be required primarily for late clearance of viral RNA from neurons.[53] However, they may also be involved in clearance of infectious virus, at least in specialized situations. For example, mice immunized with the Sindbis nonstructural protein nsp-2 do not develop a protective humoral immune response but do recover from paralysis caused by Sindbis replication in the CNS; presumably protection is T cell mediated.[54] In another study, IFN-γ–secreting T cells were required for noncytolytic clearance of virus from spinal cord and brain stem neurons but were not effective in clearance of virus from cortical neurons.[55] In contrast, T cells may also contribute to the damaging inflammatory response associated with fatal acute viral encephalomyelitis through production of IFN-γ.[56]

During self-limited infection with a non-neurotropic alphavirus, such as chikungunya, the level of viremia closely parallels the fever curve. As viremia fades and fever subsides, HI and neutralizing antibody titers start to rise, suggesting that these immune responses curtail infection. Biopsy of the maculopapular to macular rash in chikungunya infection shows lymphocytic perivascular cuffing and extravasation of erythrocytes from superficial capillaries.[57] Arthralgia may accompany early symptoms of fever and malaise (chikungunya) or may be slightly delayed and quite severe, leading to frank arthritis (Ross River). The joint fluid in the latter cases is inflammatory and contains viral antigens but no infectious virus. The pathogenesis of alphavirus-induced disease is illustrated in Figure 147-2.

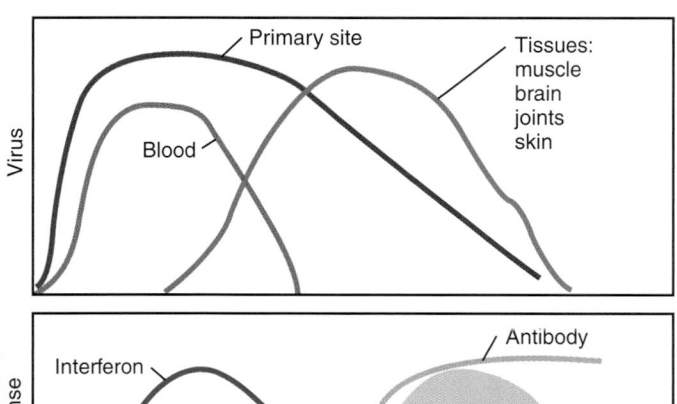

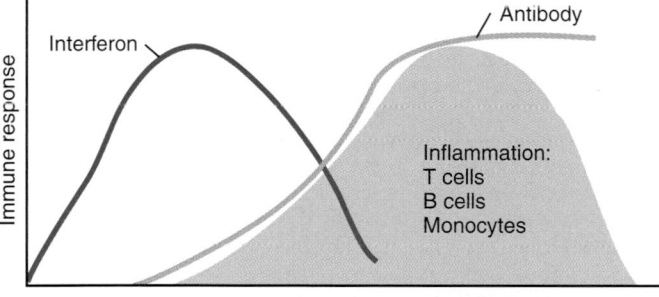

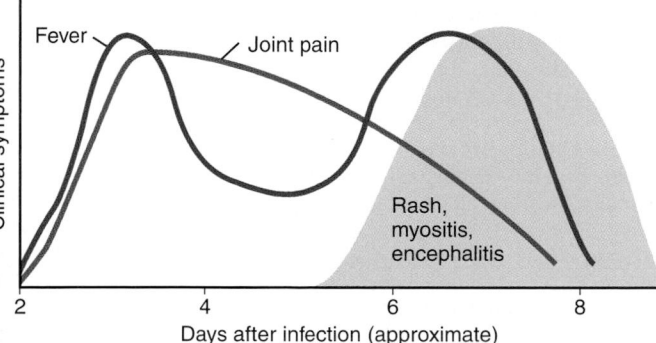

FIGURE 147-2. Schematic diagram of the pathogenesis of alphavirus-induced disease. Viremia may be accompanied by production of interferon, other proinflammatory cytokines, and fever. Virus then spreads through the blood to other target tissues. As the immune response is induced the viremia is terminated, but fever is renewed with the appearance of a mononuclear inflammatory response in the infected tissues. In infections that lead to rash and arthritis, joint pain usually appears early after infection and before the appearance of the rash. *(From Griffin D. The alphaviruses. In: Knipe DM, Howley PM, eds. Fields Virology. 4th ed. Philadelphia: Lippincott Williams & Wilkins; 2001:925.)*

CLINICAL MANIFESTATIONS

Alphaviruses Causing Encephalitis

EEE virus infection is heralded by a 5- to 10-day prodrome of headache, high fever, chills, nausea, and vomiting or diarrhea. In patients who go on to CNS involvement, initial symptoms are followed by mental confusion and somnolence often accompanied by photophobia. Seizures or convulsions occur most often in younger patients. Seizures are usually tonic-clonic but may also be of the partial-complex type. Progression to frank coma can occur rapidly. Physical examination may reveal nuchal rigidity, depressed or hyperactive reflexes, tremors, muscle twitching, spastic paralysis, bilateral papilledema, and cranial nerve palsies, which can be secondary to increased cerebrospinal fluid (CSF) pressure or directly related to inflammation. Cranial nerves VI, VII, and XII are most often affected. Infants may develop bulging fontanelles.[58,59] Other occasional findings include cyanosis secondary to depressed respiratory drive and facial, periorbital, or generalized edema.

Laboratory findings in acute EEE are as follows.[60] A polymorphonuclear leukocytosis is present in most cases to levels of 15,000 cells/mm³ or higher. Hyponatremia, when noted, may be due to the syndrome of inappropriate antidiuretic hormone. CSF protein is elevated, and 500 to 2000/mm³ cells are present, mostly lymphocytes. Red blood cells are occasionally noted as well. Hypoglycorrhachia is not present. Serologic tests are positive for antibodies to EEE virus (see later).

Neurologic sequelae include mental retardation, behavioral changes, convulsive disorders, and paralysis. These may occur in 70% of those recovering from EEE infection. Negative prognostic signs in EEE are age older than 40, rapid progression to coma, severe hyponatremia, and CSF cell counts higher than 500/mm³.[60,61] Among patients who recover, sequelae are less frequent in adults.

WEE infection is also heralded by a short prodromal phase lasting 1 to 4 days. Signs and symptoms during this period are very similar to those described for EEE. In adults, the prodromal phase may subside spontaneously with no neurologic complications. In subjects who do progress, the course of encephalitis resembles that of EEE as well, except that focal neurologic abnormalities may be less common.[59] Laboratory studies usually reveal a polymorphonuclear leukocytosis, but counts are significantly lower than those noted for EEE. The CSF protein is usually elevated, and lymphocytes and red blood cells are present. Cell counts are lower than those noted for EEE. Glucose is normal. Neurologic sequelae occur in 30% of young patients and are similar to those noted for EEE.[62] Parkinsonism is an occasional late sequela of WEE encephalitis in adults.[59]

The most common clinical manifestation of epizootic VEE infection is a febrile illness with malaise after an incubation period of 1 to 6 days. Chills, myalgia, and headache with or without photophobia, hyperesthesia, and vomiting are common. Occasionally patients complain of a sore throat. Fever may remit in a short time, with recrudescence the next day. About 4% of children and less than 1% of adults progress to severe encephalitis, which usually occurs after a few days to a week of the prodromal illness.[28] Features of encephalitis include nuchal rigidity, ataxia, convulsions, coma, and paralysis, in ascending order of severity. Laboratory studies characteristically reveal a lymphopenia, sometimes accompanied by neutropenia and mild thrombocytopenia within a day or two of onset. Serum glutamic oxaloacetic transaminase (AST) and lactate dehydrogenase enzymes are typically elevated. CSF examination reveals a few hundred lymphocytes. The overall case-fatality rate is less than 1% but approaches 20% in those who progress to encephalitis. Nearly all individuals in endemic areas contract enzootic VEE infection, as suggested by the results of serologic surveys.[28] Most seem to have experienced the influenza-like prodromal illness or to have had asymptomatic infection.

Alphaviruses Causing Fever, Rash, and Polyarthritis

Chikungunya fever is taken as the prototype of the diseases caused by this large group of alphaviruses. This is an acute viral infection characterized by a rapid transition from a state of good health to illness that includes severe arthralgia and fever.[63] The incubation period ranges from 1 to 12 days. Temperature rises abruptly to as high as 40° C and is often accompanied by shaking chills. After a few days, fever may abate and recrudesce, giving rise to a "saddleback" fever curve. Arthralgia is polyarticular, favoring the small joints and sites of previous injuries, and is most intense on arising. Patients typically avoid movement as much as possible. Joints may swell without significant fluid accumulation. These symptoms may last from 1 week to several months and are accompanied by myalgia. The rash characteristically appears on the first day of illness, but onset may be delayed. It usually arises as a flush over the face and neck, which evolves to a maculopapular or macular form that may be pruritic. The latter lesions appear on the trunk, limbs, face, palms, and soles, in that order of frequency. Petechial skin lesions have also been noted. Headache, photophobia, retro-orbital pain, sore throat with objective signs of pharyngitis, nausea, and vomiting also occur in this setting. Laboratory tests may reveal a mild leukopenia with relative lymphocytosis. The erythrocyte sedimentation rate is usually markedly elevated, and the C-reactive protein is positive.[64] Severe arthritic involvement is most commonly seen in adults, whereas children occasionally present with symptoms referable to the CNS, including seizures and convulsions. Long-term joint involvement has been reported in association with human leukocyte antigen B27.[42]

DIAGNOSIS

The epidemiology of each of the disease entities caused by alphaviruses is highly specific and provides a major clue to diagnosis. Thus, knowledge of the recent travel or outdoor exposure history of the patient is of vital importance. In certain situations, during epidemic spread of a disease, the diagnosis is obvious. In the United States, the initial signs and symptoms of EEE or WEE infection may mimic those of enteroviruses. Encephalitis caused by the flaviviruses WNV and St. Louis encephalitis virus (SLE) may occur in the same setting as encephalitis caused by WEE, although clinical disease re-

lated to SLE is more common in elderly people than in infants. Similarly, WNV encephalitis should be considered in the differential diagnosis of a viral encephalitis in areas of the United States where EEE traditionally occurs. CDC criteria for the diagnosis of an arboviral encephalitis require the presence of an acute febrile illness with encephalitis during a time when virus transmission is likely plus one of the following criteria: (1) greater than fourfold increase in viral antibody titer between acute and convalescent sera; (2) virus isolation from CSF, blood, or tissue; or (3) immunoglobulin M (IgM) positive to the virus in CSF.

For EEE, the virus can sometimes be isolated from serum during the prodrome,[58] but most cases are diagnosed by testing paired sera in HI tests or in a neutralization assay because only low-level viremia occurs in human subjects. Convalescing patients may manifest high CF antibody titers, and IgM antibodies can be detected by enzyme-linked immunosorbent assay (ELISA).[65] Sensitive nucleic acid amplification assays using the reverse transcriptase–polymerase chain reaction (RT-PCR) are under development for rapid diagnosis of EEE, WEE, VEE, and WNV infections.[66,67] Where available, such assays constitute a very rapid substitute for actual culturing of virus from a clinical specimen. Magnetic resonance imaging with specialized imaging techniques such as fluid-attenuated inversion recovery (FLAIR) and T2 weighting is of value both for diagnosis and for following the clinical course of encephalitis.[68] EEE caused focal radiographic changes involving the basal ganglia, thalamus, and brain stem, in descending order of frequency, in one study of 36 cases.[61]

Diagnostic testing for WEE follows a similar pattern except that viremia is usually not detectable. The presence of WEE in a specimen may be documented by inoculating suckling mice or embryonated eggs. In contrast, sera taken from patients with VEE infection within 48 hours of onset are almost always positive for virus. However, sera from patients with full-blown encephalitis are usually negative, and the diagnosis may be made by CF testing. ELISA for VEE-specific IgM in sera and CSF is available. IgM and IgG ELISAs using attenuated VEE as antigen are the most sensitive diagnostic tests but should be followed up with the plaque reduction neutralization assay to prove specificity.[69]

The presentation of illness caused by chikungunya virus infection may be indistinguishable from that related to Mayaro, O'nyongnyong, Ross River, or Sindbis virus infections. In addition, parvovirus infection, the prodrome of hepatitis B, juvenile rheumatoid arthritis, dengue fever, and rubella, may also be confused with chikungunya fever or with the other alphavirus infections. Patients with chikungunya fever are usually viremic for the first 48 hours, and the virus is easily isolated by in vivo or in vitro methods. Viremia may be so intense (titer $>10^7$ plaque-forming units/mL of blood) as to yield measurable amounts of hemagglutinating activity from sera.[70] Consequently, virus in sera can also often be detected by ELISA directly.[71] As previously mentioned, the decline in levels of viremia parallels a rapid rise in titers of HI and neutralizing antibodies. ELISA testing for virus-binding antibodies may detect cross-reactive immune responses to other alphaviruses.

TREATMENT AND PREVENTION

There is no specific treatment for any of the alphavirus infections. For encephalitis, supportive measures and intensive nursing care are indicated. Ribavirin and other nucleoside analogues have some in vitro activity against these viruses in tissue culture but are not in use clinically. Intravenous immune globulin was apparently effective in promoting recovery of at least one patient with acute EEE infection who had full-blown encephalitis and coma.[68]

Prevention of WEE and EEE depends primarily on control of vector mosquito populations. During outbreaks, susceptible individuals engaged in high-risk activities should be advised to avoid exposure as much as is practicable by the use of effective mosquito repellents and netting, the wearing of full-length trousers and long-sleeved shirts, and avoidance of outdoor activities at least during periods of maximal mosquito activity. Inactivated vaccines against EEE and WEE are available for limited human use. Similar veterinary vaccines are used against EEE in horses and birds and against WEE in horses. The inactivated EEE vaccine is derived from a North American virus isolate and may not be efficacious in the prevention of disease caused by the South American antigenic variant of EEE virus.[72]

Both formalin-inactivated and live, attenuated vaccines to prevent VEE infection are in limited use in humans. Efficacy of the formalin-inactivated vaccine was greatly enhanced in mice when antigens were microencapsulated in biodegradable microspheres.[73] The live, attenuated VEE strain is used in the diagnostic ELISA, and large-scale vaccination of horses with this strain is the major approach to the interdiction of VEE epizootics. A live, attenuated vaccine against chikungunya fever has been shown to be safe in volunteers. One study in which live, attenuated VEE and chikungunya fever vaccines were sequentially administered to human volunteers indicated that preexisting alphavirus immunity interferes with a subsequent neutralizing antibody response to a heterologous vaccine virus.[74]

The existing live VEE vaccine candidate is a temperature-sensitive mutant virus derived several years ago by conventional virologic methods. Newer approaches to the development of vaccines to prevent alphavirus infections have involved the use of recombinant DNA technology. VEE virus has been one focal point of this approach to vaccine development. One viable mutant virus derived from VEE "infectious DNA," which contained mutations affecting cleavage of the viral structural proteins, was avirulent in mice and produced solid mucosal immunity, possibly as a consequence of the tropism of VEE for lymphoid tissues.[75,76] This property of VEE is now viewed as a basis for efficacy of VEE DNA-based vaccines designed to induce immunity to foreign viral antigens,[77-79] especially when mucosal immune responses are considered to be of crucial importance for protection, such as for human immunodeficiency virus.[79]

REFERENCES

1. Fothergill LD, Dingle JH, Farber S, et al. Human encephalitis caused by a virus of eastern variety of equine encephalitis. N Engl J Med. 1983;219:411.
2. Beck CG, Wyckof RWG. Venezuelan equine encephalitis. Science. 1938;88:530.
3. San Martin-Barberi C, Groot H, Osborn-Mesa E. Human epidemic in Columbia caused by the Venezuelan equine encephalitis virus. Am J Trop Med Hyg. 1954;3:283.
4. Ehrenkranz NJ, Ventura AK. Venezuelan equine encephalitis virus infection in man. Annu Rev Med. 1974;25:9-14.
5. Peters CJ, Dalrymple JM. Alphaviruses. In: Fields BN, Knipe DM, eds. Virology. 2nd ed. New York: Raven Press; 1990:713-761.
6. Francki RIB, Fauquet CM, Knudson DL, Brown F. Classification and nomenclature of viruses. Arch Virol. 1991;2(Suppl):223.
7. Calisher CH, Karabatsos N. Arbovirus serogroups: Definition and geographic distribution. In: Monath TP, ed. The Arboviruses: Epidemiology and Ecology, v. 1. Boca Raton, Fla: CRC Press; 1988:19-57.
8. Powers AM, Brault AC, Shirako Y, et al. Evolutionary relationships and systematics of the alphaviruses. J Virol. 2001;75:10118-10131.
9. Anthony RP, Brown DT. Protein-protein interactions in an alphavirus membrane. J Virol. 1991;65:1187-1194.
10. Gaedigk-Nitschko K, Schlesinger MJ. The Sindbis virus 6K protein can be detected in virions and is acylated with fatty acids. Virology. 1990;175:274-281.
11. Smit JM, Klimstra WB, Ryman KD, et al. PE2 cleavage mutants of Sindbis virus: Correlation between virus infectivity and pH-dependent membrane fusion activation of the spike heterodimer. J Virol. 2001;75:11196-11204.
12. Zhang X, Fugere M, Day R, Kielian M. Furin processing and proteolytic activation of Semliki Forest virus. J Virol. 2003;77:2981-2989.
13. Yao JS, Strauss EG, Strauss JH. Interactions between PE2, E1, and 6K required for assembly of alphaviruses studied with chimeric viruses. J Virol. 1996;70:7910-7920.
14. Calisher CH, Shope RE, Brandt WE, et al. Proposed antigenic classification of registered arboviruses. I. Togaviridae. Alphavirus Intervirol. 1980;14:229-232.
15. Hahn CS, Lustig S, Strauss EG, et al. Western equine encephalitis virus is a recombinant virus. Proc Natl Acad Sci USA. 1988;85:5997-6001.
16. Weaver SC, Kang W, Shirako Y, et al. Recombinational history and molecular evolution of Western equine encephalitis complex alphaviruses. J Virol. 1997;71:613-623.
17. Brault AC, Powers AM, Chavez CL, et al. Genetic and antigenic diversity among eastern equine encephalitis viruses from North, Central, and South America. Am J Trop Med Hyg. 1999;61:579-586.
18. Monath TP. Arthropod-borne encephalitides in the Americas. Bull World Health Organ. 1979;57:513-533.
19. Del Piero F, Wilkins PA, Dubovi EJ, et al. Clinical, pathologic, immunohistochemical, and virologic findings of eastern equine encephalitis in two horses. Vet Pathol. 2001;38:451-456.
20. Shope RE, de Andrade AHP, Bensabeth G, et al. The epidemiology of EEE, WEE, SLE, and Tralock viruses. Am J Epidemiol. 1966;84:467-477.
21. Chamberlain RW. Vector relationship of the arthropod-borne encephalitides in North America. Ann NY Acad Sci. 1958;70:312-319.
22. Reisen WK, Monath TP. Western equine encephalomyelitis. In: Monath TP, ed. The Arboviruses: Epidemiology and Ecology, v. 5. Boca Raton, Fla: CRC Press; 1989: 90-137.
23. Reeves WC, Hammon W. Epidemiology of the arthropod-borne encephalitides in Kern County, California, 1943-52. Univ Calif Pub Public Health. 1962;4:257.
24. Feemster RF. Equine encephalitis in Massachusetts. N Engl J Med. 1957;257: 701-704.
25. Centers for Disease Control and Prevention. www.cdc.gov.
26. Arboviral disease in the United States, 1996-1997. MMWR Morb Mortal Wkly Rep. 1998;47:517-522.
27. Groot H. The health and economic impact of Venezuelan equine encephalitis. In: Venezuelan Encephalitis, Proceedings of the Workshop-Symposium on Venezuelan Encephalitis Virus. Washington, DC: Pan American Health Organization; 1972:244.
28. Johnson KM, Martin DH: Venezuelan equine encephalitis. Adv Vet Sci Comp Med. 1974;18:79.
29. Bowen GS, Fashinell TR, Dean PB, et al. Clinical aspects of human Venezuelan equine encephalitis in Texas. Bull Pan Am Health Org. 1976;10:46-57.
30. Scherer WF, Cupp EW, Dziem GM, et al. Mesenteronal infection threshold of an epizootic strain of Venezuelan equine encephalitis virus in Culex (Melanoconion) taeniopus mosquitoes and its implication to the apparent disappearance of this virus from an enzootic habitat in Guatemala. Am J Trop Med Hyg. 1982;31:1030-1037.
31. Powers AM, Obserste MS, Brault AC, et al. Repeated emergence of epidemic/epizootic Venezuelan equine encephalitis from a single genotype of enzootic subtype 1D virus. J Virol. 1997;71:6697-6705.
32. Brault AC, Powers AM, Holmes EC, et al. Positively charged amino acid substitutions in the E2 envelope glycoprotein are associated with the emergence of Venezuelan equine encephalitis virus. J Virol. 2002;76:1718-1730.
33. Niklasson B. Sindbis and Sindbis-like viruses. In: Monath TP, ed. The Arboviruses: Epidemiology and Ecology. Boca Raton, Fla: CRC Press; 1988:167-176.
34. Mudge PR. Clinical features of epidemic polyarthritis. Arbovirus Res Aust. 1982:158-166.
35. Pinheiro FP, LeDuc JW. Mayaro virus disease. In: Monath TP, ed. The Arboviruses: Epidemiology and Ecology. Boca Raton, Fla: CRC Press; 1988:137-150.
36. Weaver SC, Lorenz LH, Scott TW. Pathologic changes in the midgut of Culex tarsalis following infection with Western equine encephalomyelitis virus. Am J Trop Med Hyg. 1992;47:691-701.
37. Charles PC, Walters E, Margolis F, et al. Mechanism of neuro-invasion of Venezuelan equine encephalitis virus in the mouse. Virology. 1995;208:662-671.
38. Gorelkin L. Venezuelan equine encephalitis in an adult animal host. Am J Pathol. 1973;73:425-432.
39. Grieder FB, Vogel SN. Role of interferon and interferon regulatory factors in early protection against Venezuelan equine encephalitis virus infection. Virology. 1999;257:106-118.
40. Schoneboom BA, Lee JS, Grieder FB. Early expression of IFN alpha/beta and iNOS in the brains of Venezuelan equine encephalitis virus–infected mice. J Interferon Cytokine Res. 2000;20:205-215.
41. Jackson AC, Rossiter JP. Apoptotic cell death is an important cause of neuronal cell injury in Venezuelan equine encephalitis virus infection of mice. Acta Neuropathol (Berl). 1997;93:349-353.
42. Tsai TF, Monath TP. Viral diseases in North America transmitted by arthropods or from vertebrate reservoirs. In: Feigin RD, Cherry JD, eds. Textbook of Pediatric Infectious Diseases. 2nd ed. Philadelphia: WB Saunders; 1988:1417.
43. Thach DC, Kimura T, Griffin DE. Differences between C57Bl/6 and BALB/c mice in mortality and virus replication after intranasal infection with neuroadapted Sindbis virus. J Virol. 2000;74:6156-6161.
44. Dropulic B, Masters CL. Entry of neurotropic arboviruses into the central nervous system: An in vitro study using mouse brain endothelium. J Infect Dis. 1990;161: 685-691.
45. Jan JT, Chatterjee S, Griffin DE. Sindbis virus entry into cells triggers apoptosis by activating sphingomyelinase, leading to release of ceramide. J Virol. 2000;74: 6425-6432.
46. Lewis J, Oyler GA, Kazuyoshi U, et al. Inhibition of virus-induced neuronal apoptosis by Bax. Nat Med. 1999;5:832-835.
47. Havert MB, Schonfeld B, Griffin DE, Irani DN. Divergent neuronal cell death pathways activated in different target cell populations during neuroadapted Sindbis virus infection of mice. J Virol. 2000;74:5352-5356.
48. Nargi-Aizenman JL, Griffin DE. Sindbis virus–induced neuronal death is both necrotic and apoptotic and is ameliorated by N-methyl-D-aspartate receptor antagonists. J Virol. 2001;75:7114-7121.
49. Kerr DA, Larsen T, Cook SH, et al. BCL-2 and BAX protect adult mice from lethal Sindbis virus infection but do not protect spinal cord motor neurons or prevent paralysis. J Virol. 2002;76:10393-10400.
50. Griffin DE, Hardwick JM. Regulators of apoptosis on the road to persistent alphavirus infection. Annu Rev Microbiol. 1997;51:565-592.

51. Grosfeld H, Lustig S, Gozes Y, et al. Divergent envelope E2 alphavirus sequences spanning amino acids 297 to 352 induce in mice virus-specific immunity and antibodies with complemented-mediated cytolytic activity. Virology. 1992;66:1084-1090.
52. Levine B, Griffin DE. Persistence of viral RNA in mouse brains after recovery from acute alphavirus encephalitis. J Virol. 1992;66:6429-6435.
53. Kimura T, Griffin DE. The role of CD8$^+$ T cells and major histocompatibility complex class I expression in the central nervous system of mice infected with neurovirulent Sindbis virus. J Virol. 2000;74:6117-6125.
54. Gorrell MD, Lemm JA, Rice CM, Griffin DE. Immunization with nonstructural proteins promotes functional recovery of alphavirus-infected neurons. J Virol. 1997;71:3415-3419.
55. Binder GK, Griffin DE. Interferon-γ–mediated site-specific clearance of alphavirus from CNS neurons. Science. 2000;293:303-306.
56. Rowell JF, Griffin DE. Contribution of T cells to mortality in neurovirulent Sindbis virus encephalomyelitis. J Neuroimmunol. 2002;127:106-114.
57. Fourie ED, Morrison JGL. Rheumatoid arthritis syndrome after chikungunya fever. S Afr Med J. 1979;56:130-132.
58. Clarke DH. Two nonfatal human infections with the virus of eastern encephalitis. Am J Trop Med Hyg. 1961;10:67-70.
59. Baker AB. II. Western equine encephalitis. Clinical features. Neurology. 1958;8:880-881.
60. Nandalur M, Urban AW. Eastern equine encephalitis. 2002; www.emedicine.com/med/topic3155.htm.
61. Deresiewicz RL, Thaler SJ, Zamani AA. Clinical and neuroradiographic manifestations of eastern equine encephalitis. N Engl J Med. 1997;336:1867-1874.
62. Nandalur M, Urban AW. Western equine encephalitis. 2002; www.emedicine.com/med/topic3155.htm.
63. Deller JJ, Russell PK. Chikungunya disease. Am J Trop Med Hyg. 1968;17:1007-1011.
64. Kennedy AC, Fleming J, Solomon L. Chikungunya viral arthropathy: A clinical description. J Rheumatol. 1980;7:231-236.
65. Calisher CH, El-Kafrawi AO, Al-Deen Mahmud MI, et al. Complex-specific immunoglobulin M antibody patterns in humans infected with alphaviruses. J Clin Microbiol. 1986;23:155-159.
66. Linssen B, Kinney RM, Aguilar P, et al. Development of reverse transcription-PCR assays specific for detection of equine encephalitis viruses. J Clin Microbiol. 2000;38:1527-1535.
67. Lambert AJ, Martin DA, Lanciotti RS. Detection of North American eastern and western equine encephalitis viruses by nucleic acid amplification assays. J Clin Microbiol. 2003;41:379-385.
68. Golomb MR, Durand ML, Schaefer PW, et al. A case of immunotherapy-responsive eastern equine encephalitis with diffusion-weighted imaging. Neurology 2001;56:420-421.
69. Coates DM, Makh SR, Jones N, et al. Assessment of assays for the serodiagnosis of Venezuelan equine encephalitis. J Infect Dis. 1992;25:279-289.
70. Carey DE, Myers RM, DeRanitz CM, et al. The 1964 chikungunya epidemic at Vellore, South India, including observations about concurrent dengue. Trans R Soc Trop Med Hyg. 1969;63:434-435.
71. Tan R, Meegan J, LeDuc J, et al. Enzyme-linked immunosorbent assay for diagnosis of chikungunya disease. Presented at the 34th annual meeting of the American Society of Tropical Medicine and Hygiene, Miami, Fla, November 3-7, 1985.
72. Strizki JM, Repik PM. Differential reactivity of immune sera from human vaccinees with field strains of equine encephalitis virus. Am J Trop Med Hyg. 1995;53:564-570.
73. Greenway TE, Eldridge JH, Ludwig G, et al. Enhancement of protective immune responses to Venezuelan equine encephalitis virus with micro-encapsulated vaccine. Vaccine. 1995;13:1411-1420.
74. McClain DJ, Pittman PR, Ramsburg HH, et al. Immunologic interference from sequential administration of live attenuated alphavirus vaccines. J Infect Dis. 1998;177:634-641.
75. Davis NL, Brown KW, Greenwald GF, et al. Attenuated mutants of Venezuelan equine encephalitis virus containing lethal mutations in the PE2 cleavage signal combined with a second site suppressor mutation in E1. Virology. 1995;212:102-110.
76. Charles PC, Brown KW, Davis NL, et al. Mucosal immunity induced by immunization with a live attenuated Venezuelan equine encephalitis vaccine candidate. Virology. 1997;228:153-160.
77. Davis NL, Brown KW, Johnston RE. A viral vaccine vector that expresses foreign genes in lymph nodes and protects against mucosal challenge. J Virol.1996;70:3781-3787.
78. Pushko P, Parker M, Ludwig GV, et al. Replicon-helper systems from attenuated Venezuelan equine encephalitis virus: Expression of heterologous genes in vitro and immunization against heterologous pathogens in vivo. Virology. 1997;239:389-401.
79. Carey IJ, Betts MR, Irlbeck DM, et al. Humoral, mucosal, and cellular immunity in response to a human immunodeficiency virus type 1 immunogen expressed by a Venezuelan equine encephalitis virus vaccine vector. J Virol. 1997;71:3031-3038.

Rubella Virus (German Measles)

ANNE A. GERSHON

Rubella (German measles) is an acute exanthematous viral infection of children and adults. The clinical illness is characterized by rash, fever, and lymphadenopathy and resembles a mild case of measles (rubeola). Although many infections with the agent are subclinical, this virus has the potential to cause fetal infection, with resultant birth defects, and (uncommonly but especially in adults) various forms of arthritis.

Rubella virus was first isolated in 1962 by Parkman and colleagues[1] and by Weller and Neva.[2] Rubella virus is classified in the Togaviridae family[3,4] on the basis of its RNA genome, replication strategy, icosahedral capsid, and lipoprotein envelope. Rubella virus is closely related to the alphaviruses, but in contrast to alphaviruses, no vector is required for transmission of rubella virus, and it is serologically distinct from alphaviruses.[4] Therefore, rubella virus alone has been placed in a separate genus, *Rubivirus*.

On electron microscopy, rubella virus is roughly spherical. Its envelope, which has short surface projections, has a diameter of about 60 nm. The envelope surrounds the nucleocapsid, which has a diameter of about 30 nm and is composed of a helix of protein and RNA. Rubella virus matures by budding from the cell membrane.[5]

Three structural polypeptides associated with rubella virus are termed E1, E2, and C. Nonstructural proteins that are related to replication and transcription probably also exist. E1 and E2 are transmembrane glycoproteins, and C is the capsid protein that surrounds the RNA of the virion. Hemagglutinin and complement-fixing antigens are composed of varying proportions and mixtures of E1, E2, and C.[6,7]

Rubella virus is relatively unstable. It is inactivated by lipid solvents, trypsin, formalin, ultraviolet light, and extremes of pH and heat, and it is inhibited by amantadine.[8] Cytopathic effects may not be noted in all cell lines in which rubella virus replicates. However, cytopathic effects are readily observed in the rabbit kidney cell line RK-13 and in primary African green monkey cells.[6]

EPIDEMIOLOGY

Rubella was not distinguished clinically from certain other exanthematous infections until the late 19th century. It was at one time termed "third disease," when measles and scarlet fever were called "first disease" and "second disease," respectively.[9] Because postnatal rubella is such a mild illness, the disease was considered to be of only minor importance for many years. However, in 1941, when Gregg[10] recognized the link between maternal rubella and certain congenital defects, a more complete picture of disease due to rubella virus began to emerge.

Before widespread vaccine use, the incidence of clinical cases of postnatal rubella was highest in the spring, and it was traditionally recognized to be most common in children 5 to 9 years of age.[11] However, evidence suggests that rubella is now being seen with increasing frequency in an older age group because of the widespread use of rubella vaccine.[12] Rubella is only a moderately contagious illness, in contrast to measles. Therefore, in the prevaccine era, only 80% to 90% of adults were immune to rubella, whereas 98% were immune to measles.[11]

Epidemics of rubella of minor proportions occurred in the prevaccine era every 6 to 9 years, and large-scale epidemics occurred at intervals of up to 30 years. The most recent major epidemic in the United States occurred in 1964, during which some 12,500,000 persons were infected.[13] Since the licensure of a live-attenuated rubella vaccine in 1969, there have been no large rubella epidemics in countries where the vaccine is widely used. However, limited outbreaks have continued to occur in settings such as workplaces, schools, and military camps, where groups of susceptible individuals have close contact with each other.[12,14] In 2001, only 23 cases of postnatal rubella and 3 confirmed cases of congenital rubella syndrome were reported to the Centers for Disease Control and Prevention (CDC).[15] A recent increase in susceptibility to rubella has been noted among Hispanic young adults, particularly those who are recent immigrants from countries where rubella vaccine is not administered routinely or where immunization programs are still being developed. Increasing efforts to identify rubella-susceptible women before they become pregnant are strongly recommended.[15,16]

TRANSMISSION OF RUBELLA

Rubella virus is spread in droplets that are shed from respiratory secretions of infected persons. Patients are most contagious while the rash is erupting, but they may shed virus from the throat from 10 days before until 15 days after the onset of the rash. Patients with subclinical cases of illness may also transmit the infection to others.[8]

Infants with congenital rubella shed large quantities of virus from body secretions for many months and therefore may transmit the infection to those who care for them. These babies continue to excrete rubella virus despite high titers of neutralizing antibody, a puzzling phenomenon that has yet to be explained.[17] The possibility of immune tolerance due to fetal infection has been raised.[7]

Persons who receive rubella vaccine do not transmit rubella to others, although the virus may be transiently isolated from the pharynx. It may be that the quantity of virus shed is too small to be infectious.[16]

MAINTENANCE OF IMMUNITY TO RUBELLA

After an attack of rubella, lifelong protection against the disease develops in most persons. However, the factors responsible for this protection are not precisely understood. Antibody titers to rubella virus develop, but the significance of the decline of antibody titers with time remains unclear. Cell-mediated immunity to rubella virus associated with CD4+ and CD8+ T lymphocytes has also been detected by in vitro assays[6,19] months to years after an attack of rubella. The long-term persistence of humoral and cellular immunity to rubella in a group of cloistered nuns who had no opportunity for reexposure to rubella virus has been documented.[20] The persistence of specific antibody for as long as 14 years after immunization has also been demonstrated.[21,22]

Nevertheless, despite the presence of specific immunity to rubella virus, it appears that reinfection with rubella virus can occur. This had been long suspected on clinical grounds alone.[23,24] Rubella reinfections have been documented by detection of a significant boost in rubella antibody titers in naturally immune persons after reexposure to the virus. The overwhelming majority of reinfections are asymptomatic.[25] It is likely that the virus can multiply locally in the upper respiratory tract but that viremia occurs infrequently because the host's immune response eradicates the virus before it can invade the blood. However, in rare instances patients have been reported to have proven rubella reinfection occurring years after naturally acquired rubella, with symptoms indicative of viremia (e.g., arthritis, rash).[26]

Rubella reinfection occurring months or years after the receipt of rubella vaccine has also been observed. Several investigators have documented reinfections in up to 80% of persons who had received rubella vaccine previously and were subsequently exposed to rubella during an epidemic.[25,27] Most of these reinfections were not characterized by clinical illness but were identified only by a rise in antibody titer. Viremia is probably extremely rare in such cases,[27-29] although rubella virus has been recovered from throat secretions in reinfections.[25,28] In one study of eight seronegative adult vaccinees who were experimentally challenged with wild-type rubella virus, replication in the respiratory tract was found in seven subjects, and viremia was present in two.[30] However, these subjects also experienced only a mild illness or remained asymptomatic.[30]

Reinfections are more common among vaccinees than among persons who have experienced natural rubella, and they are most common among persons with hemagglutination inhibition (HAI) antibody titers of 1:64 or less.[25,27,28] It has been suggested that there may also be qualitative differences in antibody between persons with vaccine-induced immunity and those with natural immunity, because in one study, even with similar HAI titers, vaccinees were 10 times more likely to be reinfected than were those with natural immunity to rubella.[25]

Whether rubella reinfection that occurs during pregnancy can result in transmission of the virus to the fetus has been the subject of much debate. Several case reports in the older literature that ascribed fetal defects to maternal rubella reinfection actually involved primary maternal infections in all likelihood.[31,32] Viremia was documented in one woman with detectable rubella antibody before immunization.[33] Boué and colleagues[34] studied a small number of women with documented subclinical cases of rubella reinfection during pregnancy who carried their babies to term; all of the babies were found to be normal. In a number of other case reports of rubella reinfection during pregnancy, babies born (at term) to the affected mothers had symptoms suggestive of congenital rubella.[35-40] Most of these reinfections occurred years after natural infection, although some occurred years after immunization.[39,40] However, these transmissions are acknowledged to be extremely rare events, particularly considering the exceedingly low incidence of congenital rubella in the United States today (see later discussion).

In summary, it appears that persons who are immune to rubella, by virtue either of having had the natural infection or of having received rubella vaccine, may be reinfected when reexposed. However, this reinfection is usually asymptomatic and detectable only by serologic means. Viremia in reinfection appears to be a rare event.

The presence of large numbers of immune people in a community appears to be able to prevent rubella epidemics from occurring; this effect is termed "herd immunity." Although it has been documented that herd immunity does not entirely eliminate the spread of rubella, it probably plays a major role in control of this infection, which is now rare in the United States.[41]

PATHOGENESIS

The incubation period for rubella ranges from 12 to 23 days (average, 18 days). As in measles (see Chapter 157), a primary and a secondary viremia are believed to accompany rubella. Rubella virus has been detected in leukocytes of patients as early as 1 week before the onset of symptoms.[42] Also as in measles, the rubella rash appears as immunity develops and the virus disappears from the blood,[6] suggesting that the rash is immunologically mediated. Although circulating immune complexes are detectable during rubella, they do not seem to contribute to the development of rash.[6,43] Rubella virus has been isolated from involved skin,[44] but this does not preclude the possibility that the rash is secondary to an immune response to the virus.

CLINICAL MANIFESTATIONS

Age is the most important determinant of the severity of rubella. Postnatally acquired rubella is usually an innocuous infection, and, as is true for many viral illnesses, children are apt to have milder disease than are adults. In contrast, the fetus is at high risk for development of severe rubella, with serious sequelae if infected transplacentally in early pregnancy due to maternal rubella.

Postnatal Rubella

Many, if not most, cases of postnatal rubella are subclinical.[13,45] Among those patients who are symptomatic, children do not experience a prodromal phase, but adults may have a prodrome of malaise, fever, and anorexia for several days. The major clinical manifestations of postnatal rubella are adenopathy, which may last several weeks, and rash. The lymph nodes involved include the posterior auricular, posterior cervical, and suboccipital chains. On occasion, splenomegaly also

occurs.[46] These symptoms are not specific for rubella, and clinically the disease may resemble measles, toxoplasmosis, scarlet fever, roseola, parvovirus B19 infection, and certain enterovirus infections.

The rash of rubella begins on the face and moves down the body. It is maculopapular but not confluent, may desquamate during convalescence, and may be absent in some cases. An enanthem consisting of petechial lesions on the soft palate (Forscheimer's spots) has been described for rubella, but this enanthem is not diagnostic for rubella (unlike Koplik's spots in measles). The rash may be accompanied by mild coryza and conjunctivitis. Usually the rash lasts 3 to 5 days. Fever, if present, rarely lasts beyond the first day of rash.

Complications of Postnatal Rubella

The complications of postnatal rubella, in contrast to those of measles, are uncommon. Bacterial superinfections after rubella are rare.

Arthritis or arthralgia has been reported in as many as one third of women with rubella; this complication is less common in children and in men.[47] The arthritis tends to involve the fingers, wrists, and knees, and it occurs either as the rash is appearing or soon afterward. It can be rather slow to resolve, as long as 1 month. Rarely does chronic arthritis develop.

The pathogenesis of rubella arthritis is not entirely understood. The frequency of detection and the quantity of circulating immune complexes are higher in rubella vaccinees who report joint complaints than in those with no joint involvement.[43,48] Rubella virus has been isolated from joint effusions in patients with acute or recurrent rubella arthritis associated with either previous natural infection or vaccination.[49-57] Rubella virus has been isolated from peripheral blood mononuclear cells in patients with chronic arthritis.[56,58] A persistent rubella virus infection of human synovial cells cultured in vitro was reported, and this was advanced as an explanation for the pathogenesis of chronic forms of rubella arthritis.[59]

Hemorrhagic manifestations occur as a complication in approximately 1 of every 3000 cases of rubella.[46,60] In contrast to other complications of rubella, hemorrhagic manifestations occur more often in children than in adults. This complication may be secondary to both thrombocytopenia and vascular damage, and it is probably immunologically mediated.[60] Some investigators have proposed that mild thrombocytopenia often goes undetected in apparently uncomplicated rubella.[61] Thrombocytopenia may last from weeks to months and may cause serious problems if bleeding into vital areas (e.g., brain, kidney, eye) occurs.[46] Thrombocytopenic purpura as the single clinical manifestation of rubella in children has also been reported.[60]

Encephalitis is an extremely uncommon complication of rubella; its incidence during an epidemic was reported to be 1 in 5000 cases. It occurs more frequently in adults than in children, and it is associated with a mortality rate of 20% to 50%.[46,62,63] Survivors usually have no sequelae.[6] A fatal case of rubella encephalitis in a 2-month-old child whose mother had rubella in the last week of pregnancy has been reported.[64]

Mild hepatitis has been described as an unusual complication of rubella.[65]

Congenital Rubella

Rubella can be a disastrous disease in early gestation and can lead to fetal death, premature delivery, and an array of congenital defects. The incidence of congenital rubella in a given population is quite variable, depending on the number of susceptible individuals, the circulation of virus in the community, and, in recent times, the use of rubella vaccine. The rubella epidemic of 1964 left 30,000 affected infants in its wake. Between 1969 and 1979, however, an average of 39 cases per year was reported to the CDC.[66,67] Since then, an all-time low of 10 or fewer cases per year has been reported in the United States.[15,68]

The effects of rubella virus on the fetus are, to a large extent, dependent on the time of infection; in general, the younger the fetus when infected, the more severe the illness. During the first 2 months of gestation, the fetus has a 65% to 85% chance of being affected, with an outcome of multiple congenital defects or spontaneous abortion, or both.[6] Rubella during the third month of fetal life has been associated with a 30% to 35% chance of developing a single defect, such as deafness or congenital heart disease. Fetal infection during the fourth month carries a 10% risk of a single congenital defect. Occasionally, fetal damage (deafness alone) is seen if rubella occurs up to the 20th week of gestation.[69]

The specific signs and symptoms of congenital rubella may be classified as temporary (e.g., low birth weight), permanent (e.g., deafness), and developmental (e.g., myopia).[66] The most common manifestations are deafness, cataract or glaucoma, congenital heart disease, and mental retardation; a list of the major clinical manifestations is presented in Table 148-1.[66]

Prospective studies of the congenital rubella syndrome suggest that it should not be considered a static disease. Some children whose mothers had rubella during pregnancy and who, at birth, were considered normal were found to have manifestations of congenital rubella when they reached school age.[70,71] Diabetes mellitus in late childhood has also been observed 50 times more frequently in children who had congenital rubella than in normal children.[6,72] Insulin-dependent diabetes has been reported in 40% of adult survivors of congenital rubella from the 1942 epidemic.[73] Of interest, in a follow-up study of 242 children who had congenital rubella, rubella virus–induced diabetes had genetic and immunologic features similar to those observed in other forms of insulin-dependent diabetes: the frequency of the human leukocyte antigen allele HLA-DR3 was increased and that of HLA-DR2 was decreased.[74] Antibodies to pancreatic islet cells or cytotoxic surface antibodies were present in 80% of the patients with abnormalities in serum glucose concentration.[74] At autopsy of congenital rubella patients, the virus was isolated from the pancreas, which was noted to have a subnormal number of glandular cells.[74] Progressive encephalopathy resembling subacute sclerosing panencephalitis (SSPE) was observed in children with congenital rubella.[75,76] In 1991, a group of 40 adults born with the congenital rubella syndrome between 1939 and 1943 were reexamined. Although they had multiple defects involving hearing, diabetes, growth retardation, and eye and heart abnormalities, most were well adjusted socially. There was no increased incidence of malignant disease in these 50-year-old survivors.[77]

Infants with congenital rubella develop high titers of neutralizing antibody that may persist for years.[78] However, these children may eventually lose detectable antibody.[79] Reinfection with rubella has also been documented in some of these children.[80] Impairment of cell-mediated immunity to rubella antigen was found in some children with congenital rubella.[81]

TABLE 148-1 Congenital Rubella: Transient (T), Permanent (P), and Developmental (D) Manifestations

Common	Uncommon or Rare
Low birth weight (T)	Jaundice (T)
Thrombocytopenic purpura (T)	Dermatoglyphic "abnormality" (P)
Hepatosplenomegaly (T)	Glaucoma (P)
Bone "lesions" (T)	Cloudy cornea (T)
Large anterior fontanelle (T)	Severe myopia (P,D)
Meningoencephalitis (T)	Myocardial abnormalities (P)
Hearing loss (P,D)	Hepatitis (T)
Cataract (and microphthalmia) (P)	Generalized lymphadenopathy (T)
Retinopathy (P)	Hemolytic anemia (T)
Patent ductus arteriosus (P)	Rubella pneumonitis (T)
Pulmonic stenosis (P,D)	Diabetes mellitus (P,D)
Mental retardation (P,D)	Thyroid disorders (P,D)
Behavior disorders (P,D)	Seizure disorders (D)
Central language disorders (P,D)	Precocious puberty (D)
Cryptorchidism (P)	Degenerative brain disease (D)
Inguinal hernia (P)	
Spastic diplegia (P)	
Microcephaly (P)	

From Cooper LZ. Congenital rubella in the United States. In: Krugman S, Gershon A, eds. Infections of the Fetus and Newborn Infant. New York: Alan R. Liss; 1975:1. Reprinted with permission of John Wiley & Sons, Inc. Copyright © 1975. This material is used by permission of Wiley-Liss, Inc., a subsidiary of John Wiley & Sons, Inc.

A number of pathologic mechanisms have been proposed to explain certain manifestations of congenital rubella. It has been suggested that persistent infection with rubella virus leads to a mitotic arrest of cells, which in turn causes inhibition of cellular growth and, consequently, retarded organ growth.[82] Additional hypotheses put forth to explain the growth retardation associated with congenital rubella are that infection leads to angiopathy with placental and fetal vasculitis, which compromises growth,[83] and that tissue necrosis without inflammation or fibrotic damage leads to cellular damage.[84] Another possible explanation is that infection of various types of cells during gestation interferes with the normal balance of growth and differentiation, which leads to defects in organogenesis.[6] Human fibroblasts infected with rubella virus in vitro were found to produce a growth inhibitor, which might also account for fetal growth retardation.[85] An increased frequency of chromosomal breakage was found in cultured cells from children with congenital rubella, compared with cells from healthy children.[86] It has been postulated that lymphocyte abnormalities in patients with the congenital rubella syndrome may predispose them to organ-specific autoimmunity.[87]

DIAGNOSIS

Because rubella is usually a mild disease with nonspecific symptoms, it is often difficult to diagnose clinically. The disease has been confused with other infections such as scarlet fever, mild measles, infectious mononucleosis, toxoplasmosis, roseola, erythema infectiosum, and certain enteroviral infections.[88,89] Routine laboratory studies are not helpful for diagnosis because they may reveal only leukopenia and atypical lymphocytes; more specific laboratory diagnostic techniques are usually necessary.

Virus isolation from throat swabs, urine, synovial fluid, or other body secretions is an acceptable method for diagnosis. However, this technique is time-consuming and expensive, so it is usually reserved for special circumstances, such as investigation of arthritis and other conditions presumed to represent complications of postnatal rubella, and for the diagnosis of congenital rubella.[6,8] The diagnosis of congenital rubella infection has been made by isolation of virus from amniotic fluid.[90] Today, molecular methods such as reverse transcriptase–polymerase chain reaction (RT-PCR) are preferred to virus isolation.[7] Molecular studies have identified differing variants of rubella virus, but with high levels of cross-immunity.[91]

The laboratory diagnosis of postnatal rubella is most conveniently made serologically. At one time, HAI was the preferred means of measuring rubella antibody titers, but this technique has been supplanted by simpler, more accurate methods of similar sensitivity.[8,89,92-96] These include enzyme-linked immunosorbent assay (ELISA), passive latex agglutination test, and radial hemolysis test. Most of these tests may be used to measure either immunoglobulin G (IgG) or IgM antibodies. A demonstration of specific IgG on one serum sample is evidence of immunity to rubella. Acute rubella infection may be diagnosed either by a demonstration of specific IgM in one serum sample or by a fourfold or greater increase in rubella antibody titer in acute and convalescent specimens assayed in the same test.[7,97] Positive rubella IgM antibody tests have been associated not only with primary infection but also with reinfection with rubella virus.[98] This phenomenon may explain, at least in part, why apparent false-positive results on IgM-rubella ELISA testing in pregnant women have been reported.[99] Results of many of these serologic tests are available within a matter of minutes or hours and yield prompt, useful information.

For a serologic diagnosis of congenital rubella in the neonatal period, antibody to rubella virus should be measured in both infant and maternal sera. It may be necessary to perform several antibody determinations on serum from the infant to detect whether the titer of rubella antibody is falling, which indicates passively acquired maternal antibody, or rising, which suggests rubella infection. If rubella IgM is detected in a newborn infant's serum, then transplacental rubella infection has occurred. Congenital rubella infection has been diagnosed by the following tests or procedures: placental biopsy at 12 weeks, demonstration of rubella antigen with monoclonal antibody, cordocentesis and detection of RNA by in situ hybridization,[100] and PCR.[101] It may also be diagnosed by the presence of specific IgM in fetal blood, but this may not be detectable until as late as 22 weeks of gestation.[102,103]

TREATMENT

Because postnatal rubella is such a mild infection in most instances, no treatment is indicated. There is no specific therapy, but for patients with fever and arthritis or arthralgia, the treatment of symptoms is indicated. At one time, immune globulin (IG) was advocated for the prevention or modification of rubella in susceptible pregnant women who were exposed to the infection. However, it was discovered that, although IG might suppress symptoms, it would not necessarily prevent viremia.[104] Therefore, indications for the use of IG for rubella prophylaxis are few. Possibly, IG may be given to a susceptible pregnant woman who is exposed to rubella and for whom abortion is not an option if she should develop the disease. With the advent of rubella vaccine, it is now possible to immunize susceptible women of childbearing age against rubella before they become pregnant.

VACCINATION AGAINST RUBELLA

Rubella virus was isolated in 1962[1,2] and attenuated in 1966[105]; the live-attenuated vaccine was licensed for use in the United States in 1969. The rationale for use of the vaccine is to prevent congenital rubella by control of postnatal rubella. In the United States, the first strategy was to vaccinate prepubertal children, so as to minimize exposure of susceptible pregnant women to rubella. More recently, there has been an emphasis on immunization of rubella-susceptible women of childbearing age who are not pregnant. Often, this is done just after delivery of an infant; nursing mothers who are vaccinated do not cause harm to their infants. In some other countries, the approach has been to vaccinate girls against rubella as they approach puberty.

Immunization programs in the United States have dramatically reduced the transmission of rubella in young children and prevented major epidemics of rubella. There have been no such epidemics for the past 40 years, a phenomenon never previously observed in the United States. A distressing miniepidemic of congenital rubella in 21 infants occurred in 1990 in southern California. More than 55% of their mothers had a total of 22 missed opportunities for vaccination at the time of marriage or after previous delivery of a child; therefore, more than half of these cases of congenital rubella were preventable.[106]

The incidence of postnatal rubella fell to an all-time low in 1988, but by 1991 it had increased threefold. There was a concomitant increase in cases of congenital rubella syndrome during the same period, although there was still a decline of more than 98% in cases of rubella compared with the prevaccine era. The observed increase in cases was attributed to failure to immunize rather than vaccine failure.[67] With improvements in vaccine delivery since 1991, the incidence of rubella in the United States is again very low. Fewer than 300 cases were reported in 1995 and in 1996,[107] and only 23 postnatal cases were reported in 2001.[15] However, because there are still reports of minioutbreaks of rubella in colleges, the military, places of employment, and hospitals—at times with subsequent congenital rubella—there is a continued need to emphasize the importance of immunization of susceptible women of childbearing age who are not pregnant and of hospital employees, as well as infants.[105,106,108]

At present, the only rubella vaccine available in the United States is RA 27/3. This vaccine has been widely used in Europe and is more immunogenic than the previously used vaccines, HPV 77 DE5 and Cendehill, with fewer side effects. RA 27/3 vaccine also stimulates the production of secretory as well as humoral IgA, which may account for its increased immunogenic potency.[109-111]

Complications of Vaccination

Rubella vaccine may cause viremia,[112,113] and therefore the main complications are fever, adenopathy, arthritis, and arthralgia. All of the complications are more common in adults than in children, and they are most common in women older than 25 years of age.[114-116] In one study, up to 40% of such vaccinees developed joint complications[115]; however, all reactions were transient. It is uncommon for children to develop complications. In general, the incidence of joint complications, even in adults, is lower after vaccination than after natural rubella.[12,113] In 1991, a committee of the Institute of Medicine examined the issue of chronic arthritis after administration of RA 27/3 rubella vaccine and concluded that there is a rare causal relationship.[117] The risk of arthritis is increased in persons with HLA alleles DR1, DR4, and DR6.[118] Evidence in vitro indicates that wild-type strains of rubella virus can be propagated more efficiently in joint tissues than can vaccine strains.[119]

Efficacy of Vaccination

Since the introduction of rubella vaccine, the number of reported cases of clinical rubella has declined progressively. The vaccines available today, when properly administered, produce a seroconversion rate of approximately 95%.[12] Seroconversion in response to rubella vaccine is not impaired in children with upper respiratory tract infections.[120] Because antibody titers are lower after vaccination than after natural disease, the question has been raised as to whether the antibody titer, years after vaccination, will remain high enough to prevent clinical rubella. Only time and continued surveillance will provide an answer to this question, but at present there is no evidence of waning immunity,[21,22] as reflected by the low incidence of rubella in the United States. Booster injections of rubella vaccine therefore are not routinely indicated.

Effects of Rubella Vaccine on the Fetus

Since rubella vaccine was licensed in 1969, the CDC has monitored the outcome in babies born to women who were reported to have been inadvertently immunized against rubella during early pregnancy. As of late 1987, 812 such women who carried their infants to term had been included in the CDC study, with no cases of the congenital rubella syndrome attributed to rubella vaccine.[121] The observed risk of congenital rubella after immunization therefore is reported as zero; however, the theoretical maximum risk could be as high as 2%. This is in contrast to a 20% or greater risk after maternal rubella in the first trimester.[121] Of interest, the vaccine-type virus can cross the placenta, and rubella virus has been isolated from both decidua and fetal tissue at abortion after inadvertent vaccination of pregnant women.[121-125] Rubella virus was isolated from the fetus of a woman given rubella vaccine 7 weeks before conception.[126] A single case of persistent infection of a fetus whose mother was inadvertently immunized in early pregnancy has been recorded; the infant had no signs or symptoms of the congenital rubella syndrome.[127]

Based on a recent analysis of 293 normal infants born to rubella-susceptible mothers vaccinated 1 to 2 weeks before or 4 to 6 weeks after conception, for whom the theoretical risk to the fetus is 1.3%, the CDC now recommends that women avoid pregnancy for 28 days after rubella vaccination.[128] Although it is not recommended that rubella vaccine be administered to women who are pregnant, the currently recognized minimal theoretical fetal risk does not mandate automatic termination of a pregnancy. Many, if not most of such vaccinated women may wish to carry their baby to term.

REFERENCES

1. Parkman PD, Buescher EC, Artenstein MS. Recovery of rubella virus from army recruits. Proc Soc Exp Biol Med. 1962;111:225.
2. Weller TH, Neva FA. Propagation in tissue culture of cytopathic agents from patients with rubella-like illness. Proc Soc Exp Biol Med. 1962;111:215.
3. Andrewes CH. Generic names of viruses of vertebrates. Virology. 1970;40:1070.
4. Horzinek M, Maess J, Laufs R. Studies on the substructure of togaviruses. II. Analysis of equine arteritis, rubella, bovine viral diarrhea, and hog cholera viruses. Arch Gesamte Virusforsch. 1971;33:306.

5. Murphy FA, Halomen PE, Harrison AK. Electron microscopy of the development of rubella virus in BHK-21 cells. J Virol. 1968;2:1223.

6. Chandler J, Wolinsky JS, Tingle A. Rubella. In: Fields BM, Knipe DM, Chanock RM, et al., eds. Virology. 4th ed. New York: Raven Press, 2001;963-990.

7. Bellini WJ, Icenogle J. Measles and rubella virus. In: Murray PR, Baron EJ, Jorgenson JH, et al. Manual of Clinical Microbiology. Washington, DC: ASM Press; 2003:1389-1403.

8. Beor J, O'Shea S. Rubella virus. In: Lennette EH, Lennette DA, Lennette ET, eds. Diagnostic Procedures for Viral and Rickettsial Infections. 7th ed. New York: American Public Health Association; 1995:583-600.

9. Shapiro L. The numbered diseases: First through sixth. JAMA. 1971;194:680.

10. Gregg NM. Congenital cataract following German measles in the mother. Trans Ophthalmol Soc Aust. 1941;3:35.

11. Witte JJ, Karchmer AW, Case G, et al. Epidemiology of rubella. Am J Dis Child. 1969;118:107.

12. Krugman S. Present status of measles and rubella immunization in the United States: A medical progress report. J Pediatr. 1977;90:1.

13. Horstmann DM. Rubella: The challenge of its control. J Infect Dis. 1971;123:640.

14. Danovaro-Holliday MC, LeBaron CW, Allenworth C, et al. A large rubella outbreak with spread from the workplace to the community. JAMA. 2000;284:2733-2739.

15. Reef SE, Frey TK, Theall K, et al. The changing epidemiology of rubella in the 1990s: on the verge of elimination and new challenges for control and prevention. JAMA. 2002;287:464-472.

16. Sheridan E, Aitken C, Jeffries D, et al. Congenital rubella syndrome: A risk in immigrant populations. Lancet. 2002;359:674-675.

17. Cooper LZ, Green RH, Krugman S, et al. Neonatal thrombocytopenic purpura and other manifestations of rubella contracted in vitro. Am J Dis Child. 1965;110:416.

18. Halstead SB, Diwan AR. Failure to transmit rubella vaccine virus. JAMA. 1971;215:634.

19. Steele RW, Hensen SA, Vincent MM, et al. A ^{51}Cr microassay technique for cell-mediated immunity to viruses. J Immunol. 1973;110:1502.

20. Rossier E, Phipps PH, Weber JM, et al. Persistence of humoral and cell-mediated immunity to rubella virus in cloistered nuns and in schoolteachers. J Infect Dis. 1981;144:137-141.

21. Horstmann D, Schlueederberg A, Emmons JE, et al. Persistence of vaccine-induced immune responses to rubella: Comparison with natural infection. Rev Infect Dis. 1985;7(Suppl):80-85.

22. Plotkin S, Buser F. History of RA27/3 rubella vaccine. Rev Infect Dis. 1985;7(Suppl):77-78.

23. Hillenbrand FKM. Rubella in a remote community. Lancet. 1956;2:64.

24. Fry J, Dillanc JB, Fry L. Rubella 1962. Br Med J. 1962;2:833.

25. Horstmann DM, Liebhaber H, Le Bouvier GL, et al. Rubella: Reinfection of vaccinated and naturally immune persons exposed in an epidemic. N Engl J Med. 1970;283:771.

26. Wilkins J, Leedom JM, Salvotore MA, et al. Clinical rubella with arthritis resulting from reinfection. Ann Intern Med. 1972;77:930.

27. Davis WJ, Larson HE, Simsarian JP, et al. A study of rubella immunity and resistance to infection. JAMA. 1971;215:600.

28. Wilkins J, Leidom JM, Portnoy B, et al. Reinfection with rubella virus despite live vaccine-induced immunity. Am J Dis Child. 1969;118:275.

29. Forrest JM, Menser MA, Honeyman MC, et al. Clinical rubella eleven months after vaccination. Lancet. 1972;2:399.

30. Schiff G, Young B, Stefanovic GM, et al. Challenge with rubella virus after loss of detectable vaccine-induced immunity. Rev Infect Dis. 1985;7(Suppl):156-163.

31. Northrop RL, Gardner WM, Guttmann WF. Rubella reinfection during early pregnancy: A case report. Obstet Gynecol. 1972;39:524.

32. Biano S, Cochran W, Herrmann KL, et al. Rubella reinfection during pregnancy. Am J Dis Child. 1975;129:1353.

33. Balfour HH, Groth KE, Edelman CK. Rubella viraemia and antibody responses after rubella vaccination and reimmunization. Lancet. 1981;1:1078.

34. Boué A, Nicolas A, Montagron B. Reinfection with rubella in pregnant women. Lancet. 1971;1:2151.

35. Eilard T, Strannegard O. Rubella reinfection in pregnancy followed by transmission to the fetus. J Infect Dis. 1974;129:594.

36. Levine JB, Berkowitz CD, St Geme JW. Rubella virus reinfection during pregnancy leading to late-onset congenital rubella syndrome. J Pediatr. 1982;100:589.

37. Fosgren M, Carlson G, Strongert K. Case of congenital rubella after maternal reinfection. Scand J Infect Dis. 1979;11:81-93.

38. Partridge JW, Flewett TH, Whitehead JEM. Congenital rubella affecting an infant whose mother had rubella antibodies before conception. Br Med J. 1981;282:187-188.

39. Bott LM, Eizenberg DH. Congenital rubella after successful vaccination. Med J Aust. 1982;1:514-515.

40. Robinson J, Lemay M, Vaudry WL. Congenital rubella after anticipated maternal immunity: Two cases and a review of the literature. Pediatr Infect Dis J. 1994;13:812-815.

41. Klock LE, Rachelfsky GS. Failure of rubella herd immunity during an epidemic. N Engl J Med. 1973;288:69.

42. Heggie AD, Robbins FC. Rubella in naval recruits. N Engl J Med. 1964;271:231.

43. Coyle PK, Wolinsky JS, Buimovici-Klein E, et al. Rubella-specific immune complexes after congenital infection and vaccination. Infect Immun. 1982;36:498-503.

44. Heggie AD. Pathogenesis of rubella exanthem. Isolation of rubella virus from skin. N Engl J Med. 1971;285:664.

45. Buescher EL. Behavior of rubella virus in adult populations. Arch Gesamte Virusforsch. 1965;16:470.

46. Heggie AD, Robbins FC. Natural rubella acquired after birth. Am J Dis Child. 1969;118:12.

47. Johnson RE, Hall AP. Rubella arthritis. N Engl J Med. 1958;258:743.

48. Vergani D, Morgan-Capner P, Davies ET, et al. Joint symptoms, immune complexes and rubella. Lancet. 1980;1:321-322.

49. Hildebrandt HM, Maasab HF. Rubella synovitis in a one-year-old patient. N Engl J Med. 1966;274:1428.

50. Phillips CA, Behbehani AM, Johnson LW, et al. Isolation of rubella virus: An epidemic characterized by rash and arthritis. JAMA. 1965;191:615.

51. Ogra PL, Herd JK. Arthritis associated with induced rubella infection. J Immunol. 1971;107:810-813.

52. Smith CA, Petty RE, Tingle AJ. Rubella virus and arthritis. Rheum Dis Clin North Am. 1987;13:265-274.

53. Grahame R, Armstrong R, Simmons NA, et al. Isolation of rubella virus from synovial fluid in five cases of seronegative arthritis. Lancet. 1981;2:649-651.

54. Grahame R, Armstrong R, Simmons NA, et al. Chronic arthritis associated with the presence of intrasynovial rubella virus. Ann Rheum Dis. 1983;42:2-13.

55. Fraser JR, Cunningham AL, Hayes K, et al. Rubella arthritis in adults: Isolation of virus, cytology, and other aspects of synovial infection. Clin Exp Rheumatol. 1983;1:287-293.

56. Chantler JK, Tingle AJ, Petty RE. Persistent rubella virus infection associated with chronic arthritis in children. N Engl J Med. 1985;313:1117-1123.

57. Chantler JK, da Roza DM, Bonnie ME, et al. Sequential studies on synovial lymphocyte stimulation by rubella antigen, and rubella virus isolation in an adult with persistent arthritis. Ann Rheum Dis. 1985;44:564-568.

58. Chantler JK, Ford DK, Tingle AJ. Persistent rubella infection and rubella-associated arthritis. Lancet. 1982;1:1323-1325.

59. Cunningham AL, Fraser JRE. Persistent rubella virus infection of human synovial cells cultured in vitro. J Infect Dis. 1985;151:638-645.

60. Ozsoyla S, Kanra G, Savas G. Thrombocytopenic purpura related to rubella infection. Pediatrics. 1978;62:567.

61. Boyer WL, Sherman FE, Michaels RH, et al. Purpura in congenital and acquired rubella. N Engl J Med. 1965;273:1362.

62. Steen E, Torp KH. Encephalitis and thrombocytopenic purpura after rubella. Arch Dis Child. 1956;31:470.

63. Sherman FE, Michaels RH, Kenny FM. Acute encephalopathy (encephalitis) complicating rubella. JAMA. 1965;192:675.

64. Sheinis M, Sarov I, Maor E, et al. Severe neonatal rubella following maternal infection. Pediatr Infect Dis J. 1985;4:202-203.

65. Zeldis JB, Miller JG, Dienstag JL. Hepatitis in an adult with rubella. Am J Med. 1985;79:515-516.

66. Cooper LZ. Congenital rubella in the United States. In: Krugman S, Gershon A, eds. Infections of the Fetus and the Newborn Infant. New York: Alan R. Liss; 1975:1

67. Centers for Disease Control and Prevention. Increase in rubella and congenital rubella—United States. MMWR Morb Mortal Wkly Rep. 1991;40:93-99.

68. Centers for Disease Control and Prevention. Control and prevention of rubella: Evaluation and management of suspected outbreaks, rubella in pregnant women, and surveillance for congenital rubella syndrome. MMWR Morb Mortal Wkly Rep. 2001;50(Suppl):1-22.

69. Marshall WC. Rubella: Current problems and recent developments. Br J Clin Pract. 1976;30:56.

70. Menser MA, Forrest JM. Rubella: High incidence of defects in children considered normal at birth. Med J Aust. 1974;1:123.

71. Peckham CS. Clinical and laboratory study of children exposed in utero to maternal rubella. Arch Dis Child. 1972;47:571.

72. Norris JM, Dorman JS, Rewers M, Porte RE. The epidemiology and genetics of insulin-dependent diabetes mellitus. Arch Pathol Lab Med. 1987;111:905-909.

73. Menser MA, Forrest JM, Honeyman MC, et al. Diabetes, HLA antigens and congenital rubella. Lancet. 1974;2:1508-1509.

74. Ginsberg-Felner F, Witt ME, Fedun B, et al. Diabetes mellitus and auto-immunity in patients with the congenital rubella syndrome. Rev Infect Dis. 1985;7(Suppl):170-176.

75. Townsend JJ, Baringer JR, Wolinsky JS, et al. Progressive rubella panencephalitis: Late onset after congenital rubella. N Engl J Med. 1975;292:990.

76. Weil MC, Itabashi HH, Cremer NE, et al. Chronic progressive panencephalitis due to rubella virus simulating subacute sclerosing panencephalitis. N Engl J Med. 1975;292:994.

77. McIntosh ED, Menser MA. A fifty-year follow-up of congenital rubella. Lancet. 1992;340:414-415.

78. Alford CA, Neva FA, Weller TH. Virologic and serologic studies on human products of conception after maternal rubella. N Engl J Med. 1964;271:1275.

79. Hardy JB, Sever JL, Gilkeson MR. Declining antibody titers in children with congenital rubella. J Pediatr. 1969;75:213.

80. Doege TC, Kim KK. Studies of rubella and its prevention with gamma globulin. JAMA. 1967;200:584.

81. Fuccillo DA, Steele RW, Hensen SA, et al. Impaired cellular immunity to rubella virus in congenital rubella. Infect Immun. 1974;9:81.

82. Naeye RL, Blanc W. Pathogenesis of congenital rubella. JAMA. 1965;194:1277.

83. Driscoll SG. Histopathology of gestational rubella. Am J Dis Child. 1969;118:49.

84. Tondury G, Smith DW. Fetal rubella pathology. J Pediatr. 1966;68:867.

85. Plotkin SA, Vaheri A. Human fibroblasts infected with rubella virus produce a growth inhibitor. Science. 1967;154:659.

86. Nusbacher J, Hirschhorn K, Cooper LZ. Chromosomal abnormalities in congenital rubella. N Engl J Med. 1967;276:1409.

87. Rabinowe SL, George KL, Loughlin R, et al. Congenital rubella: Monoclonal antibody-defined T cell abnormalities in young adults. Am J Med. 1986;81:779-782.

88. Bell EF, Ross CA, Grist NR. ECHO 9 infection in pregnant women with suspected rubella. J Clin Pathol. 1975;28:267.

89. Black JB, Durigon E, Kite-Powell K, et al. Seroconversion to human herpesvirus 6 and human herpesvirus 7 among Brazilian children with clinical diagnoses of measles or rubella. Clin Infect Dis. 1996;23:1156-1158.

90. Levin MJ, Oxman MN, Moore MG, et al. Diagnosis of congenital rubella in utero. N Engl J Med. 1974;290:1187.

91. Frey TK, Abernathy ES, Bosma TJ, et al. Molecular analysis of rubella virus epidemiology across three continents, North America, Europe, and Asia, 1961-1997. J Infect Dis. 1998;178:642-650.

92. Chernesky M, Wyman L, Mahoney J, et al. Clinical evaluation of the sensitivity and specificity of a commercially available enzyme immunoassay for detection of rubella virus-specific immunoglobulin M. J Clin Microbiol. 1984;20:400-404.

93. Field PR, Gong CM. Diagnosis of postnatally acquired rubella by use of three enzyme-linked immunoadsorbent assays for specific immunoglobulins G and M and single radial hemolysis for specific immunoglobulin G. J Clin Microbiol. 1944;20:951-958.

94. Wittenburg RA, Roberts M, Elliott L, et al. Comparative evaluation of commercial rubella virus antibody kits. J Clin Microbiol. 1985;21:161-163.

95. Hedman K, Salonen E, Keski-Oja J, et al. Single-serum radial hemolysis to detect recent rubella infection. J Infect Dis. 1986;154:1018-1023.

96. Ferraro MJ, Kallas WM, Welch KP, et al. Comparison of a new, rapid enzyme immunoassay with a latex agglutination test for qualitative detection of rubella antibodies. J Clin Microbiol. 1987;25:1722-1724.

97. Best JM., O'Shea S, Tipples G, et al. Interpretation of rubella serology in pregnancy: Pitfalls and problems. BMJ. 2002;325:147-148.

98. Morgan-Capner P, Hodgson J, Hambling MH, et al. Detection of rubella-specific IgM in subclinical reinfection in pregnancy. Lancet. 1985;1:244-246.

99. Belin E, Safyer S, Braslow C. False positive IgM-rubella enzyme-linked immunoassay in three first trimester pregnant patients. Pediatr Infect Dis J. 1990;9:671-672.

100. Terry GM, Ho TL, Warren RC, et al. First trimester prenatal diagnosis of congenital rubella: A laboratory investigation. Br Med J. 1986;292:930-933.

101. Bosma TJ, Corbett KM, Eckstein MB, et al. Use of PCR for prenatal and postnatal diagnosis of congenital rubella. J Clin Microbiol. 1995;33:2881-2887.

102. Daffos F, Forestier F, Grangeot-Keros L, et al. Prenatal diagnosis of congenital rubella. Lancet. 1984;2:1-3.

103. Grose C, Itani O, Weiner C. Prenatal diagnosis of fetal infection: Advances from amniocentesis to cordocentesis—Congenital toxoplasmosis, rubella, cytomegalovirus, varicella virus, parvovirus and human immunodeficiency virus. Pediatr Infect Dis J. 1989;8:459-468.

104. Schiff GM. Titered lots of immune globulin: Efficacy in the prevention of rubella. Am J Dis Child. 1969;118:322.

105. Parkman PD, Meyer HM, Kirschstein RL, et al. Attenuated rubella virus. I. Development and laboratory characterization. N Engl J Med. 1966;275:569.

106. Ewert DP, Frederick PD, Moscola L. Resurgence of congenital rubella syndrome in the 1990s: Report on missed opportunities and failed prevention policies among women of childbearing age. JAMA. 1992;267:2616-2620.

107. Watson JC, Hadler SC, Dykewicz CA, et al. Measles, mumps, and rubella: Vaccine use and strategies for elimination of measles, rubella, and congenital rubella syndrome and control of mumps. Recommendations of the Advisory Committee on Immunization Practices (ACIP). MMWR Morb Mortal Wkly Rep. 1998;47(RR-8):1-57.

108. Mellinger AK, Cragan JD, Atkinson WL, et al. High incidence of congenital rubella syndrome after a rubella outbreak. Pediatr Infect Dis J. 1995;14:573-578.

109. Plotkin SA, Farquhar JD, Katz M, et al. Attenuation of RA 27/3 rubella virus in W1-38 human diploid cells. Am J Dis Child. 1969;118:178.

110. LeBouvier GL, Plotkin SA. Precepitin responses to rubella vaccine RA 27/3. J Infect Dis. 1971;123:220.

111. Ogra PL, Kerr-Grant D, Umana G, et al. Antibody response in serum and nasopharynx after naturally acquired and vaccine-induced infection with rubella virus. N Engl J Med. 1971;285:1333.

112. Modlin JF, Brandling-Bennett AD, Witte JJ, et al. A review of 5 years' experience with rubella vaccine in the United States. Pediatrics. 1975;55:20.

113. Tingle AJ, Chantler JK, Pot KH, et al. Postpartum rubella immunization: Association with development of prolonged arthritis, neurological sequelae, and chronic rubella viremia. J Infect Dis. 1985;152:606-612.

114. Horstmann DM, Liebheber H, Kohorn EI. Postpartum vaccination of rubella-susceptible women. Lancet. 1970;2:1003.

115. Lerman ST, Nankervis GA, Heggie AD, et al. Immunologic response, virus excretion and joint reactions with rubella vaccine: A study of adolescent girls and young women given live attenuated virus vaccine (HPV-77 DE5). Ann Intern Med. 1971;74:67.

116. Weibel RE, Benor DE. Chronic arthropathy and musculoskeletal symptoms associated with rubella vaccines: A review of 124 claims submitted to the National Vaccine Injury Compensation Program. Arthritis Rheum. 1996;39:1529-1534.

117. Howson CP, Katz M, Johnston RB Jr, et al. Chronic arthritis after rubella vaccination. Clin Infect Dis. 1992;15:307-312.

118. Mitchell LA, Tingle AJ, MacWilliam L, et al. HLA-DR class II associations with rubella vaccine-induced joint manifestations. J Infect Dis. 1998;177:5-12.

119. Miki NPH, Chantler JK. Differential ability of wild-type and vaccine strains of rubella virus to replicate and persist in human joint tissue. Clin Exp Rheumatol. 1992;10:3-12.

120. Dennehy PH, Saracen CL, Peter G. Seroconversion rates to combined measles-mumps-rubella-varicella vaccine of children with upper respiratory infection. Pediatrics. 1994;94:514-516.

121. Centers for Disease Control and Prevention. Rubella vaccination during pregnancy 1971-1986. MMWR Morb Mortal Wkly Rep. 1987;36:457-461.

122. Phillips CA, Maeck JVS, Rogers WA, et al. Intrauterine rubella infection following immunization with rubella vaccine. JAMA. 1970;213:624.

123. Vahieri A, Vesikari T, Oker-Blum N, et al. Isolation of attenuated rubella-vaccine virus from human products of conception and uterine cervix. N Engl J Med. 1972;286:1071.

124. Wyll SA, Herrmann K. Inadvertent rubella vaccination of pregnant women: Fetal risk in 215 cases. JAMA. 1973;225:1472.

125. Modlin JF, Herrmann K, Brandling-Bennett AD, et al. Risk of congenital abnormality after inadvertent rubella vaccination of pregnant women. N Engl J Med. 1976;294:972.

126. Fleet WF, Benz EW, Karzon DT, et al. Fetal consequences of maternal rubella immunization. JAMA. 1974;227:621.

127. Hofmann J, Kortung M, Pustowoit B, et al. Persistent fetal rubella vaccine virus infection following inadvertent vaccination during early pregnancy. J Med Virol. 2000;61:155-158.

128. Centers for Disease Control and Prevention. Notice to readers: Revised ACIP recommendation for avoiding pregnancy after receiving a rubella-containing vaccine. MMWR Morb Mortal Wkly Rep. 2001;50:1117.

CHAPTER **149**

Flaviviruses (Yellow Fever, Dengue, Dengue Hemorrhagic Fever, Japanese Encephalitis, West Nile Encephalitis, St. Louis Encephalitis, Tick-Borne Encephalitis)

THEODORE F. TSAI

DAVID W. VAUGHN

TOM SOLOMON

The *Flavivirus* genus comprises more than 60 principally arthropod-transmitted or zoonotic viruses, of which some 30 are known to cause human disease.[1] Others of the remainder have an unknown pathogenic potential but have infected humans, and several are veterinary pathogens. The agents are classified in the family Flaviviridae (from *flavus*, Latin for "yellow" and for *yellow fever virus*, the type species), together with viruses in the *Pestivirus* genus (which are of veterinary importance) and those in the genus *Hepacivirus* (hepatitis C–like viruses) on the basis of similar morphologic characteristics and genomic structures.[2] However, no antigenic relationships have been demonstrated between viruses in the respective genera.

From a global perspective, the public health burdens of flaviviral infections such as dengue, yellow fever (YF), Japanese encephalitis (JE), and tick-borne encephalitis (TBE) have been of sufficient magnitude to stimulate, at an early stage, the development of vaccines to control the diseases.[2-4] The licensure and distribution of effective vaccines for YF for more than 60 years, JE for more than 30 years, and TBE for more than 20 years have led to significant reductions in incidence and, in some locations, the effective disappearance of cases; dengue vaccines are under active development. Many of the other flaviviruses cause considerable morbidity, but their appearances as individual cases or outbreaks are infrequent or are too local in impact to have stimulated a concerted approach to prevention and control.

Flaviviral infections are important considerations in the differential diagnosis of central nervous system (CNS) infection, hemorrhagic fever, and acute febrile illnesses with arthropathy or rash, especially in returned travelers.[5,6] By evaluating the epidemiologic history, including the places and dates of travel, activities, and immunizations, in conjunction with clinical features of the illnesses and their incubation periods, the clinician can obtain important clues to pursue or exclude a diagnosis. The diseases of chief importance in this group are described later in this chapter.

HISTORY

Yellow Fever

Although the historical record and molecular taxonomic studies of viral strains have indicated an African origin of YF, the disease was first recognized in an outbreak that occurred in the New World in 1648 (Fig. 149-1A). The virus probably was introduced by *Aedes aegypti*–infested slave-trading vessels from West Africa. Through the next 2 centuries, similar outbreaks spread by saltation to port cities in the New World and in Europe. The resulting calamities were illustrated by the 1793 Philadelphia epidemic, in which one tenth of the city's population died, and by the 1878 Mississippi Valley epidemic of 100,000 cases, the cost of which equaled the national budget. Sanitary measures, especially the introduction of piped water, inadvertently served to diminish transmission of the disease, although its mosquito-borne route of spread was not demonstrated until 1900 and its viral cause not until after 1928. Theiler's development of the attenuated 17D vaccine strain in the 1930s was recognized by a Nobel Prize, but, more than 60 years later, vaccine implementation in areas with endemic transmission remains fragmentary, and outbreaks recur periodically.

Dengue

Because of dengue fever's nonspecific clinical features, the interpretation of historical records for evidence of past epidemics is open to speculation. However, Benjamin Rush's description of a 1780

Philadelphia epidemic was the earliest description in English of so-called break-bone fever. Subsequently, sporadic outbreaks were reported throughout the tropics and subtropics. Outbreaks were common in the continental United States through the early decades of the 20th century, the last large ones occurring in Florida in 1934 and in New Orleans in 1945. Clinical descriptions of dengue complicated by hemorrhages, shock, and death were reported in outbreaks in Australia in 1897, in Greece in 1928, and in Formosa in 1931. Mosquito-borne transmission of the infection by *A. aegypti* was demonstrated in 1903, and its viral etiology in 1906. While isolating the virus in 1944, Sabin demonstrated the failure of two viral strains to cross-protect humans, thus establishing the existence of dengue viral serotypes. Hammon characterized two more serotypes in 1956. After World War II, the start of a pandemic with intensified transmission of multiple viral serotypes began in Southeast Asia, leading to outbreaks of dengue hemorrhagic fever (DHF). In the last 25 years, a similar pattern of intensified viral transmission and increased DHF incidence has been established in Southwest Asia, the Americas, and Oceania, fueled by secular changes toward urbanization, population growth, and increased mobility.

Japanese Encephalitis

JE virus was isolated from a patient in a fatal case in Japan in 1934, but summertime encephalitis outbreaks leading to thousands of cases were described before that year and were called Japanese *B* encephalitis, to differentiate the disease from Von Economo's encephalitis lethargica (the qualifying *B* has fallen into disuse). Mosquito-borne transmission of the virus was established in 1938. The burden of annual epidemics led to the introduction in the mid-1960s of vaccines that effectively eliminated the disease in Japan, Korea, and Taiwan and reduced its annual incidence in China by 10-fold, from 160,000 cases in 1966 to 16,000 in 1996. Since the 1970s, the incidence of the disease has increased in countries of Southeast Asia, India, Nepal, and Sri

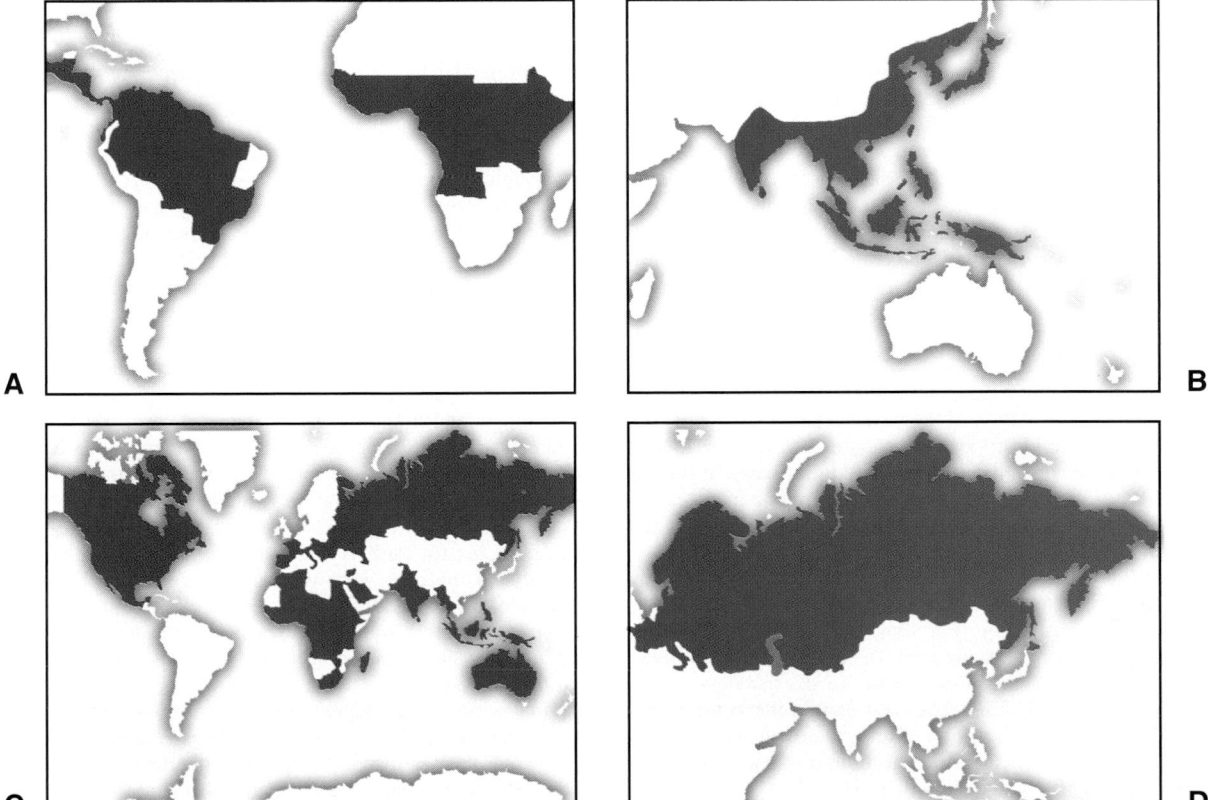

FIGURE 149-1. Geographic distribution of medically important flaviviruses. **A,** Regions with yellow fever viral transmission. **B,** Regions with Japanese encephalitis viral transmission. **C,** Countries with West Nile virus transmission. **D,** Countries with tick-borne encephalitis transmission.

Lanka, probably due in part to changes in agricultural productivity and increased recognition (see Fig. 149-1B). An estimated 35,000 to 50,000 cases and 10,000 to 15,000 deaths are reported annually, making the JE virus the most important cause of epidemic viral encephalitis worldwide. In addition, novel introductions to northern Australia in 1995 and 1998, and twice to western Pacific islands, have underscored the ability of this virus to spread. Childhood immunization programs have been established in Thailand and areas of Vietnam, India, and Sri Lanka, but a great deal more remains to be done.

West Nile Encephalitis

West Nile virus was isolated from the blood of a febrile woman in the West Nile region of Uganda in 1937, and mosquito transmission between vertebrate hosts (especially birds) was demonstrated soon afterward. Although not associated with neurologic disease at that time, the virus was shown by serologic cross-reactivity to be closely related to the then recently identified neurotropic viruses, JE virus and St. Louis encephalitis (StLE) virus. Later, sporadic cases and larger outbreaks of febrile disease (West Nile fever) were reported in the Middle East and Africa, in some instances in association with arthralgia and a rash. In the 1950s, meningeal irritation and meningoencephalitis were noted in a few patients in Israel. Outbreaks of equine and human meningoencephalitis occurred in southern France during the 1960s, and a subtype of West Nile virus (Kunjin virus) was isolated in Australasia. Since the 1990s, the epidemiology of West Nile virus has changed, with increasing frequency and severity of outbreaks in southern Europe, Russia, and the Middle East and spread of the virus to the Americas (see Fig. 149-1C). The first outbreak in the Western Hemisphere occurred in the northeastern United States in 1999. The virus rapidly spread across the continent, reaching the Pacific Coast in 2002. During 2002 and again in 2003, more than 2000 cases of CNS disease and 200 deaths were reported from the United States, with additional cases in Canada and enzootic transmission reported in Central America.

St. Louis Encephalitis

StLE was first reported as an epidemic of unknown cause in St. Louis, Missouri, in 1933, although outbreaks compatible with StLE had been described from the 1920s. A U.S. Public Health Service investigation identified the viral cause and, on the basis of epidemiologic features, surmised a mosquito-borne mode of transmission, which subsequently was proved by viral isolations from *Culex* mosquitoes in outbreaks in the Yakima Valley, Washington. With the occurrence of more than 10,000 cases in more than 50 outbreaks through 1990, the disease was the most important cause of epidemic viral encephalitis in the United States until West Nile virus became established. In 1975, there were 2900 cases of StLE in 31 states, and more than 200 cases occurred during an epidemic in Florida in 1990.

Tick-Borne Encephalitis

Descriptions of a disease compatible with TBE appeared in Austria in the early 1930s, although isolation of the virus responsible for this disease (then known as Central European encephalitis—CEE) was not reported until 1948. However, investigation of similar cases in the far eastern part of Russia in 1932 had led to descriptions of so-called Russian spring-summer encephalitis (RSSE), and in 1937 the virus was isolated from the blood of patients and from *Ixodes* tick vectors. It is now recognized that three closely related subtypes of TBE virus exist, whose names reflect the geographic areas that they principally affect: European, Siberian, and Far Eastern (see Fig. 149-1D). However, across this vast geographic area, the disease has been given a range of different names, including CEE, RSSE, Far Eastern encephalitis, and biphasic milk fever. This last name reflects the transmission of TBE virus through ingestion of unpasteurized milk from infected livestock, first confirmed during a common source epidemic leading to 660 cases in Czechoslovakia in 1951.

The incidence of TBE varies according to location and year. After the collapse of the former Soviet Union and reduced use of pesticides and vaccine against TBE, the annual incidence rose to more than 10,000 cases. In Austria, where there had been several hundred cases annually, a formalin-inactivated vaccine was introduced in the 1970s. Administration of a purified form of the vaccine in mass campaigns since the 1980s has led to a dramatic reduction in the number of cases. The TBE group serocomplex also includes viruses that are rare causes of human neurologic disease (such as Powassan virus, first isolated from a fatal case in Ontario, Canada, in 1958, and louping ill virus, first isolated from a sheep in Scotland in 1930) and viruses that produce a hemorrhagic fever syndrome (such as the Omsk hemorrhagic fever and Kyasanur Forest disease viruses).

PATHOGENS

Flaviviruses are spherical, 40 to 60 nm in diameter, and consist of a lipid envelope covered densely with surface projections comprising 180 copies of the M (membrane) and 180 copies of the E (envelope) glycoproteins.[7,8] The latter are organized as dimers, paired horizontally head to tail, on the virion surface. The viruses are unstable in the environment and are sensitive to heat, ultraviolet radiation, disinfectants (including alcohol and iodine), and acid pH. The nucleocapsid joins the capsid (C) protein to a single strand of positive-sense RNA of 11 kilobases, which includes a 10-kilobase open reading frame for a single polyprotein precursor, flanked by noncoding regions at either end. The order of protein gene products from the 5' end is C, premembrane (preM, a precursor of the mature M protein), E, and a series of seven nonstructural proteins needed in the viral replicative process: NS1, NS2A, NS2B, NS3, NS4A, NS4B, NS5.

The E protein exhibits important biologic properties, including viral-cellular attachment, endosomal membrane fusion, and the display of sites mediating hemagglutination and viral neutralization.[7] A beta sheet hinge region contains an important molecular determinant of organ tropism that determines relative neurotropism or viscerotropism.[9] Its carboxyl terminus provides a membrane anchor, and on the virion surface it is folded into three structural and corresponding antigenic domains, including an immunoglobulin-like motif that may be involved in receptor binding. Viral neutralizing epitopes are scattered on its surface; because the protein is folded, they are nonlinear and conformationally dependent. PreM protein chaperones the E protein in the cell secretory pathway, preventing its misfolding, before it is cleaved to its M form in the mature virion. NS1 is expressed on the surface of infected cells and is also excreted as a complement-fixing antigen. Although antibodies to NS1 do not neutralize the virus, they contribute to protective immunity, probably by complement and cell-mediated responses against infected cells.[10] Aside from their replicative functions, NS1, NS2A, NS3, and NS5 display epitopes mediating viral serotype and flavirviral cross-reactive human leukocyte antigen (HLA)–restricted lymphocytic responses.[11,12]

Viral attachment to unidentified cellular receptors is followed by endocytic uptake of virus-containing vesicles. Acidic-induced changes of the viral envelope lead to fusion activity, uncoating of the nucleocapsid, and viral RNA release into the cytoplasm. Glycosaminoglycans and proteoglycans have been implicated as receptors in some studies, but coreceptors may also be involved, and viral binding evidently varies with cell type.[13,14] The viral polyprotein is processed by repeated passage through the rough endoplasmic reticulum, providing the replicative complex for further viral RNA and protein synthesis and the assembly of nascent virions that mature through the Golgi and trans-Golgi network. Immature virions collect in the highly proliferated endoplasmic reticulum and secretory vesicles before release, although intracellular nucleocapsid accumulations have been observed in some virus–cell systems.

Flaviviruses are adapted to grow in a wide variety of insect, tick, and vertebrate cells and at temperatures spanning the normal temperatures of their arthropod, reptilian, mammalian, and avian hosts. Cytopathologic changes and plaque formation develop in Vero LL-CMK2, BHK-21, PS, and primary chick and duck embryo cells, whereas infection of mosquito cell lines (e.g., C6/36, AP61) is typically nondestructive and may persist.

A wide range of vertebrates, including mammals, birds, and reptiles, are naturally infected as amplifying hosts in the transmission cycle of alternating arthropod and vertebrate infection.[1] These infections are usually asymptomatic, but individual viruses may be pathogenic for domesticated or wild animals; for example, several neurotropic flaviviruses, including JE, StLE, West Nile, Kunjin, CEE, and Powassan viruses, produce encephalitis in horses, and certain CEE viral strains are neurotropic for dogs, sheep, and goats. JE virus is an important cause of swine abortion; louping ill is a manifestation of encephalitis in sheep; and YF and Kyasanur Forest disease are lethal in some monkey species. Laboratory rodents are generally susceptible to infection, with sensitivity inversely related to age.

With few exceptions, the flaviviruses can be classified by cross-neutralization assays into eight antigenic groups, of which the most important are the JE complex, consisting of JE, StLE, West Nile, and Murray Valley encephalitis viruses; the dengue complex of dengue 1 through 4 viruses; the tick-borne virus complex, including CEE, RSSE, louping ill, Powassan, Kyasanur Forest disease, and Omsk hemorrhagic fever viruses; YF virus; and a complex of non–vector-borne rodent- and bat-associated viruses.[1,15] Genetic studies largely support the antigenic classification and suggest the evolution of non–vector-borne flaviviruses from a hypothetical progenitor with the further sequential evolution of tick-borne and mosquito-borne viruses.[16,17] Genomic sequencing studies of specific viruses have facilitated the tracking of viral movements historically and in epidemics. For example, YF viral strains have been divided into East African, West African, and New World genotypes, with a close relationship between the latter two supporting the hypothesis that YF virus was introduced to the Western Hemisphere from Africa.[17] Genotypic markers have been of particular help in understanding the emergence of dengue and JE epidemics in the wake of viral introductions from other regions.[18-20] Genotypes also have been correlated with viral biologic characteristics that underlie their transmission patterns. For example, StLE viral genotypes from the eastern and western United States exhibit distinct neurovirulence and transmission characteristics that are consistent with epidemiologic observations.[21,22] On a clinical level, structural distinctions between strains associated with classic dengue and with DHF have been described, providing potential clues to molecular determinants of dengue viral virulence.[22]

EPIDEMIOLOGY

Yellow Fever

YF is transmitted in areas of sub-Saharan Africa and South America (see Fig. 149-1A). The disease has never been documented in Asia, but, in principle, anthroponotic (vector-borne person-to-person) transmission of the virus could occur there and in other A. aegypti–infested locations, including the southern United States.[3,23,24] Epidemic ("urban") YF is transmitted by A. aegypti mosquitoes; the mosquitoes are infected after feeding on viremic humans and then spread the infection in subsequent feeding attempts. The threat of epidemic transmission arises when a person with a forest-acquired infection travels to an A. aegypti–infested location while viremic.

The fluctuating global incidence of YF has been dominated by epidemics in Africa; between 1986 and 1991, they produced 20,424 reported cases and 5447 deaths. However, official reports considerably underestimated the true magnitude of those epidemics, which field studies estimated as 50-fold greater, or more than 1 million cases.[24-26] Epidemic attack rates ranged as high as 30 in 1000 persons, with case-fatality ratios of 20% to 50%. Since 2000, outbreaks in West Africa have produced more than 1000 reported cases in Burkina Faso, Cote d'Ivoire, Guinea, Ghana, and Liberia. The variable size and frequency of epidemics in recent years may reflect cyclic changes in viral activity and human immunity, acquired in recent epidemics and through vaccination in emergency campaigns and the World Health Organization's Expanded Programme of Immunization (EPI).

In South America, an annual mean of approximately 100 cases has been reported in the last 25 years, reflecting the occurrence of forest-acquired infections occurring in the greater Magdalena, Orinoco, and Amazon river basins.[27,28] In its *jungle cycle,* the virus is transmitted from tree-hole *Haemagogus* and *Sabethes* mosquitoes to forest monkeys in wandering epizootics that follow movements of the animals and of the virus to susceptible populations. Cases in humans predominate between January and March among men 15 to 45 years who are bitten incidentally by infected mosquitoes while employed as agricultural and forestry workers, soldiers, and settlers. Recent outbreaks frequently have occurred among nonimmune migrants from their coastal or Andean homes to at-risk locations in the tropical zone. An intensification of enzootic viral transmission frequently produces clusters of monkey deaths, indicating an increased transmission risk to humans. The last urban outbreak in the Western Hemisphere was reported in Trinidad in 1954, but the growth of urban areas and their reinfestation by A. aegypti have renewed concern for the emergence of epidemics, especially in cities that border forested areas. Since 1995, several patients with jungle-acquired disease have been hospitalized in Brazilian cities and in Santa Cruz, Bolivia—fortunately, without urban spread. The imminent threat of epidemic transmission has prompted mass vaccination campaigns and other control measures.[27-29]

In the moist savanna of Africa, a variety of tree-hole–breeding mosquitoes transmit infections among humans and monkeys during the end of the rainy season, leading to early infections in children and sporadic cases that are typically unrecognized. Annual infections in the range of 1% are estimated in areas of West Africa, suggesting that more than 200,000 endemic cases may occur annually.[24,30] Infections are spread readily by migration, with the potential for involvement of A. aegypti in urban areas and in dry locations where stored water provides breeding sites. During the dry season, the virus survives in infected mosquito eggs that are resistant to desiccation.

Dengue and Dengue Hemorrhagic Fever

Four serotypes of dengue virus are transmitted in the tropics, in an area roughly between 35 degrees north and 35 degrees south latitude, corresponding to the distribution of A. aegypti, the principal mosquito vector (Fig. 149-2).[31] *Aedes albopictus, Aedes polynesiensis,* and other species can transmit the virus in specific circumstances. Although enzootic transmission among forest monkeys in Asia and Africa has been described, anthroponotic viral transmission is sufficient to maintain the virus, and these animal infections could represent either epiphenomena or potentially a vestigial sylvatic cycle.[32] The intensification of dengue transmission in tropical cities, where growing populations live under crowded conditions, can be understood in view of the close relationship of A. aegypti to humans.[33,34] After the female mosquito feeds on a viremic person, viral replication in the mosquito over 1 to 2 weeks (extrinsic incubation period) occurs before it can transmit the virus on subsequent feeding attempts. Feeding attempts may occur several times a day over the insect's lifetime of 1 to 4 weeks. Mechanical transmission, without extrinsic incubation, has also been suggested. A. aegypti is adapted to breed around human dwellings, where the insects oviposit in uncovered water storage containers as well as miscellaneous containers holding water, such as vases, flower dishes, cans, automobile tires, and other discarded objects. Adult mosquitoes shelter indoors and bite during 1- to 2-hour intervals in the morning and late afternoon. In areas with endemic transmission, 1 of every 20 houses may contain an infected mosquito.[35] Cases often cluster in households, and human movements and the mosquito's peregrinations within a range of 800 m rapidly spread the infection.[36,37] In tropical areas, transmission is maintained throughout the year and intensifies at the start of the rainy season, when infected vector mosquitoes are more abundant as higher humidity lengthens their lifespan and increased temperatures shorten the extrinsic incubation period.

When the virus is introduced into susceptible populations, usually by viremic travelers, epidemic attack rates may reach 50% to 70%. Because cross-protective immunity among the serotypes is limited, epidemic transmission recurs with the introduction of novel virus types. Furthermore, because secondary infections predispose to DHF (see later discussion), the concurrent transmission of multiple viral

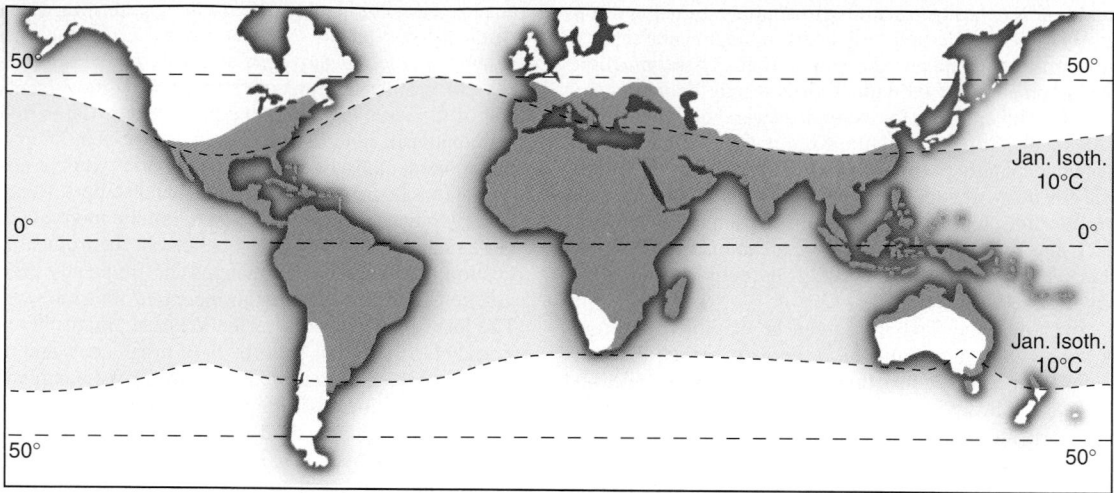

FIGURE 149-2. Approximate actual and potential distribution of *Aedes aegypti*. The band between the 10° C isotherms represents potential distribution. *(From World Health Organization. Technical Guide for Diagnosis, Treatment, Surveillance, Prevention, and Control of Dengue Haemorrhagic Fever, 2nd ed. Geneva: World Health Organization; 1997.)*

serotypes establishes the necessary conditions for endemic DHF. Under these circumstances, virtually all DHF cases occur in individuals with secondary infections, primarily children, with a relative risk of developing DHF in secondary compared with primary infection being as high as 100.[38-41] The central role of prior immunity for at least some virus types is illuminated by the phenomenon of DHF in infants, born to immune mothers, who are infected for the first time before 1 year of age. In these cases, the age distribution of disease onset parallels the expected decline of passively acquired maternal antibodies.[42-44] Outbreaks in Cuba in 1981 and 1997, in which DHF cases occurred only in the age cohort exposed during the last epidemic period (older than 3 years and older than 17 years, respectively), further underscored secondary infection as a critical precondition for DHF, at least for some serotypes.[45,46] However, anecdotal DHF cases in persons with primary infections have been reported, pointing to the contributory roles of viral strain and host factors.[47,48] Race and specific HLA haplotypes have been implicated in the risk of acquiring DHF, and a variable predominance of severe cases has been observed in girls and in children with good nutrition, indicating the contributions of both genetic and acquired host factors to susceptibility to the syndrome.[49-51]

Intensified dengue transmission in Asia after World War II evolved in the previously described pattern, resulting in novel epidemics of DHF beginning in the 1950s. Dengue infection rates in Southeast Asian areas with hyperendemic transmission are now in the range of 5% to 10%, with DHF incidence rates of 10 to 300 per 100,000 persons.[34,52] In Thailand, dengue accounts for one third of acute febrile illnesses in children seeking medical attention.[38,53] Although DHF still is principally a disease of children younger than 15 years of age, the peak age of risk has risen as dengue virus transmission has declined in some hyperendemic areas due to increased use of screens and air conditioning.

The most dramatic ascendance of dengue and DHF has occurred in the Caribbean and in Latin America, where *A. aegypti* has become widely reestablished since its near-eradication as part of YF-control efforts ending in the 1970s.[34,54-56] Before 1977, only dengue-2 and dengue-3 viruses were transmitted in the Western Hemisphere, and DHF was virtually nonexistent. Introductions of dengue-1 virus in 1977 (in Cuba and elsewhere) and dengue-4 four years later were followed by their rapid spread broadly in the region. The introduction to Cuba in 1981 of a novel dengue-2 viral strain from Southeast Asia produced the first major DHF epidemic in the hemisphere, resulting in 116,143 hospitalizations, including 10,000 for shock. Santiago de Cuba escaped the 1981 dengue-2 outbreak until a resurgence in 1997, at which time only adults infected during the 1977-1979 dengue-1 outbreak became ill.[46] Since 1989, recurrent DHF outbreaks have been re-

ported in an enlarging area within the region, including Venezuela, Colombia, Brazil, Guyana, French Guiana, Nicaragua, Honduras, Costa Rica, Puerto Rico, Guatemala, Panama, Costa Rica, El Salvador, Guadeloupe, and Mexico, resulting in several thousand DHF cases each year.[56-58] The introduction of a novel dengue-3 strain to Central America in 1994 has been anticipated as an accelerant for increased dengue incidence and severity in the region.[59]

The dissemination of dengue viruses by viremic travelers has been facilitated by the increased mobility of people living within endemic areas and internationally by burgeoning air travel. Between 1997 and 2000, a total of 390 anecdotal dengue cases were confirmed among travelers returning to the United States.[60] Incidence rates among American soldiers during World War II were as high as 300 per 1000 persons per month in the Pacific.[61] More recently, rates for those assigned temporarily to Somalia and Haiti were in the range of 1 in 1000 per month.[62] In several studies, dengue infection was documented in 7% to 45% of febrile returned travelers.[63] Small numbers of autochthonous cases acquired in Texas towns bordering Mexico were recognized in 1980, 1986, and 1995.[64]

Infection can be transmitted by accidental needlestick.[65] The high incidence of infection in endemic areas suggests that transfusion-associated cases could occur frequently, but in these same populations immunity in recipients is also high, and differentiating a transfusion-transmitted case from a natural infection would be difficult.

Japanese Encephalitis

JE is transmitted in Asia over an area spanning one third of the world's circumference, from Pakistan at the westernmost edge to far eastern Russia (see Fig. 149-1B) (Table 149-1). The disease is endemic and periodically epidemic in Southeast Asia, China, and the Asian subcontinent.[66,67] Sporadic cases are reported in tropical Asia, including the Indonesian and Philippine archipelagoes, but field studies suggest a higher incidence.[68] Twice, in 1947 and 1990, the virus was introduced to the western Pacific, resulting in outbreaks on Guam and Saipan. The virus invaded the Torres Strait islands of Australia in 1995 and the Australian mainland in 1998.[19,69,70]

Worldwide, 160,000 cases of JE were reported to the World Health Organization in 1966 and 16,000 cases in 1996, the 10-fold decline reflecting widespread childhood immunization in China, Japan, Korea, and Taiwan, as well as regional economic development and the declining emphasis on agriculture. In the latter three countries, few cases are reported currently, although enzootic viral transmission persists. In areas with endemic transmission, an annual incidence of 2.5 per 10,000 children younger than 15 years of age is estimated, with a case-

TABLE 149-1 Estimated Risk of Japanese Encephalitis by Country and Season*

Country	Affected Areas	Transmission Season	Comments
Australia[†]	Islands of Torres Strait	February-April peak; year-round transmission risk	Localized outbreak in Torres Strait in 1995 and sporadic cases in 1998 in Torres Strait and on mainland Australia at Cape York Peninsula
Bangladesh	Few data, but probably widespread	Possibly July-December, as in northern India	Outbreak reported from Tangail District, Dacca Division; sporadic cases in Rajshahi Division
Bhutan	No data	No data	—
Brunei	Presumed to be sporadic-endemic, as in Malaysia	Presumed year-round transmission	—
Cambodia	Endemic-hyperendemic countrywide	Presumed to be May-October	Cases in refugee camps on Thai border and from Phnom Penh
Democratic Republic of Korea	Presumed to be countrywide in rural areas <800 m altitude	July-October	Epidemics in 1970s; few recent data
India	Reported cases from all states except Arunachal, Dadra, Daman, Diu, Gujarat, Himachal, Jammu, Kashmir, Lakshadweep, Meghalaya, Nagar Haveli, Orissa, Punjab, Rajasthan, and Sikkim	South India: May-October in Goa, October-January in Tamil Nadu, August-December in Karnataka Second peak: April-June in Mandya District Andhra Pradesh: September-December[†] North India: July-December	Outbreaks in West Bengal, Bihar, Karnataka, Tamil Nadu, Andhra Pradesh, Kerala, Assam, Uttar Pradesh, Manipure, and Goa; urban cases reported (e.g., in Luchnow)
Indonesia	Kalimantan, Bali, Nusa, Tenggara, Sulawesi, Mollucas, Irian Jaya (Papua New Guinea), and Lombok	Probably year-round risk; varies by island; peak risks associated with rainfall, rice cultivation, and presence of pigs Peak periods of risk: November-March, June and July in some years	Endemic on Bali, Java, and possibly in Lombok; sporadic cases recognized elsewhere
Japan[†]	Rare; sporadic cases on all islands except Hokkaido	June-September, except April-December on Ryuku Islands (Okinawa)	Vaccination not routinely recommended for travel to Tokyo and other major cities; enzootic transmission without human cases observed on Hokkaido
Laos	Presumed to be endemic-hyperendemic countrywide	Presumed to be May-October	—
Malaysia	Sporadic-endemic in all states of Peninsula, Sarawak, and probably Sabah	Year-round transmission; October-February in Sarawak	Most cases from Penang, Perak, Salangor, Johore, and Sarawak
Myanmar	Presumed to be endemic-hyperendemic countrywide	Presumed to be May-October	Repeated outbreaks in Shan State in Chiang Mai valley
Nepal	Hyperendemic in southern lowlands (Terai); sporadic cases in Kathmandu valley	July-December	Vaccination not recommended for travelers visiting only high-altitude areas
Pakistan	May be transmitted in central deltas	Presumed to be June-January	Cases reported near Karachi; endemic areas overlap those for West Nile virus; lower Indus Valley might be an endemic area
Papua New Guinea	Normanby Islands and Western Province	Probably year-round risk	Localized sporadic cases
People's Republic of China[†]	Cases in all provinces except Xizang (Tibet), Xinjiang, Qinghai Temperate areas: endemic to periodically epidemic Southern China: hyperendemic Hong Kong: rare cases in new territories	Northern China: May-September Southern China: April-October (Guangxi, Yunnan, Guangdong, and southern Fujian; Sichuan, Guizhou, Hunan, and Jiangxi provinces) Hong Kong: April-October	Vaccination not routinely recommended for travelers to urban areas only
Philippines	Presumed to be endemic on all islands	Uncertain; speculations based on locations and agroecosystems West Luzon, Mindoro, Negros, Palawan: April-November Elsewhere: year-round, with greatest risk April-January	Outbreaks described in Nueva Ecija, Luzon (including January 2004), and Manila
Republic of Korea[†]	Sporadic-endemic with occasional outbreaks	July-October	Last major outbreaks were 1982-1983
Russia	Far eastern maritime areas south of Khabarousk	Peak period July-September	Sporadic transmission in rural and sylvatic cycles
Singapore	Higher rates of enzootic transmission in western rural areas of island	Year-round transmission with April peak	Vaccination not routinely recommended; two sporadic cases in 2001
Sri Lanka	Endemic in all but mountainous areas; periodically epidemic in northern and central provinces	October-January; secondary peak of enzootic transmission in May-June	Outbreaks in central (Anuradhapura) and northwestern provinces
Taiwan[†]	Endemic, sporadic cases island-wide	April-October; June peak	Cases reported in and around Taipei and the Kao-hsiung–Pingtung river basins
Thailand[†]	Hyperendemic in north; sporadic-endemic in south	May-October	Annual outbreaks in Chiang Mai Valley; sporadic cases in Bangkok suburbs
Vietnam[†]	Endemic-hyperendemic in all provinces	May-October in the North, year-round in the South	Highest rates in and near Hanoi
Western Pacific	Two epidemics reported in Guam and Saipan since 1947	Uncertain; possibly September-January	Enzootic cycle may not be sustainable; epidemics have occurred after introductions of virus

*Assessments are based on publications, surveillance reports, and personal communications. Extrapolations have been made from available data. Transmission patterns may change.

[†]Locally reported incidence rates may not reflect risks to nonimmune visitors, because high immunization rates in local populations may obscure ongoing enzootic transmission.

Modified from references 2 and 75, and updated from ProMed Mail (http://www.promedmail.org/), and following the Global Alliance for Vaccines and Immunizations, Southeast Asia and Western Pacific Regional Working Group's Japanese Encephalitis Meeting: Setting the Global Agenda on Public Health Solutions and National Needs, Bangkok, Thailand, 2002.

fatality rate of 25% and disability in 45% of surviving patients.[3,66,67] Extrapolating this incidence to the population of 700 million children younger than 15 years in the region, an estimated 175,000 JE cases, 45,000 deaths, and 78,000 cases of newly disabled children would occur annually in the absence of immunization.[68] Allowing for the countries where there is immunization, the expected number of cases annually is greater than 125,000. The fact that only one fifth of these are officially recorded probably reflects the lack of reporting from many countries where no surveillance currently exists.[68] In an era in which polio has declined to the point of eradication, JE is now preeminent among causes of pediatric CNS infections in the region.

Within temperate areas, JE is transmitted sporadically from July to September, at a relatively low incidence and with periodic seasonal epidemics. In subtropical Asia, viral transmission extends from March to October in a hyperendemic pattern, resulting in cases throughout the year and the absence of easily detected seasonal epidemics. The geographic distribution of different JE virus genotypes was postulated to explain the differences in clinical epidemiology,[69,70] but it is now thought to be best explained by the virus's evolution in the Indonesia-Malaysia region and its subsequent spread as more recently evolved genotypes.[71,72]

The virus is transmitted by *Culex tritaeniorhynchus* and related ground-pool–breeding mosquitoes to pigs and aquatic birds, which are the principal viral-amplifying hosts.[73] Viremic adult pigs are asymptomatic, but infected pregnant sows abort or deliver stillbirths. Infected horses and humans are symptomatic but incidental hosts. Because rice paddies provide favorable breeding habitats for vector mosquitoes, the risk of infection is highest in rural areas. However, both pigs and rice paddies are found at the edges of some Asian cities, resulting in isolated cases and, rarely, urban outbreaks. The mosquito vectors chiefly feed outdoors, in the evenings, and prefer animal to human hosts.

More than 99% of infections with JE virus are subclinical; consequently, in areas with endemic transmission, infections acquired naturally at an early age result in immunity in more than 80% of young adults. Cases occur chiefly in children between 2 and 10 years of age, with a slight predominance of boys. In Japan, Korea, and Taiwan, children are protected by immunizations, and cases occur principally in elderly persons, reflecting waning immunity or other biologic factors associated with senescence.[74]

Expatriate and traveler cases have been recognized since 1932, and outbreaks among American, British, and Australian soldiers in World War II, Korea, and Vietnam were considered militarily important. Travelers of all ages without naturally acquired protective antibodies are at risk for acquisition of the illness. The risk is slight, estimated to be 1 in 150,000 person-months of exposure, reflecting low vector mosquito infection rates (0.5%) and the small case/infection ratio (0.3%).[75] However, cases of JE among travelers even on short trips to southeast Asia serve as a reminder of the unpredictable risk for acquiring this disease.[76-78]

West Nile Encephalitis

West Nile virus is one of the most widely distributed arboviruses, being found across much of Africa, Europe, the Middle East, Asia, Australia (Kunjin subtype), and, more recently, the Americas[79,80] (see Fig. 149-1C). Recent outbreaks have included almost 400 confirmed cases in Romania in 1996, almost 200 cases in the Volograd region of Russia in 1999, and more than 200 cases in Israel in 2000 (Table 149-2).[80] In 1999, the virus appeared in North America for the first time, with 62 confirmed human cases and additional equine cases. It continued to spread across the continent during 2000 and 2001, with small numbers of cases (21 and 66, respectively) (Fig. 149-3). However, in 2002, there were more than 4000 cases, including ap-

TABLE 149-2 Outbreaks of West Nile Virus Infection*

Year of Outbreak	Country	No. of Suspected Cases	No. of Cases Investigated	No. of Confirmed Cases	No. of Deaths	Notes
1957	Israel	419	247	Approx. 180	4	Included first naturally occurring encephalitis cases (12 patients)
1974	South Africa	18,000	558	307	0	Estimated 18,000 cases of WN fever
1962-1966	France (Camarge)	—	—	14	1	Many horses also affected
1994	Algeria	50	18	17	8	—
1996	Romania	835	509	393	17	Continuing cases in 1997-1999
1997	Tunisia	173	129	111	8	—
1998	Democratic Republic of Congo	35	35	23	0	Military personnel newly arrived in this area
1999	USA (New York)	719	719	62	7	—
1999	Russia (Volograd Region)	826	318	183	40	—
2000	Israel	—	—	233	33	91 nonhospitalized patients with WN fever also identified
2000-2001	USA	—	—	85	24	—
2002	USA	—	—	4156	264	Approximately 3000 with CNS disease
2003	USA	—	—	9122	223	6251 WN fever, 2707 WN meningitis or encephalitis, 164 unspecified (case definition was changed to include reporting of all WN fever cases)

*Only details of selected outbreaks are shown. Criteria for hospitalization, case definitions, and diagnostic methods varied among outbreaks, and some numbers are approximations.

CNS, central nervous system; WN, West Nile.

Updated from Solomon T, Ooi MH. West Nile encephalitis. BMJ. 2003;326:865-869.

proximately 3000 involving CNS disease, with 284 deaths. In 2003, changes in the case definition led to reports of 9000 human cases, including 6251 with West Nile fever, 2707 with meningitis or encephalitis, and 223 fatal cases.

West Nile virus is transmitted in an enzootic cycle between birds, by mosquitoes (Fig. 149-4). Recent studies in the United States have demonstrated infection in at least 200 different bird species and 40 mosquito species. Members of the order Passeriformes (jays, blackbirds, finches, warblers, sparrows, and crows) appear to be important in transmission of the virus in nature; the family Corvidae (crows and blue jays) is particularly susceptible. In some areas, arrival of the virus was heralded by dying birds falling from the sky. The lack of resistance and fatal infection of avian intermediary hosts provided evidence for the novel introduction of the virus to the ecosystem of the Western hemisphere, unlike the asymptomatic infection of autochthonous birds by the closely related StLE virus. Because of their low and brief viremias, humans and horses (which also develop encephalitis) are dead-end hosts. Of the many mosquito species from which West Nile virus has been isolated, *Culex* species, particularly *Culex pipiens*, appear to be important in the enzootic cycle, although a hybrid of that species with *C. molestus* and other species (such as *Aedes* and *Ochlerotatus* species) that act as "bridging vectors" transmit the virus to humans. Transovarial transmission of the virus in mosquitoes probably provides for viral overwintering. During the 2002 outbreak in the United States, it became clear that on rare occasions viral transmission can occur via transplantation of infected organs, from infected blood products, transplacentally, and, possibly, via breast milk.[81,81a] During the height of the 2002 epidemic, the risk of infection by transfusion was estimated to be as high as 21 per 10,000 donations,[81,81a] and blood screening using real-time polymerase chain reaction (PCR) has been instituted.

The means by which West Nile virus is introduced to new areas are not completely understood. Migratory birds are thought to be important for movement of the virus from Africa into southern Europe. They may have been involved in its introduction into North America, although importation of viremic exotic birds or amphibians, travel by a viremic human, or inadvertent transport of mosquitoes are alternative explanations.[82] Molecular genetic evidence suggests a single introduction into the United States of a strain closely related to a goose isolate from an earlier outbreak in Israel.[20,83]

The majority of human infections with West Nile virus are asymptomatic. Epidemiologic surveys taken after the 1999 outbreak in New York suggested that approximately 1 in 5 people infected with West Nile virus develops fever, and only about 1 in 150 develops CNS disease.[81,81a] These are similar to the attack rates for the Romanian 1997 outbreak,[84] but they appear to be much higher than those reported from Egypt and South Africa.[85,86] In New York, Romania, and Israel, the risk of neurologic disease increased with age, which may explain, in part, the different epidemiologic patterns seen in parts of Africa. In Egypt, most of the population is infected during childhood, and neurologic disease is rare.[85] In South Africa, a large outbreak affected an estimated 18,000 people of all ages, yet only a single West Nile encephalitis (WNE) case was reported.[86]

St. Louis Encephalitis

Outbreak-associated cases of StLE have been reported from virtually all U.S. states, the provinces of Ontario and Manitoba in Canada, and Sonora State in Mexico, whereas only sporadic cases have been reported from Argentina, Brazil, Panama, Trinidad, French Guiana, Surinam, Curacao, Jamaica, and the Dominican Republic. Enzootic viral transmission has also been recognized in Alberta and British Columbia in Canada and in Ecuador, Guatemala, and Haiti and may occur elsewhere in the hemisphere.[87-89]

In the United States, the virus is transmitted to birds in three distinct cycles overlapping those of West Nile virus: by *C. pipiens* and *Culex quinquefasciatus* in the midwestern and eastern states, by *Culex nigripalpus* in Florida, and by *Culex tarsalis* in the Great Plains and farther west. Humans are infected incidentally from the enzootic cycle. Characteristics of the vectors and their respective transmission cycles define epidemiologic features in each location.

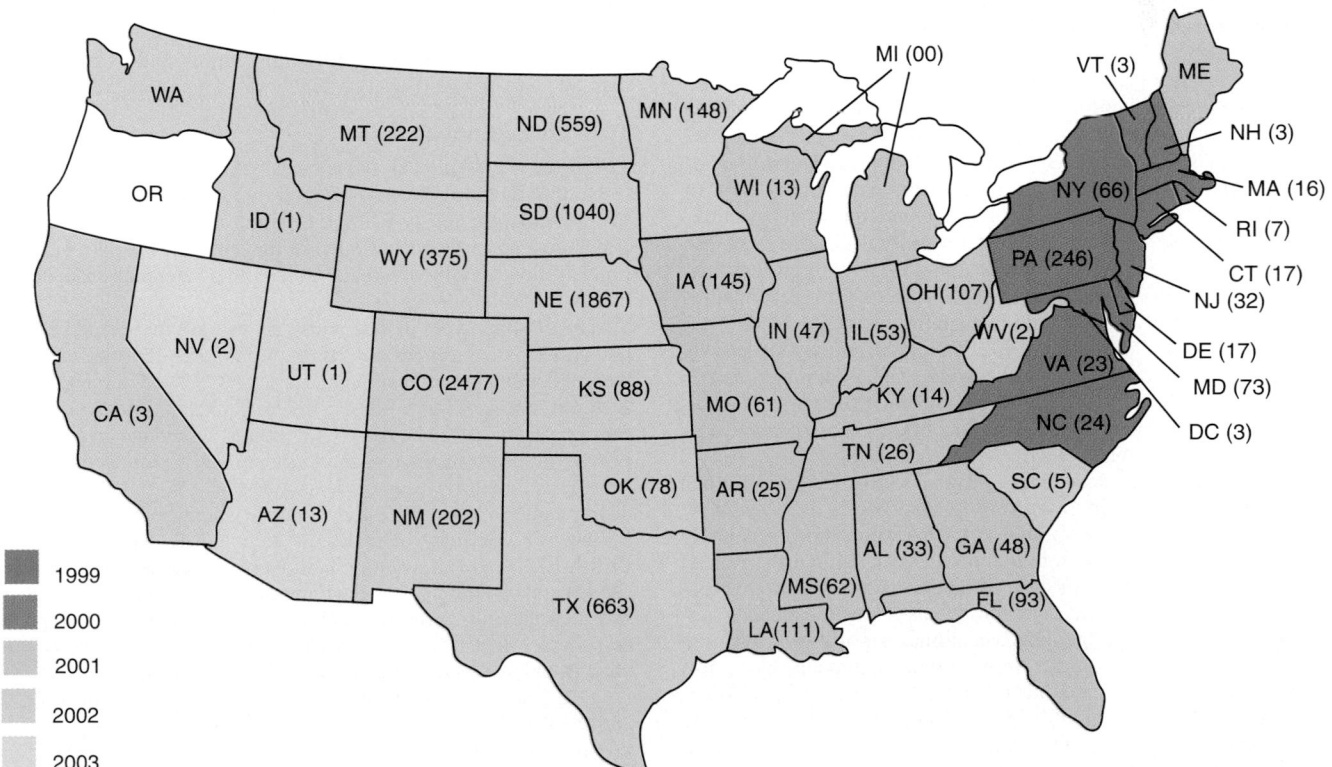

FIGURE 149-3. Human cases of West Nile fever and encephalitis by state and year of first recognition, United States, 1999-2003.

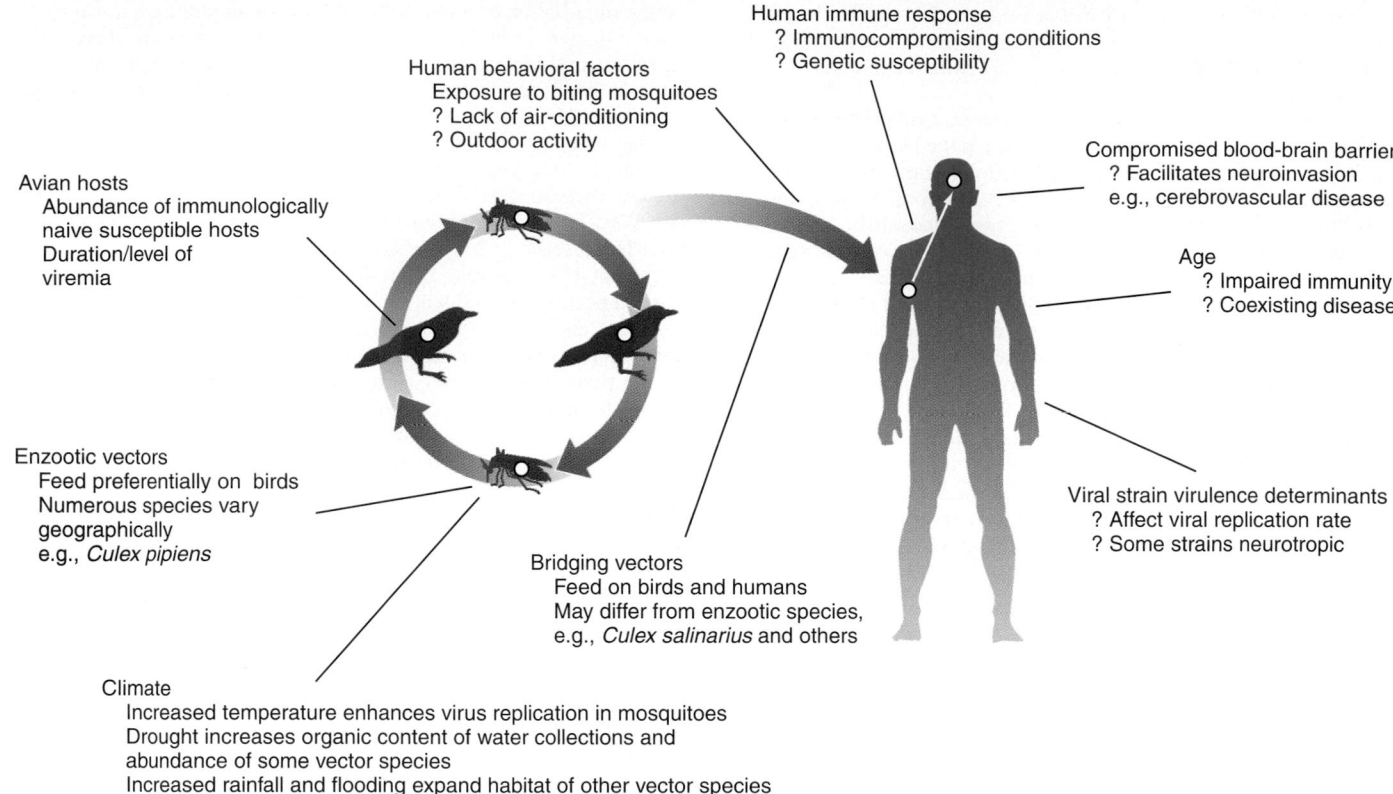

Human immune response
? Immunocompromising conditions
? Genetic susceptibility

Human behavioral factors
Exposure to biting mosquitoes
? Lack of air-conditioning
? Outdoor activity

Compromised blood-brain barrier
? Facilitates neuroinvasion
e.g., cerebrovascular disease

Avian hosts
Abundance of immunologically naive susceptible hosts
Duration/level of viremia

Age
? Impaired immunity
? Coexisting disease

Enzootic vectors
Feed preferentially on birds
Numerous species vary geographically
e.g., *Culex pipiens*

Viral strain virulence determinants
? Affect viral replication rate
? Some strains neurotropic

Bridging vectors
Feed on birds and humans
May differ from enzootic species, e.g., *Culex salinarius* and others

Climate
Increased temperature enhances virus replication in mosquitoes
Drought increases organic content of water collections and abundance of some vector species
Increased rainfall and flooding expand habitat of other vector species

FIGURE 149-4. West Nile virus transmission cycle and examples of modifying climatologic, vertebrate, mosquito, and human factors on infection and illness.

In the eastern states, StLE is transmitted periodically in localized and regional outbreaks at lengthy intervals without significant transmission in intervening years. Outbreaks in the late summer and fall occur in urban areas, often in older neighborhoods, where polluted wastewater provides breeding habitat for *C. pipiens* and *C. quinquefasciatus*, the northern and southern house mosquitoes, respectively. More than 50 epidemics, ranging in the hundreds of cases, have been recognized in small towns or cities, including Houston, Dallas, Memphis, New Orleans, Chicago, and Detroit. The largest, in 1976, led to more than 3000 cases of neurologic infection nationally, similar in scale to recent WNE outbreaks. In three outbreaks since 1991, disproportionate risk was reported among homeless persons infected with the human immunodeficiency virus (HIV), probably reflecting their increased vulnerability to mosquito bites in the evening, when the vectors are most active.[90] Between 1992 and 2000, much smaller outbreaks and sporadic cases occurred (median, 14 cases; range, 2 to 26 cases annually). The 2001 outbreak in Louisiana produced 71 cases and was a reminder of the continued enzootic transmission and epidemic potential of this virus.[91]

Outbreaks in Florida occur more diffusely in suburban and urban locations, where swales and ground pools provide breeding sites for *C. nigripalpus*.[92] In the western states, StLE is transmitted perennially and at a low level in rural areas, frequently in association with irrigated farms and pastures. Forty years ago, outbreaks in agricultural areas occurred at regular intervals; more recently, cases have been more sporadic and frequently have involved vocational exposures or have occurred in proximity to cities. Small urban outbreaks have also occurred. The decline in cases has been attributed to secular changes in land use, air-conditioning of residences, and other factors leading to reduced exposure. Diminished exposure to infection has been confirmed in rural California populations, in whom seroprevalence rates now range from 0.1 to 11%.[89]

The risk of illness is associated most strongly with advanced age, but a slightly elevated risk is also seen in infants. The importance of age is reflected in the declining ratio of asymptomatic to symptomatic infection, which ranges from 800:1 in children to 85:1 in adults older than 60 years of age (Fig. 149-5).[87,93]

Tick-Borne Encephalitis

TBE virus is classified as one species within the mammalian group of tick-borne flaviviruses and is further subdivided into three subtypes: Far Eastern (previously RSSE), Siberian (previously west-Siberian), and European (previously CEE). In this chapter, this latest classification is followed, although many of the older references use the earlier names for virus subtypes.

The three subtypes of TBE virus, as well as other related tick-borne flaviviruses, are transmitted across the Holarctic, with some evidence for their dissemination from an Asian source.[16,94,95] The Far Eastern subtype is transmitted in eastern Russia, Korea, China, and parts of Japan; the European subtype and related viral strains are found in Scandinavia, Europe, and eastern states of the former Soviet Union; and the Siberian subtype is found in western Siberia (see Fig. 149-1D). The geographic distributions overlap in Eastern Europe, where both Siberian and Far Eastern subtypes may be isolated.[96] Louping ill virus is found in the British Isles, and Powassan virus in North America and northern Asia. Closely related tick-borne flaviviruses include Turkish and Spanish sheep encephalitis viruses, which are found in southern Europe,[97] and two viruses that cause hemorrhagic fever—Kyasanur Forest disease virus in India and Omsk hemorrhagic fever virus in Siberia.

TBE has been recognized throughout Europe, except in Portugal and the Benelux countries, but endemic transmission is most intense in Austria, areas of Germany, Poland, Hungary, the former Yugoslavia, Czechoslovakia, and the Baltic states and western Russia. In these countries, incidence rates in unvaccinated popula-

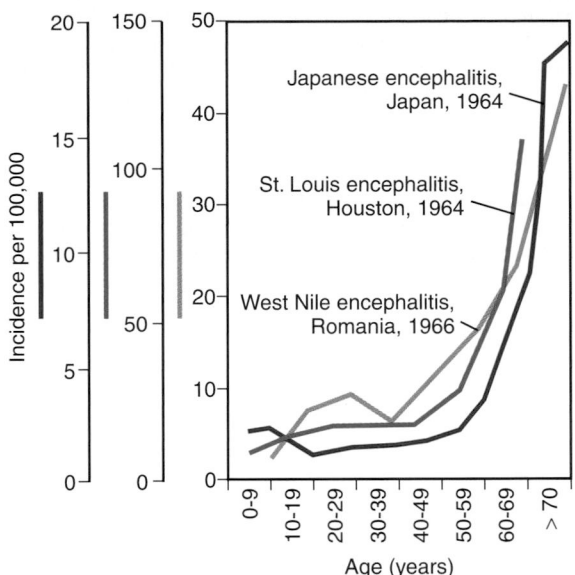

FIGURE 149-5. Age-specific incidence of St. Louis encephalitis, West Nile encephalitis, and Japanese encephalitis.

tions have approached 50 in 100,000 persons, but the risk is highly focal. In Austria, national vaccination programs have reduced the incidence of disease to less than 1 in 1000,000.[98] Sporadic cases are reported from France, Liechtenstein, Sweden, Switzerland, Italy, and Greece. In the Far East, TBE cases occur principally among people working or living in sylvatic locations in Russia, Korea, northern China, and Hokkaido Island, Japan.

The viruses are transmitted horizontally between ticks and vertebrates and through the winter by vertical transmission in the ticks and latent infections in hibernating animals. The virus passes transovarially and transtadially, from egg to larva, nymph, and adult, so all stages of the tick and both male and female ticks transmit infections to animals and humans. In addition, it appears that virus may be transmitted between ticks, as they feed on the skin of the same host, via infected host reticuloendothelial and inflammatory cells, without the need for host viremia.[99] Larval and nymphal ticks feed principally on birds and small mammals, and adult ticks on larger mammals such as roe deer, deer, domestic goats, sheep, cows, dogs, cats, and humans. Human infections are incidental to the transmission cycle. Animal movements can spread ticks and the virus to new foci.

Within the ranges of *Ixodes ricinus* and *Ixodes persulcatus*, the principal tick vectors of the European and Far Eastern subtypes, respectively, the ticks are distributed focally in sheltered microhabitats with high humidity and moderate temperatures, limited to elevations lower than 1000 m. Landscape ecology studies have characterized forest ecotones to fields or meadows, and low stands of deciduous trees and brush with a thick canopy, as high-risk biotopes that correlate with foci of human cases.[100] Transmission foci tend to be highly stable but are subject to human environmental modifications and possibly climate change.[101] In central Europe, cases occur from April until November, peaking in June and July, with a secondary rise in October.

Cases occur mainly in adults, 20 to 50 years of age, with a male predominance, reflecting occupational exposure in forestry and farming. But children at outdoor play and persons with vocational exposure while hiking, berry picking, or mushroom gathering also may be at risk, depending on the location and season. However, the risk for most persons with short-term exposures is low. Among American soldiers stationed in central Europe, no cases and a low rate of seroconversion (0.1% to 0.4%) have been reported.[102,103] Louping ill is principally an occupational disease of veterinarians, sheepherders, and butchers.[104]

TBE virus is stable at acid pH, and consumption of unpasteurized milk or milk products from infected goats, sheep, or cows previously

accounted for 10% to 20% of cases in some parts of central Europe. The possibility that Powassan virus can be transmitted from raw milk products in the United States has been suggested.[105] Slaughter or butchering of infected animals or meat is a principal mode of transmission for louping ill virus to humans and also has been reported in TBE and in outbreaks of Alkhurma virus (see later discussion).[106,107] Infection has also been acquired from infected ticks carried to households on fomites.

In addition to TBE virus, *I. ricinus* also transmits several borrelia responsible for Lyme disease (as well as *Anaplasma phagocytophilum, Babesia microti,* and several species of rickettsia), and dual infections of ticks and humans are observed. However, in at-risk areas, Lyme disease is far more common than the other diseases. This difference reflects the low proportion of virus-infected ticks (0.1% to 5%) and the 10-fold higher borrelia infection rates of ticks in the same location. This distinction may result from the brevity of viremias in animal hosts, which provide an opportunity for tick infection of only a few days; in contrast, persistent borrelia infections of rodents offer a higher likelihood of tick infection during feeding. An analogous situation obtains in the United States, where *Ixodes scapularis* transmits Lyme disease, babesiosis, human anaplasmosis, and a genotype of Powassan virus represented by deer tick virus.[108] However, *Ixodes cookei* ticks (the principal vector of Powassan virus) and *I. scapularis* differ somewhat in their host range, which may further limit opportunities for the viral and borrelial transmission cycles to intersect.

PATHOGENESIS

Yellow Fever

Early stages of YF infection can be inferred from human vaccine studies and from experimental wild-type viral infections of primates. Two days after inoculation of the attenuated 17D vaccine, levels of tumor necrosis factor α (TNF-α), interleukin-1 receptor antagonist (IL-1RA), and, to a lesser extent, interleukin-6 (IL-6) increase, with a secondary TNF-α peak 7 days later.[3,23,109,110] The cytokines are synthesized in response to local spread of the vaccine, and again as a response to viremia, which peaks between days 5 and 6.[3,23,111] TNF-α elevations correspond to declines in the lymphocyte count. After wild-type viral infection, the grippe phase of early YF presumably is associated with a similarly timed elaboration of cytokines. In experimentally inoculated rhesus monkeys, the virus replicates initially in local lymph nodes, followed rapidly by blood-borne infection of fixed macrophages, especially Kupffer cells in the liver, and further spread and replication in liver, lung, kidney, and adrenal glands, and most prolifically in regional lymph tissue, spleen, and bone marrow.[3,23] Infection by mosquito feeding, which introduces cytokines from the insect's saliva, is believed to differ from experimental needle inoculation in the outcome of local viral replication and distribution, but the importance of these factors in modulating human flaviviral infections is unknown.

Pathologic changes are most pronounced in the liver and kidneys, but widespread hemorrhages are found on mucosal surfaces, in the skin, and within various organs. Numerous petechial hemorrhages and erosion of the gastric mucosa contribute to the hematemesis that typically introduces the illness. Hepatocellular damage is characterized by a patchy midzonal distribution, sparing cells around the central vein and portal triad. The extent of lobular necrosis is variable, with an average of 60%, but, even with confluent lobular necrosis, the reticular architecture is preserved. The preservation of the reticulin network, minimal inflammatory changes, and the morphology of degenerating hepatocytes are consistent with apoptosis as the principal pathway of cell death. Early changes in infected hepatocytes consist of glycogen depletion and cloudy swelling, followed by accumulations of fat and of ceroid pigment. Necrotic cells finally undergo coagulation, with the formation of characteristic eosinophilic Councilman bodies, which correspond to apoptotic cells. Viral antigen is identified initially in Kupffer cells and appears later in hepatocytes, Councilman bodies, and endothelial cells.[112-114] Healing occurs without fibrosis.

Albuminuria and renal insufficiency reflect prerenal factors, including vomiting and myocarditis, as well as parenchymal invasion and, in advanced illness, acute tubular necrosis.[23,115] Viral antigen can be identified in the kidney and also in the heart, in which degenerative fatty infiltration of the myocardium and of the conduction system contributes to decreased output and arrhythmias.[114] Neurologic findings probably reflect metabolic disturbances, cerebral edema, and hemorrhages rather than encephalitis. The cause of the bleeding diathesis is ill-defined but probably represents a combination of reduced hepatic synthesis of clotting factors, intravascular coagulation, thrombocytopenia, and endothelial and platelet dysfunction. A combination of direct parenchymal damage and a systemic inflammatory response–like syndrome appears to contribute to shock and a fatal outcome. Neutralizing antibodies elaborated within the first week of illness clear the virus, and recovery is followed by lifelong immunity.

Heterologous flaviviral immunity (e.g., previous dengue) is believed to provide partial protection against infection, which may contribute to the absence of YF in Asia.[116] However, in contrast to the situation with DHF, antibody-mediated immune enhancement does not result. Genetic selection has been described in survivors of YF epidemics, and youth and advanced age have both been implicated as risk factors for symptomatic illness.[3,117] Hepatitis B carriage, which is prevalent in areas of Africa with endemic YF, is not a risk factor for symptomatic disease.[118]

Dengue and Dengue Hemorrhagic Fever

Most dengue virus infections are subclinical. Self-limited dengue fever is the usual clinical outcome of infection, but an immunopathologic response in some patients, usually in the setting of heterologous immunity, produces the syndrome of DHF (Fig. 149-6).[119-121]

After an infectious mosquito bite, the virus replicates in local lymph nodes and within 2 to 3 days disseminates via the blood to various tissues. Virus circulates in the blood typically for 5 days in infected monocytes/macrophages, and to a lesser degree in B cells and T cells. It also replicates in skin, reactive spleen lymphoid cells, and macrophages.[122,123] Viral antigen, possibly reflecting an uptake of immune complexes but not active viral replication, can be demonstrated more widely in liver Kupffer cells and endothelia; renal tubular cells; and alveolar macrophages and endothelia. Almost all patients are viremic at the point of clinical presentation with fever and clear the virus from the blood within days after defervescence.[124, 125] The malaise and flu-like symptoms that typify dengue probably reflect patients' cytokine response; however, myalgia, a cardinal feature of the illness, may also indicate pathologic changes in muscle, typified by a moderate perivascular mononuclear infiltrate with lipid accumulation.[126] Musculoskeletal pain (break-bone fever) conceivably could reflect viral infection of bone marrow elements, including mobile macrophages and dendritic cells (CD11b/CD18 [MAC-1]–positive) and relatively nonmotile adventitial reticular cells (nerve growth factor receptor–positive).[123] Local suppression of erythrocytic, myelocytic, and thrombocytic poiesis within 4 to 5 days is reflected in peripheral cytopenias. Histopathologic examination of skin from patients with rash discloses a minor degree of lymphocytic dermal vasculitis and, variably, viral antigen.[122,124] Elevated hepatic transaminase concentrations have been reported in most cases of dengue, with the aspartate aminotransferase (AST) level initially higher than that of alanine aminotransferase (ALT), and levels higher in DHF compared with dengue fever.[128,129] In fatal cases, histopathologic findings resemble those of early mild YF, with hypertrophy of Kupffer cells, focal ballooning and necrosis of hepatocytes in a midzonal distribution with occasional Councilman body formation, mild fatty changes, and a scant periportal mononuclear cell response.[130] Viral antigen has been demonstrated in hepatocytes, Kupffer cells, and endothelia.[123] Neurologic complications have been attributed chiefly to metabolic alterations and to focal and sometimes massive intracranial hemorrhages, but anecdotal cases and limited case series have indicated the possibility of viral CNS invasion and encephalitis.[131-133]

Shock in dengue shock syndrome (DSS) occurs after the sudden extravasation of plasma into extravascular sites, including the pleural and abdominal cavities, usually with the defervescence of fever.[134,135] The extensive increase in vascular permeability is associated with immune activation, as manifested by increased levels of plasma-soluble

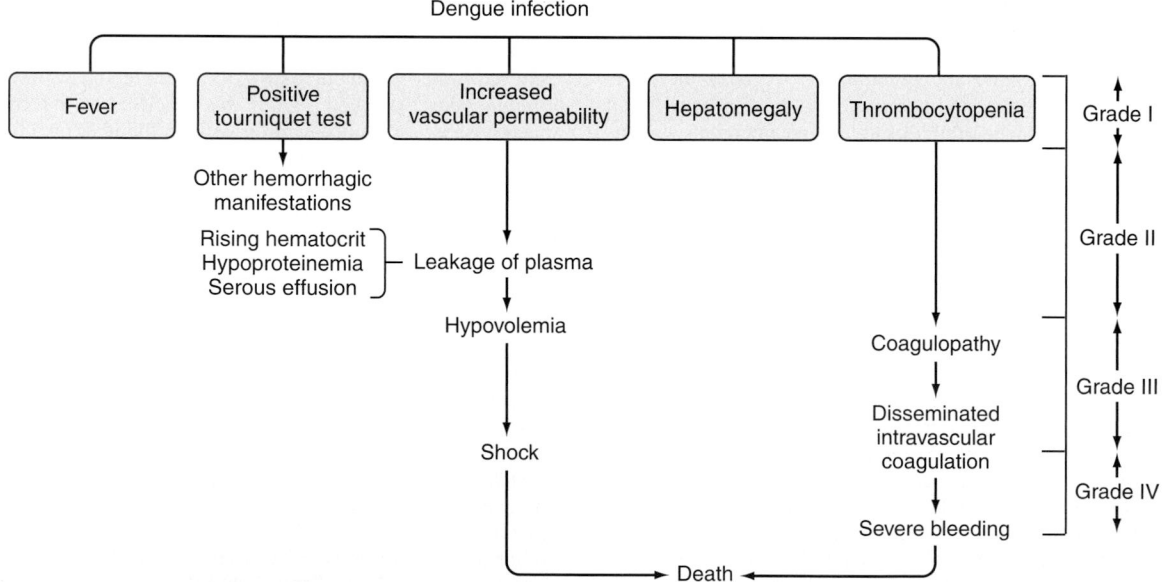

FIGURE 149-6. Clinical spectrum, pathophysiology, and classification of dengue hemorrhagic fever. At the top are key clinical findings; in the center, pathophysiologic mechanisms; and on the side, the World Health Organization classification of cases:
Grade 1: Fever accompanied by nonspecific constitutional symptoms; the only hemorrhagic manifestations are a positive tourniquet test result, easy bruising, or both.
Grade 2: Spontaneous bleeding in addition to the manifestations of grade 1, usually in the form of skin hemorrhages or other hemorrhages.
Grade 3: Circulatory failure manifested by a rapid, weak pulse and narrowing of pulse pressure or hypotension, with the presence of cold, clammy skin and restlessness.
Grade 4: Profound shock with undetectable blood pressure or pulse.
(From World Health Organization. Technical Guide for Diagnosis, Treatment, Surveillance, Prevention, and Control of Dengue Haemorrhagic Fever, 2nd ed. Geneva: World Health Organization; 1997.)

tumor necrosis factor receptor (sTNFR/75), IL-8, interferon-γ, and other mediators and local endothelial production of IL-8 RANTES with apoptotic endothelial cell death.[136-143] In addition, immune complex formation activates the complement system, with increases in C3a and C5a.[144] Levels of IL-6 and intercellular adhesion molecule-1 are depressed in parallel with hypoalbuminemia and the general loss of serum proteins. The rapid, predictable reversibility of the syndrome within 48 hours and the paucity of histopathologic correlates—usually perivascular edema with diapedesis of red cells and widespread focal hemorrhages—suggest that the inflammatory response produces a vasculopathy. Reduced cardiac output may contribute further to shock.[145] The hemorrhagic diathesis is complex and not well understood, reflecting a combination of cytokine action and vascular injury, viral antibodies' binding to platelets or cross-reacting with plasminogen and other clotting factors, reduced platelet function and survival, and a mild consumptive coagulopathy.[146-149]

The increased frequency of DHF in secondary dengue virus infections has suggested a role for heterologous antibodies in enhancing viral uptake and replication in Fc receptor–bearing cells (antibody-mediated immune enhancement).[150,151] Simultaneously, levels of TNF-α, soluble CD8, and soluble IL-2 that are higher in patients with DHF than in those with dengue fever indicate an activation of cross-reactive memory CD4+ and CD8+ T cells in response to a second infection.[136] The resulting production of IL-2, interferon-γ, and other lymphokines is reinforced by the increased abundance of infected target cells resulting from interferon-γ–mediated upregulation of Fc receptors and flaviviral-induced expression of major histocompatibility complex type I and II molecules that further activate T lymphocytes.[152] Activated infected monocytes and endothelia produce and release with their lysis TNF-α, IL-1, platelet-activating factor (PAF), IL-8, and RANTES, which act in synergy with lymphokines, histamine, and viral immune complex–induced C3a and C5a to produce the temporary vascular endothelial dysfunction that leads to plasma leakage. Paralleling the pathogenetic role of secondary enhancing antibodies in DHF, memory cellular responses to heterologous antigens also may contribute to immunopathology. While activated cells responding to cross-reactive antigens predominate over primary responses to the infecting virus, following the paradigm of original antigenic sin, they are marked for apoptosis and are ineffective in viral clearance, and they may be a source of cytokines with a negative clinical effect.[153]

Although infection with any of the serotypes can produce DHF, there is some indication for a greater propensity after second infections with certain serotypes or with specific strains of putatively greater virulence in a given partially immune population.[154-156] Trends toward an increased or fluctuating severity of illness during prolonged outbreaks have been attributed to the evolution of viral quasispecies.[157]

The rise of levels of serum neutralizing antibodies is correlated with the clearance of viremia, but immunity is associated with both humoral and cellular immune responses.[124,143] The latter are mediated by CD4+ and CD8+ cells that recognize serotype-specific, dengue serotype–cross-reactive epitopes, and flaviviral–cross-reactive epitopes.[11,158-160] The stimulation of cross-protective immunity from infection with one dengue viral serotype must be limited and brief, because infection with a second type during the same transmission season is not uncommon. Illness after infection with two serotypes (i.e., a third bout of dengue) occurs infrequently, and illness after three infections, virtually never. Repeated episodes of DHF have been recognized rarely, presumably because immune factors that promote immunopathologic responses are outweighed by immune responses that clear the infection.

Flaviviral Encephalitis

The variable and potentially lengthy incubation period of 4 to 21 days (usually 1 week) may reflect the interval for viral replication in the skin Langerhans cells and local lymph nodes, with a subsequent brief viremia before the virus invades the CNS.[161] Virus can rarely be recovered from blood, usually less than 1 week after the onset of illness and before the onset of neurologic symptoms, but sometimes later in an immunosuppressed patient. The large proportion of infections that

are asymptomatic, approximately 300 times the number of symptomatic cases, is striking and remarkably consistent among StLE, JE, and WNE (see Fig. 149-5). Subclinical infection presumably reflects the peripheral clearance of virus before neuroinvasion. In animal models of arboviral encephalitis, virus enters the CNS by crossing the vascular endothelium or through the olfactory epithelium, where the blood brain barrier is impaired. However, in humans the evidence suggests transmission across the vascular endothelium, either by passive transfer or by replication in endothelial cells.[162]

Within the brain, virions spread from cell to cell. Pathologic changes consist of meningeal congestion and inflammation, brain edema, and a widespread encephalitis with a predilection for the hippocampus and temporal cortex, thalamus, substantia nigra, cerebellum, periventricular areas of the brain stem, and anterior spinal cord. Destruction of lower motor neuron nuclei in the brain stem and the anterior horns of the cervical and upper lumbar cord is frequently seen in TBE, more so in the Far Eastern form of the disease, and less often in JE, StLE, and WNE. Focal neuronal degeneration and necrosis with neuronophagia evolve to the formation of glial nodules and, with healing, spongiform changes. Viral antigen appears in neuronal bodies and their processes and later in phagocytic cells.[163,164] Perivascular inflammatory infiltrates consist of activated CD4+ and CD8+ T cells, macrophages, and B cells. Within the cerebrospinal fluid (CSF), T cells predominate above their proportion in serum, with a correspondingly lower ratio of B and natural killer cells. T-cell activation is evidenced by the expression of HLA-DR followed by CD25 (IL2 receptor) and CD71 (transferrin receptor) and increased CSF levels of neopterin and β2-microglobulin.[165-168] A variety of processes may contribute to neuronal cell death, including apoptosis, cytoplasmic swelling, vacuolation, and membrane breakdown.

The rare recovery of virus from CSF, usually in patients with fulminant and fatal disease, is associated with the absence of intrathecal antibodies, indicating an important role of viral neutralization in recovery.[169] CD4+ and CD8+ cellular responses to JE viral N53 and N53-induced IFN-γ correlated with protection from illness and with prognosis, indicating a key role of this instructional protein in helping to stimulate an anamnestic antibody response, as well as in viral clearance of established CNS infection.[169a] On the other hand, intrathecal immune-complex formation and antineurofilament and antimyelin basic protein antibodies have also been reported in association with a poor outcome, suggesting immunopathologic injury.[170,171] Immunopathology is implicated in some animal models of flavivirus encephalitis[172] and is supported by the observation that in some immunocompromised patients infected with West Nile virus there is a delayed onset of clinical features despite high levels of viremia.[173]

The biphasic and relatively prolonged course of illness in TBE is reflected in CSF neopterin, β2-microglobulin, and intrathecal immunoglobulin G (IgG) synthesis that remains elevated for 6 weeks and pleocytosis that persists considerably longer than in other CNS infections, consistent with a protracted inflammatory reaction.[174] Although this time course alludes to a postinfectious process, pathologic changes with viral antigen in neurons, focal and perivascular infiltrates, and the recovery of virus from patients with fatal cases are consistent with a primary encephalitis.[175] Delayed CNS clearance of JE virus has also been suggested by the presence of infectious virus, antigen, or IgM antibodies in CSF several weeks after the onset of illness. JE viral antigen has been detected in peripheral blood mononuclear cells months after clinical recovery.[176,177] Clinically, subacute and progressive paralysis of the limb musculature and chronic epilepsy are well-known features of TBE,[178,179] and CNS viral persistence has been demonstrated.[180] Similar chronic symptomatic infections have been modeled in TBE virus– and West Nile virus–infected monkeys.

Advanced age is preeminent among the risk factors for development of neurologic infection. In susceptible populations, illness rates rise steeply with age, although infections uniformly attack persons of all ages, indicating age-related host factors rather than increased exposure as the risk factor (see Fig. 149-5).[1,27,84,87,93,181] The biologic basis for the age-related susceptibility is ill defined. Studies in mice indicate a critical role of the early antibody response in containing viral replication and limiting dissemination in the CNS. Although the age-related risk may simply reflect immunosenescence, other observations indicate roles for functional or structural CNS changes that facilitate neuroinvasion. As examples, in some studies, neurocysticercosis was more prevalent in patients with fatal cases of JE than in patients dying of other conditions; and in one study, hypertension was associated with an increased incidence of fatal StLE.[182-184] The interaction of concurrent viral, bacterial, or parasitic infections has been reported to alter expected outcomes of TBE and JE, related to either facilitated neuroinvasion or immune factors.[185,186] Heterologous dengue immunity has been associated with a better outcome in StLE and JE.[187,188-190]

CLINICAL FEATURES

Yellow Fever

YF illness ranges in severity from an undifferentiated, self-limited grippe to hemorrhagic fever that is fatal in 50% of cases.[3,23,115] In addition, between 5% and 50% of infections are inapparent. After an incubation period of 3 to 6 days, fever, headache, and myalgias begin abruptly, accompanied by few physical findings except conjunctival injection, facial flushing, a relative bradycardia (Faget's sign), and, on laboratory examination, leukopenia. In most cases, resolution of this *period of infection* concludes the illness, but in others, the remission of fever for a few hours to several days is followed by renewed symptoms, high fever, headache, lumbosacral back pain, nausea, vomiting, abdominal pain, and somnolence *(period of intoxication)*. Profound weakness and prostration ensue, compounded by poor oral intake and protracted vomiting, but the severe multisystemic illness is dominated by icteric hepatitis and a hemorrhagic diathesis with prominent gastrointestinal bleeding and hematemesis, epistaxis, gum bleeding, and petechial and purpuric hemorrhages. Albuminuria is a constant feature that aids in the differentiation of YF from other causes of viral hepatitis. Deepening jaundice and elevations in transaminase levels continue for several days, at the same time that azotemia and progressive oliguria ensue. Whereas direct bilirubin levels rise to 5 to 10 mg/dL, alkaline phosphatase levels are only slightly raised; not infrequently, AST may be elevated above ALT because of myocardial damage.[191] Ultimately, hypotension, shock, and metabolic acidosis develop, compounded by myocardial dysfunction and arrhythmias as late events and acute tubular necrosis in some patients. Confusion, seizures, and coma distinguish the late stages of illness, but CSF examination discloses an increased protein level without pleocytosis, consistent with cerebral edema or encephalopathy. Death usually occurs within 7 to 10 days after onset. If the patient survives the critical period of illness, secondary bacterial infections resulting in pneumonia or sepsis are common complications. Recovery has not been followed by chronic hepatitis.

Clinically, severe YF resembles other viral hemorrhagic fevers occurring in Africa and South America, so laboratory confirmation is required to make the diagnosis. Early exclusion of other causes with the potential for person-to-person spread is important to prevent nosocomial transmission. Other forms of viral hepatitis, particularly hepatitis E (which frequently appears in outbreaks), leptospirosis, malaria, typhoid, typhus, relapsing fever, acute fatty liver of pregnancy, and toxin-related hepatitis, are alternative diagnoses.

Dengue Fever and Dengue Hemorrhagic Fever

Classic dengue fever is an acute febrile disease with headaches, musculoskeletal pain, and rash, but the severity of illness and clinical manifestations vary with age. Infection is often asymptomatic or nonspecific, consisting of fever, malaise, pharyngeal injection, upper respiratory symptoms, and rash—particularly in children.[192] Dengue virus types 2 and 4 may be more likely to cause inapparent infections in flavivirus-naive persons.[125] Disease severity may be increased among infants and the elderly.[193] After an incubation period of 4 to 7 days, fever—often with chills, severe frontal headache, and retro-orbital pain—develops abruptly with a rapid progression to prostration, severe musculoskeletal and lumbar back pain, and abdominal tenderness. Anorexia, nausea, vomiting, hyperesthesia of the skin, and dysgeusia are common complaints. Initially, the skin appears flushed, but within 3 to 4 days and

with the lysis of fever, an indistinct macular and sometimes scarlatiniform rash develops, sparing the palms and soles. As the rash fades or desquamates, localized clusters of petechiae on the extensor surfaces of the limbs may remain. A second episode of fever and symptoms may ensue ("saddleback" pattern). Recovery may be followed by a prolonged period of listlessness, easy fatigability, and even depression.

Although virtually all cases are uncomplicated, minor bleeding from mucosal surfaces (usually epistaxis, bleeding from the gums, hematuria, and metrorrhagia) is not uncommon, and gastrointestinal hemorrhage and hemoptysis can occur (see Fig. 149-6).[194] In patients with preexisting peptic ulcer disease, severe, even fatal, gastric bleeding can be precipitated.[195] Subcapsular splenic bleeding and rupture, uterine hemorrhage resulting in spontaneous abortion, and severe postpartum bleeding have also been reported.[196,197] It is important to differentiate these phenomena from the bleeding diathesis that accompanies the life-threatening syndrome of hypotension and circulatory failure in DHF-DSS.

Hepatitis frequently complicates dengue fever.[128,198] In Taiwan, transaminase levels raised 10-fold above normal were observed in 11% of cases, with rare deaths due to hepatic failure. Neurologic symptoms associated with dengue fever have been reported sporadically and attributed to hemorrhages or cerebral edema, but recovery of virus from the CSF, intrathecal viral-specific IgM, and immunohistochemical evidence of infection in the brain indicate the possibility of primary dengue encephalitis in some cases.[131,133,199,200] Myositis with rhabdomyolysis has also been reported.

Vertical transmission of dengue virus to neonates whose mothers had an onset of primary or secondary dengue fever zero to 8 days before delivery has resulted in acute neonatal dengue manifesting as fever, cyanosis, apnea, mottling, hepatomegaly, and reduced platelet counts as low as 11,000/mm³.[192,201] One baby died of intracerebral hemorrhage, but others, although ill, did not have other signs of DHF, and they recovered without incident. Dengue virus was isolated from the neonates in some cases. The outcome of infection acquired earlier in pregnancy has not been addressed satisfactorily. Anecdotal reports have described spontaneous abortion (see earlier discussion) and a variety of birth defects and, in a postepidemic investigation, an increase in neural tube defects.[202] Another investigation found no increases in abnormal pregnancy outcomes.[203] In a study of cord blood samples from infants delivered 5 to 9 months after an outbreak, 4 of 59 samples had viral-specific IgM, but all the infants appeared normal.[204]

The central clinical features of DHF-DSS are hemorrhagic phenomena and hypovolemic shock caused by increased vascular permeability and plasma leakage.[134,135,205,206] The early clinical features in children who ultimately develop DHF-DSS are indistinguishable from those of ordinary dengue fever, namely, fever, malaise, headache, musculoskeletal pain, facial flushing, anorexia, nausea, and vomiting. However, with the defervescence of fever 2 to 7 days later, reduced perfusion and early signs of shock are manifested by central cyanosis, restlessness, diaphoresis, and cool, clammy skin and extremities. Abdominal pain is a common complaint. In cases with a benign course of illness, blood pressure and pulse may be maintained, but a rapid and weak pulse, narrowing of the pulse pressure to less than 20 mm Hg, and, in the most extreme cases, an unobtainable blood pressure establish the shock syndrome. The platelet count declines and petechiae appear in widespread distribution with spontaneous ecchymoses. Bleeding occurs at mucosal surfaces from the gastrointestinal tract and at venipuncture sites. The liver is palpably enlarged in up to 75% of patients, with variable splenomegaly. Increased amylase levels and sonographic evidence of pancreatic enlargement are found in up to 40% of patients. Pleural effusions can be detected in more than 80% of cases if a decubitus film is taken; in combination with an elevated hematocrit and hypoalbuminemia, reflecting hemoconcentration, these studies provide objective measures of plasma loss. However, ultrasonography has been more sensitive in detecting pleural effusions, ascites, and gallbladder edema in more than 95% of severe cases, and pararenal and perirenal effusions in 77%, as well as hepatic and splenic subcapsular and pericardial effusions.[207] The presence of pleural and peritoneal effusions is associated with severe disease. Adult respiratory distress syndrome (ARDS) may develop with capillary-alveolar leakage.[208] In untreated patients, hypoperfusion complicated by myocardial dysfunction and reduced ejection fraction results in metabolic acidosis and organ failure. With support through the critical period of illness, spontaneous resolution of vasculopathy and circulatory failure usually can be expected within 2 to 3 days, with complete recovery afterward. The duration of illness ranges from 7 to 10 days in most cases. Fatality rates have reached 50% in underserved populations, but in experienced centers, fewer than 1% of cases are fatal. Encephalopathy (often reflecting CNS hemorrhage), prolonged shock, and hepatic or renal failure infrequently complicate the illness but are associated with a poor prognosis. As would be expected in areas where dengue infects 10% of children each year, concurrent infection with bacteria, parasites, and other viral pathogens occurs frequently. Dual infections, principally gram-negative sepsis, have been reported in 1 of 200 children hospitalized with dengue, resulting in prolonged fever and hospitalization.[209] Reactivation of herpesvirus-6 infection has been reported in two thirds of patients with DHF.

Attempts to differentiate dengue fever clinically from other acute febrile illnesses are unlikely to be successful, although the diagnosis is aided if laboratory examination indicates leukopenia, neutropenia, thrombocytopenia, or mildly elevated AST levels.[6,53,157] Even when facial flushing was included as a selective criterion in a study that also included DHF patients, the only differentiating symptoms were anorexia, nausea, and vomiting. A positive tourniquet test, a requirement in the DHF case definition, is obtained more often than in children with other febrile illnesses, but its specificity is low. In comparison with chikungunya, another epidemic *A. aegypti*–borne infection, dengue patients are less likely to have conjunctivitis, rash, and musculoskeletal pain.[210] The difficulty of differentiating dengue from rubella, measles, and even influenza has been underscored by the early misrecognition of entire epidemics. The clinical differentiation of DHF from YF and other viral hemorrhagic fevers is also difficult, and diagnosis requires laboratory confirmation.

Clinical or laboratory differentiation, at the time of first presentation, of children destined to develop DHF would facilitate intervention before the sudden onset of shock. In one study, AST elevations greater than 60 U/mL, leukocyte counts less than 5000/mm³, and absolute neutrophil counts less than 3000/mm³ had higher predictive values than the tourniquet test in differentiating dengue from other febrile illnesses.[53,157] In another study, an elevated sTNFR/75 level had a sensitivity of 93% and a negative predictive value of 95% in foretelling shock.[141] Although the specificity was 34%, the choice of a 55 pg/mL cutoff errs conservatively. Increased IL-8 levels may also have prognostic value.[143] Studies to discover the pathogenic roles of other cytokines are in progress.

Japanese Encephalitis

Infection is symptomatic in fewer than 1% of cases of JE, but the illness is usually a severe encephalitis, leading frequently to coma and to a fatal outcome in 25% of cases. The spectrum of clinical illness is probably broader than is appreciated from an evaluation of hospitalized patients. JE cases are found among hospitalized children with acute pyrexia of undetermined origin, and, undoubtedly, many patients with febrile illnesses and headache or aseptic meningitis do not present to a hospital. Studies have drawn attention to patients presenting with spinal paralysis without encephalitic signs, initially misdiagnosed as poliomyelitis cases, and conversely, acute behavioral changes mimicking psychosis without motor signs.[1,2,162,211-215] The earliest symptoms are lethargy and fever and, frequently, headache, abdominal pain, nausea, and vomiting. Lethargy increases over several days, when uncharacteristic behaviors associated with an agitated delirium, unsteadiness, and abnormal motor movements may develop, advancing to progressive somnolence and coma. Although the prodrome may evolve over several days to 1 week, some children present with a sudden convulsion after a brief febrile illness.

The chief findings are high fever and altered consciousness, ranging from mild disorientation or a subtle personality change to a severe state of confusion, delirium, and coma.[1,2,162,215,216] Mutism has been a presentation in some cases. Nuchal rigidity is a variable find-

ing, present in one third to two thirds of the cases. Cranial nerve palsies resulting in facial paralysis and dysconjugate gaze are detected in one third of the cases. Muscular weakness can be associated with decreased or increased tone and can be generalized or asymmetric, with hemiparesis or unusual distributions of flaccid and spastic paralysis. Hyperreflexia, ankle clonus, and other abnormal reflexes may be elicited. Disordered movements such as nonstereotypical flailing, ataxia, or tremor may be present initially. Not uncommonly, choreoathetosis, rigidity, masked facies, and other extrapyramidal signs appear later in the illness. Focal or generalized seizures develop in up to 85% of children and 10% of adults.[216,217] Multiple seizures and status epilepticus are associated with a poor outcome. Subtle motor status epilepticus, in which the only clinical manifestation might be the twitching of a finger or eyebrow, may also occur but is easily overlooked.[217,218]

Signs of increased intracranial pressure, such as papilledema and hypertension, are detected in a minority of patients, although some fatal cases show evidence of uncal or tentorial herniation, and clinical signs consistent with brain stem herniation syndromes are not uncommon.[217] More than one third of patients in coma need ventilatory support. Fulminant cases may be rapidly fatal. More typically, improvement can be expected after 1 week with the defervescence of fever. Neurologic function is regained gradually over several weeks, with further recovery after hospital discharge over intervals of months to years. Infections from stasis ulcers, urinary tract infection, pneumonia, and bacteremia frequently complicate the lengthy recovery from coma and paralysis and may be secondary causes of death. The virulence of the infection is underscored by contemporary fatality rates of 25% in locations with intensive care facilities. Neurologic abnormalities such as seizure disorders, motor and cranial nerve paresis, cortical blindness, and movement disorders persist in up to one third of patients after 5 years. A greater proportion, perhaps even 75% of recovered children, exhibit behavioral and psychological abnormalities. Anecdotal cases of clinical relapse weeks after hospital discharge with recovery of virus from peripheral blood have alluded to delayed viral clearance or persistence, but the significance of these observations is uncertain.[177] In illness acquired during the first or second trimesters of pregnancy, the virus can infect the fetal-placental unit and precipitate abortion.[219] Cases acquired in the third trimester have not been reported to interrupt pregnancy. Congenital infections have been reported only when the virus was newly introduced to a susceptible adult population, because almost all women in endemic areas have acquired immunity. Nonimmune travelers may have an increased risk.

Laboratory studies disclose peripheral leukocytosis, as high as 30,000/mm³ with a left shift, and hyponatremia. The CSF opening pressure is elevated in approximately 50% of patients.[217] Pleocytosis ranges from less than 10 to several thousand cells per cubic millimeter, with a median of several hundred cells of a predominantly lymphocytic composition. CSF protein may be normal or elevated up to 100 mg/dL. The electroencephalogram discloses a pattern of diffuse slow waves (theta or delta) with superimposed seizure activity, including periodic lateralized epileptiform discharges (PLEDS).[217,218,220] Brain imaging reveals diffuse white matter edema and abnormal signals mainly in the thalamus (often with evidence of hemorrhage), basal ganglia, cerebellum, midbrain, pons, and spinal cord.[182a,183,221,222] Electromyography shows changes of chronic partial denervation consistent with anterior horn cell destruction.

In rural Asia, tuberculous, cerebral malaria, and bacterial meningitis (especially partially treated) are the principal alternative diagnoses.[6,68,223,223a] Typhoid fever with tremors and ataxia, dengue infection with encephalopathy, lead poisoning , heat stroke, and enterovirus 71 encephalitis have all been confused with JE. In JE-endemic areas, any encephalitis outbreak is initially assumed to be JE, but the outbreak of the previously unknown Nipah virus in Malaysia in 1999 (see Chapter 158) and an outbreak of Chandipura virus infection in India in 2003 showed how easy it is to be misled. West Nile virus and JE virus infections in particular may be mutually misrecognized, because the viruses overlap in their distribution in Southwest Asia and can produce clinically indistinguishable illnesses in contemporaneous outbreaks, and because differentiation in laboratory tests may be difficult.

West Nile Encephalitis

Most infections are asymptomatic; when symptoms do occur, they develop after an incubation period that typically lasts 2 to 6 days but may extend to 14 days, or even longer in immunosuppressed persons. In recent outbreaks, the syndrome of West Nile fever occurred in about 20% of infected individuals, who developed a sudden onset of an acute, nonspecific, flu-like illness lasting 3 to 6 days, with high fever and chills, malaise, headache, backache, arthralgia, myalgia, and retro-orbital pain, without overt neurologic signs.[79,80,162] Other nonspecific features include anorexia, nausea, vomiting, diarrhea, cough, and sore throat. In some epidemics, a flushed face, conjunctival injection, and generalized lymphadenopathy were common, and a maculopapular or pale roseolar rash was reported in about 50% of patients, more frequently in children. In one outbreak, 20% of patients with West Nile fever were reported to have hepatomegaly, and 10% had splenomegaly.[224] Myocarditis, pancreatitis, and hepatitis have also been described occasionally in severe West Nile virus infection.

Neurologic disease occurs in fewer than 1% of infected individuals. Patients typically have a febrile prodrome of 1 to 7 days, which may be biphasic, before developing neurologic symptoms (Fig. 149-7). Although in most cases the prodrome is nonspecific, 15% to 20% of patients have features suggestive of West Nile fever, including eye pain, facial congestion, or a rash; fewer than 5% have lymphadenopathy.[225] In recent outbreaks, approximately two thirds of hospitalized patients had encephalitis (with or without signs of meningeal irritation), and one third had meningitis.[84,226,227] Acute flaccid paralysis caused by virus infection of the anterior horn of the spinal cord (myelitis) has been recognized in recent outbreaks.[228-230] The clinical picture suggests poliomyelitis; paralysis is frequently

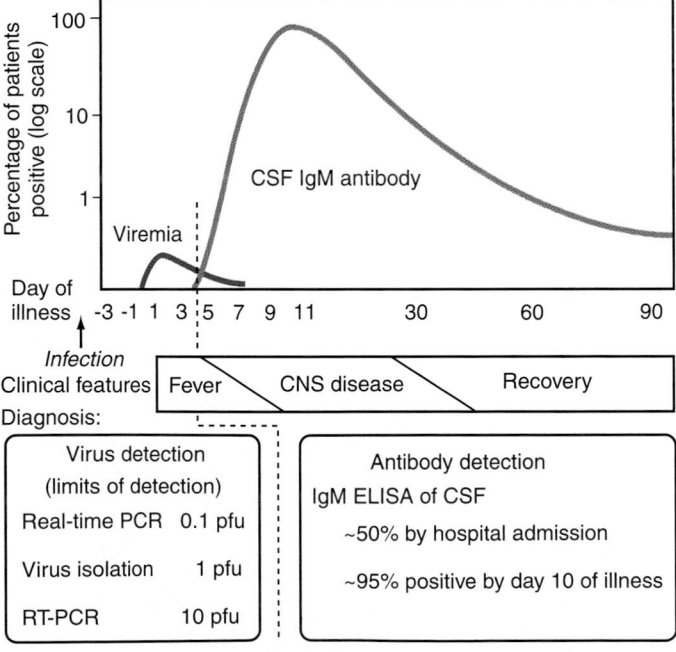

FIGURE 149-7. Schematic representation of the clinical course of West Nile encephalitis: viremia, development of antibody, and implications for diagnosis (as approximate percentage of patients). Limits of virus detection are expressed as plaque-forming units (pfu) per 100 μL; human viremia is thought to be <10 pfu/100 μL. The first day of fever is taken as the first day of illness; most patients are not admitted to hospital until day 3 to 5 of illness. CNS, central nervous system; CSF, cerebrospinal fluid; ELISA, enzyme-linked immunosorbent assay; IgM, immunoglobulin M; PCR, polymerase chain reaction; RT, reverse transcriptase. (*From Solomon T, Ooi MH. West Nile encephalitis. BMJ. 2003;326:865-869.*)

asymmetrical and may or may not be associated with meningoencephalitis. Once paralysis is established, little long-term improvement has been described. Although convulsions occurred in approximately 30% of patients in the early descriptions of WNE, they did not appear to be an important feature in the more recent outbreaks.[227,231] Other neurologic features include cranial neuropathies, optic neuritis, and ataxia. Stiffness, rigidity, spasms, bradykinesia, and tremors, associated with basal ganglia damage, have also recently been recognized in WNE.[231,232]

In recent outbreaks, overall case-fatality rates for hospitalized patients ranged from 4% to 14% but were higher in older patients.[226-227,231] Other risk factors for death include the presence of profound weakness, deep coma, failure to produce IgM antibody, impaired immunity, and coexisting illness such as hypertension or diabetes mellitus.[227,233] Neurologic sequelae are common among survivors. In one study, half of hospitalized patients still had a functional deficit at discharge,[234] and only one third had recovered fully by 1 year.

Approximately 50% of patients have a peripheral leukocytosis, and 15% have leukopenia.[227,234] Hyponatremia sometimes occurs in patients with encephalitis. Examination of the CSF typically shows a moderate lymphocytic pleocytosis, although sometimes there are no cells, or neutrophils may predominate. The protein is moderately elevated, and the glucose ratio is typically normal. Magnetic resonance imaging may show high signal intensities in the thalamus in T_2-weighted images and diffusion-weighted images in some patients (Fig. 149-8).[231,232] Electroencephalograms show diffuse slowing and, in some cases, focal seizure activity. Nerve conduction studies typically show the reduced motor axonal amplitudes consistent with anterior horn cell damage, although there may also be some slowing of conduction velocities and some changes to sensory nerves.[162]

St. Louis Encephalitis

StLE has been classified into three syndromes, characterized respectively by constitutional symptoms and headache (febrile headache), aseptic meningitis, and fatal encephalitis.[1,88,93,181,235,235a] The proportion of cases in each category is age dependent, with increasing proportions of encephalitis and fatal cases in adults, especially in the elderly. The illness usually begins with a febrile prodrome of malaise, fever, headache, and myalgias, sometimes with upper respiratory or abdominal symptoms, that evolves over several days to more than 1 week with progressive lethargy, periods of confusion, and the onset of tremors, clumsiness, and ataxia. Vomiting and diarrhea are common, and some patients complain of dysuria, urgency, and incontinence.

Altered consciousness, marked by confusion, delirium, or somnolence, is the predominant presenting feature, and generalized motor weakness is more usual than are focal signs. Indications of meningeal irritation are inconstant and are elicited more often in children. Mental clouding may be subtle and manifested only by slight disorientation. Most patients do not progress to deep coma. Tremulousness involving the eyelids, tongue, lips, and extremities is usual, and cerebellar and cranial nerve signs are common.[91,235,236] Various abnormal movements may be present, including myoclonic jerks and nystagmus. Convulsions are infrequent and signal a poor prognosis, except in children; subtle motor seizures also have been reported.[235] Most patients improve over several days; however, pneumonia, thrombophlebitis and pulmonary embolism, stroke, gastrointestinal hemorrhage, and nosocomial infection can complicate recovery. The mortality rate is 8% overall and 20% among patients older than 60 years of age. In recovered adults, asthenia, emotional lability, anxiety, irritability, forgetfulness, tremor, dizziness, and unsteadiness may persist for months, accompanied by tremor, asymmetrical deep tendon reflexes, and visual disturbances.[237] No cases of clinical relapse or progressive illness have been described. Infants and young children frequently exhibit significant neurologic sequelae when discharged, but psychomotor function is usually recovered on later follow-up.[238] Little is known of the risk or outcome of congenital infection. Pregnancy and delivery progressed normally in one case in which infection was acquired during the third trimester (T.F. Tsai, unpublished observation). HIV-positive individuals appear to be at greater risk for acquisition of StLE, but whether this is related to their immune status or to other factors (e.g., increased risk of exposure due to homelessness) is not clear.[239]

The peripheral white cell count may be slightly elevated. In some patients, microscopic hematuria, proteinuria, and pyuria have been reported. Hyponatremia due to syndrome of inappropriate secretion of antidiuretic hormone (SIADH) occurs in more than one third of patients, and the concentrations of ALT and creatine phosphokinase may be slightly elevated. One third of patients have an increased CSF opening pressure, and there is typically a moderate mononuclear pleocytosis, with an elevated protein concentration. The electroencephalogram shows diffuse slowing and seizure activity, including PLEDs. Magnetic resonance imaging may show high signal intensity in the substantia nigra.[235,240] The diagnosis should be suspected if the case is one of a cluster in the summer or early fall, especially if the patient is an elderly or homeless person. A cerebral ischemic event, heat stroke, medication or drug toxicity, or other cause of delirium or encephalopathy has frequently been the initial diagnosis in confirmed cases. Other infectious causes of aseptic meningitis or acute encephalitis, including WNE, which can be transmitted contemporaneously, cannot easily be distinguished on a clinical basis.

Tick-Borne Encephalitis

Infection leads to symptoms of TBE in only 1 in 250 persons. Three quarters of patients are able to recall a tick bite occurring a median of 8 days (range, 4 to 28 days) before symptoms developed.[174,241-243] The illness usually begins with a nonspecific grippe of fever, malaise, headache, nausea, vomiting, and myalgias that may be accompanied by fasciculation. Within 1 week, these symptoms resolve spontaneously. In the majority of patients who have the "febrile form" of the disease, there are no further symptoms,[94] but in others who progress to more severe illness, the remission of symptoms is temporary, usually 2 to 8 days (range, 1 to 20 days), before high fever, headache, and vomiting resume. The second phase may be limited to a "meningeal form" with aseptic meningitis (commonly in children), or it may manifest as a "meningoencephalitis form," a "poliomyelitic form" with poliomyelitis-like flaccid paralysis, or a "polyradiculoneuritic form" with a Guillain-Barré–like paralysis, which usually resolves spontaneously. In one series, almost 50% of hospitalized patients had meningitis, 40% had meningoencephalitis, and 10% had meningoencephalomyelitis.[244] Neurologic infections usually are benign in children, whereas severe disease occurs more often in elderly persons. The Far Eastern form of TBE is reported as more severe, with fatalities occurring in 20% of hospitalized patients and residual neurologic sequelae in up to 60% of recovered patients.[178] Although differences in hospital admission rates may have confounded some of these observations, intrinsic differences in the neurovirulence of different TBE viral subtypes have been shown in experimental animal infections.

Early prodromal symptoms may be undetected in children, whose illness in more than two thirds of cases consists of aseptic meningitis. Altered consciousness, ataxia, tremor, paresthesias, focal signs, and, less often, seizures characterize the presentation with encephalitis. Limb weakness and paralysis usually represent lower motor neuron lesions caused by myelitis or radicular neuritis; paresis may be transient, or it may evolve to permanent weakness and muscular atrophy. The shoulder girdle and upper limb musculature are affected most frequently, and urinary bladder continence and other autonomic functions can also be disturbed. Involvement of cranial nerves III, VII, IX, X, and XI produces gaze and peripheral facial paralysis and dysphagia. The outcome generally is good, especially in children, but the prognosis varies with age. A hemorrhagic syndrome has been reported in some cases and also in a laboratory-acquired louping ill infection.[245]

Approximately 1% of cases are fatal, most often in elderly persons. Sequelae are reported in up to 40% to 60% of patients, most frequently consisting of psychological disturbances such as asthenia, headache, memory loss and decreased concentration, anxiety, and emotional lability. Residual motor abnormalities include ataxia and incoordination, tremor, dysphasia, and, in fewer than 5% of cases, specific cranial or spinal muscular paralysis.[174,246] Progressive motor weakness and epilepsia partialis continua (Kozhevnikov's epilepsy) are specific syndromes that may reflect a chronic encephalitic process. Pneumonia, heart failure, and other complications associated with prolonged hospitalization have been reported.

Powassan encephalitis is a severe encephalitis with a case-fatality rate of approximately 10%. Focal features have occurred in more than 50% of reported cases; in one patient, the clinical presentation with olfactory hallucinations and temporal lobe seizures mimicked herpes encephalitis.[247,248] Significant residua of hemiplegia, quadriplegia, or aphasia, may result, and spinal paralysis with residual muscular wasting is similar to the myelitis associated with TBE.

Examination of the peripheral blood in TBE discloses leukopenia in the initial phase of illness, and leukocytosis up to 20,000/mm³ during the second phase, with a transition to leukopenia again before recovery. Thrombocytopenia can also occur in the initial viremic phase.[249] An elevated erythrocyte sedimentation rate and C-reactive protein concentration are common by the time patients present with neurologic disease, and elevated ALT and AST levels and electrocardiographic abnormalities have been reported anecdotally.[241] There is a moderate lymphocytic CSF pleocytosis (average of less than 100 leukocytes/mm³). The CSF protein level, although normal at the onset of neurologic symptoms, rises during the next 6 weeks, with an increase in the IgG index, indicating intrathecal synthesis. The albumin CSF/serum ratio, indicating disturbed blood-brain barrier permeability, can remain abnormal for as long as 1 year.[174]

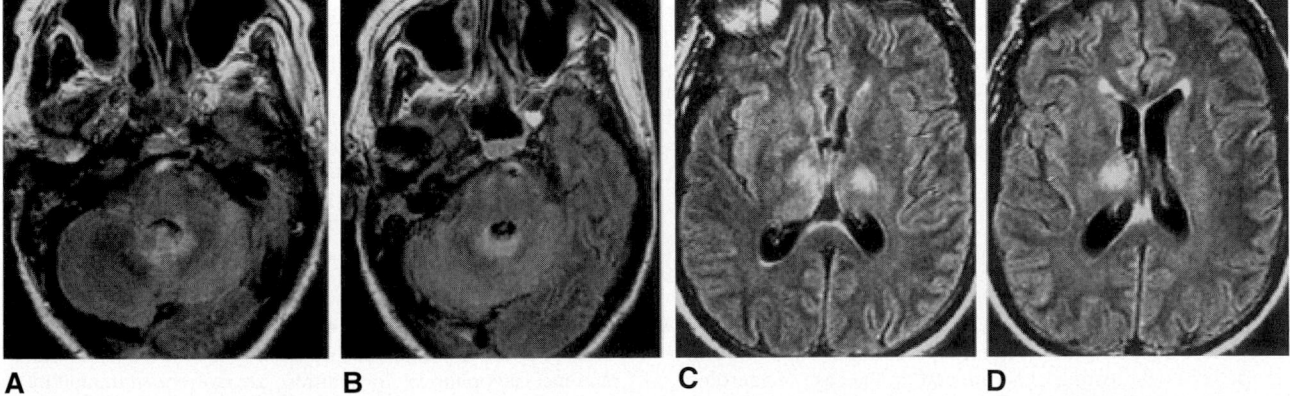

FIGURE 149-8. Magnetic resonance imaging changes in West Nile encephalitis (WNE). Fluid-attenuated inversion recovery images for a patient with WNE on day 10 of hospitalization, showing increased signal intensity in the periventricular gray matter of the fourth ventricle at the vermis of the cerebellum (**A** and **B**) and increased signal intensity in both thalami and the right caudate nucleus (**C** and **D**). (*From Solomon T, Dung NM, Kneen R, et al. Seizures and raised intracranial pressure in Vietnamese patients with Japanese encephalitis. Brain. 2002;125:1084-1093. By permission of the Oxford University Press.*)

The number and distribution of CSF lymphocytes and their cell markers differ in TBE and neuroborreliosis, a fact that may have diagnostic value in rapidly identifying patients for antibiotic treatment.[166-168] Abnormal magnetic resonance imaging signals are found most consistently in the thalami and basal ganglia.[250] Electroencephalograms show diffuse slowing in 90% of patients with encephalitis, with or without focal abnormalities.[241]

Although a history of tick bite is not given in all cases, exposure to an endemic focus during the transmission season should trigger suspicion. TBE is transmitted under the same circumstances as *Borrelia burgdorferi*, and, clinically, their radicular and aseptic meningitis syndromes can overlap. Anecdotal observations suggest that neurologic symptoms of Lyme disease may occur more often in the context of concurrent TBE, and, conversely, that TBE may be more severe in a dual infection.[167,185,186] TBE results in a more prolonged course of illness and hospitalization than do the other acute encephalitides of presumed viral origin; this pattern and the presence of spinal paralysis may aid in making the diagnosis.

LABORATORY DIAGNOSIS

Viral isolation is relevant to the diagnosis of suspected YF and dengue, because patients may present while still viremic and viral infectivity titers in blood are sufficiently high that attempts may be successful. Identifying the infective dengue viral serotype is important chiefly for public health reasons, but an individual patient also may benefit because future exposure to other serotypes places the patient at higher risk for DHF. Neurotropic flaviviruses can occasionally be isolated from blood taken within the first week of illness and before the onset of neurologic symptoms, or later if patients are immunosuppressed. In general, viral recovery from blood is successful only before an antibody response develops. Contrary to expectation, the isolation of neurotropic viruses from the CSF is usually unsuccessful except in the early stages of fulminant illness.

Tissue samples, whether from biopsy or autopsy, ideally should be divided into aliquots that are frozen at −70° C for viral isolation and fixed in buffered formalin and glutaraldehyde for light and electron microscopy. Viscerotomy liver samples are frequently taken after death as a means of postmortem YF diagnosis, but because pathologic changes are not pathognomonic, a purely histologic diagnosis should be considered presumptive and should be supplemented with immunohistochemical staining using viral-specific antibodies. Liver biopsy should never be attempted from patients with suspected YF, because they are at risk for fatal hemorrhage. StLE, West Nile, TBE, and JE viruses have been isolated from brain, lung, liver, spleen, and kidney with varied success, depending on the duration of illness and the day of death. Diverse areas of the brain and spinal cord should be sampled. StLE virus was also isolated from vitreous humor in one case. Suckling mice and C6/36 or AP61 mosquito cell cultures are the most sensitive systems for viral isolation, but Vero, LLCMK$_2$, PS, and other continuous vertebrate cell lines are also used.[251]

Multiplex PCR assays in various formats that simultaneously identify the presence of dengue virus and its serotype in serum samples are used only in specialized laboratories in the United States and several Asian and South American countries.[252] YF virus genomic sequences have also been detected in blood, but clinical experience is limited. In patients with flavivirus encephalitis, reverse transcriptase PCR of the CSF has not proved very useful, although it may have a role in the detection of TBE virus in acute serum. However, real-time (TaqMan) PCR has proved sensitive in detecting West Nile virus in the CSF and serum and has been used for screening of blood products.[81a,252]

Laboratory diagnosis of most cases, especially in travelers who come to clinical attention after viremia has cleared, depends principally on the serologic testing of serum and, in the case of neurologic infections, the CSF.[253] IgM detection by antibody capture enzyme-linked immunosorbent assay (ELISA) is the preferred technique, although some laboratories successfully detect IgM and IgG antibodies by indirect immunofluorescence assay. The assay is more than 95% sensitive when serum specimens obtained between 7 and 10 days after the onset are tested. In secondary flaviviral infections, a combination of IgM and IgG ELISAs is 100% sensitive as early as 4 to 5 days after the onset of illness. Both CSF and serum should be examined in cases of flaviviral encephalitis, because IgM may appear earlier in the CSF. If both specimens are tested, positive results are obtained in almost all patients by 10 days after the onset of illness, with, in general, a 10% increase in cumulative positivity per day (see Fig. 149-7). However, some patients die without making an antibody response.[162] Serum IgM in dengue infection declines to undetectable levels within 60 days, but antibodies persist for up to 9 months in recovered StLE and TBE patients and for longer than 16 months in some WNE patients.[254] potentially limiting the specificity of tests (see later discussion).

Heterologous reactions with other flaviviruses are problematic where numerous flaviviruses cocirculate, but in tropical Asia, where only JE and dengue viruses infect humans, the infections are easily distinguished. Circumstances are more complex in Africa and even in Australia, where more flaviviruses cocirculate. Recent vaccination against JE or YF, or recent infection with dengue or StLE virus, may cause a false-positive West Nile virus IgM antibody test result; neutralization assays such as the plaque reduction neutralization test and ELISAs that detect antibody to NS5 are more specific.[255] Fractionation of IgM before hemagglutination inhibition testing and competitive epitope-blocking ELISAs improve specificity. However, among sera from African patients, all serologic approaches frequently fail to resolve previous and recent infections. Heterologous flaviviral antibodies have become an issue even among specimens submitted in the United States for arboviral diagnosis. Previous dengue infection, reflecting prior exposures in persons who have resided abroad, is now a frequent finding that can interfere with interpretation of the serologic diagnosis of a recent flaviviral infection. These heterologous dengue antibodies frequently pose difficulties in the interpretation of tests for StLE, WNE, and Powassan encephalitis. Although neutralization tests provide the greatest specificity, they are time-consuming, are expensive to perform, and are offered only in specialized laboratories. Hemagglutination inhibition and complement fixation tests are now used infrequently, but they still have utility under some circumstances. Complement fixation antibodies are relatively specific in distinguishing between antigenic complexes, and, because they rise rather late (often 4 to 6 weeks after the onset) and decline with a half-life of 3 years, positive reactions indicate infection in the intermediate period after the disappearance of IgM antibodies. Hemagglutination inhibition and neutralizing antibodies can persist for decades after infection. Rapid immunochromatographic tests formatted as small folders to detect dengue and JE IgM and IgG have demonstrated high sensitivity and specificity in field evaluations (100% and 90%, respectively, for the dengue test) and should facilitate laboratory confirmation of cases in clinical facilities.[256]

In a patient with a compatible illness, a case is confirmed by a fourfold change in the serum antibody titer or, alternatively in encephalitis patients, by the demonstration of viral-specific IgM in CSF, reflecting intrathecal immune response. An elevated serum IgM antibody level alone is considered presumptive evidence of recent infection if high IgM prevalence rates in the population prevail because of frequent asymptomatic infections and because antibodies may persist beyond a single transmission season.

Serologic testing for StLE, West Nile, dengue, and other selected arboviruses is performed at several private laboratories, most state laboratories, the Centers for Disease Control and Prevention, the U.S. Army Medical Research Institute for Infectious Diseases, and other reference laboratories. In addition, an indirect immunofluorescence assay kit for the domestic arboviruses that includes a StLE antigen can be purchased in the United States and a TBE ELISA kit can be obtained in Europe. Dengue immunochromatographic folders and ELISA kits are sold in Asia and Australia.[256]

PREVENTION AND THERAPY

Yellow Fever

Hospitalization in an intensive care facility where the patient can be sequestered from mosquitoes is recommended to provide close clinical monitoring and supportive care and to prevent anthroponotic transmission. Blood in the acute phase of illness is potentially infectious. No antiviral therapy is available, and specific supportive interventions have not been evaluated. General support with oxygen, fluids, and pressors is indicated to treat and prevent hypotension and metabolic acidosis. Histamine type 2 (H$_2$) receptor antagonists and sucralfate may be of value in preventing or ameliorating gastric bleeding. Avoidance of sedatives and drugs dependent on hepatic metabolism is prudent, and the medication-dosing intervals should be adjusted with reduced renal function. Encephalopathy should be investigated for treatable metabolic causes, particularly hypoglycemia. Fresh-frozen plasma and vitamin K have been administered to replenish clotting factors. The effect of heparin therapy is unproved. Secondary infections should be pursued and treated.

YF is vaccine-preventable with the attenuated 17D vaccine, which produces immunity in more than 95% of recipients and long-term, possibly lifelong, protection with a single 0.5-mL subcutaneous dose.[3] Vaccination has been associated with anaphylaxis in 1 of every 116,000 doses, but the relative roles of hypersensitivity to chicken eggs and gelatin are unclear, because the vaccine is produced in chick embryos, and gelatin, which is added as a vaccine stabilizer, has been implicated in other hypersensitivity events.[256a] Equally serious, however, are rare but potentially fatal cases of vaccine-associated CNS infection or systemic illness, mimicking wild-type infection, which have been reported from the United States, Brazil, Australia, and Thailand.[257-262] Although the preponderance of the 27 known vaccine-associated encephalitis cases were reported early in the history of the vaccine's use and almost exclusively in infants, four new cases in adults have been reported more recently. In addition, 12 unprecedented cases of viscerotropic disease (6 fatal) have been reported; combinations of fulminant hepatitis, shock, renal failure, and disturbances of coagulation—all consistent with YF itself—were observed, with illness commencing several days to 3 weeks after vaccination and accompanied by detection of vaccine virus in tissues or blood in some cases. Although the rate of these serious viscerotropic illnesses cannot be estimated precisely from anecdotal reports, a range of 0.1 to 2.5 cases per million doses has been inferred from available Brazilian and U.S. data, with a suggestion that elderly persons may have a higher risk.

Despite the seriousness of these vaccine-associated events, the facts of their rarity (unknown but suggested) and the potential risks of YF (six deaths in unvaccinated travelers reported since 1996) have resulted in no change in vaccine recommendations for travelers. However, providers are admonished to ensure that the traveler's destination is an endemic area, because two cases of vaccine-associated systemic illness have occurred in persons traveling to areas free of YF. Because of the well-established risk for vaccine-associated encephalitis in infants, YF vaccine is contraindicated in infants younger than 4 months of age and is recommended for 4- to 9- month-old infants only under situations of high risk. YF and measles vaccines are coadministered at the 9-month EPI visit under World Health Organization–United Nations Children's Fund recommendations in 35 African countries; however, compliance is low. The vaccine's risk in pregnancy has not been established. Cord blood IgM viral antibodies indicating congenital infection were reported in one case without evidence of birth defects.[264,.265] In small studies, the vaccine was less immunogenic in pregnant women, asymptomatic HIV-infected adults (77% antibody response), and HIV-infected infants (17% antibody response). No adverse events were reported in the latter two studies, but a fatal CNS infection has been reported in one HIV-infected vaccinee.[263-268]

Travelers to at-risk South American and African countries should receive the vaccine at 10-year intervals to meet international requirements. The vaccine can be given concurrently with measles, oral polio, hepatitis A or B, meningococcal polysaccharide, oral or intramuscular typhoid, or oral cholera vaccines; chloroquine; or immune serum globulin.

Prevention of epidemic *A. aegypti*–borne YF follows the approach for dengue control, with the reduction of peridomestic breeding sites. In dry savanna and urban locations where drinking water frequently must be stored, the simple expedient of covering the containers or reservoirs eliminates a principal source of breeding. Surveillance of viral activity by monitoring of viral infection rates in sylvatic mosquitoes has been proposed as an early warning system for West and Central Africa, where outbreaks frequently emerge in a regionwide distribution. The discovery of intensified viral activity, even in a small number of sentinel sites, may be a sufficiently sensitive predictor of viral activity in a broader area to trigger timely and effective mass immunization. In South America, surveys to detect dead monkeys on the forest floor are conducted to monitor viral transmission and risk of its spillover to humans.

Dengue and Dengue Hemorrhagic Fever

Antipyretics may help to relieve the symptoms of dengue fever, but, to avert Reye's syndrome and hemostatic complications, aspirin should not be used. Oral rehydration is indicated to replace losses from vomiting and high fever. Attentive clinical monitoring of patients with suspected DHF-DSS and anticipatory and supportive care are lifesaving and have reduced fatality rates by 50- to 100-fold. Treatment algorithms and protocols to monitor patients by clinical and laboratory markers based on the practice at the Queen Sirikit National Institute of Child Health (formerly Bangkok Children's Hospital) have been published.[268] The critical activities are monitoring of circulation and vascular leakage by serial clinical assessments of pulse, blood pressure, skin perfusion, urine output, and hematocrit, to trigger intravenous fluid therapy. An increase in hematocrit of greater than 20% (e.g., from 35% to 42%) indicates a significant loss of intravascular volume and the urgent need for fluid resuscitation. Normal saline is administered to maintain circulation and, under continued monitoring, for recurrent shock. Shock necessitates rapid intervention with isotonic crystalloid or colloid solutions, or, if needed, plasma or whole-blood transfusions.[269] Anecdotal reports suggest that desmopressin may reduce the need for intravenous fluids and improve hemostasis; however, no controlled trials have been performed.[270] Because vascular integrity is usually restored spontaneously in 48 hours, overhydration resulting in pulmonary edema is a risk, and positive-pressure ventilation with positive end-expiratory pressure may be needed. As a result of the danger of ARDS due to capillary leakage and excessive fluid administration, DHF-DSS has been reported to be the third most common cause of ARDS in hospitalized children in Malaysia.[208] Whole blood, platelet, and fresh-frozen plasma transfusions may be needed if there is significant hemorrhage, but caution is indicated in the administration of heparin except in patients with clear signs of disseminated intravascular coagulopathy.[271-272] Preventive transfusions may be harmful and should be avoided, and invasive procedures should be minimized to avoid hemorrhagic complications. Treatment to end virus replication could be beneficial, although viremia levels usually are already decreasing dramatically at the time of presentation to health care providers.[272] In some locations, intravenous gamma globulin has been used empirically, but no benefit has been established in a controlled evaluation. Neither high-dose methylprednisolone (30 mg/kg) nor AC-17 (carbazochrome sodium sulfonate), which is believed to reduce vascular permeability, was beneficial in controlled trials.[274,275] Treatment with anti-TNF antibody has increased survivability in a lethal mouse model of dengue.[276] Secondary and concurrent infections should be investigated and treated.

Dengue prevention currently relies on public health and community-based *A. aegypti* control programs to remove and destroy mosquito-breeding sites.[36] The ubiquity of containers that potentially provide breeding habitats in urban neighborhoods and individual houses makes this a formidable challenge. Although a combination of vector surveillance, area treatment, and monitoring can be effective, it has rarely been successful for prolonged periods. Insecticidal fogging is considered unhelpful, but, in sealed houses, indoor insecticidal sprays should be effectual. Several approaches to vaccine development are being pursued. The most advanced approach is a tetravalent combination of attenuated dengue strains, and other approaches are undergoing initial clinical evaluation.[276-279] Travelers are well advised to protect themselves by using repellents and insecticidal sprays indoors.

Flaviviral Encephalitis

No specific therapy for flaviviral encephalitis has been developed. Anecdotal use of interferon-alfa in the prophylaxis and/or treatment of JE and StLE cases has been reported, but a phase III randomized double-blind, placebo-controlled trial of interferon-alfa-2a in children with JE showed that it did not improve the outcome at hospital discharge or at 3 months' follow-up.[280] A mixture of JE-virus–neutralizing monoclonal antibodies was reportedly beneficial in a clinical trial in China, but considerable experience with TBE immune globulin therapy has highlighted the potential hazards of immunotherapy.[281-283] Passive immunization appears to have been associated with exacerbation of the disease, and its use, even within the recommended interval of 96 hours after a tick bite, should be undertaken with due caution. However there were no reports of such deterioration in uncontrolled trials of immune globulin in WNE,[283,284] and a multicenter controlled trial of intravenous immunoglobulin in the treatment of WNE is underway in the United States. Corticosteroid therapy for TBE resulted in a more rapid reduction of fever but prolonged hospitalization, whereas in JE a small trial of corticosteroid treatment failed to show benefit or harm.[286] In a small controlled study, tetracycline administered as an immunomodulator was shown to reduce elaboration of proinflammatory cytokines and to hasten recovery from TBE.[287]

Supportive care should focus on controlling seizures, providing ventilatory support in respiratory failure, and monitoring and reducing cerebral edema. In many parts of Asia, mannitol or corticosteroids, or both, are given to patients with severe JE. Fluid and electrolyte administration should balance circulatory needs, the avoidance of cerebral edema, and SIADH. Secondary infections should be anticipated and treated, and careful nursing attention should be paid to minimize complications such as bed sores and contractures.

Three JE vaccines are licensed, but the inactivated cell culture–derived P-3 strain vaccine and live-attenuated SA14-14-2 vaccines are distributed only in China. Three and two doses, respectively, are administered during spring campaigns to children older than 1 year, followed by a variable number of boosters for the killed vaccine. The live vaccine, however, is highly efficacious after even one dose.[2,288,289] Both vaccines have an extensive history of safe use, with respective efficacies of 85% and 98%. An inactivated mouse brain–derived vaccine produced in Japan, Korea, Taiwan, Thailand, and Vietnam is administered in early childhood in two primary doses, with four to six additional boosters at various intervals until 15 years of age.[190] The efficacy in field trials was 91%. The vaccine has been distributed internationally to military personnel and travelers in three 1-mL doses, administered subcutaneously, on days zero, 7, and 30. Angioedema and generalized urticaria with onset up to 3 days after vaccination have occurred in approximately 0.3% of vaccinees; therefore, in travelers, the series should be completed 1 week before departure.[290] Anecdotal cases of acute disseminated encephalomyelitis temporally related to vaccination have been reported.[2] Because of vaccine side effects and the slight risk of acquiring the disease during travel, vaccination is not recommended routinely and is reserved for expatriates in Asia, persons with a high risk of exposure, and travelers spending more than 30 days during the transmission season in an endemic area (see Table 149-1). However, because individual cases have occurred in travelers with exposures as brief as a few days, more liberal use of vaccine may be appropriate in some circumstances.[76-78] The sole manufacturer of JE vaccine licensed in the United States has signaled its intent to discontinue production of that product within several years, potentially leaving no vaccine available to the U.S. civilian population (although stockpiles will have been accumulated by the Defense Department). Novel inactivated, attenuated, and genetically engineered vaccines are under study and may fill the gap, including a chimeric vaccine in clinical trials that incorporates JE virus structural proteins into a live attenuated 17D YF vaccine viral backbone.[2,4,290] To minimize the risk of

acquiring infection, travelers should avoid outdoor exposure at dusk and should use mosquito repellents and mosquito-excluding bed nets.

No human vaccines against WN or StLE viruses are licensed; however, formalin-inactivated and canarypox-vectored West Nile virus vaccines for horses are commercially available in the United States. A live-attenuated chimeric West Nile/YF17D vaccine is under clinical evaluation.[4,291]

Two inactivated TBE vaccines, derived from chick embryo cells infected with Western subtype TBE virus, are licensed in Europe and distributed with considerable uptake rates in areas that have a high transmission risk.[292] Administration in three doses over a period of 1 year, with an additional booster 3 years later, has been highly effective in reducing rates of disease. An abbreviated zero, 7, and 21- or 28-day immunization schedule also is immunogenic.[103,293] Cross-protection against the Far Eastern subtype of TBE virus has been shown in animals, but clinical efficacy against the disease has not been reported. Chiefly mild adverse events (fever and local reactions) are reported; however, neurologic adverse events including Guillain-Barré syndrome have been noted, albeit without a proven causal association, in approximately 1 of every 1 million vaccinees. The vaccine is not licensed in the United States and no longer is held as an investigational new drug by the U.S. Army. For most travelers, the risk of acquiring the disease is extremely low, and personal protective measures (e.g., avoidance of risky habitats, protective clothing, use of repellents) are appropriate. Expatriates may choose to be immunized abroad, and, for the exceptional short-term traveler with high-risk activities, preexposure prophylaxis with TBE immune globulin (0.05 mL/kg intramuscularly) is an alternative, although its efficacy is unproved and breakthrough cases and enhanced disease have been reported. Live-attenuated and naked DNA vaccines are under development.

Vector control is impractical as a means of JE prevention because of the extensive areas that must be treated. Pig immunization effectively prevents abortions in sows and can modulate the transmission of disease to humans, but wide-scale implementation is impractical. Emergency truck-mounted or aerial applications of adulticides are routinely administered in response to StLE and WNE epidemics, usually in conjunction with programs of avian or mosquito surveillance that provide early warning of increased viral transmission. Public health warnings to avoid outdoor activities in the evening and rescheduling of evening high school football games and Halloween trick-or-treat activities to daylight hours were demonstrated to reduce the risk of acquiring StLE in central Florida. In the absence of effective therapies or prophylaxis, public health interventions are the only available preventive measures. Control of TBE in defined locations by the area-wide application of acaricides has been effective in reducing vector ticks, but widespread implementation is impractical.

OTHER FLAVIVIRAL INFECTIONS

Murray Valley Encephalitis

Murray Valley encephalitis virus is a member of the antigenic complex of JE, StLE, and WNE viruses, and, like them, it is transmitted in a mosquito-avian cycle, chiefly by *Culex annulirostris*. Foci of perennial viral transmission are maintained in western Australia, where sporadic cases and small outbreaks occur. Most sporadic cases occur in aboriginal children living in areas where they are exposed to the virus, but cases have also occurred among travelers to these areas.[294,295] At infrequent intervals since the initial recognition of the disease in 1917, the virus has spread to the heavily populated southeastern river valleys, where it has produced larger outbreaks, most recently in 1981. Sporadic cases also have been recognized in Papua New Guinea. Approximately 350 cases have been reported in total, with a case-fatality rate of 20% in the most recent outbreak. The onset of encephalitis is preceded by a prodrome of headache, nausea, vomiting, photophobia, and neck stiffness, followed within 2 to 5 days by changes in sensorium, stupor, and motor signs. Coma, limb paralysis, and respiratory depression necessitating ventilatory support develop in severe cases. Recovery is followed by motor paralysis in severe cases and by milder motor disturbances and emotional and psychological symptoms in a higher proportion of survivors. Serologic diagnosis is potentially encumbered by cross-reactive antibodies to Kunjin, Kokobera, JE, Edge Hill, Alfuy, Sepik, dengue, and other flaviviruses in the region. Supportive treatment has reduced mortality and morbidity. Regional surveillance of sentinel chicken infections is maintained as an early warning system.

Rocio Encephalitis

Rocio encephalitis was recognized to be the novel cause of a series of encephalitis outbreaks that occurred from 1975 to 1977 in the Ribiera Valley and Santista lowlands in coastal Sao Paulo and Paraná States, Brazil.[295] More than 1000 cases were identified, chiefly in fishermen and others with outdoor occupations. The virus was isolated from human brain, and its relationship to StLE virus was shown antigenically and, later, by genomic sequencing. The virus is transmitted from *Psorophora* mosquitoes to birds, and human infections are incidental. Sporadic asymptomatic infections have been detected in field studies, but outbreaks have not recurred. In 1996, serologic evidence of infection was reported in Bahia State, far to the north, but the virus has not been isolated outside the original focus. A prodrome of fever, headache, malaise, vomiting, and conjunctivitis precedes the onset of altered consciousness, motor weakness, and, frequently, cerebellar signs. Neurologic infection progresses to coma in one third of cases and death in 10%. Neurologic and psychological sequelae have been reported in 20% of survivors. Supportive treatment is potentially lifesaving. Emergency applications of insecticides have been implemented in outbreak control.

Kyasanur Forest Disease

The report of an outbreak of monkey deaths and hemorrhagic fever with jaundice in 1957 in the Kyasanur Forest of Mysore (now Karnataka) State, India, triggered an investigation of what was suspected to be the much-feared introduction of YF to Asia.[296,297] The virus, isolated from dead langur monkeys and *Haemaphysalis* ticks, was shown to be a novel member of the antigenic complex of tick-borne flaviviruses that was transmitted between various ixodid ticks and forest rodents, insectivores, and monkeys. That epidemic and subsequent sporadic cases and outbreaks occurred during the dry season among peasants clearing forests for pasture, and the endemic area gradually spread and enlarged in connection with those activities. Serologic evidence of infection has also been reported in northwestern India and from the Andaman Islands. Between 1982 and 1988, 1847 cases were reported. The incubation period is 3 to 8 days, after which illness begins abruptly with fever, headache, chills, vomiting, myalgia, photophobia, and conjunctival suffusion. Facial and conjunctival hyperemia, lymphadenopathy, hepatosplenomegaly, and petechiae are found on examination. Diffuse hemorrhages from the nares, gums, and gastrointestinal tract develop, with hemorrhagic pulmonary edema in 40% of cases and renal failure in severe cases. After defervescence and a remission of symptoms for as long as 1 to 3 weeks, a second phase of illness develops, with neurologic symptoms in 15% to 50% of patients. Laboratory findings are similar to those of DHF, with leukopenia, thrombocytopenia, an elevated hematocrit reflecting hemoconcentration, and elevated hepatic transaminase levels. Patients have detectable viremias up to 12 days after the onset of illness. Between 5% and 10% of cases are fatal, and iridokeratitis has been reported in survivors. An inactivated chick embryo–derived vaccine is produced locally and distributed in response to epidemics. A related virus was recently isolated from abattoir workers in Saudi Arabia who developed a similar illness. The origin and reservoir of this virus are unknown, but it is speculated that infection may have been transmitted from imported viremic sheep at slaughter or from their infected ticks.

Omsk Hemorrhagic Fever

Omsk hemorrhagic fever virus is transmitted between *Dermacentor* ticks and small mammals in forest-steppe zones of the Omsk, Novosibirsk, Kurgan, and Tjumen regions of western Siberia, but the disease emerged in significant form only after muskrats were introduced to the region to establish a fur industry.[298] Outbreaks between 1945 and 1958 led to muskrat epizootics and 1500 human cases, chiefly among trappers, their family members, and laboratory workers. Infection is transmitted directly from infected animal tissues or by tick bite, with a peak in spring or early summer and another peak in autumn. The illness resembles Kyasanur Forest disease, but neuropsychiatric sequelae have been reported more often. The case-fatality rate is less than 3%. Inactivated TBE vaccine (produced in Russia) has been reported to offer cross-protection against the disease.

Less Commonly Recognized Flaviviral Infections

Small numbers or even single cases of the diseases listed in Table 149-3 have been reported. In some instances, experimental human infection (evaluated as cancer therapy) provides the only knowledge of their pathogenicity.

TABLE 149-3 Less Commonly Recognized Flaviviral Infections

Virus and Ref. No.	Clinical Syndrome	Geographic Distribution	Transmission Cycle	Mode of Transmission
Alkhurma[106,107]	Hemorrhagic fever, encephalitis	Saudi Arabia	Presumably tick-borne	DC, ?V
Alma-Arasan[299]	Febrile illness, meningitis	Kazakhstan	*Ixodes persulcatus*–?	V
Apoi[307]	Encephalitis	Japan	Rodent–?	L
Banzi[300]	Nonspecific febrile illness	South and East Africa	*Culex rubinotus*–rodent	V
Bussuquara[301]	Fever, arthralgias	Brazil, Colombia, Panama	*Culex melaconion* spp.–rodent	V
Edge Hill[302]	Fever, polyarthritis	Australia	*Aedes vigilax*–marsupial	V
Ilhéus[301,303]	Fever, myalgia, encephalitis	Argentina, Brazil, Colombia, Guatemala, Panama, Trinidad	*Psorophora ferox*–bird	V, E
Karshi[299]	Nonspecific febrile illness	Uzbekistan	Various ticks–rodent	V
Kokobera[304]	Fever, polyarthralgia	Australia, Papua New Guinea	*Culex annulirostris*–? Marsupial	V
Koutango[1]	Fever, rash, arthralgia	West and Central Africa	Tick–rodent	L
Kunjin[80]	Fever, polyarthralgia, encephalitis	Australia, Malaysia, Thailand	*Culex annulirostris*–bird	V
Langat[305]	Fever, encephalitis	Malaysia, Thailand, Russia	*Ixodes* tick–rodent	V
Modoc[306]	Aseptic meningitis	Western United States, Canada	Rodent–rodent	Z
Negishi[307]	Encephalitis	Japan, China, Russia	Tick–unknown	L, V
Rio Bravo[308]	Nonspecific febrile illness, meningitis	Western United States, Canada	Bat–bat	Z, L
Sepik[309]	Nonspecific febrile illness	Papua New Guinea	*Mansonia* spp.–?	V
SPH 16111–related viruses[310]	Pneumonia, encephalitis, lymphadenopathy, rash	São Paulo, Brazil	Unknown	U
Spondweni[311]	Fever, arthralgia, rash	South and West Africa	*Aedes* spp.–?	L, V
Usutu[312]	Fever, rash	South and Central Africa	*Culex* spp.–bird	V
Wesselsbron[313]	Fever, arthralgia, rash, encephalitis	Sub-Saharan Africa, Thailand	*Aedes* spp.–?	V, L, DC
Zika[314]	Fever, rash, arthralgia	West, East, and Central Africa; Indonesia, Malaysia	*Aedes* spp.–monkey	V

DC, contact with infected sheep; E, experimental infection; L, laboratory-acquired infection; U, unknown; V, vector-borne; Z, zoonotic infection.

REFERENCES

1. Burke DS, Monath TP. Flaviviruses. In: Fields BN, Howley PM, Griffin DE, et al., eds. Field's Virology. 4th ed. New York: Lippincott Williams-Wilkins; 2001;1043-1126.
2. Halstead SB, Tsai TF. Japanese encephalitis vaccines. In: Plotkin SA, Orenstein WA, eds. Vaccines. 4th ed. Philadelphia: WB Saunders; 2004:919-958.
3. Monath TP. Yellow fever vaccine. In: Plotkin SA, Orenstein WA, eds. Vaccines. 4th ed. Philadelphia: WB Saunders; 2004:815-880.
4. Chang GJ, Kuno G, Purdy DE, Davis BS. Recent advancement in flavivirus vaccine developments. Exp Rev Vaccine 2004;3:199-220.
5. Ryan ET, Wilson ME, Kain KC. Illness after international travel. N Engl J Med. 2002;347:505-516.
6. Tsai TF, Niklasson B. Arboviruses and zoonotic viruses. In: DuPont HL, Steffen R eds. Textbook of Travel Medicine and Health. 2nd ed. Hamilton, Ontario: BC Decker; 2001:290-312.
7. Heinz FX, Allison SL. Flavivirus structure and membrane fusion. Adv Virus Res. 2003;59:63-97.
8. Kuhn RJ, Zhang W, Rossmann MG, et al. Structure of dengue virus: Implications for flavivirus organization, maturation, and fusion. Cell. 2002;108:717-725.
9. Monath TP, Arroyo J, Levenbook I, et al. Single mutation in the flavivirus envelope protein hinge region increases neurovirulence for mice and monkeys but decreases viscerotropism for monkeys: Relevance to development and safety testing of live, attenuated vaccines. J Virol. 2002;76:1932-1943.
10. Co MD, Terajima M, Cruz J, et al. Human cytotoxic T lymphocyte responses to live attenuated 17D yellow fever vaccine: Identification of HLA-B35-restricted CTL epitopes on nonstructural proteins NS1, NS2b, NS3, and the structural protein E. Virology. 2002;293:151-163.
11. Brinton MA, Perelygen AA. Genetic resistance to flaviviruses. Adv Virus Res. 2003;60:43-85.
12. Stephens HA, Klaythong R, Sirikong M, et al. HLA-A and -B allele associations with secondary dengue virus infections correlate with disease severity and the infecting viral serotype in ethnic Thais. Tissue Antigens. 2002;60:309-318.
13. Wei HY, Jiang LF, Fang DY, Guo HY. Dengue virus type 2 infects human endothelial cells through binding of the viral envelope glycoprotein to cell surface polypeptides. J Gen Virol. 2003;84:3095-3098.
14. Hilgard P, Stockert R. Heparan sulfate proteoglycans initiate dengue virus infection of hepatocytes. Hepatology. 2000;32:1069-1077.
15. Van Regenmortel M, Fauquet CM, Bishop DH. Flaviviruses. In: Virus Taxonomy. Seventh Report of the International Committee on Taxonomy of Viruses. San Diego, Calif: Academic Press 2000:859-878.
16. Kuno G, Chang WJ, Tsuchiya KR, et al. Phylogeny of the genus *Flavivirus*. J Virol. 1998;72:73.
17. Chang GJ, Cropp BC, Kinney RM, et al. Nucleotide sequence variation of the envelope protein gene identifies two distinct genotypes of yellow fever virus. J Virol. 1995;69:5773.
18. Rico-Hesse R, Harrison LM, Salas RA, et al. Origins of dengue type 2 viruses associated with increased pathogenicity in the Americas. Virology. 1997;230:244.
19. Hanna JN, Ritchie SA, Phillips DA, et al. An outbreak of Japanese encephalitis in the Torres Strait, Australia, 1995. Med J Aust. 1996;165:256.
20. Lanciotti RS, Ebel GD, Deubel V, et al. Complete genome sequences and phylogenetic analysis of West Nile virus strains isolated from the United States, Europe, and the Middle East. Virology. 2002;298:96-105.
21. Trent DW, Monath TP, Bown GS, et al. Variation among strains of St Louis encephalitis virus: Basis for a genetic, pathogenic and epidemiologic classification. Ann N Y Acad Sci. 1980;354:219.
22. Rico-Hesse R. Microevolution and virulence of dengue viruses. Adv Virus Res. 2003;59:315-341.
23. Monath TP. Yellow fever: An update. Lancet Infect Dis 2001;1:11-20.
24. Barrett AD, Monath TP. Epidemiology and ecology of yellow fever virus. Adv Virus Res. 2003;61:291-315.
25. Robertson SE, Hull BP, Tomori O, et al. Yellow fever: A decade of reemergence. JAMA. 1996;276:1157.
26. Monath TP: Yellow fever: Victor, victoria? Conqueror, conquest? Epidemics and research in the last forty years and prospects for the future. Am J Trop Med Hyg. 1991;45:1.
27. de Filippis AM, Nogueira RM, Schatzmayr HG, et al. Outbreak of jaundice and hemorrhagic fever in the southeast of Brazil in 2001: Detection and molecular characterization of yellow fever virus. J Med Virol. 2002;68:620-627.
28. Vasconcelos PF, Costa ZG, Travassos Da Rosa ES, et al. Epidemic of jungle yellow fever in Brazil, 2000: Implications of climatic alterations in disease spread. J Med Virol. 2001;65:598-604.
29. Van der Stuyft P, Gianella A, Pirard M, et al. Urbanisation of yellow fever in Santa Cruz, Bolivia. Lancet. 1999;353:1558-1562.
30. Monath TP, Nasidi A. Should yellow fever vaccine be included in the expanded program of immunization in Africa? A cost-effectiveness analysis for Nigeria. Am J Trop Med Hyg. 1993;48:274.
31. World Health Organization. Technical Guide for Diagnosis, Treatment, Surveillance, Prevention, and Control of Dengue Haemorrhagic Fever. 2nd ed. Geneva: World Health Organization, 1997.
32. Wang E, Ni H, Xu R, Barrett AD, et al. Evolutionary relationships of endemic/epidemic and sylvatic dengue viruses. J Virol. 2000;74:3227-3234.
33. Reiter P, Lathrop S, Bunning M, et al. Texas lifestyle limits transmission of dengue virus. Emerg Infect Dis. 2003;9:86-89.
34. Gubler DJ. Dengue and dengue hemorrhagic fever. Clin Microbiol Rev. 1998;11:480.
35. Kuno G. Factors influencing the transmission of dengue viruses. In: Gubler DJ, Kuno G, eds. Dengue and Dengue Hemorrhagic Fever. New York: CAB International; 1997:61.
36. Reiter P, Gubler DJ. Surveillance and control of urban dengue vectors. In: Gubler DJ, Kuno G, eds. Dengue and Dengue Hemorrhagic Fever. New York: CAB International; 1997:425.
37. De Benedictis J, Chow-Shaffer E, Costero A, et al. Identification of the people from whom engorged Aedes aegypti took blood meals in Florida, Puerto Rico, using polymerase chain reaction-based DNA profiling. Am J Trop Med Hyg. 2003;68:437-446.
38. Burke DS, Nisalak A, Johnson DE, et al. A prospective study of dengue infections in Bangkok. Am J Trop Med Hyg. 1988;38:172.
39. Sangkawibha N, Rohanasuphor S, Ahandrik S, et al. Risk factors in dengue shock syndrome: A prospective study in Rayong, Thailand. I. The 1980 outbreak. Am J Epidemiol. 1984;120:653.
40. Thein S, Aung MM, Shwe TN, et al. Risk factors in dengue shock syndrome. Am J Trop Med Hyg. 1997;56:566.
41. Halstead SB. Dengue and hemorrhagic fevers of Southeast Asia. Yale J Biol Med. 1965;37:434.
42. Nguyen TH, Lei HY, Nguyen TL, et al. Dengue hemorrhagic fever in infants. J Infect Dis. 2004;189:221-232.
43. Kliks S, Nisalak A, Brandt WE, et al. Evidence that maternal dengue antibodies are important in the development of dengue hemorrhagic fever in infants. Am J Trop Med Hyg. 1988;38:411.
44. Watanaveeradej V, Endy TP, Samakoses R, et al. Transplacentally transferred maternal-infant antibodies to dengue virus. Am J Trop Med Hyg. 2003;69:123-128.
45. Kouri GP, Guzman MG, Bravo JR, et al. Dengue haemorrhagic fever/dengue shock syndrome: Lessons from the Cuban epidemic. Bull World Health Organ. 1989;67:375.
46. Guzman MG, Kouri G, Valdes L, et al. Epidemiologic studies on Dengue in Santiago de Cuba, 1997. Am J Epidemiol. 2000;152:793-799.
47. Scott RM, Nimmanitya S, Bancroft WH, et al. Shock syndrome in primary dengue infections. Am J Trop Med Hyg. 1976;25:866.
48. Rosen L. Comments on the epidemiology, pathogenesis and control of dengue. Med Trop (Mars). 1999;59:495-498.
49. Bravo JR, Guzman MG, Louri GP. Why dengue hemorrhagic fever in Cuba? I. Individual risk factors for dengue hemorrhagic fever/dengue shock syndrome. Trans R Soc Trop Med Hyg. 1987;81:816.
50. Thisyakorn U, Nimmanitya S. Nutritional status of children with dengue hemorrhagic fever. Clin Infect Dis. 1993;16:295.
51. Chiewslip P, Scott RM, Bhamarapravati N. Histocompatibility antigens and dengue hemorrhagic fever. Am J Trop Med Hyg. 1981;30:1100.
52. Halstead SB. The XXth century dengue pandemic: Need for surveillance and research. World Health Stat Q. 1992;45:292-298.
53. Kalayanarooj S, Vaughn DW, Nimmanitya S, et al. Early clinical and laboratory indicators of acute dengue illness. J Infect Dis. 1997;176:313.
54. Castleberry JS, Mahon CR. Dengue fever in the Western Hemisphere. Clin Lab Sci. 2003;16:34-38.
55. Ramirez-Ronda CH, Garcia CD. Dengue in the Western Hemisphere. Infect Dis Clin North Am. 1994;8:107.
56. Thomas SJ, Strickman D, Vaughn DW. Dengue epidemiology: Virus epidemiology, ecology, and emergence. Adv Virus Res. 2003;61:235-289.
57. International Society for Infectious Diseases. www.promedmail.org.
58. Guzman MG, Kouri G. Dengue and dengue hemorrhagic fever in the Americas: Lessons and challenges. J Clin Virol. 2003;27:1-13.
59. Guzman MG, Vazquez S, Martinez E, et al. Dengue in Nicaragua, 1994: Reintroduction of serotype 3 in the Americas. Bol Oficina Sanit Panam. 1996;12:102-110.
60. Imported dengue—United States, 1999-2000. MMWR Morb Mortal Wkly Rep. 2002;51:281-283.
61. McCoy OR, Sabin AB. Dengue. In: Coates JB, Hoff EC, Hoff PM, eds. Preventive medicine in World War II: Communicable disease. VII. Arthropodborne Diseases Other Than Malaria. Washington, DC: Office of the Surgeon General; 1946:29-62.
62. Trofa AF, DeFraites RF, Smoak BL, et al. Dengue in US military personnel in Haiti. JAMA. 1997;277:1546.
63. Jelinek T, Muhlberger N, Harms G, et al. Epidemiology and clinical features of imported dengue in Europe: Sentinel surveillance data from TropNetEurop. Clin Infect Dis. 2002;35:1047-1052.
64. Rawlings JA, Hendricks KA, Burgess CR, et al. Dengue surveillance in Texas, 1995. Am J Trop Med Hyg. 1998;59:95.
65. Langgartner J, Audebert F, Scholmerich J, Gluck T. Dengue virus infection transmitted by needle stick injury. J Infect. 2002;44:269-270.
66. Rojanasuphot S, Tsai TF, eds. Regional Workshop on Control Strategies for Japanese Encephalitis. Southeast Asian J Trop Med Public Health. 1995;26:S3.
67. Endy TP, Nisalak A. Japanese encephalitis virus: Ecology and epidemiology. Curr Top Microbiol Immunol. 2002;267:11-48.
68. Tsai TF. New initiatives for the control of Japanese encephalitis by vaccination. Minutes of a WHO/CVI meeting, Bangkok, Thailand, 13-15 October 1998. Vaccine. 2000;18(Suppl):21-25.
69. Paul WS, Moore PS, Karabatsos N, et al. Outbreak of Japanese encephalitis on the island of Saipan, 1990. J Infect Dis. 1993;167:1053.
70. Mackenzie JS, Johansen CA, Ritchie SA, et al. Japanese encephalitis as an emerging virus: The emergence and spread of Japanese encephalitis virus in Australasia. Curr Top Microbiol Immunol. 2002;267:49-73.
71. Solomon T, Ni H, Beasley DW, et al. Origin and evolution of Japanese encephalitis virus in southeast Asia. J Virol. 2003;77:3091-3098.
72. Solomon T, Winter PM. Neurovirulence and host factors in flavivirus infections: Evidence from clinical epidemiology. Arch Virol. 2004;18:161-170.
73. Rosen L. The natural history of Japanese encephalitis virus. Ann Rev Microbiol. 1986;40:395.

74. Kitaoka M. Shift of age distribution of cases of Japanese encephalitis in Japan during the period 1950 to 1967. In: Hammon WMcD, Kitaoka M, Downs WG, eds. Immunization for Japanese Encephalitis. Tokyo: Igaku-Shoin; 1972:287-291.

75. Tsai TF. Immunization Practices Advisory Committee (ACIP). Inactivated Japanese encephalitis virus vaccine: Recommendations of the ACIP. MMWR Morb Mortal Wkly Rep. 1993;42(RR-1):1-15.

76. Wittesjo B, Eitrem R, Niklasson B, et al. Japanese encephalitis after a 10-day holiday in Bali. Lancet. 1995;345:856-857.

77. Buhl MR, Black FT, Andersen PL, Laursen A. Fatal Japanese encephalitis in a Danish tourist visiting Bali for 12 days. Scand J Infect Dis. 1996;28:189.

78. Shlim DR, Solomon T. Japanese encephalitis vaccine for travelers: Exploring the limits of risk. Clin Infect Dis. 2002;35:183-188.

79. Campbell GL, Marfin AA, Lanciotti RS, Gubler DJ. West Nile virus. Lancet Infect Dis. 2002;9:519-529.

80. Solomon T, Ooi MH West Nile encephalitis. BMJ. 2003;326:865-869.

81. Pealer LN, Marfin AA, Petersen LR, et al. Transmission of West Nile virus through blood transfusion in the United States in 2002. N Eng J Med. 2003;349:1236-1245.

81a. Ravindra KV, Freifeld AG, Kalil AC, et al. West Nile virus–associated encephalitis in recipients of renal and pancreatic transplants: Case series and literature review. Clin Infect Dis. 2004;38:1257-1260.

82. Rappole JH, Derrickson SR, Hubalek Z. Migratory birds and spread of West Nile virus in the Western Hemisphere. Emerg Infect Dis. 2000;6:319-328.

83. Lanciotti RS, Roehrig JT, Deubel V, et al. Origin of the West Nile virus responsible for an outbreak of encephalitis in the northeastern United States. Science. 1999;286:2333-2337.

84. Tsai TF, Popovici F, Cernescu C, et al. West Nile encephalitis epidemic in southeastern Romania. Lancet. 1998;352:767-771.

85. Taylor R, Work T, et al. A study of the ecology of West Nile virus in Egypt. Am J Trop Med Hyg. 1956;5:579-620.

86. McIntosh BM, Jupp PG. Epidemics of West Nile and Sindbis viruses in South Africa with *Culex (culex) univittatus* Theobold as vector. S Afr J Sci. 1976;72:295-300.

87. Monath TP. Epidemiology. In: Monath TP, ed. St Louis encephalitis. Washington, DC: American Public Health Association, 1980:239.

88. Monath TP, Tsai TF. St Louis encephalitis: Lessons from the last decade. Am J Med Hyg. 1987;37:40S.

89. Reisen WK. Epidemiology of St. Louis encephalitis virus. Adv Virus Res. 2003;61:139-183.

90. Okhuysen PC, Crane JK, Pappas J. St. Louis encephalitis in patients with human immunodeficiency virus infection. Clin Infect Dis. 1993;17:140.

91. Jones SC, Morris J, Hill G, et al. St. Louis encephalitis outbreak in Louisiana in 2001. J La State Med Soc. 2002;154:303 306.

92. Meehan PJ, Wells DL, Paul W, et al. Epidemiological features of and public health response to a St. Louis encephalitis epidemic in Florida, 1990-1991. Epidemiol Infect. 2000;125:181-188.

93. Luby JP, Miller G, Gardner P, et al. The epidemiology of St Louis encephalitis in Houston, Texas, 1964. Am J Epidemiol. 1967;86:584.

94. Gritsun TS, Lashkevich VA, Gould EA. Tick-borne encephalitis. Antiviral Res. 2003;57:129-146.

95. Randolph S. Predicting the risk of tick-borne diseases. Int J Med Microbiol. 2002;291(Suppl 33):6-10.

96. Suss J. Epidemiology and ecology of TBE relevant to the production of effective vaccines. Vaccine. 2003;21(Suppl 1):S19-S35.

97. Heinz FX. Molecular aspects of TBE virus research. Vaccine. 2003;21(Suppl 1): S3-S10.

98. Kunz C. TBE vaccination and the Austrian experience. Vaccine. 2003;21(Suppl 1):S50-S55.

99. Nuttall PA, Labuda M. Dynamics of infection in tick vectors and at the tick-host interface. Adv Virus Res. 2003;60:233-272.

100. Daniel M, Kolar J, Zeman P, et al. Predictive map of *Ixodes ricinus* high-incidence habitats and a tick-borne encephalitis risk assessment using satellite data. Exp Appl Acarol. 1998;22:417.

101. Daniel M, Danielova V, Kriz B, et al. Shift of the tick *Ixodes ricinus* and tick-borne encephalitis to higher altitudes in central Europe. Eur J Clin Microbiol Infect Dis. 2003;22:327-328. Epub 2003 May 08.

102. McNeil JG, Lednar WM, Stansfield SK, et al. Central European tick-borne encephalitis: Assessment of risk for persons in the armed services and vacationers. J Infect Dis. 1985;152:650.

103. Craig SC, Pittman PR, Lewis TE, et al. An accelerated schedule for tick-borne encephalitis vaccine: The American Military experience in Bosnia. Am J Trop Med Hyg. 1999;61:874-878.

104. Davidson MM, Williams H, MacLoed JA. Louping ill in man: A forgotten disease. J Infect. 1991;23:241.

105. Woodall JP, Roz A. Experimental milk-borne transmission of Powassan virus in the goat. Am J Trop Med Hyg. 1977;26:190.

106. Zaki AM. Isolation of a flavivirus related to the tick-borne encephalitis complex from human cases in Saudi Arabia. Trans R Soc Trop Med Hyg. 1997;91:179.

107. Charrel RN, de Lamballerie X. The Alkhurma virus (family Flaviviridae, genus Flavivirus): An emerging pathogen responsible for hemorrhage fever in the Middle East. Med Trop (Mars). 2003;63:296-299.

108. Kuno G, Artsob H, Karabatsos N, et al. Genomic sequencing of deer tick virus and phylogeny of Powassan-related viruses of North America. Am J Trop Med Hyg. 2001;65:671-676.

109. Hacker UT, Jelinek T, Erhardt S, et al. In vivo synthesis of tumor necrosis factor-α in healthy humans after live yellow fever vaccination. J Infect Dis. 1998;177:774.

110. Bonnevie-Nielsen V, Heron I, Monath TP, Calisher CH. Lymphocytic 2′,5′-oligoadenylate synthetase activity increases prior to the appearance of neutralizing antibodies and immunoglobulin M and immunoglobulin G antibodies after primary and secondary immunization with yellow fever vaccine. Clin Diagn Lab Immunol. 1995;2:302-306.

111. Wheelock EF, Sibley WA. Circulating virus, interferon and antibody after vaccination with the 17-D strain of yellow fever virus. N Engl J Med. 1965;273:194-198.

112. Monath TP, Ballinger ME, Miller BR, Salaun JJ. Detection of yellow fever viral RNA by nucleic acid hybridization and viral antigen by immunocytochemistry in fixed human liver. Am J Trop Med Hyg. 1989;40:663.

113. Deubel V, Huerre M, Cathomas G, et al. Molecular detection and characterization of yellow fever virus in blood and liver specimens of a non-vaccinated fatal human case. J Med Virol. 1997;53:212.

114. DeBrito T, Sigueira SAC, Santos RTM, et al. Human fatal yellow fever: Immunohistochemical detection of viral antigens in the liver, kidney and heart. Pathol Res Pract. 1992;188:177.

115. Monath TP. Yellow fever: A medically neglected disease. Rev Infect Dis. 1987;9:165.

116. Monath TP. The absence of yellow fever in Asia: Hypotheses. A cause for concern? Virus Inform Exch Newslett. 1989;6:106-107.

117. DeVries RRP, Meera Khan P, Bernini LF, et al. Genetic control of survival in epidemics. J Immunogenet. 1979;6:271-287.

118. Monath TP, Hadler SC. Type B hepatitis and yellow fever infections in West Africa. Trans R Soc Trop Med Hyg. 1987;18:172-173.

119. Halstead SB, Shotwell H, Casals J. Studies on the pathogenesis of dengue infection in monkeys. II. Clinical laboratory responses to heterologous infection. J Infect Dis. 1973;128:15-22.

120. Halstead SB. Antibody, macrophages, dengue virus infection, shock and hemorrhage: A pathogenetic cascade. Rev Infect Dis. 1989;11:S830.

121. Halstead SB. Pathogenesis of dengue: Challenges to molecular biology. Science. 1988;239:476-481.

122. Wu SJ, Grouard-Vogel G, Sun W, et al. Human skin Langerhans cells are targets of dengue virus infection. Nat Med. 2000;6:816-820.

123. Jessie K, Fong MY, Devi S, Wong KT. Localization of dengue virus in naturally infected human tissues by immunohistochemistry and in situ hybridization. J Infect Dis. 2004;189:1411-1418.

124. Vaughn DW, Green S, Kalayanarooj S, et al. Dengue in the early febrile phase: Viremia and antibody responses. J Infect Dis. 1997;176:322.

125. Vaughn DW, Green S, Kalayanarooj S, et al. Dengue viremia titer, antibody response pattern, and virus serotype correlate with disease severity. J Infect Dis. 2000;181:2-9.

126. Malheiros SMF, Oliveira ASB, Schmidt B, et al. Dengue: Muscle biopsy findings in 15 patients. Arq Neuropsiquiatr. 1993;51:159.

127. Desruelles F, Lamaury I, Roudier M, et al. Cutaneo-mucous manifestations of dengue (in French). Ann Dermatol Venereol. 1997;124:237.

128. Kuo C-H, Tai D-I, Chang-Chien C-S, et al. Liver biochemical tests and dengue fever. Am J Trop Med Hyg. 1992;47:265.

129. Kalayanarooj S, Vaughn DW, Nimmannitya S. Early clinical and laboratory indicators of acute dengue illness. J Infect Dis. 1997;176:313-321.

130. Bhamarapravati N, Toochinda P, Boonyapaknavik V. Pathology of Thailand hemorrhagic fever. V. A study of 100 autopsy cases. Ann Trop Med Parasitol. 1967;61:500.

131. Lum LCS, Lam SK, Choy YS, et al. Dengue encephalitis: A true entity? Am J Trop Med Hyg. 1996;54:256.

132. Hommel D, Talarmin A, Deubel V, et al. Dengue encephalitis in French Guinea. Res Virol. 1998;149:235.

133. Solomon T, Dung NM, Vaughn DW, et al. Neurological manifestations of dengue infection. Lancet. 2000;355:1053-1059.

134. Monath TP Early indicators in acute dengue infection. Lancet. 1997;350:1719-1720.

135. Halstead SB. Antibody, macrophages, dengue virus infection, shock, and hemorrhage: A pathogenetic cascade. Rev Infect Dis. 1989;11(Suppl 4):S830-S839.

136. Mongkolsapaya J, Dejnirattisai W, Xu XN, et al. Original antigenic sin and apoptosis in the pathogenesis of dengue hemorrhagic fever. Nat Med. 2003;9:921-927.

137. Espina LM, Valero NJ, Hernandez JM, Mosquera JA. Increased apoptosis and expression of tumor necrosis factor-alpha caused by infection of cultured human monocytes with dengue virus. Am J Trop Med Hyg. 2003;68:48-53.

138. Gagnon SJ, Mori M, Kurane I, et al. Cytokine gene expression and protein production in peripheral blood mononuclear cells of children with acute dengue virus infection. J Med Virol. 2002;67:41-46.

139. Green S, Vaughn DW, Kalayanarooj S, et al. Elevated plasma interleukin-10 levels in acute dengue correlate with disease severity. J Med Virol. 1999;59:329-334.

140. Kurane I, Ennis FA. Cytokines in dengue virus infections: Role of cytokines in the pathogenesis of dengue hemorrhagic fever. Semin Virol. 1994;5:443.

141. Bethell DB, Flobbe K, Phuong CXT, et al. Pathophysiologic and prognostic role of cytokines in dengue hemorrhagic fever. J Infect Dis. 1998;177:778.

142. Avirutnan P, Malasit P, Seliger B, et al. Dengue virus infection of human endothelial cells leads to chemokine production, complement activation, and apoptosis. J Immunol. 1998;161:6338.

143. Rothman AL. Immunology and immunopathogenesis of dengue disease. Adv Virus Res. 2003;60:397-419.

144. Bokisch VA, Top FH Jr, Russel PK, et al. The potential pathogenic role of complement in dengue hemorrhagic shock syndrome. N Engl J Med. 1973;289:996.

145. Kabra SK, Juneja R, Madhulika, et al. Myocardial dysfunction in children with dengue haemorrhagic fever. Natl Med J India. 1998;11:59.

146. Huang YH, Lei HY, Liu HS, et al. Tissue plasminogen activator induced by dengue virus infection of human endothelial cells. J Med Virol. 2003;70:610-616.

147. Krishnamurti C, Kalayanarooj S, Cutting MA, et al. Mechanisms of hemorrhage in dengue without circulatory collapse. Am J Trop Med Hyg. 2001;65:840-847.

148. Mairuhu AT, MacGillavry MR, Setiati TE, et al. Is clinical outcome of dengue-virus infections influenced by coagulation and fibrinolysis? A critical review of the evidence. Lancet Infect Dis. 2003;3:33-41.

149. Falconar AKI. The dengue virus nonstructural-1 protein (NS1) generates antibodies to common epitopes on human blood clotting, integrin/adhesin proteins and binds to human endothelial cells: Potential implications in haemorrhagic fever pathogenesis. Arch Virol. 1997;142:897.

150. Kliks SC, Nisalak A, Brandt WE, et al. Antibody dependent enhancement of dengue virus growth in human monocytes as a risk factor for dengue hemorrhagic fever. Am J Trop Med Hyg. 1989;40:444.

151. Halsted SB. Neutralization of antibody-dependent enhancement of dengue virus. Adv Virus Res. 2003;60:421-467.

152. Mullbacher A, Lobigs M. Up-regulation of MHC class I by flavivirus-induced peptide translocation into the endoplasmic reticulum. Immunity. 1995;3:207.

153. Mongkolsapaya J, Dejnirattsai W, Xu XN, et al. Original antigenic sin in the pathogenesis of dengue hemorrhagic fever. Nature Medicine. 2003;9:21-27.

154. Vaughn DW. Invited commentary: Dengue lessons from Cuba. Am J Epidemiol. 2000;152:800-803.

155. Watts DM, Porter KR, Putvatana P, et al. Failure of secondary infection with American genotype dengue 2 to cause dengue haemorrhagic fever. Lancet. 1999;354:1431-1434.

156. Kochel TJ, Watts DM, Halstead SB, et al. Effect of dengue-1 antibodies on American dengue-2 viral infection and dengue haemorrhagic fever. Lancet. 2002;360:310-312.

157. Deparis X, Murgue B, Roche C, et al. Changing clinical and biological manifestations of dengue during the dengue-2 epidemic in French Polynesia in 1996/97: Description and analysis in a prospective study. Trop Med Int Health. 1998;3:859.

158. Mathew A, Kurane I, Green S, et al. Predominance of HLA-restricted cytotoxic T-lymphocyte responses to serotype-cross-reactive epitopes on nonstructural proteins following natural secondary dengue virus infection. J Virol. 1998;72:3999-4004.

159. Kurane I, Zeng L, Brinton MA, Ennis FA. Definition of an epitope on NS3 recognized by human CD4+ cytotoxic T lymphocyte clones cross-reactive for dengue virus types 2, 3, and 4. Virology. 1998;240:169-174.

160. Mangada MM, Endy TP, Nisalak A, et al. Dengue-specific T cell responses in peripheral blood mononuclear cells obtained prior to secondary dengue virus infections in Thai schoolchildren. J Infect Dis. 2002;185:1697-1703.

161. Chambers TJ, Diamond MS. Pathogenesis of flavivirus encephalitis. Adv Virus Res. 2003;60:273-342.

162. Solomon T, Vaughn DW. Pathogenesis and clinical features of Japanese encephalitis and West Nile virus infections. Curr Top Microbiol Immunol. 2002;267:171-194.

163. Johnson RT, Burke DS, Elwell M, et al. Japanese encephalitis: Immunocytochemical studies of viral antigen and inflammatory cells in fatal cases. Ann Neurol. 1985;18:567.

164. Desai A, Shankar SK, Ravi V, et al. Japanese encephalitis virus antigen in the human brain and its topographic distribution. Acta Neuropathol. 1995;89:368.

165. Johnson RT, Intralawan P, Puapanwatton S. Japanese encephalitis: Identification of inflammatory cells in cerebrospinal fluid. Ann Neurol. 1986;20:691.

166. Tomazic J, Ihan A. Flow cytometric analysis of lymphocytes in cerebrospinal fluid in patients with tick-borne encephalitis. Acta Neurol Scand. 1997;95:29.

167. Tomazic J, Ihan A, Strle F, et al. Immunological differentiation between tickborne encephalitis with and without concomitant neuroborreliosis. Eur J Clin Microbiol Infect Dis. 1997;16:920.

168. Holub M, Kluckova Z, Beran O, et al. Lymphocyte subset numbers in cerebrospinal fluid: Comparison of tick-borne encephalitis and neuroborreliosis. Acta Neurol Scand. 2002;106:302-308.

169. Leake CJ, Burke DS, Nisalak A, Hoke CH. Isolation of Japanese encephalitis virus from clinical specimens using a continuous mosquito cell line. Am J Trop Med Hyg. 1986;35:1045-1050.

169a. Kumar P, Sulochana P, Nirmala G, et al. Impaired T helper 1 function of nonstructural protein 3-specific T cells in Japanese patients with encephalitis with neurological sequelae. J Infect Dis. 2004;189:880-891.

170. Desai A, Ravi V, Guru SC, et al. Detection of autoantibodies to neural antigens in the CSF of Japanese encephalitis patients and correlation of findings with the outcome. J Neurol Sci. 1994;122:109.

171. Desai A, Ravi V, Chandramuki A, Gourie-Devi M. Proliferative response of human peripheral blood mononuclear cells to Japanese encephalitis virus. Microbiol Immunol. 1995;39:269.

172. Leyssen P, Paeshuyse J, Charlier N, et al. Impact of direct virus-induced neuronal dysfunction and immunological damage on the progression of flavivirus (Modoc) encephalitis in a murine model. J Neurovirol. 2003;9:69-78.

173. Iwamoto M, Jernigan DB, Guasch A, et al. Transmission of West Nile virus from an organ donor to four transplant recipients. N Engl J Med. 2003;348:2196-2203.

174. Gunther G, Haglund M, Lindquist L, et al. Tick-borne encephalitis in Sweden in relation to aseptic meningo-encephalitis of other etiology: A prospective study of clinical course and outcome. J Neurol. 1997;244:230.

175. Tomazic J, Poljak M, Popovi M, et al. Tick-borne encephalitis: Possibly a fatal disease in its acute stage. PCR amplification of TBE RNA from postmortem brain tissue (Case report). Infection. 1997;25:41.

176. Ravi V, Desai AS, Shenoy PK, et al. Persistence of Japanese encephalitis virus in the human nervous system. J Med Virol. 1993;40:326.

177. Sharma S, Mathur A, Prakash R, et al. Japanese encephalitis virus latency in peripheral blood lymphocytes and recurrence of infection in children. Clin Exp Immunol. 1991;85:85.

178. Silber LA, Soloviev VD. Far Eastern tick-borne spring-summer (spring) encephalitis. In: Davis BD, Fisher SH, eds. American Review of Soviet Medicine. New York: America-Soviet Medical Society; 1946:1.

179. Ogawa M, Okubo H, Tsuji Y, et al. Chronic progressive encephalitis occurring 13 years after Russian spring-summer encephalitis. J Neurol Sci. 1973;19:363.

180. Gritsun TS, Frolova TV, Zhankov AI, et al. Characterization of a Siberian virus isolated from a patient with progressive chronic tick-borne encephalitis. J Virol. 2003;77:25-36.

181. Zweighaft RM, Rasmussen C, Brolnitsky O, et al. St Louis encephalitis: The Chicago experience. Am J Trop Med Hyg. 1979;28:114.

182. Desai A, Shankar SK, Jayakumar PN, et al. Co-existence of cerebral cysticercosis with Japanese encephalitis: A prognostic modulator. Epidemiol Infect. 1997;118:165.

182a. Singh P, Kalra N, Ratho RK, et al. Coexistent neurocysticercosis and Japanese B encephalitis: MR imaging correlation. Am J Neuroradiol. 2001;22:1131-1136.

183. Azad R, Gupta RK, Kumar S, et al. Is neurocysticercosis a risk factor in coexistent intracranial disease? An MRI based study. J Neurol Neurosurg Psychiatry. 2003;74:359-361.

184. Broun GO. Relationship of hypertensive vascular disease to mortality in cases of St Louis encephalitis. Med Bull St. Louis Univ. 1952;4:32.

185. Cimperman J, Maraspin V, Lotri-Furlan S, et al. Double infection with tick-borne encephalitis virus and *Borrelia burgdorferi sensu laou*. Wien Klin Wochenschr. 2002;114:620-622.

186. Oksi J, Viljanen MK, Kalimo H, et al. Fatal encephalitis caused by concomitant infection with tick-borne encephalitis virus and *Borrelia burgdorferi*. Clin Infect Dis. 1993;16:392.

187. Edelman R, Schneider RJ, Chieowanich P, et al. The effect of dengue virus infection on the clinical sequelae of Japanese encephalitis: A one year follow-up study in Thailand. Southeast Asian J Trop Med Public Health. 1975;6:308-315.

188. Bond JO, Hammon WMcD. Epidemiologic studies of possible cross protection between dengue and St Louis encephalitis arboviruses in Florida. Am J Epidemiol. 1970;92:321-329.

189. Libraty DH, Nisalak A. Clinical and immunological risk factors for severe disease in Japanese encephalitis. Trans R Soc Trop Med Hyg. 2002;96:173-178.

190. Hoke CH, Nisalak A, Singawhipa N, et al. Protection against Japanese encephalitis by inactivated vaccines. N Engl J Med. 1988;319:608-614.

191. Francis TI, Moore DL, Edington GM, Smith JA. A clinicopathological study of human yellow fever. Bull World Health Organ. 1972;46:659.

192. Endy TP, Chunsuttiwat S, Nisalak A, et al. Epidemiology of inapparent and symptomatic acute dengue virus infection: A prospective study of primary school children in Kamphaeng Phet, Thailand. Am J Epidemiol. 2002;156:40-51.

193. Garcia-Rivera EJ, Rigau-Perez JG. Dengue severity in the elderly in Puerto Rico. Rev Panam Salud Publica. 2003;13:362-368.

194. Thisyakorn U, Thisyakorn C. Dengue infections with unusual manifestations. J Med Assoc Thai. 1994;77:410.

195. Tsai JC, Juo CH, Chen PC. Upper gastrointestinal bleeding in dengue fever. Am J Gastroenterol. 1991;86:33.

196. Imbert P, Sordet D, Hovette P, Touze JE. Spleen rupture in a patient with dengue fever. Trop Med Parasitol. 1993;44:327.

197. Chye JK, Lim CT, Ng KB, et al. Vertical transmission of dengue. Clin Infect Dis. 1997;25:1374.

198. Innis BL, Mhint KSA. Acute liver failure is one important cause of fatal dengue infection. Southeast Asian J Trop Med Public Health. 1990;21:658-662.

199. Hommel D, Talarmin A, Deubel V, et al. Dengue encephalitis in French Guiana. Res Virol. 1998;149:235-238.

200. Ramos C, Sanchez G, Pando RH, et al. Dengue virus in the brain of a fatal case of hemorrhagic dengue fever. J Neurovirol. 1998;4:465-468.

201. Kerdpanich A, Watanaveeradej V, Samakoses R, et al. Perinatal dengue infection. Southeast Asian J Trop Med Public Health. 2001;32:488-493.

202. Sharma JB, Gulati N. Potential relationships between dengue fever and neural tube defects in a northern district of India. Int J Gynecol Obstet. 1992;39:291-295.

203. Mirovsky J, Holub J, Nguyen BC. Influence de la dengue sur la grossesse et le foetus. Gynecol Obstet (Paris). 1965;65:673.

204. Fernandez R, Rodriguez T, Borbonet F, et al: Study of the relationship dengue-pregnancy in a group of Cuban mothers (in Spanish). Rev Cubana Med Trop. 1994;46:76.

205. Cohen SN, Halstead SB. Shock associated with dengue infection. I. The clinical and physiologic manifestations of dengue hemorrhagic fever in Thailand, 1964. J Pediatr. 1966;68:448.

206. Kautner I, Robinson MJ, Kuhnle U. Dengue virus infection: Epidemiology, pathogenesis, clinical presentation, diagnosis and prevention. J Pediatr. 1997;131:516.

207. Setiawan MW, Samsi TK, Wulur H, et al. Dengue haemorrhagic fever: Ultrasound as an aid to predict the severity of the disease. Pediatr Radiol. 1998;28:1.

208. Lum LCS, Thong MK, Cheah YK, Lam SK. Dengue-associated adult respiratory distress syndrome. Ann Trop Paediatr. 1995;15:335.

209. Pancharoen C, Thisyakorn U. Coinfections in dengue patients. Pediatr Infect Dis J. 1998;17:81.

210. Halstead SB, Nimmannitya S, Margiotta MR. Dengue and chikungunya virus infection in man in Thailand. II. Observations on disease in outpatients. Am J Trop Med Hyg. 1969;18:972.

211. Solomon T, Kneen R, Dung NM, et al. Poliomyelitis-like illness due to Japanese encephalitis virus. Lancet. 1998;351:1094.

212. Srikanth S, Ravi V, Poornima S, et al. Viral antibodies in recent onset, nonorganic psychoses: Correspondence with symptomatic severity. Soc Biol Psychiatry. 1994;36:517.

213. Misra UK, Kalita J. Anterior horn cells are also involved in Japanese encephalitis. Acta Neurol Scand. 1997;96:114.

214. Dickerson RB, Newton JR, Hansen JE. Diagnosis and immediate prognosis of Japanese B encephalitis. Am J Med. 1952;12:227.

215. Solomon T. Recent advances in Japanese encephalitis. J Neurovirol. 2003;9:274-283.
216. Kumar R, Mathur A, Kumar A, et al. Clinical features and prognostic indicators of Japanese encephalitis in children in Lucknow (India). Indian J Med Res. 1990;91:321-327.
217. Solomon T, Dung NM, Kneen R, et al. Seizures and raised intracranial pressure in Vietnamese patients with Japanese encephalitis. Brain. 2002;125:1084-1093.
218. Misra UK, Kalita J. Seizures in Japanese encephalitis. J Neurol Sci. 2001;190:57-60.
219. Chaturvedi UC, Mathur A, Chandra A, et al. Transplacental infection with Japanese encephalitis virus. J Infect Dis. 1980;141:712.
220. Misra UK, Kalita J, Jain SK, Mathur A. Radiological and neurophysiological changes in Japanese encephalitis. J Neurol Neurosurg Psychiatry. 1994;57:1484.
221. Kalita J, Misra UK, Pandey S, Dhole TN. A comparison of clinical and radiological findings in adults and children with Japanese encephalitis. Arch Neurol. 2003;60:1760-1764.
222. Kimura K, Dosaka A, Hashimoto Y, et al. Single-photon emission CT findings in acute Japanese encephalitis. Am J Neuroradiol. 1997;18:465.
223. Srey VH, Sadones H, Ong S, et al. Etiology of encephalitis syndrome among hospitalized children and adults in Takeo, Cambodia, 1999-2000. Am J Trop Med Hyg. 2002;66:200-207.
223a. Kumar A. Movement disorders in the tropics. Parkinsonism Relat Disord. 2002;9:69-75.
224. Goldblum N, Sterk VV, Paderski B. West Nile fever: The clinical features of the disease and the isolation of West Nile virus from the blood of nine human cases. Am J Hyg. 1954;59:89-103.
225. Asnis DS, Conetta R, Teixeira AA, et al. The West Nile Virus outbreak of 1999 in New York: The Flushing Hospital experience. Clin Infect Dis. 2000;30:413-418; erratum in Clin Infect Dis 2000;30:841.
226. Chowers MY, Lang R, Nassar F, et al. Clinical characteristics of the West Nile fever outbreak, Israel, 2000. Emerg Infect Dis. 2001;7:675-678.
227. Nash D, Mostashari F, Fine A, et al. The outbreak of West Nile virus infection in the New York City area in 1999. N Engl J Med. 2001;344:1807-1814.
228. Gadoth N, Weitzman S, Lehmann EE. Acute anterior myelitis complicating West Nile fever. Arch Neurol. 1979;36:172-173.
229. Leis AA, Stokic DS, Webb RM, et al. Clinical spectrum of muscle weakness in human West Nile virus infection. Muscle Nerve. 2003;28:302-308.
230. Sejvar JJ, Leis AA, Stokic DS, et al. Acute flaccid paralysis and West Nile virus infection. Emerg Infect Dis. 2003;9:788-793.
231. Sejvar JJ, Haddad MB, Tierney BC, et al. Neurologic manifestations and outcome of West Nile virus infection. JAMA. 2003;290:511-515.
232. Solomon T, Fisher AF, Beasley DW, et al. Natural and nosocomial infection in a patient with West Nile encephalitis and extrapyramidal movement disorders. Clin Infect Dis. 2003;36:E140-E145.
233. Cernescu C, Ruta SM, Tardei G, et al. A high number of severe neurologic clinical forms during an epidemic of West Nile virus infection. Rom J Virol. 1997;48:13-25.
234. Weiss D, Carr D, Kellachan J, et al. Clinical findings of West Nile virus infection in hospitalized patients, New York and New Jersey, 2000. Emerg Infect Dis. 2001;7:654-658.
235. Brinker KR, Paulson G, Monath TP, et al. St Louis encephalitis in Ohio, September 1975: Clinical and EEG studies in 16 cases. Arch Intern Med. 1979;139:561.
235a. Barrett FF, Yow MD, Phillips CA. St. Louis encephalitis in children during the 1964 epidemic. JAMA. 1965;193:381-385.
236. Wasay M, Diaz-Arrastia R, Suss RA, et al. St Louis encephalitis: A review of 11 cases in a 1995 Dallas, Tex, epidemic. Arch Neurol. 2000;57:114-118.
237. Azar GJ, Bond JO, Chappell GL, Lawton AH. Follow-up studies of St Louis encephalitis in Florida: Sensorimotor findings. Am J Public Health. 1966;56:1074.
238. Palmer RJ, Finley KH. Sequelae of encephalitis: Report of a study after the California epidemic. Calif Med. 1956;84:98-100.
239. Okhuysen PC, Crane JK, Pappas J. St. Louis encephalitis in patients with human immunodeficiency virus infection. Clin Infect Dis. 1993;17:140-141.
240. Cerna F, Mehrad B, Luby JP, et al. St. Louis encephalitis and the substantia nigra: MR imaging evaluation. Am J Neuroradiol. 1999;20:1281-1283.
241. Kaiser R. The clinical and epidemiological profile of tick-borne encephalitis in southern Germany 1994-1998: A prospective study of 656 patients. Brain. 1999;122:2067-2078.
242. Wahlberg P, Saikku G, Grummer-Korvenkontio M. Tick-borne viral encephalitis in Finland: The clinical features of Kumlinge disease during 1959-1987. J Intern Med. 1989;225:173.
243. Mickiene A, Laiskonis A, Gunther G, et al. Tickborne encephalitis in an area of high endemicity in Lithuania: Disease severity and long-term prognosis. Clin Infect Dis. 2002;35:650-658.
244. Cizman M, Rakar R, Zakotnik B, et al. Severe forms of tick-borne encephalitis in children. Wien Klin Wochenschr. 1999;111:484-487.
245. Ternovoi VA, Kurzhukov GP, Sokolov YV, et al. Tick-borne encephalitis with hemorrhagic syndrome, Novosibirsk region, Russia, 1999. Emerg Infect Dis. 2003;9:743-746.
246. Haglund M, Forsgren M, Lindh G, Lindquist L. A 10-year follow-up study of tick-borne encephalitis in the Stockholm area and a review of the literature: Need for a vaccination strategy. Scand J Infect Dis. 1996;28:217.
247. Embil J, Camfield P, Artsob H, et al. Powassan virus encephalitis resembling herpes simplex encephalitis. Arch Intern Med. 1983;143:341.
248. Conway D, Rossier E, Spence L, et al. Powassan virus encephalitis with shoulder girdle involvement. Can Dis Weekly Rep. 1976;85:2.
249. Lotric-Furlan S, Strle F: Thrombocytopenia: A common finding in the initial phase of tick-borne encephalitis. Infection. 1995;23:203.
250. Alkadhi H, Kollias SS. MRI in tick-borne encephalitis. Neuroradiology. 2000;42:753-755.
251. Tsai TF, Chandler LJ. Arboviruses. In: Murray PR, Baron EJ, Jorensen J, et al, eds. Manual of Clinical Microbiology. 8th ed. Washington, DC: American Society of Microbiology; 2003:1553-1569.
252. Lanciotti R. Molecular amplification assays for the detection of flaviviruses. Adv Virus Res. 2003;61:67-99.
253. Kuno G. Serodiagnosis of flaviviral infections and vaccinations in humans. Adv Virus Res. 2003;61:3-65.
254. Roehrig JT, Nash D, Maldin B, et al. Persistence of virus-reactive serum immunoglobulin M antibody in confirmed West Nile virus encephalitis cases. Emerg Infect Dis. 2003;9:376-379.
255. Shi PY, Wong SJ. Serologic diagnosis of West Nile virus infection. Expert Rev Mol Diagn. 2003;3:733-741.
256. Cuzzubbo AJ, Vaughn DW, Nisalak A, et al. Comparison of PanBio Dengue Duo IgM and IgG Capture ELISA and Venture Technologies Dengue IgM and IgG Dot Blot. J Clin Virol. 2000;16:135-144.
256a. Kelso JM, Mootrey GT, Tsai TF. Anaphylaxis from yellow fever vaccine. J Allergy Clin Immunol. 1999;103:698-701.
257. Vasconcelos PF, Luna EJ, Galler R, et al. Fever and multisystem organ failure associated with 17D-204 yellow fever vaccination: a report of four cases. Lancet. 2001;358:98-104.
258. Chan RC, Penney DJ, Little D, et al. Hepatitis and death following vaccination with 17D-204 yellow fever vaccine. Lancet. 2001;358:121-122.
259. Martin M, Tsai TF, Cropp B, et al. Serious adverse events associated with yellow fever 17DD vaccine in Brazil: A report of two cases. Lancet. 2001;358:91-97; erratum in Lancet 2001;358:336. Lancet 2001;358:1018.
260. Adverse events associated with 17D-derived yellow fever vaccination—United States, 2001-2002. MMWR Morb Mortal Wkly Rep. 2002;51:989-993.
261. Kitchener S. Viscerotropic and neurotropic disease following vaccination with the AD yellow fever vaccine, ARJU/AX. Vaccine. 2004;22:2103-2105.
262. Galler R, Pugachev KV, Santos CL, et al. Phenotypic and molecular analyses of yellow fever 17DD vaccine viruses associated with serious adverse events in Brazil. Virology. 2001;290:309-319.
263. Kengsakul K, Sathirapongsasuti K, Punyagupta S. Fatal myeloencephalitis following yellow fever vaccination in a case with HIV infection. J Med Assoc Thai. 2002;85:131-134.
264. Advisory Committee on Immunization Practices. Yellow fever vaccine. Recommendations of the ACIP, 2002. MMWR Morb Mortal Wkly Rep. 2002;RR-17:1-11.
265. Tsai TF, Raul R, Lynberg MC, Letson GW. Congenital yellow fever virus infection after immunization in pregnancy. J Infect Dis. 1993;168:1520.
266. Nasidi A, Monath TP, Vandenberg J, et al. Yellow fever vaccine and pregnancy: A four year prospective study. Trans R Soc Trop Med Hyg. 1993;87:337.
267. Goujon C, Tohr M, Feuillie V, et al. Good tolerance and efficacy of yellow fever vaccine among subjects who are carriers of human immunodeficiency virus (Abstract). Fourth International Conference on Travel Medicine, Acapulco, Mexico, April 23-27, 1995, p 63.
268. Sibailly TS, Wiktor SZ, Tsai TF, et al. Poor antibody response to yellow fever vaccination in children infected with human immunodeficiency virus type 1. Pediatr Infect Dis J. 1997;16:1177.
269. Dengue Haemorrhagic Fever: Diagnosis, Treatment, Prevention and Control. 2nd ed. Geneva, World Health Organization; 1997.
270. Ngo NT, Cao XT, Kneen R, et al. Acute management of dengue shock syndrome: A randomized double-blind comparison of 4 intravenous fluid regimens in the first hour. Clin Infect Dis. 2001;32:204-213.
271. Pea L, Roda L, Moll F. Desmopressin treatment for a case of dengue hemorrhagic fever/dengue shock syndrome. Clin Infect Dis. 2001;33:1611-1612.
272. Lum LC, Abdel-Latif-Yel A, Goh AY, et al. Preventive transfusion in dengue shock syndrome—is it necessary? J Pediatr. 2003;143:682-684.
273. Diamond MS, Roberts TG, Edgil D, et al. Modulation of Dengue virus infection in human cells by alpha, beta, and gamma interferons. J Virol. 2000;74:4957-4966.
274. Tassniyom S, Vasanawathana S, Dhiensiri T, et al. Failure of carbazochrome sodium sulfonate (AC-17) to prevent dengue vascular permeability or shock: A randomized, controlled trial. J Pediatr. 1997;131:525.
275. Tassniyom S, Vasanawathana S, Chirawatkul A, Rojanasuphot S. Failure of high-dose methylprednisolone in established dengue shock syndrome: A placebo-controlled, double-blind study. Pediatrics. 1993;92:111.
276. Atrasheuskaya A, Petzelbauer P, Fredeking TM, Ignatyev G. Anti-TNF antibody treatment reduces mortality in experimental dengue virus infection. FEMS Immunol Med Microbiol. 2003;35:33-42.
277. Sabchareon A, Lang J, Chanthavanich P, et al. Safety and immunogenicity of a three dose regimen of two tetravalent live-attenuated dengue vaccines in five- to twelve-year-old Thai children. Pediatr Infect Dis J. 2004;23:99-109.
278. Sun W, Edelman R, Kanesa-Thasan N, et al. Vaccination of human volunteers with monovalent and tetravalent live-attenuated dengue vaccine candidates. Am J Trop Med Hyg. 2003;69(6 Suppl):24-31.
279. Halstead SB, Deen J. The future of dengue vaccines. Lancet. 2002;360:1243-1245.
280. Jacobs M, Young P. Dengue vaccines: Preparing to roll back dengue. Curr Opin Investig Drugs. 2003;4:168-171.

281. Solomon T, Dung NM, Wills B, et al. Interferon alfa-2a in Japanese encephalitis: A randomised double-blind placebo-controlled trial. Lancet. 2003;361:821-826.

282. Arras C, Fescharek R, Gregersen JP. Do specific hyperimmunoglobulins aggravate clinical course of tick-borne encephalitis? Lancet. 1996;347:1331.

283. Kluger G, Schottler A, Waldvogel K, et al. Tickborne encephalitis despite specific immunoglobulin prophylaxis. Lancet. 1995;346:1502.

284. Shimoni Z, Niven MJ, Pitlick S, Bulvik S. Treatment of West Nile virus encephalitis with intravenous immunoglobulin. Emerg Infect Dis. 2001;7:759.

285. Agrawal AG, Petersen LR. Human immunoglobulin as a treatment for West Nile virus infection. J Infect Dis. 2003;188:1-4. Epub 2003 Jun 23.

286. Hoke CH Jr, Vaughn DW, Nisalak A, et al. Effect of high-dose dexamethasone on the outcome of acute encephalitis due to Japanese encephalitis virus. J Infect Dis. 1992;165:631.

287. Atrasheuskaya AV, Fredeking TM, Ignatyev GM. Changes in immune parameters and their correction in human cases of tick-borne encephalitis. Clin Exp Immunol. 2003;131:148-154.

288. Bista MB, Banerjee MK, Shin SH, et al. Efficacy of single-dose SA 14-14-2 vaccine against Japanese encephalitis: A case control study. Lancet. 2001;358:791-795.

289. Hennessy S, Zhengle L, Tsai TF, et al. Effectiveness of live-attenuated Japanese encephalitis vaccine (SA14-14-2): A case-control study. Lancet. 1996;347:1583.

290. Plesner AM. Allergic reactions to Japanese encephalitis vaccine. Immunol Allergy Clin North Am. 2003;23:665-697.

291. Monath TP, Guirakhoo F, Nichols R, et al. Chimeric live, attenuated vaccine against Japanese encephalitis (ChimeriVax-JE): Phase 2 clinical trials for safety and immunogenicity, effect of vaccine dose and schedule, and memory response to challenge with inactivated Japanese encephalitis antigen. J Infect Dis. 2003;188:1213-1230. Epub 2003 Oct 03.

292. Kunz C. TBE vaccination and the Austrian experience. Vaccine. 2003;21(Suppl 1):S50-S55.

293. Zent O, Jilg W, Plentz A, et al. Kinetics of the immune response after primary and booster immunization against tick-borne encephalitis (TBE) in adults using the rapid immunization schedule. Vaccine. 2003;21:4655-4660.

294. Bennett N McK. Murray Valley encephalitis, 1974: Clinical features. Med J Aust. 1976;2:446.

295. Burrow JN, Whelan PI, Kilburn CJ, et al. Australian encephalitis in the Northern Territory: clinical and epidemiological features, 1987-1996. Aust N Z J Med. 1998;28:590-596.

296. Lopes O, Sacchetta L de A, Coimbra TLM, et al. Emergence of a new arbovirus disease in Brazil. II. Epidemiologic studies on 1975 epidemic. Am J Epidemiol. 1978;108:394.

297. Pavri K. Clinical, clinicopathologic, and hematologic features of Kyasanur Forest disease. Rev Infect Dis Suppl. 1989;4S:854.

298. Prabha A, Prabhu MG, Raghuveer CV, et al. Clinical study of 100 cases of Kyasanur Forest disease with clinicopathological correlation. Indian J Med Sci. 1993;47:124.

299. Lvov DK. Arboviral zoonoses of northern Eurasia (Eastern Europe and The Commonwealth of Independent States). In: Beran GW, ed. Handbook of Zoonoses. 2nd ed. Boca Raton, Fla: CRC; 1994:237.

300. Smithburn KC, Paterson HE, Heymann CS, et al. An agent related to Uganda S virus from man and mosquitoes in South Africa. S Afr Med J. 1959;33:959.

301. Figueiredo LT The Brazilian flaviviruses. Microbes Infect. 2000;2:1643-1649.

302. Aaskov JG, Phillips DA, Wiemers MA. Possible clinical infection with Edge Hill virus. Trans R Soc Trop Med Hyg. 1993;87:452.

303. Southam CM, Moore AE. West Nile, Ilheus, and Bunyamwera infections in man. Am J Trop Med. 1951;31:724.

304. Boughton CR, Hawkes RA, Naim HM. Illness caused by a Kokobera-like virus in southeastern Australia. Med J Aust. 1986;145:90.

305. Webb HE. Leukaemia and neoplastic processes treated with Langat and Kyasanur Forest disease viruses: A clinical and laboratory study of 28 patients. BMJ. 1966;5482:258-266.

306. Reeves WC. Epidemiology and Control of Mosquito-Borne Arboviruses in California, 1943-1987. Sacramento, Calif: California Mosquito Vector Control Association; 1990.

307. Kurane I, Takasaki T, Yamada K. Trends in flavivirus infections in Japan. Emerg Infect Dis. 2000;6:569-571.

308. Sulkin SE, Burns KF, Shelton DF, Wallis C. Bat salivary gland virus: Infections of man and monkey. Tex Rep Biol Med. 1962;20:113.

309. Woodroofe GM, Marshall ID. Arboviruses from the Sepik district of New Guinea. In: John Curtin School of Medical Research Annual Report. Australian National University; 1971:90.

310. Nassar ES, Coimbra TLM, Rocco IM, et al. Human disease caused by an arbovirus closely related to Ilheus virus: Report of five cases. Intervirology. 1997;40:247.

311. Wolfe MS, Calisher CH, McGuire K. Spondweni virus infection in a foreign resident of Upper Volta. Lancet. 1982;2:1306.

312. Rapport Annuel du Centre Collaborateur OMS de Reference et de Recherche pours les Arbovirus. Dakar: Institut Pasteur; 1983.

313. Heymann CS, Kokernot RH, De Meillon B. Wesselsbron virus infections in man. S Afr Med J. 1958;32:543-545.

314. Digoutte J-P, Salaun J-J, Robin Y, et al. Les arboviroses mineures en Afrique centrale et occidentale. Med Trop (Mars). 1980;40:523-533.

CHAPTER 150

Hepatitis C

DAVID L. THOMAS

STUART C. RAY

STANLEY M. LEMON

NON-A, NON-B VIRAL HEPATITIS AND HEPATITIS C

After serologic tests for hepatitis A virus (HAV) and hepatitis B virus (HBV) were developed during the 1970s, it became evident that most cases of transfusion-associated hepatitis must be caused by yet another agent, leading to the term "non-A, non-B hepatitis."[1,2] Studies in chimpanzees confirmed that blood-borne non-A, non-B hepatitis was transmissible and was caused by a relatively small, lipid-enveloped virus.[3,4] In the late 1980s, Michael Houghton's laboratory at Chiron Corporation, working with Daniel Bradley's laboratory at the Centers for Disease Control and Prevention (CDC), identified a virally encoded antigen associated with non-A, non-B hepatitis and called the agent "hepatitis C virus" (HCV).[5] This finding rapidly led to molecular cloning of the complete viral genome[6] and other major discoveries, including recognition of the proclivity of this virus to establish persistent infection and its strong association with chronic hepatitis, cirrhosis, and hepatocellular carcinoma.

HEPATITIS C VIRUS

Virion Properties and Classification

HCV is a roughly spherical, enveloped, positive-strand RNA virus approximately 50 nm in diameter (Fig. 150-1).[7,8] Its structure, genomic organization, and replication cycle support classification as a member of the family Flaviviridae, yet it is sufficiently distinct to merit classification within a separate genus, *Hepacivirus*. Related genera include *Flavivirus* (yellow fever virus and dengue viruses) and *Pestivirus* (bovine viral diarrhea virus and classic swine fever virus). Several "GB" viruses are also in the Flaviviridae family,[9,10] although they have not yet been assigned to a particular genus. These include GB virus C (GBV-C), which was previously inappropriately considered to be a "hepatitis" virus (the so-called hepatitis G virus), and GB virus B (GBV-B), which is a true primate hepatitis virus and has the highest level of genetic relatedness to HCV of any animal virus (see Chapter 151).[11] Sucrose-gradient studies of infectious plasma and sera suggest that HCV may associate with low-density lipoproteins and, in some samples, with antibody in high-density complexes.[12-15] High- and low-density fractions may have similar viral RNA content as determined by reverse transcriptase-polymerase chain reaction (RT-PCR) assays. However, the high-density fractions are generally less infectious for chimpanzees, suggesting that infectivity is reduced by the association of the virus with immunoglobulins.[12]

Organization of the Hepatitis C Virus Genome

The genome of HCV is a positive-sense, single-stranded RNA molecule approximately 9.6 kb in length. The RNA contains a large open reading frame (ORF) encoding a single large polyprotein (approximately 3020 amino acids). A frame-shifting event occurring near the 5' end of the ORF has been suggested to shift some translating ribosomes into an alternative, truncated reading frame, giving rise to a putative "F" protein which, if it exists, is of uncertain function in the viral life cycle (see later discussion). The large ORF is flanked by highly conserved 5'and 3' untranslated regions (UTRs) that function in both translation and viral RNA replication (Fig. 150-2).[6]

Untranslated RNA Segments

The HCV 5' UTR is approximately 341 nucleotides in length, demonstrates extensive secondary and tertiary RNA structure (Fig. 150-3A),

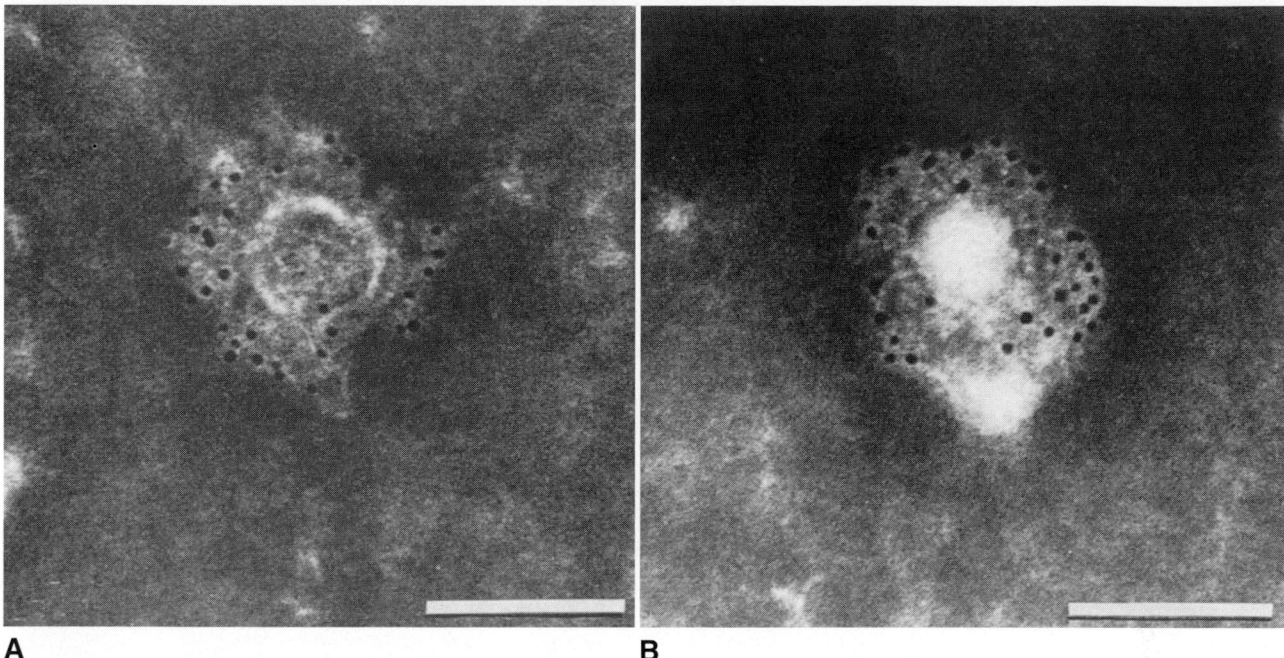

A   **B**

FIGURE 150-1. **A** and **B,** Electron microscopic images of hepatitis C virus (HCV) virions concentrated from human plasma by high speed centrifugation. The virions are identified by staining with gold-labeled antibodies to the HCV envelope proteins. *(From Kaito M, Watanabe S, Tsukiyama-Koham K, et al. Hepatitis C virus particle detected by immunoelectron microscopic study. J Gen Virol. 1994;75:1755-1760.)*

and contains two overlapping functional regions. The 125 nucleotides at the 5' end are essential for viral RNA replication, probably for recognition of the RNA by the viral replicase, whereas the remainder of the 5' UTR appears to play an accessory role in this process.[16] An overlapping segment of approximately 300 nucleotides acts as an internal ribosomal entry site (IRES), directing the cap-independent translation of the viral ORF.[16-21] The HCV IRES and the closely related IRES elements of pestiviruses are unique among eukaryotic RNAs in that they are capable of binding directly to the 40S ribosome subunit in the absence of any protein translation initiation factor.[22] The binary complex formed by the 5' UTR RNA and the 40S subunit appears to involve specific macromolecular interactions around the initiator AUG codon of HCV.[23] Thus, HCV initiates translation of its proteins via a unique prokaryotic-like mechanism that may prove to be a useful target for future antiviral drug development. The 3' UTR consists of a

relatively variable 30- to 60-nucleotide segment located downstream of the termination codon that is followed by a highly variable poly-U/UC tract of 50 to 100 nucleotides. Downstream of the poly-U/UC tract there is a highly conserved 98-base sequence known as the "3'X region" (see Fig. 150-3B).[24-26] This highly structured 3'-terminal 98-base sequence is the most conserved segment of the HCV genome. Experiments with subgenomic RNA replicons (discussed later) indicate that the 3'X region and 26 to 52 residues of the poly-U/UC tract are absolutely required for viral RNA replication.[27,28]

Polyprotein

The approximately 9.0-kb ORF encodes a polyprotein that is cotranslationally processed into at least 10 proteins. These include three structural proteins: the nucleocapsid protein, core protein (C), and two envelope proteins (E1 and E2); two proteins that play uncertain roles

FIGURE 150-2. Organization of the hepatitis C virus (HCV) genome and viral polyprotein. At the top is a schematic diagram of the genome. The boxes show the location of the individual proteins within the polyprotein encoded by the major open reading frame (ORF). Presumed structural proteins of the virus appear in purple. Below is shown the putative topology of the mature HCV proteins with respect to membranes of the endoplasmic reticulum (ER). Sites of proteolytic cleavage by cellular and viral proteinases are indicated by the triangles. Labels indicate individual proteins and major enzymatic activities that are current subjects for antiviral drug discovery efforts. The solid lines at each end of the ORF represent the 5' and 3' (left and right, respectively) untranslated segments of the genome. The location of the small ORF encoding the putative "F" (frame-shift) protein is shown. See text for additional details.

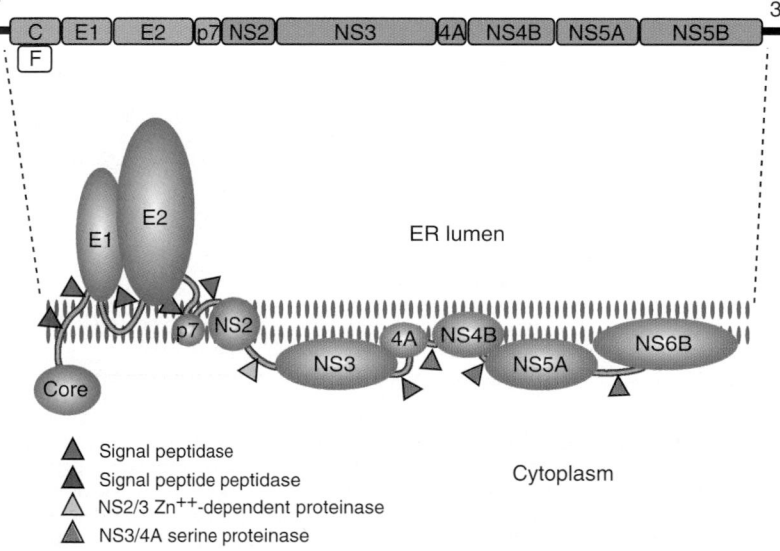

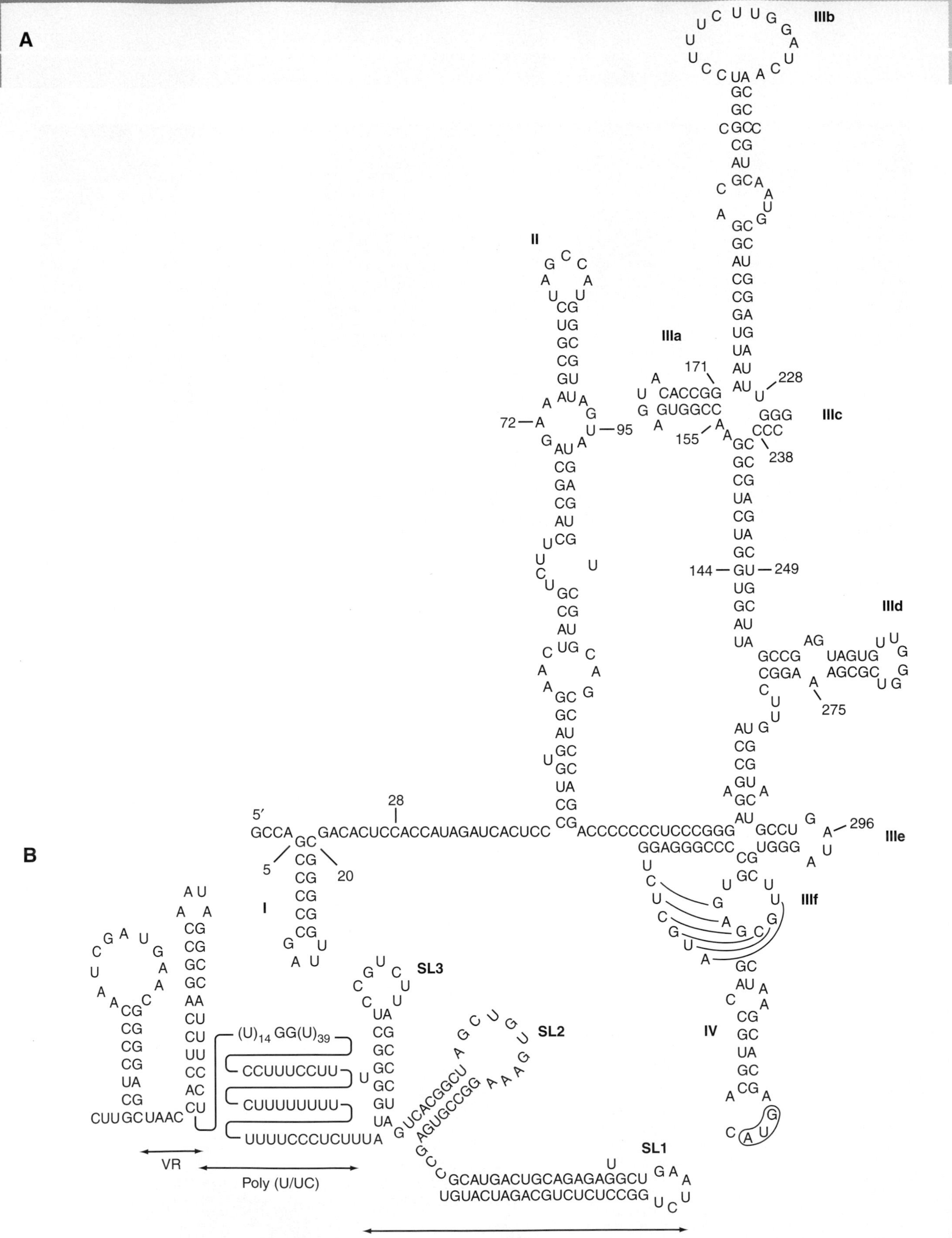

FIGURE 150-3. Secondary and tertiary RNA structures of the 5′ and 3′ untranslated segments of the genome of hepatitis C virus. **A,** The 5′ untranslated RNA segment, which contains overlapping *cis*-active replication signals and the viral internal ribosome entry site (IRES). The initiator AUG codon at the 5′ end of the major open reading frame is highlighted. Major structural domains (I through IV) are labeled, as are subdomains (IIIa through IIIf). **B,** The 3′ untranslated RNA segment, which contains three discrete domains: the variable segment (VR), the poly(U/UC) track, and the extreme 3′-terminal "3′X" sequence (which contains three putative stem-loops, SL1 through SL3). The UGA codon terminating protein translation at the 3′ end of the open reading frame is highlighted.

in particle assembly and are not required for viral RNA replication (p7 and NS2); and five nonstructural proteins that form the viral RNA replicase complex (NS3, NS4A, NS4B, NS5A, and NS5B) (see Fig. 150-2). Processing of the polyprotein is directed by both cellular and viral proteases. Four distinct signal sequences within the amino-terminal third of the polyprotein direct the translocation of the nascent protein into the endoplasmic reticulum (ER), with the result that signal peptidase cleaves the polyprotein at the C/E1, E1/E2, E2/p7, and p7/NS2 junctions. The nascent NS2/NS3 protein is an autocatalytic protease (possibly either a cysteine protease or a metalloproteinase) that acts only *in cis* to cleave the NS2/NS3 junction, whereas the NS3 protein contains a second (serine) protease activity that catalyzes the remaining *in trans* polyprotein cleavages among the nonstructural proteins. Full expression of NS3 protease activity requires formation of a complex with the NS4A protein.

Structural Proteins

The 191-amino-acid segment at the amino terminus of the HCV polyprotein is cleaved from the nascent polypeptide by signal peptidase, forming the highly basic core protein, which has RNA-binding activity.[29-32] A further cleavage occurs just upstream of the signal peptide sequence, within the membranes of the ER, and is directed by signal peptide peptidase.[33] This releases a mature core protein of about 171 amino acids into the cytoplasm of the cell. In addition to its expected role as a nucleocapsid protein, some but not all studies suggest that core may be translocated to the nucleus. Within the cytoplasm, core is found associated with the surface of small lipid droplets and mitochondria.[34,35]

A number of biologic activities have been associated with the core protein, including suppression of HBV replication, alterations in regulation of the cell cycle and transcription of cellular protooncogenes, either induction or suppression of apoptosis, and transformation of rat embryo fibroblasts.[34-44] The core protein has also been suggested to interfere with anti-HCV immune responses through a variety of mechanisms, including natural killer (NK) cell inhibition via upregulation of major histocompatibility complex (MHC) class I expression, inhibition of T-cell proliferation via interaction with complement receptor gC1qR, and interaction with the cytoplasmic tail of several cellular receptors belonging to the tumor necrosis factor (TNF) receptor family.[40,41,43,45,46] However, because HCV does not replicate well in any type of cultured cell, these data are derived largely from studies in which core was overexpressed from recombinant complementary DNA (cDNA). It is not clear whether core exerts any of these biologic effects when expressed by replicating virus within the liver, and in many cases contradictory in vitro evidence against such effects can be found in the literature. The core protein is immunogenic; both core protein and antibody to it are typically present in the serum of infected individuals (see "Laboratory Assessment of Hepatitis C Virus Infection").

Yellow fever virus and other members of the genus *Flavivirus* have a single major envelope protein and a glycosylated, cell-associated NS1 protein that can elicit neutralizing antibodies. However, HCV has two major envelope glycoproteins (E1 and E2) and no comparable NS1 protein. Signal peptidases direct cleavage of the HCV polyprotein at amino acid residues 383 and 746 (numbering based on the prototype strain HCV-1), producing the E1 and E2 proteins, respectively (see Fig. 150-2).[30] These are secreted into the ER as type 1 membrane proteins, remaining anchored to the membrane by a hydrophobic carboxyl-terminal anchor sequence. The E1 and E2 proteins are heavily glycosylated, with sugar moieties representing about 50% of the mature mass of each. The two major envelope proteins associate with each other as a noncovalent heterodimeric complex; covalently-linked complexes have also been identified but are thought to arise from misfolded forms of the proteins.[47] When expressed from recombinant heterologous viruses, E1 and E2 remain mostly localized to the ER compartment with only limited transport to the cell surface, perhaps due to ER-retention signals located in the transmembrane domain.[48-50] This suggests that, like other members of the Flaviviridae, HCV particles assemble and exit the cell by budding into intracytoplasmic vesicles, and then follow the secretory pathway for release. The envelope pro-

teins have been reported to associate with both the core and NS2 proteins, as well as lactoferrin[47,51]; the significance of the latter interaction, if any, is unknown.

A highly variable segment of approximately 30 amino acid residues near the amino terminus of E2 has been called hypervariable region 1 (HVR-1).[52-54] It is the most genetically variable segment of the envelope proteins, and it is assumed to exist as a polypeptide loop on the surface of the virion. Infected persons frequently have antibodies that react with synthetic peptides representing the HVR-1 sequences of the virus with which they are infected. The appearance of such antibodies seems to alter the quasispecies, selecting variants with HVR-1 sequences that are less reactive. This suggests that the HVR-1 harbors a neutralization epitope and that it is a site of mutations causing immune escape.[55-57] Such mutations may occur at little cost to the virus, because the extent of sequence heterogeneity within the HVR-1 indicates that there are few sequence-related constraints on its function; however, some general constraints have been observed.[58] It has been suggested that the HVR-1 may function as an immunologic decoy during infection by masking a deeper, more highly conserved structure within the envelope, such as a recognition site for the cellular receptor.[59] Importantly, deletion of this region does not eliminate the ability of the virus to infect chimpanzees, suggesting that it is not critical for viral entry or release.[60]

p7 and NS2 Proteins

The p7 and NS2 proteins may play roles in viral particle assembly or egress from the cell, but neither is required for viral RNA replication. A signal peptidase cleavage near the carboxyl terminus of E2 generates the p7 (formerly NS2A) protein (see Fig. 150-2). This is a small, 63-amino-acid, hydrophobic polypeptide that appears capable of forming a voltage-gated ion channel in a manner that suggests it may be a viroporin. This activity is inhibited in vitro by amantadine and long-alkyl-chain iminosugar derivatives, indicating a possible therapeutic target.[61-63] Its role in the life cycle of the virus is unknown, but deletion of the p7-coding region renders HCV RNA noninfectious.

The NS2 (formerly NS2B) protein is cleaved from the remainder of the polyprotein by a *cis*-acting protease that is localized to the polypeptide sequence spanning the NS2/NS3 junction. Little is known about the mechanism of cleavage, but it has been suggested that the NS2/3 protease may be a cysteine protease, or possibly a metalloproteinase. NS2 itself is a transmembrane protein, but its role in replication of the virus (other than participating in directing the NS2/NS3 cleavage) is not known.[64,65]

Nonstructural Proteins Involved in RNA Replication

Proteins spanning the region within the polyprotein from NS3 to NS5B (see Fig. 150-2) are required for RNA replication. They assemble into a membrane-associated replicase complex within the cytoplasm of infected cells. The NS3 protein possesses serine proteinase activity localized to its amino-terminal third and an RNA helicase with nucleoside triphosphatase (NTPase) activity in its carboxyl-terminal domain. The mature, fully active NS3 proteinase requires the noncovalent association of NS3 with the NS4A protein, which becomes an integral part of the proteinase structure.[66-69] Atomic-level resolution structures have been solved for both the protease and helicase domains, as well as the entire protein; both enzyme activities have been explored as targets for antiviral drug discovery efforts, and substantial progress has been made on the development of small-molecule inhibitors of the protease (see "Treatment").[66,70,71] The NS3 serine proteinase is active *in trans*, is dependent on zinc, and is responsible for the NS3/NS4A *cis* cleavage, as well as the NS4A/NS4B, NS4B/NS5A, and NS5A/NS5B cleavages that follow in the processing of the polyprotein. The carboxyl-terminal 465 amino acids of NS3 contain the NTPase and RNA helicase activity, which are likely to direct the unwinding of duplex RNA molecules at some point during the replication of the viral genome. There is evidence that the helicase has 3'-to-5' directionality and binds to the 3' poly-U/UC sequence.[72,73] No cleavage site has been identified between the NS3 proteinase and helicase, suggesting functional interdependence.[74]

NS3 protease activity has been shown to interfere with interferon-mediated signaling by blocking the virus-activated phosphorylation of interferon regulatory factor 3 (IRF3), providing a mechanism by which HCV might evade innate cellular antiviral defenses (see "Mechanisms of Persistence").[75] The multifunctional nature of NS3, including polyprotein processing, its role in the RNA replicase, and its contribution to immune evasion, is typical for the proteins of small, positive-stranded RNA viruses such as HCV. In addition, a role has been proposed for NS3 in viral pathogenesis, because NS3 expression has been shown to transform NIH 3T3 cells and to induce tumors in nude mice.[76]

The NS4A protein acts as a cofactor for the NS3 protease, as described earlier. An amino-terminal segment of the protein anchors the NS3/NS4A complex to intracellular membranes. NS4A also interacts with NS5A and therefore is a critical component of the replicase complex. NS4B is a hydrophobic, membrane-associated protein. It appears to mediate modifications of the ER membranes that occur in association with replicase assembly, and in doing so it may also inhibit normal ER-to-Golgi secretory pathways.[77,78]

NS5A is a phosphoprotein that appears to play a role in RNA replication, although its exact function remains obscure. Its phosphorylation is dependent on NS4A, with which it interacts.[79,80] Sequence polymorphisms within a short segment of NS5A called the interferon sensitivity determining region (ISDR) have been correlated with resistance to interferon therapy, and this effect may be mediated by the interaction of NS5A with the catalytic domain of interferon-induced double-stranded RNA (dsRNA)–activated protein kinase R (PKR).[81-84] Inactivation of PKR by NS5A would mitigate both the antiviral and antiproliferative activities of interferon. However, the association between ISDR polymorphisms and interferon resistance has been questioned and may be genotype specific. Furthermore, the ability of NS5A to impede PKR function during replication of the virus has been difficult to demonstrate directly because of the absence of a cell culture system that is fully permissive for viral replication.

The NS5B protein is highly conserved and contains a Gly-Asp-Asp motif that is characteristic of RNA-dependent RNA polymerases. It is considered to be the catalytic core of the replicase complex. NS5B proteins expressed from recombinant cDNA have been shown to have polymerase activity in vitro, although it has not been possible to demonstrate specificity for HCV RNA as template.[85-87] As with the enzymatic activities of the NS3 protein, the NS5B RNA polymerase has proved to be a useful target for antiviral drug development, with nucleoside analogues as well as other nonnucleoside small-molecule inhibitors now entering the development pipeline.

In addition to the polyprotein described earlier, evidence suggests that ribosomal frame shifting may generate the F protein from a short ORF found within the core region of some genotype 1 isolates.[88,89] Subjects with HCV infection, but not those with HBV infection, have been found to have serum antibody reactivity to in vitro synthesized F protein, suggesting that the protein is expressed in vivo. The role of the F protein remains speculative.

Replication

Details of the viral life cycle have been difficult to determine because there is no fully permissive cell culture system in which this process can be studied directly. However, replication-competent subgenomic RNA replicons have provided a new system for exploring aspects of viral RNA replication in cultured cells (see later discussion). Data derived from studies with replicons and reasonable analogies with other positive-strand RNA viruses suggest the following scenario (Fig. 150-4). The virus is likely to enter the cell through an interaction with one or more specific cell surface receptor molecules; suggested receptor molecules include CD81, the low-density lipoprotein (LDL) receptor, the C-type lectins DC-SIGN and L-SIGN, and human scavenger receptor class B type I (SR-BI).[90-94] After attachment, penetration, and uptake into a cellular endosome, local pH changes may alter the conformation of the envelope proteins, resulting in fusion with the endosomal membrane. The viral RNA is released into the cytoplasm, where it acts as messenger RNA, directing the cap-independent translation of the viral polyprotein. The ability to rescue infectious virus by intrahepatic inoculation of synthetic, genome-length RNA in chimpanzees, as well as the replication competence of viral RNA in transfected cells (see later discussion), provide strong proof for this step in the replication cycle.[95,96] Viral translation occurs in association with the rough ER by the process of internal ribosome entry described earlier, and the polyprotein undergoes a series of further cotranslational proteolytic cleavages, as described in the preceding section.

The core protein remains within the cytoplasm after cleavage from the signal sequence at its carboxyl terminus by signal peptide peptidase, whereas E1 and E2 are secreted into the lumen of the ER, remaining attached to the membrane and becoming heavily glycosylated. A replicase complex, composed of NS3, NS4A, NS4B, NS5A, and NS5B, forms cytoplasmic clusters of "membranous webs" derived from the ER. This replicase complex recognizes specific structures and sequences at the 3′ end of the genomic RNA and subsequently directs the synthesis of a negative-strand copy of the genome. The resulting duplex RNA most likely serves as template for the subsequent synthesis of multiple copies of the positive-strand genomic RNA, after recognition of the opposite end of the genome by the replicase. The genomic RNA is packaged into new viral particles, which are likely to

FIGURE 150-4. Putative major events in the replication of hepatitis C virus. Specific steps include (a) attachment and penetration of the virion into the hepatocyte; (b) release of viral RNA (solid blue line) into cytoplasm, possibly secondary to fusion of the viral envelope with the endosomal membrane (not shown); (c) cap-independent translation directed by the internal ribosome entry site (IRES); (d) processing of the viral polyprotein resulting in production of the core protein (light green), envelope protein (blue), and five nonstructural proteins essential for RNA replication (magenta) that form the replicase complex (light blue); (e) assembly of the replicase complex at the 3′ end of the virion RNA, followed by synthesis of a minus-strand replicative intermediate RNA (dashed red line); (f) synthesis of multiple positive-strand copies of the RNA (blue lines) from a duplex RNA template; (g) assembly of virus particles in the late endoplasmic reticulum (ER) and early Golgi compartments; and (h) release from the cell. Many of these details have yet to be confirmed by direct experimental evidence. See text for further details.

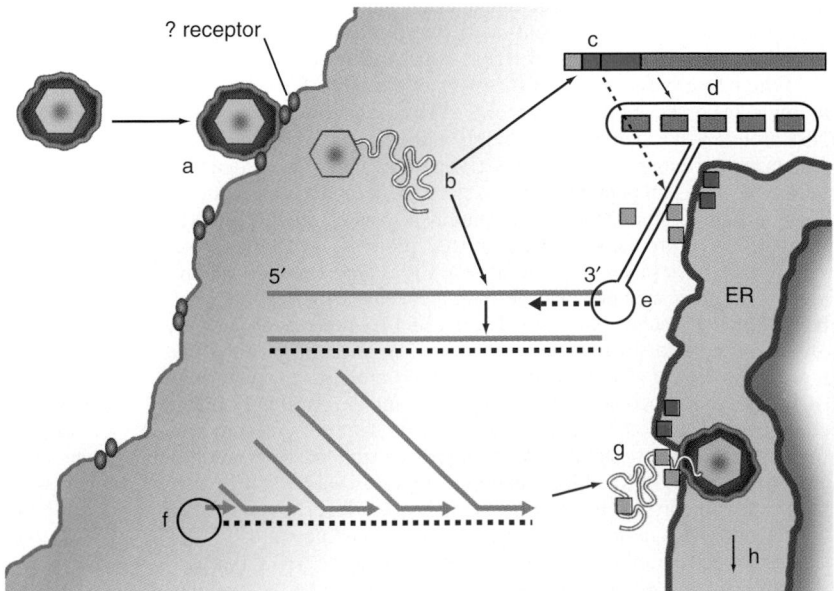

be extruded into the ER, leading to the release of the virus via the vesicular secretory pathway.

Few details of the virus life cycle have been confirmed experimentally because of the technical difficulties that beset the field, including the absence of both permissive cell lines and a readily available small animal model. Furthermore, there is much speculation but few hard data concerning the impact of HCV protein expression on the biology of the hepatocyte. Significantly, however, human hepatoma cell cultures can support ongoing replication of a high abundance of viral RNA, and express the entire viral polyprotein, without apparent effects on cell survival or gross changes in the cellular RNA transcriptome, as determined by high-density oligonucleotide microarray assays.[97]

Although the liver appears to be the primary source of virus present in blood, there are few data that directly support this conjecture. HCV-specific antigens and both negative- and positive-strand HCV RNA have been identified within hepatocytes, indicating that replication does occur in this cell type via a negative-strand intermediate, as outlined previously.[98-100] However, additional data suggest that the virus may also replicate within peripheral mononuclear cells of lymphoid or perhaps bone marrow origin (see next section).[101,102] Mathematical models of viral kinetics suggest a half-life of approximately 2.5 hours for virions in the bloodstream and that up to 1.0×10^{12} virions are produced each day in a chronically infected human.[103,104] This rate exceeds comparable estimates of the production of human immunodeficiency virus (HIV) by more than an order of magnitude.

Genetic Diversity

Quasispecies Variation

The high level of virion turnover, coupled with the absence of proofreading by the NS5B RNA polymerase, results in the relatively rapid accumulation of viral mutations. Typically, multiple HCV variants can be recovered from the plasma and liver of an infected individual at any time. As a result, like many RNA viruses, HCV exists in each infected person as a quasispecies or "swarm" of closely related but distinct genetic sequences.[54,105] For example, up to 85% of cDNA clones transcribed from viral RNAs in the blood of a recently infected individual may represent unique genetic variants.[106] During RNA replication, mutations most likely occur in an almost random fashion throughout the genome, whereas fixation of a substitution within the quasispecies population depends on how that substitution influences viral "fitness" as related to its effect on functional protein/RNA structures, the capacity for viral replication, and the host-virus interaction.

Immunologic responses appear to be important selective forces. For example, viral RNAs containing spontaneous mutations within the HVR-1 segment of the E2 protein (see earlier discussion) may be favored for survival in the host if they reduce the binding of preexisting neutralizing antibodies to the viral envelope, and they may be relatively neutral in terms of viral replication.[107-110] Significantly, agammaglobulinemic patients have slower evolution of amino acid sequence changes within HRV-1.[111,112] There is also evidence that cellular immune responses may drive the selection of specific quasispecies variants.[113] Therefore, quasispecies variants recovered from blood reflect the balance of production and selective forces.

Although the nucleotide substitutions identified in circulating virus represent only a fraction of all mutations generated during viral replication, these mutations are estimated to occur at an overall rate of 0.9 to 1.92×10^{-3} base substitutions per site per year during chronic infection.[114-116] Variation within an HCV quasispecies swarm can be described either in terms of the number of nucleotide differences between variants within a single blood sample (i.e., *genetic diversity*), or in terms of the number of distinct variants (i.e., *genetic complexity*). There is considerable interest in determining the clinical correlates of these parameters. Although much remains to be learned, it appears that genetic complexity is linked to the extent of disease and the duration of infection.[117] This is consistent with the hypothesis that immunologic responses affect both the extent of disease progression and the gener-

ation of sequence diversity. Therefore, quasispecies variation results from the persistence of infection in the face of an active but less than completely effective immune response; it is not likely, however, to be the sole cause of persistence (see "Mechanisms of Persistence"). Differences in the HCV quasispecies present in blood and liver have been described, suggesting that differences in tissue tropism may also influence genetic variation.[102,118,119]

The extent of genetic diversity varies markedly throughout the HCV genome, being highest in the segment that encodes the amino terminus of the second envelope protein, E2, within the HVR-1; almost as high in p7; and lowest in the core and NS5B genes and in the 5' and 3' UTRs of the genome.[107-110,120] High conservation at some loci suggests functional constraint; that is, mutations may be lethal or sufficiently disadvantageous to replication to be undetectable among surviving virus populations.

Hepatitis C Virus Genotypes

In addition to the impressive heterogeneity that often exists among HCV sequences present in a single infected individual (quasispecies variation), there is also remarkable genetic heterogeneity and divergence among HCV sequences recovered from different individuals (strain and genotype variation). Phylogenetic evaluation of HCV sequences recovered from multiple geographic regions suggests that there are at least six major genotypes or clades.[121] These subtypes are even more diverse than those causing the worldwide HIV-1 pandemic (Fig. 150-5). Depending on the genomic region evaluated, HCV sequences assigned to different genotypes may have less than 60% nucleotide sequence identity. This level of nucleotide sequence divergence usually correlates with substantial serotypic differences among other RNA viruses; for example, poliovirus type 1 and poliovirus type 2 are not cross-neutralizable in assays of antibody-mediated neutralization. Little is known, however, of the extent of serotypic variation among HCV strains. Despite extensive study, there is little evidence that HCV genotypes differ in transmissibility, level of replication, or rate of progression of the resulting liver disease. There are differences in response to interferon-based treatments, and these differences are likely to be magnified as new small-molecule therapeutics enter onto the clinical scene (see "Treatment").

Within individual HCV genotypes, strains can be further grouped into subgenotypes (subtypes) that typically share 75% to 85% nucleotide sequence identity within the core-E1 and NS5B regions of the genome.[121,122] In contrast, the quasispecies variants that exist within a single individual usually have 91% to 99% identity in these regions.[123]

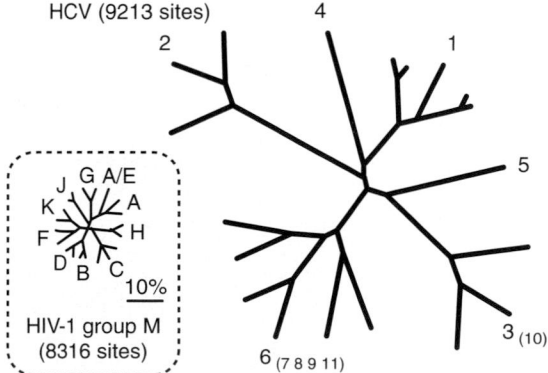

FIGURE 150-5. Phylogenetic trees for hepatitis C virus (HCV) and human immunodeficiency virus (HIV) *(inset)* derived from full-length genome nucleotide sequences. Sequences of representative strains for major genotypes were obtained from GenBank and aligned using ClustalX with minor manual adjustment; then sites containing gaps were removed, resulting in an alignment of 9213 sites for HCV and 8316 sites for HIV. Trees were inferred using the maximum likelihood HKY+G model in PAUP version 4b10 (Sinauer Associates Inc., Sunderland, MA). Tree sizes were adjusted to the same scale in terms of genetic distance.

The phylogenetic grouping of HCV strains appears to be largely independent of the segment of the genome that is analyzed.[121,124]

The geographic distribution of HCV genotypes is not fully characterized, but some trends are apparent. Within the United States, 60% to 70% of isolates are of either genotype 1a or genotype 1b (Fig. 150-6).[125,126] In contrast, genotype 4 infections are prevalent throughout Africa and the Middle East.[127] For example, more than 90% of the viral sequences recovered in an Egyptian survey were of genotype 4.[128] Genotypes 5 and 6 have been reported in South Africa and Southeast Asia.[129-131] Genotype 3 occurs in Asia but has been linked in other geographic regions to illicit drug use.[132] Differences among early proposals for genotype nomenclature may lead to some confusion in interpreting such studies. At present there is general acceptance of a uniform nomenclature, and an HCV sequence database may be accessed on the World Wide Web at http://hcv.lanl.gov.[11]

Viral Tropism

As indicated earlier, there is good evidence that HCV replicates within the hepatocyte. However, replication may also occur in other cell types. Some studies have suggested the presence of negative-strand (replicative intermediate) HCV RNA in T cells, B cells, and monocytes, especially in patients with chronic infection.[133-137] Others have suggested that this occurs rarely,[101] or not at all,[138,139] but, as mentioned previously, differences in dominant quasispecies populations in these various compartments are supportive of extrahepatic infection. Substantial evidence also supports the ability of HCV to replicate at low levels in cultured human cells of T- and B-cell origin.[140]

HCV RNA also has been detected in cutaneous lesions of persons with HCV-related cryoglobulinemia and vasculitis,[141] in renal biopsy specimens from patients with HCV-associated membranoproliferative glomerulonephritis,[142] and (with variable success) in various body fluids including saliva, semen, tears, urine, and ascitic fluid.[143-147] Unlike HBV, HCV does not replicate through a DNA intermediate and does not have the ability to integrate its genetic information into chromosomal DNA. Therefore, the detection of HCV sequences in these tissues and fluids may indicate the presence of infectious virus, though transmission via these fluids appears to be rare (see "Transmission of Hepatitis C Virus").

Experimental Models

Autonomously Replicating Viral Replicons and Genome-Length RNAs

Specially constructed subgenomic HCV RNAs (replicons) and genome-length RNAs have been shown to undergo autonomous replication in certain cultured cells. These relatively new model systems have provided novel opportunities for study of HCV RNA replication mechanisms and virus–host cell interactions. The first such replicons were dicistronic RNAs derived from molecularly cloned cDNA (Fig. 150-7).[148] The expression of a selectable antibiotic marker, such as neomycin phosphotransferase (Neo), from the upstream cistron of these dicistronic RNAs under control of the natural HCV IRES allowed the selection of stable cell clones supporting replication of the RNA after its transfection into the cells. The downstream cistron, en-

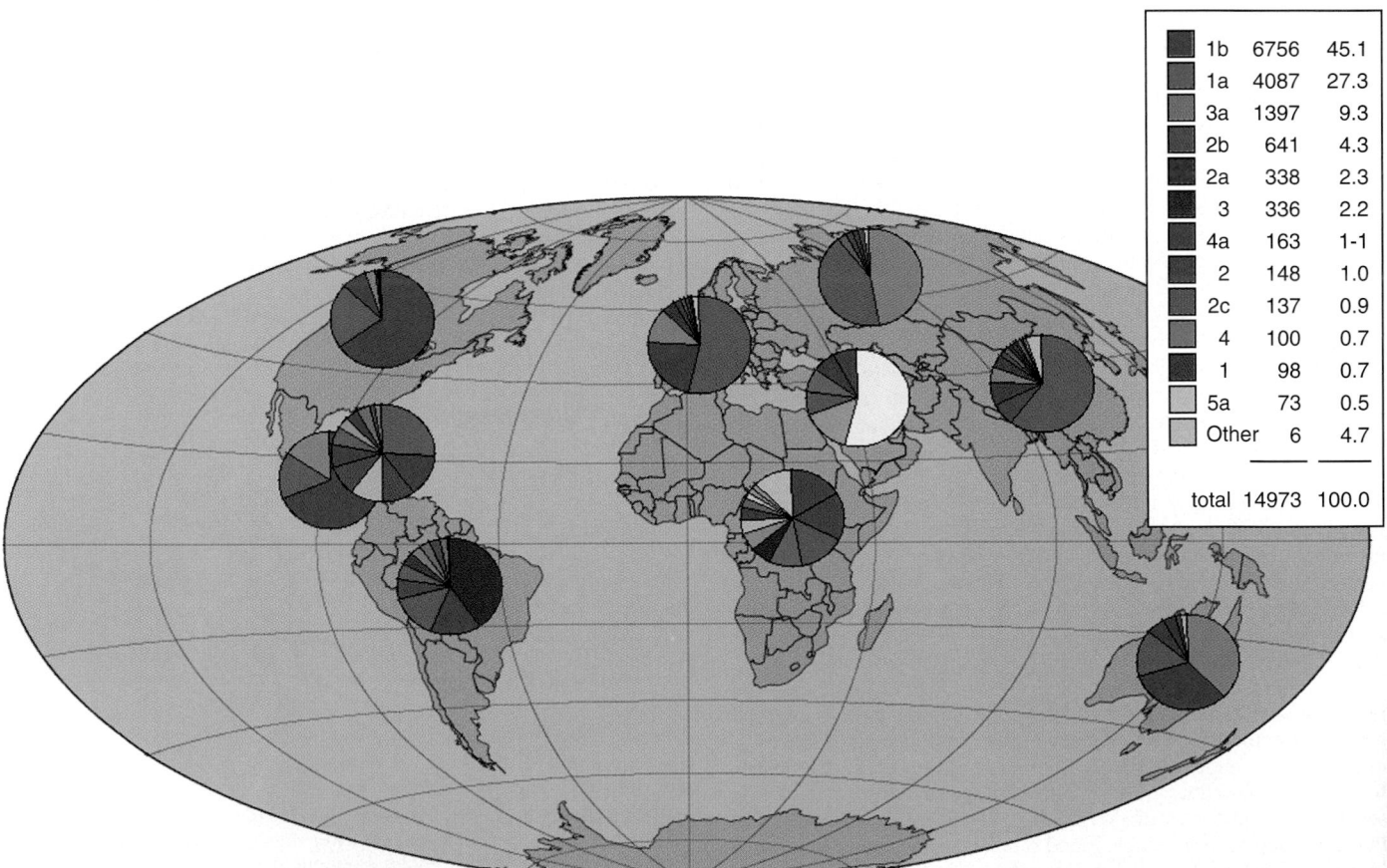

1b	6756	45.1
1a	4087	27.3
3a	1397	9.3
2b	641	4.3
2a	338	2.3
3	336	2.2
4a	163	1-1
2	148	1.0
2c	137	0.9
4	100	0.7
1	98	0.7
5a	73	0.5
Other	6	4.7
total	14973	100.0

FIGURE 150-6. Hepatitis C virus subtype distribution worldwide, based on availability in online databases because population-based sampling is not consistently available. Of 21,211 available sequences, geographic and subtype information could be determined for 12,904, which were clustered by region: Africa, Asia, the Caribbean, Central America, Europe, countries of the former Soviet Union, the Middle East, North America, Oceania, and South America. An interactive version of this map is available online at http://hcv.lanl.gov, under the Geography link (accessed April 27, 2004). *(Courtesy of Dr. Carla Kuiken, Los Alamos National Laboratory.)*

coding either the NS2-NS5B or NS3-NS5B nonstructural proteins, was placed under the translational control of a picornaviral IRES. Such RNAs demonstrate a surprisingly robust replication phenotype in cultured human hepatoma cells (Huh7 cells), but typically only after the accumulation of adaptive mutations within the HCV sequence (often in the NS5A protein) that enhance in vitro replication capacity.[149] Interestingly, such mutations appear to substantially attenuate the ability of the virus to replicate in chimpanzees.[150] Some HCV RNAs have been further adapted to growth in HeLa cells and even in cells of murine origin.[151]

Because subgenomic replicon RNAs lack the sequence encoding the structural proteins (core, E1, E2, and p7), they are not capable of producing infectious particles. However, replication-competent, selectable dicistronic RNAs that encode all of the viral proteins also have been developed, and they also do not appear to produce infectious particles despite substantial replication in hepatoma cells.[152] The nature of the apparent block in virion production in these cells is not known. Although the first replicons were made from genotype 1b strains of HCV, RNAs from other genotypes (1a and 2a) have been adapted to highly efficient replication in Huh7 cells. These subgenomic HCV replicons and genome-length RNAs appear to recapitulate the natural mechanisms of HCV RNA replication. They are proving useful for discerning differences in the susceptibility of different viral strains and genotypes to new candidate antiviral compounds and for studying mechanisms of resistance.

Propagation of Virus in Cell Cultures

No cell culture system has yet been developed that supports all steps in the virus life cycle and permits efficient replication of the virus. However, low-level HCV replication has been demonstrated in lymphoid cell lines, including a murine retrovirus-infected human T-cell line (HPB-Ma), a human T-cell leukemia virus type I–infected line (MT-2), a human B-cell line (Daudi), and others.[140,153-156] In these cell lines, replication has been shown to be sensitive to interferon, and strong evidence has been presented for transmission of the virus between cells.[157,158] The genetic diversity of the viral inoculum declines over time in such cultures, suggesting the selection of a particular variant that is favored for replication (see preceding section). Furthermore, a chimpanzee was successfully infected with culture supernatant har-

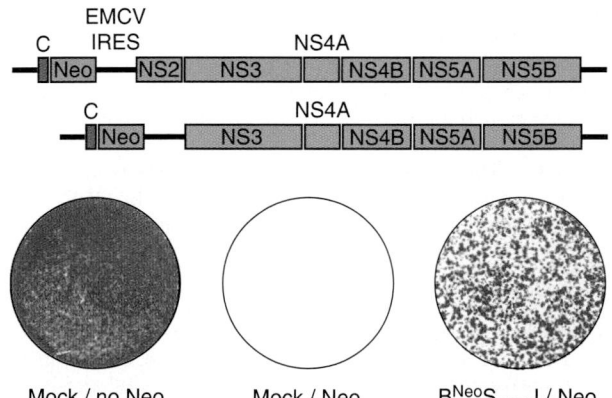

Mock / no Neo   Mock / Neo $B^{Neo}S_{1179}I$ / Neo

FIGURE 150-7. Organization of subgenomic hepatitis C virus replicons and selection of antibiotic-resistant human hepatoma cells after transfection with a neomycin phosphotransferase–expressing RNA replicon. At the top is the genetic organization of subgenomic replicons encoding the NS3-NS5B and NS2-NS5B segments of the viral polyprotein, as described by Lohmann et al.[148] Below are photographs of cultures of human hepatoma (Huh7) cells that were either mock-transfected or transfected with a subgenomic NS3-NS5B replicon RNA containing a cell-culture adaptation mutation within NS5A ($B^{Neo}S_{1179}I$). After transfection, the cells in the two plates on the right were treated with G418 (neomycin). All cultures were stained with crystal violet approximately 3 weeks later.

vested from Daudi cells 58 days after their inoculation with virus.[159] Low-level HCV replication also has been demonstrated in human hepatocytes immortalized with simian virus 40 (SV-40), primary chimpanzee hepatocytes, and primary human hepatocytes.[160,161] No one has yet recovered infectious virus after transfection of synthetic genome-length RNA into any type of cell culture, although HCV can be rescued by inoculation of the RNA into the liver of a chimpanzee.[96,162]

Animal Models

The chimpanzee, *Pan troglodytes*, is the only nonhuman animal species that has been demonstrated conclusively to be permissive for HCV replication. Percutaneous inoculation of HCV RNA–positive plasma, and in one instance saliva, has resulted in HCV infection.[163-165] Also, as noted earlier, chimpanzees have been infected by intrahepatic inoculation of synthetic genome-length RNA derived from cDNA clones.[95,96] Therefore, the chimpanzee represents a valuable model for hepatitis C infection. However, there is generally much less evidence for HCV-related disease in infected chimpanzees than in infected humans, and there may also be differences in the frequency of virus persistence and in the nature of the immunologic response.[165] Because the chimpanzee is an endangered species, the use of this animal model has been severely limited by costs, scarcity of the animals, and ethical concerns. Therefore, it is of interest that GBV-B infection of nonendangered tamarins or marmosets shows substantial promise as a surrogate animal model for hepatitis C. GBV-B has greater sequence homology with HCV than any other animal virus, replicates within the livers of these animals, and can cause both acute and chronic hepatitis with many features resembling hepatitis C.[166] A viable chimeric virus has been constructed that contains the IRES of HCV within the genetic background of GBV-B (S. Lemon et al., unpublished data, 2003). This novel virus demonstrates a robust replication phenotype in tamarins and will be especially useful for evaluating novel therapeutics, such as small interfering RNAs, that target the 5′ UTR sequences of HCV.

Several lines of transgenic mice have been established that express transgenes encoding all or some HCV proteins under the control of liver-specific promoters.[167-170] None of these transgenes contains the complete HCV genome, so none produces infectious virus. Because these animals have immunologic tolerance to the HCV proteins they express, they are useful for determining the effects of viral protein expression on hepatocyte function in the absence of an immune response. Although some of these transgenic mouse lineages appear to be free of disease, at least three mouse lines, which were established in two different laboratories, develop age-related hepatic steatosis and hepatocellular carcinoma.[168,169,171] These phenotypic effects are particularly associated with expression of the core protein, although they have also been noted in transgenic mice expressing other viral proteins, and they suggest that nonimmune mechanisms play a role in the pathogenesis of HCV-related liver injury. Transgenic mice with inducible HCV transgenes have also been developed.[172] Some data suggest that postnatal induction of HCV gene expression in these mice can lead to an immune-mediated hepatitis, indicating that such animals may be useful for investigations of the immune response to HCV proteins in vivo. In addition, salivary gland lesions similar to those observed with Sjögren's syndrome have been noted in transgenic mice expressing the envelope proteins of HCV.[173]

NATURAL HISTORY AND PATHOGENESIS

Viral Persistence

In experimentally infected chimpanzees and in humans, HCV RNA can be detected in plasma within days after exposure, often 1 to 4 weeks before liver enzyme levels rise.[163,174-176] Viremia usually peaks in the first 8 to 12 weeks of infection, then drops to lower levels and persists (Fig. 150-8).[177] In some instances, plasma HCV RNA becomes undetectable in the first few months and remains undetectable indefinitely (viral clearance); in other instances, viremia is inconsistently detected early and a stable pattern of recovery or persistence is not evident for more than 6 months.[163,178-180] Some instances of intermittent viremia may reflect reinfection, which has been observed in active injection drug users.[178] In other cases, rebounding viremia may represent escape from an initially successful immune response.[179,181] Overall, viremia persists in 50% to 85% of acutely infected persons (see "Acute Hepatitis C").[178,180,182-185]

Because of limitations in experimental models and the infrequent recognition of natural acute infection, the mechanisms of viral clearance are poorly understood. There are clinical and epidemiologic clues suggesting that host factors are critical. The role of the host in viral persistence was evident in common-source outbreaks, in which a large number of persons were accidentally infected with the same HCV inoculum and only some recovered.[186] In addition, HCV infection more often persists in African Americans than in Caucasian Americans, and more often in persons infected with HIV compared with immunocompetent persons.[187,188] Individuals also are more likely to clear HCV infection if they develop clinical symptoms (i.e., become jaundiced), which correlates with a more vigorous immune response.[178] Nonetheless, it has been difficult to define the immunologic mechanisms of HCV persistence and their genetic determinants.

Humoral Immunity

Within months after infection, antibodies are detectable in blood to multiple recombinant antigens that correspond to structural and nonstructural HCV genes. Emergence of HCV-specific antibodies does not correlate temporally with viral recovery. Indeed, although virtually all immunocompetent persons develop antibody responses to some HCV antigens, most infections persist. Viral recovery also has been described in persons with congenital agammaglobulinemia.[189] On the other hand, there are data indicating that the humoral immune response can neutralize individual variants even though it does not appear to play a major role in viral recovery. For example, there were fewer HCV infections among liver transplant recipients who received immune globulin before 1990, when it contained antibody to HCV.[190] Likewise, in a randomized controlled study, immune globulin administration was associated with a reduced incidence of sexual HCV transmission.[191] In the chimpanzee model, Farci and colleagues[55,192] demonstrated that anti-

bodies could neutralize HCV infection in chimpanzees if those antibodies were directed at the HVR-1 sequence in the E2 protein (see earlier discussion), and that the same antibodies could not neutralize an inoculum collected later that had amino acid changes in the envelope sequence. Krawczynski and co-workers[193] showed that postexposure immune globulin administration prolonged the incubation of HCV infection and, in later studies, that it was associated with early termination of infection. Persons with reduced humoral immunity also accumulate fewer amino acid mutations in the E2 sequence.[112,194]

Several functional expression systems have been described for the HCV envelope proteins, including the use of pseudotyped lentiviruses.[195,196] These pseudotyped lentivirus particles have been used to develop simple cell culture–based assays for putative neutralizing antibodies. However, there still is relatively little information available concerning the mechanisms of antibody-mediated neutralization, the extent of serotypic variation among virus strains, and the identity of important B-cell epitopes. In persons who recover from HCV infection, HCV antibody responses decline, sometimes to levels below the limits of detection by commercial assays.[165,178,197] In contrast, CD4+ T-lymphocyte responses often are maintained (see "Cellular Immunity"). Collectively, these data suggest that the humoral immune response can neutralize individual HCV variants, and can possibly limit the severity or even the risk of recurrent infection, but plays little role in recovery from infection.

Cellular Immunity

Viral recovery has been associated with a vigorous, broad cellular immune response.[179,198-203] It appears that both CD4+ T lymphocytes and CD8+ T lymphocytes play important roles in acute infection. In persons who recover, there are detectable CD4+ T-lymphocyte responses but not CD8+ T-lymphocyte responses.[179,204] In contrast, in persons with persistent infection, CD4+ T-lymphocyte responses are more difficult to detect in peripheral blood than are CD8+ T-lymphocyte responses.[204] It has been noted that some HCV-specific CD8+ T lymphocytes are unable to produce interferon-γ, a so-called "stunned" phenotype that could contribute to their inability to eradicate infection.[205,206] Thimme and colleagues[179] contrasted HCV-reactive CD38+ and CD38−CD8+ T lymphocytes and suggested that the latter, which appear to secrete interferon-γ, may clear infection through noncytolytic mechanisms, whereas the former may destroy liver cells, thereby causing hepatitis.[179] Stronger polyclonal cytotoxic T-lymphocyte (CTL) responses in the peripheral blood and liver have been associated with lower levels of circulating HCV RNA.[207,208] HCV-specific CTLs also have been found in persons who were exposed to HCV but were never known to have had HCV antibody or viremia.[209,210] Experiments carried out in chimpanzees indicate that both CD4+ and CD8+ memory T cells play critical roles in protection against reinfection with HCV. The control of second infections appears to be kinetically linked to rapid acquisition of cytolytic activity by CD8+ T cells that are resident in the liver, and it is normally associated with an expansion of circulating CD4+ and CD8+ memory T cells.[211]

Mechanisms of Persistence

Surprisingly little is known about why some cellular immune responses are broad and vigorous and others are ineffective. Coinfection with HIV or schistosomiasis has been associated with viral persistence, which in schistosomiasis also corresponded with a diminished CD4+ T-lymphocyte response.[187,212] Host differences between persons whose infections persist and those whose infections clear have been described, including the presence of certain MHC class I and II alleles.[213-216]

Innate immunity is probably extremely important in the initial containment of infection and subsequent activation of adaptive immune responses.[217] As described earlier, the NS3/4A protease directs a blockade of the viral activation of IRF3,[75] a latent cytoplasmic transcription factor that, when activated by virus infection, is translocated to the nucleus and induces the transcription of interferon-β. Interferon-β, through autocrine and paracrine mechanisms, subsequently stimulates the synthesis of interferon-α and a wide variety of

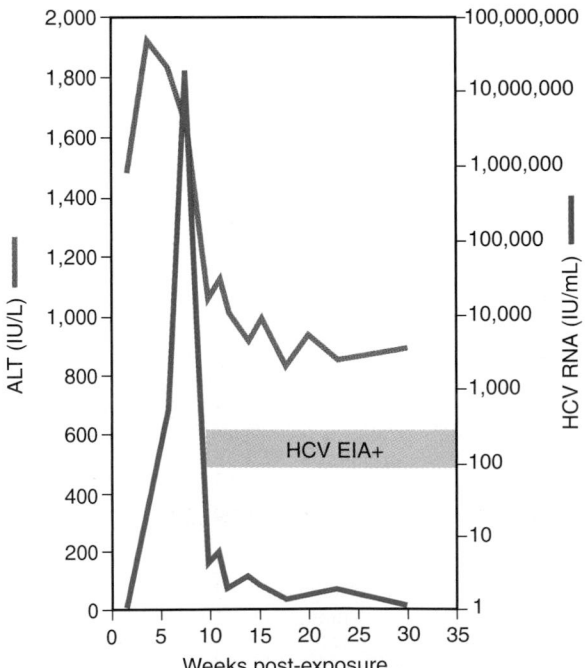

FIGURE 150-8. Course of acute hepatitis C virus (HCV) infection occurring in a health care worker after a needlestick accident (at time 0). ALT, alanine aminotransferase. *(From Sulkowski MS, Ray SC, Thomas DL. Needlestick transmission of hepatitis C. JAMA 2002;287:2406-2413.)*

other antiviral cytokines and chemokines that both inhibit viral replication and help to orchestrate the adaptive immune response. Very recent work suggests that the NS3/4A protease blockade of IRF3 activation is associated with the ability of the protease to proteolytically cleave an unknown protein within a novel intracellular signaling pathway that is independent of Toll-like receptors and that leads to IRF3 activation on viral infection. N53/4A is also capable of cleaving TRIF, a cellular regulatory molecule that serves as an adapter protein for Toll-like receptors 3 and 4, and that contributes to signaling the presence of viral infection through both IRF3 and NFκB pathways (K. Li et al., unpublished data, 2004). When infected by sendai virus, hepatoma cells supporting HCV replicons (see earlier discussion) transcribe less of the NF-κB–regulated cytokines (e.g., interleukin-6, interleukin-12), IRF3-regulated interferons, and interferon-stimulated genes (ISGs). It is therefore surprising that microarray studies have shown convincing, vigorous type 1 interferon responses within the livers of both acutely and chronically infected chimpanzees.[218,219] Further research is needed to resolve whether these interferons are produced by uninfected cells or by another mechanism.

In addition to potentially blocking the induction of interferons, HCV appears capable of impairing interferon-related effector functions. Defects in the Jak-STAT signaling pathway have been described in HCV transgenic mice.[220] In addition, the NS5A protein has been shown to bind to the catalytic domain of PKR, and this interaction may block the antiproliferative and antiviral effects of this dsRNA- and interferon-induced antiviral kinase.[83]

NK and natural killer T lymphocytes (NKT cells) are abundant in liver and, through the production of interferon-γ and other cytokines, they prime the cellular immune responses.[221] Thus, it is important that binding of the E2 protein to CD81 has been associated with inhibition of NK cell activity.[222,223] Likewise, the human leukocyte antigen allele HLA-Cw*04 and its related haplotypes, which reportedly bind to inhibitory killer immunoglobulin-like receptors on NK cells, have been associated with viral persistence.[214] Liver dendritic cells also facilitate T-cell priming, and HCV infection has been associated with impaired peripheral dendritic cell function in several studies.[224,225] Whether intrahepatic dendritic cells become infected with HCV is unknown. In addition, Crispe[217] and others have pointed out that immune responses within the liver may inherently be biased toward tolerance because of the frequent exposure of the intrahepatic environment to antigenic material borne in food.

Still other mechanisms have been suggested to reduce the susceptibility of infected cells to cytolytic attack by immune cells. The HCV core protein binds to the cytoplasmic tail of the TNF-α receptor and the lymphotoxin-β receptor.[40,41,43] This binding occurs immediately adjacent to the death domain and may modulate signal transduction through the receptor. Although the biologic effects of this interaction remain controversial, it is possible that it protects the infected cell against TNF-α–mediated apoptotic cell death. Although this has not been observed with HCV infection itself, defects in adenovirus-related, Fas-mediated apoptosis have been documented in HCV-transgenic mice, both in vivo and in hepatocyte explant cultures ex vivo.[226]

The highly glycosylated nature of the viral envelope may protect it against antibody-mediated neutralization, analogous to the "glycan shield" hypothesis for HIV-1.[227] Furthermore, the envelope may have evolved a structure (namely the HVR-1) that allows it to decoy antibodies and to protect an otherwise vulnerable, conserved receptor-binding ligand from antibody attack.[59] In addition, the virus may regulate replication to a level that is too low to disrupt cellular homeostasis and that generates only meager amounts of viral antigens.

Finally, HCV sequence variation and immune escape from both T and B cells may also contribute to viral persistence.[59,228] Mutation within the amino acid sequence of a critical epitope may allow a new quasispecies variant to evade a previously suppressive immune response, either cellular or humoral.[57,113,229] Viral escape from a CTL clone was reported in a chimpanzee with persistent infection and was shown to correlate with a single NS3 amino acid substitution.[113,181] In several studies, acutely infected persons who developed persistent infection had a more complex quasispecies.[59,228] However, because the immune response to HCV is directed against multiple epitopes simultaneously, it seems likely that quasispecies diversity is a result of, rather than the primary cause of, viral persistence. Consistent with this notion, probable escape mutations within class I MHC-restricted epitopes were observed in chimpanzees that had an inadequate CD8+ memory T-cell response due to antibody depletion of CD4+ memory cells.[211] In summary, it appears likely that many factors contribute to HCV persistence and that HCV may have evolved a variety of redundant and overlapping mechanisms of immune evasion to ensure its long-term persistence in the majority of immunologically normal persons who become infected. It is probable that additional mechanisms of viral immune evasion will be identified in the future.

Disease Progression

Although HCV infection leads to hepatic inflammation and steatosis, the major pathologic consequence of persistent HCV infection is the development of hepatic fibrosis, which may progress to life-threatening cirrhosis and a greatly increased risk of hepatocellular carcinoma. These long-term complications generally occur more than 20 years after the onset of infection, although more rapid progression has been reported.[230-232] There are wide estimates (5% to 25%) of the probability of cirrhosis occurring within 10 to 20 years after infection, and very little information is available on progression beyond 30 years (Fig. 150-9).[184,232-235] In two separate studies of women infected with HCV by contaminated Rh immune globulin, the incidence of cirrhosis during 15 to 20 years of follow-up was very low (<5%).[236-238] However, disease progression may have been limited in these cohorts by the relatively young age and exclusive female gender of the infected persons, and possibly by a lower than normal frequency of important cofactors such as alcohol ingestion (see later discussion). In another cohort of 1667 HCV-infected injection drug users who were infected at an estimated average of 14 years and were monitored an average of 8.8 years, the incidence of liver-related mortality was also low (3 per 1000 person-years).[187] Liver biopsies were performed on a random sample of 210 HCV-infected members of this cohort, and only 10% had evidence of serious liver disease (Ishak modified fibrosis scores of 3 to 6).[239]

In yet another study, Sccff and co-workers[236,240] evaluated mortality and morbidity in a cohort of patients a mean of 18 years after posttransfusion hepatitis and in control patients who had been similarly transfused but had not developed recognizable hepatitis. Overall mortality was high, reflecting the severity of underlying conditions, but was not increased in HCV-infected patients. Liver-related mortality was slightly higher in patients with posttransfusion hepatitis (3%) than in controls (1.5%), and it was estimated that approximately 10% of the patients with posttransfusion hepatitis had cirrhosis 20 years later.[236] Other studies of posttransfusion hepatitis have reported a higher rate

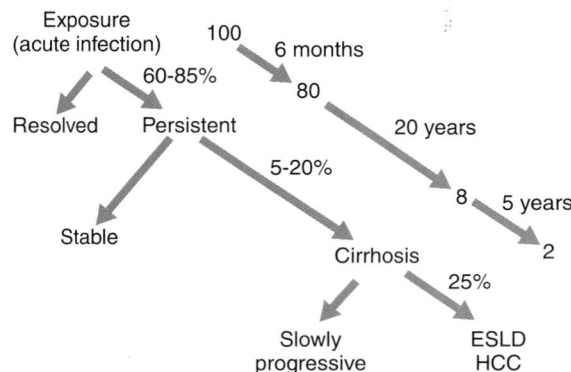

FIGURE 150-9. Natural history of hepatitis C virus (HCV) infection. Estimates of the most common outcomes of HCV infection are provided with extrapolation to the hypothetical acute infection of 100 persons (blue numbers). ESLD, end-stage liver disease (e.g., esophageal varices, ascites, hepatic encephalopathy); HCC, hepatocellular carcinoma. See text for expanded discussion.

of cirrhosis.[230,232] In a community-based study, Alberti and associates[241] tested 4820 Italian Telecom employees for HCV infection and evaluated liver disease in 78 of those who were infected. Significant hepatic histologic abnormalities were detected in 40%.

Limited data concerning progression over periods greater than 30 years come from studies involving the retrospective identification of HCV-infected persons by testing of stored sera. Seeff and co-workers[242] found 17 persons whose sera, stored from 1948 to 1954, contained HCV antibodies. Seven had already died (one of liver disease), two could not be located, and eight were contacted. Five of the eight had no evidence of liver disease, two had biochemical evidence of cirrhosis but no symptoms, and one died before evaluation from a cancer of unknown primary that involved the liver. Once cirrhosis occurs, the rates of progression to liver failure (decompensated cirrhosis) and hepatocellular carcinoma are approximately 2% to 4% and 1% to 7% per year, respectively.[243-245]

The variability and uncertainty in estimates of the frequency of life-threatening liver injury relate to limitations in basic research tools and the variable impact of environmental, host, and possibly viral factors for disease progression in different study cohorts (Table 150-1). Studies in tertiary care facilities generally predict higher rates of progression because they include a greater proportion of symptomatic subjects (referral bias). Assessment of disease is also difficult. Because HCV infection usually does not cause symptoms, it is difficult to assess the incremental progression of disease before clinical manifestation of cirrhosis or end-stage liver disease occurs (see "Clinical Manifestations of Hepatitis C Virus Infection"). Liver fibrosis can be evaluated by biopsy (see "Liver Biopsy"). A comparison of biopsy scores with estimates of the duration of infection led Poynard and associates[246] to advance the notion that fibrosis progresses linearly. In their study of 2235 persons, the median estimated rate of fibrosis progression per year was 0.133 "fibrosis units" (95% confidence interval, 0.125 to 0.143 unit/year). Given that the factors that determine progression, such as alcohol use, vary over time, it is surprising that fairly consistent results have also been reported from other studies, such as the prospective studies of Ghany and co-workers[247] (0.12 unit/year) and Wali and colleagues[248] (0.15 unit/year). However, liver biopsies are not easily obtained, especially outside referral centers, and they can misrepresent the amount of disease due to variability in sampling and interpretation.[249-251]

TABLE 150-1 Factors Associated with Cirrhosis in Persons with Hepatitis C Virus (HCV) Infection

Factor	Comment
Environmental	
Alcohol use	Importance of minimal alcohol ingestion (<20 g/day) has not been established
Host	
Human immunodeficiency virus (HIV) infection	Demonstrated in hemophiliacs; appears to be increasingly important as HIV-related survival improves
Duration of HCV infection	Cirrhosis is rare before 10 yr
Human leukocyte antigen (HLA) type	HLA-B54 is correlated with increased risk of cirrhosis, DRB1*0301 with lack of cirrhosis
Viral	
Quasispecies complexity	Cross-sectional studies cannot assess causality, and complexity may be somewhat related to duration of infection
HCV genotype 1	Genotype 1b in some but not other studies; 1b infections may be of longer duration, confounding this association
Quantitative measures of viremia (serum or plasma HCV RNA level)	Weak association, sometimes lost in multivariate analysis

The leading environmental determinant appears to be alcohol ingestion.[252-256] Although excessive alcohol ingestion and HCV infection can independently cause cirrhosis, combined exposure has a synergistic effect.[187,253,255,257] This is especially true with very heavy alcohol ingestion (>50 to 125 g/day), which in one study increased the risk of cirrhosis approximately 100-fold.[253] The mechanism underlying this synergy with an environmental toxin remains obscure, but both alcohol ingestion and HCV infection can cause microvesicular steatosis, suggesting a common pathway involving mitochondrial injury.[97,258] Coinfection with HBV may also accelerate disease progression, but persistent GBV-C infection does not appear to affect hepatitis C.[259-263] HIV infection increases the level of HCV viremia and is associated with more rapid progression of liver disease (see later discussion).[264-269] Likewise, schistosomiasis coinfection is associated with much more rapid progression of HCV-related fibrosis in Egypt.[270] Increased progression of liver disease also has been reported in patients with immunosuppression associated with agammaglobulinemia or transplantation.[271-273]

There is substantial evidence that disease progression is increased in persons who are infected at older ages. This factor alone may explain much of the variability in studies, because those involving persons infected at older ages through transfusions appear to have the highest rates of progression to cirrhosis.[187,241,246] Although there are few studies detailing the natural history of HCV infection in children, the overall rate of disease progression appears quite slow, with few notable exceptions.[274-278] Strong associations between progression of fibrosis and both older age and various forms of immunosuppression remain largely unexplained.

Hepatic Fibrosis

Liver fibrosis is the net result of a complex, tightly-regulated, dynamic process in which collagen and other proteins are deposited and removed from a matrix in the subendothelial space between hepatocytes and the sinusoidal endothelium. Accumulation of liver fibrosis occurs in response to all forms of liver injury. With viral hepatitis it begins in the periportal zone and gradually extends as so-called septa between portal areas and into lobules toward the central veins.[279] As the matrix expands and changes its composition, normal liver physiology can be disrupted and the architecture of the organ altered, although it is not clear whether this process is clinically evident before cirrhosis develops. The hepatic stellate cell (Ito cell) appears to be the chief architect of this matrix, responding to a variety of stimuli leading to various stages of activation (see Friedman's excellent review[280]).

Cytokines, reactive oxygen species, and other mediators of inflammation can initiate stellate cell activation, which can be perpetuated by autocrine and paracrine stimulation. Kupffer cells can play an important role initiating and perpetuating fibrogenesis, through production of transforming growth factor-β (TGF-β), metalloproteinases, and reactive oxygen species.[281-283] CD8+ and CD4+ T lymphocytes also appear to influence the pathogenesis of fibrosis, chiefly through stellate cell activation. In the CCl$_4$ mouse model, fibrogenesis is enhanced when Th1/CD8+ lymphocyte responses (in particular, interferon-γ) are depleted and by expression of Th2/CD4+ lymphocyte-derived cytokines such as interleukin-4.[284] These data are interesting in light of the clinical observation of greater progression of fibrosis in persons coinfected with schistosomiasis, in whom Th2-like responses predominated,[270] and of extremely rapid fibrosis progression in persons with congenital agammaglobulinemia.[271]

Nonetheless, it remains unknown why only some immunocompetent persons with chronic hepatitis C develop cirrhosis. There is little reason to believe that certain HCV variants are more virulent than others. In acute infection, the virus replicates at high level for weeks with little or no evidence of liver damage. In a few studies, cirrhosis was associated with infection with genotype 1b virus, the presence of a greater complexity of HCV quasispecies, and higher levels of viremia.[117,125,285-287] However, there is no clear correlation between the level of viremia and disease progression, such as exists in HIV infection,[288,289] and the other findings have not been confirmed.

Host genetic factors probably play a role in determining why some infected persons develop cirrhosis. Wiley and co-workers[290] reported that African Americans have slower progression of fibrosis, compared with Caucasian Americans, a finding that appeared independent of other factors and that has also been noted by others. Specific HLA alleles have been associated with differences in the progression of disease, as have polymorphisms in several genes that are believed to play a role in disease pathogenesis, including the gene for TGF-β.[291-296] With few exceptions, however, the link between these polymorphisms and the pathogenesis of disease remains unclear.

Hepatocellular Carcinoma

The risk of hepatocellular carcinoma is increased in HCV-infected persons, particularly in those with cirrhosis. In fact, there has been an increasing incidence of hepatocellular carcinoma in Western countries that has been attributed to prior increases in the prevalence of HCV infection.[297,298] Worldwide, there is considerable variation in the fraction of hepatocellular carcinoma attributed to HCV infection.[299-302] In Japan, Korea, and Southern Europe, 50% to 75% of hepatocellular carcinoma is associated with HCV infection.[303] In one Italian study, HCV infection was found in 71% of patients with liver cancer, and HBV infection in only 15%.[302]

One study in Japan reported a threefold increased incidence of hepatocellular carcinoma occurring in association with HCV infection, compared with chronic hepatitis B.[303] The mortality rate for hepatocellular carcinoma in Japan increased approximately twofold during the 1980s, and this increase could be attributed entirely to an increased incidence of HCV-associated liver cancer.[304] Reports from the Japanese Ministry of Health suggested that this relatively recent increase in the HCV-related disease burden stems from widespread illicit injection of amphetamines in the 1950s and the related spread of HCV within the Japanese population approximately 25 to 30 years before illicit injection drug use peaked in the United States. Some authorities have argued that the United States should therefore anticipate a similar increase in HCV-related cases of hepatocellular cancer, a phenomenon that is perhaps already being seen. Recent studies in the United States indicate that approximately one quarter of persons with hepatocellular carcinoma have HCV infection.[305,306] However, whereas cases of life-threatening cirrhosis appear to greatly outnumber cases of liver cancer related to HCV infection in the United States, the opposite appears to be the case at present in Japan.

As with cirrhosis, several cofactors have been proposed in the development of HCV-associated hepatocellular carcinoma. HBV coinfection appears to increase the risk of hepatocellular carcinoma in HCV-infected persons.[260,307] Infection with genotype 1b virus also has been associated with hepatocellular carcinoma, but this may reflect longer duration of infection.[301,305,308] Alcohol and tobacco use, older age, and male gender are associated with hepatocellular carcinoma among HCV-infected persons.[260,301]

Relatively little is known about how chronic HCV infection leads to cancer. The HCV genome is not reverse-transcribed to DNA and therefore cannot integrate into host cell chromosomes. Transforming activities have been associated with the core and NS3 proteins.[39,76] Strong evidence in favor of a direct or indirect transforming action of the core protein comes from studies of transgenic mice that develop such tumors in the absence of an immune response.[168,171] In addition, it is possible that NS5A promotes the development of tumors by repressing the antitumor activity of PKR.[83] However, in humans chronic HCV replication is not by itself sufficient to cause hepatocellular carcinoma, even if it is accompanied by inflammation, because liver cancer does not usually occur in the large number of persons with long-term HCV infection and no cirrhosis. Even in the transgenic mouse model, liver cancer probably occurs as a result of increased hepatocyte turnover, dysregulation of proapoptotic and antiapoptotic cellular signaling pathways, the generation of free hydroxyl radicals that are capable of damaging cellular DNA, or a combination of these factors.[97,309]

CLINICAL MANIFESTATIONS OF HEPATITIS C VIRUS INFECTION

Acute Hepatitis C

Although acute HCV infection usually is not associated with symptoms, it can cause malaise, nausea, and right upper quadrant pain, followed by dark urine and jaundice. Such infections are clinically indistinguishable in the individual patient from other types of acute viral hepatitis. Based on studies of transfusion recipients,[310,311] the incubation period for acute hepatitis C averages about 7 weeks and therefore is intermediate between those of hepatitis A and hepatitis B. However, HCV RNA can be detected in blood within days after exposure and is followed by elevations in serum levels of the liver-specific enzymes alanine aminotransferase (ALT), aspartate aminotransferase (AST), and in some cases bilirubin. Clinical symptoms and aminotransferase elevations are generally less severe than with acute hepatitis A or B. Prospective studies of transfusion recipients and injection drug users showed that more than 75% of acute hepatitis C infections are anicteric and would be missed without careful screening for ALT elevation or seroconversion.[178,310] Extrahepatic manifestations are not prominent in acute HCV infection.

Fulminant Hepatitis C

Approximately 20% of all cases of fulminant hepatitis that are thought to be caused by infectious agents are not caused by HAV or HBV. Although this would suggest a role for HCV, the frequency with which HCV causes fulminant hepatitis is controversial. HCV infection has been associated with 40% to 60% of fulminant non-A, non-B hepatitis in Japan, but it is a very uncommon cause of fulminant liver disease in Western countries.[312-314] This discordance has never been explained, but it might arise from variation in host factors or viral strains, or both. There appears to be an increased likelihood of fulminant liver disease after acute HAV infection in persons with underlying chronic hepatitis C.[315]

Chronic Hepatitis C

Between 50% and 85% of persons with acute HCV infection develop persistent infection with long-term viremia, as described earlier (viral persistence; see Fig. 150-9). Therefore, although only 1 in 6 cases of symptomatic acute viral hepatitis is caused by HCV infection, HCV is the leading infectious cause of chronic liver disease in the United States. Persistently infected individuals tend to have few symptoms that are clearly caused by HCV infection (e.g., fatigue, malaise), leading some to question whether hepatitis C is of any consequence in the majority of patients who never develop cirrhosis.[235] Many quality-of-life indices are reduced in HCV-infected patients, even in the absence of cirrhosis, and improve with successful therapy.[316,317] Nonetheless, it is not clear whether this occurs because of the infection per se, the psychological impact of having a chronic disease, or underlying depression that can be linked to illicit drug use.

Once chronic, HCV infection usually persists for decades. Serum ALT levels typically fluctuate independent of symptoms, whereas serum HCV RNA levels remain fairly constant.[182,230,318,319] The degree of inflammation present within liver biopsy specimens also varies over time.[231,320] Some individuals develop fibrosis, which typically begins in portal triads but can bridge between triads or central veins and ultimately destroy the hepatic architecture, progressing to cirrhosis.[279] There is a poor correlation between necroinflammatory liver injury, serum ALT levels, serum HCV RNA levels, and the extent of fibrosis.[321] Once cirrhosis is established, 10% to 20% of HCV-infected persons will decompensate clinically within 5 years, as evidenced by esophageal varices, ascites, coagulopathy, encephalopathy, or hepatocellular carcinoma.[243-245]

Liver histology remains the best indicator of disease stage (see "Liver Biopsy"). Hepatic histology can be especially helpful when the duration of infection is known. For example, patients infected for longer than 25 years who have little inflammation and no more than mild portal fibrosis are exceedingly unlikely to develop cirrhosis in the ensuing 5 years. This information can be useful if there are relative contraindications to treatment or if serious adverse reactions occur. However, for many patients the duration of infection is unknown and liver histology shows intermediate amounts of fibrosis and inflammation. Too little is known about the natural history of disease in such patients to reliably predict the long-term prognosis ($\geq$10 years) with only a single biopsy.

Hepatocellular Carcinoma

Primary hepatocellular carcinoma typically is a late complication of chronic hepatitis C and usually occurs in patients with cirrhosis.[301,302] HCV-related liver cancer has been particularly evident in Japan and Italy and often occurs two or more decades after infection (see previous discussion). Clinical findings can include a sudden worsening of prior symptoms and signs of cirrhosis (fatigue, ascites, jaundice), often in association with right upper quadrant pain. However, small, asymptomatic hepatocellular carcinomas are not uncommonly detected at the time of liver transplantation. Serum α-fetoprotein (AFP) levels are often very high. Ultrasonography or computed tomography reveals an intrahepatic mass, but a specific diagnosis requires liver biopsy.

Extrahepatic Manifestations of Hepatitis C Virus Infection

HCV infection is strongly associated with essential mixed cryoglobulinemia, membranoproliferative glomerulonephritis, and porphyria cutanea tarda. Up to half of HCV-infected persons have circulating cryoglobulins. However, only a small percentage develop the vasculitic syndrome of essential cryoglobulinemia (type II or type III, with circulating polyclonal immunoglobulin G [IgG] and IgM immune complexes).[322,323] Membranoproliferative glomerulonephritis may occur in association with HCV-related cryoglobulinemia, usually in the absence of vasculitis.[142,323] HCV infection is also associated with B-cell lymphoproliferative disorders.[324,325] Chronic HCV infection has also been found in 60% to 80% of persons with sporadic (but not familial) porphyria cutanea tarda.[326-328] To a lesser extent, HCV infection has been associated with Mooren corneal ulcers, Sjögren's syndrome, lichen planus, and idiopathic pulmonary fibrosis.[329] The pathogenesis of such conditions remains unknown. However, sialadenitis resembling that occurring in Sjögren's syndrome has been observed in transgenic mice expressing HCV envelope proteins.[173] Thyroid autoantibodies, Hashimoto's thyroiditis, and hypothyroidism have been associated with chronic hepatitis C in women.[330]

LABORATORY ASSESSMENT OF HEPATITIS C VIRUS INFECTION

Serology

The laboratory diagnosis of HCV infection is based principally on detection of antibodies to recombinant HCV polypeptides. The second-generation enzyme immunoassay (EIA) measured antibodies directed against NS4, core, and NS3 sequences.[331-333] The third-generation EIA that is used today includes an additional antigen from the NS5 protein and a reconfiguration of the core and NS3 antigens. The sensitivity of the third-generation assay is estimated to be 97%, and it can detect HCV antibody within 6 to 8 weeks after exposure.[334,335] These assays are measures of HCV infection, not immunity; tests for viral neutralizing antibody are not available. However, surrogate neutralizing tests have been reported that use pseudotyped lentivirus particles.[195] Assays for IgM HCV antibodies are not clinically useful.

So-called confirmatory tests are commonly used to evaluate a positive EIA result. The U.S. Food and Drug Administration (FDA) has licensed the recombinant immunoblot assay (RIBA; Ortho Diagnostic Systems, Raritan, N.J.) as a supplemental test. The RIBA generally identifies the specific antigens to which antibodies are reacting in the EIA, and it may be positive ($\geq$2 antigens), indeterminate (one antigen), or negative.[336,337] EIA- and RIBA-positive sera usually contain HCV RNA, as indicated by direct detection (see next section) and by lookback studies of donations that caused infection after transfusion.[336,338,339] EIA-positive, RIBA-indeterminate sera may also contain HCV RNA, especially if the reactivity was to core or NS3 antigens

(the c22-3 and c33-c bands). The third-generation RIBA appears to reduce the frequency of indeterminate results.[340]

The EIA is configured to optimize sensitivity, because the primary use of the assay is for screening for HCV infection. As with all tests, the predictive value of the EIA is directly related to the prevalence of infection in the population screened. Among injection drug users, HCV RNA can be detected in approximately 85% of second-generation EIA-positive sera. More than 98% of EIA-positive, RNA-negative sera from these injection drug users are RIBA-positive, indicating that most EIA-reactive samples among drug users are true positive results (D. Thomas, unpublished data, 1996). At the other extreme, up to half of all third-generation EIA-positive blood donations from otherwise healthy individuals do not have detectable HCV RNA or a positive RIBA.[340]

Direct Detection

Hepatitis C Virus RNA Testing

HCV RNA can be detected in plasma and serum by RT-PCR, transcription-mediated amplification (TMA), and branched DNA (bDNA) technologies. The FDA has approved two RT-PCR–based tests for *qualitative* detection of HCV RNA: (1) the AMPLICOR Hepatitis C Virus Test, version 2.0 and (2) the COBAS AMPLICOR Hepatitis C Virus Test, version 2.0 (Roche Molecular Systems, Branchburg, N.J.). They have lower limits of detection of approximately 50 IU/mL (see "Diagnosis").[341] In addition, the FDA has approved a TMA-based assay, VERSANT HCV RNA Qualitative Assay (Bayer Diagnostics Division, Tarrytown, N.Y.), which has a lower limit of detection of approximately 10 IU/mL.[342]

Quantification of Hepatitis C Virus RNA

There are several commercially available methods to quantify HCV RNA in sera or plasma. There is a licensed assay based on a signal amplification technique (VERSANT HCV RNA, version 3.0, Bayer Diagnostics).[343] A quantitative assay, the AMPLICOR HCV MONITOR Test Kit (Roche Diagnostic Systems), amplifies HCV RNA along with a known quantity of labeled template.[344] In persistently infected persons not receiving treatment, HCV RNA levels tend to remain stable (within 0.5 $\log_{10}$) over years.[345,346] A number of factors may affect the estimate of HCV quantity, including the assay used, time to serum separation, storage temperature, collection tube, and testing laboratory.[343,344] To improve the comparability of HCV RNA results, laboratories should report quantitative results in international units (IU), which correspond to a standardized amount of HCV RNA rather than number of viral particles.[347] Algorithms have been published for the conversion of proprietary unit values provided by commercially available assays to international units.[348]

Antigen Detection

A method has been developed that reliably detects HCV core antigen in sera by EIA (Ortho-Clinical Diagnostics, Raritan, N.J.).[348] The HCV core antigen titer corresponds closely with the HCV RNA level and, as an EIA, is technologically less demanding than other methods for direct detection of HCV infection.[349]

Genotype

Determination of the viral genotype may be useful in predicting the response to therapy. The most accurate tests involve sequencing of regions of the genome (e.g., E1, NS5), followed by phylogenetic analysis against reference sequences. One commercially available test based on direct sequencing is the Trugene HCV 5'NC Genotyping Kit (Visible Genetics, Toronto, Ontario, Canada). Another widely used test is the line probe assay, INNO-LiPA HCV II (Innogenetics, Ghent, Belgium), which is based on reverse dot-blot hybridization of a PCR amplicon to nitrocellulose strips coated with genotype-specific probes.[350,351] The line probe assay accurately identifies the genotype, which is all that is necessary for clinical decision making (discussed later), but it occasionally misclassifies the subtype. A serologic method for establishing genotype (but not subtype) also has been developed (Chiron Corporation, Emeryville, Calif.).

Clinical Application of Tests for Hepatitis C Virus

Diagnosis

HCV infection is usually diagnosed (Table 150-2) by testing for antibodies to HCV using a licensed EIA, then testing EIA-reactive sera for HCV RNA to assess whether the infection is persistent. Because most persons with persistent HCV infection have HCV RNA levels in the range of the quantitative assays, and because the quantity of HCV RNA is useful to know before providing and monitoring HCV treatment (see later discussion), it is expedient to routinely use a quantitative HCV RNA test to confirm the presence of viremia.[348] However, quantitative HCV RNA tests generally are not as sensitive as qualitative tests, so some prefer using the latter type of test for confirmation. A negative RNA test with a sensitive assay in a person found to have HCV antibodies by EIA most likely indicates that HCV infection has resolved. Other interpretations include a falsely positive EIA result, a falsely negative HCV RNA test, or, rarely, an intermittent or low-level viremia.

Although the RIBA has limited usefulness in clinical practice, it can be valuable to ascertain whether a positive EIA test in a person with nondetectable HCV RNA represents resolved prior infection or a false-positive EIA result (negative immunoblot result). In the latter scenario, no further testing is needed, which makes the RIBA useful if there is a strong suspicion that the EIA is falsely positive, such as when there are no risk factors, as is often the case for blood donors or persons tested for insurance reasons. Another approach to instances in which an EIA result is positive and an initial RNA test is negative is to repeat RNA (and ALT) testing 6 months later. If the HCV RNA result remains negative and the ALT concentration is normal, it can be assumed that the putative HCV infection has resolved or that the initial EIA was falsely positive, both situations in which further management is not required.

There are instances in which a negative EIA does not exclude HCV infection in patients with suspected liver disease, including acute HCV infection and immunosuppressed states. HCV RNA testing can be used to establish acute HCV infection, because HCV RNA is detectable 2-14 days after an exposure, whereas antibodies to HCV are detectable an average of 8 weeks later. HCV RNA testing can also be used to screen for HCV infection in persons with negative HCV EIA results who are known to have conditions associated with diminished antibody production, such as HIV infection and hemodialysis.

Pretreatment Evaluation

After HCV infection has been confirmed and appropriate counseling has been provided to reduce the risk of transmission to others, to caution against alcohol intake, and to recommend hepatitis A vaccine for those susceptible to HAV, it is appropriate to consider whether the patient is likely to benefit from specific treatment for hepatitis C (see "Selection of Patients for Treatment"). If treatment is being considered, it is appropriate to quantify the HCV RNA level, unless this was already been done to confirm infection, and to determine the HCV genotype. In addition, many authorities also recommend a liver biopsy (see next section) and screening for other underlying causes of liver disease (e.g., autoimmune liver disease, hemochromatosis, Wilson's disease, α_1-antitrypsin deficiency, and chronic hepatitis B), as well as for HIV infection if there are risk factors.

Liver Biopsy

Liver biopsy remains the only definitive method for assessing the stage of liver injury associated with HCV infection. Although biopsy may identify other causes of liver disease, such as alcohol abuse or hemochromatosis, it also provides important information on four distinct HCV-related processes: periportal necrosis (piecemeal necrosis), parenchymal injury, portal inflammation, and fibrosis.[279,320,352] Based on the sum of scores, a standardized grading system, the histologic activity index (HAI) or Knodell score, provides a numeric representation of the extent of disease that ranges from 0 to 22.[352] However, the extent of fibrosis is likely to be the most important finding in patients with chronic hepatitis C. Several alternative systems have been developed to "score" liver biopsies, and the fibrosis components are contrasted in Table 150-3.[353,354]

Although biopsy is the best available method for determining the type and extent of liver injury, there may be differences in histology when samples are taken from different sections of the liver; interobserver variance also has been described.[355-357] Complications such as serious bleeding may occur,[355,356] although with ultrasound guidance these are infrequent (probably <1%). Moreover, the histologic "snapshot" of the current state of inflammation and fibrosis that is obtained does not always predict the future course of disease. Nonetheless, most published guidelines for management of hepatitis C continue to advise routine histologic staging of the liver injury as a critical factor in deciding whether to treat, especially for persons with genotype 1 infections.[358,359] However, it is likely that the utility of the liver biopsy will diminish as treatment success improves and as treatment regimens become simpler and less toxic. Contraindications to liver biopsy include uncorrectable coagulopathy and clinical evidence of decompensated cirrhosis.

Noninvasive Markers of Hepatic Fibrosis

Given the limitations of the liver biopsy, there is substantial interest in developing noninvasive markers of hepatic fibrosis.[360-362] A large number of serum fibrosis markers have been considered, including liver-

---

TABLE 150-2 Persons Who Should Be Screened for Hepatitis C Virus (HCV) Infection*

High Prevalence	*Postexposure Testing*
Persons who ever injected illegal drugs	Persons with percutaneous or heavy mucosal exposure to HCV-positive blood
Persons with elevated aminotransferase levels	
Persons receiving hemodialysis therapy	Children born to HCV-infected women
Persons who received transfusions or organ transplants, including clotting factor concentrates produced before 1987 and transfusions or organ transplants performed before July 1992	Sexual partners of HCV-infected persons (HCV screening should be considered, although the risk of transmission during sexual intercourse is low)
Persons in settings with demonstrated high HCV prevalence and where risk factor ascertainment may be poor (e.g., inmates, patients attending inner-city clinics for sexually transmitted diseases, some university emergency departments)	

*For full recommendations regarding HCV screening, see Centers for Disease Control and Prevention. Recommendations for prevention and control of hepatitis C virus (HCV) infection and HCV-related chronic disease. MMWR Morb Mortal Wkly Rep. 1998;47(No. RR-19):1-39.

TABLE 150-3 Comparison of Systems Used to Grade Fibrosis on Liver Biopsy

Histologic Finding	Ishak[354]	METAVIR[353]	Knodell[352*]
No fibrosis	0	0	0
Expansion of some portal zones	1	1	1
Expansion of most portal zones	2	1	1
Expansion of most portal zones and occasional bridging	3	2†	
Expansion of most portal zones and marked bridging	4	3‡	3
Marked bridging and occasional nodules	5	3	
Cirrhosis	6	4	4

*The Knodell system does not use a "2" rating.
†More than one septum.
‡Portal-central septa.

related enzymes such as ALT, AST, and γ-glutamyl transferase (GGT); direct and indirect measurements of molecules made or processed by the liver, such as the prothrombin time, platelet count, and levels of serum albumin, bilirubin, γ-globulin, and apolipoprotein A_1; and markers of inflammation, fibrinolysis, fibrogenesis, or stellate cell activation (e.g., YKL-40, hyaluronic acid, procollagen III N peptide, TGF-β, $α_2$-macroglobulin, and $α_2$-globulin).

Liver enzymes are inexpensive, are readily available, and are the most studied markers.[239,363,364] In one community-based study of injection drug users in which the prevalence of serious liver disease was low, the finding of normal liver enzymes had a high negative predictive value for disease (97%).[239] Longitudinal trends in ALT and AST levels may improve their correlation with histologic disease.[239,365,366] In addition, a change in the ratio of AST to ALT has been reported to be a reliable indicator of development of cirrhosis.[367,368] Among other routine laboratory tests, decreased platelet count, reversal of the AST/ALT ratio, and prolonged prothrombin time are the earliest indicators of cirrhosis.[369,370] However, in most instances these tests are not sufficiently sensitive or specific to play a major role in clinical decision making.

The European MULTIVIRC group found that they could achieve relatively high negative and positive predictive values using a combination of six markers: $α_2$-macroglobulin, $α_2$-globulin (or haptoglobin), γ-globulin, apolipoprotein A_1, GGT, and total bilirubin.[371] However, the high negative and positive predictive values required scores that pertained, respectively, to only 12% and 34% of subjects, and the data need to be confirmed. Although there are also data suggesting that TGF-β and YKL-40 may be useful markers, there is a clear need for additional research.[372]

Significant liver disease can be detected by hepatic imaging with ultrasound, computed tomography, or magnetic resonance imaging. These modalities may detect the presence of a small, nodular liver; ascites; an enlarged spleen; intra-abdominal varices; or hepatocellular carcinoma. However, although such imaging methods are potentially useful in the management of known cirrhosis (e.g., to screen for hepatocellular carcinoma), or as a means to avoid a biopsy if cirrhosis is strongly suspected clinically, they usually offer little in regard to the initial staging of HCV infection.

Elevations in serum AFP may indicate the development of hepatocellular carcinoma in persons with HCV-related cirrhosis. A recent meta-analysis concluded that the sensitivity of serum AFP for detection of hepatocellular carcinoma was in the range of 45% to 100%, with a specificity of 70% to 95%, at thresholds of between 10 and 19 ng/mL.[373] Although the practice of screening persons with cirrhosis semiannually using ultrasound and AFP measurements is widely practiced, there is little evidence that it actually improves outcomes.

EPIDEMIOLOGY OF HEPATITIS C

HCV is most often transmitted by percutaneous exposure to blood. However, the predominant modes of transmission may change over time and may differ between, and even within, countries. In economically developed countries, most new HCV infections are related to illicit injection drug use, although blood transfusions were once important sources of infection. HCV may also be transmitted between sexual partners and from a mother to her infant, although these forms of transmission of HCV are relatively uncommon in comparison with HBV.

Prevalence of Hepatitis C Virus

HCV infection has been reported in virtually every country where it has been carefully evaluated, suggesting that HCV, unlike HIV, has a long-standing global distribution. Although there are only a few regions of the world where prevalence data are representative, it is estimated that more than 170 million persons are infected worldwide.[374] In developed nations, the HCV prevalence is typically 1% to 2% in the general population and less than 0.5% among blood donors. An estimate of hepatitis C prevalence in the United States is available from the *Third National Health and Nutrition Examination Survey*

(NHANES). Overall, the results of this survey indicated that approximately 3.9 million individuals have been infected with HCV in the United States, or 1.8% of the general population.[375] This is an underestimate of the total number of infected persons, however, because almost 2 million incarcerated persons in the United States were not included in the NHANES survey yet have been shown independently to have an extraordinarily high prevalence of infection, on the order of 20% to 40%.[376] The prevalence of HCV infection in the United States is higher among racial minority populations than among white Americans, and it is higher among African Americans than among Mexican Americans. In addition, the prevalence is increased in persons of lower socioeconomic status, in those between 30 and 50 years of age, and in men.

Although the prevalence of HCV is remarkably similar in many parts of the world, there are a few distinct geographic regions where infection is especially common. In Egypt, HCV infection occurs in 10% to 30% of the general population.[377-382] Similarly high rates of infection have been found in certain regions of Japan, Taiwan, and Italy. In such areas, HCV infection is generally more prevalent among persons older than 40 and uncommon among those younger than 20 years of age.[383-386] This cohort effect suggests that transmission occurred through a practice that has been discontinued, such as use of traditional folk remedies or reuse of needles for injection.[383,384,386-388] It is suspected that a national campaign to treat schistosomiasis infections was responsible for many of the HCV infections in Egypt,[389] although this has not been confirmed. Injection therapy for schistosomiasis was administered to entire villages in the 1970s, and needles were frequently reused. In the isolated Arahiro region of Japan, 45% of individuals older than 41 years of age were found to have HCV infection,[390] whereas the prevalence was 2% in this age group in another area of the country. Folk remedies including acupuncture and cutting of the skin with unsterilized knives were likely transmission modes.

A high prevalence of HCV infection also has been reported in some urban areas of developed countries. In Baltimore, Maryland, HCV infection was found in 18% of patients attending an inner-city emergency department and in 15% of persons attending a nearby clinic for sexually transmitted diseases.[391,392] A very high prevalence of HCV infection also was noted among incarcerated persons in California, Maryland, and Texas.[376] Undoubtedly, in these settings, prior illicit injection drug use is chiefly responsible for acquisition of the infection.

Incidence of Hepatitis C Virus Infection

In the 1980s, the annual incidence of HCV infection in the United States was approximately 15 per 100,000 persons, but since then it has declined significantly.[393,394] The CDC has estimated that at least two thirds of all community-acquired HCV infections are related to illicit injection drug use. Approximately 38% of persons with acute hepatitis C admit to such drug use within the 6 months before their illness.[395,396] An additional 44% admit to the illicit use of noninjected drugs or have other indicators of injection drug use. Sexual or household exposure to HCV is reported in approximately 10% to 15% of individuals with acute HCV infection. Transfusions, occupational exposures, and other contributing factors are infrequently identified (<4%).[397]

Transmission of Hepatitis C Virus

Biologic Basis of Transmission

HCV transmission requires that infectious virions contact susceptible cells that are permissive for replication. It is difficult with present technologies to ascertain which body fluids contain infectious hepatitis C particles. With the use of sensitive techniques, HCV RNA can be detected in blood (including serum and plasma), saliva, tears, seminal fluid, ascitic fluid, and cerebrospinal fluid.[143-147] HCV RNA–containing blood is infectious if it is inoculated intravenously (e.g., by transfusion). In addition, a chimpanzee has been infected by intravenous inoculation of saliva.[164] However, very little information is available regarding the potential infectivity of other body fluids. Furthermore, it is not clear how the virus reaches its primary site of replication within the liver without direct percutaneous inoculation into the bloodstream. As discussed earlier, it is likely that the virus is able to infect and replicate within some peripheral blood mononuclear cells.[101] However, there is little direct evidence for a primary site of replication outside the liver. Nonetheless, sexual transmission does occur (see later discussion), and infection also has been reported after conjunctival exposure.[398]

Percutaneous Transmission

Infection occurs in more than 90% of seronegative recipients who are transfused with blood from HCV-antibody positive donors.[339,399] For this reason, there is a high prevalence of HCV infection in older, multiply-transfused patients with thalassemia or hemophilia.[264,400-402] Before the introduction of nonspecific surrogate tests (serum ALT and antibody to HBV core protein) and specific EIA assays for detection of HCV infection in donated blood, approximately 17% of HCV infections in the United States were caused by transfusion.[403] Since the introduction of the EIA test, the risk of transfusion-transmitted hepatitis C has been reduced substantially (to <1 in 100,000).[404,405] The risk of transmission via transfusion is further reduced in areas, such as the United States, where donations are also screened for HCV RNA.

HCV has been transmitted by administration of contaminated blood products. Many hemophilic patients were infected by contaminated clotting factor concentrates in the past, and there have been several large outbreaks related to intravenous administration of contaminated immune globulin.[406-409] However, the risk of transmission by these products has been effectively eliminated by the introduction of solvent-detergent and other virus inactivation procedures. Transplantation of an organ from an HCV-infected donor almost always results in HCV infection in a seronegative recipient,[410-412] and in a seropositive recipient it may lead to superinfection with a second distinct viral strain.[413]

Contaminated needles, and perhaps other paraphernalia associated with illicit drug use, account for the majority of HCV infections in most developed countries. Since 1992, at least two thirds of new HCV infections in the United States have been associated with illicit drug use.[396] Worldwide, 50% to 95% of persons acknowledging drug use have HCV infection.[414-419] HCV infection generally occurs within months after initiation of illicit use of injected drugs. In one cohort, 80% of subjects acknowledging 2 or more years of injection drug use were infected with the virus, a prevalence that was higher than that of either HIV or HBV infection.[414,420] In the United States, there appears to have been a significant reduction in the incidence of HCV associated with illicit drug use since the late 1980s.[396] Although needle-exchange programs have been associated with a reduction in HCV infection in some (but not all) studies,[421,422] these programs are not sufficiently widespread to account for this nationwide trend.

HCV may be transmitted by other percutaneous exposures that are not associated with drug use but occur too infrequently to be detected in many studies. For example, tattooing has been associated with HCV infection in some studies.[423,424] Human bites, use of folk remedies such as acupuncture, and scarification rituals may also be associated with HCV infection.[425]

Nosocomial Infection

Patient-to-patient transmission of HCV is uncommon but has been documented. In one example, two patients were found to have HCV infection 8 to 10 weeks after undergoing colonoscopic procedures performed with an instrument that had been used hours earlier on an HCV-infected patient.[426] The HCV strains infecting all three patients shared a high level of nucleotide sequence identity within a variable segment of the genome, strongly suggesting a common source of infection. The nosocomial transmission of HCV within hemodialysis units and in other hospital settings also has been suggested by the identification of clusters of patients infected with closely related strains of the virus.[427-429]

Transmission of HCV to health care workers occurs after 2% to 8% of accidental needlestick exposures to HCV-infected patients.[430-432]

Studies of such accidents indicate that the risk of HCV transmission is intermediate (approximately 3% per documented exposure) between those of HIV and HBV (approximately 0.3% and 30%, respectively).[430,432,433] Although hollow-bore needlestick exposures account for most documented instances of HCV transmission, HCV infection has also been reported from blood splashed on the conjunctiva and from a solid-bore needlestick.[398] Despite these risks, the prevalence of HCV infection among dental and medical health care workers is less than or similar to that among the general population.[434-440]

HCV also may be transmitted from health care providers to patients.[441] However, in community-based studies in the United States, patients with acute HCV infection do not commonly report recent interaction with a health provider, and work restrictions are not routinely required for HCV-infected health care workers.[396] Therefore, although nosocomial exposure is a leading cause of infection in developing countries, it is rare where resources permit adherence to universal precautions.

Sexual Transmission

Although transmission of HCV during sexual intercourse has not been proven, there is mounting circumstantial evidence that it occurs. HCV RNA has been detected in semen and saliva,[143,145,146] and persons with multiple sexual partners and commercial sex workers have a high prevalence of HCV infection.[391,442-446] Acute HCV infection has been reported in instances in which sexual, but not other, exposures were recognized.[447,448] In multiple studies of families of HCV-infected patients carried out in Japan and in Europe, sexual partners of the patient generally have been the only household contacts at increased risk for infection, and the risk has increased with duration of the relationship.[449-452] HCV strains recovered from sexual partners often show a high level of nucleotide sequence identity.[191,442,450,452] Although these observations are consistent with sexual transmission, other common exposures, such as sharing of razors or needles, cannot be ruled out.

Some studies of patients attending clinics for sexually transmitted disease and some studies of commercial sex workers indicate that sexual behavior and number of partners may influence the risk of acquiring HCV infection.[391,445,453] In general, however, the association between sexual behavior and HCV infection is much weaker than for HBV or HIV infection. Moreover, a number of studies indicate that sexual transmission is not common. Studies of long-term sexual partners of HCV-infected hemophiliacs and transfusion recipients generally show little or no evidence for HCV transmission, even if unprotected sexual intercourse occurred.[454-457] In addition, HCV prevalence among homosexual men also is generally lower than for other infections such as HIV, HBV, and syphilis, for which sexual transmission is well established.[458-461] In one study, only 4.6% of a cohort of homosexual men were infected with HCV, whereas 81% were infected with HBV.[462]

Therefore, the available data suggest that HCV may be transmitted during sexual intercourse, but that this occurs much less frequently than with HBV. It is not known whether the relative infrequency of sexual transmission is caused by a paucity of infectious virions in seminal or vaginal fluids or by insufficient numbers of susceptible cells within the genital mucosa. Nonetheless, individuals in long-term monogamous relationships should be informed about the low risk of future transmission and, according to current U.S. Public Health Service Guidelines, encouraged to discuss this risk and the use of barrier precautions with their sexual partners.[394]

Maternal-Infant Transmission

HCV is uncommonly transmitted from mother to infant. Estimates of the perinatal transmission frequency vary but have ranged from zero to 8% in larger studies.[463-470] The timing of transmission is not known. However, HCV RNA has been detected within 1 month after birth in non–breast-fed infants delivered by cesarean section, suggesting that transmission occurs in utero in at least some instances.[470] Because of the passive transfer of maternal HCV antibodies, the diagnosis of infant HCV infection must be based on detection of viral RNA or on the persistence of antibody after 18 months of age. Because viremia can be intermittent in the first years of life and some HCV RNA–positive infants never develop HCV antibody, infant infection can be excluded only by repeated HCV RNA testing.

HCV RNA has been detected in breast milk.[471] However, in most studies, the risk of HCV transmission is similar in breast-fed and bottle-fed babies.[465,466,469,472-477] Neither the CDC nor the American Academy of Pediatrics recommends that HCV-infected mothers bottle-feed their babies to prevent HCV transmission.[394,478] Likewise, although one study showed a reduction in perinatal HCV transmission among women who had elective cesarean sections, this measure is not routinely recommended for HCV-infected mothers.[394]

Transmission Cofactors

Seropositive individuals who do not have detectable HCV RNA in their blood appear to be much less infectious than those who do. In a review of 2022 parenteral, sexual, and perinatal HCV exposures, HCV was transmitted only by individuals with detectable viremia.[479] Moreover, nonparenteral (e.g., perinatal) transmission of HCV is very rare if the level of viremia is low.[480] Some (but not all) studies indicate that infection with HIV may be an important cofactor for both sexual and maternal-infant transmission,[466,467,481] possibly because HIV infection is also associated with higher HCV RNA levels.[265,266,482,483]

TREATMENT OF CHRONIC HEPATITIS C

There is intense interest in developing therapeutic regimens that are capable of inhibiting HCV replication, eradicating infection, and improving the natural history of the disease. Treatment with interferon-α (typically recombinant interferon-α) appears to do all three. Incremental improvements have been made in interferon therapy by extending the duration of therapy, using interferon-alfa in combination with oral ribavirin, and, most recently, using pegylated formulations of interferon-alfa (peginterferon-alfa) with ribavirin (Fig. 150-10). Nonetheless, existing therapies are expensive, can cause significant adverse reactions, and are effective in only about half of those treated. Moreover, the cost and difficulty of administering these therapies have resulted in their being provided to only a small fraction of infected persons, underscoring the need for additional treatments that are simpler, safer, less expensive, and available for all infected persons.

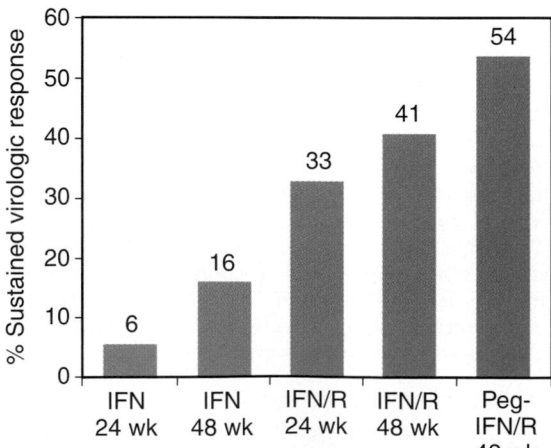

FIGURE 150-10. Improvements in response to interferon-alfa–based treatment of hepatitis C virus infection. IFN, interferon-alfa; IFN/R, interferon-alfa plus ribavirin; Peg-IFN/R, pegylated interferon-alfa plus ribavirin. Sustained virologic response rates are averages from registration trials for drugs.

Treatment Responses

Virologic Responses

The primary aim of treatment is to prevent complications of HCV infection; this is principally achieved by eradication of the infection. Although infection is rarely eradicated spontaneously once it becomes persistent (see "Viral Persistence"), HCV treatment can permanently eradicate infection such that HCV RNA is no longer detectable in blood or liver, titers of antibodies to HCV decline, and HCV-related liver pathology remits or improves.[484,485] Accordingly, treatment responses chiefly are characterized by the results of HCV RNA testing. A *sustained virologic response* (SVR) is defined as the absence of HCV RNA in serum by a sensitive test at the end of treatment and 6 months later. As discussed later, persons who achieve an SVR almost always have at least a 100-fold (i.e., 2 log$_{10}$) drop, or loss, of HCV RNA in the blood within 12 weeks after the start of therapy. This is referred to as an *early virologic response* (EVR). The term *end-of-treatment response* (ETR) refers to the absence of detectable HCV RNA at the end of treatment, and a *relapse* occurs when HCV RNA is detected again in persons who had achieved an ETR. Persons in whom HCV RNA levels remain stable with treatment are considered to be *nonresponders,* whereas those whose HCV RNA levels decline but never become undetectable are referred to as *partial responders.*

Histologic and Clinical Responses to Therapy

Studies have documented improvements in liver histology (chiefly inflammation, but in some cases fibrosis) in patients receiving interferon-alfa or peginterferon-alfa in combination with ribavirin, particularly in those patients achieving an SVR.[80,486-491] There is also a report from Japan that HCV-infected persons with cirrhosis who were randomly assigned to treatment with interferon-alfa had a reduced incidence of hepatocellular carcinoma even if they failed to achieve an SVR, an observation that, although intriguing, is difficult to interpret in the light of a very high rate of cancer among the controls in this study.[492] Whether long-term HCV therapy is ultimately beneficial in persons who do not achieve an SVR is being answered in several multicenter randomized controlled studies, including the National Institutes of Health (NIH)–sponsored Hepatitis C Antiviral Long-Term Treatment against Cirrhosis (HALT-C) study, the results of which will not be available for several years. However, anecdotal data suggest that hepatic fibrosis and even cirrhosis may be potentially reversible histologic findings if there is effective antiviral suppression.

Treatments

Interferon-α

The type 1 interferons (which include multiple types of interferon-β as well as interferon-α) comprise a heterogeneous group of cytokines that are expressed in response to viral infection. These small polypeptides (interferon-α-2b is 166 amino acid residues in length) bind to specific receptors on the surface of cells, and through signal transducer and activator of transcription (STAT) signaling pathways induce or otherwise modulate the expression of several hundred genes, many of which have antiviral and/or cellular antiproliferative activity. Interferon-stimulated genes with potential antiviral activities include, among others, ribonuclease L, 2′-5′ oligoadenylate synthetase, Mx proteins, and PKR. Interferons may alter the course of virus infections both directly and indirectly. With HCV, there is strong in vivo and in vitro evidence for a direct, interferon-mediated antiviral response, which in some cases the virus may be able to partially evade (see "Mechanisms of Persistence").[75,104] However, the exact effector mechanisms by which interferon-α exerts its antiviral effect against HCV are poorly understood. Two possibilities include the specific interruption of IRES-directed viral translation and the accelerated degradation of viral RNA. Interferon-α is also an immunomodulator, and, among other effects, it upregulates the level of expression of histocompatibility antigens on the surface of hepatocytes.

Serum levels of interferon-α peak approximately 6 hours after subcutaneous dosing and are undetectable by 16 hours. The drug is removed principally by renal catabolism and has an estimated half-life of approximately 2 hours. The correlation between serum level and biologic activity is poorly understood. Decreases in the quantity of circulating HCV RNA can be detected within 8 hours after the initiation of therapy, and a reduction of approximately 90% in the level of viremia may be evident within 48 hours.[104] However, re-bounds in viremia have been reported between doses given 48 hours apart, leading to the conjecture that longer-acting treatments might be advantageous.

Recombinant interferon-alfa-2b, interferon-alfa-2a, and consensus interferon-α (acon-1) have been approved by the FDA for the treatment of hepatitis C. The first large-scale clinical trials compared 3 million units (MiU) of interferon-α-2b given subcutaneously three times a week for 6 months versus placebo and achieved SVR rates of less than 15%.[493,494] Extension of the length of therapy to 12 to 18 months improved the SVR rates to 20% to 30%.[495] Overall, similar SVR rates have been reported with interferon-α-2a and with acon-1.[496,497]

Peginterferon-α

If an inert polyethylene glycol molecule is conjugated to interferon-alfa, the renal excretion is reduced and the half-life is increased. Two such pegylated formulations of recombinant interferon-α have been approved for treatment of HCV infection in the United States: the 12-kd peginterferon-α-2b (Peg-Intron; Schering Plough Corporation, Kenilworth, N.J.) and the 40-kd peginterferon-α-2a (Pegasys; Hoffmann-La Roche, Nutley, N.J.). Because of their prolonged half-lives, they can be administered by subcutaneous injection once weekly. In large, randomized controlled trials, higher SVR rates were achieved with the peginterferon-α products than with standard interferon-α, and even higher rates when peginterferon-α was combined with oral ribavirin given twice daily (see next section).[498-501]

Combination Therapy with Ribavirin and Interferon-α

Ribavirin is a guanosine analogue with high oral bioavailability and exceptionally broad, although not particularly potent, antiviral activity. At least four different mechanisms of action have been proposed to explain its efficacy in the treatment of HCV infection. First, ribavirin is a potent inhibitor of cellular inosine monophosphate dehydrogenase and therefore may influence intracellular nucleoside pools; second, it has been suggested that ribavirin may weakly inhibit the NS5B-encoded RNA-dependent RNA polymerase; third, ribavirin has been shown to promote the mutagenicity of RNA viruses; and, fourth, ribavirin may possibly modulate the Th1/Th2 balance in the host immune response.[502-504] Although the actual mechanisms of antiviral action in the treatment of HCV infection remain controversial, substantial data from studies with GBV-B and other positive-strand RNA viruses do suggest that the activity of ribavirin as an RNA mutagen may reduce viral fitness during treatment, leading ultimately to collapse of the replicating population of viral quasispecies through a phenomenon known as "error catastrophe."[502]

The use of orally administered ribavirin in combination with interferon-α and peginterferon-α significantly enhances the SVR rate by reducing relapse.[505-507] Administered alone, ribavirin therapy appears to reduce liver enzyme levels in 21% to 43% of patients.[508-510] However, HCV RNA levels were significantly reduced in only a few percent of patients receiving ribavirin monotherapy, suggesting that its effect on hepatitis C may be through modulation of the immune response, or that its effect on promoting RNA error catastrophe may become apparent only after substantial reduction in the viral burden (e.g., with administration of a concomitant antiviral agent such as interferon).[504,511]

The optimal treatment duration and dose of ribavirin were investigated in a multicenter randomized controlled trial in which all patients received peginterferon-alfa-2a at a dose of 180 μg while patients in the four arms received either 24 or 48 weeks of ribavirin at either 800 mg

or 1.0 to 1.2 g daily (Fig. 150-11).[512] Among patients with genotype 1 HCV, the SVR was highest in those who received the higher ribavirin dose and were treated for 48 weeks. In patients with genotypes 2 or 3, no differences were detected in SVR rates, suggesting that individuals with genotype 2 or 3 infection should be given peginterferon-alfa for only 24 weeks in combination with 800 mg of ribavirin.

Efficacy and Response Indicators

The combined use of peginterferon-alfa and ribavirin currently (in 2004) represents the standard of care for treatment of HCV infection.[358] The response to peginterferon plus ribavirin varies substantially according to pretreatment characteristics, most importantly the HCV genotype (Fig. 150-12). The highest SVR rates are reported in patients with genotype 2 or 3 HCV infection, lower pretreatment HCV RNA levels, younger age, lower body weight, and an absence of bridging fibrosis, cirrhosis, and, in some studies, steatosis.[500,501,512] In the two large, pivotal efficacy trials of pegylated interferon-α-2a and -2b, the SVRs among patients with genotype 1 infection were 42% to 46%, whereas among those with genotype 2 or 3 infection they were 76% to 82%.[500,501] In the peginterferon-α-2a study, the data were analyzed further by combining genotype and viral load.[500] Persons with genotype 1 and a high viral load who received the combination of peginterferon-α-2a and ribavirin had an SVR of 41%, whereas the rate among those with genotype 1 and a low viral load treated with the same regimen was 56%. In contrast, among persons with genotype 2 or 3 and a high viral load given peginterferon-α-2a and ribavirin, the SVR rate was 74%, whereas those with genotype 2 or 3 and a low viral load had an SVR rate of 81%. African Americans have a lower rate of response to interferon-α, which, like their lower rate of spontaneous clearance, is unexplained.[513,514]

The predictive value of the EVR has been evaluated. In the peginterferon-α-2a study, 65% of the patients who had an EVR (defined as a reduction in circulating HCV RNA greater than 2 log$_{10}$ or undetectable HCV RNA by 12 weeks after initiation of therapy) subsequently developed an SVR. More strongly predictive of outcome was failure to achieve a 2 log$_{10}$ reduction: 97% of these patients failed to

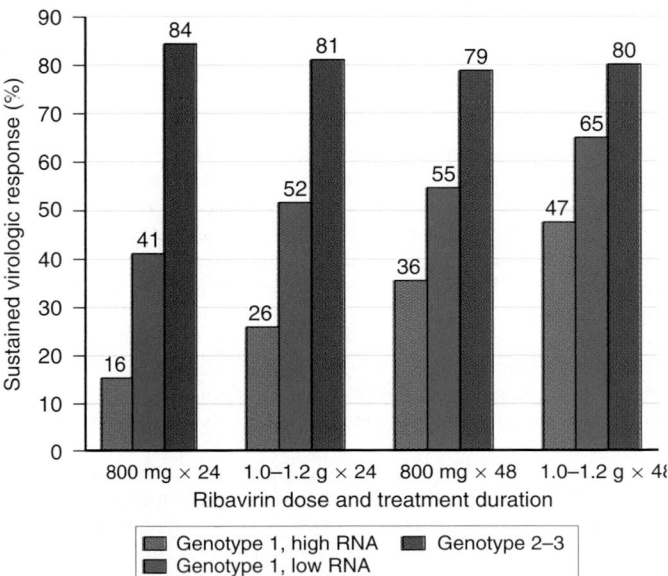

FIGURE 150-11. Sustained virologic response rates in persons taking peginterferon and ribavirin according to weeks of treatment and ribavirin dose, stratified by hepatitis C virus (HCV) genotype and HCV RNA level. *(Data from Hadzianyis SJ, Sette H Jr., Morgan TR, et al. Peginterferon-alpha2a and ribavirin combination therapy in chronic hepatitis C: A randomized study of treatment duration and ribavirin dose. Ann Intern Med. 2004;140:346-355.)*

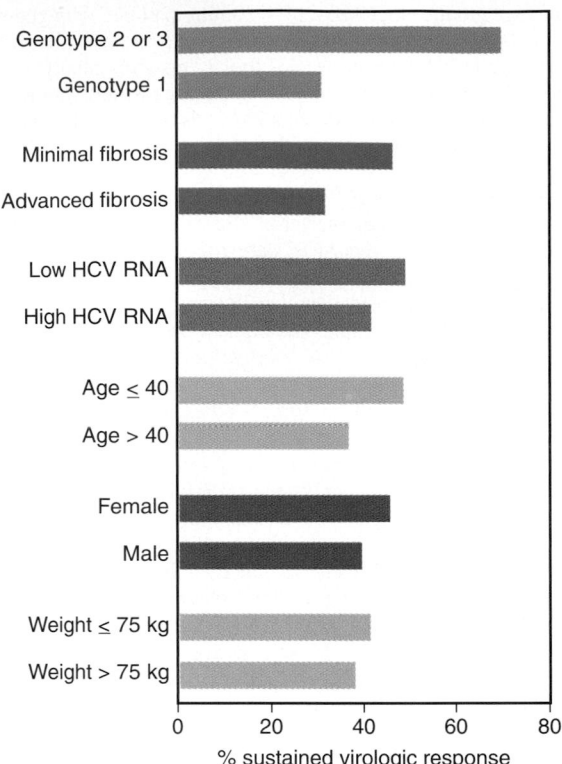

FIGURE 150-12. Factors that predict response to treatment of hepatitis C virus (HCV) infection. Sustained virologic response rates to standard interferon (IFN) plus ribavirin (RBV) therapy are provided for pairs of pretreatment factors such as genotype, age, and weight. Although overall higher rates are achieved with pegylated (PEG) IFN-alfa and RBV, similar differences are observed according to pretreatment factors.

achieve an SVR.[500] Similar data were noted in a postpublication analysis of the peginterferon-alfa-2b study.[515]

Adjunctive Therapies

Iron-reduction therapy has been associated with normalization of ALT values and a better response to interferon, but it has not gained general acceptance. The use of parenteral thymosin-α-1 in combination with interferon has been associated with an improved sustained response.[516] Amantadine, *N*-acetylcysteine, and ursodiol have also been used in the treatment of HCV infections, but there are no controlled data supporting their use.

Adverse Reactions

Adverse reactions to interferon-α are common.[517] Flu-like symptoms are experienced by most persons within 6 hours after the first dose, but they generally diminish after 1 to 2 weeks. Fatigue, depression, and cognitive changes may occur and sometimes are unacceptable, although therapy usually can be continued with counseling and antidepressant administration. Hair thinning is a common late complication of therapy. Asymptomatic retinal abnormalities occur, but their significance is not known.[518] Interferon-α also commonly causes mild-to-moderate, transient bone marrow suppression, manifested by anemia, thrombocytopenia, and especially neutropenia. These hematologic reactions may require dose reduction or administration of medications that stimulate blood cell production, or both. Ribavirin causes a 1- to 5-g/dL reduction in hemoglobin (anemia) in 90% of persons; in one registration trial, 25% of subjects had a reduction of at least 25% in hemoglobin (see excellent review by Sulkowski[519]). Ribavirin use is also associated with gout, birth defects, rash, and sinusitis.

Selection of Patients for Treatment

Initial Treatment of Chronic Hepatitis C

It may be difficult in individual patients to ascertain whether the benefits of HCV treatment outweigh the risks. Treatment is most likely to benefit those patients who are at highest risk for development of end-stage liver disease (i.e., with significant hepatic fibrosis or early cirrhosis; see earlier discussion) and those who are most likely to respond to treatment (i.e., with genotype 2 or 3 infection or a low level of viremia or both). Treatment is less likely to benefit others, such as those with minimal liver disease, those with a high risk of complications, those who are unlikely to respond, and those who might have difficulty adhering to treatment and monitoring. To the question of which patients should be treated, a recent NIH Consensus Panel concluded the following:

> *Treatment is recommended for patients with an increased risk of developing cirrhosis. These patients are characterized by detectable HCV RNA levels higher than 50 IU/mL, a liver biopsy with portal or bridging fibrosis, and at least moderate inflammation and necrosis. The majority also have persistently elevated ALT values. In some patient populations, the risks and benefits of therapy are less clear and should be determined on an individual basis or in the context of clinical trials.[358]*

Similar recommendations were made in joint guidelines from the American Association for the Study of Liver Disease and the Infectious Disease Society of America.[359] Although these recommendations place heavy emphasis on histologic evidence of disease, many experts routinely provide treatment for all patients with genotype 2 or 3 HCV infection, because response rates exceed 70% and treatment is for 6 rather than 12 months. This practice has also been supported in formal guidelines.[358,359]

It is more difficult to make treatment decisions for HCV-infected persons who have comorbid conditions such as HIV infection (discussed later), renal disease, cirrhosis, depression, alcoholism, or drug dependence. There are also few data to guide decisions for children and for persons with normal ALT values. The reader is referred to recent reviews and published guidelines for a more extensive discussion of these special situations.[358,359,520-524]

Treatment of Acute Hepatitis C

Treatment within the first 6 months after HCV infection usually results in an SVR.[525-534] The most impressive data were published by Jaeckel and colleagues,[534] who reported the efficacy of treatment with interferon-α 2b (5 MiU daily for 4 weeks, followed by 5 MiU thrice weekly for an additional 20 weeks) in preventing HCV persistence among 44 patients prospectively identified as having acute hepatitis C infection of less than 4 months' duration. For most patients, the mode of HCV acquisition was percutaneous exposure to blood (injection drug use, 9 patients; needlestick injury, 14 patients; medical procedure, 7 patients). Two thirds of the patients were icteric. The average time from estimated infection date until the start of therapy was 89 days. All 44 patients achieved an undetectable HCV RNA level after a mean of 3.2 weeks of therapy, and 43 patients completed the treatment course. One patient discontinued interferon because of adverse effects after 12 weeks. At the end of treatment and at the end of a 24-week follow-up period, 42 (98%) of the 43 patients had undetectable HCV RNA levels in serum and normal serum ALT concentrations. No serious adverse events were reported.

Although these data may be interpreted as providing a compelling justification for early treatment of HCV infection, up to half of these acutely infected persons may have spontaneously resolved their infection without any intervention. This raises the question of whether treatment could be withheld for 4 to 6 months, to assess the natural outcome, and still be as effective if instituted later. In addition, it is very unlikely that any of these acutely infected health care workers would have developed cirrhosis, if not treated, within the next 10 years, by which time better-tolerated and more-potent therapeutics could reasonably be expected. In another German study,[535] 60 patients with acute HCV (including 51 with symptomatic acute infection) were studied. Six were given therapy immediately. Of the remaining 54 patients, 37 had at least one blood specimen in which HCV RNA could not be detected, and 24 (44%) had durable recovery without treatment. Of the 30 patients without spontaneous recovery, 10 were not treated, leaving 20 who were treated beginning 3 to 6 months after the onset of symptoms. These 20 and the 6 treated immediately were given the "best available treatment," ranging from interferon-α (3 MiU thrice weekly alone) to peginterferon-α plus ribavirin; 21 (81%) of the 26 had an SVR. The authors concluded that the delayed treatment approach resulted in a 91% overall clearance rate (self-limited and treatment-related) and allowed 44% of patients to avoid unnecessary treatment.[535]

Decisions as to whether and when to treat persons with acute HCV infection need to be made on a case-by-case basis, and the optimal regimen, timing, and duration of therapy remain unclear. However, we prefer to postpone treatment for several months to see whether spontaneous recovery occurs (see previous discussion); then, for patients with persistent viremia, we use peginterferon-α plus ribavirin based on ease of administration and superior efficacy in the treatment of chronic infection.[177,536]

Retreatment

Initial treatment can fail in three ways: relapse, partial response, or nonresponse (see earlier discussion).[537] Persons who have had a relapse or only a partial response after standard interferon-α monotherapy can achieve an SVR with retreatment with a more potent regimen.[538,539] However, true nonresponders to interferon-α and ribavirin are much less likely to respond to a second course of therapy, even with peginterferon-α and ribavirin. The likelihood of achieving a response to a second course of treatment is also lower for persons with unfavorable response indicators, such as genotype 1 infection (rather than genotype 2 or 3) or African American race (rather than white). The urgency of attempting a second course of treatment is greater for persons with histologic evidence of advancing fibrosis than for those with less evidence of liver injury. Some experts advocate maintenance therapy to attenuate the progression of serious liver disease or cirrhosis in this setting. Randomized controlled studies are underway to evaluate whether maintenance interferon-α therapy is helpful in nonresponders with cirrhosis.

Specific Small-Molecule Antiviral Agents for Hepatitis C

X-ray crystallography has led to an understanding of the atomic-level resolution structures of several critical viral enzymes (NS3 protease and helicase, the NS5B polymerase). Such efforts have greatly accelerated the development of more potent and specific antiviral agents. Many compounds are now under development, but clinical data have been presented to date only for BILN 2061, a novel macrocyclic, peptidomimetic inhibitor of the NS3 serine protease. BILN 2061 potently inhibits replication of genotype 1 RNAs in hepatoma cells, having a median effective concentration (EC_{50}) of 3 to 4 nM.[540] In an initial phase I study, 31 patients with genotype 1 infection and minimal liver fibrosis were treated with placebo or with 25, 200, or 500 mg of BILN 2061 given orally twice daily for 2 days, with 10 to 14 days of follow-up. In all subjects receiving doses of 200 or 500 mg, serum HCV RNA levels decreased by 2 to 3 $\log_{10}$ copies per milliliter, becoming undetectable in some cases after only 48 hours of therapy. No differences in responsiveness were noted between interferon-naive patients and those for whom previous interferon-based therapy had failed. HCV RNA levels returned to baseline within 1 to 7 days after discontinuation of the drug. A subsequent clinical trial involving patients with non–genotype 1 infection demonstrated considerably less potent antiviral efficacy of BILN 2061, consistent with lower activity of the compound against the proteases from these other viral genotypes. This observation signals a trend that seems likely to continue with respect to genotype-specific differences in the activity of potential small-molecule inhibitors of the HCV protease and polymerase.

The possibility of cardiac toxicity in animals receiving high doses of BILN 2061 has delayed and may possibly prevent the further clinical development of this compound. Nonetheless, BILN 2061 has opened a new chapter in the therapy of chronic hepatitis C. A number of additional compounds from different chemical classes that are active against the NS3/4A protease or the NS5B polymerase are now in advanced preclinical or early clinical testing. Whether any of these will eventually make it to licensure is far from certain, but the future looks bright for more potent and less toxic antiviral therapies.

PREVENTION

Pre-exposure Prevention

The key to reducing the incidence of HCV infection is decreasing exposure to contaminated blood. The incidence of posttransfusion HCV infection has been reduced to very low levels by screening of donated blood for HCV antibody as well as surrogate markers of HCV infection.[404,405] Although the impact is more difficult to measure, nosocomial HCV transmission in developing countries should decrease with worldwide adherence to universal precautions. There is some evidence that needle-exchange programs reduce HCV transmission among illicit drug users.[421] However, more work is necessary to prevent transmission in this setting.

Efforts to develop an HCV vaccine are complicated by the extensive genetic and possibly antigenic diversity that exists among different HCV genotypes, as well as the absence of solid immunity after natural infections, as discussed earlier. Nonetheless, there is evidence that immunity can be acquired that protects against *persistent* HCV infection, both in chimpanzees and in humans. Chimpanzees that responded immunologically to an initial HCV infection, or that were immunized with an experimental vaccine, were readily infected on subsequent experimental challenge with the virus.[541] However, infection appeared to be attenuated after prior infection or immunization and rarely became persistent.[176,211,542-545] Lanford and co-workers[546] showed that such protection can even be achieved across HCV genotypes. Likewise, injection drug users who recovered from an initial HCV infection were shown to be less likely to become viremic.[188] If viremia did occur, it often was at a low level and resolved. These data suggest that a vaccine might be capable of preventing viral persistence and the significant pathologic consequences of HCV infection.

Postexposure Prevention

Early studies provided conflicting data about the extent to which HCV infection is modified by administration of pooled human immune globulin.[193,547,548] However, because HCV-seropositive donations are no longer included in the plasma pools from which immune globulin is manufactured, no benefit would be expected from products on the market today. Administration of immune globulin is not recommended after exposure to HCV in U.S. Public Health Service guidelines.[394]

An individual who has a documented exposure (e.g., a heath care worker sustaining a needlestick from a patient who is known to be infected) should be screened for HCV antibodies and have an ALT test as soon as possible after exposure to exclude prior infection.[177] Serology and ALT testing should be repeated at least once 6 months later. Some authorities also test for HCV RNA 2 to 4 weeks after exposure, because there is evidence that interferon-α may be more effective when it is used early in the course of infection rather than years later (see "Treatment of Acute Hepatitis C").[534]

HUMAN IMMUNODEFICIENCY VIRUS COINFECTION

HCV-related liver disease has become an important cause of morbidity and mortality among persons with HIV infection.[549-551] Therefore, it is important to understand the ways in which HIV infection affects the epidemiology, natural history, and management of hepatitis C.

Epidemiology and Natural History

Epidemiology of Coinfection

Because of shared routes of transmission, HCV infection is found in persons with HIV infection much more frequently than in the general population. In the United States and Europe, 15% to 30% of HIV-infected persons are coinfected with HCV.[552] However, the prevalence of HIV/HCV coinfection varies markedly depending on the route of HIV infection: 50% to 95% of HIV-infected injection drug users are coinfected, compared with fewer than 10% of HIV-infected homosexual men.[553]

There are data suggesting that HIV infection may enhance the transmissibility of HCV. The most conclusive data derive from studies comparing the rate of perinatal transmission of HCV from HIV/HCV-coinfected mothers with that from mothers infected by HCV only.[466,554] Whether the association of HIV infection with a higher HCV RNA level is the reason for more frequent perinatal (and sexual) HCV transmission is unknown.[265,483] There are fewer studies suggesting that HIV/HCV-coinfected persons are more likely to transmit HCV by sexual intercourse, but such persons appear to be much more likely to transmit HIV, rather than HCV, to their partners. In one study, HIV infection was detected in 13% of 162 female sexual partners of HIV/HCV-coinfected hemophilia patients, whereas only 3% were infected with HCV.[481] In light of the greater transmissibility of HIV by sexual intercourse, the recommendations to prevent HIV transmission through the use of barrier precautions for every act of sexual intercourse are more than satisfactory precautions to prevent spread of HCV to sexual partners.

Impact of Human Immunodeficiency Virus Infection on the Course of Hepatitis C Virus Infection

HIV infection adversely affects all phases of the natural history of HCV infection, increasing the frequency of viral persistence after acute infection, the level of viremia among persistently infected persons, the rate of progression to cirrhosis, and the proportion of persons who ultimately develop end-stage liver disease.[178,187,264,265,483,551,555-565] Darby and colleagues[555] studied mortality from liver disease and hepatocellular carcinoma among 4865 men with hemophilia who were exposed to HCV-contaminated blood products. At all ages, the cumulative risk of liver-related death after the presumed exposure to HCV was 1.4% (range, 0.7% to 3.0%) for HIV-uninfected men and 6.5% (range, 4.5% to 9.5%) for HIV-infected men. Goedert and associates[566] also found a significantly increased risk of liver disease in HIV/HCV-coinfected members of the Multicenter Hemophilia Cohort Study. In contrast, Thomas and colleagues[187] did not detect more end-stage liver disease in HIV-infected members of a study of 1667 HCV-infected current and former injection drug users. However, there were competing causes of mortality in the HIV-infected group. Overall, Graham and co-workers[558] estimated that HIV infection increases the risk of cirrhosis twofold.

Impact of Hepatitis C Virus Infection on the Course of Human Immunodeficiency Virus Infection

It remains unclear whether chronic hepatitis C affects the natural history of HIV disease.[567-571] In the Swiss cohort study, Greub and colleagues[569] reported that, among 3111 patients receiving highly active antiretroviral therapy (HAART), those with HCV coinfection had a modestly increased risk of progression to a new acquired immunodeficiency syndrome (AIDS)–defining event or death, even in the subgroup with continuous suppression of HIV replication. They also reported that the magnitude of the increase in CD4+ T lymphocytes after effective anti-HIV therapy was significantly less in HCV-infected than in HCV-uninfected persons, suggesting that HCV coinfection may blunt immune recovery. On the other hand, among 1742 patients in a Baltimore HIV Clinic, no difference was detected in the progression to AIDS or death, after adjusting for exposure to HAART and HIV suppression.[571] Likewise, Chung and associates[572] failed to detect a difference in immune restoration in HIV/HCV-coinfected participants in

a well-controlled AIDS Clinical Trial Group study, suggesting that the effect of HCV infection on progression of HIV is not large.

Hepatitis C Virus Infection and Antiretroviral Toxicity

Hepatotoxicity occurs in about one of every six persons given a new antiretroviral regimen.[573-575] In some cases, HAART-associated hepatotoxicity has been linked to liver failure and death.[576] However, in most cases it is manifested by an elevation in liver enzymes (often to greater than five times the normal value) in the absence of symptoms. Such drug-related hepatotoxicity occurs more frequently among patients with HIV/HCV coinfection.[574,575,577] Nevertheless, most HCV-coinfected patients are able to tolerate antiretroviral therapy. In fact, 88% of a large cohort of HCV-coinfected patients did not experience significant hepatotoxicity with HAART, and no irreversible outcomes were observed.[574]

The mechanisms of enhanced drug-induced hepatotoxicity among HIV/HCV-coinfected patients are unknown but may include decreased drug metabolism, HCV-specific immune reconstitution, or increased susceptibility to mitochondrial dysfunction.[97,578-581] Although there is no reason to withhold HAART from HCV-infected persons, close monitoring is advisable if cirrhosis is present. Many authorities might also avoid drugs associated with hepatocellular toxicity, such as full-dose ritonavir and possibly even dideoxyinosine (ddI) and stavudine (d4T), in persons with cirrhosis for whom equivalent antiretroviral options are available (see discussion of ribavirin ddI below).[359,582]

Pathogenesis

The biologic basis for the clinical interactions between HIV and HCV is unknown. HCV replication has been reported in monocytes and lymphocytes.[584,585] However, whereas HIV infects fewer than 1% of CD4+ T lymphocytes,[585] the frequency of HCV infection of such cells is unclear. There is no good understanding of whether direct viral interactions occur within individual cells or, if they do, whether they contribute substantially to the pathogenesis of coinfection. The immunologic effects of HIV infection are so extensive that there are several plausible means through which HIV could affect the pathogenesis of chronic hepatitis C. Infection of activated CD4+ T-lymphocytes might diminish the early cellular immune response to HCV. Bias toward a Th2-like cytokine response would also favor persistence and might increase the progression of fibrosis, as has been reported for schistosomiasis coinfection.[212] Even less is known about how HCV might alter HIV progression. It is plausible that immune activation from any source could enhance HIV progression by increasing the number of activated CD4+ T lymphocytes.[586] Cirrhosis itself, regardless of its cause, increases the incidence and severity of other infectious diseases (e.g., *Vibrio vulnificus*), and effects on HIV infection would not be surprising. The mechanisms by which these viruses interact and the pathogenesis of coinfection remain important research topics.

Diagnosis and Treatment of Hepatitis C Virus Infection in Persons Infected with Human Immuodeficiency Virus

Serologic Testing

According to U.S. Public Health Service Guidelines, all HIV-infected persons should be screened for HCV infection at entry into health care.[587] HCV screening should be performed, as described earlier (see "Diagnosis"). However, in HIV-infected persons, HCV antibody titers may decline below the level of detection, especially in those individuals with advanced immunodeficiency (CD4+ T-cell count <100/mm³).[588-591] There are also case reports of HCV *seroreversion* occurring in association with immunosuppression and of *seroconversion* associated with HAART therapy.[579,592] Therefore, although seronegative infection is uncommon in other settings,[593] HCV antibody–negative persons with HIV infection who have unexplained liver disease should be tested for HCV RNA to exclude the possibility.

The clinical value of quantitative HCV RNA testing in HIV-infected patients is not known. The results of such tests should not be interpreted based on the well-described relationship between the magnitude of HIV viremia and the rate of HIV disease progression.[289] Furthermore, although the term "viral load" is often used in reference to HCV viremia, as it is for HIV, it may be wrong to assume that the abundance of circulating HCV RNA correlates with the "load" of virus present within the liver. On the other hand, it is reasonable to assume that the results of quantitative HCV RNA tests will be predictive of the response to treatment for HCV in coinfected persons, as they are in patients infected with HCV alone (see later discussion).

Treatment of Hepatitis C Virus Infection in Persons Infected with Human Immunodeficiency Virus

There are few randomized controlled trials that have addressed the treatment of chronic hepatitis C in HIV-infected persons, and, as of early 2004, there were no drugs approved for this specific indication within the United States. However, because HCV-related morbidity and mortality are increasing threats to HIV-infected persons, treatment decisions should not be postponed until ideal studies are available. Rather, many clinical decisions need to be made on a case-by-case basis, incorporating expert opinion and available data and with close patient monitoring.

Published studies demonstrate that an SVR can be achieved in HIV/HCV-coinfected persons, even with standard interferon-α.[594-598] Soriano and colleagues[596,599] treated 90 coinfected patients (CD4+ T-cell count >200/mm³) with interferon-α for 12 months. In an intention-to-treat analysis, 18 (20%) of 90 HIV-infected patients achieved an SVR, which was associated with a pretreatment CD4+ T-cell count higher than 500/mm³. As in HIV-uninfected persons, the addition of ribavirin appears to improve response rates and is reasonably well tolerated.[600-604] Brau and co-workers treated 110 HIV/HCV-coinfected patients with interferon-α-2b in combination with ribavirin or placebo. After 12 weeks of therapy, HCV RNA was undetectable among 23% of those patients receiving combination therapy, compared with 5% of those receiving monotherapy.[601]

Given its greater efficacy in HIV-uninfected persons and data emerging from three large, randomized controlled studies, the standard of care in 2004 will most likely be combined use of peginterferon-α and ribavirin. Results presented at the 2004 Conference on Retroviruses and Opportunistic Infections showed that responses were higher in persons who received peginterferon-α than in those who received the standard interferon-α.[605-607] In one study (APRICOT[605]), 868 subjects were randomly assigned to receive either standard interferon-α-2a (3 MIU three times weekly) plus ribavirin (800 mg/day), peginterferon-α-2a (180 μg/week) plus placebo, or peginterferon-α-2a (180 μg/week) plus ribavirin (800 mg/day); the SVR rates were 12%, 20%, and 40%, respectively. For persons with genotype 1 HCV infection, the SVR rate was 29% with peginterferon-α and ribavirin, whereas for those with genotype 2 or 3 infection it was 62% (Fig. 150-13). Medication was discontinued in 25% of the subjects, in 15% because of adverse events. The median CD4+ T-cell percentage did not decline.

In an AIDS Clinical Trials Group (ACTG) 5071 study,[606] 133 adults were randomly assigned to receive either interferon (3 MiU, three times weekly) or peginterferon-α-2a (180 μg weekly) plus ribavirin (600 mg/day initially, then increased if tolerated). SVR rates in this study among subjects with genotype 1 infection were 14% for peginterferon and 6% for standard interferon; among those with other genotypes, they were 73% and 33%, respectively. Importantly, improved liver histologic activity was observed in 35% of persons who had no virologic response at week 24. No adverse effect on control of HIV replication was observed, and treatment was discontinued in only 12% of subjects.

In a third study from Europe,[607] 416 patients with HIV/HCV coinfection were randomly assigned to receive either peginterferon-α-2b (1.5 μg/kg weekly) plus ribavirin (800 mg/day) or interferon-α-2b (3 MiU three times weekly) in combination with the same dose of ribavirin. An SVR was achieved in 27% and 19% of persons in the peginterferon and standard interferon arms, respectively. In this study, 42% of patients discontinued therapy, and 31% had "severe" adverse events, including six patients with lactic acidosis syndrome and five with acute pancreatitis. Among those who were able to remain on

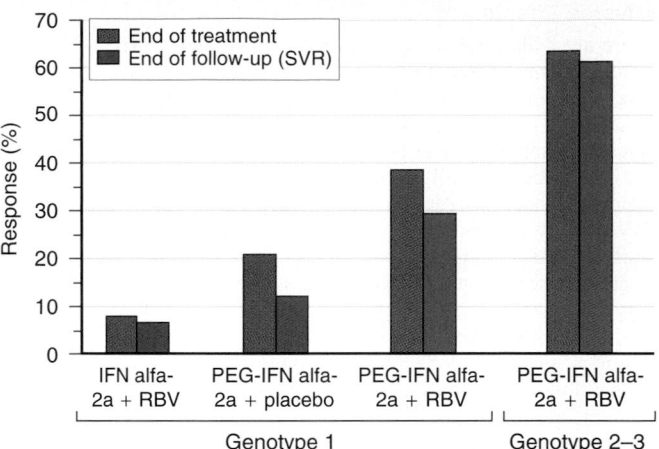

FIGURE 150-13. End-of-treatment responses and sustained virologic responses (SVR) by hepatitis C virus (HCV) genotype for human immunodeficiency virus (HIV)–infected persons treated in the multicenter APRICOT trial. Patients were treated with the indicated interferon (IFN) or pegylated interferon (PEG-IFN) formulation plus 800 mg ribavirin (RBV) or placebo for 48 weeks. (*From Torriani FJ, Rockstroh J, Rodriguez-Torres M, et al. Final results of APRICOT: A randomized, partially blinded, international trial evaluating peginterferon-alfa-2a + ribavirin vs interferon-alfa-2a + ribavirin in the treatment of HCV in HIV/HCV co-infection. Abstract 112. Eleventh Conference on Retroviruses and Opportunistic Infections, San Francisco, Clif, February 8-11, 2004.*)

treatment, the SVR rates were 35% and 26% in the peginterferon and standard interferon arms, respectively. With regard to the adverse events, it is noteworthy that 39% of patients had serious liver disease (bridging fibrosis or cirrhosis) at enrollment; and with regard to responses, 34% had genotype 3 infection.

Although it is impossible to compare results among these three studies, it is likely that lower initial ribavirin doses in the ACTG 5071 study contributed to lower SVR rates, especially in light of the results of ribavirin dose studies in HIV-negative persons.[512] Differences in enrolled participants in these studies (proportion with cirrhosis, proportion with genotype 1 infection) also probably contributed to differences in reported efficacy and safety, and the results need to be reconsidered when published in detail. Nonetheless, these preliminary data, derived from studies of both peginterferon-α-2a and peginterferon-alfa-2b, suggest that peginterferon-α plus ribavirin is currently the optimal therapy for most HIV/HCV-coinfected persons.

The optimal doses of ribavirin and peginterferon-α, and the optimal duration of HCV therapy, may eventually prove to be different from those recommended for patients who do not have HIV infection. Until there are data that indicate otherwise, however, the use of standard doses of both ribavirin and peginterferon is recommended if clinically tolerated. Although in most reported studies of HIV-infected persons treatment has continued for 48 weeks, some ongoing studies are evaluating longer courses of treatment (e.g., 18 months). Abbreviated, 24-week courses of peginterferon-alfa and ribavirin therapy for persons with genotype 2 or 3 HCV infection have not been adequately studied in persons coinfected with HIV. The negative predictive value of less than 2 $\log_{10}$ reductions in HCV RNA levels ranged from 87% to 98% in the preliminary reports of these three peginterferon/ribavirin studies in HIV/HCV-coinfected persons.[605-607] Continued treatment in persons who are not achieving virologic responses (maintenance therapy) is also being examined and, as mentioned earlier, may be especially germane to this setting in which the probability of SVR is low. Additional research is also needed to demonstrate whether administration of HAART improves SVR rates in HIV-infected persons who have CD4+ T-cell counts greater than 350/mm³.

Adverse Effects

There are additional safety concerns in treatment of HIV/HCV-coinfected patients. Ribavirin-associated anemia may be a greater problem in persons coinfected with HIV than in those with only HCV infection, because of the high prevalence of preexisting anemia and limited myeloid reserves.[608] The potential for drug interactions is also high and must be carefully considered. Ribavirin inhibits inosine-5-monophosphate dehydrogenase, an effect that potentiates ddI anti-HIV activity and increases toxicity.[609-611] Because symptomatic, even fatal, hyperlactatemia has been reported in some coinfected persons receiving ribavirin and ddI, if there are equivalent therapeutic options, it is reasonable to change ddI to another drug before starting ribavirin.[612,613] Although ribavirin may antagonize 2′,3′-dideoxynucleotides such as zidovudine, zalcitabine, and d4T *in vitro*, significant clinical interactions have not been reported.[605,611,614]

Interferon-α therapy is associated with a dose-related reduction in white blood cell count and absolute CD4+ T-cell count, but the percentage of CD4+ T cells remains essentially unchanged, and its use is not associated with the development of opportunistic infections.[615] In fact, interferon-α use is associated with a modest reduction in HIV RNA level.[605]

Selection of Patients

It is often difficult to decide whether to treat HCV infection in individual patients who are coinfected with HIV, because the increased risk of cirrhosis must be weighed against lower SVR rates and additional safety concerns. As for patients who are not infected with HIV, such decisions may be influenced by the results of liver biopsy, other factors that might reduce the benefits of treatment (e.g., stage of HIV infection, alcohol use), and comorbid conditions (e.g., depression) that might increase treatment toxicity. In our opinion, the liver biopsy provides the best information about HCV-related disease activity and fibrosis stage and can be performed as safely in HIV-infected as in HIV-uninfected individuals.[616,618] However, some authorities argue that the natural history of HCV is sufficiently accelerated in HIV-infected persons to justify treatment without prior histologic evaluation of the liver, and the practice of routinely offering HCV treatment in lieu of liver biopsy to HIV/HCV-coinfected patients is likely to increase as treatments become more successful.

If HIV treatment is indicated, antiretroviral therapy should be optimized before HCV treatment is provided, because it is reasonable to expect better results. Patients with decompensated liver disease (Child's class B or C) are not treatment candidates and should be considered for liver transplantation, which remains experimental in HIV-infected persons but can be lifesaving.[618,619]

REFERENCES

1. Feinstone SM, Kapikian AZ, Purcell RH, et al. Transfusion-associated hepatitis not due to viral hepatitis type A or B. N Engl J Med. 1975;292:767-770.
2. Prince AM, Brotman B, Grady GF, et al. Long-incubation post-transfusion hepatitis without serological evidence of exposure to hepatitis-B virus. Lancet. 1974;2:241-246.
3. Tabor E, Gerety RJ, Drucker JA, et al. Transmission of non-A, non-B hepatitis from man to chimpanzee. Lancet. 1978;1:463-466.
4. Alter HJ, Purcell RH, Holland PV, Popper H. Transmissible agent in non-A, non-B hepatitis. Lancet. 1978;1:459-463.
5. Choo QL, Kuo G, Weiner AJ, et al. Isolation of a cDNA clone derived from a blood-borne non-A, non-B viral hepatitis genome. Science. 1989;244:359-364.
6. Choo QL, Richman KH, Han JH, et al. Genetic organization and diversity of the hepatitis C virus. Proc Natl Acad Sci U S A. 1991;88:2451-2455.
7. Shimizu YK, Feinstone SM, Kohara M, et al. Hepatitis C virus: Detection of intracellular virus particles by electron microscopy. Hepatology. 1996;23:205-209.
8. Kaito M, Watanabe S, Tsukiyama-Kohara K, et al. Hepatitis C virus particle detected by immunoelectron microscopic study. J Gen Virol. 1994;75:1755-1760.
9. Simons JN, Leary TP, Dawson GJ, et al. Isolation of novel virus-like sequences associated with human hepatitis. Nat Med. 1995;1:564-569.
10. Theodore D, Lemon SM. GB virus C, hepatitis G virus, or human orphan flavivirus? Hepatology. 1997;25:1285-1286.
11. Robertson B, Myers G, Howard C, et al. Classification, nomenclature, and database development for hepatitis C virus (HCV) and related viruses: Proposals for standardization. International Committee on Virus Taxonomy. Arch Virol. 1998;143:2493-2503.
12. Hijikata M, Shimizu YK, Kato H, et al. Equilibrium centrifugation studies of hepatitis C virus: Evidence for circulating immune complexes. J Virol. 1993;67:1953-1958.
13. Kanto T, Hayashi N, Takehara T, et al. Buoyant density of hepatitis C virus recovered from infected hosts: Two different features in sucrose equilibrium density-gradient centrifugation related to degree of liver inflammation. Hepatology. 1994;19:296-302.
14. Choo SH, So HS, Cho JM, Ryu WS. Association of hepatitis C virus particles with immunoglobulin: A mechanism for persistent infection. J Gen Virol. 1995;76:2337-2341.
15. Miyamoto H, Okamoto H, Sato K, et al. Extraordinarily low density of hepatitis C virus estimated by sucrose density gradient centrifugation and the polymerase chain reaction. J Gen Virol. 1992;73:715-718.
16. Friebe P, Lohmann V, Krieger N, Bartenschlager R. Sequences in the 5′ nontranslated region of hepatitis C virus required for RNA replication. J Virol. 2001;75:12047-12057.
17. Brown EA, Zhang H, Ping LH, Lemon SM. Secondary structure of the 5′ nontranslated regions of hepatitis C virus and pestivirus genomic RNAs. Nucleic Acids Res. 1992;20:5041-5045.
18. Bukh J, Purcell RH, Miller RH. Sequence analysis of the 5′ noncoding region of hepatitis C virus. Proc Natl Acad Sci U S A. 1992;89:4942-4946.
19. Kamoshita N, Tsukiyama-Kohara K, Kohara M, Nomoto A. Genetic analysis of internal ribosomal entry site on hepatitis C virus RNA: Implication for involvement of the highly ordered structure and cell type-specific transacting factors. Virology. 1997;233:9-18.
20. Han JH, Shyamala V, Richman KH, et al. Characterization of the terminal regions of hepatitis C viral RNA: Identification of conserved sequences in the 5′ untranslated region and poly(A) tails at the 3′ end. Proc Natl Acad Sci U S A. 1991;88:1711-1715.
21. Honda M, Ping LH, Rijnbrand RC, et al. Structural requirements for initiation of translation by internal ribosome entry within genome-length hepatitis C virus RNA. Virology. 1996;222:31-42.
22. Pestova TV, Shatsky IN, Fletcher SP, et al. A prokaryotic-like mode of cytoplasmic eukaryotic ribosome binding to the initiation codon during internal translation initiation of hepatitis C and classical swine fever virus RNAs. Genes Dev. 1998;12:67-83.
23. Honda M, Brown EA, Lemon SM. Stability of a stem-loop involving the initiator AUG controls the efficiency of internal initiation of translation on hepatitis C virus RNA. RNA. 1996;2:955-968.
24. Yamada N, Tanihara K, Takada A, et al. Genetic organization and diversity of the 3′ noncoding region of the hepatitis C virus genome. Virology. 1996;223:255-261.
25. Kolykhalov AA, Feinstone SM, Rice CM. Identification of a highly conserved sequence element at the 3′ terminus of hepatitis C virus genome RNA. J Virol. 1996;70:3363-3371.
26. Tanaka T, Kato N, Cho MJ, et al. Structure of the 3′ terminus of the hepatitis C virus genome. J Virol. 1996;70:3307-3312.
27. Friebe P, Bartenschlager R. Genetic analysis of sequences in the 3′ nontranslated region of hepatitis C virus that are important for RNA replication. J Virol. 2002;76:5326-5338.
28. Yi M, Lemon SM. 3′ nontranslated RNA signals required for replication of hepatitis C virus RNA. J Virol. 2003;77:3557-3568.
29. Grakoui A, Wychowski C, Lin C, et al. Expression and identification of hepatitis C virus polyprotein cleavage products. J Virol. 1993;67:1385-1395.
30. Hijikata M, Kato N, Ootsuyama Y, et al. Gene mapping of the putative structural region of the hepatitis C virus genome by in vitro processing analysis. Proc Natl Acad Sci U S A. 1991;88:5547-5551.
31. Barba G, Harper F, Harada T, et al. Hepatitis C virus core protein shows a cytoplasmic localization and associates to cellular lipid storage droplets. Proc Natl Acad Sci U S A. 1997;94:1200-1205.
32. Yasui K, Wakita T, Tsukiyama-Kohara K, et al. The native form and maturation process of hepatitis C virus core protein. J Virol. 1998;72:6048-6055.
33. McLauchlan J, Lemberg MK, Hope G, Martoglio B. Intramembrane proteolysis promotes trafficking of hepatitis C virus core protein to lipid droplets. EMBO J. 2002;21:3980-3988.
34. Chang SC, Yen J-H, Kang H-Y, et al. Nuclear localization signals in the core protein of hepatitis C virus. Biochem Biophys Res Commun. 1994;205:1284-1290.
35. Suzuki R, Matsuura Y, Suzuki T, et al. Nuclear localization of the truncated hepatitis C virus core protein with its hydrophobic C terminus deleted. J Gen Virol. 1995;76:53-61.
36. Chen SY, Kao CF, Chen CM, et al. Mechanisms for inhibition of hepatitis B virus gene expression and replication by hepatitis C virus core protein. J Biol Chem. 2003;278:591-607.
37. Santolini E, Migliaccio G, La Monica N. Biosynthesis and biochemical properties of the hepatitis C virus core protein. J Virol. 1994;68:3631-3641.
38. Ray RB, Meyer K, Ray R. Suppression of apoptotic cell death by hepatitis C virus core protein. Virology. 1996;226:176-182.
39. Ray RB, Lagging LM, Meyer K, Ray R. Hepatitis C virus core protein cooperates with ras and transforms primary rat embryo fibroblasts to tumorigenic phenotype. J Virol. 1996;70:4438-4443.
40. Chen CM, You LR, Hwang LH, Lee YH. Direct interaction of hepatitis C virus core protein with the cellular lymphotoxin-b receptor modulates the signal pathway of the lymphotoxin-b receptor. J Virol. 1997;71:9417-9426.
41. Matsumoto M, Hsieh TY, Zhu NL, et al. Hepatitis C virus core protein interacts with the cytoplasmic tail of lymphotoxin-b receptor. J Virol. 1997;71:1301-1309.
42. Ray RB, Steele R, Meyer K, Ray R. Transcriptional repression of p53 promoter by hepatitis C virus core protein. J Biol Chem. 1997;272:10983-10986.
43. Zhu NL, Khoshnan A, Schneider R, et al. Hepatitis C virus core protein binds to the cytoplasmic domain of tumor necrosis factor (TNF) receptor 1 and enhances TNF-induced apoptosis. J Virol. 1998;72:3691-3697.
44. Shrivastava A, Manna SK, Ray R, Aggarwal BB. Ectopic expression of hepatitis C virus core protein differentially regulates nuclear transcription factors. J Virol. 1998;72:9722-9728.

45. Herzer K, Falk CS, Encke J, et al. Upregulation of major histocompatibility complex class I on liver cells by hepatitis C virus core protein via p53 and TAP1 impairs natural killer cell cytotoxicity. J Virol. 2003;77:8299-8309.
46. Kittlesen DJ, Chianese-Bullock KA, et al. Interaction between complement receptor gC1qR and hepatitis C virus core protein inhibits T-lymphocyte proliferation. J Clin Invest. 2000;106:1239-1249.
47. Yi M, Kaneko S, Yu DY, Murakami S. Hepatitis C virus envelope proteins bind lactoferrin. J Virol. 1997;71:5997-6002.
48. Op DB, Cocquerel L, Dubuisson J. Biogenesis of hepatitis C virus envelope glycoproteins. J Gen Virol. 2001;82:2589-2595.
49. Dubuisson J, Hsu HH, Cheung RC, et al. Formation and intracellular localization of hepatitis C virus envelope glycoprotein complexes expressed by recombinant vaccinia and Sindbis viruses. J Virol. 1994;68:6147-6160.
50. Ralston R, Thudium K, Berger K, et al. Characterization of hepatitis C virus envelope glycoprotein complexes expressed by recombinant vaccinia viruses. J Virol. 1993;67:6753-6761.
51. Lo SY, Selby MJ, Ou JH. Interaction between hepatitis C virus core protein and E1 envelope protein. J Virol. 1996;70:5177-5182.
52. Weiner AJ, Brauer MJ, Rosenblatt J, et al. Variable and hypervariable domains are found in the regions of HCV corresponding to the flavivirus envelope and NS1 proteins and the pestivirus envelope glycoproteins. Virology. 1991;180:842-848.
53. Kato N, Ootsuyama Y, Ohkoshi S, et al. Characterization of hypervariable regions in the putative envelope protein of hepatitis C virus. Biochem Biophys Res Commun. 1992;189:119-127.
54. Kato N, Ootsuyama Y, Tanaka T, et al. Marked sequence diversity in the putative envelope proteins of hepatitis C viruses. Virus Res. 1992;22:107-123.
55. Farci P, Shimoda A, Wong D, et al. Prevention of hepatitis C virus infection in chimpanzees by hyperimmune serum against the hypervariable region 1 of the envelope 2 protein. Proc Natl Acad Sci U S A. 1996;93:15394-15399.
56. Kato N, Sekiya H, Ootsuyama Y, et al. Humoral immune response to hypervariable region 1 of the putative envelope glycoprotein (gp70) of hepatitis C virus. J Virol. 1993;67:3923-3930.
57. Weiner AJ, Geysen HM, Christopherson C, et al. Evidence for immune selection of hepatitis C virus (HCV) putative envelope glycoprotein variants: Potential role in chronic HCV infections. Proc Natl Acad Sci U S A. 1992;89:3468-3472.
58. Penin F, Combet C, Germanidis G, et al. Conservation of the conformation and positive charges of hepatitis C virus E2 envelope glycoprotein hypervariable region 1 points to a role in cell attachment. J Virol. 2001;75:5703-5710.
59. Ray SC, Wang YM, Laeyendecker O, et al. Acute hepatitis C virus structural gene sequences as predictors of persistent viremia: Hypervariable region 1 as decoy. J Virol. 1998;73:2938-2946.
60. Forns X, Thimme R, Govindarajan S, et al. Hepatitis C virus lacking the hypervariable region 1 of the second envelope protein is infectious and causes acute resolving or persistent infection in chimpanzees. Proc Natl Acad Sci U S A. 2000;97:13318-13323.
61. Lin C, Lindenbach BD, Pragai BM, et al. Processing in the hepatitis C virus E2-NS2 region: Identification of p7 and two distinct E2-specific products with different C termini. J Virol. 1994;68:5063-5073.
62. Griffin SD, Beales LP, Clarke DS, , et al. The p7 protein of hepatitis C virus forms an ion channel that is blocked by the antiviral drug, Amantadine. FEBS Lett. 2003;535:34-38.
63. Pavlovic D, Neville DC, Argaud O, et al. The hepatitis C virus p7 protein forms an ion channel that is inhibited by long-alkyl-chain iminosugar derivatives. Proc Natl Acad Sci U S A. 2003;100:6104-6108.
64. Grakoui A, McCourt DW, Wychowski C, et al. A second hepatitis C virus-encoded proteinase. Proc Natl Acad Sci U S A. 1993;90:10583-10587.
65. Santolini E, Pacini L, Fipaldini C, et al. The NS2 protein of hepatitis C virus is a transmembrane polypeptide. J Virol. 1995;69:7461-7471.
66. Kim JL, Morgenstern KA, Lin C, et al. Crystal structure of the hepatitis C virus NS3 protease domain complexed with a synthetic NS4A cofactor peptide. Cell. 1996;87:343-355.
67. Tanji Y, Hijikata M, Satoh S, et al. Hepatitis C virus-encoded nonstructural protein NS4A has versatile functions in viral protein processing. J Virol. 1995;69:1575-1581.
68. Failla C, Tomei L, De Francesco R. Both NS3 and NS4A are required for proteolytic processing of hepatitis C virus nonstructural proteins. J Virol. 1994;68:3753-3760.
69. Lin C, Pragai BM, Grakoui A, et al. Hepatitis C virus NS3 serine proteinase: Trans-cleavage requirements and processing kinetics. J Virol. 1994;68:8147-8157.
70. Yao NH, Hesson T, Cable M, et al. Structure of the hepatitis C virus RNA helicase domain. Nat Struct Biol. 1997;4:463-467.
71. Kim JL, Morgenstern KA, Griffith JP, et al. Hepatitis C virus NS3 RNA helicase domain with a bound oligonucleotide: The crystal structure provides insights into the mode of unwinding. Structure. 1998;6:89-100.
72. Tai CL, Chi WK, Chen DS, Hwang LH. The helicase activity associated with hepatitis C virus nonstructural protein 3 (NS3). J Virol. 1996;70:8477-8484.
73. Kim DW, Kim J, Gwack Y, et al. Mutational analysis of the hepatitis C virus RNA helicase. J Virol. 1997;71:9400-9409.
74. Morgenstern KA, Landro JA, Hsiao K, et al. Polynucleotide modulation of the protease, nucleoside triphosphatase, and helicase activities of a hepatitis C virus NS3-NS4A complex isolated from transfected COS cells. J Virol. 1997;71:3767-3775.
75. Foy E, Li K, Wang C, et al. Regulation of interferon regulatory factor-3 by the hepatitis C virus serine protease. Science. 2003;300:1145-1148.
76. Sakamuro D, Furukawa T, Takegami T. Hepatitis C virus nonstructural protein NS3 transforms NIH 3T3 cells. J Virol. 1995;69:3893-3896.
77. Egger D, Wolk B, Gosert R, et al. Expression of hepatitis C virus proteins induces distinct membrane alterations including a candidate viral replication complex. J Virol. 2002;76:5974-5984.
78. Konan KV, Giddings TH Jr, Ikeda M, et al. Nonstructural protein precursor NS4A/B from hepatitis C virus alters function and ultrastructure of host secretory apparatus. J Virol. 2003;77:7843-7855.
79. Asabe SI, Tanji Y, Satoh S, et al. The N-terminal region of hepatitis C virus-encoded NS5A is important for NS4A-dependent phosphorylation. J Virol. 1997;71:790-796.
80. Kaneko T, Tanji Y, Satoh S, et al. Production of two phosphoproteins from the NS5A region of the hepatitis C viral genome. Biochem Biophys Res Commun. 1994;205:320-326.
81. Witherell GW, Beineke P. Statistical analysis of combined substitutions in nonstructural 5A region of hepatitis C virus and interferon response. J Med Virol. 2001;63:8-16.
82. Enomoto N, Sakuma I, Asahina Y, et al. Mutations in the nonstructural protein 5A gene and response to interferon in patients with chronic hepatitis C virus 1b infection. N Engl J Med. 1996;334:77-81.
83. Gale MJJ, Korth MJ, Tang NM, et al. Evidence that hepatitis C virus resistance to interferon is mediated through repression of the PKR protein kinase by the nonstructural 5A protein. Virology. 1997;230:217-227.
84. Enomoto N, Sakuma I, Asahina Y, et al. Comparison of full-length sequences of interferon-sensitive and resistant hepatitis C virus 1b: Sensitivity to interferon is conferred by amino acid substitutions in the NS5A region. J Clin Invest. 1995;96:224-230.
85. Ferrari E, Wright-Minogue J, Fang JWS, et al. Characterization of soluble hepatitis C virus RNA-dependent RNA polymerase expressed in *Escherichia coli.* J Virol. 1999;73:1649-1654.
86. Lohmann V, Körner F, Herian U, Bartenschlager R. Biochemical properties of hepatitis C virus NS5B RNA-dependent RNA polymerase and identification of amino acid sequence motifs essential for enzymatic activity. J Virol. 1997;71:8416-8428.
87. Yamashita T, Kaneko S, Shirota Y, et al. RNA-dependent RNA polymerase activity of the soluble recombinant hepatitis C virus NS5B protein truncated at the C-terminal region. J Biol Chem. 1998;273:15479-15486.
88. Xu Z, Choi J, Yen TS, et al. Synthesis of a novel hepatitis C virus protein by ribosomal frameshift. EMBO J. 2001;20:3840-3848.
89. Roussel J, Pillez A, Montpellier C, et al. Characterization of the expression of the hepatitis C virus F protein. J Gen Virol. 2003;84:1751-1759.
90. Agnello V, Abel G, Elfahal M, et al. Hepatitis C virus and other Flaviviridae viruses enter cells via low density lipoprotein receptor. Proc Natl Acad Sci U S A. 1999; 96:12766-12771.
91. Scarselli E, Ansuini H, Cerino R, et al. The human scavenger receptor class B type I is a novel candidate receptor for the hepatitis C virus. EMBO J. 2002;21:5017-5025.
92. Gardner JP, Durso RJ, Arrigale RR, et al. L-SIGN (CD 209L) is a liver-specific capture receptor for hepatitis C virus. Proc Natl Acad Sci U S A. 2003;100:4498-4503.
93. Lozach PY, Lortat-Jacob H, de Lacroix dL, et al. DC-SIGN and L-SIGN are high affinity binding receptors for hepatitis C virus glycoprotein E2. J Biol Chem. 2003;278:20358-20366.
94. Pileri P, Uematsu Y, Campagnoli S, et al. Binding of hepatitis C virus to CD81. Science. 1998;282:938-941.
95. Kolykhalov AA, Agapov EV, Blight KJ, et al. Transmission of hepatitis C by intrahepatic inoculation with transcribed RNA. Science. 1997;277:570-574.
96. Yanagi M, Purcell RH, Emerson SU, Bukh J. Transcripts from a single full-length cDNA clone of hepatitis C virus are infectious when directly transfected into the liver of a chimpanzee. Proc Natl Acad Sci U S A. 1997;94:8738-8743.
97. Okuda M, Li K, Beard MR, et al. Mitochondrial injury, oxidative stress, and antioxidant gene expression are induced by hepatitis C virus core protein. Gastroenterology. 2002;122:366-375.
98. Shimizu YK, Feinstone SM, Kohara M, et al. Hepatitis C virus: Detection of intracellular virus particles by electron microscopy. Hepatology. 1996;23:205-209.
99. Negro F, Pacchioni D, Shimizu Y, et al. Detection of intrahepatic replication of hepatitis C virus RNA by in situ hybridization and comparison with histopathology. Proc Natl Acad Sci U S A. 1992;89:2247-2251.
100. Krawczynski K, Beach MJ, Bradley DW, et al. Hepatitis C antigens in hepatocytes: Immuno-morphologic detection and identification. Gastroenterology. 1992;103:622-629.
101. Lerat H, Berby F, Trabaud MA, et al. Specific detection of hepatitis C virus minus strand RNA in hematopoietic cells. J Clin Invest. 1996;97:845-851.
102. Shimizu YK, Igarashi H, Kanematu T, et al. Sequence analysis of the hepatitis C virus genome recovered from serum, liver, and peripheral blood mononuclear cells of infected chimpanzees. J Virol. 1997;71:5769-5773.
103. Lam NP, Neumann AU, Gretch DR, et al. Dose-dependent acute clearance of hepatitis C genotype 1 virus with interferon alfa. Hepatology. 1997;26:226-231.
104. Neumann AU, Lam NP, Dahari H, et al. Hepatitis C viral dynamics in vivo and the antiviral efficacy of interferon-alpha therapy. Science. 1998;282:103-107.
105. Martell M, Esteban JI, Quer J, et al. Hepatitis C virus (HCV) circulates as a population of different but closely related genomes: Quasispecies nature of HCV genome distribution. J Virol. 1992;66:3225-3229.
106. Wang YM, Ray SC, Laeyendecker O, et al. Assessment of hepatitis C virus sequence complexity by electrophoretic mobilities of both single- and double-stranded DNAs. J Clin Microbiol. 1998;36:2982-2989.
107. Kurosaki M, Enomoto N, Marumo F, Sato C. Rapid sequence variation in the hypervariable region of hepatitis C virus during the course of chronic infection. Hepatology. 1993;18:1293-1299.
108. Kao J-H, Chen P-J, Lai M-Y, et al. Quasispecies of hepatitis C virus and genetic drift of the hypervariable region in chronic type C hepatitis. J Infect Dis. 1995;172:261-264.
109 Kato N, Ootsuyama Y, Sekiya H, et al. Genetic drift in hypervariable region 1 of the viral genome in persistent hepatitis C virus infection. J Virol. 1994;68:4776-4784.
110. Van Doorn L-J, Capriles I, Maertens G, et al. Sequence evolution of the hypervariable region in the putative envelope region E2/NS1 of hepatitis C virus is correlated with specific humoral immune responses. J Virol. 1995;69:773-778.

111. Odeberg J, Yun ZB, Söönnerborg A, et al. Variation of hepatitis C virus hypervariable region 1 in immunocompromised patients. J Infect Dis. 1997;175:938-943.
112. Booth JC, Kumar U, Webster D, et al. Comparison of the rate of sequence variation in the hypervariable region of E2/NS1 region of hepatitis C virus in normal and hypogammaglobulinemic patients. Hepatology. 1998;27:223-227.
113. Weiner A, Erickson AL, Kansopon J, et al. Persistent hepatitis C virus infection in a chimpanzee is associated with emergence of a cytotoxic T lymphocyte escape variant. Proc Natl Acad Sci U S A. 1995;92:2755-2759.
114. Ogata N, Alter HJ, Miller RH, Purcell RH. Nucleotide sequence and mutation rate of the H strain of hepatitis C virus. Proc Natl Acad Sci U S A. 1991;88:3392-3396.
115. Abe K, Inchauspe G, Fujisawa K. Genomic characterization and mutation rate of hepatitis C virus isolated from a patient who contracted hepatitis during an epidemic of non-A, non-B hepatitis in Japan. J Gen Virol. 1992;73:2725-2729.
116. Okamoto H, Kojima M, Okada S, et al. Genetic drift of hepatitis C virus during an 8.2-year infection in a chimpanzee: Variability and stability. Virology. 1992;190:894-899.
117. Honda M, Kaneko S, Sakai A, et al. Degree of diversity of hepatitis C virus quasispecies and progression of liver disease. Hepatology. 1994;20:1144-1151.
118. Cabot B, Esteban JI, Martell M, et al. Structure of replicating hepatitis C virus (HCV) quasispecies in the liver may not be reflected by analysis of circulating HCV virions. J Virol. 1997;71:1732-1734.
119. Maggi F, Fornai C, Vatteroni ML, et al. Differences in hepatitis C virus quasispecies composition between liver, peripheral blood mononuclear cells and plasma. J Gen Virol. 1997;78:1521-1525.
120. Rispeter K, Lu M, Behrens SE, et al. Hepatitis C virus variability: Sequence analysis of an isolate after 10 years of chronic infection. Virus Genes. 2000;21:179-188.
121. Simmonds P, Holmes EC, Cha T-A, et al. Classification of hepatitis C virus into six major genotypes and a series of subtypes by phylogenetic analysis of the NS-5 region. J Gen Virol. 1993;74:2391-2399.
122. Bukh J, Purcell RH, Miller RH. Sequence analysis of the core gene of 14 hepatitis C virus genotypes. Proc Natl Acad Sci U S A. 1994;91:8239-8243.
123. Bukh J, Miller RH, Purcell RH. Genetic heterogeneity of hepatitis C virus: Quasispecies and genotypes. Semin Liver Dis. 1995;15:41-63.
124. Simmonds P, Smith DB, McOmish F, et al. Identification of genotypes of hepatitis C virus by sequence comparisons in the core, E1 and NS-5 regions. J Gen Virol. 1994;75:1053-1061.
125. Zein NN, Rakela J, Krawitt EL, et al. Hepatitis C virus genotypes in the United States: Epidemiology, pathogenicity, and response to interferon therapy. Ann Intern Med. 1996;125:634-639.
126. Lau JYN, Davis GL, Prescott LE, et al. Distribution of hepatitis C virus genotypes determined by line probe assay in patients with chronic hepatitis C seen at tertiary referral centers in the United States. Ann Intern Med. 1996;124:868-876.
127. Dusheiko GM, Schmilovitz-Weiss H, Brown D, et al. Hepatitis C virus genotypes: An investigation of type-specific differences in geographic origin and disease. Hepatology. 1994;19:13-18.
128. Ray SC, Arthur RR, Carella A, et al. Genetic epidemiology of hepatitis C virus throughout Egypt. J Infect Dis. 2000;182:698-707.
129. Simmonds P. Variability of hepatitis C virus. Hepatology. 1995;21:570-583.
130. Mellor J, Walsh EA, Prescott LE, et al. Survey of type 6 group variants of hepatitis C virus in southeast Asia by using core based genotyping assay. J Clin Microbiol. 1996;34:417-423.
131. Simmonds P, Mellor J, Sakuldamrongpanich T, et al. Evolutionary analysis of variants of hepatitis C virus found in South-East Asia: Comparison with classifications based upon sequence similarity. J Gen Virol. 1996;77:3013-3024.
132. Pawlotsky J-M, Tsakiris L, Roudot-Thoraval F, et al. Relationship between hepatitis C virus genotypes and sources of infection in patients with chronic hepatitis C. J Infect Dis. 1995;171:1607-1610.
133. Chang TT, Young KC, Yang YJ, et al. Hepatitis C virus RNA in peripheral blood mononuclear cells: Comparing acute and chronic hepatitis C virus infection. Hepatology. 1996;23:977-981.
134. Moldvay J, Deny P, Pol S, et al. Detection of hepatitis C virus RNA in peripheral blood mononuclear cells of infected patients by in situ hybridization. Blood. 1994;83:269-273.
135. Navas S, Martín J, Quiroga JA, et al. Genetic diversity and tissue compartmentalization of the hepatitis C virus genome in blood mononuclear cells, liver, and serum from chronic hepatitis C patients. J Virol. 1998;72:1640-1646.
136. Ounanian A, Gueddah N, Rolachon A, et al. Hepatitis C virus RNA in plasma and blood mononuclear cells in patients with chronic hepatitis C treated with alpha-interferon. J Med Virol. 1995;45:141-145.
137. Zehender G, Meroni L, De Maddalena C, et al. Detection of hepatitis C virus RNA in CD19 peripheral blood mononuclear cells of chronically infected patients. J Infect Dis. 1997;176:1209-1214.
138. Lanford RE, Chavez D, Von Chisari F, Sureau C. Lack of detection of negative-strand hepatitis C virus RNA in peripheral blood mononuclear cells and other extrahepatic tissues by the highly strand-specific rTth reverse transcriptase PCR. J Virol. 1995;69:8079-8083.
139. Laskus T, Radkowski M, Wang LF, et al. Hepatitis C virus negative strand RNA is not detected in peripheral blood mononuclear cells and viral sequences are identical to those in serum: A case against extrahepatic replication. J Gen Virol. 1997;78:2747-2750.
140. Sung VM, Shimodaira S, Doughty AL, et al. Establishment of B-cell lymphoma cell lines persistently infected with hepatitis C virus in vivo and in vitro: The apoptotic effects of virus infection. J Virol. 2003;77:2134-2146.
141. Agnello V, Abel G. Localization of hepatitis C virus in cutaneous vasculitic lesions in patients with type II cryoglobulinemia. Arthritis Rheum. 1997;40:2007-2015.
142. Johnson RJ, Gretch DR, Yamabe H, et al. Membranoproliferative glomerulonephritis associated with hepatitis C virus infection. N Engl J Med. 1993;328:465-470.
143. Liou TC, Chang TT, Young KC, et al. Detection of HCV RNA in saliva, urine, seminal fluid, and ascites. J Med Virol. 1992;37:197-202.
144. Chen M, Yun Z-B, Sällberg M, et al. Detection of hepatitis C virus RNA in the cell fraction of saliva before and after oral surgery. J Med Virol. 1995;45:223-226.
145. Wang JT, Wang TH, Sheu JC, et al. Hepatitis C virus RNA in saliva of patients with posttransfusion hepatitis and low efficiency of transmission among spouses. J Med Virol. 1992;36:28-31.
146. Fiore RJ, Potenza D, Monno L, et al. Detection of HCV RNA in serum and seminal fluid from HIV-1 co-infected intravenous drug addicts. J Med Virol. 1995;46:364-367.
147. Mendel I, Muraine M, Riachi G, et al. Detection and genotyping of the hepatitis C RNA in tear fluid from patients with chronic hepatitis C. J Med Virol. 1997;51:231-233.
148. Lohmann V, Korner F, Koch J, et al. Replication of subgenomic hepatitis C virus RNAs in a hepatoma cell line. Science. 1999;285:110-113.
149. Blight KJ, Kolykhalov AA, Rice CM. Efficient initiation of HCV RNA replication in cell culture. Science. 2000;290:1972-1974.
150. Bukh J, Pietschmann T, Lohmann V, et al. Mutations that permit efficient replication of hepatitis C virus RNA in Huh-7 cells prevent productive replication in chimpanzees. Proc Natl Acad Sci U S A. 2002;99:14416-14421.
151. Laras A, Zacharakis G, Hadziyannis SJ. Absence of the negative strand of GBV-C/HGV RNA from the liver. J Hepatol. 1999;30:383-388.
152. Ikeda M, Yi M, Li K, Lemon SM. Selectable subgenomic and genome-length dicistronic RNAs derived from an infectious molecular clone of the HCV-N strain of hepatitis C virus replicate efficiently in cultured Huh7 cells. J Virol. 2002;76:2997-3006.
153. Shimizu YK, Iwamoto A, Hijikata M, et al. Evidence for in vitro replication of hepatitis C virus genome in a human T-cell line. Proc Natl Acad Sci U S A. 1992;89:5477-5481.
154. Nakajima N, Hijikata M, Yoshikura H, Shimizu YK. Characterization of long-term cultures of hepatitis C virus. J Virol. 1996;70:3325-3329.
155. Shimizu YK, Purcell RH, Yoshikura H. Correlation between the infectivity of hepatitis C virus in vivo and its infectivity in vitro. Proc Natl Acad Sci U S A. 1993;90:6037-6041.
156. Yoo BJ, Selby MJ, Choe J, et al. Transfection of a differentiated human hepatoma cell line (Huh7) with in vitro-transcribed hepatitis C virus (HCV) RNA and establishment of a long-term culture persistently infected with HCV. J Virol. 1995;69:32-38.
157. Mizutani T, Kato N, Ikeda M, et al. Long-term human T-cell culture system supporting hepatitis C virus replication. Biochem Biophys Res Commun. 1996;227:822-826.
158. Mizutani T, Kato N, Hirota M, et al. Inhibition of hepatitis C virus replication by antisense oligonucleotide in culture cells. Biochem Biophys Res Commun. 1995;212:906-911.
159. Shimizu YK, Igarashi H, Kiyohara T, et al. Infection of a chimpanzee with hepatitis C virus grown in cell culture. J Gen Virol. 1998;79:1383-1386.
160. Ito T, Mukaigawa J, Zuo J, et al. Cultivation of hepatitis C virus in primary hepatocyte culture from patients with chronic hepatitis C results in release of high titre infectious virus. J Gen Virol. 1996;77:1043-1054.
161. Lanford RE, Sureau C, Jacob JR, et al. Demonstration of in vitro infection of chimpanzee hepatocytes with hepatitis C virus using strand-specific RT/PCR. Virology. 1994;202:606-614.
162. Bodsworth NJ, Donovan B, Nightingale BN. The effect of concurrent human immunodeficiency virus infection on chronic hepatitis B: A study of 150 homosexual men. J Infect Dis. 1989;160:577-582.
163. Farci P, Alter HJ, Wong D, et al. A long-term study of hepatitis C virus replication in non-A, non-B hepatitis. N Engl J Med. 1991;325:98-104.
164. Abe K, Inchauspe G. Transmission of hepatitis C by saliva. Lancet. 1991;337:248.
165. Bassett SE, Brasky KM, Lanford RE. Analysis of hepatitis C virus-inoculated chimpanzees reveals unexpected clinical profiles. J Virol. 1998;72:2589-2599.
166. Martin A, Bodola F, Sangar DV, et al. Chronic hepatitis associated with GB virus B persistence in a tamarin after intrahepatic inoculation of synthetic viral RNA. Proc Natl Acad Sci U S A. 2003;100:9962-9967.
167. Kawamura T, Furusaka A, Koziel MJ, et al. Transgenic expression of hepatitis C virus structural proteins in the mouse. Hepatology. 1997;25:1014-1021.
168. Moriya K, Fujie H, Shintani Y, et al. The core protein of hepatitis C virus induces hepatocellular carcinoma in transgenic mice. Nat Med. 1998;4:1065-1067.
169. Moriya K, Yotsuyanagi H, Shintani Y, et al. Hepatitis C virus core protein induces hepatic steatosis in transgenic mice. J Gen Virol. 1997;78:1527-1531.
170. Pasquinelli C, Shoenberger JM, Chung J, et al. Hepatitis C virus core and E2 protein expression in transgenic mice. Hepatology. 1997;25:719-727.
171. Lerat H, Honda M, Beard MR, et al. Steatosis and liver cancer in transgenic mice expressing the structural and nonstructural proteins of hepatitis C virus. Gastroenterology. 2002;122:352-365.
172. Wakita T, Taya C, Katsume A, et al. Efficient conditional transgene expression in hepatitis C virus cDNA transgenic mice mediated by the Cre/loxP system. J Biol Chem. 1998;273:9001-9006.
173. Koike K, Moriya K, Ishibashi K, et al. Sialadenitis histologically resembling Sjögren syndrome in mice transgenic for hepatitis C virus envelope genes. Proc Natl Acad Sci U S A. 1997;94:233-236.
174. Shimizu YK, Weiner AJ, Rosenblatt J, et al. Early events in hepatitis C virus infection of chimpanzees. Proc Natl Acad Sci U S A. 1990;87:6441-6444.
175. Abe K, Inchauspe G, Shikata T, Prince AM. Three different patterns of hepatitis C virus infection in chimpanzees. Hepatology. 1992;15:690-695.
176. Bassett SE, Guerra B, Brasky K, et al. Protective immune response to hepatitis C virus in chimpanzees rechallenged following clearance of primary infection. Hepatology. 2001;33:1479-1487.

177. Sulkowski MS, Ray SC, Thomas DL. Needlestick transmission of hepatitis C. JAMA. 2002;287:2406-2413.

178. Villano SA, Vlahov D, Nelson KE, et al. Persistence of viremia and the importance of long-term follow-up after acute hepatitis C infection. Hepatology. 1999;29:908-914.

179. Thimme R, Oldach D, Chang KM, et al. Determinants of viral clearance and persistence during acute hepatitis C virus infection. J Exp Med. 2001;194:1395-1406.

180. Prince AM, Brotman B, Inchauspe G, et al. Patterns and prevalence of hepatitis C virus infection in posttransfusion non-A, non-B hepatitis. J Infect Dis. 1993;167:1296-1301.

181 Erickson AL, Kimura Y, Igarashi S, et al. The outcome of hepatitis C virus infection is predicted by escape mutations in epitopes targeted by cytotoxic T lymphocytes. Immunity. 2001;15:883-895.

182. Alter MJ, Margolis HS, Krawczynski K, et al. The natural history of community acquired hepatitis C in the United States. N Engl J Med. 1992;327:1899-1905.

183. Barrera JM, Bruguera M, Ercilla MG, et al. Persistent hepatitis C viremia after acute self-limiting posttransfusion hepatitis C. Hepatology. 1995;21:639-644.

184. Mattsson L, Sonnerborg A, Weiland O. Outcome of acute symptomatic non-A, non-B hepatitis: A 13-year follow-up study of hepatitis C virus markers. Liver. 1993;13:274-278.

185. Puoti M, Zonaro A, Ravaggi A, et al. Hepatitis C virus RNA and antibody response in the clinical course of acute hepatitis C virus infection. Hepatology. 1992;16:877-881.

186. Kenny-Walsh E. Clinical outcomes after hepatitis C infection from contaminated anti-D immune globulin. Irish Hepatology Research Group. N Engl J Med. 1999;340:1228-1233.

187. Thomas DL, Astemborski J, Rai RM, et al. The natural history of hepatitis C virus infection: Host, viral, and environmental factors. JAMA. 2000;284:450-456.

188. Mehta SH, Cox A, Hoover DR, et al. Protection against persistence of hepatitis C. Lancet. 2002;359:1478-1483.

189. Adams G, Kuntz S, Rabalais G, et al. Natural recovery from acute hepatitis C virus infection by agammaglobulinemic twin children. Pediatr Infect Dis J. 1997;16:533-534.

190. Feray C, Gigou M, Samuel D, et al. Incidence of hepatitis C in patients receiving different preparations of hepatitis B immunoglobulins after liver transplantation. Ann Intern Med. 1998;128:810-816.

191. Piazza M, Sagliocca L, Tosone G, et al. Sexual transmission of the hepatitis C virus and efficacy of prophylaxis with intramuscular immune serum globulin: A randomized controlled trial. Arch Intern Med. 1997;157:1537-1544.

192. Farci P, Alter HJ, Wong DC, et al. Prevention of hepatitis C virus infection in chimpanzees after antibody-mediated *in vitro* neutralization. Proc Natl Acad Sci U S A. 1994;91:7792-7796.

193. Krawczynski K, Alter MJ, Tankersley DL, et al. Effect of immune globulin on the prevention of experimental hepatitis C virus infection. J Infect Dis. 1996;173:822-828.

194. Gaud U, Langer B, Petropoulou T, et al. Changes in hypervariable region 1 of the envelope 2 glycoprotein of hepatitis C virus in children and adults with humoral immune defects. J Med Virol. 2003;69:350-356.

195. Bartosch B, Dubuisson J, Cosset FL. Infectious hepatitis C virus pseudo-particles containing functional E1-E2 envelope protein complexes. J Exp Med. 2003;197:633-642.

196. Roccasecca R, Ansuini H, Vitelli A, et al. Binding of the hepatitis C virus E2 glycoprotein to CD81 is strain specific and is modulated by a complex interplay between hypervariable regions 1 and 2. J Virol. 2003;77:1856-1867.

197. Takaki A, Wiese M, Maertens G, et al. Cellular immune responses persist and humoral responses decrease two decades after recovery from a single-source outbreak of hepatitis C. Nat Med. 2000;6:578-582.

198. Missale G, Bertoni R, Lamonaca V, et al. Different clinical behaviors of acute hepatitis C virus infection are associated with different vigor of the anti-viral cell-mediated immune response. J Clin Invest. 1996;98:706-714.

199. Lechmann M, Ihlenfeldt HG, Braunschweiger I,, et al. T- and B-cell responses to different hepatitis C virus antigens in patients with chronic hepatitis C infection and in healthy anti-hepatitis C virus-positive blood donors without viremia. Hepatology. 1996;24:790-795.

200. Diepolder HM, Gerlach JT, Zachoval R, et al. Immunodominant CD4+ T-cell epitope within nonstructural protein 3 in acute hepatitis C virus infection. J Virol. 1997;71:6011-6019.

201. Cooper S, Erickson AL, Adams EJ, et al. Analysis of a successful immune response against hepatitis C virus. Immunity. 1999;10:439-449.

202. Tsai SL, Liaw YF, Chen MH, et al. Detection of type 2-like T-helper cells in hepatitis C virus infection: Implications for hepatitis C virus chronicity. Hepatology. 1997;25:449-458.

203. Gruner NH, Gerlach TJ, Jung MC, et al. Association of hepatitis C virus-specific CD8+ T cells with viral clearance in acute hepatitis C. J Infect Dis. 2000;181:1528-1536.

204. Chang KM, Thimme R, Melpolder JJ, et al. Differential CD4 and CD8 T-cell responsiveness in hepatitis C virus infection. Hepatology. 2001;33:267-276.

205. Gruener NH, Lechner F, Jung MC, et al. Sustained dysfunction of antiviral CD8+ T lymphocytes after infection with hepatitis C virus. J Virol. 2001;75:5550-5558.

206. Wedemeyer H, He XS, Nascimbeni M, et al. Impaired effector function of hepatitis C virus-specific CD8+ T cells in chronic hepatitis C virus infection. J Immunol. 2002;169:3447-3458.

207. Nelson DR, Marousis CG, Davis GL, et al. The role of hepatitis C virus-specific cytotoxic T lymphocytes in chronic hepatitis C. J Immunol. 1997;158:1473-1481.

208. Rehermann B, Chang KM, McHutchison JG, et al. Quantitative analysis of the peripheral blood cytotoxic T lymphocyte response in patients with chronic hepatitis C virus infection. J Clin Invest. 1996;98:1432-1440.

209. Bronowicki JP, Vetter D, Uhl G, et al. Lymphocyte reactivity to hepatitis C virus (HCV) antigens shows evidence for exposure to HCV in HCV-seronegative spouses of HCV-infected patients. J Infect Dis. 1997;176:518-522.

210. Koziel MJ, Wong DKH, Dudley D, et al. Hepatitis C virus-specific cytolytic T lymphocyte and T helper cell responses in seronegative persons. J Infect Dis. 1997;176:859-866.

211. Grakoui A, Shoukry NH, Woollard DJ, et al. HCV persistence and immune evasion in the absence of memory T cell help. Science. 2003;302:659-662.

212. Kamal SM, Bianchi L, Al Tawil A, et al. et al. Specific cellular immune response and cytokine patterns in patients coinfected with hepatitis C virus and *Schistosoma mansoni*. J Infect Dis. 2001;184:972-982.

213. Minton EJ, Smillie D, Neal KR, et al. Association between MHC class II alleles and clearance of circulating hepatitis C virus. J Infect Dis. 1998;178:39-44.

214. Thio CL, Gao X, Goedert JJ, et al. HLA-Cw*04 and hepatitis C virus persistence. J Virol. 2002;76:4792-4797.

215. Thursz M, Yallop R, Goldin R, et al. Influence of MHC class II genotype on outcome of infection with hepatitis C virus. The HENCORE group. Hepatitis C European Network for Cooperative Research. Lancet. 1999;354:2119-2124.

216. Thio CL, Thomas DL, Goedert JJ, et al. Racial differences in HLA class II associations with hepatitis C virus outcomes. J Infect Dis. 2001;184:16-21.

217. Crispe IN. Hepatic T cells and liver tolerance. Nat Rev Immunol. 2003;3:51-62.

218. Su AI, Pezacki JP, Wodicka L, et al. Genomic analysis of the host response to hepatitis C virus infection. Proc Natl Acad Sci U S A. 2002;99:15669-15674.

219. Bigger CB, Brasky KM, Lanford RE. DNA microarray analysis of chimpanzee liver during acute resolving hepatitis C virus infection. J Virol. 2001;75:7059-7066.

220. Blindenbacher A, Duong FH, Hunziker L, et al. Expression of hepatitis C virus proteins inhibits interferon alpha signaling in the liver of transgenic mice. Gastroenterology. 2003;124:1465-1475.

221. Liu ZX, Govindarajan S, Okamoto S, Dennert G. NK cells cause liver injury and facilitate the induction of T cell-mediated immunity to a viral liver infection. J Immunol. 2000;164:6480-6486.

222. Tseng CT, Klimpel GR. Binding of the hepatitis C virus envelope protein E2 to CD81 inhibits natural killer cell functions. J Exp Med. 2002;195:43-49.

223. Crotta S, Stilla A, Wack A, et al. Inhibition of natural killer cells through engagement of CD81 by the major hepatitis C virus envelope protein. J Exp Med. 2002;195:35-41.

224. Bain C, Fatmi A, Zoulim F, et al. Impaired allostimulatory function of dendritic cells in chronic hepatitis C infection. Gastroenterology. 2001;120:512-524.

225. Kanto T, Hayashi N, Takehara T, et al. Impaired allostimulatory capacity of peripheral blood dendritic cells recovered from hepatitis C virus-infected individuals. J Immunol. 1999;162:5584-5591.

226. Disson O, Haouzi D, Desagher S, et al. Impaired clearance of virus-infected hepatocytes in transgenic mice expressing the hepatitis C virus polyprotein. Gastroenterology. 2004;126:859-872.

227. Wei X, Decker JM, Wang S, et al. Antibody neutralization and escape by HIV-1. Nature. 2003;422:307-312.

228. Farci P, Shimoda A, Coiana A, et al. The outcome of acute hepatitis C predicted by the evolution of the viral quasispecies. Science. 2000;288:339-344.

229. Shimizu YK, Hijikata M, Iwamoto A, et al. Neutralizing antibodies against hepatitis C virus and the emergence of neutralization escape mutant viruses. J Virol. 1994;68:1494-1500.

230. Tong MJ, El-Farra NS, Reikes AR, Co RL. Clinical outcomes after transfusion-associated hepatitis C. N Engl J Med. 1995;332:1463-1466.

231. Kiyosawa K, Sodeyama T, Tanaka E, et al. Interrelationship of blood transfusion, non-A, non-B hepatitis and hepatocellular carcinoma: Analysis by detection of antibody to hepatitis C virus. Hepatology. 1990;12:671-675.

232. Hopf U, Moller B, Kuther D, et al. Long-term follow-up of posttransfusion and sporadic chronic hepatitis non-A, non-B and frequency of circulating antibodies to hepatitis C virus (HCV). J Hepatol. 1990;10:69-76.

233. Di Bisceglie AM, Goodman ZD, Ishak KG, et al. Long-term clinical and histopathological follow-up of chronic posttransfusion hepatitis. Hepatology. 1991;14:969-974.

234. Tremolada F, Casarin C, Alberti A, et al. Long-term follow-up of non-A, non-B (type C) post-transfusion hepatitis. J Hepatol. 1992;16:273-281.

235. Koretz RL, Abbey H, Coleman E, Gitnick G. Non-A, non-B post-transfusion hepatitis: Looking back in the second decade. Ann Intern Med. 1993;119:110-115.

236. Seeff LB. Natural history of hepatitis C. Hepatology. 1997;26:21S-28S.

237. Power JP, Lawlor E, Davidson F, et al. Hepatitis C viraemia in recipients of Irish intravenous anti-D immunoglobulin. Lancet. 1994;344:1166-1167.

238. Wiese M, Berr F, Lafrenz M, et al. Low frequency of cirrhosis in a hepatitis C (genotype 1b) single-source outbreak in Germany: A 20-year multicenter study. Hepatology. 2000;32:91-96.

239. Rai R, Wilson LE, Astemborski J, et al. Severity and correlates of liver disease in hepatitis C virus-infected injection drug users. Hepatology. 2002;35:1247-1255.

240. Seeff LB, Buskell-Bales ZB, Wright EC, et al. Long-term mortality after transfusion-associated non-A, non-B hepatitis. N Engl J Med. 1992;327:1906-1911.

241. Alberti A, Noventa F, Benvegnu L, et al. Prevalence of liver disease in a population of asymptomatic persons with hepatitis C virus infection. Ann Intern Med. 2002;137:961-964.

242. Seeff LB, Miller RN, Rabkin CS, et al. 45-Year follow-up of hepatitis C virus infection in healthy young adults. Ann Intern Med. 2000;132:105-111.

243. Fattovich G, Giustina G, Degos F, et al. Morbidity and mortality in compensated cirrhosis C: A follow-up study of 384 patients. Gastroenterology. 1997;112:463-472.

244. Colombo M, De Franchis R, Del Ninno E, et al. Hepatocellular carcinoma in Italian patients with cirrhosis. N Engl J Med. 1991;325:675-680.

245. Tsukuma H, Hiyama T, Tanaka S, et al. Risk factors for hepatocellular carcinoma among patients with chronic liver disease. N Engl J Med. 1993;328:1797-1801.

246. Poynard T, Bedossa P, Opolon P. Natural history of liver fibrosis progression in patients with chronic hepatitis C. Lancet. 1997;349:825-832.

247. Ghany MG, Kleiner DE, Alter H, et al. Progression of fibrosis in chronic hepatitis C. Gastroenterology. 2003;124:97-104.

248. Wali M, Lewis S, Hubscher S, et al. Histological progression during short-term follow-up of patients with chronic hepatitis C virus infection. J Viral Hepat. 1999;6:445-452.

249. Intraobserver and interobserver variations in liver biopsy interpretation in patients with chronic hepatitis C. The French METAVIR Cooperative Study Group. Hepatology. 1994;20:15-20.

250. Feldmann G. Critical analysis of the methods used to morphologically quantify hepatic fibrosis. J Hepatol. 1995;22:49-54.

251. Westin J, Lagging LM, Wejstal R, et al. Interobserver study of liver histopathology using the Ishak score in patients with chronic hepatitis C virus infection. Liver. 1999;19:183-187.

252. Coelho-Little ME, Jeffers LJ, Bernstein DE, et al. Hepatitis C virus in alcoholic patients with and without clinically apparent liver disease. Alcohol Clin Exp Res. 1995;19:1173-1176.

253. Corrao G, Aricò S. Independent and combined action of hepatitis C virus infection and alcohol consumption on the risk of symptomatic liver cirrhosis. Hepatology. 1998;27:914-919.

254. Fong TL, Kanel GC, Conrad A, et al. Clinical significance of concomitant hepatitis C infection in patients with alcoholic liver disease. Hepatology. 1994;19:554-557.

255. Ostapowicz G, Watson KJR, Locarnini SA, Desmond PV. Role of alcohol in the progression of liver disease caused by hepatitis C virus infection. Hepatology. 1998;27:1730-1735.

256. Pessione F, Degos F, Marcellin P, et al. Effect of alcohol consumption on serum hepatitis C virus RNA and histological lesions in chronic hepatitis C. Hepatology. 1998;27:1717-1722.

257. Schiff ER. Hepatitis C and alcohol. Hepatology. 1997;26:39S-42S.

258. Monto A, Alonzo J, Watson JJ, et al. Steatosis in chronic hepatitis C: Relative contributions of obesity, diabetes mellitus, and alcohol. Hepatology. 2002;36:729-736.

259. Fong TL, Di Bisceglie AM, Waggoner JG, et al. The significance of antibody to hepatitis C virus in patients with chronic hepatitis B. Hepatology. 1991;14:64-67.

260. Chiba T, Matsuzaki Y, Abei M, et al. The role of previous hepatitis B virus infection and heavy smoking in hepatitis C virus-related hepatocellular carcinoma. Am J Gastroenterol. 1996;91:1195-1203.

261. Benvegnù L, Fattovich G, Noventa F, et al. Concurrent hepatitis B and C virus infection and risk of hepatocellular carcinoma in cirrhosis: A prospective study. Cancer. 1994;74:2442-2448.

262. Enomoto M, Nishiguchi S, Fukuda K, et al. Characteristics of patients with hepatitis C virus with and without GB virus C/hepatitis G virus co-infection and efficacy of interferon alfa. Hepatology. 1998;27:1388-1393.

263. Laskus T, Radkowski M, Wang LF, et al. Lack of evidence for hepatitis G virus replication in the livers of patients coinfected with hepatitis C and G viruses. J Virol. 1997;71:7804-7806.

264. Eyster ME, Diamondstone LS, Lien JM, et al. Natural history of hepatitis C virus infection in multitransfused hemophiliacs: Effect of coinfection with human immunodeficiency virus. The Multicenter Hemophilia Cohort Study. J Acquir Immune Defic Syndr. 1993;6:602-610.

265. Thomas DL, Shih JW, Alter HJ, et al. Effect of human immunodeficiency virus on hepatitis C virus infection among injecting drug users. J Infect Dis. 1996;174:690-695.

266. Sherman KE, O'Brien J, Gutierrez AG, et al. Quantitative evaluation of hepatitis C virus RNA in patients with concurrent human immunodeficiency virus infections. J Clin Microbiol. 1993;31:2679-2682.

267. Bierhoff E, Fischer HP, Willsch E, et al. Liver histopathology in patients with concurrent chronic hepatitis C and HIV infection. Virchows Arch Int J Pathol. 1997;430:271-277.

268. Cribier B, Schmitt C, Rey D, et al. HIV increases hepatitis C viraemia irrespective of the hepatitis C virus genotype. Res Virol. 1997;148:267-271.

269. García-Samaniego J, Soriano V, Castilla J, et al. Influence of hepatitis C virus genotypes and HIV infection on histological severity of chronic hepatitis C. Am J Gastroenterol. 1997;92:1130-1134.

270. Kamal SM, Rasenack JW, Bianchi L, et al. Acute hepatitis C without and with schistosomiasis: Correlation with hepatitis C-specific CD4(+) T-cell and cytokine response. Gastroenterology. 2001;121:646-656.

271. Bjoro K, Froland SS, Yun Z, et al. Hepatitis C infection in patients with primary hypogammaglobulinemia after treatment with contaminated immune globulin. N Engl J Med. 1994;331:1607-1611.

272. Gretch DR, Bacchi CE, Corey L, et al. Persistent hepatitis C virus infection after liver transplantation: Clinical and virological features. Hepatology. 1995;22:1-9.

273. Collier J, Heathcote J. Hepatitis C viral infection in the immunosuppressed patient. Hepatology. 1998;27:2-6.

274. Vogt M, Lang T, Frosner G, et al. Prevalence and clinical outcome of hepatitis C infection in children who underwent cardiac surgery before the implementation of blood-donor screening. N Engl J Med. 1999;341:866-870.

275. Bortolotti F, Resti M, Giacchino R, et al. Hepatitis C virus infection and related liver disease in children of mothers with antibodies to the virus. J Pediatr. 1997;130:990-993.

276. Chang M-H, Ni Y-H, Hwang L-H, et al. Long term clinical and virologic outcome of primary hepatitis C virus infection in children: A prospective study. Pediatr Infect Dis J. 1994;13:769-773.

277. Kage M, Fujisawa T, Shiraki K, et al. Pathology of chronic hepatitis C in children. Child Liver Study Group of Japan. Hepatology. 1997;26:771-775.

278. Ni YH, Chang MH, Lin KH, et al. Hepatitis C viral infection in thalassemic children: Clinical and molecular studies. Pediatr Res. 1996;39:323-328.

279. Goodman ZD, Ishak KG. Histopathology of hepatitis C virus infection. Semin Liver Dis. 1995;15:70-81.

280. Friedman SL. Liver fibrosis: From bench to bedside. J Hepatol. 2003;38(Suppl 1): S38-S53.

281. Winwood PJ, Schuppan D, Iredale JP, et al. Kupffer cell-derived 95-kd type IV collagenase/gelatinase B: Characterization and expression in cultured cells. Hepatology. 1995;22:304-315.

282. Paradis V, Scoazec JY, Kollinger M, et al. Cellular and subcellular localization of acetaldehyde-protein adducts in liver biopsies from alcoholic patients. J Histochem Cytochem. 1996;44:1051-1057.

283. Matsuoka M, Tsukamoto H. Stimulation of hepatic lipocyte collagen production by Kupffer cell-derived transforming growth factor beta: Implication for a pathogenetic role in alcoholic liver fibrogenesis. Hepatology. 1990;11:599-605.

284. Shi Z, Wakil AE, Rockey DC. Strain-specific differences in mouse hepatic wound healing are mediated by divergent T helper cytokine responses. Proc Natl Acad Sci U S A. 1997;94:10663-10668.

285. Nousbaum J-B, Pol S, Nalpas B, et al. Hepatitis C virus type 1b (II) infection in France and Italy. Ann Intern Med. 1995;122:161-168.

286. Koizumi K, Enomoto N, Kurosaki M, et al. Diversity of quasispecies in various disease stages of chronic hepatitis C virus infection and its significance in interferon treatment. Hepatology. 1995;22:30-35.

287. Gretch D, Corey L, Wilson J, et al. Assessment of hepatitis C virus RNA levels by quantitative competitive RNA polymerase chain reaction: High titer viremia correlates with advanced stage of disease. J Infect Dis. 1994;169:1219-1225.

288. Vlahov D, Graham N, Hoover D, et al. Prognostic indicators for AIDS and infectious disease death in HIV-infected injection drug users: Plasma viral load and CD4+ cell count. JAMA. 1998;279:35-40.

289. Mellors JW, Rinaldo CRJ, Gupta P, et al. Prognosis in HIV-1 infection predicted by the quantity of virus in plasma. Science. 1996;272:1167-1170.

290. Wiley TE, Brown J, Chan J. Hepatitis C infection in African Americans: Its natural history and histological progression. Am J Gastroenterol. 2002;97:700-706.

291. Aikawa T, Kojima M, Onishi H, et al. HLA DRB1 and DQB1 alleles and haplotypes influencing the progression of hepatitis C. J Med Virol. 1996;49:274-278.

292. Higashi Y, Kamikawaji N, Suko H, Ando M. Analysis of HLA alleles in Japanese patients with cirrhosis due to chronic hepatitis C. J Gastroenterol Hepatol. 1996;11:241-246.

293. Kuzushita N, Hayashi N, Moribe T, et al. Influence of HLA haplotypes on the clinical courses of individuals infected with hepatitis C virus. Hepatology. 1998;27:240-244.

294. Reynolds WF, Patel K, Pianko S, et al. A genotypic association implicates myeloperoxidase in the progression of hepatic fibrosis in chronic hepatitis C virus infection. Genes Immun. 2002;3:345-349.

295. Asti M, Martinetti M, Zavaglia C, et al. Human leukocyte antigen class II and III alleles and severity of hepatitis C virus-related chronic liver disease. Hepatology. 1999;29:1272-1279.

296. Powell EE, Edwards-Smith CJ, Hay JL, et al. Host genetic factors influence disease progression in chronic hepatitis C. Hepatology. 2000;31:828-833.

297. El Serag HB, Mason AC. Rising incidence of hepatocellular carcinoma in the United States. N Engl J Med. 1999;340:745-750.

298. Deuffic S, Poynard T, Valleron AJ. Correlation between hepatitis C virus prevalence and hepatocellular carcinoma mortality in Europe. J Viral Hepat. 1999;6:411-413.

299. Saito I, Miyamura T, Ohbayashi A, et al. Hepatitis C virus infection is associated with the development of hepatocellular carcinoma. Proc Natl Acad Sci U S A. 1990;87:6547-6549.

300. Bukh J, Miller RH, Kew MC, Purcell RH. Hepatitis C virus RNA in southern African blacks with hepatocellular carcinoma. Proc Natl Acad Sci U S A. 1993;90:1848-1851.

301. Bruno S, Silini E, Crosignani A, et al. Hepatitis C virus genotypes and risk of hepatocellular carcinoma in cirrhosis: A prospective study. Hepatology. 1997;25:754-758.

302. Simonetti RG, Camma C, Fiorello F, et al. Hepatitis C virus infection as a risk factor for hepatocellular carcinoma in patients with cirrhosis. Ann Intern Med. 1992;116:97-102.

303. Edamoto Y, Tani M, Kurata T, Abe K. Hepatitis C and B virus infections in hepatocellular carcinoma: Analysis of direct detection of viral genome in paraffin embedded tissues. Cancer. 1996;77:1787-1791.

304. Kiyosawa K, Furuta S. Hepatitis C virus and hepatocellular carcinoma. Curr Stud Hematol Blood Transfus. 1994;(61):98-120.

305. Zein NN, Poterucha JJ, Gross JB Jr, et al. Increased risk of hepatocellular carcinoma in patients infected with hepatitis C genotype 1b. Am J Gastroenterol. 1996;91:2560-2562.

306. Yu MC, Yuan JM, Ross RK, Govindarajan S. Presence of antibodies to the hepatitis B surface antigen is associated with an excess risk for hepatocellular carcinoma among non-Asians in Los Angeles County, California. Hepatology. 1997;25:226-228.

307. Kew MC, Yu MC, Kedda MA, et al. The relative roles of hepatitis B and C viruses in the etiology of hepatocellular carcinoma in southern African blacks. Gastroenterology. 1997;112:184-187.

308. Silini E, Bottelli R, Asti M, et al. Hepatitis C virus genotypes and risk of hepatocellular carcinoma in cirrhosis: A case-control study. Gastroenterology. 1996;111:199-205.

309. Nakamoto Y, Guidotti LG, Kuhlen CV, et al. Immune pathogenesis of hepatocellular carcinoma. J Exp Med. 1998;188:341-350.

310. Aach RD, Stevens CE, Hollinger FB, et al. Hepatitis C virus infection in post-transfusion hepatitis. N Engl J Med. 1991;325:1325-1329.

311. Alter HJ, Purcell RH, Shih JW, et al. Detection of antibody to hepatitis C virus in prospectively followed transfusion recipients with acute and chronic non-A, non- B, hepatitis. N Engl J Med. 1989;321:1494-1500.

312. Yanagi M, Kaneko S, Unoura M, et al. Hepatitis C virus in fulminant hepatic failure. N Engl J Med. 1991;324:1895-1896.

313. Farci P, Alter HJ, Shimoda A, et al. Hepatitis C virus-associated fulminant hepatic failure. N Engl J Med. 1996;335:631-634.

314. Wright TL, Hsu H, Donegan E, et al. Hepatitis C virus not found in fulminant non-A, non-B hepatitis. Ann Intern Med. 1991;115:111-112.
315. Vento S, Garofano T, Renzini C, et al. Fulminant hepatitis associated with hepatitis A virus superinfection in patients with chronic hepatitis C. N Engl J Med. 1998;338:286-290.
316. Foster GR, Goldin RD, Thomas HC. Chronic hepatitis C virus infection causes a significant reduction in quality of life in the absence of cirrhosis. Hepatology. 1998;27:209-212.
317. Bernstein D, Kleinman L, Barker CM, et al. Relationship of health-related quality of life to treatment adherence and sustained response in chronic hepatitis C patients. Hepatology. 2002;35:704-708.
318. Conry-Cantilena C, Vanraden MT, Gibble J, et al. Routes of infection, viremia, and liver disease in blood donors found to have hepatitis C virus infection. N Engl J Med. 1996;334:1691-1696.
319. Inglesby TV, Rai R, Astemborski J, et al. A prospective, community-based evaluation of liver enzymes in individuals with hepatitis C after drug use. Hepatology. 1999;29:590-596.
320. Perrillo RP. The role of liver biopsy in hepatitis C. Hepatology. 1997;26:57S-61S.
321. Shakil AO, Conry-Cantilena C, Alter HJ, et al. Volunteer blood donors with antibody to hepatitis C virus: Clinical, biochemical, virologic, and histologic features. Ann Intern Med. 1995;123:330-337.
322. Agnello V, Chung RT, Kaplan LM. A role for hepatitis C virus infection in type II cryoglobulinemia. N Engl J Med. 1992;327:1490-1495.
323. Misiani R, Bellavita P, Fenili D, et al. Hepatitis C virus infection in patients with essential mixed cryoglobulinemia. Ann Intern Med. 1992;117:573-577.
324. Zuckerman E, Zuckerman T, Levine AM, et al. Hepatitis C virus infection in patients with B-cell non-Hodgkin lymphoma. Ann Intern Med. 1997;127:423-428.
325. Rasul I, Shepherd FA, Kamel-Reid S, et al. Detection of occult low-grade B-cell non-Hodgkin's lymphoma in patients with chronic hepatitis C infection and mixed cryoglobulinemia. Hepatology. 1999;29:543-547.
326. Fargion S, Piperno A, Cappellini MD, et al. Hepatitis C virus and porphyria cutanea tarda: Evidence of a strong association. Hepatology. 1992;16:1322-1326.
327. Herrero C, Vicente A, Bruguera M, et al. Is hepatitis C virus infection a trigger of porphyria cutanea tarda? Lancet. 1993;341:788-789.
328. DeCastro M, Sanchez J, Herrera JF, et al. Hepatitis C virus antibodies and liver disease in patients with porphyria cutanea tarda. Hepatology. 1993;17:551-557.
329. Gumber SC, Chopra S. Hepatitis C: A multifaceted disease—Review of extrahepatic manifestations. Ann Intern Med. 1995;123:615-620.
330. Tran A, Quaranta JF, Benzaken S, et al. High prevalence of thyroid autoantibodies in a prospective series of patients with chronic hepatitis C before interferon therapy. Hepatology. 1993;18:253-257.
331. McHutchinson JG, Person JL, Govindarajan S, et al. Improved detection of hepatitis C virus antibodies in high-risk populations. Hepatology. 1992;15:19-25.
332. Nakatsuji Y, Matsumoto A, Tanaka E, et al. Detection of chronic hepatitis C virus infection by four diagnostic systems: First-generation and second-generation enzyme-linked immunosorbent assay, second-generation recombinant immunoblot assay and nested polymerase chain reaction analysis. Hepatology. 1992;16:300-305.
333. Chien DY, Choo QL, Tabrizi A, et al. Diagnosis of hepatitis C virus (HCV) infection using an immunodominant chimeric polyprotein to capture circulating antibodies: Reevaluation of the role of HCV in liver disease. Proc Natl Acad Sci U S A. 1992;89:10011-10015.
334. Couroucé A-M, Le Marrec N, Girault A, et al. Anti-hepatitis C virus (anti-HCV) seroconversion in patients undergoing hemodialysis: Comparison of second- and third-generation anti-HCV assays. Transfusion. 1994;34:790-795.
335. Vallari DS, Jett BW, Alter HJ, et al. Serological markers of posttransfusion hepatitis C viral infection. J Clin Microbiol. 1992;30:552-556.
336. van der Poel CL, Cuypers HTM, Reesink HW, et al. Confirmation of hepatitis C virus infection by new four-antigen recombinant immunoblot assay. Lancet. 1991;337:317-319.
337. Buffet C, Charnaux N, Laurent-Puig P, et al. Enhanced detection of antibodies to hepatitis C virus by use of a third-generation recombinant immunoblot assay. J Med Virol. 1994;43:259-261.
338. McGuinness PH, Bishop GA, Lien A, et al. Detection of serum hepatitis C virus RNA in HCV antibody-seropositive volunteer blood donors. Hepatology. 1993;18:485-490.
339. Vrielink H, van der Poel CL, Reesink HW, et al. Look-back study of infectivity of anti-HCV ELISA-positive blood components. Lancet. 1995;345:95-96.
340. Damen M, Zaaijer HL, Cuypers HTM, et al. Reliability of the third-generation recombinant immunoblot assay for hepatitis C virus. Transfusion. 1995;35:745-749.
341. Lau JY, Davis GL, Kniffen J, et al. Significance of serum hepatitis C virus RNA levels in chronic hepatitis C. Lancet. 1993;341:1501-1504.
342. Sarrazin C, Hendricks DA, Sedarati F, Zeuzem S. Assessment, by transcription-mediated amplification, of virologic response in patients with chronic hepatitis C virus treated with peginterferon alpha-2a. J Clin Microbiol. 2001;39:2850-2855.
343. Davis GL, Lau JYN, Urdea MS, et al. Quantitative detection of hepatitis C virus RNA with a solid-phase signal amplification method: Definition of optimal conditions for specimen collection and clinical application in interferon-treated patients. Hepatology. 1994;19:1337-1341.
344. Miskovsky EP, Carella AV, Gutekunst K, et al. Clinical characterization of a competitive PCR assay for quantitative testing of hepatitis C virus. J Clin Microbiol. 1996;34:1975-1979.
345. Gordon SC, Dailey PJ, Silverman AL, et al. Sequential serum hepatitis C viral RNA levels longitudinally assessed by branched DNA signal amplification. Hepatology. 1998;28:1702-1706.
346. Nguyen TT, Sedghi-Vaziri A, Wilkes LB, et al. Fluctuations in viral load (HCV RNA) are relatively insignificant in untreated patients with chronic HCV infection. J Viral Hepat. 1996;3:75-78.
347. Saldanha J, Lelie N, Heath A. Establishment of the first international standard for nucleic acid amplification technology (NAT) assays for HCV RNA. WHO Collaborative Study Group. Vox Sang. 1999;76:149-158.
348. Pawlotsky JM. Use and interpretation of virological tests for hepatitis C. Hepatology. 2002;36:S65-S73.
349. Bouvier-Alias M, Patel K, Dahari H, et al. Clinical utility of total HCV core antigen quantification: A new indirect marker of HCV replication. Hepatology. 2002;36:211-218.
350. Stuyver L, Rossau R, Wyseur A, et al. Typing of hepatitis C virus isolates and characterization of new subtypes using a line probe assay. J Gen Virol. 1993;74:1093-1102.
351. Stuyver L, Wyseur A, Van Arnhem W, Hernandez F, Maertens G. Second-generation line probe assay for hepatitis C virus genotyping. J Clin Microbiol. 1996;34:2259-2266.
352. Knodell RG, Ishak KG, Black WC, et al. Formulation and application of a numerical scoring system for assessing histological activity in asymptomatic chronic active hepatitis. Hepatology. 1981;1:431-435.
353. Bedossa P, Poynard T. An algorithm for the grading of activity in chronic hepatitis C. Hepatology. 1996;24:289-293.
354. Ishak K, Baptista A, Bianchi L, et al. Histological grading and staging of chronic hepatitis. J Hepatol. 1995;22:696-699.
355. Goldin RD, Goldin JG, Burt AD, et al. Intra-observer and inter-observer variation in the histopathological assessment of chronic viral hepatitis. J Hepatol. 1996;25:649-654.
356. McGill DB, Rakela J, Sinsmeister AR, Ott BJ. A 21-year experience with major hemorrhage after percutaneous liver biopsy. Gastroenterology. 1990;99:1392-1400.
357. Regev A, Berho M, Jeffers LJ, et al. Sampling error and intraobserver variation in liver biopsy in patients with chronic HCV infection. Am J Gastroenterol. 2002;97:2614-2618.
358. National Institutes of Health Consensus Development Conference Statement: Management of hepatitis C: 2002—June 10-12, 2002. Hepatology. 2002;36:S3-S20.
359. Strader DB, Wright T, Thomas DL, Seeff LB; American Association for the Study of Liver Diseases. Diagnosis, management, and treatment of hepatitis C. Hepatology. 2004;39:1147-1171.
360. Schuppan D, Stolzel U, Oesterling C, Somasundaram R. Serum assays for liver fibrosis. J Hepatol. 1995;22:82-88.
361. Wong VS, Hughes V, Trull A, et al. Serum hyaluronic acid is a useful marker of liver fibrosis in chronic hepatitis C virus infection. J Viral Hepat. 1998;5:187-192.
362. Teare JP, Sherman D, Greenfield SM, et al. Comparison of serum procollagen III peptide concentrations and PGA index for assessment of hepatic fibrosis. Lancet. 1993;342:895-898.
363. Gordon SC, Fang JW, Silverman AL, et al. The significance of baseline serum alanine aminotransferase on pretreatment disease characteristics and response to antiviral therapy in chronic hepatitis C. Hepatology. 2000;32:400-404.
364. McCormick S, Goodman ZD, Maydonovitch CL, Sjögren MH. Evaluation of liver histology, ALT elevation, and HCV-RNA titer in patients with chronic hepatitis C. Am J Gastroenterol. 1996;91:1516-1522.
365. Persico M, Persico E, Suozzo R, et al. Natural history of hepatitis C virus carriers with persistently normal aminotransferase levels. Gastroenterology. 2000;118:760-764.
366. Mathurin P, Moussalli J, Cadranel JF, et al. Slow progression rate of fibrosis in hepatitis C virus patients with persistently normal alanine transaminase activity. Hepatology. 1998;27:868-872.
367. Williams AL, Hoofnagle JH. Ratio of serum aspartate to alanine aminotransferase in chronic hepatitis: Relationship to cirrhosis. Gastroenterology. 1988;95:734-739.
368. Sheth SG, Flamm SL, Gordon FD, Chopra S. AST/ALT ratio predicts cirrhosis in patients with chronic hepatitis C virus infection. Am J Gastroenterol. 1998;93:44-48.
369. Oberti F, Valsesia E, Pilette C, et al. Noninvasive diagnosis of hepatic fibrosis or cirrhosis. Gastroenterology. 1997;113:1609-1616.
370. Matsumura H, Moriyama M, Goto I, et al. Natural course of progression of liver fibrosis in Japanese patients with chronic liver disease type C: A study of 527 patients at one establishment. J Viral Hepat. 2000;7:268-275.
371. Imbert-Bismut F, Ratziu V, et al. Biochemical markers of liver fibrosis in patients with hepatitis C virus infection: A prospective study. Lancet. 2001;357:1069-1075.
372. Kanzler S, Baumann M, Schirmacher P, et al. Prediction of progressive liver fibrosis in hepatitis C infection by serum and tissue levels of transforming growth factor-beta. J Viral Hepat. 2001;8:430-437.
373. Gebo KA, Chander G, Jenckes MW, et al. Screening tests for hepatocellular carcinoma in patients with chronic hepatitis C: A systematic review. Hepatology. 2002;36:S84-S92.
374. Hepatitis C: Global prevalence. Wkly Epidemiol Rec. 1997;72:341-344.
375. Alter MJ, Kruszon-Moran D, Nainan OV, et al. The prevalence of hepatitis C virus infection in the United States, 1988 through 1994. N Engl J Med. 1999;341:556-562.
376. Baillargeon J, Wu H, Kelley MJ, et al. Hepatitis C seroprevalence among newly incarcerated inmates in the Texas correctional system. Public Health. 2003;117:43-48.
377. Arthur RR, Hassan NF, Abdallah MY, et al. Hepatitis C antibody prevalence in blood donors in different governorates in Egypt. Trans R Soc Trop Med Hyg. 1997;91:271-274.
378. Abdel-Wahab MF, Zakaria S, Kamel M, et al. High seroprevalence of hepatitis C infection among risk groups in Egypt. Am J Trop Med Hyg. 1994;51:563-567.
379. Kamel MA, Ghaffar YA, Wasef MA, et al. High HCV prevalence in Egyptian blood donors. Lancet. 1992;340:427.
380. Darwish MA, Raouf TA, Rushdy P, et al. Risk factors associated with a high seroprevalence of hepatitis C virus infection in Egyptian blood donors. Am J Trop Med Hyg. 1993;49:440-447.
381. Hibbs RG, Corwin AL, Hassan NF, et al. The epidemiology of antibody to hepatitis C in Egypt . J Infect Dis. 1993;168:789-790.

382. El-Sayed NM, Gomatos PJ, Rodier GR, et al. Seroprevalence survey of Egyptian tourism workers for hepatitis B virus, hepatitis C virus, human immunodeficiency virus, and *Treponema pallidum* infections: Association of hepatitis C virus infections with specific regions of Egypt. Am J Trop Med Hyg. 1996;55:179-184.
383. Osella AR, Misciagna G, Leone A, et al. Epidemiology of hepatitis C virus infection in an area of southern Italy. J Hepatol. 1997;27:30-35.
384. Chiaramonte M, Stroffolini T, Lorenzoni U, et al. Risk factors in community-acquired chronic hepatitis C virus infection: A case-control study in Italy. J Hepatol. 1996; 24:129-134.
385. Nakashima K, Ikematsu H, Hayashi J, et al. Intrafamilial transmission of hepatitis C virus among the population of an endemic area of Japan. JAMA. 1995;274: 1459-1461.
386. Guadagnino V, Stroffolini T, Rapicetta M, et al. Prevalence, risk factors, and genotype distribution of hepatitis C virus infection in the general population: A community-based survey in southern Italy. Hepatology. 1997;26:1006-1011.
387. Prati D, Capelli C, Silvani C, et al. The incidence and risk factors of community-acquired hepatitis C in a cohort of Italian blood donors. Hepatology. 1997;25:702-704.
388. Noguchi S, Sata M, Suzuki H, et al. Routes of transmission of hepatitis C virus in an endemic rural area of Japan: Molecular epidemiologic study of hepatitis C virus infection. Scand J Infect Dis. 1997;29:23-28.
389. Frank C, Mohamed MK, Strickland GT, et al. The role of parenteral antischistosomal therapy in the spread of hepatitis C virus in Egypt. Lancet. 2000;355:887-891.
390. Kiyosawa K, Tanaka E, Sodeyama T, et al. Transmission of hepatitis C in an isolated area in Japan: Community-acquired infection. Gastroenterology. 1994;106:1596-1602.
391. Thomas DL, Cannon RO, Shapiro CN, et al. Hepatitis C, hepatitis B, and human immunodeficiency virus infections among non-intravenous drug-using patients attending clinics for sexually transmitted diseases. J Infect Dis. 1994;169:990-995.
392. Kelen GD, Green GB, Purcell RH, et al. Hepatitis B and hepatitis C in emergency department patients. N Engl J Med. 1992;326:1399-1404.
393. Alter MJ. Epidemiology of hepatitis C in the West. Semin Liver Dis. 1995;15:5-14.
394. Centers for Disease Control and Prevention. Recommendations for prevention and control of hepatitis C virus (HCV) infection and HCV-related chronic disease. MMWR Morb Mortal Wkly Rep. 1998;47(No. RR-19):1-39.
395. Alter MJ, Hadler SC, Judson FN, et al. Risk factors for acute non-A, non-B hepatitis in the United States and association with hepatitis C virus infection. JAMA. 1990;264:2231-2235.
396. Alter MJ. Epidemiology of hepatitis C. Hepatology. 1997;26:62S-65S.
397. Alter MJ, Mast EE, Moyer LA, Margolis HS. Hepatitis C. Infect Dis Clin North Am. 1998;12:13-26.
398. Sartori M, La Terra G, Aglietta M, et al. Transmission of hepatitis C via blood splash into conjunctiva. Scand J Infect Dis. 1993;25:270-271.
399. Esteban JI, Lopez-Talavera JC, Genesca J, et al. High rate of infectivity and liver disease in blood donors with antibodies to hepatitis C virus. Ann Intern Med. 1991; 115:443-449.
400. Lai ME, Mazzoleni AP, Argiolu F, et al. Hepatitis C virus in multiple episodes of acute hepatitis in polytransfused thalassaemic children. Lancet. 1994;343:388-390.
401. de Montalembert M, Costagliola DG, Lefrere JJ, et al. Prevalence of markers for human immunodeficiency virus types 1 and 2, human T-lymphotropic virus type I, cytomegalovirus, and hepatitis B and C virus in multiply transfused thalassemia patients. The French Study Group on Thalassaemia. Transfusion. 1992;32:509-512.
402. Brettler DB, Alter HJ, Dienstag JL, et al. Prevalence of hepatitis C virus antibody in a cohort of hemophilia patients. Blood. 1990;76:254-256.
403. Centers for Disease Control and Prevention. Public Health Service interagency guidelines for screening blood, plasma, organs, tissue and semen for evidence of hepatitis B and C. MMWR Morb Mortal Wkly Rep. 1991;40:1-23.
404. Donahue JG, Munoz A, Ness PM, et al. The declining risk of post-transfusion hepatitis C virus infection. N Engl J Med. 1992;327:369-373.
405. Blajchman MA, Bull SB, Feinman SV. Post-transfusion hepatitis: Impact of non-A, non-B hepatitis surrogate tests. Lancet. 1995;345:21-25.
406. Blanchette V, Walker I, Gill P, et al. Hepatitis C infection in patients with hemophilia: Results of a national survey. Canadian Hemophilia Clinic Directors Group. Transfus Med Rev. 1994;8:210-217.
407. Kinoshita T, Miyake K, Okamoto H, Mishiro S. Imported hepatitis C virus genotypes in Japanese hemophiliacs. J Infect Dis. 1993;168:249-250.
408. Morfini M, Mannucci PM, Ciavarella N, et al. Prevalence of infection with the hepatitis C virus among Italian hemophiliacs before and after the introduction of virally inactivated clotting factor concentrates: A retrospective evaluation. Vox Sang. 1994;67:178-182.
409. Yap PL, McOmish F, Webster ADB, et al. Hepatitis C virus transmission by intravenous immunoglobulin. J Hepatol. 1994;21:455-460.
410. Pereira BJG, Milford EL, Kirkman RL, et al. Prevalence of hepatitis C virus RNA in organ donors positive for hepatitis C antibody and in the recipients of their organs. N Engl J Med. 1992;327:910-915.
411. Terrault NA, Wright TL. Hepatitis C virus in the setting of transplantation. Semin Liver Dis. 1995;15:92-100.
412. Pereira BJG, Milford EL, Kirkman RL, Levey AS. Transmission of hepatitis C virus by organ transplantation. N Engl J Med. 1991;325:454-460.
413. Konig V, Bauditz J, Lobeck H, et al. Hepatitis C virus reinfection in allografts after orthotopic liver transplantation. Hepatology. 1992;16:1137-1143.
414. Thomas DL, Vlahov D, Solomon L, et al. Correlates of hepatitis C virus infections among injection drug users in Baltimore. Medicine (Baltimore). 1995;74:212-220.
415. Bolumar F, Hernandez-Aguado I, Ferrer L, et al. Prevalence of antibodies to hepatitis C in a population of intravenous drug users in Valencia, Spain, 1990-1992. Int J Epidemiol. 1996;25:204-209.
416. Girardi E, Zaccarelli M, Tossini G, et al. Hepatitis C virus infection in intravenous drug users: Prevalence and risk factors. Scand J Infect Dis. 1990;22:751-752.
417. Bell J, Batey RG, Farrell GC, et al. Hepatitis C virus in intravenous drug users. Med J Aust. 1990;153:274-276.
418. Van Ameijden EJ, van den Hoek JA, Mientjes GH, Coutinho RA. A longitudinal study on the incidence and transmission patterns of HIV, HBV and HCV infection among drug users in Amsterdam. Eur J Epidemiol. 1993;9:255-262.
419. Patti AM, Santi AL, Pompa MG, et al. Viral hepatitis and drugs: A continuing problem. Int J Epidemiol. 1993;22:135-139.
420. Garfein RS, Vlahov D, Galai N, et al. Viral infections in short-term injection drug users: The prevalence of the hepatitis C, hepatitis B, human immunodeficiency, and human T-lymphotropic viruses. Am J Public Health. 1996;86:655-661.
421. Hagan H, Jarlais DCD, Friedman SR, et al. Reduced risk of hepatitis B and hepatitis C among injection drug users in the Tacoma syringe exchange program. Am J Public Health. 1995;85:1531-1537.
422. Hagan H, McGough JP, Thiede H, et al. Syringe exchange and risk of infection with hepatitis B and C viruses. Am J Epidemiol. 1999;149:203-213.
423. Ko YC, Ho MS, Chiang TA, et al. Tattooing as a risk of hepatitis C virus infection. J Med Virol. 1992;38:288-291.
424. Sun DX, Zhang FG, Geng YQ, Xi DS. Hepatitis C transmission by cosmetic tattooing in women. Lancet. 1996;347:541.
425. Dusheiko GM, Smith M, Scheuer PJ. Hepatitis C virus transmission by human bite. Lancet. 1990;336:503-504.
426. Bronowicki JP, Venard V, Botté C, et al. Patient-to-patient transmission of hepatitis C virus during colonoscopy. N Engl J Med. 1997;337:237-240.
427. Allander T, Gruber A, Naghavi M, et al. Frequent patient-to-patient transmission of hepatitis C virus in a haematology ward. Lancet. 1995;345:603-607.
428. Schvarcz R, Johansson B, Nyström B, Sönnerborg A. Nosocomial transmission of hepatitis C virus. Infection. 1997;25:74-77.
429. Munro J, Biggs JD, McCruden EAB. Detection of a cluster of hepatitis C infections in a renal transplant unit by analysis of sequence variation of the NS5A gene. J Infect Dis. 1996;174:177-180.
430. Kiyosawa K, Sodeyama T, Tanaka E, et al. Hepatitis C in hospital employees with needlestick injuries. Ann Intern Med. 1991;115:367-369.
431. Ridzon R, Gallagher K, Ciesielski C, et al. Simultaneous transmission of human immunodeficiency virus and hepatitis C virus from a needle-stick injury. N Engl J Med. 1997;336:919-922.
432. Mitsui T, Iwano K, Masuko K, et al. Hepatitis C virus infection in medical personnel after needlestick accident. Hepatology. 1992;16:1109-1114.
433. Seeff LB, Wright EC, Zimmerman HJ, et al. Type B hepatitis after needle-stick exposure: Prevention with hepatitis B immune globulin. Ann Intern Med. 1978;88: 285-293.
434. Thomas DL, Gruninger SE, Siew C, et al. Occupational risk of hepatitis C infections among general dentists and oral surgeons in North America. Am J Med. 1996;100:41-45.
435. Thomas DL, Factor S, Kelen G, et al. Hepatitis B and C in health care workers at the Johns Hopkins Hospital. Arch Intern Med. 1993;153:1705-1712.
436. Gerberding JL. Incidence and prevalence of human immunodeficiency virus, hepatitis B virus, hepatitis C virus, and cytomegalovirus among health care personnel at risk for blood exposure: Final report from a longitudinal study. J Infect Dis. 1994; 170:1410-1417.
437. Kuo MY, Hahn LJ, Hong CY, et al. Low prevalence of hepatitis C virus infection among dentists in Taiwan. J Med Virol. 1993;40:10-13.
438. Campello C, Majori S, Poli A, et al. Prevalence of HCV antibodies in health-care workers from northern Italy. Infection. 1992;20:224-226.
439. Polish LB, Tong MJ, Co RL, et al. Risk factors for hepatitis C virus infection among health care personnel in a community hospital. Am J Infect Control. 1993;21:196-200.
440. Puro V, Petrosillo N, Ippolito G, et al. Occupational hepatitis C virus infection in Italian health care workers. Am J Public Health. 1995;85:1272-1275.
441. Esteban JI, Gómez J, Martell M, et al. Transmission of hepatitis C virus by a cardiac surgeon. N Engl J Med. 1996;334:555-560.
442. Thomas DL, Zenilman JM, Alter HJ, et al. Sexual transmission of hepatitis C virus among patients attending sexually transmitted diseases clinics in Baltimore: An analysis of 309 sex partnerships. J Infect Dis. 1995;171:768-775.
443. van Doornum GJJ, Hooykaas C, Cuypers MT, et al. Prevalence of hepatitis C virus infections among heterosexuals with multiple partners. J Med Virol. 1991;35:22-27.
444. Petersen EE, Clemens R, Bock HL, et al. Hepatitis B and C in heterosexual patients with various sexually transmitted diseases. Infection. 1992;20:128-131.
445. Nakashima K, Kashiwagi S, Hayashi J, et al. Sexual transmission of hepatitis C virus among female prostitutes and patients with sexually transmitted diseases in Fukuoka, Kyushu, Japan. Am J Epidemiol. 1992;136:1132-1137.
446. Utsumi T, Hashimoto E, Okumura Y, et al. Heterosexual activity as a risk factor for the transmission of hepatitis C virus. J Med Virol. 1995;46:122-125.
447. Capelli C, Prati D, Bosoni P, et al. Sexual transmission of hepatitis C virus to a repeat blood donor. Transfusion. 1997;37:436-440.
448. Healey CJ, Smith DB, Walker JL, et al. Acute hepatitis C infection after sexual exposure. Gut. 1995;36:148-150.
449. Akahane Y, Kojima M, Sugai Y, et al. Hepatitis C virus infection in spouses of patients with type C chronic liver disease. Ann Intern Med. 1994;120:748-752.
450. Kao JH, Chen PJ, Yang PM, et al. Intrafamilial transmission of hepatitis C virus: The important role of infections between spouses. J Infect Dis. 1992;166:900-903.
451. Kao JH, Hwang YT, Chen PJ, et al. Transmission of hepatitis C virus between spouses: The important role of exposure duration. Am J Gastroenterol. 1996;91:2087-2090.

452. Chayama K, Kobayashi M, Tsubota A, et al. Molecular analysis of intraspousal transmission of hepatitis C virus. J Hepatol. 1995;22:431-439.

453. Wu JC, Lin HC, Jeng FS, et al. Prevalence, infectivity, and risk factor analysis of hepatitis C virus infection in prostitutes. J Med Virol. 1993;39:312-317.

454. Bresters D, Mauser-Bunschoten ED, Reesink HW, et al. Sexual transmission of hepatitis C. Lancet. 1993;342:210-211.

455. Everhart JE, Di Bisceglie AM, Murray LM, et al. Risk for non-A, non-B (type C) hepatitis through sexual or household contact with chronic carriers. Ann Intern Med. 1990;112:544-545.

456. Brettler DB, Mannucci PM, Gringeri A, et al. The low risk of hepatitis C virus transmission among sexual partners of hepatitis C infected hemophilic males: An international, multicenter study. Blood. 1992;80:540-543.

457. Gordon SC, Patel AH, Kulesza GW, et al. Lack of evidence for the heterosexual transmission of hepatitis C. Am J Gastroenterol. 1992;87:1849-1851.

458. Melbye M, Biggar RJ, Wantzin P, et al. Sexual transmission of hepatitis C virus: Cohort study (1981-1989) among European homosexual men. BMJ. 1990;301:210-212.

459. Osmond DH, Charlebois E, Sheppard HW, et al. Comparison of risk factors for hepatitis C and hepatitis B virus infection in homosexual men. J Infect Dis. 1993;167:66-71.

460. Bodsworth NJ, Cunningham P, Kaldor J, Donovan B. Hepatitis C virus infection in a large cohort of homosexually active men: Independent associations with HIV-1 infection and injecting drug use but not sexual behaviour. Genitourin Med. 1996;72:118-122.

461. Donahue JG, Nelson KE, Munoz A, et al. Antibody to hepatitis C virus among cardiac surgery patients, homosexual men, and intravenous drug users in Baltimore, Maryland. Am J Epidemiol. 1991;134:1206-1211.

462. Zaaijer HL, Cuypers HTM, Reesink HW, et al. Reliability of polymerase chain reaction for detection of hepatitis C virus. Lancet. 1993;341:722-724.

463. Roudot-Thoraval F, Pawlotsky JM, Thiers W, et al. Lack of mother-to-infant transmission of hepatitis C virus in human immunodeficiency virus-seronegative women: A prospective study with hepatitis C virus RNA testing. Hepatology. 1993;17:772-777.

464. Reinus JF, Leikin EL, Alter HJ, et al. Failure to detect vertical transmission of hepatitis C virus. Ann Intern Med. 1992;117:881-886.

465. Ohto H, Terazawa S, Nobuhiko S, et al. Transmission of hepatitis C virus from mothers to infants. N Engl J Med. 1994;330:744-750.

466. Zanetti AR, Tanzi E, Paccagnini S, et al. Mother-to-infant transmission of hepatitis C virus. Lancet. 1995;345:289-291.

467. Lam JPH, McOmish F, Burns SM, et al. Infrequent vertical transmission of hepatitis C virus. J Infect Dis. 1993;167:572-576.

468. Novati R, Thiers V, Monforte AD, et al. Mother-to-child transmission of hepatitis C virus detected by nested polymerase chain reaction. J Infect Dis. 1992;165:720-723.

469. Wejstal R, Widell A, Mansson A-S, et al. Mother-to-infant transmission of hepatitis C virus. Ann Intern Med. 1992;117:887-890.

470. Resti M, Azzari C, Mannelli F, et al. Mother to child transmission of hepatitis C virus: Prospective study of risk factors and timing of infection in children born to women seronegative for HIV-1. Tuscany Study Group on Hepatitis C Virus Infection. BMJ. 1998;317:437-441.

471. Ogasawara S, Kage M, Kosai K, et al. Hepatitis C virus RNA in saliva and breastmilk of hepatitis C carrier mothers. Lancet. 1993;341:561.

472. Resti M, Azzari C, Lega L, et al. Mother-to-infant transmission of hepatitis C virus. Acta Paediatr. 1995;84:251-255.

473. Lin H-H, Kao J-H, Hsu H-Y, et al. Absence of infection in breast-fed infants born to hepatitis C virus-infected mothers. J Pediatr. 1995;126:589-591.

474. Manzini P, Saracco G, Cerchier A, et al. Human immunodeficiency virus infection as risk factor for mother-to-child hepatitis C virus transmission: Persistence of anti-hepatitis C virus in children is associated with the mother's anti-hepatitis C virus immunoblotting pattern. Hepatology. 1995;21:328-332.

475. Paccagnini S, Principi N, Massironi E, et al. Perinatal transmission and manifestation of hepatitis C virus infection in a high risk population. Pediatr Infect Dis J. 1995;14:195-199.

476. Ohto H, Okamoto H, Mishiro S. Vertical transmission of hepatitis C virus. Reply. N Engl J Med. 1994;331:400.

477. Kumar RM, Shahul S. Role of breast-feeding in transmission of hepatitis C virus to infants of HCV-infected mothers. J Hepatol. 1998;29:191-197.

478. American Academy of Pediatrics Committee on Infectious Diseases. Hepatitis C virus infection. Pediatrics. 1998;101:481-485.

479. Dore GJ, Kaldor JM, McCaughan GW. Systematic review of role of polymerase chain reaction in defining infectiousness among people infected with hepatitis C virus. Br Med J. 1997;315:333-337.

480. Thomas DL, Villano SA, Riester KA, et al. Perinatal transmission of hepatitis C virus from human immunodeficiency virus type 1-infected mothers. J Infect Dis. 1998;177:1480-1488.

481. Eyster ME, Alter HJ, Aledort LM, et al. Heterosexual co-transmission of hepatitis C virus (HCV) and human immunodeficiency virus (HIV). Ann Intern Med. 1991;115:764-768.

482. Telfer PT, Brown D, Devereux H, et al. HCV RNA levels and HIV infection: Evidence for a viral interaction in haemophilic patients. Br J Haematol. 1994;88:397-399.

483. Eyster ME, Fried MW, Di Bisceglie AM, Goedert JJ. Increasing hepatitis C virus RNA levels in hemophiliacs: Relationship to human immunodeficiency virus infection and liver disease. Blood. 1994;84:1020-1023.

484. Lau DT, Kleiner DE, Ghany MG, et al. 10-Year follow-up after interferon-alpha therapy for chronic hepatitis C. Hepatology. 1998;28:1121-1127.

485. Marcellin P, Boyer N, Gervais A, et al. Long-term histologic improvement and loss of detectable intrahepatic HCV RNA in patients with chronic hepatitis C and sustained response to interferon-alpha therapy. Ann Intern Med. 1997;127:875-881.

486. Poynard T, McHutchison J, Manns M, et al. Impact of pegylated interferon alfa-2b and ribavirin on liver fibrosis in patients with chronic hepatitis C. Gastroenterology. 2002;122:1303-1313.

487. Shiffman ML, Hofmann CM, Contos MJ, et al. A randomized, controlled trial of maintenance interferon therapy for patients with chronic hepatitis C virus and persistent viremia. Gastroenterology. 1999;117:1164-1172.

488. Heathcote EJ, Keeffe EB, Lee SS, et al. Re-treatment of chronic hepatitis C with consensus interferon. Hepatology. 1998;27:1136-1143.

489. Mazzella G, Accogli E, Sottili S, et al. Alpha interferon treatment may prevent hepatocellular carcinoma in HCV-related liver cirrhosis. J Hepatol. 1996;24:141-147.

490. Kasahara A, Hayashi N, Mochizuki K, et al. Risk factors for hepatocellular carcinoma and its incidence after interferon treatment in patients with chronic hepatitis C. Hepatology. 1998;27:1394-1402.

491. Serfaty L, Aumaître H, Chazouillères O, et al. Determinants of outcome of compensated hepatitis C virus-related cirrhosis. Hepatology. 1998;27:1435-1440.

492. Nishiguchi S, Kuroki T, Nakatani S, et al. Randomised trial of effects of interferon-α on incidence of hepatocellular carcinoma in chronic active hepatitis C with cirrhosis. Lancet. 1995;346:1051-1055.

493. Davis GL, Balart LA, Schiff ER, et al. Treatment of chronic hepatitis C with recombinant interferon alfa. N Engl J Med. 1989;321:1501-1506.

494. Di Bisceglie AM, Martin P, Kassianides C, et al. Recombinant interferon alfa therapy for chronic hepatitis C. N Engl J Med. 1989;321:1506-1510.

495. Poynard T, Bedossa P, Chevallier M, et al. A comparison of three interferon alfa-2b regimens for the long-term treatment of chronic non-A, non-B hepatitis. N Engl J Med. 1995;332:1457-1462.

496. Keeffe EB, Hollinger FB, Bailey R, et al. Therapy of hepatitis C: Consensus interferon trials. Hepatology. 1997;26:101S-107S.

497. Lee WM. Therapy of hepatitis C: Interferon alfa-2a trials. Hepatology. 1997;26:89S-95S.

498. Zeuzem S, Feinman SV, Rasenack J, et al. Peginterferon alfa-2a in patients with chronic hepatitis C. N Engl J Med. 2000;343:1666-1672.

499. Heathcote EJ, Shiffman ML, Cooksley WG, et al. Peginterferon alfa-2a in patients with chronic hepatitis C and cirrhosis. N Engl J Med. 2000;343:1673-1680.

500. Fried MW, Shiffman ML, Reddy KR, et al. Peginterferon alfa-2a plus ribavirin for chronic hepatitis C virus infection. N Engl J Med. 2002;347:975-982.

501. Manns MP, McHutchison JG, Gordon SC, et al. Peginterferon alfa-2b plus ribavirin compared with interferon alfa-2b plus ribavirin for initial treatment of chronic hepatitis C: A randomised trial. Lancet. 2001;358:958-965.

502. Crotty S, Cameron CE, Andino R. RNA virus error catastrophe: Direct molecular test by using ribavirin. Proc Natl Acad Sci U S A. 2001;98:6895-6900.

503. Lanford RE, Guerra B, Lee H, et al. Antiviral effect and virus-host interactions in response to alpha interferon, gamma interferon, poly(i)-poly(c), tumor necrosis factor alpha, and ribavirin in hepatitis C virus subgenomic replicons. J Virol. 2003;77:1092-1104.

504. Patterson JL, Fernandez-Larson R. Molecular mechanisms of action of ribavirin. Rev Infect Dis. 1990;12:1139-1146.

505. Davis GL, Esteban-Muir R, Rustgi VK, et al. Interferon alfa-2b alone or in combination with ribavirin for the treatment of relapse of chronic hepatitis C. N Engl J Med. 1998;339:1493-1499.

506. McHutchison JG, Gordon SC, Schiff ER, et al. Interferon alfa-2b alone or in combination with ribavirin as initial treatment for chronic hepatitis C. N Engl J Med. 1998;339:1485-1492.

507. Poynard T, Marcellin P, Lee SS, et al. Randomised trial of interferon α2b plus ribavirin for 48 weeks or for 24 weeks versus interferon α2b plus placebo for 48 weeks for treatment of chronic infection with hepatitis C virus. Lancet. 1998;352:1426-1432.

508. Bodenheimer HCJ, Lindsay KL, Davis GL, et al. Tolerance and efficacy of oral ribavirin treatment of chronic hepatitis C: A multicenter trial. Hepatology. 1997;26:473-477.

509. Dusheiko G, Main J, Thomas H, et al. Ribavirin treatment for patients with chronic hepatitis C: Results of a placebo-controlled study. J Hepatol. 1996;25:591-598.

510. Di Bisceglie AM, Conjeevaram HS, Fried MW, et al. Ribavirin as therapy for chronic hepatitis C: A randomized, double-blind, placebo-controlled trial. Ann Intern Med. 1995;123:897-903.

511. Ning Q, Brown D, Parodo J, et al. Ribavirin inhibits viral-induced macrophage production of TNF, IL-1, the procoagulant fgl2 prothrombinase and preserves Th1 cytokine production but inhibits Th2 cytokine response. J Immunol. 1998;160:3487-3493.

512. Hadziyannis SJ, Sette H Jr, Morgan TR, et al. Peginterferon-alpha2a and ribavirin combination therapy in chronic hepatitis C: A randomized study of treatment duration and ribavirin dose. Ann Intern Med. 2004;140:346-355.

513. Reddy KR, Hoofnagle JH, Tong MJ, et al. Racial differences in responses to therapy with interferon in chronic hepatitis C. Hepatology. 1999;30:787-793.

514. Theodore D, Shiffman ML, Sterling RK, et al. Intensive interferon therapy does not increase virological response rates in African Americans with chronic hepatitis C. Dig Dis Sci. 2003;48:140-145.

515. Davis GL. Monitoring of viral levels during therapy of hepatitis C. Hepatology. 2002;36:S145-S151.

516. Sherman KE, Sjögren M, Creager RL, et al. Combination therapy with thymosin alpha 1 and interferon for the treatment of chronic hepatitis C infection: A randomized, placebo-controlled double-blind trial. Hepatology. 1998;27:1128-1135.

517. Dusheiko G. Side effects of alpha interferon in chronic hepatitis C. Hepatology. 1997;26:112S-121S.

518. Manesis EK, Moschos M, Brouzas D, et al. Neurovisual impairment: A frequent complication of alpha-interferon treatment in chronic viral hepatitis. Hepatology. 1998;27:1421-1427.

519. Sulkowski MS. Anemia in the treatment of hepatitis C virus infection. Clin Infect Dis. 2003;37(Suppl 4):S315-S322.

520. Bacon BR. Treatment of patients with hepatitis C and normal serum aminotransferase levels. Hepatology. 2002;36:S179-S184.
521. Wright TL. Treatment of patients with hepatitis C and cirrhosis. Hepatology. 2002;36:S185-S194.
522. Edlin BR. Prevention and treatment of hepatitis C in injection drug users. Hepatology. 2002;36:S210-S219.
523. Peters MG, Terrault NA. Alcohol use and hepatitis C. Hepatology. 2002;36: S220-S225.
524. Jonas MM. Children with hepatitis C. Hepatology. 2002;36:S173-S178.
525. Lampertico P, Rumi M, Romeo R, et al. A multicenter randomized controlled trial of recombinant interferon-alpha 2b in patients with acute transfusion-associated hepatitis C. Hepatology. 1994;19:19-22.
526. Viladomiu L, Genesca J, Esteban JI, et al. Interferon-alpha in acute posttransfusion hepatitis C: A randomized, controlled trial. Hepatology. 1992;15:767-769.
527. Vogel W, Graziadei I, Umlauft F, et al. High-dose interferon-α_{2b} treatment prevents chronicity in acute hepatitis C: A pilot study. Dig Dis Sci. 1996;41:81S-85S.
528. Hwang SJ, Lee SD, Chan CY, et al. A randomized controlled trial of recombinant interferon alpha-2b in the treatment of Chinese patients with acute post-transfusion hepatitis C. J Hepatol. 1994;21:831-836.
529. Takano S, Satomura Y, Omata M. Effects of interferon beta on non-A, non-B acute hepatitis: A prospective, randomized, controlled-dose study. Japan Acute Hepatitis Cooperative Study Group. Gastroenterology. 1994;107:805-811.
530. Gursoy M, Gur G, Arslan H, et al. Interferon therapy in haemodialysis patients with acute hepatitis C virus infection and factors that predict response to treatment. J Viral Hepat. 2001;8:70-77.
531. Tassopoulos NC, Koutelou MG, Papatheodoridis G, et al. Recombinant human interferon alfa-2b treatment for acute non-A, non-B hepatitis. Gut. 1993;34:S130-S132.
532. Omata M, Yokosuka O, Takano S, et al. Resolution of acute hepatitis C after therapy with natural beta interferon. Lancet. 1991;338:914-915.
533. Palmovic D, Kurelac I, Crnjakovic-Palmovic J. The treatment of acute post-transfusion hepatitis C with recombinant interferon-alpha. Infection. 1994;22:222-223.
534. Jaeckel E, Cornberg M, Wedemeyer H, et al. Treatment of acute hepatitis C with interferon alfa-2b. N Engl J Med. 2001;345:1452-1457.
535. Gerlach JT, Diepolder HM, Zachoval R, et al. Acute hepatitis C: High rate of both spontaneous and treatment-induced viral clearance. Gastroenterology. 2003;125:80-88.
536. Morand P, Dutertre N, Minazzi H, et al. Lack of seroconversion in a health care worker after polymerase chain reaction-documented acute hepatitis C resulting from a needlestick injury. Clin Infect Dis. 2001;33:727-729.
537. Shiffman ML. Retreatment of patients with chronic hepatitis C. Hepatology. 2002;36:S128-S134.
538. Cheng SJ, Bonis PA, Lau J, et al. Interferon and ribavirin for patients with chronic hepatitis C who did not respond to previous interferon therapy: A meta-analysis of controlled and uncontrolled trials. Hepatology. 2001;33:231-240.
539. Cummings KJ, Lee SM, West ES, et al. Interferon and ribavirin vs interferon alone in the re-treatment of chronic hepatitis C previously nonresponsive to interferon: A meta-analysis of randomized trials. JAMA. 2001;285:193-199.
540. Lamarre D, Anderson PC, Bailey M, et al. An NS3 protease inhibitor with antiviral effects in humans infected with hepatitis C virus. Nature. 2003;426:186-189.
541. Farci P, Alter HJ, Govindarajan S, et al. Lack of protective immunity against reinfection with hepatitis C virus. Science. 1992;258:135-140.
542. Major ME, Mihalik K, Puig M, et al. Previously infected and recovered chimpanzees exhibit rapid responses that control hepatitis C virus replication upon rechallenge. J Virol. 2002;76:6586-6595.
543. Weiner AJ, Paliard X, Selby MJ, et al. Intrahepatic genetic inoculation of hepatitis C virus RNA confers cross-protective immunity. J Virol. 2001;75:7142-7148.
544. Forns X, Payette PJ, Ma X, et al. Vaccination of chimpanzees with plasmid DNA encoding the hepatitis C virus (HCV) envelope E2 protein modified the infection after challenge with homologous monoclonal HCV. Hepatology. 2000;32:618-625.
545. Choo QL, Kuo G, Ralston R, et al. Vaccination of chimpanzees against infection by the hepatitis C virus. Proc Natl Acad Sci U S A. 1994;91:1294-1298.
546. Lanford RE, Guerra B, Chavez D, et al. Cross-genotype immunity to hepatitis C. J Virol. 2004;78:1575.
547. Seeff LB, Zimmerman JH, Wright EL, et al. A randomized double-blind controlled trial of the efficacy of immune serum globulin for the prevention of post-transfusion hepatitis. A Veterans Administration Cooperative Study. Gastroenterology. 1977;72:111-121.
548. Sanchez-Quijano A, Pineda JA, Lissen E, et al. Prevention of post-transfusion non-A, non-B hepatitis by nonspecific immunoglobulin in heart surgery patients. Lancet. 1988;1:1245-1249.
549. Palella FJ Jr, Delaney KM, Moorman AC, et al. Declining morbidity and mortality among patients with advanced human immunodeficiency virus infection. HIV Outpatient Study Investigators. N Engl J Med. 1998;338:853-860.
550. Bica I, McGovern B, Dhar R, et al. Increasing mortality due to end-stage liver disease in patients with human immunodeficiency virus infection. Clin Infect Dis. 2001;32:492-497.
551. Monga HK, Rodriguez-Barradas MC, Breaux K, et al. Hepatitis C virus infection-related morbidity and mortality among patients with human immunodeficiency virus infection. Clin Infect Dis. 2001;33:240-247.
552. Sherman KE, Rouster SD, Chung RT, et al. Hepatitis C virus prevalence among patients infected with human immunodeficiency virus: A cross-sectional analysis of the U.S. Adult AIDS Clinical Trials Group. Clin Infect Dis. 2002;34:831-837.
553. Sulkowski MS, Thomas DL. Hepatitis C in the HIV infected patient. Ann Intern Med. 2002;138:197-207.
554. Gibb DM, Goodall RL, Dunn DT, et al. Mother-to-child transmission of hepatitis C virus: Evidence for preventable peripartum transmission. Lancet. 2000;356:904-907.
555. Darby SC, Ewart DW, Giangrande PL, et al. Mortality from liver cancer and liver disease in haemophilic men and boys in UK given blood products contaminated with hepatitis C. Lancet. 1997;350:1425-1431.
556. Lesens O, Deschenes M, Steben M, et al. Hepatitis C virus is related to progressive liver disease in human immunodeficiency virus-positive hemophiliacs and should be treated as an opportunistic infection. J Infect Dis. 1999;179:1254-1258.
557. Pol S, Lamorthe B, Thi NT, et al. Retrospective analysis of the impact of HIV infection and alcohol use on chronic hepatitis C in a large cohort of drug users. J Hepatol. 1998;28:945-950.
558. Graham CS, Baden LR, Yu E, et al. Influence of human immunodeficiency virus infection on the course of hepatitis C virus infection: A meta-analysis. Clin Infect Dis. 2001;33:562-569.
559. Ragni MV, Belle SH. Impact of human immunodeficiency virus infection on progression to end-stage liver disease in individuals with hemophilia and hepatitis c virus infection. J Infect Dis. 2001;183:1112-1115.
560. Soto B, Sánchez-Quijano A, Rodrigo L, et al. Human immunodeficiency virus infection modifies the natural history of chronic parenterally-acquired hepatitis C with an unusually rapid progression to cirrhosis. J Hepatol. 1997;26:1-5.
561. Garcia-Samaniego J, Rodriguez M, Berenguer J, et al. Hepatocellular carcinoma in HIV-infected patients with chronic hepatitis C. Am J Gastroenterol. 2001;96:179-183.
562. Kim WR, Gross JB, Poterucha JJ, et al. Outcome of hospital care of liver disease associated with hepatitis C in the United States. Hepatology. 2001;33:201-206.
563. Benhamou Y, Bochet M, Di M, et al. Liver fibrosis progression in human immunodeficiency virus and hepatitis C virus coinfected patients. The Multivirc Group. Hepatology. 1999;30:1054-1058.
564. Di Martino V, Rufat P, Boyer N, et al. The influence of human immunodeficiency virus coinfection on chronic hepatitis C in injection drug users: A long-term retrospective cohort study. Hepatology. 2001;34:1193-1199.
565. Serfaty L, Costagliola D, Wendum D, et al. Impact of early-untreated HIV infection on chronic hepatitis C in intravenous drug users: A case-control study. AIDS. 2001;15:2011-2016.
566. Goedert JJ, Eyster ME, Lederman MM, et al. End-stage liver disease in persons with hemophilia and transfusion-associated infections. Blood. 2002;100:1584-1589.
567. Dorrucci M, Pezzotti P, Phillips AN, et al. Coinfection of hepatitis C virus with human immunodeficiency virus and progression to AIDS. J Infect Dis. 1995;172:1503-1508.
568. Piroth L, Duong M, Quantin C, et al. Does hepatitis C virus co-infection accelerate clinical and immunological evolution of HIV-infected patients? AIDS. 1998;12:381-388.
569. Greub G, Ledergerber B, Battegay M, et al. Clinical progression, survival, and immune recovery during antiretroviral therapy in patients with HIV-1 and hepatitis C virus coinfection: The Swiss HIV Cohort Study. Lancet. 2000;356:1800-1805.
570. Staples CT Jr, Rimland D, Dudas D. Hepatitis C in the HIV (human immunodeficiency virus) Atlanta V.A. (Veterans Affairs Medical Center) Cohort Study (HAVACS): The effect of coinfection on survival. Clin Infect Dis. 1999;29:150-154.
571. Sulkowski MS, Moore RD, Mehta SH, et al. Hepatitis C and progression of HIV disease. JAMA. 2002;288:199-206.
572. Chung RT, Evans SR, Yang Y, et al. Immune recovery is associated with persistent rise in hepatitis C virus RNA, infrequent liver test flares, and is not impaired by hepatitis C virus in co-infected subjects. AIDS. 2002;16:1915-1923.
573. Martinez E, Blanco JL, Arnaiz JA, et al. Hepatotoxicity in HIV-1-infected patients receiving nevirapine-containing antiretroviral therapy. AIDS. 2001;15:1261-1268.
574. Sulkowski MS, Thomas DL, Chaisson RE, Moore RD. Hepatotoxicity associated with antiretroviral therapy in adults infected with human immunodeficiency virus and the role of hepatitis C or B virus infection. JAMA. 2000;283:74-80.
575. den Brinker M, Wit FW, Wertheim-van Dillen PM, et al. Hepatitis B and C virus co-infection and the risk for hepatotoxicity of highly active antiretroviral therapy in HIV-1 infection. AIDS. 2000;14:2895-2902.
576. Cattelan AM, Erne E, Salatino A, et al. Severe hepatic failure related to nevirapine treatment. Clin Infect Dis. 1999;29:455-456.
577. Nunez M, Lana R, Mendoza JL, et al. Risk factors for severe hepatic injury after introduction of highly active antiretroviral therapy. J Acquir Immune Defic Syndr. 2001;27:426-431.
578. Veronese L, Rautaureau J, Sadler BM, et al. Single-dose pharmacokinetics of amprenavir, a human immunodeficiency virus type 1 protease inhibitor, in subjects with normal or impaired hepatic function. Antimicrob Agents Chemother. 2000;44:821-826.
579. John M, Flexman J, French MAH. Hepatitis C virus-associated hepatitis following treatment of HIV-infected patients with HIV protease inhibitors: An immune restoration disease? AIDS. 1998;12:2289-2293.
580. Barbaro G, Di Lorenzo G, Asti A, et al. Hepatocellular mitochondrial alterations in patients with chronic hepatitis C: Ultrastructural and biochemical findings. Am J Gastroenterol. 1999;94:2198-2205.
581. Soriano V, Sulkowski M, Bergin C, et al. Care of patients with chronic hepatitis C and HIV co-infection: Recommendations from the HIV-HCV International Panel. AIDS. 2002;16:813-828.
582. Centers for Disease Control and Prevention. Guidelines for preventing opportunistic infections among HIV-infected persons—2002. Recommendations of the U. S. Public Health Service and the Infectious Diseases Society of America. MMWR Recomm Rep. 2002;14:51(RR-8):1-52.
583. Laskus T, Radkowski M, Piasek A, et al. Hepatitis C virus in lymphoid cells of patients coinfected with human immunodeficiency virus type 1: Evidence of active replication in monocytes/macrophages and lymphocytes. J Infect Dis. 2000;181:442-448.
584. Lerat H, Rumin S, Habersetzer F, et al. In vivo tropism of hepatitis C virus genomic sequences in hematopoietic cells: Influence of viral load, viral genotype, and cell phenotype. Blood. 1998;91:3841-3849.

585. Patterson BK, Till M, Otto P, et al. Detection of HIV-1 DNA and messenger RNA in individual cells by PCR-driven in situ hybridization and flow cytometry. Science. 1993;260:976-979.

586. Goletti D, Weissman D, Jackson RW, et al. Effect of *Mycobacterium tuberculosis* on HIV replication: Role of immune activation. J Immunol. 1996;157:1271-1278.

587. Centers for Disease Control and Prevention. 1999 USPHS/IDSA guidelines for the prevention of opportunistic infections in persons infected with human immunodeficiency virus: Disease-specific recommendations. USPHS/IDSA Prevention of Opportunistic Infections Working Group. U.S. Public Health Services/Infectious Diseases Society of America. MMWR. 1999;48:1-82.

588. Ragni MV, Ndimbie OK, Rice EO, et al. The presence of hepatitis C virus (HCV) antibody in human immunodeficiency virus-positive hemophilic men undergoing HCV "seroreversion." Blood. 1993;82:1010-1015.

589. Marcellin P, Martinot-Peignoux M, Elias A, et al. Hepatitis C virus (HCV) viremia in human immunodeficiency virus-seronegative and -seropositive patients with indeterminate HCV recombinant immunoblot assay. J Infect Dis. 1994;170:433-435.

590. Chamot E, Hirschel B, Wintsch J, et al. Loss of antibodies against hepatitis C virus in HIV-seropositive intravenous drug users. AIDS. 1990;4:1275-1277.

591. George SL, Gebhardt J, Klinzman D, et al. Hepatitis C virus viremia in HIV-infected individuals with negative HCV antibody tests. J Acquir Immune Defic Syndr. 2002;31:154-162.

592. Lefrère JJ, Guiramand S, Lefrère F, et al. Full or partial seroreversion in patients infected by hepatitis C virus. J Infect Dis. 1997;175:316-322.

593. Thio CL, Nolt KR, Astemborski J, et al. Screening for hepatitis C virus in human immunodeficiency virus-infected individuals. J Clin Microbiol. 2000;38:575-577.

594. Boyer N, Marcellin P, Degott C, et al. Recombinant interferon-alpha for chronic hepatitis C in patients positive for antibody to human immunodeficiency virus. J Infect Dis. 1992;165:723-726.

595. Marriott E, Navas S, Del Romero J, et al. Treatment with recombinant alpha-interferon of chronic hepatitis C in anti-HIV-positive patients. J Med Virol. 1993;40:107-111.

596. Soriano V, García-Samaniego J, Bravo R, et al. Interferon alpha for the treatment of chronic hepatitis C in patients infected with human immunodeficiency virus. Clin Infect Dis. 1996;23:585-591.

597. Mauss S, Klinker H, Ulmer A, et al. Response to treatment of chronic hepatitis C with interferon alpha in patients infected with HIV-1 is associated with higher CD4+ cell count. Infection. 1998;26:20-23.

598. Causse X, Payen JL, Izopet J, et al. Does HIV-infection influence the response of chronic hepatitis C to interferon treatment? A French multicenter prospective study. French Multicenter Study Group. J Hepatol. 2000;32:1003-1010.

599. Soriano V, Bravo R, García-Samaniego J, et al. Relapses of chronic hepatitis C in HIV-infected patients who responded to interferon therapy. AIDS. 1997;11:400-401.

600. Zylberberg H, Benhamou Y, Lagneaux JL, et al. Safety and efficacy of interferon-ribavirin combination therapy in HCV-HIV coinfected subjects: An early report. Gut. 2000;47:694-697.

601. Nasti G, di Gennaro G, Tavio M, et al. Chronic hepatitis C in HIV infection: Feasibility and sustained efficacy of therapy with interferon alfa-2b and tribavirin. AIDS. 2001;15:1783-1787.

602. Landau A, Batisse D, Piketty C, et al. Long-term efficacy of combination therapy with interferon-alpha2b and ribavirin for severe chronic hepatitis C in HIV-infected patients. AIDS. 2001;15:2149-2155.

603. Sauleda S, Juarez A, Esteban JI, et al. Interferon and ribavirin combination therapy for chronic hepatitis C in human immunodeficiency virus-infected patients with congenital coagulation disorders. Hepatology. 2001;34:1035-1040.

604. Brau N, Rodriguez-Torres M, Prokupek D, et al. Treatment of chronic hepatitis C in HIV/HCV-coinfection with interferon alpha-2b+ full-course vs. 16-week delayed ribavirin. Hepatology. 2004;39:989-998.

605. Torriani FJ, Rockstroh J, Rodriguez-Torres M, et al. Final results of APRICOT: A randomized, partially blinded, international trial evaluating peginterferon-alfa-2a + ribavirin vs interferon-alfa-2a + ribavirin in the treatment of HCV in HIV/HCV co-infection. Abstract 112. Eleventh Conference on Retroviruses and Opportunistic Infections, San Francisco, Clif, February 8-11, 2004.

606. Chung R, Andersen J, Volberding P, et al. A randomized, controlled trial of PEG-interferon-alfa-2a plus ribavirin vs interferon-alfa-2a plus ribavirin for chronic hepatitis C virus infection in HIV-co-infected persons: Follow-up results of ACTG A5071. Abstract 110. Eleventh Conference on Retroviruses and Opportunistic Infections, San Francisco, Calif, February 8-11, 2004.

607. Perrone C, Carrat F, Bani-Sadr F, et al. Final results of ANRS HC02-RIBAVIC: A randomized controlled trial of pegylated-interferon-alfa-2b plus ribavirin vs interferon-alfa-2b plus ribavirin for the initial treatment of chronic hepatitis C in HIV co-infected patients. Abstract 117LB. Eleventh Conference on Retroviruses and Opportunistic Infections, San Francisco, Calif, February 8-11, 2004.

608. Moore RD. Human immunodeficiency virus infection, anemia, and survival. Clin Infect Dis. 1999;29:44-49.

609. Baba M, Pauwels R, Balzarini J, et al. Ribavirin antagonizes inhibitory effects of pyrimidine 2′,3′-dideoxynucleosides but enhances inhibitory effects of purine 2′,3′-dideoxynucleosides on replication of human immunodeficiency virus in vitro. Antimicrob Agents Chemother. 1987;31:1613-1617.

610. Hoggard PG, Kewn S, Barry MG, et al. Effects of drugs on 2′,3′-dideoxy-2′,3′-didehydrothymidine phosphorylation in vitro. Antimicrob Agents Chemother. 1997;41:1231-1236.

611. Lafeuillade A, Hittinger G, Chadapaud S. Increased mitochondrial toxicity with ribavirin in HIV/HCV coinfection. Lancet. 2001;357:280-281.

612. Salmon-Ceron D, Chauvelot-Moachon L, Abad S, et al. Mitochondrial toxic effects and ribavirin. Lancet. 2001;357:1803-1804.

613. Vogt MW, Hartshorn KL, Furman PA, et al. Ribavirin antagonizes the effect of azidothymidine on HIV replication. Science. 1987;235:1376-1379.

614. Landau A, Batisse D, Piketty C, et al. Lack of interference between ribavirin and nucleosidic analogues in HIV/HCV co-infected individuals undergoing concomitant antiretroviral and anti-HCV combination therapy. AIDS. 2000;14:1857-1858.

615. Lane HC, Davey V, Kovacs JA, et al. Interferon-alpha in patients with asymptomatic human immunodeficiency virus (HIV) infection: A randomized, placebo-controlled trial. Ann Intern Med. 1990;112:805-811.

616. Poles MA, Dieterich DT, Schwarz ED, et al. Liver biopsy findings in 501 patients infected with human immunodeficiency virus (HIV). J Acquir Immune Defic Syndr Hum Retrovirol. 1996;11:170-177.

617. Saadeh S, Cammell G, Carey WD, et al. The role of liver biopsy in chronic hepatitis C. Hepatology. 2001;33:196-200.

618. Roland ME, Havlir DV. Responding to organ failure in HIV-infected patients. N Engl J Med. 2003;348:2279-2281.

619. Neff GW, Bonham A, Tzakis AG, et al. Orthotopic liver transplantation in patients with human immunodeficiency virus and end-stage liver disease. Liver Transpl. 2003;9:239-247.

CHAPTER **151**

Hepatitis G Virus and TT Virus

HARVEY J. ALTER

HEPATITIS G VIRUS

Discovery of GB Virus Type C and the Hepatitis G Virus

The "blind" cloning of the hepatitis C virus (HCV)[1] established a new paradigm for viral discovery. Minute quantities of unknown virus can now be vastly amplified with random primers, blindly cloned, and then detected by immunoscreening, as in the case of HCV, the hepatitis E virus (HEV), and the hepatitis G virus (HGV), or by representational difference analysis (RDA), as in the case of the GB virus (GBV) types A, B, and C.

The development of sensitive serologic assays to detect antibodies to HCV allowed for wide-scale testing of sera from previously pedigreed cases of transfusion-associated or community-acquired hepatitis that had been classified by exclusion as non-A, non-B hepatitis. It was shown that HCV was the major etiologic agent in these cases, but that 10% to 20% of cases could not be explained on this etiologic basis.[2,3] This suggested the existence of an additional human hepatitis virus, tentatively designated non-ABC. Further clinical investigations revealed that approximately 30% of the cases of chronic hepatitis[4] and the great majority of the cases of fulminant hepatitis[5] and hepatitis-associated aplastic anemia[6] were classified by serologic and molecular exclusion as non-ABC hepatitis cases. The designations *non-ABC* and *non–A–E* have been used interchangeably in the literature. The more inclusive term, *non–A–E*, indicates serologic exclusion of the five established hepatitis viruses, is used henceforth in this chapter.

With this clinical background, two independent teams initiated viral discovery programs to find and characterize the non–A–E agent or agents. Workers at the Abbott Laboratories in North Chicago, Illinois, began their investigations with a specimen designated the *GB agent*—"G.B." being the initials of a surgeon who had developed acute hepatitis in the 1960s; his serum had been inoculated into marmosets and appeared to transmit hepatitis in that model.[7] However, controversy existed as to whether the observed hepatitis was caused by a transmissible human agent or represented reactivation of an endogenous marmoset hepatitis virus. The controversy was never resolved, and the GB agent lay dormant in frozen storage until resurrected by the Abbott team in the 1990s. They began their experiments using serum from the

11th passage of the GB agent in marmosets. Employing RDA, a form of subtractive cloning, they amplified RNA from preinoculation and postinoculation marmoset sera and performed "molecular subtraction" by hybridization.[8] An exogenous and novel sequence was identified, and, with the use of overlapping clones, the full genome of the new agent was characterized.[8,9] Two novel agents were present in the GB-infected marmoset sera, and these agents were designated *GBV-A* and *GBV-B*. Using molecular amplification and GB-specific serology, it was shown that GBV-A was an endogenous marmoset agent that did not appear to be associated with hepatitis, that GBV-B was the probable causative agent of marmoset hepatitis, and that neither GBV-A nor GBV-B could be detected in human non-ABC hepatitis cases. The investigators then used degenerate primers deduced from shared sequences in GBV-A, GBV-B, and HCV and discovered a third agent, designated *GBV-C*, which has been proposed as a human agent causing non–A–E hepatitis.[10]

HGV was discovered by investigators at Genelabs, Inc. (Redwood City, Calif.), in collaboration with investigators at the Centers for Disease Control and Prevention (CDC) and the National Institutes of Health (NIH).[11] The approach used in these investigations was more akin to that used for the cloning of HCV. The cloning source was serum both from humans with presumed non–A–E hepatitis and from chimpanzees that had been inoculated with human sera. Using sequence-independent single primer amplification (SISPA), an amplification technology that does not require prior knowledge of the genomic sequence, these investigators amplified complementary DNA (cDNA), cut restriction fragments, and then cloned the fragments using an expression vector whose protein product was detected by immunoscreening.[11] The full genomic sequence was derived by "walking the genome," using overlapping clones.[12] The nucleic acid sequence in characteristic conserved regions and the general genomic organization identified the agent as a flavivirus. Subsequent analysis showed HGV to have greater than 95% global sequence and amino acid homology with GBV-C; these two agents were virtually identical and represented strain variants of a common agent.[13] In contrast, HGV and GBV-C had less than 25% homology with any other known member of the Flaviviridae family, including HCV, yellow fever virus, and dengue fever virus, and represented a new genus within that family.[13]

Because the HGV/GBV-C agent was found during investigations seeking a new hepatitis virus and because the cloning sources were patients or animals with hepatitis, it was assumed that these were hepatitis agents. The hepatitis G virus was so named because an enterically transmitted hepatitis F virus had been reported and G was the next letter available in the hepatitis alphabet. However, the hepatitis F virus was never confirmed and appears to have been spuriously classified, and the hepatitis G virus has not been conclusively shown to cause hepatitis (see later discussion).

In summary, two novel members of the family Flaviviridae were independently cloned and individually named (HGV and GBV-C), and both were reported as a cause of non–A–E hepatitis. Results of subsequent studies showed these agents to be virtually identical and cast some doubt on whether they are actually hepatitis agents. Nonetheless, HGV and GBV-C are prevalent agents with a high carrier rate among volunteer blood donors and in the general population. Although the precise transmission rate is unknown, it is apparent that HGV/GBV-C is readily transmitted by blood transfusion and that it frequently leads to persistent viremia in the infected recipient. Beyond these observations, there are many unresolved issues, including the role of nonparenteral transmission mechanisms, hepatotropism, and hepatic and extrahepatic pathogenicity. A more fundamental issue is whether this is a hepatitis virus and a significant agent in the causation of non–A–E (cryptogenic) acute and chronic hepatitis. In essence, the long-range clinical significance of the HGV/GBV-C discovery is yet to be determined.

Structure, Genomic Organization, and Virology

HGV/GBV-C is a single-stranded, positive-sense RNA virus of approximately 9.4 kb that codes for 3100 amino acids.[12,13] It is an enveloped virus and therefore is susceptible to solvent detergent inactivation. Its genomic organization is similar to that of the flaviviruses, and the agent is distantly related to HCV (25% homology), the yellow fever virus, and the pestiviruses, including bovine diarrhea virus. It is, however, sufficiently distinct from all these agents to be considered a new genus within the Flaviviridae family. HGV/GBV-C shares with other members of the Flaviviridae family a genomic structure that includes a 5′ noncoding region, followed by the structural domains for the viral envelope and then a series of nonstructural genes that extend to a 3′ noncoding region. The nonstructural genes code for proteins with enzymatic functions, including helicase, serine protease, and RNA-dependent RNA polymerase. A feature unique to HGV/GBV-C is that the core (nucleocapsid) domain, which is so important to HCV structure and function, either does not exist or exists in a severely truncated form.[14] It is interesting to speculate that the absence of the nucleocapsid may be responsible for the low pathogenicity of this agent.

HGV/GBV-C can be classified into at least four major genotypes, with type 1 predominant in West Africa, type 2 in the United States and Europe, type 3 in Asia, and type 4 in Southeast Asia.[15] Genotypes can be used for epidemiologic investigations but do not appear to have clinical relevance. Like other members of the Flaviviridae family, HGV/GBV-C also exists as a series of closely related variants, or quasispecies, but the extent of quasispecies formation is markedly less than that for HCV. This fact may explain why this agent is more readily contained by the immune system, such that viral clearance occurs in the majority of infected persons.

Detection of Hepatitis G Virus/GB Virus Type C

Most published data on HGV/GBV-C are based on the detection of viral RNA by polymerase chain reaction (PCR) assay. Originally, primers from nonstructural regions were used (NS-3 and NS-5), but these regions were less well conserved and therefore less sensitive targets than the highly conserved 5′ noncoding region. Primers from the 5′ noncoding region are now routinely employed for detection of HGV/GBV-C RNA. Currently, there is no antigen or antibody assay that accurately reflects the presence of viremia. This is in sharp contrast to HCV infection, in which infected persons readily develop antibodies to proteins expressed along the entire HCV genome, which can readily distinguish HCV carriers from controls, and where there is a core antigen assay that very closely parallels viremia. The reason for this disparity in the immune response to these two genomically similar members of the Flaviviridae family is unknown.

Whereas reliable serologic markers that coexist with viremia have been difficult to develop, antibody to the envelope protein, E2, can be easily detected and appears to be an excellent marker of recovery from HGV/GBV-C infection and a powerful epidemiologic tool.[16] During acute or chronic HGV/GBV-C infection, the only marker of that infection is the detection of viral RNA by PCR assay or another molecular amplification technique. However, after the clearance of HGV/GBV-C RNA, antibody to the E2 envelope protein can be measured. Aside from a brief overlap period during recovery, HGV/GBV-C RNA and anti-E2 antibody are mutually exclusive; the former indicates ongoing viremia and the latter recovery from prior infection.[17] In combination, these two markers reflect HGV/GBV-C exposure and provide a more extensive profile of the occurrence of this infection than would either marker alone. The relationship between HGV/GBV-C RNA and anti-E2 antibody is similar to the relationship between hepatitis B surface antigen (HBsAg) and anti-surface antibody (anti-HBs) in hepatitis B virus (HBV) infection.

Prevalence and Persistence of Hepatitis G Virus/GB Virus Type C

HGV/GBV-C prevalence in eligible U.S. volunteer blood donors ranges from 1% to 2% in most studies but has been as high as 4% in some reports.[18] Similar frequencies have been reported throughout the world. It is important to emphasize that these rates are derived from PCR measurements of viremia and not simply from detection of antibody. The prevalence of HGV/GBV-C viremia is 5- to 10-fold higher than the prevalence of HCV viremia (0.3%) that was estimated when

HCV testing was first introduced. With a combination of HGV/GBV-C RNA and anti-E2 antibody assays, both the exposure rate and the active infection rate can be estimated. The exposure rate among volunteer donors has been found to be three to six times the rate of viremia, and the rates of exposure and of viremia are considerably higher among paid blood donors.[16] Among persons at high risk for parenteral exposure, such as hemophiliacs and intravenous drug abusers, the viremia rate may be as high as 15% to 40% and the exposure rate 60% to 80%.[19,20] The large difference between the exposure rate and the active infection rate suggests that approximately three quarters of HGV/GBV-C carriers eventually clear the virus, a much greater proportion than is observed in HCV infection. Indeed, the patterns of persistent viremia versus recovery rate for HCV and HGV infections appear to be the converse of each other. In HCV infection, 15% of the patients recover and 85% become long-term carriers, whereas in HGV infection, 15% appear to be long-term carriers and almost 85% recover, although recovery may take several years.

Epidemiology of Hepatitis G Virus/GB Virus Type C

HGV/GBV-C is spread predominantly through parenteral routes, principally intravenous drug abuse and blood transfusion. However, any percutaneous exposure represents a potential means of transmitting this agent as well as other established parenterally transmitted agents, including HCV, HBV, and human immunodeficiency virus (HIV). Tattooing, acupuncture, folk medicine practices, accidental needlesticks among health care workers, and renal dialysis are among the many potential modes of inadvertent parenteral exposure. Although the reuse of needles without proper intervening sterilization is no longer practiced in most industrialized nations, such practice is a relevant concern in the developing world. Furthermore, because agents such as HGV/GBV-C and HCV can persist for a lifetime, many infected persons detected today may have been exposed in the 1940s through the 1960s, when disposable needles and instruments were not uniformly used even in industrialized societies. In those years, it is quite possible that viruses were disseminated by dental instruments, barbers' razors, manicurists' tools, mass vaccinations, and immune globulin or other drug administration. For example, it is known that HBV infected more than 50,000 soldiers from a contaminated preparation of yellow fever vaccine.[21] It is suspected that schistosomiasis vaccination and treatment may account for the high frequency of HCV infection currently observed in Egypt and that contaminated lots of Rh immune globulin accounted for outbreaks of hepatitis C in Ireland.[22] Folk medicine practitioners have been shown to spread HCV in Japan.[23] These are documented examples of HCV transmission by subtle parenteral routes, and there is no reason to think that HGV would not also be spread by each of these modalities. More recently, cocaine snorting has been proposed as a still more cryptic form of parenteral transmission. A high frequency of cocaine snorting was observed among HCV carriers who denied intravenous drug use or other established means of parenteral exposure.[24] It has been hypothesized that shared snorting devices may deposit minute amounts of one person's blood onto another's nasal membranes that have been denuded by repeated cocaine use. This mechanism of viral spread has not been proved for HCV and has not been tested for HGV/GBV-C, but it exemplifies the covert means by which blood may be spread from person to person.

The fact that HGV/GBV-C is up to five times more prevalent than HCV suggests that it may be spread by additional nonparenteral routes, particularly sexual routes. Hence, HGV/GBV-C has been sought in populations at high risk for sexually transmitted diseases. In a study of prostitutes, it was found that the frequency of HGV infection was 11%, a rate much higher than the background prevalence.[25] In addition, the prevalence of HGV/GBV-C increased in proportion to the duration of prostitution. Although such studies suggest sexual transmission, they do not establish it, because of the overlap with intravenous drug use in sexually promiscuous populations and because of the difficulty in obtaining accurate drug use histories in such populations. HGV/GBV-C infection often coexists with HIV infection, and HGV/GBV-C prevalence was found to be as high in HIV-infected patients exposed by sexual routes as in those exposed by parenteral routes. HGV/GBV-C was detected in both semen and saliva in this population, providing a mechanism for sexual transmission.[26]

A limited number of studies of the spouses of HGV-infected persons have been performed. In one study in Taiwan,[27] the spouses of 100 index cases with hepatitis C, 12 of whom were also infected with HGV/GBV-C, were tested; 14% of partners were HCV-infected, and 42% (5/12) were HGV/GBV-C–infected. Nucleotide sequence comparison and phylogenetic tree analysis of the genome in HGV/GBV-C–infected couples revealed the isolates in each partner to be closely related. These results suggested sexual transmission of HGV/GBV-C and also indicated that sexually exposed persons were at greater risk for development of HGV/GBV-C infection compared with HCV infection. Although it is probable that HGV/GBV-C infection is sexually as well as parenterally transmitted, the number of partners studied is relatively small, and it is always difficult to exclude covert means of shared parenteral exposure among spouses or other long-term sexual partners. In Japan, for example, it was found that infected partners shared folk medicine practitioners who were using contaminated instruments.[23] Partners may share razor blades or toothbrushes that are capable of transmitting small but infectious quantities of blood. Additional large, well-controlled studies are required to firmly establish sexual transmission of HGV/GBV-C. Although the genomic similarities among the isolates from sexual partners constitute convincing evidence for sexual transmission, identical viral isolates may also be acquired by partners who share a common parenteral source. The latter possibility emphasizes the difficulty in establishing proof of sexual transmission when the transmission may be real but inefficient and when the background prevalence is high. This dilemma has hampered the interpretation of data regarding the sexual transmission of HCV, and the issue remains unresolved after more than a decade of investigation.

The data for vertical transmission of HGV/GBV-C are stronger. In a study in Germany,[28] it was shown that 10 (56%) of 18 babies born to HGV/GBV-C–positive mothers were infected with HGV/GBV-C. In contrast, in this same population of women, who were intravenous drug abusers, only 1 (5%) of 19 infants born to HCV-infected mothers were infected with HCV. Sequence homology in the NS-5 region of the HGV/GBV-C isolates from 10 mother-infant pairs showed sufficient identity to confirm vertical transmission. All 10 babies remained HGV/GBV-C–positive throughout a follow-up period of 2 to 12 months, but none had any clinical or biochemical signs of liver disease.

There is no evidence for household or other casual transmission of HGV/GBV-C infection in the absence of overt or covert parenteral exposures, and there are no recommendations to change behavior patterns within the household or workplace based solely on HGV/GBV-C positivity.

Clinical Relevance of Hepatitis G Virus/GB Virus Type C

Although it is clear that HGV/GBV-C is a ubiquitous agent that is readily transmitted by blood transfusion and other parenteral means and can cause persistent infection, its clinical significance is largely unknown and is the source of considerable controversy. Because HGV/GBV-C was found during the course of investigations to uncover new hepatitis agents, and because it was found in patients and animals with unexplained hepatitis, an etiologic link between HGV/GBV-C and the coexistent hepatitis was a logical assumption. However, because the agent is so prevalent, very carefully selected controls are required to establish a causal relationship. It is relevant to examine in more detail the diseases for which HGV/GBV-C has been proposed as the etiologic agent, including acute and chronic non–A–E hepatitis (both transfusion-associated and community-acquired), fulminant hepatitis, hepatitis-associated aplastic anemia, and hepatocellular carcinoma (HCC).

Non–A–E Hepatitis

Cumulative data from studies throughout the world indicate that HGV/GBV-C RNA is found in 10% to 20% of patients with non–A–E hepatitis.[29-31] Therefore, at best, HGV/GBV-C accounts for the minority of such cases. More important, in the few studies with appropriate controls, it was shown that HGV/GBV-C is no more common in non–A–E hepatitis than it is in patients with hepatitis B or C or in patients with nonviral liver diseases, such as autoimmune hepatitis and alcoholic liver disease.[31,32] Therefore, the agent has not demonstrated appropriate specificity for non–A–E (cryptogenic) hepatitis, and whether HGV/GBV-C plays an etiologic role in these cases has been difficult to ascertain. Analyses of patients with cryptogenic hepatitis,[33] prospectively monitored transfusion recipients,[34] patients with community-acquired hepatitis,[35] and recipients with posttransplantation hepatitis[36] have all failed to demonstrate a causal association between HGV/GBV-C and the observed hepatitis. In each of these settings, it is more likely that HGV/GBV-C is merely an innocent bystander in a process caused by an as yet undiscovered infectious agent or by some noninfectious agent.

In a prospective study of transfusion recipients conducted at NIH,[34] it was found that HGV/GBV-C accounted for at most 4% of transfusion-associated hepatitis cases. However, even in this small number, causality was not established, because there was a dissociation between HGV/GBV-C RNA levels and serum alanine aminotransferase (ALT) levels (Fig. 151-1), and because cases of unknown etiology were four times more common than cases with positive tests for HGV/GBV-C. It was also shown in the NIH study[34] that, of all the HGV/GBV-C infections ($N = 82$) in prospectively monitored transfusion recipients (Fig. 151-2), 73% were not associated with any serum ALT elevation, 16% were associated with such minor and isolated serum ALT elevations that they did not meet the study criteria for hepatitis diagnosis, and 7% were HGV-HCV coinfections, in which the hepatitis was presumed to be caused by HCV. Hence, only 4% of isolated HGV/GBV-C infections were associated with hepatitis, but even in those cases causality was unlikely in view of the inconsistent relationship between serum ALT elevations and HGV/GBV-C RNA levels (see Fig. 151-1). Prospective studies in Taiwan[35] also failed to reveal an association between HGV/GBV-C and transfusion-associated hepatitis; among 25 recipients acutely infected with HGV/GBV-C in the absence of HCV, the mean peak serum ALT was only 31 U/L; 20 patients had persistently normal serum ALT levels, and the others had only low-grade, isolated serum ALT elevations insufficient to establish the diagnosis of hepatitis.

HGV/GBV-C is infrequently associated with community-acquired hepatitis. In the CDC "sentinel counties" study,[37] only 9% of the patients with acute, community-acquired non–A–E hepatitis had detectable HGV/GBV-C. By exclusion, the vast majority of cases that were not caused by HCV infection were classified as non–A–G hepatitis. The ratio of non–A–G cases to possible HGV/GBV-C cases was 10:1. Furthermore, in the few cases in which HGV/GBV-C was detected, the acute hepatitis resolved but HGV/GBV-C persisted, suggesting that the patients were chronic HGV/GBV-C carriers with a superimposed acute hepatitis of undefined cause. Therefore, although the possibility cannot be excluded, there has been no strong evidence to support HGV/GBV-C as the causal agent in either sporadic, community-acquired hepatitis cases or transfusion-associated hepatitis cases.

Further evidence against HGV/GBV-C as a hepatitis agent stems from the poor correlation between serum ALT levels and the presence of HGV/GBV-C RNA in virtually every population tested, including blood donors,[34] blood recipients,[34] dialysis patients,[38] hemophiliacs, and intravenous drug abusers.[39] This is in contrast to findings in persons with hepatitis C or hepatitis B infections; in these populations, the presence of viremia closely correlates with biochemical and histologic evidence of hepatitis. Berasain and colleagues[40] studied 1075 consecutive patients who had elevated ALT levels for longer than 6 months. The cause of the ALT elevation remained elusive after appropriate biochemical, serologic, and clinical evaluation in 109 patients (10%). HGV/GBV-C RNA was found in only one patient, and by combining PCR and liver biopsy the majority of unexplained ALT elevations were shown to be caused by cryptic forms of hepatitis B and C or by non-alcoholic steatohepatitis (NASH). Therefore, HGV/GBV-C appears to play a negligible role in the causation of hepatic inflammation.

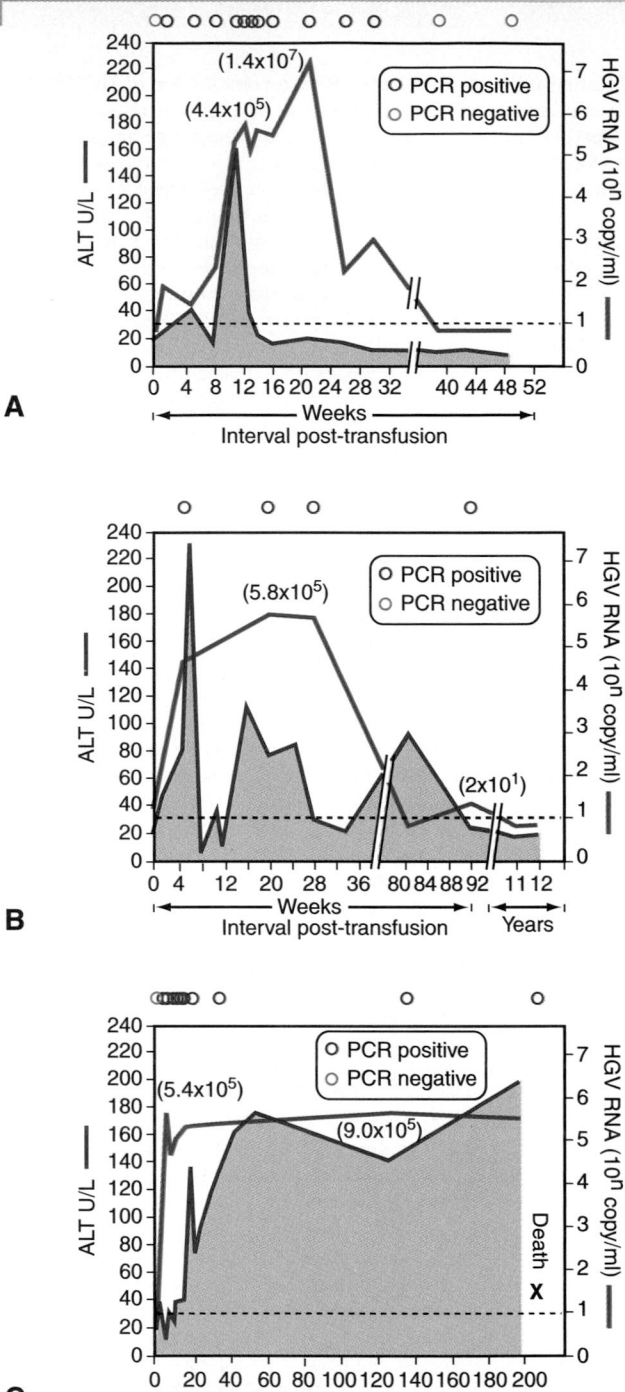

FIGURE 151-1. Hepatitis G virus (HGV) infection in three patients with transfusion-associated hepatitis. Levels of alanine aminotransferase (ALT, *shaded areas*) and HGV RNA (*blue line*) in three patients infected only with HGV are shown plotted against the time since transfusion. Qualitative results of polymerase chain reaction for HGV RNA (positive, *purple circles;* negative, *green circles*) are shown above each panel. The *dashed lines* indicate the limit of detection of HGV RNA. In each patient, the relation between the HGV RNA and ALT levels was inconsistent. In the first patient **(A),** HGV RNA continued to increase despite the normalization of ALT levels, and RNA remained detectable for at least 20 weeks after the ALT level had decreased to normal. In the second patient **(B),** HGV RNA was elevated at week 28, when the ALT level was normal, and it was undetectable at week 80, when the ALT level was rising. In the third patient **(C),** 20 weeks elapsed between the first appearance of HGV RNA and the first elevation of ALT. The numbers inside the panels show the values for HGV RNA in copies per milliliter. *(From Alter HJ, Nakatsuji Y, Melpolder J, et al. The incidence of transfusion-associated hepatitis G virus infection and its relation to liver disease. N Engl J Med. 1997;336:747. Copyright © 1997 Massachusetts Medical Society. All rights reserved.)*

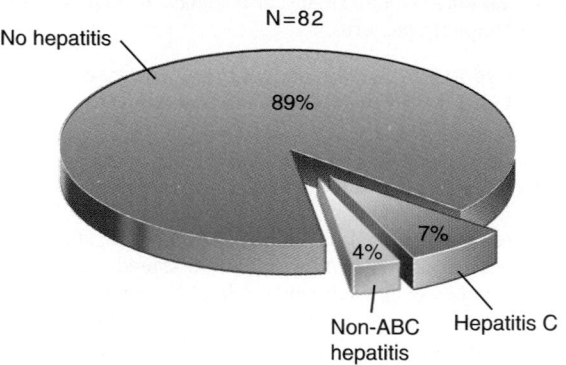

N=82

No hepatitis

89%

4%

7%

Non-ABC
hepatitis

Hepatitis C

FIGURE 151-2. Clinical outcome of acute transfusion-associated hepatitis G virus (HGV) infection. In a prospective National Institutes of Health study of transfusion-transmitted HGV infection, 35 acute HGV infections were detected among 357 transfusion recipients tested. A statistical extrapolation was then made to project the number of infections that would have been observed if the entire recipient population of 965 subjects had been tested (see Alter HJ, et al.[34] for details of the statistical analysis). The total number of HGV infections was projected to be 82. Among the 82 subjects acutely infected with HGV, 89% did not develop hepatitis (73% with no alanine aminotransferase [ALT] elevations and 16% with isolated, minor ALT elevations that did not meet the study criteria for hepatitis diagnosis), 7% had coexistent hepatitis C virus infection that was considered to be the cause of the hepatitis, and only 4% (3 patients) had non-ABC hepatitis in which HGV/GB virus type C (GBV-C) was the only virus identified. However, in these three patients, the level of HGV RNA generally did not correlate with the level of ALT (see Fig. 151-1), and HGV/GBV-C did not appear to be the causative agent.

Hepatitis C Virus Coinfection

Although it is difficult to assess whether HGV/GBV-C plays a primary role in the causation of hepatitis, the role of HGV/GBV-C in determining the clinical severity of coexistent HCV infection can be examined. Among HCV-infected persons, 10% to 20% are coinfected with HGV/GBV-C, presumably through common routes of exposure. Numerous studies[34,41-43] have shown that HGV/GBV-C has no impact on the course of coexistent hepatitis C. Peak serum ALT level, peak bilirubin level, histologic severity, severity of viremia, frequency of chronic hepatitis, and response to interferon are virtually identical in patients with combined HGV/GBV-C and HCV infection and in those with HCV infection alone. The lack of influence of HGV/GBV-C on the clinical, biochemical, histologic, or virologic course of coexistent HCV infection has been so uniform from study to study, and the number of studies has been so large (more than 30), that this conclusion appears unequivocal. However, there have been rare exceptions in which more severe histologic lesions were observed in the presence of HGV/GBV-C coinfection.[44]

Fulminant Hepatitis

Of those cases of fulminant hepatitis thought to be of viral origin, only a small number are caused by hepatitis virus A (HAV), HBV, or HCV, and most cases have remained etiologically undefined. Early studies of HGV/GBV-C prevalence in patients with fulminant hepatitis showed very high rates of infection; in one study from Japan, 50% of patients with fulminant hepatitis were HGV/GBV-C–positive.[45] However, subsequent reports from other areas of the world and additional studies from Japan showed much lower rates of HGV/GBV-C infection, and several studies of fulminant hepatitis showed that no cases were HGV/GBV-C–related.[46] This dichotomy may be explained by the fact that patients with fulminant hepatitis typically have received multiple transfusions before being tested for HGV/GBV-C. The administration of fresh-frozen plasma to correct abnormalities in clotting function is common in these patients, and it appears that such transfusions had been given before HGV/GBV-C testing in most studies that reported a

very high prevalence of this agent. Given the high prevalence of HGV/GBV-C among blood donors and the large number of fresh-frozen plasma units transfused to patients with clotting disorders associated with fulminant hepatic failure, there is a high probability that HGV infection in such patients is the result of, not the cause of, their liver failure. No study has shown a strong association between HGV/GBV-C and fulminant hepatic failure after pretest transfusion was reliably excluded.

Hepatitis-Associated Aplastic Anemia

The entity of hepatitis-associated aplastic anemia, in which severe marrow aplasia typically occurs 1 to 2 months after an episode of acute hepatitis, has been thought to be related to a single agent that could simultaneously or sequentially infect both the liver and the bone marrow and impair their respective functions. The discovery of HCV offered an intriguing candidate for the causative agent of hepatitis-associated aplastic anemia, because another flavivirus, dengue fever virus, was known to infect hematopoietic stem cells in culture. The concept that a hepatotropic flavivirus, HCV, might also infect the bone marrow and impair hematopoiesis had inherent logic. However, this did not prove to be the case, and no specific association between HCV and hepatitis-associated aplastic anemia was found.[47] The subsequent discovery of HGV/GBV-C invoked the same deductive sequence, and extensive studies were undertaken in Neal Young's laboratory at the NIH. The initial findings were promising, because a high proportion of patients with hepatitis-associated aplastic anemia were found to be infected with HGV/GBV-C. However, it was shown subsequently that the presence of HGV/GBV-C in such patients was probably related to transfusions received after the onset of aplasia.[48] The rare patients who had not received transfusions before testing were found to be HGV/GBV-C–negative, and the rate of HGV/GBV-C in the patients with aplastic anemia was no different from that in other, similarly transfused hematologic populations.[48] Safadi and associates[49] studied 17 patients with hepatitis-associated aplastic anemia and found no evidence for active infection with HAV, HBV, HCV, HDV, HEV, HGV/GBV-C, or TT virus. All patients underwent bone marrow transplantation; relapsing hepatitis was not seen in any of the cases, mitigating against, but not ruling out, a viral cause for this syndrome.

Therefore, the association between hepatitis and bone marrow failure remains unexplained. The association may be the result of infection by a single, as yet unidentified agent that infects both the liver and the bone marrow, or the aplasia may be immunologically mediated and independent of direct viral attack on hematopoietic cells. In the latter scenario, a hepatitis agent could initiate immune complex disease that either targets the marrow or contains cross-reactive antigens that make the marrow a cotarget of the antiviral immune response. Alternatively, both the hepatitis and the aplasia may be immunologically mediated, and the inciting event may or may not be viral infection. One clinical observation favoring an immunologic basis is that the marrow aplasia responds to immunosuppressive therapy in a manner similar to that observed in idiopathic aplastic anemia, a disease now considered to be immune mediated.

Hepatocellular Carcinoma

Both HCV and HBV show a significant association with HCC; indeed, infection with these two agents may be the primary underlying cause of HCC throughout the world. Epidemiologic investigations generally have failed to establish a similar association between HGV/GBV-C and HCC. A case-control study in Africa[50] compared 167 South African blacks who had HCC with 167 race-, age-, and sex-matched hospital-based control subjects. Persons infected with HGV/GBV-C did not have an increased relative risk of developing HCC (relative risk, 0.9), nor did infection with HGV/GBV-C increase the risk of tumor development in persons coinfected with HBV or HCV. In contrast, a case-control study in Los Angeles[51] showed that 8% of 144 HCC patients were HGV/GBV-C infected, compared with 2% of community controls, representing a 5.4-fold increased risk (95% confidence interval, 1.8 to 16.6). A case-control study in Italy[52] showed a significant association between HGV/GBV-C and HCC, but the possible role of

HGV/GBV-C in HCC causation seemed modest at best, because the population-attributable risk was only 4%, compared with 22% for HBV, 36% for HCV, and 52% for heavy alcohol intake. In Japan, where rates of HCC are high, the frequency of HGV/GBV-C infection was similar among patients with HCC (10%), patients with cirrhosis who did not have HCC (10%), and patients with neither HCC nor cirrhosis who were HCV infected (13%).[53] It was concluded that HGV/GBV-C was unlikely to be a major etiologic agent of HCC in Japan. A similar conclusion was reached in England.[54] Therefore, in geographic regions with a high incidence of HCC, the data do not support an important role for HGV/GBV-C in cancer causation.

Liver Transplantation

HGV/GBV-C has been found in 10% to 30% of patients undergoing liver transplantation for cryptogenic cirrhosis.[55] Similar high rates of occurrence are found in patients who received liver transplants for cirrhosis associated with hepatitis C infection or with alcohol. Therefore, there is no specific association between HGV/GBV-C infection and cryptogenic forms of end-stage liver disease. The high frequency of HGV/GBV-C infection in these patients is thought to reflect the frequency of prior parenteral exposures in patients who develop cirrhosis from any cause. Even more striking is the fact that up to 70% of liver transplant recipients test positive for HGV/GBV-C after transplantation.[56] It is probable that this high rate merely reflects additional exposure to blood products in the peritransplantation period, but the possibility of reactivation of latent HGV/GBV-C infection secondary to transplant-associated immunosuppression cannot be excluded. Despite the high frequency of viremia in this patient population, it has been repeatedly shown that HGV/GBV-C infection does not influence either the frequency or the severity of posttransplantation hepatitis in liver transplant recipients, nor does this common infection affect overall graft or patient survival.[36,55,56]

Replication of Hepatitis G Virus/GB Virus Type C in the Liver

Because the cumulative observations presented suggest that the relationship between HGV/GBV-C and non–A–E hepatitis is tenuous, and because the agent does not worsen the course of coexistent hepatitis C or B or make liver disease worse even in immunocompromised transplant recipients, the appropriateness of the appellation "hepatitis virus" could be questioned. In this regard, HGV/GBV-C has not been shown conclusively to replicate in the liver, although this issue remains unresolved. Several studies have reported finding HGV/GBV-C RNA in liver tissue using a PCR assay as the method of detection.[57,58] Madejon and colleagues[59] found genomic GBV-C RNA in seven of seven liver samples from patients with serum GBV-C RNA and also found antigenomic (negative-strand) RNA in six of these seven liver specimens. In contrast, Laskus and associates[60] studied serum and liver HGV/GBV-C RNA in 10 patients, 9 of whom were coinfected with HCV. Negative-strand HGV/GBV-C RNA was not found in the liver of any patient, whereas negative-strand HCV RNA was found in seven of nine livers from the coinfected patients. Pessoa and co-workers[61] studied patients coinfected with HGV/GBV-C and HCV in the transplantation setting and compared liver and serum RNA titers; their results did not provide evidence for hepatic replication. Studies using in situ hybridization have been limited, with generally negative results, but Mushahwar and colleagues[62] reported finding HGV/GBV-C in hepatocytes by both in situ hybridization and immunohistochemical staining. Therefore, the issue of whether this agent resides in and replicates in the liver remains controversial and constitutes an important area for further investigation.

A final observation on hepatotropism is that two laboratories have transmitted HGV/GBV-C to chimpanzees.[63,64] In neither study did the animals develop hepatitis, and no virus was found within the liver, even when serum titers were at their peak. Further, in studies of various cell lines, HGV/GBV-C was shown to replicate (presence of negative-strand RNA) in human lymphoid cells, myeloid cells, megakaryocytoid cells, and vascular endothelial cells, but not in any of several

hepatocyte cell lines.[65] Other studies also suggest that HGV/GBV-C is primarily a lymphotropic virus.[66]

Does Hepatitis G Virus/GB Virus Type C Reduce the Severity of Human Immunodeficiency Virus Infection?

Unexpectedly, several studies[67-69] have reported that HIV-infected patients who are coinfected with HGV/GBV-C fare better in terms of overall survival, interval to development of acquired immunodeficiency syndrome (AIDS), and duration of survival after the onset of AIDS. These analyses were undertaken because HIV-infected patients are frequently coinfected with HGV/GBV-C due to shared routes of transmission, but the potential ameliorative role of the HGV/GBV-C agent was unpredicted. Tillmann and co-workers[67] prospectively monitored 197 HIV-positive patients, of whom 17% tested positive for HGV/GBV-C RNA and 57% had antibodies to the HGV/GBV-C envelope protein, E2. Survival was significantly longer and progression to AIDS was slower among those testing positive for HGV/GBV-C RNA than among those testing negative ($P < .001$). Survival after AIDS was also significantly prolonged (Fig. 151-3). Similar but lesser effects were seen in those who had anti-E2 antibody. The mechanism for the protective role of HGV/GBV-C was not elucidated, but HIV viral loads were lower in those coinfected with HGV/GBV-C. Similar findings were reported by Xiang and colleagues,[68] who studied 362 HIV-infected patients, 40% of whom had HGV/GBV-C viremia. In a Cox regression analysis adjusted for treatment, CD4+ T-lymphocyte count, age, sex, race, and mode of HIV transmission, the mortality rate among those without HGV/GBV-C coinfection was significant higher than among those with coinfection (relative risk, 3.7). HIV cultures were established to study the mechanism of the HGV/GBV-C effect in vitro; it was shown that an infectious clone of HGV/GBV-C could inhibit replication of HIV and that the effect was greatest when the cultures were infected with HGV/GBV-C before the introduction of HIV. It therefore appears that HGV/GBV-C inhibits the replication of HIV, although the mechanism underlying that effect has not been elucidated. The beneficial effect of a seemingly nonpathogenic agent has raised the possibility that HGV/GBV-C might be purposefully administered to HIV-in-

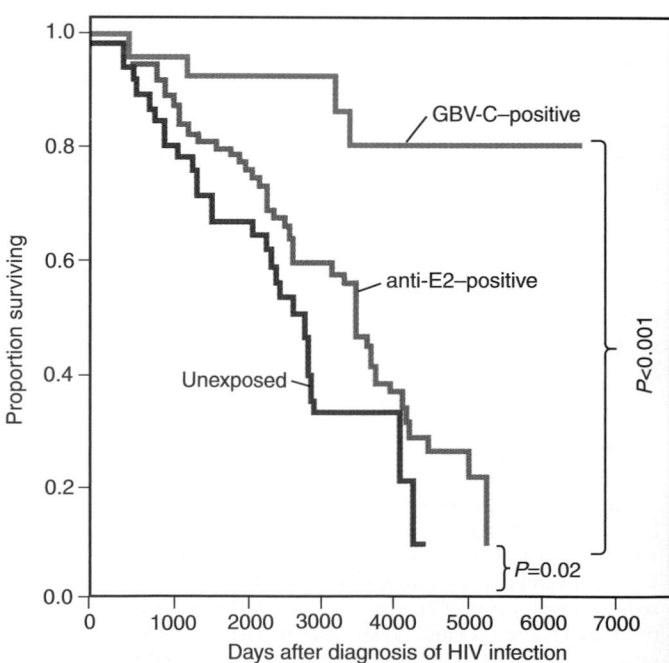

FIGURE 151-3. Survival of patients infected with the human immunodeficiency virus (HIV) according to GB virus type C (GBV-C) status. E2, envelope protein. *(From Tillmann HL, Heiken H, Knapik-Botor A, et al. Infection with GB virus C and reduced mortality among HIV-infected patients. N Engl J Med 2001;345:715-724.)*

fected patients as a therapeutic measure. However, no such trials are currently planned, and the ethical issues to be surmounted for such a trial would be considerable. Although the ameliorative effect of HGV/GBV-C in HIV infection, including an enhanced response to highly active anti-retroviral therapy (HAART),[70] has been reported from multiple centers, the association has not been found uniformly, and further studies are required to validate this surprising finding.

Future Perspectives on Hepatitis G Virus/GB Virus C

Perhaps the most significant clinical observation countermanding a role for HGV/GBV-C in liver disease is that, despite the continued transfusion of HGV/GBV-C to at least 1% and possibly up to 4% of transfusion recipients, there is no apparent hepatitis burden associated with that transmission. Posttransfusion hepatitis rates continue to decline globally and, in prospective studies in the United States and Japan, now approach zero.[71] Therefore, the designation "hepatitis virus" may have been premature, and further well-controlled clinical, molecular, and histologic studies are needed to place this virus in proper clinical perspective.

The debate regarding the clinical relevance and hepatotropism of HGV/GBV-C has broader implications as the proliferation and sophistication of molecular biology studies continue to lead to identification of new infectious agents. Each such agent will be tested for its prevalence in blood donors and for its potential to be transmitted to blood recipients. Some agents may have disease associations; others, such as HGV/GBV-C, may not have discernible disease outcomes. At present, HGV/GBV-C is a virus in search of a disease and a virus whose primary site of replication is controversial. Despite the absence of a proven disease association, its high prevalence, its persistence, and its ease of transmission by parenteral and probably nonparenteral routes dictate continued study of this agent and its potential clinical implications. The recently recognized protective effect of HGV/GBV-C in HIV infection needs to be further investigated to elucidate its underlying mechanism and to explore its therapeutic potential. The key features of HGV/GBV-C infection are summarized in Table 151-1.

TT VIRUS

Discovery and Characterization of TT Virus

In 1997, Japanese investigators described a new candidate hepatitis agent that they designated "TT virus" (TTV).[72] The virus was discovered with the use of RDA, a form of subtractive cloning. It was found in the serum of a patient with posttransfusion hepatitis and was named after the patient's initials, T.T. This designation was appealing because it could also stand for "transfusion-transmitted virus." The initial report by Nishizawa and colleagues[72] investigated five cases of transfusion-associated hepatitis and found the acute appearance of TTV in three of

the patients. There was a general correlation between DNA level and ALT level, but there were periods during which these levels diverged. Each of the three patients had mild hepatitis (peak serum ALT, <200 U/L), and all recovered from their hepatitis. It was subsequently shown that TTV had a wide range of sequence divergence; it was classified into genotypes 1 and 2, each of which has subtypes a and b.[73]

Prevalence and Epidemiology of TT Virus

Studies have shown TTV to be very prevalent in Japan and to be distributed throughout the world.[74] TTV DNA was initially found in at least 12% of Japanese blood donors; subsequently, with the use of primers for conserved regions of the genome, TTV was found in more than 90% of the general population of Japan. TTV DNA was initially found in 3% to 7.5% of U.S. blood donors—a rate almost triple that of HGV/GBV-C and one that undoubtedly would be still higher if measured with additional primers in the PCR assay. TTV is clearly transmitted by blood transfusion and is highly prevalent in populations with frequent parenteral exposures; it has been found in up to 68% of hemophiliacs, 46% of dialysis patients, and 40% of intravenous drug users,[75] figures that might be still higher depending on the assay employed.

The very high prevalence of this agent in the general population suggests that nonparenteral means of transmission may also exist. Okamoto and associates[76] reported the finding of TTV DNA in bile and feces of persons with high-level viremia. In addition, fecal supernates from TTV-infected patients transmitted TTV infection to chimps when given by the intravenous route.[77] Therefore, this agent may be spread by the fecal-oral route, although water-borne epidemics of TTV infection have not been reported. Evidence for maternal-fetal transmission of TTV is conflicting. Some studies have shown that the great majority of children born to TTV-positive mothers test positive for TTV DNA in samples obtained during the neonatal period[78]; others have shown no perinatal transmission; and still others have shown intermediate rates of vertical transmission. TTV has also been found frequently in breast milk, providing still another mechanism for spread from mother to infant.[78]

In contrast to the likelihood of frequent vertical transmission, TTV appears to be inefficiently spread by sexual routes. In one study,[79] only 3 of 41 spouses of TTV-positive index cases tested positive for TTV DNA. In two of these cases, there was close sequence homology between the partners, suggesting that TTV can be spread by sexual routes but that such transmission is inefficient.

Overall, it appears that TTV can be spread by multiple routes, including mother-to-infant in utero, breast-feeding, fecal-oral, parenteral, and perhaps sexual routes. These diverse transmission routes and a high level of viral persistence account for the extraordinarily high prevalence of this agent, particularly in Japan and other regions of the Far East.

In 2001, investigators described what was considered to be a new DNA virus distinct from TTV. This agent was called the SEN virus (SENV), after the initials of the patient in whom it was first detected. Subsequent investigations revealed that the SEN virus was a new member of the highly diverse TTV family, having less than 50% sequence homology with the prototype TTV agent.[80] Diversity within the TTV family is extensive and far greater than that shown for HCV. The SEN virus itself was shown to be diverse, and two members of the SENV subfamily (SENV-D and SENV-H) were reported to be possible agents of transfusion-associated hepatitis.[81] Although the statistical association with hepatitis was strong, it is now believed that this finding was an artifact of the small number of transfusion-associated non–A–E hepatitis cases available for study. Aside from this one report, SENV, like other members of the TTV family, has not been convincingly shown to have any disease associations.

Molecular Virology and Tissue Localization of the TT Agent

The TT virus is a nonenveloped DNA virus of relatively high density (1.31 to 1.32 g/cm^3). The TTV genome is a covalently-closed, single-stranded DNA of approximately 3.8 kb with characteristics typical of

TABLE 151-1 Features of Hepatitis G Virus/GB Virus-C Infection

Feature	Comment/Description
Taxonomic classification of agent	New genus in family Flaviviridae
Epidemiology	Globally distributed; viremia in 1 to 3% and exposure in 3 to 15% of U.S. blood donors
Replication of virus in liver	No convincing evidence
Disease associations	None established to date
Cryptogenic hepatitis or cirrhosis	Most studies have shown no relationship
Fulminant hepatitis	Early studies suggested a relationship, but this has not been confirmed in later studies
Transfusion-associated hepatitis	Insignificant role
Coinfection with hepatitis C virus	No effect on hepatitis C clinical course
Survival in HIV infection	HIV survival advantage shown in HIV-HGV/GBV-C coinfected patients

animal circoviruses, particularly the chicken anemia virus. Hence, it is tentatively classified in the family Circoviridae. A study of viral dynamics using mathematical modeling during and after interferon treatment indicated that 90% of TT virions are cleared from the plasma and replenished each day during chronic infection, and that a minimum of 3.8×10^{10} virions are generated per day.[82]

Whereas HGV/GBV-C does not appear to be hepatotropic, there is considerable evidence that TTV resides in and replicates within liver cells. Several studies have demonstrated TTV DNA within hepatocytes by in situ hybridization.[83-85] The distribution of TTV within hepatocytes has differed among studies and among patients in a single study[83-85]; cytoplasmic staining appears to be predominant.[83,85] In situ hybridization has been complemented by the finding of TTV DNA in liver tissue by PCR and, more importantly, by the demonstration of TTV replicative intermediates in liver tissue by strand-specific PCR.[84] In general, the presence of TTV in liver tissue does not correlate with histopathologic or biochemical evidence of liver disease.[85] TTV DNA has also been localized to peripheral blood mononuclear cells (PBMC), but titers are 10- to 100-fold higher in the liver, and PBMC do not appear to contain TTV replicative intermediates.[84,85]

Does TT Virus Cause Acute or Chronic Liver Disease?

As with HGV/GBV-C, the key questions are whether TTV is a primary hepatitis virus and whether it can account for cryptogenic cases of fulminant hepatitis, chronic hepatitis, cirrhosis, and hepatocellular carcinoma. The answers to these questions are not conclusive at this time, but accumulating evidence suggests that, although TTV resides in the liver, it does not cause acute or chronic hepatitis and does not worsen the course of coexisting hepatitis viral infections.

In early studies in Japan, TTV was found in up to 45% of patients with acute or chronic non–A–G hepatitis[75] and was also frequently detected in patients with fulminant hepatic failure.[86] Although the frequency of TTV infection among these patients with otherwise unexplained hepatitis was significantly higher than that in the corresponding donor population, the statistical association does not prove causality, as is evident in the case of HGV/GBV-C infection. The observed rates must be compared with those in control populations of similar age and similar parenteral exposure history who do not have liver disease, or who have liver disease of nonviral origin. The high prevalence of this agent in the general population and the ease with which TTV is parenterally transmitted make the selection of appropriate controls essential to the issue of causality. A review of 22 studies published since 2000 revealed that 17 studies (77%) showed no association between TTV infection and either fulminant hepatitis, acute hepatitis, chronic hepatitis, hepatitis-associated aplastic anemia, hepatocellular carcinoma, or asymptomatic elevations of serum ALT.[87,88] In the five studies that showed a statistical association of TTV with liver disease, there was insufficient evidence to establish causality. In addition, many studies looked at the effect of TTV infection on coexistent HCV infection and showed that the presence of TTV did not increase the severity or duration of hepatitis and did not interfere with HCV treatment responses to interferon.

One of the strongest arguments against a role for TTV as a primary agent of hepatitis is that the high prevalence in the donor population would ensure that almost all persons who receive multiple transfusions would be exposed to this agent, and yet transfusion-associated hepatitis rates continue to decline and are now approaching zero. Therefore, there is dissociation between the number of exposures and the number of hepatitis cases, although antibody data are not yet available to assess the number of susceptible persons in the recipient population. Finally, there has been almost uniformly poor correlation between the presence of TTV and elevated serum ALT levels. Clearly, further studies are needed before TTV can claim a place as the next hepatitis virus.

SUMMARY

HGV/GBV-C and TTV are newly identified viruses whose discovery was the result of sophisticated molecular biology rather than classic virology. After almost a decade of intensive investigation, neither HGV/GBV-C nor TTV has been proved to be the hepatitis agent it was originally presumed to be, nor has either been established as the cause of any disease outside the liver. This has raised the possibility that human beings harbor a normal viral flora, just as we have a bacterial flora, and that agents such as those described in this chapter may have beneficial or neutral effects rather than playing a role in disease pathogenesis. These discoveries also illustrate the need to develop new Koch's postulates to establish causality for molecularly defined agents that cannot be cultured or do not cause disease in appropriate animal models. Fredericks and Relman[89] have addressed this issue in a brilliant paper that is highly recommended. It is clear that the age of molecular virology requires a new paradigm for establishing clinical relevance.

REFERENCES

1. Choo QL, Kuo G, Weiner AJ, et al. Isolation of a cDNA clone derived from a blood-borne non-A, non-B viral hepatitis genome. Science. 1989;244:359.
2. Alter HJ, Purcell RH, Shih JW, et al. Detection of antibody to hepatitis C virus in prospectively followed transfusion recipients with acute and chronic non-A, non-B hepatitis. N Engl J Med. 1989;321:1494.
3. Alter MJ, Margolis HS, Krawczynski K, et al. The natural history of community-acquired hepatitis C in the United States. N Engl J Med. 1989; 327:1899.
4. Fiordalisi G, Zanella I, Mantero G, et al. High prevalence of GB virus C infection in a group of Italian patients with hepatitis of unknown etiology. J Infect Dis. 1996;174:181.
5. Wright TL, Hsu H, Donegan E, et al. Hepatitis C virus not found in fulminant non-A, non-B hepatitis. Ann Intern Med. 1991;115:111.
6. Zeldis JB, Dienstag JL, Gale RP. Aplastic anemia and non-A, non-B hepatitis. Am J Med. 1983;74:64.
7. Deinhardt F, Holmes AW, Capps RB, Popper H. Studies on the transmission of disease of human viral hepatitis to marmoset monkeys. I. Transmission of disease, serial passage and description of liver lesions. J Exp Med. 1967;125:673.
8. Simons JH, Pilot-Matias TJ, Leary TP, et al. Identification of two flavivirus-like genomes in the GB hepatitis agent. Proc Natl Acad Sci U S A.1995;92:3401.
9. Schlauder GG, Dawson GJ, Simons JN, et al. Molecular and serologic analysis in the transmission of the GB hepatitis agents. J Med Virol. 1995;46:81.
10. Simons JN, Leary TP, Dawson GJ, et al. Isolation of novel virus-like sequences associated with human hepatitis. Nature Med. 1995;1:564.
11. Linnen J, Wages J Jr, Zhang-Keck Z-Y, et al. Molecular cloning and disease association of hepatitis G virus: A transmissible agent. Science. 1996;271:505.
12. Okamoto H, Nakao H, Inoue T, et al. The entire nucleotide sequences of two GB virus C/hepatitis G virus isolates of distinct genotypes from Japan. J Gen Virol. 1997;78:737.
13. Erker JC, Simons JN, Muerhoff AS, et al. Molecular cloning and characterization of a GB virus C isolate from a patient with non-A-E hepatitis. J Gen Virol. 1996;77:2713.
14. Simons JN, Desai SM, Schultz DE, et al. Translation initiation in GB viruses A and C: Evidence for internal ribosome entry and implications for genome organization. Virology. 1996;70:6126.
15. Muerhoff AS, Simons JN, Leary TP, et al: Sequence heterogeneity within the 5′-terminal region of the hepatitis GB virus C genome and evidence for genotypes. J Hepatol. 1996;25:379.
16. Tacke M, Schmolke S, Schlueter V, et al. Humoral immune response to the E2 protein of hepatitis G virus is associated with long-term recovery from infection and reveals a high frequency of hepatitis G virus exposure among healthy blood donors. Hepatology. 1997;26:1626.
17. Tanaka E, Kiyosawa K, Shimoda K, et al. Evolution of hepatitis G virus infection and antibody response to envelope protein in patients with transfusion-associated non-A, non-B hepatitis. J Viral Hep. 1998;5:153.
18. Feucht HH, Zollner B, Polywka S, et al. Prevalence of hepatitis G viremia among healthy subjects, individuals with liver disease, and persons at risk for parenteral transmission. J Clin Microbiol. 1997;35:767.
19. Aikawa T, Sugai Y, Okamoto H. Hepatitis G infection in drug abusers with chronic hepatitis C. N Engl J Med. 1996;334:195.
20. Yu ML, Chuang WL, Wang LY, et al. Status and natural course of GB virus C/hepatitis G virus among high risk groups and volunteer blood donors in Taiwan. J Gastroenterol Hepatol. 2000;15:1404-1410.
21. Seeff LB, Beebe GW, Hoofnagle JH, et al. A serologic follow-up of the 1942 epidemic of post-vaccination hepatitis in the United States Army. N Engl J Med. 1987;316:965.
22. Power JP, Lawlor E, Davidson F, et al. Hepatitis C viraemia in recipients of Irish intravenous anti-D immunoglobulin. Lancet. 1994;344:1166.

23. Kiyosawa K, Tanaka E, Sodeyama T, et al. Transmission of hepatitis C in an isolated area in Japan: Community-acquired infection. Gastroenterology. 1994;106:1596.
24. Conroy-Cantilena C, Van Raden M, Gibble J, et al. Routes of infection, viremia, and liver disease in blood donors found to have hepatitis C virus infection. N Engl J Med. 1996;334:1691.
25. Kao JH, Chen W, Chen PJ, et al. GB virus-C/hepatitis G virus infection in prostitutes: Possible role of sexual transmission. J Med Virol. 1997;52:381.
26. Bourlet T, Berthelot P, Grattard F, et al. Detection of GB virus C/hepatitis G virus in semen and saliva of HIV-1 infected men. Clin Microbiol Infect. 2002;8:352-357.
27. Kao JH, Liu CJ, Chen PJ, et al. Interspousal transmission of GB virus-C/hepatitis G virus: A comparison with hepatitis C virus. J Med Virol. 1997;53:348.
28. Viazov S, Riffelmann M, Sarr S, et al. Transmission of GBV-C/HGV from drug-addicted mothers to their babies. J Hepatol. 1997;27:85.
29. Laskus T, Wang LF, Radkowski M, et al. Hepatitis G virus infection in American patients with cryptogenic cirrhosis: No evidence for liver replication. J Infect Dis. 1997;176:1491.
30. Sugai Y, Nakayama H, Fukuda M, et al. Infection with GB virus C in patients with chronic liver disease. J Med Virol. 1997;51:175.
31. Colombatto P, Ranone A, Civitico G, et al. A new hepatitis C virus-like flavivirus in patients with cryptogenic liver disease associated with elevated GGT and alkaline phosphatase serum levels. J Viral Hepat 1997;4(Suppl 1):55.
32. Guilera M, S'aiz JC, L'opez-Labrador FX, et al. Hepatitis G virus infection in chronic liver disease. Gut. 1998;42:107.
33. Di Stefano R, Ferraro D, Bonura C, et al. Are hepatitis G virus and TTV virus involved in cryptogenic liver disease? Dig Liver Dis. 2002;34:53-58.
34. Alter HJ, Nakatsuji Y, Melpolder J, et al. The incidence of transfusion-associated hepatitis G virus infection and its relation to liver disease. N Engl J Med. 1997;336:747.
35. Wang JT, Tsai FC, Lee CZ, et al. A prospective study of transfusion-transmitted GB virus C infections: Similar frequency but different clinical presentation compared with hepatitis C virus. Blood. 1996;88:1881.
36. Elkayam G, Hassoba HM, Ferrell LD, et al. GB virus C(GBV-C/HGV) and E2 antibodies in children preliver and postliver transplant. Pediatr Res. 1999;45:795-798.
37. Alter MJ, Gallagher M, Morris TT, et al. Acute non-A-E hepatitis in the United States and the role of hepatitis G virus infection. N Engl J Med. 1997;336:741.
38. Tribl B, Oesterreicher C, Pohanka E, et al. GBV-C/HGV in hemodialysis patients: Anti-E2 antibodies and GBV-C/HGV-RNA in serum and peripheral blood mononuclear cells. Kidney Int. 1998;53:212.
39. Gerolami R, Halfon P, Chambost H, et al. Prevalence of hepatitis G virus RNA in a monocentric population of French haemophiliacs. Br J Haematol. 1997;99:209.
40. Berasain C, Betes M, Panizo A, et al. Pathological and virological findings in patients with persistent hypertransaminasaemia of unknown aetiology. Gut. 2000 Sep;47(3):429-435.
41. Pawlotsky JM, Roudot-Thoraval F, Muerhoff AS, et al. GB virus C (GBV-C) infection in patients with chronic hepatitis C—Influence on liver disease and on hepatitis virus behavior: Effect of interferon alpha therapy. J Med Virol. 1998;54:26.
42. Tanaka E, Alter HJ, Nakatsuji Y, et al. Effects of hepatitis G virus infection on chronic hepatitis C. Ann Intern Med. 1996;125:740.
43. Slimane SB, Albrecht JK, Fang JWS, et al. Clinical, virological, and histological implications of GB virus-C/hepatitis G virus infection in patients with chronic hepatitis C virus infection: A multicenter study based on 671 patients. J Viral Hepat. 2000;7:51-55.
44. Moriyama M, Matsumura H, Shimizu T, et al. Hepatitis G virus coinfection influences the liver histology of patients with chronic hepatitis C. Liver 2000;20:397-404.
45. Yoshiba M, Okamoto H, Mishiro S. Detection of the GBV-C hepatitis virus genome in serum from patients with fulminant hepatitis of unknown aetiology. Lancet. 1995;346:1131.
46. Hadziyannis SJ. Fulminant hepatitis and the new G/GBV-C flavivirus. J Viral Hepat. 1997;4:15.
47. Hibbs JR, Frickhofer N, Rosenfeld SJ, et al. Aplastic anemia and viral hepatitis: Non-A, non-B, non-C? JAMA. 1992;267:2051.
48. Brown KE, Wong S, Young NS. Prevalence of GBV-C/HGV, a novel "hepatitis" virus, in patients with aplastic anaemia. Br J Haematol. 1997;97:492.
49. Safadi R, Or R, Ilan Y, et al. Lack of known hepatitis virus in hepatitis-associated aplastic anemia and outcome after bone marrow transplantation. Bone Marrow Transplant. 2001;27:183-190.
50. Lightfoot K, Skelton M, Kew MC, et al. Does hepatitis GB virus-C infection cause hepatocellular carcinoma in black Africans? Hepatology. 1997;26:740.
51. Yuan JM, Govindarin S, Ross RK, Yu MC. Chronic infection with hepatitis G virus in relation to hepatocellular carcinoma among non-Asians in Los Angeles County California. Cancer. 1999;86:936-943.
52. Tagger A, Donato F, Ribero ML, et al. A case-control study on GB virus C/hepatitis G virus infection and hepatocellular carcinoma. Brescia HCC Study. Hepatology. 1997;26:1653.
53. Kubo S, Nishiguchi S, Kuroki T, et al. Poor association of GBV-C viremia with hepatocellular carcinoma. J Hepatol. 1997;27:91.
54. Hollingsworth RC, Minton EJ, Fraser-Moodie C, et al. Hepatitis G infection: Role in cryptogenic chronic liver disease and primary liver cell cancer in the UK. J Viral Hepat. 1998;5:165.
55. Karayiannis P, Brind AM, Pickering J. Hepatitis G virus does not cause significant liver disease after liver transplantation. J Viral Hepat. 1998;5:35.
56. Berenguer M, Terrault NA, Piatak M, et al. Hepatitis G virus infection in patients with hepatitis C virus infection undergoing liver transplantation. Gastroenterology. 1996;111:1569.

57. Saito S, Tanaka K, Kondo M, et al. Plus and minus-stranded hepatitis G virus RNA in liver tissue and in peripheral blood mononuclear cells. Biochem Biophys Res Commun. 1997;237:288.
58. Kanda T, Yokosuka O, Tagawa M, et al. Quantitative analysis of GBV-C RNA in liver and serum by strand-specific reverse transcription-polymerase chain reaction. J Hepatol. 1998;29:707.
59. Madejon A, Fogeda M, Bartolome J, et al. GB virus C RNA in serum, liver, and peripheral blood mononuclear cells from patients with chronic hepatitis B, C and D. Gastroenterology. 1997;113:573.
60. Laskus T, Radkowski M, Wang LF, et al. Lack of evidence for hepatitis G virus replication in the livers of patients coinfected with hepatitis C and G viruses. J Virol. 1997;71:7804.
61. Pessoa MG, Terrault NA, Detmer J, et al. Quantitation of hepatitis G and C viruses in the liver: Evidence that hepatitis G virus is not hepatotropic. Hepatology. 1998;27:877.
62. Mushahwar IK, Erker JC, Muerhoff AS, et al. Tissue tropism of GBV-C and HCV in immunocompromised patients and protective immunity of antibodies to GB virus C second envelope (GBV-C E2) glycoprotein. Hepatologia Clinica. 1998;6(Suppl 1):23.
63. Bukh J, Kim JP, Govindarajan S, et al. Experimental infection of chimpanzees with hepatitis G virus and genetic analysis of the virus. J Infect Dis. 1998;177:855.
64. Krawczynski K. Novel hepatitis agents: The significance of clinical and experimental studies. An overview. J Gastroenterol Hepatol. 1997;12:S193.
65. Handa A, Brown KE. GB virus/hepatitis G virus replicates in human hematopoietic cells and vascular endothelial cells. J Gen Virol. 2000;81:2461-2469.
66. Tucker TJ, Smuts HE, Eedes C, et al. Evidence that GBV-C/hepatitis G virus is primarily a lymphotropic virus. J Med Virol. 2000;61:52-58.
67. Tillmann HL, Heiken H, Knapik-Botor A, et al. Infection with GB virus C and reduced mortality among HIV-infected patients. N Engl J Med. 2001;345:715-724.
68. Xiang J, Wunschmann S, Diekema DJ, et al. Effect of coinfection with GB virus C on survival among patients with HIV infection. N Engl J Med. 2001;345:707-714.
69. Yeo AE, Matsumoto A, Hisada M, et al. Effect of hepatitis G virus infection on progression of HIV infection in patients with hemophilia. Multicenter Hemophilia Cohort Study. Ann Intern Med. 2000;132:959-963.
70. Rodriguez B, Wooley J, Lederman MM, et al. Effect of GB Virus C coinfection on response to antiretroviral treatment in human immunodeficiency virus-infected patients. J Infect Dis. 2003;187:504-507.
71. Alter HJ. Posttransfusion hepatitis in the United States. In: Nishioka K, Suzuki H, Mishiro S, Oda T, eds. Viral Hepatitis and Liver Disease. Tokyo: Springer-Verlag; 1994:551.
72. Nishizawa T, Okamoto H, Konishi K, et al. A novel DNA virus (TTV) associated with elevated transaminase levels in posttransfusion hepatitis of unknown etiology. Biochem Biophys Res Commun. 1997;241:92.
73. Okamoto H, Nishizawa T, Kato N, et al. Molecular cloning and characterization of a novel DNA virus (TTV) associated with posttransfusion hepatitis of unknown etiology. Hepatol Res. 1998;10:1.
74. Simmonds P, Davidson F, Lycett C, et al. Detection of a novel DNA virus (TTV) in blood donors and blood products. Lancet. 1998;352:191.
75. Naoumov NV, Petrova EP, Thomas MG, Williams R. Presence of a newly described human DNA virus (TTV) in patients with liver disease. Lancet. 1998;352:195.
76. Okamoto H, Akahane Y, Ukita M, et al. Fecal excretion of a nonenveloped DNA virus (TTV) associated with posttransfusion non-A-G hepatitis. J Med Virol. 1998;56:128.
77. Tawara A, Akahane Y, Takahashi M, et al. Transmision of TT virus of genotype 1a to chimpanzees with fecal supernate or serum from patients with acute TTV infection. Biochem Biophys Res Commun. 2000;278:470-476.
78. Gerner P, Oettinger R, Gerner W, et al. Mother-to-infant transmission of TT virus: Prevalence, extent and mechanism of vertical transmission. Pediatr Infect Dis J. 2000;19:1074-1077.
79. Liu CJ, Kao JH, Chen W, et al. Interspousal transmission of TT virus: Low efficiency and lack of apparent risk factors. J Gastroenterol Hepatol. 2000;15:1287-1291.
80. Tanaka Y, Primi D, Wang RYH, et al. Genomic and molecular evolutionary analysis of a newly identified infectious agent (SEN Virus) and its relationship to the TT virus family. J Infect Dis. 2001;183:359-367.
81. Umemura T, Yeo AET, Sottini A, et al. SEN virus infection and its relationship to transfusion-associated hepatitis. Hepatology. 2001;33:1303-1311.
82. Maggi F, Pistello M, Vatteroni M, et al. Dynamics of persistent TT virus infection as determined in patients treated with alpha interferon for concomitant hepatitis C virus infection. J Virol. 2001;75:11999-12004.
83. Cheng J, Hada T, Liu W, et al. Investigation of TTV by in-situ hybridization in patients with chronic hepatitis. Hepatol Res. 2000;18:43-53.
84. Hu ZJ, Lang ZW, Zhou YS, et al. Clinicopathologic study of TTV infection in hepatitis of unknown etiology. World J Gastroenterol. 2002;8:288-293.
85. Ohbayashi H, Tanaka Y, Ohoka S, et al. TT virus is shown in the liver by in-situ hybridization with a PCR generated probe from the serum TTV-DNA. J Gastroenterol Hepatol. 2001;16:424-428.
86. Shibata M, Morizane T, Baba T, et al. TT virus infection in patients with fulminant hepatic failure. Am J Gastroenterol. 2000;95:3602-3606.
87. Huang YH, Wu JC, Chiang TY, et al. Detection and viral nucleotide sequence analysis of transfusion-transmitted virus infection in acute fulminant and non-fulminant hepatitis. J Viral Hepatol. 2000;7:56-63.
88. Matsumoto A, Yeo AET, Shih JWK, et al. Transfusion-associated TT virus infection and its relationship to liver disease. Hepatology. 1999;30:283-288.
89. Fredericks DN, Relman DA. Sequence-based identification of microbial pathogens: A reconsideration of Koch's postulates. Clin Microbiol Rev. 1996;9:18-33.

CHAPTER **152**

Coronaviruses, Including Severe Acute Respiratory Syndrome (SARS)–Associated Coronavirus

KENNETH McINTOSH

LARRY J. ANDERSON

The family Coronaviridae contains two genera, the *Coronaviruses* and the *Toroviruses*. The two genera appear similar on electron microscopy, and they share similar strategies of replication (along with the other member of the order Nidovirales, the *Arteriviruses*). They differ, however, in the size of their RNA genome and structural proteins, as well as the morphology of their nucleocapsids. Coronaviruses are primarily respiratory pathogens in humans and were until recently considered to cause upper respiratory tract illness and probably also some undetermined fraction of viral diarrhea. During the winter of 2002-2003, a new coronavirus, the SARS coronavirus (SARS-CoV), was found to be the cause of an acute, severe, frequently fatal respiratory disease with prominent systemic symptoms (severe acute respiratory syndrome [SARS]). The outbreak originated in southern China, probably following transmission from an animal (possibly the palm civet) in wild animal markets to humans. In retrospect, the emergence of SARS is consistent with what is known about coronaviruses as a group: they are important pathogens in animals that cause a wide variety of diseases through a wide variety of pathogenic mechanisms, and they have been noted to mutate frequently and infect new species.[1] Toroviruses are, at least as presently known, exclusively enteric pathogens, both in animals and in humans.

HISTORY

Respiratory Coronaviruses

In 1965, Tyrrell and Bynoe passaged a virus obtained from the respiratory tract of an adult with a common cold by serially culturing nasal wash fluids in human embryonic tracheal organ cultures.[2] The medium from these cultures consistently produced colds in volunteers. The agent involved, however, failed to grow in tissue culture. It was ether sensitive but not related to any of the known myxoviruses or paramyxoviruses. Subsequently, electron microscopy of fluids from infected organ cultures revealed particles that resembled the infectious bronchitis virus of chickens.[3] The particles were medium sized (80 to 150 nm), pleomorphic, membrane coated, and covered with widely spaced club-shaped surface projections. At about the same time, Hamre and Procknow[4] recovered a cytopathic agent in tissue culture from medical students with colds. This agent was also unrelated to known myxoviruses and paramyxoviruses and was ether sensitive. Subsequent electron microscopy revealed similar or identical particles[3] (Fig. 152-1).

Using techniques similar to those used by Tyrrell, McIntosh and others[5] reported the recovery of multiple strains of ether-sensitive agents from the human respiratory tract, all of which had the typical morphology of infectious bronchitis virus. At much the same time, several previously unclassified animal viruses, including mouse hepatitis virus and transmissible gastroenteritis virus of swine, were shown to have the same characteristic morphology by electron microscopy.[6,7] Very shortly thereafter the name *coronavirus* (the prefix *corona* denoting the crown-like appearance of the surface projections) was chosen to signify a new genus for this group of viruses.[8]

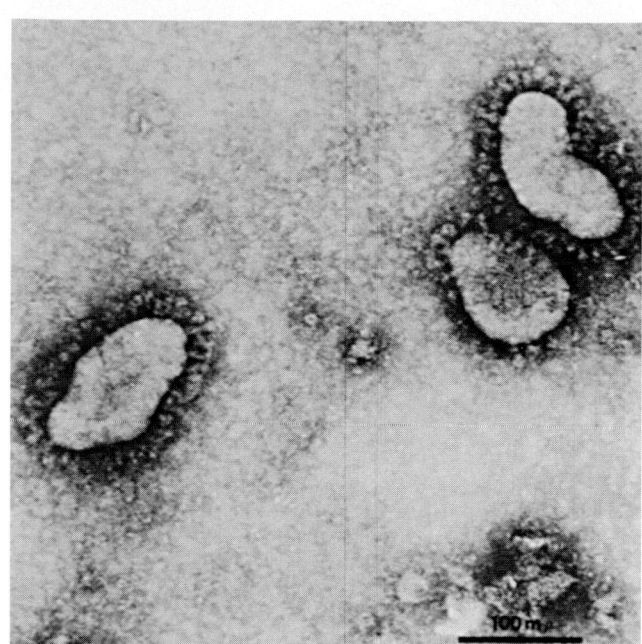

FIGURE 152-1. *Coronavirus, strain 229E, harvested from infected WI-38 cells (phosphotungstic acid stain). (From McIntosh K, Dees JH, Becker WB, et al. Recovery in tracheal organ cultures of novel viruses from patients with respiratory disease. Proc Natl Acad Sci U S A. 1967;57:933-940.)*

The number and importance of animal coronaviruses quickly grew, with the eventual identification of viruses causing diseases in rats, mice, chickens, turkeys, calves, dogs, cats, rabbits, and pigs. These diseases include infectious bronchitis and nephrosis in chickens; gastroenteritis and encephalitis in young piglets; enteritis in turkeys, dogs, and calves; hepatitis and encephalitis in mice; pneumonitis and sialodacryoadenitis in rats; and infectious peritonitis in cats. The variety of animal species infected and the severity of the associated disease have made the coronavirus one of the most important veterinary pathogens.

Severe Acute Respiratory Syndrome

SARS was first identified in Guangdong Province of China during November 2002,[9] and it spread from there first to Hong Kong and then to countries in Southeast Asia, Europe, and North America, and finally throughout the world. A coronavirus was independently and almost simultaneously isolated by several laboratories from SARS patients using African Green Monkey (Vero E6) or fetal rhesus monkey cells.[10-12] Sequencing of the entire viral RNA was quickly completed in several laboratories and demonstrated that the virus was only distantly related to all previously characterized human or animal coronaviruses.[10-14] The SARS outbreak stimulated a rapid and intense public health response coordinated by the World Health Organization (WHO), and by the end of June 2003 transmission had ceased throughout the world. When global control was formally announced in early July 2003, more than 8000 cases and more than 800 deaths had been reported.

Gastrointestinal Coronaviruses and Toroviruses

In view of the prominence of coronaviruses in animal enteric diseases, it is not surprising that coronavirus-like particles (CVLPs) have also been described in human fecal material. During the past 15 to 20 years, reports of such particles have been numerous but these particles have been difficult to characterize further, in part because they are difficult to grow in vitro.

Toroviruses were, like coronaviruses, first described in animals. They were first detected in the feces of cattle (Breda virus) and horses (Berne virus).[15,16] Shortly thereafter, Beards and colleagues[17] examined human fecal material and reported finding particles with a similar appearance that aggregated in the presence of antiserum to the bovine and equine viruses. Neither the human nor the bovine virus grows in tissue culture.

DESCRIPTION OF THE PATHOGENS

Coronaviruses

The coronavirus nucleic acid is RNA, about 30 kb in length, and of positive sense, single-stranded, polyadenylated, and infectious. The RNA, the largest known viral RNA (Fig. 152-2), codes for (in order from the 5′ end) a large polyprotein, which is cleaved by virus-encoded proteases to form several nonstructural proteins including an RNA-dependent RNA polymerase and an ATPase helicase, followed by either four or five structural proteins: a surface hemagglutinin-esterase protein (HE), present on HuCoV-OC43 and some animal coronaviruses; a surface glycoprotein (the S protein) that forms the petal-shaped surface projections and is probably responsible for the stimulation of neutralizing antibody; a small envelope protein (E); a membrane glycoprotein (M) contained within the trilamellar membrane; and a nucleocapsid protein (N) complexed with the RNA. There are several other open reading frames whose coding functions are not clear. The strategy of replication of coronaviruses is unique in that all messenger RNAs form a nested set with common polyadenylated 3′ ends, with only the unique portion of the 5′ end being translated.[1] Like other RNA viruses, mutations are common in nature. Coronaviruses are also capable of genetic recombination if two viruses infect the same cell at the same time.

All coronaviruses develop exclusively in the cytoplasm of infected cells (Fig. 152-3). They bud into cytoplasmic vesicles from membranes of the endoplasmic reticulum. These virus-filled vesicles then are either extruded by reverse pinocytosis or released from the cell when the cell is destroyed.[18] The resultant virus particles have a diameter of 70 to 80 nm by thin-section electron microscopy and 60 to 220 nm by negative staining; they are pleomorphic, with widely spaced,

petal-shaped projections 20 nm long (see Fig. 152-1). Viral antigens appear on the surface of the cell during replication.[19]

Animal and human coronaviruses have been placed into three distinct antigenic groups. Group I contains the human coronavirus 229E (HuCoV-229E) and a number of animal coronaviruses, including transmissible gastroenteritic virus of pigs, feline coronavirus, and canine coronavirus. Group II contains the human coronavirus HuCoV-OC43 and several animal coronaviruses, including mouse hepatitis virus and bovine coronavirus, and group III contains a number of avian coronaviruses, including infectious bronchitis virus of chickens.[1] The SARS coronavirus (SARS-CoV) is, based on sequence studies, distantly related to all three previously described groups, and may be placed in a fourth group that would also include the animal viruses from which it presumably was derived[13,14,20] (Fig. 152-4). The organization and types of structural and nonstructural proteins encoded in the SARS-CoV genome are typical for coronaviruses. The SARS-CoV does not encode for the HE protein present in some group II and III viruses.

A cellular receptor for group I coronaviruses (including HuCoV-229E), human aminopeptidase N, has been described.[21] An animal coronavirus, mouse hepatitis virus, which is related to strain HuCoV-OC43, uses as its receptor a member of the carcinoembryonic antigen family.[22] HuCoV-OC43 itself may use one of several cell surface molecules, including 9-O-acetylated neuraminic acid and the HLA-I molecule.[23]

Two human respiratory coronavirus strains, HuCoV-229E and HuCoV-OC43, have been adapted to growth in tissue culture or animals. All human respiratory strains studied to date are antigenically related to either 229E or OC43,[24,25] although there are probably others whose characterization has been severely limited because they have been grown only in human embryonic tracheal organ culture.[5,26]

SARS-CoV grows readily in Vero cells, especially the Vero E6 clone, producing a cytopathic effect that can include some syncytium formation. Although genomic sequence data show only a distant relatedness

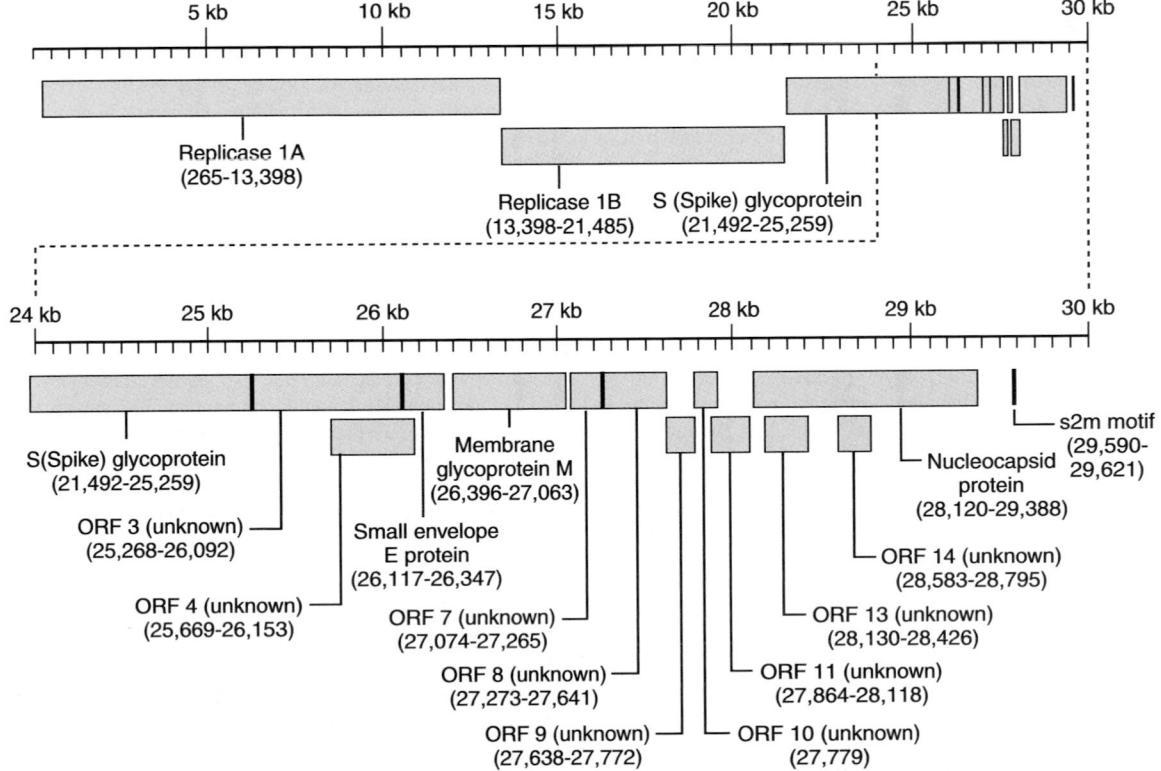

FIGURE 152-2. Map of the predicted open reading frames (ORFs) in the Tor2 severe acute respiratory syndrome (SARS) virus genome sequence. *(From Rota PA, Oberste MS, Monroe SS, et al. Characterization of a novel coronavirus associated with severe acute respiratory syndrome. Science. 2003;300:1394-1399.)*

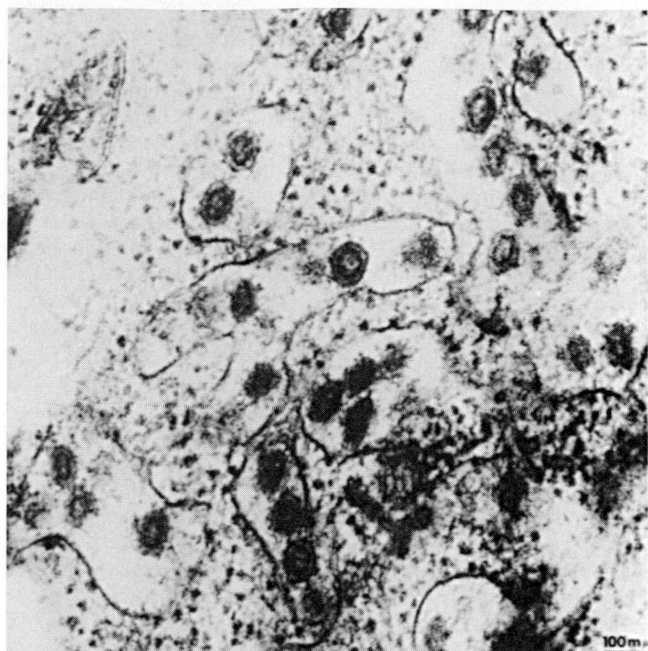

FIGURE 152-3. Coronavirus strain 229E in WI-38 cells. *(From Becker WB, McIntosh K, Dees JH, Chanock RM. Morphogenesis of avian infectious bronchitis virus and a related human virus [strain 229E]. J Virol. 1967;1:1019-1027.)*

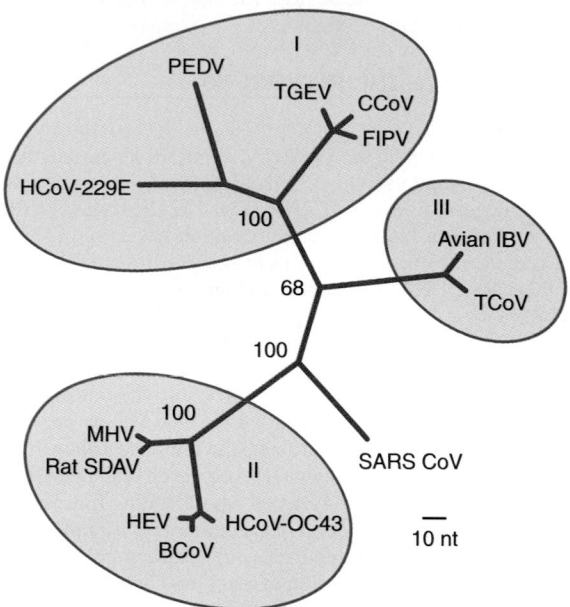

FIGURE 152-4. Estimated maximum-parsimony tree based on the sequence alignment of 405 nucleotides of the coronavirus polymerase gene open reading frame 1b comparing severe acute respiratory syndrome coronavirus with other human and animal coronaviruses. *(From Ksiazek TG, Erdman D, Goldsmith CS, et al. A novel coronavirus associated with severe acute respiratory syndrome. N Engl J Med. 2003;348:1953-1966. Copyright © 2003. Massachusetts Medical Society. All rights reserved.)*

to other coronaviruses, antisera to Group I viruses, including feline infectious peritonitis virus and HuCoV-229E, have been shown to react with SARS-CoV–infected cells.[11] SARS-CoV also contains no HE protein. The genomes of more than 30 SARS-CoV strains have been fully sequenced, and they show only slight variation, which is considered to be consistent with their epidemiologic origin and history.[27]

Enteric coronaviruses have also been difficult to cultivate in vitro. All except a few strains have been detected only by electron microscopy of human fecal material.[28-32] Some strains have been antigenically characterized by immune electron microscopy of particles in stool and found to be related to the respiratory HuCoV-OC43.[33] Several strains have been propagated in intestinal organ culture.[34,35] Two strains obtained from an outbreak of necrotizing enterocolitis in Texas and passaged in intestinal organ cultures were reported to contain four or five antigenically active proteins separable on polyacrylamide gels.[35] These proteins migrated with apparent molecular weights similar to those of well-studied coronaviruses. Antigenic relatedness to HuCoV-OC43 or other coronaviruses was not, however, demonstrable. The accumulating evidence favors the view that these two isolates, as well as the particles shown to be antigenically related to HuCoV-OC43, are members of the family Coronaviridae, although their association with human disease is not yet proved. The less well-studied strains, characterized only by their distinctive morphology on electron microscopy and called, for lack of a better name, *coronavirus-like particles*, may also be coronaviruses, but the evidence is less compelling.

Toroviruses

Toroviruses have morphology similar to that of coronaviruses. They are pleomorphic, membrane-coated viruses that are somewhat smaller and more pleomorphic than enteric coronaviruses (100 to 120 nm in their largest diameter), and their club-shaped surface projections are somewhat less distinct.[36,37] The nucleic acid–containing core of the virus assumes a doughnut shape (i.e., a torus) if viewed from a certain angle on electron microscopy.[16,37,38] Berne virus was first isolated from horses with diarrhea in the 1970s and grows in equine cell tissue culture. The human toroviruses, like the bovine toroviruses, do not grow in tissue culture.

The S glycoproteins on the surface of toroviruses have no significant sequence homology with the S proteins of coronaviruses.[39] A second surface protein with hemagglutinin-esterase activity and sequence homology to the HE proteins of both influenza C virus and mouse hepatitis virus has been found on the bovine Breda virus but not on the equine Berne virus.[40] It is not known whether this molecule exists on human toroviruses, although human toroviruses do hemagglutinate rabbit erythrocytes.[37] There is also greater than 90% identity in the 3′ end of the genome between human and animal toroviruses.[37,39] The toroviruses, like coronaviruses, contain membrane and nucleoproteins, but there is no significant sequence homology in the respective genes between the toroviruses and coronaviruses. In contrast, the toroviral replicase contains sequence similarity to that of coronaviruses, and the strategy of replication appears similar.[39]

EPIDEMIOLOGY

Respiratory Coronaviruses

Like all other known respiratory virus infections, evidence for respiratory coronavirus infections has been found wherever it has been sought; this includes North America, South America, Europe, and Asia.

In temperate climates, respiratory coronavirus infections occur more often in the winter and spring than in the summer and fall. The contribution of coronavirus infections to the total number of upper respiratory illnesses may be as high as 35% during times of peak viral activity. Overall, the proportion of adult colds produced by corona-viruses may be reasonably estimated at 15%.

In the United States, the two strains that have been extensively studied, HuCoV-OC43 and HuCoV-229E, have demonstrated periodicity, with large epidemics occurring at 2- to 3-year intervals.[41] HuCoV-229E tends to be epidemic throughout the United States, whereas strain HuCoV-OC43 tends to appear in localized outbreaks. Reinfection appears to be common and may be due to the rapid diminution of antibody levels after infection.[42] Infection occurs at all ages but is most common in children. About half of persons infected (as judged by a rise in antibody titer) become ill.

Severe Acute Respiratory Syndrome

The SARS epidemic probably began in the Guangdong Province of China in mid-November, 2002.[9] It came to worldwide attention in early March 2003 when a large number of cases of severe, acute atypical pneumonia were reported to the WHO from Hong Kong, Hanoi, and Singapore. It appeared that disease spread most often in hospitals to health care workers, visitors, and patients and among family members. Occasionally, spread was also noted in other settings including, in Hong Kong, a hotel, an apartment complex, and markets. Worldwide spread was rapid but surprisingly focal (Fig. 152-5). The largest numbers of cases were reported from China, Hong Kong, Taiwan, Singapore, and Toronto, Canada. The overall case-fatality rates in these locations ranged from 7% to 17% but persons with underlying medical conditions and those over 65 years of age had mortality rates as high as 50%.

In response to the rapid global spread and associated severe disease, the WHO coordinated a rapid and intense control program, with surveillance that used a clinical and exposure-based case definition,[43] plus implementation of stringent control measures: isolation of cases; careful attention to contact, droplet, and airborne infection control procedures; quarantine of exposed persons in some settings; and efforts to control spread between countries through travel advisories and travel alerts and, in some localities, the screening of departing and arriving passengers. Presumably as a result of these efforts, global transmission related to the initial outbreak ceased by June 2003.

It is not known if SARS will return. It is possible that SARS, like many other viruses that are transmitted via the respiratory route, spreads more efficiently during the fall, winter, or spring and that it will reappear in that setting, perhaps reintroduced from the original animal reservoir, through unrecognized ongoing transmission, or from persistent infection in humans. There are reports that SARS-CoV can be detected by polymerase chain reaction (PCR) for more than 1 month in stool specimens of persons for whom the initial illness has resolved.

Spread in human populations is thought to have occurred primarily through close contact that probably included droplet transmission and direct contact or fomite transmission. There are several instances that may have involved small-particle airborne or fecal-oral transmission. In most instances, an individual case transmitted to very few others. However, there were several well-documented instances in which one case infected up to 100 or more persons.[44] On average, it was estimated that one infected person would infect about three others and that containment measures, including quarantine, would have a major effect on the course of the epidemic.[45,46] This proved to be the case. The chain of spread was apparently broken in China, the last country to experience endemic spread, during June 2003.

The origin of the SARS epidemic is still not clear, but the absence of SARS antibody in control populations suggests that it has not previously circulated in humans to any significant degree and that the virus originated in some animal species and crossed over into the human population in southern China. The isolation of virus and detection of SARS-CoV antibodies in several masked palm civets, a raccoon dog, and a Chinese ferret-badger from a live animal market in Guangdong Province, China, suggest that animals from these markets might have been the source of the virus that infected humans.[20]

Gastrointestinal Coronaviruses

Enteric coronaviruses (or CVLPs) have been most frequently associated with gastrointestinal disease in neonates and infants younger than

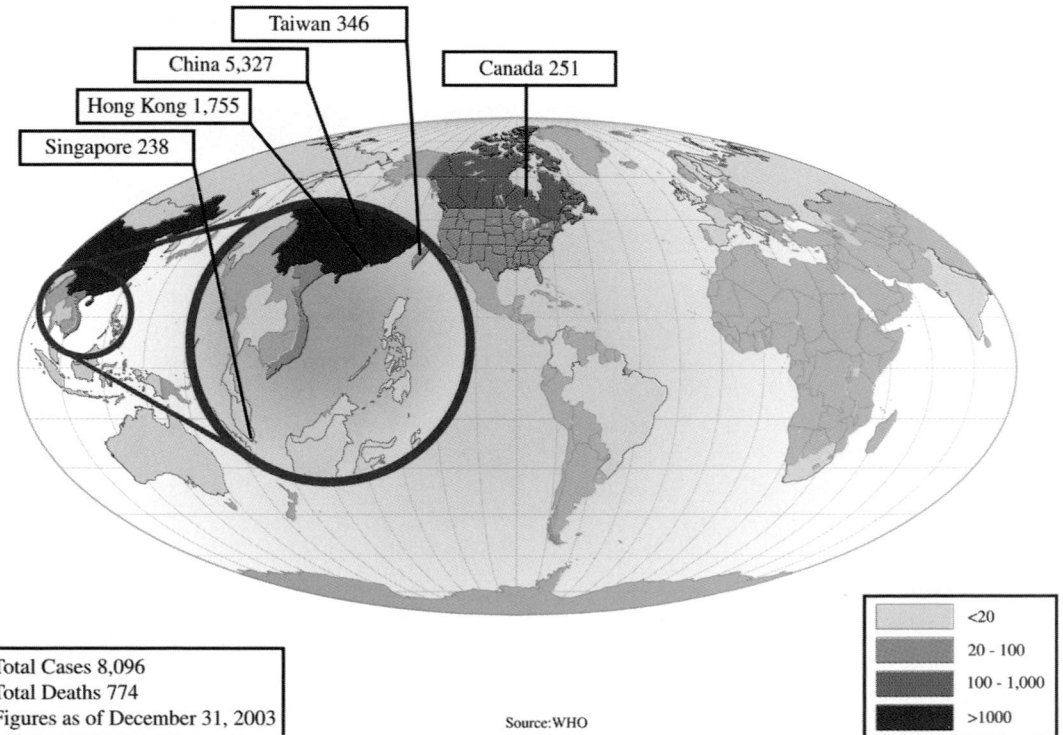

Taiwan 346
China 5,327
Hong Kong 1,755
Singapore 238
Canada 251

Total Cases 8,096
Total Deaths 774
Figures as of December 31, 2003

Source: WHO

<20
20 - 100
100 - 1,000
>1000

FIGURE 152-5. World map of countries with severe acute respiratory syndrome and number of cases as of July 3, 2003.

12 months. Particles have been found in the stools of adults with acquired immunodeficiency syndrome (AIDS).[47,48] Asymptomatic shedding is common, particularly in tropical climates[49] and in populations living in poor hygienic conditions.[50] They can be detected for prolonged periods[29,31,51] and without any apparent seasonal pattern.[52]

PATHOGENESIS

Respiratory Coronaviruses

Respiratory coronaviruses replicate in ciliated epithelial cells of the nasopharynx, probably producing both direct degeneration of the ciliated cells[53] and an outpouring of chemokines and interleukins, with a resultant common cold symptom complex similar to that produced by rhinovirus infection[54] (see Chapter 171). The incubation period is, on average, 2 days, and the peak of respiratory symptoms, as well as viral shedding, is reached at about 3 or 4 days after inoculation.[55]

The pattern of virus replication of coronaviruses is at least in part determined by virus–receptor interaction. For HuCoV-229E, the receptor is aminopeptidase N, and the known tissue distribution of this molecule is very wide,[21] including several organs in which HuCoV-229E does not normally produce disease.

Severe Acute Respiratory Syndrome

The route of infection of the SARS-CoV is probably through the respiratory tract. After an incubation period that is usually between 4 and 7 days but can be as long as 10 to 14 days, the disease usually begins, starting with fever and other systemic ("influenza-like") symptoms, and cough and dyspnea develop a few days to 1 week later.[56] Although the lung is the focus of the disease process, there are often signs of involvement in other organ systems, including diarrhea, leukopenia, thrombocytopenia, and, most notably, lymphopenia. The lymphopenia appears to be primarily from a reduction in circulating T-lymphocytes and includes CD3+, CD4+, and CD8+ T cells.[57] Virus has been detected in respiratory secretions, blood, stool, and urine specimens and in tissue from lung and kidney. Based on PCR assays, virus titer is highest during the second week of illness[58] and can often be detected into the third week of illness, sometimes for as long as several months.[12,59] The virus appears to persist longest in stool samples. In severe disease, pulmonary symptoms may worsen late in the course of the illness, with the development of adult respiratory distress syndrome (ARDS).[58] There may also be late evidence of liver and kidney involvement.

The pulmonary pathology of infection by the SARS-CoV has been described extensively.[11,60-62] There is hyaline membrane formation, interstitial infiltration with lymphocytes and mononuclear cells, and desquamation of pneumocytes in the alveolar spaces. Inclusion bodies are not usually seen, although they have been described in one report.[62] Giant cells are a constant finding and usually have macrophage markers. In bronchoalveolar wash, biopsy, and autopsy specimens, viral particles have been noted in type II pneumocytes. Later in the course of the disease process, the pathologic picture of an organizing pneumonia is seen. The pulmonary pathology of cynomolgus macaques infected experimentally with tissue culture–grown virus is very similar.[63]

Little has been published about the pathology in other organ systems.[61,62] The extrapulmonary pathologic changes found most consistently at autopsy are extensive necrosis of the white pulp of the spleen and a generalized small-vessel arteritis.[61,62]

CLINICAL MANIFESTATIONS

Respiratory Coronaviruses

The human respiratory coronaviruses cause colds in adults, and most strains were originally recovered from adults during upper respiratory tract illness. Almost all the antigenically distinct respiratory coronavirus strains have been administered to volunteers, and all these produce illness with similar characteristics.[2,55,64] A summary of these characteristics is shown in Table 152-1, in which a comparison is made with colds produced by rhinoviruses in similarly inoculated volunteers. The incubation period of coronavirus colds was longer and their duration somewhat shorter, but the symptoms were very similar. Low-grade fever was present in about one of five volunteers, and malaise after coronavirus inoculation was common. Asymptomatic infection was sometimes seen and, indeed, has been a feature of serologic surveys of natural infection of children and adults. The mechanism of respiratory tract symptoms is not clear but is probably more closely related to a release of proinflammatory mediators[65] than to cell injury. It is likely that the colds produced in volunteers are similar to those produced in adults by natural infection.[55,66]

More serious, lower respiratory tract illness is probably on occasion caused by non-SARS coronavirus infection. For example, several strains resembling HuCoV-229E have been recovered from infants with pneumonia,[67] and antibody titer rises also have been found with a frequency of 3% to 8% in this group.[67,68] An extensive survey of hos-

TABLE 152-1 Clinical Features of Colds Produced by Experimental Infection with Four Viruses

	Coronaviruses		Rhinoviruses	
Feature	229E	B814	Type 2 (HGP or PK)	DC
No. of volunteers inoculated	26	75	213	251
No. getting colds	13 (50%)	34 (45%)	78 (37%)	77 (31%)
Incubation period (days)				
Mean	3.3	3.2	2.1	2.1
Range	2-4	2-5	1-5	1-4
Duration (days)				
Mean	7	6	9	10
Range	3-18	2-17	3-19	2-26
Maximum no. of handkerchiefs used daily				
Mean	23	21	14	18
Range	8-105	8-120	3-38	33-60
Malaise (%)	46	47	28	25
Headache (%)	85	53	56	56
Chill (%)	31	18	28	15
Pyrexia (%)	23	21	14	18
Mucopurulent nasal discharge (%)	0	62	83	80
Sore throat (%)	54	79	87	73
Cough (%)	31	44	68	56
No. of volunteers with colds of indicated severity				
Mild	10 (77%)	24 (71%)	63 (80%)	36 (47%)
Moderate	2 (15%)	7 (20%)	12 (15%)	28 (36%)
Severe	1 (8%)	3 (9%)	4 (5%)	13 (17%)

Data from Bradburne AF, Bynoe ML, Tyrrell DAJ. Effects of a "new" human respiratory virus in volunteers. BMJ. 1967;3:767-769.

pitalized children in England failed to uncover a single instance of coronavirus infection.[69] However, surveys of hospitalized children using more sensitive methods, such as reverse transcriptase (RT)–PCR, have not been performed.

In one study, about one third of coronavirus infections in marine recruits were associated with pneumonia or pleural reaction, suggesting that under special circumstances non-SARS coronaviruses can also cause lower respiratory tract disease in adults.[70] The association of coronavirus infection with bouts of wheezing in asthmatic children or children with recurrent wheezy bronchitis has also been described.[71,72] Finally, six separate longitudinal serologic studies of adults with chronic pulmonary disease or asthma have each shown a significant association of coronavirus infection with exacerbations of respiratory symptoms.[73-78] In addition, it is becoming clear that elderly persons are subject to more severe respiratory disease during coronavirus infection[79] and that such infections are common. The pathogenicity of the HuCoV-229E– and HuCoV-OC43–related viruses in this population is similar to that of rhinoviruses[80,81] and probably less severe than that of influenza and respiratory syncytial viruses.[82]

This wide spectrum of severe and mild respiratory illness over a broad age range is confirmed in a recent series of patients with the CoV-OC43 sequences found in respiratory specimens during the winter 2001 in Normandy, France.[83]

Severe Acute Respiratory Syndrome

The first sign of illness in most cases of SARS is fever, usually accompanied by headache, malaise, or myalgia. This is followed, usually in a few days but up to 1 week later, by nonproductive cough and, in more severe cases, dyspnea. About 25% of patients have diarrhea. Interestingly, upper respiratory symptoms such as rhinorrhea and sore throat usually do not occur. Rash is distinctly unusual.[56,58,84,85] The chest radiograph is frequently abnormal, showing scattered air-space opacification, usually in the periphery and lower zones of the lung. Cavitation, hilar adenopathy, and reticular or nodular infiltrates are all distinctly unusual. Pleural effusions are rare.[86] Spiral computed tomography, which is more sensitive than standard radiography, demonstrates both ground-glass opacification and consolidation, often in a subpleural distribution.[87-89]

Laboratory test abnormalities are frequent. Lymphopenia is common,[58,60,84] with normal or somewhat depressed neutrophils. Reduction in lymphocytes in the blood is most marked for CD4$^+$ cells but has been seen in all T-cell phenotypes, including CD3$^+$ and CD8$^+$, as well as natural killer cells. The lymphopenia may be apparent at the onset of the illness and reaches a maximum around day 10 to 14. Creatine kinase levels may be elevated, as well as lactic dehydrogenase and aspartate aminotransferase levels.

About 25% of patients develop severe pulmonary disease that progresses to ARDS. The ARDS may resolve, or patients may die with respiratory failure. Patients over 50 years old or with underlying disease such as diabetes, cardiac disease, or chronic hepatitis are most likely to develop ARDS with SARS-CoV infection.[58,84,85,90] Overall mortality has been variously estimated but appears to be around 10%.

Pediatric disease is, interestingly, somewhat less severe than adult disease, although the features are very similar.[91,92] Disease during pregnancy may be very severe, with high mortality in both mother and fetus.[93] The long-term effects of SARS have not been described.

Gastrointestinal Coronaviruses and Toroviruses

The nature of the illness associated with enteric coronavirus infection is much less clear. One study significantly associated gastroenteritis in infants 2 to 12 months of age with the presence of CVLPs in the stool.[33] Another study, confined to infants in a neonatal intensive care unit, found highly significant associations between the presence of CVLPs in the stool and the presence of water-loss stools, bloody stools, abdominal distention, and bilious gastric aspirates.[31] A further study of symptomatic infants shedding CVLPs pointed to possible differences between rotavirus diarrhea (see Chapter 146) and CVLP-associated diarrhea: although fever and vomiting were of very similar incidence,

stools were more often positive for occult blood (18% versus 0%), less often watery (66% versus 92%), and more often mucoid (32% versus 8%).[51] Finally, coronaviruses have been associated with at least three outbreaks of necrotizing enterocolitis in newborns,[30,31,35] and the best-characterized strains[35] were isolated from infants with this illness.

The pathogenicity of human toroviruses is still in doubt, although the few controlled studies that have been done have shown a more consistent association with illness than those of enteric coronaviruses. Torovirus particles are found in the feces of both symptomatic and asymptomatic individuals, but there has been a clear excess in the former, implying a pathogenic role in diarrheal disease.[94,95]

In a study from Brazil, 20 of 91 fecal samples from children in the community with diarrhea contained torovirus antigen detectable by enzyme-linked immunosorbent assay (ELISA), and toroviruses were significantly associated with both acute and chronic diarrhea[95] ($P = 0.02$ for both). In a study from Canada, symptomatic and asymptomatic hospitalized children were sampled for fecal viruses: toroviruses were found in 35% of the former and 14.5% of the latter. In comparison to those with stools containing either rotaviruses or astroviruses, torovirus-infected children were older (mean age, 4.0 years versus 2.0 years), and their infections were more often acquired in hospital (57.6% versus 31.3%). Vomiting was less common with torovirus infection, but occult blood was more common. A large proportion of symptomatic torovirus infections were in immunocompromised children.[94]

Neurologic Syndromes

Like many other viruses, coronaviruses have been sought as possible etiologic agents in multiple sclerosis. The search has been stimulated by the capacity of JHM, a well-studied strain of mouse hepatitis virus, to produce in mice and rats a chronic demyelinating encephalitis histologically similar to multiple sclerosis.[96] There are reports of the detection in brain tissue from multiple sclerosis patients of viruses related to mouse hepatitis virus, HuCoV-OC43,[97,98] and HuCoV-229E[99] using virus isolation,[97] in situ hybridization, immunohistology,[98] and PCR.[99] Moreover, T cell lines established from patients with multiple sclerosis by stimulation with myelin basic protein or HuCoV-229E were found to be cross-reactive, suggesting that molecular mimicry might be a possible pathogenic mechanism for the disease association.[100] Nevertheless, compelling evidence is lacking to establish an etiologic or a pathogenetic association of coronaviruses with central nervous system disease in humans.

LABORATORY DIAGNOSIS

Respiratory Coronaviruses

HuCoV-229E and some closely related strains grow in human diploid cell lines. Recovery from clinical specimens often requires blind subpassage. All other human respiratory coronaviruses have been recovered from clinical specimens only in organ cultures from human embryonic tracheal or nasal epithelium. HuCoV-OC43 and HuCoV-OC38, antigenically identical to each other, were subsequently adapted first to growth in suckling mouse brain and then to tissue culture. Rapid viral diagnosis from respiratory specimens can be accomplished either by antigen detection[69,101] or, with likely greater sensitivity, by RT–PCR.[102] The latter has been used with success to detect virus in middle ear fluids.[103]

Tissue culture–grown HuCoV-OC43 and HuCoV-229E have been used in various antibody assays to study infection and disease in human populations.[73,104]

Severe Acute Respiratory Syndrome

Although SARS-CoV has been grown from respiratory tract specimens in Vero E6 and fetal rhesus monkey kidney cells, the more sensitive and rapid RT-PCR assays have been most widely used to detect infection. Virus can be detected by RT-PCR in upper and lower respiratory tract, blood, stool, and urine specimens. Early in the illness, specimens have been found to be positive in only about one third of patients.[58] Virus can be detected most frequently during the second week of illness, with stool possibly giving the highest rate of positivity.[12,58,59] The RT-PCRs are very sensitive, but the ability to detect infection appears to be limited by low titer of virus in clinical specimens. It is not yet clear what specimens or combination of specimens can best be used to rule in or out SARS-CoV infection.

Antibody tests have been developed using tissue culture grown virus and indirect immunofluorescence or ELISA. IgM antibody can be detected in most patients for a limited period of time, and IgG antibody appears first around 10 days after onset of fever and is present in essentially all cases.[58]

Gastrointestinal Coronaviruses and Toroviruses

Laboratory diagnosis of the gastrointestinal coronaviruses and of human toroviruses currently depends entirely on electron microscopy of stool specimens and detection of characteristic particles in negatively stained specimens. Such testing is best performed in laboratories with extensive prior experience.

TREATMENT

Given the severity of SARS, clinicians throughout the world empirically treated most patients with corticosteroids and intravenous or oral ribavirin.[105] It is now known that ribavirin has little or no activity against SARS-CoV in vitro, and there is no evidence that it was helpful in treating SARS cases. There is anecdotal evidence of possible benefits of steroid treatment. One large case series compared the use of corticosteroids early versus late (after 14 days) in the course of disease, and although the comparison was not randomized or contemporaneous, there was a significant difference in the rate of resolution of dyspnea and pulmonary infiltrates, which favored early treatment with corticosteroids.[9] Interferons have shown in vitro activity against SARS and were administered to a small group of patients in Canada with possibly a beneficial effect.

There is an active program to identify drugs with measurable activity against the SARS-CoV sponsored by The National Institute of Allergy and Infectious Diseases, the Centers for Disease Control and Prevention, and the Department of Defense.

PREVENTION

The containment of the global SARS outbreak is a testament to the power of the cooperation and collaboration engendered by the WHO to address a major public health threat. The rapid and intense response by the medical and public communities and the support and cooperation of the political leadership of multiple countries to implement stringent control measures appear to have succeeded in controlling SARS. Whether it will resurface and present similar problems in the future is unknown at this time.

Vaccines for animal coronaviruses have been developed and widely used with variable efficacy. In one instance, a vaccine for feline infectious peritonitis appeared to lead to enhanced disease with subsequent natural infection. If SARS does return, an effective vaccine would be extremely helpful in efforts at control, and a variety of vaccination strategies, including inactivated, subunit, and live-attenuated vaccines, are being pursued.

The high level of transmission of the SARS-CoV between patients and hospital staff in the epidemic of 2002-2003 created staffing shortages, quarantine of exposed staff, and closure of hospitals to new admissions. The issues facing hospitals as they prepare for the next epidemic of SARS or other threats posed by contagious agents are discussed in Chapter 14.

REFERENCES

1. Lai MM, Holmes KV. Coronaviridae: The Viruses and Their Replication. In: Knipe D, ed. Field's Virology. 4th ed. Philadelphia: Lippincott-Raven; 2001.
2. Tyrrell DAJ, Bynoe ML. Cultivation of a novel type of common-cold virus in organ cultures. Br Med J. 1965;1:1467-1470.
3. Almeida JD, Tyrrell DAJ. The morphology of three previously uncharacterized human respiratory viruses that grow in organ culture. J Gen Virol. 1967;1:175-178.
4. Hamre D, Procknow JJ. A new virus isolated from the human respiratory tract. Proc Soc Exp Biol Med. 1966;121:190-193.
5. McIntosh K, Dees JH, Becker WB, et al. Recovery in tracheal organ cultures of novel viruses from patients with respiratory disease. Proc Natl Acad Sci U S A. 1967;57:933-940.
6. Witte KH, Tajima M, Easterday BC. Morphologic characteristics and nucleic acid type of transmissible gastroenteritis virus of pigs. Arch Gesamte Virusforsch. 1968;23:53-70.
7. McIntosh K, Becker WB, Chanock RM. Growth in suckling-mouse brain of "IBV-like" viruses from patients with upper respiratory tract disease. Proc Natl Acad Sci U S A. 1967;58:2268-2273.
8. Tyrrell DA, Almeida JD, Cunningham CH, et al. Coronaviridae. Intervirology. 1975;5(1-2):76-82.
9. Zhao Z, Zhang F, Xu M, et al. Description and clinical treatment of an early outbreak of severe acute respiratory syndrome (SARS) in Guangzhou, PR China. J Med Microbiol. 2003;52:715-720.
10. Peiris JS, Lai ST, Poon LL, et al. Coronavirus as a possible cause of severe acute respiratory syndrome. Lancet. 2003;361:1319-1325.
11. Ksiazek TG, Erdman D, Goldsmith CS, et al. A novel coronavirus associated with severe acute respiratory syndrome. N Engl J Med. 2003;348:1953-1966.
12. Drosten C, Gunther S, Preiser W, et al. Identification of a novel coronavirus in patients with severe acute respiratory syndrome. N Engl J Med. 2003;348:1967-1976.
13. Marra MA, Jones SJ, Astell CR, et al. The Genome sequence of the SARS-associated coronavirus. Science. 2003;300:1399-1404.
14. Rota PA, Oberste MS, Monroe SS, et al. Characterization of a novel coronavirus associated with severe acute respiratory syndrome. Science. 2003;300:1394-1399.
15. Woode GN, Reed DE, Runnels PL, et al. Studies with an unclassified virus isolated from diarrheic calves. Vet Microbiol. 1982;7:221-240.
16. Weiss M, Steck F, Horzinek MC. Purification and partial characterization of a new enveloped RNA virus (Berne virus). J Gen Virol. 1983;64(Pt 9):1849-1858.
17. Beards GM, Hall C, Green J, et al. An enveloped virus in stools of children and adults with gastroenteritis that resembles the Breda virus of calves. Lancet. 1984;1:1050-1052.
18. Becker WB, McIntosh K, Dees JH, Chanock RM. Morphogenesis of avian infectious bronchitis virus and a related human virus (strain 229E). J Virol. 1967;1:1019-1027.
19. Gerna G, Battaglia M, Cereda PM, Passarani N. Reactivity of human coronavirus OC43 and neonatal calf diarrhoea coronavirus membrane-associated antigens. J Gen Virol. 1982;60(Pt 2):385-390.
20. Guan Y, Zheng BJ, He YQ, et al. Isolation and characterization of viruses related to the SARS coronavirus from animals in southern China. Science. Available at www.sciencexpress.org. Accessed September 4, 2003.
21. Yeager CL, Ashmun RA, Williams RK, et al. Human aminopeptidase N is a receptor for human coronavirus 229E. Nature. 1992;357:420-422.
22. Williams RK, Jiang GS, Holmes KV. Receptor for mouse hepatitis virus is a member of the carcinoembryonic antigen family of glycoproteins. Proc Natl Acad Sci U S A. 1991;88:5533-5536.
23. Collins AR. Human coronavirus OC43 interacts with major histocompatibility complex class I molecules at the cell surface to establish infection. Immunol Invest. 1994;23(4-5):313-321.
24. Macnaughton MR, Madge MH, Reed SE. Two antigenic groups of human coronaviruses detected by using enzyme-linked immunosorbent assay. Infect Immun. 1981;33:734-737.
25. Schmidt OW. Antigenic characterization of human coronaviruses 229E and OC43 by enzyme-linked immunosorbent assay. J Clin Microbiol. 1984;20:175-180.
26. Bradburne AF, Somerset BA. Coronavirus antibody titres in sera of healthy adults and experimentally infected volunteers. J Hyg (Lond). 1972;70:235-244.
27. Ruan YJ, Wei CL, Ee AL, et al. Comparative full-length genome sequence analysis of 14 SARS coronavirus isolates and common mutations associated with putative origins of infection. Lancet. 2003;361:1779-1785.
28. Mathan M, Mathan VI, Swaminathan SP, Yesudoss S. Pleomorphic virus-like particles in human faeces. Lancet. 1975;1:1068-1069.
29. Baker SJ, Mathan M, Mathan VI, et al. Chronic enterocyte infection with coronavirus. One possible cause of the syndrome of tropical sprue? Dig Dis Sci. 1982;27:1039-1043.
30. Chany C, Moscovici O, Lebon P, Rousset S. Association of coronavirus infection with neonatal necrotizing enterocolitis. Pediatrics. 1982;69:209-214.
31. Vaucher YE, Ray CG, Minnich LL, et al. Pleomorphic, enveloped, virus-like particles associated with gastrointestinal illness in neonates. J Infect Dis. 1982;145:27-36.
32. Maass G, Baumeister HG, Freitag N. [Viruses as causal agents of gastroenteritis in infants and young children (author's translation)]. MMW Munch Med Wochenschr. 1977;119(32-33):1029-1034.
33. Gerna G, Passarani N, Battaglia M, Rondanelli EG. Human enteric coronaviruses: Antigenic relatedness to human coronavirus OC43 and possible etiologic role in viral gastroenteritis. J Infect Dis. 1985;151:796-803.
34. Caul EO, Egglestone SI. Further studies on human enteric coronaviruses. Arch Virol. 1977;54(1-2):107-117.
35. Resta S, Luby JP, Rosenfeld CR, Siegel JD. Isolation and propagation of a human enteric coronavirus. Science. 1985;229:978-981.
36. Weiss M, Horzinek MC. The proposed family Toroviridae: Agents of enteric infections (Brief Review). Arch Virol. 1987;92(1-2):1-15.
37. Duckmanton L, Luan B, Devenish J, et al. Characterization of torovirus from human fecal specimens. Virology. 1997;239:158-168.

38. Beards GM, Brown DW, Green J, Flewett TH. Preliminary characterisation of torovirus-like particles of humans: Comparison with Berne virus of horses and Breda virus of calves. J Med Virol. 1986;20:67-78.
39. Snijder EJ, Horzinek MC. Toroviruses: Replication, evolution and comparison with other members of the coronavirus-like superfamily. J Gen Virol. 1993;74(Pt 11):2305-2316.
40. Cornelissen LA, Wierda CM, van der Meer FJ, et al. Hemagglutinin-esterase, a novel structural protein of torovirus. J Virol. 1997;71:5277-5286.
41. Monto AS. Medical reviews. Coronaviruses. Yale J Biol Med. 1974;47:234-251.
42. Callow KA, Parry HF, Sergeant M, Tyrrell DA. The time course of the immune response to experimental coronavirus infection of man. Epidemiol Infect. 1990;105:435-446.
43. CDC. Updated interim U.S. case definition of severe acute respiratory syndrome (SARS). CDC Website. 2003. Available at www.cdc.gov/ncidod/sars/casedefinition.htm.
44. Severe acute respiratory syndrome—Singapore, 2003. MMWR Morb Mortal Wkly Rep. 2003;52:405-411.
45. Lipsitch M, Cohen T, Cooper B, et al. Transmission dynamics and control of severe acute respiratory syndrome. Science. 2003;300:1966-1970.
46. Riley S, Fraser C, Donnelly CA, et al. Transmission dynamics of the etiological agent of SARS in Hong Kong: Impact of public health interventions. Science. 2003;300:1961-1966.
47. Kern P, Muller G, Schmitz H, et al. Detection of coronavirus-like particles in homosexual men with acquired immunodeficiency and related lymphadenopathy syndrome. Klin Wochenschr. 1985;63:68-72.
48. Schmidt W, Schneider T, Heise W, et al. Stool viruses, coinfections, and diarrhea in HIV-infected patients. Berlin Diarrhea/Wasting Syndrome Study Group. J Acquir Immune Defic Syndr Hum Retrovirol. 1996;13:33-38.
49. Marshall JA, Birch CJ, Williamson HG, et al. Coronavirus-like particles and other agents in the faeces of children in Efate, Vanuatu. J Trop Med Hyg. 1982;85:213-215.
50. Marshall JA, Thompson WL, Gust ID. Coronavirus-like particles in adults in Melbourne, Australia. J Med Virol. 1989;29:238-243.
51. Mortensen ML, Ray CG, Payne CM, et al. Coronaviruslike particles in human gastrointestinal disease. Epidemiologic, clinical, and laboratory observations. Am J Dis Child. 1985;139:928-934.
52. Payne CM, Ray CG, Borduin V, et al. An eight-year study of the viral agents of acute gastroenteritis in humans: Ultrastructural observations and seasonal distribution with a major emphasis on coronavirus-like particles. Diagn Microbiol Infect Dis. 1986;5:39-54.
53. Afzelius BA. Ultrastructure of human nasal epithelium during an episode of coronavirus infection. Virchows Arch. 1994;424:295-300.
54. Tyrrell DA, Cohen S, Schlarb JE. Signs and symptoms in common colds. Epidemiol Infect. 1993;111:143-156.
55. Bradburne AF, Bynoe ML, Tyrrell DA. Effects of a "new" human respiratory virus in volunteers. Br Med J. 1967;3:767-769.
56. Donnelly CA, Ghani AC, Leung GM, et al. Epidemiological determinants of spread of causal agent of severe acute respiratory syndrome in Hong Kong. Lancet. 2003;361:1761-1766.
57. Wong RS, Wu A, To KF, et al. Haematological manifestations in patients with severe acute respiratory syndrome: retrospective analysis. BMJ. 2003;326:1358-1362.
58. Peiris JS, Chu CM, Cheng VC, et al. Clinical progression and viral load in a community outbreak of coronavirus-associated SARS pneumonia: A prospective study. Lancet. 2003;361:1767-1772.
59. Ren Y, Ding HG, Wu QF, et al. [Detection of SARS-CoV RNA in stool samples of SARS patients by nest RT-PCR and its clinical value]. Zhongguo Yi Xue Ke Xue Yuan Xue Bao. 2003;25:368-371.
60. Lee N, Hui D, Wu A, et al. A major outbreak of severe acute respiratory syndrome in Hong Kong. N Engl J Med. 2003;348:1986-1994.
61. Nicholls JM, Poon LL, Lee KC, et al. Lung pathology of fatal severe acute respiratory syndrome. Lancet. 2003;361:1773-1778.
62. Ding Y, Wang H, Shen H, et al. The clinical pathology of severe acute respiratory syndrome (SARS): A report from China. J Pathol. 2003;200:282-289.
63. Kuiken T, Fouchier RA, Schutten M, et al. Newly discovered coronavirus as the primary cause of severe acute respiratory syndrome. Lancet. 2003;362:263-270.
64. Bradburne AF. Antigenic relationships amongst coronaviruses. Arch Gesamte Virusforsch. 1970;31:352-364.
65. Linden M, Greiff L, Andersson M, et al. Nasal cytokines in common cold and allergic rhinitis. Clin Exp Allergy. 1995;25:166-172.
66. Hendley JO, Fishburne HB, Gwaltney JM. Coronavirus infections in working adults. Eight-year study with 229 E and OC 43. Am Rev Respir Dis. 1972;105:805-811.
67. McIntosh K, Chao RK, Krause HE, et al. Coronavirus infection in acute lower respiratory tract disease of infants. J Infect Dis. 1974;130:502-507.
68. McIntosh K, Kapikian AZ, Turner HC, et al. Seroepidemiologic studies of coronavirus infection in adults and children. Am J Epidemiol. 1970;91:585-592.
69. McIntosh K, McQuillin J, Reed SE, Gardner PS. Diagnosis of human coronavirus infection by immunofluorescence: Method and application to respiratory disease in hospitalized children. J Med Virol. 1978;2:341-346.
70. Wenzel RP, Hendley JO, Davies JA, Gwaltney JM. Coronavirus infections in military recruits. Three-year study with coronavirus strains OC43 and 229E. Am Rev Respir Dis. 1974;109:621-624.
71. McIntosh K, Ellis EF, Hoffman LS, et al. Association of viral and bacterial respiratory infection with exacerbations of wheezing in young asthmatic children. Chest. 1973;63(suppl):43S.
72. Mertsola J, Ziegler T, Ruuskanen O, et al. Recurrent wheezy bronchitis and viral respiratory infections. Arch Dis Child. 1991;66:124-129.
73. Gill EP, Dominguez EA, Greenberg SB, et al. Development and application of an enzyme immunoassay for coronavirus OC43 antibody in acute respiratory illness. J Clin Microbiol. 1994;32:2372-2376.
74. Gump DW, Phillips CA, Forsyth BR, et al. Role of infection in chronic bronchitis. Am Rev Respir Dis. 1976;113:465-474.
75. Buscho RO, Saxtan D, Shultz PS, et al. Infections with viruses and *Mycoplasma pneumoniae* during exacerbations of chronic bronchitis. J Infect Dis. 1978;137:377-383.
76. Smith CB, Golden CA, Kanner RE, Renzetti AD. Association of viral and *Mycoplasma pneumoniae* infections with acute respiratory illness in patients with chronic obstructive pulmonary diseases. Am Rev Respir Dis. 1980;121:225-232.
77. Nicholson KG, Kent J, Ireland DC. Respiratory viruses and exacerbations of asthma in adults. BMJ. 1993;307:982-986.
78. Wiselka MJ, Kent J, Cookson JB, Nicholson KG. Impact of respiratory virus infection in patients with chronic chest disease. Epidemiol Infect. 1993;111:337-346.
79. Falsey AR, McCann RM, Hall WJ, et al. The "common cold" in frail older persons: Impact of rhinovirus and coronavirus in a senior daycare center. J Am Geriatr Soc. 1997;45:706-711.
80. El-Sahly HM, Atmar RL, Glezen WP, Greenberg SB. Spectrum of clinical illness in hospitalized patients with "common cold" virus infections. Clin Infect Dis. 2000;31:96-100.
81. Falsey AR, Walsh EE, Hayden FG. Rhinovirus and coronavirus infection-associated hospitalizations among older adults. J Infect Dis. 2002;185:1338-1341.
82. Walsh EE, Falsey AR, Hennessey PA. Respiratory syncytial and other virus infections in persons with chronic cardiopulmonary disease. Am J Respir Crit Care Med. 1999;160:791-795.
83. Vabret A, Mourez T, Gouarin S, et al. An outbreak of coronavirus OC43 respiratory infection in Normandy, France. Clin Infect Dis. 2003;36:985-989.
84. Booth CM, Matukas LM, Tomlinson GA, et al. Clinical features and short-term outcomes of 144 patients with SARS in the greater Toronto area. JAMA. 2003;289:2801-2809.
85. Lew TW, Kwek TK, Tai D, et al. Acute respiratory distress syndrome in critically ill patients with severe acute respiratory syndrome. JAMA. 2003;290:374-380.
86. Wong KT, Antonio GE, Hui DS, et al. Severe acute respiratory syndrome: Radiographic appearances and pattern of progression in 138 patients. Radiology. 2003;228:401-406.
87. Antonio GE, Wong KT, Hui DS, et al. Imaging of severe acute respiratory syndrome in Hong Kong. AJR Am J Roentgenol. 2003;181:11-17.
88. Muller NL, Ooi GC, Khong PL, Nicolaou S. Severe acute respiratory syndrome: radiographic and CT findings. AJR Am J Roentgenol. 2003;181:3-8.
89. Wong KT, Antonio GE, Hui DS, et al. Thin-section CT of severe acute respiratory syndrome: Evaluation of 73 patients exposed to or with the disease. Radiology. 2003;228:395-400.
90. Fowler RA, Lapinsky SE, Hallett D, et al. Critically ill patients with severe acute respiratory syndrome. JAMA. 2003;290:367-373.
91. Chiu WK, Cheung PC, Ng KL, et al. Severe acute respiratory syndrome in children: Experience in a regional hospital in Hong Kong. Pediatr Crit Care Med. 2003;4:279-283.
92. Hon KL, Leung CW, Cheng WT, et al. Clinical presentations and outcome of severe acute respiratory syndrome in children. Lancet. 2003;361:1701-1703.
93. Wong SF, Chow KM, de Swiet M. Severe acute respiratory syndrome and pregnancy. Br J Obstet Gynecol. 2003;110:641-642.
94. Jamieson FB, Wang EE, Bain C, et al. Human torovirus: A new nosocomial gastrointestinal pathogen. J Infect Dis. 1998;178:1263-1269.
95. Koopmans MP, Goosen ES, Lima AA, et al. Association of toroviruses with acute and persistent diarrhea in children. Pediatr Infect Dis J. 1997;16:504-507.
96. Nagashima K, Wege H, Meyermann R, ter Meulen V. Corona virus induced subacute demyelinating encephalomyelitis in rats: A morphological analysis. Acta Neuropathol (Berl). 1978;44:63-70.
97. Burks JS, DeVald BL, Jankovsky LD, Gerdes JC. Two coronaviruses isolated from central nervous system tissue of two multiple sclerosis patients. Science. 1980;209:933-934.
98. Murray RS, Brown B, Brian D, Cabirac GF. Detection of coronavirus RNA and antigen in multiple sclerosis brain. Ann Neurol. 1992;31:525-533.
99. Stewart JN, Mounir S, Talbot PJ. Human coronavirus gene expression in the brains of multiple sclerosis patients. Virology. 1992;191:502-505.
100. Talbot PJ, Paquette JS, Ciurli C, et al. Myelin basic protein and human coronavirus 229E cross-reactive T cells in multiple sclerosis. Ann Neurol. 1996;39:233-240.
101. Lina B, Valette M, Foray S, et al. Surveillance of community-acquired viral infections due to respiratory viruses in Rhone-Alpes (France) during winter 1994 to 1995. J Clin Microbiol. 1996;34:3007-3011.
102. Myint S, Johnston S, Sanderson G, Simpson H. Evaluation of nested polymerase chain reaction methods for the detection of human coronaviruses 229E and OC43. Mol Cell Probes. 1994;8:357-364.
103. Pitkaranta A, Jero J, Arruda E, et al. Polymerase chain reaction-based detection of rhinovirus, respiratory syncytial virus, and coronavirus in otitis media with effusion. J Pediatr. 1998;133:390-394.
104. Kraaijeveld CA, Reed SE, Macnaughton MR. Enzyme-linked immunosorbent assay for detection of antibody in volunteers experimentally infected with human coronavirus strain 229 E. J Clin Microbiol. 1980;12:493-497.
105. So LK, Lau AC, Yam LY, et al. Development of a standard treatment protocol for severe acute respiratory syndrome. Lancet. 2003;361:1615-1617.

CHAPTER 153

Parainfluenza Viruses

PETER F. WRIGHT

HISTORY

The five parainfluenza viruses[1-3] were first isolated from humans among the flurry of new viruses identified in the late 1950s. Initially described in association with laryngotracheobronchitis (croup) in hospitalized children, parainfluenza viruses were identified as viruses that had the property of hemadsorption of red blood cells. Subsequently, their important role in human respiratory disease in childhood and more recently in immunocompromised patients was well described. In the 1960s, mucosal immunoglobulin a (IgA) antibody was shown to have a protective role against parainfluenza viruses; they remain the viruses for which mucosal immune protection has been most clearly demonstrated. Advances in reverse genetics have led to characterization of the role of individual parainfluenza viral proteins and the rational design of vaccine candidates for prevention of human respiratory disease caused by these viruses.[4,5]

DESCRIPTION OF VIRUSES

Classification and Structure

Human parainfluenza viruses belong to the Paramyxoviridae family[6,7] and are members of the genera *Respirovirus* (parainfluenza types 1 and 3) and *Rubulavirus* (parainfluenza types 2, 4A, and 4B). They have a lipid bilayer envelope derived from the host cell, are roughly spherical with a diameter of 150 to 200 nm, have glycoprotein spikes extending from the envelope surface, and have a single-stranded, non-segmented, negative-sense ribonucleic acid (RNA) genome. The human pathogens included in this family are the five parainfluenza viruses (designated parainfluenza types 1, 2, 3, 4A, and 4B), mumps, measles, Hendra and Nipah viruses (Chapter 158),[8-10] human metapneumovirus (Chapter 156),[11] and respiratory syncytial virus (Chapter 155). Significant animal pathogens within the family include Sendai virus, simian virus type 5, Newcastle disease virus, canine distemper virus, and rinderpest.

Replication

Parainfluenza viruses attach to sialic acid–containing cellular molecules via the hemagglutinin-neuraminidase (HN) protein.[6] Sialic acid–expressing cells are widespread, and thus the specificity of attachment does not explain the respiratory tract tropism of parainfluenza viruses. The HN protein is coupled with the activated fusion (F) protein to allow cell entry of the virus.[12,13] Activation of the F protein is by proteolytic cleavage, which is mediated by cellular serine proteases. In the case of Sendai virus, F-protein cleavage may occur by a protease that is unique to a subset of respiratory cells called Clara cells.[14] The unique localization of the protease may be a factor in localization of the replication of parainfluenza viruses to the respiratory tract. Differences in tropism are striking between closely related viruses, as, for example, the respiratory localization of parainfluenza viruses contrasted to the preference of mumps for acinar tissue. Parainfluenza viruses do not appear to enter or unfold in the acid environment of the endosome, as occurs with influenza viruses. The nucleocapsid complex consists of the viral RNA and three internal proteins—nucleocapsid protein (NP), polymerase protein (L), and phosphorylated nucleocapsid–associated protein (P)—that initiate a primary transcription event to generate the messenger RNA from which viral proteins are translated. In addition, a full-length antigenome with positive-sense RNA is formed from which the genome is replicated. Diversity in expression of the P-gene–coded products leads to additional regulatory proteins whose functions are not fully defined, although some may inhibit the interferon pathway.[15] Still within the cytoplasm, virion assembly takes place in several steps. The new NP protein assembles with the genomic RNA to form a helical structure. The P- and L-protein complexes then join to form the nucleocapsid. After being synthesized in the endoplasmic reticulum and traveling a secretory pathway in the cell, the envelope proteins assemble at the cell surface with a polarity that favors the apical surface of the cell. The other major structural protein, matrix protein, plays a role in virus assembly and release from the cell surface by budding. The neuraminidase component of the HN protein may aid in release from the cell and prevention of virus aggregation by cleaving sialic acid residues to which the virus would otherwise reattach. The entire process is not efficient in that many incomplete noninfectious particles are formed that can interfere with the yield of infectious virus.

PATHOGENESIS

Tropism

Parainfluenza viruses cause acute respiratory infections. The peak of illness is associated with peak virus shedding based on observations in children infected with a partially attenuated parainfluenza type 3 vaccine candidate.[16] Parainfluenza viruses replicate exclusively in cells of the respiratory epithelial layer.[7] The epithelial layer is a complex mixture of cell types that vary as one traverses to different depths of the upper and lower respiratory tracts. Clinically, parainfluenza viruses most typically cause illness in the large airways of the lower respiratory tract manifested as laryngotracheobronchitis, or croup.[17] The reasons for this particular localization are not known. The best evidence is that parainfluenza viruses replicate in the ciliated epithelial cells that line much of the upper and lower respiratory tracts.[18,19] Not only do they grow in these superficial cells, but they are also released by budding only from the apical surface of the cell back into the mucin layer above the epithelium.[20]

As with influenza viruses, a surface protein of parainfluenza viruses, the fusion or F protein, is cleaved by a serine protease, a process required for replication of the virus. With Sendai virus, a murine virus closely related to parainfluenza virus type 1, mutations in the F protein that allow more ready cleavage lead to a mutant that will replicate throughout the body.[21] Conversely, mutants of Sendai virus that are no longer cleaved by trypsin are highly attenuated.[22] In rodent models, a protease produced by the Clara cells of the respiratory tract has been identified that mediates this cleavage in Sendai and influenza viruses.[14,23] Clara cells are secretory cells that release this protease into the respiratory tract, where it presumably acts in a paracrine fashion to cleave virus in the extracellular environment or in the process of budding from cells.[24] Early in Sendai infection, Clara cells secrete an abundance of tryptase Clara. The enzyme is found overlying the adjoining ciliated cells in which parainfluenza is replicating.[25] The human counterpart of this protein has not been identified, but serine protease activity is demonstrable in human secretions.[26]

Some of the parainfluenza viruses cause cell fusion and syncytia formation. The precise role of syncytia formation in disease is not known. It could potentially allow cell-to-cell spread without virus being exposed to neutralizing antibody in the extracellular environment.

Immune Response

Serum neutralizing antibodies directed toward epitopes on the HN and F surface proteins of parainfluenza virus are found after infection.[7,27-29] Monoclonal antibodies are preferentially formed to epitopes on the HN virus.[30] In experimental animals, antibodies raised to an HN vaccinia construct were considerably more protective than antibodies to protein F.[31] After several infections, antibodies may develop that cross-neutralize different parainfluenza strains. Cytotoxic T-cell epitopes are primarily found on the internal nucleoprotein.[32]

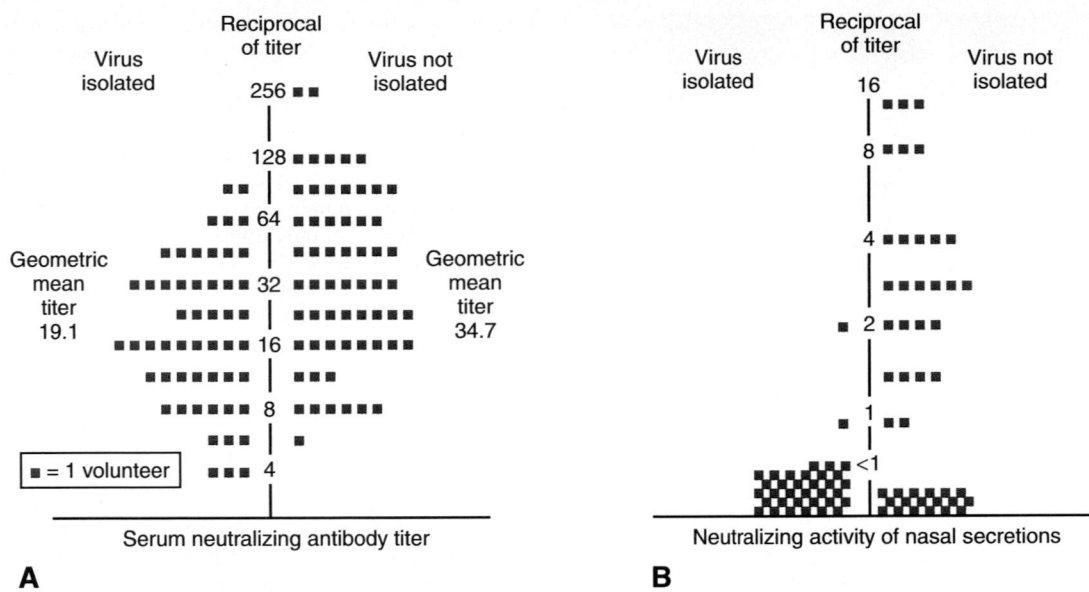

FIGURE 153-1. **A,** Serum neutralizing antibody titer before challenge with parainfluenza type 1 virus. **B,** Neutralizing activity of nasal secretions before challenge with parainfluenza type 1 virus. *(From Smith CB, Purcell RH, Bellanti JA, et al. Protective effect of antibody to parainfluenza type 1 virus. N Engl J Med. 1966:275:1145-1152. Copyright © 1996 Massachusetts Medical Society. All rights reserved.)*

In spite of these effective immune targets, children and adults are repeatedly infected with parainfluenza viruses over the course of a lifetime. Reinfection is more likely to solely involve the upper respiratory tract, with sparing of the lower respiratory tract after the first or second exposure in immunocompetent individuals.[33,34] However, symptomatic disease with lower respiratory tract involvement can be seen after reinfection with parainfluenza type 3.[35]

Antigenic variation occurs, but it is not progressive[36]; thus reinfection probably reflects a waning of immunity over time rather than antigenic drift of the virus.[37] This pattern is in obvious contrast to influenza virus, in which progressive antigenic drift is one of the major ways that the virus escapes immune surveillance.

Immunity to parainfluenza viruses, no matter how poorly sustained, can be demonstrated. Prior infection in animal models blocks virus recovery on subsequent challenge. Experimental infection of adults with wild-type viruses is modulated by the level of immunity,[38] and it is more difficult to infect seropositive children with live-attenuated vaccines than readily infect immunologically naive children.[39] In both adults and children, recovery of virus is dramatically lowered by recent past exposure to the virus.

The most important component of resistance appears to be mucosal immunity. In animal models greater protection is afforded by intranasal than by systemic administration of parainfluenza type 3 glycoproteins.[40] In addition, passive IgA antibody delivered into the respiratory tract of mice provides greater protection than does IgG.[41] In adults after an experimental parainfluenza type 1 challenge, reisolation of virus was inversely correlated with the detection of local neutralizing antibody in secretions and not with serum antibody (Fig. 153-1).[42] In children, prior natural infection blocks the replication of live-attenuated, intranasally administered virus vaccines, which replicate freely in naive children, including children in the first 6 months of life with passively acquired maternal serum antibody. However, in children the mechanisms of protection against parainfluenza viruses are less well defined than in adults. IgA antibody has the property of being transcytosed across epithelial cells from the basolateral surface to release at the apical surface into the respiratory tract.[43] It has been proposed that antibody and virus may co-localize within cells and result in intracellular inhibition of virus assembly and release.[44] Evidence that this mechanism may occur with IgA monoclonal antibodies to Sendai virus has been published.[45]

In addition to prevention of reinfection, immunity is involved in terminating primary infection. In animal models the role of CD8+ T cells is critical in virus clearance. Lymphoid cells, some of which are virus specific and some of which are bystanders, accumulate in the regional peribronchial lymph nodes during acute infection. The bystander lymphoid cells presumably contribute to the establishment of immunologic memory. The cells active in cytotoxic destruction of virally infected cells appear to accumulate in the airways and can be found in bronchoalveolar lavage fluid.[46] The severity of disease in individuals with T-cell deficits (see "Clinical Manifestations") suggests the importance of T-cell immunity in clearance of infection. It has been shown that parainfluenza virus type 3 can downregulate granzyme B, one of the perforins that mediates cytotoxicity, thus suggesting a mechanism for immune modulation by parainfluenza viruses.[47]

EPIDEMIOLOGY

A number of studies have examined the impact of respiratory viral infections in pediatric practice.[35,48,49] Parainfluenza type 3 is the most frequently recovered of the parainfluenza virus types in longitudinal studies of respiratory illness in children. Roughly half as many parainfluenza type 1 isolates are found as parainfluenza type 3 isolates and one quarter as many isolates of parainfluenza type 2 as type 3 (Table 153-1).[35] Parainfluenza viruses vary in their seasonal epidemiology by type. Parainfluenza type 3 virus is endemic, with isolation throughout the year; however, a distinct peak is seen in the spring months of April and May.[3,49] Parainfluenza virus types 1 and 2 cause annual fall epidemics of disease and often alternate in years, so an individual type may be seen only every 2 years. Parainfluenza virus types 4A and 4B are isolated so seldom that their seasonality is not well described.[50,51]

In the unique environment of overwintering on the South Pole where 20 people were isolated for 6 months, parainfluenza virus types 1 and 3 were repeatedly isolated through the quarantine period, which suggests that persistent or repeated infection was spread in this small cohort.[52] In tissue culture cells persistent parainfluenza virus type 3 infection can also be established.[53]

The early age at which parainfluenza type 3 virus is first recovered is another trait that distinguishes it from types 1 and 2. Parainfluenza

TABLE 153-1 Diagnoses, Signs, and Symptoms in Patients from Whom Parainfluenza Viruses Were Isolated

Number of Isolates	Type				
	1 (n = 77)	2 (n = 33)	3 (n = 157)	Other (n = 19)	P*
Diagnosis					
Acute otitis	38†	30	52	32	0.03
Croup	16	6	5	21	0.01
Bronchiolitis	1	9	6	0	
Signs and Symptoms					
Cough	73	67	81	77	
Hoarseness	28	18	11	39	.001
Rales/rhonchi	6	15	15	11	
Wheezing	9	12	4	5	
Temperature >38° C	33	16	38	6	0.004
Irritability	47	30	54	72	0.02

*Fisher's exact test for null hypothesis that all types are alike.
†Values are percentages of patients with the finding.
Data from Reed G, Jewett PH, Thompson J, et al. Epidemiology and clinical impact of parainfluenza virus infections in otherwise healthy infants and young children <5 years old. J Infect Dis. 1997;175:807-813

type 3 virus, like respiratory syncytial virus, is commonly seen in the first 6 months of life,[54] an age at which most viral infections are prevented or attenuated by maternal antibody. By age 5, almost all children have experienced infection with all three parainfluenza types. The impact of parainfluenza virus infections is best reflected by the peaks of hospitalization for croup that occur during biannual type 1 epidemics, which have been estimated to cause 18,000 hospitalizations nationwide.[55] In all croup cases from which virus can be isolated, about 60% of the isolates are parainfluenza.[35,49,56] The cost of a typical parainfluenza type 1 and 2 fall epidemic was estimated at $190 million for emergency department use and hospitalization.[57] Parainfluenza type 3 virus is more endemic and less associated with the distinctive clinical finding of croup, but it causes more hospitalizations for lower respiratory tract illness than does either parainfluenza type 1 or 2. Although the best studies are now 35 years old, the role of parainfluenza viruses as the second leading contributor to pediatric hospitalization for respiratory disease, after respiratory syncytial virus, is unlikely to have changed.[58] One report described 10 hospitalizations associated with isolation of parainfluenza virus type 4.[59] Nosocomial spread of parainfluenza viruses among hospitalized patients has been shown to occur.[60,61]

In adults, parainfluenza viruses have been implicated in about 10% of acute respiratory illnesses.[62] Disease is also seen in the elderly, but without the impact of respiratory syncytial virus or influenza.[63] Definition of the role of parainfluenza viruses in the elderly may require sensitive assays such as polymerase chain reaction[64] to detect the low-level shedding that typically accompanies viral infections in the elderly. Studies to date implicate parainfluenza viruses in less than 5% of acute respiratory infections in the elderly.[65,66] Nevertheless, a nursing home outbreak has been described.[67]

CLINICAL MANIFESTATIONS

Parainfluenza viruses cause a spectrum of respiratory illnesses.[68] In healthy children the majority of illnesses are upper respiratory, although 30% to 50% are associated with otitis media[69] (see Table 153-1). In a 20-year epidemiologic study at Vanderbilt University, 15% of parainfluenza isolates were associated with lower respiratory tract disease.[35] Lower respiratory tract disease was manifested as either bronchiolitis, with types 2 and 3, or croup, with type 1.[35] Croup is characterized by a

barking cough, a hoarse voice, and stridor. Radiographically, croup is distinguished by the "steeple sign" of progressive subglottic narrowing. As noted, among the virus isolates obtained from cases of croup, about 60% are parainfluenza. In some children, repeated episodes of "spasmodic" croup may occur. It is unclear whether these episodes are separate illnesses. In immunocompetent adults, clinical manifestations are primarily those of an upper respiratory tract infection.

Parainfluenza infections cause severe disease in both adult and pediatric bone marrow and lung transplant recipients.[70-73] In bone marrow transplant recipients at the University of Texas M. D. Anderson Hospital, 56% of 61 parainfluenza isolates were associated with uncomplicated upper respiratory illness; however, pneumonia developed in the remaining patients, with a mortality of 37%.[73] Similar data were reported from the University of Minnesota, which documented 27 parainfluenza infections among 1,253 bone marrow transplant recipients, 6 of which were fatal.[70] In 4 cases the virus could be isolated only with bronchoalveolar lavage. Ten percent of lung transplant patients from the same institution suffered parainfluenza infections.[71] Other immunosuppressed patients can have prolonged shedding of parainfluenza viruses, particularly parainfluenza type 3.[74] Fatal pneumonias have been described in children with severe combined immunodeficiency syndrome.[75] Rarely, parainfluenza virus types 2 and 3 have been isolated from cerebrospinal fluid in association with aseptic meningitis.[76,77]

Parainfluenza viruses have not been strongly associated with asthma in adults.[78] However, in children an IgE-mediated pathway leading to recurrent wheezing after parainfluenza infection has been proposed.[79]

DIAGNOSIS

As with many viruses, three approaches to the diagnosis of parainfluenza virus infection are currently used: viral culture, detection of viral antigen or nucleic acid, and serologic analysis. The gold standard remains the isolation of virus in tissue culture. Parainfluenza viruses are rarely isolated from healthy children, so the finding of a parainfluenza virus with an acute respiratory illness is strong proof of an association. The sensitivity of the method is greatest in primary infection, where 4 to 5 $\log_{10}$ of virus can be recovered per milliliter of nasal secretions for up to 10 days after the onset of illness.[80] In adults and older children undergoing repeated infections, the height and duration of virus shedding are much lower. In suspected lower respiratory tract disease in an immunocompromised host or transplant recipient, direct sampling of the lower respiratory tract by lung biopsy or lavage may be necessary to recover the agent.

Sensitive cell lines for parainfluenza virus include primary rhesus or cynomolgus monkey kidney cells and a monkey kidney line, LLC-MK2.[81] After primary isolation and identification by hemadsorption, the putative parainfluenza virus must be typed via immunofluorescence or hemadsorption inhibition. With parainfluenza type 2, hemadsorption cannot be relied on to identify all isolates, and immunofluorescence must be used to detect growth.[82] Critical to the success of isolating parainfluenza viruses is the way in which the specimen is collected (optimally by nasal wash or nasal aspiration), refrigerated (the specimen must be kept at 4° C), and transported (promptly to the laboratory). Rapid diagnosis does not have the sensitivity of tissue culture and entails direct immunofluorescence of exfoliated cells and enzyme-linked immunosorbent assay (ELISA) capture techniques. No commercial ELISA kits are currently available. Polymerase chain reaction amplification has been described for parainfluenza type 3 virus[83] and will distinguish type 3 from types 1 and 2 in a single multiplex assay.[61,84] Serologic tests can be used to track the age-related acquisition of infection in infancy, and comparison of antibody titers in closely timed paired sera during and after an illness is a moderately sensitive and specific, although slow way of making a diagnosis. An acute serum specimen should be obtained within 4 days of the onset of illness and a convalescent serum specimen within 2 weeks of the illness.

THERAPY

The effectiveness of specific antivirals for parainfluenza virus infection has not been established. The use of ribavirin as an aerosolized or intravenous preparation has been reported after heart and bone marrow transplantation in anecdotal cases,[85,86] but controlled studies are lacking. Aerosolized aprotinin, a protease inhibitor, reduced the mortality associated with Sendai virus infection in mice from 90% in the untreated group to 10% in the aprotinin-treated group.[87] Inhibition of tryptase Clara by surfactant and other airway protease inhibitors is another theoretical antiviral approach.[88,89] A similar effect was seen with an antibody to tryptase Clara.

In children, the weight of opinion is that aerosolized steroids have a role to play in the management of croup as a clinical illness.[90-92] In a recent study,[93] nebulized budesonide was compared with intramuscular dexamethasone and placebo in moderately severe croup in 144 children seen in the emergency department. All received racemic epinephrine and cool mist. Viral cultures were done in 133 of the patients, with parainfluenza viruses recovered from 46 of the children, 29 of whom had parainfluenza type 1. Only seven viruses other than parainfluenza were identified. Seventy-one percent of the placebo group required hospitalization versus 38% in the budesonide group and 23% in the dexamethasone group. The results in each group were significantly different from each other, and systemic steroids would seem to be the current treatment of choice. Nebulized epinephrine provides short-term relief, but return to the baseline obstruction occurs within 2 hours.[94] Its use in combination with either oral or intramuscular dexamethasone seems indicated. The value of cool mist has not been demonstrated in small controlled trials, but the clinical impression is one of improvement of children in the shower or during a ride to the hospital with exposure to cool air.[95]

PREVENTION

An inactivated whole-virus trivalent parainfluenza vaccine was explored in the late 1960s. Although it was immunogenic, it was not protective.[96] This vaccine was evaluated in parallel with an inactivated respiratory syncytial virus (RSV) vaccine that resulted in enhanced illness on natural reexposure to RSV. Because the trivalent parainfluenza vaccine did not enhance illness, development of inactivated and subunit vaccines has continued. Several subunit vaccines have been developed,[97,98] but none have entered clinical testing.

Two live-attenuated, intranasally administered parainfluenza type 3 vaccines are in development.[99] One is derived from a bovine parainfluenza type 3 virus.[100] This vaccine protects against a challenge with human parainfluenza type 3 virus in chimpanzees.[101] The bovine strain has been evaluated in phase I trials in adults, children, and infants.[101-103] It appears to be safe and immunogenic and is undergoing commercial development. In parallel, a cold-adapted parainfluenza type 3 virus vaccine was attenuated by multiple passages in tissue culture.[104] At passage 12, the virus was still insufficiently attenuated in young children.[105] After 45 passages in tissue culture cells, it was evaluated for protection in a chimpanzee challenge model[106] and subsequently in stepwise studies in young children.[107] The safety and immunogenicity profile of the cold-passaged virus are comparable to that of the bovine strain,[39] and it is undergoing further clinical evaluation. It has recently safely been given to children in the first months of life.[108] The potential for using attenuated parainfluenza type 3 strains to generate parainfluenza type 1 and 2 vaccines on the same genetic background as the type 3 strains is now being explored.[109] Critical questions that must still be answered are whether these vaccines can enable infants to mount an immune response, whether interference between strains occurs, and

what degree of protection or amelioration of illness is provided by such vaccine approaches.

REFERENCES

1. Chanock RM. Association of a new type of cytopathogenic myxovirus with infantile croup. J Exp Med. 1956;104:555-576.
2. Chanock RM, Parrott RH, Cook K, et al. Newly recognized myxovirus in children with respiratory diseases. N Engl J Med. 1958;258:207-213.
3. Andrews CH, Bang FB, Chanock RM, et al. Parainfluenza viruses 1, 2, and 3: Suggested names for recently described myxoviruses. Virology. 1959;8:129-130.
4. Durbin AP, Siew JW, Murphy BR, et al. Minimum protein requirements for transcription and RNA replication of a minigenome of human parainfluenza virus type 3 and evaluation of the rule of six. Virology. 1997;234:74-83.
5. Durbin AP, Hall SL, Siew JW, et al. Recovery of infectious human parainfluenza virus type 3 from cDNA. Virology. 1997;235:323-332.
6. Lamb RA, Kolakofsky D. Paramyxoviridae: The viruses and their replication. In: Fields BN, Knipe DM, Howley PM, eds. Virology. Philadelphia: Lippincott-Raven; 1996:1177-1204.
7. Collins PL, Chanock RM, McIntosh K. Parainfluenza viruses. In: Fields BN, Knipe DM, Howley PM, eds. Virology. Philadelphia: Lippincott-Raven; 1990:1205-1241.
8. Wang LF, Michelski WP, Yu M, et al. A novel P/V/C gene in the new member of the member of the Paramyxoviridae family, which causes lethal infection in humans, horses, and other animals. J Virol. 1998;72:1482-1490.
9. Centers for Disease Control and Prevention. Outbreak of Hendra-like virus—Malaysia and Singapore, 1998-1999. MMWR Morb Mortal Wkly Rep. 1999;48: 265-269.
10. Wong KT, Shieh WJ, Zaki SR, Tan CT. Nipah virus infection; an emerging paramyxoviral zoonosis. Springer Semin Immunopathol. 2002;24:215-228.
11. van den Hoogen BG, de Jong JC, Groen J, et al. A newly discovered human pneumovirus isolated from young children with respiratory tract disease. Nature Med. 2001;7:719-724.
12. Yao Q, Hu X, Compans RW. Association of the parainfluenza virus fusion and hemagglutinin-neuraminidase glycoproteins on cell surfaces. J Virol. 1997;71:650-656.
13. Lamb RA. Paramyxovirus fusion: A hypothesis for changes. Virology. 1993;197; 1-11.
14. He B, Paterson RG, Stock N, et al. Recovery of paramyxovirus simian virus 5 with a V protein lacking the conserved cysteine-rich domain: The multifunctional V protein blocks both interferon beta induction and interferon signaling. Virology. 2002;303:15-32.
15. Tashiro M, Yokogoshi Y, Tobita K, et al. Tryptase Clara, an activating protease for Sendai virus in rat lungs, is involved in pneumopathogenicity. J Virol. 1992;66:7211-7216.
16. Wright PF. Parainfluenza viruses 342-50. In: Belshe RB, ed. Textbook of Human Virology. 2nd ed. St. Louis: Mosby–Year Book; 1991.
17. Parrott RH, Vargosko AJ, Kim HW, et al. Clinical features of infection with hemadsorption viruses. N Engl J Med. 1959;260:731-738.
18. Heath RB. The pathogenesis of respiratory viral infection. Postgrad Med J. 1979;55:122-127.
19. Massion PP, Funari P, Ikeda S, et al. Parainfluenza (Sendai) virus infects ciliated cells and secretory cells but not basal cells of rat tracheal epithelium. Am J Respir Cell Mol Biol. 1993;9:361-370.
20. Blau DM, Compans RW. Polarization of viral entry and release in epithelial cells. Semin Virol. 1996;7:245-253.
21. Tashiro M, Yokogoshi M, Tobita K, et al. Organ tropism of Sendai virus in mice; proteolytic activation of the fusion glycoprotein in mouse organs and budding site at the bronchial epithelium. J Virol. 1990;64:3627-3634.
22. Tashiro M, Seto JT, Choosakul S, et al. Changes in specific cleavability of the Sendai virus fusion protein: Implications for pathogenicity in mice. J Virol. 1992;73:1575-1579.
23. Kido H, Yokogoshi Y, Sakai K, et al. Isolation and characterization of a novel trypsin-like protease found in rat bronchial Clara cells. J Biol Chem. 1992;267:13573-13579.
24. Sakai K, Kawaguchi Y, Kishino Y, et al. Electron immunohistochemical localization in rat bronchiolar epithelial cells of tryptase Clara, which determines the pneumotropism and pathogenes of Sendai virus and influenza virus. J Histochem Cytochem. 1993;41:89-93.
25. Sakai K, Kohri T, Tashiro M, et al. Sendai virus infection changes the subcellular localization of tryptase Clara in rat bronchiolar epithelial cells. J Eur Respir. 1994;7:686-692.
26. Morel-Barbey CL, Oeltmann TN, Edwards KM, et al. Role of respiratory tract protease in infectivity of influenza virus. J Infect Dis. 1987;155;667-672.
27. Kasel JA, Frank AL, Keitel WA, et al. Acquisition of serum antibodies to specific viral glycoproteins of parainfluenza virus 3 in children. J Virol. 1984;52:828-832.
28. Ray R, Glaze BJ, Compans RW. Role of individual glycoproteins of human parainfluenza virus type 3 in the induction of a protective immune response. J Virol. 1988;62:783-787.
29. Spriggs MK, Collins PL, Tierney E, et al. Immunization with vaccinia virus recombinates that express the surface glycoproteins of human parainfluenza virus type 3 (PIV3) protects patas monkeys against PIV3 infection. J Virol. 1988;62:1293-1296.
30. Cole GA, Katz JM, Hogg TL, et al. Analysis of the primary T-cell response to Sendai virus infection in C57BL/6 mice: CD4+ T-cell recognition is directed predominantly to the hemagglutinin-neuraminidase glycoprotein. J Virol. 1994; 68:6863-6870.
31. Spriggs MK, Murphy BR, Prince GA, et al. Expression of the F and HN glycoproteins of human parainfluenza virus type 3 by recombinant vaccinia viruses: Contribution of the individual proteins to host immunity. J Virol. 1987;61:3416-3423.

32. Al-ahdal MN, Nakamura L, Flanagan TD. Cytotoxic T-lymphocyte reactivity with individual Sendai virus glycoproteins. J Virol. 1985;54:53-57.
33. Welliver R, Wong DT, Choi TS, et al. Natural history of parainfluenza virus infection in childhood. J Pediatr. 1982;101:180-187.
34. Glezen WP, Frank AL, Taber LH, et al. Parainfluenza virus type 3: Seasonality and risk of infection and reinfection in young children. J Infect Dis. 1984;150:851-857.
35. Reed G, Jewett PH, Thompson J, et al. Epidemiology and clinical impact of parainfluenza virus infections in otherwise healthy infants and young children <5 years old. J Infect Dis. 1997;175:807-813.
36. Hetherington SV, Watson AS, Scroggs RA, et al. Human parainfluenza virus type 1 evolution combines cocirculation of strains and development of geographically restricted lineages. J Infect Dis. 1994;169:248-252.
37. van Wyke Coelingh KL, Winter C, Murphy BR. Antigentic variation in the hemagglutinin-neuraminidase protein of human parainfluenza type 3 virus. Virology. 1985;143:569-582.
38. Kapikian AZ, Chanock RM, Bethseda MD, et al. Inoculation of human volunteers with parainfluenza virus type 3. JAMA. 1961;178:537-541.
39. Karron RA, Wright PF, Newman FK, et al. A live human parainfluenza type 3 virus is attenuated and immunogenic in healthy infants and children. J Infect Dis. 1995;172:1445-1450.
40. Ray R, Glaze BJ, Moldoveanu Z, et al. Intranasal immunization of hampsters with envelope glycoproteins of human parainfluenza virus type 3. J Infect Dis. 1988; 157:648-654.
41. Manzanec MB, Lamm ME, Lyn D, et al. Comparison of IgA versus IgG monoclonal antibodies for passive immunization of the murine respiratory tract. Virus Res. 1992;23:1-12.
42. Smith CB, Purcell RH, Bellanti JA, et al. Protective effect of antibody to parainfluenza type 1 virus. N Engl J Med. 1966;275:1145-1152.
43. Mazanec MB, Coudret CL, Fletcher DR. Intracellular neutralization virus by immunoglobulin A anti-hemagglutination monoclonal antibodies. J Virol. 1995; 69:1339-1343.
44. Mazanec MB, Nerud JG, Kaetzel CS, et al. A three-tiered view of the role of IgA mucosal defense. Immunol Today. 1993;14:430-435.
45. Mazanec MB, Nerud JG, Lamm ME. Immunoglobulin A monoclonal antibodies protect against Sendai virus. J Virol. 1987;61:2624-2626.
46. Hou S, Doherty PC. Clearance of Sendai virus CD8+ T cells requires direct targeting to virus-infected epithelium. Eur J Immunol. 1995;25:111.
47. Sieg S, Xia L, Huang Y, et al. Specific inhibition of granzyme B by parainfluenza virus type 3. J Virol. 1995;69:3538-3541.
48. Glezen WP, Loda FA, Clyde WA, et al. Epidemiologic patterns of acute lower respiratory disease of children in a pediatric group practice. J Pediatr. 1971;78:397-406.
49. Knott AM, Long CE, Hall CB. Parainfluenza viral infections in pediatric outpatients: Seasonal patterns and clinical characteristics. Pediatr Infect Dis J. 1994;13:269-273.
50. Gardner SD. The isolation of parainfluenza 4 sub-types A and B in England and serological studies of their prevalence. J Hyg (Lond). 1969;67:540-545.
51. Kilgore GE, Dowdle WR. Antigenic characterization of parainfluenza 4A and 4B by the hemagglutination-inhibition test and distribution of HI antibody in human sera. Am J Epidemiol. 1970;91:306-316.
52. Muchmore HG, Parkinson AJ, Humphries JE, et al. Persistent parainfluenza virus shedding during isolation at the South Pole. Nature. 1981;289:187-189.
53. Moscona A, Galinski MS. Characterization of human parainfluenza virus type 3 persistent infection in cell culture. J Virol. 1990;64:3212-3218.
54. Moisiuk SE, Robson D, Klass L, et al. Outbreak of parainfluenza virus type 3 in an intermediate care neonatal nursery. J Pediatr Infect Dis. 1998;17:49-53.
55. Marx A, Torok TJ, Holman RC, et al. Pediatric hospitalizations for croup (laryngotracheobronchitis): Biennial increases associated with human parainfluenza virus 1 epidemics. J Infect Dis. 1997;176:1423-1427.
56. Denny FW, Murphy TF, Clyde WA Jr, et al. Croup: An 11 year study in a pediatric practice. Pediatrics. 1983;71:871-876.
57. Hendrickson KJ, Kuhn SM, Savatski LL. Epidemiology and cost of infection with human parainfluenza virus types 1 and 2 in young children. Clin Infect Dis. 1994; 18:770-779.
58. Chanock RM, Parrott RH. Acute respiratory disease in infancy and childhood: Present understanding and prospects for prevention. J Pediatr. 1965;36:21-30.
59. Rubin EE, Wuennec P, McDonald JC. Infections due to parainfluenza virus type 4 in children. Clin Infect Dis. 1993;17:998-1002.
60. Karron RA, O'Brien KL, Froehlich JL, et al. Molecular epidemiology of parainfluenza type 3 virus outbreak on a pediatric ward. J Infect Dis. 1993;167:1441-1445.
61. Mufson MA, Mocega HE, Krause HE. Acquisition of parainfluenza 3 virus infection by hospitalized children. I. Frequencies, rates, and temporal data. J Infect Dis. 1973;128:141-147.
62. Tumova B, Heinz F, Syrucek L, et al. Occurrence and aetiology of acute respiratory diseases; results of a long-term surveillance programme. Acta Virol. 1988;33:50-62.
63. Nicholson KG, Kent J, Hammersley V, et al. Acute viral infections of upper respiratory tract in elderly people living in the community: Comparative, prospective, population based study of disease burden. BMJ. 1997;315:1060-1064.
64. Echevarria JE, Erdman DD, Swierkosz EM, et al. Simultaneous detection and identification of human parainfluenza viruses 1, 2 and 3 from clinical samples by multiplex PCR. J Clin Microbiol. 1998;36:1388-1391.
65. Falsey AR, McCann RM, Hall WJ, et al. Acute respiratory tract infection in daycare centers for older persons. J Am Geriatr Soc. 1995;43:30-36.
66. Orr PH, Peeling RW, Brunka J, et al. Serology study of responses to selected pathogens causing respiratory tract infection in the institutionalized elderly. J Clin Infect Dis. 1996;23:1240-1245.
67. Glasgow KW, Tamblyn SE, Blair G. A respiratory outbreak due to parainfluenza virus type 3 in a home for the aged—Ontario. Can Commun Dis Rep. 1995;21(7):57-61.
68. Denny FW. The clinical impact of human respiratory virus infections. J Respir Crit Care Med. 1995;152(Suppl):S4-S12.
69. Henderson FW, Collier AM, Sanyal MA, et al. A longitudinal study of respiratory viruses and bacteria in the etiology of acute otitis media with effusion. N Engl J Med. 1982;306:1377-1384.
70. Wendt CH, Weisdorf DJ, Jordan CM, et al. Parainfluenza virus respiratory infection after bone marrow transplantation. N Engl J Med. 1992;326:921-926.
71. Wendt C, Fox JMK, Hertz M. Paramyxovirus infection in lung transplant recipients. J Heart Lung Transplant. 1995;14:479-485.
72. Apalsch AM, Green M, Ledesma-Medina J, et al. Parainfluenza and influenza virus infections in pediatric organ transplant recipients. Clin Infect Dis. 1995;20:394-399.
73. Lewis VA, Champlin R, Englund J, et al. Respiratory disease due to parainfluenza virus in adult bone marrow transplant recipients. J Clin Infect Dis. 1996;23:1033-1037.
74. Scully RE, Mark EJ, McNeeley WF, et al. Case records of the Massachusetts General Hospital. N Engl J Med. 1996;335:1133-1140.
75. Jarvis WR, Middleton PJ, Gelfand EW. Parainfluenza pneumonia in severe combined immunodeficiency disease. J Pediatr. 1979;93:423-425.
76. Arisoy ES, Demmler GJ, Thakar S, et al. Meningitis due to parainfluenza virus type 3: Report of two cases and review. Clin Infect Dis. 1993;17:995-997.
77. Jantausch BA, Wiedermann BL, Jeffries B. Parainfluenza virus type 2 meningitis and parotitis in an 11-year-old child. South Med J. 1995;88:230-231.
78. Sokhandan M, McFadden R, Huang YT, et al. The contribution of respiratory viruses to severe exacerbations of asthma in adults. Chest. 1995;107:1570-1575.
79. Welliver RC, Wong DT, Middleton E Jr, et al. Role of parainfluenza virus-specific IgE in pathogens of croup and wheezing subsequent to infection. J Infect Dis. 1982;101:889-896.
80. Frank AL, Taber LH, Wells CR, et al. Patterns of shedding of myxoviruses and paramyxoviruses in children. J Infect Dis. 1981;144:433-441.
81. Frank AL, Couch RB, Griffis CA, et al. Comparison of different tissue cultures for isolation and quantitation of influenza and parainfluenza viruses. J Clin Microbiol. 1979;10:32-36.
82. Henrickson KJ, Kuhn SM, Savatski, LL, et al. Recovery of human parainfluenza virus types one and two. J Virol Methods. 1994;46:189-205.
83. Karron RA, Froehlich JL, Bobo L, et al. Rapid detection of parainfluenza virus type 3 RNA in respiratory specimens: Use of reverse transcription-PCR-enzyme immunoassay. J Clin Microbiol. 1994;32:484-488.
84. Fan J, Hendrikson KJ, Savatski LL. Rapid simultaneous diagnosis of infections with respiratory syncytial viruses A and B, influenza viruses A and B, and human parainfluenza types 1,2, and 3 by multiplex quantitative reverse transcription-polymerase chain reaction-enzyme hybridization assay (Hexaplex). Clin Infect Dis. 1998; 26:1397-1402.
85. Sparrelid LP, Ekelof-Andstrom E, Aschais J, et al. Ribavirin therapy in bone marrow transplant recipients with viral respiratory tract infection. Bone Marrow Transplant. 1997;19:905-908.
86. Cobian L, Houston S, Greene J, et al. Parainfluenza virus respiratory infection after heart transplantation: Successful treatment with ribavirin. Clin Infect Dis. 1995; 21:1040-1041.
87. Hayashi T, Hotta H, Itoh M, Homma M. Protection of mice by a protease inhibitor, aprotinin, against lethal Sendai virus pneumonia. J Gen Virol 1991;72:979-982.
88. Kido H, Sakai K, Hishino Y, et al. Pulmonary surfactant is a potential endogenous inhibitor of proteolytic activation of Sendai virus and influenza A virus. FEBS Lett. 1993;322:115-119.
89. Beppu Y, Imamura Y, Tashiro M, et al. Human mucus protease inhibitor in airway fluids is a potential defensive compound against infection with influenza A and Sendai viruses. J Biochem. 1997;121:309-316.
90. Jaffee DM. The treatment of croup with glucocorticoids. N Engl J Med. 1998; 339:553-554.
91. Klassen TP, Feldman ME, Watters LK, et al. Nebulized budesonide for children with mild-to-moderate croup. N Engl J Med. 1994;331:285-290.
92. Geelhoed G. Croup. Pediatr Pulmonol. 1997;23:370-374.
93. Johnson DA, Jacobson S, Edney PC, et al. A comparison of nebulized budesonide, intramuscular dexamethasone, and placebo for moderately severe croup. N Engl J Med. 1998;339:498-503.
94. Skolnik NS. Treatment of croup: A critical review. Am J Dis Child. 1989;143: 1045-1049.
95. Bourchier D, Dawson KP, Fergusson DM. Humidification in viral croup: A controlled trial. Aust Paediatr J. 1984;20:289-291.
96. Chin J, Magoffin RL, Shearer LA, et al. Field evaluation of a respiratory syncytial virus vaccine and a trivalent parainfluenza virus vaccine in a pediatric population. Am J Epidemiol. 1969;89:449-463.
97. Homa FL, Brideau RJ, Lehman DJ, et al. Development of a novel subunit vaccine that protects cotton rats against both human respiratory syncytial virus and human parainfluenza virus type 3. J Gen Virol. 1993;74:1995-1999.
98. Ray R, Brown VE, Compans RW. Glycoproteins of human parainfluenza virus type 3: Characterization and evaluation as a subunit vaccine. J Infect Dis. 1985;152:1219-1230.
99. Murphy BR, Collins PL. Current status of respiratory syncytial virus (RSV) and parainfluenza virus type 3 (PIV3) vaccine development: Memorandum from a joint WHO/NIAID meeting. Bull World Health Organ. 1997;75:307-313.
100. van Wyke CL, Tierney EL, London WT, et al. Attenuation of bovine parainfluenza virus type 3 in nonhuman primates and its ability to confer immunity to human parainfluenza virus type 3 challenge. J Infect Dis. 1988;157:655-662.
101. Clements ML, Belshe RB, King J, et al. Evaluation of bovine, cold-adapted human, and wild-type human parainfluenza type 3 viruses in adult volunteers and in chimpanzees. J Clin Microbiol. 1991;29:1175-1182.
102. Karron RA, Wright PF, Hall SL, et al. A live attenuated bovine parainfluenza virus type 3 vaccine is safe, infectious, immunogenic, and phenotypically stable in infants and children. J Infect Dis. 1995;171:1107-1114.

103. Karron RA, Makene M, Gay K, et al. Evaluation of a live attenuated bovine parainfluenza type 3 vaccine in two- to six-month-old infants. Pediatr Infect Dis J. 1996; 15:650-654.

104. Belshe RB, Hissom FK. Cold adaption of parainfluenza virus type 3: Induction of three phenotypic markers. J Med Virol. 1982;10:235-242.

105. Choppin S, Richardson CD, Merz O, et al. The functions and inhibition of the membrane glycoproteins of paramyxoviruses and myxoviruses and the role of the measles virus M protein in subacute sclerosing panencephalitis. J Infect Dis. 1981;143:352-362.

106. Hall SL, Sarris CM, Tierney EL, et al. A cold-adapted mutant of parainfluenza virus type 3 is attenuated and protective in chimpanzees. J Infect Dis. 1993;167:958-962.

107. Belshe RB, Karron RA, Newman FK, et al. Evaluation of a live attenuated, cold-adapted parainfluenza virus type 3 vaccine in children. J Clin Microbiol. 1992;30:2064-2070.

108. Karron RA, Belshe RB, Wright PF, et al. A live human parainfluenza type 3 virus vaccine is attenuated and immunogenic in young infants. Pediatr Infect Dis. 2003;22:394-405.

109. Tao T, Durbin AP, Whitehead SS, et al. Recovery of a fully viable chimeric human parainfluenza virus (PIV) type 3 in which the hemagglutinin-neuraminidase and fusion glycoproteins have been replaced by those of PIV type 1. J Virol. 1998;72:2955-2961.

CHAPTER **154**

Mumps Virus

NATHAN LITMAN

STEPHEN G. BAUM

Mumps is an acute generalized viral infection that occurs primarily in school-aged children and adolescents. The most prominent manifestation of this disease is nonsuppurative swelling and tenderness of the salivary glands, with one or both parotid glands involved in most cases. The disease is benign and self-limited, with one third of affected persons having subclinical infection. Among the less frequent manifestations of this disease, meningitis and epididymo-orchitis are the most important. As is characteristic of many viral infections, mumps is usually a more severe illness in persons past the age of puberty than in children, and extrasalivary gland involvement more commonly occurs in older patients.

HISTORY

Hippocrates described mumps and its contagious characteristics in the fifth century BC. In the late 1700s, Hamilton emphasized the occurrence of orchitis as a manifestation of mumps. The experimental production of the disease in monkeys by Johnson and Goodpasture[1] in 1934 provided evidence that a filterable virus was present in the saliva of patients with mumps. In 1945, Habel[2] reported the cultivation of mumps virus in the chick embryo. Enders and colleagues[3] described the skin test and the development of complement-fixing antibodies after mumps in humans. A killed virus vaccine used in the early 1950s on human subjects achieved limited success,[4] and in 1966 Buynak and Hilleman[5] reported the development of an effective live virus vaccine.

The etymology of the word *mumps* is unclear. It may arise from the English noun *mump*, meaning "a lump," or from the English verb *to mump*, defined as "to be sulky"—a description of the characteristic facial expression. Alternatively, the term *mumps* has been ascribed to the mumbling speech pattern of the affected person. In the older literature, mumps may be called "epidemic parotitis."

THE AGENT

Mumps virus is a member of the Paramyxoviridae family, which includes the following genera: *Rubulavirus* (mumps virus; New Castle disease virus; human parainfluenza virus types 2, 4a, and 4b), *Respirovirus* (human parainfluenza virus types 1 and 3),

Morbillivirus (measles), *Pneumovirus* (human respiratory syncytial virus), *Metapneumovirus* (human metapneumovirus), and *Henipavirus* (Hendra virus and Nepah virus). The complete mumps virion has an irregular spherical shape, with a diameter ranging from 90 to 300 nm and averaging about 200 nm. The nucleocapsid is enclosed by an envelope that has three layers and is about 10 nm thick.[6] The external surface is regularly studded with glycoproteins possessing hemagglutinin, neuraminidase, and cell-fusion activity. The viral (V) antigen, antibodies to which are detected late in infection by the complement fixation test, is associated with this layer. The middle component of the envelope is a lipid bilayer that is acquired from the host cell as the virus buds off the cytoplasmic membrane. The innermost surface of the envelope is a nonglycosylated membrane protein that maintains the outer structure of the virus. The genome of the virus is contained in a nucleocapsid that is a helical structure composed of a continuous linear molecule of single-stranded RNA surrounded by symmetrically repeating protein subunits. The capsid protein carries RNA polymerase activity. The nucleocapsid represents the soluble (S) antigen, to which antibodies are detectable early in infection by the complement fixation test. Only one serotype of mumps virus is known.

Mumps virus is sensitive to ether by virtue of its lipid envelope. It is stable at 4° C for several days and at −65° C for months to years; however, repeated freezing and thawing may diminish viral activity.

The virus replicates in a variety of cell cultures as well as in embryonated hens' eggs.[7] In routine diagnostic virology, monkey kidney, human embryonic kidney, and HeLa cell cultures are used for primary isolation. Cytopathic effects such as the appearance of intracytoplasmic eosinophilic inclusions, rounding of cells, or fusion of cells into giant multinucleate syncytia may be noted.[8] The presence of mumps virus is usually confirmed by the hemagglutination inhibition (HAI) test, which uses convalescent serum after mumps infection to inhibit the adsorption of chick erythrocytes to mumps-infected epithelial cells.

EPIDEMIOLOGY

Mumps is endemic throughout the world. In the United States, before the licensing of live-attenuated mumps vaccine in 1967, epidemics occurred every 2 to 5 years.[9] Although the disease occurred throughout the year, the peak incidence was between January and May.[10] Epidemics have been reported in military populations and other closed communities such as prisons, boarding schools, ships, and remote islands.[11,12] Meyer[13] demonstrated that mumps is spread through the community by children in schools, with secondary spread to family members. There has been a decline of more than 99% in the annual U.S. incidence of mumps since 1967, with only 266 cases reported to the Centers for Disease Control and Prevention (CDC) in 2001; the seasonal variation that was evident in earlier years is no longer apparent.[14]

Mumps is uncommon in infants younger than 1 year of age. Resistance to infection in this age group is based on passive immunity acquired by the placental transfer of maternal antibody. In the prevaccine era, more than 50% of the cases occurred in the 5- to 9-year-old age group, and 90% occurred in children younger than 14 years of age. In 2001, 49% of the reported infections occurred in persons older than 15 years of age. In the prevaccine era, 80% to 90% of adults older than 20 years of age in the United States were immune to mumps on the basis of natural infection. At present in the United States, immunity to mumps among children and most young adults relies on prior vaccination. Men and women have the same frequency of development of parotitis with mumps infection.[15]

Humans are the only known natural host; however, monkeys and other laboratory animals have been experimentally infected.[1] Although persistent infections in cultured cells are commonly established by mumps virus,[16] a carrier state is not known to exist in humans.

PATHOGENESIS

The virus is naturally transmitted via direct contact, droplet nuclei, or fomites and enters through the nose or mouth. More intimate contact is needed to transmit mumps than for either measles or varicella. The period of peak contagion is just before or at the onset of parotitis.

Experimental mumps infection has been produced in humans and monkeys by direct instillation of the virus into Stensen's duct.[1] However, the incubation period in this experimental model is shorter than in naturally occurring disease, and initial infection of the parotid gland does not explain the fact that meningitis or other manifestations of mumps infection may occur before the onset of parotitis. It has been suggested that during the incubation period the virus proliferates in the upper respiratory tract epithelium and that viremia ensues, followed by secondary dissemination and localization to glandular and neural tissue.[17,18]

PATHOLOGY

Salivary glands from patients infected with mumps are rarely available for pathologic examination because of the usually benign course. When parotid glands have been examined, diffuse interstitial edema has been found, along with a serofibrinous exudate consisting primarily of mononuclear leukocytes. Neutrophils and necrotic debris accumulate within the ductal lumen, and the ductal epithelium shows degenerative changes. The glandular cells are relatively spared, but they may also be involved with edema and overflow of the inflammatory reaction from the interstitial tissues. The multinucleate syncytia and intracytoplasmic eosinophilic inclusions that are occasionally seen in mumps-infected tissue culture are not present in vivo. If the pancreas or the testis is involved, the microscopic picture is quite similar to that seen in the salivary glands, except that interstitial hemorrhage and polymorphonuclear leukocytes are more frequently noted in orchitis. Local areas of infarction may occur, because the vascular supply is compromised by increased pressure due to edema within an inelastic tunica albuginea. If the process has been particularly severe, atrophy of the germinal epithelium may result, with accompanying hyalinization and fibrosis.

The description of brain involvement in mumps encephalitis has most often been that of a postinfectious encephalitis characterized by perivenous demyelination, perivascular mononuclear cuffing, and a generalized increase in microglial cells, with relative sparing of neurons.[19] However, cases of what appears to be a primary mumps encephalitis have been reported that show widespread neuronolysis but without evidence of demyelination.[20]

CLINICAL MANIFESTATIONS

The incubation period of mumps averages 16 to 18 days, with a range of 2 to 4 weeks. Characteristically, the prodromal symptoms are nonspecific and include low-grade fever, anorexia, malaise, and headache. Within 1 day, the nature of the illness becomes apparent when the patient complains of an earache and tenderness can be elicited by palpation of the ipsilateral parotid. The involved gland is soon visibly enlarged and progresses to a maximum size over the next 2 to 3 days. The most severe pain accompanies the period of rapid enlargement. At its height, parotitis results in lifting of the ear lobe upward and outward. Lesser degrees of enlargement can more readily be appreciated by viewing the patient from behind. The enlarged parotid gland obscures the angle of the mandible, whereas cervical adenopathy does not hide this anatomic landmark. Usually, one parotid gland enlarges a couple of days after the other; however, mumps results in unilateral parotitis alone in one quarter of patients who have salivary gland involvement. The orifice of Stensen's duct is frequently edematous and erythematous. Trismus may result from the parotitis, and the patient may have difficulty with pronunciation and mastication. Ingestion of citrus fruits or juices typically exacerbates the pain. During the first 3 days of illness, the patient's temperature may range from normal to 40° C. After parotid swelling has reached its peak, pain, fever, and tenderness rapidly resolve, and the parotid gland returns to normal size within 1 week. Complications of parotitis are rare but are reported to include sialectasia resulting in recurrent acute and chronic sialadenitis.[21]

TABLE 154-1 Frequency of Common Clinical Manifestations of Mumps

Manifestation	Frequency (%)
Glandular	
Parotitis	60-70
Submandibular and/or sublingual sialadenitis	10
Epididymo-orchitis*	25 (postpubertal men)
Oophoritis*	5 (postpubertal women)
Neural	
Cerebrospinal fluid pleocytosis	50
Meningitis	1-10
Encephalitis	0.1
Transient high-frequency deafness	4
Other	
Electrocardiographic abnormalities	5-15
Renal function abnormalities (mild)	>60

*Rare before puberty and usually unilateral.

Involvement of the other salivary glands occurs in conjunction with parotitis in up to 10% of the cases but is rare as the sole manifestation of mumps infection (Table 154-1). Submandibular gland involvement mimics signs of anterior cervical lymphadenopathy. The sublingual glands are the least frequently inflamed during mumps infection; if involvement does occur, it is usually bilateral and may be associated with swelling of the tongue. Presternal pitting edema develops in 6% of patients with mumps, most commonly in those who have submandibular adenitis.[22] The proposed mechanism for the involvement of the tongue and presternal area is obstruction of the lymphatic drainage of those regions by enlarged salivary glands.

Central nervous system (CNS) involvement is the most common extrasalivary gland manifestation of mumps. As documentation of the remarkable neurotropism of this virus, Bang and Bang[23] reported the presence of cerebrospinal fluid (CSF) pleocytosis in 51% of 255 patients with mumps but without other evidence of meningitis. Clinical meningitis occurs in 1% to 10% of persons with mumps parotitis,[24] but only 40% to 50% of the patients with mumps meningitis confirmed by serology or viral isolation have parotitis.[24-27] Meningeal symptoms, like any of the other manifestations of mumps infection, may occur before, during, after, or in the absence of parotitis. Their time of onset averages 4 days after the appearance of salivary gland involvement but may be as early as 1 week before or as late as 2 weeks after parotitis.[23-26] Men are afflicted three times as often as women,[24-27] but the age distribution is the same as for uncomplicated mumps. Ritter[25] noted that mumps meningitis with parotitis is most frequent in the spring, whereas meningitis without parotitis is most frequent in summer.

The typical clinical features associated with viral meningitis—headache, vomiting, fever, and nuchal rigidity—are present. Lumbar puncture yields CSF containing 10 to 2000 white blood cells (WBC) per cubic millimeter. The predominating cells are usually lymphocytes, but 20% to 25% of the patients have a polymorphonuclear leukocyte predominance.[26] Protein levels are normal to mildly elevated, and 90% to 95% of patients have a CSF protein content of less than 70 mg/100 mL.[26,27] Hypoglycorrhachia (CSF glucose concentration <40 mg/100 mL) is reported in 6% to 30% of patients[26-28] and appears to be more common than in other viral meningitides. These CSF abnormalities may persist for 5 weeks or longer.[25,28] The finding of a depressed CSF glucose level with a moderate to marked pleocytosis may cause the physician to consider bacterial meningitis in the differential diagnosis, especially if neutrophils predominate, as they may early in the disease. As in other cases of meningitis, tuberculous and fungal disorders should be considered if mononuclear cells prevail in the CSF.

Abatement of fever by lysis and resolution of symptoms usually occurs 3 to 10 days after the onset of illness. The meningitis is benign, with complete recovery and an absence of sequelae. Before introduction of the live-attenuated mumps vaccine in 1967, mumps accounted for approximately 10% of the cases of aseptic meningitis in the United States. At present, aseptic meningitis is rarely attributed to mumps.

Encephalitis is reported to occur in 1 in 6000[29] to 1 in 400[30] cases of mumps. The former ratio probably represents a more accurate estimate. There appears to be a bimodal distribution of cases according to the time of onset: an early group in which onset coincides with the presence of parotitis and a larger, late group in which the condition develops 7 to 10 days after the onset of parotitis. As noted earlier, early-onset encephalitis represents direct damage to neurons as a result of viral invasion, whereas late-onset disease is a postinfectious demyelinating process related to the host response to infection. These two processes probably represent the ends of a continuum of disease. Some patients die after the primary viral invasion of the brain, and some of those who survive produce antibodies to the virus or neural breakdown products and develop an "autoimmune" reaction. The clinical features are those of a nonfocal encephalitis; in addition to marked changes in the level of consciousness, neurologic findings may include convulsions, paresis, aphasia, and involuntary movements. CSF values are similar to those observed in uncomplicated meningitis. Fever is high, with characteristic temperatures of 40° C to 41° C present. Neurologic manifestations and fever gradually resolve over a period of 1 to 2 weeks. Sequelae such as psychomotor retardation and convulsive disorders are reported,[25-27] but their frequency cannot be determined from the available data. Death has occurred in 1.4% of the reported cases.[30]

Through the mid-1960s, mumps was the leading recognized cause of viral encephalitis in the United States, being responsible for 20% to 30% of cases. However, by 1981, it represented only 0.5% of cases of viral encephalitis nationwide, and by the 1990s mumps encephalitis was rare. The major factor accounting for this change was an effective mumps immunization program.

The term *meningoencephalitis* is frequently used in describing patients with various degrees of CNS involvement.[20,24,25,28,31] This term should be eliminated in reference to mumps because it confuses a common and essentially benign condition (meningitis) with a relatively uncommon and serious illness (encephalitis) that may result in neurologic residua or death. Clearly, many patients with mumps meningitis have lethargy, as may a large percentage of persons with any viral infection (e.g., influenza). However, the presence of profound changes in level of consciousness or other findings suggestive of supratentorial involvement indicates the clear diagnosis of encephalitis, as distinct from the ambiguous designation of meningoencephalitis. Although nuchal rigidity and CSF pleocytosis may be present in patients with encephalitis, the meningeal component is a trivial aspect of this type of illness caused by mumps virus.

Transient high-frequency-range deafness was reported in 4.4% of the cases of mumps in a military population.[32] Permanent unilateral deafness occurs in 1 in 20,000 cases of mumps.[33] The onset of otologic symptoms may be gradual or abrupt; vertigo is frequently present. On subsequent testing, vestibular function has been normal.

Other neurologic syndromes rarely associated with mumps include cerebellar ataxia,[34] facial palsy,[35] transverse myelitis,[36] ascending polyradiculitis (Guillain-Barré syndrome),[37] and a poliomyelitis-like syndrome.[38] There are several well-documented cases of aqueductal stenosis and hydrocephalus developing after CNS infection caused by mumps.[39-41] Experimental and clinical reports clearly implicate mumps as the probable causative agent of this disorder.[42-44]

Epididymo-orchitis is the most common extrasalivary gland manifestation in the adult. It develops in 20% to 30% of postpubertal men with mumps infection and is bilateral in one of six of those with testicular involvement.[45,46] Although it has been reported in infancy, it is rare before puberty. Two thirds of cases occur during the first week of parotitis, and another one quarter arise during the second week.[45] However, gonadal involvement may precede parotitis, and it may be the only manifestation of mumps. The onset is abrupt, with temperatures in the range of 39° C to 41° C, chills, headache, vomiting, and

testicular pain. Genital examination reveals warmth, swelling, and tenderness of the involved testicle and erythema of the scrotum. Epididymitis is present in 85% of the cases and usually precedes the orchitis. The testis may be enlarged to three to four times its normal size. Constitutional complaints and fever usually parallel the severity of gonadal involvement. Fever resolves in 84% of the patients in 5 days or less. Pain and swelling resolve shortly after defervescence. However, tenderness may persist for longer than 2 weeks in 20% of the cases.[45] Early in convalescence, a loss of turgor may be appreciated. If testes are examined months to years later, some degree of atrophy will be noted in 50% of the patients.

The anxiety engendered by mumps orchitis is difficult to allay. The psychological fears of sexual impotence and sterility far outweigh the potential debility from testicular atrophy. Clearly, most men who have unilateral orchitis need fear nothing other than a possible cosmetic imbalance. Even those with bilateral involvement should be reassured that impotence (other than psychogenic) is not a sequela and that sterility is rare. In large surveys of infertile men, mumps is infrequently implicated as the causative disorder. Twenty-eight cases of testicular malignancy in men with atrophy of the testis due to mumps orchitis have been reported.[47]

Oophoritis develops in 5% of postpubertal women with mumps. Symptoms include fever, nausea, vomiting, and lower abdominal pain. Impaired fertility and premature menopause have been reported as a consequence of ovarian involvement but must be considered to be rare.[48]

Joint involvement during mumps is noted infrequently in adults and rarely in children.[49,50] Migratory polyarthritis is the most frequently described clinical form. Monoarticular arthritis and arthralgia have also been reported; both large and small joints are involved. Symptoms most commonly start 10 to 14 days after the onset of parotitis and may last up to 5 weeks. The process resolves spontaneously without residual joint damage.

Pancreatitis is manifested by severe epigastric pain and tenderness accompanied by fever, nausea, and vomiting. It is uncommon as a severe illness; however, many affected persons complain of mild degrees of upper abdominal discomfort.

Electrocardiographic changes appear in up to 15% of patients with mumps; the most common abnormalities are depressed ST segments, flattened or inverted T waves, and prolonged P-R intervals.[51,52] Clinically manifested myocarditis is rare; however, deaths associated with myocarditis have been reported, both during the acute illness and after a chronically progressive deteriorating course.[51,52]

Utz and colleagues[53] prospectively evaluated renal function in 20 young adult Navy servicemen admitted with mumps. These investigators discovered transient, mild to moderate abnormalities of urinary concentration, creatinine clearance, and phenolsulfonphthalein excretion in most of this group. Hughes and associates[54] reported two deaths related to mumps-associated nephritis.

A variety of other manifestations have accompanied mumps infection, but the following must be considered extremely rare: thyroiditis,[55] mastitis,[56] prostatitis,[57] hepatitis,[58] and thrombocytopenia.[59]

COMPLICATIONS

Gestational viral infections were extensively investigated in a controlled cohort study by Siegel and co-workers.[60-62] They observed excess fetal deaths when mumps developed during the first trimester; second- and third-trimester maternal mumps infections were not associated with increased fetal mortality.[60] Low birth weight (<2500 g) was identified in 7.7% of infants born to mumps-infected mothers, compared with 3.3% of a control group; however, this difference was not statistically significant. Although the number of cases was small, when the data were analyzed with respect to onset of infection, the effect on birth weight was greatest for mumps occurring in the first trimester.[61] A variety of congenital malformations have been described in pregnancies complicated by maternal mumps[63]; however, these anomalies are described in single case reports without comparison with an uninfected control population. As reported by Siegel and colleagues,[62] occurrence rates of major congenital defects were equal in both mumps and control newborn populations; even after the data were analyzed by trimester, no trends could be established. Similar results were obtained by a British team who reviewed 500 pregnancies complicated by maternal mumps.[64]

St. Geme and others[65] suggested an "embryopathic" relationship between intrauterine mumps infection and endocardial fibroelastosis (EFE) on the basis of the presence of skin test reactivity to mumps antigen in a high percentage of the EFE patients. Experimentally induced infection of the chick embryo added histopathologic support to this association.[66] Although some observers have disputed that mumps plays an etiologic role,[67] studies using polymerase chain reaction (PCR) techniques have demonstrated mumps viral RNA in more than 70% of samples of myocardium from patients with autopsy-proven EFE.[68] There has been a marked decline in the incidence of EFE in the last 3 decades, corresponding to the declining incidence of mumps.

A similar controversy exists regarding the possible role of mumps in the etiology of juvenile diabetes mellitus. A number of case reports have described cases of diabetes, either transient or permanent, that developed soon after mumps.[69,70] However, it is not clear whether this association is simply coincidental. Epidemiologic studies have demonstrated a 7-year periodicity in the incidence of both mumps and childhood diabetes, with a 3- to 4-year lag time between their respective peaks.[71] Coxsackievirus B4 has also been epidemiologically linked to diabetes.[72] Although the frequency of EFE has declined in recent years, there has been no decline in the frequency of juvenile diabetes mellitus coincident with the decreasing frequency of mumps after introduction of the mumps vaccine.

IMMUNE RESPONSES

After clinical or subclinical mumps infection, a variety of immunologic responses can be demonstrated. Complement-fixing antibodies directed against the S antigen appear rapidly; sometimes they are present at the onset of clinically apparent illness. Anti-V antibody titers rise more slowly and peak about 2 to 4 weeks after the beginning of disease.[73] Anti-S antibody titers decline rapidly over a period of several months to undetectable levels, whereas anti-V antibody titers drop more slowly and persist for years. This pattern of response provides the possibility of a serologic diagnosis of mumps from a single serum specimen. An acute-phase serum demonstrating a high anti-S with a low anti-V titer or a high anti-S with a high anti-V titer can be interpreted as evidence of current or very recent infection, respectively. The presence in serum of only anti-V antibodies would indicate a more remote infection with mumps.

Neutralizing antibodies appear during convalescence, and detectable titers persist for years. Although assays for these antibodies constitute the most reliable test to determine whether a person is immune to mumps, such assays are cumbersome and are not routinely performed. Assays for HAI antibodies, which also develop after the onset of mumps, are the simplest of the serologic studies, but results are unreliable because of potential cross-reactions with other paramyxoviruses. Enzyme-linked immunosorbent assays (ELISAs) for antibody to mumps have been developed[74,75] and are widely available.

Delayed hypersensitivity to an intradermally administered mumps skin test antigen develops between 3 weeks and 3 months after mumps.[3] The skin test was widely used in the past as a measure of immunity to mumps, as well as a test for the competence of delayed hypersensitivity. The use of mumps skin test antigen to determine immunity to mumps has been abandoned because of the variability of lots of the skin test antigen and because of false-positive and false-negative results.

Transplacental transfer of maternal mumps complement-fixing, HAI, and neutralizing antibodies has been demonstrated.[76] Titers in maternal and cord serum are almost identical. Neutralizing antibodies persist for several months, accounting for the rarity of mumps in young infants and the lack of response to immunization in this age group. One attack of mumps, whether inapparent or clinically manifested, confers lifelong immunity.

DIAGNOSIS

In most instances, the diagnosis of mumps is made on the basis of a history of exposure and of parotid swelling and tenderness accompanied by mild to moderate constitutional symptoms.

The WBC and differential counts in mumps are normal, or there may be a mild leukopenia with a relative lymphocytosis. If meningitis, orchitis, or pancreatitis is present, leukocytosis with a shift to the left is most commonly encountered. The serum amylase concentration is elevated in the presence of parotitis and may remain abnormal for 2 to 3 weeks. Serum amylase levels may also be increased in the absence of clinical salivary gland involvement. Mumps pancreatitis also increases amylase levels; differentiation from salivary gland amylase may be achieved by isoenzyme analysis or by serum pancreatic lipase determinations.

The typical CSF findings in mumps meningitis were described previously. Similar, although less marked, CSF abnormalities are present in half of the patients who have mumps parotitis without apparent CNS involvement. In a patient with aseptic meningitis, an elevated serum amylase concentration should suggest mumps infection.

Laboratory confirmation of typical mumps is unnecessary. However, if parotitis is absent or recurrent, if extrasalivary gland manifestations are prominent, or if documentation of the presence of a specific viral disorder is desired, a variety of diagnostic aids can be used.

The definitive diagnosis of mumps depends on serologic studies or viral isolation. The presence of immunoglobulin M antibodies as determined by ELISA, or a fourfold rise between acute and convalescent sera on complement fixation, HAI, ELISA, or neutralization testing, confirms the diagnosis. The HAI test can be affected by heterologous antibody responses to parainfluenza virus infection. Because parotitis can be caused by parainfluenza 3 virus,[77] serologic testing and virus isolation studies for parainfluenza 3 virus should be undertaken if the HAI test is used in the diagnosis of mumps. Immunity to mumps is usually assessed by ELISA. This assay combines ease of performance with reliability.

Virus is usually present in saliva for about 1 week, from 2 to 3 days before to 4 to 5 days after the onset of parotitis. However, virus has been isolated from saliva as early as 6 days before and as late as 9 days after the first signs of salivary gland involvement. In addition, virus may be recovered from the saliva of persons with inapparent infection and from persons who manifest only extrasalivary gland signs.[78] The virus is frequently isolated from the CSF of patients with clinical meningitis during the first 3 days of meningeal symptoms,[24] and it is present as late as the sixth day of CNS disease. Viruria has been detected during the first 2 weeks of illness; in one study, 72% of urine specimens during the first 5 days of illness yielded a positive culture.[53] Viremia has rarely been detected and has been found only during the first 2 days of illness.[17,18] Mumps viral RNA has been detected by PCR in clinical specimens from patients with mumps infection and in throat swabs of healthy children after the administration of mumps vaccine.[79-81]

DIFFERENTIAL DIAGNOSIS

A variety of entities may simulate mumps but can be easily differentiated from mumps on the basis of chronicity or associated symptoms. Infectious processes involving parotid glands are most likely to be confused with mumps because of their acute onset and associated fever. Parainfluenza 3 virus, Coxsackieviruses, and influenza A viruses have been reported to cause acute parotitis.[77,82,83] These entities can be differentiated from mumps only by viral culture or serology. Bilateral parotid swelling is often seen in children with human immunodeficiency virus (HIV) infection. Suppurative parotitis, most often caused by *Staphylococcus aureus* or gram-negative organisms, usually occurs during the postoperative period, in premature newborns, or in debilitated patients with poor oral intake. The gland is warm, hard, and extremely tender; the overlying skin is erythematous. Massage of the parotid expresses purulent drainage from Stensen's duct.

Parotid enlargement caused by drugs or metabolic disorders is usually bilateral and asymptomatic. Phenylbutazone, thiouracil, iodides, and phenothiazines have been implicated in this condition.[57] Diabetes mellitus, malnutrition, cirrhosis, and uremia are among the metabolic disorders that can cause parotid swelling.[57]

Tumors, cysts, and obstruction caused by stones or stricture are usually unilateral. Rare conditions that may mimic mumps include Mikulicz's syndrome, Parinaud's syndrome, uveoparotid fever of sarcoidosis, and Sjögren's syndrome.

THERAPY

Therapy for mumps parotitis is symptomatic and supportive. Treatment with analgesic-antipyretics such as aspirin or acetaminophen relieves pain caused by salivary gland inflammation and reduces fever. Topical application of warm or cold packs to the parotid may also relieve discomfort. Intravenous fluid administration may be necessary for patients with meningitis or pancreatitis who have persistent vomiting. Lumbar puncture may relieve the headache associated with meningitis.

Management of orchitis is purely symptomatic. Bed rest, use of narcotic analgesics, support of the inflamed testis with a "bridge," and application of ice packs make the patient feel more comfortable. An anesthetic block of the spermatic cord with 1% procaine hydrochloride may alleviate severe pain.[84] There is no convincing evidence that the use of steroids or diethylstilbestrol or incision of the tunica albuginea produces more rapid resolution of the orchitis or prevents subsequent atrophy. Interferon-alfa-2b administered to four men with bilateral mumps orchitis resulted in prompt resolution of symptoms, with no evidence of testicular atrophy or oligospermia during follow-up study.[85] Further investigation to establish the efficacy of this treatment is needed.

Gellis and colleagues[86] showed that 20 mL of mumps immune globulin administered intramuscularly to adult men with mumps reduced the incidence of orchitis from 27.4% to 7.8%. However, mumps immune globulin is no longer commercially available.

PREVENTION

Recommendations for the management of mumps include isolation until the parotid swelling has resolved to prevent the spread of infection to susceptible persons. This measure may be of little value, particularly in closed populations such as schools or hospitals,[87] because virus is present in saliva days before parotitis develops and because persons with clinically inapparent infection can shed virus.

Passive protection for exposed susceptible persons may have been afforded by mumps immune globulin, available in the past. However, Reed and colleagues[12] reported that use of mumps immune globulin during an epidemic in Alaska did not reduce clinical parotitis or inapparent infection rates and did not diminish the incidence of meningitis or orchitis.

Active immunization with the Jeryl Lynn strain of attenuated mumps virus vaccine has been available in the United States since December 1967. The vaccine is prepared in chick embryo cell culture.[5] A single subcutaneous immunization produces protective levels of mumps-neutralizing antibodies in more than 95% of vaccinees.[5] Although the antibody levels produced are lower than after natural infection, adequate titers are maintained for at least 10.5 years.[88] Adverse reactions to the vaccine are uncommon; transient suppression of tuberculin-delayed hypersensitivity has been reported, and parotitis and orchitis have been recognized rarely. In Japan, aseptic meningitis associated with mumps vaccine virus occurred in 0.05% to 0.3% of recipients of the Urabe AM 9 mumps vaccine; manifestations began 2 to 4 weeks after immunization.[89,90] Studies in the United States did not reveal evidence of an increased risk of aseptic meningitis after administration of the Jeryl Lynn strain of mumps vaccine.[91]

All children older than 12 months of age should be immunized. Vaccination should take place at 12 to 15 months and again at 5 to 12 years of age, as part of immunization with the combined live measles-mumps-rubella virus vaccine (MMR). Most states now require evidence of immunity to mumps (i.e., documented immunization, physician-diagnosed disease, or antibody studies) for school entrance and attendance (see Chapter 319). Immunization should also be considered for male adolescents and adults without a history of mumps. Male medical personnel who have no neutralizing antibodies to mumps should be immunized. Immunization after exposure may not provide protection from natural infection.

As with other live virus vaccines, mumps vaccine should not be administered to pregnant women, patients receiving immunosuppressive therapy, or persons with severe febrile illnesses, advanced malignancies, or congenital or acquired immunodeficiencies. Serious reactions to the mumps component of MMR have not been reported in limited studies in HIV-infected patients. However, a fatal case of measles pneumonitis occurred in a 21-year-old man with advanced HIV disease who was vaccinated with MMR[92]; therefore, MMR should not be administered to such patients (see Chapter 319). Individuals with HIV infection who are not severely immunocompromised may be immunized with MMR.

REFERENCES

1. Johnson CD, Goodpasture EW. An investigation of the etiology of mumps. J Exp Med. 1934;59:1.
2. Habel K. Cultivation of mumps virus in the developing chick embryo and its application to the studies of immunity to mumps in man. Pub Health Rep. 1945;60:201.
3. Enders JF, Cohen S, Kane LW. Immunity in mumps. II. The development of complement fixing antibody and dermal hypersensitivity in human beings following mumps. J Exp Med. 1945;81:119.
4. Habel K. Vaccination of human beings against mumps; vaccine administered at the start of an epidemic. I. Incidence and severity of mumps in vaccinated and control groups. Am J Hyg. 1951;54:295.
5. Buynak EB, Hilleman MR. Live attenuated mumps virus vaccine. I. Vaccine development. Proc Soc Exp Biol Med. 1966;123:768.
6. Kleiman MB. Mumps virus. In: Lennette EH, ed. Laboratory Diagnosis of Viral Infections. 2nd ed. New York: Marcel Dekker; 1992:549.
7. Deinhardt FW, Shramek GJ. Mumps virus. In: Lennette EH, Spaulding EH, Truant JP, eds. Manual of Clinical Microbiology. Washington, DC: American Society for Microbiology; 1974:703.
8. Henle G, Deinhardt F, Girardi A. Cytolytic effects of mumps virus in tissue cultures of epithelial cells. Proc Soc Exp Biol Med. 1954;87:386.
9. Centers for Disease Control and Prevention. Mumps Surveillance 1973. MMWR Morb Mortal Wkly Rep. 1974;23:431.
10. Centers for Disease Control and Prevention. Summary of notifiable diseases, United States, 1991. MMWR Morb Mortal Wkly Rep. 1991;40:3.
11. Philip RN, Reinhard KR, Lackman DB. Observations on a mumps epidemic in a "virgin" population. Am J Hyg. 1959;69:91.
12. Reed D, Brown G, Merrick R, et al. A mumps epidemic on St. George Island, Alaska. JAMA. 1967;199:967.
13. Meyer MG. An epidemiologic study of mumps; its spread in schools and families. Am J Hyg. 1962;75:259.
14. Centers for Disease Control and Prevention. Summary of notifiable diseases, United States, 2001. MMWR Morb Mortal Wkly Rep. 2003;50:1-21.
15. Centers for Disease Control. Mumps surveillance, Report No. 1. January 1968.
16. Truant AL, Hullum JV. A persistent infection of baby hamster kidney-21 cells with mumps virus and the role of temperature sensitive variants. J Med Virol. 1977;1:49.
17. Kilham L. Isolation of mumps virus from the blood of a patient. Proc Soc Exp Biol Med. 1948;69:99.
18. Overman Jr. Viremia in human mumps infection. Arch Intern Med. 1958;102:354.
19. Donohue WL, Playfair FD, Whitaker L. Mumps encephalitis. J Pediatr. 1955;47:395.
20. Taylor FB, Toreson WE. Primary mumps meningo-encephalitis. Arch Intern Med. 1963;112:216.
21. Travis LW, Hecht DW. Acute and chronic inflammatory diseases of the salivary glands, diagnosis and management. Otolaryngol Clin North Am. 1977;10:329.
22. Gellis SS, Peters M. Mumps with presternal edema. Bull Johns Hopkins Hosp. 1944;75:241.
23. Bang HO, Bang J. Involvement of the central nervous system in mumps. Acta Med Scand. 1943;113:487.
24. McLean DM, Bach RD, Larke RPB, et al. Mumps meningoencephalitis, Toronto, 1963. Can Med Assoc J. 1964;90:458.
25. Ritter BS. Mumps meningoencephalitis in children. J Pediatr. 1958;52:424.
26. Levitt LP, Rich TA, Kinde SW, et al. Central nervous system mumps. Neurology. 1970;20:829.
27. Johnstone JA, Ross CAC, Dunn M. Meningitis and encephalitis associated with mumps infection. Arch Dis Child. 1972;47:647.

28. Wilfert CM. Mumps meningoencephalitis with low cerebrospinal-fluid glucose, prolonged pleocytosis and elevation of protein. N Engl J Med. 1969;280:855.
29. Russell RR, Donald JC. The neurological complications of mumps. Br Med J. 1958;2:27.
30. Centers for Disease Control. Mumps surveillance, January 1977-December 1982. Issued September 1984.
31. Azimi PH, Shaban S, Hilty MD, et al. Mumps meningoencephalitis prolonged abnormality of cerebrospinal fluid. JAMA. 1975;234:1161.
32. Vuori M, Lahikainen EA, Peltonen T. Perceptive deafness in connection with mumps. Acta Otolaryngol. 1962;55:231.
33. Everberg G. Deafness following mumps. Acta Otolaryngol. 1957;48:397.
34. Cohen HA, Ashkenazi A, Nussinovitch M, et al. Mumps-associated acute cerebellar ataxia. Am J Dis Child. 1992;146:930-931.
35. Beardwell A. Facial palsy due to the mumps virus. Br J Clin Pract. 1969;23:37.
36. Nussinovitch M, Brand N, Frydman M, et al. Transverse myelitis following mumps in children. Acta Paediatr. 1992;81:183-184.
37. Ghosh S. Guillain-Barré syndrome complicating mumps. Lancet. 1967;1:895.
38. Lennette EH, Caplan GE, Magoffin RL. Mumps virus infection simulating paralytic poliomyelitis. Pediatrics. 1960;25:788.
39. Timmons GD, Johnson KP. Aqueductal stenosis and hydrocephalus after mumps encephalitis. N Engl J Med. 1970;283:1505.
40. Bray PF. Mumps: A cause of hydrocephalus? Pediatrics. 1972;49:446.
41. Oran B, Ceri A, Yilmaz H, et al. Hydrocephalus in mumps meningoencephalitis: Case report. Pediatr Infect Dis J. 1995;14:724-725.
42. Johnson RT, Johnson KP. Hydrocephalus following viral infection: The pathology of aqueductal stenosis developing after experimental mumps virus infection. J Neuropathol Exp Neurol. 1968;27:591.
43. Herndon RM, Johnson RT, Davis LE, et al. Ependymitis in mumps virus meningitis. Arch Neurol. 1974;30:475.
44. Uno M, Takano T, Yamano T, et al. Age-dependent susceptibility in mumps-associated hydrocephalus: Neuropathologic features and brain barriers. Acta Neuropathol (Berl). 1997;94:207-215.
45. Candel S. Epididymitis in mumps, including orchitis: Further clinical studies and comments. Ann Intern Med. 1951;34:20.
46. Lambert B. The frequency of mumps and of mumps orchitis. Acta Genet Stat Med. 1951;2(Suppl 1):1-166.
47. Kaufman JJ, Bruce PT. Testicular atrophy following mumps: A cause of testis tumour? J Urol. 1963;35:67.
48. Morrison JC, Givens JR, Wiser WL. Mumps oophoritis: A cause of premature menopause. Fertil Steril. 1975;26:655.
49. Appelbaum E, Kohn J, Steinman RE, et al. Mumps arthritis. Arch Intern Med. 1952;90:217.
50. Caranasos GJ, Felder JR. Mumps arthritis. Arch intern Med. 1967;119:394.
51. Kussy JC. Fatal mumps myocarditis. Minn Med. 1974;57:285.
52. Roberts WC, Fox SM. Mumps of the heart: Clinical and pathologic features. Circulation. 1965;32:342.
53. Utz JP, Houk VN, Alling DW. Clinical and laboratory studies of mumps. IV. Viruria and abnormal renal function. N Engl J Med. 1964;270:1283.
54. Hughes WT, Steigman AJ, Delong HF. Some implications of fatal nephritis associated with mumps. Am J Dis Child. 1966;111:297.
55. Eylan E, Zmucky R, Sheba C. Mumps virus and subacute thyroiditis: Evidence of a causal association. Lancet. 1957;1:1062.
56. Krugman S, Katz SL, Gershon AA, et al. Mumps (epidemic parotitis). In: Infectious Diseases of Children. 9th ed. St. Louis: Mosby–Year Book; 1992:260.
57. Pomeroy C, Jordan MC. Mumps. In: Hoeprich PD, Jordan MC, eds. Infectious Diseases. 4th ed. Philadelphia: JB Lippincott; 1989:801.
58. Petersdorf RG, Bennett IL. Treatment of mumps orchitis with adrenal hormones: Report of 23 cases with a note on the hepatic involvement in mumps. Arch Intern Med. 1957;99:222.
59. Graham DY, Brown CH, Benrey J, et al. Thrombocytopenia: A complication of mumps. JAMA. 1974;227:1162.
60. Siegel M, Fuerst HT, Peress NS. Comparative fetal mortality in maternal virus diseases: A prospective study on rubella, measles, mumps, chickenpox and hepatitis. N Engl J Med. 1966;274:768.
61. Siegel M, Fuerst HT. Low birth weight and maternal virus diseases: A prospective study of rubella, measles, mumps, chickenpox and hepatitis. JAMA. 1966;197:680.
62. Siegel MS. Congenital malformations following chickenpox, measles, mumps, and hepatitis: Results of a cohort study. JAMA. 1973;226:1521.
63. Gershon AA. Chickenpox, measles and mumps. In: Remington JS, Klein JO, eds. Infectious Disease of the Fetus and Newborn. Philadelphia: WB Saunders: 1990:395.
64. Manson MM, Logan WPD, Loy RM. Rubella and other virus infections in pregnancy. Reports on Public Health and Medical Subjects, No. 101. London: Ministry of Health; 1960.
65. St Geme JW, Noren GR, Adams P. Proposed embryopathic relation between mumps virus and primary endocardial fibroelastosis. N Engl J Med. 1966;275:339.
66. St Geme JW, Peralta H, Farias E, et al. Experimental gestational mumps virus infection and endocardial fibroelastosis. Pediatrics. 1971;48:821.
67. Gersony WM, Katz SL, Nadas AS. Endocardial fibroelastosis and the mumps virus. Pediatrics. 1966;37:430.
68. Ni J, Bowles NE, Kim YH, et al. Viral infection of the endocardium in endocardial fibroelastosis: Molecular evidence for the role of mumps virus as an etiologic agent. Circulation. 1997;95:133-139.
69. Dacou-Voutetakis C, Constantinidis M, Moschos A, et al. Diabetes mellitus following mumps: Insulin reserve. Am J Dis Child. 1974;127:890.
70. Hinden E. Mumps followed by diabetes. Lancet. 1962;1:1138.
71. Sultz HA, Hart BA, Zielezny M, et al. Is mumps virus an etiologic factor in juvenile diabetes mellitus? J Pediatr. 1975;86:654.
72. Gamble DR, Kinsley ML, Fitzgerald MG, et al. Viral antibodies in diabetes mellitus. Br Med J. 1969;3:627.
73. Henle G, Harris S, Henle W. The reactivity of various human sera with mumps complement fixation antigens. J Exp Med. 1948;88:133.
74. Nigro G, Nanni F, Midulla M. Determination of vaccine-induced and naturally acquired class-specific antibodies by two indirect ELISAs. J Virol Methods. 1986;13:91-106.
75. Doern GV, Robbie L, St Amand R. Comparison of the Vidas and Bio-Whittaker enzyme immunoassays for detecting IgG reactive with varicella-zoster virus and mumps virus. Diagn Microbiol Infect Dis. 1997;28:31-34.
76. Hodes D, Brunell PA. Mumps antibody placental transfer and disappearance during the first year of life. Pediatrics. 1970;45:99.
77. Zollar LM, Mufson MA. Acute parotitis associated with parainfluenza 3 virus infection. Am J Dis Child. 1970;119:147.
78. Henle G, Henle W, Wendell KK, et al. Isolation of mumps virus from human beings with induced apparent or inapparent infections. J Exp Med. 1948;88:223.
79. Boriskin YuS, Booth JC, Yamada A. Rapid detection of mumps virus by the polymerase chain reaction. J Virol Methods. 1993;42:23-32.
80. Hosoya M, Honzumi K, Sato M, et al. Application of PCR for various neurotropic viruses on the diagnosis of viral meningitis. J Clin Virol. 1998;11:117-124.
81. Nagai T, Nakayama T. Mumps vaccine virus genome is present in throat swabs obtained from uncomplicated healthy recipients. Vaccine. 2001;19:1353-1355.
82. Howlett JG, Somlo F, Kalz F. A new syndrome of parotitis with herpangina caused by the coxsackie virus. Can Med Assoc J. 1957;77:5.
83. Brill SJ, Gilfillan RF. Acute parotitis associated with influenza type A. N Engl J Med. 1977;296:1391.
84. Lyon RP, Bruyn HB. Mumps epididymo-orchitis: Treatment by anesthetic block of the spermatic cord. JAMA. 1966;196:736.
85. Erpenbach KH. Systemic treatment with interferon-alpha 2B: An effective method to prevent sterility after bilateral mumps orchitis. J Urol. 1991;146:54.
86. Gellis SS, McGuiness AC, Peters M. A study on the prevention of mumps orchitis with gamma globulin. Am J Med Sci. 1945;210:661.
87. Brunell PA, Brickman A, O'Hare D, et al. Ineffectiveness of isolation of patients as a method of preventing the spread of mumps. N Engl J Med 1968;279:1357.
88. Weibel RE, Buynak EB, McLean AA, et al. Persistence of antibody in human subjects following administration of combined liver attenuated measles, mumps, and rubella vaccines. Proc Soc Exp Biol Med. 1980;165:260.
89. Fuginaga T, Youichi M, Tamura H, et al. A prefecture-wide survey of mumps meningitis associated with measles, mumps and rubella vaccine. Pediatr Infect Dis J. 1991;10:204.
90. Sugiura A, Yamada A. Aseptic meningitis as a complication of mumps. Pediatr Infect Dis J. 1991;10:209.
91. Black S, Shinfeld H, Ray P, et al. Risk of hospitalization because of aseptic meningitis after measles-mumps-rubella vaccination in one to two year old children: An analysis of the Vaccine Safety Datalink (VSD) Project. Pediatr Infect Dis J. 1997;16:500-503.
92. Angel JA, Walpita P, Lerch RA, et al. Vaccine-associated measles pneumonitis in an adult with AIDS. Ann Intern Med. 1998;129:104.

CHAPTER **155**

Respiratory Syncytial Virus

CAROLINE BREESE HALL

CAROL A. McCARTHY

Were we but able to explain
The fiefdom of the microbe—
Why one man is his serf,
Another is his lord
When all are his domain. . . .

C. B. H.

Respiratory syncytial virus (RSV) is the major cause of lower respiratory tract illness in young children.[1-5] Its presence is witnessed in most communities in the United States by the yearly upsurge of pneumonia, bronchiolitis, and tracheobronchitis in the very young. So effectively does RSV spread that essentially all persons have experienced infection by this agent within the first few years of life. Immunity, however, is not complete, and reinfection is common. Although life-threatening infections generally occur only during the first couple of years of life, RSV infections contribute an appreciable share of the morbidity caused by acute upper respiratory tract infections and exacerbations of wheezing and bronchitis in older children and adults. The health care costs associated with these outpatient infections add appreciably to the estimated cost of $300 to $600 million for hospitalized infants with RSV infection.[6,7] Of additional concern and increasing recognition are the growing morbidity and costs associated with RSV infections in older adults.[8-11]

HISTORY

The major agent that causes outbreaks of bronchiolitis in winter and spring was discovered in 1956 when Morris and co-workers isolated a new virus from one of 14 chimpanzees suffering from colds.[12] They called this new agent *chimpanzee coryza agent* (CCA). Whether this agent was also able to infect humans was not then known, but cross-infection was suspected because one laboratory worker developed specific antibody to CCA. Subsequently, Chanock and colleagues confirmed that the agent caused respiratory illness in humans when they obtained two isolates from children that were indistinguishable from chimpanzee coryza agent.[13] These isolates were recovered from the throat swabs of a child with bronchopneumonia (Long strain) and from a child with laryngotracheobronchitis (Snyder strain). Chanock and Finberg subsequently detected rises of specific neutralizing antibody to CCA in children with respiratory illness and also discovered that such antibody was present in most children by the time they reached school age.[14] The inappropriateness of calling this virus chimpanzee coryza agent became apparent, and it was renamed *respiratory syncytial virus* to denote its clinical and laboratory manifestations. Multiple studies soon followed to support that current claim that RSV is the major agent causing outbreaks of lower respiratory disease in infants.[15-17]

DESCRIPTION

Classification

RSV belongs to the Paramyxoviridae family, which consists of five genera, three of which form the subfamily, Paramyxovirinae, consisting of Respirovirus, containing human parainfluenza types 1 and 3 viruses; Rubulavirus, containing mumps and human parainfluenza viruses types 2, 4a, and 4b; and Morbillivirus, represented by measles virus. The Pneumovirinae subfamily comprises two genera. The first is Pneumovirus, which contains RSV and the morphologically and biologically similar pneumonia virus of mice, bovine RSV, ovine RSV, and caprine RSV. The second genus in the Pneumovirinae subfamily is Metapneumovirus, to which the recently discovered human metapneumovirus has been initially assigned (see Chapter 156).[18] Distinctive features of RSV include the number and order of genes and the lack of hemagglutinin and neuraminidase activity.[19]

Characteristics

RSV is an enveloped, medium-sized (120 to 300 nm) RNA virus with a nonsegmented, single-stranded, negative-sense genome that is associated with viral proteins throughout its length, forming the nucleocapsid (Fig. 155-1). The viral envelope is a bilipid layer derived from the plasma membrane of the host cells. It has the appearance of a thistle with transmembrane surface glycoprotein spikes 11 to 12 nm in length and 6 to 10 nm apart (Fig. 155-2). Electron microscopy of ultrathin sections of infected tissue reveals RSV as pleomorphic, round, or filamentous particles budding from the cytoplasmic membrane that are fringed by the glycoprotein projections.[19]

The complete gene sequence of the A2 strain has been described (Fig. 155-3).[19,20] The viral RNA consists of 15,222 nucleotides that are transcribed into 10 monocistronic polyadenylated messenger RNAs, each of which encodes for one of the major proteins, except for M2 mRNA, which possesses two overlapping open reading frames that en-

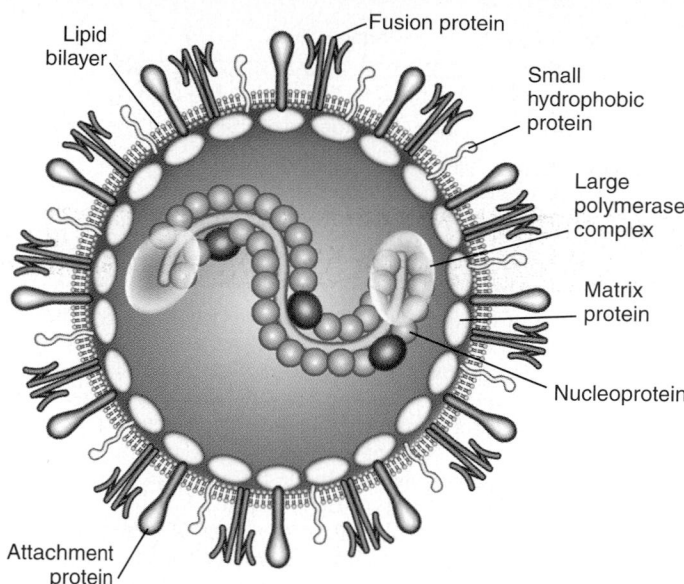

FIGURE 155-1. Structure of respiratory syncytial virus. *(Adapted 2003 with permission from the Massachusetts Medical Society. Hall CB. N Engl J Med. 2001;344:1928.)*

code for two separate proteins (M2-1 and M2-2). Three of the proteins (N, P, and L) are associated with the nucleocapsid. Of the five associated with the envelope, three (F, G, and SH) are glycosylated transmembrane surface proteins, whereas M and M2 are nonglycosylated matrix proteins. Two proteins, NS1 and NS2, are nonstructural proteins of the virion. The two glycosylated surface proteins, the F and G proteins, appear integral and important in the infectivity and pathogenesis of the virus. The fusion, or F protein, bears a structural similarity to the fusion protein of the parainfluenza viruses, consisting of two disulfide-linked fragments (F1 and F2). The F protein initiates viral penetration by fusing viral and cellular membranes and promotes viral spread by melding infected to adjacent uninfected cells, thereby resulting in the characteristic syncytia. Efficient fusion, however, appears to require the coexpression of all three of the surface glycoproteins, F, G, and SH. The largest glycoprotein, the G protein, appears primarily to mediate attachment of the virus to the host cells.

RSV withstands changes in temperature and pH relatively poorly. Only 10% of RSV remained infectious after exposing the virus to 55° C for 5 minutes.[21] At 37° C, the virus was stable for 1 hour, but only 10% of the infectivity remained after 24 hours. At 25° C, 10% infectivity was present after 48 hours, and at 4° C, 1% of the infectivity remained

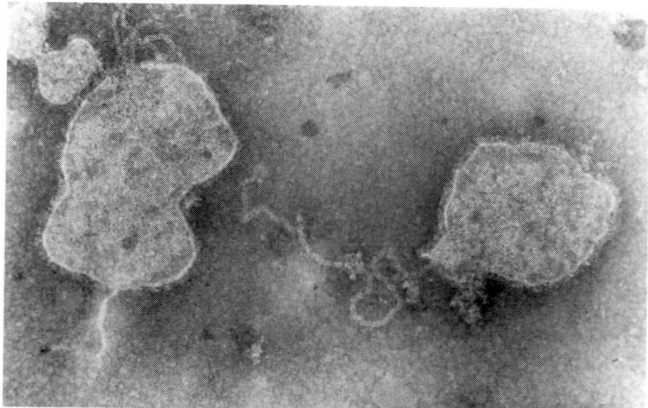

FIGURE 155-2. Negative-contrast electron micrograph of respiratory syncytial virus.

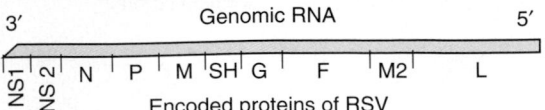

FIGURE 155-3. Simplified representation of the genomic structure of respiratory syncytial virus.

after 7 days.[21] RSV does not tolerate slow freezing and thawing. Complete loss of infectivity occurs when the virus is slowly frozen at −30° C and then thawed. When slowly frozen at −65° C, the infectivity titer fell by approximately 0.5 log. RSV also withstands an acid medium poorly, and the optimal pH is 7.5. The virus is inactivated quickly by ether, chloroform, and a variety of detergents such as 0.1% sodium deoxycholate, sodium dodecyl sulfate, and Triton X-100. Storage of RSV can be enhanced by flash freezing in an alcohol and dry ice bath and by adding glycerin or sucrose.

At room temperature, RSV in the secretions of patients may survive on nonporous surfaces, such as countertops, for 3 to 30 hours, depending on the humidity.[22] On porous surfaces, such as cloth and paper tissue, survival is generally shorter, usually less than 1 hour. The infectivity of RSV on the hands is variable from person to person but is usually less than 1 hour. The survival of RSV in the environment appears to depend in part on the drying time and on the humidity.[22]

Laboratory Propagation

RSV grows well in a variety of animal and human cell lines. For primary isolation, HEp-2 cells from an epithelial carcinoma of the larynx, HeLa cells from epithelial tissue of a cervical adenocarcinoma, and A549 cells from a type II alveolar epithelial lung carcinoma are commonly preferred (Fig. 155-4). Other cell lines that may be used but are usually less sensitive include human kidney, amnion, and diploid fibroblastic cells, and monkey kidney cells.[23] The sensitivity of all these cell lines for the growth of RSV is variable, and with serial propagation of cells, RSV growth may diminish with loss of the characteristic cytopathic effect of syncytia. Thus, the sensitivity of cell lines must be closely monitored. The degree of syncytial formation also depends on the type of cell culture, the heaviness of the cell sheet, the medium, the strain of virus, the multiplicity of infection, and its laboratory adaptation. RSV replication and syncytia formation require that

the culture media contain calcium and glutamine. On primary isolation in sensitive heteroploid cell cultures, the characteristic cytopathic effect of RSV may be first detected after an average of 3 to 5 days.[24] With strains of RSV that are adapted to tissue culture, new infectious virus may first be detected 10 to 12 hours after inoculation, but the typical syncytia do not develop until 10 to 24 hours later. The syncytia progress until the cell sheet is completely destroyed, which usually occurs within 4 days. A variable proportion of the cell sheet may also show rounding of the cells without fusion, especially in some primary cell lines.

About 90% of the inoculum is absorbed within 2 hours by standard sensitive cell lines. The viral surface glycoproteins may be detected by immunofluorescence 7 to 10 hours after inoculation. Cell-free virus may subsequently be demonstrated in the culture medium, but up to 90% of the virus remains cell associated. Release of cell-associated virus requires agitation or sonication. However, a large proportion of the virions released appear empty and would not be infectious.

Antigenic Variation

Antigenic variation among strains of RSV was previously believed to be minor on the basis of cross-neutralization assays in experimental animals. Monoclonal antibodies made it possible to detect appreciable strain differences and allowed RSV isolates to be divided into two major groups, A and B, and into subtypes within each group.[19,25,26] Group A is represented by the A2 strain and group B by the 18537 strain. Overall, the antigenic relatedness for the two strain groups is 25%. The major diversity between group A and group B resides with the G, F, SH, and NS1 proteins. The strain heterogenicity is even greater when analyzed genetically. G, the attachment protein, possesses the greatest genetic variability, and second is the SH protein. This is reflected in the relative antigenic relatedness of the G protein of each group of only 1% to 7% in comparison with 50% for the F proteins. Furthermore, the amino acid diversity of the G proteins within each group is appreciable, from 12% for group B to 20% for group A. The F, N, P, M2, NS1, and NS2 proteins are more highly conserved and demonstrate an amino acid homology of more than 87% and a nucleotide homology of more than 75%.

Strains of both groups circulate simultaneously during outbreaks, but the proportions that are A and B vary, as do the subtypes.[25-29] Antigenic and molecular analyses of the relatedness of strains circulating concurrently in a single locale, as well as in multiple areas worldwide, indicate that the strains within both groups possess genetic

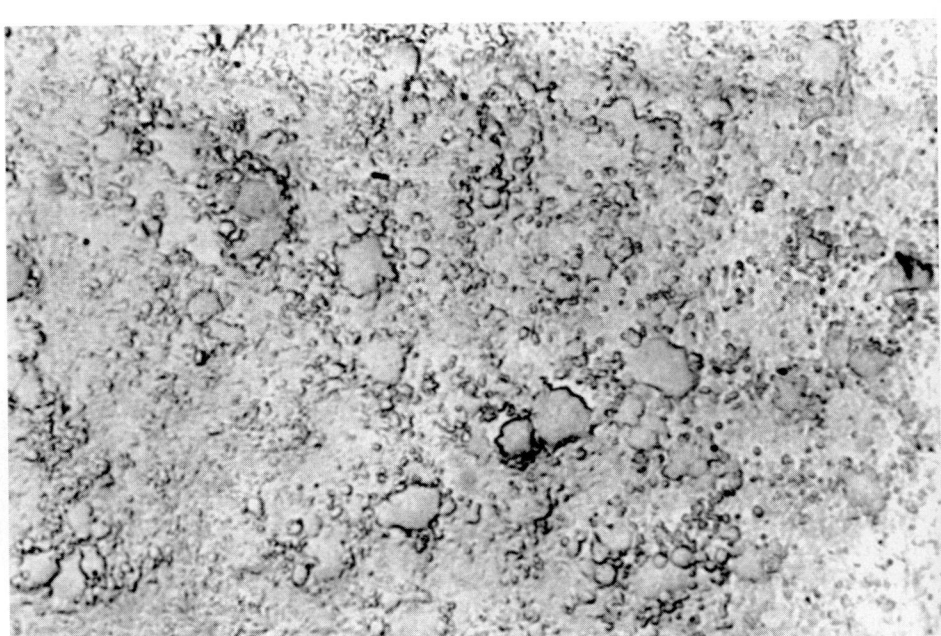

FIGURE 155-4. HEp-2 culture 4 days after inoculation with a nasal wash from an infant hospitalized with pneumonia. Multiple foci of the characteristic refractile syncytial cytopathic effect of respiratory syncytial virus are apparent.

diversity. Even in widely separated geographic areas, the cocirculating strains may have similar genotypes and parallel evolutionary lineages. Analyses of the G protein of strains collected over decades and from diverse areas suggest that the pressure of the population's immunity may play a role in the slow accumulation of the amino acid substitutions that result in strain evolution.[25-29]

Infection in Animals

A variety of animal species may be experimentally infected with RSV,[30] but natural infection with human RSV strains is limited mostly to humans and chimpanzees. Bovine strains of RSV (BRSV) have been recovered from cows with respiratory illness, potentially providing a natural animal model for the study of human RSV infection.[19,31,32] BRSV is antigenically and genetically closely related to human RSV, and their complete nucleotide sequences show 72.8% identity.[19] Antibodies directed against the F, N, P, and M proteins of either virus recognize the heterologous virus. BRSV strains also appear to consist of two major antigenic subgroups.[19,33] Ovine and caprine strains of RSV have also been recovered, and genetic analysis suggests that caprine RSV is more closely related than ovine RSV to BRSV and human RSV.[34]

The development of an animal model for infant RSV infection has been perplexing and problematic.[30] In general, animal models do not develop symptoms of lower respiratory tract disease similar to those seen in humans. Infection of the upper and lower respiratory tracts has been accomplished in a number of animal models, but, with the exception of in the chimpanzee, RSV replication in the lung is generally poor or limited, and any pulmonary abnormalities are often inconsistent. Chimpanzees infected with RSV may develop respiratory illness and shed virus. However, they do not usually develop lower respiratory tract involvement similar to that of infants and generally exhibit poor permissiveness to RSV replication on challenge.[12,35] Pneumonia has been induced in the *Cebus* monkey, and the African green monkey has been used as a model for enhanced lung abnormality induced by the formalin-inactivated vaccine.[35-37] A potential lamb model has been developed after challenge with ovine, bovine, or human RSV strains.[38-40] When human RSV was inoculated intratracheally or intranasally, tachypnea and fever were observed more frequently than in lambs given placebo.[40] Infection in ferrets has been associated with some histopathologic changes in the upper respiratory tract and in the lower respiratory tract in infant ferrets.[41] Various rodents have commonly been utilized, particularly cotton rats and mice, but even in these models, replication of RSV is only semipermissive.[19,30] Graham and colleagues have developed a mouse model that develops clinical illness and appreciable lung abnormality.[42] A number of other animals may be infected asymptomatically, including other primates, guinea pigs, minks, and chinchillas.[19,35]

EPIDEMIOLOGY

Distribution

In every geographic area studied, evidence of infection with RSV has been found. In areas of widely differing climates, RSV infections appear to have similar characteristics of ubiquity, and primary infection occurs in the very young.[3,5,43-49]

Seasonal Occurrence

RSV is singular in its ability to produce a sizable crop of infection every year.[3-5,49,50] The outbreaks occur primarily in the winter or spring in the United States, lasting for 20 or more weeks. Biannual peaks of RSV outbreaks have also been demonstrated in temperate climates. In warmer climates, the outbreaks may be more prolonged with less pronounced peaks, but they are just as regular.[51] In northern tropical areas, RSV outbreaks tend to correlate with an increase in rainfall and a decrease in temperature, whereas south of the equator the RSV season occurs when both rainfall and temperature decline. Close to the equator, RSV infections tend to occur throughout the year.[3,49,51,52]

Epidemiologic Manifestations

The spread of RSV infection within a community produces such characteristic ramifications that the presence of RSV may often be deduced without specific viral diagnosis. Characteristically, RSV produces a rise in the number of cases of bronchiolitis and pediatric pneumonia in the community and a rise in the number of hospital admissions of young children with acute lower respiratory tract disease.[4,53] The size of the outbreaks of RSV infection in general does not vary enough to change these barometers in most temperate climates, but milder outbreaks may be observed and may be followed the next season by an outbreak of greater than usual severity.

Acquisition of Infection According to Age

Experience with RSV is so universal at a young age that virtually all children have been infected in the first several years of life. All newborns passively acquire from their mothers specific antibody that is neutralizing and directed to the major surface glycoproteins of the virus.[5,54] Without natural infection, the level of antibody falls over the next 6 to 7 months to the point that little is detectable.[5] However, by 2 years of age, 95% or more of children have become seropositive.

Prevalence and Incidence

The importance of RSV in causing respiratory illnesses in children is illustrated in Table 155-1. It is the major agent recovered from young children with pneumonia and bronchiolitis.[20] The proportion of cases that are identified as caused by RSV varies according to the population examined and the methods used. During the peak period of an epidemic, RSV may be isolated from up to 89% of the young children admitted to the hospital with acute lower respiratory tract disease.[24] In contrast, RSV is rarely isolated from children without respiratory disease (see Table 155-1).[4]

From their studies in Washington, D.C., Parrott and colleagues[1,4,5] have estimated that about one half of the infants followed longitudinally were infected during their first RSV epidemic and that essentially all had become infected after experiencing two RSV epidemics. Furthermore, in 40% of these first infections, a febrile pneumonitis developed. The yearly attack rate for RSV lower respiratory tract disease has been estimated to be 23 per 1000 children younger than 1 year in middle-income families in North Carolina and 9 per 1000 in families in a Seattle prepaid medical practice.[55,56] During the second year of life, the rates were approximately the same. In children 2 to 3 years of age, the attack rates declined to 15 per 1000 in Chapel Hill and 7 per 1000 in Seattle. In 4- and 5-year-old children, the yearly attack rates were estimated to be 8 and 5 per 1000 children, respectively. Prospective studies suggest that the frequency of lower respiratory tract infection with RSV is actually much higher. In groups of infants followed closely, the attack rate for RSV lower respiratory tract diseases varied from 15% to 50%.[55,57-61] Even higher rates have been detected in a daycare center in which the children were examined almost daily.

Age, sex, and socioeconomic factors appear to influence the expression of RSV disease.[62-65] The most severe illness occurs in the youngest infants and those with underlying cardiopulmonary disease (Fig. 155-5).[66] Boys appear to have a higher incidence of lower respiratory tract disease. An increased risk of infants acquiring RSV disease, particularly lower respiratory tract disease, has been correlated

TABLE 155-1 Respiratory Illnesses Caused by Respiratory Syncytial Virus (RSV)

Syndrome	Percentage Caused by RSV	References
Bronchiolitis	43-90	1, 4, 298-300
Pneumonia	5-40	1-3, 57, 301-307
Tracheobronchitis	10-30	4, 57
Croup	3-10	3, 4, 57, 298, 302, 305, 308
Asymptomatic	0.3	4, 160

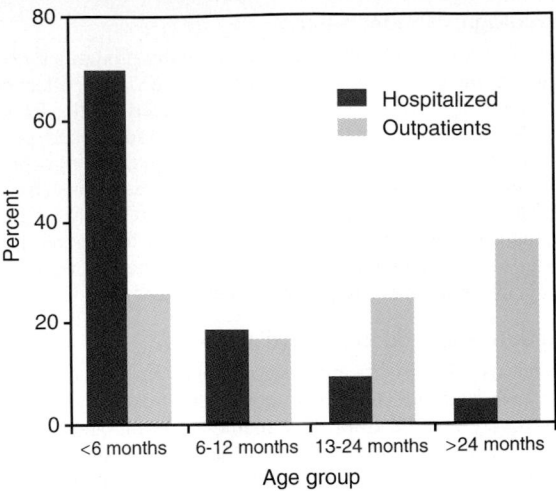

FIGURE 155-5. Difference in age distribution of inpatients and outpatients with respiratory syncytial virus infection in Rochester, New York, illustrates the effect of age on the severity of infection. Of infants requiring hospitalization, 70% were younger than 6 months. In comparison, 25% of the children treated as outpatients were younger than 6 months and 38% were older than 2 years.

with crowding, lower socioeconomic income, daycare attendance, multiple siblings, older siblings in school, and exposure to passive smoke within 6 months of onset of the RSV outbreak.

The importance of RSV as a cause of hospitalization of infants in the first year of life has been emphasized by a study indicating that RSV bronchiolitis was the leading cause of hospitalization for infants under 12 months of age for any reason.[67] Data from the Centers for Disease Control and Prevention (CDC) suggest that the rates of hospitalization for bronchiolitis associated with RSV are increasing.[68] Shay and colleagues have estimated 1.65 million hospitalizations for bronchiolitis occurred over a 17-year period in children less than 5 years of age, and 57% were among children less than 6 months of age.[68] Furthermore, annual bronchiolitis hospitalization rates increased 2.4 times, from 12.9 per 1000 children in 1980 to 31.2 per 1000 children in 1996. Assuming RSV was the cause of bronchiolitis in 50% to 80% of cases occurring in November through April, the number of hospitalizations for RSV bronchiolitis occurring in infants was estimated to be between 51,000 and 82,000 each year.[68]

Data from the Tennessee Medicaid Program emphasize that the risk for hospitalization from RSV is greatest for those in the first year of life with chronic lung disease (388 per 1000 children), followed by those with congenital heart disease (97 per 1000 children). This is compared with the rate of 30 per 1000 for normal, full-term infants.[66] Nevertheless, these normal, healthy infants accounted for 53% of all RSV hospitalizations. The associated economic burden has been considerable, estimated to be between $300 and $600 million each year in the United States for RSV pneumonia.[6,7]

Incidence of Repeated Infections

Repeated infections with RSV are common, and no age group appears protected. In a Chapel Hill daycare center, 98% of children first exposed to RSV became infected.[61] A second exposure resulted in 74% of the children becoming infected, and a third exposure only reduced the attack rate to 65%. In urban Rochester, New York, 44% of the families with young children became infected with RSV during the winter months when RSV was prevalent in the community.[69] Of the exposed family members, 46% became infected. Although the attack rate was highest in infants, between 38% and 47% of older children and adults acquired RSV infection. In the Houston family study, in which children were followed from birth, the infection rate was 68.8 per 100 children in the first year of life, and during the second year at least half were reinfected.[60]

PATHOGENESIS

In adult volunteers, experimental infection occurs after an average incubation of 5 days,[70,71] and in naturally acquired infection the average incubation period appears similar, with a range of 2 to 8 days.[16,72] Inoculation of the virus may occur through the nose or eye, and both appear to be equally sensitive portals of entry, whereas the mouth is a much less sensitive means of inoculation.[73] RSV infection is generally confined to the respiratory tract, and spread of the virus may occur during primary infection from the upper passageways to involve the entire lower respiratory tract.

In bronchiolitis, the initial pathologic findings are a lymphocytic peribronchiolar infiltration with some edema of the walls and surrounding tissue.[17,74,75] Subsequently, the characteristic proliferation and necrosis of the epithelium of the bronchioles develop. The lumina of these small airways become obstructed from the sloughed epithelium and from the increased mucus secretion. Impedance to the flow of air occurs during both inspiration and expiration but is greater in the latter when the lumen is narrowed further by the positive expiratory pressure. Hyperinflation, therefore, results from the trapping of air peripheral to the sites of partial occlusion. With complete obstruction, trapped air eventually becomes absorbed, resulting in the characteristic multiple areas of atelectasis. Young infants are particularly prone to develop such areas of atelectasis, as the collateral channels that maintain alveolar expansion in the presence of airway obstruction are not yet well developed. An increase in lung volume and expiratory resistance, therefore, occurs in bronchiolitis.[76]

Infants with lower respiratory tract disease from RSV often have pathologic evidence of both pneumonia and bronchiolitis. Patients with pneumonia demonstrate an interstitial infiltration of mononuclear cells that may be accompanied by edema and necrotic areas that lead to alveolar filling.[74,77]

Some histologic evidence of recovery is present in most patients with bronchiolitis within the first week of illness and is marked by the beginning regeneration of the bronchiolar epithelium.[74] Ciliated cells may not be present for weeks, and other morphologic alterations may persist indefinitely.

Theories of Pathogenesis

How RSV engenders these pathogenic findings remains mostly a mystery. RSV produces its most devastating illness at the time when specific antibody, maternally derived, is invariably and abundantly present. The severity of RSV infection in the young infant and in those children with high levels of circulating antibody induced by an inactivated RSV vaccine, discussed later, has suggested that immunologic mechanisms may contribute to the pathogenesis of the disease in infants.[59,78,79]

In the late 1960s, trials of the first RSV vaccine, a formalin-inactivated RSV vaccine (lot 100), were initiated.[59,78,79] Infants who received the vaccine produced both complement-fixing and neutralizing antibodies to RSV. When exposed subsequently to natural RSV infection, however, immunized children were not protected from RSV infection, and some developed an exaggerated illness characterized by severe lower respiratory tract disease requiring hospitalization. A variety of immune mechanisms have been proposed to explain the augmented disease in the vaccinees as well as the lower respiratory tract disease seen in infants with natural infection. Much attention has been given to the role of antibody in pathogenesis, including the hypothesis that an immune complex reaction may occur between the virus and passively acquired immunoglobulin G (IgG) antibody in the infant's lung, resulting in enhanced disease,[80] especially when the local defense of secretory antibody is absent. Additional hypotheses have suggested that the manifestations of RSV lower respiratory tract disease may result from RSV-specific IgE-mediated disease, or from a detrimental T-cell response, or mostly from the immunologic immaturity of the young infant.[19,81,82]

Alternatively, severe RSV infection in infancy has been explained without involving any immunologic mechanism. Exposure to large doses of virus coupled with the small lumen of the infant's airway may be sufficient to produce the severe disease seen in the young baby. The airway of the young infant is particularly vulnerable to any degree of inflammation and obstruction, because resistance to the flow of air is related inversely to the cube of the radius. Infection in the small peripheral airways of the infant, therefore, results in greater physiologic changes than in the older child, and mechanisms of compensation are less well developed.[83]

Immunity

Naturally acquired immunity to RSV infection is incomplete, variable, and not durable. Repeated infections are common, but severe disease rarely occurs after the primary encounter. Lower respiratory tract involvement may occur with repeated infections, but it is generally confined to those at either end of the age spectrum.[60,61,84,85]

The initial, innate barrier of defense against RSV infection in infants is the respiratory epithelium, which produces opsonins, collectins, and multiple cytokines.[82,86] This innate response does not evoke an immune memory. The release of cytokines results in the subsequent recruitment of effector molecules, primarily neutrophils, macrophages, natural killer cells, and eosinophils. The potential importance and variability in the endowed innate defense and susceptibility of the host are being increasingly recognized as genetic technology associates specific gene polymorphisms with the effectiveness of the inherited immunity and severe RSV disease. Severity of RSV disease has been correlated with genetic polymorphisms in genes that are integral to various components of innate immunity, including the release of specific cytokines.[87-92]

The adaptive immune response to RSV is complex. The relative contributions and interactions of different arms of the immune system in the response to either a primary or recurrent exposure are not defined. Their significance in the pathogenesis of natural disease or that seen after immunization continues to be investigated. However, most evidence suggests that an effective, nondetrimental immune response to RSV requires a fine balance of the multiple components of immunity.

Serum antibody provides some, but not complete, protection against RSV infection. Higher titers of antibody generally correlate with better resistance to infection, but no defined level of neutralizing antibody is predictive of the risk for infection, the severity of illness, or recovery in children or adults.[84,93] Higher levels of maternal antibody have been correlated with lower infection rates[54,94-96] and with less severe illness in some studies[95] but not in others.[5]

Recent studies have further defined antibody responses to specific RSV proteins and have failed to implicate humoral immunity in the pathogenesis of RSV disease, but they have increasingly shown the potential benefit and protective effects of specific humoral antibody. In particular, the trials of administration of RSV hyperimmune globulin and monoclonal antibody to high-risk infants have demonstrated protection against more severe RSV disease.[97]

Passively derived maternal antibody usually declines to undetectable levels by 6 months of age, but occasionally it may remain up to 9 to 12 months of age. During primary infection, serum IgM antibody appears within several days, but it is transient and lasts only a few weeks.[82,98] During the second week, IgG antibody appears, usually peaks in the fourth week, and begins to decline after 1 to 2 months. The IgA serum antibody response is more variable in infants. An anamnestic response involving all three immunoglobulin classes occurs after reinfection, and after about three infections the titers reach levels similar to those in adults.

The effectiveness of the antibody produced to RSV varies according to the type of antibody, its function, and its protein specificity. In general, the responses to the two large surface glycoproteins, F and G, are most important. On both of these proteins, neutralizing epitopes are present, and a fusion epitope is also present on F.[19,99,100]

Animal studies have supported the integral role of the F and G surface glycoproteins in the immune response to RSV. In rodents, administration of monoclonal antibodies to F and G proteins (but not to the internal proteins N, P, and M) or immunization with the F and G proteins has resulted in nearly complete protection against RSV challenge

in the lung but not the upper respiratory tract.[19] Also, these models have verified the broader, heterologous immunity provided by the F antibody and have demonstrated that antibody to the G protein results in little protection against challenge with a heterologous strain.[19]

In humans, the quantitative and qualitative antibody responses to these proteins are influenced by the presence of preexisting antibody and age.[101] Although infants and young children are able to produce antibodies directed against both the F and G proteins, the responses are variable, especially to the G protein in infants.[54,82,101-104] The G protein is heavily glycosylated and, therefore, is a poor immunogen in infants. Preexisting or maternal antibody appears to have more of a dampening effect on the antibody response to G than to F.

In infants, the antibody response to the F and G proteins mainly involves the subclasses IgG_1 and IgG_3 (the subclasses primarily associated with antibodies to proteins rather than to carbohydrates, which are associated with IgG_2). However, adults respond to the G protein with antibodies in both the IgG_1 and the IgG_2 subclass, and the adult response to the F protein is predominantly IgG_1.[105] Antibody to the G protein in response to primary infection in infants is of low avidity in contrast to the high-avidity anti-G antibody in adults; the high-avidity pattern was also seen in the passively derived maternal antibody.[106]

The relative degrees of protection against infection, reinfection, and illness afforded by antibodies to the F and G proteins are not well defined. However, in adults who are challenged with RSV after experiencing recent natural infection, the levels of antibodies to the F and homologous G proteins and of neutralizing antibodies to the homologous strain correlate with resistance to reinfection.[84] Symptomatic infection, however, correlates more closely with antibody to the homologous G protein. In infants with primary infection, the homologous and heterologous antibody responses to the F proteins of both A and B strains appear to be similar, but little heterologous response to the G proteins exists.[19] It has been suggested that group A strains provide better resistance to reinfection by the homologous or heterologous strain.

Local antibody production may be important in RSV infection, because the virus spreads from cell to cell, and in animal studies circulating antibody does not prevent viral replication in the nasal passages.[19,107] A number of studies have identified neutralizing activity in the nasal secretions of children with RSV infection, but a correlation with protection or with illness severity often could not be made.[59] The presence of this neutralizing activity in the secretions was associated with diminished viral shedding, but it was also present at the time of hospital admission in the secretions of infants with primary infections.[108] McIntosh and co-workers have defined the nonspecific nature of this neutralizing activity and have demonstrated that a specific IgA-antibody response does occur in infants recovering from RSV infection.[108] Although this specific IgA antibody does not neutralize the virus, its presence is correlated with diminished titers of virus. Specific IgM, IgG, and IgE antibodies may also be found in the secretions of children with RSV infections.[19,108-110] The IgM antibody appears early and disappears, and IgG appears later. The infants' secretory response to the F and G proteins is similar to their serum response in that both are diminished in younger infants and lower to the G protein.[102,104] The F protein also appears to elicit a response with a more favorable ratio of IgA to IgE.[104]

Most children with RSV infection produce a transient response to specific IgE or IgG antibody in the respiratory tract.[104,110] The length and magnitude of the specific IgE response and of the concentrations of histamine in the nasopharyngeal secretions have been correlated with wheezing during the acute illness and with subsequent episodes of bronchospasm.[110] The RSV infection of the respiratory epithelial tissue appears to result in release of cytokines and chemokines that then trigger the inflammatory responses, including IgE and eosinophils that are associated with airway bronchospasm and inflammation.[81,109-111]

Cell-mediated immunity is likely to be pivotal in the clearance of virus and in recovery, but it has not been clearly shown to have a role in protection against reinfection and illness. The central role of the cellular immune response is supported by observations that adults and children with deficiencies of cellular immunity, as well as experimentally immunosuppressed animals, have more severe disease and prolonged shedding.[112-114] The specific components of the cellular response, however, have been studied primarily in mice and to a much lesser extent in humans.

Lymphocyte transformation activity as a measure of cell-mediated immunity has been demonstrated in adults and in infants after RSV infection. Lymphocyte transformation responses have also been detected after immunization with the formalin-inactivated vaccine in those children who subsequently developed enhanced disease with natural RSV infection, and also after immunization with the RSV F glycoprotein in seropositive children.[19,82]

Cytotoxic T-lymphocyte (CTL) responses, as detected by chromium release of infected target cells, have also been identified in peripheral blood lymphocytes of both infants and adults after RSV infection.[115,116] Experimental RSV infection in volunteers has suggested that specific CTL responses correlate with an ameliorated clinical course.[115-117] During primary infection in infants, cell-mediated responses with specific CTLs have been variably produced within the first days of infection, but ameliorated disease has not been correlated with these responses. Indeed, more severe disease has been associated with depressed lymphocyte function in several T-cell subsets, as well as with depressed interleukin (IL)-12 levels and elevated IL-8 levels.[115,118-120]

Studies in mice and in humans examining both the CTL and helper T (Th)-lymphocyte responses have shown that correlations between these responses and viral clearance and clinical response are complex and sometimes contradictory. Studies in mice have produced different degrees of pathologic findings when RSV-specific CD4+ or CD8+ cells are variably depleted and passively transferred. This suggests that the combined effects of the quantity, timing, specificity, and types of T cells transferred may elicit diverse immunologic and clinical outcomes.[19,121-125]

The type of priming immunization may also influence the specificity and type of cellular immune responses. Live viral infections have been shown to evoke primarily helper T cells with a Th1 cytokine profile (IL-2, interferon-γ [IFN-γ], and tumor necrosis factor-α [TNF-α] secretion). Live RSV infection has been shown in animal models to evoke a Th1 response, and after RSV challenge, specific CTLs have been identified in the livers and spleens of mice.[121,122,126] Administration of inactivated or nonreplicating antigens, however, has been demonstrated to elicit a cytokine pattern that has predominated the Th2 profile (IL-4, IL-5, IL-10, and IL-13 secretion).

It is not clear how applicable these findings in the animal model are to infant RSV infection.[82,127] Some studies in adults and children have shown that mixed Th1- and Th2-type responses occur in association with live viral infections.[82] Furthermore, many other factors may influence the immunologic response and severity of the clinical disease. Among these are the maturity of the infant's immune response, and a genetic predisposition as shown by the increasing numbers of certain polymorphisms associated with modulating components of immunity and with more severe clinical disease.[89-91,124,128]

CLINICAL MANIFESTATIONS

Infection in Young Children

Primary infections with RSV may be manifested as lower respiratory tract disease, pneumonia, bronchiolitis, tracheobronchitis, or upper respiratory tract illness and are often accompanied by fever and otitis media. Rarely is the first infection asymptomatic.[4,60,61,69] The risk for lower respiratory tract involvement occurring with the first infection is high. Pneumonia or bronchiolitis has been estimated to occur in 30% to 71%.[5,16,19,60,61] In closed populations of infants, the proportion developing lower respiratory tract disease may be even higher, up to 89%.[72,129] Even in previously healthy outpatients, the proportion who develop lower respiratory tract disease is appreciable (Fig. 155-6).

Of the lower respiratory tract syndromes, pneumonia and bronchiolitis are the most frequent in infants.[3,4,57,60,68] Croup is the least common form of clinical illness and usually accounts for less than 5% to 10% of the cases.[57] Pneumonia and bronchiolitis are often difficult to differentiate, and many infants may appear to progress intermittently

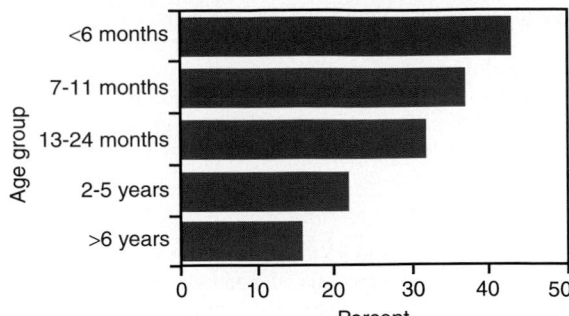

FIGURE 155-6. Proportion of outpatients according to age in Rochester, New York, 1977-1987, who were infected with respiratory syncytial virus and developed lower respiratory tract disease.

from one to the other. Wheezing, rhonchi, rales, and infiltrates on chest roentgenograms may be present in both syndromes.[55] In bronchiolitis, the infiltrates are due to atelectasis, but these often cannot be differentiated from the inflammatory shadows of pneumonia. The hallmarks of bronchiolitis, however, are wheezing and hyperaeration of the lung.

Lower respiratory tract disease is usually heralded by an upper respiratory tract infection with nasal congestion and a cough. Hoarseness and laryngitis are not prominent features. A low-grade fever, lasting for 2 to 4 days, occurs in most young children early in the course of the illness. The height or duration of the fever does not correlate with the severity of the disease and is frequently absent in the presence of lower respiratory tract involvement and at the time of hospitalization.[72] Usually after several days of upper respiratory tract signs and a deepening, more productive cough, the lower respiratory tract involvement is heralded by the onset of dyspnea, an increased respiratory rate, and retractions of the intercostal muscles. In bronchiolitis, both expiratory and inspiratory obstruction may be evident. On auscultation, the infant may have crackles and/or wheezing. These physical findings may be present intermittently and may fluctuate in intensity, indicating that repeated observations of the infant may be necessary to assess clinical severity.[130-132]

Hypoxemia is common in infants hospitalized with RSV lower respiratory tract disease and results from the diffuse viral involvement of the lung parenchyma, which causes an abnormally low ratio of ventilation to perfusion.[133-135] In one group of hospitalized infants, the mean arterial oxygen saturation on admission was 87% percent, with a range of 74% to 95%. The degree of hypoxemia is difficult to assess clinically and requires measurement of the infant's arterial oxygen saturation level.[130,131,134] In children admitted with hypoxemia, clinical improvement usually occurs before the abnormalities in the arterial oxygen saturation level have entirely resolved. In a small proportion of hospitalized infants, alveolar hypoventilation and progressive hypercarbia develop and require assisted ventilation. In most infants, however, the duration of illness is 7 to 21 days, and hospitalization, if required, averages 3 to 7 days.[134,136]

The chest radiograph may show a variety of findings, such as multiple areas of interstitial infiltration and hyperinflation.[137-141] These abnormalities, however, may be minimal despite the severity of the child's illness. Hyperaeration has been shown to be especially indicative of RSV infection, occurring in over half the children hospitalized with RSV infection, and is commonly associated with peribronchial thickening. In 15%, however, hyperaeration may be the only abnormality. Consolidation, which may be from atelectasis, has been noted in about 20% to 25% of the children, particularly in younger infants, and most commonly is subsegmental in the right upper or middle lobe.[137,138,140,142-144] Pleural fluid is rarely demonstrated.

Otitis Media

RSV replicates in the middle ear of experimentally infected animals, and otitis media is a common complication of RSV infection in young children.[69,145-149] The association between RSV infection and otitis media has been shown epidemiologically by concurrent increases in cases of otitis media during outbreaks of RSV disease.[150] In children with otitis media, RSV has been detected in middle ear fluids at rates generally varying from 20% to 60% depending on the method used. Even in children with chronic otitis media, RSV has been detected in 5% to 10% of middle ear effusions.[151,152] In children with documented RSV infection, the virus has been detected in 75% of middle ear effusions using polymerase chain reaction.[146] RSV may be recovered from the ear as the sole pathogen, but commonly it is seen in conjunction with a bacterial pathogen, usually *Streptococcus pneumoniae*.[146,148,153] Thus, whether RSV primarily causes the frequently observed otitis media accompanying RSV infection by direct viral invasion or by augmentation of obstruction of the eustachian tube in conjunction with the bacterial infection, or both, is unclear. However, clinical and experimental evidence suggests that coinfection of RSV with a bacterial pathogen may worsen the outcome of otitis media, resulting in a greater chance of treatment failure with antibiotics and persistent effusion.[146-149]

Infections in Older Children and Adults

RSV infection occurring after the first year or two of life is almost always the result of reinfection. The manifestations of repeated infection are highly variable, ranging from asymptomatic infection to lower respiratory tract involvement and severe disease in high-risk populations. In healthy individuals, repetitive infections are generally milder, and a recent RSV infection tends to ameliorate the symptoms of RSV. Nevertheless, repetitive infections can occur within a short time, even weeks. A number of RSV-specific immunologic findings that are in-

TABLE 155-3 Types of Acute Respiratory Infection in Adults Who Are Infected with Respiratory Syncytial Virus (RSV)

Type of Acute Respiratory Illness	No. of Patients	Percentage with Symptomatic RSV Infection (N = 177)	Percentage of All Patients with RSV Infection (N = 211)
Asymptomatic	34	—	16
Symptomatic	177	—	84
Upper respiratory tract	131	74	62
With fever	52	29	25
Without fever	79	45	37
Lower respiratory tract	46	26	22
Tracheobronchitis	36	20	17
Wheezing	10	6	5

From Hall CB, Long CE, Schnabel KC. Clin Infect Dis. 2001;33:792-796; copyright 2001, with permission from the Infectious Diseases Society of America.

hibitory to an adequate anamnestic response on reinfection have been postulated to contribute to this phenomenon.[118,154-159]

Most commonly, repeated or secondary infections result in an upper respiratory tract illness or tracheobronchitis (Table 155-2, and see Fig. 155-6).[57,60,69,160] When families infected with RSV have been studied, repeated infection is rarely found to be entirely asymptomatic, even in previously healthy adults.[9,69,160-162] Most family members develop signs of upper respiratory tract infection, with nasal congestion and cough (Table 155-3). Fever and earache are more common in young children than in older family members.

Although RSV infections may mimic the common cold, they tend to be more severe and prolonged than are other upper respiratory tract infections (Table 155-4, and see Table 155-3).[69,160,163] In working, healthy adults, RSV infection was symptomatic in 84%, and 22% had lower respiratory tract manifestations. In comparison to influenza infection in the same group of previously healthy adults, fever was less frequent, but ear and sinus pain and a productive cough were significantly more common. The average duration of illness was 9.5 days for

TABLE 155-2 Frequency of Signs and Symptoms in 119 Respiratory Illnesses in Family Members: Comparison of 37 Illnesses from RSV with 82 Illnesses Not Associated with the Virus

Sign or Symptom	RSV-Associated Illness (%)	RSV-Negative Illness (%)	P Value*
Nasal congestion			
Acute[†]	91.9	83	NS
Late[‡]	59.5	26	>.001
Cough			
Acute	81.1	78	NS
Late	45.9	21	<.01
Hoarseness			
Acute	35.1	26	NS
Late	2.7	4	NS
Sore throat			
Acute	32.4	37	NS
Late	2.7	5	NS
Fever			
Acute	27.0	13	>.05 to <.10
Late	5.4	1	NS
Conjunctivitis			
Acute	24.3	12	>.05 to <.10
Late	0.0	2	NS
Earache			
Acute	18.9	13	NS
Late	13.5	2	<.05
Rash			
Acute	8.1	4	NS
Late	5.4	1	NS
Asymptomatic			
Acute	—	—	NS

*Probability is derived from the chi-square test.
[†]Acute RSV illness is defined as occurring on the day RSV was first isolated plus 1 culture day before or after isolation; acute RSV-negative illness is defined as starting on the first day of symptoms plus the next culture day.
[‡]Late RSV illness is defined as occurring on the first day after the acute phase until the first asymptomatic day; late RSV-negative illness is defined as occurring on the first day after the acute phase to the first asymptomatic day.
NS, not significant; RSV, respiratory syncytial virus.
From Hall CB, Geiman JM, Biggar R, et al. Respiratory syncytial virus infections within families. N Engl J Med. 1976;294:414-417.

TABLE 155-4 Clinical Characteristics of Illness Due to Influenza or RSV among 211 Previously Healthy Adults

Characteristic	No. (%) of adults with illness due to		
	RSV (N = 177)	Influenza (N = 59)	P* Value
Sign or Symptom			
Fever (temperature >37.8° C)	50 (28)	43 (73)	<.001
Nasal congestion or rhinorrhea	157 (89)	46 (78)	<.04
Sore throat	102 (58)	32 (54)	.65
Ear pain	35 (20)	3 (5)	<.01
Headache	70 (40)	48 (81)	<.001
Sinus pain	55 (31)	8 (14)	<.01
Cough			
Nonproductive	150 (85)	47 (80)	.36
Productive	92 (52)	14 (24)	<.001
LRT signs or wheezing	28 (16)	5 (9)	.16
Work absence	67 (38)	39 (66)	<.001
Duration of Illness, Mean Days (Range)	9.5 (1-20)	6.8 (3.9-6.6)	<.001

*Values for signs and symptoms were derived by chi-square test; values for duration of illness were derived by unpaired student *t* test.
LRT, lower respiratory tract; RSV, respiratory syncytial virus.
From Hall CB, Long CE, Schnabel KC. Clin Infect Dis 2001;33:792-6. Copyright 2001 with permission from the Infectious Diseases Society of America.

RSV infection, which was significantly longer than that produced by influenza, and 38% missed work (see Table 155-4).

RSV infection may also be a major cause of prolonged cough in adults. In university students with cough persisting for 6 or more days, Harris and colleagues identified RSV infection in approximately 11%, and the cough lasted for an average of 18 to 19 days.[163] In comparison, *Bordetella pertussis* was identified in 4%, *Mycoplasma pneumoniae* in 9.5%, and *Chlamydia pneumoniae* in 8.8%. In over half of those with RSV infection, the clinical manifestations were indistinguishable from those of pertussis, and 61% were treated with a macrolide.

Viral shedding in healthy adults is generally less than that observed in young children and usually lasts for 1 to 6 days. However, serial pulmonary function testing performed in young adults with moderate clinical symptoms from RSV infection demonstrated that total pulmonary resistance was elevated, and hyperreactivity of the airway to cholinergic stimulus lasted for 8 weeks after the onset of illness.[161]

Although respiratory disease from RSV in older adults, especially those who are institutionalized, has been recognized for some time, the burden RSV places on the health care of this growing population has been appreciated only recently.[9,164-170] In long-term care facilities, 5% to 27% of respiratory infections have been estimated to be caused by RSV, and the attack rate has been estimated to be 1% to 15%.[164] Although clinical illness and mortality associated with RSV infection in this population have been reported to range from 0% to over 50%, prospective studies have estimated that pneumonia will develop in 10% of the RSV-infected patients, and 1% to 5% will succumb.[164] The severity of disease is greatest in those with underlying cardiac and pulmonary disease. Chronic obstructive pulmonary disease, cardiovascular disease, and smoking are risk factors that have been found in approximately 40% to 60% of these patients, and these rates were similar to those associated with influenza infection.[170] RSV infection is a major instigator of exacerbations of chronic obstructive pulmonary disease or cardiovascular disease, and such exacerbations may be the major epidemiologic manifestation of RSV infection in institutionalized populations. In a prospectively followed group of patients with stable chronic obstructive lung disease who had an average age of 67 years, exacerbations were associated with an identified viral pathogen in 64%.[171]

RSV was detected in 24%, which was second only to rhinoviruses as the most frequently identified agent.

In adults living independently in the community, the rates of RSV as a cause of pneumonia and hospitalization have varied considerably, as few prospective studies have been conducted in this population. Nicholson and colleagues prospectively studied acute respiratory infection occurring in older adults in the community and identified RSV as the cause in 7% of cases associated with identifiable pathogens.[167,172] In comparison, 9% were caused by influenza A or B, and 3% by the parainfluenza viruses. The morbidity associated with RSV was also similar to that with influenza, causing lower respiratory tract illness in 82% compared with 79% of patients with influenza. Among adults attending daycare facilities, 10% of acute respiratory infections have been found to be caused by RSV, a rate similar to those for influenza and coronaviruses.[173]

As a cause of community-acquired pneumonia in healthy adults of younger ages, RSV was found serologically to be the cause in 4.4% of adults admitted with a clinical diagnosis of pneumonia, which was the third most common cause identified.[9] *S. pneumoniae* accounted for 6% and influenza for 5% of cases. Of note, however, 32% of the RSV-infected patients were under 65 years of age and 44% were under 40 years of age and previously healthy. Overall, approximately 2% to 5% of pneumonia cases in adults during the entire year, and 5% to 15% of those that occur during the winter months, have been estimated to be caused by RSV.[164]

The characteristics of RSV pneumonia in these adult populations have differed clinically from those caused by influenza by a greater likelihood of wheezing, rhonchi, nasal congestion, and little or no increase in the white blood cell count in RSV-associated cases (Table 155-5).[9,164,167,172] Furthermore, RSV outbreaks in these populations tend not to be as rapid as those associated with influenza, and patients are less likely to have the high fever and gastrointestinal symptoms that frequently accompany influenza. However, the clinical findings of RSV infection in these adult populations are not sufficiently distinctive or appreciated to result in a correct diagnosis or even a suspicion of RSV infection.

Nevertheless, estimates of RSV as a cause of morbidity and mortality in adult populations underscore its potential importance.[10,166]

TABLE 155-5 Clinical Presentation of Adults Hospitalized with Lower Respiratory Infections*

Clinical Feature	RSV (%) (N = 57)	Influenza (%) (N = 65)[†]	Bacterial (%) (N = 93)[‡]	Atypical (%) (N = 89)[§]	All non-RSV (%) (N = 1528)
Reported cough	88	78**	73[¶]	83	79**
Reported fever	61	75**	77[¶]	67	64
Reported shortness of breath	82	80	73**	76	78
Reported runny nose	58	57	40[¶]	51	50
Reported sinus pain	33	31	31	30	26
Reported ear pain	19	22	20	16	16
Reported sore throat	42	40	35	39	35
Reported wheezing	79	68**	47[††]	63[¶]	62[‖]
Wheeze on physical examination	53	31[‖]	19[††]	18[††]	28[††]
Wheeze on exam or report	93	74[‖]	56[††]	68[††]	70[††]
Rhonchi on physical examination	46	29**	20[††]	26[‖]	28[‖]
Crackles on physical examination	42	52	57**	58[¶]	50
Chest radiograph "pneumonia"	40	25**	54**	60[¶]	44
Chest radiograph "clear"	27	38	16**	10[‖]	20
WBC count <12,000	67	78**	40[††]	55**	54**

*RSV-infected patients are compared with those having documented infections with influenza virus, "typical" bacterial agents, and "atypical" pneumonia agents and entire group of RSV-negative patients.

[†]Influenza A and B virus.

[‡]*Streptococcus pneumonia, Haemophilus influenzae, Streptococcus pyogenes, Neisseria meningitidis, Staphylococcus aureus, Escherichia coli,* and *Klebsiella* species.

[§]*Legionella pneumophilia, Mycoplasma pneumonia,* and *Chlamydophila pneumoniae.*

[‖].001 < p ≤ .01 vs RSV-positive group.

[¶].01 < p ≤ .05 vs RSV-positive group.

**.05 < p < .20 vs RSV-positive group.

[††]p ≤ .001 vs RSV-positive group.

RSV, respiratory syncytial virus; WBC, white blood cell.

From Dowell S, Anderson L, Gary H, et al. Respiratory syncytial virus is an important cause of community-acquired lower respiratory infection among hospitalized adults. J Infect Dis. 1996;174:456-462.

Han and colleagues have estimated that approximately 680,000 hospitalizations of older adults and 74% of their deaths are caused by pneumonia each year in the United States.[10] Approximately 2% to 9% of these cases result from RSV infection and cost 150 to 680 million dollars annually. The cost of an additional number of RSV infections in the community and in assisted living facilities has not been estimated or added to this economic burden.

Uncommon Manifestations of Infection

A variety of nonrespiratory manifestations have been associated with RSV infection in case reports. The role of RSV in producing any of these associated disorders is unclear. Central nervous system disorders, including meningitis, myelitis, ataxia, and hemiplegia, have been reported rarely.[174-176] A neuropathic strain of RSV in mice, however, has been adapted to produce encephalitis in the suckling mouse by intracerebral inoculation.[177] RSV has also been associated with cardiac abnormalities, including myocarditis and arrhythmias,[17,178,179] along with a variety of exanthems involving the trunk or face, or both.[17,174,175,178,179]

Nosocomial Infection

The characteristics of RSV make it a particularly frequent and potentially hazardous nosocomial infection that is often not recognized.[160,180-191] RSV produces outbreaks each year, with widespread infection in both children and adults, including medical personnel, whose illness may be mild enough to not cause absence from work. Furthermore, spread of the virus is facilitated by the number of young infants admitted during an outbreak who tend to shed high titers of virus for prolonged periods.[136] Introduction of infection onto a ward is almost inevitable, and a susceptible population is always present, as repeated infections are common.

In 1941, Adams described an outbreak of pneumonia that affected young hospitalized infants and resulted in the death of 28%.[192] This was probably the first description of a nosocomial outbreak of RSV infection, but it was only some 20 years later that RSV was implicated as the cause when Adams and his co-workers observed a similar outbreak in infants of illness that could then be determined to be caused by RSV.[15,193] Although recent nosocomial outbreaks of RSV in infants have not been associated with such a high mortality, fatal infection may still occur, especially in those with underlying diseases.[113,180,182,184,187,190,194] Nosocomial infections acquired by infants and older patients with underlying diseases, especially immunocompromised conditions, are almost always symptomatic and range from a febrile upper respiratory tract illness to severe lower respiratory tract involvement and death.[113,114,182-184,187,188,195,196]

How RSV spreads so effectively on hospital wards is not entirely clear. Antigenic and genomic fingerprinting of specific strains of RSV, along with reverse transcriptase–polymerase chain reaction to detect RSV in air samples, has delineated the patterns of nosocomial spread and shown that several strains and sources of RSV frequently erupt into a single nosocomial outbreak.[191] Both hospital staff and visitors appear to be important in the introduction and spread of the virus. During some nosocomial outbreaks, nearly half of hospital personnel have acquired RSV infection.[182,183,185,187,189] Transmission of the virus occurs not only as a result of infection of the medical staff but also via contaminated secretions spreading on fomites from infected patients to other patients and staff.[197,198] For example, RSV in the secretions of an infected infant can survive on countertops for more than 24 hours, and on hospital gowns, paper, tissues, and skin for 15 to 60 minutes.[22] Volunteers have been exposed to infected infants in three ways: (1) through close contact, (2) via fomites, with subsequent self-inoculation, or (3) by small-particle aerosol.[186] Volunteers exposed by either of the first two, but not the last method, became infected. This suggests that small-particle aerosols are less important in the spread of RSV than direct contact with infectious secretions via fomites or large-particle aerosols that generally traverse no more than about 3 feet.

COMPLICATIONS

Patients at High Risk for Severe Infection

Children with Underlying Diseases

Certain underlying conditions put young children at high risk for experiencing complicated RSV infection with prolonged morbidity and sequelae.[199-201] Those children who are particularly likely to require hospitalization when infected with RSV are those born prematurely and those with underlying chronic lung disease, congenital heart disease, immunosuppressive conditions, or other chronic diseases such as nephrotic syndrome.[202] An estimated one quarter to two thirds of young children identified with RSV infection have such an underlying condition and have an estimated mortality in the United States of 3% to 4%.[199-201,203]

In prospective studies conducted over a 20-year period, approximately 60% of children hospitalized with RSV lower respiratory tract disease had an underlying high-risk condition, including age less than 6 weeks (Table 155-6). Preterm gestation, with or without associated chronic lung disease, is the most frequently identified risk factor. The proportion of infants hospitalized with RSV who were preterm or had low birth weight has steadily increased in recent years.[199] During 8 years, from 1989 to 1997, the number of low-birth-weight infants (<2500 g) and very low birth weight infants (<1500 g) increased by about 12% and 20%, respectively; because this is a major risk factor, the numbers suggest that cases of severe RSV infection will continue to increase.[199]

The risk for RSV hospitalization for infants whose gestation was less than 36 weeks is approximately three times higher than that for full-term infants, and for infants under 32 weeks' gestation the risk is seven times greater.[199,202-204] The presence of chronic lung disease or bronchopulmonary dysplasia is an added risk for hospitalization that lasts through the first 2 years or more of life.[66,199,202] An estimated 17% of such infants require hospitalization for RSV during their first 2 years of life and have increased risks for admission to the intensive care unit and need for mechanical ventilation.

RSV infection also exacerbates the underlying disease in children with other forms of chronic lung disease, such as cystic fibrosis. In a prospective study aimed at determining the role of respiratory viral infections in patients with cystic fibrosis compared with their normal siblings, respiratory illnesses occurred approximately twice as fre-

TABLE 155-6 Proportions of Different Types of Underlying Conditions in 1532 Children Hospitalized* with Lower Respiratory Tract Disease from RSV

| Years | Percentage of All Children Hospitalized with RSV Infection and with Underlying Conditions of | | | | | | | |
	Prematurity (<36 wk)	Cardiac Condition	Chronic Lung Condition	Immuno-compromise	Multiple Congenital Abnormalities	Other Conditions	Age ≤ 6 wk	Total with One or More Underlying Conditions
1976-1984	21	11	3	2	5	6	26	63
1985-1992	20	7	8	2	5	3	25	57
1993-1996	28	10	9	3	4	5	24	67
1976-1996	25	8	8	2	5	5	25	63

*Study performed at Strong Memorial Hospital, Rochester, NY, 1976 to 1996.

quently in those with cystic fibrosis. RSV accounted for approximately 18% of these symptomatic infections, and 39% required hospitalization.[205] Abman and colleagues similarly showed that in the first year of life, RSV accounted for 33% of hospitalizations in children with cystic fibrosis, 43% of whom required mechanical ventilation, and the mean duration of hospitalization was 22 days.[206] Moreover, evidence of lung deterioration was greater in those children with cystic fibrosis who had been infected with RSV than in those who had not. RSV infection may cause exacerbations of cystic fibrosis and deterioration of lung function in adults as well.[207]

Children with congenital heart disease have long been noted to have an increased morbidity and mortality when infected with RSV. Congenital heart disease was the third most frequent underlying condition in infants hospitalized with RSV infection in the Palivizumab Outcomes Registry.[202] Approximately one fourth to one third of infants with congenital cardiac disease hospitalized with RSV infection required intensive care, and approximately 20% of these needed mechanical ventilation.[208-210] Infants hospitalized in the first few months of life with uncorrected cyanotic congenital heart disease are at particular peril.[200,209] The types of cardiac conditions associated with poorer prognoses have not been entirely defined, but pulmonary hypertension accompanying congenital heart disease appears to increase the risk appreciably. Recent advances in the surgical and intensive care management of these children, including early correction, have appreciably reduced the mortality from RSV infection in infants with congenital heart disease, with an estimated decrease from about 37% in the 1970s to 3% in the 1990s.[211] Nevertheless, the mortality for such infants remains three to four times greater than for infants without underlying conditions.

Immunocompromised Patients

Respiratory syncytial virus is an important cause of increased morbidity and mortality in immunosuppressed patients, especially in those with congenital immunodeficiencies, as well as those receiving immunosuppressive therapy.[112,113,194,212-214] The increasing number of highly immunosuppressed patients, particularly those undergoing transplantation of bone marrow and solid organs, has heightened awareness of RSV as an opportunistic agent in those with compromised immune function. RSV infection is usually introduced onto wards that house immunocompromised patients by medical staff or visitors who have a community-acquired RSV infection that may be mild or unrecognized. Once introduced, however, the spread may be rapid and difficult to control, and the morbidity and mortality can be appreciable.[113,194] The reported mortality in transplant units has varied considerably depending on the methods and patient populations, but it has generally been estimated to be between 30% and 100%.[194,215,216]

Factors shown to affect the severity of the RSV infection include the degree of immunosuppression and the source and timing of the transplant. More severe disease correlates with allogeneic transplantation, with occurrence of RSV infection within 2 months of receiving the transplant but before engraftment, and with the presence of acute or chronic graft-versus-host disease.[113,194,195,215-217]

RSV infection in these patients may clinically mimic other opportunistic agents and result in the correct etiology not being diagnosed or even suspected.[114] Concurrent infections by other opportunistic agents may further confound the diagnosis or retard pursuit of tests for RSV. RSV infection in these hosts is sometimes initially mild and overlooked. When lower respiratory tract involvement occurs, the chest radiograph can demonstrate a spectrum of findings similar to those associated with pathogens that are better recognized as causing opportunistic infections. Findings range from focal interstitial infiltrations, sometimes with hyperinflation or with lobar consolidation, to generalized alveolar and interstitial infiltrates, or even to a picture of acute respiratory distress syndrome.[113,194,215,216] Hypoxemia frequently accompanies any of these presentations, and progression to severe lower respiratory tract involvement may be rapid.

Some clinical and epidemiologic clues are more indicative of RSV infection than of other opportunistic pathogens. These include upper respiratory tract signs or symptoms, radiologic evidence of sinusitis, and wheezing.[194,215,216] One of the most helpful clues is the presence of an RSV outbreak in the community.

Confirmation of RSV infection by laboratory techniques is also problematic in these patients. Even when there is marked pulmonary involvement, RSV is usually shed in low titers, so viral isolation and rapid antigen detection assays using upper respiratory tract secretions are insensitive and inadequate means of diagnosis. These tests applied to bronchopulmonary lavage, however, provide a much higher yield of positive results.[194,215,216,218]

Patients with human immunodeficiency virus (HIV) infection also can have a greater morbidity from RSV infection. The severity varies according to the stage and severity of the HIV infection, but from the limited information available, RSV infection in patients with HIV generally appears to be not as severe as in those with transplants and congenital immune deficiency diseases.[219-223] In patients with HIV infection and with evidence of immunocompromise, RSV may be shed for prolonged periods, and the infection may involve the lower respiratory tract. Confounding this, however, is the observation that children with HIV infection and viral respiratory infections also have a higher rate of a bacterial coinfection.[221-223] Furthermore, the clinical outcome of respiratory viral infections has not been consistently different between children with and those without HIV infection.[223]

No definitive guidelines are currently available for optimal therapy for immunocompromised patients with RSV infection. Determining the effectiveness of the various therapeutic regimens that have been used in highly compromised patients is hampered by limited data, lack of prospective, controlled trials, and the diversity of the patient population. Furthermore, the efficacy of therapy in transplant recipients depends on the length of time between the post-transplant onset of infection and the time at which therapy is initiated.[113] The pre-engraftment stage is associated with a greater risk for lower respiratory tract involvement and mortality than is the postengraftment stage. Thus, infection occurring in the pre-eruptive stage is more likely to benefit from therapy initiated before lower respiratory tract involvement develops. At the M. D. Anderson Cancer Center, patients treated early, whether in the pre-engraftment or postengraftment stage, had a mortality of about 30% to 40%, whereas all those receiving late therapy died (Table 155-7).[113]

The therapeutic and prophylactic agents employed for RSV in highly immunocompromised patients have generally focused on immunoglobulin products and/or ribavirin as for other RSV infections in infants.[113,114,194,214,224] The immunoglobulin products have consisted of immune globulin—intravenous (IGIV), IGIV with high neutralizing titers to RSV (RSV-IGIV), and a monoclonal antibody directed against the F protein of RSV (palivizumab). Aerosolized ribavirin, alone or in combination with one of the immunoglobulin products, has also been commonly used (see "Management," later).[113,225] Most centers advise using one of these regimens, but their successes cannot be adequately compared in these variable and uncontrolled populations.

Most important, however, in the management of immunocompromised patients is prevention of RSV infection by strict adherence to infection control policies. The CDC Guidelines for Preventing Opportunistic Infection in Hematopoietic Stem Cell Transplant Recipients provides evidence-based recommendations for control of RSV infection and transmission. These guidelines emphasize preventing the introduction of community respiratory viruses, including RSV, onto units with compromised patients, along with early diagnosis.[81,226,227]

Acute Complications

Apnea is one of the most common of the acute complications in young infants hospitalized with RSV lower respiratory tract disease and is observed in approximately 20% of hospitalized infants.[81,228] Most at risk for developing apnea are preterm infants with a gestational age of 32 weeks or less, those with a history of apnea of prematurity, and infants of young postnatal age, less than 44 weeks postconception. Characteristically, the apnea occurs at the onset of the RSV infection and may be the initial sign, before respiratory symptoms are noted.

TABLE 155-7 Mortality Associated with RSV Pneumonia in Adult BMT Recipients Treated with Aerosolized Ribavirin and IGIV[*]

Timing of Therapy	Patients with Pneumonia (n)	Associated Mortality (%)
All	66	44
Early (all immunoglobulins)	46	28
Standard IGIV	27	22
"Hot lots"[†]	13	31
Monoclonal RSV antibody	3	33
RSV-IGIV	3	67
Late	9	100
No treatment	10	60
Ribavirin intolerance	1	100

[*]Study performed at the M. D. Anderson Cancer Center during the winters from 1992-1993 to 1999-2000.
[†]IGIV with high titers of RSV antibody.
BMT, bone marrow transplant; IGIV, immune globulin, intravenous; RSV, respiratory syncytial virus.
Reprinted from Champlin RE, Whimbey E. Community respiratory virus infections. Biol Blood Marrow Transplant. 2001;7:8s-10s. Copyright 2001. Reprinted with permission from the American Society Blood for Marrow Transplantation.

The apnea associated with RSV is nonobstructive and does not appear to increase the infant's risk for subsequent apneic episodes.

Infants admitted with RSV lower respiratory tract disease may be at increased risk for aspiration, which can appear clinically similar to bronchiolitis with airway hyperreactivity.[229,230] In one study of infants hospitalized with the diagnosis of RSV bronchiolitis and followed over a 12-month period, 83% developed reactive airway disease if they received neither ribavirin nor therapy for aspiration. However, the development of hyperreactive airways was reduced to 45% in infants who were given thickened feedings along with early ribavirin therapy. Furthermore, the decrease in episodes of reactive airway disease was greater in infants who received both ribavirin and thickened feedings than in those infants who received either therapy alone.[230]

Young infants hospitalized with RSV lower respiratory tract disease are frequently given antibiotics. In part, this is because of their young age, the presence of fever, and, particularly, the relatively common bacterial pneumonia–like appearance of the chest radiographic findings, especially consolidation or atelectasis. However, in the United States, a secondary bacterial infection is an unusual complication of RSV infection.[231-236] A 9-year prospective study of infants hospitalized with RSV lower respiratory tract disease identified secondary bacterial pneumonia in less than 1%. Furthermore, this complication appeared to be more frequent in infants who had been treated with broad-spectrum antibiotics.[231] In another study of young febrile children with and without bronchiolitis, bacteremia occurred in none of the 156 patients with bronchiolitis compared with 2.7% of the controls.[232] Antibiotic therapy has not been shown to improve the rate of recovery in infants with RSV lower respiratory tract disease and thus should be reserved for those with documented bacterial complications.[237] In developing countries, however, concurrent bacterial infections are much more common and may contribute appreciably to the high mortality rate from RSV.[238]

Long-Term Complications

Recurrent wheezing after RSV lower respiratory tract disease and bronchiolitis in infancy has long been recognized as a frequent sequela, occurring in approximately 50% of children.[239,240] In most children, the severity of the recurrent wheezing episodes decreases with age, although in some, pulmonary function abnormalities may persist without clinical manifestations.[111,241] The pathogenesis of the association between RSV infection and the subsequent hyperreactivity is unclear. However, research has focused on the similarities between the immune responses after RSV infection and the responses observed with reactive airway disease.[81,240,242] This link may offer a possible explanation for the immunopathogenesis of RSV disease.[81,109,243-246]

RSV infection has been shown both in vitro and in children infected with RSV to activate transcription factors that result in the release of proinflammatory cytokines, including IL-1β, IL-6, IL-10, IL-11, and the chemokines IL-8, RANTES (regulated on activation, normal T cell expressed and secreted), and macrophage inflammatory protein 1α (MIP-1α) (see section on Immunity).[81,86,243,247,248] Many studies that examine the link between RSV infection and reactive airway disease have focused primarily on cytokines that signal B cells for the production of IgE and those involved in eliciting eosinophils, monocytes, and T cells, which are also produced during an allergic response.[81,110,246] Despite the observation that these factors are elevated in RSV infection, their direct correlation with the frequency and severity of pulmonary sequela has not been proven. Although atopy does not appear to be a major predictor in determining which children will develop long-term pulmonary abnormalities,[110,111] it may increase the risk for more severe RSV disease and complications, including recurrent wheezing. In part, the conflicting data associating recurrent wheezing and RSV infection most likely result from the fact that the clinical syndrome of hyperreactive airways is engendered by many different genetic, developmental, and environmental disorders, which include atopy in some cases.[87-91,241,249]

DIAGNOSIS

The diagnosis of RSV infection is often made with reasonable accuracy on the basis of clinical and epidemiologic findings in infants with lower respiratory tract disease, but the findings are less specific in adults. A specific diagnosis may be made by viral isolation, by one of the rapid diagnostic tests, or by serology.

Although viral isolation has been the standard technique, isolation of RSV takes time, is expensive, and depends on the quality of the cell lines and the laboratory techniques. Despite this, isolation in cell culture does have the potential advantage of identifying other viral agents that may be present. The type and handling of the specimen are also important, as RSV is a relatively labile virus and requires prompt inoculation without subjecting the specimen to major temperature changes during transportation. Nasopharyngeal washes or tracheal secretions are better than nasal swabs.[250] From immunocompromised patients with positive cultures, 15% of nasopharyngeal wash specimens have been reported to be positive, compared with 71% of endotracheal secretions and 89% of bronchioalveolar washes.[251] Specific cytopathic changes usually appear within 3 to 7 days, but the range is 2 to 10 days. The use of shell vials hastens the speed of identification.[252,253]

More rapid diagnosis is necessary for infection control and to determine specific therapy. Hence, a variety of rapid direct antigen detection tests are used by most laboratories.[252,254] Direct and indirect immunofluorescent assays are highly specific but require several hours and skilled laboratory personnel. Most frequently used are the commercially available rapid detection tests using an enzyme immunoassay (EIA) method. The advantages of these tests are their rapidity, usually no more than one-half hour, their ease, their objective end point, and their relatively low cost. Their disadvantage is that their sensitivity, usually 60% to 70%, ranges from about 50% to 90%.[254] Negative tests by this method, therefore, require additional testing by another method. The specificity of EIA methods, however, is usually good, around 90% to 95%, during an RSV outbreak when the incidence of RSV infection in the community is high. Their specificity, however, falls markedly when RSV is not active in the community.

Reverse transcriptase–polymerase chain reaction (RT-PCR) for the diagnosis of RSV infections, used mostly in research laboratories, has consistently demonstrated much higher rates of specificity and sensitivity than other diagnostic methods.[254-256] The inclusion of appropriate additional primers allows the group of RSV to be concurrently determined.[257,258] Other respiratory pathogens may be simultaneously identified, and quantitation of the number of copies of the viral RNA can also be obtained.[256-258]

Serologic diagnosis of RSV infection has been more useful for epidemiologic studies than for patient management because of the delay required to obtain convalescent sera. Furthermore, young infants, older individuals with repeated infections, and immunocompromised patients may not produce a significant rise in antibody titer, depending on the assay used.[102,103,259] Serologic diagnosis is most frequently made using enzyme immunoassays and neutralization assays. These also allow detection of specific antibody classes.[260,261] Earlier diagnosis by using assays that detect specific IgM antibodies is of limited usefulness, as specific IgM antibodies are not consistently detectable in patients with proven RSV infection and may require 1 to 7 weeks to appear after the onset of illness.[9,262] Secretory class-specific antibodies to RSV in nasopharyngeal secretions may also be detected by enzyme immunoassays.[263] Because these secretory antibodies may be present earlier in infection than humoral antibodies, their detection has been used as an adjunct to diagnosis by antigen detection.[263]

MANAGEMENT

Most infants with RSV infection require no more than the usual care given to ensure comfort, fever control, and adequate fluid intake. In the hospitalized and more severely infected infants, the quality of supportive care is of prime importance.[264] Documentation of blood gases in hospitalized infants and administration of appropriate supplemental oxygen are necessary for the more severely ill. Additional therapies have primarily involved ribavirin, bronchodilating agents, corticosteroids, and antibiotics. In general, controlled studies have indicated that for most children these agents are of limited benefit, and their use should be highly selective. Despite this, these agents are administered to the majority of children hospitalized with RSV infection.[265-267]

Ribavirin (1-β-D-ribofuranosyl-1,2,4-triazole-3-carboxamide), a synthetic nucleoside, is the only currently approved specific treatment for RSV lower respiratory tract disease in hospitalized infants. The drug is administered as a small-particle aerosol for periods of 8 to 24 hours per day until improvement is evident. Shorter and intermittent periods of treatment may be beneficial.[268] Ribavirin has a broad spectrum of antiviral activity, including activity against both RNA and DNA viruses. It is generally safe and well tolerated in infants receiving aerosolized therapy, and development of resistance to ribavirin by RSV strains has not been recognized even with prolonged treatment. Although the drug has shown some clinical benefit in some studies, the days of hospitalization and short-term outcome have not been affected by ribavirin therapy. The degree of benefit relative to the considerable cost of aerosolized ribavirin must be considered on an individual basis.[97,269] Follow-up studies after ribavirin therapy have suggested that aerosolized treatment of the acute infection may provide some amelioration in the long-term pulmonary sequelae and recurrent wheezing.[270,271] Ribavirin has considerable cost and presents a potential hazard to health care personnel, which makes its use problematic. The cost and logistics are even more substantial for its use in adults, where evidence of efficacy is lacking.

Bronchodilators are commonly used to treat infants with bronchiolitis. These include oral and inhaled β₂-agonists, combined α- and β-agonists, or anticholinergics. The results have been variable, in part because the manifestations of bronchiolitis, although clinically similar to asthma, are engendered by several mechanisms of obstruction other than bronchial hyperreactivity, including mucus and inflammatory cellular material and the infant's small airway caliber.[264,272] Thus, benefit may be seen only in selected populations. In a meta-analysis of bronchodilator therapy, a firm conclusion about the benefit of bronchodilators was confounded by the heterogenicity of the populations and methods used in the studies.[272] Guidelines for the treatment of bronchiolitis have not recommended the use of bronchodilators for routine management of children under a year of age with first-time wheezing. However, because of the many variables affecting clinical presentation and patient characteristics, therapy should be selected on an individual basis.[237,273-275]

Corticosteroid therapy has mostly been studied in infants with the diagnosis of bronchiolitis, but in only some has RSV been specifically identified as the cause. The results have been conflicting.[239,264,270,273,276,277] Most trials evaluating corticosteroid therapy have been with inhaled corticosteroids. Of these, five showed no benefit during the acute phase or subsequently for recurrent wheezing, and two showed some diminished incidence of subsequent wheezing.[270] A meta-analysis of six trials of systemic corticosteroid therapy demonstrated a pooled mean reduction of 0.43 day in the duration of hospitalization and symptoms among treated infants, but four trials that excluded infants with previous wheezing showed no significant benefit.[278] These contrasting results are most likely explained by the variable methodology, the heterogeneity of the children included, and the lack of specific etiology of the bronchiolitis. Corticosteroid therapy, however, is not recommended for the routine management of infants with first-time wheezing.

The Agency for Healthcare Research and Quality reviewed 83 articles that reported various modalities of management for bronchiolitis and concluded that the evidence is currently insufficient to recommend any single agent for the treatment of bronchiolitis over good supportive care.[274] Furthermore, they stressed the need for rigorously controlled and adequately sized trials. Bronchodilating agents cited as candidates for future studies included nebulized epinephrine, nebulized salbutamol plus ipratropium bromide, nebulized ipratropium bromide, oral or parenteral corticosteroids (preferably dexamethasone), and aerosolized corticosteroids (preferably budesonide). Two potential interventions, inhaled helium-oxygen and surfactant for ventilated children, would be applicable only for severely ill children. Antibiotics should not be administered routinely for therapy or to prevent secondary bacterial infection. As secondary bacterial infection rarely occurs with RSV infection, antibiotics should be reserved for individual cases in which bacterial infection is proven or highly suspected while awaiting culture results.[231]

PREVENTION

The viper's venom,
*   the serpent's spell*
daunts not the tortoise
*   beneath his shell. . . .*

C. B. H.

Infection Control

Prevention rather than treatment is the preferable, but yet unattained, goal for the control of RSV infection. Avoiding infection at home through interruption of the transmission of the virus is unlikely to be completely effective. However, general precautions may be useful against the spread of infectious secretions on hands and fomites. These include good hand hygiene, use of hand-rub antiseptic products, and care of contaminated tissues, toys, and other objects likely to be contaminated with secretions.[279]

On hospital wards, however, strict adherence to recommended guidelines for infection control for RSV is essential and cost effective.[113,197,280] Nosocomial RSV infections remain a yearly concern, particularly on units with immunocompromised patients,[113,226] and on pediatric wards (where up to 40% of identified RSV infections are nosocomially acquired) and neonatal units (up to 70%).[180,197,281,282]

RSV may be spread by close contact and by direct inoculation of large droplets from the secretions of an infected person, as well as by indirect spread from hands that touch infectious secretions in the environment.[197,198] Careful hand hygiene by all personnel, therefore, is integral to preventing nosocomial transmission. Additional procedures aimed at preventing self-inoculation include the wearing of eye-nose goggles and gloves; gloves supplement hand hygiene by diminishing the likelihood that personnel will touch their eyes or nose. Procedures aimed at reducing the risk of introduction and spread of RSV to other personnel and patients include the wearing of gowns for close contact with infected patients, isolation or cohorting of infected patients, and the use of rapid diagnostic techniques. In addition, during the RSV season, staff with signs of respiratory illness should not care for high-risk patients, and visitors should be screened for respiratory illness. Of prime importance is that infection control procedures for RSV be reviewed yearly with all personnel, before and during the RSV season, to maintain compliance.[197]

Use of Products with Respiratory Syncytial Virus Antibody

Other available means of prophylaxis for RSV infection are primarily to be used for limited periods and for target groups most at risk for severe RSV disease. High-risk infants can be passively immunized by administration of intravenous immunoglobulin containing high levels of RSV neutralizing antibody (RSV-IGIV) or intramuscular monoclonal antibody (palivizumab).[97,202,269,283] RSV-IGIV is a polyclonal antibody preparation; when given monthly, it reduced the risk for hospitalization by 41% in high-risk children with prematurity, with or without chronic lung disease.[284,285] Palivizumab, a humanized mouse IgG monoclonal antibody that binds the F protein of RSV, was developed for monthly intramuscular administration.[286] It was shown to reduce hospitalization for RSV infection by 55% in the same high-risk groups of infants.

Current recommendations for the use of palivizumab in the United States suggest that prophylaxis should be considered for specific groups of children with chronic lung disease who are less than 24 months of age, and for preterm infants, primarily those with a gestational age of less than 28 weeks.[97,269] Although children with cyanotic heart disease were not initially recommended for prophylaxis because of concern about adverse effects in these patients in studies using RSV-IGIV, more recent studies have suggested that palivizumab is safe for children with cyanotic heart disease who meet the other criteria for RSV prophylaxis.[287]

Controversies exist about the precise definition of groups that would receive the most benefit from RSV prophylaxis, and about its relative cost effectiveness.[274,288,289] The assessment of the prophylactic use of palivizumab by the Agency for Healthcare Research and Quality confirmed its effectiveness in reducing hospitalization in high-risk infants and also noted that no data currently exist evaluating the effect of such prophylaxis on longer-term outcomes, including the sequelae of subsequent wheezing episodes, asthma, hospitalization, and pulmonary disease or functional pulmonary abnormalities.[274] Furthermore, the cost effectiveness of such prophylaxis was shown to vary widely depending on the assumed costs of hospitalization, prophylaxis, and other health care modalities. The expense of prophylaxis incurred for infants born at 32 to 35 weeks' gestation ranged from none to $328,000 in 2002 dollars. The cost per hospitalization avoided had a wide range but was typically $40,000 to $50,000. The Agency for Healthcare Research and Quality concluded that the wide variations in the methods used and results found in the analyzed studies did not permit a reliable estimate of the cost effectiveness of RSV prophylaxis for any target population.

Immunization

The optimal means of prophylaxis for RSV infection would be an effective vaccine. However, notable barriers to the development of a safe and effective vaccine against RSV exist. The vaccine must be able to protect against illness during the newborn period and at a time when specific maternal antibody is abundantly present. Furthermore, the ideal vaccine would provide better protection than natural disease, which does not confer durable immunity.

The initial alum-precipitated, formalin-inactivated vaccine developed in the 1960s produced excellent levels of serum antibody but was followed by the unfortunate event of augmented disease in the vaccinees during subsequent natural infection, as discussed previously. This past experience, however, spurred investigation into the immunopathogenesis of the abnormal response and suggested some potential criteria for the development of safe and successful candidate vaccines.

Clinical research has focused primarily on subunit vaccines, live-attenuated vaccines, and polypeptide vaccines. The two major surface glycoproteins, the F and G proteins, are the primary targets for the subunit vaccines. Three generations of the purified fusion protein (PFP) vaccines have been evaluated in clinical trials. The initial PFP-1 and PFP-2 vaccines were evaluated in trials of normal children and those with underlying diseases, including cystic fibrosis, bronchopulmonary dysplasia, and asthma. Trials in healthy adults, in older adults, and in women in their third trimester of pregnancy or postpartum have also been conducted.[290-292] These vaccines were shown to be safe and generally immunogenic, and immunogenicity was enhanced when they contained some G protein in addition to F protein.[293] This later generation of PFP continues to be investigated.

Other candidate vaccines being studied include a polypeptide vaccine (BBG2Na), which contains a conserved region of the G protein fused to the albumin-binding domain of the streptococcal G protein, and chimeric vaccines of the F and G proteins.[292,294,295] Thus far, these vaccines have been shown to be generally safe in seropositive subjects, immunogenic, and less likely to engender an augmented cytotoxic T-lymphocyte response. Additional candidate subunit vaccines are being developed that may be made more immunogenic and effective by the addition of new adjuvants or by recombinant vectors and plasmids containing complementary DNA of the F and G genes. These vaccines may boost immunity in individuals previously infected and reduce the severity of disease in those at high risk.

Live-attenuated vaccines offer the potential advantages of eliciting both systemic and mucosal immunity and a longer duration of immunity. Initial live-virus candidate vaccines were developed using cold-adapted strains from temperature-sensitive mutants. Despite promising results in adult volunteers, subsequent studies proved these initial strains to be unsuitable in young children. They resulted in unacceptable degrees of illness, were overattenuated and not protective, or were genetically unstable, with reversion to wild-type virus that was then shed.[292] New attenuated live-virus candidate vaccines have been improved by repeated rounds of chemical mutagenesis, producing mutants that are more attenuated and that provide improved stability and immunogenicity.[296]

The use of reverse genetics has resulted in generations of new candidate strains from the cold-passage and temperature-sensitive vaccines, and they contain attenuating and advantageous mutations.[297] Candidate vaccines made from full-length, RSV-complementary DNA, which produce infectious RNA transcripts, are also under investigation. Recombinant genetic engineering methods offer considerable promise for development of vaccines that would be suitable for both infants and previously infected individuals.

REFERENCES

1. Brandt C, Kim H, Arrobio J, et al. Epidemiology of respiratory syncytial virus infection in Washington, DC: III. Composite analysis of eleven consecutive yearly epidemics. Am J Epidemiol. 1973;98:355-364.
2. Chanock R, Parrott R. Acute respiratory disease in infancy and childhood: Present understanding and prospects for prevention. Pediatrics. 1965;36:21-39.
3. Glezen W, Denny F. Epidemiology of acute lower respiratory disease in children. N Engl J Med. 1973;288:498-505.
4. Kim H, Arrobio J, Brandt C, et al. Epidemiology of respiratory syncytial virus infection in Washington DC: I. Importance of the virus in different respiratory tract disease syndromes and temporal distribution of infection. Am J Epidemiol. 1973;98:216-225.
5. Parrott R, Kim H, Arrobio J, et al. Epidemiology of respiratory syncytial virus infection in Washington, DC: II. Infection and disease with respect to age, immunologic status, race, and sex. Am J Epidemiol. 1973;98:289-300.
6. Stang P, Brandenburg N, Carter B. The economic burden of respiratory syncytial virus-associated bronchiolitis hospitalizations. Arch Pediatr Adolesc Med. 2001;155:95-96.
7. Howard T, Hoffman L, Stang P, et al. Respiratory syncytial virus pneumonia in the hospital setting: Length of stay, charges, and mortality. J Pediatr. 2000;137:227-232.
8. Zambon M, Stockton J, Clewley J, et al. Contribution of influenza and respiratory syncytial virus to community cases of influenza-like illness: An observational study. Lancet. 2001;358:1410-1416.
9. Dowell S, Anderson L, Gary H, et al. Respiratory syncytial virus is an important cause of community-acquired lower respiratory infection among hospitalized adults. J Infect Dis. 1996;174:456-462.

10. Han L, Alexander J, Anderson L. Respiratory syncytial virus pneumonia among the elderly: An assessment of disease burden. J Infect Dis. 1999;179:25-30.
11. Simoes E. Overlap between respiratory syncytial virus infection and influenza. Lancet. 2001;358:1382-1383.
12. Morris J, Blount R, Savage R. Recovery of cytopathogenic agent from chimpanzees with coryza. Proc Soc Exp Biol Med. 1956;92:544-549.
13. Chanock R, Roizman B, Myers R. Recovery from infants with respiratory illness of a virus related to chimpanzee coryza agent (CCA): I. Isolation, properties and characterization. Am J Hyg. 1957;66:281-290.
14. Chanock R, Finberg L. Recovery from infants with respiratory illness of a virus related to chimpanzee coryza agent (CCA): II. Epidemiologic aspects of infection in infants and young children. Am J Hyg. 1957;66:291-300.
15. Adams J, Imagawa D, Zike K. Epidemic bronchiolitis and pneumonia related to respiratory syncytial virus. JAMA. 1961;176:1037-1039.
16. Kapikian A, Bell J, Maastrota F, et al. An outbreak of febrile illness and pneumonia associated with respiratory syncytial virus infection. Am J Hyg. 1961;74:234-248.
17. Gardner P, Turk D, Aherne W, et al. Deaths associated with respiratory tract infection in childhood. Br Med J. 1967;4:316-320.
18. van den Hoogen B, de Jong J, Groen J, et al. A newly discovered human pneumovirus isolated from young children with respiratory tract disease. Nature Med. 2001;7:719-724.
19. Collins P, Chanock R, Murphy B. Respiratory syncytial virus. In: Knipe D, Howley PM, eds. Fields' Virology. 4th ed. Philadelphia: Lippincott Williams & Wilkins; 2001:1341-1379.
20. Hall C. Respiratory syncytial virus and parainfluenza virus. N Engl J Med. 2001;344:1917-1928.
21. Hambling M. Survival of the respiratory syncytial virus during storage under various conditions. Br J Exp Pathol. 1964;45:647-655.
22. Hall C, Geiman J, Douglas RJ. Possible transmission by fomites of respiratory syncytial virus. J Infect Dis. 1980;141:98-102.
23. Walsh E, Hall C. Respiratory syncytial virus. In: Schmidt NJ, Emmons RW, eds. Diagnostic Procedures for Viral and Rickettsial Infections. 6th ed. Washington, DC: American Public Health Association; 1989:693-712.
24. Hall C, Douglas RJ. Clinically useful method for the isolation of respiratory syncytial virus. J Infect Dis. 1975;131:1-5.
25. Peret T, Hall C, Hammond G, et al. Circulation patterns of group A and B human respiratory syncytial virus genotypes in 5 communities in North America. J Infect Dis. 2000;181:1891-1896.
26. Sullender W. Respiratory syncytial virus genetic and antigenic diversity. Clin Microbiol Rev. 2000;13:1-15.
27. Hall C, Walsh E, Schnabel K, et al. Occurrence of groups A and B of respiratory syncytial virus over 15 years: Associated epidemiologic and clinical characteristics in hospitalized and ambulatory children. J Infect Dis. 1990;162:1283-1290.
28. Storch G, Anderson L, Park C, et al. Antigenic and genomic diversity within group A respiratory syncytial virus. J Infect Dis. 1991;163:858-861.
29. Choi E, Lee H. Genetic diversity and molecular epidemiology of the G protein of subgroups A and B of respiratory syncytial virus isolated over 9 consecutive epidemics in Korea. J Infect Dis. 2000;181:1547-1556.
30. Byrd L, Prince G. Animal models of respiratory syncytial virus infection. Clin Infect Dis. 1997;25:1363-1368.
31. Kinman T, Westenbrink F. Immunity to human and bovine respiratory syncytial virus. Arch Virol. 1990;112:1-25.
32. Philippou S, Otto P, Reinhold P, et al. Respiratory syncytial virus-induced chronic bronchiolitis in experimentally infected calves. Virchows Arch. 2000;436:617-621.
33. Ghildyal R, Chapman A, Peroulis I, et al. Expression and characterisation of the ovine respiratory syncytial virus (ORSV) G protein for use as a diagnostic reagent. Vet Res. 1999;30:475-482.
34. Alansari H, Potgieter L. Nucleotide sequence analysis of the ovine respiratory syncytial virus G glycoprotein gene. Virology. 1993;196:873-877.
35. Belshe R, Richardson L, London W, et al. Experimental respiratory syncytial virus infection of four species of primates. J Med Virol. 1977;1:157-162.
36. Richardson L, Belshe R, London W, et al. Evaluation of five temperature sensitive mutants of respiratory syncytial virus in primates: I. Viral shedding, immunologic response, and associated illness. J Med Virol. 1978;3:91-100.
37. Kakuk T, Soike K, Brideau R, et al. A human respiratory syncytial virus (RSV) primate model of enhanced pulmonary pathology induced with a formalin-inactivated RSV vaccine but not a recombinant FG subunit vaccine. J Infect Dis. 1993;167:553-561.
38. Wagner M, Evermann J, Gaskin J, et al. Subacute effects of respiratory syncytial virus infection on lung function in lambs. Pediatr Pulmonol. 1991;11:56-64.
39. Sharma R, Woldehiwet Z. Pathogenesis of bovine respiratory syncytial virus in experimentally infected lambs. Vet Microbiol. 1990;23:267-272.
40. Lapin C, Hiatt P, Langston C, et al. A lamb model for human respiratory syncytial virus infection. Pediatr Pulmonol. 1993;15:151-156.
41. Prince G, Porter D. The pathogenesis of respiratory syncytial virus infection in infant ferrets. Am J Pathol. 1976;82:339-352.
42. Graham B, Rutigliano J, Johnson T. Respiratory syncytial virus immunobiology and pathogenesis. Virology. 2002;297:1-7.
43. Berman S. Epidemiology of acute respiratory infections in children of developing countries. Rev Infect Dis. 1991;13:S454-S462.
44. Dowell S, Kupronis B, Zell E, et al. Mortality from pneumonia in children in the United States, 1939 through 1996. N Engl J Med. 2000;342:1399-1407.
45. Lowther S, Shay D, Holman R, et al. Bronchiolitis-associated hospitalizations among American Indian and Alaska Native children. Pediatr Infect Dis J. 2000;19:11-17.
46. Sugaya N, Mitamura K, Nirasawa M, et al. The impact of winter epidemics of influenza and respiratory syncytial virus on paediatric admissions to an urban general hospital. J Med Virol. 2000;60:102-106.
47. McIntosh K. Community-acquired pneumonia in children. N Engl J Med. 2002;346:429-437.
48. Muller-Pebody B, Edmunds W, Zambon M, et al. Contribution of RSV to bronchiolitis and pneumonia-associated hospitalizations in English children, April 1995-March 1998. Epidemiol Infect. 2002;129:99-106.
49. Stensballe L, Devasundaram J, Simoes E. Respiratory syncytial virus epidemics: The ups and downs of a seasonal virus. Pediatr Infect Dis J. 2003;22:S21-S32.
50. Centers for Disease Control and Prevention. Respiratory syncytial virus activity: United States, 2000-2001 season. MMWR Morb Mortal Wkly Rep. 2002;51:26-28.
51. Shek L, Lee B. Epidemiology and seasonality of respiratory tract virus infections in the tropics. Paediatr Respir Rev. 2003;4:105-111.
52. Anderson L, Parker R, Strikas R. Association between respiratory syncytial virus outbreaks and lower respiratory tract deaths of infants and young children. J Infect Dis. 1990;161:640-646.
53. Hall C, Douglas RJ. Respiratory syncytial virus and influenza: Practical community surveillance. Am J Dis Child. 1976;130:615-620.
54. Ward K, Lambden P, Ogilvie M, et al. Antibodies to respiratory syncytial virus polypeptides and their significance in human infection. J Gen Virol. 1983;64:1867-1876.
55. Glezen W. Pathogenesis of bronchiolitis epidemiologic considerations. Pediatr Res. 1977;11:239-243.
56. Foy H, Cooney M, Maletzky A, et al. Incidence and etiology of pneumonia, croup, and bronchiolitis in preschool children belonging to a prepaid medical care group over a four-year period. Am J Epidemiol. 1973;97:80-92.
57. Denny F, Clyde WJ. Acute lower respiratory tract infections in nonhospitalized children. J Pediatr. 1986;108:635-646.
58. Loda F, Glezen W, Clyde WJ. Respiratory disease in group day care. Pediatrics. 1972;49:428-437.
59. Kim H, Canchola J, Brandt C, et al. Respiratory syncytial virus disease in infants despite prior administration of antigenic inactivated vaccine. Am J Epidemiol. 1969;89:422-434.
60. Glezen W, Taber L, Frank A, et al. Risk of primary infection and reinfection with respiratory syncytial virus. Am J Dis Child. 1986;140:543-546.
61. Henderson F, Collier A, Clyde W, et al. Respiratory syncytial virus infections, reinfections and immunity. N Engl J Med. 1979;300:530-534.
62. Law B, Carbonell-Estrany X, Simoes E. An update on respiratory syncytial virus epidemiology: A developed country perspective. Resp Med. 2002;96:S1-S7.
63. Holberg C, Wright A, Martinez F, et al. Risk factors for respiratory syncytial virus-associated lower respiratory illnesses in the first year of life. Am J Epidemiol. 1991;133:1135-1151.
64. Jansson L, Nilsson P, Olsson M. Socioeconomic environmental factors and hospitalization for acute bronchiolitis during infancy. Acta Pediatr. 2002;91:335-338.
65. Meissner H, Welliver R, Chartrand S, et al. Prevention of respiratory syncytial virus infection in high risk infants: Consensus opinion on the role of immunoprophylaxis with respiratory syncytial virus hyperimmune globulin. Pediatr Infect Dis J. 1996;15:1059-1068.
66. Boyce T, Mellen B, Mitchel EJ, et al. Rates of hospitalization for respiratory syncytial virus infection among children in Medicaid. J Pediatr. 2000;137:865-870.
67. Leader S, Kohlhase K. Respiratory syncytial virus-coded pediatric hospitalizations, 1997-1999. Pediatr Infect Dis J. 2002;21:629-632.
68. Shay D, Holman R, Newman R, et al. Bronchiolitis-associated hospitalizations among US children, 1980-1996. JAMA. 1999;282:1440-1446.
69. Hall C, Geiman J, Biggar R, et al. Respiratory syncytial virus infections within families. N Engl J Med. 1976;294:414-419.
70. Johnson K, Chanock R, Rifkind D, et al. Respiratory syncytial virus: IV. Correlation of virus shedding, serologic response, and illness in adult volunteers. JAMA. 1961;176:663-667.
71. Kravtez H, Knight V, Chanock R, et al. Respiratory syncytial virus: III. Production of illness and clinical observations in adult volunteers. JAMA. 1961;176:657-663.
72. Sterner G, Wolontis S, Bloth B, et al. Respiratory syncytial virus: An outbreak of acute respiratory illness in a home for infants. Acta Paediat Scand. 1966;55:273-279.
73. Hall C, Douglas RJ, Schnabel K, et al. Infectivity of respiratory syncytial virus by various routes of inoculation. Infect Immun. 1981;33:779-783.
74. Aherne W, Bird T, Court S, et al. Pathological changes in virus infections of the lower respiratory tract in children. J Clin Pathol. 1970;23:7-18.
75. Urquhart G, Gibson A. RSV infections and infant deaths. Br Med J. 1970;3:110.
76. Wohl M, Stigol L, Mead J. Resistance of the total respiratory system in healthy infants and infants with bronchiolitis. Pediatrics. 1969;43:495-509.
77. Neilson K, Yunis E. Demonstration of respiratory syncytial virus in an autopsy series. Pediatr Pathol. 1990;10:491-502.
78. Fulginiti V, Eller J, Sieber O, et al. Respiratory virus immunization: I. A field trial of two inactivated respiratory virus vaccines; an aqueous trivalent parainfluenza virus vaccine, and an alum-precipitated respiratory syncytial virus vaccine. Am J Epidemiol. 1969;89:435-448.
79. Kapikian A, Mitchell R, Chanock R, et al. An epidemiologic study of altered clinical reactivity to respiratory syncytial (RS) virus infection in children previously vaccinated with an inactivated RS virus vaccine. Am J Epidemiol. 1969;89:405-421.
80. Polack F, Teng M, Collins P, et al. A role for immune complexes in enhanced respiratory syncytial virus disease. J Exp Med. 2002;196:859-865.
81. Openshaw P, Dean G, Culley F. Links between respiratory syncytial virus bronchiolitis and childhood asthma: Clinical and research approaches. Pediatr Infect Dis J. 2003;22:S58-S65.
82. Crowe J, Williams J. Immunology of viral respiratory tract infection in infancy. Paediatr Respir Rev. 2003;4:112-119.

83. Hogg J, Williams J, Richardson J, et al. Age as a factor in the distribution of lower-airway conductance and in the pathologic anatomy of obstructive lung disease. N Engl J Med. 1970;282:1283-1287.

84. Hall C, Walsh E, Long C, et al. Immunity to and frequency of reinfection with respiratory syncytial virus. J Infect Dis. 1991;163:693-698.

85. Black-Payne C. Respiratory syncytial virus infection among families and within hospitals: Infancy to the aged. Schumpert Med Q. 1992;9:203-219.

86. McNamara P, Smyth R. The pathogenesis of respiratory syncytial virus disease in childhood. Br Med Bull. 2002;61:13-28.

87. Lofgren J, Ramet M, Renko M, et al. Association between surfactant protein A gene locus and severe respiratory syncytial virus infection in infants. J Infect Dis. 2002;185:283-289.

88. Lahti M, Lofgren J, Marttila R, et al. Surfactant protein D gene polymorphism associated with severe respiratory syncytial virus infection. Pediatr Res. 2002;51:696-699.

89. Hoebee B, Rietveld E, Bont L, et al. Association of severe respiratory syncytial virus bronchiolitis with interleukin-4 and interleukin-4 receptor a polymorphisms. J Infect Dis. 2003;187:2-11.

90. Choi E, Lee H, Yoo T, et al. A common haplotype of interleukin-4 gene *IL4* is associated with severe respiratory syncytial virus disease in Korean children. J Infect Dis. 2002;186:1207-1211.

91. Hull J, Thomson A, Kwiatkowski D. Association of respiratory syncytial virus bronchiolitis with the interleukin 8 gene region in UK families. Thorax. 2000;55:1023-1027.

92. Wang S, Forsyth K. The interaction of neutrophils with respiratory epithelial cells in viral infection. Respirology. 2000;5:1-10.

93. Crowe J. Immune response of infants to infection with respiratory viruses and live attenuated respiratory virus candidate vaccines. Vaccine. 1998;16:1423-1432.

94. Ogilvie M, Vatheneo S, Radford M, et al. Maternal antibody and respiratory syncytial virus infection in infancy. J Med Virol. 1981;7:263-271.

95. Glezen W, Paredes A, Allison J, et al. Risk of respiratory syncytial virus infection for infants from low-income families in relationship to age, sex, ethnic group and maternal antibody level. J Pediatr. 1981;98:708-715.

96. Fernald G, Almond J, Henderson F. Cellular and humoral immunity in recurrent respiratory syncytial virus infections. Pediatr Res. 1983;17:753-758.

97. Meissner HC, Long SS; American Academy of Pediatrics Committee on Infectious Diseases and Committee on Fetus and Newborn. Revised indications for the use of palivizumab and respiratory syncytial virus immune globulin intravenous for the prevention of respiratory syncytial virus infections. Pediatrics. 2003;112:1447-1452.

98. Welliver R, Kaul T, Putnam T, et al. The antibody response to primary and secondary infection with respiratory syncytial virus: Kinetics of class-specific responses. J Pediatr. 1980;96:808-813.

99. Langedijk J, Meloen R, van Oirschot J. Identification of a conserved neutralization site in the first heptad repeat of the fusion protein of respiratory syncytial virus. Arch Virol. 1998;143:313-320.

100. Walsh E, Brandriss M, Schlesinger J. Immunological differences between the envelope glycoproteins of two strains of human respiratory syncytial virus. J Gen Virol. 1987;68:2169-2176.

101. Wright P, Gruber W, Peters M, et al. Illness severity, viral shedding, and antibody responses in infants hospitalized with bronchiolitis caused by respiratory syncytial virus. J Infect Dis. 2002;185:1011-1018.

102. Murphy B, Graham B, Prince G, et al. Serum and nasal-wash immunoglobulin G and A antibody response of infants and children to respiratory syncytial virus F and G glycoproteins following primary infection. J Clin Microbiol. 1986;23:1009-1014.

103. Murphy B, Alling D, Snyder M, et al. Effect of age and preexisting antibody on serum antibody response of infants and children to the F and G glycoproteins during respiratory syncytial viral infection. J Clin Microbiol. 1986;24:894-898.

104. Welliver R, Sun M, Hildreth S, et al. Respiratory syncytial virus-specific antibody responses in immunoglobulin A and E isotypes to the F and G proteins and to intact virus after natural infection. J Clin Microbiol. 1989;27:295-299.

105. Wagner D, Nelson D, Walsh E, et al. Differential immunoglobulin G subclass antibody titers to respiratory syncytial virus F and G glycoproteins in adults. J Clin Microbiol. 1987;25:748-750.

106. Meurman O, Waris M, Hedman K. Immunoglobulin G antibody avidity in patients with respiratory syncytial virus infection. J Clin Microbiol. 1992;30:1479-1484.

107. Prince G, Horswood R, Chanock R. Quantitative aspects of passive immunity to respiratory syncytial virus infection in infant cotton rats. J Virol. 1985;55:517-520.

108. McIntosh K, Master H, Orr I, et al. The immunologic response to infection with respiratory syncytial virus in infants. J Infect Dis. 1978;138:24-32.

109. Welliver R. Immunology of respiratory syncytial virus infection: Eosinophils, cytokines, chemokines, and asthma. Pediatr Infect Dis J. 2000;19:780-783.

110. Welliver R. Respiratory syncytial virus and other respiratory viruses. Pediatr Infect Dis J. 2003;22:S6-S12.

111. Martinez F. Respiratory syncytial virus bronchiolitis and the pathogenesis of childhood asthma. Pediatr Infect Dis J. 2003;22:S76-S82.

112. Hall C, Powell K, MacDonald N, et al. Respiratory syncytial virus infection in children with compromised immune function. N Engl J Med. 1986;315:77-81.

113. Champlin R, Whimbey E. Community respiratory virus infections in bone marrow transplant recipients: The M.D. Anderson Cancer Center experience. Biol Blood Marrow Transplant. 2001;7:8S-10S.

114. Nichols W, Gooley T, Boeckh M. Community-acquired respiratory syncytial virus and parainfluenza virus infections after hematopoietic stem cell transplantation: The Fred Hutchinson Cancer Research Center experience. Biol Blood Marrow Transplant. 2001;7:11S-15S.

115. Isaacs D, Bangham C, McMichael A. Cell-mediated cytotoxic response to respiratory syncytial virus in infants with bronchiolitis. Lancet. 1987;2:769-771.

116. Isaacs D, MacDonald N, Bangham C, et al. The specific cytotoxic T-cell response in adult volunteers to infection with respiratory syncytial virus. Immunol Infect Dis. 1991;1:5-12.

117. Welliver R. Immunologic mechanisms of virus-induced wheezing and asthma. J Pediatr. 1999;135:S14-S20.

118. Bont L, Heijnen C, Kavalaars A, et al. Peripheral blood cytokine responses and disease severity in respiratory syncytial virus bronchiolitis. Eur Respir J. 1999;14:144-149.

119. Bont L, Kavelaars A, Heijnen C, et al. Monocyte interleukin-12 production is inversely related to duration of respiratory failure in respiratory syncytial virus bronchiolitis. J Infect Dis. 2000;181:1772-1775.

120. Abu-Harb M, Bell F, Rao W, et al. IL-8 and neutrophil elastase levels in the respiratory tract of infants with RSV bronchiolitis. Eur Respir J. 1999;14:139-143.

121. Graham B. Pathogenesis of respiratory syncytial virus vaccine-augmented pathology. Am J Respir Crit Care Med. 1995;152:S63-S66.

122. Graham B, Johnson T, Peebles R. Immune-mediated disease pathogenesis in respiratory syncytial virus infection. Immunopharmacology. 2000;48:237-247.

123. Johnson T, Graham B. Secreted respiratory syncytial virus G glycoprotein induces interleukin-5 (IL-5), IL-13, and eosinophilia by an IL-4 independent mechanism. J Virol. 1999;73:8485-8495.

124. Tripp R, Jones L, Haynes L, et al. CX3C chemokine mimicry by respiratory syncytial virus G glycoprotein. Nat Immunol. 2001;2:732-738.

125. Tripp R, Moore D, Barskey A, et al. Peripheral blood mononuclear cells from infants hospitalized because of respiratory syncytial virus infection express T helper-1 and T helper-2 cytokines and CC chemokine messenger RNA. J Infect Dis. 2002;185:1388-1394.

126. Domachowske J, Rosenberg H. Respiratory syncytial virus infection: Immune response, immunopathogenesis, and treatment. Clin Microbiol Rev. 1999;12:298-309.

127. Bendelja K, Gagro A, Bace A, et al. Predominant type-2 response in infants with respiratory syncytial virus (RSV) infection demonstrated by cytokine flow cytometry. Clin Exp Immunol. 2000;121:332-338.

128. Smyth R, Mobbs K, O'Hea U, et al. Respiratory syncytial virus bronchiolitis: Disease severity, interleukin-8, and virus genotype. Pediatr Pulmonol. 2002;33:339-346.

129. Lee G-Y, Funk G, Chen S, et al. An outbreak of respiratory syncytial virus infection in an infant nursery. J Formosan Med Assoc. 1973;72:39-46.

130. Mulholland E, Olinsky A, Shann F. Clinical findings and severity of acute bronchiolitis. Lancet. 1990;335:1259-1261.

131. Shaw K, Bell L, Sherman N. Outpatient assessment of infants with bronchiolitis. Am J Dis Child. 1991;145:151-155.

132. Alario A, Lewander W, Dennehy P, et al. The relationship between oxygen saturation and the clinical assessment of acutely wheezing infants and children. Pediatr Emerg Care. 1995;11:331-339.

133. Wohl M. Bronchiolitis. Pediatr Ann. 1986;15:307-313.

134. Hall C, Hall W, Speers D. Clinical and physiological manifestations of bronchiolitis and pneumonia: Outcome of respiratory syncytial virus. Am J Dis Child. 1979;133:798-802.

135. Reynolds E. Arterial blood gas tensions in acute disease of lower respiratory tract in infancy. Br Med J. 1963;1:1192-1195.

136. Hall C, Douglas RJ, Geiman J. Quantitative shedding patterns of respiratory syncytial virus in infants. J Infect Dis. 1975;132:151-156.

137. Rice R, Loda F. A roentgenographic analysis of respiratory syncytial virus pneumonia in infants. Radiology. 1966;87:1021-1027.

138. Simpson W, Hacking P, Court D, et al. The radiological findings in respiratory syncytial virus infection in children: Part II: The correlation of radiological categories with clinical and virological findings. Pediatr Radiol. 1974;2:155-160.

139. Khamapirad T, Glezen W. Clinical and radiographic assessment of acute lower respiratory tract disease in infants and children. Semin Respir Infect. 1987;2:130-144.

140. Friis B, Eiken M, Hornsleth A, et al. Chest x-ray appearances in pneumonia and bronchiolitis. Acta Paediatr Scand. 1990;79:219-225.

141. Davies H, Wang E, Manson D, et al. Reliability of the chest radiograph in the diagnosis of lower respiratory infections in young children. Pediatr Infect Dis J. 1996;15:600-604.

142. Heikkinen T, Thint M, Chonmaitree T. Prevalence of various respiratory viruses in the middle ear during acute otitis media. N Engl J Med. 1999;340:260-264.

143. Pitkaranta A, Virolainen A, Jero J, et al. Detection of rhinovirus, respiratory syncytial virus, and coronavirus infections in acute otitis media by reverse transcriptase polymerase chain reaction. Pediatrics. 1998;102:291-295.

144. Sarkkinen H, Ruuskanen O, Meurman O, et al. Identification of respiratory virus antigens in middle ear fluids of children with acute otitis media. J Infect Dis. 1985;151:444-448.

145. Chonmaitree T, Howie V, Truant A. Presence of respiratory viruses in middle ear fluids and nasal wash specimens from children with otitis media. Pediatrics. 1986;77:698-702.

146. Chonmaitree T, Owen M, Patel J, et al. Effect of viral respiratory tract infection on outcome of acute otitis media. J Pediatr. 1992;120:856-862.

147. Okamoto Y, Kudo K, Shirotori K, et al. Detection of genomic sequences of respiratory syncytial virus in otitis media with effusion in children. Ann Otol Rhinol Laryngol. 1992;157:S7-S10.

148. Andrade M, Hoberman A, Glustein J, et al. Acute otitis media in children with bronchiolitis. Pediatr. 1998;101:617-619.

149. Arola M, Ziegler M, Ruuskanen O. Respiratory virus infection as a cause of prolonged symptoms in acute otitis media. J Pediatr. 1990;116:697-701.

150. Henderson F, Collier A, Sanyal M, et al. A longitudinal study of respiratory viruses and bacteria in the etiology of acute otitis media with effusion. N Engl J Med. 1982;306:1377-1383.

151. Shaw C, Obermyer N, Wetmore S, et al. Incidence of adenovirus and respiratory syncytial virus in chronic otitis media with effusion using the polymerase chain reaction. Otolaryngol Head Neck Surg. 1995;113:234-241.

152. Pitkaranta A, Jero J, Arruda E, et al. Polymerase chain reaction–based detection of rhinovirus, respiratory syncytial virus, and coronavirus in otitis media with effusion. J Pediatr. 1998;133:390-394.

153. Gronroos J, Vihma L, Salmivalli A, et al. Co-existing viral (respiratory syncytial) and bacterial (pneumococcus) otitis media in children. Acta Otolaryngol. 1968;65:505-517.

154. Bont L, Versteegh J, Swelsen W, et al. Natural reinfection with respiratory syncytial virus does not boost virus-specific T-cell immunity. Pediatr Res. 2002;52:363-367.

155. Bont L, Heijnen C, Kavelaara A, et al. Monocyte IL-10 production during respiratory syncytial virus bronchiolitis is associated with recurrent wheezing in a one-year follow-up study. Am J Respir Crit Care Med. 2000;161:1518-1523.

156. Roberts N, Prill A, Mann T. Interleukin 1 and interleukin 1 inhibitor production by human macrophages exposed to influenza virus or respiratory syncytial virus. J Exp Med. 1986;163:511-519.

157. Preston F, Beier P, Pope J. Infectious respiratory syncytial virus (RSV) effectively inhibits the proliferative T cell response to inactivated RSV in vitro. J Infect Dis. 1992;165:819-825.

158. Salkind A, McCarthy D, Nichols J, et al. Interleukin-1-inhibitor activity induced by respiratory syncytial virus: Abrogation of virus-specific and alternate human lymphocyte proliferative responses. J Infect Dis. 1991;163:71-77.

159. Looney R, Falsey A, Walsh E, et al. Effect of aging on cytokine production in response to respiratory syncytial virus infection. J Infect Dis. 2002;185:682-685.

160. Hall C. Respiratory syncytial virus infections in previously healthy working adults. Clin Infect Dis. 2001;33:792-796.

161. Hall W, Hall C, Speers D. Respiratory syncytial virus infections in adults: Clinical, virologic, and serial pulmonary function studies. Ann Intern Med. 1978;88:203-205.

162. Mlinaric-Galinovic G, Falsey A, Walsh E. Respiratory syncytial virus infection in the elderly. Eur J Clin Microbiol. 1996;15:777-781.

163. Harris J, Erdman D, Dhashemi S, et al. Respiratory syncytial virus (RSV) and persistent cough at a University Health Service. Presented at the 39th Annual Meeting of the Infectious Disease Society of America. San Francisco; 2001.

164. Falsey A, Walsh E. Respiratory syncytial virus infections in adults. Clin Microbiol Rev. 2000;13:371-384.

165. Falsey A. RSV in elderly living in chronic care facilities and in those with underlying disease. In: Respiratory Syncytial Virus in the Elderly. The 40th Annual Interscience Conference on Antimicrobial Agents and Chemotherapy (ICAAC). Toronto, Ontario. 2000.

166. Thompson W, Shay D, Weintraub E, et al. Mortality associated with influenza and respiratory syncytial virus in the United States. JAMA. 2003;289:179-186.

167. Nicholson K, Kent J, Hammersley V, et al. Acute viral infections of upper respiratory tract in elderly people living in the community: Comparative, prospective, population based study of disease burden. BMJ. 1997;315:1060-1064.

168. Walsh E, Falsey A, Hennessey P. Respiratory syncytial virus and other virus infections in persons with chronic cardiopulmonary disease. Am J Respir Crit Care Med. 1999;160:791-795.

169. Osterweil D, Norman D. An outbreak of an influenza-like illness in a nursing home. J Am Geriatr Soc. 1990;38:659-662.

170. Falsey A, Cunningham C, Barker W, et al. Respiratory syncytial virus and influenza A infections in the hospitalized elderly. J Infect Dis. 1995;172:389-394.

171. Seemungal T, Harper-Owen R, Bhowmik A, et al. Respiratory viruses, symptoms, and inflammatory markers in acute exacerbations and stable chronic obstructive pulmonary disease. Am J Respir Crit Care Med. 2001;164:1618-1623.

172. Nicholson K. RSV in community-dwelling elderly. In: Respiratory Syncytial Virus in the Elderly. The 40th Annual Interscience Conference on Antimicrobial Agents and Chemotherapy (ICAAC). Toronto, Ontario. 2000.

173. Falsey A, McCann R, Hall W, et al. Acute respiratory tract infection in daycare centers for older persons. J Am Geriatr Soc. 1995;43:30-36.

174. Cappel R, Thirty L, Clinet G. Viral antibodies in the CSF after acute CNS infections. Arch Neurol. 1975;32:629-631.

175. Wallace S, Zealley H. Neurological, electroencephalographic, and virological findings in febrile children. Arch Dis Child. 1970;45:611-623.

176. Hirayama K, Sakazaki H, Murakami S, et al. Sequential MRI, SPECT and PET in respiratory syncytial virus encephalitis. Pediatr Radiol. 1999;29:282-286.

177. Cavallaro J, Maassab H, Abrams G. An immunofluorescent and histopathological study of respiratory syncytial virus (RSV) encephalitis in suckling mice. Proc Soc Exp Biol Med. 1967;124:1059-1064.

178. Giles T, Gohd R. Respiratory syncytial virus and heart disease. JAMA. 1976;236:1128-1130.

179. Bairan A, Cherry J, Fagan L, et al. Complete heart block and respiratory syncytial virus. Am J Dis Child. 1974;127:264-265.

180. Heerens A, Marshall D, Bose C. Nosocomial respiratory syncytial virus: A threat in the modern neonatal intensive care unit. J Perinatol. 2002;22:306-307.

181. Agah R, Cherry J, Garakian A, et al. Respiratory syncytial virus (RSV) infection rate in personnel caring for children with RSV infections. Am J Dis Child. 1987;141:695-697.

182. Hall C, Douglas RJ, Geiman J, et al. Nosocomial respiratory syncytial virus infections. N Engl J Med. 1975;293:1343-1346.

183. Hall C, Geiman J, Douglas RJ, et al. Control of nosocomial respiratory syncytial viral infections. Pediatrics. 1978;62:728-731.

184. Hall C, Kopelman A, Douglas R. Neonatal respiratory syncytial viral infections. N Engl J Med. 1979;300:393-396.

185. Hall CB, Douglas RG Jr. Nosocomial respiratory syncytial virus infections: Should gowns and masks be used? Am J Dis Child. 1981;135:512-516.

186. Hall CB, Douglas RG Jr. Modes of transmission of respiratory syncytial virus. J Pediatr. 1981;99:100-103.

187. Hall C. Nosocomial viral respiratory infections: Perennial weeds on pediatric wards. Am J Med. 1981;70:670-676.

188. Hall C. The nosocomial spread of respiratory syncytial virus infections. Ann Rev Med. 1983;34:311-319.

189. Anonymous. Nosocomial infection with respiratory syncytial virus. Lancet. 1992;340:1071-1072.

190. Langley J, LeBlanc J, Wang E, et al. Nosocomial respiratory syncytial virus infection in Canadian pediatric hospitals: A pediatric investigators collaborative network on infections in Canada study. Pediatrics. 1997;100:943-946.

191. Storch G, Hall C, Anderson L, et al. Antigenic and nucleic acid analysis of nosocomial isolates of respiratory syncytial virus. J Infect Dis. 1993;167:562-566.

192. Adams J. Primary virus pneumonitis with cytoplasmic inclusion bodies: A study of an epidemic involving thirty-two infants with nine deaths. JAMA. 1941;116:925-933.

193. Adams J, Imagawa D, Zike K. Relationship of pneumonitis in infants to respiratory syncytial virus. Lancet. 1961;81:502-506.

194. Whimbey E, Ghosh S. Respiratory syncytial virus infections in immunocompromised adults. Curr Clin Top Infect Dis. 2000;20:232-255.

195. Martino R, Rámila E, Rabella N, et al. Respiratory virus infections in adults with hematologic malignancies: A prospective study. Clin Infect Dis. 2003;36:1-8.

196. Ljungman P. Respiratory virus infections in stem cell transplant patients: The European experience. Biol Blood Marrow Transplant. 2001;7:5S-7S.

197. Hall C. Nosocomial respiratory syncytial virus infections: The "cold war" has not ended. Clin Infect Dis. 2000;31:590-596.

198. Goldmann D. Epidemiology and prevention of pediatric viral respiratory infections in health-care institutions. Emerg Infect Dis. 2001;7:249-253.

199. Weisman L. Populations at risk for developing respiratory syncytial virus and risk factors for respiratory syncytial virus severity: Infants with predisposing conditions. Pediatr Infect Dis J. 2003;22:S33-S39.

200. Meissner H. Selected populations at increased risk from respiratory syncytial virus infection. Pediatr Infect Dis J. 2003;22:S40-S45.

201. Aujard Y, Fauroux B. Risk factors for severe respiratory syncytial virus infection in infants. Respir Med. 2002;96:S9-S14.

202. Romero J. Palivizumab prophylaxis of respiratory syncytial virus disease from 1998 to 2002: Results from four years of palivizumab usage. Pediatr Infect Dis J. 2003;22:S46-S54.

203. Wang E, Law B, Robinson J, et al. PICNIC (Pediatric Investigators Collaborative Network on Infections in Canada) study of the role of age and respiratory syncytial virus neutralizing antibody on respiratory syncytial virus illness in patients with underlying heart or lung disease. Pediatrics. 1997;99:470-471.

204. Stevens T, Sinkin R, Hall C, et al. Respiratory syncytial virus and premature infants born at 32 weeks' gestation or earlier. Arch Pediatr Adolesc Med. 2000;154:55-61.

205. Wang E, Prober C, Manson B, et al. Association of respiratory viral infections with pulmonary deterioration in patients with cystic fibrosis. N Engl J Med. 1984;311:1653-1658.

206. Abman S, Ogle J, Butler-Simon N. Role of respiratory syncytial virus in early hospitalizations for respiratory distress of young infants with cystic fibrosis. J Pediatr. 1988;113:826-830.

207. Efthimiou J, Hodson M, Taylor P, et al. Importance of viruses and Legionella pneumophila in respiratory exacerbations of young adults with cystic fibrosis. Thorax. 1984;39:150-154.

208. Navas L, Wang E, de Carvalho V, et al. Improved outcome of respiratory syncytial virus infection in a high-risk hospitalized population of Canadian children. J Pediatr. 1992;121:348-354.

209. MacDonald N, Hall C, Suffin S, et al. Respiratory syncytial viral infection in infants with congenital heart disease. N Engl J Med. 1982;307:397-400.

210. Altman C, Englund J, Demmler G, et al. Respiratory syncytial virus in patients with congenital heart disease: A contemporary look at epidemiology and success of preoperative screening. Pediatr Cardiol. 2000;21:433-438.

211. Fixler D. Respiratory syncytial virus infection in children with congenital heart disease: A review. Pediatr Cardiol. 1996;17:163-168.

212. Crooks B, Taylor C, Turner A, et al. Respiratory viral infections in primary immune deficiencies: significance and relevance to clinical outcome in a single BMT unit. Bone Marrow Transplant. 2000;26:1097-1102.

213. Taylor C, Osman H, Turner A, et al. Parainfluenza virus and respiratory syncytial virus infection in infants undergoing bone marrow transplantation for severe combined immunodeficiency. Commun Dis Public Health. 1998;1:202-203.

214. Small T, Casson A, Malak S, et al. Respiratory syncytial virus infection following hematopoietic stem cell transplantation. Bone Marrow Transplant. 2002;29:321-327.

215. Wendt C, Hertz M. Respiratory syncytial virus and parainfluenza virus infections in the immunocompromised host. Semin Respir Infect. 1995;10:224-231.

216. Sable C, Hayden F. Orthomyxoviral and paramyxoviral infections in transplant patients. Infect Dis Clin North Am. 1995;9:987-1003.

217. Lujan-Zilbermann J, Benaim E, Tong X, et al. Respiratory virus infection in pediatric hematopoietic stem cell transplantation. Clin Infect Dis. 2001;33:962-968.

218. Englund J, Piedra P, Whimbey E. Prevention and treatment of respiratory syncytial virus and parainfluenza viruses in immunocompromised patient. Am J Med. 1997;102:61-70.

219. Chandwani S, Borkowsky W, Krasinski K, et al. Respiratory syncytial virus infection in human immunodeficiency virus-infected children. J Pediatr. 1990;117:251-254.

220. Cane P. Analysis of linear epitopes recognised by the primary human antibody response to a variable region of the attachment (G) protein of respiratory syncytial virus. J Med Virol. 1997;51:297-304.

221. Madhi S, Schoub B, Simmank K, et al. Increased burden of respiratory viral associated severe lower respiratory tract infections in children infected with human immunodeficiency virus type-1. J Pediatr. 2000;137:78-84.
222. Madhi S, Venter M, Madhi A, et al. Differing manifestations of respiratory syncytial virus–associated severe lower respiratory tract infections in human immunodeficiency virus type 1-infected and uninfected children. Pediatr Infect Dis J. 2001;20:164-170.
223. Madhi S, Ramasamy N, Bessellar T, et al. Lower respiratory tract infections associated with influenza A and B viruses in an area with a high prevalence of pediatric human immunodeficiency type 1 infection. Pediatr Infect Dis J. 2002;21:291-297.
224. Ghosh S, Champlin R, Englund J, et al. Respiratory syncytial virus upper respiratory tract illness in adult blood and marrow transplant recipients: Combination therapy with aerosolized ribavirin and intravenous immunoglobulin. Bone Marrow Transplant. 2000;25:751-755.
225. Jafri H. Treatment of respiratory syncytial virus: Antiviral therapies. Pediatr Infect Dis J. 2003;22:S89-S93.
226. Dykewicz C. Guidelines for preventing opportunistic infections among hematopoietic stem cell transplant recipients: focus on community respiratory virus infections. Biol Blood Marrow Transplant. 2001;7:19S-22S.
227. Anonymous. Guidelines for preventing opportunistic infections among hematopoietic stem cell transplant recipients: Recommendations of CDC, the Infectious Disease Society of America, and the American Society of Blood and Marrow Transplantation. MMWR Morb Mortal Wkly Rep. 2000;49(RR10):1-128.
228. Church N, Anas N, Hall C, et al. Respiratory syncytial virus–related apnea in infants: Demographics and outcome. Am J Dis Child. 1984;138:247-250.
229. Hernandez E, Khoshoo V, Thoppil D, et al. Aspiration: A factor in rapidly deteriorating bronchiolitis in previously healthy infants? Pediatr Pulmonol. 2002;33:30-31.
230. Khoshoo V, Ross G, Kelly B, et al. Benefits of thickened feeds in previously healthy infants with respiratory syncytial virus bronchiolitis. Pediatr Pulmonol. 2001;31:301-302.
231. Hall C, Powell K, Schnabel K, et al. The risk of secondary bacterial infection in infants hospitalized with respiratory syncytial viral infections. J Pediatr. 1988;113:266-271.
232. Kuppermann N, Bank D, Walton E, et al. Risks for bacteremia and urinary tract infections in young febrile children with bronchiolitis. Arch Pediatr Adolesc Med. 1997;151:1207-1214.
233. Purcell K, Fergie J. Concurrent serious bacterial infections in 2396 infants and children hospitalized with respiratory syncytial virus lower respiratory tract infections. Arch Pediatr Adolesc Med. 2002;156:322-324.
234. Purcell R, Fergie J. Concurrent serious bacterial infections (CSBIs) in 912 infants and young children hospitalized for treatment of respiratory syncytial virus (RSV) lower respiratory tract infection (LRT) at Driscoll Children's Hospital, 2000-2002. In: Pediatric Academic Societies' Annual Meeting. Seattle; 2003.
235. Ng Y, Cox C, Atkins J, et al. Encephalopathy associated with respiratory syncytial virus bronchiolitis. J Child Neurol. 2001;16:105-108.
236. Oray-Schrom P, Phoenix C, St. Martin D, et al. Sepsis work-up of febrile infants 0-3 months infected with respiratory syncytial virus. In: 39th Annual Meeting of the Infectious Disease Society of America. San Francisco; 2001.
237. Clinical Effectiveness Committee on Bronchiolitis. Evidence based guidelines for the medical management of infants one year of age or less with a first time episode of bronchiolitis. National Guideline Clearinghouse; 1998.
238. McIntosh K. Pathogenesis of severe acute respiratory infections in the developing world: Respiratory syncytial virus and parainfluenza virus. Rev Infect Dis. 1991;13:S492-S500.
239. Wennergren G, Kristjansson S. Relationship between respiratory syncytial virus bronchiolitis and future obstructive airway diseases. Eur Respir J. 2001;18:1044-1058.
240. Piedimonte G. The association between respiratory syncytial virus infection and reactive airway disease. Resp Med. 2002;96:S25-S29.
241. Martinez F. What have we learned from the Tucson Children's Respiratory Study? Paediatr Respir Rev. 2002;3:193-197.
242. Piedimonte G. Contribution of neuroimmune mechanisms to airway inflammation and remodeling during and after respiratory syncytial virus infection. Pediatr Infect Dis J. 2003;22:S66-S75.
243. Hacking D, Hull J. Respiratory syncytial virus: Viral biology and the host response. J Infect. 2002;45:18-24.
244. Holt P, Sly P. Interactions between RSV infection, asthma, and atopy: Unraveling the complexities. J Exp Med. 2002;196:1271-1275.
245. Openshaw P, Culley F, Olszewska W. Immunopathogenesis of vaccine-enhanced RSV disease. Vaccine. 2002;20:S27-S31.
246. Welliver R, Garofalo R, Ogra P. Beta-chemokines, but neither T helper type 1 nor T helper type 2 cytokines, correlate with severity of illness during respiratory syncytial virus infection. Pediatr Infect Dis J. 2002;21:457-561.
247. Noah T, Henderson F, Wortman I, et al. Nasal cytokine production in viral acute upper respiratory infection of childhood. J Infect Dis. 1995;171:584-592.
248. Saito T, Deskin R, Casola A, et al. Respiratory syncytial virus induces selective production of the chemokine RANTES by upper airway epithelial cells. J Infect Dis. 1997;175:497-504.
249. Patino C, Martinez F. Interactions between genes and environment in the development of asthma. Allergy 2001:279-286.
250. Heikkinen T, Marttila J, Salmi A, et al. Nasal swab versus nasopharyngeal aspirate for isolation of respiratory viruses. J Clin Microbiol. 2002;40:4337-4339.
251. Englund J, Piedra P, Jewell A, et al. Rapid diagnosis of respiratory syncytial virus infections in immunocompromised adults. J Clin Microbiol. 1996:1649-1653.
252. Kellogg J. Culture vs direct antigen assays for detection of microbial pathogens from lower respiratory tract specimens suspected of containing the respiratory syncytial virus. Arch Pathol Lab Med. 1991;115:451-458.
253. Engler H, Preuss J. Laboratory diagnosis of respiratory virus infections in 24 hours of utilizing shell viral cultures. J Clin Microbiol. 1997;35:2165-2167.
254. Abels S, Nadal D, Stroehle A, et al. Reliable detection of respiratory syncytial virus infection in children for adequate hospital infection control management. J Clin Microbiol. 2001;39:3135-3139.
255. Falsey A, Formica M, Walsh E. Diagnosis of respiratory syncytial virus infection: Comparison of reverse transcription-PCR to viral culture and serology in adults with respiratory illness. J Clin Microbiol. 2002;40:817-820.
256. Kehl S, Henrickson K, Hua W, et al. Evaluation of the Hexaplex assay for detection of respiratory viruses in children. J Clin Microbiol. 2001;39:1696-1701.
257. Gueudin M, Vabret A, Petitjean J, et al. Quantitation of respiratory syncytial virus RNA in nasal aspirates of children by real-time RT-PCR assay. J Virol Methods. 2003;109:39-45.
258. Hu A, Colella M, Tam J, et al. Simultaneous detection, subgrouping, and quantitation of respiratory syncytial virus A and B by real-time PCR. J Clin Microbiol. 2003;41:149-154.
259. Falsey A, McCann R, Hall W, et al. Evaluation of four methods for the diagnosis of respiratory syncytial virus infection in older adults. J Am Geriatr Soc. 1996;44:71-73.
260. Erdman D, Anderson L. Monoclonal antibody-based capture enzyme immunoassays for specific serum immunoglobulin G (IgG), IgA, and IgM antibodies to respiratory syncytial virus. J Clin Microbiol. 1990;28:2744-2749.
261. Meddens M, Herbrink P, Lindeman J, et al. Serodiagnosis of respiratory syncytial virus (RSV) infection in children as measured by detection of RSV-specific immunoglobulins G, M, and A with enzyme-linked immunosorbent assay. J Clin Microbiol. 1990;28:152-155.
262. Vikerfors T, Grandien M, Johansson M, et al. Detection of an immunoglobulin M response in the elderly for early diagnosis of respiratory syncytial virus infection. J Clin Microbiol. 1988;26:808-811.
263. Jensen I, Thisted E, Glikmann G, et al. Secretory IgM and IgA antibodies to respiratory syncytial virus in nasopharyngeal aspirates: A diagnostic supplement to antigen detection. Clin Diagn Virol. 1997;8:219-226.
264. Panitch H. Respiratory syncytial virus bronchiolitis: Supportive care and therapies designed to overcome airway obstruction. Pediatr Infect Dis J. 2003;22:S83-S88.
265. Law B, Carvalho V. Respiratory syncytial virus infections in hospitalized Canadian children: Regional differences in patient populations and management practices. Pediatr Infect Dis J. 1993;12:659-663.
266. Kimpen J, Schaad U. Treatment of respiratory syncytial virus bronchiolitis: 1995 poll of members of the European Society for Paediatric Infectious Diseases. Pediatr Infect Dis J. 1997;16:479-481.
267. Behrendt C, Decker M, Burch D, et al. Internation variation in the management of infants hospitalized with respiratory syncytial virus. Eur J Pediatr. 1998;157:215-220.
268. Englund J, Piedra P, Jefferson L, et al. High-dose, short-duration ribavirin aerosol therapy in children with suspected respiratory syncytial virus infection. J Pediatr. 1990;117:313-320.
269. American Academy of Pediatrics Committee on Infectious Diseases and Committee of Fetus and Newborn. Prevention of respiratory syncytial virus infections: Indications for use of palivizumab and update on the use of RSV-IVIG. Pediatrics. 1998;102:1211-1216.
270. Khoshoo V, Ross G, Edell D. Effect of interventions during acute respiratory syncytial virus bronchiolitis on subsequent long term respiratory morbidity. Pediatr Infect Dis J. 2002;21:468-472.
271. Edell D, Khoshoo V, Ross G, et al. Early ribavirin treatment of bronchiolitis: Effect on long-term respiratory morbidity. Chest 2002;122:935-939.
272. Kellner J, Ohlsson A, Gadomski A, et al. Efficacy of bronchodilator therapy in bronchiolitis: A meta-analysis. Arch Pediatr Adolesc Med. 1996;150:1166-1172.
273. Clineanswers, Clineguide, Hall C. Bronchiolitis. Los Angeles: Wolters Kluwer; 2002.
274. AHRQ. Management of bronchiolitis in infants and children. Agency for Healthcare Research and Quality: Evidence Report/Technology Assessment 2003;03-E009:1-5.
275. Kellner J, Ohlsson A, Gadomski A, et al. Bronchodilators for bronchiolitis. Cochrane Database Syst Rev. 2000;3:CD001266.
276. van Woensel J, Kimpen J, Sprikkelman A, et al. Long-term effects of prednisolone in the acute phase of bronchiolitis caused by respiratory syncytial virus. Pediatr Pulmonol. 2000;30:92-96.
277. Perlstein P, Kotagal U, Bolling C, et al. Evaluation of an evidence-based guideline for bronchiolitits. Pediatrics. 1999;104:1334-1341.
278. Garrison M, Christakis D, Harvey E, et al. Systemic corticosteroids in infant bronchiolitis: A meta-analysis. Pediatrics. 2000;105:e44.
279. Centers for Disease Control and Prevention. Guideline for hand hygiene in healthcare settings: Recommendations of the Healthcare Infections Control Practices Advisory Committee and the HICPAC/SHEA/APIC/IDSA Hand Hygiene Task Force. MMWR Morb Mortal Wkly Rep. 2002;51(RR16):1.
280. Macartney K, Gorelick M, Manning M, et al. Nosocomial respiratory syncytial virus infections: The cost-effectiveness and cost-benefit of infection control. Pediatrics. 2000;106:520-526.
281. Berner R, Schwoerer F, Schumacher R, et al. Community and nosocomially acquired respiratory syncytial virus infection in a German paediatric hospital from 1988 to 1999. Eur J Pediatr. 2001;160:541-547.
282. Mlinaric-Galinovic G, Varda-Brkic D. Nosocomial respiratory syncytial virus infections in children's wards. Diagn Microbiol Infect Dis. 2000;37:237-246.
283. Sanchez P. Immunoprophylaxis of respiratory syncytial virus disease. Pediatr Infect Dis J. 2000;19:791-801.
284. PREVENT Study Group. Reduction of respiratory syncytial virus hospitalization among premature infants and infants with bronchopulmonary dysplasia using respiratory syncytial virus immune globulin prophylaxis. Pediatrics. 1997;99:93-99.
285. Wang E, Tang N. Immunoglobulin for preventing respiratory syncytial virus infection. Cochrane Database Syst Rev. 2000;2:CD001725.

286. Impact RSV Study Group, Connor E. Palivizumab, a humanized respiratory syncytial virus monoclonal antibody, reduces hospitalization from respiratory syncytial virus infection in high-risk infants. Pediatrics. 1998;102:531-537.

287. Hudak M. Palivizumab prophylaxis of RSV disease: Results of 5,097 children, 2001-2002 Outcome Registry. In: AAP National Conference and Exhibition. Boston; 2003.

288. Clark S, Beresford M, Subhedar N, et al. Respiratory syncytial virus infection in high risk infants and the potential impact of prophylaxis in a United Kingdom cohort. Arch Dis Child. 2000;83:313-316.

289. Sharland M, Bedford-Russell A. Preventing respiratory syncytial virus bronchiolitis. BMJ. 2001;322:62-63.

290. Falsey A, Walsh E. Safety and immunogenicity of a respiratory syncytial virus subunit vaccine (PFP-2) in ambulatory adults over age 60. Vaccine. 1996;14:1214-1218.

291. Englund J, Glezen W, Piedra P. Maternal immunization against viral disease. Vaccine. 1998;16:1456-1463.

292. Piedra P. Clinical experience with respiratory syncytial virus vaccines. Pediatr Infect Dis J. 2003;22:S94-S99.

293. Paradiso P, Hildreth S, Hogerman D, et al. Safety and immunogenicity of a subunit respiratory syncytial virus vaccine in children 24 to 48 months old. Pediatr Infect Dis J. 1994;13:792-798.

294. Wathen M, Kakuk T, Bridcau R, et al. Vaccination of cotton rats with a chimeric FG glycoprotein of human respiratory syncytial virus induces minimal pulmonary pathology on challenge. Pediatr Infect Dis J. 1991;163:477-482.

295. Power U, Nguyen T, Rietveld E, et al. Safety and immunogenicity of a novel recombinant subunit respiratory syncytial virus vaccine (BBG2Na) in healthy young adults. J Infect Dis. 2001;184:1456-1460.

296. Crowe J. Respiratory syncytial virus vaccine development. Vaccine. 2002;20: S32-S37.

297. Collins P, Murphy B. Respiratory syncytial virus: Reverse genetics and vaccine strategies. Virology. 2002;296:204-211.

298. Gardner P. How etiologic, pathologic, and clinical diagnoses can be made in a correlated fashion. Pediatr Res. 1977;11:254-261.

299. Jackson G, Muldoon R. Viruses causing common respiratory infections in man: III. Respiratory syncytial viruses and coronaviruses. J Infect Dis. 1973;128:674-692.

300. Henderson F, Clyde WJ, Collier A, et al. The etiologic and epidemiologic spectrum of bronchiolitis in pediatric practice. J Pediatr. 1979;95:183-190.

301. Chanock R, Kim H, Vargosko A, et al. Respiratory syncytial virus: I. Virus recovery and other observations during 1960 outbreak of bronchiolitis pneumonia, and minor respiratory diseases in children. JAMA. 1961;176:647-653.

302. Glezen W, Loda F, Clyde WJ, et al. Epidemiologic patterns of acute lower respiratory disease of children in a pediatric group practice. J Pediatr. 1971;78:397-406.

303. Murphy T, Henderson F, Clyde WJ, et al. Pneumonia: An eleven-year study in a pediatric practice. Am J Epidemiol. 1981;113:12-21.

304. Coates H, Chanock R. Clinical significance of respiratory syncytial virus. Postgrad Med. 1964;35:460-465.

305. Loda F, Clyde W, Glezen W, et al. Studies of the role of viruses, bacteria, and *M. pneumoniae* as causes of lower respiratory tract infections in children. J Pediatr. 1968;72:161-176.

306. Macasaet F, Kidd P, Bolano C, et al. The etiology of acute respiratory infections: III. The role of viruses and bacteria. J Pediatr. 1968;72:829-839.

307. Maletzky A, Cooney M, Luce R, et al. Epidemiology of viral and mycoplasmal agents associated with childhood lower respiratory illness in a civilian population. J Pediatr. 1971;78:407-414.

308. Beem M, Wright F, Manre D, et al. Association of the chimpanzee coryza agent with acute respiratory disease in children. N Engl J Med. 1960;263:523-530.

CHAPTER **156**

Human Metapneumovirus

ANN R. FALSEY

Human metapneumovirus (hMPV) is a newly discovered respiratory pathogen first described by investigators in the Netherlands in 2001.[1] This previously unidentified virus was isolated from the nasopharyngeal secretions of 28 Dutch children, and samples were collected over a 20-year period. The virus exhibited paramyxovirus-like morphology, and genetic analysis was most similar to the Pneumovirinae family of which respiratory syncytial virus (RSV) is the most prominent member. Serologic analyses indicate that infection with hMPV is nearly universal by age 5, and that the virus had been circulating for at least 50 years undetected. Although clinical data are relatively limited,

hMPV appears to account for a significant proportion of the respiratory illnesses that were not recognized as being caused by other viral pathogens.

VIRUS

Human metapneumovirus is a nonsegmented, single-stranded, negative-sense RNA virus belonging to the order Mononegavirales, family Paramyxoviridae, subfamily Pneumovirinae, and genus Metapneumovirus.[1] Consistent with the morphology of a paramyxovirus, hMPV particles are pleomorphic, spherical, or filamentous with a lipid envelope and projections on the surface as imaged by electron microscopy (Fig. 156-1).[1,2] Within the subfamily Pneumovirinae are the genera Pneumovirus and Metapneumovirus. Members of the Pneumovirus genus include human RSV and a number of animal pathogens such as bovine, ovine, and caprine RSVs, and pneumonia virus of mice.[3,4] Until recently, the only member of the Metapneumovirus genus was avian pneumovirus (APV), also known as turkey rhinotracheitis virus.[5] APV causes upper respiratory tract infection of turkeys and other avian species and was first reported in the late 1970s in South Africa. Originally classified as a pneumovirus, APV was placed into a separate new genus, Metapneumovirus, because it had a different gene number and gene order, and only 40% homology with mammalian pneumoviruses. The original genetic analysis of hMPV by van den Hoogen and colleagues indicated greatest homology with APV, with a gene order of 3'-N-P-M-F-M2-SH-G-L-5'.[1] The absence of the nonstructural interferon-inhibiting genes NS1 and NS2 showed that hMPV differed from RSV and other pneumoviruses and confirmed its classification in the Metapneumovirus genus (Fig. 156-2).[6]

The structural and functional assignments of the gene products of hMPV are presumed to be based on sequence homology with AVP. Sequence analyses of the nucleoprotein (N), phosphoprotein (P), matrix protein (M), and fusion protein (F) genes of hMPV indicate the highest identity with APV serotype C (APV-C), one of four avian pneumovirus types.[6,7] APV-C is found primarily in the United States, whereas APV serotypes A, B, and D are isolated from birds in Europe.

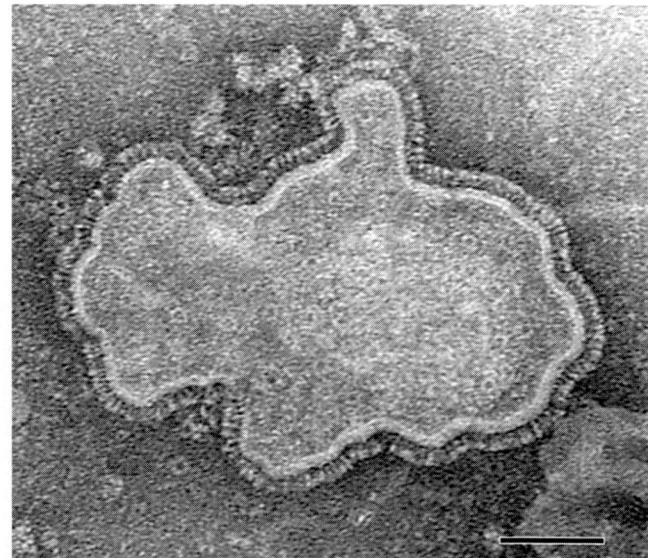

FIGURE 156-1. Negative-stain electron micrograph of human metapneumovirus. This pleomorphic form of the virus is stain penetrated, thereby permitting visualization of portions of the virus envelope and nucleocapsid. A border composed of the surface projection proteins may also be seen around the virus periphery. Phosphotungstic acid negative stain, pH 6.5. *Bar marker* represents 100 nm. *(Image courtesy of Charles Humphrey, Ph.D., research biologist, and Dean Erdman, Ph.D., Centers for Disease Control and Prevention.)*

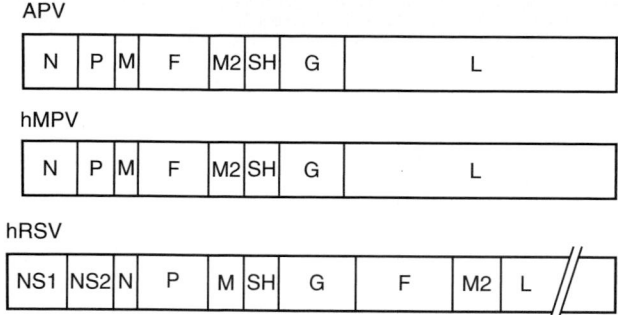

FIGURE 156-2. Schematic representation of the gene order and sequence of avian pneumovirus (APV), human metapneumovirus (hMPV), and human respiratory syncytial virus (hRSV). Gene lengths are not drawn to scale.

Sequence homology between hMPV and APV-C is 88% for the N gene, 68% for the P gene, 76% for the M gene, and 81% for the F gene.[6] Sequence homology between hMPV and APV-C for the attachment (G) gene is more variable.[4,8] The structural characteristics of the predicted G protein of APV-C are similar to those of RSV, including two mucin-like regions flanking a CX3C chemokine motif present in a conserved hydrophobic pocket.[4]

Genetic variation among hMPV isolates has been observed, and the sequences are found to cluster in two major groups.[1,9] Sequence analysis of the N, M, F, and L gene fragments from nine Dutch isolates demonstrated 99% to 100% nucleotide sequence homology between isolates within a cluster, whereas the identity between the two clusters was 81% to 88%. Sequence variation did not seem to correlate with the year of isolation. Fifteen Canadian isolates appeared similar to the Dutch viruses, and genetic analysis identified two genetic clusters.[9] Recently, two isolates representing each of the proposed major genotypes were completely sequenced.[10] The overall sequence and amino acid identities between genotypes were 80% and 90%, respectively, similar to the differences found between RSV groups A and B. The greatest diversity is found in two of the surface glycoproteins, the small hydrophobic surface (SH) and attachment (G) proteins (59% and 37% identity, respectively), which is considerably greater than the diversity observed in the RSV groups. Although it is uncertain at present whether the genetic differences between hMPV subgroups represent clinically important antigenic differences, it is reasonable to postulate that they are comparable to the genetic differences between RSV groups.[10] Phylogenetic analyses of isolates from four continents indicate that all hMPV isolates to date cluster within the same two groups.[9,11,12]

Given the close relationship between hMPV and APV-C, it is speculated that the human virus originated from birds.[1] In view of serologic data that indicate the presence of hMPV antibodies for at least 50 years, it is presumed that a zoonotic event must have taken place prior to 1958. Although current evidence links hMPV with APV, animal challenge studies indicate that hMPV is a primary human pathogen rather than an avian pathogen that incidentally affects hu-

mans. Turkeys and chickens, when inoculated with high-titer hMPV, did not exhibit clinical illness and showed no evidence of virus replication by reverse transcriptase–polymerase chain reaction (RT-PCR).[1] In contrast, four juvenile macaques that were similarly inoculated demonstrated viral replication in throat samples, and two monkeys had mild upper respiratory illness (URI).

EPIDEMIOLOGY

Human metapneumovirus is a ubiquitous pathogen that affects all age groups.[1,13-15] Seroprevalence studies from Japan and The Netherlands indicate that by age 5, most children have been infected with hMPV.[1,16] Illness caused by both RSV and hMPV appears to be common in young children, but primary infection with hMPV occurs at a slightly older age.[12,17] Whereas nearly 100% of children are infected with RSV by age 2 years, data from The Netherlands show that approximately 50% are seropositive for hMPV by age 2 and 100% by age 5.[1] In Japan, children appear to be infected at an even older age: 33% are seropositive by age 2 years and 77% by age 5.[16] Data from a Canadian study further corroborate the older age for infection with hMPV; the peak age for hospitalization with hMPV was 3 to 5 months compared with 0 to 2 months for RSV infection.[17] Among children hospitalized with respiratory illnesses, rates of hMPV detection range from 4.1% to 25% (Table 156-1).[12,17-22a] In a recent population-based study from Hong Kong, the authors estimate that 442 hospital admissions per 100,000 children less than 6 years of age are attributable to hMPV.[12] Although hMPV accounts for a significant proportion of respiratory illness in young children, its overall frequency is less than the frequencies of other childhood pathogens such as RSV and influenza (Table 156-2).

Serologic evidence and limited clinical data indicate that reinfection with hMPV occurs throughout life.[1,16] In a study of patients of all age groups visiting general practitioners in England during the 2000-2001 winter season for influenza-like illness, hMPV was detected by RT-PCR in 2.2% of nasal samples that had tested negative for other viruses.[13] Although 27% of these nasal samples were from children less than 15 years old, 89% (eight of nine) of the samples that were positive for hMPV had been obtained from adults. The infection rate in the general population was estimated at 1.3%.

In a prospective study from Rochester, New York, during two winter seasons, hMPV was identified by RT-PCR or serology in 44 of 984 (4.5%) illnesses.[14] Infections were noted in all groups studied: young adults (6.6%), healthy older adults (1.7%), high-risk adults (2.9%), and residents of long-term care facilities (5.4%). Additionally, hMPV accounted for 1.4% and 10.8% of hospitalizations for acute cardiopulmonary conditions in older persons and in adults with high-risk conditions during the two winters. In a Canadian study of patients hospitalized for respiratory diseases from 1993 to 2001, 38 isolates of hMPV were recovered retrospectively, of which 46% were in patients over age 65 years.[15]

Studies from Europe, North America, Asia, and Australia indicate that hMPV has worldwide circulation.[11-14,16-23] In temperate climates, the virus circulates predominantly in winter months and overlaps with other seasonal respiratory pathogens such as influenza and RSV.[15] In the Southern Hemisphere, hMPV circulates in the summer, and in the

TABLE 156-1 Summary of Human Metapneumovirus (hMPV) Studies in Children

Location	Authors (Ref.)	Period of Study	Child's Age	Number Tested	% hMPV	Specimens Tested
Spain	Vicente et al. (18)	11/01-2/01	<3 yr	562	4.1	Negative for other viruses
Germany	Viazov et al. (19)	1/02-5/02	<2 yr	63	17.5	All
Italy	Maggi et al. (21)	Jan-May in 2000, 2001, 2002	<2 yr	90	25	All
France	Freymuth et al. (22)	11/01-2/02	<18 yr	337	6.6	Negative for other viruses
USA	Esper et al. (20)	10/01-2/02	<5 yr	296	6.4	Negative for other viruses
Canada	Boivin et al. (17)	12/01-4/02	<3 yr	208	5.8	All
Hong Kong	Peiris et al. (12)	8/01-3/02	<18 yr	587	5.5	All
	Williams et al. (22a)	1976-2001	24 yr	248	20	Negative for other viruses

TABLE 156-2 Comparison of Percentages of Illnesses Due to Common Respiratory Viruses

	Author (Ref.); Patient Age and Number			
	Boivin et al. (17) ≤3 yr N = 208	Vicente et al. (18)*≤3 yr N = 565	Freymuth et al. (22)* ≤18 yr N = 758	Peiris et al. (12) ≤18 yr N = 587
Virus	% of Total Specimens			
hMPV	5.8	1.1	2.5	5.5
RSV	56.7	55.4	32.0	8.0
Influenza	23.6	7.8	7.6	8.0
Adenovirus	4.1	5.7	1.0	3.1
Parainfluenza	1.3	6.4	1.1	5.0

*Only specimens negative for other viruses were tested for hMPV. The percentage of hMPV is based on the number of hMPV-positive results divided by the total number of samples. Because dual infections are not accounted for, the amount of hMPV may be underestimated.
hMPV, human metapneumovirus; RSV, respiratory syncytial virus.

subtropics, peak activity is in the spring and early summer.[12] Although comprehensive studies are lacking, preliminary data suggest that hMPV intensity may exhibit yearly variation. One study of adults in the United States demonstrated a significant difference in rates of hMPV illness during the winters of 1999 and 2000 (1.5% versus 7%).[14] In addition, a 3-year study of infants in Italy found marked yearly variation in the incidence of infection: 37% in 2000, 7% in 2001, and 43% in 2002.[21] Thus, hMPV may be more like parainfluenza in its periodicity and less like RSV, which occurs predictably. There are no data on regional differences in hMPV infection during the winter.

Numerous studies from around the world confirm the presence of two major genotypes of hMPV, which, like the RSV groups, often circulate concurrently within the same community.[9,17-19] Additionally, isolates recovered from two residents of a nursing home outbreak had slightly different F gene sequences, suggesting cocirculation of different strains within the same institution.[15] The clinical significance of different genotype groups and strains of hMPV is not yet understood.

Although hMPV testing in most studies has focused on specimens yielding no other pathogens, it is not uncommon to have a dual infection of hMPV and another respiratory pathogen.[12,14,17,19-21] Rates of mixed infections range from 6% to 39%, with RSV and influenza A being the most common copathogens. The high rate of coinfection in some studies raises questions about the causal relationship between hMPV and the observed respiratory illness. Few studies have included control groups to answer this question. However, a study of Canadian children under age 3 years detected hMPV in 6% of ill patients (12 of 208) compared with 0 of 51 well children.[17] Furthermore, screening of 400 respiratory samples from infants without respiratory disease in The Netherlands by RT-PCR for hMPV revealed no positive results, suggesting that hMPV was a pathogenic virus causing respiratory symptoms.[24]

CLINICAL MANIFESTATIONS

The clinical manifestations of hMPV infection are similar to those of RSV and range from mild URI to bronchiolitis and severe pneumonia requiring mechanical ventilation.[1,15] The spectrum of disease appears to depend on the age and the health of the host.[12,14,15] As with most respiratory viruses, the clinical syndrome is not distinct. Fever, cough, and coryza are the most common symptoms. The incubation period between exposure and onset of clinical symptoms is not known. However, information from one case of nosocomial transmission suggests that the incubation period is approximately 5 to 6 days.[12]

Children

Most young children with hMPV infection exhibit fever, cough, and rhinorrhea (Table 156-3).[12,17,20] Fever appears to be more common with hMPV than with RSV, and febrile seizures were noted in 16% of patients with hMPV compared with 3.1% in RSV-infected children in one study.[12] Wheezing is also common, with rates ranging from 28%

to 83%; otitis media, conjunctivitis, pharyngitis, and laryngitis all occur with variable frequencies.[17,20,22] Less common symptoms include maculopapular truncal rash and diarrhea.[12] Notably, 2 of 26 French children with hMPV infection had diarrhea and high fever without respiratory symptoms.[22] Lymphopenia and elevated hepatic transaminase values have also been described.[12] Hypoxia and radiographic changes are common in hMPV-infected children, and abnormal chest radiographs have been found in 26% to 53% of hospitalized children.[12,20] Radiographic findings, which include peribronchial cuffing, perihilar infiltrates, patchy opacities, and hyperinflation, are similar to those in children with RSV infection. Lobar consolidation has not been described. Clinical diagnoses most frequently associated with hMPV hospitalization in children include bronchiolitis (in 47% to 84%), asthma (in 11% to 25%), and pneumonia (in 11% to 17%). The mean length of hospitalization for these children was 3 to 5 days.[12,17,20,22]

The role of hMPV in asthma and acute wheezing in childhood has not been fully elucidated. Some investigations suggest that hMPV may be a common trigger for asthma, whereas others indicate that the wheezing observed is more typical of bronchiolitis in the young child.[17,25] In a study of Chinese children, wheezing with hMPV infection was more commonly associated with a diagnosis of exacerbation of asthma than with bronchiolitis.[12] The average age of hMPV-infected children in that study was 32 months. Additionally, hMPV was detected in 8% of Finnish children (10 of 132) admitted with wheezing during the winter months, and in seven cases, hMPV was the sole pathogen identified.[23] However, Australian investigators found that rhinovirus was isolated significantly more often in children with an acute exacerbation of asthma than in those with URI.[26] On the other hand, hMPV was found more commonly in children with URI than in those with asthma. Although several respiratory viruses have been linked to childhood asthma, pathogenic mechanisms may differ. For example, children with RSV infection have high nasal concentrations of RANTES (regulated on activation, normal T cell expressed and secreted) and varying amounts of interleukin (IL)-8, whereas children with hMPV had low levels of RANTES and high concentrations of IL-8.[23]

TABLE 156-3 Comparison of Signs and Symptoms in Children with hMPV, RSV, and Influenza A

	hMPV (%)	RSV (%)	Influenza A (%)
Fever	84	57	78
Cough	84	99	96
Rhinorrhea	74	91	84
Retraction	65	95	82
Wheezing	46	59	37
Lacrimation	25	31	31
Diarrhea	5	17	9
Vomiting	25	8	10

hMPV, human metapneumovirus; RSV, respiratory syncytial virus.
Data compiled from references 12, 17, and 20.

Severity of illness can be highly variable and most likely depends, in part, on the age and overall health of the child. However, because the current literature focuses on hospitalized illnesses and large prospective studies have not been performed, the full spectrum of disease has yet to be defined. Although lower respiratory tract involvement appears common with hMPV infection, disease appears somewhat milder than that of RSV or influenza A. In a Canadian study of children less than 3 years of age, none of the hMPV-infected children were admitted to an intensive care unit, whereas 15% of those with RSV and 16% of those with influenza A required intensive care.[17] In this study, approximately 25% of the hMPV-infected children had underlying medical conditions compared with 7% of children infected with RSV. In published reports, recovery from infection is nearly universal, with the exception of immunocompromised children.[27] Coinfection with hMPV and RSV has been observed in babies with severe bronchiolitis.[28] Of children requiring mechanical ventilation for severe RSV bronchiolitis, 70% (21 of 30) were found to have hMPV by RT-PCR. These findings raise the possibility that hMPV may be a cofactor, or that mixed viral infections may be more severe. Although this is an interesting possibility, other investigators have not found dual infections to be more severe than infections with hMPV alone.[19,21]

Adults

The clinical manifestations of hMPV infection in adults, like those in children, appear to depend on age and health status. Middle-aged and healthy older adults present with influenza-like illness and common cold syndromes.[13-15] In a 2-year prospective study in New York, symptomatic infection in young adults was relatively common, and hMPV was detected in 2.9% to 9.1% of persons with respiratory illness, depending on the year.[14] Asymptomatic infection was also common, as 15% of young adults reporting no illness during the second winter had serologic evidence of infection. Clinical symptoms in young adults are not distinctive from other respiratory viral illnesses, although in one study, hoarseness was more common among hMPV-infected patients than among those with RSV(Table 156-4). Unlike in children, fever is not common in adults with hMPV illnesses.

The impact of infection in adults is greatest in older adults and high-risk patients.[13-15] When older outpatients were compared with young adults, the older adults experienced wheezing and dyspnea more often than did young adults (see Table 156-4). In addition, adults with chronic cardiopulmonary conditions were ill twice as long as healthy young adults (17 versus 9 days) and more frequently sought medical attention.[14] The demographics of those requiring hospitalization appear very similar to those of patients hospitalized with RSV or influenza. Patients are primarily older adults, and 85% have chronic

heart or lung conditions.[14] Chest radiographs reveal patchy infiltrates, with a predilection for the lower lobes, in 25% of patients. In studies of hospitalized patients, small numbers of patients have required intensive care and mechanical ventilation, and deaths have been reported.[14,15] Immunosuppression and the presence of chronic pulmonary and cardiac conditions are risk factors for poor outcome. The most common diagnoses associated with adult hospitalization are exacerbations of chronic obstructive pulmonary disease, bronchitis, and pneumonia.[14]

As is found with other common respiratory viruses such as RSV, influenza, and parainfluenza, hMPV infection is associated with severe illness and pneumonitis in immunocompromised patients.[15,27,29] Most fatalities described to date have involved patients with neoplasia. HMPV was the sole pathogen identified in a 17-month-old girl with a cough and coryza who died of progressive pneumonia while undergoing chemotherapy for acute lymphoblastic leukemia.[27] Additionally, hMPV was detected in the respiratory secretions of a bone marrow transplant recipient who became ill with a URI and died of progressive respiratory failure.[29] Finally, 83% of Canadian patients (five of six) who were immunosuppressed developed pneumonitis with hMPV, and three required intensive care.[15]

The role of hMPV in severe acute respiratory syndrome (SARS) has yet to be completely defined. Data implicating the SARS-associated coronavirus (SARS-CoV) as the primary cause of SARS are compelling (see Chapter 152).[30,31] Yet, in a number of studies of SARS, hMPV has been identified by culture, RT-PCR, or serology in a significant proportion of patients, raising the possibility that coinfection with hMPV may be a risk factor for severe disease.[32] In the first published report of SARS in Canada, five of nine patients and one asymptomatic contact of a patient with SARS were infected with hMPV. Five patients were culture positive for SARS-CoV, and four of these had evidence of dual infection with hMPV.[33] Microbiologic investigations in 12 cohorts of SARS cases in six centers throughout the world have shown marked variation in the reported rates of hMPV infection.[31] Overall, 75% of patients had evidence of SARS-CoV infection, compared with 12% who had evidence of hMPV. In 7 of the 12 cohorts, hMPV was detected; rates ranged from 2% to 36% of the patients. Using virus isolation and RT-PCR, investigators in Hong Kong found 19 (40%) of 48 patients suspected of having SARS to be infected with hMPV alone, whereas 5 (10%) were infected with SARS-CoV alone.[32] Six (13%) were infected with both viruses. Although the role of hMPV as a cofactor in SARS remains to be determined, hMPV has been identified in a significantly higher proportion of patients with SARS than of patients infected with other respiratory pathogens, and its potential role in that illness requires further study.

DIAGNOSIS

The virus probably remained unidentified for many years because the clinical syndrome is not distinct and because isolation of the virus with standard cell culture techniques is difficult. HMPV replicates very slowly, does not grow efficiently in continuous cell lines traditionally used for viral isolation, does not display hemagglutinating activity, and appears to be relatively trypsin dependent.[1] Three methods of diagnosis are used: viral culture, serology, and RT-PCR.

Viral Culture. Isolation of hMPV requires inoculation of the sample on tertiary cynomolgus monkey kidney (tMK) cells or rhesus monkey kidney (LLC-MK2) cells in medium containing trypsin. Cultures should be observed for 21 days for cytopathic effect (CPE). The characteristic CPE in LLC-MK2 cells consists of small, round, granular, and refringent cells without large syncytia, and it is usually apparent after a mean of 17 days (range, 3 to 23 days) (Fig. 156-3).[2,15] Confirmation of hMPV infection requires either immunofluorescent assays (IFA) with hMPV specific antibodies or RT-PCR of the cell supernatant. One laboratory has reported that human laryngeal tumor (HEp-2) cells were more sensitive than LLC-MK2 cells when RT-PCR was used to detect viral presence rather than CPE.[32] When cell culture supernates were tested for hMPV using RT-PCR, 38% of HEp-2 cell

TABLE 156-4 Clinical Characteristics of Young versus Older Adults with hMPV Infection			
Symptom or Sign	Older Adults* N = 13	Young Adults† N = 11	P value
Nasal congestion	11 (85%)	11 (100%)	NS
Sore throat	3 (23%)	5 (45%)	NS
Hoarseness	6 (46%)	10 (91%)	.03
Cough	13 (100%)	9 (82%)	NS
Sputum production	7 (54%)	6 (55%)	NS
Dyspnea	9 (69%)	1 (9%)	.005
Wheezing	8 (62%)	1 (9%)	.01
Rhinorrhea	9 (69%)	9 (82%)	NS
Wheezing on exam	5 (38%)	0	NS
Rales	3 (23%)	0	NS
Rhonchi	2 (15%)	0	NS
Length of illness in days (mean ± SD)	17.4±9.4	8.5±3.4	.01

*Older adults: 65 years old and older.
†Young adults: less than 40 years old.
hMPV, human metapneumovirus.
Adapted from Falsey AR, Erdman D, Anderson LJ, Walsh EE. J Infect Dis. 2003;187:785-790. Copyright 2003 University of Chicago.

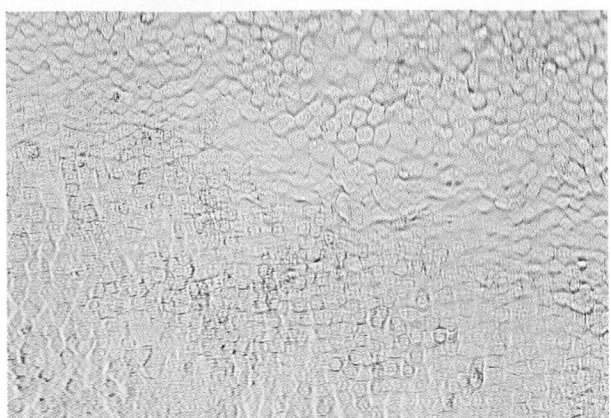

A

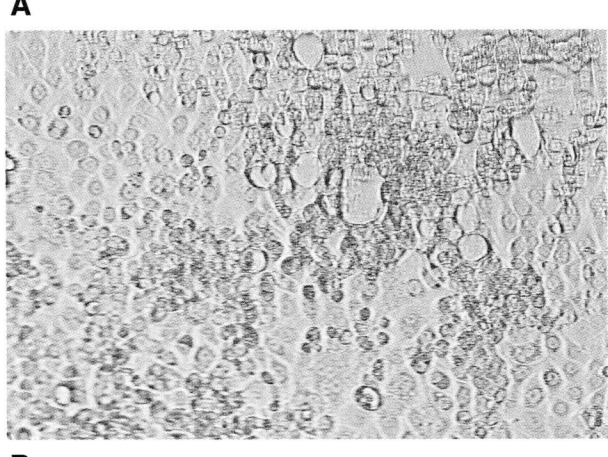

B

FIGURE 156-3. Photomicrograph of hMPV (CAN97-83) in LLC-MK2 cells. LLC-MK2 cells in a semi-confluent monolayer were infected with hMPV (provided by Dr. Guy Boivan) and allowed to grow for 11 days. **A,** Uninfected LLC-MK2 cells. **B,** Infected LLC-MK2 cells. Granular cytopathic effects, without syncytia formation, are evident.

cultures (18 of 48) showed hMPV growth compared with only 6% (three) in LLC-MK2. A comparison of different culture techniques has not been performed.

Serology. Because seropositivity is nearly universal by age 5 years, a definitive serologic diagnosis usually requires a fourfold rise in antibody titer or seroconversion. Serologic diagnosis is most often accomplished by enzyme immunoassay (EIA) using whole virus lysates of the representative strains of the two major genotypes as antigen, or IFA using hMPV-infected cells fixed to slides.[14,32]

RT-PCR. Because of the difficulty of isolating hMPV in cell culture, most investigators have relied on molecular techniques for diagnosis. The conserved regions of several genes, including those of the F, N, M, and L proteins, have been used successfully in both nested and single-round PCR.[1,17,20,32] Using primers from the M gene, Australian investigators compared two techniques for RT-PCR and found a real-time assay using the LightCycler and a fluorogenic oligoprobe was more sensitive than an enzyme-linked amplicon hybridization-based system.[34] A recent comparison of real-time PCR using different primer sets from the N, L, M, P, and F genes to detect laboratory-propagated virus, as well as clinical samples, demonstrated the greatest sensitivity with the N and L gene primers.[35] The analytic sensitivity of the N gene RT-PCR was 100 copies of viral RNA, and the sensitivity was ascribed to amplifying a more conserved gene. Because there is no gold standard for the diagnosis of hMPV, several investigators have used two different gene amplifica-

tion products to confirm infection and consider results positive only if both are successful.[12,14]

There are very limited data on the sensitivity and specificity of the various diagnostic methods. In one study, approximately half of the seropositive infections were also RT-PCR positive using the N and L gene primers.[14] RT-PCR was more likely to be positive in outpatients than in inpatients and correlated with a shorter duration of symptoms prior to evaluation.

TREATMENT AND PREVENTION

Treatment of hMPV infection is supportive because therapeutic antivirals or antibody preparations for the treatment or prevention of hMPV infection are not available. Ribavirin, a nucleoside analogue with broad antiviral activity, is approved for the treatment of serious RSV infections in young children, and polyclonal immune globulin—intravenous (IGIV) is approved for the prophylaxis of RSV infections in high-risk children (see Chapter 155).[36-38] These two agents were tested by comparing their abilities to inhibit hMPV and RSV in tissue culture and found to have equivalent antiviral activity for both viruses.[39] Recommendations for use of these agents must await data from controlled clinical trials.

The mode of transmission of hMPV is unknown, but given its close relationship with RSV, it is likely to have a similar mode of spread. Efficient transmission of RSV occurs as a result of direct contact with infected secretions via fomites or large-particle aerosols.[40] Nosocomial transmission of hMPV has been documented in two pediatric studies.[12,20] Given the difficulty of making a specific diagnosis at present, infection control policies in place for RSV should be implemented for children exhibiting symptoms of bronchiolitis when hMPV infection is a possibility. Careful hand hygiene is of primary importance, and the use of gowns and gloves can be considered.[41,42]

No vaccine is currently available for the prevention of hMPV. Reinfection occurs throughout life despite the development of an antibody response. Thus, it appears likely that hMPV leads to incomplete immunity despite the induction of serum antibody. Reinfection has been documented in one child during two consecutive winter seasons.[2] Nevertheless, efforts to produce a vaccine for hMPV are ongoing. In an animal model, immunization with a live-attenuated bovine parainfluenza virus type 3 vaccine containing the hMPV F gene was protective.[43]

REFERENCES

1. van den Hoogen BG, DeJong JC, Groen J, et al, A newly discovered human pneumovirus isolated from young children with respiratory tract disease. Nat Med. 2001;7:719-724.
2. Peret TC, Boivin G, Li Y, et al. Characterization of human metapneumoviruses isolated from patients in North America. J Infect Dis. 2002;185:1660-1663.
3. Mackie PLK. The classification of viruses infecting the respiratory tract. Paediatr Respir Rev. 2003;4:84-90.
4. Alvarez R, Lwamba HM, Kapczynski DR, et al. Nucleotide and predicted amino acid sequence-based analysis of the avian metapneumovirus type C cell attachment glycoprotein gene: Phylogenetic analysis and molecular epidemiology of U.S. pneumoviruses. J Clin Microbiol. 2003;41:1730-1735.
5. Cook JKA, Cavanagh D. Detection and differentiation of avian pneumoviruses (metapneumoviruses). Avian Pathol. 2002;31:132.
6. van den Hoogen BG, Besterbroer TM, Osterhaus AD, Fouchier RA. Analysis of the genomic sequence of a human metapneumovirus. Virology. 2002;295:119-132.
7. Jacobs JA, Njenga MK, Alvarez R, et al. Subtype B avian metapneumovirus resembles subtype A more closely than subtype C or human metapneumovirus with respect to the phosphoprotein, and second matrix and small hydrophobic proteins. Virus Res. 2003;93:171-178.
8. Toquin D, de Boisseoson C, Beven V, et al. Subgroup C avian metapneumovirus (MPV) and the recently isolated human MPV exhibit a common organization but have extensive sequence divergence in their putative SH and G genes. J Gen Virol. 2003;84:2169-2178.
9. Bastien N, Normand S, Taylor T, et al. Sequence analysis of the N, P, M and F genes of Canadian human metapneumovirus strains. Virus Res. 2003;93:51-62.

10. Biacchesi S, Skiadopoulos MH, Boivin G, et al. Genetic diversity between human metapneumovirus subgroups. Virology. 2003;315:1-9.
11. Nissen MD, Mackay IM, Withers SJ, et al. Evidence of human metapneumovirus in Australian children. Med J Aust. 2002;176:188.
12. Peiris JSM, Tang W-H, Chan K-H, et al. Children with respiratory disease associated with metapneumovirus in Hong Kong. Emerg Infect Dis. 2003;9:628-633.
13. Stockton J, Stephenson I, Fleming D, Zambon M. Human Metapneumovirus as a cause of community-acquired respiratory illness. Emerg Infect Dis. 2002;8:897-901.
14. Falsey AR, Erdman D, Anderson LJ, Walsh EE. Human metapneumovirus infections in young and elderly adults. J Infect Dis. 2003;187:785-790.
15. Boivin G, Abed Y, Pelletier G, et al. Virological features and clinical manifestations associated with human metapneumovirus: A new paramyxovirus responsible for acute respiratory-tract infections in all age groups. J Infect Dis. 2002;186:1330-1334.
16. Ebihara T, Endo R, Kikuta H, et al. Seroprevalence of human metapneumovirus in Japan. J Med Virol. 2003;70:281-283.
17. Boivin G, De Sarres G, Cote S, et al. Human metapneumovirus infections in hospitalized children. Emerg Infect Dis. 2003;9:634-640.
18. Vicente D, Cilla G, Montes M, Perez-Trallero E. Human metapneumovirus and community-acquired respiratory illness in children. Emerg Infect Dis. 2003;9:602.
19. Viazov S, Ratjen F, Scheidhauer R, et al. High prevalence of human metapneumovirus infection in young children and genetic heterogeneity of the viral isolates. J Clin Microbiol. 2003;41:3043-3045.
20. Esper F, Boucher D, Weibel C, et al. Human metapneumovirus infection in the United States: Clinical manifestations associated with a newly emerging respiratory infection in children. Pediatrics. 2003;111:1407-1410.
21. Maggi F, Pifferi M, Vatteroni M, et al. Human metapneumovirus associated with respiratory tract infections in a 3-year study of nasal swabs from infants in Italy. J Clin Microbiol. 2003;41:2987-2991.
22. Freymuth F, Vabret A, Legrand L, et al. Presence of the new human metapneumovirus in French children with bronchiolitis. Pediatr Infect Dis J. 2003;22:92-94.
22a. William JV, Harris PA, Tollefson SJ, et al. Human metapneumovirus and lower respiratory tract disease in otherwise healthy infants and children. N Engl J Med. 2004; 350:443-450.
23. Jartti T, van den Hoogen BG, Garofalo RP, Osterhaus ADME. Metapneumovirus and acute wheezing in children. Lancet. 2003;360:1394.
24. Osterhaus A, Fouchier R. Human metapneumovirus in the community. Lancet. 2003;361:890-891.
25. Crowe JE Jr, Williams JV. Immunology of viral respiratory tract infection in infancy. Paediatr Respir Rev. 2003;4:112-119.
26. Rawlinson WD, Waliuzzaman Z, Carter IW, et al. Asthma exacerbations in children associated with rhinovirus but not human metapneumovirus infection. J Infect Dis. 2003;187:1314-1318.
27. Pelletier G, Dery P, Abed Y, Boivin G. Respiratory tract reinfections by the new human Metapneumovirus in an immunocompromised child. Emerg Infect Dis. 2002;8:976-978.
28. Greensill J, McNamara PS, Dove W, et al. Human metapneumovirus in severe respiratory syncytial virus bronchiolitis. Emerg Infect Dis. 2003;9:372-375.
29. Cane PA, van den Hoogen BG, Chakrabarti S, et al. Case report: Human metapneumovirus in a haematopoietic stem cell transplant recipient with fatal lower respiratory tract disease. Bone Marrow Transplant. 2003;31:309-310.
30. Peiris JSM, Lai ST, Poon LLM, et al, SARS Study Group. Coronavirus as a possible cause of severe acute respiratory syndrome. Lancet. 2003;361:1319-1325.
31. Kuiken T, Fouchier RA, Schutten M, et al. Newly discovered coronavirus as the primary cause of severe acute respiratory syndrome. Lancet. 2003;362:263-270.
32. Chan PK, Tam JS, Lam CW, et al. Human metapneumovirus detection in patients with severe acute respiratory syndrome. Emerg Infect Dis. 2003;9:1058-1063.
33. Poutanen SM, Low DE, Henry B, et al, Canadian SARS Study Team. Identification of severe acute respiratory syndrome in Canada. N Engl J Med. 2003;348:1995-2005.
34. Mackay IM, Jacob KC, Woolhouse D, et al. Molecular assays for detection of human metapneumovirus. J Clin Microbiol. 2003;41:100-105.
35. Cote S, Abed Y, Boivin G. Comparative evaluation of real-time PCR assays for detection of the human metapneumovirus. J Clin Microbiol. 2003;41:3631-3635.
36. Hall CB, McBride JT, Gala CL, et al. Ribavirin treatment of respiratory syncytial viral infection in infants with underlying cardiopulmonary disease. JAMA. 1985;254:3047-3051.
37. Meziere A, Mollat C, Lapied R, et al. Detection of respiratory syncytial virus antigen after seventy-two hours of culture. J Med Virol. 1990;31:241-244.
38. Groothuis JR, Simoes EAF, Levin MJ, et al, Respiratory Syncytial Virus Immune Globulin Study Group. Prophylactic administration of respiratory syncytial virus immune globulin to high-risk infants and young children. N Engl J Med. 1993;329:1524-1530.
39. Wyde PR, Chetty SN, Jewell AM, et al. Comparison of the inhibition of human metapneumovirus and respiratory syncytial virus by ribavirin and immune serum globulin in vitro. Antiviral Res. 2003;60:51-59.
40. Hall CB, Douglas RG, Geiman JM. Possible transmission by fomites of respiratory syncytial virus. J Infect Dis. 1980;141:98-101.
41. Hall CB, Geiman JM, Douglas RG, Meagher MP. Control of nosocomial respiratory syncytial viral infections. Pediatrics. 1978;62:728-732.
42. Hall CB, Douglas RG, Geiman JM, Messner MK. Nosocomial respiratory syncytial virus infections. N Engl J Med. 1975;293:1343-1346.
43. Tang RS, Schickli JH, MacPhail M, et al. Effects of human metapneumovirus and respiratory syncytial virus antigen insertion in two 3′ proximal genome positions of bovine/human parainfluenza virus type 3 on virus replication and immunogenicity. J Virol. 2003;77:10819-10828.

Measles Virus (Rubeola)

ANNE A. GERSHON

Measles, an acute infection caused by rubeola virus, is highly contagious and usually seen in children. The illness is characterized by cough, coryza, fever, and a maculopapular rash that begins several days after the initial symptoms appear. There is a characteristic enanthem, Koplik's spots, that is specific for measles and that precedes the onset of rash. Recovery from measles is the rule, but serious complications of the respiratory tract and central nervous system (CNS) may occur. Measles in the United States has been dramatically controlled since the introduction of live-attenuated measles vaccine in 1963, but it remains a serious problem in developing countries.

Measles virus belongs to the genus Morbillivirus of the family Paramyxoviridae. It is closely related to the viruses causing canine and phocine distemper, rinderpest of cattle, peste des petits ruminants of goats and sheep, and morbilli of certain aquatic animals. Although these viruses are distinct agents, they share certain antigens.[1,2] Wild measles virus is pathogenic only for primates.

DESCRIPTION OF THE PATHOGEN

Morphology

On electron microscopy, measles virions are pleomorphic spheres with a diameter of 100 to 250 nm. Virions consist of an inner nucleocapsid that is a coiled helix of protein and RNA, and an envelope that bears two types of short surface projections.[2,3] These projections (peplomers) include the conical-shaped hemagglutinin (H) peplomer and the dumbbell-shaped fusion (F) peplomer. The molecular weight of the single-stranded RNA is 4.5 kd.[2] Because the entire genome has been sequenced, it is possible to differentiate between wild measles virus and vaccine-type virus.[2]

Chemical and Antigenic Composition

Measles virus is composed of six structural proteins.[2] Three, the nucleoprotein (N), the polymerase protein (P), and the large protein (L), are complexed with RNA. Three are associated with the viral envelope. The membrane envelope contains the M protein, a nonglycosylated protein associated with the inner lipid bilayer, and two glycoproteins designated H and F.[4] The F and H glycoproteins are responsible for the fusion of virus to receptors on the host cell, allowing the virus to penetrate and infect the cell. The complement regulatory protein CD46, which is widely distributed in primate tissues, serves as a receptor for the measles virus,[2,5] as does signaling lymphocyte activation molecule, or SLAM (CDw150).[6] The H glycoprotein also constitutes the antigen that mediates hemagglutination. The hemagglutination inhibition (HI) test, using red blood cells from Old World monkeys, is a major serologic test for measuring antibody to measles virus. The F glycoprotein is responsible for the membrane fusion of virus and host cell, penetration of the virus into the host cell, and hemolysis. Unlike in many other paramyxoviruses, neuraminidase is not found on the envelope of measles virus.[7] Genetic and antigenic variation of measles virus is now recognized; the sequence of genes coding for H and N is the most variable.[8] Numerous genotypes have been described.[9,10] The measles virus antigens and their role in human disease[4,11] are discussed later.

Growth of Measles Virus in Tissue Culture

Measles virus was first successfully isolated in the laboratory by Enders and Peebles in 1954.[12] The virus was initially propagated in primary human renal cells, but later it was cultivated in cultured simian kidney cell. Wild measles virus is rather difficult to propagate in vitro because it is slow growing and only a limited number of types of cell cultures are permissive for the virus.[10] Typically, cytopathic effects produced by measles virus in tissue cultures consist of stellate cells with increased refractility and, especially on passage, multinucleated syncytial giant cells containing intranuclear inclusions. In the absence of cytopathic effects, virus replication can also be detected by hemadsorption of rhesus monkey erythrocytes. Presumptive isolates of measles virus are identified by typing with monoclonal antibodies using immunofluorescence or plaque reduction tests.[2,13]

Host Range

Humans are the only natural host for wild measles virus, but monkeys may also be infected. In general, illness caused by measles virus is milder in monkeys than that in humans.[14] It has not been possible to infect small laboratory animals, such as rodents, with wild measles virus. However, newborn and suckling rodents may be infected with vaccine strains administered by the intracerebral route.[15,16]

Epidemiology

Measles has been recognized as a disease for some 2000 years, but its infectious nature was not recognized until about 150 years ago. In 1846, Panum[17] studied an epidemic of measles in the Faroe Islands and noted that the disease was contagious, that there was an incubation period of about 2 weeks, and that infection appeared to lead to lifelong immunity. The next major advance in the understanding of measles did not occur until 1954, when Enders and Peebles[12] successfully propagated wild measles virus in primary human renal tissue culture cells. This led directly to the development of a live measles vaccine, which was licensed for use in the United States in 1963.[18]

Measles is seen in every country in the world. Without a vaccine, epidemics of measles lasting 3 to 4 months could be predicted to occur every 2 to 5 years. Countries in which measles vaccine is widely used have experienced a marked decrease in the incidence of disease. For example, for many years 200,000 to 500,000 cases of measles were reported annually in the United States. Since 1963, when the vaccine was licensed, the incidence of measles in the United States has decreased by almost 99%.[19,20] This decrease has been especially pronounced since the early 1980s, when laws requiring proof of immunity to measles for school entry were enacted. The yearly incidence of measles in the United States reached a nadir in 1983, when 1497 cases were reported to the Centers for Disease Control and Prevention (CDC) in Atlanta. In the late 1980s and early 1990s, however, there was an increase in the incidence of measles; this was brought under control by increasing the rate of immunization and by routinely using two doses of measles vaccine for all children.[21-23] In 1990, more than 25,000 cases of measles and 89 measles-associated deaths were reported to the CDC.[24] In 1991, however, the number of reported cases dropped significantly, to 9643.[25] Between 1993 and 1996, fewer than 1000 annual cases in the United States were reported to the CDC.[26] In 2001, only 116 cases were reported to the CDC.[27] Using molecular techniques, it was demonstrated that transmission of indigenous measles largely ceased by 1993. Since that time, most cases of measles in the United States have resulted from international importations of measles virus.[9]

Measles has occurred in preschool children who are too young to be vaccinated.[25] Measles has also been reported in vaccinated school-aged children. About half of these cases have a history of prior vaccination, and most of these are thought to be the result of primary vaccine failure.[23,28] At present, there is minimal evidence that immunity induced by measles vaccine wanes with time.[22,28-32] The major reasons that measles has not been eliminated from the United States are failure to immunize all persons who qualify for vaccination, primary vaccine failure, and importation of measles to the United States from other countries.[9,31-34]

Spread of Infection

The measles virion is very labile; it is sensitive to acid, proteolytic enzymes, strong light, and drying.[2] The virus, however, remains infective in droplet form in air for several hours, especially under conditions of low relative humidity. This latter fact may account for the increased incidence of measles in winter.[35]

Measles is an airborne virus that is spread by direct contact with droplets from respiratory secretions of infected persons. It is one of the most communicable of the infectious diseases, most infectious during the late prodromal phase of the illness, when cough and coryza are at their peak[14]; however, the disease is probably contagious from several days before until several days after the onset of rash. Measles virus has been isolated from respiratory secretions of patients with measles only until up to 48 hours after the onset of rash.[36] Airborne spread of measles in physicians' offices[37,38] and in a sports complex[39] has been observed.

Diseases Associated with Measles Virus

Subacute sclerosing panencephalitis (SSPE) is a chronic degenerative neurologic disease that occurs several to many years after an attack of measles, particularly in children who had measles before 2 years of age. The disease was at one time more common in the rural Southeast than in other areas of the United States. A few children who received measles vaccine and who had no prior history of measles have been observed to develop SSPE. However, it is unknown whether these children might have had a subclinical case of measles before receiving vaccine. The incidence of SSPE has declined since the introduction of measles vaccine.[19,40] A single case of inclusion-body encephalitis caused by the vaccine strain was reported in 1999.[41]

Patients with SSPE have unusually high measles antibody titers, both in their serum and in their cerebrospinal fluid.[42] SSPE is caused by a persistent infection with a measles-related virus in the CNS that occurs despite a vigorous immune response on the part of the host. The pathogenesis of SSPE is extremely complex and has been ascribed to a combination of host factors and viral replicative phenomena. Although a measles-like virus has occasionally been isolated, using cocultivation techniques, from the brains of patients with SSPE at autopsy,[43,44] the infection is usually characterized by an inability to produce viral progeny.[45] This inability may be a result of defects in the formation of gene products arising from genomic mutations caused by errors of RNA replication. Originally, the inability to replicate was ascribed to failure of the infective virus to produce measles M protein.[46] Later, it was realized that this failure was related to mutations of the gene encoding this protein.[45] Now it is recognized that defects in envelope gene products H and F also occur as a result of other genomic mutations of the causative virus.[45] Host factors such as defective immunity and the ability of specific antibodies to confine the virus to intracellular multiplication are also postulated to play a role in the pathogenesis of SSPE.[45-50] Measles virus RNA was demonstrated by an in situ reverse transcriptase–polymerase chain reaction (RT-PCR) in neurons, astrocytes, oligodendrocytes, and vascular endothelial cells in the brain of a patient who died from SSPE.[51]

The evidence that multiple sclerosis, Crohn's disease, and systemic lupus erythematosus are etiologically linked with measles virus is much weaker than that for SSPE,[52-54] and measles virus infection is probably unrelated to these diseases. An etiologic role for measles virus in Paget's disease of bone has been raised as a possibility but as yet is unproven.[55-58]

PATHOGENESIS

Measles virus infects by invasion of the respiratory epithelium. Studies on volunteers inoculated with live measles virus indicate that infection may occur after instillation of virus at any point from the nose to the lower parts of the respiratory tract.[55]

On the basis of Fenner's mousepox model for exanthems[56] and on a monkey model of measles infection,[57] it has been suggested that local multiplication at the respiratory mucosa leads to a primary viremia, during which the virus spreads in leukocytes to the reticuloendothelial system.[14] As a result of necrosis of infected reticuloendothelial cells, an increased amount of virus is released, and reinvasion of leukocytes (secondary viremia) occurs.

Measles virus has been isolated from the leukocytes of patients with clinical measles.[59] The virus has also been propagated in vitro in human T and B lymphocytes and in monocytes.[60] The major infected cell in the blood is the monocyte.[2,61] Both endothelial and epithelial cells are infected. Infected tissues include thymus, spleen, lymph nodes, liver, skin, conjunctiva, and lung.[2]

After the secondary viremic phase of measles, the entire respiratory mucosa becomes involved. This accounts for the cough and coryza that are classic signs of measles. In addition, measles may directly cause croup, bronchiolitis, and pneumonia. Damage to the respiratory tract from edema and loss of cilia may predispose to secondary bacterial invasion, resulting in such complications as otitis media and pneumonia.[14]

Within a few days after generalized involvement of the respiratory tract has occurred, Koplik's spots appear and are followed by the development of a rash. Both manifestations are believed to result from similar pathologic mechanisms. On microscopic examination of skin and mucous membranes, multinucleate giant cells and other similar histologic changes are observed in both the epidermis and the oral epithelium.[62] The appearance of the measles rash coincides temporally with the appearance of serum antibody and the termination of communicability of the disease. Therefore, it has been postulated that the skin and mucous membrane manifestations of measles actually represent hypersensitivity of the host to the virus. Measles virus antigen has been demonstrated in the involved skin and mucous membranes by immunofluorescence.[62-64] Measles virus has also been isolated from the rash in its early stages.[57] If hypersensitivity is the actual cause of the rash, however, it is probably mediated by cellular rather than humoral immunity,[65] and therefore patients with agammaglobulinemia who contract measles develop a rash. Patients with deficiencies in cell-mediated immunity, on the other hand, may develop measles giant cell (Hecht's) pneumonia without a rash, after an exposure to measles or if measles vaccine is given.[66,67]

Immunity

Immunity to measles after an attack of the disease appears to be lifelong. Similarly, after measles vaccination, immunity is of many years' duration and probably lifelong in most persons.[19] How measles antibody persists for years after infection is not understood. One possible explanation is that the virus becomes latent after acute infection and provides an immunologic stimulus to antibody formation. However, latent measles virus has not been demonstrated in humans or in experimental animals. An alternative explanation for the persistence of measles antibody is that reexposure to the virus results in persistent antigenic stimulation. Reinfection with measles can occur and is almost always asymptomatic even though a boost in antibody titer can be detected.[68] Cellular immunity to measles virus probably also plays a role in the prevention of recurrent measles, because patients with agammaglobulinemia do not have multiple attacks of measles. A cell-mediated response to measles antigen in the absence of detectable measles antibody was reported in two physicians in whom no disease developed despite repeated exposures to measles.[69] Therefore, when humoral antibodies to measles are absent or of low titer, cellular immunity to the virus may protect against subsequent illness. Cellular immunity to measles virus in peripheral blood of persons with a history of measles has been shown by in vitro lymphocyte stimulation after exposure to measles antigen[70] and by demonstration of measles-specific class I and II cytotoxic T cells.[71-73] A complex interplay of cellular immunity and cytokines occurs before, during, and after measles infection in healthy persons.[74]

During infection, CD8 and CD4 T cells are activated and probably participate in the clearance of virus and the development of rash. During recovery, suppression of cell-mediated responses occurs, with elevation of suppressive cytokines such as interleukin-4, which may be responsible for depressed delayed-type hypersensitivity to tuberculin.[2,75] Effects of vaccine on the immune system that resemble the effects of naturally occurring measles have also been described.[76]

CLINICAL MANIFESTATIONS

The incubation period of measles is 10 to 14 days; it is often somewhat longer in adults than in children. A prodromal phase lasting several days begins after the incubation period. This phase probably coincides with the secondary viremia.[14] It is manifested by malaise, fever, anorexia, conjunctivitis, and respiratory symptoms such as cough and coryza, and it may resemble a severe upper respiratory tract infection. Toward the end of the prodrome, just before the appearance of the rash, Koplik's spots appear.

Koplik's spots are pathognomonic of measles. First noted by Koplik in 1896, they consist of bluish gray specks on a red base.[77] They have been likened to grains of sand, and without examination of the buccal mucosa in good light they may be overlooked. Most often they appear on the mucosa opposite the second molars. However, in severe cases, the entire mucous membrane of the mouth may be involved. This enanthem persists for several days and begins to slough as the rash appears.

The rash of measles usually begins on the face and proceeds down the body to involve the extremities last, including the palms and soles (Fig. 157-1). During the healing phase, the involved areas (except palms and soles) may desquamate. The rash is erythematous and maculopapular; as it progresses, it becomes confluent, especially on the face and the neck. The rash usually lasts about 5 days and starts to clear first on the skin that was first involved. The patient with measles is usually most ill during the first or second day of the rash. Several days after the appearance of the rash, the fever abates and the patient begins to feel better. The entire uncomplicated illness from late prodrome to resolution of the fever and rash lasts 7 to 10 days; cough may be the last symptom to disappear.

Complications

The most common complications of measles involve the respiratory tract and the CNS. Involvement of the respiratory tract is part of the virus infection itself. In addition, bacterial superinfection may occur in any area of the respiratory tract, including the middle ear.

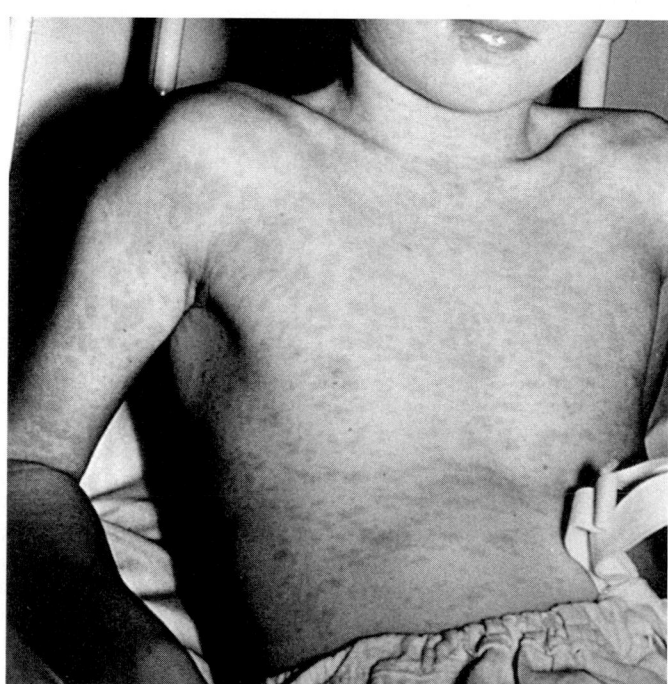

FIGURE 157-1. Typical rash on a patient with measles.

Superinfection may be secondary to local tissue damage inflicted by the virus and depression of cellular immunity. Pneumonia accompanying measles may be caused either by direct viral invasion of the lungs or by bacterial superinfection.[78] Roentgenographic evidence of pneumonia is common even during apparently uncomplicated measles.[14] Among infants who die of measles, pneumonia accounts for about 60% of the deaths, whereas among children 10 to 14 years of age, death is more often observed to be from complications of acute encephalitis.[79,80]

Encephalitis after measles in normal hosts may be acute or chronic (e.g., SSPE). Acute measles encephalitis manifests with a resurgence of fever during convalescence and frequently with headaches, seizures, and changes in the state of consciousness. Up to 50% of patients with measles but no symptoms that suggest cerebral involvement may have abnormalities detected by electroencephalography,[81] so it is believed that viral invasion of the CNS is a common feature of measles. However, only 1 in 1000 to 2000 patients with measles develops clinical signs of encephalitis. Measles encephalitis ranges from mild to severe, and a high proportion of patients who recover are left with neurologic sequelae.

Measles virus has been isolated from the brains of several persons dying of measles encephalitis.[82-85] However, virus isolation is uncommon and usually requires special virologic techniques such as cocultivation. It is hypothesized that acute measles encephalitis is caused by hypersensitivity to virus in brain tissue. Both viral antigens and host antigens are present on the surface of measles-infected cells in vitro.[86] Therefore, hypersensitivity may be directed against both viral and host (brain) antigens, which accounts for the encephalitic symptoms. Demyelination, vascular cuffing, gliosis, and infiltration of fat-laden macrophages near blood vessel walls are noted in brain tissue from patients with measles encephalitis.[2] In a laboratory study of serum and cerebrospinal fluid from 19 patients with postinfectious measles encephalitis, similarities between experimental allergic encephalomyelitis (e.g., immune responses to myelin basic protein, early destruction of myelin) were demonstrated in about 50%. There was no evidence of intrathecal synthesis of antibody against measles virus, which suggests that immunopathology, rather than viral multiplication, is involved in the pathogenesis of measles encephalitis.[87]

Transient hepatitis has also been reported during acute measles.[88]

Modified Measles

An extremely mild form of measles has been observed in persons with some degree of passive immunity to the virus. This includes some babies younger than 1 year who have passively acquired maternal antibody to measles virus, and some susceptible persons who have received immune globulin after an exposure to measles. The symptoms of modified measles are variable, and certain classic symptoms such as the prodromal period, conjunctivitis, Koplik's spots, and rash may be absent. The incubation period may be prolonged. At times, the infection is subclinical, and with a great degree of passively acquired immunity, it may be prevented completely.[68]

Atypical Measles

The syndrome of atypical measles has been described in persons who received killed measles vaccine (or killed vaccine followed soon afterward by live vaccine) and who, several years later, were exposed to wild measles virus.[89,90] Initially, these patients have an undetectable or a very low measles antibody titer. They then develop unusual manifestations of measles followed by the appearance of extremely high measles antibody titers (e.g., 1:100,000) in their serum.[91] After a prodrome of fever and pain for 1 to 2 days, the rash appears. Unlike classic measles, it begins peripherally and may be urticarial, maculopapular, hemorrhagic, vesicular, or some combination of these types. The disease may be misdiagnosed as varicella, Rocky Mountain spotted fever, Henoch-Schönlein purpura, drug eruption, or toxic shock syndrome. The patient has a high fever, edema of the extremities, interstitial pulmonary infiltrates, hepatitis, and, on occasion, a pleural effusion. The disease tends to be severe with a somewhat more prolonged course than regular measles. At least one fatality has been reported. No specific therapy is available. Measles virus has not been isolated from these patients, and they do not appear to transmit measles to others.[90]

The pathogenesis of this syndrome is believed to be one of hypersensitivity to measles virus in a partially immune host. Whether cell-mediated or humoral immune mechanisms, or both, are involved remains controversial.[90,92,93] One hypothesis concerning pathogenesis is that killed measles vaccine lacks the antigen that stimulates the immunity that prevents entry of measles virus into cells, thereby allowing measles infection to occur despite the partial immunity derived from killed vaccine.[94,95] It has been shown that killed measles vaccine does not induce antibody to the F protein, which is an antigen that facilitates spread of the virus from one cell to another by inducing cell fusion. This further supports the paradox of severe measles infection despite partial immunity.[4,95]

Recurrences of atypical measles have not been reported. Therefore, persons who received killed measles vaccine (or killed vaccine followed soon afterward by live vaccine) in the past should be reimmunized with live measles vaccine. It is important that persons who have received killed vaccine be made aware that severe local reactions can follow an injection of live vaccine.[96,97] Usually the reaction consists of tenderness and erythema around the injection site. However, severe local edema and high fever may also occur. Immunization with live vaccine is recommended because the associated risk is lower than the risk of being exposed to the wild-type virus.[98]

Measles in Immunocompromised Patients

Severe measles may occur in persons with compromised or deficient cellular immunity, such as those being treated for malignant disease and children with acquired immunodeficiency syndrome (AIDS) or any form of congenital immunodeficiency.[66,99-101] In a report of measles cases occurring in immunocompromised patients in 1989-1990, combined with some recorded in the literature, the case-fatality rate for severe measles in children and young adults was calculated to be 70% in 40 oncology patients and 40% in 11 patients infected with the human immunodeficiency virus (HIV).[102] Of the oncology patients, 40% had no rash, 58% had pneumonitis, and 20% had encephalitis. Of the HIV-infected patients, 27% had no rash, and 82% had pneumonia. Should immunocompromised patients be inadvertently exposed to measles, they may develop giant cell pneumonia without evidence of a rash.[66,99,102] In such instances, the clinical diagnosis of measles may be difficult or impossible to establish. Because these children may also have poor antibody responses, virus isolation from infected tissue (or identification of measles antigen by immunofluorescence) may be the only means of diagnosis. A chronic form of encephalitis resembling SSPE, often with a concomitant pneumonia, has also been reported in persons with deficient cellular immunity.[47,48] This entity has been classified as subacute measles encephalitis and may be confirmed by the presence of measles RNA or infectious virus in brain tissue.[103]

Malnourished children, especially in developing countries, have also been reported to develop severe measles. This may be related to poor cell-mediated immune responses resulting from malnutrition.[104] Intense exposure to the virus because of crowding may also play a role in the severity of measles in developing countries.[105,106]

Immunocompromised patients with no history of clinical measles who are exposed to the infection should be passively immunized with immunoglobulin, even if they have previously been immunized (see later discussion).

Measles in Pregnant Women and Their Offspring

Rubeola during pregnancy, in contrast to German measles (rubella), is not known to cause congenital anomalies of the fetus.[107] However, measles in pregnancy has been associated with spontaneous abortion and premature delivery.[14] Measles can be severe in pregnancy. From 1988 to 1991, when there was a resurgence of measles in the United States, a number of pregnant women developed measles. Of 13 such women hospitalized in Houston, Texas, 54% had respiratory complications requiring admission to the intensive care unit, and one died.[108] These women were thought to have primary measles pneumonia. Measles in the offspring of mothers with measles ranges from mild to severe.[109,110] It is therefore recommended that infants born to women with active measles be passively immunized with immunoglobulin at birth.

Measles in Persons with Tuberculosis

It has long been thought that tuberculosis is aggravated in persons who contract natural measles, presumably because of a depression of cell-mediated immunity by measles virus.[2] For example, the tuberculin test has been reported to become negative for about 1 month after measles or measles vaccination.[14] It seems prudent to defer measles vaccination in persons with known tuberculosis until antituberculosis therapy is underway. In geographic areas and populations where tuberculosis is rare, it is not mandatory to perform a tuberculin test on an infant before administering measles vaccine.[111]

Measles in Adults

Measles has long been regarded as an illness of childhood. When it occurs in adults, it is often a more severe illness. In a series of 3220 young adult military recruits with measles between 1976 and 1979, about 3% developed pneumonia requiring hospitalization. Bacterial superinfection of the respiratory tract occurred in 30%, and 17% had evidence of bronchospasm. In addition, 31% had laboratory evidence of hepatitis, 29% had otitis media, and 25% had sinusitis.[112] Among patients with measles reported to the CDC in 1991, the incidence of complications was higher in those older than 20 years of age than in children.[24]

DIAGNOSIS

Classic measles with cough, coryza, conjunctivitis, Koplik's spots, and a maculopapular rash beginning on the face is easily diagnosed clinically. Often there is a striking leukopenia, perhaps related to the infection and death of leukocytes. A laboratory diagnosis of measles is helpful when the clinician is unfamiliar with the illness because of the decline in cases of clinical measles since introduction of measles vaccine. A laboratory diagnosis may also be helpful in cases of possible atypical measles, or when unexplained pneumonia or encephalitis occurs in an immunocompromised patient.

Measles may be diagnosed in the laboratory by virus isolation, by the identification of measles antigen in infected tissues, or by the demonstration of a significant serologic response to measles virus. Virus isolation is technically difficult, and facilities for isolation are not always available. It is particularly useful, however, in patients with fatal pneumonia and in patients with an immunodeficiency, in whom an antibody response may be minimal. Immunofluorescent examination of cells from nasal exudates or from urinary sediment for the presence of measles antigen may be useful for rapid diagnosis of measles.[107,113] A sensitive RT-PCR method to demonstrate measles virus RNA has been described.[10,114]

The most frequently used method of laboratory diagnosis is the serologic response to the virus. A fourfold or greater increase in measles antibody titer in acute and convalescent serum specimens is considered diagnostic for measles. A number of methods are available, usually through hospital or state health department laboratories, including neutralization, complement fixation, enzyme-linked immunosorbent assay (ELISA), and HI. Neutralization, which requires propagation of the virus in vitro, is technically difficult. Therefore, this test, although sensitive, is infrequently used. Complement fixation is not an overly sensitive technique, but it is adequate for the diagnosis of acute measles. It is not useful, however, for determining the immune status to measles.

The HI test is slightly less sensitive than virus neutralization, but generally there is good correlation between the two tests. Antibodies detectable by this test persist for many years, so immune status to measles may also be determined by HI. For the diagnosis of acute or atypical measles, two serum specimens, acute and convalescent, are required. SSPE may also be diagnosed by the demonstration of high measles HI titers in serum and cerebrospinal fluid in the presence of a compatible illness.[113]

The ELISA is more sensitive and simpler to perform than HI, which is rarely performed today.[115,116] This assay can also be adapted to detect specific IgM antibody,[117] and it is therefore useful for the diagnosis of acute measles on one serum sample. An HI test that uses capillary blood collected on filter paper from finger- or heel-stick specimens has also been described and is used by some state health department laboratories.[118]

PREVENTION

Since the use of live measles vaccine, methods to prevent measles have changed dramatically. Prevention today is ideally carried out long before an anticipated exposure to measles by the administration of live vaccine during the early part of the second year of life. However, there are rare occasions when passive immunization against measles with immune globulin must be used.

Included in the group of persons for whom passive immunization is recommended are those who are at high risk for developing severe or fatal measles, who are susceptible, and who have been exposed to the infection. Such persons include children with malignant disease, particularly if they are receiving chemotherapy or radiotherapy, or both, and children with significant deficits in cell-mediated immunity, including patients with AIDS. Babies less than 1 year of age (including newborns whose mothers have measles) are also at increased risk after an exposure to measles. Because measles has been reported even after vaccination in HIV-infected children, it has been recommended that they also be passively immunized with immunoglobulin after a recognized exposure.[101,102,111,119] To be effective, passive immunization must be given within 6 days after an exposure; administration after 6 days would not be expected to influence the course of the disease.

For a healthy infant less than 1 year of age who has been exposed to measles, the modifying dose of immunoglobulin is 0.25 mL/kg intramuscularly. An infant passively immunized in this fashion should be given live measles vaccine at the age of 15 months.[111] For immunocompromised, exposed children, a larger dose of immunoglobulin is required. These children should be given immunoglobulin, 0.5 mg/kg intramuscularly, with a maximum of 15 mL.[111]

Active immunization against measles was developed in the early 1960s. Live and killed measles vaccines were licensed for use in the United States in 1963. Killed vaccine was withdrawn from the market in 1967, after the recognition of atypical measles in recipients of this vaccine. The first marketed live measles vaccine was the Edmonston B strain. This vaccine was associated with a fairly high incidence of moderately severe side reactions such as rash and fever, and it was therefore often administered along with a dose of immunoglobulin. Subsequently, more attenuated vaccines were developed from the Edmonston strain.[120] Because the incidence of vaccine reactions is low with these vaccines, immunoglobulin is no longer given along with measles vaccine.

In 1976, it was recommended that all healthy children be given live measles vaccine at 15 months of age. At present, it is recommended that children be immunized between the ages of 12 and 15 months.[111] Two doses of measles vaccine given at 15 months and again in childhood (usually as measles-mumps-rubella vaccine [MMR]) are now routinely recommended.[98,111] Properly administered measles vaccine has been associated with persistence of immunity to measles for many years.[120-122] In one study, although measles HI antibodies were no longer detectable in some subjects, antibodies were demonstrated by neutralization, and revaccination was associated with a classic booster antibody response.[121] In the general population, 95% of properly immunized children can be expected to respond serologically to measles vaccine.

Vaccination is not usually recommended for infants less than 12 months of age because the induction of immunity may be suppressed by residual transplacentally acquired antibodies. In situations in which the incidence of natural measles before the age of 1 year is high, live measles vaccine may be given at 6 to 9 months of age but should be routinely followed by additional doses.[111] Measles antibody titers are lower in women vaccinated as children than in women who have had natural measles, and the offspring of vaccinated women often lose transplacentally acquired measles antibodies before 1 year of age.[123,124] Therefore, vaccination can be routinely given as early as 12 months of age, because most women in their childbearing years today were vaccinated as children.

Transient fever and rash develop about 1 week after vaccination in 5% to 15% of children.[111] In a 1986 study of 1162 twins who were given either MMR or placebo, there were side effects (fever, irritability, drowsiness, conjunctivitis) in 0.5% to 4%.[125] Symptoms of CNS dysfunction after measles vaccine are exceedingly rare.[126] Because measles may be severe in adults, immunization of adults who were not vaccinated previously, who have no history of measles, and who were born after 1956 is recommended by the CDC.[98] A 1986 Chicago study of hospital employees, however, indicated that only 1 (0.03%) of 266 was susceptible to measles; about one third were born after 1957.[127]

A number of reasons for apparent primary vaccine failures of measles vaccine have been proposed.[19] These include improper storage of vaccine at temperatures exceeding 4° C, failure to use the proper diluent for the lyophilized vaccine, exposure of the vaccine to light or heat, and vaccination in the presence of low levels of passive antibody. The latter may occur if infants are immunized at 12 months of age or younger, if children are vaccinated 1 or 2 months after receiving an injection of immunoglobulin, if the more attenuated vaccines are given with immunoglobulin, or if live measles vaccine is administered soon after killed measles vaccine. No deleterious effects have been associated with measles revaccination. Although it is probably unusual, sustained transmission of measles has been reported in secondary schools even when 95% of the students were immune and more than 99% were immunized.[128,129]

Live measles vaccine is contraindicated in persons with deficits in cell-mediated immunity and in pregnant women. Fatal measles in children with AIDS has been reported.[119,130] Although the potential risks of measles vaccine in these children are unknown, they may be less than the disease itself. It is currently recommended that children with known asymptomatic HIV infection receive measles vaccine at the age of 15 months.[100,111] The use of measles vaccine should also be considered for children with known HIV infection who manifest symptoms if their CD4 T-cell levels are relatively well preserved, especially if they live in locations where there may be transmission of measles, such as certain inner-city areas.[111] One case of fatal measles pneumonia resulting from vaccine virus in an HIV-infected vaccinated young adult has been described, after a second dose of vaccine.[101,131] Children who have been treated for malignant disease may be given measles vaccine 3 months after they have completed their course of therapy.[111]

Serious hypersensitivity reactions to measles vaccine in persons allergic to egg protein have been reported.[132] Persons with a history of anaphylactic reactions after the ingestion of eggs should be vaccinated only with extreme caution.[132,133]

Susceptible persons who are exposed to measles, with the exception of young babies, pregnant women, and immunocompromised persons, may be given live measles vaccine to prevent disease as an alternative to immunoglobulin. If the vaccine is given shortly after exposure, clinical cases of measles may be prevented because clinical manifestations associated with measles vaccine occur in about 7 days, compared with an incubation period of 10 days for clinical measles.[14]

An experimental measles vaccine, a derivative of the original Edmonston B vaccine strain termed Edmonston-Zagreb, administered at a dose 10 to 100 times higher than usual, proved to be immunogenic in 4- to 6-month-old infants.[134] Despite its short-term safety, however, the rate of mortality from causes other than measles in these vaccinees in Senegal was significantly higher than that in children who received standard vaccine.[135] Therefore, this vaccine is no longer in use.

It has been hypothesized that the MMR vaccine is a cause of gastrointestinal inflammation and autism.[136] After extensive review, nu-

merous national committees, including the Institute of Medicine, have concluded that there is no evidence to support this hypothesis.[137-139] Unfortunately, in the United Kingdom, where there has been extensive adverse publicity about MMR, the incidence of measles has recently increased as a result of suboptimal vaccination rates.[140]

TREATMENT

Patients with measles should be given supportive therapy such as antipyretics and fluids as indicated. Bacterial superinfection should be promptly treated with appropriate antimicrobials, but prophylactic antibiotics to prevent superinfection are of no known value and are therefore not recommended.

Vitamin A, 200,000 IU administered orally to children for 2 days, has been used successfully to decrease the severity of measles.[141-143] Side effects include transient vomiting and headache.[144] Administration of vitamin A has been reported to reduce seroconversion in vaccinees and should therefore be avoided at or after immunization.[145] The efficacy of ribavirin administered intravenously or by aerosol for treatment of severe measles is unproven.[108,119,146]

REFERENCES

1. Imagawa DT. Relationships among measles, canine distemper and rinderpest viruses. Prog Med Virol. 1968;10:160.
2. Griffin, DE. Measles. In: Fields BN, ed. Virology. 4th ed. New York: Raven Press; 2001:1401-1442.
3. Waterson AP. Measles virus. Arch Gesamte Virusforsch. 1965;16:57-80.
4. Choppin PW, Richardson CD, Merz DC, et al. The functions and inhibition of the membrane glycoproteins of paramyxoviruses and myxoviruses and the role of the measles virus M protein in subacute sclerosing panencephalitis. J Infect Dis. 1981;143:352.
5. Naniche D, Varior-Krishnsnan G, Cervoni F, et al. Human membrane cofactor protein (CD46) acts as a cellular receptor for measles virus. J Virol. 1993;67:6025-6032.
6. Tatsuo H, Ono N, Tanaka, K, Yanagi Y. SLAM (CDw150) is a cellular receptor for measles virus. Nature. 2000;406:893-897.
7. Howe C, Schluederberg A. Neuraminidase associated with measles virus. Biochem Biophys Res Commun. 1970;40:606.
8. Rota JS, Rota PA, Redd SB, et al. Genetic analysis of measles viruses isolated in the United States, 1995-1996. J Infect Dis. 1998;177:204-208.
9. Rota PA, Liffick SL, Rota JS, et al. Molecular epidemiology of measles virus in the United States, 1997-2001. Emerg Infect Dis. 2002;8:902-908.
10. Bellini WJ, Icenogle J. Measles and rubella virus. In: Murray PR, Baron EJ, Jorgenson JH, et al, eds. Manual of Clinical Microbiology. Washington, DC: ASM Press; 2003:1389-1403.
11. Hall WW, Choppin PW. Measles-virus proteins in the brain tissue of patients with subacute sclerosing panencephalitis: Absence of the M protein. N Engl J Med. 1981;304:1152.
12. Enders JF, Peebles TC. Propagation in tissue cultures of cytopathogenic agents from patients with measles. Proc Soc Exp Biol Med. 1954;86:277.
13. Enders JF. Measles virus, historical review, isolation and behavior in various systems. Am J Dis Child. 1962;103:282.
14. Kempe CH, Fulginiti VA. The pathogenesis of measles virus infection. Arch Gesamte Virusforsch. 1965;16:103.
15. Burnstein T, Frankel JW, Jensen JH. Adaptation of measles virus to suckling hamsters. Fed Proc. 1958;17:507.
16. Imagawa DT, Adams JM. Propagation of measles virus in suckling mice. Proc Soc Exp Biol Med. 1958;98:567.
17. Panum P. Observations made during the epidemic of measles on the Faroe Islands in the year 1846. Med Classics. 1938-9;3:829.
18. Katz SL, Enders JF, Holloway A. The development and evaluation of an attenuated measles virus vaccine. Am J Public Health. 1962;52(Suppl):5-10.
19. Krugman S. Present status of measles and rubella immunization in the United States: A medical progress report. J Pediatr. 1977;90:1.
20. Centers for Disease Control and Prevention. Measles—United States, 1991. MMWR Morb Mortal Wkly Rep. 1992;41:1-12.
21. Schlenker TL, Bain C, Baughman AL, et al. Measles herd immunity: Association of attack rates with immunization rates in preschool children. JAMA. 1992;267:823-826.
22. Frank J, Orenstein W, Bart K, et al. Major impediments to measles elimination. Am J Dis Child. 1985;139:881.
23. Hutchins S, Markowitz L, Atkinson W, et al. Measles outbreaks in the United States 1987 through 1990. Pediatr Infect Dis J. 1996;15:31-38.
24. Public Sector Vaccination Efforts. MMWR Morb Mortal Wkly Rep. 1992;41:522.
25. Centers for Disease Control and Prevention. Measles vaccination levels among selected groups of preschool-aged children—United States. MMWR Morb Mortal Wkly Rep. 1991;40:36.

26. Centers for Disease Control and Prevention. Measles: United States. MMWR Morb Mortal Wkly Rep. 1995;45:305-307.

27. Centers for Disease Control. Measles: United States, 2000. MMWR Morb Mortal Wkly Rep. 2002;51:120-123.

28. Markowitz LE, Preblud SR, Fine PE, et al. Duration of live measles vaccine-induced immunity. Pediatr Infect Dis J. 1990;9:101-110.

29. Krugman S. Further-attenuated measles vaccine: Characteristics and use. Rev Infect Dis. 1983;5:477-481.

30. Mathias RG, Meekison WG, Arcand TA, et al. The role of secondary vaccine failures in measles outbreaks. Am J Public Health. 1989;79:475-477.

31. Gindler JS, Atkinson W, Markowitz LE, et al. Epidemiology of measles in the United States in 1989 and 1990. Pediatr Infect Dis J. 1992;841-846.

32. Anders JF, Jacobson RM, Poland G, et al. Secondary failure rates of measles vaccines: A metaanalysis of published studies. Pediatr Infect Dis J. 1996;15:62-66.

33. Frank JA, Orenstein WA, Bart KJ, et al. Major impediments to measles elimination. Am J Dis Child. 1985;39:881-888.

34. Bennish M, Arnow PM, Beem MO, et al. Epidemic measles in Chicago in 1983: Sustained transmission in the preschool population. Am J Dis Child. 1986;140:341-344.

35. De Jong JG. The survival of measles virus in air, in relation to the epidemiology of measles. Arch Gesamte Virusforsch. 1965;16:97.

36. Ruckle G, Rogers KD. Studies with measles virus: II. Isolation of virus and immunologic studies in persons who have had the natural disease. J Immunol. 1957;78:341.

37. Bloch AB, Orenstein W, Ewing WM, et al. Measles outbreak in a pediatric practice: Airborne transmission in an office setting. Pediatrics. 1985;75:767-783.

38. Remington PL, Hall W, Davis IH, et al. Airborne transmission of measles in a physician's office. JAMA. 1985;253:1574-1577.

39. Ehresmann KR, Hedberg CW, Grimm MB, et al. An outbreak of measles at an international sporting event with airborne transmission in a domed stadium. J Infect Dis. 1995;171:679-683.

40. Modlin JF, Jabbour JT, Witte JJ, et al. Epidemiologic studies of measles, measles vaccine, and subacute sclerosing panencephalitis. Pediatrics. 1977;59:505.

41. Bitnun A, Shannon P, Durward A, et al. Measles inclusion-body encephalitis caused by the vaccine strain of measles virus. Clin Infect Dis. 1999;29:855-861.

42. Connolly JH, Allen IV, Hurwitz LJ, et al. Measles-virus antibody and antigen in subacute sclerosing panencephalitis. Lancet. 1967;1:542.

43. Barbosa LH, Fuccillo DA, Sever JL, et al. Subacute sclerosing panencephalitis: Isolation of measles virus from a brain biopsy. Nature. 1969;221:974.

44. Payne FE, Baublis JV, Itabashi HH. Isolation of measles virus from cell cultures of brain from a patient with subacute sclerosing panencephalitis. N Engl J Med. 1969;281:585.

45. Cattaneo R, Schmidt A, Billeter MA, et al. Multiple viral mutations rather than host factors cause defective measles virus gene expression in a subacute sclerosing panencephalitis line. J Virol. 1988;62:1388-1397.

46. Hall WW, Lamb RA, Choppin PW. Measles and subacute sclerosing panencephalitis virus proteins: Lack of antibodies to the M protein in patients with subacute sclerosing panencephalitis. Proc Soc Natl Acad Sci U S A. 1979;76:2047-2051.

47. Aicardi J, Goutieres F, Arsenio-Nunes ML, et al. Acute measles encephalitis in children with immunosuppression. Pediatrics. 1977;59:232.

48. Breitfeld V, Hashida Y, Sherman FE, et al. Fatal measles infection in children with leukemia. Lab Invest. 1973;28:279.

49. Gerson KL, Haslam HA. Subtle immunologic abnormalities in four boys with subacute sclerosing panencephalitis. N Engl J Med. 1971;285:78.

50. Sever JL. Persistent measles infection of the central nervous system: Subacute sclerosing panencephalitis. Rev Infect Dis. 1983;4:467-473.

51. Isaacson SH, Asher DM, Goded MS, et al. Widespread, restricted low-level measles virus infection of brain in a case of subacute sclerosing panencephalitis. Acta Neuropathol. 1996;91:135-139.

52. Adams JM, Imagawa DT. Measles antibodies in multiple sclerosis. Proc Soc Exp Biol Med. 1962;111:562.

53. Tannenbaum M, Hsu K, Buda J, et al. Electron microscopic virus-like material in systemic lupus erythematosus: With preliminary immunologic observations on presence of measles antigen. J Urol. 1971;105:615.

54. Feeney M, Winwood P, Snook J. A case-control study of measles vaccination and inflammatory bowel disease. Lancet. 1997;350:764-766.

55. Kress S, Schluederberg AE, Hornick RB, et al. Studies with live attenuated measles-virus vaccine. Am J Dis Child. 1961;101:701.

56. Fenner F. The pathogenesis of the acute exanthems. Lancet. 1948;2:915.

57. Sergiev PS, Ryazantseva NE, Shroit IG. The dynamics of pathological processes in experimental measles in monkeys. Acta Virol (Engl). 1960;4:265.

58. Siris ES. Seeking the elusive etiology of Paget disease: A progress report. J Bone Miner Res. 1996;11:1599-1601.

59. Gresser I, Chany C. Isolation of measles virus from the washed leucocytic fraction of blood. Proc Soc Exp Biol Med. 1963;113:695.

60. Joseph BS, Lampert PW, Oldstone MBA. Replication and persistence of measles virus in defined subpopulations of human leukocytes. J Virol. 1975;16:1638.

61. Esolen IM, Ward BJ, Moench TR, et al. Infection of monocytes during measles. J Infect Dis. 1993;168:47-52.

62. Suringa DWR, Bank LJ, Ackerman AB. Role of measles virus in skin lesions and Koplik's spots. N Engl J Med. 1970;283:1139.

63. Kimura A, Tosaka K, Nakao T. Measles rash: I. Light and electron microscopic study of skin eruptions. Arch Virol. 1975;47:295.

64. Kimura A, Tosaka K, Nakao T. An immunofluorescent and electron microscopic study of measles skin eruptions. Tohoku J Exp Med. 1975;117:245.

65. Lackmann PJ. Immunopathology of measles. Proc R Soc Med. 1974;67:12.

66. Enders JF, McCarthy K, Mitus A, et al. Isolation of measles virus at autopsy in case of giant cell pneumonia without rash. N Engl J Med. 1959;261:875.

67. Mitus A, Holloway A, Evans AE, et al. Attenuated measles vaccine in children with acute leukemia. Am J Dis Child. 1962;103:413.

68. Krugman S, Giles JP, Friedman H, et al. Studies on immunity to measles. J Pediatr. 1965;66:471.

69. Ruckdeschel JC, Graziano KD, Mardiney MR. Additional evidence that the cell-associated immune system is the primary host defense against measles (rubeola). Cell Immunol. 1975;17:11.

70. McFarland HF, Pedone CA, Mingioli ES, et al. The response of human lymphocyte subpopulations to measles, mumps, and vaccinia virus antigens. J Immunol. 1980;125:221-225.

71. Kreth HW, ter Mulen V, Eckert G. Demonstration of HLA restricted killer cells in patients with acute measles. Med Microbiol Immunol. 1979;165:203-214.

72. Lucas CJ, Biddison WE, Nelson ID, et al. Killing of measles virus infected cells by human cytotoxic T cells. Infect Immunol. 1982;38:226-232.

73. Jacobson S, Rose JW, Flerlage ML, et al. Induction of measles virus-specific human cytotoxic T cells by purified measles virus nucleocapsid and hemagglutinin polypeptides. Viral Immunol. 1987;1:153-162.

74. Griffin DE, Ward BJ, Jauregui E, et al. Immune activation in measles. N Engl J Med. 1989;320:1667-1672.

75. Smithwick EM, Berkovich S. In vitro suppression of the lymphocyte response to tuberculin by live measles virus. Proc Soc Exp Biol Med. 1966;123:276.

76. Hussey GD, Goddard EA, Hughes J, et al. The effect of Edmonston-Zagreb and Schwartz measles vaccines on immune responses in infants. J Infect Dis. 1996;173:1320-1326.

77. Koplik H. The diagnosis of the invasion of measles from a study of the exanthemata as it appears on the buccal mucous membranes. Arch Pediatr. 1896;13:918.

78. Quiambao BP, Gatchalian SR, Halonen P, et al. Coinfection is common in measles-associated pneumonia. Pediatr Infect Dis J. 1998;17:89-93.

79. Barkin RM. Measles mortality: A retrospective look at the vaccine era. Am J Epidemiol. 1975;102:341-349.

80. Barkin RM. Measles mortality. Analysis of the primary cause of death. Am J Dis Child. 1975;129:307-309.

81. Gibbs FA, Gibbs EL, Carpenter PR, et al. Electroencephalographic changes in "uncomplicated" childhood diseases. JAMA. 1959;171:1050.

82. McLean DM, Best JM, Smith PA, et al. Viral infections of Toronto children during 1965: II. Measles encephalitis and other complications. Can Med Assoc J. 1966;94:905-910.

83. Meulen V, Müller D, Käckell Y, et al. Isolation of infectious measles virus in measles encephalitis. Lancet. 1972;2:1172.

84. Scott TF. Postinfectious and vaccinial encephalitis. Med Clin North Am. 1967;51:701.

85. Shaffer MF, Rake G, Hodes HL. Isolation of virus from a patient with fatal encephalitis complicating measles. Am J Dis Child. 1942;64:815.

86. Drzenick R, Rott R. Host-specific antigens of lipid-containing RNA viruses: Viruses as a carrier of cell-specific antigens. Int Arch Allergy. 1969;36(Suppl):146.

87. Johnson RT, Griffin D, Hirsch R, et al. Measles encephalomyelitis: Clinical and immunologic studies. N Engl J Med. 1984;310:137-141.

88. McLellan RK, Gleiner JA. Acute hepatitis in an adult with rubeola. JAMA. 1982;247:2000.

89. Rauh LW, Schmidt R. Measles immunization with killed virus vaccine. Am J Dis Child. 1965;109:232.

90. Fulginiti VA, Eller JJ, Downie AW, et al. Altered reactivity to measles virus. JAMA. 1967;202:1075.

91. Frey HM, Krugman S. Atypical measles syndrome: Unusual hepatic, pulmonary, and immunologic aspects. Am J Med. 1981;281:55.

92. Lennon RG, Isacson P, Rosales T, et al. Skin tests with measles and poliomyelitis vaccines in recipients of inactivated measles virus vaccine: Delayed dermal hypersensitivity. JAMA. 1967;200:275.

93. Bellanti JA, Sanga RL, Klutinis B, et al. Antibody responses in serum and nasal secretions of children immunized with inactivated and attenuated measles-virus vaccines. N Engl J Med. 1969;280:628.

94. Norrby E, Ruckle GE, Meulen VT. Differences in the appearance of antibodies to structural components of measles virus after immunization with inactivated and live virus. J Infect Dis. 1975;132:262.

95. Annunziato D, Kaplan M, Hall WW, et al. Atypical measles syndrome: Pathologic and serologic features. Pediatrics. 1982;70:203-209.

96. Scott TJ, Bonanno DE. Reactions to live-measles virus vaccine in children previously inoculated with killed-virus vaccine. N Engl J Med. 1967;277:248.

97. Stetler HC, Gens RD, Seastrom GR. Severe local reactions to live measles virus vaccine following an immunization program. Am J Public Health. 1983;73:899-900.

98. Centers for Disease Control and Prevention. General recommendations on immunization: Recommendations of the Immunization Practices Advisory Committee (ACIP). MMWR Morb Mortal Wkly Rep. 1994:43(RR-1).

99. Mitus A, Enders JF, Craig JM, et al. Persistence of measles virus and depression of antibody formation in patients with giant cell pneumonia after measles. N Engl J Med. 1959;261:882.

100. Centers for Disease Control and Prevention. Recommendations of the Immunization Practices Advisory Committee: Immunization of children infected with human immunodeficiency virus: Supplementary ACIP statement. MMWR Morb Mortal Wkly Rep. 1988;37:181-183.

101. Centers for Disease Control and Prevention. Measles pneumonitis following M-M-R vaccination of a patient with HIV infection. MMWR Morb Mortal Wkly Rep. 1996;45:603-606.
102. Kaplan LJ, Daum RS, Smaron M, et al. Severe measles in immunocompromised patients. JAMA. 1992;267:1237-1241.
103. Mustafa MM, Weitman SD, Winick NJ, et al. Subacute measles encephalitis in the young immunocompromised host: Report of two cases diagnosed by polymerase chain reaction and treated with ribavirin and review of the literature. Clin Infect Dis. 1993;16:654-660.
104. Katz M, Stiehm ER. Host defense in malnutrition. Pediatrics. 1977;59:490.
105. Aaby P, Bukh J, Lisse IM, et al. Measles mortality, state of nutrition, and family structure: A community study for Guinea-Bissau. J Infect Dis. 1983;147:693-701.
106. Aaby P, Bukh J, Hoff G, et al. High measles mortality in infancy related to intensity of exposure. J Pediatr. 1986;109:40-44.
107. Gershon A, Young N. Chickenpox, measles, and mumps. In: Remington J, Klein J, eds. Infectious Diseases of the Fetus and Newborn Infants. Philadelphia: Saunders; 1994:591-602.
108. Atmar RL, Englund JA, Hammill H. Complications of measles during pregnancy. Clin Infect Dis. 1992;14:217-226.
109. Bloch AB, Orenstein WA, Hinman AR. Comment. J Infect Dis. 1981;143:753-754.
110. Gazala E, Karplus M, Liberman JR, et al. The effect of maternal measles on the fetus. Pediatr Infect Dis J. 1985;4:203-204.
111. Report of the Committee on Infectious Diseases ("The Red Book"). 24th ed. Evanston, Ill: American Academy of Pediatrics; 2000.
112. Gremillion DH, Crawford GE. Measles pneumonia in young adults: An analysis of 106 cases. Am J Med. 1981;71:539-542.
113. Schiff GM. Measles (rubeola). In: Lennette EH, ed. Laboratory Diagnosis of Viral Infections. 2nd ed. New York: Marcel Dekker; 1992:535-547.
114. Matsuzono Y, Narita M, Ishiguro N, et al. Detection of measles virus from clinical samples using polymerase chain reaction. Arch Pediatr Adolesc Med. 1994;148:289-293.
115. Rice GPA, Casali P, Oldstone MBA. A new solid-phase enzyme-linked immunosorbent assay for specific antibodies to measles virus. J Infect Dis. 1983;147:1055-1059.
116. Weigle K, Murphy D, Brunell P. Enzyme-linked immunosorbent assay for evaluation of immunity to measles virus. J Clin Microbiol. 1984;19:376.
117. Mayo DR, Brennan T, Cormier DP, et al. Evaluation of a commercial measles virus immunoglobulin M enzyme immunoassay. J Clin Microbiol. 1991;29:2865.
118. Wassilak S, Bernier R, Herrmann K, et al. Measles seroconfirmation using dried capillary blood specimens in filter paper. Pediatr Infect Dis J. 1984;3:117-121.
119. Krasinski K, Borkowsky W. Measles and measles immunity in children infected with human immunodeficiency virus. JAMA. 1989;261:2512-2516.
120. Miller C. Live measles vaccine: A 21-year follow-up. Br Med J. 1987;295:22-24.
121. Krugman S. Further-attenuated measles vaccine: Characteristics and use. Rev Infect Dis. 1983;5:477-481.
122. Pederson IR, Mordhorst CH, Ewald T, et al. Long-term antibody response after measles vaccination in an isolated arctic society in Greenland. Vaccine. 1986;4:173-178.
123. Chui L, Marusyk RG, Pabst HF. Measles virus specific antibody in infants in a highly vaccinated society. J Med Virol. 1991;33:199-204.
124. Johnson CE, Nalin DR, Chui LW, et al. Measles vaccine immunogenicity in 6- versus 15-month old infants born to mothers in the measles vaccine era. Pediatrics. 1994;93:939-943.
125. Peltola H, Heinonen O. Frequency of true adverse reactions to measles-mumps-rubella vaccine. Lancet. 1986;1:939-944.
126. Weibel RE, Caserta V, Benor DE, et al. Acute encephalopathy followed by permanent brain injury or death associated with further attenuated measles vaccines: A review of claims submitted to the National Vaccine Injury Compensation Program. Pediatrics. 1998;101:383-387.
127. Chou T, Weil D, Arnow P. Prevalence of measles antibodies in hospital personnel. Infect Control. 1986;7:309-311.
128. Wassilak S, Orenstein W, Strickland P, et al. Continuing measles transmission in students despite a school-based outbreak control program. Am J Epidemiol. 1985;122:208-217.
129. Gustafson T, Lievens A, Brunell P, et al. Measles outbreak in a fully immunized secondary-school population. N Engl J Med. 1987;316:771-774.
130. Centers for Disease Control and Prevention. Measles in HIV-infected children, United States. MMWR Morb Mortal Wkly Rep. 1988;37:183-186.
131. Angel JB, Walpita P, Lerch RA, et al. Vaccine-associated measles pneumonitis in an adult with AIDS. Ann Intern Med. 1998;129:104-106.
132. Herman JJ, Radin R, Schneiderman R. Allergic reactions to measles (rubeola) vaccine in patients hypersensitive to egg protein. J Pediatr. 1983;102:196.
133. James JM, Burks AW, Robertson P, et al. Safe administration of the measles vaccine to children allergic to eggs. N Engl J Med. 1995;332:1262-1266.
134. Whittle HC, Mann G, Eccles M, et al. Immunisation of 4-6 month old Gambian infants with Edmonston-Zagreb measles vaccine. Lancet. 1984;2:834-837.
135. Garenne M, Leroy O, Beau J-P, et al. Child mortality after high-titre measles vaccines: Prospective study in Senegal. Lancet. 1991;338:903-908.
136. Uhlmann V, Martin CM, Sheils O, et al. Potential viral pathogenic mechanism for new variant inflammatory bowel disease. Mol Pathol. 2002;55:84-90.
137. Fombonne E, Chakrabarti S. No evidence for a new variant of MMR-induced autism. Pediatrics. 2001;108:E58.
138. Taylor B, Lingam R, Simmons A, et al. Autism and MMR vaccination in North London: No causal relationship. Mol Psychiatry. 2002;7(Suppl 2): S7-8.
139. Taylor B, Miller E, Lingam R, et al. Measles, mumps, and rubella vaccination and bowel problems or developmental regression in children with autism: population study. BMJ. 2002;324:393-396.
140. Coughlan S, Connell J, Cohen B, et al. Suboptimal measles-mumps-rubella vaccination coverage facilitates an imported measles outbreak in Ireland. Clin Infect Dis. 2002;35:84-86.
141. Arrieta C, Zaleska M, Stutman H, et al. Vitamin A levels in children with measles in Long Beach, California. J Pediatr. 1992;121:75-78.
142. Frieden TR, Sowell AL, Henning K, et al. Vitamin A levels and severity of measles. Am J Dis Child. 1992;146:182-186.
143. Hussey GD, Klein M. A randomized, controlled trial of vitamin A in children with severe measles. N Engl J Med. 1990;323:160-164.
144. D'Souza RM, D'Souza R. Vitamin A for preventing secondary infections in children with measles: A systematic review. J Trop Pediatr. 2002;48:72-77.
145. Semba RD, Munasir Z, Beeler J, et al. Reduced seroconversion to measles in infants given vitamin A with measles vaccination. Lancet. 1995;345:1330-1332.
146. Forni AL, Schluger NW, Roberts RB. Severe measles pneumonitis in adults: Evaluation of clinical characteristics and therapy with intravenous ribavirin. Clin Infect Dis. 1994;19:454-462.

Zoonotic Paramyxoviruses: Hendra, Nipah, and Menangle Viruses

ANNA R. THORNER

RAPHAEL DOLIN

Zoonotic paramyxoviruses have been increasingly recognized as causes of disease outbreaks. Hendra, Nipah, and Menangle viruses all emerged in Australia and Southeast Asia during the 1990s. In 1994, in Queensland, Australia, two outbreaks of a fatal illness occurred in horses and their human caretakers.[1,2] In 1997, Menangle virus caused decreased farrowing rates and stillbirths in pigs, as well as an influenza-like illness in two humans who had occupational exposure to affected pigs.[3,4] Nipah virus caused an outbreak of severe encephalitis in pig farmers in Malaysia and Singapore in 1998 and 1999 and was eventually linked to pigs.[5,6] All three viruses were transmitted to the affected animals by the *Pteropus* species of fruit bat, also known as the flying fox (Table 158-1).

VIROLOGY

Classification

Hendra, Nipah, and Menangle viruses are members of the Paramyxoviridae family, which includes the subfamilies Paramyxovirinae and Pneumovirinae. The Paramyxovirinae subfamily includes the genera Respirovirus (human parainfluenza virus types 1 and 3), Rubulavirus (mumps, Newcastle disease, and human parainfluenza types 2, 4A, and 4B), and Morbillivirus (measles). The Pneumovirinae subfamily includes the genera Pneumovirus (human respiratory syncytial virus) and Metapneumovirus. Hendra and Nipah viruses are most similar to the viruses of the Respirovirus and Morbillivirus genera, but there is significantly less sequence homology between Hendra or Nipah virus and the members of either of these genera. Hendra and Nipah virus share a high degree of sequence homology and have similar genomic organization. It has therefore been proposed that a new genus, Henipavirus, be established within the Paramyxovirinae subfamily (Fig. 158-1).[7-10] On the basis of sequence analysis, Menangle virus has been classified as a member of the Rubulavirus genus.[11]

TABLE 158-1   Epidemiologic and Clinical Features of Hendra, Nipah, and Menangle Viruses

	Hendra Virus	*Nipah Virus*	*Menangle Virus*
Geography	Australia	Malaysia, Singapore	Australia
Reservoir	Fruit bats	Fruit bats	Fruit bats
Species with clinical disease	Horses, humans	Pigs, humans, dogs	Fetal pigs, humans
Type of illness in humans	Pneumonia, encephalitis	Encephalitis, pneumonia	Influenza-like illness with rash
Number of human cases	3	276	2
Number of human fatalities	2	106	0
Year(s) of outbreaks	1994, 1999	1998-1999	1997

Structure

Hendra and Nipah Viruses

Hendra and Nipah viruses have a single-stranded, nonsegmented, negative-sense RNA genome that is fully encapsidated by protein. The virus particles range in size from 120 to 500 nm. The envelope contains two transmembrane glycoproteins: an attachment protein or cell receptor–binding glycoprotein (G), and a fusion protein (F). Thin-section electron microscopy (EM) of infected cells reveals filamentous nucleocapsids that are contained within cytoplasmic inclusions and in-corporated into virions budding from the plasma membrane. Hendra virus has a double-fringed appearance caused by projections on the surface of the viral envelope, whereas Nipah virus has only a single layer of surface projections (Fig. 158-2).[12-14]

These viruses cause the formation of syncytia in infected Vero cells. Late in Nipah virus infection, nucleocapsid aggregates are found at the periphery of infected syncytial cells, which is an unusual feature.[13] Both Nipah and Hendra virus have herringbone nucleocapsid structures, approximately 1.67 μm in length. Both viruses cause tubule-like structures to be present in the cytoplasm of infected cells, but the structures are more prevalent in cells infected by Nipah virus. These structures are unique to Hendra, Nipah, and Sendai virus, another paramyxovirus.[13] The attachment proteins (G) of Hendra and Nipah virus lack hemagglutinin and neuraminidase activity, which most other paramyxoviruses possess.[15-17]

Hendra and Nipah viruses share 68% to 92% amino acid homology in the protein-coding regions, and 40% to 67% nucleotide identity in the nontranslated regions.[7,8,10,18] Both viruses contain 18.2 kb, whereas the other members of the Paramyxovirinae subfamily are significantly smaller, ranging from 15.1 to 15.9 kb. The genomes have six transcription units that encode six major structural proteins. The six transcription units include the nucleocapsid (N), phosphoprotein (P), matrix protein (M), fusion protein (F), glycoprotein or attachment protein (G), and large protein or RNA polymerase (L). This genome arrangement is most similar to those of the Respirovirus and Morbillivirus genera.[16]

Menangle Virus

Like the other paramyxoviruses, Menangle virus consists of an enveloped, nonsegmented, negative-sense RNA genome that is tightly associated with nucleocapsid proteins.[11] EM reveals that the morphology of Menangle virus is similar to that of other members of the Paramyxoviridae family. The viral particles appear spherical or pleomorphic and range from 30 nm to 100 nm in diameter. Virus isolated from the lungs, brains, and hearts of affected piglets caused cytopathic effects, including vacuolation and syncytial formation, when grown in baby hamster kidney cells (BHK21).[4] Menangle virus, like Nipah and Hendra viruses, contains herringbone nucleocapsids. It has an envelope with a single fringe of surface projections 17 ± 4 nm in length.[4] Its genome encodes all six of the major structural proteins described earlier for Hendra and Nipah virus. Sequencing of the nucleoprotein (NP), P, M, F, and hemagglutinin-neuraminidase (HN) genes revealed that Menangle virus is a member of the Rubulavirus genus. Ultrastructural analysis also supports this classification. Unlike the other rubulaviruses, Menangle virus lacks hemagglutinin and neuraminidase activity.[4] The HN protein shares only 16% to 20% sequence homology with other Rubulavirus HN proteins. Menangle virus also lacks the hexapeptide NRKSCS, which is conserved in the other Rubulavirus and the Respirovirus HN proteins and is thought to be necessary for neuraminidase activity; only the last two amino acids in the sequence motif are conserved in the Menangle virus HN protein.[11]

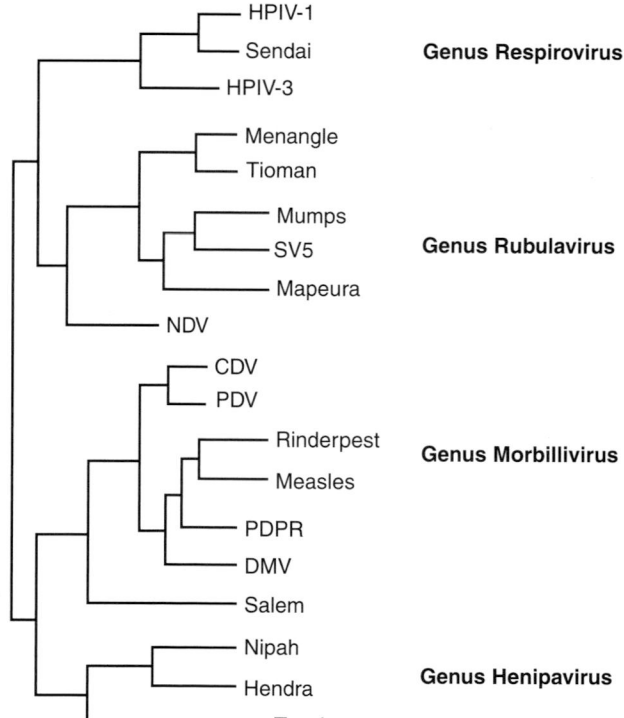

FIGURE 158-1. Phylogenetic analysis of the sequences of the open reading frame of the nucleoprotein gene from viruses in the subfamily Paramyxovirinae. A scale representing the number of nucleotide changes is shown at the bottom. HPIV-1, human parainfluenza virus type 1; HPIV-3, human parainfluenza virus type 3; SV5, simian virus 5; NDV, Newcastle disease virus; CDV, canine distemper virus; PDV, phocid distemper virus; PDPR, peste-des-petits-ruminants virus; DMV, dolphin morbillivirus. (Reprinted from Bellini WJ, Rota PA, Parashar U. Zoonotic paramyxoviruses. In: Richman DD, Whitley RJ, Haden FG, eds. Clinical Virology. Washington, DC: American Society for Microbiology; 2002:845-855, with permission; copyright 2002, American Society for Microbiology. All rights reserved.)

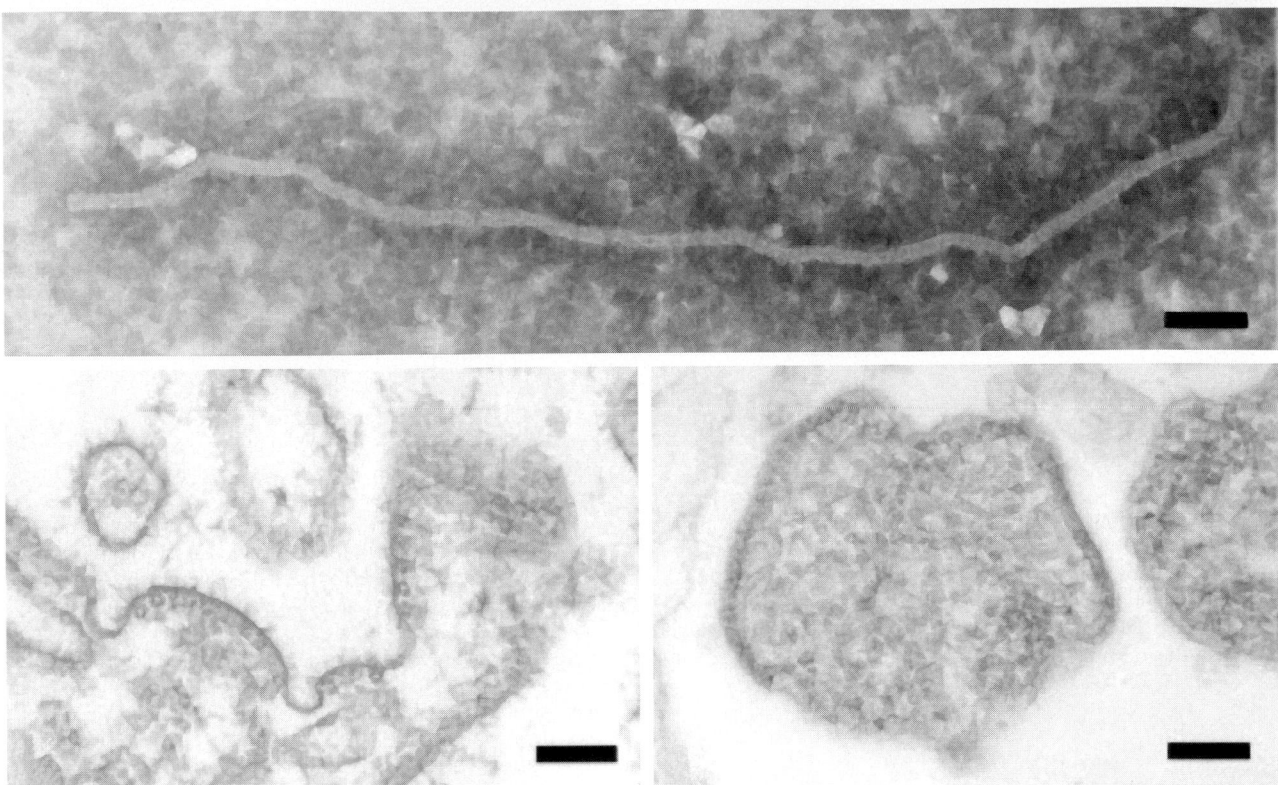

FIGURE 158-2. **Ultrastructural characteristics of Nipah virus isolate in cell culture as seen by negative stain (A) and thin-section (B and C) electron microscopy. A,** A single nucleocapsid with the typical herringbone appearance characteristic of the family Paramyxoviridae. **B,** Viral nucleocapsids, as seen in cross and longitudinal sections, aligned along the plasma membrane of Nipah virus–infected Vero E6 cells. **C,** Extracellular Nipah virus particle showing a curvilinear tangle of nucleocapsids enclosed within the viral envelope. *Scale bars,* 100 nm. *(Reprinted from Chua KB, Bellini WJ, Rota PA, et al. Nipah virus: A recently emergent deadly paramyxovirus. Science. 2000;288:1432-1435, with permission. Copyright 2000 American Association for the Advancement of Science. All rights reserved.)*

HENDRA VIRUS

Epidemiology

In September 1994, an outbreak of an acute respiratory illness occurred in thoroughbred horses in Brisbane in Queensland, Australia, to which 14 horses at a single stable succumbed. Affected horses had fever, facial swelling, severe respiratory distress, ataxia, and copious frothy nasal discharge, which was sometimes blood-tinged. The nasal discharge occurred shortly before the time of death. The index case was a pregnant mare at pasture. When she was found to be unwell, she was moved to a stable for nursing. The mare died after a 2-day illness. Over the next 2 weeks, 13 more horses died or were euthanized.[1,19] There were four nonfatal cases, two of which had mild neurologic sequelae. Three more horses were found to have seroconverted without having had signs of clinical illness. All seven of these horses were euthanized.[20] Within 1 week of the death of the index case, a horse trainer and a stablehand became ill with a severe influenza-like illness. The trainer was hospitalized and died after developing respiratory and renal failure. Infection with Hendra virus was demonstrated in both of the human cases by viral culture, immunoelectron microscopy, serology, and polymerase chain reaction (PCR) using primers derived from other paramyxoviruses.[1,12,19]

In October 1995, a second outbreak was retrospectively discovered after the death of a thoroughbred stud owner who had had relapsing encephalitis, and who was diagnosed with Hendra virus. On investigating his contacts, it was found that two horses had died on his farm in Mackay, in central Queensland, Australia, approximately 1000 km away from the first outbreak, in August 1994. The first horse was a pregnant thoroughbred horse that had developed severe respiratory distress, ataxia, and swelling of the cheeks and supraorbital fossa over a 24-hour period. The second horse had licked the face of the dead mare through a fence. The second horse, a 2-year-old colt, died 11 days later, after a 24-hour clinical course of aimless pacing, muscle trembling, and hemorrhagic nasal discharge. No epidemiologic link could be established between these two outbreaks.[2,20] The etiologic agent was originally called equine Morbillivirus, but the name was later changed to Hendra virus, after the suburb where the first outbreak was identified.

In January 1999, a single horse near Cairns, in northern Queensland, became ill with anorexia, depression, and swelling of the face, lips, and neck. The following day, she was found recumbent and with copious yellow nasal discharge. She was euthanized and was subsequently found to have Hendra virus.[20]

Outbreak Investigation

A serologic survey of wildlife species was performed in May and November 1995 that targeted species that were present at the site of the outbreaks. One hundred and sixty-eight individuals from over 16 species were tested, including rodents, marsupials, birds, amphibians, and insects, yet none were seropositive for Hendra virus. Nomadic birds and flying foxes (bats of the Pteropus genus) were then targeted as likely reservoirs, given their presence in the regions of both outbreaks and their ability to travel long distances.[21]

In April 1996, anti-Hendra virus antibodies were found in a black flying fox in central Queensland. Within weeks, antibodies were found in several other types of flying fox throughout Queensland. In September 1996, Hendra virus was isolated from the reproductive tract of a pregnant gray-headed flying fox that had become entangled on a wire fence. The bat isolate was identical to the Hendra virus that infected the horses who died in the outbreaks.[21,22] Flying foxes are thought to have subclinical infection.[20,23,24]

Pathology and Pathogenesis

The incubation period of Hendra virus in the two humans with acute infection was approximately 5 to 8 days.[1,17,19] Transmission most likely occurred through contact of infectious fluids from the pigs with the mucous membranes or nonintact skin of the humans. The horse trainer who died of acute Hendra virus infection had an interstitial pneumonia on pathology. Autopsy revealed lung congestion, edema, and hemorrhage. Histologic examination revealed focal necrotizing alveolitis with giant cells, syncytial formation, and viral inclusions.[12,19] He also had mild chronic myocarditis and regions of inflammation with necrosis in the kidney, as well as a pulmonary embolism.[19] Kidney tissue inoculated in cell culture postmortem caused syncytial formation, whereas lung, liver, and spleen tissue did not.[12,19]

Autopsy of the patient who died from relapsed encephalitis 14 months after exposure to Hendra virus–infected horses revealed a leptomeningitis with a lymphocyte and plasma cell infiltrate. There were discrete foci of necrosis in the neocortex, basal ganglia, brainstem, and cerebellum, with sparing of the subcortical white matter. Rare multinucleate endothelial cells were detected in the brain, liver, spleen, and lungs. Immunohistochemistry of brain tissue was positive for Hendra virus. EM revealed aggregates of nucleocapsids in cell remnants. Hendra virus could not be cultured from the brain.[2] The pathogenesis of disease in this patient with relapsed encephalitis remains unclear. A comparison has been made to subacute sclerosing panencephalitis (SSPE), a severe neurodegenerative disease that may occur years after infection with measles but in which infectious virus cannot be readily cultured from the brain. However, the clinical course was faster than is typical for SSPE, and the pathologic findings were quite different.

Clinical Features

Only three humans are known to have been infected with Hendra virus. One of these had an influenza-like syndrome, characterized by fever, myalgias, headache, lethargy, and vertigo. He was unwell for 6 weeks but then recovered. Another patient presented with a similar syndrome but rapidly developed respiratory distress requiring mechanical ventilation. He also had acidosis, dehydration, an arterial thrombosis in his right lower extremity, and cardiac irritability. He died 6 days after the onset of illness from an asystolic cardiac arrest. These two patients became ill approximately 1 week after the onset of illness in the first horse with Hendra virus.[1,12] The third patient diagnosed with Hendra virus died 14 months after a horse that he had cared for died from Hendra virus. This individual was a 35-year-old man who had aseptic meningitis in August 1994, after caring for two sick horses and assisting with their necropsies. He developed a sore throat, headache, drowsiness, vomiting, and neck stiffness, and he was found to have 560 white blood cells per microliter in his cerebrospinal fluid (CSF), with a polymorphonuclear predominance, and negative bacterial and viral cultures. He recovered fully, but 13 months later he developed irritability, low back pain, and a seizure. Over the following week, he had a low-grade fever and recurrent seizures. By day 7 of hospitalization, he had a right hemiplegia, brainstem signs, and a decreased level of consciousness, and he required intubation. He remained febrile and unconscious and was found by electroencephalography (EEG) to be having seizure activity despite control of clinically apparent seizures. He died 25 days after admission.[2]

Laboratory Abnormalities and Diagnostic Tests

The patient who died during an acute Hendra virus infection had thrombocytopenia and elevated levels of creatine kinase, lactate dehydrogenase, aspartate aminotransferase, alanine aminotransferase, and glutamyltransferase. He also had signs of dehydration and acidosis.[12] The patient who survived had no laboratory abnormalities.[17]

Hendra virus forms syncytia when grown in Vero cells. This cytopathic effect and the typical EM findings of the herringbone nucleocapsid and the double-fringed appearance of the surface projections of the viral envelope aid in its identification. Enzyme-linked immunosorbent assay (ELISA) can be used to detect IgM and IgG antibodies.[25] A serum neutralization assay can also be done.[21,25,26]

Treatment

Other than supportive care, such as intravenous hydration and mechanical ventilation, when indicated, no specific antiviral therapy is known to be effective in the treatment of patients with Hendra virus. In vitro data indicate that ribavirin has activity against Hendra virus.[27] It penetrates the blood-brain barrier and reaches a mean CSF-to-plasma ratio of 0.7.[28]

NIPAH VIRUS

Epidemiology

An outbreak of severe encephalitis occurred in pig farmers in the Perak state of Malaysia in September 1998.[5,6,29] By December, the outbreak had spread to pig farmers in the Negeri Sembilan state. In March 1999, 11 abattoir workers in Singapore developed an encephalitis syndrome with associated pneumonia. There was one fatality in Singapore.[30] The last cases occurred in May 1999 in the Selangor state of Malaysia.[31] There were 265 human cases of acute Nipah encephalitis in Malaysia, 105 of which were fatal.[14,32] The case-fatality rate was 40%. Of these cases, 70% occurred in individuals who worked directly with pigs.[31] The outbreak ended after more than 1 million pigs were culled.[33]

Outbreak Investigation

At the beginning of the Nipah virus outbreak, health officials in Malaysia thought that the etiologic agent was Japanese encephalitis (JE) virus. A campaign was undertaken to control the spread of disease by large-scale spraying of mosquitoes and vaccination of at-risk individuals. However, neither of these measures slowed the spread of disease.

Researchers who studied the first three patients who died cultured a virus from the CSF that caused syncytial formation in Vero cells from two of the patients. The virus stained with anti–Hendra virus antibodies by indirect immunofluorescence. An ELISA for IgM anti-Hendra antibodies was positive in the CSF of all three patients.[29]

After the outbreak of Nipah virus in abattoir workers in Singapore, a serologic survey of individuals in Singapore who could have had exposure to infected pigs was performed. Serum was tested for Nipah virus IgM, IgG, and neutralizing antibodies. Those studied included health care workers who had seen patients with Nipah virus, laboratory staff who had handled samples from infected patients, workers from two abattoirs, meat inspectors, butchers, zoo workers, and customs inspectors who had discovered a smuggled truck-load of pork from Malaysia after a ban on importation of Malaysian pigs was instituted. Of the 1469 samples tested, 22 (1.5%) had antibodies against Nipah virus. Twelve of the 22 seropositive subjects (55%) were symptomatic. All of the infected individuals were male abattoir workers. None of the subjects who had contact with horses, and none of the health care workers exposed to infected patients had detectable antibodies.[34]

A case-control study of risk factors for Nipah virus infection was performed. Using serology, clinically undetected Nipah virus was found in 10 (6%) of 166 community-farm controls (individuals from farms without reported encephalitis patients) and in 20 (11%) of 178 case-farm controls (individuals from farms with encephalitis patients). Patients with Nipah virus encephalitis had higher percentages of sick or dying pigs on their farm than did community-farm controls (59% versus 24%, $P = .001$) and were more likely to have had direct contact with pigs than the case-farm controls (86% versus 50%, $P = .005$). Of patients with Nipah virus encephalitis, 8% reported no contact with pigs.[32]

Bats were screened very quickly for the presence of anti-Nipah antibodies, as the similarity between Nipah and Hendra virus made bats an obvious candidate for the reservoir of disease. Island flying foxes

(Pteropus hypomelanus) and Malayan flying foxes *(Pteropus vampyrus)* were found to have neutralizing antibodies to Nipah virus.[26] Subsequently, viruses that caused Hendra virus–like cytopathic effect in Vero cells and stained strongly for Nipah and Hendra virus antibodies were identified from two urine samples and a sample from fruit that had been partially eaten by a fruit bat.[35]

Infection has been demonstrated serologically not just in pigs but also in cats, dogs, horses, and goats.[31,33] Of these less commonly infected species, dogs have been observed to have clinical disease.[6,20] Pigs are likely to be the source of infection for these other species.[31,33]

Pathology and Pathogenesis

Nipah virus causes a multiorgan vasculitis with a predilection for the CNS. The incubation period of Nipah virus ranges from 4 days to 2 months, although greater than 90% of patients have an incubation period of 2 weeks or less.[31,32,36] On autopsy, patients with Nipah virus infection exhibit widespread endothelial involvement, characterized by vasculitis, thrombosis, ischemia, and parenchymal necrosis. This is most marked in the central nervous system, although the lungs, heart, and kidneys are also involved. Syncytial giant cell formation is present in affected vessels. Viral inclusions are detectable both by light microscopy and by EM. Immunohistochemistry reveals the presence of Nipah virus antigens in the endothelial and smooth muscle cells of blood vessels, as well as in neurons and other affected cells.[37,38]

Nipah virus has been isolated from the respiratory secretions and urine of 8 of 20 patients with acute infection. Patients with anti-Nipah IgM had a lower chance of having the virus isolated from secretions, suggesting that shedding takes place in the early period of infection.[39] A cohort study of the health care workers in Malaysia who cared for Nipah virus encephalitis patients was performed. Serologic tests were performed on 338 health care workers exposed and 288 health care workers unexposed to patients with Nipah virus. Needlestick injuries were reported by 12 (3%), mucosal surface exposure to body fluids by 39 (11%), and skin exposure to body fluids by 89 (25%) of individuals caring for patients with Nipah virus. No cases of encephalitis occurred in either group. Three exposed and no unexposed health care workers had a positive ELISA for IgG. No IgM response and no anti-Nipah virus neutralizing antibodies were detected in either group. The researchers suggested that the IgG responses were false positives.[40] However, there was a case report of a nurse in whom magnetic resonance imaging (MRI) of the brain demonstrated the characteristic lesions of Nipah virus encephalitis, although she had no signs or symptoms of infection.[41] The authors of this report suggest that this nurse had subclinical infection and that it was transmitted nosocomially, as she had no exposures to sick animals but did care for patients with Nipah virus encephalitis. Despite limited evidence for human-to-human transmission of Hendra and Nipah viruses, they are handled with biosafety level 4 biohazard precautions in the laboratory because of the virulence of these pathogens and the lack of clinical experience with them.

The factor most likely to have enabled transmission of Hendra and Nipah virus to horses, pigs, and humans is ecologic change that brought flying foxes closer to the affected animals. Deforestation has caused flying foxes to move into suburban and urban areas to use the trees in these regions for roosting. Indeed, the pig farm that was the site of the large outbreak in Malaysia is also an orchard. Flying foxes were therefore in close proximity to the pigs. The close quarters of the pigs contributed to the rapid dissemination of Nipah virus. Transportation of pigs throughout Malaysia and exportation of pigs to Singapore resulted in further spread of disease.[20]

Phylogenetic analyses of Hendra and Nipah virus suggest that they are old viruses,[12,42] which supports the theory that their recent emergence was due to ecologic factors rather than virus mutations.

Clinical Features

Patients typically present with fever, headache, dizziness, and vomiting. More than 50% of patients have a decreased level of consciousness and brain stem dysfunction, including such signs as myoclonus, areflexia, hypotonia, hypertension, and tachycardia. Cerebellar signs are common.[31,43-45] Although neurologic dysfunction is a predominant feature, severely ill patients may have multisystem organ dysfunction, including sepsis, gastrointestinal bleeding, and renal failure.[43] Patients may also experience respiratory symptoms.[44] In the most severely affected patients, EEG revealed bilateral temporal periodic complexes of sharp and slow waves occurring every 1 to 2 seconds.[31]

MRI is sensitive for and suggestive of acute Nipah virus encephalitis, and it is far superior to computed tomography, which lacks sensitivity. The typical findings are multiple, 2- to 7-mm lesions disseminated throughout the brain but most commonly present in the subcortical and deep white matter of the cerebral hemispheres. The lesions are best seen in the T_2-weighted images, without associated cerebral edema or mass effect (Fig. 158-3A).[43,46] In a study of the MRIs of eight patients with Nipah virus, all of the patients had multiple small bilateral foci of T_2 prolongation in the subcortical and deep white matter as well as in the periventricular areas and in the corpus callosum. Five patients also had cortical involvement, three had brain stem lesions, and one patient had a thalamic lesion. In five of the patients, diffusion-weighted images (DWI) showed increased signal. Four patients had leptomeningeal enhancement and four had enhancement of the parenchymal lesions.[47] A month after the outbreak, 5 of 12 patients had widespread small foci of high signal intensity on T_1-weighted images, especially in the cerebral cortex. The DWI images showed decreased prominence or disappearance over time. At the 6-month follow-up, there was no radiographic evidence of progression or relapse.[48]

In a follow-up study of patients who survived Nipah virus infection, which was done 24 months after the outbreak, 12 patients (7.5%) developed a relapse of encephalitis. Of patients who initially had nonencephalitic disease, 10 patients (3.4%) had late-onset encephalitis, with a mean time to neurologic findings of 8.4 months. Common findings were the acute onset of fever, headache, seizures, and focal neurologic signs. Four (18%) of the 22 patients with relapsed and late-onset encephalitis died.[49] Brain MRI scans in patients with relapsed disease usually showed patchy confluent cortical gray matter lesions (see Fig. 158-3B).[43,46,49]

Laboratory Abnormalities and Diagnostic Tests

Leukopenia (11%), thrombocytopenia (30%), and elevated levels of alanine aminotransferase (33%) and aspartate aminotransferase (42%) are the most common laboratory abnormalities.[43,45] The CSF reveals a lymphocytic pleocytosis typical of viral encephalitis. During the acute illness, virus-specific antibodies are present in the serum in greater than 70% of samples, but in less than one third of CSF samples.[31] Isolation of Nipah virus from the CSF is strongly associated with mortality. Stored CSF samples from 84 patients with Nipah virus encephalitis (27 fatal and 57 nonfatal) were cultured for Nipah virus. The virus could be cultured from the CSF of 17 fatal cases and one nonfatal case.[50]

Treatment

An open-label trial of ribavirin in 140 patients with Nipah virus encephalitis showed a 36% decrease in mortality in patients who received ribavirin compared to controls. There were 45 deaths (32%) in the ribavirin group, compared to 29 deaths (54%) in the control group.[27] Although these data suggest that ribavirin is beneficial, the lack of randomized controls and the small number of patients treated make the results difficult to interpret.

MENANGLE VIRUS

Epidemiology

From April to September 1997, the farrowing rate at a commercial piggery in New South Wales, Australia, decreased from the expected 82% to 60%. The number of live piglets declined, and the rate of mummified and stillborn piglets increased. Occasional abortions also oc-

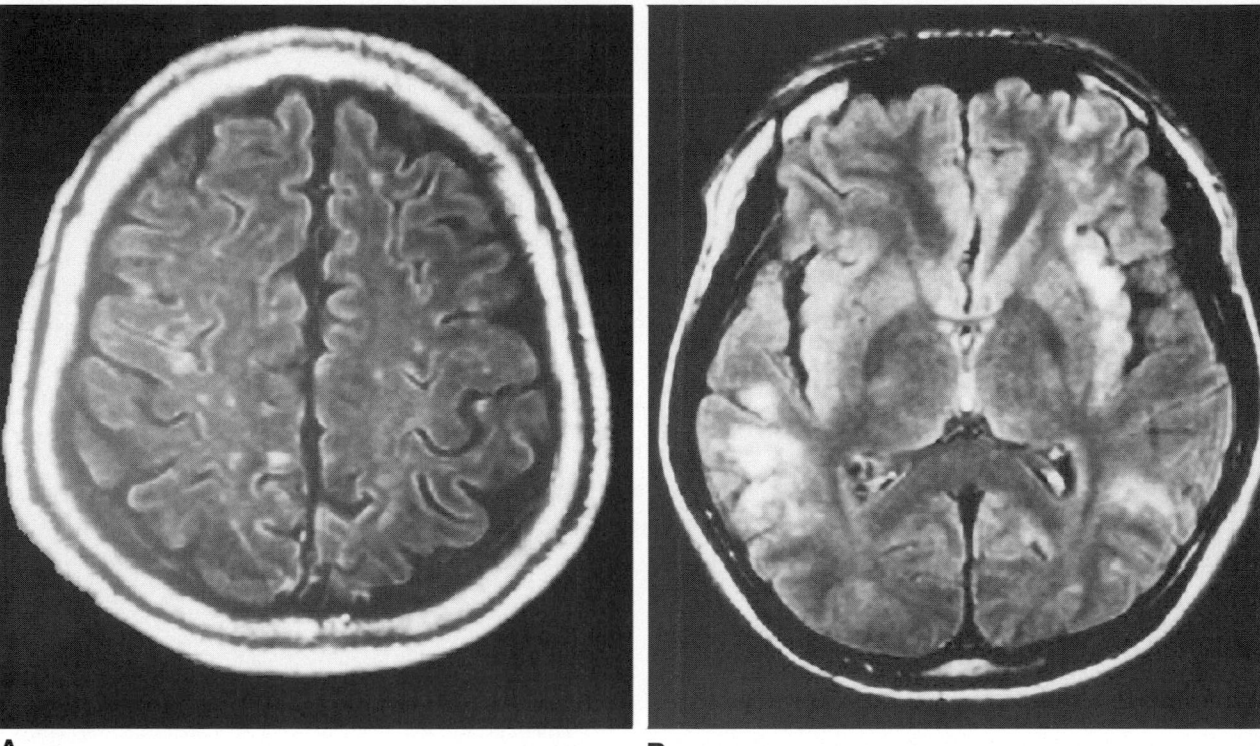

A   **B**

FIGURE 158-3. Axial magnetic resonance imaging findings in patients with acute (A) and relapsed (B) Nipah virus encephalitis with use of fluid-attenuated inversion recovery. **A,** Multiple discrete hyperintense lesions in the white and gray matter of a patient with acute Nipah virus encephalitis. **B,** Confluent lesions primarily involving the cortical gray matter in a patient with relapsed Nipah virus encephalitis. (Reprinted from Goh KJ, Tan CT, Chew NK, et al. Clinical features of Nipah virus encephalitis among pig farmers in Malaysia. N Engl J Med. 2000;342:1229-1235, with permission. Copyright 2000, Massachusetts Medical Society. All rights reserved.)

curred. The stillborn piglets had abnormalities that included severe degeneration of the brain and spinal cord, arthrogryposis, brachygnathia, and rarely, fibrinous body cavity effusions and pulmonary hypoplasia.[4] Of pigs at the affected piggery 96% had neutralizing antibodies against the virus, whereas serum and plasma samples collected from pigs at the piggery prior to May 1997 were negative.[4,51] Serum from two humans, one of whom worked at the affected piggery and one of whom worked at a piggery that had received a shipment of pigs from the affected piggery, had neutralizing antibodies. Both of these individuals had influenza-like illnesses during the weeks after exposure to likely infectious material.[4]

Outbreak Investigation

A large colony of fruit bats roosts within 200 m of the affected piggery from October to April.[4] Given the proximity of the fruit bats to the piggery and the previous Hendra virus outbreak, fruit bats were immediate targets of the investigation. Forty-two (34%) of 125 serum samples from fruit bats in New South Wales and Queensland, Australia, were positive for neutralizing antibodies against Menangle virus. Antibodies were found in several different species of fruit bat. This included samples taken from fruit bats in 1996, prior to the outbreak of disease. Antibodies were also found in fruit bats 33 km away from the affected piggery. Other species in the area, including rodents, birds, cattle, sheep, cats, and a dog, were all seronegative.[4] Two hundred and fifty-one humans who had had potential exposures to infected pigs were tested serologically. Only two of these individuals were found to have positive neutralizing antibodies, and both had an influenza-like illness with a rash at the time of the outbreak. They were also tested serologically for a broad range of viruses, bacteria, and parasites that could have caused this illness, but none of the serologic tests suggested an alternate diagnosis.[3]

Pathogenesis

Respiratory spread has been proposed as the likely mode of transmission in pigs, but it is less clear what the mode is for spread from pigs to humans. Both of the humans who were infected had exposure to body fluids of infected pigs. The first individual helped to birth pigs, and he reported that splashes of amniotic fluid and blood often occurred. He also reported having frequent minor wounds of his hands and forearms. The second patient performed autopsies on pigs without wearing gloves or protective eye wear.[3] Little is known about the pathogenesis and pathology of Menangle virus, but it is likely to have features in common with Hendra and Nipah viruses, given the ability of this virus to leap from fruit bats to pigs to humans, and given the phylogenetic relationship between Menangle virus and the Henipaviruses.

Clinical Features and Diagnostic Tests

The first individual with Menangle virus reported that in early June 1997, he had the sudden onset of malaise and chills, followed by severe headache and myalgias. He remained in bed for the next 10 days. Four days into the illness he developed a spotty erythematous rash. His physician noted that he had abdominal tenderness, lymphadenopathy, and the rash. He returned to work after 2 weeks but continued to have fatigue. He lost 10 kg during the illness. An evaluation 2 months after his illness revealed mild right lower abdominal tenderness, and an enlarged spleen on ultrasound. The liver was at the upper limit of normal. Urinalysis, complete blood count (CBC), blood chemistries, erythrocyte sedimentation rate (ESR), and C-reactive protein (CRP) were all normal.[3]

The second patient also became ill in early June 1997, with fever, chills, rigors, sweats, malaise, back pain, severe frontal headache, and photophobia. The headache lasted for 4 to 5 days. On the fourth day of illness, he noticed a spotty erythematous truncal rash, which lasted for 7 days. His acute illness lasted for about 10 days, during which time he lost 3 kg. Two months after the illness, he also underwent a clinical evaluation. His urinalysis, CBC, ESR, and CRP were normal. His blood chemistries were normal, except for mildly elevated hepatic enzymes, although he also tested positive for hepatitis C antibody. An ultrasound revealed mild hepatomegaly and a spleen size at the upper limit of normal. Both of these patients had antibodies against Menangle virus, with titers of 1:128 and 1:512.[3]

REFERENCES

1. Murray K, Rogers R, Selvey L, et al. A novel morbillivirus pneumonia of horses and its transmission to humans. Emerg Infect Dis. 1995;1:31-33.
2. O'Sullivan JD, Allworth AM, Paterson DL, et al. Fatal encephalitis due to novel paramyxovirus transmitted from horses. Lancet. 1997;349:93-95.
3. Chant K, Chan R, Smith M, et al. Probable human infection with a newly described virus in the family Paramyxoviridae. The NSW Expert Group. Emerg Infect Dis. 1998;4:273-275.
4. Philbey AW, Kirkland PD, Ross AD, et al. An apparently new virus (family Paramyxoviridae) infectious for pigs, humans, and fruit bats. Emerg Infect Dis. 1998;4:269-271.
5. Outbreak of Hendra-like virus: Malaysia and Singapore, 1998-1999. MMWR Morb Mortal Wkly Rep. 1999;48:265-269.
6. Update: outbreak of Nipah virus: Malaysia and Singapore, 1999. MMWR Morb Mortal Wkly Rep. 1999;48:335-337.
7. Yu M, Hansson E, Shiell B, et al. Sequence analysis of the Hendra virus nucleoprotein gene: Comparison with other members of the subfamily Paramyxovirinae. J Gen Virol. 1998;79:1775-1780.
8. Chan YP, Chua KB, Koh CL, et al. Complete nucleotide sequences of Nipah virus isolates from Malaysia. J Gen Virol. 2001;82:2151-2155.
9. Wang LF, Yu M, Hansson E, et al. The exceptionally large genome of Hendra virus: Support for creation of a new genus within the family Paramyxoviridae. J Virol. 2000;74:9972-9979.
10. Harcourt BH, Tamin A, Ksiazek TG, et al. Molecular characterization of Nipah virus, a newly emergent paramyxovirus. Virology. 2000;271:334-349.
11. Bowden TR, Westenberg M, Wang LF, et al. Molecular characterization of Menangle virus, a novel paramyxovirus which infects pigs, fruit bats, and humans. Virology. 2001;283:358-373.
12. Murray K, Selleck P, Hooper P, et al. A morbillivirus that caused fatal disease in horses and humans. Science. 1995;268:94-97.
13. Hyatt AD, Zaki SR, Goldsmith CS, et al. Ultrastructure of Hendra virus and Nipah virus within cultured cells and host animals. Microbes Infect. 2001;3:297-306.
14. Chua KB, Bellini WJ, Rota PA, et al. Nipah virus: A recently emergent deadly paramyxovirus. Science. 2000;288:1432-1435.
15. Yu M, Hansson E, Langedijk JP, et al. The attachment protein of Hendra virus has high structural similarity but limited primary sequence homology compared with viruses in the genus Paramyxovirus. Virology. 1998;251:227-233.
16. Wang L, Harcourt BH, Yu M, et al. Molecular biology of Hendra and Nipah viruses. Microbes Infect. 2001;3:279-287.
17. Bellini WJ, Rota PA, Parashar U. Zoonotic paramyxoviruses. In: Richman DD, Whitley RJ, Haden FG, eds. Clinical Virology. Washington, DC: American Society for Microbiology; 2002:845-855.
18. Harcourt BH, Tamin A, Halpin K, et al. Molecular characterization of the polymerase gene and genomic termini of Nipah virus. Virology. 2001;287:192-201.
19. Selvey LA, Wells RM, McCormack JG, et al. Infection of humans and horses by a newly described morbillivirus. Med J Aust. 1995;162:642-645.
20. Field H, Young P, Yob JM, et al. The natural history of Hendra and Nipah viruses. Microbes Infect. 2001;3:307-314.
21. Young PL, Halpin K, Selleck PW, et al. Serologic evidence for the presence in Pteropus bats of a paramyxovirus related to equine morbillivirus. Emerg Infect Dis. 1996;2:239-240.
22. Halpin K, Young PL, Field HE, Mackenzie JS. Isolation of Hendra virus from pteropid bats: A natural reservoir of Hendra virus. J Gen Virol. 2000;81:1927-1932.
23. Williamson MM, Hooper PT, Selleck PW, et al. Experimental Hendra virus infection in pregnant guinea-pigs and fruit bats (Pteropus poliocephalus). J Comp Pathol. 2000;122:201-207.
24. Williamson MM, Hooper PT, Selleck PW, et al. Transmission studies of Hendra virus (equine morbillivirus) in fruit bats, horses and cats. Aust Vet J. 1998;76:813-818.
25. Daniels P, Ksiazek T, Eaton BT. Laboratory diagnosis of Nipah and Hendra virus infections. Microbes Infect. 2001;3:289-295.
26. Yob JM, Field H, Rashdi AM, et al. Nipah virus infection in bats (order Chiroptera) in peninsular Malaysia. Emerg Infect Dis. 2001;7:439-441.
27. Chong HT, Kamarulzaman A, Tan CT, et al. Treatment of acute Nipah encephalitis with ribavirin. Ann Neurol. 2001;49:810-813.
28. Connor E, Morrison S, Lane J, et al. Safety, tolerance, and pharmacokinetics of systemic ribavirin in children with human immunodeficiency virus infection. Antimicrob Agents Chemother. 1993;37:532-539.
29. Chua KB, Goh KJ, Wong KT, et al. Fatal encephalitis due to Nipah virus among pig-farmers in Malaysia. Lancet. 1999;354:1257-1259.
30. Paton NI, Leo YS, Zaki SR, et al. Outbreak of Nipah-virus infection among abattoir workers in Singapore. Lancet. 1999;354:1253-1256.
31. Chua KB. Nipah virus outbreak in Malaysia. J Clin Virol. 2003;26:265-275.
32. Parashar UD, Sunn LM, Ong F, et al. Case-control study of risk factors for human infection with a new zoonotic paramyxovirus, Nipah virus, during a 1998-1999 outbreak of severe encephalitis in Malaysia. J Infect Dis. 2000;181:1755-1759.
33. Lam SK, Chua KB. Nipah virus encephalitis outbreak in Malaysia. Clin Infect Dis. 2002;34(Suppl 2):S48-51.
34. Chan KP, Rollin PE, Ksiazek TG, et al. A survey of Nipah virus infection among various risk groups in Singapore. Epidemiol Infect. 2002;128:93-98.
35. Chua KB, Koh CL, Hooi PS, et al. Isolation of Nipah virus from Malaysian Island flying-foxes. Microbes Infect. 2002;4:145-151.
36. Chew MH, Arguin PM, Shay DK, et al. Risk factors for Nipah virus infection among abattoir workers in Singapore. J Infect Dis. 2000;181:1760-1763.
37. Hooper P, Zaki S, Daniels P, Middleton D. Comparative pathology of the diseases caused by Hendra and Nipah viruses. Microbes Infect. 2001;3:315-322.
38. Wong KT, Shieh WJ, Kumar S, et al. Nipah virus infection: Pathology and pathogenesis of an emerging paramyxoviral zoonosis. Am J Pathol. 2002;161:2153-2167.
39. Chua KB, Lam SK, Goh KJ, et al. The presence of Nipah virus in respiratory secretions and urine of patients during an outbreak of Nipah virus encephalitis in Malaysia. J Infect. 2001;42:40-43.
40. Mounts AW, Kaur H, Parashar UD, et al. A cohort study of health care workers to assess nosocomial transmissibility of Nipah virus, Malaysia, 1999. J Infect Dis. 2001;183:810-813.
41. Tan CT, Tan KS. Nosocomial transmissibility of Nipah virus. J Infect Dis. 2001;184:1367.
42. Gould AR. Comparison of the deduced matrix and fusion protein sequences of equine morbillivirus with cognate genes of the Paramyxoviridae. Virus Res. 1996;43:17-31.
43. Goh KJ, Tan CT, Chew NK, et al. Clinical features of Nipah virus encephalitis among pig farmers in Malaysia. N Engl J Med. 2000;342:1229-1235.
44. Lee KE, Umapathi T, Tan CB, et al. The neurological manifestations of Nipah virus encephalitis, a novel paramyxovirus. Ann Neurol. 1999;46:428-432.
45. Chong HT, Kunjapan SR, Thayaparan T, et al. Nipah encephalitis outbreak in Malaysia, clinical features in patients from Seremban. Can J Neurol Sci. 2002;29:83-87.
46. Sarji SA, Abdullah BJ, Goh KJ, et al. MR imaging features of Nipah encephalitis. AJR Am J Roentgenol. 2000;175:437-442.
47. Lim CC, Sitoh YY, Hui F, et al. Nipah viral encephalitis or Japanese encephalitis? MR findings in a new zoonotic disease. AJNR Am J Neuroradiol. 2000;21:455-461.
48. Lim CC, Lee KE, Lee WL, et al. Nipah virus encephalitis: Serial MR study of an emerging disease. Radiology. 2002;222:219-226.
49. Tan CT, Goh KJ, Wong KT, et al. Relapsed and late-onset Nipah encephalitis. Ann Neurol. 2002;51:703-708.
50. Chua KB, Lam SK, Tan CT, et al. High mortality in Nipah encephalitis is associated with presence of virus in cerebrospinal fluid. Ann Neurol. 2000;48:802-805.
51. Kirkland PD, Love RJ, Philbey AW, et al. Epidemiology and control of Menangle virus in pigs. Aust Vet J. 2001;79:199-206.

CHAPTER **159**

Vesicular Stomatitis Virus and Related Viruses

STEVEN M. FINE

Vesicular stomatitis virus (VSV) most prominently causes a vesicular disease in domestic animals that resembles foot-and-mouth disease. Outbreaks within domestic animal herds decrease production and result in restrictions on the transport and sale of animals and animal products, which results in significant economic losses. VSV infects a high percentage of people who live in endemic areas, but VSV-associated disease in humans is generally mild, although significant morbidity can occur. In addition, because the VSV-G protein can bind to numerous cell types, VSV has earned a major role in molecular biology research involving the transduction of genetic material into cells.

CLASSIFICATION AND MORPHOLOGY

VSV is enveloped and contains a single strand of negative-sense RNA that encodes five structural proteins; the glycoprotein (G), membrane (or matrix) protein (M), nucleoprotein (N), and two internal proteins (L and P).[1,2] It belongs to the family Rhabdoviridae, genus

TABLE 159-1 Vesiculoviruses

Species	Location of Isolation
VS-Indiana	United States
VS-New Jersey	United States
VS-Alagoas	Brazil[6]
VS-Carajas	Brazil[8]
Maraba	Brazil[8]
Piry	Brazil
Cocal	Trinidad[12]
Chandipura	India[54,55]
Isfahan	Iran[7]

Adapted from Travassos da Rosa AP, Tesh RB, Travassos da Rosa JF, et al. Carajas and Maraba viruses, two new vesiculoviruses isolated from phlebotomine sand flies in Brazil. Am J Trop Med Hyg. 1984;33:999-1006; and ICTV database 2002 of the 2002 International Committee on Taxonomy of Viruses.

Vesiculovirus,[3] and it assumes the bullet morphology characteristic of the Rhabdoviridae. Approximately 1200 identical copies of the G protein cover its surface in an ordered, densely packed array of spikes, which present only one antigenic determinant accessible to neutralizing antibodies.[4,5] Of the nine confirmed and 22 tentative species of vesiculoviruses discovered thus far (Table 159-1), six cause animal or human disease: VS-New Jersey (VS-NJ), VS-Indiana (VS-I), VS-Alagoas, Chandipura, Isfahan, and Piry.[6-9]

MOLECULAR BIOLOGY

The VSV-G protein binds to the surface of most cell types. Thus, molecular biologists often replace the envelope proteins in other viral vectors with VSV-G to expand the host range of the vector. Viruses produced in cell lines expressing the VSV-G protein are thus *pseudotyped* with VSV-G on their surfaces. They can infect a large variety of cells and are therefore tremendously useful for gene transduction.[10,11] VSV is also used as an expression vector in candidate vaccines. A live-attenuated VSV vector expressing human immunodeficiency virus (HIV) *gag* and *env* genes is being tested as an HIV vaccine.

EPIDEMIOLOGY

Epizootic

In North America, VSV disease caused by VS-NJ or VS-I appears in sporadic, epizootic outbreaks in domesticated horses and cattle, mainly in the central and southwestern United States and Canada and in Mexico. Outbreaks of VS-I occurred in 1942, 1956, 1964, 1965, 1997, and 1998[12] and of VS-NJ in 1944, 1949, 1957, 1963, 1982, 1985, 1995, and 1997.[12-13a] Outbreaks typically begin in late spring, spread to adjacent or remote herds, and abate after heavy frost. The vector is not known, although insects are suspected. VSV was isolated from a mosquito during an epizootic outbreak in New Mexico[14] and from biting midges and black flies that may be responsible for long-distance transport of the virus.[15-17] The 1995 epizootic episode in the southwestern United States began in May, in horses in New Mexico, and by October had spread to 367 premises in Arizona, Colorado, New Mexico, Utah, and Wyoming. Seventy-eight percent of cases were in horses and 22% in cattle, and one case was in a llama. Production losses, quarantines, and restrictions on livestock shows, auctions, and rodeos cost an estimated $50 to $100 million.[13]

Enzootic

In parts of Central and South America and in the United States on Ossabaw Island, Georgia, outbreaks of disease from enzootic VS-NJ predictably appear near the beginning of the dry season (November) and last through March. Farms located near forests, as well as those with poultry, experience higher rates of attack.[18] One year in Costa Rica, 9% to 11% of cattle on affected farms developed disease, which constituted 2.6% of cattle overall.[18,19] Lactation and a high acute VSV antibody titer increase the risk of disease for a given animal, but other diseases do not predispose to VSV disease.[18] The reservoirs and vectors for enzootic disease are not known, but phlebotomine sand flies harbor virus in enzootic areas.[6-8,20-22] They can transmit VSV to animals as well as transovarially to a new generation of sand flies in which it can then replicate.[21,23,24] Mosquitoes can also harbor VSV and can transmit infection to animals in a laboratory setting.[25] Additionally, VSV-infected black flies feeding on uninfected mice can horizontally infect other black flies feeding on the same mouse.[17] The high prevalence of VS-NJ antibodies in cows in enzootic areas of Costa Rica (82% for VS-NJ and 17.7% for VS-I)[19] indicates a high lifetime probability of infection, and many of these infections are probably subclinical. Wild animals in enzootic areas also have VS-I and VS-NJ antibodies—VS-I mainly in arboreal and semiarboreal species and VS-NJ in bats, Carnivora, some rodents, and white-tailed deer.[26,27] Animals with high titers of neutralizing antibodies can become re-infected by other strains.[18]

Animal Disease

VSV infection causes an acute vesicular disease in horses, cattle, swine, goats, llamas, and some wild animals.[13,28] Excess salivation, with fever and blisters or vesicles in and around the mouth, nose, hooves, or teats, appears after a 2- to 8-day incubation period. Vesicles may burst and the epithelium may slough, leaving large, contiguous areas exposed and irritated. Secondary bacterial infection leading to mastitis may complicate the course, and lameness due to foot lesions can develop. A debilitating, nonvesicular manifestation with systemic symptoms, such as fever and weight loss, sometimes occurs. Most animals recover after 2 to 3 weeks,[18,29] but viral sequences may persist.[30]

Human Disease

Humans usually contract VSV during close contact with infected animals.[31,32] Human infection with VSV is usually asymptomatic or causes mild illness, but it is not always benign. Of eight animal handlers who contracted VS-I during a 1965 epizootic episode in cattle, seven reported an illness that included fever, malaise, myalgias, emesis, and pharyngitis, and two of them developed oral vesicular lesions in 24 to 48 hours. Although most had mild illness that quickly resolved, one otherwise healthy man experienced pharyngeal and buccal lesions, lymphadenopathy, and a 20-pound weight loss over 3 weeks.[29] In another case, 30 hours after self-inoculation with VS-I, a laboratory worker developed fever, chills, retro-orbital pain, myalgias, nausea, emesis, and diarrhea, which resolved in 3 days.[33]

VSV is neurotropic in baby mice,[34] and two cases of VSV meningoencephalitis have been reported in children. In one, a 3-year-old boy from Panama infected with VS-I developed fever, chills, emesis, and generalized tonic-clonic seizures and remained neurologically impaired at discharge.[9]

The vast majority of human VSV infections go unrecognized, indicating either mild or subclinical illness. In an area of Iran enzootic for Isfahan, all residents older than 5 years were seropositive in one study,[7] and in a VS-Alagoas–endemic area of Colombia, 62% to 83% of people were seropositive,[6] indicating previous infection. This relatively high rate of seropositivity, which increases with age, also occurs with other serotypes in their respective enzootic areas.[20,26,32,35]

DIAGNOSIS

VSV causes lesions that look like those of the more dangerous foot-and-mouth disease; therefore, VSV outbreaks demand urgent diagnosis. Current diagnostic methods include complement fixation, serum neutralization, enzyme-linked immunosorbent assay (ELISA), or viral isolation in tissue culture.[13] Recently developed assays, using reverse transcription and the polymerase chain reaction, ease the collection of samples, can identify viral RNA from lesions previously treated with toxic substances, and are being adapted for general use.[36]

HOST RESPONSE AND TREATMENT

Studies in mice showed that the presence of B cells and antibody responses was associated with recovery and the development of resistance to VSV; however, CD4- T cells also contribute to long-term survival, and secretion of interleukin-12 may be beneficial.[37-39] Antibody-mediated neutralization blocks virus-to-cell binding and requires 200 to 500 VSV-G-protein-specific immunoglobulin G molecules per virus particle.[2,4] Neutralizing antibodies bind to the same G-protein epitope and protect against infection with the same strain.[5,40] However, in endemic areas, up to 10% of cattle with high titers of neutralizing antibodies become infected each year with clinical symptoms. This is presumably due to mutant strains.[18]

Human infections with VSV are usually mild and generally do not require treatment. No specific treatments exist, and antiviral agents have not been evaluated in vivo. Interferon-α, interferon-β, and interferon-γ inhibit VSV growth in vitro[41-43] and protect newborn mice from lethal VSV infection.[44] Prostaglandins A_1 and A_2,[45,46] ribavirin,[47,48] and some experimental compounds[49-51] inhibit VSV in vitro. In animals, secondary bacterial infections of the mouth, teats, and hooves should be treated appropriately, and a mild, antiseptic mouthwash may relieve pain from blisters.[52] Nutritional support may help animals that stop eating.

PREVENTION AND VACCINATION

Experimental vaccination with a recombinant vaccinia vector expressing the VSV-G protein stimulated neutralizing antibody production and protected mice against lethal VSV disease after intravenous challenge. In cattle, protection was incomplete, but it correlated with high antibody titer.[53] The U.S. Department of Agriculture has approved a killed vaccine for animals, but its efficacy is unknown.[13]

REFERENCES

1. Banerjee AK, Barik S. Gene expression of vesicular stomatitis virus genome RNA. Virology. 1992;188:417-428.
2. Dietzschold B, Schneider LG, Cox JH. Serological characterization of the three major proteins of vesicular stomatitis virus. J Virol. 1974;14:1-7.
3. Knudson DL. Rhabdoviruses. J Gen Virol. 1973;20(Suppl):105-130.
4. Kelley JM, Emerson SU, Wagner RR. The glycoprotein of vesicular stomatitis virus is the antigen that gives rise to and reacts with neutralizing antibody. J Virol. 1972;10:1231-1235.
5. Bachmann MF, Rohrer UH, Kundig TM, et al. The influence of antigen organization on B cell responsiveness. Science. 1993;262:1448-1451.
6. Tesh RB, Boshell J, Modi GB, et al. Natural infection of humans, animals, and phlebotomine sand flies with the Alagoas serotype of vesicular stomatitis virus in Colombia. Am J Trop Med Hyg. 1987;36:653-661.
7. Tesh R, Saidi S, Javadian E, et al. Isfahan virus, a new vesiculovirus infecting humans, gerbils, and sandflies in Iran. Am J Trop Med Hyg. 1977;26:299-306.
8. Travassos da Rosa AP, Tesh RB, Travassos da Rosa JF, et al. Carajas and Maraba viruses, two new vesiculoviruses isolated from phlebotomine sand flies in Brazil. Am J Trop Med Hyg. 1984;33:999-1006.
9. Quiroz E, Moreno N, Peralta PH, et al. A human case of encephalitis associated with vesicular stomatitis virus (Indiana serotype) infection. Am J Trop Med Hyg. 1988;39:312-314.
10. Arai T, Matsumoto K, Saitoh K, et al. A new system for stringent, high-titer vesicular stomatitis virus G protein-pseudotyped retrovirus vector induction by introduction of Cre recombinase into stable prepackaging cell lines. J Virol. 1998;72:1115-1121.
11. Yee JK, Friedmann T, Burns JC. Generation of high-titer pseudotyped retroviral vectors with very broad host range. Methods Cell Biol. 1994;43:99-112.
12. Jonkers AH. The epizootiology of the vesicular stomatitis viruses: A reappraisal. Am J Epidemiol. 1967;86:286-291.
13. Bridges VE, McCluskey BJ, Salman MD, et al. Review of the 1995 vesicular stomatitis outbreak in the western United States. J Am Vet Med Assoc. 1997;211:556-560.
13a. Rodriquez, LL. Emergence and re-emergence of vesicular stomatitis in the United States. Virus Res. 2000;85:211-219.
14. Sudia WD, Fields BN, Calisher CH. The isolation of vesicular stomatitis virus (Indiana strain) and other viruses from mosquitoes in New Mexico, 1965. Am J Epidemiol. 1967;86:598-602.
15. Cupp EW, Mare CJ, Cupp MS, et al. Biological transmission of vesicular stomatitis virus (New Jersey) by Simulium vittatum (Diptera: Simuliidae). J Med Entomol. 1992;29:137-140.
16. Mead DG, Maré CJ, Ramberg FB. Bite transmission of vesicular stomatitis virus (New Jersey serotype) to laboratory mice by Simulium vittatum (Diptera: Simuliidae). J Med Entomol. 1999;36:410-413.
17. Mead DG, Ramberg FB, Besselsen DG, Maré CJ. Transmission of vesicular stomatitis virus (New Jersey serotype) between infected and non-infected black flies co-feeding on non-viremic deer mice. Science. 2000;287:485-487.
18. Vanleeuwen JA, Rodriguez LL, Waltner-Toews D. Cow, farm, and ecologic risk factors of clinical vesicular stomatitis on Costa Rican dairy farms. Am J Trop Med Hyg. 1995;53:342-350.
19. Rodriguez LL, Vernon S, Morales AI, et al. Serological monitoring of vesicular stomatitis New Jersey virus in enzootic regions of Costa Rica. Am J Trop Med Hyg. 1990;42:272-281.
20. Shelokov A, Peralta PH. Vesicular stomatitis virus, Indiana type: An arbovirus infection of tropical sandflies and humans? Am J Epidemiol. 1967;86:149-157.
21. Comer JA, Tesh RB, Modi GB, et al. Vesicular stomatitis virus, New Jersey serotype: Replication in and transmission by Lutzomyia shannoni (Diptera: Psychodidae). Am J Trop Med Hyg. 1990;42:483-490.
22. Corn JL, Comer JA, Erickson GA, et al. Isolation of vesicular stomatitis virus New Jersey serotype from phlebotomine sand flies in Georgia. Am J Trop Med Hyg. 1990;42:476-482.
23. Tesh RB, Chaniotis BN, Johnson KM. Vesicular stomatitis virus, Indiana serotype: Multiplication in and transmission by experimentally infected phlebotomine sandflies (Lutzomyia trapidoi). Am J Epidemiol. 1971;93:491-495.
24. Tesh RB, Chaniotis BN. Transovarial transmission of viruses by phlebotomine sandflies. Ann N Y Acad Sci. 1975;266:125-134.
25. Calisher CH, Monath TP, Sabattini MS, et al. A newly recognized vesiculovirus, Calchaqui virus, and subtypes of Melao and Maguari viruses from Argentina, with serologic evidence for infections of humans and horses. Am J Trop Med Hyg. 1987;36:114-119.
26. Tesh RB, Peralta PH, Johnson KM. Ecologic studies of vesicular stomatitis virus. I. Prevalence of infection among animals and humans living in an area of endemic VSV activity. Am J Epidemiol. 1969;90:255-261.
27. Johnson KM, Tesh RB, Peralta PH. Epidemiology of vesicular stomatitis virus: Some new data and a hypothesis for transmission of the Indian serotype. J Am Vet Med Assoc. 1969;155:2133-2140.
28. Green SL. Vesicular stomatitis in the horse. Vet Clin North Am Equine Pract. 1993;9:349-353.
29. Fields BN, Hawkins K. Human infection with the virus of vesicular stomatitis during an epizootic. N Engl J Med. 1967;277:989-994.
30. Letchworth GJ, Barrera JC, Fishel JR, et al. Vesicular stomatitis New Jersey virus RNA persists in cattle following convalescence. Virology. 1996;219:480-484.
31. Reif JS, Webb PA, Monath TP, et al. Epizootic vesicular stomatitis in Colorado, 1982: Infection in occupational risk groups. Am J Trop Med Hyg. 1987;36:177-182.
32. Brody JA, Fischer GF, Peralta PH. Vesicular stomatitis virus in Panama. Human serologic patterns in a cattle raising area. Am J Epidemiol. 1967;86:158-161.
33. Johnson KM, Vogel JE, Peralta PH. Clinical and serological response to laboratory-acquired human infection by Indiana type vesicular stomatitis virus (VSV). Am J Trop Med Hyg. 1966;15:244-246.
34. Bi Z, Barna M, Komatsu T, et al. Vesicular stomatitis virus infection of the central nervous system activates both innate and acquired immunity. J Virol. 1995;69:6466-6472.
35. Cline BL. Ecological associations of vesicular stomatitis virus in rural Central America and Panama. Am J Trop Med Hyg. 1976;25:875-883.
36. Rodriguez LL, Fitch WM, Nichol ST. Ecological factors rather than temporal factors dominate the evolution of vesicular stomatitis virus. Proc Natl Acad Sci U S A. 1996;93:13030-13035.
37. Bachmann MF, Kalinke U, Althage A, et al. The role of antibody concentration and avidity in antiviral protection. Science. 1997;276:2024-2027.
38. Thomsen AR, Nansen A, Andersen C, et al. Cooperation of B cells and T cells is required for survival of mice infected with vesicular stomatitis virus. Int Immunol. 1997;9:1757-1766.
39. Komatsu T, Barna M, Reiss CS. Interleukin-12 promotes recovery from viral encephalitis. Viral Immunol. 1997;10:35-47.
40. Bachmann MF, Hengartner H, Zinkernagel RM. T helper cell-independent neutralizing B cell response against vesicular stomatitis virus: Role of antigen patterns in B cell induction? Eur J Immunol. 1995;25:3445-3451.
41. Witter F, Barouki F, Griffin D, et al. Biologic response (antiviral) to recombinant human interferon alpha 2a as a function of dose and route of administration in healthy volunteers. Clin Pharmacol Ther. 1987;42:567-575.
42. Maheshwari RK, Friedman RM. Interferon induced inhibition of enveloped viruses. Prog Clin Biol Res. 1985;202:297-305.
43. Baxt B, Sonnabend JA, Bablianian R. Effects of interferon on vesicular stomatitis virus transcription and translation. J Gen Virol. 1977;35:325-334.
44. DeClercq E, De Somer P. Protective effect of interferon and polyacrylic acid in newborn mice infected with a lethal dose of vesicular stomatitis virus. Life Sci. 1968;7:925-933.
45. Pica F, Rossi A, Santirocco N, et al. Effect of combined alpha IFN and prostaglandin A1 treatment on vesicular stomatitis virus replication and heat shock protein synthesis in epithelial cells. Antiviral Res. 1996;29:187-198.
46. Parker J, Ahrens PB, Ankel H. Antiviral effects of cyclopentenone prostaglandins on vesicular stomatitis virus replication. Antiviral Res. 1995;26:83-96.
47. Fernandez-Larsson R, O'Connell K, Koumans E, Patterson JL. Molecular analysis of the inhibitory effect of phosphorylated ribavirin on the vesicular stomatitis virus in vitro polymerase reaction. Antimicrob Agents Chemother. 1989;33:1668-1673.
48. Toltzis P, Huang AS. Effect of ribavirin on macromolecular synthesis in vesicular stomatitis virus-infected cells. Antimicrob Agents Chemother. 1986;29:1010-1016.
49. Shuto S, Obara, T, Saito Y, et al. New neplanocin analogues: 6. Synthesis and potent antiviral activity of 6'-homoneplanocin A1. J Med Chem. 1996;39:2392-2399.

50. Spinu K, Vorozhbit V, Grushko T, et al. Antiviral activity of tomatoside from *Lycopersicon esculentum* Mill. Adv Exp Med Biol. 1996;404:505-509.
51. Muller-Decker K, Amtmann E, Sauer, G. Inhibition of the phosphorylation of the regulatory non-structural protein of vesicular stomatitis virus by an antiviral xanthate compound. J Gen Virol. 1987;68:3045-3056.
52. Animal and Plant Health Inspection Service. Precautions for Horses Diagnosed with Vesicular Stomatitis. Lakewood, Col: Colorado Department of Agriculture Animal Industry Division; 1998.
53. Mackett M, Yilma T, Rose JK, et al. Vaccinia virus recombinants: Expression of VSV genes and protective immunization of mice and cattle. Science. 1985;227:433-435.
54. Fontenille D, Traore-Lamizana M, Trouillet J, et al. First isolations of arboviruses from phlebotomine sand flies in West Africa. Am J Trop Med Hyg. 1994;50:570-574.
55. Bhatt PN, Rodrigues FM. Chandipura: A new arbovirus isolated in India from patients with febrile illness. Indian J Med Res. 1967;55:1295-1305.

CHAPTER **160**

Rhabdoviruses

THOMAS P. BLECK

CHARLES E. RUPPRECHT

Rabies is a viral disease that produces an almost uniformly fatal encephalitis in humans and most other mammals. It has been present throughout recorded history, and literature, and very likely predates the evolution of humans. Rabies remains one of the most common viral causes of mortality in the developing world. Exposure to the virus has profound medical and economic implications throughout the world, with as many as 4 million people annually receiving postexposure treatment (PET) to prevent rabies.[1] Although current technology can produce safe agents for PET, the expense involved often leads to the use of older, more dangerous vaccines in the developing world, with their attendant risk of catastrophic neurologic complications.

Rabies, Latin for "madness," derives from *rabere,* to rave, and is related to the Sanskrit word for violence, *rabhas.* The Greek term for rabies, *lyssa,* also means madness, and it provides the genus name (Lyssavirus). The Babylon Eshnuna code contains the first known mention of rabies in the 23rd century BC.[2] Democritus provided a clear description of animal rabies in about 500 BC. Wound cauterization was the preferred treatment in the 1st century AD, and this remained the only real therapy until Pasteur introduced immunization in 1885. Wound cautery was recommended for the management of rabid animal bites until the mid-twentieth century.[2] Another remedy that remains part of popular culture (with little recognition of its origin) was the hair of the dog that bit the patient.[3]

Rabies in the Western Hemisphere predated Columbus but remained rare because of low population density.[4] Bats spread the disease among cattle and humans in Central America in the early 16th century.[5] Rabies epizootics began in the northern and eastern United States in the 19th century, reflecting the importation of foxes for hunting.[6]

Rabies was diagnosed clinically only until 1903, when Adelchi Negri described the cytoplasmic inclusions that bear his name.[7] These were only pathologic marker prior to the development of the fluorescent antibody test in 1958.[8]

VIROLOGY

Classification

The Rhabdoviridae are rod-shaped, negative-sense, nonsegmented, single-stranded RNA viruses. Three genera infect animals (Lyssavirus, Vesiculovirus, and Ephemerovirus); one infects plants; and several other members are uncharacterized. Rabies (serotype 1) is the type species of the Lyssavirus genus,[6] vesicular stomatitis virus that of the Vesiculovirus genus, and bovine ephemeral fever that of the Ephemerovirus genus. Rabies is enzootic, and sometimes epizootic, in

TABLE 160-1 Members of the Lyssavirus Genus

Virus	Serotype	Reservoir
Rabies	1	Found worldwide except for a few island nations, Australia, and Antarctica
Lagos bat	2	Probably enzootic in fruit bats; no reported human cases
Mokola	3	Probably an insectivore or rodent species limited to parts of Africa; a few domestic animal and two human cases reported
Duvenhage	4	Probably insectivorous bats; cases identified in South Africa, Zimbabwe, and Senegal
European bat Lyssavirus 1 (EBLV1)	5	European insectivorous bats (probably *Eptesicus serotinus*)
European bat Lyssavirus 2 (EBLV2)	6	European insectivorous bats (probably *Myotis dasycneme*)
Australian bat Lyssavirus	7	Flying foxes and insectivorous bats

Adapted from Rupprecht CE, Smith JS, Fekadu M, Childs JE. The ascension of wildlife rabies: A cause for public health concern or intervention? Emerging Infect Dis. 1995;1:107-114.

a variety of mammals. The six other members of the genus rarely cause human disease (Table 160-1), although the pathogenic potential of Australian bat lyssavirus remains to be determined.[9] New putative lyssaviruses are being found in bats throughout the world.[10]

Vesiculoviruses share many of the virologic characteristics of the lyssaviruses. They infect a large number of animal and insect species; humans are occasionally infected by contact with animals, typically via respiratory secretions.[11] Seven vesiculoviruses are known to occasionally infect humans.[12] Another negative-sense single-stranded RNA virus, borna, produces central nervous system (CNS) infection in birds and primates, and some authors have suggested that it is related to human psychiatric disorders. In contrast to the rhabdoviruses, however, it replicates in the nucleus rather than in the cytoplasm. It is not a rhabdovirus, and its taxonomy remains uncertain.

Composition

Lyssaviruses are bullet-shaped, with an average length of 180 nm and an average diameter of 75 nm.[13] The complete virus includes a helical nucleocapsid with 30 and 35 coils between 4.2 and 4.6 nm in length.[14] This is enclosed in a lipoprotein envelope 7.5 to 10 nm thick, from which glycoprotein (G protein) spikes project 10 nm.[15] These spikes cover the surface of the virus except at the blunt end (Fig. 160-1).

The rabies genome is a single, negatively stranded RNA molecule weighing 4.6×10^3 kDa,[16] encoding five genes: N, NS (or M_1), M (or M_2), G, and L (Table 160-2).[17] Phosphorylation of the N nucleoprotein is required for efficient transcription replication of the viral RNA,[18,19] and the N nucleoprotein is potentially immunogenic.[20] It is probably required to switch from the transcription of gene products to the production of a full-length positively stranded RNA.[21] The NS phosphoprotein (also called P in more recent studies) may control the L protein, an RNA-dependent RNA polymerase.[22,23] The M, or matrix, protein is located between the nucleocapsid and the lipoprotein envelope[24]; it, in concert with the G protein, is responsible for the assembly and budding of bullet-shaped particles.[25] This M protein determines the balance between transcription and replication,[26] and it affects RNA synthesis.[27]

The G protein is involved in cellular reception and it is the antigen that induces neutralizing antibodies. Variability in this protein is responsible for serotypic differences among lyssaviruses,[28] and mutations at position 333 (substituting glutamine or isoleucine for arginine) disrupt virulence.[29] This arginine residue appears to be essential for

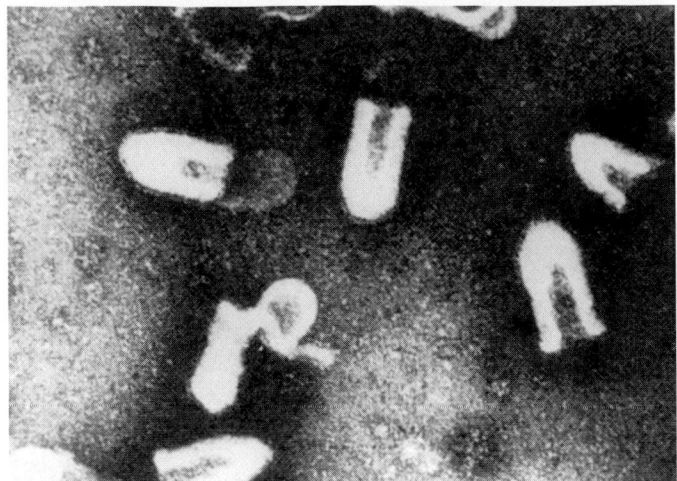

A

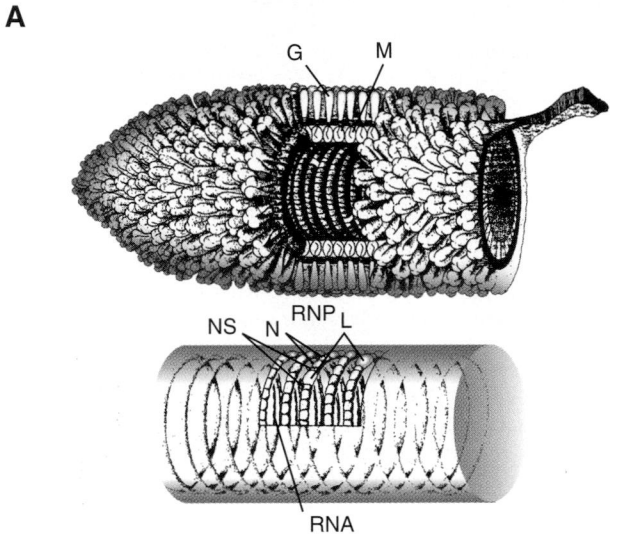

B

FIGURE 160-1. Rabies virus morphology. A, Electron micrograph of rabies virus. Original magnification, ×55,000. **B,** Schematic illustration of rabies virus *(top),* showing the surface glycoprotein (G) projections extending from the lipid envelope surrounding the RNP and the matrix protein (M) lining the envelope. The helical RNP *(bottom)* comprises the single-stranded RNA genome, plus the nucleoprotein (N), phosphoprotein (NS), and transcriptase (L). (From Dietzschold B, Rupprecht CE, Fu ZF, Koprowski H. Rhabdoviruses. In: Fields BN, Knipe DM, Howley PM, et al, eds. Fields Virology. 3rd ed. Philadelphia: Lippincott Raven; 1996:1137-1159.)

fusion of the viral envelope with neurons.[30] Molecular modifications of the G protein can increase its antigenicity.[31]

Replication Strategy

Neuronal attachment is probably mediated by more than one mechanism, including binding to a ganglioside,[32] and independently to the neural cell adhesion molecule (CD56).[33] In muscle, the virus binds to the nicotinic acetylcholine receptor.[34] Once bound to the receptor, the virus is probably internalized by receptor-mediated endocytosis. This forms a coated pit, which then fuses with a lysosome, from which the nucleocapsid escapes into the cytosol.[35] The viral envelope forms from host membranes into which the G and M proteins are inserted.[36] The envelope includes small amounts of host proteins.[23]

The virus does not tolerate a pH below 3 or above 11, and it is inactivated by ultraviolet light, sunlight, desiccation, formalin, phenol, ether, trypsin, β-propiolactone, and detergents.

TABLE 160-2 Rhabdoviral Genes and Products

Gene	Synonyms	Size (kDa)	Function
N (nucleocapsid)	—	50	—
NS (nonstructural)	M₁, P	40	Originally thought to encode a nonstructural protein but now known to produce a structural protein that is phosphorylated by kinases in the host cell and that joins with L
M (matrix)	M₂	26	Responsible for the assembly and budding of bullet-shaped particles, in concert with the G protein
G (glycoprotein)	—	65	Attachment to host cell receptors
L (large)	—	160-190	RNA-dependent RNA polymerase; required for transcription of the negatively stranded viral RNA; appears to form a complex with NS

Adapted from Rupprecht CE, Smith JS, Fekadu M, Childs JE. The ascension of wildlife rabies: A cause for public health concern or intervention? Emerging Infect Dis. 1995;1:107-114.

EPIDEMIOLOGY

Human Rabies

Rabies is currently distributed worldwide except for Antarctica and a few island nations. In 1999 (the last year for which global data are available), 99 nations reported the presence of rabies, and 42 reported its absence.[37] Worldwide, dogs account for 54% of animal rabies, terrestrial wildlife 42%, and bats 4%.

The epidemiology of human rabies reflects that of local animal rabies.[38] In developing areas where canine rabies remains common, most human cases result from dog bites. In regions where dogs are immunized, most human cases follow exposure to rabid wild animals.

The World Health Organization (WHO) estimates that 55,000 humans die of rabies annually. These probably represent an underestimate of the worldwide incidence of the disease, which may cause as many as 100,000 deaths annually.[6] An estimated 4 million persons receive PET annually, with the vast majority of persons being treated with types of vaccine that carry a risk of neurologic complications.[39] In the United States, one to four cases were reported annually in the past decade (Fig. 160-2). In countries of very low prevalence, an increasing percentage of cases are imported, occur after very long incubation periods, or lack a known source of exposure. In the United

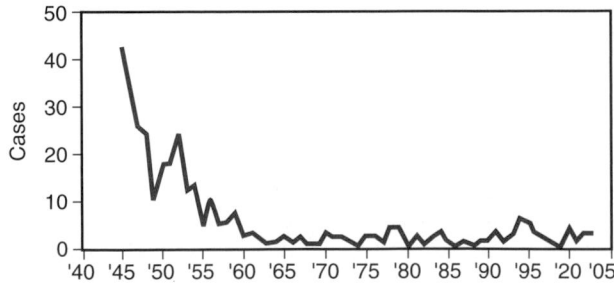

FIGURE 160-2. Reported cases of human rabies in the United States by year. *(From Centers for Disease Control and Prevention; data for 2002 and 2003 are provisional.)*

States, the sources of human cases have changed from predominantly domestic animals (1945 to 1965) to largely unknown sources (1976 to present). However, molecular biologic studies of these unknown cases indicate that most are of bat origin.

Animal Rabies

In the developing world, rabies is predominantly a problem of domestic and feral animals. The developed nations have largely eliminated rabies from domestic animals, leaving wild animals the major affected group. In the United States, the incidence of animal rabies has been increasing during the past two decades (Fig. 160-3). A resurgence of raccoon rabies in the United States began in 1977 near the Virginia–West Virginia border, and in the ensuing two decades the territory expanded to involve most of the eastern states. Over 20,000 cases of raccoon rabies have been reported, with several thousand secondary cases in dogs and other animals.[40] A single patient is known to have died from a raccoon strain of rabies; no history of animal exposure could be elicited from the patient's family or acquaintances.[41]

In New York State, the number of humans receiving PET increased from 84 in 1989 to more than 1000 in 1992.[42] The median cost per patient in Massachusetts was $2376 in 1995, with estimates of the total cost to the state as high as $6.4 million.[43]

Bats are increasingly the source of human rabies in the United States.[44] The epizoology of bat rabies is changing from typical reservoirs (e.g., the common big brown bat) to include previously rarely affected species (e.g., the silver-haired bat).[45] Fifteen of the 20 human rabies cases known to have been contracted from bats in the United States since 1980 involve the silver-haired/eastern pipistrelle bat rabies virus variant.[46] Molecular epidemiologic evidence reinforces the importance of avoiding contact with downed bats or other wildlife.[47,48] Rabies is also increasing among previously rarely affected species in other parts of the United States, such as coyotes.[49] In rare wild animal species (e.g., spotted hyenas), rabies infection may not lead to clinically apparent disease.[50] In at least one bat species (*Eptesicus serotinus*), salivary samples may contain viral RNA without detectable RNA in concurrent brain samples.[51] The implications of this finding for screening wild animals after potentially infectious human contact remain to be determined.

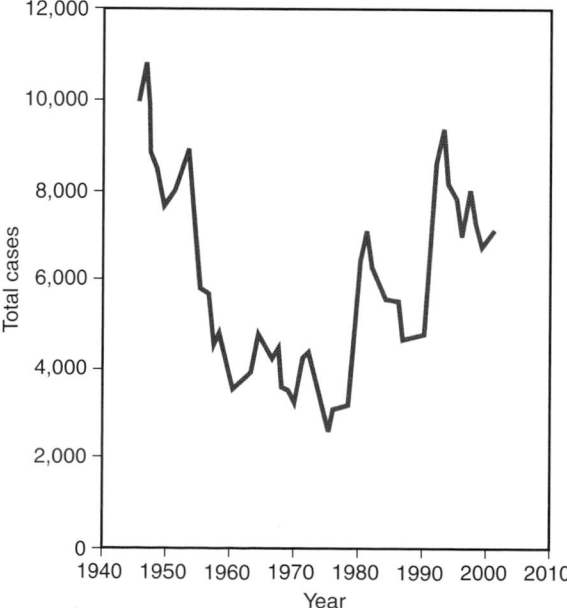

FIGURE 160-3. Reported cases of animal rabies in the United States by year. *(From Centers for Disease Control and Prevention.)*

PATHOGENESIS

Rabies infection begins with centripetal spread of the virus via peripheral nerves to the CNS, proliferation within the CNS, and centrifugal spread via peripheral nerves to many tissues.[27,52] After entering through a break in the skin, across a mucosal surface, or through the respiratory tract, virus replicates in muscle cells, and in so doing it infects the muscle spindle. It then infects the nerve that innervates the spindle and moves centrally within the axons of these neurons. Replication occurs in peripheral neurons, but not usually in glia, either peripheral or central. Virus is present in dorsal root ganglia within 60 to 72 hours of inoculation, and prior to its arrival in spinal cord neurons, confirming its transport within sensory neurons.

Some studies suggest that the neuromuscular junction is also a major site of neuronal invasion,[53] and blocking acetylcholine receptors inhibits viral attachment.[54] Partial sequence homology exists between rabies virus glycoprotein and several snake neurotoxins binding to this receptor.[55] However, rabies virus can enter neurons that do not express acetylcholine receptors, albeit with less efficiency, indicating the existence of other receptors.[56]

Natural rabies infection appears to require a period of local viral replication, perhaps to increase the inoculum, before nervous system infection occurs. Timely administration of antirabies immunoglobulin and active immunization can prevent spread of the virus into the nervous system, thereby preventing disease. Once the virus has entered peripheral nerves, current therapeutic techniques probably do not readily prevent subsequent replication and spread, and the virus quickly moves centrally. Rabies virus ascends via fast axonal transport, probably involving an interaction between the cytoplasmic dynein light chain with the rabies virus NS phosphoprotein.[57] Herpes simplex virus and tetanus toxin also make use of the microtubular transport systems.[58] After reaching the spinal cord, the virus spreads throughout the CNS, following established patterns of synaptic connectivity.[59] Virtually every neuron is infected.[35]

After CNS infection, virus spreads to the rest of the body via peripheral nerves. The high concentration of virus in saliva results from viral shedding from sensory nerve endings in the oral mucosa,[36] and it also reflects replication in the salivary glands.

The mechanisms by which rabies damages the CNS are obscure, as pathologic evidence of neuronal necrosis is frequently minimal or absent.[60] It may interfere with neurotransmission[61] and with endogenous opioid systems,[62] and the almost 30-fold increase in local nitric oxide production[63] suggests an excitotoxic mechanism. There is an inverse relationship between the concentration of G protein produced and the pathogenicity of different viral strains, and there is a monotonic relationship between pathogenicity and the induction of neuronal apoptosis.[64] The infection is also capable of inducing apoptosis in T lymphocytes,[65] which may relate to the failure of the immune response to control the disease.

Pathology

The brain in furious rabies (see later) usually appears unremarkable grossly,[66] except for the vascular congestion. The microscopic pathology of rabies is typically an encephalitis with Negri bodies (Fig. 160-4). However, not all autopsy specimens show the perivascular lymphocytic cuffing and necrosis that characterize encephalitis, and some cases look histologically like meningitis.[67] Negri bodies are concentrated in hippocampal pyramidal cells and less frequently in cortical neurons and cerebellar Purkinje cells.[66] They are round or oval, usually cosinophilic cytoplasmic inclusions between 1 and 7 μm across, and they contain viral nucleocapsids.[68] The acidophilic lyssa body is ultrastructurally identical to the Negri body.[69] Negri bodies and lyssa bodies are detected in only a relatively small percentage of the cells that are infected (as determined by immunohistochemistry).[70]

Paralytic rabies affects primarily the spinal cord, with severe inflammation and necrosis.[71] The brain stem is involved to a lesser extent. A few patients have cortical Negri bodies. Segmental demyelination

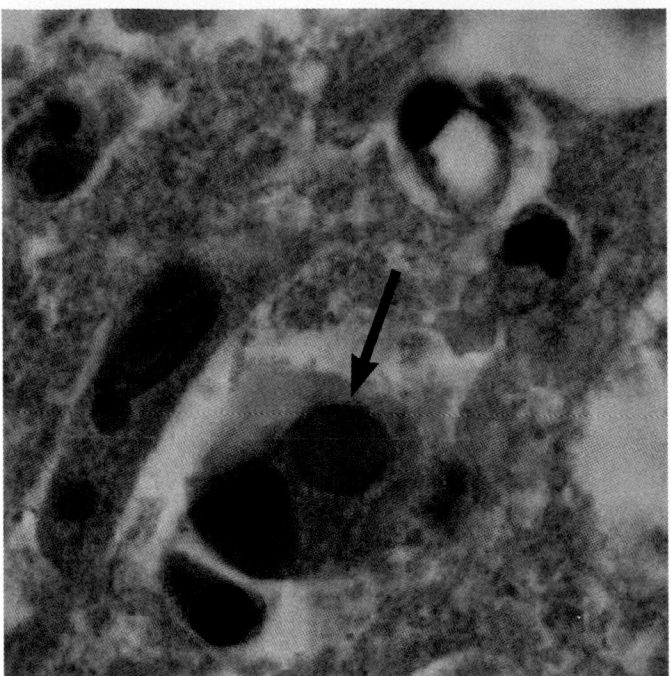

FIGURE 160-4. Negri body *(arrow)* (original magnification, ×400). *(Courtesy of Maria-Beatriz Lopes, M.D., Division of Neuropathology, University of Virginia.)*

occurs in the peripheral nerves, resembling acute inflammatory polyneuropathy (the Guillain-Barré syndrome).

Systemic pathology is most remarkable for the presence of myocarditis.[72] This cardiac disorder resembles the myocarditis that occurs in hypercatecholaminergic states such as pheochromocytoma, subarachnoid hemorrhage, and tetanus.[58] Negri bodies are found in the hearts of some patients, suggesting a direct viral role in this condition.[73] Atrial ganglioneuritis suggests that the virus reaches the myocardium via spread from the nervous system.[74]

Immune Responses

The immune response to natural rabies infection is insufficient to prevent disease. Rabies can produce immunosuppression,[75] and if unvaccinated patients develop a measurable antibody response, it occurs late in the course.[76] Patients developing a cellular immune response tend to have the encephalitic (furious) form rather than the paralytic form, and they die faster than those who do not mount such a response.[77] Differences in the host immune response appear more likely to explain whether furious or paralytic rabies develops than do differences in the strains of virus causing the natural infection.[78] Some investigators believe that interleukin-1 production in the CNS may explain the immunosuppressive effect of the virus.[79] One study suggests that the virus may persist in macrophages and emerge later to produce disease.[80] This may explain some cases with very long incubation periods, or there may be other tissue locations in which viral sequestration occurs.

CLINICAL MANIFESTATIONS

Human Rabies

Several variables affect the risk of rabies and the rate of clinical disease development after exposure to a rabid animal.[81] The viral inoculum is important, reflected by the relationship between the extent of exposure to the saliva and the rapidity of progression. A bite with prominent salivary contamination (e.g., through exposed skin) is more likely to produce rabies than a bite through thick clothing that removes saliva from the animal's teeth. Multiple bites are more likely to transmit the disease than a single bite. The location of the bite also influences the risk of rabies: bites on the face are more likely to result in disease than those on the extremities. Salivary contamination of a preexisting wound can transfer virus, as can exposure of mucous membranes or the respiratory tract to aerosolized virus.[82]

Transmission between humans has been documented only in corneal transplantation.[83] One recipient received standard PET plus interferon and did not develop rabies.[84] The reported incubation period for rabies varies from a few days to over 19 years, although 75% of patients become ill in the first 90 days after exposure.

The initial symptoms of rabies resemble those of other systemic viral infections, including fever, headache, malaise, and disorders of the upper respiratory and gastrointestinal tracts (Table 160-3).[85] Initial neurologic symptoms may include subtle changes in personality and cognition, and paresthesias or pain near the exposure site. Rabies is rarely considered early in the differential diagnosis. In one series, physicians considered rabies in only three of 21 patients on their first visit, despite an exposure history in many.[85] The prodrome typically lasts about 4 days, but up to 10 days may elapse before more specific symptoms and signs supervene.[86] Myoedema (mounding of part of the muscle struck with a reflex hammer, which then disappears in a few seconds) is present during the prodrome and persists throughout the disease.[87]

Human rabies infections are divided into two forms: furious (or encephalitic) and paralytic (or "dumb"). The furious form presents with the hydrophobia, delirium, and agitation that form the common picture of rabies. About a fifth of patients present with the paralytic form and have little clinical evidence of cerebral involvement until late in their course. The spinal cord and brain stem bear the brunt of the illness in the paralytic form. The pathogenetic distinction between the two types of rabies is unclear; it does not appear to be based on virologic or antigenic differences.[88] In either form, the symptomatic course usually runs 2 to 14 days before coma supervenes. Death occurs an average of 18 days after the onset of symptoms, but the range is broad.[85] Intensive support can prolong survival by about 50%.[89]

Some of the cases of human rabies reported in recent years have not fit into these classic forms of rabies. The diagnosis should be considered for any unexplained progressive encephalitis that ends in mortality.

Furious Rabies

Hydrophobia is the symptom most identified with furious rabies. Sir William Gowers[90] provides a seminal depiction of hydrophobia and its sequelae, in which he described

> *some discomfort about the throat, an occasional sense of choking, or a little difficulty in swallowing liquids. . . . The attempt to drink occasions some spasm in the pharynx, which increases in the course of a few hours, and spreads to the muscles of respiration, causing a short, quick inspiration, a "catch in the breath. . . ." This increases in severity to a strong inspiratory effort, in which the extraordinary muscles of respiration, sternomastoid, scaleni, etc., and even the facial muscles, take part; the shoulders are raised, and the angles of the mouth drawn outwards. As the intensity of the spasm increases, so does the readiness with which it is excited. It may be caused by the mere contact of water with the lips, and a state of cutaneous hyperæsthesia develops, so that various impressions, such as a draught of air, which normally excite a respiratory effort, bring on the spasm. The mere movement of air caused by raising the bedclothes may be sufficient. The patient is often unable to swallow the saliva, which is usually abundant and viscid, so that it hangs about the mouth and is expelled with difficulty. . . . Vomiting is common. . . . The attacks of spasm are very distressing to the patient; the mental state which they occasion increases the readiness with which they are produced; and in some cases the mere sight of water or the sound of dropping water will cause an attack. It may even be excited by visual impressions which cause a similar sensation, as*

TABLE 160-3   Durations of Different Stages of Rabies

Stage	Duration (% of Cases)	Associated Findings
Incubation period	Under 30 days (25%) 30-90 days (50%) 90 days to 1 yr (20%) More than 1 yr (5%)	None
Prodrome and early symptoms	2-10 days	Paresthesias or pain at the wound site; fever; malaise; anorexia; nausea and vomiting
Acute neurologic disease		
Furious rabies (80% of cases)	2-7 days	Hallucinations; bizarre behavior; anxiety; agitation; biting; hydrophobia; autonomic dysfunction; syndrome of inappropriate antidiuretic hormone (SIADH)
Paralytic rabies (20% of cases)	2-7 days	Ascending flaccid paralysis
Coma, death*	0-14 days	—

*Rare recoveries have been reported.

Data from Fishbein DB. Rabies in humans. In: Baer GM, ed. The Natural History of Rabies. 2nd ed. Boca Raton, Fla: CRC Press; 1991:519-549.

the reflection from a looking glass, or even a strong light. The sufferer's horror and dread of these excitants becomes intense. Thus the disturbance in the act of swallowing liquids, which constitutes . . . the first symptom and keynote of the disease, spreads, on the one hand, to mental disturbance, and on the other to extensive muscular spasm. In each of these directions further symptoms develop. The spasm, at first confined to the muscles of deglutition and respiration, spreads to the other muscles of the body, and the paroxysms, at first respiratory, afterwards become general, and assume a convulsive character, although still excited by the same causes. The convulsions may consist of general muscular rigidity, sometimes tetanoid in character, with actual opisthotonus. . . . Actual delusions occasionally supervene, and there may even be wild delirium. The mental derangement is most intense during the paroxysms of spasms, and the frenzied patient may spit his saliva at those about him, and often attempts to bite them with his teeth, making occasional strange sounds in his throat which have been thought to resemble the barking of a dog.

Hydrophobia represents an exaggerated irritant reflex of the respiratory tract, possibly arising from the nucleus ambiguus.[91] Other findings include episodic hyperactivity, seizures, and aerophobia. Hyperventilation is frequently present. Along with coma, evidence of pituitary dysfunction often develops, especially disordered water balance (either inappropriate antidiuresis or diabetes insipidus). Hyperventilation gives way to forms of periodic and ataxic respiration,[91] and eventually apnea supervenes. Cardiac arrhythmias are common, predominantly supraventricular tachycardias and bradycardias, reflecting either brain stem dysfunction or myocarditis.[92] Autonomic dysfunction is common, including pupillary dilation, anisocoria, piloerection, markedly increased salivation and sweating, and, rarely, priapism[93] or spontaneous ejaculation.[94]

With exceptions in some rare reports, patients entering coma generally die within 1 to 2 weeks despite maximal supportive care. Patients with furious rabies who receive maximal intensive care support and survive for a longer-than-expected period appear to pass through the paralytic phase before death.[89]

Paralytic (Dumb) Rabies

Patients with paralytic rabies, unlike those with the furious form, do not have hydrophobia, aerophobia, hyperactivity, and seizures. Their initial findings suggest an ascending paralysis, resembling acute inflammatory polyneuropathy (the Guillain-Barré syndrome), or a symmetric quadriparesis. Weakness may be more severe in the extremity where the virus was introduced. Meningeal signs (headache, neck stiffness) may be prominent despite a normal sensorium. As the disease progresses, the patient becomes confused and then declines into coma.

Non-neurologic Findings

In addition to the cardiac arrhythmias already mentioned, the systemic complications of rabies are similar to those of other critically ill patients. The virus disseminates to many organs,[95,96] but proof of its role in other organ dysfunction is lacking. Hypotension is usually caused by volume depletion but may reflect brain stem involvement. Gastrointestinal disturbances include bleeding, vomiting, diarrhea, and ileus.[97] Death is usually due to myocarditis, with cardiac arrhythmia or congestive heart failure as mechanisms.[98]

Animal Rabies

A complete description of the effects of rabies on behavior in all of the species that can be infected is beyond the scope of this text. WHO studies have established a crude ranking of rabies susceptibility, which is summarized in Table 160-4.[99] Descriptions of the behavioral changes of rabid animals are available elsewhere.[100,101]

DIAGNOSIS

The diagnosis of rabies poses little difficulty in a nonimmunized patient presenting with hydrophobia after a bite by a known rabid animal. The presentation in areas where domestic animals are immunized is seldom this straightforward. During the incubation period, no diagnostic studies in the patient are useful; recognition of an exposure to a potentially rabid animal should prompt prophylactic treatment. When symptoms begin, standard laboratory testing does not reliably distinguish rabies from other encephalitides. The cerebrospinal fluid (CSF) is abnormal in a minority, with a lymphocytic pleocytosis (5 to 30 cells/μL), normal glucose, and modest protein elevation (less than 100 mg/dL).[83]

TABLE 160-4   Susceptibility of Various Animal Species to Rabies

Very High	High	Moderate	Low
Wolves	Hamsters	Dogs	Opossums
Foxes	Skunks	Primates	
Coyotes	Raccoons		
Kangaroo rats	Domestic cats		
Cotton rats	Rabbits		
Jackals	Bats		
Voles	Cattle		

Data from World Health Organization. Sixth Report of the Expert Committee on Rabies: Technical Report Series 523. Geneva: World Health Organization; 1973.

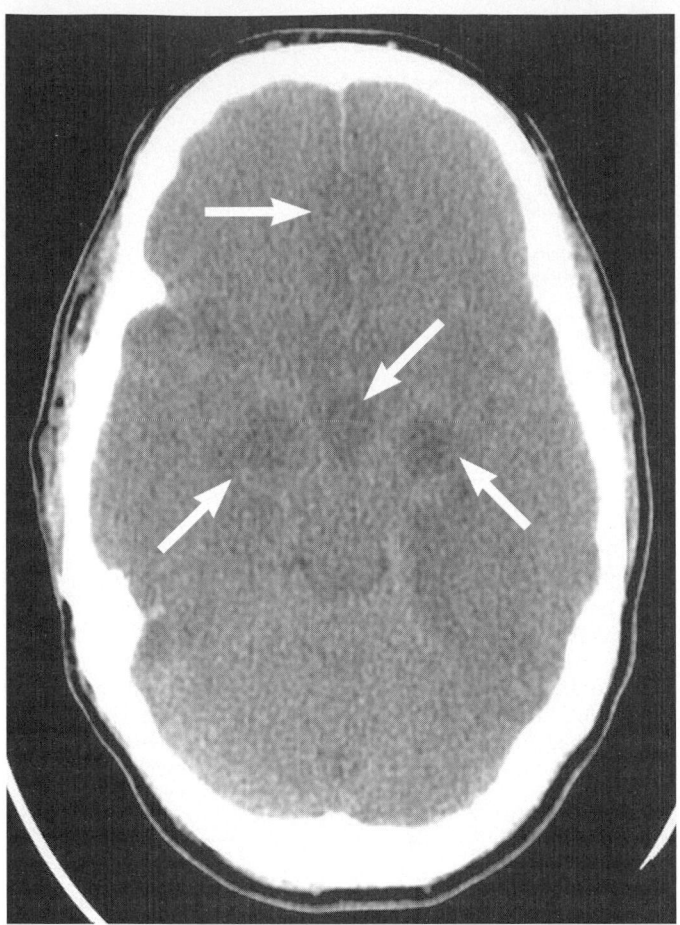

FIGURE 160-5. Noncontrast computed tomographic scan showing areas of both severe cerebral edema *(arrows)* and more widespread swelling.

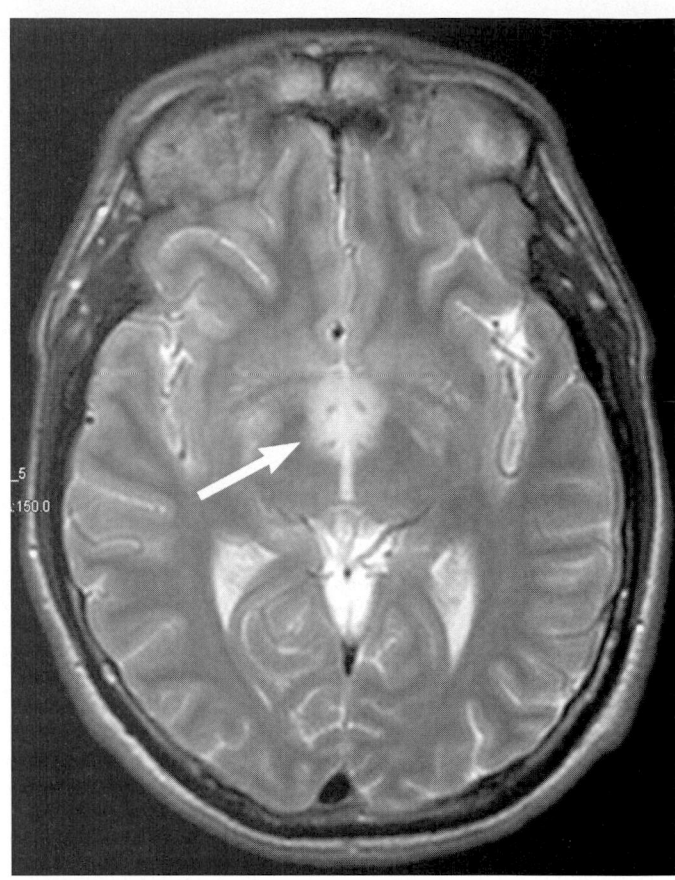

FIGURE 160-6. T$_2$-weighted MR image showing increased signal in the diencephalon *(arrow)*.

Computed tomography of the brain is usually normal early in the course,[102] unless hypoxia has supervened. Later, evidence of cerebral swelling may supervene if the patient receives prolonged critical care support (Fig. 160-5). Magnetic resonance (MR) images show areas of increased T$_2$ signal in the hippocampi, hypothalamus, brain stem, and sometimes other areas.[103] Figure 160-6 shows a T$_2$ image, highlighting involvement of the thalamus and hypothalamus. Late in the course, gadolinium enhancement may occur in the most profoundly involved areas, indicating breakdown of the blood-brain barrier. In paralytic rabies, MR imaging of the spinal cord and nerve roots may be useful.[104]

Direct fluorescent antibody (DFA) staining of biopsy or necropsy (animal or human) tissue remains the standard for the diagnosis of rabies. In humans, the procedure of choice is DFA analysis of a skin biopsy obtained from the nape of the neck, above the hairline.[105] The virus tends to localize in hair follicles. During the first week of symptoms, about 50% of samples reveal rabies virus, with an increasing percentage thereafter.[106] The reverse transcriptase–polymerase chain reaction (RT-PCR) is another diagnostic procedure of choice in suspected human rabies.[107] This test can be performed on CSF or saliva of patients, or on tissue. RT-PCR allows more specific determination of the geographic and host species origin of a particular rabies virus.[108,109] It can be successfully performed on decomposed brain material,[110] whereas older techniques failed with that material.[111] The older corneal impression test[112] is no longer in common use. Current recommendations for diagnostic testing in humans, with instructions for sample collection and submission, are available at http://www.cdc.gov/ncidod/dvrd/rabies/Diagnosis/diagnosi.htm and at http://www.cdc.gov/ncidod/dvrd/rabies/professional/Prof.forms/antem.htm, or by calling the rabies laboratory of the Centers for Disease Control and Prevention (CDC) at 404-639-1050. Diagnostic recommendations for suspected rapid animals are available at http://www.cdc.gov/ncidod/dvrd/rabies/Professional/publications/DFA_diagnosis/DFA_protocol-b.htm. In the United States, the state health department should be consulted whenever the diagnosis of rabies is suspected.

The rapid fluorescent focus inhibition test (RFFIT) is a serologic test for neutralizing antirabies antibody.[113] A few untreated patients have detectable antibody by day 6 of clinical illness, 50% by day 8, and usually 100% by day 15. Any CSF levels are diagnostically valuable, even in patients who have received PET. CSF may also be examined for the presence of specific oligoclonal bands not found in the serum as a method of confirming CNS infection.[114]

Differential Diagnosis

When considering furious rabies, the major differential consideration is another viral encephalitis. In the absence of exposure to a rabid animal, and if hydrophobia and hyperactivity are not prominent, it may be difficult to distinguish between the possibilities.[115] Because the CSF and electroencephalographic (EEG) findings in rabies may mimic those of herpes simplex encephalitis, some patients receive empiric therapy with acyclovir while awaiting a more secure diagnosis (e.g., by PCR). Tetanus is occasionally confused with rabies, because opisthotonic posturing may be seen in either.[58] However, the other symptoms of rabies, such as hydrophobia, are not seen in tetanus, and the CSF and EEG are normal in tetanus. Strychnine poisoning should be considered and can be excluded by laboratory testing.

Paralytic rabies may resemble acute inflammatory polyneuropathy, transverse myelitis, or poliomyelitis. Electromyographic studies may be useful in distinguishing rabies from polyneuropathy. In transverse myelitis, pain at the level of the lesion may be helpful, as may be the finding of a high T_2 signal lesion. A sensory level is characteristic of transverse myelitis, whereas in rabies, sensory function is typically normal.[93] Fever usually precedes weakness in poliomyelitis, and the resolution of fever with the onset of neurologic findings favors this diagnosis. A history of poliomyelitis immunization should be sought.

The sometimes prolonged incubation period of rabies recalls the slow infections of the CNS caused by conventional viruses (e.g., progressive multifocal leukoencephalopathy).[116] However, rabies requires neither a defect in host immunity nor a mutation in the virus to produce disease, distinguishing it from the agents in this group. Spongiform changes in brain tissue in rabies[117] may resemble those seen in the prion diseases.[118]

Although CNS reactions to the rabies vaccines available in developed countries are exceptionally rare, patients receiving older vaccine forms containing myelin determinants occasionally develop acute disseminated encephalomyelitis (ADEM; also called postvaccinial encephalomyelitis; see Prevention, later). ADEM is a syndrome with many precipitants other than rabies vaccine. It resembles encephalitis, or occasionally it presents as a mass lesion resembling a brain abscess. It typically begins 10 to 14 days after vaccine exposure, which would constitute an unusually brief incubation period for rabies. In the absence of viral isolation, a high RFFIT titer in spinal fluid is evidence for rabies rather than ADEM even in patients who have been immunized,[119] as is a positive RT-PCR. ADEM produces high-T_2 lesions visible by MR imaging.[120] However, differences in the distribution of the MR lesions in rabies and ADEM may aid in the differential diagnosis.[121]

Patients potentially exposed to rabies may develop a psychological reaction termed rabies hysteria.[122] They may refuse to attempt to drink water; in contrast, the patient with rabies attempts, at least initially, to drink but is halted by pharyngeal spasms.

PREVENTION

Preexposure Prophylaxis

Although control of animal rabies is central to prevention of human disease, few nations have eliminated it, and those that have been successful usually maintain quarantine procedures lest the disease reappear. Therefore, prophylactic procedures (for domestic animals and selected humans) and PET for humans remain essential. Prophylaxis for cats and dogs in many countries is required by law; in the United States, the use of 1- or 3-year vaccines is permitted, although only the 3-year vaccines are recommended.[123] Vaccination should be performed or supervised by a veterinarian; improper administration can lead to lack of immunity.[124] Measurement of animal seroconversion rates may be considered to ensure protection,[125] and immunization of livestock is recommended in areas of increasing rabies prevalence.

Vaccination of wild animals is an effective public health measure.[126] The use of vaccines effective after ingestion allows immunization of wild animals.[127] An intensive 4-year campaign in Belgium nearly eliminated rabies from the fox population.[128] This approach may also be effective in dogs.[129] Veterinary vaccines cost about $0.50 per dose in the United States. In contrast, Semple-type (grown in sheep brain cultures) human vaccines cost about $5 per course, Vero cell vaccine in France about $160 per course, and human diploid cell rabies vaccine (HDCV) in the United States more than $500 per course.[130]

Preexposure prophylaxis is confined to people with a relatively high risk of rabies exposure, such as veterinarians, laboratory workers using

rabies virus, spelunkers, and people planning to visit countries of high dog rabies prevalence where access to appropriate medical care is limited. Current recommendations for international travelers are available at the CDC website (http://www.cdc.gov/epo/mmwr/mmwr_rr.html). A series of three intramuscular or intradermal injections (days 0, 7, and 21 or 28) is sufficient; antibody response determination is not required in normal hosts. Booster doses every 2 to 3 years are usually recommended for individuals frequently at risk of exposure. An adequate antibody response is generally considered to be complete neutralization at the 1:5 level by RFFIT, which is equivalent to the 0.5 IU/mL concentration suggested by the WHO.

Postexposure Treatment

The cornerstone of rabies prevention is wound care, potentially reducing the risk of rabies by 90%.[131] Thorough washing with a 20% soap solution is as effective as the formerly recommended quaternary ammonium compounds.[132] Irrigation with a virucidal agent such as povidone-iodine is advisable.[133] After wound care, the clinician must decide whether to institute passive and active immunization. Prompt consultation with public health officials is advised, as this decision is based on the current incidence of rabies in the animal species involved in the exposure.[134] The most recent report of the Immunization Practices Advisory Committee is also an important source of information.[135] The CDC manages a 24-hour telephone system with rabies information (404-332-4555).

A healthy dog or cat in countries of low prevalence that has bitten, or otherwise transferred saliva to, a human is observed for 10 days. If the animal's behavior remains normal, the patient need not receive PET beyond proper wound care. If the animal's behavior changes, it should undergo immediate pathologic examination for evidence of rabies infection. If infection is confirmed, there is adequate time to institute PET. Wild mammal exposure, especially if the animal exhibits uncharacteristic behavior, warrants PET in most circumstances. If the animal is available for pathologic examination, and if pathologic examination of the brain does not indicate the presence of rabies virus, PET may be discontinued (Fig. 160-7). PET appears to be safe in pregnant women and should not be withheld when an indication exists.[136]

Rabies immune globulin is available in human (HRIG) and equine forms (pooled antiserum of equine origin [ARS] and purified antirabies serum of equine origin [ERIG]). These immunoglobulins are purified from the sera of hyperimmunized donors. Two HRIG preparations are available in the United States: Imogam Rabies-HT (Pasteur Merieux) and BayRab (Bayer). HRIG is given in a dose of 20 IU/kg. Previous recommendations called for half of the dose to be injected in the vicinity of the wound (see earlier) and the remainder to be injected intramuscularly in the gluteal region. However, the most recent WHO and CDC recommendations call for the entire dose to be infiltrated into the wound if anatomically feasible.[135,137] The recommended dose of ERIG is 40 IU/kg. Failure to infiltrate wounds with rabies immune globulin, or surgical closure of wounds prior to immune globulin infiltration, has been associated with the development of rabies in patients despite otherwise proper PET.[138]

Many different forms of rabies vaccine have been produced since Pasteur's original success in 1882. In some developing nations, Semple-type vaccine is still employed, but it carries a risk of central and peripheral neurologic complications in the range of 1 per 200 to 1600 vaccinees.[86] Production of vaccine in sheep CNS, a common method of Semple-type vaccine production, also carries the theoretic risk of transmitting the scrapie prion.[139] Suckling mouse brain vaccine is effective and safer, with a neurologic complication rate of approximately 1:8000.

The currently available vaccines for human use in the United States include HDCV (Imovax Rabies), vaccine grown in rhesus monkey diploid cell cultures (rabies vaccine, adsorbed [RVA]), and purified chick embryo cell vaccine (PCEC; RabAvert). These vaccines are remarkably safe and immunogenic. Local reactions (pain, swelling, or induration) are common, but systemic complaints

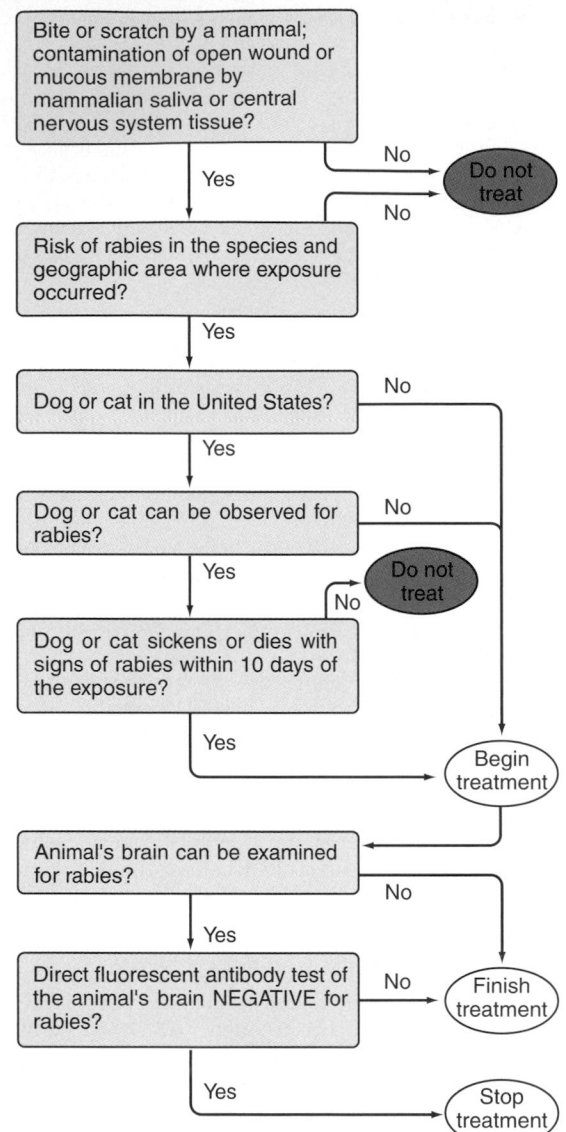

FIGURE 160-7. Algorithm for human rabies postexposure prophylaxis. In highly suspect animals, treatment should be started immediately and discontinued if fluorescent antibody test results of the animal brain are negative. In some cases when the risk is low, treatment may be delayed for up to 48 hours pending the result of fluorescent antibody testing. *(From Fishbein DB, Bernard KW. Rabies virus. In: Mandell GL, Bennett JL, Dolin R, eds. Principles and Practice of Infectious Disease. 4th ed. New York: Churchill Livingstone; 1995:1527.)*

(fever, headache, malaise, nausea, abdominal pain, or adenopathy) occur in only a minority of patients. Serious reactions have been exceedingly rare, with the Guillain-Barré syndrome reported very rarely.[140] To report a vaccine reaction, call the appropriate number (for HDCV, Aventis Pasteur at 800-VACCINE; for PCEC, Chiron Corporation at 800-244-7668). RVA is licensed to the BioPort Corporation, but is not being produced at this time. Corticosteroids should be given only to patients experiencing a life-threatening vaccine reaction, because they interfere with the development of immunity. Immunocompromised patients may not respond adequately to vaccination, and antibody titers should be measured 2 to 4 weeks after immunization.[135]

In other countries, other PET vaccines (e.g., vaccines grown in chick embryos or Vero cell cultures)[141] and regimens are often employed. Consultation with the rabies officer of the state health department may be helpful for the management of patients in whom PET has been initiated with a vaccine not approved for use in the United States.

The usual dose of HDCV or RVA for postexposure prophylaxis is 1.0 mL intramuscularly (IM) on the day of exposure (or as soon as possible thereafter), repeated on days 3, 7, 14, and 28. Other schedules are available for use; physicians not familiar with their use should consult local public health authorities and review the most recent WHO and CDC recommendations.[135,137] The varying immunogenicity of different regimens, and their interaction with the response to immunoglobulin,[142] raises the possibility of treatment failure if the recommendations are not carefully followed. If possible, the vaccine should be administered in the deltoid muscle. Gluteal injections, which may miss the muscle, have been associated with some vaccine failures. In small children, it may be given in the lateral thigh. The vaccine must not be given in the same region as the immunoglobulin. Intradermal vaccine administration (0.1 mL) was previously recommended for preexposure prophylaxis only, but in 1996 the WHO recommended it as an alternative for PET. Patients who have been previously vaccinated receive 1.0 mL IM on days 0 and 3 only, without rabies immune globulin.

A single case of a transient false-positive enzyme-linked immunosorbent assay (ELISA) for human immunodeficiency virus (HIV) after HDCV immunization was reported in 1994.[143] Subsequent screening of samples from people recently immunized against rabies revealed no similar cases,[144,145] but in view of similar phenomena with other vaccines, physicians should be aware of this possibility.

Personnel caring for patients with rabies should practice standard universal and respiratory precautions. In addition, when performing routine care duties without exposure to potentially contaminated materials, they should receive a preexposure immunization sequence and maintain a serum antirabies antibody titer of 0.5 IU/mL.[146] Exposures to potentially contaminated secretions or tissues should lead to standard PET.

TREATMENT

There is no established, specific treatment for rabies once symptoms have begun. Despite excellent intensive care, almost all patients succumb to the disease or its complications within a few weeks of onset. The three patients in the 1970s who survived, two of whom made apparently complete recoveries,[147-149] represent very unusual occurrences. Each of these patients had undergone some form of PET, and it seems likely that this treatment modified their course. Another case with partial recovery was reported in 1994 in a child who received rabies vaccine without immunoglobulin.[114] Trials of many agents have been undertaken in clinical rabies, including interferons, interferon-inducing agents, ribavirin, and cytosine arabinoside, without beneficial effects.[146] A review of issues regarding possible treatment is available.[150]

REFERENCES

1. Meslin F-X, Fishbein DB, Matter HC. Rationale and prospects for rabies elimination in developing countries. In: Rupprecht CE, Dietzschold B, Koprowski H, eds. Lyssaviruses. Berlin: Springer-Verlag; 1994:1-26.
2. Baer GM. Rabies: An historical perspective. Infect Agents Dis. 1994;3:168-180.
3. Fleming G. Rabies and hydrophobia. London: Chapman and Hall; 1872:7.
4. Blancou J, Aubert MFA, Artois M. Fox rabies. In: Baer GM, ed. The Natural History of Rabies. 2nd ed. Boca Raton, Fla: CRC Press; 1991:257-290.
5. Baer GM. Vampire bat and bovine paralytic rabies. In: Baer GM, ed. The Natural History of Rabies. 2nd ed. Boca Raton, Fla: CRC Press; 1991:389-403.
6. Rupprecht CE, Smith JS, Fekadu M, Childs JE. The ascension of wildlife rabies: A cause for public health concern or intervention? Emerging Infect Dis. 1995;1:107-114.
7. Negri A. Zur Aetiologie der Tollwuth. Die Diagnose der Tollwuth auf Grund der neuen Befunde. Z Hyg Infectionskr. 1903;44:519-540.
8. Goldwasser RA, Kissling RE. Fluorescent antibody staining of street and fixed rabies virus antigens. Proc Soc Exp Biol Med. 1958;98:219-223.

9. Guyatt KJ, Twin J, Davis P, et al. A molecular epidemiological study of Australian bat Lyssavirus. J Gen Virol. 2003;84:485-496.
10. Botvinkin AD, Poleschuk EM, Kuzmin IV, et al. Novel lyssaviruses isolated from bats in Russia. Emerg Infect Dis. 2003;9:1623-1625.
11. Reif JS, Webb PA, Monath TP, et al. Epizootic vesicular stomatitis in Colorado, 1982: Infection in occupational risk groups. Am J Trop Med Hyg. 1987;36:17-82.
12. Stoeckle MY. Rhabdoviridae. In: Mandell GM, Bennett JE, Dolin R, eds. Principles and Practice of Infectious Diseases. New York: Churchill Livingstone; 1994: 1526-1527.
13. Wunner WH. The chemical composition and molecular structure of rabies viruses. In: Baer GM, ed. The Natural History of Rabies. 2nd ed. Boca Raton, Fla: CRC Press; 1991:31-67.
14. Sokol F, Schlumberger HD, Wiktor TK, et al. Biochemical and biophysical studies on the nucleocapsid and on the RNA of rabies virus. Virology. 1969;38:651-665.
15. Dietzschold B, Rupprecht CE, Fu ZF, Koprowski H. Rhabdoviruses. In: Fields BN, Knipe DM, Howley PM, et al (eds). Fields Virology. 3rd ed. Philadelphia: Lippincott Raven; 1996:1137-1159.
16. Tordo N, Poch O, Ermine A, et al. Walking along the rabies genome: Is the large G-L intergenic region a remnant gene? Proc Natl Acad Sci U S A. 1986;83:3914-3918.
17. Bleck TP, Rupprecht CE. Rhabdoviruses. In: Richman DD, Whitley RJ, Hayden FG, eds. Clinical Virology. 2nd ed. Washington, DC: ASM Press; 2002:857-873.
18. Yang J, Koprowski H, Dietzschold B, Fang Fu Z. Phosphorylation of rabies virus nucleoprotein regulates viral RNA transcription and replication by modulating leader RNA encapsidation. J Virol. 1999;73:1661-1664.
19. Wu X, Gong X, Foley HD, et al. Both viral transcription and replication are reduced when the rabies virus nucleoprotein is not phosphorylated. J Virol. 2002;76: 4153-4161.
20. Goto H, Minimoto N, Ito H, et al. Expression of the nucleoprotein of rabies virus in *Escherichia coli* and mapping of antigenic sites. Arch Virol. 1995;140:1061-1074.
21. Blumberg BM, Giorgi C, Kolakofsky D. N protein of vesicular stomatitis virus selectively encapsidates leader RNA in vitro. Cell. 1983;32:559-567.
22. Tordo N, Poch O, Ermine A, et al. Completion of the rabies virus genome sequence determination: Highly conserved domains among the L (polymerase) proteins of unsegmented negative-strand RNA viruses. Virology. 1988;165:565-576.
23. Levy JA, Fraenkel-Conrat H, Owens RA. Virology. Englewood Cliffs, NJ: Prentice Hall; 1994:77-85.
24. Coll JM. The glycoprotein G of rhabdoviruses. Arch Virol. 1995;140:827-851.
25. Mebatsion T, Weiland F, Conzelmann KK. Matrix protein of rabies virus is responsible for the assembly and budding of bullet-shaped particles and interacts with the transmembrane spike glycoprotein G. J Virol. 1999;73:242-250.
26. Finke S, Mueller-Waldeck R, Conzelmann KK. Rabies virus matrix protein regulates the balance of virus transcription and replication. J Gen Virol. 2003;84:1613-1621.
27. Finke S, Conzelmann KK. Dissociation of rabies virus matrix protein functions in regulation of viral RNA synthesis and virus assembly. J Virol. 2003;77:12074-12082.
28. Rupprecht CE, Dietzschold B, Wunner WH, Koprowski H. Antigenic relationships of lyssaviruses. In: Baer GM, ed. The Natural History of Rabies. 2nd ed. Boca Raton, Fla: CRC Press; 1991:69-100.
29. Seif I, Coulon P, Rollin PE, Flamand A. Rabies virulence: Effect on pathogenicity and sequence characterization of rabies virus mutations affecting antigenic site III of the glycoprotein. J Virol. 1985;53:926-934.
30. Morimoto K, Ni Y-J, Kawai A. Syncytium formation is induced in the murine neuroblastoma cell cultures which produce pathogenic G proteins of the rabies virus. Virology. 1992;189:203-216.
31. Otvos A, Krivulka GR, Urge L, et al. Comparison of the effects of amino acid substitutions and the β-N- vs. α-O-glycosylation on the T-cell stimulatory activity and conformation of an epitope on the rabies virus glycoprotein. Biochim Biophys Acta. 1995;1267:55-64.
32. Kawai A, Morimoto K. Functional aspects of lyssavirus proteins. In: Rupprecht CE, Dietzschold B, Koprowski H, eds. Lyssaviruses. Berlin: Springer-Verlag; 1994:27-42.
33. Thoulouze MI, Lafage M, Schachner M, et al. The neural cell adhesion molecule is a receptor for rabies virus. J Virol. 1998;72:7181-7190.
34. Burrage TG, Tignor GH, Smith AL. Rabies virus binding at neuromuscular junctions. Virus Res. 1985;2:273-289.
35. Gosztonyi G. Reproduction of lyssaviruses: Ultrastructural composition of lyssaviruses and functional aspects of pathogenesis. In: Rupprecht CE, Dietzschold B, Koprowski H, eds. Lyssaviruses. Berlin: Springer-Verlag; 1994:43-68.
36. Murphy FA, Bauer SP, Harrison AK, Winn WC. Comparative pathogenesis of rabies and rabies-like viruses: Infection of the central nervous system and centrifugal spread to peripheral tissues. Lab Invest. 1973;29:1-16.
37. World Health Organization. World Survey of Rabies N° 35 for the year 1999. Geneva: World Health Organization, 2002. Available at http://www.who.int/emc-documents/rabies/whocdscsreph200210.html#english%20contents.
38. Turner GS. A review of the world epidemiology of rabies. Trans R Soc Trop Med Hyg. 1976;70:175-178.
39. Meslin F-X, Fishbein DB, Matter HC. Rationale and prospects for rabies elimination in developing countries. In: Rupprecht CE, Dietzschold B, Koprowski H, eds. Lyssaviruses. Berlin: Springer-Verlag; 1994:1-26.
40. Rupprecht CE, Smith JS. Raccoon rabies: The re-emergence of an epizootic in a densely populated area. Semin Virol. 1994;5:155-164.
41. Centers for Disease Control and Prevention. First human death associated with raccoon rabies: Virginia, 2003. MMWR Morb Mortal Wkly Rep. 2003;52:1102-1103.
42. Centers for Disease Control. Extension of the raccoon rabies epizootic: United States, 1992. MMWR Morb Mortal Wkly Rep. 1992;41:661-664.
43. Kreindel SM, McGuill M, Meltzer M, et al. The cost of rabies postexposure prophylaxis: One state's experience. Public Health Rep. 1998;113:247-251.
44. Krebs JW, Strine TW, Smith JS, et al. Rabies surveillance in the United States during 1994. J Am Vet Med Assoc. 1995;297:1562-1575.
45. Childs JE, Trimarchi CV, Krebs JW. The epidemiology of bat rabies in New York State, 1988-92. Epidemiol Infect. 1994;113:501-511.
46. Centers for Disease Control and Prevention. Human rabies: Connecticut, 1995. MMWR Morb Mortal Wkly Rep. 1996;45:207-209.
47. Centers for Disease Control and Prevention. Human rabies: Alabama, Tennessee, and Texas, 1994. MMWR Morb Mortal Wkly Rep. 1995;44:269-272.
48. Schmida TO. Resurgence of rabies. Arch Pediatr Adolesc Med. 1995;149:1043.
49. Clark KA, Neill SU, Smith JS, et al. Epizootic canine rabies transmitted by coyotes in south Texas. J Am Vet Med Assoc. 1994;204:536-540.
50. East ML, Hofer H, Cox JH, et al. Regular exposure to rabies virus and lack of symptomatic disease in Serengeti spotted hyenas. Proc Natl Acad Sci U S A. 2001; 98:15026-15031.
51. Echevarria JE, Avellon A, Juste J, et al. Screening of active lyssavirus infection in wild bat populations by viral RNA detection on oropharyngeal swabs. J Clin Microbiol. 2001;39:3678-3683.
52. Murphy FA, Bauer SP, Harrison AK, Winn WC. Comparative pathogenesis of rabies and rabies-like viruses: Virus spread and transit from inoculation site to the central nervous system. Lab Invest. 1973;28:361-376.
53. Watson HD, Tignor GH, Smith AL. Entry of rabies virus into the peripheral nerves of mice. J Gen Virol. 1981;56:371-382.
54. Lentz TL, Burrage TG, Smith AL, et al. Is the acetylcholine receptor a rabies virus receptor? Science. 1982;215:182-184.
55. Lentz TL, Wilson PT, Hawrot E, Speicher DW. Amino acid sequence similarity between rabies virus glycoprotein and snake venom curaremimetic neurotoxins. Science. 1984;226:847-848.
56. Kelly RM, Strick PL. Rabies as a transneuronal tracer of circuits in the central nervous system. J Neurosci Methods. 2000;103:63-71.
57. Raux H, Flamand A, Blondel D. Interaction of the rabies virus P protein with the LC8 dynein light chain. J Virol. 2000;74:10212-10216.
58. Bleck TP, Brauner JS. Tetanus. In: Scheld WM, Whitley RJ, Marra CM, eds. Infections of the Central Nervous System. 3rd ed. New York: Lippincott Williams & Wilkins; 2004:625-648.
59. Ugolini G. Specificity of rabies virus as a transneuronal tracer of motor networks: Transfer from hypoglossal motoneurons to connected second-order and higher order central nervous system cell groups. J Comp Neurol. 1995;356:457-480.
60. Jackson AC. Rabies virus infection: An update. J Neurovirol. 2003;9:253-258.
61. Charlton KM. The pathogenesis of rabies and other lyssaviral infections: Recent studies. In: Rupprecht CE, Dietzschold B, Koprowski H, eds. Lyssaviruses. Berlin: Springer-Verlag; 1994:95-119.
62. Koschel K, Munzel P. Inhibition of opiate receptor-mediated signal transmission by rabies virus in persistently infected NG-108-15 mouse neuroblastoma: Rat glioma hybrid cells. Proc Natl Acad Sci U S A. 1984;81:950-954.
63. Hooper DC, Ohnishi ST, Kean R, et al. Local nitric oxide production in viral and autoimmune diseases of the central nervous system. Proc Natl Acad Sci U S A. 1995;92:5312-5316.
64. Morimoto K, Hooper DC, Spitsin S, et al. Pathogenicity of different rabies virus variants inversely correlates with apoptosis and rabies virus glycoprotein expression in infected primary neuron cultures. J Virol. 1999;73:510-518.
65. Baloul L, Lafon M. Apoptosis and rabies virus neuroinvasion. Biochimie. 2003;85:777-788.
66. Esiri MM, Kennedy PGE. Virus diseases. In: Adams JH, Duchen LW, eds. Greenfield's Neuropathology. New York: Oxford University Press; 1992:335-399.
67. Dupont JR, Earle KM. Human rabies encephalitis: A study of forty-nine fatal cases with a review of the literature. Neurology. 1965;15:1023-1034.
68. De Brito T, Araujo MD, Tiriba A. Ultrastructure of the Negri body in human rabies. J Neurol Sci. 1973;20:363-372.
69. Sung JH, Hayano M, Mastri AR, Okagaki T. A case of human rabies and ultrastructure of the Negri body. J Neuropath Exp Neurol. 1976;35:541-559.
70. Jackson AC, Ye H, Ridaura-Sanz C, Lopez-Corella E. Quantitative study of the infection in brain neurons in human rabies. J Med Virol. 2001;65:614-618.
71. Chopra JS, Banerjee AK, Murthy JMK, Pal SR. Paralytic rabies: A clinicopathologic study. Brain. 1980;103:789-802.
72. Cohen SL, Gardner S, Lanyi C, et al. A case of rabies in man: Some problems of diagnosis and management. Br Med J. 1976;1:1041-1042.
73. Fishbein DB. Rabies in humans. In: Baer GM, ed. The Natural History of Rabies. 2nd ed. Boca Raton, Fla: CRC Press; 1991:519-549.
74. Metze K, Feiden W. Rabies virus ribonucleoprotein in the heart. N Engl J Med. 1991;324:1814-1815.
75. Wiktor TJ, Doherty PC, Koprowski H. Suppression of cell mediated immunity by street rabies virus. J Exp Med. 1977;145:1617-1622.
76. Kasempimolporn S, Hemachudha T, Khawplod P, Manatsathit S. Human immune response to rabies nucleocapsid and glycoprotein antigens. Clin Exp Immunol. 1991;84:195-199.
77. Hemachudha T, Phanuphak P, Sriwanthana B. Immunologic study of human encephalitic and paralytic rabies: A preliminary study of 16 patients. Am J Med. 1988;84:673-677.
78. Hemachudha T, Wacharapluesadee S, Lumlertdaecha B, et al. Sequence analysis of rabies virus in humans exhibiting encephalitic or paralytic rabies. J Infect Dis. 2003;188:960-966.
79. Haour F, Marquette C, Ban E, et al. Receptors for interleukin-1 in the central nervous system and neuroendocrine systems. Ann Endocrinol (Paris). 1995;56:173-179.

80. Ray NB, Ewalt LC, Lodmell DL. Rabies virus replication in primary murine bone marrow macrophages and in human and murine macrophage-like cell lines: Implications for viral persistence. J Virol. 1995;69:764-772.
81. Whitley RJ, Middlebrooks M. Rabies. In: Scheld WM, Whitley RJ, Durack DT, eds. Infections of the Central Nervous System. New York: Raven Press; 1991:127-144.
82. Constantine DG. Rabies transmission by air in bat caves. United States Public Health Service Publication; 1967.
83. Sureau P, Portnoi D, Rollin D, et al. Prévention de la transmission inter-humaine de la rage greffe de cornée. C R Seances Acad Sci. 1981;293:689-692.
84. Anderson LJ, Nicholson KG, Tauxe RV, Winkler WG. Human rabies in the United States, 1960 to 1979: Epidemiology, diagnosis, and prevention. Ann Intern Med. 1984;100:728-735.
85. Fishbein DB, Bernard KW. Rabies virus. In: Mandell GM, Bennett JE, Dolin R, eds. Principles and Practice of Infectious Diseases. New York: Churchill Livingstone; 1994:1527-1543.
86. Hemachuda T, Phanthumchinda K, Phanuphak P, Manatsathit S. Myoedema as a clinical sign in paralytic rabies. Lancet. 1987;1:1210.
87. Lopez A, Miranda P, Tejada E, Fishbein DB. Outbreak of human rabies in the Peruvian jungle. Lancet. 1992;339:408-411.
88. Gode GR, Saksena R, Batra RK, et al. Treatment of 54 clinically diagnosed rabies patients with two survivals. Indian J Med Res. 1988;88:564-566.
89. Gowers WR. A manual of diseases of the nervous system. Philadelphia: Blakiston; 1888:1237-1254.
90. Warrell DA, Davidson NM, Pope HM, et al. Pathophysiologic studies in human rabies. Am J Med. 1976;60:180-190.
91. Cheetham HD, Hart J, Coghill NF, Fox B. Rabies with myocarditis: Two cases in England. Lancet. 1970;1:921-922.
92. Hemachuda T. Human rabies: Clinical aspects, pathogenesis, and potential therapy. In: Rupprecht CE, Dietzschold B, Koprowski H, eds. Lyssaviruses. Berlin: Springer-Verlag; 1994:121-143.
93. Dutta JK. Rabies presenting with priapism (Letter). J Assoc Physicians India. 1994;42:430.
94. Jackson AC, Ye H, Phelan CC, et al. Extraneural organ involvement in human rabies. Lab Invest. 1999;79:945-951.
95. Jogai S, Radotra BD, Banerjee AK. Rabies viral antigen in extracranial organs: A post-mortem study. Neuropathol Appl Neurobiol. 2002;28:334-338.
96. Bhatt DR, Hattwick MAW, Gerdson R, et al. Human rabies: Diagnosis, complications, and prognosis. Am J Dis Child. 1974;127:862-869.
97. Warrell DA. The clinical picture of rabies in man. Trans R Soc Trop Med Hyg. 1976;701:188-195.
98. World Health Organization. Sixth report of the expert committee on rabies: Technical report series 523. Geneva: World Health Organization; 1973.
99. Baer GM, ed. The Natural History of Rabies. 2nd ed. Boca Raton, Fla: CRC Press; 1991.
100. Bleck TP, Rupprecht CE. Rabies. In: Richman DD, Whitley RJ, Hayden FG, eds. Clinical Virology. New York: Churchill Livingstone; 1997:879-897.
101. Hemachuda T. Rabies. In: McKendall RR, ed. Viral Diseases. In: Vinken PJ, Bruyn GW, Klawans HL, series eds. Handbook of Clinical Neurology. Amsterdam: Elsevier Science; 1989:383-404.
102. Houff SA, Burton RC, Wilson RW, et al. Human-to-human transmission of rabies virus by corneal transplant. N Engl J Med. 1979;300:603-604.
103. Laothamatas J, Hemachuda T, Mitrabhakdi E, et al. MR imaging in human rabies. AJNR Am J Neuroradiol. 2003;24:1102-1109.
104. Desai RV, Jain V, Singh P, et al. Radiculomyelitic rabies: Can MR imaging help? AJNR Am J Neuroradiol. 2002;23:632-634.
105. Bryceson AD, Greenwood BM, Warrell DA, et al. Demonstration during life of rabies antigen in humans. J Infect Dis. 1975;131:71-74.
106. Blenden DC, Creech W, Torres-Anjel MJ. Use of immunofluorescence examination to detect rabies virus in the skin of humans with clinical encephalitis. J Infect Dis. 1986;154:698-701.
107. Crepin P, Audry L, Rotivel Y, et al. Intravital diagnosis of human rabies by PCR using saliva and cerebrospinal fluid. J Clin Microbiol. 1998;36:1117-1121.
108. Arai YT, Yamada K, Kameoka Y, et al. Nucleoprotein gene analysis of fixed and street rabies virus variants using RT-PCR. Arch Virol. 1997;142:1787-1796.
109. Nadin-Davis SA. Polymerase chain reaction protocols for rabies virus discrimination. J Virol Methods. 1998;75:1-8.
110. Whitby JE, Johnstone P, Sillero-Zubiri C. Rabies virus in the decomposed brain of an Ethiopian wolf detected by nested reverse transcription-polymerase chain reaction. J Wildl Dis. 1997;33:912-915.
111. Albas A, Ferrari CI, da Silva LH, et al. Influence of canine brain decomposition on laboratory diagnosis of rabies. Rev Soc Bras Med Trop. 1999;32:19-22.
112. Zaidman GW, Billingsley A. Corneal impression test for the diagnosis of acute rabies encephalitis. Ophthalmology. 1998;105:249-251.
113. Smith JS, Yager PA, Baer GM. A rapid reproducible test for determining rabies neutralizing antibody. Bull WHO. 1973;48:535-541.
114. Alvarez L, Fajardo R, Lopez E, et al. Partial recovery from rabies in a nine-year-old boy. Ped Infect Dis J. 1994;13:1154-1155.
115. Whitley RJ. Viral encephalitis. N Engl J Med. 1990;323:242-250.
116. Johnson RT. Slow infections of the central nervous system caused by conventional viruses. In: Björnsson J, Carp RI, Löve A, Wisniewski HM, eds. Slow infections of the central nervous system. Ann N Y Acad Sci. 1994;724:6-13.

117. Bundza A, Charlton KM. Comparison of spongiform lesions in experimental scrapie and rabies in skunks. Acta Neuropathol. 1988;3:275-280.
118. Bleck TP, Alston SR. Prion diseases. In: Bleck TP, ed. Central Nervous System and Ocular Infections. In: Mandell GM, series ed. Atlas of Infectious Diseases. New York: Churchill Livingstone; 1995:11.1-11.16.
119. Warrell MJ, Looareesuwan S, Manatsathit S, et al. Rapid diagnosis of rabies and post-vaccinal encephalitides. Clin Exp Immunol. 1988;71:229-234.
120. Murthy JM. MRI in acute disseminated encephalomyelitis following Semple antirabies vaccine. Neuroradiology. 1998;40:420-423.
121. Mani J, Reddy BC, Borgohain R, et al. Magnetic resonance imaging in rabies. Postgrad Med J. 2003;79:352-354.
122. Fishbain DA, Barsky S, Goldberg M. Monosymptomatic hypochondriacal psychosis: Belief of contracting rabies. Int J Psychiatry Med. 1992;22:3-9.
123. Centers for Disease Control and Prevention. Compendium of animal rabies control, 1999. J Am Vet Med Assoc. 1999;214:198-202.
124. Conti LA, Tucker G, Heston S. Rabies in a dog vaccinated by its owner (Letter). J Am Vet Med Assoc. 1994;205:1250.
125. Eng TR, Fishbein DB, Talamante HE, et al. Immunogenicity of rabies vaccines used during an urban epizootic of rabies in Mexico. Vaccine. 1994;12:1259-1306.
126. Schneider LG. Rabies virus vaccines. Dev Biol Stand. 1995;84:49-54.
127. Rupprecht CE, Hanlon CA, Niezgoda M, et al. Recombinant rabies vaccines: Efficacy assessment in free-ranging animals. Onderstepoort J Vet Res. 1993;60:463-468.
128. Brochier B, Boulanger D, Costy F, Pastoret P-P. Toward rabies elimination in Belgium by fox vaccination using a vaccinia-rabies glycoprotein recombinant virus. Vaccine. 1994;12:1368-1371.
129. Matter HC, Kharmachi H, Haddad N, et al. Test of three bait types for oral immunization of dogs against rabies in Tunisia. Am J Trop Med Hyg. 1995;52:489-495.
130. Petricciani JC. Ongoing tragedy of rabies. Lancet. 1993;342:1067-1068.
131. Dean DJ. Pathogenesis and prophylaxis of rabies in man. N Y State J Med. 1963;63:3507-3513.
132. Anderson LJ, Winkler WG. Aqueous quaternary ammonium compounds and rabies treatment. J Infect Dis. 1979;139:494-495.
133. Griego RD, Rosen T, Orengo IF, Wolf JE. Dog, cat, and human bites: A review. J Am Acad Dermatol. 1995;33:1019-1029.
134. Mann JM, Burkhart MJ, Rollag OJ. Anti-rabies treatment in New Mexico: Impact of a comprehensive consultations-biologics system. Am J Public Health. 1980;70: 128-132.
135. Centers for Disease Control and Prevention. Human rabies prevention—United States, 1999: Recommendations of the Immunization Practices Advisory Committee (ACIP). MMWR Morb Mortal Wkly Rep. 1999;44(RR-1):1-40. Available at http://www.cdc.gov/ncidod/dvrd/rabies/professional/publications/ACIP/ACIP99.pdf.
136. Chutivongse S, Wilde H, Benjavongkulchai Met al. Postexposure rabies vaccination during pregnancy: Effect on 202 women and their infants. Clin Infect Dis. 1995;20:818-820.
137. World Health Organization. WHO recommendations on rabies post-exposure treatment and the correct technique of intradermal immunization against rabies. Geneva, World Health Organization; 1997. Available at http://www.who.int/emc-documents/rabies/whoemczoo966c.htm.
138. Wilde H, Sirikawin S, Sabcharoen A, et al. Failure of postexposure treatment of rabies in children. Clin Infect Dis. 1996;22:228-232.
139. Arya SC. Transmissible spongiform encephalopathies and sheep-brain derived rabies vaccines (Letter). Biologicals. 1994;22:73.
140. Bernard KW, Smith PW, Kader FJ, Moran MJ. Neuroparalytic illness and human diploid cell rabies vaccine. JAMA. 1982;248:3136-3138.
141. Hemachuda T, Mitrabhakdi E, Wilde H, et al. Additional reports of failure to respond to treatment after rabies exposure in Thailand. Clin Infect Dis. 1999;28:143-144.
142. Lang J, Simanjuntak GH, Soerjosembodo S, Koesharyono C. Suppressant effect of human or equine rabies immunoglobulins on the immunogenicity of post-exposure rabies vaccination under the 2-1-1 regimen: A field trial in Indonesia. MAS054 Clinical Investigator Group. Bull World Health Organ. 1998;76:491-495.
143. Pearlman E, Ballas S. False-positive human immunodeficiency virus screening test related to rabies vaccination. Arch Pathol Lab Med. 1994;118:805-806.
144. Plotkin SA, Loupi E, Blondeau C. False-positive positive human immunodeficiency virus screening test related to rabies vaccination (Letter). Arch Pathol Lab Med. 1995;119:679.
145. Henderson S, Leibnitz G, Turnbull M, Palmer GH. False-positive human immunodeficiency virus seroconversion is not common following rabies vaccination. Clin Diagn Lab Immunol. 2002;9:942-943.
146. Dutta JK, Dutta TK. Treatment of clinical rabies in man: Drug therapy and other measures. Clin Pharmacol Therapeut. 1994;32:594-597.
147. Hattwick MA, Weis TT, Stechschulte CJ, et al. Recovery from rabies: A case report. Ann Intern Med. 1972;76:931-942.
148. Porras C, Barboza JJ, Fuenzalida E, et al. Recovery from rabies in man. Ann Intern Med. 1976;85:44-48.
149. Rabies in a laboratory worker: New York. MMWR Morb Mortal Wkly Rep. 1977:26:183.
150. Jackson AC, Warrell MJ, Rupprecht CE, et al. Management of human rabies. Clin Infect Dis. 2003;36:60-63.

Marburg and Ebola Virus Hemorrhagic Fevers

C. J. PETERS

Filoviruses are rarely encountered and little is known about their natural history. However, because of the serious human disease they cause and our lack of predictive information about them, they demand our attention. These agents cause a severe, unrelenting viral hemorrhagic fever with high mortality. The identification of Marburg in 1967 was the first of only a handful of independent isolations of Marburg virus or the related Ebola viruses from humans.[1-4] Each episode has been characterized by the mysterious emergence of a filovirus with no traces of its origin detectable. Primates (humans, monkeys, chimpanzees, gorillas) are the only disease targets involved to date, but they are not thought to serve as reservoirs. Viral epidemics have originated from Africa and apparently from a single source in the Philippines. The name of the viral family comes from their characteristic thread-like (*filo*, Latin for "filament") morphology, and this has made their recognition in tissues or clinical samples unusually readily achieved with the electron microscope.

VIRAL CHARACTERIZATION

Filoviruses are elongated structures 80 nm in diameter. The basic length of the replicative form is 790 nm for Marburg and 970 nm for Ebola viruses, but long, branching convoluted structures are often formed (Fig. 161-1).[5,6] The 50-nm helical nucleocapsid is surrounded by a spike-studded membrane formed as the virus buds from the host cell. Inclusions of nucleocapsid aggregates can be visualized by electron microscopy of thin sections and are often visible as magenta-staining cytoplasmic structures in ordinary pathologic sections.

The virion genetic material is a single strand of negative-sense RNA of 4.2×10^6 Da that produces monocistronic messages during infection. These properties, the gene organization, virion structure, and viral sequence information place these viruses in a distinct family, Filoviridae in the order Mononegavirales. The glycoprotein gene

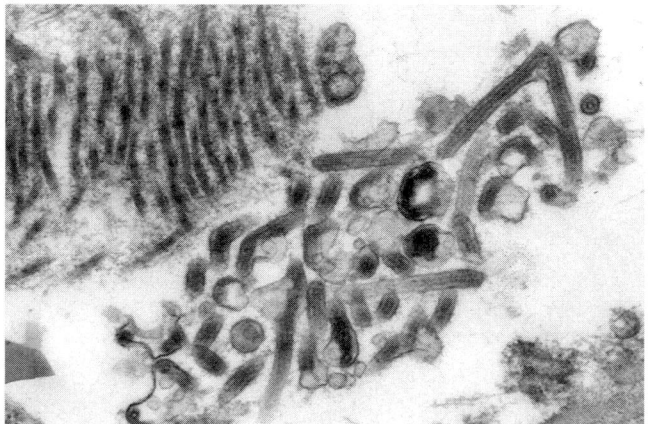

FIGURE 161-1. Ebola virus, Zaire subtype, human lung. Kikwit, Democratic Republic of the Congo, 1995. Longitudinal and cross-sections showing filamentous nucleocapsid, viral envelope, and surface projections. Original magnification, ×17,000. *(Courtesy of Cynthia Goldsmith and Pierre Rollin, Special Pathogens Branch, Centers for Disease Control.)*

codes for the 125-kDa (Ebola) or 170-kDa (Marburg) transmembrane spike protein that is highly glycosylated and is antigenically most characteristic for each virus.[5,6] Other virion proteins include a polymerase (180 kD), a nucleocapsid protein (96 to 104 kD), a matrix protein (40 kD), and three smaller proteins. Ebola viruses also code for a truncated glycoprotein species that is produced in soluble form.[7]

There are four known subtypes of Ebola that differ significantly from one another,[7] and a second Marburg subtype has been recognized. Comparison of 1172 nucleotides from the *GP* gene shows more than a 40% difference between any pair of the three subtypes from Sudan, Zaire, Ivory Coast, and Reston. Marburg viral strains differ from Ebola viruses in their genome organization, the size of their structural proteins, their glycosylation patterns, and their virion length, and they are classified as a separate genus.[6]

No serologic cross-reactivity has been demonstrated between the Marburg and Ebola viruses. The Ebola subtypes share varied degrees of cross-reactivity by the commonly used indirect fluorescent antibody or the enzyme-linked immunosorbent assay (ELISA) test.[6,8] No hemagglutinin has been demonstrated. An unusual biologic feature of filoviruses has been the difficulty in demonstrating neutralization in cell culture or animals by convalescent sera.

EPIDEMIOLOGY

Basic Ecology

There is no viral family with such a mysterious natural history. Each filovirus case or epidemic has been investigated for the source of the virus, but without success. In the case of epidemics, it has usually been possible to trace the epidemic back to a human or nonhuman primate index case, but no further. Suspects have included spiders, soft ticks, bats, and monkeys, but there is no field evidence to incriminate any of these.[1] Growth of the virus has been most commonly achieved in mammalian cells, not in arthropods or their cell culture.[6] Prolonged infection has been demonstrated in bats, suggesting the need for further study.[9]

Marburg Virus

In 1967, African green monkeys were brought from Uganda to Europe for use in vaccine production and biomedical research. They were infected with a "new" virus that resulted in deaths among the monkeys and transmission to humans. Seven deaths occurred among the 25 primary and six secondary human cases.[10] In 1980, a French engineer working in western Kenya 200 to 300 km from the site where the monkeys were shipped in 1967 developed Marburg virus disease, infecting one of the physicians caring for him[11]; again in 1987, a visitor to the same region died from Marburg virus infection.[6] Relatively nearby in western Democratic Republic of Congo, Marburg virus repeatedly infected gold miners from an unknown natural source, the only circumstance in which multiple crossovers from nature to humans have been associated with filovirus outbreaks.[4] Marburg virus circulation outside this area occurred in a traveler in Zimbabwe, who infected two persons during his medical care in South Africa.[12]

Ebola Virus (Zaire, Sudan, and Côte d'Ivoire Subtypes)

Ebola virus was first recognized in 1976, when two unrelated epidemics occurred in northern Zaire and 850 km away in southern Sudan; 88% of the patients in 318 recognized cases died in the former, and 53% of 284 in the latter.[13,14] Disease recurred in the same area of the Sudan in 1979,[14a] and the Zaire subtype virus was isolated from a patient in a solitary case in northwestern Zaire in 1977.[15] Ebola hemorrhagic fever was not recognized again for almost 2 decades. Then, in 1995-1996, an additional Ebola subtype (Côte d'Ivoire) was isolated from a human patient,[16] three separate Zaire subtype epidemics were recognized in Gabon,[17] and a major epidemic (315 cases, 81% case-fatality rate) from the Zaire subtype occurred in Kikwit, Zaire.[18] Notably, one Gabon patient made his way from Libreville, where he fell ill, to a modern hospital in South Africa.[19] In spite of the fact that his was not recognized as an Ebola infection, he transmitted the disease to only a single nurse. The secondary infection was unfortunately fatal, but the entire episode illustrates the low risk in a modern hospital setting. More recently, smoldering outbreaks of Sudan and Zaire virus subtypes have occurred in Uganda[3] and Congo,[2] respectively.

Ebola Virus (Reston Subtype)

In 1989-1991, another subtype was discovered in Reston, Virginia, among dying cynomolgus monkeys imported from Manila, Philippines.[20] This virus proved to be highly virulent for macaques, but the four animal caretakers who were infected suffered no overt disease. Fortunately, the quarantine regulations put in place after Marburg virus was first recognized in 1967 prevented the movement of infected animals outside the receiving facility. Other episodes occurred in Italy in 1992 and in the United States in 1996.[21] All these events were traced to the facility of a single exporter, but the ultimate source of the virus has never been ascertained, although Mindanao was the origin of the monkeys taken for conditioning and resale.

Transmission to Humans

In the original Marburg, Germany, importation, close contact with monkey blood or with cell cultures was present in all primary cases. Secondary cases were mainly among hospital staff and were associated with blood exposure.[10] The 1976 Zaire Ebola epidemic in particular was driven by the use of improperly sterilized needles and syringes, resulting in much of the geographic spread of infection. Interhuman spread of Ebola virus in the African epidemics was very extensive among medical staff, often resulting in closure of hospitals and clinics. Transmission to household contacts ranged between 3% and 17%, involved up to five generations of infection, and was associated with close contact with sick patients and their body fluids. The epidemics subsided with the use of properly sterilized equipment, closure of hospitals, education of the populace, and institution of mask-gown-glove precautions.[12,13,18,22] In the Reston, Virginia, epizootic among imported monkeys, there was transmission by droplet and possibly small-particle aerosol; spread to three of the humans caring for the monkeys was thought to be by droplets or small-particle aerosols, and a fourth suffered a scalpel accident during a monkey necropsy.[20]

The exact routes by which filoviruses may be spread are not intimately known. Parenteral inoculation with contaminated needles or syringes has been efficient and carries an enhanced mortality.[12] Skin or mucous membrane contact with virus-laden materials has probably been responsible for most recognized human infections. In addition to high titers of virus in blood, the skin of patients, including fibroblasts and other dermal structures, is extensively infected[23]; this probably accounts for the additional risk to those participating in traditional burial preparation of the cadaver[13] and mourners touching the cadaver.[22] Experimental studies of filoviruses establish that they are stable[24] and highly infective[25] in small-particle aerosols, and observations of inter-monkey transmission have suggested aerosol transmission. In addition, virions have been visualized in alveoli of humans and aerosol-infected monkeys.[20,26] Nevertheless, airborne infection plays a minor role, if any, in interhuman spread.

CLINICAL MANIFESTATIONS

Filovirus hemorrhagic fevers have an incubation period of 5 to 10 days (range, 2 to 19) and begin with the abrupt onset of fever, usually accompanied by myalgia and headache.[5,6,10,12-16,27] The fever is joined by some combination of nausea and vomiting, abdominal pain, diarrhea, chest pain, cough, and pharyngitis. Other common features include photophobia, lymphadenopathy, conjunctival injection, jaundice, and pancreatitis. Central nervous system involvement is often manifested by somnolence, delirium, or coma. As the disease progresses, wasting becomes evident, and bleeding manifestations such as petechiae, hemorrhages, and ecchymoses around needle puncture sites, and mucous membrane hemorrhages occur in half or more of the patients. Around day 5, most patients develop a maculopapular rash, prominent on the trunk. In the second week, the patient defervesces and improves

markedly or dies in shock with multiorgan dysfunction, often accompanied by disseminated intravascular coagulation, anuria, and liver failure. Convalescence may be protracted and accompanied by arthralgia, orchitis, recurrent hepatitis, transverse myelitis, or uveitis.[10,28]

The mortality of Marburg infection is approximately one in four, Ebola Sudan subtype one in two, and Ebola Zaire subtype 80% to 90%. Studies during epidemics suggest that subclinical infections with these viruses are uncommon, although a small percentage of the normal population has antibodies reactive in the IgG ELISA.[8,22,29,30] The limited number of Ebola Reston subtype infections observed have been subclinical.

PATHOGENESIS AND PATHOLOGY

Filovirus disease has findings that are similar in human patients and nonhuman primate models. The viremia persists throughout the acute period, and its disappearance coincides with clinical improvement and usually the appearance of antibodies in blood.[30] The effective immune response is probably not humoral, because passive convalescent antibody transfer does not protect against experimental inoculation.[6,28,31] Possible explanations for the failure to mount an effective immune response in fatal cases include the presence of a putatively immunosuppressive amino acid sequence in the filovirus glycoprotein,[32] the secretion of a soluble glycoprotein by Ebola virus–infected cells,[7] and the extensive lymphoid damage evident in postmortem examination.[26] In addition, Ebola-infected cells have a deficient response to interferon induction of the antiviral state or gene activation, which is a consequence of VP35 suppression or interferon regulatory factor 3 (IRF3).[6,33,34]

Important morphologic lesions include focal necrosis in many organs, particularly the liver, where Councilman's bodies are present, and the lymphoid organs, where prominent follicular necrosis occurs.[13,14,26] Necrotic lesions are found in conjunction with antigen and viral particles in endothelial, mononuclear, and parenchymal cells of virtually all organs. In addition to the morphologic basis for the multiorgan functional defects, cytokines are extensively activated in sick humans.[35] A major cause of the pathogenesis in experimental monkey infections is activation of tissue factor, which occurs first in monocyte/macrophages, and leads to disseminated intravascular coagulation (DIC) which precede direct viral endothelial damage.[37] Inflammatory cell infiltrates are minimal.

DIAGNOSIS

Travel to rural sub-Saharan Africa (and now perhaps the Philippines) or exposure to nonhuman primates is a historical clue. The presence of thrombocytopenia and leukopenia with elevated transaminase levels (aspartate aminotransferase levels more elevated than alanine aminotransferase levels) is characteristic of filovirus disease and some other viral hemorrhagic fevers, but a severe progressive course with abdominal pain and diarrhea should lead to suspicion of a filovirus. The rash is not seen with other viral hemorrhagic fevers, except occasionally Lassa fever.

Culture is positive during the acute stages, and seroconversion occurs around day 8 to 12. Antigen detection or polymerase chain reaction amplification of reverse transcription products provides a practical and sensitive method of diagnosis.[29,30] Negative stains of serum and thin sections of buffy coat or fixed tissue (liver, kidney) are helpful, but careful measurement of the putative virions and their internal structure is necessary to exclude artifacts.

In convalescence, virus has been isolated from semen for several weeks and from anterior chamber fluid in a case of late uveitis. Negative semen cultures should be obtained from patients before they resume unprotected sexual activity.

IgM antibodies detected in capture ELISA are useful in early convalesence.[30] IgG serologic testing has not been reliable. False-positive and irreproducible results are quite common when the indirect fluorescent antibody test is applied. For this reason, confirmation even of apparent seroconversions is desirable; only cases verified by viral isolation or from viral-isolation–verified epidemics have been included in the previous discussion. The IgG ELISA appears to have decreased this problem but still requires further verification.[6,28,29]

PREVENTION AND TREATMENT

Although some drugs have shown promise in animal studies, no antivirals are available, nor does convalescent plasma hold much promise.[6,28,31] Interferon has not been effective and may lead to fever and other symptoms that would complicate management. Whole-blood transfusions from recently convalesced patients were used in the 1995 Zaire epidemic, but a lack of concomitant controls precluded evaluation of their efficacy, and retrospective analysis taking into account the day of initial treatment and other variables suggested they were not useful.[37] A DNA vaccine prepared against GP induces protective cellular immunity against Zaire strain challenge in guinea pigs but not in monkeys.[31] A prototype adenovirus vaccine expressing this antigen has successfully protected monkeys and is in phase I studies in humans.[38]

Prevention of epidemics rests on early recognition of initial cases and prompt institution of barrier nursing.[18] Increased clinical awareness should lead to the institution of barrier nursing, which can be done with means appropriate to the African health care setting.[39] Fatal cases can be recognized readily by immunohistochemical staining of postmortem skin samples, obviating the need for cold preservation of samples and providing a safe and inexpensive diagnostic modality in these high-mortality diseases.[23]

Management of the patient should be supportive, with minimal trauma and careful maintenance of hydration, realizing the possibility of myocardial compromise and increased lung vascular permeability. Replacement of coagulation factors and platelets is indicated. Heparin or other treatment of DIC should be undertaken if laboratory evidence shows it to be present, and if adequate hematologic support is available. In the very severe monkey model, a recombinant inhibitor of the tissue factor–activated factor VII complex improves survival and should be considered in human therapy.[40]

At the community level, properly sterilized injection equipment, protection from body fluids and skin contact during preparation of the dead, and routine barrier nursing precautions are probably adequate in most cases.[18,19] In the United States, where more aggressive therapeutic procedures may be practiced, strict isolation, barrier nursing, staff training to avoid parenteral exposures, and, when practical, respirator protection should be routine.[41]

Extensive quarantine precautions are now in place to prevent the movement of infected monkeys into the United States and to prevent contamination of vaccines or cell cultures. Nevertheless, the potential for the emergence of filoviruses as a significant public health problem exists,[1] and concern by U.S. clinicians is warranted when suspicious cases with an epidemiologic link to Africa or nonhuman primates occur.

Note: Useful sources for information of the basic biology of filoviruses are the books that followed the Marburg outbreak[10] and the 1976 Ebola outbreak[42]; a 1999 journal supplement with much of the 1995 Kikwit, Zaire, outbreak and other data[28] (available at http://www.journals.uchicago.edu/JID/journal/contents/v179nS1.html); and a 1999 review volume.[5] These compendia have been referenced freely here to limit the size of the reference list.

REFERENCES

1. Murphy FA, Peters CJ. Ebola virus: Where does it come from and where is it going? In: Krause RM, ed. Emerging Infections. New York: Academic Press; 1998;375-410.
2. Anonymous. Outbreak(s) of Ebola haemorrhagic fever in the Republic of the Congo, January-April 2003. Wkly Epidemiol Rec. 2003;78:285-289.
3. Centers for Disease Control and Prevention. Outbreak of Ebola hemorrhagic fever-Uganda, August 2000-January 2001. JAMA. 2001;285:1010-1012.
4. Zeller H. Lessons from the Marburg virus epidemic in Durba, Democratic Republic of the Congo (1998-2000). Med Trop. 2000;60:23-26
5. Klenk H-D, ed. Marburg and Ebola Viruses. Curr Top Microbiol Immunol. 1999;235:1-225.
6. Sanchez A, Khan AS, Zaki SR, et al. Filoviridae: Marburg and Ebola viruses. In: Knipe DM, Howley PM, eds. Fields' Virology. 4th ed. Philadelphia: Lippincott, Williams, and Wilkins; 2001;1279-1304.
7. Sanchez A, Trappier SG, Mahy BWJ, et al. The virion glycoproteins of Ebola viruses are encoded in two reading frames and are expressed through transcriptional editing. Proc Natl Acad Sci U S A. 1996;93:3602.
8. Ksiazek TG, Rollin PE, Jahrling PB, Peters CJ. Enzyme-linked immunosorbent assays for the detection of antibodies to Ebola viruses. J Infect Dis. 1999;179(Suppl 1):S192-S198.
9. Swanepoel R, Leman PA, Burt FJ, et al. Experimental inoculation of plants and animals with Ebola virus. Emerg Infect Dis. 1996;2:321-325.
10. Martini GA, Siegert R, eds. Marburg Virus Disease. Berlin: Springer-Verlag; 1971: 1-230.
11. Smith DH, Johnson BK, Isaacson M, et al. Marburg virus disease in Kenya. Lancet. 1982;1:816-820.
12. Gear JSS, Cassel GA, Gear AJ, et al. Outbreak of Marburg virus disease in Johannesburg. Br Med J. 1975;4:489-493.
13. World Health Organization. Ebola haemorrhagic fever in Zaire, 1976: Report of an international commission. Bull World Health Organ. 1978;56:271-293.
14. World Health Organization. Ebola haemorrhagic fever in Sudan, 1976: Report of a WHO/international study team. Bull World Health Organ. 1978;56:247-270.
14a. Baron RC, McCormick JB, Zubeir OA. Ebola hemorrhagic fever in southern Sudan: Hospital dissemination and intrafamilial spread. Bull World Health Organ. 1983;6:997-1003.
15. Heymann DL, Weisfeld JS, Webb PA, et al. Ebola hemorrhagic fever: Tandala, Zaire, 1977-1978. J Infect Dis. 1980;142:372-376.
16. Formenty P, Hatz C, Stoll A, et al. Human infection due to Ebola Côte d'Ivoire: Clinical and biological presentation. J Infect Dis. 1999;179(Suppl 1):S48-S53.
17. Georges A, Leroy EB, Renaut AA, et al. Recent Ebola outbreaks in Gabon from 1994 to 1997: Epidemiological and health control issues. J Infect Dis. 1999;179(Suppl 1): S65-S75.
18. Khan AS, Kweteminga TF, Heymann DH, et al. The reemergence of Ebola hemorrhagic fever (EHF), Zaire, 1995. J Infect Dis. 1999;179(Suppl 1):S76-S86.
19. Richards, GA, Murphy S, Jobson R, et al. Unexpected Ebola virus in a tertiary setting: Clinical and epidemiologic aspects. Crit Care Med. 2000;28:240-244.
20. Peters CJ, Johnson ED, Jahrling PB, et al. Filoviruses. In: Morse S, ed. Emerging Viruses. New York: Oxford University Press; 1991:159-175.
21. Rollin PE, Williams J, Bressler D, et al. Ebola (subtype Reston) virus among quarantined non-human primates recently imported from the Philippines to the United States. J Infect Dis. 1999;179(Suppl 1):S108-S114.
22. Dowell SF, Mukunu R, Ksiazek TG, et al. Transmission of Ebola hemorrhagic fever: A study of risk factors in family members, Kikwit, Zaire 1995. J Infect Dis. 1999;179(Suppl 1):S87-S91.
23. Zaki S, Greer PW, Shieh WJ, et al. A novel immunohistochemical assay for detection of Ebola virus in skin: Implications for diagnosis and surveillance of Ebola hemorrhagic fever. J Infect Dis. 1999;179(Suppl 1):S36-S37.
24. Belanov YF, Muntyanov VP, Kryuk VD, et al. Retention of Marburg virus infecting capability on contaminated surfaces and in aerosol particles (in Russian). Vopr Virusol. 1996;41:32-34.
25. Bazhutin NB, Belanov EF, Spiridonov VA, et al. The influence of the methods of experimental infection with Marburg virus on the features of the disease process in green monkeys. Vopr Virusol. 1992;37:153-156.
26. Zaki SR, Goldsmith CS. Pathologic features of filovirus infections in humans. Curr Top Microbiol Immunol. 1999;235:97-116.
27. Bwaka MA, Bonnet M, Calain P, et al. Ebola hemorrhagic fever in Kikwit, Democratic Republic of Congo (former Zaire): Clinical observations. J Infect Dis. 1999;179(Suppl 1):S1-S7.
28. Peters CJ, LeDuc JW, ed. Ebola: The virus and the disease. J Infect Dis. 1999;179(Suppl 1):S1-S288.
29. Busico KM, Marshall KL, Ksiazek TG, et al. Prevalence of IgG antibodies to Ebola virus in individuals during an Ebola outbreak, Democratic Republic of the Congo, 1995. J Infect Dis. 1999;179(Suppl 1):S102-S107.
30. Ksiazek TG, Rollin PE, Williams AJ, et al. Clinical virology of Ebola hemorrhagic fever (EHF): Virus, virus antigen, and IgG and IgM antibody findings among EHF patients in Kikwit, Democratic Republic of the Congo, 1995. J Infect Dis. 1999;179(Suppl 1):S177-S187.
31. Xu L, Sanchez A, Yang Z, et al. Genetic immunization for Ebola virus infection. Nat Med. 1998;4:37.
32. Volchkov VE, Blinov VM, Netesov SV. The envelope glycoprotein of Ebola virus contains an immunosuppressive-like domain similar to oncogenic retroviruses. FEBS Lett. 1992;305:181-184.
33. Harcourt BH, Sanchez A, Offerman MK. Ebola virus selectively inhibits responses to interferons, but not to IL-1beta in endothelial cells. J Virol. 1999;73:3491-3496.
34. Basler CF, Mikulasova A, Martinez-Sobrido L, et al. The Ebola virus VP35 protein inhibits activation of interferon regulatory factor 3. J Virol. 2003;77:7945-7956.
35. Villinger F, Rollin PE, Brar SS, et al. Markedly elevated levels of IFN-gamma/alpha, IL-2, IL-10 and TNF-alpha associated with fatal Ebola virus infection. J Infect Dis. 1999;179(Suppl 1):S188-S191.
36. Geisbert TW, Young HA, Jahrling PB, et al. Pathogenesis of Ebola hemorrhagic fever in primate models: Evidence that hemorrhage is not a direct effect of virus-induced cytolysis of endothelial cells. Am J Pathol. 2003;163:2371-2382.
37. Sadek RF, Kilmarx PH, Khan AS, et al. Outbreak of Ebola hemorrhagic fever, Zaire, 1995: A closer numerical look. J Infect Dis. 1999;179(Suppl 1):S24-S27.
38. Sullivan NJ, Geisbert TW, Geisbert JB, et al. Accelerated vaccination for Ebola virus haemorrhagic fever in non-human primates. Nature. 2003;424:681-684.

39. Lloyd ES, Zaki SR, Rollin PE, et al. Long-term disease surveillance in Bandundu region, Democratic Republic of the Congo: A model for early detection and prevention of Ebola hemorrhagic fever. J Infect Dis. 1999;179(Suppl 1):S274-S280.

40. Geisbert TW, Hensley LE, Jahrling PB, et al. Treatment of Ebola virus infection with a recombinant inhibitor of factor VIIa/tissue factor: A study in rhesus monkeys. Lancet. 2003;362:1953-1958.

41. Centers for Disease Control and Prevention. Update: Management of patients with suspected viral hemorrhagic fever—United States. MMWR Morb Mortal Wkly Rep. 1995;44:475-479.

42. Pattyn SR, ed. Ebola Virus Haemorrhagic Fever. Amsterdam: Elsevier North-Holland; 1978.

CHAPTER 162

Influenza Virus

JOHN J. TREANOR

Influenza is an acute, usually self-limited, febrile illness caused by infection with influenza type A or B virus that occurs in outbreaks of varying severity almost every winter. The attack rates during such outbreaks may be as high as 10% to 40% over a 5- to 6-week period. The most common clinical manifestations are fever, malaise, and cough. The two most important features of influenza are the epidemic nature of the disease and the mortality that results in part from its pulmonary complications.

HISTORY

Influenza virus has been causing recurrent epidemics of febrile respiratory disease every 1 to 3 years for at least the past 400 years.[1,2] Although the disease is not associated with a characteristic manifestation such as rash, the high attack rate, the explosive nature of the epidemic, and the frequency of cough allow the identification of some past epidemics. For example, Sydenham's account of an epidemic that occurred in 1679 is a clear description of influenza.[3] Hirsch tabulated 299 outbreaks occurring at an average interval of 2.4 years between 1173 and 1875.[1] As discussed later, severe epidemics of worldwide scope occur less often and are referred to as pandemics. The first recorded pandemic that clearly fits the description of influenza occurred in 1580, although others may have occurred earlier. Since then, 31 pandemics have been described. The greatest pandemic in recorded history occurred in 1918-1919 when, during three "waves" of influenza, 21 million deaths were recorded worldwide, among them 549,000 in the United States.[4]

The modern understanding of influenza was ushered in by Smith and associates when they isolated influenza A virus in ferrets in 1933.[5] Influenza B virus was isolated by Francis in 1939[6] and influenza C virus by Taylor in 1950.[7] The discovery by Burnet in 1936 that influenza virus could be grown in embryonated hens' eggs allowed extensive study of the properties of the virus and the development of inactivated vaccines.[8] Animal cell culture systems for the growth of influenza viruses were developed in the 1950s.[9] The phenomenon of hemagglutination, which was discovered by Hirst in 1941, led to simple and inexpensive methods for the measurement of virus and specific antibody.[10]

Evidence of the protective efficacy of inactivated vaccines was developed in the 1940s.[11,12] Vaccines have been in widespread use in various parts of the world since, but usually for only selected segments of a population. The use of live vaccines for influenza was first suggested shortly after the virus was discovered,[13] but the first live vaccine was not licensed in the United States until 2003, approximately 70 years later. Finally, four antiviral agents in two classes have been approved for prevention and treatment of influenza. These include the so-called M2 inhibitors, amantadine in the mid-1960s, rimantadine in 1993, and the neuraminidase inhibitors zanamivir and oseltamivir in 2000. Although the M2 inhibitors are active against only influenza A, the neuraminidase inhibitors are clinically active against both influenza A and B viruses.

THE VIRUSES

Classification

Influenza viruses belong to the family Orthomyxoviridae and are classified into three distinct types, influenza A, influenza B, and influenza C virus, on the basis of major antigenic differences. In addition, there are significant differences in genetic organization, structure, host range, epidemiology, and clinical characteristics between the three influenza virus types (Table 162-1). However, all three viruses share certain features that are fundamental to their biologic behavior, including the presence of a host-cell derived envelope, envelope glycoproteins of critical importance in virus entry and egress from cells, and a segmented genome of negative sense (i.e., opposite of message sense), single-stranded RNA. The standard nomenclature for influenza viruses includes the influenza type, place of initial isolation, strain designation, and year of isolation. For example, the influenza A virus isolated by Francis[14] from a patient in Puerto Rico in 1934 is given the strain designation A/Puerto Rico/8/34, sometimes referred to as PR8 virus. Influenza A viruses are further divided into subtypes on the basis of their hemagglutinin (H) and neuraminidase (N) activity (e.g., H1N1 or H3N2).

Morphologic Characteristics

The morphologic characteristics of all influenza virus types, subtypes, and strains are similar. Electron microscopic studies estimate their size to be 80 to 120 nm in diameter and show them to be enveloped viruses covered with surface projections or spikes. They may exist as spherical or elongated filamentous particles as well (Fig. 162-1). The latter predominate in newly isolated strains, whereas most laboratory-adapted strains consist almost entirely of spherical particles. The filamentous forms vary in length but may be up to 40 nm long. A schematic diagram of an influenza A virus is shown in Figure 162-2.

Eight structural proteins have been identified in influenza A viruses. The surface spikes are glycoproteins that possess either hemagglutinin (HA) or neuraminidase (NA) activity. Each rod-shaped HA spike measures approximately 4 nm in diameter by 14 nm in length. They can be removed from the intact virion by sodium dodecyl sulfate, by bromelain, or by chymotrypsin. Each spike is a trimer

TABLE 162-1 Differences among Influenza A, B, and C Viruses

	Influenza A	Influenza B	Influenza C
Genetics	8 gene segments	8 gene segments	7 gene segments
Structure	10 viral proteins	11 viral proteins	9 viral proteins
	M2 unique	NB unique	HEF unique
Host range	Humans, swine, equine, avian, marine mammals	Humans only	Humans and swine
Epidemiology	Antigenic shift and drift. Drift is generally linear	Antigenic drift only. More than one variant may cocirculate	Antigenic drift only. Multiple variants
Clinical features	May cause large pandemics with significant mortality in young persons	Severe disease generally confined to older adults or persons at high risk; pandemics not seen	Mild disease without seasonality

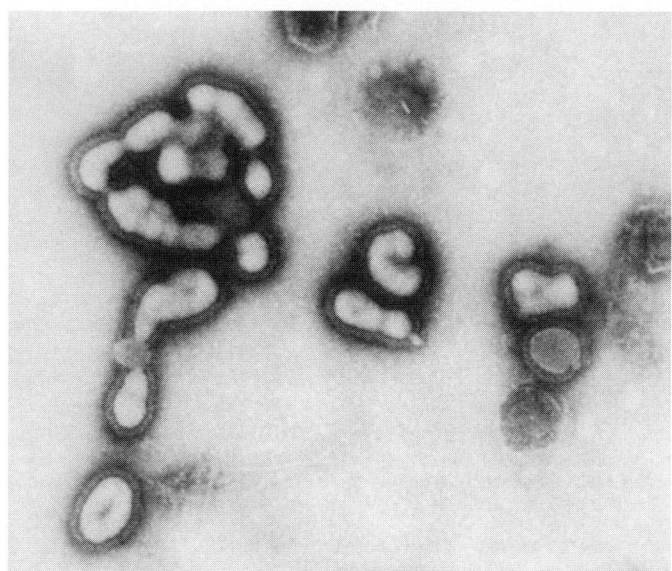

FIGURE 162-1. Electron micrograph of influenza A/USSR/77 H1N1 (×189,000).

TABLE 162-2 Genes and Protein Products of Influenza A Virus

RNA Segment Number	Gene Product Description	Name of Protein	Proposed Functions
1	PB1	Basic polymerase 1	RNA transcriptase
2	PB2	Basic polymerase 2	Cap binding, endonucleolytic cleavage
3	PA	Acidic polymerase	Unknown
4	HA	Hemagglutinin	Viral attachment to cell membranes; membrane fusion
5	NA	Neuraminidase	Cleaves sialic acid from cell surface; released from membranes; prevents aggregation
6	NP	Nucleoprotein	Encapsidates RNA; regulation of transcription/replication
7	M	Matrix	Surrounds viral core; controls nuclear transport
	M2	Matrix 2	Ion channel; required for uncoating
8	NS1	Nonstructural	Antagonizes type I interferons, may be involved in regulation of mRNA transport from nucleus
	NEP (NS2)	Nuclear export protein (?structural)	Transport of newly assembled RNP from nucleus to cytoplasm

composed of three HA polypeptides, each with a molecular weight of 75,000 to 80,000, resulting in a trimer with a molecular weight of approximately 224,640.[15] The HA is synthesized as a monomer (HA_0), which is cleaved by host-cell proteases into HA_1 and HA_2 components that remain linked together. Antigenic sites and sites for binding to cells are located in the globular head of the molecule.

The viral NA is an enzyme that catalyzes the removal of terminal sialic acids (*N*-acetyl neuraminic acid) from sialic acid–containing glycoproteins. The NA spike is shaped like a mushroom rather than a

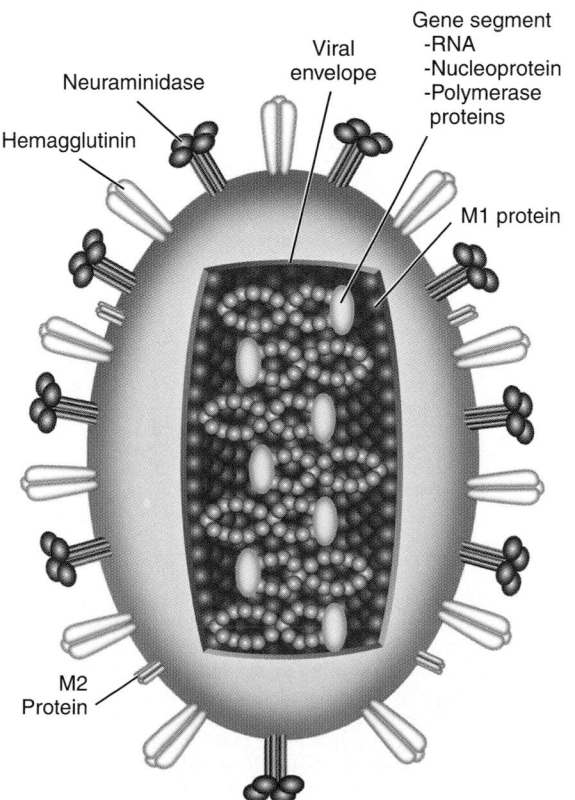

FIGURE 162-2. Schematic model of an influenza A virus.

rod and has a molecular weight of 240,000. The intact NA consists of a tetramer of NA polypeptides, each with a molecular weight of 58,000. As in HA, the antigenic sites and the enzyme active site are located in the mushroom-shaped head.

At least 15 highly divergent, antigenically distinct HAs have been described in influenza A viruses (H1 to H15), as well as at least nine distinct NAs (N1 to N9). A third integral membrane protein, the M2 protein, is also present in small amounts on the viral envelope.

Interior to the envelope is the matrix, or M1, protein.[16] This protein is believed to provide stability to the virion. Within the envelope are eight physically discrete nucleocapsid segments (Table 162-2). Each nucleocapsid is composed of a single segment of genomic RNA intimately associated with the viral nucleoprotein (NP), with the three polymerase proteins PB1, PB2, and PA bound to one end. These so-called internal viral proteins are important targets for cross-reactive, viral-specific cytotoxic T lymphocytes (CTL). Two nonstructural viral proteins, NS1 and NS2 (also referred to as the nuclear export protein, or NEP), are also found within infected cells. Small amounts of NEP may be present within virions.

EPIDEMIOLOGY

Disease Impact

Influenza epidemics are regularly associated with excess morbidity and mortality,[17] usually expressed in the form of excess rates of pneumonia and influenza-associated hospitalizations and deaths during epidemics.[17,18] Pneumonia and influenza deaths fluctuate annually in a predictable fashion with peaks in the winter and troughs in the summer. Observed pneumonia- and influenza-related death rates are compared with an expected baseline derived from a time-series regression model,[19] which allows calculation of excess mortality due to influenza epidemics. A tabulation of levels of excess pneumonia and influenza

TABLE 162-3 Estimated Excess Pneumonia- and Influenza-Related Deaths and Excess Mortality of All Causes during Influenza Epidemics

Year	Percent of Isolates That Were of the Following (Sub) Type			Pneumonia- and Influenza-Related Excess Deaths (Range)	All-Cause Excess Deaths (Range)
	H3N2	H1N1	B		
1972/73	90	0	10	7900 (5500-10,300)	18,300 (1200-35,000)
1973/74	20	0	80	0 0	0 0
1974/75	100	0	0	6500 (4100-8900)	15,100 (0-32,100)
1975/76	70	0	30	11,800 (9200-14,400)	24,600 (3400-45,900)
1976/77	5	0	95	0 0	0 0
1977/78	60	26	14	8300 (6000-10,500)	46,200 (19,800-72,700)
1978/79	0	98	2	0 0	0 0
1979/80	2	1	97	5100 (3500-6700)	17,300 (600-34,100)
1980/81	77	23	0	11,700 (9100-14,200)	47,200 (27,800-66,600)
1981/82	1	24	75	2100 (600-3700)	0 0
1982/83	79	10	11	4700 (2800-6700)	9600 (0-19,200)
1983/84	5	50	45	3500 (1600-5400)	8200 (0-17,600)
1984/85	97	0	3	8100 (6600-9600)	36,200 (17,700-54,700)
1985/86	24	0	76	6700 (4900-8500)	34,000 (6800-61,200)
1986/87	—	—	—	1800 (1100-2500)	16,800 (1900-31,700)
1987/88	0	80	20	7400 (5600-9100)	33,400 (12,900-53,800)
1988/89	45	45	10	5100 (3600-6600)	10,500 (800-20,200)
1989/90	90	1	9	10,100 (8500-11,700)	43,600 (27,600-59,600)
1990/91	4	3	93	4200 (2400-6100)	23,000 (0-46,000)
1991/92	19	81	0	6600 (5600-7700)	41,700 (19,600-63,700)

Data from Table 153-3 in Treaner JL. Influenza virus. In: Mandell GL, Bennett JE, Dolin R, eds. Mandell, Douglas, and Bennett's Principles and Practice of Infectious Diseases, ed. 5. Philadelphia: Saunders; 2000:1826; and Simonsen L, Clarke MJ, Williamson DW, et al. The impact of influenza epidemics on mortality. Introducing a severity index. Am J Public Health. 1947;87:1944-1950.

deaths (i.e., deaths in which specific International Classification of Diseases [ICD]-9 codes are recorded as the cause of death) attributable to influenza epidemics[20] is shown in Table 162-3, compared with the estimated percentage of isolates which were typed as influenza A (H3N2), A (H1N1), or B in each year. Significant levels of excess mortality are reported in most years. Generally, the level of excess mortality is highest in years when influenza A (H3N2) viruses predominate, but influenza B and to a lesser extent H1N1 viruses also can be associated with excess mortality. Because not all influenza-related deaths are manifested as pneumonia, the pneumonia and influenza mortality statistics probably underestimate the true impact of influenza on the population. Table 162-3 also lists the all-cause excess mortality, defined as deaths due to any cause, above a similarly derived baseline, that occur during periods of influenza epidemic activity. Although less precise than the pneumonia- and influenza-related deaths, all-cause mortality is probably a more accurate reflection of the total burden of influenza. Recent studies suggest that even higher levels of mortality might be attributable to influenza, potentially as high as 51,000 deaths annually in the United States.[21]

Mortality is only the most severe manifestation of influenza impact, and similar techniques can be used to estimate excess morbidity due to influenza epidemics.[22] Data from the Tecumseh Community Health Study have been used to estimate that influenza is responsible for from 13.8 to 16.0 million excess respiratory illnesses per year in the United States among individuals less than 20 years of age, and for 4.1 to 4.5 million excess illnesses in older individuals.[22]

Influenza is usually associated with a U-shaped epidemic curve. Attack rates are generally highest in the young, whereas mortality is generally highest among older adults (Fig. 162-3).[17,23] Excess morbidity and mortality are particularly high in those with certain high-risk medical conditions, including adults and children with cardiovascular and pulmonary conditions such as asthma, or those requiring regular medical care because of chronic metabolic disease, renal dysfunction, hemoglobinopathies, or immunodeficiency.[24] Influenza-related death rates in nursing home residents with comorbid conditions are as high as 2.8% per year.[25]

Influenza also results in more severe disease and significant mortality in individuals with human immunodeficiency virus (HIV) infection,[26,27] in those with iatrogenic immunosuppression,[28] and in women

in the second or third trimester of pregnancy.[29] Influenza is being increasingly recognized as an important health problem in young children. Rates of influenza-related hospitalizations are particularly high in healthy children under 2 years of age, where rates approach those of older children with high-risk conditions.[30-32] In addition, a high rate of secondary complications, particularly otitis media and pneumonia, oc-

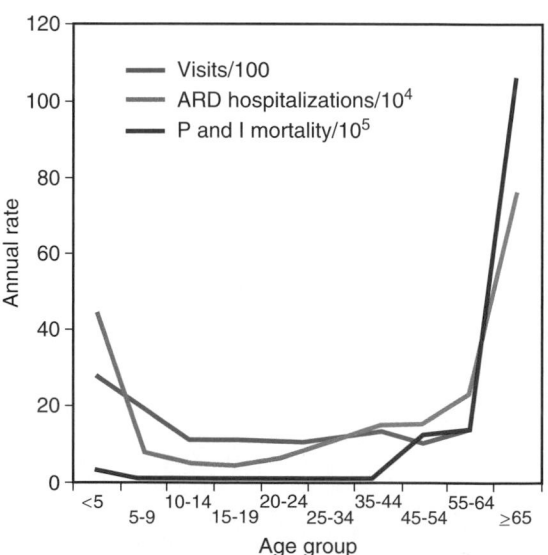

FIGURE 162-3. Typical epidemic curve in the interpandemic era, showing the rates of medically attended illness (*green line*, rate per 100), hospitalizations for acute respiratory disease (*blue line*, rate per 10,000), and pneumonia- and influenza-related mortality (*red line*, rate per 100,000) by age for several seasons of influenza in Houston, Texas. Attack rates and hospitalizations occur at both extremes of age, but mortality occurs largely in those older than 65 years. (*Data from Glezen WP, Keitel WA, Taber LH, et al. Age distribution of patients with medically attended illnesses caused by sequential variants of influenza A/H1N1: Comparison to age-specific infection rates, 1978-1989. Am J Epidemiol. 1991;133:296-304.*)

cur in children with influenza infection.[33] Disease impact is particularly severe in both adults and children with chronic pulmonary diseases, especially asthma.[34-36] It should be recognized that although complication rates are higher in older adults and debilitated persons, the majority of individuals hospitalized during influenza epidemics were ambulatory and leading productive lives prior to their acute illness.[24]

Much of the impact of influenza is related to the malaise and consequent disability that it produces, even in young, healthy individuals. It has been estimated that a typical case of influenza, on average, is associated with 5 to 6 days of restricted activity, 3 to 4 days of bed disability, and about 3 days lost from work or school.[37,38] The average number of medical visits for cases in which medical attention was sought was from 1.1 to 3.6, depending on year of the outbreak and age of the patient. It is worth noting that direct medical costs of illness account for only about 20% or the total expenses of a case of influenza, with a major proportion (30% to 50%) of the economic impact due to loss of productivity. In one study, influenza in schoolchildren resulted in 37 missed school days by children and 20 days of missed work by parents, per 100 children.[39] Influenza is also associated with decreased job performance in working adults[40,41] and reduced levels of independent functioning in older adults.[42]

Epidemic Influenza

An epidemic is an outbreak of influenza confined to one location, such as a city, town, or country. In a given community, epidemics of influenza A virus infection have a characteristic pattern. A graphic description of an epidemic due to an A/Victoria/75/H3N2-like virus that occurred in 1976 in Houston, Texas, is shown in Figure 162-4. Such localized epidemics begin rather abruptly, reach a sharp peak in 2 to 3 weeks, and last 5 to 6 weeks.[43] Reports of increased numbers of children with febrile respiratory illness are often the first indication of influenza, although on occasion, an outbreak in a nursing home is the very first indication of influenza in a community. Outbreaks in children are usually soon followed by the occurrence of influenza-like illnesses among adults. The next event is increased hospital admissions for patients with pneumonia, exacerbation of chronic obstructive pulmonary disease, croup, and congestive heart failure. Increased school and industrial absenteeism also occurs, but these events are insensitive and late indicators of influenza in a community.[43] Although an increased number of deaths due to pneumonia is a highly specific indicator of influenza, it invariably lags behind the other indications because of two factors: the time from the onset of illness to time of death and the delay involved in reporting deaths to public health officials.[44] During epidemics, average overall attack rates are estimated to be 10% to 20%, but in selected populations or age groups, attack rates of 40% to 50% are not unusual.[45] The factors that lead to termination of an outbreak in any given location are unclear, because usually the outbreak ceases before the supply of susceptible individuals is exhausted.

In temperate climates in either hemisphere, epidemics occur almost exclusively in the winter months (generally October to April in the Northern Hemisphere, and May to September in the Southern Hemisphere), whereas influenza may be seen year round in the tropics. The reasons for these seasonal changes are not entirely clear. Modeling studies suggest that the effect can mostly be explained by postulating seasonal effects on virus transmissibility.[46] Such effects could be the result of more favorable environmental conditions for virus survival,[47] or of behavioral changes that increase transmission, such as indoor crowding. In large countries such as the United States or Australia, regional differences in the time occurrence of influenza outbreaks are also apparent. It is not uncommon to have major outbreaks occurring in some communities or regions while others are experiencing modest activity or none whatsoever.

Usually, a single strain of influenza virus will prevail during an epidemic of influenza, and other respiratory viruses decrease in frequency.[45,48] However, this is not always the case, and occasionally two different strains within a single subtype (e.g., A/Victoria/3/75/H3N2 and A/Texas/1/77/H3N2)[49] or two different influenza A subtypes (H1N1 and H3N2) circulate simultaneously. Furthermore, concomi-

tant outbreaks of influenza A and B or simultaneous outbreaks of influenza A and respiratory syncytial virus have been demonstrated.[50] In many years, the end of the influenza epidemic season is characterized by a brief spike in cases due to a new strain. These limited outbreaks, which have been referred to as a "herald wave," often predict the predominant strain in the next influenza season.[51]

Pandemic Influenza

In contrast to the familiar pattern of epidemic influenza, pandemics are severe outbreaks that rapidly progress to involve all parts of the world and are associated with the emergence of a new virus to which the overall population possesses no immunity. Characteristics of pandemics include extremely rapid transmission with concurrent outbreaks throughout the globe; the occurrence of disease outside the

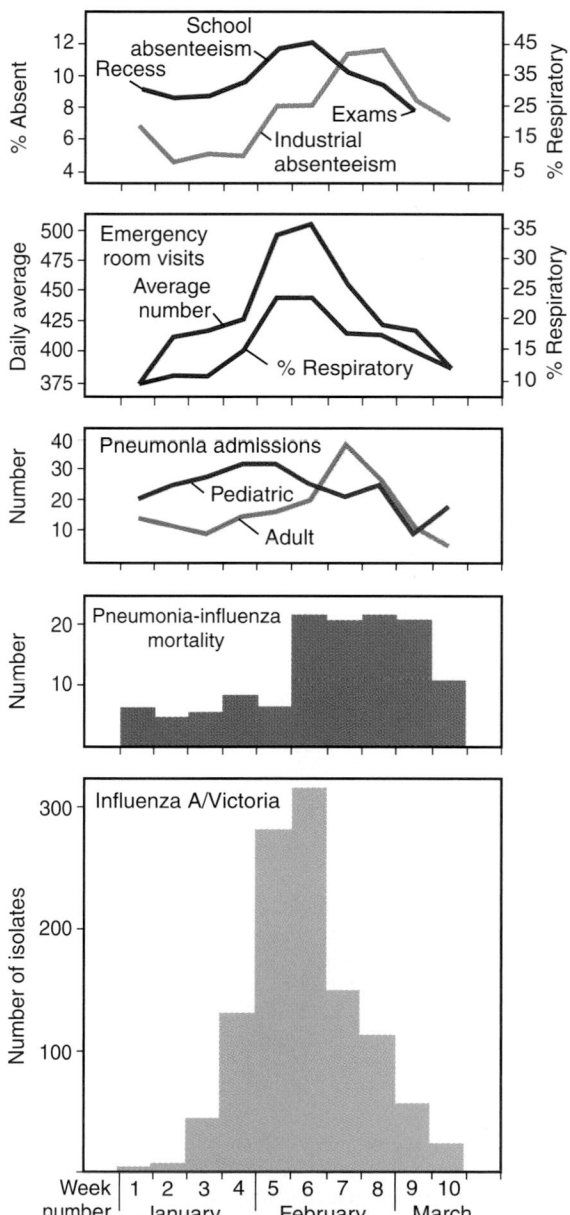

FIGURE 162-4. Correlation of the nonvirologic indexes of epidemiologic influenza with the number of isolates of A/Victoria virus according to week, Houston, 1976. (Industrial absenteeism is determined by the percentage with respiratory complaints.) *(From Glezen WP, Couch RB. Interpandemic influenza in the Houston area, 1974-1976. N Engl J Med. 1978;298:587-593, with permission.)*

usual seasonality, including during the summer months; high attack rates in all age groups, with high levels of mortality particularly in healthy young adults[52]; and multiple waves of disease immediately before and after the main outbreak. The interval between pandemics is quite variable and unpredictable, but it is likely that pandemics of influenza will continue to occur in the future.

Antigenic Variation

One of the unique and most remarkable features of influenza virus is the frequency with which changes in antigenicity occur; these changes are referred to as antigenic variation. Alteration of the antigen structure of the virus leads to infection with variants to which little or no resistance is present in the population at risk. The phenomenon of antigenic variation helps explain why influenza continues to be a major epidemic disease of humans.

Antigenic variation involves principally the two external glycoproteins of the virus, HA and NA, and is referred to as antigenic drift or antigenic shift, depending on whether the variation is small or great.

Antigenic Drift

Antigenic drift refers to relatively minor antigenic changes that occur frequently (every year or every few years) within the HA and/or NA of the virus. It is generally accepted that the mechanism of antigenic drift, which has been studied more intensively for the HA, is one of gradual accumulation of amino acid changes in one or more of the five identified major antigenic sites on the HA molecule.[53] Because antibody generated by exposure to previous strains does not neutralize the antigenic variant as effectively as it did the wild type, immunologic selection takes place, and the variant supplants previous strains as the predominant virus in the epidemic. Support for this thesis comes from experimental work demonstrating that antigenic variants (generated by drift) can be produced in cell cultures in the presence of limiting amounts of antibody, and these variants have similar single amino acid sequences in the HA.[54-57]

Comparison of the HA gene sequences of influenza viruses isolated in successive years reveals differences in the patterns of HA evolution between influenza A, B, and C viruses. Generally, a single lineage, or relatively few lineages, of influenza A virus circulate in humans, and the accumulation of point mutations in the HA is linear, with each strain replacing the previously circulating one. This is particularly true of H3 influenza A viruses.[53,58] In contrast, multiple lineages of influenza C virus cocirculate, as shown by sequence comparisons of the HEF gene. The evolution of influenza B viruses is somewhere between these two examples, with relatively few lineages of the HA gene (but more than one) cocirculating.[59] Relatively less information is available regarding the evolution of NA gene sequences, but these appear to follow a similar pattern.[60]

Antigenic Shift

The major antigenic shifts that herald pandemic influenza presumably result from a different mechanism. These viruses are "new" viruses to which the population has no immunity. There is very little or no serologic relationship between the HA (or NA) antigens of the "old" and "new" viruses; hence, in nomenclature, each receives a different designation. The schema shown in Figure 162-5 ties together the concepts of antigenic shift and antigenic drift in relation to population immunity.[61] When a new virus, here called HxNx, to which antibody is lacking, is introduced into a population, pandemic influenza results. After one or more waves of pandemic influenza, the proportion of immune individuals in the population increases. This situation favors the emergence of viruses with antigenic changes in the HA and/or NA, whose spread through the partially immune population is thus facilitated. This phenomenon is repeated with subsequent epidemics due to strains of influenza A/HxNx that exhibit some antigenic drift. After 10 to 30 years of circulation of variants with this given subtype, the level of immunity in the population to all variants within the subtype is very high, and the conditions for the spread of a new virus, HyNy, become favorable, with the emergence of a new pandemic of influenza.

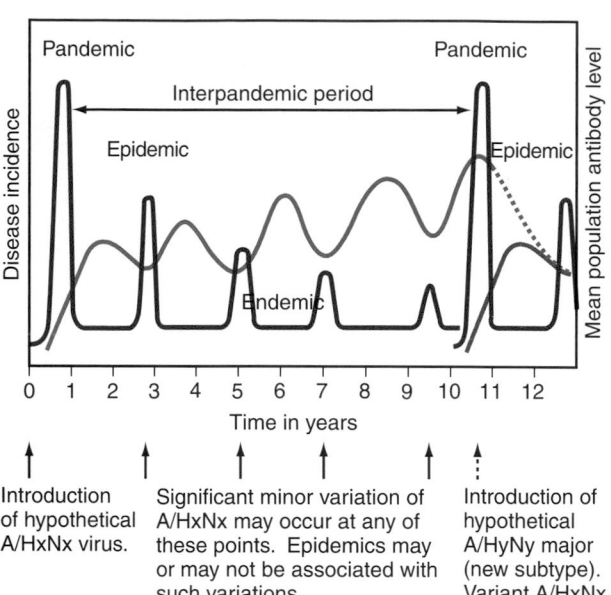

FIGURE 162-5. Schema of the occurrence of influenza pandemics and epidemics in relation to the level of immunity in the population. A/HxNx and A/HyNy represent influenza viruses with completely different hemagglutinins and neuraminidases. *(Modified from Kilbourne ED. The epidemiology of influenza. In: Kilbourne ED, ed. The Influenza Viruses and Influenza. New York: Academic Press; 1975:483, with permission.)*

The pattern of replacement of HA and NA subtypes during the most recent century of pandemics is shown in Figure 162-6 and is based both on virus isolation and serologic studies of individuals who lived through previous pandemics. Such studies suggest that the pandemic of 1889 was associated with viruses of an H2N2 type, followed by a pandemic in 1901 caused by an H3N8-type virus.[62] Virologic and polymerase chain reaction (PCR) studies have shown that the "Spanish" pandemic of 1918 (mentioned previously) was caused by an H1N1 virus, which in turn was supplanted in the "Asian" pandemic of 1957 by H2N2 viruses. In 1968, the "Hong Kong" pandemic was caused by viruses of the H3N2 subtype. In 1977, viruses of the H1N1 subtype were reintroduced through an unknown mechanism. These viruses are genetically identical to the H1N1 viruses that were circulating in 1950. Since 1977, influenza A viruses of both the H1N1 and H3N2 subtypes have cocirculated.

The degree of genetic difference between subtypes, 30% or greater, precludes their arising by simple point mutation, and the origin of new pandemic strains has been the subject of intense interest and study, for obvious reasons. The most plausible explanation for their origin takes into account three features of this phenomenon: that the virus has a segmented genome, that pandemics occur only with influenza A viruses, and that influenza A viruses, but not other influenza viruses, maintain a large reservoir of genetic diversity in animals.

Influenza A viruses infect a variety of species, including man, swine, horses, marine mammals, and in particular, birds. In fact, no less than 15 unique HA subtypes (H1 to H15)[63] and nine NA subtypes (N1 to N9)[64] have been identified in avian influenza viruses. Fortunately, avian influenza A viruses themselves appear to be relatively restricted in their ability to replicate in humans.[65] The precise molecular mechanisms responsible for the host-range preferences of avian influenza A viruses are not completely known, but several fac-

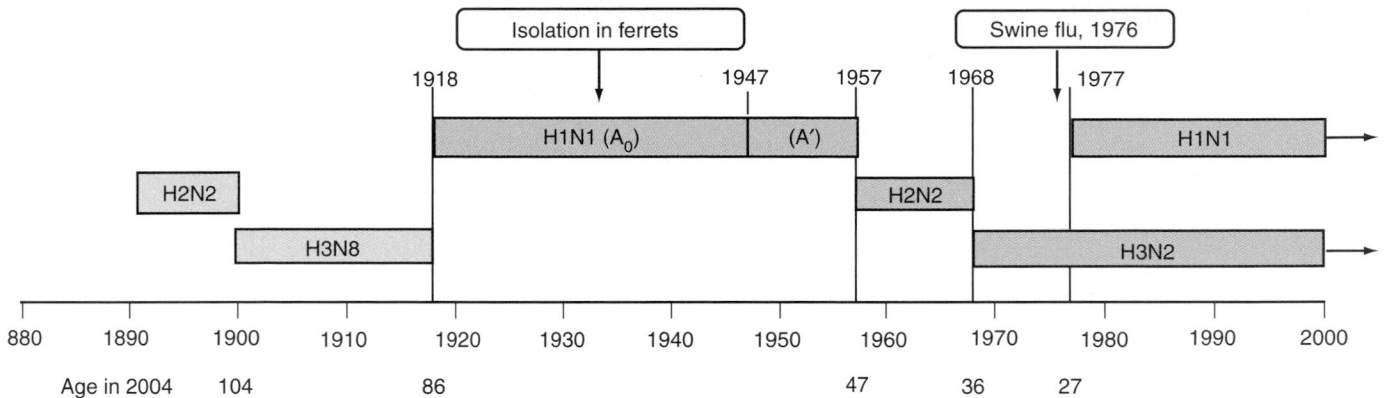

FIGURE 162-6. Recent pandemics of influenza. The duration of circulation of viruses of various subtypes is shown by the boxes. Because the nature of influenza epidemics prior to 1918 is known only by serologic means, those boxes are *shaded tan*. Below the time line is given the ages of individuals in 2004 who were alive during the various epidemic periods of earlier influenza subtypes. For example, individuals currently living who are between the ages of 47 and 86 probably experienced their first influenza A infection as an H1N1 virus. Individuals who are 36 years of age or younger have never been infected with H2N2 viruses.

tors probably play a role. The divergent evolution of the genes of these viruses in avian hosts could have resulted in less efficient interactions between undefined viral and mammalian host cell components. The relative attenuation of avian-human influenza reassortants for man[66] supports a role for non-HA genes in this restriction. In addition, the HAs of avian and mammalian influenza viruses display a different host-cell receptor specificity, with avian viruses preferring receptors containing sialic acid–galactose linkages of the $\alpha 2 \rightarrow 3$ variety, and mammalian viruses tending toward $\alpha 2 \rightarrow 6$ linkages.

Extensive sequence analysis has suggested at least two mechanisms by which avian viruses can circumvent these barriers to interspecies transmission. These studies have shown significant sequence similarity between the HA, NA, and PB1 gene segments of the pandemic H2N2 virus and avian viruses,[67,68] and between the H3 and PB1 gene segments of the pandemic H3N2 virus and avian viruses,[67,69] suggesting that in some circumstances, new pandemic viruses arise by reassortment between avian viruses, which provide novel surface glycoproteins, and human viruses, which provide genes allowing efficient replication in humans. Reassortment would be facilitated by the presence of a third species that is susceptible to infection with both avian and human viruses, such as the pig. Avian-to-swine transmission has been demonstrated previously in nature,[70,71] and naturally occurring avian–human reassortant viruses have been recovered in pigs.[72] However, there are likely to be constraints on what types of reassortants are viable; in particular, it has been suggested that the hemagglutinins of recent human influenza A viruses are not compatible with the matrix genes of current avian viruses,[73] and phenomena of this type may limit the possibilities for generation of pandemic viruses by reassortment.

A second mechanism would involve adaptation of avian viruses to the human host by evolution in swine, and this is supported by sequence analysis showing that the 1918 pandemic was most likely the result of direct introduction of a swine influenza A virus into humans.[74] Recently, it has been shown that avian H1N1 viruses introduced into swine populations are evolving in these animals and have switched receptor specificity to a more mammalian type.[75] This type of evolution is very likely facilitated by the presence of both types of receptors in pig tracheal epithelia.[75]

Finally, avian viruses might also be directly introduced into human populations without prior reassortment or adaptation in an intermediate host. Avian viruses of three different hemagglutinin subtypes, H5, H7, and H9, have caused human disease, and in the case of the H5 and H7 viruses, some illnesses have been severe or even fatal.[76-78] In 1997, an outbreak of H5N1 infection occurred in Hong Kong, in which 18 people were hospitalized and six died. A second outbreak in February 2003 involved two cases and one fatality.[79] Additional human cases of H5N1 were reported in early 2004, from Vietnam and Thailand.[80] A large outbreak of H7N7 infection in The Netherlands in April of 2003 involved 87 human cases. Most of the individuals had illness restricted to conjunctivitis, but one fatality associated with severe pulmonary involvement occurred.[81] Human infection with avian H9N2 virus has also been reported.[82] Human infection appears to take place in the context of intense exposure to infected bird droppings in live bird markets or in agricultural settings. However, despite the presence of virus in the respiratory tract of infected individuals, person-to-person transmission appears to occur rarely, if ever.[83] The specific barrier to transmission is unclear, but there is considerable concern that eventually these introductions will result in generation of a transmission-competent virus.

PATHOGENESIS AND HOST RESPONSE

Cellular Pathogenesis

Influenza virus infection is acquired by a mechanism involving the transfer of virus-containing respiratory secretions from an infected to a susceptible person.[84] A number of lines of evidence indicate that small-particle aerosols (<10 μm mass median diameter) are the predominant factor in such person-to-person transmission. First, large amounts of virus are present in respiratory secretions of infected persons at the time of illness and are thus available for dispersion in small-particle aerosols created by sneezing, coughing, and talking.[84] Second, the explosive nature and simultaneous onset in many persons suggest that a single infected person can transmit virus to a large number of susceptible individuals. Furthermore, influenza virus type A has been shown to be relatively stable in small-particle aerosols at a variety of relative humidities and temperatures, but survival appears to be favored by low relative humidity and low environmental temperature.[85] In experimental influenza in volunteers, inoculation with small-particle aerosols produces an illness that more closely mimics natural disease than does inoculation with large drops into the nose.[86,87] Finally, in such experimental infections, doses of 137 to 300 times the median tissue-culture infective dose ($TCID_{50}$) are required to infect by nasal drops, whereas 0.6 to 3.0 $TCID_{50}$ (i.e., a 100-fold lower dose) is infectious by the aerosol route.[86,87]

Once virus is deposited on the respiratory tract epithelium, it can attach to and penetrate columnar epithelial cells if not prevented from doing so by specific secretory antibody (IgA), by nonspecific mucoproteins to which virus may attach, or by the mechanical action of the mucociliary apparatus. After adsorption, virus replication begins, leading to cell death through several mechanisms. There is a dramatic shutoff of host-cell protein synthesis that occurs at several levels. Newly synthesized cellular mRNAs are degraded (probably because cleavage by the virus cap endonuclease renders these transcripts susceptible to hydrolysis by cellular nuclease),[88] whereas translation of already-synthesized cytoplasmic mRNAs is blocked at both initiation and elongation.[89] Finally, expression of the influenza virus PA protein has been shown to induce generalized degradation of coexpressed proteins through an unknown mechanism.[90] Ultimately, the loss of critical cellular proteins very likely contributes to cell death.

In addition to effects leading to cell necrosis, infection of cells with influenza A and B viruses causes cell death by apoptosis,[91,92] a form of cell death characterized by fragmentation of nuclear DNA. Bronchiolar epithelial and alveolar cells harvested from experimentally infected mice also exhibit apoptotic changes, suggesting that this mechanism of cell death may be important in the pathogenesis of influenza in vivo.[93] The specific mechanism by which influenza virus induces apoptosis is unclear, but it may be related to induction of Fas antigen by double-stranded RNA during virus replication.[94] An unusual viral protein of influenza A viruses, encoded by a second open reading frame in the PB1 gene and therefore referred to as PB1-F2, also plays a role in induction of apoptosis by poisoning mitochondria.[95]

Virus release continues for several hours before cell death ensues. Released virus then may initiate infection in adjacent and nearby cells, so within a few replication cycles, a large number of cells in the respiratory tract are releasing virus and dying as a result of the virus replication. The time between the incubation period and the onset of illness and virus shedding varies from 18 to 72 hours depending in part on the inoculum dose.[84,96]

Influenza virus infection of peripheral blood mononuclear cells, including polymorphonuclear leukocytes (PMNs), lymphocytes, and monocytes, is nonproductive, but it is associated with measurable defects in cellular function that may be relevant to the pathogenesis of influenza-related infectious complications. These include defects in PML chemotaxis and phagocytosis[97] as well as decreased proliferation

and costimulation by mononuclear cells.[98,99] The effects are mediated by virus replication and possibly by a direct toxic effect of certain virus proteins, including hemagglutinin, neuraminidase,[100,101] and nucleoprotein.[102] It has been noted that the short portion of the sequence of the influenza A virus NP is homologous to a naturally occurring peptide found in normal bronchoalveolar lavage fluid that inhibits PMN chemotaxis and oxidative burst.[103]

Virus Shedding

Quantitation of virus in respiratory tract specimens reveals a characteristic pattern (Fig. 162-7). Virus is first detected just before the onset of illness (within 24 hours), rapidly rises to a peak of 3.0 to 7.0 $\log_{10}$ $TCID_{50}$/mL, remains elevated for 24 to 48 hours, and then rapidly decreases to low titers.[84,104] Usually, virus is no longer detectable after 5 to 10 days of virus shedding. However, because of the relative lack of immunity in the young, more prolonged shedding of higher titers of virus is seen in children.[105]

The severity of illness correlates temporally with quantities of virus shed in experimental influenza in volunteers, thus suggesting that a major mechanism in the production of illness is cell death resulting from viral replication.[84] Although the clinical manifestations of influenza are dominated by systemic symptoms, viral replication is limited to the respiratory tract. Instead, systemic symptoms are probably due to the release of potent cytokines, such as type I interferons, tumor necrosis factor, and interleukins (ILs), by infected cells and responding lymphocytes.[104]

Histopathology

Bronchoscopy of individuals with typical, uncomplicated acute influenza has revealed diffuse inflammation of the larynx, trachea, and bronchi, with mucosal injection and edema.[106,107] Biopsy in these cases has revealed a range of histologic findings, from vacuolization of columnar cells with cell loss, to extensive desquamation of the ciliated columnar epithelium down to the basal layer of cells (Fig. 162-8).[107,108]

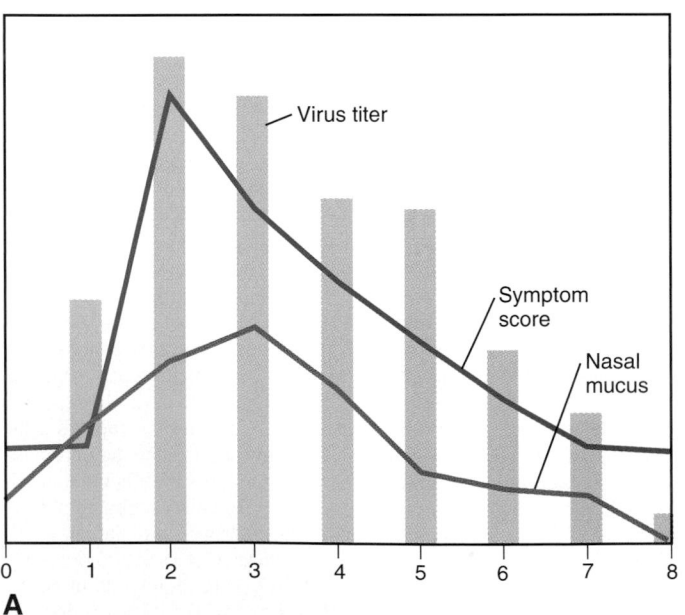
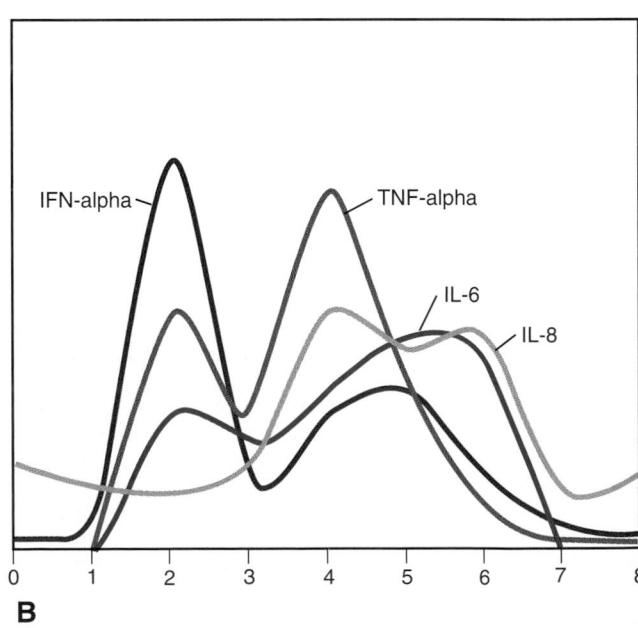

Day post inoculation with A/Texas/91 (H1N1) virus

FIGURE 162-7. Time course of virus shedding, symptoms, and cytokine responses of healthy adults after experimental inoculation with wild-type A/Texas/36/91 virus by nasal drops. **A,** Mean $\log_{10}$ virus titer (tissue-culture infective dose [$TCID_{50}$]/mL nasal secretions), clinical symptom scores, and nasal mucus weights (in grams). **B,** Nasal cytokine levels measured by enzyme-linked immunosorbent assay (ELISA) (pg/mL lavage fluid, corrected for collection efficiency). In both graphs, multiple measurements have been combined for illustration, so that the y-axes are relative values only. Peak values reported in each assay are approximately as follows: virus titer, 3.6 $\log_{10}$ $TCID_{50}$/mL nasal secretions; symptom score, 7.0; nasal mucus weight, 7.0 g; interleukin (IL)-6, 450 pg/mL; interferon (IFN)-α, 150 pg/mL; tumor necrosis factor (TNF)-α, 270 pg/mL; IL-8, 9000 pg/mL. *(Data from Hayden FG, Fritz R, Lobo MC, et al. Local and systemic cytokine responses during experimental human influenza A virus infection: Relation to symptom formation and host defense. J Clin Invest. 1998;101:643-649.)*

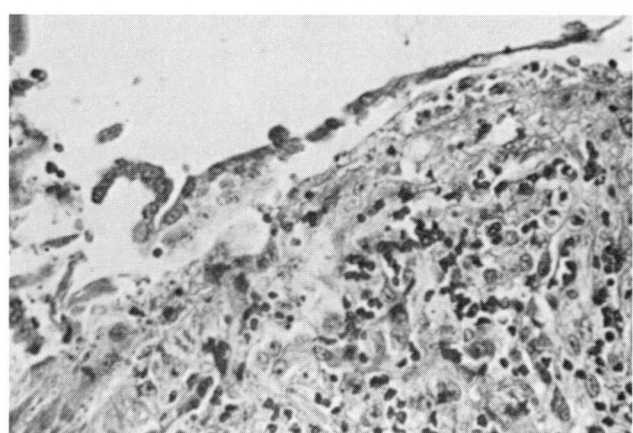

FIGURE 162-8. A small bronchus in acute influenza A infection shows ulceration and attempted regeneration of epithelium (H&E, ×100). *(Courtesy of I. D. Stuard, Reading, Pa.)*

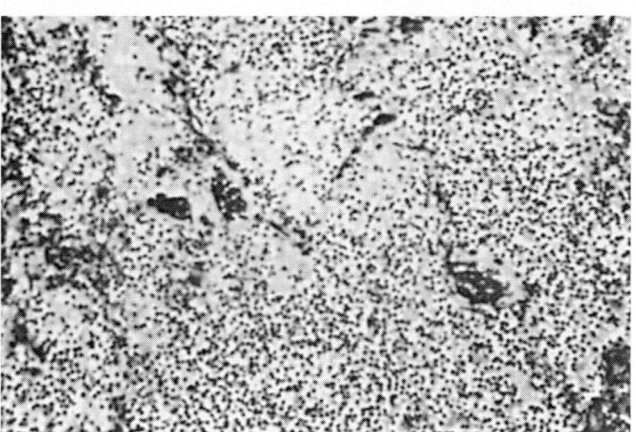

FIGURE 162-10. Lung parenchyma in secondary bacterial infection *(Streptococcus pneumoniae)* complicating influenza A virus infection. Note the marked intra-alveolar polymorphonuclear cell exudate (H&E, ×400). *(Courtesy of I. D. Stuard, Reading, Pa.)*

Individual cells show shrinkage, pyknotic nuclei, and a loss of cilia. Viral antigen can be demonstrated in epithelial cells[109] but is not seen in the basal cell layer.[110] Generally, the tissue response becomes more prominent as one moves distally in the airway.[107] Epithelial damage is accompanied by cellular infiltrates primarily composed of lymphocytes and histiocytes.[107] Histologic findings on autopsy in more severe cases show extensive necrotizing tracheobronchitis, with ulceration and sloughing of the bronchial mucosa,[108,111] extensive hemorrhage, hyaline membrane formation, and a paucity of PMN infiltration (Fig. 162-9). Patients with secondary bacterial pneumonia have the changes characteristic of bacterial pneumonia in addition to the tracheobronchial findings of influenza (Fig. 162-10). Recovery is associated with rapid regeneration of the epithelial cell layer and with pseudometaplasia.

Pathophysiology

Abnormalities of pulmonary function are frequently demonstrated in otherwise healthy, nonasthmatic young adults with uncomplicated (nonpneumonic) acute influenza. Demonstrated defects include diminished forced flow rates, increased total pulmonary resistance, and decreased density-dependent forced flow rates consistent with generalized increased resistance in airways less than 2 mm in diameter,[112,113] as well as increased responses to bronchoprovocation.[112] In addition, abnormalities of carbon monoxide diffusing capacity[114] and increases

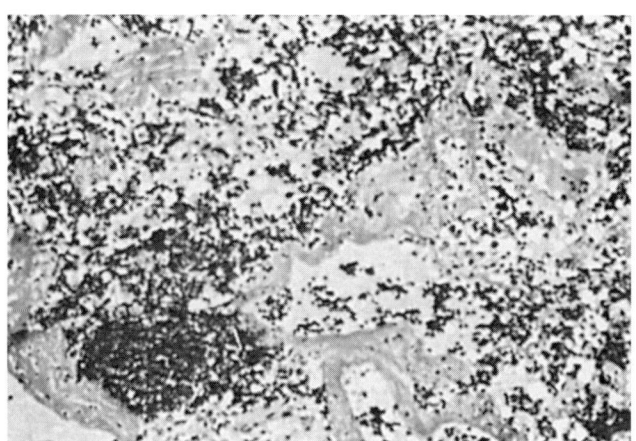

FIGURE 162-9. Lung parenchyma in primary influenza viral pneumonia shows extensive hemorrhage, acellular hyaline membrane lining alveolar ducts and alveoli, and a paucity of inflammatory cells within the alveoli (H&E, ×400). *(Courtesy of I. D. Stuard, Reading, Pa.)*

in the alveolar-arterial oxygen gradient[115] have been seen. Of note, pulmonary function defects can persist for weeks after clinical recovery. Influenza in asthmatics[116] or in patients with chronic obstructive disease[117] may result in acute declines in forced expiratory vital capacity (FVC) or forced expiratory volume in 1 second (FEV$_1$). Individuals with acute influenza may be more susceptible to bronchoconstriction from air pollutants such as nitrates.[118]

Primary viral pneumonia is an uncommon but frequently severe complication of acute influenza. In this situation, virus infection reaches the lung either by contiguous spread from the upper respiratory tract or by inhalation. The trachea and bronchi contain bloody fluid, and the mucosa is hyperemic.[119] Tracheitis, bronchitis, and bronchiolitis are seen, with loss of normal ciliated epithelial cells. Submucosal hyperemia, focal hemorrhage, edema, and cellular infiltrate are present. The alveolar spaces contain varying numbers of neutrophils and mononuclear cells admixed with fibrin and edema fluid. The alveolar capillaries may be markedly hyperemic with intra-alveolar hemorrhage. Acellular hyaline membranes line many of the alveolar ducts and alveoli.[119] Pathologic findings seen by biopsy of lung in nonfatal cases are similar to those described in fatal cases.[120]

Bacterial superinfection is a well-recognized complication of viral pneumonia and accounts for a large proportion of the morbidity and mortality of viral lower respiratory tract disease, especially in adults. Consequently, the spectrum of disease and pathophysiology of bacterial superinfection has been studied intensively, and a number of factors have been identified in viral respiratory disease that could play a role in increasing the risk of bacterial infection.[121] Uncomplicated influenza is associated with significant abnormalities in ciliary clearance mechanisms.[122,123] In addition, increased adherence of bacteria to virus-infected epithelial cells has been demonstrated.[124,125] The disruption of the normal epithelial cell barrier to infection, and loss of mucociliary clearance undoubtedly enhance bacterial pathogenesis.[107,126] In addition, influenza infection may upregulate certain cell surface receptors involved in bacterial adherence.[127] Alterations in PMNs and mononuclear cells, described earlier, may also contribute to enhanced bacterial infection.[98,128,129]

Viral Factors That Influence Pathogenicity

Clinical characteristics of illness during the 1918 influenza pandemic differed from those of subsequent pandemics, with higher mortality rates in young adults. The viral factors, if any, that might have been responsible for this behavior remain unknown. Extensive analysis of genetic sequences recovered from preserved specimens of material from victims of the pandemic have not revealed obvious differences between the 1918 influenza virus and more conventional influenza viruses, but investigations are continuing. Since that time, there has been little direct evidence for major inherent differences in viral strains as regards to pathogenic potential in humans. Instead, the severity of epidemics is most likely determined largely by the status of immunity in the population. However, in certain situations, individual viral proteins have been demonstrated to have a significant impact on pathogenicity. This is particularly true for the HA and NS1 proteins.

An essential feature of influenza A virus replication is that proteolytic cleavage of the HA is required to generate infectious virus, and this plays a role in the most clear-cut demonstration of the role of an individual influenza virus protein in pathogenicity. Infection of fowl with avian influenza viruses can result in a relatively avirulent, asymptomatic infection limited to the respiratory and gastrointestinal mucosa, or in a virulent, rapidly progressive, fatal systemic infection with involvement of the brain and other visceral organs. Comparison of the HAs of virulent and avirulent strains of H5 subtype and H7 subtype influenza A viruses has shown that the structure of the HA cleavage site is critical in determining the virulence phenotype in this model. Proteases capable of cleaving the HA of avirulent viruses, such as tryptase Clara,[130] are restricted in distribution to cells of the respiratory and gastrointestinal mucosa, thereby limiting replication to these areas. However, addition of several basic amino acids to the cleavage site,[131] coupled with the absence of a nearby glycosylation site,[132] renders the hemagglutinin capable of being cleaved by ubiquitous cellular furin-like proteases[133] and allows these viruses to escape the confines of the mucosa and replicate systemically in chickens.[134]

As described previously, human infections with H5 and H7 viruses can be fatal, and as it turns out, these viruses also have the highly cleavable form of hemagglutinin. Although some of these viruses also have a high level of lethality in mice, to date there has been no evidence of replication of these viruses outside the respiratory tract in man. Thus, the potential role of HA cleavability in pathogenesis in humans is currently unknown. Interestingly, evaluation of the nucleotide sequence of the HA from the 1918 pandemic virus did not reveal this virus to have the highly cleavable type of HA.[74]

Both influenza A and influenza B viruses use the NS1 protein as a mechanism to circumvent the host type-I interferon response. The NS gene antagonizes the action of type-I interferons through an unknown mechanism, and absence of the NS1 protein renders the virus incapable of growth in interferon-competent systems. The NS gene of the H5 avian viruses appears to be especially potent in this regard, and this may provide a partial explanation for its enhanced virulence in mice. Recent reports have suggested that H5 viruses associated with fatal cases in humans have changes in nucleotide sequences in the N51 gene that result both in increased resistance to the action of interferon and in the ability to induce proinflammatory cytokines.[135] In contrast, when the NS gene of the 1918 pandemic human virus was placed in the background of an avirulent influenza virus and administered to mice, more attenuated disease, rather than enhanced disease, was the result, suggesting the effect is host specific.

Multiple additional animal models have been described in which it is possible to generate influenza viruses with altered levels of pathogenicity. A variety of classic genetic and molecular biologic techniques have been used to evaluate the role of specific viral genes or gene products in determining the virulence of influenza viruses in these models. An exhaustive review of these studies is beyond the scope of this chapter, but they have generally shown that virulence is a multigenic trait whose specific basis varies with the virus strains and the models used.[136-139]

Immunology

Epidemiologic and experimental observations in humans have shown that infection with influenza virus results in long-lived resistance to reinfection with the homologous virus.[140] In addition, variable degrees of cross-protection within a subtype have been observed, but infection induces essentially no protection across subtypes,[141] or between types A and B. Infection induces both systemic and local antibody, as well as cytotoxic T-cell responses, each of which plays a role in recovery from infection and resistance to reinfection.

Antibody Responses

Systemic Antibody Responses. Infection with influenza virus results in the development of antibody to the influenza virus envelope glycoproteins HA and NA, as well as to the structural M and NP proteins. Some individuals may develop antibody to the M2 protein as well.[142] As measured by enzyme-linked immunosorbent assay (ELISA), serum IgM, IgA, and IgG antibody to the HA appear simultaneously within 2 weeks of inoculation of virus.[143] The antibody response is more rapid after reinfection. The development of anti-NA antibodies parallels that of hemagglutinin-inhibiting (HAI) antibodies.[144] However, whereas responses to the HA develop after primary infection, responses to the NA appear to require previous infection.[141] Peak antibody responses are seen at 4 to 7 weeks after infection and decline slowly thereafter; titers can still be detected years after infection even without reexposure.

Antibody to the HA can be measured by standard HAI tests or a variety of ELISAs, and it neutralizes virus infectivity.[145] Because of the cost and requirement for cell cultures for the neutralizing test, the HAI test is the primary method of detecting antigenic relatedness among hemagglutinins of influenza viruses. Antihemagglutinin antibody protects against both disease and infection with the homologous virus.[146] Although there is no exact correlation, serum HAI titers of 1:40 or greater, or serum neutralizing titers of 1:8 or greater, are associated with protection against infection; HAI titers of 1:20 or 1:10 are associated with lesser degrees of protection. Higher levels of antibody may be required for complete protection in older adults.[147,148]

Protection in clinical studies has been shown to be primarily strain specific, but some degree of protection is present against strains showing antigenic drift within a subtype, depending on the degree of drift.[149,150] For example, Foy and colleagues showed that influenza A vaccine (A/Hong Kong/68/H3N2) induced protection against the drift variant A/England/72/H3N2 virus that persisted for 3 years.[149] Generally, antibody that is present in low quantity, or that is primarily directed against a heterologous strain of influenza, may only modify the severity of illness and not prevent infection.

Antibody to the NA can be measured by NA inhibition or ELISA. In contrast to anti-HA antibody, anti-NA antibody does not neutralize virus infectivity but instead reduces efficient release of virus from infected cells, resulting in decreased plaque size in in vitro assays[151] and in reductions in the magnitude of virus shedding in infected animals.[152,153] Observations on the relative protection of those with anti-N2 antibody during the A/Hong Kong/68 (H3N2) pandemic,[144,154] as well as experimental challenge studies in humans,[155] have shown that anti-NA antibody can be protective against disease and results in decreased virus shedding and severity of illness, but that it is infection permissive.[156] Passive transfer studies in mice have also suggested that antibody to the M2 protein of influenza A viruses may have a similar effect to that of anti-NA antibody.[157]

Antibody to internal viral proteins such as M or NP can be measured by the complement fixation (CF) test. These antibodies are cross-reactive among type A viruses, but they are non-neutralizing and do not appear to play a role in protective immunity. They disappear much more rapidly (in weeks to months) than do neutralizing, HAI, or anti-NA antibodies, primarily because they are predominantly IgM rather than IgG, and thus they may be useful for diagnosis of recent infection.

Mucosal Antibody Responses. The majority of studies of mucosal responses to influenza in humans have concentrated on measurement of HA responses by ELISA or by neutralization tests, because nonspecific inhibitors of hemagglutination present in nasal mucus interfere with the standard HAI test. These studies have demonstrated significant mucosal responses to infection with wild-type virus or live-attenuated influenza vaccines. Both IgA and IgG are found in nasal secretions. Nasal HA-specific IgG is predominantly IgG$_1$, and its levels correlate well with serum levels of HA-specific IgG$_1$, suggesting that nasal IgG originates by passive diffusion from the systemic compartment.[158] Nasal HA-specific IgA is predominantly polymeric and IgA$_1$, suggesting local synthesis. Serum HA-specific IgA is also mostly polymeric IgA$_1$. The origin of serum IgA after mucosal infection is unclear but may derive from seeding of peripheral lymphoid tissue by memory cells derived from the mucosa.[146]

Studies in mice and ferrets have emphasized the importance of local IgA antibody in resistance to infection, particularly in protection of the upper respiratory tract. Polymeric IgA was shown to be specifically transported into the nasal secretions of mice and to protect against nasal challenge. Protection could be abrogated by intranasal administration of antiserum against IgA but not IgM or IgG.[159] Local antibody has also been shown to play a role in protection against antigenic variants in mice.[160] Studies in humans have also suggested that the resistance to reinfection induced by virus infection is mediated predominantly by local HA-specific IgA, whereas that induced by parenteral immunization with inactivated virus depends also on systemic IgG.[155,161] Almost all persons with nasal neutralizing antibody titers of 1:4 or greater are protected against influenza.[162,163] Importantly, either mucosal or systemic antibody alone can be protective if present in high enough concentrations, and optimal protection occurs when both serum and nasal antibodies are present.[164]

Cellular Responses

Antibody responses to the HA are T-cell dependent[165-167] and class II restricted. CD4$^+$ cells provide help (Th) to B cells for production of antibody to the HA and NA. Both CD4$^+$ cells that recognize epitopes on the HA molecule, and CD4$^+$ cells that recognize epitopes on M, NP, or PB2 may provide help for HA antibody production.[168] The epitopes on HA recognized by Th cells are distinct from those recognized by neutralizing antibody,[169] and they may be cross-reactive within a subtype. Influenza-specific Th cells also promote the generation of virus-specific CD8$^+$ cytotoxic T lymphocytes.[170,171]

Recently, it has been recognized that Th responses can be further classified as type 1 (Th1) or type 2 (Th2) responses on the basis of the profile of cytokines produced on in vitro challenge. Influenza virus infection of mice generates a strong Th1-type response.[172] Th2-type cytokines (IL-4, IL-5, IL-6, IL-10) have been also described in the lungs of mice infected with influenza virus.[173,174] Circumstantial evidence suggests that protective immune responses to influenza are associated with Th1-like responses. Adoptive transfer of anti-influenza T-cell clones secreting cytokines of the Th2 type fails to promote viral clearance,[175] and administration of interferon-γ delays viral clearance and development of CTL in influenza virus–infected mice.[176] Of note, blockade of gamma interferon by interferon antibody does not affect development of CTL responses but results in reduced migration of PMNs to the lung in the murine model.[177] In addition, administration of IL-4 to infected mice promotes Th2-type responses and results in markedly delayed viral clearance.[178]

Influenza virus–infected cells can be lysed by antibody in the presence of complement, by antibody-dependent cellular cytotoxicity,[179] or by the action of cytotoxic T (Tc) lymphocytes. Generally, Tc lymphocytes express CD8$^+$ and recognize class I HLA. Such cells may recognize either HA or internal proteins such as M, NP, or PB2.[180] Therefore, Tc lymphocytes may be subtype specific or, in the case of those that recognize internal proteins, may be broadly cross-reactive, lysing cells infected with influenza A but not influenza B virus.[181,182] In addition, class II restricted cells may exhibit cytotoxic activity similar to that shown by class I restricted cells.[182]

Extensive adoptive transfer experiments have shown that virus-specific Tc lymphocytes can mediate recovery from influenza virus infection,[183-188] including both HA-specific and cross-reactive Tc. However, studies in mice lacking major histocompatibility complex (MHC) class I have shown that Tc lymphocytes are not absolutely required for recovery.[189-191]

Tc lymphocyte responses to influenza also develop in humans after influenza virus infections, generally peaking on about day 14 after infection.[192] Although not studied extensively, the presence of virus-specific prechallenge, class I–restricted Tc lymphocytes has been shown to correlate with reductions in the duration and level of virus replication in adults with low levels of serum HA and NA antibody who were challenged with influenza A virus.[193] The role of Tc lymphocytes directed against internal viral proteins in protection against severe disease in humans is unclear, as the internal virus proteins were shared between viruses causing the pandemics of 1957 and 1968 and the viruses in circulation immediately prior to these pandemics.[68,194] Memory Tc-lymphocyte responses may play a role in ameliorating the severity of disease and speeding recovery after infection, as suggested by the finding of more severe influenza in individuals with severe defects in cell-mediated immunity.[28]

CLINICAL FINDINGS

Uncomplicated Influenza

Typical uncomplicated influenza often begins with an abrupt onset of symptoms after an incubation period of 1 to 2 days. Many patients can pinpoint the hour of onset.[84,195-197] Initially, systemic symptoms predominate, including feverishness, chilliness or frank shaking chills, headaches, myalgia, malaise, and anorexia. In more severe cases, prostration is observed. Usually, myalgia or headache is the most troublesome symptom, and the severity is related to the height of the fever. Myalgia may involve the extremities or the long muscles of the back. In children, calf muscle myalgia may be particularly prominent. Severe pain in the eye muscles can be elicited by gazing laterally, and arthralgia but not frank arthritis is commonly observed. Other ocular symptoms include tearing and burning. The systemic symptoms usually persist for 3 days, the typical duration of fever. Respiratory symptoms, particularly a dry cough, severe pharyngeal pain, and nasal obstruction and discharge, are usually also present at the onset of illness but are overshadowed by the systemic symptoms. The predominance of systemic symptoms is a major feature distinguishing influenza from other viral upper respiratory infections. Hoarseness and a dry or sore throat may also be present, but these symptoms tend to appear as systemic symptoms diminish, and thus they become more prominent as the disease progresses, persisting 3 to 4 days after the fever subsides. Cough is the most frequent and troublesome of these symptoms and may be accompanied by substernal discomfort or burning. Older adults may simply present with high fever, lassitude, and confusion without the characteristic respiratory complaints, which may not occur at all. In addition, there is a wide range of symptomatology in healthy adults, ranging from classic influenza to mild illness or asymptomatic infection.

Fever is the most important physical finding. The temperature usually rises rapidly to a peak of 100° to 104° F, and occasionally to 106° F, within 12 hours of onset, concurrent with the development of systemic symptoms. Fever is usually continuous but may be intermittent, especially if antipyretics are administered. On the second and third days of illness, the temperature elevation is usually 0.5° to 1.0° F lower than on the first day, and as the fever subsides, the systemic symptoms diminish. Typically, the duration of fever is 3 days, but it may last 4 to 8 days. In a small number of cases, a second fever spike occurs on the third or fourth day and results in a biphasic fever curve.

Early in the course of illness, the patient appears toxic, the face is flushed, and the skin is hot and moist. The eyes are watery and reddened. A clear nasal discharge is common, but nasal obstruction is uncommon. The mucous membranes of the nose and throat are hyperemic, but exudate is not observed. Small, tender cervical lymph nodes are often present. Transient scattered rhonchi or localized areas of rales are found in less than 20% of cases. A convalescent period of 1, 2, or more weeks to full recovery then ensues. Cough, lassitude, and malaise are the most frequent symptoms during this period.

Available data suggest that illness associated with influenza B virus infection closely resembles that described for influenza A, although some have suggested that influenza B illness may be somewhat milder than influenza A illness.[198,199] In contrast, influenza C infection, when it occurs, causes afebrile common colds and rarely, if ever, produces the influenza syndrome.[200] It does not occur in epidemics.

At the extremes of age, there are prominent differences in influenza. Influenza attack rates are higher in children than in adults.[23,201] Maximal temperatures tend to be higher among children, and cervical adenopathy is more frequent among children than among adults.[96] Croup associated with influenza virus infection occurs only among children.[202-204] Among older adults, fever remains a very frequent finding, although the height of the febrile response may be lower than among children and young adults. Pulmonary complications are far more frequent in older adults than in any other age group.

Complications of Influenza

Pulmonary Complications

Two manifestations of pneumonia associated with influenza are well recognized: primary influenza viral pneumonia and secondary bacterial infection. In addition, less distinct and milder pulmonic syndromes often occur during an outbreak of influenza that may represent tracheobronchitis, localized viral pneumonia, or possibly mixed viral and bacterial pneumonia. Comparative features of these clinical syndromes are shown in Table 162-4. Studies to determine the interaction between virus and bacteria have helped researchers understand the different clinical patterns described here.[205]

Primary Influenza Viral Pneumonia. The syndrome of primary influenza viral pneumonia was first well documented in the 1957-1958 outbreak.[106,119] However, it is clear that many deaths of young healthy adults in the 1918-1919 outbreak were the result of this syndrome. In outbreaks since 1918, primary influenza viral pneumonia has occurred predominantly among persons with cardiovascular disease, especially rheumatic heart disease with mitral stenosis, and to a lesser extent in others with chronic cardiovascular and pulmonary disorders. The illness begins with a typical onset of influenza, followed by a rapid progression of fever, cough, dyspnea, and cyanosis. Physical examination and chest radiographs reveal bilateral findings consistent with the adult respiratory disease syndrome but no consolidation. Blood gas studies show marked hypoxia, Gram stain of the sputum fails to reveal significant bacteria, and bacterial culture yields sparse growth of normal flora, whereas viral cultures yield high titers of influenza A virus. Such patients do not respond to antibiotics and mortality is high. At autopsy, findings consist of tracheitis, bronchitis, diffuse hemorrhagic pneumonia, hyaline membranes lining alveolar ducts and alveoli, and a paucity of inflammatory cells within the alveoli (see Figs. 162-9 and 162-10). At the present time, late in the interpandemic era, severe primary influenza viral pneumonia is rare.

Secondary Bacterial Pneumonia. Secondary bacterial pneumonia often produces a syndrome that is clinically indistinguishable from that occurring in the absence of influenza.[206,207] The patients (most often older adults or those with chronic pulmonary, cardiac, and metabolic or other disease) have a classic influenza illness followed by a period of improvement lasting usually 4 to 14 days. Recrudescence of fever is associated with symptoms and signs of bacterial pneumonia such as cough, sputum production, and an area of consolidation detected on physical examination and a chest radiograph. Gram staining and culture of sputum reveal a predominance of a bacterial pathogen, most often *Streptococcus pneumoniae* or *Haemophilus influenzae,* and, notably, an increased frequency of *Staphylococcus aureus,* which is otherwise an uncommon cause of community-acquired pneumonia. Such patients usually respond to specific antibiotic therapy. Analysis of different radiographic patterns of pneumonia indicates that a variety of abnormalities can occur in all ages.[208,209]

During an outbreak of influenza, many patients do not clearly fit into either of the aforementioned categories.[210] The disease is not relentlessly progressive, and yet the fever pattern may not be biphasic. These patients may have primary viral, secondary bacterial, or mixed viral and bacterial infection of the lung. In more recent epidemics, in which surveillance cultures of hospitalized patients have been carried out, most patients with pneumonia and influenza presented early, while they were still culture positive for influenza virus. Most responded to antibiotics without the use of antivirals. In addition, milder forms of influenza viral pneumonia involving only one lobe or segment have been described that do not invariably lead to death, and that are more likely to be confused with pneumonia caused by *Mycoplasma pneumoniae* than to pneumonia produced by bacterial infection.

In children, pneumonia may occur, but it is less common than in adults. Bronchitis may also occur as a result of influenza A or B virus infection, but respiratory syncytial virus and parainfluenza virus type 3 are more important causes of bronchiolitis.

Pulmonary Complications in Immunosuppressed Patients. In patients with HIV infection, influenza has not been recognized as a major clinical problem, although disease of greater severity has been noted in some patients[211] and pneumonic complications of influenza have occurred. Additional studies are required to better define the importance of influenza virus infection in HIV-infected patients.

Influenza has been noted to cause severe disease with an increased incidence of pneumonia in immunosuppressed children with cancer compared with age-matched individuals without immunosuppression.[212] Severe disease associated with pneumonia and death has been reported, particularly in bone marrow transplant recipients and leukemic patients.[28,213,214] Relatively more immunosuppressed individuals early after transplantation appear to be at greater risk.[214] However, for reasons that are not completely clear, influenza has not appeared to be quite the problem in this population that other respiratory viruses, particularly paramyxoviruses, are. Influenza virus shedding can be quite prolonged in immunosuppressed children,[215] particularly those with HIV and low CD4+ counts.[216] Because of the prolonged, unchecked replication of influenza viruses in these individuals, resistance to antiviral drugs eventually occurs in many treated patients.[215,217]

Other Pulmonary Complications. In addition to pneumonia, other pulmonary complications of influenza have been recognized.

TABLE 162-4 Comparative Features of Pulmonary Complications of Influenza

	Primary Viral Pneumonia	*Secondary Bacterial Pneumonia*	*Mixed Viral and Bacterial Pneumonia*	*Localized Viral Pneumonia*
Setting	Cardiovascular disease; pregnancy; young adult (Hsw1N1)	Age >65 yr; pulmonary disease	Any associated with A or B	?Normal
Clinical history	Relentless progression from classic 3-day influenza	Improvement, then worsening after 3-day influenza	Features of both primary and secondary pneumonia	Continuation of classic 3-day syndrome
Physical examination	Bilateral findings, no consolidation	Consolidation	Consolidation	Area of rales
Sputum bacteriology	Normal flora	*Pneumococcus, Staphylococcus, Haemophilus influenzae*	*Pneumococcus, Staphylococcus, H. influenzae*	Normal flora
Chest radiography	Bilateral findings	Consolidation	Consolidation	Segmental infiltrate
White blood cell count	Leukocytosis with a shift to the left	Leukocytosis with a shift to the left	Leukocytosis with a shift to the left	Usually normal
Isolation of influenza virus	Yes	No	Yes	Yes
Response to antibiotics	No	Yes	Often	No
Mortality	High	Low	Variable	Very low

Croup. Significant numbers of cases of croup occur in influenza A and B outbreaks.[202,203] Croup associated with influenza A virus appears to be more severe but less frequent than that associated with parainfluenza virus types 1 or 3 or respiratory syncytial virus infections (see Chapters 153 and 155).

Exacerbation of Chronic Pulmonary Disease. Acute exacerbation of chronic bronchitis, a phenomenon that is associated with other respiratory disease–causing viruses and bacteria,[218-220] is common. Studies by Monto and Ross have shown that such infections result in a permanent loss of pulmonary function.[221] Another major illness that is exacerbated is asthma. Often, stable asthmatics will worsen to status asthmaticus as a result of influenza.[222,223] Another illness exacerbated by influenza is cystic fibrosis. In children afflicted with this entity, influenza infections may lead to severe complications.[224]

Frequency of Pulmonary Involvement. The findings of persistent physiologic changes in the lower respiratory tract with uncomplicated influenza discussed earlier suggest that viral invasion of the lower respiratory tract is common in uncomplicated influenza and may help to explain the relatively long convalescence. The frequency of overt involvement of the respiratory tract has been answered in part by Fry.[208,209,225] In five successive epidemics, he showed that the overall rate of chest complications (tracheobronchitis or pneumonia) was 9.5% of cases. From the ages of 5 to 50, the rate was low (4% to 8%), but it increased progressively after the age of 60, reaching a level of 73% in those over 70 years of age. Foy et al. studied seven successive epidemics of influenza A infection and showed that six of the seven were associated with at least a doubling of pneumonia rates among adults.[226] Still others have studied rates of admission to the hospital and have shown a lower impact on hospitalization.[226-228]

Nonpulmonary Complications

Most of the complications of influenza have been evaluated in years when there were sizable outbreaks.[119,229-231] However, as antigenic variation of a subtype evolves and as the exposure of the population to vaccine and to virus occurs, the full-blown influenza syndrome becomes a less frequent manifestation. Nonetheless, infection rates may remain high, and consequences of infection in severely compromised older adult patients remain significant.

Myositis. Myositis and myoglobinuria with tender leg muscles and elevated serum creatine phosphokinase (CPK) levels have been reported, mostly in children after influenza A or B infection, most commonly after the latter,[232-235] but they can occur in adults as well. Symptoms may be sufficiently severe to interfere with walking, but neurologic changes are not evident.

Cardiac Complications. Both myocarditis and pericarditis have been rarely associated with influenza A or B virus infection.[236] Some investigators have associated influenza with myocardial infarction. However, neither myocarditis nor pericarditis is commonly observed at autopsy among those who died of primary influenza viral pneumonia.[119] In patients with cardiac disease, the acquisition of influenza provides a significant risk of death.[230,237,238]

Toxic Shock Syndrome. In recent outbreaks of influenza A or B, a toxic shock–like syndrome has occurred in previously healthy children or adults, presumably because viral infection changed colonization and replication characteristics of the toxin-producing staphylococcus.[239,240]

Central Nervous Complications. Guillain-Barré syndrome has been reported to occur after influenza A infection, as it has after numerous other infections, but no definite etiologic relationship has been established. In addition, cases of transverse myelitis and encephalitis have occurred rarely.[241,242] An etiologic association of these syndromes with influenza virus infection has only infrequently been proven, and influenza infection accounts at most for only a small proportion of cases of each of these symptoms. Early reports of deaths associated with influenza A infection in children and young adults during the 2003-2004 season, have implicated encephalitis as a prominent feature.[243]

Reye's Syndrome. Reye's syndrome is associated with many viral infections, prominently including influenza and varicella in children. The classic manifestation is a change in mental status occurring several days after a typical respiratory illness. Manifestations range from lethargy to delirium, obtundation, seizures, and respiratory arrest. Lumbar puncture reveals normal protein values and normal cell counts, confirming the presence of encephalopathy rather than encephalitis or meningoencephalitis. The most frequent laboratory abnormality is elevation of the blood ammonia value, which occurs in almost all patients. Reye's syndrome is almost exclusively seen in children who have been given aspirin to treat febrile illnesses due to influenza and other viruses, and it is important to use other antipyretics such as nonsteroidal anti-inflammatory drugs in this situation. Children who require continuous aspirin therapy are an important target group for influenza vaccination to reduce the risks of Reye's syndrome.

DIAGNOSIS

Virus Isolation

Virus isolation or detection of viral antigen in respiratory secretions is the technique of greatest utility in the setting of acute illness. Virus can be isolated readily from nasal swab specimens, throat swab specimens, nasal washes, or combined nose and throat swab specimens. The general consensus is that throat swab alone is probably less sensitive for detection than other samples. Virus can also be isolated from sputum samples, if these are being produced.[244] Samples should be placed into containers of viral transport medium and transported to the laboratory as soon as possible, although the virus survives overnight if the specimen is kept on ice. Specimens for influenza are inoculated onto rhesus monkey kidney, cynomolgus monkey kidney, or Madin-Darby canine kidney cell cultures, where virus is detected by cytopathic effect or hemadsorption. Less commonly, embryonated eggs can be used for virus isolation. Over 90% of positive cultures can be detected within 3 days of inoculation[245] and the remainder by 5 to 7 days.

Rapid Diagnosis

A variety of techniques have been employed to speed the process. The most widely used tests are based on immunologic detection of viral antigen in respiratory secretions. For influenza, such tests include the Directigen Flu A+B (Becton-Dickenson), Flu OIA (BioStar), and QuickVue Influenza A+B test (Quidel Corporation). In each of these tests, a sample of respiratory secretions is treated with a mucolytic agent and then tested, either on a filter paper (Directigen), in an optical device (Flu OIA), or with a dipstick (QuickVue) in which reaction with specific antibody results in a color change. In a slight variation of this strategy, the ZstatFlu (ZymeTx) test detects the presence of viral neuraminidase activity in the sample using a chromogenic substrate; this test is based on the same chemistry used to develop neuraminidase inhibitors. All of the tests are designed to detect both influenza A and influenza B, are relatively simple to perform, and can provide results within 30 minutes. Currently, both the QuickVue and Zstat tests are eligible for Clinical Laboratory Improvement Amendment of 1998 (CLIA) waiver. Additional tests are in development, and updated information is available at http://www.cdc.gov/flu/professionals/labdiagnosis.htm.

The reported sensitivities of each test in comparison to cell culture have ranged between 40% and 80%, and they are somewhat dependent on the nature of the samples tested and the patients from whom they were derived.[246-251] In general, sensitivities in adults and older adult patients tend to be lower than those reported in young children, who shed much larger quantities of virus in nasal secretions and therefore have much higher concentrations of antigen in their samples.[252] Similarly, sensitivity is likely to be higher early in the course of illness, when viral shedding is maximal. The sensitivity of some tests for detection of influenza B viruses may be lower than that for influenza A viruses.[247,251] Reported specificities have ranged from 85% to 100%. It is important to note in this regard that in each of these studies, a portion of samples that are negative by culture and positive by rapid test are confirmed as positive by PCR (see later).[245] Although all types of respiratory samples can be used in such tests, the sensitivity appears to be better with nasopharyngeal swabs and aspirates than with throat swabs or gargles.[246,253]

As no published comparative data are currently available that conclusively demonstrate superiority of one test over another, decisions regarding a specific test are generally made on the basis of convenience, cost, and the familiarity of the operator with the technique. In most medical centers, the cost is approximately $20 per diagnostic test.

A variety of approaches to direct detection of viral nucleic acids in clinical specimens have also been explored for rapid diagnosis, including nucleic acid hybridization and PCR amplification. PCR in particular has the advantage of being potentially more sensitive than cell culture, and it may allow detection of virus in samples in which the virions have lost viability. In addition, it is possible to devise multiplex techniques so that a single test can detect a number of different agents.[254] However, as PCR techniques are more labor intensive and technically demanding, and they require specialized laboratory equipment, they generally have not supplanted antigen detection for rapid diagnosis.

Serology

Serologic tests, such as complement fixation and hemagglutination inhibition, can be used to retrospectively establish a diagnosis of influenza infection. Because most individuals have been previously infected with influenza viruses, a single serum is generally not adequate, and paired serum specimens, consisting of an acute and a convalescent sera obtained 10 to 20 days later, should be submitted for testing.

Epidemiologic Diagnosis

A diagnosis can also be made on epidemiologic grounds. That is, when the presence of influenza virus is confirmed in a region or community, healthy adults with acute influenza-like illness most commonly have influenza. In fact, several studies have shown that the accuracy of a clinical diagnosis in healthy adults in the setting of an influenza outbreak is as high as 80% to 90%.[255-257] In an analysis of symptoms in young adults being assessed for entry into studies of influenza virus treatment, the best multivariate predictors of laboratory-confirmed influenza virus infection were cough and fever,[256] with an increasing predictive value with increasing levels of fever. However, the predictive value of such a symptom complex may be less in older adults[258] and in children.[259] In nursing homes, the presence of cocirculating pathogens (such as respiratory syncytial virus) that can result in identical symptoms can clearly complicate the ability to make a clinical diagnosis of influenza specifically.[260,261]

Role of Rapid Diagnosis in Clinical Decision Making

The optimal use of rapid diagnostic tests in patient management is yet to be defined. Such tests are most clearly useful in the rapid identification of outbreaks within institutions or in the community, where the testing of multiple specimens can compensate for the relative lack of sensitivity of the test for any single specimen. The utility of rapid testing in other situations depends on a number of factors beyond the specific performance of the test, including the extent of influenza epidemic activity (i.e., the a priori likelihood of infection) and the potential consequences of a positive or negative result.

TREATMENT

Uncomplicated Influenza

Four antiviral drugs are currently available for the prevention and treatment of influenza. A comparison of the basic pharmacology and antiviral activity of these agents is given in Table 162-5, and they are described in detail later. Certain general principles apply regardless of the specific form of therapy chosen. It is important to recognize that individuals with an intact immune system who have had previous influenza infections rapidly limit the replication of these viruses. Therefore, the opportunity to impact viral replication with antiviral agents is limited, and effective use of these agents requires early initiation of therapy. No studies have ever demonstrated a benefit of antiviral therapy begun after 48 hours or more of symptoms, and the greatest effect is typically seen when therapy is started in the first 24 hours. The question of whether delayed therapy may be useful in selected populations, such as immunosuppressed individuals, remains unanswered.

M2 Inhibitors: Amantadine and Rimantadine

Mechanism of Action and Activity

The M2 inhibitors amantadine and rimantadine are related primary symmetrical amines and are active against all strains of influenza A virus in a variety of cell culture systems and animal models.[262] In cell culture, inhibitory levels for influenza A virus range from 0.2 to 0.4 μg/mL for amantadine, and from 0.1 to 0.4 μg/mL for rimantadine.[263]

The antiviral activity of these drugs is the result of inhibition of the M2 ion channel activity of susceptible viruses. The function of the M2 ion channel in viral replication is to acidify the interior of the virion, disrupting the interaction between the matrix and nucleoproteins, and allowing the ribonucleoproteins to be transported to the nucleus, where replication occurs.[264] Thus, the antiviral effect is primarily manifested in cell culture as inhibition of virus uncoating.[265,266] Similar ion channels have been described for influenza B and C viruses; however, at clinically achievable levels, these drugs are active against only influenza A.

TABLE 162-5 Antiviral Agents for Influenza				
	Amantadine	*Rimantadine*	*Zanamivir*	*Oseltamivir*
Protein target	M2	M2	Neuraminidase	Neuraminidase
Activity	A only	A only	A and B	A and B
Side effects	CNS (13%) GI (3%)	GI (6%) GI (3%)	?Bronchospasm	GI (9%)
Metabolism	None	Multiple (hepatic)	None	Hepatic
Excretion	Renal	Renal + others	Renal	Renal (tubular secretion)
Drug interactions	Antihistamines, anticholinergics	None	None	Probenecid (increased levels of oseltamivir)
Dose adjustments needed	≥65 yr old CrCl < 50 mL/min	≥65 yr old CrCl < 10 mL/min	None	CrCl < 30 mL/min Severe liver dysfunction
Contraindications	Acute-angle glaucoma	Severe liver dysfunction	Underlying airways disease	
FDA Approved Indications				
Therapy	Adults and children ≥ year of age	Adults only	Adults and children ≥ 7 years of age	Adults and children ≥ 1 year of age
Prophylaxis	Yes	Yes	No	Adults and children ≥ 13 years of age

CNS, central nervous system; CrCl, creatinine clearance; FDA, U.S. Food and Drug Administration; GI, gastrointestinal.

Pharmacology and Side Effects

Although the mechanism of action and spectrum of activity for amantadine are similar to those for rimantadine, there are important pharmacokinetic differences between the two drugs.[267] Amantadine does not undergo metabolic change and is excreted unchanged in the urine with a half-life of 12 to 18 hours. This leads to rapid accumulation of amantadine in two settings: in patients with renal failure and in older adults with reduced renal function because of age. In older adults, it is recommended that the dosage of amantadine be reduced to no more than 100 mg daily and perhaps even to 100 mg every other day after the first few days, although extensive evidence of the efficacy for these lower doses is not available. By contrast, rimantadine undergoes extensive metabolism. Less than 15% of the drug is excreted in the urine unchanged, and the remainder is excreted as metabolic products.[268] A dosage reduction to a maximum of 100 mg/day in older adults is also recommended for rimantadine.

The most common side effects of amantadine are minor and reversible central nervous system (CNS) side effects such as insomnia, dizziness, and difficulty in concentrating.[269-271] These side effects may be more troublesome in older adults, in whom confusion is noted in about 18% of recipients.[272] In addition, amantadine use has been associated with seizures in individuals with prior seizure disorder.[273] Minor gastrointestinal complaints have also been reported. The CNS effects of amantadine are increased when these drugs are co-administered with anticholinergics or antihistamines. In addition, trimethoprim-sulfamethoxazole may inhibit tubular secretion of amantadine and increase the potential for CNS toxicity.[274] There are no other known significant drug interactions with amantadine. However, co-administration of amantadine with drugs known to have CNS side effects may exacerbate those effects and thus should be avoided.

Rimantadine is associated with a considerably reduced rate of CNS side effects, and in comparative studies of long-term administration, the rate of CNS side effects was not significantly different from the rate with placebo.[271] There are no known drug interactions that significantly affect the levels or metabolism of rimantadine.

Efficacy

Both amantadine and rimantadine are effective in the therapy of experimentally induced and naturally occurring influenza A. Amantadine treatment of H3N2 influenza A during the 1968 pandemic within the first 48 hours of illness was associated with decreases in the duration of fever by about 24 hours[275] and with a greater proportion of subjects considered to be "rapid resolvers."[276,277] In addition, treated individuals had more rapid decreases in individual symptoms of cough, sore throat, and nasal obstruction.[278] Treatment with amantadine results in significantly more rapid improvement in small airways dysfunction in healthy adults with uncomplicated H3N2 influenza.[112,270]

Additional trials of amantadine therapy were performed when H1N1 viruses reappeared in the late 1970s, with similar results. Early amantadine therapy of influenza A/USSR/77 in otherwise healthy adults was shown to result in a more rapid decrease in fever, and in a higher frequency of subjects reporting improved symptoms at 48 hours compared with placebo.[269] In addition, treated subjects were less likely to shed virus at 48 hours. In a second study conducted in young adults infected with A/Brazil/78, amantadine therapy was associated with a more rapid decrease in symptoms compared with aspirin therapy,[279] and with decreased virus shedding.

Studies of rimantadine therapy of acute influenza in otherwise healthy adults with uncomplicated influenza have shown levels of benefit essentially identical to those seen with amantadine. Treatment of adults with H1N1[269] and H3N2[280] influenza A resulted in improved symptoms, decreased fever, and reduced virus shedding compared with placebo. When rimantadine and amantadine were directly compared in a randomized trial,[269] the efficacies of the two drugs were essentially identical.

Neither amantadine nor rimantadine has been subjected to extensive efficacy evaluation in high-risk subjects. One placebo-controlled study carried out with nursing home residents showed more rapid reduction in fever and in symptoms in rimantadine recipients. Furthermore, physicians who were caring for these patients, but who were blinded to study drug status, prescribed significantly fewer antipyretics, antitussives, and antibiotics and obtained fewer chest radiographs for the rimantadine recipients.[281]

Rimantadine has also been evaluated in the treatment of influenza A in children, and shown to reduce the level of virus shedding early in infection when compared with acetaminophen.[282,283] More variable effects on clinical symptom scores have been seen, with one study showing a decrease in scores and fever compared with acetaminophen,[282] and the other, in which illness was relatively mild, showing no significant difference.[283] However, rimantadine is not currently licensed for treatment of children in the United States.

Drug Resistance

Drug resistance has been a factor in limiting the more widespread use of these antiviral agents.[284] Although resistant viruses are seen in less than 1% of unexposed individuals,[285,286] they emerge fairly frequently in treated individuals,[287,288] particularly children.[282] Resistance is the result of single point mutations in the membrane-spanning region of the M2 protein, and it confers complete cross-resistance between amantadine and rimantadine.[289] Resistant virus can be transmitted to, and can cause disease in, susceptible contacts.[287,288,290] Prolonged shedding of resistant viruses may occur in immunocompromised patients, particularly children, and may continue even after therapy is terminated,[291] consistent with the relative fitness of these resistant viruses. Although vaccination combined with amantadine treatment can decrease the generation and transmission of resistant viruses,[292,293] the problem of drug resistance remains an important consideration and has limited enthusiasm for more widespread use of these agents.

Neuraminidase Inhibitors: Zanamivir and Oseltamivir

Knowledge of the crystal structure of neuraminidase complexed with its substrate, sialic acid,[294] has allowed the development of a series of sialic acid analogues with neuraminidase-inhibiting activity.[295]

Mechanism of Action and Activity

The neuraminidase inhibitors act by inhibiting the functioning of the influenza virus neuraminidase. This enzyme cleaves terminal sialic acid from sialic acid–containing glycoproteins that serve as host cell receptors for attachment of influenza viruses. As virus replication proceeds within the cell, neuraminidase is synthesized and transported to the cell surface, where it removes the sialic acid from these cell surface glycoproteins. Destruction of these receptors by neuraminidase is critical in allowing newly formed viruses to subsequently egress from the cell and spread to other cells. Studies with mutant, neuraminidase-deficient viruses have shown that in the absence of a functional neuraminidase, virus remains attached to the host cell and to other virions.[296,297] In addition, neuraminidase may be important in facilitating the penetration of virus through secretions in the respiratory tract, which are rich in sialic acid–containing macromolecules.[64]

Neuraminidase inhibitors are active against influenza viruses at millimolar concentrations or less. Activity against clinical isolates assessed in plaque inhibition tests ranges from concentrations of 0.01 to 16 μM. Influenza B viruses are approximately 10-fold less sensitive than influenza A viruses, but they are still sensitive well within clinically achievable concentrations. Among the influenza viruses sensitive to neuraminidase inhibitors are avian viruses with all nine known neuraminidase subtypes.

Pharmacology and Side Effects

Although zanamivir and oseltamivir have identical mechanisms of action and similar profiles of antiviral activity, they have different pharmacologic properties. Zanamivir (4-guanidino-Neu5Ac2en) is a polar molecule that is not orally bioavailable. Therefore, effective use of this agent requires local administration. The drug is currently supplied as a dry powder for oral inhalation, using the Diskhaler device (GlaxoSmithKline) also used commonly for a variety of asthma-related medications. Oseltamivir carboxylate is an orally bioavailable ethyl ester prodrug of oseltamivir phosphate, a carbocyclic transition-state–based inhibitor of the influenza virus neuraminidase.[298]

Oseltamivir is rapidly absorbed from the gastrointestinal tract and is converted in the liver by hepatic esterases to the active metabolite, oseltamivir carboxylate. The metabolite is excreted unchanged in the urine by tubular secretion, with a serum half life of 6 to 10 hours. Administration of the drug with food may improve tolerability without impacting drug levels. Zanamivir is not bioavailable by the oral route and must be administered topically to be effective. The drug is supplied in blister packs in which each blister contains 5 mg of zanamivir and 20 mg of lactose carrier. The standard dose is therefore two inhalations twice a day. It is estimated that approximately 4 mg of drug is actually delivered with each inhalation. Intravenous dosing of zanamivir has also been studied, although this formulation is not currently available for clinical use. In one small study, an intravenous dose of 600 mg twice daily was well tolerated and was effective in preventing experimental infection of adults with influenza A (H1N1) virus.[299]

Both drugs have been well tolerated in clinical trials. The major adverse effects reported for oseltamivir have been gastrointestinal upset, probably irritation due to rapid release of the drug in the stomach. Rates of nausea can be substantially reduced if the drug is taken with food. The most commonly reported adverse effects in individuals treated with zanamivir have been diarrhea, nausea, and nasal signs and symptoms, which have occurred at essentially the same rate as in placebo recipients. In one study in which zanamivir was used in influenza-infected patients with asthma or chronic obstructive pulmonary disease, the frequency of significant changes in FEV_1 or peak flow rates was higher in zanamivir than in placebo recipients. For this reason, individuals with these pulmonary conditions should have ready access to a rapidly acting bronchodilator when using zanamivir, in the event that the drug precipitates bronchospasm.

The dose of oseltamivir should be reduced to 75 mg once daily in individuals with renal impairment (i.e., with creatinine clearance of less than 30 mL/min). No data are available regarding the use of the drug in individuals with more significant levels of renal impairment. Likewise, no information is available regarding the use of oseltamivir in individuals with hepatic impairment. Clinically significant drug interactions have not been reported. Because oseltamivir is eliminated by tubular secretion, probenecid increases serum levels of the active metabolite approximately twofold. However, dosage adjustments are not necessary in individuals taking probenecid. Co-administration of cimetidine, amoxicillin, or acetaminophen has no effect on serum levels of oseltamivir or oseltamivir carboxylate.[300]

Although significant increases in the serum half-life of zanamivir are seen in the presence of renal failure, the small amounts of the drug that are absorbed systemically suggest that dosage adjustments would not be necessary. Studies of the pharmacokinetics of the drug in the presence of impaired hepatic function have not been reported.

Efficacy

Zanamivir and oseltamivir, the two available neuraminidase inhibitors, have shown very similar results in clinical trials. Both drugs were initially evaluated in the human experimental challenge model. Studies in which oseltamivir was administered 28 hours after experimental infection showed reductions in viral shedding, reduced symptom scores, and decreased frequencies of middle ear abnormalities compared with placebo.[301] Zanamivir given by drops or spray as late as 50 hours after infection also demonstrated reduced viral shedding, symptom scores, nasal mucus weights, and middle ear abnormalities.[302,303] Similar effects are seen with oseltamivir in adults experimentally infected with influenza B virus.[304]

In studies of naturally occurring, uncomplicated influenza in healthy adults, therapy with oseltamivir initiated within the first 36 hours of symptoms resulted in 30% to 40% reductions in the duration of symptoms and severity of illness and reduced rates of prolonged coughing.[305,306] In addition, early therapy is associated with a significantly earlier return to work or other normal activities. Similarly, in healthy adults, early therapy of uncomplicated influenza A or B with inhaled zanamivir has been shown to result in a reduction of approximately 0.8 to 1.5 days in the duration of influenza symptoms, and an earlier return to normal activities.[307,308] Early treatment of healthy adults with zanamivir may also reduce the frequency of complications, with reductions in the use of antibacterials and in hospitalization.[309]

Both oseltamivir and zanamivir have been evaluated as therapy for children, but only oseltamivir is currently licensed for pediatric use. Administration of oseltamivir liquid at a dose of 2 mg/kg per dose twice daily for 5 days was well tolerated and resulted in a 36-hour reduction in the duration of symptoms in children with influenza A.[310] In addition, the use of oseltamivir was associated with a 44% reduction in the frequency of otitis media complicating influenza, and with reductions in antibiotic prescriptions in influenza-infected children. Similarly, therapy of children 5 to 12 years old with symptomatic influenza A and B virus infection who were treated within 36 hours with inhaled zanamivir (10 mg twice a day) resulted in relief of symptoms 1.25 days earlier than did placebo recipients, and a more rapid return to normal activities.[311]

Neuraminidase inhibitor therapy of influenza in adults with risk factors for influenza complications has not been evaluated extensively. However, both drugs have shown trends toward efficacy in such populations.[308,312] The results of meta-analyses of the pooled data from subsequent phase III studies have indicated that early treatment with inhaled zanamivir is associated with a median reduction of illness of 2.5 days in older adult and high-risk subjects, and a 3-day earlier return to normal activities.[313] In these pooled analyses, early treatment of high-risk adults and older adults resulted in a 43% reduction in the rates of complications requiring antimicrobials.

Drug Resistance

Because the neuraminidase inhibitors interact with highly conserved residues within the influenza virus neuraminidase, it has been hypothesized that antiviral resistance will be a relatively limited problem. In fact, truly resistant viruses have been infrequently isolated from immunologically intact individuals treated with neuraminidase inhibitors in clinical trials to date.[314,315] Viruses with reduced susceptibility to oseltamivir have been isolated from 1% of adult and 5.5% of pediatric recipients.[316] Resistant viruses have been recovered more commonly from immunosuppressed children.[217]

Viruses resistant to the in vitro antiviral activity of these agents have been isolated after passage in cell culture. Analysis of these viruses has revealed two basic mechanisms of resistance, and it illustrates the interactive roles of the viral HA and NA in binding to and release from infected cells. Mutations within the catalytic framework of the NA that abolish binding of the drugs have been described.[317,318] Depending on the location of the mutation, these viruses may be specifically resistant to only one inhibitor. Resistance mutations in the NA may be associated with altered characteristics of the enzyme with significantly reduced activity.[319,320]

A second type of mutation associated with cell cultured resistant viruses involves mutations in the receptor binding region of the hemagglutinin. HA mutations associated with resistance to neuraminidase inhibitors reduce the affinity of the HA for its receptor, allowing cell-to-cell spread of virus in the absence of NA activity.[317,321] It is even possible to generate inhibitor-dependent viruses, in which the affinity for the receptor is apparently so low that NA activity must be inhibited to allow the virus to bind at all. Resistant viruses with HA mutations exhibit cross-resistance to these drugs in cell culture but may retain susceptibility in animal models. Many of these viruses also exhibit reduced virulence in animals.

As expected, resistant viruses appear to have significantly reduced fitness, with reduced levels of replication, attenuation in animals, and reduced ability to be transmitted from animal to animal.[322-324] These characteristics probably contribute to the relatively low frequency with which these viruses are detected clinically.

Treatment of Complications

Supportive care, including fluid and electrolyte management, is important. Supplemental oxygen, intubation, tracheotomy, assisted ventilation, and the use of positive end-expiratory pressure may have a role depending on the severity of the illness.[325] For patients with proven or suspected bacterial supra-infection, appropriate antibiotics for the specific organism should be administered. Because of the rapidly advancing nature of many cases of pneumonia occurring during an influenza epidemic, therapy to cover the potential pathogens, including *S. pneumoniae* and *H. influenzae,* and possibly *S. aureus,* is indicated if an etiologic diagnosis cannot be made from a Gram stain of the sputum.

There have been no controlled studies of antiviral therapy for the treatment of influenza viral pneumonia, so their use for this condition is based on extrapolation from anecdotal case reports of benefit and on data indicating an effect of amantadine on peripheral airways resistance in uncomplicated influenza.[112,270] In a small controlled study, there was no difference in outcome between hospitalized adults treated with the combination of rimantadine and zanamivir and those treated with rimantadine alone, although both drugs were well tolerated.[326]

PREVENTION

Vaccines

Inactivated Influenza Vaccine

The most effective measure available for the control of influenza is the annual administration of inactivated influenza vaccines. Chemically inactivated influenza virus vaccines were first licensed in the United States in 1943. The original vaccine, which consisted of formalin-inactivated whole virions grown in embryonated chicken eggs, was demonstrated to have a protective efficacy of 70% in healthy adults.[11] Since then, although there have been several important advances in the techniques for producing vaccine, the basic vaccine strategy has remained the same. The development of the zonal gradient centrifuge allowed more efficient production and more highly purified vaccines from which reactogenic contaminants had been removed.[327] Treatment of the whole virus with solvents to create "split" vaccines, or with detergents to create "subunit" vaccines, has resulted in a vaccine with fewer adverse reactions, particularly fever, than the whole-cell vaccine.[328] The efficiency of vaccine production has also been improved through the development of techniques to create so called high-yield reassortant strains adapted to grow in high yield from hens' eggs.[329] The current vaccine is generally formulated as a trivalent preparation, containing one example each of influenza A (H1N1) virus, A (H3N2) virus, and influenza B virus thought to be most likely to cause disease in the upcoming season on the basis of epidemiologic and antigenic analysis of currently circulating strains. Since the late 1970s, the vaccine has been standardized to contain at least 15 μg of each hemagglutinin (HA) antigen as assessed by single radial immunodiffusion (SRID).[330]

Safety. Influenza vaccine is generally very well tolerated in adults. Rates of mild local soreness after administration of inactivated influenza vaccine have been documented to be in the range of 60% to 80% in multiple studies.[331-334] Local side effects are slightly more common in women than in men.[331] Systemic reactions, including malaise, flulike illnesses, and fever, are relatively uncommon. Rates of transient, low-grade fever have varied from 2% to 10% of recipients in these studies; these rates are only marginally increased above the rates in placebo recipients.[331,335] Although whole-virus and split-product vaccines are similarly reactogenic in adults,[336] whole-virus vaccines are associated with fever in children[337] and are no longer available in the United States. Fever occurs in approximately 8% to 11% of vaccinated children and may be associated with other systemic symptoms such as myalgia, arthralgia, headache, and malaise.[338]

Severe, life-threatening, immediate hypersensitivity reactions to parenteral inactivated vaccine have been rare. However, hypersensitivity to hens' eggs, in which the vaccine virus is grown, is a contraindication to vaccination. Generally, if persons can eat eggs or egg-containing products, vaccination is safe. Although vaccine is usually not administered to patients with a genuine anaphylactic hypersensitivity to egg products, such individuals can be desensitized and safely vaccinated if necessary.[339-341]

During the 1976 National Immunization Program against swine influenza, 45 million persons received influenza vaccine. In the first 4 to 6 weeks after vaccination, the incidence of Guillain-Barré syndrome (GBS) among vaccinees exceeded that among persons who did not receive the vaccine.[342] The estimated risk of acquiring GBS during that vaccination program was 1 in 100,000 vaccinations; the mortality for those with GBS was 5% (i.e., 1 in 2,000,000 vaccinations), and another 5% to 10% had some residual neurologic abnormality.[342] The relationship between inactivated influenza vaccines other than the Swine/New Jersey/76 vaccine and GBS is less clear-cut. National surveillance conducted since 1976 has generally not identified increased rates of this syndrome after vaccination.[343] However, very slight increases in the risk of GBS were seen after the 1992-1993 and 1993-1994 vaccines, representing an excess of approximately one case per million persons vaccinated.[344]

Immune Response. Increases in HAI antibody are seen in about 90% of healthy adult recipients of vaccine.[336,345,346] Only a single dose of vaccine is required in individuals who were previously vaccinated or who experienced prior infection with a related subtype, but a two-dose schedule is required in unprimed individuals.[337,347] Primed individuals generally respond with antibody that recognizes a broader range of antigenic variants than do unprimed individuals.[348] Serum antibodies peak between 2 and 4 months after vaccination but fall quickly, reaching near baseline before the next influenza season.[349] Mucosal anti-influenza antibodies are not generated efficiently by parenteral inactivated influenza vaccine.[350,351] Cytotoxic T-lymphocyte or cellular immune responses have been reported after administration of parenteral inactivated influenza vaccine to individuals primed by previous infection.[352] It has recently been reported that human leukocyte antigen (HLA) type is significantly associated with influenza vaccine responsiveness.[353]

Groups of adults with potentially decreased responses to inactivated influenza vaccine include older adults,[354-356] individuals on immunosuppressive therapy,[357] those with renal disease,[358] and some transplant recipients.[359-362] To be maximally effective, immunizations should be given before transplantation, should avoid the nadir of white counts, and should include vaccination of close contacts.[363] The responsiveness to influenza vaccination in HIV-infected individuals is related to the degree of immunosuppression.[364,365] Most patients with chronic lung disease respond reasonably well to vaccination, and steroids at doses commonly used to treat reactive airways disease do not appear to preclude vaccine responses.[366,367]

Efficacy and Effectiveness. Inactivated influenza vaccine has been shown to be effective in the prevention of influenza A in controlled studies conducted in young adults, with levels of protection of 70% to 90% when there is a good antigenic match between the vaccine and the epidemic virus.[150,368,369] In a recent randomized controlled trial,[370] the efficacy of trivalent inactivated influenza vaccine (TIV) for preventing culture-proven influenza A illness in adults was 76% (95% confidence interval [CI], 58% to 87%) for H1N1 and 74% (95% CI, 52% to 86%) for H3N2. A subanalysis of efficacy in children in this trial demonstrated efficacy of 91% and 77% in preventing symptomatic, culture-positive influenza A H1N1 and A H3N2 illness, respectively, compared with placebo.[371] Vaccination of working adults is also associated with decreased absenteeism from work or school and is significantly cost effective,[372] but these benefits do not extend to years when there is not a good match between vaccine and circulating viruses.[373] In children, TIV has reduced the rates of otitis media in some,[374,375] but not all,[376] studies.

Relatively few prospective trials of protective efficacy have been conducted in high-risk populations. In one placebo-controlled prospective trial in an older adult population, inactivated vaccine was approximately 58% effective in preventing laboratory-documented influenza.[377] In addition, numerous retrospective case-control studies are available that have documented the effectiveness of inactivated influenza vaccines in older adults.[24,378-382] Vaccine is protective against influenza- and pneumonia-related hospitalization in older adults, and it is accompanied by a decrease in all-cause mortality.[383] Vaccine has also been shown to be protective in limited studies in other high-risk groups, including those with HIV infection.[384] It has recently been shown that inactivated vaccine administered to older adults and persons with coronary artery disease can reduce the rates of coronary events or stroke during the influenza season.[385,386]

Live-Attenuated (Cold-Adapted) Influenza Vaccine

Recently, the first live-attenuated influenza vaccines for use in humans, the cold-adapted influenza vaccine–trivalent (CAIV-T), was licensed for use in the United States in the age group from 5 to 49 years. The use of live-attenuated viruses as influenza vaccines offers several potential advantages over parenteral inactivated vaccines, including induction of a mucosal immune response that closely mimics the response induced by natural influenza virus infection.[387] In addition, the potential superiority of such vaccines in protection of the upper respiratory tract[388] might be useful in strategies using vaccine to limit transmission of influenza. In practical terms, the use of the nasal, rather than the parenteral, route of administration might be more acceptable to patients, particularly in certain age groups.

Development of these vaccines takes advantage of the principle of reassortment to generate rapidly attenuated vaccines for new antigenic variants (Fig. 162-11).[389,390] In this case, the master vaccine viruses are the cold-adapted influenza A/Ann Arbor/6/60 (H2N2) and B/Ann Arbor/1/66 viruses, developed by Dr. John Maassab at the University of Michigan in the 1960s.[391] The process of cold adaptation is the repetitive passage of a virus at gradually decreasing temperature until a virus is isolated that replicates efficiently at a low temperature at which the replication of the original wild-type virus is significantly restricted.[392]

Genetic analysis of the cold-adapted A/Ann Arbor/6/60 virus has demonstrated multiple mutations in all six of the so-called internal, or non-HA or NA, gene segments, and analysis of single gene reassor-

tants has shown that at least three of these gene segments (PB1, PB2, and PA) participate in the attenuation of the virus in animals and humans.[393,394] Recent studies have also implicated the NP gene in this phenotype.[395] The basis of attenuation of the B/Ann Arbor/1/66 virus has been worked out less completely. Mutations in five of the six internal gene segments have been described,[396] and analysis of laboratory-derived revertant viruses has implicated the PA gene segment as playing an important role in attenuation.[397,398]

Safety. CAIV-T or closely related formulations of CAIV have been well tolerated in adults,[370,399-403] with rates of mild nasal symptoms (runny nose, nasal congestion, or coryza) and sore throat occurring at rates slightly in excess of those in placebo recipients. These vaccines have also been shown to be safe and well tolerated in children,[371,404-414] although children under 8 years have had slightly increased but variable rates of low-grade fever, runny nose, and abdominal symptoms in the 7 days after vaccination compared with placebo recipients. However, when considering all the pediatric studies in aggregate, no consistent symptom was significantly more common in CAIV recipients compared with placebo recipients. In older children, 11 to less than 16 years of age, sore throat was observed slightly more frequently in CAIV recipients than in recipients of inactivated influenza.[371]

Safety has also been demonstrated in high-risk individuals who would not be able to tolerate even minor lower respiratory tract inflammation. No significant vaccine-related adverse events were seen in studies of children with cystic fibrosis[415,416] or asthma,[417,418] and vaccinated children with asthma did not experience significant changes in FEV_1, use of beta-adrenergic rescue medications or asthma symptom scores compared with placebo recipients.[418] CAIV has also been well tolerated in adults with chronic obstructive airway disease.[419-421] Vaccine is very well tolerated in older adults, although in one study vaccine recipients had a 13% excess of sore throats compared with those who received placebo.[399]

Young children with advanced HIV infection were reported to have difficulty clearing wild-type influenza virus from the respiratory tract, and there have been several reports of very prolonged virus shedding in highly immunosuppressed individuals,[215] including children with

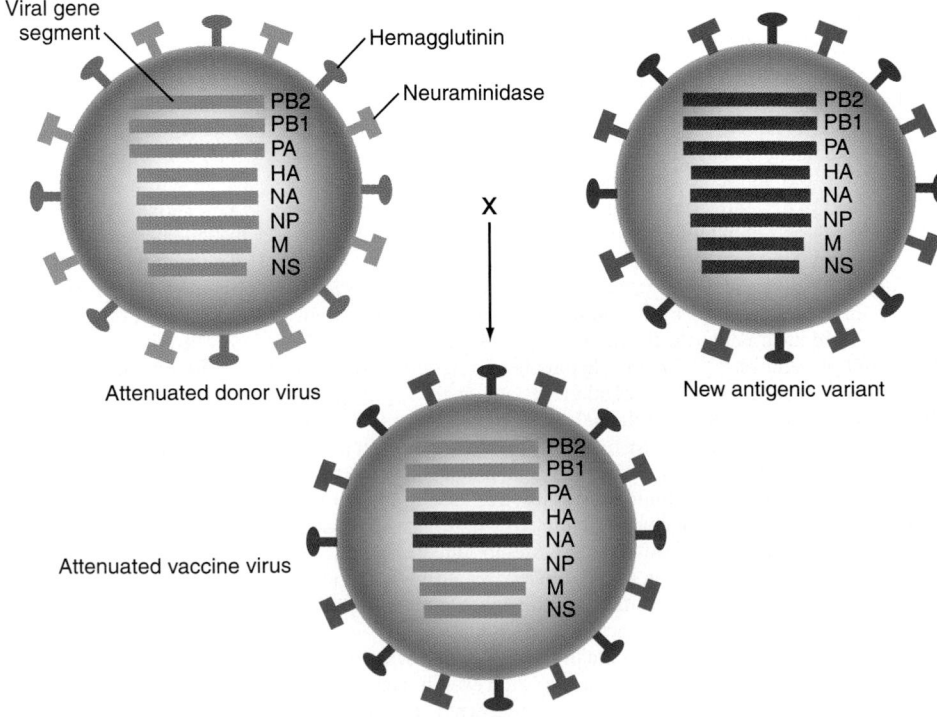

FIGURE 162-11. Genetic reassortment is used to generate new live-attenuated vaccine viruses. The genetic basis of attenuation of the "master donor virus" is encoded in gene segments other than the hemagglutinin (HA) or neuraminidase (NA). Using either mixed infection in cell culture or reverse genetics techniques, the genes encoding the HA and NA of new antigenic variants can be inserted into the background of the master donor virus to rapidly create a new attenuated vaccine virus.

Viral gene segment

Hemagglutinin

Neuraminidase

PB2
PB1
PA
HA
NA
NP
M
NS

Attenuated donor virus

X

PB2
PB1
PA
HA
NA
NP
M
NS

New antigenic variant

PB2
PB1
PA
HA
NA
NP
M
NS

Attenuated vaccine virus

acquired immunodeficiency syndrome (AIDS). However, in small studies in adults[400] and children[408] with HIV who did not have manifestations of AIDS, CAIV-T was well tolerated and not associated with prolonged shedding.

Shedding of CAIV does occur in vaccinated adults and particularly in children. Therefore, it is possible that live CAIV viruses could be transmitted to susceptible contacts. However, this does not appear to happen frequently. No transmission of CAIV from vaccine recipients to susceptible contacts was detected in studies of young children involved in daycare-like settings where CAIV and placebo recipients played together for up to 8 hours a day for 7 to 10 days after vaccination.[390,422] In the largest study, 197 children between 8 and 36 months of age in a daycare setting were randomized to receive trivalent CAIV or placebo, and CAIV was detected in one placebo recipient; thus, the estimates of transmissibility in this age group were 0.6% to 2.0%.[423] Importantly, samples of vaccine virus recovered from vaccinated volunteer subjects have all retained the attenuated phenotype and genotype.[423,424] Administration of CAIV to health care workers is not recommended because of potential transmission of virus to patients. The high cost of the vaccine has also restricted its use in institutional settings.

Immune Response. Studies of the immunogenicity of cold-adapted reassortant vaccines have been carried out in children, adults, and older adults. The results of these studies are consistent with the hypothesis that the replication of cold-adapted vaccines in the upper respiratory tract, and hence their immunogenicity, is influenced by the susceptibility of the host at the time of vaccination. The frequency and magnitude of immune responses to vaccination are therefore highest in young children, intermediate in adults, and lowest in older adult subjects who have been repeatedly infected with influenza viruses throughout their lifetime. In addition, the mucosally administered CAIV is generally more effective than parenterally administered inactivated influenza vaccine at inducing nasal HA-specific IgA, whereas inactivated vaccine usually induces higher serum titers of HAI and HA-specific IgG antibody.[425]

Most susceptible children demonstrate measurable serum and mucosal HA-specific antibody responses.[306,307,409,410,412,414,416,426] Mucosal responses have been demonstrated in up to 85% of young children after CAIV-T.[427] In contrast, adults generally have a low rate of serum antibody response after CAIV,[370,402,403] and relatively lower rates of mucosal responses.[428] Even in those prescreened to have low prevaccination vaccine-specific influenza antibody, the rates of serum antibody responses to intranasal CAIV in adults and older adults are low.[403,429] However, the significance of these findings is unclear, as protection can be demonstrated in some circumstances in the absence of detectable mucosal responses,[430] and the specific levels of mucosal antibody required for protection are unknown.

Although not studied extensively, limited data suggest that cold-adapted influenza vaccines may induce antibody and cytotoxic T cells with more broadened recognition within a subtype than seen after inactivated vaccine.[431,432] However, these responses have been more difficult to measure in young children.[433]

Efficacy and Effectiveness. CAIV-T was demonstrated to be efficacious in the prevention of influenza in a 2-year, randomized, placebo-controlled trial conducted in 1314 children 15 to 74 months of age. Efficacy against culture-confirmed influenza illness in the first year of this trial was 95% against influenza A/H3N2 and 91% against influenza B. In the second year of the trial, the H3 component of the vaccine (A/Wuhan/93) was not a close match with the predominant H3 virus that season, A/Sydney/95. However, the efficacy of CAIV against this variant was 86% (95% CI, 75% to 92%),[405] suggesting that CAIV can induce protective immunity against drift variants. The efficacy in children is also supported by smaller trials using bivalent preparations of CAIV-T.[371,412]

Efficacy of CAIV-T against naturally acquired influenza in adults has not been demonstrated directly. However, its efficacy was demonstrated in an experimental infection study in which adults were given either trivalent live intranasal CAIV, parenteral trivalent inactivated influenza vaccine, or placebo, and then experimentally infected with wild-type influenza A/H1N1, A/H3N2, or B virus.[403] The combined efficacy of CAIV-T in preventing laboratory-documented influenza illness was 85%, consistent with observations from other experimental infection studies conducted with monovalent CAIV.[161,388,434,435] In addition, in a large, 5-year field trial in Nashville, Tennessee,[370] the efficacy of bivalent CAIV was 85% (95% CI, 70% to 92%) against A/H1N1 illness and 58% (95% CI, 29%-75%) against A/H3N2 illness. Use of CAIV-T in adults has also been shown to reduce rates of severe febrile illness of any cause during the influenza season.[401]

No studies of the protective efficacy of CAIV alone have been conducted in older adults because of the possibly reduced immunogenicity of the vaccine in this age group. However, the combination of local live-attenuated influenza vaccine and parenteral inactivated vaccine administered together was shown to result in an approximately 60% decrease in cases of laboratory-confirmed influenza in an older adult nursing home population, compared with inactivated vaccine alone.[436]

Recommendations for Vaccine Use

The main goal of the strategy for use of influenza vaccine is to reduce complications by targeting vaccine to those individuals at highest risk of influenza-related hospitalizations or death. Table 162-6 lists those groups for whom annual influenza vaccination is currently recommended,[437] including older adults and adults and children with chronic conditions known to increase the risk of influenza complications. The age at which annual vaccination is recommended has been lowered from 65 to 50. The rationale for this recommendation is to achieve higher vaccination rates in adults with high-risk conditions, a large proportion of whom are between 50 and 65 years old.

Recommendations for annual vaccination of healthy children are also being considered. The Advisory Committee on Immunization Practices (ACIP) has recommended that practitioners vaccinate all children 6 to 23 months of age with the influenza vaccine,[437] because of the high rates of influenza-related hospitalizations and medically attended illness in this age group. An additional benefit of widespread vaccination of young children could be reductions in rates of influenza in other groups, because children play an important role in the propagation of influenza epidemics in a community.[438] Relatively little direct evidence supports the use of influenza vaccine to prevent transmission, but in one study, mass vaccination of school-aged children resulted in reduced rates of influenza in teachers and parents compared with a control community where children were not vaccinated.[439] Vaccination of children in daycare has been reported to reduce the rates

TABLE 162-6 Groups Targeted for Influenza Immunization

Persons at Increased Risk for Complications
- Persons aged ≥65 years
- Residents of nursing homes and other chronic-care facilities
- Adults and children with chronic pulmonary or cardiovascular diseases, including asthma
- Adults and children with chronic metabolic diseases (including diabetes mellitus), renal dysfunction, hemoglobinopathies, or immunosuppression (including HIV)
- Children and adolescents receiving long-term aspirin therapy
- Women who will be in the second or third trimester of pregnancy during the influenza season
- Children aged 6 mo-23 mo

Persons Aged 50-64 Years
- Recommended for this entire age group to increase vaccination rates among persons in this age group with high-risk conditions

Persons Who Can Transmit Influenza to Those at High Risk
- Physicians, nurses, and other personnel in both hospital and outpatient-care settings, including medical emergency response workers
- Employees of nursing homes and assisted living and other chronic-care facilities who have contact with patients or residents
- Persons who provide home care to persons in groups at high risk
- Household contacts (including children) of persons in groups at high risk
- Household contacts of children aged 0-23 months

of febrile respiratory illnesses in unvaccinated household contacts.[440] In addition, it has been observed that influenza-related mortality rates among older adults have increased in Japan, coincident with discontinuation of that country's policy of universal vaccination of school children.[441] Such observations suggest that expanding the population of children targeted for annual influenza immunization could be a reasonable approach to reducing the impact of influenza in the whole community.

For similar reasons, vaccination of individuals who are in close contact with persons with high-risk conditions is strongly recommended, including health care workers. At a minimum, such a policy would reduce workplace absences and prevent disruptions in care.[442] In addition, there is supportive evidence that vaccination of health care workers reduces mortality in patients, at least among residents of nursing homes, independently of the vaccination status of the patients themselves.[443,444]

Except for the influenza pandemics of 1918-1919 and 1957-1958, influenza in pregnancy has not been associated with increased mortality or fetal loss.[445] However, the increased physiologic demands of pregnancy could be associated with enhanced severity of influenza, and recent studies suggest that there is a significant increase in hospitalizations for cardiorespiratory conditions among women in the third trimester of pregnancy during influenza season.[29] There has been a considerable experience with the use of influenza vaccine in pregnancy, and it appears to be safe in this situation. Therefore, current recommendations are to administer vaccine to women who will be in the second or third trimester (i.e., at >14 weeks' gestation) during influenza season.[446] A secondary benefit of this strategy could be the provision of antibody to the infant, depending on the timing of maternal immunization.[447] Because of the high rate of spontaneous fetal loss during the first trimester, vaccination should generally be avoided during this period, unless the pregnant woman has other high-risk medical conditions, in which case vaccine should be administered regardless of the stage of pregnancy.

The duration of protective immunity appears to be limited, particularly in older adults,[448] and in most years, one or more of the vaccine components are updated to keep pace with antigenic drift in circulating viruses. Thus, current inactivated vaccines must be administered yearly. In some situations, yearly administration has been reported to result in decreased effectiveness.[449] Recent studies suggest that prior immunization does not adversely affect immune responses to vaccination or the protection afforded by inactivated vaccine, at least in healthy adults.[450]

Chemoprophylaxis

All four of the available antiviral agents are effective at preventing influenza prophylaxis, provided drug is administered continuously throughout the period of exposure. Several schemes for such prophylaxis have been evaluated, including seasonal prophylaxis, where drug is administered throughout the influenza epidemic season, generally 4 to 6 weeks; family prophylaxis, where drug is administered to family members for a short period of time after recognition of an index case in the family; and outbreak-initiated prophylaxis in institutions, which could be considered to be a variation on the theme of family prophylaxis. In addition, short-term antiviral prophylaxis can be considered for high-risk individuals who are vaccinated during the influenza season.

Seasonal Prophylaxis

Seasonal prophylaxis with amantadine has been shown to result in protection rates of 70%[451] to 90%[271] against H1N1 viruses, and 68% against H3N2 viruses.[452] Seasonal prophylaxis with amantadine has also been effective in children, in whom an approximately 90% reduction in laboratory-confirmed illness due to influenza A H2N2 was reported.[453,454] Significantly fewer studies of prophylaxis with rimantadine have been performed. However, when rimantadine and amantadine were directly compared in seasonal prophylaxis in healthy adults, the levels of protection were approximately equal.[271]

Both zanamivir and oseltamivir have also been shown to be protective in seasonal prophylaxis. In healthy adults, inhaled zanamivir was shown to have about 67% efficacy for prevention of confirmed influenza,[455] and in a similar study, the efficacy of oral oseltamivir was 74%.[456] Both drugs were well tolerated on prolonged use. However, only oseltamivir is approved for prophylaxis (for individuals 2 and 3 years of age.)

Relatively less information is available about the use of any of the influenza antivirals for prophylaxis in older adult or high-risk populations. In one study, seasonal prophylaxis was highly effective in preventing laboratory-documented influenza in older adult residents of retirement communities.[457] Importantly, 80% of the subjects had previously been vaccinated, and prophylaxis resulted in a 91% reduction in influenza in this group. Thus, vaccine and chemoprophylaxis had an additive protective effect in older adults.

Family Prophylaxis

Results of outbreak prophylaxis in the family setting have yielded conflicting results depending on whether the index case does or does not receive concurrent therapy. When the index case was not treated with amantadine, protection of family contacts was seen for both drugs.[458-460] However, if the index case was treated with amantadine at the same time that contacts received prophylaxis, no protection was seen,[287,461] presumably because of the generation and transmission of resistant virus in this setting.[456] In contrast, use of oseltamivir[462] or zanamivir[463] is associated with 80% protection without the development or transmission of resistant virus. Generally, drug is administered to contacts for 5 to 7 days after recognition of the index case. It is important to realize that treated individuals remain susceptible to infection from outside the family after such prophylaxis is discontinued.

Outbreak Prophylaxis

Probably one of the most common uses of antiviral agents for influenza is to terminate the transmission of influenza within institutions such as nursing homes during outbreaks. Although this has not been subject to formal, placebo-controlled study, many anecdotal reports support the efficacy of amantadine,[273,464,465] zanamivir,[466] and oseltamivir[467,468] in this setting. When M2 inhibitors are used for outbreak prophylaxis, individuals who are receiving treatment with amantadine should be isolated from those who are receiving prophylaxis. Failure to adhere to this practice is associated with the development and transmission of resistant viruses within the institution.[290,469] One preliminary report has suggested that prophylactic administration of zanamivir was successful in terminating an outbreak of influenza in a nursing home in which cases continued to occur despite amantadine prophylaxis.[470]

REFERENCES

1. Hirsch A. Handbook of Geographical and Historical Pathology. 2nd ed. London: New Sydenham Society; 1883.
2. Thomson D, Thomson R. Influenza. New York: Ann Pickett-Thomas Research Labs; 1933.
3. Sydenham T. Influenza: of the epidemic diseases. In: Major RH, ed. Classical Descriptions of Disease. Springfield, Ill: Charles C Thomas; 1955:201.
4. Crosby AW. Epidemic and Peace, 1918. Part IV. Westport, Conn: Greenwood Press; 1976.
5. Smith W, Andrewes CH, Laidlaw PP. A virus obtained from influenza patients. Lancet. 1933;2:66-68.
6. Francis T Jr. A new type of virus from epidemic influenza. Science. 1940;92:405-408.
7. Taylor RM. A further note on 1233 ("influenza C") virus. Arch Gesamte Virusforsch. 1951;4:485-495.
8. Burnet FM. Influenza virus on the developing egg: I. Changes associated with the development of an egg-passage strain of virus. Br J Exp Pathol. 1936;17:282-295.
9. Mogabgab WJ, Green IJ, Dierkhising OC. Primary isolation and propagation of influenza virus in cultures of human embryonic renal tissue. Science. 1954;120:320-321.
10. Hirst GK. The agglutination of red cells by allantoic fluid of chick embryos infected with influeza virus. Science. 1941;94:22-23.
11. Francis T Jr, Salk JE, Pearson HE, Brown PN. Protective effect of vaccination against influenza A. Proc Soc Exp Biol Med. 1944;55:104-105.
12. Francis T Jr, Pearson HE, Salk JE, Brown PN. Immunity in human subjects artificially infected with influenza virus type B. Am J Public Health. 1944;34:317-334.

13. Smorodintseff, AA, Tushinsky MD, Drobyshevskaya AI, et al. Investigation of volunteers infected with the influenza virus. Am J Med Sci. 1937;194:159-170.

14. Francis T Jr. Transmission of influenza by a filterable virus. Science. 1934;80: 457-459.

15. Wilson IA, Skehel JJ, Wiley DG. Structure of the hemagglutinin membrane glycoprotein of influenza virus at 3A resolution. Nature. 1981;289:366.

16. Kendal AP, Galphin JC, Palmer EL. Replication of influenza virus at elevated temperature: Production of virus-like particles with reduced matrix protein content. Virology. 1977;76:186.

17. Glezen WP. Serious morbidity and mortality associated with influenza epidemics. Epidemiol Rev. 1982;4:24-44.

18. Perrotta DM, Decker M, Glezen WP. Acute respiratory disease hospitalizations as a measure of impact of epidemic influenza. Am J Epidemiol. 1985;122:468-476.

19. Liu KJ, Kendal AP. Impact of influenza epidemics on morality in the United States from October 1972 to May 1985. Am J Public Health. 1987;77:712-716.

20. Simonsen L, Clarke MJ, Williamson DW, et al. The impact of influenza epidemics on mortality: Introducing a severity index. Am J Public Health. 1997;87:1944-1950.

21. Thompson WW, Shay DK, Weintraub E, et al. Mortality associated with influenza and respiratory syncytial virus in the United States. JAMA. 2003;289:179-186.

22. Sullivan KM, Monto AS, Longini IM. Estimates of the US health impact of influenza. Am J Public Health. 1993;83:1712-1716.

23. Glezen WP, Keitel WA, Taber LH, et al. Age distribution of patients with medically attended illnesses caused by sequential variants of influenza A/H1N1: Comparison to age-specific infection rates, 1978-1989. Am J Epidemiol. 1991;133:296-304.

24. Barker WH, Mullooly JP. Impact of epidemic type A influenza in a defined adult population. Am J Epidemiol. 1980;112:798-813.

25. Ellis SE, Coffey CS, Mitchel EF Jr, et al. Influenza- and respiratory syncytial virus-associated morbidity and mortality in the nursing home population. J Am Geriatr Soc. 2003;51:761-7.

26. Neuzil KM, Reed GW, Mitchel EF Jr, Griffin MR. Influenza-associated morbidity and mortality in young and middle-aged women. JAMA. 1999;281:901-907.

27. Lin JC, Nichol KL. Excess mortality due to pneumonia or influenza during influenza seasons among persons with acquired immunodeficiency syndrome. Arch Intern Med. 2001;161:441-446.

28. Whimbey E, Eling LS, Couch RB, et al. Influenza A virus infection among hospitalized adult bone marrow transplant recipients. Bone Marrow Transplant. 1994;13:437-40.

29. Neuzil KM, Reed GW, Mitchel EF, et al. The impact of influenza on acute cardiopulmonary hospitalizations in pregnant women. Am J Epidemiol. 1998;148: 1094-1102.

30. Neuzil KM, Mellen BG, Wright PF, et al. The effect of influenza on hospitalizations, outpatient visits, and courses of antibiotics in children. N Engl J Med. 2000;342: 225-231.

31. Izurieta HS, Thompson WW, Kramarz P, et al. Influenza and the rates of hospitalization for respiratory disease among infants and young children [see comments]. N Engl J Med. 2000;342:232-239.

32. Chiu SS, Lau YL, Chan KH, et al. Influenza-related hospitalizations among children in Hong Kong. N Engl J Med. 2002;347:2097-20103.

33. Silberry GK. Complications of influenza infection in children. Pediatr Ann. 2000;29:683-690.

34. Neuzil KM, Wright PF, Mitchel EF Jr, Griffin MR. The burden of influenza illness in children with asthma and other chronic medical conditions. J Pediatr. 2000;137: 856-864.

35. Glezen WP, Greenberg SB, Atmar RL, et al. Impact of respiratory virus infections on persons with chronic underlying conditions. JAMA. 2000;283:499-505.

36. Griffin MR, Coffey CS, Neuzil KM, et al. Winter viruses: Influenza- and respiratory syncytial virus-related morbidity in chronic lung disease. Arch Intern Med. 2002;162:1229-1236.

37. Schoenbaum SC. Impact of influenza in persons and populations. In: Brown LE, Hampson AW, Webster RG, eds. Options for the Control of Influenza: III. New York: Elsevier Science B.V.; 1996:17-25.

38. Kavet J. A perspective on the significance of pandemic influenza. Am J Public Health. 1977;67:1063-1070.

39. Neuzil KM, Hohlbein C, Zhu Y. Illness among schoolchildren during influenza season: Effect on school absenteeism, parental absenteeism from work, and secondary illness in families. Arch Pediatr Adolesc Med. 2002;156:986-991.

40. Keech M, Scott AJ, Ryan PJJ. The impact of influenza and influenza-like illness on productivity and healthcare resource utilization in a working population. Occup Med (Lond). 1998;48:85-90.

41. Smith AP, Thomas M, Brockman P, et al. Effect of influenza B virus infection on human performance. Br Med J. 1993;306:760-761.

42. Barker WH, Borisute H, Cox C. A study of the impact of influenza on the functional status of frail older people. Arch Intern Med. 1998;158:645-650.

43. Glezen WP, Couch RB. Interpandemic influenza in the Houston area, 1974-1976. N Engl J Med. 1978;298:587-593.

44. Glezen WP, Payne AA, Snyder DN, Downs TD. Mortality and influenza. J Infect Dis. 1982;146:313-321.

45. Monto AS, Kioumehr F. The Tecumseh study of respiratory illness: IX. Occurrence of influenza in the community, 1966-1971. Am J Epidemiol. 1975;102:553-559.

46. Yorke MA, Nathanson N, Pianigiani G, Martin J. Seasonality and the requirements for perpetuation and eradication of viruses in populations. Am J Epidemiol. 1979;109:103-123.

47. Schaffer FL, Soergel ME, Straube DC. Survival of airborne influenza virus: Effects of propagating host, relative humidity, and composition of spray fluids. Arch Virol. 1976;54:263-273.

48. Hall CB, Douglas RG Jr. Respiratory syncytial virus and influenza: Practical community surveillance. Am J Dis Child. 1976;130:615-620.

49. Kendal AP, Schieble J, Cooney MK, et al. Co-circulation of two influenza A (H3N2) antigenic variants detected by virus surveillance in individual communities. Am J Epidemiol. 1978;108:308-311.

50. Falsey AR, Cunningham CK, Barker WH, et al. A comparison of respiratory syncytial virus and influenza infection in the hospitalized elderly. In: Annual meeting of the Infectious Disease Society of America, 1993. New Orleans, La; 1993.

51. Glezen WP, Couch RB, Six HR. The influenza herald wave. Am J Epidemiol. 1982;116:589-598.

52. Simonsen L, Clarke MJ, Schonberger LB, et al. Pandemic versus epidemic influenza mortality: A pattern of changing age distribution. J Infect Dis. 1998;178:53-60.

53. Wilson IA, Cox NJ. Structural basis of immune recognition of influenza virus hemagglutinin. Ann Rev Immunol. 1990;8:737-771.

54. Webster RG, Laver WG, Air GM, et al. The mechanism of antigenic drift in influenza viruses: Analysis of Hong Kong (H3N2) variants with monoclonal antibodies to the hemagglutinin molecule. Ann N Y Acad Sci. 1980;354:142-161.

55. Lai CJ, Markoff LJ, Sveda MM, et al. Genetic variation of influenza A viruses as studied by recombinant DNA techniques. Ann N Y Acad Sci. 1980;354:162-171.

56. Hauptmann R, Clarke LD, Mountford RC, et al. Nucleotide sequence of the haemagglutinin gene of influenza virus A/England/321/77. J Gen Virol. 1983;64(Pt 1): 215-220.

57. Webster RG, Laver WG. Determination of the number of nonoverlapping antigenic areas on Hong Kong (H3N2) influenza virus hemagglutinin with monoclonal antibodies and the selection of variants with potential epidemiological significance. Virology. 1980;104:139-148.

58. Hay AJ, Gregory V, Douglas AR, Lin YP. The evolution of human influenza viruses. Philos Trans R Soc Lond B Biol Sci. 2001;356:1861-1869.

59. Yamashita M, Krystal M, Fitch WM, Palese P. Influenza B virus evolution: Co-circulating lineages and comparison of evolutionary patterns with those of influenza A and C viruses. Virology. 1988;163:112-122.

60. Xu X, Cox NJ, Bender CA, et al. Genetic variation in the neuraminidase genes of influenza A (H3N2) viruses. Virology. 1996;224:175-183.

61. Kilbourne ED. Influenza. New York: Plenum; 1987.

62. Masurel N, Marine WM. Recycling of Asian and Hong Kong influenza A virus hemagglutinins in man. Am J Epidemiol. 1973;97:44-49.

63. Rohm C, Zhou N, Suss J, et al. Characterization of a novel influenza hemagglutinin, H15: Criteria for determination of influenza A subtypes. Virology. 1996;217:508-515.

64. Colman PM, Ward CW. Structure and diversity of influenza virus neuraminidase. Curr Top Microbiol Immunol. 1985;11:177-255.

65. Beare AS, Webster RG. Replication of avian influenza viruses in humans. Arch Virol. 1991;119:37-42.

66. Murphy BR, Sly DL, Tierney EL, et al. Reassortant virus derived from avian and human influenza A viruses is attenuated and immunogenic in monkeys. Science. 1982;218:1330-1332.

67. Kawaoka Y, Krauss S, Webster RG. Avian-to-human transmission of the PB1 gene of influenza A viruses in the 1957 and 1968 pandemics. J Virol. 1989;63: 4603-4608.

68. Treanor J, Kawaoka Y, Miller R, et al. Nucleotide sequence of the avian influenza A/Mallard/NY/6750 virus polymerase genes. Virus Res. 1989;14:257-270.

69. Bean WJ, Schell M, Katz J, et al. Evolution of the H3 hemagglutinin from human and nonhuman hosts. J Virol. 1992;66:1129-1138.

70. Shu LL, Zhou NN, Sharp GB, et al. An epidemiological study of influenza viruses among Chinese farm families with household ducks and pigs. Epidemiol Infect. 1996;117:179-188.

71. Zhou N, He S, Zhang T, et al. Influenza infection in humans and pigs in southeastern China. Arch Virol. 1996;141:649-661.

72. Castrucci MR, Donatelli I, Sidoli I, et al. Genetic reassortment between avian and human influenza A viruses in Italian pigs. Virology. 1993;193:503-506.

73. Scholtissek C, Stech J, Krauss S, Webster RG. Cooperation between the hemagglutinin of avian viruses and the matrix protein of human influenza A viruses. J Virol. 2002;76:1781-1786.

74. Taubenberger JK, Reid AH, Krafft AE, et al. Initial genetic characterization of the 1918 "Spanish" influenza virus. Science. 1997;275:1793-1796.

75. Ito T, Couceiro JN, Kelm S, et al. Molecular basis for the generation in pigs of influenza A viruses with pandemic potential. J Virol. 1998;72:7367-7373.

76. Subbarao K, Klimov A, Katz J, et al. Characterization of an avian influenza A (H5N1) virus isolated from a child with a fatal respiratory illness. Science. 1998;279:393-396.

77. Suarez DL, Perdue ML, Cox N, et al. Comparisons of highly virulent H5N1 influenza A viruses isolated from humans and chickens from Hong Kong. J Virol. 1998;72:6678-6688.

78. Yuen KY, Chan PKS, Peiris M, et al. Clinical features and rapid viral diagnosis of human disease associated with avian influenza A H5N1 virus. Lancet. 1998;351: 467-471.

79. Tam JS. Influenza A (H5N1) in Hong Kong: An overview. Vaccine. 2002;20(Suppl 2): 577.

80. Centers for Disease Control and Prevention. Health Alert Network Update. Jan 23, 2004.

81. Centers for Disease Control and Prevention. Health Alert Network Update. May 28, 2003.

82. Peiris, M. Yuen K, Leung CW, et al. Human infection with H9N2. Lancet. 1999;354:916.

83. Katz JM, Lim W, Bridges CB, et al. Antibody response in individuals infected with avian influenza A (H5N1) viruses and detection of anti-H5 antibody among household and social contacts. J Infect Dis. 1999;180:1763-1770.

84. Douglas RG Jr. Influenza in man. In: Kilbourne ED, ed. The Influenza Viruses and Influenza. New York: Academic Press; 1975:395-447.

85. Hemmes HJ, Winkler DC, Kool SM. Virus survival as a seasonal factor in influenza and poliomyelitis. Nature. 1960;188:430.

86. Alford RH, Kasel JA, Gerone PJ, Knight V. Human influenza resulting from aerosol inhalation. Proc Soc Exp Biol Med. 1966;122:800-804.

87. Little JW, Douglas RG Jr, Hall WJ, Roth FK. Attenuated influenza produced by experimental intranasal inoculation. J Med Virol. 1979;3:177-188.

88. Katze M, Krug R. Metabolism and expression of RNA polymerase II transcripts in influenza virus infected cells. Mol Cell Biol. 1984;4:2198-2206.

89. Katze M, DeCorato D, Krug R. Cellular mRNA translation is blocked at both initiation and elongation after infection by influenza virus or adenovirus. J Virol. 1986;60:1027-1039.

90. Sanz-Esquerro JJ, De La Luna S, Ortin J, Nieto A. Individual expression of the influenza virus PA protein induces degradation of coexpressed proteins. J Virol. 1995;69:2420-2426.

91. Hinshaw VS, Olsen CW, Dybdahl-Sissoko N, Evans D. Apoptosis: A mechanism of cell killing by influenza A and B viruses. J Virol. 1994;68:3667-3673.

92. Takizawa T, Shigeru M, Higuchi Y, et al. Induction of programmed cell death (apoptosis) by influenza virus infection in tissue culture cells. J Gen Virol. 1993;74:2347-2355.

93. Mori I, Komatsu T, Takeuchi K, et al. In vivo induction of apoptosis by influenza virus. J Gen Virol. 1995;76:2869-2873.

94. Takizawa T, Fukuda R, Miyawaki T, et al. Activation of the apoptotic *Fas* antigen-encoding gene upon influenza virus infection involving spontaneously produced beta-interferon. Virology. 1995;209:288-296.

95. Chen W, Calvo PA, Malide D, et al. A novel influenza A virus mitochondrial protein that induces cell death. Nat Med. 2001;7:1306-1312.

96. Jordan WS, Denny FW, Badger GF. A study of illness in a group of Cleveland families: XVII. The occurrence of Asian influenza. Am J Hyg. 1958;68:160.

97. Larson HE, Parry RP, Tyrrell DAJ. Impaired polymorphonuclear leucocyte chemotaxis after influenza virus infection. Br J Dis Chest. 1980;74:56-62.

98. Roberts NJ, Steigbigel RT. Effect of in vitro virus infection on response of human monocytes and lymphocytes to mitogen stimulation. J Immunol. 1978;121:1052-1058.

99. Roberts NJ, Prill AH, Mann TN. Interleukin 1 and interleukin 1 inhibitor production by human macrophages exposed to influenza virus or respiratory syncytial virus: Respiratory syncytial virus is a potent inducer of inhibitory activity. J Exp Med. 1986;163:511-519.

100. Suzuki H, Kurita T, Kakinuma K. Effects of neuraminidase on O_2 consumption and release of O_2 and H_2O_2 from phagocytosing human polymorphonuclear leukocytes. Blood. 1982;60:446-453.

101. Cassidy LF, Lyles DS, Abramson JS. Depression of polymorphonuclear leukocyte functions by purified influenza virus hemagglutinin and sialic acid-binding lectins. J Immunol. 1989;142:4401-4406.

102. Cooper JA Jr, Carcelen R, Culbreth R. Effects of influenza A nucleoprotein on polymorphonuclear neutrophil function. J Infect Dis. 1996;173:279-284.

103. Cooper JA Jr, Culbreth RR. Characterization of a neutrophil inhibitor peptide harvested from human bronchiolar lavage: Homology to influenza A nucleoprotein. Am J Resp Cell Molec Biol. 1996;15:207-215.

104. Hayden FG, Fritz R, Lobo MC, et al. Local and systemic cytokine responses during experimental human influenza A virus infection: Relation to symptom formation and host defense. J Clin Invest. 1998;101:643-649.

105. Hall CB, Douglas RG Jr. Nosocomial influenza infection as a cause of intercurrent fevers in infants. Pediatrics. 1975;55:673.

106. Martin CM, Kunin CM, Gottlieb LS, et al. Asian influenza A in Boston, 1957-1958. Arch Intern Med. 1959;103:516-531.

107. Walsh JJ, Dietlein LF, Low FN, et al. Bronchotracheal response in human influenza. Arch Intern Med. 1961;108:376-388.

108. Hers JFP, Mulder J, Masurel N, et al. Studies on the pathogenesis of influenza virus pneumonia in mice. J Pathol Bacteriol. 1962;83:207-217.

109. Guarner J, Shieh WJ, Dawson J, et al. Immunohistochemical and in situ hybridization studies of influenza A virus infection in human lungs. Am J Clin Pathol. 2000;114:227-233.

110. Mulder J, Hers JF. Influenza. Groningen, Netherlands: Wolters-Noordhoff; 1979.

111. Oseasohn R, Adelson L, Kaji M. Clinicopathologic study of 33 fatal cases of Asian influenza. N Engl J Med. 1959;260:509.

112. Little JW, Hall WJ, Douglas RG Jr, et al. Airway hyperreactivity and peripheral airway dysfunction in influenza A infection. Am Rev Respir Dis. 1978;118:295-303.

123. Hall WJ, Douglas RG Jr, Hyde RW, et al. Pulmonary mechanics after uncomplicated influenza A infection. Am Rev Respir Dis. 1976;113:141-147.

114. Horner GJ, Gray FD Jr. Effect of uncomplicated, presumptive influenza on the diffusing capacity of the lung. Am Rev Respir Dis. 1973;108:866-869.

115. Johanson WGJ, Pierce AK, Sanford JP. Pulmonary function in uncomplicated influenza. Am Rev Respir Dis. 1969;100:141-146.

116. Kondo S, Abe K. The effects of influenza virus infection on FEV1 in asthmatic children. Chest. 1991;100:1235-1238.

117. Smith CB, Kanner RE, Goldern CA, et al. Effect of viral infections on pulmonary function in patients with chronic obstructive pulmonary diseases. J Infect Dis. 1980;141:271-279.

118. Utell MJ, Aquilina AT, Hall WJ, et al. Development of airway reactivity to nitrates in subjects with influenza. Am Rev Respir Dis. 1980;121:233-241.

119. Louria DB, Blumenfeld HL, Ellis JT, et al. Studies on influenza in the pandemic of 1957-1958: II. pulmonary complications of influenza. J Clin Invest. 1959;38:213-265.

120. Yelandi AV, Colby TV. Pathologic features of lung biopsy specimens from influenza pneumonia cases. Hum Pathol. 1994;25:47-53.

121. Greenberg SB. Viral pneumonia. Infect Dis Clin North Am. 1991;5:603-621.

122. Levandowski RA, Gerrity TR, Garrard CS. Modifications of lung clearance mechanisms by acute influenza A infection. J Lab Clin Med. 1985;106:428-432.

123. Camner P, Jarstrand C, Philipson K. Tracheobronchial clearance in patients with influenza. Am Rev Respir Dis. 1973;108:131-135.

124. George RC, Broadbent DA, Drasar BS. The effect of influenza virus on the adherence of *Haemophilus influenzae* to human cells in tissue culture. Br J Exp Pathol. 1983;64:655-659.

125. Babiuk LA. Viral-bacterial synergistic interactions in respiratory infections in applied virology. In: Kurstak E, Al-Nakib W, Kurstak C, eds. Applied Virology. New York: Academic Press; 1984:431.

126. Ramphal R, Fischschweiger W, Shands JWJ, Small PA. Murine influenzal tracheitis: A model for the study of influenza and tracheal epithelial repair. Am Rev Respir Dis. 1979;120:1313-1324.

127. McCullers JA, Rehg JE. Lethal synergism between influenza virus and *Streptococcus pneumoniae:* Characterization of a mouse model and the role of platelet-activating factor receptor. J Infect Dis. 2002;186:341-350.

128. Cassidy LF, Lyles DS, Abramson JS. Synthesis of viral proteins in polymorphonuclear leukocytes infected with influenza A virus. J Clin Microbiol. 1988;26:1267-1270.

129. Abramson JS, Wheeler JG, Parce JW, et al. Suppression of endocytosis in neutrophils by influenza A virus in vitro. J Infect Dis. 1986;154:456-463.

130. Kido H, Yokogoshi Y, Sakai K, et al. Isolation and characterization of a novel trypsin-like protease found in rat bronchiolar Clara cells: A possible activator of the viral fusion glycoprotein. J Biol Chem. 1992;267:13573-13579.

131. Kawaoka Y, Webster RG. Sequence requirements for cleavage activation of influenza virus hemagglutinin expressed in mammalian cells. Proc Natl Acad Sci U S A. 1988;85:324-328.

132. Kawaoka Y, Webster RG. Interplay between carbohydrate in the stalk and the length of the connecting peptide determined the cleavability of influenza virus hemagglutinin. J Virol. 1989;63:3296-3300.

133. Stieneke-Grober A, Vey M, Angliker H, et al. Influenza virus hemagglutinin with multibasic cleavage site is activated by furin, a subtilisin-like endoprotease. EMBO J. 1992;11:2407-2414.

134. Horimoto T, Kawaoka Y. Reverse genetics provides direct evidence for a correlation of hemagglutinin cleavability and virulence of an avian influenza A virus. J Virol. 1994;68:3120-3128.

135. Cheung CY, Poon LL, Lau AS, et al. Induction of proinflammatory cytokines in human macrophages by influenza A(H5N1) viruses: A mechanism for the unusual severity of human disease? Lancet. 2002;360:1831-1837.

136. Brown EG. Increased virulence of a mouse-adapted variant of influenza A/FM/1/47 virus is controlled by mutations in genome segments 4, 5, 7, and 8. J Virol. 1990;64:4523-4533.

137. Li S, Schulman J, Itamura S, Palese P. Glycosylation of neuraminidase determines the neurovirulence of influenza A/WSN/33 virus. J Virol. 1993;67:6667-6673.

138. Schlesinger RW, Bradshaw GL, Barbone F, et al. Role of hemagglutinin cleavage and expression of M1 protein in replication of A/WS/33, A/PR/8/34, and WSN influenza viruses in mouse brain. J Virol. 1989;63:1695-1703.

139. Brown EG, Liu H, Kit LC, et al. Pattern of mutation in the genome of influenza A virus on adaptation to increased virulence in the mouse lung: Identification of functional themes. Proc Natl Acad Sci U S A. 2001;98:6883-6888.

140. Noble GR. Epidemiologic and clinical aspects of influenza. In: Beare AS, ed. Basic and Applied Influenza Research. Boca Raton, Fla: CRC Press; 1982:1179.

141. Couch RB, Kasal JA. Immunity to influenza in man. Ann Rev Microbiol. 1983;37:529-549.

142. Black RA, Rota PA, Gorodkova N, et al. Antibody response to the M2 protein of influenza A virus expressed in insect cells. J Gen Virol. 1993;74:143-146.

143. Murphy BR, Nelson DL, Wright PF, et al. Secretory and systemic immunologic response in children infected with live attenuated influenza A virus. Infect Immun. 1982;36:1102-1108.

144. Murphy BR, Kasel JA, Chanock RM. Association of serum antineuraminidase antibody with resistance to influenza in man. N Engl J Med. 1972;286:1329-1332.

145. Virelizier J-L. Host defenses against influenza virus: The role of anti-hemagglutinin antibody. J Immunol. 1975;115:434-439.

146. Murphy BR, Clements ML. The systemic and mucosal immune response of humans to influenza A virus. Curr Top Microbiol Immunol. 1989;146:107-116.

147. Betts RF, O'Brien D, Menegus M, et al. A comparison of the protective benefit of influenza (FLU) vaccine in reducing hospitalization of patients infected with FLU A or FLU B. Clin Infect Dis. 1993;17:573.

148. Arden NH, Patriarca PA, Kendal AP. Experiences in the use and efficacy of inactivated influenza vaccine in nursing homes. In: Kendal A, ed. Options for the Control of Influenza. Keystone, Colo: Liss; 1986:155-168.

149. Foy HM, Cooney MK, McMahan R, et al. Single-dose monovalent A2 Hong Kong influenza vaccine: Efficacy 14 months after immunization. JAMA. 1971;217:1067-1071.

150. Meiklejohn G, Eickhoff TC, Graves P. Antigenic drift and efficacy of influenza virus vaccines, 1976-1977. J Infect Dis. 1978;138:618-624.

151. Webster RG, Reay PA, Laver WG. Protection against lethal influenza with neuraminidase. Virology. 1988;164:230-237.

152. Schulman JL, Khakpour M, Kilbourne ED. Protective effects of specific immunity to viral neuraminidase on influenza virus infection of mice. J Virol. 1968;2:778-786.

153. Schulman JL, Khakpour M, Kilbourne ED. Protective effects of hemagglutinin and neuraminidase antigens on influenza virus: Distinctiveness of hemagglutinin antigens of Hong Kong—68 virus. J Virol. 1968;2:778.

154. Monto AS, Kendal AP. Effect of neuraminidase antibody on Hong Kong influenza. Lancet. 1973;7804:623-625.

155. Clements ML, Betts RF, Tierney EL, Murphy BR. Serum and nasal wash antibodies associated with resistance to experimental challenge with influenza A wild-type virus. J Clin Microbiol. 1986;24:157-160.

156. Johansson BE, Grajower B, Kilbourne ED. Infection-permissive immunization with influenza virus neuraminidase prevents weight loss in infected mice. Vaccine. 1993;11:1037-1039.

157. Treanor JJ, Tierney EL, Zebedee SL, et al. Passively transferred monoclonal antibody to the M2 protein inhibits influenza A virus replication in mice. J Virol. 1990;64:1375-1377.

158. Wagner DK, Clements ML, Reimer CB, et al. Analysis of immunoglobulin G antibody responses after administration of live and inactivated influenza A vaccine indicates that nasal wash immunoglobulin G is a transudate from serum. J Clin Microbiol. 1987;25:559-562.

159. Renegar KB, Small PAJ. Passive transfer of local immunity to influenza virus by IgA antibody. J Immunol. 1991;146:1972-1978.

160. Liew FY, Russell SM, Appleyard G, et al. Cross-protection in mice infected with influenza A virus by the respiratory route is correlated with local IgA antibody rather than serum antibody or cytotoxic T-cell activity. Eur J Immunol. 1984;14:409-413.

161. Clements ML, Betts RF, Tierney EL, Murphy BR. Resistance of adults to challenge with influenza A wild-type virus after receiving live or inactivated virus vaccine. J Clin Microbiol. 1986;23:73-76.

162. Wenzel RP, Hendley JO, Sande MA, Gwaltney JM Jr. Revised (1972-1973) bivalent influenza vaccine: Serum and nasal antibody responses to parenteral vaccination. JAMA. 1973;226:435-438.

163. Kilbourne ED, Butler WT, Rossen RD. Specific immunity in influenza: Summary of influenza workshop: III. J Infect Dis. 1973;127:220.

164. Couch RB, Douglas RGJ, Rossen R, et al. Role of secretory antibody in influenza. In: Dayton DH Jr, Small PA Jr, Chanock RM, et al, eds. The Secretory Immunologic System. Washington, DC: U.S. General Printing Office; 1969:93.

165. Virelizier J-L, Allison AC, Shild GC. Antibody responses to antigenic determinants of influenza virus hemagglutinin: II. Original antigenic sin: A bone marrow-derived lymphocyte memory phenomenon modulated by thymus-derived lymphocytes. J Exp Med. 1974;140:1571-1578.

166. Burns WH, Billups LC, Notkins AL. Thymus dependence of viral antigens. Nature. 1975;256:654-656.

167. Lucas SJ, Barry DW, Kind P. Antibody production and protection against influenza in immunodeficient mice. Infect Immun. 1978;20:115-119.

168. Lamb JR, Woody JN, Hartzman RD, Eckels DD. In vitro influenza virus-specific antibody production in man: Antigen specific and HLA-restricted induction of helper activity mediated by cloned human T lymphocytes. J Immunol. 1982;129:1465-1470.

169. Hackett CJ, Deitzschold B, Gerhard W, et al. Influenza virus site recognized by a murine helper T-cell specific for H1 strains: Localization to a nine amino acid sequence in the hemagglutinin molecule. J Exp Med. 1983;158:294-302.

170. Biddison WE, Sharrow SO, Shearer GM. T-cell subpopulations required for the human cytotoxic T lymphocyte response to influenza virus: Evidence for T-cell help. J Immunol. 1981;127:487-491.

171. Reiss CS, Burakoff SJ. Specificity of the helper T-cell for the cytotoxic T lymphocyte response to influenza viruses. J Exp Med. 1981;154:541.

172. Topham DJ, Tripp RA, Sarawar SR, et al. Immune CD4+ T-cells promote the clearance of influenza virus from major histocomptibility complex class II -/- respiratory epithelium. J Virol. 1996;70:1288-1291.

173. Baumgarth N, Brown L, Jackson D, Kelso A. Novel features of the respiratory tract T-cell response to influenza virus infection: Lung T-cells increase expression of gamma interferon mRNA in vivo and maintain high levels of mRNA expression for interleukin-5 (IL-5) and IL-10. J Virol. 1994;68:7575-7581.

174. Sarawar SR, Carding SR, Allan W, et al. Cytokine profiles in bronchoalveolar lavage cells from mice with influenza pneumonia: Consequences of CD4+ and CD8+ T-cell depletion. Reg Immunol. 1993;5:142-150.

175. Graham MB, Braciale VL, Braciale TJ. Influenza virus-specific CD4+ T helper type 2 T lymphocytes do not promote recovery from experimental virus infection. J Exp Med. 1994;180:1273-1282.

176. Sarawar SR, Sangster M, Coffman RL, Doherty PC. Administration of anti-IFN-g antibody to B2-microglobulin-deficient mice delays influenza virus clearance but does not switch the response to a T helper cell 2 phenotype. J Immunol. 1994;153:1246-1253.

177. Baumgarth N, Kelso A. In vivo blockade of gamma interferon affects the influenza virus-induced humoral and the local cellular immune response in lung tissue. J Virol. 1996;70:4411-4418.

178. Moran TM, Isobe H, Fernandez-Sesma A, Shulman JL. Interleukin-4 causes delayed virus clearance in influenza virus-infected mice. J Virol. 1996;70:5230-5235.

179. Hashimoto G, Wright PF, Karzon DT. Antibody-dependent cell-mediated cytotoxicity against influenza virus-infected cells. J Infect Dis. 1983;148:785-794.

180. Fleischer B, Becht H, Rott R. Recognition of viral antigens by human influenza A virus-specific T lymphocyte clones. J Immunol. 1985;165:2800-2804.

181. Braciale TJ. Immunologic recognition of influenza virus-infected cells: II. Expression of influenza A matrix protein on the infected cell surface and its role in recognition by cross-reactive cytotoxic T cells. J Exp Med. 1977;146:673-689.

182. Yewdell JW, Hackett CJ. The specificity and function of T lymphocytes induced by influenza A viruses. In: Krug R, ed. The Influenza Viruses. New York: Plenum Press; 1989:361-429.

183. Lin Y-L, Askonas BA. Biologic properties of an influenza A virus-specific killer T cell clone: Inhibition of virus replication in vivo and induction of delayed-type hypersensitivity reactions. J Exp Med. 1981;154:225-234.

184. Lukacher AE, Braciale VL, Braciale TJ. In vivo effector function of influenza virus-specific cytotoxic T lymphocyte clones is highly specific. J Exp Med. 1984;160:814-826.

185. Taylor PM, Askonas BA. Influenza nucleoprotein-specific cytotoxic T-cell clones are protective in vivo. Immunology. 1986;58:417-420.

186. Yap KL, Ada GL, McKenzie IFC. Transfer of specific cytotoxic T lymphocytes protects mice inoculated with influenza virus. Nature. 1978;273:238-239.

187. MacKenzie CD, Taylor PM, Askonas BA. Rapid recovery of lung histology correlates with clearance of influenza virus by specific CD8+ cytotoxic cells. Immunology. 1989;67:375-381.

188. Reiss CS, Schulman JL. Cellular immune responses of mice to influenza virus infection. Cell Immunol. 1980;56:502-506.

189. Eichelberger M, Allan W, Zijlstra M, et al. Clearance of influenza virus respiratory infection in mice lacking class I major histocompatibility complex-restricted T cells. J Exp Med. 1991;174:875-880.

190. Scherle PA, Palladino G, Gerhard W. Mice can recover from pulmonary influenza virus infection in the absence of class-I restricted cytotoxic T cells. J Immunol. 1992;148:212-217.

191. Epstein SL, Misplon JA, Lawson CM, et al. Beta 2-microglobulin-deficient mice can be protected against influenza A infection by vaccination with vaccinia-influenza recombinants expressing hemagglutinin and neuraminidase. J Immunol. 1993;150:5484-5493.

192. Ennis FA. Some newly recognized aspects of resistance against and recovery from influenza. Arch Virol. 1982;73:207-217.

193. McMichael AJ, Gotch FM, Noble GR, Beare PAS. Cytotoxic T-cell immunity to influenza. N Engl J Med. 1983;309:13-17.

194. Treanor JJ, Murphy B. Genes involved in the restriction of replication of avian influenza A viruses in primates. In: Kurstak E, ed. Virus Variability, Epidemiology, and Control. New York: Plenum; 1990:159-176.

195. Jordan WS, Gordon I, Dorrance WR. A study of illness in a group of Cleveland families: VII. Transmission of acute nonbacterial gastroenteritis to volunteers: Evidence for two different etiologic agents. J Exp Med. 1953;98:461-475.

196. Kilbourne ED, Loge JP. Influenza A prime: A clinical study of an epidemic caused by a new strain of virus. Ann Intern Med. 1950;33:371-382.

197. Stuart-Harris CH. Twenty years of influenza epidemics. Am Rev Respir Dis. 1961;83:54-75.

198. Nigg C, Ecklund CM, Wilson DE. Study of epidemics of influenza B. Am J Hyg. 1942;35:265-275.

199. Blaine WB, Luby JP, Martin SM. Severe illness with influenza B. Am J Med. 1980;68:181-189.

200. Mogabgab WJ. Virus association with upper respiratory illnesses in adults. Ann Intern Med. 1963;59:306-311.

201. McIntosh K, Halonon P, Ruuskanen O. Report of a workshop on respiratory viral infection: Epidemiology, diagnosis, treatment and prevention. Clin Infect Dis. 1993;16:151-164.

202. Glezen WP, Loda FA, Clyde WA Jr, et al. Epidemiologic patterns of acute lower respiratory disease of children in a pediatric group practice. J Pediatr. 1971;78:397-406.

203. Howard JB. Influenza A2 virus as a cause of croup requiring tracheostomy. J Pediatr. 1972;81:1148-1150.

204. Glezen WP, Paredes A, Taber LH. Influenza in children. JAMA. 1980;243:1345-1349.

205. Scheiblauer H, Reinacher M, Tashiro M, Rott R. Interactions between bacteria and influenza A virus in the development of influenza pneumonia. J Infect Dis. 1992;166:783-791.

206. Schwarzmann SW, Adler JL, Sullivan RFJ, Marine WM. Bacterial pneumonia during the Hong Kong influenza epidemic of 1968-1969. Arch Intern Med. 1971;127:1037-1041.

207. Bisno AL, Griffin JP, VanEpps KA. Pneumonia and Hong Kong influenza: A prospective study of the 1968-1969 epidemic. Am J Med Sci. 1971;261:251-274.

208. Fry J. Lung involvement in influenza. Br Med J. 1951;2:1374.

209. Fry J. Influenza A (Asian) 1957: Clinical and epidemiological features in a general practice. Br Med J. 1958;1:259.

210. Kay D, Rosenbluth M, Hook EW. Endemic influenza: II. The nature of the disease in the post-pandemic period. Am Rev Respir Dis. 1962;85:9.

211. Safrin S, Rush JD, Mills J. Influenza in patients with human immunodeficiency virus infection. Chest. 1990;98:33-37.

212. Kempe A, Hall CB, MacDonald NE, et al. Influenza in children with cancer. J Pediatr. 1989;115:33-39.

213. Hirschhorn LR, McIntosh K, Anderson KG, Dermody TS. Influenzal pneumonia as a complication of autologous bone marrow transplantation (Letter). Clin Infect Dis. 1992;14:786-787.

214. Yousuf HM, Englund J, Couch R, et al. Influenza among hospitalized adults with leukemia. Clin Infect Dis. 1997;24:1095-1099.

215. Klimov AI, Rocha E, Hayden FG, et al. Prolonged shedding of amantadine-resistant influenzae A viruses by immunodeficient patients: Detection by polymerase chain reaction-restriction analysis. J Infect Dis. 1995;172:1352-1355.

216. Evans KM, Kline MW. Prolonged influenza A infection responsive to rimantadine therapy in a human immunodeficiency virus-infected child. Pediatr Infect Dis J. 1995;14:332-334.

217. Gubareva LV, Matrosovich MN, Brenner MK, et al. Evidence for zanamivir resistance in an immunocompromised child infected with influenza B virus. J Infect Dis. 1998;178:1257-1262.

218. Carilli AD, Gohd RS, Gordon W. A virologic study of chronic bronchitis. N Engl J Med. 1964;270:123-127.

219. Stark JE, Heath RB, Curwen MP. Infection with influenza and parainfluenza viruses in chronic bronchitis. Thorax. 1965;20:124.

220. Stenhouse AC. Rhinovirus infection in acute exacerbation of chronic bronchitis: A controlled prospective study. Br Med J. 1967;3:461.

221. Monto AS, Ross HW. The Tecumseh study of respiratory illness: X. Relation of acute infections to smoking, lung function, and chronic symptoms. Am J Epidemiol. 1978;107:57-64.

222. Clementsen P, Jensen CB, Hannoun C, et al. Influenza A virus potentiates basophil histamine release caused by endotoxin-induced complement activation: Examination of normal individuals and patients with intrinsic asthma. Allergy. 1988;43:93-99.

223. Lin CY, Kuo YC, Liu WT, Lin CC. Immunomodulation of influenza virus infection in the precipitating asthma attack. Chest. 1988;93:1234-1238.

224. Ferson MJ, Morton JR, Robertson PW. Impact of influenza on morbidity in children with cystic fibrosis. J Paedtr Child Health. 1991;27:308-311.

225. Fry J. Influenza, 1959: The story of an epidemic. Br Med J. 1959;2:135-147.

226. Foy HM, Cooney MK, Allan I, Kenny GE. Rates of pneumonia during influenza epidemics in Seattle, 1964 to 1975. JAMA. 1979;241:253-258.

227. Jones A, MacFarlane J, Pugh S. Antibiotic therapy, clinical features and outcome of 36 adults presenting to hospital with proven influenza: Do we follow guidelines? Postgraduate Medical J. 1991;67:988-990.

228. Fedson DS, Wajda A, Nicol JP, Roos LL. Disparity between influenza vaccination rates and risks for influenza-associated hospital discharge and death in Manitoba in 1982-1983. Ann Intern Med. 1992;116:550-555.

229. Tillett HE, Smith JW, Clifford RE. Excess morbidity and mortality associated with influenza in England and Wales. Lancet. 1980;1:793-795.

230. Barker WH, Mullooly JP. Pneumonia and influenza deaths during epidemics: Implications for prevention. JAMA. 1982;142:85-89.

231. Choi K, Thacker SB. Mortality during influenza epidemics in the United States, 1967-1978. Am J Public Health. 1982;72:1280-1287.

232. Middleton PJ, Alexander RM, Szymanski MT. Severe myositis during recovery from influenza. Lancet. 1970;2:533.

233. Simon NM. Acute myoglobinuria associated with type A2 influenza. JAMA. 1970;212:1704-1707.

234. Dietzman DE, Schaller JG, Ray CG, Reed ME. Acute myositis associated with influenza B infection. Pediatrics. 1976;57:255-258.

235. Minow RA, Gorbach S, Johnson BL Jr, Dornfeld L. Myoglobinuria associated with influenza A infection. Ann Intern Med. 1974;80:359-361.

236. Greco TP, Askenase PW, Kashgarian M. Postviral myositis: Myxovirus-like structures in affected muscle. Ann Intern Med. 1977;86:193-198.

237. Glezen WP, Decker M, Perrotta DM. Survey of underlying conditions of persons hospitalized with acute respiratory disease during influenza epidemics in Houston, 1978-1981. Am Rev Respir Dis. 1987;136:550-555.

238. Bainton D, Jones GR, Hole D. Influenza and ischemic heart disease: A possible trigger for acute myocardial infarction. Int J Epidemiol. 1978;7:231.

239. MacDonald KL, Osterholm MT, Hedberg CW, et al. Toxic shock syndrome: A newly recognized complication of influenza and influenza like illness. JAMA. 1987;257:1053-1058.

240. Sperber SJ, Francis JB. Toxic shock during an influenza outbreak. JAMA. 1987;257:1086-1089.

241. Edelen JS, Bender TR, Chin TDY. Encephalopathy and pericarditis during an outbreak of influenza. Am J Epidemiol. 1974;100:79-83.

242. Bayer WH. Influenza B encephalitis. West J Med. 1987;147:466-468.

243. Centers for Disease Control and Prevention. Severe Morbidity and mortality associated with influenza in children and young adults—Michigan, 2003. MMWR Morb Mortal Wkly Rep. 2003;52:834-840.

244. Kimball AM, Foy HM, Cooney MK, et al. Isolation of respiratory syncytial and influenza viruses from the sputum of patients hospitalized with pneumonia. J Infect Dis. 1983;147:181-184.

245. Newton DW, Mellen CF, Baxter BD, et al. Practical and sensitive screening strategy for detection of influenza virus. J Clin Microbiol. 2002;40:4353-4356.

246. Covalciuc KA, Webb KH, Carlson CA. Comparison of four clinical specimen types for detection of influenza A and B viruses by optical immunoassay (FLU OIA test) and cell culture methods. J Clin Microbiol. 1999;37:3971-3974.

247. Noyola DE, Clark B, O'Donnell FT, et al. Comparison of a new neuraminidase detection assay with an enzyme immunoassay, immunofluorescence, and culture for rapid detection of influenza A and B viruses in nasal wash specimens. J Clin Microbiol. 2000;38:1161-1165.

248. Boivin G, Hardy I, Kress A. Evaluation of a rapid optical immunoassay for influenza viruses (FLU OIA test) in comparison with cell culture and reverse transcription-PCR. J Clin Microbiol. 2001;39:730-732.

249. Herrmann B, Larsson C, Zweygberg BW. Simultaneous detection and typing of influenza viruses A and B by a nested reverse transcription-PCR: Comparison to virus isolation and antigen detection by immunofluorescence and optical immunoassay (FLU OIA). J Clin Microbiol. 2001;39:134-138.

250. Landry ML, Ferguson D. Suboptimal detection of influenza virus in adults by the Directigen Flu A+B enzyme immunoassay and correlation of results with the number of antigen-positive cells detected by Cytospin immunofluorescence. J Clin Microbiol. 2003;41:3407-3409.

251. Cazacu AC, Greer J, Taherivand M, Demmler GJ. Comparison of lateral-flow immunoassay and enzyme immunoassay with viral culture for rapid detection of influenza virus in nasal wash specimens from children. J Clin Microbiol. 2003;41:2132-2134.

252. Chan KH, Maldeis N, Pope W, et al. Evaluation of the Directigen FluA+B test for rapid diagnosis of influenza virus type A and B infections. J Clin Microbiol. 2002;40:1675-1680.

253. Ryan-Pourier KA, Katz JM, Webster RG, Kawaoka Y. Application of Directigen FLU-A for the detection of influenza A virus in human and non-human specimens. J Clin Microbiol. 1992;30:1072-1075.

254. Coiras MT, Perez-Brena P, Garcia ML, Casas I. Simultaneous detection of influenza A, B, and C viruses, respiratory syncytial virus, and adenoviruses in clinical samples by multiplex reverse transcription nested-PCR assay. J Med Virol. 2003;69:132-144.

255. Boivin G, Hardy I, Tellier G, Maziade J. Predicting influenza infections during epidemics with use of a clinical case definition. Clin Infect Dis. 2000;31:1166-1169.

256. Monto AS, Gravenstein S, Elliott M, et al. Clinical signs and symptoms predicting influenza infection. Arch Intern Med. 2000;160:3243-3247.

257. Zambon M, Hays J, Webster A, et al. Diagnosis of influenza in the community: Relationship of clinical diagnosis to confirmed virologic, serologic, or molecular detection of influenza. Arch Intern Med. 2001;161:2116-2122.

258. Walsh EE, Cox C, Falsey AR. Clinical features of influenza A virus infection in older hospitalized persons. J Am Geriatr Soc. 2002;50:1498-1503.

259. Ruest A, Michaud S, Deslandes S, Frost EH. Comparison of the Directigen Flu A+B test, the QuickVue influenza test, and clinical case definition to viral culture and reverse transcription-PCR for rapid diagnosis of influenza virus infection. J Clin Microbiol. 2003;41:3487-3493.

260. Falsey AR. Noninfluenza respiratory virus infection in long-term care facilities. Infect Control Hosp Epidemiol. 1991;12:602-608.

261. Drinka PJ, Gravenstein S, Krause P, et al. Non-influenza respiratory viruses may overlap and obscure influenza activity. J Am Geriatr Soc. 1999;47:1087-1093.

262. Dolin R. Amantadine and rimantadine. Antimicrob Agents Annu. 1988;3:361-370.

263. Douglas RG Jr. Prophylaxis and treatment of influenza. N Engl J Med. 1990;322:443-450.

264. Bui M, Whittaker G, Helenius A. Effect of M1 protein and low pH on nuclear transport of influenza virus ribonucleoproteins. J Virol. 1996;70:8391-8401.

265. Richman DD, Yazaki P, Hostetler KY. The intracellular distribution and antiviral activity of amantadine. Virology. 1981;112:81-90.

266. Richman DD, Hostetler KY, Yazaki PJ, Clark S. Fate of influenza A virion proteins after entry into subcellular fractions of LLC cells and the effect of amantadine. Virology. 1986;151:200-210.

267. Hayden FG, Minocha A, Spyker DA, Hoffman HE. Comparative single-dose pharmacokinetics of amantadine hydrochloride and rimantadine hydrochloride in young and elderly adults [published erratum appears in Antimicrob Agents Chemother. 1986;30:579]. Antimicrob Agents Chemother. 1985;28:216-221.

268. Wills RJ, Farolino DA, Choma N, Keigher N. Rimantadine pharmacokinetics after single and multiple doses. Antimicrob Agents Chemother. 1987;31:826-828.

269. Van Voris LP, Betts RF, Hayden FG, et al. Successful treatment of naturally occurring influenza A/USSR/77 H1N1. JAMA. 1981;245:1128-1131.

270. Little J, Hall W, Douglas RG Jr, et al. Amantadine effect on peripheral airways abnormalities in influenza. Ann Intern Med. 1976;85:177-182.

271. Dolin R, Reichman RC, Madore HP, et al. A controlled trial of amantadine and rimantadine in the prophylaxis of influenza A in humans. N Engl J Med. 1982;307:580-584.

272. Keyser LA, Karl M, Nafziger AN, Bertino JS Jr. Comparison of central nervous system adverse effects of amantadine and rimantadine used as sequential prophylaxis of influenza A in elderly nursing home patients. Arch Intern Med. 2000;160:1485-1488.

273. Atkinson WL, Arden NH, Patriarca PA, et al. Amantadine prophylaxis during an institutional outbreak of type A (H1N1) influenza. Arch Intern Med. 1986;146:1751-1756.

274. Speeg KV, Leighton JA, Maldonado AL. Case report: Toxic delirium in a patient taking amantadine and trimethoprim-sulfamethoxazole. Am J Med Sci. 1989;298:410-412.

275. Galbraith AW, Oxford JS, Schild GC, et al. Therapeutic effect of 1-adamantanamine hydrochloride in naturally occurring influenza A2/Hong Kong infection. Lancet. 1971;1:113-115.

276. Togo Y, Hornick RB, Felitti VJ, et al. Evaluation of the therapeutic efficacy of amantadine in patients with naturally occurring A2 influenza. JAMA. 1970;211:1149-1156.

277. Hornick RB, Togo Y, Mahler S, Iezzoni D. Evaluation of amantadine hydrochloride in the treatment of A2 influenzal disease. Bull World Health Organ. 1969;41:671-676.

278. Knight V, Fedson D, Baldini J, et al. Amantadine therapy of epidemic influenza A2/Hong Kong. Antimicrob Agents Chemother. 1969:370-371.

279. Younkin SW, Betts RF, Roth FK, Douglas RG Jr. Reduction in fever and symptoms in young adults with influenza A/Brazil/78 H1N1 infection after treatment with aspirin or amantadine. Antimicrob Agents Chemother. 1983;23:577-582.

280. Hayden FG, Monto AS. Oral rimantadine hydrochloride therapy of influenza A virus H3N2 subtype infection in adults. Antimicrob Agents Chemother. 1986;29:339-341.

281. Betts RF, Treanor J, Braman P, et al. Antiviral agents to prevent or treat influenza in the elderly. J Respir Dis. 1987;8:S56-S59.

282. Hall CB, Dolin R, Gala CL, et al. Children with influenza A infection: Treatment with rimantadine. Pediatrics. 1987;80:275-282.

283. Thompson J, Fleet W, Lawrence E, et al. A comparison of acetaminophen and rimantadine in the treatment of influenza A infection in children. J Med Virol. 1987;21:249-255.

284. Monto AS, Arden NH. Implications of viral resistance to amantadine in control of influenza A. Clin Infect Dis. 1992;15:362-367.

285. Belshe RB, Burk B, Newman F, et al. Resistance of influenza A virus to amantadine and rimantadine: Results of one decade of surveillance. J Infect Dis. 1989;159:430-435.

286. Ziegler T, Hemphill ML, Ziegler ML, et al. Low incidence of rimantadine resistance in field isolates of influenza A viruses. J Infect Dis. 1999;180:935-939.

287. Hayden FG, Belshe RB, Clover RD, et al. Emergence and apparent transmission of rimantadine-resistant influenza A virus in families. N Engl J Med. 1989;321:1696-1702.

288. Hayden FG, Sperber SJ, Belshe RB, et al. Recovery of drug-resistant influenza A virus during therapeutic use of rimantadine. Antimicrob Agents Chemother. 1991;35:1741-1747.

289. Hay AJ, Wolstenholme AJ, Skehel JJ, Smith MH. The molecular basis of the specific anti-influenza action of amantadine. EMBO J. 1985;4:3021-3024.

290. Degelau J, Somani SK, Cooper SL, et al. Amantadine-resistant influenza A in a nursing facility. Arch Intern Med. 1992;152:390-392.

291. Boivin G, Goyette N, Bernatchez H. Prolonged excretion of amantadine-resistant influenza A virus quasi species after cessation of antiviral therapy in an immunocompromised patient. Clin Infect Dis. 2002;34:E23-25.

292. Webster RG, Kawaoka Y, Bean WJ, et al. Chemotherapy and vaccination: A possible strategy for the control of highly virulent influenza virus. J Virol. 1985;55:173-176.

293. Webster RG, Kawaoka Y, Bean WJ. Vaccination as a strategy to reduce the emergence of amantadine- and rimantadine-resistant strains of A/Chick/Pennsylvania/83 (H5N2) influenza virus. J Antimicrob Chemother. 1986;18(Suppl B):157-164.

294. Varghese JN, Laver WG, Colman PM. Structure of the influenza glycoprotein antigen neuraminidase at 2.9A resolution. Nature. 1983;303:35-40.

295. von Itzstein M, Wu W-Y, Kok GB, et al. Rational design of potent sialidase-based inhibitors of influenza virus replication. Nature. 1993;363:418-423.

296. Garcia-Sastre A, Palese P. The cytoplasmic tail of the neuraminidase protein of influenza A virus does not play an important role in the packaging of this protein into viral envelopes. Virus Res. 1995;37:37-47.

297. Mitnaul LJ, Castrucci MR, Murti KG, Kawaoka Y. The cytoplasmic tail of influenza A virus neuraminidase (NA) affects NA incorporation into virions, virion morphology, and virulence in mice but is not essential for virus replication. J Virol. 1996;70:873-879.

298. Kim CU, Lew W, Williams MA, et al. Influenza neuraminidase inhibitors possessing a novel hydrophobic interaction in the enzyme active site: Design, synthesis, and structural analysis of carbocyclic sialic acid analogues with potent anti-influenza activity. J Am Chem Soc. 1997;119:681-690.

299. Calfee DP, Peng AW, Cass LMR, et al. Protective efficacy of intravenous zanamivir in experimental human influenza. In: Proceedings of 38th International Conference on Antimicrobial Agents and Chemotherapy. San Diego, Calif: American Society for Microbiology; 1998:A332.

300. Hill G, Cihlar T, Oo C, et al. The anti-influenza drug oseltamivir exhibits low potential to induce pharmacokinetic drug interactions via renal secretion-correlation of in vivo and in vitro studies. Drug Metab Dispos. 2002;30:13-19.

301. Hayden FG, Treanor JJ, Fritz RS, et al. Use of the oral neuraminidase inhibitor oseltamivir in experimental human influenza: Randomized controlled trials for prevention and treatment. JAMA. 1999;282:1240-1246.

302. Hayden FG, Lobo M, Hussey EK, Eason CU. Efficacy of intranasal GG167 in experimental human influenza A and B virus infection. In: Brown LE, Hampson AW, Webster RG, eds. Options for the Control of Influenza III. London: Elsevier Science B.V.; 1996:718-725.

303. Walker JB, Hussey EK, Treanor JJ, et al. Effects of the neuraminidase inhibitor Zanamivir on otologic manifestations of experimental human influenza. J Infect Dis. 1997;176:1417-1422.

304. Hayden FG, Robson R, Jennings LC, et al. Efficacy of oral oseltamivir in experimental human influenza B virus infection. In: 37th Annual Meeting of the Infectious Diseases Society of America. Philadelphia; 1999:A677.

305. Treanor JJ, Hayden FG, Vrooman PS, et al. Efficacy and safety of the oral neuraminidase inhibitor oseltamivir in treating acute influenza: A randomized, controlled trial. JAMA. 2000;283:1016-1024.

306. Nicholson KG, Aoki FY, Osterhaus AD, et al. Efficacy and safety of oseltamivir in treatment of acute influenza: A randomized controlled trial. Lancet. 2000;355:1845-1850.

307. Hayden FG, Osterhaus AD, Treanor JJ, et al. Efficacy and safety of the neuraminidase inhibitor zanamivir in the treatment of influenzavirus infections. N Engl J Med. 1997;337:874-880.

308. MIST (Management of Influenza in the Southern Hemisphere Trialists) Study Group. Randomised trial of efficacy and safety of inhaled zanamivir in treatment of influenza A and B virus infections. Lancet. 1998;352:1877-1881.

309. Kaiser L, Wat C, Mills T, et al. Impact of oseltamivir treatment on influenza-related lower respiratory tract complications and hospitalizations. Arch Intern Med. 2003;163:1667-1672.

310. Whitley RJ, Hayden FG, Reisinger KS, et al. Oral oseltamivir treatment of influenza in children. Pediatr Infect Dis J. 2001;20:127-133.

311. Hedrick JA, Barzilai A, Behre U, et al. Zanamivir for treatment of symptomatic influenza A and B infection in children five to twelve years of age: A randomized controlled trial. Pediatr Infect Dis J. 2000;19:410-417.

312. McClellan K, Perry CM. Oseltamivir: A review of its use in influenza. Drugs. 2001;61:263-283.

313. Lalezari J, Campion K, Keene O, Silagy C. Zanamivir for the treatment of influenza A and B infection in high-risk patients: A pooled analysis of randomized controlled trials. Arch Intern Med. 2001;161:212-217.

314. Covington E, Mendel DB, Escarpe P, et al. Phenotypic and genotypic assay of influenza virus neuraminidase indicates a low incidence of viral drug resistance during treatment with oseltamivir. J Clin Virol. 2000;18:P326.

315. Barnett JM, Cadman A, Gor D, et al. Zanamivir susceptibility monitoring and characterization of influenza virus clinical isolates obtained during phase II clinical efficacy studies. Antimicrob Agents Chemother. 2000;44:78-87.

316. Jackson HC, Roberts N, Wang Z, et al. Management of influenza: Use of antivirals and resistance in perspective. Clin Drug Invest. 2000;447-454.

317. Gubareva LV, Bethell R, Hart GJ, et al. Characterization of mutants of influenza A selected with the neuraminidase inhibitor 4-guanidino-Neu5Ac2en. J Virol. 1996;70:1818-1827.

318. Gubareva LV, Robinson MJ, Bethell RC, Webster RG. Catalytic and framework mutations in the neuraminidase active site of influenza viruses that are resistant to 4-guanidino-neu5ac2en. J Virol. 1997;71:3385-3390.

319. McKimm-Breschkin JL, Sahasrabudhe A, Blick TJ, et al. Mutations in a conserved residue in the influenza virus neuraminidase active site decreases sensitivity to neu5acen-derived inhibitors. J Virol. 1998;72:2456-2462.

320. Goto H, Bethell RC, Kawaoka Y. Mutations affecting the sensitivity of the influenza virus neuraminidase to 4-guanidino-2,4-dideoxy-2,3-dehydro-N-acetylneuraminic acid. Virology. 1997;238:265-272.

321. Blick TJ, Sahasrabudhe A, McDonald M, et al. The interaction of neuraminidase and hemagglutinin mutations in influenza virus in resistance to 4-guanidino-neu5ac2en. Virology. 1998;246:95-103.

322. Ives JA, Carr JA, Mendel DB, et al. The H274Y mutation in the influenza A/H1N1 neuraminidase active site following oseltamivir phosphate treatment leave virus severely compromised both in vitro and in vivo. Antiviral Res. 2002;55:307-317.

323. Carr J, Ives J, Kelly L, et al. Influenza virus carrying neuraminidase with reduced sensitivity to oseltamivir carboxylate has altered properties in vitro and is compromised for infectivity and replicative ability in vivo. Antiviral Res. 2002;54:79-88.

324. Herlocher ML, Carr J, Ives J, et al. Influenza virus carrying an R292K mutation in the neuraminidase gene is not transmitted in ferrets. Antiviral Res. 2002;54:99-111.

325. Winterbauer RH, Ludwig WR, Hammer SP. Clinical course, management, and long-term sequelae of respiratory failure due to influenza viral pneumonia. Johns Hopkins Med J. 1977;141:148.

326. Kaiser L, Henry D, Flack NP, et al. Short-term treatment with zanamivir to prevent influenza: Results of a placebo-controlled study. Clin Infect Dis. 2000;30:587-589.

327. Peck FB Jr. Purified influenza vaccine. JAMA. 1968;10:2277-2282.

328. Wright PF, Dolin R, LaMontagne JR. Summary of clinical trials of influenza vaccine II. J Infect Dis. 1976;134:633-638.

329. Kilbourne ED, Schulman JL, Schild GC, et al. Correlated studies of a recombinant influenza-virus vaccine: I. Derivation and characterization of virus and vaccine. J Infect Dis. 1971;124:449-462.

330. Wood JM. Standardization of inactivated influenza vaccine. In: Nicholson KG, Webster RG, Hay AJ, eds. Textbook of Influenza. London: Blackwell Science; 1998:333-345.

331. Nichol KL, Margolis KL, Lind A, et al. Side effects associated with influenza vaccination in healthy working adults: A randomized, placebo-controlled trial. Arch Intern Med. 1996;156:1546-1550.

332. Scheifele DW, Bjornson G, Johnston J. Evaluation of adverse events after influenza vaccination in hospital personnel. CMAJ. 1990;142:127-130.

333. Aoki FY, Yassi A, Cheang M, et al. Effects of acetaminophen on adverse effects of influenza vaccination in health care workers. CMAJ. 1993;149:1425-1430.

334. al-Mazrou A, Scheifele DW, Soong T, Bjornson G. Comparison of adverse reactions to whole-virion and split-virion influenza vaccines in hospital personnel. CMAJ. 1991;145:213-218.

335. Margolis KL, Poland GA, Nichol KL, et al. Frequency of adverse reactions after influenza vaccination. Am J Med. 1990;88:27-30.

336. LaMontagne JR, Noble GR, Quinnan GV, et al. Summary of clinical trials of inactivated influenza vaccine-1978. Rev Infect Dis. 1983;5:723-736.

337. Wright PF, Thompson J, Vaughn WT, et al. Trials of influenza A/New Jersey/76 virus vaccine in normal children: An overview of age-related antigenicity and reactogenicity. J Infect Dis. 1977;136(Suppl):S731-S741.

338. Gross PA, Ennis FA, Gaerlan PF, et al. A controlled double-blind comparison of reactogenicity, immunogenicity, and protective efficacy of whole-virus and split-product influenza vaccines in children. J Infect Dis. 1977;136:623-632.

339. Davies R, Pepys J. Egg allergy, influenza vaccine, and immunoglobulin E antibody. J Allergy Clin Immunol. 1976;57:373-383.

340. Murphy DR, Strunk RC. Safe administration of influenza vaccine in asthmatic children hypersensitive to egg proteins. J Pediatr. 1985;106:931-933.

341. Bierman CW, Shapiro GG, Pierson WE, et al. Safety of influenza vaccination in allergic children. J Infect Dis. 1977;136:S652-S655.

342. Schonberger LB, Bregman DJ, Sullivan-Bolyai JZ, et al. Guillain-Barré syndrome following vaccination in the national influenza immunization program, United States, 1976-1977. Am J Epidemiol. 1979;110:105-123.

343. Kaplan JE, Katona P, Hurwitz ES, Schonberger LB. Guillain-Barré syndrome in the United States, 1979-1980 and 1980-1981: Lack of an association with influenza vaccination. JAMA. 1982;248:698-700.

344. Lasky T, Tarracciano GJ, Magder L, et al. The Guillain-Barré syndrome and the 1992-1993 and 1993-1994 influenza vaccines. N Engl J Med. 1998;339:1797-1802.

345. Cate TR, Couch RB, Parker D, Baxter B. Reactogenicity, immunogenicity, and antibody persistence in adults given inactivated influenza virus vaccines—1978. Rev Infect Dis. 1983;5:737-747.

346. Quinnan GV, Schooley R, Dolin R, et al. Serologic responses and systemic reactions in adults after vaccination with monovalent A/USSR/77 and trivalent A/USSR/77, A/Texas/77, B/Hong Kong/72 influenza vaccines. Rev Infect Dis. 1983;5:748-757.

347. Wright PF, Cherry JD, Foy HM, et al. Antigenicity and reactogenicity of influenza A/USSR/77 virus vaccine in children: A multicentered evaluation of dosage and toxicity. Rev Infect Dis. 1983;5:758-764.

348. Levandowski RA, Regnery HL, Staton E, et al. Antibody responses to influenza B viruses in immunologically unprimed children. Pediatrics. 1991;88:1031-1036.

349. Lerman SJ, Wright PJ, Patil KD. Antibody decline in children following A/New Jersy/76 influenza virus immunization. J Pediatr. 1980;96:271-274.

350. Zahradnik JM, Kasel JA, Martin RR, et al. Immune responses in serum and respiratory secretions following vaccination with a live cold-recombinant (CR35) and inactivated A/USSR/77 (H1N1) influenza virus vaccine. J Med Virol. 1983;11:277-285.

351. Bokstad KA, Eriksson J-C, Cox RJ, et al. Parenteral vaccination against influenza does not induce a local antigen-specific immune response in the nasal mucosa. J Infect Dis. 2002;185:878-884.

352. Ennis FA, Yi-Hua Q, Schild GC. Antibody and cytotoxic T lymphocyte responses of humans to live and inactivated influenza vaccines. J Gen Virol. 1982;58:273-281.

353. Gelder CM, Lambkin R, Hart KW, et al. Associations between human leukocyte antigens and nonresponsiveness to influenza vaccine. J Infect Dis. 2002;185:114-117.

354. Powers DC, Belshe RB. Effect of age on cytotoxic T lymphocyte memory as well as serum and local antibody responses elicited by inactivated influenza vaccine. J Infect Dis. 1993;197:584-592.

355. Nicholson KG, Baker DJ, Chakraverty P, et al. Immunogenicity of inactivated influenza vaccine in residential homes for elderly people. Age Ageing. 1992;21: 182-188.

356. Remarque EJ, van Beek WC, Ligthart GJ, et al. Improvement of the immunoglobulin subclass response to influenza vaccine in elderly nursing-home residents by the use of high-dose vaccines. Vaccine. 1993;11:649-654.

357. Abu-Shakra M, Press J, Varsano N, et al. Specific antibody response after influenza immunization in systemic lupus erythematosus. J Rheumatol. 2002;29:2555-2557.

358. Pabico RC, Douglas RG Jr, Betts RF, et al. Influenza vaccination of patients with glomerular diseases: Effects on creatinine clearance, urinary protein excretion, and antibody response. Ann Intern Med. 1974;81:171-177.

359. Pabico RC, Douglas RG Jr, Betts RF, et al. Antibody response to influenza vaccination in renal transplant patients: Correlation with allograft function. Ann Intern Med. 1976;85:431-436.

360. Stiver HG, Graves P, Meiklejohn G, et al. Impaired serum antibody response to inactivated influenza A and B vaccine in renal transplant recipients. Infect Immun. 1977;16:738-741.

361. Kumar SS, Ventura AK, VanderWerf B. Influenza vaccination in renal transplant recipients. JAMA. 1978;239:840-842.

362. Duchini A, Hendry RM, Nyberg LM, et al. Immune response to influenza vaccine in adult liver transplant recipients. Liver Transpl. 2001;7:311-313.

363. Duchini A, Goss JA, Karpen S, Pockros PJ. Vaccinations for adult solid-organ transplant recipients: Current recommendations and protocols. Clin Microbiol Rev. 2003;16:357-364.

364. Nelson KE, Clements ML, Miotti P, et al. The influence of human immunodeficiency virus (HIV) infection on antibody responses to influenza vaccines. Ann Intern Med. 1988;109:383-388.

365. Kroon FP, van Dissel JT, de Jong JC, et al. Antibody response after influenza vaccination in HIV-infected individuals: A consecutive 3-year study. Vaccine. 2000;18:3040-3049.

366. Kubiet MA, Gonzalez-Rothi RJ, Cottey R, Bender BS. Serum antibody response to influenza vaccine in pulmonary patients receiving corticosteroids. Chest. 1996;110:367-370.

367. Park CL, Frank AL, Sullivan M, et al. Influenza vaccination of children during acute asthma exacerbation and concurrent prednisone therapy. Pediatrics. 1996;98: 196-200.

368. Meiklejohn G. Viral respiratory disease at Lowry Air Force Base in Denver, 1952-1982. J Infect Dis. 1983;148:775-783.

369. Ruben FL. Prevention and control of influenza: Role of vaccine. Am J Med. 1987;82:31-33.

370. Edwards KM, Dupont WD, Westrich MK, et al. A randomized controlled trial of cold-adapted and inactivated vaccines for the prevention of influenza A disease. J Infect Dis. 1994;169:68-76.

371. Neuzil KM, Dupont WD, Wright PF, Edwards KM. Efficacy of inactivated and cold-adapted vaccines against influenza A infection, 1985 to 1990: The pediatric experience. Pediatr Infect Dis J. 2001;20:733-740.

372. Nichol KL, Lind A, Margolis KL, et al. The effectiveness of vaccination against influenza in healthy, working adults. N Engl J Med. 1995;333:889-893.

373. Bridges CB, Thompson WW, Meltzer MI, et al. Effectiveness and cost-benefit of influenza vaccination of healthy working adults: A randomized controlled trial [see comments]. JAMA. 2000;284:1655-1663.

374. Heikkinen T, Ruuskanen O, Waris M, et al. Influenza vaccination in the prevention of acute otitis media in children. Am J Dis Child. 1991;145:445-448.

375. Clements DA, Langdon L, Bland C, Walter E. Influenza A vaccine decreases the incidence of otitis media in 6- to 30-month-old children in day care. Arch Pediatr Adolesc Med. 1995;149:1113-1117.

376. Hoberman A, Greenberg DP, Paradise JL, et al. Effectiveness of inactivated influenza vaccine in preventing acute otitis media in young children: A randomized controlled trial. JAMA. 2003;290:1608-1616.

377. Govaert TM, Thijs CT, Masurel N, et al. The efficacy of influenza vaccination in elderly individuals: A randomized double-blind placebo-controlled trial. JAMA. 1994;272:1956-1961.

378. Paul WS, Cowan J, Jackson GG. Acute respiratory illness among immunized and nonimmunized patients with high-risk factors during a split season of influenza A and B. J Infect Dis. 1988;157:633-639.

379. Patriarca PA, Weber JA, Parker RA, et al. Efficacy of influenza vaccine in nursing homes: Reduction in illness and complications during an influenza A (H3N2) epidemic. JAMA. 1985;253:1136-1139.

380. Saah AJ, Neufeld R, Rodstein M, et al. Influenza vaccine and pneumonia mortality in a nursing home population. Arch Intern Med. 1986;146:2353-2357.

381. Patriarca PA, Weber JA, Parker RA, et al. Risk factors for outbreaks of influenza in nursing homes: A case-control study. Am J Epidemiol. 1986;124:114-119.

382. Gross PA, Quinnan GV, Rodstein M, et al. Association of influenza immunization with reduction in mortality in an elderly population: A prospective study. Arch Intern Med. 1988;148:562-565.

383. Fedson DS, Wajda A, Nicol JP, et al. Clinical effectiveness of influenza vaccination in Manitoba. JAMA. 1993;270:1956-1961.

384. Tasker SA, Treanor JJ, Paxton WB, Wallace MR. Efficacy of influenza vaccination in HIV-infected persons: A randomized, double-blind, placebo-controlled trial. Ann Intern Med. 1999;131:430-433.

385. Gurfinkel EP, de la Fuente RL, Mendiz O, Mautner B. Influenza vaccine pilot study in acute coronary syndromes and planned percutaneous coronary interventions: The FLU Vaccination Acute Coronary Syndromes (FLUVACS) Study. Circulation. 2002;105:2143-2147.

386. Nichol KL, Nordin J, Mullooly J, et al. Influenza vaccination and reduction in hospitalizations for cardiac disease and stroke among the elderly. N Engl J Med. 2003;348:1322-1332.

387. Johnson PR, Feldman S, Thompson JM, et al. Immunity to influenza A virus infection in young children: A comparison of natural infection, live cold-adapted vaccine, and inactivated vaccine. J Infect Dis. 1986;154:121-127.

388. Clements ML, Betts RF, Murphy BR. Advantage of live attenuated cold-adapted influenza A virus over inactivated vaccine for A/Washington/80 (H3N2) wild-type virus infection. Lancet. 1984;1:704-708.

389. Chanock RM, Murphy BR. Use of temperature-sensitive and cold-adapted mutant viruses in the immunoprophylaxis of acute respiratory tract disease. Rev Infect Dis. 1980;2:421-432.

390. Wright PF, Karzon DT. Live attenuated influenza vaccines. Prog Med Virol. 1987;34:70-88.

391. Maassab HF. Biologic and immunologic characteristics of cold-adapted influenza virus. J Immunol. 1969;102:728-732.

392. Maassab HF, DeBorde DC. Development and characterization of cold-adapted viruses for use as live virus vaccines. Vaccine. 1985;3:335-369.

393. Snyder MH, Betts RF, DeBorde D, et al. Four viral genes independently contribute to attenuation of live influenza A/Ann Arbor/6/60 (H2N2) cold-adapted reassortant virus vaccines. J Virol. 1988;62:488-495.

394. Subbarao EK, Perkins M, Treanor JJ, Murphy BR. The attenuation phenotype conferred by the M gene of the influenza A/Ann Arbor/6/60 cold-adapted virus (H2N2) on the A/Korea/82 (H3N2) reassortant virus results from a gene constellation effect. Virus Res. 1992;25:37-50.

395. Jin H, Lu B, Zhou H, et al. Multiple amino acid residues confer temperature sensitivity to human influenza virus vaccine strains (FluMist) derived from cold-adapted A/Ann Arbor/6/60. Virology. 2003;306:18-24.

396. DeBorde DC, Donabedian AM, Herlocher ML, et al. Sequence comparison of wild-type and cold-adapted B/Ann Arbor/1/66 influenza virus genes. Virology. 1988;163:429-443.

397. Donabedian AM, DeBorde DC, Maassab HF. Genetics of cold-adapted B/Ann Arbor/1/66 influenza virus reassortants: The acidic polymerase (PA) protein gene confers temperature sensitivity and attenuated virulence. Microbiol Pathol. 1987;3:97-108.

398. Donabedian AM, DeBorde DC, Cook S, et al. A mutation in the PA protein gene of cold-adapted B/Ann Arbor/1/66 influenza virus associated with reversion of temperature sensitivity and attenuated virulence. Virology. 1988;163:444-451.

399. Jackson LA, Holmes SJ, Mendelman PM, et al. Safety of a trivalent live attenuated intranasal vaccine, FluMist, administered in addition to parenteral trivalent inactivated influenza vaccine to seniors with chronic medical conditions. Vaccine. 1999;17:1905-1909.

400. King JC, Treanor J, Fast PE, et al. Comparison of the safety, vaccine virus shedding, and immunogenicity of influenza virus vaccine, trivalent, types A and B, live cold-adapted, administered to human immunodeficiency virus (HIV)-infected and non-HIV-infected adults. J Infect Dis. 2000;181:725-728.

401. Nichol KL, Mendelman PM, Mallon KP, et al. Effectiveness of live, attenuated intranasal influenza virus vaccine in healthy, working adults: A randomized controlled trial. JAMA. 1999;282:137-144.

402. Keitel WA, Couch RB, Quarles JM, et al. Trivalent attenuated cold-adapted influenza virus vaccine: Reduced viral shedding and serum antibody responses in susceptible adults. J Infect Dis. 1993;167:305-311.

403. Treanor JJ, Kotloff K, Betts RF, et al. Evaluation of trivalent, live, cold-adapted (CAIV-T) and inactivated (TIV) influenza vaccines in prevention of virus infection and illness following challenge of adults with wild-type influenza A (H1N1), A (H3N2), and B viruses. Vaccine. 1999;18:899-906.

404. Belshe RB, Mendelman PM, Treanor J, et al. The efficacy of live attenuated cold-adapted trivalent, intranasal influenzavirus vaccine in children. N Engl J Med. 1998;358:1405-1412.

405. Belshe RB, Gruber WC, Mendelman PM, et al. Efficacy of vaccination with live attenuated, cold-adapted, trivalent, intranasal influenza virus vaccine against a variant (A/Sydney) not contained in the vaccine. J Pediatr. 2000;136:168-175.

406. Zangwill KM, Droge J, Mendelman P, et al. Prospective, randomized, placebo-controlled evaluation of the safety and immunogenicity of three lots of intranasal trivalent influenza vaccine among young children. Pediatr Infect Dis J. 2001;20:740-746.

407. King JC Jr, Lagos R, Bernstein DI, et al. Safety and immunogenicity of low and high doses of trivalent live cold-adapted influenza vaccine administered intranasally as drops or spray to healthy children. J Infect Dis. 1998;177:1394-1397.

408. King JC Jr, Fast PE, Zangwill KM, et al. Safety, vaccine virus shedding and immunogenicity of trivalent, cold-adapted, live attenuated influenza vaccine administered to human immunodeficiency virus-infected and noninfected children. Pediatr Infect Dis J. 2001;20:1124-1131.

409. Swierkosz EM, Newman FK, Anderson EL, et al. Multidose, live attenuated, cold-recombinant, trivalent influenza vaccine in infants and young children. J Infect Dis. 1994;169:1121-1124.

410. Belshe RB, Swierkosz EM, Anderson EL, et al. Immunization of infants and young children with live attenuated trivalent cold-recombinant influenza A H1N1, H3N2, and B vaccine. J Infect Dis. 1992;165:727-732.

411. Gruber WC, Kirschner K, Tollefson S, et al. Comparison of monovalent and trivalent live attenuated influenza vaccines in young children. J Infect Dis. 1993;168:53-60.

412. Gruber WC, Belshe RB, King JC, et al. Evaluation of live attenuated influenza vaccines in children 6-18 months of age: Safety, immunogenicity, and efficacy. J Infect Dis. 1996;173:1313-1319.

413. Wright PF, Bhargava M, Johnson PR, et al. Simultaneous administration of live attenuated influenza A vaccines representing different serotypes. Vaccine. 1985;3: 305-308.

414. Gruber WC, Darden PM, Still JG, et al. Evaluation of bivalent live attenuated influenza A vaccines in children 2 months to 3 years of age: Safety, immunogenicity and dose-response. Vaccine. 1997;15:1379-1384.

415. King JC Jr, Gross PA, Denning CR, et al. Comparison of live and inactivated influenza vaccine in high risk children. Vaccine. 1987;5:234-238.

416. Gruber WC, Campbell PW, Thompson JM, et al. Comparison of live attenuated and inactivated influenza vaccines in cystic fibrosis patients and their families: Results of a 3-year study. J Infect Dis. 1994;169:241-247.

417. Miyazaki C, Nakayama M, Tanaka Y, et al. Immunization of institutionalized asthmatic children and patients with psychomotor retardation using live attenuated cold-adapted reassortment influenza A H1N1, H3N2, and B vaccines. Vaccine. 1993;11:853-858.

418. Redding G, Walker RE, Hessel C, et al. Safety and tolerability of cold-adapted influenza virus vaccine in children and adolescents with asthma. Pediatr Infect Dis J. 2002;21:44-48.

419. Gorse GJ, Belshe RB, Munn NJ. Safety of and serum antibody response to cold-recombinant influenza A and inactivated trivalent influenza virus vaccines in older adults with chronic diseases. J Clin Microbiol. 1986;24:336-342.

420. Gorse GJ, Belshe RB, Munn NJ. Local and systemic antibody responses in high-risk adults given live attenuated and inactivated influenza A virus vaccines. J Clin Microbiol. 1988;26:911-918.

421. Atmar RL, Bloom K, Keitel W, et al. Effect of live attenuated, cold recombinant (CR) influenza virus vaccines on pulmonary function in healthy and asthmatic adults. Vaccine. 1990;8:217-224.

422. Wright PF, Johnson PR, Karzon DT. Clinical experience with live, attenuated vaccines in children. In: Kendal AP, Patriarca PA, eds. Options for the Control of Influenza. New York: Alan R Liss; 1986:243-253.

423. Vesikari T, Karvonen A, Korhonen T, et al. A randomized, double-blind, placebo-controlled trial of the safety, transmissibility and phenotypic stability of a live, attenuated, cold adapted influenza virus vaccine (CAIV-T) in children attending day care. In: 41st Interscience Conference on Antimicrobial Agents and Chemotherapy. Chicago, Ill: American Society of Microbiology Press; 2001:Abstract G-450.

424. Cha TA, Kao K, Zhao J, et al. Genotypic stability of cold-adapted influenza virus vaccine in an efficacy clinical trial. J Clin Microbiol. 2000;38:839-845.

425. Beyer WEP, Palache AM, de Jong JC, Osterhaus AD. Cold-adapted live influenza vaccine versus inactivated vaccine: Systemic vaccine reactions, local and systemic antibody response, and vaccine efficacy—A meta-analysis. Vaccine. 2002;20:1340-1353.

426. Edwards KM, Snyder MH, Thompson JM, et al. In vitro production of anti-influenza virus antibody after simultaneous administration of H3N2 and H1N1 cold-adapted vaccines in seronegative children. Vaccine. 1986;4:50-54.

427. Boyce TG, Gruber WC, Coleman-Dockery SD, et al. Mucosal immune response to trivalent live attenuated intranasal influenza vaccine in children. Vaccine. 1999;18:82-88.

428. Clements ML, Murphy BR. Development and persistence of local and systemic antibody responses in adults given live attenuated or inactivated influenza A virus vaccine. J Clin Microbiol. 1986;23:66-72.

429. Powers DC, Fries LF, Murphy BR, et al. In elderly persons live attenuated influenza A virus vaccines do not offer an advantage over inactivated virus vaccine in inducing serum or secretory antibodies or local immunologic memory. J Clin Microbiol. 1991;29:498-505.

430. Belshe RB, Gruber WC, Mendelman PM, et al. Correlates of immune protection induced by live attenuated, cold-adapted, trivalent, intranasal influenza virus vaccine. J Infect Dis. 2000;181:1133-1137.

431. Gorse GJ, Belshe RB. Enhancement of anti-influenza A virus cytotoxicity following influenza A vaccination in older, chronically ill adults. J Clin Microbiol. 1990;28:2539-2550.

432. Clover RD, Crawford S, Glezen WP, et al. Comparison of heterotypic protection against influenza A/Taiwan/86 (H1N1) by attenuated and inactivated vaccines to A/Chile/83-like viruses. J Infect Dis. 1991;163:300-304.

433. Mbawuike IN, Piedra PA, Cate TR, Couch RB. Cytotoxic T lymphocyte responses of infants after natural infection or immunization with live cold-recombinant or inactivated influenza A virus vaccine. J Med Virol. 1996;50:105-111.

434. Keitel WA, Couch RB, Cate TR, et al. Cold-recombinant influenza B/Texas/1/84 virus vaccine: Attenuation, immunogenicity, and efficacy against homotypic challenge. J Infect Dis. 1990;161:22-26.

435. Clements ML, Snyder MH, Sears SD, et al. Evaluation of the infectivity, immunogenicity, and efficacy of live cold-adapted influenza B/Ann Arbor/1/86 reassortant virus in adult volunteers. J Infect Dis. 1990;161:869-877.

436. Treanor JJ, Mattison HR, Dumyati G, et al. Protective efficacy of combined live intranasal and inactivated influenza A virus vaccines in the elderly. Ann Intern Med. 1992;117:625-633.

437. Centers for Disease Control and Prevention. Prevention and control of influenza: Recommendations of the advisory committee on immunization practice. MMWR Morb Mortal Wkly Rep. 2003;52(RR-8):1-26.

438. Fox JP, Cooney MK, Hall CE, Foy JM. Influenza virus infections in Seattle families, 1975-1979: II. Pattern of infection in invaded households and relation of age and prior antibody to occurrence of infection and related illness. Am J Epidemiol. 1982;116:228-242.

439. Monto AS, Davenport FM, Napier JA, Francis T Jr. Modification of an outbreak of influenza in Tecumseh, Michigan. J Infect Dis. 1970;122:16-25.

440. Hurwitz ES, Haber M, Chang A, et al. Effectiveness of influenza vaccination of day care children in reducing influenza-related morbidity among household contacts. JAMA. 2000;284:1677-1682.

441. Reichert TA, Sugaya N, Fedson DS, et al. The Japanese experience with vaccinating schoolchildren against influenza. N Engl J Med. 2001;344:889-896.

442. Wilde JA, McMillan JA, Serwint J, et al. Effectiveness of influenza vaccine in health care professionals: A randomized trial [see comments]. JAMA. 1999;281:908-913.

443. Potter J, Stott DJ, Roberts MA, et al. Influenza vaccination of health care workers in long-term-care hospitals reduces the mortality of elderly patients. J Infect Dis. 1997;175:1-6.

444. Carman WF, Elder AG, Wallace LA, et al. Effects of influenza vaccination of health-care workers on mortality of elderly people in long-term care: A randomised controlled trial [see comments]. Lancet. 2000;355:93-97.

445. Freeman DW, Barno A. Deaths from Asian influenza associated with pregnancy. Am J Obstet Gynecol. 1959;78:1172-1175.

446. Centers for Disease Control and Prevention. Prevention and control of influenza: Recommendations of the advisory committee on immunization practices (ACIP). MMWR Morb Mortal Wkly Rep. 1998;47(RR-6):1-26.

447. Englund JA, Mbawuike IN, Hammill H, et al. Maternal immunization with influenza or tetanus toxoid vaccine for passive antibody protection in young infants. J Infect Dis. 1993;168:647-656.

448. MacKenzie JS. Influenza subunit vaccine: Antibody response to one and two doses of vaccine and length of response, with particular reference to the elderly. Br Med J. 1977;1:200-202.

449. Hoskins TW, Davies JR, Smith AJ, et al. Assessment of inactivated influenza A vaccine after three outbreaks of influenza A at Christ's Hospital. Lancet. 1979;1:33-35.

450. Keitel WA, Cate TR, Couch RB. Efficacy of sequential annual vaccination with inactivated influenza vaccine. Am J Epidemiol. 1988;127:353-364.

451. Monto AS, Gunn RA, Bandyk MG, King CL. Prevention of Russian influenza by amantadine. JAMA. 1979;241:1003-1007.

452. Oker-Blom N, Hovi T, Leinikki P, et al. Protection of man from natural infection with influenza A2 Hong Kong virus by amantadine: A controlled field trial. Br Med J. 1970;3:676-678.

453. Quilligan JJ, Harayama M, Baernstein HD Jr. The suppression of A2 influenza in children by the chemoprophylactic use of amantadine. J Pediatr. 1966;69:572-575.

454. Finklea JF, Hennessy AV, Davenport FM. A field trial of amantadine prophylaxis in naturally occurring acute respiratory illness. Am J Epidemiol. 1967;85: 403-412.

455. Monto AS, Robinson DP, Herlocher ML, et al. Zanamivir in the prevention of influenza among healthy adults: A randomized controlled trial. JAMA. 1999;282:31-35.

456. Hayden FG, Atmar RL, Schilling M, et al. Use of the selective oral neuraminidase inhibitor oseltamivir to prevent influenza. N Engl J Med. 1999;341:1336-1346.

457. Peters PH Jr, Gravenstein S, Norwood P, et al. Long-term use of oseltamivir for the prophylaxis of influenza in a vaccinated frail older population. J Am Geriatr Soc. 2001;49:1025-1031.

458. Galbraith AW, Oxford JS, Schild GC. Protective effect of 1-adamantanamine hydrochloride on influenza A2 in the family environment. Lancet. 1969;2:1026-1028.

459. Clover RD, Crawford SA, Abell TD, et al. Effectiveness of rimantadine prophylaxis of children within families. Am J Dis Child. 1986;140:706-709.

460. Crawford SA, Clover RD, Abell TD, et al. Rimantadine prophylaxis in children: A follow-up study. Pediatr Infect Dis J. 1988;7:379-383.

461. Galbraith AW, Oxford JS, Schild GC, Watson GI. Study of 1-adamantanamine hydrochloride used prophylactically during the Hong Kong influenza epidemic in the family environment. Bull World Health Organ. 1969;41:677-682.

462. Welliver R, Monto AS, Carewicz O, et al. Effectiveness of oseltamivir in preventing influenza in household contacts: A randomized controlled trial. JAMA. 2001;285:748-754.

463. Hayden FG, Gubareva LV, Monto AS, et al. Inhaled zanamivir for the prevention of influenza in families. N Engl J Med. 2000;343:1282-1289.

464. Arden NH, Patriarca PA, Fasano MB, et al. The roles of vaccination and amantadine prophylaxis in controlling an outbreak of influenza A(H3N2) in a nursing home. Arch Intern Med. 1988;148:865-868.

465. Patriarca PA, Arden NH, Koplan JP, Goodman RA. Prevention and control of type A influenza infections in nursing homes: benefits and costs of four approaches using vaccination and amantadine. Ann Intern Med. 1987;107:732-740.

466. Schilling M, Povinelli L, Krause P, et al. Efficacy of zanamivir for chemoprophylaxis of nursing home influenza outbreaks. Vaccine. 1998;16:1771-1774.

467. Parker R, Loewen N, Skowronski D. Experience with oseltamivir in the control of a nursing home influenza B outbreak. Can Commun Dis Rep. 2001;27:37-40.

468. Bowles SK, Lee W, Simor AE, et al. Use of oseltamivir during influenza outbreaks in Ontario nursing homes, 1999-2000. J Am Geriatr Soc. 2002;50:608-616.

469. Mast EE, Harman MW, Gravenstein S, et al. Emergence and possible transmission of amantadine-resistant viruses during nursing home outbreaks of influenza A(H3N2). Am J Epidemiol. 1991;134:988-997.

470. Lee C, Loeb M, Phillips A, et al. Use of zanamivir to control an outbreak of influenza A. In: 39th Interscience Conference on Antimicrobial Agents and Chemotherapy. San Francisco; 1999:A283.

CHAPTER 163

California Encephalitis, Hantavirus Pulmonary Syndrome, and Bunyavirid Hemorrhagic Fevers

C. J. PETERS

The family Bunyaviridae comprises more than 200 animal viruses classified into four major genera (*Bunyavirus, Phlebovirus, Nairovirus,* and *Hantavirus*) readily distinguished by genetic, morphologic, biochemical, and immunologic characteristics.[1] The circulation of the viruses in nature via arthropod-vertebrate cycles or chronic infection of vertebrates leads to disease distributions that are determined by ecologic circumstances, can be highly focal, and depend on weather and climatic variables. Caused by viruses in the genus *Bunyavirus,* California encephalitis (CE) is the common childhood central nervous system (CNS) disease reported every year, making CE second in importance only to St. Louis encephalitis among the mosquito-borne viral diseases in the United States. La Crosse (LAC) virus is responsible for most cases of CE, although a number of other antigenically related viruses compose the CE group, including California[2] and Jamestown Canyon[3] viruses. Although not endemic in the Americas, Rift Valley fever (RVF),[4] Crimean-Congo hemorrhagic fever (CCHF),[5] and Hantaan (HTN)[6] viruses cause serious and fatal acute disease with hemorrhagic manifestations (hemorrhagic fever with renal syndrome [HFRS]) on other continents. Relatives of HTN virus, isolated initially in Korea in 1978, are present in wild rodents throughout Eurasia, where they also cause HFRS, and other relatives in the Americas (e.g., Sin Nombre virus [SNV]) are implicated as causes of severe pulmonary edema and shock.[6,7] Salient features of these agents including genus assignment and associated diseases are summarized in Table 163-1. Emphasis in the following presentation is given primarily to LAC and SNV viruses with comparative properties for HTN, RVF, and CCHF viruses where appropriate. A few emerging agents are mentioned.

VIRAL CHARACTERIZATION

Structure, Genetics, and Antigenic Relationships

Bunyaviridae are spherical, lipid membrane-enclosed viruses 90 to 110 nm in diameter. They contain three negative-sense RNA segments that code for six or fewer proteins. The molecular weights of the proteins and RNA vary by genus, but the small RNA codes for a viral nucleoprotein and the middle RNA codes for two glycosylated envelope proteins.[8] Nonstructural proteins are usually found, and the large RNA is thought to encode a viral polymerase present in the lipid enveloped viruses. In general, the G1 or G2 protein, or both, are responsible for viral neutralization, fusion of infected cells, and hemagglutination.[8,9] The nucleocapsid protein is thought to be the most important source of immunologic relationships observed within and across genera of the family. In general, the fluorescent antibody (FA) test is the most cross-reactive with hemagglutination inhibition and particularly the neutralization tests providing greater specificity. The latter is of greatest use in distinguishing individual viruses. Increasingly enzyme-linked immunosorbent assay (ELISA) tests are used for diagnosis of acute or resolving (immunoglobulin M [IgM]) or retrospective (IgG) infections.

Morphogenesis

Viral morphogenesis usually occurs intracellularly, with virions maturing by budding from the Golgi complex and endoplasmic reticulum into vesicles. Exceptions include RVF virus, which also buds through the outer cell membrane of hepatocytes, and SNV, which matures at the cytoplasmic membrane.[10]

EPIDEMIOLOGY

Basic Ecology and Distribution

California Encephalitis Viruses

LAC virus is medically the most significant CE virus in the United States, and its principal vector is *Aedes triseriatus,* a forest-dwelling, tree hole–breeding mosquito of the north-central and northeastern regions of the country. LAC virus is maintained in this mosquito via transovarial transmission supplemented by intraspecific venereal transmission and amplification during summer by mosquitoes feeding on viremic chipmunks, squirrels, foxes, and woodchucks.[11,12]

Female mosquitoes infected by any of these mechanisms are capable of transmitting virus via a bite. The virus survives during the win-

TABLE 163-1   Some Characteristics of Severe Diseases Caused by Bunyaviridae

Disease	Genus and Viruses	Vector	Transmission to Humans	Disease Pattern and Annual Incidence	Major Clinical Features
California encephalitis	*Bunyavirus* La Crosse California encephalitis Jamestown Canyon	*Aedes triseriatus* Transovarial transmission, amplification by chipmunks	Mosquito bite	Summer-fall. Northern United States: 60-130 cases	Meningoencephalitis, seizures, cerebral edema
Rift Valley fever	*Phlebovirus* Rift Valley fever	*Aedes mcintoshi* Transovarial transmission Horizontal transmission in other arthropods	Mosquito bite. Aerosol or contact with fresh carcasses, domestic animals	Endemic in rainy season sub-Saharan Africa: hundreds of cases. Occasional epidemics associated with exceptional rainfall	Acute febrile illness with occasional retinitis, hemorrhagic fever, or encephalitis
Crimean-Congo hemorrhagic fever	*Nairovirus* Crimean-Congo hemorrhagic fever	*Hyalomma* ticks Amplified by hares, domestic animals	Tick bite, contact with blood of humans or domestic animals	Spring-summer. Former Soviet Union, Middle East, Africa: 50-200 cases	Severe hemorrhagic fever
Hemorrhagic fever with renal syndrome	*Hantavirus* Hantaan Dobrava Seoul Puumala	Chronic infection of striped field mouse, yellow-necked mouse, rat, or bank vole	Aerosols from rodent excreta	Endemic and epidemic. Season depends on local conditions. Asia, Europe: 100,000 cases	Fever, shock, bleeding, renal failure
Hantavirus pulmonary syndrome	*Hantavirus* Sin Nombre Others	Chronic infection of deer mouse	Aerosols from rodent excreta	Discovered 1993. Dozens of cases annually in North and South America	Fever, shock, pulmonary edema

ter in mosquito eggs.[13] LAC virus and human encephalitis were first recognized in the upper Mississippi and Ohio River valleys. Most cases have been reported from Wisconsin, Minnesota, Iowa, Indiana, Ohio, and Illinois.[14,15] However, recognition of the disease in West Virginia and Georgia[14] has led to an understanding that viral transmission occurs throughout the eastern United States; indeed, studies in Tennessee suggest recent extension into that state.[15] Other vectors are not of major importance except focally. The recently introduced Asian mosquito *Aedes albopictus* is an efficient vector and is capable of horizontal and vertical transmission in the laboratory.[16] Its strongly anthropophilic biting habits and its documented extension into areas where LAC virus is endemic raise concern, particularly since the virus has been isolated from field collections of *A. albopictus*.[17]

Other CE viruses have distinct ecologic cycles based on an element of transovarial transmission in mosquitoes, and human disease is uncommon and usually, but not always, mild.[2,3]

Rift Valley Fever and Crimean-Congo Hemorrhagic Fever

RVF virus is maintained in sub-Saharan Africa via transovarial transmission in certain floodwater-breeding *Aedes* mosquitoes, notably *Aedes mcintoshi*.[18] Infected eggs can remain dormant but viable in soil for years while awaiting heavy rains for subsequent hatching. Other mosquitoes are important during epizootics and epidemics; large domestic ungulates such as sheep or cattle serve as amplifiers because they experience high viremia during infection.[19] In 1977, the virus was introduced into Egypt, producing widespread epidemic disease in humans and domestic animals; it has reappeared in the 1990s. After an extensive epidemic in Kenya in 1997-1998, it was introduced into the Arabian peninsula, where it also caused epidemic disease in animals and humans.[20,21] It is likely that other receptive areas such as North America could experience the same fate if an introduction should occur.[4]

CCHF virus is transmitted by ticks. The principal vectors belong to the genus *Hyalomma*. Immature stages feed on hares, hedgehogs, and ground-feeding birds, whereas adults parasitize large wild and domestic animals. This virus is widely distributed in the southwestern Russia, the Balkans, the Middle East, central Asia, western China, and Africa.[5]

Hantaviruses

These agents are fundamentally parasites of wild rodents and perhaps insectivores.[6] As such, hantaviruses are the exception to the general rule that Bunyaviridae members are arthropod-borne viruses. Although many rodent species worldwide have been shown to be infected, each of the presently recognized viral species has a single major rodent host species. This species become chronically infected despite an immune response that eliminates viremia, and they excrete virus in urine and saliva for weeks or months.[22,23] Mechanisms of intraspecific transmission depend largely on horizontal transmission between sexually mature animals.[6,23] HTN virus, the cause of severe hemorrhagic fever with renal syndrome (HFRS) in Korea, China, and eastern Russia, is carried by the striped field mouse, *Apodemus agrarius*.[6] *A. agrarius* is found in or near cultivars of humans; rodent breeding seasons and human agricultural practices result in fall and spring disease peaks.[8,24,25] Dobrava virus associated with *Aedes flavicollis* is the major cause of severe HFRS in the Balkans, and related viruses cause similarly severe disease in other areas of the former Soviet Union. Another hantavirus, Seoul virus, is found worldwide in *Rattus norvegicus*. Although the virus is found wherever the reservoir sewer rat occurs, disease has rarely, if ever, been identified in the United States.

Bank voles, *Clethrionomys glareolus*, are the reservoir-vectors of Puumala virus, the cause of a milder form of HFRS termed nephropathia epidemica in Scandinavia, the western former Soviet Union, and Europe. These small rodents are found in forests and agricultural hedgerows, have highly fluctuating populations, and disperse into rural and suburban gardens and dwellings particularly in the fall and winter of years when their populations reach peaks.[24,25]

Many native North and South American rodents (family Muridae, subfamily Sigmodontinae) host phylogenetically distinct hantaviruses associated with hantavirus pulmonary syndrome (HPS).[26] HPS is a disease of the Americas and is probably more important in South America than in North America. The most important North American virus is SNV. The reservoir of SNV is the deer mouse, *Peromyscus maniculatus*, a species that is widespread in the United States and readily enters homes and other structures. On the East Coast, the closely related New York virus is a chronic infection of the white-footed mouse, *Peromyscus leucopus*. Somewhat more distantly related viruses are Bayou and Black Creek Canal viruses found in the southern United States and Florida, respectively, and associated with a degree of renal failure in their clinical picture. The most important South American virus is Andes virus, which is a common cause of disease in Argentina and Chile and which is the only hantavirus that has caused person-to-person transmission.[26]

Transmission to Humans

California Encephalitis Viruses

LAC virus transmission occurs through the bite of female mosquitoes that have viral infection of their salivary glands. Human infection occurs mainly during the summer and early fall in persons entering forested areas for recreation or those living near forests. Members of *Aedes triseriatus* range a considerable distance from forest across open terrain in search of a blood meal and breed effectively in some manufactured containers such as abandoned tires, bringing the mosquito range closer to human habitation.[27]

Rift Valley Fever and Crimean-Congo Hemorrhagic Fever

RVF in Africa has two main modes of transmission. It is recognized as a disease of farmers, veterinarians, and abattoir workers who have close contact with blood shed from sick domestic livestock or fresh carcasses containing a high concentration of virus.[19] Another major route of transmission to humans is from mosquito bites, particularly during epidemics. Infrequent years of heavy precipitation trigger the dormant transovarially infected eggs, and other secondary vectors widely disseminate virus.[4,19] CCHF virus infects humans principally by the bite of adult *Hyalomma* ticks. Milkers and shepherds are frequent victims. Asymptomatically viremic sheep and cattle have been implicated in transmission to abattoir workers, even outside known endemic areas,[28] and it is also hazardous to crush infected ticks. Highly infectious blood from patients also has caused several alarming nosocomial hospital outbreaks with fatalities in medical personnel, particularly when the correct diagnosis of the index case was not suspected.[29-31]

Hantaviruses

Aerosols of virus-contaminated rodent urine or perhaps feces are thought to represent the principal vehicle for the transmission of hantaviruses; disease has also followed the bite of infected rodents (saliva contains virus).[6,32] Infections from *Apodemus* or *Clethrionomys* are acquired principally by persons visiting or working in forests and on farms. Depending on the circumstances, the incidence may be highest in summer or in fall and early winter. Disease is maximal in "high-rodent" years, when suburban residents may be exposed to dispersing infected rodents.[6,24-26,33]

Infection with Seoul virus from *Rattus norvegicus* may occur on farms or in residential areas. Indeed, cases of HFRS, traced to non-traveling residents of urban Seoul, Korea, were the first clues to the existence of the virus. Rat-borne disease has striking seasonal prevalence (winter-spring) in China and Russia.[33] In addition, infection, human disease, and even death have been linked to infected laboratory rats in Korea, Japan, Belgium, France, and the United Kingdom.[32] Rat colonies are apparently infected by the introduction of infected laboratory rats or by contact with wild rats bearing the virus. The United States has been spared this problem because rat stocks imported for research are cesarean delivered and barrier maintained.

Deer mice are numerous and readily enter human dwellings and outbuildings, particularly when mouse populations are high or in autumn when food and cover are scarce. Abundant rodent populations led to a large number of cases in the southwestern United States in summer 1993 and resulted in the first discovery of the virus. Most hantavirus epidemic years have been associated with increased rodent populations.[6,25,26]

CLINICAL MANIFESTATIONS

California Encephalitis Viruses

Infection of humans by CE viruses is most commonly asymptomatic. After an incubation period of 3 to 7 days, however, individuals may experience mild febrile illness, encephalitis, or meningoencephalitis. More than 90% of acute CNS disease caused by LAC virus occurs in children younger than 15 years; males are affected more often than females, and the mortality in acute CNS disease is about 1%.[1,14,34-36] LAC infection has caused encephalitis in an immunocompromised adult with a presentation resembling herpes encephalitis.[35] Clinically and pathologically, CE is difficult to distinguish from other acute viral infections of the CNS. It can range in severity from mild aseptic meningitis to a severe disease mimicking herpes encephalitis. Computed tomography scans are abnormal in a minority of cases, magnetic resonance imaging is sometimes positive, and either can yield focal images[14]; the electroencephalogram is usually abnormal and often focally so, even with periodic lateralizing epileptiform discharges that lead to a suspicion of herpes encephalitis.[36] Fever, headache, nausea, and vomiting are present in most patients. Lethargy, aphasia, incoordination, and focal motor abnormalities, even paralysis, may be present, but the outstanding serious finding is convulsions, which occur in about one half of cases. The spinal fluid generally shows a modest pleocytosis (<100 white blood cells/mm^3) that occasionally is largely granulocytic and exhibits a normal or slightly increased protein concentration. Peripheral leukocytosis in excess of 15,000 white blood cells/mm^3 is not uncommon. Although most patients make uneventful recoveries, abnormal electroencephalographic findings 1 to 5 years later are present in 75%, emotional lability is persistent in 10%, and epilepsy is a chronic problem in 6% to 10% of all diagnosed cases. Frank neurologic deficit is uncommon but does occur.[34] Thus, the residua of La Crosse encephalitis may be more serious than is generally appreciated.

Rift Valley Fever and Crimean-Congo Hemorrhagic Fever

RVF infection in humans causes undifferentiated febrile disease in the great majority of instances. Perhaps 10% of patients experience macular and perimacular retinitis and vasculitis that may cause a permanent loss of vision. In as much as 1% of infections, fulminant disease with hemorrhage, jaundice, and hepatitis may develop at the end of a 3- to 6-day febrile episode with a high mortality.[37] Other infections (<1%) lead to severe, frequently fatal encephalitis directly related to viral invasion of the CNS.

CCHF is a severe hemorrhagic fever with shock, disseminated intravascular coagulation, frequent extensive bleeding, and severe thrombocytopenia.[5,29-31] The virus infects the reticuloendothelial system and frequently involves hepatocytes extensively, leading to icteric hepatitis.[38] Mortality rates range from 20% to 35%.

Hantaviruses

Hemorrhagic Fever with Renal Syndrome

The hallmarks of clinical infection by HTN, Dobrara, Seoul, and Puumala viruses as well as other Eurasian hantaviruses are fever, thrombocytopenia, and acute renal insufficiency pathologically typical of acute interstitial nephritis. The incubation period, typically 2 weeks, may vary from 5 to 42 days. In the severe form of HFRS exemplified by HTN virus infection, patients who survive full-blown disease progress through febrile (toxic), hypotensive, oliguric, and polyuric clinical stages and may require weeks or months to recover from general asthenia.[39-41]

In the toxic phase, patients complain of headache, abdominal and lower back pain, dizziness, and, often, blurred vision.[37-39] Conjunctival injection and petechiae occur over the upper trunk and soft palate. An erythematous flush that blanches on pressure is characteristically seen on the torso and face. Leukocyte levels are normal or more likely elevated, often exceeding 20,000/mm^3. The differential count shows a left shift, immature myeloid cells, and atypical lymphocytes as well, confirming the decreased thrombocyte count. At the end of the febrile period (4 to 7 days), many patients experience severe clinical shock. Those surviving then must endure varied grades of renal insufficiency that can include anuria, oliguria, mucosal bleeding diathesis, electrolyte and acid-base abnormalities, hypertension, and pneumonitis complicated by pulmonary edema. After 3 to 10 days, polyuria begins with its attendant stresses on the fluid and electrolyte balance. The fatality rate in Asian HFRS averages about 5%: one third during the shock phases and two thirds (cerebrovascular accidents and pulmonary edema) during the renal phases of illness. Hemodynamic changes result from massive acute capillary leak syndrome of uncertain cause and equally poorly understood shock-inducing mechanisms. The renal lesions, predominantly in medullary tubules, are possibly related to systemic and intrarenal hemodynamic factors and the influence of immunopathologically released kinins and cytokines.[42]

The milder form of HFRS caused by Puumala virus and often referred to as nephropathia epidemica is rarely hemorrhagic and is fatal in less than 1% of clinical cases. Abdominal pain and hyposphenuria may be manifestations. Up to 90% of Puumala virus infections are asymptomatic. Proteinuria, creatinine level elevation, and leukocytosis, although common, are much less severe than for HTN virus infection.

Seoul virus also causes a mild to moderately severe HFRS in Eurasia with more prominent hepatic involvement than classic HFRS.[39]

Hantavirus Pulmonary Syndrome

HPS begins with a febrile prodrome followed by a severe increase in pulmonary vascular permeability and shock.[42-44] If hypoxia is managed and shock is not fatal, the vascular leak reverses in a few days and recovery is apparently complete. The first symptoms are fever of sudden onset and generalized myalgia. This prodrome resembles the initial phases of HFRS and may also be accompanied by abdominal pain and gastrointestinal disturbances.[43] About 4 to 5 days later (range, 1 to 10 days), the patient presents with respiratory symptoms, which usually consist of modest cough and dyspnea. Examination may be unrevealing, but generally fever, tachycardia, and tachypnea are present, perhaps with mild hypotension. Laboratory abnormalities commonly found at this time or developing within 1 to 2 days thereafter are an elevated hematocrit; leukocytosis, left shift, or both; abnormal (atypical) lymphocytes and immature myeloid cells on smear; mild thrombocytopenia; a prolonged activated partial thromboplastin time; and mildly elevated aspartate aminotransferase or lactate dehydrogenase levels. Mild increases in serum creatinine levels and proteinuria occur in some cases,[26] but the severe renal lesions seen in HFRS are not a regular feature of this syndrome.[42,45] Respiratory involvement can progress from mild desaturation and interstitial pulmonary edema to florid pulmonary edema with respiratory failure in a matter of hours.[44,46] HPS should be suspected when an otherwise healthy adult develops unexplained pulmonary edema or is suspected of adult respiratory distress syndrome without one of the known causes of adult respiratory distress syndrome being present; thrombocytopenia or a falling platelet count is a particularly useful finding early in the course.[44]

The histopathologic findings of interstitial infiltrates of T lymphocytes and alveolar pulmonary edema without marked necrosis or polymorphonuclear leukocyte involvement correlate with the rapid resolution of the lesion and suggest that the major abnormality may be the induction of a functional vascular permeability increase via an immunopathologic mechanism.[45,47]

DIAGNOSIS

The diagnosis of CE is immunologic because virus is not present in blood or secretions during the phase of clinical CNS disease. The diagnosis can be rapidly and specifically achieved with ELISA tests for antiviral IgM antibodies in blood and cerebrospinal fluid, which are usually, but not always, positive at the time of admission.[14,48] A licensed indirect FA test is available for IgG and IgM antibodies to LAC and is useful in the diagnosis.[15] Virtually all hantavirus patients have both IgM and IgG ELISA antibodies present when admitted to the hospital.[4,6,40] Hantaviruses can be recovered only with difficulty in cell culture or animal hosts,[24] but the agent can be detected in blood or tissues by reverse transcription–polymerase chain reaction or in tissues by immunohistochemical staining.[6,7,9,45,47]

RVF and CCHF viruses are readily recovered from the blood of acutely ill patients in cell cultures or suckling mice. Antigen detection ELISA is useful in diagnosis, particularly of severe cases. The polymerase chain reaction provides additional sensitivity with no loss of specificity. Antibodies detectable by a variety of methods generally appear within 5 to 14 days of onset and coincide with clinical improvement. ELISA detection of IgM antibodies is a reliable definitive method.[5,6,19,28,29] Because of the aerosol hazard to laboratory personnel, acute samples must be handled with care, and attempts to isolate these two agents should be restricted to facilities with maximal containment.

PREVENTION AND TREATMENT

With the exception of RVF, for which there is an investigational inactivated vaccine and an investigational live attenuated vaccine,[49] prevention of these diseases is accomplished only by personal means (avoidance of rodent contact; use of mosquito and tick repellents) and perhaps in the case of La Crosse virus by the elimination of manufactured containers leading to mosquito breeding together with aerial spraying of slow-release insecticides over forested areas of known high *A. triseriatus* reproduction.[50]

Ribavirin, a guanosine analogue, was effective in the treatment of HFRS in a double-blind placebo-controlled study in China using the intravenous dosing regimen established for Lassa fever (see Chapter 164). Studies in vitro and in laboratory animals suggest that ribavirin also might be effective in the treatment of severe RVF and CCHF, and clinical experience with the drug in CCHF supports its use.[51,52] An open-label trial of ribavirin failed to show any marked efficacy in HPS patients, perhaps because death typically occurs within 24 to 48 hours of hospitalization.[45,53] Effective supportive care is important in all of the severe bunyavirid diseases. Careful management of coma, cerebral edema, and seizures is critical in CE patients; there is danger in too vigorous use of phenobarbital in children with status epilepticus.[14,36,54] LAC virus is sensitive in vitro to ribavirin, and treatment of one unusual case diagnosed with brain biopsy has been reported.[54] Early management of hantavirus patients should avoid excessive administration of fluids in these febrile, hemoconcentrated, hypotensive patients. Vascular leak leads to extravasation into retroperitoneal tissues (HFRS) or lung (HPS); cardiotonic drugs should be used early because of the hemodynamic profile of decreased cardiac output and increased systemic vascular resistance.[42] Patients with Asian HFRS may require hemodialysis or peritoneal dialysis during the oliguric phase, and plasma protein or whole blood, or both, may be useful in treating hemorrhage or shock, or both, in this and other hemorrhagic fevers. Heparin is not recommended for the treatment of presumptive or incipient disseminated intravascular coagulation in HFRS. Patients with mild HFRS due to Puumala virus rarely require dialysis.

OTHER BUNYAVIRIDAE OF CONCERN

Jamestown Canyon Virus

This California group Bunyavirus is more important than was previously recognized and has been implicated in encephalitis in several adults.[2] Antibodies are not often sought in encephalitis patients and

cross-react with other CE antigens in some tests. It is distributed widely across North America and is transmitted by *Culiseta inornata* and several species of *Aedes* mosquitoes, and often-burgeoning populations of white-tailed deer are suspected as the vertebrate amplifier.

Oropouche Virus

Another Bunyavirus (Simbu group) has caused epidemics in towns and cities of Brazil, Panama, and Peru but also has a much wider distribution in the forest.[55] Infection of humans results in an abrupt onset of fever, chills, headache, myalgia, and often vomiting and arthralgia. Aseptic meningitis has been reported in some cases. The disease is self-limiting, but prolonged asthenia and arthralgia may occur. The natural forest cycle is unknown, but in urban areas the rainy season leads to breeding of biting midges, and epidemics involve thousands of humans.

Toscana Virus

The classic sand fly fevers (Sicilian and Naples viruses) are acute febrile illnesses with headache and myalgias and were common in the broad European and Asian range of their vector, *Phlebotomus papatasi,* until DDT campaigns against malaria virtually eliminated this sand fly in much of Europe. Another sand fly, *Phlebotomus perniciosus,* spreads the related but distinct *Phlebovirus toscana,* which appears to be an important cause of febrile disease, aseptic meningitis, and mild encephalitis in both adults and children in the Tuscany area, where it may be a more common cause of aseptic meningitis than enteroviruses.[56,57] CNS infections are common in the circum-Mediterranean distribution of the vector in Europe from Cyprus to Portugal and are often causes of disease in returning travelers.[56,58,59]

Garissa Virus

During the 1997-1998 RVF outbreak in Kenya, a virus belonging to the *Bunyavirus* genus was isolated from putative hemorrhagic fever cases and reverse transcription–polymerase chain reaction was positive in 12 sera. The virus was found to have the S and L RNA segments of Bunyamwera virus, but the M segment was derived from another *Bunyavirus.* Thus, this virus should be considered in other VHF epidemics and is a cautionary example of the emergence of novel pathogens through viral reassortment.[60]

REFERENCES

1. Peters CJ, Le Duc JW. Bunyaviridae: Bunyaviruses, phleboviruses, and related viruses. In: Belshe RB, ed. Textbook of Human Virology. St. Louis: Mosby-Year Book; 1991:571.
2. Eldridge BF, Glaser C, Pedrin RE, Chiles RE. The first reported case of California encephalitis in more than 50 years. Emerg Infect Dis. 2001;7:451-452.
3. Huang CW, Campbell L, Grady I, et al. Diagnosis of Jamestown Canyon encephalitis by polymerase chain reaction. Clin Infect Dis. 1999;28:1294-1297.
4. Peters CJ. Emergence of Rift Valley fever. In: Saluzzo JF, Dodet B, eds. Factors in the Emergence of Arbovirus Diseases. Paris: Elsevier; 1997:253.
5. Swanepoel R. Crimean-Congo haemorrhagic fever. In: Palmer SR, Soulsby EJL, Simpson DIH, eds. Zoonoses. Oxford: Oxford University Press; 1998:461-470.
6. Peters CJ, Mills JN, Spiropoulou C, et al. Hantaviruses. In: Guerrant RL, Walker DH, Weller PF, eds. Tropical Infectious Diseases: Principles, Pathogens, and Practice. New York: WB Saunders; 1999:1189-1212.
7. Nichol ST, Spiropoulou CF, Morzunov S, et al. Genetic identification of a hantavirus associated with an outbreak of acute respiratory illness. Science. 1993;262:914-917.
8. Schmaljohn CS. Bunyaviridae: The viruses and their replication. In: Knipe DM, Howley PM, eds. Fields Virology. Philadelphia: Lippincott, Williams, & Wilkins; 2001:1635-1668.
9. Dantas JR, Okuno Y, Tanishira O, et al. Viruses causing hemorrhagic fever with renal syndrome (HFRS) grouped by immunoprecipitation and hemagglutination inhibition. Intervirology. 1987;27:161.
10. Goldsmith CS, Elliott LH, Peters CJ, Zaki SR. Ultrastructural characteristics of Sin Nombre virus, causative agent of hantavirus pulmonary syndrome. Arch Virol. 1995;140:2107.
11. Thompson WH: Vector-virus relationship. In: Calisher CH, Thompson WH, eds. California Serogroup Viruses, Proceedings of an International Symposium. New York: Alan R Liss; 1983:57.
12. Yuill TM. The role of mammals in the maintenance and dissemination of La Crosse virus. In: Calisher CH, Thompson WH, eds. California Serogroup viruses, Proceedings of an International Symposium. New York: Alan R Liss; 1983:77.
13. Watts DM, Thompson WH, Yuill TM, et al. Overwintering of La Crosse virus in Aedes triseriatus. Am J Trop Med Hyg. 1974;23:694.

14. McJunkin JE, Khan RR, Tsai TF. California-La Crosse encephalitis. Infect Dis Clin North Am. 1998;12:83.
15. Jones TF, Erwin PC, Craig AS, et al. Serological survey and active surveillance for La Crosse virus infections among children in Tennessee. Clin Infect Dis. 2000;31:1284-1287.
16. Cully JF, Streit TG, Geard PB. Transmission of La Crosse virus by four strains of Aedes albopictus and from the eastern chipmunk (Tamias striatus). J Am Mosquito Control Assoc. 1992;8:237.
17. Gerhardt RR, Gottfried KL, Apperson CS, et al. First isolation of La Crosse virus from naturally infected Aedes albopictus. Emerg Infect Dis. 2001;7:807-811.
18. Lithicum KJ, Davies FG, Kairo A, et al. Rift Valley fever virus (family Bunyaviridae, genus Phlebovirus). Isolation from Diptera collected during an interepizootic period in Kenya. J Hyg (Lond). 1985;95:197.
19. Swanepoel R, Coetzer JAW. Rift Valley fever. In: Coetzer JAW, Thomson GR, Tustin RC, eds. Infectious Diseases of Livestock With Special Reference to Southern Africa. Cape Town: Oxford University Press; 1994:688.
20. Woods CW, Karpati AM, Grein T, et al. An outbreak of Rift Valley fever in Northeastern Kenya, 1997-98. Emerg Infect Dis. 2002;8:138-144.
21. Fagbo SF. The evolving transmission pattern of Rift Valley fever in the Arabian Peninsula. Ann N Y Acad Sci. 2002;969:201-204.
22. Lee HW, Lee PW, Baek LJ, et al. Intraspecific transmission of Hantaan virus, etiotogic agent of Korean hemorrhagic fever, in the rodent Apodemus agrarius. Am J Trop Med Hyg. 1981;30:1106.
23. Hutchinson KL, Rollin PE, Peters CJ. Pathogenesis of a North American hantavirus, Black Creek Canal virus, in experimentally infected Sigmodon hispidus. Am J Trop Med Hyg. 1998;59:58.
24. Korpela H, Lahdevirta J. The role of small rodents and patterns of living in the epidemiology of nephropathia epidemica. Scand J Infect Dis. 1978;10:303.
25. Niklasson B, Hornfeldt B, Lindkvist A, et al. Temporal dynamics of Puumala virus antibody prevalence in voles and of nephropathia epidemica incidence in humans. Am J Trop Med Hyg. 1995;53:134.
26. Peters CJ. Hantavirus pulmonary syndrome in the Americas. In: Scheld WM, Craig WA, Hughes JM, eds. Emerging Infections II. Washington, DC: ASM Press; 1998:7-64.
27. Mather TN, DeFoliart GR. Dispersion of gravid Aedes triseriatus (Diptera: Culcicidae) from woodlands into open terrain. J Med Entomol. 1984;21:384.
28. Rodriguez LL, Maupin GO, Ksiazek TG, et al. Molecular investigation of a multi-source outbreak of Crimean-Congo hemorrhagic fever in the United Arab Emirates. Am J Trop Med Hyg. 1997;57:512.
29. Burney MI, Ghafoor A, Saleen M, et al. Nosocomial outbreak of viral hemorrhagic fever-Congo virus in Pakistan, January 1976. Am Trop Med Hyg. 1980;29:941.
30. Van Eeden PJ, Joubert JR, van de Wal BW, et al. A nosomial outbreak of Crimean-Congo haemorrhagic fever at Tygerberg hospital. I. Clinical features. S Afr Med J. 1985;68:711
31. Papa A, Bino S, Llagami A, et al. Crimean-Congo hemorrhagic fever in Albania, 2001. Eur J Clin Microbiol Infect Dis. 2002;21:603-606.
32. Kawamata J, Yamanouchi T, Dohmae K, et al. Control of laboratory acquired hemorrhagic fever with renal syndrome (HFRS) in Japan. Lab Anim Sci. 1987;37:431.
33. Chen HX, Qiu FX, Dong BJ, et al. Epidemiologic studies in hemorrhagic fever with renal syndrome in China. J Infect Dis. 1986;154:394.
34. McJunkin JE, los Reyes EC, Irazuzta JE, et al. La Crosse encephalitis in children. N Engl J Med. 2001;344:801-807.
35. Wurtz R, Paleologos N. La Crosse encephalitis presenting like herpes simplex encephalitis in an immunocompromised adult. Clin Infect Dis. 2000;31:1113-1114.
36. Deering WM. Neurological aspects and treatment of La Crosse encephalitis. In: Calisher CH, Thompson WH, eds. California Serogroup Viruses. Proceedings of an International Symposium. New York: Alan R Liss; 1983:187.
37. Al Hazmi M, Ayoola EA, Abdurahman M, et al. Epidemic Rift Valley fever in Saudi Arabia: a clinical study of severe illness in humans. Clin Infect Dis. 2003;36:245-252.
38. Burt FJ, Swanepoel R, Shieh W-J, et al. Immunohistochemical and in situ localization of Crimean-Congo hemorrhagic fever virus in human tissues and pathogenic implications. Arch Pathol Lab Med. 1997;121:839.
39. Lee JS, Cho BY, Lee MC, et al. Clinical features of serologically proven Korean hemorrhagic fever patients. Seoul J Med. 1980;21:163.
40. Earle DP. Symposium on epidemic hemorrhagic fever. Am J Med. 1954;16:617.
41. Bruno P, Harrison HL, Brown J, et al. The protean manifestations of hemorrhagic fever with renal syndrome. A retrospective review of 26 cases from Korea. Ann Intern Med. 1990;113:385.
42. Peters CJ, Simpson G, Levy H. Spectrum of hantavirus infection: Hemorrhagic fever with renal syndrome and hantavirus pulmonary syndrome. Annu Rev Med. 1999;50:531-545.
43. Duchin JS, Koster F, Peters CJ, et al. Hantavirus pulmonary syndrome: Clinical description of disease caused by a newly recognized hemorrhagic fever virus in the southwestern United States. N Engl J Med. 1994;330:949.
44. Moolenaar RL, Dalton C, Lipman HB, et al. Clinical features that differentiate hantavirus pulmonary syndrome from three other acute respiratory illnesses. Clin Infect Dis. 1995;21:643.
45. Peters CJ, Khan AS: Hantavirus pulmonary syndrome: The new American hemorrhagic fever. Clin Infect Dis. 34:1224-1231, 2002.
46. Ketai LH, Williamson MR, Telepak RJ, et al. Hantavirus pulmonary syndrome: Radiographic findings in 16 patients. Radiology. 1994;191:665.
47. Zaki SR, Greer PW, Coffield LM, et al. Hantavirus pulmonary syndrome: Pathogenesis of an emerging infectious disease. Am J Pathol. 1995;146:552.
48. Calisher CH, Pretzman CI, Muth DJ, et al. Serodiagnosis of La Crosse virus infections in humans by detection of immunoglobulin M class antibodies. J Clin Microbiol. 1986;12:667.
49. Pittman PR, Liu CT, Cannon TL, et al. Immunogenicity of an inactivated Rift Valley fever vaccine in humans: A 12-year experience. Vaccine. 1999;18:181-189.
50. Francy DB. Mosquito control for prevention of California (La Crosse) encephalitis. In: Calisher CH, Thompson WH, eds. California Serogroup Viruses. Proceedings of an International Symposium. New York: Alan R Liss; 1983:365.
51. Peters CJ, Reynolds JA, Slone TW, et al. Prophylaxis of Rift Valley fever with antiviral drugs, immune serum, an interferon inducer, and a macrophage activator. Antiviral Res. 1986;6:285.
52. Mardani M, Jahromi MK, Naieni KH, Zeinali M. The efficacy of oral ribavirin in the treatment of crimean-congo hemorrhagic fever in Iran. Clin Infect Dis. 2003;36:1613-1618.
53. Chapman LE, Mertz GJ, Peters CJ, et al. Intravenous ribavirin for hantavirus pulmonary syndrome: Safety and tolerance during one year of open label experience. Antiviral Ther. 1999;4:211-219.
54. McJunkin JE, Khan R, de los Reyes EC, et al. Treatment of severe La Crosse encephalitis with intravenous ribavirin following diagnosis by brain biopsy. Pediatrics. 1997;99:261.
55. Watts DM, Phillips I, Callahan JD, et al. Oropouche virus transmission in the Amazon River basin of Peru. Am J Trop Med Hyg. 1997;56:148.
56. Nicoletti L, Ciufolini MG, Verani P. Sandfly fever viruses in Italy (Review). Arch Virol. 1996;(suppl 11):41.
57. Nicoletti L, Verani P, Caciolli S, et al. Central nervous system involvement during infection by Phlebovirus Toscana of residents in natural foci in central Italy (1977-1988). Am J Trop Med Hyg. 1991;45:429.
58. Braito A, Ciufolini MG, Pippi L, et al. Phlebotomus-transmitted toscana virus infections of the central nervous system: A seven-year experience in Tuscany. Scand J Infect Dis. 1998;30:505-508.
59. Echevarria JM, de Ory F, Guisasola ME, et al. Acute meningitis due to Toscana virus infection among patients from both the Spanish Mediterranean region and the region of Madrid. J Clin Virol. 2003;26:79-84.
60. Bowen MD, Trappier SG, Sanchez AJ, et al. A reassortant bunyavirus isolated from acute hemorrhagic fever cases in Kenya and Somalia. Virology. 2001;291:185-190.

CHAPTER **164**

Lymphocytic Choriomeningitis Virus, Lassa Virus, and the South American Hemorrhagic Fevers

C. J. PETERS

The arenavirus family is characterized by single-stranded RNA, a unique morphology, and the usual use of rodents as virus reservoirs. These viruses include lymphocytic choriomeningitis (LCM) virus, Lassa virus, and American viruses that belong to the Tacaribe complex. The viruses can be divided into two major phylogenetic and antigenic groups corresponding to (1) LCM, Lassa, and close relatives from Old World rodents (family Muridae, subfamily Murinae) and (2) the Tacaribe complex from New World or American rodents (family Muridae, subfamily Sigmodontinae); the correspondence between the phylogeny of the hosts and of the viruses suggests a long association and coevolution.[1,2] The New World complex can be further divided into three distinct clades designated A, B, and C. Tacaribe virus isolated from bats is the only member of the family that is not known to be a chronic, inapparent infection of rodents. Significant human disease is associated with several of the viruses (Table 164-1). The family prototype, LCM virus, was first isolated in 1933 during serial monkey passage of human material obtained from a fatal infection in the first documented epidemic of St. Louis encephalitis.[3] Junin, Machupo, Lassa, Guanarito, and Sabia viruses were first recovered during investigations of human disease in 1958,[4] 1963,[5] 1969,[6] 1989,[7] and 1990,[8] respectively.

TABLE 164-1 Arenaviruses and Human Disease

Virus	Disease	Geography	Reservoir	Pathogenesis	Specific Therapy	Prevention
Lymphocytic choriomeningitis	Aseptic meningitis; other organ involvement	North and South America, Europe, and wherever *Mus* is introduced	*Mus domesticus* and *Mus musculus* (house mice)	Systemic infection; when CNS invasion occurs, immunopathologic CNS disease follows	None	House mouse control and avoidance, particularly by pregnant women; monitor mouse and hamster suppliers
Lassa	Lassa fever	West Africa, particularly Sierra Leone, Guinea, Liberia, and Nigeria	*Mastomys huberti, Mastomys erythroleucus* (multimammate mouse)	Vascular leak, multiorgan dysfunction, shock; bleeding and CNS involvement occur but not as common as in South American diseases	Intravenous ribavirin	Rodent avoidance and control in houses may be of ancillary benefit; strict isolation of hospitalized patients
Junin	Argentine HF	Argentine pampas	*Calomys musculinis*	As Lassa fever, except encephalopathy and thrombocytopenia are common, as is hemorrhage	Convalescent plasma Ribavirin probably efficacious	Effective live-attenuated vaccine
Machupo	Bolivian HF	Bolivia, Beni Department	*Calomys callosus*	As Argentine HF	Ribavirin or convalescent plasma	Elimination of rodents from home; laboratory evidence for cross-protection by Junin vaccine
Guanarito	Venezuelan HF	Venezuela, Portuguese State	*Zygodontomys brevicauda*	As Argentine HF	Unknown; ribavirin or convalescent plasma suggested	Unknown; rodent control?
Sabia	Brazilian HF	Brazil	Unknown	Resembles Argentine HF; patient in single naturally occurring case had severe hepatitis	Unknown; ribavirin suggested	Unknown

CNS, central nervous system; HF, hemorrhagic fever.

VIRAL CHARACTERIZATION

Virions are round, oval, or pleomorphic particles averaging about 110 to 130 nm in diameter but ranging from 50 to 300 nm.[9] The viral envelope is formed by budding from the viral glycoprotein-bearing host plasma membrane. The surface of the particle bears 6- to 10-nm spikes, and the interior shows variable numbers of characteristic dense granules, 20 to 25 nm in diameter, which have been shown to be host cell ribosomes (Fig. 164-1). These unique structures resembling grains of sand are responsible for the family name (Latin, *arenosos*, or "sandy"). Arenaviruses contain a segmented RNA genome with 31- and 22-S strands. Host ribosomal RNA of 28, 18, and 4 to 6 S is also present but apparently is not biologically functional.

The S, or small, RNA of arenaviruses codes for three virion proteins in a unique manner. The 60- to 70-kDa nucleocapsid protein (N) is read first in a conventional negative sense, and later a glycoprotein precursor polypeptide (GPC) is transcribed from genomic sense messenger RNA. This pattern has been termed *ambisense*. The GPC protein is then glycosylated and cleaved to form the spike glycoproteins G1 and G2, typically of molecular weights 35 to 45 and 40 to 60 kDa. Arenavirus L, or large, RNA is also ambisense and codes for a viral polymerase of about 200 kDa and a zinc-finger protein.[2] The Z protein is a virion component important in budding[10] and other intracellular functions.

Epitopes mediating neutralization and antibody-complement cell lysis have been localized to the glycoproteins, particularly G1, which is also more genetically and antigenically variable among viral species.[11,12] The most serologically cross-reactive protein is N, which is usually measured in the diagnostic indirect fluorescent antibody (IFA) test. Protective T-cell epitopes are coded by the genes for N and GPC and probably other proteins as well.[12] Old World and clade C New World viruses attach to host cells via α-dystroglycan or possibly other receptors. Arenaviruses then fuse, interiorize, and uncoat within an acidic compartment.[11,13,14] Replication is usually not accompanied by overt cytopathic effects.

EPIDEMIOLOGY AND EPIZOOTOLOGY

Arenaviruses are parasites of rodents. They exhibit high species specificity, and a single rodent species is the reservoir for a given agent. Chronic viral infection without obvious disease occurs with the release of virus into excreta, especially urine, resulting in transmission to humans. Among rodents, both vertical transmission and horizontal intraspecific spread, are important to varied degrees.[2] Thus, human arenaviral disease is determined by viral pathogenicity, by the geographic distribution of a particular reservoir rodent, and by rodent-human ecologic factors that permit contact with excreted virus particularly in aerosolized urine.

Lymphocytic Choriomeningitis

Although LCM virus infection may occur worldwide, human infection has been conclusively demonstrated only in Europe and the Americas.[15] Moreover, in regions where the virus is known to exist, infection in the two closely related nonoverlapping reservoir species, *Mus domesticus* and *Mus musculus,* is highly focal. Studies conducted in Baltimore, Boston, and Washington, D.C., revealed a spotty distribution of virus-positive mice in houses.[16,17] Similarly, in Germany, much higher murine infection rates prevail in the west-central than in the southern or northern portions of the country.[18]

Human cases of LCM are most common in autumn. This pattern is the result of seasonal population densities of rodents and the movement of mice into homes and barns with cold weather. In addition, seasonal variation in infection rates of Mus or differential survival of excreted virus related to the temperature and relative humidity may be involved. It has been shown that aerosolized arenaviruses survive better at lower humidity.[19] Situations associated with wild mouse infection of humans include substandard housing such as mobile homes or inner city dwellings, the cleaning of rodent-infested barns or outbuildings, and the autumn entry of wild mice into dwellings. Most human LCM infections occur among young adults, although persons of all ages have been affected.

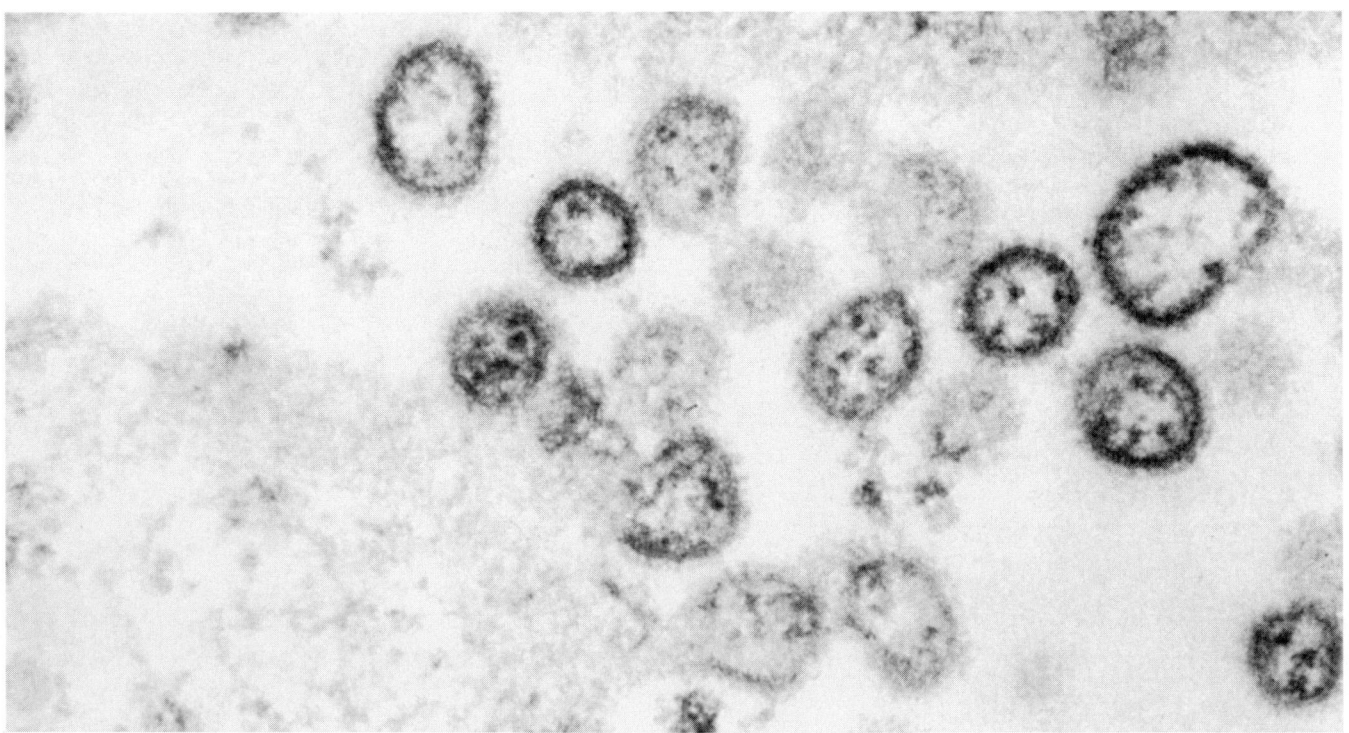

FIGURE 164-1. Electron micrograph of Lassa virus in the first Vero cell passage envelope; electron-dense interior granules can be seen (original magnification, ×121,000).

The mode of transmission in most sporadic human infections is not definitely known; however, experimental and epidemiologic observations implicate aerosols, direct contact with rodents, and rodent bites (in that order) as the most likely vehicles.[2,16,20,21] The incubation period of human LCM disease is variable, but it most often ranges from 5 to 10 days. Patients not seeking medical care for the nonspecific febrile illness that begins at this time, but who may later present with acute meningitis, generally are found to have been exposed 2 to 3 weeks before the onset of nervous system signs.

Although most sporadic LCM cases are attributed to contact with infected wild mice, outbreaks of disease have been traced to infected laboratory mice or Syrian hamsters (*Mesocricetus auratus*). Several of these were the result of the introduction of LCM virus into hamsters through infected tumor cell lines.[21] A recent epidemic resulted from chronic infection of nude, athymic mice by stored infected hamster tumors.[22] Other outbreaks in the United States and Europe resulted from exposure in the home to pet hamsters obtained from breeders with infected stock.[23,24]

Lassa Fever

Lassa fever is a disease of West Africa; however, with the contemporary ease of international travel, it may occur anywhere in the world. This disease is distinguished from other arenaviral diseases by its occasional ability to spread from person to person. Lassa fever was initially recognized in a Nigerian hospital where three nurses developed illness successively.[25] Since then, extensive transmission with occasional nosocomial outbreaks have been reported from Nigeria, Liberia, Sierra Leone, and Guinea. Serologic studies and occasional cases have shown its presence in every country of West Africa between Nigeria and Senegal. West Africa, however, represents only a small part of the range of *Mastomys* rodents, which serve as viral reservoirs, and different species of these are found throughout the continent south of the Sahara Desert. Further work is needed to define the species of the genus *Mastomys*, but clearly at least two species are infected in Sierra Leone,[26,27] probably *Mastomys huberti* and *Mastomys erythroleucus*. Isolation of Lassa-like viruses of reduced pathogenicity for laboratory animals and presumably for humans from related rodents elsewhere in Africa may provide a partial explanation for the observed regional boundaries of Lassa fever, through understanding of rodent–virus genetic interactions.

Most of the nosocomial outbreaks of Lassa fever have occurred during the dry season (January to April). Endemic transmission occurs throughout the year, with more cases during dry than during wet periods.[26,28] All ages and both sexes are infected equally; in some villages in Sierra Leone, infection rates may reach 10% to 20% per year. Based on serologic data, there may be 20 mild or inapparent infections for each hospitalized case.[26] In contrast, retrospective studies among white missionaries suggest, but do not yet prove, that moderately severe or even fatal illness usually follows infection.[29] Outbreaks typically include a few health care workers because of their close exposure to patients and infectious body fluids without barrier nursing precautions and because of their residence in the endemic area.

The modes of Lassa virus transmission are not precisely known, but they are almost certainly multiple. Endemic transmission is related to infected rodents by aerosol and direct contact, and most probably to person-to-person spread in homes.[30] Capture of rodents as a supplemental food source is another high risk factor for infection, until the rodents are cooked. *Mastomys* are common rodents in houses and in the nearby bush. In some areas they are found in virtually all homes with high infection rates,[30] but in others infection is less intensive and infected rodents tend to cluster in individual houses,[31,32] not unlike the distribution of LCM virus in urban *Mus*.[17] Given the pervasive nature of *Mastomys*, control campaigns cannot be expected to prevent the disease, although model intensive efforts in a village in Sierra Leone resulted in a temporary fourfold reduction in transmission to humans. During nosocomial outbreaks, parenteral inoculation of body fluids (e.g., surgery or autopsy accidents), contact with infected body fluids, and aerosols generated by patients have all been incriminated.[28] Tertiary and quaternary cases in

outbreaks are less numerous than are secondary cases, which suggests that only the unusual patient is very infectious.

The incubation period varies from 3 to 16 days (usually 7 to 12 days) when infection is transmitted from person to person. It is assumed to be similar in rodent-transmitted infection.

South American Hemorrhagic Fevers

The South American hemorrhagic fevers (HFs) are local public health problems in Argentina, Bolivia, and Venezuela and are caused by Junin, Machupo, and Guanarito viruses. Another lethal arenavirus, Sabia virus, has been discovered in Brazil, but its health impact and reservoir are not yet known.[8]

In Argentina, the principal reservoir rodent is *Calomys musculinus*.[33] Argentine HF initially occurred mainly in an expanding zone within the rich agricultural pampas of northern Buenos Aires province. Now cases are found within an enlarged zone encompassing two more provinces and putting 5 million people at risk. *Calomys* populations reach their highest density in the cornfields during the austral fall (February to May); the disease thus affects principally men engaged in harvesting corn. Roughly 200 to 2000 cases are reported annually, and the numbers did not change substantially despite the change from manual to mechanized harvesting techniques. Introduction of effective vaccination has had a marked impact on the incidence of the disease, which has fallen below 100 annually.[34] Infectious aerosols are thought to be the most common mode of transmission, although food contamination and the direct contact of abraded fingers with blood and tissues of rodents crushed by machinery may also occur.

Bolivian HF is restricted to the tropical savanna of the Beni Department in northeastern Bolivia. The small reservoir rodent *Calomys callosus*[35] freely enters homes and gardens in this region, and most infections are house acquired. The incidence of cases is greatest from April to July (late rainy and early dry season), but the dominant feature of the epidemiologic pattern is that of small outbreaks in different villages and ranches with several years of quiescence thereafter. In town epidemics, all ages and both sexes are equally affected. On remote ranches and in fields, adult male patients predominate. Transmission is thought to occur by aerosols from infected rodents or possibly by contact with food contaminated by infectious rodent urine. Both nosocomial[36] and person-to-person[37] transmission have occurred, although these routes are not usual.

The mechanisms underlying the annual variations in both Bolivian and Argentine HF incidence as well as the extension of the endemic zone in Argentina are unknown. Rodent population density correlates with horizontal spread among rodents and human infection.[38]

In the Portuguese state of Venezuela, cases of HF were noted in September 1989. The causative agent, named Guanarito virus for the municipality where most of the cases were found,[7] has the cane mouse (*Zygodontomys brevicauda*)[39] as reservoir. The main affected population was settlers moving into cleared forest areas to practice smallhold agriculture. The carrier rodents are well adapted to open grasslands and readily invaded fields, pastures, and peridomestic habitats.

Sabia virus has caused a single natural human infection that was fatal, as well as two laboratory infections.[8,40]

After parenteral exposures, the incubation period of South American HF may be only 2 to 6 days. The estimated interval after natural exposure to either Junin or Machupo viruses (and presumably Guanarito and Sabia viruses as well) ranges from 5 to 19 days, with a mode of 7 to 12 days.

Other Arenaviruses

Several African viruses related to Lassa and LCM viruses have been discovered (Mopeia, Mobala, Ippy), but no human disease, and in many cases no human infection, has been identified. They are attenuated for nonhuman primates and guinea pigs.[1,2,41] Similarly, there is a growing group of viruses in the Tacaribe complex that have not been associated with human disease in both South America (Amapari, Flexal, Cupixni, Allpahuayo, Latino, Oliveros, Parana, Pichinde, and Pirital) and North America (Tamiami, Bear Canyon,[42] and Whitewater

Arroyo[43]).[1,2] Some have caused human infections in the laboratory without inducing disease (Pichinde virus), but most are under continuing study, including the Whitewater Arroyo virus possibly associated with fatal human disease in the western United States.[44]

PATHOGENESIS

Rodents

Arenavirus infection of rodent hosts is chronic but clinically benign. The age of the host, route of infection, and strain of virus are important variables. In natural murine infections with LCM virus, the newborn or fetal animal becomes chronically viremic but has normal growth and fertility; despite widespread infection of many organs, there is no inflammatory response. Peripheral inoculation of adult mice results in a transient immunizing infection.

Laboratory-manipulated strains of LCM virus exhibit different pathogenicity for inbred strains of laboratory mice, and this infection has been extremely important in studying viral immunopathology and CD8+ T-cell function. Infection of newborn mice results in chronic viremic infection in which T-cell immunity is suppressed. Depending on the murine genotype, different quantities of antiviral antibodies are produced and complex with viral antigens, leading to the development of chronic glomerulonephritis.[45] The artificial intracerebral inoculation of adult mice produces an acute fatal choriomeningitis with extensive mononuclear cell infiltrate mediated by immune cytotoxic T cells.[46]

The responses of natural reservoir *Calomys* rodents experimentally infected with Junin or Machupo virus somewhat resemble the mouse–LCM virus outcomes.[2,33,35] The differences are that lethal infection is not inducible by any route at any age, that antigen–antibody complexes are not demonstrable, and that some adult rodents develop chronic viremic infection exactly like that observed in very young mice inoculated with LCM. In addition, chronic infection with Machupo virus induces a microcytic hemolytic anemia (Coombs negative) that results in chronic splenomegaly, a useful field marker for infection.

Mastomys rodents infected with Lassa virus similarly show no acute signs, do not develop inflammatory responses, and exhibit chronic infection or an effective immune response depending on age.[47] Field studies suggest that carrier *Mastomys* have little or no antibody but have sufficiently large quantities of virus to be readily detected in antigen tests.[31]

Arenavirus infection of nonreservoir rodents results in benign, self-limited infection and immunity. Guinea pigs, however, may experience severe acute disease and provide useful models for arenaviral HFs.[41]

Nonhuman Primates

Monkeys are good but not perfect models for the pathogenesis and experimental therapy of arenavirus infections in humans.[3,19,41,47-49] Macaque monkeys are readily infected by the inhalation of LCM virus, and the resulting disease resembles HF rather than central nervous system disease. Marmosets are also susceptible to fatal disease from LCM virus, including zoo animals fed infected newborn mice.[48]

Lassa virus induces a fatal disease in rhesus monkeys infected by small-particle aerosols, establishing the aerosol infectivity of the virus; the monkeys also have a pathologic appearance similar to that of humans.[19,43,49] Machupo and Junin viruses are also pathogenic for nonhuman primates, and these models as well as the less expensive guinea pig models have provided considerable information on the pathogenesis of human HF.[41,47,49,50]

Humans

Few data are available regarding the histopathology of fatal cases of human LCM infection, which is commonly lethal. Two fatal cases associated with early studies of the virus in monkeys displayed hemorrhagic necrosis much more typical of other arenavirus HFs[51]; they are regarded as aberrant human infections with this agent. A single fatal human encephalitis case was particularly well studied, and the patient showed a marked neuronal pattern of viral infection.[52]

Fatal Lassa virus infection in humans shows relatively few lesions. Variable necrosis with little or no inflammatory response has been observed in liver, spleen, and adrenal glands.[53] Focal liver necrosis is always found, but in no instance was the hepatic abnormality sufficient to cause death.[54] The degree of histologic change rarely seems sufficient to explain the clinical severity of the disease on a morphologic basis. Studies in animal models suggest that direct viral infection of endothelial cells as well as mediators possibly released from infected macrophages may be extremely important in causing the vascular dysfunction and shock of these viral HFs.[50,55] Immunopathologic events seem less likely to be involved because immunosuppression fails to ameliorate the disease in animal models.[56]

Patients dying of Argentine or Bolivian HF have few prominent findings. There is no vasculitis and virtually no inflammatory response in any organ, but a pattern of small focal hemorrhages is present, primarily in mucosal surfaces. Hepatic necrosis, on the average, is more severe in Lassa than in Junin or Machupo infections, but Councilman-like bodies are readily discernible in all three diseases. Bronchopneumonia, either primary viral or more commonly secondary bacterial, is often found as well.

Argentine HF virus patients exhibit extremely high concentrations of circulating endogenous interferon-α that reach a maximum at 6 to 12 days of illness. The highest levels were observed in fatal cases.[57] Experimental and clinical studies support the concept that interferons may prove to be detrimental rather than beneficial in arenavirus infections.[58] High levels of circulating proinflammatory cytokines are present as well.[59]

At autopsy, tissues of humans and monkeys infected by Lassa, Junin, or Machupo virus contain large amounts of virus, viral antigen, and, in some instances, virions as in liver in Lassa infection. Spleen, nodes, and bone marrow are major replication sites for Junin and Machupo viruses, whereas Lassa virus is found in many viscera and, notably, in the placentas of pregnant women. Prominent infection of mesothelial surfaces may well be important in the frequent development of serous effusions.[55]

The paucity of histologic lesions in fatal cases and the lack of evidence of immunopathology suggest cytokines as candidates for the mediators of arenavirus HF.[60] The high levels seen in Lassa[61,62] and AHF[57,59] as well as the induction of cytokines by in vitro infection of monocytes[63] lend support to this idea, but the data are not entirely consistent and require further clinical and experimental studies.

CLINICAL MANIFESTATIONS

Clinically apparent infections with all the arenaviruses are similar in presenting manifestations. Fever is typically insidious in onset and is accompanied by headache and significant myalgia and malaise. Relative bradycardia is common, as is dysesthesia, particularly hyperesthesia of the skin. Thereafter, the various diseases pursue different courses.

Lymphocytic Choriomeningitis Virus

LCM virus infections are most commonly febrile illnesses with headache and systemic symptoms and are associated with leukopenia and thrombocytopenia.[2,15,16,20-22,64] After 3 to 5 days of nonspecific illness, occasionally with lymphadenopathy and a maculopapular rash, the fever subsides, but it frequently recurs in 2 to 4 days with several days of even more severe headache. Patients may exhibit frank meningitis during this second febrile period. Cerebrospinal fluid (CSF) pressure usually is elevated, occasionally even with papilledema, the protein concentration ranges from 50 to 300 mg/dL, and several hundred lymphocytes per cubic millimeter are commonly observed. Hypoglycorrachia is found in less than one third of the cases. Encephalomyelitic infection may present as encephalitis, psychosis, paraplegia, or disturbances of cranial, sensory, or autonomic nervous function. Ependymal inflammation has resulted in transient aqueductal stenosis.

Occasionally, patients develop orchitis, myocarditis, arthritis, or alopecia. Orchitis develops 1 to 3 weeks after the onset of the illness; it is usually unilateral and painful and resolves within 2 weeks. Myocarditis is revealed by electrocardiographic changes and labile tachycardia during and after the second febrile period. Arthritis occurs occasionally during convalescence, principally affects the metacarpophalangeal and proximal interphalangeal joints, and is marked by minimal swelling and redness; it generally resolves within a few weeks.

The second febrile episode as well as some of the complications of convalescence have long been thought to represent immunopathologic phenomena. Antibodies detectable by immunofluorescence appear at about this time, and the lymphocytes in the CSF presumably are analogues of the T lymphocytes that cause LCM disease in the intracerebrally inoculated adult mouse.[64]

Lassa Fever

Most Lassa virus infections in Africa are mild or subclinical.[26] Severe multisystem disease occurs only in 5% to 10% of infections. Case-fatality rates in hospitalized patients average 15% to 25%.[65,66] Clinical manifestations are varied and differential diagnosis difficult.[25,29,61,65-67] In a case-control study of patients hospitalized with Lassa fever in Sierra Leone, the frequencies of selected findings were as follows: retrosternal chest pain, 74%; sore throat, 60%; back pain, 62%; cough, 62%; abdominal pain, 50%; vomiting, 49%; diarrhea, 26%; conjunctivitis, 25%; facial edema, 10%; and proteinuria, 43%. Mucosal bleeding at any time was noted in just 17% of patients. These findings were present in many febrile patients not infected with Lassa virus, which rendered a clinical diagnosis in many instances impossible. A combination of fever, pharyngitis, retrosternal pain, and proteinuria correctly predicted 70% of laboratory-confirmed Lassa fever cases and 80%, by exclusion, of the control illnesses.[60] Central nervous system involvement has been described with encephalopathy, encephalitis, meningeal signs, and convalescent cerebellar syndromes.[66,68,69]

Lassa virus infection also causes serious disease and death in children, although manifestations may be even more protean or clinically confusing than among adults.[70] Four cases (three were fatal) of a distinctive syndrome consisting of severe generalized edema, abdominal distention, and bleeding were recorded in children younger than 2 years in Liberia.[71]

Concentrations of virus and serum aspartate transaminase in the blood at admission are highly reliable, objective predictors of the outcome of infection. Patients with at least 10^3 median tissue culture infective doses of virus per milliliter and 150 IU of aspartate transaminase per liter experienced a mortality rate of 78%, whereas 83% of those with lower values survived.[72,73] The clinical manifestations associated with death, however, generally occur during the second week of illness. These consist of hypotension, peripheral vasoconstriction, reduced urinary output, facial and pulmonary edema, and, in some cases, pleural effusions and ascites. These events, often accompanied by minor hemorrhages from mucosal surfaces, strongly suggest a lesion of diffuse capillary leakage. Myocardial depression may contribute to the circulatory defect.

Patients who do not develop a capillary leak syndrome may experience other complications during the second or third week of illness. Chief among these is eighth-nerve deafness, which may be unilateral or bilateral and has been seen in almost one third of hospitalized cases.[74] Some of the patients have mild lesions or will improve, but village surveys confirm a major impact of Lassa infection on hearing loss in the community. About 3% to 5% of male patients suffer pericarditis detected by auscultation that resolves clinically in 7 to 10 days; all such patients survive. Less common complications include uveitis and orchitis. Many hospitalized Lassa fever patients undergo some degree of transient alopecia during convalescence.

South American Hemorrhagic Fevers

Argentine and Bolivian HFs are remarkably similar clinically, and the mortality rate in each is about 15% to 30%.[33,75,76] Reported Venezuelan HF cases have been somewhat more severe, although this probably reflects case ascertainment.[7] The onset of the illness is insidious, with progressive fever, malaise, and myalgia often centered over the lower back. There may be epigastric pain, retro-orbital pain, dizziness, photophobia, and constipation. Conjunctival injection, flushing of the face and upper portion of the trunk, and orthostatic hypotension also are common. An exanthema consisting of petechiae or small vesicles, or both, on the palate and fauces is present in most patients, as are skin petechiae, particularly in the axilla, and generalized lymphadenopathy. Early diagnosis is facilitated by the frequent findings of dizziness, leukopenia, thrombocytopenia, tremor, and early signs of hemorrhage such as petechial rash.

Fever is unremitting, and some patients become progressively ill with one of a combination of syndromes of vascular or neurologic disease. Vascular disease consists of (1) increasing evidence of a capillary leak syndrome; (2) proteinuria, rising hematocrit, and the onset of gingival, gastrointestinal, nasal, and other membrane hemorrhages; (3) narrowing pulse pressure; and (4) vasoconstriction and clinical shock. There may be signs of pulmonary infiltration due to a vascular leak or to secondary bacterial infection, which is a common complication, or both. Such patients are extremely difficult to manage. Plasma expanders may precipitate refractory pulmonary edema. Neurologic disease is common and is heralded by the development of hyporeflexia followed by gait abnormalities, palmomental reflex, tremors of the tongue and upper extremities, and other cerebellar signs. If these changes are followed by clonic seizures and coma, the prognosis is extremely grave.

Convalescence requires several weeks but occurs without sequelae. Alopecia and nail furrows are very common, as is postural hypotension for 1 to 2 weeks.

Intrauterine Infection

Arenaviruses readily invade the fetus, whether in their natural reservoir, laboratory animals, or humans. In Lassa fever, pregnant women often abort and have a high mortality rate,[77] and similar observations have been made in Argentine and Bolivian HFs. LCM virus infection of pregnant women leads to fetal infection, hydrocephalus, microcephaly, or chorioretinitis, or all of these.[78-81] Because viral antibody rates indicate that about 5% of adults in large cities of the United States have been infected with LCM virus, congenital infection may be more common than appreciated.[2,82]

DIAGNOSIS

The diagnosis of past infection with arenaviruses is best done through serologic tests with enzyme-linked immunosorbent assay (ELISA) because of the sensitivity of the test. Until more data are obtained confirming ELISA specificity, cell culture plaque-reduction neutralization tests should be used as a supplement because of their known sensitivity and specificity.

The diagnosis of acute illness, by contrast, has features unique to each agent. In the case of LCM, virus is found in the blood early and in the CSF late in disease. The most sensitive test is to inoculate young adult mice in the brain.[15] Fluorescent immunostaining of inoculated cell cultures reveals virus earlier than mouse inoculation in most instances. IgM ELISA of serum and CSF is an effective method of diagnosis and is supplanting IFA and other serologic tests.[83]

Virus can be recovered from the blood of acutely ill patients in all arenavirus HFs, but titers are highest in Lassa fever. The viremic interval ranges from 3 to 20 days, with Lassa fever being the most persistent. Patients with LCM and Lassa fever who exhibit meningeal signs have increased protein, leukocytes, and virus in spinal fluids.[16,68,69,72]

Lassa fever virus is easily isolated from blood during the first 7 to 10 days of illness by inoculating cell cultures.[72,84] Junin virus was recovered from 96% of patients by cocultivation of patients' blood mononuclear cells with Vero cell cultures, whereas cell cultures or suckling mice were only about 50% positive when whole blood was tested.[85] Isolation of some strains of Machupo virus is difficult, but others are readily recovered in cell culture.[5,36] Throat swabs are frequently positive in patients with Lassa fever and LCM, and late shedding of Lassa virus is often observed, even up to 67 days.[72,86] Biopsy or autopsy specimens of lymphoid tissues, marrow, and liver usually yield virus, often in concentrations greatly exceeding those found in blood.

Serodiagnosis of Lassa fever by detection of IgM antibodies by IFA or ELISA is rapid and quite sensitive.[72,84,87] In Sierra Leone, 75% of patients were positive on IFA on admission (mean duration of illness, 8.5 days). In recent studies, either Lassa antigen or IgM antibodies were detectable in the blood of virtually all acutely ill patients, and the degree of antigenemia was correlated with poor prognosis. Antibodies detectable by IFA appear about 2 weeks after the onset of LCM illness.[83]

Reverse transcription of extracted RNA followed by polymerase chain reaction amplification has been used successfully in all the arenavirus infections and is highly sensitive provided broadly reactive primers are chosen and cross-contamination with plasmids is avoided.[1,2,88]

PREVENTION AND TREATMENT

Arenavirus infection may be prevented by interdicting transmission from rodents to humans, from person to person, and from infected specimens to laboratory workers or by passive or active immunization. Community rodent control completely halted a major outbreak of Bolivian HF[89]; elimination of infected laboratory hamsters controlled LCM outbreaks.[21,22] A household rodent control study of Lassa infection, however, gave disappointing results.[30]

Person-to-person spread within hospitals has been a problem with Lassa fever. In endemic situations such as in Sierra Leone, partial spatial isolation of patients and the use of "enteric precautions" such as gloves, gowns, and careful disposal of patient wastes and fomites have generally served to prevent nosocomial outbreaks. Segregation of patients on the basis of the risk of death and likely content of virus in blood and body fluids by measuring aspartate transaminase levels should be of value. Rarely hospital outbreaks appear to have been caused by infectious aerosols.[28,36] Thus, wherever practical, it is advisable to place patients in single rooms with isolated negative-pressure airflow and to provide medical staff with goggles and positive-pressure filtered air respirators or absolute filter respirators.[90] All potentially contaminated refuse or specimens should be double-bagged and the outer bag rinsed with 0.6% sodium hypochlorite before removal from the patient's room. Isolation of patients should continue until multiple blood and urine specimens are virus negative. Condoms should be used for a period in convalescence because of the occasional sexual transmission of arenavirus HF. In the recognized cases of Lassa fever that have been exported from Africa, no secondary transmission has yet been detected in contacts or in medical staff, indicating that a conservative approach to isolation provides a reasonable standard of safe care in most cases.

Laboratory-acquired infection is a major problem because all arenaviruses are infectious as aerosols. Several infections, some fatal, have occurred in laboratory workers. Thus, it is imperative that work with all arenaviruses except LCM be conducted in special laboratories with BSL 4 containment. Clinical pathologic tests, particularly in Lassa fever patients, also present problems. Aerosols must be minimized or contained. Acid treatment inactivates virus for leukocyte counts, and alcohol fixation is useful for blood smears; heating serum at 60°C for 1 hour is feasible for measuring heat-stable substances.[91]

There are no licensed arenavirus vaccines. However, field trials with a live-attenuated Argentine HF vaccine showed greater than 95% efficacy and virtually no side effects.[92] More than 250,000 doses have been used in the endemic area and the vaccine continues to be safe and protective (D. Enria and J. Barrera, personal communication, 2004). Although wider vaccination would be desirable, regulatory standards have not been

developed for additional lots of vaccine. Work in laboratory animals suggests the Junin vaccine would be efficacious against Machupo, but not Guanarito or Sabia, viruses. Vaccinia-vectored Lassa genes have given protection to experimental animals and suggest the possibility of such a vaccine for use in humans,[84,93] but the immunology of the Old World arenaviruses is complicated, and additional work is required.[40]

Convalescent human plasma was proved to be effective in the treatment of Argentine HF (16% placebo versus 1% treated mortality rates) provided adequate amounts of neutralizing antibodies were given before the ninth day of illness.[94] Cerebellar signs, usually transient and possibly the result of virus multiplication in the central nervous system, occurred in 10% of those receiving this treatment. Immune plasma treatment of Lassa fever has not been as successful, and experiments in animals suggest that this may be related to the fact that neutralizing antibodies after Lassa fever (as well as LCM[83]) appear weeks after recovery and are generally of low titer and avidity.[41]

Ribavirin, a purine nucleoside with broad-spectrum antiviral properties, was found to be highly effective in monkeys lethally infected with Lassa and other arenaviruses.[41] The intravenous administration of this compound to Lassa patients admitted to the hospital in Sierra Leone with aspartate transaminase elevations of at least 150 IU reduced the mortality rate from 55% to 5% if treatment was begun before day 7 of the disease.[73] A positive effect on survival was achieved, however, at all stages of infection. After a 30-mg/kg loading dose, patients were given 15 mg/kg every 6 hours for 4 days and then 7.5 mg/kg 3 times daily for 6 additional days. Reversible anemia, not requiring transfusions, was the only adverse effect associated with treatment. Ribavirin has been used with apparent success in aborting a Sabia laboratory infection,[40] in treating Bolivian HF patients,[37] and in late therapy of Argentine HF patients.[94] Given the similarities to Lassa virus and similar preclinical test efficacy, the drug should be considered for any serious arenavirus infection. Close contacts of patients with arenavirus infections or possible bioterrorist exposures should not be given prophylactic ribavirin but rather be monitored for the appearance of fever.[95] Ribavirin therapy should be begun expectantly if fever is confirmed. Intravenous ribavirin is not licensed in the United States and arenavirus treatment is not a U.S. Food and Drug Administration–recognized indication for the oral drug.

Supportive care may be lifesaving in HFs. Fluid balance should be maintained orally as long as possible. Cautious volume replacement therapy with the judicious use of colloid should be started before the appearance of clinical shock, and electrolyte balance should be maintained.

The reader who desires to delve more deeply into arenaviruses should consult one of the following as a starting point. The biology of arenaviruses, including clinical descriptions, has been reviewed in an excellent volume published in 1993[96] and more recently in two slim but thorough collections of reviews in 2002.[97,98]

REFERENCES

1. Bowen MD, Peters CJ, Nichol ST. The phylogeny of New World (Tacaribe complex) arenaviruses. Virology. 1996;219:285-290.
2. Enria D, Bowen M, Mills JN, et al. Arenaviruses. In: Guerrant RL, Walker DH, Weller PF, eds. Tropical Infectious Diseases: Principles, Pathogens, and Practice. Philadelphia: Churchill Livingstone; 1999:Chapter 111.
3. Armstrong C, Lillie RD. Experimental lymphocytic choriomeningitis of monkeys and mice produced by a virus encountered in studies of the 1933 St Louis encephalitis epidemic. Public Health Rep. 1934;49:1019-1027.
4. Parodi AS, Greenway DJ, Rugiero HR. Sobre la etiologia del brote epidemico de Junin. El Dia Medico. 1958;30:2300-2301.
5. Johnson KM, Wiebenga NH, Mackenzie RB, et al. Virus isolations from human cases of hemorrhagic fever in Bolivia. Proc Soc Exp Biol Med. 1965;118:113-118.
6. Buckley SM, Casals J. Lassa fever, a new virus disease of man from West Africa. III. Isolation and characterization of the virus. Am J Trop Med Hyg. 1970;19:680-691.
7. Salas R, de Manzione N, Tesh RB, et al. Venezuelan hemorrhagic fever. Lancet. 1991;338:1033-1036.
8. Coimbra TLM, Nassar ES, Burattini MN, et al. New arenavirus isolated in Brazil. Lancet. 1994;343:391-392.
9. Murphy FA, Whitfield SG. Morphology and morphogenesis of arenaviruses. Bull World Health Organ. 1975;52:409-419.
10. Strecker T, Eichler R, Meulen J, et al. Lassa virus Z protein is a matrix protein sufficient for the release of virus-like particles. J Virol. 2003;77:10700-10705.

11. Burns JW, Buchmeier MJ. Glycoproteins of the arenaviruses. In: Salvato MS, ed. The Arenaviridae. New York: Plenum; 1993:17-31.
12. Klavinskas LS, Whitton JL, Oldstone MBA. Molecular anatomy of the cytotoxic T-lymphocyte responses to lymphocytic choriomeningitis virus. In: Salvato MD, ed. The Arenaviridae. New York: Plenum; 1993:225-242.
13. Cao W, Henry MD, Borrow P, et al. Identification of alpha-dystroglycan as a receptor for lymphocytic choriomeningitis virus and lassa fever virus. Science. 1998;282:2079-2081.
14. Spiropoulou CF, Kunz S, Rollin PE, et al. New World arenavirus clade C, but not clade A and B viruses, utilizes alpha-dystroglycan as its major receptor. J Virol. 2002;76:5140-5146.
15. Lehmann-Grube F. Lymphocytic Choriomeningitis Virus. New York: Springer; 1971.
16. Farmer TW, Janeway CA. Infection with the virus of lymphocytic choriomeningitis. Medicine (Balt). 1942;2:11.
17. Childs JC, Glass GE, Korch GW, et al. Lymphocytic choriomeningitis virus infection and house mouse (Mus musculus) distribution in urban Baltimore. Am J Trop Med Hyg. 1992;47:27-34.
18. Ackermann R, Bloedhorn H, Kupper B, et al. Über die Verbreiting des Virus der lymphocytaren Choriomeningitis unter den Mausen in Westdeutschland. I. Utersuchungen uberwiegend an Hausmauden (Mus musculus). Zentrabl Bakteriol. 1964;194:407.
19. Stephenson EH, Larson EW, Dominik JW. Effect of environmental factors on aerosol induced Lassa virus infection. J Med Virol. 1984;14:295.
20. Hinman AR, Fraser DW, Douglas RG, et al. Outbreak of lymphocytic choriomeningitis virus infection in medical center personnel. Am J Epidemiol. 1975;101:103.
21. Baum SG, Lewis AM, Rowe WP, et al. Epidemic nonmeningitic lymphocytic choriomeningitis virus infection. N Engl J Med. 1966;274:934.
22. Dykewitz CA, Dato VM, Fisher-Hoch SF, et al. Lymphocytic choriomeningitis outbreak associated with nude mice in a research institute. JAMA. 1992;267:1349-1353.
23. Biggar RJ, Woodall JP, Walter PD, et al. Lymphocytic choriomeningitis outbreak associated with pet hamsters: Fifty-seven cases from New York State. JAMA. 1975;232:494.
24. Ackermann R, Stille W, Blumenthal W, et al. Syrische Goldhamster als Ubertrager von lymphozytarer Choriomeningitis. Dtsch Med Wochenschr. 1972;97:1725.
25. Frame JD, Baldwin JM Jr, Gocke DJ, et al. Lassa fever, a new virus disease of man from West Africa. I. Clinical description and pathological findings. Am J Trop Med Hyg. 1970;19:670.
26. McCormick JB, Webb PA, Krebs JW, et al. A prospective study of the epidemiology and ecology of Lassa fever. J Infect Dis. 1987;155:437.
27. Robbins CB, Van Der Straeten E. Comments on the systematics of Mastomys Thomas 1915 with the description of a new West African species. Senckenbergiana Biol. 1989;69:1-14.
28. Monath TP. Lassa fever: Review of epidemiology and epizootology. Bull World Health Organ. 1975;52:577.
29. Frame JD. Surveillance of Lassa fever in missionaries stationed in West Africa. Bull World Health Organ. 1975;52:593.
30. Keenlyside RA, McCormick JB, Webb PA, et al. Case-control study of Mastomys natalensis and humans in Lassa virus-infected households in Sierra Leone. Am J Trop Med Hyg. 1983;32:829-837.
31. Demby AH, Inapogui A, Kargbo K, et al. Lassa fever in Guinea: II. Distribution and prevalence of Lassa virus infection in small mammals. Vector Borne Zoonotic Dis. 2001;1:283-297.
32. Keenlyside RA, McCormick JB, Webb PA, et al. Case-control study of Mastomys natalensis and humans in Lassa virus-infected households in Sierra Leone. Am J Trop Med Hyg. 1983;32:829-837.
33. Sabattini MS, Maiztegui JI. Fiebre hemorragica argentina. Medicina (Buenos Aires). 1970;30(suppl):111.
34. Enria DA, Barrera Oro JG. Junin virus vaccines. Curr Top Microbiol Immunol. 2002;263:239-261.
35. Johnson KM, Kuns ML, Mackenzie RB, et al. Isolation of Machupo virus from wild rodent Calomys callosus. Am J Trop Med Hyg. 1966;15:103.
36. Peters CJ, Kuehne RW, Mercado R, et al. Hemorrhagic fever in Cochabamba, Bolivia. 1971. Am J Epidemiol. 1974;99:425-433.
37. Kilgore PE, Peters CJ, Mills JN, et al. Prospects for the control of Bolivian hemorrhagic fever. Emerg Infect Dis. 1995;1:97-100.
38. Mills JN, Ellis BA, McKee KT, et al. A longitudinal study of Junin virus activity in the rodent reservoir of Argentine hemorrhagic fever. Am J Trop Med Hyg. 1992;47:749-763.
39. Fulhorst CF, Bowen MD, Salas RA, et al. Isolation and characterization of Pirital virus, a newly discovered South American arenavirus. Am J Trop Med Hyg. 1997;56:548-553.
40. Barry M, Russi M, Armstrong L, et al. Treatment of a laboratory-acquired Sabia virus infection. N Eng J Med. 1995;333:294-296.
41. Peters CJ, Jahrling PB, Liu CT, et al. Experimental studies of arenaviral hemorrhagic fevers. Curr Top Microbiol Immunol. 1987;134:5.
42. Fulhorst CF, Bennett SG, Milazzo ML, et al. Bear Canyon virus: An arenavirus naturally associated with the California mouse (Peromyscus californicus). Emerg Infect Dis. 2002;8:717-721.
43. Fulhorst CF, Bowen MD, Ksiazek TG, et al. Isolation and characterization of Whitewater Arroyo virus, a novel North American arenavirus. Virology. 1996;224:114-120.
44. Fatal illnesses associated with a new world arenavirus—California, 1999-2000. MMWR Morb Mortal Wkly Rep 2000;49:709-711.
45. Oldstone MBA, Dixon FJ. Pathogenesis of chronic disease associated with persistent lymphocytic choriomeningitis infection. II. Relationship of the antilymphocytic choriomeningitis virus immune response to tissue injury in chronic lymphocytic choriomeningitis disease. J Exp Med. 1970;131:1.
46. Nathanson N, Monjan AA, Panitch HS, et al. Virus-induced cell-mediated immunopathological disease. In: Notkins AL, ed. Viral Immunology and Immunopathology. New York: Academic Press; 1975:357-391.
47. Walker DH, Wulff H, Lange JV, et al. Comparative pathology of Lassa virus infection in monkeys, guinea pigs, and Mastomys natalensis. Bull World Health Organ. 1975;52:523.
48. Montali RJ, Scanga CA, Perkikoff D, et al. A common-source outbreak of callitrichid hepatitis in captive tamarins and marmosets. J Infect Dis. 1993;167:946-950.
49. McKee KT Jr, Mahlandt BG, Maiztegui JI, et al. Experimental Argentine hemorrhagic fever in rhesus monkeys: Viral strain-dependent clinical response. J Infect Dis. 1985;152:218.
50. Peters CJ. Pathogenesis of viral hemorrhagic fevers. In: Nathanson N, Ahmed R, Gonzalez-Scarano F, et al, eds. Viral Pathogenesis. Philadelphia: Lippincott-Raven; 1997:779-799.
51. Smadel JE, Green RH, Paltauf RM, et al. Lymphocytic choriomeningitis: Two human fatalities following an unusual febrile illness. Proc Soc Exp Biol Med. 1942;49:683.
52. Warkel RL, Rinaldi CF, Bancroft WH, et al. Fatal acute meningoencephalitis due to lymphocytic choriomeningitis virus. Neurology. 1973;23:198-202.
53. Walker DH, McCormick JB, Johnson KM, et al. Pathologic and virologic study of fatal Lassa fever in man. Am J Pathol. 1982;107:349.
54. McCormick JB, Walker DB, King IJ, et al. Lassa virus hepatitis: A study of fatal Lassa fever in humans. Am J Trop Med Hyg. 1986;35:401.
55. Zaki SR, Peters CJ. Viral hemorrhagic fevers. In: Connor DH, Chandler FW, Schwartz DA, et al, eds. The Pathology of Infectious Diseases. Norwalk, CT: Appleton & Lange; 1997:347-364.
56. Kenyon RH, Green DE, Peters CJ. Effect of immuno-suppression on experimental Argentine hemorrhagic fever in guinea pigs. J Virol. 1985;53:75-80.
57. Levis SC, Saavedra MC, Ceccoli C, et al. Correlation between endogenous interferon and the clinical evolution of patients with Argentine hemorrhagic fever. J Interferon Res. 1985;5:383.
58. Vilcek J. Adverse effects of interferon in virus infections, autoimmune diseases and acquired immunodeficiency. Prog Med Virol. 1984;30:62.
59. Marta RF, Montero VF, Hack CE, et al. Proinflammatory cytokines and elastase-alpha-1antitrypsin in Argentine hemorrhagic fever. Am J Trop Med Hyg. 1999;60:85-89.
60. Vanzee BE, Douglas RG, Betts RF, et al. Lymphocytic choriomeningitis in university hospital personnel. Am J Med. 1975;58:803-807.
61. Schmitz H, Kohler B, Laue T, Drosten C, Veldkamp PJ, Gunther S et al. Monitoring of clinical and laboratory data in two cases of imported Lassa fever. Microbes Infect 2002;4:43-50.
62. Mahanty S, Bausch DG, Thomas RL, et al. Low levels of interleukin-8 and interferon-inducible protein-10 in serum are associated with fatal infections in acute Lassa fever. J Infect Dis. 2001;183:1713-1721.
63. Lukashevich IS, Maryankova R, Vladyko AS, et al. Lassa and Mopeia virus replication in human monocytes/macrophages and in endothelial cells: Different effects on IL-8 and TNF-alpha gene expression. J. Med Virol. 1999;59:552-560.
64. Peters CJ. Arenavirus diseases. In: Porterfield JS, ed. Kass Handbook of Infectious Diseases. Exotic Viral Infections. New York: Chapman and Hall Medical; 1995: 227-246.
65. Monson MH, Frame JD, Jahrling PB, et al. Endemic Lassa fever in Liberia. I. Clinical and epidemiological aspects of Curran Lutheran Hospital, Zorzor, Liberia. Trans R Soc Trop Med Hyg. 1984;78:549.
66. McCormick JB, King IJ, Webb PA, et al. A case-control study of the clinical diagnosis and course of Lassa fever. J Infect Dis. 1987;155:445.
67. Bausch DG, Demby AH, Coulibaly M, et al. Lassa fever in Guinea: I. Epidemiology of human disease and clinical observations. Vector Borne Zoonotic Dis. 2001;1: 269-281.
68. Solbrig MV. Lassa virus and central nervous system diseases. In: Salvato MS, ed. The Arenaviridae. New York: Plenum; 1993:325-330.
69. Gunther S, Weisner B, Roth A, et al. Lassa fever encephalopathy: Lassa virus in cerebrospinal fluid but not in serum. J Infect Dis. 2001;184:345-349.
70. Webb PA, McCormick JB, King IJ, et al. Lassa fever in children in Sierra Leone, West Africa. Trans R Soc Trop Med Hyg. 1986;80:577.
71. Monson MH, Cole AK, Frame JD, et al. Pediatric Lassa fever: A review of 33 Liberian cases. Am J Trop Med Hyg. 1987;36:408.
72. Johnson KM, McCormick JB, Webb PA, et al. Clinical virology of Lassa fever in hospitalized patients. J Infect Dis. 1987;155:456.
73. McCormick JB, King IB, Webb PA, et al. Lassa fever: Effective therapy with ribavirin. N Engl J Med. 1986;314:20.
74. Cummins D, McCormick JB, Bennett D, et al. Acute sensorineural deafness in Lassa fever. JAMA. 1990;264:2093-2096.
75. Maiztegui JI. Clinical and epidemiological patterns of Argentine haemorrhagic fever. Bull World Health Organ. 1975;52:567.
76. Stinebaugh BJ, Schloeder FX, Johnson KM, et al. Bolivian hemorrhagic fever: A report of four cases. Am J Med. 1966;40:217.
77. Price ME, Fisher-Hoch SP, Craven RB, et al. A prospective study of maternal and fetal outcome in acute Lassa fever infection during pregnancy. BMJ. 1988;297: 584-587.
78. Barton LL, Budd SC, Morfitt WS, et al. Congenital lymphocytic choriomeningitis virus infection in twins. Pediatr Infect Dis J. 1993;12:942-946.

79. Ackermann R, Korver G, Turss R, et al. Pranatale Infektion mit dem Virus der lymphozytaren Choriomeningitis. Dtsch Med Wochenschr. 1974;99:629-632.

80. Wright R, Johnson D, Neumann M, et al. Congenital lymphocytic choriomeningitis virus syndrome: A disease that mimics congenital toxoplasmosis or cytomegalovirus infection. Pediatrics. 1997;100:E9.

81. Barton LL, Mets MB, Beauchamp CL. Lymphocytic choriomeningitis virus: Emerging fetal teratogen. Am J Obstet Gynecol 2002;187:1715-1716.

82. Childs JE, Glass GE, Ksiazek TG, et al. Human-rodent contact and infection with lymphocytic choriomeningitis and Seoul viruses in an inner-city population. Am J Trop Med Hyg. 1991;44:117-121.

83. Lehmann-Grube F, Kallay M, Ibscher B, Schwartz R. Serologic diagnosis of human infections with lymphocytic choriomeningitis virus: Comparative evaluation of seven methods. J Med Virol. 1979;4:125-136.

84. Bausch DG, Rollin PE, Demby AH, et al. Diagnosis and clinical virology of Lassa fever as evaluated by enzyme-linked immunosorbent assay, indirect fluorescent-antibody test, and virus isolation. J Clin Microbiol. 2000;38:2670-2677.

85. Ambrosio AM, Enria DA, Maiztegui JI. Junin virus isolation from lymphomononuclear cells of patients with Argentine hemorrhagic fever. Intervirology. 1986;25:97.

86. Emond RTD, Bannister B, Lloyd G, et al. A case of Lassa fever: Clinical and virological findings. BMJ. 1982;285:1001.

87. Nicklasson BS, Jahrling PB, Peters CJ. Detection of Lassa virus antigens and Lassa virus-specific immunoglobulins G and M by enzyme-linked immunosorbent assay. J Clin Microbiol. 1984;20:239.

88. Park JY, Peters CJ, Rollin PE, et al. Development of an RT-PCR assay for diagnosis of lymphocytic choriomeningitis virus (LCMV) infection and its use in a prospective surveillance study. J Med Virol. 1997;51:107-114.

89. Mackenzie RB. Epidemiology of Machupo virus infection. I. Pattern of human infection, San Joaquin, Bolivia, 1962-1965. Am J Trop Med Hyg. 1965;14:808.

90. CDC (1995) update: Management of patients with suspected viral hemorrhagic fever-United States. MMWR Morb Mortal Wkly Rep. 44:475-479.

91. Mitchell SW, McCormick JB. Physicochemical inactivation of Lassa, Ebola, and Marburg viruses and effect on clinical laboratory analyses. J Clin Microbiol. 1984;20:486.

92. Maiztegui JI, McKee KT, Barrera Oro JG, et al. Protective efficacy of a live attenuated vaccine against Argentine hemorrhagic fever. J Infect Dis. 1998;177;277-283.

93. Auperin DD. Construction and evaluation of recombinant virus vaccines for Lassa fever. In: Salvato MS, ed. The Arenaviridae. New York: Plenum; 1993:259-280.

94. Enria D, Maiztegui JI. Antiviral treatment of Argentine hemorrhagic fever. Antiviral Res. 1994;23:23-31.

95. Borio L, Inglesby T, Peters CJ, et al. Hemorrhagic fever viruses as biological weapons: medical and public health management. JAMA. 2002;287:2391-2405.

96. Salvato MS, ed. The Arenaviridae. New York: Plenum; 1993.

97. Oldstone MB, ed. Arenaviruses. I. The epidemiology molecular and cell biology of arenaviruses. Curr Top Microbiol Immunol. 2002;262:1-197.

98. Oldstone MB, ed. Arenaviruses. II. The molecular pathogenesis of arenavirus infections. Curr Top Microbiol Immunol. 2002;263:1-268.

CHAPTER **165**

Human T-Cell Lymphotropic Virus Types I and II

WILLIAM BLATTNER

MANHATTAN CHARURAT

The human T-cell lymphotropic virus type I (HTLV-I), the first recognized human retrovirus, was described in 1979 by Poiesz and Gallo and co-workers,[1,2] who isolated retroviral particles with type C morphology and budding from fresh cultured lymphocytes of a 28-year-old black man with a diagnosis of cutaneous T-cell lymphoma. The long-standing search for a human homologue to cancer-causing retroviruses of animals, first discovered at the beginning of the twentieth century, ended at a time when most researchers had abandoned this quest and focused instead on viral transforming genes that occur as oncogenes in human tumors. Human T-cell lymphotropic virus type II (HTLV-II) was identified 2 years later.[3] The techniques used to isolate and characterize these viruses provided the intellectual and technical basis for the discovery of

the human immunodeficiency virus (HIV) in 1983,[4,5] which was shown to be the cause of acquired immunodeficiency syndrome (AIDS) in 1984.[6]

Within the taxa of DNA and RNA reverse-transcribing viruses, the HTLV viruses, along with bovine leukemia virus (BLV), are classified in the subfamily Retroviridae within the genus *Deltaretrovirus* (formerly termed *Oncovirus*).[7] The oncogenic properties of these viruses and their molecular structure distinguish them from retroviruses HIV-1 and HIV-2, which are members of the genus *Lentivirus*. Both oncoviruses and lentiviruses are capable of prolonged asymptomatic infection. In vitro, however, HIV-1 and HIV-2 have cytopathic effects on human T cells, whereas HTLV-I and HTLV-II are capable of transforming T cells, resulting in immortalized cell lines.

HTLV-I has been shown to be associated with adult T-cell leukemia/lymphoma (ATL) as well as a unique form of progressive neurologic disease known as HTLV-I–associated myelopathy (HAM), also known as tropical spastic paraparesis (TSP). HTLV-II is less clearly linked to human diseases but has been associated with scattered cases of leukemia/lymphoma and neurologic disease.[8]

STRUCTURE AND MOLECULAR ORGANIZATION

HTLV-I and HTLV-II are approximately 100 nm in diameter, with a thin electron-dense outer envelope and an electron-dense, roughly spherical core (Fig. 165-1). Its genomic structure is illustrated in Figure 165-2. The total provirus genome consists of roughly 9,000 nucleotides with two flanking identical sequences termed *long terminal repeats* (LTRs) at the 5′ and 3′ ends of the genome, which mediate proviral integration and contain *cis*-acting regulatory elements important for viral transcription, viral mRNA processing, and reverse transcription. Retroviral genes generally code for large overlapping polyproteins that are processed by a virally encoded protease and cellular proteases into functional peptide products. The HTLV viruses share with other replication-competent retroviruses the three main genomic regions of *gag* (group-specific antigen), *pol* (protease/polymerase/integrase), and *env* (envelope) (Table 165-1). However, unlike other vertebrate leukemia viruses, these Deltaretroviruses have an additional region called pX that contains four small open reading frames (ORFs): pX-I, pX-II, pX-III, and pX-IV.[9] The pX ORFs III and IV encode two transcriptional regulatory proteins, the Tax and Rex proteins, which are

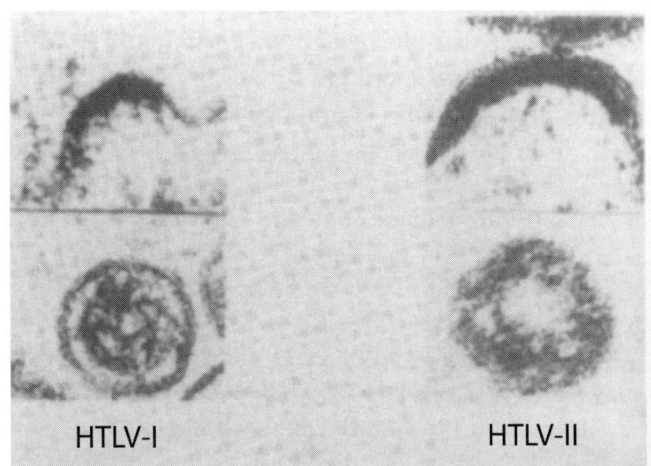

FIGURE 165-1. Electron micrographs of human T-cell lymphotropic virus type I (HTLV-I) and II. HTLV-I and -II have a diameter of approximately 100 nm. The budding particles are shown for each virus (*top*), and the mature virion (*bottom*). The HTLV-I and -II viruses have a roughly spherical electron-dense core.

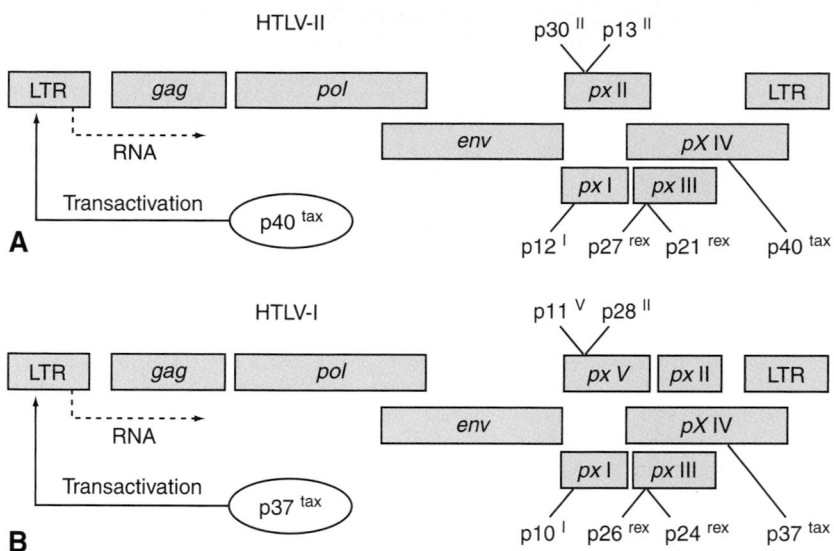

FIGURE 165-2. Genomic structures of **(A)** human T-cell lymphotropic virus type I (HTLV-I) and **(B)** HTLV-II. *gag*, group-specific antigen, whose products form the skeleton of the virion (matrix, capsid, nucleocapsid, nucleic acid binding protein); *pol/pro*, gene for reverse transcriptase, integrase, and protease; *env*, envelope gene; *tax*, transactivator gene; *rex*, viral regulatory gene involved in promoting genomic RNA production.

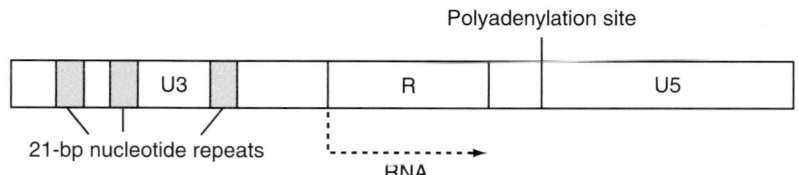

FIGURE 165-3. Structure of the long terminal repeat (LTR) organized into three regions: (1) U5, R, and U3, which house the polyadenylation site; (2) Rex-responsive elements (RxREs); (3) 21-bp enhancer transactivating response elements, which are involved in controlling viral gene expression.

TABLE 165-1 **Major Structural and Regulatory Proteins of Human T-Cell Lymphotropic Virus (HTLV) Type I**

Viral Gene	Gene Product (Protein Size [kDa])	Function
LTR		Regulation of viral gene expression, integration of provirus into host genetic material, and regulation of virion production
gag	p15	Nucleocapsid is a small basic protein found in the virion in association with the genome RNA characterized by zinc-finger motifs associated with nucleic acid binding.
gag	p19	Matrix protein forms close linkage to internal surface of viral envelope via myristic acid.
gag	p24	Capsid protein forms the major internal structural feature of the core shell of the virion.
gag	p53	Precursor protein for other gag
pol	Integrase	Integrates viral DNA into the host-cell chromosomes
pol	Reverse transcriptase (95 kDa)	Reverse transcriptase generates a double-stranded DNA from the RNA genome.
pro	Protease (p14)	Cleaves Gag and Gag-Pol polypeptides into proteins of the mature virion.
env	gp46	Envelope surface glycoprotein attached to surface lipid bilayer involved in virion binding to target cell
env	p21e	Envelope transmembrane protein
pX	Tax (p40)	Transactivator for enhanced transcription of viral and cellular gene products
pX	Rex (p27/p21)	Regulator of expression of virion proteins for HTLV stabilizes viral mRNAs and modulates the splicing and transport from the nucleus of viral RNA.
pX	ORF I (p12^I)	Activation of STAT5 and interference with major histocompatibility complex class I trafficking; elevation of cytoplasmic calcium, which is antecedent to T-cell activation
pX	ORF II (p30^{II}, p13^{II})	Inhibition of acetyltransferase activity of P/CAF on histones and stabilization of p53. p13″ localizes to the mitochondria; p30″ localizes to the nucleolus.

P/CAF, P^{300}/CREB binding protein-associated factor.

involved in regulation of virus expression. As shown in Figure 165-2, two overlapping reading frames are involved in the expression of both of these gene products translated from a doubly spliced mRNA involving the initiation codon from *env* and the remaining sequences from the pX region. HIV-1 uses a similar strategy for expressing Tat and Rev proteins that share similar regulatory functions. Despite similar function, the Tax and Rex proteins bear little amino acid homology with the corresponding proteins encoded by the transcriptional and post-transcriptional regulators Tat and Rev in HIV-1 and HIV-2, respectively. The pX ORFs I and II code for other accessory and regulatory genes whose protein products appear to involve cell cycle regulation.[10]

The LTR is organized into three regions: (1) U5, R, U3; (2) Rex-responsive elements (RxREs), and (3) 21–base pair (bp) response element. The U3 region contains sequences that control transcription of the provirus (Fig. 165-3). The 21-bp repeats are necessary for *trans*-activating transcriptional activation involving tax protein. The U3 region also contains sequences responsible for termination and polyadenylation of mRNAs. In addition, the 5′ part of the U3 region encodes the carboxyl terminus of the tax protein. Comparisons of the LTRs of HTLV-I and HTLV-II reveal that these elements are critical for viral gene expression. The R and U5 regions are unusually long in comparison to other retroviruses. These regions form the leader sequence encoded at the 5′ end of the mRNAs.

Gag and Pol

The Gag proteins function as structural proteins of the nucleocapsid, capsid, and matrix, also named p15, p24, and p19 Gag proteins, respectively. The *pol* gene encodes for several enzymes: protease that cleaves Gag and Gag/Pol polypeptides into proteins of the mature virion; reverse transcriptase that generates a double-stranded DNA from the RNA genome; and integrase that integrates viral DNA into the host-cell chromosomes. The polymerase region contains the largest open-reading frame in the HTLV genome, potentially able to encode an 896–amino acid product for HTLV-I and a 982–amino acid product for HTLV-II. The polymerase genes of HTLV-I and HTLV-II share only 56% homology based on their predicted amino acid sequences. The *env* gene encodes the major components of the viral coat: the surface glycoprotein of 46,000 molecular weight (MW) (gp46) and the 21,000-MW transmembrane glycoprotein (gp2l). Although HTLV-I and HTLV-II share the same overall genetic organization, they show some diversity at the nucleotide level, exhibiting a variable degree of amino acid homology between viral capsid and envelope proteins. There is 65% overall nucleotide homology between sequenced HTLV-I and HTLV-II isolates. Homology is lowest within the LTRs (30%) and is highest within the 3′ Tax and Rex regulatory genes (75% to 80%).[11-13]

Production of the Gag proteins derives from the translation of the full-length mRNA, which yields a large precursor polypeptide that is subsequently cleaved by the virally coded protease. For the Pol proteins, production depends on translation made possible when the stop codon of the *gag* gene is bypassed, leading to a large polypeptide including *gag-* and *pol-*related proteins, which are subsequently cleaved into functional proteins by the viral protease. Production of the Env surface and transmembrane proteins involves translation of a spliced message (see Fig. 165-2) that results in an envelope precursor, cleaved into the subunits. The precursor proteins have characteristic molecular weights that Western blot (WB) analysis can detect immunologically.

Tax

HTLV-I Tax is a 40-kilodalton (kDa) protein (p40), and HTLV-II Tax is a 37-kDa protein (p37).[14,15] These proteins localize primarily to the nucleus of infected cells, although small amounts of Tax have been found in the cytoplasm. The Tax proteins are responsible for enhanced transcription of viral and cellular gene products and are essential for transformation of human T lymphocytes.[16] The Tax viral regulatory protein for HTLV-1, like its counterpart, Tat of HIV-1, plays an important role in promoting viral growth and disease

pathogenesis. Both promote *trans*-acting, transcriptional activation of the LTR, but the effect of Tax appears to be mediated via expression of cellular growth factors that are abundantly activated by Tax through its *trans*-activation properties. This *trans*-activation of cellular genes by Tax not only facilitates viral replication but also has emerged as a cofactor in disease pathogenesis. The *tax* gene is responsible for the *trans*-activation of virus transcription via *tax*-responsive elements of a number of regulatory enhancers such as the 21-bp enhancer, the nuclear factor-κB (NF-κB) binding site, and serum-responsive element. Such promoter interactions lead to activation of a number of cellular genes such as those encoding interleukin (IL)-2 and the IL-2 receptor (IL-2R), which promote cell proliferation. Additionally, *tax* activates the proto-oncogenes c-*fos* and c-*erg*, as well as the gene for granulocyte-macrophage colony-stimulating factor, an array of early response genes, the human lymphotoxin gene, and parathyroid hormone–related protein gene, whereas it *trans*-represses the β-polymerase gene. Overproduction of interferon-γ via this pathway has been implicated in promoting chronic inflammation that characterizes diseases such as HAM/TSP.[17] The mechanism by which Tax interacts with a variety of cell regulatory elements involves nuclear regulatory elements (the NF-κB pathway); Tax also operates cytoplasmically through the induction of nuclear translocation of active transcriptional factors but not via pathways typical of other oncoviral proteins that target tumor suppressor genes.[18]

Rex Proteins

The *rex* gene of HTLV-I and HTLV-II encodes two protein species in each virus. In HTLV-I, a 27-kDa protein (p27) and a 21-kDa protein (p21) appear to result from the use of alternative initiator methionine codons. In HTLV-II, however, a 26-kDa protein appears to be formed by phosphorylation of a serine residue in a 24-kDa protein.[19] Unlike the products of *tax* gene, *rex* does not directly regulate RNA transcription but instead appears to act chiefly at a post-transcriptional level to regulate viral gene expression. The Rex (regulator of expression of virion proteins for HTLV) stabilizes viral mRNA and is essential for export of full-length *gag/pol* and single-spliced *env* mRNA from the nucleus to cytoplasm.[20] This function is analogous to that of Rev in HIV-1 and HIV-2.[21-23] Rex localizes to the nucleus and specifically to the nucleoli of infected cells.[24,25] Phosphorylated Rex binds with high affinity to *cis*-acting RNA sequences, called Rex-responsive elements, in the viral mRNA.[26-28] This interaction facilitates the export of mRNA. Rex binding may also inhibits mRNA splicing by preventing early steps in spliceosome assembly.[29] As a consequence of the accumulation of Rex in the cell, there is an accumulation of unspliced and single-spliced mRNA, favoring the production of structural proteins (Gag and Env). This is accompanied by a decrease in the levels of double-spliced mRNA encoding Tax and Rex. Rex accumulation may also inhibit *tax*, thus slowing viral transcription.[30] A fine balance between *tax* and *rex* expression and function may dictate the rate of viral replication within infected cells.

Other Proteins Encoded by the pX Region

pX ORF I, produced by a similar double-splicing mechanism to the gene products of pX ORF III and IV, codes for a hydrophobic 12-kDa protein, p12^I, and pX ORF II results in the production of two nuclear proteins, p13^{II} and p30^{II}.[10] In addition to activating nuclear factor of activated T cells[31] (NFAT), p12^I localizes in the endoplasmic reticulum and *cis*-Golgi apparatus and elevates cytoplasmic calcium that is antecedent to T-cell activation and essential for establishing persistent infection.[32] Other major structural and regulatory proteins of HTLV-I are summarized in Table 165-1. The gene products of pX ORF I and II also appear to impact cell proliferation and modulate host immune responses to HTLV-1 infection.[33] Tax and the ORF I and II gene products may play an integral role in pathogenesis of HTLV-associated diseases through its effects on cyclins that regulate cell growth.

BIOLOGY

The replication strategy of the HTLVs involves a life cycle typical of all members of the Retroviridae (Fig. 165-4), whereby the RNA genome undergoes reverse transcription into a DNA provirus that integrates into the host genome. Subsequently, new virions are produced via this integrated DNA template under the regulation of viral regulatory genes. During infection, HTLV-I is preferentially expressed in human CD4+ T-helper cells. This tropism appears to be mediated by transcriptional factors. The receptor for HTLV-I has not yet been identified, but it is believed to be expressed on many cell types[34] because HTLV-I infects a wide range of cells in vitro, including endothelial cells and fibroblasts.[35] Additionally, a number of animal species can be infected either experimentally (mice, rats, rabbits, and New World primate species) or naturally (Old World primates).[36] The natural host range for HTLV is thus humans and Old World non-human primates.

Although HTLV-I can infect a number of different cell types, its growth and propagation are supported mainly by CD4+ cells involving undefined postinfection transcriptional factors. In addition to CD4+ cells, HTLV-II frequently targets CD8+ cells.[37] CD8+ cells are also a target of HTLV-I but at a lower frequency, and they are detected by real-time quantitative polymerase chain reaction (PCR) and intracellular protein staining of T cells from patients with HAM/TSP.[38]

Based on epidemiologic data demonstrating that HTLV-I transmission is strongly cell-associated and through in vitro studies where cocultivation is required for efficient infection of target cells, transmission of HTLV is mediated by live cells and not via cell-free body fluids. For this reason, HTLV-I is not an easily transmitted virus and universal precautions such as are recommended for HIV-1 are applicable for inactivation and protection from potentially infectious blood or bodily secretions. Because HTLV-I is highly cell associated, the means for viral attachment are not well characterized but, as for other retroviruses, fusion of the virion with the cell membrane results in uncoating of the diploid RNA genome of the virus (see Fig. 165-4). Recent work by Igakura and co-workers,[39] however, challenged this mechanism by indicating that additional cell surface adhesion proteins and cell–cell contacts/interface ("virologic synapse") are important for facilitating virus transmission. Cytoskeletal reorganization in the infected cells and segregation of virus particles to the interface between the infected and uninfected cells can be observed by immunofluorescence microscopy.

Once in the cell, the virally encoded RNA-dependent DNA polymerase (reverse transcriptase) complexed to the genomic RNA of the virus transcribes viral RNA into double-stranded DNA. This double-stranded viral cDNA is transported to the nucleus as a ribonucleoprotein complex that includes the p24 capsid protein as well as integrase and reverse transcriptase. There the cDNA, through a complex process

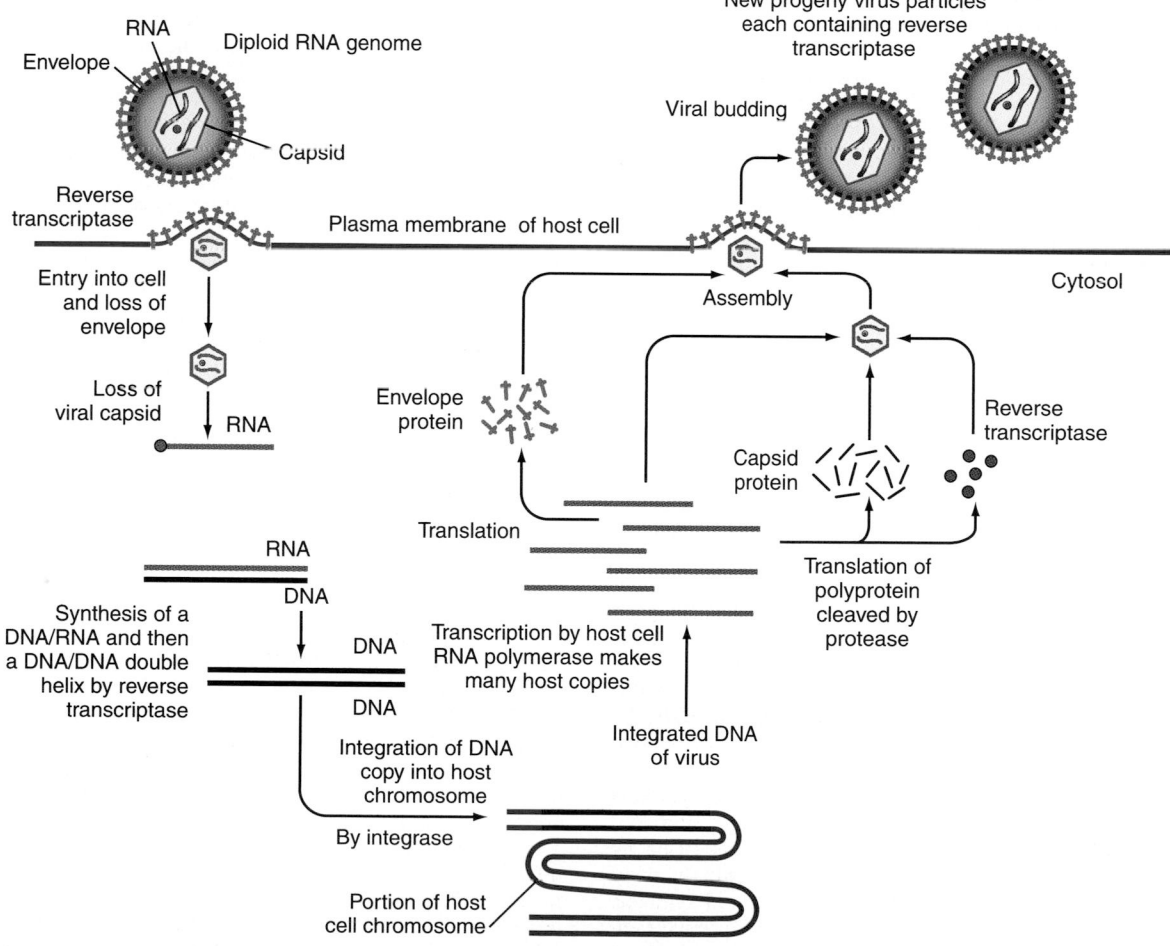

FIGURE 165-4. Life cycle of human T-cell lymphotropic virus type I (HTLV-I). Virus infection involves initial binding to cell surface of target CD4 cell, uncoating, and release of viral genetic material. Virally encoded reverse transcriptase creates a DNA copy that is integrated into the host genome under the influence of viral integrase. Viral replication involves production of both genomic RNA and poly proteins that are cleaved by the viral protease resulting in virion assembly at the cell surface. See text for details. *(Adapted from Alberts B, Bray D, Johnson A, et al, eds. Essential Cell Biology: An Introduction to the Molecular Biology of the Cell. New York: Garland Science Publishing; 2004. Reproduced by permission of Garland Science/Taylor & Francis Books, Inc.)*

mediated by the viral integrase, is inserted into the host genome. The genomic integration of HTLV-I establishes a lifelong infection and is integral to both the virus replication cycle and amplification.

Elements in the viral LTR (see Fig. 165-3) are essential to integration and replication; they form the sites for covalent attachment of the provirus to cellular DNA and provide important regulatory components for transcription. Additional key regulatory elements of HTLV are *tax*, which activates transcription of the viral genome, and *rex*, which modulates the processing of the viral RNA expressing unspliced forms of the viral mRNA. When the DNA provirus is expressed (transcribed by a cellular RNA polymerase), viral genomic and mRNA and subsequently viral proteins are made by the cell. Under the influence of Rex, which stabilizes viral mRNAs and regulates their splicing and transport, new genomic RNA is assembled at the cell membrane and packaged for release *(budding)*. During the budding process, the envelope incorporates some of the cell's lipid bilayer, producing an infectious virion of about 100 nm (see Figs. 165-1 and 165-4).

LABORATORY DETECTION

No gold standard exists for diagnosis of HTLV infection.

Virus Isolation

Direct detection of virus by culture is intensive, expensive, and time consuming, often requiring several weeks for results. The ability to culture retroviruses has been improved by co-cultivation of patients' T cells with human peripheral blood mononuclear cells (PBMCs) that have been stimulated in vitro with mitogens (e.g., phytohemagglutinin) and growth factors (e.g., IL-2), as well as by removal of patient CD8+ suppressor cells from the co-culture. The number of infected cells present in the blood of an infected individual is generally relatively low: less than or equal to 1:100 to 10,000 PBMCs for HTLV. The ability to isolate HTLV is dependent on viral load, immune status, and stage of disease. In infants and children, the small volume of blood available for culture and the low virus load make virus isolation especially challenging.

Serologic Assays and Antigen Detection

The primary test for HTLV-I /II infection is detection of the presence of antibody. A variety of techniques are used to detect antibodies to HTLV-I. Because HTLV infection is a chronic process, almost all HTLV-I antibody–positive patients are also virus positive. The epidemiology of HTLV-I/II has been largely defined through the use of antibody testing. Samples are first screened with one of several assays that use whole virus lysates, sometimes enriched with recombinant antigens. The most widely used assay for detection of HTLV-I in the United States is the enzyme-linked immunosorbent assay (ELISA) technique, using whole disrupted virus.[40] These assays have performed with high sensitivity but poor type specificity due to cross-reactivity between HTLV-I and HTLV-II.[41] The problem of cross-reactivity has been resolved by WB technology, which uses a combination of whole virus and recombinantly produced peptides; this technique can confirm positivity by screening samples and antibody to distinguish between the two virus types in one assay[42,43] (Fig. 165-5).

For HTLV-I and -II, a combination of ELISA confirmed by WB is the standard approach, although alternative strategies using immunofluorescence assays and agglutination approaches are also used by some investigators.[44-46] The most recent screening assays with lysate of both virus and WB technology that includes the addition of synthetic peptides to both confirm positively and distinguish virus type have enhanced such studies.[45-47] A modified WB has been developed that contains both group-specific conserved motifs from the transmembrane protein and type-specific motifs from the external glycoproteins (recombinant gp46 [rgp46]) of HTLV-I (MTA1) and HTLV-II (K55). They have been coated onto the strips, which allows a simultaneous confirmation and differentiation of both HTLV-I and -II in 98% of the cases.[48]

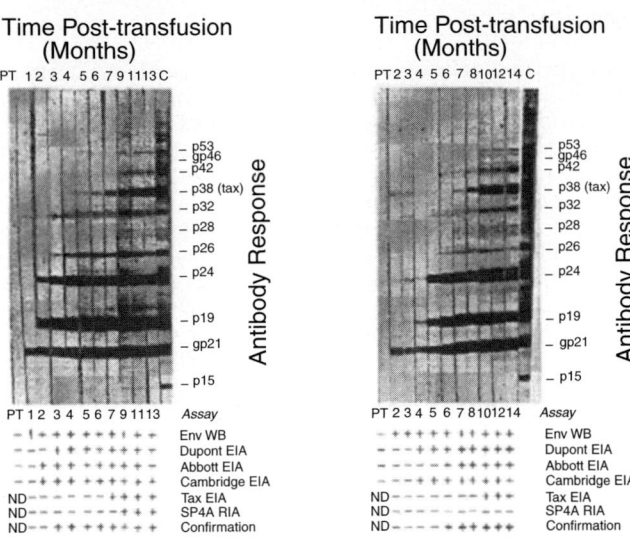

FIGURE 165-5. During seroconversion, antibodies for envelope and core antigen are detected at varying time points, usually 6 weeks after exposure. ND, not done; PT, pretransfusion.

The criterion for WB positivity is the presence of reactivity to both a *gag* and an *env* gene product, and in the case of *env* this usually entails a recombinantly produced antigen because of the paucity of HTLV envelope antigens in whole virus preparations. Because the virus is highly cell associated, additional tests are sometimes needed to demonstrate antibody to the *env*-encoded components of the virus. The *env* antibodies are selectively picked up by radioimmunoprecipitation assay, a more difficult procedure based on virus-infected whole cells. Confirmation by immunofluorescence assay is often used for the particle agglutination assay widely used in Japan. Titration to allow quantification of antibody is possible with modifications to the ELISA and particle agglutination tests. In tropical countries, especially in Africa, repeatable ELISA reactive samples exhibit a high frequency of indeterminate WB results. The interpretation of WB results such as reactivities to *gag*-encoded proteins (p19, p24, or p53) without reactivity to *env*-encoded glycoproteins (gp21, gp46) remains to be resolved to avoid overestimating the rate of HTLV-I/II seroprevalence in these regions.[49-51] In these cases, PCR proves to be a useful technique for distinguishing virus type and quantifying viral presence.

Nucleic Acid Detection

PCR assays have been developed to distinguish virus type and to quantify viral presence. In PCR, proviral DNA is amplified enzymatically and subsequently detected using a system of specific nucleotide primers and probes.[52] The limits of detection are about 10 molecules of DNA in 1 mg of human DNA (about 1 infected cell in 100,000 PBMC).[53] With some modification, the technique can also be used to detect viral RNA in infected cells that helps to identify actively replicating virus. Although exquisitely sensitive in the best laboratories, PCR remains a research technique; it is under consideration for use as a screening assay as new technologies are evolving. The sensitivity and specificity of PCR for the diagnosis of retroviral infections have been recently confirmed in a multicenter study, but further refinement may be necessary in pediatric populations. It has proved especially valuable in enigmatic situations. PCR is also useful in cases of sero-indeterminate WBs (i.e., cases from Africa and Melanesia). It can determine if such cases represent a new exogenous retrovirus, are the expression of endogenous sequences with *gag* homologies, are cross-reactive epitopes present on parasitic antigens such as the malaria virus, or are an immunogenetically restricted immune response to HTLV-I.

The PCR technique has also been useful to facilitate epidemiologic studies by providing a precise tool to distinguish virus type and to quantify viral presence.[52,54] For example, because virus-positive antibody-negative individuals could be missed by antibody tests, the true prevalence of virus may be underestimated. In fact, several surveys using PCR have not detected large numbers of virus-positive antibody-negative individuals, although some instances have been reported.[55-57]

Cellular Assays

In the research setting, detection of cellular immune responses to HTLV-I involves standard cytotoxic T-lymphocyte (CTL) assays using chromium release by either leukemic cells or transformed cells treated with HTLV-I peptides or infected with recombinant virus.[58-60] More recently, flow cytometry–based assays adapting tetramer technology have provided a much more precise measure of cell-specific CTL quantities. In these assays, PBMCs can be directly quantitated by the ability of major histocompatibility complex (MHC) class I–restricted tetramers to bind Tax peptides. The assay, however, is restricted to the human leukocyte antigen (HLA)-A 02 haplotype at this time because reagents are available only for this class of tetramer.[61]

SEROLOGIC EPIDEMIOLOGY

Geographic Distribution and Patterns

Endemic clusters of HTLV-I seropositivity or infection are present in southern Japan, the islands of the Ryukyu Chain, including Okinawa, and some isolated villages in the north of Japan among aboriginal Ainu populations; most of the seropositives in northern Japan are among immigrants from endemic areas in the south.[62-64] Rates of infection among persons over 40 years of age exceed 15% in these areas.[63-65] China, Taiwan, Korea, and Vietnam are largely free of infection[66]; the high rates (>15%) in Melanesia are attributed to the E strain.[67] Another major endemic focus of HTLV-I infection occurs in the Caribbean, where rates of seropositivity in Jamaica, Trinidad and Tobago, Martinique, Barbados, St. Lucia, Haiti, and the Dominican Republic range between 5% and 14%.[68-70] Foci of seropositivity are present in South and Central America, including Brazil (>15% in Bahia), Colombia, Venezuela, Guyana, Surinam, Panama, and Honduras. One survey in Chile identified pockets of HTLV-I in persons of non-African descent, which raises the possibility of a trans-Pacific viral passage.[71] Study of DNA from pre-Columbian mummies have confirmed that the molecular characteristics of this Chilean virus are closely related to the virus from Japan.[72] In Trinidad and Tobago, seropositivity (5% to 14%) is restricted almost exclusively to persons of African descent, even though individuals of Indo-Asian ethnic background have shared a common environment for over a century.[70] In Jamaica, varying rates of seropositivity occur in different regions, with the highest rates (10%) of positivity observed in the lowland, high-rainfall areas.[73] Seropositivity is found more frequently in persons of lower socioeconomic class and persons who lack formal education.[69,74-77] Men and women attending clinics for sexually transmissible infections have the highest rate of seropositivity (>15%).[75] The rate in blood donors is lower (1% to 5%).[78,79]

In the United States, large-scale blood supply screening has documented rates of HTLV-I/II of 0.43 per 1,000; approximately half of the positives result from HTLV-II infection.[78,79] In a significant proportion of HTLV-I–positive cases, the donor either has links to an endemic area or a history of risk-related behaviors, such as injecting drugs.[78] Smaller regional surveys and studies of military populations show similar patterns: persons of African ancestry have higher rates of seropositivity. Migrant populations from Okinawa to Hawaii, from the Caribbean to the United States, and from the Caribbean to the United Kingdom are at risk of HTLV positivity, as are those who experience exposure through sexual contact or blood transfusion in viral endemic areas.[74,80-84]

Surveys from the Ivory Coast, Ghana, Nigeria, Zaire, Kenya, and Tanzania document that rates of HTLV-I seropositivity are similar to those in the Caribbean region (5% to 14%).[85,86]

In Europe, occasional infections are detected among migrants from endemic areas. Middle East surveys have been largely negative, with the exception of Iranian Jews from northeastern Iran (Mashhad) and emigrants from that area now residing in Israel and New York.[87,88] Surveys in southern India and Indonesia have identified some HTLV-I positives; the Seychelles in the Indian Ocean are highly endemic for HTLV-I (>15%).[89]

HTLV-II has a more restricted distribution than HTLV-I, primarily occurring in the Americas and parts of West and Central Africa.[90-92] A major reservoir exists in injection drug users in the United States and southern Europe, with rates ranging from 10% to 15% and higher.[93,94] Amer-Indians residing in North, Central, and South America have varying rates of positivity for HTLV-II (5% to 30%). Pockets of infection are present among the Seminoles in south Florida and the Pueblo and Navajo in New Mexico but not among various tribes in Alaska.[95-97] In Central America, the Guaymi Indians residing in northeastern Panama near the Costa Rican border have high seropositive rates (>15%), but this does not hold true for the Guaymi living in southwest Panama.

MOLECULAR EPIDEMIOLOGY

Human T-Cell Lymphotropic Virus Type I

Phylogenetic analysis has been used to classify HTLV-I into five major molecular and geographic subtypes[98] (Fig. 165-6): (1) a cosmopolitan (C) subtype isolated all over the world (endemic to Caribbean, South America), (2) a Japanese (J) subtype, (3) a West African (WA) subtype, (4) a Central African (CA) subtype, and (5) a Melanesian (M) subtype (Papua New Guinea, Melanesia, and Australian aborigines). HTLV-I isolates from different parts of the world show a high degree of nucleotide sequence conservation, in contrast to HIV-1 and HIV-2, in which considerable genomic variability occur. Isolates of HTLV-I from Japan, the West Indies, the Americas, and Africa share 97% or greater homology.[99-101] Even the most divergent HTLV-I, isolated in Melanesia, is 92% homologous with a prototypic Japanese isolate.[102] The majority of the nucleotide differences are single point mutations that do not correlate with specific disease patterns. Studies of the LTR by restriction fragment length polymorphisms covering the major HTLV-I endemic area (and including new specimens) have demonstrated that variations are more linked to the geographic origin of the infected individuals and not to the patient's clinical status.[103-105] The genetic variability of HTLV-I appears to reflect the geographic origin, and hence possibly the migration patterns of ancient populations carrying the virus.

An African origin of HTLV-I is supported by the occurrence of HTLV-I clusters in Africa[50,85,106] and among persons of African descent residing in the Caribbean but not among other migrant populations residing in the region.[70] On the other hand, clusters of HTLV-I in southern Japan and northeastern Iran and the isolation of a closely related virus in aboriginal peoples of Papua New Guinea, Northern Australia, and the Solomon Islands make the origin of this class of virus more difficult to discern.[67-70,107-109] Speculation exists regarding the spread of HTLV-I, possibly through the African slave trade: for example, there is a high degree of homology between viruses isolated from West Africa and those from the Caribbean.[98] The difference between Japanese and Caribbean isolates varies by as much as 2%, indicating a close homology but distinctive origin,[9,110] whereas a variant African strain was isolated from Zaire that differs from the West African strain by about 3% to 4%.[71,102,111] The most significant variant HTLV-I viruses have been isolated from seropositive individuals in various parts of Melanesia.[112] The original isolate was obtained from an unacculturated hunter-gatherer tribe, the Hagahai, residing in the highlands of Papua New Guinea. Their only contact with the outside world had occurred within weeks of the original blood sample collection. These viruses differ by as much as 9% to 10% from the prototype Japanese strain and by as much as 4% to 6% from the viruses isolated in Australia and the Solomon Islands.[108,112,113] In some cases, these strains have been isolated

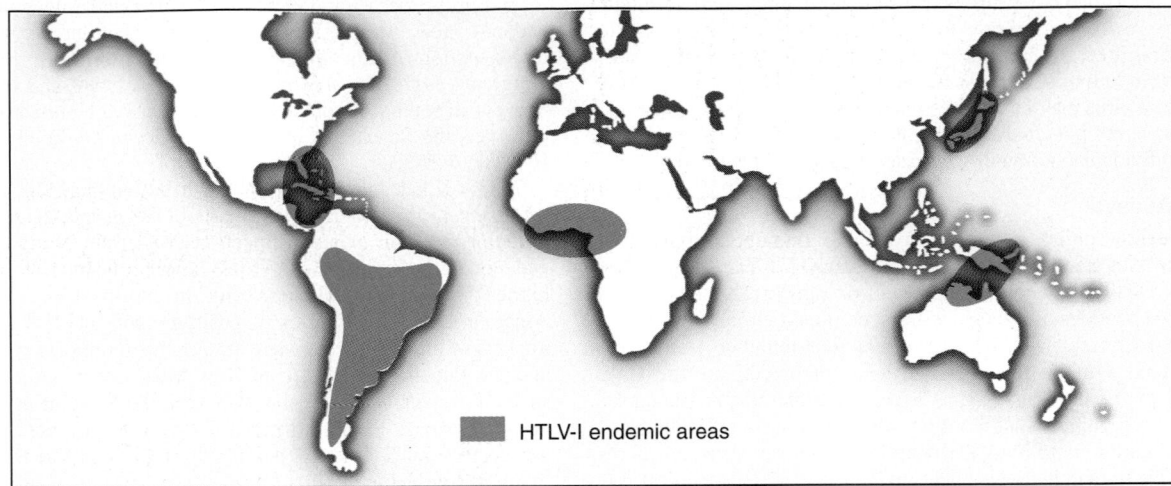

FIGURE 165-6. Geographic distribution of five molecular subtypes of human T-cell lymphotropic virus type I (HTLV-I). HTLV-I is endemic to some regions of the world, especially southwest Japan, the Caribbean islands, the countries surrounding the Caribbean basin, parts of South America, parts of Central Africa and Papua New Guinea.

from persons with adult T-cell leukemia and HTLV-associated myelopathy, suggesting that despite genetic differences the virus has pathogenic potential.[103,114]

Human T-Cell Lymphotropic Virus Type II

Compared with HTLV-I, the origin of HTLV-II is less certain. HTLV-II is documented in intravenous drug users in the United States and Italy.[94,115-119] A natural reservoir has recently been detected among various Amer-Indian populations residing in the United States and Central and South America.[95,97,120-127] It has also been shown to be endemic in South America (Brazil) and Southeast Asia (Vietnam). In 1986, the prevalence of HTLV-II infections in intravenous drug users (IVDUs) in the borough of Queens in New York City was shown to be 18%. The presence of HTLV-II infection in culturally and geographically distinct Indian groups in North America, Central America (Panama), and South America (Argentina, Brazil, Colombia, and Chile) led to the speculation that HTLV-II may have originated in the New World. However, the degree of homology between HTLV-I and HTLV-II supplemented by the finding of HTLV-II infection among certain groups in Africa supports a common geographic origin in Africa. Based on the relative divergence of nucleotide sequences of the env, gag, and LTR regions,[124,128-130] HTLV-II is classified into three subtypes: HTLV-IIa (previously known as HTLV-II Mo), HTLV-IIb (formerly HTLV-II NRA), and HTLV-IIc.[131] Molecular epidemiologic studies have shown that HTLV-IIa is the predominant infection in IVDUs in urban North America.[132] HTLV-IIb is the predominant subtype in Indian groups in Panama, Colombia, and Argentina. HTLV-IIc appears to be confined to urban Brazilian and Indian populations.

Virus isolates from these populations have revealed that HTLV-IIa and HTLV-IIb differ molecularly by approximately 2% to 4%.[133,134] The Tat protein of HTLV-IIb is 25 amino acids longer and is a more potent transactivator of the HTLV-II LTR than the corresponding HTLV-IIa protein.[130] The in vivo significance of this functional difference is not known. On the other hand, HTLV-IIc has LTR and env sequences related to HTLV-IIa and tax sequences similar to those of HTLV-IIb.[124]

MODES OF TRANSMISSION

Table 165-2 summarizes the routes, modes, and co-factors associated with HTLV-I and -II transmission. Modes of viral transmission have been well characterized for HTLV-I. The available evidence suggests

that routes of transmission of HTLV-II are similar to those of HTLV-I. A discrete cellular receptor for both HTLV-I and HTLV-II has yet to be isolated but appears to reside on chromosome 17.[135-137] The three major reported routes of HTLV-I transmission are mother-to-child transmission, sexual transmission, and parenteral transmission.

Mother-to-Child Transmission

In contrast to mother-to-child transmission of HIV, wherein up to 30% of offspring of positive mothers acquire infection by the transplacental and/or perinatal route, breast-feeding is the predominant route of mother-to-child HTLV-I and HTLV-II transmission[138-141] and occurs through ingestion of infected milk-borne lymphocytes.[142] Both HTLV-I and HTLV-II viruses have been detected in breast milk.[143-145] In Japanese intervention trials,[139] while 20% of breastfed infants seroconvert to HTLV-I, only 1% to 2% of bottle-fed infants of HTLV-I–positive mothers become infected.[146] In prospective studies from Jamaica, a similar rate of transmission has been documented.[143]

TABLE 165-2 Transmission of Human T-Cell Lymphotropic Virus (HTLV) Types I and II

	HTLV Type I	HTLV Type II
Mode of Transmission		
Mother to infant		
Transplacental	Low efficiency	Not known
Breast milk	High efficiency	Probable but not quantified
Sexual		
Male to female	Most efficient	Yes but not quantified
Female to male	Efficient	Yes but not quantified
Male to male	Efficient	Not known
Parenteral		
Blood transfusion	Very efficient	Very efficient
Intravenous drug use	Efficient	More efficient
Cofactors of Transmission		
Elevated virus load		
Mother to infant	Yes	Not known
Heterosexual	Yes	Not known
Ulcerative genital lesions	Yes	Not known
Cellular transfusion products	Yes	Yes
Sharing of needles and paraphernalia	Yes	Yes

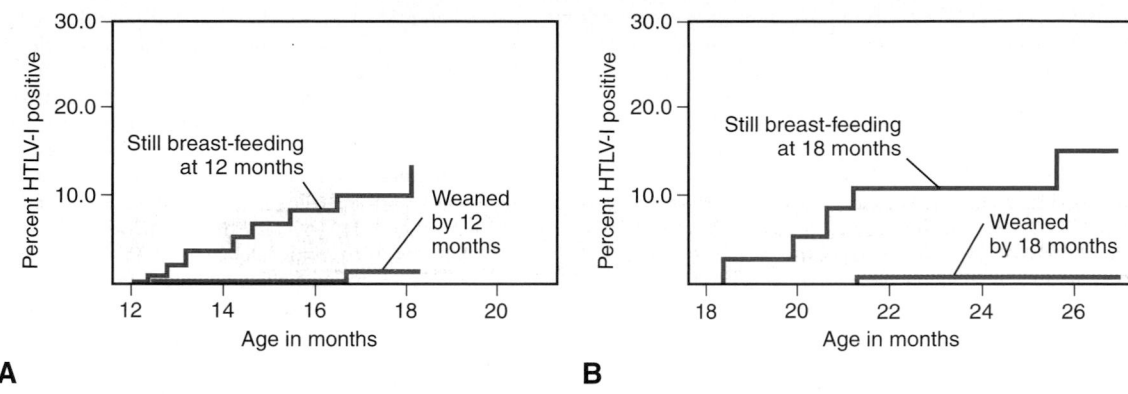

FIGURE 165-7. Incidence of human T-cell lymphotropic virus type I (HTLV-I) infection among children who were still HTLV-I negative **(A)** at 12 months and **(B)** at 18 months. The values are stratified according to whether a child had been weaned at 12 months (n = 84) or 18 months (n = 88) or was still being breast-fed beyond that age (n = 64 in A, n = 37 in B). *(From Wiktor SZ, Pate EJ, Rosenberg PS, et al. Mother-to-child transmission of human T-cell lymphotropic virus type I associated with prolonged breast-feeding. J Hum Virol. 1997;1:37-44, with permission.)*

During the first 6 months of life, maternal antibodies are present; in serial WBs, all bands often disappear before new bands appear as a result of neonatal infection. In some cases, breast-feeding had ceased up to several months before seroconversion, but study of cells from exposed but nonseroconverting children identified none with latent HTLV-I viral infection. The major predictor of maternal-to-child transmission is the viral load of the mother as measured by antibody titer and viral antigen level on short-term culture.[147,148] The presence of antibody to the tax[149,150] and/or env antigen has also been associated with transmission.[143,151,152] Transmission of HTLV-I has been shown to be inhibited by passive immunization with antibody against HTLV-I.[153]

Furthermore, the duration and timing of breast-feeding were strongly associated with the efficiency of transmission.[138,140,142,154,155] In a prospective study conducted in Jamaica,[142] among children born from HTLV-I–positive mothers in follow-up for more than 2 years, 32% of children breastfed for 12 months or longer were HTLV-I seropositive compared with 9% of those breastfed for less than 12 months (data shown in Fig. 165-7). These data strongly suggest that limiting the duration of breast-feeding to less than 12 months might significantly reduce mother-to-child transmission of HTLV-I. Follow-up studies indicated that seroconversion typically occurs in infants at the age of 1 to 3 years, with approximately 2% to 5% of HTLV-I infections resulting from maternal-to-child transmission in the first few years of life.[156,157] In many studies, no infants or children became newly infected after 2 years of age.[141] The early life infection may have considerable significance for subsequent risk for disease, particularly adult T-cell leukemia.[158]

HTLV-II transmission from mother to child is still controversial, as prospective surveys are still under investigation.[159] For instance, in studies of intravenous drug–using mothers who are HTLV-II positive, none transmitted the virus to their bottle-fed infants, whereas among Indians of the Gran Chaco (Argentina) and Kayapo (Brazil), a high rate (30% and 46%, respectively) of mother-to-child transmission was observed.[160] Among the Guaymi Indians of Panama, there is a 1% to 2% prevalence among preadolescent children.[161] This is consistent with early life infection and an excess of seropositive children when the mother is seropositive compared with the virtual absence of seropositive children when the mother is negative.[156,162]

Sexual Transmission

Sexual transmission of HTLV-I is bidirectional, with male-to-female transmission considered to be four times more likely than female-to-male transmission.[75,163] In a 10-year follow-up study of discordant couples, women had a 60% likelihood of being infected compared with only 0.4% for men.[75] Male-to-male sexual transmission was also supported by the higher prevalence of HTLV-I among men who have sex with men (15%) compared with the general population prevalence of 2.4%.[164] HIV-1 shares these routes of infection but appears to be an order of magnitude more infectious than HTLV-I.[164,165] This might reflect differences in viral load or the fact that HTLV-I is highly cell associated, whereas HIV-1 is both cell associated and cell free.

Several markers of sexual activity are associated with HTLV-I transmission. In one study of a sexually transmitted disease clinic in Jamaica, seropositivity in women was associated with a large number of sexual partners; no such association was observed among men.[75] In a study of homosexual men in Trinidad,[164] however, the number of lifetime partners was positively associated. Serologic evidence of HTLV-I infection has been associated with ulcerative (syphilis, herpes simplex virus type 2, and chancroid) and nonulcerative (gonorrhea and *Chlamydia*) sexually transmitted diseases.[75,165-167] These data suggest that the difference in HTLV-I prevalence between men and women may result from the low efficiency of female-to-male transmission and a potential role for cofactors that interrupt normal mucosal barriers and promote transmission. However, female-to-male transmission can occur in the absence of detectable cofactors.[168,169]

There are also other risk factors associated with sexual transmission. For HTLV-I, elevated antibody titer appears to correlate with virus load.[75,170] This has also been more directly shown by quantitative PCR.[171] In addition, the presence of anti-tax antibody has been shown to be associated with heightened transmission, possibly related to a state of virus proliferation induced by tax and measured indirectly by anti-tax antibody.[170] Host-related factors may also play a more important role than do virus-specific factors in determining HTLV-I viral load. A study evaluating the sequence of the gp46-coding region among 13 infected patients and their partners revealed that, although the gp46 sequences were identical within each married couple, the level of HTLV-I proviral DNA in the spouses often differed.[172]

Virus-positive mononuclear cells have been detected in semen.[173] This finding, coupled with the higher probability of male-to-female transmission, suggests that seminal fluid is a likely vehicle for transmission. More recently, the presence of HTLV-I DNA was found in cervicovaginal secretions from infected sex workers in Peru.[174,175] In the latter study, cervical shedding of HTLV-I DNA was detected in two thirds of the women and was highly correlated with the presence of cervicitis (30 polymorphonuclear cells within cervical mucus per ×100 microscopic field). Whether HTLV-I is a cause or an effect of cervicitis remains to be clarified. It is plausible that cervicitis, which is associated with cervical microulcerations, coinfections, and increased lymphocytes, results in shedding of cell-associated HTLV-I.

Sexual transmission of HTLV-II has been difficult to study because of the frequent coincidence of intravenous drug use in the study populations. In virtually all studies of female prostitutes, intravenous drug use was the major risk factor for seropositivity.[171,176] Preliminary analyses of the Guaymi in Panama and Amer-Indians residing in New Mexico report an excess concordance for seropositivity among married couples; this pattern is consistent with that observed in cross-sectional studies of HTLV-I suggesting seroconversion.[177] In a recent serosurvey of Guaymi Indians, both univariate and multivariate analyses demonstrated that among women, early age at first intercourse (younger than 13 years), number of lifetime sexual partners, and number of long-term sexual relationships were significantly associated with HTLV-II positivity.[178] Among men, intercourse with prostitutes was associated with HTLV-II seropositivity.

Parenteral Transmission

Parenteral transmission, through either transfusion or injection drug use, is another major mode of HTLV transmission. Because the HTLV viruses are cell associated, transmission via transfusion of cellular components (e.g., whole blood, packed cells, and platelet concentrates) is highly efficient. Seroconversion rates of 44% to 63% have been reported in recipients of HTLV-I–infected cellular components in endemic areas.[179-182] However, seroconversion has not been associated with plasma or cryoprecipitate; donor units of whole blood or packed cells are less likely to be associated with transmission the longer they are stored in the blood bank, presumably because of the loss of white blood cell viability.[180] In retrospective surveys,[180,183] the rate of transmission decreased to near zero when blood components were stored for more than 14 days compared with 47% transmission for a storage period of 14 days or less.

Transmission of HTLV-II has been well documented in 50% of the recipients of known units of positive blood.[184] Parenteral drug abuse has been associated with transmission of HTLV-I and -II, but most HTLV-positive drug abusers are HTLV-II infected. This suggests a difference in transmission efficiency of the two viruses among drug abusers.[88] Risk factors for seroconversion include sharing of drug abuse paraphernalia and "booting," which involves blood exposure (notably the use of an eye dropper rather than a syringe), a common

practice before the wide availability of disposable syringes.[185] This circumstance may help to explain the exceptionally high rates of seropositivity in older drug users, as this method was associated with a larger exchange of blood during the sharing of equipment. Transmission involving "casual contact" does not appear to occur.

Although rare, the only documented illness linked to HTLV-I or -II transfusion transmission is HAM/TSP.[146] ATL has not been reported in association with transfusion. In recognition of this risk, testing of donated blood for HTLV viruses has been routine in the United States since 1988.[40] HTLV seroprevalence is generally low among hemophiliacs unless they were multiply transfused with cellular blood products before the institution of routine screening.[186,187] In developing countries, however, blood transfusions remain a major risk factor for HTLV infection. Routine screening of donated blood in the United States led to the recognition that HTLV infection is more common than was previously thought, with roughly 0.05% noted in two large studies of 600,000 U.S. volunteers.[79] Among U.S. blood donors who are confirmed HTLV positive, approximately half are HTLV-I positive and the other half are HTLV-II positive. A case of HTLV-I infection in several transplant recipients sharing the same donor have also been documented.[188] Genomic sequencing revealed 100% homology in these cases.

In 1993, the Centers for Disease Control and Prevention issued guidelines for counseling persons infected with HTLV-I and HTLV-II. Seropositive persons are advised not to donate blood, semen, body organs, or other tissues and not to share needles or syringes, not to breast-feed infants, and to use latex condoms to prevent sexual transmission. They are also advised to communicate their HTLV-positive status to their physician. Health care and laboratory workers who experience a needle stick or skin or mucous membrane exposure in the absence of protective barriers have never been documented to have acquired HTLV-I or -II infection.[189] A single Japanese health care worker who experienced a "microtransfusion" when a loaded syringe punctured his foot has been documented to have seroconverted to HTLV-I.

Demographic Patterns

HTLV-I–associated ATL rarely occurs in the pediatric age group, but cases have been reported in 5- and 6-year-old children.[65] Most ATL cases occur in middle age, between the late 30s and late 50s (Fig. 165-8) rather than in the older age groups that are typical of B-cell lymphomas in developed countries. HTLV-I is the major single cause of lymphoma before age 50 in viral endemic areas. Compared with Japan, where the peak occurrence is between 50 and 60 years of age, cases in the Caribbean and Brazil among persons of African descent peak approximately a decade earlier, and immigrants from these regions to nonen-

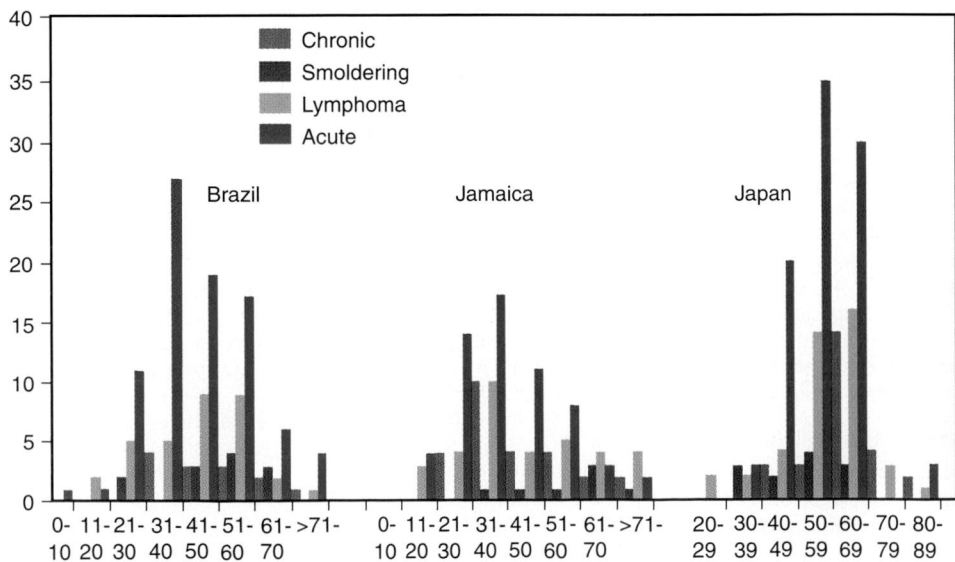

FIGURE 165-8. Age distribution for adult T-cell leukemia/lymphoma (ATL) patients compared with the age-specific prevalence of ATL in patients from Brazil, Japan, and Jamaica (the Caribbean). *(Courtesy of Barry Haralad and Dr. Maria Pombo-Oliveira.)*

demic areas sustain this differential in the age-specific incidence of this disease.[62,69] The male-to-female ratio for ATL cases is approximately 1:1, which contrasts with the excess of infections among females in adulthood (see later). Virtually all ATL patients have a seropositive mother, and the decline in attributable risk for ATL after age 50 argues that early-life exposure to HTLV-1 contributes substantially to subsequent risk of lymphoid malignancy with a latency of decades.

For HTLV-II there is also a characteristic age-dependent rise in seroprevalence.[122] However, recent data from studies of endemic populations of Amer-Indians document that, although the shape of the curve resembles that for HTLV-I, there are no differences between male and female patients at any age.[161,190] In intravenous drug–using populations, unusually high rates of seropositivity in older age groups have been linked to the sharing of primitive "eyedropper" injection equipment, raising the possibility of a "cohort effect" resulting from changes in injection techniques.[93] There is no evidence for the frequent occurrence of a virus-positive antibody-negative state.

IMMUNOLOGY OF HUMAN T-CELL LYMPHOTROPIC VIRUS INFECTIONS

Humoral Immune Responses

Antibodies to the various antigens of HTLV-I occur at high levels in carriers and among patients with ATL and HAM/TSP. During primary infection, the pattern of antibody responses (see Fig. 165-5) demonstrates that the first specific antibodies to emerge after primary HTLV infection are directed against the Gag proteins. Over several weeks to months, anti-envelope antibodies appear, and about 50% of infected individuals develop detectable antibodies to p40 Tax protein.[170,191] Antibody titers vary from patient to patient and are significantly higher in patients with HAM/TSP and among those at risk for this disease. The antibody titers correlate with the proviral burden.[143,192] This may explain the paradoxical finding of high antibody titers among women who transmit HTLV-I to their infants through prolonged breast-feeding. The explanation for this paradox is that transplacental maternal antibodies appear to protect the infant from infection in the first months of life, but subsequently the infant becomes infected via maternal virus transmitted via breast milk. Other than this apparent protection afforded the baby through passive antibody transfer from an in-fected mother at birth, there are few data to suggest that humoral immune responses play a role in protection from disease or that they induce immune injury. The high titers observed in patients with HAM/TSP and ATL seem to reflect immune responses in the context of high viral burden observed in these conditions rather than indicate a direct correlate of disease risk.

Cellular Immunity

CTLs targeted at viral antigens play an essential role in the regulation of viral expression.[193] Among chronic carriers, infected individuals mount a strong cell-mediated immune response to the virus and up to 1% of CD8-positive CTLs can recognize at least one epitope of HTLV virus.[58,59,61,194-196] Freshly isolated cells have substantial expression of activation markers, indicating that these cells have recently encountered the Tax antigen.[59,61,193] A proposed model of this viral interaction with the host cell–mediated immune response is shown in Figure 165-9. In this model the dynamic equilibrium between viral replication and immune destruction is mediated through Tax overexpression, causing CD4 target cell proliferation, and a robust cell-mediated response to the antigen in particular, causing CTL-mediated lysis of these HTLV-I–infected CD4 cells.[59,61,196,197] As a consequence of ongoing Tax proliferation, there is a cell-associated expansion of HTLV-I genome containing CD4$^+$ cells and a compensatory expansion of CD8$^+$ CTLs. As the number of CD4$^+$ cells containing the HTLV-I genome expand, HTLV-I antigens are expressed on the cell surface and become targets for CD8$^+$-mediated cytotoxic killing. The role for CD8$^+$-mediated cell killing as the primary means of viral suppression may explain the epidemiologic observation that recipients of infected blood products who are also receiving exogenous immunosuppressive medications are more susceptible to HTLV-1 infection. The blunting of cell-mediated immune responses by exogenous immunosuppression dampens the host capacity to clear initial virus infection.[198]

The role of CD4$^+$-mediated T-helper 1 (Th1) responses in upregulating the CTL response is not well characterized. However, an association between class I HLA haplotypes and protection against HAM/TSP suggests that carriers of certain antigen-presenting motifs augment the efficient control of HTLV-I–containing cells. Thus, carriers of the HLA-A 02 haplotype are less likely to develop HAM/TSP. Because carriers at risk for this disease and patients with HAM/TSP

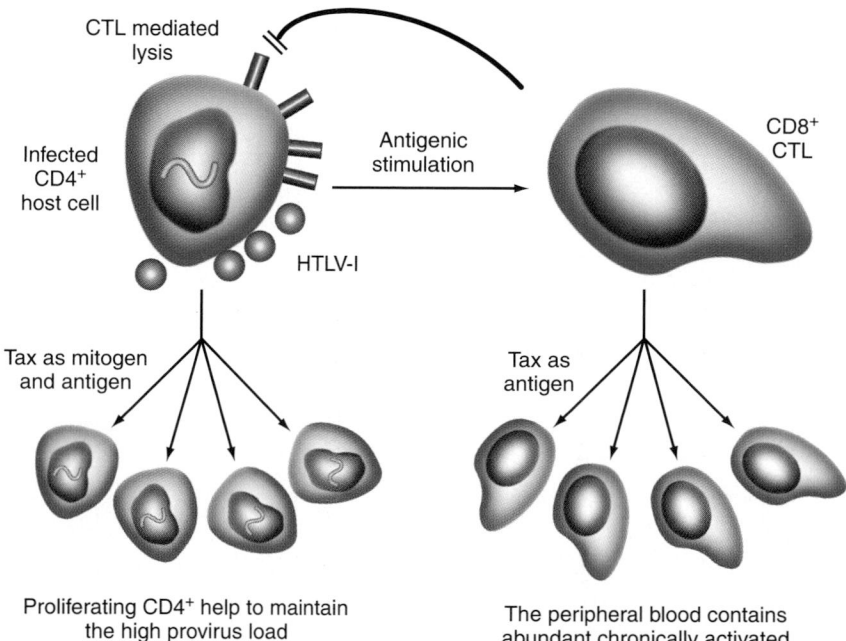

FIGURE 165-9. A model of CD8$^+$ cytotoxic T-lymphocyte–mediated control of human T-cell lymphotropic virus type I (HTLV-I) infection. HTLV-I infects CD4$^+$ T lymphocytes with expansion of infection primarily via cell replication. As HTLV-I–specific antigens, particularly tax, are expressed, a robust CD8$^+$ cytotoxic T-lymphocyte response is generated. The inability of some persons to control HTLV-I expansion is thought to contribute to disease pathogenesis. See text for details. *(From Bangham CRM. HTLV-1 infections. J Clin Pathol. 1999;53:581-586, with permission.)*

CTL mediated lysis

Infected CD4$^+$ host cell

HTLV-I

Antigenic stimulation

CD8$^+$ CTL

Tax as mitogen and antigen

Proliferating CD4$^+$ help to maintain the high provirus load

Tax as antigen

The peripheral blood contains abundant chronically activated CTL specific to HTLV-I have high viral loads and are less likely to be HLA-A 02 positive, it is postulated that such patients are less able to mount a strong cell-mediated immune response.[196,199-201]

CLINICAL MANIFESTATIONS OF HUMAN T-CELL LYMPHOTROPIC VIRUS INFECTIONS

Clinical disease associated with HTLV-I is rare; it develops in approximately 3% to 5% of carriers over their lifetime. The risk of developing disease is related to age, means of infection, and the immune competency of the host. Acute seroconversion is associated with no clinical syndrome; the time from infection to seroconversion can vary from 1 to 2 months, as seen with transfusion cases. The time from seroconversion to disease can vary from 18 weeks with HAM/TSP to many decades with ATL. As summarized in Table 165-3, there are a wide range of clinical conditions that are linked to HTLV-I, some of which result from virally induced cell transformation, as in the case of ATL, whereas others appear to result from the indirect effects of virus-induced immunologic perturbation.

Human T-Cell Lymphotropic Virus Type I–Associated Malignancies

ATL was first recognized in 1977, before the discovery of HTLV-I, as an aggressive leukemia/lymphoma of mature T lymphocytes with varied clinical manifestations: generalized lymphadenopathy, visceral involvement, hypercalcemia, cutaneous skin involvement, lytic bone lesions, and peripheral blood involvement with cells manifesting pleotropic features ("flower cells") in a large number of cases.[202] The skin lesions seen in ATL are varied and include localized or diffuse papules, nodules (Fig. 165-10), plaques (Fig. 165-11), erythematous patches, and diffuse erythroderma. Biopsy of skin lesions reveals dermal or epidermal infiltration with malignant lymphocytes. So-called Pautrier's microabscesses may also be noted in the dermis, as in mycosis fungoides. Biopsy of bone lytic lesions reveals osteoclast activation and bone resorption (Fig. 165-12), often without infiltration by ATL cells. It has been suggested that Tax transactivation and production of parathyroid hormone–related protein and other cytokines are responsible for hypercalcemia, osteoclast activation, and lytic bone lesions seen in this disorder.[203,204] The lifetime risk of development of ATL in HTLV-I carriers is estimated at 1% to 4%.[205] The latent period from infection to actual development of disease is estimated to be 30 to 50 years.[206]

The Lymphoma Study Group in Japan[207] has classified ATL into four clinical types based on clinical features and cell morphology: smoldering (5%), chronic (19%), lymphoma/leukemia (19%), and acute (57%) types. Transformation from the smoldering or chronic phase to the acute form can occur at any point during the course of the disease progression. Figure 165-13 shows the characteristic morphologic features of the leukemia cells observed for the three clinical types.

1. *Smoldering ATL*—characterized by 5% or more abnormal T cells in the peripheral blood (see Fig. 165-13, 1) with a normal total lymphocyte count, the presence of skin lesions, and, occasionally, pulmonary involvement. There is no hypercalcemia, lymphadenopathy, or other visceral involvement. Serum lactate dehydrogenase (LDH) levels may be elevated. This phase is often indolent and can last for years. Smoldering ATL may clinically resemble mycosis fungoides/Sézary syndrome with cutaneous involvement presenting as erythema or as infiltrative plaques or tumors, and Pautrier's microabscesses may be observed.
2. *Chronic ATL*—characterized by an absolute lymphocytosis ($\geq 4 \times 10^9$/L) with a T-cell lymphocytosis ($>3.5 \times 10^9$/L) that resembles chronic T-lymphocytic leukemia. LDH may be increased up to twice the normal limit. Cells from chronic ATL patients are relatively uniform in size and nuclear configuration (see Fig. 165-13, 2). Patients may have lymphadenopathy, hepatomegaly, splenomegaly, and skin and pulmonary involvement. No hypercalcemia, ascites, pleural effusion, or involvement of the central nervous system (CNS), bone, or gastrointestinal tract is present. The median survival time for patients with chronic ATL is 24 months.
3. *Lymphoma/leukemia ATL*—characterized by lymphadenopathy in the absence of lymphocytosis. Lymph node involvement with ATL

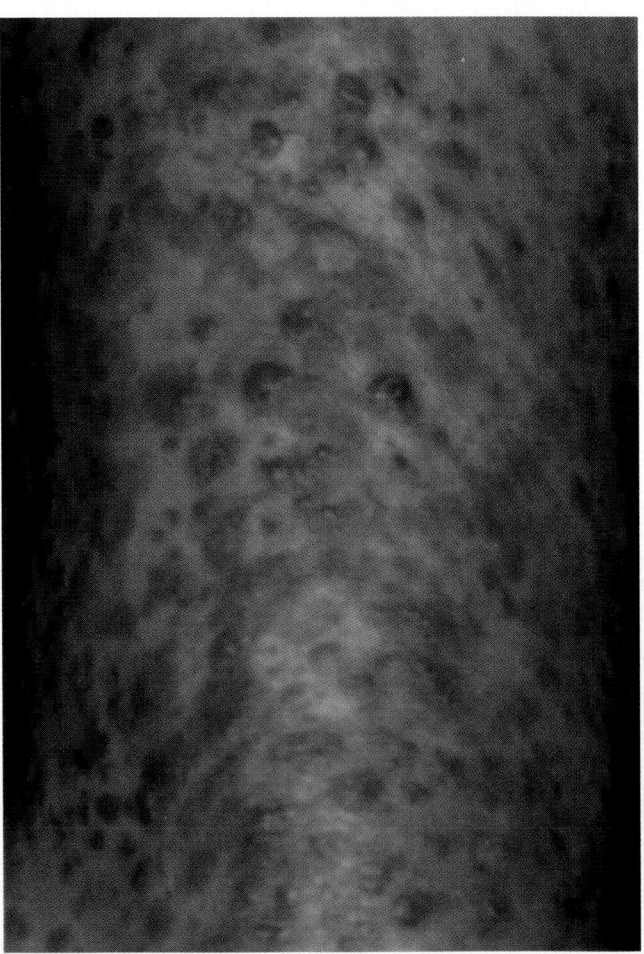

FIGURE 165-10. Multiple skin papules and nodules in a patient with adult T-cell leukemia.

TABLE 165-3 Human T-Cell Lymphotropic Virus (HTLV)–Associated Diseases

Disease	HTLV Type I	HTLV Type II
Children		
Infective dermatitis	++++	No
Persistent lymphadenopathy	++	No
Adults		
Adult T-cell leukemia/lymphoma	++++	No
HTLV-associated myelopathy	++++	+++
Infective dermatitis	+++	No
Polymyositis	++	Unknown
Uveitis	+++	Unknown
HTLV-associated arthritis	++	Unknown
Sjögren's syndrome	++	Unknown
Strongyloidiasis	++	Unknown
Pulmonary infiltrative pneumonitis	++	Unknown
Invasive cervical cancer	+	Unknown
Small cell carcinoma of lung	+	Unknown

++++, very strong evidence; +++, strong evidence; ++, possible association; +, weak association; No, evidence does not support association; Unknown, no data to support association or lack of association.

must be histologically proved. The median survival time is approximately 10 months.

4. *Acute ATL*—distinguished by increased numbers of leukemic T cells with characteristic pleomorphic morphology (see Fig. 165-13, 3), skin lesions, systemic lymphadenopathy, hepatosplenomegaly, and metabolic disorders, especially hypercalcemia. Lytic bone lesions and visceral involvement are common. Acute ATL has a poor prognosis, with a median survival time of 6.2 months.

Most patients with the acute and lymphoma types die within 6 months of diagnosis (Fig. 165-14), particularly if hypercalcemia is a presenting sign.[208] In general, the smoldering type is the least aggressive; the chronic type has a relatively poor prognosis, with death occurring within a few years of diagnosis.[207] The cause of death is usually an explosive growth of tumor cells, hypercalcemia, bacterial sepsis, and other infections observed in patients with immunodeficiency. Sometimes ATL presents as a T-cell non-Hodgkin's lymphoma with no other clinical features of ATL save for monoclonal integration of HTLV-I in the proviral DNA of the tumor cells. These cases are termed lymphoma-type ATL and are indistinguishable from peripheral T-cell lymphomas.

The malignant T cells of ATL are mature (terminal deoxynucleotide transferase–negative [TdT⁻]) and CD4⁺CD8⁻ and have increased IL-2R α-chain (CD25/TAC antigen) expression.[209-211] All subtypes have a monoclonal integration of HTLV-I proviral DNA into the cellular genome, indicating that the malignant T cells are monoclonal and originated from a single HTLV-I–infected T cell.[212] The site of integration, although constant for a given patient, varies between individual patients and does not appear to be related to the pathogenesis of the virus.

Pneumocystis jirovecii pneumonia, cryptococcal meningitis, disseminated fungal infections, and other opportunistic infections are often present[213] and contribute to a rapid progression to death for patients with acute and lymphoma-type ATL. The fact that *Strongyloides stercoralis* appears to be a common concurrent infection[214-216] has led to speculation that *Strongyloides* infection may be a cofactor in the development of ATL. The state of immune compromise resulting from HTLV-I infection is not due to the type of immune ablation observed in HIV-1, even though CD4 cells are infected by HTLV-I; rather, the immunodeficiency is associated with rapidly proliferating malignancy, and the pattern of opportunistic infections is typical for those reported in patients with aggressive non-Hodgkin's lymphomas. The diagnosis of ATL is based on testing serum for HTLV-I antibodies in patients with the characteristic features of T-cell malignancy. Proviral HTLV-I can also be detected in the blood leukemia cells or in biopsy specimens from the patient, but such studies require a laboratory with specialized expertise. In some cases of ATL from patients from high-risk areas with typical clinical features, antibody is absent but a defective integrated virus with a retained *tax* function can be detected with sophisticated molecular probes.[217]

HTLV-I has also been associated with isolated cases of other malignancies. In one case of small cell cancer of the lung, viral sequences were monoclonally integrated into the tumor cells. There is a statistically increased prevalence of HTLV-I antibodies in patients with invasive carcinoma of the cervix, but this could result from shared sexual risk factors rather than a direct effect of HTLV-I in carcinogenesis.[218] Surveys of hospitalized Japanese patients with a variety of malignancies show elevated rates of HTLV-I infections compared with "normal populations," but here, too, biases such as blood transfusion might have influenced the association.

Differential diagnosis of ATL include other T-cell malignancies such as non-Hodgkin's lymphoma, mycosis fungoides, and Sézary syndrome. Recent studies have shown that mycosis fungoides is an indolent T-cell lymphoma that is distinguished from other lymphomas by its initial appearance. ATL should be suspected in any patient from an endemic population with a T-cell malignancy. The presence of circulating "flower cells," hypercalcemia, and skin lesions is highly suggestive. Leukemic cells are characteristically TdT⁻, CD4⁺, and CD25⁺. Laboratory detection and confirmation can be based on testing for

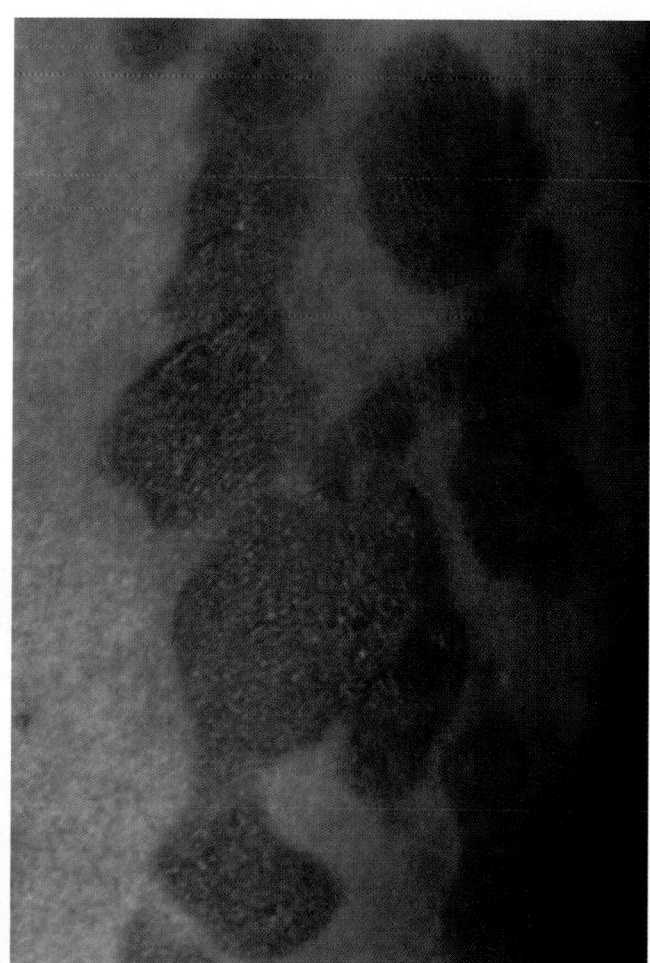

FIGURE 165-11. Multiple red plaques in a patient with adult T-cell leukemia.

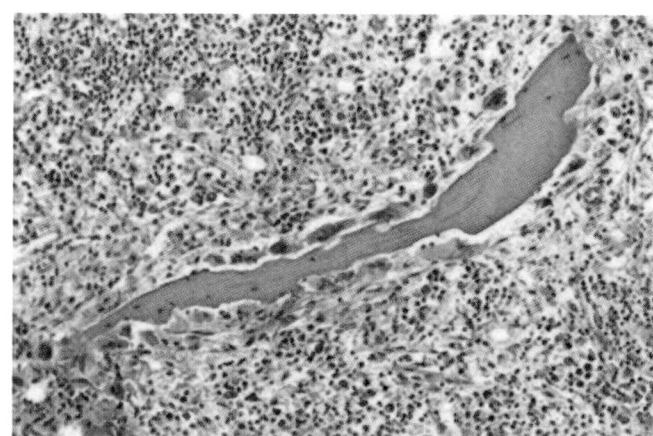

FIGURE 165-12. Microscopic examination of lytic bone lesions reveals osteoclast proliferation and bone resorption.

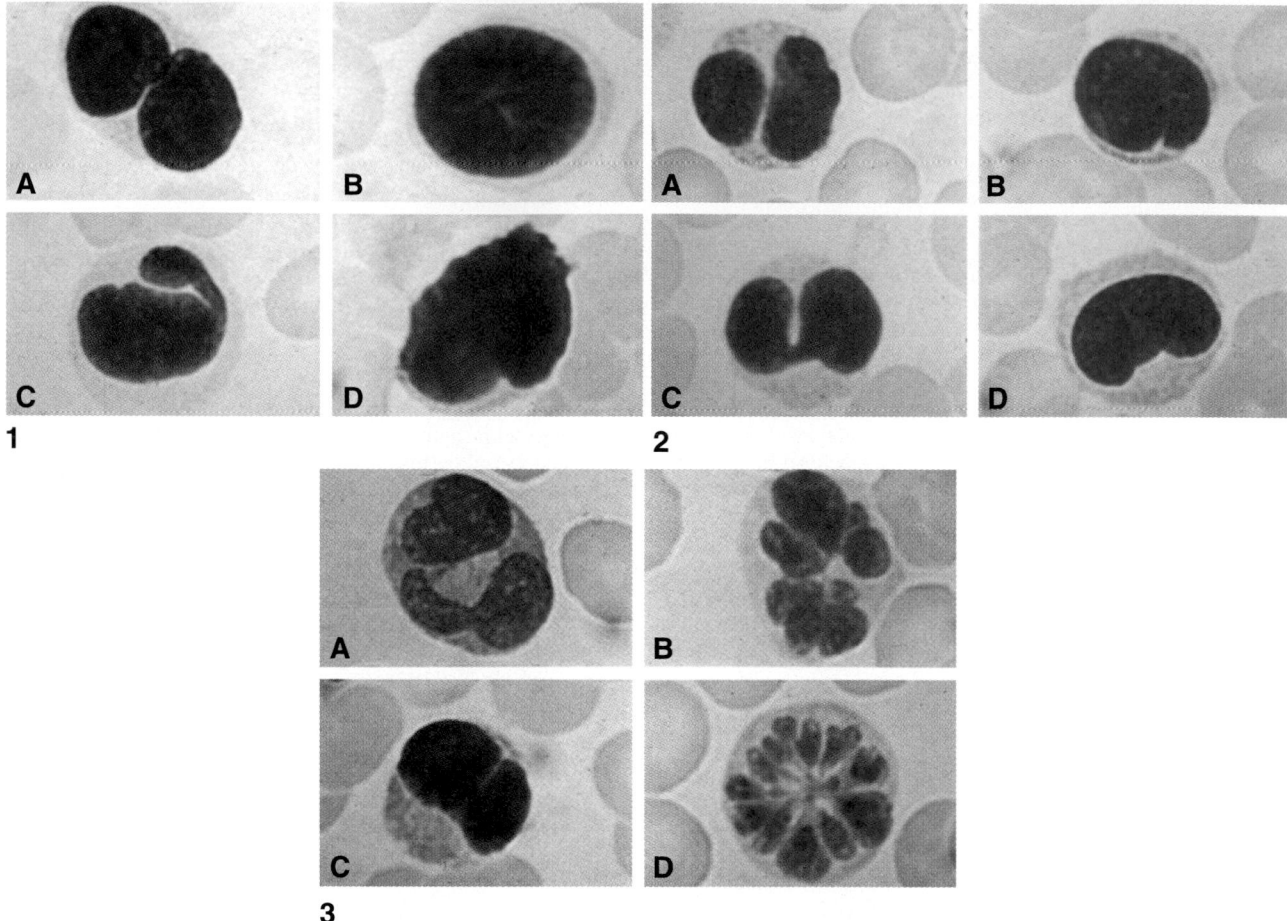

FIGURE 165-13. Photomicrographs of typical peripheral blood leukemic cells from (1) smoldering adult T-cell leukemia/lymphoma (ATL), (2) chronic ATL, and (3) acute ATL. Details of the features are discussed in text.

1. Smoldering ATL. The ATL cells are relatively large (mean diameter, 15 μm in these patients and they do not have cytoplasmic granules or vacuoles. The lobulated nuclei are bifoliate or trifoliate. Most of the nuclei exhibit indentations or clefts.
2. Chronic ATL. Cells from chronic ATL patients are relatively uniform in size and nuclear configuration. They are smaller than those from acute or smoldering ATL (mean diameter, 13 μm), they rarely contain small vacuoles, and they do not contain azurophilic granules. Cells in this type of ATL also exhibit lobular division of their nuclei. Most of the lobulated nuclei are bifoliate or trifoliate **(A, C).** Many cells also exhibit deep nuclear indentation rather than lobulation **(B, D).**
3. Acute ATL. Numerous abnormal lymphocytes, which vary considerably in size (mean diameter, 15 μm) and cytoplasmic basophility, are seen in acute ATL. Cells from 30% of these patients contain small vacuoles, but not azurophilic granules. Most of the cells characteristically exhibit lobular division of their nuclei; most nuclei are multifoliate **(A, B, D)**, although **C** shows a bifoliate nucleus separated by a deep indentation. Cells with such a nuclear configuration are known as flower cells. These leukemic cells show relatively coarsely clumped chromatin and are not morphologically homogeneous.

anti–HTLV-I antibody or demonstrating via Southern blotting of monoclonal integration of proviral DNA in the malignant cells.

Human T-Cell Lymphotropic Virus Type I–Associated Neurologic Disease

HAM/TSP (or chronic progressive myelopathy) is a chronic progressive demyelinating disease that affects the spinal cord and white matter of the CNS.[219-222] The lifetime incidence of HAM/TSP in HTLV-I carriers is estimated to be less than 5%.[223] While mainly affecting adults, particularly females, cases occasionally occur in children under the age of 10. The overrepresentation of females probably reflects the predominance of infections among adult females due to sexually acquired infection. This association is consistent with the hypothesis that HAM/TSP has a shorter incubation period than does ATL, where the male-to-female ratio is 1.[224] The typical time of onset is in the fourth decade of life. Additionally, HAM/TSP has been linked to blood transfusion, and some cases are acutely progressive.[146,225,226] Familial clusters have also been reported.

The onset of disease is often subtle, and the florid clinical picture of HAM/TSP is not always seen at first presentation. A single symptom or physical sign may be the only evidence of early HAM/TSP. Symptoms often begin with a stiff gait,[224] progressing (usually slowly) to increasing spasticity and lower extremity weakness,[227] back pain, urinary incontinence,[228,229] and impotence in men. Patients may complain of sensory symptoms such as tingling, "pins and needles," and burning. Vibration sense is frequently impaired.[230] Hyperreflexia of lower limbs, often with clonus and Babinski's sign, may be detected. Hyperreflexia of upper limbs as well as positive Hoffmann's and Trömner's signs are also frequent. Exaggerated jaw jerk is seen in some patients. Ataxia may develop.

Nuclear magnetic resonance images may be normal or show atrophy of the spinal cord and nonspecific lesions in the brain.[228,231-233] The syndrome is significantly different from classic multiple sclerosis. HAM/TSP follows a slow course, without the waxing and waning of symptoms, without the changes in affect, and without the multiple nuclear magnetic resonance scan abnormalities characteristic of multiple

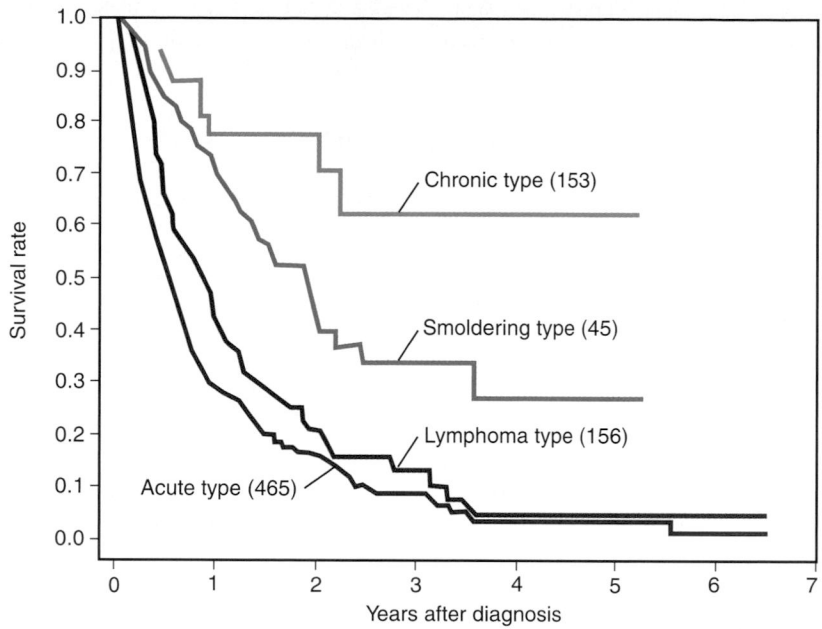

FIGURE 165-14. Survival patterns of different adult T-cell leukemia/lymphoma (ATL) subtypes after polychemotherapy. Acute and lymphoma-type ATL have the poorest prognosis after chemotherapy (see text). *(From Tsukasaki K, Ikeda S, Murata K, et al. Characteristics of chemotherapy-induced clinical remission in long survivors with aggressive adult T-cell leukemia/lymphoma. Leuk Res. 1993;17:157-166, with permission.)*

sclerosis. Varying degrees of brain parenchymal degeneration have also been described, with reactive astrocytosis and perivascular mononuclear cell infiltration.[220] These mononuclear cells are predominantly CD8+ lymphocytes,[221,234] suggesting that an immune mechanism may play a role in the development of HAM. High frequency of cytolytic T cells with specificity directed against MHC class I–restricted epitopes derived from the Tax protein has also been observed.[235]

It is possible that HTLV-I induces an autoimmune-like process through molecular mimicry (an autoimmune model) or through indirect effects on immune function (a cytotoxic model). In the former model, it is postulated that HTLV-I infection activates autoreactive T cells, which then cause autoimmune destruction within the CNS.[236,237] In the latter model, it is postulated that HTLV-I infects glial cells, which subsequently induces a cytotoxic immune response against these cells, leading to demyelination.[234]

HAM/TSP patients characteristically have HTLV-I antibodies or antigens in the blood and cerebrospinal fluid (CSF). CSF may show mild lymphocytic pleocytosis; lobulated lymphocytes with morphologic similarity to ATL cells ("flower cells") (see Fig. 165-13) also may be present in the blood and CSF.[227] Mild to moderate increases in protein may be observed in the CSF, and oligoclonal bonds with specific reactivity to HTLV-I antigens are detected.[224,227] Elevated levels of lymphokines such as IL-6, tumor necrosis factor-α, and IL-2 are elevated in the CSF. However, attempts to document the presence of HTLV-I in the demyelinated lesion have not demonstrated a direct role of the virus in the target cell.

Differential diagnoses of HAM include multiple sclerosis, toxic neuropathies, malnutrition, and HIV or syphilis infection. The diagnosis is suspected in unexplained CNS disease with loss of pyramidal tract functions and is confirmed by testing sera for HTLV-I antibodies. In contrast to lymphocytes in ATL, HTLV-I–infected lymphocytes in HAM are oligoclonal or polyclonal, rather than monoclonal.

Other Diseases Associated with Human T-Cell Lymphotropic Virus Type I

Polymyositis of skeletal muscle is frequently associated with HTLV-I seropositivity in viral endemic areas. These cases are indistinguishable from polymyositis seen in HTLV-I nonendemic areas. A large joint polyarthropathy has been reported in Japan

among elderly patients.[238,239] A distinguishing feature of these cases is the presence of HTLV-I–producing cells in the synovial infiltrate. Recently a unique form of uveitis has been observed in HTLV-I–positive individuals. These cases account for about 30% to 40% of idiopathic uveitis in HTLV-I endemic areas.[240] The first evidence of an association of HTLV-I infection with uveitis was reported by Ohba and colleagues[241] in Japan, who detected ocular involvement in patients with ATL, HAM/TSP, and asymptomatic carriers. The ocular manifestations were then classified into three groups: (1) opportunistic infections and tumor infiltration in ATL patients; (2) ocular alterations in HAM/TSP patients, including Sjögren's syndrome, retinal pigmentary degeneration, optic atrophy, vitreous opacities, cotton-wool spots, and retinal vasculitis; and (3) HTLV-I uveitis in asymptomatic carriers. Proviral DNA of HTLV-I was identified in 60% of T cells from intraocular fluid of these patients.[241,242] HTLV-I–associated infiltrative pneumonitis has also been reported in some individuals in Japan.[243,244]

The association of HTLV-I with parasitic infestations (e.g., *Strongyloides*) refractory to treatment has also been interpreted to suggest that HTLV-I may have immunosuppressive effects.[215,245,246] A variety of subclinical perturbations in hematologic markers such as depressed hemoglobin and lymphopenia have been reported in healthy HTLV-I carriers.[247]

The infective dermatitis (rash) syndrome was first shown to be HTLV-I associated in Jamaica.[248] It appears to represent the first childhood HTLV-I syndrome. Patients are born of HTLV-I–positive mothers and experience a syndrome of "failure to thrive." They are prone to refractory generalized eczema and infection with saprophytic *Staphylococcus* and *Streptococcus* bacteria that are suppressed by chronic antibiotic therapy and recur when the therapy is stopped. This syndrome usually emerges early in life, in the first few years after birth, and in cases followed for many years that persist into adulthood. Anecdotal cases emerging in adolescence suggest that some infective dermatitis cases may result from infection at older age. It is postulated that infective dermatitis is an immunodeficiency syndrome induced by HTLV-I. Interestingly, some patients go on to develop ATL and HAM/TSP.[249,250] Further study of the pathogenesis of this syndrome should provide valuable insights into the pathogenesis of HTLV-I–associated diseases.

Other possible pediatric consequences of HTLV-I infection include the persistent lymphadenopathy syndrome, which has been identified among offspring of HTLV-I–positive women.[143,251] Its relationship to HTLV-I is unclear because the virus has not been detected in many children with this syndrome. It is possible that it represents an immunologic response to the virus, because some children with the syndrome have seroconverted later than most children exposed through breast-feeding. Others are persistently virus antibody negative but show a modest elevation in CD8 cells.

Whether coinfection with HTLV-I and HIV-1 results in a more rapid progression to AIDS is controversial. Further data from prospectively followed cohorts are needed to clarify this association. It is noteworthy that coinfected persons have increased CD4 counts but still develop opportunistic infections.

Diseases Associated with Human T-Cell Lymphotropic Virus Type II

HTLV-II remains an orphan virus without clear disease association other than an emerging link to HAM/TSP. The original isolations of HTLV-II came from patients diagnosed with T-cell hairy cell leukemia. In one of these cases, the tumor involved B cells, whereas HTLV-II was in the T cells. HTLV-II has been associated with certain rare hematologic malignancies, including atypical hairy cell leukemia,[3,252] and with some cases of large granular lymphocytic leukemia[253] and mycosis fungoides.[254] It is possible that these leukemias are the same entity. Systematic surveys have not identified a clear association of this type of lymphoid malignancy with HTLV-II, suggesting that these patients may be coincidentally infected. Prospective studies of blood donors who are HTLV-II infected have shown that they are at increased risk for HAM/TSP,[255] although the incidence is lower than that reported for HTLV-I carriers.[8,226] HTLV-II viral load appears to be lower in these patients than does the HTLV-I load.[226,256] One prospective study of HTLV-II–positive drug users showed an excess of asthma-related deaths and an increased frequency of skin and soft tissue infections.[257] In contrast to the possible association between HTLV-I and accelerated HIV-1 progression, some studies of persons coinfected with HIV-1 and HTLV-II suggest a protective effect, especially among those with high HTLV-II levels, possibly as a result of chemokine overproduction.[258] HTLV-II has also been linked with neurodegenerative disorders characterized by spastic paraparesis and varying degrees of ataxia.[8,259] The virus has been isolated from a patient with a chronic progressive neurologic disease indistinguishable from HAM/TSP.[260]

TREATMENT

There is no antiviral therapy for HTLV-I that has been proved to be successful. Hypothetically, some drugs that target HIV-1 reverse transcriptase might have antiviral effects on HTLV-I, but this has not been systematically studied. Furthermore, the exact role of HTLV-I in disease pathogenesis has not been clearly defined. In adult T-cell leukemia, the role of active viral replication is far from clear, because the tumor cell harbors many oncogenic mutations in cell regulatory genes that may not be reversible by treating the virus. HAM/TSP, with its high viral load and substantial cell-mediated immune response to HTLV-I, would appear to be a better candidate for antiviral treatment; however, therapy that targets the immune response itself may afford an equally attractive avenue for experimental treatment. Because of the shared routes of exposure, there is a potential opportunity to investigate the impact of antiviral therapy on persons coinfected with HTLV-I or -II and HIV-1, but such studies have not been undertaken to determine if, for example, viral load of HTLV-I or -II is modulated by anti–HIV-1 therapy. It is noteworthy, however, that a recent report indicated that high viral load of HTLV-II was protective against HIV-1 disease progression.

The mechanism appears to involve heightened production of CC chemokines (β chemokines) in relationship to HTLV-II infection, blocking HIV-1 infection.[258] Further systematic study of this relationship is warranted.

Adult T-Cell Leukemia

ATL patients are treated with antitumor chemotherapy, using therapies that are routinely used for non–HTLV-I–positive lymphoproliferative diseases. Patients with chronic and smoldering ATL are not treated or are given prednisone with or without cyclophosphamide. Patients with these more indolent forms of ATL, when treated with aggressive therapy, have a high rate of complicating infections resulting from the damaging effects of therapy on the bone marrow. The acute and lymphoma types of ATL are aggressive high-grade lymphomas with a generally poor prognosis, although some patients do respond to multidrug regimens with prolonged remission.[207,213,261] In Japan, large trials of vincristine, cyclophosphamide, prednisolone, and doxorubicin (VEPA) or VEPA-M (addition of methotrexate), as well as more complex 9- and 10-drug regimens, have shown some success but poor long-term survival.[261,262] Although initial response rates, even for the poorest risk categories, are over 50% and complete remissions are achieved in 20% of patients, these responses can be short lived, with relapses occurring in weeks to months.[261] Significant prognostic factors include poor performance status at diagnosis, age over 40 years, extensive disease, hypercalcemia, and high serum LDH level. Approximately 13% to 15% of patients with such aggressive cases experience a long-term survival (>2 years), which in one study was associated with several factors: complete remission, longer time to remission, and total doxorubicin dose. Relapses in these long-term survivors often occurred in the CNS and proved refractory to subsequent therapy. Studies using combinations of doxorubicin and etoposide have resulted in complete remission rates of 40%.

Experimental approaches that use monoclonal antibodies to IL-2R linked with cell toxins selectively targeted to the leukemic cells are being tested, with some evidence of at least partial responses.[211,263] Interferons have inhibitory effects on HTLV-I in vitro but produce complete remission in less than 10% of cases in vivo.[264,265] Preliminary data on a small number of cases in phase I trials using a combination of antiretrovirals and interferons have reported remission in some cases.[266,267] Recent laboratory-based studies, however, have demonstrated that this regimen does not cause direct cytotoxic killing of the leukemia cells and does not directly counteract virus-specific pathways of leukemogenesis.[268] Recently adopted therapy approaches for high-grade lymphomas such as allogeneic bone marrow transplantation and autologous stem cell transplantation have resulted in remission. One case showed reappearance of cells harboring the integration of HTLV-I previously observed in his leukemia cells, but the patient continues in clinical remission, suggesting a possible reversion to the preleukemic carrier state.[269]

Human T-Cell Lymphotropic Virus Type I–Associated Myelopathy and Tropical Spastic Paraparesis

Treatment of HAM/TSP with corticosteroids,[222,270] cyclophosphamide,[271] and interferon-α[272,273] benefits some patients, particularly when given early in clinical course or to some with rapidly progressive disease. Treatment with danazol, an androgenic steroid, has reversed urinary and fecal incontinence in some cases, but not the spastic limb disease or the underlying neurologic deficit.[274] Experimental studies such as the use of anti-TAC antibodies directed against CD25 IL-2R α-chain concurrently with zidovudine[275,276] and therapies currently being implemented for multiple sclerosis may be of value because the mechanism of immune pathogenesis may be shared between the two diseases. Given the emerging picture of disease pathogenesis with inability to control high viral expression, therapy with antiviral drugs would appear a promising avenue for research. However, such studies will be dependent on identifying agents that target cell-associated virus with sufficient specificity to block the HTLV-I reverse transcriptase and other viral specific targets.

PREVENTION

Guidelines for prevention and counseling have been developed for HTLV-I and HTLV-II by a Centers for Disease Control and Prevention Working Group.[277] Standard prevention approaches address each of the major avenues of transmission and are similar for both viruses: screen blood, eliminate breast-feeding by known infected mothers (or, where not feasible, limit breast-feeding to the first 6 months of life), and advise use of condoms.

The value of blood donor screening has been well documented in Japan, where up to 15% of HTLV-I infections have been eliminated. In areas where the infection is not endemic, such as the United States, the cost-effectiveness of screening has been questioned, but because of the risk for HAM/TSP in the transfusion setting, all blood bank units in the United States are screened. However, because HTLV-I is transmitted only in blood units containing cells and not in plasma, plasma donations are not screened for HTLV-I.

In the United States, the official policy is that pregnant women who are HTLV-I positive should not breastfeed their infants. However, in developing countries where safe alternatives to breast-feeding may not be available, limiting breast-feeding to the first 6 months may afford some protection via maternal antibodies. The use of condoms is recommended for couples who are serodiscordant for HTLV infection. Given the relatively low frequency of sexual transmission for each sexual encounter, couples who desire a pregnancy could plan to have unprotected sex during periods of maximal fertility. Such decisions require careful discussion between physician and patient, and there are no absolute guidelines in this particular area.

Counseling seropositive patients involves a clear discussion of the distinction of HTLV from HIV. In addition, HTLV virus type should be defined by serologic methods, and the distinctions in disease associations of the two virus types should be emphasized. On a population level, prevention measures that have been developed for HIV infection are also applicable against HTLV. Because the populations at risk for HIV are also at risk for HTLV-I in viral endemic areas (e.g., persons at risk for sexually transmitted diseases, persons with high rates of partner exchange, commercial sex workers, etc.), HIV prevention guidelines also benefit those at risk for HTLV-I. Thus prevention measures that promote condom use, treatment of sexually transmitted infections, and decrease of high-risk exposures also prevent HTLV-I infection.

There is no therapy for HTLV-I infection and thus no chemoprophylaxis. Passive immunoprophylaxis is hypothetically effective as noted later in animal studies but has no practical clinical application given the low risk for transmission except through sexual, breast-feeding, and transfusion exposure where other prevention methods are more applicable. Although vaccines against HTLV-I are feasible, due to the low attack rate for disease, there has been no impetus to develop or market an HTLV-I vaccine. This decision is based on the observation that although the incidence of disease is not dissimilar to the estimated incidence of hepatocellular carcinoma in hepatitis B antigen carriers, there is no acute morbidity comparable for HTLV-I as there is for hepatitis B–induced acute hepatitis.

Experimentally, vaccines containing whole virus and recombinant HTLV-I envelope antigens have successfully prevented HTLV-I infection in monkey and rabbit models. Protection correlates with the presence of neutralizing antibodies, indicating that humoral immunity can be an effective barrier against infection even when the challenge is cell associated.[278] The HTLV-I envelope is relatively highly conserved and neutralizing antibody appears to protect against challenge with even major strain variants, consistent with the conclusion that a single serotype protects against all variants. Thus, a synthetic vaccine against one HTLV-I isolate could protect against other HTLV-I isolates. A vaccine that induces cell-mediated immune responses in nonhuman primate studies has also been shown to be effective. Whether a vaccine will ever be implemented in human populations in endemic areas has been questioned.

SUMMARY

The study of HTLV-I and -II represents an important chapter in the history of contemporary medicine. In the years since the discovery of the first human leukemia virus, significant progress has been made in the understanding of the epidemiology and modes of transmission of HTLV. The mechanisms for HTLV transmission have been found to be similar to those for HIV but less efficient. Knowledge of HTLV-associated diseases has expanded since the discovery of the relationship between HTLV-I and ATL and between HTLV-I and HAM/TSP and includes a growing array of syndromes of altered immunity and malignant potential. Based on current knowledge, mortality resulting directly from the effects of the virus is probably between 5% and 10% among carriers during their lifetime, and morbidity may be twice as high.

HTLV viruses offer new avenues for expanding knowledge of disease causation and provide a conceptual model for exploring disease pathogenesis. Additional examples of viruses of this class with shared properties of long latency, low-level replication, and cellular tropism to other tissues are candidate agents for unexplained autoimmune, immunodeficiency, and neurologic diseases, and some human malignancies. Critical to this process will be the development of techniques for detecting and growing these putative viruses. The complete pathogenesis of diseases induced by these viruses remains unclear. With approximately 10 to 20 million people estimated to be infected by HTLV-I,[279] coupled with the lack of effective therapy, preventive strategies such as screening of blood supply and avoidance of or limited breast-feeding represent the global approach to control the spread of the virus. Such measures, however, are not always readily applicable in the developing countries.

REFERENCES

1. Poiesz BJ, Ruscetti FW, Gazdar AF, et al. Detection and isolation of type C retrovirus particles from fresh and cultured lymphocytes of a patient with cutaneous T-cell lymphoma. Proc Natl Acad Sci U S A. 1980;77:7415-7419.
2. Poiesz BJ, Ruscetti FW, Reitz MS, et al. Isolation of a new type C retrovirus (HTLV) in primary uncultured cells of a patient with Sezary T-cell leukaemia. Nature. 1981;19(294):268-271.
3. Kalynaraman VS, Sarngadharan MG, Robert-Guroff M, et al. A new subtype of human T-cell leukemia virus (HTLV-II) associated with a T-cell variant of hairy cell leukemia. Science. 1982;218:571-573.
4. Barre-Sinoussi F, Chermann J-C, Rey F, et al. Isolation of a T-lymphotropic retrovirus from a patient at risk for acquired immune deficiency syndrome (AIDS). Science. 1983;220:868-871.
5. Gallo RC, Sarin PS, Gelmann EP, et al. Isolation of human T-cell leukemia virus in acquired immune deficiency syndrome (AIDS). Science. 1983;220:865-867.
6. Gallo R, Salahuddin SZ, Popovic M, et al. Frequent detection and isolation of cytopathic retroviruses (HTLV-III) from patients with AIDS and at risk for AIDS. Science. 1984;224:500-503.
7. van Regenmortel MHV, Fauquet CM, Bishop DHL, et al. Virus Taxonomy: The Classification and Nomenclature of Viruses. The Seventh Report of the International Committee on Taxonomy of Viruses. San Diego; Academic Press; 2000.
8. Hjelle B, Appenzeller O, Mills R, et al. Chronic neurodegenerative disease associated with HTLV-II infection. Lancet. 1992;339:645-646.
9. Seiki M, Hattori S, Hirayama Y, Yoshida M. Human adult T-cell leukemia virus: Complete nucleotide sequence of the provirus genome integrated in leukemia cell DNA. Proc Natl Acad Sci U S A. 1983;80:3618-3622.
10. Lairmore MD, Albrecht B, D'Souza C, et al. In vitro and in vivo functional analysis of human T cell lymphotropic virus type 1 pX open reading frames I and II. AIDS Res Hum Retroviruses. 2000;16:1757-1764.
11. Shimotohno K, Takahashi Y, Shimizu N, et al. Complete nucleotide sequence of an infectious clone of human T-cell leukemia virus type II: An open reading frame for the protease gene. Proc Natl Acad Sci U S A. 1985;82:3101-3105.

12. Haseltine WA, Sodroski J, Patarca R, et al. Structure of 3′ terminal region of type II human T lymphotropic virus: Evidence for new coding region. Science. 1984;225:419-421.

13. Shimotohno K, Wachsman W, Takahashi Y, et al. Nucleotide sequence of the 3′ region of an infectious human T-cell leukemia virus type II genome. Proc Natl Acad Sci U S A. 1984;81:6657-6661.

14. Slamon DJ, Shimotohno K, Cline MJ, et al. Identification of the putative transforming protein of the human T-cell leukemia viruses HTLV-I and HTLV-II. Science. 1984;226:61-65.

15. Lee TH, Coligan JE, Sodroski JG, et al. Antigens encoded by the 3′-terminal region of human T-cell leukemia virus: Evidence for a functional gene. Science. 1984;226:57-61.

16. Ross TM, Pettiford SM, Green PL. The tax gene of human T-cell leukemia virus type 2 is essential for transformation of human T lymphocytes. J Virol. 1996;70:5194-5202.

17. Umehara F, Izumo S, Ronquillo AT, et al. Cytokine expression in the spinal cord lesions in HTLV-I-associated myelopathy. J Neuropathol Exp Neurol. 1994;53:72-77.

18. Yoshida M. Multiple viral strategies of HTLV-1 for dysregulation of cell growth control. Annu Rev Immunol. 2001;19:475-496.

19. Green PL, Xie YM, Chen IS. The Rex proteins of human T-cell leukemia virus type II differ by serine phosphorylation. J Virol. 1991;65:546-550.

20. Kiyokawa T, Seiki M, Iwashita S, et al. p27x-III and p21x-III, proteins encoded by the pX sequence of human T-cell leukemia virus type I. Proc Natl Acad Sci U S A. 1985;82:8359-8363.

21. Ahmed YF, Hanly SM, Malim MH, et al. Structure-function analyses of the HTLV-I Rex and HIV-1 Rev RNA response elements: Insights into the mechanism of Rex and Rev action. Genes Dev. 1990;4:1014-1022.

22. Hanly SM, Rimsky LT, Malim MH, et al. Comparative analysis of the HTLV-I Rex and HIV-1 Rev trans-regulatory proteins and their RNA response elements. Genes Dev. 1989;3:1534-1544.

23. Itoh M, Inoue J, Toyoshima H, et al. HTLV-1 rex and HIV-1 rev act through similar mechanisms to relieve suppression of unspliced RNA expression. Oncogene. 1989;4:1275-1279.

24. Nosaka T, Siomi H, Adachi Y, et al. Nucleolar targeting signal of human T-cell leukemia virus type I rex-encoded protein is essential for cytoplasmic accumulation of unspliced viral mRNA. Proc Natl Acad Sci U S A. 1989;86:9798-9802.

25. Siomi H, Shida H, Nam SH, et al. Sequence requirements for nucleolar localization of human T cell leukemia virus type I pX protein, which regulates viral RNA processing. Cell. 1988;55:197-209.

26. Bogerd HP, Tiley LS, Cullen BR. Specific binding of the human T-cell leukemia virus type I Rex protein to a short RNA sequence located within the Rex-response element. J Virol. 1992;66:7572-7575.

27. Grassmann R, Berchtold S, Aepinus C, et al. In vitro binding of human T-cell leukemia virus rex proteins to the rex-response element of viral transcripts. J Virol. 1991;65:3721-3727.

28. Yip MT, Dynan WS, Green PL, et al. Human T-cell leukemia virus (HTLV) type II Rex protein binds specifically to RNA sequences of the HTLV long terminal repeat but poorly to the human immunodeficiency virus type 1 Rev-responsive element. J Virol. 1991;65:2261-2272.

29. Bakker A, Li X, Ruland CT, et al. Human T-cell leukemia virus type 2 Rex inhibits pre-mRNA splicing in vitro at an early stage of spliceosome formation. J Virol. 1996;70:5511-5518.

30. Watanabe CT, Rosenblatt JD, Bakker A, et al. Negative regulation of gene expression from the HTLV type II long terminal repeat by Rex: Functional and structural dissociation from positive posttranscriptional regulation. AIDS Res Hum Retroviruses. 1996;12:535-546.

31. Albrecht B, D'Souza CD, Ding W, et al. Activation of nuclear factor of activated T cells by human T-lymphotropic virus type 1 accessory protein p12(I). J Virol. 2002;76:3493-3501.

32. Ding W, Albrecht B, Kelley RE, et al. Human T-cell lymphotropic virus type 1 p12(I) expression increases cytoplasmic calcium to enhance the activation of nuclear factor of activated T cells. J Virol. 2002;76:10374-10382.

33. Franchini G. HTLV and immortalization/transformation: Current concepts and clinical relevance. AIDS Res Hum Retroviruses. 2001;17(suppl 1):S-5.

34. Trejo SR, Ratner L. The HTLV receptor is a widely expressed protein. Virology. 2000;268:41-48.

35. Richardson JH, Edwards AJ, Cruickshank JK, et al. In vivo cellular tropism of human T-cell leukemia virus type 1. J Virol. 1990;64:5682-5687.

36. Kinoshita K, Yamanouchi K, Ikeda S, et al. Oral infection of a common marmoset with human T-cell leukemia virus type-I (HTLV-I) by inoculating fresh human milk of HTLV-I carrier mothers. Jpn J Cancer Res. 1985;76:1147-1153.

37. Ijichi S, Ramundo MB, Takahashi H, Hall WW. In vivo cellular tropism of human T cell leukemia virus type II (HTLV-II). J Exp Med. 1992;176:293-296.

38. Nagai M, Brennan MB, Sakai JA, et al. CD8+ T cells are an in vivo reservoir for HTLV-I. Blood. 2001;98:1858-1861.

39. Igakura T, Stinchcombe JC, Goon PK, et al. Spread of HTLV-I between lymphocytes by virus-induced polarization of the cytoskeleton. Science. 2003;299:1713-1716.

40. Centers for Disease Control and Prevention. Licensure of screening tests for antibody to human T-lymphotropic virus type 1. MMWR Morb Mortal Wkly Rep. 1988;37:736.

41. Madeleine MM, Wiktor SZ, Goedert JJ, et al. HTLV-I and HTLV-II world-wide distribution: Reanalysis of 4,832 immunoblot results. Int J Cancer. 1993;54:255-260.

42. Lipka JJ, Miyoshi I, Hadlock KG, et al. Segregation of human T cell lymphotropic virus type I and II infections by antibody reactivity to unique viral epitopes. J Infect Dis. 1992;165:268-272.

43. Centers for Disease Control and Prevention. Update: Serologic testing for human T-lymphotrophic virus type 1—United States. MMWR Morb Mortal Wkly Rep. 1992;41:259.

44. Roberts BD, Foung SK, Lipka JJ, et al. Evaluation of an immunoblot assay for serological confirmation and differentiation of human T-cell lymphotropic virus types I and II. J Clin Microbiol. 1993;31:260-264.

45. Kleinman SH, Kaplan JE, Khabbaz RF, et al. Evaluation of a p21e-spiked Western blot (immunoblot) in confirming human T-cell lymphotropic virus type I or II infection in volunteer blood donors. The Retrovirus Epidemiology Donor Study Group. J Clin Microbiol. 1994;32:603-607.

46. Lipka JJ, Santiago P, Chan L, et al. Modified Western blot assay for confirmation and differentiation of human T cell lymphotropic virus types I and II. J Infect Dis. 1991;164:400-403.

47. Blomberg J, Robert-Guroff M, Blattner WA, Pipkorn R. Type- and group-specific continuous antigenic determinants of HTLV. Use of synthetic peptides for serotyping of HTLV-I and -II infection. J Acquir Immune Defic Syndr. 1992;5:294-302.

48. Horal P, Hall WW, Svennerholm B, et al. Identification of type-specific linear epitopes in the glycoproteins gp46 and gp21 of human T-cell leukemia viruses type I and type II using synthetic peptides. Proc Natl Acad Sci U S A. 1991;88:5754-5758.

49. Gallo D, Diggs JL, Hanson CV. Evaluation of two commercial human T-cell lymphotropic virus Western blot (immunoblot) kits with problem specimens. J Clin Microbiol. 1994;32:2046-2049.

50. Garin B, Gosselin S, De The G, Gessain A. HTLV-I/II infection in a high viral endemic area of Zaire, Central Africa: Comparative evaluation of serology, PCR, and significance of indeterminate Western blot pattern. J Med Virol. 1994;44:104-109.

51. Gessain A, Mathieux R. HTLV-I "indeterminate" Western blot patterns observed in sera from tropical regions: The situation revisited. J Acquir Immune Defic Syndr Hum Retrovirol. 1995;9:316-319.

52. Heneine W, Khabbaz RF, Lal RB, Kaplan JE. Sensitive and specific polymerase chain reaction assays for diagnosis of human T-cell lymphotropic virus type I (HTLV-I) and HTLV-II infections in HTLV-I/II-seropositive individuals. J Clin Microbiol. 1992;30:1605-1607.

53. Saiki RK, Gelfand DH, Stoffel S, et al. Primer-directed enzymatic amplification of DNA with a thermostable DNA polymerase. Science. 1988;239:487-491.

54. Defer C, Coste J, Descamps F, et al. Contribution of polymerase chain reaction and radioimmunoprecipitation assay in the confirmation of human T-lymphotropic virus infection in French blood donors. Retrovirus Study Group of the French Society of Blood Transfusion. Transfusion. 1995;35:596-600.

55. Pate EJ, Wiktor SZ, Shaw GM, et al. Lack of viral latency of human T-cell lymphotropic virus type I. N Engl J Med. 1991;325:284.

56. Saito S, Ando Y, Furuki K, et al. Detection of HTLV-I genome in seronegative infants born to HTLV-I seropositive mothers by polymerase chain reaction. Jpn J Cancer Res. 1989;80:808-812.

57. Rios M, Khabbaz RF, Kaplan JE, et al. Transmission of human T cell lymphotropic virus (HTLV) type II by transfusion of HTLV-I-screened blood products. J Infect Dis. 1994;170:206-210.

58. Daenke S, Kermode AG, Hall SE, et al. High activated and memory cytotoxic T-cell responses to HTLV-1 in healthy carriers and patients with tropical spastic paraparesis. Virology. 1996;217:139-146.

59. Parker CE, Daenke S, Nightingale S, Bangham CR. Activated, HTLV-1-specific cytotoxic T-lymphocytes are found in healthy seropositives as well as in patients with tropical spastic paraparesis. Virology. 1992;188:628-636.

60. Parker CE, Nightingale S, Taylor GP, et al. Circulating anti-Tax cytotoxic T lymphocytes from human T-cell leukemia virus type I-infected people, with and without tropical spastic paraparesis, recognize multiple epitopes simultaneously. J Virol. 1994;68:2860-2868.

61. Hanon E, Hall S, Taylor GP, et al. Abundant tax protein expression in CD4+ T cells infected with human T-cell lymphotropic virus type I (HTLV-I) is prevented by cytotoxic T lymphocytes. Blood. 2000;95:1386-1392.

62. Kajiyama W, Kashiwagi S, Nomura H, et al. Seroepidemiologic study of antibody to adult T-cell leukemia virus in Okinawa, Japan. Am J Epidemiol. 1986;123:41-47.

63. Hinuma Y, Komoda H, Chosa T, et al. Antibodies to adult T-cell leukemia-virus-associated antigen (ATLA) in sera from patients with ATL and controls in Japan: A nation-wide sero-epidemiologic study. Int J Cancer. 1982;29:631-635.

64. Tajima K. The 4th nation-wide study of adult T-cell leukemia/lymphoma (ATL) in Japan: Estimates of risk of ATL and its geographical and clinical features. The T- and B-cell Malignancy Study Group. Int J Cancer. 1990;45:237-243.

65. Mueller N, Tachibana N, Stuver SO, et al. Epidemiologic perspectives of HTLV-I. In: Blattner WA, ed. Human Retrovirology: HTLV. Philadelphia: Lippincott-Raven; 1990:281-293.

66. Geng L, Zai N, Xiao Y, et al. Search for human T-lymphotropic virus type I carriers among northeastern Chinese. J Dermatol Sci. 1998;18:30-34.

67. Yanagihara R, Jenkins CL, Alexander SS, et al. Human T lymphotropic virus type I infection in Papua New Guinea: High prevalence among the Hagahai confirmed by Western analysis. J Infect Dis. 1990;162:649-654.

68. Bartholomew C, Saxinger WC, Clark JW, et al. Transmission of HTLV-I and HIV among homosexual men in Trinidad. JAMA. 1987;257:2604-2608.
69. Blattner WA, Saxinger C, Riedel D, et al. A study of HTLV-I and its associated risk factors in Trinidad and Tobago. J Acquir Immune Defic Syndr. 1990;3: 1102-1108.
70. Bartholomew C, Charles W, Saxinger C, et al. Racial and other characteristics of human T cell leukemia/lymphoma (HTLV-I) and AIDS (HTLV-III) in Trinidad. Br Med J. 1985;290:1243-1246.
71. Cartier L, Araya F, Castillo JL, et al. Southernmost carriers of HTLV-I/II in the world. Jpn J Cancer Res. 1993;84:1-3.
72. Li HC, Fujiyoshi T, Lou H, et al. The presence of ancient human T-cell lymphotropic virus type I provirus DNA in an Andean mummy. Nat Med. 1999;5:1428-1432.
73. Maloney EM, Murphy EL, Figueroa JP, et al. Human T-lymphotropic virus type I (HTLV-I) seroprevalence in Jamaica. II. Geographic and ecologic determinants. Am J Epidemiol. 1991;133:1125-1134.
74. Blattner WA, Nomura A, Clark JW, et al. Modes of transmission and evidence for viral latency from studies of human T-cell lymphotrophic virus type I in Japanese migrant populations in Hawaii. Proc Natl Acad Sci U S A. 1986;83:4895-4898.
75. Murphy EL, Figueroa JP, Gibbs WN, et al. Sexual transmission of human T-lymphotropic virus type I (HTLV-I). Ann Intern Med. 1989;111:555-560.
76. Murphy EL, Figueroa JP, Gibbs WN, et al. Human T-lymphotropic virus type I (HTLV-I) seroprevalence in Jamaica: I. Demographic determinants. Am J Epidemiol. 1991;133:1114-1124.
77. Chen YM, Ting ST, Lee CM, et al. Community-based molecular epidemiology of HTLV type I in Taiwan and Kinmen: Implication of the origin of the cosmopolitan subtype in northeast Asia. AIDS Res Hum Retroviruses. 1999;15:229-237.
78. Williams AE, Fang CT, Slamon DJ, et al. Seroprevalence and epidemiological correlates of HTLV-I infection in U.S. blood donors. Science. 1988;240:643-646.
79. Lee HH, Swanson P, Rosenblatt JD, et al. Relative prevalence and risk factors of HTLV-I and HTLV-II infection in US blood donors. Lancet. 1991;337: 1435-1439.
80. Dosik H, Denic S, Patel N, et al. Adult T-cell leukemia/lymphoma in Brooklyn. JAMA. 1988;259:2255-2257.
81. Cruickshank JK, Richardson JH, Morgan OS, et al. Screening for prolonged incubation of HTLV-I infection in British and Jamaican relatives of British patients with tropical spastic paraparesis. BMJ. 1990;300:300-304.
82. Catovsky D, Greaves MF, Rose M, et al. Adult T-cell lymphoma-leukaemia in Blacks from the West Indies. Lancet. 1982;1:639-643.
83. Ho GY, Nomura AM, Nelson K, et al. Declining seroprevalence and transmission of HTLV-I in Japanese families who immigrated to Hawaii. Am J Epidemiol. 1991;134:981-987.
84. Blattner WA, Kalynaraman VS, Robert-Guroff M, et al. The human type-C retrovirus, HTLV, in Blacks from the Caribbean region, and relationship to adult T-cell leukemia/lymphoma. Int J Cancer. 1982;30:257-264.
85. Delaporte E, Dupont A, Peeters M, et al. Epidemiology of HTLV-I in Gabon (Western Equatorial Africa). Int J Cancer. 1988;42:687-689.
86. Verdier M, Denis F, Sangare A, et al. Prevalence of antibody to human T cell leukemia virus type 1 (HTLV-1) in populations of Ivory Coast, West Africa. J Infect Dis. 1989;160:363-370.
87. Farid R, Etemadi M, Baradaran H, Nikkin B. Seroepidemiology and virology of HTLV-I in the city of Mashhad, northeastern Iran. Serodiagn Immunother Infect Dis. 1993;5:251.
88. Sidi Y, Meytes D, Shohat B, et al. Adult T-cell lymphoma in Israeli patients of Iranian origin. Cancer. 1990;65:590-593.
89. Lavanchy D, Bovet P, Hollanda J, et al. High seroprevalence of HTLV-I in the Seychelles. Lancet. 1991;337:248-249.
90. Gessain A, De The G. What is the situation of human T cell lymphotropic virus type II (HTLV-II) in Africa? Origin and dissemination of genomic subtypes. J Acquir Immune Defic Syndr Hum Retrovirol. 1996;13(suppl 1):S228-S235.
91. Gessain A, Mauclere P, Froment A, et al. Isolation and molecular characterization of a human T-cell lymphotropic virus type II (HTLV-II), subtype B, from a healthy Pygmy living in a remote area of Cameroon: An ancient origin for HTLV-II in Africa. Proc Natl Acad Sci U S A. 1995;92:4041-4045.
92. Goubau P, Liu HF, De Lange GG, et al. HTLV-II seroprevalence in pygmies across Africa since 1970. AIDS Res Hum Retroviruses. 1993;9:709-713.
93. Lee HH, Weiss SH, Brown LS, et al. Patterns of HIV-1 and HTLV-I/II in intravenous drug abusers from the middle Atlantic and central regions of the USA. J Infect Dis. 1990;162:347-352.
94. Biggar RJ, Buskell-Bales Z, Yakshe PN, et al. Antibody to human retroviruses among drug users in three east coast American cities. 1972-1976. J Infect Dis. 1991;163: 57-63.
95. Levine PH, Jacobson S, Elliott R, et al. HTLV-II infection in Florida Indians. AIDS Res Hum Retroviruses. 1993;9:123-127.
96. Biggar RJ, Taylor ME, Neel JV, et al. Genetic variants of human T-lymphotrophic virus type II in American Indian groups. Virology. 1996;216:165-173.
97. Hjelle B, Scalf R, Swenson S. High frequency of human T-cell leukemia-lymphoma virus type II infection in New Mexico blood donors: Determination by sequence-specific oligonucleotide hybridization. Blood. 1990;76:450-454.
98. Vidal AU, Gessain A, Yoshida M, et al. Phylogenetic classification of human T cell leukemia/lymphoma virus type I genotypes in five major molecular and geographical subtypes. J Gen Virol. 1994;75(Pt 12):3655-3666.

99. Gessain A, Gallo RC, Franchini G. Low degree of human T-cell leukemia/lymphoma virus type I genetic drift in vivo as a means of monitoring viral transmission and movement of ancient human populations. J Virol. 1992;66:2288-2295.
100. Komurian F, Pelloquin F, De The G. In vivo genomic variability of human T-cell leukemia virus type I depends more upon geography than upon pathologies. J Virol. 1991;65:3770-3778.
101. Malik KT, Even J, Karpas A. Molecular cloning and complete nucleotide sequence of an adult T cell leukaemia virus/human T cell leukaemia virus type I (ATLV/HTLV-I) isolate of Caribbean origin: Relationship to other members of the ATLV/HTLV-I subgroup. J Gen Virol. 1988;69(Pt 7):1695-1710.
102. Gessain A, Yanagihara R, Franchini G, et al. Highly divergent molecular variants of human T-lymphotropic virus type I from isolated populations in Papua New Guinea and the Solomon Islands. Proc Natl Acad Sci U S A. 1991;88:7694-7698.
103. Song KJ, Nerurkar VR, Pereira-Cortez AJ, et al. Sequence and phylogenetic analyses of human T cell lymphotropic virus type I from a Brazilian woman with adult T cell leukemia: Comparison with virus strains from South America and the Caribbean basin. Am J Trop Med Hyg. 1995;52:101-108.
104. Yang YC, Hsu TY, Liu MY, et al. Molecular subtyping of human T-lymphotropic virus type I (HTLV-I) by a nested polymerase chain reaction-restriction fragment length polymorphism analysis of the envelope gene: Two distinct lineages of HTLV-I in Taiwan. J Med Virol. 1997;51:25-31.
105. Voevodin A, al Mufti S, Farah S, et al. Molecular characterization of human T-lymphotropic virus, type 1 (HTLV-1) found in Kuwait: Close similarity with HTLV-1 isolates originating from Mashhad, Iran. AIDS Res Hum Retroviruses. 1995;11: 1255-1259.
106. Wiktor SZ, Piot P, Mann JM, et al. Human T cell lymphotropic virus type I (HTLV-I) among female prostitutes in Kinshasa, Zaire. J Infect Dis. 1990;161:1073-1077.
107. Yanagihara R, Nerurkar VR, Ajdukiewicz AB. Comparison between strains of human T lymphotropic virus type I isolated from inhabitants of the Solomon Islands and Papua New Guinea. J Infect Dis. 1991;164:443-449.
108. May JT, Stent G, Schnagl RD. Antibody to human T-cell lymphotropic virus type I in Australian aborigines. Med J Aust. 1988;149:104.
109. Meytes D, Schochat B, Lee H, et al. Serological and molecular survey for HTLV-I infection in a high-risk Middle Eastern group. Lancet. 1990;336:1533-1535.
110. Schulz TF, Calabro ML, Hoad JG, et al. HTLV-1 envelope sequences from Brazil, the Caribbean, and Romania: Clustering of sequences according to geographic origin and variability in an antibody epitope. Virology. 1991;184:483-491.
111. Hahn BH, Shaw GM, Popovic M, et al. Molecular cloning and analysis of a new variant of human T-cell leukemia virus (HTLV-ib) from an African patient with adult T-cell leukemia-lymphoma. Int J Cancer. 1984;34:613-618.
112. Sherman MP, Saksena NK, Dube DK, et al. Evolutionary insights on the origin of human T-cell lymphoma/leukemia virus type I (HTLV-I) derived from sequence analysis of a new HTLV-I variant from Papua New Guinea. J Virol. 1992;66:2556-2563.
113. Bastian I, Gardner J, Webb D, Gardner I. Isolation of a human T-lymphotropic virus type I strain from Australian aboriginals. J Virol. 1993;67:843-851.
114. Ajdukiewicz A, Yanagihara R, Garruto RM, et al. HTLV-1 myeloneuropathy in the Solomon Islands. N Engl J Med. 1989;321:615-616.
115. Robert-Guroff M, Weiss SH, Giron JA, et al. Prevalence of antibodies to HTLV-I, -II, and -III in intravenous drug abusers from an AIDS endemic region. JAMA. 1986;255:3133-3137.
116. Lee H, Swanson P, Shorty VS, et al. High rate of HTLV-II infection in seropositive i.v. drug abusers in New Orleans. Science. 1989;244:471-475.
117. Cantor KP, Weiss SH, Goedert JJ, Battjes RJ. HTLV-I/II seroprevalence and HIV/HTLV coinfection among U.S. intravenous drug users. J Acquir Immune Defic Syndr. 1991;4:460-467.
118. Khabbaz RF, Hartel D, Lairmore M, et al. Human T lymphotropic virus type II (HTLV-II) infection in a cohort of New York intravenous drug users: An old infection? J Infect Dis. 1991;163:252-256.
119. Calabro ML, Luparello M, Grottola A, et al. Detection of human T lymphotropic virus type II/b in human immunodeficiency virus type 1-coinfected persons in southeastern Italy. J Infect Dis. 1993;168:1273-1277.
120. Lairmore MD, Jacobson S, Gracia F, et al. Isolation of human T-cell lymphotropic virus type 2 from Guaymi Indians in Panama. Proc Natl Acad Sci U S A. 1990;87:8840-8844.
121. Heneine W, Kaplan JE, Gracia F, et al. HTLV-II endemicity among Guaymi Indians in Panama. N Engl J Med. 1991;324:565.
122. Maloney EM, Biggar RJ, Neel JV, et al. Endemic human T cell lymphotropic virus type II infection among isolated Brazilian Amerindians. J Infect Dis. 1992;166: 100-107.
123. Ishak R, Harrington WJ Jr, Azevedo VN, et al. Identification of human T cell lymphotropic virus type IIa infection in the Kayapo, an indigenous population of Brazil. AIDS Res Hum Retroviruses. 1995;11:813-821.
124. Eiraku N, Novoa P, da Costa FM, et al. Identification and characterization of a new and distinct molecular subtype of human T-cell lymphotropic virus type 2. J Virol. 1996;70:1481-1492.
125. Ferrer JF, Esteban E, Dube S, et al. Endemic infection with human T cell leukemia/lymphoma virus type IIB in Argentinean and Paraguayan Indians: Epidemiology and molecular characterization. J Infect Dis. 1996;174:944-953.
126. Ferrer JF, Del Pino N, Esteban E, et al. High rate of infection with the human T-cell leukemia retrovirus type II in four Indian populations of Argentina. Virology. 1993;197:576-584.

127. Ijichi S, Tajima K, Zaninovic V, et al. Identification of human T cell leukemia virus type IIb infection in the Wayu, an aboriginal population of Colombia. Jpn J Cancer Res. 1993;84:1215-1218.

128. Lee H, Idler KB, Swanson P, et al. Complete nucleotide sequence of HTLV-II isolate NRA: Comparison of envelope sequence variation of HTLV-II isolates from U.S. blood donors and U.S. and Italian i.v. drug users. Virology. 1993;196:57-69.

129. Takahashi H, Zhu SW, Ijichi S, et al. Nucleotide sequence analysis of human T cell leukemia virus, type II (HTLV-II) isolates. AIDS Res Hum Retroviruses. 1993;9:721-732.

130. Pardi D, Kaplan JE, Coligan JE, et al. Identification and characterization of an extended Tax protein in human T-cell lymphotropic virus type II subtype b isolates. J Virol. 1993;67:7663-7667.

131. Lewis MJ, Novoa P, Ishak R, et al. Isolation, cloning, and complete nucleotide sequence of a phenotypically distinct Brazilian isolate of human T-lymphotropic virus type II (HTLV-II). Virology. 2000;271:142-154.

132. Switzer WM, Pieniazek D, Swanson P, et al. Phylogenetic relationship and geographic distribution of multiple human T-cell lymphotropic virus type II subtypes. J Virol. 1995;69:621-632.

133. Hall WW, Takahashi H, Liu C, et al. Multiple isolates and characteristics of human T-cell leukemia virus type II. J Virol. 1992;66:2456-2463.

134. Kubo T, Zhu SW, Ijichi S, et al. Molecular characterization of human T-cell leukemia virus, type II (HTLV-II). AIDS Res Hum Retroviruses. 1994;10:465.

135. Sommerfelt MA, Williams BP, Clapham PR, et al. Human T cell leukemia viruses use a receptor determined by human chromosome 17. Science. 1988;242:1557-1559.

136. Tajima Y, Tashiro K, Camerini D. Assignment of the possible HTLV receptor gene to chromosome 17q21-q23. Somat Cell Mol Genet. 1997;23:225-227.

137. Gavalchin J, Fan N, Waterbury PG, et al. Regional localization of the putative cell surface receptor for HTLV-I to human chromosome 17q23.2-17q25.3. Virology. 1995;212:196-203.

138. Ando Y, Nakano S, Saito K, et al. Transmission of adult T-cell leukemia retrovirus (HTLV-I) from mother to child: Comparison of bottle- with breast-fed babies. Jpn J Cancer Res. 1987;78:322-324.

139. Hino S, Katamine S, Kawase K, et al. Intervention of maternal transmission of HTLV-1 in Nagasaki, Japan. Leukemia. 1994;8(suppl 1):S68-S70.

140. Kinoshita K, Amagasaki T, Hino S, et al. Milk-borne transmission of HTLV-I from carrier mothers to their children. Jpn J Cancer Res. 1987;78:674-680.

141. Ando Y, Matsumoto Y, Nakano S, et al. Long-term follow up study of vertical HTLV-I infection in children breast-fed by seropositive mothers. J Infect. 2003;46:177-179.

142. Wiktor SZ, Pate EJ, Rosenberg PS, et al. Mother-to-child transmission of human T-cell lymphotropic virus type I associated with prolonged breast-feeding. J Hum Virol. 1997;1:37-44.

143. Wiktor SZ, Pate EJ, Murphy EL, et al. Mother-to-child transmission of human T-cell lymphotropic virus type I (HTLV-I) in Jamaica: Association with antibodies to envelope glycoprotein (gp46) epitopes. J Acquir Immune Defic Syndr. 1993;6:1162-1167.

144. Kinoshita K, Hino S, Amagaski T, et al. Demonstration of adult T-cell leukemia virus antigen in milk from three sero-positive mothers. Gann. 1984;75:103-105.

145. Heneine W, Woods T, Green D, et al. Detection of HTLV-II in breastmilk of HTLV-II infected mothers. Lancet. 1992;340:1157-1158.

146. Gout O, Baulac M, Gessain A, et al. Rapid development of myelopathy after HTLV-I infection acquired by transfusion during cardiac transplantation. N Engl J Med. 1990;322:383-388.

147. Ureta-Vidal A, Angelin-Duclos C, Tortevoye P, et al. Mother-to-child transmission of human T-cell-leukemia/lymphoma virus type I: Implication of high antiviral antibody titer and high proviral load in carrier mothers. Int J Cancer. 1999;82:832-836.

148. Manns A, Miley WJ, Wilks RJ, et al. Quantitative proviral DNA and antibody levels in the natural history of HTLV-I infection. J Infect Dis. 1999;180:1487-1493.

149. Hirata M, Hayashi J, Noguchi A, et al. The effects of breastfeeding and presence of antibody to p40tax protein of human T cell lymphotropic virus type-I on mother to child transmission. Int J Epidemiol. 1992;21:989-994.

150. Sawada T, Tohmatsu J, Obara T, et al. High risk of mother-to-child transmission of HTLV-I in p40tax antibody-positive mothers. Jpn J Cancer Res. 1989;80:506-508.

151. Hino S, Katamine S, Miyamoto T, et al. Association between maternal antibodies to the external envelope glycoprotein and vertical transmission of human T-lymphotropic virus type I. Maternal anti-env antibodies correlate with protection in non-breast-fed children. J Clin Invest. 1995;95:2920-2925.

152. Yoshinaga M, Yashiki S, Oki T, et al. A maternal risk factor for mother-to-child HTLV-I transmission: Viral antigen-producing capacities in culture of peripheral blood and breast milk cells. Jpn J Cancer Res. 1995;86:649-654.

153. Takahashi K, Takezaki T, Oki T, et al. Inhibitory effect of maternal antibody on mother-to-child transmission of human T-lymphotropic virus type I. The Mother-to-Child Transmission Study Group. Int J Cancer. 1991;49:673-677.

154. Hino S, Yamaguchi K, Katamine S, et al. Mother-to-child transmission of human T-cell leukemia virus type-I. Jpn J Cancer Res. 1985;76:474-480.

155. Tsuji Y, Doi H, Yamabe T, et al. Prevention of mother-to-child transmission of human T-lymphotropic virus type-I. Pediatrics. 1990;86:11-17.

156. Nyambi PN, Ville Y, Louwagie J, et al. Mother-to-child transmission of human T-cell lymphotropic virus types I and II (HTLV-I/II) in Gabon: A prospective follow-up of 4 years. J Acquir Immune Defic Syndr Hum Retrovirol. 1996;12:187-192.

157. Kusuhara K, Sonoda S, Takahashi K, et al. Mother-to-child transmission of human T-cell leukemia virus type I (HTLV-I): A fifteen-year follow-up study in Okinawa, Japan. Int J Cancer. 1987;40:755-757.

158. Sugiyama H, Doi H, Yamaguchi K, et al. Significance of postnatal mother-to-child transmission of human T-lymphotropic virus type-I on the development of adult T-cell leukemia/lymphoma. J Med Virol. 1986;20:253-260.

159. Andersson S, Dias F, Mendez PJ, et al. HTLV-I and -II infections in a nationwide survey of pregnant women in Guinea-Bissau, West Africa. J Acquir Immune Defic Syndr Hum Retrovirol. 1997;15:320-322.

160. Black FL, Biggar RJ, Neel JV, et al. Endemic transmission of HTLV type II among Kayapo Indians of Brazil. AIDS Res Hum Retroviruses. 1994;10:1165-1171.

161. Vitek CR, Gracia FI, Giusti R, et al. Evidence for sexual and mother-to-child transmission of human T lymphotropic virus type II among Guaymi Indians, Panama. J Infect Dis. 1995;171:1022-1026.

162. Wilks R, Hanchard B, Morgan O, et al. Patterns of HTLV-I infection among family members of patients with adult T-cell leukemia/lymphoma and HTLV-I associated myelopathy/tropical spastic paraparesis. Int J Cancer. 1996;65:272-273.

163. Stuver SO, Tachibana N, Okayama A, et al. Transmission of human T cell leukemia/lymphoma virus type I among married couples in southwestern Japan: An initial report from the Miyazaki Cohort Study. J Infect Dis. 1993;167:57-65.

164. Bartholomew C, Saxinger WC, Clark JW, et al. Transmission of HTLV-I and HIV among homosexual men in Trinidad. JAMA. 1987;257:2604-2608.

165. Figueroa JP, Ward E, Morris J, et al. Incidence of HIV and HTLV-1 infection among sexually transmitted disease clinic attenders in Jamaica. J Acquir Immune Defic Syndr Hum Retrovirol. 1997;15:232-237.

166. Nakashima K, Kashiwagi S, Kajiyama W, et al. Sexual transmission of human T-lymphotropic virus type I among female prostitutes and among patients with sexually transmitted diseases in Fukuoka, Kyushu, Japan. Am J Epidemiol. 1995;141:305-311.

167. Figueroa JP, Morris J, Brathwaite A, et al. Risk factors for HTLV-I among heterosexual STD clinic attenders. J Acquir Immune Defic Syndr Hum Retrovirol. 1995;9:81-88.

168. Brodine SK, Oldfield EC III, Corwin AL, et al. HTLV-I among U.S. Marines stationed in a hyperendemic area: Evidence for female-to-male sexual transmission. J Acquir Immune Defic Syndr. 1992;5:158-162.

169. Brodine SK, Hyams KC, Molgaard CA, et al. The risk of human T cell leukemia virus and viral hepatitis infection among US Marines stationed in Okinawa, Japan. J Infect Dis. 1995;171:693-696.

170. Chen YM, Okayama A, Lee TH, et al. Sexual transmission of human T-cell leukemia virus type I associated with the presence of anti-Tax antibody. Proc Natl Acad Sci U S A. 1991;88:1182-1186.

171. Kaplan JE, Khabbaz RF, Murphy EL, et al. Male-to-female transmission of human T-cell lymphotropic virus types I and II: Association with viral load. The Retrovirus Epidemiology Donor Study Group. J Acquir Immune Defic Syndr Hum Retrovirol. 1996;12:193-201.

172. Iga M, Okayama A, Stuver S, et al. Genetic evidence of transmission of human T cell lymphotropic virus type 1 between spouses. J Infect Dis. 2002;185:691-695.

173. Nakano S, Ando Y, Ichijo M, et al. Search for possible routes of vertical and horizontal transmission of adult T-cell leukemia virus. Gann. 1984;75:1044-1045.

174. Belec L, Georges-Courbot MC, Georges A, et al. Cervicovaginal synthesis of IgG antibodies to the immunodominant 175-199 domain of the surface glycoprotein gp46 of human T-cell leukemia virus type I. J Med Virol. 1996;50:42-49.

175. Zunt JR, Dezzutti CS, Montano SM, et al. Cervical shedding of human T cell lymphotropic virus type I is associated with cervicitis. J Infect Dis. 2002;186:1669-1672.

176. Khabbaz RF, Onorato IM, Cannon RO, et al. Seroprevalence of HTLV-1 and HTLV-2 among intravenous drug users and persons in clinics for sexually transmitted diseases. N Engl J Med. 1992;326:375-380.

177. Hjelle B, Cyrus S, Swenson SG. Evidence for sexual transmission of human T lymphotropic virus type II. Ann Intern Med. 1992;116:90-91.

178. Maloney EM, Armien B, Gracia F, et al. Risk factors for HTLV-II infection among the Guaymi Indians. J Infect Dis. 1999;180:876-879.

179. Okochi K, Sato H, Hinuma Y. A retrospective study on transmission of adult T cell leukemia virus by blood transfusion: Seroconversion in recipients. Vox Sang. 1984;46:245-253.

180. Kleinman S, Swanson P, Allain JP, Lee H. Transfusion transmission of human T-lymphotropic virus types I and II: Serologic and polymerase chain reaction results in recipients identified through look-back investigations. Transfusion. 1993;33:14-18.

181. Sullivan MT, Williams AE, Fang CT, et al. Transmission of human T-lymphotropic virus types I and II by blood transfusion. A retrospective study of recipients of blood components (1983 through 1988). The American Red Cross HTLV-I/II Collaborative Study Group. Arch Intern Med. 1991;151:2043-2048.

182. Kamihira S, Nakasima S, Oyakawa Y, et al. Transmission of human T cell lymphotropic virus type I by blood transfusion before and after mass screening of sera from seropositive donors. Vox Sang. 1987;52:43-44.

183. Donegan E, Busch MP, Galleshaw JA, et al. Transfusion of blood components from a donor with human T-lymphotropic virus type II (HTLV-II) infection. The Transfusion Safety Study Group. Ann Intern Med. 1990;113:555-556.

184. Cohen ND, Munoz A, Reitz BA, et al. Transmission of retroviruses by transfusion of screened blood in patients undergoing cardiac surgery. N Engl J Med. 1989;320:1172-1176.

185. Sakashita A, Hattori T, Miller CW, et al. Mutations of the p53 gene in adult T-cell leukemia. Blood. 1992;79:477-480.

186. Dekaban G, Inwood M, Waters D, et al. Absence of human T-lymphotropic virus types I and II infection in an Ontario hemophilia population. Transfusion. 1992;32:513-516.

187. Canavaggio M, Leckie G, Allain JP, et al. The prevalence of antibody to HTLV-I/II in United States plasma donors and in United States and French hemophiliacs. Transfusion. 1990;30:780-782.
188. Gonzalez-Perez MP, Munoz-Juarez L, Cardenas FC, et al. Human T-cell leukemia virus type I infection in various recipients of transplants from the same donor. Transplantation. 2003;75:1006-1011.
189. Amin RM, Jones B, Rupert M. Risk of retroviral infection among retrovirology laboratory and health care workers (Abstract). General Meeting of the American Society of Microbiology, New Orleans, LA, 1992.
190. Proietti F, Viahov D, Alexander S, et al. Correlates of HTLV-II/HIV-1 seroprevalence and incidence of HTLV-II infection among intravenous drug users. Int Conf AIDS. 1992;8:C310.
191. Manns A, Murphy EL, Wilks R, et al. Detection of early human T-cell lymphotropic virus type I antibody patterns during seroconversion among transfusion recipients. Blood. 1991;77:896-905.
192. Cho I, Sugimoto M, Mita S, et al. In vivo proviral burden and viral RNA expression in T cell subsets of patients with human T lymphotropic virus type-1-associated myelopathy/tropical spastic paraparesis. Am J Trop Med Hyg. 1995;53:412-418.
193. Jacobson S, Gupta A, Mattson D, et al. Immunological studies in tropical spastic paraparesis. Ann Neurol. 1990;27:149-156.
194. Bieganowska K, Hollsberg P, Buckle GJ, et al. Direct analysis of viral-specific CD8+ T cells with soluble HLA-A2/Tax11-19 tetramer complexes in patients with human T cell lymphotropic virus-associated myelopathy. J Immunol. 1999; 162:1765-1771.
195. Elovaara I, Koenig S, Brewah AY, et al. High human T cell lymphotropic virus type 1 (HTLV-1)-specific precursor cytotoxic T lymphocyte frequencies in patients with HTLV-1-associated neurological disease. J Exp Med. 1993;177:1567-1573.
196. Jacobson S, Shida H, McFarlin DE, et al. Circulating CD8+ cytotoxic T lymphocytes specific for HTLV-I pX in patients with HTLV-I associated neurological disease. Nature. 1990;348:245-248.
197. Jacobson S, Reuben JS, Streilein RD, Palker TJ. Induction of CD4+, human T lymphotropic virus type-1-specific cytotoxic T lymphocytes from patients with HAM/TSP. Recognition of an immunogenic region of the gp46 envelope glycoprotein of human T lymphotropic virus type-1. J Immunol. 1991;146:1155-1162.
198. Manns A, Wilks RJ, Murphy EL, et al. A prospective study of transmission by transfusion of HTLV-I and risk factors associated with seroconversion. Int J Cancer. 1992;51:886-891.
199. Bangham CRM, Kermode AG, Hall SE. The cytotoxic T-lymphocyte response to HTLV-I: The main determinant of disease? Semin Virol. 1996;7:41-48.
200. Kubota R, Kawanishi T, Matsubara H, et al. HTLV-I specific IFN-gamma+ CD8+ lymphocytes correlate with the proviral load in peripheral blood of infected individuals. J Neuroimmunol. 2000;102:208-215.
201. Jeffery KJ, Usuku K, Hall SE, et al. HLA alleles determine human T-lymphotropic virus-I (HTLV-I) proviral load and the risk of HTLV-I-associated myelopathy. Proc Natl Acad Sci U S A. 1999;96:3848-3853.
202. Uchiyama T, Yodoi J, Sagawa K, et al. Adult T-cell leukemia: Clinical and hematologic features of 16 cases. Blood. 1977;50:481-492.
203. Richard V, Lairmore MD, Green PL, et al. Humoral hypercalcemia of malignancy: Severe combined immunodeficient/beige mouse model of adult T-cell lymphoma independent of human T-cell lymphotropic virus type-1 tax expression. Am J Pathol. 2001;158:2219-2228.
204. Mori N, Ejima E, Prager D. Transactivation of parathyroid hormone-related protein gene expression by human T-cell leukemia virus type I tax. Eur J Haematol. 1996;56(1-2):116-117.
205. Tajima K, Kuroishi T. Estimation of rate of incidence of ATL among ATLV (HTLV-I) carriers in Kyushu, Japan. Jpn J Clin Oncol. 1985;15:423-430.
206. Murphy EL, Hanchard B, Figueroa JP, et al. Modelling the risk of adult T-cell leukemia/lymphoma in persons infected with human T-lymphotropic virus type I. Int J Cancer. 1989;43:250-253.
207. Shimoyama M. Diagnostic criteria and classification of clinical subtypes of adult T-cell leukaemia-lymphoma. A report from the Lymphoma Study Group (1984-87). Br J Haematol. 1991;79:428-437.
208. Gibbs WN, Lofters WS, Campbell M, et al. Non-Hodgkin lymphoma in Jamaica and its relation to adult T-cell leukemia-lymphoma. Ann Intern Med. 1987;106:361-368.
209. Hattori T, Uchiyama T, Toibana T, et al. Surface phenotype of Japanese adult T-cell leukemia cells characterized by monoclonal antibodies. Blood. 1981;58:645-647.
210. Waldmann TA, Greene WC, Sarin PS, et al. Functional and phenotypic comparison of human T cell leukemia/lymphoma virus positive adult T cell leukemia with human T cell leukemia/lymphoma virus negative Sezary leukemia, and their distinction using anti-Tac. Monoclonal antibody identifying the human receptor for T cell growth factor. J Clin Invest. 1984;73:1711-1718.
211. Waldmann TA, White JD, Goldman CK, et al. The interleukin-2 receptor: A target for monoclonal antibody treatment of human T-cell lymphotrophic virus I-induced adult T-cell leukemia. Blood. 1993;82:1701-1712.
212. Yoshida M, Seiki M, Yamaguchi K, Takatsuki K. Monoclonal integration of human T-cell leukemia provirus in all primary tumors of adult T-cell leukemia suggests causative role of human T-cell leukemia virus in the disease. Proc Natl Acad Sci U S A. 1984;81:2534-2537.
213. Bunn PA, Schechter GP, Jaffe E, et al. Clinical course of retrovirus-associated adult T-cell lymphoma in the United States. N Engl J Med. 1983;309:257-264.
214. Newton RC, Limpuangthip P, Greenberg S, et al. *Strongyloides stercoralis* hyperinfection in a carrier of HTLV-I virus with evidence of selective immunosuppression. Am J Med. 1992;92:202-208.
215. Nakada K, Yamaguchi K, Furugen S, et al. Monoclonal integration of HTLV-I proviral DNA in patients with strongyloidiasis. Int J Cancer. 1987;40:145-148.
216. Sato Y, Shiroma Y. Concurrent infections with strongyloides and T-cell leukemia virus and their possible effect on immune responses of host. Clin Immunol Immunopathol. 1989;52:214-224.
217. Ijichi S, Izumo S, Eiraku N, et al. An autoaggressive process against bystander tissues in HTLV-I-infected individuals: A possible pathomechanism of HAM/TSP. Med Hypotheses. 1993;41:542-547.
218. Strickler HD, Rattray C, Escoffery C, et al. Human T-cell lymphotropic virus type I and severe neoplasia of the cervix in Jamaica. Int J Cancer. 1995;61:23-26.
219. Osame M, Usuku K, Izumo S, et al. HTLV-I associated myelopathy, a new clinical entity. Lancet. 1986;1:1031-1032.
220. Akizuki S, Setoguchi M, Nakazato O, et al. An autopsy case of human T-lymphotropic virus type I-associated myelopathy. Hum Pathol. 1988;19:988-990.
221. Bhigjee AI, Wiley CA, Wachsman W, et al. HTLV-I-associated myelopathy: Clinicopathologic correlation with localization of provirus to spinal cord. Neurology. 1991;41:1990-1992.
222. Ohama E, Horikawa Y, Shimizu T, et al. Demyelination and remyelination in spinal cord lesions of human lymphotropic virus type I-associated myelopathy. Acta Neuropathol (Berl). 1990;81:78-83.
223. Kaplan JE, Osame M, Kubota H, et al. The risk of development of HTLV-I-associated myelopathy/tropical spastic paraparesis among persons infected with HTLV-I. J Acquir Immune Defic Syndr. 1990;3:1096-1101.
224. Vernant JC, Maurs L, Gessain A, et al. Endemic tropical spastic paraparesis associated with human T-lymphotropic virus type I: A clinical and seroepidemiological study of 25 cases. Ann Neurol. 1987;21:123-130.
225. Osame M, Janssen R, Kubota H, et al. Nationwide survey of HTLV-I-associated myelopathy in Japan: Association with blood transfusion. Ann Neurol. 1990;28:50-56.
226. McFarlin DE. Neurological disorders related to HTLV-I and HTLV-II. J Acquir Immune Defic Syndr. 1993;6:640-644.
227. Osame M, Matsumoto M, Usuku K, et al. Chronic progressive myelopathy associated with elevated antibodies to human T-lymphotropic virus type I and adult T-cell leukemia-like cells. Ann Neurol. 1987;21:117-122.
228. Gessain A, Gout O. Chronic myelopathy associated with human T-lymphotropic virus type I (HTLV-I). Ann Intern Med. 1992;117:933-946.
229. Shibasaki H, Endo C, Kuroda Y, et al. Clinical picture of HTLV-I associated myelopathy. J Neurol Sci. 1988;87:15-24.
230. Roman GC, Roman LN. Tropical spastic paraparesis. A clinical study of 50 patients from Tumaco (Colombia) and review of the worldwide features of the syndrome. J Neurol Sci. 1988;87:121-138.
231. Gout O, Gessain A, Bolgert F, et al. Chronic myelopathies associated with human T-lymphotropic virus type I. A clinical, serologic, and immunovirologic study of ten patients in France. Arch Neurol. 1989;46:255-260.
232. Levin MC, Lehky TJ, Flerlage AN, et al. Immunologic analysis of a spinal cord-biopsy specimen from a patient with human T-cell lymphotropic virus type I-associated neurologic disease. N Engl J Med. 1997;336:839-845.
233. Tournier-Lasserve E, Gout O, Gessain A, et al. HTLV-I, brain abnormalities on magnetic resonance imaging, and relation with multiple sclerosis. Lancet. 1987;2:49-50.
234. Moore GR, Traugott U, Scheinberg LC, Raine CS. Tropical spastic paraparesis: A model of virus-induced, cytotoxic T-cell-mediated demyelination? Ann Neurol. 1989;26:523-530.
235. Koenig S, Woods RM, Brewah YA, et al. Characterization of MHC class I restricted cytotoxic T cell responses to tax in HTLV-1 infected patients with neurologic disease. J Immunol. 1993;151:3874-3883.
236. Hollsberg P, Hafler DA. Seminars in medicine of the Beth Israel Hospital, Boston. Pathogenesis of diseases induced by human lymphotropic virus type I infection. N Engl J Med. 1993;328:1173-1182.
237. Levin MC, Lee SM, Kalume F, et al. Autoimmunity due to molecular mimicry as a cause of neurological disease. Nat Med. 2002;8:509-513.
238. Morgan OS, Rodgers-Johnson P, Mora C, Char G. HTLV-1 and polymyositis in Jamaica. Lancet. 1989;2:1184-1187.
239. Nishioka K, Maruyama I, Sato K, et al. Chronic inflammatory arthropathy associated with HTLV-I. Lancet. 1989;1:441.
240. Mochizuki M, Tajima K, Watanabe T, Yamaguchi K. Human T lymphotropic virus type 1 uveitis. Br J Ophthalmol. 1994;78:149-154.
241. Ohba N, Matsumoto M, Sameshima M, et al. Ocular manifestations in patients infected with human T-lymphotropic virus type I. Jpn J Ophthalmol. 1989;33:1-12.
242. Sagawa K, Mochizuki M, Masuoka K, et al. Immunopathological mechanisms of human T cell lymphotropic virus type I (HTLV-I) uveitis. Detection of HTLV-I-infected T cells in the eye and their constitutive cytokine production. J Clin Invest. 1995;95:852-858.
243. Sugimoto M, Nakashima H, Kawano O, et al. Bronchoalveolar T-lymphocytosis in HTLV-1-associated myelopathy. Chest. 1989;95:708.
244. Mita S, Sugimoto M, Nakamura M, et al. Increased human T lymphotropic virus type-1 (HTLV-1) proviral DNA in peripheral blood mononuclear cells and bronchoalveolar lavage cells from Japanese patients with HTLV-1-associated myelopathy. Am J Trop Med Hyg. 1993;48:170-177.

245. Robinson RD, Lindo JF, Neva FA, et al. Immunoepidemiologic studies of *Strongyloides stercoralis* and human T lymphotropic virus type I infections in Jamaica. J Infect Dis. 1994;169:692-696.

246. Nakada K, Kohakura M, Komoda H, Hinuma Y. High incidence of HTLV antibody in carriers of *Strongyloides stercoralis*. Lancet. 1984;1:633.

247. Ho GY, Nelson K, Nomura AM, et al. Markers of health status in an HTLV-I-positive cohort. Am J Epidemiol. 1992;136:1349-1357.

248. LaGrenade L, Hanchard B, Fletcher V, et al. Infective dermatitis of Jamaican children: A marker for HTLV-I infection. Lancet. 1990;336:1345-1347.

249. Hanchard B, LaGrenade L, Carberry C, et al. Childhood infective dermatitis evolving into adult T-cell leukaemia after 17 years. Lancet. 1991;338:1593-1594.

250. Tsukasaki K, Yamada Y, Ikeda S, Tomonaga M. Infective dermatitis among patients with ATL in Japan. Int J Cancer. 1994;57:293.

251. Wiktor SZ, Pate EJ, Murphy EL, et al. Mother-to-child transmission of human T-cell lymphotropic virus type I (HTLV-I) in Jamaica: Association with antibodies to envelope glycoprotein (gp46) epitopes. J Acquir Immune Defic Syndr. 1993;6:1162-1167.

252. Rosenblatt JD, Golde DW, Wachsman W, et al. A second isolate of HTLV-II associated with atypical hairy-cell leukemia. N Engl J Med. 1986;315:372-377.

253. Loughran TP Jr, Coyle T, Sherman MP, et al. Detection of human T-cell leukemia/lymphoma virus, type II, in a patient with large granular lymphocyte leukemia. Blood. 1992;80:1116-1119.

254. Zucker-Franklin D, Hooper WC, Evatt BL. Human lymphotropic retroviruses associated with mycosis fungoides: Evidence that human T-cell lymphotropic virus type II (HTLV-II) as well as HTLV-I may play a role in the disease. Blood. 1992;80:1537-1545.

255. Murphy EL, Fridey J, Smith JW, et al. Prevalence of HTLV-II and HTLV-I associated myelopathy (HAM) in a cohort of seropositive blood donors. AIDS Res Hum Retroviruses. 1994;10:473.

256. Bhagavati S, Ehrlich G, Kula RW, et al. Detection of human T-cell lymphoma/leukemia virus type I DNA and antigen in spinal fluid and blood of patients with chronic progressive myelopathy. N Engl J Med. 1988;318:1141-1147.

257. Modahl LE, Young KC, Varney KF, et al. Injection drug users seropositive for human T-lymphotropic virus type II (HTLV-II) are at increased risk for pneumonia. J Acquir Immune Defic Syndr Hum Retrovirol. 1995;10:260.

258. Ciancianaini P, Magnani G, Barchi E, et al. Serological and clinical follow-up of an Italian IVDU cohort of HTLV-II/HIV-1 co-infected patients. Evidence of direct relationship between CD4 count and HTLV-II proviral load. AIDS Res Hum Retroviruses. 2001;17[S1]:S-70.

259. Harrington WJ Jr, Sheremata W, Hjelle B, et al. Spastic ataxia associated with human T-cell lymphotropic virus type II infection. Ann Neurol. 1993;33:411-414.

260. Jacobson S, Lehky T, Nishimura M, et al. Isolation of HTLV-II from a patient with chronic, progressive neurological disease clinically indistinguishable from HTLV-I-associated myelopathy/tropical spastic paraparesis. Ann Neurol. 1993;33:392-396.

261. Tsukasaki K, Ikeda S, Murata K, et al. Characteristics of chemotherapy-induced clinical remission in long survivors with aggressive adult T-cell leukemia/lymphoma. Leuk Res. 1993;17:157-166.

262. Taguchi H, Kinoshita KI, Takatsuki K, et al. An intensive chemotherapy of adult T-cell leukemia/lymphoma: CHOP followed by etoposide, vindesine, ranimustine, and mitoxantrone with granulocyte colony-stimulating factor support. J Acquir Immune Defic Syndr Hum Retrovirol. 1996;12:182-186.

263. Waldmann TA, White JD, Carrasquillo JA, et al. Radioimmunotherapy of interleukin-2R alpha-expressing adult T-cell leukemia with Yttrium-90-labeled anti-Tac. Blood. 1995;86:4063-4075.

264. Matsushima M, Yoneyama A, Nakamura T, et al. A first case of complete remission of beta-interferon sensitive adult T-cell leukemia. Eur J Haematol. 1987;39:282-287.

265. Saigo K, Shiozawa S, Shiozawa K, et al. Alpha-interferon treatment for adult T cell leukemia: Low levels of circulating alpha-interferon and its clinical effectiveness. Blut. 1988;56:83-86.

266. Ezaki K, Hirano M, Ohno R, et al. A combination trial of human lymphoblastoid interferon and bestrabucil (KM2210) for adult T-cell leukemia-lymphoma. Cancer. 1991;68:695-698.

267. Gill PS, Harrington W, Kaplan MH, et al. Treatment of adult T-cell leukemia-lymphoma with a combination of interferon alfa and zidovudine. N Engl J Med. 1995;332:1744-1748.

268. Bazarbachi A, Nasr R, El-Sabban ME, et al. Evidence against a direct cytotoxic effect of alpha interferon and zidovudine in HTLV-I associated adult T cell leukemia/lymphoma. Leukemia. 2000;14:716-721.

269. Tajima K, Amakawa R, Uehira K, et al. Adult T-cell leukemia successfully treated with allogeneic bone marrow transplantation. Int J Hematol. 2000;71:290-293.

270. Matsuo H, Nakamura T, Tsujihata M, et al. Plasmapheresis in treatment of human T-lymphotropic virus type-I associated myelopathy. Lancet. 1988;2:1109-1113.

271. Matsuo H, Nakamura T, Shibayama K, et al. Long-term follow-up of immunomodulation in treatment of HTLV-I-associated myelopathy. Lancet. 1989;1:790.

272. Izumo S, Goto I, Itoyama Y, et al. Interferon-alpha is effective in HTLV-I-associated myelopathy: A multicenter, randomized, double-blind, controlled trial. Neurology. 1996;46:1016-1021.

273. Shibayama K, Nakamura T, Nagasato K, et al. Interferon-alpha treatment in HTLV-I-associated myelopathy. Studies of clinical and immunological aspects. J Neurol Sci. 1991;106:186-192.

274. Harrington WJ, Sheremata WA, Snodgrass SR, et al. Tropical spastic paraparesis/HTLV-1-associated myelopathy (TSP/HAM): Treatment with an anabolic steroid danazol. AIDS Res Hum Retroviruses. 1991;7:1031-1034.

275. Gout O, Gessain A, Iba-Zizen M, et al. The effect of zidovudine on chronic myelopathy associated with HTLV-1. J Neurol. 1991;238:108-109.

276. Sheremata WA, Benedict D, Squilacote DC, et al. High-dose zidovudine induction in HTLV-I-associated myelopathy: Safety and possible efficacy. Neurology. 1993;43:2125-2129.

277. Centers for Disease Control and Prevention and the U.S.P.H.S. Working Group. Guidelines for counseling persons infected with human T-lymphotropic virus type I (HTLV-I) and type II (HTLV-II). Ann Intern Med. 1993;118:448-454.

278. Dearden C, Matutes E, Catovsky D. Deoxycoformycin in the treatment of mature T-cell leukaemias. Br J Cancer. 1991;64:903-906.

279. Franchini G. Molecular mechanisms of human T-cell leukemia/lymphotropic virus type I infection. Blood. 1995;86:3619-3639.

280. Bangham CRM. HTLV-1 infections. J Clin Pathol. 1999;53:581-586.

CHAPTER 166

Human Immunodeficiency Viruses

FARLEY R. CLEGHORN

MARVIN S. REITZ, Jr.

MIKULAS POPOVIC

ROBERT C. GALLO

Infection with human immunodeficiency virus type 1 (HIV-1) and its end stage, acquired immunodeficiency syndrome (AIDS), is the major public health challenge of modern times, with over 25 million persons already dead and over 50 million living with HIV/AIDS, the majority of whom are without access to therapy.[1] AIDS was first recognized in the United States in 1981 with reports of unexplained opportunistic infections, including *Pneumocystis jirovecii* (formerly *Pneumocystis carinii*) pneumonia and Kaposi's sarcoma (KS), among homosexual men in New York and San Francisco.[1-3] On the basis of the epidemiologic features, association with the loss of CD4+ lymphocytes and immunosuppression, and likely infectious etiology, a new human retrovirus was postulated as a causal agent. The field of retrovirology had markedly advanced just a decade earlier with the description of reverse transcriptase (RT) and with the discovery of human T-cell lymphotropic virus types I and II (HTLV-I and HTLV-II), the first two known human retroviruses, in 1979 and 1981 (reported in 1980 and 1982, respectively).[4,5] The discovery of interleukin-2 or T-cell growth factor[6,7] allowed the culture of blood T lymphocytes from early cases of AIDS; by 1984, the detection, isolation, and propagation of HIV-1, the third human retrovirus, had led to the development of a diagnostic test, an increasingly detailed understanding of the molecular biology of this virus, and, most important, the introduction of a rational basis for antiviral therapy.[8-14] After a long era of expanding research, new therapeutic combinations (RT and protease inhibitors), combined with the ability to measure circulating viral RNA and resistance to drugs, have led to a dramatically improved clinical course for persons fortunate enough to have access to therapy. Within a brief period, technologic advances have provided a clearer understanding of viral dynamics and the disease process, focusing attention on viral replication, host immune responses, and T-cell dynamics while confirming and elaborating the causal role of the virus. Equally dramatic has been the elucidation of how HIV enters cells, utilizing both the CD4 molecule and a chemokine receptor as a dual-receptor system, as well as the mapping of the three-dimensional structure of the viral envelope protein. Contemporary retrovirology is largely devoted to the study of HIV-1 and of HIV-associated diseases. The molecular and cellular biology of this virus is now better understood than that of almost any other in history: research on HIV has shown that rational antiviral therapy is possible, thereby pointing the way toward therapy for other viral diseases. However, this knowledge has yet to be translated into greater progress in the areas of prevention, therapy, vaccines, and immune reconstitution for much of the developing world, where most HIV is transmitted.

Viruses are obligate intracellular parasites, and every aspect of the virus is in some way relevant to virus-host relationships. This chapter outlines the life cycle, the molecular and cellular biology, the structure, and the regulation of HIV-1 and includes some discussion of pathogenesis and outcome of infection. Although the division of the chapter into sections is useful for organization of the information presented, in reality these subjects cannot be separated from one another; from the perspective of both virus and host, the process of infection is a continuous series of connected interactions.

ORIGIN AND CLASSIFICATION OF HUMAN RETROVIRUSES

Current knowledge places retroviral infection of humans as zoonoses that originated in primate-to-human species–jumping events. For HIV-1 and HIV-2, these events occurred in Central and West Africa, most likely at multiple times, with the more recent attaining major epidemic significance. Simian immunodeficiency virus of chimpanzees (SIV_{cpz}) is the immediate precursor to HIV-1.[15] It now appears likely that similar species-jumping events occurred between certain types of monkeys and chimpanzees.[16]

Retroviruses have been classified, by a number of different biologic features, into at least seven genera.[17] Oncogenic retroviruses occur in all classes of vertebrates. The first infectious agents that produced cancer in chickens were isolated by Ellerman and Bang (1908)[18] and by Peyton Rous (1911).[19] These workers were considerably ahead of their time, and the biologic systems to culture and study these viruses were not yet described. Rous eventually won a Nobel Prize for his work in 1966. The pioneering work of Ludwig Gross in the 1950s stimulated renewed interest by demonstrating that oncogenic viruses could produce tumors in mammals,[20] but for the next three decades it remained orthodoxy for most scientists that human retroviruses did not exist. We now know that the pathogenic human retroviruses include *lenti* viruses (HIV-1 and -2) and *onc* viruses (HTLV-I and -II). The human endogenous retrovirus (HERV-K) has not been shown to be infectious; that is, it lacks a true viral nature. Also, it has not been shown to cause any disease.[21]

Retroviruses use as a replication strategy the transcription of viral RNA into linear double-stranded DNA with subsequent integration into the host genome. The characteristic enzyme used for this process, an RNA-dependent DNA polymerase that reverses the flow of genetic information, is known as RT. The discovery of this enzyme helped to initiate the modern era of molecular biology. This enzyme is error prone; with the massive turnover of virions in the infected host, these errors accumulate in the viral DNA, accounting for the relatively high mutability of HIV-1. The lifestyle of the retrovirus therefore involves two forms: a DNA provirus and an RNA-containing infectious virion. The basic structure, genetic organization, and life cycle of HIV-1 are similar to those of most retroviruses but have some unique additional features.

The study of retroviral infection at the cellular level has made continuing contributions to the development of molecular biology and medicine. Experimental observation and vision led to a hypothesis that challenged the "central dogma" of molecular biology—namely, that genetic information must necessarily flow from DNA to RNA.[22-25] The discovery that a retroviral transforming gene, v-*src*, was also present in the host cellular genome, c-*src*, demonstrated the cellular origin of retroviral oncogenes and opened oncology to the molecular exploration of the control of cell growth. The discovery of HTLV-I and its etiologic association first with adult T-cell leukemia, an aggressive T-cell lymphoma,[5] and later with a neurologic disease, tropical spastic paraparesis/HTLV-I–associated myelopathy (TSP/HAM),[26] were pivotal events in modern medicine. Although there is relatively little variation among HTLV-I isolates, HTLV-II, the second human retrovirus, is 50% identical to HTLV-I at the genomic level.[4] Similarly, HIV-2, the fourth human retrovirus, was identified as a serologic variant of HIV-1, the third human retrovirus, and was isolated from patients in western Africa.[27,28] Some types of SIV are so closely related to HIV-2 that they may form an overlapping continuum with recent common ancestors. HIV-2 is known to infect several monkey species, including the sooty mangabey, its natural host, and SIV has been known to be transmitted, albeit rarely, to laboratory workers. SIVs and SIV/HIV hybrids have been used extensively to study animal models of immunodeficiency.[29] Other species, including cats (feline leukemia virus [FeLV] and feline immunodeficiency virus [FIV]) and cattle (bovine leukemia virus [BLV] and bovine immunodeficiency virus [BIV]), harbor retroviruses analogous to those of humans and some African primates. HIV-related retroviruses, known as lentiretroviruses, also include the ungulate

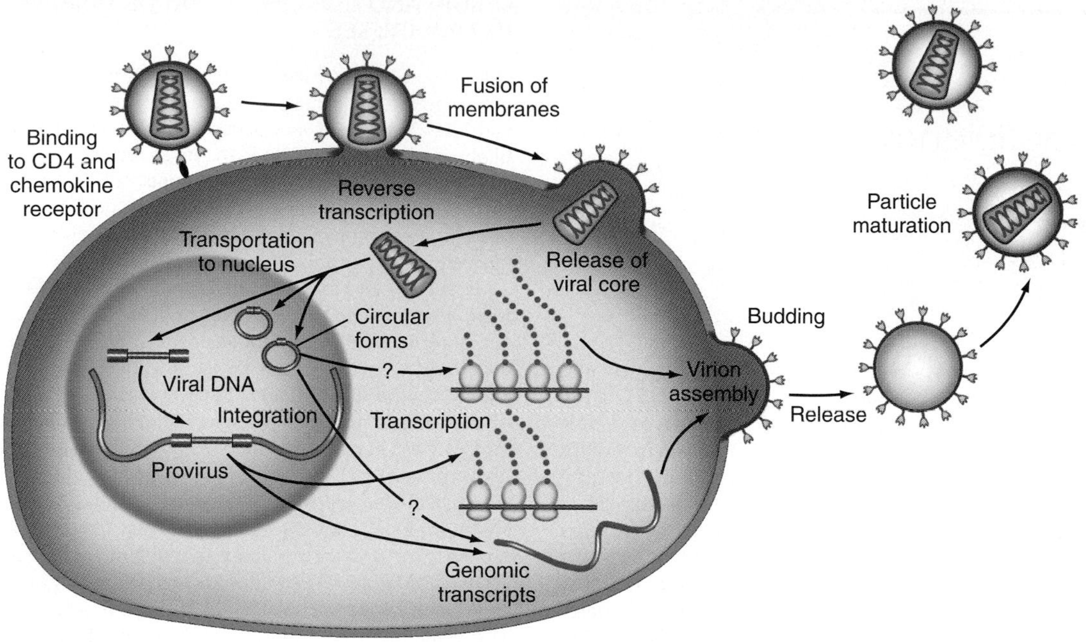

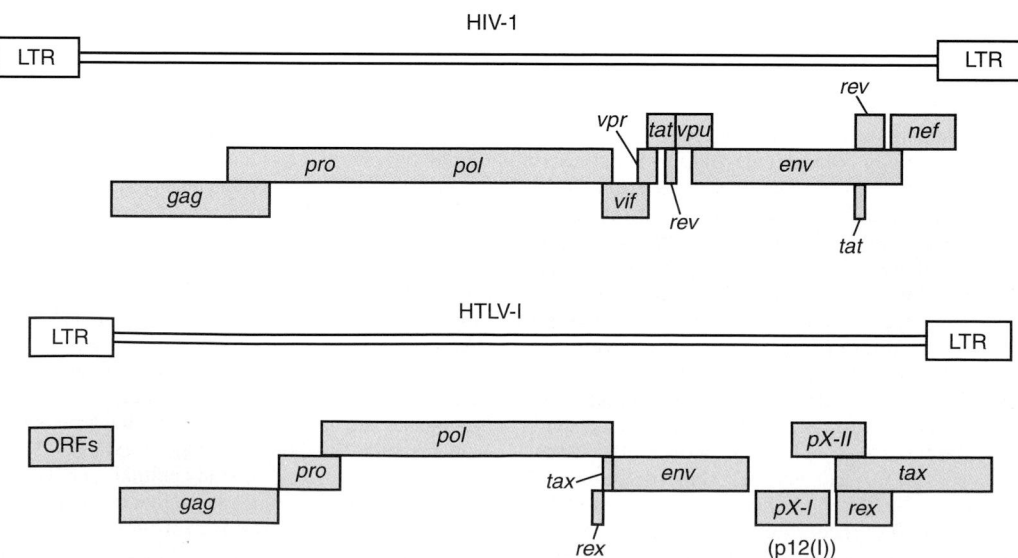

FIGURE 166-1. The life cycle of human immunodeficiency virus type 1 (HIV-1).

viruses, maedi-visna virus of sheep, caprine arthritis-encephalitis virus, and equine infectious anemia virus.

As RNA viruses, retroviruses have the survival advantage of great genetic diversity. As viruses with a DNA intermediate in their replication cycle, they also have the advantage of latency, as do many DNA viruses, but even more so because the DNA provirus is integrated into the chromosomal DNA of the infected cell. As a CD4$^+$ T-cell and macrophage-tropic virus, HIV also has the advantage of reducing the effectiveness of the host immune response.

Retroviruses are typically 100 nm in diameter and contain two single strands of RNA, which permits recombination between the strands (Fig. 166-1). The typical genome is approximately 10 kilobases (kb) or less in size and contains three major structural genes: namely *gag, pol,* and *env.* HIV-1 also contains several additional genes; these "extra" genes were first described in HTLV-I. In both viruses, some of these extra genes are essential to viral replication, whereas others may modulate interactions of the virus with its host. Figure 166-2 outlines the genome composition of HIV-1 and HTLV-I.

In addition to infectious and endogenous retroviruses, a number of other elements that utilize RT have been described. These "retro" elements also constitute a diverse group of related entities that inhabit the genomes of all eukaryotic and many prokaryotic organisms. It is possible that all of these elements evolved from one ancient RT gene, as proposed by Temin.[29a] These include retrotransposons (Alu-like sequences and processed pseudo-genes), which function as mobile DNA elements that may jump to other regions of the genome; retrotransposon-containing long interspersed nucleic acid repeat (LINE) elements; long terminal repeat (LTR)-containing elements; and para-retroviruses (hepadnavirus) that use RT. Large-scale genomic sequencing has revealed that a huge proportion of many eukaryote genomes consist of

FIGURE 166-2. Genomic organization of human retroviruses. A comparison of the genomes of human T-cell lymphotropic virus type I (HTLV-I) and human immunodeficiency virus (HIV) is shown. Studies of HTLV genes and gene products laid the foundation for an understanding of their functional homologues subsequently found in HIV (e.g., *tat* and *rev*), although there is little sequence homology of these genes between HTLV and HIV.

transposable elements.[30] These mobile DNA sequences range in size from hundreds to thousands of base pairs—short interspersed nucleic acid repeat elements (SINEs) or LINEs—and may "jump" from one location to another. As yet unknown mechanisms must be present to control these elements. A number of diseases have been associated in humans with gene disruption by insertion.[31] (Comprehensive reviews of the expanse of retrovirus biology are available.[32,33])

VIRAL TRANSMISSION AND LIFE CYCLE

Biology of Transmission

The infectious life cycle of HIV can be described both at the molecular, single-cell level and at the level of an organism infected with a "swarm" of closely related viral species. Multiple variables, including route of exposure, dose, immunogenetic background, and concomitant infections, influence the probability of transmission. The biologic events during exposure and successful infection of the host are only partially elucidated. The most common modes of infection are sexual transmission at the genital or colonic mucosa, exposure to other infected fluids such as blood or blood products, transmission from mother to infant, and, occasionally, accidental occupational exposure. Transmitted viruses typically utilize the interaction of the viral glycoprotein gp120 with the cellular receptor CD4 and the chemokine receptor CCR5 to gain cell entry, thus selecting for macrophage-tropic *non–syncytia-forming* variants.[34] This finding explains why persons who lack a functional CCR5 receptor are relatively resistant to infection by sexual transmission. Non–macrophage-tropic strains, also called *syncytia-inducing* (SI), are typically found late in infection. These strains use another chemokine receptor, CXCR4, to facilitate entry and are apparently not readily transmitted from person to person. In a model of acute infection in the macaque, the first cellular targets of intravaginal inoculation of the virus are Langerhans cells, tissue dendritic cells in the lamina propria, which then fuse with lymphocytes. However, direct infection of T cells has also been described. Infected cells can be found in draining lymph nodes within 2 days and in plasma by 5 days.[35]

In HIV-1–infected persons, there is a rapid rise in the degree of plasma viremia within days, with high viral titers and widespread dissemination, probably targeting lymphoid organs and the central nervous system (CNS). This acute stage of HIV infection is sometimes manifested as a transient symptomatic illness characterized by a maculopapular rash and flu-like symptoms. This phase is followed by a marked reduction in virus to steady-state levels, probably owing to vigorous antivirus cellular responses. The immune response probably accounts for the mononucleosis-like acute syndrome seen in approximately half of the patients. Initially, perhaps within hours of infection, at least three HIV inhibitory chemokines (notably the chemokines MIP 1α, MIP 1β, and RANTES [regulated on activation, normal T cell expressed and secreted]) may be produced. As is the case for many infections with viruses that establish chronic infections, this response is at least partially successful in controlling replication. Levels of HIV-1–specific cytotoxic T lymphocytes (CTLs) are inversely correlated with plasma viral RNA levels.[36] High levels of potent CTL virus-specific cells targeted to the viral Env protein and soluble factors produced by these cells early in infection may correlate with the decline of virus, even before a neutralizing antibody can be detected.[37]

A great deal of variability in peak viral RNA plasma levels is seen during the first 120 days after infection. By 3 to 6 months after infection, viral levels reach a temporary steady state, sometimes called a *viral set point*. This level is highly correlated with subsequent disease progression in that lower viral steady-state level is correlated with slower disease progression. Thus, early in the course of infection, virus-host interactions are established that are predictive of subsequent disease.[38]

Intervention to control infection during this initial period has been shown to decrease the risk of subsequent infection in health care workers after needle-stick exposure.[39] Treatment of infected mothers and exposed neonates has also shown a dramatic effect in decreasing the incidence of maternal-fetal transmission. The theory underlying the use of antiretroviral prophylaxis following sexual exposure is biologically plausible, and even in common use, but lacks direct proof of efficacy in controlled studies.[40]

Life Cycle

The life cycle of HIV-1 can be considered in two distinct phases (see Fig. 166-1). The initial early events include viral attachment, entry into the cytoplasm, reverse transcription, entry into the nucleus, and integration of the double-stranded DNA (the provirus). The second phase occurs over the lifetime of the infected cell as viral and cellular proteins regulate the production of viral proteins and new infectious virions.

Infection is initiated by the binding of the virion gp120 Env protein to the CD4 molecule found on some T cells, macrophages, and microglial cells. Both SIV and HIV-2 also utilize this molecule. CD4 was first identified as a viral receptor in a number of studies showing the susceptibility of CD4-bearing cells to infection and the ability to block infection with anti-CD4 monoclonal antibodies in culture. Transfection of human CD4⁻ HeLa cells with CD4 DNA rendered them permissive for infection.[41] Successful in vitro experiments blocking this interaction with soluble CD4 used laboratory strains adapted to cell lines and led to therapeutic attempts using immunoglobulin CD4, which were not successful. Subsequent experiments showed that primary isolates were not sensitive to soluble CD4 and highlighted the necessity of using primary rather than laboratory-adapted isolates in studying virus-host interactions.

Early experiments demonstrated that, as with other lentiretroviruses, macrophages could also be infected with HIV, but strains differed in their ability to infect either T-cell lines or monocytes.[42] Binding to CD4 is not sufficient for entry of HIV into either human or nonhuman cells, and the fact that small changes in the V3 loop of envelope gp120 (see later) could determine tropism of the virus for either macrophage or T-cell lines suggested that a second receptor was present. The first important clue for the basis of this tropism was the unexpected finding that a group of chemokines (RANTES, MIP-1α, and MIP-1β) isolated from CD8⁺ T cells inhibited macrophage-tropic but not T-cell line–adapted strains.[43] This discovery at once explained the nature of a long-sought CD8 viral suppressor factor and suggested a previously unexpected role for chemokine receptors. The independent identification of an orphan chemokine receptor, CXCR4, as the second receptor for T-cell line–tropic strains[44] resulted in a rapid series of reports demonstrating CCR5 to be the principal second receptor for macrophage-tropic strains and CXCR4 for T-cell line–adapted strains.[45-49] Crystallographic evidence indicates that CD4 binds in a recessed pocket on gp120, which includes a deep cavity that binds to phenylalanine-43 of CD4. Previous mutagenesis studies had shown this phenylalanine to be a crucial residue for binding.[50] Recent studies also indicate a role for sugar molecules, glycosaminoglycans, in the binding of gp120, which influences interactions with the chemokine receptor.[51]

Events that occur immediately after viral entry—collectively, the disassembly process—are not simply the reverse of viral assembly. For example, recent studies have shown that HIV-1 must incorporate a cellular protein, cyclophilin A, which binds to the viral capsid protein p24. Failure to incorporate this cellular protein results in a profound postentry block during the next viral entry. Coincidentally, cyclophilin (peptidyl-prolyl isomerase) is the binding protein for cyclosporine, an inhibitor of T-cell activation, suggesting that activation-related cellular processes may be enlisted in viral disassembly.[52,53] In addition, Vif and Nef, accessory viral proteins, may also be required.[54]

The process of reverse transcription begins in the cytoplasm, as DNA synthesis is initiated from the transfer RNA primer bound to the viral genomic RNA just downstream of the 5′ LTR. Reverse transcription proceeds in an orderly fashion in a similar manner in all retroviruses.[55] Briefly, the transcription complex begins at the 5′ end, copies the U5 and R regions of the 5′ LTR, and then jumps to the 3′ end of the RNA, where the newly synthesized R region DNA binds to the R region of the 3′ LTR. Reverse transcription continues through the U3 region of the 3′ LTR and then through the remainder of the viral RNA, which gives a complete minus strand of DNA. The RNA is degraded by the viral ribonuclease H, except for two resistant purine-rich tracts in the middle and toward the 3′ end of the viral RNA. These then serve as the primers for formation of the DNA plus strand.[56]

Retroviruses are positive-stranded RNA viruses. No viral message is encoded directly from virion RNA; the virus particle lacks RNA polymerase and transcriptional factors, and during the process of reverse transcription, the positive-strand RNA produced from the viral genomic template is destroyed by the RNase H function of the RT. Because reverse transcription takes place in the cytoplasm, local concentrations of nucleotides may be a limiting factor, particularly in nondividing cells. This is the rationale for using the ribonucleoside reductase inhibitor hydroxyurea to limit viral replication.[57,58]

During the formation of double-stranded DNA, the uncoated nucleoprotein complex, termed the preintegration complex, is imported into the nucleus.[59] This is an energy-requiring process that uses nuclear localization signals present on viral Gag, Vpr, and integrase (IN) proteins. Unlike most retroviruses, which integrate into the host cellular DNA as the nuclear membrane is disrupted during cell division, HIV-1 can be imported into the nucleus and integrate into nondividing cells. This may be especially important in the infection of monocytes and macrophages, which are essentially nondividing cells.

IN-negative mutants of HIV do not integrate and do not produce infectious virus.[60,61] Integration does not appear to be site directed. However, HIV preferentially integrates into or near active genes, particularly those that are activated following infection by HIV-1.[62] Integration of the provirus appears to be an essential step in every replication cycle. In eukaryotes, integration is typical only of retroviruses and retrotransposable elements.[17] Unintegrated viral DNA may survive, particularly in quiescent cells. This may provide a stable intermediate form in cells that are temporarily not permissive for infection; if cell activation occurs when these forms are present, viral infection may then proceed to completion.

Integration of viral DNA establishes a linear copy of the viral genome in the genome of the cell, and replication of the virus occurs along with replication of the cell. Synthesis of new viral RNA genomes and proteins is accomplished in a highly regulated manner utilizing host cell enzymes. Integration is generally for the life of the cell and, with the cell and its progeny, for the life of the organism. It is at this point in the life cycle that differences in the natural history of different retroviruses emerge. HIV infection may be unusual in that a high level of viral production from several different cellular compartments is maintained throughout the course of infection. The high number of replication cycles that occur in a single infection allows for the generation of variants and selection by drugs or the immune system. The half-life of virus-producing CD4+ T cells is approximately 0.7 day, and the generation time of HIV-1 in vivo, approximately 2 days.[63] HIV-1 pathogenesis is the result of a complex interplay between the virus and the immune system, particularly the mechanisms responsible for T-cell homeostasis and regeneration. Protracted loss of CD4+ T cells results from early viral destruction of selected memory T-cell populations, followed by a combination of profound increases in overall memory T-cell turnover, damage to the thymus and other lymphoid tissues, and physiologic limitations in peripheral CD4+ T-cell renewal.[64] Equally important are indirect hematopoietic and immunoregulatory effects of viral components described later in this chapter.

Once integration has occurred, virus production depends on the presence of cellular and viral factors required for activation of viral promoters. External factors, including coinfection with other agents, production of inflammatory cytokines, and cellular activation, may enhance viral replication.[65] The molecular mechanisms regulating virus production include cellular pathways involving factors, such as the nuclear factor-κB (NF-κB) family of inducible transcription factors, that result in a cascade of events leading to viral genome expression.[66,67]

A unique feature of HIV-1 is that expression of different viral RNA species is temporally regulated. Using cellular enzymes, such as RNA polymerase II, transcription of the provirus is initiated at the viral promoter, at the junction of the U3-R regions in the LTR, as a single complete message. The viral messenger RNA (mRNA) and genomic RNA transcripts, processed by cellular machinery, are spliced, capped, polyadenylated, and transported to the cytoplasm for translation into viral proteins (see Fig. 166-2). Differential splicing of this complete RNA, controlled in part by the viral protein Rev, determines the type of message and protein that is produced. Early after infection, activated cells produce 2-kb mRNAs for viral regulatory proteins that can be detected by Northern blot analysis[68]; using even more sensitive reverse transcription–polymerase chain reaction (PCR) techniques, expression can be detected within 6 hours.[69] These messages represent the unique doubly spliced RNA for Tat, Rev, and Nef proteins. The Tat protein induces a markedly enhanced activity of the viral promoter, chiefly by increasing RNA elongation, resulting in further increased RNA and protein production. The Rev protein serves to decrease the production of double-spliced messages. With the accumulation of Rev protein, there is a switch to enhanced expression of unspliced and singly spliced mRNAs that code for the late viral proteins. These proteins include the virion proteins Gag, Pol, and Env and Vpu, Vpr, and Vif, as well as genomic RNA. The delayed transit from early to late viral genes is probably due to the requirement for a threshold amount of Rev needed to bind and form multimers of the protein complexed with the Rev regulatory element (RRE) located in all of the incompletely spliced mRNAs. Packaging of the genomic RNA within a virus particle requires the presence of a specific packaging signal located between the major splice donor at the 5′ end of the genome and the initiation codon for Gag. In the absence of this signal, mature particles are formed that are devoid of RNA. The incorporation of genomic RNA requires two "zinc-finger" domains found in the p7 Gag protein. Assembly of mature viral particles occurs at the cell membrane with the association of the matrix protein p17 with the cytoplasmic domain of the envelope transmembrane protein gp41, which in turn binds to the viral gp120 on the outer surface. Assembled virions include the viral envelope proteins, cell membrane and associated cellular proteins, a matrix composed mainly of Gag p17, and an inner core containing RNA, RT, IN, and core proteins p7 and p24, as well as Vpr and p6 proteins. The mature viral particle characteristically buds from the cell surface into the surrounding media, completing the life cycle of the virus. Budding of HIV-1 virions occurs at highly specialized membrane microdomains known as lipid rafts.[70] These domains are characterized by a distinct lipid composition that includes high concentrations of cholesterol, sphingolipids, and glycolipids.

THE PATHOGEN

The mature infectious virus particle buds from a cell membrane forming a sphere with an outer lipid bilayer and a nucleocapsid with a dense, cone-shaped core (Fig. 166-3). The core appears to be attached to the viral outer envelope at its narrow end.[71] The outer membrane contains 72 spiked knobs, which are assembled as trimers of the outer envelope protein gp120 bound to the transmembrane portion, gp41. The viral membrane is cholesterol rich and includes cellular proteins.[72]

Each mature virion is composed of two molecules of single-stranded RNA surrounded by three *gag* gene cleavage products: the p17 matrix protein; the p24 major capsid protein, which forms the capsid shell; and the p7 nucleoprotein, which binds tightly to the viral RNA. The matrix contains the myristoylated matrix protein p17, which is critical for virion formation and is localized between the capsid protein p24 of the viral core and envelope. The p7 protein binds the two positive-strand copies of complete viral RNA attached at the packaging site, and it also binds to p24. A number of other viral proteins required for the early phases of infection are incorporated with the virion (Fig. 166-4): protease, which is essential for viral assembly; RT and IN, which are needed after entry for viral DNA synthesis and integration; tRNA^lys at the 5′ end of the RNA, which serves as the primer for initiation of negative-strand DNA synthesis; and Vpr. The latter is a small protein that contains a nuclear localization signal and is associated with the nucleocapsid in large quantities. The virus encodes at least five other regulatory and/or accessory genes of diverse function. Some have

FIGURE 166-3. Structure of the HIV-1 virion. The viral envelope is formed from the host cell membrane, into which the HIV-1 envelope proteins gp41 and gp120 have been inserted and may include several host cell proteins, most significantly the major histocompatibility complex class II proteins. The matrix between the envelope and the core is formed predominantly from Gag protein p17. The core contains the viral RNA, closely associated with Gag protein p7, in addition to RT and integrase. It has also been shown that virions contain complementary DNA, as shown, synthesized by the RT. The major structural proteins of the core are Gag proteins p24 and p6. Also present within the virion is the protease and two cleavage products from the Gag precursor protein (p1 and p2, not shown) of undetermined position within the virion. Vpr is also packaged in the virion and is thought to be localized within the core, as shown.

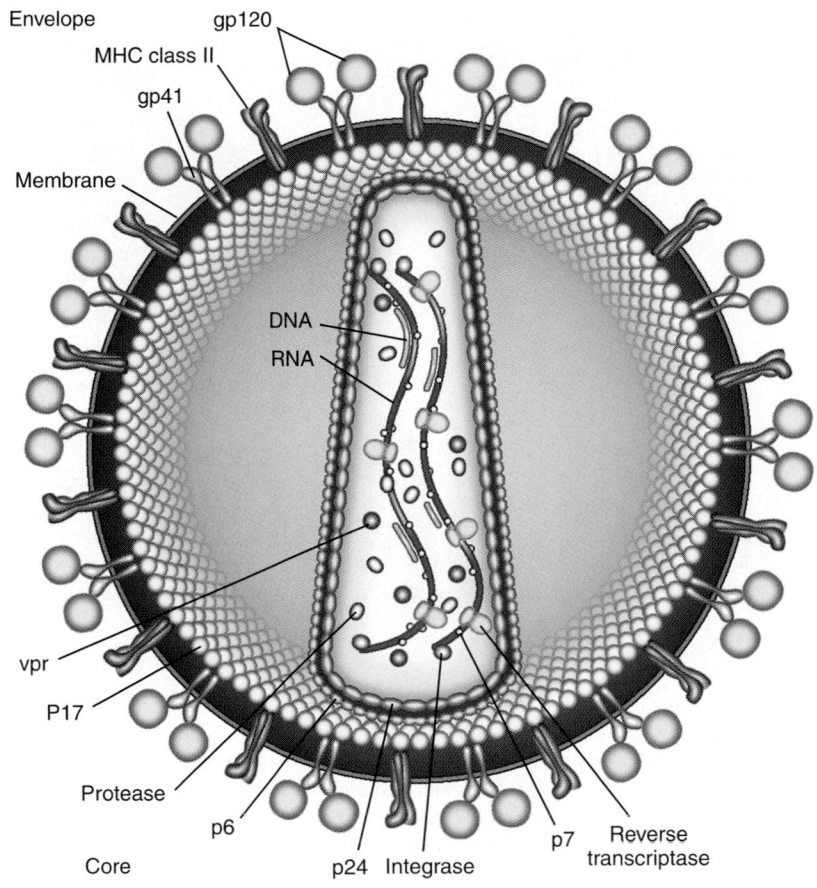

been discussed already, and most are present in the infected cell but not in the mature virion. A list of HIV genes and associated proteins is presented in Table 166-1.

Genetic Organization

The HIV-1 proviral DNA integrated into the host cell is 9.7 kb in length and follows the basic genomic structure common to most retroviruses: *gag-pol-env* genes flanked by two complete viral LTRs (see Fig. 166-2). The provirus is symmetrically flanked at either end by the viral LTR and by cellular sequences representing the site of integration. These LTRs contain transcriptional regulatory sequences, RNA processing signals, packaging sites, and the integration sites. The 5′ end begins with the *gag* gene, which encodes core and matrix proteins; the *pol* gene, which begins in an overlapping frame encod-

TABLE 166-1 Genes and Gene Products of Human Immunodeficiency Virus (HIV)-1 and HIV-2

Gene	Proteins	Size (kDa)	Function/Properties
gag	p17		Matrix protein; interacts with gp41
	p24		Core protein
	p6		Core protein; binds to Vpr
	p7		Nucleocapsid; binds to RNA
	p1		
	p2		
pol	Protease	10	Proteolytic cleavage of Gag and Pol
	Reverse transcriptase	66, 51	Polymerase and RNase H activity (p66 only)
	Integrase	32	Integration into chromosome
env	gp120		Envelope; viral entry into cell
	gp41		Transmembrane protein; cell fusion
vif	Virion infectivity protein	23	Efficient cell-free transmission
vpr	Viral protein R	18	Enhances viral replication in primary cells, virion-associated protein; G₂/M phase arrest; nuclear localization
tat	*Trans*-activator of transcription	14	Major viral *trans*-activator, immune suppression
rev	Regulator of expression of virion protein	19	Enhances expression of unspliced and singly spliced RNAs
*vpu**	Viral protein U	15-16	Enhances virion release from cells; downregulates CD4 and MHC class I surface expression
nef	Negative regulatory factor	27	Inhibits or enhances viral replication depending on strain and cell type; Downregulates CD4; MHC class I; Antiapoptosis
vpx†	Virion protein x	25	Packaged into the virion

*HIV-1 only.
†HIV-2 only.
MHC, major histocompatibility complex; RNase H, ribonuclease H.

FIGURE 166-4. Following entry, formation of the reverse transcription complex and reverse transcription human immunodeficiency virus infection involves the formation of the pre-integration complex, consisting of the newly synthesized viral DNA and several HIV proteins—the matrix protein (p17), integrase, reverse transcriptase, and viral protein R (vpr).

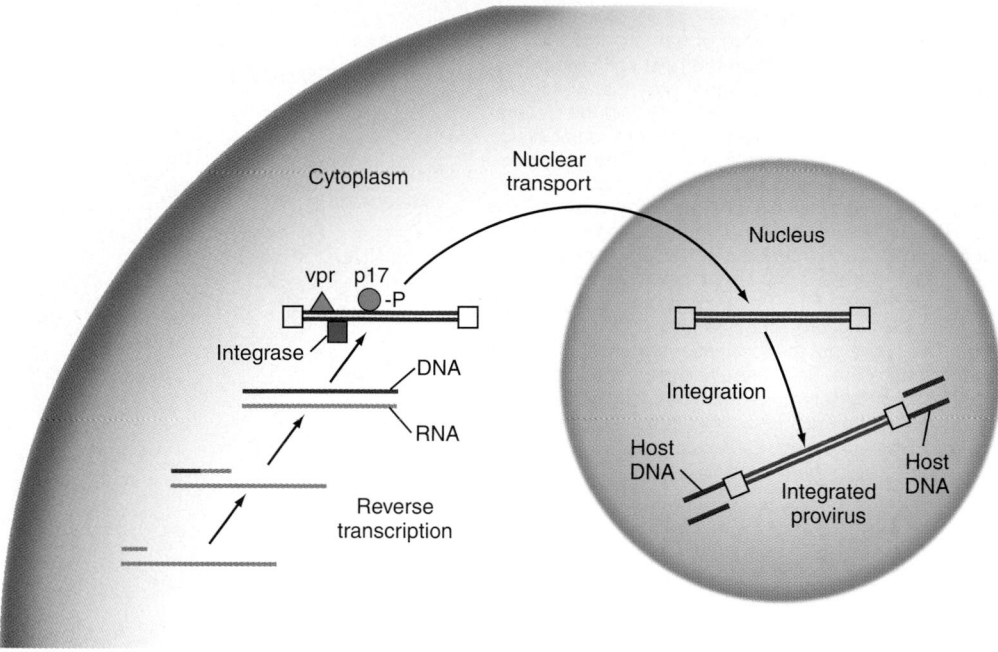

ing viral protease, RT, and IN; and then the *env* gene, which encodes the outer and transmembrane envelope proteins. A complex series of open reading frames encode the accessory proteins. *vif* is partly contained within the *pol* coding region and partly downstream, and *vpr* is located downstream from *vif*. The first coding exons for *tat* and *rev* are co-linear and located between *vpr* and *env*, and their second exons, located in the *env* gene, are joined to the first exons by RNA splicing. The *vpu* gene is co-linear with the 5′ region of the *env* gene. *nef* is located downstream from the *env* gene and extends into the downstream LTR sequence.

Transcription of a single unspliced RNA is initiated at the 5′ end by the cellular RNA polymerase II. The unspliced mRNA serves as a template for translation of the Gag and Gag-Pol precursor polypeptides. This message is also spliced to produce single-spliced transcripts for Vif, Vpr, and Vpu proteins and the Env precursor polypeptide, and doubly spliced transcripts for Tat and Rev. The precursor polyproteins are then cleaved by cellular or viral enzymes; the Gag and Gag-Pol precursors are cleaved by the viral protease, which is itself transcribed from the unspliced viral message. The Env precursor polypeptide is cleaved by cellular proteases (Fig. 166-5).

FIGURE 166-5. The role of RNA splicing in the life cycle of human immunodeficiency virus type 1 (HIV-1). The early mRNA transcripts of HIV-1 are doubly spliced and produce viral regulatory proteins Tat, Rev, and Nef. The function of HIV Rev is to facilitate the expression of the late transcripts of HIV-1. These can be divided into two categories: unspliced and singly spliced. The unspliced HIV-1 mRNA has two functions: it is translated into the structural precursor polyproteins for the *gag* and *pol* gene products and is incorporated into virions as genomic RNA. The different singly spliced mRNAs of HIV-1 are translated into the envelope proteins gp120 and gp41, as well as Vif, Vpr, and Vpu.

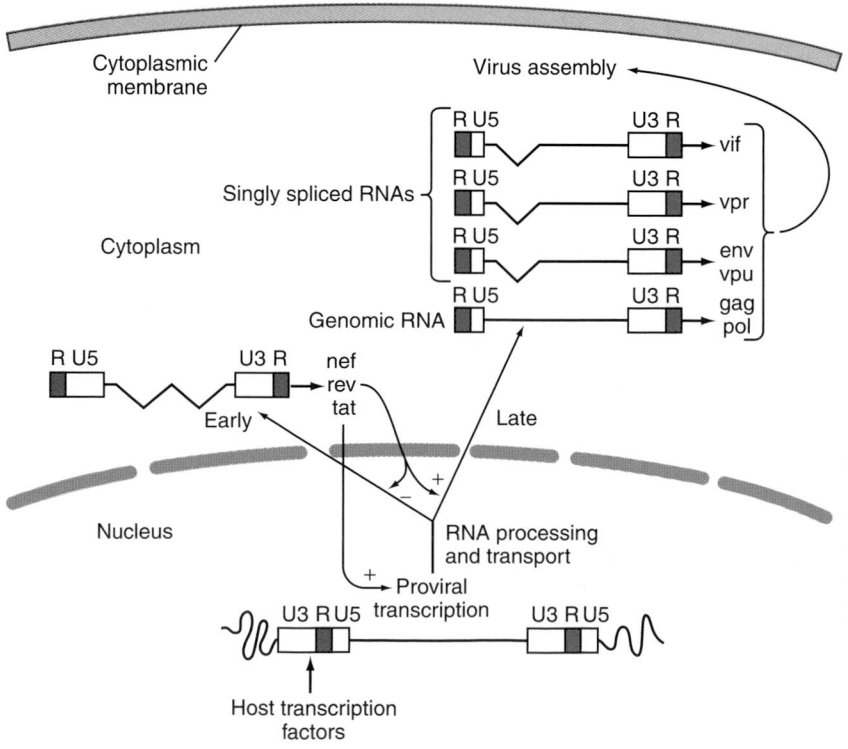

VIRION STRUCTURAL PROTEINS

Gag Proteins

The cleavage of the Gag precursor protein by viral protease produces the structural components of the virus that interact with other viral proteins, RNA, and cellular proteins. To form the virus capsid structure, one large protein is made from the viral mRNA. This 55-kDa polyprotein—a Gag precursor protein sometimes called p55—is cleaved into at least five structural proteins by the viral 34-kb protease encoded at the 5′ end of the *pol* gene. Lack of protease function, either through inhibition by drugs or following transfection of the p55 gene into a cell that lacks protease, results in the formation of noninfectious viral particles.[73]

The p55 protein can be seen on Western blot preparations made from whole cell lysates but not on those made from mature virions. During or shortly after self-assembly, the viral protease is activated and the precursor is cleaved into three principal proteins and two smaller peptides. These proteins undergo extensive post-translational modification by cellular enzymes. After translation, the initiating methionine residue is removed, and p17 is myristoylated; p17 and p24 are phosphorylated by cellular kinases, and p7 (the nucleocapsid protein, or NC) binds to two zinc ions to form the zinc-fingers that bind to RNA. Although the virus depends on cellular systems for many functions, it requires the virally encoded protease for the cleavage of the Gag proteins. Gag proteins are sufficient to form particles when expressed from transfected cells. These self-assembled particles are noninfectious. The p17 matrix protein, MA (molecular weight, 17,000), contains about 130 amino acids and is myristoylated on a glycine at its amino terminus by the host cell enzyme *N*-myristoyl transferase.[74] The first 31 amino acids target the myristoylated protein to the cell membrane, and nonmyristoylated proteins form noninfectious capsids. In addition to viral assembly at the cell surface, MA may function as part of the preintegration complex targeting viral DNA to the cell nucleus and enabling HIV-1 to infect and integrate into nondividing cells such as macrophages.[75] p17 has extracellular functions via binding to a receptor on peripheral blood mononuclear cells (PBMCs), including T cells, and increases their production of proinflammatory cytokines and counteracts the inhibitory activity of interleukin-4 (IL-4) on these cells.[76]

The p24 capsid protein, CA, is produced by two cleavages to form a 240–amino acid hydrophobic protein that forms the major subunits of the viral capsid and self-associates to form dimers and higher-order structures. This protein binds the cellular cyclophilins, a process that may be important for viral replication.[77] A major homology region of 29 amino acids is shared with many retroviruses.[78,79] p24 Gag is typically the easiest protein to detect using sera from infected patients, and serologic detection in infected animals gave the name *group antigen* (Gag) to these proteins. The carboxyl-terminal sequences encode a 70–amino acid hydrophilic protein, NC, that binds both viral RNA and the capsid p24 protein, intertwining approximately one molecule with four to six nucleotides of RNA.[80] A zinc-finger domain binds RNA, whereas the NC recognizes the packaging site on Gag.[81,82] Two small proteins of unknown function, p2 and p1, are also found in the viral core.

Viral Enzymes

Pol Gene Products

The *pol* gene encodes three enzymes: protease, RT, and IN. These proteins are synthesized from the same mRNA as the Gag proteins through a ribosomal translational frameshift. The cleavage of the 160-kDa precursor polyprotein is essential for viability. It has been estimated that there are about 2000 copies of each Gag protein and 100 copies of each Pol protein in each virion.

Protease

Protease is a 10-kDa 99–amino acid protein that is fully active as a dimer. It is autocatalytically cleaved from the precursor protein during the viral assembly process. Site-specific mutagenesis has demonstrated that noninfectious particles containing uncleaved Gag and Gag-Pol proteins are produced if this enzyme is inactivated. The similarity of viral protease to other aspartyl proteases such as angiotensin-converting enzyme (ACE) greatly facilitated the design of potent antiviral drugs, including inhibitors of dimerization and molecules that bind to the active catalytic site.[73,83]

Reverse Transcriptase

Viral RT is an RNA-dependent DNA polymerase. This highly versatile enzyme is capable of synthesizing DNA copies from both RNA and DNA templates and degrading viral RNA from RNA-DNA hybrids. RT and its RNase H activity are required for viral replication. The protein is first cleaved from the precursor polyprotein to form a p66 homodimer and, after a second cleavage, forms a p66-p51 heterodimer with identical amino-terminal ends.

The structure of the RT heterodimer has been used to reveal the enzymatic mechanism of reverse transcription and the molecular basis of resistance to antiviral drugs.[84] The p66 and p51 assemble in an unusual head-to-tail heterodimer. Four domains of the p66 protein are similar in shape to a clenched right hand and therefore are designated as the fingers, palm, and thumb. These are joined to the RNase H domain. The cleft between them contains the highly conserved catalytic site Tyr-Met-Asp-Asp. Although the p51 subunit is derived from the same protein, it maintains a different conformation.[85,86]

RT plays a major role in the generation of genetic diversity in retroviruses. The fidelity of the enzyme has been determined for a variety of retroviruses by measuring misincorporation rates on defined templates. For HIV-1, this rate ranges from 1:1700 to 1:4000 misincorporations per nucleotide per replication, somewhat higher than for other retroviruses, and considerably greater than for the host cell polymerases. For the 9.7-kb HIV-1 genome, the in vivo error rate is estimated to be one misincorporation per replication cycle.[87]

Variants produced by RT generate sequence diversity that may emerge under the selective pressure of immune responses or antiviral drugs and may allow virus to change cell tropism. However, the same lack of fidelity also allows nucleoside analogues to be preferentially incorporated into viral rather than cellular DNA.[88,89]

Integrase

IN is a 288–amino acid, 32-kDa viral enzyme that mediates the linkage of double-stranded viral DNA into the host cell genome. Integration occurs following the translocation of a large complex derived from the viral core from the cytoplasm into the nucleus. IN is part of this complex and catalyzes the cleavage of viral DNA and ligation to host cell DNA.[90] A large central acidic domain of IN is highly conserved in retroviruses and retrotransposons. Once integrated, the provirus can be considered for most purposes to be a stable genetic element remaining for the life of the cell and, through cellular replication, for the life of the individual.

Envelope Glycoproteins and Viral Fusion

The *env* gene of HIV-1 encodes a single-spliced viral RNA transcript that encodes both Vpu and a 160-kDa precursor that is synthesized in the late stages of viral replication; this 850–amino acid polyprotein is cleaved by cellular proteases at amino acids 512 and 513 to form the external gp120 and the transmembrane gp41. Proteolytic cleavage is essential for viral infectivity. There is extensive *N*-linked glycosylation on asparagine residues with high-mannose complex oligosaccharide groups. Selective removal of glycosylation sites reduces infectivity. The extensive variation among different strains of HIV-1 and the ability of the virus to evolve during the course of a single infection and to rapidly adapt to drugs and immunologic attack present problems in therapy and vaccine development. Most of the variability among strains of HIV occurs in the envelope sequence in five variable domains of gp120, designated V1 through V5 (comprising amino acids 128 to 152, 182 to 195, 300 to 330, 395 to 415, and 460 to 467, respectively).[91] The third variable region, called the V3 loop (formed by joining two cysteine residues), is a dominant antibody-neutralizing domain of gp120 and plays an important role in determining viral tropism. Four regions that are relatively invariant have been designated C1 through C4 (amino acids 33 to 60, 87 to 126, 231 to 276, and 460 to 467). These regions presumably maintain essential viral structures.

Although some structure-function relationships have been deduced from secondary structure, biochemical, mutagenic, and immunologic analyses, the solution of the crystal structure of the gp120 protein and of part of the gp41 protein has literally put a new face on the virus, with implications for cell fusion mechanisms and immune evasion. The crystal structure of gp120 at 2.5-Å resolution reveals a cavity-laden gp120–CD4 interface and a conserved binding site for the chemokine receptor with evidence for a conformational change on CD4 binding. gp120 is visualized as two domains joined by a bridge. The V3 loop, together with conserved regions that remain unexposed until CD4 binding occurs, is the principal determinant of chemokine receptor variability. An understanding of the structural basis that enables HIV to evade humoral responses while maintaining function may help in vaccine design.[92-94]

Virus–Cell Fusion

The viral envelope ultimately must be understood as a fusion machine allowing viral entry into target cells. Fusion depends on the sequential binding of gp120 to the CD4 and chemokine receptors, but the fusogenic machinery is located in gp41. The fusion peptide that is inserted into the target cell membrane is formed at the new amino terminus created by proteolytic cleavage of the gp160 precursor protein.[95] However, this hydrophobic tip must be kept in an inactive state until juxtaposed to the target cell membrane. Premature triggering of the fusion peptide would result in an inactive virus. The core structure of gp41 has been crystallized from peptide fragments.[96]

The core structure that mediates the fusion-active state between virus and cell is formed from a trimer of gp41 molecules composed of two α-helical regions within gp41 that form a six-helix bundle characteristic of "coiled coils." The crystallized complex shows striking structural homology with the low pH-induced fusogenic conformation of the influenza virus hemagglutinin protein (HA), which contains three antiparallel helices packed in a central trimeric coiled coil. The conformational change in HIV-1 is not mediated by endocytic uptake into the low pH compartment as it is for HA, however. Probably, the binding to the second receptor triggers the conformational change, which leads to cell fusion and virus uptake. The transition from a loop structure to a coiled-coil state is the basis for the "spring-loaded" model of activation for membrane fusion. The fusion-active state has been identified using synthetic viral peptides to block fusion following triggering[97] (Fig. 166-6). Synthetic peptides that span all or part of these domains can inhibit HIV cell fusion and infection.[98]

Viral Regulatory and Accessory Genes

In addition to the structural genes, HIV has six accessory genes: *tat* (coding for the *trans*-activator of transcription), *rev* (encoding the regulator of viral expression), *vif* (encoding the virion infectivity factor), *vpr* (encoding the viral protein R), *vpu* (encoding viral protein U), and *nef* (encoding the "negative" regulatory factor, which was a misnomer). These genes enable the virus to manipulate host cell processes and to achieve efficient replication under host-selec-

tive pressure, thus contributing to disease progression.[54] Expression of Nef in infected macrophages has been shown to activate T cells through the CD2 stimulatory pathway, rendering the T cells susceptible to infection.[99] Of these genes, only *tat* and *rev* are necessary for high levels of viral expression in culture. Tat protein augments viral RNA by increasing transcription, primarily by permitting elongation of otherwise blocked short nascent RNA chains. Rev regulates the splicing and transport of RNA. Vif appears to be required for efficient cell-free transmission of virus. Vif has been shown[100] to block the effects of APOBEC3G, a deoxycytidine deaminase. APOBEC3G acts on newly synthesized viral DNA to induce its degradation and hypermutation and may represent a general antiretroviral defense mechanism.[101] Nef has been found to be crucial to virulence and immune evasion and downregulates surface expression of CD4, presumably to allow efficient expression of gp120 on the cell surface. As mentioned earlier, expression of Nef in macrophages may be important in rendering neighboring T cells permissive to infection. Vpr also downregulates surface expression of CD4. Vpr is the only accessory protein found abundantly in the mature virion.

As a presumed example of convergent evolution, *tax* and *rex* genes present in HTLV-I (and related viruses) encode two proteins, Tax (*trans*-activator of transcription) and Rex (regulator of viral expression); these genes function analogously to *tat* and *rev*. Similar genes are present in HIV-2, which lacks *vpu* but has *vpx*, which encodes a unique protein Vpx (viral protein X). Accessory genes that are formed by complex splicing arrangements are not generally found in all retroviruses, suggesting that retroviruses should be classified as either simple or complex, depending on the presence or absence of these genes.[17]

Early in infection, a *rev*-independent pathway removes "introns" from the viral transcript. The multiply spliced messages of *tat* and *rev* are transported and translated and, as proteins, are shuttled back to the nucleus. As Tat acts and Rev accumulate in the nucleus, additional unspliced and single-spliced messages for *gag, gag-pol,* and *env* and viral accessory genes *vpu, vpr,* and *vif* are transported out of the nucleus.[102]

The Tat protein is translated from a transcript that contains three exons, the first of which is noncoding. The *tat* reading frame overlaps both the *rev* and *env* genes. Tat is a small nuclear (14 to 16 kDa) protein that varies in size, containing 86 to 102 amino acids, depending on the strain of HIV-1. The first 72 amino acids contained in the second exon are required for full activity, whereas all of the length variation occurs at the carboxyl-terminal end of the protein.[103] Tat binds to the Tat activation response element (TAR) region found in all HIV-1 mRNAs, in conjunction with cellular factors, to stabilize the nascent mRNA and enhance its rate of elongation up to 1000-fold. However, Tat activation is downregulated after periods of several hours, suggesting that these cellular cofactors may be present in limited amounts and that negative regulatory factors may downmodulate Tat function.

The Tat protein has three functional domains. A highly conserved cysteine-rich domain between amino acids 22 and 37 contains seven

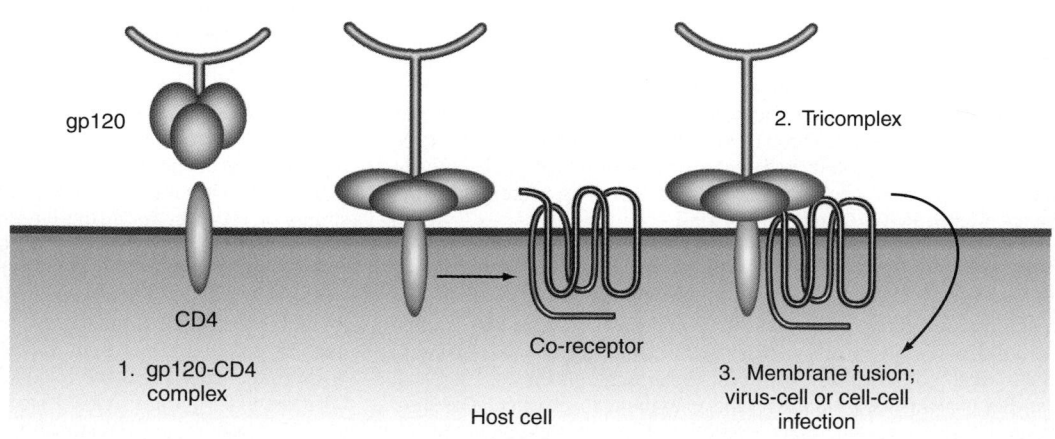

FIGURE 166-6. The human immunodeficiency virus type 1 (HIV-1) infection process at the cell surface. Upon first infection and after initial binding of gp120 of HIV to the cell surface CD4 molecule, an envelope conformational change occurs which fosters binding to the chemokine coreceptor (e.g., CCR5 or CXCR4). This interaction involves specific portions of gp120 including the V3 region.

cysteine residues and two zinc-finger motifs, as is characteristic of a number of DNA-binding proteins. Loss of any one of six cysteines results in loss of activity. The interaction of Tat with TAR is mediated through a basic domain between nucleic acids 48 and 56. One requirement for Tat activity is the CDC2-like kinase CD9, which phosphorylates the carboxyl-terminal domain of RNA polymerase II. However, Tat must first interact with a host cell factor, which is cell specific and limits Tat activation in nonhuman cells. This factor, encoded on chromosome 12, has been identified as a novel 87-kDa cyclin C–related protein named cyclin T.[104] Overexpression of this protein, along with CD4 and chemokine receptors, may permit virus infection and expression in nonpermissive cells.

Tat also contains an RGD (arginine-glycine-aspartate) motif at amino acids 78 to 80 that is common to proteins that bind to integrin receptors. This feature is consistent with the finding that Tat may be secreted by cells into the media and induce extracellular effects. Binding of HIV-1 Tat to cells derived from KS lesions, mediated in part through the RGD motif, enhances the growth of these cells. Extracellular Tat by itself has been shown to induce KS-like lesions in nude mice.[105]

All three functional domains of Tat are highly conserved among HIV-1 isolates. HIV-2/SIV Tat has an additional 30 amino acids in the amino-terminal sequence but lacks the RGD region. Tat should be an inviting target for blocking viral replication, although in some instances cellular factors may allow virus to be expressed without Tat.[106] Extracellular Tat may also be immunosuppressive, as well as promoting increased HIV replication.[107] Both Tat and interferon (IFN)-α inhibit antigen-stimulated T-cell proliferation, and specific anti-Tat and/or anti–IFN-α antibodies prevent generation of HIV-1–induced suppressor cells. It is possible that high titer anti-Tat and/or anti–IFN-α antibodies, neutralizing extracellular Tat, and/or IFN-α, including those induced by vaccines, antagonize HIV-1–induced immunosuppression.[108]

Tat can affect the expression of heterologous and cellular genes, including the promoters of the human polyomaviruses, human papillomaviruses, and cytokines, such as tumor necrosis factor (TNF)-α and IL-2. The first exon of Tat has been shown to downregulate major histocompatibility complex (MHC) class I expression. The demonstration that another viral protein, Nef, also functions to downregulate this protein suggests that these proteins are important because the immune system is exerting significant selective pressure on the virus. It also illustrates how single viral proteins may have multiple or complex functions that contribute to immunosuppression.

The *rev* gene encodes a serine phosphorylated protein, Rev, that ranges in size from 106 to 123 amino acids but is most commonly 116 amino acids in length, with a molecular weight of 19 kDa. This protein is translated from a unique doubly spliced mRNA, with the second splice acceptor located downstream of the Tat translation initiation site.[109] Expression of Rev results in the accumulation of viral structural proteins encoded by the Gag, Pol, Env, Vpu, Vpr, and Vif mRNAs. In contrast, multiple-spliced viral messages for Tat, Rev, and Nef are efficiently expressed without Rev protein. In the absence of Rev, most viral mRNAs are processed to the double-spliced form, thereby limiting the production of virions. Rev protein accumulates in the nucleolus and shuttles back and forth to the cytoplasm. Although it binds to unspliced genomic RNA, it does not appear in the mature virion. Rev binds to a unique RNA element located in the Env coding region of HIV-1 RNA. This Rev regulatory element, RRE, is found in all unspliced and singly spliced mRNAs.

Rev contains at least two functional domains: an arginine-rich region at amino acids 35 to 50, which is conserved and required for nucleolar localization and specific RRE binding, and a multimerization domain. After initial RRE binding, multiple additional Rev molecules bind to each other, and this oligomerization is required for activity.[110]

The *nef* gene product is a 206–amino acid myristoylated protein that inserts into the cell membrane. The Nef protein may have many different properties that depend in part on the experimental methodology used to analyze them. The original observation that T-cell–tropic, Nef-deleted viruses replicated to high levels led to the name *negative factor*. Downregulation of CD4 requires myristoylation and membrane targeting of Nef to the cytoplasmic domain of CD4 and increases CD4 endocytosis. The protection of HIV-1–infected cells by Nef protein against killing by CTL correlates with downregulation of MHC class I.[111] Nef appears to be important in maintaining high virus loads associated with rapid progression to immunodeficiency. As mentioned earlier, Nef leads to activation of T cells when it is expressed in macrophages.

Viruses with Nef deleted appear to be less virulent than wild-type viruses but equally infectious, both in tissue culture and in rhesus macaques. The possible role of Nef as a virulence factor has led to the use of Nef-deleted virus as a potential live vaccine in rhesus macaques. These "attenuated" viruses were able to protect against infection by challenge with other virulent SIV strains. However, the Nef-deleted viruses are not entirely benign and are themselves able to cause disease in both newborn animals and adults.[112,113]

The immune response to Nef may exert considerable selection pressure. When T cells capable of CTL activity against Nef were transferred to HIV-infected patients, a Nef-deleted variant emerged, and although there was apparent successful immunologic intervention, the patient's disease progressed.[114] Nef-deleted viruses detected in several human clusters have been associated with little or no disease, raising the possibility that they represent less virulent viruses.[115] However, long-term follow-up of these cases demonstrates that definite, albeit slower, disease progression does indeed occur.[116]

Vif is a 193–amino acid viral protein of 23 to 27 kDa with no N-linked glycosylation sites. The infectivity of Vif deletion mutants is decreased up to 1000-fold in some cell lines compared with that of wild-type virus. The deleted virus is capable of cell entry and initiating reverse transcription, but double-stranded DNA is not produced. As mentioned earlier, Vif likely blocks the activity of deoxycytidine deaminase APOBEC3G.[100]

Vpr is a 96–amino acid protein translated from a single-spliced mRNA and, like Vif, is dependent on Rev function. Vpr is abundantly present in the mature virion associated with capsid protein. Expression of p55 Gag and Vpr in transfected cells is sufficient for incorporation and export of viral proteins. The protein plays a role in the nuclear localization of the preintegration complex.[117,118] In addition, in transfected human muscle cells, Vpr blocks proliferation and induces differentiation, suggesting a nuclear role for Vpr in regulation of gene expression. Vpr causes arrest of cell cycle progression at the G_2/M interface, presumably through an effect on cyclin CDC2 activity, which correlates with the ability to activate HIV transcription.[119,120] In addition, Vpr causes massive ruptures in cell nuclei.[121] A gene encoding a second homologous protein, VpX, is found in HIV-2 and several SIV strains but not in nonprimate lentiviruses.

Vpu is an amphipathic integral membrane protein.[122] The first 27 amino acids are hydrophobic, whereas the remainder of this small, 81–amino acid 16-kDa protein is hydrophilic. A single-spliced message overlaps with the *env* gene in a different reading frame.[123] The protein forms oligomeric complexes localized to the perinuclear region. Cells infected with Vpu-defective mutants show large accumulations of intracellular vesicles, in contrast with those infected with wild-type virus. Vpu along with Nef is associated with the rapid degradation of CD4, which may in part eliminate CD4-gp160 intracellular complexes that interfere with virus production. The CD4 cytoplasmic tail is required for targeting the degradation of CD4 by Vpu. Vpu has structural similarities to the influenza virus M2 protein, an ion channel protein that modulates the pH of the *trans*-Golgi.[124]

Virus Regulation and the Long Terminal Repeat

The LTR of all retroviruses is located at each end of the provirus as a direct repeat containing U3, R, and U5 region. It functions as a eukaryotic transcription unit (Fig. 166-7). The U3 region contains the viral promoter and enhancer elements; the R region includes the mRNA initiation site (+1) used by all viral messages and ends at the polyadenylation site. The function of the U5 region is not well understood. It separates the R region from the tRNA primer binding site used to initiate reverse transcription. HIV-1 uses tRNA[lys] as a primer. Once the virus has formed a double-stranded DNA copy, it depends entirely on cellular machinery for transcription and translation.

However, the control of virus expression results from a complex set of interactions between viral elements and cellular proteins. Small changes in these regions may result in profound differences in virus behavior. cis-Acting control elements of the virus (TAR, TATAA, SP1, and enhancer and negative regulatory regions, located within the U3 and R regions) interact with cellular and viral proteins. These interactions, which occur at both the DNA and the RNA levels, are crucial in controlling the level of viral expression in both resting and activated cells.[125]

The TATAA box, located at −27 (relative to the RNA initiation site), binds the critical cellular transcription factor TFIID to initiate transcription. The promoter region, the binding site of the cellular polymerase, lies farther 5′ (between −45 and −77) and contains three binding sites for the cellular SP1 transcription factor.[126]

An enhancer element is still further 5′, mapping to nucleotides −82 to −105, and contains a consensus sequence also found in the κ-immunoglobulin, IL-2, and IL-2R enhancer regions. This region binds an inducible cellular transcription factor, NF-κB. Although originally described in B lymphocytes, this factor or family of factors is also expressed in activated T cells and stimulates HIV expression.[66,67]

In addition to NF-κB, other factors have been shown to increase HIV-1 promoter activity by interactions in the region. These include cellular cytokines, such as TNF-α and IL-1, and heterologous viral proteins, such as HTLV-I Tax. Such observations indicate molecular mechanisms by which other viruses could interact with HIV; however, the relevance of such interactions in vivo is not known.

Farther 5′ are the binding sites for additional cellular factors (AP-1, NFAT-1) that lie within a negative regulatory element (NRE). Removing this region from a functional provirus enhances virus expression, again suggesting that viral production is carefully modulated in both a negative and positive manner.

The R region of the LTR codes for the 5′ untranslated leader sequence shared by all HIV-1 mRNAs and for the TAR, essential for the activity of the potent virally coded HIV-1 trans-activating protein, Tat. The TAR is available in the LTR transcript as a unique stem loop structure. Of interest, the structure of the HIV-2 LTR is significantly different from that of the HIV-1 LTR and may contribute to distinctly different biologic activities of these two human retroviruses.

VIRUS-HOST INTERACTIONS

Viral Receptors, Chemokines, Receptors, and Tropism

Chemokines and their receptors constitute a complex signaling system essential for orchestrating inflammatory responses. Over 40 chemokines are grouped into two principal families, C-C and C-X-C; there are at least 14 known seven-transmembrane spanning, pertussis toxin–sensitive, G protein–coupled chemokine receptors. These molecules have been exploited by bacterial and viral pathogens as their receptors to gain entry to or activate cells, and virally encoded antagonists often subvert chemokine function.[127,128]

The revelation that chemokine receptors are essential for HIV cell fusion brings together several distinct areas of viral research: how CD8+ cell–derived factors suppress HIV-1 replication, the mechanisms of cell entry and viral tropism, and host genetic determinants of infection. Three CC (or β) cytokines released by CD8+ T cells—RANTES, MIP-1α, and MIP-1β—bind to the CCR5 receptor and potently suppress HIV macrophage-tropic virus.[43,129] The first co-receptor identified, the CXCR4 molecule, known at the time only as an "orphan receptor," was discovered using a complementary DNA (cDNA) screening approach for receptor activity mediating cell–cell fusion.[44] A group of reports followed, showing that a recently identified receptor, CCR5, that could use the identified suppressor molecules as ligands, was the main co-receptor for primary isolates and macrophage-tropic strains.[45,49] The number of receptors that may function as co-receptors continues to expand. Dual tropic strains are able to use both co-receptors. The role of other receptors, such as CX3CR1, expressed in the brain, or CCR8, expressed in the thymus, is not known. Some strains of monocyte-tropic virus may use CCR2 or CCR3. Chemokine co-receptor use may be a determinant of viral virulence and disease progression.[130] Additionally, recent evidence points to the critical role of cholesterol in the cell membrane in HIV-1 co-receptor function; removal of cellular cholesterol-rendered primary cells and cell lines highly resistant to HIV-1–mediated syncytium formation and to infection by both CXCR4- and CCR5-specific viruses.[131]

A mutant CCR5 gene that codes for a receptor that is unable to bind virus has been found in exposed but uninfected persons, strongly suggesting that a functional CCR5 protein is required for infection.[132] Homozygosity for this mutant[133] is a strong protective factor, but rare infections by CCR5-independent viruses have been documented in a person with hemophilia and in another person following sexual transmission. Heterozygous adults and children are not protected from infection but may take a longer time to develop disease.[134,135]

Pathogenesis, T-Cell Depletion, and Viral Load

Understanding the rates of HIV-1 production and associated loss of T cells has been dramatically advanced by the ability to measure the changes produced by potent new drug combinations. HIV-1 production and T-cell turnover constitute a continuous dynamic process.[136,137] Mathematical modeling of virus production has suggested that a continuous battle is being waged between the virus and the host. Production of billions of virions and T-cell turnover estimated at a billion cells per day may help to account for the very rapid emergence of

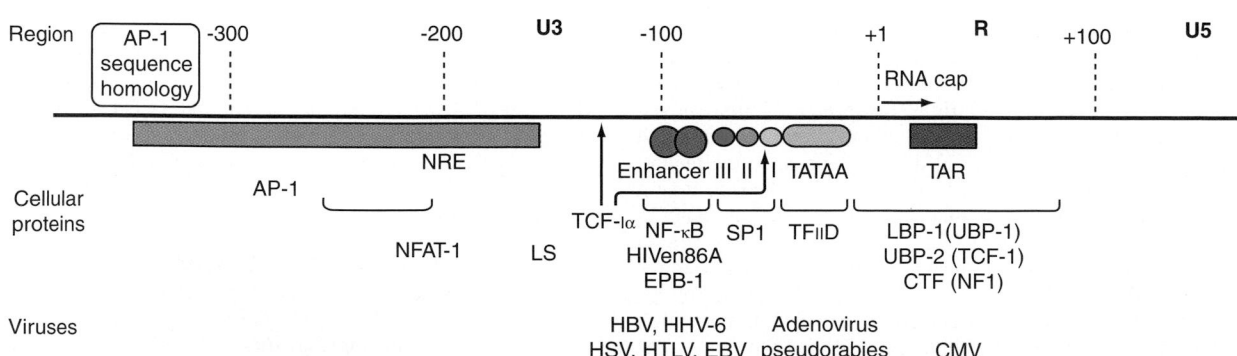

FIGURE 166-7. The human immunodeficiency virus type 1 (HIV-1) long terminal repeat (LTR). Like other retroviruses, the LTR of HIV-1 is composed of three regions: U3, R, and U5. Integrated proviral DNA is flanked by two complete LTRs, whereas genomic viral RNA transcripts contain partial LTRs at either end, the 5′ end containing the R and U5 regions, and the 3′ end containing the U3 and R regions. The untranslated 5′ (U3) region contains the major regulatory domains of the LTR, including an NRE and the major binding sites for cellular enhancers of HIV-1 transcription, NF-κB and SP1. A number of cellular as well as viral proteins interact directly or indirectly with the LTRs. The R region of the LTR includes the TAR, which (as RNA) binds the HIV-1 transcriptional activator, Tat, and a number of cellular factors that also enhance transcriptional activity.

viral variants and the fluctuating and progressive nature of T-cell depletion. Virus may be distributed across different cellular compartments with different rates of turnover and production. Even in the steady state that may occur during periods of clinical latency, hordes of virus freshly infecting T cells lead to a highly activated immune system that is attempting both to control virus replication and to renew itself.[138] The increase in CD4+ cells with highly active antiretroviral therapy (HAART) is probably due to a combination of initial redistribution of memory T cells and a continuous but slow repopulation with newly produced naive T cells.[139]

Although no similar measure of T-cell turnover in uninfected individuals is available, bromodeoxyuridine labeling of CD4+ and CD8+ populations in SIV-infected macaques suggested a generalized state of activation and rapid T-cell turnover compared with uninfected animals.[139a]

The mathematical models that have been proposed, although useful, grossly oversimplify the real dynamics of infection. Several pathologic mechanisms, including indirect viral killing and activation-induced apoptosis, have been suggested. For example, circulating Tat protein, along with abnormally high levels of IFN-α in HIV-infected people, appears to suppress cell-mediated immunity.[107] Uninfected CD8+ cells turn over as rapidly as CD4+ cells but are not initially depleted.[140] The eventual loss of noninfected CD8+ T cells may be mediated by gp120 binding to CXCR4.[141] Eventually, viral escape from immune control and emergence of T-cell–tropic viruses utilizing CXCR4 may lead to immunodeficiency.[142] All of these models incorporate two common assumptions: a demonstrated quantitative association between virus production and T-cell depletion, and a compartmentalization of virus production and cell turnover at different rates.

The significance of virus integration for the natural history of HIV-1 infection has been vividly demonstrated by the effects of combination therapy on virus production from different populations of cells and has helped to define what is meant by latent infection. Potent antiretroviral regimens that include a combination of RT and protease inhibitors can produce sustained reductions of plasma viral RNA to below detectable limits.[143] Patients with detectable viral plasma RNA, even if the level is greatly reduced, have viral loads in their lymph nodes similar to those in the nodes of patients who did not receive treatment, reflecting ongoing viral replication and emergence of drug resistance.[144] However, even in persons with no detectable plasma RNA, viral DNA could be detected in lymph nodes and PBMCs, and virus could be grown from PBMCs after removal of CD8+ cells and activation. Furthermore, no new mutations associated with drug resistance were detected from these isolates recovered after 2 years of therapy. This strongly suggests that virus persisted in a long-lived and latently infected T-cell population. This pool of latently infected cells is probably established very early during primary HIV-1 infection. Even though plasma viremia could be suppressed, initiation of HAART therapy as early as 10 days after onset of symptoms did not prevent generation of latently infected CD4+ lymphocytes.[145] Although the frequency of these cells is low, on the order of 16 per million PBMCs, the fact that virus may survive by hiding out in these cells may represent a significant factor in long-term therapy and shape strategies to eliminate virus.[146,147]

Like the impairment or killing of infected cells, there are several distinct mechanisms by which bystander cells can be affected that can be demonstrated in vitro. For example, HIV-1–infected PBMCs either taken directly from patients or obtained through infection of normal PBMCs with HIV-1 in vitro led to marked impairment of proliferative responses even though only a small fraction of T cells are infected.[148–150] Other indirect (bystander) effects include (1) impaired hematopoiesis leading to cytopenias of several blood cell lines, (2) impaired thymopoiesis, (3) anergy and apoptosis of uninfected immune cells, likely through increased levels of cytokines such as TNF-α, IFN-α, and transforming growth factor-beta (TGF-β), and (4) hyperactivation and apoptosis of uninfected immune cells by the effects of extracellular Tat.

Viral Variation: Genetic and Phenotypic Variation

One of the most striking characteristics of HIV-1 is its remarkable variability, contributing to phenotype diversity, and resulting in altered cell tropism, immune escape, and resistance to RT and protease inhibitors.[151] As a consequence of the underlying variation by mutation, high rates of virus turnover and selection of viral variants cause viral evolution in individual hosts with time, as well as among populations of infected individuals. On the basis of phylogenetic analysis, HIV strains can be separated into major (M) subgroups A through J and a more distant group O. Within the M group are multiple subtypes A, B, C, D, F, G, H, J, and K and two circulating recombinant forms, CRF 01 AE/B and CRF 02 A/G.[152] In an individual case, the initial infection transmits a limited range of variants, generally of a single group, and subsequent exposure following infection rarely results in infection with a second variant. Therefore, most affected persons appear to be infected with a single strain that evolves into a swarm of related viruses or quasispecies during the course of infection.[153] By the time a person has been infected for several years, viruses emerge that are able to use the CXCR4 receptor. This phenotypic change is associated with progressive disease. Most of the variation is neutral and not adaptive. Although the mutation rate per base pair per cycle is presumed to be equal throughout the genome, diversity is greatest within distinct regions of the envelope gp120, presumably owing to selection. Neutral variation has resulted in grouping of the viruses into clades that may represent geographic distribution and transmission of virus rather than functional differences. HIV is going through rapid epidemiologic change even as the virus is being studied. Thus, genetic relatedness of viruses can be used to track transmission of the virus as well as the relatedness of different viruses. This information is often presented in the form of a viral phylogenetic tree.[154,155]

Human Immunodeficiency Virus–Related Neurologic Disease

HIV crosses the blood-brain barrier relatively early in its natural history. More than half of all HIV-infected patients, including children, develop neurologic disease during the course of infection. Disease may be caused directly by HIV infection of the nervous system or secondarily by infection or tumors associated with immunodeficiency. Primary neurologic disease can occur at any time during the course of infection and anywhere along the CNS neuraxis; the AIDS dementia complex (ADC), vacuolar neuropathy, and peripheral neuropathy are the most frequent presentations[156,157] (see Chapter 120). Where antiretroviral therapy is relatively common, peripheral neuropathy and HIV-associated cognitive dysfunction (including AIDS dementia) account for the greatest burden of neurologic disease in HIV/AIDS.

AIDS-dementia complex is a progressive disorder that can be manifested as signs and symptoms of behavioral, cognitive, or motor dysfunction in any combination. Examination of brain tissue and spinal cord shows high levels of HIV-1 mRNA and expression of viral proteins in microglial cells and macrophages in 90% of symptomatic patients. The extent of virus expression correlates with the severity of clinical disease and increases with time. Viral levels measured in the cerebrospinal fluid (CSF) reflect active production of virus. High levels ($>10^6$ copies/mL) suggest high viral loads in the CNS and may be independent of levels found in the peripheral circulation.[158] Vacuolar myelopathy is a unique degeneration of the spinal cord that may be found in 20% of AIDS patients. Although the etiology and role of the virus in this disorder are still unclear, the disorder is associated with dementia and bears the same pathologic hallmark of multinucleated cells. HIV-1 is also associated with a diverse group of peripheral neuropathies, and the virus can be demonstrated in the dorsal root ganglia and peripheral nerves.

In vitro studies of human brain cultures have shown that HIV-1 is efficiently expressed only in microglial cells and that the ability to infect these cells is the same as for the macrophage. Infection of microglial cells, probably derived from circulating macrophages, requires binding to CD4 and the presence of a chemokine receptor (CCR3 or CCR5) that mediates fusion with macrophage-tropic strains.[158] Of great interest, neurologic symptoms and virologic evidence of CSF infection can be found during primary HIV infection prior to seroconversion. This supports the idea that the CNS is seeded with virus very early and possibly continually during the course of infection.

The pathologic mechanism responsible for neurologic degeneration is not known. However, several mechanisms have been proposed. Most of these involve toxicity associated with HIV-1 proteins or release of cellular products from infected cells. For example, gp120 has been shown to be toxic to neurons in vitro, and TNF-α is toxic to oligodendrocytes, the myelin-forming cells of the CNS. Tat and Nef have also been shown to be neurotoxic. It should be noted that the damage seen in AIDS dementia is not cell type–specific, but generalized, affecting all of the cells within a given area of the brain, and that the lesions are widely distributed. Thus, pathology is not limited to infected cells. Clusters of HIV-1–infected microglial cells form nodules and characteristic multinucleated syncytia, with loss of surrounding tissue, resulting in spongiform lesions. Imaging often demonstrates a degree of brain atrophy.[159] Antiviral therapy can produce a dramatic reversal of dementia, particularly in children. The use of these agents, many of which cross the blood-brain barrier, has been particularly effective in the incidence of opportunistic infections in the brain and meninges; however, the incidence of ADC has been relatively unaffected by their use and may even have increased.[160,161]

MALIGNANCIES AND HUMAN IMMUNODEFICIENCY VIRUS

Although cancer is not common in the young adults most frequently exposed to HIV, KS has been recognized as a defining clinical presentation of AIDS. Previously known as a rare and usually indolent vascular tumor, the incidence of KS in patients with HIV infection may be 10% to 20%, more than 10,000 times that in the general population. Several forms of KS have been described: classic KS; endemic KS, non–HIV associated; transplantation-associated KS; and AIDS-associated KS. The tumor appears to be a vascular proliferation characterized by the presence of spindle cells, vascular channels, and a mixed cellular infiltrate.[162] The "malignant" cell is most likely a population of activated endothelial cells, which are sometimes clonal and sometimes not. These cells themselves and factors produced from them, such as basic fibroblast growth factor and vascular endothelial cell growth factor, can induce vascular lesions in nude mice. The HIV protein Tat can bind to KS spindle cells and stimulate their growth.[163] Although the importance of immunodeficiency and viral proliferation in the etiology of KS is well established, the mechanism is not certain, and KS may occur early in the course of HIV infection. Within the group of HIV-infected individuals, KS occurs predominantly in homosexuals and bisexuals, leading to the hypothesis that a previously undescribed infectious agent might cause KS. Using modern culture techniques, two new human herpesviruses—HHV-6 and HHV-7—were isolated from T cells in 1986. In 1994, using DNA subtraction hybridization, DNA representing a novel herpesvirus was obtained from KS lesions, which led to the isolation of HHV-8[164] (see Chapter 137). Also known as KS herpesvirus, it is related to other gamma herpesviruses such as Epstein-Barr virus (EBV). HHV-8 has also been identified in an EBV-transformed B-cell line and from a unique form of B-cell lymphoma known as body cavity lymphoma. This large virus contains many genes that interact with host cells, including several chemokine and cytokine homologues that can induce vascular growth.[165] Seroepidemiologic studies have made a strong association between this virus and KS. HHV-8 was found to be associated with all forms of KS, and seroconversion precedes the appearance of KS in HIV-infected persons. The prevalence of HHV-8 is far greater than the incidence of KS, however, and the relationship of the virus to the disease is not likely to be simple. A review discusses this and other aspects of KS that are not clear at present.[166] The incidence of KS in AIDS continues to decrease and established lesions may respond to HAART only.

B-cell lymphoma is the second most common cancer associated with AIDS, occurring in approximately 3% to 4% of individuals as their first AIDS-defining diagnosis. The most common site is in the brain (primary brain lymphoma). However, in contradistinction to KS, lymphoma appears to be a late manifestation of HIV disease, with rates rising directly with length of time infected. Up to 16% of AIDS patients eventually die from this condition.

Also in contradistinction to KS, non-Hodgkin's lymphoma (NHL) appears to occur approximately at equal rates in all HIV-1 risk groups. In 53,042 AIDS patients from 21 European countries, approximately 2.6% of injection drug users, 3.2% of transfusion recipients, 3.4% of homosexual men, 3.9% of hemophiliacs, and 2.6% of individuals who acquired HIV through heterosexual contact eventually developed AIDS-related lymphoma.[167]

In the United States, data from the Multi-State AIDS-Cancer Match Registry demonstrated a significantly increased risk of lymphoma among patients with a prior AIDS diagnosis, compared with population control subjects who had not been diagnosed with AIDS.[168] The relative risk of all NHL was increased approximately 113-fold. While the greatest risk is for NHL, there is a 10-fold increase of Hodgkin's disease in the infected group as well.

These tumors are predominantly extranodal and often of high grade, with small cell noncleaved histologic features[169] (see Chapter 121). EBV is found in almost all primary CNS tumors, but high rates of dysregulated B-cell turnover may account for increased cellular turnover, which predisposes to lymphoma. Rates of EBV-associated primary brain lymphoma have fallen off markedly in the era of HAART, but the same cannot be said for systemic lymphoma, which appears to be increasing in frequency as people live longer with HIV.[170]

Several other rare tumors, including leiomyosarcoma, have also been reported.[172] Cervical cancer, almost universally associated with human papillomavirus infection, is accepted as an AIDS-defining illness.[173] High rates of anal intraepithelial neoplasia (AIN) have been documented among HIV-infected homosexual men, and routine screening for AIN is being considered, using the same methodology as Pap smears, with samples obtained through anoscopy.[174] However, the incidence of common cancers does not appear to be greatly increased among HIV patients. Most of the cancers seen appear to be associated directly or indirectly with viral proliferation, suggesting that the role of the immune system may be more directly related to viral expression than to immune control of tumor.

CONCLUSION

Antiretroviral therapy directed at HIV-1 has continued to develop rapidly (see Chapter 124). Significant advances in the ability to treat individual cases, propelled by an understanding of the biology of the virus, have led to the control of viral replication and have altered the course of disease progression. At present, patients have been maintained on combination therapy for several years, with a low rate of relapse due to development of resistance and low viral burdens. Immune restoration and long-term biologic control or complete eradication of the viral burden with minimal toxicity remain elusive goals, while intense efforts continue to focus on new anti-HIV therapies. As we have learned, retroviral disease has important social aspects that, as much as viral biology, determine the extent of viral transmission and the dimensions of the epidemic; this results in a series of epidemics, each with a unique sociobiology. Moreover, despite remarkable progress, the full social and economic effects of the global HIV epidemic are materializing very vividly in sub-Saharan Africa, with devastating losses of population life expectancy and productivity (see Chapter 113). Renewed emphasis on the development of an effective anti-HIV vaccine that might either stem an ongoing epidemic or ameliorate the course of disease has produced encouraging results in primates, and human trials are beginning (see Chapter 126). The history of retrovirology has been filled with remarkable, often serendipitous discoveries based on scientific imagination supported by technologic advances. There is every reason to expect that continued advances will deepen our understanding of fundamental biologic processes and that we will meet the challenges presented by HIV and the inevitability of the emergence of new pathogens.

ACKNOWLEDGMENT

This update is based on a previous chapter co-authored by Howard Streicher, PhD, of the National Cancer Institute. We gratefully acknowledge his support.

REFERENCES

1. Masur H, Michelis MA, Greene JB, et al. An outbreak of community-acquired *Pneumocystis carinii* pneumonia: Initial manifestations of cellular immune dysfunction. N Engl J Med. 1981;305:1431.
2. Gottlieb MS, Schroff R, Schanker HM, et al. *Pneumocystis carinii* pneumonia and mucosal candidiasis in previously healthy homosexual men: Evidence of a new acquired cellular immunodeficiency. N Engl J Med. 1981;305:1425.
3. Durack DT. Opportunistic infections and Kaposi's sarcoma in homosexual men. N Engl J Med. 1981;305:1465.
4. Kalyanaraman VS, Sarngadharan MG, Robert-Guroff M, et al. A new subtype of human T-cell leukaemia virus (HTLV-II) associated with a T-cell variant of hairy cell leukaemia. Science. 1982;218:571.
5. Poiesz BJ, Ruscetti FW, Reitz MS, et al. Isolation of a new type-C retrovirus (HTLV) in primary uncultured cells of a patient with Sézary T-cell leukaemia. Nature. 1981;294:268.
6. Morgan DA, Ruscetti FW, Gallo R. Selective in vitro growth of T lymphocytes from normal human bone marrows. Science. 1976;193:1007-1008.
7. Mier JW, Gallo RC. Purification and some characteristics of human T-cell growth factor from phytohemagglutinin-stimulated lymphocyte-conditioned media. PNAS 1980;77:6134-6138.
8. Gallo RC, Montagnier L. AIDS in 1988. Sci Am. 1988;259:41.
9. Barre-Sinoussi F, Chermann JC, Rey F, et al. Isolation of a T-lymphotrophic retrovirus from a patient at risk for acquired immune deficiency syndrome (AIDS). Science. 1983;220:868.
10. Gallo RC, Salahuddin SZ, Popovic M, et al. Human T-lymphotropic retrovirus, HTLV-III, isolated from AIDS patients and donors at risk for AIDS. Science. 1984;224:500.
11. Popovic M, Sarngadharan MG, Read E, et al. A method for the detection, isolation, and continuous production of cytopathic human T-lymphotropic retroviruses of the HTLV family (HTLV-III) from patients with AIDS and pre-AIDS. Science. 1984;224:497.
12. Schupbach J, Popovic M, Gilden RV, et al. Serological analysis of a subgroup of human T-lymphotropic retroviruses (HTLV-III) associated with AIDS. Science. 1984;224:503.
13. Sarngadharan MG, Popovic M, Bruch L, et al. Antibodies reactive with human T-lymphotropic retroviruses (HTLV-III) in the serum of patients with AIDS. Science. 1984;224:506.
14. Mitsuya H, Weinhold KJ, Furman PA, et al. 3′-Azido-2′-deoxythymidine (BW A509U): An antiviral agent that inhibits the infectivity and cytopathic effect of human T-lymphotrophic virus type III/lymphadenopathy associated virus in vitro. Proc Natl Acad Sci U S A. 1985;82:7096.
15. Santiago ML, Lukasik M, Kamenya S, et al. Foci of endemic simian immunodeficiency virus infection in wild-living eastern chimpanzees (Pan troglodytes schweinfurthii). J Virol. 2003;77:7545-7562.
16. Bailes E, Gao F, Bibollet-Ruche R, et al. Hybrid origin of SIV in chimpanzees. Science 2003;300:1713.
17. Coffin J. Retrovirology: An overview. In: Wormser G, ed. AIDS and Other Manifestations of HIV Infection. Philadelphia: Lippincott-Raven; 1998:41.
18. Ellerman V, Bang O. Experimentelle leukamie bei huhnem. Centralbl Bacteriol. 1908;46:595.
19. Rous P. Transmission of a malignant new growth by means of a cell-free filtrate. JAMA. 1911;56:198.
20. Gross L. Development and serial cell-free passage of a highly potent strain of mouse leukemia virus. Proc Soc Exp Biol Med. 1957;76:27.
21. Boller K, Konig H, Sauter M, et al. Evidence that HERV-K is the endogenous retrovirus sequence that codes for the human teratocarcinoma-derived retrovirus HTDV. Virology. 1993;196:349.
22. Temin HM. The effects of actinomycin D on growth of Rous sarcoma virus in vitro. Virology. 1963;20:577.
23. Temin HM. The participation of DNA in Rous sarcoma virus production. Virology. 1964;23:486.
24. Temin H, Mizutani S. RNA-dependent DNA polymerase in virions of Rous sarcoma virus. Nature. 1970;226:1211.
25. Baltimore D. Viral RNA-dependent DNA polymerase. Nature. 1970;226:1209.
26. Gessain A, Barin F, Vernanat J. Antibodies to human T-lymphotropic virus type-I in patients with tropical spastic paraparesis. Lancet. 1985;2:407.
27. Kanki PJ, Barin F, M'Boup M, et al. New human T-lymphotropic retrovirus related to simian T-lymphotropic retrovirus type III (STLV-III). Science. 1986;232:238.
28. Clavel F, Guetard D, Brun-Vezinet F, et al. Isolation of a new human retrovirus from West African patients with AIDS. Science. 1986;233:343.
29. Weiss R. Retroviral zoonoses. Nat Med. 1998;4:391.
29a. Temin HM. The protovirus hypothesis: Speculations on the significance of RNA-directed DNA synthesis for normal development and for carcinogenesis. J Natl Cancer Inst. 1971;46:3-7.
30. Kidwell MG, Lisch DR. Hybrid genetics: Transposons unbound. Nature. 1998;393:22.
31. Kobayashi K, Nakahori Y, Miyake M, et al. An ancient retrotransposal insertion causes Fukuyama-type congenital muscular dystrophy. Nature. 1998;394:388.
32. Coffin J, Hughs S, Varmus H. Retroviruses. Cold Spring Harbor, NY: Cold Spring Harbor Laboratory Press; 1998.
33. Gallo RC. Human retroviruses after 20 years: A perspective from the past and prospects for their future control [erratum in Immunol Rev. 2002;188:183]. Immunol Rev. 2002;185:236-265.
34. Miedema F, Meyaard L, Koot M, et al. Changing virus-host interactions in the course of HIV-1 infection. Immunol Rev. 1994;140:35.
35. Kahn JO, Walker BD. Acute human immunodeficiency virus type 1 infection. N Engl J Med. 1998;339:33.
36. Ogg GS, Jin X, Bonhoeffer S, et al. Quantitation of HIV-1-specific cytotoxic T lymphocytes and plasma load of viral RNA. Science. 1998;279:2103.
37. Musey L, Hughes J, Schacker T, et al. Cytotoxic T-cell responses, viral load, and disease progression in early human immunodeficiency virus type 1 infection. N Engl J Med. 1997;337:1267.
38. Schacker TW, Hughes JP, Shea T, et al. Biological and virologic characteristics of primary HIV infection. Ann Intern Med. 1998;128:613.
39. Cardo DM, Culver DH, Ciesielski CA, et al. A case-control study of HIV seroconversion in health care workers after percutaneous exposure. Centers for Disease Control and Prevention Needle-stick Surveillance Group. N Engl J Med. 1997;337:1485.
40. Katz MH, Gerberding JL. The care of persons with recent sexual exposure to HIV. Ann Intern Med. 1998;128:306.
41. Maddon PJ, McDougal JS, Clapham PR, et al. HIV infection does not require endocytosis of its receptor, CD4. Cell. 1988;54:865.
42. Gartner S, Markovits P, Markovitz DM, et al. The role of mononuclear phagocytes in HTLV-III/LAV infection. Science. 1986;233:215.
43. Cocchi F, DeVico AL, Garzino-Demo A, et al. Identification of RANTES, MIP-1α, and MIP-1β as the major HIV-suppressive factors produced by CD8⁺ T cells. Science. 1995;270:1811.
44. Feng Y, Broder CC, Kennedy PE, Berger EA. HIV-1 entry cofactor: Functional cDNA cloning of a seven-transmembrane, G protein-coupled receptor. Science. 1996;272:872.
45. Deng H, Liu R, Ellmeirer W, et al. Identification of a major co-receptor for primary isolates of HIV-1. Nature. 1996;381:661.
46. Choe H, Farzan M, Sun Y, et al. The β-chemokine receptors CCR3 and CCR5 facilitate infection by primary HIV-1 isolates. Cell. 1996;85:1135.
47. Dragic T, Litwin V, Allaway GP, et al. HIV-1 entry into CD4⁺ cells is mediated by the chemokine receptor CC-CKR-5. Nature. 1996;381:667.
48. Alkhatib G, Combadiere C, Broder CC, et al. CC CKR5: A RANTES, MIP-1α, MIP-1β receptor as a fusion cofactor for macrophage-tropic HIV-1. Science. 1996;272:1955.
49. O'Brien S. AIDS: A role for host genes. Hosp Pract. 1998;33:53.
50. Wyatt R, Sodroski J. The HIV-1 envelope glycoprotein: Fusogens, antigens, and immunogens. Science. 1998;280:1884.
51. Reitter JN, Means RE, Desrosiers RC. A role for carbohydrates in immune evasion in AIDS. Nat Med. 1998;4:679.
52. Sherry B, Zybarth G, Alfano M, et al. Role of cyclophilin A in the uptake of HIV-1 by macrophages and T lymphocytes. Proc Natl Acad Sci U S A. 1998;95:1758.
53. Braaten D, Franke EK, Luban J. Cyclophilin A is required for an early step in the life cycle of human immunodeficiency virus type 1 before the initiation of reverse transcription. J Virol. 1996;70:3551.
54. Emerman M, Malim MH. HIV-1 regulatory/accessory genes: Keys to unraveling viral and host cell biology. Science. 1998;280:1880.
55. Wong-Staal F. Human immunodeficiency viruses and their replication. In: Fields BN, ed. Virology. 2nd ed. New York: Raven Press; 1990:1529.
56. Peliska JA, Benkovic SJ. Mechanism of DNA strand transfer reactions catalyzed by HIV-1 reverse transcriptase. Science. 1992;258:1112.
57. Lori F, Malykh A, Cara A, et al. Hydroxyurea as an inhibitor of human immunodeficiency virus-type 1 replication. Science. 1994;266:801.
58. Rutschmann O, Opravil M, Iten A, et al. A placebo-controlled trial of didanosine plus stavudine, with and without hydroxyurea, for HIV infection. AIDS. 1998;12:F71.
59. Farnet CM, Hasseltine WA. Determination of viral proteins present in the human immunodeficiency virus type 1 preintegration complex. J Virol. 1991;65:1910.
60. Wiskerchen M, Muesing MA. Human immunodeficiency virus type 1 integrase: Effects of mutations on viral ability to integrate direct viral gene expression from unintegrated viral DNA templates, and sustain propagation in primary cells. J Virol. 1995;69:376.
61. Cara A, Cereseto A, Lori F, Reitz MS Jr. HIV-1 protein expression from synthetic circles of DNA mimicking the extrachromosomal forms of viral DNA. J Biol Chem. 1996;271:5393.
62. Schroder AR, Shinn P, Chen H, et al. HIV-1 integration in the human genome favors active genes and local hotspots. Cell. 2002;110:521-529.
63. Markowitz M, Louie M, Hurley A, et al. A novel antiviral intervention results in more accurate assessment of human immunodeficiency virus type 1 replication dynamics and T-cell decay in vivo. J Virol. 2003;77:5037-5038.
64. Douek DC, et al. T cell dynamics in HIV-1 infection. Annu Rev Immunol. 2003;21:265-304. Epub 2001 Dec 19.
65. Honda Y, Rogers L, Nakata K, et al. Type I interferon induces inhibitory 16-kDa CCAAT/enhancer binding protein (C/EBP) beta, repressing the HIV-1 long terminal repeat in macrophages: Pulmonary tuberculosis alters C/EBP expression, enhancing HIV-1 replication. J Exp Med. 1998;188:1255.
66. Kawakami K, Scheidereit C, Roeder RG. Identification and purification of a human immunoglobulin enhancer-binding protein (NF-κB) that activates transcription from a human immunodeficiency virus type 1 promoter in vitro. Proc Natl Acad Sci U S A. 1988;85:4700.
67. Nabel G, Baltimore D. An inducible transcription factor activates expression of human immunodeficiency virus in T cells. Nature. 1987;326:711.

68. Kim SY, Byrn R, Groopman J, Baltimore D. Temporal aspects of DNA and RNA synthesis during human immunodeficiency virus infection: Evidence for differential gene expression. J Virol. 1989;63:3708.

69. Klotman ME, Kim S, Buchbinder A, et al. Kinetics of expression of multiply spliced RNA in early human immunodeficiency virus type 1 infection of lymphocytes and monocytes. Proc Natl Acad Sci U S A. 1991;88:5011.

70. Liao Z, Cimakasky LM, Hampton R, et al. Lipid rafts and HIV pathogenesis: Host membrane cholesterol is required for infection by HIV type 1. AIDS Res Hum Retroviruses. 2001;17:1009-1019.

71. Hoglund S, Ofverstedt LG, Nilsson A, et al. Spatial visualization of the maturing HIV-1 core and its linkage to the envelope. AIDS Res Hum Retroviruses. 1992;8:1.

72. Arthur LO, Bess JW Jr, Sowder RC II, et al. Cellular proteins bound to immunodeficiency viruses: Implications for pathogenesis and vaccines. Science. 1992;258:1935.

73. Flexner C. HIV-protease inhibitors. N Engl J Med. 1998;338:1281.

74. Bryant M, Ratner L. Myristoylation-dependent replication and assembly of human immunodeficiency virus I. Proc Natl Acad Sci U S A. 1990;87:523.

75. Bukrinsky MI, Haggerty S, Dempsey MP, et al. A nuclear localization signal within HIV-1 matrix protein that governs infection of non-dividing cells. Nature. 1993;365:666.

76. DeFrancesco MA, Baronio M, Fiorentini S, et al. IIIV-1 matrix protein p17 increases the production of proinflammatory cytokines and counteracts IL-4 activity by binding to a cellular receptor. Proc Natl Acad Sci U S A. 2002;99:9972-9977.

77. Luban J, Bossolt KL, Franke EK, et al. Human immunodeficiency virus type 1 Gag protein binds to cyclophilins A and B. Cell. 1993;73:1067.

78. Mammano F, Ohagen A, Hoglund S, Gottlinger HG. Role of the major homology region of human immunodeficiency virus type 1 in virion morphogenesis. J Virol. 1994;68:4927.

79. Dorfman T, Bukovsky A, Ohagen A, et al. Functional domains of the capsid protein of human immunodeficiency virus type 1. J Virol. 1994;68:8180.

80. Karpel RL, Henderson LE, Oroszlan S. Interactions of retroviral structural proteins with single-stranded nucleic acids. J Biol Chem. 1987;262:4961.

81. South TL, Blake PR, Sowder RC III, et al. The nucleocapsid protein isolated from HIV-1 particles binds zinc and forms retroviral-type zinc fingers. Biochemistry. 1990;29:7786.

82. Sakaguchi K, Zambrano N, Baldwin ET, et al. Identification of a binding site for the human immunodeficiency virus type 1 nucleocapsid protein. Proc Natl Acad Sci U S A. 1993;90:5219.

83. Roberts NA, Martin JA, Kinchington D, et al. Rational design of peptide-based HIV proteinase inhibitors. Science. 1990;248:358.

84. Huang H, Chopra R, Verdine G, Harrison S. Structure of a covalently trapped catalytic complex of HIV-1 reverse transcriptase: Implications for drug resistance. Science. 1998;282:1669.

85. Arnold E, Jacobo-Molina A, Nanni R, et al. Structure of HIV-1 reverse transcriptase/DNA complex at 7 Å resolution showing active site locations. Nature. 1993;357:85.

86. Kohlstaedt L, Wang JM, Friedman J, et al. The structure of HIV-1 reverse transcriptase. In: Skalka A, Goff S, eds. Reverse Transcriptase. Cold Spring Harbor, NY: Cold Spring Harbor Laboratory Press; 1993:223.

87. Lukashov VV, Goudsmit J. HIV heterogeneity and disease progression in AIDS: A model of continuous virus adaptation. AIDS. 1998;12:S43.

88. Pavlakis G. The molecular biology of human immunodeficiency virus type 1. In: DeVita V, Hellman S, Rosenberg S, eds. AIDS: Biology, Treatment, and Prevention. Philadelphia: Lippincott-Raven; 1997:45.

89. Varmus H. Retroviruses. Science. 1988;240:1427.

90. Bukrinsky MI, Sharova N, McDonald TL, et al. Association of integrase, matrix, and reverse transcriptase antigens of human immunodeficiency virus type 1 with viral nucleic acids following acute infection. Proc Natl Acad Sci U S A. 1993;90:6125.

91. Starcich BR, Hahn BH, Shaw GM, et al. Identification and characterization of conserved and variable regions in the envelope gene of HTLV-III/LAV, the retrovirus of AIDS. Cell. 1986;45:637.

92. Kwong PD, Wyatt R, Robinson J, et al. Structure of an HIV gp120 envelope glycoprotein in complex with the CD4 receptor and a neutralizing human antibody. Nature. 1998;393:648.

93. Wyatt R, Kwong PD, Desjardins E, et al. The antigenic structure of the HIV gp120 envelope glycoprotein. Nature. 1998;393:705.

94. Balter M. Revealing HIV's T cell passkey. Science. 1998;280:1833.

95. White JM. Membrane fusion. Science. 1992;258:917.

96. Chan DC, Fass D, Berger JM, Kim PS. Core structure of gp41 from the HIV envelope glycoprotein. Cell. 1997;89:263.

97. Furuta RA, Wild CT, Weng Y, Weiss CD. Capture of an early fusion-active conformation of HIV-1 gp41 (erratum, Nat Struct Biol. 1998;5:612). Nat Struct Biol. 1998;5:276.

98. Wild CT, Shugars DC, Greenwell TK, et al. Peptides corresponding to a predictive alpha-helical domain of human immunodeficiency virus type 1 gp41 are potent inhibitors of virus infection. Proc Natl Acad Sci U S A. 1994;91:9770.

99. Swingler S, Brichacek B, Jacque JM, et al. HIV-1 Nef intersects the macrophage CD40L signalling pathway to promote resting-cell infection. Nature 2003;424:213-219.

100. Sheehy AM, Gaddis NC, Choi JD, Malim MH. Isolation of a human gene that inhibits HIV-1 infection and is suppressed by the viral Vif protein. Nature. 2002;418:646-650.

101. Harris RS, Bishop KN, Sheehy AM, et al. DNA deamination mediates innate immunity to retroviral infection. Cell 2003;113:803-809.

102. Garrett ED, Tiley LS, Cullen BR. Rev activates expression of the human immunodeficiency virus type 1 vif and vpr gene products. J Virol. 1991;65:1653.

103. Fischer AG, Feinberg MB, Josephs SF, et al. The trans-activator gene of HTLV-III is essential for virus replication. Nature. 1986;320:367.

104. Wei P, Garber ME, Fang SM, et al. A novel CDK-9-associated C-type cyclin interacts directly with HIV-1 Tat and mediates its high-affinity, loop-specific binding to TAR RNA. Cell. 1998;92:451.

105. Ensoli B, Gendelman R, Markham P, et al. Synergy between basic fibroblast growth factor and HIV-1 Tat protein in induction of Kaposi's sarcoma. Nature. 1994;371:674.

106. Luznik L, Kraus G, Guatelli J, et al. Tat-independent replication of human immunodeficiency viruses. J Clin Invest. 1995;95:328.

107. Zagury D, Lachgar A, Chams V, et al. Interferon alpha and Tat involvement in the immunosuppression of uninfected T cells and C-C chemokine decline in AIDS. Proc Natl Acad Sci U S A. 1998;31:3581.

108. Gallo RC, Burny A, Zagury D. Targeting Tat and IFN(alpha) as a therapeutic AIDS vaccine. DNA Cell Biol. 2002;21:611-618.

109. Sodroski J, Goh WC, Rosen C, et al. A second post-transcriptional trans-activator gene required for HTLV-III replication. Nature. 1986;321:412.

110. Malim MH, Bohnlein S, Hauber J, Cullen BR. Functional dissection of the HIV Rev trans-activator-derivation of a trans-dominant repressor of Rev function. Cell. 1989;58:205.

111. Collins KL, Chen BK, Kalams SA, et al. IIIV-1 Nef protein protects infected primary cells against killing by cytotoxic T lymphocytes. Nature. 1998;391:397.

112. Hofmann-Lehmann R, et al. Live attenuated, nef-deleted SIV is pathogenic in most adult macaques after prolonged observation. AIDS. 2003;17:157-166.

113. Jekle A, Schramm B, Jayakumar P, et al. Coreceptor phenotype of natural human immunodeficiency virus with nef deleted evolves in vivo, leading to increased virulence. J Virol. 2002;76:6966-6973.

114. Koenig S, Conley AJ, Brewah YA, et al. Transfer of HIV-1-specific cytotoxic T lymphocytes to an AIDS patient leads to selection for mutant HIV variants and subsequent disease progression. Nat Med. 1995;1:330.

115. Deacon NJ, Tsykin A, Solomon A, et al. Genomic structure of an attenuated quasi-species of HIV-1 from a blood transfusion donor and recipients. Science. 1995;270:988.

116. Birch MR, Learmont JC, Dyer WB, et al. An examination of signs of disease progression in survivors of the Sydney Blood Bank Cohort (SBBC). J Clin Virol. 2001;22:263-270.

117. Oberste MS, Gonda MA. Conservation of amino-acid sequence motifs in lentivirus Vif proteins. Virus Genes. 1992;6:95.

118. Heinzinger NK, Bukrinsky MI, Haggerty SA, et al. The Vpr protein of human immunodeficiency virus type 1 influences nuclear localization of viral nucleic acids in non-dividing host cells. Proc Natl Acad Sci U S A. 1994;91:7311.

119. Felzien LK, Woffendin C, Hottiger MO, et al. HIV transcriptional activation by the accessory protein, VPR, is mediated by the p300 co-activator. Proc Natl Acad Sci U S A. 1998;95:5281.

120. Poon B, Grovit-Ferbas K, Stewart SA, Chen ISY. Cell cycle arrest by Vpr in HIV-1 virions and insensitivity to antiretroviral agents. Science. 1998;281:266.

121. de Noronha CM, Sherman MP, Lin HW, et al. Dynamic disruptions in nuclear envelope architecture and integrity induced by HIV-1 Vpr. Science. 2001;294:1105-1108.

122. Maldarelli F, Chen MY, Willey RL, Strebel K. Human immunodeficiency virus type 1 Vpu protein is an oligomeric type I integral membrane protein. J Virol. 1993;67:5056.

123. Schwartz S, Felber BK, Fenyo EM, Pavlakis GN. Env and Vpu proteins of human immunodeficiency virus type 1 are produced from multiple bicistronic mRNAs. J Virol. 1990;64:5448.

124. Pinto LH, Holsinger LJ, Lamb RA. Influenza virus M2 protein has ion channel activity. Cell. 1992;69:517.

125. Fan H. Influences of the long terminal repeats on retrovirus pathogenicity. Semin Virol. 1990;1:165.

126. Jones KA, Peterlin BM. Control of RNA initiation and elongation at the HIV-1 promoter. Annu Rev Biochem. 1994;63:717.

127. Pease JE, Murphy P. Microbial corruption of the chemokine system: An expanding paradigm. Semin Immunol. 1998;10:169.

128. Premack BA, Schall TJ. Chemokine receptors: Gateways to inflammation and infection. Nat Med. 1996;2:1174.

129. Garzino-Demo A, DeVico AL, Cocchi F, Gallo RC. Beta-chemokines and protection from HIV type 1 disease. AIDS Res Hum Retroviruses. 1998;14:S177.

130. Connor RI, Sheridan KE, Ceradini D, et al. Change in co-receptor use correlates with disease progression in HIV-1-infected individuals. J Exp Med. 1997;185:621.

131. Nguyen DH, Hildreth JE. Evidence for budding of human immunodeficiency virus type 1 selectively from glycolipid-enriched membrane lipid rafts. J Virol. 2000;74:3264-3272.

132. Liu R, Paxton WA, Choe S, et al. Homozygous defect in HIV-1 co-receptor accounts for resistance of some multiply-exposed individuals to HIV infection. Cell. 1996;86:367.

133. O'Brien TR, Goedert JJ. Chemokine receptors and genetic variability: Another leap in HIV research. JAMA. 1998;279:317.

134. Misrahi M, Teglas JP, N'Go N, et al. CCR5 chemokine receptor variant in HIV-1 mother-to-child transmission and disease progression in children. French Pediatric HIV Infection Study Group. JAMA. 1998;279:277.

135. Wei X, Ghosh SK, Taylor ME, et al. Viral dynamics in human immunodeficiency virus type 1 infection. Nature. 1995;373:117.

136. Ho DD, Neumann AU, Perelson AS, et al. Rapid turnover of plasma virions and CD4$^+$ lymphocytes in HIV-1 infection. Nature. 1995;373:123.

137. Coffin JM. HIV population dynamics in vivo: Implications for genetic variation, pathogenesis, and therapy. Science. 1995;267:483.

138. Pakker NG, Notermans DW, deBoer RJ, et al. Biphasic kinetics of peripheral blood T cells after triple combination therapy in HIV-1 infection: A composite of redistribution and proliferation. Nat Med. 1998;4:208.

139. Mohri H, Bonhoeffer S, Monard S, et al. Rapid turnover of T lymphocytes in SIV-infected rhesus macaques. Science. 1998;279:1223.

139a. DeBoer RJ, Mohri H, Ho DD, Perelson AS. Turnover rates of B cells, T cells and NK cells in simian immunodeficiency virus infected and uninfected rhesus macaques. J Immunol. 2003;170:2479-2487.

140. Herbein G, Mahlnecht U, Batliwalla F, et al. Apoptosis of CD8$^+$ T cells is mediated by macrophages through interaction of HIV gp120 with chemokine receptor CXCR4. Nature. 1998;395:189.

141. Zagury D. A naturally unbalanced combat. Nat Med. 1997;3:156.

142. Gulick RM, Mellors JW, Havlir D, et al. Treatment with indinavir, zidovudine, and lamivudine in adults with human immunodeficiency virus infection and prior anti-retroviral therapy. N Engl J Med. 1997;337:734.

143. Wong JK, Gunthard HF, Havlir DV, et al. Reduction of HIV-1 in blood and lymph nodes following potent antiretroviral therapy and the virologic correlates of treatment failure. Proc Natl Acad Sci U S A. 1997;94:12574.

144. Chun TW, Engel D, Berrey MM, et al. Early establishment of a pool of latently infected, resting CD4$^+$ T cells during primary HIV-1 infection. Proc Natl Acad Sci U S A. 1998;95:8869.

145. Wong JK, Hezareh M, Gunthard HF, et al. Recovery of replication-competent HIV despite prolonged suppression of plasma viremia. Science. 1997;278:1291.

146. Finzi D, Hermankova M, Pierson T, et al. Identification of a reservoir for HIV-1 in patients on highly active antiretroviral therapy. Science. 1997;278:1295.

147. Zagury D. Long-term cultures of HTLV-III. Science 1986;231:850-853.

148. Gougeon ML, et al. Evidence of a process of death of lymphocytes by apoptosis in patients infected with HIV. CR Acad Sci Paris 1993;III(series 312):529-537.

149. Oyaizu N, McCloskey TW, Coronesi M, et al. Accelerated apoptosis in peripheral blood mononuclear cells from HIV-1 infected patients and in CD cross-linked PBMCs from normal individuals. Blood. 1993;82:3392-3400.

150. Wong-Staal F, Shaw GM, Hahn BH, et al. Genomic diversity of human T-lymphotropic virus type III (HTLV-III). Science. 1985;229:759.

151. McCutchan FE. Understanding the genetic diversity of HIV-1. AIDS. 2000;14(suppl 3):S31-S44.

152. Wolinsky SM, Wike CM, Korber BT, et al. Selective transmission of human immunodeficiency virus type-1 variants from mothers to infants. Science. 1992;225:1134.

153. Korber B, Theiler J, Wolinsky S. Limitations of a molecular clock applied to considerations of the origin of HIV-1. Science. 1998;280:1868.

154. Meyers G, Berzofsky JA, Korber B, et al. Human Retroviruses and AIDS. Los Alamos, NM: Los Alamos National Laboratory; 1992.

155. Glass JD, Johnson RT. Human immunodeficiency virus and the brain. Annu Rev Neurosci. 1996;19:1.

156. Berger J, Levy R. AIDS and the Nervous System. Philadelphia: Lippincott-Raven; 1997.

157. Wiley CA, Soontornniyomkij V, Radhakrishnan L, et al. Distribution of brain HIV loads in AIDS. Brain Pathol. 1998;8:277.

158. Westmoreland SV, Rottman JB, Williams KC, et al. Chemokine receptor expression on resident and inflammatory cells in the brain of macaques with simian immunodeficiency virus encephalitis. Am J Pathol. 1998;152:659.

159. Budka H. Neuropathology of human immunodeficiency virus infection. Brain Pathol. 1991;1:163.

160. Foudranine N, Hoetelmans R, Lange J, et al. Cerebrospinal-fluid HIV-1 RNA and drug concentrations after treatment with lamivudine plus zidovudine or stavudine. Lancet. 1998;351:1547.

161. Dore GJ, Correll PK, Li Y, et al. Changes to AIDS dementia complex in the era of highly active antiretroviral therapy. AIDS. 1999;13:1249-1253.

162. Safai B. Tumors in HIV infection. In: Wormser G, ed. AIDS and Other Manifestations of HIV Infection. Philadelphia: Lippincott-Raven; 1998:295.

163. Ensoli B, Barillari G, Salahuddin SZ, et al. Tat protein of HIV stimulates growth of cells derived from Kaposi's sarcoma lesions of AIDS patients. Nature. 1990;345:84.

164. Chang Y, Cesarman E, Pessin MS, et al. Identification of herpesvirus-like DNA sequences in AIDS-associated Kaposi sarcoma. Science. 1994;266:1865.

165. Arvanitakis L, Geras-Raaka E, Varma A, et al. Human herpesvirus KSHV encodes a constitutively active G-protein-coupled receptor linked to cell proliferation. Nature. 1997;385:347.

166. Gallo RC. The enigmas of Kaposi's sarcoma. Science. 1998;282:1837.

167. Serraino D, Salamina G, Franceschi S, et al. The epidemiology of AIDS-associated non-Hodgkin's lymphoma in the World Health Organization European Region. Br J Cancer. 1992;66:912-916.

168. Cote TR, Biggar RJ, Rosenberg PS, et al. Non-Hodgkin's lymphoma among people with AIDS: Incidence, presentation and public health burden. Int J Cancer. 1997;73:645.

169. Beral V, Peterman T, Berkelman R, Jaffe H. AIDS-associated non-Hodgkin's lymphoma. Lancet. 1991;337:805.

170. Flinn I, Ambinder R. AIDS primary central nervous system lymphoma. Curr Opin Oncol. 1966;8:373.

171. Levine A. HIV-related cancers: Emerging Trends and Management Issues, Presentations from the 7th Annual Clinical Care Options Symposium. Clinical Care Options for HIV Online Journal. 1997;3:1-20.

172. McClain KL, Leach CJ, Jenson HB, et al: Association of Epstein-Barr virus with leiomyosarcomas in young people with AIDS. N Engl J Med. 1995;332:12.

173. Williams AB, Darragh TM, Vranizan K, et al. Anal and cervical human papillomavirus infection and risk of anal and cervical intraepithelial abnormalities in human immunodeficiency virus-infected women. Obstet Gynecol. 1994;83:205.

174. Palefsky JM. Human papillomavirus-associated malignancies in HIV-positive men and women. Curr Opin Oncol. 1995;7:437-441.

Introduction to the Enteroviruses

JOHN F. MODLIN

PHYSICAL CHARACTERISTICS OF ENTEROVIRUSES

The genus *Enterovirus* belongs to the family Picornaviridae, a large family of morphologically identical single-strand RNA viruses that share a common genomic and structural organization.[1] The enteroviruses are icosahedral, approximately 30 nm in diameter, and nonenveloped. The virion capsid is composed of 60 structural subunits that are formed from four polypeptides with an aggregate molecular weight of 80 to 140 kDa. The capsid encloses a linear, single-stranded RNA genome approximately 7.4 kb in length. The RNA is infectious and either may serve as a template for the synthesis of additional RNA or may be encapsidated to form progeny virions. The RNA functions as a monocistronic messenger whose translational product, a "polyprotein" of molecular weight of 250 kDa, is coded for by a single open reading frame involving about 90% of the entire genome. The polyprotein subsequently undergoes specific cleavages to form the structural polypeptides, an RNA polymerase, viral-coded proteases, and additional polypeptides necessary for intracellular replication.

Enteroviruses are stable at pH 3 to 10, distinguishing them from other picornaviruses (including rhinoviruses), which are unstable below pH 6. After initial replication in the oropharynx, enteroviruses, unlike rhinoviruses, survive transit through the acidic environment of the stomach and reach the lower intestinal tract, where they replicate more extensively. Lacking a lipid envelope, enteroviruses are resistant to ether, chloroform, and alcohol. However, they are readily inactivated by ionizing radiation, formaldehyde, and phenol.[1] Molar $MgCl_2$ reduces the thermolability of enteroviruses across a wide range of temperatures, allowing live, attenuated oral poliomyelitis vaccines to maintain potency when refrigeration is suboptimal or unavailable.

CLASSIFICATION OF ENTEROVIRUSES

The enteroviruses are conventionally divided into five subgenera: polioviruses, group A coxsackieviruses, group B coxsackieviruses, echoviruses, and "newer" enteroviruses, based on differences in host range and pathogenic potential[2,3] (Table 167-1). The subgenera each contain a number of unique enterovirus serotypes that are distinguished from one another on the basis of neutralization by specific antisera. The 72 serotypes originally identified have been reduced to 64 through the recognition of some redundant serotypes and reclassification of others. Some enterovirus isolates considered "nontypable" by reference laboratories may represent previously nondescribed serotypes.[4]

Mutation in the capsid coding region of the genome over time has resulted in variable neutralization among epidemiologically unrelated isolates of the same serotype[5] and has sometimes obscured the determination of serotype with reference sera raised against prototypic strains isolated decades earlier.[4,6,7] A new classification scheme has recently been adopted that divides all non-polio enteroviruses into four groups designated A through D based on homology within the RNA region coding for the VP1 capsid protein, which contains the major epitopes associated with neutralization.[8,9] Isolates of the same serotype characteristically diverge in the VP1 region by less than 25% and 12%, respectively, within corresponding nucleotide and amino acid sequences.[8]

TABLE 167-1 Conventional Classification and Host Range of Human Enterovirus

Species	Serotypes	Host Range		
		Primates	Newborn Mice	Cell Culture
Polioviruses*	1-3	++	0	++
Group A coxsackieviruses[†,‡]	1-24	0	+++	±
Group B coxsackieviruses[†,§]	1-6	0	+++	++
Echoviruses[‖]	1-34	0	0	++
Enteroviruses[¶,**]	68-72	Variable	Variable	+

*Polioviruses generally replicate only in primates or primate cell cultures, although rare strains such as the type 2 Lansing strain have been adapted to rodents. Although polioviruses multiply in the alimentary tract of some subhuman primates, the hallmark of these viruses is the characteristic histopathologic lesions produced by direct inoculation of the central nervous system.

[†]The coxsackieviruses were first recovered from the feces of children with poliomyelitis in the town of Coxsackie, New York,[138] but unlike polioviruses, they produce paralysis and death in experimentally infected suckling mice.

[‡]All group A coxsackieviruses produce generalized myositis of skeletal muscle and flaccid hind limb paralysis in suckling mice[139] and coxsackievirus A7 is pathogenic for the primate central nervous system. However, most group A coxsackieviruses, except serotypes A9 and A16, grow poorly in cell culture. Coxsackievirus A23 has been reclassified as echovirus 9, leaving 23 coxsackievirus serotypes.

[§]The group B coxsackieviruses are distinguished by their ability to produce focal myositis and generalized infection of the myocardium, brown fat, pancreas, and central nervous system in suckling mice that results in spastic paralysis. The group B coxsackieviruses are commonly isolated in cultured primate cells.

[‖]The echoviruses (enteric cytopathic human orphan) viruses were originally discovered in fecal specimens of healthy children.[140,141] They cause cytopathic effects in primate cell culture but are generally nonpathogenic for suckling mice (except for echovirus 21) and primates. Echovirus 10 has been reclassified as reovirus 1 and echovirus 28 as rhinovirus 1. Echovirus 34 is a variant of coxsackievirus A24. Echoviruses 22 and 23 have been assigned to the genus *Parechovirus* as parechovirus serotypes 1 and 2, respectively.[82] Therefore a total of 29 serotypes of the original 34 serotypes of echovirus remain.

[¶]The human enteroviral serotypes recognized since 1970 are designated by serial numbers only.[142] Four new serotypes (enteroviruses 68 to 71) have been discovered since the adoption of this simplified taxonomic scheme.

**Hepatitis A virus was briefly classified as enterovirus 72, until genetic sequence data led to reclassification of this virus as a hepadnavirus.[143]

MOLECULAR BIOLOGY OF ENTEROVIRUSES AND THEIR REPLICATION

The RNA genomes of naturally occurring polioviruses, attenuated polioviruses, and many non-polio enteroviruses have been fully sequenced, and the replication of polioviruses in primate cells has been studied in extensive detail.[10] Poliovirus type 1 RNA has been reverse transcribed and the complementary DNA sequences cloned and transfected into cultured cells, resulting in progeny virions.[11,12] The molecular structure and intracellular replicative events appear to be similar for all the human enteroviruses.

The enteroviral genome incorporates approximately 7450 nucleotides divided into three regions: a 5' end region of 743 nucleotides, a continuous-coding region of about 6625 nucleotides, and a 3' poly(A) end region of variable length. The 5' terminus is covalently linked to a small virus-coded protein of approximately 7 kDa (VPg) that is required for the initiation of RNA synthesis. Removal of the poly(A) 3' terminus renders the RNA noninfectious. The most conserved regions of the genome are the 5' noncoding region and those coding for the VPg protein and the RNA polymerase.[13] The regions coding for the structural proteins are less conserved, and there is considerable variation within the regions that code for epitopes that bind neutralizing antibody.

Host cell susceptibility to enteroviral infection is defined by the presence of specific membrane receptor proteins that bind enteroviruses generally along taxonomic lines[14,15] (Table 167-2). The three poliovirus serotypes share a common receptor, a member of the immunoglobulin superfamily that is coded on human chromosome 19.[16-18] Both decay-accelerating factor (DAF, or CD55), a complement regulatory protein, and intercellular adhesion molecule 1 (ICAM-1) play a role in coxsackievirus A21 cell entry.[19] The group B coxsackieviruses also interact with two different cell membrane proteins, the 49-kDa coxsackievirus-adenovirus receptor (CAR) and DAF.[20,21] The presence of CAR permits binding and cell entry by all six coxsackievirus B serotypes,[21] whereas antibodies to DAF block binding and infection by serotypes 1, 3, and 5.[20,22,23] DAF also appears to be a major echovirus receptor, binding many echovirus serotypes,[24,25] whereas echovirus serotypes 1 and 8 bind to the α_2-subunit of the very late antigen (VLA) integrin molecule.[26,27]

Penetration, uncoating, and release of the nucleic acid into the cytoplasm occur within minutes at 37° C. RNA synthesis begins within 30 minutes, leading to an exponential increase of minus-strand complementary and plus-strand progeny RNA until 2.5 hours after infection, when there is a switch to a linear accumulation of mainly progeny RNA. The viral polymerase-regulated RNA-dependent RNA synthesis results in production of about 2×10^5 molecules of progeny RNA per cell, of which 50% is used as message. A polyprotein with a molecular mass of about 250 kDa is synthesized from the single open reading frame, which is first cleaved into three polypeptides. The 5' product, P1, undergoes subsequent cleavages to form four capsid proteins. Cleavage of P2 and P3 results in eight nonstructural proteins whose known functions include polymerase activity, proteolytic cleavage of the translational products, and inhibition of host cell protein synthesis.

The complete virion contains 60 copies of each of the four structural proteins. Synthesis of the capsid proceeds by aggregation of five copies each of VP1, VP3, and VP0 (a precursor of VP2 and VP4) into subunits and assembly of 12 of these pentamers into the complete dodecahedral capsid shell. Encapsidation of the viral RNA is associated with a final cleavage of the VP0 protein to VP2 and VP4. The latter is an internal protein closely associated with the RNA. For polioviruses, VP1 is the dominantly exposed protein, containing at least two epitopes that induce neutralizing antibodies. VP2 and VP3 are partially exposed and antigenic.

Host protein and RNA synthesis are severely compromised by 3 hours after infection. After about 6 to 7 hours, virions are visible by electron microscopy within the cytoplasm, and they are subsequently

TABLE 167-2 Enterovirus Cell Membrane Receptors

Enterovirus Serotype	Receptor Protein
Polioviruses 1-3	Poliovirus receptor (PVR)
Coxsackieviruses A13, A18, A21	Intercellular adhesion molecule 1 (ICAM-1)
Coxsackieviruses B1-B6	Coxsackie adenovirus receptor (CAR)
Coxsackieviruses B1, B3, B5	Decay accelerating factor (DAF)
Echoviruses 1, 8	VLA-2 ($\alpha_2\beta_1$)
Echoviruses 6, 7, 11, 12, 13, 20, 21, 29, 33	DAF
Enterovirus 70	DAF

released by lysis of the cell, which results in a yield of 10^4 to 10^5 virions per cell. The number of infectious virions is 10- to 1000-fold lower.

PATHOGENESIS AND IMMUNITY IN ENTEROVIRAL INFECTIONS

Pathogenesis

The pathogenesis of poliovirus infection has been extensively investigated in primates experimentally infected with neurovirulent strains and in humans infected with vaccine strains,[28-31] and it is widely assumed that the early pathophysiologic events of non-polio enterovirus infections are similar. Studies of coxsackievirus infection in mice have also produced much information about the influence of various host and environmental factors on the ability of the virus to replicate in the heart, brain, and other organs and about the mechanism of vertical transmission of enteroviruses from infected pregnant animals to their offspring.

Enteroviruses infect humans via direct or indirect contact with virus shed from the gastrointestinal tract or upper respiratory tract. Ingested virus implants and replicates in susceptible tissues of the pharynx or distal part of the gut. The precise site of viral entry and initial replication in the gastrointestinal tract is not established, although enteroviruses have been demonstrated within the mucosal M cells, which are implicated in the uptake from the lumen of gastrointestinal reoviruses.[32] Enteroviral replication in ileal lymphoid tissue is detectable 1 to 3 days after the ingestion of virus. Polioviruses replicate most efficiently in the lower intestines, especially the distal portion of the small bowel. Humans ingesting more than 10^6 $TCID_{50}$ of attenuated poliovirus regularly shed virus in both oropharyngeal secretions and feces, whereas lower infecting doses ($<10^5$ $TCID_{50}$) result only in fecal shedding.[28] Moreover, the quantity of virus recoverable from the tonsils is much less than that in Peyer's patches, where it may reach 10^7 to 10^8 $TCID_{50}$/g. The maximal duration of viral excretion is 3 to 4 weeks from the pharynx and 5 to 6 weeks in the feces.

After multiplication in submucosal lymphatic tissues, enteroviruses pass to regional lymph nodes (cervical, mesenteric) and give rise to a "minor viremia" that is transient and not usually detectable. During this low-grade viremia, virus spreads to reticuloendothelial tissue such as the liver, spleen, bone marrow, and deep lymph nodes. In subclinical infections, which are the most common, viral replication at this point ceases or is contained by host defense mechanisms. However, in a minority of infected persons, further replication of virus occurs in these reticuloendothelial sites leading to a sustained ("major") viremia that coincides with the onset of the "minor illness" of poliomyelitis and probably the nonspecific febrile illnesses associated with other enterovirus infections. Prodromal viremia has been demonstrated with wild strains of poliovirus[31,33] and echovirus 9[34] but is uncommon with Sabin vaccine strains except for type 2.[35]

The major viremia results in dissemination to target organs such as the central nervous system, heart, and skin. In these tissues, necrosis and inflammatory lesions are observed, whereas histopathologic lesions are generally not seen in the gut as a result of earlier replicative events. In target organs, the degree of inflammatory change and tissue necrosis corresponds to the titer of infectious virus present. The severity of infection in experimental animals can be enhanced by induced exercise, cold exposure, malnutrition, pregnancy, and immune suppression with corticosteroids or radiation.

Mutation of Enteroviruses during Natural Infection

Enteroviruses undergo a high rate of mutation during replication in the human gastrointestinal tract and transcription errors occur with a frequency of 1 per 10^4 bases, approximately one error per genome. As a result, single-site mutations are commonly observed in the 5′ noncoding region of attenuated polioviruses within days of feeding to young infants, a change associated with longer excretion and increased neurovirulence.[36,37] Serial isolates of the same enterovirus serotype excreted by patients with B-cell immunodeficiency syn-

dromes for many years undergo continuous genetic variation, which can be detected by oligonucleotide fingerprinting[38,39] or RNA sequencing[40] and permit estimation of the duration of infection. RNA sequencing has led to the detection of oral poliovirus vaccine (OPV)-derived virulent polioviruses causing outbreaks of paralytic disease among underimmunized populations in several locations.[41-44]

Dual infection of the same cell with different enteroviral strains may produce recombinant progeny virus, especially when the parent strains share the same serotype. Intertypic recombinants are less frequent but can be demonstrated in 1 per 10^4 to 1 per 10^5 infectious virions in vitro[45] and also in the feces of infants fed trivalent OPV.[43] Interestingly, the vaccine-derived virulent polioviruses isolated to date are OPV viruses that have recombined with non-polio enteroviruses.[41]

Immunity and the Immune Response

Immunity to enteroviral infections is serotype specific. Antibody-mediated immune mechanisms operate both in the alimentary tract to prevent mucosal infection and in the blood to prevent dissemination to target organs. Circulating antibodies play the most important role in preventing enteroviral disease. Small concentrations of type-specific neutralizing antibodies prevent poliovirus viremia and paralysis in experimentally infected primates,[46] and passive immunity to paralytic disease in humans can be achieved by the administration of immune serum globulin before exposure to neurovirulent polioviruses.[47,48] However, passively administered immune globulin does not modify the outcome of established central nervous system poliovirus disease[49]; at this late stage of infection, patients have detectable neutralizing antibody. There is no proven role for immune globulin treatment of other systemic enterovirus infections.

Immunoglobulin A (IgA) antibody appears in nasal and alimentary secretions 2 to 4 weeks after the administration of live-attenuated OPV and persists for at least 15 years.[30] However, mucosal immunity is relative: on reexposure to infectious virus, high titers of secretory IgA antibodies prevent or substantially reduce poliovirus shedding, while lower titers are associated with more extensive oropharyngeal replication of virus and longer viral shedding.[30] The elaboration of virus-specific IgA antibodies by the small intestine appears to depend on local immunocompetent tissues, not those of the pharynx. This principle was elegantly demonstrated by experiments in which infants with double-barrel colostomies were fed live-attenuated poliovirus through the colostomy.[50] Although they developed serum IgA, IgG, and IgM antibodies to poliovirus, secretory IgA antibodies were elaborated only in the distal loop of the colostomy and not in the pharynx or proximal loop. When subsequently challenged with OPV, they shed virus from the pharynx but not from the distal segment of the bowel and then proceeded to develop IgA antibodies in pharyngeal secretions. Antibodies to enteroviruses are present in the colostrum and milk of immune women, and this may interfere with the replication of OPV virus given to breastfed neonates.[51] Maternal antibodies passively acquired either transplacentally or via milk prevent or modify enteroviral infections of early infancy.[51,52]

As early as 1 to 3 days after enteroviral challenge, IgM humoral antibodies are produced that predominate in serum during the first month and disappear within 2 to 3 months.[30] IgG antibody, which is generally detected by 7 to 10 days after infection, is mostly of the IgG_1 and IgG_3 subtypes.[53] Neutralizing IgG antibodies in serum persist for life after natural infection with enteroviruses. Humoral antibodies also have an important role in the recovery from enteroviral infection, as evidenced by the development of persistent infections in persons with significant B-cell immunodeficiency.[54] Nonetheless, there is both clinical and laboratory evidence that humoral antibody alone is not sufficient to limit enteroviral replication in target organs. Data from several laboratories indicate that macrophage function is also a critical component of the immune response to enteroviral infection.[55,56] Macrophages predominate in the early stages and probably play a significant role in viral clearance because ablation of macrophage function in experimental animals markedly enhances the severity of coxsackievirus B infections.[55] However, inhibition of T-lymphocyte function has little effect on virus replication in vivo[57] and persons with abnormal cell-mediated immunity are not predisposed to serious or prolonged enterovirus infections unless they have accompanying B-cell dysfunction.

Even though T lymphocytes do not contribute to the inhibition of enteroviral replication, there is growing evidence that certain immunopathologic events after enterovirus infection are mediated by T-cell activity. In the murine myocarditis model, expression of proinflammatory cytokines and an acute inflammatory infiltration follows peak viral replication,[58-62] and induction of natural killer cell activity and T-lymphocyte immune responses contributes to necrosis of infected cardiac myocytes[57,63,64] (see Chapter 77). An inflammatory response may persist long after viral replication has ceased, and ongoing cardiac damage may be mediated by virus-induced antibodies against cardiac antigens[65] or by cytotoxic T-lymphocyte–mediated myocyte lysis.[61,63,66,67]

EPIDEMIOLOGY OF ENTEROVIRAL INFECTIONS

Endemic and Epidemic Behavior

Enteroviruses are distributed worldwide. Infection rates vary with the season, geography, and age and socioeconomic status of the population sampled. Enteroviral infections occur throughout the year, but in temperate climates infections are strikingly more prevalent in the summer and autumn months (June to October in the Northern Hemisphere).[68-70] This seasonal periodicity, which has never been satisfactorily explained, is repeatedly observed each year in cities of the northern United States but is less pronounced in Atlanta and Miami and disappears altogether in the tropics, where enteroviruses are endemic the year round. Climate also affects the frequency and abundance of enteroviruses isolated from healthy children. For example, several surveys of southern and southwestern cities of the United States have indicated that 7% to 15% of children sampled during the year excreted enteroviruses in feces, whereas comparable populations in New York, Buffalo, and Minneapolis had annual excretion rates less than 5%.[71]

Age and Socioeconomic Status

Three fourths of enteroviral infections reported to the World Health Organization occur in children younger than 15 years.[72] In the United States, attack rates for both infection and illness with non-polio enteroviruses are highest in infants younger than 1 year.[73,74] During the annual peak period of enteroviral transmission in Rochester, New York, the incidence of infection was found to be 12.8% during the first month of life.[75] Rates of symptomatic enteroviral infection drop after the second month of life[76] but remain higher for infants and toddlers compared with older children and adults. Enteroviral infections are more prevalent among lower socioeconomic class children, probably because of crowding, poor hygiene, and opportunities for fecal contamination. Simultaneous infection by more than one serotype is common under these circumstances. A study of infants in Karachi, Pakistan, revealed that 80% yielded rectal swabs with at least one enterovirus. Of the positives, nearly half yielded two enteroviruses and occasional subjects as many as four.[77]

The frequency with which particular serotypes of enteroviruses cause infection varies markedly. Wild-type polioviruses now circulate only in a diminishing number of developing countries (see Chapter 168), whereas vaccine strains are commonly isolated throughout the world because of widespread OPV use. In urban areas of the United States, usually one to three non-polio enteroviral serotypes predominate each season, and these vary from one region to another. Some prevalent serotypes are continuously isolated from year to year,[7,69,78] while other serotypes may emerge, or reemerge after years of relative inactivity, such as occurred with echovirus 30 in the early 1990s.[78,79] Occasional epidemics are global, such as the one caused by echovirus 9 in the late 1950s and the explosive pandemics of acute hemorrhagic conjunctivitis due to enterovirus 70 and coxsackievirus A24 that have

occurred over the past three decades. The reasons why individual serotypes of enteroviruses appear and disappear and behave as either endemic or epidemic pathogens are not well understood. Some epidemic strains such as echovirus 9 may spread rapidly and exhaust susceptible individuals in the population beyond a "critical mass" necessary for continued transmission, whereas those strains appearing endemically over several years may be less contagious. Periodic reappearances of the same enteroviral serotype occur in which the new strain is poorly neutralized by antisera to earlier strains[80,81] or varies significantly from earlier strains by certain well-characterized genetic markers.[82]

During the 2-year period of 2000-2001, 10 serotypes represented 85% of all enterovirus isolates (submitted from state and local public health laboratories to the National Enterovirus Surveillance System of the Centers for Disease Control and Prevention).[7] Echoviruses represent slightly more than half of these clinical isolates, and group B coxsackieviruses represent about one fourth[7] (Table 167-3). It is likely that group A coxsackieviruses are underrepresented in these data because only a few serotypes such as A9 and A16 grow readily in cell culture.[83] Infection with some serotypes, such as coxsackievirus B6 and enteroviruses 68 and 69, is rarely recognized.

Molecular Epidemiology

The study of enteroviral epidemiology is enhanced by the application of several molecular genetic methods including two-dimensional oligonucleotide gel electrophoresis of viral RNA (*fingerprinting*), Southern blotting, and amplification and identification of defined RNA sequences with the polymerase chain reaction (PCR). These methods have been used to unambiguously differentiate live vaccine and naturally occurring poliovirus strains[84,85] and to trace the routes of spread of poliovirus type 1,[86] coxsackievirus A24,[87] and enterovirus 70[88,89] by determining the degree of RNA relatedness among epidemiologically distinct isolates, and to demonstrate the reemergence of an epidemic coxsackievirus B5 strain in 1983 that had remained dormant in the United States for 16 years.[90]

Genomic RNA sequencing has proved the most adept in characterizing the evolutionary relationships among poliovirus isolates of the same serotype. "Genotypes" are distinguished from one another by the divergence of more than 15% among the RNA nucleotides in the homologous portions of the genome that are sequenced.[85] The application of genomic sequencing has demonstrated the relatedness of the outbreak of poliovirus type 1 in Finland in 1984-1985 to strains circulating in the Mediterranean region,[91] detected circulating OPV-derived polioviruses in Haiti,[41] and has traced the pandemic spread of acute he-

TABLE 167-3 Most Common Enterovirus Serotypes Submitted by State and Local Public Health Laboratories to Centers for Disease Control and Prevention, 2000-2001

Enterovirus Serotype	Percentage
Echovirus 18	22.0
Echovirus 13	20.8
Coxsackievirus B5	11.9
Coxsackievirus B2	6.3
Echovirus 6	6.1
Echovirus 11	4.5
Coxsackievirus A9	4.0
Echovirus 9	3.3
Coxsackievirus B4	3.2
Echovirus 4	3.1
Coxsackievirus B3	2.4
Coxsackievirus B1	2.0
Echovirus 30	1.8
Echovirus 25	1.2
Enterovirus 71	1.1
Total	93.5

From Centers for Disease Control and Prevention. Enterovirus surveillance—United States, 2000-2001. Morb Mortal Wkly Rep. 2002;51:1047.

morrhagic conjunctivitis caused by both enterovirus 70 and coxsackievirus A24 in the 1980s.[88,92,93]

Transmission

Because viral shedding from the gastrointestinal tract is more prolonged than is shedding from the upper respiratory tract, the fecal-oral route is commonly thought to be the predominant mode of enteroviral transmission. Notable exceptions to this pattern occur, however. Respiratory-oral spread is probably important in the transmission of poliovirus in settings of good hygiene and also in the spread of coxsackievirus A21, which causes upper respiratory infections,[94] and perhaps other coxsackieviruses, which are frequently shed simultaneously from both the upper respiratory tract and in the feces.[95] Enterovirus 70, the agent of acute hemorrhagic conjunctivitis, is spread by fomites, fingers, and ophthalmologic instruments contaminated with virus in tears.[96] Although direct spread of enteroviruses from person to person is likely, the mechanisms of transmission by direct and indirect contact have not been studied under experimental conditions. Vigorous washing with soap and water reduces but does not eliminate infectious poliovirus from the hands.[97] Although enteroviruses have been isolated from flies, cockroaches, food exposed to naturally infected flies, and dog feces, transmission by these vehicles has never been demonstrated. Sampling of sewage in most cities, especially in summer months, usually yields several enteroviral serotypes.[98] Clams in seawater polluted by sewage concentrate enteroviruses 10- to 60-fold. Nevertheless, except for hepatitis A, waterborne epidemics of enteroviral diseases attributed to shellfish ingestion have never been demonstrated.

Longitudinal studies have shown substantial clustering of enterovirus infections in families.[95] Once the virus has been introduced into the household, secondary attack rates for infection among susceptible family members (those lacking type-specific antibody) are 90% to 100% for wild-type polioviruses and approximately 75% for coxsackieviruses.[95] Secondary attack rates for echoviruses are less than 50%, probably because these viruses tend to be shed only in feces and for shorter periods. Infants in diapers who shed virus in the feces are the most efficient disseminators of infection. Mothers and infant siblings are at greater risk of acquiring infection than are fathers and teenaged siblings.[95] For all enteroviruses, the period of maximal contagiousness corresponds to the period of maximal viral excretion in the feces.

When reinfection with the same enterovirus serotype occurs, the duration of excretion of virus is considerably shorter than in the primary infection.[95,99]

Incidence of Infection and Illness

Approximately 95% of infections due to wild-type polioviruses and at least 50% to 80% of non-polio enteroviral infections are completely asymptomatic. Even symptomatic infections usually produce undifferentiated febrile illnesses lasting but a few days, often accompanied by symptoms of upper respiratory tract infection.[100] These illnesses may be caused by virtually any enteroviral serotype and are clinically indistinguishable from infection by many other viral agents. Disease syndromes considered characteristic of enteroviruses, such as aseptic meningitis or pericarditis, are in fact unusual manifestations of infection; a 4-year longitudinal family-based study in New York City detected 291 enteroviral infections, none with "characteristic" illnesses, and only 6 with exanthems.[95]

The risk of some enterovirus-related clinical syndromes varies with age and sex. Aseptic meningitis is most commonly recognized in very young infants, whereas some other illnesses such as pleurodynia and myopericarditis are seen predominantly in adolescents and young adults. Symptomatic enteroviral infections in elderly persons are uncommon. Among young children, boys are at greater risk of illness (but not infection) than are girls.[74] Aseptic meningitis and poliomyelitis occur nearly twice as often in boys. After puberty, the reverse is true, perhaps because women have greater exposure than men

to children shedding virus.[95,101] Pregnancy also may enhance the severity of enteroviral infections. The incidence of paralytic poliomyelitis was two to three times higher in pregnant women than in age-matched nonpregnant women in Boston before the control of poliomyelitis.[102] There are also clinical and epidemiologic data that demonstrate that enteroviral illnesses are more frequent[103] and more severe[104] in persons who exercise vigorously before the onset of symptoms. Although these data are anecdotal, they are supported by considerable evidence that exercise enhances the severity of coxsackievirus B infection in the murine model.[105]

Although the incidence and prevalence of non-polio enteroviral infections have been accurately measured in selected populations and they are undeniably common, the overall incidence in the United States is unknown. Viral isolations tend to be reported only from patients with symptomatic illness, especially the "characteristic" syndromes, for which reporting is incomplete. Serologic surveys encompassing all known enteroviral serotypes are not feasible. Antibody prevalence rates measured for a few serotypes indicate that after the decline of passively acquired maternal antibodies after the age of 6 months, the fraction of immune persons in the population rises progressively with age until 15% to 90% of the adult population have type-specific neutralizing antibodies for each serotype tested, depending on the serotype and the socioeconomic class of the population surveyed.[74,95]

Incubation Period and Period of Communicability

The incubation period for illness due to enteroviral infections can rarely be determined precisely. Because the source of infection is often an asymptomatic person who transmits virus as readily as one who is ill, the time of exposure is usually unknown. Although the incubation period may range from 2 days to 2 weeks, it is usually 3 to 5 days. Patients with enteroviral illnesses typically excrete virus in throat secretions or feces for several days before the onset of symptoms and continue to excrete virus in feces for several weeks thereafter. The period of communicability is therefore potentially long. However, the period of maximal communicability is believed to be early in illness, when viral shedding is greatest.

LABORATORY DIAGNOSIS OF ENTEROVIRAL INFECTIONS

The laboratory diagnosis of enteroviral infection is accomplished by cell culture, PCR, or retrospectively by serologic methods. Cell culture is performed by many academic medical center and public health laboratories and remains the standard method for virus isolation, and the method to which other techniques are compared. However, because cell culture is laborious and relatively slow, it is likely to be gradually supplanted by more rapid and sensitive PCR-based assays and genomic sequencing in the future.

Viral Isolation

A presumptive diagnosis of enteroviral infection can usually be reported by the laboratory within 2 to 5 days following identification of a characteristic cytopathic effect (CPE) in any of three or four appropriately chosen cell lines.[106] Primary monkey kidney cell lines and human embryonic fibroblast cell lines support the growth of most polioviruses, group B coxsackieviruses, and echoviruses. The inclusion of buffalo green monkey kidney cells and human rhabdomyosarcoma cells enhances the recovery of group B coxsackieviruses and echoviruses, respectively.[106] Only a few serotypes of the group A coxsackieviruses (e.g., A9, A16) grow readily in routinely used cell lines. Although the use of specialized cell lines such as rhabdomyosarcoma[107] or guinea pig embryo[108] may aid the recovery of some group A coxsackieviruses in cell culture, inoculation of newborn mice remains the method of choice for recovery of this subgroup of enteroviruses.[83]

Isolates demonstrating CPE may be confirmed as enteroviruses with the use of a monoclonal antibody to a broadly reactive VP1 epitope.[109]

The serotype of an enterovirus isolated in cell culture may be determined by neutralization with type-specific antisera. Unless a small number of serotypes is suspected, this serotypic identification requires the use of the Lim Benyesh-Melnick intersecting antiserum pools,[6] a time-consuming assay that is performed mainly by research and reference laboratories. Because the equine sera that constitute the Lim Benyesh-Melnick pools were harvested against enterovirus strains prevalent more than 30 years ago, their ability to identify contemporary isolates has gradually diminished.[4,6,7]

The opportunity to recover a virus in cell culture is optimized by sampling of multiple sites. Late in the course of enteroviral illnesses, viral cultures of feces are useful because the lower intestine may be the only site from which the agent is still being excreted. An etiologic diagnosis can be confirmed by the isolation of virus from cerebrospinal fluid, pericardial fluid, tissue, or blood, depending on the clinical syndrome. Isolation of virus from the upper respiratory tract or stool is considered by some to be less definitive, because intercurrent asymptomatic enterovirus infections etiologically unrelated to the observed illness may produce a false-positive result. However, in developed countries, background rates of asymptomatic infection are generally low enough that isolation of an enterovirus from a throat or stool specimen is strong evidence of causation.

Polymerase Chain Reaction and Genomic Sequencing

Reverse transcription–PCR is a rapid, sensitive, and specific method of detecting enterovirus RNA in clinical specimens. Most reported PCR protocols amplify a highly conserved portion of the 5' nontranslated region of the genome, enabling the detection of most enteroviruses.[110,111] Subgroup-specific primers distinguish the polioviruses from other enteroviruses.[112,113] With cerebrospinal fluid specimens from patients with aseptic meningitis, PCR detects enteroviral RNA in 66% to 86%, compared with viral isolation rates of approximately 30%.[114-116] Experience with non–cerebrospinal fluid specimens is more limited. PCR has detected enteroviral RNA from throat swabs, serum, urine, and stool. Two reports suggest that the sensitivity with urine specimens is somewhat lower than with other specimens.[117,118] PCR has detected enteroviral RNA in a minority of endomyocardial biopsy specimens from cases of acute myopericarditis.[119,120]

Further characterization of enteroviruses isolated in cell culture or detected by PCR can be accomplished by sequencing the portions of the capsid-coding regions of the viral RNA. This method is used to assign non-polio enterovirus isolates to one of four classes according to the new classification scheme (see earlier, Classification of Enteroviruses) and accurately predict serotype.[4,8,121,122]

Serology

The microneutralization test is the most widely used method for the determination of antibodies to enteroviruses. Because microneutralization is serotype specific, it has limited usefulness in the routine diagnosis of non-polio enteroviral infections because of the low feasibility of testing with multiple live viral antigens, and because methods based on neutralization are relatively insensitive, poorly standardized, and labor intensive. Type-specific immunoassays are more versatile methods that are now offered in commercial laboratories for assay of antibodies against the more common enteroviral serotypes. Serum IgM antibody to the group B coxsackieviruses can often be detected early in the course of illness, but positive test results are not serotype-specific and may occur during infections with enteroviruses of other classes.[123] Epitopes on capsid proteins have been described that are common to many different enteroviral serotypes,[124,125] and monoclonal antibodies are reported to detect VP1 capsid antigens common to many enteroviruses.[109,126] However, identification of a common antigen that is sufficiently immunogenic to form the basis of a broadly reactive serologic assay has not been reported.

TREATMENT AND PREVENTION OF ENTEROVIRAL INFECTIONS

Most enterovirus infections are self-limited and do not require antiviral therapy. Exceptions may include acute myocarditis, and infections in neonates and B-cell–deficient hosts that may be life threatening. The therapeutic options for these more serious infections are quite limited. Serum immune globulin and intravenous immune globulin have been given to individual, persistently infected B-cell–deficient patients with mixed results[54,127] and have been used in nonrandomized trials in children with myocarditis with uncertain effect.[128]

An effective antiviral drug to treat serious enterovirus infections has not been licensed even though several agents have shown activity against enteroviruses in animal models and in early clinical trials.[129] The most promising of these are compounds that bind to a pocket in the viral capsid altering virus attachment and uncoating.[130] The best studied of the capsid-binding drugs is pleconaril, which inhibits replication of most enterovirus serotypes at concentrations of less than 0.1 μg/mL in vitro[131] and which has favorable pharmacologic and safety profiles[132] (see Chapter 38). Placebo-controlled trials of pleconaril in patients with enterovirus meningitis have shown significant reductions in the duration and severity of headache and other symptoms and a shorter period of viral shedding when the drug was administered within 24 hours of symptom onset.[133-136] Uncontrolled experience with pleconaril for B-cell–deficient patients with persistent enterovirus infections and patients with potentially fatal infections, including neonates and persons of all ages with acute myocarditis, suggests substantial clinical benefit.[137] The drug has been previously available for compassionate use, but that program has now ended.

The preexposure administration of immune globulin is known to reduce the risk of paralytic poliomyelitis.[48] It is very likely that immune globulin would also prevent non-polio enterovirus disease as well, but this strategy is rarely applicable to clinical practice. The successful vaccine approach against paralytic poliomyelitis is detailed in Chapter 168. In the setting of a community epidemic or a patient hospitalized with enteroviral illness, simple hygienic measures such as hand washing and careful disposal or autoclaving of potentially infected feces and secretions should be practiced. Gown and mask procedures or isolation of the patient except in the newborn nursery is unwarranted. Pregnant women, especially those near term, should be advised to avoid contact with patients suspected of having enteroviral illness.

REFERENCES

1. Melnick JL. Portraits of viruses: The picornaviruses. Intervirology. 1983;20:61.
2. Melnick JL. Discovery of the enteroviruses and the classification of poliovirus among them. Biologicals. 1993;21:305.
3. King AMQ, Brown F, Christian P, et al. Picornaviridae. In: Van Regenmortel MHV, Fauquet CM, Bishop DHL, eds. Seventh Report of the International Committee on Taxonomy of Viruses. New York: Academic Press; 2000.
4. Oberste MS, Maher K, Flemister MR, et al. Comparison of classic and molecular approaches for the identification of untypable enteroviruses. J Clin Microbiol. 2000;38:1170.
5. Melnick JL. Enteroviruses: Polioviruses, coxsackieviruses, echoviruses, and newer enteroviruses. In: Fields BN, Knipe DM, Howley PM, et al, eds. Fields Virology. Philadelphia: Lippincott-Raven; 1996.
6. Melnick JL, Wimberly IL. Lyophilized combination pools of enterovirus equine antisera. New LBM pools prepared from reserves of antisera stored frozen for two decades. Bull WHO. 1985;63:543.
7. Centers for Disease Control and Prevention. Enterovirus surveillance—United States, 2000-2001. Morb Mortal Wkly Rep. 2002;51:1047.
8. Oberste MS, Maher K, Kilpatrick DR, et al. Typing human enteroviruses by partial sequencing of VP1. J Clin Microbiol. 1999;37:1288.
9. Norder H, Bjerregaard L, Magnius LO. Homotypic echoviruses share aminoterminal VP1 sequence homology applicable for typing. J Med Virol. 2001;63:35.
10. Rueckert RR. Picornaviridae and their replication. In: Fields BN, Knipe DM, eds. Virology. New York: Raven Press; 1990:507.
11. Racaniello VR, Baltimore D. Cloned poliovirus complementary DNA is infectious in mammalian cells. Science. 1981;214:916.

12. Racaniello VR, Baltimore D. Molecular cloning of poliovirus cDNA and determination of the complete nucleotide sequence of the viral genome. Proc Natl Acad Sci U S A. 1981;78:4887.

13. Werner G, Rosenwirth B, Bauer E, et al. Molecular cloning and sequence determination of the genomic regions encoding protease and genome-linked protein of three picornaviruses. J Virol. 1986;57:1084.

14. Holland JJ. Receptor affinities as major determinants of enterovirus tissue tropisms in humans. Virology. 1961;15:312.

15. Rotbart HA, Kirkegaard K. Picornavirus pathogenesis: Viral access, attachment and entry into susceptible cells. Semin Virol. 1992;3:483.

16. Mendelsohn CL, Johnson B, Lionetti KA, et al. Transformation of a human poliovirus receptor gene into mouse cells. Proc Natl Acad Sci U S A. 1986;83:7845.

17. Mendelsohn CL, Wimmer E, Racaniello VR. Cellular receptor for poliovirus: Molecular cloning, nucleotide sequence, and expression of a new member of the immunoglobulin super family. Cell. 1989;56:855.

18. Miller DA, Miller OJ, Vaithilingam GD, et al. Human chromosome 19 carries a poliovirus receptor gene. Cell. 1974;1:167.

19. Shafren DR, Dorahy DJ, Ingham RA, et al. Coxsackievirus A21 binds to decay-accelerating factor but requires intracellular adhesion molecule 1 for cell entry. J Virol. 1997;71:4736.

20. Shafren DR, Bates RC, Agrez MV, et al. Coxsackieviruses B1, B3, and B5 use decay accelerating factor as a receptor for cell attachment. J Virol. 1995;69:3873.

21. Bergelson JM, Cunningham JA, Droguett G, et al. Isolation of a common receptor for coxsackie B viruses and adenoviruses 2 and 5. Science. 1997;275:1320.

22. Crowell RL, Field AK, Schleif WA, et al. Monoclonal antibody that inhibits infection of HeLa and rhabdomyosarcoma cells by selected enteroviruses through receptor blockade. J Virol. 1986;57:438.

23. Hsu K-HL, Lonberg-Holm K, Alstein B, et al. A monoclonal antibody specific for the cellular receptor for the group B coxsackieviruses. J Virol. 1988;62:1647.

24. Bergelson JM, Chan M, Solomon K, et al. Decay-accelerating factor (CD55), a glycosylphosphatidylinositol-anchored complement regulatory protein, is a receptor for several echoviruses. Proceedings of the National Academy of Sciences (USA). 1994;91:6245.

25. Modlin JF, Bergelson J, Wieland-Alter W. Unpublished data.

26. Bergelson JM, Shepley MP, Chan BMC, et al. Identification of the integrin VLA-2 as a receptor for echovirus 1. Science. 1992;255:1718.

27. Bergelson JM, St. John N, Kawaguchi S, et al. Infection by echoviruses 1 and 8 depends on the a2 subunit of human VLA-2. J Virol. 1993;67:6847.

28. Sabin AB. Behavior of chimpanzee-avirulent poliomyelitis viruses in experimentally infected human volunteers. Am J Med Sci. 1955;230:1.

29. Sabin AB. Pathogenesis of poliomyelitis: Reappraisal in light of new data. Science. 1956;123:1151.

30. Ogra PL, Karzon DT. Formation and function of poliovirus antibody in different tissues. Prog Med Virol. 1971;13:157.

31. Horstmann DM, McCollum RW. Poliomyelitis virus in human blood during the "minor" illness and asymptomatic infection. Proc Soc Exp Biol Med. 1953;82:434.

32. Wolf JL, Rubin DH, Finberg R, et al. Intestinal M cells: A pathway for entry of reovirus into the host. Science. 1981;212:471.

33. Davis DC, Melnick JL. Two additional examples of viremia in asymptomatic poliomyelitis infection. Pediatrics. 1957;20:975.

34. Yoshioka I, Horstmann DM. Viremia in infection due to echo virus type 9. N Engl J Med. 1961;262:224.

35. Horstmann DM, Opton EM, Klemperer R, et al. Viremia in infants vaccinated with oral poliovirus vaccine (Sabin). Am J Hyg. 1964;79:47.

36. Minor PD, John A, Ferguson M, et al. Antigenic and molecular evolution of the vaccine strain of type 3 poliovirus during the period of excretion by a primary vaccinee. J Gen Virol. 1986;67:693.

37. Jameson BA, Bonin J, Wimmer E, et al. Natural variants of the Sabin type 1 vaccine strains of poliovirus and correlation with a poliovirus neutralization site. Virol. 1985;143:337.

38. Yoneyama T, Hagiwara A, Hara M, et al. Alteration in oligonucleotide fingerprint patterns of the viral genome in poliovirus type 2 isolated from paralytic patients. Infect Immun. 1982;37:46.

39. O'Neil KM, Pallansch MA, Winkelstein JA, et al. Chronic group A coxsackievirus infection in agammaglobulinemia: Demonstration of genomic variation of serotypically identical isolates persistently excreted from the same patient. J Infect Dis. 1988;157:183.

40. Kew OM, Sutter RW, Nottay BK, et al. Prolonged replication of a type 1 vaccine-derived poliovirus in an immunodeficient patient. J Clin Microbiol. 1998;36:2893.

41. Kew O, Morris-Glasgow V, Landaverde M, et al. Outbreak of poliomyelitis in Hispaniola associated with circulating type 1 vaccine-derived poliovirus. Science. 2002;296:356.

42. Centers for Disease Control and Prevention. Circulation of a type 2 vaccine-derived poliovirus—Egypt, 1982-1993. Morb Mortal Wkly Rep. 2001;50:41.

43. Centers for Disease Control and Prevention. Public health dispatch: Acute flaccid paralysis associated with circulating vaccine-derived poliovirus—Philippines, 2001. Morb Mortal Wkly Rep. 2001;50:874.

44. Centers for Disease Control and Prevention. Poliomyelitis—Madagascar, 2002. Morb Mortal Wkly Rep. 2002;51:622.

45. Tolskaya EA, Romanova LI, Kolesnikova MS, et al. Intertypic recombination in poliovirus: Genetic and biochemical studies. Virology. 1983;124:121.

46. Bodian D, Nathanson N. Inhibitory effects of passive antibody on virulent poliovirus excretion and on immune response in chimpanzees. Bull Johns Hopkins Hosp. 1960;107:143.

47. Hammon WM, Coriell LI, Stokes J Jr. Evaluation of Red Cross gamma globulin as a prophylactic agent for poliomyelitis. JAMA. 1952;150:139.

48. Stevens KM. Estimate of molecular equivalent of antibody required for prophylaxis and therapy of poliomyelitis. J Hyg. 1959;57:198.

49. Bahlke AM, Perkins JE. Treatment of preparalytic poliomyelitis with gamma globulin. JAMA. 1945;129:1146.

50. Ogra PL, Karzon DT. Distribution of poliovirus antibody in serum, nasopharynx, and alimentary tract following segmental immunization of the lower alimentary tract with poliovaccine. J Immunol. 1969;102:1423.

51. Warren RJ, Lepow ML, Bartsch GE, et al. The relationship of maternal antibody, breast feeding, and age to the susceptibility of newborn infants to infection with attenuated poliovirus. Pediatrics. 1964;34:4.

52. Modlin JF, Polk BF, Horton P, et al. Perinatal echovirus 11 infection: Risk of transmission during a community outbreak. N Engl J Med. 1981;305:368.

53. Torfason EG, Reimer CB, Keyserling HL. Subclass restriction of human enterovirus antibodies. J Clin Microbiol. 1987;25:1376.

54. McKinney RE, Katz SL, Wilfert CM. Chronic enteroviral meningoencephalitis in agammaglobulinemic patients. Rev Infect Dis. 1987;9:334.

55. Rager-Zisman B, Allison AC. The role of antibody and host cells in the resistance of mice against infection by coxsackie B-3 virus. J Gen Virol. 1973;19:329.

56. Woodruff J. Lack of correlation between neutralizing antibody production and suppression of coxsackie B-3 replication in target organs: Evidence for involvement of mononuclear inflammatory cells in host defense. J Immunol. 1979;123:31.

57. Woodruff JF, Woodruff JJ. Involvement of T lymphocytes in the pathogenesis of coxsackievirus B3 heart disease. J Immunol. 1974;113:1726.

58. Rabin ER, Hassan SA, Jenson AB, et al. Coxsackie virus B3 myocarditis in mice. Am J Pathol. 1964;44:775.

59. Woodruff JF, Kilbourne ED. The influence of quantitated post-weanling undernutrition on coxsackievirus B-3 infection of adult mice: I. Viral persistence and increased severity of Lesions. J Infect Dis. 1970;121:137.

60. Woodruff JF. Viral myocarditis. Am J Pathol. 1980;101:427.

61. Kawai C. From myocarditis to cardiomyopathy: Mechanisms of inflammation and cell death: Learning from the past for the future. Circulation. 1999;99:1091.

62. Schmidtke M, Gluck B, Merkle I, et al. Cytokine profiles in heart, spleen, and thymus during the acute stage of experimental coxsackievirus B3-induced chronic myocarditis. J Med Virol. 2000;61:518.

63. Huber SA, Job LP, Woodruff JF. In vitro culture of coxsackievirus group B, type 3 immune spleen cells on infected endothelial cells and biological activity of the cultured cells in vivo. Infect Immun. 1984;43:567.

64. Godeny EK, Gauntt CJ. Murine natural killer cells limit coxsackievirus B3 replication. J Immunol. 1987;139:913.

65. Gauntt CJ. Roles of the humoral immune response in coxsackievirus-B-induced disease. In: Tracy S, Chapman NM, Mahy BWJ, eds. The Coxsackie B Viruses, v. 223. Berlin: Springer; 1997:259.

66. Liao O, Sindhwani R, Rojkind M, et al. Antibody-mediated autoimmune myocarditis depends on genetically determined target organ sensitivity. J Exp Med. 1995;181:1123.

67. Schwimmbeck PL, Huber SA, Schultheiss H-P. Roles of T cells in coxsackievirus B-induced disease. In: Tracy S, Chapman NM, Mahy BWJ, eds. The Coxsackie B Viruses, v. 223. Berlin: Springer; 1997:283.

68. Gelfand HM. The occurrence in nature of the Coxsackie and ECHO viruses. Prog Med Virol. 1961;3:193.

69. Moore M. Enteroviral disease in the United States. J Infect Dis. 1982;146:103.

70. Berlin LE, Rorabaugh ML, Heldrich F, et al. Aseptic meningitis in infants less than two years of age: Diagnosis and etiology. J Infect Dis. 1993;168:888.

71. Gelfand HM, Holgium AH, Marchetti GE, et al. A continuing surveillance of enterovirus infections in healthy children in six United States cities. I. Viruses isolated during 1960 and 1961. Am J Hyg. 1963;78:358.

72. Grist NR, Bell EJ, Assad F. Enteroviruses in human disease. Prog Med Virol. 1978;24:114.

73. Dagan R, Powell KR, Hall CB, et al. Identification of infants unlikely to have serious bacterial infection although hospitalized for suspected sepsis. J Pediatr. 1985;107:855.

74. Froeschle JE, Feorino PM, Gelfand HM, et al. A continuing surveillance of enterovirus infections in healthy children in six United States cities. II. Surveillance enterovirus isolates from cases of acute central nervous system disease. Am J Epidemiol. 1966;83:455.

75. Jenista JA, Dalzell LE, Davidson PW, et al. Outcome studies of neonatal enterovirus infection. Pediatr Res. 1984;18:230A.

76. Rorabaugh ML, Berlin LE, Heldrich F, et al. Aseptic meningitis among infants less than two years of age: Acute illness and neurologic complications. Pediatrics. 1993;92:206.

77. Parks WP, Queiroga LT, Melnick JL. Studies of infantile diarrhea in Karachi, Pakistan. II. Multiple virus isolations from rectal swabs. Am J Epidemiol. 1967;85:469.

78. Strikas RA, Anderson LJ, Parker RA. Temporal and geographic patterns of isolates of nonpolio enteroviruses in the United States. J Infect Dis. 1986;153:346.

79. Centers for Disease Control and Prevention. Enterovirus surveillance—United States, 1990. Morb Mortal Wkly Rep. 1990;39:788.

80. Hovi T, Cantell K, Huovilainen A, et al. Outbreak of paralytic poliomyelitis in Finland: Widespread circulation of antigenically altered poliovirus type 3 in a vaccinated population. Lancet. 1986;1:1427.

81. Huovilainen A, Hovi T, Kinnunen L, et al. Evolution of poliovirus during an outbreak: Sequential type 3 poliovirus isolates from several persons show shifts of neutralization determinants. J Gen Virol. 1987;68:1373.

82. Auvinen P, Hyypia T. Echoviruses include genetically distinct serotypes. J Gen Virol. 1990;71:2133.

83. Lipson SM, Walderman R, Costello P, et al. Sensitivity of rhabdomyosarcoma and guinea pig embryo cell cultures to field isolates of difficult-to-cultivate group A coxsackieviruses. J Clin Microbiol. 1986;26:1298.

84. Yang CF, De L, Holloway BP, et al. Detection and identification of vaccine related polioviruses by the polymerase chain reaction. Virol Res. 1991;20:159.

85. Kew OM. Applications of molecular epidemiology to the surveillance of poliomyelitis, Poliomyelitis vaccines: Re-evaluating policy options. Washington, DC: National Academy of Sciences; 1988.

86. Hatch MH, Marchetti GE, Nottay BK, et al. Strain characterization studies of poliovirus type 1 isolates from poliomyelitis cases in the United States in 1979. Dev Biol Stand. 1981;47:307.

87. Lin K H, Wang H L, Sheu M M, et al. Molecular epidemiology of a variant of coxsackievirus A24 in Taiwan: Two epidemics caused by phylogenetically distinct viruses from 1985 to 1989. J Clin Microbiol. 1993;31:1160.

88. Takeda N, Miyamura K, Ogino T, et al. Evolution of enterovirus type 70: Oligonucleotide mapping analysis of RNA genome. Virology. 1984;134:375.

89. Miyamura K, Tanimura M, Takeda N, et al. Evolution of enterovirus 70 in nature: All isolates were recently derived from a common ancestor. Arch Virol. 1986;89:1.

90. Hamby BB, Pallansch MA, Kew OM. Reemergence of an epidemic coxsackie B5 genotype. J Infect Dis. 1987;156:288.

91. Poyry T, Kinnunen L, Kapsenberg J, et al. Type 3 poliovirus/Finland/1984 is genetically related to common Mediterranean strains. J Gen Virol. 1990;71:2535.

92. Lin K-H, Chern C-L, Chu P-Y, et al. Genetic analysis of recent Taiwanese isolates of a variant of coxsackievirus A24. J Med Virol. 2001;64:269.

93. Ishiko H, Shimada T, Yonaha M, et al. Molecular diagnosis of human enteroviruses by phylogeny-based classification by use of the VP4 sequence. J Infect Dis. 2002;185:744.

94. Couch RB, Douglas RG, Lindgren KM, et al. Airborne transmission of respiratory infection with coxsackievirus A type 21. Am J Epidemiol. 1970;91:78.

95. Kogon A, Spigland I, Frothingham TE, et al. The Virus Watch Program: A continuing surveillance of viral infections in metropolitan New York families. Am J Epidemiol. 1969;89:51.

96. Hierholzer JC, Hilliard KA, Esposito JJ. Serosurvey for "acute hemorrhagic conjunctivitis" virus (enterovirus 70) antibodies in the southeastern United States, with review of the literature and some epidemiologic implications. Am J Epidemiol. 1975;102:533.

97. Schurmann W, Eggers HJ. An experimental study on the epidemiology of enteroviruses: Water and soap washing of poliovirus 1-contaminated hands, its effectiveness and kinetics. Med Microbiol Immunol. 1985;174:221.

98. Horstmann DM, Emmons J, Gimpel L, et al. Enterovirus surveillance following a communitywide oral poliovirus vaccination program: A seven year study. Am J Epidemiol. 1973;97:173.

99. Modlin JF, Halsey NA, Thoms ML, et al. Humoral and mucosal immunity in infants induced by three sequential IPV-OPV immunization schedules. J Infect Dis. 1997;75:S228.

100. Johnson KM, Bloom HH, Forsyth B, et al. The role of enteroviruses in respiratory disease. Am Rev Respir Dis. 1963;88:240.

101. Siegel M, Greenberg M, Bodian J. Presence of children in the household as a factor in the incidence of paralytic poliomyelitis in adults. N Engl J Med. 1957;257:958.

102. Weinstein L, Aycock WL, Feemster RF. Relation of sex, pregnancy, and menstruation to susceptibility in poliomyelitis. N Engl J Med. 1951;245:54.

103. Baron RC, Hatch MH, Kleeman K, et al. Aseptic meningitis among members of a high school football team. An outbreak associated with echovirus 16 infection. JAMA. 1982;248:1724.

104. Josselson J, Pula T, Sadler JH. Acute rhabdomyolysis associated with echovirus 9 infection. Arch Intern Med. 1980;140:1671.

105. Gatmaitan BG, Chason JL, Lerner AM. Augmentation of the virulence of murine coxsackievirus B-3 myocardiopathy by exercise. J Exp Med. 1970;131:1121.

106. Dagan R, Menegus MA. A combination of four cell types for rapid detection of enteroviruses in clinical specimens. J Med Virol. 1986;19:219.

107. Schmidt NJ, Ho H, Lennette EH. Propagation and isolation of group A coxsackieviruses in RD cells. J Clin Microbiol. 1975;2:183.

108. Landry ML, Madore HP, Fong CKY, et al. Use of guinea pig embryo cell cultures for isolation and propagation of group A coxsackieviruses. J Clin Microbiol. 1981;13:588.

109. Trabelsi A, Grattard F, Nejmeddine M, et al. Evaluation of an enterovirus group-specific anti-VP1 monoclonal antibody, 5D8/1, in comparison with neutralization and PCR for rapid identification of enteroviruses in cell culture. J Clin Microbiol. 1995;33:2454.

110. Rotbart HA, Sawyer MH, Fast S, et al. Diagnosis of enteroviral meningitis by using PCR with a colorimetric microwell detection assay. J Clin Microbiol. 1994;32:2590.

111. Halonen P, Rocha E, Hierholzer J, et al. Detection of enteroviruses and rhinoviruses in clinical specimens by PCR and liquid-phase hybridization. J Clin Microbiol. 1995;33:648.

112. Abraham R, Chonmaitree T, McCombs J, et al. Rapid detection of poliovirus by reverse transcription and polymerase chain amplification: Application for differentiation between poliovirus and non-poliovirus enteroviruses. J Clin Microbiol. 1993;31:395.

113. Kilpatrick DR, Nottay B, Yang C-F, et al. Group-specific identification of polioviruses by PCR using primers containing mixed-base or deoxyinosine residues at positions of codon degeneracy. J Clin Microbiol. 1996;34:2990.

114. Sawyer M, Holland D, Aintablian N, et al. Diagnosis of enteroviral central nervous system infection by polymerase chain reaction during a large community outbreak. Pediatr Infect Dis J. 1994;13:177.

115. Yerly S, Gervaix A, Simonet V, et al. Rapid and sensitive detection of enteroviruses in specimens from patients with aseptic meningitis. J Clin Microbiol. 1996;34:199.

116. Pozo F, Casas I, Tenorio A, et al. Evaluation of a commercially available reverse transcription-PCR assay for diagnosis of enteroviral infection in archival and prospectively collected cerebrospinal fluid specimens. J Clin Microbiol. 1998;36:1741.

117. Nielsen LP, Modlin JF, Rotbart HA. Detection of enteroviruses by polymerase chain reaction in urine samples from patients with aseptic meningitis. Pediatr Infect Dis J. 1996;15:625.

118. Rotbart HA, Ahmed A, Hickey S, et al. Diagnosis of enterovirus infection by PCR of multiple specimen types. Pediatr Infect Dis J. 1997;16:409.

119. Weiss LM, Movahed LA, Billingham ME, et al. Detection of coxsackievirus B3 RNA in myocardial tissues by polymerase chain reaction. Am J Pathol. 1991;138:497.

120. Jin O, Sole MJ, Butany JW, et al. Detection of enterovirus RNA in myocardial biopsies from patients with myocarditis and cardiomyopathy using gene amplification by polymerase chain reaction. Circulation. 1990;82:8.

121. Oberste MS, Maher K, Kilpatrick DR, et al. Molecular evolution of the human enteroviruses: Correlation of serotype with VP1 sequence and application to picornavirus classification. J Virol. 1999;73:1941.

122. Oberste MS, Maher K, Pallansch MA. Molecular phylogeny of all human enterovirus serotypes based on comparison of sequences at the 5' end of the region coding VP2. Virol Res. 1998;58:35.

123. Pozzetto B, Gaudin OG, Aouni M, et al. Comparative evaluation of immunoglobulin M neutralizing antibody response in acute-phase sera and virus isolation for the routine diagnosis of enterovirus infection. J Clin Microbiol. 1989;27:705.

124. Romero J, Putnak JR, Wimmer E. Use of poliovirus proteins VP3 and 2C as group antigens for the detection of enterovirus infections by indirect immunofluorescence. Pediatr Res. 1986;20:319.

125. Romero JR, Putnak JR, Wimmer E. Enteroviral capsid protein VP3 as a group antigen for the enteroviruses. Pediatr Res. 1988;23:380A.

126. Yousef GE, Brown IN, Mowbray JF. Derivation and biochemical characterization of an enterovirus group-specific monoclonal antibody. Intervirology. 1987;28:163.

127. Mease PJ, Ochs HD, Wedgewood RJ. Successful treatment of echovirus meningoencephalitis and myositis-fasciitis with intravenous immune globulin therapy in a patient with X-linked hypogammaglobulinemia. N Engl J Med. 1981;304:1278.

128. Drucker NA, Colan SD, Lewis AB, et al. Gamma-globulin treatment of acute myocarditis in the pediatric population. Circulation. 1994;89:252.

129. Schiff GM, Sherwood JR. Clinical activity of pleconaril in an experimentally induced coxsackievirus A21 respiratory infection. J Infect Dis. 2000;181:20.

130. Zhang A, Nanni RG, Oren DA, et al. Three-dimensional structure-activity relationships for antiviral agents that interact with picornavirus capsids. Semin Virol. 1992;3:453.

131. Pevear DC, Fancher MJ, Felock PJ, et al. Conformational change in floor of the human rhinovirus canyon blocks adsorption to HeLa cell receptors. J Virol. 1989;63:2002.

132. Rotbart HA. Treatment of picornavirus infections. Antiviral Res. 2002;53:83.

133. Rotbart HA. Pleconaril treatment of enterovirus and rhinovirus infections. Infect Med. 2000;17:488.

134. Sawyer MH, Saez-Llorenz X, Aviles CL, et al. Oral pleconaril reduces the duration and severity of enterviral meningitis in children, Pediatric Academic Societies Annual Meeting, San Francisco, CA, 1999. Society for Pediatric Research.

135. Shafran SD, Halota W, Gilbert D, et al. Pleconaril is effective for enterovirus meningitis in adolescents and adults: A randomized placebo-controlled multicenter trial, 39th Interscience Conference on Antimicrobial Agents and Chemotherapy, San Francisco, CA, 1999.

136. Weiner LB, Rotbart HA, Gilbert DL, et al. Treatment of "enterovirus" meningitis with pleconaril (VP 63843), an antipicornavirus agent, 37th Interscience Conference on Antimicrobial Agents and Chemotherapy, Toronto, 1997. American Society for Microbiology.

137. Rotbart HA. Pleconaril therapy of potentially life-threatening enterovirus infections, 36th Annual Meeting of the Infectious Disease Society of America, Denver, CO, 1998. Infectious Disease Society of America.

138. Dalldorf G, Sickles G. An unidentified, filtrable agent isolated from the feces of children with paralysis. Science. 1948;108:61.

139. Melnick JL, Shaw EW, Curnen EC. A virus from patients diagnosed as non-paralytic poliomyelitis or aseptic meningitis. Proc Soc Exp Biol Med. 1949;71:344.

140. Melnick JL, Agren K. Poliomyelitis and coxsackie viruses isolated from normal infants in Egypt. Proc Soc Exp Biol Med. 1952;81:621.

141. Ramos-Alvarez M, Sabin AB. Characteristics of poliomyelitis and other enteric viruses recovered in tissue culture from healthy American children. Proc Soc Exp Biol Med. 1954;87:655.

142. Rosen L, Melnick J, Schmidt NJ, et al. Subclassification of enteroviruses and ECHO virus type 34. Arch Ges Virusforsch. 1970;30:89.

143. Cohen JI, Ticehurst JR, Purcell RH, et al. Complete nucleotide sequence of wild-type hepatitis A virus: Comparison with different strains of hepatitis A and other picornaviruses. J Virol. 1987;61:50.

Poliovirus

JOHN F. MODLIN

Polioviruses are the cause of poliomyelitis, a systemic infectious disease that predominantly affects the central nervous system (CNS) causing paralysis. The name of the disease (*polios,* "gray"; *myelos,* "marrow" or "spinal cord"), now commonly shortened to polio, is descriptive of the pathologic lesions that involve neurons in the gray matter, especially in the anterior horn of the spinal cord. Older, less commonly used names for the disease include *infantile paralysis* and *Heine-Medin disease.* Paralytic poliomyelitis has been completely controlled in the United States and other developed countries through immunization with inactivated poliovirus vaccine (IPV) or live-attenuated oral poliovirus vaccine (OPV), or both, and global eradication is anticipated to occur early in the 21st century.

HISTORY

Evidence of poliomyelitis exists from antiquity, and clinical reports of sporadic cases were published as early as 1840.[1] There is little record of epidemic poliomyelitis until the late 19th century, when outbreaks were first recorded in Scandinavia, western Europe, and the United States. Karl Oskar Medin, a Swedish physician, characterized the natural history and neurologic complications of poliomyelitis in 1890 after an outbreak in Scandinavia, and Charles Caverly, a graduate of Dartmouth College, wrote the first description of epidemic poliomyelitis in the United States, an outbreak of 132 cases near Rutland, Vermont, in 1894.[2] In 1908, Landsteiner and Popper[3] demonstrated that polio was caused by a "filterable virus" when they transmitted disease to monkeys from human spinal cord homogenates. However, scientific progress remained somewhat limited until the landmark discovery in 1949 by Enders, Weller, and Robbins[4] that poliovirus could be propagated in vitro in cultures of human embryonic tissues of nonneural origin. This discovery facilitated experimental investigation of the pathogenesis of the disease and the development of vaccines. Bodian and colleagues[5] first recognized the three distinct serotypes of poliovirus. By 1952, Bodian[6] and Horstmann[7] had independently discovered that viremia occurred early in infection, which explained the systemic phase of the illness.

Salk[8] reported in 1953 that human subjects could be successfully immunized with formalin-inactivated poliovirus, a discovery that rapidly led to an extensive field trial and licensure of IPV in 1955. The incidence of poliomyelitis fell sharply once IPV was widely available, and introduction of the Sabin strain live-attenuated OPVs in 1961-1962 led to still further reductions in disease incidence.[9] Universal polio immunization ultimately resulted in eradication of disease due to naturally occurring (wild-type) polioviruses in the United States by 1979 and, under the leadership of the Pan American Health Organization, in the entire Western Hemisphere by 1991. Endemic poliomyelitis has since been controlled by all except a few nations and now is limited to a few areas in sub-Saharan Africa and the Indian subcontinent.[10]

POLIOMYELITIS IN THE UNITED STATES

The first half of the 20th century witnessed sporadic epidemic disease occurring every few years without regular periodicity. By the early 1950s, epidemic polio occurred regularly in the United States with approximately 25 cases per 100,000 population reported annually. Accompanying the increased incidence was a shift in the affected age groups. In 1920, 90% of the cases occurred in infants younger than 5 years ("infantile paralysis"). In the early 1950s, the peak incidence was in 5- to 9-year-olds and more than one third of the cases occurred

in persons older than 15 years. Abundant epidemiologic evidence supports the explanation that in the endemic period before 1900, polioviruses were ubiquitous and resulted in mostly unapparent infections that conferred widespread immunity in early childhood; with rising standards of hygiene in the 20th century, infection frequently was delayed until a later age, when the pool of susceptible people was large enough to permit the spread of epidemic disease. This concept presupposes that the appearance of epidemics of paralytic poliomyelitis was a result of a higher ratio of paralysis to inapparent infections among children old enough to have lost the protection of passively acquired maternal antibody.[11]

The introduction of IPV, and later OPV, produced sudden, dramatic reductions in the incidence of paralytic poliomyelitis in the developed countries of the world. In the United States, the attack rate fell from 17.6 cases of poliomyelitis (paralytic and nonparalytic) per 100,000 population in 1955 to 0.4 case per 100,000 in 1962. During the next two decades, the rate of disease continued to fall until 1979, when the last case of endemic, naturally occurring poliomyelitis was reported, indicating that indigenous transmission of naturally occurring polioviruses had completely ceased in the United States.[12] This fade-out of naturally occurring strains has been attributed to the widespread use of OPV and to a reduction in the number of susceptible persons to a level insufficient to allow perpetuation of wild-type strains during periods when transmission is naturally low (i.e., winter and spring).[11] From 1979 to 1997, the only cases of poliomyelitis reported in the United States were the rare cases caused by OPV viruses or imported from other countries. None of the imported cases resulted in secondary spread of poliomyelitis.

PATHOPHYSIOLOGY

Virology

Polioviruses are prototypic members of the genus *Enterovirus* (see Chapter 167). Three poliovirus serotypes are distinguished from one another by neutralization with type-specific antisera. Infection confers type-specific, lifelong immunity to disease but little or no immunity to infection or disease caused by heterologous serotypes.[13] Before the introduction of poliovirus vaccines, most paralytic disease was caused by type 1.[14] Naturally occurring (wild-type) polioviruses, live-attenuated OPV viruses, and virulent polioviruses derived from OPV strains (vaccine-derived polioviruses [VDPVs]) may circulate in different populations, depending on whether endemic transmission of wild-type polioviruses has been eliminated, on whether OPV is used, and on the vaccine-induced immunity rates in the population.

Humans are the only natural host and reservoir of polioviruses, although experimental infections and disease can be produced in other primates, and polioviruses can be adapted to replicate in subprimate mammals. Naturally occurring strains vary over a 10^7-fold range in neurovirulence.[15] Rhesus and cynomolgus monkeys are readily paralyzed by most naturally occurring strains, although much higher doses or more virulent strains are required to paralyze chimpanzees and humans. In contrast, polioviruses are more infectious for the human gut than for the gut of lower primates.

Attenuated OPV strains are occasionally able to paralyze rhesus and cynomolgus monkeys but only when injected in high doses directly into the CNS. In addition to low neurovirulence, vaccine strains can often be distinguished from naturally occurring strains by their temperature sensitivity and by subtle antigenic differences. The genomes for each of the attenuated Sabin vaccine strains have been fully sequenced as well as the genomes of each of the naturally occurring parental strains. The RNA sequences of the vaccine strains differ from the sequences of their naturally occurring parents by less than 1%, with the smallest difference occurring between the type 3 vaccine and parent strains. For all three serotypes, analogous nucleotide substitutions in the 5'-noncoding region appear to be associated with diminished ability to replicate in the gastrointestinal tract, and with reduced neurovirulence.[16-18] Attenuating mutations also map to capsid proteins for individual serotypes.

In contrast, VDPVs represent OPV viruses that have been permitted to circulate due to low population immunity for long periods of time and, by continuous mutation, acquire biologic properties that are indistinguishable from those of naturally occurring wild-type polioviruses.[19-21] VDPVs that circulated in Hispaniola for approximately 2 to 3 years were shown to have diverged from the RNA sequence of parent OPV strain RNA sequence by 2% and to have acquired the temperature-sensitive phenotype and neurovirulence associated with wild-type polioviruses.[20]

Pathogenesis

The early events in the pathogenesis of poliomyelitis are similar to other enterovirus infections that are described in Chapter 167. After implantation at a mucosal site and replication in the gut and adjacent lymphoid tissues, polioviruses may disseminate to susceptible reticuloendothelial tissues via a "minor" viremia. In asymptomatic infections, the virus is contained at this point and elicits the formation of type-specific antibodies. In a few infected persons, replication in the reticuloendothelial system gives rise to a "major viremia," which corresponds temporally with the "minor illness" and causes the symptoms associated with abortive poliomyelitis. At this point, the course of poliomyelitis deviates from other enteroviral diseases in the capacity of polioviruses to infect neurons in the gray matter of the brain and spinal cord. Although the preponderance of evidence indicates that viremia precedes paralysis in both experimental primates and humans,[22,23] the exact routes by which the CNS becomes infected remain uncertain. A study in transgenic mice expressing the human poliovirus receptor suggests that polioviruses spread from muscle to CNS via peripheral nerve fibers, rather than directly from the blood stream.[24] Neuropathologic studies and animal experiments indicate that spread is neural once the virus reaches the CNS.[25,26]

Poliovirus principally affects motor and autonomic neurons. Neuronal destruction is accompanied by an inflammatory infiltrate of polymorphonuclear leukocytes, lymphocytes, and macrophages. These lesions are characteristically distributed throughout the gray matter of the anterior horn of the spinal cord and the motor nuclei of the pons and medulla.[25] The mesencephalon, cerebellar roof nuclei, and precentral gyrus of the cerebral cortex are less severely involved. Clinical symptoms depend on the severity of lesions rather than on their distribution, which is similar in essentially all cases; almost all fatal cases have involvement of both the spinal cord and the cranial nerve nuclei and brain stem, even in the absence of bulbar signs. The dorsal root ganglia are commonly involved pathologically, but this does not result in sensory deficits. Polioviruses can be recovered from the spinal cord for only the first few days after the onset of paralysis, but the inflammatory lesions may persist for months.

CLINICAL FEATURES

Incubation Period

Best estimates of the incubation period of poliomyelitis are 9 to 12 days (range, 5 to 35 days) measured from presumed contact until the onset of the prodromal symptoms, and 11 to 17 days (range, 8 to 36 days) until the onset of paralysis.[27]

Clinical Manifestations of Infection

The manifestations of infection by polioviruses range from unapparent illness to severe paralysis and death. Usual estimates of the ratio of unapparent to clinically recognized polio infection vary between 60:1 and 1000:1.[11,28] Figure 168-1 depicts the time course for the clinical manifestations of poliovirus infection. At least 95% of infections are asymptomatic or unapparent and can be recognized only by the isolation of poliovirus from feces or oropharynx or by a rise in antibody titer. *Abortive poliomyelitis*, which occurs in 4% to 8% of infections, is characterized by a 2- to 3-day period of fever, which may be accompanied by headache, sore throat, listlessness, anorexia, vomiting, or abdominal pain. Because the neurologic examination is normal, abortive poliomyelitis cannot be distinguished from other viral infections and can be clinically suspected only during an epidemic. *Nonparalytic poliomyelitis* differs from abortive poliomyelitis by the presence of signs of meningeal irritation. The disease is identical to meningitis caused by other enteroviruses. The systemic manifestations of nonparalytic poliomyelitis are generally more severe than in abortive poliomyelitis.

Spinal Paralytic Poliomyelitis

Frank paralysis occurs in roughly 0.1% of all poliovirus infections. In children there is frequently a biphasic course with *minor* and *major* illnesses. The minor illness, coinciding with viremia, corresponds to the symptoms of abortive poliomyelitis and lasts 1 to 3

FIGURE 168-1. Schema of the clinical and subclinical forms of poliomyelitis, showing presence of virus and antibodies in relation to the development and persistence of the infection. *(From Paul JR. History of Poliomyelitis. New Haven, CT: Yale University Press; 1971.)*

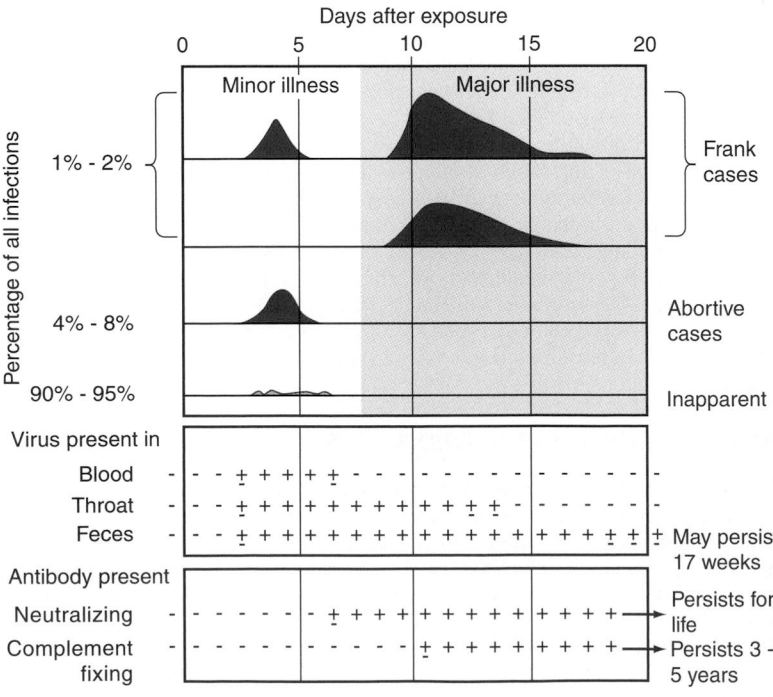

days. The patient then appears to be recovering and remains symptom-free for 2 to 5 days before the abrupt onset of the major illness. The preparalytic symptoms and signs of the major illness are those of meningitis, with headache, fever, malaise, vomiting, neck stiffness, and cerebrospinal fluid (CSF) pleocytosis. The temperature is generally 37° C to 39° C and is often is accompanied by chills. This biphasic pattern (seen in perhaps one third of the children) is rarely observed in adults, who usually have a single phase but a more prolonged prodrome of symptoms before the more gradual onset of paralysis.[29,30] The major illness is heralded by severe myalgias and occasionally localized cutaneous hyperesthesia, paresthesias, involuntary muscle spasm, or muscular fasciculations. The meningismus and muscle pain are present for 1 to 2 days before frank weakness and paralysis ensue. The severity of the disease varies from weakness of a single portion of one muscle to complete quadriplegia. The paralysis is flaccid; deep tendon reflexes are initially hyperactive and then become absent. The most characteristic feature of the paralysis is its asymmetrical distribution, which affects some muscle groups while sparing others. Proximal muscles of the extremities tend to be more involved than distal muscles, the legs are more commonly involved than the arms, and the large muscle groups of the hand are at greater risk than the small ones. Any combination of limbs may be paralyzed, but the most common pattern is involvement of one leg, followed by one arm, or both legs and both arms. Quadriplegia is almost never observed in infants.[30] Although occasional cases progress from the onset of weakness to complete quadriplegia and bulbar involvement in a few hours, more commonly the paralysis extends over 2 to 3 days. Progression of paralysis almost invariably halts when the patient becomes afebrile.[29] Paralysis of the bladder is usually associated with paralysis of the legs. It occurs in about one quarter of the adults but is uncommon in children. Sensory loss in poliomyelitis is very rare,[31] and its occurrence should strongly suggest some other diagnosis (e.g., Guillain-Barré syndrome).

Bulbar Paralytic Poliomyelitis

Bulbar poliomyelitis results from paralysis of muscle groups innervated by the cranial nerves, especially those of the soft palate and pharynx, which may present as dysphagia, nasal speech, and sometimes dyspnea. The frequency of the bulbar form of the disease has varied in different epidemics from 5% to 35% of paralytic cases. The ninth and tenth cranial nerves are most commonly involved, and pharyngeal paralysis with pooling of secretions often is the only obvious sign.[32] Patients usually are extremely anxious and agitated about their inability to swallow and breathe. Involvement of the circulatory and respiratory centers of the medulla represent the most serious form of bulbar poliomyelitis.

Polioencephalitis

Encephalitis, manifested primarily by confusion and disturbances of consciousness, is an uncommon form of poliomyelitis occurring principally in infants. It is the only type of poliomyelitis in which seizures are common. In contrast to spinal paralytic polio, there may be spastic paralysis indicating the presence of upper motor neuron involvement. The illness is not clinically distinguishable from other forms of viral encephalitis.

COMPLICATIONS

The most important complication of paralytic poliomyelitis is respiratory compromise caused by paralysis of the respiratory muscles including the diaphragm and intercostal muscles, by airway obstruction from involvement of the cranial nerve nuclei, or by lesions of the medullary respiratory center.[33] Myocarditis has been documented by the presence of inflammatory infiltrates in cardiac tissue obtained postmortem and isolation of poliovirus from myocardium,[34,35] but myocardial dysfunction is rarely recognized clinically. Gastrointestinal events such as hemorrhage, paralytic ileus, and gastric dilatation may complicate acute paralysis.[36]

Risk Factors

Several preexisting factors and provocative events are known to influence the likelihood that an individual, once infected with poliovirus, develops paralysis. Before puberty, poliovirus infections occur equally in boys and girls, although paralysis is more common in boys. Among adults, women are at greater risk of infection but are not necessarily at greater risk of paralysis.[37,38] Both the incidence and the severity of poliomyelitis may be increased in pregnant women.[38,39] Not only are women of childbearing age more likely to be exposed to infections in young children,[37] but also late pregnancy may be associated with increased susceptibility to more serious illness.

Strenuous exercise substantially increases both the incidence and the severity of paralytic poliomyelitis.[40,41] Exercise during the minor illness or the prodrome has no effect, but it is detrimental when it occurs during the first 3 days of the major illness.[41] Both epidemiologic[42,43] and experimental[44,45] studies have confirmed that poliomyelitis tends to localize in a limb that has been the site of an intramuscular injection or injury within 2 to 4 weeks before the onset of infection. This association holds for both naturally occurring disease and vaccine-associated paralytic poliomyelitis.[46] Tonsillectomy increases the risk of bulbar poliomyelitis whether the procedure is performed just before poliovirus infection or in the remote past.[47,48] Because the ninth and tenth cranial nerves supply the fauces, the spread of virus from damaged nerve endings may explain the effect.

DIFFERENTIAL DIAGNOSIS

Sporadic cases of acute motor neuron disease that is indistinguishable from poliomyelitis may be caused by other enteroviruses, especially enterovirus 71 (see Chapter 167) or by West Nile virus infection[49,50] (see Chapter 149). Few other diseases are confused with paralytic poliomyelitis, except Guillain-Barré syndrome, which, unlike poliomyelitis, produces symmetrical, bilateral ascending paralysis with loss of sensation in the majority of cases that may progress over a period of 1 to 2 weeks. In acute poliomyelitis, pleocytosis and a minimally elevated protein concentration are present, whereas in Guillain-Barré syndrome, the protein level is elevated with absent or minimal pleocytosis (the "albuminocytologic dissociation").

LABORATORY DIAGNOSIS

Abnormalities of the CSF are not distinguishable from those of other viral diseases that cause aseptic meningitis. Polioviruses usually can be isolated from throat secretions in the first week of illness and from feces often for several weeks. Unlike other enteroviruses that cause aseptic meningitis, polioviruses rarely are isolated from the CSF. In sporadic cases of poliomyelitis occurring in areas of low incidence, it is important to characterize virus isolates as either wild-type (naturally occurring strains) or vaccine-like by means of phenotypic and genotypic methods, methodologies that are available only in public health reference laboratories. Isolation from CSF (or brain and spinal cord in fatal cases), although uncommon, is especially valuable in evaluating vaccine-associated paralytic poliomyelitis, because recovery of fecal virus is expected for several weeks following receipt of OPV and only a CNS virus isolate with vaccine characteristics provides conclusive evidence of the etiologic association.

In the absence of a viral isolate, the diagnosis of poliovirus infection can be established serologically by testing paired acute and convalescent sera by neutralization against antigens of the three serotypes. Serologic tests cannot distinguish between wild-type virus and vaccine virus infection.

PROGNOSIS

Muscular paralysis usually progresses or extends for only 1 to 3 days after its onset, but occasionally for as long as 1 week.[51] Permanent weakness is observed in approximately two thirds of patients with paralytic poliomyelitis. Complete recovery is less likely when acute paralysis is severe, and patients requiring mechanical ventilation because of spinal respiratory paralysis rarely recover without some sequelae. Some estimate of the eventual outcome can be made after 1 month, when most reversible damage has disappeared. Very little additional return of function can be expected beyond 9 months. Recovery from pharyngeal paralysis usually is evident by 10 days and is eventually complete. Bulbar poliomyelitis is rarely responsible for permanent sequelae in surviving patients.

Available mortality figures date from the era of epidemic poliomyelitis, a period when critical care medicine was less advanced than it is today. The reported overall mortality for acute paralytic poliomyelitis during this period was 5% to 10%, but was substantially higher with bulbar involvement.[52]

MANAGEMENT

Specific antiviral agents for the treatment of poliomyelitis are not available, and therefore management is supportive and directed to relief of symptoms. In the acute phase of paralytic poliomyelitis, patients should be hospitalized. Bed rest is essential to prevent augmentation or extension of paralysis. Hot moist packs applied to muscles are helpful in relieving pain and spasm. Physical therapy should be initiated once the progression of paralysis has ceased.

Paralysis of the respiratory muscles necessitates mechanical ventilation before hypoxia develops, generally when the vital capacity falls to less than 50%. Tank respirators used in the past to treat this form of paralysis are available in few hospitals; despite their advantage of avoiding tracheal intubation, they have been replaced by positive-pressure ventilators, which permit easier access to the patient. Pooling of secretions in the pharynx in mild bulbar poliomyelitis, if it is unaccompanied by spinal respiratory paralysis, can be managed with postural drainage and suction. Severe bulbar paralysis necessitates tracheal intubation. Weakness or paralysis of the bladder may necessitate catheterization.

Management of long-term physical and psychiatric sequelae of paralytic poliomyelitis is beyond the scope of this book. The reader is referred to excellent older references on these topics.[53,54]

POSTPOLIOMYELITIS SYNDROME

Some patients who partially or fully recover from paralytic poliomyelitis experience a new onset of muscle weakness, pain, atrophy, and fatigue many years after the acute illness.[55] Typically, the involved muscles are the same as those affected during the original illness, but weakness may also occur in previously unaffected limb muscles. Progression of new symptoms is gradual, and, as a result, affected individuals are seldom severely disabled.[56] Population-based studies suggest that the syndrome affects 20% to 30% of previously paralyzed patients.[57] The risk of postpoliomyelitis syndrome peaks between 25 and 35 years after acute poliomyelitis.[57] Although the cause is unknown, some authorities believe that late progression of muscle weakness is a result of physiologic attrition of motor units innervating muscles and muscle groups already less innervated as a result of earlier acute infection.[58]

POLIOVIRUS IMMUNIZATION

Poliovirus Vaccines

Both IPV and live-attenuated OPV have been used effectively for more than 30 years in controlling paralytic poliomyelitis. The introduction of Salk IPV in 1955 led to an immediate and dramatic reduction in both epidemic and endemic poliomyelitis. The IPV available for the first several years possessed relatively low potency, accounting for the observation that as many as 17% of children with paralytic poliomyelitis in 1959 had received three or more doses of IPV.[59] Meanwhile live-attenuated OPV strains were developed by multiple passage of polioviruses in monkey kidney cell culture and selection of mutants with low virulence for primates.[60] Successful field trials of the Sabin OPV vaccine strains were carried out in the United States and

many foreign countries from 1955 to 1959, and OPV was introduced for routine use in 1962 as separate monovalent vaccines; the trivalent product became available in 1964. OPV was quickly accepted by the pediatric and public health community because of several advantages, including superior immunogenicity; lower cost; ease of administration; spread of vaccine virus to unimmunized, susceptible persons; and induction of gastrointestinal immunity. Because of these properties, OPV is used almost exclusively in developing countries. However, OPV also causes rare cases of vaccine-associated paralytic poliomyelitis (VAPP). Once it was clear that the risk of VAPP outweighed the advantages of OPV, the United States reintroduced a more potent IPV into the routine childhood immunization schedule in 1997 and moved to exclusive use of IPV in 2000.[61] Other developed countries have also adopted IPV for routine polio immunization.

Inactivated Poliovirus Vaccine

IPV is prepared by the inactivation of poliovirus seed strains by the method originally developed by Jonas Salk (i.e., 1:1000 formalin treatment for 12 to 14 days at 37° C). The potency of IPV has been "enhanced" in the past two decades by the adoption of continuous cell lines and microcarrier systems for vaccine production. Enhanced-potency IPV was introduced in Europe and Canada in the early 1980s and licensed in the United States in 1987. The preparation now available (IPOL; Aventis Pasteur) is produced in monkey kidney cells and contains 40-, 8-, and 32-Da antigen units, respectively, for poliovirus serotypes 1, 2, and 3. Four doses of IPV are recommended at 2 months, 4 months, 6 to 18 months, and 4 to 6 years of age.[61] A very similar IPV is formulated in combination with other routinely recommended childhood vaccines as Pediarix (GlaxoSmithKline).

The currently licensed IPV formulations are more immunogenic than those available before 1987. Seroconversion rates are equal to, and mean antibody titers are superior to, those of OPV when given according to the same schedule. Neutralizing antibodies are detectable to all three types in 99% of recipients after two doses and in 100% after the third dose.[62,63] A large boost in antibody titer follows the third dose.[63] After three doses, mean titers to types 1 and 3 are higher than in OPV-immunized children, whereas mean titers to type 2 are equivalent. Detectable antibody persists at protective levels for at least 5 years, although mean titers decline more rapidly than after OPV.[64] The efficacy of IPV after one or two doses may be lower than for an equivalent number of OPV doses. A case-control study in Senegal indicated protection rates of 36% and 89% for recipients of one and two doses, respectively.[65]

IPV-immunized children develop little or no measurable secretory antibody.[66] When challenged with live polioviruses, IPV-immunized children shed the challenge virus in their feces at a higher rate and a higher titer and for a longer period than do OPV-immunized children,[67,68] indicating a greater potential for asymptomatic infection and transmission of circulating polioviruses to unimmunized contacts. Although this is widely considered to be a disadvantage of IPV, there is evidence that the universal use of IPV results in partial protection that extends to unvaccinated persons in the community, albeit less than the protection provided by OPV.[69-71]

Live-Attenuated Poliovirus Vaccine

OPV is no longer distributed in the United States. Most trivalent OPV preparations made in other countries meet the World Health Organization Expanded Program on Immunization minimum potency standard of $10^{6.0}$, $10^{5.0}$, and $10^{5.5}$ $TCID_{50}$ for poliovirus types 1, 2, and 3, respectively.[72] Because the more efficient replication of type 2 OPV virus regularly interferes with the replication of types 1 and 3,[73] a primary series of three doses is required to ensure seroconversion to all three serotypes.

Infants in developed countries experience seroconversion rates of 50%, 85%, and 30% to serotypes 1, 2, and 3, respectively, after the first OPV dose.[74] Two months after the second dose, more than 86% of infants have serum antibody to all three poliovirus serotypes, and 2 months after the third dose, the prevalence of antibody to all three types is more than 96%.[63,75] Detectable serum antibody to all three types persists in 84% to 98% of vaccinees 5 years after primary immunization.[76] Reexposure to vaccine viruses probably contributes to the maintenance of antibody levels in the population.[77,78] Secretory immunoglobulin A poliovirus antibody appears in oropharyngeal and duodenal secretions 1 to 3 weeks after OPV immunization[66] and persists for at least 5 to 6 years.[79] Challenge studies suggest that the intestinal immunity induced by OPV is similar to intestinal immunity after natural infection.[80] The efficacy of OPV was never tested when natural polioviruses were circulating in the United States. During a type 1 poliovirus outbreak in Taiwan, OPV efficacy was estimated to be 82%, 96%, and 98% for one, two, and three or more doses, respectively.[81]

Nonimmune OPV recipients shed vaccine viruses in the feces for 1 to 6 weeks and from the oropharynx for 1 to 3 weeks. The spread of OPV virus to unimmunized children is considered to be advantageous, especially in areas in which vaccine acceptance levels are low. The importance of this "back door" method of protecting the community is uncertain. A seroprevalence study in Houston and Detroit found that 11% to 42% of 11- to 35-month-old children had antibody, despite receiving no prior OPV.[82]

Vaccine-Associated Paralytic Poliomyelitis

The only disadvantage of OPV is the rare occurrence of VAPP, which affects approximately 1 person per 2.6 million OPV doses distributed.[83] Before 1997, an average of eight cases of VAPP were reported annually in the United States.[83,84] Approximately 45% of VAPP cases are recent OPV vaccinees, most of whom develop paralysis 7 to 21 days after the first feeding of OPV.[83] A similar number of VAPP cases occur among parents, other family members, babysitters, or other associates of the family who develop paralysis 20 to 29 days after the administration of OPV to a close contact. For immunocompetent patients, the clinical features and outcome of VAPP differ little from disease caused by naturally occurring polioviruses. More than 80% of recipient and contact cases are associated with the first dose of OPV. OPV virus types 3 and 2 are more common causes of vaccine-associated paralysis than type 1.[83]

Approximately one fourth of reported VAPP cases occur in children and adults who are immune deficient.[85] Most of these patients have transient or hereditary B-cell immunodeficiency, severe combined immunodeficiency syndrome, or common variable immunodeficiency. The risk of VAPP among newborn infants with a congenital B-cell immunodeficiency disorder is estimated to be 2000-fold higher than for immunocompetent infants.[29] However, there is little evidence that immunodeficiency states that predominantly affect T-cell function, rather than B-cell function, increase the risk of VAPP. Although one Romanian infant infected with human immunodeficiency virus (HIV) is reported to have developed VAPP,[86] there has been no evidence of neurologic complications among thousands of HIV-infected infants known to have received OPV in the United States and elsewhere.[87,88] Similarly, VAPP is not known to complicate hematologic malignancies, bone marrow transplantation, or solid organ transplantation.

Certain clinical features distinguish VAPP in immunodeficient patients from VAPP in those who are immunocompetent. The interval between the last OPV dose and onset of neurologic disease is unusually long, with a typical range of 1 to 8 months, but it has been documented to be as long as 7 years.[89] The illness is protracted and characterized by chronic meningitis, progressive neurologic dysfunction suggesting involvement of both upper and lower motor neurons, and progression of paralysis over several weeks.[90,91] Immunodeficient patients also have a much higher risk of dying from VAPP than immunocompetent patients. Although fewer than 20% of surviving VAPP patients excrete polioviruses for longer than 6 months,[89] fecal excretion of virus has been estimated to occur for as long as 9 years in one immunodeficient patient.[92] The majority of VAPP cases in immunocompromised children and adults have been associated with type 2 OPV virus.[85]

The mechanism by which the OPV viruses cause rare cases of paralytic disease is not completely understood. It is well known that OPV virus readily undergoes mutation during the brief period of intestinal replication and that isolates can be recovered that are neurovirulent for primates.[15] Most OPV recipients shed polioviruses that have reverted to the naturally occurring genotype at a specific locus in the 5′ noncoding region of the genome that is strongly associated with attenuation for each of the three OPV serotypes.[93] However, because the attenuated Sabin strains differ from their virulent parent strains at multiple genetic loci, other mutational events probably contribute to reversion to full neurovirulence.[94-98]

USE OF POLIOMYELITIS VACCINES IN THE DEVELOPING WORLD

OPV is used almost exclusively in underdeveloped nations because of its lower cost and ease of administration. The superior secretory immunity in the gastrointestinal tract induced by OPV is considered an advantage because of high rates of exposure to wild-type polioviruses. Transmission of OPV virus from immunized to nonimmune contacts, an event that is thought to be aided by poor sanitation and crowded living conditions, is also considered an advantage of OPV. The WHO Expanded Program on Immunization (EPI) calls for an OPV dose at birth and for three additional OPV doses in the first year of life at 6, 10, and 14 weeks of age.[99,100] Passively acquired maternal antibody present in the infant's circulation and in maternal colostrum blunts the immune response to the birth dose in some infants. However, infants who receive OPV at birth are more likely to have antibody to all three poliovirus types at 4 months of age.[101]

Unfortunately, many infants in tropical countries are left unprotected even if they receive the entire OPV series. Low seroconversion rates to three OPV doses have been documented in many locations,[102-104] averaging 73%, 90%, and 70% for types 1, 2, and 3, respectively.[105] This poor response appears to have contributed to poliomyelitis outbreaks in several countries with relatively high immunization rates.[104,106,107] Although the reasons for the lower potency of OPV in tropical areas remains incompletely understood, both vaccine formulation and the effect of concurrent diarrheal illnesses have emerged as important factors. In the past, OPV vaccines distributed in many countries only marginally met EPI minimal potency standards. Patriarca and colleagues[106] demonstrated that a twofold increase in antigen content increased the type 3 seroconversion rate from 16% to 42% among type 3–seronegative Brazilian children given one dose of trivalent OPV. Diarrheal disease at the time of immunization also reduces seroconversion rates to OPV. Studies conducted in Brazil[108] and in Bangladesh[109] have shown reduced seroconversion rates to types 2 and 3 OPV among infants with diarrhea at the time of OPV feeding, whereas the response to type 1 was not affected. The impact of diarrhea on seroconversion persists despite the administration of three or four OPV doses.

Although IPV has been shown to be highly immunogenic among children in developing areas,[110,111] the costs associated with production and delivery, and the requirement for injection, have made the sole use of IPV an undesirable alternative for developing countries. However, IPV has been used as a supplement to OPV immunization in Israel, where type 1 poliovirus continued to cause epidemic disease in the Gaza Strip despite relatively good rates of OPV coverage,[104,112] and in Côte d'Ivoire, where IPV administered at 9 months markedly enhanced seroconversion rates among infants given OPV at 2, 3, and 4 months of age.[113]

POLIOMYELITIS IN DEVELOPING NATIONS AND GLOBAL ERADICATION

Even after the introduction of polio vaccines, poliomyelitis was regarded as an epidemic disease of wealthier nations and was ignored in developing countries. However, lameness surveys of schoolchildren in the 1960s and 1970s in more than 20 nations revealed lower limb paralysis prevalence rates of 2 to 11 per 1000, figures that reflect poliomyelitis incidence rates that equal or exceed those of the peak epidemic years in the United States.[99,114] Most cases of paralytic poliomyelitis in developing countries occur in children between the ages of 6 months and 2 years. The majority of cases are caused by type 1 poliovirus.

In 1974, the World Health Organization founded the EPI, which provided monetary and technical support for basic immunization against several childhood diseases including polio and created a worldwide standard polio immunization policy.[99] There was considerable progress in controlling poliomyelitis, but vaccines still failed to reach many children because of interrupted supplies, disruptions in the cold chain necessary to maintain the potency of OPV, civil strife, and poor political support. In 1983, an international conference held in Bellagio, Italy, soon after smallpox eradication articulated the feasibility of worldwide poliomyelitis eradication.[115] The Pan American Health Organization resolved in 1985 to eradicate poliomyelitis from the Western Hemisphere, a goal that was achieved within 6 years, and in 1988, the World Health Assembly set a goal of global eradication of poliomyelitis by the year 2000.[116,117]

The WHO Global Poliomyelitis Eradication Program has adopted several successful strategies to control and ultimately eradicate polio from most regions of the world including encouragement of routine childhood immunization, national immunization days (NIDs), improvement of laboratory capabilities, intensified surveillance, and rapid response to identified outbreaks.[117,118] NIDs are highly coordinated nationwide or regionwide events in which all children younger than 5 years, regardless of immunization history, receive two doses of OPV given 1 month apart, which has been particularly successful in many areas in rapidly controlling poliomyelitis.[119,120] Seroconversion rates during these mass campaigns are higher than for routine immunization,[121] possibly because of the spread of OPV virus, or because they are conducted during the dry season, when diarrheal disease is less prevalent.

By 2002, the reported worldwide incidence of poliomyelitis had declined to approximately 1900 cases per year, and wild-type polioviruses were contained within seven countries in sub-Saharan Africa and south Asia.[10] Furthermore, naturally occurring type 2 polioviruses are no longer circulating anywhere.[122] With a provisional total of 700 cases occurring in the year 2003, and barring unforeseen setbacks, eradication may be achieved by the end of 2004.

VACCINE-DERIVED POLIOMYELITIS

An outbreak of 21 cases of paralytic poliomyelitis on the island of Hispaniola during 2000 and 2001 was found to be caused by a virulent strain genetically related to the type 1 Sabin OPV vaccine strain.[20] This occurrence led to the discovery that type 2 VDPVs had also circulated in Egypt from 1982 to 1993 in association with at least 32 polio cases.[21] Subsequently, VDPVs were implicated in smaller outbreaks of paralytic disease in the Philippines and Madagascar.[123,124] The VDPVs isolated so far have RNA sequences that vary by more than 1.0% from the corresponding OPV parent strain and have acquired in vitro and in vivo virulence markers characteristic of wild-type poliovirus strains, including virulence in transgenic mice bearing the human poliovirus receptor.[20]

The VDPV outbreaks have occurred among underimmunized children living in economically deprived regions where low immunization rates have permitted VDPV to circulate for long periods of time and, by continuous mutation, acquire biologic properties that are indistinguishable from naturally occurring wild-type polioviruses.

POSTERADICATION

Active surveillance for virulent polioviruses (both wild-type and VDPV) is necessary in the posteradication period. Possible sources might include continued circulation among persons living in very remote locations, persons who excrete polioviruses for long periods because of congenital or acquired immunodeficiency, escape from a laboratory facility, or intentional reintroduction into the human population as a result of a bioterrorist event. The likelihood of reintroduction from an infected immunodeficient person is considered to be very low, because most such persons actually excrete polioviruses for a short period of time, and those who excrete for longer periods have

a higher risk of death from either poliomyelitis or their underlying immunodeficiency.[89] An OPV stockpile will be maintained to counter the threat of reintroduction of wild polioviruses, and containment of existing laboratory poliovirus stocks is now under way.[125,126]

The discovery of VDPV has profoundly influenced plans for cessation of poliovirus immunization following global eradication of poliomyelitis. Although several strategies have been considered, it is likely that all OPV use will be discontinued simultaneously in a coordinated manner at an opportune time after eradication is certified by the World Health Organization.[126] Countries that can afford to continue vaccination with IPV will probably elect to do so for an indefinite period of time.

REFERENCES

1. Paul JR. History of Poliomyelitis. New Haven: Yale University Press; 1971.
2. Vermont State Department of Public Health. Infantile Paralysis in Vermont. Brattleboro, VT: Vermont Printing Co; 1924.
3. Landsteiner K, Popper E. Mikroscopische präparate von einem menschlichen und zwei affenrückemarken. Wien Klin Wochenschr. 1908;21:1830.
4. Enders JF, Weller TH, Robbins FC. Cultivation of the Lansing strain of poliomyelitis virus in cultures of various human embryonic tissue. Science. 1949;109:85.
5. Bodian D, Morgan IM, Howe HA. Differentiation of three types of poliomyelitis virus. III. The grouping of fourteen strains into three immunological types. Am J Hyg. 1949;49:234.
6. Bodian D. Pathogenesis of poliovirus in normal and passively immunized primates after virus feeding. Fed Proc. 1952;11:462.
7. Horstmann DM. Poliomyelitis in the blood of orally infected monkeys and chimpanzees. Proc Soc Exp Biol Med. 1952;79:417.
8. Salk JE. Studies in human subjects on active immunization against poliomyelitis. I. A preliminary report of experiments in progress. JAMA. 1953;151:1081.
9. Live Poliovirus Vaccines. First and Second International Conferences on Live Poliovirus Vaccines, Washington, DC: World Health Organization; 1959, 1960.
10. Centers for Disease Control and Prevention. Progress towards global eradication of poliomyelitis, 2002. MMWR Morb Mortal Wkly Rep. 2003;52:366.
11. Nathanson N, Martin JR. The epidemiology of poliomyelitis: Enigmas surrounding its appearance and disappearance. Am J Epidemiol. 1979;110:672.
12. Kim-Farley RJ, Bart KJ, Schonberger LB, et al. Poliomyelitis in the USA: Virtual elimination of disease caused by wild virus. Lancet. 1984;2:1315.
13. Bodian D. Second attacks of paralytic poliomyelitis in human beings in relation to immunity, virus types and virulence. Am J Hyg. 1951;54:174.
14. Shelokov A, Habel K, McKinstry DW. Relation of poliomyelitis virus types to clinical disease and geographic distribution: A preliminary report. Ann N Y Acad Sci. 1955;61:998.
15. Sabin AB. Properties and behavior of orally administered attenuated poliovirus vaccine. JAMA. 1957;164:1216.
16. Omata T, Kohara M, Kuge S, et al. Genetic analysis of the attenuation phenotype of poliovirus type 1. J Virol. 1986;58:348.
17. Pollard SR, Dunn G, Cammack N, et al. Nucleotide sequence of a neurovirulent variant of the type 2 oral poliovirus vaccine. J Virol. 1989;63:4949.
18. Westrop GD, Wareham KA, Evans D, et al. Genetic basis of attenuation of the Sabin type 3 oral poliovirus vaccine. J Virol. 1989;63:1338.
19. Centers for Disease Control and Prevention. Outbreak of poliomyelitis—Dominican Republic and Haiti, 2000. MMWR Morb Mortal Wkly Rep. 2000;49:1094.
20. Kew O, Morris-Glasgow V, Landaverde M, et al. Outbreak of poliomyelitis in Hispaniola associated with circulating type 1 vaccine-derived poliovirus. Science. 2002;296:356.
21. Centers for Disease Control and Prevention. Circulation of a type 2 vaccine-derived poliovirus—Egypt, 1982-1993. MMWR Morb Mortal Wkly Rep. 2001;50:41.
22. Bodian D. Viremia in experimental poliomyelitis. I. General aspects of infection after intravascular inoculation with strains of high and low invasiveness. Am J Hyg. 1954;60:339.
23. Bodian D. Emerging concept of poliomyelitis infection. Science. 1955;122:105.
24. Ren R, Costantini F, Gorgacz EJ, et al. Transgenic mice expressing a human poliovirus receptor: A new model for poliomyelitis. Cell. 1990;63:353.
25. Bodian D, Howe HA. An experimental study of the role of neurones in the dissemination of poliomyelitis virus in the nervous system. Brain. 1940;63:135.
26. Jubelt B, Gallez-Hawkins G, Narayan O, et al. Pathogenesis of human poliovirus infection in mice. II. Age dependency of paralysis. J Neuropathol Exp Neurol. 1980;39:138.
27. Horstmann DM, Paul JR. The incubation period in human poliomyelitis and its implications. JAMA. 1947;135:11.
28. Melnick JL, Ledinko N. Social serology: Antibody levels in a normal young population during an epidemic of poliomyelitis. Am J Hyg. 1951;54:354.
29. Horstmann DM. Clinical aspects of acute poliomyelitis. Am J Med. 1949;6:592.
30. Weinstein L, Shelokov A, Seltser R, et al. A comparison of the clinical features of poliomyelitis in adults and children. N Engl J Med. 1952;246:297.
31. Plum F. Sensory loss with poliomyelitis. Neurology. 1956;6:166.
32. Baker AB. Bulbar poliomyelitis: Its mechanism and treatment. Am J Med. 1949;6:614.

33. Ibsen B. The clinical diagnosis and evaluation of respiratory problems in patients with acute poliomyelitis. In: Poliomyelitis Papers and Discussions, Fourth International Poliomyelitis Conference. Philadelphia: JB Lippincott; 1958.

34. Weinstein L. Cardiovascular disturbances in poliomyelitis. Circulation. 1957;15:735.

35. Galpine JF, Wilson WCM. Occurrence of myocarditis in paralytic poliomyelitis. Br Med J. 1959;2:1379.

36. Neu H. Gastrointestinal complications in poliomyelitis. In: Poliomyelitis Papers and Discussions, Fourth International Poliomyelitis Conference. Philadelphia: JB Lippincott; 1958.

37. Siegel M, Greenberg M, Bodian J. Presence of children in the household as a factor in the incidence of paralytic poliomyelitis in adults. N Engl J Med. 1957;257:958.

38. Weinstein L, Aycock WL, Feemster RF. Relation of sex, pregnancy, and menstruation to susceptibility in poliomyelitis. N Engl J Med. 1951;245:54.

39. Anderson GW, Anderson G, Skaar A, et al. Poliomyelitis in pregnancy. Am J Hyg. 1952;55:127.

40. Russell WR. Paralytic poliomyelitis: The early symptoms, and the effect of physical activity on the course of disease. Br Med J. 1949;1:465.

41. Horstmann DM. Acute poliomyelitis. Relation of physical activity at the time of onset to the course of the disease. JAMA. 1950;142:236.

42. Greenberg M, Abramson H, Cooper HM, et al. The relation between recent injections and paralytic poliomyelitis in children. Am J Public Health. 1952;42:142.

43. Sutter RW, Patriarca PA, Suleiman AM, et al. Attributable risk of DTP (diphtheria and tetanus toxoids and pertussis vaccine) injection in provoking paralytic poliomyelitis during a large outbreak in Oman. J Infect Dis. 1992;165:444.

44. Bodian D. Viremia in experimental poliomyelitis. II. Viremia and the mechanism of the "provoking" effect of injections or trauma. Am J Hyg. 1954;60:358.

45. Trueta J, Hodes R. Provoking and localizing factors in poliomyelitis. Lancet. 1954;1:998.

46. Strebel PM, Nedelcu N-I, Baughman AL, et al. Intramuscular injections within 30 days of immunization with oral poliovirus vaccine—a risk factor for vaccine-associated paralytic poliomyelitis. N Engl J Med. 1995;332:500.

47. Eley RC, Flake CG. Acute anterior poliomyelitis following tonsillectomy and adenoidectomy: With special reference to the bulbar form. J Pediatr. 1938;13:63.

48. Paffenbarger RS. The effect of prior tonsillectomy on incidence and clinical type of acute poliomyelitis. Am J Hyg. 1957;66:131.

49. Sejvar JJ, Leis AA, Stokic DS, et al. Acute flaccid paralysis and West Nile virus infection. Emerg Infect Dis. 2003;9:788.

50. Li J, Loeb JA, Shy ME, et al. Asymmetric flaccid paralysis: A neuromuscular presentation of West Nile virus infection. Ann Neurol. 2003;53:703.

51. Russell WR, Fischer-Williams M. Recovery of muscular strength after poliomyelitis. Lancet. 1954;1:330.

52. Ferris Jr BG, Auld PAM, Cronkhite L, et al. Life threatening poliomyelitis, Boston, 1959. N Engl J Med. 1960;262:371.

53. Weinstein L. Diagnosis and treatment of poliomyelitis. Med Clin North Am. 1948;32:1377.

54. Bennett RI. Care of the after effects of poliomyelitis. Am J Med. 1949;6:620.

55. Dalakas MC, Sever JL, Madden DL, et al. Late postpoliomyelitis muscular atrophy: Clinical, virologic, and immunologic studies. Rev Infect Dis. 1984;6(2):S562.

56. Dalakas MC, Elder G, Hallet M, et al. A long-term follow-up study of patients with post-poliomyelitis neuromuscular symptoms. N Engl J Med. 1986;314:959.

57. Ramlow J, Alexander M, LaPorte R, et al. Epidemiology of the post-polio syndrome. Am J Epidemiol. 1992;136:769.

58. Johnson RT. Late progression of poliomyelitis paralysis: Discussion of pathogenesis. Rev Infect Dis. 1984;6:S568.

59. Melnick JL. Advantages and disadvantages of killed and live poliomyelitis vaccines. Bull WHO. 1978;56:21.

60. Sabin AB. Oral polio vaccine: History of its development and use and current challenge to eliminate poliomyelitis from the world. J Infect Dis. 1985;151:420.

61. Centers for Disease Control and Prevention. Poliomyelitis prevention in the United States. MMWR Morb Mortal Wkly Rep. 2000;49:1.

62. Simoes EA, John TJ. The antibody response of seronegative infants to inactivated poliovirus vaccine of enhanced potency. Dev Biol Stand. 1986;14:127.

63. McBean AM, Thoms ML, Albrecht P, et al. The serologic response to oral polio vaccine and enhanced potency inactivated polio vaccines. Am J Epidemiol. 1988;128:615.

64. Swartz TA, Roumiantzeff M, Peyron L, et al. Use of a combined DTP-polio vaccine in a reduced schedule. Dev Biol Stand. 1986;65:159.

65. Robertson SE, Traverso HP, Drucker JA, et al. Clinical efficacy of a new, enhanced-potency, inactivated poliovirus vaccine. Lancet. 1988;1:897.

66. Ogra PL, Karzon DT, Righthand F. Immunoglobulin response in serum and secretions after immunization with live and inactivated poliovaccine and natural infection. N Engl J Med. 1968;279:893.

67. Onorato IM, Modlin JF, McBean AM, et al. Mucosal immunity induced by enhanced potency IPV and OPV. J Infect Dis. 1991;163:1.

68. Modlin JF, Halsey NA, Thoms ML, et al. Humoral and mucosal immunity in infants induced by three sequential IPV-OPV immunization schedules. J Infect Dis. 1997;75:S228.

69. Fox JP, Elveback L, Scott W, et al. Herd immunity: Basic concept and relevance to public health immunization practices. Am J Epidemiol. 1971;94:179.

70. Stickle G. Observed and expected poliomyelitis in the United States, 1958-1961. Am J Public Health. 1964;54:1222.

71. Schaap GJP, Bijkerk H, Coutinho RA, et al. The spread of wild poliovirus in the well-vaccinated Netherlands in connection with the 1978 epidemic. Prog Med Virol. 1984;29:124.

72. Expanded Programme on Immunization. Poliomyelitis surveillance and vaccine efficacy. Week Epidemiol Record WHO. 1988;63:249.

73. Robertson HE, Acker MS, Dillenberg HO, et al. Community-wide use of a "balanced" trivalent oral poliovirus vaccine (Sabin). Can J Public Health. 1962;53:179.

74. Cohen-Abbo A, Culley BS, Reed GW, et al. Seroresponse to trivalent oral poliovirus vaccine as a function of dosage interval. Pediatr Infect Dis J. 1995;14:100.

75. Hardy GE, Hopkins CC, Linneman CC, et al. Trivalent oral poliovirus vaccine: A comparison of two infant immunization schedules. Pediatrics. 1970;45:444.

76. Krugman RD, Hardy GE, Sellers C. Antibody persistence after primary immunization with trivalent oral poliovirus vaccine. Pediatrics. 1977;60:80.

77. Bass JW, Halsted SB, Fischer GW, et al. Oral polio vaccine: Effect of booster vaccination one to 14 years after primary series. JAMA. 1978;239:2252.

78. Nishio O, Ishihara Y, Sakae K, et al. The trend of acquired immunity with live poliovirus vaccine and the effect of revaccination: Follow-up of vaccinees for ten years. Dev Biol Stand. 1984;12:1.

79. Ogra PL. Mucosal immune response to poliovirus vaccines in childhood. Rev Infect Dis. 1984;6:S361.

80. Ghendon YUZ, Sanakoyeva II. Comparison of the resistance of the intestinal tract to poliomyelitis virus (Sabin's strains) in a person after naturally and experimentally acquired immunity. Acta Virol (Praha). 1961;5:265.

81. Kim-Farley RJ, Rutherford G, Lichfield P, et al. Outbreak of paralytic poliomyelitis, Taiwan. Lancet. 1984;2:1322.

82. Chen RT, Hausinger S, Dajani AS, et al. Seroprevalence of antibody against poliovirus in inner-city preschool children. JAMA. 1996;275:1639.

83. Strebel PM, Sutter RW, Cochi SL, et al. Epidemiology of poliomyelitis in the United States one decade after the last reported case of indigenous wild virus-associated disease. Clin Infect Dis. 1992;14:568.

84. Prevots DR, Sutter RW, Strebel PM, et al. Completeness of reporting for paralytic poliomyelitis, United States, 1980 through 1991. Arch Pediatr Adolesc Med. 1994;148:479.

85. Sutter RW, Prevots DR. Vaccine-associated paralytic poliomyelitis among immunodeficient persons. Infect Med. 1994;11:426.

86. Ion-Neldescu N, Dobrescu A, Strebel PM, et al. Vaccine-associated paralytic poliomyelitis and HIV infection (Letter). Lancet. 1994;343:51.

87. von Reyn CF, Clements CJ, Mann JM. Human immunodeficiency virus infection and routine childhood immunisation. Lancet. 1987;ii:669.

88. Onorato IM, Markowitz LE, Oxtoby MJ. Childhood immunization, vaccine-preventable diseases and infection with human immunodeficiency virus. Pediatr Infect Dis J. 1988;7:588.

89. Khetsuriani N, Prevots DR, Quick L, et al. Persistence of vaccine-derived polioviruses among immunodeficient persons with vaccine-associated paralytic poliomyelitis. J Infect Dis. 2003;188:1845.

90. Davis LE, Bodian D, Price D, et al. Chronic progressive poliomyelitis secondary to vaccination of an immunodeficient child. N Engl J Med. 1977;297:241.

91. Wyatt HV. Poliomyelitis in hypogammaglobulinemics. J Infect Dis. 1973;128:802.

92. Kew OM, Sutter RW, Nottay BK, et al. Prolonged replication of a type 1 vaccine-derived poliovirus in an immunodeficient patient. J Clin Microbiol. 1998;36:2893.

93. Minor P, Dunn G, Begg N, et al. Poliovirus vaccination schedules and reversion to virulence. Presented at the 33rd Conference on Antimicrobial Agents and Chemotherapy, New Orleans, 1993.

94. Stanway G, Hughes PJ, Mountford RC, et al. Comparison of the complete nucleotide sequences of the genomes of the neurovirulent poliovirus P3/Leon/37 and its attenuated Sabin vaccine derivative P3/Leon 12a1b. Proc Natl Acad Sci U S A. 1984;81:1539.

95. Evans DM, Dunn G, Minor PD, et al. Increased neurovirulence associated with a single nucleotide change in a noncoding region of the Sabin type 3 poliovaccine genome. Nature. 1985;314:548.

96. Minor PD, John A, Ferguson M, et al. Antigenic and molecular evolution of the vaccine strain of type 3 poliovirus during the period of excretion by a primary vaccinee. J Gen Virol. 1986;67:693.

97. Almond JW. The attenuation of poliovirus neurovirulence. Annu Rev Microbiol. 1987;41:154.

98. Almond JW, Westrop GD, Evans DM, et al. Studies on the attenuation of the Sabin type 3 oral polio vaccine. J Virol Methods. 1987;17:183.

99. Henderson RH. The Expanded Programme on Immunization of the World Health Organization. Rev Infect Dis. 1984;6:475.

100. Expanded Programme on Immunization Global Advisory Group. WHO Week Epidemiol Rec. 1985;60:13.

101. Dong D-X, Hu X-M, Liu W-J, et al. Immunization of neonates with trivalent oral poliomyelitis vaccine (Sabin). Bull WHO. 1986;64:853.

102. Domok I, Balayan MS, Fayinka OA, et al. Factors affecting the efficacy of live poliovirus vaccine in warm climates. Bull WHO. 1974;51:333.

103. Hanlon P, Hanlon L, Marsh V, et al. Serological comparisons of approaches to polio vaccination in the Gambia. Lancet. 1987;1:800.

104. Lasch EE, Abed Y, Abdulla K, et al. Successful results of a program combining live and inactivated poliovirus vaccines to control poliomyelitis in Gaza. Rev Infect Dis. 1984;6:467.

105. Patriarca PA, Wright PF, John TJ. Factors affecting the immunogenicity of oral poliovirus vaccine in developing countries. Rev Infect Dis. 1991;13:926.

106. Patriarca PA, Laender F, Palmeira G, et al. Randomised trial of alternative formulations of oral poliovaccine in Brazil. Lancet. 1988;1:429.

107. WHO Collaborative Study Group on Oral and Inactivated Poliovirus Vaccines. Combined immunization of infants with oral and inactivated poliovirus vaccines: Results of a randomized trial in the Gambia, Oman, and Thailand. J Infect Dis. 1997;175:S215.

108. Posey DL, Linkins RW, Couto Oliveria MJ, et al. The effect of diarrhea on oral poliovirus vaccine failure in Brazil. J Infect Dis. 1997;175:S258.

109. Myaux JA, Unicomb L, Besser RE, et al. Effect of diarrhea on the humoral response to oral polio vaccination. Pediatr Infect Dis J. 1996;15:204.

110. Swartz TA, Ben-Porath E, Ben-Yshai Z, et al. A controlled trial with inactivated poliovaccine. Dev Biol Stand. 1981;47:199.

111. Simoes EAF, Padmini B, Steinhoff MC, et al. Antibody response of infants to two doses of inactivated poliovirus vaccine of enhanced potency. Am J Dis Child. 1985;139:977.

112. Lasch EE, Abed Y, Marcus O, et al. Combined live and inactivated poliovirus vaccine to control poliomyelitis in a developing country—five years after. Dev Biol Stand. 1986;65:137.

113. Morinere BJ, van Loon FPL, Rhodes PH, et al. Immunogenicity of a supplemental dose of oral versus inactivated poliovirus vaccine. Lancet. 1993;341:1545.

114. Ofusu-Amaah S. The challenge of poliomyelitis in tropical Africa. Rev Infect Dis. 1984;6:318.

115. Rockefeller Foundation. Protecting the world's children: Vaccines and immunization, Bellagio, Italy. 1984. Rockefeller Foundation.

116. World Health Organization. Global eradication of poliomyelitis by the year 2000. Week Epidemiol Record WHO. 1988;63:161.

117. Hull HF, Ward NA, Hull BP, et al. Paralytic poliomyelitis: Seasoned strategies, disappearing disease. Lancet. 1994;343:1331.

118. Wright PF, Kim-Farley RJ, de Quadros CA, et al. Strategies for the global eradication of poliomyelitis by the year 2000. N Engl J Med. 1991;325:1774.

119. John TJ. Poliomyelitis in India: Prospects and problems of control. Rev Infect Dis. 1984;6:438.

120. Sabin AB. Strategies for elimination of poliomyelitis in different parts of the world with use of oral poliovirus vaccine. Rev Infect Dis. 1984;6:391.

121. Richardson G, Linkins R, Eames M, et al. Immunogenicity of oral poliovirus vaccine administered in mass campaigns versus routine immunization programmes. Bull WHO. 1995;73:769.

122. Centers for Disease Control and Prevention. Apparent global interruption of wild poliovirus type 2 transmission. MMWR Morb Mortal Wkly Rep. 2001;50:222.

123. Centers for Disease Control and Prevention. Public health dispatch: Acute flaccid paralysis associated with circulating vaccine-derived poliovirus—Philippines, 2001. MMWR Morb Mortal Wkly Rep. 2001;50:874.

124. Centers for Disease Control and Prevention. Poliomyelitis—Madagascar, 2002. MMWR Morb Mortal Wkly Rep. 2002;51:622.

125. Dowdle WR, Gary HE, Sanders R, et al. Can post-eradication laboratory containment of wild polioviruses be achieved? Bull WHO. 2002;80:311.

126. Technical Consultative Group to the World Health Organization on the Global Eradication of Poliomyelitis. "Endgame" issues for the global polio eradication initiative. Clin Infect Dis. 2002;34:72.

CHAPTER **169**

Coxsackieviruses, Echoviruses, and Newer Enteroviruses

JOHN F. MODLIN

This chapter covers human disease caused by the group A coxsackieviruses, group B coxsackieviruses, echoviruses, and newer enteroviruses, which, as members of the genus *Enterovirus*, share many characteristics with polioviruses, including structure, physicochemical properties, mode of replication, pathogenesis, and epidemiology (described in Chapters 167 and 168). More than 90% of infections caused by the non-polio enteroviruses are asymptomatic or result only in undifferentiated febrile illness.[1] When disease occurs, the spectrum and severity of clinical manifestations vary with the age, gender, and immune status of the host and with the subgroup, serotype, and even the intratypic enterovirus strain.

Some clinical syndromes (viral meningitis and some exanthems) are caused by many enterovirus serotypes, some are predominately caused by certain enterovirus subgroups (e.g., pleurodynia and myocarditis by the group B coxsackieviruses), and other diseases are mostly associated with individual enterovirus serotypes. Infections caused by the four serotypes representing the subgenus of newer enteroviruses are considered at the end of this chapter.

CENTRAL NERVOUS SYSTEM INFECTIONS

Acute Aseptic Meningitis

Acute aseptic meningitis is a syndrome characterized by signs and symptoms of meningeal irritation and cerebrospinal fluid (CSF) pleocytosis in the absence of bacteria or fungi (see Chapter 80). Most community-acquired aseptic meningitis cases are caused by viruses; of these, group B coxsackieviruses and echoviruses together cause more than 90% of cases.[2] Group A coxsackieviruses cause relatively fewer cases.[2] Although many enterovirus serotypes are reported to cause aseptic meningitis, historically the group B coxsackievirus serotypes 2 through 5 and echovirus serotypes 4, 6, 9, 11, 16, and 30 have been the most frequently implicated. On occasion, another echovirus serotype may cause widespread outbreaks; for example, echovirus 13 caused outbreaks of aseptic meningitis throughout Europe and the United States in 2000 and 2001,[3] and echovirus 33 caused widespread disease in New Zealand during the winter of 2000.[4] Infection with certain serotypes, particularly the group B coxsackieviruses and echovirus 30, may be more likely to be accompanied by aseptic meningitis than infection with other common enterovirus serotypes.[5]

Clinical Manifestations

Infants younger than 3 months have the highest rates of clinically recognized aseptic meningitis, in part because lumbar punctures are routinely performed for evaluation of fever in this age group.[6] Only a minority of these infants have clinical manifestations suggestive of neurologic disease.[5]

The severity of disease in older children and adults with aseptic meningitis varies widely. The onset may be gradual or abrupt, and the typical patient has a brief prodrome of fever and chills. Headache is usually a prominent complaint. Meningismus, when present, varies from mild to severe. Kernig's and Brudzinski's signs are present in only about one third of patients. Pharyngitis and other symptoms of upper respiratory tract infections are often present. The illness is sometimes biphasic, as in poliomyelitis; these patients present with a prodromal illness with fever and myalgias, followed by defervescence and absence of symptoms for a few days, and then experience abrupt recurrence of fever with headache and other signs of meningismus. Complications such as febrile seizures, complex seizures, lethargy, coma, and movement disorders occur early in the course of aseptic meningitis in 5% to 10% of patients.[6,7] Adults may experience a more prolonged period of fever and headache than infants and children do, and some adult patients may take weeks to return to normal activity.[8]

Laboratory Diagnosis

The clinical diagnosis of aseptic meningitis depends on routine examination of CSF. The CSF is clear and under normal or mildly increased pressure. The total CSF cell count is usually 10 to 500/mm³ but may occasionally exceed 1000/mm³. Cell counts less than 10/mm³ may occur in a small minority of cases.[2,9-12] Differential cell counts of the CSF often reveal an increased proportion of neutrophils, but the differential invariably shifts to a predominance of lymphocytes during the initial 1 to 2 days of illness. By 24 hours after the initial evaluation, the CSF differential should have fewer than 50% neutrophils.[13,14] In general, the CSF glucose concentration is normal and the CSF protein concentration is normal or slightly elevated. However, the glucose content may be lower than normal in 18% to 33% of cases,[15-17] and values less than 40 mg/dL may occur.[6,16] Uncommonly, it may be difficult to exclude bacterial meningitis on the basis of the CSF profile alone. In some cases, the CSF findings may closely mimic those of tuberculous meningitis.[18]

Enteroviruses can be detected in CSF and other specimens by cell culture and by polymerase chain reaction (PCR) genomic amplification. Cell culture yields an isolate that can be serotyped for clinical or epidemiologic purposes. However, culture requires multiple cell lines, is labor intensive, and typically takes 3 to 7 days to yield a viral isolate.[19,20] The overall sensitivity of virus isolation from the CSF of patients with aseptic meningitis is 30% to 35%,[2,21-25] although higher figures have been reported during some echovirus outbreaks.[9,12,26]

Concomitant culture of serum, upper respiratory secretions, urine, and stool enhances the likelihood of virus recovery. The introduction of PCR has improved the speed and sensitivity of enterovirus detection in CSF.[27] For confirmed or suspected enteroviral meningitis cases, PCR sensitivity ranges from 66% to over 90%.[25,28-30]

Differential Diagnosis

Bacterial meningitis is the most important disease to be distinguished from enteroviral aseptic meningitis. Although some clinical features of bacterial meningitis that is incompletely treated with antibiotics may overlap those of enteroviral aseptic meningitis when therapy has been instituted before lumbar puncture, several studies have demonstrated that pretreatment of bacterial meningitis alters the CSF minimally; even when some parameters are altered by therapy (i.e., change from polymorphonuclear to lymphocytic pleocytosis), others continue to indicate bacterial disease (i.e., low glucose or high protein concentration).[31-33] Arboviruses, lymphocytic choriomeningitis virus, leptospirosis, Lyme borreliosis, and acute human immunodeficiency virus syndrome account for most of the remaining cases of infectious aseptic meningitis. Mumps virus infection was a common cause of aseptic meningitis before the introduction of mumps vaccine in the United States. Aseptic meningitis also occurs with other infectious and noninfectious diseases (see Chapter 80), but the etiology is usually suggested by other clinical features.

Management and Prognosis

Although hospitalization is not necessary for all cases and indeed may not be feasible during summer epidemics of enterovirus infections, it is advisable when disturbances in consciousness, muscle weakness, or a petechial rash suggests the possibility of a more serious illness. Pyogenic bacterial meningitis should be excluded by lumbar puncture. When bacterial meningitis cannot be excluded because of prior antibiotic treatment, administration of appropriate antibiotics is advisable after performing Gram stains and bacterial cultures. CSF PCR testing may be useful in deciding whether to continue administration of antibiotics if the test can be reported within 1 to 2 days.

In most cases, treatment consists only of relief of symptoms. Analgesics are usually given to older children and adults to alleviate headache. Pleconaril, an orally administered enteroviral capsid-stabilizing drug, reduced the duration of headache and other symptoms in a clinical trial.[34,35] It was formerly available for compassionate use but is no longer being developed by the pharmaceutical sponsor (also see Chapter 36).[36,37] Antiviral therapy may provide significant symptomatic relief to adults and older children, who may experience lassitude and easy fatigability for weeks after the acute illness.[8] Treatment studies of infants and young children, who generally experience a shorter duration of symptoms, have been inconclusive.[36]

In one large study of enteroviral aseptic meningitis, subtle disturbances in motor function such as limitation of passive motion, muscle spasm, and poor coordination were observed during convalescence.[7] These abnormalities slowly resolve and are rarely detectable 1 year after infection. In young children, fever and signs of meningeal irritation subside in a few days to 1 week. Infants younger than 3 months may have fewer symptoms of illness and fewer complications than older infants.[6] Although some investigators have suggested that enteroviral meningitis in the first year of life may result in permanent neurologic sequelae,[37,38] studies of larger numbers of children using more rigorous methods indicate that the long-term prognosis for the youngest infants is also excellent.[39,40]

Encephalitis

Encephalitis is a well-described, although unusual manifestation of coxsackievirus and echovirus central nervous system (CNS) infection. Symptoms of encephalitis sometimes complicate the course of aseptic meningitis. Rarely, full-blown encephalitis dominates the clinical illness in the presence or absence of meningeal involvement. The enteroviruses account for less than 5% of all encephalitis cases and for 11% to 22% of all cases that are proved to be viral.[21,41-43] Numerous

serotypes have been implicated as causes of encephalitis; coxsackievirus types A9, B2, and B5 and echovirus types 6 and 9 are the serotypes reported most often, but the evidence linking each of these serotypes to encephalitis is highly variable. In a minority of cases, a specific etiology has been proved by isolating virus from brain tissue or CSF; in others, the cause of encephalitis has been inferred by isolating virus from a non-neurologic site or by serology.

In perinatally acquired enterovirus infection, encephalitis is often only one manifestation of generalized viral disease, but beyond the neonatal period signs and symptoms are generally limited to the CNS. Children and young adults are most frequently affected. Clinical manifestations have ranged from lethargy, drowsiness, and personality change to seizures, paresis, and coma. Children with focal encephalitis present with partial motor seizures, hemichorea, and acute cerebellar ataxia,[44-47] features that in some cases have suggested a diagnosis of herpes simplex virus encephalitis.[45,48] Group A coxsackieviruses have been conspicuous among the agents isolated from infants and children with focal enteroviral encephalitis.[45]

The CSF findings in enteroviral encephalitis are similar to those in aseptic meningitis. Abnormalities on an electroencephalogram usually reflect the extent and severity of brain involvement. Most patients with coxsackievirus and echovirus encephalitis beyond the neonatal period recover fully, although permanent neurologic sequelae and rare deaths occur.[21,44,49,50]

Paralysis and Other Neurologic Complications of Coxsackievirus and Echovirus Infections

Sporadic cases of flaccid motor paralysis have been associated with several coxsackievirus and echovirus serotypes and with enterovirus 71. The latter has been associated with large outbreaks of poliomyelitis-like disease in Russia and eastern Europe and in Thailand and Taiwan. Brain stem encephalitis and noncardiogenic pulmonary edema were also associated with enterovirus 71 infections in those outbreaks. Coxsackievirus A7, which is neuropathogenic in monkeys, and enterovirus 71 have each caused disease with sufficient frequency to be recognized as the etiologic agent in outbreaks of paralysis.[51-55] Coxsackievirus A9 was found to be the etiology of 3.1% of poliomyelitis cases in New Delhi, India, over a period of 7 years.[56] In sporadic cases, the serotypes that are most often implicated have been coxsackieviruses A7, A9, and B1 to B5 and echoviruses 6 and 9. Less frequently implicated serotypes are coxsackieviruses A4, A5, and A10 and echoviruses 1 to 4, 7, 11, 14, 16 to 18, and 30.[57-60]

Paralytic disease caused by the non-polio enteroviruses other than enterovirus 71 is characteristically less severe than poliovirus-associated paralysis. In fact, muscle weakness is more common than flaccid paralysis, and the paresis is not usually permanent. Cranial nerve involvement has occasionally resulted in complete unilateral oculomotor palsy.[61,62] Guillain-Barré syndrome has been reported in a small number of patients in association with coxsackievirus serotypes A2, A5, and A9 and with echovirus serotypes 6 and 22.[22,63,64] In a few cases, the implicated virus has been isolated from CSF or the brain stem.[64] Transverse myelitis was reported in one patient who had a rise in neutralizing antibody to coxsackievirus B4[63] and in another who had echovirus 5 recovered from CSF.[65] Systemic coxsackievirus B2 disease has been reported with many of the clinical features of Reye's syndrome.[66] Furthermore, several children with well-documented Reye's syndrome have had a variety of enteroviruses isolated concurrently from multiple sites, including the brain and CSF[67,68]; however, a clear etiologic or epidemiologic link between enterovirus infection and Reye's syndrome has not been established. Opsoclonus-myoclonus, or the "dancing eyes" syndrome, has been reported in two children with concurrent coxsackievirus B3 infection.[69]

EXANTHEMS

Coxsackieviruses and echoviruses cause a variety of exanthems, which are sometimes associated with enanthems. With the exception of hand-foot-and-mouth (HFM) disease, these rashes are not sufficiently distinctive to permit a reliable etiologic diagnosis on clinical grounds alone. Virus can be isolated from the vesicular lesions of patients with HFM disease, and therefore these lesions appear to be a direct result of viral invasion of the skin after viremia. No attempts at isolation of virus from the skin in cases of maculopapular and petechial exanthems have been reported; consequently, it is not known whether these lesions are also caused by the virus directly or by immunopathologic mechanisms.

Enteroviral exanthems themselves cause little morbidity. They are important as sentinels of the prevalence of coxsackieviruses and echoviruses in the community and because they are often confused with other infective exanthems, some of which have more serious implications. Rashes caused by enteroviruses may be grouped according to the type of exanthem that they mimic: (1) rubelliform or morbilliform, (2) roseoliform, (3) vesicular, and (4) petechial. Some overlap between these types of exanthems may be observed in different patients infected with the same enterovirus or even among different morphologic lesion types in the same patient.

Rubelliform and Morbilliform Exanthems

Fine maculopapular rashes resembling rubella but occurring during summer epidemics are common manifestations of echovirus infection. High attack rates have been noted with echovirus 9, the most common serotype associated with rubelliform rash. In one epidemic, 57% of persons younger than 5 years with illness caused by echovirus 9 had rash, 41% of those 5 to 9 years old had rash, but rash affected only 6% of those older than 10 years.[26] The rash, which characteristically appears simultaneously with fever, begins on the face and then spreads to the neck, chest, and extremities. Usually, innumerable faint pink macules 1 to 3 mm in diameter that do not itch or desquamate are present. The illness may be distinguished from rubella by the absence of pruritus and posterior cervical lymphadenopathy.[70,71] In occasional patients with an enanthem resembling Koplik spots and a blotchy eruption, the disease may be confused with measles, but the coryza and conjunctivitis characteristic of that disease are absent.[72] Other serotypes associated with rubelliform rash include echoviruses 2, 4, 11, 19, and 25, and coxsackievirus A9.

Roseoliform Exanthems

These enterovirus exanthems are distinctive not in their appearance but in their timing; as in roseola, the rash does not appear until defervescence. The prototype is the "Boston exanthem," the first of the enterovirus exanthems to be recognized and now known to be caused by echovirus 16.[73,74] Multiple cases often occur sequentially in families, rash developing in as many as one quarter of the children in a household. The mean age of those affected is 3 years. Most children are mildly ill with low-grade fever and pharyngitis. The fever lasts 24 to 36 hours and then declines simultaneously with the appearance of discrete, nonpruritic, salmon-pink macules and papules approximately 1 cm in diameter on the face and upper part of the chest. The extremities are less commonly involved. The duration of the rash is 1 to 5 days. Other enterovirus serotypes (coxsackievirus B1 and B5 and echovirus 11 and 25) have also been associated with roseola-like illness.[73,75,76] Exanthem subitum (roseola infantum), a common, nonseasonal exanthem in which the rash typically develops as the fever declines, is caused by human herpesvirus 6 (see Chapter 136).

Herpetiform Exanthems

Hand-Foot-and-Mouth Disease

Coxsackievirus A16 is the most common cause of a distinctive vesicular eruption known as HFM disease or vesicular stomatitis with exanthem, although many other enteroviruses are also associated with HFM disease, including coxsackieviruses A4, A5, A6, A7, A9, A10, A24, B2 to B5, and echovirus 18.[77-80] Another prominent cause of HFM disease is enterovirus 71, which has caused large outbreaks in Southeast Asia associated with severe CNS disease and deaths.[80-82]

Children younger than 10 years are often affected, and spread to other family members occurs commonly. Most patients complain of sore throat or sore mouth, and affected young children may refuse to eat. Temperatures of 38° C to 39° C last 1 to 2 days and are accompanied in essentially all cases by vesicles in the oral cavity occurring chiefly on the buccal mucosa and tongue. Several lesions may coalesce to form bullae, which frequently ulcerate by the time they are seen by a physician. Peripherally distributed cutaneous lesions occur in roughly 75% of patients.[83] These lesions are most common on the hands and feet, where either the extensor surfaces or the palms and soles may be involved. They also occur more proximally on the extremities and sometimes on the buttocks or genitalia. Disseminated lesions have been described in an infant with preexisting atopic eczema and have been given the sobriquet "eczema coxsackium" by analogy with eczema herpeticum and eczema vaccinatum.[84]

The skin lesions of HFM disease are tender and consist of mixed papules and clear vesicles with a surrounding zone of erythema. Skin biopsy demonstrates subepidermal lesions with a mixed lymphocytic and polymorphonuclear inflammatory response and acantholysis of the overlying epidermis.[85] Eosinophilic nuclear inclusions and intracytoplasmic picornavirus particles can be seen microscopically within cells surrounding dermal vessels.[86]

The vesicular lesions of HFM disease superficially resemble those caused by herpes simplex or varicella-zoster virus. Patients with HFM disease invariably have lesions of the oral mucosa. In contrast, oral lesions are less common in patients with chickenpox; moreover, these patients generally appear more ill, and their cutaneous lesions are more extensive and centrally distributed, generally with sparing of the palms and soles. Patients with primary herpetic gingivostomatitis also usually appear more ill and have a higher fever and cervical lymphadenopathy; lesions are usually confined to the oral cavity and do not involve the extremities. The enanthem of herpangina also resembles HFM disease, but it occurs in the posterior oropharynx and typically involves the fauces and soft palate.

Other Herpetiform Exanthems

Generalized vesicular eruptions are reported to be caused by coxsackievirus A9[87] and echovirus 11.[88] The eruptions caused by coxsackievirus A9 are similar to the lesions of HFM disease, but they occur in crops on the head, trunk, and extremities. Unlike chickenpox, the vesicles do not evolve to form pustules and scabs. The vesicular eruptions caused by echovirus 11 have occurred in immunocompromised adult patients.[88] An acute eruption resembling dermatomal zoster in which echovirus 6 was isolated from the bullous lesions has been reported.[89]

Petechial Exanthems and Other Cutaneous Manifestations

Petechial and purpuric rashes have been described with echovirus 9[26,90] and coxsackievirus A9[91] infections. When these rashes have a hemorrhagic component, the illness is easily confused with meningococcal disease, especially if aseptic meningitis occurs simultaneously. Occasionally, cutaneous eruptions of coxsackievirus A9 disease have an urticarial nature.[87] One child was reported to have papular acrodermatitis (Gianotti-Crosti syndrome) in association with coxsackievirus A16 infection.[92]

ACUTE RESPIRATORY DISEASE

Many enterovirus serotypes cause undifferentiated febrile illnesses ("summer grippe") with sore throat and occasionally cough or coryza. Enteroviruses account for most viruses recovered from children with summertime upper respiratory tract infections.[93,94] Enterovirus upper respiratory tract illnesses are generally clinically indistinguishable from disease caused by other agents such as rhinoviruses and *Mycoplasma pneumoniae*, unless accompanied by aseptic meningitis, exanthem, or other clinical features suggesting enterovirus infection.

The best characterized enteroviral respiratory pathogens are coxsackieviruses A21 and A24, which produce illness resembling the common cold, except for a higher incidence of fever.[95,96] Outbreaks of coxsackievirus A21 illness are reported predominantly in military populations. Although epidemics in civilians have not been recognized, sporadic infections presumably account for antibody prevalence rates of 70% in persons older than 50 years.[95] Unlike most other enteroviruses, coxsackievirus A21 is more readily recovered from throat swabs than from feces. In volunteers receiving small-particle aerosols of the virus, illness has included not only coryza and sore throat but also tracheobronchitis and pneumonia.[97] Among the echoviruses, serotype 11 is the most firmly established and (possibly) the most common cause of respiratory disease,[95] although serotypes 4, 8, 9, 20, 22, and 25 appear to be responsible for similar illnesses. Echovirus 11 produces sore throat, coryza, cough, and sometimes fever. It has also been associated with croup. The spectrum of group B coxsackievirus disease includes coryza, laryngotracheobronchitis, bronchiolitis, and pneumonia.[63,98] Pneumonia, which may be interstitial or a patchy bronchopneumonia, has occurred in children[99] and rarely in adults.[100]

Severe lower respiratory tract enterovirus infections are uncommon, although some enteroviruses, notably echoviruses 6, 9, 11, and 33 and enterovirus 71, have been isolated post mortem from infants and young children with severe pneumonia.[4,80,101-103]

Herpangina

Herpangina (herpes = vesicular eruption; angina = quinsy, or inflammation of the throat) is a well-characterized vesicular enanthem of the fauces and soft palate that is accompanied by fever, sore throat, and pain on swallowing. Herpangina is usually seen in the setting of summer outbreaks involving children 3 to 10 years old and, less commonly, adolescents and young adults. Sporadic illnesses are less common. Group A coxsackieviruses (serotypes 1 to 10, 16, and 22) are the most common viruses recovered from patients with herpangina. Other serotypes that have been isolated far less commonly from persons with herpangina include group B coxsackieviruses 1 to 5, echoviruses 3, 6, 9, 16, 17, 25, and 30, and enterovirus 71.[82,104]

Clinical Manifestations

The illness begins suddenly with fever. Vomiting, myalgia, and headache are common at the onset but generally do not persist. Sore throat and pain on swallowing are the most prominent symptoms and precede appearance of the enanthem by several hours to a day. Casual inspection of the throat reveals erythema and mild exudate of the tonsils, which leads to a diagnosis of pharyngitis or tonsillitis if the characteristic enanthem is missed. The enanthem begins as punctate macules, which evolve over a 24-hour period to 2- to 4-mm erythematous papules that vesiculate and then ulcerate centrally. The lesions, which usually number two to six but rarely a dozen, are moderately painful. They are located on the soft palate, most frequently on the free-hanging margin between the tonsils and the uvula. Less commonly, they are on the tonsils, the posterior pharyngeal wall, or the buccal mucosa. The fever subsides in 2 to 4 days, but the ulcers may persist for up to a week. Patients with herpangina do not appear very ill and require only symptomatic treatment for sore throat.

A variant of the syndrome, acute lymphonodular pharyngitis, has been described in association with coxsackievirus A10 infection.[105] Lesions occur in the same distribution as herpangina but consist of tiny nodules of packed lymphocytes that eventually recede without undergoing vesiculation or ulceration.

Differential Diagnosis

Herpangina is most often confused with bacterial tonsillitis or other viral causes of pharyngitis, but these infections do not produce vesicular lesions. Furthermore, the lesions of herpangina occur in the posterior of the oral cavity, whereas other vesicular enanthems such as primary herpetic gingivostomatitis and HFM disease characteristically occur in the anterior oral cavity, especially on the inner aspects of the lips, the buccal mucosa, and the tongue. Gingivitis, prominent systemic toxicity, and cervical lymphadenitis are additional features of primary herpes simplex infection that are not seen in herpangina. In

HFM disease, lesions also occur on the extremities in most cases. Aphthous stomatitis is characterized by larger ulcerative lesions of the lips, tongue, and buccal mucosa; a history of multiple recurrences is common, and the disease usually occurs in older children, adolescents, and adults. Typical cases can be confidently diagnosed on clinical grounds, but confirmation may be obtained by isolation of the etiologic agent from the throat or feces.

MYOSITIS

Epidemic Pleurodynia

Epidemic pleurodynia is an acute enteroviral disease characterized by fever and sharp, spasmodic pain in the chest or upper part of the abdomen.

Pleurodynia was first described in 1872 by Daae and by Homann during an outbreak of "acute muscular rheumatism spread by contagion" in Norway. Other reports subsequently appeared in Scandinavia; in particular, Ejnar Sylvest, a Danish general practitioner, in 1933 described his experience with the disease on the island of Bornholm in the Baltic Sea. His monograph received worldwide attention after it was translated into English in 1934.[106] Over the years, many synonyms for the disease have been used, among which are epidemic myalgia, epidemic benign dry pleurisy, devil's grippe, Drangedal disease, Bamle's disease, Bornholm's disease, and Sylvest's disease. Little has been added to Sylvest's descriptions of the disease and its epidemiology, pathogenesis, and complications.

The etiologic role of group B coxsackieviruses, the most important cause of epidemic pleurodynia, was established in 1949.[107,108] Other agents rarely implicated in pleurodynia include echoviruses 1, 6, 9, 16, and 19 and group A coxsackieviruses 4, 6, 9, and 10.[59,60,109,110]

Epidemiology

Published reports of major epidemics have come primarily from Europe and North America. These epidemics have been reported at infrequent intervals, often 10 to 20 years, and attack rates have been higher in sparsely populated areas than in cities. Persons with pleurodynia are somewhat older than those with most other diseases caused by coxsackieviruses and echoviruses. Multiple family members may be attacked almost simultaneously or in rapid succession separated by several days.

Pathogenesis

Pleurodynia is a disease of muscle, not of the pleura or peritoneum. Although pleurodynia probably results from direct viral invasion of muscles after viremia, direct virologic evidence supporting this hypothesis is lacking. Tenderness mimicking spontaneously occurring pain can be elicited by pressure on affected muscles in most cases; in addition, palpable, often visible muscle swelling is a subtle finding in some cases.[106] A pleural friction rub has been rare or absent in most epidemics, although this sign has occasionally been noted in 7% or more of those afflicted.[111,112]

Clinical Manifestations

Pleurodynia has no prodrome and begins with an abrupt onset of spasmodic pain, typically over the lower part of the rib cage or the upper abdominal region. Fever with a temperature to 39.5° C peaks within 1 hour after the onset of each paroxysm and subsides as the pain recedes. Sore throat and headache may occur, but cough and coryza are notably absent. Aseptic meningitis and orchitis occur in a small number of patients with pleurodynia, generally less than 10%.[106,113,114] Pericarditis and pneumonia are rare.[111]

The intensity of the pain varies considerably. It is variously described as sticking, a "stitch" in the side, lancinating, stabbing, constricting, or viselike. Patients asked to localize the pain are likely to indicate a broad area with the palm of the hand rather than a specific point with the finger. The most common location is the vicinity of the costal margin on one or both sides or occasionally the subxiphoid region. Approximately half the patients, especially adults, have pain primarily in muscles of the thorax, especially the intercostals, the trapezius, and occasionally the erector spinae or pectoralis major. In the other half, pain is primarily in the upper part of the abdomen, especially the hypochondrium (internal and external obliques and transversus abdominis) or the epigastrium (rectus abdominis). Periumbilical pain and pain in the lower abdominal quadrants are also seen, especially in children, in whom abdominal localization of pain is the rule.[96,112] A few patients experience pain in neither the chest nor the abdomen but instead in the neck or limbs[113]; in these cases, the diagnosis can be made only by association with other typical cases in the family. Whatever the localization of the pain, it is usual for an individual patient to experience this pain in only one or two areas of the body.

Although the location and severity vary, it is the spasmodic and paroxysmal character of the pain that is its hallmark. If the pain is mild and the patient ambulatory, the patient stoops forward or leans to the side to splint the chest. With more severe pain, the patient lies still in bed and appears acutely ill and apprehensive. Chest pain limits deep inspiration, and respirations are shallow and rapid. Auscultation of the chest reveals no abnormalities. Motion also produces pain, and patients resist being turned in bed.

Pain can be elicited by pressure on the involved muscles in most patients. Swelling is seen or felt only occasionally and by careful, sequential observations; it is detected most readily when the rectus abdominis or erector spinae is involved. Involvement of the muscles of the hypochondrium does not cause discrete swelling, but spasm of these muscles leads to loss of the upper superficial abdominal reflexes.

Most patients are ill for 4 to 6 days. Children have milder disease than adults, and adults are often confined to bed. The first paroxysm is the most severe, and subsequent paroxysms are shorter and accompanied by less fever. Although dull aching of involved muscles usually persists between bouts of sharp pain, the patient may look and feel entirely healthy between paroxysms. About one quarter of patients experience multiple recurrences, often after they have been free of pain for a day or more and have felt well enough to return to work or school.[106,113] In about half of these persons, recurrence of pain is at the same site; in the remainder, a new site is attacked. Late relapses occur in some patients after they have been free of symptoms for a month or more.[113]

Diagnosis

The severity, location, and other characteristics of the pain are so protean that pleurodynia is readily confused with many other illnesses. Pain in the chest may mimic pneumonia, pulmonary infarction, myocardial ischemia, and the preeruptive phase of zoster. Abdominal pain in epidemic pleurodynia may resemble that in acute abdomen of a variety of causes. Normal auscultatory examination of the chest, together with the characteristic spasmodic and relapsing character of the pain, is helpful in excluding pneumonia. A negative chest radiographic film is also helpful, although pleural effusions may rarely be present.

Management and Prognosis

Analgesics and the application of heat to affected muscles are useful in relieving pain in most cases; in some, opiate analgesics are required for adequate pain control. Despite the distressing tendency of the disease to relapse, all patients eventually recover completely. Debility out of all proportion to the apparent severity of the illness is occasionally observed for several months during convalescence.[106,114]

Other Skeletal Myositis

Other enteroviruses have been implicated as a cause of acute myositis in some patients,[115-122] although the diagnosis has rarely been proved virologically. Echovirus 11 has been recovered from clinically involved skeletal muscle of a 3-month-old infant with a fatal systemic infection.[115] In other cases, coxsackievirus A9, group B coxsackievirus types 2 and 6, and echovirus 9 have been etiologically linked to myositis on the basis of serology, recovery of virus from the throat or feces, or demonstration of viral antigen in muscle by immunofluorescence. Both generalized polymyositis and focal myositis have been noted, the latter sometimes localized to the thighs. Clinical myositis is manifested by fever, chills, weakness, hypotonia, tenderness, and edema of the involved muscle groups. Myoglobinemia, myoglobinuria, and an elevated creatine phosphokinase level are often found. Most reported patients have recovered rapidly.

A dermatomyositis-like illness occurs in B-cell–deficient immunocompromised patients with persistent enterovirus infections (see later).

MYOPERICARDITIS

Because enteroviruses rarely, if ever, attack the pericardium alone without involving the subepicardial myocardium, the term *myopericarditis* best describes the disease caused by these viruses when they affect the heart (see Chapter 77).[123] Clinically, however, the signs of either myocarditis or pericarditis often predominate. In older children and adults, the severity of myopericarditis varies from asymptomatic cardiac involvement to severe disease with intractable heart failure and death. The myocarditis that occurs with generalized enterovirus infection in the newborn is discussed separately in the later section on neonatal infections.

An epidemic of coxsackievirus B5 myopericarditis occurred in Finland in autumn 1965 when 18 patients were admitted to a single hospital.[124] Epidemic myopericarditis appears to be exceptional, however, and most reported cases beyond the neonatal period have been sporadic, probably because involvement of the heart is a relatively uncommon manifestation of illness even during substantial enterovirus epidemics.

Etiology and Pathogenesis

Enteroviruses appear to be the most common viral agents and account for at least half of all cases of acute myopericarditis.[125-128] However, the strength of the evidence linking a given enterovirus serotype with myopericarditis varies considerably. Proof of causation exists for all group B coxsackievirus serotypes, group A coxsackievirus types 4 and 16, and echovirus types 9 and 22 by demonstration of infectious virus or viral antigen in myocardium or pericardial fluid.[60,129-132] The evidence is less substantive for group A coxsackievirus types 1, 2, 5, 8, and 9 and echovirus types 1 to 4, 6 to 8, 11, 14, 19, 25, and 30.[128-131,133-142] These serotypes have been recovered from noncardiac sources during an episode of acute myopericarditis, some with a significant increase in antibody titer to the homotypic virus.

Many other viruses and bacteria have been associated with myopericarditis, although adenovirus,[143-145] influenza A virus,[146] mumps virus,[147] and vaccinia virus[148] are the principal nonenterovirus agents that have been detected directly in pericardial fluid or myocardial tissue. The weight of clinical evidence suggests that *M. pneumoniae*, respiratory syncytial virus, Epstein-Barr virus, varicella-zoster virus, and measles virus also cause myopericarditis.

Group B coxsackieviruses and other enteroviruses reach the heart during the viremia that follows replication in the gastrointestinal or respiratory tract (see Chapter 167). Experimental studies in a murine model strongly suggest that virus replication occurs in myocytes and results in scattered myocyte necrosis followed by focal infiltration of polymorphonuclear leukocytes, lymphocytes, plasma cells, and macrophages.[149] A chronic inflammatory response persists for weeks to months when replicating virus is no longer present in the heart, and this lingering response has been a subject of keen interest. Some investigators consider the late-phase inflammatory response to be due to virus-induced, cytotoxic T-lymphocyte destruction of myocytes.[150] Others have postulated the development of a myocardial neoantigen[151] or cross-reactivity between viral and myocardial cell antigens.[152] Healing is accompanied by a variable degree of interstitial fibrosis and evidence of myocyte loss.

Clinical Manifestations

Enteroviral myocarditis occurs at all ages but has a special predilection for physically active adolescents and young adults. The incidence in males is at least twice that in females.[125,128] In two thirds of cases, an upper respiratory tract illness precedes the onset of cardiac manifestations by 7 to 14 days.[128] The most common symptoms are dyspnea, chest pain, fever, and malaise, each of which occurs in about 60% to 90% of cases.[124,128,153-155] Pain in the precordial area is usually dull, but it may resemble angina pectoris or be sharp, pleuritic, and exacerbated by recumbency when pericarditis is present. A pericardial friction rub, often transient, has been observed in 35% to 80% of cases. Enlargement of the cardiac silhouette on chest radiograph films, present in about 50%, may be due to either pericardial effusion or cardiac dilatation. A gallop rhythm and other signs of frank congestive heart failure are observed in roughly 20%.[154,155]

Electrocardiographic abnormalities are invariably present. With pericarditis or mild myocarditis, which are the most common, these abnormalities consist of ST segment elevations or nonspecific ST segment and T wave abnormalities. More severe myocardial disease may lead to the development of Q waves, ventricular tachyarrhythmias, and all degrees of heart block. Echocardiography may confirm the presence of acute ventricular dilatation or a diminished cardiac ejection fraction. Serum levels of myocardial enzymes are frequently elevated. Other clinical manifestations of systemic enteroviral disease sometimes occur with myopericarditis and include aseptic meningitis, pleurodynia, hepatitis, and orchitis.

Acute myocardial infarction associated with chest pain, arrhythmias, and congestive heart failure may be difficult to distinguish from myopericarditis. Patients suspected of having acute myocardial infarction sometimes have evidence of concurrent group B coxsackievirus infection,[156-158] and focal myocarditis has been proved in at least one case of acute coxsackievirus B5 infection.[159] Furthermore, some patients presenting with suspected myocardial infarction who have normal coronary angiographic studies have been shown to have myocarditis by radiolabeled antimyosin antibody cardiac scanning.[160]

Diagnosis

Although coxsackieviruses have been isolated on numerous occasions from pericardial fluid or heart muscle at autopsy[125] or by open biopsy procedures,[161] in practice these specimens are rarely available. Diagnosis by virus isolation from myocardium obtained by percutaneous, transvenous biopsy of the right ventricle is theoretically feasible but has not yet been reported. Cardiac tissue infrequently yields a viral isolate when cultured, and only a small number of specimens yield a positive PCR result for enteroviral RNA.[162,163] In the absence of identification of virus in cardiac tissue, the diagnosis often rests on circumstantial evidence provided by recovery of the agent from the oropharynx or feces or on serologic evidence of recent infection by a group B coxsackievirus.

Management

Supportive treatment consists of bed rest, pain relief, and medical management of arrhythmias and heart failure.[164] Although one study reported improved cardiac function and a trend toward increased survival for children with acute myocarditis who received intravenous immune globulin (IGIV) compared with historical controls,[165] randomized trials of immunosuppressive therapy, including IGIV, prednisone, and other drugs, have failed to show any consistent treatment effect.[166-168] Compassionate release of the experimental antiviral agent pleconaril has been associated with favorable outcomes in a small number of patients,[169] but controlled studies have not been done.

Course and Prognosis

Persistent electrocardiographic abnormalities (10% to 20%), cardiomegaly (5% to 10%), and chronic congestive heart failure are indications of permanent myocardial injury that occur overall in about one third of adult patients identified with acute myopericarditis; these abnormalities may ultimately lead to a diagnosis of dilated cardiomyopathy.[128,154,155] Chronic constrictive pericarditis has occurred after intervals of 5 weeks to 1 year.[170-172]

The prognosis for children with acute myocarditis is better than for adults. Fewer than 15% of children die during the acute illness from intractable heart failure or uncontrolled arrhythmias, and fewer than 10% develop persistent or recurrent compromise from dilated car-

diomyopathy requiring cardiac transplantation.[173] The risk of developing long-term cardiac sequelae may be higher for children with less severe acute myocarditis.[174]

Dilated Cardiomyopathy

Chronic dilated cardiomyopathy, which is second only to ischemic heart disease as a cause of chronic congestive heart failure, is the final result of multiple infectious and noninfectious cardiac insults,[175] including up to one third of cases of acute myopericarditis and, in some instances, unrecognized past enterovirus infection.[128,154,155] Some investigators have detected enterovirus RNA in cardiac tissue months to years after the onset of dilated cardiomyopathy, but others who have searched with similar methods have not detected enteroviral RNA.[176-182]

COXSACKIEVIRUS AND ECHOVIRUS DISEASE IN THE NEWBORN INFANT

The human neonate is uniquely susceptible to coxsackievirus and echovirus disease. Although many enterovirus serotypes cause the same self-limited clinical syndromes in neonates as they do in older persons (e.g., aseptic meningitis, exanthems), some serotypes are capable of producing fulminant, frequently fatal disease in the newborn infant. Group B coxsackievirus serotypes 2 to 5 and echovirus 11 are most frequently associated with overwhelming systemic neonatal infections. Rare cases of serious neonatal disease are reported with group A coxsackievirus serotypes 3, 9, and 16.[183-185]

Epidemiology

Although most neonatal enteroviral infections are directly transmitted from the mother, some infections are acquired by a nosocomial route. The first description of group B coxsackievirus disease in newborn infants followed outbreaks occurring in newborn nurseries in South Africa, Zimbabwe, and the Netherlands.[186] Many nursery outbreaks of neonatal echovirus infection have been recorded, with the severity of neonatal disease varying according to the viral serotype.[187,188] Introduction of infection into the nursery has been traced to an infected mother or to ill hospital personnel. Infant-to-infant spread within nurseries probably occurs by the hands of personnel engaged in mouth care, gavage feeding, and other activities requiring close direct contact.[189]

Because most neonatal enterovirus infections are sporadic rather than nosocomial, the incidence and severity of neonatal enteroviral infection generally reflect the occurrence of enteroviral disease in the community. Although many cases occur sporadically during the enterovirus season, clusters of vertically transmitted neonatal infection sometimes occur during community outbreaks with a single enterovirus serotype.[190,191]

Pathophysiology

Most newborns with life-threatening enterovirus disease are infected by vertical transmission from the infected mother in the perinatal period.[187,192] Approximately 60% to 70% of women who bear infected infants have a febrile illness during the last week of pregnancy.[10,187] Experimental evidence indicates that the fetus is relatively protected by the placenta during maternal infection,[192,193] but the newborn has a high risk of infection,[104,194] perhaps as a result of exposure to either virus-positive cervical secretions[195,196] or viremic maternal blood.[197] Although most vertically transmitted enterovirus infections are probably acquired during delivery, some infants are infected before delivery, as evidenced by the recovery of virus from cord blood[195] and the development of disease within the first 2 days of life.[187,198]

When a newborn infant is infected, it is presumed that enteroviruses spread systemically through the blood stream. Tropism for and replication within specific organs of the neonatal host appear to depend on both virus and host factors. Experimental evidence suggests that some neonatal tissues are innately more susceptible to infection with some enteroviruses than the corresponding tissues from an adult host.[199] In addition, the neonatal immune system is insufficient to control the replication and spread of virulent enteroviruses. Both premature and term human infants respond adequately to enterovirus infection with humoral neutralizing antibody.[200] However, macrophage function, which does not mature sufficiently until several weeks of age in the human neonate, is necessary to limit initial enteroviral replication.[201,202]

The outcome of neonatal infection is also strongly influenced by the presence or absence of passively acquired maternal antibody specific for the infecting enterovirus serotype.[193,194,203] Thus, the timing of maternal infection in relation to the development of maternal immunoglobulin G (IgG) antibody and delivery of the infant may be the most critical factor in determining the outcome of neonatal enterovirus infection.

Clinical Manifestations

Symptoms develop in most neonates with generalized coxsackievirus and echovirus disease between 3 and 7 days of life.[187,198] A small number have signs of illness in the delivery room or within the first 1 to 2 days of life[187,198]; conversely, the onset of fatal infection has been documented in infants as old as 3 months.[115] Male infants and premature infants are overrepresented among infants with serious illness. Early symptoms are generally mild and nonspecific and include listlessness, anorexia, and transient respiratory distress. Fever may or may not be present. Approximately one third of cases have a biphasic illness with a period of 1 to 7 days of apparent wellbeing interspersed between the initial symptoms and the appearance of more serious manifestations.

Generalized enterovirus disease in the newborn most often occurs in one of two characteristic clinical syndromes, either myocarditis or fulminant hepatitis. Neonatal myocarditis, which is often accompanied by encephalitis and sometimes by hepatitis, is characteristically a manifestation of group B coxsackievirus infection[60,186] and less commonly echovirus 11 infection.[141,204] Fulminant hepatitis is characterized by hypotension, profuse bleeding, jaundice, and multiple organ failure. Echovirus 11 is responsible for a large proportion of cases, but welldocumented cases of severe hepatitis in neonates have resulted from echovirus serotypes 4, 6, 7, 9, 12, 14, 19, 20, 21, 31, and 33.[187,205-209]

Myocarditis

Signs of neonatal myocarditis include rapid onset of heart failure, respiratory distress, tachycardia often exceeding 200 beats/min, cardiomegaly, and electrocardiographic evidence of myocardial injury and arrhythmias. Cyanosis and circulatory collapse develop rapidly in severely affected infants. Fatal cases are often accompanied by disseminated viral infection involving other organs in a pattern resembling that seen in experimentally infected suckling mice; these organs, in order of frequency, are the CNS, liver, pancreas, and adrenal gland. Most affected neonates are lethargic, and seizures, a bulging fontanelle, and CSF pleocytosis indicate the presence of meningoencephalitis. Enlargement of the liver is more often due to congestive heart failure than to viral hepatitis.

Although initial reports suggested that most cases of neonatal coxsackievirus myocarditis ended fatally, accumulated experience now indicates that the mortality is less than 50%. Death usually occurs within 1 week of onset. Myocardial function rapidly improves in surviving infants after defervescence, generally by 1 week, although in a few infants convalescence is prolonged for several weeks. Pathologic data are limited to information obtained at postmortem examination. Infants dying of myocarditis have enlarged, dilated hearts, extensive myonecrosis, and a variable degree of cardiac inflammation. Lymphocytic infiltration of the brain, meninges, lungs, liver, pancreas, and adrenal glands may also be found.

Hepatitis

The initial symptoms of severe neonatal hepatitis syndrome are lethargy, poor feeding, and increasing jaundice. These nonspecific symptoms may initiate an evaluation and therapy for bacterial sepsis. However, within 1 to 2 days, the jaundice progresses and ecchymoses, bleeding from puncture sites, and signs of metabolic acidosis develop. From this stage, many infected infants rapidly progress downhill with uncontrollable hemorrhage, hepatic failure, acute renal failure, and

generalized seizures. Hepatic transaminases rise rapidly to extremely high levels and thrombocytopenia develops. Markedly prolonged prothrombin times and partial thromboplastin times are indicative of profound hepatic failure.

More than half of infants with severe neonatal echovirus hepatitis die within days after the onset of symptoms despite therapy with blood products and intensive supportive care. Some ultimately fatal cases survive for 2 to 3 weeks with supportive care.[190] Postmortem findings include massive hepatic necrosis and extensive hemorrhage into the cerebral ventricles, pericardial sac, renal medullae, and interstitial spaces of many solid organs.[210] Inflammation is commonly limited to the liver and adrenal glands, with sparing of the heart, brain, meninges, and other organs. The long-term prognosis for surviving infants is not well known, although hepatic fibrosis and chronic hepatic insufficiency develop in some early in life.

Pneumonia

Several cases of enterovirus pneumonia occurring in the first few days of life have been reported, all of them fatal and caused by echovirus types 6,[101] 9,[102] and 11,[103] and group A coxsackievirus type 3.

Diagnosis and Differential Diagnosis

The diagnosis of neonatal coxsackievirus and echovirus infection is most rapidly made by detection of viral RNA by PCR or isolation of virus in cell culture. Because virus is usually present in the infected neonate in high titer, recovery from oropharyngeal secretions, feces, and urine is relatively rapid; virus may also be recovered from blood, CSF, ascitic fluid, and multiple tissues obtained at biopsy or autopsy. Because infected infants make humoral antibody to the virus, the diagnosis can also be made by serologic means when a specific enterovirus serotype is suspected.

Neonatal myocarditis is sometimes mistaken for congenital heart disease because in both conditions murmurs and evidence of congestive heart failure may be present. However, fever and electrocardiographic evidence of acute myocardial injury are absent in patients with congenital heart disease. The early features of myocarditis and severe hepatitis resemble those of bacterial sepsis. Because of liver and CNS involvement in either syndrome, visceral dissemination with perinatally acquired herpes simplex virus in the absence of cutaneous lesions may be suspected.

Management

Management of neonatal enteroviral disease is supportive. Infants in congestive heart failure require judicious fluid management and administration of inotropic agents and diuretics. The profuse bleeding that results from hepatic failure necessitates frequent replacement therapy with packed red blood cells, platelets, and fresh frozen plasma. Vitamin K should be administered intravenously in pharmacologic doses. Large doses of IGIV, which have been reported to improve outcome in at least one case,[211] may be justified given the extremely poor prognosis.

CHRONIC MENINGOENCEPHALITIS IN AGAMMAGLOBULINEMIC AND OTHER IMMUNOCOMPROMISED PATIENTS

The enteroviruses have been responsible for persistent, sometimes fatal infections of the CNS in patients with hereditary or acquired defects in B-lymphocyte function; most reported patients are children with X-linked agammaglobulinemia.[212] Persistent skeletal muscle involvement causes a dermatomyositis-like syndrome in more than half of these patients, and some also have chronic hepatitis.

Etiologic Agents

Most cases have been caused by echoviruses; single cases caused by group A coxsackievirus serotypes 4, 11, and 15 and by group B coxsackievirus serotypes 2 and 3 are recorded.[212,213] Several enterovirus infections have been detected by PCR testing of CSF and other specimens when the serotype could not be identified.[214,215]

Clinical Manifestations

Nervous system manifestations may be totally absent, or mild nuchal rigidity, headache, lethargy, papilledema, seizure disorders, motor weakness, tremors, and ataxia may be present. These neurologic abnormalities may fluctuate in severity, disappear, or steadily progress. The CSF exhibits lymphocytic pleocytosis and a higher protein concentration than is usually seen in cases of acute enteroviral aseptic meningitis. An enterovirus can be repeatedly recovered from the CSF over a period of months to years, usually in high titer. In some cases, virus is isolated only intermittently from the CSF or detected only by PCR. For unknown reasons, it is usually more difficult to find virus in the feces than in the CSF. Enteroviruses have been recovered from many other sites in these patients, including the brain, lung, liver, spleen, kidney, myocardium, pericardial fluid, skeletal muscle, and bone marrow.[212] Some patients have been infected with more than one enterovirus serotype, either concurrently[216] or sequentially.[212,213] The etiology of the chronic muscle and soft tissue inflammation is not fully understood, but isolation of echovirus from muscle in one case suggests a role for direct virus infection.[217]

In many patients, possibly most, the disease ends fatally. Autopsy findings have included chronic meningitis and encephalitis, with lymphocytic perivascular cuffing, focal loss of neurons, and gliosis of both gray and white matter. However, widespread destruction of motor neurons such as that seen in poliomyelitis has not been observed.

Prophylaxis and Therapy

Prophylactic use of standard immune serum globulin does not completely prevent chronic enterovirus infection. IGIV, which has now replaced immune serum globulin for routine replacement therapy for patients with B-cell immunodeficiency, may prove more effective because much higher serum IgG concentrations can be maintained. Use of IGIV in the treatment of chronic enterovirus meningitis has been ineffective, even when using IGIV lots with relatively high concentrations of specific antibody. Some patients have experienced clinical improvement when IGIV has been injected directly into the ventricles,[212] but relapse of infection may occur even after long-term intraventricular IGIV therapy. The use of the experimental antiviral drug pleconaril holds more promise, but the reported experience with it is uncontrolled and limited to a small number of patients.[218]

Infections in Bone Marrow Transplant Recipients

Bone marrow allograft recipients have profoundly suppressed immunologic responses during the immediate post-transplantation period, including suppression of the ability to mount a humoral immune response. In some recipients, enterovirus infections have developed in the post-transplantation period that were disseminated, prolonged, and contributed to fatal outcomes.[219-221] In addition, Townsend and colleagues observed considerable morbidity and mortality during an outbreak of coxsackievirus A1 diarrheal illness in a bone marrow transplantation unit.[222] During this outbreak, virus-induced diarrhea was difficult to distinguish from graft-versus-host enteritis.

ACUTE HEMORRHAGIC CONJUNCTIVITIS

Acute hemorrhagic conjunctivitis (AHC) is a contagious ocular infection characterized by pain, swelling of the eyelids, and subconjunctival hemorrhage that generally resolves spontaneously within a week. Epidemic or pandemic disease has now occurred in most parts of the world.

Etiologic Agents

Enterovirus 70 has been responsible for tens of millions of cases of AHC since 1969. A variant of coxsackievirus A24 causes a similar but geographically more restricted disease that has afflicted hundreds of thousands of persons. Some epidemics of conjunctivitis in the Far East have involved both viruses sequentially or concurrently. Although the relative contribution of these two agents has not always been defined, it is clear that enterovirus 70 has accounted for greater total morbidity.

Epidemiology

AHC appeared to emerge as a new disease in 1969 with explosive, pandemic spread from simultaneous foci in Ghana and Indonesia.[223] The initial epidemic caused by enterovirus 70 spread along the coast of West Africa and ultimately involved many countries on the African continent by 1973, as well as England, the former Soviet Union, Holland, France, and Yugoslavia.[224,225] Meanwhile, a new strain of coxsackievirus A24 was identified as the etiology of more than 60,000 cases of AHC in Singapore in 1970.[226-228] In 1971 the disease again appeared in Singapore, but this time the epidemic was caused by enterovirus 70. Subsequently, both viruses circulated in Southeast Asia and the Indian subcontinent, causing large seasonal outbreaks.[229-232] Although the geographic distribution of AHC is wide, large-scale epidemics have occurred predominantly in crowded coastal areas of tropical countries during the hot, rainy season.[233]

Outbreaks in economically developed countries and temperate climates have been much more limited. AHC in the West has been mostly confined to seasonal outbreaks in Central America and the Caribbean. The disease did not appear in the United States until September 1981, when enterovirus 70 conjunctivitis was first reported in Key West, Florida. Within weeks, approximately 2500 cases occurred, largely among disadvantaged blacks in Miami.[234] With the exception of a few imported cases, AHC activity has not since been noted in the United States.[235] Coxsackievirus A24 AHC cases first appeared in the Western Hemisphere in Trinidad, Jamaica, St. Croix, Panama, and Mexico in 1986.[236] Approximately 31,000 cases occurred in Puerto Rico in 1987.[237]

Patterns of Transmission

AHC is highly contagious and spreads rapidly. Unlike most other enterovirus infections, AHC is transmitted primarily from fingers or fomites directly to the eye rather than by respiratory secretions or fecal contamination. Both enterovirus 70 and coxsackievirus A24 can be regularly recovered from the conjunctivae early in the illness but only infrequently recovered from throat secretions or feces. Both appear to be naturally occurring, temperature-sensitive viruses whose optimal replication at 33° C to 35° C reflects their adaptation to the temperature of the conjunctiva.[238,239] Virus shedding is quantitatively greater from the eye than from the gut, and rapid serial transmission at approximately 24-hour intervals is consistent with direct spread of virus from hand to eye. During a 1980 enterovirus 70 outbreak in Singapore, the secondary attack rate within affected households was 72.6%.[240] Contagion is favored by crowding and unsanitary living conditions. AHC occurs substantially more often among the poor than among others living in the same country.[241,242] Reuse of water for bathing and sharing of towels are implicated as factors contributing to the spread of infection. Limited outbreaks of AHC in Europe have been primarily nosocomial, particularly in ophthalmology clinics, where infection appears to have been spread directly by physicians' fingers or by instruments.

Postepidemic antibody prevalence rates of nearly 50% have been observed in Ghana and Indonesia but only 6% in affected populations of Japan. These findings are consistent with less explosive spread of AHC in economically developed regions. Antibody prevalence rates are highest in children younger than 10 years, whereas attack rates for clinical disease are greatest in young adults, which indicates that many infections in children must be unapparent or mild.[243,244]

Clinical Manifestations

AHC begins abruptly, and the illness reaches its peak within 24 hours. It usually occurs first in one eye and then a few hours later in the other. The main symptoms are a burning, foreign body sensation, ocular pain, photophobia, swelling of the eyelids, and watery discharge.[234] Constitutional symptoms such as fever, malaise, and headache are observed in 20% of cases. The most distinctive sign is subconjunctival hemorrhage, which is present in 70% to 90% of patients with AHC caused by enterovirus 70,[244] but it is much less frequent in cases caused by coxsackievirus A24.[227,228,230] The hemorrhages may be pinpoint or occupy the entire bulbar conjunctiva and are precipitated by everting the upper lid or by rubbing the eyes (Fig. 169-1).

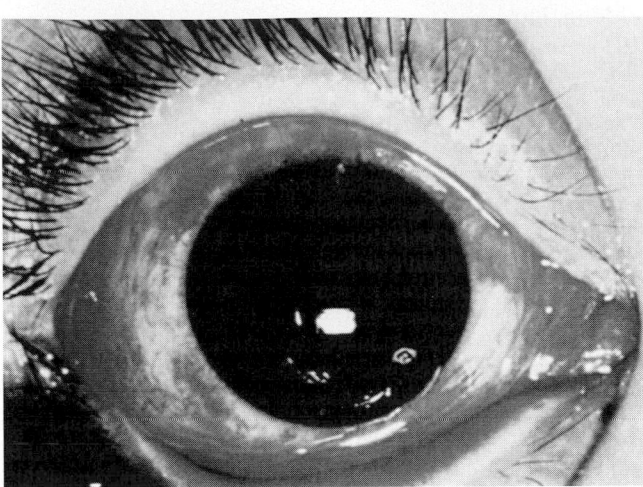

FIGURE 169-1. Acute hemorrhagic conjunctivitis due to enterovirus 70. *(From Kono R, Uchida Y. Acute hemorrhagic conjunctivitis. Ophthalmol Dig. 1977;39:14.)*

Conjunctival edema is said to be more common in elderly people; hemorrhage is more profuse in young patients.[244] Small follicles appear on the tarsal conjunctiva after 3 to 5 days in 90% of patients. In most cases, corneal erosion or a fine punctate epithelial keratitis can be demonstrated by slit-lamp examination after staining with fluorescein. The ocular discharge is serous or seromucoid and contains abundant neutrophils in the first 24 hours. Preauricular lymph nodes are often enlarged and tender by the second day of illness. Recovery is usually noticeable by the second or third day and is complete in most cases in 10 days, although discoloration from the hemorrhages sometimes persists for many days.

Complications

In severe cases of AHC, keratitis occasionally persists for several weeks but almost never leads to permanent scarring. Uveitis has not been reported. Conjunctivitis may be complicated by secondary bacterial infection.

More than 200 cases of acute motor paralysis have been reported in persons who have recently recovered from AHC in India, Thailand, Taiwan, and Senegal.[231,245-248] This complication is clinically indistinguishable from poliomyelitis except for its temporal association with AHC, which it generally follows by 2 to 5 weeks. A "minor illness" with fever and constitutional symptoms usually precedes the onset of neurologic manifestations by 1 to 3 days. Radicular pain and paresthesias are prominent early symptoms preceding the onset of asymmetrical paralysis of the limbs. Bulbar paralysis complicates as many as one half of cases; respiratory failure has been observed rarely. The CSF abnormalities are those of aseptic meningitis.

Neurologic complications of AHC have been reported only during epidemics caused by enterovirus 70 and not those caused by coxsackievirus A24. Enterovirus 70 has not been recovered from the CSF and has been recovered only once from feces.[245] However, high titers of specific neutralizing antibody to enterovirus 70 have been demonstrated in the CSF of virtually all patients with motor paralysis but not in patients with AHC alone.[248] Neuroparalytic disease has been reproduced clinically and pathologically in monkeys by inoculation of enterovirus 70 into the spinal cord.[223,249]

Differential Diagnosis

AHC is not likely to be confused with other causes of conjunctivitis during major epidemics. Small outbreaks or sporadic cases may be mistaken for adenovirus infection causing epidemic keratoconjunctivitis (see Chapter 139). The incubation period of epidemic keratoconjunctivitis is longer, usually 5 to 7 days compared with 1 day for AHC. In AHC, the conjunctivitis reaches its peak several hours after onset and lasts less than 1 week, whereas symptoms from epidemic keratoconjunctivitis are maximal after several days and sometimes last for 2 or 3 weeks. Early in the illness, pain and subconjunctival hemorrhage are characteristic of AHC but are uncommon in epidemic keratoconjunctivitis. Follicular deposits on the conjunctiva are much more prominent in epidemic keratoconjunctivitis, as are subepithelial corneal opacities persisting after the conjunctivitis has subsided.

Laboratory Diagnosis

Enterovirus 70 and coxsackievirus A24 can be recovered from conjunctival swabs or scrapings of patients with AHC during the first 3 days of illness.[226,250] Isolation rates exceeding 90% from conjunctival scrapings have been reported for coxsackievirus A24, but recovery rates for enterovirus 70 have been somewhat lower.[241] Less than 5% of fecal specimens or throat swabs have been positive for either virus. Rising antibody titers can be demonstrated in paired sera from patients with conjunctivitis.

Treatment and Prevention

Treatment of conjunctivitis is symptomatic. Antimicrobial agents are not indicated. Contagion can be prevented by careful hand washing, use of separate towels, and sterilization of ophthalmologic instruments.

ILLNESSES IN WHICH THE ETIOLOGIC ROLE OF ENTEROVIRUSES IS MINOR OR POORLY DEFINED

Gastrointestinal Diseases

The liver and the pancreas are both affected in mice infected with group B coxsackieviruses. In humans, acute hepatitis occurring beyond the neonatal period is described in association with group B coxsackievirus and echovirus infections.[251-256] Most cases have been mild and self-limited. Prospective studies indicated that 2% to 20% of patients with acute pancreatitis have concurrent enterovirus infection.[257,258] Group B coxsackievirus types 1 to 5 and echovirus types 6, 11, 22, and 30 are all reported to cause acute pancreatitis.[257-260]

Coxsackieviruses and echoviruses, possibly as a result of their replication in the small bowel, are frequently cited as causes of nonbacterial diarrhea or gastroenteritis. However, conflicting results have been obtained in several studies that compared rates of enteroviral isolation from children with acute diarrheal illness versus matched healthy control subjects.[60,261-263] The consensus of these reports favors a variable, generally small excess of enteroviral infections in subjects with diarrhea. Evidence is somewhat stronger that certain echoviruses, particularly types 11, 14, and 18, have occasionally been responsible for epidemic diarrhea in young infants.[60,262,264] Most of these studies were performed before the discovery of toxigenic *Escherichia coli*, rotaviruses, enteric adenoviruses, and caliciviruses, now established as major causes of diarrheal illness. In light of this new knowledge, additional epidemiologic investigations encompassing all these agents are required before the contribution of enteroviruses to diarrheal disease can be accurately assessed. Nonetheless, their role is probably minor. Similarly, the hemolytic-uremic syndrome has been temporally associated with coxsackieviruses A4, B2, and B4 and with echovirus 22 (now parechovirus 1),[265-267] and coxsackievirus B5 has been reported in association with acute renal failure in five patients.[268] Now that a strong link between enterohemorrhagic *E. coli* infection and the hemolytic-uremic syndrome exists, the relationship between enterovirus infection and acute renal disease is questionable.

Other Diseases

Orchitis has been observed in adolescent boys during infection with coxsackievirus A9, group B coxsackieviruses 2, 4, and 5, and echovirus 6,[269-273] including coxsackievirus B5 isolation from a testicular biopsy specimen in one case.[269] Splenomegaly and a heterophile-negative mononucleosis-like syndrome have also been reported.[60] Echoviruses have been associated with acute arthritis, including echovirus 11, which was recovered from synovial fluid in one case.[274,275] In separate case reports, echovirus 25[276,277] and an untyped enterovirus resembling a group A coxsackievirus[277] have been recovered from the gastrointestinal tracts of children with acute infectious lymphocytosis; however, further evidence of an etiologic association is lacking.

Diabetes Mellitus

A gradually accumulating body of epidemiologic, clinical, and experimental evidence suggests an intriguing link between the group B coxsackieviruses and type 1 insulin-dependent diabetes mellitus (IDDM). The reader is referred to several excellent reviews for more detailed analyses.[259,278-282]

The observation that new-onset IDDM cases occur in seasonal patterns[283,284] and sometimes in clusters or small outbreaks[282,285,286] has been cited as evidence for the role of viral disease in the pathophysiology of IDDM. The peak occurrence of new IDDM cases is late in the calendar year, 1 to 2 months later than peak enterovirus activity. However, the occurrence of enterovirus infection and IDDM during the same season could be independent, and at least two studies found no increase in new onset of IDDM after outbreaks of group B coxsackievirus disease.[287,288] Cross-sectional studies in which the prevalence of group B coxsackievirus antibody has been compared in children with IDDM and control subjects are inconclusive. In general, studies that used hospital or neighborhood controls have found a positive association, whereas those using sibling controls have not.[278,280]

Two major theories of the pathophysiology of virus-induced IDDM exist and are not necessarily mutually exclusive. The "direct hit" hypothesis, which posits destruction of pancreatic islets by direct virus infection, derives support from murine studies in which enteroviruses cause specific destruction of β cells in the islets of Langerhans,[259,289] from detection of enterovirus RNA in serum at the onset of IDDM,[290,291] and from postmortem isolation of coxsackievirus serotypes B4[292] and B5[293] from the pancreatic tissue of children dying of ketoacidosis as their initial manifestation of IDDM. Demonstration of group B coxsackievirus IgM antibody in the serum of children with recent-onset IDDM supports the direct-infection hypothesis, although inconsistency regarding this finding has been noted across different studies.[294-298]

A second theory focuses on acute viral infection as a trigger for an autoimmune response to pancreatic islet cells; the autoimmune response is induced by the similarity between viral and islet cell antigens, which may be related to a past viral insult, genetic predisposition, or both.[299] This concept is supported by the induction of chronic islet cell inflammation in genetically susceptible mice by enterovirus infection,[300] by the observation that most children with IDDM have humoral anti–islet cell antibodies at diagnosis, and by one study demonstrating a temporal association between the development of islet cell antibodies and seroconversion to group B coxsackievirus infection.[301] Some investigations suggest that molecular mimicry between a nonstructural coxsackievirus protein and a β-cell enzyme may permit autoimmune destruction of pancreatic islet cell tissue.[302] Although persistent enterovirus infection is also considered a possible mechanism of islet cell damage, no evidence is widely accepted that enteroviruses are capable of persisting in an immunocompetent human host.

INFECTIONS CAUSED BY THE NEWER ENTEROVIRUSES

Four new enteroviruses, serotypes 68 to 71, have been recognized since adoption of the simplified classification scheme described in Chapter 167. Enterovirus 68, recovered from the stool of an asymptomatic child, has yet to be associated with a disease and is therefore considered an "orphan" virus.[303] Enterovirus 69 has been isolated from the throat secretions of infants with bronchiolitis and pneumonia.[304] These two viruses have been little studied, and only a handful of isolates from California and Mexico have been recovered. Enterovirus 70 is recognized as the major cause of AHC, a distinctive infection affecting persons in warm, humid coastal areas in many parts of the

world (see "Acute Hemorrhagic Conjunctivitis"). Enterovirus 71, the most recently discovered enterovirus serotype, has been recognized as a cause of cutaneous and CNS disease in scattered locations throughout the world since 1969.

Enterovirus 71 Infections

Enterovirus 71 is an enterovirus related to coxsackievirus A16 that causes skeletal myositis in suckling mice and myelitis with paralysis in cynomolgus monkeys.[305,306] The virus was first isolated from young children with encephalitis and aseptic meningitis in California in 1969.[307] The first infections outside California occurred in 1972 in New York State[308] and in Melbourne, Australia.[309] In both locations, HFM disease was a prominent feature of the illness. Subsequent clusters of enterovirus 71 disease were reported in Sweden, Australia, Japan, Hong Kong, Bulgaria, Hungary, France, and many locations in the United States.[310-316] Large outbreaks involving genetically separate groups of enterovirus 71 have occurred in Australia, Malaysia, Singapore, and Taiwan during the past decade.[80,82,317,318]

Most recognized human infections have been observed in patients with aseptic meningitis or HFM disease, but several outbreaks have also produced serious CNS complications in young children. Enterovirus 71 is unique among the non-polio enteroviruses as a cause of epidemic paralysis, in which localized outbreaks have involved small numbers of patients over several years[307,309,319,320] and regional epidemics have involved hundreds to thousands of persons within a single season.[53,54,82,314,321] Many infants and young children have developed a brain stem encephalitis associated with high mortality related to rapid cardiovascular collapse and pulmonary edema.[55,80,317] Other less common manifestations attributed to enterovirus 71 infection include generalized maculopapular rash,[309] interstitial pneumonia,[80] and myocarditis.[54,80]

Enterovirus 71 has been isolated from a number of clinical specimens, including vesicle fluid, feces, oropharyngeal secretions, urine, and CSF. Isolation rates are highest from vesicle swabs and lowest from the CSF.[53,54,315] Primary isolation has been most successful in African green monkey kidney cell culture and in suckling mice. Even under optimal conditions, a cytopathic effect may take 5 to 8 days to develop and then progress slowly and incompletely.

Treatment of enterovirus 71 infection is symptomatic and supportive. Widespread distribution of oral polio vaccine during the Bulgarian epidemic was postulated to have dampened the spread of enterovirus 71 disease by virtue of gastrointestinal interference, but proof of a significant effect of oral polio vaccine is lacking. An inactivated enterovirus 71 vaccine was prepared for use during this epidemic but not administered to humans.

REFERENCES

1. Kogon A, Spigland I, Frothingham TE, et al. The Virus Watch Program: A continuing surveillance of viral infections in metropolitan New York families. Am J Epidemiol. 1969;89:51.
2. Berlin LE, Rorabaugh ML, Heldrich F, et al. Aseptic meningitis in infants less than two years of age: Diagnosis and etiology. J Infect Dis. 1993;168:888.
3. Echovirus type 13—United States, 2001. MMWR Morb Mortal Wkly Rep. 2001;50:777.
4. Huang QS, Carr JM, Nix WA, et al. An echovirus type 33 outbreak in New Zealand. Clin Infect Dis. 2003;37:650.
5. Dagan R, Jenista J, Menegus MA. Association of clinical presentation, laboratory findings, and virus serotypes with the presence of meningitis in hospitalized infants with enterovirus infection. J Pediatr. 1988;113:975.
6. Rorabaugh ML, Berlin LE, Heldrich F, et al. Aseptic meningitis among infants less than two years of age: Acute illness and neurologic complications. Pediatrics. 1993;92:206.
7. Lepow ML, Coyne N, Thompson LB, et al. A clinical, epidemiologic and laboratory investigation of aseptic meningitis during the four-year period, 1955-1958. II. The clinical disease and its sequelae. N Engl J Med. 1962;266:1188.
8. Rotbart H, Brennan PJ, Fife KH, et al. Enterovirus meningitis in adults. Clin Infect Dis. 1998;27:896.
9. Haynes RE, Cramblett HG, Kronfol HJ. Echovirus 9 meningoencephalitis in infants and children. JAMA. 1969;208:1657.
10. Lake AM, Lauer BA, Clark JC, et al. Enterovirus infections in neonates. J Pediatr. 1976;89:787.

11. Wenner HA, Abel D, Olson LC, et al. A mixed epidemic associated with echovirus types 6 and 11. Am J Epidemiol. 1981;114:369.
12. Wilfert CM, Lauer BA, Cohen M, et al. An epidemic of echovirus 18 meningitis. J Infect Dis. 1975;131:75.
13. Amir J, Harel L, Frydman M, et al. Shift in cerebrospinal polymorphonuclear cell percentage in the early stage of aseptic meningitis. J Pediatr. 1991;119:938.
14. Feigin RD, Shackelford PG. Value of repeat lumbar puncture in the differential diagnosis of meningitis. N Engl J Med. 1973;289:571.
15. Avner E, Satz J, Plotkin SA. Hypoglycorrhachia in young infants with viral meningitis. J Pediatr. 1975;87:883.
16. Singer JI, Mauer PR, Riley JP, et al. Management of central nervous system infections during an epidemic of enteroviral aseptic meningitis. J Pediatr. 1980;96:559.
17. Sumaya CV, Corman LI. Enteroviral meningitis in early infancy: Significance in community outbreaks. Pediatr Infect Dis J. 1982;3:151.
18. Malcom BS, Eiden JJ, Hendley JO. Echovirus type 9 meningitis simulating tuberculous meningitis. Pediatrics. 1980;65:725.
19. Chonmaitree T, Ford C, Sanders C, et al. Comparison of cell cultures for rapid isolation of enteroviruses. J Clin Microbiol. 1988;26:2576.
20. Dagan R, Menegus MA. A combination of four cell types for rapid detection of enteroviruscs in clinical specimens. J Med Virol. 1986;19:219.
21. Lennette EH, Magoffin R, Knouf EG. Viral central nervous system disease: An etiologic study conducted at the Los Angeles County General Hospital. JAMA. 1962;179:687.
22. Lepow ML, Carver DH, Wright HT, et al. A clinical, epidemiologic and laboratory investigation of aseptic meningitis during the four-year period, 1955-1958. I. Observations concerning etiology and epidemiology. N Engl J Med. 1962;266:1181.
23. Marier R, Rodriguez W, Chloupek RJ, et al. Coxsackievirus B5 infection and aseptic meningitis in neonates and children. Am J Dis Child. 1975;129:321.
24. Torphy DE, Ray GC, Thompson RS, et al. An epidemic of aseptic meningitis due to echovirus type 30: Epidemiologic features and clinical and laboratory findings. Am J Public Health. 1970;60:1447.
25. Yerly S, Gervaix A, Simonet V, et al. Rapid and sensitive detection of enteroviruses in specimens from patients with aseptic meningitis. J Clin Microbiol. 1996;34:199.
26. Sabin AB, Krumbiegel ER, Wigand R. ECHO type 9 virus disease. Am J Dis Child. 1958;96:197.
27. Rotbart HA. Nucleic acid detection systems for enteroviruses. Clin Microbiol Rev. 1991;4:156.
28. Schlesinger Y, Sawyer MH, Storch GA. Enteroviral meningitis infancy: Potential role for polymerase chain reaction in patient management. Pediatrics. 1994;94:157.
29. Rotbart HA, Sawyer MH, Fast S, et al. Diagnosis of enteroviral meningitis by using PCR with a colorimetric microwell detection assay. J Clin Microbiol. 1994;32:2590.
30. Sawyer M, Holland D, Aintablian N, et al. Diagnosis of enteroviral central nervous system infection by polymerase chain reaction during a large community outbreak. Pediatr Infect Dis J. 1994;13:177.
31. Mandal BK. The dilemma of partially treated bacterial meningitis. Scand J Infect Dis. 1976;8:185.
32. Converse GM, Gwaltney JMJ, Strasburg DA, et al. Alteration of cerebrospinal fluid findings by partial treatment of bacterial meningitis. J Pediatr. 1973;83:220.
33. Dalton HP, Allison MJ. Modification of laboratory results by partial treatment of bacterial meningitis. Am J Clin Pathol. 1968;49:410.
34. Weiner LB, Rotbart HA, Gilbert DL, et al. Treatment of "enterovirus" meningitis with pleconaril (VP 63843), an antipicornavirus agent. 37th Interscience Conference on Antimicrobial Agents and Chemotherapy, Toronto, 1997. American Society for Microbiology.
35. Shafran SD, Halota W, Gilbert D, et al. Pleconaril is effective for enterovirus meningitis in adolescents and adults: A randomized placebo-controlled multicenter trial. 39th Interscience Conference on Antimicrobial Agents and Chemotherapy, San Francisco, 1999.
36. Abzug MJ, Cloud G, Bradley J, et al. Double blind placebo-controlled trial of pleconaril in infants with enterovirus meningitis. Pediatr Infect Dis J. 2003;22:335.
37. Farmer K, MacArthur BA, Clay MM. A follow-up study of 15 cases of neonatal meningoencephalitis due to Coxsackie virus B5. J Pediatr. 1975;87:568.
38. Sells CJ, Carpenter RL, Ray CG. Sequelae of central-nervous-system enterovirus infections. N Engl J Med. 1975;293:1.
39. Bergman I, Painter MJ, Wald ER, et al. Outcome in children with enteroviral meningitis during the first year of life. J Pediatr. 1987;110:705.
40. Rorabaugh ML, Berlin LE, Rosenberg L, et al. Absence of Neurodevelopmental Sequelae from Aseptic Meningitis. Baltimore: Society for Pediatric Research; 1992.
41. Meyer HM, Johnson RT, Crawford IP, et al. Central nervous system syndromes of viral etiology. A study of 713 cases. Am J Med. 1960;29:334.
42. Glaser CA, Gilliam S, Schnurr D, et al. In search of encephalitis etiologies: Diagnostic challenges in the California Encephalitis Project, 1998-2000. Clin Infect Dis. 2003;36:731.
43. Kolski H. Etiology of acute childhood encephalitis at the Hospital for Sick Children, Toronto, 1994-95. Clin Infect Dis. 1998;26:398.
44. Chalhub E, Devivo D, Siegel BA, et al. Coxsackie A9 focal encephalitis associated with acute infantile hemiplegia and porencephaly. Neurology. 1977;27:574.
45. Modlin JF, Dagan R, Berlin LE, et al. Focal encephalitis with enterovirus infections. Pediatrics. 1991;88:841.
46. Peters ACB, Vielvoye GJ, Versteeg J, et al. Echo 25 focal encephalitis and subacute hemichorea. Neurology. 1979;29:676.
47. Roden VJ, Cantor HE, O'Connor DM, et al. Acute hemiplegia of childhood associated with Coxsackie A9 viral infection. J Pediatr. 1975;86:56.
48. Whitley RJ, Cobbs CG, Alford CA, et al. Diseases that mimic herpes simplex encephalitis. JAMA. 1989;262:234.
49. Klapper PE, Bailey AS, Longson M, et al. Meningoencephalitis caused by coxsackievirus group B type 2: Diagnosis confirmed by measuring intrathecal antibody. J Infect. 1984;8:227.
50. Price RA, Garcia JH, Rightsel WA. Choriomeningitis and myocarditis in an adolescent with isolation of Coxsackie B5 virus. Am J Clin Pathol. 1970;53:825.
51. Voroshilova MK, Chumakov MP. Poliomyelitis-like properties of AB-IV-Coxsackie A7 group of viruses. Prog Med Virol. 1959;2:106.
52. Grist NR, Bell EJ. Enteroviral etiology of the paralytic poliomyelitis syndrome. Arch Environ Health. 1970;21:382.
53. Gilbert GL, Dickson KE, Waters M-J, et al. Outbreak of enterovirus 71 infection in Victoria, Australia, with a high incidence of neurologic involvement. Pediatr Infect Dis J. 1988;7:484.
54. Shindarov LM, Chumakov MP, Voroshilova MK, et al. Epidemiological, clinical, and pathophysiological characteristics of epidemic poliomyelitis-like disease caused by enterovirus 71. J Hyg Epidemiol Microbiol Immunol. 1979;23:284.
55. Huang C-C, Liu C-C, Chang Y-C, et al. Neurologic complications in children with enterovirus 71 infection. N Engl J Med. 1999;341:936.
56. Santhanam S, Choudhury DS. Coxsackie A-9 in the etiology of poliomyelitis-like diseases. Indian J Pediatr. 1985;52:405.
57. Assaad F, Cockburn WC. Four year study of WHO virus reports on enteroviruses other than poliovirus. Bull World Health Organ. 1972;46:329.
58. Godtfredsen A, Hansen B. A case of mild paralytic disease due to ECHO virus type 11. Acta Pathol Microbiol Scand. 1961;53:111.
59. Grist NR, Bell EJ. The epidemiology of enteroviruses. Scot Med J. 1975;20:27.
60. Kibrick S. Current status of Coxsackie and ECHO viruses in human disease. Prog Med Virol. 1964;6:27.
61. Hertenstein JR, Sarnat HB, O'Connor DM. Acute unilateral oculomotor palsy associated with ECHO 9 viral infection. J Pediatr. 1976;89:79.
62. Steigman AJ, Lipton MM. Fatal bulbospinal paralytic poliomyelitis due to ECHO 11 virus. JAMA. 1960;174:178.
63. Dery P, Marks MI, Shapera R. Clinical manifestations of coxsackievirus infections in children. Am J Dis Child. 1974;128:464.
64. Geer J. Coxsackie virus infections in Southern Africa. Yale J Biol Med. 1961;34:289.
65. Barak Y, Schwartz JF. Acute transverse myelitis associated with ECHO type 5 infection (Letter). Am J Dis Child. 1988;142:128.
66. Kaul A, Cohen ME, Broffman S, et al. Reye-like syndrome associated with Coxsackie B2 virus infection. J Pediatr. 1979;94:67.
67. Alvira MM, Mendoza M. Reye's syndrome: A viral myopathy? N Engl J Med. 1975;292:1297.
68. Brunberg JA, Bell WE. Reye syndrome. Arch Neurol. 1974;30:304.
69. Kuban KC, Ephros MA, Freeman RL, et al. Syndrome of opsoclonus-myoclonus caused by Coxsackie B3 infection. Ann Neurol. 1983;13:69.
70. Bell EJ, Ross CAC, Grist NR. Echo 9 infection in pregnant women with suspected rubella. J Clin Pathol. 1975;28:267.
71. Lerner AM, Klein JO, Levin HS, et al. Infections due to Coxsackie virus group A, type 9, in Boston, 1959, with special reference to exanthems and pneumonia. N Engl J Med. 1960;263:1265.
72. Annunziato D. Koplik spots and echo 9 virus (Letter). NY State J Med. 1987;87:667.
73. Hall CB, Cherry JD, Hatch MH, et al. The return of Boston exanthem: Echovirus 16 infections in 1974. Am J Dis Child. 1977;131:323.
74. Neva FA. A second outbreak of Boston exanthem disease in Pittsburgh during 1954. N Engl J Med. 1956;254:838.
75. Cherry JD, Lerner AM, Klein JO, et al. Coxsackie B5 infections with exanthems. Pediatrics. 1963;31:455.
76. Moritsugu Y, Sawada K, Hinohara M, et al. An outbreak of type 25 echovirus infection with exanthem in an infant home near Tokyo. Am J Epidemiol. 1968;87:599.
77. Hughes RO, Roberts C. Hand, foot, mouth disease associated with Coxsackie A9 virus. Lancet. 1972;2:751.
78. Lindenbaum JE, Van Dyck PC, Allen RG. Hand, foot and mouth disease associated with coxsackievirus group B. Scand J Infect Dis. 1975;7:161.
79. Robinson CR, Doane FW, Rhodes AJ. Report of an outbreak of febrile illness with pharyngeal lesions and exanthem. Can Med Assoc J. 1958;79:615.
80. Chan KP, Goh KT, Chong CY, et al. Epidemic hand, foot and mouth disease caused by enterovirus 71, Singapore. Emerg Infect Dis. 2003;9:78.
81. Wang S-M, Liu C-C, Tseng H-W, et al. Clinical spectrum of enterovirus 71 infection in children in southern Taiwan, with an emphasis on neurological complications. Clin Infect Dis. 1999;29:184.
82. Ho M, Chen E-R, Hsu K-H, et al. An epidemic of enterovirus 71 infection in Taiwan. N Engl J Med. 1999;341:929.
83. Adler JL, Mostow SR, Mellin II, et al. Epidemiologic investigation of hand, foot, and mouth disease: Infection caused by coxsackievirus A16 in Baltimore, June through September 1968. Am J Dis Child. 1970;120:309.
84. Nahmias AJ, Froeschle JE, Feorino PM, et al. Generalized eruption in a child with eczema due to coxsackievirus A16. Arch Dermatol. 1968;97:147.
85. Miller GD. Hand-foot-and-mouth disease. JAMA. 1968;203:827.
86. Kimura A, Abe M, Nakao T. Light and electron microscopic study of skin lesions in patients with hand, foot, and mouth disease. Tohoku J Exp Med. 1977;122:237.
87. Cherry JD, Lerner AM, Klein JO, et al. Coxsackie A9 infections with exanthems with particular reference to urticaria. Pediatrics. 1963;31:819.
88. Deseda-Tous J, Byatt PH, Cherry JD. Vesicular lesions in adults due to echovirus 11 infections. Arch Dermatol. 1977;113:1705.
89. Meade RH, Chang TW. Zosterlike eruption due to echovirus 6. Am J Dis Child. 1979;133:283.
90. Frothingham TE. ECHO virus type 9 associated with three cases simulating meningococcemia. N Engl J Med. 1958;259:484.

91. Cherry JD, Jahn CL. Virologic studies of exanthems. J Pediatr. 1966;68:204.
92. James WD, Odom RB, Hatch MH. Gianotti-Crosti–like eruption associated with coxsackievirus A16 infection. J Am Acad Dermatol. 1982;6:862.
93. Kepfer P, Hable DA, Smith TF. Viral isolation rates during summer from children with acute upper respiratory tract disease and healthy children. Am J Clin Pathol. 1974;61:1.
94. Rotbart HA, McCracken GH, Whitley RJ, et al. The clinical significance of enteroviruses in serious summer febrile illnesses of children. Pediatr Infect Dis J. 1999;18:869.
95. Jackson GG, Muldoon RL. Viruses causing common respiratory infections in man. II. Enteroviruses and paramyxoviruses. J Infect Dis. 1973;128:387.
96. Johnson KM, Bloom HH, Forsyth B, et al. The role of enteroviruses in respiratory disease. Am Rev Respir Dis. 1963;88:240.
97. Couch RB, Cate TR, Gerone PJ, et al. Production of illness with a small particle aerosol of Coxsackie A21. J Clin Invest. 1965;44:535.
98. Eckert HL, Portnoy B, Salvatore MA, et al. Group B Coxsackie virus infection in infants with acute lower respiratory disease. Pediatrics. 1967;39:526.
99. Flewett TH. Histological study of two cases of Coxsackie B virus pneumonia in children. J Clin Pathol. 1965;18:743.
100. Jahn CL, Felton OL, Cherry JD. Coxsackie B1 pneumonia in an adult. JAMA. 1964;189:236.
101. Boyd MT, Jordan SW, Davis LE. Fatal pneumonitis from congenital echovirus type 6 infection. Pediatr Infect Dis J. 1987;6:1138.
102. Cheeseman SH, Hirsch MS, Keller EW, et al. Fatal neonatal pneumonia caused by echovirus type 9 (Letter). Am J Dis Child. 1977;131:1169.
103. Toce SS, Keenan WJ. Congenital echovirus 11 pneumonia in association with pulmonary hypertension. Pediatr Infect Dis J. 1988;7:360.
104. Cherry JL, Soriano F, Jahn CL. Search for perinatal enterovirus infection. Am J Dis Child. 1968;116:245.
105. Steigman AJ, Lipton MM, Braspennickx H. Acute lymphonodular pharyngitis: A newly described condition due to Coxsackie A virus. J Pediatr. 1962;61:331.
106. Sylvest E. Epidemic Myalgia: Bornholm Disease. London: Oxford University Press; 1934:155.
107. Curnen EC, Shaw EW, Melnick JL. Disease resembling nonparalytic poliomyelitis associated with virus pathogenic for infant mice. JAMA. 1949;141:894.
108. Weller TH, Enders JF, Buckingham M, et al. Etiology of epidemic pleurodynia: Study of two viruses isolated from typical outbreak. J Immunol. 1950;65:337.
109. Bell EJ, Grist NR. ECHO viruses, carditis, and acute pleurodynia. Am Heart J. 1971;82:133.
110. Madhaven HN, Bedninath S, Chanraseker S. A case of pleurodynia associated with Coxsackie virus type A9. J Assoc Physicians India. 1977;25:491.
111. Bain HW, McLean DM, Walker SJ. Epidemic pleurodynia (Bornholm disease) due to Coxsackie B-5 virus: The interrelationship of pleurodynia, benign pericarditis, and aseptic meningitis. Pediatrics. 1961;27:889.
112. Disney ME, Howard EM, Wood BSB. Bornholm disease in children. Br Med J. 1953;1:1351.
113. Warin JF, Davies JBM, Sanders FK, et al. Oxford epidemic of Bornholm disease, 1951. Br Med J. 1953;1:1345.
114. Gordon RB, Lennette EH, Sandrock RS. The varied clinical manifestations of Coxsackie viral infections. Arch Intern Med. 1959;103:63.
115. Halfon N, Spector SA. Fatal echovirus type 11 infections. Am J Dis Child. 1981;135:1017.
116. Fukuyama Y, Ando T, Yokota J. Acute fulminant myoglobinuric polymyositis with picornavirus-like crystals. J Neurol Neurosurg Psychiatry. 1977;40:775.
117. Gyorkey F, Cabral GA, Gyorkey PK, et al. Coxsackievirus aggregates in muscle cells of a polymyositis patient. Intervirology. 1978;10:69.
118. Schiraldi O, Iandolo E. Polymyositis accompanying coxsackie virus B2 infection. Infection. 1978;6:32.
119. Josselson J, Pula T, Sadler JH. Acute rhabdomyolysis associated with echovirus 9 infection. Arch Intern Med. 1980;140:1671.
120. Jehn UW, Fink MW. Myositis, myoglobinemia, and myoglobinuria associated with enterovirus echo 9 infection. Arch Neurol. 1980;33:457.
121. Bowles NE, Dubowitz V, Sewry CA, et al. Dermatomyositis, polymyositis, and Coxsackie-B-virus infection. Lancet. 1987;1:1004.
122. De Renck J, De Coster W, Inderadjaja N. Acute viral polymyositis with predominant diaphragm involvement. J Neurol Sci. 1977;33:453.
123. Smith WG. Adult heart disease due to the Coxsackie virus group B. Br Heart J. 1966;28:204.
124. Helin M, Savola J, Lapinleimu K. Cardiac manifestations during a Coxsackie B5 epidemic. Br Med J. 1968;2:97.
125. Grist NR. Coxsackie virus infections of the heart. In: Waterson AP, ed. Recent Advances in Clinical Virology. Edinburgh: Churchill Livingstone; 1977:141.
126. Grist NR, Bell EJ. A six-year study of coxsackievirus B infections in heart disease. J Hyg (Lond). 1974;73:165.
127. Ayutha PSN, Jayavasu JJ, Pongpanich B. Coxsackie group B virus and primary myocardial disease in infants and children. Am Heart J. 1974;88:311.
128. Sainani GS, Krompotic E, Slodki SJ. Adult heart disease due to the Coxsackie virus B infection. Medicine (Baltimore). 1968;47:133.
129. Russell SJM, Bell EJ. Echoviruses and carditis. Lancet. 1970;1:784.
130. Grist NR, Bell EJ. Coxsackieviruses and the heart. Am Heart J. 1969;77:295.
131. Lerner AM, Wilson FM. Virus myocardiopathy. Prog Med Virol. 1973;15:63.
132. Woodruff JF. Viral myocarditis. Am J Pathol. 1980;101:427.
133. Grist NR, Bell EJ. Coxsackie virus and heart diseases. Br Med J. 1968;3:556.
134. Grist NR, Bell EJ, Assad F. Enteroviruses in human disease. Prog Med Virol. 1978;24:114.
135. Meehan WF, Bertrand CA. Ventricular tachycardia associated with echovirus infection. JAMA. 1970;212:1701.
136. Schleissner LA, Fiala M, Imagawa DT, et al. Application of systolic time intervals to acute cardiomyopathy with echovirus 2. Chest. 1976;69:563.
137. Kanra G, Dogruel N, Tinaztepe K, et al. Myocarditis caused by echovirus 11 virus. Turk J Pediatr. 1978;20:24.
138. Lewes D, Rainford DJ, Lane WF. Symptomless myocarditis and myalgia in viral and *Mycoplasma pneumoniae* infections. Br Heart J. 1974;36:924.
139. Van Loon GR, Masson AM. Viral pericarditis. Can Med Assoc J. 1968;99:163.
140. Bell EJ, Grist NR. Echoviruses, carditis, and acute pleurodynia. Lancet. 1970;1:326.
141. Berkovich S, Rodriguez-Torres R, Lin J-S. Virologic studies in children with acute myocarditis. Am J Dis Child. 1968;115:207.
142. Johnson RT, Portnoy B, Rogers NG, et al. Acute benign pericarditis: Virologic study of 34 patients. Arch Intern Med. 1961;108:823.
143. Shimizu C, Rambaud C, Cheron G, et al. Molecular identification of viruses in sudden infant death associated with myocarditis and pericarditis. Pediatr Infect Dis J. 1995;14:584.
144. Martin AB, Webber S, Fricker FJ, et al. Acute myocarditis. Rapid diagnosis by PCR in children. Circulation. 1994;90:330.
145. Lozinski GM, Davis GG, Krous HF, et al. Adenovirus myocarditis: Retrospective diagnosis by gene amplification from formalin-fixed, paraffin-embedded tissues. Hum Pathol. 1994;25:831.
146. Hildebrandt HM, Massab HF, Willis PW. Influenza virus pericarditis. Am J Dis Child. 1962;104:579.
147. Fatal mumps myocarditis in England. MMWR Morb Mortal Wkly Rep. 1980;27:425.
148. Caldera R, Sarrut S, Mallet R, et al. Existetil des complications cardiaques de la vaccine? Semin Hop Paris. 1961;37:1281.
149. Woodruff JF, Woodruff JJ. Involvement of T lymphocytes in the pathogenesis of coxsackievirus B3 heart disease. J Immunol. 1974;113:1726.
150. Rose NR, Wolfgram LJ, Herskowitz A, et al. Postinfectious autoimmunity: Two distinct phases of coxsackievirus B3–induced myocarditis. Ann NY Acad Sci. 1986;475:146.
151. Paque RE, Strauss DC, Nealon TJ, et al. Fractionation and immunologic assessment of KCl-extracted cardiac antigens in coxsackievirus B3 viral–induced myocarditis. J Immunol. 1979;123:358.
152. Gauntt CJ, Arizpe HM, Higdon AL, et al. Anti-coxsackievirus B3 neutralizing antibodies with pathological potential. Eur Heart J. 1991;12:124.
153. Sainani GS, Dekate MP, Rao CP. Heart disease caused by coxsackievirus B infection. Br Heart J. 1975;37:819.
154. Smith WG. Coxsackie B myopericarditis in adults. Am Heart J. 1970;80:34.
155. Koontz CH, Ray CG. The role of Coxsackie group B virus infections in sporadic myopericarditis. Am Heart J. 1971;82:750.
156. Woods JD, Nimmo MJ, MacKay-Scollay EM. Acute transmural myocardial infarction associated with active Coxsackie virus B infection. Am Heart J. 1975;89:283.
157. Lau RC. Coxsackie B virus–specific IgM responses in coronary care unit patients. J Med Virol. 1986;18:193.
158. Griffiths PD, Hannington G, Booth JC. Coxsackie B virus infection and myocardial infarction. Lancet. 1980;1:1387.
159. Desaneto A, Bullington JD, Bullington RH, et al. Coxsackie B5 heart disease. Demonstration of inferolateral wall myocardial necrosis. Am J Med. 1980;68:295.
160. Narula J, Khaw BA, Dec GW, et al. Brief report: Recognition of acute myocarditis masquerading as acute myocardial infarction. N Engl J Med. 1993;328:100.
161. Sutton GC, Harding HB, Truehart RP, et al. Coxsackie B4 myocarditis in an adult: Successful isolation of virus from ventricular myocardium. Aerospace Med. 1967;38:66.
162. Jin O, Sole MJ, Butany JW, et al. Detection of enterovirus RNA in myocardial biopsies from patients with myocarditis and cardiomyopathy using gene amplification by polymerase chain reaction. Circulation. 1990;82:8.
163. Weiss LM, Movahed LA, Billingham ME, et al. Detection of coxsackievirus B3 RNA in myocardial tissues by polymerase chain reaction. Am J Pathol. 1991;138:497.
164. Feldman AM, McNamara D. Myocarditis. N Engl J Med. 2000;343:1388.
165. Drucker NA, Colan SD, Lewis AB, et al. γ-Globulin treatment of acute myocarditis in the pediatric population. Circulation. 1994;89:252.
166. Latham RD, Mulrow JP, Virmani R, et al. Recently diagnosed idiopathic dilated cardiomyopathy: Incidence of myocarditis and efficacy of prednisone therapy. Am Heart J. 1989;117:876.
167. Mason JW, O'Connell JB, Herskowitz A, et al. A clinical trial of immunosuppressive therapy for myocarditis. N Engl J Med. 1995;333:269.
168. Garg A, Shaiu J, Guyatt G. The ineffectiveness of immunosuppressive therapy in lymphocytic myocarditis: An overview. Ann Intern Med. 1998;129:317.
169. Rotbart HA. Pleconaril therapy of potentially life-threatening enterovirus infections. 36th Annual Meeting of the Infectious Disease Society of America, Denver, 1998. Infectious Disease Society of America.
170. Gibbons JE, Goldbloom RB, Dobell ARC. Rapidly developing pericardial constriction in childhood following acute nonspecific pericarditis. Am J Cardiol. 1965;15:863.
171. Howard EJ, Maier HC. Constrictive pericarditis following acute Coxsackie viral pericarditis. Am Heart J. 1968;75:247.
172. Matthews JD, Cameron SJ, George M. Constrictive pericarditis following Coxsackie virus infection. Thorax. 1970;25:624.
173. Lee KJ, McCrindle BW, Bohn DJ, et al. Clinical outcomes of acute myocarditis in childhood. Heart. 1999;82:226.
174. McCarthy RE III, Boehmer JP, Hruban RH, et al. Long-term outcome of fulminant myocarditis as compared with acute (nonfulminant) myocarditis. N Engl J Med. 2000;342:690.

175. Codd MB, Sugrue DD, Gersh BJ, et al. Epidemiology of idiopathic dilated and hypertrophic cardiomyopathy. A population-based study in Olmsted County, Minnesota, 1975-1984. Circulation. 1989;80:564.

176. Weiss LM, Liu XF, Chang KL, et al. Detection of enteroviral RNA in idiopathic dilated cardiomyopathy and other human cardiac tissues. J Clin Invest. 1991;90:156.

177. Andreoletti L, Hober D, Decoene C, et al. Detection of enteroviral RNA by polymerase chain reaction in endomyocardial tissue of patients with chronic cardiac diseases. J Med Virol. 1996;48:53.

178. Giacca M, Severini GM, Mestroni L, et al. Low frequency of detection by nested polymerase chain reaction of enterovirus ribonucleic acid in endomyocardial tissue of patients with idiopathic dilated cardiomyopathy. J Am Coll Cardiol. 1994;24:1033.

179. de Leeuw N, Melchers WJG, Balk AHMM, et al. No evidence for persistent enterovirus infection in patients with end-stage idiopathic dilated cardiomyopathy. J Infect Dis. 1998;178:256.

180. Griffin LD, Kearney D, Ni J, et al. Analysis of formalin-fixed and frozen myocardial autopsy samples for viral genome in childhood myocarditis and dilated cardiomyopathy with endocardial fibroelastosis using polymerase chain reaction (PCR). Cardiovasc Pathol. 1995;4:3.

181. Grasso M, Arbustini E, Silini E, et al. Search for coxsackievirus B3 RNA in idiopathic dilated cardiomyopathy using gene amplification by polymerase chain reaction. Am J Cardiol. 1992;69:658.

182. Muir P, Nicholson F, Illavia SJ, et al. Serological and molecular evidence of enterovirus infection in patients with end-stage dilated cardiomyopathy. Heart. 1996;76:243.

183. Baker DA, Phillips CA. Maternal and neonatal infection with coxsackievirus. Obstet Gynecol. 1980;55:12.

184. Talsma M, Vegting M, Hess J. Generalized Coxsackie A9 infection in a neonate presenting with pericarditis. Br Heart J. 1984;52:683.

185. Wright HT, Landing BH, Lennette EH, et al. Fatal infection in an infant associated with Coxsackie virus group A, type 16. N Engl J Med. 1963;268:1041.

186. Gear JHS, Measroch V. Coxsackievirus infection of the newborn. Prog Med Virol. 1973;15:42.

187. Modlin JF. Perinatal echovirus infection: Insights from a literature of 61 cases of serious infection and 16 outbreaks in nurseries. Rev Infect Dis. 1986;8:918.

188. Modlin JF, Kinney JS. Perinatal enterovirus infections. In: Aronoff SC, Hughes WT, Kohl S, et al, eds. Advances in Pediatric Infectious Diseases, v. 2. Chicago: Year Book Medical Publishers; 1986:57.

189. Kinney JS, McCray E, Kaplan JE, et al. Risk factors associated with echovirus 11 infection in a newborn nursery. Pediatr Infect Dis J. 1986;5:192.

190. Modlin JF. Fatal echovirus 11 disease in premature neonates. Pediatrics. 1980;66:775.

191. Piraino FF, Sedmak G, Raab K. Echovirus 11 infections of newborns with mortality during the 1979 enterovirus season in Milwaukee, Wis. Public Health Rep. 1982;97:346.

192. Modlin JF, Kinney JS. Perinatal enterovirus infections. In: Aronoff SC, Hughes WT, Kohl S, et al, eds. Advances in Pediatric Infectious Diseases, v. 2. Chicago: Year Book Medical Publishers; 1987.

193. Modlin JF, Bowman M. Perinatal transmission of Coxsackie B3 virus in a murine model. J Infect Dis. 1987;156:21.

194. Modlin JF, Polk BF, Horton P, et al. Perinatal echovirus 11 infection: Risk of transmission during a community outbreak. N Engl J Med. 1981;305:368.

195. Jones MJU, Kolb M, Votava HJ, et al. Intrauterine echovirus type 11 infection. Mayo Clin Proc. 1980;55:509.

196. Reyes MP, Ostrea EM, Roskamp J, et al. Disseminated neonatal echovirus 11 disease following antenatal maternal infection with a virus-positive cervix and virus negative gastrointestinal tract. J Med Virol. 1983;12:155.

197. Yoshioka I, Horstmann DM. Viremia in infection due to echo virus type 9. N Engl J Med. 1961;262:224.

198. Kaplan MH, Klein SW, McPhee J, et al. Group B coxsackievirus infections in infants younger than three months of age: A serious childhood illness. Rev Infect Dis. 1983;5:1019.

199. Kunin CM. Virus-tissue union and the pathogenesis of enterovirus infections. J Immunol. 1962;88:556.

200. Eichenwald HF, Kotsevalov O. Immunologic responses of premature and full-term infants to infection with certain viruses. Pediatrics. 1960;25:829.

201. Rager-Zisman B, Allison AC. The role of antibody and host cells in the resistance of mice against infection by Coxsackie B-3 virus. J Gen Virol. 1973;19:329.

202. Woodruff J. Lack of correlation between neutralizing antibody production and suppression of Coxsackie B-3 replication in target organs: Evidence for involvement of mononuclear inflammatory cells in host defense. J Immunol. 1979;123:31.

203. Berry PJ, Nagington J. Fatal infection with echovirus 11. Arch Dis Child. 1982;57:22.

204. Drew JH. Echo 11 virus outbreak in a nursery associated with myocarditis. Aust J Pediatr. 1973;9:90.

205. Georgieff MK, Johnson DE, Thompson TR, et al. Fulminant hepatic necrosis in an infant with perinatally acquired echovirus 21 infection. Pediatr Infect Dis J. 1987;6:71.

206. Spector SA, Straube RC. Protean manifestations of perinatal enterovirus infection. West J Med. 1983;138:847.

207. Speer ME, Yawn DH. Fatal hepatoadrenal necrosis in the neonate associated with echovirus types 11 and 12 presenting as a surgical emergency. J Pediatr Surg. 1984;19:591.

208. Wreghitt TG, Gandy GM, King A, et al. Fatal neonatal echo 7 virus infection (Letter). Lancet. 1984;2:465.

209. Chambon M, Delage C, Bailly J-L, et al. Fatal hepatic necrosis in a neonate with echovirus 20 infection: Use of the polymerase chain reaction to detect enterovirus in liver tissue. Clin Infect Dis. 1997;24:523.

210. Mostoufizadeh G, Lack EE, Gang DL, et al. Postmortem manifestations of echovirus 11 sepsis in five newborn infants. Hum Pathol. 1983;14:819.

211. Johnston JM, Overall JC. Intravenous immunoglobulin in disseminated neonatal echovirus 11 infection. Pediatr Infect Dis J. 1989;8:254.

212. McKinney RE, Katz SL, Wilfert CM. Chronic enteroviral meningoencephalitis in agammaglobulinemic patients. Rev Infect Dis. 1987;9:334.

213. O'Neil KM, Pallansch MA, Winkelstein JA, et al. Chronic group A coxsackievirus infection in agammaglobulinemia: Demonstration of genomic variation of serotypically identical isolates persistently excreted from the same patient. J Infect Dis. 1988;157:183.

214. Webster ADB, Rotbart HA, Warner T, et al. Diagnosis of enterovirus brain disease in hypogammaglobulinemic patients by polymerase chain reaction. Clin Infect Dis. 1993;17:657.

215. Rotbart HA, Kinsella JP, Wasserman RL. Persistent enterovirus infection in culture-negative meningoencephalitis: Demonstration by enzymatic amplification. J Infect Dis. 1990;161:787.

216. Webster ADB. Echovirus disease in hypogammaglobulinaemic patients. Clin Rheum Dis. 1984;10:189.

217. Mease PJ, Ochs HD, Wedgewood RJ. Successful treatment of echovirus meningoencephalitis and myositis-fasciitis with intravenous immune globulin therapy in a patient with X-linked hypogammaglobulinemia. N Engl J Med. 1981;304:1278.

218. Rotbart HA, Webster ADB. Treatment of potentially life-threatening enterovirus infections with pleconaril. Clin Infect Dis. 2001;32:228.

219. Biggs DD, Toorkey BC, Carrigan DR, et al. Disseminated echovirus infection complicating bone marrow transplantation. Am J Med. 1990;88:421.

220. Aquino VM, Farah RA, Lee ME, et al. Disseminated Coxsackie A9 infection complicating bone marrow transplantation. Pediatr Infect Dis J. 1996;15:1053.

221. Galama JMD, de Leeuw N, Wittebol S, et al. Prolonged enteroviral infection in a patient who developed pericarditis and heart failure after bone marrow transplantation. Clin Infect Dis. 1996;22:1004.

222. Townsend TR, Bolyard EA, Yolken RH, et al. Outbreak of Coxsackie A1 gastroenteritis: A complication of bone-marrow transplantation. Lancet. 1982;1:820.

223. Kono R. Apollo 11 disease or acute hemorrhagic conjunctivitis: A pandemic of a new enterovirus infection of the eyes. Am J Epidemiol. 1975;101:383.

224. Kono R, Sasagawa A, Ishii K, et al. Pandemic of new type of conjunctivitis. Lancet. 1972;ii:1191.

225. Mirkovic RR, Kono R, Yin-Murphy M, et al. Enterovirus type 70: The etiologic agent of pandemic acute hemorrhagic conjunctivitis. Bull World Health Organ 1973;49:341.

226. Mirkovic RR, Schmidt NJ, Yin-Murphy M, et al. Enterovirus etiology of the 1970 Singapore epidemic of acute conjunctivitis. Intervirology. 1974;4:119.

227. Yin-Murphy M, Lim KH, Yo YM. A coxsackievirus type A24 epidemic of acute conjunctivitis. Southeast Asian J Trop Med Public Health. 1976;7:1.

228. Yin-Murphy M, Lim KH. Picornavirus epidemic conjunctivitis in Singapore. Lancet. 1972;2:857.

229. Higgins PG, Scott RJ, Davies PM, et al. A comparative study of viruses associated with acute hemorrhagic conjunctivitis. J Clin Pathol. 1974;27:292.

230. Christopher S, Theogaraj S, Godbole S, et al. An epidemic of acute hemorrhagic conjunctivitis due to coxsackievirus A24. J Infect Dis. 1982;146:16.

231. Kono R, Miyamura K, Tajiri E, et al. Neurologic complications associated with acute hemorrhagic conjunctivitis virus infection and its serologic confirmation. J Infect Dis. 1974;129:590.

232. Ray I, Roy IS, Sarkhar JK, et al. Laboratory investigations of an epidemic of conjunctivitis in Calcutta: A preliminary report. Bull Calcutta Sch Trop Med. 1972;20:1.

233. Hierholzer JC, Hilliard KA, Esposito JJ. Serosurvey for "acute hemorrhagic conjunctivitis" virus (enterovirus 70) antibodies in the southeastern United States, with review of the literature and some epidemiologic implications. Am J Epidemiol. 1975;102:533.

234. Sklar VE, Patriarca PA, Onorato IM, et al. Clinical findings and results of treatment in an outbreak of acute hemorrhagic conjunctivitis in southern Florida. Am J Ophthalmol. 1983;95:45.

235. Kuritsky JN, Weaver JH, Bernard KW, et al. An outbreak of acute hemorrhagic conjunctivitis in central Minnesota. Am J Ophthalmol. 1983;96:449.

236. Acute hemorrhagic conjunctivitis caused by coxsackievirus A24—Caribbean. MMWR Morb Mortal Wkly Rep. 1987;36:245.

237. Acute hemorrhagic conjunctivitis caused by coxsackievirus A24 variant—Puerto Rico. MMWR Morb Mortal Wkly Rep. 1988;37:123.

238. Miyamura K, Tanimura M, Takeda N, et al. Evolution of enterovirus 70 in nature: All isolates were recently derived from a common ancestor. Arch Virol. 1986;89:1.

239. Stanton GJ, Langford MP, Baron S. Effect of interferon, elevated temperature, and cell type on replication of acute hemorrhagic conjunctivitis viruses. Infect Immun. 1977;18:370.

240. Goh KT, Doraisingham S, Yin-Murphy M. An epidemic of acute conjunctivitis caused by enterovirus-70 in Singapore in 1980. Southeast Asian J Trop Med Public Health. 1981;12:473.

241. Arnow PM, Hierholzer JC, Higbee J, et al. Acute hemorrhagic conjunctivitis: A mixed virus outbreak among Vietnamese refugees on Guam. Am J Epidemiol. 1977;105:69.

242. Onorato IM, Morens DM, Schonberger LB, et al. Acute hemorrhagic conjunctivitis caused by enterovirus type 70: An epidemic in American Samoa. Am J Trop Med Hyg. 1985;34:984.

243. Kono R, Sasagawa A, Miyamura K, et al. Serologic characterization and seroepidemiologic studies on acute hemorrhagic conjunctivitis (AHC) virus. Am J Epidemiol. 1975;101:444.

244. Kono R, Uchida Y. Acute hemorrhagic conjunctivitis. Ophthalmol Dig. 1977;39:14.

245. Kono R, Miyamura K, Tajiri E, et al. Virological and serological studies of neurological complications of acute hemorrhagic conjunctivitis in Thailand. J Infect Dis. 1977;135:706.

246. Hung TS, Sung SM, Liang HC, et al. Radiculomyelitis following acute hemorrhagic conjunctivitis. Brain. 1976;99:771.

247. Katiyar BC, Misra S, Singh RB, et al. Adult polio-like syndrome following enterovirus 70 conjunctivitis (natural history of the disease). Acta Neurol Scand. 1983;67:263.

248. Wadia NH, Katrak SM, Misra VP, et al. Polio-like motor paralysis associated with acute hemorrhagic conjunctivitis in an outbreak in 1981 in Bombay. J Infect Dis. 1983;147:660.

249. Kono R, Uchida N, Sasagawa A, et al. Neurovirulence of acute hemorrhagic conjunctivitis virus in monkeys. Lancet. 1973;1:61.

250. Yin-Murphy M. Simple tests for the diagnosis of picornavirus epidemic conjunctivitis (acute haemorrhagic conjunctivitis). Bull World Health Organ. 1976;54:675.

251. Lansky LL, Krugman S, Huq G. Anicteric Coxsackie B hepatitis. J Pediatr. 1979;94:64.

252. Leggiadro RJ, Chwatsky DN, Zucker SW. Echovirus 3 infection associated with anicteric hepatitis. Am J Dis Child. 1982;136:744.

253. O'Shaughnessey WJ, Buechner HA. Hepatitis associated with a Coxsackie B5 virus infection during late pregnancy. JAMA. 1962;179:71.

254. Morris JA, Elisberg BL, Pond WL, et al. Hepatitis associated with Coxsackie virus group A, type 4. N Engl J Med. 1962;267:1230.

255. Sun NC, Smith VM. Hepatitis associated with myocarditis: Unusual manifestation of infection with Coxsackie virus group B, type 3. N Engl J Med. 1966;274:190.

256. Gregor GR, Geller SA, Walker GF, et al. Coxsackie hepatitis in an adult with ultrastructural demonstration of the virus. Mt Sinai J Med. 1975;42:575.

257. Arnesjo B, Eden T, Ihse I, et al. Enterovirus infections in acute pancreatitis—A possible etiologic connection. Scand J Gastroenterol. 1976;11:645.

258. Imrle CW, Ferguson JC, Sommerville RG. Coxsackie and mumps virus infection in a prospective study of acute pancreatitis. Gut. 1977;18:53.

259. Craighead JE. The role of viruses in the pathogenesis of pancreatic disease and diabetes mellitus. Prog Med Virol. 1975;19:162.

260. Ursing B. Acute pancreatitis in Coxsackie B infection. Br Med J. 1973;3:524.

261. Ramos-Alverez M, Olarte J. Diarrheal diseases of children. Am J Dis Child. 1964;107:218.

262. Steinhoff MC. Viruses and diarrhea—A review. Am J Dis Child. 1978;132:302.

263. Yow DM, Melnick JL, Blattner JR, et al. Enteroviruses in infantile diarrhea. Am J Hyg. 1963;77:283.

264. Patel JR, Daniel J, Mathan VI. An epidemic of acute diarrhoea in rural southern India associated with echovirus type 11 infection. J Hyg (Lond). 1985;95:483.

265. Oregan S, Robitaille P, Mongeau J, et al. The hemolytic-uremic syndrome associated with echo 22 infection. Clin Pediatr. 1980;19:125.

266. Glasgow LA, Balduzzi P. Isolation of Coxsackie virus group A, type 4, from a patient with hemolytic uremic syndrome. N Engl J Med. 1965;273:754.

267. Ray CG, Tucker VL, Harris DJ, et al. Enteroviruses associated with the hemolytic-uremic syndrome. Pediatrics. 1970;46:378.

268. Aronson MD, Phillips CA. Coxsackievirus B5 infections in acute oliguric renal failure. J Infect Dis. 1975;132:303.

269. Craighead JE, Mahoney EM, Carver DH, et al. Orchitis due to Coxsackie virus group B, type 5. N Engl J Med. 1962;267:498.

270. Welliver RC, Cherry JD. Aseptic meningitis and orchitis associated with echovirus 6 infection. J Pediatr. 1978;92:239.

271. Ager EA, Felsenstein WC, Alexander ER, et al. An epidemic of illness due to Coxsackie virus group B, type 2. JAMA. 1964;187:251.

272. Willems WR, Hornig C, Bauer H, et al. A case of Coxsackie A9 virus infection with orchitis. J Med Virol. 1978;3:137.

273. Murphy AM, Simmul R. Coxsackie B4 virus infections in New South Wales during 1962. Med J Aust. 1964;2:443.

274. Blotzer JW, Myers AR. Echovirus-associated polyarthritis. Report of a case with synovial fluid and synovial histologic characterization. Arthritis Rheum. 1978;21:978.

275. Kujala G, Newman JH. Isolation of echovirus type 11 from synovial fluid in acute monocytic arthritis. Arthritis Rheum. 1985;28:98.

276. Van der Sar A. Acute infectious lymphocytosis with echovirus type 25. West Ind Med J. 1979;28:185.

277. Norwitz MS, Moore GT. Acute infectious lymphocytosis: An etiologic study of an outbreak. N Engl J Med. 1968;279:399.

278. Barrett-Connor E. Is insulin-dependent diabetes mellitus caused by coxsackievirus B infection? A review of the epidemiologic evidence. Rev Infect Dis. 1985;7:207.

279. Craighead JE, Huber SA, Sriram S. Animal models of picornavirus-induced autoimmune disease: Their possible relevance to human disease. Lab Invest. 1990;63:432.

280. Banatvala JE. Insulin-dependent (juvenile-onset, type 1) diabetes mellitus Coxsackie B viruses revisited. Prog Med Virol. 1987;34:33.

281. Yoon JW. The role of viruses and environmental factors in the induction of diabetes. Curr Top Microbiol Immunol. 1990;164:95.

282. Rewers M, Atkinson M. The possible role of enteroviruses in diabetes mellitus. In: Rotbart HA, ed. Human Enterovirus Infections. Washington, DC: American Society for Microbiology; 1995:353.

283. Gamble DR, Taylor KW. Seasonal incidence of diabetes mellitus. Br Med J. 1969;3:631.

284. Gleason RE, Kahn CB, Funk IB, et al. Seasonal incidence of insulin-dependent diabetes in Massachusetts, 1964-1973. Int J Epidemiol. 1982;11:39.

285. Rewers M, LaPorte R, Walczak M, et al. Apparent epidemic of insulin-dependent diabetes mellitus in midwestern Poland. Diabetes. 1987;36:106.

286. Huff JC, Hierholzer JC, Farris WA. An "outbreak" of juvenile diabetes mellitus: Consideration of a viral etiology. Am J Epidemiol. 1974;100:277.

287. Hierholzer JC, Farris WA. Follow-up of children infected in a coxsackievirus B3 and B4 outbreak: No evidence of diabetes mellitus. J Infect Dis. 1974;129:741.

288. Dippe SE, Bennett PH, Miller M, et al. Lack of causal association between Coxsackie B4 virus infection and diabetes. Lancet. 1975;1:1314.

289. Hartig PC, Madge GE, Webb SR. Diversity within a human isolate of Coxsackie B4: Relationship to viral-induced diabetes mellitus. J Med Virol. 1983;11:23.

290. Andreoletti L, Hober D, Hober-Vandenberghe C, et al. Detection of Coxsackie B virus RNA sequences in whole blood samples from adult patients at the onset of type I diabetes mellitus. J Med Virol. 1997;52:121.

291. Clements GB, Galbraith DN, Taylor KW. Coxsackie B virus infection and onset of childhood diabetes. Lancet. 1995;346:221.

292. Yoon JW, Austin M, Onodera T, et al. Virus-induced diabetes mellitus: Isolation of a virus from the pancreas of a child with diabetic ketoacidosis. N Engl J Med. 1979;300:1173.

293. Gladish R, Hofmann W, Waldherr R. Myocarditis and insulitis in coxsackievirus infection. Z Kardiol. 1976;65:835.

294. Helfand RF, Gary HE Jr., Freeman CY, et al. Serologic evidence of an association between enteroviruses and onset of type 1 diabetes mellitus. J Infect Dis. 1995;172:1206.

295. D'Alessio DJ. A case-control study of group B coxsackievirus immunoglobulin M antibody prevalence and HLA-DR antigens in newly diagnosed cases of insulin-dependent diabetes mellitus. Am J Epidemiol. 1992;135:1331.

296. Gamble DR, Cumming H. Coxsackie B virus and juvenile-onset diabetes. Lancet. 1985;2:455.

297. Tuvemo T, Dahlquist G, Frisk G, et al. The Swedish childhood diabetes study. III. IgM against Coxsackie B viruses in newly diagnosed type 1 (insulin-dependent) diabetic children—No evidence of increased antibody frequency. Diabetologia. 1989;32:745.

298. Frisk G, Fohlman J, Kobbah M, et al. High frequency of Coxsackie-B-virus–specific IgM in children developing type I diabetes during a period of high diabetes morbidity. J Med Virol. 1985;17:219.

299. Oldstone MBA. Molecular mimicry and autoimmune disease. Cell. 1987;50:819.

300. See DM, Tilles JG. Pathogenesis of virus-induced diabetes in mice. J Infect Dis. 1995;171:1131.

301. Hiltunen M, Hyoty H, Knip M, et al. Islet cell antibody seroconversion in children is temporally associated with enterovirus infections. J Infect Dis. 1997;175:554.

302. Solimena M, De Camilli P. Coxsackieviruses and diabetes. Nat Med. 1995;1:25.

303. Rosen L, Schmidt NJ, Kern J. Toluca 1, a newly recognized enterovirus. Arch Ges Virusforsch. 1973;40:132.

304. Schieble JH, Fox VL, Lennette EH. A probable new human picornavirus associated with respiratory disease. Am J Epidemiol. 1967;85:297.

305. Hagiwara A, Yoneyama T, Takami S, et al. Genetic and phenotypic characteristics of enterovirus 71 isolates from patients with encephalitis and with hand, foot, and mouth disease. Arch Virol. 1984;79:273.

306. Hashimoto I, Hagiwara A, Kodama H. Neurovirulence in cynomolgus monkeys of enterovirus 71 isolated from a patient with hand, foot, and mouth disease. Arch Virol. 1978;56:257.

307. Schmidt NJ, Lennette EH, Ho HH. An apparently new enterovirus isolated from patients with disease of the central nervous system. J Infect Dis. 1974;129:304.

308. Deibel R, Gross L, Collins DN. Isolation of a new enterovirus. Proc Soc Exp Biol Med. 1975;148:203.

309. Kennett ML, Birch CJ, Lewis FA, et al. Enterovirus type 71 infection in Melbourne. Bull World Health Organ. 1974;51:609.

310. Tagaya I, Takayama R, Hagiwara A. A large-scale epidemic of hand, foot and mouth disease associated with enterovirus 71 infection in Japan in 1978. Jpn J Med Sci Biol. 1981;34:191.

311. Bloomberg J, Lycke E, Ahlfors K, et al. New enterovirus type associated with epidemic of aseptic meningitis and/or hand, foot, and mouth disease. Lancet. 1974;2:122.

312. Moses EB, Narian JP, Hatch MH, et al. Isolation of echovirus type 11 and enterovirus type 71 in a day care winter outbreak. J Arkansas Med Soc. 1987;83:469.

313. Sohier R. Enterovirus type 71 surveillance: France. WHO Wkly Epidemiol Rec. 1979;54:219.

314. Nagy G, Takatsy S, Kukan E, et al. Virological diagnosis of enterovirus type 71 infections: Experiences gained during an epidemic of acute CNS diseases in Hungary in 1978. Arch Virol. 1982;71:217.

315. Chumakov MP, Voroshilova MK, Shindarov L, et al. Enterovirus 71 isolated from cases of poliomyelitis-like disease in Bulgaria. Arch Virol. 1979;60:329.

316. Alexander JP, Baden L, Pallansch MA, et al. Enterovirus 71 infections and neurologic disease—United States, 1977-1991. J Infect Dis. 1994;169:905.

317. Lum LCS, Wong KT, Lam SK, et al. Fatal enterovirus 71 encephalomyelitis. J Pediatr. 1998;133:795.

318. Cardosa MJ, Perera D, Brown BA, et al. Molecular epidemiology of human enterovirus 71 strains and recent outbreaks in the Asia-Pacific region: Comparative analysis of the VP1 and VP4 genes. Emerg Infect Dis. 2003;9:461.

319. Chonmaitree T, Menegus MA, Schervish-Swierkosz EM, et al. Enterovirus 71 infection: Report of an outbreak with two cases of paralysis and a review of the literature. Pediatrics. 1981;67:489.

320. Samuda GM, Chang WK, Yeung CY, et al. Monoplegia caused by enterovirus 71: An outbreak in Hong Kong. Pediatr Infect Dis J. 1987;6:206.

321. Miwa C, Ohtani M, Watanabe H, et al. Epidemic of hand, foot and mouth disease in Gifu prefecture in 1978. Jpn J Med Sci Biol. 1980;33:167.

CHAPTER 170

Hepatitis A Virus

BETH P. BELL

DAVID A. ANDERSON

STEPHEN M. FEINSTONE

Hepatitis A is generally an acute, self-limiting infection of the liver by an enterically transmitted picornavirus, hepatitis A virus (HAV). Infection may be asymptomatic or result in acute hepatitis. Rarely, fulminant hepatitis can ensue. Although the duration and severity of symptoms vary widely, hepatitis A infections never cause chronic liver disease.

HISTORY

The earliest accounts of contagious jaundice are from ancient China.[1] Although the symptoms that were described are similar to those currently found in people with hepatitis A, it should be remembered that a number of other infections produce similar symptoms. The earliest outbreaks of hepatitis that were almost certainly hepatitis A were documented in Europe in the 17th and 18th centuries, especially during periods of war. From 1855, the disease became known as "catarrhal jaundice" because the pathologists Bamberger and Virchow believed that the disease was caused by blockage of the common bile duct by a plug of inspissated mucus.[2] The first suggestion that the disease was caused by an infectious agent was made by McDonald, who unable to demonstrate the involvement of enteric bacteria, suggested that the infection might be caused by a virus.[3] Shortly thereafter, Cockayne proposed that the sporadic and the epidemic forms of jaundice were manifestations of the same disease.[4] In 1923, Blumer analyzed a large number of epidemics of hepatitis in the United States and identified its predilection for young adults and children and peak incidence in winter and fall.[5] The first indication of the existence of a second form of hepatitis came in 1833, when an outbreak of hepatitis was observed in shipyard workers who were vaccinated against smallpox with a particular batch of human glycerinated lymph. The disease, which became known as "serum hepatitis," was assumed to be due to a blood-borne infectious agent. During the 1920s and 1930s, other outbreaks that appeared to be associated with the administration of serum or blood were described.

Analysis of epidemics of hepatitis during World War II confirmed the existence of two epidemiologically and etiologically distinct forms of the disease that MacCallum called *infectious hepatitis* and *serum hepatitis*.[6-8] Experimental transmission studies in volunteers soon clarified the major features of the two diseases. Hepatitis A had an incubation period of between 15 and 49 days and was transmitted by the fecal-oral route.[7,9,10] Later studies demonstrated that the virus could be detected in feces or blood during the acute infection, that infection could be transmitted experimentally by both the oral and parenteral routes, and that infection was followed by long-term immunity and could be prevented by prior administration of normal human immune globulin (IG).[5,6,11] In addition, the disease was shown to be associated with a filterable agent resistant to heating at 56° C for 30 minutes and resistant to diethyl ether. In the 1950s and 1960s, Krugman and colleagues[12] expanded these observations by a series of studies in human volunteers that further defined the incubation period, period of infectivity, and period of viremia, and they developed standardized reagents representing hepatitis A and hepatitis B. In 1973, Feinstone and colleagues[13] detected 27-nm virus-like particles in the stools of volunteers infected with hepatitis A and demonstrated that they were aggregated by convalescent but not by preinfection serum, thus indicating that the particles represented the etiologic agent of the disease. The identification of HAV, transmission of the disease to marmosets and chimpanzees, propagation of HAV in cell culture, and molecular cloning of the viral genome ushered in a new era of research that culminated almost two decades later in the development and licensing of effective vaccines.[14-20]

CLASSIFICATION AND PHYSICOCHEMICAL AND BIOLOGIC PROPERTIES OF HEPATITIS A VIRUS

HAV is a member of the Picornaviridae family, which includes the enteroviruses and rhinoviruses of humans, as well as the apthoviruses (foot-and-mouth disease viruses) of hoofed animals and cardioviruses (encephalomyocarditis virus) of mice. Although originally classified as Enterovirus type 72,[21] HAV now has its own genus, *Heparnavirus*, within the Picornaviridae family.[22]

Structure

HAV is a 27- to 28-nm spherical, nonenveloped virus (Fig. 170-1)[13] with a surface structure suggesting icosahedral symmetry.[23] Purification of virus from clinical samples or tissue culture yields three distinct populations of particles[24]: mature hepatitis A virus virions that band at 1.32 to 1.34 g/cm^3 in CsCl and sediment at approximately 160 S (similar to enteroviruses and cardioviruses), a lower-density fraction that bands at about 1.27 g/cm^3 in CsCl and sediments at 70 to 80 S and may represent empty capsids or particles with incomplete genomes, and a high-density fraction (1.4 g/cm^3) that may represent particles with a more open virion structure that allows increased penetration and binding of CsCl to the viral particle. These high-density particles have been shown to contain RNA but tend to be less stable than mature virions.[25,26]

Resistance to Physical and Chemical Agents

HAV is more resistant to heat than other picornaviruses[27] and may be incompletely inactivated (depending on the conditions) by exposure to 60° C for 10 to 12 hours.[28,29] Complete inactivation in food requires heating to greater than 85° C for at least 1 minute.[30,31] HAV may survive for days to weeks in shellfish, water, soil, or marine sediment.[32] Outbreaks of hepatitis A have been reported after ingestion of steamed shellfish, suggesting that the internal temperature achieved by steaming sometimes may be insufficient to destroy the virus.[33] However, HAV can be reliably inactivated by autoclaving (121° C for 30 minutes).[34]

The virus is resistant to most organic solvents and detergents as well as pH as low as 3.[34-36] HAV can be inactivated by many common disinfecting chemicals, including hypochlorite (bleach), and quaternary ammonium formulations containing 23% HCl found in many toilet bowl cleaners.[34] Currently licensed vaccines are inactivated by 1:4000 formalin at room temperature for at least 15 days to exceed complete inactivation by at least 3-fold. As a result of several outbreaks of hepatitis A in hemophiliacs who received factor VIII concentrates that had been treated by a solvent detergent method for inactivation of lipid-enveloped viruses, interest has focused on techniques capable of inactivating nonenveloped viruses without compromising the biologic activity of the proteins of interest.[37] Currently, the most promising techniques are dry heat (80° C for 24 hours), ultraviolet irradiation, or γ-irradiation.[38] Sequential ultrafiltration through 35-nm and 15-nm membranes[39] and pasteurization at 60° C for 10 hours[40] have been validated for inactivation or removal of HAV in commercial albumin and factor VIII preparations.

Genome and Proteins

Although HAV was believed to be a picornavirus and indirect tests suggested an RNA genome, molecular cloning and sequence analysis demonstrated that the HAV genome is composed of single-stranded, positive-sense linear RNA of 7478 nucleotides (strain HM175) and a molecular weight of approximately 2.25×10^6, with an overall structure and gene order typical of picornaviruses.[19,41,42]

The 5′ end of the genome does not have a cap structure but instead has a small, covalently bound protein termed VPg.[43] The genome itself has a long 5′ untranslated region (UTR) beginning with UU, as found in all picornaviruses. This 5′ UTR folds to form a highly ordered secondary structure known as an internal ribosome entry site (IRES) that directs the initiation of translation at the appropriate internal AUG codon, being the AUG after nucleotide 734 in the case of HAV[42]

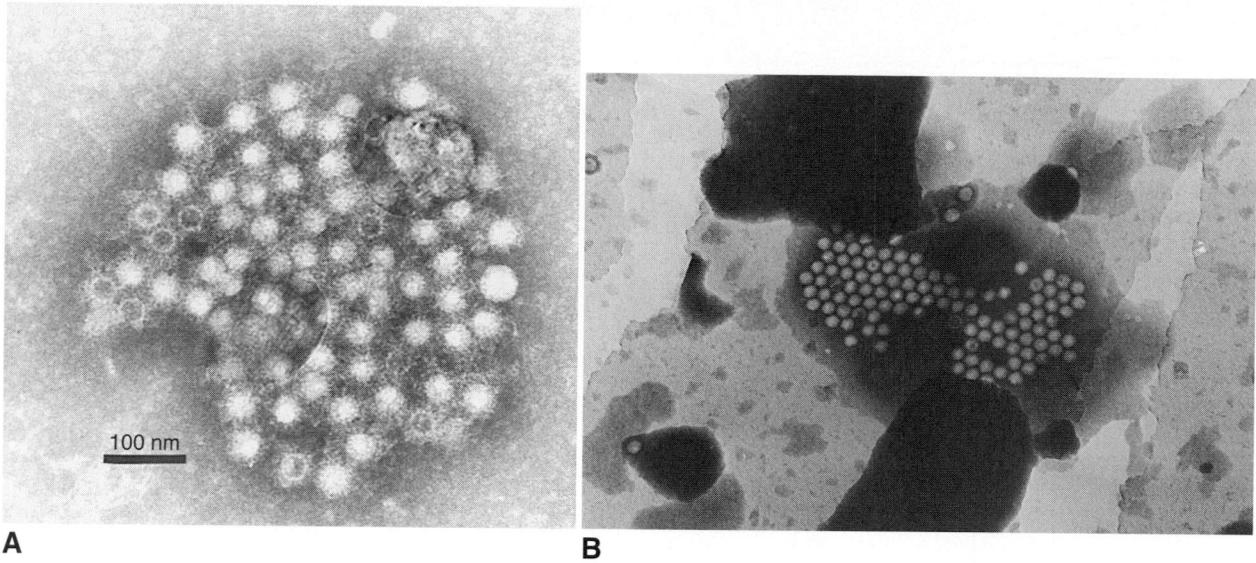

A   **B**

FIGURE 170-1. Electron micrographs of hepatitis A virus particles **(A)** aggregated by antibody, 27 to 28 nm in diameter, and **(B)** highly concentrated, purified hepatitis A virus from human feces.

(Fig. 170-2). This AUG codon begins a single long open reading frame of 6681 nucleotides that encodes a polyprotein 2227 amino acid residues in length. The coding region of picornaviruses has been arbitrarily divided into three parts termed P1, P2, and P3, and the peptides that are ultimately cleaved from the translation products of these regions are referred to as 1A, 1B, 1C, 2A, 2B, 2C, and so forth, in order of translation from the 5′ to the 3′ end of the genome.[44] The HAV genome ends with a 3′ noncoding region of 63 nucleotides that is followed by a poly(A) tail. The four capsid proteins of mature virus particles are coded by the first 2373 nucleotides (P1) and the nonstructural proteins by the remainder (P2 and P3).

The mature HAV particle is composed of four capsid polypeptides as detected first by sodium dodecyl sulfate–polyacrylamide gel elec-

trophoresis and by molecular cloning and nucleic acid sequencing. By analogy with other picornaviruses, these proteins, which are coded within the P1 region, are referred to as virion proteins (VP): VP1 = peptide 1D (molecular weight, 32,800 Da), VP2 = 1B (24,800 Da), VP3 = 1C (27,300 Da), and VP4 = 1A (2500 Da).[45,46] A VP0 protein (1AB) that is the precursor to VP4 and VP2 can also be detected, especially from cell cultures where immature virions (provirions) accumulate in large amounts for HAV relative to other picornaviruses.[47] The VP4 molecule must be liberated during the maturation cleavage of VP0, which converts provirions to virions (see later), but VP4 has never been experimentally determined to be within the virion particle and, at just 23 amino acids, is about one third the size of the VP4 proteins of other picornaviruses.

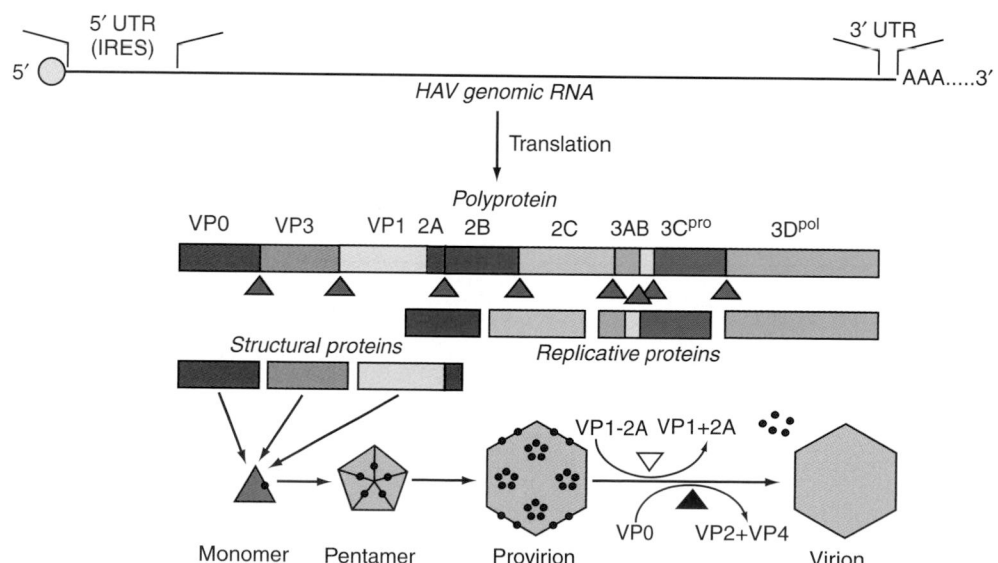

FIGURE 170-2. Organization of the RNA genome of hepatitis A virus, polyprotein cleavage, and viral assembly. The 7.5-kb positive-strand RNA is covalently attached to VPg (5′ end) and has a poly(A) tail. The 5′ untranslated region (UTR) of 734 nucleotides functions as an internal ribosome entry site (IRES) to initiate translation (*vertical arrow*) of the precursor polyprotein of 2227 amino acids. Regions of the polyprotein are indicated according to standard nomenclature. The single viral protease, 3C^pro, cleaves itself from the polyprotein, and subsequently cleaves elsewhere in the polyprotein to yield the structural protein precursors VP0, VP3, and VP1-2A (PX) and replicative proteins 2B, 2C, 3A, 3B, and 3D (RNA-dependent RNA polymerase). VP0, VP3, and VP1-2A probably remain associated as a monomer and then form pentamers that are a stable precursor in capsid formation. Assembly of 12 pentamers together with RNA forms the provirion, after which 2A is susceptible to cleavage by host cell protease(s) (*open arrowhead*). The final maturation cleavage of VP0 to VP2 and VP4 (*solid arrowhead*) is dependent on the encapsidated viral RNA.

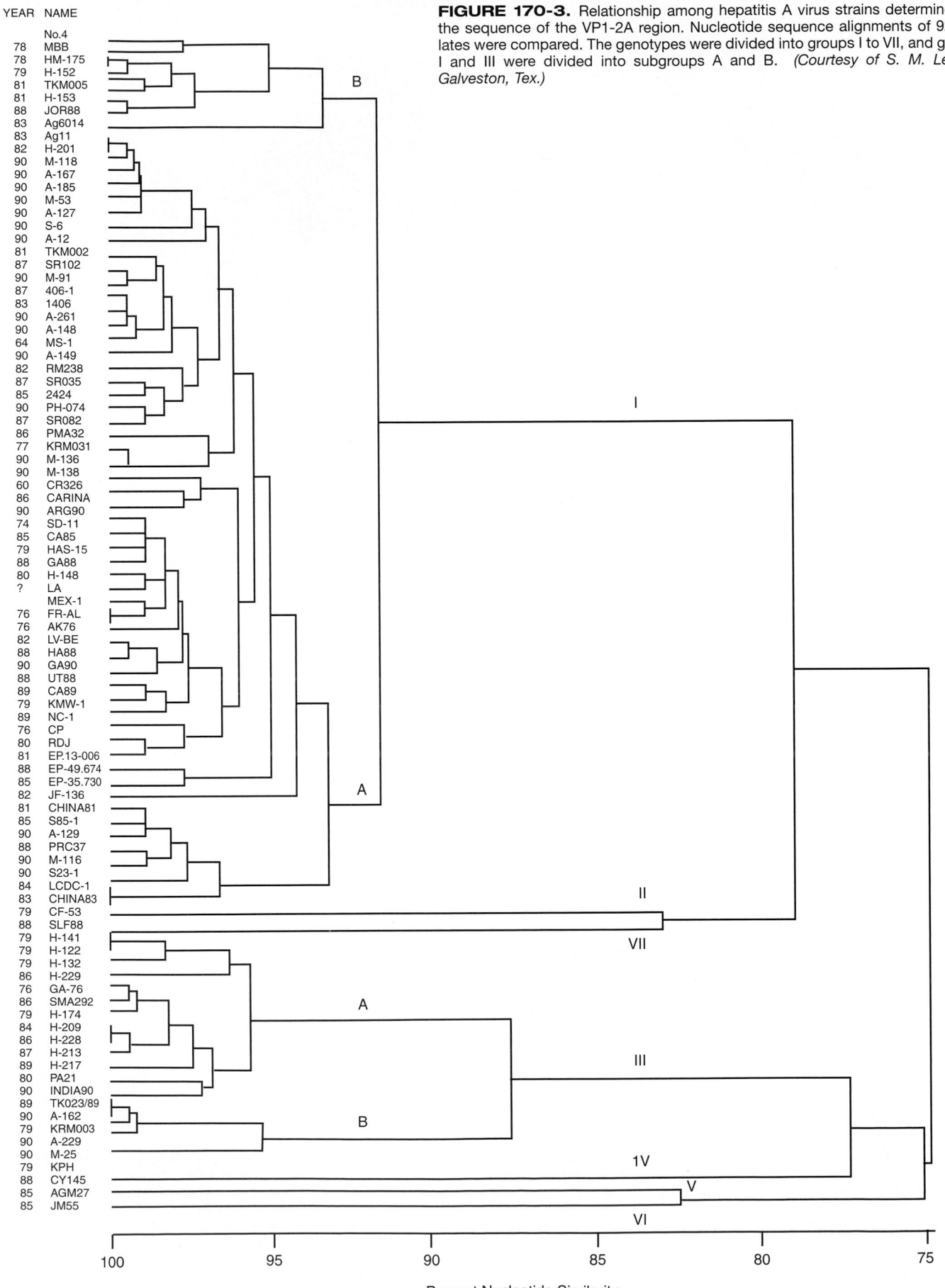

FIGURE 170-3. Relationship among hepatitis A virus strains determined by the sequence of the VP1-2A region. Nucleotide sequence alignments of 92 isolates were compared. The genotypes were divided into groups I to VII, and groups I and III were divided into subgroups A and B. *(Courtesy of S. M. Lemon, Galveston, Tex.)*

Percent Nucleotide Similarity

Assembly of HAV particles proceeds through several steps (see Fig. 170-2). Cleavage of the polyprotein by the 3C protease yields three capsid-related proteins, VP0, VP3, and VP1-2A (also known as PX), that constitute a monomer and subsequently assemble into pentameric subunits.[48,49] Twelve copies of the pentamer then associate with viral RNA to form provirions, or without viral RNA to form empty capsids (procapsids). The involvement of the VP1-2A precursor in assembly is unique to HAV,[48] and it has been shown that the 2A extension is essential for proper processing and assembly of the pentameric subunit.[50,51] Following assembly, 2A is removed from VP1 by cellular proteases,[52,53] and in the final maturation step VP0 is cleaved to yield VP2 and VP4.[47] The VP0 cleavage is dependent on the presence of viral RNA in the particle and procapsids therefore fail to cleave VP0, but in HAV these procapsids are quite stable and indeed have the same antigenic structure as mature virions.

Antigenic Composition

Although a variety of genotypes of HAV have been identified by analysis of genome sequences (Fig. 170-3), there appears to be only one serotype.[54-56] This view is supported by the observation that immune serum globulin prepared in developed countries and monovalent vaccines prepared from strains originating in Australia, Central America, or Europe protect travelers from disease equally well irrespective of their destination.

Neutralization sites for HAV are located primarily on the structural proteins VP1 and VP3, with possibly a minor contribution from VP2.[54,55,57] The antigenic structure of the virus has been analyzed by the use of monoclonal antibodies in competition binding assays[54,55] and the generation of neutralization escape mutants,[58] which together support the hypothesis that the separate capsid proteins contribute to closely related and partly overlapping antigenic sites.

Although many strains of HAV have been described on the basis of different growth characteristics, nucleotide sequence, or geographic origin, polyclonal and monoclonal antibodies directed against the major antigenic determinant appear to be capable of detecting strains of HAV isolated in different parts of the world, thus confirming the presence of only one major serotype.[54,55,57] Comparison of nucleic acid sequences in the region around the VP1/2A junction (see Fig. 170-3) from viruses isolated in different parts of the world indicates that HAV strains can be differentiated into four genotypes (I, II, III, and VII). Three additional types (IV, V, and VI) have been identified in monkeys and may be viruses of simian origin.[55,59-61] Strains recovered from patients in the United States were closely related to each other, whereas viruses recovered in western Europe belonged to three genotypes, thus suggesting importation from other geographic regions.[42,62] Although individual strains of HAV have differences at the molecular level that may be useful for epidemiologic studies, a high degree of identity in nucleic acid (up to 90%) and amino acid sequence (up to 98%) is generally seen between strains.[62]

Biology of Hepatitis A Virus in Cell Culture

HAV was first propagated in marmoset liver explant cultures and a cloned line of fetal rhesus monkey kidney cells (FRhK-6) with a strain of virus (CR326) that had been adapted by multiple passages in *Saguinus mystax* and *Saguinus labiatus* marmosets.[16] Many HAV strains have subsequently been isolated from clinical material, although the procedure may take several weeks. Until recently, only epithelial or fibroblast cells of primate origin have been shown to support growth of the virus.[17,18,63] However, in a systematic search for cells that would support HAV replication, growth was detected in cells of guinea pig, dolphin, and porcine origin.[64]

The major characteristics of HAV in cell culture are slow growth and low yields relative to other picornaviruses.[65] In addition, the virus remains largely cell associated, does not usually produce a cytopathic effect, and readily leads to persistently infected cell lines.[66] Rapidly replicating variants of HAV have been selected that induce cytopathic effects in some cell lines; these variants have proved extremely useful for virus titrations and studies of inactivation kinetics and virus replication.[67-69]

Although a number of HAV strains have been adapted to cell culture,[70,71] the process is unreliable, so in vitro cultivation has not been used for confirmation of diagnosis in environmental studies. A variety of methods are used for detection and quantification, including immunofluorescence or immunoperoxidase staining of infected cells, radioimmunoassay or enzyme immunoassay of culture harvests, radioimmunofocus assay, plaque assay using a cytopathic strain of HAV, molecular hybridization assay, and polymerase chain reaction (PCR).[62,72-74]

The kinetics of viral replication and biosynthetic events have been studied in cells infected with cell culture–adapted strains of HAV and reveal a number of differences from most other picornaviruses. Following attachment to cells, the uncoating of virus is delayed for more than 8 hours[75,76]; this exceeds the duration of an entire growth cycle for many picornaviruses. The delayed uncoating appears to be related to the protracted maturation cleavage of VP0 to VP2 and VP4, as virions are uncoated more rapidly than provirions.[77] Accumulation of new viral RNA can be detected from as early as 12 hours after infection of BS-C-1 cells with a fast-growing, cytopathic variant of strain HM175, but levels of viral replicative intermediates (double-stranded RNAs) remain much lower than in cells infected with other picornaviruses.[75] As outlined above, translation of the viral polyprotein is directed by the IRES within the 5′ UTR, but the IRES of HAV is extraordinarily inefficient with initiation at around 1% of that seen for the IRES of encephalomyocarditis virus (EMCV).[78]

The initial proteolytic processing of HAV polyprotein is accomplished by the viral 3C protease, and assembly of viral particles proceeds via monomers and pentamers[48] (see Fig. 170-2). After infection of cell cultures with rapidly replicating and cytopathic variants of HAV, pentamers are first detected at 9 hours postinfection and reach peak levels around 18 hours even though the amount of viral RNA (and presumably viral translation) increases beyond this time.[49] These cells continue to produce virus for 2 to 3 days before cell death, whereas most HAV variants progress to a persistent infection with reduced levels of virus production over many weeks and subsequent cell passages.[66]

Repeated passage in cell culture has been used to apply mutation pressure to HAV to alter the phenotype. For example, HAV variants have been selected that grow more rapidly or are resistant to neutralization by monoclonal antibodies.[79] Attenuated strains of HAV have been selected by multiple tissue culture passages, and cold adaptation has been achieved by passage at reduced temperature.[80,81] Some of the mutations responsible for these altered phenotypes have been identified by molecular cloning and sequencing of the mutant. Mutations within the 5′ untranslated region and mutations within the 2B and 2C coding regions of HAV RNA have been shown to enhance virus replication in vitro.[82-84] However, mutations within the VP1-2A and 2C proteins appear to be most important for attenuation of virulence.[85] Although evidence of extrahepatic viral replication in humans in tissues other than the liver is sparse, some cells of the gastrointestinal tract are probably susceptible to HAV.[86] Animal studies have demonstrated some evidence of replication in the oropharynx or tonsillar tissue and the upper portion of the small intestine.[86,87]

Most viruses initiate infection by first binding to a specific cell surface receptor molecule or in many cases may require binding to both receptors and co-receptors to facilitate virus entry and uncoating. Identification of a specific receptor for HAV remained elusive for many years; however, Kaplan and colleagues succeeded in the isolation of one specific receptor molecule, havcr-1, first in cells of simian origin[88] and later in human cells.[89] This molecule is a novel mucin-like class I integral membrane glycoprotein of 451 amino acids, with the amino-terminal, cysteine-rich domain responsible for binding to HAV.[89] Because this molecule is expressed on cells from many tissues that are not susceptible to HAV infection, it is likely that specific co-receptors contribute to the organ tropism of HAV. However, havcr-1 has some ability to neutralize particles of HAV directly,[90] which is consistent with roles in both attachment and uncoating of virus.

It remains possible that HAV may use other pathways for cell entry in addition to havcr-1. Recent studies have demonstrated that the asialoglycoprotein receptor can also mediate infection of cells with HAV when the virus is first complexed with specific immunoglobulin A (IgA), leading to the interesting hypothesis that IgA may play a role as both carrier and targeting molecule during infection and transmission, particularly in relapsing cases of HAV.[91]

Host Range

Humans are considered to be the only important reservoir of HAV. However, the existence of extrahuman reservoirs of infection remains possible. In 1961, Hillis[92] described an outbreak of hepatitis A among chimpanzee handlers who apparently contracted the infection from the chimpanzees. Epidemiologic data suggested that the animals had become infected during captivity, but before their importation into the United States. Interestingly, although epidemics of hepatitis were recognized in American primate handlers, the disease was rarely seen in Africa, presumably because most handlers were already immune.

In 1962, Deinhardt and colleagues[93] demonstrated liver function abnormalities in chimpanzees that were inoculated with human feces or acute-phase sera known to have transmitted hepatitis A to humans. In 1967, they inoculated tamarins (*Saguinus nigricollis*) with sera from patients who were judged to have hepatitis A and were able to transmit infection.[94] These results were confirmed in other species of tamarins and later in chimpanzees.[14]

Widespread screening of nonhuman primates has revealed antibodies to HAV in chimpanzees, gorillas, orangutans, gibbons, macaques, owl monkeys, pig tail monkeys, rhesus monkeys, and several species of South American tamarin monkeys.[14,95-97] It is unclear whether such primates may serve as reservoirs of infection, or rather as transient hosts after exposure to HAV from human sources. However, both the PA21[61] and AGM-27 strains of HAV appear to be a true simian viruses.[98] Interestingly, the AGM-27 virus produces attenuated disease in chimpanzees and has been the subject of some study as a potential live attenuated vaccine.[99]

EPIDEMIOLOGY

Modes of Transmission

HAV replicates in the liver, is excreted in bile, and is found in highest concentrations in stool. Thus, fecal excretion is the primary source of virus. In experimental studies, infectivity of stools has been demonstrated for 14 to 21 days before to 8 days after onset of jaundice, but the highest concentrations occur during the 2-week period before jaundice develops or liver enzymes become elevated, followed by a rapid decline after the appearance of jaundice[100-102] (Fig. 170-4). Data from epidemiologic studies also suggest that peak infectivity occurs during the 2 weeks before the onset of symptoms.[103] Shedding of HAV in stool may continue for longer periods in infected infants and children than adults. HAV RNA has been detected in stool of infected newborns for up to 6 months after infection.[104] Excretion in older children and adults has been demonstrated 1 to 3 months after clinical illness.[104,105] Although chronic shedding of HAV does not occur, the virus has been detected in stool during relapsing illness.[106]

During the period of viremia, which begins during the prodrome and extends through the period of liver enzyme elevation (see Fig. 170-4), HAV concentrations in serum are several orders of magnitude lower than in stool.[86,107-109] However, in experiments conducted in nonhuman primates, HAV was several orders of magnitude more infectious when administered by the intravenous compared with the oral route, and animals were successfully infected with low concentrations of HAV administered via the intravenous route.[110] Although HAV may occasionally be detected in saliva in experimentally infected animals,[86] transmission by saliva has not been demonstrated.

Enzyme immunoassays and PCR may detect defective as well as infectious viral particles. Thus, the detection of HAV antigen in the stool by enzyme immunoassays or HAV RNA in the serum or stool by PCR does not mean that an infected person is necessarily infectious, and it is likely that the period of infectivity is shorter than the period during which HAV RNA is detectable. For practical purposes, both children and adults with hepatitis A can be assumed to be noninfectious 1 week after jaundice appears.

Person to Person

Person-to-person transmission by the fecal-oral route is the primary means of HAV transmission in the United States and throughout the world.[111,112] Most transmission occurs among close contacts, particularly in households and extended family settings.[113] Young children have the highest rates of infection and are often the source of infection for others, because infections in this age group are often asymptomatic and standards of hygiene are generally lower among young children compared with adults.[113-115]

Foodborne and Waterborne

HAV can remain infectious in the environment for long periods of time,[116] allowing for common-source outbreaks and sporadic cases to occur from exposure to fecally contaminated food or water. Many uncooked foods have been recognized as the source of outbreaks. Cooked foods also can transmit HAV if the cooking is inadequate to kill the virus or if the food is contaminated after cooking, as commonly occurs in outbreaks associated with infected food handlers.[117-120] Contaminated shellfish were responsible for a large outbreak in Shanghai, China, in 1988[121] and have been implicated as the source of cases in Italy[122] but have rarely been associated with outbreaks in the United States in recent years.[123-126] Waterborne outbreaks of hepatitis A are uncommon in developed countries.

Blood-borne

Transfusion-related hepatitis A is rare because HAV does not result in chronic infection, and, in the developed world, blood donors have been screened for many years for elevated aminotransferase levels.

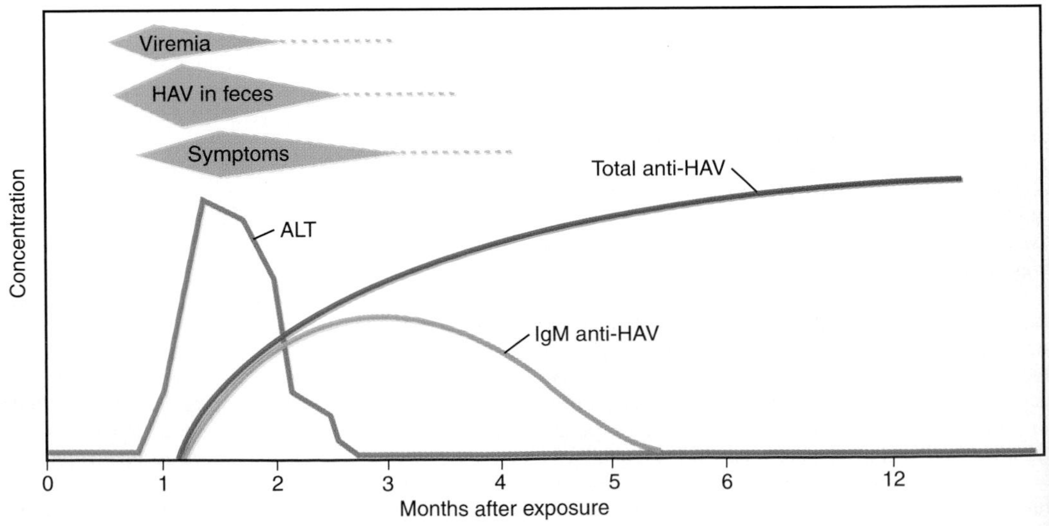

FIGURE 170-4. Clinical, virologic, and serologic events associated with hepatitis A virus (HAV) infection. ALT, alanine aminotransferase.

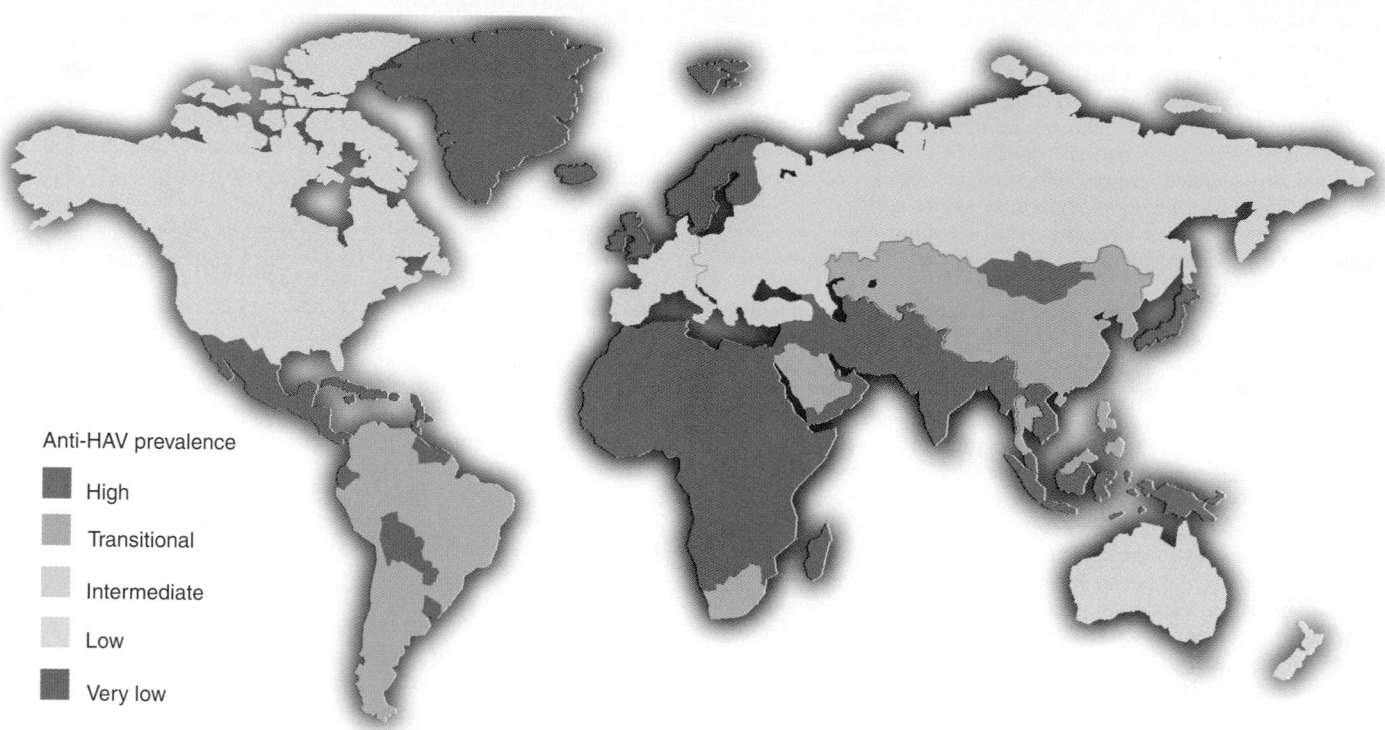

Anti-HAV prevalence

■ High

■ Transitional

■ Intermediate

■ Low

■ Very low

FIGURE 170-5. World map indicating patterns of endemicity of hepatitis A virus infection, generalized from available data. The patterns of high, transitional, intermediate, low, and very low endemicity are shown.

However, transmission by transfusion of blood or blood derivatives collected from donors during the viremic phase of their infection has been reported, including outbreaks in Europe and the United States among patients who received factor VIII and factor IX concentrates prepared using solvent-detergent treatment to inactivate lipid-containing viruses.[37,109,127-129] HAV is resistant to solvent-detergent treatment, and contamination presumably occurred from plasma donors with hepatitis A who donated during the incubation period.

Vertical

Two published case reports describe intrauterine transmission of HAV during the first trimester, resulting in fetal meconium peritonitis.[130,131] After delivery, both infants were found to have a perforated ileum. The risk of transmission from pregnant women who develop hepatitis A in the third trimester of pregnancy to newborns appears to be low.[132] However, newborns who acquire infection in this manner are usually asymptomatic, and an outbreak among hospital staff related to exposure to such an infant has been reported.[133]

Worldwide Disease Patterns

Hepatitis A occurs worldwide, but major geographical differences exist in endemicity and resulting epidemiologic features (Fig. 170-5). The degree of endemicity is closely related to hygienic and sanitary conditions and other indicators of the level of development. In less-developed areas, especially when there is limited access to clean water and inadequate disposal of human feces, HAV infects most people early in life, when infection is rarely clinically apparent (Fig. 170-6). When high standards of hygiene and sanitation apply, the majority of adults remain susceptible. Distinct patterns of HAV infection can be described, each characterized by particular age-specific anti-HAV prevalence and hepatitis A incidence, and prevailing environmental (hygienic and sanitary) and socioeconomic conditions[111,134] (see Fig. 170-6).

In areas of high endemicity, represented by the least-developed countries (i.e., parts of Africa, Asia, Central and South America), poor hygienic and sanitary conditions allow HAV to spread readily (see Fig. 170-5). Infection is nearly universal in early childhood, when asymp-

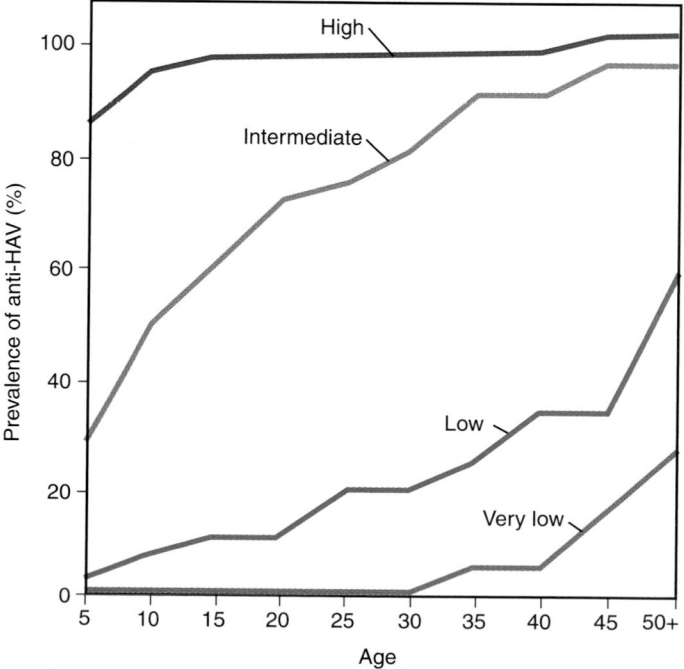

FIGURE 170-6. Patterns of hepatitis A virus infection worldwide. The purple line represents age-specific prevalence of anti-HAV in areas of high endemicity; the yellow line, in areas of intermediate endemicity; the blue line, in areas of low endemicity; and the brown line, in areas of very low endemicity.

tomatic infection predominates, and essentially the entire population is infected before reaching adolescence, as demonstrated by the age-specific prevalence of anti-HAV[135,136] (see Fig. 170-6). Susceptible adults in these areas are at high risk of hepatitis A, but reported disease rates are generally low and outbreaks are rare because most adults are immune. High endemicity patterns can also be seen in some ethnic or geographically defined groups within highly developed countries, such as aboriginal children in the north of Australia.[137]

In areas of moderate endemicity, HAV is not transmitted as readily because of better sanitary and living conditions, and the predominant age of infection is older than in areas of high endemicity[138] (see Figs. 170-5 and 170-6). Paradoxically, the overall incidence and average age of reported cases are often higher than in highly endemic areas because high levels of virus circulate in a population that includes many susceptible older children, adolescents, and young adults, who are likely to develop symptoms with HAV infection.[139] Large common-source food- and water-associated outbreaks can occur, because of the relatively high rate of virus transmission and large number of susceptible persons, especially among those of higher socioeconomic level. Such an outbreak occurred in Shanghai in 1988, with over 300,000 cases associated with consumption of clams harvested from water contaminated with human sewage.[121] Nevertheless, person-to-person transmission in community-wide epidemics continues to account for much of the disease in these countries.

Shifts in age-specific prevalence patterns that reflect a transition from high to intermediate endemicity are occurring in many parts of the world (see Fig. 170-5). A feature of this transitional pattern is striking variations in hepatitis A epidemiology between countries, and within countries and cities, with some areas displaying a pattern typical of high endemicity, and others of intermediate endemicity.[53,111,140-148] Considerable hepatitis A–related morbidity and associated costs occur with this transition, even in developing countries.[149,150] For example, hepatitis A was the etiology of the fulminant hepatitis of two thirds of children presenting to two hospitals in Argentina during a 15-year period, and, in one of these hospitals performing liver transplantations, one third of liver transplantations among children were performed for fulminant hepatitis A.[149]

In the United States, Canada, western Europe, and other developed countries, the endemicity of HAV infection is low (see Fig. 170-5). Relatively fewer children are infected, the incidence of disease is generally low, and disease often occurs in the context of community-wide and child care center outbreaks.[112,151-154] Population-based seroprevalence surveys show a gradual increase in the prevalence of anti-HAV with increasing age, primarily reflecting declining incidence, changing endemicity, and resultant lower childhood infection rates over time. Some countries (e.g., Scandinavia) currently have very low endemicity, with most cases occurring in defined risk groups such as travelers returning from endemic areas and users of injection drugs.[155]

Epidemiology in the United States

Hepatitis A epidemiology in the United States can be divided into two time periods, before and after implementation of national recommen-

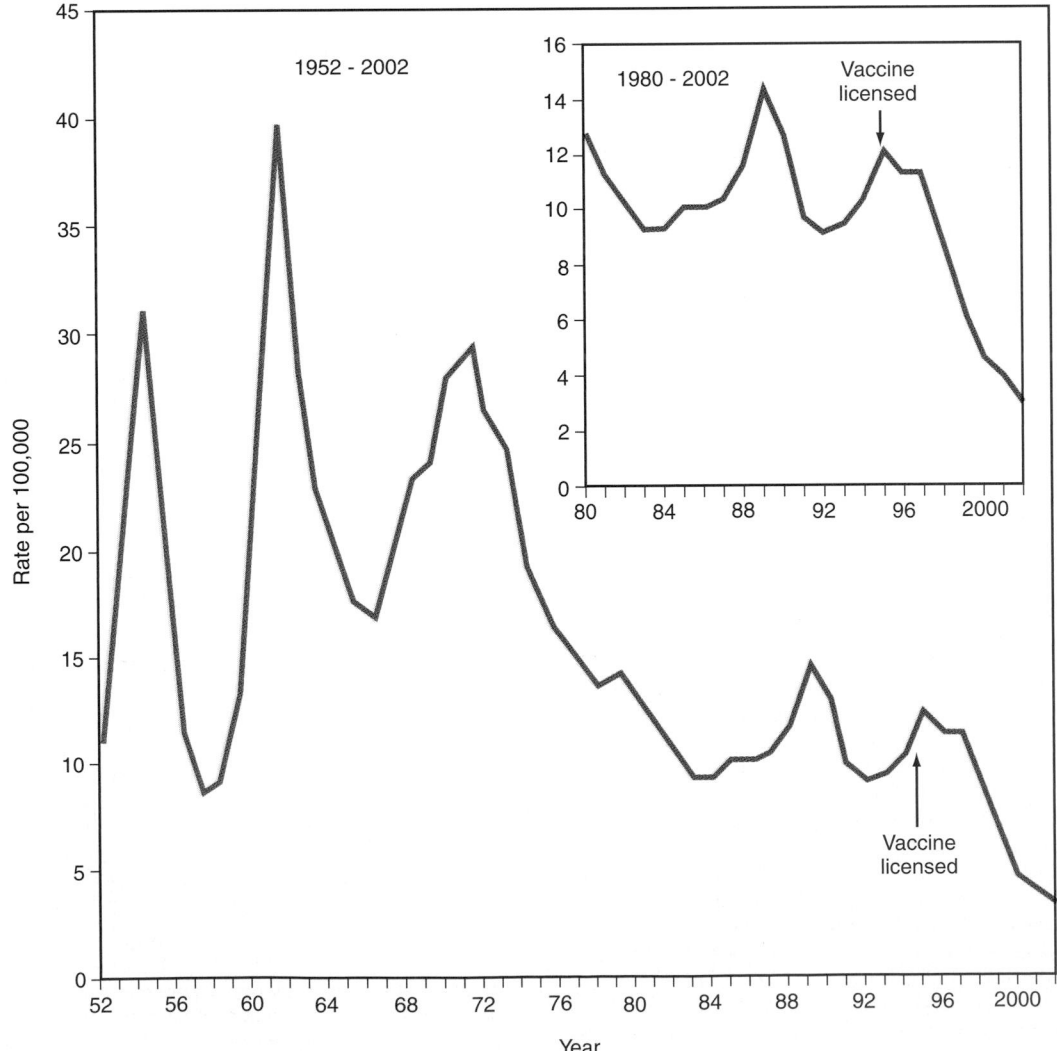

FIGURE 170-7. Hepatitis A incidence, United States, 1952-2002. *(From the Centers for Disease Control and Prevention, National Notifiable Diseases Surveillance System, Atlanta. 2002 Data are provisional.)*

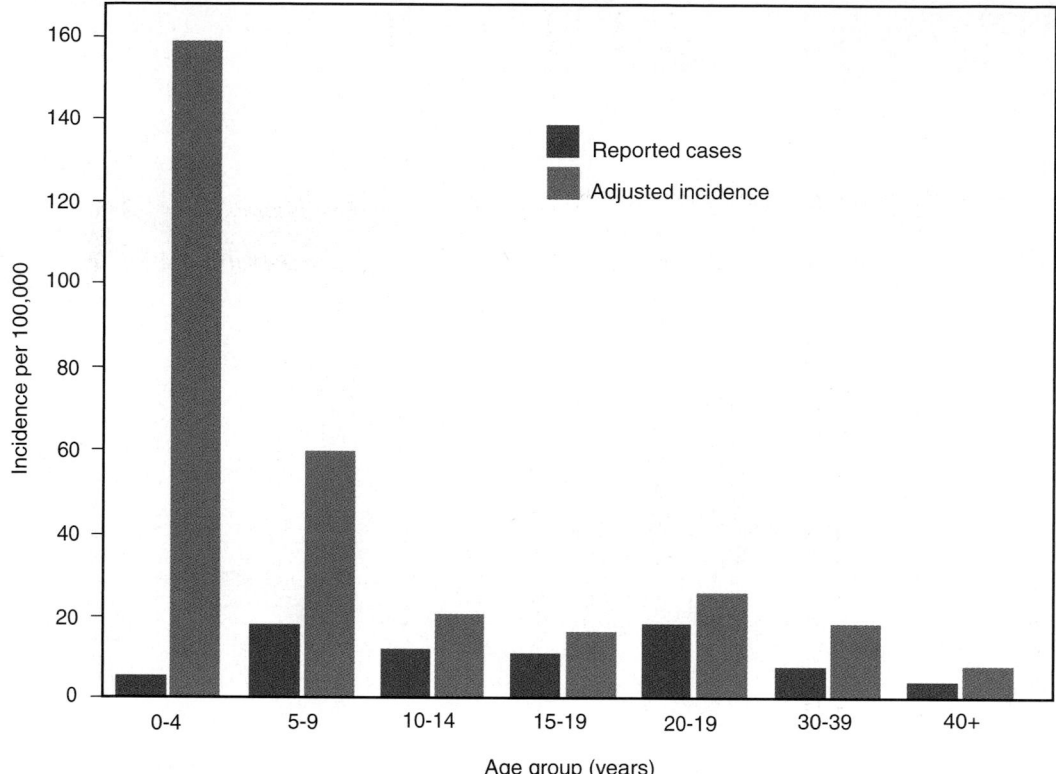

FIGURE 170-8. Reported and adjusted incidence of hepatitis A in the United States, 1980-1999. The purple bars represent reported age-specific incidence and the brown bars represent age-specific incidence after adjusting for anicteric infections. *(Modified from Armstrong GL, Bell BP. Hepatitis A virus infections in the United States: Model-based estimates and implications for childhood immunization. Pediatrics. 2002;109:839-845.)*

dations for use of hepatitis A vaccine. In general, hepatitis A incidence has been cyclic, with peaks every 10 to 15 years (Fig. 170-7). Throughout the 1980s and early 1990s in the United States, approximately 25,000 to 35,000 hepatitis A cases were reported annually to Centers for Disease Control and Prevention,[156] but incidence models indicate that many more infections occurred. One such analysis estimated an average of 271,000 infections per year during 1980-1999, 10.4 times the reported number of cases.[115]

With the availability in the United States of hepatitis A vaccines beginning in the mid-1990s, hepatitis A became one of the most frequently reported vaccine-preventable diseases.[156] Recommendations for use of hepatitis A vaccine were made by the Advisory Committee on Immunization Practices (ACIP) in 1996 and 1999[157,158] (see later Disease Control Strategies). National hepatitis A rates have been declining precipitously over the past several years; in 2002 a provisional total of 8,795 cases were reported, yielding a historically low rate of 2.9 per 100,000 (see Fig. 170-7). This remarkable decline incidence is reflected in other fundamental shifts in hepatitis A epidemiology, as described later.

Variation by Age and Race or Ethnicity

Historically, the highest hepatitis A rates were reported among children 5 to 14 years of age, with approximately one third of cases occurring among children younger than 15 years.[159] Because many young children have unrecognized or asymptomatic infection, a relatively smaller proportion of infections among children than adults are detected by public health disease surveillance systems. Incidence models indicate that during 1980-1999, more than half of HAV infections occurred among children younger than 10 years old, the majority of which were in children 0 to 4 years old[115] (Fig. 170-8). Hepatitis A incidence rates among children have declined more sharply than among adults following the implementation of routine vaccination of children in some areas in recent years, and in 2002 rates were similar among adults and children (Fig. 170-9).

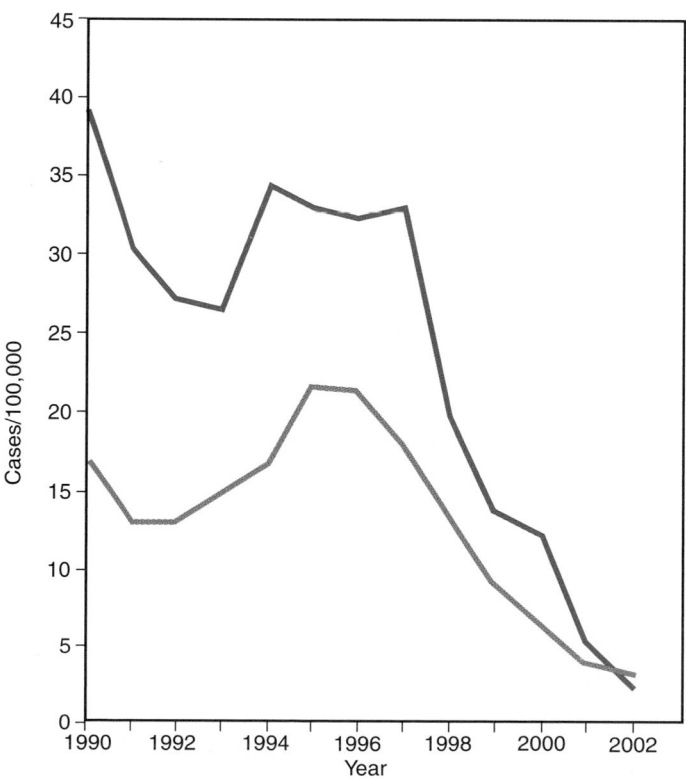

FIGURE 170-9. Hepatitis A incidence by age group, United States, 1990-2002. The blue line represents incidence among children aged 2 to 18 years and the yellow line represents incidence among persons older than 18 years. *(From the Centers for Disease Control and Prevention, National Notifiable Diseases Surveillance System, Atlanta, GA. 2002 Data are provisional.)*

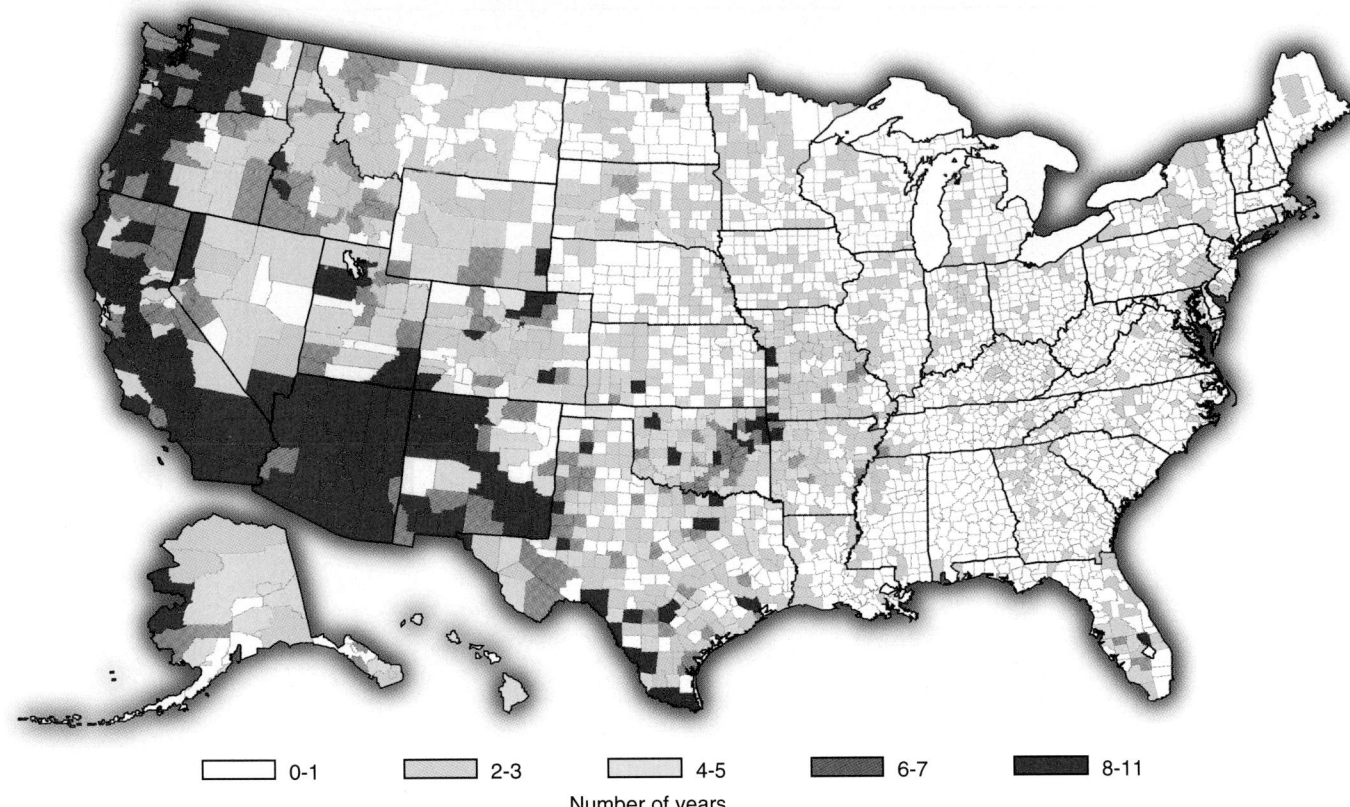

0-1   **2-3**   **4-5**   **6-7**   **8-11**

Number of years

FIGURE 170-10. Number of years that reported hepatitis A incidence exceeded 10 cases per 100,000*, by county for 1987-1997. (*Approximately the national average during 1987-1997.)

Among racial and ethnic groups, before the use of hepatitis A vaccine rates among American Indians and Alaska Natives were more than 10 times the rate in other racial/ethnic groups, and rates among Hispanics were approximately three times higher than among non-Hispanics.[157] However, by 2000, hepatitis A incidence among American Indians and Alaska Natives had declined by 97% compared with the beginning of the decade, and was lower than the overall U.S. rate (see "Disease Control Strategies").[160]

Results of the Third National Health and Nutrition Examination Survey, conducted during 1988 to 1994, indicated that about one third of the U.S. population had serologic evidence of prior HAV infection.[158] Anti-HAV prevalence was related directly to age, ranging from 9% among children 6 to 11 years of age to 75% among persons older than 70 years of age and was related inversely to income. Anti-HAV prevalence was highest among Mexican-Americans (70%), compared with non-Hispanic blacks (39%) and whites (23%).

TABLE 170-1 Occurrence of Hepatitis A in States with Average Reported Incidence of ≥10 Cases per 100,000 Population—1987-1997*

State	Rate (per 100,000)*,†	Cumulative Average No. of Cases/yr‡	Cumulative Cases (%)	Cumulative Population (%)§
Arizona	48	1,852	7	2
Alaska	45	2,137	8	2
Oregon	40	3,297	12	3
New Mexico	40	3,916	14	4
Utah	33	4,519	16	5
Washington	30	6,007	21	7
Oklahoma	24	6,786	24	8
South Dakota	24	6,953	25	8
Idaho	21	7,172	26	9
Nevada	21	7,449	27	10
California	20	13,706	50	22
Missouri	19	14,706	54	24
Texas	16	17,587	64	31
Colorado	16	18,138	56	33
Arkansas	14	18,483	67	34
Montana	11	18,576	68	34
Wyoming	11	18,627	68	34

*The overall U.S. rate during 1987-1997 was 10.8/100,000 population.
†Children living in areas (states, counties, communities) where the rate was ≥20 cases per 100,000 population should be routinely vaccinated. Children living in areas where the rate was ≥10 cases per 100,000 population should be considered for routine vaccination.
‡Approximately 37% of cases were among persons younger than 20 years.
§1997 Estimate, U.S. Census.

Geographic Variation

Analysis of national surveillance data shows striking regional variation in hepatitis A incidence, with the highest rates and majority of cases consistently occurring in a limited number of states and counties concentrated in the western and southwestern United States (Fig. 170-10). Despite year-to-year fluctuations, rates in these areas consistently remained above the national average. Cases among residents of the 11 states with consistently elevated rates, representing 22% of the U.S. population, in which the average annual hepatitis A incidence was greater than 20 cases per 100,000 during 1987-1997 (twice the national average of about 10 per 100,000) accounted for an average of 50% of reported cases (Table 170-1). An additional 18% of cases occurred among residents of states with average annual rates above the national average but less than twice the national average during this time (see Table 170-1). These geographic variations have essentially disappeared, presumably due, at least in part, to implementation of vaccination recommendations (see section on disease control strategies).[158]

Potential Sources of Infection

Based on data from disease surveillance systems, the most commonly reported potential source of infection is household or sexual contact with a person who has hepatitis A (15% to 25% of reported cases)[112,159] (Fig. 170-11). Historically, approximately 10% to 15% of reported cases occurred among children and employees of child care centers and members of their households. However, this may have overestimated disease truly attributable to exposure in these settings because these cases are ascribed to child care center–related contact without requiring a known contact with hepatitis A or even identifying a case of hepatitis A in the center.[112,159] International travel (5% to 7%) and suspected foodborne or waterborne outbreaks (2% to 5%) each account for a small proportion of cases.[152,159] Cyclic outbreaks occur among men who have sex with men and users of injecting and noninjecting drugs.[112,160-164] Historically during outbreak years, these exposures could account for 10% of nationally reported cases and, with the large declines in incidence among children and their adult contacts, have accounted for an even larger proportion of cases. Nearly 50% of patients with hepatitis A do not have a recognized source of infection[159] but may be contacts of persons, especially children, with asymptomatic infection.

Community-Wide Epidemics

Historically, most cases of hepatitis A in the United States occurred in the context of community-wide epidemics, during which infection is transmitted from person to person in households and extended family settings.[112] These epidemics generally spread throughout the community, and no single risk factor or risk group can be identified that can account for the majority of cases.[112] Once initiated, they often persist for several years and have proved difficult to control,[165] even when at-

tempts were made to rapidly vaccinate some portion of the population.[166,167] Children have played an important role in sustaining HAV transmission during these epidemics. Serologic studies of members of households with an adult case without an identified source have found that 25% to 40% of contacts younger than 6 years old had serologic evidence of recent HAV infection[113] (Centers for Disease Control and Prevention, unpublished data). In one of these studies, 52% of households of adults without an identified source of infection included a child less than 6 years old, and the presence of a young child was associated with household transmission of HAV.[113]

Specific Groups and Settings

Child Care Centers, Schools, and Institutions

Outbreaks in child care centers have been recognized for many decades. They rarely occur in centers that do not have children in diapers and are more common in larger centers.[168,169] As has been recognized since the 1970s, outbreaks can be sustained among children with asymptomatic infection and often are not recognized until adult contacts (usually parents) become ill.[168,170] Despite the occurrence of outbreaks when HAV is introduced into a child care center, studies of child care center employees do not show a significantly increased prevalence of HAV infection compared with control populations.[171] Occasionally, outbreaks in child care centers can be the source of more extensive transmission within a community.[169,172,173] However, it is likely that most disease within child care centers reflects disease transmission from the community. Hepatitis A cases among children in schools usually reflect disease that has been acquired in the community, although multiple cases among children within a school may indicate a common-source outbreak.[174] Historically, HAV infection was endemic in institutions for the developmentally disabled, but with smaller facilities and improved conditions, the incidence and prevalence of infection have decreased and outbreaks rarely are reported in the United States.[175]

Users of Illicit Drugs

During the two past decades, outbreaks have been reported with increasing frequency among illicit drug users in North America, Australia, and Europe.[163,164,176-178] In the United States, these outbreaks, particularly in the past decade, have frequently involved users of injected and noninjected methamphetamine, who may account for up to 30% of reported cases in these communities during outbreaks.[112,164,178,179] Cross-sectional serologic surveys have demonstrated that injection drug users have higher prevalence of anti-HAV than the general U.S. population.[180,181] Transmission among injection drug users probably occurs through both percutaneous and fecal-oral routes.[178]

Men Who Have Sex with Men

Hepatitis A outbreaks among men who have sex with men have been reported frequently, most recently in urban areas in the United States, Canada, England, and Australia, and may occur in the context of an outbreak in the larger community.[112,161,162,182-184] Seroprevalence surveys have not consistently demonstrated an elevated prevalence of anti-HAV compared with a similarly aged general population.[181,185] Some studies conducted during outbreaks and seroprevalence surveys among men who have sex with men have identified specific sex practices associated with illness, whereas others have not demonstrated such associations.[161,181,183]

Transfusions and Other Health Care Settings

Transfusion-related hepatitis A is rare. The risk of infection in patients with hemophilia is not known, but results of one serologic survey of hemophiliac patients suggest they may be at increased risk,[186] and outbreaks have been reported in Europe and the United States among patients who received factor VIII and factor IX concentrates.[128,187] Outbreaks have also been reported in neonatal intensive care units following transmission to hospital staff from a neonate with asymptomatic HAV infection acquired from a blood transfusion.[104,188,189]

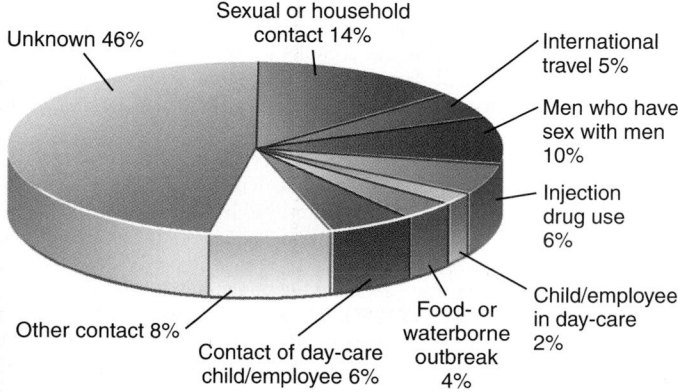

FIGURE 170-11. Risk factors for hepatitis A among reported cases, United States, 1990-2000. *(From the Centers for Disease Control and Prevention, Viral Hepatitis Surveillance Program, Atlanta, GA.)*

Unknown 46%
Sexual or household contact 14%
International travel 5%
Men who have sex with men 10%
Injection drug use 6%
Child/employee in day-care 2%
Food- or waterborne outbreak 4%
Contact of day-care child/employee 6%
Other contact 8%

Transmission also was reported in association with an experimental treatment with lymphocytes incubated in serum from a donor with HAV infection.[190]

Nosocomial transmission from adult patients to health care workers is rare because most patients with hepatitis A are hospitalized after the onset of jaundice, when infectivity is low,[101] but it has been reported in association with fecal incontinence of the patient.[191,192] Health care workers have not been found to have an increased prevalence of anti-HAV compared with control populations in serologic surveys conducted in the United States.[193]

International Travel

Hepatitis A is a common infection among travelers from developed countries who travel to regions with high, transitional, or intermediate endemicity[194-196] (see Fig. 170-5). In prospective studies of American and European travelers, the risk of infection for those who did not receive immunoglobulin was found to be 3 to 5 per 1000 per month of stay, of the same order of magnitude as that for malaria, 10 to 100 times greater than that for typhoid, and 1000 times greater than that for cholera.[197,198] The risk may be higher among travelers staying in areas with poor hygienic conditions,[199] varies according to the region and the length of stay, and appears to be increased even among travelers who reported observing protective measures and staying in urban areas or luxury hotels (Centers for Disease Control and Prevention, unpublished data). Travelers who acquire hepatitis A during their trip may also transmit to others on their return.[200]

Foodborne and Waterborne

Foodborne hepatitis A outbreaks are recognized relatively infrequently in the United States.[119] They are most commonly associated with contamination of food during preparation by a food handler with HAV infection.[118,117,201,202] Implicated foods include those not cooked after handling, such as sandwiches and salads, as well as partially cooked foods.[203-206] Food contaminated before retail distribution, such as lettuce or fruits contaminated at the growing or processing stage, has been increasingly recognized as the source of hepatitis A outbreaks.[123,174,207-210] Waterborne hepatitis A outbreaks are rare and related to sewage contamination or inadequate treatment of water.[211-213]

Although results of some serologic surveys conducted among sewage workers in Europe indicated a possible elevated risk of HAV infection, findings have not been consistent.[214-216] In published reports of three serologic surveys conducted among U.S. sewage workers and appropriate comparison populations, no substantial or consistent increase in prevalence of anti-HAV was found among sewage workers.[217-219] No work-related instances of HAV transmission have been reported among sewage workers in the United States.

PATHOGENESIS

Although HAV shares many virologic characteristics with enteroviruses, it has several differentiating features that influence the pathogenesis and clinical expression of the disease. HAV is resistant to heat, solvents, and acid and grows slowly in living cells, where it has been shown to be relatively noncytolytic and to have little effect on the rate of host protein synthesis.

Incubation Period

Determination of the incubation period of disease is imprecise because the early symptoms of hepatitis are often vague and nonspecific. Jaundice may not be noticed by the patient, so the most useful marker of the onset of the disease is a change in urine color, which is almost always recognized by the patient and is the most common reason for seeking medical attention. The range of incubation is between 2 and 7 weeks, with a mean of about 4 weeks. Although HAV can be transmitted orally or parenterally, the incubation period is independent of the route of inoculation.[177] Experiments in primates and observations in humans suggest that the incubation period is dependent on the infectious dose.[178]

Site of Viral Replication

HAV is generally transmitted by the fecal-oral route. Because the virus is acid resistant, it probably passes through the stomach, replicates lower in the intestine,[85,152,179] and is then transported to the liver, which is the major site of replication.[85,180,181] Evidence of replication in the oropharynx has been obtained in chimpanzees.[84] HAV, like many other picornaviruses, is highly organ specific with little evidence of significant replication outside the liver. Virus is shed from infected liver cells into the hepatic sinusoids and canaliculi, passes into the intestine, and is excreted in feces. In humans as well as in nonhuman primates, HAV has been detected in the liver, bile, and feces.[182-184] The first indirect evidence that virus may replicate in the gut was the detection of co-proantibodies in the feces,[185,186] followed by the demonstration of hepatitis A antigen in duodenal lining cells.[85] Nonetheless, the major pathology is restricted to the liver.

Pathogenesis

HAV is generally not cytopathic in cell culture, and histopathologic findings in experimental animals and humans do not show widespread hepatocyte necrosis, although the vast majority of hepatocytes at the peak of viral replication appear to be infected by immunohistochemical staining. Therefore, immune mechanisms have been invoked to explain the pathogenesis of the disease.[187] It has been postulated that liver cell damage occurs through a cell-mediated immune response, whereas circulating antibodies are probably more important in limiting the spread of virus to uninfected liver cells and other organs. This hypothesis is consistent with observations in animal models and humans. For example, intravenous inoculation of marmosets with a large dose of HAV resulted in mildly abnormal liver function test results and detectable hepatitis A antigen in hepatocytes within 1 week. Enzyme levels stabilized or even declined until the third week after inoculation, when a second, higher peak was observed coincident with the appearance of serum antibodies.[188] One explanation is that the early mild hepatitis was due to a direct viral effect but the second, more severe episode was due to an immune response. The presence of large quantities of virus in hepatocytes before the onset of hepatitis also argues against a major direct cytopathic effect of HAV.[44,152] It has been suggested that virally elicited T cells target infected liver cells and induce immunopathology. In human studies, Vallbracht found that lymphocytes from convalescing patients produced cytotoxic effects against autologous epidermal cell lines infected with HAV and that CD8+ T-cell clones demonstrated cytotoxic activity against autologous fibroblasts infected with hepatitis A. These findings are consistent with the hypothesis that CD8+ T lymphocytes mediate liver cell damage.[187,189] Furthermore, natural killer cells have been demonstrated to be capable of lysing HAV-infected tissue culture cells.[190]

Although liver damage occurs at the time that circulating antibodies become detectable, it has not been proved that the pathology is antibody dependent.[191] Circulating immune complexes containing HAV and specific IgM antibodies have been found during infection. However, immunoglobulin and complement deposits were not found at the sites of liver cell damage, and resolution of disease occurred even when antibody levels were rising and hepatitis A antigen could still be detected in the liver.[192,193]

Over the past two decades, there has been a reported dramatic increase in childhood asthma prevalence, which some have hypothesized might be related to be due to improved hygienic conditions leading to fewer childhood infections.[220] At least one study has shown that the prevalence of asthma is lower in children who are seropositive for antibody to HAV.[221] A trait associated with asthma, the T-cell and airway phenotype regulator (TAPR), which controls the development of airway hyperreactivity, is a member of the T-cell membrane proteins (TIMs). The human homolog of TIM-1 is the HAV receptor.[89,222] This potential association between atopic airway disease and hepatitis A is interesting, but appropriate studies that could evaluate a causal relationship have not been conducted.

CLINICAL FEATURES

Hepatitis A is an acute or a subclinical infection of the liver. Although the clinical expression of infection varies widely, the disease is self-limited, sometimes subclinical, but typically is symptomatic with jaundice. The most important determinant of the likelihood of clinical expression is the age at which infection occurs.[223] The vast majority of infections in children younger than 5 years are silent, and the proportion of symptomatic infections increases with age. The ratio of anicteric to icteric cases has been reported to vary from 12:1 to 1:3.5, depending on the age at which infection occurs.[224] In modeling studies, the estimated average probability of jaundice increased from 7% among children younger than 5 years to 37% among children 5 to 9 years old and to greater than 70% among adolescents and adults. In the Greenland epidemic of 1970-1974, the frequency of clinically recognizable hepatitis increased from 1% in children younger than 1 year to 24% in 15-year-olds.[225,226] Similar low rates of clinical symptoms have been noted in children involved in outbreaks in day care centers in the United States[227]; however, adults infected in these outbreaks usually became jaundiced.

Symptoms

Patients with hepatitis A often describe a mild illness—the prodrome (see Fig. 170-4)—that appears 1 to 7 days before the onset of dark urine, although longer periods have been recorded.[223,194] These symptoms are not usually severe enough to cause the patient to seek medical attention or to stay home from work. In the early stages, flulike symptoms are common; fever (up to 40° C) may be accompanied by chills, mild headache, malaise, and fatigue. Loss of appetite is a common symptom, with patients reporting that the sight or smell of food, especially fatty foods, is nauseating. Vomiting may occur but is neither severe nor protracted, and weight loss is common. In addition, patients with hepatitis A often lose their taste for tobacco. Occasionally, children may experience atypical with symptoms such as diarrhea, cough, coryza, or arthralgia.

The first specific sign of disease and the one that causes most patients to seek medical attention is the onset of dark urine. Bilirubinuria is usually followed within a few days by pale or clay-colored feces and yellow discoloration of the sclera, skin, and mucous membranes. The return of color to the stool occurs 2 or 3 weeks after the onset of illness and is an indication of resolution of disease. Itching, a sign of cholestasis, occurs in less than 50% of patients but may be severe enough to require antipruritics or corticosteroids.

On physical examination, the patient's liver may be enlarged and sometimes tender. In adults the liver can be enlarged up to 14 cm in the vertical axis and has a firm consistency. The spleen is palpable in 5% to 15% of patients. Spider nevi may appear on the trunk and usually disappear during convalescence. Other physical findings occur rarely.

The duration of illness varies, but by the third week most patients feel better, have lost their hepatomegaly, and have normal or nearly normal levels of serum alanine aminotransferase (ALT) and aspartate aminotransferase (AST). In many patients the appearance of jaundice is associated with rapid resolution of symptoms. In a study of 59 patients in the United States, about two thirds recovered within 2 months, 85% within 3 months, and nearly all by 6 months.[228]

The clinical course and histologic findings do not differ in pregnancy.[229,230] Intrauterine transmission of HAV during the first trimester that resulted in fetal meconium peritonitis has been described in two case reports.[130,131] At delivery, both infants has a perforated ileum. No evidence has suggested more severe infection or subsequent loss of immunity occurs in the presence of human immunodeficiency virus infection. Although not demonstrated in all published studies, on balance it appears that HAV infection in persons with chronic liver disease may be more severe and more likely to result in fulminant hepatitis A.[231,232]

Complications

Recognized complications of hepatitis A include cholestasis, prolonged and relapsing disease, fulminant hepatitis, triggering of chronic active autoimmune hepatitis, and autoimmune extrahepatic disease.

Cholestatic hepatitis, characterized by fever, pruritus, and prolonged jaundice, has been reported as an occasional complication. Cholestasis developed in 4 of 59 (7%) patients in a hospital-based study.[228] In a detailed description of six patients, peak serum bilirubin levels of 12 to 29 mg/dL were recorded, and jaundice lasted for 12 to 18 weeks. In each case, peak ALT levels were below 500 IU/L.[233] Liver biopsies revealed centrilobular cholestasis and portal inflammation. Although the prognosis is universally favorable, a short, rapidly tapered course of corticosteroids may be used to reduce symptoms and hasten resolution.

Relapsing disease has been reported as an occasional complication in both adults and children.[228,234,235] It is reported that between 3% and 20% of cases relapse after a typical initial course. Typically, symptoms decrease but may not completely resolve during the recovery phase, and the relapse disease is usually milder than the first. In the study of Tong and colleagues,[228] the mean ALT level was 3500 mIU/mL and the mean bilirubin level was 4.9 mg/dL during the first peak and 1554 mIU/mL and 2.5 mg/dL, respectively, during the second. Viral excretion during the relapse has been detected. Although the pathogenesis of relapses has not been elucidated, it is important to recognize that these cases resolve without sequelae, although some clinicians have given corticosteroids to hasten recovery.[235,236]

Extrahepatic manifestations of hepatitis A rarely include cardiac involvement, although patients with acute hepatitis may have bradycardia and electrocardiograms may show prolongation of the PR interval and some mild T-wave depression. These changes resolve rapidly during convalescence.[237] HAV infection rarely causes pathology of other organs, but occasional cases of postviral encephalitis, Guillain-Barré syndrome, cholecystitis, acute pancreatitis, acute renal failure secondary to interstitial nephritis, aplastic or hemolytic anemia, agranulocytosis, thrombocytopenic purpura, or pancytopenia have been reported. Several cases of arthritis, vasculitis, and cryoglobulinemia have also been reported.[238-240] Some patients may become depressed, and, occasionally, the depression may be severe enough to require treatment, but it is usually mild and self-limited.

The clinical course of hepatitis A is usually benign. Although severe disease is occasionally observed, especially in older patients, long-term sequelae in recovered patients have not been observed. During the 1988 Shanghai epidemic, complications were unusual, mostly involving cholestasis[241] (Table 170-2). Death from hepatitis A is well documented, but unusual. In the Shanghai epidemic that involved primarily adolescents and young adults, 47 deaths were registered among 310,746 cases (0.015%).[241] This is consistent with surveillance data reported to the Centers for Disease Control and Prevention; in 2001, for example, 18 deaths were identified among approximately 4900 cases, yielding a case-fatality ratio of 0.4% (Table 170-3).[159] In general, the severe clinical manifestations and outcomes (e.g., hospitalizations, fulminant hepatic failure, death) are more common among older adults but also occur among children[159,242,243] (see Table 170-3).

The most serious complication of hepatitis A is fulminant hepatic failure, defined by the appearance of severe acute liver disease with hepatic encephalopathy in a previously healthy person.[244,245] Danger signs include excitability, irritability, insomnia, confusion, and severe vomiting. Laboratory and clinical evidence of deteriorating liver function, especially prolonged prothrombin times, correlates with the histologic picture of almost complete destruction of the hepatic parenchyma, with only a reticulin framework and portal tracts remaining. Occasionally, small groups of surviving hepatocytes can be seen close to the portal tracts, which may represent foci of regeneration. Surprisingly, little indication of a vigorous inflammatory response has been noted. Fulminant hepatitis A is a rare occurrence in

TABLE 170-2 Clinical Manifestations of 8647 Hospitalized Patients, 1988 Shanghai Epidemic

Symptom	Percent	Clinical Findings	Percent	Complications	Percent
Jaundice	84	Hepatomegaly	87	Cholestasis	1.6-5.3
Weight loss	82	Splenomegaly	9	Upper gastrointestinal bleeding	0.5-1.2
Malaise	80	Skin rashes	3	Thrombocytopenic purpura	<0.1 (6 cases)
Fever	76	Mild edema	2	Guillain-Barré syndrome	<0.1 (4 cases)
Nausea	69	Petechia	2	Pure red cell aplasia	<0.1 (3 cases)
Vomiting	47	Cardiac arrhythmias	0.8	Autoimmune hemolytic anemia	<0.1 (2 cases)
Abdominal pain	37			Tranverse mylelitis, optic neuritis	<0.1 (1 case each)
Arthralgia	6				

Data summarized from Yao G. Clinical spectrum and natural history of viral hepatitis A in a 1988 Shanghai epidemic. In: Hollinger FB, Lemon SM, Margolis HS, eds. Viral Hepatitis and Liver Disease. Baltimore: Williams & Wilkins; 1991:76-78.

TABLE 170-3 Hospitalizations and Deaths, by Age, for Reported Hepatitis A Cases, United States, 2001

	Age of Cases											
	<5 yr (n = 189)		5-14 yr (n = 668)		15-39 yr (n = 2306)		40-59 yr (n = 1267)		60+ yr (n = 466)		All (N = 4896)	
	No.	%	No.	%	No.	%	No.	%	No.	%	No.	%
Died from hepatitis	1	0.5	2	0.3	2	0.1	5	0.4	8	1.7	18	0.4
Hospitalized for hepatitis	25	13.2	103	15.4	503	21.8	302	23.8	143	30.7	1,076	22.0

Includes all cases with nonmissing relevant data, from among the total of 10,615 reported cases of hepatitis A.
From the Centers for Disease Control and Prevention, National Notifiable Diseases Surveillance System, Atlanta, GA.

the developed world, accounting for 4.5% of cases of fulminant hepatitis in a prospective series of U.S. cases.[245] Spontaneous survival from fulminant hepatits A occurs more commonly than from fulminant hepatitis of other causes.[245]

LABORATORY DIAGNOSIS

Hepatitis A is not clinically distinguishable from other forms of viral hepatitis, although the diagnosis may be suspected in a patient with typical symptoms during an outbreak. Liver function tests (see Fig. 170-4), especially serum levels of ALT and AST, are sensitive measures of parenchymal liver damage but are not specific for hepatitis A. In the study by Tong and co-workers,[228] the peak mean ALT level was 1952 mIU/mL and the mean peak AST was 1442 mIU/mL, with the highest ALT level being 9711 mIU/mL, although values greater than 20,000 mIU/mL have been observed. The ALT levels returned to normal by a mean of 7.4 weeks (range, 1 to 29 weeks). Although elevated ALT levels are detected in patients with severe hepatitis, high levels are not necessarily correlated with an adverse outcome. Alkaline phosphatase levels are usually only mildly elevated, and persisting elevated levels suggest hepatitis-associated cholestasis.[233] The highest bilirubin level in the Tong study was 38 mg/dL and the peak levels of serum bilirubin were positively correlated with age. Elevated levels of total serum IgM, a mild lymphocytosis, and occasional atypical mononuclear cells are commonly found in patients with acute hepatitis A but are not diagnostic of the disease.[228,246]

The diagnosis of acute hepatitis A is most commonly confirmed by detection of specific IgM in a single acute-phase serum sample.[247] The hepatitis A-specific IgM antibody is usually present at the initial evaluation and may be detectable at the time of the first rise in ALT. IgM anti-HAV can be detected in nearly 100% of patients with acute hepatitis A at their first clinical examination and remains positive in most

for 3 to 6 months and for as long as 12 months in up to 25% of patients. False-positive tests are rare and should be suspected when IgM anti-HAV is found to persist for more than 1 year. Assays for total antibody to the virus are of little diagnostic value because IgG persists for many years and may be related to a past infection. Antibodies to naturally acquired HAV are primarily directed against the virion and do not react well with the individual peptides that make up the virion capsid. Low levels of antibodies to nonstructural proteins are found in the serum of convalescing patients and have been used to distinguish the antibody response to natural infection from the response to a killed virus preparation.[248,249]

HAV or viral antigen can be detected in the stools of patients 1 to 2 weeks before symptoms develop, but such detection has little place in routine clinical diagnosis because the tests are not widely available and shedding is often complete before the patient seeks medical attention.[73,74] Nucleic acid–based diagnostic techniques, primarily PCR or other nucleic acid amplification assays, have been used in research laboratories when a highly sensitive test for the presence of HAV is required. PCR has been very useful in the study of environmental samples.[250,251] In response to several outbreaks of hepatitis A associated with pooled plasma products, screening by nucleic acid testing (NAT) of plasma pools intended for manufacture into various plasma components has been instituted by most plasma fractionators for process testing. While these NAT are now commercially available for testing of plasma, they are not recommended for use as diagnostics for patients with acute hepatitis. The performance of these assays in the diagnostic situation has not been evaluated. The use of PCR for identifying HAV in stool samples has also not been validated as a diagnostic. Many stools have inhibitors of PCR, which could result in false-negative results. Until sufficient studies with NAT have been performed, the use of these types of assays for diagnosis cannot be recommended outside of the research setting.

Liver biopsy is rarely indicated to establish a diagnosis in acute hepatitis because this procedure is associated with a small, but finite, risk and the histopathology is not usually diagnostic. In one study done in Japan, where biopsy for acute hepatitis was routine, 86 patients with serologically established acute hepatitis A were evaluated for quantitative and qualitative light microscopic features, together with biopsy samples from 78 patients with acute hepatitis B and from 76 patients with acute hepatitis non-A, non-B. Hepatitis A was characterized by more pronounced portal inflammation than was hepatitis non-A, non-B, but less conspicuous parenchymal changes such as focal necrosis, Kupffer cell proliferation, acidophil bodies, and ballooning. Nonspecific reactive hepatitis with slightly raised serum transaminase levels was often seen during recovery from hepatitis A and needs to be distinguished from the longer-lasting cases of acute hepatitis B and C.[252,253] Hepatitis A antigen and HAV particles can be detected in the cytoplasm of infected cells by immunostaining techniques or thin-section electron microscopy.[254,255]

IMMUNITY

The high prevalence of antibody in older individuals in countries that now have a low incidence of hepatitis A suggests that anti-HAV IgG usually persists for life. Second attacks of hepatitis A have not been documented in the field and have not been induced experimentally. In two sets of experiments involving a total of 19 volunteers, reinoculation with HAV 6 to 9 months after the initial illness failed to induce disease.[5,256]

Passive immunization with immune serum globulin provides complete protection against hepatitis A, suggesting that serum antibody alone is sufficient to prevent infection. It has been difficult to judge the effect of mucosal immunity because IgA antibodies in saliva or feces are either not detected or are present at very low levels.[257] The antibody response to HAV infection is generally brisk and high titered. Both IgG and IgM can usually be detected at the time of the first expression of clinical illness (see Fig. 170-11). Neutralizing antibody as measured by in vitro tissue culture assays can also be detected early in disease. Because HAV is not usually cytopathic, a radioimmunofocus reduction test was devised that is equivalent to a plaque reduction assay.[258] This highly sensitive test was shown to correlate closely, although it is about 100-fold more sensitively than total antibody radioimmunoassay. With this assay, both IgM and IgG have been shown to possess neutralizing activity. It has also been demonstrated that patients convalescing from hepatitis A may have very high titers of in vitro neutralizing antibody. Serum dilutions of 1:100,000 to 1:500,000 or more are not uncommon.

The role of T lymphocytes in protection from HAV infection has not been fully elucidated. Undoubtedly, T-cell responses do occur, and CD8+ cytotoxic T lymphocytes and possibly natural killer cells are important in pathogenesis.[259-261]

PREVENTION

The most effective method to control hepatitis A and other enteric infections is through improved standards of hygiene and sanitation, especially the provision of clean water. Good hygienic practices with particular emphasis on hand washing and restriction of activities of workers who are ill are of primary importance in the food preparation industry. These general measures are most important to prevent hepatitis A transmission from person to person in families and hospitals. Nosocomial infections have been reported but are not common and transmission usually is from a patient who is not suspected of having hepatitis A.[262,263] Hence, hospitalized patients need only enteric isolation (see Chapter 298). Private rooms, gowns, and masks are not necessary unless the patient is incontinent. Gloves should be worn when handling any material potentially contaminated with feces. Frequent hand washing, whether gloves are worn or not, should be emphasized. Hospital personnel in general do not have a higher prevalence of antibody to HAV than matched controls do. However, several outbreaks of hepatitis A in hospital nurseries have been reported with transmission to staff.[263-265]

Travelers to developing countries should be advised to eat only properly cooked food and be careful of uncooked vegetables and shellfish. Even in the vaccine era, the maxim to prevent traveler's diarrhea, "boil it, cook it, peel it, or forget it," also applies to hepatitis A prevention.

Improvements in sanitary systems, although technologically possible, may not be practical in large parts of the world. In more developed areas, sudden deterioration in living conditions because of war or political or economic instability can rapidly degrade sanitary systems. In the developed world, hepatitis A remains a risk associated with travel to exotic areas. Therefore, considerable effort has been expended in the development of hepatitis A vaccines.

Passive Immunization

Before the licensing of hepatitis A vaccines, the mainstay of hepatitis A immunoprophylaxis had been passive immunization with pooled IG, which has been known in the past as gamma globulin or immune serum globulin. Even with the availability of vaccines, IG still has importance in hepatitis A prophylaxis. IG has proved useful for the prevention of hepatitis A in travelers, Peace Corps volunteers, and military personnel and even in postexposure prophylaxis in common-source or family outbreaks. However, IG has never been successful in altering the epidemiology of hepatitis in a high-risk community because of the transient nature of the protection, coverage rates, and perhaps lack of herd immunity.

IG is manufactured by cold ethanol precipitation from large pools of plasma collected from tens of thousands of donors.[266] At present, the individual plasma units used in these pools are screened for hepatitis B virus (HBV), hepatitis C virus (HCV), and human immunodeficiency virus (HIV) by the appropriate serologic assays. Mini-pools of plasma are tested by NAT for HCV and HIV and the product itself undergoes at least one specific viral inactivation step in its manufacturing process. Because the prevalence of antibody to HAV in the population has been declining, concern has been voiced that antibody levels against HAV in IG preparations might drop below effective levels. Although no standard for anti-HAV levels exists in IG preparations in the United States even though prophylaxis against hepatitis A is the primary use for this product, anti-HAV levels remain adequate at this time to provide short-term protection.[267] Eventually, the manufacture of IG from selected antibody-positive donors may need to be considered to develop a hyperimmune globulin for hepatitis A prevention analogous to other agent-specific hyperimmune globulins.[268] With the licensure of inactivated hepatitis A vaccines, the use of IG for preexposure prophylaxis has been largely eliminated, but IG still has a role in the prevention of hepatitis A after exposure has already occurred, when an exposure is expected before the vaccine would become effective, and in children younger than 2 years, for whom the vaccine has not been approved.

The efficacy of IG was first demonstrated in an outbreak at a summer camp in 1944 and has been confirmed many times since.[269,270] Several studies have demonstrated the effectiveness of IG in preexposure settings such as among travelers, military personnel,[271] and Peace Corps workers.[272] The rate of HAV infections in Peace Corps volunteers dropped from 1.6 to 2.1 cases per 100 per year before mandatory IG every 4 months to 0.1 to 0.3 case per 100 per year after the institution of a mandatory program.[272] Active prophylaxis with the recently licensed killed vaccines has largely supplanted the use of IG in this setting. Nevertheless, when administered before exposure or within 2 weeks after exposure, IG is more than 85% effective in preventing hepatitis A.[269,273,274] Whether IG completely prevents infection or leads to asymptomatic infection and the development of persistent anti-HAV (passive-active immunity) probably is related to the amount of time that has elapsed between exposure and IG administration.[275,276]

Active Immunization

Active Immunization with hepatitis A vaccines has developed along classic lines similar to the path followed for polio vaccines. Like poliovirus, the initial breakthrough came with the in vitro cultivation of HAV in cell lines suitable for vaccine production.[16] Formalin-inactivated, cell culture–produced, whole-virus vaccines have now been approved in much of the world.

Two HAV killed vaccines have been approved for use in the United States and widely throughout the world. A third vaccine has now been licensed in Europe, and several other similar inactivated vaccines have been developed and registered, at least in their country of manufacture.[289,290] Both widely licensed vaccines are produced from highly cell culture–adapted virus strains that have also been shown to be highly attenuated in humans, which gives them an extra measure of safety.[291] The entire nucleotide sequences of both the wild-type and the vaccine variant of strain HM175 have been determined.[41,292] A full-length, infectious cDNA clone of the cell culture–adapted virus was made,[41] and the mutations responsible for cell culture adaptation and attenuation have been determined by the molecular construction of chimeric viruses.[288,293] It was found that substitutions and deletions in the 5′ noncoding region and substitutions in the 2B/2C coding regions are highly important for cell culture adaptation and attenuation of virulence. However, mutations throughout the genome contributed to improved in vitro replication.[83]

Both licensed vaccines, Havrix (GSK) and Vaqta (Merck), are grown in MRC-5 cells, purified, inactivated by formalin, and formulated with alum as an adjuvant. Both vaccines begin to be effective about 2 weeks after a single intramuscular dose. For individuals who expect repeated exposure or require long-term protection, a booster dose is recommended 6 to 12 months after the initial vaccination.

Clinical trials indicate that inactivated hepatitis A vaccines are safe, highly immunogenic and provide durable protection against infection; the protection is expected to last at least 10 years for those receiving the primary vaccine plus the booster.[105,289,294,295] In one study, 1037 healthy seronegative children 2 to 16 years of age in a community experiencing yearly outbreaks of hepatitis A received either a single dose of formalin-inactivated vaccine (n = 519) or placebo (n = 518). No cases of hepatitis occurred in the vaccinated group, except for a few that appeared within 3 weeks of vaccination. These cases represented patients who were already incubating the infection at the time of vaccination. In the period from 21 days to 103 days, 34 cases of hepatitis A were observed, all in the placebo group indicating a 100% vaccine protective efficacy during that period of observation.[296,297] Vaccination of children at 2 years of age has continued in this community since the time of the original trial. Despite the reintroduction of HAV from unvaccinated individuals joining the community, no new outbreaks have occurred over a 9-year span. In a large field trial of an inactivated vaccine involving over 40,000 children in Thailand, the vaccine was found to be at least 80% effective in comparison to placebo and was without serious adverse reactions.[105]

While the absolute level of antibody required to protect against infection has not been rigorously established, it is accepted based on comparisons with protective antibody levels associated with passive immunization with IG that antibody concentrations of 10 to 20 mIU/mL (depending on the assay used) are protective.[294,298,299] The licensed inactivated hepatitis A vaccines have all been shown to be highly and rapidly immunogenic. They induce seroconversions to protective levels of antibody in as little as 2 weeks after the initial dose.[300,301] Therefore, travelers, military personnel, or others who had no previous vaccine could be vaccinated as little as 2 weeks before their expected exposure instead of receiving IG.[302] The level of antibody after vaccination varies with the dose and schedule of the vaccine. However, after a single dose of vaccine, antibody titers are higher than titers produced by known protective levels of IG but are generally lower than titers measured after natural infection.[303-305] The quality of the antibody response after vaccination has also been studied by comparing antibodies detected by radioimmunoassay, radioimmunoprecipitation, and in vitro neutralization in sera from persons passively immunized with IG and in persons immunized by vaccine. With the antibody normalized between the two groups by radioimmunoassay, the IG recipients had higher neutralization titers but negligible radioimmunoprecipitation titers compared with the group who was vac-

cinated.[305] However, it has also been shown that IG prepared from the serum of vaccinees could protect a chimpanzee from HAV challenge when the titer of antibody achieved by passive immunization in the chimpanzee was similar to that found in humans receiving IG prophylaxis.[306] It must also be understood that there are no direct correlations between in vitro neutralization assays and seroprotection. Regardless of the results of antibody measurements following vaccination, clinical trials have demonstrated that the vaccine is highly effective within a month after the first dose.

Certain factors may reduce the response to the vaccine. Only about 75% of HIV-positive vaccinees developed protective levels of antibody, and those that responded had lower antibody titers than vaccinees without HIV.[307] The final antibody concentrations achieved in patients with chronic liver disease were also lower than in normal subjects, but the seroprotection rates were about the same. The common recommended schedule of a single dose followed by a booster dose 6 to 12 months later produces very high levels of antibody, well in excess of that achieved after passive immunization with IG that are known to be effective. After the booster dose, it is estimated that protective levels of antibody will persist for at least 20 years.[308] Because the incubation period for hepatitis A is usually 4 weeks and the anamnestic responses observed after the 12-month booster are rapid and robust, it has been suggested that vaccinees who have seroconverted will be protected even if their antibody levels have fallen below protective levels.[294] Long-term follow-up studies will have to be performed to confirm this hypothesis.

Live attenuated vaccines based on the CR326 and the HM175 strains have also been tested in primates and to a limited extent in humans, and the H2 strain has been used in extended clinical studies in China.[277-281] Both CR326 and HM175 strains have been evaluated as candidate live vaccines and found to be highly attenuated in humans.[279,282] For both strains, an inoculum dose of greater than 10^6 tissue culture infective doses was required to induce an antibody response in volunteers. Even at high doses in the volunteers, it was not possible to prove that the vaccine virus replicated because no vaccine virus was ever isolated from the volunteers and the only evidence for replication was seroconversion, which could have been induced by the antigenic mass contained in the inoculum rather than new antigen produced by replication.

The entire nucleotide sequences of both the wild type and the vaccine variant of HM175 have been determined.[283,284] A full-length, infectious cDNA clone of the cell culture–adapted virus was made,[285] and the mutations responsible for cell culture adaptation and attenuation were determined by the molecular construction of chimeric viruses.[286-288] It was found that substitutions and deletions in the 5′ noncoding region and substitutions in the 2B/C coding regions are highly important for cell culture adaptation and attenuation of virulence. However, mutations throughout the genome contributed to improved in vitro replication.[85] It may be difficult to develop a live vaccine that is both adequately immunogenic and attenuated because the properties of replication and pathogenesis may be closely linked.

RECOMMENDATIONS FOR PREVENTION

Passive Immunization

Immune globulin is recommended to prevent hepatitis A after exposure in certain settings (Table 170-4). Household and sexual contacts of patients with hepatitis A should receive IG as soon as possible but no later than 2 weeks after exposure.[158] Casual contacts such as school classmates or co-workers who have not had close physical contact usually do not require IG. Aggressive use of IG is indicated to control hepatitis A outbreaks in child care centers when a child or an employee is diagnosed with hepatitis A.[158,170] Outbreaks in other settings (e.g., hospitals, facilities for developmentally disabled persons) are rare. When a food handler is identified with hepatitis A, IG should be administered to other food handlers at the food establishment and can be considered

TABLE 170-4 Recommendations for Hepatitis A Postexposure Prophylaxis

Time Since Exposure	Future Exposure Likely or Other Indication for Vaccination*	Recommended Prophylaxis
<2 wk	No	IG 0.02 mL/kg
<2 wk	Yes	IG 0.02 mL/kg and initiate hepatitis A vaccine series†
>2 wk	No	None
>2 wk	Yes	Initiate hepatitis A vaccine series

*See Table 170-6.

†Children <2 years of age (for whom vaccine is not licensed) and persons with a contraindication to vaccination should receive immune globulin (IG) 0.06 mL/kg, repeated every 5 months during exposure.

for patrons if certain other conditions exist.[117,158,119] Once cases are identified that are associated with a food service establishment, it generally is too late to administer IG to patrons because the 2-week postexposure period during which IG is effective will have passed.

IG also may be used for preexposure prophylaxis for persons who are traveling to countries with high, transitional, or intermediate hepatitis A endemicity, instead of or in addition to hepatitis A vaccine (Tables 170-5 and 170-6).[158] Travelers who need optimal protection earlier than 4 weeks after the first dose of vaccine should also receive IG with the first vaccine dose (0.02 mL/kg), at a different injection site. IG should be given to travelers younger than 2 years of age, because hepatitis A vaccine is not licensed for children in this age

TABLE 170-5 Recommendations for Hepatitis A Preexposure Immunoprophylaxis

Age (yr)	Exposure Duration	Recommended Prophylaxis
<2	Short term (<3 mo)	IG 0.02 mL/kg
<2	3-5 mo	IG 0.06 mL/kg
<2	>5 mo	IG 0.06 mL/kg repeated every 5 mo
>2	Short or long term	Hepatitis A vaccine
		Hepatitis A vaccine and IG (0.02 mL/kg) if exposure is expected in less than 2-4 weeks
		Substitute IG as above if vaccine is contraindicated or refused

IG, immune globulin.

group, to prevent the rare severe cases that occur, and to prevent transmission to others after returning from abroad.[158] Economic analyses have shown that, in general, hepatitis A vaccine becomes more cost effective than IG as the number of expected trips to endemic areas or the duration of each trip increases.[309,310] IG also can be used for preexposure prophylaxis for travelers who are allergic to vaccine or components.

The usual dose of IG is a single intramuscular injection of 0.02 or 0.06 mL per kg (see Table 170-4). The lower dose is adequate to provide protection for up to 3 months and the higher dose is effective for up to 5 months.[311] Readministration every 5 months is necessary for extended trips, and hepatitis A vaccine, if not contraindicated, is probably a better choice for such travelers. Intramuscular preparations of IG should never be given intravenously, and the intravenous preparations of IG are not intended for hepatitis A prevention and are formulated at a lower globulin concentration.

IG does not interfere with the immune response to oral polio virus or yellow fever vaccine or, in general, to inactivated vaccines. However, IG can interfere with the immune response to some live attenuated vaccines (e.g., measles, mumps, rubella vaccine [MMR], varicella vaccine) (see Chapter 319). Administration of MMR should be delayed for at least 3 months, and of varicella vaccine for at least 5 months after administration of IG. IG should not be given within 2 weeks after the administration of MMR or within 3 weeks of varicella vaccine, unless the benefits of IG administration are greater than the benefits of vaccination.[312]

Serious adverse events from IG are rare. Because anaphylaxis has been reported after repeated administration to persons with immunoglobulin A deficiency, these persons should not receive IG.[313] Pregnancy or lactation is not a contraindication to IG administration. For infants and pregnant women, a preparation that does not include thimerosal is preferable.

Active Immunization

Inactivated hepatitis A vaccine is indicated for susceptible persons 2 years of age or older at increased risk of hepatitis A, and for any person wishing to obtain immunity.

Prevaccination serologic testing may be considered to reduce costs by not vaccinating persons with prior immunity, such as older adolescents and adults in certain population groups with a high prevalence of infection (e.g., persons born in areas of high hepatitis A endemicity), but should take into account the cost of testing, vaccine cost, and the likelihood that the person will return for vaccination.[314] Vaccination of immune people is not harmful. Postvaccination testing is not indicated because of the high rate of vaccine response. Furthermore, testing methods that can detect the low anti-HAV concentrations generated by immunization are not licensed for use in the United States.

TABLE 170-6 Recommendations for Routine Preexposure Use of Hepatitis A Virus (HAV) Vaccine*

Group	Comments
Children living in communities with consistently elevated hepatitis A rates	Includes Alaska, Arizona, California, Idaho, Nevada, New Mexico, Oklahoma, Oregon, South Dakota, Utah, Washington, and selected areas in other states†‡
International travelers§	Immune globulin may be given in addition to or instead of vaccine; children <2 years old should receive immune globulin
Men who have sex with men	Includes adolescents
Illicit drug users	Includes adolescents
Persons with chronic liver disease	Increased risk of fulminant hepatitis A with HAV infection
Persons receiving clotting factor concentrates	
Persons who work with HAV in research laboratory settings	

*Hepatitis A vaccine is not licensed for children <2 years old.

†Where the average reported hepatitis A incidence during 1987-1997 was ≥20/100,000 population (approximately twice the national average).

‡Routine vaccination can also be considered for children living in Arkansas, Colorado, Missouri, Montana, Texas, Wyoming, and selected areas in other states where the average reported incidence during 1987-1997 was ≥10/100,000 population but <20/100,000.

§Persons traveling to Canada, western Europe, Japan, Australia, or New Zealand are at no greater risk than in the United States.

From Centers for Disease Control and Prevention. Prevention of hepatitis A through active or passive immunization. Recommendations of the Advisory Committee on Immunization Practices. MMWR Morb Mortal Wkly Rep. 1999;48(RR-12):1-37.

Disease Control Strategies

Soon after hepatitis A vaccines became available in the United States, it was recognized that a strategy of widespread routine vaccination of children had the potential to achieve a sustained reduction in the overall incidence of hepatitis A in the United States, by preventing infection among individuals in age groups that accounted for at least one-third of cases and eliminating a major source of infection for others. However, hepatitis A vaccines could not be readily incorporated into the routine infant schedule because they are not currently licensed for children younger than 2 years. To overcome these logistical barriers to widespread use of hepatitis A vaccines among children, a novel vaccination strategy was developed, based on distinct features of hepatitis A epidemiology and experience gathered from demonstration projects and other research, involving incremental implementation of routine childhood hepatitis A vaccination.

Recommendations for use of hepatitis A vaccine were first issued by the ACIP of the U.S. Public Health Service, the American Academy of Pediatrics (AAP), and other groups in 1996, and updated in 1999 (Table 170-7; see also Tables 170-5 and 170-6).[157,158,315] The initial recommendations, published in 1996 soon after vaccines became available in the United States, called for routine vaccination of children living in communities with the highest hepatitis A rates (e.g., American Indian and Alaska Native communities).[157] Although apparently effective in reducing disease rates in communities covered by the 1996 recommendations, implementation of these recommendations had little impact on overall disease incidence nationwide because only a small proportion of nationally reported cases occurred among persons in such communities. In 1999 the recommendation for routine vaccination of children was extended to include those living in states, counties, and communities with consistently elevated hepatitis A rates (see Tables 170-1 and 170-6),[158] with an average reported incidence of more than 10 cases per 100,000 population in 1987-1997.

Recommended Groups and Settings

Children Living in Areas with Consistently Elevated Hepatitis A Rates

Children living in areas where rates of hepatitis A have been consistently elevated should be routinely vaccinated, beginning at or after 2 years of age (see "Epidemiology"; Tables 170-1 and 170-6). Various vaccination strategies can be used, including vaccinating one or more single-age cohorts of children or adolescents, vaccination of children in selected settings (e.g., daycare), or vaccination of children and adolescents over a wide range of ages in a variety of settings, such as when they seek health care for other purposes.

TABLE 170-7 Recommended Doses and Schedules for Inactivated Hepatitis A Vaccines

Age (yr)	Vaccine	Dose	Volume (mL)	No. of Doses	Schedule (mo)*
2-18	HAVRIX	720 ELU†	0.5	2	0, 6-12
	VAQTA	25 U‡	0.5	2	0, 6-18
≥19	HAVRIX	1440 ELU	1.0	2	0, 6-12
	VAQTA	50 U‡	1.0	2	0, 6-18
>15	AVAXIM‖	160 antigen units	0.5	2	0, 6-12
1-15	AVAXIM‖	80 antigen units	0.5	2	0, 6-12
≥2	EPAXAL‖	24 IU§	0.5	2	0. 6-12

*0 months represents timing of initial dose; subsequent numbers represent months after the initial dose.
†Enzyme-linked immunosorbent assay (ELISA) units.
‡Units.
§International units.
‖Not licensed in the United States.

Persons at Increased Risk of Hepatitis A Infection or Severe Consequences

Men Who Have Sex with Men. Adolescent and adult men who have sex with men should be vaccinated, regardless of reported level of sexual activity.[158,161] Prevaccination serologic testing is not necessary for vaccination of adolescents and young adults, but could be considered for older adults.

Users of Illicit Drugs. Vaccination is recommended for users of injected and noninjected illegal drugs. Prevaccination testing could be considered for adults; the need might depend on the particular characteristics of the population of drug users, including the type and duration of drug use.[180,181,316]

International Travelers. Susceptible persons who travel to or work in countries where hepatitis A is endemic should be vaccinated or receive IG before departure. Hepatitis A vaccination is preferred, particularly for persons who plan frequent travel or will live in an endemic area. The first dose should be administered as soon as travel is considered. Travelers who need optimal protection earlier than 4 weeks after the first dose of vaccine should also receive IG with the first vaccine dose (0.02 mL/kg), at a different injection site. Prevaccination serologic testing should be considered for older travelers or younger travelers who were born in a country in which hepatitis A is endemic.

Regular Recipients of Blood or Plasma-Derived Products. The risk of hepatitis A from a blood transfusion or from plasma derivatives is extremely low, but both have been reported.[41,282] Individuals who receive these products regularly should be immunized against diseases transmitted via blood-borne means with available vaccines. Many recipients of factor VIII, for instance, have been infected by hepatitis C virus or even hepatitis B virus, and they should not undergo another infection of their liver. Presently, these products are treated by a viral inactivation process often based on solvents or heat. Because HAV is resistant to organic solvents and is relatively resistant to heat, cases of hepatitis A associated with factor VIII have caused the manufacturers to begin to develop new methods that would eliminate infectious HAV from their products. Nevertheless, vaccination of this group remains prudent.

Persons with Chronic Liver Disease. Although individuals with chronic liver disease may not be at increased risk for hepatitis A, acute hepatitis A infections in such patients can have very serious or fatal consequences.[317] Therefore, it is recommended that all such persons, no matter the etiology of their liver disease, be vaccinated against hepatitis A.

Other Groups and Settings. Persons who work with HAV in research settings and persons who have clotting factor disorders should also be vaccinated.[158]

Although hepatitis A outbreaks occur in child care centers, their frequency is not high enough to warrant routine vaccination of attendees or staff to prevent them, and there is little experience using vaccine to control outbreaks when they occur.[318] When outbreaks are recognized, aggressive use of IG is effective in limiting transmission.[168] In areas where routine vaccination of children is recommended, previously unvaccinated children can be vaccinated when they receive postexposure prophylaxis with IG.[158] In addition, child care center attendees can be a readily accessible target population for ongoing routine vaccination programs.

The frequency of outbreaks in hospitals, institutions, and schools is not high enough to warrant routine vaccination of persons in these settings, and there are no data with respect to using vaccine to control outbreaks in these settings. Although persons who work as food handlers are not at increased risk of hepatitis A because of their occupation, they may transmit HAV to others when they contract hepatitis A.[201] To reduce the frequency of evaluations of food handlers with hepatitis A and the need for postexposure prophylaxis of patrons, public health officials in some jurisdictions have instituted measures to promote hepatitis A vaccination of food handlers.[319] However, because transmission from infected food handlers accounts for a very small proportion of cases nationwide, vaccination of food handlers is not likely to affect overall disease incidence, and has not been found to be cost effective.[320]

Community-Wide Outbreaks. There has been considerable interest in using hepatitis A vaccine to control ongoing community-wide epidemics. Implementation of routine vaccination of children, which is recommended for most areas that include communities that experience these outbreaks, will prevent them in the future. Because of logistical difficulties, accelerated vaccination as an additional measure to control outbreaks should be undertaken with caution.[158] Efforts are probably better directed towards sustained routine vaccination of children to maintain high levels of immunity and prevent future epidemics.

IMPLEMENTATION OF PREVENTION STRATEGIES

Communities with the Highest Hepatitis A Rates

Hepatitis A epidemics typically occurred every 5 to 10 years in these communities.[321] Few cases occur among persons older than 15 years; seroprevalence data indicate that 30% to 40% of children acquire infection by 5 years of age, and almost all persons have been infected by early adulthood.[322-325] Demonstration projects conducted soon after hepatitis A vaccines became available showed that routine vaccination of children living in these communities was feasible, and that when relatively high vaccination coverage was achieved and sustained, ongoing epidemics were interrupted, and a reduction in disease incidence was sustained.[321,326] For example, a 1992-1993 community-wide epidemic among Alaska Natives in one rural area was ended within 4 to 8 weeks of vaccinating approximately 80% of children and young adults.[326]

Following publication in 1996 of recommendations for routine vaccination of children in these areas to prevent such outbreaks, surveys indicated vaccination coverage of 50% to 80% among preschool and school-aged American Indian and Alaska Native children, suggesting that recommendations were being implemented.[160] By 2000, hepatitis A incidence among American Indians and Alaska Natives had declined by 97% compared with the beginning of the decade, and was lower than the overall U.S. rate (Fig. 170-12).[160] A decline of this magnitude has not been observed in the previous 30 years of surveillance, and suggests a fundamental alteration in hepatitis A epidemiology in American Indian and Alaska Native

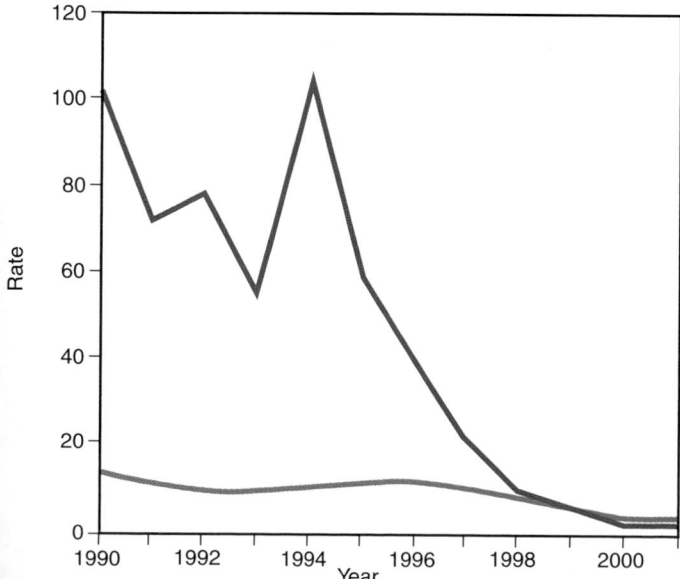

FIGURE 170-12. Hepatitis A incidence, United States, and American Indians and Alaska Natives, 1990-2001. The purple line represents the rate among American Indians and Alaska Natives; the brown line represents the overall U.S. rate. *(From the Centers for Disease Control and Prevention, National Notifiable Diseases Surveillance System, Atlanta, GA.)*

Communities with Consistently Elevated Rates

Areas with consistently elevated rates, in which routine hepatitis A vaccination of children was recommended, were defined using average rates during a baseline period of 1987-1997 (see Table 170-1). Overall, national hepatitis A rates have been falling precipitously over the past several years (Fig. 170-13). The provisional 2002 rate in states with consistently elevated rates represents a decline of approximately 85%, compared to the average rate during the baseline period and approaches, for the first time, the rate in states in which no statewide routine vaccination of children is recommended, where the rate has decreased by 50% compared with the baseline period.[327] Rates have declined most dramatically among children 2 to 18 years old.

At least 2 million pediatric doses of hepatitis A vaccine were purchased in the public sector alone each year since 2000. Thus, the precipitous decrease in hepatitis A rates in states likely reflects, at least in part, the impact of routine vaccination of children. However, because hepatitis A incidence is cyclic, additional years of data are needed to verify that low rates are sustained and attributable to vaccination, and for a definitive determination of the overall impact of this strategy of routine childhood vaccination in selected, higher incidence areas.

DIRECTIONS FOR THE FUTURE

At the present, hepatitis A vaccination is generally not indicated in developing countries, particularly those with highest endemicity where infection in early childhood is nearly universal and disease is uncommon. Although vaccination strategies could be devised directed at areas within transitional or intermediate endemicity countries where a sizeable proportion of adults are likely to be susceptible, such as urban areas with good water and sanitation facilities, the relative cost effectiveness of hepatitis A vaccination compared with other major health public health priorities has not been evaluated. However, the global disease burden associated with hepatitis A will increase in the coming years, particularly in these areas, as a larger proportion of the population remains susceptible to HAV infection into adolescence and adulthood, because of continuing improvements in standards of living and sanitary and hygienic conditions.[111] If vaccine was available at a low cost and vaccination was shown to be cost effective, some countries in which a significant susceptible adolescent and adult population has developed might find it useful to include hepatitis A in their vaccination programs.

In the United States, vaccination of successive cohorts of children should eventually result in a sustained reduction in disease incidence nationwide, providing the opportunity to eliminate HAV transmission. To achieve this goal, vaccination of young children nationwide will be needed. Advances in hepatitis A vaccine development, such as the availability of a vaccine that can be used in the first 2 years of life and of combination vaccines that include hepatitis A vaccine, would facilitate this effort.

HAV has been considered as a target for eradication, but international bodies have not made this recommendation, primarily because of considerations of cost and feasibility.[328] At present, the disease can best be controlled by improving living conditions in the developing world and the wise application of the existing vaccines in other areas.

THERAPY AND GENERAL MANAGEMENT

There is no specific therapy are available for hepatitis A, and management is supportive without hospitalization. In the rare event of fulminant hepatitis, hospitalization and symptomatic supportive treatment become necessary.[243] Identification of patients requiring liver transplantation is difficult because as many as 60% of patients, especially children, with fulminant hepatic failure caused by hepatitis A survive.[329] Transplantation is used for the management of carefully selected patients who have a poor prognosis with medical management alone. The survival rate is reported to be 80%, although reinfection has been reported.[330,331]

FIGURE 170-13. Hepatitis A incidence rates by county, United States, 1987-1997 and 2002. The top map represents the average incidence during 1987-1997; the bottom map represents 2002 incidence. *(From the Centers for Disease Control and Prevention, National Notifiable Diseases Surveillance System, Atlanta, GA. 2002 data are provisional.)*

1987 - 97 average incidence

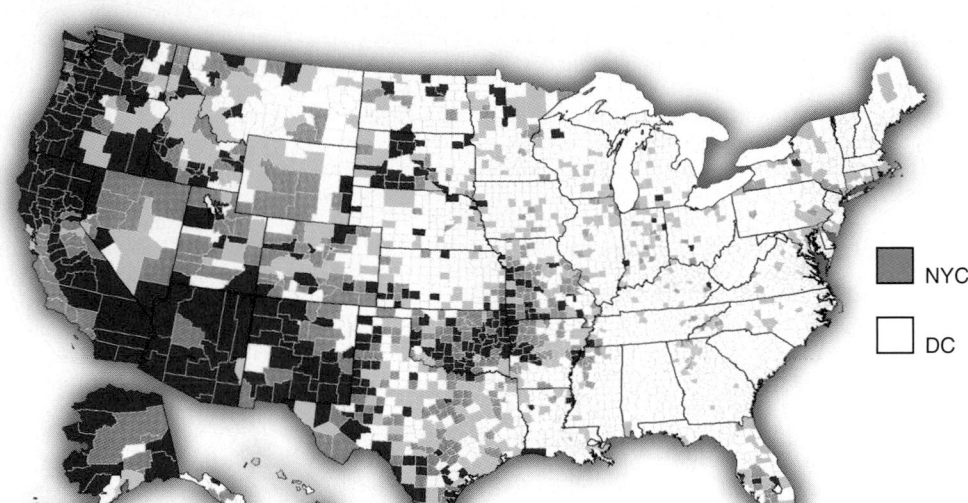

2002 incidence

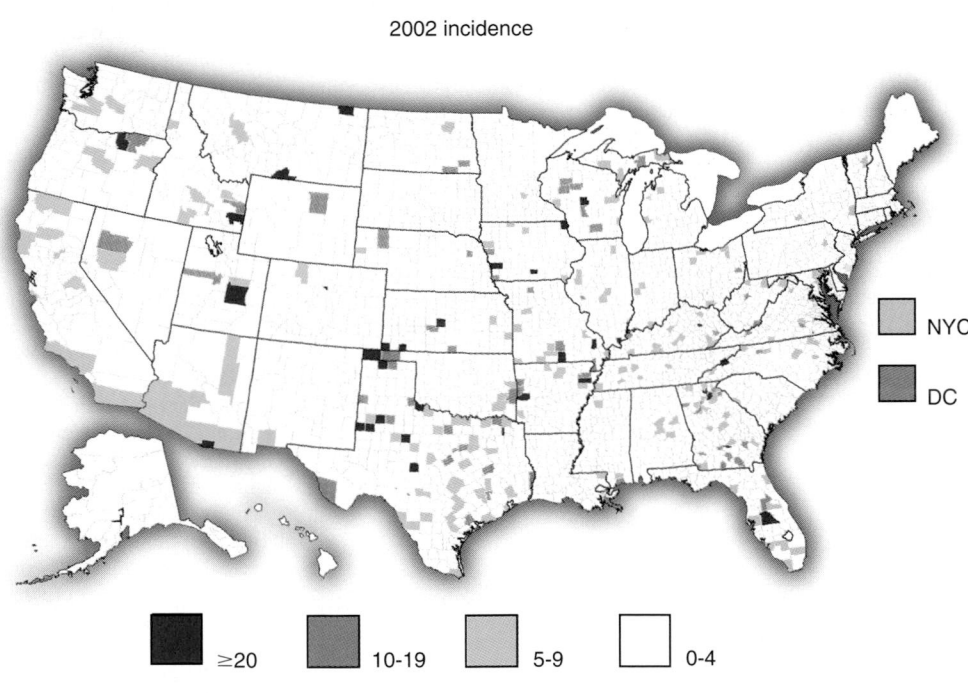

≥20   10-19   5-9   0-4

Rate per 100,000

In most patients with hepatitis A, admission to the hospital is not indicated, provided that patients have access to good care. If hospitalized, fecally incontinent patients, patients with diarrhea, and small children should be given a separate room and toilet. The necessity for bed rest seems to have been overstated because no objective evidence has been provided that bed rest or restriction of physical activity affects the outcome of disease. Dietary restrictions, including prohibition of even modest amounts of alcohol, also seem to have little effect on outcome. Nevertheless, recommendation of abstention from alcohol has become conventional because alcohol has been linked with relapse of jaundice.[332] Whatever the clinical presentation of any given case of hepatitis A, it is important to recognize that all cases, except the rare event of fulminant hepatitis A, will resolve without any chronic sequelae.

REFERENCES

1. Zuckerman AJ. The history of viral hepatitis from antiquity to the present. In: Deinhardt F, Deinhardt J (eds). Viral Hepatitis: Laboratory and Clinical Science. New York: Marcel Dekker; 1983:3-32.
2. Virchow R. Ueber das Vorkommen und den Nachweis des Hepatogenen, Insbesondere des Katarrhalischen Icterus. Virchows Arch (Pathol Anat). 1865;32:117.
3. McDonald S. Acute yellow atrophy of the liver. Edinb Med J. 1907;1:83.
4. Cockayne EA. Catarrhal jaundice, sporadic and epidemic, and its relation to acute yellow atrophy of the liver. Q J Med. 1912;6:1-29.
5. Havens WP Jr. Immunity in experimentally induced infectious hepatitis. J Exp Med. 1946;84:403.
6. Havens WP Jr, Paul JR. Prevention of infectious hepatitis with gamma globulin. JAMA. 1997;129:270-272.
7. Neefe JR, Gellis SS, Stokes J Jr. Homologous serum hepatitis and infectious (epidemic) hepatitis; studies in volunteers bearing on immunological and other characteristics of the etiological agents. Am J Med. 1946;1:9.
8. MacCallum FO. Early studies on viral hepatitis. Br Med Bull. 1972;28:105-108.

9. Havens WPJ, Ward R, Drill VA, et al. Experimental production of hepatitis by feeding icterogenic materials. Proc Soc Exp Biol Med. 1944;57:206-208.
10. MacCallum FO. Transmission of infective hepatitis to human volunteers. Lancet. 1944;2:228.
11. Gellis SS, Stokes J Jr, Brother GM, et al. The use of immune globulin (gamma globulin) in infectious (epidemic) hepatitis in the Mediterranian theatre of operations. JAMA. 1945;128:1062.
12. Krugman S. Viral hepatitis: Overview and historical perspectives. Yale J Biol Med. 1976;49:199-203.
13. Feinstone SM, Kapikian AZ, Purcell RH. Hepatitis A. detection by immune electron microscopy of a viruslike antigen associated with acute illness. Science. 1973;182:1026-1028.
14. Maynard JE, Lorenz D, Bradley DW, et al. Review of infectivity studies in nonhuman primates with virus-like particles associated with MS-1 hepatitis. Am J Med Sci. 1975;270:81-85.
15. Dienstag JL, Feinstone SM, Purcell RH, et al. Experimental infection of chimpanzees with hepatitis A virus. J Infect Dis. 1975;132:532-545.
16. Provost PJ, Hilleman MR. Propagation of human hepatitis A virus in cell culture in vitro. Proc Soc Exp Biol Med. 1979;160:213-221.
17. Frosner GG, Deinhardt F, Scheid R, et al. Propagation of human hepatitis A virus in a hepatoma cell line. Infection. 1979;7:303-305.
18. Daemer RJ, Feinstone SM, Gust ID, et al. Propagation of human hepatitis A virus in African green monkey kidney cell culture: primary isolation and serial passage. Infect Immun. 1981;32:388-393.
19. Ticehurst JR, Racaniello VR, Baroudy BM, et al. Molecular cloning and characterization of hepatitis A virus cDNA. Proc Natl Acad Sci U S A. 1983;80:5885-5889.
20. Andre FE, D'Hondt E, Delem A, et al. Clinical assessment of the safety and efficacy of an inactivated hepatitis A vaccine: Rationale and summary of findings. Vaccine. 1992;10 (Suppl 1):S160-S168.
21. Melnick JL. Properties and classification of hepatitis A virus. Vaccine. 1992;10(Suppl 1):S24-S26.
22. Pringle CR. Virus taxonomy-San Diego. 1998. Arch Virol. 1998;143:1449-1459.
23. Luo M, Rossmann MG, Palmenberg AC. Prediction of three-dimensional models for foot-and-mouth disease virus and hepatitis A virus. Virology. 1988;166:503-514.
24. Coulepis AG, Locarnini SA, Westaway EG, et al. Biophysical and biochemical characterization of hepatitis V virus. Intervirology. 1982;18:107-127.
25. Lemon SM, Jansen RW, Newbold JE. Infectious hepatitis A virus particles produced in cell culture consist of three distinct types with different buoyant densities in CsCl. J Virol. 1985;54:78-85.
26. Siegl G, Frosner GG. Characterization and classification of virus particles associated with hepatitis A. I. Size, density, and sedimentation. J Virol. 1978;26:40-47.
27. Murphy P, Nowak T, Lemon SM, et al. Inactivation of hepatitis A virus by heat treatment in aqueous solution. J Med Virol. 1993;41:61-64.
28. Nissen E, Konig P, Feinstone SM, et al. Inactivation of hepatitis A and other enteroviruses during heat treatment (pasteurization). Biologicals. 1996;24:339-341.
29. Murphy P, Nowak T, Lemon SM, et al. Inactivation of hepatitis A virus by heat treatment in aqueous solution. J Med Virol. 1993;41:61-64.
30. Parry JV, Mortimer PP. The heat sensitivity of hepatitis A virus determined by a simple tissue culture method. J Med Virol. 1984;14:277-283.
31. Favero MS, Bond WW. Disinfection and sterilization. In: Zuckerman AJ, Thomas HC, eds. Viral hepatitis, scientific basis, and clinical management. New York, Churchill Livingston;1993:565-575.
32. Sobsey MD. Survival and persistence of hepatitis A virus in environmental samples. In: Zuckerman AJ (ed). Viral hepatitis and liver disease. Alan R. Liss, New York, 1988, p 124.
33. Millard J, Appleton H, Parry JV. Studies on heat inactivation of hepatitis A virus with special reference to shellfish. Part 1. Procedures for infection and recovery of virus from laboratory-maintained cockles. Epidemiol Infect. 1987;98:397-414.
34. Peterson DA, Hurley TR, Hoff JC, et al. Effect of chlorine treatment on infectivity of hepatitis A virus. Appl Environ Microbiol. 1983;45:223-227.
35. Siegl G, Weitz M, Kronauer G. Stability of hepatitis A virus. Intervirology. 1984;22:218-226.
36. Peterson DA, Hurley TR, Hoff JC, et al. Effect of chlorine treatment on infectivity of hepatitis A virus. Appl Environ Microbiol. 1983;45:223-227.
37. Mannucci PM, Gdovin S, Gringeri A, et al. Transmission of hepatitis A to patients with hemophilia by factor VIII concentrates treated with organic solvent and detergent to inactivate viruses. The Italian Collaborative Group. Ann Intern Med. 1994;120:1-7.
38. Hart H, Jones J, Cubie H, et al. Distribution of hepatitis A antibody over a process for the preparation of a high-purity factor VIII concentrate. Vox Sang. 1994;67(Suppl 1):51-55.
39. Johnston A, MacGregor A, Borovec S, et al. Inactivation and clearance of viruses during the manufacture of high purity factor IX. Biologicals. 2000;28:129-136.
40. Borovec S, Broumis C, Adcock W, et al. Inactivation kinetics of model and relevant blood-borne viruses by treatment with sodium hydroxide and heat. Biologicals. 1998;26:237-244.
41. Cohen JI, Rosenblum B, Ticehurst JR, et al. Complete nucleotide sequence of an attenuated hepatitis A virus: Comparison with wild-type virus. Proc Natl Acad Sci U S A. 1987;84:2497-2501.
42. Cohen JI, Ticehurst JR, Feinstone SM, et al. Hepatitis A virus cDNA and its RNA transcripts are infectious in cell culture. J Virol. 1987;61:3035-3039.
43. Weitz M, Baroudy BM, Maloy WL, et al. Detection of a genome-linked protein (VPg) of hepatitis A virus and its comparison with other picornaviral VPgs. J Virol. 1986;60:124-130.
44. Ruckert RR, Wimmer E. Systematic nomenclature of picornavirus proteins. J Virol. 1984;50:957-959.

45. Tratschin JD, Siegl G, Frosner GG, et al. Characterization and classification of virus particles associated with hepatitis A. III. Structural proteins. J Virol. 1981;38:151-156.
46. Updike WS, Tesar M, Ehrenfeld E. Detection of hepatitis A virus proteins in infected BS-C-1 cells. Virology. 1991;185:411-418.
47. Bishop NE, Anderson DA. RNA-dependent cleavage of VP0 capsid protein in provirions of hepatitis A virus. Virology. 1993;197:616-623.
48. Anderson DA, Ross BC. Morphogenesis of hepatitis A virus: Isolation and characterization of subviral particles. J Virol. 1990;64:5284-5289.
49. Borovec SV, Anderson DA. Synthesis and assembly of hepatitis A virus-specific proteins in BS-C-1 cells. J Virol. 1993;67:3095-3102.
50. Probst C, Jecht M, Gauss-Muller V. Intrinsic signals for the assembly of hepatitis A virus particles. Role of structural proteins VP4 and 2A. J Biol Chem. 1999;274:4527-4531.
51. Cohen L, Benichou D, Martin A. Analysis of deletion mutants indicates that the 2A polypeptide of hepatitis A virus participates in virion morphogenesis. J Virol. 2002;76:7495-7505.
52. Graff J, Richards OC, Swiderek KM, et al. Hepatitis A virus capsid protein VP1 has a heterogeneous C terminus. J Virol. 1999;73:6015-6023.
53. Lagos R, Potin M, Munoz A, et al. [Serum antibodies against hepatitis A virus among subjects of middle and low socioeconomic levels in urban area of Santiago, Chile]. Rev Med Chil. 1999;127:429-436.
54. Lemon SM, Chao SF, Jansen RW, et al. Genomic heterogeneity among human and nonhuman strains of hepatitis A virus. J Virol. 1987;61:735-742.
55. Stapleton JT, Lemon SM. Neutralization escape mutants define a dominant immunogenic neutralization site on hepatitis A virus. J Virol. 1987;61:491-498.
56. Lemon SM, Binn LN. Serum neutralizing antibody response to hepatitis A virus. J Infect Dis. 1983;148:1033-1039.
57. Lemon SM, Binn LN. Antigenic relatedness of two strains of hepatitis A virus determined by cross-neutralization. Infect Immun. 1983;42:418-420.
58. Ping LH, Lemon SM. Antigenic structure of human hepatitis A virus defined by analysis of escape mutants selected against murine monoclonal antibodies. J Virol. 1992;66:2208-2216.
59. Robertson BH, Khanna B, Nainan OV, et al. Epidemiologic patterns of wild-type hepatitis A virus determined by genetic variation. J Infect Dis. 1991;163:286-292.
60. Robertson BH, Jansen RW, Khanna B, et al. Genetic relatedness of hepatitis A virus strains recovered from different geographical regions. J Gen Virol. 1992;73:1365-1377.
61. Brown EA, Jansen RW, Lemon SM. Characterization of a simian hepatitis A virus (HAV): Antigenic and genetic comparison with human HAV. J Virol. 1989;63:4932-4937.
62. Jansen RW, Siegl G, Lemon SM. Molecular epidemiology of human hepatitis A virus defined by an antigen-capture polymerase chain reaction method. Proc Natl Acad Sci U S A. 1990;87:2867-2871.
63. Gauss-Muller V, Frosner GG, Deinhardt F. Propagation of hepatitis A virus in human embryo fibroblasts. J Med Virol. 1981;7:233-239.
64. Dotzauer A, Feinstone SM, Kaplan G. Susceptibility of nonprimate cell lines to hepatitis A virus infection [published erratum appears in J Virol. 1994;68:6829]. J Virol. 1994;68:6064-6068.
65. Siegl G. Replication of hepatitis A virus and processing of proteins. Vaccine. 1992;10(Suppl 1):S32-S35.
66. de Chastonay J, Siegl G. Replicative events in hepatitis A virus-infected MRC-5 cells. Virology. 1987;157:268-275.
67. Anderson DA. Cytopathology, plaque assay, and heat inactivation of hepatitis A virus strain HM175. J Med Virol. 1987;22:35-44.
68. Cromeans T, Sobsey MD, Fields HA. Development of a plaque assay for a cytopathic, rapidly replicating isolate of hepatitis A virus. J Med Virol. 1987;22:45-56.
69. Cromeans T, Fields HA, Sobsey MD. Replication kinetics and cytopathic effect of hepatitis A virus. J Gen Virol. 1989;70:2051-2062.
70. Binn LN, Lemon SM, Marchwicki RH, et al. Primary isolation and serial passage of hepatitis A virus strains in primate cell cultures. J Clin Microbiol. 1984;20:28-33.
71. Siegl G, deChastonay J, Kronauer G. Propagation and assay of hepatitis A virus in vitro. J Virol Methods. 1984;9:53-67.
72. Mathiesen LR, Fauerholdt L, Moller AM, et al. Immunofluorescence studies for hepatitis A virus and hepatitis B surface and core antigen in liver biopsies from patients with acute viral hepatitis. Gastroenterology. 1979;77:623-628.
73. Hollinger FB, Bradley DW, Maynard JE, et al. Detection of hepatitis A viral antigen by radioimmunoassay. J Immunol. 1975;115:1464-1466.
74. Purcell RH, Wong DC, Moritsugu Y, et al. A microtiter solid-phase radioimmunoassay for hepatitis A antigen and antibody. J Immunol. 1976;116:349-356.
75. Anderson DA, Ross BC, Locarnini SA. Restricted replication of hepatitis A virus in cell culture: Encapsidation of viral RNA depletes the pool of RNA available for replication. J Virol. 1988;62:4201-4206.
76. Wheeler CM, Fields HA, Schable CA, et al. Adsorption, purification, and growth characteristics of hepatitis A virus strain HAS-15 propagated in fetal rhesus monkey kidney cells. J Clin Microbiol. 1986;23:434-440.
77. Bishop NE, Anderson DA. Uncoating kinetics of hepatitis A virus virions and provirions. J Virol. 2000;74:3423-3426.
78. Brown EA, Zajac AJ, Lemon SM. In: vitro characterization of an internal ribosomal entry site (IRES) present within the 5' nontranslated region of hepatitis A virus RNA. comparison with the IRES of encephalomyocarditis virus. J Virol. 1994;68:1066-1074.
79. Ping LH, Jansen RW, Stapleton JT, et al. Identification of an immunodominant antigenic site involving the capsid protein VP3 of hepatitis A virus. Proc Natl Acad Sci U S A. 1988;85:8281-8285.
80. Karron RA, Daemer R, Ticehurst J, et al. Studies of prototype live hepatitis A virus vaccines in primate models. J Infect Dis. 1988;157:338-345.
81. Provost PJ, Banker FS, Giesa PA, et al. Progress toward a live, attenuated human hepatitis A vaccine. Proc Soc Exp Biol Med. 1982;170:8-14.

82. Emerson SU, Huang YK, McRill C, et al. Mutations in both the 2B and 2C genes of hepatitis A virus are involved in adaptation to growth in cell culture. J Virol. 1992;66:650-654.

83. Emerson SU, Huang YK, Purcell RH. 2B and 2C mutations are essential but mutations throughout the genome of HAV contribute to adaptation to cell culture. Virology. 1993;194:475-480.

84. Funkhouser AW, Purcell RH, D'Hondt E, et al. Attenuated hepatitis A virus: Genetic determinants of adaptation to growth in MRC-5 cells. J Virol. 1994;68:148-157.

85. Emerson SU, Huang YK, Purcell RH. 2B and 2C mutations are essential but mutations throughout the genome of HAV contribute to adaptation to cell culture. Virology. 1993;194:475-480.

86. Cohen JI, Feinstone S, Purcell RH. Hepatitis A virus infection in a chimpanzee: Duration of viremia and detection of virus in saliva and throat swabs. J Infect Dis. 1989;160:887-890.

87. Karayiannis P, Jowett T, Enticott M, et al. Hepatitis A virus replication in tamarins and host immune response in relation to pathogenesis of liver cell damage. J Med Virol. 1986;18:261-276.

88. Kaplan G, Totsuka A, Thompson P, et al. Identification of a surface glycoprotein on African green monkey kidney cells as a receptor for hepatitis A virus. EMBO J. 1996;15:4282-4296.

89. Feigelstock D, Thompson P, Mattoo P, et al. The human homolog of HAVcr-1 codes for a hepatitis A virus cellular receptor. J Virol. 1998;72:6621-6628.

90. Silberstein E, Dveksler G, Kaplan GG. Neutralization of hepatitis A virus (HAV) by an immunoadhesin containing the cysteine-rich region of HAV cellular receptor-1. J Virol. 2001;75:717-725.

91. Hornei B, Kammerer R, Moubayed P, et al. Experimental hepatitis A virus infection in guinea pigs. J Med Virol. 2001;64:402-409.

92. Hillis WD. Viral hepatitis: A vulnerable foe. Mil Med. 1978;143:86-93.

93. Deinhardt F. Hepatitis in primates. Adv Virus Res. 1976;20:113-157.

94. Deinhardt F, Holmes AW, Capps RB, et al. Studies on the transmission of human viral hepatitis to marmoset monkeys. J Exp Med. 1967;125:673-689.

95. Coursaget P, Drucker J, Maupas P, et al. Epidemiological and serological study of hepatitis A virus outbreaks in France: A comparison between immunoadherence and radioimmunoassay. J Hyg (Lond). 1981;86:155-162.

96. LeDuc JW, Escajadillo A, Lemon SM. Hepatitis A virus among captive Panamanian owl monkeys (Letter). Lancet. 1981;2:1427-1428.

97. Hilleman MR, Provost PJ, Villarejos VM, et al. Infectious hepatitis (hepatitis A) research in nonhuman primates. Bull Pan Am Health Organ. 1977;11:140-152.

98. Emerson SU, Tsarev SA, Purcell RH. Biological and molecular comparisons of human (HM-175) and simian (AGM-27) hepatitis A viruses. J Hepatol. 1991;13(Suppl 4):S144-S145.

99. Emerson SU, Tsarev SA, Govindarajan S, et al. A simian strain of hepatitis A virus, AGM-27, functions as an attenuated vaccine for chimpanzees. J Infect Dis. 1996;173:592-597.

100. Feinstone SM, Kapikian AZ, Purcell RH. Hepatitis A. detection by immune electron microscopy of a viruslike antigen associated with acute illness. Science. 1973;182:1026-1028.

101. Skinhoj P, Mathiesen LR, Kryger P. Faecal excretion of hepatitis A virus in patients with symptomatic hepatitis A infection. Ann Intern Med. 1987;106:221-226.

102. Tassopoulos NC, Papaevangelou GJ, Ticehurst JR, et al. Fecal excretion of Greek strains of hepatitis A virus in patients with hepatitis A and in experimentally infected chimpanzees. J Infect Dis. 1986;154:231-237.

103. Krugman S, Ward R, Giles JP. Infectious hepatitis: Detection of virus during the incubation period and in clinically inapparent infection. N Engl J Med. 1959;261:729-734.

104. Rosenblum LS, Villarino ME, Nainan OV, et al. Hepatitis A outbreak in a neonatal intensive care unit: Risk factors for transmission and evidence of prolonged viral excretion among preterm infants. J Infect Dis. 1991;164:476-482.

105. Innis BL, Snitbhan R, Kunasol P, et al. Protection against hepatitis A by an inactivated vaccine. JAMA. 1994;271:1328-1334.

106. Sjogren MH, Tanno H, Fay O, et al. Hepatitis A virus in stool during clinical relapse. Ann Intern Med. 1987;106:221-226.

107. Bower WA, Nainan OV, Han X, et al. Duration of viremia in hepatitis A virus infection. J Infect Dis. 2000;182:12-17.

108. Krugman S, Ward R, Giles WP. The natural history of infectous hepatitis. Am J Med. 1962;32:717-728.

109. Lemon SM. The natural history of hepatitis A. the potential for transmission by transfusion of blood or blood products. Vox Sang. 1994;67(Suppl 4):19-23.

110. Purcell RH, Wong DC, Shapiro M. Relative infectivity of hepatitis A virus by the oral and intravenous routes in 2 species of nonhuman primates. J Infect Dis. 2002;185:1668-1771.

111. Bell BP. Global epidemiology of hepatitis A. implications for control strategies. In: Margolis HS, Alter MJ, Liang JT, et al, eds. Viral Hepatitis and Liver Disease. London: International Medical Press; 2002:359-365.

112. Bell BP, Shapiro CN, Alter MJ, et al. The diverse patterns of hepatitis A epidemiology in the United States: Implications for vaccination strategies. J Infect Dis. 1998;178:1579-1584.

113. Staes CJ, Schlenker TL, Risk I, et al. Sources of infection among persons with acute hepatitis A and no identified risk factors during a sustained community-wide outbreak. Pediatrics. 2000;106:E54.

114. Smith PF, Grabau JC, Werzberger A, et al. The role of young children in a community-wide outbreak of hepatitis A. Epidemiol Infect. 1997;118:243-252.

115. Armstrong GL, Bell BP. Hepatitis A virus infections in the United States: Model-based estimates and implications for childhood immunization. Pediatrics. 2002;109:839-845.

116. McCaustland KA, Bond WW, Bradley DW, et al. Survival of hepatitis A virus in feces after drying and storage for 1 month. J Clin Microbiol. 1982;16:957-958.

117. Carl M, Francis DP, Maynard JE. Food-borne hepatitis A: Recommendations for control. J Infect Dis. 1983;148:1133-1135.

118. Massoudi MS, Bell BP, Paredes V, et al. An outbreak of hepatitis A associated with an infected foodhandler. Public Health Rep. 1999;114:157-164.

119. Fiore A. Foodborne hepatitis A. Clin Infect Dis. 2004;38:705-715.

120. Centers for Disease Control and Prevention. Foodborne hepatitis A: Alaska, Florida, North Carolina, Washington. MMWR Morb Mortal Wkly Rep. 1990;39:228-232.

121. Halliday ML, Kang LY, Zhou TK, et al. An epidemic of hepatitis A attributable to the ingestion of raw clams in Shanghai, China. J Infect Dis. 1991;164:852-859.

122. Mele A, Rastelli MG, Gill ON, et al. Recurrent epidemic hepatitis A associated with consumption of raw shellfish probably controlled through public health measures. Am J Epidemiol. 1980;130:540-546.

123. Desenclos JC, Klontz KC, Wilder MH, et al. A multistate outbreak of hepatitis A caused by the consumption of raw oysters. Am J Public Health. 1991;81:1268-1272.

124. Wang JY, Hu SL, Liu HY, et al. Risk factor analysis of an epidemic of hepatitis A in a factory in Shanghai. Int J Epidemiol. 1990;19:435-438.

125. Germinario C, Lopalco PL, Chicanna M, et al. From hepatitis B to hepatitis A and B prevention: The Puglia (Italy) experience. Vaccine. 2000;18(Suppl):S83-S85.

126. Mele A, Stroffolini T, Palumbe F, et al. Incidence and risk factors for hepatitis A in Italy: Public health indications from a 10-year surveillance. J Hepatol. 1997;26:743-747.

127. Hollinger FB, Khan NC, Oefinger PE, et al. Posttransfusion hepatitis type A. JAMA. 1983;250:2313-2317.

128. Soucie JM, Robertson BH, Bell BP, et al. Hepatitis A virus infections associated with clotting factor concentrate in the United States. Transfusion. 1998;38:573-579.

129. Benjamin RJ. Nucleic acid testing: Update and applications. Semin Hematol. 2001;38:11-16.

130. Leikin E, Lysikiewicz A, Garry D, et al. Intrauterine transmission of hepatitis A virus. Obstet Gynecol. 1996;88:690-691.

131. McDuffie RS Jr, Bader T. Fetal meconium peritonitis after maternal hepatitis A. Am J Obstet Gynecol. 1999;180:1031-1032.

132. Tong MJ, Thursby M, Rakela J, et al. Studies on the maternal-infant transmission of the viruses which cause acute hepatitis. Gastroenterology. 1981;80:999-1004.

133. Watson JC, Fleming DW, Borella AJ, et al. Vertical transmission of hepatitis A resulting in an outbreak in a neonatal intensive care unit. J Infect Dis. 1993;167:567-571.

134. Hadler SC. Global impact of hepatitis A virus infection: changing patterns. In: Hollinger FB, Lemon SM, Margolis HS, eds. Viral Hepatitis and Liver Disease. Baltimore; Williams & Wilkins; 1991:14-20.

135. Coursaget P, Lebouleux D, Gharbi Y, et al. Etiology of acute sporadic hepatitis in adults in Senegal and Tunisia. Scand J Infect Dis. 1995;27:9-11.

136. Tsega E, Mengesha B, Hansson BG, et al. Hepatitis A, B, and delta infection in Ethiopia: A serologic survey with demographic data. Am J Epidemiol. 1986;123:344-351.

137. Bowden FJ, Currie BJ, Miller NC, et al. Should aboriginals in the "top end" of the Northern Territory be vaccinated against hepatitis A? Med J Aust. 1994;161:372-373.

138. Cianciara J. Hepatitis A shifting epidemiology in Poland and Eastern Europe. Vaccine. 2000;18(Suppl 1):S68-S70.

139. Green MS, Block C, Slater PE. Rise in the incidence of viral hepatitis in Israel despite improved socioeconomic conditions. Rev Infect Dis. 1989;11:464-469.

140. Gdalevich M, Grotto I, Mandel Y, et al. Hepatitis A antibody prevalence among young adults in Israel: The decline continues. Epidemiol Infect. 1998;121:477-479.

141. Innis BL, Snitbhan R, Hoke CH, et al. The declining transmission of hepatitis A in Thailand. J Infect Dis. 1991;163:989-995.

142. Kunasol P, Cooksley G, Chan VF, et al. Hepatitis A virus: Declining seroprevalence in children and adolescents in Southeast Asia. Southeast Asian J Trop Med Public Health. 1998;29:255-262.

143. Pinho JR, Sumita LM, Moreira RC, et al. Duality of patterns in hepatitis A epidemiology: A study involving two socioeconomically distinct populations in Campinas, Sao Paulo State, Brazil. Rev Inst Med Trop Sao Paulo. 1998;40:105-106.

144. Poovorawan Y, Vimolkej T, Chongsrisawat V, et al. The declining pattern of seroepidemiology of hepatitis A virus infection among adolescents in Bangkok, Thailand. Southeast Asian J Trop Med Public Health. 1997;28:154-157.

145. Das K, Jain A, Gupta S, et al. The changing epidemiological pattern of hepatitis A in an urban population of India: Emergence of a trend similar to the European countries. Eur J Epidemiol. 2000;16:507-510.

146. Tapia-Conyer R, Santos JI, Cavalcanti AM, et al. Hepatitis A in Latin America: A changing epidemiologic pattern. Am J Trop Med Hyg. 1999;61:825-829.

147. Tufenkeji H. Hepatitis A shifting epidemiology in the Middle East and Africa. Vaccine. 2000;18(Suppl 1):S65-S67.

148. Wang LY, Cheng YW, Chou SJ, et al. Secular trend and geographical variation in hepatitis A infection and hepatitis B carrier rate among adolescents in Taiwan: An island-wide survey. J Med Virol. 1993;39:1-5.

149. Ciocca M. Clinical course and consequences of hepatitis A infection. Vaccine. 2000;18(Suppl 1):S71-S74.

150. Shah U, Habib Z, Kleinman RE. Liver failure attributable to hepatitis A virus infection in a developing country. Pediatrics. 2000;105:436-438.

151. Gil A, Gonzalez A, Dal Re R, et al. Prevalence of antibodies against varicella zoster, herpes simplex (types 1 and 2), hepatitis B and hepatitis A viruses among Spanish adolescents. J Infect. 1998;36:53-56.

152. Shapiro CN, Coleman PJ, McQuillan GM, et al. Epidemiology of hepatitis A. seroepidemiology and risk groups in the USA. Vaccine. 1992;10(Suppl 1):S59-S62.

153. Prodinger WM, Larcher C, Solder BM, et al. Hepatitis A in western Austria: The epidemiological situation before the introduction of active immunisation. Infection. 1994;22:53-55.

154. Termorshuizen F, Dorigo-Zetsma JW, de Melker HE, et al. The prevalence of antibodies to hepatitis A virus and its determinants in the Netherlands: A population-based survey. Epidemiol Infect. 2000;124:459-466.

155. Bottiger M, Christenson B, Grillner L. Hepatitis A immunity in the Swedish population. A study of the prevalence of markers in the Swedish population. Scand J Infect Dis. 1997;29:99-102.

156. Centers for Disease Control and Prevention. Summary of notifiable diseases, United States, 2000. MMWR Morb Mortal Wkly Rep. 2002;49:1-102.

157. Centers for Disease Control and Prevention. Prevention of hepatitis A through active or passive immunization: Recommendations of the Advisory Committee on Immunization Practices (ACIP). MMWR Recomm Rep. 1996;45:1-30.

158. Centers for Disease Control and Prevention. Prevention of hepatitis A through active or passive immunization: Recommendations of the Advisory Committee on Immunization Practices (ACIP). MMWR Recomm Rep. 1999;48:1-37.

159. Centers for Disease Control and Prevention. Hepatitis Surveillance Report No. 58. Atlanta: The Centers; 2003.

160. Bialek S, Thoroughman D, Hu D, et al. Hepatitis A incidence and hepatitis A vaccination among American Indians and Alaskan Natives, 1990-2001. Am J Public Health. 2004.

161. Cotter SM, Sansom S, Long T, et al. Outbreak of hepatitis A among men who have sex with men: Implications for hepatitis A vaccination strategies. J Infect Dis. 2003;187:1235-1240.

162. Friedman MS, Blake PA, Koehler JE, et al. Factors influencing a communitywide campaign to administer hepatitis A vaccine to men who have sex with men. Am J Public Health. 2000;90:1942-1946.

163. Harkess J, Gildon B, Istre GR. Outbreaks of hepatitis A among illicit drug users, Oklahoma, 1984-87. Am J Public Health. 1989;79:463-466.

164. Hutin YJ, Bell BP, Marshall KL, et al. Identifying target groups for a potential vaccination program during a hepatitis A communitywide outbreak. Am J Public Health. 1999;89:918-921.

165. Shaw FE Jr, Sudman JH, Smith SM, et al. A community-wide epidemic of hepatitis A in Ohio. Am J Epidemiol. 1986;123:1057-1065.

166. Craig AS, Sockwell DC, Schaffner W, et al. Use of hepatitis A vaccine in a community-wide outbreak of hepatitis A. Clin Infect Dis. 1998;27:531-535.

167. Averhoff F, Shapiro CN, Bell BP, et al. Control of hepatitis A through routine vaccination of children. JAMA. 2001;286:2968-2973.

168. Hadler SC, Webster HM, Erben JJ, et al. Hepatitis A in day-care centers. A community-wide assessment. N Engl J Med. 1980;302:1222-1227.

169. Venczel LV, Desai MM, Vertz PD, et al. The role of child care in a community-wide outbreak of hepatitis A. Pediatrics. 2001;108:E78.

170. Shapiro CN, Hadler SC. Hepatitis A and hepatitis B virus infections in day-care settings. Pediatr Ann. 1991;20:435-441.

171. Jackson LA, Stewart LK, Solomon SL, et al. Risk of infection with hepatitis A, B or C, cytomegalovirus, varicella or measles among child care providers. Pediatr Infect Dis J. 1996;15:584-589.

172. Desenclos JC, MacLafferty L. Community wide outbreak of hepatitis A linked to children in day care centres and with increased transmission in young adult men in Florida 1988-9. J Epidemiol Community Health. 1993;47:269-273.

173. Hadler SC, Erben JJ, Matthews D, et al. Effect of immunoglobulin on hepatitis A in day-care centers. JAMA. 1983;249:48-53.

174. Hutin YJ, Pool V, Cramer EH, et al. A multistate, foodborne outbreak of hepatitis A. National Hepatitis A Investigation Team. N Engl J Med. 1999;340:595-602.

175. Szmuness W, Purcell RH, Dienstag JL, et al. Antibody to hepatitis A antigen in institutionalized mentally retarded patients. JAMA. 1977;237:1702-1705.

176. Shaw DD, Whiteman DC, Merritt AD, et al. Hepatitis A outbreaks among illicit drug users and their contacts in Queensland, 1997. Med J Aust. 1999;170:584-587.

177. O'Donovan D, Cooke RP, Joce R, et al. An outbreak of hepatitis A amongst injecting drug users. Epidemiol Infect. 2001;127:469-473.

178. Hutin YJ, Sabin KM, Hutwanger LC, et al. Multiple modes of hepatitis A virus transmission among methamphetamine users. Am J Epidemiol. 2000;152:186-192.

179. Vong S, Fiore AE, Haight DO, et al. Vaccination in the county jail as a strategy to reach high risk adults during a community-based hepatitis A outbreak among methamphetamine drug users. Vaccine. 2004.

180. Ivie K, Spruill C, Bell BP. Prevalence of hepatitis A virus infection among illicit drug users, 1993-1994. Antiviral Therapy. 2000;5(Suppl 1):A.7.

181. Villano SA, Nelson KE, Vlahov D, et al. Hepatitis A among homosexual men and injection drug users: More evidence for vaccination. Clin Infect Dis. 1997;25:726-728.

182. Stokes ML, Ferson MJ, Young LC. Outbreak of hepatitis A among homosexual men in Sydney. Am J Public Health. 1997;87:2039-2041.

183. Henning KJ, Bell E, Braun J, et al. A community-wide outbreak of hepatitis A risk factors for infection among homosexual and bisexual men. Am J Med. 1995;99:132-136.

184. Centers for Disease Control and Prevention. Hepatitis A among homosexual men-United States, Canada, and Australia. MMWR Morb Mortal Wkly Rep. 1992;41:155, 170-155, 164.

185. Katz MH, Hsu L, Wong E, et al. Seroprevalence of and risk factors for hepatitis A infection among young homosexual and bisexual men. J Infect Dis. 1997;175:1225-1229.

186. Mah MW, Royce RA, Rathouz PJ, et al. Prevalence of hepatitis A antibodies in hemophiliacs: Preliminary results from the Southeastern Delta Hepatitis Study. Vox Sang. 1994;67(suppl 1):21-22.

187. Mannucci PM, Santagostino E, Di Bona E, et al. The outbreak of hepatitis A in Italian patients with hemophilia: Facts and fancies. Vox Sang. 1994;67(Suppl 1):31-35.

188. Klein BS, Michaels JA, Rytel MW, et al. Nosocomial hepatitis A. A multinursery outbreak in Wisconsin. JAMA. 1984;252:2716-2721.

189. Noble RC, Kane MA, Reeves SA, et al. Posttransfusion hepatitis A in a neonatal intensive care unit. JAMA. 1984;252:2711-2715.

190. Weisfuse IB, Graham DJ, Will M, et al. An outbreak of hepatitis A among cancer patients treated with interleukin-2 and lymphokine-activated killer cells. J Infect Dis. 1990;161:647-652.

191. Goodman RA. Nosocomial hepatitis A. Ann Intern Med. 1985;103:452-454.

192. Papaevangelou GJ, Roumeliotou-Karayannis AJ, Contoyannis PC. The risk of nosocomial hepatitis A and B virus infections from patients under care without isolation precaution. J Med Virol. 1981;7:143-148.

193. Gibas A, Blewett DR, Schoenfeld DA, et al. Prevalence and incidence of viral hepatitis in health workers in the prehepatitis B vaccination era. Am J Epidemiol. 1992;136:603-610.

194. Steffen R, Rickenbach M, Wilhelm U, et al. Health problems after travel to developing countries. J Infect Dis. 1987;156:84-91.

195. Steffen R. Risk of hepatitis A in travellers. Vaccine. 1992;10(Suppl 1):S69-S72.

196. Mele A, Sagliocca L, Palumbo F, et al. Travel-associated hepatitis A effect of place of residence and country visited. J Public Health Med. 1991;13:256-259.

197. Steffen R, Kane MA, Shapiro CN, et al. Epidemiology and prevention of hepatitis A in travelers. JAMA. 1994;272:885-889.

198. Steffen R. Hepatitis A in travelers: The European experience. J Infect Dis. 1995;171(suppl 1):S24-S28.

199. Lange WR, Frame JD. High incidence of viral hepatitis among American missionaries in Africa. Am J Trop Med Hyg. 1990;43:527-533.

200. Christenson B. Epidemiological aspects of acute viral hepatitis A in Swedish travellers to endemic areas. Scand J Infect Dis. 1985;17:5-10.

201. Dalton CB, Haddix A, Hoffman RE, et al. The cost of a food-borne outbreak of hepatitis A in Denver, Colo. Arch Intern Med. 1996;156:1013-1016.

202. Lowry PW, Levine R, Stroup DF, et al. Hepatitis A outbreak on a floating restaurant in Florida, 1986. Am J Epidemiol. 1989;129:155-164.

203. Latham RH, Schable CA. Foodborne hepatitis A at a family reunion: Use of IgM-specific hepatitis A serologic testing. Am J Epidemiol. 1982;115:640-645.

204. Mishu B, Hadler SC, Boaz VA, et al. Foodborne hepatitis A: Evidence that microwaving reduces risk? J Infect Dis. 1990;162:655-658.

205. Parkin WE, Marzinsky P, Griffin MR. Foodborne hepatitis A associated with cheeseburgers. J Med Soc N J. 1983;80:612-615.

206. Weltman AC, Bennett NM, Ackman DA, et al. An outbreak of hepatitis A associated with a bakery, New York, 1994: The 1968 "West Branch, Michigan' outbreak repeated. Epidemiol Infect. 1996;117:333-341.

207. Dentinger CM, Bower WA, Nainan OV, et al. An outbreak of hepatitis A associated with green onions. J Infect Dis. 2001;183:1273-1276.

208. Rosenblum LS, Mirkin IR, Allen DT, et al. A multitocal outbreak of hepatitis A traced to commercially distributed lettuce. Am J Public Health. 1990;80:1075-1079.

209. Niu MT, Polish LB, Robertson BH, et al. Multistate outbreak of hepatitis A associated with frozen strawberries. J Infect Dis. 1992;166:518-524.

210. Reid TM, Robinson HG. Frozen raspberries and hepatitis A. Epidemiol Infect. 1987;98:109-112.

211. Bloch AB, Stramer SL, Smith JD, et al. Recovery of hepatitis A virus from a water supply responsible for a common source outbreak of hepatitis A. Am J Public Health. 1990;80:428-430.

212. De Serres G, Cromeans TL, Levesque B, et al. Molecular confirmation of hepatitis A virus from well water: Epidemiology and public health implications. J Infect Dis. 1999;179.37-43.

213. Bergeisen GH, Hinds MW, Skaggs JW. A waterborne outbreak of hepatitis A in Meade County, Kentucky. Am J Public Health. 1985;75:170-164.

214. Lerman Y, Chodick G, Aloni H, et al. Occupations at increased risk of hepatitis A: A 2-year nationwide historical prospective cohort. Am J Epidemiol. 1999;150:312-320.

215. Glas C, Hotz P, Steffen R. Hepatitis A in workers exposed to sewage: A systematic review. Occup Environ Med. 2001;58:762-768.

216. Poole CJ, Shakespeare AT. Should sewage workers and carers for people with learning disabilities be vaccinated against hepatitis A? BMJ. 1993;306:1102.

217. Trout D, Mueller C, Venczel L, et al. Evaluation of occupational transmission of hepatitis A virus among wastewater workers. J Occup Environ Med. 2000;42:83-87.

218. Weldon M, Van Engdom MJ, Hendricks KA, et al. Prevalence of antibody to hepatitis A virus in drinking water workers and wastewater workers in Texas from 1996 to 1997. J Occup Environ Med. 2000;42:821-826.

219. Venczel L, Brown S, Frumkin H, et al. Prevalence of hepatitis A virus infection among sewage workers in Georgia. Am J Ind Med. 2003;43:172-178.

220. Umetsu DT, McIntire JJ, Akbari O, et al. Asthma: An epidemic of dysregulated immunity. Nat Immunol. 2002;3:715-720.

221. Matricardi PM, Rosmini F, Panetta V, et al. Hay fever and asthma in relation to markers of infection in the United States. J Allergy Clin Immunol. 2002;110:381-386.

222. McIntire JJ, Umetsu SE, Akbari O, et al. Identification of Tapr (an airway hyperreactivity regulatory locus) and the linked Tim gene family. Nat Immunol. 2001;2:1109-1116.

223. Koff RS. Clinical manifestations and diagnosis of hepatitis A virus infection. Vaccine. 1992;10(Suppl 1):S15-S17.

224. Mathiesen LR. The hepatitis A virus infection. Liver. 1981;1:81-109.

225. Skinhoj P. Natural history of viral hepatitis in Greenland. Am J Med Sci. 1975;270:305-307.

226. Skinhoj P, Mikkelsen F, Hollinger FB. Hepatitis A in Greenland: Importance of specific antibody testing in epidemiologic surveillance. Am J Epidemiol. 1977;105:140-147.

227. Hadler SC, McFarland L. Hepatitis in day care centers: Epidemiology and prevention. Rev Infect Dis. 1986;8:548-557.

228. Tong MJ, el-Farra NS, Grew MI. Clinical manifestations of hepatitis A: Recent experience in a community teaching hospital. J Infect Dis. 1995;171(Suppl 1):S15-S18.

229. Mishra L, Seeff LB. Viral hepatitis, A through E, complicating pregnancy. Gastroenterol Clin North Am. 1992;21:873-887.

230. Zhang RL, Zeng JS, Zhang HZ. Survey of 34 pregnant women with hepatitis A and their neonates. Chin Med J (Engl). 1990;103:552-555.

231. Vento S, Garofano T, Renzini C, et al. Fulminant hepatitis associated with hepatitis A virus superinfection in patients with chronic hepatitis C. N Engl J Med. 1998;338:286-290.

232. Bianco E, Stroffolini T, Spada E, et al. Case fatality rate of acute viral hepatitis in Italy: 1995-2000. An update. Dig Liver Dis. 2003;35:404-408.

233. Gordon SC, Reddy KR, Schiff L, et al. Prolonged intrahepatic cholestasis secondary to acute hepatitis A. Ann Intern Med. 1984;101:635-637.

234. Sjogren MH, Tanno H, Fay O, et al. Hepatitis A virus in stool during clinical relapse. Ann Intern Med. 1987;106:221-226.

235. Cobden I, James OF. A biphasic illness associated with acute hepatitis A virus infection. J Hepatol. 1986;2:19-23.

236. Bornstein JD, Byrd DE, Trotter JF. Relapsing hepatitis A: A case report and review of the literature. J Clin Gastroenterol. 1999;28:355-356.

237. Scully LJ, Ryan AE. Urticaria and acute hepatitis A virus infection. Am J Gastroenterol. 1993;88:277-278.

238. Kano Y, Kokaji T, Shiohara T. Photo-accentuated eruption and vascular deposits of immunoglobulin A associated with hepatitis A virus infection. Dermatology. 2000;200:266-269.

239. Inman RD, Hodge M, Johnston ME, et al. Arthritis, vasculitis, and cryoglobulinemia associated with relapsing hepatitis A virus infection. Ann Intern Med. 1986;105:700-703.

240. Ilan Y, Hillman M, Oren R, et al. Vasculitis and cryoglobulinemia associated with persisting cholestatic hepatitis A virus infection. Am J Gastroenterol. 1990;85:586-587.

241. Yao G. Clinical spectrum and natural history of viral hepatitis A in a 1988 Shanghai epidemic. In: Hollinger FB, Lemon SM, Margolis HS, eds. Viral Hepatitis and Liver Disease. Baltimore: Williams & Wilkins; 1991:76-78.

242. Willner IR, Uhl MO, Howard SC, et al. Serious hepatitis A: An analysis of patients hospitalized during an urban epidemic in the United States. Ann Intern Med. 1998;128:111-114.

243. Hoofnagle JH, Carithers RL Jr, Shapiro C, et al. Fulminant hepatic failure: Summary of a workshop. Hepatology. 1995;21:240-252.

244. Hann JN, Warnock TH, Shepherd RW, et al. Fulminant hepatitis A in indigenous children in north Queensland. Med J Aust 2000;172;19-21.

245. Schiodt V, Davern TJ, Shakil O, et al. Viral hepatitis-related acute liver failure. Am J Gastroenterol. 2003;98:448-453.

246. Norkrans G, Nilsson LA, Frosner G, et al. Serum immunoglobulin levels in hepatitis non-A, non-B: A comparison with hepatitis A and B. Infection. 1980;8:98-100.

247. Hoofnagle JH, Di Bisceglie AM. Serologic diagnosis of acute and chronic viral hepatitis. Semin Liver Dis. 1991;11:73-83.

248. Robertson BH, Jia XY, Tian H, et al. Antibody response to nonstructural proteins of hepatitis A virus following infection. J Med Virol. 1993;40:76-82.

249. Summers DF, Ehrenfeld E. Host antibody response to viral structural and nonstructural proteins after hepatitis A virus infection. J Infect Dis. 1992;165:273-280.

250. Tsai YL, Sobsey MD, Sangermano LR, et al. Simple method of concentrating enteroviruses and hepatitis A virus from sewage and ocean water for rapid detection by reverse transcriptase-polymerase chain reaction. Appl Environ Microbiol. 1993;59:3488-3491.

251. Le Guyader F, Dubois E, Menard D, et al. Detection of hepatitis A virus, rotavirus, and enterovirus in naturally contaminated shellfish and sediment by reverse transcription-seminested PCR. Appl Environ Microbiol. 1994;60:3665-3671.

252. Abe H, Beninger PR, Ikejiri N, et al. Light microscopic findings of liver biopsy specimens from patients with hepatitis type A and comparison with type B. Gastroenterology. 1982;82:938-947.

253. Kobayashi K, Hashimoto E, Ludwig J, et al. Liver biopsy features of acute hepatitis C compared with hepatitis A, B, and non-A, non-B, non-C. Liver. 1993;13:69-72.

254. Mathiesen LR, Drucker J, Lorenz D, et al. Localization of hepatitis A antigen in marmoset organs during acute infection with hepatitis A virus. J Infect Dis. 1978;138:369-377.

255. Shimizu YK, Mathiesen LR, Lorenz D, et al. Localization of hepatitis A antigen in liver tissue by peroxidase-conjugated antibody method: Light and electron microscopic studies. J Immunol. 1978;121:1671-1679.

256. Neefe JR, Stokes J Jr, Gellis SS. Homologous serum hepatitis and infectious (epidemic) hepatitis: Experimental study of immunity and cross immunity in volunteers; preliminary report. Am J Med Sci. 1945;210:561-575.

257. Stapleton JT, Lange DK, LeDuc JW. The role of secretory immunity in hepatitis A virus infection. J Infect Dis. 1991;163:7-11.

258. Lemon SM, Binn LN, Marchwicki RH. Radioimmunofocus assay for quantitation of hepatitis A virus in cell cultures. J Clin Microbiol. 1983;17:834-839.

259. Baba M, Takegawa M, KAITO M, et al. Propagation of hepatitis A virus in a renal cell line JTC-12 P3 of cynomolgus monkey origin. Acta Virol (Praha). 1993;37:209-222.

260. Baba M, Fukai K, Hasegawa H, et al. The role of natural killer cells and lymphokine activated killer cells in the pathogenesis of hepatic injury and hepatitis A. J Clin Lab Immunol. 1992;38:1-14.

261. Pinto MA, Marchevsky RS, Pelajo-Machado M, et al. Inducible nitric oxide synthase (iNOS) expression in liver and splenic T lymphocyte rise are associated with liver histological damage during experimental hepatitis A virus (HAV) infection in Callithrix jacchus. Exp Toxicol Pathol. 2000;52:3-10.

262. Doebbeling BN, Li N, Wenzel RP. An outbreak of hepatitis A among health care workers: risk factors for transmission. Am J Public Health. 1993;83:1679-1684.

263. Petrosillo N, Raffaele B, Martini L, et al. A nosocomial and occupational cluster of hepatitis A virus infection in a pediatric ward. Infect Control Hosp Epidemiol. 2002;23:343-345.

264. Rosenblum LS, Villarino ME, Nainan OV, et al. Hepatitis A outbreak in a neonatal intensive care unit: Risk factors for transmission and evidence of prolonged viral excretion among preterm infants. J Infect Dis. 1991;164:476-482.

265. Watson JC, Fleming DW, Borella AJ, et al. Vertical transmission of hepatitis A resulting in an outbreak in a neonatal intensive care unit. J Infect Dis. 1993;167:567-571.

266. Cohn E, Oncley J, Strong LE. Chemical, clinical, and immunological studies on the products of human plasma fractionation. The characterization of the protein fractions of human plasma. J Clin Invest. 1944;23:417-432.

267. Lerman Y, Shohat T, Ashkenazi S, et al. Efficacy of different doses of immune serum globulin in the prevention of hepatitis A: A three-year prospective study. Clin Infect Dis. 1993;17:411-414.

268. Smallwood LA, Tabor E, Finlayson JS, et al. Antibodies to hepatitis A virus in immune serum globulin (Letter). Lancet. 1980;2:482-483.

269. Stokes J, Neefe JR. The prevention and attenuation of infectious hepatitis by gamma globulin. JAMA. 1945;127:144-145.

270. Stapleton JT. Passive immunization against hepatitis A. Vaccine. 1992;10(Suppl 1):S45-S47.

271. Weiland O, Niklasson B, Berg R, et al. Clinical and subclinical hepatitis A occurring after immunoglobulin prophylaxis among Swedish UN soldiers in Sinai. Scand J Gastroenterol. 1981;16:967-972.

272. Pierce PF, Cappello M, Bernard KW. Subclinical infection with hepatitis A in Peace Corps volunteers following immune globulin prophylaxis. Am J Trop Med Hyg. 1990;42:465-469.

273. Kluge I. Gamma globulin in the prevention of viral hepatitis: A study of the effect of medium-size doses. Acta Med Scand. 1963;174:469-477.

274. Mosley JW, Reisler DM, Brachott D, et al. Comparison of two lots of immune serum globulin for prophylaxis of infectious hepatitis. Am J Epidemiol. 1968;87:539-550.

275. Stokes N. The prevention and attenuation of infectious hepatitis by gamma globulin. JAMA. 1945;127:144-145.

276. Lemon SM. Type A viral hepatitis. New developments in an old disease. N Engl J Med. 1985;313:1059-1067.

277. Mao JS. Development of live, attenuated hepatitis A vaccine (H2-strain). Vaccine. 1990;8:523-524.

278. Karron RA, Daemer R, Ticehurst J, et al. Studies of prototype live hepatitis A virus vaccines in primate models. J Infect Dis. 1988;157:338-345.

279. Sjogren MH, Purcell RH, McKee K, et al. Clinical and laboratory observations following oral or intramuscular administration of a live attenuated hepatitis A vaccine candidate. Vaccine. 1992;10(Suppl 1):S135-S137.

280. Midthun K, Ellerbeck E, Gershman K, et al. Safety and immunogenicity of a live attenuated hepatitis A virus vaccine in seronegative volunteers. J Infect Dis. 1991;163:735-739.

281. Mao JS, Dong DX, Zhang HY, et al. Primary study of attenuated live hepatitis A vaccine (H2 strain) in humans. J Infect Dis. 1989;159:621-624.

282. Cho MW, Ehrenfeld E. Rapid completion of the replication cycle of hepatitis A virus subsequent to reversal of guanidine inhibition. Virology. 1991;180:770-780.

283. Cohen JI, Ticehurst JR, Purcell RH, et al. Complete nucleotide sequence of wild-type hepatitis A virus: Comparison with different strains of hepatitis A virus and other picornaviruses. J Virol. 1987;61:50-59.

284. Cohen JI, Rosenblum B, Ticehurst JR, et al. Complete nucleotide sequence of an attenuated hepatitis A virus: Comparison with wild-type virus. Proc Natl Acad Sci U S A. 1987;84:2497-2501.

285. Cohen JI, Ticehurst JR, Feinstone SM, et al. Hepatitis A virus cDNA and its RNA transcripts are infectious in cell culture. J Virol. 1987;61:3035-3039.

286. Funkhouser AW, Purcell RH, D'Hondt E, et al. Attenuated hepatitis A virus: Genetic determinants of adaptation to growth in MRC-5 cells. J Virol. 1994;68:148-157.

287. Cohen JI, Rosenblum B, Feinstone SM, et al. Attenuation and cell culture adaptation of hepatitis A virus (HAV): A genetic analysis with HAV cDNA. J Virol. 1989;63:5364-5370.

288. Emerson SU, Huang YK, McRill C, et al. Molecular basis of virulence and growth of hepatitis A virus in cell culture. Vaccine. 1992;10(Suppl 1):S36-S39.

289. Vidor E, Fritzell B, Plotkin S. Clinical development of a new inactivated hepatitis A vaccine. Infection. 1996;24:447-458.

290. Gluck R, Mischler R, Brantschen S, et al. Immunopotentiating reconstituted influenza virus virosome vaccine delivery system for immunization against hepatitis A. J Clin Invest. 1992;90:2491-2495.

291. Sjogren MH, Purcell RH, McKee K, et al. Clinical and laboratory observations following oral or intramuscular administration of a live attenuated hepatitis A vaccine candidate. Vaccine. 1992;10(Suppl 1):S135-S137.

292. Cohen JI, Ticehurst JR, Purcell RH, et al. Complete nucleotide sequence of wild-type hepatitis A virus: Comparison with different strains of hepatitis A virus and other picornaviruses. J Virol. 1987;61:50-59.

293. Cohen JI, Rosenblum B, Feinstone SM, et al. Attenuation and cell culture adaptation of hepatitis A virus (HAV): A genetic analysis with HAV cDNA. J Virol. 1989;63:5364-5370.

294. Nalin DR, Kuter BJ, Brown L, et al. Worldwide experience with the CR326F-derived inactivated hepatitis A virus vaccine in pediatric and adult populations: An overview. J Hepatol. 1993;18(Suppl 2):S51-S55.

295. Werzberger A, Mensch B, Kuter B, et al. A controlled trial of a formalin-inactivated hepatitis A vaccine in healthy children. N Engl J Med. 1992;327:453-457.

296. Werzberger A, Mensch B, Kuter B, et al. A controlled trial of a formalin-inactivated hepatitis A vaccine in healthy children. N Engl J Med. 1992;327:453-457.

297. Werzberger A, Kuter B, Shouval D, et al. Anatomy of a trial: A historical view of the Monroe inactivated hepatitis A protective efficacy trial. J Hepatol. 1993;18(Suppl 2):S46-S50.

298. Clemens R, Safary A, Hepburn A, et al. Clinical experience with an inactivated hepatitis A vaccine. J Infect Dis. 1995;171(Suppl 1):S44-S49.

299. Dagan R, Amir J, Mijalovsky A, et al. Immunization against hepatitis A in the first year of life: Priming despite the presence of maternal antibody. Pediatr Infect Dis J. 2000;19:1045-1052.

300. Shouval D, Ashur Y, Adler R, et al. Single and booster dose responses to an inactivated hepatitis A virus vaccine: Comparison with immune serum globulin prophylaxis. Vaccine. 1993;11(Suppl 1):S9-S14.

301. van Damme P, Mathei C, Thoelen S, et al. Single dose inactivated hepatitis A vaccine: Rationale and clinical assessment of the safety and immunogenicity. J Med Virol. 1994;44:435-441.

302. Hoke CH Jr, Binn LN, Egan JE, et al. Hepatitis A in the US Army: Epidemiology and vaccine development. Vaccine. 1992;10(Suppl 1):S75-S79.

303. Fujiyama S, Iino S, Odoh K, et al. Time course of hepatitis A virus antibody titer after active and passive immunization. Hepatology. 1992;15:983-988.

304. Fujiyama S, Odoh K, Kuramoto I, et al. Current seroepidemiological status of hepatitis A with a comparison of antibody titers after infection and vaccination. J Hepatol. 1994;21:641-645.

305. Lemon SM, Murphy PC, Provost PJ, et al. Immunoprecipitation and virus neutralization assays demonstrate qualitative differences between protective antibody responses to inactivated hepatitis A vaccine and passive immunization with immune globulin. J Infect Dis. 1997;176:9-19.

306. Purcell RH, D'Hondt E, Bradbury R, et al. Inactivated hepatitis A vaccine: Active and passive immunoprophylaxis in chimpanzees. Vaccine. 1992;10(Suppl 1):S148-S151.

307. Hess G, Clemens R, Bienzle U, et al. Immunogenicity and safety of an inactivated hepatitis A vaccine in anti-HIV positive and negative homosexual men. J Med Virol. 1995;46:40-42.

308. Bell BP. Hepatitis A vaccine. Semin Pediatr Infect Dis. 2002;13:165-173.

309. Van Doorslaer E, Tormans G, van Damme P, et al. Cost effectiveness of alternative hepatitis A immunisation strategies. Pharmacoeconomics. 1995;8:5-8.

310. Fenn P, McGuire A, Gray A. An economic evaluation of vaccination against hepatitis A for frequent travelers. J Infect. 1998;36:17-22.

311. Lerman Y, Shohat T, Ashkenazi S, et al. Efficacy of different doses of immune serum globulin in the prevention of hepatitis A: A three-year prospective study. Clin Infect Dis. 1993;17:411-414.

312. Centers for Disease Control and Prevention. General recommendations on immunization. Recommendations of the Advisory Committee on Immunization Practices (ACIP). MMWR Recomm Rep. 1994;43:1-38.

313. Ellis EF, Henney CS. Adverse reactions following administration of human gamma globulin. J Allergy. 1969;43:45-54.

314. Bryan JP, Nelson M. Testing for antibody to hepatitis A to decrease the cost of hepatitis A prophylaxis with immune globulin or hepatitis A vaccines. Arch Intern Med. 1994;154:663-668.

315. American Academy of Pediatrics: Hepatitis A. In: Pickering LK, ed. Red Book: Report of the Committee on Infectious Diseases, ed. 25. Elk Grove Village, IL: The Academy; 2000:280-289.

316. Ochnio JJ, Patrick D, Ho M, et al. Past infection with hepatitis A virus among Vancouver street youth, injection drug users and men who have sex with men: Implications for vaccination programs. Can Med Assoc J. 2001;165:293-297.

317. Bell BP. Hepatitis A and hepatitis B vaccination of patients with chronic liver disease. Acta Gastroenterol Belg. 2000;63:359-365.

318. Bonanni P, Colombai R, Franchi G, et al. Experience of hepatitis A vaccination during an outbreak in a nursery school of Tuscany, Italy. Epidemiol Infect. 1998;121:377-380.

319. Thorburn KM, Bohorques R, Stepak P, et al. Immunization strategies to control a community-wide hepatitis A epidemic. Epidemiol Infect. 2001;127:461-467.

320. Meltzer JI, Shapiro CN, Mast EE, et al. The economics of vaccinating restaurant workers against hepatitis A. Vaccine. 2001;19:2138-2145.

321. Centers for Disease Control and Prevention. Hepatitis A vaccination programs in communities with high rates of hepatitis A. MMWR Morb Mortal Wkly Rep. 1997;46:600-603.

322. Shaw FE Jr, Shapiro CN, Welty TK, et al. Hepatitis transmission among the Sioux Indians of South Dakota. Am J Public Health. 1990;80:1091-1094.

323. Dentinger CM, Heinrich NL, Bell BP, et al. A prevalence study of hepatitis A virus infection in a migrant community: Is hepatitis A vaccine indicated? J Pediatr. 2001;138:705-709.

324. Bulkow LR, Wainwright RB, McMahon BJ, et al. Secular trends in hepatitis A virus infection among Alaska Natives. J Infect Dis. 1993;168:1017-1020.

325. Leach CT, Koo FC, Hilsenbeck SG, et al. The epidemiology of viral hepatitis in children in South Texas: Increased prevalence of hepatitis A along the Texas-Mexico border. J Infect Dis. 1999;180:509-513.

326. McMahon BJ, Beller M, Williams J, et al. A program to control an outbreak of hepatitis A in Alaska by using an inactivated hepatitis A vaccine. Arch Pediatr Adolesc Med. 1996;150:733-739.

327. Samandari T, Wesley A, Bell BP. Quantifying the impact of hepatitis A immunization in the United States, 1995-2001. Vaccine. 2004.

328. Goodman RA, Foster KL, Trowbridge FL, et al. Global disease elimination and eradication as public health strategies. Proceedings of a conference held in Atlanta, Georgia, USA, 23-25 February, 1998. Bull World Health Organ. 1998;76:1-162.

329. O'Grady J. Management of acute and fulminant hepatitis A. Vaccine. 1992;10(Suppl 1):S21-S23.

330. Fagan E, Yousef G, Brahm J, et al. Persistence of hepatitis A virus in fulminant hepatitis and after liver transplantation. J Med Virol. 1990;30:131-136.

331. Gane E, Sallie R, Saleh M, et al. Clinical recurrence of hepatitis A following liver transplantation for acute liver failure. J Med Virol. 1995;45:35-39.

332. Mijch AM, Gust ID. Clinical, serologic, and epidemiologic aspects of hepatitis A virus infection. Semin Liver Dis. 1986;6:42-45.

CHAPTER **171**

Rhinovirus

JACK M. GWALTNEY, Jr.

Since antiquity, people have been plagued with colds[1]; however, it was only in 1914 that the first direct evidence of the infectious nature of colds was reported by Kruse. He produced colds in volunteers by intranasal instillation of bacteria-free filtrates of nasal secretions from cold sufferers.[2] In the 1940s and 1950s, Dingle and colleagues[3] and a British research team headed by Andrewes[4] examined many facets related to the etiology and epidemiology of colds. At a later date, the nasal secretions used by Andrewes and Tyrrell for human transmission studies were shown to contain rhinoviruses.

Pelon and associates[5] and Price[6] independently isolated a new virus in 1956, which was later designated rhinovirus 1A. A significant advance in the isolation and characterization of rhinoviruses was the use by Ketler and co-workers[7] of the highly sensitive human embryonic lung cells developed by Hayflick and Moorhead.[8] By 1963, the number of known rhinovirus immunotypes had increased so rapidly that no single laboratory could characterize the rhinovirus group. Beginning in 1967, a collaborative program directed by Kapikian and associates[9] established a uniform classification system for the known rhinovirus immunotypes 1 to 55. In 1971 other immunotypes were added, which brought the total to 89,[10] and in 1986 the addition of 11 new immunotypes increased the number to 100.[11] The viral genome[12-14] and the x-ray crystallographic structure of the viral shell[15] were characterized in 1984 and 1985, respectively.

Epidemiologic studies have shown that rhinoviruses are the major known cause of the common cold.[16-18] There is also evidence that they have a role in acute sinus infections,[19] otitis media,[20] exacerbations of chronic bronchitis,[21-23] and attacks of asthma.[24,25] Discovery of the rhinoviruses established that the common cold is a complex syndrome produced by a large number of antigenically distinct viruses and that controlling colds with vaccines is not feasible. Recent work in the field has focused on the role that inflammatory mediators play in rhinovirus pathogenesis and on developing new methods of chemoprophylaxis and chemotherapy.

DESCRIPTION OF THE PATHOGEN

Classification

Rhinoviruses are one of five genera of the picornavirus family[26] and share basic properties with enteroviruses, including 40% to 60% homology between their genomes.[27] Rhinoviruses are distinguished from enteroviruses by their susceptibility to inactivation by acid and a higher density in cesium chloride gradients.[28] Rhinovirus serotypes are divided into three subgroups on the basis of receptor specificity.[28] The "major group," which contains 91 of the viral immunotypes, uses the intercellular adhesion molecule 1 (ICAM-1) receptor. ICAM-1 is a member of the immunoglobulin superfamily and maps to chromosome 19. The remaining types, the "minor" receptor group with one exception, use the low-density lipoprotein receptor. Attachment of type 87 is inhibited by treatment with neuraminidase, and its receptor is believed to be a sialoprotein.

Morphology and Structure

The overall size of the virus when fully hydrated is approximately 30 nm[28] (Table 171-1). Like other picornaviruses, rhinovirus contains four structural proteins (VP1, VP2, VP3, and VP4), which form a nonenveloped capsid with icosahedral symmetry. The high degree of cesium binding suggests that the capsid structure is less densely packed than in other picornaviruses. Water forms an important part of

TABLE 171-1 Characteristics of Rhinovirus

Size: 20-27 nm
Shape: nonenveloped capsid with icosahedral symmetry constructed from 60 repeated protomers
Molecular weight: 8.16×10^6 Da
Density: higher in cesium chloride gradient than other members of the picornavirus group are, which suggests a more open capsid structure
Nucleic acid: single-stranded RNA with positive polarity containing approximately 7000 nucleotides
Optimal growth temperature 33-35° C; growth restricted at 37° C
Replication: virus synthesis and maturation in cell cytoplasm
Antigenicity: type specific

the internal structure of the virus, and when dried the virus shrinks approximately 30% and loses infectivity. The atomic structure of the viral shell is composed of 60 repeated subunits (protomers) organized as 12 pentamers and containing the four viral proteins (Fig. 171-1). A deep cleft or canyon on the viral surface separates the five VP1 subunits clustered about the pentamer axis from the adjacent VP2 and VP3 subunits. The canyon is highly conserved among serotypes and is thought to provide a conformationally sensitive region of the capsid that plays an important role in the steps following attachment, leading to release of viral RNA.[29] At the base of the canyon is a hydrophobic "pocket" that is the binding site for molecules with antiviral activity called "capsid binders."

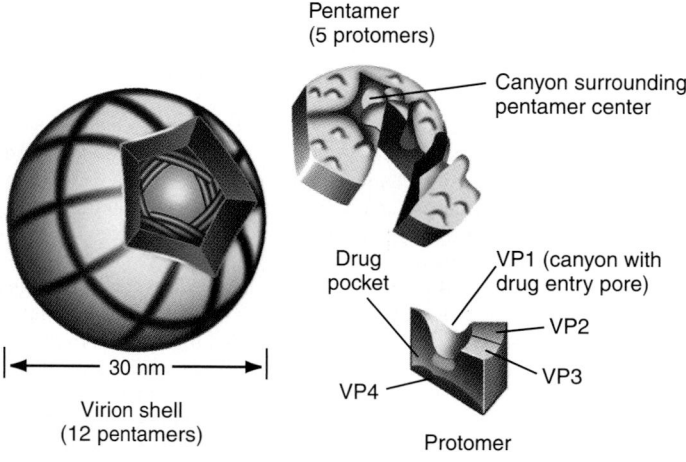

A

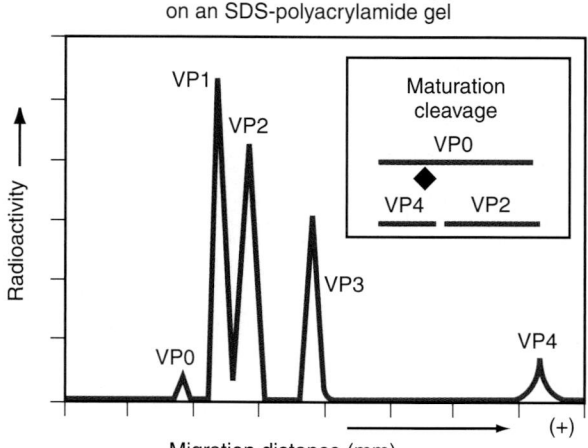

B

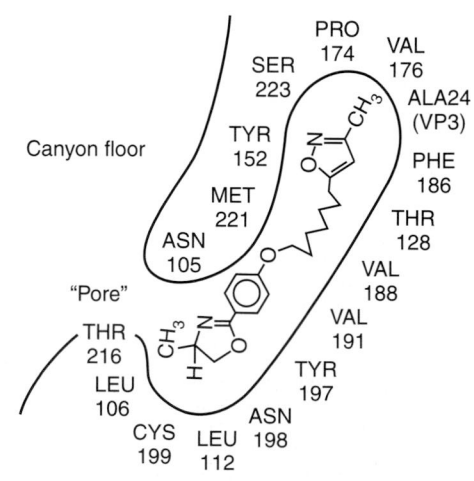

C

D

FIGURE 171-1. Key features of a human rhinovirus (HRV). **A,** The virion shell consists of 12 pentamers, one of which has been removed to show the approximate location of the RNA packed tightly into a central cavity. Each pentamer, in turn, consists of five wedge-shaped subunits, called protomers. The canyon (stippled) is shown in only 1 of the 12 pentamers. **B,** The virion contains four major proteins (VP1, -2, -3, and -4) plus traces of another, VP0, representing residual precursor following the maturation cleavage (see *inset*) required for acquisition of infectivity. **C,** Transverse section through the center of a pentamer depicting entry of its cellular receptor (intercellular adhesion molecule 1 [ICAM-1]) and the location of the drug-binding pocket just beneath the canyon floor. An ion, located at each pentamer center in HRV-1A, -14, and -16, is tentatively identified as calcium, which is necessary for attachment of some rhinoviruses. **D,** Detail showing orientation of a capsid binder (WIN 52084) and identity of amino acid residues lining the canyon floor and drug-binding pocket in a single protomer. In HRV-14 the drug prevents attachment of its receptor, ICAM-1. *(Courtesy of Dr. Roland R. Ruckert.)*

The rhinovirus genome contains a single strand of positive-sense RNA about 7200 bases long that is organized in essentially the same way as that of poliovirus.[28] A single large polyprotein containing nearly 2200 amino acids represents about 90% of the total genome. Rhinovirus RNA has genes that code for the four capsid proteins, VPg, a small protein at the 5′ end, an RNA polymerase, and a protease. Rhinovirus multiplication occurs in the cytoplasm and is similar to the model developed for poliovirus.

Biologic Characteristics

Heating, ultraviolet light, and desiccation cause rhinovirus to lose its native antigenicity and acquire a new set of surface determinants called the coreless or heated antigen.[28] Rhinovirus is sensitive to acidic pH less than 5 and to alkaline pH exceeding 9. Capsid-binding drugs, such as chalcones, stabilize rhinovirus against heat inactivation. Neutralization of rhinovirus by antibody results from steric hindrance of the virus-receptor interaction. Halogens or sodium dodecyl sulfate in the presence of organic acid such as malate and citrate inactivate rhinovirus at room temperature.

Human rhinovirus infects only humans and some higher primates and grows in cell cultures derived from these species. The optimal temperature for rhinovirus replication, 33° to 35° C, corresponds to the temperature found in the nose and large airways.[30] At a core body temperature of 37° C, virus yields fall by as much as 90% of maximum.[31] The relatively low temperature range for optimal rhinovirus growth may explain why generalized infection as manifested by viremia has not been observed with rhinovirus.[32,33] Also, temperature may be one of the factors inhibiting viral replication in the intestinal tract. Gastrointestinal secretions may likewise have an adverse effect on virus survival.[34] Replication in cell culture requires approximately 8 hours but may vary with the condition of culture.[28] Although rhinovirus multiplication takes place primarily in the cells of the nasal passages,[35] it has been recovered from sinus[36] and middle ear[37] aspirates, and replicative strand RNA has been identified in bronchial epithelial cells.[38] Evidence suggests that the adenoidal area is an important location for initiation of infection.[39] In support is the finding that lymphoepithelial cells located in the crypts of the adenoid have been shown by immunohistochemistry to contain heavy concentrations of ICAM-1.[40] Infection also spreads to the ciliated epithelial cells of the nasal passages but appears to be spotty in location.[39,41,42] Rhinovirus survives on skin and environmental surfaces for at least several hours after contamination of these sites.[43]

Antigenic Characteristics

Four major immunogenic neutralization sites are present within each rhinovirus protomer. Rhinoviruses have been numbered 1 to 100 and subtype 1A on the basis of these surface antigens.[9-11] Identification is based on neutralization of viral growth with hyperimmune animal antiserum containing 20 units of antibody. The native antigenic structure of the virus can be altered by exposure to pH 5 at 56° C or to 2 mol/L urea.[44] The configurational change in the capsid that results from such treatments produces an altered state of antigenicity characterized by reactivity with heterologous rhinovirus types. The altered, or C-antigenic, state does not stimulate protective antibody.

With antisera against the 100 numbered rhinovirus immunotypes, it has been possible to identify most strains recovered in more recent epidemiologic studies.[11,45,46] Thus, it does not appear that new immunotypes of rhinovirus are emerging at a rapid rate. However, antigenic differences have been found in strains of the same type recovered several years apart[47,48]; also, intertypes have been discovered,[49] which suggests that some antigenic drift of rhinoviruses does take place. With a cloned stock of rhinovirus type 2, it has been shown that escape from neutralization by monoclonal antibody can occur with a single amino acid substitution in the viral shell.[50]

EPIDEMIOLOGY

Distribution and Prevalence

Rhinoviruses have a worldwide distribution. In a given geographic area, the different antigenic types circulate in a random fashion with no pattern other than for current types to be slowly replaced by strains of different antigenic types.[51] Infections begin to occur in early childhood and continue throughout life.[52-54] Studies of the prevalence of rhinovirus antibody show rapid acquisition of antibody during childhood and adolescence, with a peak prevalence in young adults,[55] which probably reflects their exposure to young children. Antibody prevalence then declines slightly and remains relatively constant throughout adulthood. A slight decrease in the prevalence of antibody in older adults probably results from lessened viral exposure. Rhinoviruses are also encountered in military populations, where they are a cause of respiratory disease in military recruits.[56-58]

Seasonal Pattern of Infection

In temperate climates, rhinoviruses have a well-established seasonal pattern, with fall and spring peaks of infection. Most characteristic in the United States is an early fall outbreak of rhinovirus colds, which annually initiates the respiratory disease season.[17,59] In adults with colds in the eastern United States, rhinovirus infection rates are highest in September. In some years and some locations, however, a fall rhinovirus outbreak has not been observed.[46] A second, less prominent peak of rhinovirus infection occurs in March, April, and May. Rhinoviruses also account for a relatively high proportion of summer colds. In the winter months, rhinovirus activity is low; coronaviruses and possibly undiscovered agents are thought to account for most colds at that time. In tropical areas, rhinovirus outbreaks have been encountered in the rainy season[52] and, in the arctic, during cold weather.[60] The reasons for the seasonal pattern of rhinovirus infection are not well understood. Volunteers exposed to thermal cold have not shown increased susceptibility to experimental rhinovirus colds.[61] Seasonal changes in living conditions, such as the opening of schools and crowding indoors, are believed to be important in initiating fall rhinovirus outbreaks. Also, rhinoviruses survive better under conditions of high relative humidity, which occurs from late spring to midfall in temperate areas.[62]

Infection and Illness Rates

Rhinovirus colds are one of the most common infections in humans. In longitudinal studies, rhinovirus has been recovered in cell culture from 25% of adults with colds[17] and detected by culture combined with polymerase chain reaction in 50%.[63] Infection rates range from 1.2 infections per person-year in children younger than 1 year[64] to 0.7 in young adults.[17,65] Infection rates in men and women are similar. In illness surveillance studies at the workplace, not in persons seeking medical care, cigarette smokers had rhinovirus illness rates similar to those of nonsmokers, although their illnesses were more severe.[17,66] From 70% to 88% of rhinovirus infections are associated with symptomatic respiratory illness, for an apparent-to-inapparent infection ratio of approximately 3:1.[17,57,65-67]

Serum neutralizing antibody is a major factor in determining rhinovirus infection rates. The relative risk of infection in persons with serum antibody titers of less than 1:2 is 174 when compared with persons with titers of 1:32 or 1:64. Lack of antibody also increases the risk of illness, but to a lesser degree.[68] Work has shown that chronic stress[69] and the number of social ties[70] also affect the risk of rhinovirus illness. However, in antibody-free subjects (<1:2), lack of chronic stress or the presence of abundant social ties did not protect against infection after rhinovirus challenge.

Transmission

A major site for rhinovirus transmission is the home,[71-73] and the most frequent introducer of infection is a school-aged child. Secondary infections are most common in young siblings and mothers. From 1- to

5-day intervals are seen between the onset of cases occurring in families. Secondary attack rates in family members have ranged from 25% to 70% and have varied with the immune status of the person exposed to the invading virus. Equally important locations for rhinovirus spread are schools and day care centers.[74,75] In some outbreaks, up to 77% of children in a nursery school became infected when a new serotype was introduced into the classroom.[76] Mixing of different rhinovirus types in a school population provides an efficient way for the virus to be disseminated in a community.

Epidemiologic observations suggest that efficient rhinovirus transmission depends on some type of close contact that allows exposure to infectious secretions over a short distance. Studies in volunteers have shown that spread of infectious nasal secretions from hand to hand, followed by autoinoculation of the nasal and conjunctival mucosa, is an efficient means of viral transmission.[77] Contamination of the hands with nasal secretions containing rhinovirus is a common occurrence in people with natural colds. These individuals may then pass virus to the hands of others with whom they have contact. Finger-to-nose and finger-to-eye contact occurs frequently in the course of normal behavior and provides a means for accidental self-inoculation of susceptible persons. Also, rhinovirus has been recovered from objects in the homes of persons with colds,[77] and infection has been transmitted to volunteers by means of contaminated plastic tiles.[78] In one field study entailing regular treatment of the hands with a virucidal lotion, persons using the active treatments had fewer rhinovirus colds than did those using a placebo lotion.[79] The findings of that study provide direct evidence that the hand contamination/self-inoculation route of rhinovirus transmission occurs under natural conditions.

Experimental rhinovirus infection has also been transmitted through the air in either large- or small-particle aerosols.[80] However, under ordinary indoor conditions of 70° F and 40% relative humidity, rhinovirus in aerosol is inactivated rapidly.[80a] The development of a re-liable aerosol model demonstrates the feasibility of that route of rhinovirus transmission. Further studies designed to interrupt spread of natural infection by the different routes are needed to determine their relative importance.[79]

PATHOGENESIS

A basic feature of rhinovirus pathogenesis is the susceptibility of the nose of nonimmune individuals to the virus; experimental challenge resulted in up to a 95% infection rate.[81] Under experimental conditions, one median tissue culture infective dose ($TCID_{50}$) of rhinovirus placed in the nose leads to infection and illness.[82] Newly produced virus can be recovered from the nasal secretions of volunteers by 8 to 10 hours after nasal inoculation.[83] Viral shedding increases to peak levels on the second and third day, at which time nasal secretions contain 10 to 1000 $TCID_{50}$/mL of virus.[32] As mentioned earlier, replication occurs primarily in the nasal passages[79] but virus has been cultured from sinus[36] and middle ear aspirates,[37] and replicative strand RNA has been identified in bronchial epithelial cells.[38]

During the acute illness, large quantities of protein including fibrinogen are released from the mucous membrane of the nose. Cross-linked fibrin has been identified in the nasal fluid of persons with colds.[84] Over the first 5 days of experimental rhinovirus infection, mean ($\pm$SD) nasal fluid weight was 23 ($\pm$22) g.[85] Also at this time, ciliated epithelial cells containing rhinovirus antigen are present in nasal mucus, but their numbers are low and do not correlate with the severity of illness in individual cases.[42]

Clinical manifestations of illness appear as early as 8 to 10 hours after viral inoculation into the nose.[83,86] The specific mechanisms by which rhinovirus produces disease are not fully understood. Histologic examination of nasal biopsy specimens from volunteers with experimental infections has failed to show consistent pathologic

TABLE 171-2 Possible Inflammatory Pathways in Rhinovirus Colds

Mediator	Physiologic Actions That May Be Responsible for Cold Symptoms	Possible Links to Pathogenesis
Histamine	Dilatation of small vessels Increased permeability of postcapillary venules Stimulation of secretion of exocrine glands (goblet cells) Stimulation of nerve endings	Intranasal inhalation causes sneezing, rhinorrhea, nasal obstruction, and sore throat Increased histamine levels in nasal secretions from experimental colds First-generation antihistamines reduce sneezing and rhinorrhea in natural and experimental rhinovirus colds
Kinins	Vasodilatation (arterioles) Increased permeability of small venules Stimulation of pain nerve endings Stimulation of the release of histamine from mast cells	Intranasal inhalation causes rhinorrhea, nasal obstruction, and sore throat Increased kinin levels in nasal secretions from natural and experimental rhinovirus colds
Prostaglandins	E and D_2 cause vasodilatation E_2 causes pain when injected intradermally E_1 and E_2 act synergistically with bradykinin and histamine to increase vascular permeability $F_{2\alpha}$ causes bronchoconstriction (especially in asthmatics)	Intranasal inhalation causes rhinorrhea (D_2, $F_{2\alpha}$), nasal obstruction (D_2), sore throat ($F_{2\alpha}$), cough ($F_{2\alpha}$) Increased levels of stable metabolite of prostacyclin, 6-keto-PGF_1, in nasal secretions from experimental rhinovirus colds (preliminary data) Naproxen reduces headache, malaise, myalgia, and cough in experimental rhinovirus colds
Interleukin-1	Recruitment of inflammatory cells (neutrophils and lymphocytes) Increased responsiveness of some cells to bradykinin Increased vascular permeability Release of prostanoids, platelet-activating factor, and other inflammatory mediators	Increased interleukin-1 levels in nasal secretions from experimental rhinovirus colds
Interleukin-8	Recruitment of neutrophils	Increased interleukin-8 levels in nasal secretions from experimental rhinovirus colds
Interleukin-6	Stimulates acute-phase response Causes fever	Increased interleukin-6 levels in nasal secretions from experimental rhinovirus colds
Interleukin-16	Predominant lymphocyte chemoattractant in asthma	Increased levels in rhinovirus-infected human bronchial epithelial cells
RANTES	Acts on macrophages and eosinophils Chemoattractant for eosinophils and T lymphocytes	Increased levels in rhinovirus-infected human bronchial epithelial cells Increased concentrations in nasal aspirates of children with natural rhinovirus colds
Parasympathetic nervous system	Stimulates secretion of seromucous glands	Intranasal and oral treatment with parasympatholytic compounds reduces nasal secretions in experimental rhinovirus colds

changes.[39,87,88] These studies suggest that damage to the epithelium is slight and that the infection serves as a trigger for the release of chemical mediators and activation of neurologic reflexes, which are the ultimate cause of the clinical illness. The role of inflammatory pathways in the pathogenesis of rhinovirus colds has been investigated by measuring mediator concentrations in respiratory secretions, by blocking mediator and reflex activity by specific compounds, and by challenging volunteers with selected mediators applied to the upper airway. By these approaches, several mediators, including bradykinin and lysyl-bradykinin,[86,89] prostaglandin,[89,90] histamine,[89,91,92] RANTES (regulated on activation, normal T cell expressed and secreted),[38] and interleukins 1, 6, 8, and 16[38,92-94] have been associated with rhinovirus colds (Table 171-2). Also, parasympathetic[95] and α-adrenergic[96] pathways have been implicated in some of the symptoms of rhinovirus colds.

IMMUNITY

Rhinovirus infection stimulates the appearance of serum neutralizing antibody in up to 80% of persons with natural colds.[66,97] The neutralizing activity is associated with serum fractions containing immunoglobulin A (IgA) and IgG.[98,99] After recent experimental infections, rhinovirus-neutralizing activity has also been associated with serum IgM. In addition, neutralizing activity is present in nasal secretions, where it is associated primarily with the 9S and 11S fractions of IgA.[100] During rhinovirus colds, transudation of considerable amounts of serum immunoglobulin occurs in nasal secretions.[101,102]

After an infection in which antibody has been stimulated, most persons appear to be immune to reinfection with the same serotype.[66,72,103] Longitudinal studies have shown the persistence of serum antibody for years,[53] and it is probable that most rhinovirus colds confer long-lasting immunity. Antibody responses do not follow all infections, however. Also, in volunteers, protection associated with preexisting antibody can be overcome by a large virus challenge.[104] Therefore, it is evident that recurrent infections with the same rhinovirus type do occur.

It has been suggested that the primary immune mechanism in rhinovirus infection is the neutralizing antibody present in nasal secretions rather than that in serum. However, because nasal and serum antibody are found in close association,[98,105] it has been difficult to provide a definite answer to this question.[106-108]

CLINICAL MANIFESTATIONS

Signs and Symptoms of Rhinovirus Colds

Rhinoviruses produce a typical common cold. The median length of illness in young adults is 7 days, but symptoms last up to 2 weeks in one quarter of cases.[66] Complaints fall into nasal, pharyngeal, lower respiratory tract, and general categories; however, the individual symptoms may be the result of different pathogenic mechanisms so that combining the groups is not a good idea. On average, the symptoms of rhinovirus colds have a consistent pattern[109] (Fig. 171-2). However, wide variations occur in individual patients, and it is not possible to distinguish rhinovirus infections from other causes of upper respiratory illness on clinical grounds alone.

In adults with uncomplicated rhinovirus colds, fever is uncommon, and other systemic complaints are of low-grade severity. In most cases, rhinorrhea and nasal obstruction are the most prominent complaints. A sore or scratchy throat is also frequently present. Cough and hoarseness occur in approximately 30% and 20% of cases, respectively, and become more prominent in the later phase of illness. In cigarette smokers, the frequency and duration of cough are prolonged. In the average case, nasal and pharyngeal symptoms subside rapidly during the third and fourth day of illness.

On examination, the end of the nose may have a red color, and clear or mucoid nasal secretions are frequently present. Nasal obstruction is often more obvious to the patient than to the physician unless special methods are used to measure resistance to nasal airflow. A glistening appearance of the nasal membrane is often seen. The pharyngeal mucosa may show mild edema and erythema, but marked inflammation or exudate does not occur. Rhonchi may be heard on examination of the chest. In many patients with a moderate degree of subjective discomfort, the nose and throat show few objective changes at the time of examination.

Rhinoviruses also cause the common cold in children. Available evidence is conflicting on the role of rhinoviruses in viral pneumonia, croup, and bronchiolitis. The prevailing opinion is that rhinoviruses do not commonly cause these illnesses in children.[110-113] Rhinovirus infections have also been reported in immunosuppressed adults and children with fatal pneumonia. In one of these patients, rhinovirus antigen was reported to be present in the cytoplasm of hyperplastic alveolar lining cells.[114] In other cases, rhinovirus was isolated from bronchoalveolar lavage fluid.[115] In the latter cases, the question of contamination of the specimens with upper respiratory tract secretions could not be resolved, so that the existence of rhinovirus pneumonia as a clinical entity remains open.[116]

Viral Sinusitis

It is now understood that the occurrence of disease in the paranasal sinuses is part of the illness identified as the common cold. Evidence for this comes from sinus imaging studies performed in adults and children with colds in which up to 87% of adults and 88% of children had abnormalities in the sinuses.[117-120] Some cases were of rhinoviral etiology. The abnormalities in the sinus cavities and ostia were due to the presence of highly viscous exudate, which in some cases contained air bubbles.[121] The source of the exudate may in part be due to the propulsion of nasal fluid into the sinus cavities by nose blowing during colds[121] and in part to exocytosis of mucus from the goblet cells lining the sinus cavity. Rhinovirus has been recovered from sinus aspirates, but it is not clear if infection of the sinus cavity occurs in all cases where exudate is present. The contribution of the sinus involvement to the signs and symptoms of a cold is unclear, but in one small study, volunteers with experimental rhinovirus colds who had sinus abnormalities on magnetic resonance imaging had higher nasal mucus weights than those without this finding[117] (see Chapter 55).

Viral Otitis Media

Rhinovirus infection is commonly associated with abnormalities in eustachian tube function and middle ear pressure.[122-124] Eustachian tube dysfunction was measured in up to 80% of adults with experimental rhinovirus infection. Abnormalities in middle ear pressure were seen in up to 75% of volunteers with experimental rhinovirus colds and in up to 76% of patients with natural rhinovirus colds. Middle ear effusion developed in only 10% of adults[125] but presumably is more common in children because of closely spaced colds and the smaller size of the eustachian tube. Rhinovirus has been recovered alone and in combination with bacteria in middle ear aspirates from patients with acute otitis media[126,127] and rhinovirus RNA has been identified by reverse transcription–polymerase chain reaction.[128]

COMPLICATIONS OF RHINOVIRUS COLDS

Bacterial Sinusitis

Acute community-acquired bacterial sinusitis has been reported to complicate 0.5% to 2.2% of common respiratory diseases.[3,129] Viral rhinosinusitis is believed to be the major risk factor for the development of acute bacterial sinusitis. Sinus aspirate cultures have yielded rhinovirus in association with bacterial pathogens such as *Streptococcus pneumoniae* and unencapsulated strains of *Haemophilus influenzae*. Presumably, both viruses and bacteria are propelled into the nose by nose blowing during colds[121] (see Chapter 54).

Bacterial Otitis Media

Two percent of common respiratory disease is complicated by bacterial otitis media.[3] Rhinovirus has been implicated in the pathogenesis of bacterial otitis media by creating inflammatory obstruction of the eustachian tube and abnormal middle ear pressure.[122-125] Respiratory viruses, including rhinovirus, have been recovered directly from the middle ear fluid of patients with otitis media,[126,127] and rhinovirus RNA

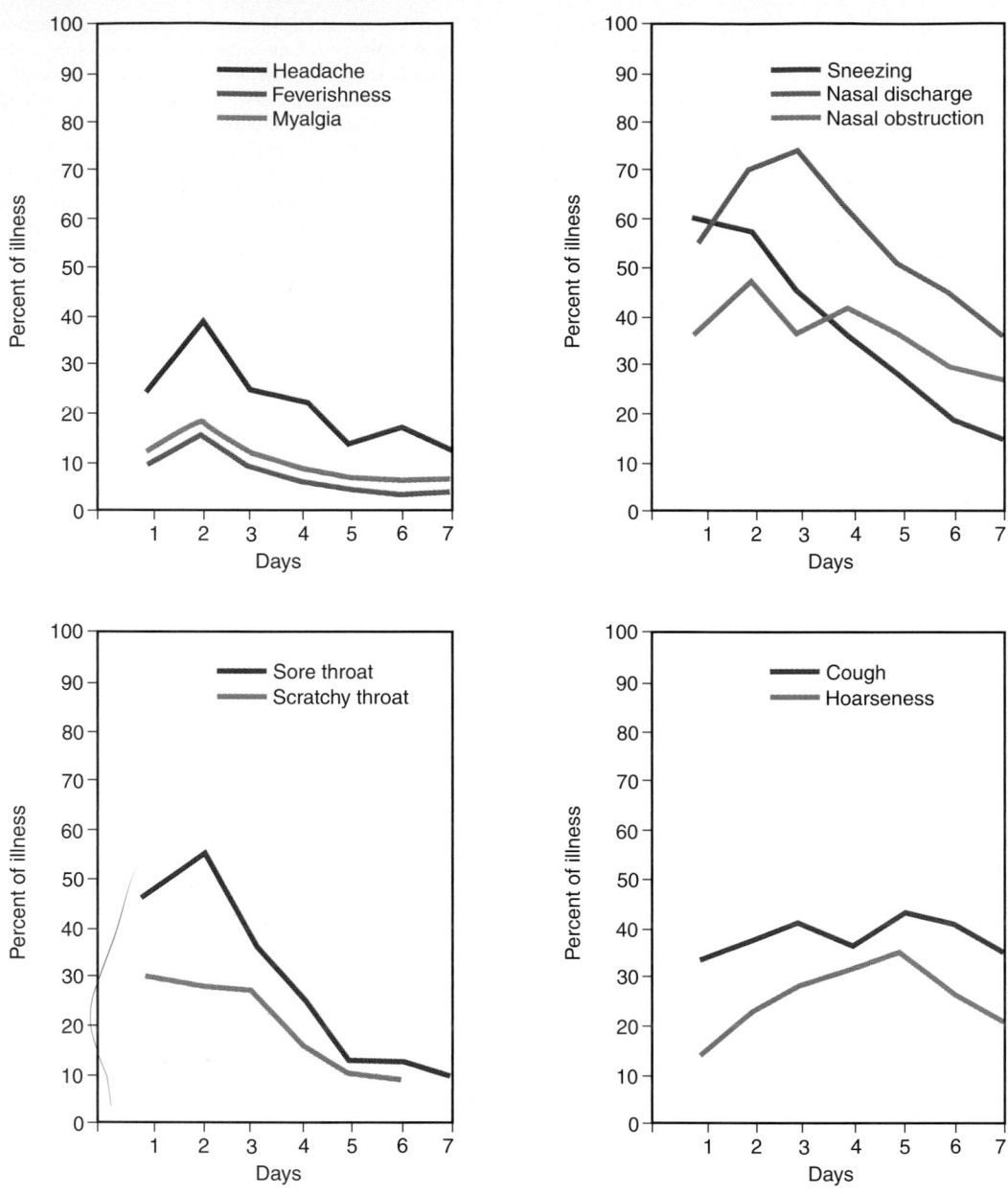

FIGURE 171-2. Rhinovirus cold symptoms (139 adults with natural infection).

has been detected in middle aspirates.[128] In some cases, *S. pneumoniae* and *H. influenzae* were recovered in combination with viruses. Microorganisms presumably reach the middle ear as a result of nose blowing during colds[114] (see Chapter 54).

Acute Infectious Episodes in Patients with Chronic Bronchitis

Rhinoviruses have been implicated in acute infectious exacerbations in patients with chronic bronchitis.[21-23,130] In a longitudinal study in patients with chronic obstructive pulmonary disease, viral infections were documented in 23% of hospitalized cases, and rhinovirus was the most frequently identified agent.[130] There is recent evidence that rhinovirus infects the tracheobronchial tree based on the identification of replicative strand RNA in bronchial epithelial cells of volunteers with experimental rhinovirus colds.[38] Mild alterations in ventilation have been measured in some persons with chronic bronchitis with rhinovirus infection.[131] Secondary bacterial infection may also play a role in this condition.

Precipitation of Asthma

Rhinovirus infection is an important cause of attacks of asthma in children and adults.[132-134] Rhinovirus was isolated from 31% of 70 wheezing children older than 2 years admitted to a pediatric emergency department and was associated with allergen-specific IgE.[135] Picornavirus RNA has been detected during 50% of 292 symptomatic episodes in children with wheezing or persistent cough.[136] The mechanisms by which rhinovirus infections induces wheezing[132,137] appear to represent a complex process involving cellular inflammation, cytokines, and mediators. Rhinovirus infection has been shown to induce production of interleukins 6, 8, and 16 and RANTES[38] and increases 5-lipoxygenase and cyclooxygenase-2 concentrations.[138] Experimental rhinovirus infection leads to a decrease in forced expiratory volume in 1 second and an increase in histamine sensitivity in some, but not all, young adults with mild to moderate asthma.[139] Evidence indicates that rhinovirus infection induces bronchial inflammation and hyperresponsiveness.

DIAGNOSIS

Clinical

Rhinovirus colds have similar and indistinguishable characteristics from colds due to other respiratory viruses.[66] Clinical diagnosis should focus on excluding cases of noninfectious rhinitis and identifying cases with secondary bacterial infection of the sinus and middle ear. Patients with a history of acute respiratory symptoms lasting longer than 7 to 10 days without improvement should be suspected of having acute bacterial sinusitis. Erythema and bulging of the ear drum and the presence of pus behind the drum suggest acute bacterial otitis media (see Chapters 50, 54, and 55).

Viral Identification

Rhinoviruses grow well in several cell culture systems, particularly human embryonic lung (WI-38 and MRC-5 strains) and M-HeLa cells. However, unexplained variation in the sensitivity of these cells can cause problems in testing if not recognized.[140,141] Viral growth is optimum at 33° to 34° C, and cultures must be incubated in a roller drum to achieve maximum cytopathic change. Rhinovirus cytopathic effect is usually evident in 2 to 6 days (Fig. 171-3). Polymerase chain reaction with nucleic acid probes has been used with increasing frequency to detect rhinovirus.[38,136,142] With this method, the use of proper controls is required to prevent false-positive results. Because the specificity of the viral antigen of each type prevents serologic identification of members of the group as a whole, viral identification has been the only practical method of diagnosis.

Identification of the antigenic type of an unknown rhinovirus by neutralization requires a large battery of antisera, and it is best accomplished with a system of intersecting antiserum pools.[143] A microtitration system can be used for preliminary identification.[144,145] Final proof of antigenic type is demonstrated by neutralization of the $TCID_{10-300}$ of virus by 20 units of antibody using monovalent hyperimmune animal serum.

Serology

A neutralization test can be used for the serodiagnosis of rhinovirus infection if the infecting type is known. However, the multiplicity of rhinovirus types prevents the use of serologic techniques for routine diagnosis. For measuring neutralizing antibody in human serum, it is

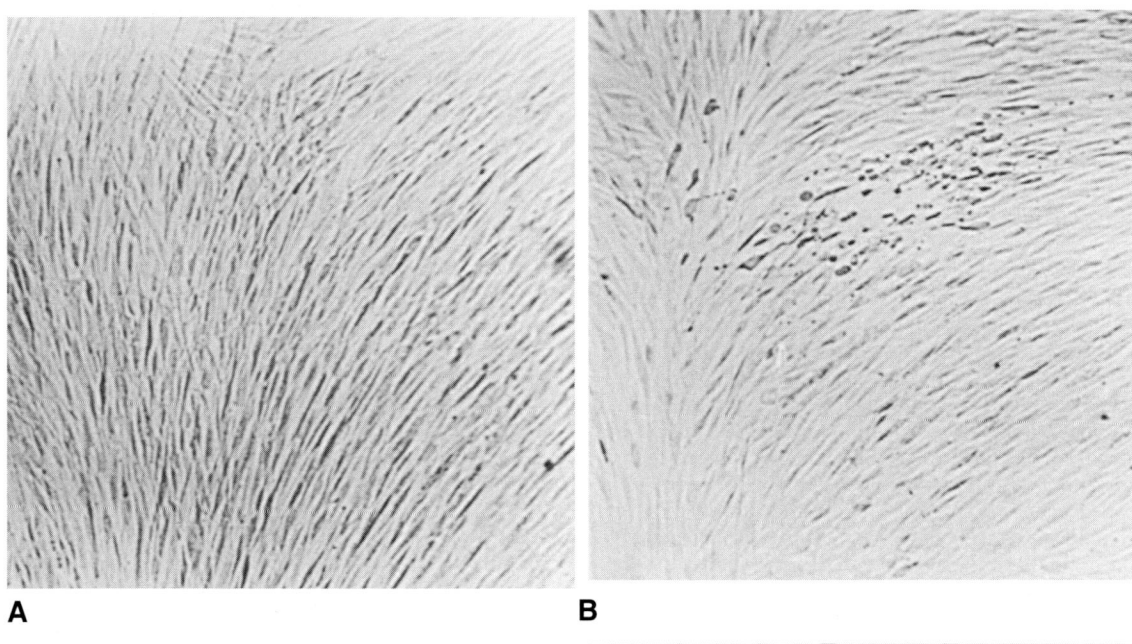

A

B

FIGURE 171-3. Rhinovirus cytopathic effect in human embryonic lung cells (WI-38). **A,** Uninfected cell cultures (original magnification, ×160). **B,** Cytopathic effect of rhinovirus type 39 at 48 hours. **C,** Cytopathic effect at 72 hours.

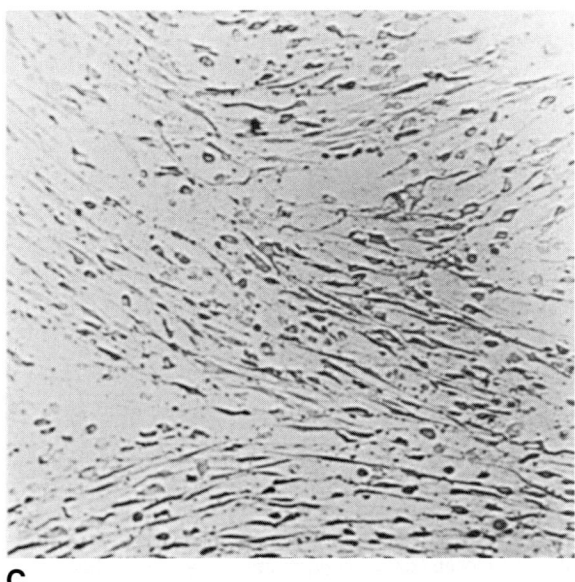

C

necessary to use small doses of virus (TCID$_{3\text{-}30}$) if the test is to have satisfactory sensitivity.[146]

TREATMENT AND PREVENTION

Symptomatic Therapy

A combination of a first-generation antihistamine and a nonsteroidal anti-inflammatory drug (NSAID) is effective treatment for rhinovirus colds. Treatment should be started as early as symptoms are recognized and continued every 12 hours until symptoms subside (see Chapter 50). Antibiotics have no place in therapy because they neither ameliorate the viral illness nor reduce the frequency of bacterial complications.

Rest, hydration, saline gargles, and cough suppressants may also be useful. If needed, oral decongestants may be used on a regular basis during the acute stage of illness. Topical decongestants tend to cause "rebound" nasal obstruction and sore throat. The regular application of a petrolatum-based ointment helps prevent painful maceration of the nares. Patients with secondary bacterial sinusitis or otitis media require appropriate antimicrobial therapy.

Prospects for Vaccines and Antivirals

Studies of the molecular structure of the rhinovirus shell[29] confirm that rhinovirus is a difficult candidate for vaccine development. The most conserved region of the viral capsid lies in the bottom of the surface cleft, where it is inaccessible to antibody. Experimental rhinovirus vaccines made against one immunotype of virus have reduced the rate of symptomatic illness and viral shedding but not the overall rate of infection of volunteers given an experimental challenge with rhinovirus.[105,147] Because of the large number of rhinovirus immunotypes, the prospects for an effective rhinovirus vaccine are not good.

Chemical compounds with in vitro activity against rhinovirus continue to be discovered.[148,149] However, on reaching human testing, even those showing good promise in cell culture, such as the capsid binders, have shown only modest clinical benefit when used alone.[150] Pleconaril, an orally active antipicornavirus compound that binds in the hydrophobic pocket of the rhinovirus surface capsid, had a small effect on the duration of colds in controlled studies (1 day more rapid alleviation of symptoms).[150a] Treatment was associated with slight increases in rates of nausea and vomiting. A Food and Drug Administration advisory committee recommended against its approval as a treatment for colds. Also, soluble ICAM-1, although effective in blocking rhinovirus infection in cell culture, has proved to be difficult to adapt to use in humans.[151] The most promising results have been obtained with recombinant interferon-alfa-2 applied topically in the nose. Given prophylactically in doses of approximately 5 million units a day, interferon-alfa-2 has been highly effective in preventing experimental infection and illness.[152] When used in short courses for contact prophylaxis in two studies in families, topical interferon-alfa-2 reduced the overall rate of colds in treated persons by 40% and virtually eliminated colds caused by rhinovirus.[153,154] However, when used in the treatment of volunteers with experimental rhinovirus colds, interferon-alfa-2 reduced viral shedding but had only a modest effect on symptomatic illness.[152] Intranasal interferon, when applied for periods of longer than a few days, has the disadvantage of causing local side effects consisting of nasal irritation and pinpoint mucosal ulcerations. However, this side effect is avoided with the short courses of administration used in contact prophylaxis and combined antiviral-antimediator treatment described later.

Combined Antiviral-Antimediator Treatment

Another approach to the treatment of rhinovirus colds is based on the observed failure of antivirals such as interferon and capsid binders to have therapeutic efficacy when given alone and on an understanding of the key role of inflammatory mediators in pathogenesis. The treatment consists of a combination of an antiviral agent for reducing viral replication and selected compounds that block inflammatory pathways. In controlled trials, in subjects with experimental rhinovirus colds this approach had shown promise.[155,156] Intranasal interferon-alfa-2b was used as the antiviral in association with an oral NSAID and either intranasal ipratropium or oral chlorpheniramine at the onset of symptoms. With the combination therapy, viral shedding and progression of illness were attenuated and clinically useful reductions were observed in sneezing, rhinorrhea, nasal mucus weights, nasal tissue use, sore throat, cough, and headache. The treatments were well tolerated.

Environmental Measures to Control Infection

If the hand contact/self-inoculation route is one means by which rhinovirus spreads under natural conditions, persons can protect themselves by hand washing and avoiding finger-to-eye and finger-to-nose contact. Until further knowledge is gained on this question, it seems expedient to take such precautions, particularly when a member of the household has a respiratory illness. It may be possible to develop additional approaches to hand[79] and environmental[78] disinfection that are effective in interrupting the spread of rhinovirus colds. Because aerosol spread may be another route of rhinovirus transmission,[80] covering coughs and sneezes with disposable nasal tissues is also recommended.

REFERENCES

1. Gwaltney JM Jr. Historical eras of the common cold. In: Sande MA, Root RK, eds. Contemporary Issues in Infectious Diseases, v. 10, Viral Infections: Diagnosis, Treatment and Prevention. New York: Churchill Livingstone; 1992:1-13.
2. Kruse W. Die Erreger von Husten and Schupfen. Munchen Med Wochenschr. 1914;61:1547.
3. Dingle JH, Badger GF, Jordan WS Jr. Illness in the Home. A Study of 25,000 Illnesses in a Group of Cleveland Families. Cleveland: Western Reserve University; 1964.
4. Andrewes C. The Common Cold. New York: WW Norton; 1965.
5. Pelon W, Mogabgab WJ, Phillips IA, et al. A cytopathogenic agent isolated from naval recruits with mild respiratory illness. Proc Soc Exp Biol Med. 1957;94:262.
6. Price WH. The isolation of a new virus associated with respiratory clinical disease in humans. Proc Natl Acad Sci U S A. 1956;42:892.
7. Ketler A, Hamparian VV, Hilleman MR. Characterization and classification of ECHO 28-rhinovirus-coryzavirus agents. Proc Soc Exp Biol Med. 1962;110:821.
8. Hayflick L, Moorhead PS. The serial cultivation of human diploid cell strains. Exp Cell Res. 1961;25:585.
9. Kapikian AZ, Conant RM, Hamparian VV, et al. Rhinoviruses: A numbering system. Nature. 1967;213:761.
10. Kapikian AZ, Conant RM, Hamparian VV, et al. A collaborative report: Rhinoviruses-extension of the numbering system. Virology. 1971;43:524.
11. Hamparian VV, Colonno RJ, Cooney MK, et al. A collaborative report: Rhinoviruses-extension of the numbering system from 89 to 100. Virology. 1987;159:191.
12. Callahan PL, Mizutani S, Colonno RJ. Molecular cloning and complete sequence determination of RNA genome of human rhinovirus 14. Proc Natl Acad Sci U S A. 1985;82:732.
13. Stanway G, Hughes PJ, Mountford RC, et al. The complete nucleotide sequence of a common cold virus; human rhinovirus 14. Nucleic Acids Res. 1984;12:7859.
14. Skern T, Sommergruber W, Blaas D, et al. Human rhinovirus 2: Complete nucleotide sequence and proteolytic processing signals in the capside protein region. Nucleic Acids Res. 1985;12:2111.
15. Rossmann MG, Arnold E, Erickson JW, et al. The structure of a human common cold virus (rhinovirus 14) and its functional relations to other picornaviruses. Nature. 1985;317:145.
16. Hamre D, Procknow JJ. Viruses isolated from natural common colds among young adult medical students. Am Rev Respir Dis. 1963;88:277.
17. Gwaltney JM Jr, Hendley JO, Simon G, et al. Rhinovirus infections in an industrial population. I. The occurrence of illness. N Engl J Med. 1966;275:1261.
18. Monto AS, Ullman BM. Acute respiratory illness in an American community: The Tecumseh study. JAMA. 1974;227:164.
19. Evans FO, Sydnor JB, Moore WEC, et al. Sinusitis of the maxillary antrum. N Engl J Med. 1975;293:735.
20. Buchman CA, Doyle WJ, Skoner D, et al. Otologic manifestations of experimental rhinovirus infection. Laryngoscope. 1994;104:1295-1299.
21. Eadie MB, Stott EJ, Grist RN. Virological studies in chronic bronchitis. BMJ. 1966;2:671.
22. McNamara MJ, Phillips IA, Williams OB. Viral and Mycoplasma pneumoniae infections in exacerbations of chronic lung disease. Am Rev Respir Dis. 1969;100:19.
23. Stenhouse AC. Rhinovirus infection in acute exacerbations of chronic bronchitis: A controlled prospective study. BMJ. 1967;3:461.
24. Hilleman MR, Reilly CM, Stokes J Jr, et al. Clinical epidemiologic findings in coryzavirus infections. Am Rev Respir Dis. 1963;88(Suppl):S274.
25. Minor TE, Dick EC, DeMeo AN, et al. Viruses as precipitants of asthmatic attacks in children. JAMA. 1974;227:292.
26. Wildy P. Classification and nomenclature of viruses. In: Melnick JL, ed. Monographs in Virology. Basel: Karger; 1971.
27. Palmenberg AC. Sequence alignments of picornaviral capsid proteins. In: Semler BL, Ehrenfeld E, eds. Molecular Aspects of Picornavirus Infection and Detection. Washington, DC: American Society for Microbiology; 1987:211-241.

28. Gwaltney JM Jr, Heinz BA. Rhinovirus. In Richman DD, Whitley RJ, Hayden FG, eds. Clinical Virology. Washington, DC: ASM Press; 2002:995-1018.
29. Smith TJ, Baker TS. Picornavirus epitopes, canyons, and pockets. Adv Virus Res. 1999;52:1-23.
30. Halperin SA, Eggleston PA, Hendley JO, et al. Pathogenesis of lower respiratory tract symptoms in experimental rhinovirus infection. Am Rev Respir Dis. 1983;128:806.
31. Stott EJ, Killington RA. Rhinoviruses. Annu Rev Microbiol. 1972;26:503.
32. Douglas RG Jr, Cate TR, Gerone PJ, et al. Quantitative rhinovirus shedding patterns in volunteers. Am Rev Respir Dis. 1966;94:159.
33. Douglas RG Jr, Rossen RD, Butler WT, et al. Rhinovirus neutralizing antibody in tears, parotid saliva, nasal secretions and serum. J Immunol. 1967;99:297.
34. Cate TR, Douglas RG Jr, Johnson KM, et al. Studies on the inability of rhinovirus to survive and replicate in the intestinal tract of volunteers. Proc Soc Exp Biol Med. 1967;124:1290.
35. Gwaltney JM Jr. Epidemiology of the common cold. Ann N Y Acad Sci. 1980;353:54.
36. Hamory BH, Sande MA, Sydnor A Jr, et al. Etiology and antimicrobial therapy of acute maxillary sinusitis. J Infect Dis. 1979; 139:197-202.
37. Gwaltney JM Jr. Viral vaccines in the control of otitis media. Pediatr Infect Dis J. 1989;8:S78-S79.
38. Papadopoulos NG, Bates PJ, Bardin PG, et al. Rhinoviruses infect the lower airway. J Infect Dis. 2000;181:1875-1884.
39. Winther B, Gwaltney JM Jr, Mygind N, et al. Sites of rhinovirus recovery after point inoculation of the upper airway. JAMA. 1986;256:1763.
40. Winther B, Greve JM, Gwaltney JM Jr, et al. Surface expression of intercellular adhesion molecule 1 on epithelial cells in the human adenoid. J Infect Dis. 1997;25:574-583.
41. de Arruda E III, Mifflin TE, Gwaltney JM Jr, et al. Localization of rhinovirus replication in vitro with in situ hybridization. J Med Virol. 1991;34:38-44.
42. Turner RB, Hendley JO, Gwaltney JM Jr. Shedding of infected ciliated epithelial cells in rhinovirus colds. J Infect Dis. 1982;145:849-853.
43. Hendley JO, Wenzel RP, Gwaltney JM Jr. Transmission of rhinovirus colds by self-inoculation. N Engl J Med. 1973;288:1361.
44. Lonberg-Holm K, Yin FH. Antigenic determinants of infective and inactivated human rhinoviruses type 2. J Virol. 1973;12:114.
45. Krilov L, Pierik L, Keller E, et al. The association of rhinoviruses with lower respiratory tract disease in hospitalized patients. J Med Virol. 1986;19:345.
46. Monto AS, Bryan ER, Ohmit S. Rhinovirus infections in Tecumseh, Michigan: Illness frequency and number of serotypes. J Infect Dis. 1987;156:43.
47. Schieble JH, Lennette EH, Fox VL. Antigenic variation of rhinovirus type 22. Proc Soc Exp Biol Med. 1970;133:329.
48. Stott EJ, Walker M. Antigenic variation among strains of rhinovirus type 51. Nature. 1969;224:1311.
49. Halfpap LM, Cooney MK. Isolation of rhinovirus intertypes related to either rhinoviruses 12 and 78 or 36 and 58. Infect Immun. 1983;40:213.
50. Speller SA, Sanger DV, Clarke BE, Rowlands DJ. The nature and spatial distribution of amino acid substitutions conferring resistance to neutralizing monoclonal antibodies in human rhinovirus type 2. J Gen Virol. 1993;74:193-200.
51. Hamre D. Rhinoviruses. In: Melnick JL, ed. Monographs in Virology 1. Basel: Karger; 1968.
52. Monto AS, Johnson KM. A community study of respiratory infections in the tropics. II. The spread of six rhinovirus isolates within the community. Am J Epidemiol. 1968;88:55.
53. Taylor-Robinson D. Studies on some viruses (rhinoviruses) isolated from common colds. Arch Ges Virusforsch. 1963;13:281.
54. Tyrrell DAJ. Rhinoviruses. In: Gard S, Hallauer C, Myer KF, eds. Virology Monographs 2. New York: Springer-Verlag; 1968.
55. Hamparian VV, Conant RM, Thomas DC. Rhinovirus Reference Laboratory, Annual Contract Progress Report to the National Institute of Allergy and Infectious Diseases. Contract No. 69-2062. Bethesda, MD: National Institutes of Health; Dec 1, 1969-Nov 30, 1970.
56. Forsyth BR, Bloom HH, Johnson KM, et al. Patterns of illness in rhinovirus infection of military personnel. N Engl J Med. 1963;269:602.
57. Johnson KM, Bloom HH, Forsyth BR, et al. Relationship of rhinovirus infection to mild upper respiratory disease. II. Epidemiologic observations in male military trainees. Am J Epidemiol. 1965;81:131.
58. Rosenbaum MJ, DeBerry P, Sullivan EJ, et al. Epidemiology of the common cold in military recruits with emphasis on infections by rhinovirus type 1A, 2, and two unclassified rhinoviruses. Am J Epidemiol. 1971;93:183.
59. Monto AS, Cavallaro JJ. The Tecumseh study of respiratory illness. II. Patterns of occurrence of infection with respiratory illness pathogens, 1965-1969. Am J Epidemiol. 1971;94:280.
60. Wulff H, Nobel GR, Maynard JE, et al. An outbreak of respiratory infection in children associated with rhinovirus types 16 and 29. Am J Epidemiol. 1969;90:304.
61. Douglas RG Jr, Lindgren KM, Couch RB. Exposure to cold environment and rhinovirus common cold: Failure to demonstrate effect. N Engl J Med. 1968;279:743.
62. Gwaltney JM Jr, The Jeremiah Metzger Lecture. Climatology and the common cold. Trans Am Clin Climatolog Assoc. 1984;96:159-175.
63. Mäkelä MJ, Puhakka T, Ruuskanen O, et al. Viruses and bacteria in the etiology of the common cold. J Clin Microbiol. 1998;36:539-542.
64. Cooney MK, Hall CE, Fox JP. The Seattle virus watch. 3. Evaluation of isolation methods and summary of infections detected by virus isolations. Am J Epidemiol. 1972;96:286.
65. Hamre D, Connelly AP Jr, Procknow J. Virologic studies of acute respiratory disease in young adults. IV. Virus isolations during four years of surveillance. Am J Epidemiol. 1966;83:238.

66. Gwaltney JM Jr, Hendley JO, Simon G, et al. Rhinovirus infections in an industrial population. II. Characteristics of illness and antibody response. JAMA. 1967;202:494.
67. Fox JP, Hall CE, Cooney MK, et al. The Seattle virus watch. II. Objectives, study population and its observation, data processing and summary of illnesses. Am J Epidemiol. 1972;96:270.
68. Mufson MA, Bloom HH, Forsyth BR, et al. Relationship of rhinovirus to mild upper respiratory disease. III. Further epidemiologic observations in military personnel. Am J Epidemiol. 1966;83:379.
69. Cohen S, Gwaltney JM Jr, Doyle WJ, et al. State and trait negative affect as predictors of objective and subjective symptoms of a common cold. J Personality Soc Psychol. 1995;68:159-171.
70. Cohen S, Doyle WJ, Skoner DP, et al. Social ties and susceptibility to the common cold. JAMA. 1997;227:1940-1944.
71. Dick EC, Blumer CR, Evans AS. Epidemiology of infections with rhinovirus types 43 and 55 in a group of University of Wisconsin student families. Am J Epidemiol. 1967;86:386.
72. Hendley JO, Gwaltney JM Jr, Jordan WS Jr. Rhinovirus infections in an industrial population. IV. Infections within families of employees during two fall peaks of respiratory illness. Am J Epidemiol. 1969;89:184.
73. Monto AS. A community study of respiratory infections in the tropics. III. Introduction and transmission of infections within families. Am J Epidemiol. 1968;88:69.
74. Periera MA, Andrews BE, Gardner SD. A study on the virus aetiology of mild respiratory infections in the primary school child. J Hyg. 1967;64:475.
75. Kendall EJC, Bynoe ML, Tyrrell DAJ. Virus isolations from common colds occurring in a residential school. BMJ. 1962;2:82.
76. Beem MO. Acute respiratory illness in nursery school children: A longitudinal study of the occurrence and respiratory viruses. Am J Epidemiol. 1969;90:30.
77. Gwaltney JM Jr, Moskalski PB, Hendley JO. Hand to hand transmission of rhinovirus colds. Ann Intern Med. 1978;88:463.
78. Gwaltney JM Jr, Hendley JO. Transmission of experimental rhinovirus infection by contaminated surfaces. Am J Epidemiol. 1982;116:828.
79. Hendley JO, Gwaltney JM Jr. Mechanisms of transmission of rhinovirus infections. Epidemiol Rev. 1988;10:242.
80. Dick EC, Jennings LC, Mink KA, et al. Aerosol transmission of rhinovirus colds. J Infect Dis. 1987;156:442.
80a. Karim YG, Ijaz MK, Sattar SA, Johnson-Lussenburg CM. Effect of relative humidity on the airborne survival of rhinovirus 14. Can J Microbiol. 1985;31:1058-1061.
81. Gwaltney JM Jr., Hayden FG. Response to psychological stress and susceptibility to the common cold (Letter to the Editor). N Engl J Med. 1992;326:644-645.
82. Douglas RG Jr. Pathogenesis of rhinovirus common colds in human volunteers. Ann Otol Rhinol Laryngol. 1970;79:563.
83. Harris JM II, Gwaltney JM Jr. The incubation periods of experimental rhinovirus infection and illness. Clin Infect Dis. 1996;23:1286-1290.
84. Winther B, Gwaltney JM Jr, Humphries JE, Hendley JO. Cross-linked fibrin in the nasal fluid of patients with the common cold. Clin Infect Dis. 2002;34:708-710.
85. Parekh IIII, Cragun KT, Hayden FG, et al. Nasal mucus weights in experimental rhinovirus infection. Am J Rhinol. 1992;6:107-110.
86. Naclerio RM, Proud D, Kagey-Sobotka A, et al. Kinins are generated during experimental rhinovirus colds. J Infect Dis. 1988;157:133-142.
87. Douglas RG Jr, Alford BR, Couch RB. A traumatic nasal biopsy for studies of respiratory virus infection in volunteers. Antimicrob Agents Chemother. 1968;8:340.
88. Winther B, Farr B, Turner RB, et al. Histopathologic examination and enumeration of polymorphonuclear leukocytes in the nasal mucosa during experimental rhinovirus colds. Acta Otolaryngol Suppl (Stockh). 1984;413:19.
89. Doyle WJ, Boehm S, Skoner DP. Physiologic responses to intranasal dose-response challenges with histamine, methacholine, bradykinin, and prostaglandin in adult volunteers with and without nasal allergy. J Allergy Clin Immunol. 1990;86:924-935.
90. Sperber SJ, Hendley JO, Hayden FG, et al. Effects of naproxen on experimental rhinovirus colds. A randomized, double-blind, controlled trial. Ann Intern Med. 1992;117:37-41.
91. Gaffey MJ, Gwaltney JM Jr, Sastre A, et al. Intranasal and oral antihistamine treatment of experimental rhinovirus colds. Am Rev Respir Dis. 1987;136:556-560.
91a. Gwaltney JM Jr, Druce HM. Efficacy of brompheniramine maleate treatment for rhinovirus colds. Clin Infect Dis. 1997;25:1188.
92. Proud D, Gwaltney JM Jr, Hendley JO, et al. Increased levels of interleukin-1 are detected in nasal secretions of volunteers during experimental rhinovirus colds. J Infect Dis. 1994; 171:1007-1013.
93. Zhu Z, Tang W, Ray A, Wu Y, et al. Rhinovirus stimulation of interleukin-6 in vivo and in vitro: Evidence for NF-κB-dependent transcriptional activation. J Clin Invest. 1996;97:421-430.
94. Turner RB, Weingand K, Yeh CH, Leedy D. Association between interleukin-8 concentration in nasal secretions and severity of symptoms of experimental rhinovirus colds. Clin Infect Dis. 1998;26:840-846.
95. Gaffey MJ, Hayden FG, Boyd JC, et al. Ipratropium bromide treatment of experimental rhinovirus infection. Antimicrob Agents Chemother. 1988;32:1644-1647.
96. Sperber SJ, Sorrentino JV, Riker DK, et al. Evaluation of an alpha agonist alone and in combination with a nonsteroidal anti-inflammatory agent in the treatment of experimental rhinovirus cold. Bull N Y Acad Med. 1989;65:145-160.
97. Gwaltney JM Jr, Jordan WS Jr. Rhinoviruses and respiratory disease. Bacteriol Rev. 1964;28:409.
98. Cate TR, Rossen RD, Douglas RG Jr, et al. The role of nasal secretion and serum antibody in the rhinovirus common cold. Am J Epidemiol. 1966;84:352.
99. Rossen RD, Douglas RG Jr, Cate TR, et al. The sedimentation behavior of rhinovirus neutralizing activity in nasal secretion and serum following the rhinovirus common cold. J Immunol. 1966;97:532.

100. Knopf HLS, Perkins JC, Bertran DM, et al. Analysis of the neutralizing activity in nasal wash and serum following intranasal vaccination with inactivated type 13 rhinovirus. J Immunol. 1970;104:566.

101. Butler WT, Waldmann TA, Rossen RD, et al. Changes in IgA and IgG concentrations in nasal secretions prior to the appearance of antibody during viral respiratory infection in man. J Immunol. 1970;105:584.

102. Rossen RD, Kasel JA, Couch RB. The secretory immune system: Its relation to respiratory viral infection. In: Melnick JL, ed. Progress in Medical Virology. Basel: Karger; 1971:194.

103. Cate TR, Couch RB, Johnson KM. Studies with rhinoviruses in volunteers: Production of illness, effect of naturally acquired antibody, and demonstration of a protective effect not associated with serum antibody. J Clin Invest. 1964;43:56.

104. Hendley JO, Edmondson WP Jr, Gwaltney JM Jr. Relation between naturally acquired immunity and infectivity of two rhinoviruses in volunteers. J Infect Dis. 1971;125:243.

105. Mufson MA, Ludwig WM, James HD Jr, et al. Effect of neutralizing antibody on experimental rhinovirus infection. JAMA. 1963;186:578.

106. Perkins JC, Tucker DN, Knopf HLS, et al. Comparison of protective effect of neutralizing antibody in serum and nasal secretions in experimental rhinovirus type 13 illness. Am J Epidemiol. 1969;90:519.

107. Perkins JC, Tucker DN, Knopf HLS, et al. Evidence for protective effect of an inactivated rhinovirus vaccine administered by the nasal route. Am J Epidemiol. 1969;90:319.

108. Gwaltney JM Jr. Rhinoviruses. In: Evans AS, ed. Viral Infections of Humans: Epidemiology and Control. 4th ed. New York: Plenum; 1997:815-838.

109. Rao SR, Hendley JO, Hayden FG, Gwaltney JM Jr. Symptom expression in natural and experimental rhinovirus colds. Am J Rhinol. 1995;9:49-52.

110. Bloom HH, Forsyth BR, Johnson KM, et al. Relationship of rhinovirus infection to mild upper respiratory disease. 1. Results of a survey in young adults and children. JAMA. 1963;186:38.

111. Glezen WP, Loda FA, Clyde WA, et al. Epidemiologic patterns of acute lower respiratory disease of children in a pediatric group practice. J Pediatr. 1971;78:397.

112. Mufson MA, Krause HE, Mocega HE, et al. Viruses, *Mycoplasma pneumoniae* and bacteria associated with lower respiratory tract disease among infants. Am J Epidemiol. 1970;91:192.

113. Portnoy B, Eckert HL, Salvatore MA. Rhinovirus infection in children with acute lower respiratory disease: Evidence against etiological importance. Pediatrics. 1965;35:899.

114. Imakita M, Shiraki K, Yutani C, Ishibashi-Udea H. Pneumonia caused by rhinovirus. Clin Infect Dis. 2000; 30:611-612.

115. Ghosh S, Champlin R, Couch R, et al. Rhinovirus infections in myelosuppressed adult blood and marrow transplant recipients. Clin Infect Dis. 1999;29:528-532.

116. Kaiser L, Hayden FG. Editorial Response: Rhinovirus pneumonia—A clinical entity? Clin Infect Dis. 1999;29:533-535.

117. Turner BW, Cail WS, Hendley JO, et al. Physiologic abnormalities in the paranasal sinuses during experimental rhinovirus colds. J Allergy Clin Immunol. 1992;90:474-478.

118. Gwaltney JM Jr, Phillips CD, Miller RD, Riker DK. Computed tomographic study of the common cold. N Eng J Med. 1994;330:25-30.

119. Kristo A, Uhari M, Luotonen J. Parnasal sinus findings in children during respiratory infection evaluated with magnetic resonance imaging. Pediatrics. 2003;111:586-589.

120. Puhakka T, Mäkelä MJ, Alanen A, et al. Sinusitis in the common cold. J Allergy Clin Immunol. 1998;102:403-408.

121. Gwaltney JM Jr, Hendley JO, Phillips CD, et al. Nose blowing propels nasal fluid into the paranasal sinuses. Clin Infect Dis. 2000;30:387-391.

122. McBride TP, Doyle WJ, Hayden FG, et al. Alterations of eustachian tube, middle ear and nose in rhinovirus infections. Arch Otolaryngol Head Neck Surg. 1989;115:1054-1059.

123. Elkhatieb A, Hipskind G, Woerner D, Hayden FG. Middle ear abnormalities during natural rhinovirus colds in adults. J Infect Dis. 1993;168:618-621.

124. Doyle WJ, Alper CM, Buchman CA, et al. Illness and otological changes during upper respiratory virus infection. Laryngoscope. 1999;109:324-328.

125. Buchman CA, Doyle WJ, Skoner D, et al. Otologic manifestations of experimental rhinovirus infection. Laryngoscope. 1994; 104:1295-1299.

126. Gwaltney JM Jr. Virology of middle ear. Ann Otol Rhinol Laryngol. 1971;80:365.

127. Arola M, Ruuskanen O, Ziegler T, et al. Clinical role of respiratory virus infection in acute otitis media. Pediatrics. 1990;86:848.

128. Pitkaranta A, Jero J, Arruda E, et al. Polymerase chain reaction-based detection of rhinovirus, respiratory syncytial virus, and coronavirus in otitis media with effusion. J Pediatr. 1998;133:390-394.

129. Gwaltney JM Jr. Acute community-acquired sinusitis. Clin Infect Dis. 1996;23:1209-1223.

130. Greenberg SB, Allen M, Wilson J, Atmar RL. Respiratory viral infections in adults with and without chronic obstructive pulmonary disease. Am J Respir Crit Care Med. 2000;171:167-173.

131. Smith CB, Kanner RE, Golden CA, et al. Effect of viral infections on pulmonary function in patients with chronic obstructive pulmonary diseases. J Infect Dis. 1980;141:271.

132. Gern JE, Busse WW. Association of rhinovirus infections with asthma. Clin Microbiol Rev. 199;12:9-18.

133. Rakes GP, Arruda E, Ingram JM, et al. Rhinovirus and respiratory syncytial virus in wheezing children requiring emergency care. IgE and eosinophil analyses. Am J Respir Crit Care Med. 1999;159:785-790.

134. Rawlinson WD, Waliuzzaman Z, Carter IW, et al. Asthma exacerbations in children associated with rhinovirus but not human metapneumovirus infection. J Infect Dis. 2003;187:1314-1318.

135. Duff AL, Pomeranz ES, Gelber LE, et al. Risk factors for acute wheezing in infants and children: Viruses, passive smoke, and IgE antibodies to inhalant allergens. Pediatrics. 1993;92:535-540.

136. Johnston SL, Sanderson G, Pattemore PK, et al. Use of polymerase chain reaction for diagnosis of picornavirus infection in subjects with and without respiratory symptoms. J Clin Microbiol. 1993;31:111-117.

137. Mygind N, Gwaltney JM, Winther B, Hendley O. The common cold and asthma. Allergy 1999;54:146-159.

138. Seymour ML, Gilby N, Bardin PG, et al. Rhinovirus infection increases 5-lipoxygenase and cyclooxygenase-2 in bronchial biopsy specimens from nonatopic subjects. J Infect Dis. 2002;185:540-544.

139. Halperin SA, Eggleston PA, Beasley P, et al. Exacerbations of asthma in adults during experimental rhinovirus infection. Am Rev Respir Dis. 1985;132:976.

140. Brown PK, Tyrrell DAJ. Experiments on the sensitivity of strains of human fibroblasts to infection with rhinovirus. Br J Exp Pathol. 1964;45:571.

141. Gwaltney JM Jr, Edmonson WP Jr. Etiology and Epidemiology of Acute Respiratory Disease. Annual Progress Report to the Commission on Acute Respiratory Disease of the Armed Forces Epidemiological Board. Contract No. DADA 49-007-MD-1000, September 15, 1968.

142. Arruda E, Hayden FG. Detection of human rhinovirus RNA in nasal washings by PCR. Mol Cell Probes. 1993;7:373-379.

143. Kenny GE, Cooney MK, Thompson DJ. Analysis of serum pooling schemes for identification of large numbers of viruses. Am J Epidemiol. 1970;91:439.

144. Gwaltney JM Jr. Micro-neutralization test for identification of rhinovirus serotypes. Proc Soc Exp Biol Med. 1966;122:1137.

145. Kriel RL, Wulff H, Chin TDY. Micro-neutralization test for determination of rhinovirus and coxsackievirus A antibody in human diploid cells. Appl Microbiol. 1969;17:611.

146. Douglas RG Jr, Fleet WF, Cate TR, et al. Antibody to rhinovirus in human sera. I. Standardization of a neutralization test. Proc Soc Exp Biol Med. 1968;127:497.

147. Douglas RG Jr, Couch RB. Parenteral inactivated rhinovirus vaccine: Minimal protective effect. Proc Soc Exp Biol Med. 1972;139:899.

148. Arruda E, Hayden FG. Clinical studies of antiviral agents for picornaviral infections. In: Jeffries DJ, De Clercq E, eds. Antiviral Chemotherapy. New York: John Wiley & Sons; 1995:321-355.

149. Gaudernak E, Seipelt J, Triendl A. Antiviral effects of pyrrolidine dithiocarbamate on human rhinovirus. J Virol. 2002;76:6004-6015.

150. Hayden FG, Herrington DT, Coats TL, et al. Efficacy and safety of oral pleconaril for treatment of colds due to picornavirus in adults: Results of 2 double-blind, randomized, placebo-controlled trials. Clin Infect Dis. 2003;36:1523-1532.

150a. Hayden FG, Coats T, Kim K, et al. Oral pleconaril treatment of picornavirus-associated viral respiratory illness in adults: Efficacy and tolerability in Phase II clinical trials. Antivir Ther. 2002;7:53.

151. Turner RB, Wecker MT, Pohl G, et al. Efficacy of tremacamra, a soluble intercellular adhesion molecule-1, for experimental rhinovirus infection: A randomized clinical trial. JAMA. 1999;281:1797-1804.

152. Hayden FG. Use of interferons for prevention and treatment of respiratory viral infections. In: Mills J, Corey L, eds. Antiviral Chemotherapy: New Directions for Clinical Application and Research. New York: Elsevier; 1986:28.

153. Hayden FG, Albrecht JK, Kaiser DL, et al. Prevention of natural colds by contact prophylaxis with intranasal alpha₂-interferon. N Engl J Med. 1986;314:71.

154. Douglas RM, Moore BW, Miles HB, et al. Prophylactic efficacy of intranasal alpha₂-interferon against rhinovirus infections in the family setting. N Engl J Med. 1986;314:65.

155. Gwaltney JM Jr. Combined antiviral and antimediator treatment of rhinovirus colds. J Infect Dis. 1992;166:776-782.

156. Gwaltney JM Jr, Winther B, Patrie JT, Hendley JO. Combined antiviral-antimediator treatment for the common cold. J Infect Dis. 2002;186:147-154.

CHAPTER **172**

Noroviruses and Other Caliciviruses

JOHN J. TREANOR

RAPHAEL DOLIN

Acute gastrointestinal disease is an exceedingly common and widespread illness throughout the world. According to the National Health Interview Survey, the incidence of acute gastroenteritis in American families is 6.0% per year, with an estimated 21.2 days lost from work or school per 100 persons annually.[1] Approximately 612,000 hospitalizations and 3000 deaths in adults are estimated to occur annually due to acute gastroenteritis in the United States.[2] Worldwide, it has been estimated that acute diarrheal disease accounts for nearly 5 million deaths in children younger than 5 years.[3] Although the etiology of much of this disease remains unknown, evidence suggests that many cases result from viral infections.[4,5] Two new virus families, the Caliciviridae and the Astroviridae (see Chapter 173), have emerged as important causes of gastroenteritis in adults and children.

HISTORY

The failure to isolate causative agents, bacterial or viral, from apparently infectious outbreaks of diarrhea or vomiting, or both, led to the widely held assumption that undetected viruses were responsible for such disease. In 1945, Reimann and co-workers[6] transmitted disease to volunteers by administering bacteria-free filtrates of throat washings and/or stool filtrates from naturally occurring cases. Gordon[7] and Jordan[8] and their associates also induced disease in normal volunteers with bacteria-free material. These studies described two transmissible agents of subbacterial size, the Marcy and FS agents, that appeared to be antigenically distinct. However, these workers were unable to detect viral agents in vitro with techniques available at that time. Despite extensive virologic investigations in laboratories throughout the world, relatively little progress was made in this area until 1972 when the Norwalk virus, the prototype of this group, was described and partially characterized.[9,10] This virus was initially detected in diarrheal stools obtained from an outbreak of gastroenteritis in Norwalk, Ohio, that involved students in an elementary school and family contacts. Subsequently, additional viruses with similar properties were described, including the Hawaii,[11] Montgomery County (MC),[12] Taunton,[13] and Snow Mountain[14] viruses, also named by the geographical region in which they were first recognized. All of these viruses had a similar small, round structured morphology on electron microscopy, were of a similar size and density, did not grow in any in vitro propagation system, and were responsible for acute gastroenteritis, commonly in epidemic form with high secondary attack rates.[4] At the same time, viruses with more readily identifiable morphology on electron microscopy, referred to as *human caliciviruses*,[15] were observed in the stools of individuals, primarily children, with gastroenteritis.

A major advance in this field occurred when polymerase chain reaction (PCR) techniques were applied to amplify the genome of the Norwalk virus from virion-containing stool samples.[16,17] These studies identified the Norwalk virus as a member of the Caliciviridae family and allowed determination of the complete nucleotide sequence of this virus.[18] Subsequent molecular studies have clearly identified all of these viruses as caliciviruses and established them as extremely common causes of gastrointestinal disease in both adults and children worldwide.

VIROLOGY

The name *calicivirus* is derived from the characteristic appearance of the viral particles under the electron microscope, which consists of a scalloped border with "cuplike" indentations on its surface (Fig. 172-1), from which the Latin name *chalice* or *calyx* is derived.[19,20] Caliciviruses have been detected in a variety of animal species, including marine mammals, swine, felines, and rabbits, as well as humans. Although many animal caliciviruses replicate efficiently in cell culture, no practical in vitro method has been described for the propagation of noroviruses or sapoviruses responsible for gastroenteritis. Therefore, these viruses were originally grouped together based on physical properties determined by electron microscopic visualization or physicochemical manipulation, or both, of infectious inocula. Because of the small numbers of virions characteristically found in stool samples, it is sometimes necessary to enhance electron microscopic visualization of the particles through the addition of immune serum, which obscures the typical morphologic features (Fig. 172-2).

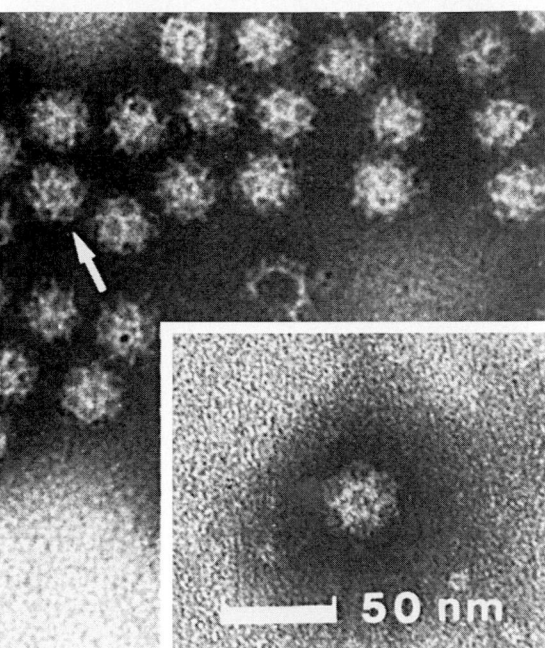

FIGURE 172-1. Calicivirus particles *(arrow)* in a fecal extract from a child with gastroenteritis. *(Inset* is higher magnification of particle indicated by arrow.) *(From Chiba S, Sakuma Y, Kogasaka R, et al. An outbreak of gastroenteritis associated with calicivirus in an infant home. J Med Virol. 1979;4:249-254. Reprinted by permission of Wiley-Liss, Inc., a subsidiary of John Wiley & Sons, Inc. Copyright © 1979 Wiley-Liss, Inc.)*

Characteristics of the noroviruses include a single-stranded positive-sense RNA genome with a polyadenlylated 3′ tail[18,21] and a single capsid polypeptide of 59- to 62-kDa molecular mass.[22] The virions are 26 to 34 nm in diameter, have cubic symmetry with a buoyant density in CsCl of 1.34 to 1.41 g/mL, and are relatively heat and acid stable and ether resistant.[10]

The genomic organization of the Norwalk virus is shown in Figure 172-3.[18] Three long open reading frames (ORFs) are present. The first

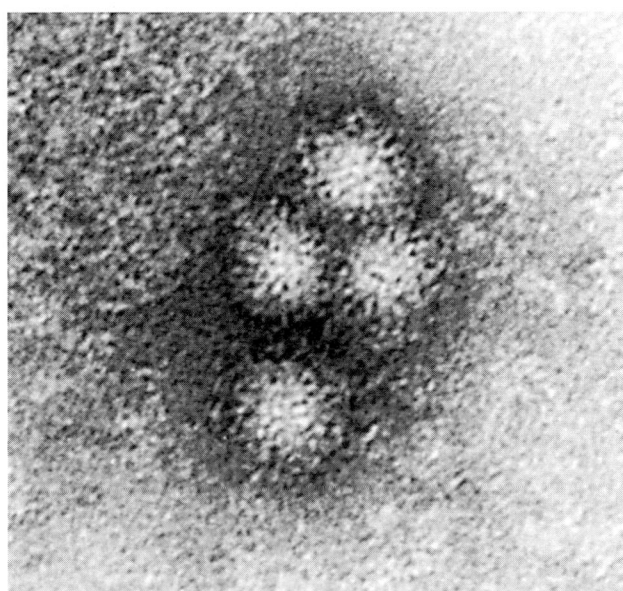

FIGURE 172-2. Snow Mountain agent in stool filtrate from a volunteer with experimentally induced disease as visualized by immune electron microscopy. Particles are 27 nm in diameter and are stained with 2% phosphotungstic acid.

FIGURE 172-3. Genomic organization of the Norwalk virus. The three open reading frames (ORFs) present on the positive strand are shown with the predicted sizes of their polypeptide products. Above this map are indicated regions of amino acid similarity to domains of known function in the picornavirus genome. The size of the genome in kilobases is shown at the top. *(From Jiang X, Wang M, Wang K, Estes MK. Sequence and genomic organization of Norwalk virus. Virology. 1993;195:51-61.)*

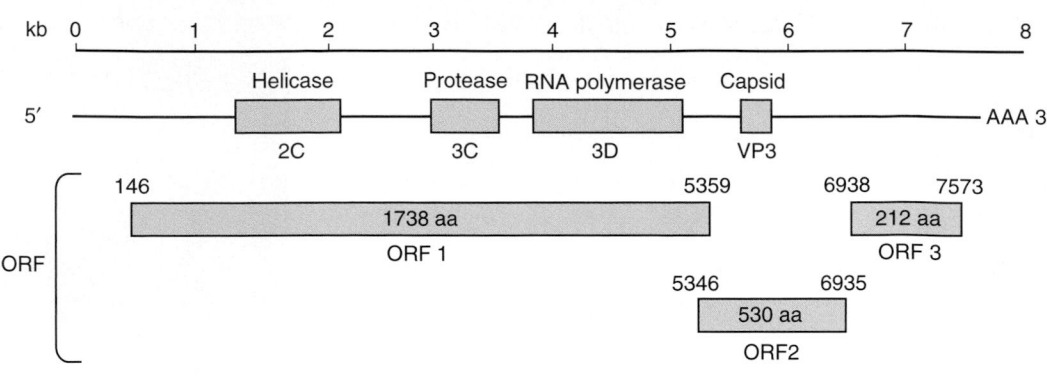

ORF encodes a protein of approximately 57-kDa molecular weight. It has been suggested that this protein is the viral RNA polymerase and also has helicase and protease functions, based on sequence homology with other RNA viruses.[18] The second ORF encodes the viral capsid protein of 58-kDa molecular weight.[23] Based on work done with animal caliciviruses, it is likely that this protein is encoded by a subgenomic mRNA in infected cells. When expressed in insect cells by a recombinant baculovirus, the capsid protein spontaneously assembles into virus-like particles (VLPs), which are immunogenic and react specifically with convalescent human sera.[23] The three-dimensional structure of these empty capsids has been studied by electron cryomicroscopy, which suggests that the capsid has icosahedral symmetry with T = 3.[24] The x-ray structure of these VLPs shows that the capsid contains two domains, a shell (S) domain and a protruding (P) domain that may be involved in binding to susceptible cells.[25] Finally, the third ORF encodes a protein of predicted 22.5-kDa molecular weight,[18] which currently has no known function but which may represent a minor structural protein.[26]

Genetic analysis of a large number of human and animal caliciviruses has led to the creation of four genera within the Caliciviridae: the vesiviruses, which cause vesicular diseases in swine, cats, and marine mammals; the lagoviruses, which cause hemorrhagic diseases in rabbits; and two genera responsible for gastroenteritis in humans, the noroviruses and the sapoviruses.[27] The prototypic norovirus is the Norwalk virus, and the prototypic sapovirus is the Sapporo virus. In addition to sequence differences, the four genera differ in minor details of genome organization.

The noroviruses have been further subdivided based on phylogenetic analysis into at least three genogroups designated GI, GII, and GIII, and additional gene clusters are recognized within the genogroups.[28] The GI genogroup includes the Norwalk virus, whereas the Snow Mountain and Hawaii viruses belong to genogroup GII. Genogroup GIII viruses have been identified only as diarrheal agents in pigs and cows.

Because of the lack of a convenient in vitro propagation system, antigenic characterization of these viruses is less straightforward. Not unexpectedly, predicted amino acid homology within the capsid region is less than that within the polymerase region.[29] Thus, phylogenetic trees based on capsid sequence have a slightly different structure than those based on polymerase structure.[30] Virus-like particles have been generated by expression of the capsid regions of many of the noroviruses, including Norwalk[23] and Desert Sheild[31] viruses (genogroup GI) and MX,[32] Lordsdale,[33] Snow Mountain,[30] Hawaii,[34] and Toronto[35] viruses (genogroup GII), as well as the prototype sapovirus Sapporo.[36] In general, hyperimmune animal sera raised against capsids are very specific. However, tests of postinfection human sera have suggested a significant degree of cross-reactivity among viruses within a genogroup.

The most clear-cut antigenic distinction between these viruses is between the Norwalk and Hawaii viruses, because these agents have been compared through cross-challenge experiments in human subjects.[37] In these studies, infection with the Norwalk virus provided short-term protection against re-challenge with the Norwalk virus but not against the Hawaii virus, and vice versa. Because this type of experiment is the closest analog to virus neutralization that is available, this is the best evidence that there are at least two distinct norovirus serotypes, roughly corresponding to the GI and GII genogroups described earlier.

The role of antigenic variation in the epidemiology of these viruses remains an area of continued investigation. Generally, antibody to viruses within genogroup II appear to be more common than that to viruses within genogroup I.[38] Typically, a large number of diverse genotypes cocirculate,[39-41] with significant variation from year to year in the predominant genotypes of viruses associated with illness.[42,43] However, occasionally a single predominant strain arises that is responsible for the majority of cases over a widespread distribution.[44] The causes of this phenomenon are unknown.

EPIDEMIOLOGY

Infection with noroviruses is exceedingly widespread and common. In developed countries, serum antibody to the noroviruses is first noted at ages 3 to 4 years, with antibody prevalence gradually rising to greater than 50% by the fifth decade of life.[45-48] Studies using recombinant Norwalk antigen have suggested that significant increases in antibody prevalence occur in infancy, on entry into primary schools, and in young adulthood.[49] Seroepidemiologic studies of the sapoviruses carried out in Japan, Southeast Asia, and the United Kingdom indicate that antibody is acquired in early childhood and can be detected in up to 90% of older children and adults.[50-52] Antibody appears to be acquired more rapidly in developing countries[45] and may be rare or nonexistent in some isolated populations.[45,53] Transmission of noroviruses occurs year round but with a higher incidence of disease in the winter months in temperate climates.[54]

The experimental induction of illness in normal volunteers suggests that the major route of person-to-person transmission is fecal-oral. Epidemiologic reports have also implicated vomitus as a vehicle of transmission,[55,56] and virus has been detected in vomitus on electron microscopy[57] and PCR.[58] Airborne transmission has also occasionally been implicated,[59,60] but limited attempts to experimentally transmit virus with nasopharyngeal washings from an ill volunteer were unsuccessful.[10] It has been estimated that fewer than 100 viral particles are required for infection of a susceptible individual.[61]

Incubation periods are generally 24 to 48 hours, although ranges from 18 to 72 hours have been observed. Virus shedding in stools is maximal over the first 24 to 48 hours after illness.[12,14] In volunteer studies, virus has been rarely detected beyond 72 hours after the onset of vomiting or diarrhea[12,14] by these techniques. However, virus can be detected for up to 3 weeks after illness using sensitive enzyme-linked immunosorbent assay techniques[62] or PCR.[63,64] The clinical significance of the prolonged detection of virus in stools in unclear, but epidemiologic data have implicated individuals who are postsymptomatic in the transmission of illness.[65]

Noroviruses were first recognized in association with point-source outbreaks of gastroenteritis, and such outbreaks remain the most common situation in which noroviruses have been implicated as etiologic agents. There are several features that are characteristics of such outbreaks and that may be useful in empirical diagnosis. These include a short-lived illness of 2 to 3 days' duration with vomiting as a prominent symptom in a majority of affected individuals, an incubation period of 24 to 48 hours, high secondary attack rates, and lack of identifiable pathogens on routine examinations of stool samples.[66] The application of modern diagnostic techniques has shown that the frequency of norovirus infection in such outbreaks is extremely high.[39]

Outbreaks of norovirus gastroenteritis are particularly common in closed settings such as in hospitals, nursing homes, ships, and the military.[67-69] Secondary transmission is a prominent feature of such outbreaks. Although most of these outbreaks will terminate spontaneously after 1 to 2 weeks, some may be quite prolonged. For example, up to 12 recurrent outbreaks of norovirus gastroenteritis have been reported on cruise ships despite stringent attempts to determine the source and disinfect the ship between cruises.[70]

Almost any type of food that has contact with contaminated water may serve as a vehicle for outbreaks of norovirus gastroenteritis. This includes drinking contaminated water, or even swimming in pools or lakes in which ill individuals have also been swimming,[71,72] indicative of the highly infectious nature of these viruses. Of note, these viruses appear to be relatively resistant to inactivation by chlorine.[56] Because such products as shellfish or contaminated commercial ice[73] can be distributed to multiple sites, these outbreaks can encompass a wide geographic area.[74] Contamination of foodstuffs has been traced to both presymptomatic[75] and postsymptomatic[65] food handlers, complicating infection control recommendations.

Shellfish, such as clams and oysters, are filter feeders and efficiently concentrate microorganisms from contaminated water. When consumed, these foods are very frequently implicated in the transmission of enteric viruses in general and of norovirus gastroenteritis in particular.[76] Because noroviruses are relatively resistant to heat inactivation, steaming of shellfish does not entirely eliminate the risk of transmission.[77,78]

Recommendations for evaluation and control of nosocomial outbreaks[61] include identification and elimination of common sources and the use of handwashing and barrier methods to prevent secondary transmission. Exclusion of ill employees may be important in limiting the spread of nosocomial outbreaks.[79] These methods have generally been found to be more effective in limiting the spread of outbreaks from unit to unit within an institution than in terminating an outbreak in an individual unit once it has begun.[80,81] The Viral Gastroenteritis Section of the Centers for Disease Control and prevention is available for advice regarding such outbreaks (404-639-3607).

Although noroviruses were initially recognized primarily in association with outbreaks of acute gastroenteritis mostly involving adults, there has been an increasing recognition of the role of these viruses as causes of sporadic gastroenteritis in children in various parts of the world.[15,19,82-86] Toronto virus has been reported to be the second most common virus detected in the stools of young children with gastroenteritis.[87] The frequency of norovirus gastroenteritis has been estimated at between 10% and 100% that of rotavirus in children where direct comparisons have been made.[88-90] In one study, 49% of prospectively followed Finnish infants and children seroresponded to norovirus over a 2-year period.[91] Sapoviruses and noroviruses have also been detected in community-wide, day care,[92] and nosocomial outbreaks of gastroenteritis in children.[93]

PATHOGENESIS

Because convenient animal models for gastroenteritis induced by the Norwalk viruses are not available, information about the pathogenesis of this illness is based largely on studies of experimentally induced disease in normal volunteers. Acute infection with Norwalk and Hawaii viruses results in a reversible histopathologic lesion in the jejunum,[11,94-96] with apparent sparing of the stomach[97] and rectum (Fig. 172-4). The villi are blunted, but the mucosa is otherwise intact. Round cells and polymorphonuclear leukocytic infiltration are seen in the lamina propria. On electron microscopy, the epithelial cells are similarly intact, microvilli are shortened, and widened intercellular spaces are noted. These histopathologic changes appear within 24 hours after virus challenge, are present at the height of illness, and persist for a variable period of time after the illness. The histopathologic changes have generally cleared within 2 weeks after the onset of illness, although some jejunal changes have been noted as late as 6 weeks after challenge. Histopathologic changes have been described in both clinical and subclinical cases of infection[95,96] and appear to be indistinguishable between Norwalk virus– and Hawaii virus–induced disease.

Diarrhea induced by the Norwalk virus is associated with a transient malabsorption of D-xylose and fat[98] and with decreased activity of brush-border enzymes, including alkaline phosphatase and trehalase.[94] Absorption and brush-border enzyme levels return to normal values within 2 weeks after challenge. During acute illness, a variable amount of intestinal fluid is produced, but infection with Norwalk and Hawaii agents has not been associated with detectable enterotoxin production. Adenylate cyclase levels in jejunal biopsy specimens appear to be normal during infection.[99] Thus, the precise mechanisms of virus-induced diarrhea, vomiting, or both remain unknown at the present. Calicivirus infections of animals have been associated with atrophy of the small intestinal mucosa along with a mild inflammatory infiltrate in the lamina propria.[100,101]

The noroviruses have been demonstrated to bind to several blood group antigens, which are complex carbohydrate structures expressed on a variety of cells including gastrointestinal epithelial cells.[102,103] The specific antigens recognized appear to vary by genogroup, with genogroup GI noroviruses preferentially binding to blood group antigens of A and O secretors and genogroup GII viruses binding predominantly to A and B secretors.[104] The binding domain for these antigens has been localized to a pocket within the P2 domain of the viral capsid.[105]

These blood group antigens probably serve either as receptors for the noroviruses or some other function critical for viral infection, because blood group is closely linked to susceptibility to norovirus gastroenteritis. Specifically, nonsecretors appear to be quite resistant to infection even when challenged with large amounts of Norwalk virus.

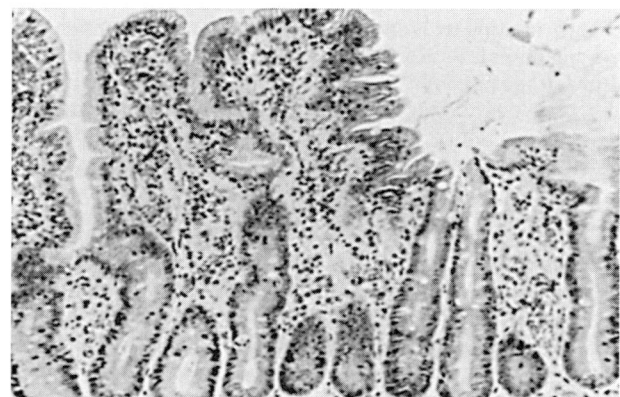

FIGURE 172-4. Light micrograph of a jejunal mucosal biopsy specimen from a volunteer with Hawaii virus–induced disease 48 hours after challenge. Blunted villi and inflammatory cell infiltrate in the lamina propria are present (hematoxylin-eosin stain; original magnification, ×140).

Individuals of blood group type B also are somewhat resistant.[106,107] These findings may represent an explanation for observations of a poorly defined long-term resistance to infection seen in previous challenge studies, in which some individuals consistently remained well despite repeated challenge with virus.[108]

IMMUNE RESPONSE

Infection with the Norwalk virus results in the induction of virus-specific serum immunoglobulin G (IgG), IgA, and IgM antibody,[109-112] even in the presence of previous exposure. IgA and IgM responses appear to be relatively short lived, whereas elevations in Norwalk-specific serum IgG persist for months.[111,112] In addition to recognizing the infecting strain of norovirus, serum antibody responses to infection may recognize other variants within the same genogroup, although generally to lower titer.[113] Such heterologous antibody responses are more common within a genogroup than between genogroups.[110,114] Serum IgM and IgA antibody may be more specific for the infecting strain of virus.[110,115] Using baculovirus-expressed capsid proteins, it has been demonstrated that responses to viruses within genogroup GI may be more specific than responses to infection with viruses within genogroup GII.[116] Heterologous responses have also been seen in individuals infected with the sapoviruses.[51] These broad responses are in contrast to the extremely specific antibody response of animals hyperimmunized with capsid antigen[117] and may in part reflect the extensive prior exposure of most adults to related viruses. It is not clear that such heterologous responses are significant from the point of view of protection against reinfection.

Mucosal immune responses have not been studied extensively, but jejunal IgA synthesis has been shown to be elevated in biopsy specimens obtained 2 weeks after challenge with the Norwalk agent,[118] and fecal IgA responses after Norwalk infection have also been reported.[119] Limited studies of cell-mediated immune responses in these infections indicate that acute illness is associated with a transient lymphopenia that involves thymus-derived, bone marrow–derived, and null cell subpopulations.[120] Antigen-specific cellular responses to the capsid have been demonstrated in peripheral blood after experimental infection and are predominantly of the Th1 type.[121] Such responses are also cross reactive within genogroup.

Parameters defining protective immunity to the Norwalk viruses are poorly understood. After infection with Norwalk virus, most individuals manifest resistance to reinfection that persists for at least 4 to 6 months.[108,122] Multiple exposure appears to increase this resistance.[122] This short-term resistance does not appear to extend to other, antigenically distinct viruses.[37] Infection-induced resistance eventually wanes, and after 2 to 3 years, such individuals are susceptible to reinfection with the same virus.[108]

Studies of the role of serum antibody in mediating this protection have yielded conflicting results. In most studies in adults, infection and illness induced by Norwalk-like agents occur in the presence of a wide range of preexisting serum antibody levels, which thus correlate poorly with protection.[110,122] However, after repeated experimental exposure of adults[122] and in epidemiologic studies of norovirus and sapovirus in children,[123-125] there has been a better correlation between the presence of serum antibody and protection from illness. Protection may also be related to other host defense factors such as a local mucosal antibody. However, direct measurements of intestinal antibody have failed to show a correlation with protection from Norwalk-induced illness,[126] and the presence of prechallenge Norwalk-specific fecal IgA was also not protective against challenge.[63] Studies of related animal viruses have also suggested a role for innate immunity in resistance to norovirus infection.[127]

CLINICAL MANIFESTATIONS

Clinical characteristics of illness induced by the noroviruses appear to be similar in both naturally occurring and experimentally induced disease (Fig. 172-5), and there are no apparent differences in clinical

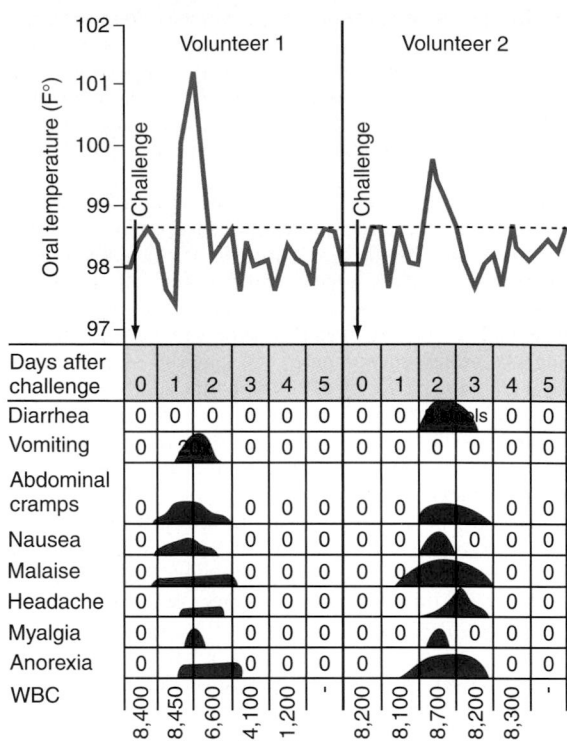

FIGURE 172-5. Clinical response of two normal volunteers after the oral administration of the Norwalk agent. The height of the shaded curve is proportional to the severity of the sign or symptom. *(From Dolin R, Reichman RC, Fauci AS. Lymphocyte populations in acute viral gastroenteritis. Infect Immunol. 1976;14:422-428, with permission.)*

findings between genogroups. However, clinically evident sapovirus infections appear to be largely restricted to children younger than 5 years[64] and may be somewhat milder than that seen with norovirus infection.[90] The onset of symptoms can be either gradual or abrupt, and most persons complain first of abdominal cramps and/or nausea. Generally both vomiting and diarrhea occur, although either can be present alone. Myalgias, malaise, and occasional headaches are also seen. Low-grade fever (with temperatures of 101° to 102° F) occurs in approximately half of cases. Diarrheal stool is generally moderate in amounts, with four to eight nonbloody stools being produced over a period of 24 hours. Disease manifestations generally last 48 to 72 hours and remit without sequelae.

DIAGNOSIS

A clinical diagnosis of norovirus-related illness can be suspected on the basis of epidemiologic information and on the absence of other documented pathogens. However, the signs and symptoms of illness are not sufficiently characteristic to enable a diagnosis to be made on clinical grounds alone. Routine laboratory tests are also generally not helpful in making a specific diagnosis of norovirus infection. Peripheral white blood cell counts are normal or slightly elevated with a relative polymorphonuclear leukocytosis and lymphopenia but with otherwise unremarkable white cell morphology. The results of liver function tests, blood urea nitrogen and creatinine determinations, and urinalysis are generally within normal limits. The absence of fecal leukocytes, as determined by microscopic examination of stools stained with methylene blue,[128] is a useful tool with which to exclude infection with enteroinvasive pathogens such as *Shigella*.

Specific diagnosis requires laboratory confirmation. Because these agents currently cannot be cultivated in vitro, a variety of methods have been developed to detect virus directly in stool samples.[129] Immune electron microscopy, in which immune sera is used to aggregate and highlight virions in stool suspensions (see Fig. 172-2), was the method used to originally identify these viruses.[14,130] The technique has the advantage of being readily adaptable to the detection of new virus types and can be used both for the detection of virus and for antibody determination but cannot be used conveniently for routine screening.

The expression of the capsid antigens has provided a way to generate high-titer animal hyperimmune sera for diagnostic purposes. Antigen detection immunoassays using such reagents have been reported for the noroviruses. These assays suggest are extremely sensitive for detection of homologous virus but lack sensitivity for detection of antigenic variants.[117] An alternative strategy has been to use panels of monoclonal antibodies instead of hyperimmune sera. One such test (IDEAI; Dako Cytomation) is commercially available and is reported to have sensitivity and specificity comparable or slightly greater than that of electron microscopy for both genogroup GI and GII viruses.[131]

Nucleic acid detection techniques such as PCR have also been used extensively for detection of noroviruses and sapoviruses.[132-136] The success of this strategy depends on the ability to remove inhibitors of reverse transcription from the samples, and the choice of primers in relatively conserved regions of the genome to widen the scope of viruses detected.[137,138] Conversely, carefully selected primers within relatively more divergent regions can be used to genotypically differentiate virus strains.[139] Highly sensitive molecular techniques such as PCR may be particularly useful for detecting contamination of food and environmental samples.[58,140-144]

Immunoassay techniques have also been adapted for the detection of antibody to these viruses and are useful for the serologic diagnosis of infection. Because virus excretion in stools is limited and collection of stool samples in outbreaks can be problematic, serologic techniques are often used for diagnostic purposes.[145] Serum antibody titer rises can be detected within 10 to 14 days after the onset of illness.[146,147]

TREATMENT AND PREVENTION

Oral fluid replacement with isotonic liquids is generally adequate to replace fluid losses. Rarely, parenteral intravenous therapy may be required if severe vomiting and diarrhea develop. Symptomatic treatment of headache, myalgias, and nausea with analgesics and antiemetics may provide relief. In one study, the administration of bismuth subsalicylate reduced gastrointestinal symptoms in Norwalk-induced disease in normal volunteers but had no effect on the number or character of stools or on virus shedding.[148] Although antiperistaltic agents are frequently prescribed to control diarrhea, their effect on the disease course and on excretion of virus has not been rigorously evaluated.

There are multiple obstacles to successful development of a vaccine to prevent norovirus gastroenteritis.[149] As described earlier, infection does not appear to induce long-term protective immunity, although short-term protection has been demonstrated. The likely presence of multiple antigenic types is also a challenge, and progress has been further hampered by lack of in vitro propagation systems and a suitable animal model. However, some progress has been made using virus-like particles. Norwalk VLPs have been shown to be immunogenic when administered orally to human volunteers, inducing serum IgG, mucosal IgA, and cellular responses that resemble those seen after infection, although of substantially lower magnitude.[150,151] In addition, Norwalk virus has proved to be an excellent model to evaluate expression of vaccine antigens in plants as a method for oral immunization.[152]

These illnesses also appear to be reasonable targets for the application of broadly protective antiviral measures such as antiviral chemoprophylaxis and/or therapy. Because outbreaks are often associated with waterborne or food-borne spread, efforts to reduce potential sources of contamination represent additional important control measures.

REFERENCES

1. Adams PF, Hendershot GE, Marano MA. Current estimates from the National Health Interview Survey, 1996. National Center for Health Statistics, Vital Health Stat 10(200). 1999.
2. Mounts AW, Holman RC, Clarke MJ, et al. Trends in hospitalizations associated with gastroenteritis among adults in the United States, 1979-1995. Epidemiol Infect. 1999;123:1-8.
3. Snyder SD, Merson MH. The magnitude of the global problem of acute diarrheal disease: A review of active surveillance data. Bull WHO. 1982;60:605-613.
4. Dolin R, Treanor J, Madore HP. Novel agents of viral enteritis in humans. J Infect Dis. 1987;155:365-375.
5. Blacklow NR, Greenberg HB. Viral gastroenteritis. N Engl J Med. 1991;325:252-264.
6. Reimann HA, Price AH, Hodges JH. The cause of epidemic diarrhea, nausea, and vomiting (viral dysentery?). Proc Soc Exp Biol Med. 1945;59:8-9.
7. Gordon I, Ingraham HS, Korns RF. Tansmission of epidemic gastroenteritis to human volunteers by oral administrationof fecal filtrate. J Exp Med. 1947;86:409-422.
8. Jordan WS, Gordon I, Dorrance WR. A study of illness in a group of Cleveland families. VII. Transmission of acute nonbacterial gastroenteritis to volunteers: Evidence for two different etiologic agents. J Exp Med. 1953;98:461-475.
9. Kapikian AZ, Gerin JL, Wyatt RG, et al. Density in cesium chloride of the Norwalk agent: Determination by ultracentrifugation and immune elecron microscopy. Proc Soc Exp Biol Med. 1973;142:874-877.
10. Dolin R, Blacklow NR, DuPont H, et al. Biological properties of Norwalk agent of acute infectious nonbacterial gastroenteritis. Proc Soc Exp Biol Med. 1972;140:578-583.
11. Dolin R, Levy AG, Wyatt RG, et al. Viral gastroenteritis induced by the Hawaii agent: Jejunal histopathology and serologic response. Am J Med. 1975;59:768-771.
12. Thornhill TS, Wyatt RG, Kalica AR, et al. Detection by immune electron microscopy of 26-27 nm virus-like particles associated with two family outbreaks of gastroenteritis. J Infect Dis. 1977;138:20-27.
13. Caul EO, Ashley C, Pether JVS. Norwalk-like particle in epidemic gastroenteritis in the U.K. Lancet. 1979;2:1292.
14. Dolin R, Reichman RC, Roessner KD, et al. Detection by immune electron microscopy of the Snow Mountain agent of acute viral gastroenteritis. J Infect Dis. 1982;146:184-189.
15. Flewett TH, Davies H. Caliciviruses (Letter). Lancet. 1976;1:311.
16. Jiang X, Graham DY, Wang K, Estes MK. Norwalk virus genome cloning and characterization. Science. 1990;250:1580-1583.
17. Matsui S, Kim JP, Greenberg HB, et al. The isolation and characterization of a Norwalk virus-specific cDNA. J Clin Invest. 1991;87:1456-1461.
18. Jiang X, Wang M, Wang K, Estes MK. Sequence and genomic organization of Norwalk virus. Virology. 1993;195:51-61.
19. Chiba S, Sakuma Y, Kogasaka R, et al. An outbreak of gastroenteritis associated with calicivirus in an infant home. J Med Virol. 1979;4:249-254.
20. Chiba S, Sakuma Y, Kagasaka R, et al. Fecal shedding of virus in relation to the days of illness in infantile gastroenteritis due to calicivirus. J Infect Dis. 1980;142:247-249.
21. Hardy ME, Estes MK. Completion of the Norwalk virus genome sequence. Virus Genes. 1996;12:287-290.
22. Greenberg HB, Valdesuso J, Kalica AR. Proteins of Norwalk virus. J Virol. 1981;37:994-999.
23. Jiang X, Wang M, Graham DY, Estes MK. Expression, self-assembly, and antigenicity of the Norwalk virus capsid protein. J Virol. 1992;66:6527-6532.
24. Prasad BV, Rothnagel R, Jiang X, Estes MK. Three-dimensional structure of baculovirus-expressed Norwalk virus capsids. J Virol. 1994;68:5117-5125.
25. Prasad BV, Hardy ME, Dokland T, et al. X-ray crystallographic structure of the Norwalk virus capsid. Science. 1999;286:287-290.
26. Glass PJ, White LJ, Ball JM, et al. Norwalk virus open reading frame 3 encodes a minor structural protein. J Virol. 2000;74:6581-6591.
27. Green KY, Ando T, Balayan MS, et al. Taxonomy of the caliciviruses. J Infect Dis. 2000;181(Suppl 2):S322-S330.
28. Ando T, Noel JS, Fankhauser RL. Genetic classification of "Norwalk-like viruses. J Infect Dis. 2000;181(Suppl 2):S336-S348.
29. Lew JF, Kapikian AZ, Valdesuso J, Green KY. Molecular characterization of the Hawaii virus and other Norwalk-like viruses: Evidence for genetic polymorphism among human caliciviruses. J Infect Dis. 1994;170:535-142.
30. Hardy ME, Kramer SF, Treanor JJ, Estes MK. Human calicivirus genogroup II capsid sequence diversity revealed by analysis of the prototype Snow Mountain agent. Arch Virol. 1997;142:1469-1479.
31. Lew JF, Kapikian AZ, Jiang X, et al. Molecular characterization and expression of the capsid protein of a Norwalk-like virus recovered from a Desert Sheild troop with gastroenteritis. Virology. 1994;200:319-325.
32. Jiang X, Matson DO, Ruiz-Palacios GM, et al. Expression, self-assembly, and antigenicity of a Snow Mountain agent-like calicivirus capsid protein. J Clin Microbiol. 1995;33:1452-1425.
33. Dingle KE, Lambden PR, Caul EO, Clarke IN. Human enteric *Caliciviridae*: the complete genome sequence and expression of virus-like particles from a genetic group II small round structured virus. J Gen Virol. 1995;76:2349-2355.
34. Green KY, Kapikian AZ, Valdesuso J, et al. Expression and self-assembly of recombinant capsid protein from the antigenically distinct Hawaii human calicivirus. J Clin Microbiol. 1997;35:1909-1914.
35. Leite JP, Ando T, Noel JS, et al. Characterization of Toronto virus capsid protein expressed in baculovirus. Arch Virol. 1996;141:865-875.
36. Numata K, Hardy mME, Nakata S, et al. Molecular characterization of morphologically typical human calicivirus Sapporo. Arch Virol. 1997;142:1537-1552.

37. Wyatt RG, Dolin R, Blacklow NR, et al. Comparison of three agents of acute infectious nonbacterial gastroenteritis by virus challenge in volunteers. J Infect Dis. 1974;129:709-714.
38. Cubitt WD, Green KY, Payment P. Prevalence of antibodies to the Hawaii strain of human calicivirus as measured by a recombinant protein based immunoassay. J Med Virol. 1998;54:135-139.
39. Fankhauser RL, Noel JS, Monroe SS, et al. Molecular epidemiology of "Norwalk-like viruses" in outbreaks of gastroenteritis in the United States. J Infect Dis. 1998;178:1571-1578.
40. Fankhauser RL, Monroe SS, Noel JS, et al. Epidemiologic and molecular trends of "Norwalk-like viruses" associated with outbreaks of gastroenteritis in the United States. J Infect Dis. 2002;186:1-7.
41. Gonin P, Couillard M, d'Halewyn MA. Genetic diversity and molecular epidemiology of Norwalk-like viruses. J Infect Dis. 2000;182:691-697.
42. Lewis DC, Hale A, Jiang X, et al. Epidemiology of Mexico virus, a small round-structured virus in Yorkshire, United Kingdom, between January 1992 and March 1995. J Infect Dis. 1997;175:951-954.
43. Vinje J, Altena SA, Koopmans MP. The incidence and genetic variability of small round-structured viruses in outbreaks of gastroenteritis in the Netherlands. J Infect Dis. 1997;176:1374-1378.
44. Noel JS, Fankhauser RL, Ando T, et al. Identification of a distinct common strain of "Norwalk-like viruses" having a global distribution. J Infect Dis. 1999;179:1334-1344.
45. Greenberg HB, Valdesuso J, Kapikian AZ, et al. Prevalence of antibody to the Norwalk virus in various countries. Infect Immun. 1979;26:270-273.
46. Dolin R, Roessner KD, Treanor J, et al. Radioimmunoassay for detection of Snow Mountain agent of viral gastroenteritis. J Med Virol. 1985;19:11-18.
47. Hinkula J, Ball JM, Lofgren S, et al. Antibody prevalence and immunoglobulin IgG subclass pattern to Norwalk virus in Sweden. J Med Virol. 1995;47:52-27.
48. Numata K, Nakata S, Jiang X, et al. Epidemiologic study of Norwalk virus infections in Japan and Southeast Asia by enzyme-linked immunosorbent assays with Norwalk virus capsid protein produced by the baculovirus expression system. J Clin Microbiol. 1994;32:121-126.
49. Gray JJ, Jiang X, Morgan-Capner P, et al. Prevalence of antibodies to Norwalk virus in England: Detection by enzyme-linked immunosorbent assay using baculovirus-expressed Norwalk virus capsid antigen. J Clin Microbiol. 1993;31:1022-1025.
50. Sakuma Y, Chiba S, Kogasaka R, et al. Prevalence of antibody to human calicivirus in general population of northern Japan. J Med Virol. 1981;7:221-225.
51. Cubitt WD, Blacklow NR, Herrmann JE. Antigenic relationships between human caliciviruses and Norwalk virus. J Infect Dis. 1987;156:806-814.
52. Nakata S, Chiba S, Terashima H, et al. Prevalence of antibody to human calicivirus in Japan and Southeast Asia determined by radioimmunoassay. J Clin Microbiol. 1985;22:519-521.
53. Gabbay YB, Glass RI, Monroe SS, et al. Prevalence of antibodies to Norwalk virus among Amerindians in isolated Amazonian communities. Am J Epidemiol. 1994;139:728-733.
54. Mounts AW, Ando T, Koopmans M, et al. Cold weather seasonality of gastroenteritis associated with Norwalk-like viruses. J Infect Dis. 2000;181(Suppl 2):S284-S287.
55. Chadwick PR, McCann R. Transmission of a small round structured virus by vomiting during a hospital outbreak of gastroenteritis. J Hosp Infect. 1994;26:251-259.
56. Patterson W, Haswell P, Fryers PT, Green J. Outbreak of small round structured virus gastroenteritis arose after kitchen assistant vomited. Commun Dis Rep CDR Rev. 1997;7:R101-R103.
57. Greenberg HB, Wyatt RG, Kapikian AZ. Norwalk virus in vomitus. Lancet. 1979;1:55.
58. Kilgore PE, Belay ED, Hamlin DM, et al. A university outbreak of gastroenteritis due to a small round-structured virus. Application of molecular diagnostics to identify the etiologic agent and patterns of transmission. J Infect Dis. 1996;173:787-793.
59. Sawyer LA, Murphy JJ, Kaplan JE, et al. 25- to 30-nm virus particle associated with a hospital outbreak of acute gastroenteritis with evidence for airborne transmission. Am J Epidemiol. 1988;127:1261-1271.
60. Caul EO. Small round structured viruses: Airborne transmission and hospital control. Lancet. 1994;343:1240-1242.
61. Centers for Disease Control and Prevention. Norwalk-like viruses: public health impact and outbreak management. MMWR Morb Mortal Wkly Rep. 2001;50(RR-9):1-17.
62. Graham DY, Jian X, Tanaka T, et al. Norwalk virus infection of volunteers: New insights based on improved assays. J Infect Dis. 1994;170:34-43.
63. Okhuysen PC, Jiang X, Ye L, et al. Viral shedding and fecal IgA response after Norwalk virus infection. J Infect Dis. 1995;171:566-569.
64. Rockx B, De Wit M, Vennema H, et al. Natural history of human calicivirus infection: A prospective cohort study. Clin Infect Dis. 2002;35:246-253.
65. Patterson T, Hutching P, Palmer S. Outbreak of SRSV gastroenteritis at an international conference traced to food handled by a post-symptomatic caterer. Epidemiol Infect. 1993;111:157-162.
66. Kaplan JE, Feldman R, Campbell DS, et al. The frequency of a Norwalk-like pattern of illness in outbreaks of acute gastroenteritis. Am J Public Health. 1982;72:1329-1332.
67. Khan AS, Moe CL, Glass RI, et al. Norwalk virus-associated gastroenteritis traced to ice consumption aboard a cruise ship in Hawaii: Comparison and application of molecular method-based assays. J Clin Microbiol. 1994;31:318-322.
68. Bourgeois AL, Gardiner CH, Thornton SA, et al. Etiology of acute diarrhea among United States military personnel deployed to South America and west Africa. Am J Trop Med Hyg. 1993;48:243-248.
69. Hyams KC, Bourgeois AL, Merrell BR, et al. Diarrheal disease during Operation Desert Shield. N Engl J Med. 1991;325:1423-1428.
70. Ho MS, Glass RI, Monroe SS. Viral gastroenteritis aboard a cruise ship. Lancet. 1989;2:961-965.

71. Baron RC, Murphy FD, Greenberg HB. Norwalk gastrointestinal illness: An outbreak associated with swimming in a recreational lake with secondary person-to-person transmission. Am J Epidemiol. 1982;115:163-172.
72. Koopman JS, Eckert EA, Greenberg HB. Norwalk virus enteric illness acquired by swimming exposure. Am J Epidemiol. 1982;115:173-177.
73. Cannon RO, Poliner JR, Hirschhorn RB, et al. A multistate outbreak of Norwalk virus gastroenteritis associated with consumption of commercial ice. J Infect Dis. 1991;164:860-863.
74. Hedberg CW, Osterholm MT. Outbreaks of food-borne and waterborne viral gastroenteritis. Clin Microbiol Rev. 1993;6:199-210.
75. Lo SV, Connolly AM, Palmer SR, et al. The role of the pre-symptomatic food handler in a common source outbreak of food-borne SRSV gastroenteritis in a group of hospitals. Epidemiol Infect. 1994;113:513-521.
76. Stafford R, Strain D, Heymer M, et al. An outbreak of Norwalk virus gastroenteritis following consumption of oysters. Commun Dis Intell. 1997;21:317-320.
77. McDonnell S, Kirkland KB, Hlady WG, et al. Failure of cooking to prevent shellfish-associated viral gastroenteritis. Arch Intern Med. 1997;157:111-116.
78. Kirkland KB, Meriwether RA, Leiss JK, Mac Kenzie WR. Steaming oysters does not prevent Norwalk-like gastroenteritis. Public Health Rep. 1996;111:527-530.
79. Rodriguez EM, Parrott C, Rolka H, et al. An outbreak of viral gastroenteritis in a nursing home: Importance of excluding ill employees. Infect Control Hosp Epidemiol. 1996;17:587-592.
80. Augustin AK, Simor AE, Shorrock C, McCausland J. Outbreaks of gastroenteritis due to Norwalk-like virus in two long-term care facilities for the elderly. Can J Infect Control. 1995;10:111-113.
81. Russo PL, Spelman DW, Harrington GA, et al. Hospital outbreak of Norwalk-like virus. Infect Control Hosp Epidemiol. 1997;18:576-579.
82. Kjeldsberg E. Small spherical viruses in faeces from gastroenteritis patients. Acta Pathol Microbiol Immunol Scand. 1977;85:351-354.
83. Spatt HC, Marks MI, Gomersall M, et al. Nosocomial infantile gastroenteritis associated with mini-rotavirus and calicivirus. J Pediatr. 1978;93:922-926.
84. Oishi I, Maeda A, Yamazaki K, et al. Calicivirus detected in outbreaks of acute gastroenteritis in school children. Biken J. 1980;23:163-168.
85. Steele AD, Phillips J, Smit TK, et al. Snow mountain-like virus identified in young children with winter vomiting disease in South Africa. J Diarrh Dis Res. 1997;15:177-182.
86. Levett PN, Gu M, Luan B, et al. Longitudinal study of molecular epidemiology of small round-structured viruses in a pediatric population. J Clin Microbiol. 1996;34:1497-1501.
87. Middleton PJ, Szymanski MT, Petric M. Viruses associated with acute gastroenteritis in young children. Am J Dis Child. 1977;131:733.
88. Wolfaardt M, Taylor MB, Booysen HF, et al. Incidence of human calicivirus and rotavirus infection in patients with gastroenteritis in South Africa. J Med Virol. 1997;51:290-296.
89. Pang XL, Honma S, Nakata S, Vesikari T. Human caliciviruses in acute gastroenteritis of young children in the community. J Infect Dis. 2000;181(Suppl 2):S288-S294.
90. Sakai Y, Nakata S, Honma S, et al. Clinical severity of Norwalk virus and Sapporo virus gastroenteritis in children in Hokkaido, Japan. Pediatr Infect Dis J. 2001;20:849-853.
91. Lew JF, Valdesuso J, Vesikari T, et al. Detection of Norwalk virus or Norwalk-like virus infections in Finnish infants and young children. J Infect Dis. 1994;169:1364-1367.
92. Grohmann G, Glass RI, Gold J, et al. Outbreak of human calicivirus gastroenteritis in a day-care center in Sydney, Australia. J Clin Microbiol. 1991;29:544-550.
93. Struve J, Bennet R, Ehrnst AE, et al. Nosocomial calicivirus gastroenteritis in a pediatric hospital. Pediatr Infect Dis J. 1994; 13:882-885.
94. Agus SG, Dolin R, Wyatt RG, et al. Acute infectious nonbacterial gastroenteritis: Intestinal histopathology. Ann Intern Med. 1973;79:18-25.
95. Schreiber DS, Blacklow NR, Trier JS. The mucosal lesion of the proximal small intestine in acute infectious nonbacterial gastroenteritis. N Engl J Med. 1973;288:1318-1323.
96. Schreiber DS, Blacklow NR, Trier JS. The small intestinal lesion induced by Hawaii agent acute infectious nonbacterial gastroenteritis. J Infect Dis. 1974;129:705-708.
97. Widerlite L, Trier J, Blacklow N, et al. Structure of the gastric mucosa in acute infectious nonbacterial gastroenteritis. Gastroenterology. 1975;70:321-325.
98. Blacklow NR, Dolin R, Feson DS, et al. Acute infectious nonbacterial gastroenteritis: Etiology and pathogenesis. Ann Intern Med. 1972;76:993-1000.
99. Levy AG, Widerlite L, Schwartz CJ, et al. Jejunal adenylate cyclase activity in human subjects during viral gastroenteritis. Gastroenterology. 1976;70:321-325.
100. Woode GN, Bridger JC. Isolation of small viruses resembling astroviruses and caliciviruses from acute enteritis of calves. J Med Microbiol. 1978;11:441-452.
101. Saif LJ, Bohl EH, Theil KW, et al. Rotavirus-like, calicivirus-like, and 23-nm virus-like particles associated with diarrhea in young pigs. J Clin Microbiol. 1980;12:105-111.
102. Marionneau S, Ruvoen N, Le Moullac-Vaidye B, et al. Norwalk virus binds to histo-blood group antigens present on gastroduodenal epithelial cells of secretor individuals. Gastroenterology. 2002;122:1967-1977.
103. Hutson AM, Atmar RL, Marcus DM, Estes MK. Norwalk virus-like particle hemagglutination by binding to histo-blood group antigens. J Virol. 2003;77:405-415.
104. Huang P, Farkas T, Marionneau S, et al. Noroviruses bind to human ABO, Lewis, and secretor histo-blood group antigens: Identification of 4 distinct strain-specific patterns. J Infect Dis. 2003;188:19-31.
105. Tan M, Huang P, Meller J, et al. Mutations within the P2 domain of Norovirus capsid affect binding to human histo-blood group antigens: Evidence for a binding pocket. J Virol. 2003;77:12562-12571.
106. Hutson AM, Atmar RL, Graham DY, Estes MK. Norwalk virus infection and disease is associated with ABO histo-blood group type. J Infect Dis. 2002;185:1335-1337.

107. Lindesmith L, Moe C, Marionneau S, et al. Human susceptibility and resistance to Norwalk virus infection. Nat Med. 2003;9:548-553.

108. Parrino TA, Schreiber DS, Trier JS, et al. Clinical immunity in acute gastroenteritis caused by Norwalk agent. N Engl J Med. 1977;291:86-89.

109. Cukor G, Nowak NA, Blacklow NR. Immunoglobulin M responses to the Norwalk virus of gastroenteritis. Infect Immun. 1982;37:463-468.

110. Treanor JJ, Jiang X, Madore HP, Estes MK. Subclass-specific serum antibody responses to recombinant Norwalk virus capsid antigen (rNV) in adults infected with Norwalk, Snow Mountain, or Hawaii viruses. J Clin Microbiol. 1993;31:1630-1634.

111. Erdman DD, Gary GW, Anderson LJ. Development and evaluation of an IgM capture enzyme immunoassay for diagnosis of recent Norwalk virus infection. J Virol Methods. 1989;24:57-66.

112. Erdmann DD, Gary GW, Anderson LJ. Serum immunoglobulin A response to Norwalk virus infection. J Clin Microbiol. 1989;27:1417-1418.

113. Farkas T, Thornton SA, Wilton N, et al. Homologous versus heterologous immune responses to Norwalk-like viruses among crew members after acute gastroenteritis outbreaks on 2 US Navy vessels. J Infect Dis. 2003;187:187-193.

114. Madore HP, Treanor JJ, Buja R, Dolin R. Antigenic relatedness among the Norwalk-like agents by serum antibody rises. J Med Virol. 1990;32:96-101.

115. Hale AD, Lewis DC, Jiang X, Brown DW. Homotypic and heterotypic IgG and IgM antibody responses in adults infected with small round structured viruses. J Med Virol. 1998;54:305-312.

116. Noel JS, Ando T, Leite JP, et al. Correlation of patient immune responses with genetically characterized small round-structured viruses involved in outbreaks of nonbacterial acute gastroenteritis in the United States, 1990 to 1995. J Med Virol. 1997;53:372-383.

117. Jiang X, Wang J, Estes MK. Characterization of SRSVs using RT-PCR and a new antigen ELISA. Arch Virol. 1995;140:363-374.

118. Agus S, Falchuk ZM, Sessoms CS, et al. Increased jejunal IgA synthesis in vitro during acute infectious nonbacterial gastroenteritis. Am J Digest Dis. 1974;19:127-131.

119. Okhuysen P, Jiang X, Tenjaria G, et al. Detection of Norwalk specific fecal IgA in challenged volunteers utilizing ELISA with baculovirus expressed Norwalk particles as coating antigens. Abstract 1392. In: 32nd Interscience Conference on Antimicrobial Agents and Chemotherapy, 1992. Anaheim, CA: American Society for Microbiology; 1992:343.

120. Dolin R, Reichman RC, Fauci AS. Lymphocyte populations in acute viral gastroenteritis. Infect Immunol. 1976;14:422-428.

121. Lindesmith L, Moe C, LePendu J, et al. Cellular and humoral immunity following Snow Mountain virus challenge. 2004.

122. Johnson PC, Mathewson JJ, DuPont HL, Greenberg HB. Multiple-challenge study of host susceptibility to Norwalk gastroenteritis in US adults. J Infect Dis. 1990;161:18-21.

123. Black RE, Greenberg HB, Kapikian AZ, et al. Acquisition of serum antibody to Norwalk virus and rotavirus and relation to diarrhea in a longitudinal study of young children in rural Bangladesh. J Infect Dis. 1982;145:483-489.

124. Ryder RW, Singh N, Reeves WC, et al. Evidence of immunity induced by naturally acquired rotavirus and Norwalk virus infection on two remote Panamanian islands. J Infect Dis. 1985;135:20-27.

125. Nakata S, Chiba A, Terashima H, et al. Humoral immunity in infants with gastroenteritis caused by human calicivirus. J Infect Dis. 1985;152:274-279.

126. Greenberg HB, Wyatt RG, Kalica AR, et al. New insights in viral gastroenteritis. Perspect Virol. 1981;11:163-187.

127. Karst SM, Wobus CE, Lay M, et al. STAT1-dependent innate immunity to a Norwalk-like virus. Science. 2003;299:1575-1578.

128. Harris JC, DuPont HL, Hornick RB. Fecal leukocytes in diarrheal illness. Ann Intern Med. 1972;76:697-703.

129. Atmar RL, Estes MK. Diagnosis of noncultivatable gastroenteritis viruses, the human caliciviruses. Clin Microbiol Rev. 2001;14:15-37.

130. Kapikian Z, Wyatt RG, Dolin R, et al. Visualization of 27 nm particle associated infectious nonbacterial gastroenteritis. J Virol. 1972;10:1075-1081.

131. Richards AF, Lopman B, Gunn A, et al. Evaluation of a commercial ELISA for detecting Norwalk-like virus antigen in faeces. J Clin Virol. 2003;26:109-115.

132. Jiang X, Wang J, Graham DY, Estes MK. Detection of Norwalk virus in stool by polymerase chain reaction. J Clin Microbiol. 1992;30:2529-2534.

133. De Leon R, Matsui SM, Baric RS, et al. Detection of Norwalk virus in stool specimens by reverse transcriptase-polymerase chain reaction and nonradioactive oligoprobes. J Clin Microbiol. 1992;30:3151-3157.

134. Willcocks MM, Silcock JG, Carter MJ. Detection of Norwalk virus in the UK by the polymerase chain reaction. FEMS Microbiol Lett. 1993;112:7-12.

135. Moe CL, Gentsch J, Ando T, et al. Application of PCR to detect Norwalk virus in fecal specimens from outbreaks of gastroenteritis. J Clin Microbiol. 1994;32:642-648.

136. Honma S, Nakata S, Sakai Y, et al. Sensitive detection and differentiation of Sapporo virus, a member of the family Caliciviridae, by standard and booster nested polymerase chain reaction. J Med Virol. 2001;65:413-417.

137. Jiang X, Huang PW, Zhong WM, et al. Design and evaluation of a primer pair that detects both Norwalk- and Sapporo-like caliciviruses by RT-PCR. J Virol Methods. 1999;83:145-154.

138. Kojima S, Kageyama T, Fukushi S, et al. Genogroup-specific PCR primers for detection of Norwalk-like viruses. J Virol Methods. 2002;100:107-114.

139. Ando T, Monroe SS, Gentsch JR, et al. Detection and differentiation of antigenically distinct small round-structured viruses (Norwalk-like viruses) by reverse transcription-PCR and southern hybridization. J Clin Microbiol. 1995;33:64-71.

140. Atmar RL, Metcalf TG, Neill FH, Estes MD. Detection of enteric viruses in oysters by using the polymerase chain reaction. Appl Environ Microbiol. 1993;59:631-635.

141. Gouvea V, Santos N, Timenetsky M, Estes MK. Identification of Norwalk virus in artificially seeded shellfish and selected foods. J Virol Methods. 1994;8:177-187.

142. Beller M, Ellis A, Lee SH, et al. Outbreak of viral gastroenteritis due to a contaminated well: International consequences. JAMA. 1997;278:563-568.

143. Le Guyader F, Neill FH, Estes MK, et al. Detection and analysis of a small round-structured virus strain in oysters implicated in an outbreak of acute gastroenteritis. Appl Environ Microbiol. 1996;62:4268-4272.

144. Shieh Y, Monroe SS, Fankhauser RL, et al. Detection of Norwalk-like virus in shellfish implicated in illness. J Infect Dis. 2000;181(Suppl 2):S360-S366.

145. Gary GW, Anderson LJ, Keswick BH, et al. Norwalk virus antigen and antibody response in an adult volunteer study. J Clin Microbiol. 1987;25:2001-2003.

146. Brinker JP, Blacklow NR, Estes MK, et al. Detection of Norwalk virus and other genogroup 1 human caliciviruses by a monoclonal antibody, recombinant-antigen-based immunoglobulin M capture enzyme immunoassay. J Clin Microbiol. 1998;36:1064-1069.

147. Brinker JP, Blacklow NR, Jiang X, et al. Immunoglobulin M antibody test to detect genogroup II Norwalk-like virus infection. J Clin Microbiol. 1999;37:2983-2986.

148. Steinhoff MC, Douglas RG Jr, Greenberg HB, Callahan DR. Bismuth subsalyscylate therapy of viral gastroenteritis. Gastroenterology. 1980;78:1495-1499.

149. Estes MK, Ball JM, Guerrero RA, et al. Norwalk virus vaccines: Challenges and progress. J Infect Dis. 2000;181(Suppl 2):S367-S373.

150. Ball JM, Graham DY, Opekun AR, et al. Norwalk virus-like particles given orally to volunteers: Phase I study. Gastroenterology. 1999;117:40-48.

151. Tacket CO, Sztein MB, Losonsky G, et al. Humoral, mucosal, and cellular immune responses to oral Norwalk virus-like particles in volunteers. Clin Immunol. 2003;108:241-247.

152. Tacket CO, Mason HS, Losonsky G, et al. Human immune responses to a novel norwalk virus vaccine delivered in transgenic potatoes. J Infect Dis. 2000;182:302-305.

Astroviruses and Picobirnaviruses

JOHN J. TREANOR

RAPHAEL DOLIN

In addition to caliciviruses several newly described viruses have been implicated as agents of gastroenteritis in adults and children. The greatest evidence exists for the role of the astroviruses. Other viruses that may be responsible for some cases of gastroenteritis include the toroviruses (see Chapter 152) and the picobirnaviruses.

ASTROVIRUSES

Astroviruses are members of a new virus family, the Astroviridae, and are now recognized as important causes of gastroenteritis in children and adults. Together with the Caliciviridae (see Chapter 172), these small ribonucleic acid (RNA) viruses are probably responsible for much of the presumably viral gastroenteritis that had previously been of unknown etiology.

Virology

Astroviruses are small RNA viruses that are found in a wide variety of animal species including humans. The virions are nonenveloped, display cubic symmetry, and are approximately 28 to 30 nm in diameter. Under the electron microscope, the particles in stool samples have a characteristic morphology that consists of round smooth edges with multiple triangular electron-lucent areas and an electron-dense center that results in the appearance of a five- or six-pointed star from which the virus derives its name (Fig. 173-1).[1] Analysis of virus grown in cell culture has shown the virus particles to exhibit a layer of 10-nm spike-like projections on the surface.[2] The human astroviruses have a density of 1.35 to 1.37 g/mL in cesium chloride (CsCl), and contain a positive-sense, single-stranded 35 S RNA genome with a 3′ polyadenylated tail.[3] The genomic organization includes three open reading frames (ORFs): ORF1a encodes the protease region; ORF1b encodes the polymerase; and ORF2 encodes the capsid protein(s).[4,5] The capsid is translated from a subgenomic polyadenylated RNA in infected

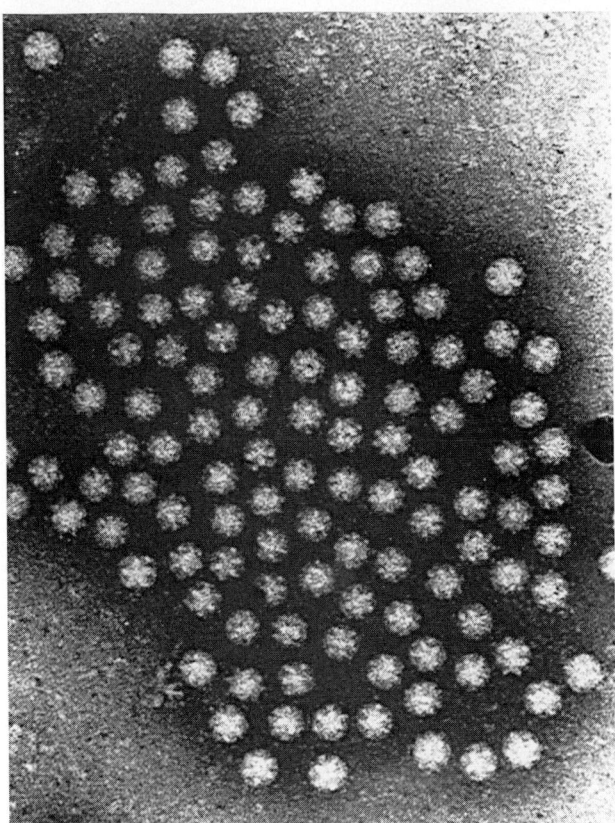

FIGURE 173-1. Astrovirus in the intestinal contents of gnotobiotic lambs. Particles are 30 nm in diameter. *(From Snodgrass DR, Gray W, with permission.)*

TABLE 173-1 Detection of Astroviruses in Children with Diarrhea

| Geographic Location | Percent of Samples in Which Astroviruses Were Detected in Subjects | | |
	With Illness	Without Illness	Reference
Baltimore	2.7	1.4	55
Phoenix	4.0	2.4	24
Providence	6.8	0.0	43
Thailand	8.6	2.0	56
Guatemala	7.3	2.4	35
Korea	1.9	2.2	57
Peru	2.9	2.5	57

cells.[6,7] The number of viral structural proteins appears to vary with the serotype, with between one and three reported for the human viruses,[8,9] possibly reflecting differences in the processing of the capsid precursor.[10] Generation of an infectious cDNA clone has recently been reported,[11] which will likely add significantly to studies of the molecular biology of these viruses.

Astrovirus serotypes can be distinguished by immunofluorescence or plaque neutralization techniques,[12,13] whereas considerable cross-reactivity exists by enzyme immunoassay[14] due to the presence of a group antigen. At least eight serotypes of human astroviruses have been recognized,[15-17] denoted HastV-1 to HastV-8. All eight serotypes are widely distributed throughout the world.[16,17] Further characterization of these viruses has been greatly enhanced by the development of methods for their adaptation to and propagation in cell culture systems.[14,18,19]

Epidemiology

Astroviruses have been detected in the stools of between 2% and 9% of children with diarrhea brought to medical attention in a variety of settings (Table 173-1). Outbreaks have been described in schools, day care settings, and pediatric wards.[20-25] Illness has most often been seen in individuals younger than the age of 2 years, although outbreaks in healthy adults[26,27] and in elderly populations[28] have also been described. Astroviruses have also been detected in the stools of immunosuppressed patients with diarrhea, including human immunodeficiency virus (HIV)–infected patients,[29] following bone marrow transplantation,[30] and in children with hematologic malignancy.[31] However, the severity of illness in HIV-infected children with astrovirus is no greater than that seen in other children.[32,33]

A winter predilection has been noted in temperate climates,[9,34] whereas infection occurs throughout the year in tropical climates,[35] similar to the pattern reported for rotaviruses. Transmission is pre-

sumably by the fecal-oral route. Seroprevalence studies in the United States and elsewhere have shown that more than 90% of children have antibody to HastV-1 by age 9,[36] suggesting that infection, largely asymptomatic, is common. Serosurveys of this type have generally identified antibody to HastV-1 more commonly than to the other serotypes.[36-38]

Pathogenesis

The pathogenesis of astrovirus-induced illness is not well understood. Astrovirus infections in animals have been associated with small intestinal villus shortening and with mild inflammatory infiltrates in the lamina propria.[39,40] Astrovirus infection may result in decreased intestinal disaccharidase activity and subsequent osmotic diarrhea,[41] similar to the mechanism postulated for rotavirus. Stool filtrates that contain astroviruses readily infect volunteers after oral administration but induce illness very infrequently,[8,42] which suggests that astroviruses may be less "pathogenic" in adults than are the noroviruses.

Clinical Illness

Illness attributed to astroviruses consists primarily of diarrhea, headache, malaise, and nausea, whereas vomiting appears to be less common. In general, the symptoms are similar to those seen in rotavirus infection in children, but are milder, and children with astrovirus gastroenteritis are less likely to be dehydrated than those with rotavirus.[43] Low-grade fever is frequently present. The incubation period of illness has been estimated to be 3 to 4 days, and in the absence of coexisting pathogens disease manifestations usually last 5 days or less, with occasional longer duration. The duration of virus shedding as assessed by polymerase chain reaction (PCR) may be longer than by enzyme immunoassay (EIA), as long as 35 days.[44]

Diagnosis, Treatment, and Prevention

In contrast to other recently described viral agents of gastroenteritis, astroviruses are often shed in large amounts in stool and can be readily detected by electron microscopy even without immune aggregation. Detection of astroviruses in cell culture has been carried out by immune electron microscopy or by immunofluorescence, and an enzyme immunoassay technique[45] that detects the astrovirus group antigen has been used widely in epidemiologic studies. Nucleic acid hybridization[46] and PCR-based[47] detection techniques have also been reported. PCR is significantly more sensitive than enzyme immunoassay.[44]

Illness associated with these agents is generally self-limited, and treatment, if required at all, is supportive and directed at maintaining hydration and electrolyte balance. Epidemiologic observations suggest that infection is associated with at least short-term protection against reinfection with the same serotype,[48] raising the possibility of vaccine strategies at some point in the future. Infection is also associated with the development of astrovirus-specific Th1-type CD4 cells in the gut mucosa.[49]

PICOBIRNAVIRUSES

The picobirnaviruses (PBVs) are small icosahedral viruses with a segmented double-stranded RNA genome of either two or three segments. Their exact taxonomic position is unclear, and they derive their name from the observation that they (usually) have a *bi*-segmented double-stranded RNA genome similar to the *Bi*rnaviridae, but are smaller (pico), with a virion size of 30 to 40 nm.[50] They were first observed in the stools of humans[51] in the course of studies using polyacrylamide gel electrophoresis (PAGE) to detect rotavirus. Picobirnavirus genomes have been found in the stools of a variety of animals and in children and adults with diarrhea, including HIV-infected adults.[29,52,53] However, the role of these viruses as causative agents of gastroenteritis is unclear, because the prevalence of PBVs in stools of individuals with and without diarrhea is similar.[54]

Toroviruses are newly described viral agents that cause gastroenteritis. They are members of the Coronaviridae family and are discussed in Chapter 152.

REFERENCES

1. Snodgrass DR, Gray W. Detection and transmission of 30 nm virus particles (astroviruses) in the faeces of lambs with diarrhoea. Arch Virol. 1977;55:287-291.
2. Risco C, Carrascosa JL, Pedregosa AM, et al. Ultrastructure of human astrovirus serotype 2. J Gen Virol. 1995;76(Pt 8):2075-2080.
3. Herring AJ, Gray EW, Snodgrass DR. Purification and characterization of bovine astrovirus. J Gen Virol. 1981;53:47-55.
4. Jiang B, Monroe SS, Koonin EV, et al. RNA sequence of astrovirus: Distinctive genomic organization and a putative retrovirus-like ribosomal frameshifting signal that directs the viral replicase synthesis. Proc Nat Acad Sci. U S A 1993;90:10539-10543.
5. Willcocks MM, Brown TDK, Madeley CR, Carter MJ. The complete sequence of a human astrovirus. J Gen Virol. 1994;75:1785-1788.
6. Monroe SS, Stine SE, Gorelkin L, et al. Temporal synthesis of proteins and RNAs during human astrovirus infection of cultured cells. J Virol. 1991;65:641-648.
7. Matsui SM, Kim JP, Greenberg HB, et al. Cloning and characterization of human astrovirus immunoreactive epitopes. J Virol 1993;67:1712-1715.
8. Midthun K, Greenberg HB, Kurtz JB, et al. Characterization and seroepidemiology of a type 5 astrovirus associated with an outbreak of gastroenteritis in Marin County, California. J Clin Microbiol. 1993;31:955-962.
9. Monroe SS, Glass RI, Noah N, et al. Electron microscopic reporting of gastrointestinal viruses in the United Kingdom, 1985-1987. J Med Virol. 1991;33:193-198.
10. Belliot G, Laveran H, Monroe SS. Capsid protein composition of reference strains and wild isolates of human astroviruses. Virus Res. 1997;49:49-57.
11. Geigenmuller U, Ginzton NH, Matsui SM. Construction of a genome-length cDNA clone for human astrovirus serotype 1 and synthesis of infectious RNA transcripts. J Virol 1997;71:1713-1717.
12. Kurtz JB, Lee TW. Human astrovirus serotypes (Letter). Lancet. 1984;2:1405.
13. Hudson RW, Herrmann JE, Blacklow NR. Plaque quantitation and virus neutralization assays for human astroviruses. Arch Virol. 1989;108:33-38.
14. Herrmann JE, Hudson RW, Perron-Henry DM, et al. Antigen characterization of cell-cultivated astrovirus serotypes and development of astrovirus-specific monoclonal antibodies. J Infect Dis. 1988;158:182-185.
15. Lee TW, Kurtz JB. Prevalence of human astrovirus serotypes in the Oxford region 1976-1992, with evidence for two new serotypes. Epidemiol Infect. 1994;112:187-193.
16. Noel JS, Lee TW, Kurtz JB, et al. Typing of human astroviruses from clinical isolates by enzyme immunoassay and nucleotide sequencing. J Clin Microbiol. 1995;33:797-801.
17. Taylor MB, Walter J, Berke T, et al. Characterisation of a South African human astrovirus as type 8 by antigenic and genetic analyses. J Med Virol. 2001;64:256-261.
18. Willcocks MM, Carter MJ, Laidler FR, Madeley CR. Growth and characterisation of human faecal astrovirus in a continuous cell line. Arch Virol. 1990;113:73-81.
19. Yamashita T, Kobayashi S, Sakae K, et al. Isolation of cytopathic small round viruses with BS-C-1 cells from patients with gastroenteritis. J Infect Dis. 1991;164:954-957.
20. Madeley CR, Cosgrove BP. 28 nm particles in faeces in infantile gastroenteritis (Letter). Lancet. 1975;2:451.
21. Ashley CR, Caul EO, Paver WK. Astrovirus-associated gastroenteritis in children. J Clin Pathol. 1978;31:939-343.
22. Kurtz JB, Lee TW, Pickering D. Astrovirus associated gastroenteritis in a children's ward. J Clin Pathol 1977;30:948-52.
23. Konno T, Suzuki H, Ishida N, et al. Astrovirus-associated epidemic gastroenteritis in Japan. J Med Virol. 1982;9:11-17.
24. Lew JF, Moe CL, Monroe SS, et al. Astrovirus and adenovirus associated with diarrhea in children in day care settings. J Infect Dis. 1991;164:673-678.
25. Esahli H, Breback K, Bennet R, et al. Astroviruses as a cause of nosocomial outbreaks of infant diarrhea. Pediatr Infect Dis J. 1991;10:511-515.
26. Oishi I, Yamazaki K, Kimoto T, et al. A large outbreak of acute gastroenteritis associated with astrovirus among students and teachers in Osaka, Japan. J Infect Dis. 1994;170:439-443.
27. Belliot G, Laveran H, Monroe SS. Outbreak of gastroenteritis in military recruits associated with serotype 3 astrovirus infection. J Med Virol. 1997;51:101-106.
28. Gray JJ, Wreghitt TG, Cubitt WD, Elliot PR. An outbreak of gastroenteritis in a home for the elderly associated with astrovirus type 1 and human calicivirus. J Med Virol. 1987;23:377-381.
29. Grohmann GS, Glass RI, Pereira HG, et al. Enteric viruses and diarrhea in HIV-infected patients. Enteric Opportunistic Infections Working Group. N Engl J Med. 1993;329:14-20.
30. Cox GJ, Matsui SM, Lo RS, et al. Etiology and outcome of diarrhea after marrow transplantation: A prospective study. Gastroenterology. 1994;107:1398-1407.
31. Coppo P, Scieux C, Ferchal F, et al. Astrovirus enteritis in a chronic lymphocytic leukemia patient treated with fludarabine monophosphate. Ann Hematol. 2000;79:43-45.
32. Liste MB, Natera I, Suarez JA, et al. Enteric virus infections and diarrhea in healthy and human immunodeficiency virus-infected children. J Clin Microbiol. 2000;38:2873-2877.
33. Giordano MO, Martinez LC, Rinaldi D, et al. Diarrhea and enteric emerging viruses in HIV-infected patients. AIDS Res Hum Retrovir. 1999;15:1427-1432.
34. Lew JF, Glass RI, Petric M, et al. Six-year retrospective surveillance of gastroenteritis viruses identified at ten electron microscopy centers in the United States and Canada. Pediatr Infect Dis J. 1990;9:709-714.
35. Cruz JR, Bartlett AV, Herrmann JE, et al. Astrovirus-associated diarrhea among Guatemalan ambulatory rural children. J Clin Microbiol. 1992;30:1140-1144.
36. Mitchell DK, Matson DO, Cubitt WD, et al. Prevalence of antibodies to astrovirus types 1 and 3 in children and adolescents in Norfolk, Virginia. Pediatr Infect Dis J. 1999;18:249-254.
37. Kriston S, Willcocks MM, Carter MJ, Cubitt WD. Seroprevalence of astrovirus types 1 and 6 in London, determined using recombinant virus antigen. Epidemiol Infect. 1996;117:159-164.
38. Koopmans MP, Bijen MH, Monroe SS, Vinje J. Age-stratified seroprevalence of neutralizing antibodies to astrovirus types 1 to 7 in humans in the Netherlands. Clin Diagn Lab Immunol. 1998;5:33-37.
39. Snodgrass DR, Angus KW, Gray EW, et al. Pathogenesis of diarrhoea caused by astrovirus infection in lambs. Arch Virol. 1979;60:217-226.
40. Woode GN, Bridger JC. Isolation of small viruses resembling astroviruses and caliciviruses from acute enteritis of calves. J Med Microbiol. 1978;11:441 452.
41. Thouvenelle ML, Haynes JS, Sell JL, Reynolds DL. Astrovirus infection in hatchling turkeys: Alterations in intestinal maltase activity. Avian Dis. 1995;39:343-348.
42. Kurtz JB, Lee TW, Craig JW, et al. Astrovirus infection in volunteers. J Med Virol. 1979;3:221-230.
43. Dennehy PH, Nelson SM, Spangenberger S, et al. A prospective case-control study of the role of astrovirus in acute diarrhea among hospitalized young children. J Infect Dis. 2001;184:10-15.
44. Mitchell DK, Monroe SS, Jiang X, et al. Virologic features of an astrovirus diarrhea outbreak in a day care center revealed by reverse transcriptase-polymerase chain reaction. J Infect Dis. 1995;172:1437-1444.
45. Herrmann JE, Nowak NA, Perron-Henry DM, et al. Diagnosis of astrovirus gastroenteritis by antigen detection with monoclonal antibodies. J Infect Dis 1990;161:226-229.
46. Willcocks MM, Carter MJ, Silcock JG, Madeley CR. A dot-blot hybridization procedure for the detection of astrovirus in stool samples. Epidemiol Infect. 1991;107:405-410.
47. Major ME, Eglin RP, Easton AJ. 3' terminal nucleotide sequence of human astrovirus type 1 and routine detection of astrovirus nucleic acid and antigens. J Virol Methods. 1992;3:217-225.
48. Naficy AB, Rao MR, Holmes JL, et al. Astrovirus diarrhea in Egyptian children. J Infect Dis. 2000;182:685-690.
49. Molberg O, Nilsen EM, Sollid LM, et al. CD4⁺ T cells with specific reactivity against astrovirus isolated from normal human small intestine [see comments]. Gastroenterology. 1998;114:115-122.
50. Chandra R. Picobirnavirus, a novel group of undescribed viruses of mammals and birds: A minireview. Acta Virol. 1997;41:59-62.
51. Pereira HG, Fialho AM, Flewett TH, et al. Novel viruses in human faeces. Lancet. 1988;2:103-104.
52. Giordano MO, Martinez LC, Rinaldi D, et al. Detection of picobirnavirus in HIV-infected patients with diarrhea in Argentina. J Acquir Immune Defic Syndr Hum Retrovirol. 1998;18:380-383.
53. Gonzalez GG, Pujol FH, Liprandi F, et al. Prevalence of enteric viruses in human immunodeficiency virus seropositive patients in Venezuela. J Med Virol. 1998;55:288-292.
54. Gallimore CI, Appleton H, Lewis D, et al. Detection and characterisation of bisegmented double-stranded RNA viruses (picobirnaviruses) in human faecal specimens. J Med Virol. 1995;45:135-140.
55. Kotloff KL, Herrmann JE, Blacklow NR, et al. The frequency of astrovirus as a cause of diarrhea in Baltimore children. Pediatr Infect Dis J. 1992;11:587-589.
56. Herrmann JE, Taylor DN, Echeverria P, Blacklow NR. Astroviruses as a cause of gastroenteritis in children. N Engl J Med. 1991;324:1757-1760.
57. Moe CL, Allen JR, Monroe SS, et al. Detection of astrovirus in pediatric stool samples by immunoassay and RNA probe. J Clin Microbiol. 1991;29:2390-2395.

CHAPTER **174**

Hepatitis E Virus

ROBERT H. PURCELL

SUZANNE U. EMERSON

Hepatitis E virus (HEV) causes an acute, self-limiting hepatitis. This recently classified virus is enterically transmitted, although other routes of transmission may exist. Infection with HEV may be asymptomatic or may cause hepatitis varying in degree of severity from mild to fulminant disease. Fulminant hepatitis E has been reported most frequently in pregnant women. Hepatitis E is the most common form of acute hepatitis in adults in highly endemic regions of Asia, but the disease is rarely diagnosed in industrialized countries, including the United States.

HISTORY

Evidence for an enterically transmitted form of viral hepatitis distinct from viral hepatitis A came from serologic studies of waterborne epidemics of hepatitis in India in the late 1970s. Khuroo, and Wong and colleagues, demonstrated that patients involved in such epidemics of hepatitis in the Kashmir region and in Delhi, India, respectively, lacked serologic evidence of recent hepatitis A virus (HAV) infection.[1,2] In fact, all the patients were found to have immunoglobulin G (IgG)–class but not IgM-class antibodies to HAV, indicating that they had been infected with HAV in the past and were presumably immune to reinfection. Therefore, they concluded that another agent must have caused the hepatitis. Three years later, Balayan and co-workers confirmed the existence of a new hepatitis virus by transmitting hepatitis to a volunteer from a patient involved in an outbreak of enterically transmitted non-A, non-B hepatitis in central Asia.[3] The volunteer (one of the authors of the paper) had preexisting antibody to HAV, developed a severe hepatitis, shed virus-like particles in his feces, and developed antibodies to the virus-like particles during convalescence. Balayan and co-workers also inoculated cynomolgus monkeys with the new virus and again demonstrated hepatitis virus–like particles, and an immune response to the particles in this primate species.[3]

The new form of non-A, non-B hepatitis came to be known as epidemic non-A, non-B hepatitis or enterically transmitted non-A, non-B hepatitis. Subsequently, the name of the disease was changed to *hepatitis E* to conform with the accepted nomenclature for the other types of viral hepatitis, and the virus was designated *hepatitis E virus.*[4-6]

VIRUS

Molecular Virology

HEV is a spherical, nonenveloped particle that is approximately 30 to 32 nm in diameter (Fig. 174-1).[7,8] It has an indefinite surface structure that is intermediate between that of the Norwalk agent (a member of the Caliciviridae family) and that of HAV (a member of the Picornaviridae family).[9] It is believed to have an icosahedral symmetry.[8,10] The buoyant density of HEV is 1.35 to 1.40 g/cm³ in CsCl.[3,11] Its sedimentation coefficient is 183 S.[12] The virus appears to be relatively stable to environmental and chemical agents.[13] HEV contains a ribonucleic acid (RNA) genome enclosed within a capsid that is composed of one or possibly two proteins, but direct analysis of purified virions has not been possible to date.[14]

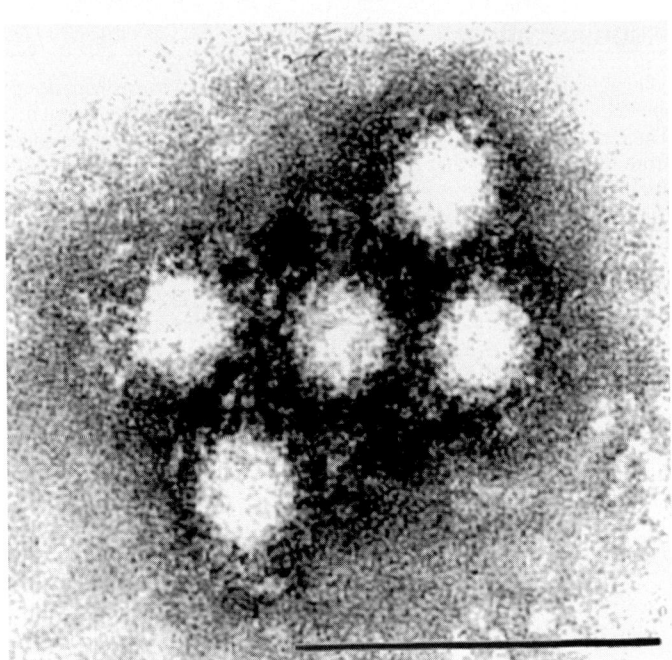

FIGURE 174-1. Antibody-coated hepatitis E virus particles detected in the feces of a patient with hepatitis E in Pakistan (immune electron microscopy). *(Modified from Ticehurst J, Popkin TJ, Bryan JP, et al. Association of hepatitis E virus with an outbreak of hepatitis in Pakistan: Serologic responses and pattern of virus excretion. J Med Virol. 1992;36:84-92.)*

The genome of HEV is a single-stranded positive-sense RNA molecule approximately 7.2 kb in length followed by a polyadenylated tract (Fig. 174-2).[14,15] The genome consists of a short 5′ nontranslated region that is capped,[16,17] three open reading frames (ORFs), each in a different coding frame, and a short 3′ nontranslated region that is terminated by a stretch of adenosine residues. ORF1, the largest ORF, is believed to encode the nonstructural protein or proteins of the virus. Based on the identification of characteristic amino acid motifs,[18] the following genetic elements have been identified, in order, from the 5′ to the 3′ end of the ORF: a methyltransferase, presumably involved in capping the 5′ end of the viral genome; the "Y" domain, a sequence of unknown function that is found in certain other viruses, including rubella virus; a papain-like cysteine protease, a type of protease found predominantly in alphaviruses and rubella virus[19]; a proline-rich "hinge" that may provide flexibility and that contains a region of hypervariable sequence[20,21]; an "X" domain of unknown function that has been found adjacent to papain-like protease domains in the polyproteins of other positive-strand RNA viruses[19]; a domain containing helicase-like motifs similar to those found in viruses containing type I (superfamily 3) helicases[22,23]; and an RNA-dependent polymerase, with motifs most closely related to those found in viruses containing an RNA polymerase of superfamily 3.[24] There is evidence that the putative protease is not functional.[25] Methyltransferase and guanylyltransferase activities have been demonstrated with expressed recombinant protein from the 5′ (methyltransferase) portion of this ORF, as has replicase activity with expressed recombinant protein from the 3′ (polymerase) portion of the ORF.[26,27] Infection of nonhuman primates with RNA from a circular deoxyribonucleic acid (cDNA) clone demonstrated the cap was required for infection in vivo and identified a *cis*-reactive element.[17] ORF2 is approximately 2000 nucleotides in length and begins approximately 40 nucleotides 3′ of the termination of ORF1 and consists of a 5′ signal sequence, which is a 300-nucleotide region rich in codons for arginine, possibly representing an RNA-binding site,[14] and three potential glycosylation sites.[28] Although glycosylation of one or more of these sites has been demonstrated in vitro, it has not

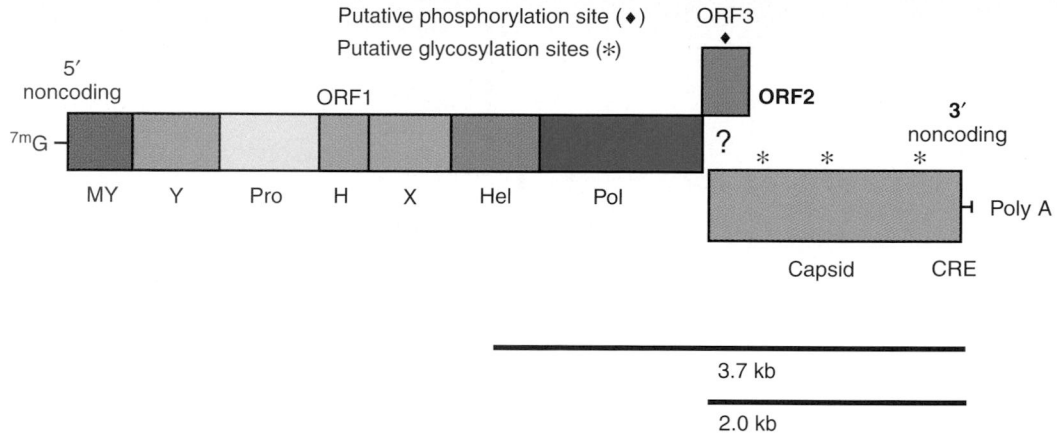

FIGURE 174-2. Organization of hepatitis E virus genome. The approximately 7.2-kb genome encodes three open reading frames (ORFs). The nonstructural proteins are encoded within the large 5′ ORF (see text for details). The capsid protein is encoded by the 3′ ORF (ORF2). The small overlapping third ORF (ORF3) encodes an immunogenic protein of unknown function. There is a short capped 5′ noncoding region and a short polyadenylated (Poly A) 3′ noncoding region. A *cis*-reacting element (CRE) overlaps the 3′ end of ORF2 and the 3′ noncoding region. It is essential for replication. Two subgenomic messenger ribonucleic acids (RNAs) have been identified but the exact dimensions and functions are unknown.

been established whether they are glycosylated in the mature virus.[29] The protein encoded by ORF2 is the capsid protein of HEV.[14,30-32] Dimerization of ORF2 protein may be important for its function.[30-32] ORF3, less than 400 nucleotides in length, overlaps ORF1 by one nucleotide at its 5′ end and overlaps ORF2 by more than 300 nucleotides at its 3′ end. The function of ORF3 is unknown,[20] but expressed recombinant protein has been reported to be a phosphoprotein, to bind to the cellular cytoskeleton, and to interact with ORF2 and with a number of cellular tyrosine kinases in vitro.[33-36]

Classification

Because the morphology and genomic organization of HEV resemble those of the caliciviruses, it was classified as a member of the family Caliciviridae.[37] However, the sequence of HEV is not closely related to that of any other virus, including the caliciviruses. It most resembles the sequence of rubella virus, a member of the virus family Togaviridae, as well as the sequence of beet necrotic yellow vein virus, a plant furovirus.[38] In addition, its codon usage most resembles that of rubella virus, and the sequences of the putative RNA polymerase and helicase of HEV resemble those of superfamily 3 viruses (rubella, other alphaviruses, and so forth) rather than those of superfamily 1 (caliciviruses, picornaviruses, and so forth).[14] For these and other reasons, HEV has been removed from the family Caliciviridae and recently reclassified in its own genus (*Hepevirus*) and family (Hepeviridae).[39]

Geographic Distribution and Genetic Variation

Hepatitis E has been clinically important primarily in developing countries of Southeast and Central Asia, the Middle East, and North Africa.[5,40] Epidemic hepatitis E has also been reported in Mexico.[41] Individual cases of hepatitis E have been reported occasionally in industrialized countries, including the United States.[42] Strains of HEV recovered from within one geographic region generally are genetically similar and characteristic of that region and differ from strains indigenous to other regions.[43-50] However, the overall heterogeneity of HEV strains is not great, and all human strains recovered to date appear to belong to the same serotype.[7,8,12,51-54] The genomes of several HEV strains from Asia, North Africa, Mexico, and the United States have been entirely or partially sequenced.[14,15,21,43-49,52,55-61] On the basis of analysis of these sequences, HEV strains can be classified into five major genotypes: (1) Asian-African human strains, (2) Mexican-African strains, (3) U.S. human and swine strains, (4) Asian human and swine strains, and (5) Australian and North

American avian strains (Fig. 174-3).[47,50,60] The Asian-African genotype 1 strains can be subdivided into closely related Northern and Central Asian strains, Southeast and Southern Asian strains, and North African strains.[43-46,48,49] The Asian strains are more closely related to one another than they are to the African strains. Strains of HEV with sequences resembling those of Southern and Southeast Asian strains have been recovered in North Africa, South Africa, the Middle East, and the Mediterranean region, but these are thought to have been introduced, as in other regions of the world, from Asia in recent times by recreational travelers, religious pilgrims, or laborers.[62-66] Each of the other genotypes is significantly different from the Asian strains and from each other. Genotype 2–like strains have been recovered only from an epidemic in Mexico and from isolated cases in Nigeria. Genotype 3 comprises a genetically heterogeneous group of strains that have been recovered from humans with hepatitis E in the United States, the Netherlands, Austria, Spain, Argentina, and Japan and from swine in the United States, Canada, several European countries, New Zealand, Japan, and Taiwan (from swine recently imported from the United States). Genotype 4 strains have been recovered from human cases of hepatitis E in China, Taiwan, and Japan and from swine in China, Taiwan, Japan, and India.[46,67-70] Genotype 5 strains differ from other strains in nucleotide identity by 48% to 60% depending on the region sequenced and are enzoonotic in chicken flocks in the United States.[60,71,72] Each of the four major genetic groups of human HEV has nucleotide deletions or insertions, or both, that are unique to the respective group. The ORF1 sequences of the four major genotypes differ from each other in nucleotide sequence identity by about 20%, whereas sequence identity within each group differs by no more than 5% to 10%.[43,44,47,50] Thus, genetic heterogeneity appears to be regionally distributed, suggesting that HEV is an ancient virus, but its distribution has been modified by mass movements of people and their animals. Undoubtedly, the genetic complexity of HEV will continue to expand as new data are collected.

Antigenic Composition

HEV encodes multiple antigens that are reactive in a variety of assays, including immunoelectronmicroscopy,[3] immunofluorescence,[73,74] enzyme-linked immunosorbent assay (ELISA),[53,75] and Western blot.[53,76-80] On the basis of antibody mapping with synthetic peptides, a number of linear epitopes have been identified on HEV-encoded proteins.[79,81-84] At least 12 such epitopes have been identified among the nonstructural proteins encoded by ORF1; these were con-

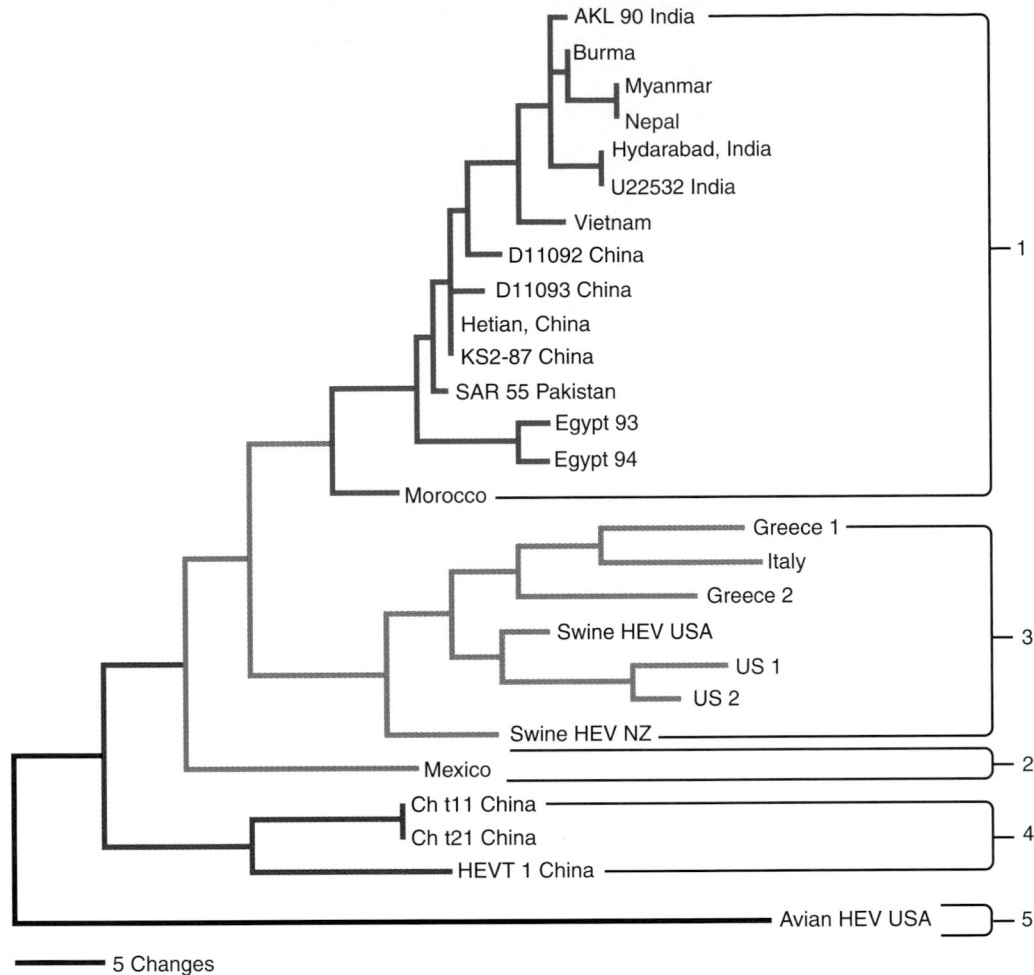

FIGURE 174-3. Genetic diversity of hepatitis E virus strains. Five major genotypes have been identified. Genotype 1 is found in Asia, the Middle East, and North Africa. Genotype 2 has been found in Mexico and Nigeria. Genotype 3 has been recovered from humans in North and South America, Europe, and Japan and from swine in North America, Europe, Asia, and New Zealand. Genotype 4 has been recovered from humans and swine in Asia. Genotype 5 has been recovered from chickens in North America and Australia. *(Modified from Haqshenas G, Shivaprasad HL, Woolcock PR, et al. Genetic identification and characterization of a novel virus related to human hepatitis E virus from chickens with hepatitis-splenomegaly syndrome in the United States. J Gen Virol. 2001;82:2449-2462.)*

centrated in the RNA polymerase.[83] Of greater diagnostic importance are epitopes encoded by the other two ORFs. Three major antigenic sites, found respectively in the amino-terminal, central, and carboxyl-terminal regions of the gene product of ORF2 (capsid protein), have been reported.[83,85-87] One immunoreactive antigenic site consisting of conformational epitopes has been localized to the carboxyl-terminal region.[86,87] Similarly, a major epitope is found in the carboxyl-terminal 30 amino acids of the gene product of ORF3.[85] Although epitopes located in ORF2 are relatively highly conserved among different HEV strains, the epitope in ORF3 is relatively poorly conserved. Thus, diagnostic tests based on ORF2 epitopes appear to be more broadly reactive than those based on ORF3 epitopes, but this has not been a universal finding.[77,81,88-93] Although synthetic peptides based on the demonstrated linear epitopes of ORFs 2 and 3 have been useful in diagnostic tests,[82] longer recombinant proteins, especially those expressed from ORF2, have proved to be more sensitive for detection of anti-HEV in natural infections of humans and experimental infections of nonhuman primates.[53,75,93-96] Specifically, antibodies detected with large expressed ORF2 proteins appear to be longer lasting than antibodies detected with synthetic peptides, especially those peptides representing ORF3.[97,98] This is probably because large expressed proteins of ORF2, which can form dimers and virus-like particles, detect antibodies to conformational epitopes.[32,53,86,99] However, full-length

protein expressed from ORF2 was found to detect acute-phase anti-HEV better than late convalescent antibody.[100] An artificial mosaic protein containing selected epitopes of ORF2 and ORF3 coupled together may be an exception because it provides a sensitive detection assay.[101,102] Neutralizing antibody to HEV appears to be directed against epitopes in the carboxyl terminus of ORF2 that have yet to be fully identified.[87,103,104] Neutralization assays have been reported but are difficult to perform.[105]

Epidemiology

HEV is an important human pathogen in Southeast and Central Asia, the Middle East, and North and West Africa. Epidemic hepatitis E has been reported in Mexico, and rare-to-occasional cases of hepatitis E have been identified in a number of industrialized countries, including the United States.[47] The more spectacular form of the disease, epidemic hepatitis E, is actually a relatively uncommon occurrence, and by far the majority of the cases occur as endemic or sporadic disease.[3,41,63,76,78,91,106-140] Endemic hepatitis E is limited to a band of developing countries, often in tropical or subtropical regions. In much of Asia, HEV is the single most frequent cause of acute hepatitis in adults[141]; in parts of the Middle East and North Africa, it is second only to hepatitis B (Fig. 174-4).[63,130] Most of the cases reported in industrialized countries occur in travelers recently returned from an en-

FIGURE 174-4. Importance of hepatitis E virus (HEV) in the etiology of viral hepatitis in regions where the virus is endemic. HEV is the most important cause of sporadic hepatitis among adults (and the second most important cause among children) in Asia and the second most important cause among adults (after hepatitis B virus) in the Middle East and North Africa. Hepatitis of unknown etiology is important in both regions. *(Adapted from Das K, Agarwal A, Andrew R, et al. Eur J Epidemiol. 2000;16:937-940 and Ghabrah TM, Strickland GT, Tsarev S, et al. Clin Infect Dis 1995;21:621-627.)*

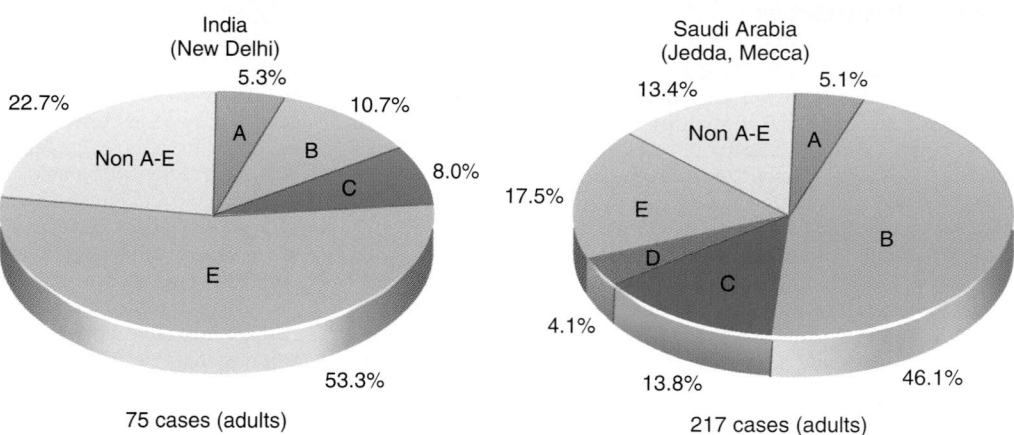

India (New Delhi)
A 5.3%
B 10.7%
C 8.0%
E 53.3%
Non A-E 22.7%
75 cases (adults)

Saudi Arabia (Jedda, Mecca)
A 5.1%
Non A-E 13.4%
E 17.5%
D 4.1%
C 13.8%
B 46.1%
217 cases (adults)

demic area.[42,63,114,142-156] However, rare cases of hepatitis E that appear to have been contracted locally do occur in industrialized countries (see later).

Although there are still questions about the relative sensitivity and specificity of serologic tests for anti-HEV, a more complete picture of the worldwide distribution and seroprevalence of HEV infection is emerging. Surprisingly, the prevalence of antibody to HEV in developing and documented endemic regions is much lower than expected (3% to 27%),[79,90,91,117,155,157-190] with a few exceptions,[191] and the prevalence of anti-HEV in nonendemic regions has been much higher than anticipated (1% to 28%).[79,90,116,136,192-203] In many, but not all, studies, the prevalence of anti-HEV in infants and children has been much lower than expected for a virus transmitted by the fecal-oral route.[91,116,117,157] The greatest incremental increase in the prevalence of anti-HEV has generally been found among young adults, the age group at the highest risk of clinical disease (Figs. 174-5 and 174-6).[91,116,157,204,205] In older adults from regions where the virus is endemic, the prevalence of anti-HEV is relatively constant (10% to 40%), with little or no difference in the prevalence between men and women.[91,116,157] Although such a pattern of age-specific anti-HEV might suggest a cohort effect representing the disappearance of HEV from endemic regions as was seen for HAV previously,[5] similar age-specific anti-HEV patterns have been reported for sera collected 10 years apart from the same population residing in an area that is highly endemic for HEV (see Fig. 174-5).[157] Thus, HEV appears to have epidemiologic characteristics that are quite different from those of most viruses, such as HAV, that are transmitted by the fecal-oral route.

Young children are susceptible to infection with HEV, because clinical disease has occurred with a similar frequency in all age groups in some epidemics[117] and sporadic clinical hepatitis E in children has been reported.[78,110,111-113,117,204,206-212] A male preponderance of cases has been observed in some but not all epidemics.[213] In areas where the disease is endemic, waterborne epidemics of hepatitis E are more likely to occur during the rainy season, when flooding of rivers occurs.[204] The famous Delhi epidemic of hepatitis E, occurring in the winter of 1955 to 1956, resulted from rechanneling of the flooded Yamuna River, causing raw sewage from a drainage ditch to be drawn into the intake pipes of a malfunctioning water treatment plant (see Fig. 174-6).[213] In the Kashmir region of India, epidemics of hepatitis E have followed the spring thaws, when feces accumulated over the winter have been washed into melting rivers.[214]

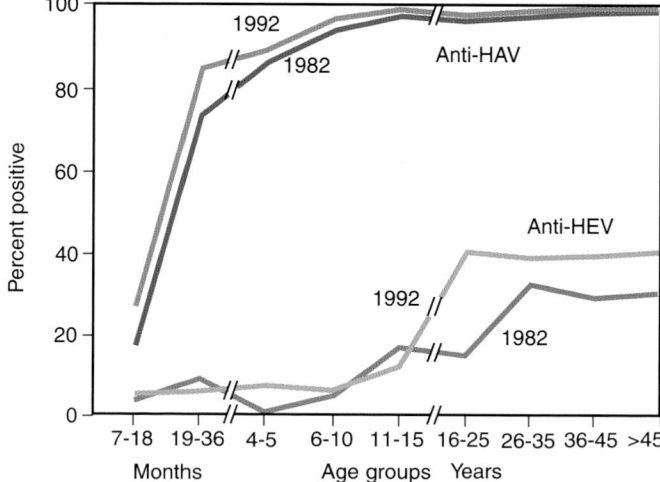

FIGURE 174-5. Age-specific prevalences of antibodies to hepatitis A virus and hepatitis E virus in a population residing in Pune, India. Antibodies were measured by enzyme-linked immunosorbent assay (ELISA). Infection with hepatitis A virus occurred at an earlier age and in a higher proportion of the population than infection with hepatitis E virus. *(Modified from Arankalle VA, Tsarev SA, Chadha MS, et al. Age-specific prevalence of antibodies to hepatitis A and E viruses in Pune, India, 1982 and 1992. J Infect Dis. 1995;171:447-450.)*

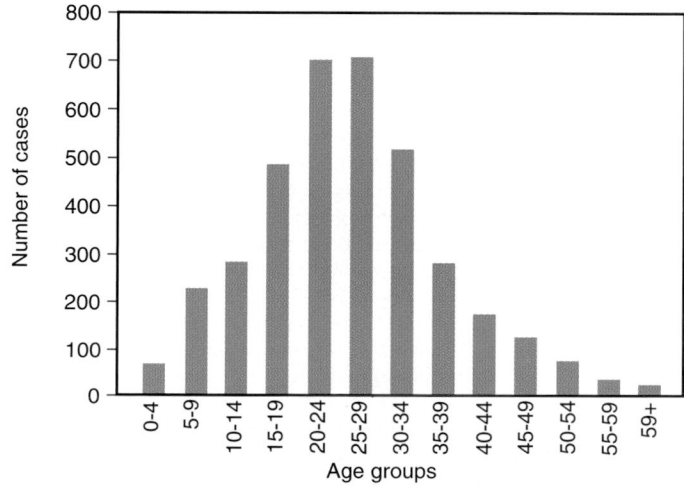

FIGURE 174-6. The age-specific clinical attack rate of hepatitis in a large, waterborne epidemic of hepatitis in Delhi, India, 1955 to 1956. The epidemic was caused by hepatitis E virus. *(Modified from Viswanathan R. Epidemiology. Indian J Med Res. 1957;45:1-29. Copyright © 1957 Indian Council of Medical Research.)*

Modes of Transmission

Most epidemics of hepatitis E have been waterborne,* but a few food-borne epidemics have been reported from China,[222-225] and cases of suspected hepatitis E have been epidemiologically linked to the consumption of raw or uncooked shellfish.[226] The epidemiologic risk factors associated with most sporadic cases of hepatitis E have not been identified. Person-to-person spread from patients to contacts appears to be relatively uncommon, at least in most studies.[110,113,227-229] However, one hospital-related outbreak has been reported.[230] The relatively rapid acquisition of anti-HEV during puberty raises the question of whether HEV might be sexually transmitted. However, there is no direct evidence for this. The duration of infectivity after exposure to HEV is not fully known, but viral RNA can be detected in the feces as early as 1 week and as late as 5 weeks after inoculation in experimental infections of nonhuman primates,[21] and protracted viremia of up to 45 to 112 days has been detected by polymerase chain reaction (PCR) in naturally infected patients.[231,232] HEV was detected in the feces of one experimentally infected volunteer as early as 4 weeks after exposure, persisted for 2½ weeks, and disappeared at approximately the time of onset of jaundice.[3] Viremia was detected as early as day 22 in a second volunteer, which was approximately 1 week earlier than the virus was detected in feces.[233]

Thus, there is a relatively long period of viremia and fecal shedding of HEV, principally during the period before the onset of disease.[231,232] Transmission of the other enterically transmitted hepatitis virus, HAV, by contaminated blood or blood products has been reported to occur occasionally,[234] suggesting that similar transmission of HEV might occur if blood or plasma were donated during the incubation period of hepatitis E. However, there is little or no conclusive seroepidemiologic evidence for the transmission of HEV by blood or blood products, and the risk appears to be low.[164,235-252]

Host Range, Experimental Transmission to Animals

Chimpanzees, Old World monkeys (rhesus, cynomolgus, pigtail macaques, African green monkeys), New World monkeys (owl monkeys, squirrel monkeys, tamarins),[8,40,53,206,253,254] swine,[255-258] rodents,[259-261] and sheep[262] have been reported to be susceptible to experimental infection with HEV. Extensive studies in primates have confirmed the utility of these animals, especially chimpanzees, rhesus monkeys, and cynomolgus monkeys, for experimental transmission of human strains of HEV. The susceptibility of swine, rats, and mice to infection with human HEV strains has been difficult to confirm, probably because of genotype-dependent or strain-dependent variations in transmissibility of HEV isolates.[256,263-265] The transmissibility of genotypes 1 and 2 HEV strains to these animals has been especially difficult to confirm. However, a genotype 3 strain of human origin is readily transmissible to swine and genotypes 3 and 4 strains recovered from swine have been transmitted to nonhuman primates, suggesting that these latter genotypes may be spread zoonotically (V. A. Arankalle, personal communication).[266] Seroepidemiologic studies of swine handlers further suggest that exposure to swine is a risk factor for acquiring HEV infection.[267-269]

Transmission of human strains of HEV to rodents also remains controversial. However, a high proportion of urban rats, as well as indigenous rodent species, has antibody to HEV.[265,270,271] Transmissible HEV-like agents have been recovered and serially propagated in laboratory rats (R. H. Purcell, unpublished). Although they have not yet been sequenced, in part because they replicate at a very low titer, they appear to be quite different from human strains of HEV and they appear not to be transmissible to nonhuman primates. Infection of rats with rat HEV does not appear to be associated with significant disease. Avian HEV comprising genotype 5 is genetically distant from the other HEV genotypes. It naturally infects chickens and produces a disease known as big liver and spleen disease and hepatitis-splenomegaly syndrome.[60,72] Avian HEV appears not to be transmissible to nonhuman primates and probably is not a risk to humans.

Antibodies to HEV have been detected in wild rhesus monkeys, bonnet macaques, and langurs in India and in Japanese macaques in Japan.[272,273] Similarly, captive rhesus monkeys within North American breeding colonies acquire antibody to HEV in a pattern strongly suggestive of endemic infection.[274,275] However, a virus has not yet been recovered from these animals, and it is not clear whether rhesus monkeys are infected with a unique simian HEV or whether human strains of HEV are circulating in these animals. Seronegative rhesus monkeys and cynomolgus monkeys as well as chimpanzees are highly susceptible to experimental infection with human strains of HEV. The course of infection in experimentally infected primates is similar to that in humans.[254] The incubation period to peak liver enzyme levels is generally 3 to 8 weeks but can be quite variable, depending on the dose of virus administered.[51,53,276,277] Peak viremia and peak shedding of virus in the feces occur during the incubation period and early acute phase of disease.[3,52,278,279] The detection of HEV antigens in the liver parallels the detection of viremia in the serum and feces,[73,278] and histologic changes in the liver generally parallel biochemical evidence of hepatitis.[279] As in humans, hepatitis E in nonhuman primates is acute and self-limiting. Unlike experimental hepatitis caused by the other human hepatitis viruses, experimental hepatitis E is dose dependent: High doses of virus are associated with histologic and biochemical evidence of hepatitis, whereas lower doses of virus (<1000 infectious doses) are more likely to be associated with a normal histologic appearance and normal serum liver enzyme values.[94] As in hepatitis A, the immune response in primates to HEV appears during the late incubation period or early acute phase of infection and is characterized by a brisk IgM and IgG anti-HEV response. Viremia may persist after the appearance of anti-HEV, which suggests that the virus coexists with antibody in immune complexes in the blood.[280] Infection with HEV protects nonhuman primates from hepatitis E after reexposure to the virus.[52,281,282] Evidence for fetal wastage was detected in one but not in a second study of experimental HEV infection of pregnant rhesus monkeys.[274,283] Antibody to HEV has been detected in several species of wild and domestic animals, including wild cynomolgus, rhesus and bonnet macaques, and langurs[273,284]; captive rhesus monkeys[274]; domestic swine and cattle[271,285]; dogs[271]; and wild rats and mice.[260,271,285]

Hepatitis E Virus Infection in Animals

In addition to the transmission of human strains of HEV to nonhuman primates, its transmission to swine, rats, mice, and sheep has also been reported.[255,257-259,261,262] Although reported in the literature, the transmission of human strains of HEV to domestic swine and laboratory rats and mice has been difficult to confirm.[256,263-265] In contrast, an HEV strain isolated from young domestic swine in the United States was experimentally transmissible to other swine and, furthermore, to nonhuman primates.[49,256] This virus was genetically distinct from all previously recovered human strains and probably represents the first recognized nonhuman strain of HEV.[275] Interestingly, two isolates of HEV from human hepatitis E patients in Tennessee and Minnesota, respectively, were shown to be closely related to swine HEV, and one of these was experimentally transmitted to swine.[47,50,286] Because swine HEV and the two human U.S. isolates were genetically very similar (including sharing specific nucleotide insertions), and because they came from the same geographic region, it is possible that all three of the viruses are of swine origin. Additionally, strains isolated from a pig and from a hepatitis E patient in Japan shared 99% nucleotide sequence identity.[287]

Because the epidemiology of HEV is somewhat unusual and because antibodies to HEV have been discovered in several species of animals, it has been proposed that animals may serve as a reservoir for HEV[260,288] and that environmental conditions can expose humans to animal feces containing HEV. The discovery that two HEV strains recovered from patients with hepatitis E in the United States were very closely related to swine HEV that was endemic to the same geographic region[47,50] supports the hypothesis that zoonoses of HEV may occur occasionally. However, the failure to prove conclusively the transmission of bona fide human strains of HEV to animals makes this an un-

*See references 1, 2, 41, 106, 119, 123, 175, 176, 205, 213, 215-221.

likely explanation for most cases of hepatitis E, whether epidemic or endemic. Indeed in India, genotype 1 circulates in humans, whereas genotype 4 circulates in swine in the same region.[69]

The transmission of animal viruses to humans via transplantation of animal organs and tissues to humans is a potential threat. The prospects for such transmissions have been greatly increased with improvements in procedures to control immediate and delayed rejection of animal organs by the human immune system. With the control of rejection a possibility, there is growing interest in the xenotransplantation of animal organs and tissues because of the shortage of suitable clinical materials of human origin. Swine are currently the donors of choice, although these animals harbor a number of viruses.[50,289] The discovery of swine HEV has added another virus to the list of viruses that must be excluded from swine herds before tissues and organs from those herds can be considered for xenotransplantation.

PATHOGENESIS

Incubation Period

The incubation period from exposure to the onset of clinical disease is approximately 28 to 40 days, based on analysis of waterborne epidemics in which the time of exposure was identified.[213] In experimental HEV transmission studies in humans, liver enzyme values peaked 42 to 46 days after ingestion of the virus.[3] In experimental infection of pregnant rhesus monkeys, the incubation period in one study was as short as 1 to 2 weeks,[283] but this was not observed in another similar study in which the incubation period averaged 4 to 5 weeks.[274] An incubation period of 4 to 6 weeks is in good agreement with the results of numerous experimental infections of nonhuman primates. The first appearance of viremia, detected by reverse transcriptase–polymerase chain reaction (RT-PCR), occurred 3 weeks after ingestion of the virus in one volunteer,[233] but viremia after intravenous exposure of nonhuman primates has been as short as 9 days.[21]

Viral Replication

HEV has been reported to replicate in cell culture.[105,259,290-292] However, because HEV does not replicate well in cell culture, its replicative pathway is not fully understood. The mechanisms of attachment to susceptible cells, entry, and uncoating are unknown, but it is assumed that the virus attaches to receptor sites on hepatocytes and possibly cells in the intestinal tract. After uncoating, the positive-sense, polyadenylated genome of HEV is probably directly translated via cellular mechanisms that recognize capped RNA. Translated ORF1 is probably cleaved by cellular proteases. The motif of a papain-like protease has been detected in the sequence of ORF1,[18] but a functional protease has not been demonstrated.[25] Replicative intermediate negative-strand RNA is probably synthesized by the viral RNA polymerase that is encoded by the 3′ region of ORF1. The viral polymerase probably also synthesizes subsequent strands of positive-sense full-length RNA, as well as at least two subgenomic messenger RNAs of 3.7- and 2.0-kb length, respectively.[14,293] Assembly and transport of HEV out of the cell are poorly understood. The gene product of ORF2 has been identified as the capsid protein; it contains hydrophobic, signal-like sequences at its amino-terminal end[20] as well as an arginine-rich region that probably binds the genomic RNA.[14] The gene product of ORF3 also contains a hydrophobic, signal-like sequence at its amino-terminal end, but it is not known whether this small immunogenic protein is incorporated into the virion.[20] Nothing is known about whether release of the virus from infected cells is an active process or the result of virus-mediated cell death, but virus is found in the bile during the acute phase of infection, and bile may be the principal source of HEV in the feces.[21,283,294]

Pathology

Although all viral hepatitis is histologically similar, the histologic changes in the liver of patients with hepatitis E are somewhat characteristic.[217] Histologic changes include focal necrosis associated with minimal infiltration. The lesions are not localized to a particular zone of the lobule. Inflammation is modest and consists of Kupffer cells and polymorphonuclear leukocytes in focal lesions that resemble drug-associated toxic hepatitis. Cholestatic hepatitis is a frequent finding and is characterized by ballooning hepatocytes, cytoplasmic cholestasis, and focal cytolytic necrosis. "Pseudoglandular" modification of the hepatocyte plates has been a prominent finding in some epidemics (Fig. 174-7). HEV replication has been found also in bile epithelial cells in rhesus monkeys and in many extrahepatic sites in swine.[295,296] The lack of a temporal relationship between viral replication in the liver and histopathologic and biochemical evidence of hepatitis suggests that HEV, like the other hepatitis viruses, is not cytopathogenic and that the pathogenesis of hepatitis E is immunologically mediated, but this remains speculative.[297]

The average severity of HEV infections is somewhat greater than that of hepatitis A infections. Thus the mortality of hepatitis E has been reported to be as high as 1%, whereas hepatitis A has a mortality of up to 0.2%.[298] However, the mortality of hepatitis E in pregnant women has been as high as 20%, with incremental increases in the mortality rate with each succeeding trimester of pregnancy.[122,299-307] In one study, the mortality rate in the first, second, and third trimesters of pregnancy were 1.5%, 8.5%, and 21.0%, respectively, and mother-to-child transmission was 50% in another study but 100% in a third (Fig. 174-8).[125,306,307] However, although frequently reported, a high mortality among pregnant women has not been detected in all studies, suggesting that the observation may be in part artifactual.[308,309] Nevertheless, none of the other four recognized hepatitis viruses appears to cause such severe hepatitis in pregnancy,[310,311] except perhaps for hepatitis B.[312,313] Acute hepatitis E superimposed on chronic hepatitis B has also been reported in pregnant and nonpregnant patients with fulminant hepatitis.[134] Superinfection of patients with hepatitis B

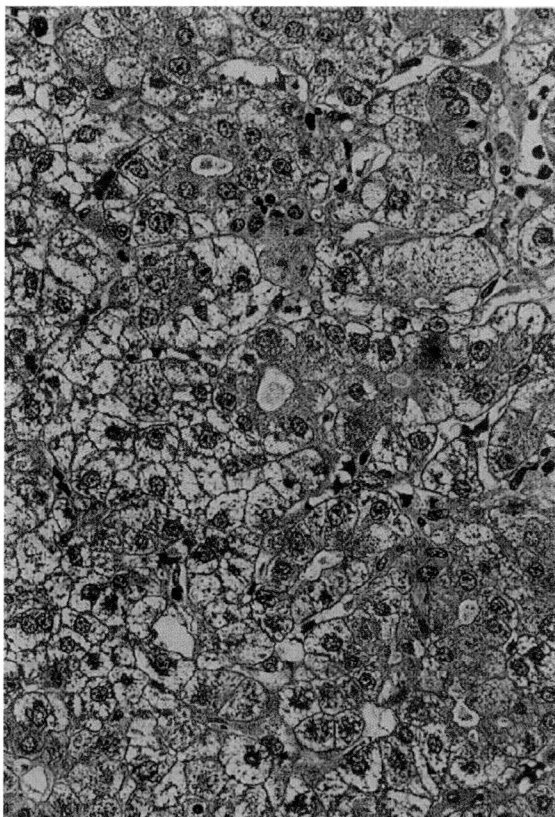

FIGURE 174-7. Liver biopsy from a 30-year-old Pakistani patient with acute hepatitis E (H&E, ×100). The specimen demonstrates acinar transformation ("pseudoglandular" alteration) and cholestasis within the lumen. Hepatocytes demonstrate "ballooning" and degeneration. *(Courtesy of M. Sjogren.)*

FIGURE 174-8. The outcome of acute hepatitis E in pregnant women, United Arab Emirates. All women positive for anti–hepatitis E virus (HEV) were screened for viremia and 30% were acutely infected (anti-HEV appears early during acute infection); the other 70% had evidence of a previous HEV infection. All of the acutely infected women had evidence of hepatitis E, and 43% had severe disease; 22% had fulminant hepatitis and half of these died. (*Adapted from Kumar RM, Uduman S, Rana S, et al. Eur J Obstet Gyn Reprod Bio. 2001; 100:9-15.*)

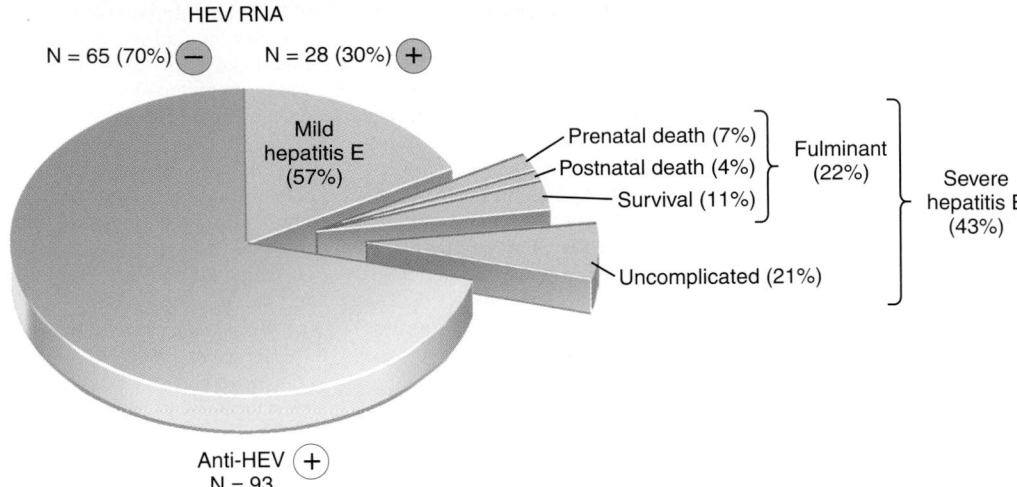

or with chronic liver disease can lead to increased morbidity and mortality.[314,315] Fulminant non-A, non-B hepatitis occurring in nonendemic areas or in nonpregnant women in India appeared not to be caused by HEV in some studies.[304,316] However, HEV has been detected in fulminant hepatitis cases in Japan.[317]

Immune Response

Specific IgM and IgG immune responses to HEV occur early in the infection, usually by the onset of clinical illness. In this respect, hepatitis E resembles hepatitis A, and a serologic diagnosis usually can be made at the time of presentation of the patient. Anti-HEV IgM disappears after several months, whereas anti-HEV IgG persists.[107] IgG anti-HEV appears to diminish in titer at a more rapid rate than antibody to hepatitis A, raising questions about the duration of immunity after hepatitis E. However, anti-HEV has been detected as long as 12 to 14 years after infection.[93,318,319] Anti-HEV of the IgA class has also been detected in the serum of naturally infected individuals.[320] The significance of such antibody is unknown. All isolates of HEV to date are serologically related. Regarding the human HEV genotypes 1 through 4, convalescent antibody produced in response to infection with one strain probably protects against subsequent exposure to all other strains[7,8,12,51-54] but it is not known whether this is true for the avian or other recently discovered unclassified HEV strains. Little is known about the cell-mediated immune response to HEV in humans, but lymphocytes of patients with acute hepatitis E show sensitization to HEV peptides.[321]

CLINICAL MANIFESTATIONS

Symptoms

Hepatitis E cannot be differentiated from other types of viral hepatitis on the basis of clinical presentation (Fig. 174-9).[5,63,78] Clinically, the severity of HEV infections may range from unapparent to fulminant.[5,107,214,228,322] However, most patients experience abdominal pain and tenderness, nausea, vomiting, and fever.[323] Serologic tests have confirmed that clinical disease can occur in individuals of all ages, including children.[78,110,112,113,117,207] Hepatitis E never progresses to chronicity, but prolonged persistence of anti-HEV IgM (21 months) was reported in one patient.[91] Recurrent (bimodal) hepatitis E has not been reported, except in experimentally infected nonhuman primates.[284] In contrast, recurrent hepatitis A is relatively common (see Chapter 170).[324]

As noted earlier, in experimental infections of nonhuman primates, the clinical presentation of hepatitis E is dose dependent: The severity of infection is directly related to the infectivity titer of challenge virus.[94] It is not known whether such a clinical-infectious dose rela-

tionship exists for naturally infected humans, but if so, it could explain how HEV can be maintained in a population with little or no clinical disease.

Complications

The only complications of hepatitis E are those related to severe hepatitis in pregnancy and in those with chronic liver disease. In addition to the apparent high mortality of infected pregnant women, a high incidence of fetal wastage has been reported.[122,325-327] In one study of 10 consecutive pregnant women presenting with hepatitis E in India, 6 developed fulminant hepatitis and 2 died.[328] Of the 8 infants available for study, 2 died, one of which had massive hepatic necrosis. Five of the infants had elevated levels of liver enzymes and HEV viremia in cord blood or early postnatal serum samples, as detected by RT-PCR. In another study of 28 pregnant women with hepatitis E in the United Arab Emirates, 43% had severe disease with a mortality rate of 11%.[307] Of 26 offspring, all had clinical hepatitis E, and 4% died.

LABORATORY DIAGNOSIS

Hepatitis E is the most likely cause of waterborne epidemics of hepatitis occurring in developing countries in which HAV infection is still highly endemic. However, in developing countries in which improved public health has resulted in a high prevalence of young adults who remain susceptible to HAV infection, waterborne epidemics may be caused by HAV or HEV. In such epidemics, unusually severe hepatitis in pregnant women should suggest hepatitis E. Clinical hepatitis E is rare in industrialized countries and is usually associated with recent travel from a region in which hepatitis E is endemic.[42] However, because cases of indigenous hepatitis E have been reported from a number of industrialized countries, including the United States, HEV must be considered as a possible, albeit rare, cause in all cases of acute viral hepatitis.[47,50,275,286,329-333]

Serologic Tests

As with all types of viral hepatitis, serologic tests are necessary to establish a diagnosis. Hepatitis E can usually be diagnosed by the detection of anti-HEV of the IgM class in a serum sample obtained during the acute phase of disease. Antibody of the IgG class may also be present (see Fig. 174-9). Commercial tests for IgM and IgG are available in Europe, Asia, and Canada but not in the United States. These include tests based on ELISA and Western blot technology and utilize synthetic peptides or recombinant antigens expressed from ORF2 or ORF3, or both, of the viral genome. The assays vary widely in sensitivity and specificity.[93] In general, assays based on antigens derived from ORF2 of the virus, with or without antigens from ORF3, perform

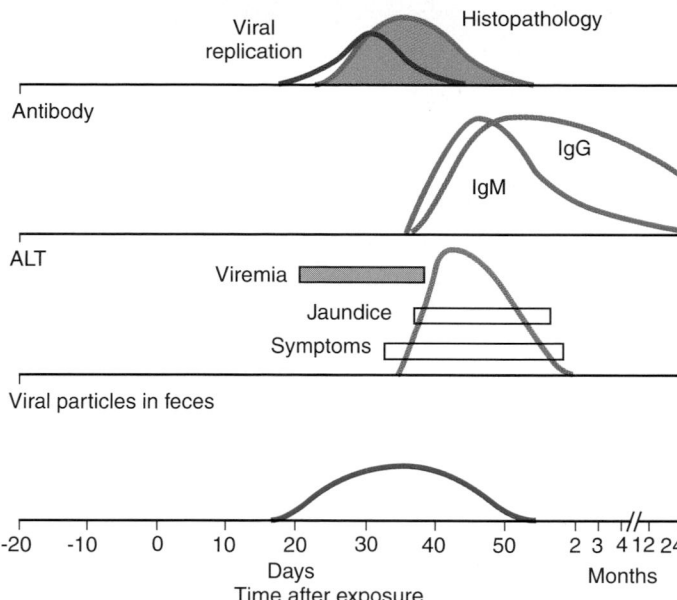

FIGURE 174-9. Diagram of clinical and serologic events in a typical case of acute hepatitis E. Antibody patterns are based on enzyme-linked immunosorbent assay (ELISA) results; viremia and fecal shedding are based on polymerase chain reaction data. *(Modified from Purcell RH, Hoofnagle JH, Ticehurst J, et al. Hepatitis viruses. In: Schmidt NJ, Emmons RW, eds. Diagnostic Procedures for Viral, Rickettsial and Chlamydial Infections. 6th ed. Washington, DC: American Public Health Association; 1989:957-1065.)*

much better than assays based solely on antigens derived from ORF3. Tests based on ELISA methods perform slightly better than Western blot assays. Based on field studies with the best of these assays, anti-HEV IgM can be detected in up to 96% of acute infections if a serum sample is obtained 1 to 4 weeks after the onset of disease.[76,97,101,107,112,117,334,335] By 3 months after the onset of the acute phase, anti-HEV IgM is no longer detectable in at least 50% of hepatitis E patients.[106,117,135] Anti-HEV of the IgM class reaches peak titers (1:1000-1:10,000) during the first 4 weeks of disease.[106,107,336,337] A rising titer of anti-HEV IgG is also diagnostic. Peak titers of anti-HEV IgG (1:1000-1:100,000) are detected 2 to 4 weeks after the onset of disease and diminish relatively rapidly thereafter.[90,106,107] Thus a very high titer of anti-HEV IgG may also suggest recent infection.[92] Some cases of hepatitis E appear not to have a serologic response to the virus: acute-phase feces from well-studied seronegative cases of viral hepatitis associated with waterborne epidemics of hepatitis E have transmitted HEV to nonhuman primates (R. H. Purcell and S. U. Emerson, unpublished data). The infected primates had hepatitis E with a typical serologic response to the virus. It is not known why these patients remained seronegative or whether they would be susceptible to a second case of hepatitis E after reexposure to the virus.

Molecular Tests

Molecular approaches to studying the epidemiology of HEV are promising. However, because HEV does not cause chronic infections, the value of molecular approaches has been limited to the study of acute infections.[232,313,338-340] Molecular tools such as RT-PCR have been useful in identifying modes of transmission and estimating the duration of infectivity in cases of hepatitis E.[21,66,231-233] However, a positive result for HEV RNA by RT-PCR is not the equivalent of demonstrating infectivity, because RT-PCR is generally more sensitive than infectivity for measuring HEV. Also, RT-PCR has been useful for monitoring for HEV in sewage.[332,341,342]

Genomic RNA of HEV can be detected in acute-phase feces and blood by RT-PCR in most naturally infected humans and experimentally infected nonhuman primates during the acute phase of the disease (see Fig. 174-9).[21,232,253] The virus can often be detected in the bile at this time.[6,21,206,283,343] HEV may be detected in blood and feces of primates for up to 5 weeks after the onset of disease.[21] Primers for RT-PCR must be selected carefully because HEV is genetically heterogeneous. Primers located in highly conserved regions of the genome or degenerate primers must be used to ensure detection of all recognized variants of HEV.

IMMUNITY

Because the immunopathogenesis of hepatitis E is poorly understood, the role of immunity in preventing reinfection is speculative. It has been suggested that infection with HEV during childhood results in an unapparent infection with subsequent rapid loss of anti-HEV and immunity and that clinical disease results from reexposure of such individuals as young adults.[209] This can be neither confirmed nor refuted at present. However, when nonhuman primates that are convalescent from experimental hepatitis E are rechallenged with the same or distantly related HEV strains, they are protected against a second case of hepatitis E.[7,8,12,51-54] Furthermore, a correlation was found between the presence of anti-HEV IgG and resistance to clinical hepatitis in cohorts exposed to HEV in waterborne epidemics.[107,219,335] The success of passive and active immunoprophylaxis under experimental conditions (see later) argues for antibody-mediated immunity after HEV infection.

PREVENTION

General Sanitation

The role of improved sanitation and public hygiene in the control of hepatitis E is somewhat hard to assess. Clearly, industrialized countries with a generally high level of public sanitation do not experience epidemics of waterborne hepatitis E or significant endemic or sporadic disease, although hepatitis A continues to be an important cause of clinical disease in some of these countries, for example, the United States. In developing countries, even where the prevalence of antibody to HAV is extremely high, the prevalence of antibody to HEV is much lower.[167,173,177,180,181,184,187,202,344] These observations suggest that HEV is either much less readily spread or much less stable than HAV in the environment, or that other factors are involved. It is difficult at present to assess the importance of animal reservoirs for the maintenance of HEV in the environment, but this clearly needs to be studied. Regardless of mechanisms of transmission, however, improved sanitation is important in controlling infectious diseases that have fecal-oral transmission as a prominent part of their epidemiology.

Immunoprophylaxis

Attempts to prevent hepatitis E by the administration of normal immune globulin have generally been unsuccessful or uncertain, even when the immune globulin was manufactured from pooled plasma obtained from areas endemic for hepatitis E.[41,218,228,345,346] Failure of such globulin to protect may be related to the relatively low prevalence and titer of anti-HEV in such populations. One study failed to demonstrate protection of nonhuman primates after administration of convalescent serum obtained from a volunteer who had been experimentally infected with HEV 4 years earlier, but the authors failed to demonstrate anti-HEV in the infused monkeys at the time of challenge with HEV, and they employed a very large but unquantified intravenous dose of challenge virus.[347] Such a study may have little relevance to predicting the efficacy of immune globulin with a high titer of anti-HEV administered to individuals with exposure to relatively small doses of HEV acquired by the natural route of infection. In contrast, infusion of nonhuman primates with convalescent serum or plasma from other primates experimentally infected with HEV has protected them against hepatitis E.[280,348] However, infection was not necessarily prevented, probably because relatively large doses of HEV were administered intravenously. These studies suggest that passively acquired anti-HEV does modify hepatitis E and may be useful for passive immunoprophylaxis in pregnant women during epidemics. Monoclonal antibodies (Mabs) that neutralize HEV have been recovered from chimpanzees.[103] These "humanized" Mabs can prevent hepatitis E in nonhuman primates and may be useful for immunoprophylaxis and immunotherapy in humans.

There are no commercially available vaccines for the prevention of hepatitis E. However, attempts to protect primates against experimental hepatitis E by vaccination with recombinant HEV-derived proteins have yielded encouraging results.[280,349-353] Among the most extensively tested are proteins expressed from baculovirus in insect cells. The full-length (72-kDa) protein encoded by ORF2 is spontaneously processed in insect cells to a protein of approximately 50 to 60 kDa by proteolytic cleavage of the amino- and carboxyl-terminal portions of the protein.[53,96,99,354-356] The resultant protein is more soluble than the full-length protein, can form virus-like particles, and is highly immunogenic in nonhuman primates.[53,99,350-352] It is also useful as an antigen for ELISA.[53,99] This protein, when combined with alum adjuvant, protected against hepatitis E after challenge with homologous or heterologous HEV.[280,350-352,357,358] The vaccine generally did not protect against infection, possibly because the challenge virus was administered intravenously and at a high dose. However, when a smaller challenge dose was administered, the vaccine also protected against infection.[357] Clinical trials of the insect cell–produced candidate hepatitis E vaccine are in progress, but a commercial vaccine is not expected to be available for several years.[359]

Other approaches to vaccine development for hepatitis E have also been attempted.[350,360] Following DNA vaccination with the ORF2 gene, two of four macaques were protected against HEV infection.[360] Co-delivery of cytokine genes is reported to augment the immune response to ORF2 DNA.[361]

THERAPY

There is no specific therapy for hepatitis E. Patients should be treated symptomatically as for hepatitis A. Because hepatitis E does not progress to chronicity, attempts to treat with antiviral agents are not warranted.

REFERENCES

1. Khuroo MS. Study of an epidemic of non-A, non-B hepatitis. Possibility of another human hepatitis virus distinct from post-transfusion non-A, non-B type. Am J Med. 1980;68:818-824.
2. Wong DC, Purcell RH, Sreenivasan MA, et al. Epidemic and endemic hepatitis in India: Evidence for non-A/non-B hepatitis virus etiology. Lancet. 1980;2:876-878.
3. Balayan MS, Andjaparidze AG, Savinskaya SS, et al. Evidence for a virus in non-A, non-B hepatitis transmitted via the fecal-oral route. Intervirology. 1983;20:23-31.
4. Bradley DW. Hepatitis non-A, non-B viruses become identified as hepatitis C and E viruses. In: Melnick JL, ed. Progress in Medical Virology. Basel: Karger; 1990: 101-135.
5. Purcell RH, Ticehurst JR. Enterically transmitted non-A, non-B hepatitis: Epidemiology and clinical characteristics. In: Zuckerman A, ed. Viral Hepatitis and Liver Disease. New York: Alan R Liss; 1988:131-137.
6. Reyes GR, Purdy MA, Kim JP, et al. Isolation of a cDNA from the virus responsible for enterically transmitted non-A, non-B hepatitis. Science. 1990;247:1335-1339.
7. Bradley DW. Enterically-transmitted non-A, non-B hepatitis. Br Med Bull. 1990;46:442-461.
8. Ticehurst J. Identification and characterization of hepatitis E virus. In: Hollinger FB, Lemon SM, Margolis H, eds. Hepatitis and Liver Disease. Baltimore: Williams & Wilkins; 1991:501-513.
9. Kapikian AZ, Chanock RM. Norwalk group of viruses. In: Fields BN, ed. Virology. New York: Raven; 1985:1495-1517.
10. Xing L, Kato K, Li T, et al. Recombinant hepatitis E capsid protein self-assembles into a dual-domain T = 1 particle presenting native virus epitopes. Virology 1999;265:35-45.
11. Favorov MO, Goldberg EZ, Gurov AV, et al. Some physicochemical properties of non-A, non-B hepatitis virus with the fecal-oral mechanism of transmission and specific diagnosis of the disease (in Russian). Vopr Virusol. 1989;1:47-50.
12. Bradley DW, Andjaparidze AG, Cook EH Jr, et al. Etiologic agent of enterically-transmitted non-A, non-B hepatitis. J Gen Virol. 1988;69:731-738.
13. Jothikumar N, Aparna K, Kamatchiammal S, et al. Detection of hepatitis E virus in raw and treated wastewater with the polymerase chain reaction. Appl Environ Microbiol. 1993;59:2558-2562.
14. Tam AW, Smith MM, Guerra ME, et al. Hepatitis E virus (HEV): Molecular cloning and sequencing of the full-length viral genome. Virology. 1991;185:120-131.
15. Huang C-C, Nguyen D, Fernandez J, et al. Molecular cloning and sequencing of the Mexico isolate of hepatitis E virus (HEV). Virology. 1992;191:550-558.
16. Kabrane-Lazizi Y, Meng XJ, Purcell RH, Emerson SU. Evidence that the genomic RNA of hepatitis E virus is capped. J Virol. 1999;73:8848-8850.
17. Emerson SU, Zhang M, Meng XJ, et al. Recombinant hepatitis E virus genomes infectious for primates: Importance of capping and discovery of a cis-reactive element. Proc Natl Acad Sci U S A. 2001;98:15270-15275.
18. Koonin EV, Gorbalenya AK, Purdy MA, et al. Computer-assisted assignment of functional domains in the nonstructural polyprotein of hepatitis E virus: Delineation of an additional group of positive-strand RNA plant and animal viruses. Proc Natl Acad Sci U S A. 1992;89:8259-8263.
19. Gorbalenya AK, Koonin EV, Lai MM-C. Putative papain-related proteases of positive-strand RNA viruses. FEBS Lett. 1991;288:201-205.
20. Reyes GR, Huang C-C, Yarbough PO, et al. Hepatitis E virus. J Hepatol. 1991;13:S155-S161.
21. Tsarev SA, Emerson SU, Reyes GR, et al. Characterization of a prototype strain of hepatitis E virus. Proc Natl Acad Sci U S A. 1992;89:559-563.
22. Gorbalenya AK, Koonin EV, Donchenko AP, et al. Two related superfamilies of putative helicases involved in replication, recombination, repair and expression of DNA and RNA genomes. Nucleic Acids Res. 1989;17:4713-4730.
23. Gorbalenya AK, Koonin EV, Donchenko AP, et al. A novel superfamily of nucleoside triphosphate-binding motif-containing proteins which are probably involved in duplex unwinding in DNA and RNA replication and recombination. FEBS Lett. 1988;239:16-24.
24. Koonin EV. The phylogeny of RNA-dependent RNA polymerases of positive-strand RNA viruses. J Gen Virol. 1991;72:2197-2206.
25. Ropp SL, Tam AW, Beames B, et al. Expression of the hepatitis E virus ORF1. Arch Virol. 2000;145:1321-1337.
26. Magden J, Takeda N, Li T, et al. Virus-specific mRNA capping enzyme encoded by hepatitis E virus. J Virol. 2001;75:6249-6255.
27. Agrawal S, Gupta D, Panda SK. The 3' end of hepatitis E virus (HEV) genome binds specifically to the viral RNA-dependent polymerase (RdRp). Virology 2001;282: 87-101.
28. Bradley DW, Purdy MA. Molecular and serological characteristics of hepatitis E virus. In: Nishioka K, Suzuki H, Mishiro S, et al, eds. Viral Hepatitis and Liver Disease. Tokyo: Springer-Verlag; 1993:42-45.
29. Jameel S, Zafrullah M, Ozdener MH, et al. Expression in animal cells and characterization of the hepatitis E virus structural proteins. J Virol. 1996;70:207-216.
30. Tyagi S, Jameel S, Lal SK. The full-length and N-terminal deletion of ORF2 protein of hepatitis E virus can dimerize. Biochem Biophys Res Commun. 2001;286: 214-221.
31. Xiaofang, L, Zafrullah M, Ahmad F, Jameel S. A C-terminal hydrophobic region is required for homo-oligomerization of the hepatitis E virus capsid (ORF2) protein. J Biomed Biotechnol. 2001;1:122-128.
32. Zhang JZ, Ng MH, Xia NS, et al. Conformational antigenic determinants generated by interactions between a bacterially expressed recombinant peptide of the hepatitis E virus structural protein. J Med Virol. 2001;64:125-132.
33. Zafrullah M, Ozdener MH, Panda SK, et al. The ORF3 protein of hepatitis E virus is a phosphoprotein that associates with the cytoskeleton. J Virol. 1997;71:9045-9053.
34. Korkaya H, Jameel S, Gupta D, et al. The ORF3 protein of hepatitis E virus binds to Src homology 3 domains and activates MAPK. J Biol Chem. 2001;276:42389-42400.
35. Tyagi S, Korkaya H, Zafrullah M, et al. The phosphorylated form of the ORF3 protein of hepatitis E virus interacts with its non-glycosylated form of the major capsid protein, ORF2. J Biol Chem. 2002;277:22759-22769.
36. Tyagi S, Jameel S, Lal SK. Self-association and mapping of the interaction domain of hepatitis E virus ORF3 protein. J Virol. 2001; 75:2493-2498.
37. Cubitt W, Bradley D, Carter M, et al. Caliciviridae. Arch Virol Suppl. 1995;10: 359-363.
38. Fry KE, Tam AW, Smith MM, et al. Hepatitis E virus (HEV): Strain variation in the nonstructural gene region encoding consensus motifs for an RNA-dependent RNA polymerase and an ATP/GTP binding site. Virus Genes. 1992;6:173-185.
39. Virus Taxonomy: Classification and Nomenclature of Viruses. Eighth Report of the International Committee on Taxonomy of Viruses. In press.
40. Mast EE, Alter MJ. Epidemiology of viral hepatitis: An overview. Semin Virol. 1993;4:273-283.
41. Velazquez O, Stetler HC, Avila C, et al. Epidemic transmission of enterically transmitted non-A, non-B hepatitis in Mexico, 1986-1987. JAMA. 1990;263:3281-3285.
42. Centers for Disease Control and Prevention. Hepatitis E among US travelers, 1989-1992. MMWR Morb Mortal Wkly Rep. 1993;42:1-4.
43. Chatterjee R, Tsarev S, Pillot J, et al. African strains of hepatitis E virus that are distinct from Asian strains. J Med Virol. 1997;53:139-144.
44. Van Cuyck-Gandre H, Zhang HY, Tsarev SA, et al. Characterization of hepatitis E virus (HEV) from Algeria and Chad by partial genome sequence. J Med Virol. 1997;53:340-347.
45. Gouvea V, Snellings N, Cohen SJ, et al. Hepatitis E virus in Nepal: Similarities with the Burmese and Indian variants. Virus Res. 1997;53:87-96.
46. Huang R, Nakazono N, Ishii K, et al. Existing variations on the gene structure of hepatitis E virus strains from some regions of China. J Med Virol. 1995;47:303-308.
47. Schlauder GG, Dawson GJ, Erker JC, et al. The sequence and phylogenetic analysis of a novel hepatitis E virus isolated from a patient with acute hepatitis reported in the United States. J Gen Virol. 1998;79:447-456.
48. Yin SR, Purcell RH, Emerson SU. A new Chinese isolate of hepatitis E virus: Comparison with strains recovered from different geographical regions. Virus Genes. 1994;9:23-32.

49. Yin SR, Tsarev SA, Purcell RH, et al. Partial sequence comparison of eight new Chinese strains of hepatitis E virus suggests the genome sequence is relatively stable. J Med Virol. 1993;41:230-241.

50. Meng XJ, Halbur PG, Shapiro MS, et al. Genetic and experimental evidence for cross-species infection by the swine hepatitis E virus. J Virol. 1998;72:9714-9721.

51. Bradley DW, Krawczynski K, Cook EH, et al. Enterically transmitted non-A, non-B hepatitis: Serial passage of disease in cynomolgus macaques and tamarins and recovery of disease-associated 27- to 34-nm viruslike particles. Proc Natl Acad Sci U S A. 1987;84:6277-6281.

52. Bradley DW, Krawczynski K, Cook EH Jr, et al. Enterically transmitted non-A, non-B hepatitis: Etiology of disease and laboratory studies in nonhuman primates. In: Zuckerman AJ, ed. Viral Hepatitis and Liver Disease. New York: Alan R Liss; 1988:138-147.

53. Tsarev SA, Tsareva TS, Emerson SU. ELISA for antibody to hepatitis E virus (HEV) based on complete open-reading frame-2 protein expressed in insect cells: Identification of HEV infection in primates. J Infect Dis. 1993;168:369-378.

54. Yin S, Bao Z, Tian X, et al. Protection of rhesus monkeys from challenge with hepatitis E virus. Bull Acad Mil Med Sci. 1992;16:115-118.

55. Aye TT, Uchida T, Ma XZ, et al. Complete nucleotide sequence of a hepatitis E virus isolated from the Xinjiang epidemic (1986-1988) of China. Nucleic Acids Res. 1992;20:3512.

56. Aye TT, Uchida T, Ma X, et al. Sequence and gene structure of the hepatitis E virus isolated from Myanmar. Virus Genes. 1993;7:95-110.

57. Bi SL, Purdy MA, McCaustland KA, et al. The sequence of hepatitis E virus isolated directly from a single source during an outbreak in China. Virus Res. 1993;28:233-247.

58. Hsieh SY, Yang PY, Ho YP, et al. Identification of a novel strain of hepatitis E virus responsible for sporadic acute hepatitis in Taiwan. J Med Virol. 1998;55:300-304.

59. Schlauder GG, Desai SM, Zanetti AR, et al. Novel hepatitis E virus (HEV) isolates from Europe: Evidence for additional genotypes of HEV. J Med Virol. 1999;57:243-251.

60. Haqschenas G, Shivaprasad HL, Woolcock PR, et al. Genetic identification and characterization of a novel virus related to human hepatitis E virus from chickens with hepatitis-splenomegaly syndrome in the United States. J Gen Virol. 2001;82:2449-2462.

61. Hijikata M, Hayashi S, Trinh NT, et al. Genotyping of hepatitis E virus from Vietnam. Intervirology. 2002;45:101-104.

62. Al-Kandari S, Nordenfelt E, Al-Nakib B, et al. Acute non-A, non-B hepatitis in Kuwait. Scand J Infect Dis. 1987;19:611-616.

63. Ghabrah T, Strickland T, Tsarev S, et al. Acute viral hepatitis in Saudi Arabia: Seroepidemiological analysis, risk factors, clinical manifestations, and evidence for a sixth hepatitis agent. Clin Infect Dis. 1995;21:621-627.

64. Glynn MJ, Rashid A, Antao AJO, et al. Imported epidemic non-A, non-B hepatitis in Qatar. J Med Virol. 1985;17:371-375.

65. Skidmore SJ, Yarbough PO, Gabor KA, et al. Imported hepatitis E in UK. Lancet. 1991;337:1541.

66. Pina S, Jofre J, Emerson SU, et al. Characterization of a strain of infectious hepatitis E virus isolated from sewage in a non-endemic area. Appl Environ Microbiol. 1998;64:4485-4488.

67. Takahashi M, Nishizawa T, Miyajima H, et al. Swine hepatitis E virus strains in Japan form four phylogenetic clusters comparable with those of Japanese isolates of human hepatitis E virus. J Gen Virol. 2003;84:851-862.

68. Wang YC, Zhang HY, Xia NS, et al. Prevalence, isolation, and partial sequence analysis of hepatitis E virus from domestic animals in China. J Med Virol. 2002;67:516-521.

69. Arankalle VA, Chobe LP, Joshi MV, et al. Human and swine hepatitis E viruses from Western India belong to different genotypes. J Hepatol. 2002;36:417-425.

70. Hsieh SY, Meng XJ, Wu YH, et al. Identity of a novel swine hepatitis E virus in Taiwan forming a monphyletic group with Taiwan isolates of human hepatitis E virus. J Clin Microbiol. 1999;37:3828-3834.

71. Huang FF, Haqshenas G, Shivaprasad HL, et al. Heterogeneity and seroprevalence of a newly identified avian hepatitis E virus from chickens in the United States. J Clin Microbiol. 2002;40:4197-4202.

72. Haqshenas G, Huang FF, Fenaux M, et al. The putative capsid protein of the newly identified avian hepatitis E virus shares antigenic epitopes with that of swine and human hepatitis E viruses and chicken big liver and spleen disease virus. J Gen Virol. 2002;83:2201-2209.

73. Krawczynski K, Bradley DW. Enterically transmitted non-A, non-B hepatitis: Identification of virus-associated antigen in experimentally infected cynomolgus macaques. J Infect Dis. 1989;159:1042-1049.

74. Purdy MA, Carson D, McCaustland KA, et al. Viral specificity of hepatitis E virus antigens identified by fluorescent antibody assay using recombinant HEV proteins. J Med Virol. 1994;44:212-214.

75. Yarbough PO, Tam AW, Gabor K, et al. Assay development of diagnostic tests for hepatitis E. Viral Hep Liv Dis. 1994;367-370.

76. Favorov MO, Fields HA, Purdy MA, et al. Serologic identification of hepatitis E virus infections in epidemic and endemic settings. J Med Virol. 1992;36:246-250.

77. He J, Tam AW, Yarbough PO, et al. Expression and diagnostic utility of hepatitis E virus putative structural proteins expressed in insect cells. J Clin Microbiol. 1993;31:2167-2173.

78. Hyams KC, Purdy MA, Kaur M, et al. Acute sporadic hepatitis E in Sudanese children: Analysis based on a new Western blot assay. J Infect Dis. 1992;165:1001-1005.

79. Paul DA, Knigge MF, Ritter A, et al. Determination of hepatitis E virus seroprevalence by using recombinant fusion proteins and synthetic peptides. J Infect Dis. 1994;169:801-806.

80. Purdy MA, McCaustland KA, Krawczynski K, et al. Expression of a hepatitis E virus (HEV)-trpE fusion protein containing epitopes recognized by antibodies in sera from human cases and experimentally infected primates. Arch Virol. 1992;123:335-349.

81. Coursaget P, Buisson Y, Depril N, et al. Mapping of linear B cell epitopes on open reading frame 2- and 3-encoded proteins of hepatitis E virus using synthetic peptides. FEMS Microbiol Lett. 1993;109:251-256.

82. Favorov MO, Khudyakov YE, Fields HA, et al. Enzyme immunoassay for the detection of antibody to hepatitis E virus based on synthetic peptides. J Virol Methods. 1994;46:237-250.

83. Kaur M, Hyams KC, Purdy MA, et al. Human linear B-cell epitopes encoded by the hepatitis E virus include determinants in the RNA-dependent RNA polymerase. Proc Natl Acad Sci U S A. 1992;89:3855-3858.

84. Qi Z, Cui D, Pan W, et al. Synthesis and application of hepatitis E virus peptides to diagnosis. J Virol Methods. 1995;55:55-66.

85. Yarbough PO, Tam AW, Fry KE, et al. Hepatitis E virus: Identification of type-common epitopes. J Virol. 1991;65:5790-5797.

86. Riddell MA, Li F, Anderson DA. Identification of immunodominant and conformational epitopes in the capsid protein of hepatitis E virus by using monoclonal antibodies. J Virol. 2000;74:8011-8017.

87. Schofield DJ, Purcell RH, Nguyen HT, Emerson SU. Monoclonal antibodies that neutralize HEV recognize an antigenic site at the carboxy terminus of an ORF2 protein vaccine. Vaccine. 2003;22:257-267.

88. Khudyakov YE, Khudyakova NS, Fields HA, et al. Epitope mapping in proteins of hepatitis E virus. Virology. 1993;194:89-96.

89. Khudyakov YE, Khudyakova NS, Jue DL, et al. Comparative characterization of antigenic epitopes in the immunodominant region of the protein encoded by open reading frame 3 in Burmese and Mexican strains of hepatitis E virus. J Gen Virol. 1994;75:641-646.

90. Dawson GJ, Chau KH, Cabal CM, et al. Solid-phase enzyme-linked immunosorbent assay for hepatitis E virus IgG and IgM antibodies utilizing recombinant antigens and synthetic peptides. J Virol Methods. 1992;38:175-186.

91. Lee S-D, Wang Y-J, Lu R-H, et al. Seroprevalence of antibody to hepatitis E virus among Chinese subjects in Taiwan. Hepatology. 1994;19:866-870.

92. Ghabrah TM, Tsarev S, Yarbough PO, et al. Comparison of tests for antibody to hepatitis E virus. J Med Virol. 1998;55:134-137.

93. Mast EE, Alter MJ, Holland PV, et al. Evaluation of assays for antibody to hepatitis E virus by a serum panel. Hepatology. 1998;27:857-861.

94. Tsarev SA, Tsareva TS, Emerson SU, et al. Infectivity titration of a prototype strain of hepatitis E virus in cynomolgus monkeys. J Med Virol. 1994;43:135-142.

95. He J, Ching WM, Yarbough P, et al. Purification of a baculovirus-expressed hepatitis E virus structural protein and utility in an enzyme-linked immunosorbent assay. J Clin Microbiol. 1995;33:3308-3311.

96. Zhang Y, McAtee P, Yarbough P, et al. Expression, characterization, and immunoreactivities of a soluble hepatitis E virus putative capsid protein species expressed in insect cells. Clin Diagn Lab Immunol. 1997;4:423-428.

97. Koshy A, Grover S, Hyams K, et al. Short-term IgM and IgG antibody responses to hepatitis E virus infection. Scand J Infect Dis. 1996;28:439-441.

98. Li F, Zhuang H, Kolivas S, et al. Persistent and transient antibody responses to hepatitis E virus detected by Western immunoblot using open reading frame 2 and 3 and glutathione S-transferase fusion proteins. J Clin Microbiol. 1994;32:2060-2066.

99. Li TC, Yamakawa Y, Suzuki K, et al. Expression and self-assembly of empty viruslike particles of hepatitis E virus. J Virol. 1997;71:7202-7213.

100. Li F, Torresi J, Locarnini S, et al. Amino-terminal epitopes are exposed when full-length open reading frame 2 of hepatitis E virus is expressed in Escherichia coli, but carboxy-terminal epitopes are masked. J Med Virol. 1997;52:289-300.

101. Favorov MO, Khudyakov YE, Mast EE, et al. IgM and IgG antibodies to hepatitis E virus (HEV) detected by an enzyme immunoassay based on an HEV-specific artificial recombinant mosaic protein. J Med Virol. 1996;50:50-58.

102. Obriadina A, Meng J, Ulanova T, et al. A new enzyme immunoassay for the detection of antibody to hepatitis E virus. J Gastroenterol Hepatol. 2002;17(Suppl 3):S360-S264.

103. Schofield DJ, Glamann J, Emerson SU, Purcell RH. Identification by phage display and characterization of two neutralizing chimpanzee monoclonal antibodies to the hepatitis E virus capsid protein. J Virol. 2000;74:5548-5555.

104. Meng J, Dai X, Chang JC, et al. Identification and characterization of the neutralization eptiope(s) of the hepatitis E virus. Virology. 2001;288:203-211.

105. Meng J, Dubreuil P, Pillot J. A new PCR-based seroneutralization assay in cell culture for diagnosis of hepatitis E. J Clin Microbiol. 1997;35:1373-1377.

106. Arankalle VA, Chadha MS, Tsarev SA, et al. Seroepidemiology of water-borne hepatitis in India and evidence for a third enterically-transmitted hepatitis agent. Proc Natl Acad Sci U S A. 1994;91:3428-3432.

107. Bryan JP, Tsarev SA, Iqbal M, et al. Epidemic hepatitis E in Pakistan: Patterns of serologic response and evidence that antibody to hepatitis E virus protects against disease. J Infect Dis. 1994;170:517-521.

108. Chauhan A, Dilawari JB, Jameel S, et al. Common aetiological agent for epidemic and sporadic non-A, non-B hepatitis. Lancet. 1992;339:1509-1510.

109. Coursaget P, Krawczynski K, Buisson Y, et al. Hepatitis E and hepatitis C virus infections among French soldiers with non-A, non-B hepatitis. J Med Virol. 1993;39:163-166.

110. El-Zimaity DMT, Hyams KC, Imam IZE, et al. Acute sporadic hepatitis E in an Egyptian pediatric population. Am J Trop Med Hyg. 1993;48:372-376.

111. Favorov MO, Kuzin SN, Yashina TL, et al. Characteristics of viral non-A non-B hepatitis with fecal-oral mode of infection transmission in Southern Uzbekistan (in Russian). Vopr Virusol. 1988;34:436-442.

112. Goldsmith R, Yarbough PO, Reyes GR, et al. Enzyme-linked immunosorbent assay for diagnosis of acute sporadic hepatitis E in Egyptian children. Lancet. 1992;339:328-331.

113. Hyams KC, McCarthy MC, Kaur M, et al. Acute sporadic hepatitis E in children living in Cairo, Egypt. J Med Virol. 1992;37:274-277.

114. Koshy A, Richards AL, Al-Mufti S, et al. Acute sporadic hepatitis E in Kuwait. J Med Virol. 1994;42:405-408.

115. Krawczynski K, Bradley D, Ajdukiewicz A, et al. Virus-associated antigen and antibody of epidemic non-A, non-B hepatitis: Serology of outbreaks and sporadic cases. In: Shikata T, Purcell RH, Uchida T, eds. Viral Hepatitis C, D, and E. New York: Elsevier Science; 1991:229-236.

116. Lok ASF, Kwan W-K, Moeckli R, et al. Seroepidemiological survey of hepatitis E in Hong Kong by recombinant-based enzyme immunoassays. Lancet. 1992;340:1205-1208.

117. Mushahwar IK, Dawson GJ, Bile KM, et al. Serological studies of an enterically transmitted non-A, non-B hepatitis in Somalia. J Med Virol. 1993;40:218-221.

118. Saguanwongse S, Pojanagaroon B, Jayavasu C. Detection of 27-32 nm virus-like particles in stools of non-A, non-B hepatitis patients in Thailand by immunoelectron microscopy. Southeast Asian J Trop Med Public Health. 1990;21:265-268.

119. Skidmore SJ, Yarbough PO, Gabor KA, et al. Hepatitis E virus: The cause of a waterbourne hepatitis outbreak. J Med Virol. 1992;37:58-60.

120. Song DY, Zhuang H, Li Z, et al. Hepatitis E in Hetian city: Analysis of 562 cases. Chung Hua Nei Ko Tsa Chih. 1992;31:275-277.

121. Ticehurst J, Popkin TJ, Bryan JP, et al. Association of hepatitis E virus with an outbreak of hepatitis in Pakistan: Serologic responses and pattern of virus excretion. J Med Virol. 1992;36:84-92.

122. Tsega E, Hansson B-G, Krawczynski K, et al. Acute sporadic viral hepatitis in Ethiopia: Causes, risk factors, and effects on pregnancy. Clin Infect Dis. 1992;14:961-965.

123. Uchida T, Aye TT, Ma X, et al. An epidemic outbreak of hepatitis E in Yangon of Myanmar: Antibody assay and animal transmission of the virus. Acta Pathol Japonica. 1993;43:94-98.

124. Zaaijer HL, Yin MF, Lelie PN. Seroprevalence of hepatitis E in the Netherlands. Lancet. 1992;340:681.

125. Zhuang H, Cao X-Y, Liu C-B, et al. Enterically transmitted non-A, non-B hepatitis in China. In: Shikata T, Purcell RH, Uchida T, eds. Viral Hepatitis C, D, and E. New York: Elsevier Science; 1991:277-285.

126. Tsai JF, Jeng JE, Chang WY, et al. Antibodies to hepatitis E virus among Chinese patients with acute hepatitis in Taiwan. J Med Virol. 1994;43:341-344.

127. Tan D, Im S, Yao J, et al. Acute sporadic hepatitis E virus infection in southern China. J Hepatol. 1995;23:239-245.

128. Jardi R, Buti M, Rodriguez-Frias F, et al. Hepatitis E infection in acute sporadic hepatitis in Spain. Lancet. 1993;341:1355-1356.

129. John R, Abraham P, Kurien G, et al. Sporadic hepatitis E in southern India. Trans R Soc Trop Med Hyg. 1997;91:392.

130. Gomatos P, Mounir M, Arthur R, et al. The etiology of community-acquired viral hepatitis in Cairo, Egypt: Diagnosis of HEV infections. Egypt J Med Microbiol. 1996;5:223-229.

131. Gunaid AA, Nasher TM, el-Guneid AM, et al. Acute sporadic hepatitis in the Republic of Yemen. J Med Virol. 1997;51:64-66.

132. Cacopardo B, Russo R, Preiser W, et al. Acute hepatitis E in Catania (Eastern Sicily) 1980-1994. The role of hepatitis E virus. Infection. 1997;25:313-316.

133. Corwin A, Dai T, Duc D, et al. Acute viral hepatitis in Hanoi, Viet Nam. Trans R Soc Trop Med Hyg. 1996;90:647-648.

134. Coursaget P, Buisson Y, N'gawara MN, et al. Role of hepatitis E virus in sporadic cases of acute and fulminant hepatitis in an endemic area (Chad). Am J Trop Med Hyg. 1998;58:330-334.

135. Chow WC, Lee AS, Lim GK, et al. Acute viral hepatitis E: Clinical and serological studies in Singapore. J Clin Gastroenterol. 1997;24:235-238.

136. Buti M, Jardi R, Cotrina M, et al. Hepatitis E virus infection in acute hepatitis in Spain. J Virol Methods. 1995;55:49-54.

137. Arif M, Qattan I, Ramia S. Possible aetiological role of hepatitis E virus in acute non-A, non-B, non-C hepatitis in Saudi Arabia. Trans R Soc Trop Med Hyg. 1996;90:645-646.

138. Lynch M, O'Flynn N, Cryan B, et al. Hepatitis E in Ireland. Eur J Clin Microbiol Infect Dis. 1995;14:1109.

139. Heath T, Burrow J, Currie B, et al. Locally acquired hepatitis E in the Northern Territory of Australia. Med J Aust. 1995;162:318-319.

140. Hyams KC, Yarbough PO, Gray S, et al. Hepatitis E virus infection in Peru. Clin Infect Dis. 1996; 2:719-720.

141. Pattanayak S. Magnitude of the problem of hepatitis and directions for research, prevention and control. New Delhi: World Health Organization, WHO Regional Office for South-East Asia; 1986:1-13.

142. Smalley D, Brewer S, Dawson G, et al. Hepatitis E virus infection in an immigrant to the United States. South Med J. 1996;89:994-996.

143. Skidmore SJ, Sherratt LM. Hepatitis E infection in the UK. J Viral Hepat. 1996;3:103-105.

144. Wu JC, Sheen IJ, Chiang TY, et al. The impact of travelling to endemic areas on the spread of hepatitis E virus infection: Epidemiological and molecular analyses. Hepatology. 1998;27:1415-1420.

145. Smalligan R, Lange W, Frame J, et al. The risk of viral hepatitis A, B, C and E among North American missionaries. Am J Trop Med Hyg. 1995;53:233-236.

146. Janisch T, Preiser W, Berger A, et al. Emerging viral pathogens in long-term expatriates (I): Hepatitis E virus. Trop Med Int Health. 1997;2:885-891.

147. Gambel JM, Drabick JJ, Seriwatana J, et al. Seroprevalence of hepatitis E virus among United Nations Mission in Haiti (UNMIH) peacekeepers, 1995. Am J Trop Med Hyg. 1998;58:731-736.

148. Drabick J, Gambel J, Gouvea V, et al. A cluster of acute hepatitis E infection in United Nations Bangladeshi Peacekeepers in Haiti. Am J Trop Med Hyg. 1997;57:449-454.

149. Clayson E, Innis B, Myint KS, et al. Short report: Relative risk of hepatitis A and E among foreigners in Nepal. Am J Trop Med Hyg. 1995;52:506-507.

150. Burans J, Sharp T, Wallace M, et al. Threat of hepatitis E virus infection in Somalia during Operation Restore Hope. Clin Infect Dis. 1994;18:100-102.

151. Alecci A, Bonciani M, Tola T. Prevalence of anti-HEV among Italian soldiers sent in East Africa for "Restore Hope" mission. Eur J Epidemiol. 1997;13:735.

152. De Cock KM, Bradley DW, Sandford NL, et al. Epidemic non-A, non-B hepatitis in patients from Pakistan. Ann Intern Med. 1987;106:227-230.

153. Fletcher J. A traveler returning from Nepal with hepatitis E. Med J Aust. 1993;159:563.

154. Moaven LD, Fuller AJ, Doultree JC, et al. A case of acute hepatitis E in Victoria. Med J Aust. 1993;159:124-125.

155. Roberts JK, Whitlock RT. Hepatitis E in a traveler to Bangladesh. Ann Intern Med. 1992;117:93.

156. Zaaijer HL, Kok M, Lelie PN, et al. Hepatitis E in the Netherlands: Imported and endemic. Lancet. 1993;341:826.

157. Arankalle VA, Tsarev SA, Chadha MS, et al. Age-specific prevalence of antibodies to hepatitis A and E viruses in Pune, India, 1982 and 1992. J Infect Dis. 1995;171:447-450.

158. Pujol FH, Favorov MO, Marcano T, et al. Prevalence of antibodies against hepatitis E virus among urban and rural populations in Venezuela. J Med Virol. 1994;234-236.

159. Thomas DL, Mahley RW, Badur S, et al. Epidemiology of hepatitis E virus infection in Turkey. Lancet. 1993;341:1561-1562.

160. Tsega E, Krawczynski K, Hansson B-G, et al. Outbreak of acute hepatitis E virus infection among military personnel in Northern Ethiopia. J Med Virol. 1991;34:232-236.

161. Pawlotsky JM, Belec L, Gresenguet G, et al. High prevalence of hepatitis B, C, and E markers in young sexually active adults from the Central African Republic. J Med Virol. 1995;46:269-273.

162. Rioche M, Dubreuil P, Kouassi-Samgare A, et al. [Incidence of sporadic hepatitis E in Ivory Coast based on still problematic serology] (in French). Bull World Health Organ. 1997;75:349-354.

163. Focaccia R, Sette H Jr, Conceicao OJG. Hepatitis E in Brazil. Lancet. 1995;346:1165.

164. Cengiz K, Ozyilkan E, Coar AM, et al. Seroprevalence of hepatitis E in hemodialysis patients in Turkey. Nephron. 1996;74:730.

165. Blitz-Dorfman L, Monsalve F, Atencio R, et al. Serological survey of markers of infection with viral hepatitis among the Yukpa Amerindians from western Venezuela. Ann Trop Med Parasitol. 1996;90:655-657.

166. Arif M, Qattan I, Al-Faleh F, et al. Epidemiology of hepatitis E virus (HEV) infection in Saudi Arabia. Ann Trop Med Parasitol. 1994;88:163-168.

167. Aubry P, Niel L, Niyongabo T, et al. Seroprevalence of hepatitis E virus in an adult urban population from Burundi. Am J Trop Med Hyg. 1997;57:272-273.

168. Aubry P, Larouze B, Niyongabo T, et al. [Markers of hepatitis C and E virus in Burundi] (in French). Bull Soc Pathol Exot. 1997;90:150-152.

169. Abdelaal M, Zawawi TH, al Sobhi E, et al. Epidemiology of hepatitis E virus in male blood donors in Jeddah, Saudi Arabia. Isr J Med Sci. 1998;167:94-96.

170. Brahm J, Hurtado C, Moraga M, et al. [Hepatitis E virus infection in Chile: preliminary report] (in Spanish). Rev Med Chil. 1996;124:947-949.

171. Bernal MC, Leyva A, Garcia F, et al. Seroepidemiological study of hepatitis E virus in different population groups. Eur J Clin Microbiol Infect Dis. 1995;14:954-958.

172. Benjelloun S, Bahbouhi B, Bouchrit N, et al. Seroepidemiological study of an acute hepatitis E outbreak in Morocco. Res Virol. 1997;148:279-287.

173. Cruells MR, Mescia G, Gaibisso R, et al. [Epidemiological study of hepatitis A and E viruses in different populations in Uruguay] (in Spanish). Gastroenterol Hepatol. 1997;20:295-298.

174. Chow WC, Ng HS, Lim GK, et al. Hepatitis E in Singapore—A seroprevalence study. Singapore Med J. 1996;37:579-581.

175. Corwin A, Putri M, Winarno J, et al. Epidemic and sporadic hepatitis E virus transmission in west Kalimantan (Borneo), Indonesia. Am J Trop Med Hyg. 1997;57:62-65.

176. Corwin A, Jarot K, Lubis I, et al. Two years' investigation of epidemic hepatitis E virus transmission in West Kalimantan (Borneo), Indonesia. Trans R Soc Trop Med Hyg. 1995;89:262-265.

177. Darwish MA, Faris R, Clemens JD, et al. High seroprevalence of hepatitis A, B, C, and E viruses in residents in an Egyptian village in The Nile Delta: A pilot study. Am J Trop Med Hyg. 1996;54:554-558.

178. Grabow WOK, Favorov MO, Khudyakova NS, et al. Hepatitis E seroprevalence in selected individuals in South Africa. J Med Virol. 1994;44:384-388.

179. Ibarra H, Reidemann S, Reinhardt G, et al. [Prevalence of hepatitis E virus antibodies in blood donors and other population groups in southern Chile] (in Spanish). Rev Med Chil. 1997;125:275-278.

180. Ibarra H, Reidemann S, Siegel F, et al. Hepatitis E virus in Chile. Lancet. 1994;344:1501.

181. Kamel M, Troonen H, Kapprell HP, et al. Seroepidemiology of hepatitis E virus in the Egyptian Nile Delta. J Med Virol. 1995;47:399-403.

182. Langer BCA, Frösner GG, von Brunn A. Epidemiological study of viral hepatitis types A, B, C, D, and E among Inuits in West Greenland. J Viral Hepat. 1997;4:339-349.

183. Poovorawan Y, Theamboonlers A, Chumdermpadetsuk S, et al. Prevalence of hepatitis E virus infection in Thailand. Ann Trop Med Parasitol. 1996;90:189-196.

184. Perez OM, Morales W, Paniagua M, et al. Prevalence of antibodies to hepatitis A, B, C, and E viruses in a healthy population in Leon, Nicaragua. Am J Trop Med Hyg. 1996;55:17-21.

185. Parana R, Cotrim HP, Cortey-Boennec ML, et al. Prevalence of hepatitis E virus IgG antibodies in patients from a referral unit of liver diseases in Salvador, Bahia, Brazil. Am J Trop Med Hyg. 1997;57:60-61.

186. Tucker T, Kirsch R, Louw S, et al. Hepatitis E in South Africa: Evidence for sporadic spread and increased seroprevalence in rural areas. J Med Virol. 1996;50:117-119.

187. Talarmin A, Kazanji M, Cardoso T, et al. Prevalence of antibodies to hepatitis A, C, and E viruses in different ethnic groups in French Guiana. J Med Virol. 1997;52:430-435.

188. Mouzin E, Beilke M. Hepatitis E virus infection in Peru. Clin Infect Dis. 1996;22:719-720.

189. Ritter A, Flacke H, Vornwald A, et al. A seroprevalence study of hepatitis E in Europe and the Middle East. Viral Hepat Liver Dis. 1994;432-434.

190. Pang L, Alencar FEC, Cerutti C, et al. Hepatitis E infection in the Brazilian Amazon. Am J Trop Med Hyg. 1995;52:347-348.

191. Fix AD, Abdel-Hamid M, Purcell RH, et al. Prevalence of antibodies to hepatitis E in two rural Egyptian communities. Am J Trop Med Hyg. 2000;62:519-523.

192. Zanetti AR, Dawson GJ. The Study Group of Hepatitis E. Hepatitis type E in Italy: A seroepidemiological survey. J Med Virol. 1994;42:318-320.

193. Mast E, Kuramoto I, Favorov M, et al. Prevalence of and risk factors for antibody to hepatitis E virus seroreactivity among blood donors in northern California. J Infect Dis. 1997;176:34-40.

194. Thomas DL, Yarbough P, Vlahov D, et al. Seroreactivity to hepatitis E virus in areas where the disease is not endemic. J Clin Microbiol. 1997;35:1244-1247.

195. Bernal Reyes R, Licona Sols JE. Seroepidemiologa de la hepatitis E en el Estado de Hidalgo. Rev Gastroenterol Mex. 1996;61:233-238.

196. Bernal W, Smith HM, Williams R. A community prevalence study of antibodies to hepatitis A and E in inner-city London. J Med Virol. 1996;49:230-234.

197. Peng CF, Lin MR, Chue PY, et al. Prevalence of antibody to hepatitis E virus among healthy individuals in Southern Taiwan. Microbiol Immunol. 1995;39:733-736.

198. Pazdiora P, Nemecek V, Topolcan O. [Initial results of monitoring hepatitis E virus antibodies in selected population groups in the West Bohemia region] (in Czech). Epidemiol Mikrobiol Imunol. 1996;45:117-118.

199. Queiros L, Condeco J, Tender A, et al. [The seroprevalence for hepatitis E viral antibodies in the northern region of Portugal] (in Portuguese). Acta Med Port. 1997;10:447-453.

200. Quiroga J, Cotonat T, Castillo I, et al. Hepatitis E virus seroprevalence in acute viral hepatitis in a developed country confirmed by a supplemental assay. J Med Virol. 1996;50:16-19.

201. Stroffolini T, Menchinelli M, Dambruoso V, et al. Prevalence of hepatitis E in a central Italian town at high endemicity for hepatitis C virus. Ital J Gastroenterol. 1996;28:523-525.

202. Trautwein C, Kiral G, Tillmann HL, et al. Risk factors and prevalence of hepatitis E in German immigrants from the former Soviet Union. J Med Virol. 1995;45:429-434.

203. Moaven L, Asten M, Crofts N, et al. Seroepidemiology of hepatitis E in selected Australian populations. J Med Virol. 1995;45:326-330.

204. Clayson E, Shrestha M, Vaughn D, et al. Rates of hepatitis E virus infection and disease among adolescents and adults in Kathmandu, Nepal. J Infect Dis. 1997;176:763-766.

205. Clayson E, Vaughn D, Innis B, et al. Association of hepatitis E virus with an outbreak of hepatitis at a military training camp in Nepal. J Med Virol. 1998;54:178-182.

206. Jameel S, Durgapal H, Habibullah CM, et al. Enteric non-A, non-B hepatitis: Epidemics, animal transmission, and hepatitis E virus detection by the polymerase chain reaction. J Med Virol. 1992;37:263-270.

207. Arankalle VA, Chadha MS, Mehendale SM, et al. Outbreak of enterically transmitted non-A, non-B hepatitis among schoolchildren. Lancet. 1988;2:1199-1200.

208. Schlauder G, Dawson G, Mushahwar I, et al. Viraemia in Egyptian children with hepatitis E virus infection. Lancet. 1993;341:378.

209. Aggarwal R, Shahi H, Naik S, et al. Evidence in favour of high infection rate with hepatitis E virus among young children in India. J Hepatol. 1997;26:1425-1430.

210. Ripabelli G, Sammarco ML, Campo T, et al. Prevalence of antibodies against enterically transmitted viral hepatitis (HAV and HEV) among adolescents in an inland territory of central Italy. Eur J Epidemiol. 1997;13:45-47.

211. Chadha MS, Walimbe AM, Chobe LP, Arankalle VA. Comparison of etiology of sporadic acute and fulminant viral hepatitis in hospitalized patients in Pune, India during 1978-81 and 1996-97. Indian J Gastroenterol. 2003;22:11-15.

212. Puddar U, Thapa BR, Prasad A, Singh K. Changing spectrum of sporadic acute viral hepatitis in Indian children. J Trop Pediatr. 2002; 48:210-213.

213. Viswanathan R. Epidemiology. Indian J Med Res. 1957;45:1-29.

214. Khuroo MS. Hepatitis E. The enterically transmitted non-A, non-B hepatitis. Indian J Gastroenterol. 1991;10:96-100.

215. Rab MA, Bile MK, Mubarik MM, et al. Water-borne hepatitis E virus epidemic in Islamabad, Pakistan: A common source outbreak traced to the malfunction of a modern water treatment plant. Am J Trop Med Hyg. 1997;57:151-157.

216. Iqbal M, Ahmed A, Qamar A, et al. An outbreak of enterically transmitted non-A non-B hepatitis in Pakistan. Am J Trop Med Hyg. 1989;40:438-443.

217. Ramalingaswami V, Purcell R. Waterborne non-A, non-B hepatitis. Lancet. 1988;1:571-573.

218. Tandon BN, Joshi YK, Jain SK, et al. An epidemic of non-A non-B hepatitis in north India. Indian J Med Res. 1982;75:739-744.

219. Viswanathan R. Infectious hepatitis in Delhi (1955-1956): A critical study; epidemiology. Indian J Med Res. 1957;45:1-29.

220. Coursaget P, Buisson Y, Enogat N, et al. Outbreak of enterically-transmitted hepatitis due to hepatitis A and hepatitis E viruses. J Hepatol. 1998;28:745-750.

221. Corwin A, Khiem H, Clayson E, et al. A waterborne outbreak of hepatitis E virus transmission in southwestern Viet Nam. Am J Trop Med Hyg. 1996;54:559-562.

222. Bai F, Zhaorigetai, Wu BR. A foodborne outbreak of non-A, non-B hepatitis. Neimenggu Med J. 1987;7:157-158.

223. Meng H, Yiang XC, He SC, et al. A food-borne outbreak of non-A, non-B hepatitis. Chin J Prevent Med. 1987;21:28-30.

224. Qin SM, Wang HL, Chen LY, et al. A preliminary report of an out-break of non-A, non-B hepatitis. Chin J Infect Dis. 1984;2:272-273.

225. Shi GR, Li SQ, Qian L, et al. The epidemiolgical study on a food-borne outbreak of non-A, non-B hepatitis. J Chin Med Univ. 1987;16:150-151.

226. Caredda F, Antinori S, Re T, et al. Clinical features of sporadic non-A, non-B hepatitis possibly associated with faecal-oral spread. Lancet. 1985;2:414-145.

227. Aggarwal R, Naik SR. Hepatitis E: Intrafamilial transmission versus waterborne spread. J Hepatol. 1994;21:718-723.

228. Cao X-Y, Ma X-Z, Liu Y-Z, et al. Epidemiological and etiological studies on enterically transmitted non-A, non-B hepatitis in the south part of Xinjiang. In: Shikata T, Purcell RH, Uchida T, eds. Viral Hepatitis C, D, and E. New York: Elsevier Science; 1991:297-312.

229. Arankalle VA, Chadha MS, Mehendale SM, Tungatkar SP. Epidemic hepatitis E: Serological evidence for lack of intrafamilial spread. Indian J Gastroenterol. 2000;19:24-28.

230. Robson SC, Adams S, Brink N, et al. Hospital outbreak of hepatitis E. Lancet. 1992;339:1424-1425.

231. Nanda SK, Ansari IH, Acharya SK, et al. Protracted viremia during acute sporadic hepatitis E virus infection. Gastroenterology. 1995;108:225-230.

232. Clayson E, Myint KS, Snitbhan R, et al. Viremia, fecal shedding, and IgM and IgG responses in patients with hepatitis E. J Infect Dis. 1995; 172:927-933.

233. Chauhan A, Jameel S, Dilawari JB, et al. Hepatitis E virus transmission to a volunteer. Lancet. 1993;341:149-150.

234. Mannucci PM, Gdovin SL, Gringeri A, et al. Transmission of hepatitis A to patients with hemophilia by factor VIII concentrates treated with organic solvent and detergent to inactivate viruses. Ann Intern Med. 1994;120:1-7.

235. Mannucci PM, Gringeri A, Santagostino E, et al. Low risk of transmission of hepatitis E virus by large-pool coagulation factor concentrates. Lancet. 1994;343:597-598.

236. Klarmann D, Kreuz W, Kornhuber B. Low prevalence of hepatitis E virus antibodies in hepatitis C virus-positive patients with coagulation disorders. Transfusion. 1995;35:969-970.

237. Psichogiou M, Tzala E, Boletis J, et al. Hepatitis E virus infection in individuals at high risk of transmission of non-A, non-B hepatitis and sexually transmitted diseases. Scand J Infect Dis. 1996;28:443-445.

238. Barzilai A, Schulman S, Karetnyi Y, et al. Hepatitis E virus infection in hemophiliacs. J Med Virol. 1995;46:153-156.

239. Zaaijer HL, Mauser-Bunschoten EP, Veen JH, et al. Hepatitis E virus antibodies among patients with hemophilia, blood donors, and hepatitis patients. J Med Virol. 1995;46:244-246.

240. Wang CW, Tschen SY, Schalasta G, et al. Anti-hepatitis E virus markers in hemodialysis patients. Nephron. 1996;72:343-345.

241. Psichogiou M, Tassopoulos N, Papatheodoridis G, et al. Hepatitis E virus infection in a cohort of patients with acute non-A, non-B hepatitis. J Hepatol. 1995;23:668-673.

242. Pohjanpelto P, Ebeling F, Rasi V, et al. Hepatitis E virus: No evidence of parenteral transmission in Finland. Thromb Haemost 1995;74:1379-1387.

243. Psichogiou M, Vaindirli E, Tzala E, et al. Hepatitis E virus (HEV) infection in haemodialysis patients. Nephrol Dial Transplant. 1996;11:1093-1095.

244. Knodler B, Hiller J, Loliger CC, et al. [Hepatitis E antibodies in blood donors, hemodialysis patients and in normal people] (in German). Beitr Infusionsther Transfusionsmed. 1994;32:124-127.

245. Gessoni G, Manoni F. Hepatitis E virus infection in north-east Italy: Serological study in the open population and groups at risk. J Viral Hepat. 1996;3:197-202.

246. Fabrizi F, Lunghi G, Bacchini G, et al. Hepatitis E virus infection in haemodialysis patients: A seroepidemiological survey. Nephrol Dial Transplant. 1997;12:133-136.

247. Dalekos GN, Zervou E, Elisaf M, et al. Antibodies to hepatitis E virus among several populations in Greece: Increased prevalence in a hemodialysis unit. Transfusion. 1998;38:589-595.

248. Wang C-H, Flehmig B, Jahn G, et al. Hepatitis E virus in haemodialysis (Letter to Editor). Vox Sang. 1997;73:54-55.

249. Sylvan S, Jacobson S, Christenson B. Prevalence of antibodies to hepatitis E virus among hemodialysis patients in Sweden. J Med Virol. 1998;54:38-43.

250. Buffet C, Laurent-Puig P, Chandot S, et al. A high hepatitis E virus seroprevalence among renal transplantation and haemophilia patient populations. J Hepatol. 1996;24:122-125.

251. Arankalle VA, Chobe LP. Hepatitis E virus: Can it be transmitted parenterally? J Viral Hepat. 1999;6:161-164.

252. Aggarwal R, Kini D, Sofat S, Naik SR, Krawczynski K. Duration of viraemia and faecal viral excretion in acute hepatitis E. Lancet. 2000;356:1081-1082.

253. McCaustland KA, Krawszynski K, Ebert JW, et al. Hepatitis E virus infection in chimpanzees: a retrospective analysis. Arch Virol. 2000;145:1909-1918.

254. Purcell RH, Emerson SU. Animal models of hepatitis A and E. ILAR J. 2001;42:161-177.

255. Balayan MS, Usmanov RK, Zamyatina NA, et al. Brief report: Experimental hepatitis E infection in domestic pigs. J Med Virol. 1990;32:58-59.

256. Meng XJ, Halbur PG, Haynes JS, et al. Experimental infection of pigs with the newly identified swine hepatitis E virus (swine HEV), but not with human strains of HEV. Arch Virol. 1998;143:1405-1415.

257. Usmanov RK, Balaian MS, Dzhumalieva DI, et al. [Experimental hepatitis E infection in piglets] (in Russian). Vopr Virusol. 1991;36:212-216.

258. Usmanov RK, Balaian MS, Kazachkov I, et al. [Further study of experimental hepatitis E in piglets] (in Russian). Vopr Virusol. 1994;39:208-212.

259. Huang RT, Li DR, Wei J, et al. Isolation and identification of hepatitis E virus in Xinjiang, China. J Gen Virol. 1992;73:1143-1148.

260. Karetnyi YV, Dzhumalieva DI, Usmanov RK, et al. Probable involvement of rodents in the spread of viral hepatitis E. Zh Mikrobiol Epidemiol Immunobiol. 1993;4: 52-56.

261. Maneerat Y, Clayson E, Myint K, et al. Experimental infection of the laboratory rat with the hepatitis E virus. J Med Virol. 1996;48:121-128.

262. Usmanov RK, Balaian MS, Dvoinikova OV, et al. [Experimental infection of lambs with hepatitis E virus] (in Russian). Vopr Virusol. 1994;39:165-168.

263. Bradley DW. Hepatitis E: Epidemiology, aetiology and molecular biology. Rev Med Virol. 1992;2:19-28.

264. Platt KB, Yoon K-J, Zimmerman JJ. Susceptibility of swine to hepatitis E virus and its significance to human health. Swine Research Report. Ames, Iowa: Iowa State University Press; 1998:125-126.

265. Kabrane-Lazizi Y, Fine JB, Elm J, et al. Evidence for wide-spread infection of wild rats with hepatitis E virus in the United States. Am J Trop Med Hygiene. 1999;61:331-335.

266. Meng XJ, Halbur PG, Shapiro MS, et al. Genetic and experimental evidence for cross-species infection by swine hepatitis E virus. J Virol.1998;72:9714-9721.

267. Meng XJ, Wiseman B, Elvinger F, et al. Prevalence of antibodies to hepatitis E virus in veterinarians working with swine and in normal blood donors in the United States and other countries. J Clin Microbiol. 2002;40:117-122.

268. Withers MR, Correa MT, Morrow M, et al. Antibody levels to hepatitis E virus in North Carolina swine workers, non-swine workers, swine, and murids. Am J Trop Med Hyg. 2002;66:384-388.

269. Drobeniuc J, Favorov MO, Shapiro CN, et al. Hepatitis E virus antibody prevalence among persons who work with swine. J Infect Dis. 2001;184:1594-1597.

270. Favorov MO, Kosoy MY, Tsarev SA, et al. Prevalence of antibody to hepatitis E virus among rodents in the United States. J Infect Dis. 2000;181:449-455.

271. Arankalle VA, Joshi MV, Kulkarni AM, et al. Prevalence of anti-hepatitis E virus antibodies in different Indian animal species. J Viral Hepat. 2001;8:223-227.

272. Hirano M, Ding X, Tran HT, et al. Prevalence of antibody against hepatitis E virus in various species of non-human primates: Evidence of widespread infection in Japanese monkeys (Macaca fuscata). Jpn J Infect Dis. 2003;56:8-11.

273. Arankalle VA, Goverdhan MK, Banerjee K. Antibodies against hepatitis E virus in Old World monkeys. J Viral Hepat. 1994;1:125-129.

274. Tsarev SA, Tsareva TS, Emerson SU, et al. Experimental hepatitis E in pregnant rhesus monkeys: Failure to transmit hepatitis E virus (HEV) to offspring and evidence of naturally acquired antibodies to HEV. J Infect Dis. 1995;172:31-37.

275. Purcell RH, Tsarev SA. Seroepidemiology of hepatitis E. In: Buisson Y, Coursaget P, Kane M, eds. Enterically-Transmitted Hepatitis Viruses. Joué-lès-Tours, France: La Simarre; 1996:153-166.

276. Ticehurst J, Rhodes LL, Krawczynski K, et al. Infection of owl monkeys (Aotus trivirgatus) and cynomolgus monkeys (Macaca fascicularis) with hepatitis E virus from Mexico. J Infect Dis. 1992;165:835-845.

277. Uchida T, Win KM, Suzuki K, et al. Serial transmission of a putative causative virus of enterically transmitted non-A, non-B hepatitis to Macaca fascicularia and Macaca mulatta. Jpn J Exp Med. 1990;60:13-21.

278. Longer CF, Denny SL, Caudill JD, et al. Experimental hepatitis E: Pathogenesis in cynomolgus macaques (Macaca fascicularis). J Infect Dis. 1993;168:602-609.

279. Tsarev SA, Emerson SU, Tsareva TS, et al. Variation in course of hepatitis E in experimentally infected cynomolgus monkeys. J Infect Dis. 1993;167:1302-1306.

280. Tsarev SA, Tsareva TS, Emerson SU, et al. Successful passive and active immunization of cynomolgus monkeys against hepatitis E. Proc Natl Acad Sci U S A. 1994;91:10198-10202.

281. Arankalle VA, Favorov MO, Chadha MS, et al. Rhesus monkeys infected with hepatitis E virus (HEV) from the former USSR are immune to subsequent challenge with an Indian strain of HEV. Acta Virol. 1993;37:515-518.

282. Arankalle VA, Chadha MS, Chobe LP, et al. Cross-challenge studies in rhesus monkeys employing different Indian isolates of hepatitis E virus. J Med Virol. 1995;46:358-363.

283. Arankalle VA, Chadha MS, Banerjee K, et al. Hepatitis E virus infection in pregnant rhesus monkeys. Indian J Med Res. 1993;97:4-8.

284. Balayan MS. HEV infection: Historical perspectives, global epidemiology, and clinical features. In: Hollinger FB, Lemon SM, Margolis H, eds. Viral Hepatitis and Liver Disease. Baltimore: Williams & Wilkins; 1991:498-501.

285. Clayson ET, Snitbhan R, Ngarmpochana M, et al. Evidence that the hepatitis E virus (HEV) is a zoonotic virus: Detection of natural infections among swine, rats, and chickens in an area endemic for human disease. In: Buisson Y, Coursaget P, Kane M, eds. Enterically-Transmitted Hepatitis Viruses. Joué-lès-Tours, France: La Simarre; 1996:329-335.

286. Kwo P, Schlauder G, Carpenter H, et al. Acute hepatitis E by a new isolate acquired in the United States. Mayo Clin Proc. 1997;72:1133-1136.

287. Nishizawa T, Takahashi M, Mizuo H, et al. Characterization of Japanese swine and human hepatitis E virus isolates of genotype IV with 99% identity over the entire genome. J Gen Virol. 2003;84:1245-1251.

288. Meng XJ. Novel strains of hepatitis E virus identified from humans and other animal species: Is hepatitis E a zoonosis? J Hepatol. 2000;33:842-845.

289. Weiss RA. Transgenic pigs and virus adaptation. Nature. 1998;391:327-328.

290. Tam AW, White R, Yarbough PO, et al. In vitro infection and replication of hepatitis E virus in primary cynomolgus macaque hepatocytes. Virology. 1997;238:94-102.

291. Kazachkov YA, Balayan MS, Ivannikova TA, et al. Hepatitis E virus in cultivated cells. J Arch Virol. 1992;127:399-402.

292. Wei S, Walsh P, Huang R, To SS. 93G, a novel sporadic strain of hepatitis E virus in South China isolated by cell culture. J Med Virol. 2000;61:311-318.

293. Xia X, Huang R, Li D. [Studies on the subgenomic RNAs of hepatitis E virus] (in Chinese). Wei Sheng Wu Xue Bao 2000;41:622-627.

294. Humphrey C, Cook EH, McCaustland K, et al. Enterically-transmitted non-A, non-B hepatitis (ET-NANBH): Isolation of infectious virus from gall bladder bile. Abstract FP4. The II International Symposium on Viral Hepatitis and Hepatocellular Carcinoma. Taipei, Taiwan, ROC, 1988.

295. Kawai HF, Koji T, Iida F, et al. Shift of hepatitis E virus RNA from hepatocytes to biliary epithelial cells during acute infection of rhesus monkey. J Viral Hepat. 1999;6:287-297.

296. Williams TP, Kasorndorkbua C, Halbur PG, et al. Evidence of extrahepatic sites of replication of the hepatitis E virus in a swine model. J Clin Microbiol. 2001;39:3040-3046.

297. Soe S, Uchida T, Suzuki K, et al. Enterically transmitted non-A, non-B hepatitis in cynomolgus monkeys: Morphology and probable mechanism of hepatocellular necrosis. Liver. 1989;9:135-145.

298. Purcell RH, Jafri MW, Ticehurst J, et al. Hepatitis viruses. In: Schmidt NJ, Emmons RW eds. Diagnostic Procedures for Viral, Rickettsial and Chlamydial Infections. 6th ed. Washington, DC: American Public Health Association; 1989: 957-1065.

299. Hamid SS, Jafri MW, Khan H, et al. Fulminant hepatic failure in pregnant women: Acute fatty liver or acute viral hepatitis? J Hepatol. 1996;25:20-27.

300. Khuroo MS, Teli MR, Skidmore S, et al. Incidence and severity of viral hepatitis in pregnancy. Am J Med. 1981;70:252-255.

301. Jaiswal SB, Chitnis DS, Asolkar MV, et al. Aetiology and prognostic factors in hepatic failure in central India. Trop Gastroenterol. 1996;17:217-220.

302. Kar P, Budhiraja S, Narang A, et al. Etiology of sporadic acute and fulminant non-A, non-B viral hepatitis in north India. Indian Soc Gastroenterol. 1997;16:43-45.

303. Khuroo MS, Kamili S. Aetiology, clinical course and outcome of sporadic acute viral hepatitis in pregnancy. J Viral Hepat. 2003;10:61-69.

304. Jaiswal SP, Jain AK, Naik G, et al. Viral hepatitis during pregnancy. Int J Gynaecol Obstet. 2001;72:103-108.

305. Jain A, Kar P, Madan K, et al. Hepatitis C virus infection in sporadic fulminant viral hepatitis in North India: cause or co-factor? Eur J Gastroenterol Hepatol. 1999;11:1231-1237.

306. Singh S, Mohanty A, Joshi YK, et al. Mother-to-child transmission of hepatitis E virus infection. Indian J Pediatr. 2003;70:37-39.

307. Kumar RM, Uduman S, Rana S, et al. Sero-prevalence and mother-to-infant transmission of hepatitis E virus among pregnant women in the United Arab Emirates. Eur J Obstet Gyn Reprod Biol 2001:100:9-15.

308. Hussaini SH, Skidmore SJ, Richardson P, et al. Severe hepatitis E infection during pregnancy. J Viral Hepat. 1997;4:51-54.

309. Arankalle VA, Chadha BM, Dama BM, et al. Role of immune serum globulins in pregnant women during an epidemic of hepatitis E. J Viral Hepat. 1998;5:199-204.

310. Mishra L, Seeff LB. Viral hepatitis, A through E, complicating pregnancy. Gastroenterol Clin North Am. 1992;21:873-887.

311. Michielsen PP, Van Damme P. Viral hepatitis and pregnancy. Acta Gastroenterol Belg. 1999;62:21-29.

312. Nayak NC, Panda SK, Datta R, et al. Aetiology and outcome of acute viral hepatitis in pregnancy. J Gastroenterol Hepatol. 1989;4:345-352.

313. Acharya SK, Dasarathy S, Kumer TL, et al. Fulminant hepatitis in a tropical population: Clinical course, cause, and early predictors of outcome. Hepatology 1996;23:1448-1455.

314. Hamid SS, Atiq M, Shehzad F, et al. Hepatitis E virus superinfection in patients with chronic liver disease. Hepatology. 2002;36:474-478.

315. Shang Q, Yu J, Xiao D, et al. [The effects of hepatitis E virus superinfection on patients with chronic hepatitis B: a clinico-pathological study] (in Chinese). Zhonghua Nei Ke Za Zhi. 2002;41:656-659.

316. Kuwada SK, Patel VM, Hollinger FB, et al. Non-A, non-B fulminant hepatitis is also non-E and non-C. Am J Gastroenterol. 1994;89:57-61.

317. Ohnishi S, Kang JH, Maekubo H, et al. A case report: Two patients with fulminant hepatitis E in Hokkaido, Japan. Hepatol Res. 2003;25:213-218.

318. Khuroo MS, Kamili S, Dar MY, et al. Hepatitis E and long-term antibody status. Lancet. 1993;341:1355

319. Chadha MS, Walimbe AM, Arankalle VA. Retrospective serological analysis of hepatitis E patients: A long-term follow-up study. J Viral Hepat. 1999;6:457-461.

320. Chau KH, Dawson GJ, Bile KM, et al. Detection of IgA class antibody to hepatitis E virus in serum samples from patients with hepatitis E virus infection. J Med Virol. 1993;40:334-338.

321. Naik S, Aggarwal R, Naik SR, et al. Evidence for activation of cellular immune responses in patients with acute hepatitis E. Indian J Gastroenterol. 2002;21:149-52.

322. Balayan MS. New form of hepatitis with fecal-oral mode of spread. Soc Med Rev J Virol. 1987;2:235-261.

323. Mast EE, Purdy MA, Krawczynski K. Hepatitis E. Baillieres Clin Gastroenterol. 1996;10:227-242.

324. Glikson M, Galun E, Oren R, et al. Relapsing hepatitis A: Review of 14 cases and literature survey. Medicine. 1992;71:14-23.

325. Malkani PK, Grewal AK. Observations on infectious hepatitis in pregnancy. Indian J Med Res. 1957;(Jan):77-84.

326. Song D-Y, Zhuang H, Kang X-C, et al. Hepatitis E in Hetian city: A report of 562 cases. In: Hollinger FB, Lemon SM, Margolis H, eds. Viral Hepatitis and Liver Disease. Baltimore: Williams & Wilkins; 1991:528-529.

327. Reyes GR. Overview of the epidemiology and biology of the hepatitis E virus. In: Willson RA, ed. Viral Hepatitis. New York: Marcel Dekker; 1997:239-258.
328. Khuroo MS, Kamili S, Jameel S. Vertical transmission of hepatitis E virus. Lancet. 1995;345:1025-1026.
329. Tsang TH, Denison EK, Williams HV, et al. Acute hepatitis E infection acquired in California. Clin Infect Dis. 2000;30:618-619.
330. Schlauder GG, Frider B, Sookoian S, et al. Identification of 2 novel isolates of hepatitis E virus in Argentina. J Infect Dis. 2000;182:294-297.
331. Takahashi M, Nishizawa T, Okamoto H. Identification of a genotype III swine hepatitis E virus that was isolated from a Japanese pig born in 1990 and that is most closely related to Japanese isolates of human hepatitis E virus. J Clin Microbiol. 2003;41:1342-1343.
332. Pina S, Buti M, Cotrina M, et al. HEV identified in serum from humans with acute hepatitis and in sewage of animal origin in Spain. J Hepatol. 2000;33:826-833.
333. Schlauder GG, Mushahwar IK. Genetic heterogeneity of hepatitis E virus. J Med Virol. 2001;65:282-292.
334. Ke WM, Tan D, Li JG, et al. Consecutive evaluation of immunoglobulin M and G antibodies against hepatitis E virus. J Gastroenterol. 1996;31:818-822.
335. Bryan JP, Iqbal M, Tsarev S, et al. Epidemic of hepatitis E in a military unit in Abbotrabad, Pakistan. Am J Trop Med Hyg. 2002;67:662-668.
336. Seriwatana J, Shrestha MP, Scott RM, et al. Clinical and epidemiological relevance of quantitating hepatitis E virus-specific immunoglobulin M. Clin Diagn Lab Immunol. 2002;9:1072-1078.
337. Yu C, Engle RE, Bryan JP, et al. Detection of immunoglobulin M antibodies to hepatitis E virus by class capture enzyme immunoassay. Clin Diagn Lab Immunol. 2003;10:579-586.
338. Chobe LP, Chadha MS, Banerjee K, et al. Detection of HEV RNA in faeces, by RT-PCR during the epidemics of hepatitis E in India (1976-1995). J Viral Hepat. 1997;4:129-133.
339. Van Cuyck-Gandre H, Caudill JD, Zhang HY, et al. Short report: Polymerase chain reaction detection of hepatitis E virus in north African fecal samples. Am J Trop Med Hyg. 1996;54:134-135.
340. Ray R, Aggarwal R, Salunke PN, et al. Hepatitis E virus genome in stools of hepatitis patients during large epidemic in north India. Lancet. 1991;338:783-784.
341. Vaidya SR, Chitambar SD, Arankalle VA. Polymerase chain reaction-based prevalence of hepatitis A, hepatitis E and TT viruses in sewage from an endemic area. J Hepatol. 2002;37:131-136.
342. Clemente-Casares P, Pina S, Buti M, et al. Girones R. Hepatitis E virus epidemiology in industrialized countries. Emerging Infect Dis, 2003;9:448-454.
343. Uchida T, Suzuki K, Komatsu K, et al. Occurrence and character of a putative causative virus of enterically-transmitted non-A, non-B hepatitis in bile. Jpn J Exp Med. 1990;60:23-29.
344. Arif M. Enterically transmitted hepatitis in Saudi Arabia: An epidemiological study. Ann Trop Med Parasitol. 1996;90:197-201.
345. Joshi YK, Babu S, Sarin S, et al. Immunoprophylaxis of epidemic non-A non-B hepatitis. Indian J Med Res. 1985;81:18-19.
346. Khuroo MS, Dar MY. Hepatitis E: Evidence for person-to-person transmission and inability of low dose immune serum globulin from an Indian source to prevent it. Indian J Gastroenterol. 1992;11:113-116.
347. Chauhan A, Dilawari JB, Sharma R, et al. Role of long-persisting human hepatitis E virus antibodies in protection. Vaccine. 1998;16:755-756.
348. Pillot J, Turkoglu S, Dubreuil P, et al. Cross-reactive immunity against different strains of the hepatitis E virus transferable by simian and human sera. C R Acad Sci III. 1995;318:1059-1064.
349. Purdy MA, McCaustland KA, Krawczynski K, et al. Preliminary evidence that a trpE-HEV fusion protein protects cynomolgus macaques against challenge with wild-type hepatitis E virus (HEV). J Med Virol. 1993;41:90-94.
350. Fuerst TR, Yarbough PO, Zhang Y, et al. Prevention of hepatitis E using a novel ORF-2 subunit vaccine. In: Buisson Y, Coursaget P, Kane M, eds. Enterically-Transmitted Hepatitis Viruses. Joué-lès-Tours, France: La Simarre; 1996:384-392.
351. Tsarev SA, Tsareva TS, Emerson SU, et al. Recombinant vaccine against hepatitis E: Dose response and protection against heterologous challenge. Vaccine. 1997;15:1834-1838.
352. Tsarev SA, Tsareva TS, Emerson SU, et al. Prospects for prevention of hepatitis E. In: Buisson Y, Coursaget P, Kane M, eds. Enterically-Transmitted Hepatitis Viruses.
353. Emerson SU, Purcell RH. Recombinant vaccines for hepatitis E. Trends Mol Med. 2001;7:462-266.
354. Robinson R, Burgess W, Emerson SU, et al. Structural characterization of recombinant hepatitis E ORF2 proteins in baculovirus-infected insect cells. Protein Expr Purif. 1998;12:75-84.
355. McAtee C, Zhang Y, Yarbough P, et al. Purification of a soluble hepatitis E open reading frame 2-derived protein with unique antigenic properties. Protein Expr Purif. 1996;8:262-270.
356. McAtee C, Zhang Y, Yarbough P, et al. Purification and characterization of a recombinant hepatitis E protein vaccine candidate by liquid chromatography-mass spectrometry. J Chromatogr B Biomed Sci Appl. 1996;685:91-104.
357. Purcell RH, Nguyen H, Shapiro M, et al. Pre-clinical immunogenicity and efficacy trial of a recombinant hepatitis E vaccine. Vaccine. 2003;21:2607-2615.
358. Zhang M, Emerson SU, Nguyen H, et al. Recombinant vaccine against hepatitis E: duration of protective immunity in rhesus macaques. Vaccine. 2002;20:3285-3291.
359. Safary A. Perspectives of vaccination against hepatitis E. Intervirology. 2001:44:162-166.
360. Kamili S, Spelbring J, Krawczynski K. DNA vaccination against hepatitis E virus infection in cynomolgus macaques. J Gastroenterol Hepatol. 2002;17:S365-S369.
361. Tuteja R, Li TC, Takeda N, Jameel S. Augmentation of immune responses to hepatitis E virus ORF2 DNA vaccination by codelivery of cytokine genes. Viral Immunol. 2000;13:169-178.

CHAPTER 175

Prions and Prion Diseases of the Central Nervous System (Transmissible Neurodegenerative Diseases)

KENNETH L. TYLER

The concept of "atypically slow infections" was introduced in 1954 by Sigurdsson,[1] based on his observations of the naturally occurring diseases of visna, maedi, and scrapie in sheep, which first had been described in the 18th century. He suggested that these "slow infections" were progressive pathologic processes caused by a transmissible agent that remained clinically silent during a prolonged incubation period lasting months to years, after which progressive clinical disease appeared, usually ending in profound disability or death.

After the initial reports describing the clinical and pathologic features of kuru appeared (see later), Hadlow[2] remarked on the similarities in the neuropathology of kuru and scrapie, triggering the search for the potential transmissibility of kuru, a feature previously known to be characteristic of scrapie. The key similarities between kuru and scrapie that drew Hadlow's attention were the presence in both disorders of profound neuronal degeneration and intense reactive astrogliosis in the absence of an associated inflammatory response.

Kuru became the prototype of a new group of human neurologic disorders that have been linked by (1) common pathologic features, (2) the capability of infected brain material to transmit the disease, and (3) molecular and genetic data indicating that the accumulation of abnormal host proteins—prions—is central to their pathogenesis. This group of diseases now includes the human diseases Creutzfeldt-Jakob disease (CJD), new variant CJD (nvCJD), Gerstmann-Sträussler-Scheinker syndrome (GSS), and fatal familial insomnia (FFI) and the animal diseases scrapie, bovine spongiform encephalopathy (BSE), transmissible mink encephalopathy, chronic wasting disease (CWD) of elk and deer, feline spongiform encephalopathy, and exotic ungulate encephalopathy.[3-16] These disorders frequently are referred to as *prion diseases* or *transmissible neurodegenerative diseases.*

In 1982, Prusiner[17] proposed the name *prion* for the agent responsible for the transmissible neurodegenerative diseases. The term *prion* initially was chosen to emphasize the hypothesis that the causative agents in these diseases were *pro*teinaceous *in*fectious particles that could be distinguished from viruses and viroids by their apparent lack of nucleic acid.[17,18] Subsequently a prion has been defined as a "small infectious pathogen containing protein" that is "resistant to procedures that modify or hydrolyze nucleic acids"[19] or as a "proteinaceous infectious protein that lacks nucleic acid."[7,11] The pathogenesis of this group of diseases has been hypothesized to involve the generation and accumulation of a pathologic isoform of the normal form of the prion protein with subsequent neuronal dysfunction. The exact mechanism leading to the conversion of the normal prion protein to its pathologic isoform, the process that allows for accumulation of the pathologic proteins, and the mechanism by which they lead to neuronal cell death are subjects of active investigation and in some cases continued controversy (see later).

Human prion diseases share many fundamental properties. First, their major pathologic manifestations are confined almost exclusively to the central nervous system (CNS). Second, the diseases typically have long incubation times that, at least in the case of kuru, may exceed 30 years.[20,21] Third, the diseases seem to be inexorably progressive and ultimately fatal. Fourth, the neuropathologic hallmarks of the prion diseases are similar, although not identical, and often include reactive astrocytosis, minimal inflammatory response, and neuronal degeneration often, but not invariably, accompanied by vacuoles within cells and in the surrounding neuropil (status spongiosus or spongioform degeneration). Finally, each of these diseases seems to be associated with aberrant accumulation of a pathologic isoform of the prion protein.

MOLECULAR BIOLOGY AND PROPERTIES OF PRIONS

The bulk of investigations of prions have involved the scrapie agent, which can be taken as the unofficial prototype for the group. Purification of material from brains of animals infected with scrapie resulted in the identification of a protease-resistant protein, designated the *prion protein (PrP)*. PrP seems to be the major, and likely exclusive, component of prions, the agents responsible for prion diseases. Systematic studies of the resistance and susceptibility of prions to a wide variety of physical and chemical agents have been done in an effort to glean information concerning their fundamental composition and structure.[9-16,22-24] Prions are extraordinarily resistant to inactivation by agents that hydrolyze, modify, or shear nucleic acids, including nucleases, ultraviolet radiation, and nucleophiles.[25,26] Hybridization studies using probes derived from the PrP gene sequence (see later) also indicate that there are fewer than 0.004 PrP gene sequence per median infective dose (ID_{50}) unit of prion infectivity.[27] These results have been interpreted as indicating that prions do not contain nucleic acid, although some investigators continue to insist that it is possible for prions to contain an extremely small amount (e.g., <50 nucleotides) of nucleic acid or nucleic acid protected within a densely packed protein shell.[6,28-32] Salient properties of prions are summarized in Table 175-1.

TABLE 175-1   Properties of Cellular (PrPc) and Scrapie (PrPSc) Prion Proteins

Feature	Protein	
	PrPc (Normal Isoform)	*PrPSc (Scrapie Isoform)*
Form	Monomer	Oligomer or Polymer
Secondary structure	α-Helix (42%) β-sheet (3%)	α-Helix (30%) β-sheet (43%)
Proteinase K digestion	Sensitive	Resistant
Detergent extraction	Soluble	Insoluble; forms rods, fibrils
Predominant cellular localization	Cell surface	Vesicles (acidic compartment)
Presence in normal brain	Yes	No
Presence in scrapie-infected brain	+	+++
Synthesis rate ($T_{1/2}$)	Rapid (<0.1 hr)	Slow (1-3 hr)
Degradation rate ($T_{1/2}$)	Rapid (5 hr)	Slow (>24 hr)

$T_{1/2}$, half-life.
After Johnson RT. Viral Infections of the Nervous System. 2nd ed. Philadelphia: Lippincott-Raven; 1998.

In contrast to the difficulty in inactivating scrapie prions with manipulations that alter or hydrolyze nucleic acids is the relative ease in reducing infectivity of prions with agents that digest, denature, or chemically modify proteins.[18] These agents include a variety of proteolytic enzymes, denaturing agents, detergents, organic solvents, chaotropic salts, and urea. These studies suggest that protein is an integral component of prions and is required for their infectivity.

Initial attempts to characterize prions were hampered severely by the difficulty in conducting bioassays to measure infectivity and the fact that studies required the use of large animals, such as sheep or goats. Subsequent purification of prions has been facilitated greatly by the transmission of scrapie and other prion diseases to small rodents, including mice[33] and Syrian hamsters,[34] and by the development of improved bioassays.[35] One of the most commonly employed bioassays, the incubation time interval assay, is based on the assumption that as the infective dose of prions in a test inoculum increases, the incubation time to the development of illness decreases.[36,37] Although the accuracy of this type of assay has been questioned,[38] its use dramatically facilitated development of improved purification procedures for prions.

Using a variety of purification strategies, it has been possible to increase the specific infectivity (ID_{50} units per mg of protein) in scrapie preparations more than 4000-fold over the initial starting material.[39] As noted previously, the major, and perhaps exclusive, component in these purified preparations is a hydrophobic protein with a molecular mass of 27 to 30 kD, which has been designated *PrP 27-30*.[40,41] It subsequently was shown that PrP 27-30 is the protease-resistant core generated by removal of approximately 67 amino acids from the amino-terminus of a larger protein of molecular mass 33 to 35 kD, designated *PrP 33-35* or *PrP^Sc* (see later).[27,42] A protein similar to PrP^Sc, designated *PrP^C*, is present in the brains of normal (uninfected) animals. PrP^Sc differs from PrP^C in many biologic and chemical properties, including increased resistance to protease digestion and capacity to polymerize into abnormal structures referred to as *prion rods* or *scrapie-associated fibrils* (see Table 175-1).[11,43-46]

Purification of PrP^Sc from the brains of scrapie-infected animals allowed the amino acid sequence of its amino-terminal amino acids to be determined. This sequence was used to generate a series of oligonucleotide probes that were used to screen a cDNA library containing 150,000 colonies derived from scrapie-infected hamster brain. This strategy ultimately led to the cloning and sequencing of the gene encoding PrP. This was a crucial discovery because it indicated that the PrP was encoded by a host gene rather than contained within the infectious agent itself.[27] The PrP gene has been mapped to the short arm of human chromosome 20 and the homologous region of mouse chromosome 2.[47] The PrP gene is either identical to or extremely closely linked to genes (*Prn-i, Sinc*) that control the incubation time to onset of illness in inbred strains of mice infected with scrapie.[48,49] This relationship provides additional evidence for the key role played by PrP in the pathogenesis of prion diseases.

The PrP gene[3,11,27,50,51] begins with a guanine-cytosine–rich promoter region. After a 10-kb intron, there is a long open reading frame contained within a single exon. This open reading frame encodes a large 253–amino-acid (human) or 254–amino-acid (mouse, hamster) protein[27,50] that encompasses PrP 33-35. The carboxyl-terminal 23 amino acids of PrP are removed during biosynthesis, and a phosphatidylinositol glycolipid anchor is added.[52] An amino-terminal signal sequence of 22 amino acids also is removed by host cell proteases, presumably within either the rough endoplasmic reticulum or the lysosomes.[53] There are two asparagine-linked oligosaccharides, which subsequently are sialylated within the Golgi apparatus, and a single disulfide bond.[54] No differences have been detected in the organization of the PrP gene in healthy and scrapie-infected animals.[55]

The topologic orientation of PrP^C in the cell membrane remains to be definitively established because the protein contains two transmembrane-spanning domains[56] and a glycosyl phosphatidylinositol[52] anchor. Most models of PrP^C suggest that it is attached to the cell surface by the glycosyl phosphatidylinositol anchor. The protein seems to transit rapidly (half-life 1 to 6 hours) from the cell surface via clathrin-mediated endocytosis,[58] although some PrP^C may be recycled to the cell surface.[59] A secreted form of PrP^C also has been found in cell cultures.[60] PrP^Sc accumulates within cells, rather than being located on the cell surface similar to its normal counterpart. PrP^Sc is found in cytoplasmic vacuoles and secondary lysosomes.[11,51,53,57,61] It has been suggested that conversion of PrP^C to PrP^Sc occurs in caveolae-like membranous domains.[62] A key step in the synthesis of the abnormal isoform PrP^Sc may occur during transit of PrP between the Golgi apparatus, where the protein is sialylated, and its subsequent entry into lysosomes.[53]

Various forms of PrP may be synthesized at the endoplasmic reticulum. It has been suggested that some of these topologic isoforms may be neurotoxic,[63] and expression of some forms in transgenic mice can lead to neurodegenerative disease.[64] Retrograde transport of PrP^C from the endoplasmic reticulum into the cytosol results in the appearance of PrP^Sc-like aggregates, suggesting that aberrant cell trafficking of PrP^C could play a key role in PrP^Sc formation.[63] The exact mechanisms by which accumulation of PrP^Sc results in neuronal dysfunction are unknown, however. Rodent neuronal cultures exposed to peptides encompassing part or all of amino acids 106 to 126 of the PrP undergo apoptotic cell death, suggesting that PrP or its derivatives may be directly neurotoxic.[65,66] This neurotoxicity does not occur in cells devoid of PrP^C.[67]

Levels of messenger RNA (mRNA) encoding PrP^C seem to vary during development, and amounts of the protein differ in different tissues. Levels of PrP are greatest in the CNS and are substantially higher in neurons than in glial cells.[68] These levels suggest that PrP^C may play a role in neuronal development; however, the function of PrP^C in normal cells is unknown. It was suggested previously that the chicken prion protein co-purified with a protein having acetylcholine receptor–inducing activity (ARIA),[69,70] but more recent evidence indicates that PrP and ARIA protein are distinct from one another.[71]

PrP^C shares approximately 26% sequence homology and is structurally similar to a copper-binding protein, "doppel," which is a 179–amino acid protein encoded by a gene (*PRND*) approximately 16 kb downstream of the gene encoding PrP (*PRNP*).[72-74] PrP^C, similar to doppel, also functions as a copper-binding protein.[75] It has been suggested that PrP^C and doppel are paralogues that arose from an ancient gene duplication with PrP encoded by the *PRNP* gene and doppel encoded by the *PRND* gene, representing the two known members of the *PRN* gene family. Doppel expression is limited to the testis and endothelial cells in the developing CNS, and the protein is not found in the mature CNS. Ectopic overexpression of doppel in the CNS results in cerebellar degeneration due to apoptotic death of cerebellar granule cells.[72-74] The physiologic role of doppel, similar to that of PrP^C, is unknown. Among the candidate functions for PrP^C are a role in regulating cuproenzymes, such as superoxide dismutase activity (found in some studies but not others); cell adhesion; laminin binding; neurite genesis; and synaptic function (found in some studies but not others).[76-79]

Transgenic mice with a disrupted PrP gene show normal early development and do not have detectable abnormalities in the CNS or elsewhere.[80-82] These mice may show alterations in circadian rhythms and sleep-wake cycles.[83] Initial studies suggested that mice also developed progressive ataxia associated with loss of cerebellar Purkinje cells as they aged; this ataxia seems to have been due to aberrant overexpression of doppel in the cerebellum rather than due to loss of PrP^C.[72,74,84] These findings are of interest given the prominence of insomnia in the human prion disease FFI and of cerebellar disease in patients with GSS, kuru, and some forms of CJD (see later on). Older mice harboring high copy numbers of wild-type PrP transgenes develop neurologic illness characterized clinically by truncal ataxia, hindlimb paralysis, and tremors and pathologically by necrotizing myopathy, demyelinating polyneuropathy, and focal CNS vacuolization.[85]

The expression of the PrP gene does not differ between healthy and scrapie-infected animals.[27,50] Despite this fact, PrP^Sc clearly accumulates in scrapie-infected animals. Although expression of PrP^C mRNA does increase during normal development, the PrP gene is constitutively expressed in adult animals,[27,50] and PrP^C levels do not increase during adult life in uninfected animals. These findings, combined with differences in the biologic properties of PrP^C and PrP^{Sc}, have led to the conclusion that in infected animals, PrP^C undergoes a post-translational modification resulting in its conversion to the abnormal PrP^{Sc} isoform. The conformational change that results from the conversion of the normal cellular prion protein (PrP^C) to the abnormal disease-associated isoform (PrP^{Sc}) is associated with a marked decrease in the protein's α-helical content and a corresponding increase in the amount of β-pleated sheet.[11,86,87] Evidence suggests that this conversion occurs predominantly within certain subcellular compartments, including caveolae-like membranous domains.[62]

The identification of specific mutations in patients with familial prion diseases (see later) provided the impetus to develop transgenic mice expressing mutant forms of the *PRNP* gene. Transgenic mice with the proline-to-leucine (P102L) mutation found in GSS patients within the mouse *PRNP* gene (MoPrP-P101L) develop spongiform changes in the CNS, gliosis, neuronal loss, and PrP$^+$ plaques.[88] These mice develop clinical features of scrapie. When brain extracts from these diseased mice are inoculated into transgenic mice, these mice develop neuropathologic changes consistent with scrapie but not overt clinical disease.[89,90]

Transgenic mice with a variety of additional mutations in codons 113, 115, and 118 of the *PRNP* gene also develop spontaneous neurodegeneration that can be transmitted to hamsters and transgenic mice.[7] Transgenic mice also have been created carrying transgenes with deletions in individual regions of the *PRNP* gene encoding areas of putative important secondary structures in PrP.[91] Transgenic mice with transgene deletions in the amino-terminal part of PrP remain healthy, whereas mice with deletions in either of the two carboxyl-terminal α-helices develop neurodegenerative disease. The disease differs from typical prion disease, however, and is characterized by enlarged neurons with prominent cytoplasmic inclusions.

Studies with transgenic mice also have led to the hypothesis that there is another, as yet unidentified, host factor—"protein X"—that binds to PrP^C and facilitates its conversion to PrP^{Sc}.[92,93] It has been suggested that PrP^C and PrP^{Sc} molecules bind together through a site in the amino-terminal portion of PrP, whereas the X factor binds near the carboxyl terminus of PrP.[17,93-95] Studies using conformation-sensitive monoclonal antibodies and Fab fragments suggest that it is at the amino-terminal amino acid residues (amino acids 90 to 112) of PrP that the most striking conformational changes occur during its conversion to PrP^{Sc}.[7,95,96] Overexpression of a PrP with deletions in a nearby region (amino acids 114 to 121) inhibits accumulation of PrP^{Sc} in scrapie-infected neuroblastoma cells—effectively behaving as a dominant negative mutant.[97] Three mutations in patients with familial prion diseases (GSS) are known to occur within these regions (e.g., P102L, P105L, A117V), but most do not. Mutations elsewhere in the protein also may influence PrP^C-to-PrP^{Sc} conversion, perhaps by destabilizing PrP structure.

The accumulation of PrP^{Sc} in infected animals after experimental inoculation and in spontaneously occurring prion disease indicates that prions are capable of replication. The mechanism by which PrP replicates and by which scrapie infectivity increases is unknown, although many possibilities have been suggested.[7,11,51] It has been proposed that the combination of a single PrP^{Sc} molecule with a single PrP^C molecule results in a heterodimeric intermediate that subsequently is transformed into two PrP^{Sc} molecules. This interaction is consistent with data from studies of transgenic mice.[98,99] This process continues through successive cycles in which newly created PrP^{Sc} combines in exponentially increasing numbers with PrP^C molecules.[11,22,23,51] Many additional models of prion replication also have been proposed.[12,51,100,101]

Many studies indicate that when inoculated into the CNS, PrP^{Sc} disseminates by spreading within the axons of nerve cells,[101-103] possibly by slow axonal transport. Intriguingly, more recent studies suggest that follicular dendritic cells and B cells may play a crucial role in the neuroinvasion of scrapie, although the mechanism by which this occurs is unclear.[104] Immunodeficient mice with defects in B cells and resulting severe defects in follicular dendritic cell organization, but not mice with isolated T-cell defects, fail to develop scrapie after in-

traperitoneal challenge.[101] It has been suggested that after peripheral inoculation, prions may undergo an initial period of replication in lymphoreticular tissues[101] before neuroinvasion, which, as noted, seems to occur via axonal transport.

PRION DISEASES

Kuru

Kuru was the first of the human prion diseases to be studied in detail (Table 175-2).[4,105-115] It was originally endemic within the Fore linguistic tribal group of the Eastern Highlands of Papua New Guinea. Epidemiologic studies suggest that the disease likely was transmitted through the practice of ritual endocannibalism at funeral feasts[113]; no one born since the cessation of this practice has developed kuru. The mean incubation period was 10 to 13 years, with 90% of cases occurring within 21 to 27 years of exposure. Incubation period was likely related to exposure dose and was shorter in women than men and shorter in older women than younger women, reflecting the likelihood of participation in cannibalistic practices.[116]

Kuru remains important conceptually, even as it disappears as a clinical entity, as an example of human-to-human transmission of a prion disease and an example of the potential of prion diseases to be transmitted via the oral route. Kuru typically begins insidiously with a prodrome of headaches and arthralgia. This prodrome is followed by the development of an inexorably progressive neurologic disease resulting in death within 3 months to 2 years of onset, usually from intercurrent pneumonia and malnutrition. The cardinal clinical features include cerebellar ataxia, action tremor, and involuntary movements (choreoathetosis, myoclonic jerks, and coarse fasciculations), followed in the later stages of the illness by progressively worsening dementia.[6,10,11,13,14,16,115] Cranial nerve abnormalities, motor weakness, and sensory loss are absent or occur only in the late stages of the disease.

Although laboratory tests, including electroencephalogram (EEG), cerebrospinal fluid (CSF) analysis for 14-3-3 and other pathologic proteins, and magnetic resonance imaging (MRI), can provide important clues to assist in the premortem diagnosis of many prion diseases (see later), the lack of "modern" cases of kuru has made it impossible to gauge accurately the frequency with which these tests would be abnormal in kuru. When kuru was prevalent, laboratory tests rarely were helpful in making the diagnosis and largely served to exclude other diagnostic possibilities. The CSF did not show pleocytosis or elevated protein concentration; 14-3-3 protein analysis has not been done on any significant number of specimens. EEG did not show the characteristic periodic sharp wave complexes (PSWCs) typical of CJD (see later on).[114] No neuroimaging studies are available on patients with kuru. In a study of brain material obtained from 18 patients with kuru, 95% of the tissue preparations transmitted the infection to primates.[4]

Neuropathologic examination of kuru brains shows neuronal loss and astrogliosis with the accumulation of PrP^{Sc}.[112,117] One of the pathologic hallmarks of kuru is the presence of PrP^{Sc}-reactive plaques, predominantly in cerebellar tissue. These plaques are usually unicentric, located in the granular layer of the cerebellum, and often associated with microglial cells. Plaques resembling those seen in kuru and irregular plaques or other depositions of PrP^{Sc} immunoreactive material can be seen in patients with GSS (see later) and some subtypes of familial CJD (fCJD), including patients with *PRNP* gene base-pair insertions and the E200K/199V mutation, and FFI patients with the D178N/129M genotype. Molecular analyses of the gene encoding the prion protein (*PRNP*) and of the characteristics of the PrP^{Sc} derived from brain material from kuru patients are limited. To date, there have been no reports of mutations in the *PRNP* gene in kuru patients. Kuru cases show, however, a higher than expected incidence of methionine/methionine (M/M) homozygosity at polymorphic codon 129, of the *PRNP* gene[118] (see later). Conversely, older women who potentially were exposed to infected brain material during the era of cannibalism and survived without developing kuru show a higher than expected frequency of heterozygosity at codon 129, leading to the suggestion that this heterozygosity may have played a protective role against the

TABLE 175-2 Clinical and Epidemiologic Features of Human Prion Diseases

Disease	Clinical Features	Source of Infection	Geographic Distribution and Prevalence	Useful Ancillary Tests	Duration of Illness
sCJD	Dementia, myoclonus	Unknown	Worldwide; 1/1 million/yr; 85-95% of CJD cases	EEG—PSWCs; CSF 14-3-3; MRI/DWI	
fCJD	Dementia, myoclonus	Genetic (*PRNP* mutations)	Worldwide—geographic clusters; >100 known families; 5-15% of CJD cases	Gene testing; EEG—PSWC rare; MRI/DWI (?)	Mean ≈15 mo
iCJD	Incoordination, dementia (late)	Cadaver dural grafts, human pituitary hormones, corneal transplantation, neurosurgical instruments, EEG depth electrodes	<1% of CJD cases in toto: ≈115-200 cases (cadaver dural grafts), ≈140-200 cases (human pituitary hormones), ≈4 cases (corneal transplantation); ≈5 cases (neurosurgical instruments), 2 cases (EEG depth electrodes)		1 mo-10 yr incubation period: 1.5-18 yr for dural grafts, 6-30 yr for growth hormone, 12-28 mo for neurosurgical cases and electrodes
nvCJD	Mood and behavioral abnormalities, paresthesias, dementia	Linked to BSE in cattle	United Kingdom; ≈150 cases	Tonsil biopsy may show PrPSc	14 mo
Kuru	Incoordination, ataxia, tremors, dementia (late)	Linked to cannibalism	Fore tribes of Papua New Guinea (≈2600 known cases)	EEG—no PSWCs; CSF 14-3-3 often negative; MRI (?)	3-24 mo
GSS	Incoordination, chronic progressive ataxia, corticospinal tract signs, dementia (late), myoclonus (rare)	90% genetic (*PRNP* mutations)	Worldwide; >50 families; 1-10/100 million/yr	Gene testing	2-6 yr (mean ≈57 mo)
FFI	Disrupted sleep > intractable insomnia; autonomic hyperactivation; myoclonus, ataxia; corticospinal tract signs; dementia	*PRNP* gene mutation (D178L); very rare sporadic cases	≈27 families in Europe, United Kingdom, U.S., Finland, Australia, China, Japan	EEG—PSWCs only rarely positive; MRI—no DWI abnormalities; CSF 14-3-3 positive in ≈50%	8 mo-6 yr (mean ≈18 mo)

BSE, bovine spongiform encephalopathy; CSF, cerebrospinal fluid; DWI, diffusion-weighted imaging; EEG, electroencephalogram; fCJD, familial Creutzfeldt-Jakob disease; FFI, fatal familial insomnia; GSS, Gerstmann-Sträussler-Scheinker syndrome; iCJD, iatrogenic Creutzfeldt-Jakob disease; MRI, magnetic resonance imaging; nvCJD, new variant Creutzfeldt-Jakob disease; PSWCs, periodic sharp wave complexes; sCJD, sporadic Creutzfeldt-Jakob disease.

transmission of prion diseases in the Fore and other ancient populations practicing cannibalism.[119] It has been suggested, not without controversy, that the wide geographic prevalence of codon 129 heterozygosity is indirect evidence that cannibalism may have been more widespread among ancient human populations than previously believed, although environmental exposure to prion diseases from other sources (e.g., tainted animal meat) also would have provided a survival benefit for maintaining codon 129 heterozygosity.

Creutzfeldt-Jakob Disease

In the early 1920s, the German neurologists Creutzfeldt and Jakob separately described a puzzling series of cases of neurodegenerative disease.[120,121] The neuropathologist Spielmeyer was the first to use the eponym *Creutzfeldt-Jakob disease,* a designation now solidified by historical usage, although modern review of the available pathologic material from Creutzfeldt and Jakob's original cases suggests that many were examples of other diseases, and only a few of the original cases likely would be diagnosed as CJD today. CJD is a rare disease, with a prevalence and incidence of approximately 1 case per 1 million population worldwide. It is the most commonly encountered of the human prion diseases and has been responsible for much of the current knowledge concerning the clinical, pathologic, and laboratory features of these diseases (see Table 175-2).[3,4,8,10,13,16] Most (85% to 95%) cases are sporadic. Familial cases, although accounting for only a few patients, have proved to be invaluable in establishing the role played by the PrP gene in the pathogenesis of this disease (see later). fCJD is inherited in autosomal dominant fashion, although the penetrance may be variable.

CJD shows no gender predilection. Mean age at onset is 57 to 62 years, although patients 17 to 20 years old[122-124] and older than 80 years old with classic CJD have been reported.[122,125] Early onset of CJD should prompt a thorough search for iatrogenic sources of infection, such as administration of cadaver human growth or gonadotropic

hormone or the transplantation of potentially infected human material, and is a characteristic of some cases of nvCJD and some cases of fCJD (see later).

Despite fears to the contrary, CJD is not contagious. Examples of iatrogenic person-to-person spread are exceedingly rare,[123,126] but such spread has followed transplantation of dural grafts,[126-130] corneal transplantation,[126,130-133] liver transplantation,[134] use of dura mater material in radiographic embolization procedures,[135,136] and use of contaminated neurosurgical instruments or stereotactic depth electrodes.[126,130,137-139] Although the numbers are evolving constantly as new cases are identified, a review in 2000 identified 143 cases of iatrogenic CJD (iCJD) associated with human pituitary hormone administration, 114 cases associated with cadaver lyophilized dural transplants, 7 cases associated with contaminated neurosurgical instruments or intracortically implanted EEG depth electrodes, and 3 cases associated with cadaver corneal transplantation.[126,130] In the case of dura mater grafts, most implicated grafts have been the product (Lyodura) of a single German commercial producer (Braun). More cases (67 of 114) have been reported from Japan than from all other countries worldwide.[126,127,129,130] Cases have occurred in at least 15 additional countries, however, including at least 10 cases from Canada and the United States. The incubation period in these cases has ranged from 16 months to 19 years (median 6 to 8 years). The common clinical presentation includes memory disturbance (68%), disorientation (56%), cerebellar ataxia (56%), and visual disturbances (51%), with a smaller subset of patients (12% to 28%) having abnormal behavior, hallucinations, dysarthria, or paresthesias. Myoclonus was not seen in any patients in one review of 57 cases.[128]

At least 114 cases of iCJD have been reported in young patients who received cadaver human growth hormone for the treatment of endocrine disorders, including panhypopituitarism,[126,130,140-145] with at least 4 additional cases in women receiving cadaver pituitary gonadotropin for infertility,[126,146,147] practices that now have been discontinued. Patients with human growth hormone–associated CJD typically received injections of growth hormone prepared from pools of 15,000 pituitary glands, several times weekly for several years. CJD developed after a variable incubation period (range 3 to 22 years, median 12 to 13 years), and patients often presented with a clinical picture reminiscent of kuru. One more recently reported patient received human growth hormone in low dose on one occasion for diagnostic purposes and developed iCJD 38 years later, suggesting that even longer incubation periods are possible in cases with low inoculum exposure.[148] Ataxia and associated incoordination and extrapyramidal features often are prominent, and dementia may be minimal or absent in the early stages.

The first reported case of iCJD in a corneal transplant recipient was a 56-year-old woman, who developed CJD 18 months after a transplant for Fuchs's corneal dystrophy and died 8 months later.[131] A second case occurred in a 63-year-old woman who developed CJD 15 months after receiving a corneal transplant for a traumatic corneal injury and died 40 months later.[129] A third case occurred in a 46-year-old woman who received transplants at ages 15 and 33 years for keratoconus and developed CJD 30 years after her first transplant, dying after a 14-month illness.[129,133] Another case was a 28-year-old man who had received two corneal transplants at ages 6 months and 1 year, who developed CJD 25 years later and died after a 23-month illness.[129] It is important to emphasize the rarity of these reports in light of the enormous number of corneal transplants performed annually (approximately 40,000/year in the United States alone). No case of corneal transplant–related iCJD has been reported in the United States in nearly 3 decades.

Five cases of iCJD have followed surgery with contaminated neurosurgical instruments, four from the United Kingdom[137] and one from France.[138] The incubation period after surgery ranged from 12 to 28 months (median 17 months). In two cases from Switzerland,[139] intracortically implanted stereotactic depth electrodes for EEG monitoring were implicated. The incubation period was 16 and 20 months in the two affected patients. Documented cases of neurosurgical transmission are remarkably rare, despite the large number of neurosurgical procedures performed.[126,130] Several hospitals in the United States, Canada, and United Kingdom have reported incidents in which neurosurgical instruments inadvertently were reused in other patients after having been used initially for diagnostic brain biopsies in patients who subsequently were found to have CJD. Despite these medical mishaps, no patient so exposed is known to have developed iCJD, although the time since surgery in most of these instances is insufficient to exclude absolutely the possibility that this may occur in the future. The Joint Commission on Accreditation of Healthcare Organizations has issued a Sentinel Event Alert concerning this risk.[149] Hospitals should be aware of this potential and should establish guidelines for the handling, quarantine, and tracking of neurosurgical instruments in patients undergoing brain biopsy for dementia or other unknown neurodegenerative illnesses. In such cases, disposable instruments can be used if practicable, reducing the need for quarantine and tracking.

Animal transmission studies suggest that whole blood, serum, or buffy coat derived from patients with CJD or animals experimentally inoculated with prions can contain low levels of infectivity.[150,151] BSE has been transmitted between sheep by large-volume blood transfusion.[152] This fact has raised legitimate concerns about the risk of transmitting CJD via transfusion of blood or blood products.[153,154] Despite fears to the contrary, however, there have been no documented cases in which CJD has been transmitted by transfusion of blood or blood products,[155] and a history of preceding transfusion does not seem to increase the risk for CJD in epidemiologic studies.[155-158]

Epidemiologic studies have tried to calculate odds ratios for various potential risk factors for CJD.[155-158] A family history of CJD (odds ratio 19.1) or dementia (odds ratio 2.3) or a medical history of psychotic disease (odds ratio 9.9)[155,158] enhanced the risk of CJD. The risk associated with surgical procedures in general or neurosurgical procedures in particular has differed among different studies. In one case-control study,[156] the odds ratio for surgical procedures was 2.1; two

other studies failed to find a statistically significant increased risk,[157,158] although in one study,[158] the odds ratio associated with brain surgery was 1.8. Blood transfusion has been examined repeatedly as a potential risk factor, with no evidence to date that it increases risk of developing CJD.[155-158] Dietary exposure to cooked animal meats is not a risk factor for CJD,[155] although consumption of raw meat (odds ratio 1.6) or brain (odds ratio 1.7) may be associated with some increased risk.[158] Working or living on a farm for more than 10 years (odds ratio 2.7) was related to increased risk of CJD in one study,[156] as was frequent exposure to leather products (odds ratio 1.9) or to fertilizer containing hoof and horn by-products (odds ratio 2.3) in another study.[158]

Isolated cases of CJD have occurred in approximately 24 physicians and other health care workers,[159] including 2 neurosurgeons, 1 pathologist, 9 nurses, and 2 histology technicians. Despite the natural concern these reports produce among some health care professionals, the incidence of CJD in this group does not exceed what would be expected by chance alone. There have been no documented reports of clear-cut transmission of disease from patients to hospital or mortuary staff. Similarly, although isolated cases of conjugal CJD have been reported, there does not seem to be any increased risk to spouses or other family members from exposure to CJD. As noted earlier, the presence of familial cases of CJD seems invariably to result from genetic factors rather than person-to-person spread of illness.

CJD typically manifests as a rapidly progressive dementia with associated myoclonus, although these characteristics are hardly apparent in the original descriptions of the disease.[160,161] There is a great deal of variability in the clinical manifestations of CJD, and this has led to attempts to describe a variety of clinical subtypes, including subtypes with predominance of visual (Heidenhain[162]), cerebellar (Brownell and Oppenheimer[163]), thalamic (Stern[164]), and striatal (Garcin and coworkers[165]) features.[166] The primary importance of these syndromes is that they indicate CJD may predominantly affect particular brain regions disproportionately.

In most patients, CJD begins with mental deterioration, which may be manifested as dementia, behavioral disturbances, or other deficits in higher cortical function.[4,13,16,167,168] In about one third of patients, predominant initial visual or cerebellar symptoms may overshadow dementia. Mental deterioration typically is rapidly progressive, and the average duration of illness from onset of symptoms to death is 7 to 9 months. Unusual cases of longer duration have been described.[169] In addition to profound and rapidly progressive mental deterioration, another almost invariant feature of the disease is the presence of myoclonus. Myoclonus may be absent at disease onset, only to appear with increasing severity as the disease progresses. Myoclonus frequently is aggravated or induced by stimulation, including startle. Extrapyramidal symptoms and signs, including hypokinesia and rigidity, and cerebellar signs and symptoms, including nystagmus, tremor, and ataxia, ultimately develop in about two thirds of patients. About 40% to 80% of patients have signs of corticospinal tract dysfunction, including hyperreflexia, spasticity, and extensor plantar responses. Of CJD patients, 50% have prominent visual disturbances, which can include visual field cuts, cortical blindness, and visual agnosia. Rare cases have been reported in which isolated myoclonic alien hand syndrome has been the initial manifestation of CJD and has preceded the appearance of dementia and startle myoclonus.[170]

Certain neurologic disturbances occur only rarely as prominent features in CJD, and their presence should prompt consideration of other diagnostic possibilities. Although seizures occur in 10% to 20% of cases, they rarely are a dominant feature and typically are amenable to therapy. Seizures have not been prominent in fCJD cases with the possible exception of patients with the P102L and A117V mutations and GSS and the D178N/129M mutation and FFI (see later). Some patients have vague sensory complaints, including pruritus, but prominent sensory signs are unusual except in nvCJD (see later). Cranial nerve involvement is never prominent, although isolated cases with involvement of the pupils; extraocular movements; and trigeminal, auditory, and vestibular systems have been reported.[171] One family with the E200K mutation has prominent supranuclear gaze palsy. CJD does not typically affect the peripheral nervous system to any significant degree; however, demyelinating peripheral neuropathy occurs in transgenic mice overexpressing wild-type PrP.[85] Neuropathy has been described in rare patients with fCJD and the E200K mutation[172] and in isolated cases of sporadic CJD.[173,174] One study found, however, clinical evidence of peripheral neuropathy in approximately 20% of cases examined, and electrophysiologic abnormalities in 88% of 16 surveyed cases of sCJD.[175] The most common findings were abnormalities consistent with axonal neuropathy (nine cases), mixed axonal and demyelinating neuropathy (four cases), and motor neuronopathy (one case). Nonetheless, the presence of significant peripheral neuropathy or amyotrophy should prompt a careful search for alternative diagnoses in patients with suspected CJD.

Rare cases of CJD also have been reported in which the clinical features indicated prominent autonomic nervous system involvement. These features included hypohidrosis, bowel dysfunction, abnormal pupillary responses to autonomic drugs, abnormal diurnal blood pressure variation, and electrocardiogram abnormalities.[176] Autonomic hyperactivity also is a cardinal feature in FFI (see later).

A subgroup of patients (10%) develop prominent lower motor neuron signs and symptoms, including prominent muscular atrophy and fasciculations.[177] These patients frequently have a slowly progressive illness of longer duration—atypical for classic CJD. In contrast to classic CJD, this "amyotrophic" variant of CJD is only rarely transmissible to primates,[178,179] suggesting that most cases are not truly cases of prion disease but probably are related more closely to syndromes of amyotrophic lateral sclerosis plus dementia). Lower motor neuron, features including prominent atrophy and fasciculations, also occasionally have been described in patients with fCJD and the D178N/129V and E200K mutations and in GSS patients with the P102L and A117V mutations (see later).

Routine laboratory and diagnostic tests are rarely helpful in establishing the diagnosis of CJD but may be useful in excluding other diagnostic possibilities. Complete blood count, differential count, and sedimentation rate all are normal. A few patients have had abnormalities in liver function.[179,180]

In patients with CJD, the CSF is acellular and has a normal glucose concentration and a normal or mildly elevated protein content. The presence of a significant pleocytosis or hypoglycorrhachia should prompt a search for other diagnostic possibilities. Several studies have suggested that the presence of specific proteins in CSF may serve as useful diagnostic tests for CJD. The first evidence for this possibility came when abnormalities were noted in the CSF protein profile of patients with CJD after two-dimensional isoelectric focusing.[181-183] One of the abnormal CSF proteins is the 14-3-3 protein. Specific Western immunoblot and enzyme-linked immunosorbent assays for CSF 14-3-3 protein have been developed.[184-187] Testing for CSF 14-3-3 protein is available at the National Prion Disease Pathology Surveillance Center (http://www.cjdsurveillance.com/) and through the Laboratory of CNS Studies at the National Institutes of Neurological Disorders and Stroke. The sensitivity and specificity of detecting CSF 14-3-3 protein are controversial. Early studies reported elevated 14-3-3 protein in 95% to 97% of patients with definite sCJD and in 93% of patients with probable sCJD.[185] Using quantitative rather than qualitative assays may improve diagnostic accuracy.[186,187] CSF 14-3-3 levels also may increase progressively during the course of disease. In one study, the specificity of detecting CSF 14-3-3 levels greater than 8 ng/mL was 100% compared with only 49% when a cutoff of 4 ng/mL was used.[186] In a second study, a cutoff value of 8.3 ng/mL had a sensitivity of 93% and specificity of 98%.[187] As would be expected, the higher cutoff levels led to decreased sensitivity (61% at 8 ng/mL compared with 94% at 4 ng/mL). Studies using immunoblots rather than quantitative detection of 14-3-3 have produced widely varying estimates of specificity. In one study, only 17 of 32 (53%) patients with autopsy-confirmed sCJD had a positive 14-3-3 protein,[188] but in another prospective study of 112 patients with suspected CJD, the specificity was 87%.[189] Detection of CSF 14-3-3 is even less sensitive in patients with fCJD or nvCJD

compared with sCJD, with only approximately 50% of cases having detectable CSF 14-3-3 (see later).

False-positive 14-3-3 protein elevations are an issue of concern if this test is to be used to assist in diagnosis of sCJD. Among the diseases that can enter into the differential diagnosis of sCJD, elevations in CSF 14-3-3 protein have been found in frontotemporal dementia, Alzheimer's disease, vascular dementia, dementia with Lewy bodies, metabolic encephalopathy, intracerebral metastatic cancer and carcinomatous meningitis, paraneoplastic encephalitis, hypoxic encephalopathy, and herpes simplex encephalitis.[190-192]

Levels of a variety of proteins, including neuron-specific enolase, S100 glial protein, and tau protein,[186,192a-194] may be elevated in the CSF of patients with CJD, although it is unknown which of these abnormalities are sensitive and specific enough to be clinically useful. Detection of neuron-specific enolase levels greater than 30 ng/mL has a reported sensitivity of 87% and specificity of 66%, whereas with use of a higher cutoff value (35 ng/mL), sensitivity decreases to 80%, but specificity increases to 83%.[186] It has been suggested that finding elevations of CSF neuron-specific enolase (>35 ng/mL) or S100 (>8 ng/mL) in combination with the 14-3-3 protein may add to the sensitivity and specificity of the 14-3-3 test. The sensitivity of CSF neuron-specific enolase levels greater than 30 ng/mL is 87%, but specificity increases from 66% to 77% when this is combined with a 14-3-3 level greater than 4 ng/mL with no change in sensitivity.[186] The CSF S100 protein assay alone (>8 ng/mL) has been reported to have 84% specificity and 91% sensitivity for the diagnosis of sCJD.[192a] A serum version of the S100 test has been developed and has been reported in an initial study to have a sensitivity of 78% and a specificity of 81% for the diagnosis of CJD using a cutoff value of 213 pg/mL or greater.[191] Similar to other surrogate markers of CJD, this test has the disadvantage that elevated values can be found in a variety of neurologic diseases, including Alzheimer's disease, Parkinson's disease, multi-infarct dementia, meningoencephalitis, hypoxic brain injury, multiple sclerosis, and Wernicke's disease.[192a] It also has been suggested that finding elevated levels of tau (>1300 pg/mL)[193] or phosphorylated tau protein in CSF[194] has a sensitivity of 92% to 94% and a specificity of 90% to 97% in detection of sCJD, suggesting that this may be another useful CSF biomarker in disease diagnosis.

Computed tomography (CT) scan results may be abnormal in CJD, but the changes are nonspecific and nondiagnostic.[195-197] The presence of profound and rapidly progressive dementia in association with a CT scan without evidence of significant atrophy should suggest the possibility of CJD, however, because patients with advanced Alzheimer's disease typically have prominent atrophy. In some patients with CJD, serial CT scans[198,199] may show rapidly progressing cerebral atrophy and associated ex vacuo ventricular enlargement. Rapidly evolving CT scan changes such as these are encountered only rarely in other forms of dementia.

MRI is more sensitive than CT in detecting abnormalities in patients with CJD.[200-206] Protocols for obtaining MRI in patients with suspected CJD have been suggested.[204] Ideally the basic imaging sequences should include T_2 and proton density axial images at 3-mm slice thickness. Whenever available, diffusion-weighted imaging (DWI) and fluid-attenuated inversion recovery images also should be obtained because both seem to be more sensitive in detecting abnormalities then either proton density or T_2-weighted images. The most common abnormalities on standard images are increased T_2 signals in the striatum.[201,205,206] Increased signal intensity in the basal ganglia has been reported to have 67% sensitivity and 93% specificity for diagnosis of sCJD.[205] Many studies have suggested that DWI sequences are the most sensitive sequences for detecting abnormalities in patients with sCJD.[204,207-209] DWI sequences may show symmetrical increases in signal intensity in the cortex, basal ganglia, thalamus, and cingulate gyrus.[204,208-211] The cortical abnormalities often appear as multifocal or contiguous, ribbon-like areas of increased signal along gyri associated with decreased apparent diffusion coefficient values.[209,210] In one small study of 12 patients with rapidly progressive dementia, including 5 found subsequently to have sCJD at autopsy, the sensitivity and specificity of DWI abnormalities were reportedly 100%.[207] Abnormalities tend to increase in distribution and intensity over time, and apparent diffusion coefficient values progressively decline,[210] findings that can help distinguish the changes of CJD from changes of infarction or vasculitis. Although studies are extremely limited, similar DWI abnormalities also can be seen in patients with fCJD.[212] In one case presented as the first report of DWI abnormalities in iCJD, the possible iatrogenic cause was based solely on the patient's history of having received three cadaver corneal transplants 2 to 6 years previously, although there was no evidence the donors had CJD.[213] This case hardly can be considered an example of iCJD based on the information provided. The neuropathologic substrate for DWI abnormalities has not been characterized fully yet, although these abnormalities correlate with areas of severe neuropathologic change, including spongiform degeneration.[214]

Studies evaluating other imaging techniques, such as positron emission tomography (PET)[215] and single-photon emission computed tomography (SPECT),[216] are too few to determine the sensitivity or specificity of these tests. Fluorodeoxyglucose PET typically shows decreased glucose use in involved cortical areas, and SPECT shows decreased perfusion that may be global or confined to involved brain regions. Magnetic resonance spectroscopy has been reported in two patients, both of whom showed reduced *N*-acetyl aspartate-to-creatine ratios within the basal ganglia and thalami.[217]

Patients with CJD often have characteristic abnormalities on EEG,[199,218-222] and this test may be extremely helpful as a diagnostic tool. The classic EEG pattern, which ultimately appears in 67% to 95% of patients, consists of a slow background interrupted by generalized, bilaterally synchronous biphasic or triphasic PSWCs.[218,221,223] These occur at intervals of 0.5 to 2.5 seconds and have a duration of 100 to 600 msec. PSWCs may be absent early in disease, may disappear in the terminal stages, and often are more dramatic during periods of alertness, but they may disappear during sleep or under the influence of certain drugs, including barbiturates, benzodiazepines, topiramate, and methylphenidate.[224,225] It has been suggested that the presence of PSWCs, identified according to strict criteria in blinded EEG readings, has a sensitivity of approximately 65% and a specificity of 74% to 86% for the diagnosis of CJD.[221,222,226] In addition to changes in the waking EEG, many patients have almost complete absence of the rapid eye movement (REM) stage and other disturbances in sleep architecture.[228] Abnormalities in sleep architecture also are a cardinal clinical feature of FFI (see later). Obtaining serial EEGs in patients suspected of having CJD may be extremely useful if PSWCs are absent on an initial EEG study.[219,220] Lack of this typical EEG pattern in a patient whose illness has lasted for more than 4 months should cast doubt on the diagnosis of CJD. Typical periodic EEG abnormalities may be absent, however, in cases of fCJD[227] and generally are not seen in GSS, FFI, or nvCJD (see later).

Examination of brain material remains the gold standard for diagnosis of prion diseases, including CJD. The National Prion Disease Pathology Surveillance Center at Case Western Reserve University, Cleveland, Ohio, assists clinicians and pathologists in analyzing fixed brain material for characteristic histopathology and the presence of PrP^Sc and performs PrP^Sc immunohistochemistry and prion isoform analysis on frozen brain tissue from patients with suspected prion diseases. Instructions for shipping material are available at their website (http://www.cjdsurveillance.com/). Neuropathologic features of neuronal loss, reactive gliosis, and neuronal vacuolation (spongiform change), with an absence of inflammatory changes, typically are present in such cases and are consistent with the diagnosis. CJD occasionally may coexist with Alzheimer's disease, with patients showing the characteristic neuropathologic features of both disorders.[229,230]

The availability of monoclonal and polyclonal antibodies against prion proteins has allowed for the identification of PrP^Sc by Western immunoblot assay in brain material obtained at autopsy or by biopsy.[231] Immunologic tests seem to be sensitive and specific and have largely replaced demonstration of transmissibility to animals as the standard for diagnosis. A variety of techniques have been devel-

oped to immunostain for PrP^Sc in paraffin-embedded brain material or in cryostat preparations blotted onto nitrocellulose membranes ("histoblots"). Hydrolytic autoclaving or proteolysis disrupts the normal PrP^C isoform but leaves abnormal and still immunoreactive PrP^Sc. With these techniques, a variety of PrP staining patterns have been identified in CJD brain tissue. This tissue may show positive PrP staining limited to plaques or a more diffuse staining pattern that co-localizes with synaptic markers (e.g., synaptophysin) throughout the gray matter or a combination of both patterns.[232] In sCJD, pathologic and immunocytochemical changes typically are limited to brain. One more recent report suggests that PrP^Sc immunoreactivity also can be found at autopsy in neuroepithelial cells in olfactory mucosal epithelium of patients with sCJD.[233] In cases of fCJD, distinct neuropathologic and immunostaining features may correlate with particular PrP gene mutations or isoforms.[234,235]

Using a variety of analytical techniques, including examination of PrP^Sc glycosylation pattern and size of proteinase K digestion patterns, at least four types of PrP^Sc have been identified in brain material from patients with human prion diseases.[234] Molecular classification of PrP^Sc isoform may be helpful in characterizing different clinical phenotypes of disease when used in conjunction with information about the patient's genotype at polymorphous codon 129 of the *PRNP* gene. The particular PrP^Sc isoform identified is related closely to disease type and to the genotype at polymorphous *PRNP* codon 129.[234] In one study, 98% of patients with sporadic CJD and 129M homozygosity had either isoform type 1 or isoform type 2.[234] All sCJD patients with valine homozygosity at codon 129 (129V) had either type 2 or type 3 isoforms. By contrast, the 30 nvCJD cases tested all had the 129M polymorphism and the type 4 PrP^Sc isoform. It was suggested initially that iCJD cases were associated with a type 3 isoform, but subsequent analysis of more cases have indicated this also is found commonly in sCJD. Additional clinical correlations that have emerged have suggested that patients with type 1 isoforms (all of whom also were 129M homozygotes) have shorter duration of disease, and patients with type 3 isoforms and 129MV have longer disease duration. Type 2 129V homozygous cases and type 3 cases also are less likely to have characteristic EEG abnormalities than patients with type 1 or type 2 and 129M homozygosity. Type 1 and type 2 cases also show variations in the degree and distribution of spongiform changes and PrP^Sc.[234]

Several attempts have been made to use the various available clinical, laboratory, and neuropathologic tests to develop diagnostic criteria for sCJD.[226,236-239] It has been suggested that patients exhibiting appropriate clinical signs and symptoms, including EEG abnormalities, can be classified on this basis alone as having "probable" CJD. To achieve a "definite" diagnosis, these features must be combined with morphologic evidence of CJD, including (1) typical neuropathologic findings on light microscopic examination of frozen or formalin-fixed brain tissue (e.g., spongiform degeneration, neuronal loss, astrogliosis, PrP^Sc+ plaques); (2) positive immunohistochemical staining for PrP^Sc after appropriate pretreatment of tissue with guanidine thiocyanate, autoclaving, or related techniques; or (3) positive histoblotting of tissue for PrP^Sc after proteinase K treatment. Although no longer used with any frequency, demonstration of animal transmission from brain material also can be accepted as evidence for definite CJD. Finally, in patients with the appropriate clinical manifestations, demonstration of a *PRNP* gene mutation can be taken as definitive evidence of CJD (see later). It is crucial to recognize, however, that *PRNP* mutations occur only in the relatively few (<10%) prion diseases that are familial (fCJD, GSS, FFI; see later). Genetic techniques are highly specific but insensitive when used for diagnosis of isolated cases of prion disease.

Several studies have assessed the accuracy of premortem diagnosis of CJD. Masters and colleagues[236] proposed a series of clinical criteria for diagnosis of sCJD. Definitive diagnosis required neuropathologic confirmation of spongiform encephalopathy in a patient with a progressive dementia and the presence of at least one of the following clinical features: myoclonus, pyramidal signs, extrapyramidal signs, or PSWCs on EEG. Cases were considered *probable*

CJD if they met these criteria but lacked neuropathologic confirmation. These criteria have low specificity (18%). In an attempt to enhance specificity, several modifications of these original criteria have been made.[226,237-239] Subsequent criteria have accepted immunocytochemical identification of PrP[Sc] in tissue specimens or in immunoblots of brain homogenates or the demonstration of scrapie-associated fibrils in prepared brain material as providing neuropathologic confirmation of diagnosis. The combination of neuropathologic confirmation of diagnosis and the clinical and laboratory criteria discussed subsequently for probable CJD enabled patients to be classified as having *definite* CJD. No currently available criteria for sCJD allow the diagnosis to be considered definite without neuropathologic confirmation at biopsy or autopsy. Patients were classified as having probable CJD if they had a progressive dementia, PSWCs on EEG, and at least *two* of the following clinical criteria: (1) myoclonus, (2) pyramidal or extrapyramidal signs or both, (3) akinetic mutism, and (4) visual or cerebellar signs (sometimes considered individually as separate clinical criteria) or both. *Possible* CJD was diagnosed in patients in whom the criteria for probable CJD were met but who lacked characteristic EEG findings. In one autopsy study validating these criteria, of 95 cases of CJD meeting these probable criteria, 95% were shown to have CJD (95% specificity), and there was a 98% positive predictive value.[239] The 5% (5 cases) incorrectly diagnosed included 4 cases of Alzheimer's disease and 1 patient with CNS lymphoma. By contrast, of 21 autopsy cases of possible CJD, only 52% were found to have CJD. The remaining 48% (10 cases) had Alzheimer's disease (4 cases), vascular dementia (2 cases), encephalitis (2 cases), unclassified dementia (1 case), and hypoxic encephalopathy (1 case).[239]

The specificity of laboratory tests, including detection of CSF 14-3-3 protein, PSWCs on EEG, and characteristic hyperintense signals in the basal ganglia on MRI, has been variably reported (see earlier). In one study,[226] specificity of 14-3-3 and MRI abnormalities were estimated at 93% with specificity of EEG abnormalities at 86%. The sensitivity of these tests ranged from approximately 65% for EEG and MRI to 95% for detection of 14-3-3 protein (although, as noted, the 14-3-3-data have varied considerably in different studies). Another study suggested that inclusion of 14-3-3 protein detection as a criterion for probable CJD would not increase substantially sensitivity or specificity of existing diagnostic criteria.[239] Despite the high specificity of available diagnostic clinical criteria and associated ancillary testing, some patients ultimately prove to have alternate diagnoses, including rapidly progressive forms of Alzheimer's disease, frontotemporal dementia, and dementia with Lewy bodies. Perhaps of more concern are patients with treatable or at least potentially treatable disorders that can mimic sCJD, including toxic and metabolic encephalopathies, nonconvulsive status epilepticus, cerebral vasculitis, CNS Whipple's disease, Hashimoto's encephalitis, paraneoplastic encephalitis, and intravascular lymphoma.

Genetics of Creutzfeldt-Jakob Disease

Mutations in the gene encoding the prion protein (*PRNP*) are not found in patients with nonfamilial sCJD or the rare cases of kuru, sporadic GSS, or sporadic FFI.[235,240] An exception has been a single Japanese case of apparently sCJD, in which a double mutation involving codons 180 and 232 was found (Table 175-3).[241] Many reports indicate that polymorphisms at codon 129 of the PrP gene may play a role in disease expression and susceptibility in sCJD, nvCJD, and iCJD. Although 51% of normal persons exhibit methionine-valine heterozygosity at codon 129 of the PrP gene (Met/Val), with the remainder showing homozygosity for methionine or valine (37% Met/Met, 12% Val/Val), it has been reported that 95% of patients who develop nonfamilial sCJD and 100% of patients with nvCJD exhibit homozygosity at this locus.[242] Similarly, five of seven studied cases of growth hormone–related CJD showed homozygosity for valine or methionine at codon 129 (four Val/Val, one Met/Met).[243] Particular patterns of codon 129 polymorphism in patients with sCJD also may be associated with specific patterns of PrP[Sc] immunostaining in brain tissues.[244]

TABLE 175-3 Common *PRNP* Gene Point Mutations Associated with Human Prion Diseases

Codon[†]	Designation	Normal AA	Mutant AA	Common Clinical Phenotype
102	P102L	Pro	Leu	GSS
105	P105L	Pro	Leu	GSS
117	A117V	Ala	Val	GSS
131	G131V	Gly	Val	GSS
145	Y145*	Tyr	STOP	GSS
160	Q160*	Gln	STOP	CJD (?)
178	D178N	Asp	Asn	CJD, FFI[‡]
180	V180I	Val	Ile	CJD
183	T183A	Thr	Ala	CJD, FTD
187	H187R	His	Arg	GSS
188	T188A	Thr	Ala	CJD (?)
188	T188K	Thr	Lys	CJD (?)
188	T188R	Thr	Arg	CJD (?)
196	E196K	Glu	Lys	CJD
198	F198S	Phe	Ser	GSS (+ NFT)
200	E200K	Glu	Lys	CJD
202	D202N	Asp	Asn	GSS
203	V203I	Val	ILeu	CJD
208	R208H	Arg	His	CJD
210	V210I	Val	Ile	CJD
211	E211Q	Glu	Gln	CJD
212	Q212P	Gln	Pro	GSS
217	Q217R	Gln	Arg	GSS (+ NFT)
232	M232R	Met	Arg	CJD
232	M232T	Met	Thr	GSS
238	P238S	Pro	Ser	CJD (?)

[†]Octapeptide repeats of 24, 48, 96, 120, 144, 168, and 216 total base pairs inserted between codons 51 through 91 have been associated with CJD and a repeat of 192 bp within this region with GSS. Homozygosity for valine or methionine at polymorphic codon 129 is associated with an increased susceptibility to iatrogenic CJD, new variant CJD, and sporadic CJD.

[‡]In the presence of the D178N mutation, valine homozygosity at polymorphic codon 129 (129V) is associated with CJD and methionine homozygosity at codon 129 (129M) is associated with FFI.

AA, amino acid; CJD, Creutzfeldt-Jakob disease; FFI, fatal familial insomnia; FTD, autosomal dominant frontotemporal dementia; GSS, Gerstmann-Sträussler-Scheinker syndrome; NFT, neurofibrillary tangles.

See the article by Kovacs et al[235] and text discussion for details.

At least 30 distinct mutations in the *PRNP* gene are known to be associated with the inherited prion diseases, including fCJD, GSS, and FFI[7,11,13,14] (see Table 175-3). Specific mutations in the PrP gene frequently, but not invariably, are associated with particular clinical and pathologic disease phenotypes. It seems that particular mutations may influence the age at onset and duration of disease; the prominence of certain clinical features, including dementia, myoclonus, and ataxia; the presence of typical EEG abnormalities; the degree of spongiform neuropathologic change; and the regional distribution and pattern of accumulation of PrP[Sc] within the brain.

Perhaps the most commonly encountered mutation in fCJD is a lysine-for-glutamic acid substitution in codon 200 (E200K). This mutation has been found in geographic clusters of fCJD in Slovakia and Chile and among Sephardic Jews in Greece, Libya, Tunisia, and Israel.[244] At least one family with this particular mutation presented with a disease resembling progressive supranuclear palsy that was not associated with myoclonus or EEG abnormalities typical of CJD.[245] It has been reported that immunostaining for PrP[Sc] in fCJD cases with this mutation tends to show PrP accumulation in a dense synaptic pattern in the gray matter rather than within plaques.[232]

Additional mutations reported in fCJD include an asparagine-for-aspartic acid mutation in codon 178 (D178N)[246] and an isoleucine-for-valine substitution in codon 210 (V210I).[11] The D178N mutation has been described in kindreds from Finland and Europe.[246] Some of these patients have had disease characterized by earlier age at onset, longer duration of illness, and absence of typical periodic EEG changes.[247] Mutations in this codon also have been described in patients with GSS and FFI (see later). It has been suggested that the phenotype expression of the codon 178 mutation may be influenced by the nature of the associated codon 129 polymorphism. Patients with homozygosity for valine at codon 129 present with fCJD, whereas patients with homozygosity for methionine at codon 129 present with FFI (see later). In addition to mutations resulting in amino-acid substitutions in the PrP gene, many base-pair insertions have been described within the PrP gene in cases of fCJD.[248,249]

New Variant Creutzfeldt-Jakob Disease

Beginning in 1995, cases of a new variant of CJD were reported from the United Kingdom,[250-253] with a total of 141 cases reported to the United Kingdom Creutzfeldt-Jakob Disease Surveillance Unit as of April 2004 (see http://www.cjd.ed.ac.uk/ for latest case totals), with eight additional cases from France (six),[254-256] Ireland (one), and Italy (one).[257] One case also has been reported from the United States, a 22-year-old patient living in Florida at the time of disease onset, who had resided in the United Kingdom from 1979 through 1992.[258] During this same period (1995 to 2004) in the United Kingdom, there were 522 reported cases of sCJD, 41 cases of fCJD and GSS, and 24 cases of iCJD. Retrospective review of available autopsy material suggests that nvCJD did emerge as a new disease entity in 1995; no current evidence suggests that cases occurred earlier.[259] Initial fears that there would be a large epidemic of cases of nvCJD have been unfounded, and estimates for the total number of expected cases now typically range between 200 and 3000, with the lower part of this range seeming more likely.[260-263] The largest number of annual cases (28) was reported in 2000, with a subsequent steady decline in case number in each subsequent year (2001, 20; 2002, 17; 2003, 18; 2004, through April, 30)[260,261] (see also http://www.cjd.ed.ac.uk/).

The epidemiologic, clinical, and pathologic features of the nvCJD cases sets them apart from typical sCJD.[251-253,264] Patients with nvCJD have been considerably younger than patients with sCJD, with a mean age at onset of 26 years (range 12 to 74 years)[253] compared with 65 years for sCJD. The duration of illness in nvCJD is longer (average 14 months) than in sCJD (average 4.5 months). The patients with nvCJD frequently presented with sensory disturbances and psychiatric manifestations, both of which are unusual in sCJD. Among the sensory symptoms were pain, dysesthesias, or paresthesias involving the face, hands, feet, and legs or in a hemisensory distribution. Only one of five patients who underwent electromyography and nerve conduction studies was found to have abnormalities; these consisted of mild denervation in the tibialis anterior and an absent peroneal F wave. One French patient had clear clinical and neurophysiologic evidence of a polyneuropathy.[254] Psychiatric manifestations frequently were present early in these patients with nvCJD[253,265] and commonly included early (within 4 months of onset) symptoms of dysphoria, withdrawal, anxiety, irritability, insomnia, and loss of interest in usual activities. As the disease progressed, impairment of memory and concentration and a tendency toward aggressive behavior appeared. In the later (>6 months after onset) stages of disease, disorientation and agitation were common.[253] Symptoms of depression included apathy, withdrawal, weight loss, and insomnia and often prompted a psychiatric referral and an initial diagnosis of psychiatric illness. Neurologic signs and symptoms were uncommon in the early stages of illness (within 4 months of onset). As disease progressed, the most frequent neurologic signs included dysarthria and gait disturbance and less commonly sensory symptoms, including pain, paresthesias, and numbness. In the later stages of disease (>6 months after onset), prominent neurologic signs (seen in >50%) included hyperreflexia, myoclonus, incoordination or other cerebellar signs, up-gaze paralysis, and incontinence.[253] Of patients, 25% to 50% had chorea, dysphagia, hypertonia, clonus, extensor plantar responses, and primitive reflexes.

In a detailed analysis of the psychiatric symptoms in these patients,[265] it was noted that psychiatric symptoms were a consistent and early clinical feature in nvCJD. Psychiatric symptoms persisted until they were obscured by dementia. Most patients were found to have depression, personality change, withdrawal, and insomnia. Anorexia and

weight loss accompanied depressive symptoms. Twelve of 14 patients had transient delusions. These often occurred near the onset of illness, were detailed and complex in nature, and lasted hours or 1 to 2 days. Auditory hallucinations occurred in 5 of 14 cases, and visual hallucinations occurred in 8 of 14 cases. Psychiatric medication was not of sustained benefit, although in 3 of 14 patients, transient improvement was noted.

Neuroimaging results are accumulating now for increased numbers of patients with nvCJD. In early reports based on the first cases, it was noted that 8 of 11 CT scans and 8 of 14 MRI scans were essentially unremarkable. Three additional patients had mild cerebral atrophy as their only MRI abnormality. Two patients had increased T_2 signal in the posterior thalamus (pulvinar), as did single French and Italian patients.[252,254,255,257,266] Subsequent studies have suggested that increased T_2 signal in the pulvinar of the thalami may be seen in 70% of cases, suggesting it may be a valuable diagnostic clue.[204,267,268] Similar findings also can occur in sCJD and are not pathognomonic of nvCJD.[269] It has been suggested that in patients with nvCJD the pulvinar hyperintensity is typically bilateral and of greater intensity than any signal seen elsewhere in the thalamus, basal ganglia, or cortex. By contrast, in patients with sCJD who have increased signal in the pulvinar, it is typically less intense than signal elsewhere. SPECT has been performed in a few patients with nvCJD and can show widespread abnormal areas of cerebral perfusion.[270] Use of magnetic resonance spectroscopy has been reported in a single patient with nvCJD; it showed decreased N-acetyl aspartate-to-creatine ratios in the pulvinar region of the posterior thalamus.[217] Patients with nvCJD do not show the periodic EEG changes characteristic of sCJD.[254] Many patients had nonspecific abnormalities, including slowing, which worsens as the disease progresses. Initial EEG findings were normal in 29% (4 of 14) of patients and remained so in 3 patients despite the presence of impressive cognitive and neurologic abnormalities.[252] CSF 14-3-3 protein has been found in approximately 50% of cases.[267] None of the patients tested to date have had mutations in the PRNP gene, but all have shown homozygosity for methionine at polymorphic codon 129 (129M).[234,252] Homozygosity for methionine or valine at this codon previously has been reported to occur with increased frequency in sCJD and iCJD (discussed earlier).

The neuropathologic features of nvCJD are strikingly different than those of sCJD.[251] The most characteristic differences between the neuropathology of nvCJD and sCJD seem to be the prominent involvement of the cerebellum in almost all cases of nvCJD compared with only a subset of cases with sCJD (Brownell-Oppenheimer variant and GSS cases). nvCJD cases also show typical spongiform change, neuronal loss, and astrogliosis in cortex, basal ganglia, and thalamus, but these do not distinguish nvCJD from sCJD. nvCJD cases also had prominent ("florid") PrPSc+ amyloid plaques distributed throughout the cerebrum and cerebellum and, to a lesser extent, the basal ganglia and thalamus. These plaques had a dense eosinophilic center and pale periphery and were surrounded by spongiform change in the neuropil. The plaques stain strongly positive for PrPSc.[251] In many respects, the nvCJD plaques share similarities with but are not identical to the plaques seen in kuru and GSS. Patients with nvCJD also seem to have a consistent pattern of electrophoretic mobility of PrPSc protein (type 4 isoform) that is distinct from the mobility patterns encountered in sCJD and is similar to the pattern seen in BSE PrPSc.[234,271,272]

Additional evidence for a BSE-nvCJD link comes from the close neuropathologic similarities ("signature") between the two diseases, including the presence of florid PrPSc+ plaques throughout the brain and the distribution and intensity of vacuolation in different brain regions ("lesion profile"). Transgenic mice expressing bovine PrP develop indistinguishable neurologic illness and neuropathologic changes after a similar incubation period when injected with brain material from either cattle with BSE or humans with nvCJD, and this differs from the pattern and incubation time seen after inoculation with scrapie.[273] In addition, the PrPSc protein isoforms isolated from the brains of the BSE-inoculated or nvCJD-inoculated mice show an identical fragment size and glycosylation pattern, which differs from that seen after scrapie inoculation.[274] These data provide strong evidence supporting the hypothesis that nvCJD arose from human infection with BSE.

An increasingly compelling body of evidence indicates that nvCJD is the result of bovine-to-human transmission of BSE.[271,273-276] From an epidemiologic viewpoint, cases of nvCJD followed a massive epidemic of BSE in the United Kingdom with a lag period that is consistent with the known inoculation period of prions. During the BSE epidemic, the first cases of which were recognized retrospectively as early as April 1985, it was estimated that several hundred thousand BSE-infected cattle might have entered the human food chain.[264,277-279] The number of BSE-infected cattle peaked during 1992 to 1993 and subsequently declined steadily. This decline has been attributed to bans on using ruminant protein for ruminant feeds (July 1988) and on using bovine brain, spinal cord, and other specified offals as feed for nonruminant animals and poultry (September 1990). Another ban prohibited use of certain bovine tissues for human consumption (November 1989).[264,277,278] It has been suggested that the BSE epidemic was triggered by changes in the rendering process, particularly the abandonment of the use of organic solvents.[264,280]

To date, definitive diagnosis of nvCJD has depended on neuropathologic analysis of brain tissue obtained at necropsy or by brain biopsy. In addition to brain, PrP^{Sc} has been found in spinal cord, retina and proximal optic nerve, tonsils, thymus, spleen, liver, appendix, and lymph nodes of patients with nvCJD.[281] It has been suggested that analysis of PrP from extraneural lymphoreticular tissue, such as the tonsil, might provide a less invasive method than brain biopsy for definitive diagnosis of nvCJD.[282] Highly sensitive immunoblotting assays now are available that enable detection of small quantities of PrP^{Sc} from patients with nvCJD.[283] Tonsil tissue obtained at necropsy from a patient who had confirmed nvCJD showed abnormal PrP staining in germinal centers. PrP isolated from tonsil tissue showed protease-resistant PrP by Western immunoblot assay, and the PrP^{Sc} protein had a glycosylation pattern similar to that described with nvCJD. Similar efforts to identify abnormal PrP in lymphoreticular tissues from patients with GSS were not successful.[284] In a more recent study, 9 of 9 tonsil, 10 of 10 spleen, and 7 of 8 lymph node necropsy specimens were positive for PrP^{Sc} by immunohistochemistry in patients with nvCJD, and none of these tissues was positive in patients with iatrogenic, sporadic, or inherited prior disease.[285] In another autopsy study, 19 of 20 (95%) of appendices removed at autopsy from patients with nvCJD tested positive for PrP,[286] although a subsequent report found only 1 positive case among 4 tested (25%).[287] If subsequent studies confirm the sensitivity and specificity of tonsil and lymphoreticular tissue biopsy for diagnosis of nvCJD, this may become an important diagnostic tool.

Diagnosis of nvCJD should be considered when patients with a history of residence in a BSE endemic area, such as the United Kingdom, develop a progressive neurodegenerative disease with early psychiatric symptoms, including depression, anxiety, apathy, withdrawal, or delusions, associated with neurologic signs and symptoms of prominent sensory abnormalities, including painful paresthesias; ataxia; movement disorders such as myoclonus, chorea, or dystonia; or frank dementia. When present, increased T$_2$ signal in the pulvinar on MRI can help support the diagnosis. The absence of PSWCs helps distinguish nvCJD from sCJD. Evidence of PrP^{Sc} in extraneural lymphoid tissue, such as tonsil or appendix, also is strongly suggestive because PrP^{Sc} is not found in these extraneural areas in healthy individuals or in patients with other prion diseases. Definitive diagnosis ultimately requires demonstration of PrP^{Sc} with florid plaques in the brain and cerebellum. In one series of 15 suspected nvCJD cases in which an alternative diagnosis was discovered subsequently at autopsy or biopsy, the most common alternatives were sCJD (6 cases), possible or confirmed cerebral vasculitis (3 cases), Alzheimer's disease (2 cases), limbic encephalitis (1 case), encephalitis (1 case), and cerebrovascular disease (1 case).[267]

Gerstmann-Sträussler-Scheinker Syndrome

GSS first was described in 1936,[288] although it was not recognized as a transmissible neurodegenerative disease related to CJD until 1981.[289] GSS is an exceedingly rare human prion disease, with an incidence of 1 to 10 cases per 100 million population per year (see Table 175-2). Most reported cases are familial, with an autosomal dominant pattern of inheritance and virtually complete penetrance. Approximately 24 independent kindreds have been identified worldwide to date. Rare sporadic cases occur that are unassociated with *PRNP* gene mutations.[290]

The basic clinical features are those of a midlife progressive spinocerebellar degeneration with associated dementia.[13,16,291-294] The average duration of disease is 5 to 6 years (range 3 months to 13 years), with mean age at onset of 43 to 48 years (range 24 to 66 years). In typical cases, cerebellar features dominate the clinical picture, with dementia a late or minor accompaniment. In most patients, when dementia does occur, the features are those of a global dementia with impairment in intelligence, memory, attention, and cognitive skills.[295,296] Some patients have prominent mood disorders ranging from apathy to increased irritability and aggressiveness, or simply emotional lability. Cerebellar dysfunction manifests as gait ataxia, incoordination including dysmetria and dysdiadochokinesia, clumsiness, tremor, dysarthria, and nystagmus. Signs of corticospinal (pyramidal) tract dysfunction, including hyperreflexia, spasticity, and extensor plantar responses, are common and in rare cases may produce a clinical phenotype closer to familial spastic paraplegia than a cerebellar degeneration, as seen in some patients with the P105L mutation. Some families also have more prominent dementia, extrapyramidal signs (choreoathethosis, myoclonus), or other findings.[294,297,298] One Native American family with the F198S mutation has members with prominent parkinsonian features. In contrast to CJD, myoclonus is only rarely a prominent feature in GSS and often is absent. Some of the clinical heterogeneity of the disease may be the result of the variable phenotypic effects of different PrP gene mutations associated with the disease (see later), although even within families containing the same *PRNP* gene mutation there can be significant phenotypic variability in presentation (e.g., CJD-like versus GSS-like) and age of onset,[299] a variability seen even in monozygotic twins.[300]

Laboratory tests are rarely helpful in the diagnosis but may be valuable in excluding other diagnostic possibilities. Similar to kuru and nvCJD, but in contrast to sCJD, the EEG in GSS does not usually show PSWCs except in patients with more rapidly progressive disease and an associated P102L mutation. The EEG may show nonspecific slowing or be normal.[292] CT scans may be normal or show evidence of cerebellar or brain stem atrophy. MRI studies have been limited,[292,301] but some patients have had decreased T$_2$ signal in the striatum, substantia nigra, and red nucleus. PET studies using fluorodeoxyglucose have been performed in some affected patients. Typical findings include decreased fluorodeoxyglucose uptake in temporoparietal cortices in patients with dementia and in cerebellar cortices in patients with prominent ataxia consistent with severe hypometabolism.[302]

Definitive diagnosis requires the examination of brain material. Similar to the other prion diseases, GSS may be transmitted to animals by brain material from infected cases,[289] although the frequency of transmission seems to be considerably lower than that reported for kuru and sCJD and almost exclusively in patients with the P102L mutation. Neuropathologic findings are typical of other prion diseases except that virtually all patients have widespread multicentric amyloid plaques reminiscent of those seen in kuru (kuru plaques). Within the cerebellum, where plaque concentration typically is the most dense, plaques typically are found in the molecular layer, often are multicentric, and are associated with a microglial reaction. The degree of spongiform change is variable, ranging from substantial and severe, as in the original GSS families, to completely absent. Atypical kindreds have been reported in whom prion amyloid plaques are prominent throughout the telencephalon and not limited to the cerebellum and in whom neurofibrillary tangles are prominent.[302] Cases of this type may have been mischaracterized previously as familial Alzheimer's disease. The availability of immunostaining now allows the amyloid plaques associated with prion diseases to be distinguished clearly from the senile plaques characteristic of Alzheimer's disease. Prion plaques immunostain with antibodies against PrP^Sc and do not stain with antibodies to β-amyloid protein, whereas senile plaques have the opposite characteristics.

Many PrP gene mutations have been identified in patients with familial GSS (see Table 175-3). The most common is a leucine-for-proline substitution on codon 102 (P102L). This mutation was found in descendants of the original family described by Gerstmann, Sträussler, and Scheinker.[298] Transgenic mice with this codon 102 mutation spontaneously develop a neurodegenerative disease indistinguishable from scrapie, although the multicentric amyloid plaques characteristic of GSS are found only inconsistently.[89,90,304] In the case of the GSS P102L mutation, the phenotype also may be influenced by the nature of the amino acids present at the polymorphic codon 129. Most reported patients with classic GSS and the P102L mutation also are homozygous for methionine at codon 129 (129M).[294,297,305] Additional mutations found have included A117V, a stop (amber) mutation at codon 145 (Y145STOP), F198S, D202N, Q212P, Q217R, E219L, and 92 bp inserts between codons 51 and 91 of the *PRNP* gene (see Table 175-3). It has been suggested that GSS associated with the P102L mutation may present predominantly as ataxia with severe spongiform degeneration,[294] whereas patients with GSS A117V, Y145STOP, and F198S mutations may have more prominent dementia associated with neurofibrillary degeneration. It is important to recognize that many of the clinical and pathologic phenotypes show significant variation and heterogeneity not only between families with similar mutations, but also among members of the same family.[300,302,302a,305,306]

Fatal Familial Insomnia

FFI first was reported as a human prion disease in 1986,[307-310] although there is clinical and pathologic overlap between FFI and cases previously described as "thalamic dementia"[311] (see Table 175-2). Onset of disease is in middle or late life (36 to 62 years, mean 51 ± 7 years), with an average disease duration of 18 ± 17 months (range 8 to 72 months).[310] There is no predilection for either sex. Most cases have been associated with a D178N mutation in the *PRNP* gene and show an autosomal dominant pattern of inheritance with high penetrance (see later). Approximately seven cases of apparently fatal sporadic insomnia have been reported that were associated with neuropathologic changes, including a PrP deposition pattern indistinguishable from FFI,[312-314] and in some cases documented transmissibility to animals.[314] Although the first reports of FFI all were in Italian families, currently a total of approximately 27 families with FFI have been reported from the United Kingdom, Europe, United States, Finland, Australia, China, and Japan, indicating the disease occurs worldwide.[310]

In this unusual disorder, patients present with progressive sleep disturbance insomnia evolving into intractable insomnia, associated with autonomic hyperactivity (increased sweating, tearing, salivation, mild nocturnal hyperthermia, increased heart rate and blood pressure), and later develop motor disturbances that can include ataxia, myoclonus, spasticity, hyperreflexia, and dysarthria.[307,308,310] Monitoring of daily rest and activity patterns in affected patients often shows a loss of normal circadian rest-activity rhythm.[315] Mental status abnormalities resemble a progressive confusional state more than a classic dementia and can include hallucinations, delirium, decreased attention, and memory disorders.[310,316,317] Early impairment of attention, vigilance, and memory and a progressive dreamlike or confusional state are characteristic neurobehavioral deficits.[317] These features seem to be distinct from the typical features of classic cortical and subcortical dementias and the Wernicke-Korsakoff syndrome.[317]

Patients manifest a wide variety of autonomic and circadian abnormalities, including elevation in resting body core temperature, blood pressure, and heart rate and exaggerated blood pressure and heart rate responses to postural changes, Valsalva maneuver, and isometric exercise.[310] Plasma levels of norepinephrine, epinephrine, and cortisol often are elevated, and the normal circadian fluctuations in levels of these hormones and of prolactin and somatotropin (growth hormone) and melatonin are lost.[310]

Abnormalities in sleep architecture are a characteristic and early feature of disease. Initially, total sleep time is reduced and fragmented substantially, and its normal cyclical organization is disrupted.[310,318,319] Sleep studies show an early reduction in sleep spindles and K complexes. Non-REM sleep may be entirely absent, and REM sleep that remains may not be associated with characteristic loss of muscle tone.[318] These residual abnormal REM periods often are associated with vivid dreams, which the patient may try and enact, owing to the absence of the normal REM-associated muscle atonia. It has been suggested that increased activity of serotoninergic systems may account for some of the sleep abnormalities in FFI.[320,321] As the ability to sleep vanishes, the patient remains in an exhausted state of perpetual wakefulness that is associated with marked increase in energy expenditure from the associated motor overactivity and results in metabolic exhaustion and progressive cachexia.[310,315,322]

Differential diagnosis of FFI includes other organic causes of insomnia and associated motor and autonomic hyperactivity. Common causes of this syndrome include delirium tremens and other toxic-metabolic disorders and Morvan's fibrillary chorea, although these diseases are not familial. Morvan's fibrillary chorea is an exceedingly rare disorder that manifests with abnormal involuntary movements and a limbic encephalitis associated with the presence of autoantibodies that bind to voltage-gated potassium channels on neurons.[323,324]

EEG abnormalities can occur in FFI, although the PSWCs characteristic of CJD do not typically occur. Some patients with long-standing illness may develop a periodic EEG pattern in the late stages of disease.[310,319] MRI is generally nonspecific, and abnormalities characteristic of CJD, including increased signal in the basal ganglia and abnormal patterns on DWI, have not been reported in FFI. Some patients show ventricular enlargement and cortical and cerebellar atrophy, especially at late stages of the disease. PET scans using fluorodeoxyglucose show severely reduced glucose use in the thalamus and, to a lesser extent, in the cortex, basal ganglia, and cerebellum, the hypometabolism correlating with regions of greatest neuronal loss.[325-327] CSF 14-3-3 protein has been detected in approximately 50% of cases, a sensitivity that makes it of limited diagnostic utility for FFI.[310]

Neuropathologic changes, including significant (>50%) neuronal loss and reactive gliosis, are found consistently in the anterior ventral and mediodorsal nuclei of the thalamus, the inferior olives, and less strikingly the cerebellar and cerebral cortex.[307-310,328,329] Spongiform degeneration is not usually present in cases with a short disease duration (<18 months) but has been reported as a later feature in some cases.[310] Immunostaining of brain material for PrP^Sc is positive,[307] although the concentration of protein is 5 to 10 times less than that seen in sCJD, with cases of shorter duration having less intense staining with less involvement of cortex than patients with long-standing disease.[329,330]

Similar to the other human prion diseases, FFI is transmissible to experimental animals.[331] Most reported cases have been associated with an asparagine-for-aspartic acid substitution in codon 178 (D178N) (see Table 175-3).[310] The D178N mutation also has been associated with a more classic CJD phenotype. As discussed earlier, polymorphism at codon 129 seems to determine the phenotypic expression of D178N mutations. Patients who exhibit homozygosity for methionine at codon 129 (M129) develop FFI, patients who exhibit heterozygosity develop an FFI-like illness with longer symptom duration, and patients who show homozygosity for valine (V129) develop fCJD.[310,332-334] The PrP isoforms in D178N/M129 and D178N/V129 patients differ in the size of their proteinase K–resistant fragments and their glycosylation pattern.[329] There is one report of a patient with a lysine mutation at codon 200 and associated homozygosity for methionine at codon 129 who developed CJD associated with severe insomnia.[335] At autopsy, this patient was found to have FFI-like pathologic changes in the thalamus, supporting the idea that these changes are responsible for the dysregulation in sleep patterns. Mice with knockout mutations in the *PRNP* gene show altered circadian activity rhythms and patterns, including sleep fragmentation, suggesting that PrP may play a role in the normal regulation of these processes.[83]

Chronic Wasting Disease

The appearance of cases of nvCJD linked to spread of infection from BSE-infected cattle to humans (see earlier) has raised the possibility that similar transmission could occur from deer and elk infected with CWD to humans. CWD first was identified in the United States in 1967 and subsequently found to be endemic in captive deer in northeastern Colorado and later in captive and free-ranging deer in Colorado and southeastern Wyoming.[336] Export of infected animals from captive herds has resulted in spread of CWD to captive herds in at least nine additional states (Kansas, Nebraska, Oklahoma, New Mexico, Montana, Illinois, Minnesota, Wisconsin, and South Dakota) and at least one Canadian province (Saskatchewan). Prevalence of CWD in mule deer in the endemic regions of Colorado is approximately 5%; the prevalence in elk is substantially less (<1%). There is one report of early-onset CJD in three individuals younger than age 30 with a history of regular deer and elk hunting and subsequent regular consumption of deer or elk meat.[337] Investigation did not document definite exposure to CWD-infected animals, and the PrP^{Sc} isoform and pattern of staining in brain tissues in the patients tested appeared more consistent with sCJD than with a variant form of prion disease. Another report described three men age 55 to 66 who were avid hunters and regularly consumed deer meat at the same "wild game feasts" in northern Wisconsin who all died between 1993 and 1999 of neurodegenerative diseases.[338] At autopsy, only one of the three patients was found to have CJD, and the pattern was believed to be consistent with sCJD. A third report in abstract form of two additional cases with strong exposure histories to CWD-infected animals also did not find evidence to support transmission; one patient was found to have fCJD, and the other was found to have Alzheimer's disease.[339] The Division of Viral and Rickettsial Diseases of the Centers for Disease Control and Prevention has an active program in place to monitor the occurrence of emerging forms of CJD in the United States.[340]

TREATMENT OF PRION DISEASES

Kuru, CJD, GSS, and FFI seem to be invariably fatal diseases. There is no known effective form of therapy. Treatments with agents such as idoxuridine, acyclovir, interferon, polyanions, and amphotericin B all have been unsuccessful.[341] Anecdotal reports of stabilization or improvement after treatment with amantadine, vidarabine, and methisoprinol have not been confirmed by other studies.[341] Following reports that acridine, bis-acridine, and phenothiazine derivatives inhibited PrP^{Sc} formation in neuroblastoma cells,[342,343] quinacrine was tested in unblinded and noncontrolled studies in isolated cases of sCJD. Some patients treated with quinacrine reportedly showed transient improvements before reverting to their previous states and dying of progressive disease.[344] Treatment is not benign because the drug has resulted in serious hepatotoxicity. A British court approved the administration of pentosan polysulfate, an anticoagulant, intracerebrally to two patients with nvCJD, although no results of this experimental trial have been reported.[344] There also are unpublished reports of a reduction in cognitive decline in a clinical trial of the N-methyl-D-aspartate antagonist flupirtine.[344a]

The availability of animal models of prion disease and cell culture systems including neuroblastoma cells permanently infected with prions may provide better models for screening new antiprion drugs. The anion Congo red has been shown to delay disease onset in rodent models of prion disease and to reduce the accumulation of PrP^{Sc} in infected neuroblastoma cells.[345] The anthracycline IDX inhibits prion disease in Syrian hamsters,[346] and glycerol and dimethyl sulfoxide interfere with the formation of PrP^{Sc} in cell culture.[347] There also are reports that preincubation of scrapie brain homogenates with tetracycline or doxycycline reduces their infectivity and prolongs the incubation time and the survival of infected Syrian hamsters.[348] Intriguing results also have been obtained suggesting that dominant-negative inhibition of PrP^{Sc} formation by transgenic expression of a prion protein with the Q167R or Q218K polymorphism,[349] vaccination with recombinant PrP,[350] and treatment with anti-PrP monoclonal antibodies[351] all can delay disease onset or in some cases prevent development of prion disease after challenge in mice. It remains to be seen whether these strategies are adaptable to humans and, if so, whether they would be equally efficacious.

HANDLING OF POTENTIALLY INFECTIOUS MATERIAL

As noted earlier, there is no evidence that prion diseases are contagious in the usual sense of the term, although instances of person-to-person spread have been documented. Iatrogenic cases have required the direct inoculation, implantation, or transplantation of infectious material. Kuru seems to have been transmitted by ingestion, and this has been suggested as a possible route of infection in cases of nvCJD. Kuru, CJD, and BSE have been transmitted to primates and rodents by the oral route, although this route is inefficient.[352] As might be expected, repeated oral inoculations are more effective in transmitting infection than single doses.[353] Nonetheless, there is no evidence that ingestion is an important route of spread for CJD, GSS, or FFI, and its importance in nvCJD remains to be established.

Based on animal studies,[4,8] the highest concentrations of the infectious agent in human tissues can be expected to occur in the brain, dura mater, spinal cord, and eye. Other organs or body fluids occasionally found to contain infectious material include CSF, lymphoreticular organs, kidney, spleen, and lung. The infectious agent almost never is found in blood, and no cases of blood transfusion–associated CJD have been documented; transfusion does not seem to be a major risk factor for the acquisition of CJD in epidemiologic studies (see earlier). There are no reported isolations of infectious material from human feces, saliva, sputum, tears, vaginal secretions, semen, or milk.[4,8]

From a practical viewpoint, it seems that the universal system of precautions now widely employed in most health care settings is adequate for dealing with patients suspected of having prion diseases. Gloves should be worn for handling blood, CSF, urine, feces, and material soiled by these fluids and for the performance of invasive procedures, including venipuncture and lumbar puncture. Masks, gowns, and protective eyewear should be worn if extensive exposure to blood, CSF, body fluids, or neural tissue is anticipated. Gloves should be discarded after single patient use, and hands should be washed thoroughly. Potentially infectious material should be placed in appropriate containers, bagged to reduce the risk of accidental spills, and marked clearly. Persons transporting this material should wear gloves. Care should be taken to avoid self-inoculation with needles, surgical instruments, or other sharp objects. Specific guidelines and precautions also have been suggested for special situations, such as the performance of neuropathologic autopsies in suspected cases of CJD.[354]

Controversy continues concerning the best procedures for fully sterilizing instruments, tissues, or other materials known to contain prions. Compounds known to reduce prion infectivity most consistently and effectively include chlorine (at concentrations of ≥10,000 ppm), guanidine thiocyanate (at concentrations of 3 to 4 M), and sodium hydroxide (at concentrations of 1 to 2 N).[355,356] The Committee on Health Care Issues of the American Neurological Association has suggested either steam autoclaving (1 hour at 132°C) or immersing potentially contaminated instruments or materials into 1 N sodium hydroxide (1 hour at room temperature).[356] More rigorous decontamination protocols for steam autoclaving (4.5 hours at 121°C and 15 psi) and 1 N sodium hydroxide immersion (three treatments of 30 minutes each) also have been suggested. The treatment of surgical instruments by these procedures may damage them severely so that they are unusable,[357] suggesting that whenever possible it is better to use disposable instruments rather than depend on sterilization for either prion inactivation or instrument preservation. Prion infectivity is not reduced reliably by exposure to ultraviolet light, alcohol solutions, liquid disinfectant (Lysol), iodine, formaldehyde, formalin, glutaraldehyde, or ammonia.[355] Pretreatment of scrapie-infected brain tissue with formaldehyde inhibited the inactivating effects of autoclaving, suggesting that this type of treatment not only is ineffective, but also to be avoided.[355] More recent studies have suggested that concentrated (≥3 to 4 M) guanidine thiocyanate solutions may be highly effective as disinfectants.[358]

REFERENCES

1. Sigurdsson B. Rida, a chronic encephalitis of sheep: With general remarks on infections which develop slowly and some of their special characteristics. Br Vet J. 1954;110:341-354.
2. Hadlow WJ. Neuropathology and the scrapie-kuru connection. Brain Pathol. 1995;5:27-31.
3. Prusiner SB. Genetic and infectious prion diseases. Arch Neurol. 1993;50:1129-1153.
4. Brown P, Gibbs CJ Jr, Rodgers-Johnson P, et al. Human spongiform encephalopathy: The National Institutes of Health series of 300 cases of experimentally transmitted disease. Ann Neurol. 1994;35:513-529.
5. Goldfarb LG, Brown P. The transmissible spongiform encephalopathies. Annu Rev Microbiol. 1995;46:57-65.
6. Haywood AM. Transmissible spongiform encephalopathies. N Engl J Med. 1997;337:1821-1828.
7. Prusiner SB. Prion diseases and the BSE crisis. Science. 1997;278:245-251.
8. Asher DM. Slow viral infections. In: Scheld WM, Whitley RJ, Durack DT, eds. Infections of the Central Nervous System. 2nd ed. New York: Lippincott-Raven; 1997:199-221.
9. Prusiner SB. Prions. Proc Natl Acad Sci U S A. 1998;95:13363-13383.
10. Prusiner SB. Shattuck lecture—neurodegenerative diseases and prions. N Engl J Med. 2001;344:1516-1526.
11. Prusiner SB. Prions. In: Knipe DM, Howley PM, eds. Fields Virology. 4th ed. New York: Lippincott Williams & Wilkins; 2001:3063-3087.
12. Jackson GS, Collinge J. The molecular pathology of CJD: Old and new variants. J Clin Pathol Mol Pathol. 2001;54:393-399.
13. Sy MS, Gambetti P, Wong B-S. Human prion diseases. Med Clin North Am. 2002;86:551-571.
14. McKintosh E, Tabrizi SJ, Collinge J. Prion diseases. J Neurovirol. 2003;9:183-193.
15. DeArmond SJ, Prusiner SB. Perspectives on prion biology, prion disease pathogenesis, and pharmacologic approaches to treatment. Clin Lab Med. 2003;23:1-41.
16. Tyler KL. Prions and prion diseases of the central nervous system. Curr Clin Topics Infect Dis. 1999;19:226-251.
17. Prusiner SB. Novel proteinaceous infectious particles cause scrapie. Science. 1982;216:136-144.
18. Prusiner SB. The prion hypothesis. In: Prusiner SB, McKinley MP, eds. Prions. San Diego: Academic Press; 1987:17-36.
19. Prusiner SB. Terminology. In: Prusiner SB, McKinley MP, eds. Prions. San Diego: Academic Press; 1987:37-53.
20. Klitzman RL, Alpers MP, Gajdusek DC. The natural incubation period of kuru and the episodes of transmission in three clusters of patients. Neuroepidemiology. 1985;3:3-20.
21. Prusiner SB, Gajdusek DC, Alpers MP. Kuru with incubation periods exceeding two decades. Ann Neurol. 1982;12:1-9.
22. Prusiner SB. Molecular biology and pathogenesis of prion diseases. Trends Biochem Sci. 1997;21:482-487.
23. Prusiner SB. Prions and neurodegenerative diseases. N Engl J Med. 1987;317:1571-1581.
24. Gajdusek CD. Infectious amyloids: Subacute spongiform encephalopathies as transmissible cerebral amyloidoses. In: Fields BN, Knipe DM, Howley PM, eds. Fields Virology. 3rd ed. New York: Lippincott-Raven; 1996:2851-2890.
25. Bellinger-Kawahara C, Diener TO, McKinley MP, et al. Purified scrapie prions resist inactivation by procedures that hydrolyze, modify, or shear nucleic acids. Virology. 1987;160:271-274.
26. Bellinger-Kawahara C, Cleaver JE, Diener TO, et al. Purified scrapie prions resist inactivation by UV irradiation. Virology. 1987;61:159-166.
27. Oesch B, Westaway D, Walchli M, et al. A cellular gene encodes scrapie PrP 27-30 protein. Cell. 1985;40:735-746.
28. Kimberlin RH, Hope J. Genes and genomes in scrapie. Trends Genet. 1987;3:117-118.
29. Kimberlin RH, Walker CA. Scrapie: How much do we really understand? Neuropathol Appl Neurobiol. 1986;12:131-147.
30. Bruce ME, Dickinson AG. Biological evidence that scrapie agents have an independent genome. J Gen Virol. 1987;68:79-89.
31. Rohwer RG. The scrapie agent: "A virus by any other name." Curr Top Microbiol Immunol. 1991;172:195-232.
32. Narang HK, Asher DM, Gajdusek DC. Evidence that DNA is present in abnormal tubulofilamentous structures found in scrapie. Proc Natl Acad Sci U S A. 1988;85:3575-3579.
33. Chandler RL. Encephalopathy in mice produced by inoculation with scrapie brain material. Lancet. 1961;1:1378-1379.
34. Manuelidis EE, Manuelidis L, Pincus IH, et al. Transmission, from man to hamster, of Creutzfeldt-Jakob disease with clinical recovery (Letter). Lancet. 1978;2:40-42.
35. Prusiner SB, McKinley MP, Bolton DC, et al. Methods for assay, purification and characterization. In: Maramorosch K, Koprowski H, eds. Methods in Virology, v. 8. New York: Academic Press; 1984:293-345.
36. Prusiner SB, Groth DF, Cochran SP, et al. Molecular properties, partial purification and assay by incubation time period measurements of the hamster scrapie agent. Biochemistry. 1980;19:4883-4891.
37. Prusiner SB, Cochran SP, Groth DF, et al. Measurement of the scrapie agent using an incubation time interval assay. Ann Neurol. 1982;11:353-358.
38. Lax AJ, Millson GC, Manning EF. Can scrapie titres be calculated accurately from incubation periods? J Gen Virol. 1983;64:971-973.
39. Gabizon R, McKinley MP, Groth D, et al. Immunoaffinity purification and neutralization of scrapie prion infectivity. Proc Natl Acad Sci U S A. 1988;85:6617-6621.
40. McKinley MP, Bolton DC, Prusiner SB. A protease-resistant protein is a structural component of the scrapie prion. Cell. 1983;35:57-62.
41. Bolton DC, McKinley MP, Prusiner SB. Molecular characteristics of the major scrapie prion protein. Biochemistry. 1984;23:5898-5905.
42. Meyer RK, McKinley MP, Bowman KA, et al. Separation and properties of cellular and scrapie prion proteins. Proc Natl Acad Sci U S A. 1986;83:2310-2314.
43. Merz PA, Rohwer RG, Kascsak R, et al. Infection-specific particle from the unconventional slow virus diseases. Science. 1984;225:437-440.
44. Prusiner SB, McKinley MP, Bowman KA, et al. Scrapie prions aggregate to form amyloid-like birefringent rods. Cell. 1983;35:349-358.
45. Merz PA, Kascsak R, Rubenstein R, et al. Antisera to scrapie-associated fibril protein and prion protein decorate scrapie-associated fibrils. J Virol. 1987;61:42-49.
46. Merz PA, Somerville RA, Wisniewski HM, et al. Scrapie associated fibrils in Creutzfeldt-Jakob disease. Nature. 1983;306:474-478.
47. Sparkes RS, Simon M, Cohn VH, et al. Assignment of the human and mouse prion protein genes to homologous chromosomes. Proc Natl Acad Sci U S A. 1986;83:7358-7362.
48. Westaway D, Goodman P, Mirenda C, et al. Distinct prion proteins in short and long scrapie incubation period mice. Cell. 1987;51:651-662.
49. Carlson GA, Kingsbury DT, Goodman P, et al. Linkage of prion protein and scrapie incubation time genes. Cell. 1986;46:503-511.
50. Chesebro B, Race R, Wehrly K, et al. Identification of scrapie prion protein-specific mRNA in scrapie-infected and uninfected brain. Nature. 1985;315:331-333.
51. Prusiner SB. Molecular biology of prion diseases. Science. 1991;252:1515-1522.
52. Stahl N, Borchelt DR, Hsiao KK, et al. Scrapie prion protein contains a phosphatidylinositol glycolipid. Cell. 1987;51:229-240.
53. Taraboulos A, Raeber AJ, Borchelt DR, et al. Synthesis and trafficking of prion proteins in cultured cells. Mol Biol Cell. 1992;3:851-863.
54. Bolton DC, Meyer RK, Prusiner SB. Scrapie PrP 27-30 is a sialoglycoprotein. J Virol. 1985;53:596-606.
55. Basler K, Oesch B, Scott M, et al. Scrapie and cellular PrP isoforms are encoded by the same chromosomal gene. Cell. 1986;46:417-428.
56. Hay B, Barry RA, Leberburg I, et al. Biogenesis and transmembrane orientation of the cellular isoform of the scrapie prion protein. Mol Cell Biol. 1987;7:914-920.
57. Borchelt DR, Scott M, Taraboulos A, et al. Scrapie and cellular prion proteins differ in their kinetics of synthesis and topology in cultured cells. J Cell Biol. 1990;110:743-752.
58. Shyng SL, Heuser JE, Harris DA. A glycolipid-anchored prion protein is endocytosed via clathrin-coated pits. J Cell Biol. 1994;125:1239-1250.
59. Shyng SL, Huber MT, Harris DA. A prion protein cycles between the cell surface and an endocytic compartment in cultured neuroblastoma cells. J Biol Chem. 1993;21:15922-15928.
60. Hay B, Prusiner SB, Lingappa VR. Evidence of a secretory form of the cellular prion protein. Biochemistry. 1987;26:8110-8115.
61. Borchelt DR, Taraboulos A, Prusiner SB. Evidence for synthesis of scrapie prion proteins in endocytic pathway. J Biol Chem. 1992;267:16188-16199.
62. Vey M, Pikuhn S, Wille H, et al. Subcellular colocalization of the cellular and scrapie prion protein in caveolae-like membranous domains. Proc Natl Acad Sci U S A. 1996;93:14945-14949.
63. Ma J, Wollman R, Lindquist S. Neurotoxicity and neurodegeneration when PrP accumulates in the cytosol. Science. 2002;298:1781-1785.
64. Hegde RS, Mastrianni J, Scott M, et al. A transmembrane form of the prion protein in neurodegenerative disease. Science. 1998;279:827-834.
65. Forloni G, Angeretti N, Chiesa R, et al. Neurotoxicity of a prion protein fragment. Nature. 1993;362:543-546.
66. Brown DR, Schmidt B, Kretzschmar HA. Role of microglia and host prion protein in neurotoxicity of a prion protein fragment. Nature. 1996;380:345-347.
67. Brandner S, Isenmann S, Raeber A, et al. Normal host prion protein necessary for scrapie-induced neurotoxicity. Nature. 1996;379:339-343.
68. Kretzschmar HA, Prusiner SB, Stowring LE, et al. Scrapie prion proteins are synthesized in neurons. Am J Pathol. 1986;122:1-5.
69. Harris DA, Falls DL, Johnson FA, et al. A prion-like protein from chicken brain copurifies with an acetylcholine receptor-inducing activity. Proc Natl Acad Sci U S A. 1991;88:7664-7668.
70. Harris DA, Lele P, Snider WD. Localization of the mRNA for a chicken prion protein by in situ hybridization. Proc Natl Acad Sci U S A. 1993;90:4309-4313.
71. Falls DL, Rosen KM, Corfas G, et al. ARIA, a protein that stimulates acetylcholine receptor synthesis, is a member of the neu ligand family. Cell. 1993;72:801-815.
72. Moore RC, Mastrangelo P, Bouzamondo E, et al. Doppel-induced cerebellar degeneration in transgenic mice. Proc Natl Acad Sci U S A. 2001;98:15288-15293.
73. Legname G, Nelken P, Guan Z, et al. Prion and doppel proteins bind granule cells of the cerebellum. Proc Natl Acad Sci U S A. 2002;99:16285-16290.
74. Mo H, Moore RC, Cohen FE, et al. Two different neurodegenerative diseases caused by proteins with similar structure. Proc Natl Acad Sci U S A. 2001; 98:2352-2357.
75. Brown DR, Qin K, Herms JW, et al. The cellular prion protein binds copper in vivo. Nature. 1997;390:684-687.
76. Schmitt-Ulms G, Legname G, Baldwin MA, et al. Binding of neural cell adhesion molecules (N-CAMs) to the cellular prion protein. J Mol Biol. 2001;314:1209-1225.
77. Rieger R, Edenhofer F, Lasmezas CI, et al. The human 37-kDa laminin receptor precursor interacts with prion protein in eukaryotic cells. Nat Med. 1997;3:1383-1388.

78. Lledo P-M, Tremblay P, DeArmond SJ, et al. Mice deficient for prion protein exhibit normal neuronal excitability and synaptic transmission in the hippocampus. Proc Natl Acad Sci U S A. 1996;93:2403-2407.

79. Graner E, Mercadante AF, Zanata SM, et al. Cellular prion protein binds laminin and mediates neuritogenesis. Brain Res Mol Brain Res. 2000;76:85-92.

80. Bueler H, Fischer M, Lang Y, et al. Normal development and behavior of mice lacking the normal cell surface PrP protein. Nature. 1992;356:577-582.

81. Bueler H, Aguzzi A, Sailer A, et al. Mice devoid of PrP are resistant to scrapie. Cell. 1993;73:1339-1347.

82. Prusiner SB, Groth D, Serban A, et al. Ablation of the prion protein (PrP) gene in mice prevents scrapie and facilitates production of anti-PrP antibodies. Proc Natl Acad Sci U S A. 1993;90:10608-10612.

83. Tobler I, Gaus SE, Deboer T, et al. Altered circadian activity rhythms and sleep in mice devoid of prion protein. Nature. 1996;380:639-642.

84. Sakaguchi S, Katamine S, Nishida N, et al. Loss of cerebellar Purkinje cells in aged mice homozygous for a disrupted PrP gene. Nature. 1996;380:528-531.

85. Westaway D, DeArmond SJ, Cayetano-Canlas J, et al. Degeneration of skeletal muscle, peripheral nerves, and the central nervous system in transgenic mice overexpressing wild-type prion proteins. Cell. 1994;76:117-129.

86. Pan KM, Baldwin M, Nguyen J, et al. Conversion of alpha-helices into beta-sheets features in the formation of the scrapie prion proteins. Proc Natl Acad Sci U S A. 1993;90:10962-10966.

87. Riek R, Hornemann S, Wider G, et al. NMR structure of the mouse prion protein domain PrP(121-231). Nature. 1996;382:180-182.

88. Hsiao KK, Scott M, Foster D, et al. Spontaneous neurodegeneration in transgenic mice with mutant prion protein. Science. 1990;250:1587-1590.

89. Hsiao KK, Groth D, Scott M, et al. Serial transmission in rodents of neurodegeneration from transgenic mice expressing mutant prion protein. Proc Natl Acad Sci U S A. 1994;91:9126-9130.

90. Telling GC, Haga T, Torchia M, et al. Interactions between wild-type and mutant prion proteins modulate neurodegeneration in transgenic mice. Genes Dev. 1996;10:1736-1750.

91. Muramoto T, DeArmond SJ, Scott M, et al. Heritable disorder resembling neuronal storage disease in mice expressing prion protein with deletion of an alpha-helix. Nat Med. 1997;3:750-755.

92. Telling GC, Scott M, Mastrianni J, et al. Prion propagation in mice expressing human and chimeric PrP transgenes implicates the interaction of cellular PrP with another protein. Cell. 1995;83:79-90.

93. Kaneko K, Zulianello L, Scott M, et al. Evidence for protein X binding to a discontinuous epitope on the cellular prion protein during scrapie prion propagation. Proc Natl Acad Sci U S A. 1997;94:10069-10074.

94. Kaneko K, Vey M, Scott M, et al. COOH-terminal sequence of the cellular prion protein directs subcellular trafficking and controls conversion into the scrapie isoform. Proc Natl Acad Sci U S A. 1997;94:2333-2338.

95. Peretz D, Williamson RA, Matsunaga Y, et al. A conformational transition at the N terminus of the prion protein features in formation of the scrapie isoform. J Mol Biol. 1997;273:614-622.

96. Kocisco DA, Lansbury PT, Caughey B. Partial unfolding and refolding of scrapie-associated prion protein: Evidence for a critical 16-kDa C-terminal domain. Biochemistry. 1996;35:13434-13442.

97. Holscher C, Delius H, Burkle A. Overexpression of the nonconvertible PrPC D114-121 in scrapie-infected mouse neuroblastoma cells leads to trans-dominant inhibition of wild-type PrPSc accumulation. J Virol. 1998;72:1153-1159.

98. Prusiner SB, Scott M, Foster M, et al. Transgenetic studies implicate interaction between homologous PrP isoforms in scrapie prion replication. Cell. 1990;63:673-686.

99. Scott M, Groth D, Foster D, et al. Propagation of prions with artificial properties in transgenic mice expressing chimeric PrP genes. Cell. 1993;73:979-988.

100. Weissmann C. A 'unified theory' of prion propagation. Nature. 1991;352:679-683.

101. Aguzzi A, Heppner FL. Pathogenesis of prion diseases: A progress report. Cell Death Differentiation. 2000;7:889-902.

102. DeArmond SJ, Yang SL, Lee A, et al. Three scrapie prion isolates exhibit different accumulation patterns of the prion protein scrapie isoform. Proc Natl Acad Sci U S A. 1993;90:6449-6453.

103. Beekes M, McBride PA, Baldauf E. Cerebral targeting indicates vagal spread of infection in hamsters fed with scrapie. J Gen Virol. 1998;79:601-607.

104. Klein MA, Frigg R, Flechsig E, et al. A crucial role for B cells in neuroinvasive scrapie. Nature. 1997;390:687-690.

105. Zigas V. Laughing Death: The Untold Story of Kuru. Clifton, NJ: Humana Press; 1990.

106. Zigas V, Gajdusek DC. Kuru: Clinical study of a new syndrome resembling paralysis agitans in natives of the Eastern Highlands of Australian New Guinea. Med J Aust. 1957;2:745-754.

107. Gajdusek DC, Gibbs CJ Jr, Alpers MP. Experimental transmission of a kuru syndrome to chimpanzees. Nature. 1966;209:794-796.

108. Gajdusek DC, Zigas V. Degenerative disease of the central nervous system in New Guinea: The endemic occurrence of "kuru" in the native population. N Engl J Med. 1957;257:974-978.

109. Gajdusek DC, Zigas V. Clinical, pathological and epidemiological study of an acute progressive degenerative disease of the central nervous system among natives of the Eastern Highlands of New Guinea. Am J Med. 1959;26:442-469.

110. Scrimgeour EM, Masters CL, Alpers MP, et al. A clinico-pathologic study of a case of kuru. J Neurol Sci. 1983;59:265-275.

111. Hornabrook RW. Kuru: A subacute cerebellar degeneration—the natural history and clinical features. Brain. 1968;91:53-74.

112. Klatzo I, Gajdusek DC, Zigas V. Pathology of kuru. Lab Invest. 1959;8:799-847.

113. Alpers MP. Epidemiology and ecology of kuru. In: Prusiner SB, Hadlow WJ, eds. Slow Transmissible Diseases of the Nervous System. New York: Academic Press; 1979:67-90.

114. Cobb WA, Hornabrook RW, Sanders S. The EEG of kuru. Electroencephalogr Clin Neurophysiol. 1973;34:419-427.

115. Liberski PP, Gajdusek DC. Kuru: Forty years later, a historical note. Brain Pathol. 1997;7:555-560.

116. Huillard d'Aignaux JN, Cousens SN, Maccario J, et al. The incubation period of kuru. Epidemiology. 2002;13:402-408.

117. Hainfellner JA, Liberski PP, Guiroy DC, et al. Pathology and immunocytochemistry of a kuru brain. Brain Pathol. 1997;7:547-553.

118. Lee HS, Brown P, Cervenakova L, et al. Increased susceptibility to Kuru of carriers of the PRNP methionine/methionine genotype. J Infect Dis. 2001;183:192-196.

119. Mead S, Stumpf MP, Whitfield J, et al. Balancing selection at the prion protein gene consistent with prehistoric kurulike epidemics. Science. 2003;300:640-643.

120. Creutzfeldt HG. Uber eine eigenartige herdfoermige Erkrankung des Zentralnervensystems. Z Gesamte Neurol Psychiatry. 1920;57:1-18.

121. Jakob A. Uber eigenartige Erkrankungen des Zentralnervensystems mit bemerkenswertem anatomischen Befund. Z Gesamte Neurol Psychiatry. 1921;64:147-228.

122. Brown P, Cathala F, Rabertas RB, et al. The epidemiology of Creutzfeldt-Jakob disease: Conclusions of a 15 year investigation in France and review of the world literature. Neurology. 1987;37:895-909.

123. Packer RJ, Cornblath DR, Gonatas NK, et al. Creutzfeldt-Jakob disease in a 20-year-old woman. Neurology. 1980;30:492-496.

124. Monreal J, Collins GH, Masters CL, et al. Creutzfeldt-Jakob disease in an adolescent. J Neurol Sci. 1981;52:341-350.

125. de Silva R, Findlay C, Awad I, et al. Creutzfeldt-Jakob disease in the elderly. Postgrad Med J. 1997;73:557-559.

126. Brown P, Preece M, Brandel J-P, et al. Iatrogenic Creutzfeldt-Jakob disease at the millennium. Neurology. 2000;55:1075-1081.

127. Creutzfeldt-Jakob disease associated with cadaveric dura mater grafts—Japan, January 1979–May 1996. MMWR Morb Mortal Wkly Rep. 1998;46:1066-1069.

128. Hoshi K, Yoshino H, Urata J, et al. Creutzfeldt-Jakob disease associated with cadaveric dura mater grafts in Japan. Neurology. 2000;55:718-721.

129. Lang CJG, Heckmann JG, Neundorfer B. Creutzfeldt-Jakob disease via dural and corneal transplants. J Neurol Sci. 1998;160:128-139.

130. Blattler T. Implications of prion diseases for neurosurgery. Neurosurg Rev. 2002;25:195-203.

131. Duffy P, Wolf J, Collins G, et al. Possible person to person transmission of Creutzfeldt-Jakob disease (Letter). N Engl J Med. 1974;290:692-693.

132. Allan B, Tuft S. Transmission of Creutzfeldt-Jakob disease in corneal grafts. BMJ. 1997;315:1553-1554.

133. Heckmann JG, Lang CJ, Petruch F, et al. Transmission of Creutzfeldt-Jakob disease via a corneal transplant. J Neurol Neurosurg Psychiatry. 1997;63:388-390.

134. Creange A, Gray F, Cesaro P, et al. Creutzfeldt-Jakob disease after liver transplantation. Ann Neurol. 1995;38:269-272.

135. Antoine JC, Michel D, Bertholon P, et al. Creutzfeldt-Jakob disease after extracranial dura mater embolization for nasopharyngeal angiofibroma. Neurology. 1997;48:1451-1453.

136. Defebvre L, Destee A, Caron J, et al. Creutzfeldt-Jakob disease after embolization of intercostal arteries with cadaveric dura mater suggesting a systemic transmission of the prion agent. Neurology. 1997;48:1470-1471.

137. Will RG, Matthews WB. Evidence for case-to-case transmission of Creutzfeldt-Jakob disease. J Neurol Neurosurg Psychiatry. 1982;45:235-238.

138. El Hachimi KH, Chaunu M-P, Cervenakova L, et al. Putative neurosurgical transmission of Creutzfeldt-Jakob disease with analysis of donor and recipient:agent strains. C R Acad Sci (Paris). 1997;320:319-328.

139. Bernoulli C, Siegfried J, Baumgartner G, et al. Danger of accidental person-to-person transmission of Creutzfeldt-Jakob disease by surgery. Lancet. 1977;1:478-479.

140. Brown P. The decline and fall of Creutzfeldt-Jakob disease associated with human growth hormone therapy. Neurology. 1988;38:1135-1137.

141. Ellis CJ, Katifi H, Weller RO. A further British case of growth hormone induced Creutzfeldt-Jakob disease. J Neurol Neurosurg Psychiatry. 1992;55:1200-1202.

142. Gibbs CJ Jr, Asher DM, Brown PW, et al. Creutzfeldt-Jakob disease infectivity of growth hormone derived from human pituitary glands (Letter). N Engl J Med. 1993;328:358-359.

143. Markus HS, Duchen LW, Parkin EM, et al. Creutzfeldt-Jakob disease in recipients of human growth hormone in the United Kingdom: A clinical and radiographic study. QJM. 1992;82:43-51.

144. Frasier SD. The not-so-good old days: Working with pituitary growth hormone in North America, 1956 to 1985. J Pediatr. 1997;131:S1-S4.

145. Villemeur TB, Deslys J-P, Pradel A, et al. Creutzfeldt-Jakob disease from contaminated growth hormone extracts in France. Neurology. 1996;47:690-695.

146. Cochius JI, Hyman N, Esiri MM. Creutzfeldt-Jakob disease in a recipient of human pituitary-derived gonadotrophin: A second case. J Neurol Neurosurg Psychiatry. 1992;55:1094-1095.

147. Dumble LJ, Klein RD. Creutzfeldt-Jakob legacy for Australian women treated with human pituitary gonadotropins (Letter). Lancet. 1992;340:847-848.

148. Croes EA, Roks G, Jansen GH, et al. Creutzfeldt-Jakob disease 38 years after diagnostic use of human growth hormone. J Neurol Neurosurg Psychiatry 2002;72:792-793.

149. Joint Commission on Accreditation of Healthcare Organizations. Sentinel event alert: Exposure to Creutzfeldt-Jakob disease. Issue 20, 2001. Available at: 〈http://www.jcaho.com/about+us/news+letters/sentinel+event+alert/sea_20.htm〉.

150. Manuelidis EE, Kim JH, Mericangas JR, et al. Transmission to animals of Creutzfeldt-Jakob disease from human blood. Lancet. 1985;2:896-897.
151. Manuelidis EE, Gorgacs EJ, Manuelidis L. Viremia in experimental Creutzfeldt-Jakob disease. Science. 1978;200:1069-1071.
152. Hunter N, Foster J, Chong A, et al. Transmisison of prion diseases by blood transfusion. J Gen Virol. 2002;83:2897-2905.
153. Ricketts MN, Brown P. Transmissible spongiform encephalopathy update and implications for blood safety. Clin Lab Med 2003;23:129-137.
154. Foster PR. Prions and blood products. Ann Med. 2000;32:501-513.
155. Wientjens DPWM, Davinipour Z, Hofman A, et al. Risk factors for Creutzfeldt-Jakob disease: A reanalysis of case-controlled studies. Neurology. 1996;46:1287-1291.
156. Collins S, Law MG, Fletcher A, et al. Surgical treatment and risk of sporadic Creutzfeldt-Jakob disease: A case-control study. Lancet. 1999;353:693-697.
157. Zerr I, Brandel J-P, Masullo C, et al. European surveillance on Creutzfeldt-Jakob disease: A case control study for medical risk factors. J Clin Epidemiol. 2000;53:747-754.
158. van Duijn CM, Delasnerie-Laupretre N, Masullo C, et al. Case-control study of risk factors of Creutzfeldt-Jakob disease in Europe during 1993-95. Lancet 1998;351:1081-1085.
159. Berger JR, David NJ. Creutzfeldt-Jakob disease in a physician: A review of the disorder in health care workers. Neurology. 1993;43:205-206.
160. Creutzfeldt HG. Über eine eigenartige herdformige Erkrankung des Zentralnervensystems (Vorlaufige Mitteilung). Z Neurol Psychiatr. 1920;57:1-18.
161. Jakob A. Über eigenartige Erkrankungen des Zentralnervensystems mit bemerkenswetem anatomischen Befunde (spastische Pseudosklerose-Encephalomyelopathie mit disseminierten Degenerationsherden). Dtsch Z Nervenheilk. 1921;70:132-146.
162. Heidenhain A. Klinische und anatomische Untersuchungen über eine eigenartige Erkrankung des Zentralnervensystems im Praesenium. Z Neurol Psychiatr. 1929;118:49-114.
163. Brownell B, Oppenheimer DR. An ataxic form of subacute presenile polioencephalopathy (Creutzfeldt-Jakob disease). J Neurol Neurosurg Psychiatry. 1965;28:350-361.
164. Stern K. Severe dementia associated with bilateral symmetrical degeneration of the thalamus. Brain. 1939;62:157-171.
165. Garcin R, Brion S, Khochneviss AA. Le syndrome de Creutzfeldt-Jakob et les syndromes corticostries du presenium (a l'occasion de 5 observations anatomo-cliniques). Rev Neurol (Paris). 1963;109:419-441.
166. Kirschbaum WR. Jakob-Creutzfeldt Disease. New York: Elsevier; 1968.
167. Brown P, Cathala F, Castaigne P, et al. Creutzfeldt-Jakob disease: Clinical analysis of a consecutive series of 230 neuropathologically verified cases. Ann Neurol. 1986;20:597-602.
168. Cathala F, Baron H. Clinical aspects of Creutzfeldt-Jakob disease. In: Prusiner SB, McKinley MP, eds. Prions: Novel Infectious Pathogens Causing Scrapie and Creutzfeldt-Jakob Disease. Orlando: Academic Press; 1987:467-509.
169. Brown P, Rodgers-Johnson P, Cathala F, et al. Creutzfeldt-Jakob disease of long duration: Clinicopathological characteristics, transmissibility, and differential diagnosis. Ann Neurol. 1984;16:295-304.
170. MacGowan DJ, Delanty N, Petito F, et al. Isolated myoclonic alien hand as the sole presentation of pathologically established Creutzfeldt-Jakob disease: A report of two patients. J Neurol Neurosurg Psychiatry. 1997;63:404-407.
171. Guiroy DC, Shankar SK, Gibbs CJ, et al. Neuronal degeneration in the trigeminal ganglia in Creutzfeldt-Jakob disease. Ann Neurol. 1989;25:102-106.
172. Antoine JC, Laplanche JL, Mosnier JF, et al. Demyelinating peripheral neuropathy with Creutzfeldt-Jakob disease and mutation at codon 200 of the prion protein gene. Neurology. 1996;46:1123-1127.
173. Esiri MM, Gordon WI, Collinge J, et al. Peripheral neuropathy in Creutzfeldt-Jakob disease. Neurology. 1997;48:784.
174. Kovacs T, Aranyi Z, Szirmai I, et al. Creutzfeldt-Jakob disease with amyotrophy and demyelinating polyneuropathy. Arch Neurol 2002;59:1811-1814.
175. Newiadomska M, Kulczycki J, Wochnik-Dyjas D, et al. Impairment of the peripheral nervous system in Creutzfeldt-Jakob disease. Arch Neurol. 2002;59:1430-1436.
176. Nomura E, Harada T, Kurokawa K, et al. Creutzfeldt-Jakob disease associated with autonomic nervous system dysfunction in the early stage. Intern Med. 1997;36:492-496.
177. Salazar AM, Masters CL, Gajdusek DC, et al. Syndromes of amyotrophic lateral sclerosis and dementia: Relation to transmissible Creutzfeldt-Jakob disease. Ann Neurol. 1983;14:17-26.
178. Gibbs CJ Jr, Gajdusek DC, Asher DM, et al. Creutzfeldt-Jakob disease (spongiform encephalopathy): Transmission to chimpanzee. Science. 1968;161:388-389.
179. Roos R, Gajdusek DC, Gibbs CJ Jr. The clinical characteristics of transmissible Creutzfeldt-Jakob disease. Brain. 1973;96:1-20.
180. Tanaka M, Iizuko O, Yuasa T. Hepatic dysfunction in Creutzfeldt-Jakob disease. Neurology. 1992;42:1249.
181. Blisard KS, Davis LE, Harrington MG, et al. Pre-mortem diagnosis of Creutzfeldt-Jakob disease by detection of abnormal cerebrospinal fluid proteins. J Neurol Sci. 1990;99:75-81.
182. Harrington MG, Merril CR, Asher DM, et al. Abnormal proteins in the cerebrospinal fluid of patients with Creutzfeldt-Jakob disease. N Engl J Med. 1986;315:279-283.
183. Zerr I, Bodemer M, Otto M, et al. Diagnosis of Creutzfeldt-Jakob disease by two-dimensional electrophoresis of cerebrospinal fluid. Lancet. 1996;348:846-849.
184. Hsich G, Kenney K, Gibbs CJ, et al. The 14-3-3 brain protein in cerebrospinal fluid as a marker for transmissible spongiform encephalopathies. N Engl J Med. 1996;335:924-930.
185. Zerr I, Bodemer M, Gefeller O, et al. Detection of 14-3-3 protein in the cerebrospinal fluid supports the diagnosis of Creutzfeldt-Jakob disease. Ann Neurol. 1998;43:32-40.
186. Aksamit AJ, Preissner CM, Homburger HA. Quantitation of 14-3-3 and neuron-specific enolase proteins in CSF in Creutzfeldt-Jakob disease. Neurology. 2001;57:728-730.
187. Kenney K, Brechtel C, Takahashi H, et al. An enzyme-linked immunosorbent assay to quantify 14-3-3 protein in the cerebrospinal fluid of suspected Creutzfeldt-Jakob disease patients. Ann Neurol. 2000;48:395-398.
188. Geschwind MD, Martindale J, Miller D, et al. Challenging the clinical utility of the 14-3-3 protein for the diagnosis of sporadic Creutzfeldt-Jakob disease. Arch Neurol. 2003;60:813-816.
189. Lemstra A, van Meegen MT, Vreyling JP, et al. 14-3-3 testing in diagnosing Creutzfeldt-Jakob disease. Neurology. 2000;55:514-516.
190. Chapman T, McKeel DW, Morris JC. Misleading results with the 14-3-3 assay for the diagnosis of Creutzfeldt-Jakob disease. Neurology. 2000;55:1396-1397.
191. Burkhard PR, Sanchez J-C, Landis T, et al. CSF detection of the 14-3-3 protein in unselected patients with dementia. Neurology. 2001;56:1528-1533.
191a. Tschampa HJ, Neumann M, Zerr I, et al. Patients with Alzheimer's disease and dementia with Lewy bodies mistaken for Creutzfeldt-Jakob disease. J Neurol Neurosurg Psychiatry. 2001;71:33-39.
192. Roseman H, Meiner Z, Kahana E, et al. Detection of 14-3-3 protein in the CSF of genetic Creutzfeldt-Jakob disease. Neurology. 1997;49:593-595.
192a. Otto M, Stein H, Szudra A, et al. S-100 protein concentration in the cerebrospinal fluid of patients with Creutzfeldt-Jakob disease. J Neurol. 1997;244:566-570.
193. Otto M, Wiltfang J, Cepek L, et al. Tau protein and 14-3-3 protein in the differential diagnosis of Creutzfeldt-Jakob disease. Neurology. 2002;58:192-197.
194. Van Everbroeck B, Green AJ, Vanmechelen E, et al. Phosphorylated tau in cerebrospinal fluid as a marker for Creutzfeldt-Jakob disease. J Neurol Neurosurg Psychiatry. 2002;73:79-81.
195. Galvez S, Cartier L. Computed tomographic findings in 15 cases of Creutzfeldt-Jakob disease with histological verification. J Neurol Neurosurg Psychiatry. 1984;47:1244-1246.
196. Berciano J, Diez C, Polo JM, et al. CT appearance of panencephalopathic and ataxic type of Creutzfeldt-Jakob disease. J Comput Assist Tomogr. 1991;15:332-334.
197. Kovanen J, Erkinjuntti T, Livanainen M, et al. Cerebral MR and CT imaging in Creutzfeldt-Jakob disease. J Comput Assist Tomogr. 1985;9:125-128.
198. Schelnska GK, Walter GF. Serial computed tomography findings in Creutzfeldt-Jakob disease. Neuroradiology. 1989;31:303-306.
199. Hayashi R, Hanyu N, Kuwabara T, et al. Serial computed tomographic and electroencephalographic studies in Creutzfeldt-Jakob disease. Acta Neurol Scand. 1992;85:161-165.
200. Milton WJ, Atlas SW, Lavi E, et al. Magnetic resonance imaging of Creutzfeldt-Jakob disease. Ann Neurol. 1991;29:438-440.
201. Yamamoto K, Morimatsu M. Increased signal in basal ganglia and white matter on magnetic resonance imaging in Creutzfeldt-Jakob disease. Ann Neurol. 1992;32:114.
202. Finkenstaedt M, Szudra A, Zerr I, et al. MR imaging of Creutzfeldt-Jakob disease. Radiology. 1996;199:793-798.
203. Zeidler M, Will RG, Ironside JW, et al. Magnetic resonance imaging is not a sensitive test for Creutzfeldt-Jakob disease. BMJ. 1996;312:844.
204. Collie DA, Sellar RJ, Zeidler M, et al. MRI of Creutzfeldt-Jakob disease: Imaging features and recommended MRI protocol. Clin Radiol. 2001;56:726-739.
205. Schroter A, Zerr I, Henkel K, et al. Magnetic resonance imaging in the clinical diagnosis of Creutzfeldt-Jakob disease. Arch Neurol. 2000;57:1751-1757.
206. Uemura Y, O'uchi T, Sakamoto Y, et al. High signal of the striatum in sporadic Creutzfeldt-Jakob disease: Sequential changes on T2-weighted MRI. Neuroradiology. 2002;44:314-318.
207. Demaerel P, Sciot R, Robberecht W, et al. Accuracy of diffusion-weighted MR imaging in the diagnosis of sporadic Creutzfeldt-Jakob disease. J Neurol. 2003;250:222-225.
208. Bahn MM, Kido DK, Lin W, et al. Brain magnetic resonance diffusion abnormalities in Creutzfeldt-Jakob disease. Arch Neurol. 1997;54:1411-1415.
209. Mao-Draayer Y, Braff SP, Nagle KJ, et al. Emerging patterns of diffusion-weighted MR imaging in Creutzfeldt-Jakob disease: Case report and review of the literature. AJNR Am J Neuroradiol. 2002;23:550-556.
210. Murata T, Shiga Y, Higano S, et al. Conspicuity and evolution of lesions in Creutzfeldt-Jakob disease at diffusion-weighted imaging. AJNR Am J Neuroradiol. 2002;23:1164-1172.
211. Demaerel P, Baert AL, Vanopdenbosch L, et al. Diffusion-weighted magnetic resonance imaging in Creutzfeldt-Jakob disease. Lancet. 1997;349:847-848.
212. Nitrini R, Medonca RA, Huang N, et al. Diffusion-weighted MRI in two cases of familial Creutzfeldt-Jakob disease. J Neurol Sci. 2001;184:163-167.
213. Rabinstein AA, Whiteman ML, Shebert RT. Abnormal diffusion-weighted magnetic resonance imaging in Creutzfeldt-Jakob disease following corneal transplantation. Arch Neurol. 2002;59:637-639.
214. Mittal S, Farmer P, Kalina P, et al. Correlation of diffusion-weighted magnetic resonance imaging with neuropathology in Creutzfeldt-Jakob disease. Arch Neurol. 2002;59:128-134.
215. Henkel K, Zerr I, Hertel A, et al. Positron emission tomography with [(18)F]FDG in the diagnosis of Creutzfeldt-Jakob disease. J Neurol. 2002;249:699-705.
216. Watanabe N, Seto H, Shimuzu M, et al. Brain SPECT of Creutzfeldt-Jakob disease. Clin Nucl Med. 1996;21:236-241.
217. Pandya HG, Coley SC, Wilkinson ID, Griffiths PD. Magnetic resonance spectroscopic abnormalities in sporadic and variant Creutzfeldt-Jakob disease. Clin Radiol. 2003;58:148-153.

218. Levy RS, Chiappa KH, Burke CJ, et al. Early evolution and incidence of electroencephalographic abnormalities in Creutzfeldt-Jakob disease. J Clin Neurophysiol. 1986;3:1-21.
219. Aguglia U, Farnarier G, Tinuper P, et al. Subacute spongiform encephalopathy with periodic paroxysmal activities: Clinical evolution and serial EEG findings in 20 cases. Clin Electroencephalogr. 1987;18:147-158.
220. Chiofalo N, Fuentes A, Galvez S. Serial EEG findings in 27 cases of Creutzfeldt-Jakob disease. Arch Neurol. 1980;37:143-145.
221. Steinhoff BJ, Racker S, Herrendorf G, et al. Accuracy and reliability of periodic sharp wave complexes in Creutzfeldt-Jakob disease. Arch Neurol. 1996;53:162-166.
222. Zerr I, Pocchiari M, Collins S, et al. Analysis of EEG and CSF 14-3-3 proteins as aids to the diagnosis of Creutzfeldt-Jakob disease. Neurology. 2000;55:811-815.
223. Traub RD, Pedley TA. Virus induced electrotonic coupling: Hypothesis on the mechanism of periodic EEG discharges in Creutzfeldt-Jakob disease. Ann Neurol. 1981; 10:405-410.
224. Elliott F, Gardner-Thorpe C, Barwick DD, et al. Jakob-Creutzfeldt disease: Modification of clinical and electroencephalographic activity with methylphenidate and diazepam. J Neurol Neurosurg Psychiatry. 1974;37:879-887.
225. Floel A, Reilmann R, Ludemann P. Anticonvulsants for Creutzfeldt-Jakob disease. Lancet 2003;361:224.
226. Poser S, Mollenhauer B, Kraub A, et al. How to improve the clinical diagnosis of Creutzfeldt-Jakob disease. Brain. 1999;122:2345-2351.
227. Tietjen GE, Drury I. Familial Creutzfeldt-Jakob disease without periodic EEG activity. Ann Neurol. 1990;28:585-588.
228. Donnet A, Farnarier G, Gambarelli D, et al. Sleep electroencephalogram at the early stage of Creutzfeldt-Jakob disease. Clin Electroencephalogr. 1992;23:118-125.
229. Brown P, Jannotta F, Gibbs CJ Jr, et al. Coexistence of Creutzfeldt-Jakob disease and Alzheimer's disease in the same patient. Neurology. 1990;40:226-228.
230. Muramoto T, Kitamoto T, Koga H, et al. The coexistence of Alzheimer's disease and Creutzfeldt-Jakob disease in a patient with dementia of long duration. Acta Neuropathol. 1992;84:686-689.
231. Castellani R, Parchi P, Madoff L, et al. Biopsy diagnosis of Creutzfeldt-Jakob disease by Western blot: A case report. Brain Pathol. 1997;28:623-626.
232. Kitamoto T, Doh-ura K, Muramoto T, et al. The primary structure of the prion protein influences the distribution of abnormal prion protein in the central nervous system. Am J Pathol. 1992;141:271-277.
233. Zanusso G, Ferrari S, Cardone F, et al. Detection of pathological prion protein in the olfactory epithelium in sporadic Creutzfeldt-Jakob disease. N Engl J Med. 2003;348:711-719.
234. Hill AF, Joiner S, Wadsworth DF, et al. Molecular classification of sporadic Creutzfeldt-Jakob disease. Brain. 2003;126:1333-1346.
235. Kovacs GG, Trabattoni G, Hainfellner JA, et al. Mutations of the prion protein gene: Phenotypic spectrum. J Neurol. 2002;249:1567-1582.
236. Masters CL, Harris JO, Gajdusek DC, et al. Creutzfeldt-Jakob disease: Patterns of worldwide occurrence and significance of familial and sporadic clustering. Ann Neurol. 1979;5:177-188.
237. Budka H, Aguzzi A, Brown P, et al. Neuropathological diagnostic criteria for Creutzfeldt-Jakob disease (CJD) and other human spongiform encephalopathies (prion diseases). Brain Pathol. 1995;5:459-466.
238. Kretzschmar H, Ironside J, DeArmond SJ, et al. Diagnostic criteria for sporadic Creutzfeldt-Jakob disease. Arch Neurol. 1996;53:913-920.
239. Brandel J-P, Delasnerie-Laupretre N, Laplanche J-L, et al. Diagnosis of Creutzfeldt-Jakob disease: Effect of clinical criteria on disease estimates. Neurology. 2000;54:1095-1099.
240. Goldfarb LG, Brown P, Goldgaber D, et al. Creutzfeldt-Jakob disease and kuru patients lack a mutation consistently found in the Gerstmann-Sträussler-Scheinker syndrome. Exp Neurol. 1990;108:247-250.
241. Hitoshi S, Nagura H, Yamagouchi H, et al. Double mutations at codon 180 and codon 232 of the PrP gene in an apparently sporadic case of Creutzfeldt-Jakob disease. J Neurol Sci. 1993;93:208-212.
242. Palmer MS, Dryden AJ, Hughes JT, et al. Homozygous prion protein genotype predisposes to sporadic Creutzfeldt-Jakob disease (Letter). Nature. 1991;352:340-342.
243. Collinge J, Palmer MS, Dryden AJ. Genetic predisposition to iatrogenic Creutzfeldt-Jakob disease. Lancet. 1991;337:1441-1442.
244. Meiner Z, Gabizon R, Prusiner SB. Familial Creutzfeldt-Jakob disease: Codon 200 prion disease in Libyan Jews. Medicine. 1997;76:227-237.
245. Bertoni JM, Brown P, Goldfarb LG, et al. Familial Creutzfeldt-Jakob disease (codon 200 mutation) with supranuclear palsy. JAMA. 1992;268:2413-2415.
246. Goldfarb LG, Brown P, Haltia M, et al. Creutzfeldt-Jakob disease cosegregates with codon 178 Asn PRNP mutation in families of European origin. Ann Neurol. 1992;31:274-281.
247. Brown P, Goldfarb LG, Kovanen J, et al. Phenotypic characteristics of familial Creutzfeldt-Jakob disease associated with the codon 178 Asn PRNP mutation. Ann Neurol. 1992;31:282-285.
248. Brown P, Goldfarb LG, McCombie WR, et al. Atypical Creutzfeldt-Jakob disease in an American family with an insert mutation in the PRNP amyloid precursor gene. Neurology. 1992;42:422-427.
249. Collinge J, Brown J, Hardy J, et al. Inherited prion disease with a 144 base pair gene insertion: 2. Clinical and pathological features. Brain. 1992;115:687-710.
250. Britton TC, Al-Sarraj S, Shaw C, et al. Sporadic Creutzfeldt-Jakob disease in 1 16-year-old in the UK. Lancet. 1995;346:1155.
251. Will RG, Ironside JW, Zeidler M, et al. A new variant of Creutzfeldt-Jakob disease in the UK. Lancet. 1996;347:921-925.
252. Zeidler M, Stewart GE, Barraclough CR, et al. New variant Creutzfeldt-Jakob disease: Neurological features and diagnostic tests. Lancet. 1997;350:903-907.
253. Spencer MD, Knight RSG, Will RG. First hundred cases of variant Creutzfeldt-Jakob disease: Retrospective case note review of early psychiatric and neurological features. BMJ. 2002;324:1479-1482.
254. Chazot G, Broussolle E, Lapras CL, et al. New variant Creutzfeldt-Jakob disease in a 26-year-old French man. Lancet. 1996;347:1181.
255. Streichenberger N, Jordan D, Verejan I, et al. The first case of new variant Creutzfeldt-Jakob disease in France: Clinical data and neuropathological findings. Acta Neuropathol. 2000;99:704-708.
256. Deslys J-P, Lasmezas CI, Streichenberger N, et al. New variant Creutzfeldt-Jakob disease in France. Lancet. 1997;349:30-31.
257. La Bella V, Collinge J, Pocchiari M, et al. Variant Creutzfeldt-Jakob disease in an Italian woman. Lancet. 2002;360:997-998.
258. Wiersma S, Cooper S, Knight R, et al. Probable variant Creutzfeldt-Jakob disease in a US resident—Florida, 2002. JAMA. 2002;288:2965-2966.
259. Hillier CEM, Salmon RL, Neal JW, et al. Possible underascertainment of variant Creutzfeldt-Jakob disease: A systematic study. J Neurol Neurosurg Psychiatry. 220;72:304-309.
260. Venters GA. New variant Creutzfeldt-Jakob disease: The epidemic that never was. BMJ. 2001;323:858-861.
261. Andrews NJ, Farrington CP, Ward HJT, et al. Deaths from variant Creutzfeldt-Jakob disease in the UK. Lancet. 2003;361:751-752.
262. d'Aignaux JN, Cousens SN, Smith PG. Predictability of the UK variant Creutzfeldt-Jakob disease epidemic. Science. 2001;294:1729-1731.
263. Valleron A-J, Boelle P-Y, Will R, et al. Estimation of epidemic size and incubation time based on age characteristics of cCJD in the United Kingdom. Science. 2001;294:1726-1728.
264. Schonberger L. New variant Creutzfeldt-Jakob disease and bovine spongiform encephalopathy. Infect Dis Clin North Am. 1998;12:111-121.
265. Zeidler M, Johnstone EC, Bamber RWK, et al. New variant Creutzfeldt-Jakob disease: Psychiatric features. Lancet. 1997;350:908-910.
266. Coulthard A, Hall K, English PT, et al. Quantitative analysis of MRI signal intensity in new variant Creutzfeldt-Jakob disease. Br J Radiol. 1999;72:742-748.
267. Will RG, Zeidler M, Stewart GE, et al. Diagnosis of new variant Creutzfeldt-Jakob disease. Ann Neurol. 2000;47:575-582.
268. Zeidler M, Sellar RJ, Collie DA, et al. The pulvinar sign on magnetic resonance imaging in variant Creutzfeldt-Jakob disease. Lancet. 2000;355:1412-1418.
269. Martindale J, Geschwind MD, De Armond S, et al. Sporadic Creutzfeldt-Jakob disease mimicking variant Creutzfeldt-Jakob disease. Arch Neurol. 2003;60:767-770.
270. deSilva R, Patterson J, Hadley D, et al. Single photon emission computed tomography in the identification of new variant Creutzfeldt-Jakob disease: Case reports. BMJ. 1998;316:593-594.
271. Collinge J, Sidle KCL, Meads J, et al. Molecular analysis of prion strain variation and the aetiology of 'new variant' CJD. Nature. 1996;383:685-690.
272. Parchi P, Capellari S, Chen SG, et al. Typing prion isoforms. Nature. 1997;386:232.
273. Bruce ME, Will RG, Ironside JW, et al. Transmissions to mice indicate that 'new variant' CJD is caused by BSE agent. Nature. 1997;389:498-501.
274. Scott MR, Will R, Ironside J, et al. Compelling transgenetic evidence for transmission of bovine spongiform encephalopathy to humans. Proc Natl Acad Sci U S A. 1999;96:15137-15142.
275. Hill AF, Desbruslais M, Joiner S, et al. The same prion strain causes vCJD and BSE. Nature. 1997;389:448-450.
276. Lasmezas CI, Deslys J-P, Demalmay R, et al. BSE transmission to macaques. Nature. 1996;381:743-744.
277. Collee JG, Bradley R. BSE: A decade on—part 2. Lancet. 1997;349:715-721.
278. Collee JG, Bradley R. BSE: A decade on—part 1. Lancet. 1997;349:636-641.
279. Anderson RM, Donnelly CA, Ferguson NM, et al. Transmission dynamics and epidemiology of BSE in British cattle. Nature. 1996;382:779.
280. Nathanson N, Wilesmith J, Griot C. Bovine spongiform encephalopathy (BSE): Causes and consequences of a common source epidemic. Am J Epidemiol. 1997;145:959.
281. Ramasamy I, Law M, Collins S, et al. Organ distribution of prion proteins in variant Creutzfeldt-Jakob disease. Lancet Infect Dis. 2003;3:214-222.
282. Hill AF, Zeidler M, Ironside J, et al. Diagnosis of new variant Creutzfeldt-Jakob disease by tonsil biopsy. Lancet. 1997;349:99-100.
283. Wadsworth JDF, Joiner S, Hill AF, et al. Tissue distribution of protease resistant prion protein in variant Creutzfeldt-Jakob disease using a highly sensitive immunoblotting assay. Lancet. 2001;358:171-180.
284. Kawashima T, Furukawa H, Doh-ura K, et al. Diagnosis of new variant Creutzfeldt-Jakob disease by tonsil biopsy. Lancet. 1997;350:68-69.
285. Hill AF, Butterworth RJ, Joiner S, et al. Investigation of variant Cruetzfeldt-Jakob disease and other human prion diseases with tonsil biopsy samples. Lancet. 1999;353:183-189.
286. Hilton DA, Ghani AC, Conyers L, et al. Accumulation of prion protein in tonsil and appendix: Review of tissue samples. BMJ. 2002;325:633-634.
287. Joiner S, Linehan J, Brandner S, et al. Irregular presence of abnormal prion protein in appendix in variant Creutzfeldt-Jakob disease. J Neurol Neurosurg Psychiatry. 2002;73:597-598.
288. Gerstmann J, Sträussler E, Scheinker I. Über eine eigenarte hereditär-familiäre Erkrankung des Zentralnervensystems: Zugleich ein Beitrag zur Frage des vorzeitgen lokalen Alterns. Z Neurol Psychiatr. 1936;154:736-762.
289. Masters CL, Gajdusek DC, Gibbs CJ Jr. Creutzfeldt-Jakob disease virus isolations from the Gerstmann-Sträussler-Scheinker syndrome: With an analysis of the various forms of amyloid plaque deposition in the virus-induced spongiform encephalopathies. Brain. 1981;104:559-588.

290. Liberski P, Barcikowska M, Cervenakova L, et al. A case of sporadic Creuztfeldt-Jakob disease with a Gerstmann-Straussler-Scheinker phenotype but no alterations in PRNP gene. Acta Neuropathol. 1998;96:425-430.

291. Brown P, Goldfarb LG, Brown WT, et al. Clinical and molecular genetic study of a large German kindred with Gerstmann-Straussler-Scheinker syndrome. Neurology. 1991;41:375-379.

292. Farlow MR, Yee RD, Dlouhy SR, et al. Gerstmann-Straussler-Scheinker disease: I. Extending the clinical spectrum. Neurology. 1989;39:1446-1452.

293. Kuzuhara S, Kanazawa I, Sasaki H, et al. Gerstmann-Straussler-Scheinker's disease. Ann Neurol. 1983;14:216-225.

294. Ghetti B, Dlouhy SR, Giaccone G, et al. Gerstmann-Straussler-Scheinker disease and the Indiana kindred. Brain Pathol. 1995;5:61-75.

295. Unverzagt FW, Farlow MR, Norton J, et al. Neuropsychological function in patients with Gerstmann-Straussler-Scheinker disease from the Indiana kindred (F198S). J Int Neuropsychol Soc. 1997;3:169-178.

296. Lyketsos CG, Kraus M. The dementia of Gerstmann-Straussler-Scheinker syndrome: Clinical variability demonstrated by two case reports. J Neuropsychiatry Clin Neurosci. 1995;7:239-242.

297. Itoh Y, Yamada M, Hayakawa M, et al. A variant of Gerstmann-Straussler-Scheinker disease carrying codon 105 mutation with codon 129 polymorphism of the prion protein gene: A clinicopathological study. J Neurol Sci. 1994;127:77-86.

298. Hainfellner JA, Brantner-Inthaler S, Cervenakova L, et al. The original Gerstmann-Straussler-Scheinker family of Austria: Divergent clinicopathological phenotypes but constant PrP genotype. Brain Pathol. 1995;5:201-211.

299. Goldfarb LG, Brown P, Vrbovska A, et al. An insert mutation in the chromosome 20 amyloid precursor gene in a Gerstmann-Straussler-Scheinker family. J Neurol Sci. 1992;111:189-194.

300. Hamasaki S, Shirabe S, Tsuda R, et al. Discordant Gerstmann-Straussler-Scheinker disease in monozygotic twins. Lancet. 1998;353:1358-1359.

301. Wimberger D, Uranitsch K, Schindler E, et al. Gerstmann-Straussler-Scheinker syndrome: MR findings. J Comput Assist Tomogr. 1993;17:326-327.

302. Amano N, Yagishita S, Yokoi S, et al. Gerstmann-Straussler syndrome—a variant type: Amyloid plaques and Alzheimer's neurofibrillary tangles in cerebral cortex. Acta Neuropathol. 1992;84:15-23.

302a. Tanaka Y, Minematsu K, Moriyasu H, et al. A Japanese family with a variant of Gerstmann-Straussler-Scheinker disease. J Neurol Neurosurg Psychiatry. 1997;62:454-457.

303. Kretzschmar HA, Honold G, Seitelberger F, et al. Prion protein mutation in family first described by Gerstmann, Straussler, Scheinker (Letter). Lancet. 1991;337:1160.

304. Hsiao KK, Scott M, Foster D, et al. Spontaneous neurodegeneration in transgenic mice with mutant prion protein. Science. 1990;250:1587-1590.

305. Barbanti P, Fabbrini G, Salvatore M, et al. Polymorphism at codon 129 or codon 219 of PRNP and clinical heterogeneity in a previously unrecognized family with Gerstmann-Straussler-Scheinker disease (PrP-P102L mutation). Neurology. 1996;47:734-741.

306. Tranchant C, Sergeant N, Wattez A, et al. Neurofibrillary tangles in Gerstmann-Straussler-Scheinker syndrome with the A117V prion gene mutation. J Neurol Neurosurg Psychiatry. 1997;63:240-246.

307. Medori R, Tritschler H-J, LeBlanc A, et al. Fatal familial insomnia, a prion disease with a mutation at codon 178 of the prion protein gene. N Engl J Med. 1992;326:444-449.

308. Manetto V, Medori R, Cortelli P, et al. Fatal familial insomnia: Clinical and pathologic study of five new cases. Neurology. 1992;42:312-319.

309. Lugaresi E, Medori R, Montagna P, et al. Fatal familial insomnia and dysautonomia with selective degeneration of thalamic nuclei. N Engl J Med. 1986;315:997-1003.

310. Montagna P, Gambetti P, Cortelli P, et al. Familial and sporadic fatal insomnia. Lancet Neurol. 2003;2:167-176.

311. Petersen BB, Tabaton M, Berg L, et al. Analysis of the prion protein gene in thalamic dementia. Neurology. 1992;42:1859-1863.

312. Parchi P, Capellari S, Chin S, et al. A subtype of sporadic prion disease mimicking fatal familial insomnia. Neurology. 1999;52:1757-1763.

313. Mastrianni JA, Nixon R, Layzer R, et al. Prion protein conformation in a patient with sporadic fatal insomnia. N Engl J Med. 1999;340:1630-1638.

314. Scaravilli F, Cordery RJ, Kretzschmar H, et al. Sporadic familial insomnia: A case study. Ann Neurol. 2000;48:665-668.

315. Plazzi G, Schutz Y, Cortelli P, et al. Motor overactivity and loss of motor circadian rhythm in fatal familial insomnia. Sleep. 1997;20:739-742.

316. Galassi R, Morreale A, Montagna P, et al. Fatal familial insomnia: A neuropsychological study of a disease with thalamic degeneration. Cortex. 1992;28:175-187.

317. Gallassi R, Morreale A, Montagna P, et al. Fatal familial insomnia: Behavioral and cognitive features. Neurology. 1996;46:935-939.

318. Sforza E, Montagna P, Tinuper P, et al. Sleep-wake cycle abnormalities in fatal familial insomnia: Evidence of the role of the thalamus in sleep regulation. Electroencephalogr Clin Neurophysiol. 1995;94:398-405.

319. Tinuper P, Montagna P, Medori R, et al. The thalamus participates in the regulation of the sleep-waking cycle: A clinicopathological study in fatal thalamic degeneration. Electroencephalogr Clin Neurophysiol. 1989;73:117-123.

320. Wanschitz J, Kloppel S, Jaris C, et al. Alteration of the serotonergic nervous system in fatal familial insomnia. Ann Neurol. 2000;48:788-791.

321. Cortelli P, Polinsky R, Montagna P, et al. Alteration of the serotoninergic system in fatal familial insomnia. Ann Neurol. 2001;50:421-422.

322. Almer G, Hainfellner JA, Brucke T, et al. Fatal familial insomnia: A new Austrian family. Brain. 1999;122:5-16.

323. Liguori R, Vincent A, Clover L, et al. Morvan's syndrome: Peripheral and central nervous system and cardiac involvement with antibodies to voltage-gated potassium channels. Brain. 2001;124:2417-2426.

324. Barber PA, Anderson NE, Vincent A. Morvan's syndrome associated with voltage-gated K+ channel antibodies. Neurology. 2000;54:771-772.

325. Perani D, Cortelli P, Lucignani G, et al. [18F]FDG PET in fatal familial insomnia: The functional effects of thalamic lesions. Neurology. 1993;43:2565-2569.

326. Cortelli P, Perani D, Parchi P, et al. Cerebral metabolism in fatal familial insomnia: Relation to duration, neuropathology, and distribution of protease-resistant prion protein. Neurology. 1997;49:126-133.

327. Bar KJ, Hager F, Nenadic I, et al. Serial positron emission tomographic findings in an atypical presentation of fatal familial insomnia. Arch Neurol. 2002;59:1815-1818.

328. Gambetti P, Parchi P, Petersen RB, et al. Fatal familial insomnia and familial Creutzfeldt-Jakob disease: Clinical, pathological and molecular features. Brain Pathol. 1995;5:43-51.

329. Parchi P, Castellani R, Cortelli P, et al. Regional distribution of protease-resistant prion protein in fatal familial insomnia. Ann Neurol. 1995;38:21-29.

330. Brown P, Kenney K, Little BW, et al. Intracerebral distribution of infectious amyloid protein in spongiform encephalopathy. Ann Neurol. 1995;38:245-253.

331. Tateishi J, Brown P, Kitamoto T, et al. First experimental transmission of fatal familial insomnia. Nature. 1995;376:434-435.

332. Goldfarb LG, Petersen RB, Tabaton M, et al. Fatal familial insomnia and familial Creutzfeldt-Jakob disease: Disease phenotype determined by a DNA polymorphism. Science. 1992;258:806-808.

333. Monari L, Chen SG, Brown P, et al. Fatal familial insomnia and familial Creutzfeldt-Jakob disease: Different prion proteins determined by a DNA polymorphism. Proc Natl Acad Sci U S A. 1994;91:2839-2842.

334. Gambetti P. Fatal familial insomnia and familial Creutzfeldt-Jakob disease: A tale of two diseases with the same genetic mutation. Curr Top Microbiol Immunol. 1996;207:19-25.

335. Chapman J, Arlazoroff A, Goldfarb LG, et al. Fatal insomnia in a case of familial Creutzfeldt-Jakob disease with the codon 200(Lys) mutation. Neurology. 1996;46:758-761.

336. Yam P. Shoot this deer. Sci Am. 2003;288:38-43.

337. Belay ED, Gambetti P, Schonberger LB, et al. Creutzfeldt-Jakob disease in unusually young patients who consumed venison. Arch Neurol. 2001;58:1673-1678.

338. Davis JP, Kazmierczak J, Wegner M, et al. Fatal degenerative neurologic illnesses in men who participated in wild game feasts—2002. MMWR Morb Mortal Wkly Rep. 2003;52:125-127.

339. Anderson CA, Bosque PJ, Filley CM, et al. Colorado surveillance program for chronic wasting disease transmission to humans: Two negative cases. Neurology. 2003;60(Suppl 1):A310.

340. Belay ED, Maddox RA, Gambetti P, et al. Monitoring the occurrence of emerging forms of Creutzfeldt-Jakob disease in the United States. Neurology. 2003;60:176-181.

341. Brown P. Drug therapy in human and experimental transmissible spongiform encephalopathy. Neurology. 2002;58:1720-1725.

342. Korth C, May BCH, Cohen FE, et al. Acridine and phenothiazine derivatives as pharmacotherapeutics for prion disease. Proc Natl Acad Sci U S A. 2001;98:9836-9841.

343. May BCH, Fafarman AT, Hong SB, et al. Potent inhibition of scrapie prion replication in cultured cells by bis-acridines. Proc Natl Acad Sci U S A. 2003;100:3416-3421.

344. Follette P. Prion disease treatment's early promise unravels. Science. 2003;299:191-192.

344a. Otto M, Cepek L, Ratzka P, et al. Efficacy of flupirtine on cognitive function in patients with CJD: A double-blind study. Neurology. 2004;62:714-718.

345. Caspi S, Halimi M, Yanai A, et al. The anti-prion activity of Congo red: Putative mechanism. J Biol Chem. 1998;273:3484-3489.

346. Tagliavini F, McArthur RA, Canciani B, et al. Effectiveness of anthracycline against experimental prion disease in Syrian hamsters. Science. 1997;276:1119-1122.

347. Tatzelt J, Prusiner SB, Welch WJ. Chemical chaperones interfere with the formation of scrapie prion protein. EMBO J. 1996;15:6363-6373.

348. Forloni G, Iussich S, Awan T, et al. Tetracyclines affect prion infectivity. Proc Natl Acad Sci U S A. 2002;99:10849-10854.

349. Perrier V, Kaneko K, Safar J, et al. Dominant-negative inhibition of prion protein replication in transgenic mice. Proc Natl Acad Sci U S A. 2002;99:13079-13084.

350. Sigurdsson EM, Brown DR, Daniels M, et al. Immunization delays the onset of prion disease in mice. Am J Pathol. 2002;161:13-17.

351. White AR, Enever P, Tayebl M, et al. Monoclonal antibodies inhibit prion replication and delay the development of prion disease. Nature. 2003;422:8083.

352. Gibbs CJ Jr, Amyx HL, Bacote A, et al. Oral transmission of kuru, Creutzfeldt-Jakob disease and scrapie to non-human primates. J Infect Dis. 1980;142:205-208.

353. Diringer H, Roehmel J, Beekes M. Effect of repeated oral infection of hamsters with scrapie. J Gen Virol. 1998;79:609-612.

354. Ironside J, Bell JE. The "high risk" neuropathological autopsy in AIDS and Creutzfeldt-Jakob disease: Principles and practice. Neuropathol Appl Neurobiol. 1996;22:388-393.

355. Rutala WA, Weber DJ. Creutzfeldt-Jakob disease: Recommendations for disinfection and sterilization. Clin Infect Dis. 2001;32:1348-1356.

356. Committee on Health Care Issues ANA. Precautions in handling tissues, fluids and other contaminated materials from patients with documented or suspected Creutzfeldt-Jakob disease. Ann Neurol. 1986;19:75-77.

357. McDonnell G, Burke P. The challenge of prion decontamination. Clin Infect Dis. 2000;36:1152-1154.

358. Manuelidis L. Decontamination of Creutzfeldt-Jakob disease and other transmissible agents. J Neurovirol. 1997;3:62-65.

CHAPTER **176**

Introduction to Chlamydial Diseases

WALTER E. STAMM
ROBERT B. JONES
BYRON E. BATTEIGER

Chlamydiae are obligate intracellular bacteria with a unique biphasic life cycle.[1] Although there is currently disagreement in the field as to the most appropriate taxonomic classification of these organisms, in the current schema they are classified in the order Chlamydiales, which contains only one family, the Chlamydiaceae, and one genus, *Chlamydia*. Within this genus four species are recognized currently, *C. pecorum*,[2] *C. psittaci, C. trachomatis,* and *C. pneumoniae*. All except *C. pecorum* have been associated with human disease (Table 176-1). Although the chlamydiae were originally classified taxonomically on the basis of their phenotypic properties, Everett, Bush, and Anderson have proposed, based on sequence analysis of 16Sr ribonucleic acid (RNA), that there is sufficient divergence between the *C. trachomatis*–group organisms and the *C. psittaci* and *C. pneumoniae*–group organisms to divide these groups at the genus level into *Chlamydia* and *Chlamydophila*, respectively. Both the new and the older classifications are currently in use in the literature. From a clinician's perspective, the most important conclusions from this debate are that (1) all Chlamydiales belong to a distinct bacterial division that is widely separated from other bacterial divisions and has a direct phylogenetic root that diverges very early in the evolution of eubacteria and (2) the known *Chlamydia* species, namely, *C. trachomatis, C. pneumoniae, C. pecorum,* and *C. psittaci* form coherent and distinct groups based on both phenotypic characteristics and rRNA sequence comparisons. Based on ribosomal RNA sequencing, the current species *C. psittaci* contains four distinct genetic groups of strains that may eventually be proposed as separate species.[3,5] Deoxyribonucleic acid (DNA) sequence homology confirms these insights.[6,7] The multiple strains of *C. psittaci* exhibit from less than 10% to 60% homology with each other and from less than 5% to approximately 20% homology with *C. trachomatis* strains. The human strains of *C. trachomatis* are almost 100% homologous with each other and approximately 30% with the mouse biovar. The latter does not cause human disease, and it has also been suggested that the mouse biovar should be classified as a separate species.[5,6] *C. pneumoniae* shows 10% or less homology with either of the other two species and so far appears to consist of only a single strain, TWAR.[8,9]

C. trachomatis has been the most extensively studied species because of its association with ocular trachoma and its importance as a sexually transmitted pathogen. Three biovars have been identified, namely, the trachoma biovar associated with oculogenital disease, the lymphogranuloma venereum biovar associated with proctitis and systemic infections, and the mouse pneumonitis biovar, which appears to contain only a single strain. *C. pneumoniae* may be even more prevalent a human pathogen than *C. trachomatis*. This species was only recognized in 1992,[10] and the full extent and spectrum of disease attributable to it remain to be defined. Current evidence suggests, however, that *C. pneumoniae* is an extremely common pathogen on a global basis, most likely infecting nearly everyone and often causing recurrent infections throughout life. Most of these infections initially involve the upper or lower respiratory tract, but recent evidence also suggests that the organism may infect macrophages within the respiratory tract that later transport chlamydiae via the blood stream to other distant sites. This likely includes the vascular endothelium, where endothelial cells, smooth muscle cells, and macrophages may be infected. There are multiple strains of *C. psittaci* that primarily infect birds and other nonhuman mammalian hosts. Transmission to humans occasionally occurs, usually after exposure to avian strains.[11]

Chlamydiae are prokaryotes that all share a common biology and life cycle. The organisms grow only within a specialized vacuole in eukaryotic cells called the *inclusion* (Fig 176-1). They have extremely small genomes (e.g., 894 protein coding genes for *C. trachomatis*) and are auxotrophic for many amino acids and nucleotides, depending on the host cell for these molecules. They exhibit morphologic and structural similarities to gram-negative bacteria, including a trilaminar outer membrane that contains lipopolysaccharide and several membrane proteins that are structurally and functionally analogous to those found in *Escherichia coli*. Chlamydiae appear to lack classic peptidoglycan,[1,12] a macromolecule that provides most prokaryotes with structural rigidity and osmotic stability, despite the fact that the chlamydial genome contains all the genes necessary for peptidoglycan synthesis.[13]

All chlamydiae have a unique life cycle that utilizes an extracellular infectious form, the elementary body (EB), and an intracellular replicative form, the reticulate body (RB). The extracellular form, the EB, exhibits extensive disulfide cross-linking between cysteine residues both within and between outer membrane proteins.[14,15] The result is an almost sporelike structure that is metabolically inert. The life cycle is initiated when an EB attaches to a susceptible epithelial cell. A number of candidate chlamydial adhesins have been proposed, and putative membrane protein candidates have been identified in the chlamydial genome,[16] but the precise identity of adhesins and associated epithelial cell receptors remains uncertain. The EB enters the epithelial cell by receptor-mediated endocytosis via clathrin-coated pits,[16,17] but evidence also exists for other mechanisms, including pinocytosis via noncoated pits and the use of heparin-like bridging molecules.[16] It is likely that chlamydiae exploit several adhesin-ligand entry mechanisms. A unique feature of all chlamydiae is their ability to inhibit lysosomal fusion by undefined mechanisms, allowing the infecting EB to reside in a protected membrane-bound vesicle called an *inclusion*. The EB, which is approximately 350 nm in diameter, then undergoes reorganization into the much larger replicative form, the reticulate body (RB), which is about 800 to 1000 nm in diameter.[18] The initial events triggering this reorganization have not been defined precisely, but early events include new synthesis of chlamydial proteins, reduction of disulfide bonds so that membrane proteins are no longer cross-linked,[15] and activation of an adenosine triphosphatase.[19] During growth and replication, chlamydiae obtain high-energy phosphate compounds from the host cell.[20] They also require some amino acids from the host cell but are able to synthesize others. RBs are osmotically unstable and incapable of infecting another cell. They divide by binary fission to produce an enlarging inclusion (Fig. 176-2) that eventually fills the infected cells. The intracellular regulatory signals that control EB-to-RB and RB-to-EB conversion are not known.[21] Condensation of RBs into EBs leads to extensive shedding of membrane blebs containing lipopolysaccharide[22] and compaction of the chromatin into an electron-dense nucleoid. The latter is mediated by a histone-like protein and is associated with a decrease in transcription.[23] Depending on the species, the cell membrane proteins are cross-linked either during condensation or later during cell lysis and release. Release of the organisms from infected cells apparently can be accomplished by cell lysis,[24] by extrusion of intact inclusions,[25] or by a process resembling exocytosis.[26] The release of the infectious elementary bodies permits infection of new cells and the potential for transmission to a new host.

TABLE 176-1 Comparative Aspects of Chlamydial Species Causing Human Infections

Species	Serovars	Natural Host	Transmission	Tropism	Acute Infection	Long-Term Complications	Prevention/ Control
C. trachomatis	A-C	Human	Hands/eye, fomites, flies	Conjunctiva	Conjunctivitis	Blindness	SAFE strategy
C. trachomatis	D-K	Human	Sexual, perinatal	Anogenital mucosa: urethral, cervix, rectum	Nongonococcal urethritis, mucopurulent cervicitis	PID, TFI, EP, SARA, CA	Screen, treat
C. trachomatis	L1, L2, L3	Human	Sexual	Genital mucosa, lymphocyte, monocyte	Genital ulcers, lymphadenopathy	LGV	None
C. pneumoniae	One	Human	Direct/ indirect respiratory droplets	Respiratory epithelium	Upper respiratory infection, community-acquired pneumonia	Atherosclerotic cardiovascular disease?, asthma?	None
C. psittaci	Many	Birds, mammals	Aerosol, respiratory	Systemic	Community-acquired pneumonia	Hepatitis	Identify and eliminate animal reservoir

CA, cancer; EP, ectopic pregnancy; PID, pelvic inflammatory disease; SARA, sexually acquired reactive arthritis; TFI, tubal factor infertility.

Numerous advances in our understanding of the chlamydiae and their cell biology are emerging now that seven chlamydial genomes have been sequenced. For example, a new family of polymorphic outer membrane proteins (POMPs) has been identified. In addition, chlamydiae express proteins that localize in the cytoplasmic surface of the inclusion membrane, the prototype of which is IncA.[31] Such exported proteins may be involved in the trafficking of inclusions into the exocytic pathway,[32,33] the trafficking of host cell lipids into chlamydial membranes,[34] and the inhibition of apoptosis.[30] Such proteins are hypothesized to enter the host cell from the inclusion by a type III secretion mechanism,[35] similar to systems used by *Yersinia* and other gram-negative species to inject effector proteins into eukaryotic cells. *C. trachomatis* has been shown to possess type III secretion genes,[13,35] including potential effectors like phosphatases and kinases used by other bacteria to influence eukaryotic cell signaling. On electron microscopy, chlamydial forms possess surface projections[36] that are outwardly similar to structures in *Salmonella* known to be composed of type III secretion components. It is speculated that the surface projections of chlamydiae may constitute the chlamydial type III secretion apparatus.[37]

Chlamydiae primarily infect columnar epithelial cells, but recent studies indicate that a wide range of cells can be productively infected, including endothelial cells, smooth muscle cells, lymphocytes, and monocyte/macrophages. In macrophages, some strains of *C. psittaci* exhibit productive growth.[38] Conversely, macrophages restrict the growth of both the lymphogranuloma venereum and trachoma biovars

of *C. trachomatis,* although they are more permissive for lymphogranuloma venereum.[39] Human polymorphonuclear leukocytes ingest and destroy *C. trachomatis* and *C. psittaci* fairly efficiently. However, a small proportion of organisms remain viable and potentially able to perpetuate infection.[40] Infection of host epithelial cells causes secretion of a variety of cytokines, including interleukin (IL)-6 and tumor necrosis factor (TNF).

The chlamydial genome has a molecular mass of only 660×10^6 daltons, which is smaller than that of any other prokaryote except *Mycoplasma* spp.[13] The complete genome sequence of *C. trachomatis* serovar D, 1.043 million base pairs, was the first chlamydial genome to be completed.[13] Based on the sequence, certain metabolic pathways are missing from this small genome, including amino acid and purine-pyrimidine biosynthesis, anaerobic fermentation, and transformation competence proteins.[41] However, complete glycolytic and glycogen degrading pathways are present, and a full synthetic capacity for fatty acids, phospholipids, lipopolysaccharide, and peptidoglycan is represented.[13] The subsequent completion of six additional chlamydial genomes has demonstrated that there are striking similarities among the chlamydiae both in terms of gene content and order. This may indicate that there is little opportunity for horizontal genetic exchange between chlamydiae and other microorganisms. This might be expected given the intracellular location of its replicative cycle. However, gene exchange could occur via plasmids or bacteriophage, which some chlamydiae have.

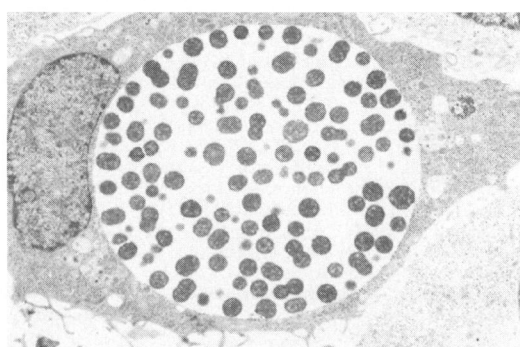

FIGURE 176-1. Electron photomicrograph of *Chlamydia trachomatis* growing in tissue culture. The larger reticulate bodies (RBs) have more diffuse chromatin. One of the RBs appears to be dividing, and the trilaminar outer membrane is evident in some areas. EB, elementary body. *(Photo courtesy of Robert Suchland, Seattle, Washington.)*

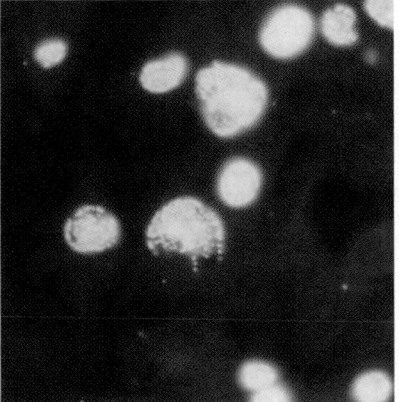

FIGURE 176-2. *Chlamydia trachomatis* inclusions in a McCoy cell monolayer stained with a genus reactive mouse monoclonal antibody followed by fluorescein conjugated rabbit anti-mouse immunoglobulin. *(Photo courtesy of Robert Suchland, Seattle, Washington.)*

C. pneumoniae does not appear to contain any extrachromosomal genetic material,[8] whereas some strains of *C. psittaci*[42] and most strains of *C. trachomatis* contain a plasmid of approximately 7.5 kb. Slight sequence variations exist between plasmids from different strains within *C. trachomatis* and more extensive variations among the plasmids from *C. psittaci*.[43] Although the extensive conservation implies a critical function and, based on sequence homology with *E. coli* genes, it has been suggested that it may play a role in DNA replication,[44] the function of the plasmid remains unknown.

Phenotypically, the three chlamydial species that cause human disease differ antigenically, metabolically, and in host cell preference, antibiotic susceptibility, and inclusion morphology. Shared antigenic determinants are present in the lipopolysaccharide and some of the membrane proteins.[1,8] In addition, several outer-membrane proteins contain species and subspecies determinants. Strain-specific determinants reside primarily in the major outer-membrane protein. All strains of *C. trachomatis* are sensitive to sulfonamides, whereas *C. pneumoniae* and most strains of *C. psittaci* are not. The morphology of the elementary and reticulate bodies of *C. psittaci* and *C. trachomatis* are very similar to each other. Also, the RBs of all four species appear identical. However, the elementary bodies of *C. pneumoniae* are often pear shaped, with a relatively large periplasmic space that contains some electron-dense structures that are not seen in the other two species and whose function is unknown.[8] *C. psittaci* forms multiple small inclusions in a single infected cell, with each infective EB forming its own inclusion. In cells infected with multiple *C. trachomatis* EBs, the organism-containing vesicles usually fuse so that each infected cell contains only one or two inclusions.[22] However, nonfusogenic variants of *C. trachomatis* have been described whose inclusions appear to lack IncA.[45] The inclusions of *C. pneumoniae* resemble those of *C. psittaci* but are less variable in shape. Only *C. trachomatis* accumulates glycogen in its inclusions, a property that allows their staining with iodine.

Despite the relative uniformity of their life cycle, genomes, and physiology, chlamydiae exhibit a wide range of host and tissue tropism, modes of transmission, and disease causation. *C. trachomatis* and *C. pneumoniae* appear to be exclusively human pathogens, except for the mouse pneumonitis biovar of *C. trachomatis,* which does not infect humans. Lymphogranuloma venereum strains of *C. trachomatis* as well as those associated with oculogenital disease are generally spread by sexual contact, during birth, or by autoinoculation of the eye with infected genital secretions. The strains associated with ocular trachoma are spread by fingers, by fomites, and on the feet of flies. Transfer of respiratory secretions by droplets or hands is probably the primary mode of transmission of *C. pneumoniae*.[10]

Most chlamydial species produce an initial acute infection often limited to the mucosal epithelium and generally producing minimal or no symptoms. Many such infections may spontaneously resolve but others appear to persist in an asymptomatic state. Initial infections by LGV strains of *C. trachomatis* or by *C. psittaci* are generally more invasive, producing severe or systemic infections, or both, in the initial phase.

The natural history of chlamydial infections is unknown or only poorly defined in most cases. However, a growing body of data suggests that chronic asymptomatic or persistent infections are frequent. This appears to be the case for *C. psittaci* in animals[6] and for both *C. trachomatis*[45-47] and *C. pneumoniae*[48] in humans. Reinfections with *C. trachomatis* or *C. pneumoniae* also appear to be frequent, suggesting that infection-induced immunity is incompletely protective or short lived, or both. Chronic persistent infection or exogenous reinfection is thought to play an important role in inducing the immunopathologic responses that are important in producing the major complications associated with chlamydial infections, namely, blinding trachoma or upper genital tract fibrosis and inflammation causing pelvic inflammatory disease (PID), infertility, and ectopic pregnancy. Moreover, considerable data now suggest that chronic endovascular *C. pneumoniae* infections may play a role in atherosclerosis and coronary artery disease.[10,49]

REFERENCES

1. Moulder JW. Looking at chlamydiae without looking at their hosts. Am Soc Microbiol News. 1984;50:353-362.
2. Fukushi H, Hirai K. 1989. Proposal of *Chlamydia pecorum* sp. nov. for *Chlamydia* strains derived from ruminants. Int J Syst Bacteriol. 1992;42:306-308.
3. Everett KDE, Bush RM, Andersen AA. Emended description of the order Chlamydiales, proposed of Parachlamydiaceae fam. nov and Simkaniaceae fam. nov, each containing one monotypic genus, revised taxonomy of the family Chlamydiaceae, including a new genus and five new species and standards for the identification of organisms. Int J Syst Bacteriol. 1999;49:415-440.
4. Weisburg WG, Hatch TP, Woese CR. Eubacterial origin of chlamydiae. J Bacteriol. 1986;167:570-574.
5. Pudjiatmoko, Fukushi H, Ochiai Y, et al. Phylogenetic analysis of the genus *Chlamydia* based on 16S rRNA gene sequences. Int J Syst Bacteriol. 1997;47:425-431.
6. Moulder JW. Interaction of chlamydiae and host cells in vitro. Microbiol Rev. 1991;55:143-190.
7. Herring AJ. The molecular biology of chlamydia—A brief overview. J Infect. 1992;25(Suppl 1):1-10.
8. Kalman S, Mitchell W, Marathe R, et al. Comparative genomes of *Chlamydia pneumoniae* and *Chlamydia trachomatis*. Nat Genet. 1999;21:385-389.
9. Pettersson B, Andersson A, Leitner T, et al. Evolutionary relationships among members of the genus *Chlamydia* based on 16S ribosomal DNA analysis. J Bacteriol. 1997;179:4195-4205.
10. Kuo CC, Jackson LA, Campbell LA, Grayston JT. *Chlamydia pneumoniae*. Clin Microbiol Rev. 1995;8:451-61.
11. Yung AP, Grayson ML. Psittacosis—A review of 135 cases. Med J Aust. 1988;148:228-233.
12. Fox A, Robers JC, Gilbart J, et al. Muramic acid is not detectable in *Chlamydia psittaci* or *Chlamydia trachomatis* by gas chromatography–mass spectrometry. Infect Immun. 1990;58:835-837.
13. Stephens RS, Kalman S, Lammel C, et al. Genome sequence of an obligate intracellular pathogen of humans: *Chlamydia trachomatis*. Science. 1998;282:754-759.
14. Newhall WJV, Jones RB. Disulfide-linked oligomers of the major outer membrane protein of chlamydiae. J Bacteriol. 1983;154:998-1001.
15. Hatch TP, Miceli M, Sublett JE. Synthesis of disulfide-bonded outer membrane proteins during the developmental cycle of *Chlamydia psittaci* and *Chlamydia trachomatis*. J Bacteriol. 1986;165:379-385.
16. Rockey DD. Chlamydial interactions with host cells. In: Schachter J, Christiansen G, Clarke IN, et al, eds. Chlamydial Infections: Proceedings of the Tenth International Symposium on Human Chlamydial Infection. International Chlamydial Symposium, San Francisco. 2002;35-45.
17. Wyrick PB, Choong J, Davis CH, et al. Entry of genital *Chlamydia trachomatis* into polarized human epithelial cells. Infect Immun. 1989;57:2378-2389.
18. Schachter J, Caldwell HD. Chlamydiae. Ann Rev Microbiol. 1980;34:285-309.
19. Peeling R, Peeling J, Brunham R. High-resolution ³¹P nuclear magnetic resonance study of *Chlamydia trachomatis:* Induction of ATPase activity in elementary bodies. Infect Immun. 1989;57:3338-3344.
20. Hatch TP, Al-Hossainy E, Silverman JA. Adenine nucleotide and lysine transport in *Chlamydia psittaci*. J Bacteriol. 1982;150:662-670.
21. Kaul R, Wenman WM. Cyclic AMP inhibits developmental regulation of *Chlamydia trachomatis*. J Bacteriol. 1986;168:722-777.
22. Stirling P, Richmond SJ. Production of outer membrane blebs during chlamydial replication. FEMS Microbiol Lett. 1980;9:103-105.
23. Barry CE, Hayes SF, Hackstadt T. Nucleoid condensation in *Escherichia coli* that express a chlamydial histone homolog. Science. 1992;256:377-379.
24. Todd WJ, Storz J. Ultrastructural cytochemical evidence for the activation of lysosomes in the cytocidal effect of *Chlamydia psittaci*. Infect Immun. 1975;12:638-646.
25. De la Maza LM, Peterson EM. Scanning electron microscopy of McCoy cells infected with *Chlamydia trachomatis*. Exp Mol Pathol. 1982;36:217-226.
26. Todd WJ, Caldwell HD. The interaction of *Chlamydia trachomatis* with host cells: Ultrastructural studies of the mechanism of release of a biovar II strain from HeLa 229 cells. J Infect Dis. 1985;151:1037-1044.
27. Fan T, Lu H, Hu H, et al. Inhibition of apoptosis in chlamydia-infected cells: Blockade of mitochondrial cytochrome c release and caspase activation. J Exp Med. 1998;187:487-496.
28. Read TD, Brunham RC, Shen C, et al. Genome sequences of *Chlamydia trachomatis* MoPn and *Chlamydia pneumoniae*. AR 39. Nucleic Acids Res. 2000;28:1397-1406.
29. Read TD, Myers GS, Brunham RC, et al. Genome sequence of *Chlamydophila caviae*: examining the role of niche-specific genes in the evolution of the Chlamydiaceae. Nucleic Acids Res. 2003;31:2134-2147.
30. Read TD, Fraser CM, Hsia R-C, et al. Comparative analysis of Chlamydia bacteriophages reveals variation localized to a putative receptor binding domain. Microb Comp Genomics. 2000;5:223-231.
31. Rockey DD, Grosenbach D, Hruby DE, et al. *Chlamydia psittaci* IncA is phosphorylated by the host cell and is exposed on the cytoplasmic face of the developing inclusion. Mol Microbiol. 1997;24:217-228.
32. Hackstadt T, Scidmore MA, Rockey DD. Lipid metabolism in *Chlamydia trachomatis*-infected cells: Directed trafficking of Golgi-derived sphingolipids to the chlamydial inclusion. Proc Natl Acad Sci U S A. 1995;92:4877-4881.
33. Heinzen RA, Scidmore MA, Rockey DD, Hackstadt T. Differential interaction with endocytic and exocytic pathways distinguish parasitophorous vacuoles of *Coxiella burnetii* and *Chlamydia trachomatis*. Infect Immun. 1996;64:796-809.

34. Wylie JL, Hatch GM, McClarty G. Host cell phospholipids are trafficked to and then modified by *Chlamydia trachomatis*. J Bacteriol. 1997;179:7233-7242.

35. Hsia R-C, Pannekoek Y, Ingerowski E, Bavoil PM. Type III secretion genes identify a putative virulence locus of *Chlamydia*. Mol Microbiol. 1997;25:351-359.

36. Matsumoto A. Structural characteristics of chlamydial bodies. In: Barron AL, ed. Microbiology of Chlamydia. Boca Raton, Fla: CRC Press; 1998:21-46.

37. Bavoil PB, Hsia R-C. Type III secretion in *Chlamydia*: A case of deja vu? Mol Microbiol. 1998;28:860-862.

38. Wyrick PB, Brownridge EA. Growth of *Chlamydia psittaci* in macrophages. Infect Immun. 1978;19:1054-1060.

39. Kuo C-C. Cultures of *Chlamydia trachomatis* in mouse peritoneal macrophages: Factors affecting organism growth. Infect Immun. 1978;20:439-445.

40. Register KB, Morgan PA, Wyrick PB. Interaction between *Chlamydia* spp. and human polymorphonuclear leukocytes in vitro. Infect Immun. 1986;52:664-670.

41. Rockey DD, Lenart J, Stephens RS, Genome sequencing and our understanding of chlamydiae. Infect Immun. 2000;68:5473-5479.

42. McClenaghan M, Honeycombe JR, Bevan BJ, et al. Distribution of plasmid sequences in avian and mammalian strains of *Chlamydia psittaci*. J Gen Microbiol. 1988;134:559-565.

43. Comanducci M, Ricci S, Cevenini R, et al. Diversity of the *Chlamydia trachomatis* common plasmid in biovars with different pathogenicity. Plasmid. 1990;23:149-154.

44. Hatt C, Ward ME, Clarke IN. Analysis of the entire nucleotide sequence of the cryptic plasmid of *Chlamydia trachomatis* serovar L1. Evidence for involvement in DNA replication. Nucleic Acids Res. 1988;16:4053-4067.

45. Suchland RJ, Rockey DD, Bannantine JP, Stamm WE. Isolates of *Chlamydia trachomatis* that occupy nonfusogenic inclusions lack IncA, a protein localized to the inclusion membrane. Infect Immun. 2000;68:360-367.

46. Campbell LA, Patton DL, Moore DE, et al. Detection of *Chlamydia trachomatis* deoxyribonucleic acid in women with tubal infertility. Fertil Steril. 1993;59:45-50.

47. Dean D, Suchland RJ, Stamm WE. Evidence for long-term persistence of *Chlamydia trachomatis* by omp1 genotyping. J Infect Dis. 2000;182:909-916.

48. Hammerschlag MR, Chirgwin K, Roblin PM, et al. Persistent infection with *Chlamydia pneumoniae* following acute respiratory illness. Clin Infect Dis. 1992;14:178-182.

49. Kalayoglu MV, Libby P, Byrne GI. *Chlamydiae pneumoniae* as an emerging risk factor in cardiovascular disease. JAMA. 2002;288:2724-2731.

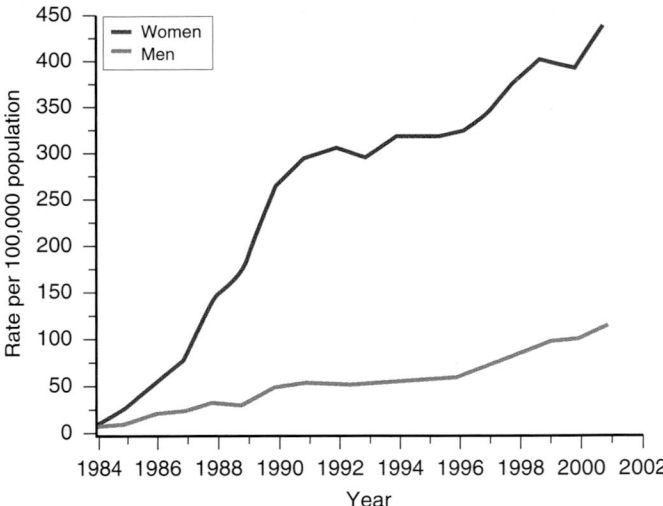

FIGURE 177-1. Reported incidence of *Chlamydia trachomatis* in the United States. *(Data from Centers for Disease Control and Prevention. Sexually Transmitted Disease Surveillance 2001 Supplement, Chlamydia Prevalence Monitoring Project. Atlanta, Ga: Centers for Disease Control and Prevention; 2002.)*

CHAPTER **177**

Chlamydia trachomatis (Trachoma, Perinatal Infections, Lymphogranuloma Venereum, and Other Genital Infections)

WALTER E. STAMM
ROBERT B. JONES
BYRON E. BATTEIGER

*C*hlamydia trachomatis* infections, which are among the most common of bacterial infections, impose a tremendous burden on humans globally.[1-4] It has been estimated that worldwide at least 500 million people are affected by ocular trachoma and some 7 million to 9 million are blind as a result.[5] Ocular trachoma is considered the most common cause of preventable blindness worldwide. Although the disease has disappeared from many parts of the developed world coincident with improved sanitation, access to water, and reduced crowding, it remains common in many developing parts of the world. Genital tract infections with *C. trachomatis* are even more prevalent and have as major complications pelvic inflammatory disease (PID), ectopic pregnancy, infertility, and infant pneumonia. Because of a lack of universal testing and reporting, reliable incidence and prevalence data are not available (Fig. 177-1). However, the Centers for Disease Control and Prevention (CDC) estimated that there are approximately 4 mil-

lion new *C. trachomatis* infections per year in the United States.[6] The World Health Organization (WHO) estimated that 90 million cases occur annually on a global basis. On the basis of selective screening of target populations of sexually active young women, the proportion infected ranges from 8% to 40%, with a median of about 15%.[7] Approximately 10% of sexually active asymptomatic men are infected.[8,9] Prevalence studies demonstrate that the disease is most prevalent in adolescents and is found worldwide.

LIFE CYCLE

As discussed in the preceding chapter, chlamydiae have a unique biphasic life cycle. The elementary body, which is the transmissible form of the organism capable of extracellular survival, attaches to a susceptible epithelial cell to initiate the cycle (Fig. 177-2). Neither the eukaryotic receptors nor the chlamydial surface structures responsible for attachment and entry have been fully defined, although possible candidates have been identified.[10-13] The two primary candidates are the major outer-membrane protein (MOMP) and the chlamydial 60-kD cysteine-rich protein OmcB.[12] It may well be that different chlamydial species and serovars utilize different and perhaps multiple means for initial attachment and entry. Stephens and co-workers have demonstrated a potential role for a heparin sulfate–like compound that may serve as a molecular bridge between chlamydiae and host cells.[13] MOMP has been shown to bind to heparin in a concentration-dependent manner and thus may serve as a heparin-binding adhesin for chlamydiae. Glycosylation of MOMP may be important in facilitating binding to eukaryotic cells.

C. trachomatis can enter cells by phagocytosis, pinocytosis, or receptor-mediated endocytosis.[10] The last is the pathway by which eukaryotic cells internalize and transport macromolecules to specific sites within the cell. Convincing data that receptor-mediated endocytosis is also the pathway primarily used by the trachoma biovar of *C. trachomatis* come from experiments using polarized human genital epithelial cells.[14] In this model, infecting chlamydial elementary bodies are found predominantly in clathrin-coated pits and vesicles that are associated with receptor-mediated endocytosis.[15] The clathrin-coated pit invaginates and becomes an endocytic vesicle containing the chlamydial elementary body.[14]

The elementary body has stores of adenosine triphosphate (ATP) and an adenosine triphosphatase (ATPase)[16] that is activated in the

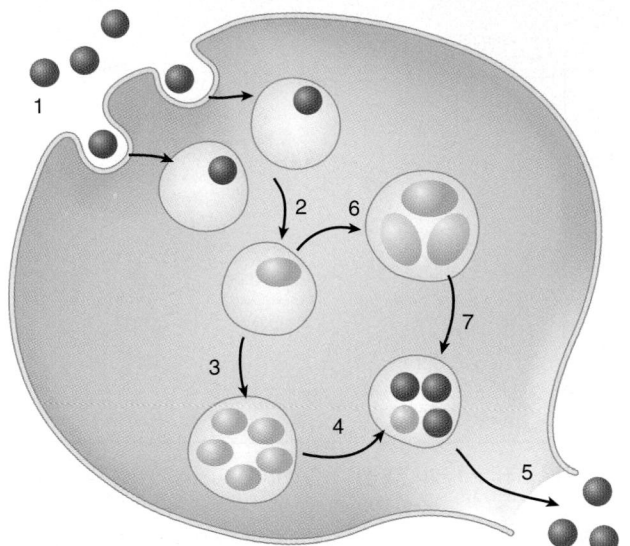

FIGURE 177-2. Life cycle of *Chlamydia trachomatis* in cell culture. (1) Electron dense elementary bodies (EBs) attach to and are taken up by epithelial cells. (2) Inclusions fuse and EBs differentiate into reticulate bodies (RBs). (3) RBs divide by binary fission. (4) RBs re-form into EBs. (5) EBs released, often with cell death, to infect other cells. (6) Alternate course under stressful conditions (i.e., IFN-γ exposure) leading to large, metabolically inactive persistent forms. (7) With removal of stress, return to replication and infectious state.

presence of reducing agents.[17] ATPase activation and reduction of the disulfide bonds that cross link membrane proteins are early events in reorganization of elementary bodies into reticulate bodies.[17,18] The MOMP is a porin that is extensively cross linked by disulfide bonds both internally and with two other cysteine-rich membrane proteins in elementary bodies but not in reticulate bodies.[19,20] Reduction of these bonds may be a key factor in initiation of reorganization.

The reticulate body is the intracellular and replicative form of the organism. As it divides it fills the endosome, now a cytoplasmic inclusion, with its progeny and with glycogen. When an epithelial cell is infected with more than one elementary body of *C. trachomatis*, the endosomes usually fuse so that each cell eventually contains only one inclusion (see Fig 177-2). The yield of new infectious units per host cell ranges from less than 100 to more than 1000,[21] representing the equivalent of 8 to 12 doublings of a single organism. Synthesis of specific proteins is temporally regulated throughout the life cycle. Proteins thought to be associated with conversion of elementary to reticulate bodies are synthesized early,[22] followed by the MOMP and then late in the cycle by the other cysteine-rich proteins[20] and DNA-binding proteins.[23] Regulation of the cycle appears at least in part to be at a transcriptional level. Growth cycle–specific messenger RNA (mRNA) has been identified[24] and multiple promoters for several different genes described.[25] Binding of subunits of RNA polymerase to the different promoters may serve as a key regulatory mechanism.[25] Two of the DNA-binding proteins of *C. trachomatis* have extensive sequence homology with eukaryotic histone H$_1$. They are expressed concomitantly with nucleoid condensation and cessation of transcription as the reticulate body forms an elementary body. They may provide global regulation of gene expression rather than conventional transcriptional regulation.[26]

Studies have demonstrated the complex and intimate array of interactions between chlamydia and the infected host cell throughout the life cycle.[11] These activities include endocytosis, tyrosine phosphorylation events, cytoskeletal rearrangement, and alterations in host cell macromolecular biosynthesis.[27] Chlamydiae have been found to possess a type III secretion apparatus comparable to that found in other gram-negative bacteria. The system probably serves as

a means of transporting chlamydial proteins outside the inclusion membrane, where they may regulate host cell transcription, perhaps facilitating key events such as regulation of vesicular transport or inhibition of fusion of the chlamydial inclusion with host cell lysosomes. Using a shigella expression system, Subtil and colleagues demonstrated that chlamydial Inc proteins can be secreted by the type III secretion apparatus.[28]

In cell culture, the entire life cycle takes between 48 and 72 hours, with some strains or serovars growing faster than others. In particular, strains of the lymphogranuloma venereum (LGV) biovar usually complete their life cycle more rapidly than those of the trachoma biovar. At the end of the cycle, an inclusion containing elementary bodies of the LGV biovar ruptures inside the cell, causing cell lysis and death with release of the elementary bodies.[21] The same sequence of events can occur with trachoma biovar strains, but their inclusions can also be released intact without killing the host cell by a process similar to exocytosis.[11] This difference in effect on host cells is paralleled by more efficient cell-to-cell spread by LGV strains in cell culture and their propensity to cause more invasive disease in vivo.

Largely on the basis of work done in cell culture systems, a modification of the chlamydial life cycle has been proposed incorporating a persistent state.[29] In cell culture systems, a state of persistence can be induced by exposure of chlamydia-infected cells to interferon-γ (IFN-γ), to penicillin, or to tryptophan depletion. Under these conditions, viable chlamydiae undergo a growth cycle arrest characterized by lack of replication, conversion of reticulate to elementary bodies, or viability. During persistence, enlarged atypical reticulate bodies are seen; synthesis of MOMP and the 60-kD cystine-rich proteins is reduced but synthesis of the chlamydial 60-kD heat shock protein continues. Removal of the IFN-γ or other inciting factor results in reestablishment of the normal life cycle and chlamydial viability.[29] Although chlamydial persistence seemingly fits with current understanding of the epidemiology and biology of chlamydial infections, further study of whether and how often persistence actually occurs in vivo is needed.

ANTIGENIC AND CHEMICAL COMPOSITION

Isolates of *C. trachomatis* from the LGV and trachoma biovars were originally classified into 15 serovars (see Chapter 176, Table 176-1) on the basis of antigenic cross-reactivity in the microimmunofluorescence test of Wang and Grayston.[30] Three serovars, L$_1$, L$_2$, and L$_3$, are associated either with clinical LGV or with proctocolitis in homosexual men and are rarely recovered under other circumstances. These strains rarely produce asymptomatic infection. The remaining 12 serovars are associated with oculogenital disease: strains A, B, Ba, and C with ocular trachoma and strains D through K with genital tract disease and with inclusion conjunctivitis. Occasionally, serovars B and Ba have been isolated from the genital tract, but A and C have not. Cross-reactivity patterns originally revealed two subgroups within the oculogenital group: B complex (B, Ba, D, E, L$_1$, and L$_2$) and C complex (C, J, H, I, A, K, and L$_3$). Serovars F and G bridge the two complexes, although they are more closely related to the B complex.[29] These relationships were subsequently confirmed and further defined by monoclonal antibodies that identified genus-, species-, subspecies-, and serovar (strain)-specific antigens and by defining the molecular sequence of the MOMP genes for prototype strains.[31] In addition, they led to recognition of three new serovars (Da, Ia, and L$_{2a}$).[32]

The molecular basis for chlamydial tissue tropism is partly understood for the trachoma and the genital serovars of *C. trachomatis*.[33] Thus, all of the trachoma serovar strains tested to date (both wild type and reference strains) lack a functional tryptophan synthase gene because of either mutational inactivation (serovars A and C) or loss of the entire operon (serovar C). In contrast, all genital isolates retain functional enzymes that can synthesize tryptophan from indole.[33]

The epitopes reactive with species-, subspecies-, and serovar-specific antibodies are located in four variable sequence regions of the MOMP.[34] The serovar-specific epitopes are found mostly in variable sequence regions 1 and 2, whereas the more broadly shared epitopes cluster in variable region 4.[34] However, some serovars contain more than one serovar-specific epitope, and serovar-specific epitopes are found in variable region 4 as well.[35] Classification of strains on the basis of nucleotide sequencing of the MOMP gene (*OMP1*) has revealed variation within serovars[36,37] that may reflect immunologic pressure[38] and that has been useful in defining the molecular epidemiology of trachoma[39] and genital infection.[40] Genus-reactive epitopes have been demonstrated in the MOMP,[41] the 60-kD cysteine-rich protein,[41] and in a 60-kD heat shock protein (HSP60).[42] However, the immunodominant genus-reactive epitope is in lipopolysaccharide. Chlamydial lipopolysaccharide is closely related to the lipopolysaccharide of other gram-negative bacteria, in particular to the deep rough (Re) mutants of *Salmonella minnesota* and *Salmonella typhimurium*. However, it contains a 3-deoxy-D-manno-octulosonic acid trisaccharide in a 2, 4 and 2, 8 linkage, with the latter being unique to the genus *Chlamydia*.[43]

The chlamydial genome of serovar D has been sequenced, and the data are available on the Internet.[44] A partial sequence of the LGV serovar has also been completed. Previously, a number of individual genes had been cloned and sequenced, including the genes for the MOMP,[45] the 60-kD cysteine-rich outer-membrane protein,[46] the 60-kD heat shock protein,[42] enzymes involved in lipopolysaccharide synthesis,[43] and the S7 and S12 ribosomal proteins.[47] Information derived from comparative genomic analysis includes confirmation of the antigenic relationships predicted by serologic and monoclonal antibody studies[48] and a molecular basis for some of the antigenic variation observed within serovars.[49,50] In addition, sequence analysis of 16S ribosomal RNA genes has confirmed the eubacterial nature of chlamydiae and established their singularity (see Chapter 176).[51] By this measure their closest relatives are the *Planctomyces*, an obscure group of bacteria that also lack peptidoglycan.

PATHOGENESIS

The mechanisms by which *C. trachomatis* induces inflammation and tissue destruction are poorly understood. The LGV biovar of *C. trachomatis* gains entrance through breaks in the skin or infects epithelial cells of the mucous membranes of the genital tract or rectum. It is then carried by lymphatic drainage to the regional lymph nodes, where it multiplies inside mononuclear phagocytes.[52] Bacteremic spread may also occur and the central nervous system may be infected. The characteristic histopathology is that of granuloma formation with development of small abscesses that may become necrotic or coalesce into suppurative foci.[53]

The target cells of the trachoma biovar of *C. trachomatis* are the squamocolumnar epithelial cells of the endocervix and upper genital tract in women and the conjunctiva, urethra, and rectum in men and women. In men, the epididymis and perhaps the prostate can be infected, whereas in infants the columnar epithelial cells of the respiratory tract are also commonly infected.[52] Regardless of the site, the initial response to infection appears to be primarily a polymorphonuclear leukocyte response.[54-56] Epithelial cells infected in vitro produce interleukin-8 and other proinflammatory cytokines, stimulating the initial neutrophilic response.[57] Lipopolysaccharide may be the predominant chlamydial antigen capable of inducing proinflammatory cytokines.[58]

The initial neutrophilic infiltration is followed by tissue infiltration with lymphocytes, macrophages, plasma cells, and eosinophils.[52] In ocular and genital infections, plasma cells are generally present in large numbers,[59,60] whereas in infant pneumonia, eosinophils and neutrophils predominate.[55] In ocular and genital disease with the trachoma biovar, lymphoid follicles (aggregates of lymphocytes and macrophages in the submucosa) form as the acute inflammation begins to subside. There is thinning or loss of epithelium overlying the follicles, and they may become necrotic as the disease progresses.[52] They are clinically apparent in the conjunctiva as raised avascular lesions. Epithelial proliferation leads to formation of papillae and papillary hypertrophy. As the infection then begins to resolve, fibrosis and scarring occur.

Initial infection of the eye in humans[52] and of the eye[60] and genital tract in monkeys[61] resolves with little or no residual tissue damage. However, in both settings recurrent infection produces an accelerated and more intense inflammatory response with scarring and tissue damage. The potentially important role of reinfection in chlamydial disease was first recognized during human trachoma vaccine trials in which volunteers were immunized and then subsequently challenged with live organisms.[62,63] In these and other studies in humans and monkeys, limited serovar-specific protection against infection could be induced. However, when infection did occur after immunization, it was more severe than in unvaccinated persons, and the increased severity was not serovar specific.[1,63]

Multiple episodes of reinfection or persistent infection appears to be required for the development of ocular trachoma, and much of the inflammation and tissue damage appears to be due to the host immune response to the organism.[63] Thus, marked inflammation can be induced in the eyes of previously infected monkeys by application of an extract of *C. trachomatis* containing the chlamydial 60-kD heat shock protein (cHSP60).[64] Furthermore, the presence of serum antibodies reactive with HSP60 is associated with ectopic pregnancy and infertility in women as well as with persistent upper genital tract infection and with perihepatitis.[65-67] There is considerable sequence homology between cHSP60 and analogous proteins from other species including humans,[68,69] and human sera reactive with cHSP60 also react with an analogous human protein.[68,70] Consequently, it has been suggested that the pathogenesis of chlamydial disease may be in part autoimmune, with cHSP60 being the sensitizing antigen.[69-71] In mice the antibody response to HSP60 is restricted at the major histocompatibility locus[72]; that is, the genetic background of the mouse regulates the response. If the same is true in humans, it might explain some of the variability observed in both the antibody response and morbidity in infected individuals.[72] More recent data have confirmed the relationship between antibody response to cHSP60 and risk of PID[73] and scarring trachoma.[74]

Chlamydiae are able to induce cytokine production, one consequence of which is the production of IFN-γ.[75] IFN-γ inhibits chlamydial replication[76] and in animal models shortens the duration of infection.[77] In cell culture systems it induces a dose-related persistent infection in which synthesis of cHSP60 continues out of proportion to structural membrane components.[29] However, subsequent removal of the IFN-γ allows the infectious organisms to be rescued and viable once again. If such persistent infections occur in people (see later discussion), cyclic changes in inhibitory cytokines, chlamydial replication, antigen production, and hypersensitivity response could explain the chronic inflammation and scarring often associated with chlamydial infections.[78]

IMMUNITY

Natural infection with *C. trachomatis* appears to confer little protection against reinfection, and the limited protection that is conferred is short lived. Multiple or persistent infections are an essential factor in the pathogenesis of ocular trachoma.[79] Moreover, rates of recurrent infection are also quite high in young sexually active individuals with genital tract infections: 29% over a 3½-year period in men and women attending a sexually transmitted disease clinic[80] and 38.4% in adolescent women who were observed prospectively for up to 2 years.[81] However, other data suggest that genital tract infections confer at least partial immunity against reinfection. In women with endocervical infection, the presence of secretory immunoglobulin A (IgA) correlated inversely with the numbers of organisms shed.[82] Men experiencing their first episode of nongonococcal urethritis (NGU) are more likely to have *C. trachomatis* recovered from their urethra than men with a prior history of NGU.[83] Also, individuals at risk for a chlamydial infection who have either a prior history of any sexually transmitted disease or a documented chlamydial infection within the preceding 6 months are at lower risk for a chlamydial infection than those without such a history.[84] In the trachoma vaccine trials mentioned earlier, partial serovar-specific immunity could be elicited, but protection lasted for only 1 to 2 years.[63,79]

In mouse models, CD4 lymphocytes of the Th1 type that traffic to the genital mucosa are crucial for restriction of intracellular growth and resolution of infection.[85] Antibodies directed at epitopes on the MOMP are neutralizing and may play a role in reducing acquisition of infection.[86] Antibodies may also influence the severity of upper genital tract pathology in the mouse.[87] Both antibody and cell-mediated mechanisms are important in protective immunity in the guinea pig model.[88] It is possible that antigen presentation in natural mucosal infection may be relatively ineffective in producing strong protective immunity because dendritic cells pulsed in vitro with inactivated chlamydiae are capable of conferring protective immunity in the mouse model.[89] The current consensus is that CD4+ T cells and B cells are most critical in mediating recall immunity to *C. trachomatis* infection and CD8+ T cells are less important. The latter may exert antichlamydial activity by production of IFN-γ rather than by cytotoxic activity. Because of the combination of protective and deleterious effects seen with whole organism infection or vaccination, present vaccine development efforts have been directed at defining relevant epitopes that could be used as components in some form of synthetic or genetically engineered vaccine.[90] Studies of DNA vaccines utilizing the *omp1* gene of the mouse pneumonitis strain of *C. trachomatis* showed reduced organism burden and mortality in a mouse pneumonia model,[91] but similar studies have not demonstrated an influence on the course of experimental genital infection in mice.[92]

LABORATORY DIAGNOSIS

Among *C. trachomatis* infections, only classic trachoma can be diagnosed on clinical grounds alone and then only in the proper epidemiologic setting. Although other chlamydial infections are often associated with specific clinical syndromes, syndromic diagnosis is imprecise and laboratory confirmation is required for definitive diagnosis. Laboratory procedures of value include cytologic examination for intracytoplasmic inclusions, isolation of *C. trachomatis* in cell culture, demonstration of chlamydial antigen by enzyme-linked immunosorbent assay or by immunofluorescent staining, and demonstration of nucleic acid by direct hybridization or by amplification techniques.[93]

Cytologic Diagnosis

In infant inclusion conjunctivitis and in ocular trachoma, typical intracytoplasmic inclusions can often be identified in Giemsa-stained cell scrapings from the conjunctiva. However, the technique is relatively insensitive in mild disease, with inclusion-bearing cells found in 10% to 30% of scrapings collected from patients with active trachoma.[94] Stained scrapings are positive in infants with neonatal conjunctivitis and in adults with inclusion conjunctivitis in as many as 90% and 50%, respectively. Cytology has also been used to evaluate endocervical scrapings, including those obtained for Papanicolaou smears. However, interpretation is difficult, and sensitivity and specificity have been low.[95] Cytologic diagnosis has largely been replaced by the much more sensitive and specific nucleic acid amplification tests.

Isolation in Cell Culture

C. trachomatis grows well in a variety of cell lines that can be maintained in culture. Most commonly used are McCoy or HeLa cells, which are grown either on glass cover slips in 12-mm-diameter vials or on the bottom of polystyrene microtiter plate wells.[96] Incubation in cell culture ranges from 40 to 72 hours, depending on the cell type and biovar. Intracytoplasmic inclusions can be detected after staining with Giemsa, Macchiavello, or Gimenez stains or by immunofluorescence. Inclusions can also be detected in McCoy cells by staining with iodine, which stains glycogen.[94] However, immunofluorescent staining with monoclonal antibodies is clearly the most sensitive and specific means of detecting inclusions and has largely replaced other methods (see Chapter 176, Fig. 176-2).[97] The quantity of infectious chlamydiae

in a specimen is usually expressed as inclusion-forming units. Proper handling of clinical specimens before cell culture inoculation is critical for optimal recovery of organisms but limits the utility of this method.[98] For example, specimens must be maintained at 4° C and inoculated into tissue culture within 24 hours from the time they are obtained.[99] Alternatively, they can be frozen and stored at −70° C before inoculation, but this results in loss of some organisms and in false-negative results in some specimens containing low numbers of inclusion-forming units.[100] Sensitivity of the culture method is enhanced by blind passage of monolayers after incubation or by inoculation of multiple monolayers with a single specimen.[98] Although its specificity approaches 100%, even under optimal conditions the sensitivity of culture is estimated at between 70% and 80% in experienced laboratories and may be as low as 40% to 50% in some settings.[101] These estimates have been derived from studies comparing the results of culture with those of the more sensitive nucleic acid amplification tests.[93] Because of its high specificity, cell culture is recommended when testing is being used to establish the presence or absence of infection in situations with legal implications (e.g., rape or sexual assault).[6]

The numbers of viable organisms shed by infected individuals and the isolation rates in cell culture parallel each other. Both are affected by the clinical situation.[102] For example, the highest isolation rates and highest numbers of recoverable inclusion-forming units are found in ocular infections such as active trachoma and neonatal or adult inclusion conjunctivitis. Rates are lower in mild or chronic ocular disease. In genital infections, many more organisms are usually recovered from the endocervix than from the male urethra, and even fewer are recovered from the female urethra.[103] More organisms generally accompany infections associated with symptoms or signs, and higher inclusion counts are also generally seen in younger patients.[104] When women at risk for infection have cultures of both the endocervix and urethra, as opposed to the endocervix alone, the increase in identification of infected women is approximately 20%[103]; that is, 20% of infected women have positive urethral and negative endocervical cultures. In LGV, the organism can be recovered by culture from bubo pus in approximately 30% of cases and less frequently from sites such as the cervix or the urethra.[105] In appropriate clinical settings, *C. trachomatis* has been recovered from the nasopharynx and rectum,[106] bronchoalveolar lavage fluid and lung biopsy tissue,[107] endometrium, fallopian tubes,[108] epididymis,[109] peritoneal cavity,[110] and donor semen.[111]

Antigen Detection and Nucleic Acid Hybridization

Given the limited availability and variable sensitivity of *C. trachomatis* cultures as well as the technical impediments associated with their use, considerable effort has been directed at developing better diagnostic tests for chlamydia.[112] Several tests that do not require culture for detection of chlamydiae are commercially available. These tests are based on either (1) antigen detection by direct fluorescent antibody (DFA) staining, (2) antigen detection by enzyme-linked immunosorbent assay, or (3) detection of chlamydial ribosomal RNA by hybridization with a DNA probe. Published evaluations have been based primarily on MicroTrak DFA (Syva Co., Palo Alto, Calif.) and Chlamydiazyme (Abbott Laboratories, North Chicago, Ill.), although a number of similar tests have been approved by the Food and Drug Administration.[6] Most studies evaluating these tests have reported sensitivities greater than 70% and specificities of 97% to 99% in populations of men and women with a prevalence of infection of 5% or more.[6] These performance characteristics offer acceptable positive and negative predictive values for most diagnostic purposes.[6] In general, nonculture tests are more reliable in patients who are symptomatic and shedding large numbers of organisms than in patients who are asymptomatic and may be shedding fewer organisms.[102,112] All of these tests require invasive collection procedures (i.e., a cervical swab in women or a urethral swab in men) and cannot utilize urines or self-collected vaginal swabs because of low sensitivity with these approaches when used with these tests.

In low-prevalence populations (i.e., less than 5% infected), a significant proportion of positive test results are false positives. For example, if 1000 patients have a prevalence of 3%, 30 are infected. A test with a sensitivity of 80% and a specificity of 99% detects 24 of the infected people but falsely identifies 10 (1% of 1000) uninfected as infected. Consequently, the interpretation of a positive test result must be handled with care in counseling patients, and verification is desirable in this situation. Verification of a positive test result can be accomplished by (1) culture, (2) a second nonculture test that identifies a different chlamydial antigen or nucleic acid sequence than the first test, or (3) a blocking antibody or competitive probe.[6] However, as noted earlier, only culture should be used if there are potential legal consequences associated with misdiagnosis of a chlamydial infection.[6]

Each of these tests and formats has its own advantages and disadvantages. DFA allows assessment of the quality of the specimen (by observation of the presence of epithelial cells) in addition to the presence or absence of organisms but requires a highly skilled microscopist for proper interpretation.[112] Tests using antibodies directed against the MOMP are species specific, whereas those using antilipopolysaccharide antibodies can cross react with other bacteria, including other species of chlamydiae.[6] Performance of the enzyme immunoassay tests requires personnel with fewer skills, but these tests generally take longer to perform. To differentiate false-positive from true-positive reactions, some manufacturers now provide reagents for the test to be repeated on the same specimen with blocking antibody present.[113] The DNA hybridization techniques are relatively easy to perform and interpret. Although considerably fewer comparative data have been published on the DNA hybridization techniques than on the other formats, their sensitivity and specificity generally appear similar to those of the enzyme immunoassay tests.[114,115]

Amplification Tests

Nucleic acid amplification tests (NAATs) based on the detection of chlamydial DNA or RNA using amplification procedures such as polymerase chain reaction (PCR), ligase chain reaction (LCR), or chlamydial ribosomal RNA using transcription-mediated amplification are now available. A review of studies establishes that these tests are considerably more sensitive than culture and are nearly as specific.[93,116-119] These tests have provided a major breakthrough in chlamydial diagnosis as they are the first tests that exceed culture in their sensitivity. In general, these tests are 15% to 20% more sensitive than high-quality culture systems but they may be up to 40% to 50% more sensitive than some culture or enzyme immunoassay tests (Table 177-1). Moreover, the NAATs can be used to detect *C. trachomatis* in urine or in self-collected vaginal swab specimens,[120] with a sensitivity comparable to that obtained with urogenital swab specimens. Thus,

these tests make noninvasive testing for chlamydial infections possible for the first time.[119,121] Studies of military recruits,[122] adolescents,[123] high school students,[124] job training participants,[125] and juvenile detainees demonstrate the utility of these tests in diagnosing infection without pelvic examination or collection of swab specimens and outside traditional screening sites. Such testing makes both population-based research projects and community-based prevention programs feasible. However, the NAATs are expensive and may not be affordable by health departments for comprehensive screening. In addition, they may be technically demanding for some routine laboratory settings, leading to erroneous false-positive or false-negative results. What remains to be determined is the most cost-effective way to employ NAATs in screening situations to ensure the greatest impact on the public health consequences of undiagnosed chlamydial infections. Considerations include selective screening, pooling of specimens, and combined use of less expensive enzyme immunoassays followed by NAAT confirmation. Approaches to development of appropriate quality control procedures must also be delineated.

The choice of the most appropriate NAAT or approach to screening depends on the clinical setting, the facilities available, and the relative cost.

Serology

Chlamydial serologic tests are of limited value in the diagnosis of most common oculogenital chlamydial infections. A complement fixation test is commercially available that measures antibodies against group-reactive antigens (i.e., lipopolysaccharide) in people infected with *C. trachomatis*, *C. pneumoniae*, or *C. psittaci*. Virtually 100% of individuals with LGV or psittacosis have complement-fixing antibody titers greater than 1:16 after infection.[126] Patients with LGV often present 3 to 4 weeks after the onset of their illness, at which time their antibody titer is stable. Consequently, in an appropriate clinical setting a complement fixation titer of 1:64 or greater is strongly supportive of a diagnosis of LGV, although confirmation requires a fourfold or greater titer rise between acute and convalescent specimens.[126] The complement fixation test may also become positive, however, in patients with recently acquired *C. pneumoniae* infections or some patients with oculogenital infections and thus it lacks specificity. Titers are low or nonexistent in this test among most patients with chlamydial urethritis, cervicitis, or conjunctivitis, and thus it has little diagnostic utility in these settings.

The other serologic test that is available primarily in research laboratories is the microimmunofluorescence test. In its most common format, elementary bodies from each of the 15 serovars are employed as antigens, and antibodies against cell wall components of the organisms are detected.[30] When done in an experienced laboratory, this test is more sensitive than the complement fixation test and because the target MOMP antigens are species specific, it can differentiate infections caused by *C. trachomatis*, *C. pneumoniae*, and *C. psittaci*. The test, when used on acute and convalescent sera, demonstrates a fourfold rise in antibody in the majority of adult patients with eye or genital infection. Titers are especially high in women with PID or perihepatitis, in whom its diagnostic sensitivity may be highest. Likewise, anti-*Chlamydia* IgM is present in approximately 30% of infants with neonatal inclusion and in nearly all infants with chlamydial pneumonia.[126] Consequently, an IgM titer of 1:32 or greater in the microimmunofluorescence test can be diagnostic of infant chlamydial pneumonia in an appropriate clinical setting.

Anti-*Chlamydia* IgM is uncommon in adults with genital tract infection. The prevalence of anti-*Chlamydia* IgG is high in sexually active adults (30% to 60%), even in those who do not have an active infection, and is probably due to past infection. There may be an association between chlamydia-specific serum IgA and active disease. However, the sensitivity, specificity, and predictive values of this test are not high enough to make it clinically useful in the diagnosis of active disease.[127] Thus, chlamydial serologies are not recommended for diagnosis of active disease except in suspected cases of LGV, psittacosis, and infants with pneumonia.

TABLE 177-1 Comparative Performances of Selected Diagnostic Tests in the Detection of *Chlamydia trachomatis*

Test	Sensitivity Relative to Expanded Gold Standard* (%)	Specificity (%)	Detectability Level (Elementary Bodies)
Enzyme immunoassay	40-60	99.5[†]	1000-10,000
Nonamplified genetic probe	40-65	99.0	1000-10,000
Direct fluorescent antibody	50-80	99.8	50-1000
Cell culture	50-90	99.9	10-100
Nucleic acid amplification tests	Cervix 81-100 F urine 80-96 M urine 90-96	99.7	1-10

*Defined using a combination of different test methodologies, including culture, direct fluorescent antibody, and polymerase chain reaction (PCR) or ligase chain reaction (LCR) directed against a target sequence distinct from that used in the routine PCR or LCR assays.

[†]Specificity using confirmatory assays.

F, female; M, male.

CLINICAL MANIFESTATIONS

C. trachomatis infections can be divided into four clinical categories: (1) classic ocular trachoma, (2) LGV, (3) other oculogenital diseases in adults, and (4) perinatal infections.

Ocular Trachoma

Ocular trachoma has been recognized since antiquity. Therapy for trachoma and its complications was described in China in the 27th century BC and in Egypt in the 19th century BC.[1] In areas in which trachoma is endemic, the first infection usually occurs early in life (generally before age 2), and active disease persists for several years. Although initial infections may resolve spontaneously, they are frequently complicated by reinfection or by superimposed bacterial conjunctivitis. In its initial stages, trachoma manifests as a chronic follicular conjunctivitis with papillary hypertrophy and inflammatory infiltration. As the disease progresses, scarring of the conjunctiva occurs, and there is involvement of the cornea. In addition, as the inner surface of the lids becomes scarred, the eyelashes turn in and abrade the cornea, resulting in ulceration, scarring, and visual loss. Children with mild disease are left with some conjunctival scarring and pannus formation (fibrovascular infiltrate), whereas others develop badly scarred conjunctivae and corneas. The latter may not occur until well into adult life.[128] The WHO's simplified grading scheme for trachoma is presented in Table 177-2.

Treatment

In endemic areas, the primary reservoir is children with ocular infection.[129] Transmission occurs by hand-to-eye contact between children and their caregivers or by contact with the feet of flies who feed on the exudate from children with active conjunctivitis.[130,131] Hygienic factors that seem to be particularly important in control of disease include facial cleanliness, access to water, and reduction of household fly density. Topical antibiotic therapy is of only marginal benefit,[128] perhaps because extraocular sites such as the nasopharynx and rectum are colonized in children with trachoma.[130] Systemic antibiotic therapy is effective in individuals and possibly in communities in which the incidence of disease is relatively low.[128] However, compliance with erythromycin is poor, and doxycycline is contraindicated in young children. Trials of mass treatment with azithromycin at the village level indicate that both infection and clinical disease are markedly decreased at 6 and 12 months after such treatment.[132-135] Programs involving lid surgery teams for the prevention of blindness related to lid deformities that cause continuing corneal damage are also of value.[128] Because of the importance of hygienic factors, there is a strong historic link between improvement in socioeconomic conditions and disappearance of endemic trachoma.

The WHO has initiated a program to eliminate blinding trachoma by the year 2020.[131] The objective is not necessarily to eliminate the trachoma serovars of chlamydiae (A, B, Ba, and C) but to eliminate or at least markedly reduce clinically active disease. The key elements of the S-A-F-E strategy are surgery for deformed eyelids; periodic mass treatment of villages with the antibiotic azithromycin; face washing and hygiene; and environmental improvements to control flies by such techniques as building latrines outside villages. In a study done in Nepal, a once-annual treatment of all children 1 to 10 years old with azithromycin was associated with a marked reduction in both clinically evident trachoma and evidence of chlamydial infection by PCR.[133] In some areas, trachoma appears to be disappearing coincident with economic gains and without the introduction of specific control programs.

Lymphogranuloma Venereum

LGV is a sexually transmitted disease caused by the LGV serovars of *C. trachomatis*. It is endemic in Africa, India, Southeast Asia, South America, and the Caribbean and occurs as a sporadic disease elsewhere. There are three distinct stages in classic LGV. The first stage is formation of a primary lesion, usually on genital mucosa or adjacent skin. *C. trachomatis* cannot infect squamous epithelial cells, and when the primary lesion occurs on the external genitalia or in the vagina the organism probably gains entry through minute lacerations or abrasions.[105] The primary lesion is usually a small papule or herpetiform ulcer that produces few or no symptoms and is generally not noticed. It appears between 3 and 30 days after acquisition of infection[53] and heals rapidly without leaving a scar. Initial infection can also be intraurethral, producing a symptomatic urethritis, or cervical, producing cervicitis.

The secondary stage occurs days to weeks after the primary lesion and is characterized by lymphadenopathy and systemic symptoms. The lymph nodes involved are those that drain the area of the primary lesion and thus depend on its location. In men, the primary lesion is usually on the penis or in the urethra, and thus the inguinal lymph nodes are the main ones affected. Lymphadenopathy is unilateral in two thirds of patients.[53] Similarly, when the site of primary infection is vulvar, inguinal and femoral nodes are affected. When the primary infection is rectal, the affected nodes are the deep iliac, and when it is upper vaginal or cervical, the obturator and iliac nodes are infected.[104]

Inguinal lymphadenopathy, however, is the most characteristic manifestation of the secondary stage and the one most frequently recognized. Initially the lymph nodes are discrete and tender with overlying erythema, but because of extensive periadenitis the inflammatory process spreads from the lymph nodes into the surrounding tissue, forming an inflammatory mass. Abscesses within the mass coalesce, forming a bubo that may rupture spontaneously with development of loculated abscesses, fistulas, or sinus tracts.[136]

Systemic manifestations are often associated with this phase, including fever, headache, and myalgias. Meningitis may occur, and in some cases the organism has been recovered from blood or cerebrospinal fluid.[104] Rupture of the fluctuant inflammatory mass (bubo) relieves pain and fever,[105] although sinus tracts may continue to drain thick, yellowish pus for several weeks or months before fully resolving.[136] Excised inguinal nodes often have a characteristic inflammatory response, with central stellate coalescing abscesses that contain neutrophils and necrotic debris surrounded by a zone of palisaded epithelioid cells, macrophages, and occasional multinucleated giant cells. Surrounding this, there is an outer layer of lymphocytes and plasma cells. With time, the nodal architecture is effaced and replaced by progressive fibrosis. This histopathologic presentation is suggestive of the diagnosis of LGV or cat-scratch disease but is not unique to these entities.

Healing leaves some scarring in the inguinal region but does not result in significant sequelae in most cases. Relapse occurs in approximately 20% of untreated cases.[105] Only about one third of buboes become fluctuant and rupture. The others harden and form inguinal masses, which gradually involute over time.[136] Femoral nodes are also frequently affected, and the division between the femoral and inguinal nodes by the inguinal ligament produces the "groove" sign described as characteristic of LGV.[105] Inguinal or femoral lymphadenopathy may be misdiagnosed as inguinal hernia, whereas deep iliac node involve-

---

TABLE 177-2 World Health Organization Simplified Grading Scheme for Trachoma

Trachomatous inflammation—follicular (TF): There are five or more follicles in the upper tarsal conjunctiva (follicles must be at least 0.05 mm in diameter).

Trachomatous inflammation—intense (TI): Pronounced inflammatory thickening of the tarsal conjunctiva, which obscures half of the normal deep tarsal vessels.

Trachomatous conjunctival scarring (TS): The presence of easily visible scars in the tarsal conjunctiva.

Trachomatous trichiasis (TT): At least one eyelash rubs on the eyeball. Evidence of recent removal of inturned lashes was also graded as trichiasis.

Corneal opacity (CO): Easily visible corneal opacity present over the pupil, which was so dense that at least part of the pupil margin was blurred when seen through the opacity.

Adapted from Thylefors B, Dawson CR, Jones BR, et al. A simple system of the assessment of trachoma and its complications. Bull World Health Organ. 1987;65:477-483.

ment may raise a question of appendicitis. Only 20% to 30% of women present with inguinal lymphadenopathy as their primary manifestation. Other common presentations in women and in homosexual or bisexual men are symptoms consistent with proctitis, proctocolitis, or complaints of lower abdominal and back pain related to involvement of deep pelvic and lumbar lymph nodes.[136]

In the third stage, complications include *esthiomene* (Greek, "eating away"), which refers to hypertrophic chronic granulomatous enlargement with ulceration of the external genitalia (either the vulva or scrotum and penis).[136] Lymphatic obstruction may also lead to elephantiasis of the male or female genitalia.

The differential diagnosis of inguinal lymphadenopathy in the age group likely to be infected includes herpes simplex virus, syphilis, chancroid, and occasionally lymphoma.[137] Mild leukocytosis, with an increase in monocytes and eosinophils, frequently accompanies early bubonic and anogenital rectal LGV.[105] Significant polymorphonuclear leukocytosis suggests bacterial adenitis or superinfection with pyogenic bacteria. The diagnosis can be made on the basis of a positive chlamydial serology, isolation of LGV from infected tissue, or histopathology. A skin test (the Frei test) has been used in the past but is no longer available.[105,138] *C. trachomatis* can be recovered from bubo aspirates, genital tissue, or rectal tissue in only about 30% of cases.[105] The utility of newer diagnostic techniques such as PCR has not been extensively studied but limited experience indicates high sensitivity. Histopathologic changes in LGV are not specific but, when combined with serologic results in an appropriate clinical setting, are usually sufficient to make a presumptive diagnosis.

LGV manifesting as inguinal lymphadenopathy can be distinguished from genital herpes by the presence of the multiple painful ulcers at the site of the primary herpes infection, in contrast to the painless primary lesion of LGV, and by matting of the lymph nodes in LGV. Also, lymphadenopathy is frequently bilateral in herpes but not in LGV. A diagnosis of syphilis is suggested by a primary lesion with indurated margins (chancre) and bilateral and nontender inguinal lymphadenopathy. Large ulcers that are multiple and extremely tender in association with lymphadenopathy suggest chancroid. The pseudobuboes that occur in granuloma inguinale are nodules in the skin and subcutaneous tissue, with lymph node involvement being the result of secondary infection.[53] However, the clinical presentation of sexually transmitted agents causing inguinal lymphadenopathy clearly overlaps, and appropriate laboratory tests are usually required to distinguish among them. When an ulcer is present, a darkfield examination should be performed for *Treponema pallidum* and serologic tests for syphilis obtained.[53,105,137]

Treatment of Lymphogranuloma Venereum

Although sulfonamides have in vitro activity against *C. trachomatis* and some clinical efficacy, they do not produce bacteriologic cures reliably.[138] Tetracycline, doxycycline, minocycline, chloramphenicol, erythromycin, and rifampin have been used with good effect in the treatment of primary and secondary stages of LGV.[105,139,140] Few comparative studies of therapy have been done, but current recommendations by the CDC are for 21 days of doxycycline, 100 mg twice daily, with erythromycin or sulfisoxazole listed as alternative regimens.[141] In addition, fluctuant buboes should be aspirated to prevent rupture and sinus tract formation.[105] Antibiotic therapy results in rapid abatement of constitutional symptoms but has only a limited effect on bubo resolution.[105] Effects on late complications such as strictures are variable.[53,105]

Oculogenital Disease in Adults

C. trachomatis serovars D through K produce a wide variety of oculogenital infections (Fig. 177-3).

Inclusion Conjunctivitis

In the adult, chlamydial eye infection manifests as an acute follicular conjunctivitis, often with a foreign body sensation in the eye. Symptoms are usually unilateral. The clinical picture in the first 2 weeks is dominated by hyperemia and a mucoid discharge that be-

comes purulent.[142] This is followed by lymphoid follicle formation (frequently with corneal lesions and epithelial keratitis[143,144]), as well as invasion of the cornea by blood vessels (pannus), and is indistinguishable from early ocular trachoma. Preauricular lymphadenopathy and otitis media may be present.[143] Untreated or improperly treated, the condition may persist for many months but usually resolves without complications.[145] Scarring similar to that seen in mild trachoma may occur in occasional cases.

Slightly more than half of adults with inclusion conjunctivitis have documented concurrent genital tract infections with *C. trachomatis*.[145,146] In such individuals, the presumed mode of transmission is autoinoculation with infected genital secretions or, in some cases, direct inoculation from an infected partner. More difficult to explain is the acquisition of infection by individuals who do not have concurrent genital tract infections. Spread between individuals from eye to eye by transfer of infected secretions without sexual contact may also occur and account for some cases.[146] Many such cases may be due to asymptomatic or unrecognized genital infection. Although as many as 9% of patients with keratoconjunctivitis who are 16 to 20 years of age have chlamydial ocular infection, eye involvement is still seen in less than 1% of individuals with proven genital tract infection.[145,146]

The differential diagnosis is primarily conjunctivitis caused by adenovirus or other viruses.[144] A definitive diagnosis can be made only by demonstration of the organism by culture, PCR, or other test. The condition responds promptly to the administration of appropriate systemic antibiotics, with decrease in discharge, hyperemia, and symptoms from keratitis within 48 hours.[142] Evaluation and treatment of the patient and partners for genital tract infection should also be undertaken.

Urogenital Infections

The risk of aquisition of *C. trachomatis* with a single episode of sexual intercourse with an infected partner is not known. However, it appears to be substantially less than that for *Neisseria gonorrhoeae*.[147] On the basis of extrapolation of data from partner notification programs and from couples with discordant cell culture–proven infection, the transmission probability has been estimated as 0.39 from men to women and as 0.32 from women to men.[148] More recently, transmission probability has been estimated as approximately 0.68 in both directions, based on results of a more sensitive diagnostic test, PCR.[149] However, these estimates are based on the average frequency of intercourse among pairs

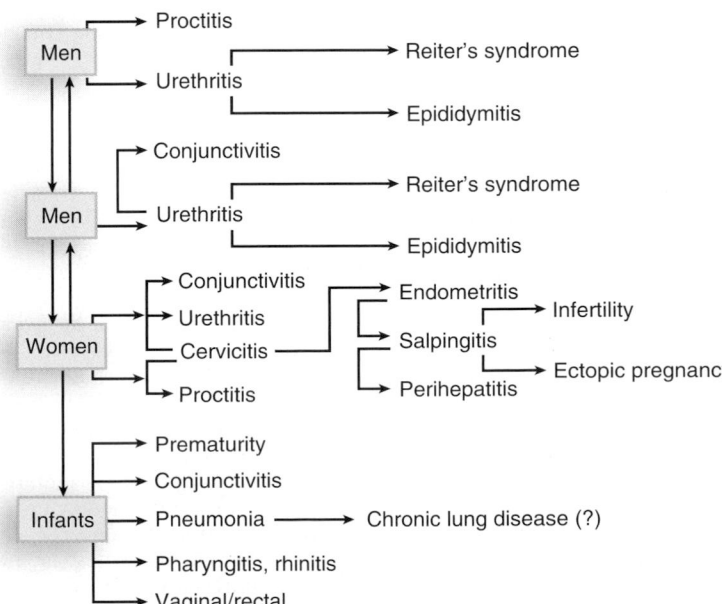

FIGURE 177-3. Clinical manifestations of *C. trachomatis* and patterns of transmission.

rather than a single encounter. Partners of asymptomatic individuals identified through a screening program are less likely to be infected than partners of symptomatic individuals,[150] and in one study, recent exposure to a new partner was much more strongly associated with gonococcal than with chlamydial infection.[151] Furthermore, in adolescents, chlamydial infection is strongly associated with frequency of intercourse, both in those reporting only one lifetime partner and in those reporting more than one lifetime partner.[152] Thus, in contrast to gonococcal infections, genital infections with *C. trachomatis* have more characteristics of a prevalent than an incident disease. Most individuals infected with *N. gonorrhoeae* develop symptoms and seek care quickly, whereas many men and most women infected with *C. trachomatis* are either asymptomatic or minimally symptomatic and are diagnosed as a result of screening or because a contact is symptomatic.[151]

C. trachomatis is recovered more often from women who acquire gonorrhea than from similarly exposed women who do not acquire gonorrhea.[153] In individuals with gonorrhea the recurrence rate of *C. trachomatis* infection with the same serovar is significantly greater than can be explained by variables related to likely exposure.[154] Furthermore, individuals infected with both *C. trachomatis* and *N. gonorrhoeae* shed larger numbers of *C. trachomatis* than those infected with *C. trachomatis* alone.[102] These data suggest that acquisition of a gonococcal infection either reactivates a persistent chlamydial infection or increases the susceptibility of the host to acquisition of chlamydiae.

Urethritis

There is little information on the natural history of untreated urethral infection. Only one of eight infected men who were observed without treatment for a minimum of 21 days developed symptomatic urethritis.[155] Although asymptomatic infections are common in men, *C. trachomatis* is also the cause of between 30% and 50% of cases of symptomatic NGU and an even higher proportion of cases of postgonococcal urethritis.[156] Other causes of NGU include *Ureaplasma urealyticum*, *Trichomonas vaginalis*, *Mycoplasma genitalium*, and herpes simplex virus.[158] *C. trachomatis* can also be recovered from approximately 20% of men with gonococcal urethritis.[159] When men who are dually infected are treated only with single-dose therapy for their gonorrhea, most develop postgonococcal urethritis, which manifests as a persistence or recurrence of their urethritis. In the United States the incidence of NGU exceeds that of gonococcal urethritis by ratios greater than 2 to 1 in most sexually transmitted diseases clinics, with even higher ratios in many private practice settings.[7] Risk factors for chlamydial urethritis in men include age younger than 20 years, black race, and heterosexual orientation.[160]

The incubation period for symptomatic chlamydial urethritis is usually between 7 and 14 days, in contrast to that for gonococcal urethritis, which is approximately 4 days. Patients present with dysuria and urethral discharge, which is usually white, gray, or sometimes clear, in contrast to the more purulent discharge observed with gonococcal urethritis.[160] The discharge may be so slight as to be demonstrable only after penile stripping or only in the morning. Some patients may deny the presence of discharge but may note stained underwear in the morning resulting from scant discharge overnight. However, there is sufficient overlap between the signs and symptoms of gonococcal urethritis and NGU that a reliable distinction between them cannot be made on clinical grounds alone. An average of four or more polymorphonuclear leukocytes per oil immersion field (1000×) in a Gram stain of an endourethral swab specimen establishes a diagnosis of urethritis.[161] The absence of organisms with the typical morphology of *N. gonorrhoeae* and the subsequent failure to culture *N. gonorrhoeae* establish a diagnosis of NGU. In adolescent males, more than 10 leukocytes per high-power field in the initial 15 to 20 mL of a first-catch urine specimen is also strongly suggestive of urethritis,[162] as is a positive urine leukocyte esterase test result.[163] The primary complications of chlamydial urethritis in men are (1) epi-

didymitis; (2) sexually reactive arthritis, including Reiter's syndrome; and (3) transmission to women.

Epididymitis and Prostatitis

C. trachomatis and *N. gonorrhoeae* are the most frequent causes of epididymitis in men younger than 35 years, whereas Enterobacteriaceae (primarily *Escherichia coli*) are the usual pathogens in men older than 35.[164] In the younger men, urethritis is usually also present but may be asymptomatic and demonstratable only on examination. However, its absence does not exclude chlamydial infection or gonorrhea as the etiologic agent. Most men with *E. coli* as the etiologic agent, in addition to being older, have other risk factors for urinary tract infection, including recent catheterization, urologic surgery, or rectal insertive intercourse. Chlamydial epididymitis is often associated with oligospermia during the acute phase,[164] but there are no data indicating that future fertility is impaired. In addition, epididymitis is usually unilateral, and attempts to correlate chlamydial infections with male factor infertility have been unsuccessful.[165] A presumptive diagnosis of NGU can be confirmed as chlamydial in etiology utilizing a first void urine specimen tested by a NAAT (Table 177-3).

Typically, epididymitis arises with a unilateral swollen epididymis or testicle or both, dysuria, fever, and in some cases shaking chills. Many patients can be managed in the outpatient setting but others require hospitalization for parenteral antibiotics, scrotal elevation, analgesia, and observation. The diagnosis of testicular torsion should always be considered in young men with acute onset of severe unilateral scrotal pain and should be ruled out with radionuclide studies.

The role of chlamydia in prostatic infection remains controversial. From available data, it does not appear to play a role in acute prostatitis; these cases are mainly attributable to *E. coli*, other gram-negative rods, or enterococci. Its role in chronic nonbacterial prostatitis remains more controversial. Although some investigators have recovered *C. trachomatis* from prostatic expressate or biopsies of such patients, convincing evidence that chlamydia plays an etiologic role in chronic nonbacterial prostatitis has yet to be developed and antibiotic therapy is not recommended.[166]

Proctitis and Proctocolitis

Although asymptomatic rectal carriage of *C. trachomatis* occurs in both infants[106] and adults,[167] *C. trachomatis* is also a common cause of symptomatic proctitis and proctocolitis in homosexual men.[168] Proctitis can result from direct inoculation of the rectum in either men or women through anal intercourse or secondary spread of secretions from the cervix. In LGV, lymphatic spread from the posterior vaginal wall or cervix through lymphatics may occur.[105,169] Severity and extent of disease are related to the infecting serovars. In infection with serovars D through K, the primary manifestations are anal pruritus and a mucous rectal discharge that may become mucopurulent. The infection remains superficial, is limited to the rectum, and closely resembles gonococcal proctitis. In many patients, infection is asymptomatic. Leukocytes are usually present on rectal Gram stain even in asymptomatic patients with *C. trachomatis* infection.[168,170] With the LGV strains, rectal pain, tenesmus, rectal bleeding, and fever are present. The disease extends into the colon. The rectal and colonic mucosa become ulcerated, and a granulomatous inflammatory process is present in the bowel wall, with both noncaseating granulomas and crypt abscesses. As the disease related to LGV strains progresses, muscle layers are replaced by fibrous tissue, which contracts to form rectal strictures. Sinus tract formation can lead to rectovaginal fistulas in women.[136,169] The inflammatory process as seen on sigmoidoscopy may be localized to one segment or may occur at several different levels concurrently. Involvement of the distal rectal mucosa can lead to perirectal abscesses and anal fissures. Outgrowths of lymphatic tissue resembling hemorrhoids occur as a result of lymphatic obstruction. The clinical and histologic similarity between LGV strain infection and other inflammatory bowel diseases, such as Crohn's disease, can lead to misdiagnosis and inappropriate therapy.[168]

TABLE 177-3 Clinical Characteristics of Common *Chlamydia trachomatis* Infections

	Infection	Symptoms and Signs	Presumptive Diagnosis	Definitive Diagnosis	Treatment
Men	Nongonococcal urethritis	Urethral discharge, dysuria	Urethral leukocytosis; no gonococci seen	Urine or urethral NAAT	Azithromycin, 1 g PO (single dose) *or* Doxycycline, 100 mg PO bid, for 7 days
	Epididymitis	Unilateral epididymal tenderness, swelling; pain; fever, presence of NGU	Urethral leukocytosis; pyuria on urinalysis	Urine or urethral NAAT	Outpatient: levofloxacin, 500 mg bid for 10 days *or* Ceftriaxone, 1 g IM, plus doxycycline, 100 mg PO, bid, for 10 days
	Proctitis	Rectal pain, discharge, bleeding; history of receptive anal intercourse	≥ 1 PMN/OIF on rectal Gram stain; no gonococci seen	Urine or urethral NAAT; urine culture	Doxycycline, 100 mg PO bid, for 7 days
	Conjunctivitis	Ocular pain, redness, discharge; simultaneous genital infection	Gram stain of conjunctival swab negative for bacterial pathogens; PMNs on smear	Rectal culture or DFA (NAAT untested)	Azithromycin, 1 g PO (single dose) *or* Doxycycline, 100 mg PO bid., for 7 days
	Cervicitis	Mucopurulent cervical discharge; simultaneous genital infection	≥ 20 PMN/OIF on cervical Gram stain	Urine or cervical NAAT	Azithromycin, 1 g PO (single dose) *or* Doxycycline, 100 mg PO bid, for 7 days
	Urethritis	Dysuria, frequency; no hematuria	Pyuria on UA; negative urine Gram stain and culture	Urine, cervical, or urethral NAAT	Azithromycin, 1 g PO (single dose) *or* Doxycycline, 100 mg PO bid, for 7 days
Women	Salpingitis	Lower abdominal pain, adnexal pain, cervical motion tenderness	Evidence of mucopurulent cervicitis	Urine or cervical NAAT	Outpatient: Ofloxacin, 400 mg bid, PO, plus metronidazole, 500 mg PO, bid, for 14 days *or* Ceftriaxone, 250 g IM plus doxycycline, 100 mg PO, bid, for 14 days
Adult	Conjunctivitis	Ocular pain, redness, discharge; simultaneous genital infection	Gram stain of conjunctival swab negative for bacterial pathogens; PMNs on smear	DFA or NAAT on conjunctival swab	Azithromycin, 1 g PO (single dose) *or* Doxycycline, 100 mg PO bid, for 7 days
Newborn	Conjunctivitis	Ocular pain, redness, discharge; simultaneous genital infection	Gram stain of conjunctival swab negative for bacterial pathogens; PMNs on smear	DFA or NAAT on conjunctival swah; vagina, rectum, pharynx also often positive	Erythromycin base 50 mg/kg/day, orally divided into four doses daily for 14 days, evaluate and treat parents as well.
	Pneumonia	Staccato cough, tachypnea, hyperinflation	Diffuse interstitial infiltrate, eosinophilia	Nasopharyngeal NAATs or culture; MIF serology (IgM)	Erythromycin base 50 mg/kg/day, orally divided into four doses daily for 14 days, evaluate and treat parents as well.

DFA, direct fluorescent antibody; IgM, immunoglobulin M; MIF, microimmunofluorescence; NAAT, nucleic acid amplification test; NGU, nongonococcal urethritis; OIF, oil immersion field; PMN, polymorphonuclear neutrophil; UA, urinalysis.

Sexually Reactive Arthritis

Reactive arthritis by definition is an immune-mediated inflammatory response in the joints to a primary infection at a distant mucosal site.[171] Although enteric infections such as salmonella, shigella, campylobacter, or yersinia can provoke reactive arthritis, chlamydial infections appear to be a very common triggering event as well. Approximately 1% of men presenting with NGU develop an acute aseptic arthritis syndrome referred to as sexually reactive arthritis. One third of these have the full complex of Reiter's syndrome, namely arthritis, conjunctivitis, urethritis, and skin lesions.[172] In men with untreated Reiter's syndrome who have urethritis, *C. trachomatis* can be recovered from the urethra in as many as 69% at the onset of the acute arthritis.[173] Reiter's syndrome patients have elevated synovial and serum antibody levels to *C. trachomatis*,[173] and it has been reported that patients who develop Reiter's syndrome after chlamydial urethritis have antibodies in sera and synovial fluid directed against cHSP60.[174] Approximately 80% of Reiter's syndrome patients also have the histocompatibility marker HLA-B27.[172] Furthermore, in addition to Reiter's syndrome, there appears to be an association between chlamydial infection, HLA-B27, and undifferentiated oligoarthritis.[175]

Synovial lymphocytes from Reiter's syndrome patients show higher proliferative responses in vitro to chlamydial antigens than do peripheral blood lymphocytes from the same patients or synovial fluid lymphocytes from control patients.[171] These and other data suggest that *C. trachomatis* may be present in the joints of afflicted patients but in a form that either cannot be cultured or is very difficult

to culture. Early reports suggested that *C. trachomatis* could be recovered by culture from the synovial membranes of at least some patients with Reiter's syndrome,[176,177] but more recent studies have not confirmed this even with improvements in isolation technique.[171] However, organisms with morphology consistent with *Chlamydia* have been identified in the synovium of Reiter's syndrome patients by electron microscopy, immunocytochemical staining,[171,173] and molecular hybridization and amplification techniques,[171] suggesting that *Chlamydia* may persist in some form in the synovial membranes of patients with Reiter's syndrome. Similar studies have been done with enteric organisms associated with reactive arthritis. Chlamydial DNA was found in synovial biopsies together with mRNA detected by reverse transcriptase PCR, suggesting that the detectable forms and DNA represent viable, persistent organisms.[178] These persistent chlamydiae exhibit aberrant gene expression, with no *OMP1* mRNA detected but with detectable cHSP60 mRNA.[178] A double-blind study comparing lymecycline (tetracycline-L-methylene lysine) and placebo in patients with reactive arthritis suggested that 3 months of treatment was efficacious in arthritis associated with chlamydial infection but not in reactive arthritis associated with other causes.[179] Furthermore, when patients with Reiter's syndrome were treated for genitourinary infections with antichlamydial antibiotics, the incidence of arthritic relapses was significantly reduced compared with that observed in patients left untreated or treated with penicillin.[180] These data have led some to suggest that patients with Reiter's syndrome should receive prompt antichlamydial therapy for arthritic recurrences and any genitourinary complaints suggestive of a chlamydial infection.[181]

Genital Infection in Women

Although most infected women are asymptomatic, it is women who suffer the most serious consequences of genital chlamydial infections. Risk factors for infection vary in different population groups, but in most circumstances being a sexual partner of a man with either gonococcal urethritis or NGU confers a risk of infection in excess of 30%.[7,159] In the United States, higher prevalence rates in sexually active individuals have been associated with younger age, African American ethnicity, unmarried status, new or multiple sexual partners, and oral contraceptive use.[6,7,182] Higher rates are also seen in the southeastern part of the country. Young age is the single factor most strongly associated with increased risk of chlamydial infection among sexually active females. In addition, young age is associated with an increased risk of repeated infection[183] and with an associated increased risk of PID, ectopic pregnancy, and infertility.[184] Oral contraceptives may truly increase susceptibility or ease detection because of an increase in cervical ectopy in exposed susceptible cells. Alternatively, oral contraceptive use may be a surrogate marker for increased sexual activity.[182] In some studies,[185] but not others,[151] a recent change of sexual partners and increased numbers of partners have also been associated with increased prevalence.

The natural history of endocervical infection with *C. trachomatis* in women is not known. In most animal models, including primates, an immune response is mounted after infection or reinfection, and the organism can no longer be cultured.[186] It is likely that this occurs in a substantial proportion of infected women as well, or the women may inadvertently receive effective antichlamydial therapy for some other indication. However, other data suggest that chlamydiae can persist in an asymptomatic state for prolonged periods of time in the female genital tract. In 14 infected college women who were observed for a minimum of 15 months without specific treatment, 7 remained infected.[187] Likewise, 68 of 85 (80%) infected adolescent women who remained asymptomatic were still infected when reevaluated 2 months or more after their initial evaluation.[188] Other examples of persistent infection in humans include a case of LGV from which the organism was recovered after 20 years,[189] persistence of organisms in the synovium of patients with Reiter's syndrome,[171,178] detection of chlamydial DNA in fallopian tube biopsy specimens from infertile women,[190] infants persistently infected for up to 28 months,[191] young women persistently infected with genetically identical strains for up to 5 years,[192] and recovery of *C. trachomatis* from the fallopian tubes and endometrium of infertile women in circumstances in which recent acquisition of infection was unlikely.[108]

Cervicitis and Urethritis

Mucopurulent cervicitis caused by *C. trachomatis* has been called the female counterpart of male NGU. Approximately 70% of women with endocervical infection have no symptoms or have only mild symptoms such as vaginal discharge, bleeding, mild abdominal pain, or dysuria.[7] Dysuria may reflect concurrent urethral infection. A vaginal discharge in such women is attributable to endocervical rather than vaginal infection because *C. trachomatis* cannot infect the squamous epithelium of the adult vagina. However, it can cause vaginitis before puberty when the vagina is lined with transitional cell epithelium. On examination, the cervix may appear normal or may exhibit edema, erythema, and hypertrophy with a mucopurulent discharge from the os.[54] Studies employing colposcopy emphasize the follicular nature of the cervicitis as well as erythema, ectopy, and easily induced mucosal bleeding.[193]

The acute urethral syndrome is defined as dysuria and frequency with fewer than 10^5 organisms per milliliter of urine.[194] In one study of 59 women with this syndrome, 42 also had pyuria and 11 of the 42 were infected with *C. trachomatis*, as were 3 of 66 women without symptoms and 1 of 35 women with cystitis related to *E. coli*. Most of the remainder of the women with pyuria and the urethral syndrome had low urine concentrations of *E. coli* or *Staphylococcus saprophyticus* demonstrated by culture of urine obtained by suprapubic aspiration.[194] Women with this clinical syndrome respond to appropriate antibiotics such as doxycycline. *C. trachomatis* has also been isolated from the Bartholin glands in women with bartholinitis. Although case-control studies have found an association between cervical dysplasia or neoplasia and *C. trachomatis* infection,[195,196] considerable evidence now supports the role of specific oncogenic types of human papillomavirus in the etiology of cervical cancer. Further, in prospective studies of women with human papillomavirus infections, concurrent chlamydial infection had little apparent effect on the course of their cervical lesions.[197] It is still possible that *C. trachomatis* may play an important role as a cofactor in the development of cervical neoplasia. Studies indicating that specific strains of *C. trachomatis* may be associated with cervical cancer support such a role.[198]

Of potentially far greater concern is the possible association between chlamydial cervicitis and acquisition of human immunodeficiency virus (HIV) infection by women.[199] In a case-control study of female prostitutes in Zaire, the adjusted odds ratio for HIV seroconversion with *C. trachomatis* infection was 3.6 with a 95% confidence interval of 1.4 to 9.1. Other data also support the idea that infections with *C. trachomatis* and other sexually transmitted agents increase shedding of HIV in genital secretions,[200] although not all studies have demonstrated this.[200] However, that infection with agents that produce genital mucosal inflammation would increase the risk of acquisition of HIV is not surprising and has substantial public health implications for control of the spread of HIV among heterosexuals.[200]

Endometritis and Salpingitis

The proportion of women with endocervical *C. trachomatis* infections who develop acute salpingitis has been estimated to be 8% but probably varies by population group.[7] Eighteen of 109 (16.5%) infected asymptomatic adolescent women observed for 2 months or more became symptomatic, but only 2 (1.8%) developed clinical PID.[188] However, when women infected with both *C. trachomatis* and *N. gonorrhoeae* were treated for gonorrhea with penicillin only, 6 of 20 (30%) developed acute salpingitis during a 7-day follow-up interim.[201] The broader term *pelvic inflammatory disease* is preferable to *salpingitis*, as the clinical entity usually encompasses clinically suspected endometritis, salpingitis, peritonitis, or a combination of these, and the presence of salpingitis has not been confirmed pathologically or by direct visual inspection of the fallopian tubes in most patients (e.g., laparoscopically).[202] The proportion of women presenting with acute PID from whom chlamydiae can be isolated from the urogenital tract ranges between 5% and 51%, depending on the population studied and the techniques used, but is most often approximately 20%.[7] Histologic evidence of plasma cell endometritis is present in most cases of laparoscopically verified salpingitis, suggesting early spread of the infection from the cervix to the endometrium in most patients.[203] Endometritis is also present in 40% of women with mucopurulent cervicitis and presumably progresses to salpingitis if untreated.[59]

The spectrum of PID associated with *C. trachomatis* infection ranges from acute, severe disease resembling gonococcal salpingitis, with associated perihepatitis and ascites, to completely or largely asymptomatic or "silent" salpingitis.[204] Subclinical, undiagnosed salpingitis appears to be far more common than acute disease. When women with chlamydial salpingitis are compared with women with gonococcal or with nongonococcal nonchlamydial salpingitis, the chlamydial group are more likely to experience a chronic, subacute course with a longer duration of abdominal pain before seeking medical care. Yet, they have as much or more tubal inflammation at laparoscopy.[205] In a prospective study of women randomly assigned to normal care or to chlamydial screening, routine screening of asymptomatic women for chlamydial infection followed by treatment of those identified as infected reduced the incidence of PID in a health maintenance organization setting.[206]

Infertility and Ectopic Pregnancy

The long-term consequences of both acute PID and silent, subclinical disease are tubal infertility, ectopic pregnancy, and chronic pelvic pain syndrome.[204] In developed countries, infertility affects approximately one in six couples, with tubal occlusion being a factor in 10% to 30%.[202] The mechanisms responsible for the tubal occlusion are not understood. In the case of *Chlamydia*, presumably they involve a combination of chronic inflammation and scarring induced by either recurrent or persistent infection. In a nonhuman primate model, repeated endocervical infections followed by a direct tubal inoculation of *C. trachomatis* produced peritubular adhesions as well as plasma cell endometritis.[207] Furthermore, women with nongonococcal salpingitis are more likely to have an adverse reproductive outcome than women with gonococcal salpingitis.[208]

In a prospective study of women who underwent laparoscopy for suspected PID,[209] those with verified salpingitis were observed for a mean of 94 months. Sixteen percent of the patients and 2.7% of the control subjects failed to conceive. Ten percent of patients and none of the control subjects had confirmed tubal factor infertility. Tubal factor infertility increased with increasing severity of infection as judged at the time of the index laparoscopy from 0.6% after a case of mild PID to 21.4% after a case of severe PID. It also increased with number of episodes of PID, from 8% after one episode to 19% after two and 40% after three. The ectopic pregnancy rate was 9.1% among patients versus 1.4% among control subjects.[209]

Most women with infertility related to tubular disease do not have a prior history of a sexually transmitted disease or of PID. However, a strong association between tubal infertility and serologic evidence of prior chlamydial infection has been a consistent observation in multiple studies.[7] Furthermore, *Chlamydia* has been recovered from fallopian tube biopsies in women undergoing microtuboplasty for surgical correction of damaged tubes,[108,110] and chlamydial DNA and antigens have been demonstrated by in situ hybridization in the fallopian tubes of infertile women from whom *Chlamydia* could not be recovered by culture.[210]

Case-control studies have also shown a strong association between ectopic pregnancy and serologic evidence of past chlamydial infection,[7] and in one study 22% of women experiencing ectopic pregnancy had histologic evidence of plasma cell salpingitis as well as antichlamydial antibodies.[211] Moreover, 81% of women experiencing ectopic pregnancy who had high titers of antichlamydial antibodies had specific antibody to cHSP60,[67] suggesting that hypersensitivity induced by this protein may play a role in tubal damage. In addition, presence of cHSP60 antibodies predicted a two- to threefold increased risk of PID.[73] However, further studies are needed to define the role of persistent, as opposed to prior, infection in ectopic pregnancy.

Pregnancy Complications

Women experiencing recurrent spontaneous abortions were found to have high titers of antichlamydial IgG but negative endocervical cultures for *C. trachomatis*,[212] raising the possibility that prior or persistent *C. trachomatis* infection of the endometrium may be associated with some spontaneous abortions. Existing data on the effect of *C. trachomatis* infections on pregnancy outcome are conflicting. Several studies[213] found no association between adverse outcome and *C. trachomatis* infection, although a subset of women with IgM antibody against *C. trachomatis* (indicating recent infection) had infants with lower birth weight than those of women lacking specific IgM.[214] Other investigators found an association between chlamydial infection and prematurity and premature rupture of the membranes.[215,216]

In one large treatment study, a comparison of pregnancy outcomes was carried out in 1110 women who were infected with *C. trachomatis* but not treated, 1323 infected women who were treated with erythromycin, and 9111 uninfected, untreated women.[217] There was a significant association between treatment and a decrease in premature rupture of the membranes with an odds ratio of 0.56 (0.37 to 0.85). In addition, there was a trend toward increased perinatal survival with an odds ratio of 2.21 (0.89 to 5.49, *p* <.08).

Pregnancy outcomes have also been compared in 244 treated women who were cured of a *C. trachomatis* infection and 79 treated women who had a persistent or recurrent infection.[218] Successful treatment was found to decrease the frequency of premature rupture of the membranes and small-for-gestational-age infants.

These studies suggest that identification and treatment of *C. trachomatis* infection in pregnancy are likely to improve pregnancy outcome as well as prevent infant infection. However, more definitive data are needed. A major difficulty in such studies is the potential interaction of many infections that may influence pregnancy outcomes, including mycoplasmas, urinary tract infections and vaginal colonization with gram-negative rods, herpesviruses such as cytomegalovirus, trichomonas, and bacterial vaginosis. Studies need to evaluate and analyze all of these factors comprehensively, which make such studies both large and complex.[219]

Other Infections

Pneumonia caused by *C. trachomatis* is primarily a disease of infants, although there have been isolated reports of *C. trachomatis* pneumonia in immunocompromised patients.[220] In addition, pulmonary infection may occur in laboratory workers exposed to relatively high concentrations of LGV serovars. Previously reported serologic associations with community-acquired pneumonia[221] probably reflected cross-reacting antibody with then-unrecognized *C. pneumoniae*. *C. trachomatis* has also been associated in case reports or in case-control studies serologically with meningoencephalitis,[222] myocarditis,[223] and endocarditis.[224]

Treatment of Genital and Ocular Infections in Adults

The antibiotics that have excellent activity against *Chlamydia* in cell culture include the tetracyclines, macrolides and related compounds, rifampin, and some of the fluoroquinolones.[225] Although chlamydiae lack peptidoglycan, ampicillin and penicillin, both of which penetrate eukaryotic cells to a limited degree, have some activity, whereas cephalosporins and aminocyclitols do not. Considerable clinical data are available on the treatment of uncomplicated urogenital tract infections in both men and women. These data have been utilized to develop guidelines for the prevention and management of *C. trachomatis* infections.[6] For many years, standard therapy for uncomplicated genital tract infection has been doxycycline, 100 mg orally, twice daily for 7 days, with erythromycin as the first alternative. However, azithromycin given as a single 1-g dose has been found to be as effective as a 7-day course of doxycycline[226] and is the recommended regimen in the most recent guidelines for the treatment of sexually transmitted diseases from the CDC. This is the only antimicrobial agent effective against *C. trachomatis* infection as single-dose therapy, which eliminates lack of compliance as a source of treatment failure. However, studies indicate that there may be early recurrences of chlamydial infection in as many as 5% to 13% of adolescents treated with azithromycin.[227,228] Reinfection probably accounts for some of these early recurrences, but persistent infection despite treatment may have occurred in some cases.[228] As yet, antimicrobial resistance among wild-type chlamydiae has not been demonstrated to be a clinically important problem.[229] Resistance can be induced in the laboratory to fluoroquinolones and other drugs, however. Azithromycin has also been shown to be effective in the treatment of the NGU syndrome, whether related to *C. trachomatis*, genital mycoplasmas, or neither.[230] Ofloxacin at a dose of 300 mg twice daily for 7 days has been approved by the U.S. Food and Drug Administration for uncomplicated *C. trachomatis* infections. However, it should not be used in adolescents younger than 18 years or in pregnant women.[6] Azithromycin is considerably more expensive than doxycycline, and relative costs are a consideration in choice of therapy. Given the excellent efficacy achieved with doxycycline in compliant patients, it may be preferable in such groups. Cost-effectiveness studies have suggested that despite its higher purchase price, azithromycin is cost-effective in the long run because of complications averted with improved compliance.

Pregnant women unable to tolerate erythromycin at the standard dose of 500 mg four times a day for 7 days can be treated with 250 mg four times a day for 14 days or amoxicillin, 500 mg orally, three times a day for 7 to 10 days. There are fewer treatment failures in women who are able to complete a full course of erythromycin than in women who take amoxicillin.[231] However, amoxicillin appears to be more effective overall because of a lower frequency of side effects and better compliance.[231,232] Clindamycin is only partially effective in eradicating *C. trachomatis* in men with NGU,[233] but it appears to be as efficacious as erythromycin in both pregnant[234] and nonpregnant women.[235] Doxycycline and ofloxacin are contraindicated in pregnancy. Azithromycin has not been approved for use in pregnancy, and its safety and efficacy have not been extensively studied. However, small trials of azithromycin versus erythromycin in pregnancy suggest that it may be effective and well tolerated, and many clinicians now use the drug in this setting.[236]

Clinical conditions in which the likelihood of a chlamydial infection is high enough to warrant presumptive treatment for *C. trachomatis* in both the patient and sexual partners are NGU (heterosexual men), PID, epididymitis in men younger than 35, and gonococcal infection in either men or women.[6] Presumptive treatment of mucopurulent cervicitis alone is more controversial, and current guidelines suggest diagnostic testing with treatment based on test results as a reasonable approach.[141]

Proctitis in homosexual men and the acute urethral syndrome in women may be managed either by presumptive therapy or therapy based on test results. Empirical therapy of both proctitis and epididymitis should include treatment for gonorrhea, for example, ceftriaxone, 250 mg intramuscularly, in a single dose, followed by 7 to 10 days of doxycycline, 100 mg orally twice daily.[141] When chlamydial infection is proved or strongly suspected, partners with whom the person has had recent sexual contact should be treated.[6]

The management of PID, even when gonorrhea is present, should always include therapy directed against *C. trachomatis* as well as *N. gonorrhoeae* and anaerobic bacteria. Some experts recommend that initial therapy should be parenteral, followed by oral administration after initial improvement.[141] Recommended regimens include cefoxitin or cefotetan along with doxycycline, with the latter continued for a total of 14 days, or, alternatively, clindamycin and an aminoglycoside, again followed by doxycycline to complete a total of 14 days of therapy. An alternative to doxycycline is to continue clindamycin orally at a dose of 450 mg four times a day to complete 14 days of therapy.[141] Outpatient regimens include initial, single-dose, intramuscular therapy with a second- or third-generation cephalosporin plus 14 days of doxycycline. Alternatively, ofloxacin, 400 mg orally twice daily, plus oral metronidazole may be given.[141]

Few comparative data exist on the treatment of adult inclusion conjunctivitis, but tetracycline and its congeners (e.g., doxycycline) are effective when given for a 2- to 3-week period of time.[237] Erythromycin is an effective alternative.

Perinatal Infections

Neonatal Inclusion Conjunctivitis

Before the introduction of perinatal ocular prophylaxis for gonorrhea, it was assumed that all neonatal conjunctivitis was gonococcal in origin. However, even after prophylaxis for gonorrhea was introduced, neonatal conjunctivitis continued to occur, and conjunctival scrapings from neonates with conjunctivitis were shown to contain cells with cytoplasmic inclusions identical to those seen in patients with ocular trachoma. Subsequently, inclusions were demonstrated in cells from the cervix of the mother and the urethra of the father of an infected infant and in urethral scrapings from men with NGU. Infant infection is usually acquired during passage through an infected birth canal. Exceptions include occasional infants who seem to have acquired an infection perinatally in spite of birth by cesarean section[238] and infants who acquire the organism postnatally from an infected caregiver by hand-to-eye contact. Between 22% and 44% of infants born to infected women develop neonatal conjunctivitis, although approximately 60% have serologic evidence of infection.[239] The usual incubation period is 5 to 12 days from birth, although the onset may be as late as 6 weeks of age.[240] Typically, a watery ocular discharge appears, which becomes progressively more purulent. The eyelids swell and the conjunctivae become erythematous and thickened. At birth, the conjunctiva lacks a lymphoid layer, and so follicles do not develop initially but may become apparent after 3 to 6 weeks.

The progression of the disease is very similar to that described for adults, with spontaneous resolution occurring in most untreated infants after 3 to 12 months.[241] However, mild or subclinical infection may persist for several years,[191] and late sequelae such as scars and corneal lesions occur in a small proportion of cases.[242] A mucopurulent rhinitis, and in female infants vulvovaginitis, is often associated with the conjunctivitis. The primary differential diagnosis in a newborn is gonococcal ophthalmia, which is uncommon in children who receive ocular prophylaxis at birth but does still occur.[243] Ocular prophylaxis does not seem to be effective against *C. trachomatis* infection even when erythromycin or tetracycline is applied topically.[243]

Infant Pneumonia

Between 11% and 20% of infants born to infected mothers develop pneumonia caused by *C. trachomatis*.[244] Infected infants usually become symptomatic before 8 weeks of age with nasal obstruction or discharge or both, tachypnea, and cough.[245] Presentation for care is usually between 4 and 11 weeks, and, characteristically, the infants have been symptomatic for 3 or more weeks before presentation. Most are only moderately ill and are afebrile.[246] A history of conjunctivitis is present in approximately one half of infants and middle ear abnormalities in more than half.[245] Paroxysms of staccato coughing that interfere with sleeping and eating are sometimes present. Auscultation may reveal scattered crackles, but breath sounds are usually good and wheezing absent. Chest radiographs show bilateral interstitial infiltrates with hyperinflation (Fig. 177-4).[245] Peripheral eosinophilia, arterial hypoxemia, and elevated serum immunoglobulins are characteristic.[245-247] *C. trachomatis* can usually be recovered from nasopharyngeal swab specimens and antichlamydial IgM titers are elevated.[244]

Untreated, the course is protracted, often lasting weeks to months.[246] Especially in very young infants, the initial respiratory manifestations of *C. trachomatis* infection may be more severe and include prolonged spells of apnea or respiratory failure.[248,249] Although published reports emphasize more serious disease, it is likely that most patients with *C. trachomatis* infant pneumonia are treated as outpatients, often without laboratory confirmation of diagnosis. However, follow-up for as long as 8 years of children who had chlamydial pneumonia in the first 6 months of life has demonstrated a higher than normal frequency of obstructive airway disease (by pulmonary function testing) and of physician-diagnosed asthma.[250,251] Thus, long-term respiratory sequelae may be significant.

Perinatally acquired *C. trachomatis* infection may persist in the nasopharynx, urogenital tract, or rectum for more than 2 years.[191] Consequently, differentiating infection acquired at birth from infection related to sexual abuse may be particularly difficult in younger children. In older children, oropharyngeal infection with *C. trachomatis* needs to be differentiated from that with *C. pneumoniae*. For this reason and because of problems with specificity with the nonculture tests, cell culture testing using *C. trachomatis*–specific fluorescent antibody to detect inclusions should be used for diagnosis of infections in the genitalia, rectum, or pharynx in children.[141]

Prevention and Treatment of Infant Infections

Topical treatment of inclusion conjunctivitis is not recommended primarily because of difficulty in application and failure to eliminate concurrent nasopharyngeal carriage.[252] The latter can result in either recurrent conjunctivitis, pneumonia, or both.[252] Recommended therapy is oral erythromycin in doses of 50 mg/kg of body weight per day in four divided doses for 10 to 14 days. The efficacy of therapy is approximately 80%, and a second course may be required.[253] The course

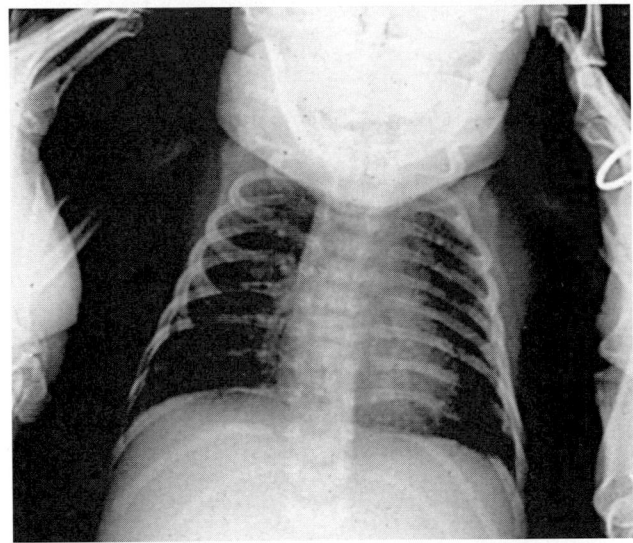

A

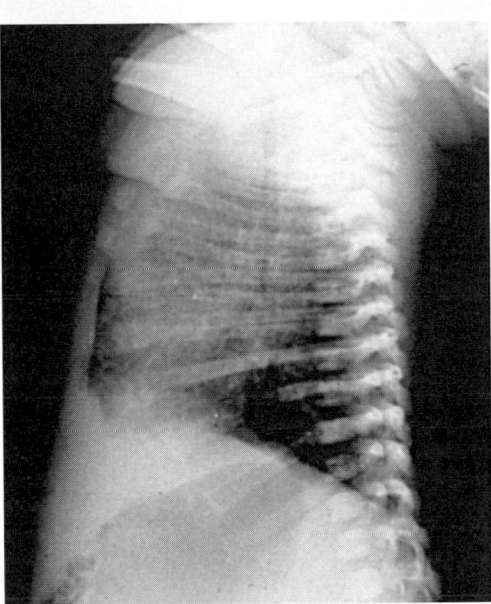

B

FIGURE 177-4. A and **B,** Chest radiographs of a 2-month-old infant with *Chlamydia trachomatis* pneumonia demonstrate typical patchy interstitial infiltrates and flattened diaphragms. *(Courtesy of Dr. John Gaebler, Indianapolis, Ind.)*

of therapy for *C. trachomatis* pneumonia is the same as that for conjunctivitis, and the efficacy is also approximately 80%. Mothers of infants with *C. trachomatis* should be evaluated and treated appropriately, as should their sexual partners.

Prenatal screening for chlamydia and treatment of infected women is approximately 90% effective in preventing their infants from acquiring infection.[253] However, in populations at high risk for reinfection, particularly adolescents, reacquisition of infection after the first trimester is frequent,[254] and repeated prenatal screening may be warranted in this population.

PREVENTION STRATEGIES

Primary prevention strategies involve (1) inducing behavioral changes that reduce the risk of acquisition of chlamydial infections as well as other sexually transmitted diseases and (2) identification and treatment

TABLE 177-4 Screening for Chlamydial Infection, U.S. Preventive Services Task Force, 2001

Screen all sexually active women ≤25
Screen other high-risk* women
Screen pregnant women ≤ 25
Screen older high-risk* pregnant women
Insufficient evidence to recommend male screening at present

*High-risk women as defined in various populations can include women ≤ 25, unmarried, African American, prior sexually transmitted disease, new or multiple sexual partners, cervical ectopy, inconsistent use of barrier contraceptives.

of persons with genital infection before they can transmit the infection. Behaviors that reduce risk of infection include delaying age of first intercourse, decreasing numbers of partners, and use of condoms. The use of vaginal microbicides such as vaginal sponges containing the spermicide nonoxynol 9 may be of value.[6,255-257] Nonoxynol 9 has in vitro activity against *C. trachomatis*[258] and in two controlled trials was shown to reduce male-to-female transmission.[255,256] However, a more recent controlled trial showed that nonoxynol 9 did not reduce the rate of male-to-female new chlamydia infection,[259] and nonoxynol 9 exhibits in vitro toxicity to cervical cells[258] and increases the likelihood of vaginal yeast infection.[256] Other microbicides are under development that may be more effective and less toxic than nonoxynol 9.

Programs that appear effective in reducing transmission of *C. trachomatis* include screening of high-risk populations for asymptomatic infections and partner notification and treatment. Indications for screening women have been published and are summarized in Table 177-4.

Because of the high frequency of repeated chlamydial infections within the first several months after treatment of an initial infection,[228,260] more frequent (e.g., every 6 months) screening of asymptomatic sexually active adolescents may be important in some populations.[261] The feasibility of employing noninvasive screening (i.e., urine testing or use of self-collected vaginal swabs) of sexually active young men and women has been proved using NAATs (PCR, LCR), particularly in nontraditional settings such as high schools, military intake centers, juvenile detention centers, and other nonclinic sites in the community.[122-124,262] Also promising is the potential use of the leukocyte esterase test to identify asymptomatic adolescent men with pyuria for further evaluation with more expensive amplification tests.[163,263] The benefits of screening women have been clearly demonstrated and include a declining prevalence of infection and of PID in the screened population over time. A randomized trial of screening using selective screening criteria in a health maintenance organization demonstrated a 60% reduction in PID among screened women over 12 months of follow-up.[206]

Notification and treatment of sexual partners are also effective in reducing infection and can be shown to be cost-effective in spite of the resources required.[264,265] Innovative approaches to improve the effectiveness of sex partner management are under study, including provision of empirical single-dose antibiotic therapy through the index case and solicitation of mailed-in urine or swabs for NAAT testing. In Sweden, where there is an extensive educational and control program using the previously mentioned elements, there has been a dramatic decline in chlamydial infections over the last decade.[265,266] In addition, in selected areas in the United States that have many of these elements in place, such as the states of Washington[267] and Wisconsin[257] and the city of Indianapolis,[268] significant declines in the prevalence of *C. trachomatis* infection have been observed.

REFERENCES

1. Schachter J, Dawson CR. Human Chlamydial Infections. Littleton, Mass: PSG Publishing; 1978:63-96.
2. Institute of Medicine Committee on Prevention and Control of Sexually Transmitted Diseases. In: Eng T, Butler E, eds. The Hidden Epidemic: Confronting Sexually Transmitted Diseases. Washington, DC: National Academy Press; 1997:1-411.

3. Centers for Disease Control and Prevention. Sexually Transmitted Disease Surveillance 2000. Atlanta, Ga: Division of Sexually Transmitted Diseases, National Center for HIV, STD, and TB Prevention; 2001:7-13.

4. Tracking the Hidden Epidemics: Trends in STDs in the United States 2000. Atlanta, Ga: Centers for Disease Control and Prevention; 2001:1-31.

5. Thylefors B. Development of trachoma control programs and the involvement of national resources. Rev Infect Dis. 1985;7:774-776.

6. Centers for Disease Control and Prevention. Sexually Transmitted Disease Surveillance 2001 Supplement, Chlamydia Prevalence Monitoring Project. Atlanta, Ga: Centers for Disease Control and Prevention; 2002.

7. Cates W Jr, Wasserheit JN. Genital chlamydial infections: Epidemiology and reproductive sequelae. Am J Obstet Gynecol. 1991;164:1771-1781.

8. Podgore JK, Holmes KK, Alexander ER. Asymptomatic urethral infections due to Chlamydia trachomatis in male U.S. military personnel. J Infect Dis. 1982;146:828.

9. Karam GH, Martin DH, Flotte TR, et al. Asymptomatic Chlamydia trachomatis infections among sexually active men. J Infect Dis. 1986;154:900-903.

10. Rockey DD. Chlamydial interactions with host cells. In: Schachter J, Christiansen G, Clarke IN, et al, eds. Chlamydial Infections: Proceedings of the 10th International Symposium on Human Chlamydial Infection, International Chlamydia Symposium, San Francisco; 2002:35-44.

11. Duensing TD, Wing JS, van Putten JP. Sulfated polysaccharide–directed recruitment of mammalian host proteins: A novel strategy for microbial pathogenesis. Infect Immun. 1999;67:4463-4468.

12. Stephens RS. The cellular paradigm of chlamydial pathogenesis. Trends Microbiol. 2003;11:44-51.

13. Stephens RS, Koshiyama K, Lewis E, Kubo A. Heparin-binding outer membrane of chlamydiae. Mol Microbiol. 2001;40:691-699.

14. Wyrick PB, Choong J, Davis CH, et al. Entry of genital Chlamydia trachomatis into polarized human epithelial cells. Infect Immun. 1989;57:2378-2389.

15. Hodinka RL, Davis CH, Choong J, et al. Ultrastructural study of endocytosis of Chlamydia trachomatis by McCoy cells. Infect Immun. 1988;56:1456-1463.

16. Tipples G, McClarty G. The obligate intracellular bacterium Chlamydia trachomatis is auxotrophic for three of the four ribonucleoside triphosphates. Mol Microbiol. 1993;8:1105-1114.

17. Peeling R, Peeling J, Brunham R. High-resolution ^{31}P nuclear magnetic resonance study of Chlamydia trachomatis: Induction of ATPase activity in elementary bodies. Infect Immun. 1989;57:3338-3344.

18. Hatch TP, Miceli M, Sublett JE. Synthesis of disulfide-bonded outer membrane proteins during the developmental cycle of Chlamydia psittaci and Chlamydia trachomatis. J Bacteriol. 1986;165:379-385.

19. Bavoil P, Ohlin A, Schachter J. Role of disulfide bonding in outer membrane structure and permeability in Chlamydia trachomatis. Infect Immun. 1984;44:479-485.

20. Newhall WJ 5th. Biosynthesis and disulfide cross-linking of outer membrane components during the growth cycle of Chlamydia trachomatis. Infect Immun. 1987;55:162-168.

21. Moulder JW. Interaction of chlamydiae and host cells in vitro. Microbiol Rev. 1991;55:143-190.

22. Gerard HC, Krausse-Opatz B, Wang Z, et al. Expression of C. trachomatis genes encoding products required for DNA synthesis and cell division during active vs. persistent infection. Mol Microbiol. 2001;41:731-741.

23. Nicholson TL, Olinger L, Chong K, et al. Global stage-specific gene regulation during the developmental cycle of Chlamydia trachomatis. J Bacteriol. 2003;185:3179-3189.

24. Crenshaw RW, Fahr MJ, Wichlan DG, et al. Developmental cycle–specific host-free RNA synthesis in Chlamydia spp. Infect Immun. 1990;58:3194-3201.

25. Rockey DD, Stephens RS. Genome sequencing and our understanding of Chlamydia. Infect Immun. 2000;68:5473-5479.

26. Barry CE, Hayes SF, Hackstadt T. Nucleoid condensation in Escherichia coli that express a chlamydial histone homolog. Science. 1992;256:377-379.

27. Bavoil PM, Hsia R, Ojicius DM. Closing in on Chlamydia and its intracellular bag of tricks. Microbiology. 2000;146:2723-2731.

28. Subtil A, Blocker A, Dantry-Varsat A. Type III secretion system in Chlamydia species: Identified members and candidates. Microbes Infect. 2000;2:367-369.

29. Beatty WL, Byrne GL, Morrison RP. Morphologic and antigenic characterization of IFN-γ mediated persistent C. trachomatis infection in vitro. Proc Natl Acad Sci USA. 1993;90:3998-4002.

30. Wang SP, Grayston JT. Microimmunofluorescence antibody responses in Chlamydia trachomatis infection, a review. In: Mardh PA, Holmes KK, Oriel JD, et al, eds. Chlamydial Infections. Amsterdam: Elsevier Biomedical Press; 1982:301-316.

31. Wang SP, Kuo CC, Barnes RC, et al. Immunotyping of Chlamydia trachomatis with monoclonal antibodies. J Infect Dis. 1985;152:791-800.

32. Wang SP, Grayston JT. Three new serovars of Chlamydia trachomatis: Da, Ia, and L2a. J Infect Dis. 1991;163:403-405.

33. Fehlner-Gardiner C, Roshick C, Carlson JH, et al. Molecular basis defining human C. trachomatis tissue tropism: A possible role for tryptophan synthase. J Biol Chem. 2002;13:468-476.

34. Stephens RS, Wagar EA, Schoolnik GK. High-resolution mapping of serovar-specific and common antigenic determinants of the major outer membrane protein of Chlamydia trachomatis. J Exp Med. 1988;167:817-831.

35. Batteiger BE. The major outer membrane protein of a single Chlamydia trachomatis serovar can possess more than one serovar-specific epitope. Infect Immun. 1996;64:542-547.

36. Dean D, Millman K. Molecular and mutation trends analyses of omp1 alleles for serovar E of Chlamydia trachomatis. J Clin Invest. 1997;99:475-483.

37. Stothard DR, Boguslawski G, Jones RB. Phylogenetic analysis of the Chlamydia trachomatis major outer membrane protein and examination of potential pathogenic determinants. Infect Immun. 1998;66:3618-3625.

38. Brunham RC, Plummer FA, Stephens RS. Bacterial antigenic variation, host immune response, and pathogen-host coevolution. Infect Immun. 1993;61:2273-2276.

39. Hayes LJ, Pecharatana S, Bailey RL, et al. Extent and kinetics of genetic change in the omp1 gene of Chlamydia trachomatis in two villages with endemic trachoma. J Infect Dis. 1995;172:268-272.

40. Brunham RC, Kimani J, Bwayo J, et al. The epidemiology of Chlamydia trachomatis within a sexually transmitted diseases core group. J Infect Dis. 1996;173:950-956.

41. Mondesire RR, Maclean IW, Shewen PE, et al. Identification of genus-specific epitopes on the outer membrane complexes of Chlamydia trachomatis and Chlamydia psittaci immunotypes 1 and 2. Infect Immun. 1989;57:2914-2918.

42. Yuan Y, Lyng K, Zhang YX, et al. Monoclonal antibodies define genus-specific, species-specific, and cross-reactive epitopes of the chlamydial 60-kilodalton heat shock protein (hsp60): Specific immunodetection and purification of chlamydial hsp60. Infect Immun. 1992;60:2288-2296.

43. Belunis CJ, Mdluli KE, Raetz CRH, et al. A novel 3-deoxy-D-manno-octulosonic acid transferase from Chlamydia trachomatis required for expression of the genus-specific epitope. J Biol Chem. 1992;267:18702-18707.

44. Stephens RS, Kalman S, Fenner C, Davis R. Chlamydia Genome Project. http://chlamydia-www.berkeley.edu:4231; 1998.

45. Stephens RS, Mullenbach G, Sanchez Pescador R, et al. Sequence analysis of the major outer membrane protein gene from Chlamydia trachomatis serovar L2. J Bacteriol. 1986;168:1277-1282.

46. Allen JE, Stephens RS. Identification by sequence analysis of two-site posttranslational processing of the cysteine-rich outer membrane protein 2 of Chlamydia trachomatis serovar L2. J Bacteriol. 1989;171:285-291.

47. Wagar EA, Pang M. The gene for the S7 ribosomal protein of Chlamydia trachomatis: Characterization within the chlamydial str operon. Mol Microbiol. 1992;6:327-335.

48. Yuan Y, Zhang YX, Watkins NG, et al. Nucleotide and deduced amino sequences for the four variable domains of the major outer membrane proteins of the 15 Chlamydia trachomatis serovars. Infect Immun. 1989;57:1040-1049.

49. Dean D, Patton M, Stephens RS. Direct sequence evaluation of the major outer membrane protein gene variant regions of Chlamydia trachomatis subtypes D', I', and L2'. Infect Immun. 1991;59:1579-1582.

50. Lampe MF, Schland RJ, Stamm WE. Nucleotide sequence of the variable domains within the major outer membrane protein gene from serovariants of Chlamydia trachomatis. Infect Immun. 1993;61:213-219.

51. Weisburg WG, Hatch TP, Woese CR. Eubacterial origin of chlamydiae. J Bacteriol. 1986;167:570-574.

52. Kuo CC. Host response. In: Barron AL, ed. Microbiology of Chlamydia. Boca Raton, Fla: CRC Press; 1988:193-208.

53. Schachter J, Dawson CR. Human Chlamydial Infections. Littleton, Mass: PSG Publishing; 1978:45-62.

54. Brunham RC, Paavonen J, Stevens CE, et al. Mucopurulent cervicitis: The ignored counterpart in women of urethritis in men. N Engl J Med. 1984;311:1-6.

55. Griffin M, Pushpanathan C, Andrews W. Chlamydia trachomatis pneumonitis: A case study and literature review. Pediatr Pathol. 1990;10:843-852.

56. Braley AE. Inclusion blennorrhea. Am J Ophthalmol. 1938;21:1203-1207.

57. Rasmussen SJ, Eckmann L, Quayle AJ, et al. Secretion of proinflammatory cytokines by epithelial cells in response to Chlamydia infection suggests a central role for epithelial cells in chlamydial pathogenesis. J Clin Invest. 1997;99:77-87.

58. Ingalls RR, Rice PA, Qureshi N, et al. The inflammatory cytokine response to Chlamydia trachomatis infection is endotoxin mediated. Infect Immun. 1995;63:3125-3130.

59. Paavonen J, Kiviat N, Brunham RC, et al. Prevalence and manifestations of endometritis among women with cervicitis. Am J Obstet Gynecol. 1985;152:280-286.

60. Patton DL, Taylor HR. The histopathology of experimental trachoma: Ultrastructural changes in the conjunctival epithelium. J Infect Dis. 1986;153:870-878.

61. Patton DL, Kuo CC, Wang SP, et al. Distal tubal obstruction induced by repeated Chlamydia trachomatis salpingeal infections in pigtailed macaques. J Infect Dis. 1987;155:1292-1299.

62. Grayston JT, Wang SP, Lin HM, et al. Trachoma vaccine studies in volunteer students of the National Defense Medical Center. II. Response to challenge eye inoculation of egg grown trachoma virus. Chin Med J (Republic of China). 1961;8:312-318.

63. Grayston JT, Wang S. New knowledge of chlamydiae and the diseases they cause. J Infect Dis. 1975;132:87-105.

64. Taylor HR, Maclean IW, Brunham RC, et al. Chlamydial heat shock proteins and trachoma. Infect Immun. 1990;58:3061-3063.

65. Brunham RC, Peeling R, Maclean I, et al. Chlamydia trachomatis–associated ectopic pregnancy: Serologic and histologic correlates. J Infect Dis. 1992;165:1076-1081.

66. Eckert LO, Hawes SE, Wölner-Hanssen P, et al. Prevalence and correlates of antibody to chlamydial heat shock protein in women attending sexually transmitted disease clinics and women with confirmed pelvic inflammatory disease. J Infect Dis. 1997;175:1453-1458.

67. Money DM, Hawes SE, Eschenbach DA, et al. Antibodies to the chlamydial 60 kd heat-shock protein are associated with laparoscopically confirmed perihepatitis. Am J Obstet Gynecol. 1997;176:870-877.

68. Cerrone MC, Ma JJ, Stephens RS. Cloning and sequence of the gene for heat shock protein 60 from Chlamydia trachomatis and immunological reactivity of the protein. Infect Immun. 1991;59:79-90.

69. Morrison RP, Belland RJ, Lyng K, et al. Chlamydial disease pathogenesis: 57 kD chlamydial hypersensitivity antigen is a stress response protein. Exp Med. 1989;170:1271-1283.
70. Yi Y, Zhong G, Brunham RC. Continuous B cell epitopes in *Chlamydia trachomatis* heat shock protein 60. Infect Immun. 1993;61:1117-1120.
71. Domeika M, Domeika K, Paavonen J, et al. Humoral immune response to conserved epitopes of *Chlamydia trachomatis* and human 60-kDa heat-shock protein in women with pelvic inflammatory disease. J Infect Dis. 1998;177:714-719.
72. Zhong G, Brunham RC. Antibody responses to chlamydial heat shock proteins hsp60 and hsp70 are H2 linked. Infect Immun. 1992;60:3143-3149.
73. Peeling RW, Kimani J, Plummer F, et al. Antibody to chlamydial hsp60 predicts an increased risk for chlamydial pelvic inflammatory disease. J Infect Dis. 1997;175:1153-1158.
74. Peeling RW, Bailey RL, Conway DJ, et al. Antibody response to the 60-kDa chlamydial heat-shock protein is associated with scarring trachoma. J Infect Dis. 1998;177:256-259.
75. Zhong G, Peterson EM, Czarniecki CW, et al. Role of endogenous gamma interferon in host defense against *Chlamydia trachomatis* infections. Infect Immun. 1989;57:152-157.
76. Rothermel CD, Byrne GI, Havell EA. Effect of interferon on the growth of *Chlamydia trachomatis* in mouse fibroblasts (L cells). Infect Immun. 1983;39:362-370.
77. Rank RG, Ramsey KH, Pack EA, et al. Effect of gamma interferon on resolution of murine chlamydial genital infection. Infect Immun. 1992;60:4427-4429.
78. Morrison RP. New insights into a persistent problem—Chlamydial infections. J Clin Invest. 2003;111:1647-1649.
79. Grayston JT, Wang SP, Yeh LJ, et al. Importance of reinfection in the pathogenesis of trachoma. Rev Infect Dis. 1985;7:717-725.
80. Katz BP, Caine VA, Batteiger BE, et al. A randomized trial to compare 7- and 21-day tetracycline regimens in the prevention of recurrence of infection with *Chlamydia trachomatis*. Sex Transm Dis. 1991;18:36-40.
81. Blythe MJ, Katz BP, Batteiger BE, et al. Recurrent genitourinary chlamydial infections in sexually active female adolescents. J Pediatr. 1992;121:487-493.
82. Brunham RC, Kuo CC, Cles L, et al. Correlation of host immune response with quantitative recovery of *Chlamydia trachomatis* from the human endocervix. Infect Immun. 1983;39:1491-1494.
83. Alani MD, Darougar S, Burns DC, et al. Isolation of *Chlamydia trachomatis* from the male urethra. Br J Vener Dis. 1977;53:88-92.
84. Katz BP, Batteiger BE, Jones RB. Effect of prior sexual transmitted disease on the isolation of *Chlamydia trachomatis*. Sex Transm Dis. 1987;14:160-164.
85. Igietseme JU, Ramsey KH, Magee DM, et al. Resolution of murine chlamydial genital infection by the adoptive transfer of a biovar-specific, Th1 clone. Reg Immunol. 1994;5:317-324.
86. Su H, Feilzer K, Caldwell HD, Morrison RP. *Chlamydia trachomatis* genital tract infection of antibody-deficient gene knockout mice. Infect Immun. 1997;65:1993-1999.
87. Cotter TW, Meng Q, Shen ZL, et al. Protective efficacy of major outer membrane protein specific immunoglobulin A (IgA) and IgG murine monoclonal antibodies in a murine model of *Chlamydia trachomatis* genital tract infection. Infect Immun. 1995;63:4704-4714.
88. Igietseme JU, Black CM, Caldwell HD. *Chlamydia* vaccines—Strategies and status. Biodrugs. 2002;16:19-35.
89. Su H, Messer R, Whitmire W, et al. Vaccination against chlamydial genital tract infection after immunization with dendritic cells pulsed ex vivo with nonviable Chlamydiae. J Exp Med. 1998;188:809-818.
90. de la Maza LM, Peterson EM. Vaccines for *Chlamydia trachomatis* infections. Curr Opin Investig Drugs. 2002;3:980-986.
91. Zhang D, Yang X, Berry J, et al. DNA vaccination with the major outer membrane protein gene induces acquired immunity to *Chlamydia trachomatis* (mouse pneumonitis) infection. J Infect Dis. 1997;176:1035-1040.
92. Pal S, Barnhart KM. Abai AM, et al. Immunization of mice with expression plasmids containing DNA sequences corresponding to the *C. trachomatis* MOPN MOMP failed to protect against a genital challenge. In: Stephens RS, Byrne GI, Christiansen G, et al, eds. Chlamydial Infections: Proceedings of the Ninth International Symposium on Human Chlamydial Infection. International Chlamydial Symposium, San Francisco; 1998:438-441.
93. Black CM. Current methods of laboratory diagnosis of *Chlamydia trachomatis* infections. Clin Microbiol Rev. 1997;10:160-184.
94. Schachter J, Dawson CR. Human Chlamydial Infections. Littleton, Mass: PSG Publishing; 1978:181-219.
95. Dorman SA, Danos LM, Wilson DJ, et al. Detection of chlamydial cervicitis by Papanicolaou-stained smears and culture. Am J Clin Pathol. 1983;79:421-425.
96. Yoder BL, Stamm WE, Koester CM, et al. Microtest procedure for isolation of *Chlamydia trachomatis*. J Clin Microbiol. 1981;13:1036-1039.
97. Stamm WE, Tam M, Koester M, et al. Detection of *Chlamydia trachomatis* inclusions in McCoy cell cultures with fluorescein-conjugated monoclonal antibodies. J Clin Microbiol. 1983;17:666-668.
98. Jones RB, Van Der Pol B, Katz BP. Effect of differences in specimen processing and passage technique on recovery of *Chlamydia trachomatis*. J Clin Microbiol. 1989;27:894-898.
99. Mahony JB, Chernesky MA. Effect of swab type and storage temperature on the isolation of *Chlamydia trachomatis* from clinical specimens. J Clin Microbiol. 1985;22:865-867.
100. Lin JL, Jones WE, Yan L, et al. Underdiagnosis of *Chlamydia trachomatis* infection: Diagnostic limitations in patients with low-level infection. Sex Transm Dis. 1992;19:259-265.
101. Stamm WE. *Chlamydia trachomatis*—The persistent pathogen: Thomas Parran Award Lecture. Sex Transm Dis. 2001;28:684-689.
102. Barnes RC, Katz BP, Rolfs RT, et al. Quantitative culture of endocervical *Chlamydia trachomatis*. J Clin Microbiol. 1990;28:774-780.
103. Jones RB, Katz BP, Van Der Pol PB, et al. Effect of blind passage and multiple sampling on recovery of *Chlamydia trachomatis* from urogenital specimens. J Clin Microbiol. 1986;24:1029-1033.
104. Geisler WM, Suchland RJ, Whittington WLH, Stamm WE. Quantitative culture of *Chlamydia trachomatis*: Relationship of inclusion-forming units produced in culture to clinical manifestations and acute inflammation in urogenital disease. J Infect Dis. 2001;184:1350-1354.
105. Perine PL, Osoba AO. Lymphogranuloma venereum. In: Holmes KK, Mardh PA, Sparling PF, et al. eds. Sexually Transmitted Diseases. 2nd ed. New York: McGraw-Hill; 1990:195-204.
106. Schachter J, Grossman M, Holt J, et al. Infection with *Chlamydia trachomatis*: Involvement of multiple anatomic sites in neonates. J Infect Dis. 1979;139:232-234.
107. Moncada JV, Schachter J, Wofsy C. Prevalence of *Chlamydia trachomatis* lung infection in patients with acquired immune deficiency syndrome. J Clin Microbiol. 1986;23:986.
108. Shepard MK, Jones RB. Recovery of *Chlamydia trachomatis* from endometrial and fallopian tube biopsies in women with infertility of tubal origin. Fertil Steril. 1989;52:232-238.
109. Berger RE, Alexander ER, Monda GD, et al. *Chlamydia trachomatis* as a cause of acute "idiopathic" epididymitis. N Engl J Med. 1978;298:301-304.
110. Henry-Suchet J, Catalan F, Loffredo V, et al. *Chlamydia trachomatis* associated with chronic inflammation in abdominal specimens from women selected for tuboplasty. Fertil Steril. 1981;36:599-605.
111. Sherman JK, Jordan GW. Cryosurvival of *Chlamydia trachomatis* during cryopreservation of human spermatozoa. Fertil Steril. 1985;43:664-666.
112. Stamm WE. Diagnosis of *Chlamydia trachomatis* genitourinary infections. Ann Intern Med. 1988;108:710-717.
113. Moncada J, Schachter J, Bolan G, et al. Confirmatory assay increases specificity of the Chlamydiazyme test for *Chlamydia trachomatis* infection of the cervix. J Clin Microbiol. 1990;28:1770-1773.
114. Clarke LM, Sierra MF, Daidone BJ, et al. Comparison of the Syva MicroTrak enzyme immunoassay and Gen-Probe PACE 2 with cell culture for diagnosis of cervical *Chlamydia trachomatis* infection in a high-prevalence female population. J Clin Microbiol. 1993;31:968-971.
115. Chapin-Robertson K. Use of molecular diagnostics in sexually transmitted diseases. Critical assessment. Diagn Microbiol Infect Dis. 1993;16:173-184.
116. Ossewaarde JM, Rieffe M, Rozenberg-Arska M, et al. Development and clinical evaluation of polymerase chain reaction test for detection of *Chlamydia trachomatis*. J Clin Microbiol. 1992;30:2122-2128.
117. Viscidi RP, Bobo L, Hook EW, et al. Transmission of *Chlamydia trachomatis* among sex partners assessed by polymerase chain reaction. J Infect Dis. 1993;168:488-492.
118. Dille BJ, Butzen CC, Birkenmeyer LG. Amplification of *Chlamydia trachomatis* by ligase chain reaction. J Clin Microbiol. 1993;31:729-731.
119. Mahony JB, Luinstra KE, Waner J, et al. Interlaboratory agreement study of a double set of PCR plasmid primers for detection of *Chlamydia trachomatis* in a variety of genitourinary specimens. J Clin Microbiol. 1994;32:87-91.
120. Hook EW III, Smith K, Mullen C, et al. Diagnosis of genitourinary *Chlamydia trachomatis* infections by using the ligase chain reaction on patient-obtained vaginal swabs. J Clin Microbiol. 1997;35:2133-2135.
121. Bauwens JE, Clark AM, Loeffelholz MJ, et al. Diagnosis of *Chlamydia trachomatis* urethritis in men by polymerase chain reaction assay of first-catch urine. J Clin Microbiol. 1993;31:3013-3016.
122. Gaydos CA, Howell MR, Pare B, et al. *Chlamydia trachomatis* infections in female military recruits. N Engl J Med. 1998;339:739-744.
123. Rietmeijer CA, Yamaguchi KJ, Ortiz CG, et al. Feasibility and yield of screening urine for *Chlamydia trachomatis* by polymerase chain reaction among high-risk male youth in field-based and other nonclinic settings. Sex Transm Dis. 1997;24:429-435.
124. Cohen DA, Nsuami M, Etame RB, et al. A school-based chlamydia control program using DNA amplification technology. Pediatrics. 1998;101:E1.
125. Lifson AR, Halcon LL, Hannan P, et al. Screening for sexually transmitted infections among economically disadvantaged youth in a national job training program. J Adolesc Health. 2001;28:190-196.
126. Schachter J. Chlamydiae. In: Rose NR, Friedman H, eds. Manual of Clinical Immunology. 2nd ed. Washington, DC: American Society for Microbiology; 1980:700-706.
127. Mattila A, Miettinen A, Heinonen PK, et al. Detection of serum antibodies to *Chlamydia trachomatis* in patients with chlamydial and nonchlamydial pelvic inflammatory disease by the IPAzyme *Chlamydia* and enzyme immunoassay. J Clin Microbiol. 1993;31:998-1000.
128. Dawson CR, Schachter J. Strategies for treatment and control of blinding trachoma: Cost effectiveness of topical or systemic antibiotics. Rev Infect Dis. 1985;7:768-773.
129. Baral K, Osaki S, Shresta B, et al. Reliability of clinical diagnosis in identifying infectious trachoma in a low prevalence area of Nepal. Bull World Health Organ. 1999;11:461-466.
130. Taylor HR, Siler JA, Mkocha HA, et al. The natural history of endemic trachoma: A longitudinal study. Am J Trop Med Hyg. 1992;46:552-559.
131. Bailey R, Lietman T. The SAFE strategy for the elimination of trachoma by 2020—Will it work? Bull World Health Organ. 2001;79:233-236.
132. Kuper H, Solomon AW, Buchan J, et al. A critical review of the SAFE strategy for preventing blinding trachoma. Lancet Infect Dis. 2003;3:372-379.

133. Gaynor BD, Miao Y, Cevallos V, et al. Eliminating trachoma in areas with limited disease. Emerg Infect Dis. 2003;9:596-598.
134. Baily RL, Arullendraw P, Whittle HC, Mabey DC. Randomized controlled trial of single-dose azithromycin in treatment of trachoma. Lancet. 1993;342:453-456.
135. Schachter J, West SK, Mabey D, et al. Azithromycin in control of trachoma. Lancet. 1999;354:630-635.
136. D'Aunoy R, von Haam E. General reviews: Venereal lymphogranuloma. Arch Pathol. 1939;27:1032-1082.
137. Perine PL, Stamm WE. Lymphogranuloma venereum. In: Holmes KK, Sparing PF, et al, eds. Sexually Transmitted Diseases. 3rd ed. New York: McGraw-Hill; 1999; 423-432.
138. Coutts WE. Lymphogranuloma venereum: A general review. Bull World Health Organ. 1950;2:545-562.
139. Greenblatt RB. Antibiotics in treatment of lymphogranuloma venereum and granuloma inguinale. Ann NY Acad Sci. 1952;55:1082-1089.
140. Greaves AB, Hilleman MR, Taggart SR, et al. Chemotherapy in bubonic lymphogranuloma venereum: A clinical and serological evaluation. Bull World Health Organ. 1957;16:277-289.
141. Centers for Disease Control and Prevention. Sexually transmitted diseases treatment guidelines 2002. MMWR Recomm Rep. 2002; 51:1-80.
142. Schachter J, Dawson CR. Human Chlamydial Infections. Littleton, Mass: PSG Publishing; 1978:97-109.
143. Dawson CR, Schachter J. TRIC agent infections of the eye and genital tract. Am J Ophthalmol. 1967;63(Suppl):1288-1298.
144. Stenson S. Adult inclusion conjunctivitis: Clinical characteristics and corneal changes. Arch Ophthalmol. 1981;99:605-608.
145. Rönnerstam R, Persson K, Hansson H, et al. Prevalence of chlamydial eye infection in patients attending an eye clinic, a VD clinic, and in healthy persons. Br J Ophthalmol. 1985;69:385-388.
146. Stenberg K, Mardh PA. Genital infection with Chlamydia trachomatis in patients with chlamydial conjunctivitis: Unexplained results. Sex Transm Dis. 1991;18:1-4.
147. Lycke E, Löwhagen GB, Hallhagen G, et al. The risk of transmission of genital Chlamydia trachomatis infection is less than that of genital Neisseria gonorrhoeae infection. Sex Transm Dis. 1980;7:6-10.
148. Katz BP, Caine VA, Jones RB. Estimation of transmission probabilities for chlamydial infection. In: Bowie WR, Caldwell HD, Jones RP, et al, eds. Chlamydial Infections. Cambridge: Cambridge University Press; 1990:567-570.
149. Quinn TC, Gaydos C, Shepherd M, et al. Epidemiologic and microbiologic correlates of Chlamydia trachomatis infection in sexual partnerships. JAMA. 1996;276: 1737-1742.
150. Ramstedt K, Forssman L, Giesecke J, et al. Epidemiologic characteristics of two different populations of women with Chlamydia trachomatis infection and their male partners. Sex Transm Dis. 1991;18:205-210.
151. Hook EW 3d, Reichart CA, Upchurch DM, et al. Comparative behavioral epidemiology of gonococcal and chlamydial infections among patients attending a Baltimore, Maryland, sexually transmitted disease clinic. Am J Epidemiol. 1992;136:662-672.
152. Blythe MJ, Katz BP, Orr DP, et al. Historical and clinical factors associated with Chlamydia trachomatis genitourinary infection in female adolescents. J Pediatr. 1988;112:1000-1004.
153. Oriel JD, Ridgway GL. Studies of the epidemiology of chlamydial infection of the human genital tract. In: Mardh PA, Holmes KK, Piot P, et al, eds. Chlamydial Infections. Amsterdam: Elsevier Biomedical Press; 1982:425-428.
154. Batteiger BE, Fraiz J, Newhall WJ, et al. Association of recurrent chlamydial infection with gonorrhea. J Infect Dis. 1989;159:661-669.
155. Stamm WE, Cole B. Asymptomatic Chlamydia trachomatis urethritis in men. Sex Transm Dis. 1986;13:163-165.
156. Bowie WR, Alexander ER, Holmes KK. Etiologies of postgonococcal urethritis in homosexual and heterosexual men: Roles of Chlamydia trachomatis and Ureaplasma urealyticum. Sex Transm Dis. 1978;5:151-154.
157. Bowie WR, Wang SP, Alexander ER, et al. Etiology of nongonococcal urethritis. Evidence for Chlamydia trachomatis and Ureaplasma urealyticum. J Clin Invest. 1977;59:735-742.
158. Krieger JN, Verdon M, Siegel N, et al. Risk assessment and laboratory diagnosis of trichomoniasis in men. J Infect Dis. 1992;166:1362-1366.
159. Nettleman MD, Jones RB, Roberts SD, et al. Cost effectiveness of culturing for Chlamydia trachomatis. A study in a clinic for sexually transmitted diseases. Ann Intern Med. 1986;105:189-196.
160. Stamm WE, Koutsky LA, Benedetti JK, et al. Chlamydia trachomatis urethral infections in men. Prevalence, risk factors, and clinical manifestations. Ann Intern Med. 1984;100:47-51.
161. Bowie WR. Approach to men with urethritis and urologic complications of sexually transmitted diseases. Med Clin North Am. 1990;74:1543-1557.
162. Adger H, Sweet RL, Shafer MA, et al. Screening for Chlamydia trachomatis and Neisseria gonorrhoeae in adolescent males: Value of first-catch urine examination. Lancet. 1984;2:944-945.
163. Shafer MA, Schachter J, Moscicki AB, et al. Urinary leukocyte esterase screening test for asymptomatic chlamydial and gonococcal infections in males. JAMA. 1989;262:2562-2566.
164. Berger RE, Alexander ER, Harnisch JP, et al. Etiology, manifestations and therapy of acute epididymitis: Prospective study of 50 cases. J Urol. 1979;121:750-754.
165. Ruijs GJ, Kauer FM, Jager S, et al. Is serology of any use when searching for correlations between Chlamydia trachomatis infection and male infertility? Fertil Steril. 1990;53:131-136.
166. Shortliffe LMD, Sellers RG, Schachter J. The characterization of the nonbacterial prostatitis: Search for an etiology. J Urol. 1992;148:1461-1466.
167. Jones RB, Rabinovitch RA, Katz BP, et al. Recovery of Chlamydia trachomatis from the pharynx and rectum of heterosexual patients at risk for genital infection. Ann Intern Med. 1985;6:757-762.
168. Quinn TC, Goodell SE, Mkrtichian E, et al. Chlamydia trachomatis proctitis. N Engl J Med. 1981;305:195-200.
169. Annamunthodo H. Rectal lymphogranuloma venereum in Jamaica. Ann R Coll Surg Engl. 1961;28:141-159.
170. Stamm WE. Chlamydia trachomatis infections of the adult. In: Holmes KK, Mardh PA, Sparling PF, et al, eds. Sexually Transmitted Diseases. 3rd ed. New York: McGraw-Hill; 1999:407-422.
171. Rahman MU, Hudson AP, Schumacher HR Jr. Chlamydia and Reiter's syndrome (reactive arthritis). Rheum Dis Clin North Am. 1992;18:67-79.
172. Keat A, Thomas BJ, Taylor-Robinson D. Chlamydial infection in the aetiology of arthritis. Br Med Bull. 1983;39:168-174.
173. Keat A. Extragenital Chlamydia trachomatis infection as sexually-acquired reactive arthritis. J Infect. 1992;25(Suppl 1):47-49.
174. Inman RD, Morrison RP. Immunoblot analysis of reactivity to chlamydial 57-kD heat shock protein in Reiter's syndrome (Abstract). Arthritis Rheum. 1990;33:S26.
175. Sieper J, Braun J, Brandt J, et al. Pathogenetic role of Chlamydia, Yersinia and Borrelia in undifferentiated oligoarthritis. J Rheumatol. 1992;19:1236-1242.
176. Schachter J. Isolation of Bedsoniae from human arthritis and abortion tissues. Am J Ophthalmol. 1967;63(Suppl):1082-1086.
177. Vilppula AH, Yli-Kerttula UI, Ahlroos AK, Terho PE. Chlamydial isolation and serology in Reiter's syndrome. Scand J Rheumatol. 1981;10:181-185.
178. Gerard HC, Branigan PJ, Schumacher HR Jr, Hudson AP. Synovial Chlamydia trachomatis in patients with reactive arthritis/Reiter's syndrome are viable but show aberrant gene expression. J Rheumatol. 1998;25:734-742.
179. Lauhio A, Leirisalo-Repo M, Lähdevirta J, et al. Double-blind, placebo-controlled study of three-month treatment with lymecycline in reactive arthritis, with special reference to Chlamydia arthritis. Arthritis Rheum. 1991;34:6-14.
180. Bardin T, Enel C, Cornelis F, et al. Antibiotic treatment of venereal disease and Reiter's syndrome in a Greenland population. Arthritis Rheum. 1992;35:190-194.
181. Bardin T, Schumacher HR. Should we treat postvenereal Reiter's syndrome by antibiotics (Editorial)? J Rheumatol. 1991;18:1780-1782.
182. Washington AE, Gove S, Schachter J, et al. Oral contraceptives, Chlamydia trachomatis infection, and pelvic inflammatory disease. JAMA. 1985;253:2246-2250.
183. Hillis SD, Nakashima A, Marchbanks PA, et al. Risk factors for recurrent Chlamydia trachomatis infections in women. Am J Obstet Gynecol. 1994;170:801-806.
184. Hillis SD, Owens LM, Marchbanks PA, et al. Recurrent chlamydial infections increase the risks of hospitalization for ectopic pregnancy and pelvic inflammatory disease. Am J Obstet Gynecol. 1997;176:103-107.
185. Handsfield HH, Jasman LL, Roberts PL, et al. Criteria for selective screening for Chlamydia trachomatis infection in women attending family planning clinics. JAMA. 1986;255:1730-1734.
186. Wolner-Hanssen P, Patton DL, Holmes KK. Protective immunity in pigtailed macaques after cervical infection with Chlamydia trachomatis. Sex Transm Dis. 1991;18:21-25.
187. McCormack WM, Alpert S, McComb DE, et al. Fifteen-month follow-up study of women infected with Chlamydia trachomatis. N Engl J Med. 1979;300:123-125.
188. Rahm VA, Gnarpe H, Odlind V. Chlamydia trachomatis among sexually active teenage girls. Lack of correlation between chlamydial infection, history of the patient and clinical signs of infection. Br J Obstet Gynaecol. 1988;95:916-919.
189. Dan M, Rotmensch HH, Eylan E, et al. A case of lymphogranuloma venereum of 20 years' duration. Br J Vener Dis. 1980;56:344-346.
190. Campbell LA, Patton DL, Moore DE, et al. Detection of Chlamydia trachomatis deoxyribonucleic acid in women with tubal infertility. Fertil Steril. 1993;59:45-50.
191. Bell TA, Stamm WE, Wang SP, et al. Chronic Chlamydia trachomatis infections in infants. JAMA. 1992;267:400-402.
192. Dean D, Suchland RJ, Stamm WE. Evidence for long-term persistence of C. trachomatis by Omp-1 genotyping. J Infect Dis. 2000;182:909-916.
193. Dunlop EMC, Garner A, Darougar S, et al. Colposcopy, biopsy, and cytology results in women with chlamydial cervicitis. Genitourin Med. 1989;65:22-31.
194. Stamm WE, Wagner KF, Amsel R, et al. Causes of the acute urethral syndrome in women. N Engl J Med. 1980;303:409-415.
195. Hare MJ, Taylor-Robinson D, Cooper P. Evidence for an association between Chlamydia trachomatis and cervical intraepithelial neoplasia. Br J Obstet Gynaecol. 1982;89:489-492.
196. Schachter J, Hill EC, King EB, et al. Chlamydia trachomatis and cervical neoplasia. JAMA. 1982;248:2134-2138.
197. Yliskoski M, Tervahauta A, Saarikoski S, et al. Clinical course of cervical human papillomavirus lesions in relation to coexistent cervical infections. Sex Transm Dis. 1992;19:137-139.
198. Anttila T, Saikku P, Koskela P, et al. Serotypes of C. trachomatis and risk for development of cervical squamous cell carcinoma. JAMA. 2001;285:47-51.
199. Laga M, Manoka A, Kivuvu M, et al. Nonulcerative sexually transmitted diseases as risk factors for HIV-1 transmission in women: Results from a cohort study. AIDS. 1993;7:95-102.
200. Centers for Disease Control and Prevention. HIV prevention through early detection and treatment of other sexually transmitted diseases—United States. MMWR Morb Mortal Wkly Rep. 1998;47(RR-12):2-4.
201. Stamm WE, Guinan ME, Johnson C, et al. Effect of treatment regimens for Neisseria gonorrhoeae on simultaneous infection with Chlamydia trachomatis. N Engl J Med. 1984;310:545-549.
202. Cates W Jr, Rolfs RT Jr, Aral SO. Sexually transmitted diseases, pelvic inflammatory disease, and infertility: An epidemiologic update. Epidemiol Rev. 1990;12:199-220.

203. Paavonen J, Aine R, Teisala K, et al. Comparison of endometrial biopsy and peritoneal fluid cytologic testing and laparoscopy in the diagnosis of acute pelvic inflammatory disease. Am J Obstet Gynecol. 1985;151:645-650.

204. Paavonen J. Genital *Chlamydia trachomatis* infections in the female. J Infect. 1992;25(Suppl 1):39-45.

205. Svenssen L, Westrom L, Ripa KT, et al. Differences in some clinical and laboratory parameters in acute salpingitis related to culture and serologic findings. Am J Obstet Gynecol. 1980;138:1017-1021.

206. Scholes D, Stergachis A, Heidrich FC, et al. Prevention of pelvic inflammatory disease by screening for cervical chlamydial infection. N Engl J Med. 1996;334:1362-1366.

207. Patton DL, Wölner-Hanssen P, Cosgrove SJ, et al. The effects of *Chlamydia trachomatis* on the female reproductive tract of the *Macaca nemestrina* after a single tubal challenge following repeated cervical inoculations. Obstet Gynecol. 1990;76:643-650.

208. Brunham RC, Binns B, Guijon F, et al. Etiology and outcome of acute pelvic inflammatory disease. J Infect Dis. 1988;158:510-517.

209. Weström L, Joesoef R, Reynolds G, et al. Pelvic inflammatory disease and fertility: A cohort study of 1,844 women with laparoscopically verified disease and 657 control women with normal laparoscopic results. Sex Transm Dis. 1992;19:185-192.

210. Campbell LA, Patton DL, Moore DE, et al. Detection of *Chlamydia trachomatis* deoxyribonucleic acid in women with tubal infertility. Fertil Steril. 1993;59:45-50.

211. Brunham RC, Binns F, McDowell J, et al. *Chlamydia trachomatis* infection in women with ectopic pregnancy. Obstet Gynecol. 1986;67:722-726.

212. Witkin SS, Ledger WJ. Antibodies to *Chlamydia trachomatis* in sera of women with recurrent spontaneous abortions. Am J Obstet Gynecol. 1992;167:135-139.

213. McGregor JA, French JI. *Chlamydia trachomatis* infection during pregnancy. Am J Obstet Gynecol. 1991;164:1782-1789.

214. Berman SM, Harrison HR, Boyce WT, et al. Low birth weight, prematurity, and postpartum endometritis: Association with prenatal cervical *Mycoplasma hominis* and *Chlamydia trachomatis* infections. JAMA. 1987;257:1189-1194.

215. Gravett MG, Nelson HP, DeRouen T, et al. Independent associations of bacterial vaginosis and *Chlamydia trachomatis* infection with adverse pregnancy outcome. JAMA. 1986;256:1899-1903.

216. Martius J, Krohn MA, Hillier SL, et al. Relationships of vaginal *Lactobacillus* species, cervical *Chlamydia trachomatis*, and bacterial vaginosis to preterm birth. Obstet Gynecol. 1988;71:89-95.

217. Ryan GM Jr, Abdella TN, McNeeley SG, et al. *Chlamydia trachomatis* infection in pregnancy and effect of treatment on outcome. Am J Obstet Gynecol. 1990;162:34-39.

218. Cohen I, Vielle IC, Calkins BM. Improved pregnancy outcome following successful treatment of chlamydial infection. JAMA. 1990;263:3160-3163.

219. Hillier SL, Nugent RP, Eschenbach DA, et al. Association between bacterial vaginosis and preterm delivery of a low birth-weight infant. The Vaginal Infections and Prematurity Study Group. N Engl J Med. 1995;333:1737-1742.

220. Meyers JD, Hackman RC, Stamm WE. *Chlamydia trachomatis* infection as a cause of pneumonia after human marrow transplantation. Transplantation. 1983;36:130-134.

221. Komaroff AL, Aronson MD, Schachter J. *Chlamydia trachomatis* infection in adults with community-acquired pneumonia. JAMA. 1981;245:1319-1322.

222. Myhre EB, Mardh PA. *Chlamydia trachomatis* infection in a patient with meningoencephalitis. N Engl J Med. 1981;304:910-911.

223. Grayston JT, Mordhorst CH, Wang SP. Childhood myocarditis associated with *Chlamydia trachomatis* infection. JAMA. 1981;246:2823-2837.

224. van der Bel-Kahn JM, Watanakunakorn C, Menefee MG, et al. *Chlamydia trachomatis* endocarditis. Am Heart J. 1978;95:627-636.

225. Suchland RJ, Geisler WM, Stamm WE. Methodologies and cell lines used for antimicrobial susceptibility testing of *Chlamydia* spp. Antimicrob Agents Chemother. 2003;47:636-642.

226. Martin DH, Mroczkowski TF, Dalu ZA, et al. A controlled trial of a single dose of azithromycin for the treatment of chlamydial urethritis and cervicitis. N Engl J Med. 1992;327:921-925.

227. Hillis SD, Coles B, Litchfield B, et al. Doxycycline and azithromycin for prevention of chlamydial persistence or recurrence one month after treatment in women: A use-effectiveness study in public health settings. Sex Transm Dis. 1998;25:5-11.

228. Fortenberry JD, Brizendine EJ, Katz BP, et al. Subsequent STDs among adolescent women with *C. trachomatis*, *N. gonorrhoeae* or *T. vaginalis*. Sex Transm Dis. 1999;26:26-32.

229. Stamm WE, Geisler WM, Suchland RJ. Assessment of antimicrobial resistance in *C. trachomatis* strains associated with treatment failure or same strain recurrence. In: Schachter J, Christiansen G, Clarke IN, et al, eds. Chlamydial Infections, Proceedings of The Tenth International Symposium on Human Chlamydial Infections. International Chlamydial Symposium, San Francisco; 2002.

230. Stamm WE, Hicks CB, Martin DH, et al. Azithromycin for empirical treatment of the nongonococcal urethritis syndrome in men: A randomized double-blind study. JAMA. 1995;274:545-549.

231. Magat AH, Alger LS, Nagey DA, et al. Double-blind randomized study comparing amoxicillin and erythromycin for the treatment of *Chlamydia trachomatis* in pregnancy. Obstet Gynecol. 1993;81:745-749.

232. Crombleholme WR, Schachter J, Grossman M, et al. Amoxicillin therapy for *Chlamydia trachomatis* in pregnancy. Obstet Gynecol. 1990;75:752-756.

233. Bowie WR, Yu JS, Jones HD. Partial efficacy of clindamycin against *Chlamydia trachomatis* in men with nongonococcal urethritis. Sex Transm Dis. 1986;13:76-80.

234. Alger LS, Lovchik JC. Comparative efficacy of clindamycin versus erythromycin in eradication of antenatal *Chlamydia trachomatis*. Am J Obstet Gynecol. 1991;165:375-381.

235. Campbell WF, Dodson MG. Clindamycin therapy for *Chlamydia trachomatis* in women. Am J Obstet Gynecol. 1990;162:343-347.

236. Wehbeh HA, Ruggeirio RM, Shahem S, et al. Single-dose azithromycin for *Chlamydia* in pregnant women. J Reprod Med. 1998;43:509-514.

237. Viswalingam ND, Daroughar S, Yearsley P. Oral doxycycline in the treatment of adult chlamydial ophthalmia. Br J Ophthalmol. 1986;70:301-304.

238. Shariat H, Young M, Abedin M. An interesting case presentation: A possible new route for perinatal acquisition of chlamydia. J Perinatol. 1992;12:300-302.

239. Hammerschlag MR. Chlamydial infections in infants and children. In: Holmes KK, Mardh PA, Sparling PF, et al, eds. Sexually Transmitted Diseases. 3rd ed. New York: McGraw-Hill; 1999;1155-1164.

240. Chandler JW, Alexander ER, Pheiffer TA, et al. *Ophthalmia neonatorum* associated with maternal chlamydial infections. Trans Am Acad Ophthalmol Otolaryngol. 1977;83:302-308.

241. Schachter J, Dawson CR. Human Chlamydial Infections. Littleton, Mass: PSG Publishing; 1978:111-120.

242. Persson K, Rönnerstam R, Svanberg L, et al. Neonatal chlamydial eye infection: An epidemiological and clinical study. Br J Ophthalmol. 1983;67:700-704.

243. Hammerschlag MR, Cummings C, Roblin PM, et al. Efficacy of neonatal ocular prophylaxis for the prevention of chlamydial and gonococcal conjunctivitis. N Engl J Med. 1989;320:769-772.

244. Schachter J, Grossman M, Sweet RL, et al. Prospective study of perinatal transmission of *Chlamydia trachomatis*. JAMA. 1986;255:3374-3377.

245. Tipple MA, Beem MO, Saxon EM. Clinical characteristics of the afebrile pneumonia associated with *Chlamydia trachomatis* infection in infants less than six months of age. Pediatrics. 1979;63:192-197.

246. Beem MO, Saxon EM. Respiratory tract colonization and a distinctive pneumonia syndrome in infants infected with *Chlamydia trachomatis*. N Engl J Med. 1977;296:306-310.

247. Harrison HR, English MG, Lee CK, et al. *Chlamydia trachomatis* infant pneumonitis: Comparison with matched controls and other infant pneumonitis. N Engl J Med. 1978;288:702-708.

248. Wheeler WB, Kurachek SC, Lobas JG, et al. Acute hypoxemic respiratory failure caused by *Chlamydia trachomatis* and diagnosed by flexible bronchoscopy. Am Rev Respir Dis. 1990;142:471-473.

249. Broadbent R, O'Leary L. Chlamydial infections in young infants—A cause for concern. NZ Med J. 1988;101:44-45.

250. Brasfield DM, Stagno S, Whitley RJ, et al. Infant pneumonitis associated with cytomegalovirus, *Chlamydia*, *Pneumocystis*, and *Ureaplasma*: Follow-up. Pediatrics. 1987;79:76-83.

251. Weiss SG, Newcomb RW, Beem MO. Pulmonary assessment of children after chlamydial pneumonia of infancy. J Pediatr. 1986;108:659-664.

252. Heggie AD, Jaffe AC, Stuart LA, et al. Topical sulfacetamide vs oral erythromycin for neonatal chlamydial conjunctivitis. Am J Dis Child. 1985;139:564-566.

253. Pereira LH, Embil JA, Haase DA, et al. Cytomegalovirus infection among women attending a sexually transmitted disease clinic: Association with clinical symptoms and other sexually transmitted diseases. Am J Epidemiol. 1990;131:683-692.

254. Oh MK, Cloud GA, Baker SL, et al. Chlamydial infection and sexual behavior in young pregnant teenagers. Sex Transm Dis. 1993;20:45-50.

255. Louv WC, Austin H, Alexander WJ, et al. A clinical trial of nonoxynol 9 for preventing gonococcal and chlamydial infections. J Infect Dis. 1988;158:518-523.

256. Rosenberg MJ, Rojanapithayakorn W, Feldblum PJ, et al. Effect of contraceptive sponge on chlamydial infection, gonorrhea, and candidiasis. A comparative clinical trial. JAMA. 1987;257:2308-2312.

257. Addiss DG, Vaughn ML, Ludka D, et al. Decreased prevalence of *Chlamydia trachomatis* infection associated with a selective screening program in family planning clinics in Wisconsin. Sex Transm Dis. 1993;20:28-35.

258. Patton DL, Wang SK, Kuo CC. In vitro activity of nonoxynol 9 on HeLa 229 cells and primary monkey cervical epithelial cells infected with *Chlamydia trachomatis*. Antimicrob Agents Chemother. 1992;36:1478-1482.

259. Roddy RE, Zekeng L, Ryan KA, et al. A controlled trial of nonoxynol 9 film to reduce male-to-female transmission of sexually transmitted diseases. N Engl J Med. 1998;339:504-510.

260. Burstein GR, Gaydos CA, Diener-West M, et al. Incident *Chlamydia trachomatis* infection among inner-city adolescents. JAMA. 1998;280:521-526.

261. Orr DP, Fortenberry JD. Screening adolescents for sexually transmitted infections. JAMA. 1998;280:654-655.

262. Screening tests to detect *C. trachomatis and N. gonorrheal* infections—2002. MMWR Recomm Rep. 2002;51:1-38.

263. Bowden FJ. Reappraising the value of urine leukocyte esterase testing in the age of nucleic acid amplification. Sex Transm Dis. 1998;25:322-326.

264. Katz BP, Danos CS, Quinn TS, et al. Efficiency and cost effectiveness of field follow-up for patients with *Chlamydia trachomatis* infection in a sexually transmitted diseases clinic. Sex Transm Dis. 1988;15:11-16.

265. Ripa T. Epidemiologic control of genital *Chlamydia trachomatis* infections. Scand J Infect Dis. 1990;69(Suppl):157-167.

266. Herrmann BF, Johansson AB, Mardh PA. A retrospective study of efforts to diagnose infections by *Chlamydia trachomatis* in a Swedish county. Sex Transm Dis. 1991;18:233-237.

267. Britton JF, Delisle S, Fine D. STDs and family planning clinics: A regional program for *Chlamydia* control that works. Am J Gynecol Health. 1992;3:80-87.

268. Jones RB. Treatment of *Chlamydia trachomatis* infections of the urogenital tract. In: Bowie WR, Caldwell HD, Jones RP, et al, eds. Chlamydial Infections. Cambridge: Cambridge University Press; 1990;509-518.

CHAPTER 178

Chlamydophila (Chlamydia) psittaci (Psittacosis)

DAVID SCHLOSSBERG

Psittacosis is a systemic infection that frequently causes pneumonia. Its relationship to bird exposure has been known for more than a hundred years. In 1879, Ritter studied an outbreak in Switzerland and called it pneumotyphus.[1] Morange applied the term *psittacosis* (from the Greek word for parrot) in 1892 after studying cases associated with sick parrots. In 1930, the organism was identified in several laboratories, by Bedson in the United Kingdom, Kromwede in the United States, and Levinthal in Germany.[2]

The name psittacosis has persisted, even though the term *ornithosis* more accurately depicts the potential for all birds to spread this infection. In fact, even mammals, including humans, are rare sources of psittacosis.

The causative agent of psittacosis is *Chlamydophila psittaci.* Under a recently proposed classification, *C. psittaci* would now be grouped with *Chlamydophila pneumoniae, Chlamydophila pecorum, Chlamydophila abortus, Chlamydophila caviae,* and *Chlamydophila felis* in the genus *Chlamydophila* of the family Chlamydiaceae.[3]

EPIDEMIOLOGY

C. psittaci is common in birds and domestic animals. Infection is therefore a hazard to pet owners, pet shop employees, poultry farmers (turkey-associated psittacosis has the highest attack rate in psittacosis epidemics), workers in abattoirs and processing plants (psittacosis is the most common abattoir-associated pneumonia), and veterinarians. However, anyone in contact with an infected bird or animal is at risk. Human cases occur both sporadically and as outbreaks.[4]

Most patients with psittacosis have had some contact with a bird, usually as a pet. In fact, importation of exotic birds (sometimes illegal) has been correlated with an increase in human psittacosis in the United States, Sweden, England, and Wales. Often the bird was recently acquired or was ill. Bird contact may achieve surprising levels of intimacy. Patients have acquired psittacosis by kissing their parrot or by performing mouth-to-mouth resuscitation on a dying bird. Other patients have had more trivial or transient exposure, such as visits to public bird parks, transporting pigeons by car, passing through a room in which infected birds were sitting, sharing a stage with a parrot, or guarding crates of pigeons at a railroad depot. Still, some patients (25%) have had no avian exposure.[5]

Birds transmit the infection to their nestlings, which in turn shed the organism during periods of both illness and good health. In bird populations studied, there is a baseline prevalence of 5% to 8% of *C. psittaci* carriage. This may increase to 100% when birds are subjected to the stress of shipping, crowding, and breeding.[2,5]

It is likely that all birds are susceptible. More than 130 avian species have been documented as hosts of *C. psittaci.*[2] These include members of the parrot family (macaws, cockatoos, parakeets, budgerigars), finches (canaries, bullfinches, goldfinches, sparrows), poultry (hens, ducks, geese, turkeys), pigeons, pheasants, egrets, seagulls, and puffins.

Infection may appear in birds years after exposure. Infected birds may be asymptomatic or obviously sick. In the latter case, birds may exhibit shivering, depression, anorexia, emaciation, dyspnea, and diarrhea, frequently with closed eyes and ruffled feathers. Spontaneous relapse and remittance of the illness may occur, although it is during periods of illness that infected birds excrete the largest numbers of organisms. Discharge from their beaks and eyes and feces and urine are all infective; their feathers and the dust around their cage become contaminated.

The infection is generally spread by the respiratory route, by direct contact or aerosolization of infective discharges or dust. Rarely, the bird may spread the infection by a bite. If untreated, 10% of infected birds become chronic asymptomatic carriers.[5]

Strains from turkeys and psittacine birds are the most virulent for humans. Although most human exposure comes from avian strains of *C. psittaci,* disease has occurred in ranchers after exposure to infected tissues from parturient cows, goats, and sheep. Endocarditis has been attributed to avian and nonavian strains, and cats have spread feline pneumonitis to humans and other mammals. The growing practice of pet-associated therapy in nursing homes has produced a new epidemiologic risk for psittacosis.[6]

Human-to-human[7] and nosocomial[8] transmissions are rare and it is therefore thought unnecessary to isolate patients in the hospital or to give antibiotic prophylaxis to contacts. However, cases acquired from humans tend to be more severe than avian-acquired disease. Environmental sanitation is important because the organism is resistant to drying and can remain viable for months at room temperature.[2,5]

CLINICAL FINDINGS

The disease begins after an incubation period of 5 to 15 days. Onset may be insidious or abrupt, and the clinical manifestations tend to be nonspecific. Several syndromes may result. The infection may be subclinical, or it may resemble a nonspecific viral illness with fever and malaise, or a mononucleosis-like syndrome with fever, pharyngitis, hepatosplenomegaly, and adenopathy. A typhoidal form manifests as fever, bradycardia, malaise, and splenomegaly. Finally, the presentation most suggestive of the etiology is that of atypical pneumonia, with nonproductive cough, fever, headache, and chest film abnormalities more dramatic than would be suggested by the physical findings. The illness ranges in severity from an inapparent or mild disease to a fatal systemic illness with prominent respiratory symptoms.

Because many patients have an illness with nonspecific findings, the list of initial diagnoses for which patients have been referred to hospitals is extensive. This list reflects the various organ systems that may be involved in *C. psittaci* infection and includes the diagnoses of pneumonia, meningitis, gastroenteritis, hepatitis, urinary tract infection, endocarditis, vasculitis, septicemia, malaria, brucellosis, fever of unknown origin, pulmonary embolism, myocardial infarction, tonsillitis, pancreatic carcinoma, and polymyositis.[6,9]

The most common symptom is fever, occurring in 50% to 100% of patients. Cough has been reported in 50% to 100%, but often it appears late in the illness and is not present initially. Headache, myalgias, and chills are reported in 30% to 70% of patients. The nonspecificity of these signs and symptoms may be puzzling until cough supervenes. Even then, the long list of other signs and symptoms that occur in less than half the patients may be particularly confusing: diaphoresis, photophobia, tinnitus, ataxia, deafness, anorexia, nausea and vomiting, abdominal pain, diarrhea, constipation, sore throat, dyspnea, hemoptysis, epistaxis, arthralgia, and rash. Chest soreness is reported, but true pleuritic pain is rare.[4,5,9,10]

The signs most frequently reported are fever, pharyngeal erythema, rales or other abnormalities on chest auscultation, and hepatomegaly. These occur in more than half of the cases. Fewer than half the patients show the signs of somnolence, confusion, tachycardia, relative bradycardia, pleural rub, splenomegaly (this occurs toward the end of the first week and is helpful diagnostically), adenopathy, palatal petechiae, herpes labialis, Horder's spots (see later on), and muscle tenderness.[4,5,9]

Specific end-organ involvement reflects the systemic nature of psittacosis. The organ most commonly involved in humans is the lung. This is manifested clinically by cough, dyspnea, and a variety of nonspecific auscultatory findings on physical examination. Occasionally, the pneumonitis may progress to acute respiratory distress syndrome

(ARDS). Cardiac manifestations include pericarditis (rarely with effusion and tamponade), myocarditis, idiopathic dilated cardiomyopathy,[11] and "culture-negative" endocarditis. *C. psittaci* endocarditis is associated with preexisting heart disease and may cause valvular destruction. Arterial embolism to major vessels occurs rarely. The source of these emboli and the mechanism are unknown; some are attributed to endocarditis or mural thrombi.[12]

Hepatitis may develop, sometimes with jaundice. Anemia may result from hemolysis (both Coombs test positivity and cold agglutinins are reported) and from a reactive hemophagocytosis, in which case pancytopenia may be present. Disseminated intravascular coagulation (DIC) also complicates psittacosis.[13,14] Reactive arthritis occurs 1 to 4 weeks after the initial illness. Although most of the described cases are polyarticular, monoarticular arthritis has also been described.

Neurologic abnormalities include cranial nerve palsy (including sensorineural hearing loss), cerebellar involvement, transverse myelitis, confusion, meningitis, encephalitis, transient focal neurologic signs, and seizures. Results of cerebrospinal fluid examination on lumbar puncture are usually normal; a small number of white cells (predominantly lymphocytes) may be seen, and the protein on occasion is greatly elevated.[15-19]

Dermatologic phenomena include Horder's spots, which are a pink blanching maculopapular eruption resembling the rose spots of typhoid fever. Also described are erythema multiforme, erythema marginatum, erythema nodosum, and urticaria, as well as acrocyanosis, subungual splinter hemorrhages, and superficial venous thromboses. The kidney may develop an acute glomerulonephritis or acute tubulointerstitial nephritis, as well as acute tubular necrosis. Psittacosis has severe consequences in pregnancy and often causes DIC, hepatic dysfunction, and placentitis with fetal compromise.[20,21]

Also noted as complications of psittacosis are phlebitis, pancreatitis, and thyroiditis. Bacteremia has been demonstrated in a patient with a sarcoid-like illness.

There is no documented protection after infection, and second infections have been seen in spite of elevated levels of complement-fixing antibodies.[2] Treated birds can be reinfected also.

LABORATORY FINDINGS

The total white blood cell count is usually normal or slightly elevated. Two thirds of patients have a leftward shift. Eosinophilia has been seen in convalescence. Results on liver function testing are mildly abnormal in 50% of cases and may suggest cholestasis. Culture of the organism is possible from blood in the first 4 days of illness and from sputum in the first 2 weeks. However, although the organism can be isolated in cell culture and by animal inoculation, these methods are dangerous, and serologic diagnosis is preferred (see later).

Appearance on the chest film is abnormal in approximately 75% of patients (range, 50% to 90%) and is usually more abnormal than auscultation would predict. The most frequent finding is consolidation in a single lower lobe, seen in 90% of the abnormal chest films. However, a variety of patterns have been reported, including a homogeneous ground-glass appearance, a patchy reticular pattern radiating from the hila, segmental or lobar consolidation with or without atelectasis, a miliary pattern, and unilateral or bilateral hilar enlargement. These chest film findings may take as long as 20 weeks to resolve, with the occurrence of resolution by 6 weeks on average. Pleural effusions are seen in up to 50% of cases but are usually small and asymptomatic.[4] As noted, hilar enlargement may be present but never as the sole manifestation of disease.

PATHOLOGIC FINDINGS

Birds show involvement predominantly in the liver, spleen, and pericardium, but in humans the lung is most frequently and characteristically involved. The trachea and bronchi become inflamed, with widespread mucous plugging. The inflammation spreads from respiratory bronchioles to the alveoli in a lobular pattern. Alveolar and then interstitial exudate accumulates; this is composed of mononuclear cells with a few polymorphonuclear leukocytes, red blood cells, epithelial cells, and fibrin. There is hyperplasia, proliferation, and desquamation of alveolar lining cells, which contain basophilic intracytoplasmic inclusions. Hilar lymph nodes swell, and the lungs become rubbery and solid. The classic sequence of congestion, edema, and red and then gray hepatization is seen.

The brain is congested and edematous, with diffuse arachnoiditis. Meningeal exudate contains macrophages with intracytoplasmic inclusions. The heart shows monocytic infiltration, edema, fatty degeneration, and subendocardial hemorrhage. The pathologic findings in acute glomerulonephritis include hyaline glomerular occlusion, with subepithelial electron-dense deposits on electron microscopy. The liver may show nonspecific hepatitis or granulomas. Infected placental tissue shows intervillositis with trophoblastic cytoplasmic inclusions.[20] In emboli, polymorphonuclear leukocytes, platelets, and fibrin are seen, but not organisms or chlamydial antigen.[14]

DIAGNOSIS

Culture from sputum, pleural fluid, and clotted blood is possible but dangerous, and direct identification in tissue specimens is not standardized, so diagnosis depends on serology. The Centers for Disease Control and Prevention (CDC)[5] considers a *confirmed* case one with a compatible clinical illness plus laboratory confirmation by one of the following: a titer of 1:16 with microimmunofluorescence (MIF) IgM, culture from respiratory secretions, or a fourfold or greater rise in either complement-fixing (CF) or MIF antibody to a titer of 1:32 in specimens drawn 2 weeks apart. A *probable* case is one associated with a compatible illness linked epidemiologically to a confirmed human case or a titer of at least 1:32 in a single specimen by CF or MIF. There are false-positive and false-negative reactions. Also, the complement fixation test is only genus specific and does not distinguish *C. psittaci* from *C. trachomatis* or *C. pneumoniae*, both of which are common pathogens. MIF testing has greater sensitivity and specificity and is therefore preferable to the CF, but cross-reactions still occur. Thus serologic testing remains imperfect. In addition, antibiotic therapy can delay or diminish the antibody response. Polymerase chain reaction (PCR) can distinguish *C. psittaci* from other chlamydia but is not routinely available.

TREATMENT

The treatment of choice is tetracycline hydrochloride, 500 mg PO four times daily, or doxycycline, 100 mg PO twice daily, for 10 to 21 days. Some observers recommend the longer course to prevent relapse, but this is controversial. Erythromycin therapy is the alternative treatment but may be less efficacious in severe cases and may not protect the fetus in therapy of pregnant patients.

Anecdotal reports suggest possible efficacy of azithromycin and chloramphenicol, and some of the newer quinolones demonstrate activity in vitro and in animal models. For example, an in vitro study of 10 strains of *C. psittaci* demonstrated a moxifloxacin minimal inhibitory concentration (MIC) range of 0.06 to 0.125 mg/L; the minimal bactericidal concentration (MBC) range was identical. MIC$_{50}$ was 0.06 mg/L, and MIC$_{90}$ was 0.125 mg/L.[22] In a mouse model of psittacosis, sitafloxacin, sparfloxacin, and tosufloxacin showed promising therapeutic potency, with in vitro MIC ranges of 0.031 to 0.063 mg/L for sitafloxacin and sparfloxacin and 0.125-0.125 mg/L for tosufloxacin. MBC ranges were identical to those of the corresponding MIC. The authors also studied ofloxacin (MIC range, 0.5 to 1.0 mg/L; MBC, 0.5 to 2.0 mg/L) and ciprofloxacin (MIC range, 1.0 to 2.0 mg/L; MBC, 1.0 to 4.0 mg/L).[23] The utility of these latter agents awaits further clinical evaluation.

Most patients respond within 24 hours subjectively. Without treatment, the fatality rate is approximately 20%; with treatment, it drops to 1%. The best therapy for endocarditis is valve replacement and prolonged antimicrobial therapy.[5,12]

PREVENTION

Infected birds should be treated with tetracycline, chlortetracycline, or doxycycline for at least 45 consecutive days. The U.S. Department of Agriculture (USDA) requires that imported birds be quarantined for 30 days to prevent introduction of Newcastle disease. During this period, birds are treated with chlortetracycline. The USDA recommends that importers continue treatment for an additional 15 days, but this is not always done, and if treated for fewer than 45 days, some infected birds will continue to shed the organism.[5]

DIFFERENTIAL DIAGNOSIS

The list of considerations in the differential diagnosis is extensive, and the diagnostic possibilities depend on the presentation. A typhoidal picture suggests the mononucleosis syndrome, typhoid fever, brucellosis, tularemia, influenza, or subacute bacterial endocarditis. Respiratory signs and symptoms plus headache and myalgias should orient the clinician to causes of atypical pneumonia, such as viral pneumonia, Q fever, legionellosis, and infection with mycoplasma and *C. pneumoniae.*

Helpful clues to a diagnosis of psittacosis, when present, are relative bradycardia, rash, hemoptysis, epistaxis, and splenomegaly.

REFERENCES

1. Harris RL, Williams TW. Contribution to the question of pneumotyphus: A discussion of the original article by J. Ritter in 1880. Rev Infect Dis. 1985;7:119-122.
2. Macfarlane JT, Macrae AD. Psittacosis. Med Bull. 1983;39:163-167.
3. Everett KD, Bush RM, Andersen AA. Emended description of the order Chlamydiales, proposal of Parachlamydiaceae fam. nov. and Simkaniaceae fam. nov., each containing one monotypic genus, revised taxonomy of the family Chlamydiaceae, including a new genus and five new species and standards for the identification of organisms. Int J Syst Bacteriol. 1999;49:415-440.
4. Schlossberg D, Delgado J, Moore MM, et al. An epidemic of avian and human psittacosis. Arch Intern Med. 1993;153:2594-2596.
5. Centers for Disease Control and Prevention. Compendium of measures to control *Chlamydia psittaci* infection among humans (psittacosis) and pet birds (avian chlamydiosis). MMWR Recomm Rep. 2000 Jul 14;49(RR-8):3-18.
6. Guay DR. Pet-assisted therapy in the nursing home setting: Potential for zoonosis. Am J Infect Control. 2001;29(3):178-186.
7. Ito I, Ishida T, Mishima M, et al. Familial cases of psittacosis: Possible person-to-person transmission. Intern Med. 2002;41(7):580-583.
8. Hughes C, Maharg P, Rosario P, et al. Possible nosocomial transmission of psittacosis. Infect Control Hosp Epidemiol. 1997;18:165-168.
9. Yung AP, Grayson ML. Psittacosis: A review of 135 cases. Med J Aust. 1988;148:228-233.
10. Schaffner W, Drutz DJ, Duncan GW, et al. The clinical spectrum of endemic psittacosis. Arch Intern Med. 1967;119:433-443.
11. Schinkel AFL, Bax JJ, van der Wall EE, Jonkers GJPM. Echocardiographic follow-up of *Chlamydia psittaci* myocarditis. Chest. 2000;117:1203-1205.
12. Patel RT, Jekinson LR, Wheeler MH, et al. Arterial embolism associated with psittacosis. J Royal Soc Med. 1991;84:374-375.
13. Timmerman R, Bieger R. Haemolytic anemia due to cold agglutinins caused by psittacosis. Neth J Med. 1989;34:306-309.
14. Wong KF, Chan JKC, Chan CH, et al. Psittacosis-associated hemophagocytic syndrome. Am J Med. 1991;91:204-205.
15. Zumla A, Lipscomb G, Lewis D. Sixth cranial nerve palsy complicating psittacosis. J Neurol Neurosurg Psychiatry. 1988;51:1462.
16. Newton P, Lalvani A, Conlon CP. Psittacosis associated with bilateral 4th cranial nerve palsies. J Infect. 1996;32:63-65.
17. Crook T, Bannister B. Acute transverse myelitis associated with *Chlamydia psittaci* infection. J Infect. 1996;32:151-152.
18. Brewis C, McFerran J. Farmer's ear: Sudden sensorineural hearing loss due to *Chlamydia psittaci* infection. J Laryngol Otol. 1997;111:855-857.
19. Shee CD. Cerebellar disturbance in psittacosis. Postgrad Med J. 1988;64:382-383.
20. Hyde SR, Benirschke K. Gestational psittacosis: Case report and literature review. Mod Pathol. 1997;10:602-607.
21. Jorgensen DM. Gestational psittacosis in a Montana sheep rancher. Emerg Infect Dis. 1997;3:191-194.
22. Donati M, Rodriguez FM, Olmo A, et al. Comparative in vitro activity of moxifloxacin, minocycline and azithromycin against *Chlamydia* spp. J Antimicrob Chemother. 1999;43(6):825-827.
23. Miyashita N, Niki Y, Matsushima T. In vitro and in vivo activities of sitafloxacin against *Chlamydia* spp. Antimicrob Agents Chemother. 2001;45:3270-3272.

CHAPTER **179**

Chlamydophila (Chlamydia) pneumoniae

LISA A. JACKSON

Chlamydophila (Chlamydia) pneumoniae, the most recently identified of the three chlamydial species pathogenic for humans, shares with *Chlamydia trachomatis* and *Chlamydophila psittaci* the unique chlamydial developmental cycle but differs from those two species in terms of several important characteristics. Unlike *C. trachomatis, C. pneumoniae* is not sexually transmitted but is spread by aerosolized respiratory secretions, and, unlike *C. psittaci,* it is not a zoonosis. *C. pneumoniae* isolates show relatively limited genotypic or phenotypic variation, and to date only a single serovar or strain of *C. pneumoniae* is recognized. *C. pneumoniae* is a common cause of acute respiratory infection, including bronchitis and pneumonia. In the last 15 years, explorations of a possible association of *C. pneumoniae* and atherosclerotic cardiovascular disease have become an increasingly important focus of *C. pneumoniae* research.

HISTORY

In 1965, the first *C. pneumoniae* isolate was cultivated from a conjunctival swab specimen obtained from a child enrolled in a trachoma vaccine trial in Taiwan.[1] Inoculation of that specimen in the yolk sac of an embryonated chicken egg, which was at that time the only method available for growth of chlamydiae, allowed identification of the isolate as a *Chlamydia* species but was not optimal for further morphologic characterization. It was not until 1971, when cell culture methods became available, that the retained Taiwan isolate was observed to form round, dense inclusions in host cells. These inclusions were more similar in appearance to those of *C. psittaci* than to those of *C. trachomatis* and, unlike *C. trachomatis* inclusions, did not stain with iodine; therefore, the isolate was believed to be a variant of *C. psittaci.*[1]

On the basis of this assumption, further explorations of a possible association of the Taiwan isolate with respiratory infection were initiated. The first link with human disease was obtained when serologic testing of banked serum specimens obtained during a 1977 epidemic of mild pneumonia in northern Finland suggested that the Taiwan isolate organism was the etiologic agent.[2] The role of *C. pneumoniae* as a human pathogen was more firmly established in 1983, when the first respiratory isolate was obtained from a throat swab from a university student in Seattle with pharyngitis.[3] The strain name TWAR was derived from the laboratory identifiers assigned to the first conjunctival (TW-183) and respiratory (AR-39) isolates. In 1989, DNA sequence analysis, as well as morphology by electron microscopy, established the organism as a separate species of a genus designated first as *Chlamydia.* In 1999, analysis of 16S and 23S ribosomal RNA gene sequences indicated that *C. psittaci, C. pneumoniae,* and several other species should be placed in a new genus, *Chlamydophila.*[4] That proposal is followed here, although the reclassification is controversial in the *C. pneumoniae* community.

MICROBIOLOGY

As described in Chapter 176, Chlamydiaceae are obligate intracellular bacteria that have a unique biphasic developmental cycle. Chlamydiae have cell walls; replicate by binary fission; contain DNA, RNA, and ribosomes; and synthesize some proteins. They cannot, however, synthesize adenosine triphosphate or guanosine triphosphate and must rely on the host cell for energy sources. The small, dense elementary body is the metabolically inactive infectious form of the organism. Elementary bodies have a rigid cell wall resulting from disulfide cross-

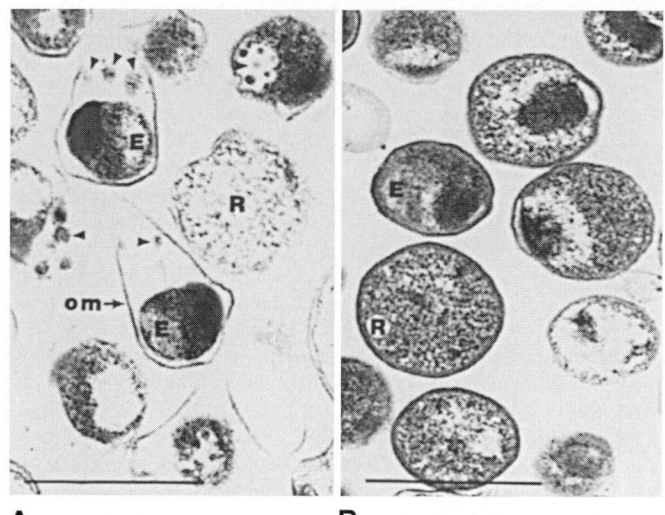

FIGURE 179-1. Electron micrograph of (**A**) *C. pneumoniae* and (**B**) *C. trachomatis* (bar = 0.5 m). E, elementary body; om, outer membrane; R, reticulate body; *arrowhead*, small electron-dense bodies of undetermined function. *(From Grayston JT, Kuo C-C, Campbell LA, et al. Chlamydia pneumoniae sp. nov. for Chlamydia sp. strain TWAR. Int J Syst Bacteriol. 1989;39:88-90.)*

linking of envelope proteins, allowing survival outside the host cell. After infection of a susceptible host eukaryotic cell by receptor-mediated endocytosis, the elementary bodies differentiate into reticulate bodies, which are the larger, metabolically active form of the organism. Inside the host cell, the reticulate bodies divide by binary fission, forming a microcolony referred to as a chlamydial inclusion that is visible by light or electron microscopy (Fig. 179-1). During this process, chlamydial antigens are released onto the surface of the host cell, stimulating a host immune response. After a period of growth and division, the reticulate bodies reorganize and condense to form new elementary bodies, which are released from the host cell to initiate new infectious cycles.

As demonstrated in Figure 179-1, *C. pneumoniae* has a characteristic pear-shaped elementary body surrounded by a periplasmic space that is morphologically distinct from the round elementary body of *C. trachomatis*. It is assumed that this shape indicates that the *C. pneumoniae* elementary body has a less rigid cell wall than the other *Chlamydia* and *Chlamydophila* species. The pear shape may also have functional significance, as ultrastructural studies have demonstrated that the *C. pneumoniae* elementary bodies first attach to host cells by the pointed end, then secure other binding sites on the host cells by forming cell wall protrusions, enter host cells by invaginating the host cell membrane, and form vacuolated endocytic vesicles. By electron microscopy, small, electron-dense bodies of unknown function have also been identified in the periplasmic space.

C. pneumonia can persist in tissues for prolonged periods of time after initial infection. In such persistent states, the normal life cycle just described may be interrupted. Such an alteration has been documented by in vitro studies in which cells infected with *C. pneumoniae* are treated with interferon-γ. After this treatment, aberrant, greatly enlarged, reticulate bodies are seen in the chlamydial inclusions by electron microscopy.[5] These reticulate bodies are nondividing and do not mature into infectious elementary bodies in the usual time cycle. In the persistent state, genes required for bacterial cell division are not expressed or are expressed only at an extremely low level while genes required for chromosomal DNA replication and partition continued to be expressed, indicating bacterial metabolic activity.[5] It is possible that an effect of *C. pneumoniae* in the pathogenesis of chronic diseases such as atherosclerosis or asthma, if present, may be mediated by chronically persistent forms of the organism in human tissues.

C. pneumoniae isolates have 94% to 100% DNA homology with each other but less than 10% homology with *C. trachomatis* or *C. psittaci*. All *C. pneumoniae* isolates tested are immunologically similar, and representative strains from different countries have been examined by molecular fingerprinting and found to be very similar.[6] In contrast to the other *Chlamydia* species, at this time *C. pneumoniae* has only one immunotype or serovar.

LABORATORY TESTING

A variety of methods can be used to identify the presence of *C. pneumoniae* in tissues and secretions, including isolation of the organism in cell culture, nucleic acid amplification methods such as polymerase chain reaction (PCR), and antigen detection methods such as immunohistochemistry. These tests are used primarily in the research setting and are commercially available only from a limited number of research laboratories. In the clinical setting, the diagnosis of acute *C. pneumoniae* infection is typically based on results of serologic testing to identify anti–*C. pneumoniae* immunoglobulin G (IgG) and IgM antibodies.

Detection of *Chlamydia pneumoniae*

Culture

C. pneumoniae can be isolated in cell culture, but the organism is fastidious and slow growing and so culture is not a sensitive method for detection of the presence of *C. pneumoniae* in clinical specimens. For this reason, isolation is not usually attempted for documentation of infection in the clinical setting but can be useful for research purposes.

C. pneumoniae has been isolated from pharyngeal swabs, bronchoalveolar lavage fluid, and tissue biopsy specimens. Sputum is toxic to cell cultures and therefore is not a suitable specimen for isolation. The swabs used for collection of pharyngeal specimens should have a Dacron tip and an aluminum or plastic shaft, as swabs with calcium alginate or cotton tips and those with wooden shafts may inhibit the growth of the organism. After collection of the specimen, swabs should be placed in chlamydial transport medium (sucrose-phosphate-glutamic acid [SPG] buffer solution) for transport to the laboratory. Bronchoalveolar lavage and pleural fluid samples should be collected in SPG at a ratio of specimen to medium of 1:2. All specimens that can be processed in the laboratory within 24 hours should be held refrigerated at 4° C and shipped on wet ice. Samples that cannot be processed within 24 hours should be held at 4° C for 1 to 4 hours before freezing to −65° C or −70° C, as more rapid freezing decreases the titer of viable organisms. After inoculation, the culture cells are incubated and later stained with a fluorescent-labeled antibody specific to *Chlamydophila (Chlamydia)* to visualize the bacterial inclusions within the host cells.

Polymerase Chain Reaction

Detection of *C. pneumoniae* DNA by PCR testing of respiratory specimens, vascular tissue pathologic specimens, serum, and peripheral blood mononuclear cells has been reported. This method is potentially much more sensitive for detection of *C. pneumoniae* than culture and holds promise for use in both the clinical and research settings. At least 18 different PCR assays using various *C. pneumoniae*–specific primers have been developed, 4 of which met validation criteria established by a group of experts in the field.[7] None of the assays have been commercially standardized or approved by the Food and Drug Administration (FDA), limiting their application outside the research setting. Specimens for PCR testing should be collected and transported in accordance with the preceding recommendations for culture specimens.

Antigen Detection

C. pneumoniae has also been detected in tissue sections using monoclonal antibodies labeled with a peroxidase (immunohistochemistry) or a fluorescent (immunofluorescence) marker. Antigen detection testing has the advantage of preserving tissue morphology because tissue sections are tested intact and are not homogenized as they are for culture and PCR testing. This permits localization of the infectious agent to specific areas within tissues or to within specific types of host cells. Interpretation of the staining pattern to distinguish localization of the organism from background or nonspecific staining is subjective, however, and results can vary depending on factors including the level of experience of the reader.

Serologic Testing

Serologic Assays

Several types of serologic assays are available for detection of antibodies to *C. pneumoniae*. Complement fixation detects genus-specific antibodies against chlamydial lipopolysaccharides but does not differentiate between infection caused by *C. pneumoniae*, *C. psittaci*, or *C. trachomatis*. Whole-inclusion fluorescence tests are available as commercial kits, but they also are not species specific and have not been widely evaluated. Several enzyme immunoassay (EIA) kits are commercially available, although none have been approved by the FDA for use in the United States. The sensitivity and specificity of these EIA tests are not well defined.

The microimmunofluorescence (MIF) test detects anti–*C. pneumoniae* specific antibodies and is the standard serologic assay for this organism.[8] The assay uses purified formalinized elementary bodies from *C. pneumoniae* that have been fixed onto glass slides as distinct dots of antigen. Small drops of sera are placed over the antigen dots and incubated. During this process, anti–*C. pneumoniae* antibodies present in the serum sample bind with *C. pneumoniae* antigen on the slide. After the slides are dried, fluorescein conjugates of antihuman IgG or IgM are applied and then rinsed. These conjugates bind to the antibodies linked to the *C. pneumoniae* antigen. The presence of anti–*C. pneumoniae* antibodies in the serum is then recognized by the pattern of fluorescence of the conjugated anti-IgG or IgM. False-positive IgM reactions may occur because of circulating rheumatoid factor; therefore, absorption of sera with an antihuman IgG reagent before testing is recommended.

Limitations of the MIF assay include its technical complexity, the subjective interpretation of the results, and the fact that the reagents have not been standardized. Moderate to large degrees of interlaboratory variation have been reported.[9]

Diagnostic Criteria for Acute Infection

Anti–*C. pneumoniae* IgM antibodies are produced transiently after acute primary infection, and detection of anti–*C. pneumoniae* IgM antibodies at a titer of 16 or higher is considered indicative of an acute *C. pneumoniae* infection. Because IgM antibodies appear approximately 2 to 3 weeks after the onset of illness, detectable levels may not be present in specimens obtained early in the course of illness. In addition, *C. pneumoniae* infection does not appear to induce protective immunity consistently and reinfection is common and may in fact be substantially more common than primary infection in older persons. In cases of reinfection, IgM antibody may not appear. For these reasons, failure to detect anti–*C. pneumoniae* IgM in a serum specimen obtained in the context of an acute respiratory illness does not exclude *C. pneumoniae* as a possible cause.

Anti–*C. pneumoniae* IgG antibodies are also produced after exposure to the organism, and detectable levels persist for months to years. After primary infection, the IgG response occurs at about 6 to 8 weeks; after reinfection, a more rapid response, within 1 to 2 weeks, occurs. Detection of a fourfold change in IgG antibody titer between paired serum specimens obtained at least 3 weeks apart provides the most reliable indication of an acute infection. It is recognized that the requirement for testing of a convalescent specimen allows only a retrospective diagnosis of acute infection and is not optimal for management of patients. Interpretation of the significance of elevated IgG titers detected in a single acute specimen is problematic, however, because of the high background IgG antibody prevalence in adults. High

IgG titers have been consistently documented among adults who are asymptomatic. The diagnosis of acute infection based on a single IgG titer is therefore not recommended, and if single IgG titers are reported, they should be interpreted with caution.[7]

Issues with Classification of Persistent Infection

In determining the cause of pneumonia or other acute respiratory syndrome, diagnostic testing is used to ascertain whether the patient was recently infected with the organism of interest. Coincident infection may be demonstrated, for example, by a fourfold or greater change in IgG antibody titer between acute and convalescent specimens. In contrast, when evaluating the possible contribution of an infectious agent in the development or exacerbation of a chronic condition, such as asthma or atherosclerotic cardiovascular disease, the time frame of interest can be much longer. Often the hypothesis is that organisms persisting after a remote past exposure, rather than those recently introduced in the context of an acute infection, have contributed to the pathogenesis of the disease. Assuming that some but not all past infections persist, to evaluate the persistent infection hypothesis there is a need to distinguish persons with persistent infection from persons who had past infections that resolved without persistence.

In research studies evaluating the possible association of *C. pneumoniae* infection and chronic conditions such as atherosclerotic cardiovascular disease, varying levels of anti–*C. pneumoniae* IgG or IgA antibody titers have frequently been used as presumptive markers of persistent, or chronic, infection status. It has been proposed that high IgA titers may be a better marker of chronic *C. pneumoniae* infection than IgG titers because serum IgA has a half-life of less than 7 days, whereas IgG has a half-life of weeks to months, and thus the presence of IgA is more indicative of persistent antigenic stimulation by an ongoing infection. However, the establishment of any serologic criteria for classification of persistent infection requires validation of those criteria by comparison with a "gold standard" of persistent infection. In the case of the association of *C. pneumoniae* and atherosclerotic disease, such a gold standard could be the presence of *C. pneumoniae* in a coronary atheroma. Identification of the organism in coronary specimens requires invasive testing, and therefore these comparisons are difficult to perform on a large scale. In addition, testing of the typically limited vascular specimen samples available from an individual patient might not be reflective of the infection status of other vascular areas from that person. Reported comparisons of IgG seropositivity and detection of *C. pneumoniae* in vascular specimens by PCR suggest that IgG titers are not highly correlated with vascular infection.[10] Thus, there are currently no serologic markers that have been proved valid in identifying persons with persistent *C. pneumoniae* infection, which is a limitation to research efforts in this field.

EPIDEMIOLOGY

Seroprevalence and Seroconversion

Much of the current information on the epidemiology of *C. pneumoniae* infection is derived from serologic studies using the MIF test for detection of *C. pneumoniae*–specific IgG antibodies to identify persons with past exposure to the organism. These studies indicate that exposure to *C. pneumoniae* is common and occurs throughout the world, with seroprevalence rates of more than 50% among adults in the United States and many other countries. As shown in Figure 179-2, seropositivity rates are very low among children younger than 5 years but then rise rapidly in the school-age years. By early adulthood, approximately 50% of persons are seropositive. This rate continues to gradually increase with age, reaching approximately 75% in elderly persons. Because antibody titers decline with time, the persistently high seropositivity rates documented in the older age groups suggest that repeated infections occur over time, with subsequent rises in anti–*C. pneumoniae* IgG titers.

Studies of age-specific rates of seroconversion show a similar trend. Testing of banked serum samples from a long-term study of

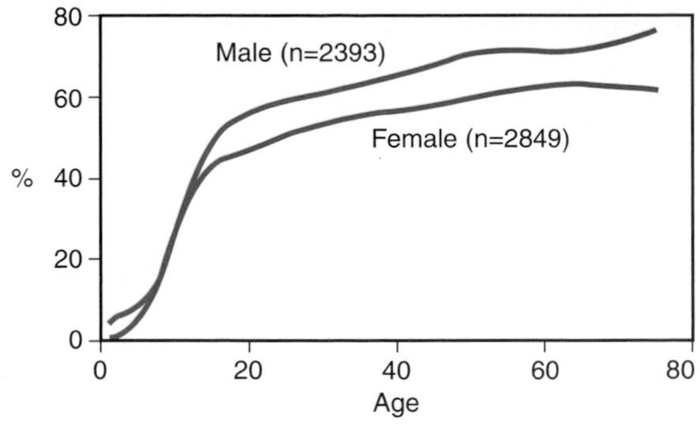

FIGURE 179-2. *Chlamydia pneumoniae* age-specific microimmuno-fluorescence seropositivity (immunoglobulin G titer ≥ 8) rates among 5242 persons in Seattle. *(From Grayston JT. Infections caused by* Chlamydia pneumoniae *strain TWAR. Clin Infect Dis. 1992;15:757-763.)*

TABLE 179-1 Rate of Serologic Evidence of Acute Infection with *Chlamydia pneumoniae* by Age Group, Longitudinal Studies of Seattle Families, 1975-1979

Age (yr)	No. of Acute Rises*	No. of Person-Years	Incidence†
0-4	0	27	
5-9	14	151	9.3
10-14	15	242	6.2
15-19	2	91	2.2
>19	6	394	1.5

*Greater than or equal to a fourfold rise in antibody titer between consecutive specimens.
†Rate per 100 person-years at risk.
Adapted from Aldous MB, Grayston JT, Wang S-P, et al. Seroepidemiology of *Chlamydia pneumoniae* TWAR infection in Seattle families, 1966-1979. J Infect Dis 1992;166:646-649.

Seattle families, in which blood samples were obtained at regular intervals, indicated that children in the 5- through 9-year-old age group had the highest rate of a fourfold or higher rise in antibody titer between consecutive specimens, with the next highest rate among children in the 10- through 14-year-old age group (Table 179-1). The available clinical information suggested that many persons who seroconverted were asymptomatic during that period. Reinfection was also documented in that some persons had a fourfold or greater antibody rise in more than one set of paired specimens obtained during the study. In addition, most of the seroconversions in adults were among persons previously identified as seropositive.

In children, seropositivity rates do not vary by sex, but among adults, rates among men are significantly higher than among women (see Fig. 179-2). Although this finding has been replicated in multiple settings, to date a satisfactory explanation for this difference has not been elucidated.

Asymptomatic Infection

C. pneumoniae has been detected in pharyngeal specimens from persons without concurrent respiratory symptoms. In one study of 1211 schoolchildren in Germany, *C. pneumoniae* was detected by PCR in throat swabs from 5.6% of the children tested.[11] The rate of detection among children who had respiratory symptoms, such as sore throat or cough, at the time of specimen collection (5.4%) was not significantly different from the rate of detection from asymptomatic children (6.0%). Detection of *C. pneumoniae* DNA in throat swabs from asymptomatic adults has also been reported,[12] and asymptomatic seroconversion of IgG antibody status has also been documented.

Whether detection of *C. pneumoniae* is invariably associated with a detectable serologic response is controversial. Although, in most cases, detection of the organism by isolation or PCR testing of pharyngeal swabs is associated with a subsequent rise in serologic titer detectable by the MIF test, *C. pneumoniae* has been detected in pharyngeal swab specimens from persons reported to be persistently seronegative.[13] This appears to be less common in adults than in young children.

Acute Respiratory Infection

C. pneumoniae is a significant cause of pneumonia in both the hospital and outpatient settings. Results of hospital-based studies have indicated that the organism accounts for 2% to 10% of cases of community-acquired pneumonia among adults.[14] For example, findings from a population-based active surveillance study of adults hospitalized with community-acquired pneumonia in Ohio indicate that 8.9% of cases met a definition of *C. pneumoniae* infection that included either a fourfold rise in IgG antibody titer between paired specimens, a single IgG titer of 512 or higher, or a single IgM titer of 16 or higher, and 2% of cases met a more restrictive definition of *C. pneumoniae* infec-

tion that included only a fourfold rise in IgG antibody titer between paired specimens.[15] The incidence of pneumonia caused by *C. pneumoniae* among the study population was estimated to be 23.8 per 100,000 population on the basis of the broader serologic criteria and 7.4 per 100,000 population on the basis of the more restrictive criteria. The projected number of annual cases of patients hospitalized with pneumonia caused by *C. pneumoniae* among the U.S. adult population was 88,400 to 108,000 based on the broader serologic criteria and 18,700 to 37,700 based on the more restrictive criteria. The highest rate of pneumonia related to *C. pneumoniae* was in the 65- through 79-year-old age group (Fig. 179-3); however, the organism accounted for the highest proportion of cases in the 18- through 34-year-old age-group (Fig. 179-4). Unlike *Streptococcus pneumoniae* infections, which demonstrated peak rates in the winter months, rates of *C. pneumoniae* infection did not vary significantly by season, which is consistent with other reports.

In a prospective study of 90 adults with community-acquired pneumonia at a teaching hospital in Spain that included serologic testing of paired serum specimens as well as PCR testing of lung aspirates, *C. pneumoniae* was the third most commonly identified cause of pneumonia, accounting for 13% of cases.[16] These results are similar to those obtained in a population-based study of adults in Finland.[17] In that study, which included ambulatory and hospitalized

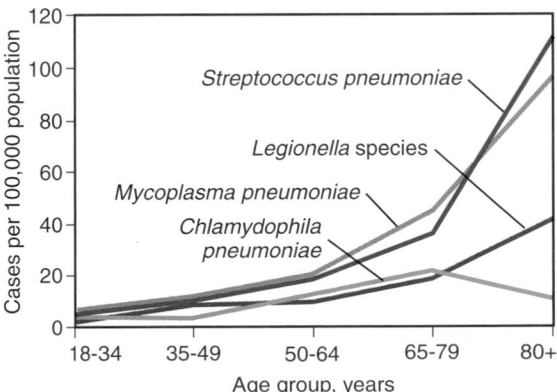

FIGURE 179-3. Age-specific rates of hospital admissions for community-acquired pneumonia caused by *Chlamydophila pneumoniae*, *Mycoplasma pneumoniae*, *Streptococcus pneumoniae*, and *Legionella*, from a population-based study. *C. pneumoniae* infection was defined by a fourfold or greater rise in titer between acute and convalescent serum specimens. *(Adapted from Marston BJ, Plouffe JF, File TM, et al. Incidence of community-acquired pneumonia requiring hospitalization: Results of a population-based active surveillance study in Ohio. Arch Intern Med. 1997;157:1709-1718.)*

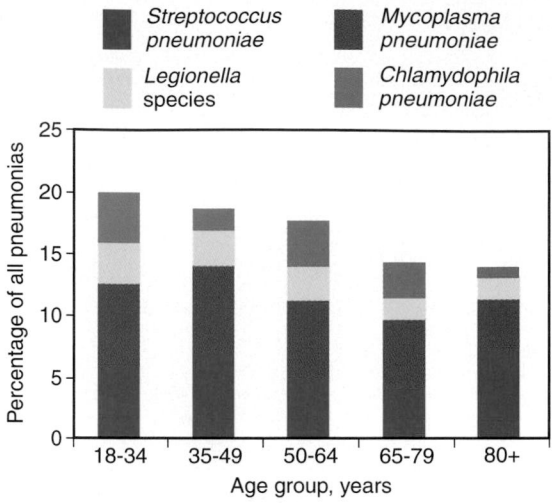

FIGURE 179-4. Percentage of hospital admissions for community-acquired pneumonia attributed to *Chlamydophila pneumoniae*, *Mycoplasma pneumoniae*, *Streptococcus pneumoniae*, and *Legionella*, by age group, from a population-based study. *C. pneumoniae* infection was defined by a fourfold or greater rise in titer between acute and convalescent serum specimens. *(Adapted from Marston BJ, Plouffe JF, File TM, et al. Incidence of community-acquired pneumonia requiring hospitalization: Results of a population-based active surveillance study in Ohio. Arch Intern Med. 1997;157:1709-1718.)*

cases, *C. pneumoniae* infection, as defined by change in titer between acute and convalescent specimens or by detection of IgM antibodies in a single specimen, was found in 13% of adults with community-acquired pneumonia.

Most respiratory infections caused by *C. pneumoniae* do not result in hospitalization, and therefore higher rates of infection are found in the ambulatory setting. Testing of sera obtained during a study of children and adults with pneumonia at Group Health Cooperative of Puget Sound during 1963 through 1975, in which more than 80% of cases were not hospitalized, identified *C. pneumoniae* as the etiologic agent in 8% of cases, with a corresponding incidence of 100 per 100,000 population.[18] In that population, the highest rates of pneumonia related to *C. pneumoniae* were among elderly persons, which differed from the pattern seen with *Mycoplasma pneumoniae* infection, with peak rates among children.

C. pneumoniae is infrequently documented as a cause of acute lower respiratory tract infection in infants[19] but is an important cause of pneumonia among older children, especially in the outpatient setting.[13,18] Among children with moderate to severe acute lower respiratory tract infection, coinfections with *C. pneumoniae* and other agents, such as *S. pneumoniae* or influenza A, have been reported. Evidence of coinfection, particularly with *S. pneumoniae*, is also not uncommon among adults hospitalized with pneumonia.[14]

C. pneumoniae is also a significant cause of bronchitis and upper respiratory infections. Among adults, *C. pneumoniae* accounts for approximately 5% of cases of bronchitis and sinusitis but is a less frequent cause of pharyngitis, generally accounting for only approximately 1% of cases.

Epidemic Disease

C. pneumoniae is primarily a cause of endemic disease; however, outbreaks of respiratory infection have been reported in nursing homes, schools, and among military recruits and families. More sustained increases, persisting for months to years, in rates of respiratory infection attributed to *C. pneumoniae* among members of communities[2] or countries[20] have also been reported.

CLINICAL MANIFESTATIONS

Acute Respiratory Infection

Pneumonia and bronchitis are the most common clinical syndromes associated with *C. pneumoniae* infection. Upper respiratory infections, including sinusitis and pharyngitis, may also occur, either in isolation or in conjunction with a lower respiratory infection. The incubation period of infection related to *C. pneumoniae* is about 21 days, which is longer than the incubation period of many other respiratory pathogens.

As with the other bacterial causes of atypical pneumonia, *M. pneumoniae* and *Legionella pneumophila*, the clinical manifestations of acute respiratory infection with *C. pneumoniae* are nonspecific.[21] Upper respiratory symptoms, such as rhinitis, sore throat, or hoarseness, may be reported initially. These symptoms may then diminish over days to weeks, followed by the onset of cough, which is a predominant symptom in *C. pneumoniae* respiratory infections, thus at times producing a biphasic pattern of illness symptoms.

The duration from onset of symptoms to presentation for medical evaluation tends to be longer for infections with *C. pneumoniae* than for those caused by other respiratory agents.[21-23] Patients with *C. pneumoniae* infection are also reported to be less likely to give a history of fever, or to have an elevated temperature documented, on clinical presentation than patients with respiratory infection caused by other agents. In addition to having a gradual onset, symptoms related to *C. pneumoniae* respiratory infections may be prolonged, with cough and malaise persisting for several weeks or months despite appropriate antibiotic therapy.

A single, subsegmental, patchy infiltrate is the classic radiographic appearance associated with atypical pneumonias and is commonly seen with *C. pneumoniae* infection. However, this pattern is also common in cases of pneumonia caused by typical bacterial pathogens, including *S. pneumoniae*.[24] In addition, other radiographic features, such as lobar or sublobar consolidation, interstitial infiltrates, bilateral involvement, pleural effusion, and hilar adenopathy, may be demonstrated with *C. pneumoniae* infection, although less frequently.[24,25] Therefore, the pattern of infiltrates on chest radiography is not a reliable indicator of the probable etiologic agent for cases of community-acquired pneumonia.[24,25] As with other atypical pathogens, the white blood cell count is usually not elevated with *C. pneumoniae* infection[21] and other laboratory findings are nonspecific.

Infection in Hosts with Altered Defense Mechanisms

C. pneumoniae has been identified as a cause of lower respiratory infection in immunocompromised patients, including persons infected with human immunodeficiency virus. However, whether immunocompromised persons are at increased risk for infection with *C. pneumoniae*, or more severe disease as a consequence of infection, is not well defined. *C. pneumoniae* has also been identified as a cause of acute respiratory exacerbations in patients with cystic fibrosis and has been associated with acute chest syndrome in children with sickle cell disease.

Other Syndromes

The organism has been isolated from adults and children with otitis media, often in conjunction with isolation of other bacterial pathogens. Other reported clinical syndromes include endocarditis, lumbosacral meningoradiculitis, and erythema nodosum. A case of Guillain-Barré syndrome after infection with *C. pneumoniae* has been reported. The organism has been associated serologically with encephalitis in children and adults. A multisystem febrile illness in a 10-year-old boy with pneumonia, pericarditis, pleuritis, and hepatosplenomegaly was documented to be due to *C. pneumoniae* by serology and by PCR detection of the organism in lymph node and liver biopsy samples.[23]

Several chronic diseases have been presumptively associated with *C. pneumoniae* infection, the best example of which is atherosclerotic cardiovascular disease, as further described later. *C. pneu-

moniae has been associated with the development of adult-onset asthma[26] as well as with acute exacerbations among adults with asthma[25] and with reactive airway disease in children.[27] An association with sarcoidosis was suggested by detection of the organism in sarcoid skin granuloma specimens in one report; however, it was not detected by PCR in lung biopsy specimens from 33 patients with sarcoid in another report. *C. pneumoniae* has also been implicated in reactive arthritis, and a serologic association with lung cancer has been reported.

TREATMENT

In the clinical setting, *C. pneumoniae* diagnostic tests are not commonly performed, and if they are performed, testing of acute and convalescent serum specimens can provide only a retrospective indication of acute infection. For these reasons, most respiratory infections possibly caused by *C. pneumoniae* are treated empirically without diagnostic confirmation. Established guidelines for treatment of lower respiratory tract infections in adults and children typically include agents active against *C. pneumoniae*. If *C. pneumoniae* infection is strongly suspected or is confirmed, consideration can be given to use of a more specific course of therapy.

Erythromycin, tetracycline, and doxycycline are active in vitro against *C. pneumoniae* and have traditionally been recommended as first-line therapy for suspected *C. pneumoniae* infections. Newer macrolide-like antibiotics, such as azithromycin and clarithromycin, are also active in vitro and achieve high intracellular concentrations. These agents are better tolerated than erythromycin and so may be considered as either first-line agents or alternatives to erythromycin and the tetracyclines for treatment of infections believed to be due to *C. pneumoniae*. Although older quinolones such as ofloxacin are not highly active against *C. pneumoniae*, the newer quinolone agents, such as gatifloxacin and gemifloxacin, are active in vitro. The organism is not susceptible to β-lactam drugs, including penicillin and ampicillin, or to sulfa drugs.

Many of the studies evaluating antibiotic treatment of *C. pneumoniae* respiratory infections estimated effectiveness of treatment on the basis of symptomatic response to treatment rather than the microbiologic criteria of eradication of the organism. In the original report documenting *C. pneumoniae* as a cause of respiratory infection, many patients treated with 1 g of erythromycin orally per day for 5 to 10 days continued to have persistent symptoms, suggesting that this therapy was inadequate. On this basis, a treatment course of either 2 g of tetracycline per day for 7 to 10 days or 1 g/day for 21 days was recommended.

The results of several clinical trials that have included nasopharyngeal culture positivity as an end point have been reported. These types of studies allow estimation of the microbiologic efficacy of antimicrobial therapy against *C. pneumoniae* infections, as evidenced by isolation of the organism from pharyngeal swab specimens. The first such trial was a randomized controlled trial of a 10-day course of treatment with either clarithromycin or erythromycin suspension among children 3 to 12 years of age with radiographically demonstrated community-acquired pneumonia.[13] Of the 33 patients with *C. pneumoniae* isolated from pretreatment nasopharyngeal cultures, bacteriologic eradication was documented in 79% (15 of 19) of those treated with clarithromycin and 86% (12 of 14) of those treated with erythromycin. All of the children with persistent infection improved clinically, with complete resolution of the chest radiographs.

Two studies of azithromycin for treatment of community-acquired pneumonia have reported similar findings. In a study of children 6 months through 16 years of age, *C. pneumoniae* was eradicated after treatment in 19 of the 23 (83%) children with *C. pneumoniae* isolated from pretreatment nasopharyngeal cultures. In an open study of a 5-day course of azithromycin in adults, *C. pneumoniae* infection was identified by culture in 10 of 48 (21%) patients at enrollment. Seven of the 10 patients were culture negative after treatment. All patients improved clinically.

In aggregate, these studies indicate that *C. pneumoniae* is eradicated from the nasopharynx from most but not all patients treated with antimicrobial agents with in vitro activity against *C. pneumoniae*. A clinical response to treatment appears to occur even with persistence of the organism, however. These studies also suggest that azithromycin and clarithromycin are likely to be at least as effective as doxycycline or erythromycin therapy for *C. pneumoniae* respiratory infections. In adults, there is also a role for use of newer quinolone agents for empirical treatment of respiratory infections potentially caused by *C. pneumoniae*.

Azithromycin also appears to be effective in prophylaxis among persons at high risk for infection. High rates of respiratory infections occur among military recruits in training camps, and in this setting weekly azithromycin prophylaxis was estimated to be 58% effective in preventing infections attributed to *C. pneumoniae* on the basis of changes in antibody titer from specimens obtained before and after the training period.[28]

VACCINES

There are currently no vaccines available for prevention of chlamydial infection in humans. There are long-standing efforts to develop vaccines to prevent ocular and genital *C. trachomatis* infection, and work has been initiated for *C. pneumoniae*. Vaccine development efforts are hampered by the fact that anti–*C. pneumoniae* IgG antibodies do not appear to be protective, because IgG-seropositive persons may be repeatedly infected. Studies in an experimental mouse infection model indicate that cell-mediated immune responses, especially the action of CD8+ cells, are of crucial importance for protective immunity. In addition, the immunodominant antigen for a protective *C. pneumoniae* immune response has not been identified. One potentially promising approach is the use of DNA vaccines, which are being evaluated in animal models.[29]

CHLAMYDIA PNEUMONIAE AND ATHEROSCLEROSIS

Exploration of a possible influence of *C. pneumoniae* vascular infection on the pathogenesis of atherosclerotic cardiovascular disease is the most active current area of *C. pneumoniae* research. This topic has been the focus of hundreds of scientific publications since the possibility of an association was first suggested in 1988 by the results of a seroepidemiologic study among Finnish men.[30] Soon after that, the presence of the organism in coronary atheroma was initially identified by electron microscopy and then confirmed by PCR testing and immunohistochemistry.[31] These initial findings have spurred multiple other investigations using a variety of experimental and nonexperimental approaches.

Most, but not all, hypotheses for an effect of *C. pneumoniae* infection on atherosclerosis indicate a role for organisms persisting in cardiovascular tissue. Such persistent organisms may induce an inflammatory response that initiates or exacerbates the disease process. Inflammation is believed to be an important component of all stages of the atherosclerotic disease process, and thus there are multiple pathways by which an infectious agent could potentially influence pathogenesis.

C. pneumoniae has been detected in cardiovascular specimens, including coronary and carotid artery specimens, by electron microscopy, PCR, and immunohistochemistry, with prevalence rates ranging from 0% to 80% or more in published studies. Higher rates of detection have been correlated with more advanced atherosclerotic changes, and the organism is very infrequently detected in normal arteries without atherosclerotic changes. Using reverse transcriptase PCR, *C. pneumoniae*–specific RNA has been demonstrated in atheroma, implying that the bacteria detected are viable, which has been confirmed by isolation of the organism from coronary and carotid plaque specimens.[32,33] Although the presence of *C. pneumoniae* in atherosclerotic plaque is well documented, this evidence does not establish whether infection plays a causal role in the disease or whether the organism simply exists within the tissues as an "innocent bystander."

A number of different approaches have been used to evaluate whether *C. pneumoniae* causes atherosclerotic disease or its complications, and each method has strengths and limitations (Table 179-2). These approaches, including human studies, animal studies, and in vitro cellular studies, are described further in the following.

Human Studies

Seroepidemiologic Studies

A large number of seroepidemiologic assessments have been performed, in which the relationship between serologic criteria, including varying anti–*C. pneumoniae* IgA and IgG antibody titers, and the risk of cardiovascular outcomes, such as acute myocardial infarction, has been evaluated. Study designs of these evaluations have included cohort, case-control, and cross-sectional studies. Some of the studies have indicated an association between serologic criteria and risk of cardiovascular disease,[30,34] whereas others have not found such an association.[35,36] Two meta-analyses by Danesh and colleagues suggest that neither *C. pneumoniae* IgA titers nor IgG titers are strongly predictive of coronary heart disease.[37,38] A consistent limitation of all seroepidemiologic studies, however, is the uncertain correlation, as previously described in this chapter, between serologic criteria and the presence of endovascular infection. This factor complicates the interpretation of the results of either positive or negative serologic studies.

TABLE 179-2   Strengths and Limitations of Different Research Methods for Evaluation of the Possible Association of *Chlamydia pneumoniae* Infection and Atherosclerotic Cardiovascular Disease

Method	Description	Examples (References)	Strengths	Limitations
C. pneumoniae detection	Testing of atherosclerotic vascular specimens using PCR, immunohistochemistry, or isolation to identify the presence of C. pneumoniae.	59-61	Indicates the presence of the organism in arterial atheroma.	Cannot establish a causal association between the presence of the organism in tissue and disease. Estimates of the prevalence of the organism in plaque specimens are limited by the interlaboratory variability in detection rates.
Seroepidemiologic studies	Results of serologic testing are used to define infection status. The risk of cardiovascular outcomes among persons defined as infected and uninfected by serologic criteria are compared in study designs including cohort, case-control, and cross-sectional studies.	30, 35, 36, 38	Study designs can include prospective as well as retrospective assessments. Large sample sizes are possible. A variety of clinical cardiovascular outcomes, such as acute myocardial infarction, as well as subclinical outcomes, such as intimal medial carotid artery thickness, can be assessed. This potentially allows the evaluation of the association of C. pneumoniae infection with different stages of atherosclerosis.	Uncertain correlation between serologic status and endovascular infection with C. pneumoniae. Comparability of study results is limited by differences in the criteria used to define infection status as well as by interlaboratory variability of serologic assays.
Retrospective antibiotic studies	Observational studies that look back in time to evaluate the association of antibiotics taken in the course of usual clinical care with risk of subsequent cardiovascular outcomes.	40-43, 62	Large sample sizes are possible. A variety of cardiovascular outcomes can be evaluated. Much less costly than prospective clinical trials.	Evaluations restricted to the types of antibiotics and the relatively limited durations of therapy typically employed in usual clinical care. There may be differences between persons who happen to have received antibiotic treatment and those who did not that may be related to the association of treatment and disease risk. An effect of antibiotic treatment, if seen, may be due to an effect of antibiotics on factors other than C. pneumoniae infection.
Antibiotic treatment trials	Randomized placebo-controlled trials prospectively evaluating risk of cardiovascular events among persons assigned to receive antibiotic treatment and those assigned to the placebo group.	49, 53, 63-67	Random assignment to antibiotic treatment ensures that the characteristics of the treated and untreated groups are balanced. Specific antibiotics and long durations of therapy can be evaluated.	Large trials are expensive to conduct. Extremely large sample sizes would be required to evaluate an effect of antibiotic treatment on the primary prevention of cardiovascular events among persons without known atherosclerotic disease. Therefore, antibiotic trials have focused on evaluations of secondary prevention among persons with known disease and therefore evaluate only the later stages of atherosclerosis. An effect of antibiotic treatment, if seen, may be due to an effect of antibiotics on factors other than C. pneumoniae infection.
Animal studies	Rabbits or mice genetically predisposed to development of atherosclerotic-like aortic lesions are infected with C. pneumoniae.	54-56	Allow identification of the temporal relationship between infection and disease. Short time frame for disease occurrence. Effect of antibiotic treatments can be evaluated	Uncertain generalizability of the results to humans. Only early stages of atherosclerotic-like changes can be evaluated in the murine and rabbit models, as the animals do not develop plaque rupture or thrombotic complications.
Cellular studies	In vitro studies of the effect of C. pneumoniae infection on cellular mechanisms.	57, 58, 68	Allows exploration of specific pathogenic factors. Identification of effect of antibiotic therapy on cellular mechanisms.	Uncertain generalizability to in vivo systems.

PCR, polymerase chain reaction.

Detection of *C. pneumoniae* DNA in Peripheral Blood Mononuclear Cells

Chlamydophila pneumoniae DNA has been detected by PCR in peripheral blood mononuclear cells in blood specimens from persons with and without known cardiovascular disease. The reported prevalence of detection of the organism in these specimens in different studies has varied widely, from 0% to 59% in different study populations.[39] Because *C. pneumoniae* are transported from the respiratory tract to other parts of the body by circulating macrophages, it is possible that testing of peripheral blood mononuclear cells may provide a marker of persistent, active, *C. pneumoniae* infection. At this time, however, the relationship between detection of *C. pneumoniae* DNA in circulating mononuclear cells and the presence of either cardiovascular disease or endovascular *C. pneumoniae* infection is uncertain.

Antibiotic Treatment Evaluations

Evaluation of the association of antibiotic treatment and risk of cardiovascular events is a way to assess indirectly the hypothesis that *C. pneumoniae* infection plays a causal role in the atherosclerotic disease process. If the use of an antibiotic active against *C. pneumoniae* is associated with a reduction in cardiovascular disease risk, it is possible that the reduction in disease risk was mediated by the suppression or eradication of *C. pneumoniae* infection. Using this approach, it is not necessary to attempt to discern the infection status of individuals; rather the relevant comparison is between antibiotic-treated and untreated persons. These evaluations can be conducted either retrospectively, using existing data on antibiotic use and the occurrence of cardiovascular events, or prospectively in the context of randomized clinical trials.

Retrospective evaluations of existing data sources are attractive because they can be performed relatively quickly and at low cost and they avoid the need for subjects to be put at risk for adverse effects of investigational treatment for the purpose of the study. These studies are, however, limited to evaluation of the relatively short courses of antibiotics prescribed in the context of usual clinical practice. In addition, as with all observational studies, the results may be influenced by differences in the characteristics of persons who receive or do not receive antibiotic treatment that are related to the risk of disease.

The retrospective antibiotic studies reported to date have varied widely in terms of the study design, populations evaluated, and antibiotics assessed. Although some have reported a beneficial effect of receipt of antibiotics active against *C. pneumoniae* on the risk of acute cardiovascular events,[40] this effect has not been consistently demonstrated.[41-43] Therefore, in aggregate, these studies do not provide strong support for an effect of routine use of antibiotics effective against *C. pneumoniae* on risk of cardiovascular outcomes. However, the studies are not suitable for the evaluation of the effect of larger doses of antibiotics or longer durations of therapy than are usually prescribed in the context of routine clinical care.

Prospective clinical trials allow the evaluation of prolonged courses of antibiotic treatment among persons randomly assigned to antibiotic treatment or placebo. The first reported prospective trial was a small nonblinded and nonrandomized intervention study by Gupta and colleagues that included only 60 *C. pneumoniae*–seropositive subjects and, based on a very high event rate in the untreated group, demonstrated a significant reduction in risk of cardiovascular outcomes among persons who received the study intervention of 3 to 6 days of azithromycin treatment.[44] These results were not replicated in a subsequent evaluation by Muhlestein and co-workers of 302 *C. pneumoniae*–seropositive subjects who were randomly assigned to 3 months of weekly therapy with azithromycin or placebo.[45]

In an evaluation of patients treated with 28 days of roxithromycin or placebo immediately after a percutaneous coronary stent procedure, no effect of antibiotic treatment was found in the primary analysis of angiographically demonstrated restenosis among all subjects.[46] However, in a subanalysis stratified by *C. pneumoniae* IgG antibody titer at baseline, there was a trend toward a reduction in risk for angiographic restenosis among patients with higher baseline titers, and a significant protective effect of treatment against the need for subsequent revascularization of the stented vessel was found among subjects with baseline titers of 512 or greater (odds ratio, 0.32; 95% confidence interval, 0.13 to 0.81).

Two studies have evaluated the effect of antibiotics on the rate of expansion of abdominal aortic aneurysms. One small study found a nonsignificant decrease in this rate with doxycycline treatment,[47] and the other found a similar difference with roxithromycin treatment that did reach statistical significance.[48] One study has reported reduced progression of carotid atherosclerosis, as measured by ultrasonography, among *C. pneumoniae*–seropositive patients treated with roxithromycin for 30 days.[49]

In the coming months, several large-scale trials, including thousands of subjects and tens of thousands of person-years of follow-up per study, of antibiotics for the secondary prevention of cardiac events are to be reported.[50-52] The results of those studies should provide more definitive evidence regarding the potential for this type of intervention to reduce the risk of cardiovascular outcomes among persons with known atherosclerotic cardiovascular disease.

It should be noted that interpretation of the results of antibiotic treatment studies is not necessarily straightforward. A limitation of all antibiotic studies is that an effect of antibiotics, if seen, may not represent an effect against *C. pneumoniae* infection specifically. It is possible that antibiotics may have nonspecific anti-inflammatory actions or have an effect on coronary plaque stabilization that could lead to a reduction in risk of cardiac events whether or not *C. pneumoniae* is involved in the disease process. Such an effect may be suggested by the results of the South Thames Trial of Antibiotics in Myocardial Infarction and Unstable Angina (STAMINA), in which patients with acute myocardial infarction or unstable angina were randomly assigned to receive a 1-week course of either the combination of amoxicillin, metronidazole, and omeprazole or the combination of azithromycin, metronidazole, and omeprazole, or placebo.[53] At 12 weeks, there was a 36% reduction in risk of cardiovascular events in patients who were randomly assigned to the treatment groups compared with the placebo group, but there was no difference between the amoxicillin and azithromycin treatment groups. Because *C. pneumoniae* is not susceptible to amoxicillin, the results of this one trial suggest an activity of antibiotic treatment independent of an action against *C. pneumoniae*.

Similarly, evidence for a lack of effect of antibiotic therapy in these trials may not indicate a true lack of association between *C. pneumoniae* infection and atherosclerosis. Failure of an adequately powered study to demonstrate a reduction in risk of cardiac events in the antibiotic treatment group indicates that there was no evidence that the course of antibiotics used in the study modified disease risk in that particular study population. One explanation for the lack of effect of the antibiotic intervention would be that *C. pneumoniae* does not play a role in the disease process. An alternative explanation would be that *C. pneumoniae* infection influenced the risk of cardiovascular disease but that this effect was not modifiable by antibiotic treatment, either because the effect occurred early in life, before initiation of therapy, or because the optimal type of antibiotic or dose or duration of therapy was not used. Thus, although the antibiotic treatment trials will provide important information related to whether antibiotics can alter the risk of cardiovascular disease in older adults, they will not provide all of the information needed to answer directly the question of whether *C. pneumoniae* infection plays a causal role in the initiation or progression of atherosclerotic cardiovascular disease in humans.

Animal Model Studies

Animal studies allow experimental manipulation of infection and treatment in ways that would not be possible in humans. Two animal models used for *C. pneumoniae* research are apolipoprotein E (apoE)–deficient knockout mice and New Zealand white rabbits. Both of these animals can develop atherosclerotic-like changes in the aortic arch, and the size of the lesions can be quantified to allow comparison between infected and uninfected animals.

Results of studies using apoE-deficient knockout mice indicate that *C. pneumoniae* can be detected in aortic plaque specimens after intranasal inoculation, that the organism persists in aortic plaque for at least 20 weeks after initial infection, and that infection appears to accelerate the progression of the atherosclerotic process in these animals. Studies of New Zealand white rabbits found that animals infected intranasally with *C. pneumoniae* later showed changes in the aorta consisting of intimal thickening or fibrolipid plaques and that *C. pneumoniae* could be detected in the plaque specimens by immunocytochemistry. In addition, a study of New Zealand white rabbits intranasally inoculated with either *C. pneumoniae* or saline and then randomly assigned to a 7-week course of treatment with azithromycin or to no treatment found that the infected, untreated animals had significantly larger areas of plaque involvement of the thoracic aorta than the uninfected control animals.[54] In contrast, the infected, azithromycin-treated rabbits did not demonstrate this increase, with mean areas of plaque involvement that were not significantly different from those of the uninfected controls, suggesting that treatment with azithromycin ameliorated the infection-induced acceleration in atherosclerotic plaque development. Subsequent studies suggest that antibiotic therapy is most effective if initiated early, within 1 week, after infection.[55,56]

These models are useful, particularly in assessing the effect of timing of antibiotic treatment with the effect of infection on enhanced atherosclerosis. The models are, however, limited by the fact that although the animals can develop inflammatory aortic lesions, they cannot be used to model the late occlusive complications of atherosclerotic disease in humans, such as stroke or coronary thrombosis. Further, the generalizability of animal models to the human condition is necessarily limited. This would be true to some extent even of studies evaluating infection in large animals such as primates.

In Vitro Cellular Studies

In vitro studies have the potential to evaluate the influence of *C. pneumoniae* infection on specific aspects of the complex mechanisms involved in the atherosclerotic disease process (Fig. 179-5). *C. pneumoniae* has been shown to infect readily human vascular smooth muscle, endothelial, and monocyte-macrophage cell lines. Effects of *C. pneumoniae* infection on these cell types that are consistent with an interaction with the atherosclerotic disease process have been demonstrated by multiple in vitro studies. For example, *C. pneumoniae* has been shown to facilitate the adhesion of infected monocytes to human coronary artery endothelial and smooth muscle cells, which could influence the early stages of atheroma development.[57]

Infection of human monocyte-derived macrophages with *C. pneumoniae* exposed to native low-density lipoprotein (LDL) has also been demonstrated to induce transformation of those cells into lipid-laden foam cells.[58] Further, exposure of the infected macrophages to both LDL and heparin, which binds to LDL and interferes with its uptake by the macrophage native LDL receptor, blocks this transformation, suggesting that *C. pneumoniae*–induced foam cell formation results from dysregulation of native LDL uptake or metabolism, or both. *C. pneumoniae* infection of cultured endothelial cells has also been shown to stimulate tissue factor, or procoagulant, activity and enhance platelet adhesion. These and other evaluations of the influence of *C. pneumoniae* infection on the cellular mechanisms involved in atherosclerosis tend to support the possibility that the infection may play a role in the disease process.

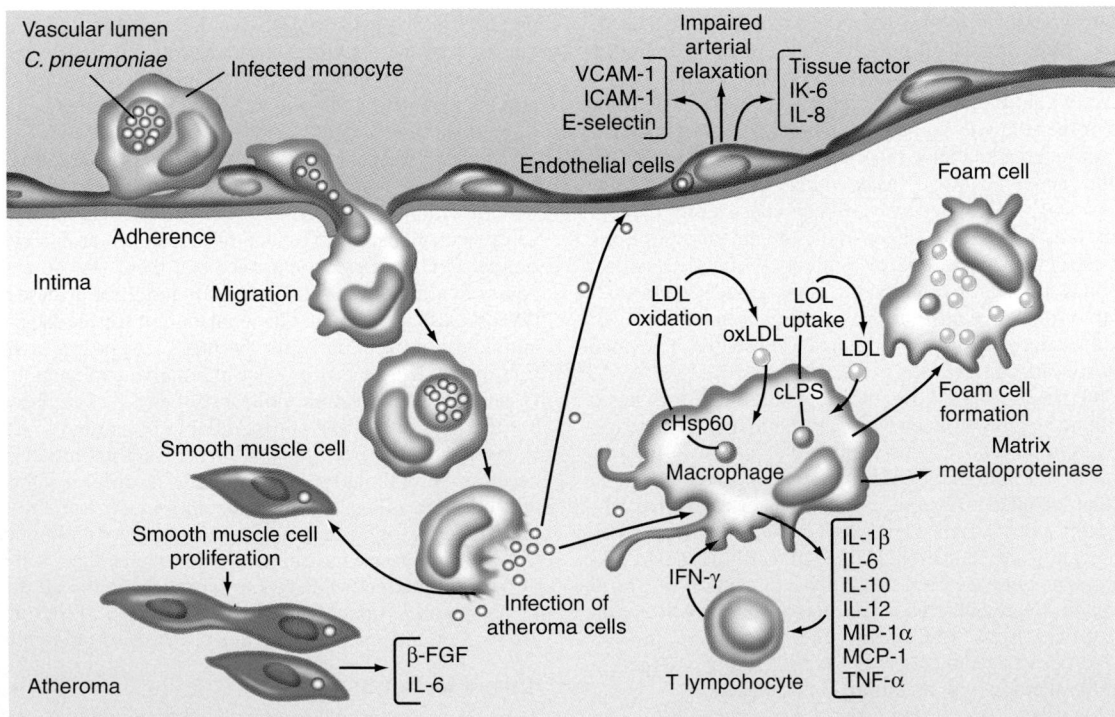

FIGURE 179-5. Cellular mechanisms by which *C. pneumoniae* may promote atherosclerosis. cHsp60, 60-kD chlamydial heat shock protein; cLPS, chlamydial lipopolysaccharide; FGF, fibroblast growth factor; ICAM, intercellular adhesion molecule; IFN, interferon; IL, interleukin; LDL, low-density lipoprotein; MCP, monocyte chemoattractant protein; MIP, macrophage inflammatory protein; TNF, tumor necrosis factor; VCAM, vascular cell adhesion molecule. *(From Kalayoglu MV, Libby P, Byrne GI. Chlamydia pneumoniae* as an emerging risk factor in cardiovascular disease. JAMA. 2002;288:2724-2731. Copyright ©2002 American Medical Association. All rights reserved.)

REFERENCES

1. Kuo CC, Chen HH, Wang SP, Grayston JT. Identification of a new group of *Chlamydia psittaci* strains called TWAR. J Clin Microbiol. 1986;24:1034-1037.
2. Saikku P, Wang SP, Kleemola M, et al. An epidemic of mild pneumonia due to an unusual strain of *Chlamydia psittaci*. J Infect Dis. 1985;151:832-839.
3. Grayston JT, Kuo CC, Wang SP, Altman J. A new *Chlamydia psittaci* strain, TWAR, isolated in acute respiratory tract infections. N Engl J Med. 1986;315:161-168.
4. Everett KD, Bush RM, Anderson AA. Emended description of the order Chlamydiales, proposal of Parachlamydiaceae fam. nov. and Simkaniaceae fam. nov, each containing one monotypic genus, revised taxonomy of the family Chlamydiaceae, include a new genus and five new species and standards for the identification of organisms. Int J Syst Bacteriol. 1999;49:415-440.
5. Byrne GI, Ouellette SP, Wang Z, et al. *Chlamydia pneumoniae* expresses genes required for DNA replication but not cytokinesis during persistent infection of HEp-2 cells. Infect Immun. 2001;69:5423-5429.
6. Kaltenboeck B, Kousoulas KG, Storz J. Structures of and allelic diversity and relationships among the major outer membrane protein (ompA) genes of the four chlamydial species. J Bacteriol. 1993;175:487-502.
7. Dowell SF, Peeling RW, Boman J, et al. Standardizing *Chlamydia pneumoniae* assays: Recommendations from the Centers for Disease Control and Prevention (USA) and the Laboratory Centre for Disease Control (Canada). Clin Infect Dis. 2001;33:492-503.
8. Wang S. The microimmunofluorescence test for *Chlamydia pneumoniae* infection: Technique and interpretation. J Infect Dis. 2000;181(Suppl 3):S421-S425.
9. Peeling RW, Wang SP, Grayston JT, et al. *Chlamydia pneumoniae* serology: Interlaboratory variation in microimmunofluorescence assay results. J Infect Dis. 2000;181(Suppl 3):S426-S429.
10. Maass M, Gieffers J, Krause E, et al. Poor correlation between microimmunofluorescence serology and polymerase chain reaction for detection of vascular *Chlamydia pneumoniae* infection in coronary artery disease patients. Med Microbiol Immunol (Berl). 1998;187:103-106.
11. Schmidt SM, Muller CE, Mahner B, Wiersbitzky SK. Prevalence, rate of persistence and respiratory tract symptoms of *Chlamydia pneumoniae* infection in 1211 kindergarten and school age children. Pediatr Infect Dis J. 2002;21:758-762.
12. Hyman CL, Augenbraun MH, Roblin PM, et al. Asymptomatic respiratory tract infection with *Chlamydia pneumoniae* TWAR. J Clin Microbiol. 1991;29:2082-2083.
13. Block S, Hedrick J, Hammerschlag MR, et al. *Mycoplasma pneumoniae* and *Chlamydia pneumoniae* in pediatric community-acquired pneumonia: Comparative efficacy and safety of clarithromycin vs. erythromycin ethylsuccinate. Pediatr Infect Dis J. 1995;14:471-477.
14. Grayston JT, Diwan VK, Cooney M, Wang SP. Community- and hospital-acquired pneumonia associated with *Chlamydia* TWAR infection demonstrated serologically. Arch Intern Med. 1989;149:169-173.
15. Marston BJ, Plouffe JF, File TM Jr, et al. Incidence of community-acquired pneumonia requiring hospitalization. Results of a population-based active surveillance study in Ohio. The Community-Based Pneumonia Incidence Study Group. Arch Intern Med. 1997;157:1709-1718.
16. Ruiz-Gonzalez A, Falguera M, Nogues A, Rubio-Caballero M. Is *Streptococcus pneumoniae* the leading cause of pneumonia of unknown etiology? A microbiologic study of lung aspirates in consecutive patients with community-acquired pneumonia. Am J Med. 1999;106:385-390.
17. Jokinen C, Heiskanen L, Juvonen H, et al. Microbial etiology of community-acquired pneumonia in the adult population of 4 municipalities in eastern Finland. Clin Infect Dis. 2001;32:1141-1154.
18. Grayston JT. Infections caused by *Chlamydia pneumoniae* strain TWAR. Clin Infect Dis. 1992;15:757-761.
19. Jantos CA, Wienpahl B, Schiefer HG, et al. Infection with *Chlamydia pneumoniae* in infants and children with acute lower respiratory tract disease. Pediatr Infect Dis J. 1995;14:117-122.
20. Grayston JT, Mordhorst C, Bruu AL, et al. Countrywide epidemics of *Chlamydia pneumoniae*, strain TWAR, in Scandinavia, 1981-1983. J Infect Dis. 1989;159:1111-1114.
21. Kauppinen MT, Saikku P, Kujala P, et al. Clinical picture of community-acquired *Chlamydia pneumoniae* pneumonia requiring hospital treatment: A comparison between chlamydial and pneumococcal pneumonia. Thorax. 1996;51:185-189.
22. Thom DH, Grayston JT, Wang SP, et al. *Chlamydia pneumoniae* strain TWAR, *Mycoplasma pneumoniae*, and viral infections in acute respiratory disease in a university student health clinic population. Am J Epidemiol. 1990;132:248-256.
23. Grayston JT. *Chlamydia pneumoniae* (TWAR) infections in children. Pediatr Infect Dis J. 1994;13:675-684; quiz 685.
24. Kauppinen MT, Lahde S, Syrjala H. Roentgenographic findings of pneumonia caused by *Chlamydia pneumoniae*. A comparison with streptococcus pneumonia. Arch Intern Med 1996;156:1851-1856.
25. McConnell CT Jr, Plouffe JF, File TM, et al. Radiographic appearance of *Chlamydia pneumoniae* (TWAR strain) respiratory infections. CBPIS Study Group. Community-based Pneumonia Incidence Study. Radiology. 1994;192:819-824.
26. Hahn DL, Dodge RW, Golubjatnikov R. Association of *Chlamydia pneumoniae* (strain TWAR) infection with wheezing, asthmatic bronchitis, and adult-onset asthma. JAMA. 1991;266:225-230.
27. Emre U, Roblin PM, Gelling M, et al. The association of *Chlamydia pneumoniae* infection and reactive airway disease in children. Arch Pediatr Adolesc Med. 1994;148:727-732.
28. Gray GC, McPhate DC, Leinonen M, et al. Weekly oral azithromycin as prophylaxis for agents causing acute respiratory disease. Clin Infect Dis. 1998;26:103-110.
29. Penttila T, Vuola JM, Puurula V, et al. Immunity to *Chlamydia pneumoniae* induced by vaccination with DNA vectors expressing a cytoplasmic protein (Hsp60) or outer membrane proteins (MOMP and Omp2). Vaccine. 2000;19:1256-1265.
30. Saikku P, Leinonen M, Mattila K, et al. Serological evidence of an association of a novel *Chlamydia*, TWAR, with chronic coronary heart disease and acute myocardial infarction. Lancet. 1988;2:983-986.
31. Shor A, Kuo CC, Patton DL. Detection of *Chlamydia pneumoniae* in coronary arterial fatty streaks and atheromatous plaques. S Afr Med J. 1992;82:158-161.
32. Ramirez JA. Isolation of *Chlamydia pneumoniae* from the coronary artery of a patient with coronary atherosclerosis. The *Chlamydia pneumoniae*/Atherosclerosis Study Group. Ann Intern Med. 1996;125:979-982.
33. Jackson LA, Campbell LA, Kuo CC, et al. Isolation of *Chlamydia pneumoniae* from a carotid endarterectomy specimen. J Infect Dis 1997;176:292-295.
34. Thom DH, Grayston JT, Siscovick DS, et al. Association of prior infection with *Chlamydia pneumoniae* and angiographically demonstrated coronary artery disease. JAMA. 1992;268:68-72.
35. Nieto FJ, Folsom AR, Sorlie PD, et al. *Chlamydia pneumoniae* infection and incident coronary heart disease: the Atherosclerosis Risk in Communities Study. Am J Epidemiol. 1999;150:149-156.
36. Ridker PM, Kundsin RB, Stampfer MJ, et al. Prospective study of *Chlamydia pneumoniae* IgG seropositivity and risks of future myocardial infarction. Circulation. 1999;99:1161-1164.
37. Danesh J, Whincup P, Lewington S, et al. *Chlamydia pneumoniae* IgA titres and coronary heart disease; prospective study and meta-analysis. Eur Heart J. 2002;23:371-375.
38. Danesh J, Whincup P, Walker M, et al. *Chlamydia pneumoniae* IgG titres and coronary heart disease: Prospective study and meta-analysis. BMJ. 2000;321:208-213.
39. Smieja M, Mahony JB, Petrich A, et al. Association of circulating *Chlamydia pneumoniae* DNA with cardiovascular disease: A systematic review. BMC Infect Dis. 2002;2:21.
40. Meier CR, Derby LE, Jick SS, et al. Antibiotics and risk of subsequent first-time acute myocardial infarction. JAMA. 1999;281:427-431.
41. Jackson LA, Smith NL, Heckbert SR, et al. Lack of association between first myocardial infarction and past use of erythromycin, tetracycline, or doxycycline. Emerg Infect Dis. 1999;5:281-284.
42. Pilote L, Green L, Joseph L, et al. Antibiotics against *Chlamydia pneumoniae* and prognosis after acute myocardial infarction. Am Heart J. 2002;143:294-300.
43. Luchsinger JA, Pablos-Mendez A, Knirsch C, et al. Relation of antibiotic use to risk of myocardial infarction in the general population. Am J Cardiol. 2002;89:18-21.
44. Gupta S, Leatham EW, Carrington D, et al. Elevated *Chlamydia pneumoniae* antibodies, cardiovascular events, and azithromycin in male survivors of myocardial infarction. Circulation. 1997;96:404-407.
45. Anderson JL, Muhlestein JB, Carlquist J, et al. Randomized secondary prevention trial of azithromycin in patients with coronary artery disease and serological evidence for *Chlamydia pneumoniae* infection: The Azithromycin in Coronary Artery Disease: Elimination of Myocardial Infection with Chlamydia (ACADEMIC) study. Circulation. 1999;99:1540-1547.
46. Neumann F, Kastrati A, Miethke T, et al. Treatment of *Chlamydia pneumoniae* infection with roxithromycin and effect on neointima proliferation after coronary stent placement (ISAR-3): A randomised, double-blind, placebo-controlled trial. Lancet. 2001;357:2085-2089.
47. Mosorin M, Juvonen J, Biancari F, et al. Use of doxycycline to decrease the growth rate of abdominal aortic aneurysms: A randomized, double-blind, placebo-controlled pilot study. J Vasc Surg. 2001;34:606-610.
48. Vammen S, Lindholt JS, Ostergaard L, et al. Randomized double-blind controlled trial of roxithromycin for prevention of abdominal aortic aneurysm expansion. Br J Surg. 2001;88:1066-1072.
49. Sander D, Winbeck K, Klingelhofer J, et al. Reduced progression of early carotid atherosclerosis after antibiotic treatment and *Chlamydia pneumoniae* seropositivity. Circulation. 2002;106:2428-2433.
50. Dunne MW. Rationale and design of a secondary prevention trial of antibiotic use in patients after myocardial infarction: The WIZARD (weekly intervention with Zithromax. J Infect Dis. 2000;181(Suppl 3):S572-S578.
51. Mawhorter SD, Lauer MA. Is atherosclerosis an infectious disease? Cleve Clin J Med. 2001;68:449-458.
52. Jackson LA. Description and status of the azithromycin and coronary events study (ACES). J Infect Dis. 2000;181(Suppl 3):S579-S581.
53. Stone AF, Mendall MA, Kaski JC, et al. Effect of treatment for *Chlamydia pneumoniae* and *Helicobacter pylori* on markers of inflammation and cardiac events in patients with acute coronary syndromes: South Thames Trial of Antibiotics in Myocardial Infarction and Unstable Angina (STAMINA). Circulation. 2002;106:1219-1223.
54. Muhlestein JB, Anderson JL, Hammond EH, et al. Infection with *Chlamydia pneumoniae* accelerates the development of atherosclerosis and treatment with azithromycin prevents it in a rabbit model. Circulation. 1998;97:633-636.
55. Rothstein NM, Quinn TC, Madico G, et al. Effect of azithromycin on murine arteriosclerosis exacerbated by *Chlamydia pneumoniae*. J Infect Dis. 2001;183:232-238.
56. Fong IW, Chiu B, Viira E, et al. Influence of clarithromycin on early atherosclerotic lesions after *Chlamydia pneumoniae* infection in a rabbit model. Antimicrob Agents Chemother. 2002;46:2321-2326.

57. Kaul R, Wenman WM. *Chlamydia pneumoniae* facilitates monocyte adhesion to endothelial and smooth muscle cells. Microb Pathog. 2001;30:149-155.

58. Kalayoglu MV, Byrne GI. Induction of macrophage foam cell formation by *Chlamydia pneumoniae*. J Infect Dis. 1998;177:725-729.

59. Grayston JT, Kuo CC, Coulson AS, et al. *Chlamydia pneumoniae* (TWAR) in atherosclerosis of the carotid artery. Circulation. 1995;92:3397-3400.

60. Maass M, Bartels C, Kruger S, et al. Endovascular presence of *Chlamydia pneumoniae* DNA is a generalized phenomenon in atherosclerotic vascular disease. Atherosclerosis. 1998;140(Suppl 1):S25-S30.

61. Wong YK, Gallagher PJ, Ward ME. *Chlamydia pneumoniae* and atherosclerosis. Heart. 1999;81:232-238.

62. Jackson LA, Smith NL, Heckbert SR, et al. Past use of erythromycin, tetracycline, or doxycycline is not associated with risk of first myocardial infarction. J Infect Dis. 2000;181(Suppl 3):S563-S565.

63. Gupta S, Leatham EW, Carrington D, et al. Elevated *Chlamydia pneumoniae* antibodies, cardiovascular events, and azithromycin in male survivors of myocardial infarction. Circulation. 1997;96:404-407.

64. Anderson JL, Muhlestein JB, Carlquist J, et al. Randomized secondary prevention trial of azithromycin in patients with coronary artery disease and serological evidence for *Chlamydia pneumoniae* infection: The Azithromycin in Coronary Artery Disease: Elimination of Myocardial Infection with Chlamydia (ACADEMIC) study. Circulation. 1999;99:1540-1547.

65. Mosorin M, Juvonen J, Biancari F, et al. Use of doxycycline to decrease the growth rate of abdominal aortic aneurysms: A randomized, double-blind, placebo-controlled pilot study. J Vasc Surg. 2001;34:606-610.

66. Vammen S, Lindholt JS, Ostergaard L, et al. Randomized double-blind controlled trial of roxithromycin for prevention of abdominal aortic aneurysm expansion. Br J Surg. 2001;88:1066-1072.

67. Muhlestein JB, Anderson JL, Carlquist JF, et al. Randomized secondary prevention trial of azithromycin in patients with coronary artery disease: Primary clinical results of the ACADEMIC study. Circulation. 2000;102:1755-1760.

68. Kalayoglu MV, Byrne GI. A *Chlamydia pneumoniae* component that induces macrophage foam cell formation is chlamydial lipopolysaccharide. Infect Immun. 1998;66:5067-5072.

CHAPTER **180**

Introduction to *Mycoplasma* Diseases

STEPHEN G. BAUM

Mycoplasma organisms are ubiquitous as pathogens and colonizing agents in the plant, animal, and insect kingdoms.[1] They represent the smallest known free-living forms, but because they have fastidious growth requirements, they are often difficult to culture on a cell-free medium. On the other hand, the presence of several species of *Mycoplasma* as commensals in animals and on human oral and genital mucosa has in the past produced frequent contamination of cell cultures.[2] Such contamination has in turn led to the false implication of mycoplasmas as causative agents in many human diseases, both trivial and life threatening. Knowledge of the true range of diseases that these organisms cause is, however, expanding rapidly with the advent of immunohistochemical and nucleic acid probe techniques used to detect mycoplasmas directly in tissue specimens.

DESCRIPTION OF THE ORGANISM

Mycoplasma organisms are prokaryotes that lack a cell wall. They are bounded by a cell membrane containing sterols, substances not found in either bacteria or viruses. Because of their small size (150 to 250 nm) and deformable membrane, they are able to pass through filters with pore sizes that retain bacteria.[3] Therefore, when first discovered, they were thought to be viruses.[4] However, their ability to grow in cell-free medium and the fact that they contain both RNA and DNA clearly set them apart from this class of microorganisms. For a time, mycoplasmas were thought to be L *(Lister)* forms of bacteria, which, like mycoplasmas, do not have cell walls. However, like the bacteria from

which they derive, L-forms lack sterols in their membranes and under certain conditions can be made to revert to their walled parental forms.[5] DNA homology studies have failed to demonstrate any significant relationship between mycoplasmas and known bacteria, although mycoplasmas probably devolved from gram-positive bacteria through reductive evolution[1] (Table 180-1).

The small size of these organisms suggests that they require many exogenous nutrients for growth, including vitamins, amino acids, nucleic acid precursors, and, in particular, lipids. The latter are provided by the addition of serum or cholesterol to growth medium. Energy is supplied by carbohydrate metabolism. Some nonfermenting mycoplasmas derive energy from amino acid (arginine) metabolism. As its name implies, *Ureaplasma* can split urea, but it is unclear whether urea splitting is the sole source of energy for these organisms.[6]

Most mycoplasmas grown on agar form colonies with a dense central zone and a less dense peripheral zone. The resultant colony has been likened to the shape of a fried egg (Fig. 180-1A). An important exception is *Mycoplasma pneumoniae*, the most significant human pathogen of the genus. This mycoplasma forms no peripheral halo, and colonies have been likened to a mulberry (see Fig. 180-1B).

Other characteristics of *Mycoplasma* growth in vitro include absorption of erythrocytes from a number of animal species and

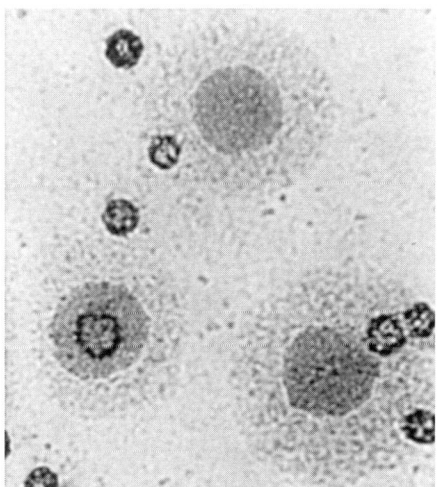

A

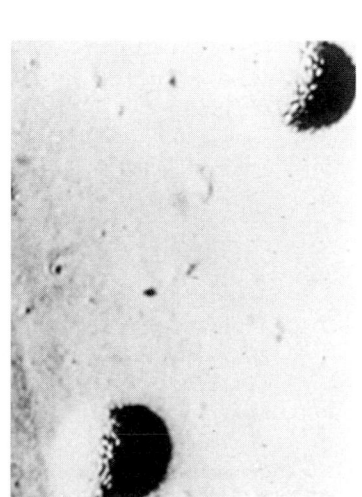

B

FIGURE 180-1. Photomicrograph of colonies of mycoplasma growing on agar medium. **A,** *Mycoplasma salivarium* colonies growing with "fried egg" appearance. **B,** *Mycoplasma pneumoniae* colonies with "mulberry" colony formation.

TABLE 180-1   Characteristics Defining Mycoplasmas

General
    Prokaryotic
    Small size: 150-250 nm
    No cell wall
    Trilayered cell membrane
    Most are aerobic
    Fastidious growth requirements
    Form "fried egg" colonies on agar
Differentiation from bacteria and L-forms
    Sterols in membrane
    No DNA homology with known bacteria
    Low guanine + cytosine content
    Low-molecular-weight genome ($4.5 \times 10^8 - 1 \times 10^9$ Da)
    No reversion to walled forms
Differentiation from viruses
    Contain both DNA and RNA
    Free living: cell-free growth on defined media in vitro
    Extracellular parasitism in vivo

Modified from Couch RB. *Mycoplasma* diseases: Introduction. In: Mandell GL, Douglas RG Jr, Bennett JE, eds. Principles and Practice of Infectious Diseases. New York: Churchill Livingstone; 1990:1445-1446.

hemolysis of erythrocytes in blood agar through the elaboration of hydrogen peroxide.

TAXONOMY AND DISTRIBUTION

Mycoplasmas have now been assigned taxonomically to their own class, Mollicutes, which has three main families: Mycoplasmataceae, which encompasses organisms infecting and colonizing humans and animals; Spironoplasmataceae, the plant mycoplasmas; and Acholeplasmataceae, most of which are isolated primarily from birds. A fourth family, Anaeroplasmataceae, consists of strict anaerobes that have been isolated from bovine and ovine rumen; they are not known to infect humans. A fifth family, Entomoplasmataceae, infects insects and plants. It is likely that all complex living organisms are or can be colonized by mycoplasmas.

The family Mycoplasmataceae is composed of two genera responsible for human infection: *Mycoplasma* and *Ureaplasma;* the genus *Mycoplasma* has at least 13 species that infect humans, as listed in Figure 180-2.[1,7] Ureaplasmas were previously referred to as T-strain mycoplasmas because of the tiny colonies that they formed on agar.[8]

Based on studies of 16SrRNA homology, increasing numbers of unculturable organisms are being classified as mycoplasmas.[9]

PATHOGENESIS

Mycoplasmas appear to cause infection primarily as extracellular parasites. They attach to the surface of ciliated and nonciliated epithelial cells. Some mycoplasmas, such as *M. penetrans* and *M. genitalium*, have special attachment organelles, but many that effectively penetrate cells, such as *M. fermentans* and *M. hominis*, do not.[1] Subsequent events are unclear but may include direct cytotoxicity of such elaborated substances as hydrogen peroxide,[10] or they may cause cytolysis via an inflammatory response mediated through chemotaxis of mononuclear cells, upregulation or downregulation of inflammatory cytokines, or antigen–antibody reactions.[11,12]

Mycoplasma organisms are very common contaminants of tissue cultures.[2,13] In this situation they are most often intracellular parasites. This fact may contribute to the difficulty in eradicating mycoplasmas from contaminated cultures. Their presence has been shown to markedly alter both cellular and viral molecular events, a fact that has

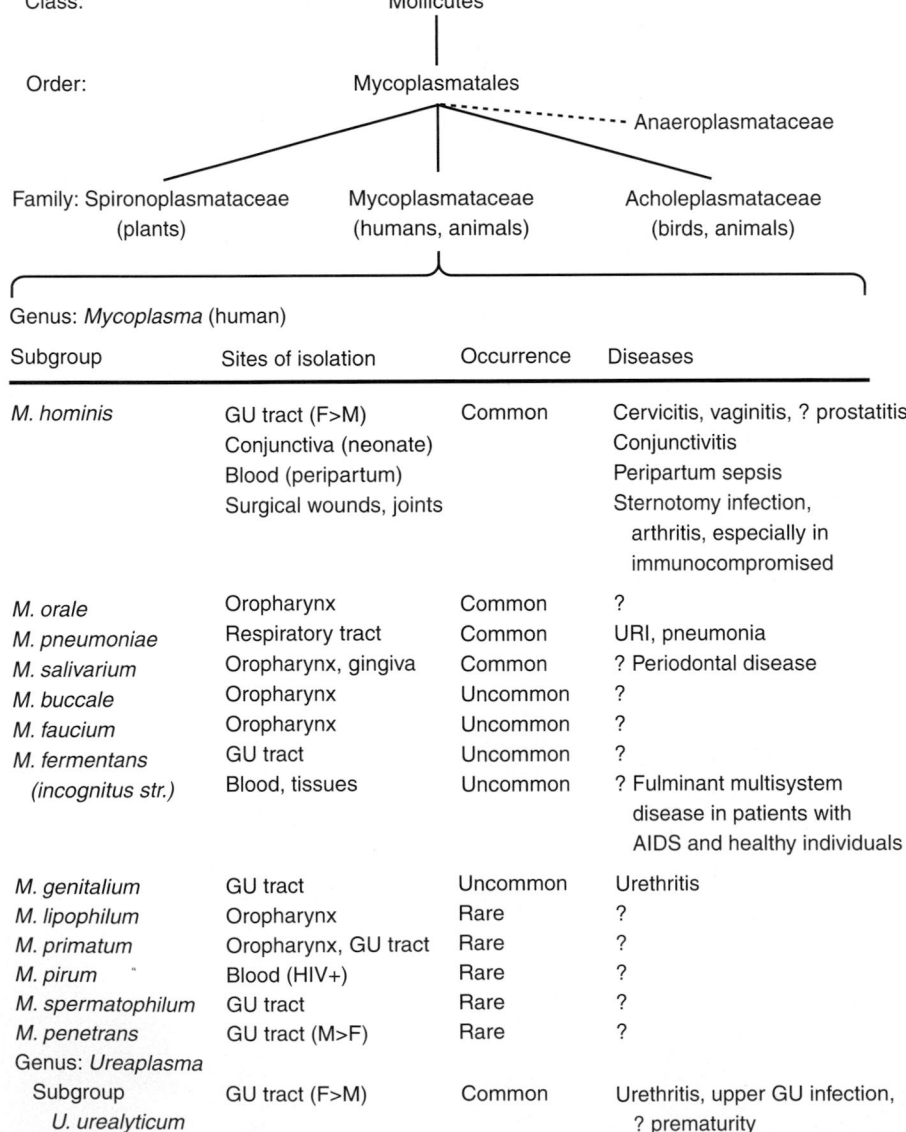

FIGURE 180-2. Taxonomy and distribution of the class Mollicutes. AIDS, acquired immunodeficiency syndrome; F, female; GU, genitourinary; HIV, human immunodeficiency virus; M, male; URT, upper respiratory infection. (Modified from Somerson NL, Cole BC. The mycoplasma flora of human and nonhuman primates. In: Tully JG, Whitcomb RF, eds. The Mycoplasmas, v. 2. New York: Academic Press; 1979;191-216. With permission from Elsevier.)

prompted some to question many of the molecular biologic results derived from tissue culture experiments.[2] A more complete discussion of mycoplasma molecular biology and pathogenesis in provided in a comprehensive review by Razin and associates.[1]

MYCOPLASMA ORGANISMS RECENTLY ASSOCIATED WITH HUMAN DISEASE

Mycoplasma fermentans (Incognitus Strain)

Mycoplasma incognitus (a variant of *M. fermentans*), *Mycoplasma penetrans,* and *Mycoplasma pirum* have been associated with severe disease in healthy people and those with acquired immunodeficiency syndrome (AIDS).[16,17] *M. fermentans* was first isolated by Lo and colleagues from the blood, organs, and Kaposi's sarcoma lesions of patients with AIDS and has since been reported to cause fulminant multisystem infection in presumably healthy patients.[17] The organism was first believed to be a virus,[14,15] then was identified as the mycoplasma *M. penetrans,*[18] and ultimately was shown by immunohistochemistry, DNA homology, electron microscopy, and in situ hybridization to be a mycoplasma closely related to *M. fermentans.*[17,18] The organism has been identified at the advancing margins of lesions in the liver, brain, spleen, lymph nodes, and thymus of infected patients.[19] *M. penetrans* has been isolated from the urogenital tract and *M. pirum* from the blood of patients with human immunodeficiency virus (HIV) infection.[15]

Cultivation of these organisms directly from patient material on cell-free medium has proved to be difficult, and prior animal and tissue culture passage is required. This difficulty in direct culturing has fueled a controversy over whether these organisms are pathogens or contaminants in these patients.

The organism is sensitive in vitro to tetracycline, chloramphenicol, clindamycin, lincomycin, and the quinolones. Sensitivity to the macrolides appears to be very limited.[23]

Animal *Mycoplasma* Organisms as Human Pathogens

Case reports have recently appeared of human infections caused by mycoplasmas previously thought to infect only animals. One such report describes fatal septicemia caused by *Mycoplasma arginini* in an immunocompromised slaughterhouse worker. This organism is often found in the respiratory tracts of cattle, sheep, and goats.[24]

Genital *Mycoplasma* Organisms Causing Nongenital Infection

A number of publications indicate that the genital mycoplasmas (*Mycoplasma hominis, Mycoplasma genitalium,* and *Ureaplasma urealyticum*) can cause serious infections involving the respiratory tract, heart, blood stream, central nervous system, sternotomy wounds, and prosthetic valves and joints of infants and adults.[25-35] The urogenital *Mycoplasma* organisms are discussed in detail in Chapter 182.

REFERENCES

1. Razin S, Yogev D, Naot Y. Molecular biology and pathogenicity of mycoplasmas. Microbiol Mol Biol Rev. 1998;62:1094-1156.
2. Barile MF, Hopps HE, Grabowski MW, et al. The identification and sources of mycoplasmas isolated from contaminated cell cultures. Ann N Y Acad Sci. 1973;25: 251-264.
3. Elford WJ. Ultrafiltration methods and their application in bacteriological and pathological studies. Br J Exp Pathol. 1929;10:126.
4. Eaton MD, Meiklejohn G, van Herick W, et al. Studies on the etiology of primary atypical pneumonia. II. Properties of the virus isolated and propagated in chick embryos. J Exp Med. 1945;82:317.
5. Madoff S. Introduction to the bacterial L forms. In: Madoff S, ed. The L Forms of Bacteria. New York: Marcel Dekker; 1986:1-20.
6. Rodwell AW, Mitchell A. Nutrition, growth and reproduction. In: Barile MF, Razin S, eds. The Mycoplasmas, v. 1. New York: Academic; 1979:103-139.
7. Taylor-Robinson D. Infections due to species of *Mycoplasma* and *Ureaplasma*: An update. Clin Infect Dis. 1996;23:671-684.
8. Razin S, Freundt EA. The mycoplasmas. In: Krieg NR, Holt JG, eds. Bergey's Manual of Systematic Microbiology, v. 1. Baltimore: Williams & Wilkins; 1984: 740-793.
9. Neimark HC, Kocan KM. The cell wall-less rickettsia *Eperythrozoon wenyoni* is a mycoplasma. FEMS Microbiol Lett. 1997;156:287-291.
10. Clyde WA Jr. *Mycoplasma pneumoniae* infections of man. In: Tully JG, Whitcomb RF, eds. The Mycoplasmas, v. 2. New York: Academic; 1979:275-306.
11. Chmura K, Lutz RD, Chiba H, et al. *Mycoplasma pneumoniae* antigens stimulate interleukin-8. Chest. 2003;123(suppl):425.
12. Tanaka H, Narita M, Teramoto S, et al. Role of interleukin-18 and T-helper type 1 cytokines in the development of *Mycoplasma pneumoniae* pneumonia in adults. Chest. 2002;121:1493-1497.
13. Somerson NL, Cole BC. The mycoplasma flora of human and nonhuman primates. In: Tully JG, Whitcomb RF, eds. The Mycoplasmas, v. 2. New York: Academic; 1979:191-216.
14. *Mycoplasma incognitus:* A workshop. Am J Trop Med Hyg. 1990;42:399.
15. Lo SC, Dawson MS, Newton PB III, et al. Association of the virus-like infectious agent originally reported in patients with AIDS with acute fatal disease in previously healthy non-AIDS patients. Am J Trop Med Hyg. 1989;41:364.
16. Wang R Y-H, Shih J W-K, Grandinetti T, et al. High frequency of antibodies to *Mycoplasma penetrans* in HIV-infected patients. Lancet. 1992;340:1312.
17. Hawkins RE, Rickman LS, Vermund SH, et al. Detection of amplified *Mycoplasma fermentans* DNA in blood. J Infect Dis. 1992;165:581.
18. *Mycoplasma incognitus*: A workshop. Am J Trop Med Hyg. 1990;42:399.
19. Lo SC, Dawson M, Wong DM. Identification of *Mycoplasma incognitus* infection in patients with AIDS: An immunohistochemical, in-situ hybridization and ultrastructural study. Am J Trop Med Hyg. 1989;41:601.
20. Chowdhury IH, Munakata T, Koyanagi Y, et al. *Mycoplasma* can enhance HIV replication in vitro: A possible co-factor responsible for the progression of AIDS. Biochem Biophys Res Commun. 1990;170:1365.
23. Taylor-Robinson D, Bébeár C. Antibiotic susceptibilities of mycoplasmas and treatment of mycoplasmal infections. J Antimicrob Chemother. 1997;40:622-630.
24. Yechouron A, Lefebvre J, Robson HG. Fatal septicemia due to *Mycoplasma arginini:* A new human zoonosis. Clin Infect Dis. 1992;15:434.
25. Cassell GH, Waites KB, Krouse DT. Perinatal mycoplasmal infections. Clin Perinatol. 1991;18:241.
26. Alonso-Vega C, Wauters N, Vermeylen D, et al. A fatal case of *Mycoplasma hominis* meningoencephalitis in a full-term newborn. J Clin Microbiol. 1997;35:286-287.
27. Cohen JI, Sloss LJ, Kundsin R, et al. Prosthetic valve endocarditis caused by *Mycoplasma hominis.* Am J Med. 1989;86:819.
28. Mohiuddin AA, Coren J, Harbeck RJ, et al. *Ureaplasma urealyticum* chronic osteomyelitis in a patient with hypogammaglobulinemia. J Allergy Clin Immunol. 1991;87:104.
29. Parides GC, Bloom JW, Ampel NM, et al. *Mycoplasma* and *Ureaplasma* in bronchoalveolar lavage fluids from immunocompromised hosts. Diagn Microbiol Infect Dis. 1988;9:55.
30. Smeller H, Wellborne F, Barile MF, et al. Prosthetic joint infection with *Mycoplasma hominis.* J Infect Dis. 1986;153:174.
31. Baseman JB, Dallo SF, Tully JG, et al. Isolation and characterization of *Mycoplasma genitalium* strains from the human respiratory tract. J Clin Microbiol. 1988;26:2266.
32. Cassell GH, Crouse DT, Waites KB, et al. Does *Ureaplasma urealyticum* cause respiratory disease in newborns? Pediatr Infect Dis J. 1988;7:535.
33. Couch RB. *Mycoplasma* diseases: Introduction. In: Mandell GL, Douglas RG Jr, Bennett JE, eds. Principles and Practice of Infectious Diseases. New York: Churchill Livingstone; 1990:1445-1446.
34. Sielaff TD, Everett JE, Shumway SJ, et al. *Mycoplasma hominis* infections occurring in cardiovascular surgical patients. Ann Thorac Surg. 1996;61:99-103.
35. Luttrell LM, Kanj SS, Corey GR, et al. *Mycoplasma hominis* septic arthritis: 2 Case reports and review. Clin Infect Dis. 1994;19:1067-1070.

Mycoplasma pneumoniae and Atypical Pneumonia

STEPHEN G. BAUM

The term and concept of atypical pneumonia arose at the onset of the antibiotic era. In the early 1940s, sulfonamides and then penicillins were introduced into clinical practice. At that time, it was recognized that some cases of pneumonia did not respond to these antibiotics and that these were the pneumonias that could not be attributed by Gram stain or culture to a known bacterial cause. The condition was designated primary atypical pneumonia (PAP). The prefix *primary* indicated that no causative agent could be determined.

In the intervening years, with the advent of virology and better techniques for identifying fastidious bacterial and protozoan agents, it has become clear that the atypical pneumonia syndrome can be caused by influenza virus, adenovirus, respiratory syncytial virus, cytomegalovirus, *Chlamydia, Legionella, Pneumocystis carinii, Mycoplasma pneumoniae,* the newly described coronavirus variant causing severe acute respiratory syndrome (SARS),[1] and probably many other agents. Because we now can identify many of the agents, the prefix *primary* should be discarded. In addition, some of these agents do respond to antimicrobial drugs.

Despite the identification of multiple causes, atypical pneumonias share two unifying features. The first is a nonlobar, patchy, or interstitial pattern on chest radiography, and the other is the failure to identify a causative organism on Gram stain or culture of sputum as routinely performed. Because the organisms involved are difficult to identify at the time the patient presents to the physician, it is unlikely that the term *atypical pneumonia* will disappear from the infectious diseases or pulmonary medicine lexicon any time soon.

HISTORY

From the time of the description of the atypical pneumonia syndrome in the mid-1940s until the early 1960s, the cause of this syndrome was in question. Bacteria other than the pneumococcus, viruses such as influenza, and other as yet unidentified agents were all implicated at one time or another. However, one organism, *M. pneumoniae,* is probably responsible for more cases of this syndrome than is any other single organism.

In 1945, Eaton and colleagues described an agent that passed through virus filters and caused focal areas of pneumonia when inoculated in several species of rodents.[2] The agent, initially thought to be a virus, could be serially passaged in chick embryos but could not be grown in culture. The relation of this agent to the PAP syndrome was suggested by the fact that human serum from some patients recovering from PAP neutralized the agent.[3] Serum from about 50% to 70% of these patients also was found by Finland and colleagues to agglutinate red blood cells when a mixture of the two was exposed to the cold (4° C).[4] This cold agglutination reaction became and has remained the laboratory hallmark of the disease (see "Immunology," later). When serum from patients with PAP caused by a known etiologic agent (e.g., influenza virus) was used, cold agglutinins were not demonstrable and there was no neutralization of Eaton agent.[5] This provided a link between Eaton agent and a proportion of PAP cases of unknown cause. However, serum from this same group of patients also had antibodies to *Streptococcus* MG. This and other nonspecific antibody formation in these patients served to confuse matters for a time and to detract from the evidence that Eaton agent was a major cause of PAP.

By 1946, the disease could be transmitted to human volunteers by ultrafiltrates from patients, but this transmissibility did not necessarily tie the syndrome to Eaton agent rather than to a virus, because passage of the chick embryo isolate to humans had not been attempted.[5] This link came in 1961 with the evidence that convalescent serum from volunteers inoculated with PAP ultrafiltrate neutralized Eaton's chick embryo "virus."[6] Subsequently, evidence that Eaton agent was a mycoplasma came from Clyde,[7] who grew the agent in tissue culture, Goodburn and Marmion,[8] who described its morphology, and Chanock and co-workers,[9] who, in 1962, were the first to grow the organism on cell-free artificial medium. The ultimate proof of the role of Eaton agent in PAP was the demonstration that the organism isolated in cell-free culture produced the syndrome in volunteers.[10]

Because Eaton agent passed through virologic filters and could be grown only in chick embryos, it was believed throughout most of two decades after its discovery that the agent was a virus. In the early 1960s, it was established that the organism had many characteristics in common with those that caused pneumonia in cattle, hence the transiently used term *pleuropneumonia-like organism.*[11] These organisms were soon shown to be mycoplasmas[12] of the class Mollicutes, described in Chapter 180.

DESCRIPTION OF THE ORGANISM

M. pneumoniae exhibits most of the characteristics described for this family of organisms. It is capable of growth on cell-free defined medium, setting it apart from all but one *(Legionella)* of the common causative organisms of the atypical pneumonia syndrome. *M. pneumoniae,* unlike most of the other human mycoplasmas, grows well aerobically and ferments glucose as its primary energy source, producing acid.[9,13]

This organism is also unusual among human mycoplasmas in being able to reduce the dye tetrazolium from a blue to a yellow color, adsorb guinea pig and chick erythrocytes to growing colonies, and lyse red blood cells incorporated into the growth agar by means of the elaboration of hydrogen peroxide. Detection of each of these unique characteristics has been used to establish presumptive identification of this organism in culture.

M. pneumoniae is a short rod (about 10×200 nm) and has at one end an organelle that is responsible for attachment of the organism to cell membranes.[14] The major protein of this organelle (P1) has been purified, and it has been suggested that this peptide would serve well as an antigen for a vaccine.[15] This protein may also confer on *M. pneumoniae* its affinity for respiratory epithelium. *M. pneumoniae* is prokaryotic and is bounded by a trilamellar membrane containing sterols. It divides by binary fission, with a doubling time of more than 6 hours.[16] This long doubling time makes culturing of *M. pneumoniae* a slow process (5 to 20 days), compared with bacteria.[13] Colonies of *M. pneumoniae* differ in morphology from those of other mycoplasmas. They have no outer halo and grow in a dense mulberry shape (see Fig. 180-1 in Chapter 180). Because they lack a cell wall, mycoplasmas including *M. pneumoniae* are not affected by β-lactam antibiotics and are not visible on Gram staining.

EPIDEMIOLOGY

Most cases of mycoplasma respiratory infection occur singly or as family outbreaks. In closed populations such as military recruit camps and boarding schools, mycoplasma can cause miniepidemics and may represent from 25% to 75% of pneumonias in such settings.[17] Serologically based epidemiologic studies throughout the world have documented the high incidence of mycoplasma respiratory infection. In the United States, it is estimated that each year at least one case of mycoplasma pneumonia occurs for each 1000 persons, or more than 2 million cases annually. The incidence of mycoplasma nonpneumonic respiratory infection may be 10 to 20 times this high.[18,19] The highest attack rates are in children 5 to 20 years old, but *M. pneumoniae* infection can occur at any age and may cause particularly severe disease in neonates.[20]

A few studies have reported a peak incidence in the fall in temperate climates.[21-23] This is not surprising given the peak age-related incidence and the fact that late summer and fall represent the time of return to schools. Most surveys, however, show little or no seasonal preponderance in sporadic cases. Distribution of the disease is worldwide.[24,25]

There appears to be an age-related incidence of upper versus lower respiratory tract infection caused by *M. pneumoniae.* Children younger than 3 years of age develop primarily upper respiratory tract infection,[26] whereas those 5 to 20 years old tend to develop bronchitis and pneumonia. In older adults, pneumonia is relatively common in infected patients.[27]

TRANSMISSION

M. pneumoniae infection is spread from one patient to another by respiratory droplets produced by coughing. Relatively close association with the index case appears to be required. The disease is usually introduced into families by a young child, and in some studies most of the adults who were infected were the parents of young children.[28,29]

As opposed to most viral respiratory infections, which are clinically manifest 1 to 3 days after infection, mycoplasma has an incubation period of 2 to 3 weeks.[29] Therefore, a careful history showing several weeks between cases within a family may give an important clue as to mycoplasmal etiology. In experimental situations, the incubation period seemed to be shorter (7 to 10 days), but this may have resulted from the use of large inocula to induce disease.[10]

Organisms can be cultured from the sputum of infected individuals for weeks to months after clinically effective treatment,[30] and the extent of the effect of treatment of an index case on subsequent transmission to family members is unclear.

CLINICAL DISEASE

In view of the very high incidence of mycoplasma pneumonia when studied epidemiologically in large populations, it would appear that specific, confirmed diagnosis of this entity is not often accomplished in individual clinical practice. There are probably three reasons for this. The first is that mycoplasma pneumonia is usually self-limited and rarely fatal. This fact dampens the zeal to establish the cause of infection. Second, mycoplasmas are relatively fastidious and slow growing; therefore, culture results, if obtained at all, often return after the patient is well. Finally, there is deficient knowledge of the epidemiology and clinical manifestations of infection, so that the diagnosis is often not considered.

Respiratory Infection

Epidemiologic studies indicate that most *M. pneumoniae* infections lead to clinically apparent disease rather than to subclinical infection. Most of these infections involve only the upper respiratory tract. After a 2- to 3-week incubation period, the disease has an insidious onset composed of fever, malaise, headache, and cough. The latter is the clinical hallmark of *M. pneumoniae* infection (Fig. 181-1). The frequency and severity of cough increase over the next 1 to 2 days and may become debilitating. The gradual onset of symptoms is in contradistinction to the often acute presentation of respiratory infection caused by influenza or adenovirus.

In 5% to 10% of patients, depending somewhat on age, the infection progresses to tracheobronchitis or pneumonia. In these cases, the original manifestations persist and the cough becomes more severe. It is usually relatively nonproductive but may yield white or occasionally blood-flecked sputum. Gram staining of this sputum reveals evidence of inflammatory cells but no predominant bacterial species. With continued cough, the patient may develop parasternal chest soreness due to muscle strain, but true pleuritic pain is unusual. Fever is usually at the level of 101° to 102° F and may be associated with chilly sensations. As opposed to pneumonia caused by *Streptococcus pneumoniae*, that caused by *M. pneumoniae* rarely involves true shaking chills. In comparison with influenza, which can also manifest as an atypical pneumonia syndrome, myalgias and gastrointestinal complaints of nausea and vomiting are unusual. Diarrhea, sometimes a concomitant of adenoviral pneumonia (see Chapter 139), is uncommon in mycoplasmal infection.

On physical examination, the general appearance is that of a patient who is not terribly ill. In fact, this disease is the paradigm of the term *walking pneumonia*. The pharynx may be injected and erythematous, usually without the marked cervical adenopathy seen in group A streptococcal pharyngitis. *M. pneumoniae* is not a common cause of isolated pharyngitis in the pediatric or adult population.[29] Much has been made of the finding of bullous myringitis in this disease. This abnormality was associated with experimentally induced *M. pneumoniae* infection in about 20% of volunteers.[31] However, true bullous myringitis in naturally occurring mycoplasma disease is rare. In a study of a pediatric population, otitis was rarely associated with isolation of mycoplasma and, on the contrary, was often associated with bacterial and viral upper respiratory tract pathogens.[32,33] The important synthesis of these data is that the absence of myringitis, bullous or otherwise, should not dissuade one from a diagnosis of mycoplasma pneumonia.

Examination of the chest in patients with mycoplasma pneumonia is often unrevealing, even in those patients with severe, productive cough. There may be no auscultative or percussive findings, or only minimal rales may be present. Disparity between physical findings and radiographic evidence of pneumonia in this condition may be the greatest of any of the atypical pneumonia syndromes. Although wheezing can occur in this disease, in one study of asthmatic patients the presence of wheezing had a negative correlation with the isolation of *M. pneumoniae*, compared with viral respiratory pathogens.[34] *M. pneumoniae* also does not seem to be a common pathogen in patients with preexisting chronic obstructive lung disease.[28] Bacterial superinfection following *M. pneumoniae* respiratory infection is rare.

FIGURE 181-1. Major clinical and laboratory manifestations of mycoplasmal pneumonia. ELISA, enzyme-linked immunosorbent assay. *(Adapted from Baum SG Mycoplasmal infections. In: Wyngaarden JB, Smith LH Jr, eds. Cecil Textbook of Medicine. 17th ed. Philadelphia; WB Saunders; 1985:1506.)*

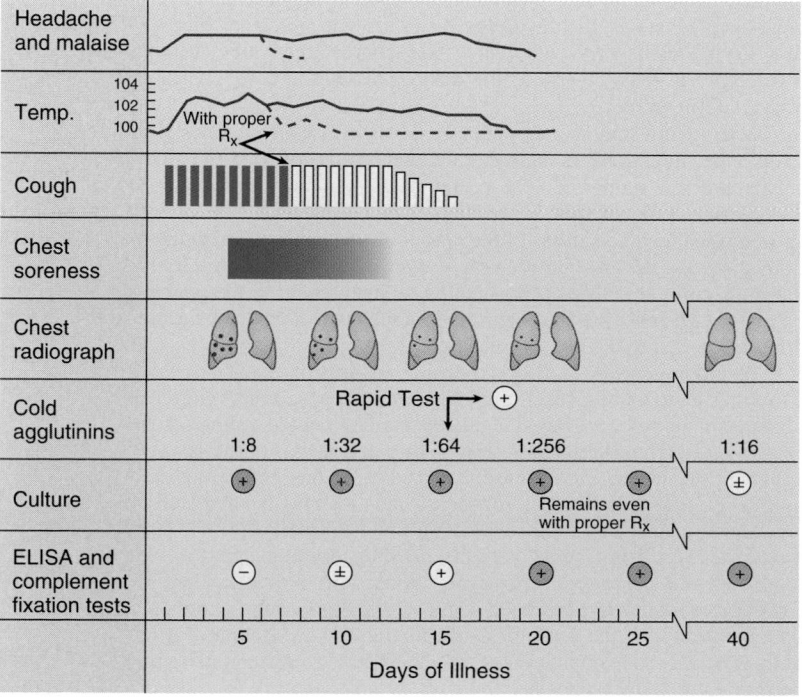

Pleural effusion (usually small) occurs in 5% to 20% of patients with *M. pneumoniae* infection.[35,36] This low incidence of pleural inflammation is consistent with the rarity of pleuritic pain. If effusion is present, thoracentesis reveals serous fluid that is exudative with minimal inflammatory reaction. The cell differential count in the fluid is variable,[37] and bloody effusions are rare. It is unusual to isolate *M. pneumoniae* from effusions when they do occur, but several reports of such isolation exist.[38]

Although pneumonia is usually mild and self-limited, fulminant, severe, and lethal cases have been reported in normal young adults and may be underdiagnosed.[39]

Extrapulmonary Involvement

Abnormalities in almost every organ system have been described as examples of the extrapulmonary manifestations of *M. pneumoniae* infection. The frequency of these extrapulmonary manifestations varies greatly from one report to another and is much less common when viewed as part of a prospective epidemiologic study rather than as the sum of isolated case reports. The lesson from this appears to be that the high prevalence of mycoplasma infection in most populations predisposes to the reporting of many concurrent but perhaps unrelated events as if they were part of the mycoplasmal disease. Therefore, single case reports, particularly those confirmed only by serologic response, have not been included in this chapter. Several clinical syndromes have been reported with sufficient frequency to provide some support for a causal relationship.

Dermatologic Involvement

A wide variety of transient dermatologic conditions have been reported in conjunction with mycoplasma pneumonia. These include macular, morbilliform, and papulovesicular eruptions as well as erythema nodosum and urticaria.[40,41] Again, the variety and high incidence of these rashes in the absence of mycoplasma infection makes it difficult to define the relationships, if any, among these occurrences. Further, the role that concurrent antibiotic therapy plays in the development of the exanthems seen during *M. pneumoniae* infection is unknown.

One skin condition that occurs often enough in concert with *M. pneumoniae* infection to provide some basis for relatedness is erythema multiforme major, or Stevens-Johnson syndrome (Fig. 181-2A). This has been reported in up to 7% of patients with mycoplasma pneumonia.[42-44] Erythema multiforme major consists of erythematous vesicles, plaques, and bullae involving the skin, with particular localization at mucocutaneous junctions. The conjunctivae may also be involved,[45] as may organs of the gastrointestinal and genitourinary tracts and the joints.[42]

These manifestations have been associated in isolated cases with many other infections, including some that can manifest as the atypical pneumonia syndrome. These include legionnaires' pneumonia,[46] adenovirus conjunctivitis,[47] and influenza B infection.[48] However, among possible associations of Stevens-Johnson syndrome with infectious diseases, the association with *M. pneumoniae* infection is by far the most common.[49] This complication tends to occur in the younger patients with mycoplasma pneumonia and has a definite male predominance (2:1 to 4:1) in this disease.

The pathogenesis of this syndrome in any of the diseases in which it occurs is unclear. It has long been supposed that immunity plays a major role,[50,51] but several reports have noted culture of *M. pneumoniae* from the lesions.[44,52,53] The relationship to the level of cold agglutinins in this disease is variable. It has been suggested that development of Stevens-Johnson syndrome may be the result of augmented sensitivity to antibiotics in the presence of *M. pneumoniae* infection,[54] but some patients develop erythema multiforme major in the absence of prior or concurrent antibiotic therapy. Corticosteroid therapy has been suggested for this complication, but data in support of the usefulness of this therapy are lacking.[55] Most patients clear the lesions in 1 to 2 weeks without scarring unless impetiginization supervenes.

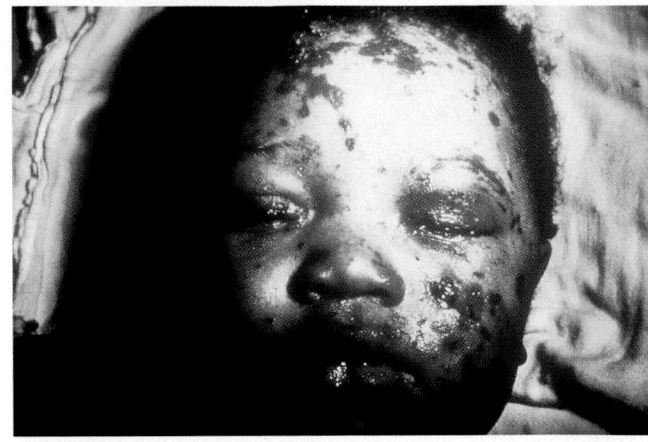

A

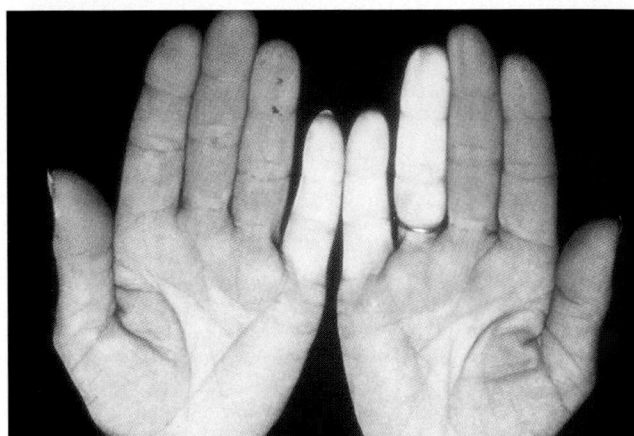

B

C

FIGURE 181-2. A, Stevens-Johnson syndrome in a child with *Mycoplasma pneumoniae* infection. **B,** Raynaud's phenomenon in a young woman with *M. pneumoniae* infection and high titers of cold agglutinins. **C,** Necrosis of distal extremities in a patient with sickle cell disease who contracted *M. pneumoniae* infection accompanied by very high cold agglutinin titers.

Raynaud's Phenomenon

Although transient reversible vasospasm of the digits on exposure to the cold is not technically a dermatologic syndrome, it is manifested in the skin (see Fig. 181-2B). This phenomenon occurs in many people, usually women, without any association with infection. It has been reported in patients with acute mycoplasma pneumonia whether or not these patients manifested this syndrome before infection.[41,56] Although the pathophysiology of this phenomenon in *M. pneumoniae* infection is unclear, it may be related to in vivo action of cold agglutinins (see "Immunology," later).[57,58] Other vascular complications reported in *M. pneumoniae* infection include internal carotid artery occlusion and cerebral infarction.[59]

Cardiac Complications

Of all the extrapulmonary manifestations of *M. pneumoniae* infection other than exanthems, cardiac abnormalities are the most commonly reported. Most studies have involved hospitalized patients, so the true incidence of cardiac changes may be underestimated.[60-62] The signs and symptoms suggesting involvement of the heart are arrhythmia, congestive failure, chest pain, and electrocardiographic abnormalities, particularly conduction defects. One report suggests that a loud third heart sound may be the only clue to cardiac involvement.[63] Although cardiac abnormalities have been reported in as many as 10% of cases of *M. pneumoniae* infection, other reports indicate a much lower prevalence. Cardiac abnormalities are more common as the age of the patients studied increases. Cardiac complications prolong illness and have led to death[64] but generally do not appear to appreciably increase mortality. The mechanism of heart damage is unknown, but *M. pneumoniae* has been isolated from the pericardial fluid of one patient.[65]

Neurologic Complications

Proof of involvement of the central nervous system in mycoplasma pneumonia is somewhat tenuous. Aseptic meningitis and meningoencephalitis,[66,67] transverse myelitis,[68] brain stem dysfunction,[69] Guillain-Barré syndrome,[70] and peripheral neuropathy have all been reported. In aggregate, these central nervous system manifestations occur no more frequently than 1 per 1000 cases and are more often noted in hospitalized patients.[71] The cerebrospinal fluid findings in these cases are variable, but cellular response is usually minimal, with slightly elevated protein and normal to slightly depressed glucose. Most often, diagnosis of mycoplasma-related central nervous system involvement is made on exclusion of other causes, presence of antecedent or intercurrent respiratory illness, and a rise in antibody titer to *M. pneumoniae* in the serum.[67] Occasionally, mycoplasma-specific antibodies have been demonstrated in the cerebrospinal fluid, but these titers have paralleled serum antibody titers.

Neurologic complications are usually reversible when associated with mycoplasma infection, but the mortality of patients with central nervous system involvement is higher than that of others. Although *M. pneumoniae* has been isolated from a few of these patients,[72] polymerase chain reaction (PCR) failed to detect *M. pneumoniae* DNA in the cerebrospinal fluid of 11 patients deemed to have *M. pneumoniae*–related central nervous system disease on serologic grounds.[73] Therefore, immune mechanisms of neural damage have been suggested.[74] Some mycoplasmas elaborate a neurotoxin, but this has not been described for *M. pneumoniae*.[75]

Musculoskeletal, Renal, and Hematopoietic Complications

Polyarthralgias are common in mycoplasma pneumonia, but arthritis is rare.[76] Although immune mechanisms have been postulated for this complication, there have been a few reports of isolation of *M. pneumoniae* from joint fluid.[77,78] When present, arthritis may be monoarticular or migratory. Several of the cases of frank arthritis have been reported in patients with hypogammaglobulinemia. Nonhuman mycoplasmas probably cause arthropathy in several animal species (see Chapter 180).

Renal complications associated with immune complex deposition and high-titer cold agglutinins have been reported (see "Immunology," later).[79] There are several case reports of *M. pneumoniae*–associated aplastic anemia.[80]

Conditions Leading to Increased Susceptibility

Several reports have emphasized the unusually high severity of *M. pneumoniae* infection in patients with sickle cell disease[81] or sickle-related hemoglobinopathies.[82,83] These patients may develop large pleural effusions and marked respiratory distress. Functional asplenia and its attendant opsonization deficiencies may contribute to overwhelming infection with *M. pneumoniae*, as they do to *S. pneumoniae* infection. It is interesting in this regard that some patients with sickle cell disease and *M. pneumoniae* infection who develop extremely high cold agglutinin titers may experience digital necrosis, as they do with *S. pneumoniae*. One such patient is shown in Figure 181-2C, and a hypothesis on pathogenesis is given in the discussion on cold agglutinins later under "Immunology."

Patients with immune deficiency syndromes have been the subjects of case reports of *M. pneumoniae* infection.[84] Because mycoplasma infections are so common in normal children, the contribution of the immune deficiency is unclear. *M. pneumoniae* does not seem to be a very common opportunistic agent in the acquired immunodeficiency syndrome (AIDS),[84] but another mycoplasma, *Mycoplasma fermentans* (*incognitus* strain), has been identified in these patients.[85]

Unusually severe *M. pneumoniae* infection has also been reported in children with Down syndrome.[86] All of these patients survived infection.

IMMUNOLOGY

Mycoplasmas are active in stimulating several components of the immune system. They can act as polyclonal T-cell and B-cell activators[87,88] and can cause capping of lymphocytes.[89] Macrophages can also be stimulated by some mycoplasmas in vitro.[90] *M. pneumoniae* is capable of inducing several cytokines, including granulocyte-macrophage colony-stimulating factor[91] and interferon,[92] and several pro-inflammatory interleukins.[13,93]

In the course of *M. pneumoniae* infection, several classes of antibody are produced. Some of these fulfill the desired role of antibody production in infection—neutralization of the agent[94]—and others appear to be autoantibodies. The latter include agglutinins to lung, brain, cardiolipins, and smooth muscle.[73,92] The best studied of these autoagglutinins are the cold isohemagglutinins.

In 1943, Finland and colleagues described the presence of cold agglutinins in 50% to 70% of patients with Eaton agent pneumonia.[4,95,96] These agglutinins were capable of clumping erythrocytes at 4° C. Agglutination was reversible by warming the serum–erythrocyte mixture to 37° C and, unlike hemagglutination by myxoviruses and paramyxoviruses, was repeatable with the same sample, indicating that receptor-destroying enzyme (neuraminidase) played no role in the dissociation at 37° C (see Fig. 181-3).

Cold agglutinins in *M. pneumoniae* infection have been shown to be oligoclonal immunoglobulin M (IgM) antibodies directed against an altered "I" antigen on the surface of erythrocytes of *M. pneumoniae*–infected patients.[97] The I antigen is one of the blood group antigens, but unlike the A and B isoantigens it seems to be common to almost all mature erythrocytes. Fetal erythrocytes have "i" antigen instead. Like other IgM antibodies, the mycoplasma-induced cold agglutinins develop early in the disease (7 to 10 days) and therefore are often present by the time the patient seeks medical attention. The titer of these agglutinins peaks at 2 to 3 weeks and persists for 2 to 3 months.

There are several theories as to the factors triggering formation of cold agglutinins in mycoplasma pneumonia. One is that the organism alters the I antigen so as to make it antigenic to the patient. Hydrogen peroxide elaborated by *M. pneumoniae* could be responsible for this alteration. One study indicates that the I antigen in a sialated state may serve as a receptor for *M. pneumoniae* and that the cold agglutinins are directed at the modified receptor.[98] Other studies indicate that the cold agglutinins are directed at mycoplasma substructures themselves and merely cross-react with the I antigen on red cells.[99] The role in pathogenesis that these antibodies play is unclear. Given their apparent target, they could either contribute to cytolysis and exacerbate infection or interfere with cell-to-cell spread by blocking or disrupting the cell receptor for the mycoplasma.

There is a report of chronic renal failure associated with *M. pneumoniae*–induced cold agglutinins. Fluctuating severity of the renal failure correlated with variations in cold agglutinin titer; respiratory infection associated with complement-fixing antibodies to *M. pneumoniae* preceded the renal failure. There were no immunohistologic analyses done in this case, and the role of cold agglutinins in this patient's renal disease remains speculative.[79,80] High titers of cold agglutinins also have been associated with hemolysis, presumably as a result of the activation of complement-mediated erythrocyte destruction.[4] The direct Coombs test is positive in many of these patients.[100,101] Although clinically significant hemolysis is uncommon, subclinical levels of red cell destruction are common.

One syndrome in some patients with mycoplasma pneumonia that could be related to cold agglutinins is Raynaud's phenomenon, described previously. A unifying hypothesis would relate capillary obstruction in extremities exposed to the cold to erythrocyte autoagglutination in the microcirculation of these patients with high-titer cold agglutinins. In support of this hypothesis is the severe vascular damage that occurs in patients with sickle cell disease who contract mycoplasma pneumonia accompanied by high titers of cold agglutinins. The extremities of one such patient, who had a cold agglutinin titer greater than 1:20,000, are shown in Figure 181-2C. The hypothetical pathogenesis of vasculopathy in this condition would then extend from reversible in vivo cold agglutination in microvasculature exposed to the cold (Raynaud's), to irreversible vascular damage in patients who have underlying microvascular compromise that is exacerbated and leads to digital necrosis (sickle cell disease).

M. pneumoniae infection leads to the production of complement-fixing antibodies as well. These arise early in the disease (2 to 3 weeks) and persist for 2 to 3 months. Assay of *M. pneumoniae*–specific complement-fixing antibodies has been the standard for retrospective serologic confirmation of infection with this organism.

Clearly, antibody production of both IgG and IgA classes plays a part in protection against the disease.[94] However, second cases of *M. pneumoniae* infection have been reported in apparently immunocompetent individuals.[102] Polymorphonuclear leukocytes and pulmonary macrophages also play a role in containing infection, but they appear to have relative difficulty in clearing the organism, in comparison with the cellular killing of most bacteria.[103]

PATHOLOGY AND PATHOPHYSIOLOGY

Because of two fortunate aspects of mycoplasma pneumonia—its low severity and low mortality—there is relatively little information on pathologic findings in this disease, and knowledge rests on relatively few specimens. As stated previously, sickle cell disease, sickle-related hemoglobinopathies, and hypogammaglobulinemia predispose to increased severity and to mortality. Some of the available pathologic data therefore may be influenced by the pathophysiology of these underlying conditions.

When deaths have occurred, they have been in cases of diffuse pneumonia, adult respiratory distress syndrome, thromboembolism, and disseminated intravascular coagulopathy.[39,104-106]

A clinicopathologic presentation described a previously healthy man who succumbed to *M. pneumoniae* infection; autopsy revealed diffuse alveolar pneumonia with hyaline membrane formation and multiple pulmonary infarctions. Other evidence of diffuse intravascular coagulopathy included thrombosis and infarction of kidneys, liver, spleen, and brain.[107] Other pathologic findings have included myocarditis[108] and diffuse interstitial fibrosis.[109]

In nonfatal cases in which lung biopsy was performed, the inflammatory process involved primarily the trachea, bronchioles, and peribronchial tissues.[41,110] The lumen of the respiratory tree was filled with purulent exudate rich in polymorphonuclear leukocytes. The lining of the bronchial and bronchiolar walls showed metaplastic cells, and the walls themselves were infiltrated with monocytic elements, especially plasma cells. There was widening of the peribronchial septa and hyperplasia of type II pneumocytes.

Tracheal organ culture has demonstrated that, on inoculation of *M. pneumoniae*, first ciliary action is stopped, and then loss of cilia and complete desquamation of ciliated epithelial cells into the lumen occur.[111] This sloughing of cells is doubtless responsible for the cough that defines the clinical presentation. Histologic findings in human lung biopsy mirror the findings of ciliated cell damage seen in the animal experiments.[110]

Several characteristics of *M. pneumoniae* probably play a direct role in the respiratory pathogenicity of this organism. The first is the relatively great affinity of *M. pneumoniae* for respiratory epithelial cells. Attachment appears to be between a terminal organelle at one end of the filamentous organism[13,14] and a sialated glycoprotein (I-FI) on the surface of both respiratory epithelium and erythrocytes,[112-114] which acts as a receptor. The mycoplasmal terminal adhesin protein (P1) has been purified, and antibodies to the protein have been analyzed.[15] *M. pneumoniae* attaches to ciliated epithelial cells at the base of cilia and appears to produce most of its physiologic and cytolytic changes while remaining extracellular. Hydrogen peroxide, which only *M. pneumoniae* of all the human mycoplasmas produces, may be responsible for some in vivo cell damage, as it is for the hemolysis seen when the organisms are grown on blood agar plates. Cytokine upregulation probably plays a role in inflammation-related cell destruction.[13,93]

DIAGNOSIS

PCR performed on a throat swab specimen serves as a specific and rapid diagnostic method.[115-118] Table 181-1 lists identifying properties of *M. pneumoniae*.

Although a cold agglutination phenomenon is not unique to patients with mycoplasma pneumonia, and although many patients with mycoplasma pneumonia never develop demonstrable cold agglutinins, this assay has remained an often used acute laboratory confirmatory test for this disease. Patients with other types of atypical pneumonias may have cold agglutinins. In the diagnostic serology laboratory, cold agglutinins are demonstrated by combining the patient's serum and type O (to avoid A-B incompatibility) erythrocytes. The mixture is incubated at 4° C for several minutes, and the presence or absence of hemagglutination is noted. If there is macroscopic red cell clumping, the patient's serum is serially diluted and the test is repeated. The highest dilution causing hemagglutination at 4° C is reported as the cold agglutinin titer. A titer of 1:32 or greater is highly suggestive of infection with *M. pneumoniae*. Other diseases that can give rise to cold agglutinins are mononucleosis caused by Epstein-Barr virus (anti-i),[119] cytomegalovirus (anti-I),[120] some other viral diseases, and lymphoma.

Because the results of this test as performed in a laboratory will not be available for at least a day, and in some cases a week, it is important to know that there is a rapid bedside version of this test that can be performed easily by any health care provider. In this test, 1 mL of the patient's blood is drawn into a tube containing anticoagulant. The type of tube used to collect specimens for prothrombin determination is preferred. Before cooling, examination shows a smooth coating of the tube by red cells, as shown in Figure 181-3A. The blood is cooled to 4° C by placing it on liquid ice or in a standard refrigerator. After 3 to 4 minutes, the tube is examined for the presence of macroscopic

TABLE 181-1 Identifying Properties of *Mycoplasma pneumoniae*

Slow growth on cell-free media
Both aerobic and anaerobic growth
"Mulberry" rather than "fried egg" colonies
Ferments glucose as major nutritional source, producing acid
Hemadsorption to colonies
Hemolysis by hydrogen peroxide
Affinity for respiratory epithelium
Infection leads to cold agglutinin formation
Resistance to cell wall inhibitors
Inhibited by macrolides, tetracyclines, and quinolones

agglutination (see Fig. 181-3B). The tube is then rewarmed to 37° C in an incubator, or by exposure to body heat, and reexamined. The agglutination should dissociate at 37° C, and the appearance of the tube is again as shown in Figure 181-3A. This temperature-associated agglutination and dissociation can be repeated many times on the same sample. A positive result in the "bedside" test correlates with a laboratory titer of 1:64 or greater and is therefore less sensitive than the laboratory test. It can be accomplished in minutes, however, and, if positive, it is highly suggestive of mycoplasma-related cold agglutination. The presence of cold agglutinins can also artifactually give rise to macrocytic indices as measured by the Coulter counter method. This is secondary to in vitro clumping of erythrocytes. In this case, the red cell distribution width would be high, indicating heterogeneity in measured red cell size.

Laboratory confirmation of *M. pneumoniae* infection has depended on demonstration of cold agglutinins or complement-fixing antibodies. The former, although appearing relatively early in the disease, are both insensitive and nonspecific indicators of *M. pneumoniae* infection. Complement-fixing antibodies, although far more specific, do not arise early enough in infection to be helpful in guiding diagnostic and therapeutic decisions. They are useful primarily in epidemiologic studies or to provide intellectual satisfaction in having made a good clinical diagnosis.

Likewise, culture of *M. pneumoniae* is an elaborate and time-consuming procedure requiring specialized media (see Chapter 180). Mycoplasmas are fastidious in their growth requirements. Because of this and the relative infrequency of requests for culture, most hospital microbiology laboratories are not set up to culture mycoplasmas. If culture is attempted, a number of transport media are available for temporary support of viability. These are similar to virus transport media in that they contain peptide broth, serum albumin, and antibiotics to retard bacterial overgrowth. Culture media are poorly defined in that they contain serum as a source of sterols and preformed nucleic acid precursors. Both liquid and solid media are inoculated. *M. pneumoniae* isolation takes advantage of the fact that this mycoplasma ferments glucose to produce acid, which can be detected by a color change in a dye indicator. In addition, this organism can reduce the dye tetrazolium, resulting in a color change from blue to yellow. *M. pneumoniae* on agar produces a "mulberry" colony as opposed to a "fried egg" appearance, as shown in Figure 180-1 in Chapter 180. Further identification can be obtained by showing that the colonies hemolyze red cells via hydrogen peroxide production[121] and can hemadsorb chick and guinea pig erythrocytes. Specific direct immunofluorescence of colonies can be used for ultimate identification.[122] Culture requires 1 to 2 weeks for definitive results. Although there are methods using pH and dye indicators that provide presumptive results more rapidly, even these require at least 4 to 5 days.

Therefore, there has been considerable interest in developing rapid diagnostic tests with high sensitivity and specificity for *M. pneumoniae*. These assays fall into three categories: detection of *M. pneumoniae*–specific immunoglobulins in serum and detection of *M. pneumoniae*–specific antigens or of mycoplasmal nucleotide sequences directly in clinical specimens.

Diagnostically, the most useful *M. pneumoniae*–specific immunoglobulin to detect is IgM, as it is most likely to indicate recent infection. An enzyme-linked immunoassay has been developed to detect IgM and IgG directed against *M. pneumoniae*.[123] Both immunoglobulins were chosen as targets of the assay because adults with *M. pneumoniae* infection may elaborate only an IgG response. When used in patients with positive assays for complement-fixing antibodies, the enzyme immunoassay had a specificity of more than 99% and a sensitivity of 98%. Specificity was retained but sensitivity dropped to only 46% when IgG alone was the target. Variations on this theme detect IgM antibodies directed at specific *M. pneumoniae* antigens.[124] The tests are simple to perform and have high sensitivity and specificity but are limited in that they do not become positive until 1 to 2 weeks into the infection. One study compared three assays designed to detect antimycoplasma IgM: a particle agglutination test, a mu-capture enzyme-linked immunosorbent assay, and indirect immunofluorescence.[125] All three assays were about equally sensitive when compared with a standard complement fixation assay, but the particle agglutination assay appeared to give more false-positive results. In that all of these tests are designed to detect IgM antibody, they may all be negative early (less than 7 to 10 days) into infection. Therefore, they do not provide the desired confirmation early enough to guide initial therapy in many cases.

Detection of *M. pneumoniae* antigens directly in sputum specimens has been accomplished with the use of an antigen-capture, indirect enzyme immunoassay.[126] The specificity of the assay was high, the reagents reacting only with *M. pneumoniae* and *M. genitalium*. Sensitivity was also relatively high (91%) when the assay was used on sputum and nasopharyngeal aspirates from patients who were shown either by culture or serologically to have *M. pneumoniae* infection.[127]

Detection of *M. pneumoniae*–specific nucleotide sequences directly in clinical material has been accomplished with the use of test kits developed commercially and in-house by large reference laboratories. The test, which can be completed in 2 hours, uses radioiodine-labeled DNA complementary to *M. pneumoniae* ribosomal RNA. When compared in one study with culture as the gold standard of proven infection, the nucleotide assay detected 89% of the culture-positive specimens; specificity was also 89%.[128] In a second comparative study, although the probe assay showed excellent sensitivity (95%) and good specificity (85%) compared with culture and serology when sputum was used, sensitivity and specificity on throat washings were considerably lower.[129] The manufacturer of the kit recommends that throat swabs be used for the assay.

A

B

FIGURE 181-3. Bedside cold agglutinin test for confirmation of mycoplasmal pneumonia. **A,** Patient's blood before exposure to the cold. **B,** Patient's blood after 3-minute exposure to 4° C. On rewarming the sample to 37° C, the appearance reverts to that shown in **A.**

In a third study, the probe was not as sensitive as indirect enzyme immunoassay when seropositivity rather than culture was used as the benchmark for infection.[127] A comparison of immunologic and molecular biologic diagnostic tests has been published.[130]

TREATMENT

Despite the number and variety of tests for the rapid diagnosis of *M. pneumoniae* infection, most cases are encountered in the ambulatory setting, and institution of antimicrobial therapy remains empirical and based on clinical recognition of the syndrome.

Antimicrobial therapy is not necessary for mycoplasmal upper respiratory tract infection, and the mycoplasmal etiology of this syndrome probably most often goes undiagnosed. Pneumonia due to mycoplasma is self-limited and not life threatening in most cases. However, treatment with effective antimicrobials can markedly shorten the illness and, by reducing cough and the number of organisms per unit volume of sputum, can perhaps reduce the spread of infections in contacts.

As would be predicted by the lack of a cell wall, *M. pneumoniae* is unaffected by treatment with β-lactam antibiotics such as the penicillins and cephalosporins. Aminoglycosides are effective in vitro but have not been evaluated for efficacy in vivo.

The mainstays of treatment for *M. pneumoniae* respiratory tract infection are macrolides and tetracyclines. Use of either of these antimicrobials shortens the duration of illness. The radiographic findings may take a week or longer to resolve, even with appropriate therapy (see Fig. 181-1). In addition, studies have shown that organisms may continue to be culturable from the sputum for several weeks after a complete course of clinically effective treatment.[30] This may be a result of the fact that, although *M. pneumoniae* causes respiratory disease as an extracellular parasite, it has the capacity to reside intracellularly as well. This intracellular residence may make it difficult to eradicate the organism in vivo, as it does in cell cultures. The effect of therapy on extrapulmonary manifestations is unknown.

Although the tetracyclines are very active against *M. pneumoniae,* their use is precluded in young children because of adverse effects of the drug on developing teeth and bones. Furthermore, erythromycin is poorly tolerated by many people because of its gastrointestinal side effects. These include nausea, vomiting, abdominal pain, and diarrhea. There is anecdotal information that administration of histamine type 2 (H$_2$)-blocking drugs can reduce these adverse effects, but there is no information on possible changes in macrolide absorption by concurrent use of these agents. Erythromycin also raises theophylline levels, a consideration in the few asthmatic patients who may be still taking this drug.

Because of the adverse effects of erythromycin and tetracycline, there is considerable interest in the antimycoplasmal efficacy of other agents. Doxycycline is somewhat better tolerated than tetracycline and can be administered in two daily doses rather than three. In vitro, doxycycline is as effective as tetracycline against *M. pneumoniae* but, again, is contraindicated in children.

Several other classes of antimicrobials have been found to have significant in vitro and in vivo activity against *M. pneumoniae* and other *Mycoplasma* species. These include the fluoroquinolones,[131-133] broad-spectrum macrolides (azithromycin, clarithromycin),[134] ketolides (telithromycin),[134] and streptogramins (quinupristin-dalfopristin).[135] There are no good data on the optimal duration of therapy needed to minimize carriage and relapse with these agents.

The macrolides are more active in vitro than the tetracyclines. Fluoroquinolones are more active than the tetracyclines but are at least 100 times less active than the macrolides. Nevertheless, the fluoroquinolones have adequate activity for treatment of these infections. The streptogramins are also less active than the macrolides but more active than the tetracyclines.[134,135] There is a significant cost differential in the use of these drugs. The newer macrolides and quinolones are 50 to 60 times more expensive than the tetracyclines and 6 to 10 times more costly than erythromycin. No erythromycin-resistant strains of

M. pneumoniae have been found. Quinolones are relatively contraindicated in children because of their adverse effects on weight-bearing joints in young animals.[132]

Recommended therapy would include doxycycline 100 mg every 12 hours, or azithromycin 500 mg on day 1, and then 250 mg every 24 hours. The usual duration of therapy is 7 to 14 days.

PREVENTION

Because of outbreaks of *M. pneumoniae* respiratory infection among military recruits, there was for a time great enthusiasm and activity to produce a vaccine to protect against this organism.[136] The vaccines did induce specific antibody responses, but protection against infection was limited to no more than 50% of vaccine recipients.[137,138] Live vaccines using attenuated wild-type and temperature-sensitive mutant mycoplasma have proved no more effective.[139,140]

In one study, volunteers who received vaccine but did not mount an antibody response developed more severe disease when rechallenged with wild-type mycoplasma than did nonvaccinated personnel.[141] Although *M. pneumoniae* continues to be perhaps the leading cause of the atypical pneumonia syndrome in closed populations, the enthusiasm for vaccine development for this disease appears to have waned. Vaccine development technology involving DNA expression-library immunization has proved successful in animal studies with nonhuman mycoplasmas.[142] These methods may breathe new life into *M. pneumoniae* vaccine development.

Examination of the effects of prophylactic antibiotic use in family members exposed to mycoplasma has shown a decrease in clinical disease in these patients, but seroconversion was not prevented.[143] A study showed that azithromycin prophylaxis, given as a 500-mg loading dose and 250 mg/day on days 2 through 5, significantly reduced the secondary attack rate of *M. pneumoniae* infection in a long-term care facility.[144]

REFERENCES

1. Drosten C, Gunther S, Preiser W, et al. Identification of a novel coronavirus in patients with severe acute respiratory syndrome. N Engl J Med. 2003;348:1967-1976.
2. Eaton MD, Meikeljohn G, van Herick W, et al. Studies on the etiology of primary atypical pneumonia: II. Properties of the virus isolated and propagated in chick embryos. J Exp Med. 1945;82:317.
3. Eaton MD, van Herick W, Meikeljohn G. Studies on the etiology of primary atypical pneumonia: III. Specific neutralization of the virus by human serum. J Exp Med. 1945;82:329.
4. Finland M, Peterson OL, Allen HE, et al. Cold agglutinins: I. Occurrence of cold isohaemagglutinins in various conditions. J Clin Invest. 1945;24:451.
5. Marmion BP. Eaton agent—Science and scientific acceptance: A historical commentary. Rev Infect Dis. 1990;12:338.
6. Chanock RM, Mufson MA, Bloom HH, et al. Eaton agent pneumonia. JAMA. 1961;175:213.
7. Clyde WA Jr. Demonstration of Eaton's agent in tissue culture. Proc Soc Exp Biol Med. 1961;107:715.
8. Goodburn GM, Marmion BP. Study of properties of Eaton's primary atypical pneumonia organism. J Gen Microbiol. 1962;29:271.
9. Chanock RM, Hayflick L, Barile MF. Growth on artificial medium of an agent associated with atypical pneumonia and its identification as a PPLO. Proc Natl Acad Sci U S A. 1962;48:41.
10. Chanock RM, Rifkind D, Dravetz HM, et al. Respiratory disease in volunteers infected with Eaton agent: A preliminary report. Proc Natl Acad Sci U S A. 1961;47:887.
11. Marmion BP, Goodburn GM. Effect of an organic gold salt on Eaton's primary atypical pneumonia organism and other observations. Nature. 1961;189:247.
12. Conference on Newer Respiratory Disease Viruses, US Public Health Service. Bethesda, Md: National Institutes of Health; 1962:198.
13. Razin S, Yogev D, Naot Y. Molecular biology and pathogenicity of mycoplasmas. Microbiol Mol Biol Rev. 1998;62:1094-1156.
14. Powell DA, Hu PC, Wilson M, et al. Attachment of *Mycoplasma pneumoniae* to respiratory epithelium. Infect Immun. 1976;13:959.
15. Hirschberg L, Holme T, Krook A. Human antibody response to the major adhesin of *Mycoplasma pneumoniae:* Increase in titers against synthetic peptides in patients with pneumonia. APMIS. 1991;99:515.
16. Furness G, Pipes FJ, McMurtrey MJ. Analysis of the life cycle of *Mycoplasma pneumoniae* by synchronized division and by ultraviolet and X irradiations. J Infect Dis. 1968;118:7.
17. Mogabgab WJ. *Mycoplasma pneumoniae* and adenovirus respiratory illness in military and university personnel, 1959-1966. Am Rev Respir Dis. 1968;97:345.

18. Foy HM, Kenny GE, Cooney MK, et al. Long term epidemiology of infections with *Mycoplasma pneumoniae*. J Infect Dis. 1979;139:681.
19. Chanock RM. Mycoplasma infections of man. N Engl J Med. 1965;273:1199.
20. Hers JF, Masurel N. Infection with *Mycoplasma pneumoniae* in civilians in the Netherlands. Ann N Y Acad Sci. 1967;143:447.
21. Foy HM, Kenny GE, McMahan R, et al. *Mycoplasma pneumoniae* pneumonia in an urban area. JAMA. 1970;214:1966.
22. Foy HM, Alexander ER. *Mycoplasma pneumoniae* infections in childhood. Adv Pediatr. 1969;16:301.
23. Denny FW, Clyde WA, Glenzen WP. *Mycoplasma pneumoniae* disease: Clinical spectrum, pathophysiology, epidemiology and control. J Infect Dis. 1971;123:74.
24. Noah ND. *Mycoplasma pneumoniae* infections in the United Kingdom—1967-73. Br Med J. 1974;2:544.
25. Toma S. Isolation of *Mycoplasma pneumoniae* from respiratory tract specimens in Ontario. Can Med Assoc J. 1987;137:48.
26. Fernald GW, Collier AM, Clyde WA. Respiratory infections due to *Mycoplasma pneumoniae* in infants and children. Pediatrics. 1975;55:327.
27. McIntosh JC, Gutierrez HH. *Mycoplasma* infections. In: Smith TF, ed. Immunology and Allergy Clinics of North America: Respiratory Infections. Philadelphia: WB Saunders; 1993:43.
28. Alexander ER, Foy HM, Kenny GE, et al. Pneumonia due to *Mycoplasma pneumoniae*. N Engl J Med. 1966;275:131.
29. Foy HM, Grayston JT, Kenny GE, et al. Epidemiology of *Mycoplasma pneumoniae* infection in families. JAMA. 1966;197:859.
30. Smith CB, Friedewald WT, Chanock RM. Shedding of *Mycoplasma pneumoniae* after tetracycline and erythromycin therapy. N Engl J Med. 1967;276:1172.
31. Ritkind D, Chanock R, Kravetz H, et al. Ear involvement (myringitis) and primary atypical pneumonia following inoculation of volunteers with Eaton agent. Am Rev Respir Dis. 1962;85:479.
32. Klein JO, Teele DW. Isolation of viruses and mycoplasmas from middle ear effusions: A review. Ann Otol Rhinol Laryngol. 1976;85:140.
33. Sobeslavsky O, Syrucek L, Bruckaya M, et al. The etiologic role of *Mycoplasma pneumoniae* in otitis media in children. Pediatrics. 1965;35:652.
34. Nagayama Y, Sakurai N, Yamamota K, et al. Isolation of *Mycoplasma pneumoniae* from children with lower-respiratory-tract infections. J Infect Dis. 1988;157:911.
35. Mansel JK, Rosenow EC III, Smith TF, et al. *Mycoplasma pneumoniae* pneumonia. Chest. 1989;95:639.
36. Fine NL, Smith LR, Sheedy PF. Frequency of pleural effusions in mycoplasmal and viral pneumonias. N Engl J Med. 1970;283:790.
37. Tuazon CV, Murray HW. Atypical pneumonias. In: Pennington JE, ed. Respiratory Infections: Diagnosis and Management. New York: Raven Press; 1989:341.
38. Loo VG, Richardson S, Quinn P. Isolation of *Mycoplasma pneumoniae* from pleural fluid. Diagn Microbiol Infect Dis. 1991;14:443.
39. Chan ED, Welsh CH. Fulminant *Mycoplasma pneumoniae* pneumonia. West J Med. 1995;162:133-142.
40. Cherry JD, Hurwitz ES, Welliver RC. *Mycoplasma pneumoniae* infections and exanthems. J Pediatr. 1975;87:369.
41. Murray HW, Masur H, Senterfit LB, et al. The protean manifestations of *Mycoplasma pneumoniae* in adults. Am J Med. 1975;58:229.
42. Levy M, Shear NH. *Mycoplasma pneumoniae* infections and Stevens-Johnson syndrome. Clin Pediatr (Phila). 1991;30:42.
43. Sanders DY, Johnson HW. Stevens-Johnson syndrome associated with *Mycoplasma pneumoniae* infection. Am J Dis Child. 1971;121:243.
44. Lyell A, Dick HM, Gordon AM, et al. Mycoplasmas and erythema multiforme. Lancet. 1967;2:1116.
45. Arstikaitis MJ. Ocular aftermath of Stevens-Johnson syndrome. Arch Ophthalmol. 1973;90:376.
46. Anderson R, Bergan T, Halvorsen K, et al. Legionnaires' disease combined with erythema multiforme in a 3 year old boy. Acta Pediatr Scand. 1981;70:427.
47. Kierman JP, Schanzlin DJ, Leveille AS. Stevens-Johnson syndrome associated with adenovirus conjunctivitis. Am J Ophthalmol. 1981;92:543.
48. Baine WB, Luby JB, Martin SM. Severe illness with influenza B. Am J Med. 1980;68:181.
49. Tay Y-K, Huff JC, Weston WL. *Mycoplasma pneumoniae* infection is associated with Stevens-Johnson syndrome, not erythema multiforme (von Hebra). J Am Acad Dermatol. 1996;35:757-760.
50. Kazmierowski JA, Wuepper KD. Erythema multiforme: Clinical spectrum and immunopathogenesis. Springer Semin Immunopathol. 1981;4:45.
51. Goldsmith DP. The erythema syndromes: Erythema multiforme and the Stevens-Johnson syndrome. Pract Pediatr. 1980;3:1.
52. Stutman HR. Stevens-Johnson syndrome and *Mycoplasma pneumoniae*: Evidence for cutaneous infection. J Pediatr. 1987;111:845.
53. Meseguer MA, de Rafael L, Vidal ML. Stevens-Johnson syndrome with isolation of *Mycoplasma pneumoniae* from skin lesions. Eur J Clin Microbiol. 1986;5:167.
54. McCormack JG. *Mycoplasma pneumoniae* and the erythema multiforme–Stevens-Johnson syndrome. J Infect. 1981;3:32.
55. Easterly NB. Corticosteroids for erythema multiforme? Pediatr Dermatol. 1989;6:229.
56. Feizi T, Maclean H. Sommerville RG, et al. Studies on an epidemic of respiratory disease caused by *Mycoplasma pneumoniae*. Br Med J. 1967;1:457.
57. Schubothe H. The cold hemagglutinin disease. Semin Hematol. 1966;3:27.
58. Furioli J, Bourdon C, Le Loc'h H. *Mycoplasma pneumoniae* infection: Manifestation in a 3 year old child by Raynaud's phenomenon. Arch Fr Pediatr. 1985;42:313.
59. Visudhiphan P, Chiemchanya S, Sirinavin S. Internal carotid artery occlusion associated with *Mycoplasma pneumoniae* infection. Pediatr Neurol. 1992;8:237.
60. Sands MJ, Satz JE, Soloff LA. Pericarditis and perimyocarditis associated with active *Mycoplasma pneumoniae* infection. Ann Intern Med. 1977;86:544.
61. Ponka A. Carditis associated with *Mycoplasma pneumoniae* infection. Acta Med Scand. 1979;11:1.
62. Karjalainen J, Heikkila J, Nieminen MS, et al. Etiology of mild acute infectious myocarditis. Relation to clinical features. Acta Med Scand. 1983;213:65.
63. Karjalainen J. A loud third heart sound and asymptomatic myocarditis during *Mycoplasma pneumoniae* infection. Eur Heart J. 1990;11:960.
64. Sands MJ Jr, Rosenthal R. Progressive heart failure and death associated with *Mycoplasma pneumoniae*. Chest. 1982;81:763.
65. Meseguer MA, Perez-Molina J, Fernández-Bustamante E, et al. *Mycoplasma pneumoniae* pericarditis and cardiac tamponade in a ten-year-old girl. Pediatr Infect Dis J. 1996;15:829-831.
66. Yesnick L. Central nervous system complications of primary atypical pneumonia. Arch Intern Med. 1956;97:93.
67. Lerer RJ, Kalavsky SM. Central nervous system disease associated with *Mycoplasma pneumoniae* infection: Report of five cases and review of the literature. Pediatrics. 1973;52:658.
68. Mills RW, Schoolfield L. Acute transverse myelitis associated with *Mycoplasma pneumoniae* infection: A case report and review of the literature. Pediatr Infect Dis J. 1992;11:228.
69. Ong ELC, Ellis ME, Yuill GM. Neurologic complication of *Mycoplasma pneumoniae* infection. Respir Med. 1989;83:441.
70. Steele JC, Gladstone RM, Thanasophon S, et al. *Mycoplasma pneumoniae* as a determinant of the Guillain-Barré syndrome. Lancet. 1969;2:719.
71. Koskiniemi M. CNS manifestations associated with *Mycoplasma pneumoniae* infections: Summary of cases at the University of Helsinki and review. Clin Infect Dis. 1993;17(Suppl 1):S52-S57.
72. Abramovitz P, Schvartzman P, Harel D, et al. Direct invasion of the central nervous system by *Mycoplasma pneumoniae*: A report of two cases. J Infect Dis. 1987;155:482.
73. Fink CG, Sillis M, Read SJ, et al. Neurologic disease associated with *Mycoplasma pneumoniae* infection: PCR evidence against a direct invasive mechanism. Clin Mol Pathol. 1995;48:51-54.
74. Kusunoki S, Shiina M, Kanazawa I. Anti-Gal-C antibodies in GBS subsequent to mycoplasma infection: Evidence for molecular mimicry. Neurology. 2001;57:736-738.
75. Thomas L, Alen F, Bitensky MW, et al. The neurotoxin of *Mycoplasma neurolyticum*. J Exp Med. 1966;124:1967.
76. Ponka A. Arthritis associated with *Mycoplasma pneumoniae* infection. Scand J Rheumatol. 1979;8:27.
77. Davis CP, Cochran S, Lisse J, et al. Isolation of *Mycoplasma pneumoniae* from synovial fluid samples in a patient with pneumonia and polyarthritis. Arch Intern Med. 1988;148:969.
78. Johnston CLW, Webster ADB, Taylor-Robinson D, et al. Primary late-onset hypogammaglobulinaemia associated with inflammatory polyarthritis and septic arthritis due to *Mycoplasma pneumoniae*. Ann Rheum Dis. 1983;442:108.
79. Vitullo BV, O'Regan S, de Chadarevian JP, et al. *Mycoplasma pneumoniae* associated with acute glomerulonephritis. Nephron. 1978;21:284.
80. Stephan JL, Galambrun C, Pozzetto B, et al. Aplastic anemia after *Mycoplasma pneumoniae*: A report of two cases. J Pediatr Hematol Oncol. 1999;21:299-302.
81. Shulman ST, Barlett J, Clyde WA, et al. The unusual severity of mycoplasmal pneumonia in children with sickle-cell disease. N Engl J Med. 1972;287:164.
82. Solanki DL, Berdoff RL. Severe mycoplasma pneumonia with pleural effusions in a patient with sickle cell-hemoglobin C (SC) disease. Am J Med. 1979;66:707.
83. Chusid MJ, Lachman BS, Lazerson J. Severe mycoplasma pneumonia and vesicular eruption in SC hemoglobinopathy. J Pediatr. 1978;93:449.
84. Foy HM. Infections caused by *Mycoplasma pneumoniae* and possible carrier state in different populations of patients. Clin Infect Dis. 1993;17(Suppl 1):S37-S46.
85. Lo SC, Dawson M, Wong DM. Identification of *Mycoplasma incognitus* infection in patients with AIDS: An immunohistochemical, in-situ hybridization and ultrastructural study. Am J Trop Med Hyg. 1989;41:601.
86. Orlieck SL, Walker MS, Kuhls TL. Severe mycoplasma pneumonia in young children with Down syndrome. Clin Pediatr (Phila). 1992;31:409.
87. Biberfeld G, Gronowicz E. *Mycoplasma pneumoniae* is a polyclonal B-cell activator. Nature. 1976;261:238.
88. Naot Y, Tully JG, Ginsburg H. Lymphocyte activation by various mycoplasma strains and species. Infect Immun. 1977;18:310.
89. Stanbridge EJ, Weiss RL. Mycoplasma capping on lymphocytes. Nature. 1978;276:583.
90. Dietz JN, Cole BC. Direct activation of the J774.1 murine macrophage cell line by *Mycoplasma arthritidis*. Infect Immun. 1981;37:811.
91. Mahkoul N, Merchav S, Tatarsky I, et al. Mycoplasma-induced in vitro production of interleukin-2 and colony-stimulating activity. Isr J Med Sci. 1987;23:480.
92. Capobianchi MR, Lorino G, Lun MT, et al. Membrane interactions involved in the induction of interferon-alpha by *Mycoplasma pneumoniae*. Antiviral Res. 1987;8:115.
93. Tanaka H, Mitsuo N, Shin T, et al. Role of interleukin-18 and T-helper type 1 cytokines in the development of *Mycoplasma pneumoniae* pneumonia in adults. Chest. 2002;121:1493-1497.
94. Brunner H, Greenberg HB, James WD, et al. Antibody to *Mycoplasma pneumoniae* in nasal secretions and sputa of experimentally infected human volunteers. Infect Immun. 1973;8:612.
95. Peterson OL, Ham TH, Finland M. Cold agglutinins (auto-haemagglutinins) in primary atypical pneumonias. Science. 1943;97:167.
96. Turner JC. Development of cold agglutinins in atypical pneumonia. Nature. 1943;151:419.

97. Feizi T, Taylor-Robinson D. Cold agglutinin anti-I and *Mycoplasma pneumoniae*. Immunology. 1967;13:405.
98. Konig AL, Kreft H, Hengge U. Coexisting anti-I and anti-FI/Gd cold agglutinins in infections by *Mycoplasma pneumoniae*. Vox Sang. 1988;55:176.
99. Costea N, Yakulis VJ, Heller P. Inhibition of cold agglutinins (anti-I) by *M. pneumoniae* antigens. Proc Soc Exp Biol Med. 1972;139:476.
100. Feizi T. Cold agglutinins, the direct Coombs' test and serum immunoglobulins in *Mycoplasma pneumoniae* infection. Ann N Y Acad Sci. 1967;143:801.
101. Jacobson LB, Longstreth GF, Edington TS. Clinical and immunologic features of transient cold agglutinin hemolytic anemia. Am J Med. 1973;54:514.
102. Foy HM, Kenny GE, Sefi R, et al. Second attacks of pneumonia due to *Mycoplasma pneumoniae*. J Infect Dis. 1977;135:673.
103. Erb P, Bredt W. Interaction of *Mycoplasma pneumoniae* with alveolar macrophages: Viability of adherent and ingested mycoplasmas. Infect Immun. 1979;25:11.
104. Koletsky RJ, Weinstein AJ. Fulminant mycoplasma pneumonia infection: Report of a fatal case and a review of the literature. Am Rev Respir Dis. 1980;122:491.
105. Nilsson IM, Rausing A, Dennenberg T, et al. Intravascular coagulation and acute renal failure in a child with mycoplasma infection. Acta Med Scand. 1971;189:359.
106. Meyers BR, Hirshman SZ. Fatal infections associated with *Mycoplasma pneumoniae*: Discussion of three cases with necropsy findings. Mt Sinai J Med. 1972;39:258.
107. Scully RE, ed. Case records of the Massachusetts General Hospital: Mycoplasma pneumonia with diffuse alveolar damage and disseminated intravascular coagulation. N Engl J Med. 1992;326:324.
108. Pickens S, Catterall JR. Disseminated intravascular coagulation and myocarditis associated with *Mycoplasma pneumoniae* infection. Br Med J. 1978;23:1526.
109. Kaufman JM, Cuvelier CA, Van der Staeten M. Mycoplasma pneumonia with fulminant evolution into diffuse interstitial fibrosis. Thorax. 1980;35:140.
110. Rollin S, Colby T, Clayton F. Open lung biopsy in mycoplasma pneumonia. Arch Pathol Lab Med. 1986;110:34.
111. Hu PC, Collier AM, Baseman JB. Interaction of virulent *Mycoplasma pneumoniae* with hamster tracheal organ cultures. Infect Immun. 1976;14:217.
112. Brunner H, Feldner J, Bredt W. Effect of monoclonal antibodies to the attachment tip on experimental *Mycoplasma pneumoniae* infection of hamsters. Isr J Med Sci. 1984;20:878.
113. Baseman JB, Banai M, Kahane I. Sialic acid residues mediate *Mycoplasma pneumoniae* attachment to human and sheep erythrocytes. Infect Immun. 1982;38:389.
114. Hengge VR, Kirschfink M, Konig AL, et al. Characterization of I/F1 glycoprotein as a receptor for *Mycoplasma pneumoniae*. Infect Immun. 1992;60:79.
115. Van Kuppeveld FJ, Johansson KE, Galoma JM, et al. 16S mRNA based polymerase chain reaction compared with culture and serologic methods for diagnosis of *Mycoplasma pneumoniae* infection. Eur J Clin Microbiol Infect Dis. 1994;13:401-405.
116. Ramirez JA, Ahkee S, Tolentino A, et al. Diagnosis of *Legionella pneumophila*, *Mycoplasma pneumoniae* or *Chlamydia pneumoniae* lower respiratory infection using the polymerase chain reaction on a single throat swab specimen. Diagn Microbiol Infect Dis. 1996;24:7-14.
117. Shelhamer JH, Gill VJ, Quinn TC, et al. The laboratory evaluation of opportunistic pulmonary infections. Ann Intern Med. 1996;124:585-599.
118. Schluger NW, Rom WN. The polymerase chain reaction in the diagnosis and evaluation of pulmonary infections. Am J Respir Crit Care Med. 1995;152:11-16.
119. Rosenfield RE, Schmidt PJ, Calvo RC, et al. Anti-i, a frequent cold agglutinin in infectious mononucleosis. Vox Sang. 1965;10:631.
120. Lind K, Spencer ES, Anderson HK. Cold agglutinin production and cytomegalovirus infection. Scand J Infect Dis. 1974;6:109.
121. Clyde WA Jr. Hemolysis in identifying Eaton's pleuropneumonia-like organism. Science. 1963;139:55.
122. Del Giudice RA, Robillard NF, Carski TR. Immunofluorescence identification of mycoplasma on agar by use of incident illumination. J Bacteriol. 1967;93:1205.
123. Uldum SA, Jensen JS, Søndergard-Anderson J, et al. Enzyme immunoassay for detection of immunoglobulin M (IgM) and IgG antibodies to *Mycoplasma pneumoniae*. J Clin Microbiol. 1992;30:1198.
124. Cimolai N, Cheong ACH. IgM anti-PI immunoblotting: A standard for the rapid serologic diagnosis of *Mycoplasma pneumoniae* infection in pediatric care. Chest. 1992;102:477.
125. Barker CE, Sillis M, Wreghitt TG. Evaluation of Serodia, Myco II particle agglutination test for detecting *Mycoplasma pneumoniae* antibody: Comparison with mu-capture ELISA and indirect fluorescence. J Clin Pathol. 1990;43:163.
126. Marmion BP, Williamson J, Worswick DA, et al. Experience with newer techniques for the laboratory detection of *Mycoplasma pneumoniae* infection: Adelaide, 1978-1992. Clin Infect Dis. 1993;17(Suppl 1):S90-S99.
127. Harris R, Marmion BP, Varkanis G, et al. Laboratory diagnosis of *Mycoplasma pneumoniae* infection: 2. Comparison of methods for the direct detection of specific antigen or nucleic acid sequences in respiratory exudates. Epidemiol Infect. 1988;101:685.
128. Dular R, Kajioka R, Kusatiya S. Comparison of Gen-Probe commercial kit and culture technique for the diagnosis of *Mycoplasma pneumoniae* infection. J Clin Microbiol. 1988;26:1068.
129. Kleemola MSR, Karjalainen JE, Raty RKH. Rapid diagnosis of *Mycoplasma pneumoniae* infection: Clinical evaluation of a commercial probe test. J Infect Dis. 1990;162:70.
130. Baum SG. Mycoplasma infection: Immunologic and molecular biologic diagnostic techniques. In: Rose NR, de Macario EC, Folds JD, et al, eds. Manual of Clinical Laboratory Immunology: Infections Caused by Bacteria, Mycoplasmas, Chlamydiae and Rickettsiae. Washington, DC: American Society for Microbiology; 1997:547-557.
131. Rylander M, Hallander HO. In vitro comparison of the activity of doxycycline, tetracycline, erythromycin and a new macrolide, CP 62993, against *Mycoplasma pneumoniae*, *Mycoplasma hominis* and *Ureaplasma urealyticum*. Scand J Infect Dis. 1988;53(Suppl):12.
132. Martin SJ, Meyer JM, Chuck SK, et al. Levofloxacin and sparfloxacin: New quinolone antibiotics. Ann Pharmacother. 1998;32:320-336.
133. Ridgway GL, Salman H, Robbins MJ, et al. The in vitro activity of grepafloxacin against *Chlamydia* spp., *Mycoplasma* spp., *Ureaplasma urealyticum* and *Legionella* spp. J Antimicrob Chemother. 1997;40(Suppl A):31-34.
134. Taylor-Robinson D, Bébeár C. Antibiotic susceptibilities of mycoplasmas and treatment of mycoplasmal infections. J Antimicrob Chemother. 1997;40:622-630.
135. Izumikawa K, Hirakata Y, Yamaguchi T, et al. In vitro activities of quinupristin-dalfopristin and the streptogramin RPR 106972 against *Mycoplasma pneumoniae*. Antimicrob Agents Chemother. 1998;42:698-699.
136 Mogabgab WJ. Protective effects of inactive *Mycoplasma pneumoniae* vaccine in military personnel. Am Rev Respir Dis. 1968;97:359.
137. Wenzel RP, Craven RB, Davies JA, et al. Field trial on an inactivated *Mycoplasma pneumoniae* vaccine: I. Vaccine efficacy. J Infect Dis. 1976;134:571.
138. Smith CB, Friedewald WT, Chanock RM. Inactivated *Mycoplasma pneumoniae* vaccine. JAMA. 1967;199:353.
139. Couch RB, Cate TR, Chanock RM. Infection with artificially propagated Eaton agent (*Mycoplasma pneumoniae*). JAMA. 1964;187:442.
140. Greenberg H, Helms CM, Brunner H, et al. Asymptomatic infection of adult volunteers with a temperature sensitive mutant of *Mycoplasma pneumoniae*. Proc Natl Acad Sci U S A. 1974;71:4015.
141. Smith CB, Chanock RM, Friedewald WTK, et al. *Mycoplasma pneumoniae* infections in volunteers. Ann N Y Acad Sci. 1967;143:471.
142. Barry M, Lai WC, Johnston SA. Protection against mycoplasma infection using expression-library immunization. Nature. 1995;377:632-635.
143. Jensen KE, Senterfit LB, Scully WE, et al. *Mycoplasma pneumoniae* infections in children: An epidemiological appraisal in families treated with oxytetracycline. Am J Epidemiol. 1967;86:419.
144. Klausner JD, Passaro D, Rosenberg J. Enhanced control of an outbreak of *Mycoplasma pneumoniae* pneumonia with azithromycin prophylaxis. J Infect Dis. 1998;177:161-166.

CHAPTER **182**

Genital Mycoplasmas: *Mycoplasma genitalium*, *Mycoplasma hominis*, and *Ureaplasma* Species

GEORGE E. KENNY

The microbial flora of the human genital tract is complex, including organisms that are difficult to cultivate and detect and most likely organisms that have yet to be discovered.[1] Mycoplasmas and ureaplasmas fit into the difficult-to-grow category. So far, eight species of mycoplasmas and ureaplasmas have been identified in the genital tract (Table 182-1). Although six species are classified in the genus *Mycoplasma*, they are far more heterogeneous than their classification implies. *Mycoplasma genitalium* has the smallest genome of any mycoplasma (580 kb) and is closely related to *Mycoplasma pneumoniae* in spite of its much larger genome (816 kb).[2] Metabolically, they are also diverse. *Mycoplasma hominis*, *Mycoplasma primatum*, and *Mycoplasma spermatophilum* metabolize arginine to ornithine with the production of ammonia but do not utilize glucose. *M. genitalium* utilizes glucose with the production of acid but does not utilize arginine. *Mycoplasma fermentans* and *Mycoplasma penetrans* utilize both arginine and glucose. *Ureaplasma urealyticum* and *Ureaplasma parvum* are the most unusual because they both require and hydrolyze urea with the production of energy, CO_2, and NH_3.[2] No other microorganism has such a requirement. They are further unusual in that they grow only in medium that is pH 6.5 or lower. The features that mycoplasmas and ureaplasmas have in common are small size (0.2 to 0.3

TABLE 182-1 The Human Genital Ureaplasmas and Mycoplasmas[2]

Species	Prevalence in Genital Tract of Healthy Persons	Substrate Utilization	Atmosphere for Isolation	pH for Growth	Growth from Specimens
Ureaplasma urealyticum	++++	Urea	Indifferent	6.0-6.5	Rapid (2-4 days)
Ureaplasma parvum	++++	Urea	Indifferent	6.0-6.5	Rapid (2-4 days)
Mycoplasma hominis	+++	Arginine	Indifferent	6.5-8.0	Rapid (2-5 days)
Mycoplasma genitalium	Unknown	Glucose	Aerobic	7.0-7.5	Very slow (30-60 days)
Mycoplasma fermentans	+?	Glucose and arginine	Anaerobic	7.0-8.0	Slow (5-10 days)
Mycoplasma penetrans	Rare	Glucose and arginine	?	7.0-8.0?	?
Mycoplasma spermatophilum	Rare	Arginine	?	7.0-8.0?	?
Mycoplasma primatum	rare	Arginine	?	7.0-8.0?	?

μm), small genome (580 to 1170 kb),[2] no cell wall, and a requirement for a highly enriched medium containing animal serum. The generation times in broth culture are 1 to 2 hours for ureaplasmas and most mycoplasmas, but *M. genitalium* grows very slowly with initial estimates of its doubling time being 12 hours or more.[3]

PREVALENCE OF GENITAL MYCOPLASMAS IN HEALTHY PERSONS

M. hominis and ureaplasmas have been most studied because of their relative ease of cultivation. Ureaplasmas are highly prevalent in the genital tracts of healthy sexually active women with infection rates of 60% to 70%.[4] *U. parvum* strains account for 70% of ureaplasmas detected.[5] The prevalence of ureaplasmas in the male urethra is lower at 10% to 20%.[6] Infants can be infected with ureaplasmas at birth. The organisms persist for a while and disappear by age 2.[7] Ureaplasmas become prevalent with the onset of sexual activity in both males and females. Taken as a whole, the high prevalence of ureaplasmas and *M. hominis* in healthy persons indicates that they are not prime pathogens. However, we cannot exclude the possibility that a specific serovar or biovar might have a more significant role in disease. We do not know how long an individual serovar or biovar persists in carriers or if there are changes in types over time. *M. penetrans* has been found in persons with human immunodeficiency virus infection.[8] *M. spermatophilum* has been reported from several persons.

MYCOPLASMAS AND NONGONOCOCCAL URETHRITIS IN MEN

The diagnosis of nongonococcal urethritis (NGU) arose when it was recognized that urethritis persisted in some cases after treatment with penicillin and elimination of gonococci. Mycoplasmas and ureaplasmas have no cell walls and thus are not susceptible to antimicrobial agents, such as penicillin, that target the cell wall of bacteria. Ureaplasmas were discovered in the late 1950s and were suspected of having a role in NGU because of their prevalence, resistance to penicillin, susceptibility to tetracyclines, and the fact that they were sexually transmitted. However, another group of bacteria, the chlamydiae, were subsequently found to have a large role in NGU, accounting for as much as 30% of disease.[6,9] There was some evidence that ureaplasmas were involved in cases of urethritis in young men experiencing their first sexual encounters.[10] With the advent of simple and effective polymerase chain reaction (PCR) methods, it now appears clear that *M. genitalium* may account for as much as 15% to 20% of NGU.[3,6,11-13] Chlamydiae and *M. genitalium* are independent agents of NGU.[6,14] Detection of *M. genitalium* is not associated with the presence of other mycoplasmas and ureaplasmas. Ureaplasmas and *M. hominis* are found as often in the control populations as they are in NGU cases, indicating that they do not have a prime role in NGU. If chlamydiae are associated with 30% of NGU and *M. genitalium* with 20%, then these two organisms are the major cause of NGU.

MYCOPLASMAL INFECTIONS IN WOMEN

The high prevalence of ureaplasmas in the vagina of healthy sexually active women (~66%)[4,6,15] indicates that they are commensals and normal flora. *M. hominis* is less prevalent at about 10% in healthy women. Concentrations of *M. hominis* are high in bacterial vaginosis.[16] Studies of the association of *M. genitalium* with genital diseases in women are just beginning, and only a few case-control studies have been carried out. *M. genitalium* was detected in 7% of 719 women with mucopurulent cervicitis.[17] The relative risk was 3.3-fold, indicating that *M. genitalium* may have a role in cervicitis. Similar results were obtained for endometritis, in which 16% of cases were positive for *M. genitalium* with 2% positive in the control subjects.[16] In a study of pelvic inflammatory disease,[18] 13% of 45 cases had *M. genitalium* compared with none in 37 control subjects. Twenty-seven percent were positive for *Chlamydia trachomatis.* Only one patient had both chlamydiae and *M. genitalium,* indicating that the two agents were independent. There is serologic evidence that as many as 40% of women with pelvic inflammatory disease showed antibody increases to *M. genitalium.*[14] Overall, *M. genitalium* is associated with a proportion of the same diseases that *C. trachomatis* is associated with. On premature rupture of membranes, there is invasion of the uterus not only by ureaplasmas but also by the numerous bacterial species normally found in the vagina.[16]

Cultivation and Detection

Mycoplasma medium for isolation contains peptones, yeast extract, and 20% serum. Horse serum is most frequently used, although some formulations call for fetal calf serum. *M. hominis* grows readily on both agar plates and broth cultures. *M. genitalium* grows slowly, with the prototype strain G37 producing colonies in 6 days or more (Fig. 182-1). *M. hominis* forms microscopically visible colonies in 2 to 5 days. It occasionally forms minute colonies on conventional blood agar. In broth cultures, *M. hominis* forms only a faint haze. Growth in broth is usually detected visually by identifying the alkaline products of arginine hydrolysis with a pH indicator. Minute ureaplasmal colonies appear in 2 to 5 days on special medium of pH 6.5 or lower. In broth culture, the alkaline reaction from hydrolysis of urea is used to monitor growth. *M. fermentans* is isolated best on mycoplasma agar or broth under anaerobic or microaerophilic conditions. Initial isolation may take 10 days or more. Detection of growth in broth cultures is by utilization of either glucose or arginine. *M. spermatophilum* and *M. penetrans* have seldom been isolated in clinical studies. Overall, diagnosis of mycoplasmal and ureaplasmal infections by culture is slow and difficult compared with isolation of *Neisseria gonorrhoeae.* As a consequence, the PCR has been developed for these organisms[19-22] and is probably the assay of choice. Determining the quantity of organisms present has proved useful for assessing the disease-causing ability of mycoplasmas and ureaplasmas.[10,23] Real-time PCR addresses this problem.

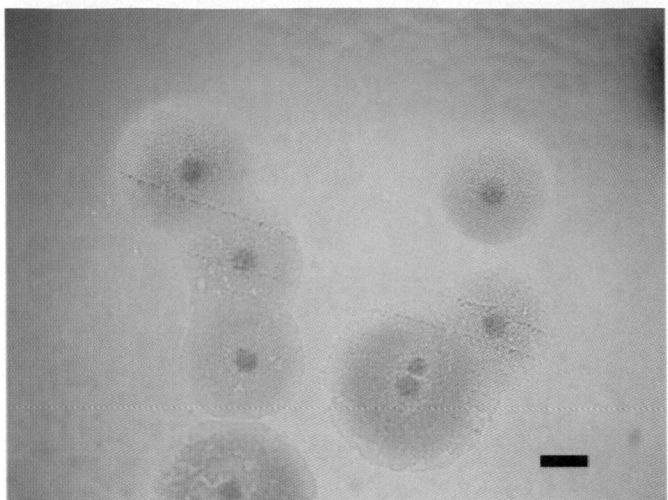

FIGURE 182-1. Light micrograph of *Mycoplasma genitalium* strain G37 on H agar[39] after 14 days of incubation. Bar = 100 μm.

Detection of *Mycoplasma genitalium*

The initial isolation of *M. genitalium* on SP-4 medium was reported in 1981.[24] No subsequent isolates were recovered from the genital tract until 1996, when Jensen and colleagues[3] reported isolation of the organism on agar using tissue culture as an enrichment culture for eventual growth on Friis medium. Because there still is no reliable medium for the direct isolation of *M. genitalium*, detection is carried out by PCR. Urine appears to be as good a sample in men as urethral swabs and is much easier to collect . In women, vaginal or cervical swabs are used. The most commonly used primers are directed at the 110-kD attachment protein.[6,19,21] Because PCR contamination is a major problem, strains may be genotyped, which permits identification of specific strains and excludes the possibility of contamination with strains of known sequence.[25] Culture is important for obtaining organisms for susceptibility testing and is a topic of continuing research.

INFECTIONS OUTSIDE THE GENITAL TRACT

M. hominis and ureaplasmas appear to be opportunists when they infect beyond the lower genital tract. Both are associated with mild self-limiting postpartum fevers.[26] *M. hominis* has been recovered from a variety of extragenital diseases[23,27,28] including infection of the kidneys, joints, surgical wounds, and other sites, particularly in immuno-compromised individuals.[28] *M. fermentans* is a rare isolate from the genital tract. It has been associated with rheumatoid arthritis, but proof that it is an independent cause is lacking. It was thought to be a co-factor in the development of the acquired immunodeficiency syndrome (AIDS). However, the organism can be detected as often in the blood stream of healthy persons as in those with AIDS.[20] The significance of the frequent detection of *M. fermentans* DNA in the blood stream from apparently healthy persons is not understood and may be a promising avenue for further study.

Serodiagnosis

The procedures used by mycoplasmologists to determine antibody levels include indirect immunofluorescence, Western blotting, enzyme-linked immunosorbent assay (ELISA), and metabolic inhibition testing. The metabolic inhibition test relies on the ability of patients' serum to prevent growth of mycoplasmas as evidenced by the failure to produce a metabolic product. A major problem for diagnosis of *M. genitalium* infections is its strong cross-reactivity with *M. pneumoniae*. A cloned *M. genitalium*–specific protein[29] may have utility for specific measurement of antibodies, which could be carried out by ELISA.

Interpretation of Laboratory Results

Ureaplasmas or *M. hominis* detected in the vagina or male urethra can best be interpreted as normal flora. Detection of *M. genitalium* from these sites implies potential disease that should be treated with the same concern as chlamydial infections. Detection of ureaplasmas or mycoplasmas in the blood stream, joints, wound lesions, and other extragenital sites is significant Mycoplasmas and ureaplasmas should be looked for in putatively infected sites where conventional bacteria cannot be found. Overall, detection of mycoplasmas by conventional culture is slow; it takes 2 to many days to detect any colonies and several more days to identify species. More widespread use of PCR will facilitate timely diagnosis of mycoplasmal infections.

Susceptibility to Antimicrobial Agents

Mycoplasmas in general are susceptible to tetracyclines and quinolones.[30-34] Because they have no cell wall, they are not susceptible to penicillins or cephalosporins. The susceptibilities of *M. genitalium* parallel those of *M. pneumoniae* in that both are highly susceptible to macrolides.[33,34] *M. hominis* is intrinsically resistant to erythromycin and other macrolides[30] but moderately susceptible to josamycin and lincomycin.

Ureaplasmas show limited susceptibility to erythromycin and other macrolides[30] but are resistant to lincomycin. Because macrolide susceptibility is less as pH decreases,[30] macrolides are less effective in the acid environment of genital tract. In vitro, azithromycin and clarithromycin are significantly more active than erythromycin.[30]

Some clinical strains of both ureaplasmas and *M. hominis* show high-level tetracycline resistance because of the transposon TetM.[35,36] Treatment with azithromycin but not tetracycline has resulted in clearance of *M. genitalium* from persons with NGU.[37] Treatment of extragenital *M. hominis* infections is difficult. Tetracycline resistance is becoming more common and tetracycline is bacteriostatic so that infections tend to recur even with susceptible strains. The mutation rate for quinolone resistance is high in *M. hominis*, and resistant strains have already been recognized.[32] Approved quinolones with the highest in vitro activity relative to achievable blood levels should be used to minimize chances for mutation because mutation to high-level resistance is a multistep process.[38]

REFERENCES

1. Krieger JN, Riley DE, Roberts MC, Berger RE. Prokaryotic DNA sequences in patients with chronic idiopathic prostatitis. J Clin Microbiol. 1996;34:3120.
2. Razin S, Yogev D, Naot Y. Molecular biology and pathogenicity of mycoplasmas. Microbiol Mol Biol Rev. 1998;62:1094.
3. Jensen JS, Hansen HT, Lind K. Isolation of *Mycoplasma genitalium* strains from the male urethra. J Clin Microbiol. 1996;34:286.
4. Tsunoe H, Tanaka M, Nakayama H, et al. High prevalence of *Chlamydia trachomatis*, *Neisseria gonorrhoeae* and *Mycoplasma genitalium* in female commercial sex workers in Japan. Int J STD AIDS. 2000;12:790.
5. Abele-Horn M, Wolf C, Dressel P, et al. Association of *Ureaplasma urealyticum* biovars with clinical outcome for neonates, obstetric patients and gynecological patients with pelvic inflammatory disease. J Clin Microbiol. 1997;35:1199.
6. Totten PA, Schwartz MA, Sjostrom KE, et al. Association of *Mycoplasma genitalium* with nongonococcal urethritis in heterosexual men. J Infect Dis. 2001;183:269.
7. Foy HM, Kenny GE, Levinsohn EM, et al. Acquisition of mycoplasmata and T-strains during infancy. J Infect Dis. 1970;121:579.
8. Hussain AI, Robson WLM, Kelley R, et al. *Mycoplasma penetrans* and other mycoplasmas in urine of human immunodeficiency virus–positive children. J Clin Microbiol. 1999;37:1518.
9. Johannisson G, Enstrom Y, Lowhagen GB, et al. Occurrence and treatment of *Mycoplasma genitalium* in patients visiting STD clinics in Sweden. Int J STD AIDS. 2000;11:324.
10. Bowie WR, Wang SP, Alexander ER. Etiology of non-gonococcal urethritis. Evidence for *Chlamydia trachomatis* and *Ureaplasma urealyticum*. J Clin Invest.1977;59:735.
11. Keane FE, Thomas BJ, Gilroy CB, et al. The association of *Chlamydia trachomatis* and *Mycoplasma genitalium* with non-gonococcal urethritis: Observations on heterosexual men and their female partners. Int J STD AIDS. 2000;11:439.
12. Jensen JS, Orsum R, Dohn B, et al. *Mycoplasma genitalium*: A cause of male urethritis? Genitourin Med. 1993;69:265.
13. Mena L, Wang X, Mroczkowski TF, Martin DH. *Mycoplasma genitalium* infections in asymptomatic men and men with urethritis attending a sexually transmitted diseases clinic in New Orleans. J Clin Infect Dis. 2002;35:1167.
14. Taylor-Robinson D, Gilroy CB, Hay PE. Occurrence of *Mycoplasma genitalium* in different populations and its clinical significance. Clin Infect Dis. 1993;17(Suppl 1): S66.

15. Taylor-Robinson D. *Ureaplasma urealyticum, Mycoplasma hominis,* and *Mycoplasma genitalium.* In Mandell GL, Bennet JE, Dolin R, eds. Principles and Practice of Infectious Diseases. 5th ed. Philadelphia: Churchill Livingstone; 2000:2027.

16. Germain M, Krohn MA, Hillier SL, Eschenbach DA. Genital flora in pregnancy and its association with intrauterine growth retardation. J. Clin Microbiol. 1994;32:2162.

17. Manhart LE, Critchlow CW, Holmes KK, et al. Mucopurulent cervicitis and *Mycoplasma genitalium.* J Infect Dis. 2003;187:650.

18. Simms I, Eastick K, Mallinson H, et al. Associations between *Mycoplasma genitalium, Chlamydia trachomatis,* and pelvic inflammatory disease. Sex Transm Infect. 2003;79:154.

19. Jensen JS, Uldum SA, Sondergard-Andersen J, et al. Polymerase chain reaction for detection of *Mycoplasma genitalium* in clinical samples. J Clin Microbiol. 1991;29:46.

20. Kovacic R, Launay V, Tuppin P, et al. Search for the presence of six *Mycoplasma* species in peripheral blood mononuclear cells of subjects seropositive and seronegative for human immunodeficiency virus. J Clin Microbiol. 1996;34:1808.

21. Palmer HM, Gilroy CB, Claydon EJ, Taylor-Robinson D. Detection of *Mycoplasma genitalium* in the genitourinary tract of women by the polymerase chain reaction. Int J STD AIDS. 1991;4:261.

22. Yoshida T, Macda S-I, Deguchi T, et al. Rapid detection of *Mycoplasma genitalium, Mycoplasma hominis, Ureaplasma parvum,* and *Ureaplasma urealyticum* organisms in genitourinary samples by PCR–microtiter plate hybridization assay. J Clin Microbiol. 2003;41:1850.

23. Heggie AD, Bar-Shain D, Boxerbaum B, et al. Identification and quantification of ureaplasmas colonizing the respiratory tract and assessment of their role in the development of chronic lung disease in preterm infants. Pediatr Infect Dis J. 2001;20:854.

24. Tully J, Taylor-Robinson D, Cole RM, Rose DL. A newly discovered mycoplasma in the human genital tract. Lancet. 1981;1:1288.

25. Kokotovic B, Friis NF, Jensen JS, Ahrens P. Amplified-fragment length polymorphism fingerprinting of *Mycoplasma* species. J Clin Microbiol. 1999;37:3300.

26. Eschenbach DA. *Ureaplasma urealyticum* as a cause of postpartum fever. Pediatr Infect Dis J. 1986;5(6 Suppl):S258.

27. Madoff S, Hooper DC. Nongenitourinary infections caused by *Mycoplasma hominis* in adults. Rev Infect Dis. 1988;3:602.

28. Meyer RD, Clough W. Extragenital *Mycoplasma hominis* infections in adults: Emphasis on immunosuppression. Clin Infect Dis.1993;17(Suppl 1):S243.

29. Clausen HF, Fedder J, Drasbek M, et al. Serological investigation of *Mycoplasma genitalium* in infertile women. Hum Reprod. 2001;16:866.

30. Kenny GE, Cartwright FD. Susceptibilities of *Mycoplasma hominis, M. pneumoniae* and *Ureaplasma urealyticum* to GAR 936, dalfopristin, dirithromycin, evernimicin, gatifloxacin, linezolid, moxifloxacin, quinupristin-dalfopristin and telithromycin compared to their susceptibilities to reference macrolides, tetracyclines and quinolones. Antimicrob Agents Chemother. 2001;45:3604.

31. Cakan H, Polat E, Kocazeybek B, et al. Assessment of antibiotic susceptibility of *Ureaplasma urealyticum* from prostitutes and outpatient clinic patients using the E-test and agar dilution method. Chemotherapy. 2003;49:39.

32. Bebear CM, Renaudin H, Charron A, et al. In vitro activity of trovafloxacin compared to those of five antimicrobials against mycoplasmas including *Mycoplasma hominis* and *Ureaplasma urealyticum* fluoroquinolone-resistant isolates that have been genetically characterized. Antimicrob Agents Chemother. 2000;44:2557.

33. Hannan PC. Comparative susceptibilities of various AIDS-associated and human mycoplasmas and strains of *Mycoplasma pneumoniae* to 10 classes of antibiotics in vitro. J Med Microbiol. 1998;47:1115.

34. Taylor-Robinson D, Bebear C. Antibiotic susceptibilities of mycoplasmas and treatment of mycoplasmal infections. J Antimicrob Chemother. 1997;40:622.

35. Roberts MC, Kenny GE. Dissemination of the tetM tetracycline resistance determinant to *Ureaplasma urealyticum.* Antimicrob Agents Chemother. 1986;29:350.

36. Roberts MC, Koutsky LA, Holmes KK, et al. Tetracycline-resistant *Mycoplasma hominis* strains contain streptococcal tetM sequences. Antimicrob Agents Chemother. 1985;28:141.

37. Falk L, Fredlund H, Jensen JS. Tetracycline treatment does not eradicate *Mycoplasma genitalium.* Sex Transm Infect. 2003;79:318.

38. Kenny GE, Young PA, Cartwright FD, et al. Sparfloxacin selects gyrase mutations in first-step *Mycoplasma hominis* mutants whereas ofloxacin selects topoisomerase IV mutations. Antimicrob Agents Chemother. 1999;43:2493.

39. Kenny GE, Kaiser GG, Cooney MK, Foy HM. Diagnosis of *Mycoplasma pneumoniae* pneumonia: Sensitivities and specificities of serology with lipid antigen and isolation of the organism on soy peptone medium for identification of infections. J Clin Microbiol. 1999;37:1518.

CHAPTER **183**

Introduction
to Rickettsioses
and Ehrlichioses

DIDIER RAOULT

BACTERIOLOGY

The definition of the Rickettsiaceae family has been mainly based on unspecific phenotypic characters. Basically, small gram-negative bacteria, associated (or not) with arthropods and necessitating (or not) eukaryotic cells from growth, were considered Rickettsiaceae. Over the past 20 years, generalization of the use of gene sequencing and genetic phylogeny deeply changed this classification.[1] The *Rickettsia* genus did not change, but a new genus, *Orientia*, was created from an independent branch of its phylum. The Ehrlichia group was recently reclassified[2] into four genera—*Ehrlichia* and *Anaplasma* being asso-

ciated with ticks, *Neorickettsia* with helminths, and *Wolbachia* with both arthropods and helminths. The *Bartonella* genus is a close neighbor in the alpha group of proteobacteria and now comprises the former *Rochalimaea* species, *Grahamella*, and *Wolbachia melophagi*. *Coxiella* and *Rickettsiella* are now in the gamma group of proteobacteria closely related to *Legionella* species and *Francisella tularensis* (into which *Wolbachia persica* is integrated). Even more distant *Eperythrozoon* and *Haemobartonella*, two intraerythrocytic animal pathogens, are closely related to *Mycoplasmas* issued from the gram-positive lineage (Fig. 183-1). We limit this chapter to the Rickettsiales (*Rickettsia* and *Anaplasma* genera). These are intracellular alpha proteobacteria associated with eukaryotic hosts (arthropods or helminths). Based on antigenic and genetic data, Rickettsiae are traditionally divided into three groups (Table 183-1): the spotted fever group accounts for most tick-borne rickettsiosis, but *R. felis* is the agent of flea-borne spotted fever[3,4] and *R. akari* is the agent of Rickettsialpox. The typhus group comprises two human pathogens transmitted by insects. Epidemic typhus is caused by *R. prowazekii* and is transmitted by the body louse. Murine typhus is caused by *R. typhi* and is transmitted by rat and cat fleas. The scrub typhus group is composed of *Orientia tsutsugamushi* only and is transmitted by "chiggers."

HISTORY AND EMERGING DISEASES

New genetic tools, as well as the use of cell culture assays, have allowed the discovery of many new rickettsioses and ehrlichioses over the past 20 years (Table 183-2).[5] Three ehrlichioses and 10 rickettsioses have been described since 1980. Only one erhlichiosis and nine rickettsioses were known before that time. Three major conditions determined the discovery of these diseases. Some were discovered after clinical description in countries where spotted fever had been unknown (Japan and *R. japonica*, Flinder's Island and *R. honei*, Russia and

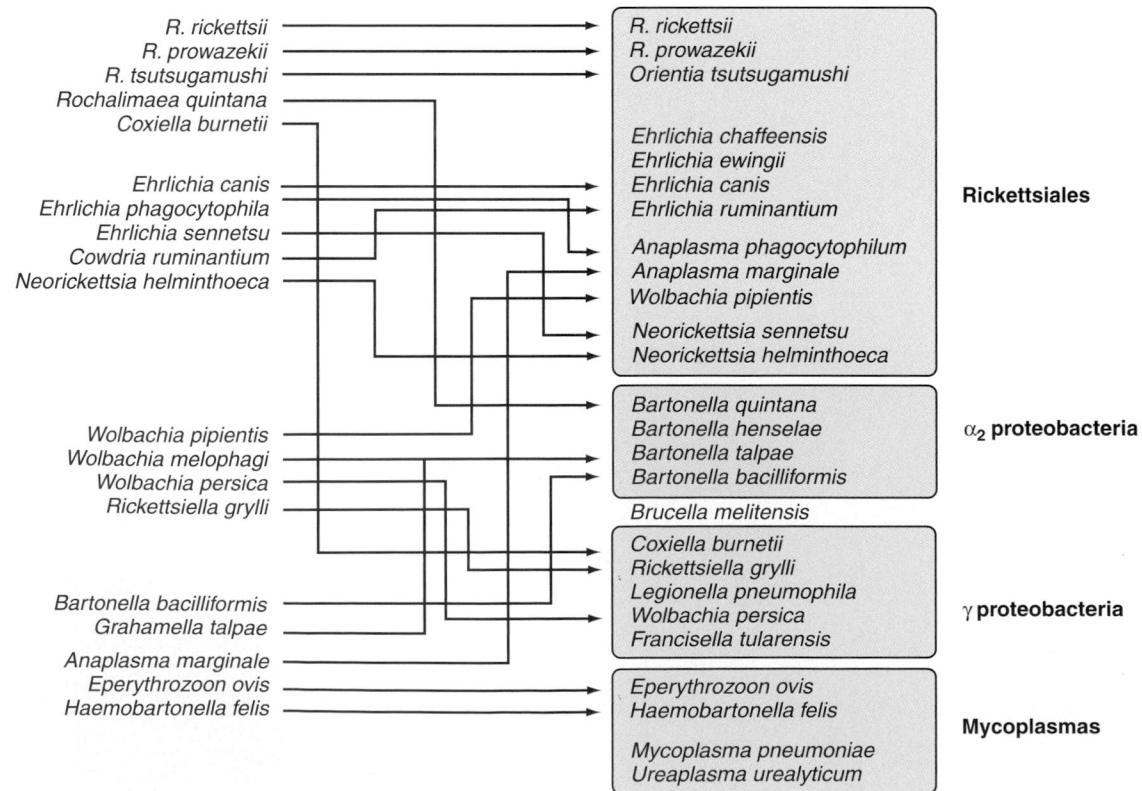

FIGURE 183-1. Classification and Taxonomy of Rickettsiaceae. Most changes were performed with the use of 16 S r RNA sequence-based phylogeny. (*Left column, Krieg NR, Holt JG. Bergey's Manual of Systematic Bacteriology, vol 1. Baltimore: Williams & Wilkins; 1984. Right column, Garrity G. Bergey's Manual of Systematic Bacteriology, vol 2. London: Springer Verlag; 1984.*)

TABLE 183-1 Rickettsioses and Ehrlichioses of Humans and Their Vectors

	Tick-borne	Flea-borne	Louse-borne	Mite-borne	Helminth-borne
Rickettsiae					
Spotted fever group	R. rickettsii	R. felis		R. akari	
	R. conorii				
	R. japonica				
	R. sibirica				
	R. australis				
	R. slovaca				
	R. africae				
	R. honei				
	R. aeschlimanii				
	R. helvetica				
Typhus group		R. typhi	R. prowazekii		
Orientia				O. tsutsugamushi	
Anaplasma	A. phagocytophila				
Wolbachia spp.		W. pipientis†			Wolbachia spp.‡
Ehrlichia	E. chaffeensis				
	E. ewingii				
	E. canis*				
Neorickettsia					N. sennetsu§

*A single asymptomatic patient was reported as infected.
†This symbiont was found in fleas that were biting patients.
‡Wolbachia species are believed to cause inflammation during filariasis.
§In monocytic patients, it is believed that ehrlichiosis is transmitted by the eating of raw fish parasitized by worms.

TABLE 183-2 Historical Data on Diseases Caused by *Rickettsia* Species (first and senior authors)

Year	Discovery	Authors	Year	Discovery	Authors
1760	Description of exanthematic typhus	Boissier de Sauvage	1981	Ehrlichia chaffeensis	Anderson
1879	First report of scrub typhus	Nagayo	1984	Japanese spotted fever	Mahara
1899	Description of RMSF	Maxcy	1985	Culture of R. heilongjianghensis	Udida and Walker
1906	Isolation of R. rickettsii	Ricketts	1987	First case of human erhlichiosis in United States	Maeda and McDade
1909	Role of body lice in typhus	Nicolle (Nobel prize)	1989	Culture of R. japonica	Lov
1909	Description of MSF	Conor et al	1990	First human cases of granulocytic erhlichioses	Bakken
1910	Serology test based on *Proteus*	Wilson	1990	Isolation of R. africae	Kelly
1911	Isolation of R. prowazekii	Nicolle	1991	Flinder's Island spotted fever	Stewart
1914	Tick role in MSF	Wilson	1992	Molecular identification of *Ehrlichia ewingii*	Anderson
1916	Weil Felix test	Weil and Felix	1992	First case of infection by R. africae	Kelly and Raoult
1921	Identification of R. typhi	Mooser	1992	Culture and identification of R. conorii	Tarasevitch and Raoult
1925	Description of the tâche noire in MSF	Pieri	1992	Culture of R. honei	Baird et al
1930	First isolation of *Orientia tsutsugamushi* (R. orientalis)	Nagayo	1993	Culture and identification of R. sibirica and R. mongolotimonae	Yu and Raoult
1930	Role of chiggers in scrub typhus	Kawarimura	1994	First case of flea-borne spotted fever	Schriefer and Azad
1930	Role of fleas in murine typhus	Dyer	1996	Infection by R. sibirica and R. mongolotimonae	Raoult et al
1932	Isolation of R. conorii	Brumpt			
1935	Description of Siberian tick typhus	Shmatikov et al	1997	First infection by R. slovaca	Raoult et al
			1997	Culture of R. aeschlimanii	Beati and Raoult
1938	Isolation of R. sibirica	Krontovuka et al	1999	Astrakhan fever	Tarasevitch and Raoult
1940	R. phagocytophila	Gordon			
1946	Description of Rickettsialpox	Huebner	1999	First human cases of infection with E. ewingii	Buller
1946	Isolation of R. akari	Huebner			
1946	Isolation of R. australis	Plotz and Smadel	2000	Role of *Wolbachia* in filariasis	Taylor
1946	Queensland tick typhus	Plotz and Smadel	2000	First case of acute infection by R. helvetica	Fournier and Raoult
1956	Ehrlichia sennetsu	Kobayashi			
1968	Isolation of R. slovaca	Brezina et al	2000	Culture of R. felis	Raoult et al
1974	Culture of R. conorii	Goldwasser	2002	First case of infection by R. aeschlimanii	Raoult et al
1979	Isolation of R. helvetica	Burgdorfer and Peter	2004	First case of infection by R. parkeri	Paddock et al

MSF, Mediterranean spotted fever; RMSF, Rocky Mountain spotted fever.

Astrakhan fever). Some were recognized by bacterial identification based on culture and polymerase chain reaction (PCR) in places where the new pathogen was confounded with another known rickettsial pathogen (*Rickettsia africae, Rickettsia mongolotimonae,* and *Rickettsia aeschlimanii* with *Rickettsia conorii, Rickettsia felis* with *Rickettsia typhi, Anaplasma phagocytophilum* and *Ehrlichia ewingii* with *Ehrlichia chaffeensis*). Some were identified through association by physicians and microbiologists when an atypical unknown disease (*Ehrlichia chaffeensis, Rickettsia slovaca, Rickettsia helvetica*) was being explored.[5]

Some old diseases such as epidemic typhus or scrub typhus apparently reemerged because of lack of social control or ecologic changes. These diseases, which were the more deadly rickettsioses for the human species, remain a threat and should be controlled.

Wolbachia, a symbiont of human filarial worms, has been shown to play a major role in the pathology and clinical manifestations of filariasis. It introduces a completely new concept in infectious diseases.[6] It appears that inflammatory reactions of patients during the disease and during the treatment of filariasis are caused by the release of lipopolysaccharide-like molecules from the symbiotic *Wolbachia.*

Many rickettsiae were found in their vectors long before a particular disease could be associated with them. The denomination *nonpathogenic rickettsia* that is used for bacteria found only in ticks is misleading.[5] Among famous pathogens first classified as nonpathogenic rickettsiae were *Legionella pneumophila; Coxiella burnetii,* the agent of Q fever; *R. parkeri,*[6a] and *R. africae.* Ticks may well be the reservoir of many other human pathogens. Several rickettsiae have been found in ticks throughout the world, the pathogenic potential of which remains unknown.

PATHOPHYSIOLOGY

Rickettsia and *Ehrlichia* are host-associated pathogens. However, it may be possible for them to be grown axenically in the future. These pathogens depend on their environment for the supply of many nutriments. *Rickettsia* species escape rapidly from the phagosome to multiply within the cytoplasm. Spotted fever rickettsiae, which are motile in the cytoplasm through actin polymerization,[7] invade neighboring cells. *R. prowazekii* is devoid of such motility and is released only by destruction of the host cell. No virulence factor has been definitively identified, but I suspect that phospholipase D may play a key role in cellular invasion. The target cell of *Rickettsia* is the vascular endothelial cell, except for *R. akari* and *O. tsutsugamushi,* which multiply in monocytic cells. *E. chaffeensis* multiplies in monocytic cells; *A. phagocytophilum* and *E. ewingii* multiply in polymorphonuclear cells. Some animal ehrlichiae are multiplying in blood platelets.

GENETICS

The complete gene sequences of *R. prowazekii*[8] and *R. conorii*[9] have recently been published. Analysis shows that *R. prowazekii* is genetically a subset of bigger *R. conorii* and that it comprises many degraded genes. The genomes of *R. rickettsii* and *R. typhi* and the bacteria of the *Anaplasma* phylum are currently sequenced; this may provide elucidation for some questions about the way of life and pathogenicity of Rickettsiales.

EPIDEMIOLOGY

The geographic and temporal distribution of rickettsioses and ehrlichioses is mainly determined by their vectors (see Table 183-1). Louse-transmitted diseases occur worldwide. The human louse is common to all humans. Lice parasitize poor people, preferentially in cold places and during wars. Common fleas such as cat and dogs fleas (*Ctenocephalides felis* and *Ctenocephalides canis*) and rat fleas (*Xenopsylla cheopis* and *Pulex irritans*) are reported worldwide, as are their transmitted diseases—murine typhus and flea-borne spotted fever (caused by *R. felis*). Tick species are highly dependent on their envi-

ronment; very few are found worldwide with the exception of *Rhipicephalus sanguineus*—the dog tick, vector of *R. conorii* (in the Old World) and of *Ehrlichia canis* (worldwide). Therefore, tick-transmitted diseases are usually restricted to parts of the world where they can be transmitted by the local fauna. Among rickettsioses and ehrlichioses transmitted by ticks, only *A. phagocytophilum* is currently found both in Europe and in the United States.

Tick behavior may determine the targeted human population and the seasonality. It may also influence the clinical presentation. For example, *Amblyomma* ticks are aggressive hunting ticks. They frequently attack in groups. This behavior explains grouped cases and several inoculation eschars per patient. *Dermacentor* species wait for their host in an ambush strategy, falling onto a hairy host from a height of 1 meter.[10] Therefore, they bite frequently in the hair, and children are a primary target. As a consequence, *Dermacentor*-transmitted rickettsioses, such as Rocky Mountain spotted fever (RMSF), and infections by *R. slovaca* more frequently involve children than do other rickettsial diseases.[11] Wide variations in the annual incidence of tick-transmitted diseases, such as RMSF and Mediterranean spotted fever, have been observed. A worldwide increase was noticed during the 1970s, followed by a decrease in the 1980s, which is not understood.[12] It was hypothesized that this was caused by increased exposure, better use of diagnostic tests, or a shift from effective to ineffective empirically prescribed antibiotics.

CLINICAL FINDINGS

Fever, rash, and headache were considered for years the diagnostic clue for rickettsial diseases. Indeed, this remains a major triad, but spotless RMSF has been reported, and many of the newly described rickettsial diseases have no rash.[13] Major findings in rickettsioses and ehrlichioses include fever in a patient with exposure to a potential vector that may be associated with rash, inoculation eschar, or localized lymphadenopathy (Table 183-3). Biologically, neutropenia, thrombocytopenia, and moderate increases in transaminases are common. This may prompt a diagnostic test and eventually treatment with doxycycline.

The severity of these diseases varies with the causative agent and the host. Some *Rickettsia* species have more severe potential, such as *R. rickettsii, R. prowazekii,* and *O. tsutsugamushi.* Some variations in the same disease are seen between regions for scrub typhus and RMSF.

Host factors also play a role in severity. Old age, alcoholism, and deficit in glucose-6-phosphate dehydrogenase have been associated with more severe disease.[14] In such patients, a multiple organ dysfunction syndrome can be observed that usually leads to a fatal outcome. Gangrene of the extremities can also be observed in such cases.

DIAGNOSIS

Culture remains extremely difficult for these organisms, and diagnosis mainly relies on serology and PCR. The reference technique for serology is immunofluorescence. Many cross-reactions are observed, and precise species determination of the infecting agent may be difficult. Testing of several antigens on the same slide to compare reactivity may help in discriminating among cross-reacting agents. Western blot may be more specific in early sera. Cross-absorption may help to resolve these problems, but it is technically demanding and expensive.[5]

PCR has been widely used. It is an appropriate tool for the diagnosis of ehrlichioses with the use of blood samples. As for rickettsioses, biopsies of skin lesions are preferable (because biopsies can also be used for immunohistochemistry[15,16]). PCR may be of value for the serum testing of patients with rickettsial disease.[17] PCR testing should include controls because it is very easy for specimens to become contaminated. The amplicon must be tested by another technique to assure its specificity, including enzyme restriction cutting, sequencing, or hybridization.

TABLE 183-3 Clinical Findings and Target Cells for Ehrlichioses and Rickettsioses

Disease	Rash	Rash Specificity	Eschar	Enlarged Lymph Nodes	Target Cells
Rocky Mountain spotted fever	90%	45% purpuric	Very rare	No	Endothelial cells
Mediterranean spotted fever	97%	10% purpuric	72%	Rare	Endothelial cells
Siberian tick typhus	100%	Macular	77%	Yes	Endothelial cells
Queensland tick typhus	100%	Vesicular	65%	Yes	Endothelial cells
Israeli spotted fever	100%	Macular	Rare	No	Endothelial cells
Flinder's Island spotted fever	85%	8% purpuric	28%	Yes	Endothelial cells
Astrakhan fever	100%	Macular	23%	No	Endothelial cells
African tickbite fever	30%	Vesicular	100% multiple	Yes	Endothelial cells
Japanese spotted fever	100%	Macular	90%	No	Endothelial cells
Rickettsia mongolotimonae	Yes	Macular	Yes (could be multiple)	No	Endothelial cells
Rickettsia slovaca	No	Macular	Yes	Yes	Endothelial cells
Rickettsia helvetica	No	—	No	No	Endothelial cells
Rickettsia heilongjianghensis	Yes	Macular	Yes	Yes	Endothelial cells
Rickettsia aeschlimanii	Yes	—	Yes	No	Endothelial cells
Rickettsialpox	100%	Vesicular	100%	Yes	Macrophages/monocytes
Epidemic typhus	50%	Macular	No	No	Endothelial cells
Murine typhus	50%	Macular	No	No	Endothelial cells
Scrub typhus	30%	Macular	50% (could be multiple)	Yes	Macrophages/monocytes
Monocytic ehrlichioses	36%	Macular	No	25%	Macrophages/monocytes
Granulocytic erhlichioses	<10%	Macular	No	No	Polymorphonuclear cells
Infection by *Ehrlichia ewingii*	—	—	—	—	Polymorphonuclear cells

TREATMENT

The most useful drug in children and in adults is doxycycline. It can be prescribed in short courses (1 day for typhus, scrub typhus, and Mediterranean spotted fever). Dental problems should not be a problem for children if fewer than three courses of doxycycline are prescribed during childhood. Chloramphenicol should not be prescribed because it is insufficient for ehrlichioses[18] and less active than doxycycline for RMSF.[19] Quinolones, which have been disappointingly inactive in cases of typhus and scrub typhus despite good in vitro efficacy (see Chapters 187 and 188), are not sufficient for ehrlichioses.

REFERENCES

1. Roux V, Raoult D. Phylogenetic analysis and taxonomic relationships among the genus *Rickettsia*. In: Raoult D, Brouqui P, eds. Rickettsiae and Rickettsial Diseases at the Turn of the Third Millennium. Marseille: Elsevier; 1999:52-66.
2. Dumler JS, Barbet AF, Bekker CPJ, et al. Reorganisation of genera in the families *Rickettsiaceae* and *Anaplasmataceae* in the order *Rickettsiales*: Unification of some species of *Ehrlichia* with *Anaplasma*, *Cowdria* with *Ehrlichia* and *Ehrlichia* with *Neorickettsia*; descriptions of six new species combinations and designation of *Ehrlichia equi* and 'HGE agent' as subjective synonyms of *Ehrlichia phagocytophila*. Int J Syst Evol Microbiol. 2001;51:2145-2165.
3. La Scola B, Meconi S, Fenollar F, et al. Emended description of *Rickettsia felis* (Bouyer et al, 2001), a temperature-dependent cultured bacterium. Int J Syst Evol Microbiol. 2002;52:2035-2041.
4. Bouyer DH, Stenos J, Crocquet-Valdes P, et al. *Rickettsia felis*: Molecular characterization of a new member of the spotted fever group. Int J Syst Evol Microbiol. 2001;51:339-347.
5. Raoult D, Roux V. Rickettsioses as paradigms of new or emerging infectious diseases. Clin Microbiol Rev. 1997;10:694-719.
6. Cross HF, Haarbrink M, Egerton G, et al. Severe reactions to filarial chemotherapy and release of *Wolbachia* endosymbionts into blood. Lancet. 2001;358:1873-1875.
6a. Paddock CD, Sumner JW, Comer JA, et al. *Rickettsia parkeri*: A newly recognized cause of spotted fever rickettsiosis in the United States. Clin Infect Dis. 2004;38:805-811.
7. Teysseire N, Chiche-Portiche C, Raoult D. Intracellular movements of *Rickettsia conorii* and *R. typhi* based on actin polymerization. Res Microbiol. 1992;143:821-829.
8. Andersson SG, Zomorodipour A, Andersson JO, et al. The genome sequence of *Rickettsia prowazekii* and the origin of mitochondria. Nature. 1998;396:133-140.
9. Ogata H, Audic S, Renesto-Audiffren P, et al. Mechanisms of evolution in *Rickettsia conorii* and *R. prowazekii*. Science. 2001;293:2093-2098.
10. Parola P, Raoult D. Ticks and tickborne bacterial diseases in humans: An emerging infectious threat. Clin Infect Dis. 2001;32:897-928.
11. Raoult D, Lakos A, Fenollar F, et al. Spotless rickettsiosis caused by *Rickettsia slovaca* and associated with *Dermacentor* ticks. Clin Infect Dis. 2002;34:1331-1336.
12. Walker DH, Raoult D. *Rickettsia rickettsii* and other spotted fever group rickettsiae (Rocky Mountain spotted fever and other spotted fevers). In: Mandell GL, Bennett JE, Dolin R, eds. Principles and Practice of Infectious Diseases. 4th ed. New York: Churchill Livingstone; 1995:1721-1727.
13. Sexton DJ, Kaye KS. Rocky mountain spotted fever. Med Clin North Am. 2002;86:351-360, VII, VIII.
14. Walker DH. The role of host factors in the severity of spotted fever and typhus rickettsioses. Ann N Y Acad Sci. 1990;590:10-19.
15. La Scola B, Raoult D. Diagnosis of Mediterranean spotted fever by cultivation of *Rickettsia conorii* from blood and skin samples using the centrifugation-shell vial technique and by detection of *R. conorii* in circulating endothelial cells: A 6 year follow-up. J Clin Microbiol. 1996;34:2722-2727.
16. Walker DH, Feng H-M, Ladner S, et al. Immunohistochemical diagnosis of typhus rickettsioses using an anti-lipopolysaccharide monoclonal antibody. Mod Pathol. 1997;10:1038-1042.
17. Raoult D, Fournier PE, Fenollar F, et al. *Rickettsia africae*, a tick-borne pathogen in travelers to sub-Saharan Africa. N Engl J Med. 2001;344:1504-1510.
18. Maurin M, Bryskier A, Raoult D. Antibiotic susceptibilities of *Parachlamydia acanthamoeba* in amoebae. Antimicrob Agents Chemother. 2002;46:3065-3067.
19. Paddock CD, Holman RC, Krebs JW, Childs JE. Assessing the magnitude of fatal Rocky Mountain spotted fever in the United States: Comparison of two national data sources. Am J Trop Med Hyg. 2002;67:349-354.

CHAPTER **184**

Rickettsia rickettsii and Other Spotted Fever Group Rickettsiae (Rocky Mountain Spotted Fever and Other Spotted Fevers)

DAVID H. WALKER

DIDIER RAOULT

The spotted fevers comprise a large group of tick-, mite-, and flea-borne zoonotic infections that are caused by closely related rickettsiae.[1] These include Rocky Mountain spotted fever, boutonneuse fever, African tick-bite fever, North Asian tick typhus, Queensland tick typhus, Flinders Island spotted fever, Japanese spotted fever, *Rickettsia slovaca* infection, flea-borne spotted fever, and rickettsialpox. Rickettsiae are in many places of the world emerging or reemerging pathogens.[2-6] Associated diseases have a broad spectrum of severity; the most virulent, Rocky Mountain spotted fever, has a case-fatality rate of 23% unless treated early and appropriately. Even young and previously healthy people may die with Rocky Mountain spotted fever. In recent years, the wide distribution and potential severity of the other spotted fevers have been recognized, especially in Europe, Africa, Australia, China, and Japan. Early diagnosis remains deceptively difficult.

ROCKY MOUNTAIN SPOTTED FEVER

The Pathogen

Rocky Mountain spotted fever (RMSF) was first described in Idaho in the late 19th century.[7] Ricketts established the infectious nature of the illness and demonstrated the role of ticks as the vector in western Montana in 1906.[8] Wolbach in 1919 clearly identified the etiologic rickettsiae within endothelial cells.[9]

The causative agent, *Rickettsia rickettsii,* belongs to the spotted fever group of rickettsiae, which are genetically closely related. Traditional classification according to differences in surface antigenic proteins is being replaced by phylogenetic analysis.[1] Some presumably nonpathogenic rickettsiae also belong to this group. Spotted fever group (SFG) rickettsiae are obligately intracellular bacteria that reside in the cytosol and less often in the nuclei of host cells. These rickettsiae are small, measuring approximately 0.3 by 1.0 μm. They have one of the smallest bacterial genomes ranging between 1.1 and 1.6 MB. The cell wall, which has the ultrastructural appearance of a gram-negative bacterium, contains peptidoglycan and lipopolysaccharide (LPS). Rickettsiae are difficult to stain with ordinary bacterial stains but are conveniently stained by the Gimenez method or with acridine orange. They have not been cultivated in cell-free medium. Growth requires living host cells, such as the yolk sac of embryonated eggs, experimental animals, or cell culture (e.g., Vero, HEL, and L-929 cells). Rickettsiae have undergone remarkable genome reduction with exploitation of their cytosolic environment by being highly adapted for intracellular survival with effective transport systems for adenosine triphosphate (ATP), amino acids, and phosphorylated sugars, as well as their own independent metabolic enzymes. Among the protein antigens of *R. rickettsii,* two surface proteins (OmpA [190-kDa] and OmpB [135-kDa]) contain conformational epitopes that are targets of humoral immunity and are the antigenic basis for serotyping; other antigens are shared among the SFG.[10] The LPS of SFG rickettsiae contains highly immunogenic antigens that are strongly cross-reactive among all members of the group; they cross-react to a lesser extent with *Rickettsia typhi* and *Rickettsia prowazekii*. However, antibodies to LPS do not provide protection against infection. T lymphocytes (particularly CD8 cells) are important effectors of immune clearance of rickettsiae, and interferon-γ and tumor necrosis factor-α activate infected endothelial cells to kill intracellular rickettsiae.[11-13] Natural killer (NK) cells activated in the early innate immune response secrete interferon-γ that dampens the rickettsial burden; cytotoxic T lymphocytes are crucial to the clearance of rickettsial infection.[14,15] OmpA and OmpB cell wall proteins are important immunogens.[16-19]

Epidemiology

The role of a tick bite in the transmission of RMSF was demonstrated by McCalla and Brereton and reported in 1908[7]; a tick obtained from a patient suffering from RMSF transmitted the disease to two volunteers. The seasonal distribution of RMSF parallels tick activity. The tick is both the vector and the main reservoir.[20] *Dermacentor variabilis,* the American dog tick, is the prevalent vector in the eastern two thirds of the United States and the Far West; *Dermacentor andersoni,* the Rocky Mountain wood tick, in the western states; *Rhipicephalus sanguineus,* in Mexico; and *Amblyomma cajennense,* in South America (see Chapter 295 for illustrations of ticks). Causes for the variation in infection rates among populations of ticks are not clear, although in *Dermacentor,* only a small portion of ticks (generally 4%) carry any rickettsiae, and fewer than one in 1000 ticks carry virulent *R. rickettsii*. One limiting factor is the deleterious effect that *R. rickettsii* has on ticks; another is the inhibition of establishment of transovarial transmission of *R. rickettsii* by the presence of another

Rickettsia species in the tick. Humidity, climatic variations, human activities altering the vegetation and fauna, and the use of insecticides have been suspected to play a role in the fluctuation of tick populations and the prevalence of human rickettsiosis.

R. rickettsii is transmitted trans-stadially (stage to stage) and transovarially in ticks, thus maintaining the agent in nature. Horizontal transmission through vertebrate hosts would also appear to occur to a small degree and to be a necessary factor for the maintenance of *R. rickettsii* in nature.[20] In most mammals, rickettsemia is of very short duration and low titer, allowing for infection of only a small proportion of feeding ticks. Of the three tick stages—larva, nymph, and adult—only adult *Dermacentor* ticks feed on humans. The prevalence of pathogenic rickettsiae in various populations of ticks is variable. Many rickettsiae of unknown pathogenicity have been isolated and characterized in the United States, including *R. bellii, R. montanensis, R. rhipicephali, R. peacockii,* and *R. parkeri*.[21,22]

The tick transmits the disease to humans during a prolonged period of feeding that may last for 1 to 2 weeks. The bite is painless and frequently goes unnoticed. After the attached tick has fed for 6 to 10 hours, rickettsiae begin to be injected from the salivary glands. An even longer period may be required for reactivation of rickettsial virulence in unfed ticks. Humans can also be infected by exposure to infective tick hemolymph during the removal of ticks from persons or domestic animals, especially when the tick is crushed between the fingers.

Although *R. rickettsii* has rarely been recovered from feral animals, serum antibodies are detected in many of these animals, and the prevalence of antibodies in dogs correlates with the prevalence of human cases in the particular area.

Laboratory-acquired infection[23] transmitted by infectious aerosols or parenteral inoculation of *R. rickettsii* may be prevented by careful technique and the use of biohazard containment hoods, masks, and gloves. *R. rickettsii* is covered by the Select Agents Act, which restricts its possession, investigation, transfer, and shipment, owing to its potential use as an aerosol-transmitted agent of bioterrorism.[24]

The considerable fluctuation in the annual number of patients with RMSF in the United States (Fig. 184-1) may reflect cyclic changes in the ecology of the tick/rickettsia relationship or tick populations.[25,26] The increased infection rate that occurred between 1966 and 1981 may have several hypothetical explanations—an increase in the infected tick population or tick contact with humans, an increase in interest of physicians in the disease, and the development of more sensitive and specific serologic tools. The fall in incidence in 1949 followed the introduction of effective antibiotics, and increased incidence in the 1970s coincided with a decline in the use of tetracycline as a first-choice antibiotic for many other infections. These correla-

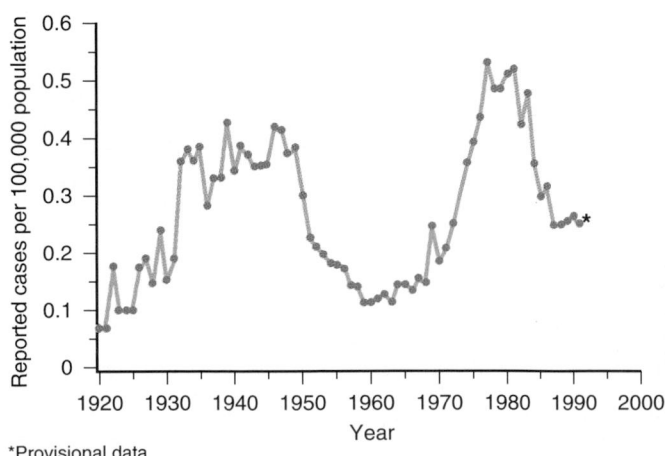

*Provisional data

FIGURE 184-1. Rocky Mountain spotted fever rates per year in the United States from 1920 to 1991.

tions imply a substantial occurrence of undiagnosed cases aborted by early treatment.

From the 1870s until 1931, RMSF was recognized as existing only in the western United States. At present, the prevalence of the disease is higher in the South Atlantic states (0.65 per 100,000 inhabitants) and in the East South Central region (0.49 per 100,000) than in the Rocky Mountain states (Fig. 184-2).[26] Local prevalence in highly endemic areas such as North Carolina has been as high as 14.59 per 100,000.[27] Moreover, although the incidence of infection may be decreasing in one area, it is increasing simultaneously in another region. The report of a focus in the South Bronx emphasizes that the ecologic conditions that permit the establishment of RMSF are widely distributed.[28] Most cases are diagnosed during late spring and summer. However, especially in the southern states, a few cases occur during the winter.

In the southern states, incidence is highest among children and patients who are known to be exposed more often to ticks than are matched controls. In the western states, owing to transmission by the wood tick *D. andersoni,* a higher proportion of adult males contract the disease because of occupational exposure. The case-fatality rates are significantly higher for progressively older age groups.[29] The disease also occurs in Central and South America, where it is currently largely unrecognized and possibly misdiagnosed as dengue or other febrile exanthems.[3,30,31]

Serosurveys of humans have been conducted to evaluate the prevalence of the disease.[25] The specificity of the assays has been questioned because of cross-reactivity of *R. rickettsii* with other rickettsiae and other bacteria, some of the methods employed, and the selection of minimal significant titers. A prospective study of soldiers under conditions of intense tick exposure revealed a high rate of asymptomatic seroconversion. The exact *Rickettsia* species or other antigenic stimulus of the antibody response remains to be determined, but *R. amblyommii* would appear a more likely agent than *R. rickettsii.*

Pathogenesis

Rickettsiae introduced into the skin apparently spread via lymphatics and small blood vessels to the systemic and pulmonary circulation, where, by means of OmpA, OmpB, and rickettsial phospholipase, they attach to, and induce phagocytosis through, their target cells—the vascular endothelium—to establish numerous disseminated foci of infection.[32-35] After entry by induced phagocytosis, the rickettsiae

escape rapidly from the phagosome into the cytosol and less frequently invade the nucleus. Rickettsiae proliferate intracellularly by binary fission and are released from infected cells via long, thin cell projections either extracellularly or into the adjoining cell.[36,37] The movement of spotted fever rickettsiae within the cytoplasm, into projections invaginating into the nucleus, and into cell projections from which they are released is caused by propulsion by the host cell's actin filaments.[38] The consequence of cell-to-cell spread in the body is a focal network of hundreds of contiguous infected endothelial cells corresponding to the lesions (e.g., maculopapular rash). The presence of greater quantities of rickettsiae in damaged cells supports the concept of direct cell injury.[36] No convincing data support endotoxin or exotoxin as a pathogenic mechanism. In vitro studies suggest that rickettsial injury to the host cell may be caused by free radical–induced damage to host cell membranes, rickettsial phospholipase activity, and protease activity.[39-43] The major pathophysiologic effect of endothelial cell injury is increased vascular permeability, which in turn results in edema, hypovolemia, hypotension, and hypoalbuminemia.[44] Hyponatremia is the result of secretion of antidiuretic hormone as an appropriate response to hypovolemia.[45] High quantities of rickettsiae infecting the pulmonary microcirculation are associated with increased vascular permeability and cause noncardiogenic pulmonary edema.[46,47] Vascular injury and the subsequent host lymphohistiocytic response correspond to the distribution of rickettsiae and include interstitial pneumonia, interstitial myocarditis, perivascular glial nodules of the central nervous system, and similar vascular lesions in the rash, gastrointestinal tract, pancreas, liver, skeletal muscles, and kidneys. However, even severe vascular injury rarely leads to clinically significant hemorrhage. Platelets are consumed locally in numerous foci of infection; consequently, thrombocytopenia is observed in 32% to 52% of patients.[48,49] A procoagulant state occurs, including endothelial injury, release of procoagulant components, activation of the coagulation cascade with thrombin generation, platelet activation, increased antifibrinolytic factors, consumption of natural anticoagulants, activation of the kallikrein-kinin system, and secretion of coagulation-promoting cytokines.[50-57] These studies are supported by numerous studies of endothelial cells in culture, such as the demonstration that tissue factor is secreted by *Rickettsia*-infected endothelial cells,[58,59] but true disseminated intravascular coagulation occurs only rarely, and occlusive vascular thrombosis is not the basic pathophysiologic event.[53,60]

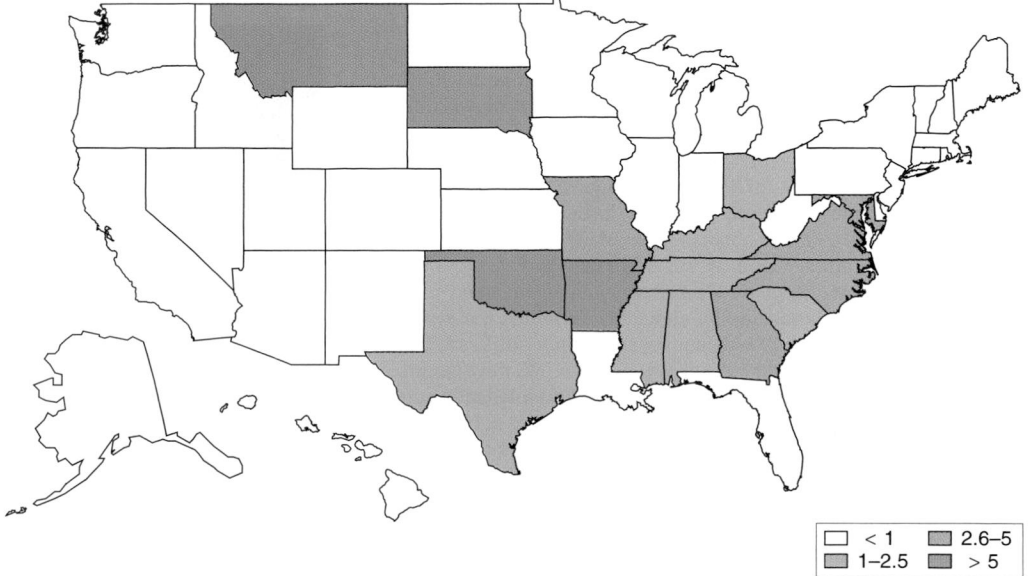

FIGURE 184-2. Reported Rocky Mountain spotted fever cases per 1,000,000 population per year in the United States from 1981 to 1991.

☐ < 1	▨ 2.6–5
▨ 1–2.5	▨ > 5

doxycycline be used for suspected RMSF in children of all ages because of the life-threatening nature of RMSF and the unlikelihood that a single course of doxycycline would stain the teeth.[80] Avoidance of therapeutic delay is critical for the prognosis.[29,81] Severely ill patients require intensive supportive care. Fluid maintenance is critical for maintenance of organ perfusion. Because of increased vascular permeability and risk of extravasation of fluid into pulmonary alveoli, a Swan-Ganz catheter may be needed to monitor hemodynamics in some patients. Glucocorticoids are sometimes given to severely ill patients, but no documentation of efficacy has occurred, and they are not recommended, although in experimentally infected dogs treated simultaneously with doxycycline, no detrimental effects of prednisolone treatment were noted.[82]

Prevention

Although no vaccine is available currently, immunodominant surface proteins have been identified, and the major surface protein antigens (OmpA and OmpB) of *Rickettsia rickettsii* and *Rickettsia conorii* are candidate vaccine antigens. Immunization of guinea pigs with OmpA provided protective immunity against a virulent challenge, and protective fragments of OmpB have been identified.[16-19] A vaccine may be developed that would protect against all SFG rickettsiae, but currently, no vaccine is available for any of the SFG rickettsiae.

Currently, the best means of prevention remains the avoidance of contact with ticks through the use of repellents and protective clothing. In the hot weather usually associated with the tick season, these techniques are often impractical. Regular checks of the body, including scalp, pubic, and axillary hair, allow removal of the tick before rickettsial transmission. To remove an attached tick, one should use forceps to detach the intact tick without leaving mouth parts in the skin. The tick-bite wound should be cleansed.

OTHER SPOTTED FEVER GROUP RICKETTSIOSES

Among the eleven other SFG *Rickettsia* species reported with convincing evidence to have caused infection of humans *(R. conorii, R. sibirica, R. japonica, R. australis, R. honei, R. africae, R. parkeri, R. slovaca, R. aeschlimanii, R. felis,* and *R. akari),* the first nine are transmitted by tick bite. *R. felis* is maintained transovarially in fleas and is presumably transmitted by them. The last, *R. akari,* is discussed in Chapter 185. In addition, numerous distinct species and serotypes of SFG rickettsiae (e.g., *R. massiliae, R. helvetica, R. montanensis, R. rhipicephali,* and *R. parkeri*) have been identified only in ticks.[1] Some of these may prove to be pathogenic for humans, even if they cause only a short nonexanthematous febrile illness or asymptomatic seroconversion.[83] *R. conorii* infection has been designated by many geographic names: Marseilles fever, Mediterranean spotted fever, Kenya tick typhus, Israeli tick typhus, Astrakhan spotted fever, and Indian tick typhus. *R. conorii,* a typical SFG rickettsia with high genetic homology with *R. rickettsii,* appears to have greater intraspecies antigenic and genetic diversity than does *R. rickettsii.*[1,2] SFG cross-reactive protein and LPS antigens are detected, and cross-protection is shared among SFG rickettsiae.[10,84] Conformational antigens on the surface proteins of SFG rickettsiae also contain species- and even strain-specific epitopes; for example, some strain-specific epitopes of *R. conorii* strains cause Israeli tick typhus and Astrakhan spotted fever.[85]

During the 1970s and 1980s, an increased incidence of spotted fever rickettsioses was noted in many parts of the world, particularly in Spain, France, Italy, Israel, and Australia. Spotted fever rickettsioses have also been described recently in China, Thailand, Japan, Mexico, Australia, and sub-Saharan Africa.[2-6,86,87] Historically, boutonneuse fever was first described by Conor and Bruch in 1909 in Tunisia, although the *tache noire* ("black spot"), that is, the eschar at the site of the bite, was not described until 1923 by Pieri in Marseille. *R. conorii* has been identified in India, Pakistan, Israel, Russia, Georgia, Ukraine, Ethiopia, Kenya, South Africa, Morocco, and southern Europe. The epidemiology of boutonneuse fever and ecology of *R. conorii* are closely related to ticks, particularly *Rhipicephalus sanguineus.*

R. conorii is maintained transovarially in ticks and is transmitted to humans by tick bite. The frequent absence of a history of tick bite is likely due to transmission by immature larvae and nymphs, which are often not noticed. Cases occur mainly in warm months with peak incidences in July, August, and September in many Mediterranean locations. Imported cases occur in travelers returning to the United States and northern Europe from southern Europe and Africa. The pathogenic basis for tissue injury in the spotted fevers is well elucidated in the tache noire or eschar at the site of the infective tick bite. Dermal and epidermal necrosis and perivascular edema are the consequences of endothelial injury by *R. conorii.*[88] Necropsies of fatal cases of boutonneuse fever reveal disseminated vascular infection and injury by *R. conorii,* including meningoencephalitis and vascular lesions in kidneys, lungs, gastrointestinal tract, liver, pancreas, heart, spleen, and skin.[89,90] Hepatic biopsy specimens reveal focal hepatocellular necrosis and granuloma-like lesions.[91] Boutonneuse fever can be a severe illness, particularly in patients with underlying conditions such as diabetes mellitus or cardiac insufficiency, alcoholism, old age, and G6PD deficiency. The disease is milder in children. In France, Israel, and Spain, the death rate among hospitalized patients ranges from 1.4% to 5.6%, similar to that of RMSF.[92] Boutonneuse fever is associated with a procoagulant state,[51-54,93] and 9.6% of cases are complicated by deep venous thrombosis late in the course.[94] Plasma levels of tumor necrosis factor rise during infection.[57] After a mean incubation period of 7 days, fever, myalgias, and headache characterize the onset (see Table 184-1). Careful clinical examination may reveal a tache noire, which facilitates the clinical diagnosis.

Rickettsia sibirica has been documented in Russia, China, Mongolia, and Pakistan, as well as in France and South Africa, where human infections have been caused by the mongolotimonae strain. This strain has also been found in ticks in Central Africa. Spotted fever group rickettsiae have been isolated from six species of ticks in northern Asia, as well as from wild mammals. Transovarial transmission is an important mechanism of survival of *R. sibirica* in nature. Recently, North Asian tick typhus was diagnosed among paleontologists doing field research in Mongolia. *Rickettsia australis* is limited to eastern Australia, and *Rickettsia honei,* the etiologic agent of the newly recognized Flinder's Island spotted fever, has been associated with human infection only in Australia, although it is present also in ticks in Thailand. A vesicular rash has been reported in a few patients with spotted fever rickettsiosis in Australia.

Strains of *Rickettsia japonica,* the etiologic agent of Japanese spotted fever, have also been found in ticks in China (designated there as "*Rickettsia heilongjiang*" and "*Rickettsia hulinii*").[95] Although Japanese spotted fever has been described as a typically moderate SFG rickettsial illness (fever 100%, rash 100%, and eschar 90%), more severe illness, including meningoencephalitis, respiratory failure, and shock associated with elevated proinflammatory cytokines, does occur.[96,97] The agent of the SFG rickettsioses of southeastern Asia has yet to be determined.

Rickettsia africae is prevalent throughout sub-Saharan Africa, where the vector ticks—*Amblyomma hebraeum* and *Amblyomma variegatum*—are present.[86,98] The identification of *R. africae* infections in Guadaloupe, West Indies, apparently conforms to the distribution of *A. variegatum.*[3,86,99] African tick-bite fever is the only tick-transmitted rickettsiosis in which several inoculation eschars are observed in a high proportion of cases.[86,98] *R. africae,* the most frequently imported rickettsiosis, is often observed in patients who have hunted or traveled in the bush in southern Africa. The attack rate in an exposed group can be quite high.[98] Patients with African tick-bite fever typically have headache, fever, and myalgia, as well as acute-stage elevations of serum tumor necrosis factor-α, interleukin (IL)-6, IL-8, IL-13, gamma interferon, regulated upon activation normal T cell expressed and secreted (RANTES), and macrophage inflammatory protein 1-α.[100] Rash may be vesicular, maculopapular, sparse, or even absent in more than half of patients. Distinctive features include frequent regional lymphadenitis that drains the region of the eschars and, in a small portion of patients, aphthous stomatitis. The infection is very common among native Africans in whom it is frequently suspected to be malaria or typhoid fever. Infection with the closely related *R. parkeri* has been documented in the United States.[100a]

Human infections with *R. slovaca* have been recognized in Europe.[101,102] *R. slovaca* is transmitted to humans most often by the bite of adult *Dermacentor marginatus* ticks during winter and early spring. The illness is characterized by an eschar, typically on the scalp, and enlarged, sometimes tender, draining cervical lymph nodes. Fewer than half of patients manifest a fever, and rash occurs rarely, although the eschar site may have persistent alopecia. The occurrence of persistent asthenia in a small fraction of patients, despite response to antirickettsial treatment otherwise, and the often weak serologic response suggest that other factors or agents might also be involved. The fact that SFG rickettsiae can cause an eschar in an otherwise healthy person[103]—the mildest manifestation of illness, short of asymptomatic seroconversion—has been demonstrated for *R. aeschlimanii*.[104]

R. felis, an SFG rickettsia occupying the unusual niche of a flea host, has been cultivated by growth at a temperature below 30° C.[105,106] *R. felis* infections have been documented by PCR in the United States, Mexico, Brazil, and Germany and by serology in France and Brazil.[107-110] The cat flea host, *Ctenocephalides felis*, is cosmopolitan, suggesting a worldwide distribution. *R. felis* has been identified in North and South America, Europe, and Asia. Presumably the agents of a dengue-like SFG rickettsiosis in the Yucatan, six *R. felis* infections documented by PCR have manifested fever in all cases, maculopapular rash (four cases), headache (three cases), neurologic involvement (photophobia, stupor, and meningismus in one case each), myalgia (two cases), abdominal pain (two cases), vomiting (two cases), eschar with lymphadenopathy (one case), and cough with radiologic infiltrates (one case). Pitfalls associated with ascribing an illness to a causative agent by PCR are emphasized in the dubious association of *R. helvetica* with sarcoidosis and chronic myopericarditis.[111,112]

The diagnosis may be established by immunohistologic demonstration of *R. conorii* in skin biopsy, and PCR can be applied to blood or skin biopsy for *R. conorii*, *R. africae*, *R. slovaca*, or *R. japonica*.[71-76,88,89,113] A novel approach that can be used to diagnose boutonneuse fever before the onset of rash is immunofluorescent detection of *R. conorii* in circulating endothelial cells captured by immunomagnetic beads coated with a monoclonal antibody to the human endothelial cell surface.[70,74,114] Timely diagnosis can also be established by isolating *R. conorii* in a shell vial cell culture system.[70] During the convalescent phase, production of antibodies to SFG rickettsiae is demonstrated by the use of microimmunofluorescence, latex agglutination, enzyme immunoassay, Western blot, or complement fixation.

Successful treatment is achieved with doxycycline (200 mg/day), tetracycline (25 mg/kg/day), chloramphenicol (2 g/day for 7-10 days), or ciprofloxacin (1.5 g/day for 5-7 days).[115-117] Single-dose treatment with 200 mg doxycycline has been proposed, as has treatment with josamycin, a macrolide compound, for children and pregnant women, or with clarithromycin or azithromycin for children with mild disease.[118]

REFERENCES

1. Yu XJ, Walker DH. Family I. Rickettsiaceae. In: Garrity GM, ed. Bergey's Manual of Systematic Bacteriology. 2nd ed, v. 2. Baltimore: Williams & Wilkins; in press.
2. Raoult D, Roux V. Rickettsioses as paradigms of new or emerging infectious diseases. Clin Microbiol Rev. 1997;10:694-719.
3. Zavala-Velazquez JE, Yu X, Walker DH. Unrecognized spotted fever group rickettsiosis masquerading as dengue fever in Mexico. Am J Trop Med Hyg. 1996;55:157-159.
4. Sirisanthana T, Pinyopornpanit V, Sirisanthana V, et al. First cases of spotted fever group rickettsiosis in Thailand. Am J Trop Med Hyg. 1994;50:682-686.
5. Cohen MAH, Cheng AFB, Leung NWY. A fatal case of rickettsial spotted fever in Hong Kong—Lion Rock fever. J Hong Kong Med Assoc. 1989;41:185-186.
6. Mahara F. Japanese spotted fever: Report of 31 cases and review of the literature. Emerg Infect Dis. 1997;3:105-111.
7. Harden VA. Rocky Mountain Spotted Fever: History of a Twentieth Century Disease. Baltimore and London: The Johns Hopkins University Press; 1990.
8. Ricketts HT. A micro-organism which apparently has a specific relationship to Rocky Mountain spotted fever. JAMA. 1909;52:379-380.

9. Wolbach SB. Studies on Rocky Mountain spotted fever. J Med Res. 1919;41:2-197.
10. Xu WB, Raoult D. Taxonomic relationships among spotted fever group rickettsiae as revealed by antigenic analysis with monoclonal antibodies. J Clin Microbiol. 1998;36:887-896.
11. Feng H-M, Walker DH. Mechanisms of intracellular killing of *Rickettsia conorii* in infected human endothelial cells, hepatocytes, and macrophages. Infect Immun. 2000;68:6729-6736.
12. Feng H-M, Popov VL, Yuoh G, et al. Role of T-lymphocyte subsets in immunity to spotted fever group rickettsiae. J Immunol. 1997;158:5314-5320.
13. Feng H-M, Popov VL, Walker DH. Depletion of interferon gamma and tumor necrosis factor alpha in mice with *Rickettsia conorii*-infected endothelium: Impairment of rickettsicidal nitric oxide production resulting in fatal, overwhelming rickettsial disease. Infect Immun. 1994;62:1952-1960.
14. Billings AN, Feng H-M, Olano JP, et al. Rickettsial infection in murine models activates an early anti-rickettsial effect mediated by NK cells and associated with production of gamma interferon. Am J Trop Med Hyg. 2001;65:52-56.
15. Walker DH, Olano JP, Feng H-M. Critical role of cytotoxic T lymphocytes in immune clearance of rickettsial infection. Infect Immun. 2001;69:1841-1846.
16. Sumner JW, Sims KG, Jones DC, et al. Protection of guinea-pigs from experimental Rocky Mountain spotted fever by immunization with baculovirus-expressed *Rickettsia rickettsii* rOmpA protein. Vaccine. 1995;13:29-35.
17. Vishwanath S, McDonald GA, Watkins NG. A recombinant *Rickettsia conorii* vaccine protects guinea pigs from experimental boutonneuse fever and Rocky Mountain spotted fever. Infect Immun. 1990;58:646-653.
18. Crocquet-Valdes PA, Diaz-Montero CM, Feng H-M, et al. Immunization with a portion of rickettsial outer membrane protein A stimulates protective immunity against spotted fever rickettsiosis. Vaccine. 2002;20:979-988.
19. Díaz-Montero CM, Feng H-M, Crocquet-Valdes PA, Walker DH. Identification of protective components of two major outer membrane proteins of spotted fever group rickettsiae. Am J Trop Med Hyg. 2001;65:371-378.
20. McDade JE, Newhouse VF. Natural history of *Rickettsia rickettsii*. Annu Rev Microbiol. 1986;40:287-309.
21. Philip RN, Casper EA, Anacker RL, et al. *Rickettsia bellii* sp. nov.: A tick borne rickettsia, widely distributed in the United States, that is distinct from the spotted fever and typhus biogroups. Int J Syst Bacteriol. 1983;33:94-106.
22. Niebylski ML, Schrumpf ME, Burgdorfer W, et al. *Rickettsia peacockii* sp. nov., a new species infecting wood ticks, *Dermacentor andersoni*, in western Montana. Intern J Syst Bacteriol. 1997;47:446-452.
23. Johnson JE, Kadull PJ. Rocky Mountain spotted fever acquired in a laboratory. N Engl J Med. 1967;227:842-846.
24. Walker DH. Principles of the malicious use of infectious agents to create terror: Reasons for concern for organisms of the genus *Rickettsia*. Ann NY Acad Sci. 2003;990:739-742.
25. Walker DH, Fishbein DB. Epidemiology of rickettsial diseases. Eur J Epidemiol. 1991;7:237-245.
26. Treadwell TA, Holman RC, Clarke MJ, et al. Rocky Mountain spotted fever in the United States, 1993-1996. Am J Trop Med Hyg. 2000;63:21-26.
27. Wilfert CM, McCormack JN, Kleeman K, et al. Epidemiology of Rocky Mountain spotted fever as determined by active surveillance. J Infect Dis. 1984;150:469-479.
28. Salgo MP, Telzak EE, Currie B, et al. A focus of Rocky Mountain spotted fever within New York City. N Engl J Med. 1988;318:1345-1348.
29. Childs JE, Paddock CD. Passive surveillance as an instrument to identify risk factors for fatal Rocky Mountain spotted fever: Is there more to learn? Am J Trop Med Hyg. 2002;66:450-457.
30. Galvao MA, Dumler JS, Mafra CL, et al. Fatal spotted fever rickettsiosis, Minas Gerais, Brazil. Emerg Infect Dis. 2003;9:1402-1405.
31. Ripoll CM, Remondegui CE, Ordonez G, et al. Evidence of rickettsial spotted fever and ehrlichial infections in a subtropical territory of Jujuy, Argentina. Am J Trop Med Hyg. 1999;61:350-354.
32. Walker DH, Valbuena GA, Olano JP. Pathogenic mechanisms of diseases caused by *Rickettsia*. Ann NY Acad Sci. 2003;990:1-11.
33. Li H, Walker DH. rOmpA is a critical protein for the adhesion of *Rickettsia rickettsii* to host cells. Microb Pathog. 1998;24:289-298.
34. Uchiyama T. Role of major surface antigens of *Rickettsia japonica* in the attachment to host cells. In: Raoult D, Brouqui P, eds. Rickettsiae and Rickettsial Diseases at the Turn of the Third Millennium. Paris: Elsevier; 1999:182-188.
35. Silverman DJ, Santucci LA, Meyers N, et al. Penetration of host cells by *Rickettsia rickettsii* appears to be mediated by a phospholipase of rickettsial origin. Infect Immun. 1992;60:2733-2740.
36. Walker DH, Cain BG. The rickettsial plaque: Evidence for direct cytopathic effect of *Rickettsia rickettsii*. Lab Invest. 1980;43:388-396.
37. Schaechter M, Bozeman FM, Smadel JE. Study on the growth of rickettsiae. II. Morphologic observations of living rickettsiae in tissue culture cells. Virology. 1957;3:160-172.
38. Teysseire N, Chiche-Portiche C, Raoult D. Intracellular movements of *Rickettsia conorii* and *R. typhi* based on actin polymerization. Res Microbiol. 1992;143:821-829.
39. Santucci LA, Gutierrez PL, Silverman DJ. *Rickettsia rickettsii* induces superoxide radical and superoxide dismutase in human endothelial cells. Infect Immun. 1992;60:5113-5118.
40. Eremeeva ME, Dasch GA, Silverman DJ. Quantitative analyses of variations in the injury of endothelial cells elicited by 11 isolates of *Rickettsia rickettsii*. Clin Diagn Lab Immunol. 2001;8:788-795.

41. Eremeeva ME, Silverman DJ. Effects of the antioxidant α-lipoic acid on human umbilical vein endothelial cells infected with *Rickettsia rickettsii*. Infect Immun. 1998;66:2290-2299.

42. Walker DH, Firth WT, Ballard JG, et al. Role of phospholipase-associated penetration mechanism in cell injury by *Rickettsia rickettsii*. Infect Immun. 1983;40:840-842.

43. Walker DH, Tidwell RR, Rector TM, et al. Effect of synthetic protease inhibitors of the amidine type on cell injury by *Rickettsia rickettsii*. Antimicrob Agents Chemother. 1984;25:582-585.

44. Harrell GT, Aikawa JK. Pathogenesis of circulatory failure in Rocky Mountain spotted fever. Alteration in the blood volume and the thiocyanate space at various stages of the disease. Arch Intern Med. 1949;83:331-347.

45. Kaplowitz LG, Robertson GL. Hyponatremia in Rocky Mountain spotted fever: Role of antidiuretic hormone. Ann Intern Med. 1983;98:334-335.

46. Walker DH, Crawford CG, Cain BG. Rickettsial infection of the pulmonary microcirculation: The basis for interstitial pneumonitis in Rocky Mountain spotted fever. Hum Pathol. 1980;11:263-272.

47. Lankford HV, Glauser FL. Cardiopulmonary dynamics in a severe case of Rocky Mountain spotted fever. Arch Intern Med. 1980;140:1357-1360.

48. Helmick CG, Bernard KW, D'Angelo LJ. Rocky Mountain spotted fever: Clinical, laboratory, and epidemiological features of 262 cases. J Infect Dis. 1984;150:480-486.

49. Kaplowitz LG, Fischer JJ, Sparling PF. Rocky Mountain spotted fever: A clinical dilemma. In: Remington JB, Swartz HN, eds. Current Clinical Topics in Infectious Diseases. v. 2. New York: McGraw-Hill; 1981:89-108.

50. Rao AK, Schapira M, Clements ML, et al. A prospective study of platelets and plasma proteolytic systems during the early stages of Rocky Mountain spotted fever. N Engl J Med. 1988;318:1021-1028.

51. Davi G, Giammarresi C, Vigneri S, et al. Demonstration of *Rickettsia conorii*-induced coagulative and platelet activation in vivo in patients with Mediterranean spotted fever. Thromb Haemost. 1995;74:631-634.

52. George F, Brouqui P, Boffa M-C, et al. Demonstration of *Rickettsia conorii*–induced endothelial injury in vivo by measuring circulating endothelial cells, thrombomodulin, and von Willebrand factor in patients with Mediterranean spotted fever. Blood. 1993;82:2109-2116.

53. Elghetany TM, Walker DH. Hemostatic changes in Rocky Mountain spotted fever and Mediterranean spotted fever. Am J Clin Pathol. 1999;112:159-168.

54. Vicente V, Espana F, Tabernero D, et al. Evidence of activation of the protein C pathway during acute vascular damage induced by Mediterranean spotted fever. Blood. 1991;78:416-422.

55. Vicente V, Estelles A, Moraleda JM, et al. Fibrinolytic changes during acute vascular damage induced by Mediterranean spotted fever. Fibrinolysis. 1993;7:324-329.

56. Yamada T, Harber P, Pettit GW, et al. Activation of the kallikrein-kinin system in Rocky Mountain spotted fever. Ann Intern Med. 1978;88:764-768.

57. Oristrell J, Amengual MJ, Font-Creus B, et al. Plasma levels of tumor necrosis factor-α in patients with Mediterranean spotted fever: Clinical and analytical correlations. Clin Infect Dis. 1994;19:1141-1143.

58. Teysseire N, Arnoux D, George F, et al. Von Willebrand factor release and thrombomodulin and tissue factor expression in *Rickettsia conorii*-infected endothelial cells. Infect Immun. 1992;60:4388-4393.

59. Sporn LA, Haidaris PJ, Shi R, et al. *Rickettsia rickettsii* infection of cultured human endothelial cells induces tissue factor expression. Blood. 1994;83:1527-1534.

60. Schmaier AH, Srikanth S, Elghetany MT, et al. Hemostatic/fibrinolytic protein changes in C3H/HeN mice infected with *Rickettsia conorii*. Thromb Haemost. 2001;86:871-879.

61. Walker DH, Gay RM, Valdes-Dapena M. The occurrence of eschars in Rocky Mountain spotted fever. J Am Acad Dermatol. 1981;4:571-576.

62. Rosenblum MJ, Masland RL, Harrell GT. Residual effects of rickettsial disease on the central nervous system. Arch Intern Med. 1952;90:444-445.

63. Walker DH, Mattern WD. Acute renal failure in Rocky Mountain spotted fever. Arch Intern Med. 1979;139:443-448.

64. Donohue JF. Lower respiratory tract involvement in Rocky Mountain spotted fever. Arch Intern Med. 1980;140:223-227.

65. Feltes TF, Wilcox WD, Feldman WE, et al. M-mode echocardiographic abnormalities in Rocky Mountain spotted fever. South Med J. 1984;787:1130-1132.

66. Walker DH, Hawkins HL, Hudson P. Fulminant Rocky Mountain spotted fever. Its pathologic characteristics associated with glucose-6-phosphate dehydrogenase deficiency. Arch Pathol Lab Med. 1983;107:121-125.

67. Dalton MJ, Clarke MJ, Holman RC, et al. National surveillance for Rocky Mountain spotted fever, 1981-1992: Epidemiologic summary and evaluation of risk factors for fatal outcome. Am J Trop Med Hyg. 1995;52:405-413.

68. Archibald LK, Sexton DJ. Long-term sequelae of Rocky Mountain spotted fever. Clin Infect Dis. 1995;20:1122-1125.

69. Kirkland KB, Marcom PK, Sexton DJ, et al. Rocky Mountain spotted fever complicated by gangrene: Report of six cases and review. Clin Infect Dis. 1993;16:629-634.

70. LaScola B, Raoult D. Diagnosis of Mediterranean spotted fever by cultivation of *Rickettsia conorii* from blood and skin samples using the centrifugation-shell vial technique and by detection of *R. conorii* in circulating endothelial cells: A 6-year follow-up. J Clin Microbiol. 1996;34:2722-2727.

71. Walker DH, Burday MS, Folds JD. Laboratory diagnosis of Rocky Mountain spotted fever. South Med J. 1980;73:1443-1447.

72. Kaplowitz LG, Lange JV, Fischer JJ, et al. Correlation of rickettsial titers, circulating endotoxin, and clinical features in Rocky Mountain spotted fever. Arch Intern Med. 1983;143:1149-1151.

73. Dumler JS, Gage WR, Pettis GL, et al. Rapid immunoperoxidase demonstration of *Rickettsia rickettsii* in fixed cutaneous specimens from patients with Rocky Mountain spotted fever. Am J Clin Pathol. 1990;93:410-414.

74. LaScola B, Raoult D. Laboratory diagnosis of rickettsioses: Current approaches to diagnosis of old and new rickettsial diseases. J Clin Microbiol. 1997;35:2715-2727.

75. Tzianabos T, Anderson BE, McDade JE. Detection of *Rickettsia rickettsii* DNA in clinical specimens using polymerase chain reaction technology. J Clin Microbiol. 1989;27:2866-2868.

76. Sexton DJ, Kanj SS, Wilson K, et al. The use of a polymerase chain reaction as a diagnostic test for Rocky Mountain spotted fever. Am J Trop Med Hyg. 1994;50:59-63.

77. Walker DH, Sexton D: *Rickettsia rickettsii*. In: Yu VL, Merigan TC, Barriere SL, eds. Antimicrobial Therapy and Vaccines. 2nd ed. Baltimore: Williams & Wilkins; 2002:899-906.

78. Rolain JM, Maurin M, Vestris G, et al. In vitro susceptibilities of 27 rickettsiae to 13 antimicrobials. Antimicrob Agents Chemother. 1998;42:1537-1541.

79. Holman RC, Paddock CD, Curns AT, et al. Analysis of risk factors for fatal Rocky Mountain spotted fever: Evidence for superiority of tetracyclines for therapy. J Infect Dis. 2002;184:1437-1444.

80. American Academy of Pediatrics, Committee on the Control of Infectious Diseases. Rocky Mountain spotted fever. In: Pickering LK, ed. 2000 Red Book: Report of the Committee on Infectious Diseases. 25th ed. Elk Grove Village, Ill: American Academy of Pediatrics; 2000:491-493.

81. Kirkland KB, Wilkinson WE, Sexton DJ. Therapeutic delay and mortality in cases of Rocky Mountain spotted fever. Clin Infect Dis. 1995;20:1118-1121.

82. Breitschwerdt EB, Davidson MG, Hegarty BC, et al. Prednisolone at anti-inflammatory or immunosuppressive dosages in conjunction with doxycycline does not potentiate the severity of *Rickettsia rickettsii* infection in dogs. Antimicrob Agents Chemother. 1997;41:141-147.

83. Fournier P-E, Grunnenberger F, Jaulhac B, et al. Evidence of *Rickettsia helvetica* infection in humans, Eastern France. Emerg Infect Dis. 2000;6:389-392.

84. Vishwanath S. Antigenic relationships among the rickettsiae of the spotted fever and typhus groups. FEMS Microbiol Lett. 1991;81:341-344.

85. Walker DH, Feng H, Saada JI, et al. Comparative antigenic analysis of spotted fever group rickettsiae from Israel and other closely related organisms. Am J Trop Med Hyg. 1995;52:569-576.

86. Raoult D, Fournier P-E, Fenollar F, et al. *Rickettsia africae*, a tick-borne pathogen in travelers to sub-Saharan Africa. N Engl J Med. 2001;344:1501-1510.

87. Stewart RS. Flinders Island spotted fever: A newly recognized endemic focus of tick typhus in Bass Strait. Med J Aust. 1991;154:94-99.

88. Walker DH, Occhino C, Tringali GR, et al. Pathogenesis of rickettsial eschars. The tache noire of boutonneuse fever. Hum Pathol. 1988;19:1449-1454.

89. Walker DH, Gear JM. Correlation of the distribution of *Rickettsia conorii*, microscopic lesions, and clinical features in South African tick bite fever. Am J Trop Med Hyg. 1985;34:361-371.

90. Walker DH, Herrero-Herrero JI, Ruiz-Beltran R, et al. The pathology of fatal Mediterranean spotted fever. Am J Clin Pathol. 1987;87:669-672.

91. Walker DH, Staiti A, Mansueto S, et al. Frequent occurrence of hepatic lesions in boutonneuse fever. Acta Trop. 1986;43:175-181.

92. Raoult D, Zuchelli P, Weiller PJ, et al. Incidence, clinical observations and risk factors in the severe form of Mediterranean spotted fever among patients admitted to the hospital in Marseilles 1983-1984. J Infect. 1986;12:111-116.

93. Vicente V, Alberca I, Ruiz R, et al. Coagulation abnormalities in patients with Mediterranean spotted fever. J Infect Dis. 1986;153:128-131.

94. Raoult D, Weiller PJ, Chagnon A, et al. Mediterranean spotted fever: Clinical, laboratory and epidemiological features of 199 cases. Am J Trop Med Hyg. 1986;35:845-850.

95. Zhang JZ, Fan MY, Wu YM, et al. Genetic classification of "*Rickettsia heilongjiang*" and "*Rickettsia hulinii*," two Chinese spotted fever group rickettsiae. J Clin Microbiol. 2000;38:3498-3501.

96. Iwasaki H, Mahara F, Takada N, et al. Fulminant Japanese spotted fever associated with hypercytokinemia. J Clin Microbiol. 2001;39:2341-2343.

97. Araka M, Takatsuka K, Kawamura J, Kanno Y. Japanese spotted fever involving the central nervous system. Two case reports and a literature review. J Clin Microbiol. 2002;40:3874-3876.

98. Jensenius M, Fournier P-E, Vene S, et al. African tick bite fever in travelers to rural sub-equatorial Africa. Clin Infect Dis. 2003;36:1411-1417.

99. Parola P, Vestris G, Martinez D, et al. Tick-borne rickettsiosis in Guadeloupe, the French West Indies: Isolation of *Rickettsia africae* from *Amblyomma variegatum* ticks and serosurvey in humans, cattle, and goats. Am J Trop Med Hyg. 1999;60:888-893.

100. Jensenius M, Ueland T, Fournier PE, et al. Systemic inflammatory responses in African tick-bite fever. J Infect Dis. 2003;187:1332-1336.

100a. Paddock CD, Sumner JW, Comer JA, et al. *Rickettsia parkeri*: A newly recognized cause of spotted fever rickettsiosis in the United States. Clin Infect Dis. 2004;38:805-811.

101. Raoult D, Lakos A, Fenollar F, et al. Spotless rickettsiosis caused by *Rickettsia slovaca* and associated with *Dermacentor* ticks. Clin Infect Dis. 2002;34:1331-1336.

102. Casola C, Enea M, Lucht F, Raoult D. First isolation of *Rickettsia slovaca* from a patient, France. Emerg Infect Dis. 2003;9:135.

103. Mansueto S, Tringali G, Leo RD, et al. Demonstration of spotted fever group rickettsiae in the *tache noire* of a healthy person in Sicily. Am J Trop Med Hyg. 1984;33:479-482.

104. Pretorius A-M, Birtles RJ. *Rickettsia aeschlimanii*: A new spotted fever group rickettsia, South Africa. Emerg Infect Dis. 2002;8:874.

105. Bouyer DH, Stenos J, Crocquet-Valdes P, Moron CG, et al. *Rickettsia felis*: Molecular characterization of a new member of the spotted fever group. Int J Syst Evol Bacteriol. 2001;51:339-347.

106. La Scola B, Meconi S, Fenollar F, et al. Emended description of *Rickettsia felis* (Bouyer et al, 2001), a temperature-dependent cultured bacterium. Int J Syst Evol Bacteriol. 2002;52:2035-2041.

107. Zavala-Velazquez JE, Ruiz-Sosa JA, Sanchez-Elias RA, et al. *Rickettsia felis* rickettsiosis in Yucatán. Lancet. 2000;356:1079-1080.
108. Schriefer ME, Sacci JB Jr, Dumler JS, et al. Identification of a novel rickettsial infection in a patient diagnosed with murine typhus. J Clin Microbiol. 1994;32:949-954.
109. Raoult D, La Scola B, Enea M, et al. A flea-associated rickettsia pathogenic for humans. Emerg Infect Dis. 2001;7:73-81.
110. Richter J, Fournier P-E, Petridou J, et al. *Rickettsia felis* infection acquired in Europe and documented by polymerase chain reaction. Emerg Infect Dis. 2002;8:207-208.
111. Nilsson K, Lindquist O, Pahlson C. Association of *Rickettsia helvetica* with chronic perimyocarditis in sudden cardiac death. Lancet. 1999;354:1169-1173.
112. Nilsson K, Pahlson C, Lukinius A, et al. Presence of *Rickettsia helvetica* in granulomatous tissue from patients with sarcoidosis. J Infect Dis. 2002;185:1128-1130.
113. Furuya Y, Katayama T, Yoshida Y, et al. Specific amplification of *Rickettsia japonica* DNA from clinical specimens by PCR. J Clin Microbiol. 1995;33:487-489.
114. Drancourt M, George F, Brouqui P, et al. Diagnosis of Mediterranean spotted fever by indirect immunofluorescence of *Rickettsia conorii* in circulating endothelial cells isolated with monoclonal antibody-coated immunomagnetic beads. J Infect Dis. 1992;166:660-663.
115. Raoult D, Maurin M. *Rickettsia* species. In: Yu VL, Merigan TC, Barriere SL, eds. Antimicrobial Therapy and Vaccines. 2nd ed. Baltimore: Williams & Wilkins; 2002:568-574.
116. Raoult D, Gallais H, De Micco C, et al. Ciprofloxacin therapy for Mediterranean spotted fever. Antimicrob Agents Chemother. 1986;30:606-607.
117. Ruiz-Beltran R, Herrero-Herrero JI. Evaluation of ciprofloxacin and doxycycline in the treatment of Mediterranean spotted fever. Eur J Clin Microbiol Infect Dis. 1992;11:427-431.
118. Cascio A, Colomba C, Di Rosa D, et al. Efficacy and safety of clarithromycin as a treatment for Mediterranean spotted fever in children: A randomized controlled trial. Clin Infect Dis. 2001;33:409-411.

CHAPTER **185**

Rickettsia akari
(Rickettsialpox)

DIDIER RAOULT

Rickettsialpox is a worldwide mite-borne rickettsiosis with a vesicular eruption. It is caused by *Rickettsia akari*, associated with mice, and transmitted by its ectoparasite, the mite *Liponyssoides sanguineus*.

ETIOLOGY

R. akari is classified among spotted fever group rickettsiae based on antigenic and genetic data. It differs from these in that it is transmitted by the bite of a mite. *R. akari* is transmitted through infected mice (*Mus musculus*) to *L. sanguineus,* the mouse mite. The epidemiology of rickettsialpox is therefore linked to house mice. Another vector (perhaps the tick or flea) is suspected in that the seroprevalence of *R. akari* is high in New York City dogs.[1] The target cell of *R. akari* is the macrophage and not the endothelial cell as with other rickettsiae.[2]

EPIDEMIOLOGY

Rickettsialpox was initially described in New York City and has been since reported in eastern Europe, Korea, and South Africa.[3] The recent bioterrorist attack with anthrax directed the attention of physicians to skin eschars and rash and allowed the identification of 34 cases of rickettsialpox in New York City[3] from February of 2001 to August of 2002. The patients were suspected of suffering cutaneous anthrax or smallpox. The usual yearly incidence in New York City is 5 cases. A surprisingly high seroprevalence of *R. akari* was recently reported in intravenous drug users from Baltimore.[4] Because this disease is not actively sought, its overall prevalence is completely unknown.

TABLE 185-1 Clinical and Epidemiologic Findings

Series	Paddock et al[3]	Greenberg et al[7]	Kass et al[5]
Number of cases	34	144	13
Year	2003	1947	1994
Fever	97%	100%	100%
Mice at residence or work	67%	—	—
Eschars	90%	99.8%	100%
Any rash	100%	100%	100%
Vesicular rash	—	—	92%
Fever + eschars + rash	92%	—	100%
Hospitalization	32%	—	—
Headache	NA	90%	100%

CLINICAL MANIFESTATIONS

The typical triad of the disease, which includes fever, rash, and eschar,[5] was found in 92% of patients recently investigated in New York City (Table 185-1). Indeed, the disease is recognized by only a few physicians; in the New York City cases, half of patients were identified by a single physician, and 75% by three. The incubation period is approximately 7 days. Eschar is the clinical hallmark of the disease.[6] It starts as a primary papule; a vesicle then appears in the center, and, when it dries, it leaves a brown or dark eschar (Fig. 185-1). Palpable regional lymph nodes draining this eschar are common and are usually tender.[7] The rash usually appears on the third or fourth day. It is papular at the beginning and becomes vesicular in many patients. The vesicles dry, and each leaves a black crust. Patients typically have 20 to 40 skin lesions. Palm and soles are not involved. The disease is benign, and patients usually recover. A transient leukopenia can be documented, as can thrombocytopenia. A case was described of a human immunodeficiency virus (HIV)-positive patient who recovered.[8]

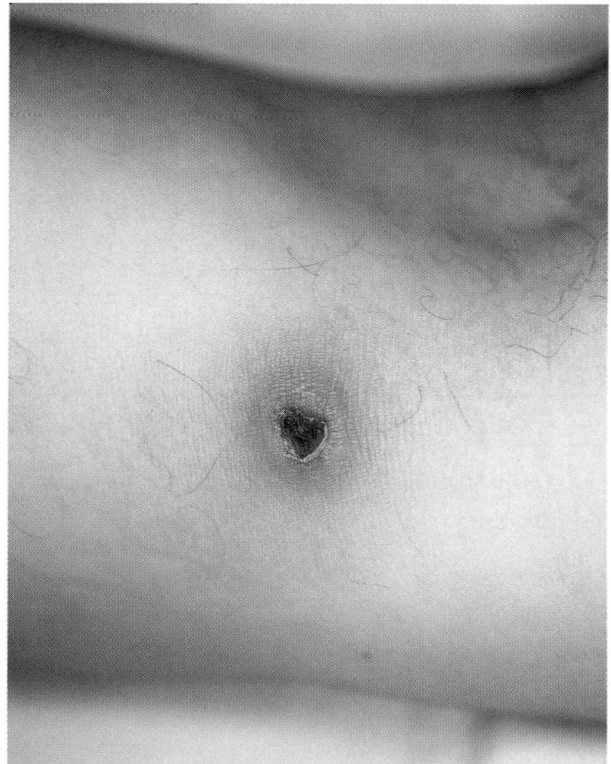

FIGURE 185-1. Picture of a patient with Rickettsialpox in 2002. *(Courtesy of C. Paddock.)*

DIAGNOSIS

Serology is the easiest tool that can be used for diagnosis. Cross-reactions have been noted between *R. akari* and *Rickettsia rickettsii*, so the use of homologous antigens that are more sensitive is preferable. Immunoglobulin (Ig)M and IgG are detected 7 to 15 days after onset. Immunohistochemistry is of value with skin biopsies and was considered the most efficient tool in the recent New York City series. A nested polymerase chain reaction (PCR) assay that used DNA sequences that coded for a 17-kDa antigen was used on fresh tissues.[3] Isolation from skin biopsy could be performed on Vero cells in specialized laboratories. Consideration of *R. akari* in the differential diagnosis is critical in that its eschar can be misdiagnosed as inoculation anthrax. Moreover, it is one of the few infections that causes vesicular rashes, along with smallpox, varicella, herpes zoster, herpes simplex, and some other rickettsioses (e.g., Queensland tick typhus and African tick-bite fever).

TREATMENT[9]

The basic treatment for Rickettsialpox is doxycycline, as is the case for other rickettsial diseases (200 mg/day for 7 days). The alternative treatment is chloramphenicol. However, *R. akari* is susceptible to many antibiotics, including azithromycin. This should be tested as an alternative treatment because it has proved to be effective in the treatment of other rickettsioses.

REFERENCES

1. Comer JA, Vargas MC, Poshni I, Childs JE. Serologic evidence of *Rickettsia akari* infection among dogs in a metropolitan city. J Am Vet Med Assoc. 2001;218:1780-1782.
2. Walker DH, Hudnall SD, Szaniawski WK, Feng H-M. Monoclonal antibody-based immunohistochemical diagnosis of rickettsialpox: The macrophage is the principal target. Mod Pathol. 1999;12:529-533.
3. Paddock CD, Zaki SR, Koss T, et al. Rickettsialpox in New York City: A persistent urban zoonosis. Ann N Y Acad Sci. 2003;990:36-44.
4. Comer JA, Tzianabos T, Flynn C, et al. Serologic evidence of rickettsialpox (*Rickettsia akari*) infection among intravenous drug users in inner-city Baltimore, Maryland. Am J Trop Med Hyg. 1999;60:894-898.
5. Kass EM, Szaniawski WK, Levy H, et al. Rickettsialpox in a New York City hospital, 1980 to 1989. N Engl J Med. 1994;15:1612-1617.
6. Brettman LR, Lewin S, Holzman RS, et al. Rickettsialpox: Report of an outbreak and a contemporary review. Medicine (Baltimore). 1981;60:363-372.
7. Greenberg M, Pellitteri O, Klein IF, Huebner RJ. Rickettsialpox—a newly recognized rickettsial disease. II. Clinical observations. JAMA. 1947;133:901-906.
8. Sanders S, Di Costanzo D, Leach J, et al. Rickettsialpox in a patient with HIV infection. J Am Acad Dermatol. 2003;48:286-289.
9. Raoult D, Maurin M. *Rickettsia akari* (Rickettsialpox). In: Yu VL, Weber R, Raoult D, eds. Antimicrobial Therapy and Vaccine. 2nd ed. New York: Apple Trees Production, LLC; 2002:889-892.

CHAPTER **186**

Coxiella burnetii (Q Fever)

THOMAS J. MARRIE
DIDIER RAOULT

Q fever is an acute (on occasion chronic) febrile illness that occurs worldwide. The most common animal reservoirs for this zoonosis are cattle, sheep, and goats. These domestic ungulates, when infected, shed the desiccation-resistant organisms in urine, feces, milk, and especially in birth products. The placenta of infected sheep contains up to 10^9 organisms per gram of tissue. Humans are infected by inhalation of contaminated aerosols and after an incubation period of 20 days (range, 14 to 39 days) become ill with severe headache, fever, chills, fatigue, and myalgia. Other signs and symptoms depend upon the organs that are involved. In contrast to other rickettsial infections, rash rarely occurs in acute Q fever. The rash in chronic Q fever (endocarditis) is that of palpable purpura related to an immune complex vasculitis. Other differences between Q fever and the usual rickettsial infections are the aerosol route of infection and the lack of cross-reacting antibodies to *Proteus* X strain (the Weil-Felix reaction).

THE PATHOGEN

Coxiella burnetii, the etiologic agent of Q fever, is a highly pleomorphic coccobacillus with a gram-negative cell wall (Fig. 186-1). It measures 0.3 to 0.7 μm long,[1] but unlike true rickettsiae, it enters the cell by a passive mechanism. Within host cells, it survives within the phagolysosome—the low pH of this environment is necessary for the metabolic functioning of *C. burnetii*. Large and small variants exist, and a spore stage has been described.[2] This spore stage explains the ability of *C. burnetii* to withstand harsh environmental conditions.[3] It survives for 7 to 10 months on wool at 15° C to 20° C, for more than 1 month on fresh meat in cold storage, and for more than 40 months in skim milk at room temperature.[4] Although it is destroyed by 2% formaldehyde, the organism has been isolated from infected tissues stored in formaldehyde for up to 4 to 5 months. It has also been isolated from fixed "paraffinized" tissues. Either 1% Lysol or 5% hydrogen peroxide kills *C. burnetii*.

C. burnetii undergoes phase variation.[4] In nature and in laboratory animals it exists in the phase I state, in which organisms react with late (45 days) convalescent guinea pig sera and only slightly with early (21 days) sera.[4] Repeated passage of phase I virulent organisms in embryonated chicken eggs leads to gradual conversion to phase II avirulent forms by chromosomal deletions.[5] There is no morphologic difference between the two phases, although they differ in the sugar composition of their lipopolysaccharides,[6] in their buoyant density in cesium chloride, and in their affinity for hematoxylin and basic fuchsin dyes. *C. burnetii* lipopolysaccharide is nontoxic to chicken embryos at doses higher than 80 μg per embryo, in contrast to *Salmonella typhimurium* smooth- and rough-type lipopolysaccharide, which is toxic in nanogram amounts.[7]

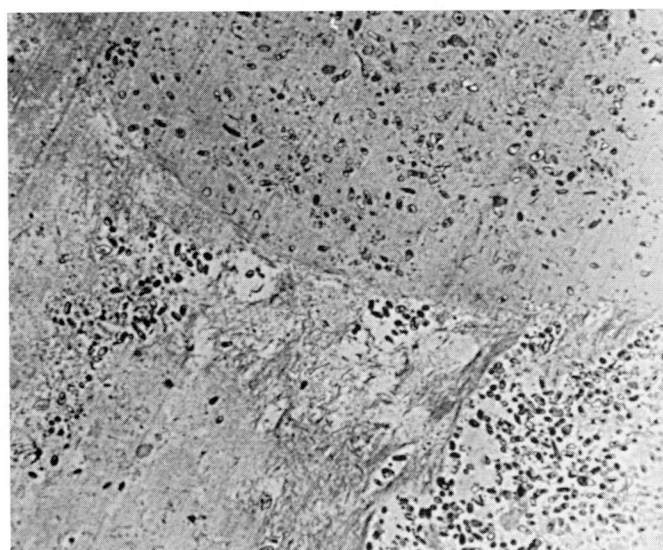

FIGURE 186-1 Transmission electron micrograph of a vegetation from a patient with Q fever endocarditis. Many *Coxiella burnetii* cells are evident. The electron-dense material within each cell is DNA. (Original magnification, ×46,665.)

Plasmids have been found in both phase I and phase II cells.[8] Some strains are plasmidless. No specific role in pathogenesis has been associated with the presence of a plasmid.[9]

The genome of *C. burnetii* consists of 1,995,275 base pairs.[10] The genome contains many genes with potential roles in adhesion, invasion, intracellular trafficking, and host cell modulation.[10] A difference from other intracellular bacteria is the observation that the genome of *C. burnetii* contains 32 insertion sequences dispersed in the chromosome.[10]

EPIDEMIOLOGY

Humans become infected by inhalation of small-particle aerosols containing *C. burnetii*. The resulting illness has been termed Q fever. In August 1935, Derrick, a medical officer of health in Queensland, Australia, investigated a febrile illness that affected 20 of 800 employees of a Brisbane meat works.[11] He coined the term *Q* (or query) *fever* for this illness, which he had no diagnosis for but suspected was a new disease. Burnet and Freeman showed that the microorganism isolated from the blood and urine of Derrick's patients was a rickettsia.[12] At about the same time Davis and Cox isolated a microorganism from ticks (*Dermacentor andersoni*) collected near Nine Mile Creek, Montana.[13] Later Dyer[14,15] showed that *Rickettsia burnetii* (Burnet and Freeman's organism) was the same as *Rickettsia diaporica* (Cox's organism)—it is now known as *Coxiella burnetii*.

C. burnetii has been identified in arthropods, fish, birds, rodents, marsupials, and livestock.[1] Worldwide, the most common animal reservoirs are cattle, sheep, and goats.[16] A variety of other animals may be infected by *C. burnetii* including horses, dogs, swine, camels, water buffalo, pigeons, ducks, geese, turkeys, several species of wild birds, squirrels, deer mice, harvest mice, cats, and rabbits. The epidemiology of *C. burnetii* varies from country to country. For example, collared doves have been suspected of carrying *C. burnetii* from western Europe to Ireland. In Nova Scotia, exposure to infected parturient cats has resulted in several outbreaks of Q fever.[17,18]

Q fever has been reported from at least 51 countries on five continents.[5] It is usually an occupational disease affecting those with direct contact with infected animals, such as farmers, veterinarians, and abattoir workers.[5] However, indirect contact with infected animals has resulted in outbreaks of Q fever, as in Switzerland, where more than 350 persons who lived along a road over which sheep traveled from mountain pastures developed Q fever.[19] Exposure to contaminated straw, manure, or dust from farm vehicles resulted in Q fever in British residents who lived along a road traveled by these vehicles.[20] Exposure may be even more indirect, as in the case of laundry workers who developed Q fever after handling contaminated laundry.[21] Ingestion of contaminated raw milk,[22] exposure to infected parturient cats,[17] and the skinning of infected wild rabbits are also ways in which Q fever may be acquired. *C. burnetii* has also been isolated from human milk[23] and human placentas.[24] *C. burnetii* is known to undergo reactivation during pregnancy in animals other than humans. It is likely that this happens in humans as well, and Q fever complicating human pregnancy is probably underdiagnosed.[25] Laboratory exposure to *C. burnetii*[26] and transport of infected sheep through hospitals to research laboratories have resulted in large outbreaks of Q fever.[27,28]

Rarely, Q fever has been transmitted by blood transfusion.[29] Transmission has occurred during an autopsy[30] but has not been documented during clinical care of infected patients. There is one report of apparent human-to-human transmission of Q fever among members of a household.[31]

PATHOGENESIS

The most likely sequence of events in the cycle of transmission of *C. burnetii* to humans is that the organism is maintained in ticks or other arthropods. These ectoparasites infect domestic and other animals including a variety of small mammals by bite or through contamination of the skin by infected feces. Infected domestic ungulates are usually asymptomatic, although abortion or stillbirth may result. The heavily infected placenta contaminates the environment at the time of parturition. Air samples are positive for up to 2 weeks after parturition, and viable organisms are present in the soil for periods of up to 150 days.[32-34] Humans are infected by the inhalation of contaminated aerosols. The microorganisms proliferate in the lung or lungs, and blood-stream invasion follows. This invasion results in the onset of systemic symptoms and a variety of clinical manifestations depending on the dose of the microorganism inhaled and probably the characteristics of the infecting strain.[35] In the healthy host, multiplication of *C. burnetii* is controlled by macrophages, and granulomas are formed. In some people the macrophages cannot kill *C. burnetii*, seemingly because of the secretion of interleukin-10 (IL-10).[36] Patients with chronic Q fever have increased levels of IL-10 secreted by stimulated blood monocytes. Patients with cancer, valve lesions, arterial aneurysms, or pregnancy are at risk for chronic Q fever if infected with *C. burnetii*.[9]

CLINICAL MANIFESTATIONS

Humans are the only animals known to develop illness regularly as a result of *C. burnetii* infection.[37] In one large series of 207 patients, the mortality rate was 2.4%.[38] There are several clinical syndromes.

1. A self-limited febrile illness (2 to 14 days)
2. Pneumonia
3. Endocarditis
4. Hepatitis
5. Osteomyelitis
6. Q fever in the immunocompromised host
7. Q fever in infancy
8. Neurologic manifestations—encephalitis, aseptic meningitis, toxic confusional states, dementia, extrapyramidal disease

Self-Limited Febrile Illness

Self-limited febrile illness is probably the most common form of Q fever. In many areas 11% to 12% of individuals have antibodies to *C. burnetii*—most do not recall pneumonia or other severe illness.[39] It is likely that the age at which infection occurs and the dose of the agent determine whether or not Q fever is a mild self-limited febrile illness.[40,41] There is also a suggestion that some infections may be totally asymptomatic.[42] The proportion of all Q fever infections that represent "asymptomatic" seroconversion is unknown. In the south of Spain, 21% (108 of 505) of adults who had fever of more than 1 week's and less than 3 weeks' duration had Q fever.[43] There was no radiographic evidence of pneumonia among these individuals.

Pneumonia

There are three presentations of this form of Q fever: atypical pneumonia, rapidly progressive pneumonia, and pneumonia as an incidental finding in a patient with a febrile illness. The last presentation is probably the most common form of Q fever pneumonia.

Atypical pneumonia is a clinical term used to describe pneumonia characterized by a dry nonproductive cough with blood and sputum cultures negative for conventional bacterial pathogens.[44] Cough is a symptom in only 28% of patients with radiographically confirmed Q fever pneumonia. This illness may be of gradual or sudden onset.[45] Fever occurs in all patients. A severe headache is present in about 75% of patients and is a useful clue to the diagnosis. Other symptoms and the frequency with which they occur are fatigue, 98%; chills, 88%; sweats, 84%; myalgia, 68%; nausea, 49%; vomiting, 25%; pleuritic chest pain, 28%; and diarrhea, 21%. On occasion, diarrhea may be a presentation of Q fever.[46]

Physical examination of the chest is often unremarkable. The most common physical finding is inspiratory crackles.[45] Patients with rapidly progressive pneumonia usually have the physical signs of pulmonary consolidation. About 5% of patients have splenomegaly. Fever and severe headache suggest central nervous system infection, and lumbar puncture is often performed. The spinal fluid is usually normal; however, *C. burnetii* has been isolated from the spinal fluid under such circumstances.[47] The rapidly progressive form of Q fever pneumonia mimics legionnaires' disease and the pneumonic form of tularemia, and indeed, all the causes of rapidly progressive pneumonia enter the differential diagnosis.

The radiographic picture of Q fever pneumonia is variable (Fig. 186-2). Nonsegmental and segmental pleural-based opacities are common.[48-50] Multiple rounded opacities are very suggestive of Q fever that follows exposure to infected cat placentas (see Fig. 186-2).[48] Pleural effusion is found in 35% of cases and is usually small but on occasion may be large.[49] Atelectasis, an increase in reticular markings, and hilar adenopathy may occur. In one series, the resolution time ranged from 10 to 70 days, with a mean of 30 days.[49]

C. burnetii pneumonia is rarely fatal, and in such instances there is usually a coexisting condition that contributes to the mortality.[50] Information regarding the histology of this form of pneumonia in humans is limited. Pierce and co-workers found small coccobacilli within alveolar macrophages on transbronchial biopsy in a patient with Q fever.[51] A fatal case of pneumonia in a 43-year-old man was characterized by severe intra-alveolar hemorrhagic and focal necrotizing pneumonia with associated necrotizing bronchitis. Histiocytes, lymphocytes, and plasma cells were in the alveoli. This was thought to be Q fever pneumonia on the basis of organisms seen with a modified

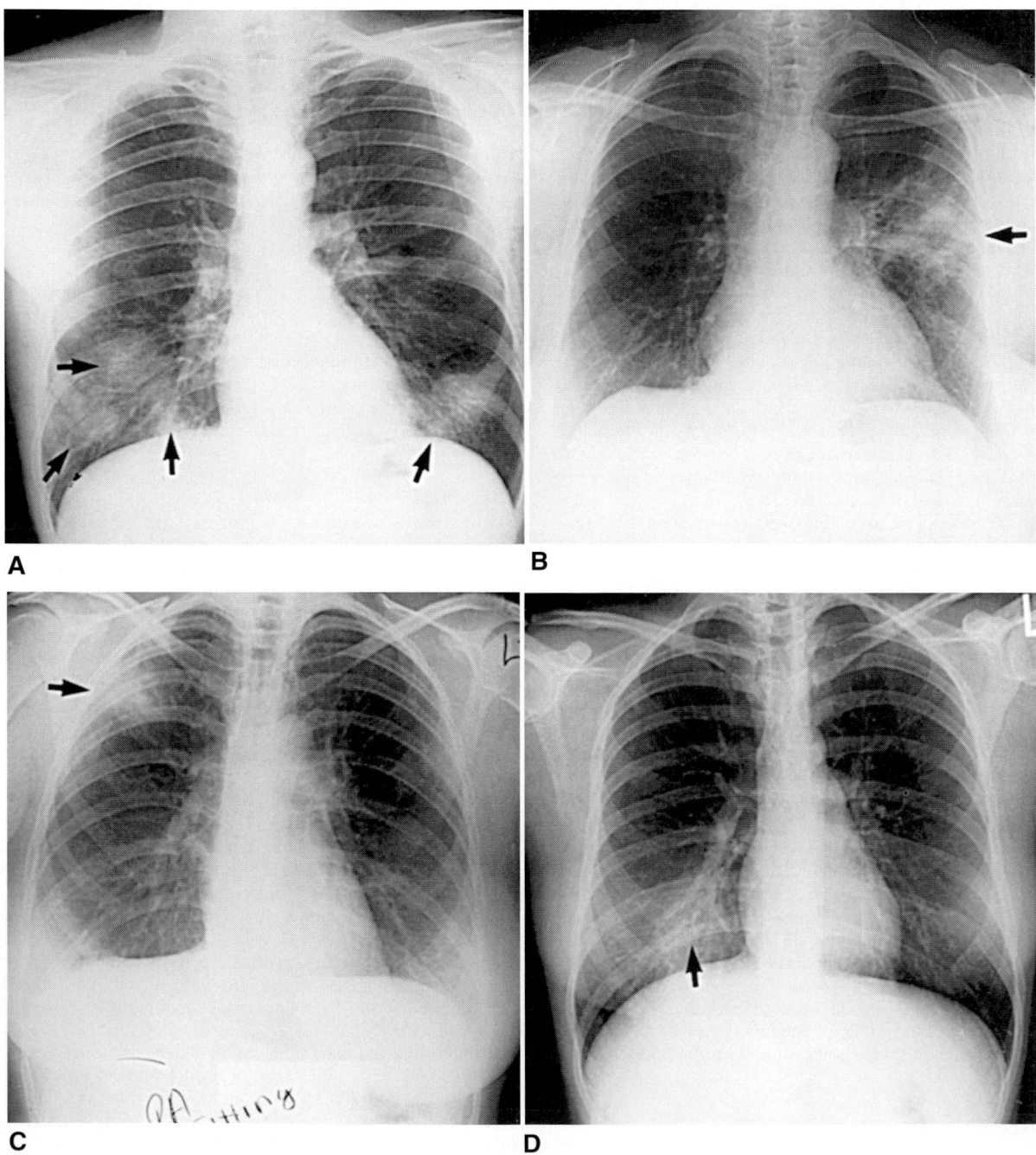

FIGURE 186-2. Radiographic manifestations of Q fever pneumonia. All four patients are members of one family who developed Q fever after exposure to the infected products of feline conception. Their cat gave birth to kittens in their house. **A,** Multiple rounded opacities. **B,** Left upper lobe opacity. **C,** Pleural-based opacity involving the right upper lobe. **D,** Right lower lobe opacity. In an endemic area A is characteristic of cat-related Q fever pneumonia, and C is suggestive of this diagnosis. However, **B** and **D** are not at all distinctive and could be due to any pulmonary pathogen.

Giemsa stain.[52] A resolving, *C. burnetii* pneumonia lesion was characterized by an inflammatory pseudotumor—a lung mass composed of mixtures of macrophages, giant cells, plasma cells, and lymphocytes. The bronchiolar epithelium was focally absent, regenerated, or hyperplastic.[53] The changes that result from the inoculation of the lungs of rhesus monkeys resemble those reported from humans. The resulting consolidation was peribronchial or peribronchiolar.[54] The interstitial infiltrate had more lymphocytes than monocytes (Fig. 186-3).

The white blood cell count is usually normal, but one third of patients have an increased count. A slight elevation (two to three times normal) of the hepatic transaminase levels occurs in almost all patients. The serum bilirubin level is usually normal; however, jaundice may occur. Rarely, the syndrome of inappropriate secretion of antidiuretic hormone occurs.[55]

The treatment of choice for *C. burnetii* pneumonia is tetracycline.[56] Chloramphenicol has been used to treat Q fever.[51] Yeaman and associates performed antibiotic susceptibility testing of *C. burnetii* by using persistently infected L929 fibroblast cells.[57] The most effective agents were quinolones (difloxacin, ciprofloxacin, oxolinic acid) and rifampin. Chloramphenicol, doxycycline, and trimethoprim were somewhat effective, whereas tetracycline, gentamicin, streptomycin, erythromycin, sulfamethoxazole, penicillin G, and polymyxin B were ineffective. A macrolide or doxycycline is usually the drug of choice for the treatment of atypical pneumonia. Although others have reported an apparent response of *C. burnetii* pneumonia to macrolides,[58-61] we have observed that all of our cases of rapidly progressive pneumonia caused by *C. burnetii* have failed to respond to erythromycin therapy despite dosages of up to 4 g/day. The addition of rifampin, 300 mg twice daily orally, resulted in cure. When tested in vitro, no antibiotic compound is bactericidal against *C. burnetii*.[62] When several strains were tested, some variation in antibiotic susceptibilities was observed.[63] Doxycycline is usually effective but some strains may be resistant; co-trimoxazole (trimethoprim-sulfamethoxazole), chloramphenicol, and rifampin are consistently efficient. New macrolide compounds such as the ketolide telithromycin are effective.[64] Erythromycin and quinolones have inconsistent in vitro activities.

The diagnosis of Q fever (*C. burnetii*) pneumonia is confirmed serologically because most laboratories do not have the facilities required to isolate *C. burnetii*.[65] The development of primers derived from the *C. burnetii* superoxide dismutase gene has allowed the amplification of *C. burnetii* DNA in clinical specimens using polymerase chain reaction.[66] The microagglutination,[67] complement fixation,[68] and microimmunofluorescence tests[69] as well as the enzyme-linked immunosorbent assay[70] have all been used in the serologic diagnosis of this illness. The complement fixation test is most commonly used.

A fourfold rise in titer between acute and convalescent samples is diagnostic of Q fever. Cross-reactions have been reported between antibodies to *Bartonella* and *Legionella micdadei* and antibodies to *C. burnetii*.[71] Some authors have advocated using the indirect immunofluorescence test to detect antibodies to immunoglobulin M (IgM) so that a single serum specimen may be used in the diagnosis of acute Q fever.[72] A titer of 1:50 or higher has a high positive predictive value.[73] However, IgM antibodies may persist for up to 678 days,[74] and in one study[75] 3% of 162 patients still had a significant IgM antibody level 1 year after the infection.

C. burnetii is highly infectious, and tissues from patients with Q fever should be processed under biosafety level 3 conditions.

Chronic Q Fever

It is now recognized that chronic Q fever has a variety of manifestations—endocarditis, infection of a vascular prosthesis, infection of aneurysms, osteomyelitis, hepatitis, interstitial pulmonary fibrosis, prolonged fever, and purpuric eruptions.[76]

Endocarditis

Endocarditis is the prime manifestation of "chronic" Q fever.[77-96] Usually, abnormal or prosthetic cardiac valves are affected[95]; however, any part of the vascular tree may become infected,[94] including clot in a left ventricular aneurysm. Such patients have a defective cell-mediated immune response to *C. burnetii*.

The incidence of Q fever endocarditis is increasing, but this may reflect increased recognition of this entity. Turck and colleagues reported 16 cases of chronic Q fever diagnosed between 1968 and 1973; their review of the world's literature yielded 55 cases.[77] Siegman-Igra and associates reported on 408 cases of Q fever from 17 countries in their 1997 review.[96] From 1975 to 1980, 79 cases of Q fever endocarditis were reported to the Public Health Laboratory Service Communicable Disease Surveillance Center in England.[90] Indeed, from 1975 to 1981, *C. burnetii* accounted for 3% of all cases of endocarditis reported in England and Wales.[89] In France, 229 cases of Q fever endocarditis were diagnosed.[38] The clinical presentation is that of culture-negative endocarditis; however, fever is frequently absent. Q fever endocarditis is rare in children.[93]

Marked clubbing of the fingers and hypergammaglobulinemia are frequently present. Splenomegaly and hepatomegaly are found in slightly more than half the patients. A purpuric rash related to leukocytoclastic vasculitis occurs in about 20%. The erythrocyte sedimentation rate is usually increased; anemia and microscopic hematuria are also found. Arterial emboli complicate the course of one third of the patients.

The vegetations in chronic Q fever differ in both gross and microscopic appearance from those seen in pyogenic bacterial endocarditis. Figures 186-4 and 186-5 show the gross appearance of the vegetations

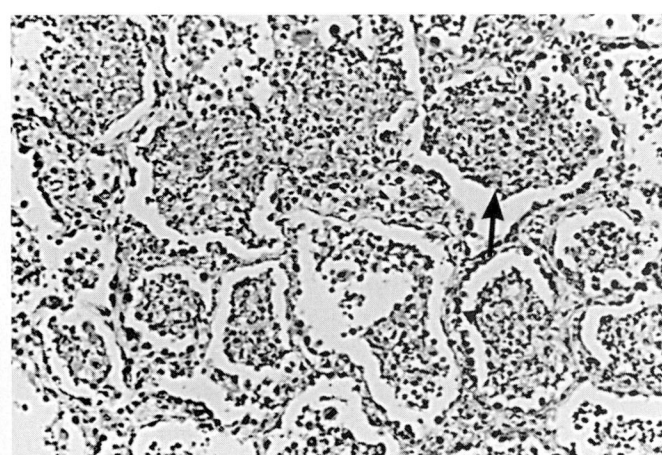

FIGURE 186-3. Photomicrograph of an open lung biopsy specimen from a patient with Q fever pneumonia. The alveolar spaces are filled with an inflammatory exudate consisting of lymphocytes and macrophages (*arrow*). Note the hyperplasia of the alveolar lining cells (*arrowhead*). (Magnification, ×500.)

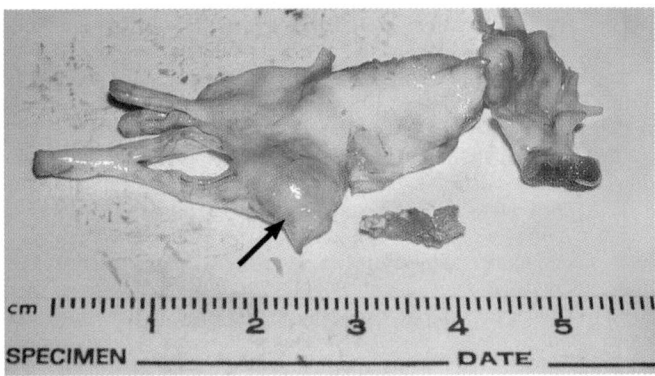

FIGURE 186-4. Mitral valve of a patient with Q fever endocarditis. The nodule (*arrow*) was full of *C. burnetii* organisms within foamy macrophages. (*From Raoult D, Raza A, Marrie TJ. Q fever endocarditis and other forms of chronic Q fever. In: Marrie TJ, ed. Q Fever—The Disease. Boca Raton, Fla: CRC Press; 1990:179-199, with permission.*)

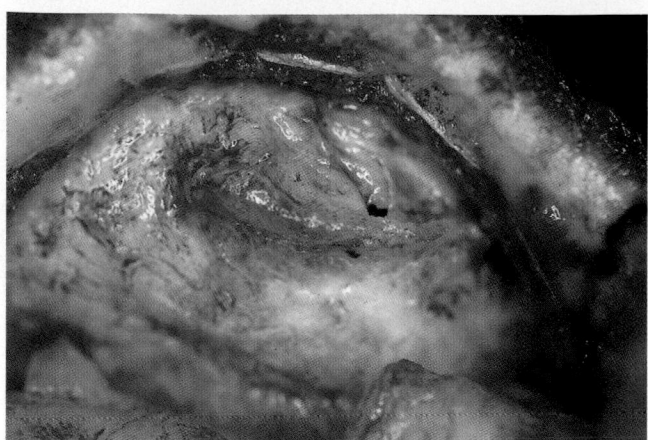

FIGURE 186-5. Q fever endocarditis on bioprosthetic valve leaflet. The ridge in the center of the photograph is the area infiltrated with *C. burnetii. (From Raoult D, Raza A, Marrie TJ. Q fever endocarditis and other forms of chronic Q fever. In: Marrie TJ, ed. Q Fever—The Disease. Boca Raton, Fla: CRC Press; 1990:179-199, with permission.)*

in Q fever endocarditis. Microscopically, there is a subacute and chronic inflammatory infiltrate. Many large foamy macrophages are present. Characteristic microorganisms are readily seen with electron microscopy (see Fig. 186-1).

The confirmation of the diagnosis in most instances is serologic. A complement fixation titer of 1:200 or greater to phase I antigen is said to be diagnostic of chronic Q fever, although not all patients in the series of Turck and co-workers had this titer.[77] In acute Q fever, complement fixation antibody titers to phase I antigen do not reach this level.

Studies reported high titers of IgA antibodies to phase I antigen in chronic Q fever (endocarditis and granulomatous hepatitis),[73,97] whereas another study found that patients with acute Q fever also produced IgA antibodies to phase I antigen, albeit in low titer.[74] Fournier and colleagues used a phase I IgG antibody titer of 1:800 or greater by microimmunofluorescence as diagnostic of Q fever endocarditis.[98] Indeed, they and others have proposed that this be added as a major criterion to the Duke Endocarditis Service criteria for the diagnosis of infective endocarditis.[99,100]

Antibody titers fall slowly with treatment. Western immunoblotting of serum samples from patients with chronic Q fever shows that there are IgG antibodies to 12 to 15 antigens of phase I *C. burnetii,* whereas serum from patients with acute Q fever reacts with 7 to 10 *C. burnetii* antigens.[101] Antibodies to antigens of molecular masses 50, 80, and 160 kD were present only in serum from patients with chronic Q fever.

There is no agreement on the type and duration of antimicrobial therapy for Q fever endocarditis.[74,75] Some authorities recommend that treatment be continued indefinitely.[74] A consensus is emerging that combination antibiotic therapy is necessary to treat chronic Q fever.[102] We have used doxycycline in combination with ciprofloxacin or rifampin for 2 years to treat this infection. Others have used doxycycline with either pefloxacin or ofloxacin with success.[102] Maurin and co-workers found that the bactericidal effect of doxycycline was enhanced when alkalinization of the phagolysosome was accomplished with chloroquine or amantadine.[62] Raoult and Marrie used doxycycline and hydroxychloroquine to treat patients with Q fever endocarditis with success.[103] Hydroxychloroquine is given in a dose of 200 mg/day, and the dose is adjusted to maintain a serum concentration between 0.8 and 1.2 μg/mL. Antibody titers should be determined every 6 months during therapy and every 3 months for the first 2 years after the cessation of therapy. Successful therapy is accompanied by a falling erythrocyte sedimentation rate, correction of anemia, and resolution of hyperglobulinemia. Valve replacement is frequently necessary but should be dictated by the patient's hemodynamic status.

Patients are considered cured when the IgG phase I antibody titer is less than 1:800 and IgM and IgA antibody titers are less than 1:50 by microimmunofluorescence. The release of IL-10 and transforming growth factor-β from unstimulated peripheral blood mononuclear cells is markedly increased in Q fever endocarditis.[104] IL-10 and transforming growth factor-β impair the function of macrophages and monocytes. IL-10 counteracts the shift to a protective helper T-cell 1 pattern and also favors the survival of intracellular bacteria.

Hepatitis

Hepatitis is the most common manifestation of *C. burnetii* infection in France.[38,105,106] In the United States, 61.9% of all cases of Q fever are manifested as hepatitis. Also, hepatitis is more frequent in sheep- and goat-breeding areas. In Nova Scotia, there have been no cases diagnosed as Q fever hepatitis.

There are three presentations of Q fever hepatitis[62,107-112]:

1. An infectious hepatitis–like picture
2. Fever of unknown origin with characteristic granulomas on liver biopsy
3. As an incidental finding in a patient with acute Q fever pneumonia

In patients with fever of unknown origin related to Q fever, the typical "doughnut granuloma" is seen on liver biopsy.[108,109] This is a granuloma with a dense fibrin ring surrounded by a central lipid vacuole. These granulomas are highly suggestive of Q fever but may be seen in Hodgkin's disease and infectious mononucleosis. *C. burnetii* has been isolated from the liver of patients with Q fever hepatitis, but the organism has not been visualized within the hepatic parenchyma.[77] Antibiotic treatment for 2 weeks is probably sufficient. The rare cases of Q fever hepatitis with a serologic profile suggestive of chronic Q fever should be treated for longer than 2 weeks. There are no data on which to base a recommendation for the exact duration of therapy. These patients should be observed with serial antibody titers.

Neurologic Manifestations

Severe headache is the most common manifestation[113-116] and probably represents central nervous system infection, although there is little evidence of serious brain involvement in Q fever.[113] Aseptic meningitis or encephalitis or both complicate 0.2% to 1.3% of cases of Q fever.[114] A review of 16 cases of Q fever meningoencephalitis revealed that eight patients had an elevated cerebrospinal fluid white blood cell level, ranging from 18 to 1392 cells/mm³.[117] In all but one case, mononuclear cells predominated. The protein level was usually increased, and the glucose level was normal.[117] The electroencephalogram was abnormal in five of the six patients in whom this investigation was carried out.

In a study from Plymouth, Reilly and co-workers reported an astoundingly high 22% incidence of neurologic complications among 103 patients, of whom 46 had acute Q fever, 5 had chronic Q fever, and 52 had past infections.[118] Six of the 45 patients with acute Q fever had residual neurologic impairment—weakness, recurrent meningismus, blurred vision, residual paresthesias, and sensory loss involving the left leg.

The meningoencephalitis of Q fever may be accompanied by seizures and coma.[119]

Behavioral disturbance, cerebellar symptoms and signs, cranial nerve palsies, extrapyramidal disease, and the Miller-Fisher variant of the Guillain-Barré syndrome (areflexia and ophthalmoparesis) have been reported to complicate acute Q fever. Demyelinating polyradiculoneuritis developed in a 71-year-old man 10 weeks after the onset of *C. burnetii* pneumonia.[120]

Q Fever in the Immunocompromised Host

Q fever has been reported infrequently as an infection in the immunocompromised host[121-125]; however, this may be a reflection of infrequent consideration of Q fever in this group of patients. Indeed, when Raoult and co-workers examined serum samples from 500 individuals positive for human immunodeficiency virus, they found that 10.4% of the 500 had IgG antibodies to *C. burnetii* in a titer of 1:25 or greater, compared with 4.1% of 925 apparently healthy blood donors ($p < .001$).[125] They also found that over the 3 years from 1987 to 1989, 5 of 68 (7.3%) patients hospitalized with Q fever were positive for human immunodeficiency virus. They estimated that in individuals positive for human immunodeficiency virus, the number of cases of Q fever was 13 times higher and these patients were symptomatic more frequently than the general population.

In a review of all cases of chronic Q fever in France from 1982 to 1990, the investigators noted that 20% of 84 patients were immuno-compromised.[76] These were patients with cancer, chronic myeloid leukemia, acquired immunodeficiency syndrome, renal transplanta-tion, corticosteroid therapy, renal dialysis, postpartum state, and chronic alcoholism.

C. burnetii infection resulted in a fatal interstitial pneumonia in an 11-year-old boy with chronic granulomatous disease.[126]

Other Manifestations of Q Fever

Vertebral osteomyelitis is an uncommon manifestation of *C. burnetii* infection.[127] Q fever may also occur in infancy, when it has caused pneumonia, febrile seizures, pyrexia of unknown origin, malaise, and meningeal irritation.[128] Hematologic manifestations include bone mar-row necrosis,[129] histiocytic hemophagocytosis,[130] and hemolytic ane-mia,[131] and on occasion this disease may simulate lymphoma.[132] Other hematologic manifestations include transient hypoplastic anemia,[133] reactive thrombocytosis, rarely thrombocytopenia, and splenic rup-ture.[134] Optic neuritis[135] and erythema nodosum[136] have also rarely been reported in association with *C. burnetii* infection. In the past, it was thought Kawasaki disease might be a variant of Q fever.[137,138] Support for this concept has not materialized. Q fever during preg-nancy may result in abortion when the infection occurs during the first trimester.[139] Administration of co-trimoxazole for the duration of the pregnancy prevents abortion and neonatal infection. However, it does not prevent evolution to chronic infection.

PREVENTION

Vaccination of those at risk for infection (e.g., abattoir workers, veterinarians) should be carried out as soon as a safe vaccine is available.[140,141] An investigational inactivated vaccine, made from infected egg yolk sacs, has been used to protect laboratory work-ers handling live *C. burnetii*. Vaccine may be requested under Investigational New Drugs from the Commanding Officer, U.S. Army Medical Research Institute for Infectious Diseases, Fort Detrick, Frederick, MD 21701-5011.

Using only seronegative sheep in research facilities prevents out-breaks in these institutions. Because of the lack of person-to-person spread, there is no need to isolate patients hospitalized with Q fever.[142] Simple measures, such as the consumption of only pasteurized milk, serve to eliminate cases of Q fever that are transmitted in this manner. In Cyprus, the incidence of *C. burnetii* infection among sheep and goats was reduced by a program in which aborted material was de-stroyed, affected dams isolated, and the premises disinfected.[143] Control of ectoparasites on cattle, sheep, and goats is also important in the control of Q fever.[143]

REFERENCES

1. Baca OG, Paretsky D. Q fever and *Coxiella burnetii:* A model for host-parasite inter-action. Microbiol Rev. 1983;47:127-149.
2. McCaul TF, Williams JC. Development cycle of *Coxiella burnetii:* Structure and mor-phogenesis of vegetative and sporogenic differentiations. J Bacteriol. 1981;147:1063-1076.
3. Sawyer LA, Fishbein DB, McDade JE. Q fever: Current concepts. Rev Infect Dis. 1987;9:935-946.
4. Q fever. In: Christie AB. Infectious Diseases, Epidemiology and Clinical Practice. Edinburgh: Churchill Livingstone; 1974:876-891.
5. Hoover TA, Culp DW, Vodkin MH, et al. Chromosomal DNA deletions explain phe-notypic characteristics of two antigenic variants, phase II and RSA 514 (crazy), of the *Coxiella burnetii* nine mile strain. Infect Immun. 2002;70:6726-6733.
6. Schramek S, Mayer H. Different sugar compositions of lipopolysaccharides isolated from phase I and pure phase II cells of *Coxiella burnetii*. Infect Immun. 1982;38:53-57.
7. Hackstadt T, Peacock MG, Hitchcock PJ, Cole RL. Lipopolysaccharide variation in *Coxiella burnetii:* Intrastrain heterogeneity in structure and antigenicity. Infect Immun. 1985;48:359-365.
8. Samuel JE, Frazier ME, Mallavia LP. Correlation of plasmid type and disease caused by *Coxiella burnetii*. Infect Immun. 1985;49:775-777.
9. Maurin M, Raoult D. Q fever. Clin Microbiol Rev. 1999;12:518-553.
10. Seshadri R, Paulsen IT, Eisen JA, et al. Complete genome sequence of the Q-fever pathogen *Coxiella burnetii*. Proc Natl Acad Sci U S A. 2003;100:5455-5460.
11. Derrick EH. "Q" fever, new fever entity: Clinical features, diagnosis and laboratory investigation. Med J Aust. 1937;2:281-299.
12. Burnet FM, Freeman M. Experimental studies on the virus of "Q" fever. Med J Aust. 1937;2:299-305.
13. Davis G, Cox HR. A filter-passing infectious agent isolated from ticks: Isolation from *Dermacentor andersoni*, reactions in animals, and filtration experiments. Public Health Rep. 1939;53:2259-2267.
14. Dyer RE. A filter-passing infectious agent isolated from ticks. IV. Human infection. Public Health Rep. 1939;53:2277-2283.
15. Dyer RE. Similarity of Australian Q fever and a disease caused by an infectious agent isolated from ticks in Montana. Public Health Rep. 1939;54:1229-1237.
16. Babudieri B. Q fever: A zoonosis. Adv Vet Sci. 1959;5:81-181.
17. Langley JM, Marrie TJ, Covert A, et al. Poker players' pneumonia. An urban outbreak following exposure to a parturient cat. N Engl J Med. 1988;319:354-356.
18. Marrie TJ, Durant H, Williams JC, et al. Exposure to parturient cats is a risk factor for acquisition of Q fever in Maritime Canada. J Infect Dis. 1988;158:101-108.
19. Q fever outbreak—Switzerland. MMWR Morb Mortal Wkly Rep. 1984;33:355-361.
20. Salmon MM, Howells B, Glencross EJF, et al. Q fever in an urban area. Lancet. 1982;1:1002-1004.
21. Oliphant JW, Gordon DA, Meis A, et al. Q fever in laundry workers presumably trans-mitted from contaminated clothing. Am J Hyg. 1949;49:76-82.
22. Bell JA, Beck MD, Huebner RJ. Epidemiologic studies of Q fever in southern California. JAMA. 1950;142:868-872.
23. Kumar A, Yadav MP, Kakkar S. Human milk as a source of Q fever infection in breast-fed babies. Indian J Med Res. 1981;73:510-512.
24. Syrucek L, Sobeslavsky O, Gutvirth I. Isolation of *Coxiella burnetii* from human pla-centas. J Hyg Epidemiol Microbiol Immunol. 1958;2:29-35.
25. Raoult D, Fenollar F, Stein, A. Q fever during pregnancy: Diagnosis, treatment and follow-up. Arch Intern Med. 2002;162:701-704.
26. Johnson JE II, Kadull PJ. Laboratory acquired Q fever. A report of fifty cases. Am J Med. 1966;41:391-403.
27. Hall CJ, Richmond SJ, Caul EO, et al. Laboratory outbreak of Q fever acquired from sheep. Lancet. 1982;1:1004-1006.
28. Meiklejohn G, Reimer LG, Graves PS, Helmick C. Cryptic epidemic of Q fever in a medical school. J Infect Dis. 1981;144:107-114.
29. Editorial comment on Q fever transmitted by blood transfusion—United States. Can Dis Wkly Rep. 1977;3:210.
30. Harman JB. Q fever in Great Britain: Clinical account of eight cases. Lancet. 1949;2:1028-1030.
31. Mann JS, Douglas JG, Inglis JN, Leitch AG. Q fever: Person to person transmission within a family. Thorax. 1986;41:974-975.
32. Welsh HH, Lennette EH, Abinanti FR, Win JF. Air-borne transmission of Q fever: The role of parturition in the generation of infective aerosols. Ann NY Acad Sci. 1958;70:528-540.
33. Lennette EH, Welsh HH. Q fever in California. X. Recovery of *Coxiella burnetii* from the air of premises harbouring infected goats. Am J Hyg. 1951;54:44-49.
34. Welsh HH, Lennette EH, Abinanti FR, et al. Q fever studies XXI. The recovery of *Coxiella burnetii* from the soil and surface water of premises harbouring infected sheep. Am J Hyg. 1959;70:14-20.
35. Baca OG. Pathogenesis of rickettsial infections. Emphasis on Q fever. Eur J Epidemiol. 1991;7:222-228.
36. Honstettre A, Imbert G, Ghigo E, et al. Dysregulation of cytokines in acute Q fever: Role of interleukin-10 and tumor necrosis factor in chronic evolution of Q fever. J Infect Dis. 2003;187:956-962.
37. Stoker MGP, Marmion BP. The spread of Q fever from animals to man. The natural history of a rickettsial disease. Bull World Health Organ. 1955;13:781-806.
38. Raoult D. Rickettsial diseases. Medicine (Baltimore). 1996;24:71-75.
39. Clark WH, Romker MS, Holmes MA, et al. Q fever in California. VIII. An epidemic of Q fever in a small rural community in northern California. Am J Hyg. 1951;54:25-34.
40. Gonder JC, Kishimoto RA, Kastello MR, et al. Cynomolgus monkey model for ex-perimental Q fever infection. J Infect Dis. 1979;139:191-196.
41. Tigertt WD, Benenson AS, Goscheneur WS. Airborne Q fever. Bacteriol Rev. 1961;25:285-293.
42. Luoto L, Casey ML, Pickens EG. Q fever studies in Montana. Detection of asympto-matic infection among residents of infected dairy premises. Am J Epidemiol. 1965;81:356-369.
43. Viciana P, Pachon J, Cuello JA, et al. Fever of indeterminate duration in the commu-nity. A seven year study in the south of Spain. Abstract 683. Presented at the 32nd Interscience Conference on Antimicrobial Agents and Chemotherapy, October 11-14, 1992. American Society for Microbiology, Washington, DC.
44. Cunha BA, Quintiliani R. The atypical pneumonias. A diagnostic and therapeutic ap-proach. Postgrad Med. 1979;66:95-102.
45. Feinstein M, Yesner R, Marks JL. Epidemic of Q fever among troops returning from Italy in the spring of 1945. 1. Clinical aspects of the epidemic at Fort Patrick Henry, Virginia. Am J Hyg. 1946;44:72-87.

46. Lim KCL, Kang JYU. Q fever presenting with gastroenteritis. Med J Aust. 1980;1:327.

47. Robins FC. Q fever in the Mediterranean area: Report of its occurrence in Allied troops. Am J Hyg. 1946;12:51-71.

48. Gordon JD, MacKeen AD, Marrie TJ, et al. The radiographic features of epidemic and sporadic Q fever pneumonia. J Can Assoc Radiol. 1984;35:293-296.

49. Millar JK. The chest film findings in 'Q' fever—A series of 35 cases. Clin Radiol. 1978;329:371-375.

50. Perin TL. Histopathologic observations in a fatal case of Q fever. Arch Pathol. 1949;47:361-365.

51. Pierce TH, Yucht SC, Gorin AB, et al. Q fever pneumonitis: Diagnosis by transbronchoscopic lung biopsy. West J Med. 1979;130:453-455.

52. Urso FP. The pathologic findings in rickettsial pneumonia. Am J Clin Pathol. 1975;64:335-342.

53. Janigan DT, Marrie TJ. An inflammatory pseudotumor of the lung in Q fever pneumonia. N Engl J Med. 1983;30:86-88.

54. Lille RD, Perrin TL, Armstrong C. An institutional outbreak of pneumonitis. III. Histopathology in man and rhesus monkeys in the pneumonitis due to the virus of "Q fever." Public Health Rep. 1941;56:1419-1425.

55. Biggs BA, Douglas JG, Grant IWB, et al. Prolonged Q fever associated with inappropriate secretion of anti-diuretic hormone. J Infect. 1984;8:61-63.

56. Turck WPG. Q fever. In: Braude AL, Davis CE, Fierer J, eds. Medical Microbiology and Infectious Diseases. Philadelphia: WB Saunders; 1981:932-937.

57. Yeaman MR, Mitscher LA, Baca OG. In vitro susceptibility of Coxiella burnetii to antibiotics, including several quinolones. Antimicrob Agents Chemother. 1987;31:1079-1084.

58. D'Angelo LJ, Hetherington R. Q fever treated with erythromycin. Br Med J. 1979;2:305-306.

59. Ellis ME, Dunbar EM. In vivo response of acute Q fever to erythromycin. Thorax. 1982;37:867-868.

60. Kofteridis D, Gikas A, Spiradakis G, et al. Clinical response of Q fever infection to macrolides. Abstract 4.3. Presented at the Fourth International Conference on Macrolides, Azalides, Streptogramins and Ketolides, Barcelona, Spain, January 12-23, 1998:47.

61. Kuzman I, Schonwald S, Culig J, et al. The efficacy of azithromycin in the treatment of Q fever: A retrospective study. Abstract 4.31. Presented at the Fourth International Conference on Macrolides, Azalides, Streptogramins and Ketolides, Barcelona, Spain, January 21-23, 1998:47.

62. Maurin M, Benoliel A, Bongrand P, Raoult D. Phagolysosomal alkalinization and the bactericidal effect of antibiotics: The Coxiella burnetii paradigm. J Infect Dis. 1992;166:1097-1102.

63. Raoult D, Bres P, Drancourt M, Vestris G. In vitro susceptibilities of Coxiella burnetii, Rickettsia rickettsii, and Rickettsia conorii to the fluoroquinolone Sparfloxacin. Antimicrob Agents Chemother. 1991;35:88-91.

64. Rolain JM, Maurin M, Bryskier A, Raoult D. In vitro activities of telithromycin (HMR 3647) against Rickettsia rickettsii, Rickettsia conorii, Rickettsia africae, Rickettsia typhi, Rickettsia prowazekii, Coxiella burnetii, Bartonella henselae, Bartonella quintana, Bartonella bacilliformis, and Ehrlichia chaffeensis. Antimicrob Agents Chemother. 2000;44:1391-1393.

65. Huebner RJ, Jellison WL, Beck MD. Q fever, a review of current knowledge. Ann Intern Med. 1949;30:495-509.

66. Stein A, Raoult D. Detection of Coxiella burnetii by DNA amplification using polymerase chain reaction. J Clin Microbiol. 1992;30:2462-2466.

67. Fiset P, Ormsbee RA, Silberman R, et al. A microagglutination technique for detection and measurement of rickettsial antibodies. Acta Virol. 1969;13:60-66.

68. Murphy AM, Field PR. The persistence of complement-fixing antibodies to Q fever (Coxiella burnetii) after infection. Med J Aust. 1970;1:1148-1150.

69. Field PR, Hunt JG, Murphy AM. Detection and persistence of specific IgM antibody to Coxiella burnetii by enzyme-linked immunosorbent assay: A comparison with immuno-fluorescence and complement fixation tests. J Infect Dis. 1983;148:477-487.

70. Peter O, Dupuis G, Burgdorfer W, et al. Evaluation of the complement fixation and indirect immunofluorescence test in the early diagnosis of primary Q fever. Eur J Clin Microbiol. 1985;4:394-396.

71. Maurin M, Raoult D. Q fever. Clin Microbiol Rev. 1999;12:518-553.

72. Hunt JG, Field PR, Murphy AM. Immunoglobulin responses to Coxiella burnetii (Q fever): Single-serum analysis of acute infection using an immunofluorescence technique. Infect Immun. 1983;39:977-981.

73. Tissot-Dupont H, Thirion X, Raoult D. Q fever serology: Cutoff determination for microimmunofluorescence. Clin Diagn Lab Immunol. 1994;1:189-196.

74. Worswick D, Marmion BP. Antibody response in acute and chronic Q fever and in subjects vaccinated against Q fever. J Med Microbiol. 1985;119:281-296.

75. Dupuis G, Peter O, Peacock M, et al. Immunoglobulin responses in acute Q fever. J Clin Microbiol. 1985;22:484-487.

76. Brouqui P, Dupont HT, Drancourt M, et al. Chronic Q fever: Ninety-two cases from France; including 27 cases without endocarditis. Arch Intern Med. 1993;153:642-649.

77. Turck WPG, Howitt G, Turnberg LA, et al. Chronic Q fever. Q J Med. 1976;45:193-217.

78. Wilson HG, Neilson GH, Galea EG, et al. Q fever endocarditis in Queensland. Circulation. 1976;53:680-684.

79. Grist NR. Q fever endocarditis. Am Heart J. 1968;75:845-846.

80. Robson AO, Shimin CDGL. Chronic Q fever. 1. Clinical aspects of a patient with endocarditis. Br Med J. 1959;2:980-953.

81. Varma MPS, Adgey AAJ, Connolly JH. Chronic Q fever endocarditis. Br Heart J. 1980;43:695-699.

82. Tobin MH, Cahill N, Gearty G, et al. Q fever endocarditis. Am J Med. 1982;72:396-400.

83. Kimbrough RC III, Ormsbee RA, Peacock M, et al. Q fever endocarditis in the United States. Ann Intern Med. 1979;91:400-402.

84. Ross PJ, Jacobson J, Muir JR. Q fever endocarditis of porcine xenograft valves. Am Heart J. 1983;105:151-153.

85. Wiley RF, Matthews MB, Peutherere JF, Marion BP. Chronic cryptic Q fever infection of the heart. Lancet. 1979;2:270-272.

86. Subramanya NI, Wright JS, Khan MAR. Failure of rifampicin and co-trimoxazole in Q fever endocarditis. Br Med J (Clin Res Ed). 1982;203:343-344.

87. Marmion BP. Subacute rickettsial endocarditis: An unusual complication of Q fever. J Hyg Epidemiol Microbiol Immunol. 1952;6:79-84.

88. Applefield MM, Bellingsley LN, Tucker JH, Fiset P. Q fever endocarditis: A case occurring in the United States. Am Heart J. 1977;93:669-670.

89. Palmer SR, Young SEJ. Q fever endocarditis in England and Wales, 1975-81. Lancet. 1982;2:1148-1149.

90. Chronic Q fever (Editorial). J Infect. 1984;8:1-4.

91. Haldane EV, Marrie TJ, Faulkner RS, et al. Endocarditis due to Q fever in Nova Scotia: Experience with five patients in 1981-1982. J Infect Dis. 1983;148:978-985.

92. Raoult D, Etienne J, Massip P, et al. Q fever endocarditis in the south of France. J Infect Dis. 1987;155:570-573.

93. Laufcr D, Lew PD, Oberhansli I, et al. Chronic Q fever endocarditis with massive splenomegaly in childhood. J Pediatr. 1986;108:535-539.

94. Raoult D, Piquet PH, Gallais H, et al. Coxiella burnetii infection of a vascular prosthesis. N Engl J Med. 1986;315:1358-1359.

95. Tellez A, Sainz C, Echevarria C, et al. Q fever in Spain: Acute and chronic cases, 1981-1985. Rev Infect Dis. 1988;10:198-202.

96. Siegman-Igra Y, Kraufman O, Keysary A, et al. Q fever endocarditis in Israel and a worldwide review. Scand J Infect Dis. 1997;29:41-49.

97. Peacock MG, Philip RN, Williams JC, Faulkner RS. Serological valuation of Q fever in humans: Enhanced phase I titers of immunoglobulins G and A are diagnostic for Q fever endocarditis. Infect Immun. 1983;41:1089-1098.

98. Fournier PE, Casalta JP, Habib G, et al. Verification of the diagnostic criteria proposed by the Duke Endocarditis Service to permit improved diagnosis of Q fever endocarditis. Am J Med. 1996;100:629-633.

99. Durack DT, Lukes AS, Bright DK. New criteria for diagnosis of infective endocarditis: Utilization of specific echocardiographic findings. Am J Med. 1994;96:200-209.

100. Li JS, Sexton DJ, Mick N, et al. Proposed modifications to the Duke criteria for the diagnosis of infective endocarditis. Clin Infect Dis. 2000;30:633-638.

101. Blondeau JM, Williams JC, Marrie TJ. The immune response to phase I and phase II Coxiella burnetii antigens as measured by Western immunoblotting. Ann NY Acad Sci. 1990;590:187-202.

102. Levy PY, Drancourt M, Etienne J, et al. Comparison of different antibiotic regimens for therapy of 32 cases of Q fever endocarditis. Antimicrob Agents Chemother. 1991;35:533-537.

103. Raoult D, Marrie T. Q fever. Clin Infect Dis. 1995;20:489-496.

104. Capo C, Zaffran Y, Zugun F, et al. Production of interleukin-10 and transforming growth factor β by peripheral blood mononuclear cells in Q fever endocarditis. Infect Immun. 1996;64:4143-4147.

105. Hofmann CER, Heaton JW Jr. Q fever hepatitis. Clinical manifestations and pathological findings. Gastroenterology. 1982;83:474-479.

106. Dupont HL, Hornick EV, Levin HA, et al. Q fever hepatitis. Ann Intern Med. 1971;74:198-206.

107. Qizilbash AH. The pathology of Q fever as seen on liver biopsy. Arch Pathol Lab Med. 1983;107:364-367.

108. Travis LB, Travis WD, Li C-Y, et al. Q fever. A clinicopathologic study of five cases. Arch Pathol Lab Med. 1986;110:1017-1020.

109. Weir WRC, Bannister B, Chambers S, et al. Chronic Q fever associated with granulomatous hepatitis. J Infect. 1980;8:56-60.

110. Pellegrin M, Delsol G, Auvergnat JC, et al. Granulomatous hepatitis in Q fever. Hum Pathol. 1980;11:51-57.

111. Voigt JJ, Delsol G, Fabre J. Liver and bone marrow granulomas in Q fever. Gastroenterology. 1983;84:887-888.

112. Alkan WJ, Ewenchik Z, Eschar J. Q fever and infectious hepatitis. Am J Med. 1965;38:54-61.

113. Harrell GT. Rickettsial involvement of the central nervous system. Med Clin North Am. 1953;37:395-422.

114. Bernit E, Pouget J, Janbon F, et al. Neurological involvement in acute Q fever. A report of 29 cases and review of the literature. Arch Intern Med. 2002;162:693-700.

115. Gomez-Aranda F, Diaz JKP, Acebol MR, et al. Computed tomographic brain scan findings in Q fever encephalitis. Neuroradiology. 1984;26:329-332.

116. Marrie TJ. Pneumonia and meningo-encephalitis due to Coxiella burnetii. J Infect. 1985;11:59-61.

117. Marrie TJ, Raoult D. Rickettsial infections of the central nervous system. Semin Neurol. 1992;12:213-224.

118. Reilly S, Northwood JL, Caul EO. Q fever in Plymouth, 1972-88. A review with particular reference to neurological manifestations. Epidemiol Infect. 1990;105:391-408.

119. Drancourt M, Raoult D, Xeridat B, et al. Q fever meningoencephalitis in five patients. Eur J Epidemiol. 1991;7:134-138.

120. Bonetti B, Monaco S, Ferrari S, et al. Demyelinating polyradiculoneuritis following Coxiella burnetii infection (Q fever). Ital J Neurol Sci. 1991;12:415-417.

121. Heard SR, Ronalds CJ, Heath RB. Coxiella burnetii infection in immunocompromised patients. J Infect. 1985;11:15-18.

122. Kanfer E, Farraj N, Price C, et al. Q fever following bone-marrow transplantation. Bone Marrow Transplant. 1988;3:165-166.

123. Loudon MM, Thompson EN. Severe combined immunodeficiency syndrome, tissue transplant, leukemia and Q fever. Arch Dis Child. 1988;63:207-209.

124. Raoult D, Brouqui P, Gastraut JA, Marchou B. Acute and chronic Q fever in patients with cancer. Clin Infect Dis. 1992;14:127-130.
125. Raoult D, Levy P-Y, Dupont HT, et al. Q fever and HIV infection. AIDS. 1993;7:81-86.
126. Meis JFGM, Weemaes CRM, Horrevorts AM, et al. Rapidly fatal Q-fever pneumonia in a patient with chronic granulomatous disease. Infection. 1992;20:287-289.
127. Ellis ME, Smith CC, Moffatt MAJ. Chronic or fatal Q-fever infection: A review of 16 patients seen in north-east Scotland (1967-1980). Q J Med. 1983;205:54-66.
128. Richardus JH, Dumas AM, Huisman J, Schaap GJ. Q fever in infancy: A review of 18 cases. Pediatr Infect Dis. 1985;4:369-373.
129. Brada M, Bellingham AJ. Bone marrow necrosis and Q fever. Br Med J. 1980;210:1108-1109.
130. Estrov Z, Bruck R, Shtalrid M, et al. Histiocytic hemophagocytosis in Q fever. Arch Pathol Lab Med. 1984;108:7.
131. Cardellach F, Font J, Agusti AGN, et al. Q fever and hemolytic anemia. J Infect Dis. 1983;148:769.
132. Ramos HS, Hodges RE, Meroney WH. Q fever: Report of a case simulating lymphoma. Ann Intern Med. 1957;47:1030-1035.
133. Hitchins R, Cobcroft RG, Hocker G. Transient severe hypoplastic anemia in Q fever. Pathology. 1986;18:254-255.
134. Baumbach A, Brehm B, Sauer W, et al. Spontaneous splenic rupture complicating acute Q fever. Am J Gastroenterol. 1992;87:1651-1653.
135. Schuil J, Richardus JH, Baarsma GS, et al. Q fever as a possible cause of bilateral optic neuritis. Br J Ophthalmol. 1985;69:580-583.
136. Conger J, Mallolas J, Mensa J, et al. Erythema nodosum and Q fever. Arch Dermatol. 1987;123:867.
137. Swaby ED, Fisher-Hoch S, Lambert HP, et al. Is Kawasaki disease a variant of Q fever? Lancet. 1980;2:146.
138. Weir WRC, Bouchet VA, Mitford E, et al. Kawasaki disease in European adult associated with serological response to *Coxiella burnetii*. Lancet. 1985;2:504.
139. Raoult D, Fenollar F, Stein, A. Q fever during pregnancy: Diagnosis, treatment and follow-up. Arch Intern Med. 2002;162:701-704.
140. Ascher MS, Berman MA, Ruppaner R. Initial clinical and immunologic evaluation of a new phase I Q fever vaccine and skin test in humans. J Infect Dis. 1983;148:214-242.
141. Marmion BP, Ormsbee RAD, Kyrkou M, et al. Vaccine prophylaxis of abattoir-associated Q fever. Lancet. 1984;2:1411-1414.
142. Grant CG, Ascher MS, Bernard KW, et al. Q fever and experimental sheep. Infect Control. 1985;6:122-123.
143. Polydorou K. Q fever control in Cyprus—Recent progress. Br Vet J. 1985;141:427-430.

CHAPTER **187**

Rickettsia prowazekii (Epidemic or Louse-Borne Typhus)

DIDIER RAOULT

DAVID H. WALKER

Rickettsia prowazekii is the only rickettsia that can cause devastating, naturally occurring epidemics capable of killing a substantial proportion of human populations infested with body lice. Epidemics are associated with conditions that prevent bathing and washing of clothes in hot water, such as war and poverty, natural disasters such as earthquakes and floods, displacement of populations, jails, and lack of hygiene. A continued problem in impoverished, louse-infested populations, epidemic typhus threatens to reemerge as it did during the Civil War in Burundi; an estimated 100,000 persons suffered from typhus in 1997.[1]

Based on his observations of an Italian epidemic in 1528, epidemic typhus was described vividly by Hieronymus Fracastorius as a previously unknown, life-threatening disease: A petechial rash appeared 4 to 7 days after the onset of fever and was accompanied by stupor and delirium. The word *typhus* indeed is derived from the Greek *typhos*, meaning smoky or hazy, which describes the state of confusion accompanied by stupor. Luis de Toro described the same course and signs of an illness that occurred among soldiers on the Iberian Peninsula in 1557, also noting winter seasonality and association with contact with clothing of the ill. During an epidemic of typhoid fever in

Philadelphia in 1836, Gerhard distinguished these diseases by the presence of intestinal lesions in typhoid patients. In 1909, Charles Nicolle experimentally established the fact that typhus was a transmissible infection with the human body louse as its vector. Investigations between 1910 and 1922 by Ricketts, von Prowazek, da Rocha-Lima, and Wolbach employed microscopy, xenodiagnosis in lice, and histochemistry to establish that the agent was a bacterium that proliferated in human endothelial cells and louse gut epithelium but could not be cultured axenically.[2]

In 1896 and 1910, Nathan Brill described series of patients in New York with a mild febrile illness that was shown by Hans Zinsser in 1934 to be a rickettsial infection.[3,4] Zinsser hypothesized correctly that the illness is a recrudescence of long latent *R. prowazekii*. The distinction of *Rickettsia typhi* as a separate agent that causes an endemic, clinically similar disease transmitted to humans by fleas from a zoonotic cycle involving rats was established by the work of Neill (1917),[5] Mooser (1928),[6] Maxcy (1929),[7] and Dyer (1931).[8] The feared specter of epidemic louse-borne typhus receded with (1) the success of a killed-rickettsia vaccine in preventing the deaths of allied soldiers during World War II, (2) the effectiveness of insecticides in curtailing epidemics by louse control, and (3) the effective treatment of illness with tetracyclines and chloramphenicol. Currently, epidemics of typhus are increasingly recognized, lice resistant to various insecticides have been detected, antibiotic-resistant rickettsiae have been developed, and aerosol-transmitted, weaponized *R. prowazekii* is a biothreat. Moreover, in 1975, *R. prowazekii* was identified in a highly prevalent zoonotic cycle in flying squirrels in the eastern United States, which represents the likely evolutionary origin of the organism.[9]

ETIOLOGY

The causative agent of louse-borne typhus, *R. prowazekii*, is an obligately intracellular, small (1×0.3 μm) coccobacillus. Its 1.1-Mb genome has undergone considerable reduction in that many biosynthetic functions are provided by its milieu in the resource-rich host cell cytosol to which the organism has adapted by evolutionary selection for transport mechanisms for adenosine triphosphate (ATP), amino acids, and phosphorylated sugars.[10] Its gram-negative cell wall contains an abundant 135-kDa, immunodominant, tetragonally arranged, S-layer surface protein, lipopolysaccharide, and peptidoglycan.[11] It possesses an extracellular dormant form that remains infectious in louse feces for months.

EPIDEMIOLOGY

Typhus has affected the outcomes of wars from the 1500s until the end of the 19th century. During the Russian campaign of 1812, typhus was responsible for the deaths of as many as half of the 700,000 troops of Napoleon. During World War I, the Bolshevik revolution, and its aftermath, an estimated 30 million cases of typhus occurred in the Soviet Union alone, with 3 million deaths.[12] During World War II, epidemics of typhus occurred in eastern Europe, North Africa, concentration camps, and southern Italy, where DDT was used against lice to abort an epidemic in Naples in 1944.

R. prowazekii is transmitted between patients by the human body louse (*Pediculus humanus corporis*), which is strictly adapted to humans, lives in the clothes, and takes a blood meal five times a day.[13] Lice become infected while feeding on the blood of rickettsemic patients. *R. prowazekii* enters the louse gut epithelial cells and replicates by binary fission until the massively infected cells burst[14] and are released into the louse feces 5 to 7 days after ingestion. Lice are not adapted to an elevated body temperature and leave febrile patients for a new host. Rickettsia-laden louse feces are deposited on the skin and clothes and are introduced into the new host by scratching into the louse-bitten skin or by rubbing into mucous membranes such as the conjunctiva; they are also transmitted through inhalation.

Persons who recover from typhus fever remain latently infected and are susceptible to reactivation of the infection and rickettsemia

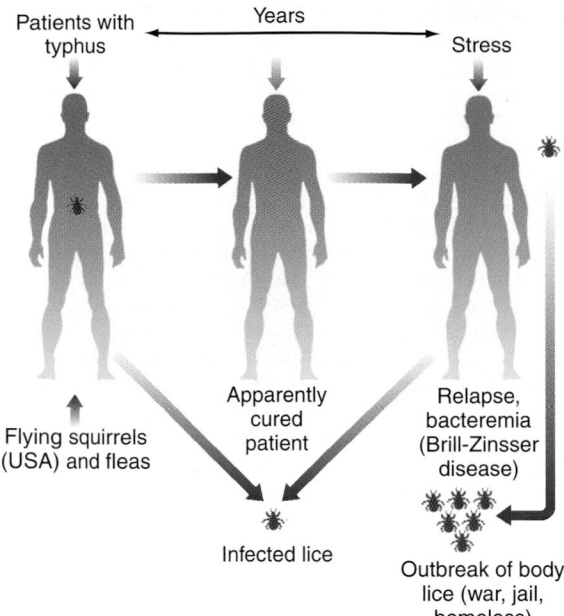

FIGURE 187-1. Transmission of typhus.

that can infect body lice and ignite an epidemic under circumstances of crowding, extreme poverty, cold climate, and poor hygiene; this can lead to a high prevalence of louse infestation (Fig. 187-1). The louse population can expand rapidly (11% per day).[13] Lice are currently prevalent in poor countries, are spreading in the former USSR, and are found on homeless persons in developed countries. In France, 35% of members of the homeless population have lice. Risk factors for reactivation of latent infection in humans have not been determined, but waning immunity, poor nutrition, alcoholism, and stress have been hypothesized as potentially important.

Typhus is endemic in the Peruvian Andes, Burundi, and Rwanda, and recently, cases have been diagnosed in Russia, in patients from Algeria and Senegal, and in a homeless person in France.[1,15-18] Given the geographic distribution of latent typhus infection from known historic epidemics, the neglect with which this disease has been handled, and the unavailability of laboratory diagnostic methods, the current epidemiology of louse-borne typhus, particularly in marginal populations of mountainous areas in Asia, South and Central America, and Africa, is unknown.

An extrahuman reservoir of *R. prowazekii* exists in a large portion of Southern flying squirrels (*Glaucomys volans*), which are distributed from Florida to Maine and westward to Minnesota and east Texas.[9] In stark contrast with the louse/human cycle in which 15% of humans die and 100% of lice suffer rickettsial destruction of the intestine with extravasation of the red blood meal into the hemocoele and death, *R. prowazekii* causes subclinical rickettsemia in flying squirrels and no ill effects on the squirrel's own species of lice and fleas.[19] Infections are apparently transmitted to humans by flying squirrel fleas or mucous membrane or inhalation exposure to the feces of the flea or louse. These illnesses occur mainly during winter when flying squirrels enter buildings.

PATHOGENESIS

After inoculation into the skin, *R. prowazekii* spreads throughout the body via the blood stream. Rickettsiae enter mainly through endothelial cells and, to a lesser extent, through macrophages by induced phagocytosis; they escape from the phagosome into the cytosol, where they proliferate until the cell bursts.[20] *R. prowazekii* lacks actin-based mobility that mediates cell-to-cell spread of spotted fever group rickettsiae. The principal pathophysiologic effects of rickettsial infection include increased vascular permeability and pe-

techial hemorrhage. Thrombosis occurs in only a tiny minority of foci of vascular infection and injury, and ischemic necrosis is a rare consequence.[2] Although a model of cytotoxicity is mediated by rickettsial phospholipase activity, the actual rickettsial pathogenic mechanism in vivo is not known.[21] The most important vital target organs are the brain and the lung. The petechial maculopapular rash is a manifestation of cutaneous vascular infection by *R. prowazekii*. Classic pathologic lesions comprise swollen, infected endothelial cells in the microcirculation with adjacent perivascular infiltration by lymphocytes and macrophages, which represents the effector host cellular immune response.[2,22]

CLINICAL MANIFESTATIONS

Experiments in human volunteers during the preantibiotic era demonstrated that after an incubation period of 8 to 16 days (mean, 11.1 days) and a prodrome of 2 days, rash developed in 79% of subjects an average of 4 days after onset of illness, and the fever lasted for 12 days. In an epidemic in Poland after World War I, a prodrome of 1 day or longer occurred in 88%, followed by fever (100%), headache (89%), chills (74%), myalgias (54%), rash (an entry criterion of the study), conjunctival injection (87%), and rales (74%).[2] Erythematous 2- to 6-mm macules appeared most often on the trunk on day 5 and later on the extremities. Without the availability of antibiotics, the course was characterized by marked delirium (48%), severe cough (38%), hemorrhagic rash (34%), gangrene (4%), coma (6%), death (13%) a median of 12.5 days after onset, or defervescence a median of 14 days after onset. Recent series from Ethiopia and Burundi demonstrated lower recognition of rash in darkly pigmented skin; marked myalgia; variable incidence of stupor, cough, and conjunctivitis (Table 187-1); and a lower case-fatality rate caused by effective antimicrobial treatment in many patients.[1,19] Indeed, the illness in Burundi was locally called *sutama*, denoting the crouching position that one assumed to mitigate the severe muscle pain.

Onset is usually abrupt with rigors, malaise, and severe headache. The tongue is dry, and the patient is constipated. The rash progresses through macules that disappear on pressure to maculopapules with petechiae. The face, palms, and soles are usually spared. Even in darkly pigmented patients, cutaneous lesions are often visible in the axilla. Chest radiographs frequently reveal interstitial pneumonia. Cases have not occurred in settings in which clinical laboratory abnormalities have been studied extensively, except for the Ethiopian series, which demonstrated values characteristic of disseminated rickettsial vascular injury and increased vascular permeability (Table 187-2).[23]

Flying squirrel–associated typhus cases have generally been less severe with no fatalities recorded. Patients have developed fever (100%), headache (81%), maculopapular rash (66%), confusion (44%), and myalgia (42%).[24-26]

TABLE 187-1 Clinical Manifestations of Epidemic Typhus

Place	Burundi[*]	Ethiopia[†]
Number of cases	102	60
Fever > 39° C	100%	100%
Headaches	100%	100%
Any rash	25%	38%
Purpuric rash	11%	33%
Stupor	81%	35%
Coma	4%	—
Cough	70%	38%
Nausea/vomiting	57%	43%
Conjunctivitis	15%	53%
Diarrhea	13%	—
Splenomegaly	8%	13%
Photophobia	—	33%
Myalgias	100%	70%

[*]Fournier PE, Ndihokubwayo JB, Guidran J, et al. Human pathogens in body and head lice. Emerg Infect Dis. 2002;8:1515-1518.
[†]Perine PL, Chandler BP, Krause DK, et al. A clinico-epidemiological study of epidemic typhus in Africa. Clin Infect Dis. 1992;14:1149-1158.

TABLE 187-2 Clinical Laboratory Findings in Patients with Epidemic Typhus

White blood cell count	Low, 3%; elevated, 14%
Thrombocytopenia	43%
Increased serum AST	63%
Increased serum ALT	35%
Increased serum LDH	82%
Increased serum CPK	31%
Increased BUN	31%
Decreased serum protein	38%

ALT, alanine transaminase; AST, aspartate transaminase; BUN, blood urea nitrogen; CPK, creatine phosphokinase; LDH, lactate dehydrogenase. Based on Perine PL, Chandler BP, Krause DK, et al. A clinico-epidemiological study of epidemic typhus in Africa. Clin Infect Dis. 1992;14:1149-1158.

Brill's clinical description of recrudescent typhus in 1910 was that of an illness resembling nonfatal typhus, with onset characterized by chills, intense headache, fever, myalgia, nausea, and sometimes vomiting.[3] Patients are prostrate with apathy, dulled sensorium, and persistent headache as an overriding symptom. Between the fifth and seventh days of illness, a maculopapular rash appears on the back and abdomen and spreads rapidly. Congested conjunctivae and constipation are prominent features in many cases. The untreated illness lasts about 2 weeks. Brill stated, "In the case of an epidemic of typhus fever, in my opinion, it would be simply impossible to say that these cases which I have described were not mild typhus fever." Twenty-four years later, Hans Zinsser isolated rickettsiae from the blood of similar patients—louse-free immigrants from typhus-endemic regions of Europe; thus, the eponymic designation, Brill-Zinsser disease, began to be used to refer to recrudescent typhus.[4]

DIAGNOSIS

In the midst of a recognized epidemic, the patient with a late-stage florid rash or even one with fever, severe headache, and myalgia without a rash would likely be diagnosed with louse-borne typhus. The diagnosis of louse-borne typhus early in an outbreak when only a few cases have been reported is more challenging. The most important differential diagnosis is typhoid fever.[16] The prominent cough and crackles often suggest a diagnosis of pneumonia. Neurologic signs and cerebrospinal fluid (CSF) pleocytosis may lead to consideration of viral or bacterial meningoencephalitis. Nausea, vomiting, and abdominal tenderness raise the diagnostic possibilities of viral or bacterial enterocolitis or acute surgical abdomen. Jaundice and elevated hepatic enzymes suggest viral hepatitis. The hemorrhagic rash may lead to diagnostic consideration of arenaviral and filoviral hemorrhagic fevers.[27] Other differential diagnoses include malaria, leptospirosis, arboviral and enteroviral infections, meningococcemia, measles, rubella, secondary syphilis, toxic shock syndrome, infectious mononucleosis, trench fever, relapsing fever, and other rickettsioses.

Other circumstances under which *R. prowazekii* infection should be considered involve immigrants from regions where epidemic typhus has been prevalent, persons who have been exposed to flying squirrels, and homeless persons.[17,24,27] It is very unlikely that cases of aerosol-transmitted typhus in a bioterrorist attack would be diagnosed clinically before the onset of rash, if even then.[28]

The laboratory diagnosis of louse-borne typhus generally relies on the detection of antibodies with a fourfold rise in titer in convalescence. Usually, a diagnostic titer is detected during the second week of illness. The standard serologic method is indirect immunofluorescence assay, and an immunoglobulin (Ig) G titer of 128 or an IgM titer of 32 confirms the diagnosis. Enzyme immunoassays that yield reliable results have also been developed. Although *Proteus vulgaris* OX-19 agglutination (Weil-Felix reaction) has been demonstrated to be poorly sensitive and nonspecific, it may be useful when it is the only method that is available in an underdeveloped country. Antibodies stimulated by *R. prowazekii* react with shared antigens of *R. typhi,* allowing for diagnostic detection of cross-reactive antibodies. A fourfold higher titer against *R. prowazekii* than *R. typhi* distinguishes epidemic typhus from murine typhus in fewer than half of cases.[29] The predominance of IgG antibodies and the absence of IgM and Weil-Felix antibodies in recrudescent typhus is controversial.[30]

Although serodiagnosis is retrospective, methods that are capable of establishing a diagnosis during the acute stage of infection, namely, polymerase chain reaction (PCR) and immunohistochemical detection of *R. prowazekii* in blood or tissue, respectively, are seldom available in locations where typhus epidemics occur.[31,32] Feasibility has been demonstrated for serodiagnosis on blood spotted onto filter paper and for rickettsial isolation or PCR detection in lice removed from the patient, either of which can be sent to a referral laboratory by mail.[33,34] Rickettsiae may also be isolated most effectively from blood, buffy coat, plasma, or tissue in shell vial cell culture.[35]

TREATMENT

The treatment of choice for all patients who are not allergic to tetracyclines and who are not pregnant is doxycycline 100 mg twice daily for 7 to 10 days.[36] Under chaotic epidemic conditions and in other situations in which doxycycline availability is limited, a single dose of 200 mg of doxycycline is effective, although a small portion of patients may relapse.[37] Chloramphenicol (60 to 75 mg/kg/day in four divided doses) and tetracycline (25 to 50 mg/kg/day in four divided doses) are also effective. Other antibiotics, including β-lactams, aminoglycosides, and sulfonamides, are ineffective. Although fluoroquinolones, rifampin, and some of the newer macrolides show inhibition of growth of *R. prowazekii* in cell culture, none has been proved to be efficacious clinically. Administration of quinolones has been associated with treatment failure.[27]

PREVENTION

Control of body lice is the mainstay in the prevention of epidemic typhus. When an outbreak of lice appears, the first step is to change all garments and wash them in hot water. Introducing regular washing of clothes will stop outbreaks. Only when this is impossible is delousing using insecticides such as Lindane in powder form useful. Application of 30 to 50 g of 1% permethrin dusting powder per adult both inside and outside of clothing and on bedding may be repeated every 6 weeks to kill lice.

No vaccine is currently available for the prevention of typhus.

REFERENCES

1. Raoult D, Ndihokubwayo JB, Tissot-Dupont H, et al. Outbreak of epidemic typhus associated with trench fever in Burundi. Lancet. 1998;352:353-358.
2. Wolbach SB, Todd JL, Palfrey FW. The Etiology and Pathology of Typhus. Cambridge, Mass: Harvard University Press; 1922.
3. Brill NE. An acute infectious disease of unknown origin. Am J Med Sci. 1910;139:484.
4. Zinsser H. Varieties of typhus virus and the epidemiology of the American form of European typhus fever (Brill's disease). Am J Hyg. 1934;20:513.
5. Neill MH. Experimental typhus fever in guinea pigs. Public Health Rep. 1917;21:1105-1108.
6. Mooser H. Experiments relating to the pathology and the etiology of Mexican typhus (Tabardillo). J Infect Dis. 1928;43:241-260.
7. Maxcy KF. Typhus fever in the United States. Public Health Rep. 1929;44:1735-1743.
8. Dyer RE. Typhus fever. A virus of the typhus type derived from fleas collected from wild rats. Public Health Rep. 1931;46:334-338.
9. Bozeman FM, Masiello SA, Williams MS, et al. Epidemic typhus rickettsiae isolated from flying squirrels. Nature 1975;255:545-547.
10. Andersson SG, Zomorodipour A, Andersson JO, et al. The genome sequence of *Rickettsia prowazekii* and the origin of mitochondria. Nature. 1998;396:133-140.
11. Moron CG, Bouyer DH, Yu X-J, et al. Phylogenetic analysis of the *rompB* genes of *Rickettsia felis* and *Rickettsia prowazekii* European-human and North American flying-squirrel strains. Am J Trop Med Hyg. 2000;62:598-603.
12. Patterson KD. Typhus and its control in Russia, 1870-1940. Med Hist. 1993;37:361.
13. Raoult D, Roux V. The body louse as a vector of reemerging human diseases. Clin Infect Dis. 1999;29:888-911.
14. Houhamdi L, Fournier PE, Fang R, et al. An experimental model of human body louse infection with *Rickettsia prowazekii.* J Infect Dis. 2000;186:1639-1646.

15. Fournier PE, Ndihokubwayo JB, Guidran J, et al. Human pathogens in body and head lice. Emerg Infect Dis. 2002;8:1515-1518.

16. Niang M, Brouqui P, Raoult D. Epidemic typhus imported from Algeria. Emerg Infect Dis. 1999;5:716-718.

17. Raoult D, Foucault C, Brouqui P. Infections in the homeless. Lancet Infect Dis. 2001;1:77-84.

18. Tarasevich I, Rydkina E, Raoult D. Outbreak of epidemic typhus in Russia. Lancet. 1998;352:1151.

19. Sonenshine DE, Bozeman FM, Williams MS, et al. Epizootiology of epidemic typhus (*Rickettsia prowazekii*) in flying squirrels. Am J Trop Med Hyg. 1978;27:339-349.

20. Walker TS. Rickettsial interactions with human endothelial cells in vitro: Adherence and entry. Infect Immun. 1984;44:205.

21. Walker DH, Feng H-M, Popov VL. Rickettsial phospholipase A$_2$ as a pathogenic mechanism in a model of cell injury by typhus and spotted fever group rickettsiae. Am J Trop Med Hyg. 2001;65:936-942.

22. Turco J, Winkler HH. Role of nitric oxide synthase pathway in inhibition of growth of interferon-sensitive and interferon-resistant *Rickettsia prowazekii* stains in L929 cells treated with tumor necrosis factor alpha and gamma interferon. Infect Immun. 1993;61:4317.

23. Perine PL, Chandler BP, Krause DK, et al. A clinico-epidemiological study of epidemic typhus in Africa. Clin Infect Dis. 1992;14:1149-1158.

24. Centers for Disease Control. Epidemic typhus associated with flying squirrels—United States. MMWR. 1982;31:555-561.

25. Duma RJ, Sonenshine DE, Bozeman M, et al. Epidemic typhus in the United States associated with flying squirrels. JAMA. 1981;245:2318-2323.

26. McDade JE, Shepard CC, Redus MA, et al. Evidence of *Rickettsia prowazekii* infections in the United States. Am J Trop Med Hyg. 1980;29:277-284.

27. Birg ML, La Scola B, Roux V, et al. Isolation of *Rickettsia prowazekii* from blood by shell vial cell culture. J Clin Microbiol. 1999;37:3722-3724.

28. Zanetti G, Francioli P, Tagan D, et al. Imported epidemic typhus. Lancet. 1998;352:1709.

29. Walker DH. Principles of the malicious use of infectious agents to create terror: Reasons for concern for organisms of the genus *Rickettsia*. Ann NY Acad Sci. 2003;990:1-4.

30. LaScola B, Rydkina L, Ndihokubwayo JB, et al. Serological differentiation of murine typhus and epidemic typhus using cross-absorption and Western blotting. Clin Diagn Lab Immunol. 2000;7:612-616.

31. Eremeeva ME, Balayeva NM, Raoult D. Serological response of patients suffering from primary and recrudescent typhus: Comparison of complement fixation reaction, Weil-Felix Test, microimmunofluorescence, and immunoblotting. Clin Diagn Lab Immunol. 1995;1:318-324.

32. Carl M, Tibbs CW, Dobson ME, et al. Diagnosis of acute typhus infection using the polymerase chain reaction. J Infect Dis. 1990;161:791-793.

33. Walker DH, Feng H-M, Ladner S, et al. Immunohistochemical diagnosis of typhus rickettsioses using an anti-lipopolysaccharide monoclonal antibody. Mod Pathol. 1997;10:1038-1042.

34. Fenollar F, Raoult D. Diagnosis of rickettsial diseases using samples dried on blotting paper. Clin Diagn Lab Immunol. 1999;6:483-488.

35. Roux V, Raoult D. Body lice as tools for diagnosis and surveillance of reemerging diseases. J Clin Microbiol. 1999;37:596-599.

36. Maurin M, Raoult D. *Rickettsia prowazekii*. In: Mann J, Crabbe MJC, eds. Bacteria and Antibacterial Agents. Baltimore: Williams & Wilkins; 2001:558-561.

37. Perine PL, Krause DW, Awoke A, et al. Single-dose doxycycline treatment of louse-borne relapsing fever and epidemic typhus. Lancet. 1974;2:742-744.

CHAPTER **188**

Rickettsia typhi (Murine Typhus)

J. STEPHEN DUMLER

DAVID H. WALKER

Since 1926, when Maxcy successfully differentiated among typhus fevers and identified murine typhus as a distinct clinical and epidemiologic entity, and 1931, when Dyer isolated a new typhus group *Rickettsia* from rats and fleas, murine typhus has been recognized as a worldwide zoonotic problem.[1] Often underrecognized and believed to be clinically mild, murine typhus may occur in epidemics or with high prevalence in certain geographic regions.[2-8] Illness may be severe, with death occurring in a small proportion of individuals. The association with both rat and cat fleas is now well established; with fluctuations in human seroprevalence, the changing ecology of this zoonosis complicates both clinical recognition and laboratory diagnosis.[9,10]

ETIOLOGY

Rickettsia typhi, the causative agent of murine typhus, is an obligate intracellular bacterium that infects endothelial cells in mammalian hosts and midgut epithelial cells in the flea host.[9] A new rickettsial agent, *Rickettsia felis,* has been recognized to share some antigenic and genetic components with *R. typhi* but is best characterized as a spotted fever group rickettsia.[11] As typical for the genus *Rickettsia*, *R. typhi* contains rickettsial outer membrane protein B (OmpB),[12] a member of the Sca protein family, a surface array protein similar to that present in other gram-negative bacteria and in gene D,[13] and a gene that encodes a 17-kDa predicted lipoprotein. Moreover, it lacks the presence of rickettsial outer membrane protein A (OmpA), a characteristic of spotted fever group rickettsiae. Epitopes present on OmpB, the major protein antigen, are unique for the species. In addition, *R. typhi* contains an invasin-related hemolysin gene, *tlyC.*[14] These organisms are well adapted for intracellular life, and within the host cell, *R. typhi* stimulates host actin polymerization poorly and remains relatively nonmotile,[15] allowing accumulation to significant numbers before the occurrence of mechanical host cell lysis and spread.

EPIDEMIOLOGY

Murine typhus is found worldwide and is especially prevalent in tropical and subtropical seaboard regions, where the most important rat reservoirs (*Rattus* spp.) and flea vectors (*Xenopsylla cheopis*) are found.[1,9,16] An important vector in some areas (south Texas and southern California) is the cat flea (*Ctenocephalides felis*), and opossums have been implicated as a potential reservoir in these areas.[7,9,16,17] Thus, residents and visitors to these urban and suburban regions are at risk when flea-bearing animals bring infected fleas into close proximity to humans.

Murine typhus persists at a low level in the United States, where most cases are seen in south Texas and southern California. Yet outbreaks are well documented around the world, especially in regions with inadequate vector and reservoir control.[1,8,17-19] In fact, among Khmers displaced into temporary shelters at the Thai-Cambodian border, 70% of patients with unexplained fever had murine typhus, and the calculated attack rate was approximately 172 in 100,000 adult patients during this period.[8] Most patients are adults, although persons of all ages may become ill. Cases are recognized year round, with a peak prevalence from April through June in Texas[7] and during the warm months of summer and early fall elsewhere.[1,20,21] It is worth remembering that murine typhus can occur in travelers returning from endemic regions throughout the world.[22-24]

The disease is transmitted after the inoculation of infected flea feces into a pruritic flea-bite wound. Because predominantly gut epithelial cells are infected in the flea vector, a reservoir of infected fleas is maintained mostly by horizontal transmission from flea to vertebrate host to uninfected flea.[25] Once infected, the flea maintains the rickettsial infection for the duration of its life. *R. typhi* may also infect the flea reproductive organs and foregut tissues, which explains the low levels of transovarial (vertical) transmission and occasional direct inoculation via flea bite.[26] The longevity of fleas is unaffected by gut epithelial cell or disseminated *R. typhi* infection.[9]

PATHOLOGY AND PATHOGENESIS

Few accurate descriptions of the histopathology of murine typhus have been provided, despite the fact that the case-fatality rate ranges between 1% and 4%.[7,27] Pathologic findings indicate a systemic endothelial infection similar to epidemic typhus and Rocky Mountain spotted fever.[28-30] Lymphohistiocytic vasculitis may affect any organ, and in fatal cases, interstitial pneumonitis, interstitial nephritis, interstitial myocarditis, meningoencephalitis, and portal triaditis may be present. Rickettsiae may be demonstrated in many organs and are especially numerous in foci of vasculitis.[28] This underlying vasculitic lesion and the rickettsia-induced vascular injury account for most of the clinicopathologic abnormalities. As vascular injury accumulates, a substantial loss of intravascular volume, albumin, and electrolytes occurs, and leukocytes and platelets are consumed at foci of infection. With multifocal heavy infection and attendant inflammation, vascular and parenchymal injury may yield localized symptoms, signs, or laboratory findings related to the sites of infection and injury. The induction of hypovolemia insufficiently corrected by normal homeostatic mechanisms further exacerbates compromise of tissue perfusion and may lead to prerenal azotemia. Mild to moderate hepatic injury is a frequent finding in murine typhus and probably results from multifocal infection of hepatic sinusoidal and portal endothelium with "bystander" hepatocyte damage.[7,31] With extensive rickettsial vascular injury and hypoperfusion secondary to transvascular volume loss, the result may be renal failure, respiratory failure, central nervous system abnormalities, or multiorgan failure.[7,28]

Immunity to *R. typhi* is mediated mainly by cell-mediated immunity with CD8 T lymphocytes, gamma interferon, and, most likely, cytotoxic T-lymphocyte activity, which plays important roles, and antibody, which plays an adjunctive role.[32-36] OmpB is a prominent vaccine candidate.[35,37]

CLINICAL MANIFESTATIONS

Signs and Symptoms

Usually only a small proportion of patients with murine typhus recall a flea bite or flea exposure, and an incubation period of approximately 1 to 2 weeks may transpire before an abrupt onset of illness occurs.[7,20,21] The presentation is often nonspecific, and fever (96%), severe headache (45%-88%), chills (44%-87%), myalgia (33%), and nausea (33%) are the most frequently reported early findings.[7] Rash is noted in only 18% of patients at presentation, and over the course of the illness, between 50% and 80% will develop this sign.[7,20,21] As the illness progresses, most patients continue with fever and can have frequent gastrointestinal (nausea 48%, vomiting 40%, and anorexia 35%) or respiratory involvement (cough in 35%).[7,20,21] Some studies record the presence of hepatomegaly and splenomegaly in up to 24% and 10% of patients, respectively.[38,39] Neurologic signs and symptoms have been reported to occur in up to 45% of patients, usually manifested as confusion, stupor, seizures, or localized findings such as ataxia.[7,40,41]

The absence of rash or lack of petechiae should not dissuade one from a diagnosis of murine typhus. In fact, when rash is identified, it is described as macular or maculopapular in 78%, and petechiae are noted in less than 10%.[7] These lesions are most often distributed on the trunk (88% of cases), but involvement of the extremities (>45%) is not infrequent. The initial rash distribution is equally frequent on the extremities and on the trunk. On occasion, the rash may also be present on the palms and soles.[7]

The clinical course of murine typhus is usually uncomplicated, and childhood murine typhus is often mild, with one series reporting only nighttime fever with normal daytime activities.[42] However, occasional patients develop central nervous system abnormalities, renal insufficiency, hepatic insufficiency, respiratory failure requiring intubation, or hematemesis. Patients are ill enough that 10% require admission to an intensive care facility, and up to 4% of hospitalized adult patients die from the infection.[7]

Once the diagnosis has been considered and appropriate therapy begun, most patients defervesce rapidly (median 3 days). Findings associated with severe illness include a high leukocyte count and an elevated blood urea nitrogen level, creatinine level, and blood urea nitrogen-to-creatinine ratio. Advanced age and a prolonged interval before the administration of specific antirickettsial therapy are also significantly correlated with severity.[7] One report suggests a link between hemolytic disorders such as glucose-6-phosphate dehydrogenase deficiency, hemoglobinopathy, and thalassemia and more severe hepatic involvement, including jaundice.[31] A trend toward more severe infection is also noted in patients treated with trimethoprim-sulfamethoxazole.

Laboratory Features

Early mild leukopenia (which coincides with thrombocytopenia) is seen in one fourth to one half of patients during the first 7 days of illness. Subsequently, leukocytosis develops in less than one third.[7,43,44] Prothrombin times are occasionally prolonged, but true disseminated intravascular coagulation with hypofibrinogenemia is very infrequently documented. The most frequent laboratory abnormality in murine typhus, a mild to moderate elevation in serum aspartate aminotransferase levels, is present in the vast majority (67%-92%), and related indices of hepatic and cellular injury (levels of alanine aminotransferase, alkaline phosphatase, lactate dehydrogenase) are often elevated in parallel.[7,31,43,44] Rickettsia-induced vascular damage frequently leads to hypoproteinemia (45%) and hypoalbuminemia (89%) and is probably responsible in large part for multiple serum electrolyte abnormalities, especially mild hyponatremia (60%) and hypocalcemia (79%). Even in the presence of symptomatic central nervous system abnormalities, cerebrospinal fluid examination may be normal or may reveal pleocytosis and increased protein concentration, resembling the findings in viral or leptospiral meningoencephalitis.[7,45]

DIAGNOSIS

Early diagnosis of murine typhus is still based mostly on clinical suspicion. Because early and specific antirickettsial therapy is indicated to avoid severe or potentially fatal infections, treatment should not be withheld while laboratory confirmation is awaited. The predominant method of laboratory confirmation is serologic. Because antibodies are infrequently detected during acute illness, serologic diagnosis is retrospective. Obsolete Weil-Felix agglutination reactions have proved insensitive and are intrinsically nonspecific, and as such, should not be used to establish a definitive diagnosis.[46] Instead, sensitive serologic tests that use specific *R. typhi* antigens such as indirect fluorescent antibody or solid-phase immunoassay[47] are preferable. With the use of a sensitive and specific test such as indirect fluorescent antibody assay, diagnostic titers are present in approximately 50% of murine typhus patients within 1 week and in nearly all within 15 days after the onset of illness.[7] Because typhus group rickettsiae share antigens, routine serologic evaluation does not distinguish between epidemic typhus and murine typhus.[48] In occasional sera, reactions against both typhus and spotted fever groups are observed, creating further serodiagnostic difficulties.

Although it affords a definitive diagnosis, culture is rarely attempted owing to a reputation of biohazard and difficulty; however, in the age of routine viral isolation and universal precautions, rickettsial isolation must be reconsidered a valuable adjunct to diagnosis. A shell vial assay for the isolation of spotted fever group rickettsiae has been successfully used to confirm infection during the acute phase of illness. This method could be easily adapted for the isolation of *R. typhi* and the confirmation of murine typhus.[49] For rickettsial isolation from peripheral blood, anticoagulated, sterile specimens should be obtained before antirickettsial therapy is initiated and should be processed immediately. If a delay is unavoidable, specimens should be stored for no longer than 48 hours at 4° C or can be frozen at −70° C until culture is attempted.

Recently described methods for laboratory confirmation of rickettsiosis include the immunohistologic demonstration of *R. typhi* in tissues[28,50] and polymerase chain reaction amplification of rickettsial nucleic acids in peripheral blood.[51] However, none of these methods has been adequately evaluated for the diagnosis of murine typhus; thus, sensitivities, specificities, and predictive values are unknown.

The reduction noted in the prevalence of murine typhus has seen a parallel decrease in accurate early diagnosis, owing to lack of consideration of the possibility of murine typhus. Most patients are initially investigated for fever of undetermined origin, and less often, patients are investigated for suspected pneumonia, cerebrovascular accident, gastroenteritis, or neoplasm, among other diagnoses.[7,27]

Despite the occasional presence of findings that suggest alternative diagnoses because of isolated organ system involvement, an early clue toward the successful diagnosis of murine typhus is recognition of the systemic manifestations associated with fever. Other rickettsioses may cause considerable difficulty in the differential diagnosis; Rocky Mountain spotted fever is the most frequent. Murine typhus and Rocky Mountain spotted fever may be distinguished on the basis of the history, clinical presentation, and serologic tests. Many patients with murine typhus are exposed to flea vectors in urban or suburban regions,[2,10,52] and a small proportion (1%-40%) report a flea bite or exposure, whereas patients with Rocky Mountain spotted fever often acquire illness after rural exposure or documented tick bites and more often develop rash and petechiae. The distribution of rash is of little help in individual cases. The likelihood of monocytotropic ehrlichiosis or human anaplasmosis is diminished if leukopenia and thrombocytopenia are minimal or absent, although serum hepatic transaminase levels may be elevated in both murine typhus and the ehrlichioses. Murine typhus, Rocky Mountain spotted fever, and ehrlichiosis/anaplasmosis occur during warm seasons in which the vector arthropods are most active. In contrast, the louse vector of epidemic typhus is most active and is likely to spread its rickettsial agent in cooler seasons when layers of clothing are worn, persons are crowded indoors, and personal hygiene diminishes. Differentiation of the sporadic cases of sylvatic typhus, caused by *Rickettsia prowazekii*, from murine typhus may be exceedingly difficult, but the former illness is suggested when exposure to potential reservoirs (e.g., flying squirrels) is elicited in the history.

The differential diagnosis of murine typhus is quite long because of its usually nonspecific presentation. Aside from the rickettsioses and the ehrlichioses, alternative diagnoses that may need to be considered include meningococcemia, measles, typhoid fever, bacterial and viral meningitis, secondary syphilis, leptospirosis, toxic shock syndrome, and Kawasaki syndrome.

TREATMENT AND PREVENTION

The preferred drug for treatment of *R. typhi* infection is a tetracycline, such as doxycycline. Clinical trials of fluoroquinolones in the treatment of spotted fever group rickettsioses in Europe and individual case reports suggest that ciprofloxacin, ofloxacin, and pefloxacin may be effective alternatives.[53,54] However, at least one report of murine typhus poorly responsive to ciprofloxacin has been reported.[55] In vitro, the fluoroquinolones, sparfloxacin, temofloxacin, and clinafloxacin, as well as azithromycin and clarithromycin, inhibit rickettsial growth at concentrations achieved routinely in human therapy.[56,57] Whether such results may be extrapolated for broad treatment of human infections with *R. typhi* awaits clinical study. The current recommendation is for administration of doxycycline 100 mg orally twice daily. In severely ill patients, intravenous doxycycline or chloramphenicol is effective, the latter given as 50 to 75 mg/kg/day in four divided doses. Oral chloramphenicol is not currently available in the United States. Corticosteroids are occasionally used for severe central nervous system disease, but no controlled study to evaluate their efficacy has been performed. Infected pregnant patients must be evaluated individually, and either chloramphenicol (early trimester) or doxycycline (late trimester) may be used if necessary. Antimicrobial therapy should be continued until 2 to 3 days after defervescence. After initiation of therapy, patients become afebrile at a median interval of 3 days. Single-dose doxycycline therapy was effective in nearly 80% of patients in one study[38] but is not routinely advocated because relapse may occur.

Prevention is directed primarily toward the control of flea vectors and potential flea hosts.[9] Because the potential for epidemic spread is associated with foci of infected flea infestations, all suspected cases of murine typhus should be promptly reported to local public health authorities. Although it is usually considered a mild illness, murine typhus may be fatal or severe if misdiagnosed or inadequately treated. Unfortunately, no vaccine of proven effectiveness exists for murine

typhus. Recovery from natural infection confers solid, long-lasting immunity to reinfection.

REFERENCES

1. Azad AF. Epidemiology of murine typhus. Annu Rev Entomol. 1990;35:553-569.
2. Marshall GS. *Rickettsia typhi* seroprevalence among children in the Southeast United States. Tick-Borne Infections in Children Study (TICKS) Group. Pediatr Infect Dis J. 2000;19:1103-1104.
3. Tay ST, Ho TM, Rohani MY, Devi S. Antibodies to *Orientia tsutsugamushi*, *Rickettsia typhi* and spotted fever group rickettsiae among febrile patients in rural areas of Malaysia. Trans R Soc Trop Med Hyg. 2000;94:280-284.
4. Lledó L, Gonzalez MI, Saz JV, Beltrán M. Prevalence of antibodies to *Rickettsia typhi* in an area of the center of Spain. Eur J Epidemiol. 2001;17:927-928.
5. Daniel SA, Manika K, Arvanmdou M, Antoniadis A. Prevalence of *Rickettsia conorii* and *Rickettsia typhi* infections in the population of northern Greece. Am J Trop Med Hyg. 2002;66:76-79.
6. Boostrom A, Beier MS, Macaluso JA, et al. Geographic association of *Rickettsia felis*-infected opossums with human murine typhus, Texas. Emerg Infect Dis. 2002;8:549-554.
7. Dumler JS, Taylor JP, Walker DH. Clinical and laboratory features of murine typhus in south Texas, 1980 through 1987. JAMA. 1991;266:1365-1370.
8. Duffy PE, Le Buillouzic H, Gass RF, et al. Murine typhus identified as a major cause of febrile illness in a camp for displaced Khmers in Thailand. Am J Trop Med Hyg. 1990;43:520-526.
9. Azad AF, Radulovic S, Higgins JA, et al. Flea-borne rickettsioses: Ecologic considerations. Emerg Infect Dis. 1997;3:319-327.
10. Comer JA, Paddock CD, Childs JE. Urban zoonoses caused by *Bartonella*, *Coxiella*, *Ehrlichia*, and *Rickettsia* species. Vector Borne Zoonotic Dis. 2001;1:91-118.
11. Bouyer DH, Stenos J, Crocquet-Valdes P, et al. *Rickettsia felis*: Molecular characterization of a new member of the spotted fever group. Int J Syst Evol Microbiol. 2001;51:339-347.
12. Radulovic S, Higgins JA, Jaworski DC, et al. Isolation, cultivation, and partial characterization of the ELB agent associated with cat fleas. Infect Immun. 1995;63:4826-4829.
13. Sekeyova Z, Roux V, Raoult D. Phylogeny of *Rickettsia* spp. inferred by comparing sequences of 'gene D,' which encodes an intracytoplasmic protein. Int J Syst Evol Microbiol. 2001;51:1353-1360.
14. Radulovic S, Troyer JM, Beier MS, et al. Identification and molecular analysis of the gene encoding *Rickettsia typhi* hemolysin. Infect Immun. 1999;67:6104-6108.
15. Van Kirk LS, Hayes SF, Heinzen RA. Ultrastructure of *Rickettsia rickettsii* actin tails and localization of cytoskeletal proteins. Infect Immun. 2000;68:4706-4713.
16. Traub R, Wisseman CL Jr, Farhang-Azad A. The ecology of murine typhus: A critical review. Trop Dis Bull. 1978;75:237-317.
17. Irons JV, Bohls SW, Thurman DC, et al. Probable role of the cat flea, *Ctenocephalides felis*, in the transmission of murine typhus. Am J Trop Med. 1944;24:359-362.
18. Fan MY, Walker DH, Yu SR, et al. Epidemiology and ecology of rickettsial diseases in the People's Republic of China. Rev Infect Dis. 1987;9:823-840.
19. Dupont HT, Brouqui P, Faugere B, Raoult D. Prevalence of antibodies to *Coxiella burnetii*, *Rickettsia conorii*, and *Rickettsia typhi* in seven African countries. Clin Infect Dis. 1995;21:1126-1133.
20. Bernabeu-Wittel M, Pachon J, Alarcon A, et al. Murine typhus as a common cause of fever of intermediate duration: A 17-year study in the south of Spain. Arch Intern Med. 1999;159:872-876.
21. Gikas A, Doukakis S, Pediaditis J, et al. Murine typhus in Greece: Epidemiological, clinical, and therapeutic data from 83 cases. Trans R Soc Trop Med Hyg. 2002;96:250-253.
22. Abramson MA, Sexton DJ. Diagnosis: Murine typhus (*Rickettsia typhi*). Clin Infect Dis. 1995;21:991.
23. Hassan ISA, Ong ELC. Fever in the returned traveller. Remember murine typhus! J Infect. 1995;31:173-174.
24. Parola P, Vogelaers D, Roure C, et al. Murine typhus in travelers returning from Indonesia. Emerg Infect Dis. 1998;4:677-680.
25. Azad AF, Traub R. Transmission of murine typhus rickettsiae by *Xenopsylla cheopis*, with notes on experimental infection and effects of temperature. Am J Trop Med Hyg. 1985;34:555-563.
26. Azad AF, Traub R, Baqar S. Transovarial transmission of murine typhus rickettsiae in *Xenopsylla cheopis* fleas. Science. 1985;227:543-545.
27. Miller ES, Beeson PB. Murine typhus fever. Medicine. 1946;25:1-15.
28. Walker DH, Parks FM, Betz TB, et al. Histopathology and immunohistologic demonstration of the distribution of *Rickettsia typhi* in fatal murine typhus. Am J Clin Pathol. 1989;91:720-724.
29. Binford CH, Ecker HD. Endemic (murine) typhus. Report of autopsy findings in three cases. Am J Clin Pathol. 1947;17:797-806.
30. Wolbach SB, Todd JL, Palfrey FW. The Etiology and Pathology of Typhus. Cambridge, Mass: Harvard University Press; 1922.
31. Silpapojakul K, Mitarnun W, Ovartlarnporn B, et al. Liver involvement in murine typhus. Q J Med. 1996;89:623-629.
32. Walker DH, Popov VL, Feng H-M. Establishment of a novel endothelial target mouse model of a typhus group rickettsiosis: Evidence for critical roles for gamma interferon at CD8 T lymphocytes. Lab Invest. 2000;80:1361-1372.
33. Crist AE, Wisseman CL, Murphy JR. Characteristics of lymphoid cells that adoptively transfer immunity to *Rickettsia mooseri* infection in mice. Infect Immun. 1984;44:55-60.

34. Rollwagen FM, Dasch GA, Jerrells TR. Mechanisms of immunity to rickettsial infection: Characterization of a cytotoxic effector cell. J Immunol. 1985;136:1418-1421.

35. Bourgeois AL, Dasch GA. The species-specific surface protein antigen of *Rickettsia typhi:* Immunogenicity and protective efficacy in guinea pigs. In: Burgdorfer W, Anacker RL, eds. Rickettsiae and Rickettsial Diseases. New York: Academic Press; 1981.

36. Murphy JR, Wisseman CL Jr, Fiset P. Mechanisms of immunity in typhus infection: Analysis of immunity to *Rickettsia mooseri* infection in guinea pigs. Infect Immun. 1980;27:730-738.

37. Dasch GA, Bourgeois AL, Rollwagen FM. The surface protein antigen of *Rickettsia typhi:* In vitro and in vivo immunogenicity and protective efficacy in mice. In: Raoult D, Brouqui P, eds. Rickettsia and Rickettsial Diseases at the Turn of the Third Millennium. Paris: Elsevier; 1999:116-122.

38. Silpapojakul K, Chayakul P, Krisanapan S. Murine typhus in Thailand: Clinical features, diagnosis and treatment. Q J Med. 1993;86:43-47

39. Tselentis Y, Babalis TL, Chrysanthis D, et al. Clinicoepidemiological study of murine typhus on the Greek island of Evia. Eur J Epidemiol. 1992;8:268-272.

40. Stuart BM, Pullen RL. Endemic (murine) typhus fever: Clinical observations of 180 cases. Ann Intern Med. 1945;23:520-536.

41. Samra Y, Shaked Y, Maier MK. Delayed neurologic display in murine typhus. Report of two cases. Arch Intern Med. 1989;149:949-951.

42. Silpapojakul K, Chupuppakarn S, Yuthasompob S, et al. Scrub and murine typhus in children with obscure fever in the tropics. Pediatr Infect Dis J. 1991;10:200-203.

43. Fergie JE, Purcell K, Wanat D. Murine typhus in South Texas children. Pediatr Infect Dis J. 2000;19:535-538.

44. Whiteford SF, Taylor JP, Dumler JS. Clinical, laboratory, and epidemiologic features of murine typhus in 97 Texas children. Arch Pediatr Adolesc Med. 2001;155:396-400.

45. Silpapojakul K, Ukkachoke C, Krisanapan S, Silpapojakul K. Rickettsial meningitis and encephalitis. Arch Intern Med. 1991;151:1753-1757.

46. Hechemy KE, Stevens RW, Sasowski S, et al. Discrepancies in Weil-Felix and microimmunofluorescence test results for Rocky Mountain spotted fever. J Clin Microbiol. 1979;9:292-293.

47. Kelly DJ, Chan CT, Paxton H, et al. Comparative evaluation of a commercial enzyme immunoassay for the detection of human antibody to *Rickettsia typhi.* Clin Diagn Lab Immunol. 1995;2:356-360.

48. La Scola B, Rydkina L, Ndihokubwayo JB, et al. Serological differentiation of murine typhus and epidemic typhus using cross-adsorption and Western blotting. Clin Diagn Lab Immunol. 2000;7:612-616.

49. Marrero M, Raoult D. Centrifugation-shell vial technique for rapid detection of Mediterranean spotted fever rickettsia in blood culture. Am J Trop Med Hyg. 1989;40:197-199.

50. Walker DH, Feng H-M, Ladner S, et al. Immunohistochemical diagnosis of typhus rickettsioses using an anti-lipopolysaccharide monoclonal antibody. Mod Pathol. 1997;10:1038-1042.

51. Carl M, Tibbs CW, Dobson ME, et al. Diagnosis of acute typhus infection using the polymerase chain reaction. J Infect Dis. 1990;161:791-793.

52. Sorvillo FJ, Gondo B, Emmons R, et al. A suburban focus of endemic typhus in Los Angeles County: Association with seropositive domestic cats and opossums. Am J Trop Med Hyg. 1993;48:269-273.

53. Raoult D, Drancourt M. Antimicrobial therapy of rickettsial diseases. Antimicrob Agents Chemother. 1991;35:2457-2462.

54. Strand Ö, Strömberg A. Case report. Ciprofloxacin treatment of murine typhus. Scand J Infect Dis. 1990;22:503-504.

55. Laferl H, Fournier PE, Seiberl G, et al. Murine typhus poorly responsive to ciprofloxacin: A case report. J Travel Med. 2002;9:103-104.

56. Keren G, Itzhaki A, Oron C, Keysary A. Evaluation of the anti-rickettsial activity of fluoroquinolones. Drugs. 1995;49(Suppl 2):208-210.

57. Keysary A, Itzhaki A, Rubinstein E, et al. The in-vitro anti-rickettsial activity of macrolides. J Antimicrob Chemother. 1996;38:727-731.

CHAPTER **189**

Scrub Typhus

DIDIER RAOULT

Scrub typhus is a rickettsiosis caused by *Orientia tsutsugamushi* and transmitted by a chigger bite. It is a rural disease prevalent in a wide part of the world. Its distribution is documented in a triangle limited by northern Japan, eastern Australia, and eastern Russia that includes the Indian subcontinent, western Russia, China, and the Far East. It has been known in the Far East for more than 1500 years. One billion people live in the endemic area. As many as 1 million may be infected yearly (Fig. 189-1).

ETIOLOGY

O. tsutsugamushi is a rickettsial organism formerly named *Rickettsia tsutsugamushi* (until 1995).[1] This bacterium exhibits a wide heterogenicity that may lead to the defining of several species in this genus. Major serotypes have been identified and must be included in serologic tests to detect scrub typhus, including serotypes Gilliam, Karp, Kato, Boryon, and Kawazaki. These antigens exhibit enough cross-reactivity to detect all cases of scrub typhus. *O. tsutsugamushi* is transmitted by the bite of thrombiculid mite larvae (chiggers). It is transmitted transovarially in mites and generates a deviation of the sex ratio in infected females that favors females. Seasonality of the disease is determined by the appearance of larvae. In temperate zones, scrub typhus season is observed mainly in autumn but also in spring.

EPIDEMIOLOGY

The disease has been known since ancient times. The first description was documented in 313 AD in China. Scrub typhus is a common disease in endemic areas. Chiggers are prevalent in rural areas, and local residents as well as tourists are exposed to their bite. In the past, military personnel, during wars in the Far East, were frequently infected, and it may have been one of the first infections they experienced. In Vietnam, during the war, it was the second or third most common cause of fever in American soldiers.[2,3] Its current prevalence is not known, but in Thailand, along with leptospirosis, it is one of the two most frequent infections reported in hospitalized patients. It is also common in India but is apparently grossly underreported.

CLINICAL MANIFESTATIONS

The major symptoms of scrub typhus include fever, mental changes, headache, inoculation eschar, and lymphadenopathy (Table 189-1).[4,5] Ten or more days after exposure, the onset of the disease is abrupt with fever, headache, and myalgia. Ability to differentiate the eschar from the mite bite, as with tick-borne disease, highly depends on the inves-

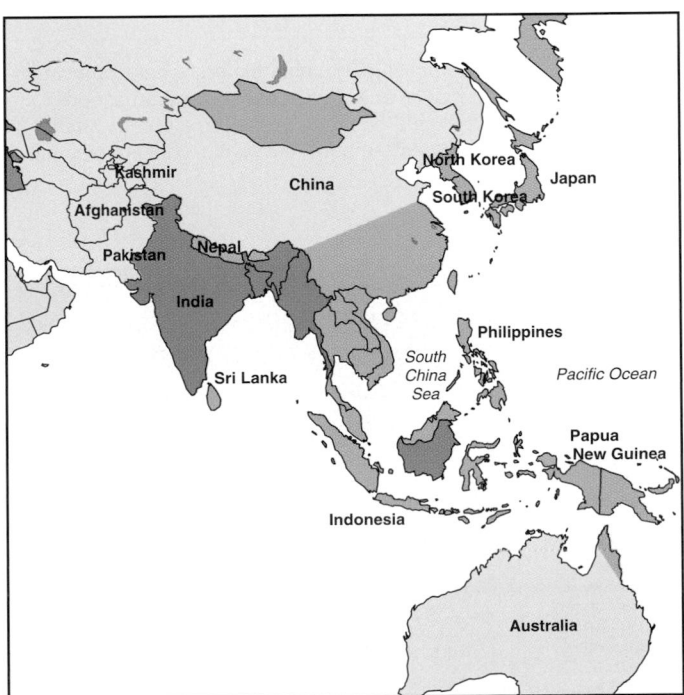

FIGURE 189-1. Geographic distribution of scrub typhus. Darker colors have a higher incidence.

tigators. In a survey in Japan, where it was considered prevalent in 50% of cases, a trained physician found it in 100% of cases.[6] The patient can have several eschars. The rash is macular, pale, and transient and is easily missed. Lymph nodes may be tender and are sometimes limited to the site proximal to the mite bite. Hepatomegaly and splenomegaly can be observed. Mental changes are usual and range from slight intellectual blunting to coma or delirium.[4]

In severe cases, evolution to a multiple organ dysfunction syndrome with hemorrhage can be observed. After apparent recovery, relapses frequently occur and may also follow short treatment courses. Relapse is usually less severe than the first attack. Surprisingly, scrub typhus has been reported to lead to a diminution of viral load in human immunodeficiency virus (HIV)-1 infected patients and to help restore the immune status of infected patients.[7] A wide variation in prevalence of cutaneous symptoms has been noted, as well as in severity and fatality rate. This varies with published series, year of publication, and country and population studied. The fatality rate during scrub typhus before the advent of chemotherapy was widely variable[6] from 3% in Taiwan to 60% on the northern coast of Japan. It is still a life-threatening disease despite efficient treatment. During pregnancy, scrub typhus frequently leads to spontaneous abortion.[8]

Biologically, lymphocyte count is decreased and the T4:T8 ratio is diminished. Liver enzymes are increased in 60% of cases. Thrombocytopenia may be sufficient to cause bleeding.

DIAGNOSIS

Serology is the preferred diagnostic tool. Immunofluorescence and immunoperoxidase are the most reliable. Five strains must be tested: Kawazaki, Karp, Gilliam, Kato, and Boryon. Weil-Felix tests detect cross-reacting antibodies to *Proteus mirabilis* OX-K. The Weil-Felix test is still used because of its low cost. Isolation of *O. tsutsugamushi* can be done in cell culture or in inoculated mice. The organism is visualized in the spleens of infected mice by Giemsa (or Diff Quick) staining (not by Gimenez stain as is used for *Rickettsia*). Polymerase chain reaction amplification of blood, skin, or lymph node samples is useful. Usually, the primers are selected from the gene that codes for the 56-kDa protein gene.[9]

TREATMENT[10]

Doxycycline and chloramphenicol remain the preferred treatment approaches. Doxycycline given in a single dose or for short periods (3 to 7 days) is effective. It should be recommended for use in children as well. Parola and associates[10] report that some patients responded poorly to doxycycline and chloramphenicol. Alternative drugs, including rifampin (600–900 mg/day) and azithromycin (500 mg the first day and 250 mg/day later), can also be prescribed in pregnant women. Ciprofloxacin, in experience with parturient women in India, is ineffective and should not be used.[8]

Prevention is limited to the use of repellents during travel in rural areas of endemic countries.

REFERENCES

1. Tamura A, Ohashi N, Urakami H, Miyamura S. Classification of *Rickettsia tsutsugamushi* in a new genus, *Orientia* gen nov, as *Orientia tsutsugamushi* comb. nov. Int J Syst Bacteriol. 1995;45:589-591.
2. Deller JJ, Russell PK. An analysis of fevers of unknown origin in American soldiers in Vietnam. Ann Intern Med. 1967;66:1129-1143.
3. Berman SJ, Irving GS, Kundin WD, et al. Epidemiology of the acute fevers of unknown origin in South Vietnam: Effect of laboratory support upon clinical diagnosis. Am J Trop Med Hyg. 1973;22:796-801.
4. Tattersall RN. *Tsutsugamushi* fever on the India-Burma border. Lancet. 1945;2:392-394.
5. Berman SJ, Kundin WD. Scrub typhus in South Vietnam. A study of 87 cases. Ann Intern Med. 1973;79:26-30.
6. Kawamura AJ, Tanaka H, Tamura A. Tsutsugamushi Disease. Tokyo: University of Tokyo Press; 1995.
7. Watt G, Kantipong P, de Souza M, et al. HIV-1 suppression during acute scrub-typhus infection. Lancet. 2000;356:475-479.
8. Mathai E, Rolain JM, Verghese L, et al. Scrub typhus in pregnancy as a cause of abortions in India is not prevented by ciprofloxacin. Trans R Soc Trop Med Hyg. 2004. In press.
9. Furuya Y, Yoshida Y, Katayama T, et al. Specific amplification of *Rickettsia tsutsugamushi* DNA from clinical specimens by polymerase chain reaction. J Clin Microbiol. 1991;29:2628-2630.
10. Parola P, Watt G, Brouqui P. *Orientia tsutsugamushi* (scrub typhus). In: Yu VL, Weber R, Raoult D, eds. Antimicrobial Therapy and Vaccine. 2nd ed. New York: Apple Trees Production, LLC; 2002:883-887.

CHAPTER **190**

Ehrlichia chaffeensis (Human Monocytotropic Ehrlichiosis), *Anaplasma phagocytophilum* (Human Granulocytotropic Anaplasmosis), and Other Ehrlichieae

DAVID H. WALKER

J. STEPHEN DUMLER

Until 1987, infections by members of the family Anaplasmataceae, including the genera *Ehrlichia, Anaplasma,* and *Neorickettsia,* were known mainly as veterinary diseases (Table 190-1). Canine ehrlichiosis was first described in 1935 by Donatien and Lestoquard in Algeria. This disease is produced by *Ehrlichia canis* transmitted to dogs by *Rhipicephalus sanguineus* ticks. The disease was characterized by fever associated with the presence of clusters of small Giemsa-stained organisms in circulating monocytes. *Ehrlichia* spp. generally have a tick vector and tropism for either macrophages or granulocytes where they grow within cytoplasmic, membrane-bound vacuoles. Consequently, *Ehrlichia* was recognized as distinct from other genera of obligate intracellular bacteria of medical importance (*Rickettsia, Coxiella,* and *Chlamydia*). In 1937, the genus *Ehrlichia* was suggested

TABLE 189-1 Scrub Typhus: Prevalence of Signs and Symptoms

Authors	Berman and Kundin[5]	Tattersall[4]
Year	1973	1945
Number of cases	87	500
Location	South Vietnam	India/Burma
Population	Soldiers	Soldiers and local
Fever	100%	
Mental changes		100%
Headache	100%	100%
Cough	45%	68%
Myalgia	32%	
Nausea	28%	
Adenopathy	85%	92%
Eschar	46%	11%
Splenomegaly	43%	47%
Rash	34%	64%
Conjunctivitis and conjunctival suffusion	29%	
Case-fatality rate		6%

TABLE 190-1 Ehrlichiae Causing Medical and Veterinary Diseases

Etiologic Agent	Mammalian Host	Major Target Cell	Vector/Transmission
Ehrlichia chaffeensis	Humans, deer, dogs, coyotes	Macrophages	Ticks *(Amblyomma americanum, Dermacentor variabilis,* and *Ixodes pacificus)*
Ehrlichia ewingii	Dogs, humans, deer	Granulocytes	Ticks *(A. americanum, D. variabilis)*
Ehrlichia muris	Humans, *Apodemus* mice, vole	Unknown	Ticks *(Ixodes persulcatus, Haemaphysalis flava)*
Ehrlichia canis	Dogs, humans	Macrophages	Ticks *(Rhipicephalus sanguineus)*
Ehrlichia ruminantium	Cattle, wild ruminants	Endothelial cells	Ticks *(Amblyomma variegatum)*
Anaplasma phagocytophilum	Humans, white-footed mice, wood rats, bank voles, wood mice, yellow-necked mice, horses, dogs, cats, sheep, cattle, white-tailed deer, roe deer, red deer, fallow deer	Granulocytes	Ticks *(Ixodes scapularis, Ixodes pacificus, Ixodes ricinus, Ixodes persulcatus)*
Anaplasma platys	Dogs	Platelets, macrophages	
Anaplasma marginale	Cattle, wild ruminants	Erythrocytes	Unknown
Neorickettsia sennetsu	Humans	Macrophages	Ticks *(Boophilus, Rhipicephalus,* and others)
Neorickettsia risticii	Horses	Macrophages, enterocytes, mast cells	Possibly ingestion of raw fish
			Unknown
Neorickettsia helminthoeca	Dogs	Macrophages	
			Ingestion of fluke-infested salmon

in honor of the German bacteriologist Paul Ehrlich.[1] Subsequent phylogenetic studies have shown that two other economically important veterinary pathogens, *Anaplasma marginale* (described in 1910) and *Ehrlichia* (formerly *Cowdria*) *ruminantium* (described in 1925), are also ehrlichiae.[2] The first human disease demonstrated to have an ehrlichial etiology was sennetsu neorickettsiosis, an infectious mononucleosis–like illness recognized to have occurred only in western Japan and Malaysia.[3] Although human infections caused by all members of the reorganized family Anaplasmataceae have been generically referred to as "ehrlichiosis" and the causative agents are referred to as "ehrlichiae," it is increasingly apparent that the clinical manifestations and etiologic agents are distinct.[2]

The first diagnosed case of human ehrlichiosis in the United States occurred in a 51-year-old man who became ill in April 1986, 12 to 14 days after tick bites in rural Arkansas.[4] His severe course of illness was characterized by fever, hypotension, confusion, acute renal failure requiring hemodialysis, pancytopenia, coagulopathy, cutaneous and gastrointestinal hemorrhages, and hepatocellular injury. The diagnosis of ehrlichial infection was documented by observation of 2-to 5-μm morulae (cytoplasmic vacuoles containing ehrlichial organisms) in 1% to 2% of circulating leukocytes (Fig. 190-1). Electron microscopy demonstrated that the inclusions represented membrane-bound vacuoles containing up to 40 bacteria with a diameter of 0.2 to 0.8 μm and a gram-negative cell wall. Moreover, the patient's serum contained antibodies reactive at a high titer with *E. canis,* which is genetically and antigenically closely related to the subsequently identified *Ehrlichia chaffeensis,*[5] the etiologic agent of human monocytotropic ehrlichiosis (HME). In 1994, *Anaplasma phagocytophilum* was identified as the causative agent of a distinctly different infection, now called human anaplasmosis or human granulocytotropic anaplasmosis (HGA).[6,7]

ETIOLOGY

Members of the family Anaplasmataceae are defined not only by their phenotypic characteristics and their host affinities (see Table 190-1) but also by their genetic similarities and differences. These are small (0.5 μm) gram-negative bacteria. Their clustered inclusion-like appearance in the host cell vacuoles is called a morula, from the Latin word for mulberry.

The taxonomic relationships of *Ehrlichia, Anaplasma, Neorickettsia, Wolbachia, Orientia, Rickettsia, Coxiella,* and *Chlamydia* have been clarified by molecular genetic and metabolic

studies.[2] The evolutionary relationships determined by 16S ribosomal RNA gene (*rrs*) and *groESL* comparisons indicate that *Ehrlichia, Anaplasma, Neorickettsia, Wolbachia, Orientia,* and *Rickettsia* evolved from a common ancestor[2,5]; in contrast, *Coxiella* and *Chlamydia* are phylogenetically unrelated to ehrlichiae. Ehrlichiae and chlamydiae superficially resemble one another in that both reside within cytoplasmic vacuoles. Unlike chlamydiae, however, ehrlichiae are able to synthesize adenosine triphosphate by metabolism of glutamine, a metabolic characteristic shared with members of the genus *Rickettsia.* Within the phylogeny of ehrlichiae are four genera that are actually very different from one another.[2] *E. chaffeensis* shares many antigens and genetic sequences with the canine pathogens, *E. canis* and *Ehrlichia ewingii*[8]; *Ehrlichia muris* found in Japanese wild mice, voles, and ticks; and the ruminant pathogen, *E. ruminantium.*[5,8-10] A second genus includes a human granulocytotropic organism,

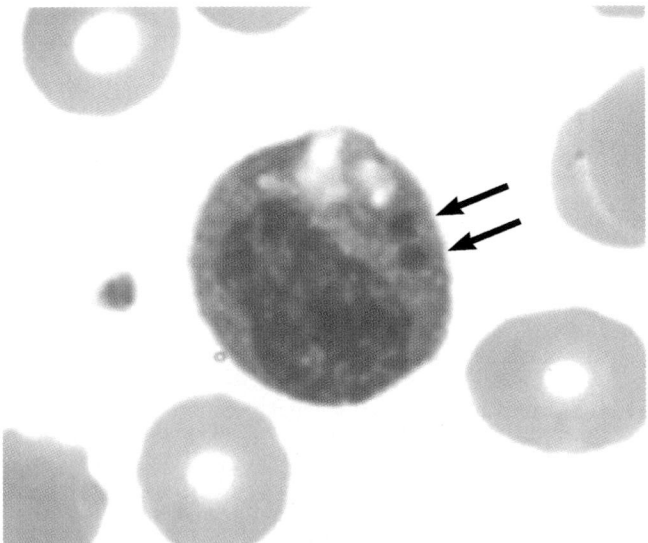

FIGURE 190-1. Peripheral blood smear (buffy coat preparation) showing intracellular inclusions (*arrows*) in mononuclear cells of a patient with human monocytotropic ehrlichiosis. (Wright stain, original magnification, ×400.)

A. phagocytophilum, that is related genetically to *Anaplasma platys* and *A. marginale.*[2,7] The third contains *Neorickettsia sennetsu,* which is closely related to *Neorickettsia risticii, Neorickettsia helminthoeca,* and an unnamed organism found in Japanese fish flukes.[11,12] The fourth genus, *Wolbachia,* contains bacterial endosymbionts of invertebrates, including insects and helminths—some of which may contribute to disease in human filariasis.[13] Contemporary methods are both discovering and characterizing ehrlichieae at a greatly accelerating pace.

Ehrlichia and *Anaplasma* have two ultrastructural forms, a larger reticulate cell and a smaller, dense-core cell, and the cell wall differs from that of *Rickettsia* spp., with thinner outer and inner leaflets reflecting the absence of lipopolysaccharide and lipooligosaccharide.[14] Genes coding for the enzymes required for the biosynthesis of peptidoglycan are not present in the *Ehrlichia chaffeensis* genome. The genomes of these obligately intracellular bacteria are small, ranging from 1.2 to 1.6 Mb to as low as 900 kb for *Neorickettsia.* Bacteria in the Anaplasmataceae family possess multiple genes that are members of the pfam01617.8, Surface_Ag_2 gene family, encoding major surface porin proteins responsible for antigenic variation and host cell adhesion in genera as diverse as *Neisseria, Brucella,* and *Pseudomonas.* *E. chaffeensis, E. canis,* and *A. phagocytophilum* have gene families that encode more than 20 paralogous, surface-exposed pfam01617.8 proteins of 22 to 30 kD (p28s) for *Ehrlichia* and of 41 to 49 kD (major surface protein-2 [Msp2]) for *A. phagocytophilum.*[15-17] In accordance with the pfam01617.8 predictions, roles for *A. phagocytophilum* Msp2 in binding to surfaces of neutrophils and in antigenic variation have been shown.[18,19] Interstrain antigenic diversity is based upon the presence of three hypervariable regions in the *Ehrlichia* p28 family, and Msp2 of *Anaplasma* is characterized by conserved domains that flank a hypervariable region.[9,15,16,20-23] Analysis of *Ehrlichia p28* genes has revealed evolution of three main genetic strains.[24] Reinfection with a different strain has been reported in a liver transplant recipient.[25] Among the other major protein antigens of *E. chaffeensis* and *A. phagocytophilum,* a 58-kD analogue of the GroEL stress protein and other proteins share antigens and genetic homology with many other ehrlichiae.[9,26] In addition, *E. chaffeensis* and *E. canis* have a 19- to 21-kD major surface protein and two antigenic glycoproteins. One of the glycoproteins comprises approximately 50% O-linked carbohydrates, is surface exposed, contains two to five tandem repeat regions, and plays a role in adhesion to the target cell.[27,28] An orthologue of this protein is also found in *A. phagocytophilum,* but it is undetermined whether it has a role in target cell adhesion.[29]

EPIDEMIOLOGY OF HUMAN MONOCYTIC EHRLICHIOSIS

Human ehrlichioses in the United States are tick-borne zoonoses.[6,30-45] The vast majority of patients give a history of tick exposure during the month before the onset of illness. The seasonality of HME with peak incidence in May to July reflects the tick-transmitted epidemiology. Exposures are predominantly rural and suburban and involve recreational, peridomestic, occupational, and military activities. More than 75% of patients are male. Documented cases of HME have been reported in 47 states particularly in the south-central and southeastern United States. This region conforms to the distribution of the Lone Star tick, *Amblyomma americanum,* which along with white-tailed deer maintains the ehrlichiae in nature by acquiring *E. chaffeensis* during feeding as a larva or nymph on persistently infected deer and subsequently transmitting ehrlichiae to nonimmune deer.[32] The pathogen is transmitted transstadially from larvae to nymphs and from nymphs to adults, but, as with related species, *E. chaffeensis* is unlikely to be transmitted transovarially.[46] On the other hand, HME cases reported in western states suggest the likelihood of travel-acquired infections as well as additional vectors, including *Dermacentor variabilis* and *Ixodes pacificus,* which have been found to be naturally infected.[30,47-49] Organisms closely related to *E. chaffeensis* and evidence of human ehrlichial infections have also been reported in eastern Asia.[50]

In a prospective study of hospitalized patients in Georgia, 11% with fever of undetermined cause were demonstrated by seroconver-

sion to have HME.[39] In Oklahoma, the state with the highest incidence of Rocky Mountain spotted fever, HME is at least as prevalent. In the Piedmont of North Carolina, where many cases of Rocky Mountain spotted fever occur, a prospective study identified an even greater number of cases of HME.[40] An active, prospective, 3-year study in Cape Girardeau, Missouri revealed an annual incidence of 11 cases per 100,000 population, with one family physician's practice having 100 cases per 100,000 population.[41]

Currently, most infections are not diagnosed. HME is a life-threatening disease with hospitalization in 41% to 63% of cases; thus, it is suspected that asymptomatic seroconversion reflects exposure to another *Ehrlichia* or *Anaplasma* species or other antigenic stimulus.[51] *E. canis* has been isolated from the blood of an asymptomatic persistently infected person in South America.[52] There is a potential for transfusion-transmitted HME.[53]

Epidemiology and Epizootiology of Human Granulocytic Anaplasmosis

HGA has a seasonal occurrence with a bimodal distribution peaking in July and again in November in accordance with the activity of nymphal and adult stages of *Ixodes scapularis* ticks, respectively, in the eastern United States.[43] Although risk for HGA is associated with outdoor activity, a substantial proportion of cases occurs in suburban areas of northeastern and upper midwestern cities.[43,45] HGA cases are concentrated in southern New England, New York State, northwest Wisconsin, eastern Minnesota, and northern California. The distribution is identical to that of Lyme disease owing to the shared *Ixodes* spp. tick vectors. In Europe, HGA has been documented in Slovenia, Sweden, and the Czech Republic, and serologic evidence from many other European and Asian countries suggests a worldwide distribution for *A. phagocytophilum* and its tick vectors.[54]

The incidence of HGA is not known; however, active case collection yielded an incidence of 14 to 16 cases per 100,000 population in the upper Midwest between 1990 and 1995, with rates as high as 24 to 58 cases per 100,000 population in certain northwest Wisconsin counties in 1994 to 1995 and in Connecticut in 1997 to 1999.[43,44] Cross-sectional seroprevalence studies have shown that approximately 15% of the population in northwestern Wisconsin, 1% of Connecticut residents, and 12% of the entire population of Sweden's Koster Islands have antibodies reactive with *A. phagocytophilum* in the absence of antecedent evidence for HGA.[55,56] A similar seroprevalence exists in New York State but is attributed to nonspecificity in the analytical method.[57] The demonstration of mildly affected patients who recover spontaneously, even in the absence of specific therapy, suggests that HGA may frequently be subclinical or asymptomatic.[58]

Between 6% and 21% of patients with HGA also have serologic evidence of *Borrelia burgdorferi* or *Babesia microti* infection, both agents also transmitted by *Ixodes* spp. tick bites.[55,59-61] Concurrent human granulocytic ehrlichiosis and Lyme disease, documented by isolation of both agents, has been reported.[62] Whether concurrent infection by these agents allows increased severity, prolonged duration of illness, or more frequent and severe sequelae has yet to be determined.[63]

A. phagocytophilum is transmitted to humans by the bites of nymphal and adult *I. scapularis* in the eastern United States, *I. pacificus* in California, *Ixodes ricinus* ticks in Europe, and presumably *Ixodes persulcatus* in Asia. Although transstadial transmission of the infectious agent occurs, *A. phagocytophilum* is not maintained transovarially, and thus natural maintenance requires horizontal (tick-mammal-tick) transmission.[35,64] A major proven reservoir host is the white-footed mouse, *Peromyscus leucopus*; however, other small mammals and ruminants have been found naturally infected or have serologic evidence of infection, including voles, wood rats, white-tailed deer, red deer, and roe deer.[35,65-68] Current serologic evidence suggests that larval ticks acquire *A. phagocytophilum* after feeding upon small mammals infected earlier in the season by nymphal ticks. White-footed mice develop immunity to *A. phagocytophilum* after a period of bacteremia that may last from several days to weeks and may reduce transmission.[35,65,69-70] Small mammals are not adversely affected by the infection, and some may become persistently infected.[35,69] The contribution of persistently infected ruminants and cervids as reservoir hosts requires further investigation.[71]

PATHOGENESIS AND PATHOLOGY

Pathology and Pathogenesis of Human Monocytotropic Ehrlichiosis

After entering the skin by tick bite inoculation and being spread presumably through lymphatic and blood vessels, ehrlichiae invade their target cells of the hematopoietic and lymphoreticular systems. Morulae of *E. chaffeensis* have been observed mainly in macrophages and monocytes, less frequently in lymphocytes, and rarely in polymorphonuclear leukocytes.[4,72-76] Ehrlichial morulae have been identified in peripheral blood, bone marrow, hepatic sinusoids, lymph nodes, splenic cords, splenic sinusoids, splenic periarteriolar lymphoid sheaths, cerebrospinal fluid (CSF) macrophages, and macrophages within perivascular lymphohistiocytic infiltrates in organs such as the kidney, appendix, and heart.

The best studied tissue in HME is bone marrow, largely owing to the frequency of leukopenia, thrombocytopenia, and anemia. Frequent findings include granulomas, myeloid hyperplasia, and megakaryocytosis.[72] Erythrophagocytosis and plasmacytosis occur in smaller proportions of patients with HME. Focal hepatocellular necrosis; hepatic granulomas including ring granulomas; cholestasis; splenic and lymph node necrosis; diffuse mononuclear phagocyte hyperplasia of the spleen, liver, lymph node, and bone marrow; perivascular lymphohistiocytic infiltrates of various organs including kidney, heart, liver, meninges and brain; and interstitial mononuclear cell pneumonitis have also been observed.[74-76] It is worthy of emphasis that endothelial injury and thrombosis have not been described. Analysis of the mechanisms of thrombocytopenia in acute canine ehrlichiosis reveals increased platelet destruction with splenic sequestration and consequent accelerated release of platelets from bone marrow when counts are less than 100,000/μL. The observation of erythrophagocytosis, myeloid hyperplasia, and megakaryocytosis in the bone marrow of patients with HME suggests peripheral consumption of blood elements and a compensatory response.

Although *E. chaffeensis* causes a direct cytopathic effect when grown in cell culture, it appears that the host responses account for some of the clinical manifestations.[77,78] The toxic shock manifestations of HME are likely to be the systemic effects of proinflammatory cytokines including tumor necrosis factor-γ. Interferon-γ stimulates macrophage killing of *E. chaffeensis* through the sequestration of iron, and opsonization with immune serum enhances the destruction of ehrlichieae by macrophages.[79,80] *E. chaffeensis* circumvents host defenses by inhibiting the fusion of infected phagosomes with lysosomes, inhibiting the signal transduction pathway of interferon-γ–mediated antiehrlichial activity, and increasing transferrin receptor delivery of iron to the ehrlichial vacuole.[81,82] Ehrlichial infection is controlled by a combination of CD4 and CD8 T lymphocytes, antibodies, interferon-α, and tumor necrosis factor-α. The disease caused by *E. chaffeensis* is partly determined by host immunologic and inflammatory responses.

Pathology and Pathogenesis of Human Granulocytotropic Anaplasmosis

A. phagocytophilum are observed predominantly in neutrophils in the peripheral blood and tissues from infected individuals.[43,45,76,83] The most dramatic histopathologic findings involve the presence of opportunistic pathogens, especially severe fungal and viral infections. Similar changes are well documented in ruminants with tick-borne fever caused by *A. phagocytophilum* infection. Experimental tickborne fever is associated with impairment of T-lymphocyte proliferation to mitogens; decreased circulating CD4, CD8, and CD5 cells; weak antibody responses to vaccines; and impairment of neutrophil recruitment and phagocytosis.[84] Other pathologic findings in humans

and animal models include normocellular or hypercellular bone marrow, erythrophagocytosis in mononuclear phagocytic organs, hepatic apoptosis and periportal lymphohistiocytic infiltrates, focal splenic necrosis, and mild interstitial pneumonitis and pulmonary hemorrhage.[76,85] Vasculitis, endothelial injury, granulomas, and meningeal inflammation have not been described.

A. phagocytophilum disseminate to bone marrow and spleen after a tick bite. In the bone marrow, progenitors of myeloid and monocytic lineages are infected.[86] The ehrlichiae attach to host cell surface platelet selectin ligand-1 (PSGL-1), and perhaps other ligands, and enter an endosome that avoids lysosomal fusion.[87,88] Within this vacuole, the ehrlichiae survive and divide. In vitro, *A. phagocytophilum* survive by deactivation of neutrophils through inhibition of *rac2* transcription, downregulation of phagocyte oxidase activity, delay of apoptosis, ineffective binding to and transmigration of activated endothelium, and inhibition of phagocytic activity.[89-93] Yet, infection also paradoxically stimulates neutrophil activation with chemokine secretion and degranulation.[92,94] Increased proinflammatory activity allows the recruitment of additional host neutrophil cells and localized tissue injury when neutrophils are unable to generate effective antimicrobial responses that may further exacerbate inflammatory stimulation. These findings are consistent with the dissociation of bacterial burden and histopathologic evidence of tissue injury in the mouse model, suggesting a role for host immunity in disease.[95] Approximately 25% and 100% of patients develop specific antibodies detectable at presentation and after 30 days, respectively.[43]

CLINICAL MANIFESTATIONS

Human Monocytotropic Ehrlichiosis

Signs and Symptoms

Thousands of cases of HME have been diagnosed. The clinical picture in immunocompetent patients is of a mild to severe multisystemic illness with a median duration of 23 days (Table 190-2).[4,36-42,74,75,96-98] In severely immunocompromised patients, *E. chaffeensis* acts as an opportunistic pathogen and can cause a fatal overwhelming infection.[99-103] The median incubation period is 7 days. Symptoms at onset of illness include fever, chills, headache, myalgia, and malaise.

TABLE 190-2 Clinical and Laboratory Abnormalities in Human Monocytic Ehrlichial and Granulocytic Anaplasmosis

Sign, Symptom, or Laboratory Finding	HME Patients with Abnormal Findings (%)	HGA Patients with Abnormal Findings (%)
Fever	97	94-100
Headache	81	61-85
Chills or rigors	67	39-98
Myalgia	68	78-98
Malaise	84	98
Nausea	48	39
Anorexia	66	37
Vomiting	37	34
Diarrhea	25	22
Abdominal pain	22	
Rash	36	2-11
Cough	26	29
Dyspnea	23	
Lymphadenopathy	25	
Confusion	20	17
Leukopenia	60	50-59
Thrombocytopenia	68	59-92
Elevated AST	86	69-91
Elevated ALT	80	61
Elevated urea nitrogen	38	
Elevated creatinine	29	70

ALT, alanine aminotransferase; AST, aspartate aminotransferase; HGA, human granulocytotropic anaplasmosis; HME, human monocytotropic ehrlichiosis.

Later in the course, patients often develop nausea, anorexia, vomiting, and weight loss. Physical signs are not striking. Fewer than half of patients have a rash, which is maculopapular and may be petechial. Rash has been observed more frequently in children. Adult patients with severe illness are more likely to have a cough, diarrhea, confusion, and lymphadenopathy, whereas pediatric patients may develop edema of the hands or feet. Severe complications include adult respiratory distress syndrome (18% require mechanical ventilation), acute renal insufficiency, central nervous system (CNS) abnormalities including meningoencephalitis, coagulopathy, gastrointestinal hemorrhage, and even death.[36,42,73-76,97-99,104] CSF pleocytosis usually contains a predominance of lymphocytes and increased protein concentration and may demonstrate the presence of infected cells.[73] Nearly half of patients with chest roentgenographic evaluation have infiltrates.

Important laboratory features are thrombocytopenia, mild to moderate leukopenia, and elevations of serum hepatic transaminases (see Table 190-2).[36,42] The nadir of leukopenia is usually between 1300 and 4000 cells/μL. Neutropenia, lymphopenia, or both combined account for the leukopenia. Thrombocytopenia occurs concurrently with leukopenia and is usually between 50,000 and 140,000 platelets/μL although occasionally severe (<20,000 platelets/μL).[36]

Course

The clinical course of illness ranges from mild illness to a fatal outcome. The patients from whom E. chaffeensis has been isolated reflect this clinical variation in severity. A 72-year-old man had a near-fatal multisystemic febrile illness with CNS involvement, acute renal failure requiring hemodialysis, respiratory failure requiring intubation, and a 4.5-week hospitalization.[73] A 21-year-old soldier was ill for 4 days with fever, headache, pharyngitis, nausea, vomiting, cervical lymphadenopathy, and splenomegaly.[105] He defervesced 24 to 48 hours after initiation of tetracycline treatment and did not require hospitalization. The higher incidence in older patients suggests the importance of host factors in disease severity. A virulent form of HME occurs in human immunodeficiency virus–infected individuals that is often associated with overwhelming infection, a toxic shock– or sepsis-like syndrome, and fatality.[99,101,103] Immune compromise related to corticosteroid therapy or immunosuppression with organ transplantation is also associated with increased severity.[25,102]

The median duration of hospitalization is about a week. Convalescence is often prolonged. Persistent infection has been documented in only one patient with HME.[75] Fatalities have occurred in approximately 3%.[76] Many patients treated with doxycycline or tetracycline recover rapidly. On the other hand, most patients receiving no effective antiehrlichial treatment have had uncomplicated complete recovery.

Diagnosis

A diagnosis based on epidemiologic and clinical factors offers the opportunity to administer empirical antiehrlichial treatment. However, the physician's index of suspicion must be high or an early diagnosis is not made. Patients presenting with fever, leukopenia, thrombocytopenia, elevated serum transaminases, and a history of recent tick bite in endemic regions from May through July should be considered as possibly having HME. No absolute clinical criteria distinguish HME from Rocky Mountain spotted fever, although patients with ehrlichiosis are less likely to have a rash and more likely to have leukopenia (median white blood cell count, 3500/μL). Although the first recognized case of HME was diagnosed by visualization of ehrlichial morulae in circulating leukocytes, morulae have been observed subsequently in less than 7% of patients with HME, most often in immunocompromised patients with overwhelming ehrlichiosis.[106]

The "gold standard" for etiologic diagnosis of infectious disease, cultivation of the agent, has been achieved in one large series of cases of HME,[107] but culture is a research approach at the present time.[20,103,105,108] Specialized methods employing unique cell lines may require longer than 1 month to detect ehrlichieae.

At present, the major diagnostic criterion for human ehrlichiosis is serologic, as determined by indirect immunofluorescence assay (IFA) with E. chaffeensis–infected cells. To be considered positive, the patient's sera must show a fourfold or greater rise or fall in antibody titer during the course of the disease, with a minimal peak titer of 64.[36,109]

IFA shows a peak geometric mean titer of 1280 at 6 weeks after onset.[109] Only 22% of the sera tested in the first week of illness have a titer of 80 or greater. Among sera from patients tested in the second week, 68% are diagnostic. Sera tested 4 or more weeks after the onset of illness should demonstrate seroconversion.

Immunohistologic demonstration of ehrlichial morulae provides a timely specific diagnosis.[72,74,75,110] Unfortunately, a patient's sample that is readily available and reliably contains demonstrable organisms has not been identified. Thus, this approach is relatively unused. A polymerase chain reaction (PCR) method employing E. chaffeensis–specific primers for amplification and detection of ehrlichial DNA from peripheral blood appears to be the most sensitive technique for a timely laboratory diagnosis of active infection.[30,111]

Differential Diagnosis

Early in the course of the disease, when the patient presents with fever, headache, myalgia, and malaise, the differential diagnoses may include various viral syndromes, Rocky Mountain spotted fever, upper respiratory illness, sepsis, and urinary tract infection. If nausea, vomiting, and anorexia are prominent symptoms, gastroenteritis is often included. If cough is prominent, pneumonia is often considered. CNS signs and symptoms with CSF pleocytosis suggest viral or bacterial meningoencephalitis. On obtaining a history of recent tick bite, the physician may consider tick-borne febrile illnesses such as Rocky Mountain spotted fever, relapsing fever, tularemia, Lyme borreliosis, Colorado tick fever, and babesiosis. Other diagnostic considerations include meningococcemia, toxic shock syndrome, leptospirosis, hepatitis, enteroviral infection, influenza, murine typhus, Q fever, typhoid fever, bacterial sepsis, endocarditis, Kawasaki disease, collagen-vascular diseases, and leukemia. A comparison of the ehrlichioses and Rocky Mountain spotted fever is presented in Table 190-3.

TABLE 190-3 Comparison of Ehrlichiosis and Anaplasmosis in the United States with Rocky Mountain Spotted Fever (RMSF)

Similarities
History of tick attachment
Incubation period of about 1 week between tick bite and onset of symptoms
Peak incidence in late spring and summer
Acute onset with headache, fever, myalgia, and malaise; cough, dyspnea, and vomiting present less commonly
Severe cases may have coagulopathy, azotemia, and encephalopathy
WBC count usually not elevated, platelet count often low, AST (SGOT) may be increased
Diagnosis by acute and convalescent serology
Treatment—a tetracycline (chloramphenicol may not be effective for ehrlichioses)

Differences
RMSF—rash is present in 90% of patients and is petechial in about half the cases
Ehrlichiosis and anaplasmosis—rash is present in less than half of adult patients with HME and rarely in HGA, is maculopapular, and is rarely petechial
Leukopenia and absolute lymphopenia and neutropenia are common in hospitalized patients with HME and neutropenia in those with HGA, but are uncommon in RMSF
Inclusions (morulae) may be seen rarely in monocytes and macrophages of patients with HME, occasionally in neutrophils of patients with HGA, but not with RMSF
Vasculitis, the pathologic hallmark of RMSF, is not observed in the ehrlichioses or anaplasmosis

AST, aspartate aminotransferase; HGA, human granulocytic anaplasmosis; HME, human monocytotropic ehrlichiosis; SGOT, serum glutamate oxaloacetate transaminase; WBC, white blood cell.

Doxycycline is the drug of choice, even in pregnant patients and children, and is administered to adults at a dose of 100 mg twice daily until the patient has become afebrile and clinically improved. Courses of treatment of 7 to 10 days have yielded a favorable outcome in many patients. *E. chaffeensis* has been demonstrated to be susceptible to rifampin and resistant to fluoroquinolones in cell culture; at present there are no clinical studies to support the use of rifampin.

Ehrlichiosis Caused by *Ehrlichia ewingii* and *Ehrlichia muris*

Ehrlichiosis ewingii has been diagnosed in Missouri, Tennessee, and Oklahoma, and *E. ewingii* has been identified in *A. americanum* ticks in North Carolina and Florida as well as in deer in Missouri.[112] The majority of infections have been reported in immunocompromised patients. Clinical manifestations are similar to those of HME with the impression that overall the illness is not as severe with fewer complications, and no deaths have been reported.[106] Diagnosis requires PCR with species-specific primers or with DNA sequencing of amplicons of broad range PCR. Sera of patients with ehrlichiosis ewingii react with *E. chaffeensis* IFA antigens but do not react with the 28-kD proteins of *E. chaffeensis* in Western immunoblots.

E. muris has been detected in *I. persulcatus* ticks in the Perm region of Russia, where 86 patients with an acute febrile illness had antibody titers of 1:80 to 1:1200 against the antigenically related *E. chaffeensis.*[113,114] In Japan, where *E. muris* is found in *Apodemus* mice and *Haemaphysalis flava* ticks, antibodies were present in 1% of humans in a large serosurvey.[115] No human illness has been reported.

Human Granulocytotropic Anaplasmosis (Formerly Human Granulocytic Ehrlichiosis)

Signs, Symptoms, and Course

HGA is not a reportable illness in most states; however, more than 1300 cases have been identified by the Centers for Disease Control and Prevention in the United States since 1990. A smaller number of cases have been documented in Europe, where disease manifestations seem less severe.[54] Male patients outnumber female patients by 2 to 1, and the median age ranges from 43 to 60 years in different series.[43,45,54,116] After an incubation period of approximately 1 to 2 weeks, HGA arises as a mild to severe illness with fever, headache, malaise, and myalgias in the majority of patients.[43,45,54,116] Nausea, vomiting, diarrhea, cough, arthralgias, stiff neck, and confusion are present in less than half of patients, and less than 10% have rash. The majority of doxycycline-treated patients are well within 7 days, and if untreated the median duration of illness is 9 days (range 1 to 60 days).[116] Severe

manifestations include respiratory insufficiency, a septic shock–like illness, rhabdomyolysis, hemorrhage, and opportunistic infections.[43,45,83,117,118] Meningoencephalitis and CSF pleocytosis are exceedingly rare in documented cases of HGA; however, neurologic sequelae may include facial diplegia, brachial plexopathy, and demyelinating polyneuropathy.[119-121] At least four patients have died after HGA, including three after severe opportunistic fungal or viral infections.[76,85]

Laboratory features observed in a substantial portion of cases include thrombocytopenia, leukopenia, mild anemia, and increases in serum hepatic aminotransferase activities within the first 7 days of illness.[43,45] Neutropenia with a left shift and relative lymphocytosis may occur. Leukocyte, erythrocyte, and platelet counts return to normal by 14 days, but the left shift may persist for longer.[122] Doxycycline therapy reverses the decline in leukocyte and platelet counts and blunts the degree of left shift usually within 5 to 7 days; anemia responds more slowly.

Diagnosis

Unlike the rarity of morulae in circulating mononuclear cells in HME, between 20% and 80% of patients with HGA are reported have ehrlichial morulae identified in peripheral blood neutrophils (Fig. 190-2).[43,45] Culture of *A. phagocytophilum* is promising but usually requires 1 week or more, whereas PCR amplification of *A. phagocytophilum* nucleic acids from blood is between 54% and 86% sensitive, highly specific, and may be performed in a timely manner.[123-125] Serologic diagnosis is most often achieved retrospectively by detection of antibodies reactive with *A. phagocytophilum* in infected tissue culture cells.[43,45,119,126-129] By current criteria, a titer of at least 80 is considered significant, but a fourfold rise provides more definitive evidence for infection owing to the fact that 15% to 16% of the population in the upper Midwest and New York State have preexisting serologic reactions. Immunoglobulin M testing may be useful as reactions are demonstrated only during the first 45 to 60 days, but this test lacks sensitivity.[128] A role for Western immunoblot confirmation or use of recombinant antigens for serodiagnosis is not currently defined.[126,127]

TREATMENT AND PREVENTION

Doxycycline, 100 mg twice a day, or tetracycline, 25 mg/kg/day in four equally divided doses, has been used successfully. Susceptibility testing of *A. phagocytophilum* in cell culture systems confirms that doxycycline and the rifamycins are bactericidal and reveals that chloramphenicol is not effective.[130,131] The clinical effectiveness of rifampin has not yet been evaluated, but it has been used in pregnancy.[132] *Ehrlichia,* but not *Anaplasma* species, have a mutation in *gyrA* that leads to in vitro resistance to fluoroquinolones.[133]

PREVENTION OF EHRLICHIOSIS AND ANAPLASMOSIS

At present, prevention of human ehrlichiosis and anaplasmosis must rely on avoidance of exposure to ticks, regular careful search of the body for ticks when exposure occurs, and prompt removal of ticks from the body. Although *A. phagocytophilum* may be transmitted within 4 hours of a tick bite, no analysis of prophylactic antibiotic therapy has been conducted.[134]

SENNETSU NEORICKETTSIOSIS

Physicians outside the Far East are unlikely to see a patient with sennetsu neorickettsiosis. *N. sennetsu* was isolated in 1953 from the blood, bone marrow, and lymph node of a 25-year-old man who had fever, severe headaches, myalgia, anorexia, lymphadenopathy, and an increased quantity of atypical lymphocytes in his peripheral blood.[135] Organisms isolated in mice were inoculated into human volunteers, who developed a syndrome resembling infectious mononucleosis. Neorickettsiae were recovered from their blood samples.

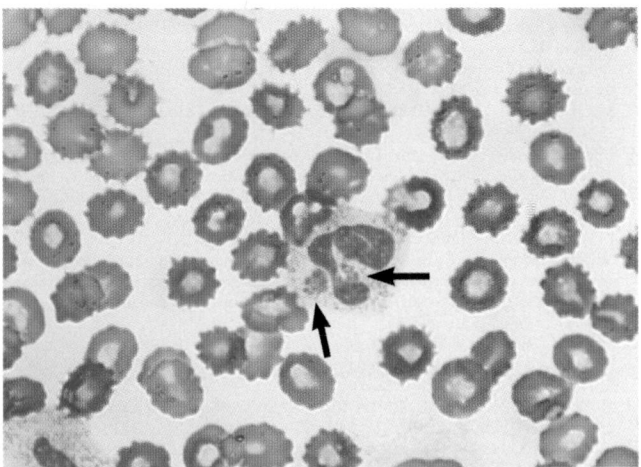

FIGURE 190-2. Peripheral blood smear showing intracellular inclusion within a neutrophil of a patient with human granulocytic anaplasmosis (*arrows*). (Wright stain, ×1000.)

The average incubation period of 14 days is followed by sudden onset of chills and a fever that lasts for 2 weeks unless treated effectively.[3] Patients also complain of headache and myalgia. Postauricular and posterior cervical lymphadenopathy appears 5 to 7 days after onset. Hepatosplenomegaly occurs in one third to one half of patients. Aseptic meningitis is observed only occasionally and rash very rarely. Early in the illness leukopenia occurs; in the late febrile and convalescent phases, absolute lymphocytosis is observed with 10% or greater atypical lymphocytes. Mild to moderate elevations occur in serum transaminases. Laboratory diagnosis can be made by inoculation of mice and by demonstration of specific serum antibody by IFA or complement fixation test. Treatment with one of the tetracycline antimicrobials, including doxycycline or minocycline, results in defervescence after 1 to 2 days.

REFERENCES

1. Silverstein AM. On the naming of rickettsiae after Paul Ehrlich. Bull Hist Med. 1998;72:731-733.
2. Dumler JS, Barbet AF, Bekker CP, et al. Reorganization of genera in the families Rickettsiaceae and Anaplasmataceae in the order Rickettsiales: Unification of some species of Ehrlichia with Anaplasma, Cowdria with Ehrlichia and Ehrlichia with Neorickettsia, descriptions of six new species combinations and designation of Ehrlichia equi and 'HGE agent' as subjective synonyms of Ehrlichia phagocytophila. Int J Syst Evol Microbiol. 2001;51:2145-2165.
3. Tachibana N. Sennetsu fever: The disease, diagnosis, and treatment. In: Leive L, ed. Microbiology 1986. Washington, DC: American Society for Microbiology; 1986:205-208.
4. Maeda K, Markowitz N, Hawley RC, et al. Human infection with Ehrlichia canis, a leukocytic Rickettsia. N Engl J Med. 1987;316:853-856.
5. Anderson BE, Dawson JE, Jones DC, et al. Ehrlichia chaffeensis, a new species associated with human ehrlichiosis. J Clin Microbiol. 1991;29:2838-2842.
6. Bakken JS, Dumler JS, Chen SM, et al. Human granulocytic ehrlichiosis in the upper Midwest United States. A new species emerging? JAMA. 1994; 272:212-218.
7. Chen S-M, Dumler JS, Bakken JS, et al. Identification of a granulocytotropic Ehrlichia species as the etiologic agent of human disease. J Clin Microbiol. 1994;32:589-595.
8. Anderson BE, Greene CE, Jones DC, et al. Ehrlichia ewingii sp. nov., the etiologic agent of canine granulocytic ehrlichiosis. Int J Syst Bacteriol. 1992;42:299-302.
9. Chen S-M, Dumler JS, Feng H-M, et al. Identification of the antigenic constituents of Ehrlichia chaffeensis. Am J Trop Med Hyg. 1993;50:52-58.
10. Wen BH. Ehrlichia muris sp. nov., identified on the basis of 16S rRNA base sequences and serological, morphological, and biological characteristics. Int J Syst Bacteriol. 1995;45:250-254.
11. Pretzman C, Ralph D, Stothard DR, et al. 16S rRNA gene sequence of Neorickettsia helminthoeca and its phylogenetic alignment with members of the genus Ehrlichia. Int J Syst Bacteriol. 1995;45:207-211.
12. Wen B, Rikihisa Y, Yamamoto S, et al. Characterization of the SF agent, an Ehrlichia sp. isolated from the fluke Stellantchasmus falcatus, by 16S rRNA base sequence, serological, and morphological analyses. Int J Syst Bacteriol. 1996;46:149-154.
13. Taylor MJ. Wolbachia endosymbiotic bacteria of filarial nematodes. A new insight into disease pathogenesis and control. Arch Med Res. 2002;33:422-424.
14. Popov VL, Han VC, Chen S-M, et al. Ultrastructural differentiation of the genogroups in the genus Ehrlichia. J Med Microbiol. 1998;47:235-251.
15. Ohashi N, Zhi N, Zhang Y, et al. Immunodominant major outer membrane proteins of Ehrlichia chaffeensis are encoded by a polymorphic multigene family. Infect Immun. 1998;66:132-139.
16. Yu X, McBride JW, Zhang X, Walker DH. Characterization of the complete transcriptionally active Ehrlichia chaffeensis 28 kDa outer membrane protein multigene family. Gene. 2000;248:59-68.
17. Asanovich KM, Bakken JS, Madigan JE, et al. Antigenic diversity of granulocytic Ehrlichia isolates from humans in Wisconsin and New York and a horse in California. J Infect Dis. 1997;176:1029-1034.
18. Park J, Choi KS, Dumler JS. Major surface protein 2 of Anaplasma phagocytophilum facilitates adherence to granulocytes. Infect Immun. 2003;71:4018-4025.
19. IJdo JW, Wu C, Telford SR 3rd, Fikrig E. Differential expression of the p44 gene family in the agent of human granulocytic ehrlichiosis. Infect Immun. 2002;70: 5295-5298.
20. Chen S-M, Yu X-J, Popov VL, et al. Genetic and antigenic diversity of Ehrlichia chaffeensis: Comparative analysis of a novel human strain from Oklahoma and previously isolated strains. J Infect Dis. 1997;175:856-863.
21. Zhi N, Ohashi N, Rikihisa Y. Multiple p44 genes encoding major outer membrane proteins are expressed in the human granulocytic ehrlichiosis agent. J Biol Chem. 1999;274:17828-17836.
22. IJdo JW, Sun W, Zhang Y, et al. Cloning of the gene encoding the 44-kilodalton antigen of the agent of human granulocytic ehrlichiosis and characterization of the humoral response. Infect Immun. 1998;66:3264-3269.
23. Caspersen K, Park JH, Patil S, Dumler JS. Genetic variability and stability of Anaplasma phagocytophila msp2 (p44). Infect Immun. 2002;70:1230-1234.
24. Sumner JW, Childs JE, Paddock CD. Molecular cloning and characterization of the Ehrlichia chaffeensis variable-length PCR target: An antigen-expressing gene that exhibits interstrain variation. J Clin Microbiol. 1999;37:1447-1453.
25. Liddell AM, Sumner JW, Paddock CD, et al. Reinfection with Ehrlichia chaffeensis in a liver transplant recipient. Clin Infect Dis. 2002;34:1644-1647.
26. Sumner JW, Nicholson WL, Massung RF. PCR amplification and comparison of nucleotide sequences from the groESL heat shock operon of Ehrlichia species. J Clin Microbiol. 1997;35:2087-2092.
27. McBride JW, Yu XJ, Walker DH. Glycosylation of homologous immunodominant proteins of Ehrlichia chaffeensis and Ehrlichia canis. Infect Immun. 2000;68:13-18.
28. Popov VL, Yu X, Walker DH. The 120 kDa outer membrane protein of Ehrlichia chaffeensis: Preferential expression on dense-core cells and gene expression in Escherichia coli associated with attachment and entry. Microb Pathog. 2000;28: 71-80.
29. Storey JR, Doros-Richert LA, Gingrich-Baker C, et al. Molecular cloning and sequencing of three granulocytic Ehrlichia genes encoding high-molecular-weight immunoreactive proteins. Infect Immun. 1998;66:1356-1363.
30. Anderson BE, Sumner JW, Dawson JE, et al. Detection of the etiologic agent of human ehrlichiosis by polymerase chain reaction. J Clin Microbiol. 1992;30:775-780.
31. Anderson BE, Sims KG, Olson JG, et al. Amblyomma americanum: A potential vector of human ehrlichiosis. Am J Trop Med Hyg. 1993;49:239-244.
32. Ewing SA, Dawson JE, Kocan AA, et al. Experimental transmission of Ehrlichia chaffeensis (Rickettsiales: Ehrlichieae) among white-tailed deer by Amblyomma americanum (Acari: Ixodidae). J Med Entomol. 1995;32:368-374.
33. Lockhart JM, Davidson WR, Stallknecht DE, et al. Site-specific geographic association between Amblyomma americanum (Acari: Ixodidae)) infestations and Ehrlichia chaffeensis–reactive (Rickettsiales: Ehrlichieae) antibodies in white-tailed deer. J Med Entomol. 1996;33:153-158.
34. Lockhart JM, Davidson WR, Dawson JE, et al. Temporal association of Amblyomma americanum with the presence of Ehrlichia chaffeensis reactive antibodies in white-tailed deer. J Wildl Dis. 1995;31:119-124.
35. Telford SR III, Dawson JE, Katavolos P, et al. Perpetuation of the agent of human granulocytic ehrlichiosis in a deer tick–rodent cycle. Proc Natl Acad Sci U S A. 1996;93:6209-6214.
36. Fishbein DB, Dawson JE, Robinson LE. Human ehrlichiosis in the United States, 1985-1990. Ann Intern Med. 1994;120:736-743.
37. Fishbein DB, Sawyer LA, Holland CJ, et al. Unexplained febrile illnesses after exposure to ticks. JAMA. 1987;257:3100-3104.
38. Harkess JR, Ewing SA, Crutcher JM, et al. Human ehrlichiosis in Oklahoma. J Infect Dis. 1989;159:576-579.
39. Fishbein DB, Kemp A, Dawson JE, et al. Human ehrlichiosis: Prospective active surveillance in febrile hospitalized patients. J Infect Dis. 1989;160:803-809.
40. Carpenter CF, Gandhi TK, Kong LK, et al. The incidence of ehrlichial and rickettsial infection in patients with unexplained fever and recent history of tick bite in central North Carolina. J Infect Dis. 1999;180:900-903.
41. Olano JP, Walker DH. Human ehrlichioses. Med Clin North Am. 2002;86:375-392.
42. Eng TR, Harkess JR, Fishbein DB, et al. Epidemiologic, clinical, and laboratory findings of human ehrlichiosis in the United States, 1988. JAMA. 1990;264:2251-2258.
43. Bakken JS, Krueth J, Wilson-Nordskog C, et al. Clinical and laboratory characteristics of human granulocytic ehrlichiosis. JAMA. 1996;275:199-205.
44. Ijdo JW, Meek JI, Cartter ML, et al. The emergence of another tickborne infection in the 12-town area around Lyme, Connecticut: Human granulocytic ehrlichiosis. J Infect Dis. 2000;181:1388-1393.
45. Aguero-Rosenfeld M, Horowitz HW, Wormser GP, et al. Human granulocytic ehrlichiosis (HGE): A series from a single medical center in New York State. Ann Intern Med. 1996;125:904-908.
46. Groves MG, Dennis GL, Amyx HL, et al. Transmission of Ehrlichia canis to dogs by ticks (Rhipicephalus sanguineus). Am J Vet Res. 1975;36:937-940.
47. Dawson JE, Warner CK, Standaert S, et al. The interface between research and the diagnosis of an emerging tick-borne disease, human ehrlichiosis due to Ehrlichia chaffeensis. Arch Intern Med. 1996;156:137-142.
48. Morais JD, Dawson JE, Green C, et al. First European case of ehrlichiosis. Lancet. 1991;338:633-634.
49. Uhaa IJ, Maclean JD, Greene CR, et al. A case of human ehrlichiosis acquired in Mali: Clinical and laboratory findings. Am J Trop Med Hyg. 1992;46:161-164.
50. Heo EJ, Park JH, Koo JR, et al. Serologic and molecular detection of Ehrlichia chaffeensis and Anaplasma phagocytophila (human granulocytic ehrlichiosis agent) in Korean patients. J Clin Microbiol. 2002;40:3082-3085.
51. Yevich SJ, Sanchez JL, DeFraites RF, et al. Seroepidemiology of infections due to spotted fever group rickettsiae and Ehrlichia species in military personnel exposed in areas of the United States where such infections are endemic. J Infect Dis. 1995;171:1266-1273.
52. Perez M, Rikihisa Y, Wen B. Ehrlichia canis–like agent isolated from a man in Venezuela: Antigenic and genetic characterization. J Clin Microbiol. 1996;34: 2133-2139.
53. McKechnie DB, Slater KS, Childs JE, et al. Survival of Ehrlichia chaffeensis in refrigerated, ADSOL-treated RBCs. Transfusion. 2000;40:1041-1047.
54. Blanco JR, Oteo JA. Human granulocytic ehrlichiosis in Europe. Clin Microbiol Infect. 2002;8:763-772.

55. Magnarelli LA, Dumler JS, Anderson JF, et al. Coexistence of antibodies to tick-borne pathogens of babesiosis, ehrlichiosis, and Lyme borreliosis in human sera. J Clin Microbiol. 1995;33:2054-2057.
56. Dumler JS, Dotevall L, Gustafson R, et al. A population-based seroepidemiological study of human granulocytic ehrlichiosis (HGE) and Lyme borreliosis on the west coast of Sweden. J Infect Dis. 1997;175:720-722.
57. Aguero-Rosenfeld ME, Donnarumma L, Zentmaier L, et al. Seroprevalence of antibodies that react with *Anaplasma phagocytophila*, the agent of human granulocytic ehrlichiosis, in different populations in Westchester County, New York. J Clin Microbiol. 2002;40:2612-2615.
58. Petrovec M, Furlan SL, Zupanc TA, et al. Human disease in Europe caused by a granulocytic *Ehrlichia* species. J Clin Microbiol. 1997;35:1556-1559.
59. Pancholi P, Kolbert CP, Mitchell P, et al. *Ixodes dammini* (*scapularis*) as a potential vector of human granulocytic ehrlichiosis. J Infect Dis. 1995;172:1007-1012.
60. Mitchell PD, Reed KD, Hofkes JM. Immunoserologic evidence of coinfection with *Borrelia burgdorferi*, *Babesia microti*, and human granulocytic *Ehrlichia* species in residents of Wisconsin and Minnesota. J Clin Microbiol. 1996;34:724-727.
61. Brouqui P, Dumler JS, Lenhard R, et al. Serologic evidence of human granulocytic ehrlichiosis in Europe. Lancet. 1995;346:782-783.
62. Nadelman RB, Horowitz HW, Chen HT, et al. Simultaneous human granulocytic ehrlichiosis and Lyme borreliosis. N Engl J Med. 1997;337:27-30.
63. Belongia EA. Epidemiology and impact of coinfections acquired from *Ixodes* ticks. Vector Borne Zoonotic Dis. 2002;2:265-273.
64. MacLeod JR, Gordon WS. Studies in tick-borne fever of sheep. I. Transmission by the tick, *Ixodes ricinus*, with a description of the disease produced. Parasitology. 1933;25:273-285.
65. Walls JJ, Greig B, Neitzel DF, Dumler JS. Natural infection of small mammal species in Minnesota with the agent of human granulocytic ehrlichiosis. J Clin Microbiol. 1997;35:853-855.
66. Nicholson WL, Muir S, Sumner JW. Serologic evidence of infection with *Ehrlichia* spp. in wild rodents (Muridae: Sigmodontinae) in the United States. J Clin Microbiol. 1998;36:695-700.
67. Liz JS, Sumner JW, Pfister K, Brossard M. PCR detection and serological evidence of granulocytic ehrlichial infection in roe deer (*Capreolus capreolus*) and chamois (*Rupicapra rupicapra*). J Clin Microbiol. 2002;40:892-897.
68. Magnarelli LA, Ijdo JW, Stafford KC 3rd, Fikrig E. Infections of granulocytic ehrlichiae and *Borrelia burgdorferi* in white-tailed deer in Connecticut. J Wildl Dis. 1999;35:266-274.
69. Hodzic E, Ijdo JW, Feng S, et al. Granulocytic ehrlichiosis in the laboratory mouse. J Infect Dis. 1998;177:737-745.
70. Levin ML, Fish D. Immunity reduces reservoir host competence of *Peromyscus leucopus* for *Ehrlichia phagocytophila*. Infect Immun. 2000;68:1514-1518.
71. Belongia EA, Reed KD, Mitchell PD, et al. Prevalence of granulocytic *Ehrlichia* infection among white-tailed deer in Wisconsin. J Clin Microbiol. 1997;35:1465-1468.
72. Dumler JS, Dawson JE, Walker DH. Human ehrlichiosis: Hematopathology and immunohistologic detection of *Ehrlichia chaffeensis*. Hum Pathol. 1993;24:391-396.
73. Dunn BE, Monson TP, Dumler JS, et al. Identification of *Ehrlichia chaffeensis* morulae in cerebrospinal fluid mononuclear cells. J Clin Microbiol. 1992;30:2207-2210.
74. Dumler JS, Brouqui P, Aronson J, et al. Identification of *Ehrlichia* in human tissue. N Engl J Med. 1991;325:1109-1110.
75. Dumler JS, Sutker WL, Walker DH. Persistent infection with *Ehrlichia chaffeensis*. Clin Infect Dis. 1993;17:903-905.
76. Walker DH, Dumler JS. Human monocytic and granulocytic ehrlichioses. Discovery and diagnosis of emerging tick-borne infections and the critical role of the pathologist. Arch Pathol Lab Med. 1997;121:785-791.
77. Lee EH, Rikihisa Y. Absence of tumor necrosis factor alpha, interleukin-6 (IL-6), and granulocyte-macrophage colony-stimulating factor expression but presence of IL-1β, IL-8, and IL-10 expression of human monocytes exposed to viable or killed *Ehrlichia chaffeensis*. Infect Immun. 1996;64:4211-4219.
78. Lee EH, Rikihisa Y. Anti–*Ehrlichia chaffeensis* antibody complexed with *E. chaffeensis* induces potent proinflammatory cytokine mRNA expression in human monocytes through sustained reduction of IκB-α and activation of NF-κB. Infect Immun. 1997;65:2890-2897.
79. Barnewall RE, Rikihisa Y. Abrogation of gamma interferon–induced inhibition of *Ehrlichia chaffeensis* infection in human monocytes with iron-transferrin. Infect Immun. 1994;62:4804-4810.
80. Winslow GM, Yager E, Shilo K, et al. Antibody-mediated elimination of the obligate intracellular bacterial pathogen *Ehrlichia chaffeensis* during active infection. Infect Immun. 2000;68:2187-2195.
81. Barnewall RE, Rikihisa Y, Lee EH. *Ehrlichia chaffeensis* inclusions are early endosomes which selectively accumulate transferrin receptor. Infect Immun. 1997;65:1455-1461.
82. Lee EH, Rikihisa Y. Protein kinase A–mediated inhibition of gamma interferon–induced tyrosine phosphorylation of Janus kinases and latent cytoplasmic transcription factors in human monocytes by *Ehrlichia chaffeensis*. Infect Immun. 1998;66:2514-2522.
83. Hardalo CJ, Quagliarello V, Dumler JS. Human granulocytic ehrlichiosis in Connecticut: Report of a fatal case. Clin Infect Dis. 1995;21:910-914.
84. Larsen HJS, Overnes G, Waldeland H, et al. Immunosuppression in sheep experimentally infected with *Ehrlichia phagocytophila*. Res Vet Sci. 1994;56:216-224.
85. Lepidi H, Bunnell JE, Martin ME, et al. Comparative pathology, and immunohistology associated with clinical illness after *Ehrlichia phagocytophila*–group infections. Am J Trop Med Hyg. 2000;62:29-37.
86. Klein MB, Miller JS, Nelson CM, et al. Primary bone marrow progenitors of both granulocytic and monocytic lineages are susceptible to infection with the agent of human granulocytic ehrlichiosis. J Infect Dis. 1997;176:1405-1409.
87. Herron MJ, Nelson CM, Larson J, et al. Intracellular parasitism by the human granulocytic ehrlichiosis bacterium through the P-selectin ligand, PSGL-1. Science. 2000;288:1653-1656.
88. Webster P, Ijdo JW, Chicoine LM, Fikrig E. The agent of human granulocytic ehrlichiosis resides in an endosomal compartment. J Clin Invest. 1998;101:1932-1941.
89. Carlyon JA, Chan WT, Galan J, et al. Repression of rac2 mRNA expression by *Anaplasma phagocytophila* is essential to the inhibition of superoxide production and bacterial proliferation. J Immunol. 2002;169:7009-7018.
90. Banerjee R, Anguita J, Roos D, Fikrig E. Cutting edge: Infection by the agent of human granulocytic ehrlichiosis prevents the respiratory burst by down-regulating gp91phox. J Immunol. 2000;164:3946-3949.
91. Yoshiie K, Kim HY, Mott J, Rikihisa Y. Intracellular infection by the human granulocytic ehrlichiosis agent inhibits human neutrophil apoptosis. Infect Immun. 2000;68:1125-1133.
92. Choi K-S, Garyu J, Park J, Dumler JS. Diminished adhesion of *Anaplasma phagocytophilum*–infected neutrophils to endothelial cells is associated with reduced expression of leukocyte surface selectin. Infect Immun. 2003;71:4586-4594.
93. Whist SK, Storset AK, Larsen HJ. Functions of neutrophils in sheep experimentally infected with *Ehrlichia phagocytophila*. Vet Immunol Immunopathol. 2002;86:183-193.
94. Klein MB, Hu S, Chao CC, Goodman JL. The agent of human granulocytic ehrlichiosis induces the production of myelosuppressing chemokines without induction of proinflammatory cytokines. J Infect Dis. 2000;182:200-205.
95. Martin ME, Caspersen K, Dumler JS. Immunopathology and ehrlichial propagation are regulated by interferon-gamma and interleukin-10 in a murine model of human granulocytic ehrlichiosis. Am J Pathol. 2001;158:1881-1888.
96. Harkess JR, Stucky D, Ewing SA. Neurologic abnormalities in a patient with human ehrlichiosis. South Med J. 1990;83:1341-1343.
97. Moskovitz M, Fadden R, Min T. Human ehrlichiosis: A rickettsial disease associated with severe cholestasis and multisystemic disease. J Clin Gastroenterol. 1991;13:86-90.
98. Schutze GE, Jacobs RF. Human monocytic ehrlichiosis in children. Pediatrics. 1997;100:10-17.
99. Paddock CD, Suchard DP, Grumbach KL, et al. Brief report: Fatal seronegative ehrlichiosis in a patient with HIV infection. N Engl J Med. 1993;329:1164-1167.
100. Fichtenbaum CJ, Peterson LR, Weil GJ. Ehrlichiosis presenting as a life-threatening illness with features of the toxic shock syndrome. Am J Med. 1993;95:351-357.
101. Barenfanger J, Patel PG, Dumler JS, et al. Identifying human ehrlichiosis. Lab Med. 1996;27:372-374.
102. Marty AM, Dumler JS, Imes G, et al. Ehrlichiosis mimicking thrombotic thrombocytopenic purpura. Case report and pathological correlation. Hum Pathol. 1995;26:920-925.
103. Paddock CD, Sumner JW, Shore GM, et al. Isolation and characterization of *Ehrlichia chaffeensis* strains from patients with fatal ehrlichiosis. J Clin Microbiol. 1997;35:2496-2502.
104. Ratnasamy N, Everett ED, Roland WE, et al. Central nervous system manifestations of human ehrlichiosis. Clin Infect Dis. 1996;23:314-319.
105. Dawson JE, Anderson BE, Fishbein DB, et al. Isolation and characterization of an *Ehrlichia* sp. from a patient diagnosed with human ehrlichiosis. J Clin Microbiol. 1991;29:2741-2745.
106. Paddock CD, Folk SM, Shore GM, et al. Infections with *Ehrlichia chaffeensis* and *Ehrlichia ewingii* in persons coinfected with human immunodeficiency virus. Clin Infect Dis. 2001;33:1586-1594.
107. Standaert SM, Yu T, Scott MA, et al. Primary isolation of *Ehrlichia chaffeensis* from patients with febrile illnesses: Clinical and molecular characteristics. J Infect Dis. 2000;181:1082-1088.
108. Dumler JS, Chen S-M, Asanovich K, et al. Isolation and characterization of a new strain of *Ehrlichia chaffeensis* from a patient with nearly fatal monocytic ehrlichiosis. J Clin Microbiol. 1995;33:1704-1711.
109. Dawson JE, Fishbein DB, Eng TR, et al. Diagnosis of human ehrlichiosis with the indirect fluorescent antibody test: Kinetics and specificity. J Infect Dis. 1990;162:91-95.
110. Yu X-J, Brouqui P, Dumler JS, et al. Detection of *Ehrlichia chaffeensis* in human tissue by using a species-specific monoclonal antibody. J Clin Microbiol. 1993;31:3284-3288.
111. Everett ED, Evans KA, Henry RB, et al. Human ehrlichiosis in adults after tick exposure. Diagnosis using polymerase chain reaction. Ann Intern Med. 1994;120:730-735.
112. Arens MQ, Liddell AM, Buening G, et al. Detection of *Ehrlichia* spp. in the blood of wild white-tailed deer in Missouri by PCR assay and serologic analysis. J Clin Microbiol. 2003;41:1263-1265.
113. Ravyn M, Korenberg E, Oeding J, Kovaleskii Y. Monocytic *Ehrlichia* in *Ixodes persulcatus* ticks from Perm, Russia. Lancet. 1999;353:722-723.
114. Vorobyeva NN, Korenberg E, Grigoryan YV. Diagnostics of tick-borne diseases in the endemic region of Russia. Wien Klin Wochenschr. 2002;114:610-612.
115. Kawahara M, Ito T, Suto C, et al. Comparison of *Ehrlichia muris* strains isolated from wild mice and ticks and serologic survey of humans and animals with *E. muris* as antigen. J Clin Microbiol. 1999;37:1123-1129.
116. Bakken JS, Dumler JS. Human granulocytic ehrlichiosis. Clin Infect Dis. 2000;31:554-560.

117. Wong S, Grady LJ. *Ehrlichia* infection as a cause of severe respiratory distress (Letter). N Engl J Med. 1996;334:273.
118. Shea KW, Calio AJ, Klein NC, et al. *Ehrlichia equi* infection associated with rhabdomyolysis. Clin Infect Dis. 1996;22:605.
119. Horowitz HW, Marks SJ, Weintraub M, et al. Brachial plexopathy associated with human granulocytic ehrlichiosis. Neurology. 1996;46:1026-1029.
120. Bakken JS, Erlemeyer SA, Kanoff RJ, et al. Demyelinating polyneuropathy associated with human granulocytic ehrlichiosis. Clin Infect Dis. 1998;27:1323-1324.
121. Lee FS, Chu FK, Tackley M, et al. Human granulocytic ehrlichiosis presenting as facial diplegia in a 42-year-old woman. Clin Infect Dis. 2000;31:1288-1291.
122. Bakken JS, Aguero-Rosenfeld ME, Tilden RL, et al. Serial measurements of hematologic counts during the active phase of human granulocytic ehrlichiosis. Clin Infect Dis. 2001;32:862-870.
123. Goodman JL, Nelson C, Vitale B, et al. Direct cultivation of the causative agent from patients with human granulocytic ehrlichiosis. N Engl J Med. 1996;334:209-215.
124. Edelman DC, Dumler JS. Evaluation of an improved PCR diagnostic assay for human granulocytic ehrlichiosis. Mol Diagn. 1996;1:41-49.
125. Horowitz HW, Aguero-Rosenfeld ME, McKenna DF, et al. The clinical and laboratory spectrum of culture proven human granulocytic ehrlichiosis: Comparison with culture negative cases. Clin Infect Dis. 1998;27:1314-1317.
126. Ijdo JW, Zhang Y, Hodzic E, et al. The early humoral response in human granulocytic ehrlichiosis. J Infect Dis. 1997;176:687-692.
127. Ravyn MD, Goodman JL, Kodner CB, et al. Immunodiagnosis of human granulocytic ehrlichiosis by using culture-derived human isolates. J Clin Microbiol. 1998;36:1480-1488.
128. Walls JJ, Aguero-Rosenfeld M, Bakken JS, et al. Inter- and intralaboratory comparison of *Ehrlichia equi* and human granulocytic ehrlichiosis (HGE) agent strains for serodiagnosis of HGE by the immunofluorescent-antibody test. J Clin Microbiol. 1999;37:2968-2973.
129. Bakken JS, Haller I, Riddell D, et al. The serological response of patients infected with the agent of human granulocytic ehrlichiosis. Clin Infect Dis. 2002;34:22-27.
130. Maurin M, Bakken JS, Dumler JS. Antibiotic susceptibilities of *Anaplasma* (*Ehrlichia*) *phagocytophilum* strains from various geographic areas in the United States. Antimicrob Agents Chemother. 2003;47:413-415.
131. Klein MB, Nelson CM, Goodman JL. Antibiotic susceptibility of the newly cultivated agent of human granulocytic ehrlichiosis: Promising activity of quinolones and rifamycins. Antimicrob Agents Chemother. 1997;41:76-79.
132. Buitrago MI, Ijdo JW, Rinaudo P, et al. Human granulocytic ehrlichiosis during pregnancy treated successfully with rifampin. Clin Infect Dis. 1998;27:213-215.
133. Maurin M, Abergel C, Raoult D. DNA gyrase–mediated natural resistance to fluoroquinolones in *Ehrlichia* spp. Antimicrob Agents Chemother. 2001;45:2098-2105.
134. des Vignes F, Piesman J, Heffernan R, et al. Effect of tick removal on transmission of *Borrelia burgdorferi* and *Ehrlichia phagocytophila* by *Ixodes scapularis* nymphs. J Infect Dis. 2001;183:773-778.
135. Misao T, Kobayashi Y. Studies on infectious mononucleosis (glandular fever). I. Isolation of etiologic agent from blood, bone marrow, and lymph node of a patient with infectious mononucleosis by using mice. Kyushu J Med Sci. 1955;6:145-152.

SECTION F

BACTERIAL DISEASES

CHAPTER 191

Introduction to Bacteria and Bacterial Diseases

MARTIN J. BLASER

TABLE 191-1 Disease Mechanisms Involved in Bacterial Infections

Mechanism	Examples
Pyogenic infection	Pneumococcal pneumonia, staphylococcal abscess
Granulomatous infection	Pulmonary tuberculosis, brucellosis, syphilis
Intoxication (augmentation of host physiology)	Cholera (*Vibrio cholerae*)
Intoxication (tissue destruction)	Gas gangrene (*Clostridium perfringens*), diphtheria (*Corynebacterium diphtheriae*)
Immunologic mediation	Guillain-Barré syndrome following *Campylobacter jejuni* infection; Reiter's syndrome following shigellosis
Neoplasia	Adenocarcinoma of the stomach as a consequence of *Helicobacter pylori* persistence

Bacteria, the oldest forms of life on earth, are remarkably diverse and exist in astounding number. Diseases caused by bacteria include some of the most common infections in the world, as well as some of humankind's most important scourges, past, present, and probably future. At the same time, each of us is colonized by more bacterial cells than we have human cells in our bodies. Generally, this is a peaceful, even productive (symbiotic) relationship, but occasionally even these well-tolerated residents of the human biosphere cause disease.[1,2]

We are surrounded and ever exposed to bacteria, including those that evolved to live well with us (e.g., *Bacteroides* species), as well as those whose evolution has promoted the tendency to cause disease (e.g., *Mycobacterium* tuberculosis) and death (e.g., *Bacillus anthracis*). In consequence, and not surprisingly, many of the presently recognized infectious diseases are caused by bacteria. It also may be safely predicted that many important illnesses not yet recognized or widespread ("emerging" infectious diseases), will be found to be caused by bacteria,[3] as will some of the chronic inflammatory diseases of unknown cause (see later). Therefore, knowledge of pathogenic bacteria, the diseases to which they lead, and current preventive and therapeutic strategies is critical for all physicians, especially for specialists in infectious diseases.

CLASSIFICATION OF BACTERIA

Bacteria have been classified according to phenotype, including size, shape, staining properties, and biochemical properties, since the beginning of microbiology. In recent years, classification has been dominated by genotype, especially relying on conserved molecules like 16S ribosomal RNA.[4] Although there is a considerable degree of overlap between phenotype and genotype, as would be expected, dichotomies do occur. In the future, taxonomy, understanding of pathogenesis, and diagnostics will be increasingly based on genotype. Thus, physicians and other students of infectious diseases must broaden their knowledge of molecular biology and taxonomy. As bacteriology advances in its differentiation of genera and species, as subspecies diversity is increasingly appreciated,[5] as variation within individual hosts is better understood, and as the evolution of pathogens is better outlined,[6] a grounding in evolutionary biology and ecology also will become more critical.

VARIATION IN BACTERIAL INFECTIONS

Because all organs of the body are subject to bacterial infection, a recitation of these sites would be exhaustive and thus not useful. However, at the least, bacterial infections may be considered as varying in etiology, in mechanisms, and in time frame. Infections may be caused by gram-positive or gram-negative bacilli or cocci; these were the first recognized bacterial agents of disease. However, this simple taxonomy does not fully account for other etiologic bacterial agents including *Mycobacterium* species, treponemes, mycoplasma, rickettsia, chlamydia, and actinomyces, all of which are Eubacteria. Each of these types of organisms has particular stereotypic features that characterize its interactions with hosts, but exceptions and variation abound. In recent years, Archaea, a widespread and ancient group of prokaryotes, most closely resembling bacteria, have been isolated from human specimens[7]; whether they play roles in human diseases is not yet known.

The mechanisms by which bacteria cause disease are quite varied (Table 191-1). There is no universal mechanism or principle, as the causative organism need not even be present in the human body. For example, food poisoning is commonly due to the ingestion of "preformed" toxin produced by *Clostridium botulinum* or *Staphylococcus aureus* when they are growing in food, not in the host. The scope of bacterial infections includes interactions across time frames that vary from minutes to decades, or longer (Table 191-2). The descendents of the organisms that we each acquire from our mother as a newborn can be the cause of our death in old age (e.g., due to a perforated diverticulum), to carry the argument to the farthest extreme. Each bacterial infection is unique, which increases the difficulty in our grasping the underlying concepts; this complexity also makes the practice of infectious diseases so intellectually satisfying!

POLYMORPHISM AND BACTERIAL INFECTION

From the earliest days of microbiology, when it was recognized that some organisms of the same species were encapsulated and many were not, it has been clear that pathogenic bacteria are polymorphic. With the development of antisera came the recognition that apparently identical organisms showed variation; this information became the basis for typing schemes based on capsular, somatic (O-)antigen, or flagellar antigenic differences. Such polymorphisms enabled better classification of virulent (and avirulent) meningococci, pneumococci, and *Escherichia coli,* for example, and have led to diagnostics, therapeutic antisera, and vaccines. But in recent years, especially, has come the understanding that once bacteria begin to multiply in a host, their own populations become polymorphic.[8] Antigenic variation is one subtheme of that phenomenon and has been known since the studies of *Borrelia recurrentis,* the cause of relapsing fever, for example. Increasingly, with the tools provided by the sequencing of whole bacterial genomes, we are learning just how polymorphic are bacteria, often considered as "clonal" organisms, and how dynamic their changes in relation to individual hosts.[9]

In parallel, we have been learning more about human genetic polymorphisms and their relationship to bacterial diseases. Medical science is rapidly advancing from phenotypes (e.g., blood groups) to genotypes (e.g., alleles of the IL-1β promoter). The genetic composition of each individual helps determine its response to bacterial infections and thus the outcome. Increasingly, these host characteristics will become the focus of the information that clinicians will need

TABLE 191-2 Variation in Time Courses for Representative Bacterial Infections

Time Frame	Disease	Representative Causative Organism	Clinical Manifestations	Mechanisms
Minutes	Food poisoning	*Clostridium perfringens*	Vomiting, diarrhea	Pre-formed enterotoxin
Hours	Necrotizing fasciitis	*Streptococcus pyogenes*	Devitalization of muscle, sepsis	Bacterial spread across tissue planes
Days	Anthrax	*Bacillus anthracis*	Cough, chest pain, fever, dyspnea	Resistance to macrophage killing
Weeks	Lung abscess	Oral anaerobes	Cough, fever, chest pain	Necrotizing pyogenic process
Months	Subacute bacterial endocarditis	β-Hemolytic streptococci	Fever, anemia, stroke, heart failure	Infection of immunologically privileged site
Years	Whipple's disease	*Tropheryma whipplei*	Fever, diarrhea, weight loss	(??) Resistance to macrophage killing
Decades (persistence)	Osteomyelitis	*S. aureus*	Fever, wound discharge, pain	Pyogenic infection of devitalized tissue (± foreign body)
Decades (latency)	Pulmonary tuberculosis	*Mycobacterium tuberculosis*	Cough, fever, weight loss	Reactivation of latent focus into active granulomatous process
Decades (oncogenesis)	Gastric adenocarcinoma (intestinal type)	*Helicobacter pylori*	Mass lesion, abdominal pain, cachexia	Persistent inflammation, selection for cell cycle abnormalities

when considering prevention, differential diagnosis, and therapy of bacterial infections.[10]

BACTERIA AS "NEW" CAUSES FOR "OLD" DISEASES

The finding that an indigenous bacterium, *Helicobacter pylori,* plays pathogenetic roles in two important illnesses, peptic ulcer disease and gastric cancer,[11] advances a new paradigm: that many of the diseases that we consider diseases of unknown cause may in fact be "infectious diseases."[3] This idea, which gained prominence with the relationship of streptococcal pharyngitis to rheumatic fever, has been growing over the past decade, and other examples have been recognized. For example, after an episode of enteritis due to *Campylobacter jejuni,* the Guillain-Barré syndrome may develop.[12] Similarly, nearly 20 years ago, it was recognized that acute infection with enterohemorrhagic *E. coli* may lead to the hemolytic uremic syndrome.[13] Thus, acute, transient, and self-limited infections of the respiratory or gastrointestinal tracts may trigger cardiac, neurologic, or systemic diseases, with consequences lasting for months or permanently. Importantly, the disease locus (e.g., kidney, peripheral nervous system, heart) may be distant from the original infection at a mucosal surface. How many other examples of parallel phenomena may be present? The uncovering of clinical and epidemiologic associations has allowed work to identify the pathogenetic mechanisms, which provide new paradigms for autoimmunity.[14] Could a more persistent bacterial pathogen trigger multiple sclerosis, or Graves' disease?

Diseases such as sarcoidosis, ulcerative colitis, Crohn's disease, Wegener's granulomatosis, and thyroiditis are chronic inflammatory diseases for which a bacterial role in causation is not improbable. Despite a long inconclusive history, new data again point to *Mycobacteria* being present in sarcoidosis.[15]

BACTERIAL EVOLUTION

The study of infectious diseases is a dynamic field, at least in part because of the changing nature of the pathogens we consider. An obvious and absolutely critical aspect of bacterial evolution is the acquisition of resistance to antimicrobial agents. As the prescribing of antimicrobial therapies flourishes, whether they address important, controversial, or even trivial indications, antimicrobial resistance by our pathogens and indigenous organisms continues to grow.[16-18] Understanding resistance patterns is pivotal to understanding proper therapeutic approaches.[16] Also importantly, understanding the biology, epidemiology, and mechanisms for resistance leads to the ways we will need to prevent and curtail resistance in the populations of microbes that infect us, as well as those that colonize us, which may provide reservoirs for resistance.[17] Physicians, especially those who are specialists in infectious diseases, must be at the forefront of efforts to reduce the development of resistance.

Interestingly, considerations of resistance are useful for understanding other important aspects in the evolution of infectious diseases; we live in a world of natural selection. Resistance is among the easiest phenotypes to detect and understand, but bacteria continue to be selected on the basis of differences in the soaps we use (also a function of resistance), the sizes of our families and other social groups, the presence of daycare centers and jet planes, and by our changing dietary habits (functions of transmission).[19] Study of bacterial infections provides a rich school, not only for the physician but also for the student of human evolutionary biology.[20,21]

BACTERIA AS THERAPEUTICS

Since Metchnikoff and earlier, physicians have sought ways to harness bacteria to fight disease. At present, the highly lethal exotoxin of *C. botulinum* is being used as a therapeutic agent for both medical and cosmetic purposes. The BCG vaccine, an attenuated form of *Mycobacterium tuberculosis,* is used as adjuvant therapy for bladder cancer. Although at first glance such harnessing of bacteria for useful purposes seems extraordinary, it in fact makes great sense. The bacteria that live with us, or that attack us, often "know" us well; their evolution has selected for organisms that exploit chinks in our armor.[22] They are skilled cell biologists, immunologists, and physiologists. Similarly, they are great competitors with one another. Bacteria have potential utility as probiotics to treat disease.[23] Prebiotics, nutrients that provide substrate for particular bacteria or biochemical processes, extend the concept by another step.[24] Understanding the clinical manifestations and pathogenesis of bacterial infections will lead to new approaches to medicine—new therapeutics and new preventives. Predictably, each of the new treatments will lead to new complications. A thorough grounding in knowledge about bacterial infections will enable physicians to develop such new therapeutics, and to predict and treat the expected complications.

REFERENCES

1. Relman DA. The human body as microbial observatory. Nat Genet. 2002;30:131-133.
2. Kroes I, Lepp PW, Relman DA. Bacterial diversity within the human subgingival crevice. Proc Natl Acad Sci U S A. 1999;96:14547-14552.
3. Blaser MJ. Bacteria and diseases of unknown cause. Ann Intern Med. 1994;121:144-145.
4. Woese C. Microbiology in transition. Proc Natl Acad Sci U S A. 1994;91:1601-1603.
5. Caldwell HD, Wood H, Crane D, et al. Polymorphisms in *Chlamydia trachomatis* tryptophan synthase genes differentiate between genital and ocular isolates. J Clin Invest. 2003;111:1757-1769.
6. Walder MK, Mekalanos JJ. Lysogenic conversion by a filamentous phase encoding cholera toxin. Science. 1996;272:1910-1914.
7. Eckburg PB, Lepp PW, Relman DA. Archaea and their potential role in human disease. Infect Immun. 2003;71:591-596.
8. Blaser MJ, Musser JM. Bacterial polymorphisms and disease in humans. J Clin Invest. 2001;107:391-392.
9. Blaser MJ, Berg DE. *Helicobacter pylori* genetic diversity and risk of human disease. J Clin Invest. 2001;107:767-773.

10. Rossouw M, Nel HJ, Cooke GS, et al. Association between tuberculosis and a polymorphic NF$_k$B binding site in the interferon γ gene. Lancet. 2003;361:1871-1872.
11. Blaser MJ. The changing relationships of *Helicobacter pylori* and humans: Implications for health and disease. J Infect Dis. 1999;179:1523-1530.
12. Rees JH, Soudain SE, Gregson NA, Hughes RAC. *Campylobacter jejuni* infection and Guillain-Barré syndrome. N Engl J Med. 1995;333:1374-1379.
13. Karmali MA, Petric MA, Lim C, et al. The association between idiopathic hemolytic uremic syndrome and infection by verotoxin-producing *Escherichia coli*. J Infect Dis. 1985;151:775-782.
14. Ang CW, Noordzij PG, de Klerk MA, et al. Ganglioside mimicry of *Campylobacter jejuni* lipopolysaccharides determines antiganglioside specificity in rabbits. Infect Immun. 2002;70:5081-5085.
15. Drake WP, Pei Z, Pride DT, et al. Molecular analysis of sarcoidosis and control tissues for DNA from *Mycobacterium* species. Emerg Infect Dis. 2002;8:1334-1341.
16. Lonks JR, Garau J, Gomez L, et al. Failure of macrolide antibiotic treatment in patients with bacteremia due to erythromycin-resistant *Streptococcus pneumoniae*. Clin Infect Dis. 2002;35:556-564.
17. Sjolund M, Andersson DI, Blaser MJ, Engstrand L. Long-term persistence of resistant Enterococcus species after antibiotic treatment to eliminate *Helicobacter pylori*. Ann Intern Med. 2003;139:483-487.
18. Fenton KA, Ison C, Johnson AP, et al. Ciprofloxacin resistance in *Neisseria gonorrhoeae* in England and Wales in 2002. Lancet. 2003;361:1867-1868.
19. Wilson ME. Infectious diseases: An ecological perspective. BMJ 1995;331:1681-1684.
20. Ghose C, Perez-Perez GI, Dominguez-Bello MG, et al. East Asian genotypes of *Helicobacter pylori*: Strains in Amerindians provide evidence for its ancient human carriage. Proc Natl Acad Sci U S A. 2002;99:15107-15111.
21. Falush D, Wirth T, Linz B, et al. Traces of human migration in *Helicobacter pylori* populations. Science. 2003;299:1582-1585.
22. Collin M, Olsen A. Extracellular enzymes with immunomodulating activities: Variations on a theme in *Streptococcus pyogenes*. Infect Immun. 2003;71:2983-2992.
23. Kalliomaki M, Salminen S, Poussa T, et al. Probiotics and prevention of atopic disease: 4-Year follow-up of a randomised placebo-controlled trial. Lancet. 2003;361:1869-1870.
24. Tannock G, ed. Probiotics and Prebiotics: Where Are We Going? Wymondham, UK: Caister Academic Press, 2002:1-336.

Staphylococcus aureus (Including Staphylococcal Toxic Shock)

PHILIPPE MOREILLON
YOK-AI QUE
MICHEL P. GLAUSER

Staphylococcus aureus can produce a wide variety of diseases, from relatively benign skin infections such as folliculitis and furunculosis to deep-seated and life-threatening conditions, including cellulitis, deep abscesses, osteomyelitis, pneumonia, sepsis, and endocarditis.[1]

In addition to producing many kinds of infections in which the organism is physically present at the infected site, *S. aureus* is capable of producing "distant" diseases, which are mediated by the secretion of toxins.[2] The toxins can be produced directly by bacteria colonizing the skin or mucosal surfaces or indirectly by microorganisms colonizing food or beverages. The direct route is exemplified by the staphylococcal scalded skin syndrome (SSSS),[3] which is due to mucosal or wound colonization by *S. aureus* producing exfoliative toxin A or B (ETA or ETB), as well as by the staphylococcal toxic shock syndrome (TSS),[4] related to the production of toxin shock syndrome toxin 1 or exotoxin B or C. The indirect route is exemplified by *S. aureus* food intoxication. In this case, the toxin is ingested with the contaminated dish and disease follows shortly thereafter in the form of vomiting and diarrhea. Food intoxication is due to staphylococcal toxins called enterotoxins.[5] These toxins are heat stable. Cooking may kill the contaminants but does not denature the toxins. Hence, subsequent culture of the dish may fail to grow the culprit bacterium.

The heterogeneity of these diseases and the unique ability of *S. aureus* to develop resistance to virtually any new antibacterial agent reflect the extraordinary capacity of this organism to adapt and survive in a great variety of environments. Over the past 30 years, molecular and genetic dissection of *S. aureus* has revealed a great number of surface adhesins, which mediate adherence to and colonization of target tissues, and secreted enzymes and toxins that are responsible for invasion and distant disease (Table 192-1).[1,6] The development of genomics and the availability of the complete nucleotide sequence of several *S. aureus* genomes have helped to complete this portrait. Approximately 50% of the *S. aureus* genome shares homology with notoriously nonpathogenic *Bacillus subtilis*, indicating that the two organisms are quite close and have evolved from a common ancestor.[7,8] Homology searches on the chromosome have revealed numerous new surface-attached and secreted factors that might represent additional pathogenic factors. Most interestingly, *S. aureus* harbor a large number of mobilizable exogenous DNA stretches, including insertion sequences, transposons, bacteriophages, and pathogenicity islands[8-10] (also referred to as genomic islands[11]), that contain specific determinants responsible for disease and antibiotic resistance.[8,11] The presence of these exogenous elements attests to the high capacity of *S. aureus* to undergo horizontal gene transfer and exchange genetic elements with other organisms, including both staphylococcal and nonstaphylococcal genera. Because gene exchange is a key player of evolution, this peculiar genetic plasticity is a likely explanation for the success of *S. aureus* as both a colonizer and disease-producing microbe. In the case of superantigens (see "Superantigens"), one of the trading partners is suspected to be *Streptococcus pyogenes*.[4]

THE MICROORGANISM

Members of the *Staphylococcus* genus are gram-positive cocci (0.5 to 1.5 μm in diameter) that occur singly and in pairs, tetrads, short chains, and irregular grapelike clusters. Ogston[12] introduced the name "staphylococcus" (from the Greek *staphylé*, a "bunch of grapes") to describe "micrococci" responsible for inflammation and suppuration. Staphylococci are nonmotile, non–spore forming, usually catalase positive, and are often uncapsulated or have a limited capsule (Fig. 192-1). Most species are facultative anaerobes.[7,13]

Staphylococci were formerly classified in a common genus with micrococci. However, the organisms are quite different in several aspects including major differences in their guanine-cytosine (G + C) content (staphylococci have a low G + C content of 30 to 39%, whereas micrococci have a high G + C content of 63% to 73%), in their cell wall structure (staphylococci have peptidoglycan-bound teichoic acids, whereas micrococci have no teichoic acids), and in the cytochrome and menaquinone composition of their respiratory chain.[7,13] Staphylococci are closer to *Bacillus* and streptococci and belong to the broad *Bacillus-Lactobacillus-Streptococcus* cluster.

The genus *Staphylococcus* contains 32 species, 16 of which are found in humans (Table 192-2). Only a few of them are pathogenic in the absence of predisposing host conditions such as immunosuppression or the presence of a foreign body. The most virulent ones include *S. aureus* and *Staphylococcus lugdunensis* in humans and *S. aureus* and *Staphylococcus intermedius* in animals. Although *Staphylococcus epidermidis* and *Staphylococcus saprophyticus* are commonly responsible for device-related and urinary tract infections, they produce substantially less devastating disease syndromes than *S. aureus*. Pathogenic staphylococci harbor some unique features when compared with their less disease-producing congeners (see Table 192-2). These include coagulase and clumping factor (or fibrinogen-binding protein), which are of laboratory diagnostic value because they help to discriminate rapidly between coagulase-positive (e.g., *S. aureus*) and coagulase-negative staphylococci (see Table 192-2).

Habitat

Staphylococci are ubiquitous colonizers of the skin and mucosa of virtually all animals including mammals and birds.[7] Some species have

penicillin-binding protein 2A (PBP2A) in methicillin-resistant staphylococci, or specific genes by direct molecular probing by polymerase chain reaction (PCR) amplification.[31-33,34] Diagnostic PCR is mostly based on amplifying the genes coding for the 16S or 23S ribosomal RNAs (rRNAs).[32,35] Because these genes are polyallelic (five to six copies per cell),[8] they increase the chance of primer attachment and PCR amplification when bacteria in the sample are scarce. The primers are targeted against highly conserved rRNA gene sequences that bracket an intervening species-specific region. After amplification, the intervening sequence is either determined and compared with existing databases or hybridized against an array containing specific probes for known bacteria.[35,36] The techniques are powerful but have some limitations. For instance, they apply only to otherwise sterile sites and may be confounding in the case of polymicrobial infection.

Molecular diagnosis plays an important role in the case of culture-negative infection, which is often the case when antibiotic treatment has been started before clinical samples were collected.[35,37] In such conditions, particular culture techniques should be applied to inactivate or wash out the contaminating drug and the period of incubation should be prolonged (for up to 2 weeks in the case of blood cultures). It is important to make the diagnostic laboratory aware of possible contaminating antibiotics so that all measures can be taken to detect the microbe.

A wealth of molecular techniques are currently being developed and proposed for routine utilization. Aside from direct species diagnosis, several molecular probing systems help directly detect antibiotic resistance determinants. The future of these tools is probably microchip technology, with which amplified samples are probed against microarrays allowing concomitant species and resistance determination for numerous bacteria.[34,36] However, although the methods are fast and elegant, they require relatively sophisticated technical skills and do not provide the live organism for further characterization. Thus, they represent a useful complementary tool, not a replacement for standard microbial culture.

PATHOGENESIS I: REGULATION AND VIRULENCE DETERMINANTS

S. aureus is extremely well equipped with surface factors and secreted proteins that mediate host colonization and disease.[1] The principal determinants of this armamentarium are listed in Table 192-1. In addition to these features, *S. aureus* is equipped with regulatory systems that sense the environmental conditions and respond by fine-tuning the expression of given metabolic and virulence determinants (for a review see references 6 and 38). Some aspects of this subtle adaptation machinery are described subsequently.

Regulation

The *agr* System

The paradigm of *S. aureus* virulence gene regulation is *agr*, which stands for accessory gene regulator and is schematized in Figure 192-2.[39] *agr* functions as a quorum-sensing control that reacts to bacterial density, allowing the preferential expression of surface adhesins during the exponential phase of growth (low cell density) and switching to the expression of exoproteins during the postexponential and stationary growth phases (high cell density).[38,39] The switch is composed of two divergent operons (see Fig. 192-2). On the left hand, promoter P2 drives the transcription of a series of components comprising (1) a transmembrane protein (AgrB); (2) an autoinducing peptide precursor (AgrD), which is processed and exported by membrane-spanning AgrB; (3) a transmembrane sensor (AgrC), which is the cognate receptor of the AgrD-derived autoinducing peptide; and (4) a transcription regulator (AgrA) that can be activated by AgrC. At low cell density (exponential growth phase), the P2 promoter is off and the operon is transcribed at a low level. As cell growth proceeds, the concentrations of both bacteria and extracellular autoinducing peptide increase in the milieu, thereby augmenting the chance of au-

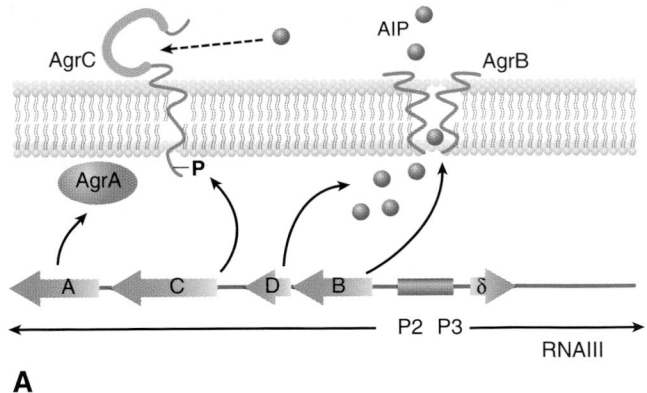

A

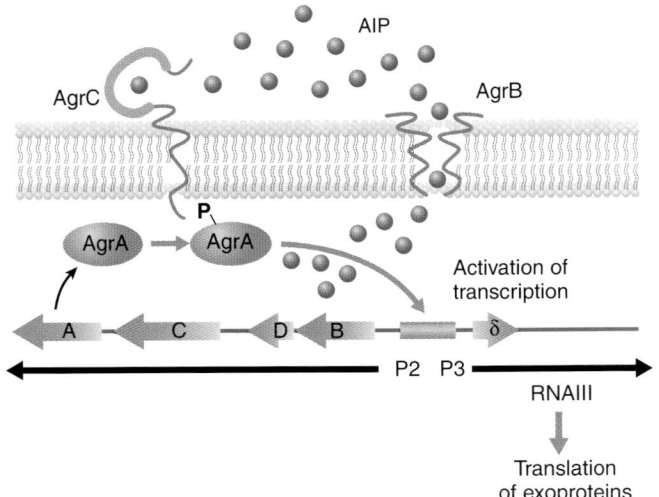

B

FIGURE 192-2. Schematic representation of the *Staphylococcus aureus* global regulatory system *agr* (accessory gene regulator). **A,** The system at rest. It consists of two divergent operons, transcribed from promoters P2 and P3, respectively. Promoter P2 encodes the putative membrane protein AgrB, the precursor of the autoinducing peptide (AIP) AgrD, which is processed by AgrB; the transmembrane receptor AgrC; and the response regulator AgrA. Promoter P3 encodes δ-hemolysin and RNAIII. At low bacterial density, P2 and P3 are off and only a small amount of AIP is secreted because of promoter leakiness (A). As bacterial growth proceeds and bacterial density increases (**B**), there is an increasing chance of AIP encountering its cognate receptor AgrC. Upon contact, AgrC undergoes a conformational change and phosphorylates (or dephosphorylates) the response regulator AgrA. Activated AgrA activates the transcription from both P2 and P3, resulting in positive feedback. δ-Hemolysin is a membrane-active protein toxic for eukaryotic cells. RNAIII is an intracellular regulator that acts in *trans* and regulates the expression of many virulence genes, including numerous toxins (see Table 192-1). Although *agr* is pivotal in quorum-sensing regulation of gene expression, it is not the only regulator of pathogenic determinants in *S. aureus. sar, saeRS, rot,* and other systems may affect the expression of *agr* itself or affect virulence genes directly (e.g., *sar*), or both (see Table 192-1).

toinducing peptide to make contact with its cognate AgrC receptor. Upon contact, AgrC activates the response regulator AgrA, a process that may involve AgrA phosphorylation or dephosphorylation.[38]

Activated AgrA is a DNA-binding protein that turns on the transcription from both promoter P2—generating a positive feedback on the system—and promoter P3, which drives the transcription of δ-hemolysin and of a peculiar effector called RNAIII. RNAIII has a reciprocal effect, activating the expression of most secreted proteins while downregulating the expression of surface-bound factors (see Table 192-1). RNAIII has a complex three-dimensional structure and a long half-life (up to 15 minutes). It is believed to regulate gene expression in several ways, including regulation at the translational level by blocking the messenger RNA ribosome-binding site of the target genes.

Other Regulatory Systems, *sae, srrAB, sigmaB, sar,* and RAP

The *agr* locus was the first two-component regulatory system affecting virulence genes that was described in *S. aureus*.[39] Since then, at least three additional two-component regulatory systems affecting global gene expression have been described. These include *sae* (for *S. aureus* exoproteins),[40] *arlS* (for autolysis-related locus sensor),[41] and *srrAB* (for staphylococcal respiratory response).[42] They affect gene expression either directly or indirectly by interfering with *agr*.

sae was identified by transposon mutation in a pleiotropic mutant defective in synthesis of exoproteins other than those regulated by *agr* (for instance, coagulase; see Table 192-1). *sae* acts independently of *agr* and responds to environmental stimuli such as high salt, low pH, glucose, and subinhibitory antibiotic concentrations. *arlS* and *srrAB* interfere with autolysis and growth in microaerobic conditions, respectively.

srrAB represses the expression of TSS toxin-1 and protein A in microaerobic conditions,[42] an observation that may be relevant for the pathogenesis of tampon-related TSS (see "Toxic Shock Syndrome").[4] Both *arlS* and *srrAB* interact reciprocally with *agr*.

Sigma factors (σ) are a second major mechanism of response to environmental stimuli. They are activated directly within the cell. *S. aureus* possesses one sigma factor homologous to the *B. subtilis* σ^B. σ^B responds to a variety of stresses including temperature, energy depletion, and chemical stimuli.[43] σ^B acts mostly through the global regulatory network but also has some direct effect by activating the expression of coagulase and fibronectin-binding proteins at the early growth stage and downregulating certain secreted proteins in the stationary phase. Increasing the production of surface adhesins suggests that σ^B-defective mutants could be less virulent than wild-type strains. However, this is not the case in rat and murine experimental infection.[44] Thus, σ^B might play a role in other situations.

sar stands for staphylococcal accessory regulator.[45] *sar* is an important locus that encodes a DNA-binding protein, SarA, that positively controls *agr*[6,46] and maybe also *sae* and *arlS*.[38] In addition, *sar* directly regulates adhesin genes (see Table 192-1). SarA is the prototype of a growing family of DNA-binding proteins that may drive a number of transcriptional activities including the expression of housekeeping genes as well as phage-related genes. Homologues of SarA include SarS, SarT, and Rot.[6]

Other factors influencing *agr* are the RNAIII-activating protein (RAP) and target of RAP (TRAP) protein.[47,48] The RAP-TRAP complex is proposed to be a two-component regulatory system that activates *agr*. It consists of (1) an autoinducer (RAP), which is a homologue of ribosomal protein L2; (2) an unknown transmembrane sensor (possibly *svrA*)[49]; and (3) an intracellular protein called TRAP that becomes phosphorylated through RAP. Interestingly, a peptide called RIP, isolated from *Staphylococcus xylosus*, is an inhibitory analogue of the active portion of RAP and was reported to block *agr* activation.[47,50] This could open new perspective in antistaphylococcal therapy.

Although this intricate network underlines the subtlety of the bacterial response to environmental stresses, it also suggests that dissecting out the role of each of these pathways in disease is an almost impossible task. The regulatory network must be considered as a metabolic hub that integrates both external and internal information and responds in the most appropriate way. Some of these circuitries are likely to complement each other. Interrupting one of them might be compensated by others, thus introducing biases in the observed phenotype. In this complex system, *agr* appears to be a central switch toward which many other regulators converge.

Role in Pathogenesis

Because these regulators can affect the expression of multiple determinants at the same time, it was logical to study both their effect in experimental infection and their relation to disease epidemiology. Inactivating the function of *agr* alone decreased pathogenicity in experimental models of tissue destruction (e.g., subcutaneous abscesses), in which exoprotein production is likely to be important.[51] On the other hand, *agr* inactivation did not influence much the course of experimental endocarditis, in which bacterial surface adhesins are critical for valve colonization.[52] The logic of this result is that *agr* inhibits adhesin production in late exponential phase, whereas the negative mutant does not (see Table 192-1). Therefore, although the negative mutant is hampered in exoprotein production, it is still fully equipped with surface-bound colonizing determinants. On the other hand, inactivating *sar* decreased infectivity in experimental endocarditis[52] because the inactivated mutant has decreased expression of surface fibronectin-binding proteins (see Table 192-1), which were shown to be important in experimental endocarditis.[53]

The implication of *agr* and *sar* in disease has stimulated the search for inhibitors of the *agr* loop, acting either on the autoinducing peptide or on the RAP pathway.[50,51,54] Implementation of these strategies for future prevention or treatment of *S. aureus* infection is a subject of active research.

Ecologic and Epidemiologic Implication of *agr*

Genetic and functional experiments revealed the existence of at least four *agr* groups in *S. aureus*, which were characterized by specific variations in all three AgrB, AgrD, and AgrC proteins: the processor-transporter, the autoinducing peptide precursor, and the receptor, respectively.[55] Whereas the autoinducing peptide of a given type stimulated signaling by members of the same group, it either cross-inhibited (e.g., group I and group IV) or cross-activated (e.g., group I and group II) members of other groups. This suggested that certain antagonistic *agr* groups could be mutually exclusive when trying to colonize simultaneously the same niche. However, studies regarding this hypothesis gave conflicting results. In particular, patients with cystic fibrosis colonized with *S. aureus* can successfully harbor organisms from two antagonistic *agr* groups.[56]

Although *agr* and other global regulators control the timely expression of pathogenic genes, they are not bona fide pathogenic factors themselves. The *agr* locus has homologues in numerous nonpathogenic staphylococci. A phylogenic study of nonpathogenic species indicated that variations in *agr* genes followed parallel variations in housekeeping rRNA genes.[57] This finding indicates that *agr* types are not selected by the capacity of one organism to exclude another but rather represent a clonal marker of distinct staphylococcal strains that were evolving in distinct environments.

This clonal relation was confirmed when *agr* groups were compared with other epidemiologic markers. Most *S. aureus* producing the TSS toxin-1 or the Panton-Valentine toxin (see "Secreted Enzymes and Hemolysins"), or both, belong to *agr* group III. The vancomycin-intermediate strains belong to *agr* group II, and the ETA-producing strains belong to group IV. Thus, global regulators were originally meant to control the expression of useful metabolic genes. How exogenous virulent genes, which were acquired later, succeeded in taking advantage of such systems remains a fascinating question in evolutionary genetics.

Cell Surface Determinants Involved in Pathogenesis

Figure 192-3 depicts the surface constituents believed to be involved in the bacteria-host relationship. Their structure and function regarding *S. aureus* pathogenesis are discussed later.

Biofilm

Biofilm is an extracellular polysaccharidic network that gathers bacterial communities within a mechanically cohesive scaffold. It is very common in the bacterial world. Biofilm-producing staphylococci were

FIGURE 192-3. Schematic representation of the gram-negative (left) and gram-positive (right) bacterial envelopes. Gram-negative bacteria have a very thin peptidoglycan (PGN) as well as an outer membrane (OM), made of lipopolysaccharide (LPS), which is not present in gram-positive bacteria. Gram-positive bacteria have a very thick peptidoglycan as well as teichoic acids (TA) and lipoteichoic acids (LTA) that are not present in gram-negative bacteria. Caps, capsule; Lprot, lipoprotein; Mb, plasma membrane; PO, porin.

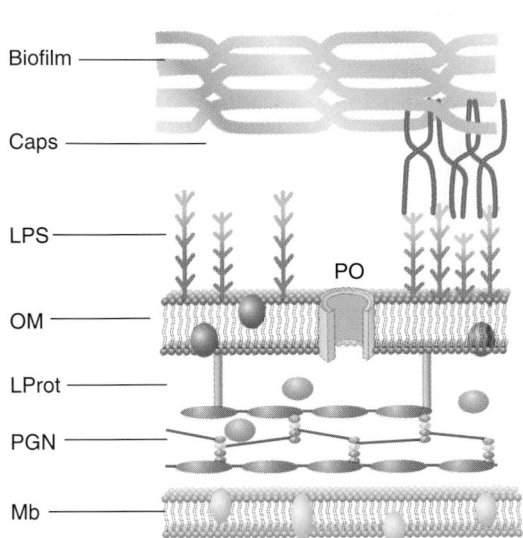
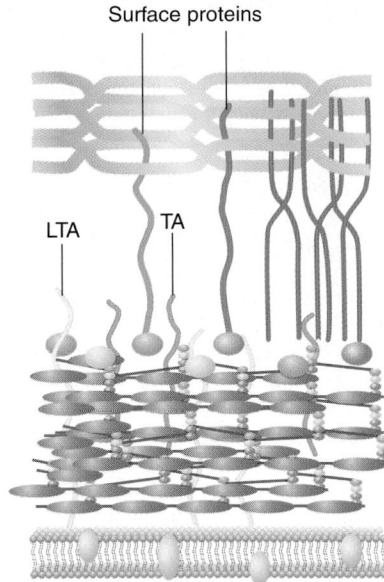

Gram Negative   **Gram Positive**

described mainly in coagulase-negative species, in which they are implicated in colonization and persistence on catheters and biomaterials. Colonization is thought to evolve in two steps, starting with nonspecific adherence of individual cells to the materials and followed by growth and biofilm formation. This process is associated with the production of the polysaccharide PIA, for polysaccharide intercellular adhesin, which is constituted of β-1,6-glucosamine chains that are N-substituted with succinate residues.[58] PIA is synthesized by an operon called *ica* composed of a regulator (*icaR*) and biosynthetic (*icaADBC*) genes.[59]

An *ica* homologue and the ability to produce biofilm were also described in *S. aureus*.[60] Its role in colonizing amorphous surfaces might be identical to that demonstrated in coagulase-negative staphylococci. However, its role in experimental pathogenesis is debated.[61] It is possible that biofilm production is a relatively ancestral mode of colonization, especially used by poorly pathogenic bacteria. The presence of more effective adherence factors in *S. aureus* could mask the contribution of biofilm to colonization. Ideally, the effect of *S. aureus* biofilm should be tested in mutants deficient in other surface colonization factors (e.g., MSCRAMMs, see later).

Capsule

More than 90% of clinical isolates of *S. aureus* elaborate polysaccharidic capsules, among which 11 serotypes have been reported.[62] Capsule type 1 and type 2 *S. aureus* produce large quantities of polysaccharides and appear mucoid on culture plates. However, they are rarely found in human clinical samples. In contrast, capsule type 5 and type 8 *S. aureus* are responsible for up to 75% of clinical infections. Type 5 and type 8 capsules are made of various sugars including mannose and fucose. They are both antiphagocytic and can increase virulence in several animal models.[63] Antibodies against these capsular types are protective in animal models of sepsis, and naturally occurring antibodies are detected in normal human serum. A conjugate vaccine directed against type 5 and type 8 capsules demonstrated some efficacy in hemodialysis patients.[64] Thus, the capsule is an antiphagocytic constituent that might be a promising target for vaccination.

Surface Adhesins

S. aureus carry several surface adhesins (Table 192-3; see Table 192-1), which confer adherence to a variety of host proteins. They are reassembled under the acronym MSCRAMM, for microbial surface component reacting with adherence matrix molecules.[65] Most of them are covalently bound to the cell wall peptidoglycan. Wall anchoring obeys

a conserved mechanism in gram-positive bacteria.[66] It involves a membrane-bound enzyme called sortase, which recognizes a conserved amino acid motif (LPXTG) at the carboxyl-terminal end of wall-attached proteins. Sortase covalently binds the threonine (T) residue of LPXTG to a free acceptor in the peptidoglycan side chain—usually a glycine in *S. aureus* (Fig. 192-4). Eleven surface proteins were characterized by their in vitro adherence properties, and screening the staphylococcal genome for LPXTG-containing species has revealed 10 additional ones.[67,68] Two of these new proteins, encoded by the *sasG* and *sasH* genes, respectively, seem significantly associated with invasive staphylococcal disease.[67]

All these MSCRAMMs have a relatively similar type of architecture. An amino-terminal signal sequence is followed by variable functional domains that carry the binding activity, themselves followed by a series of repeated sequences, an LPXTG wall-anchoring domain, and a membrane-spanning domain, which is cleaved off during wall anchoring by the enzyme sortase (see Fig. 192-4). Putative MSCRAMMs and their proven in vitro or in vivo implications are listed in Table 192-3. Some of the most relevant species for invasive disease include clumping factor A (ClfA) and fibronectin-binding protein A (FnBPA) in experimental endocarditis,[53] collagen-binding protein in osteoarthritis,[69] protein A as an antiphagocytic factor and in osteoarthritis and lethality in rodents,[70,71] and the MHC class II analog protein (MAP) or the extracellular adherence protein (EAP) as an immunomodulator subverting the T-cell response in mice.[72]

In this kind of in vivo investigation, the results depend highly on the experimental model used. As with regulatory elements, a difficulty comes from the fact that *S. aureus* harbor many MSCRAMMs at their surface. Thus, inactivating only one of them might pass undetected because its function might be complemented by others. Such a situation may result in underestimating the importance of a given factor in disease. To circumvent this limitation, the suspected gene can be transferred and expressed in a surrogate bacterium devoid of the redundant *S. aureus* background. The recombinant organism is then tested for increased adherence or infectivity, or both, in vitro and in vivo. Such experiments were useful in assessing the specific pathogenic role of ClfA and FnBPA in experimental endocarditis.[53]

MSCRAMMs are present in all *S. aureus* isolates. Although implicated in pathogenesis, they are encoded on the chromosome and do not belong to the described pathogenicity (or genomic) islands (see later).[9-11] This suggests that they arose and became stabilized in the genome earlier than mobile elements in the evolution of *S. aureus*.

TABLE 192-3 Potential *Staphylococcus aureus* MSCRAMMs Belonging to the LPXTG Anchoring Domain Family of Wall-Associated Proteins

Gene	Protein	Function	Potential Implication in Disease
spa	Protein A	Binds antibody Fc fragment	Experimental sepsis
			Experimental osteoarthritis
clfA	Clumping factor A	Binding to fibrinogen	Experimental endocarditis
clfB	Clumping factor B	Binding to fibrinogen	—
cna	Collagen binding protein	Binding to collagen	Experimental osteomyelitis
fna	Fibronectin-binding protein A	Binding to fibronectin	Experimental endocarditis
			Cell invasion
fnb	Fibronectin-binding protein B	Binding to fibronectin	—
sdrC	Serine-aspartate repeat protein	Binding to fibrinogen	—
sdrD	Serine-aspartate repeat protein	Possible binding to fibrinogen	—
sdrE	Serine-aspartate repeat protein	Possible binding to fibrinogen	—
pls	Plasmin-sensitive protein	Binding to nasal mucosal cells	Colonization of nasal mucosa
fmtB	Factor affecting methicillin resistance in the presence of Triton X-100	Putative cell wall building	Affects the expression of methicillin resistance
sasA	*S. aureus* surface protein A	Undetermined	—
sasB	*S. aureus* surface protein B	Undetermined	—
sasC	*S. aureus* surface protein C	Undetermined	—
sasE	*S. aureus* surface protein E	Undetermined	—
sasF	*S. aureus* surface protein F	Undetermined	—
sasG	*S. aureus* surface protein G	Binding to nasal mucosal cells	Associated with invasive disease
sasH	*S. aureus* surface protein H	Undetermined	Associated with invasive disease
sasI	*S. aureus* surface protein I	Undetermined	—
sasJ	*S. aureus* surface protein J	Undetermined	—
sasK	*S. aureus* surface protein K	Undetermined	—

MSCRAMM, microbial surface component reacting with adherence matrix molecules.

Adapted from Roche FM, Massey R, Peacock SJ, et al. Characterization of novel LPXTG-containing proteins of *Staphylococcus aureus* identified from genome sequences. Microbiology. 2003;149:643-654, Mazmanian SK, Ton-That H, Schneewind O. Sortase-catalysed anchoring of surface proteins to the cell wall of *Staphylococcus aureus*. Mol Microbiol. 2001;40:1049-1057, and Roche FM, Meehan M, Foster TJ. The *Staphylococcus aureus* surface protein SasG and its homologues promote bacterial adherence to human desquamated nasal epithelial cells. Microbiology. 2003;149:2759-2767.

Teichoic Acids and Lipoteichoic Acids

Teichoic acids represent up to 50% of the dry weight of purified staphylococcal walls. It is constituted of polyribitol-phosphate polymers cross-linked to *N*-acetylmuramic acid residues of the peptidoglycan (see Fig. 192-3) and decorated with D-alanine and *N*-acetylglucosamine residues.[73] Teichoic acids play an important physiologic role in the cell wall metabolism and are likely to be a site of attachment of cell wall–active enzymes and other proteins.[74] Whether teichoic acids have a direct role in staphylococcal pathogenesis is unclear. They have not been clearly defined as adhesins and do not trigger inflammation by the host innate immune system.[75]

Lipoteichoic acids are the plasma membrane–bound counterparts of teichoic acids. They have a similar general structure except for the fact that they contain polyglycerol phosphates and are linked to a diacylglycerol moiety that serves as a plasma membrane anchor.

Lipoteichoic acids have been implicated in inflammation by triggering the release of cytokines by macrophages and other players of the innate immune system. In particular, it was shown that the stereochemistry of the D-alanine decorations and the presence of the diacylglycerol lipid anchor were determinant for host recognition and subsequent inflammation.[73] It was also shown that lipoteichoic acids and purified peptidoglycan could synergize for host recognition and inflammation, the ultimate role of which is bacterial eradication. Although vital for the bacterium, lipoteichoic acids and peptidoglycan are susceptible to host defense mechanisms because they are recognized by host immunity. Thus, they are not strictly pathogenic factors.

Peptidoglycan

Peptidoglycan is a highly conserved constituent of both the gram-positive and gram-negative envelopes. It is constituted of glycan

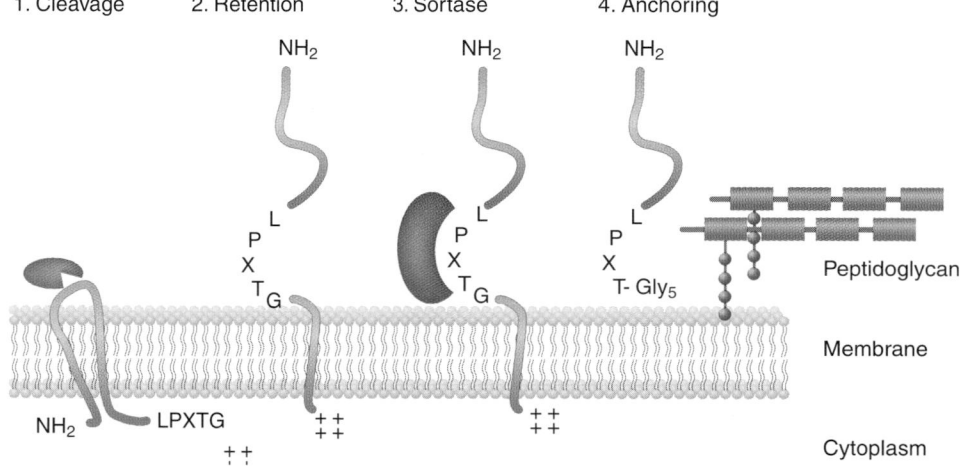

FIGURE 192-4. Anchoring of gram-positive surface proteins to the peptidoglycan through sortase-mediated processing of the LPXTG consensus motif. During membrane translocation, the N-terminal leader sequence is clipped off. The protein is then transiently retained on the cell surface through a membrane-anchor domain, rich in positively charged amino acids at its intracellular carboxyl-terminal portion. The LPXTG consensus region is then processed by sortase that clips between threonine and glycine (T-G) and transfers the covalent bond to a glycine acceptor in the peptidoglycan meshwork. (Adapted from Fischetti VA, Pancholi V, Schneewind O. Conservation of a hexapeptide sequence in the anchor region of surface proteins from gram-positive cocci. Mol Microbiol. 1990;4:1603-1605; Mazmanian SK, Ton-That H, Schneewind O. Sortase-catalysed anchoring of surface proteins to the cell wall of *Staphylococcus aureus*. Mol Microbiol. 2001;40:1049-1057.)

1. Cleavage 2. Retention 3. Sortase 4. Anchoring

chains made of N-acetylglucosamine and N-acetylmuramic acid disaccharide subunits, in which the N-acetylmuramate moiety is linked to highly conserved pentapeptide or tetrapeptide stems (L-alanine-D-isoglutamine-L-lysine-D-alanine-[D-alanine]) (Fig. 192-5). The L-lysine in position 3 is typical of staphylococci and streptococci but can be substituted for diaminopimelic acid in many other microbes including gram-negative bacteria. Peptidoglycan is a thick structure in gram-positive bacteria (10 layers), whereas it is thin (1 or 2 layers) in their gram-negative counterparts.[76]

The chains of disaccharide-peptide are cross-linked through peptide bridges between the penultimate D-alanine and the diamino acid L-lysine located in position 3 of a neighboring stem peptide. In S. aureus, the interpeptide bridge typically contains a polyglycine linking piece, comprising one to five glycine residues. The addition of glycines to the wall precursors is driven by the femABC and fhmB genes (Fig. 192-6).[77] These determinants are implicated in the plasticity of the wall and are indirectly implicated in staphylococcal resistance to both methicillin and vancomycin (see "Antibiotic Resistance").

Peptidoglycan is the major scaffold for anchoring most MSCRAMMs. Hence, it plays an indirect role in pathogenesis. On the other hand, it is recognized by the innate immune system and triggers cytokine release and inflammation, as do lipoteichoic acids.[75] Thus, it is probably important for the microorganisms to hide these structures from host recognition, an objective that can be achieved by producing antiphagocytic components such as a capsule or protein A.[63,70]

Because peptidoglycan is a critical cell structure, its assembly is the target of antibiotics such as β-lactams and glycopeptides (e.g., vancomycin). Modification of peptidoglycan synthesis is a response of resistant staphylococci to attack by these drugs (see "Antibiotic Resistance").

Secreted Enzymes and Hemolysins

S. aureus produce a number of exoenzymes, membrane-active proteins (hemolysins and leukocidins), and toxins that are involved in disease mechanisms (see Table 192-1).[2-4] Exoenzymes encompass proteases and lipases, which are destructive to host tissues and use-

FIGURE 192-5. Peptidoglycan assembly in wild-type *Staphylococcus aureus* (**A**) and in methicillin-resistant *S. aureus* (MRSA) (**B**). **A**, Cell wall precursors consist of the disaccharide pentapeptides N-acetylglucosamine-N-acetylmuramic acid-L-ala-D-glu-L-lys-D-ala-D-ala. After membrane translocation, the precursors are handled by membrane penicillin-binding proteins (PBPs). High-molecular-weight PBPs are bifunctional enzymes that perform both a transglycosidase step, linking the incoming N-acetylglucosamine (G) to a muramic acid (M) in the nascent wall, and a transpeptidase step, linking the penultimate D-ala to a glycine acceptor in the nascent wall. In *S. aureus,* the lysine in position 3 of the stem peptide is almost always decorated with a pentaglycine side chain (orange bars). Penicillin is a mechanism-based inhibitor of the transpeptidase domain of PBPs. **B**, MRSA carry an additional PBP called PBP2A, which has very low affinity for most available β-lactam drugs. Therefore, when β-lactams are present, they block the normal PBPs but not PBP2A. PBP2A has only a transpeptidase domain and must "hijack" the transglycosidase domain of normal PBP2 in order to be active.[122]

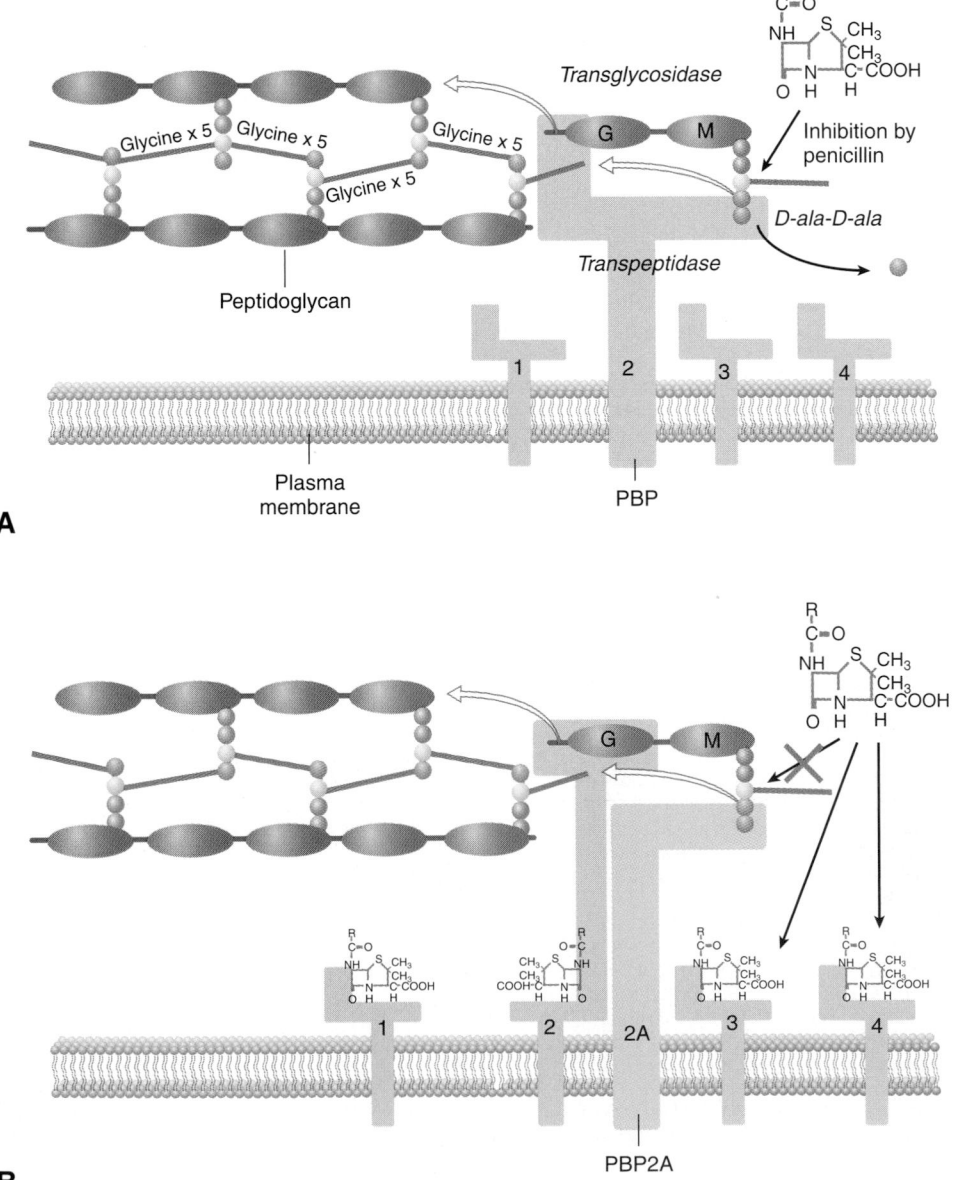

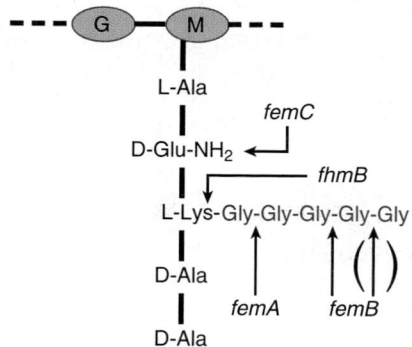

FIGURE 192-6. In order to be functional, penicillin-binding protein 2A (PBP2A) requires that the cell provide fully decorated precursors, containing both a pentaglycine side chain and an amidated glutamine. Inactivation of the *femB*, *femA*, and *fhmB* genes blocks the addition of pentaglycines and thus decreases the expression of methicillin-resistance even though PBP2A is present in the bacterial membrane. Inactivation of *femC* has a similar effect. (Adapted from Berger-Bächi B. Expression of resistance to methicillin. Trends Microbiol. 1994;2:389-393.)

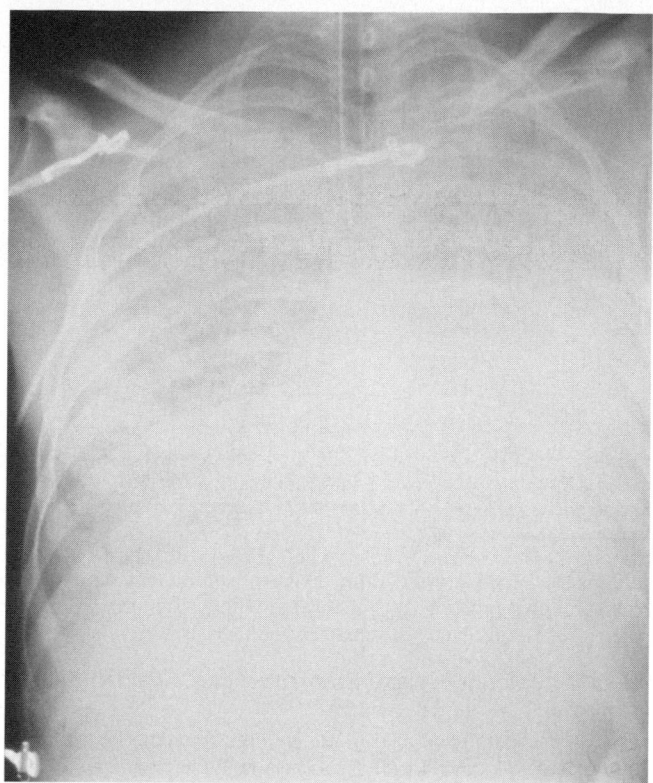

FIGURE 192-7. Fulminant hemorrhagic pneumonia in a 20-year-old patient infected with a Panton-Valentine toxin–producing *Staphylococcus aureus*.

ful for conveying nutrients to the invading bacterium. Their pathogenic role has not been much studied in animal models, but their contribution to disease is apparent.

Hemolysins

S. aureus has a minimum of four hemolysins referred to as α-, β-, γ-, and δ-hemolysin.[7,13] They can lyse erythrocytes and other eukaryotic cells. The α- and δ-hemolysins are secreted in nontoxic soluble forms and multimerize on eukaryotic membranes to form lytic pores.[2] α-Hemolysin was shown to be important in experimental endocarditis.[78]

β-Hemolysin is distinctive because it is a sphingomyelinase that damages membranes by enzymatic alteration of their lipid content. γ-Hemolysin is also peculiar. It is composed of two types of proteins called S and F, for slow and fast elution in chromatography. It can lyse white blood cells in addition to other cells and is sometimes referred to as "leukocidin." It is encoded by two distinct operons, one encoding a unique HlgA (S protein) and the other encoding one S protein (HglC) and one F protein (HglB). S and F proteins must assemble to form membrane-perforating complexes. Therefore, this class of hemolysins is also referred to as "synergohymenotropic" toxins. Active γ-hemolysin exists in two bioactive forms, HlgA-HglB and HlgA-HglC. The α-, β-, δ-, and γ-hemolysins are present in most *S. aureus* isolates. They are all encoded on the chromosome and are subject to *agr* regulation (see Table 192-1).

Panton-Valentine Toxin

A few homologues of γ-hemolysin have been described. One of them was reported in 1932 by Panton and Valentine.[79] The toxin is encoded by two genes, *lukS* and *lukF*, products of which can assemble either between themselves or with the components of γ-hemolysin, thus producing chimera structures. Like the other hemolysins, Panton-Valentine (PVL) toxin is apparently regulated by *agr* (see Table 192-1). Unlike the other hemolysins, PVL is encoded by a mobile phage (ϕSLT) that can transfer PVL to other strains. Also unlike the other hemolysins, PVL is present in only 2% of *S. aureus* clinical isolates.

PVL-producing *S. aureus* appeared to be associated with furunculosis or severe hemorrhagic pneumonia, or both, in young adults and children,[80] as well as with a few clusters of skin infections related to community-acquired MRSA (CA-MRSA).[21] By contrast, PVL-producing *S. aureus* are rarely responsible for other infections

such as osteomyelitis, septicemia, and endocarditis.[80] The reason for clustering in young patients is unclear. It could be linked to an age-related permissive milieu or a permissive immunologic window. Nevertheless, the connection is important; a young adult suffering recurrent boils and presenting with pneumonia deserves particular attention because the mortality rate associated with the hemorrhagic lung disease is very high (Fig. 192-7).

Exfoliative Toxins and Staphylococcal Scalded Skin Syndrome

SSSS is a superficial skin disorder that varies from local blistering to impressive generalized scalding (Fig. 192-8). It was originally described by the German physician Baron Gotfried Ritter von Rittershain, who published a series of 297 cases in young children in 1878.[81] Hence, it is sometimes referred to as "Ritter's" disease. SSSS clusters in newborns and infants younger than 1 year and rarely in adults. It is typically due to mucosal or skin colonization (e.g., umbilical cord) with a toxigenic *S. aureus* producing either ETA or ETB, encoded by the *eta* and *etb* genes, respectively. The toxin genes are located either on a phage (*eta*)[11] or on a plasmid (*etb*).

The cases of SSSS often evolve as small epidemics caused by clonally related strains, usually in nurseries. Nasal carriage of the organism may be found among the medical staff, and all caretakers should be screened for this possibility. A recent study indicates that the proportion of *S. aureus* carrying *eta* or *etb* in overall staphylococcal nasal carriers or clinical isolates is low (0% to 2% of isolates),[82] which may explain the rarity of the disease and its clustering in favorable milieus.[83]

The toxins act by a direct effect on the strata granulosum of the keratinized epidermis. The mucosas are never involved. This consideration is important for the differential diagnosis from more severe Lyell's syndrome, which usually involves the mucosa.[3] Lyell's syndrome, or toxic

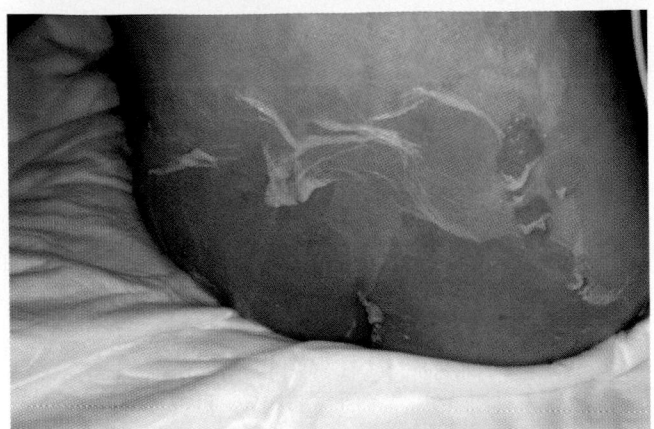

FIGURE 192-8. Staphylococcal scalded skin syndrome. Blisters are the expression of a toxin-related (exfoliative toxin A or B) distant disease and usually do not contain the microorganisms.

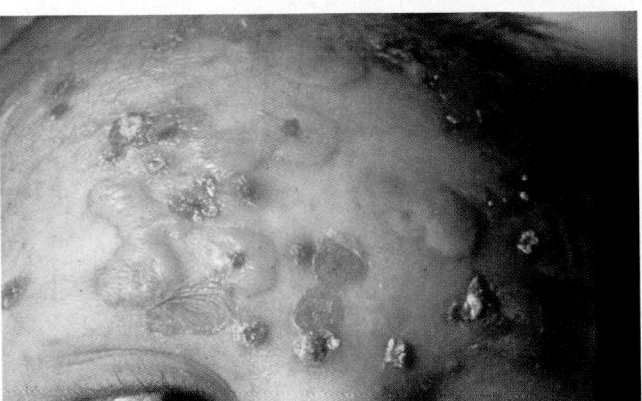

FIGURE 192-9. Localized staphylococcal scalded skin syndrome, also called bullous impetigo. The disease is due to the local production of exfoliative toxins and bacteria may be found in the blister liquid.

epidermal necrolysis, results from cleavage within the dermis or at the dermoepidermal junction. It is associated with a reaction to more than 100 drugs and sometimes vaccination, and there is a high fatality rate.

Molecular Pathogenesis of Staphylococcal Scalded Skin Syndrome

The molecular pathogenesis of SSSS is sophisticated. The toxin is released by staphylococci locally, passes though the body, and localizes at the level of the strata granulosum because of the local occurrence of a specific cell membrane ganglioside (GM4). GM4 is present only in the skin of young children and in adults with peculiar skin diseases, which may explain the clustering of SSSS in these populations. GM4-like gangliosides are present in the skin of suckling mice and can inhibit the effect of the toxin when coincubated before injection into susceptible animals.[84] The toxin demonstrates a serine protease activity but only after it has reached the skin. This suggests that a locally induced conformational change is required for activity. Extensive research has led to the following model (reviewed in reference 3). The secreted toxin is targeted to the skin of susceptible patients because of its strong affinity for GM4. Binding to GM4 triggers its internalization into keratinocytes, where the toxin reaches the keratohyalin granules. The serine protease domain becomes activated locally either by partial proteolysis or by attachment to an as yet unknown inducing coreceptor. The definitive targets of the protease or other enzymatic activities of the toxin are as yet unclear.

Clinical Aspects

There are two forms of SSSS, a generalized form and a localized form. In the generalized form, the toxin spreads throughout the body and localizes at the level of the skin, where it produces generalized scalding (see Fig. 192-8). The skin is easily detached by mere rubbing (Nikolsky's sign). The blister liquid is clear. Because scalding is the expression of a distantly secreted toxin, the responsible staphylococci are usually not found in the lesions. The disease is self-limited and wanes within 4 to 7 days. This period probably parallels the appearance of specific antitoxin immunoglobulins. Indeed, in addition to age-related expression of GM4 in the skin, the presence of antitoxin antibodies in older children and adults explains the restriction of SSSS to the younger age groups.

The localized form of SSSS is sometimes referred to as bullous impetigo (Fig. 192-9). It results from local spread of the toxin around a colonized wound in individuals who already have some immunity against the toxin. This is the case in newborns (often around the umbilicus), in infants still benefiting from passive maternal immunity, and in older individuals who are already immunized. The presence of antibodies hinders distant dissemination of the toxin but not local spread around the colonized area. The presence of GM4 or related fac-

tors is likely to be necessary. Unlike that in the generalized form, scalding is localized and the blister liquid often contains bacteria and sometimes white blood cells.

Patients may have general symptoms including fever and lethargy, especially in the generalized form. Treatment includes general measures such as antiseptic wound dressing and fluid support, specific antibiotic therapy to eradicate the causative agent, and screening and decontamination of caretakers, especially in nurseries. If it is appropriately handled, the prognosis for children with SSSS is usually good, with a mortality below 5%. In contrast, mortality can be very high in adults (>50%) and is usually associated with their underlying condition.

As mentioned, the differential diagnosis from Lyell's syndrome (toxic epidermal necrolysis) is critical because the etiology, treatment, and prognosis of the diseases are different. In doubtful cases, skin biopsy is useful to provide a definitive answer.

Superantigens

Toxic shock syndrome toxin-1 (TSST-1) and staphylococcal enterotoxins (SEs) are the paradigm of a large family of pyrogenic exotoxins called superantigens (SAgs).[2,4,5] SAgs are proteins that do not activate the immune system through normal contact between antigen-presenting cells and T lymphocytes. Normally, antigens are taken up by antigen-presenting cells, hydrolyzed, and presented as restricted peptides to cognate T lymphocytes. The peptides are expressed within a grove on the major histocompatibility complex (MHC) class II receptor on the surface of the antigen-presenting cell. Cognate T cells recognize the peptide–MHC class II complex by specific contacts with the five variable domains of the α- and β-chains of their T-cell receptor (Vβ, Dβ, Jβ, Vα, Jα).[85]

SAgs can bypass this highly specific interaction. They attach to an external portion of the Vβ domains from large quantities of lymphocytes and directly wedge them to the MHC class II receptors of antigen-presenting cells. This nonspecific contact activates up to 20% of the total pool of T cells compared with approximately 1 per 10,000 during "normal" antigen presentation. The consequence is a massive burst of cytokine release, which drives an overwhelming inflammatory response resulting in endotoxin-like shock, including endothelial leakage, hemodynamic shock, multiorgan failure, and possibly death.

S. aureus can produce a large number of SAgs. Aside from TSST-1, they produce at least 15 different enterotoxins (staphylococcal enterotoxin A [SEA], B, C_n, D, E, G, H, I, J, K, L, M, N, O), to which genomic analyses have added an equivalent number of SAg homologues called staphylococcal exotoxins, denominated SET1 to SET15.[86,87]

Although there is quite some variation in the primary structure of many SAgs, they all share a common architecture as demonstrated by crystallography. They consist of A and B globular domains, which are made of β-sheet barrels and α-helices and rejoined by a discrete linking piece. In TSST-1 the region binding to the Vβ chain of the T-cell receptor has been mapped at the A-B hinge region.

A genealogy of SAgs was constructed on the basis of their sequence homologies. The SAgs studied were segregated into five groups.[4] Group I was represented only by TSST-1. Group III contained only staphylococcal SAgs (SEA, E, J, D, and H) and group IV only streptococcal SAgs (SPE C, J, G and SME Z). Groups II and V contained both staphylococcal and streptococcal SAgs. Group II contained staphylococcal SEB, C, and G and streptococcal SSA and SPE A, and group V contained staphylococcal SEI, K, L, and P and streptococcal SPE H. This underlines the likelihood of horizontal gene transfer between these two genera, a fact that is becoming increasingly apparent through genome comparisons.[2,4,8,88]

Toxic Shock Syndrome

TSS has been sporadically reported as staphylococcal scarlet fever since 1927.[89] Interest in TSS increased dramatically in the early 1980s, when a number of staphylococcal TSS cases occurred in young women using high-absorbency tampons during their menses.[90] The disease was shown to be associated with a toxin, called TSST-1, that was secreted locally by toxigenic strains. TSST-1 can cross the mucosal membrane—which is apparently not the case for all SAgs—and then disseminate throughout the body. There are two clinical forms of TSS: menstrual TSS and nonmenstrual TSS.

Menstrual Toxic Shock Syndrome

The disease starts within 2 days of the beginning or the end of menses and is primarily associated with the use of high-absorbency tampons. Clinical signs include high fever, capillary leak syndrome with hypotension and hypoalbuminemia, generalized nonpitting edema, and a morbilliform rash, followed by desquamation after a few days. The toxin is produced locally, and blood cultures are typically negative. The responsible organism was represented by a single clone in most reported cases.

The disease proceeds by SAg-induced hyperactivation of the immune system (see earlier). Toxin production is regulated by *agr* (see Table 192-1). Moreover, its expression requires certain conditions, including (1) an elevated protein level, (2) a relatively neutral pH (6.5 to 8), (3) an elevated partial pressure of CO_2, and (4) an elevated partial pressure of O_2.[42] All four conditions are met when menstruation is combined with the usage of high-absorbency tampons. The high protein concentration and neutral pH are provided by blood proteins and their buffering capacity. The high partial pressure of CO_2 is ensured by the higher than atmospheric CO_2 content of blood. Eventually, the high concentration in O_2 is introduced into the vaginal anaerobic flora by the high-absorbency tampon. Thus, the O_2 brought in by the tampon might be the trigger that modifies an otherwise equilibrated ecosystem and stimulates the production of TSST-1 by colonizing staphylococci.

TSST-1–producing *S. aureus* are found in up to 20% of isolates from both carrier and clinical specimens.[82] The fact that TSST-1 expression has special requirements may partially explain the comparatively low prevalence of the disease (about 0.5 to 10 per 100,000 patients per year between normal incidence and tampon-related peaks).[4]

Nonmenstrual Toxic Shock Syndrome

Nonmenstrual TSS has attracted less attention than menstrual TSS. In addition to TSST-1, nonmenstrual TSS can be due to enterotoxins SEB and SEC, which are *agr* regulated (see Table 192-1). Responsible organisms may colonize virtually any site in the body, including surgical wounds (surgical TSS), lung (influenza-associated TSS), mucosa or skin (recalcitrant desquamative syndrome in patients with acquired immunodeficiency syndrome [AIDS]),[91] contraceptive diaphragms, and dialysis catheters in patients undergoing chronic peritoneal dialysis. The development of general symptoms with high fever and cutaneous rash should suggest the possibility of nonmenstrual TSS in such patients.

A special feature of wound colonization is that the affected tissues often do not appear inflammatory. This appearance is believed to result from the toxin itself, which is able to prevent the influx of professional macrophages.

Predisposing Factors

In addition to using high-absorbency tampons and being colonized by a toxigenic strain, most TSS-susceptible patients lack specific antibodies to block the responsible SAg. In one study, antibody titers considered protective against TSST-1 (>100) were detected in 30% of 2-year-old children and in more than 90% of women and men 25 years of age. Low or negative titers of anti-TSST-1 antibodies (<5) were found in acute-phase sera from 90.5% of patients with menstrual TSS, and less than 50% of them developed positive titers of anti-TSST-1 antibody during convalescence.[4,92] Hence, some patients remain susceptible to recurrent TSS.

An interesting feature of SAgs is that they trigger primarily a CD_4^+ T-cell response, which results in a helper T cell Th1 cytokine release response without a significant Th2 response. A consequence of the dominant Th1 response is decreased antibody expression, which could explain the relative lack of antibody response of patients with TSS. An additional explanation for the anergy could be SAg-induced apoptosis of responsive T cells, which could account for the prolonged anergy toward the deleterious toxin.[88]

Diagnosis

The diagnosis of TSS is based on a constellation of clinical and laboratory signs as proposed by the Centers for Disease Control and Prevention (Table 192-4).[93] Table 192-4 also proposes additional laboratory features, such as isolating a toxin-producing organism in order to broaden the diagnostic tools.[4] The criteria for streptococcal TSS, caused by toxigenic *Streptococcus pyogenes* isolates, are presented for comparison. Although both syndromes are due to similar kinds of SAgs, they differ in two important aspects. First, in contrast to staphylococcal TSS, streptococcal TSS is almost always associated with the presence of streptococci in deep-seated infections, such as erysipelas or necrotizing fasciitis, which has been referred to as "flesh-eating dis-

---

TABLE 192-4 Diagnostic Criteria for Staphylococcal and Streptococcal Toxic Shock Syndrome

*Staphylococcal Toxic Shock Syndrome**	*Streptococcal Toxic Shock Syndrome*
Fever	Isolation of group A streptococci from:
Hypotension	A sterile site for a definite case
Diffuse macular rash with subsequent desquamation	A nonsterile site for a probable case
Three of the following organ systems involved:	Hypotension
Liver	Two of the following symptoms:
Blood	Renal dysfunction
Renal	Liver involvement
Mucous membranes	Erythematous macular rash
Gastrointestinal	Coagulopathy
Muscular	Soft tissue necrosis
Central nervous system	Adult respiratory distress syndrome
Negative serologies for measles, leptospirosis, and Rocky Mountain spotted fever as well as negative blood or cerebral spinal fluid cultures for organisms other than *S. aureus*	

*Proposed revision of diagnostic criteria for staphylococcal toxic shock syndrome (TSS) includes (1) isolation of *S. aureus* from a mucosal or normally sterile site, (2) production of TSS-associated superantigen by isolate, (3) lack of antibody to the implicated toxin at the time of acute illness, and (4) development of antibody to the toxin during convalescence.

Adapted from McCormick JK, Yarwood JM, Schlievert PM. Toxic shock syndrome and bacterial superantigens: An update. Annu Rev Microbiol. 2001;55:77-104.

ease." Second, whereas the mortality in adequately treated staphylococcal TSS is about 5%, the mortality in streptococcal TSS is close to 50%, and treatment requires urgent and generous surgical débridement of infected tissues and sometimes amputation.

Treatment and Prevention

Treatment of staphylococcal TSS consists of eliminating the causative agent by antibiotic treatment and appropriate drainage of affected tissues if necessary. Otherwise, supportive care including intravenous fluid and vasopressors may be necessary. The immunologic gap allowing the toxin to be active in susceptible patients suggests that passive immunotherapy such as intravenous immunoglobulin (IVIG) could be effective. A large case-control study involving patients with streptococcal TSS showed that IVIG combined with antibiotic and supportive therapy may have significantly reduced the fatality rate.[94] Because the mortality in staphylococcal TSS is relatively low, immunotherapy is usually not warranted and is reserved for life-threatening cases of streptococcal TSS.

Prevention is aimed at avoiding the use of hyperabsorbent tampons as well as preventing staphylococcal colonization of wound and mucosa. In the case of nasal carriage, prevention is achieved by topical application of antibacterials such as mupirocin. In the case of extranasal colonization, additional complete body washing with antiseptics such as chlorhexidine is recommended for at least 1 week.[15,95] Control cultures should be taken thereafter.

Because up to 20% of natural *S. aureus* colonizers carry the TSST-1 gene,[82] the risk of recolonization with another strain is high. Immunization with a TSST-1 vaccine could circumvent this problem.[96] However, vaccines might be incompletely effective in certain patients who are intrinsically anergic to the toxins.

Enterotoxins and Food Poisoning

S. aureus harbor up to 15 enterotoxins, which are defined as SAgs able to produce gastrointestinal symptoms including vomiting and diarrhea in primate models.[2,5] Although many of these toxins have potential SAg activity, not all of them have a clear role in human disease. As mentioned, SEB and SEC are associated with nonmenstrual TSS. Likewise, SEA, SEB, and SEC are the most frequent enterotoxins associated with food poisoning.

Foodborne disease is a major public health problem and may account for 6 million to 8 million cases per year in the United States.[97] *S. aureus* food poisoning follows ingestion of toxins that have been released into contaminated food stocks or beverages. The toxins are heat stable and thus are not denatured by cooking. The disease typically starts 2 to 6 hours after ingestion with general malaise, nausea, vomiting, abdominal pain, and diarrhea. There is no fever, but the symptoms may be distressing enough to justify hospital consultation in about 10% of patients. The symptoms resolve spontaneously within 6 to 12 hours and the prognosis is excellent, except in the case of severe dehydration in young children and elderly patients

Although the mode of action of SAgs at the level of T lymphocytes is known, their mechanism at the surface of the intestinal mucosa is unclear. TSST-1 and SEB, which may produce TSS, can traverse the mucosa by transcytosis.[98] On the other hand, SEA, which is one of the major causes of food intoxication, apparently can not. Thus, symptoms could be related to some kind of local toxicity.

Other Implications of Superantigens

Although SAgs can result in dramatic subversion of the host immune system, they are not ultimate bacterial weapons because they affect only a restricted subgroup of anergic patients. In addition, bacteria may have evolved their Sag toxin repertoire in parallel in order to escape immunity. Such evolution could explain the more than 30 SAgs and Sag homologues discovered on the *S. aureus* chromosome.[8,11,87] Many of these genes are physically contiguous, suggesting that they could have arisen by duplication, maybe for the purpose of diversity. The versatility of SAgs is further supported by the discovery that one of them, SEH, develops its SAg activity by binding to the Vα rather

than the Vβ domains of the T-cell receptor, thus expanding different sets of T-cell lineages than classic SAgs.[99]

The clinical relevance of this multiplicity of toxins is not entirely understood. Toxin genes are dispensable elements that are not needed for growth in rich media and in the absence of competition. Some SAgs (e.g., TSST-1, SEA, SEB, and SEC) obviously provide a way for the bacterium to escape host immunity. Carrying multiple toxin variants may be an additional advantage for survival in specific niches. For instance, SAgs are postulated to have been involved in the etiology of psoriasis and atopic dermatitis,[100] in which toxin-induced skin modification could promote bacterial survival. SAgs may also be involved in the Kawasaki syndrome.[100] On the other hand, food poisoning is more difficult to understand because the organism is not present at the time of disease. An alternative is that toxin multiplicity could serve to broaden the spectrum of potential animal hosts for *S. aureus*.

PATHOGENESIS II: PATHOGENICITY (GENOMIC) ISLANDS AND MOVABLE ELEMENTS

Genome comparisons indicate that about 50% of predicted proteins encoded by the *S. aureus* chromosome are highly homologous to those of *B. subtilis*.[7,8] This suggests that both organisms inherited most of their genes from a common ancestor and diverged later on. Most homologous genes are housekeeping determinants needed for growth and division. Divergent genes comprise sporulation genes, which are present only in *B. subtilis*, and pathogenic genes, which are present only in *S. aureus*.

A salient feature of the *S. aureus* genome is the presence of a large number of mobile elements that often carry pathogenic or drug resistance determinants, or both (see Table 192-1).[8-11,87] These comprise insertion sequences, transposons, viruses, and pathogenicity (or genomic) islands (see Table 192-1). Insertion sequences may move throughout the chromosome and turn off or turn on target genes by disruption or restitution of open reading frames or transcription activation by intrinsic promoters. Transposons often carry resistance determinants against antibiotics or heavy metals. Viruses mostly carry single pathogenic determinants such as ETA[8] and PVL leukocidin[11,101] and can transmit these determinants by infecting other strains.

Pathogenicity or genomic islands are continuous structures that vary in size from about 15 to 70 kb and can harbor many virulence or resistance genes. They mostly contain heterologous DNA, indicating exogenous acquisition. A common feature of these elements is that they are bracketed by direct or inverted repeats and carry recombinase genes. The repeats serve as attachment sites (*att*) for integration into homologous regions of the bacterial chromosome. The recombinase, which is often an integrase, catalyses chromosomal integration.[102]

Mobilization of Pathogenicity (Genomic) Islands

A seminal study demonstrated that *S. aureus* pathogenicity island 1 (SaPI1) could be mobilized from the bacterial chromosome by ϕ80α and ϕ11 and transferred into naïve recipients thereafter.[102] During productive phage infection, SaPI1 is first excised from the chromosome, owing to the phage Xis function, amplified in the cytoplasm (up to 120 copies in the case of ϕ80α), encapsidated, and ready for infection of naïve recipients. After entering a new *Staphylococcus*, SaPI1 undergoes Campbell-like site-specific integration into the chromosome using both its *att* site and its own integrase. Such phage mobilization was observed with other pathogenicity islands (e.g., SaPI2)[10] and is likely to be a general mechanism of gene transfer for these large elements.

Staphylococcus aureus Pathogenicity Islands, Types, and Nomenclature

Several SaPIs were described before complete staphylococcal genomes were available.[9,10] SaPI1 and SaPI2 harbor the gene for TSST-1 and are responsible for most cases of TSS (one SaPI2-containing clone in particular). SaPI3 and SaPI4 contain numerous enterotoxin genes. SaPIbov encodes a bovine version of TSST, and

SaPIbap encodes a bovine adherence protein that may play a role in bovine mastitis.

The analysis of complete staphylococcal genomes has confirmed the existing SaPIs and revealed additional features.[8,11,87] As new islands are being discovered, their nomenclature is being revisited.[11] Structures resembling SaPIs but containing determinants other than toxin genes are apparent. These include antibiotic resistance genes (see SCCmec later), other types of SCC elements containing capsule genes,[103] and SaPIs containing adherence proteins (SaPIbap).[9] It was proposed to rename these multigene exchange cassettes using the more general denomination "genomic" islands and abbreviate them as "νSa," where ν stands for island, Sa for *S. aureus*, and additional numbers refer to their chromosomal insertion site.[11] In this proposed nomenclature, former SaPI2 corresponds to νSaα and former SaPI3 to νSaβ. The other SaPIs might be different in the strains in which they were originally described and the strain MW2 (a community MRSA) that was completely sequenced.[11] The increasing list of staphylococcal virulence genes and the fact that they are located on movable elements underline once more the extraordinary versatility of this organism and raise fundamental questions regarding its chromosomal evolution.[87]

The Resistance Island SCCmec

By analogy to pathogenicity (or genomic) islands, MRSA contain one resistance island called SCCmec, where SCC stands for staphylococcal cassette chromosome and mec for the genetic element conferring resistance to methicillin.[104] SCCmec is an exogenous piece of DNA that may vary between 15 to 60 kb and is absent from methicillin-susceptible staphylococci. Its boundaries are demarcated by direct and inverted repeats, which allow integration at a homologous site into the chromosome. The SCCmec critical genes are the recombinases ccrA and ccrB, which can mediate mobilization of the whole element, and the mecA gene, which mediates β-lactam resistance. The rest of SCCmec contains various additional determinants and is referred to as "J" for junkyard.[103]

mecA encodes a particular penicillin-binding protein called PBP2A, which has a very low affinity for methicillin and most other β-lactam drugs.[105] Hence, PBP2A is responsible for the intrinsic resistance of MRSA to almost all β-lactams (see "Mechanism of Methicillin Resistance"). The mecA gene is preceded or not by the mecRI and mecI regulatory determinants, which are homologues of the blaRI and blaI regulators of penicillinase (bla) genes. mecRI (and blaRI) encodes a membrane receptor, and mecI (and blaI) encodes a gene repressor. In the presence of penicillin, the extracellular portion of the membrane mecRI (blaRI) receptor triggers an autocatalytic cleavage of its intracytoplasmic portion. The liberated intracytoplasmic peptide acts as a metalloprotease, which further cleaves the mecI (blaI) repressor, thus derepressing gene expression.[106] The mecA gene is bracketed by one or two copies of IS431, which are believed to serve as a gene collector and may promote the local insertion of additional determinants, such as antibiotic resistance genes.[103]

Four types of SCCmec were discriminated on the basis of the structure of their ccrA-B and mecA complexes.[103,107,108] These four types are likely to mirror major original MRSA clones. Notably, types I, II, and III were shown to belong to hospital clones. They harbor multiple resistance determinants, they have relatively large sizes (35 to 60 kb), and therefore they are difficult to mobilize. A fourth type (type IV) of SCCmec has been identified as typical of CA-MRSA.[108] It is much smaller (about 15 kb) than its hospital congeners, does not carry multiple antibiotic resistance genes, and may be easier to mobilize. On the other hand, its seems to be associated with other elements in the same bacterium, including the PVL toxin that is encoded by a virus and multiple staphylococcal exotoxin (set) genes that are located on the νSaβ island or former SaPI3.[11] Together, these elements may make the organism particularly fit and virulent. It is unlikely that these particular CA-MRSA have arisen from hospital MRSA that permeated the community. It is more likely that CA-MRSA have emerged independently, having acquired their SCCmec from coagulase-negative staphylococcal donors,[109] and been allowed to evolve either because of the widespread use of β-lactams or because it provides another, as yet undetermined advantage to the bacterium.

ANTIBIOTIC RESISTANCE

S. aureus have developed resistance to virtually all antibiotic classes available for clinical use. These encompass cell wall inhibitors such as β-lactams and glycopeptides, ribosomal inhibitors including macrolide-lincosamide-streptogramin B (MLS$_B$), aminoglycosides, tetracyclines, fusidic acid, and the new oxazolidinones, the RNA polymerase inhibitor rifampin, the DNA gyrase blocking quinolones, and the antimetabolite trimethoprim-sulfamethoxazole.[110,111] The main resistance mechanisms are summarized in Table 192-5. Some of them are discussed in the following.

β-Lactams

β-Lactams inhibit bacterial growth by interfering with cell wall assembly. They bind to the active site of a series of membrane-bound enzymes responsible for inserting the peptidoglycan precursors into the nascent wall (see Fig. 192-5).[112,113] Certain of these enzymes are bifunctional and carry both a transglycosidase and a transpeptidase activity. Transpeptidation takes place at the D-ala-D-ala terminus of the precursor. It hydrolyzes the covalent bond between the penultimate and the terminal D-ala and then transfers it to a free NH$_2$ terminus (a glycine in *S. aureus*) of neighboring stem peptides. The terminal D-ala is released and a new stem peptide cross-link is created (see Fig. 192-5A).

Penicillin and other β-lactams are steric analogues of the cell wall D-ala-D-ala terminus of the precursors. They compete with it for binding to the active site of the membrane-bound transpeptidase and act as "mechanism-based" inhibitors. Hence the term penicillin-binding protein (PBP) coined for these enzymes.

Resistance to Penicillin

The most common mechanism of *S. aureus* resistance to β-lactams involves penicillinase, which is encoded by the bla gene usually carried on a plasmid. The gene is inducible and preceded by the blaRI and blaI regulatory determinants (see SCCmec earlier). Penicillinase is a secreted enzyme that hydrolyzes penicillin and other penicillinase-susceptible compounds into inactive penicilloic acid.[112] Penicillinase-producing *S. aureus* emerged rapidly after penicillin was introduced as a therapeutic agent in the mid 1940s. They are now prevalent both in the hospital and in the community, where they represent close to 80% of the isolates.[110,114]

The minimal inhibitory concentration (MIC) of penicillin G for fully susceptible *S. aureus* is approximately 0.01 mg/L. In contrast, the MIC of penicillinase-stable drugs such as nafcillin or cephalosporins is 10-fold greater. Thus, penicillin G remains one of the best choices against penicillin-susceptible staphylococci.

Hospital-Acquired Methicillin-Resistant *Staphylococcus aureus*

The first penicillinase-stable β-lactams such as cephalosporins and semisynthetic methicillin and nafcillin became available in the late 1950s. Ironically, the first MRSA was described at about the same time.[115] The prevalence of MRSA progressively increased thereafter.[19,116] One survey of the National Nosocomial Infections Surveillance System reported that the hospital prevalence of MRSA increased from 2.1% in 1975 to 35% in 1991.[117] It is now as high as 70% in certain centers, but great geographic variations exists. In a survey from the SENTRY Antimicrobial Surveillance Program (1997 to 1999), the MRSA prevalence varied as follows: western Pacific region, 46%; United States, 34.2%; Latin America, 34.9%; Europe, 26.3%; Canada, 5.7%. Methicillin resistance varied greatly among countries within a region. In western Pacific countries, percentages of MRSA ranged from 23.6% (Australia) to more than 70% in Japan and Hong Kong. In European centers, these percentages varied from less than 2% in the Netherlands to 54.4% in Portugal.[118]

TABLE 192-5 Mechanisms of *Staphylococcus aureus* Resistance to Major Classes of Antibiotics

Antimicrobials	Resistance Mechanisms			Resistance Gene		
	Target Modification[(a)]	Drug Inactivation[(b)]	Decreased Accumulation[(c)]	Nature*	Origin	Location[†]
β-Lactams						
Penicillinase-S	Yes [(a)]	Yes [(b)]	No	Penicillinase [(b)]	Acquired	Plasmid
				PBP2A [(a)]	Acquired	SCC*mec* (chromosome)
Penicillinase-R	Yes [(a)]	No	No	PBP2A [(a)]	Acquired	SCC*mec* (chromosome)
Glycopeptides						
Intermediate-R	Yes [(a)]	No	No	Mutations in wall-building genes [(a)]	Intrinsic	Chromosome
Fully-R	Yes [(a)]	No	No	*vanA* and *vanH* [(a)]	Acquired	Tn*1546* (chromosome)
Macrolide-Lincosamide-Streptogramin B						
Macrolides	Yes [(a)]	No	Yes [(c)]	*erm* [(a)]	Acquired	Plasmid or chromosome
				msrA [(c)]	Acquired	Plasmid
Lincosamide[‡]	Yes [(a)]	Yes [(b)]	No	*erm* [(a)]	Acquired	Plasmid or chromosome
				linA ′ [(b)]	Acquired	Plasmid or chromosome
Streptogramin B[‡]	No	Yes [(b)]	Yes [(c)]	*erm* [(a)]	Acquired	Plasmid or chromosome
				vgb [(b)] (rare)	Acquired	Plasmid or chromosome
				msrA [(c)] (rare)	Acquired	Plasmid or chromosome
Streptogramin A	No	Yes [(b)]	Yes [(c)]	*vat, vatA* [(b)] (rare)	Acquired	Plasmid or chromosome
				vga, vgaB [(c)] (rare)	Acquired	Plasmid or chromosome
Quinupristin-dalfopristin	Yes [(a)]	Yes [(b)]	Yes [(c)]	Combinations of above (rare)		
Other Classes						
Linezolid	Yes [(a)]	No	No	Mutation in 23S rRNA gene [(a)]	Intrinsic	Chromosome
Tetracyclines	Yes [(a)]	No	Yes [(c)]	*tet*(M), tet(O) [(a)]	Acquired	Plasmid or chromosome
				tet(K) and *tet*(L) [(c)]	Acquired	Plasmid or chromosome
Gentamicin	No	Yes [(b)]	Yes [(c)]	*aac*(6′)-*aph*(2″) [(b)]	Acquired	Plasmid or chromosome
				Respiratory chain mutants [(c)]		Chromosome
Chloramphenicol	No	Yes [(b)]	No	*cat* [(b)]	Acquired	Plasmid or chromosome
Fusidic acid	Yes [(a)]	No	Yes [(c)]	*fusA* mutation [(a)]	Intrinsic	Chromosome
				pUB101 [(c)]	Acquired	Plasmid
Rifampin	Yes [(a)]	No	No	*rpoβ* mutation [(a)]	Intrinsic	Chromosome
Fluoroquinolones	Yes [(a)]	No	Yes [(c)]	*grlA* and *gyrA* [(a)]	Intrinsic	Chromosome
				norA [(c)]	Intrinsic	Chromosome
Trimethoprim	Yes [(a)]	No	No	*dfrA* mutation [(a)]	Intrinsic	Chromosome
				dfrA [(a)]	Acquired	Plasmid or chromosome (acts by mutation or overproduction)
Sulfamethoxazole	Yes [(a)]	No	No	*dpsA* [(a)]	Intrinsic	Chromosome
					Acquired	Plasmid (probable) (acts by mutation or overproduction)

*PBP2A, penicillin-binding protein 2A; *vanA* and *vanH*, vancomycin resistance A and H genes (see text for details); *erm*, erythromycin resistance methylase, mainly *ermA* (chromosome, transposons Tn554) and *ermC* (plasmid); *linA* ′, lincosamide nucleotidyl transferase; *vgb*, virginiamycin hydrolysis; *msrA*, macrolide-streptogramin resistance, ABC transporter; *vat* and *vatA*, acetyl transferase genes; *vga* and *vgaB*, streptogramin A efflux gene, ABC transporter; *tet*(M) and *tet*(O), responsible for ribosomal modification and protection; *tet*(K) and *tet*(L), responsible for active efflux of tetracyclines; *aac*(6′)-*aph*(2″), bifunctional aminoglycoside acetyltransferase and phosphortransferase determinant, present on transposons Tn*4001; cat*, chloramphenicol acetyltransferase; *fusA*, gene encoding elongation factor G (EF-G); pUB101, plasmid encoding penicillin resistance (penicillinase), cadmium resistance, and a protein (Far1) conferring impermeability to fusidic acid; *rpoβ*, gene encoding the β-subunit of RNA polymerase; *grlA* and *gyrA*, genes encoding the DNA topoisomerase and gyrase, respectively; *norA*, gene encoding a staphylococcal efflux pump; *dfrA*, dihydrofolate reductase gene; *dpsA*, dihydropteroate synthase; (a) target modification; (b) drug inactivation; (c) decreased drug accumulation.
†SCC*mec*, staphylococcal cassette chromosome *mec* (see text for details).
‡The *erm* gene must be induced or constitutively expressed in order to confer resistance to lincosamides and streptogramins B. Only macrolides are good inducers. Lincosamides and streptogramins do not induce resistance but are inactive against constitutively macrolide-lincosamide-streptogramin B (MLS$_B$)-resistant strains.
R, resistant; S, susceptible.

Community-Acquired Methicillin-Resistant *Staphylococcus aureus*

Although originally confined to the hospital environment, MRSA have emerged in community-acquired infection clusters (CA-MRSA).[19-22] At first it was thought that these had emerged from hospital clones that had escaped their original milieu and permeated the community. The scenario was formally similar to the one that is widely accepted for the emergence of community-acquired penicillinase-producing *S. aureus* strains in the early 1950s.

However, clinical and molecular epidemiology indicates that we are facing two separate evolutions. On the one hand, hospital isolates are multiresistant and clonal and are associated with risk factors including recent hospitalization or surgery, living in a nursing home, and having an indwelling catheter or device. On the other hand, CA-MRSA are pauciresistant and more polyclonal[103] and produce skin disease and severe pneumonia in otherwise healthy people. Eventually, although both

hospital MRSA and CA-MRSA harbor an SCC*mec* carrying the *mecA* gene, their SCC*mec*s are of quite different sizes and most likely of different origin.[103,108,119] Thus, the two types of organisms are not alike. Practically, MRSA in patients at risk are likely to be of the multiresistant hospital type, whereas those in patients without risks are likely to be more susceptible but more invasive.

Mechanism of Methicillin Resistance

The main mechanism of methicillin resistance is mediated not by penicillinase but by the newly acquired PBP2A, encoded by *mecA*.[105] The few staphylococci expressing borderline methicillin resistance related to the overexpression of penicillinase[120] are not clinically relevant. Because of its low β-lactam affinity, PBP2A can take over the cell wall assembly when normal staphylococcal PBPs are blocked by these compounds (see Fig. 192-5B).[121] However, although this confers high intrinsic resistance to virtually all β-lactams, PBP2A has a special requirement for peculiar cell wall precursors. These must contain a pentaglycine decorating side chain attached to the L-lysine in position 3 of their stem peptide as well as other specificities such as an amidated D-glutamine in position 2 of the peptide (see Fig. 192-6).

Providing this adequate substrate to PBP2A requires the functionality of numerous accessory genes implicated in the normal wall-building machinery.[77,122] These include more than 20 accessory determinants,[122] some of which (*femABC* and *fhmB*) are responsible for adding the glycine residues critical for the PBP2A function.[77] Any alteration in these elements decreases the expression of methicillin resistance in spite of the fact that PBP2A is present.

Another fragile aspect of PBP2A is that it carries only a transpeptidase domain and is missing a transglycosidase activity (see Fig. 192-5B). Thus, to assemble the peptidoglycan successfully, PBP2A needs to "hijack" the transglycosidase domain of a normal staphylococcal PBP, namely, PBP2.[123] This is a salient example of heterologous protein cooperation in antibiotic resistance but also represents the Achilles heel of the system. Because most β-lactams can readily block the normal staphylococcal PBPs, further drug development needs only to target additional PBP2A to be effective. Both experimental work and crystallographic evidence indicate that such an approach is feasible.[124] Indeed, successful treatment of experimental endocarditis related to MRSA was achieved with an array of older and newer β-lactams with good PBP2A affinity.[125,126] This approach is a driving force for the development of new anti-MRSA compounds.[127]

Glycopeptides

Two types of resistance to glycopeptides were reported in clinical isolates of *S. aureus:* (1) intermediate resistance (MIC of vancomycin = 8 to 32 mg/L) and (2) high-level resistance (MIC of vancomycin >32 mg/L). Both phenotypes result from different mechanisms and may be of different clinical and epidemiologic relevance.

Intermediate Resistance to Glycopeptides

S. aureus isolates with intermediate resistance have emerged in several countries.[128-130] In 1997 Hiramatsu and colleagues[128] first described an isolate, called Mu50, that was recovered from a 4-month-old child suffering from MRSA sternal wound infection following cardiac surgery. The infection did not respond to vancomycin treatment. The organism had an MIC of vancomycin of 8 mg/L, as detected by standard broth dilution methods. The National Committee for Clinical Laboratory Standards (NCCLS) limits for vancomycin susceptibility and resistance are less than 4 mg/L and greater than 32 mg/L, respectively.[131] Therefore, the phenotype formally corresponded to intermediate resistance. The same authors reported a second MRSA with reduced glycopeptide susceptibility, called Mu3, that was clonally related to Mu50 and appeared to be a precursor of it.[132] In contrast to Mu50, only a small fraction of the Mu3 bacterial population ($<10^{-6}$ colony-forming units) was able to grow on agar plates containing 6 to 8 mg/L of vancomycin, the majority of the population being inhibited by such a drug concentration. However, selecting the most resistant subclones on antibiotic-containing plates reselected for the Mu50 phenotype. Mu50-like organisms are referred to as GISA or VISA, for glycopeptide- or vancomycin-intermediate *S. aureus,* and Mu3-like organisms are referred to as hGISA (or hVISA) for heterogeneous GISA or VISA.

Intermediate glycopeptide resistance arises from chromosomal mutations that affect the structure of the wall peptidoglycan.[130,133] In susceptible strains, glycopeptides inhibit cell wall assembly by binding to the D-ala-D-ala terminus of cell wall precursors, thus blocking transpeptidation. GISA harbor a thickened cell wall that contains an increased number of free, uncross-linked D-ala-D-ala terminals. This increased amount of free D-ala-D-ala is thought to act as a lure and traps glycopeptide molecules before they reach their target.

Although GISA may cause glycopeptide treatment failure, their low level of resistance and sometimes heterogeneous phenotype make them difficult to detect in the laboratory. Hence, their epidemiologic meaning is difficult to appraise. Special techniques such as screening on vancomycin-containing plates (4 mg/L) and population analysis profiles are needed to detect these phenotypes.[134]

Full Resistance to Glycopeptides

Full vancomycin resistance (MIC > 32 mg/L) has been known for more than a decade in *Enterococcus* spp.[135] In these organisms, glycopeptide resistance results from the acquisition of either Tn*1546* or Tn*1547*, two transposons encoding for a series of genes modifying the D-ala-D-ala terminus of the bacterial peptidoglycan precursor—the target of glycopeptide compounds—to D-ala-D-lactate. The modified D-ala-D-lactate–containing precursor has a low affinity for the glycopeptides and thus confers resistance. Tn*1546*, encoding the so-called VanA resistance phenotype, could be transferred to *S. aureus* experimentally.[136] Thus, it is not surprising that fully vancomycin-resistant *S. aureus* (VRSA) expressing the VanA phenotype have emerged among human clinical isolates.[137] Although these organisms are still rare, they must be taken very seriously. They indicate that the enterococcal mobile element has passed into the staphylococcal world and may become established similarly to the other mobilizable elements described previously.

Macrolide-Lincosamide-Streptogramin B Antibiotics

This group comprises separate classes of antibiotics—macrolides, lincosamides, and streptogramins B—that all bind to the bacterial ribosome and block protein synthesis. Resistance proceeds by any of the three classic mechanisms: modification of the bacterial drug target, modification-inactivation of the drug itself, and decreasing intracellular accumulation of the drug.

Ribosome Modification

Ribosome modification and drug efflux are the most frequent resistance mechanisms in *S. aureus*.[138,139] Ribosome modification is mediated by the *erm* gene (for erythromycin methylase), which encodes a methylase that adds one or two methyl groups to the 23S rRNA. This addition results in a steric alteration that greatly decreases the affinity of the drug for its target. The *erm* determinants belong to a family of methylase genes preferentially located on mobile elements such as transposons (e.g., Tn*554* and *ermA*) or plasmids (e.g., pE194 and *ermC*). An additional sophistication in *S. aureus* is that the expression of *erm* is inducible.[139] The *erm* product is synthesized only in the presence of inducing drugs. Thus, the bacterium does not waste metabolic energy in the absence of antibiotic pressure. Among MLS$_B$ drugs, only macrolides are good *erm* inducers. However, once induced, the gene product confers cross-resistance to the other members of the group, including lincosamides and streptogramins B (but not streptogramins A; see later). Moreover, mutations resulting in constitutive *erm* expression, and hence global MLS$_B$ resistance, occur at high frequency (10^{-7} to 10^{-8}). Therefore, an *erm*-inducible isolate—that is, resistant to erythromycin but susceptible to lincosamides (e.g., clindamycin) and streptogramins B—should never be treated with clindamycin because it selects for constitutive MLS$_B$ mutants that are resistant to the whole group of compounds. A double disc diffusion test, called the D-test, has been devised for detecting these strains in the routine laboratory.[140]

Drug Efflux

Active macrolide efflux has been reported in both streptococci and staphylococci.[141-143] In *Streptococcus pyogenes* and *Streptococcus pneumoniae,* efflux is mediated by the *mefA* and *mefE* genes, respectively, which are members of the major facilitator transporter group and export only macrolides (M-resistance phenotype). *S. aureus* and coagulase-negative staphylococci may contain *msrA*, which belongs to the complex ATP-binding cassette (ABC) transporter set of genes,[141] and confers resistance to both macrolides and streptogramins B (MS-resistance phenotype). In contrast to major facilitators, ABC transporters utilize ATP hydrolysis as a source of energy for active efflux. The *msrA* complex is located on a plasmid and is frequently observed in MLS$_B$-resistant coagulase-negative staphylococci. It can be transferred into *S. aureus*,[141] but its clinical relevance to MLS$_B$ resistance is unclear. Of note, lincosamides are not subject to efflux by these pumps.

TABLE 192-6 Coresistance Patterns of Methicillin-Resistant *Staphylococcus aureus* (MRSA), by Region, among All MRSA Isolates Recovered during 1997 to 1999 (*n* = 4788): Percentage of MRSA Isolates Resistant to Indicated Antimicrobial

	Region				
Antibiotics	*United States*	*Canada*	*Latin America*	*Europe*	*Western Pacific*
Gentamicin	35.5	25.9	91.2	71.7	74.0
Rifampin	7.7	4.9	23.4	44.4	10.5
Chloramphenicol	4.7	4.9	57.9	9.4	9.6
Ciprofloxacin	88.6	60.5	89.6	89.5	88.1
Tetracycline	15.6	14.8	63.8	57.2	82.0
Clindamycin	79.2	63.0	88.0	73.5	79.3
Erythromycin	92.7	75.3	93.0	82.6	94.7
TMP-SMZ	26.0	16.0	65.4	23.0	35.8

TMP-SMZ, trimethoprim-sulfamethoxazole.

Adapted from Diekema DJ, Pfaller MA, Schmitz FJ, et al. Survey of infections due to *Staphylococcus* species: Frequency of occurrence and antimicrobial susceptibility of isolates collected in the United States, Canada, Latin America, Europe, and the Western Pacific region for the SENTRY Antimicrobial Surveillance Program, 1997-1999. Clin Infect Dis. 2001;32(Suppl 2):S114-132.

Constitutive MLS_B resistance associated or not with drug efflux is extremely frequent (>90%) in hospital MRSA (Table 192-6). Therefore, MLS_B drugs should never be considered against such organisms. The only exception is the newer quinupristin-dalfopristin combination (streptogramin B and A), which is discussed in the alternative treatment section later.

Quinolones

Quinolones are an important class in the anti-infective armamentarium. They originated in the 1960s as a by-product of the synthesis of antimalarial quinines. Fluorinated derivatives such as ciprofloxacin, norfloxacin, and ofloxacin appeared in the 1980s. They had very low MICs (of the order of 0.01 mg/L) for most gram-negative pathogens. However, their MIC for gram-positive bacteria was relatively high (0.25 to 2 mg/L for *Staphylococcus* spp. and *Streptococcus* spp.)[144] and close to their therapeutic concentrations in human serum (2 mg/L for peak concentration of ciprofloxacin).[145] Using these borderline active drugs against problematic gram-positive pathogens such as MRSA facilitated the selection for resistant derivatives. The prevalence of quinolone resistance in hospital MRSA is now close to 90% (see Table 192-6),[110] making all quinolones—including the newer ones (see later)—inappropriate against such isolates.

Mechanisms of Resistance

Quinolone resistance results from chromosomal mutations (see Table 192-5). It proceeds by two types of mechanisms including overexpression of the efflux pump NorA[146] and structural mutations in the quinolone targets topoisomerase IV (*grlA* and *grlB*) and gyrase (*gyrA* and *gyrB*) genes.[147] Resistance is acquired stepwise. A first *grlA* mutation, occurring at frequencies of 10^{-7} to 10^{-8}, produced a moderate increase in MIC (e.g., from 0.5 to 2 mg/L of ciprofloxacin) that is still considered in the susceptible range (4 mg/L).[131] However, this first mutation paves the way to a second mutation in the *gyrA* gene, which combined with the *grlA* mutation results in high-level resistance. Because the initial *grlA* mutation jeopardizes the efficacy of quinolones, it is critical to avoid selecting it at first. Therefore, it is important to detect first-level quinolone resistance in the diagnostic laboratory before attempting treatment with such compounds.

Older quinolones readily select for such alterations, yielding highly resistant organisms after only a few serial exposures to the drug.[148] Newer quinolones with improved anti–gram-positive activity (levofloxacin, moxifloxacin, gatifloxacin, garenoxacin) are less selective. However, they still carry the risk of selection, particularly in bacteria that have already acquired a first degree (*grlA* mutant) of ciprofloxacin resistance (MIC = 2 to 8 mg/L).

A series of pharmacokinetic-pharmacodynamic criteria were established to predict both quinolone efficacy and resistance. Efficacy was predicted by ratios of peak drug level to MIC greater than 8 and ratios of area under the curve to MIC greater than 100.[149] Moreover, a mutant prevention concentration (MPC) was defined as a drug concentration in body fluids that is at least two to four times above the MIC.[150] Although based on experimental work, such criteria might be useful to appraise the risk of quinolone failure in problematic situations.

ALTERNATIVE TREATMENTS

Treatment of infections with hospital (multiresistant) MRSA may be problematic. It is important to test the activity of all available drugs against the isolate in order to establish whether some of them can still be used. It is also important to evaluate the severity of the disease because not all drugs are equally appropriate in serious conditions. Superficial and non–life-threatening infections probably respond to a variety of drugs, including trimethoprim-sulfamethoxazole, to which MRSA are sometimes susceptible, combined or not with other substances such as rifampin. On the other hand, there is a notorious lack of good alternatives in the case of deep-seated or life-threatening infection. Vancomycin is the first choice in such situations. However, poor response to vancomycin may occur in a substantial proportion of patients[151,152] because of the relatively poor bactericidal activity of the drug or development of resistance, or both. Combining an aminoglycoside with vancomycin increases its bactericidal activity. However, both kidney toxicity and ototoxicity are a matter of concern. Adding rifampin to vancomycin led to rather inconclusive results.[153] Other strategies are based either on relatively new compounds or on empirical-compassionate approaches that require expert supervision.

Quinupristin-Dalfopristin and Linezolid

The two newer compounds available for clinical use are the protein ribosome inhibitors quinupristin-dalfopristin and linezolid. Both compounds have proved efficacious against problematic *S. aureus* infections, but no large double-blind studies demonstrating their superiority to standard therapy are available.

Quinupristin-dalfopristin is a combination of a streptogramin B and a streptogramin A.[154] Streptogramin A is structurally different from streptogramin B and its activity is not altered by the product of *erm* genes. Quinupristin and dalfopristin are synergistic and are active against both MLS_B-susceptible and MLS_B-resistant staphylococci. The combination is highly bactericidal against MLS_B-susceptible isolates but tends to be less bactericidal in the case of constitutive MLS_B resistance, which is practically always the case in hospital MRSA (see Table 192-6). It is important to give relatively large quantities of the compound (7.5 mg/kg every 8 hours) to ensure efficacy against such organisms. Experimental data indicate that combining quinupristin-dalfopristin with a β-lactam increases its activity against MRSA, even though the β-lactam is inactive on its own.[155] This strategy is awaiting further clinical demonstration.

Linezolid belongs to the new oxazolidinone family of molecules.[156] It has no cross-resistance with other drugs and is globally active against all multiresistant gram-positive pathogens. An incontestable advantage of linezolid is its good bioavailability after oral absorption, which allows its use for intravenous-oral switch therapy. Its disadvantage is that it is essentially bacteriostatic and may not be the first choice in severe diseases such as infective endocarditis.

As with quinupristin-dalfopristin, there are no large controlled studies describing the activity of linezolid in deep-seated infections, such as osteomyelitis. Hence, both quinupristin-dalfopristin and linezolid are alternatives rather than the first choice when vancomycin is active. As with other drugs, both compounds have toxic limitations. Quinupristin-dalfopristin causes phlebitis at the infusion site and must be administered through central catheter. Linezolid may be hematotoxic, and blood counts should be followed on a weekly basis. Moreover, anecdotal cases of resistance selection during therapy have also been reported for both drugs.

Daptomycin is a cyclic lipopeptide antibiotic active against MRSA. The drug is given intravenously once every 24 hours and has been approved by the Food and Drug Administration for *S. aureus* soft tissue infections (see Chapter 29).

PREVENTION AND PERSPECTIVES

Prevention of *S. aureus* infection is mainly based on both bacterial decolonization of chronic carriers with local antiseptics and the development of new vaccines and antiadhesin strategies (see also "Carriage of *Staphylococcus aureus*").

Perspectives on antistaphylococcal strategies encompass development of new antimicrobial drugs, development of molecules that interfere with pathogenesis, and development of vaccines. Current antibacterial development includes β-lactams with improved PBP2A affinity, membrane-active daptomycin, ramoplanin (a glycolipodepsipeptide), tetracycline analogues, glycylcyclines, newer glycopeptides, peptide-deformylase inhibitors, and bacteriolytic enzymes such as lysostaphin. Antipathogenesis strategies include molecules aimed at blocking *agr*-type regulatory loops and surface adhesin blockage (see "Pathogenesis I"). Vaccination is an important area of research in both the human and veterinary fields. Experimental vaccines have been raised by a variety of means—including DNA vaccines—and against constituents as diverse as the capsule, specific surface adhesins, PBP2A, and the RAP autoinducing protein. Most of these vaccines conferred some protection in experimental models, and one trial with a conjugated capsular vaccine gave promising results in hemodialysis patients.[64] However, no approved antistaphylococcal vaccine is available for clinical utilization yet.

CLINICAL ASPECTS AND EPIDEMIOLOGY

S. aureus is a leading cause of community-acquired infections and the first cause of nosocomially acquired bacteremia, along with coagulase-negative staphylococci.[157,158] The economic cost associated with *S. aureus* infections was estimated for New York City in 1995 as $435.5 million.[159] The average length of hospital stay of *S. aureus*–infected patients was close to 20 days, compared with an overall average of 9 days for other patients. The direct cost for *S. aureus*–infected patients was $32,100, compared with an overall average cost of $13,263. Moreover, the mortality rate associated with invasive *S. aureus* infections is high, ranging from 19% to 34%.[18,160-162] However, great variations may be observed among studies.[163] In a Canadian population-based survey, the annual incidence of invasive staphylococcal infections was 28.4 cases per 100,000 population and the annual rate of mortality 4.9 cases per 100,000 population, resulting in a mortality rate of 15%.[18]

Predictors of mortality were evaluated in the case of bacteremia (Table 192-7). Predictors of an increased risk of mortality at 30 days included lower respiratory tract infection (relative risk = 5.8), diabetes mellitus (relative risk = 2.4), and age older than 65 years (relative risk = 2, 95% confidence interval 1 to 3.8).[160] Other predictors included an uneradicated infection focus (relative risk = 6.7), the presence of septic shock (relative risk = 3.7), and an insufficient dosage (<4 g daily) of penicillinase-stable penicillins (relative risk = 3.7).[161] Combined with the problem of multiple antibiotic resistance, these numbers underline the high social and economic burden of this particular organism.

Clinical Spectrum

Aside from toxin-related diseases (see "Pathogenesis I"), *S. aureus* are responsible for an array of infections in which they are directly responsible for tissue inflammation and destruction. These range from relatively benign superficial skin and soft tissue infections to severe and life-threatening conditions, including deep tissue abscesses, joint and bone infections, pneumonia, bacteremia, and endovascular infections. In a survey from the SENTRY Antimicrobial Surveillance Program—which collects data from the United States, Canada, Latin America, Europe, and the western Pacific—the distribution of *S. aureus* infections was as follows: (1) 39.2% of skin and soft tissue infections; (2) 23.2% of lower respiratory tract infections; (3) 22% of blood-stream infections, including infective endocarditis; and (4) 15.6% of other infections, including infections of the urinary tract, brain, and abdominal cavity.[118]

S. aureus are a leading cause of nosocomial infections including surgical wound infections (28%)[164] as well as pneumonia (28%).[165] In

TABLE 192-7 Univariate Analysis of Significant (P ≤ .1) Predictive Factors for Death among Patients with Invasive *Staphylococcus aureus* Infections

| Factor | Fatality Rate | | Relative Risk | |
	With Factor	Without Factor	(95% CI)	P Value
Male sex	36/152	10/95	2.3 (1.2-4.3)	.01
Age older than 65 years	28/104	18/143	2.1 (1.3-3.7)	<.01
Heart disease	29/115	17/132	2.0 (1.0-3.4)	.01
Rheumatoid arthritis	3/5	43/242	3.4 (1.6-7.3)	.05
History of stroke	6/16	40/231	2.2 (1.1-4.3)	.1
Catheter-associated infection	0/28	46/219	0.0	.004
Soft tissue infection	4/60	42/187	0.3 (0.1-0.8)	.007
Bone and joint infections	2/43	44/204	0.2 (0.1-0.9)	<.01
Respiratory focus	21/50	25/197	3.3 (2.0-5.4)	<.001
Bacteremia without focus	12/29	34/218	2.7 (1.6-4.5)	<.0.1
Positive blood culture	42/162	4/85	5.5 (2.0-14.8)	<.001
Empirical antibiotic treatment within 8 hr	37/174	6/61	2.2 (1.0-4.9)	.05
More than four medications at presentation	28/96	18/150	2.4 (1.4-4.1)	<.01

CI, confidence interval.
Adapted from Laupland KB, Church DL, Mucenski M, et al. Population-based study of the epidemiology of and the risk factors for invasive *Staphylococcus aureus* infections. J Infect Dis. 2003;187:1452-1459, and Mylotte JM, Tayara A. *Staphylococcus aureus* bacteremia: Predictors of 30-day mortality in a large cohort. Clin Infect Dis. 2000;31:1170-1174.

TABLE 192-8 Risk of Invasive *Staphylococcus aureus* Infection, Associated with Selected Underlying Conditions, in Adults 20 Years Old or Older

Underlying Condition	No. of Patients with ISA Infection (n = 226)	Annual Incidence, per 100,000	Relative Risk (95% Confidence Interval)	P Value
Hemodialysis	24	7692	257.2 (161.0-393.6)	<.001
Peritoneal dialysis	3	4918	150.0 (30.5-441.1)	<.001
Human immunodeficiency virus infection	4	778	23.7 (6.4-61.4)	<.001
Solid organ transplantation	3	683	20.7 (4.2-61.3)	<.001
Heart disease	114	362	20.6 (15.8-27.0)	<.001
Cancer	47	348	12.9 (9.1-17.8)	<.001
Illicit intravenous drug use	13	321	10.1 (5.3-17.7)	<.001
Alcohol abuse	31	241	8.2 (5.4-12.0)	<.001
Diabetes mellitus	48	192	7.0 (5.0-9.7)	<.001
Stroke	16	200	6.4 (3.6-10.6)	<.001
Chronic obstructive pulmonary disease	26	120	3.9 (2.5-5.9)	<.001
Systemic lupus erythematosus	2	80	2.4 (0.3-8.7)	.3
Rheumatoid arthritis	5	74	2.2 (0.7-5.3)	.1

ISA, invasive *Staphylococcus aureus*.
Adapted from Laupland KB, Church DL, Mucenski M, et al. Population-based study of the epidemiology of and the risk factors for invasive *Staphylococcus aureus* infections. J Infect Dis. 2003;187:1452-1459.

the community, they are the first cause of osteomyelitis (in 50% to 70% of cases)[166-169] and a major cause of bacteremia (15% to 23.5%)[157,158,170,171] and endocarditis, in which they account for up to 38% of native valve endocarditis, 69% of endocarditis in intravenous drug users, and 21% and 20% of early and late prosthetic valve endocarditis, respectively.[172]

Risk Factors for *Staphylococcus aureus* Infection

Certain populations of patients have a significantly greater risk of invasive staphylococcal infection than the normal population (Table 192-8).[18] They are represented by hemodialysis patients (relative risk = 257, 95% confidence interval 161 to 393), followed by peritoneal dialysis patients (relative risk = 150), patients with human immunodeficiency virus (HIV) infection (relative risk = 23.7), intravenous drug users (relative risk = 10.1), patients suffering from diabetes mellitus (relative risk = 7), and alcohol abusers (relative risk = 8.2).

Less frequent predisposing factors encompass chemotactic defects and defects in phagocytosis. Chemotactic defects include those in patients suffering from Job's syndrome, the Chédiak-Higashi syndrome, the Wiskott-Aldrich syndrome, and Down syndrome. Job's syndrome is a condition involving recurrent eczema with repeated skin infections and cold abscesses. The Chédiak-Higashi syndrome is defined clinically by albinism and recurrent *S. aureus* infections and cytologically by giant granules in phagocytic and other cells. Acquired chemotactic defects are also relatively rare and include rheumatoid arthritis and diabetic ketoacidosis. Opsonic defects, whether inherited or acquired, are predisposing factors for all kinds of pyogenic infections and are not specific for *S. aureus*. They are exemplified by selective or combined hypogammaglobulinemias and various kinds of complement defects.

However, one of the most important factors that independently adds to these predisposing conditions is chronic *S. aureus* carriage (see later).[15,173] Although patients with recurrent *S. aureus* infections should be tested for possible immune defects, it is of utmost importance to screen them for *S. aureus* nasal or cutaneous carriage. Positive cases should be decontaminated by using mupirocin ointment or other means (Table 192-9).

Antibiotic Resistance

The problem of antibiotic-resistant *S. aureus* is extremely challenging. Staphylococci are commonly resistant to penicillin and its penicillinase-susceptible derivatives. They are becoming increasingly resistant to methicillin and multiple other drugs. Moreover, they are now becoming resistant to last-resort glycopeptides. In a meta-analysis, methicillin resistance was associated with approximately twofold higher hospital costs as well as increased mortality.[163] The epidemiology and mechanisms of resistance are discussed in more detail under "Antibiotic Resistance."

Carriage of *Staphylococcus aureus*

Three patterns of carriage can be distinguished: (1) persistent carriers, (2) intermittent carriers, and (3) noncarriers. Approximately 20% of healthy people are persistent carriers, 60% are intermittent carriers, and 20% are noncarriers.[15,173] Most infants become colonized shortly after birth, but carriage decreases with age (63.8% at 1 month, 28.2% at 6 months).[174] In many people the pattern of carriage changes between the ages of 10 and 20 years.[175] Cross-sectional surveys reported carriage rates between 20% and 55%.[176] For instance, the prevalence of *S. aureus* nasal carriage was 30.5% in a study from Italy.[177]

The primary reservoirs of *S. aureus* are the anterior nares, but the organism can be isolated from multiple sites. Some subgroups of patients are at increased risk for carriage. They include patients with insulin-dependent diabetes, patients undergoing hemodialysis or peritoneal dialysis, intravenous drug users, patients with recurrent *S. aureus* skin infections, HIV-positive patients, and healthy patients receiving repeated injections for allergies.[15,173,178]

TABLE 192-9 Example of Decontaminating Scheme for Patients Colonized or Infected with Methicillin-Resistant *Staphylococcus aureus*

Protective measures
Put patient in "contact isolation" (one or several contaminated patients in a single room with restricted access).
Use protective gown and gloves.
Use protective mask and glasses if risk of spray with contaminated liquids.
Clean hands with alcoholic chlorhexidine solution at glove removal and between patients.
Leave any disposable objects in the room and discard for sterilization in special containers.

Decontamination measures
Apply nasal mupirocin ointment (2%) every 8 hr for 5 to 7 days.
Apply chlorhexidine-based oral spray three to four times a day for 5 to 7 days.
Take daily shower or bathe thoroughly with chlorhexidine-based soap for 5 to 7 days.
In the case of dental prostheses, clean and soak daily in chlorhexidine-based solution for 5 to 7 days.

Control cultures and decision
Culture swabs of any contaminated sites 48 and 96 hr after the end of treatment.
Keep isolation measures until laboratory results are available.
If no MRSA are present in control cultures, consider decontaminated. Relief isolation and swab weekly for follow-up cultures.
If MRSA are present in control cultures, pursue isolation measures and repeat whole decontamination scheme.

MRSA, methicillin-resistant *Staphylococcus aureus*.
Adapted from current recommendations at the University Hospital of Lausanne (CHUV), Switzerland.

Although the mechanism of colonization is incompletely solved, it is becoming evident that the nasal reservoir of the patients themselves is a most important source of infection.[179] Up to 80% of cases of *S. aureus* bacteremia are due to the strain isolated from the patients' anterior nares.[16] Moreover, a significant reduction in the rate of infection was achieved after nasal decolonization with a mupirocin ointment in both surgical and dialysis patients.[15,173,180,181] Therefore, it may be important to screen patients at risk for *S. aureus* carriage because they have a greater probability of infection.[18]

Carriage of Methicillin-Resistant *Staphylococcus aureus*

MRSA colonization is particularly important in the hospital environment. Factors associated with it include prior antibiotic exposure, prolonged hospitalization, surgery, admission to an intensive care unit, living in a nursing home, and close proximity to a patient colonized or infected with MRSA.[182-184]

Measures to control the spread of MRSA include swab screening of the anterior nares, isolating colonized and infected patients until complete decontamination, and implementing permanent hygiene precautions such as hand washing and antisepsis, the efficacy of which has been demonstrated.[185] Eradicating MRSA nasal carriage from health care workers with mupirocin ointment is effective.[186] On the other hand, decontaminating colonized or infected patients appears more difficult. Most decontamination regimens recommend a 1-week daily total body washing with a chlorhexidine-based soap plus nasal mupirocin application (see Table 192-9). Control cultures should be performed thereafter.

Infection control measures should also involve the laboratory. Determining the clonality of MRSA recovered from several patients is important to differentiate sporadic cases of MRSA infection from more problematic MRSA epidemics. There are several techniques for typing a given organism at the molecular level. Currently, the technique most commonly used for MRSA surveys is pulsed-field gel electrophoresis.

Decolonization of Nasal Carriers

Three regimens have been envisioned: (1) systemic antibiotics, (2) local antibiotics or disinfectants, and (3) bacterial interference. Results obtained with systemic antibiotics, such as rifampin and trimethoprim-sulfamethoxazole, were disappointing because of the emergence of resistance and significant failure rates.

Local disinfection appeared more successful. Application of a mupirocin (2%) into the anterior nares is highly efficacious in eliminating *S. aureus* in both healthy carriers and carriers belonging to at-risk groups.[187-191] Mupirocin is a topical antibiotic with broad-spectrum activity against gram-positive bacteria, including *S. aureus* and MRSA. It is well tolerated when applied twice daily for up to 5 days. Low-level resistance (MIC 8 to 256 mg/L) and high-level resistance (MIC > 512 mg/L) exist but are uncommon and usually follow prolonged administration.[192,193] Currently, intranasal application of mupirocin is the standard for *S. aureus* decolonization of carrier patients (see Table 192-9).

Bacterial interference is an old concept in which a nonpathogenic staphylococcus is used to outcompete a pathogenic species on the patient.[194] However, several complications occurred and the project was abandoned.[195] The concept may become resurgent in the light of research on the global regulator *agr* (see "Pathogenesis I"). However, no applicable strategy has emerged from this research yet. Other promising alternatives include the cell wall lytic enzyme lysostaphin,[196] bacteriophage-derived cell wall autolysins,[197] and an extract from the Australian native plant *Melaleuca alternifolia*.[198]

CLINICAL SYNDROMES

In general, infection (or disease) begins with the colonization of target tissues by the microbes. *S. aureus* mainly colonize the anterior nares. Further infection results from more specific invasion processes, during which bacteria interact directly or indirectly (e.g., through toxins) with the host. When they have broken through the natural skin barrier, bacteria can disseminate to more profound, normally sterile sites. Thus, any localized infection has the potential to become the seeding site of a more severe infection, either by contiguous extension or by distant spread through the blood circulation.

Staphylococcus aureus Toxin-Related Diseases

Toxin-related diseases typically include SSSS, staphylococcal TSS, and staphylococcal food poisoning. These syndromes and their pathogenesis are described under "Pathogenesis I." They are mediated by a variety of *S. aureus* toxins that carry SAg activity. Because the disease is toxin mediated, the bacteria responsible for the symptoms are often not found in the diseased area or in blood cultures.

S. aureus produce more than 20 different toxins with SAg activity (see "Pathogenesis I"). In addition, they produce cytotoxins that can lyse eukaryotic cells. One of these cytotoxins, PVL toxin, was shown to be associated with recurrent boils in young adults and occasional severe hemorrhagic pneumonia in young adults and children (see Fig. 192-7).[80] The toxin is carried by a virus and has a low prevalence among clinical isolates or isolates from healthy carriers (about 2%). Therefore, recurrent boils may be associated with chronic carriage of such strains.

Skin and Soft Tissue Infections

The basic pathologic lesion induced by *S. aureus* is a pyogenic exudate or an abscess. *S. aureus* infections of the skin and soft tissues encompass several clinical entities, which are classified according to the anatomic structure involved (Fig. 192-10): (1) infection of the epidermis is represented by impetigo; (2) infection of the superficial dermis by folliculitis; (3) infection of the deep dermis by furuncles, carbuncles, and hidradenitis suppurativa; and (4) infection of subcutaneous cellular tissues by erysipelas, cellulitis, and fasciitis.

Superficial infections can often be treated by local care and rarely require general antibiotics. On the other hand, deeper infections such as lymphangitis, lymphadenitis, cellulitis, and necrotizing fasciitis are severe diseases that may be life threatening. They require general antibacterial therapy and sometimes surgical drainage and débridement.

Impetigo

Impetigo is a superficial staphylococcal skin infection that affects mostly children, usually on exposed areas of the body (e.g., on the face and the legs). Although *Streptococcus pyogenes* was usually considered the causative agent, most cases of impetigo are now due to *S. aureus*. *Streptococcus pyogenes* is found in only 20% of cases, often in association with *S. aureus*.

The disease usually starts as a red macula that evolves into vesicles containing cloudy fluid based on the area of erythema (Fig. 192-11). The vesicles rapidly rupture and leave a yellowish, thick, wet crust with a diameter exceeding 1 cm that is surrounded by erythema. Most affected children present with multiple lesions of various ages. General symptoms are absent, but a local inflammatory lymph node reaction is a rule. At the beginning, the differential diagnosis includes other vesicular eruptions, such as herpes simplex. However, the evolution is typical and rapidly differentiates the diseases. Gram stain and culture make the diagnosis and suggest antibiotic treatment.

Although of mild severity, the disease is extremely contagious and the affected child should be kept apart from other children until an effective treatment has been applied. Localized lesions can be handled with topical antibiotics such as mupirocin or fusidic acid. Extensive lesions should be treated with general antibiotherapy covering both *S. aureus* and *Streptococcus pyogenes*. The combination of amoxicillin and clavulanate is an appropriate choice. An alternative is to combine a penicillinase-stable antistaphylococcal penicillin (e.g., nafcillin, oxacillin, or flucloxacillin), which is active against staphylococci but not very active against streptococci, with penicillin G, which is one of the first choices against *Streptococcus pyogenes*. Other drugs such as macrolides should be used with caution because of the risk of one of the microorganisms being resistant. Indeed, 20% to 50% of

FIGURE 192-10. Skin anatomy delineating the various levels at which *Staphylococcus aureus* infection can occur (see text for details).

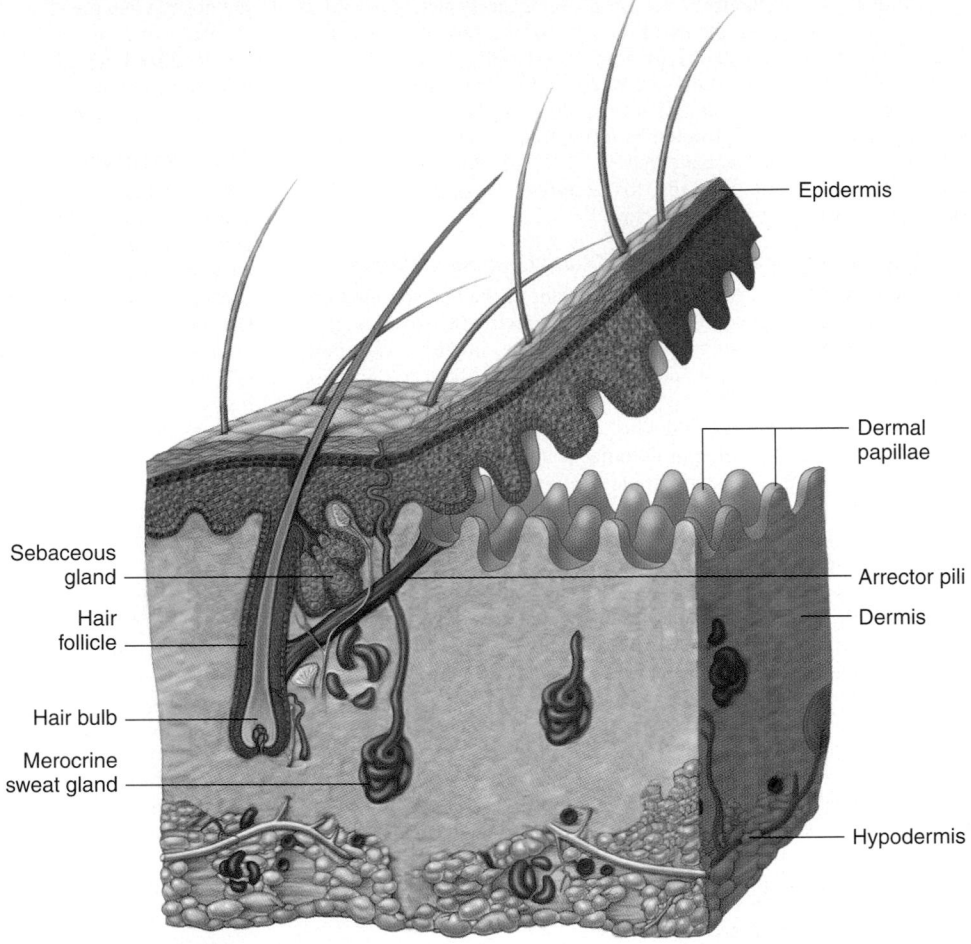

Streptococcus pyogenes are resistant to macrolides in many industrialized countries.

Folliculitis

Folliculitis is defined as a pyoderma involving the hair follicle and its immediate surroundings. It is manifest as a series of raised, painful reddish lesions with indurated bases, each centered on a hair follicle. Extensive folliculitis of the bearded area of the face is called *sycosis barbae*. General symptoms are usually absent, and local antiseptic measures are the treatment of choice.

Furuncles and Carbuncles

Furuncles (boils) represent an extension of the infectious process involving the hair follicle and are located, by definition, on the hairy areas of the body, with a predilection for the face, neck, axillae, and buttocks. The disease starts as a painful red nodule and rapidly evolves into a hot, painful, raised, and indurated lesion with a diameter of 1 to 2 cm. Its evolution is characterized by the appearance of a yellowish area in its center. On rupture (either spontaneous or surgical), it liberates a small amount of yellowish, creamy discharge of purulent and necrotic material. Secondary foci related to autoinoculation are frequent. General symptoms are normally absent. Local treatment is usually sufficient. In case of recurrent episodes, testing for nasal carriage and appropriate eradication may be necessary. In this regard, it is worth remembering the association between young adults and furunculosis, PVL toxin–producing *S. aureus,* and the risk of severe hemorrhagic pneumonia (see earlier and "Pathogenesis I").[80] Young patients with boils and the onset of septic symptoms raise suspicion of severe *S. aureus* disease including not only pneumonia but also fasciitis and arthritis (our unpublished observation).

Another remarkable situation is that in which furuncles are located around the nares or upper lip. Such lesions may lead to life-threatening septic thrombophlebitis of the cavernous sinus. Therefore, they must be treated with high-dose parenteral antibiotics.

Carbuncles are deep-seated infections that involve several hair follicles and result from the coalescence and spreading of the infectious process into the depths of subcutaneous tissue. They are usually localized at the base of the neck. The disease leads to the development of a central necrotic crater, which heals by the development of a hard hypertrophic violaceous scar. Fever and malaise are generally present. Carbuncles may be a source of bacteremia and require systemic antibiotherapy.

Hidradenitis Suppurativa

This is a pyogenic infection of the apocrine sweat glands that is manifest as crops of furuncles developing in the axillary, perineal, and genital areas. Following spontaneous drainage, hypertrophic scarring may occur. As in furunculosis, treatment is primarily limited to local care and disinfection. Administration of an oral antimicrobial is indicated only in the case of general symptoms.

Mastitis

From 1% to 3% of nursing mothers may suffer various staphylococcal breast infections. These may vary from a painful erythematous nodule to a frank canalicular abscess. The infection develops most commonly during the second or the third week of the puerperium. High fever and general symptoms may be present. Beside topical treatment, acute mastitis mandates the use of oral antibiotics. In the case of abscess formation, incision and drainage rapidly control the infection.

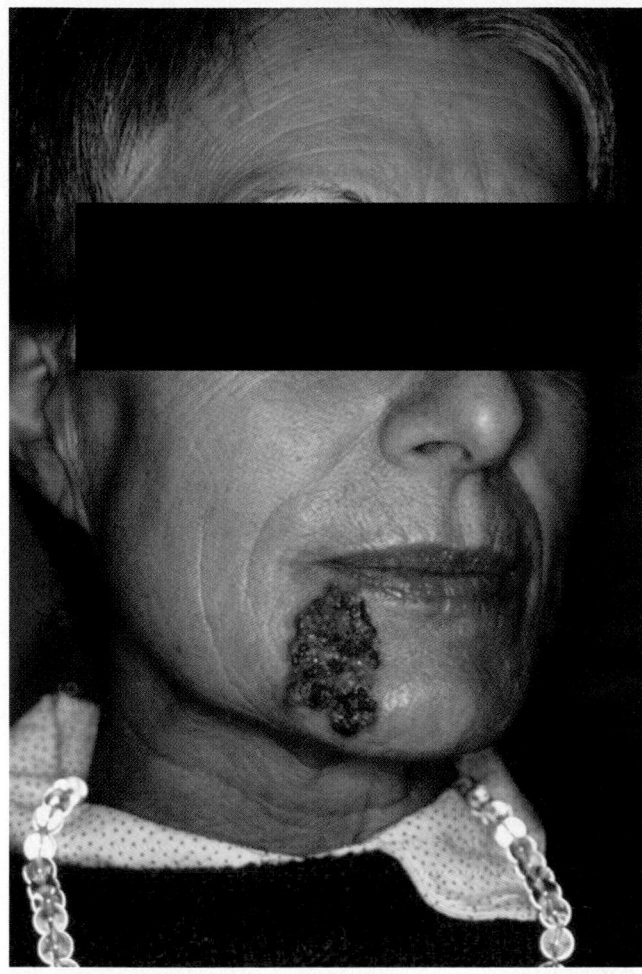

FIGURE 192-11. Infective skin lesions in staphylococcal impetigo.

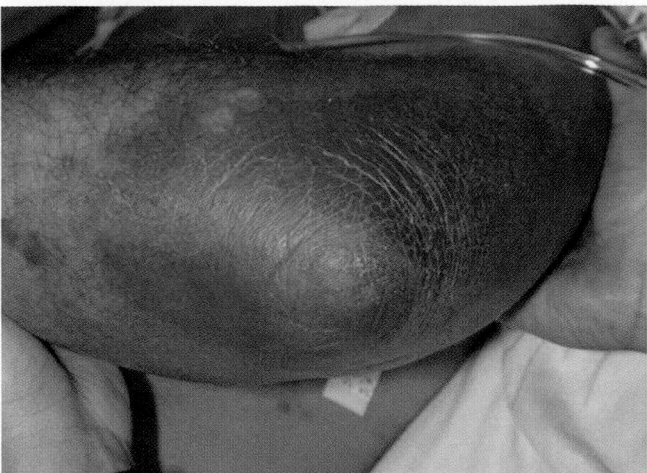

FIGURE 192-12. *Staphylococcus aureus* cellulitis of the elbow in a cancer patient with low neutrophil counts. The pain was disproportional to the visual appearance of the lesion. The patient was bacteremic.

Wound Infection

Because *S. aureus* is a skin colonizer, it is a major cause of surgical wound infection.[164] Postsurgical wound infections are characterized by progressive edema, erythema, and pain around the surgical incision two or more days after surgery. General symptoms are frequently associated. Careful inspection of the wound, ulcer, or lesion is essential. If deeper structures are not involved, release of the stitches, repeated cleansing, and antibiotic coverage for 7 to 10 days are usually curative. If the infection involves deeper structures (e.g., bone) or foreign material (e.g., prosthetic devices), prolonged parenteral antibiotherapy (4 to 6 weeks) may be necessary, and removal of the foreign material is warranted.

The evolution of wound infection is highly dependent on the patient's comorbidities. Healing may be delayed particularly in patients with vascular insufficiency and diabetes.

Erysipelas, Cellulitis, and Fasciitis

Superficial or deep extension of infection may result in erysipelas, cellulitis, or fasciitis. Erysipelas and fasciitis are commonly due to *Streptococcus pyogenes,* but this etiology is not exclusive. Fasciitis can arise from hematogenous seeding. An important common feature of all three entities is severe pain. In staphylococcal erysipelas, pain and tenderness are usual. In the case of cellulitis or fasciitis, severe pain complaints are disproportionate to the visible anatomic lesions (Fig. 192-12). Hence, high fever, severe local pain, and relatively meager clinical findings at visible examination are highly suggestive of one of these entities. This consideration is important because emergency surgical drainage is indicated in the case of fasciitis, and prompt intervention may be delayed because of the confounding picture.

Erysipelas appears as a geographically delineated erythematous and swollen area of the skin. It often complicates skin ulcers such as in varicose limbs. As in impetigo, it may be due to mixed *Streptococcus pyogenes* and *S. aureus* infection. Clinical signs of sepsis with high fever are present. The diagnosis is clinical and microbiologic. Local sampling by puncture may be attempted and blood must be drawn for cultures. Prompt empirical treatment should be started with parenteral antibiotics covering at least both staphylococci and streptococci. Currently, the classic first and second choices remain β-lactams and glycopeptides.

In patients with underlying conditions, such as diabetic foot, mixed pictures of erysipelas and cellulitis may occur. These may be due to gram-negative bacteria as well, including *Pseudomonas aeruginosa.* Therefore, the spectrum of empirical treatment should be broadened to cover these agents until the microbiologic results are available. If gram-negative bacteria or MRSA are suspected, adding an aminoglycoside or vancomycin, or both, to a broad-spectrum β-lactam may be warranted.

Cellulitis involves deeper anatomic structures and does not produce the typical geographic skin lesion of erysipelas (see Fig. 192-12). Therefore, it is more confusing and may be mistaken for nonspecific lesions such as trauma. Pain and fever are important signs. Cellulitis may be due to multiple other organisms, including gram-negative bacteria, especially in immunocompromised patients. Therefore, microbiologic sampling (including blood cultures) should be promptly followed by broad-spectrum antibiotherapy with both anti–gram-positive and anti–gram-negative coverage. Magnetic resonance imaging (MRI) or ultrasound imaging is useful to delineate the extension of the lesion and the involvement of other structures.

Necrotizing fasciitis is the most severe condition, which paradoxically presents the least superficial signs at visual observation of the skin and soft tissues. The pain may be so intense that it requires opiate administration for relief. The condition is often due to *Streptococcus pyogenes,* but *S. aureus* may be involved, especially in the presence of the PVL toxin (our unpublished observation). Gram-negative bacteria, including *Pseudomonas aeruginosa,* may be responsible, especially in immunocompromised patients, and must be considered in the choice of initial empirical treatment.

Whatever its cause, fasciitis is an absolute emergency that necessitates immediate and generous surgical débridement and drainage. The evolution is a matter of minutes rather than hours and may rapidly result in amputation or death. Prompt clinical diagnosis and multidisciplinary evaluation are warranted. Imaging may help delineate the lesions, but urgent surgical exploration and fasciotomy are essential. High-dose and broad-spectrum antibiotherapy is required, which can be readjusted after isolating the bacterial pathogen. In the case of *Streptococcus pyogenes* and severe refractory shock, IVIG has been proposed (see also "Pathogenesis I").[94]

Staphylococcus aureus Bacteremia

The incidence of *S. aureus* blood-stream infection has substantially increased over the past decades.[199] It is usually divided in two categories: hospital-acquired bacteremia, in which positive blood cultures occur more than 2 days after hospital entry, and community-acquired bacteremia, occurring in the community or before 2 days of hospitalization. However, with modern management of patients and the increasing number of community patients who have underlying conditions, these two categories are progressively overlapping more. Hence, community-acquired bacteremia may be more appropriately referred to as "community-onset" bacteremia and the predisposing factors of the patient considered as additional information for prognosis.

Community-Onset Bacteremia

A study categorized patients with community-onset *S. aureus* bacteremia as having (1) health care–associated bacteremia, (2) underlying medical conditions, and (3) no underlying medical condition, depending on their health care dependence or predisposing diseases, or both.[200] The overall incidence of bacteremia was 17 per 100,000 population per year. The "no underlying medical condition" subgroup accounted for only 5% (11 of 201) of the total cases. All the other patients (190 of 201) had some predisposing factors, including the presence of intravascular catheters. Most cases (35%) were associated with indwelling devices, followed by bacteremia without a focus (18%), cellulitis (17%), and endocarditis (13%). Bacteremia in patients with no underlying medical condition was always associated with a detectable infectious focus, including skin and soft tissue infection, osteomyelitis, arthritis, and possible endocarditis.

Similarly, MRSA were found in 16% of all the patients with pre-existing conditions but not in patients without an underlying medical condition. These MRSA were multiply antibiotic resistant and did not match the new CA-MRSA types described in healthy patients (see "Antibiotic Resistance"). These MRSA were probably remnant organisms from previous hospital stays.

Thus, community-onset *S. aureus* bacteremia must be interpreted in the context of the patient's condition. Health care–related bacteremia is comparable to hospital-acquired bacteremia, with a great proportion of device-related infections and multiresistant organisms. Bacteremia in patients without underlying conditions resembles former classic community-acquired bacteremia, caused by antibiotic-susceptible organisms, always associated with the detectable focus and, if not, with infective endocarditis.

Compared with that of other organisms, the frequency of *S. aureus* as a cause of bacteremia in both hospital-acquired and community-onset bacteremia is high.[199] In one study, it was the most frequent (18%) cause of community-onset bacteremia and came before *Escherichia coli* (15%), coagulase-negative staphylococci (12%), and pneumococci (7%).[201] The associated mortality was 10% to 20%[200,201] but varied as a function of underlying conditions (see Table 192-7).[160] Of note, patients receiving hemodialysis are at particularly high risk for staphylococcal endocarditis and represent a quasi-new at-risk group for this disease.[202]

Nosocomial Bacteremia

S. aureus is one of the leading causes of nosocomial bacteremia.[199] The condition is often preceded by invasive medical procedures in contaminated sites, wound infection, and nosocomial *S. aureus* pneumonia. However, it is mostly associated with the presence of intravascular or urinary catheters. Complications involve peripheral metastatic foci, which can be revealed later in time. Nosocomial *S. aureus* bacteremia enters in the differential diagnosis of any hospital-related febrile or septic episodes. Notably, one study suggests that up to 13% of cases of *S. aureus* nosocomial bacteremia may become complicated with infective endocarditis, even in the absence of cardiac risk factors.[203]

Treatment

Treatment of *S. aureus* bacteremia depends on the nature of the primary focus and the presence or not of metastatic lesions. Tunnel infections around implanted vascular catheters require immediate removal. Catheter-acquired *S. aureus* bacteremia in the absence of a tunnel infection sometimes responds to 10 to 14 days of antibiotic therapy through all the ports of the catheter without catheter removal.[204,205]

Skin and soft tissue infections usually respond to a 14-day course of antibiotic treatment. Deeper infections such as arthritis and osteomyelitis and endocarditis must be treated with antibiotics for 4 to 6 weeks.

Staphylococcus aureus Endocarditis

Infective endocarditis on a native valve is one of the most severe complications of *S. aureus* bacteremia. The disease can be lethal with appropriate antibiotics whether or not the valve is replaced. *S. aureus* endocarditis typically follows an acute course with multiple peripheral septic emboli, valve destruction, myocarditis, and mixed cardiogenic and septic shock (Figs. 192-13 and 192-14). Appropriate care requires a multidisciplinary evaluation, including infectious disease and microbiology experts, cardiologists, intensive care specialists, cardiac surgeons, and sometimes neurologists.

Epidemiology

In a meta-analysis, the median incidence of overall infective endocarditis cases was 3.6 per 100,000 population per year (range 0.3 to 22.4) and increased with age.[172] In spite of improving general health

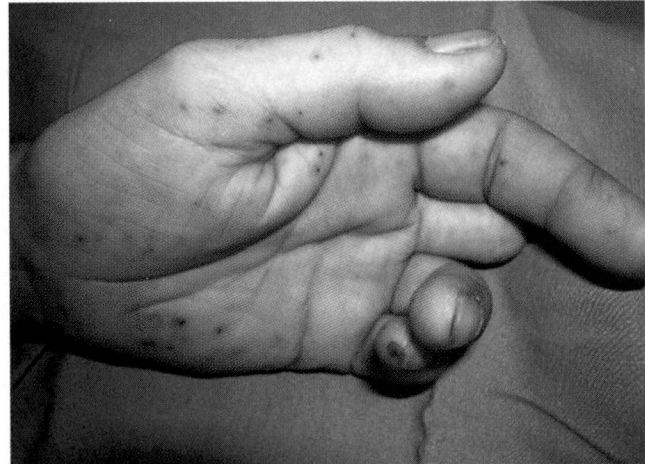

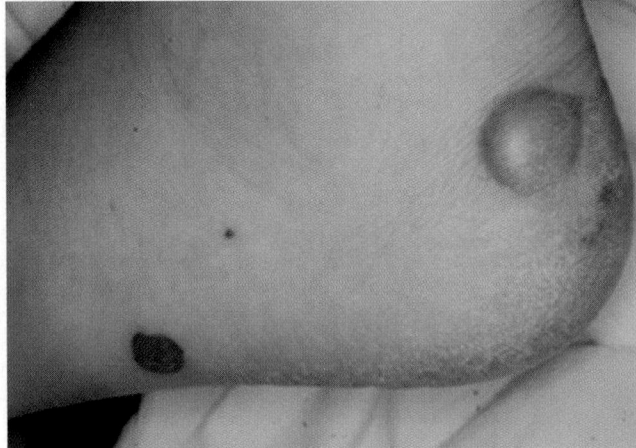

FIGURE 192-13. Embolic skin lesions (Janeway spots) in the framework of an acute mitral valve endocarditis caused by *Staphylococcus aureus*.

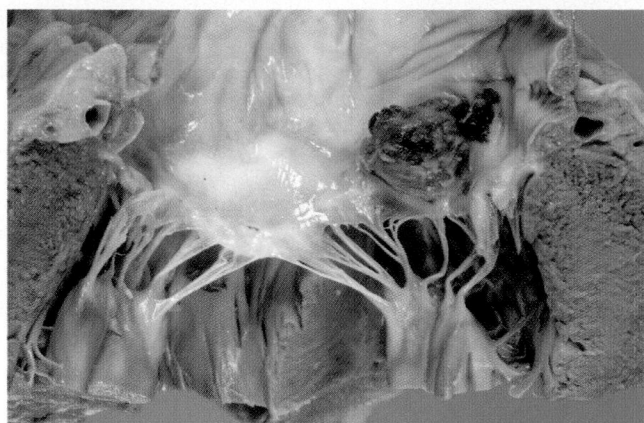

FIGURE 192-14. *Staphylococcus aureus* endocarditis of the mitral valve. The picture shows a large ulcerovegetative lesion on the anterior leaflet. (Courtesy of Drs. A. Lobrinus and I. Letovanec, Pathology Institute, Lausanne University.)

care, the incidence of endocarditis did not decrease over the past 20 years. This persistence is due to a changing pattern of the disease. Patients with classic risk factors such as rheumatic heart disease are being replaced by new at-risk groups, including intravenous drug users, elderly people with valve sclerosis, patients with intravascular prostheses, patients with nosocomially acquired infective endocarditis, and patients receiving hemodialysis.[202] In parallel, the historical predominance of streptococcal endocarditis is being replaced by staphylococcal valve infection. *S. aureus* is responsible for more than 30% of cases of native valve endocarditis, 69% of cases of endocarditis in intravenous drug users, and about 20% of cases of both early and late prosthetic valve endocarditis.[172] It is one of the most commonly isolated pathogens in this disease.

Pathogenesis

The pathogenesis of *S. aureus* endocarditis has been reviewed.[206] There is a close relation between certain *S. aureus* surface adhesins and host proteins present on the surface of damaged or inflamed valves. Physically damaged endothelia are covered by a meshwork of fibrin, platelets, and numerous host matrix proteins. *S. aureus* harbor surface adhesins that interact with host proteins and are critical for valve colonization and infection. They include fibrinogen-binding protein A (ClfA) and FnBPA (see Table 192-1).[53]

In the case of physically intact but inflamed endothelia, *S. aureus* fibronectin-binding proteins may be of primary importance. During inflammation, endothelial cells express integrins of the β_1 family,[207] which can bind plasma fibronectin at the luminal pole of the cell. The resulting fibronectin coat functions as a ligand surface for circulating *S. aureus* that express fibronectin-binding proteins. The contact between the adhesin and its ligand triggers the active internalization of *S. aureus* by endothelial cells as well as by other cells.[208] Once internalized, *S. aureus* may either persist locally, being protected from host defenses and antimicrobial therapy, or multiply and secrete hemolysins (see Table 192-1), which lyse the host cell and allow bacteria to spread both locally and to distant organs. This second scenario probably explains many cases of infective endocarditis on anatomically "normal" valves.

The Role of Platelets

One additional factor in the pathogenesis of endocarditis is the ability of bacteria to resist killing by platelet microbicidal peptides.[209] These are cationic peptides that are contained in the α-granules of thrombocytes and are released upon platelet activation. They kill numerous gram-positive organisms by perturbing their membrane potential. Experimental evidence indicates that platelet-resistant mutants of staphylococci or streptococci have an increased ability to produce en-

docarditis in animals. In addition, clinical studies indicate that isolates of *S. aureus* recovered from patients with endocarditis are more often resistant to platelet-induced killing than *S. aureus* isolated from other infected sites.[210] Thus, platelets play an important role in innate defenses against the disease.

Platelets have a dual role in endovascular infections, however. On the one hand, numerous experimental studies have shown that they contributed to the growth of cardiac vegetations and possible embolization. On the other hand, they may be beneficial because they release platelet microbicidal peptides. This finding raises the question of whether drugs to inhibit platelet aggregation might be useful in the disease. The issue has been studied both in thrombocytopenic animals and in animals given antiaggregant therapy. Thrombocytopenic animals had an increased propensity to develop experimental endocarditis caused by streptococci.[211] Paradoxically, anticoagulant therapy (with acetosalicylic acid) decreased the severity of endocarditis caused by *S. aureus.*

The contradiction between these results has an explanation. It appears that acetosalicylic acid has a direct antistaphylococcal effect, which might overcome its negative effect on platelet-induced killing.[212] The mechanism of the antistaphylococcal effect was mediated by acetosalicylate-induced modulation of the global regulators Sar and SigB, which resulted in decreased expression of fibronectin-binding protein and α-hemolysin.[212] Thus, acetosalicylic acid highlights the potential benefit of interfering with pathogenic gene regulation in *S. aureus* (see "Pathogenesis I").

Although acetosalicylic acid provides some benefit in *S. aureus* experimental endocarditis, its clinical use is not recommended in humans because antiaggregants increase the risk of secondary bleeding at the site of septic emboli and mycotic aneurysms, including hemorrhagic stroke.[213]

Host Defenses and Prevention

The role of host defenses is marginal in infective endocarditis. When staphylococci have colonized the valves, their intrinsic procoagulant activities (e.g., fibrinogen polymerization by coagulase and platelet activation by fibrinogen-binding protein) trigger further deposition of platelets and fibrin on top of the microorganisms, thus providing a protective niche inside the vegetation. Moreover, *S. aureus* can be internalized into endothelial cells through bridging with fibronectin (see earlier). Both cases result in failure of professional phagocytes to eradicate the organisms.

Killing by T cell–mediated effectors is not operative in endocarditis. The only alternative is antibody-mediated protection, which could act before colonization by blocking *S. aureus* surface adhesins or by increasing the speed of blood clearance by opsonization, or both. Active research is dedicated to such an approach, but few promising results are available yet. The limitation of preventive vaccines in endocarditis might be the very short delay (1 to 2 minutes) between blood invasion and valve colonization, which leaves a very small window for antibody activity.

Clinical Features

S. aureus endocarditis often arises as an acute septic syndrome with fever, tachycardia, and hypotension. Dyspnea may be present from congestive heart failure or from septic pulmonary emboli in the case of right-sided endocarditis (Fig. 192-15). General signs such as arthralgia or myalgia, back pain, and pleuritic pain are present in 10% to 50% of cases. Specific signs include a new cardiac murmur, usually of valve regurgitation, in approximately 90% of cases; septic emboli in the form of petechiae and Janeway lesions; and central nervous system manifestations in up to one third of the patients (see Fig. 192-13).

Cardiac failure is a major indication for emergency valve replacement. A defect in atrioventricular conduction may represent a mycotic aneurysm of the sinus of Valsalva, usually the noncoronary cusp. Transesophageal echocardiography is useful in detecting this complication. Large vegetations have been associated with an increased risk of embolization. However, the risk of embolization decreases rapidly within the first days of efficacious therapy.

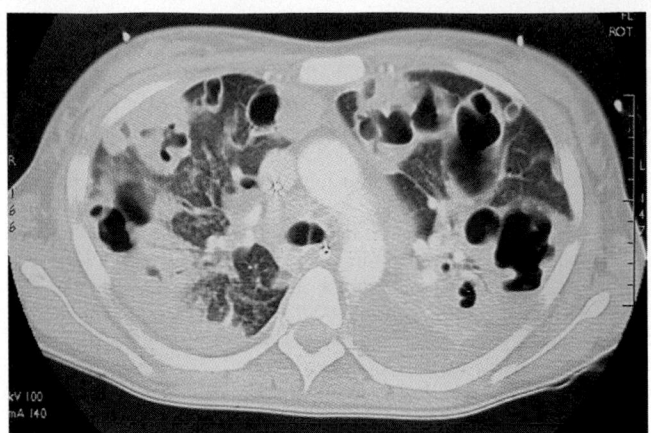

FIGURE 192-15. Chest computed tomographic scan of a 30-year-old intravenous drug addict with tricuspid valve *Staphylococcus aureus* endocarditis and bilateral lung abscesses and empyema.

Vascular Complications

Septic emboli from broken-off vegetations can occlude the coronary or peripheral arteries (see Fig. 192-13). Small skin lesions from immune-related vasculitis are a delayed sign of relatively chronic infection and not a usual feature of acute *S. aureus* endocarditis. Mycotic aneurysms are found in up to 15% of patients with bacterial endocarditis and probably more frequently in *S. aureus* endocarditis. They may arise from direct invasion of the arterial wall by the infecting organisms, from septic embolization of the vasa vasorum, or from the deposition of immune complexes that trigger local inflammation and weakening of the arterial wall.

Neurologic Complications

Neurologic manifestations, mainly septic emboli and mycotic aneurysms, may occur in up to 40% of cases. However, because patients who have no neurologic symptoms do not undergo specific in-

vestigations, the true incidence of neurologic events during endocarditis may be underestimated. Lesions include cerebral infarctions, arteritis, abscesses, mycotic aneurysms, intracerebral or subarachnoid hemorrhage, encephalomalacia, cerebritis, and meningitis. Controlling the infection is essential because embolization sharply decreases thereafter. Recurrent embolization after the onset of efficacious therapy may be an indication for urgent valve replacement. This decision is difficult because anticoagulation during extracorporeal circulation and after valve replacement puts patients at increased risk for secondary intracerebral hemorrhage. Therefore, the tendency is often to postpone emergency surgery and wait for the patient to stabilize. On the other hand, ongoing studies suggest that earlier intervention, within the first 72 hours of stroke, may be beneficial in selected patients.

Diagnosis

Criteria for the diagnosis of infective endocarditis changed with the use of echocardiography and are discussed in detail in Chapter 74.[214-216] In *S. aureus* endocarditis the first two blood cultures are positive in more than 90% of cases. The volume of blood cultures is critical because persistent bacteremia in infective endocarditis is often low level, representing 1 to 100 bacteria per milliliter of blood. For each culture, 8 to 12 mL of blood should be drawn with careful antiseptic precaution.

Treatment options are listed in Table 192-10 (reviewed in reference 172).

Management of Right-Sided Endocarditis in Injection Drug Users

Although standard treatment of left-sided *S. aureus* endocarditis requires 4 to 6 weeks of antibiotherapy (see Table 192-10), the duration of treatment for right-sided endocarditis can be considerably shortened in injection drug users.[217] Right-sided endocarditis involves a somewhat different physiopathology and is easier to cure or can heal spontaneously in experimental models.[218] Moreover, the prognosis is less severe than that of left-sided valve infection. Regimens proved appropriate for a 2-week treatment of right-sided endocarditis were nafcillin or cloxacillin combined with an effective aminoglycoside to which the organism is susceptible (gentamicin, tobramycin, or amikacin given every 8 hours).[217] If an aminoglycoside is contraindi-

TABLE 192-10   Suggested Treatment for Native Valve and Prosthetic Valve Endocarditis Caused by Staphylococci

Antibiotic	Frequency, Dosage, and Route	Duration (weeks)	Comments
Native Valves			
A. Methicillin-susceptible staphylococci			
Flucloxacillin (non-USA) or oxacillin, or nafcillin	2 g IV q4h	4-6	The benefit of gentamicin addition is not demonstrated
with gentamicin (optional)	1 mg/kg IV or IM q8h	3-5 days	
Cefazolin (or other first-generation cephalosporins)	2 g IV q8h	4-6	Alternative for patients allergic to penicillins (not in
with gentamicin (optional)	1 mg/kg IV or IM q8h	3-5 days	case of immediate-type penicillin hypersensitivity)
Vancomycin	15 mg/kg IV q12h	4-6	Recommended for patients with life-threatening β-lactam allergy
B. Methicillin-resistant staphylococci			
Vancomycin	15 mg/kg IV q12h	4-6	
Prosthetic Valves			
*A. Methicillin-susceptible staphylococci**			
	2 g IV q4h	≥6	Rifampin increases the hepatic metabolism of numerous drugs, including warfarin
	300 mg PO or IV q8h	≥6	
Flucloxacillin (non-USA) or oxacillin,	1 mg/kg IV or IM q8h	2	
or nafcillin with rifampin and gentamicin			
Vancomycin plus rifampin and gentamicin	15 mg/kg IV q12h	≥6	Recommended for β-lactam–allergic patients
	300 mg PO or IV q8h	≥6	
	1 mg/kg IV or IM q8h	2	
B. Methicillin-resistant staphylococci			
Vancomycin plus rifampin and gentamicin	15 mg/kg IV q12h	≥6	
	300 mg PO or IV q8h	≥6	
	1 mg/kg IV or IM q8h	2	

*Rifampin plays a special role in prosthetic device infection because it helps kill bacteria attached to foreign material. Rifampin should never be used alone because it selects for resistance at a high frequency (about 10^{-6}).

Adapted with modifications from Moreillon P, Que YA. Infective endocarditis. Lancet. 2004;363:135-149, and Wilson WR, Karchmer AW, Dajani AS, et al. Antibiotic treatment of adults with infective endocarditis due to streptococci, enterococci, staphylococci, and HACEK microorganisms. JAMA. 1995;274:1706-1713.

cated, ciprofloxacin may be substituted if the organism is susceptible. Another proposed regimen that may allow intravenous-oral switch therapy is ciprofloxacin plus rifampin.[219] Today, new anti–gram-positive quinolones, combined with rifampin, might be even more effective. Some authors would not start rifampin until effective therapy has been given for 3 days, hoping to reduce the chance of secondary rifampin resistance (see Chapter 74).

Glycopeptides (vancomycin or teicoplanin) combined with aminoglycosides resulted in an unacceptable proportion of failures. Thus, glycopeptides should not be used for short-course treatment.

Contraindications to short-course therapy in injection drug users include (1) a slow clinical or microbiologic response (>96 hours) to the initial antibiotic treatment; (2) complicated right-sided endocarditis with heart failure, valve vegetations greater than 2 cm, acute respiratory failure, empyema, or septic metastatic foci outside the lung; (3) therapy with glycopeptides or first-generation cephalosporins; (4) right-sided endocarditis caused by MRSA or polymicrobial infection; and (5) severe immunosuppression (<200 CD4+ cells/μL) or AIDS.[217]

Meningitis

In a review of 43 hematogenous and 61 postoperative cases of *S. aureus* meningitis in Denmark,[220] hematogenous cases were part of an overwhelming disseminated infection. Among the hematogenous cases, 21% had concomitant endocarditis and 12% had osteomyelitis. In contrast, postoperative meningitis was related to local surgery and often associated (in 89% of cases) with the presence of local foreign materials. The mortality was lower in postoperative cases (18% [11 of 61]) than in hematogenous cases (56% [24 of 43]), as were problems with general symptoms, mental status, and sequelae. Thus, hematogenous *S. aureus* meningitis is a severe disease that warrants a search for another deep-seated initial infected focus.

Pericarditis

Purulent pericarditis may result from contiguous contamination during surgery, local extension of a paravalvular infection, or embolization of septic material in the coronary arteries. An autopsy study has shown that up to 22% of cases of pericarditis were due to *S. aureus*.[221] Sudden chest pain with septic conditions and possibly tamponade or global cardiac dysfunction during staphylococcal infection should suggest the possibility of this potentially lethal complication. Echocardiography to determine the status of both the pericardial space and the valves is useful before pericardiocentesis and possible emergency surgery for drainage or valve repair and replacement, or both.

Pulmonary Infections

Epidemiology

S. aureus is responsible for less than 10% of microbiologically confirmed cases of community-acquired pneumonia[222] but accounts for 20% to 30% of cases of hospital-acquired pneumonia.[165] *S. aureus* community-acquired pneumonia occurs primarily in elderly patients (older than 75 years) admitted from nursing homes[223] but also in patients with predisposing factors such as diabetes and alcoholism and typically during influenza virus epidemics.[224] Lethality is high, especially when it is associated with acute respiratory distress syndrome or septic shock.

In the hospital, *S. aureus* is becoming the pathogen most frequently responsible for nosocomial pneumonia. It was responsible for 13% of cases between 1981 and 1986, 16% between 1986 and 1989, and 19% between 1990 and 1996, according to the National Nosocomial Infections Surveillance System.[225] In one study, it was the single most frequent pathogen isolated (in 28% of cases) from patients with nosocomial pneumonia in 2000.[165]

Clinical Spectrum

The clinical manifestations of *S. aureus* pneumonia are frequently indistinguishable from those of pneumonia caused by other pathogens, although the pneumonia caused by *S. aureus* is typically a necrotizing infection with rapid progression to tissue destruction and cavitation. It may result either from airborne contamination or aspiration or from hematogenous seeding during bacteremia or right-sided endocarditis. In both cases, the pulmonary infection can lead to local complications, such as abscesses and pleural empyema.

S. aureus remains one of the most common causes of pleural empyema and still accounts for about one third of the cases.[226] Acute empyema usually arises by direct extension from *S. aureus* pneumonia or lung abscess. It is also often seen as a complication of thoracic surgery. Computed tomography or ultrasonography confirms the clinical suspicion. Demonstration of a pleural air-fluid level in the absence of a previous thoracentesis suggests a bronchopleural fistula, another feared complication of *S. aureus* infection. Figure 192-15 demonstrates multiple lung abscesses and pleural effusion in a young patient with right-sided endocarditis.

A necrotizing pneumonia caused by PVL leukocidin–positive *S. aureus* was recognized as a new clinical entity with a poor prognosis. It occurs in otherwise healthy children and young adults and is preceded by an influenza-like syndrome. It is characterized by fever, hemoptysis, and leukopenia and rapidly progress to acute respiratory distress syndrome. The lethality rate is high.[21,80]

Treatment

Treatment of *S. aureus* pneumonia is determined by the general picture of the disease. The less complicated cases without overt tissue destruction and without associated deep-seated infections respond to appropriate antibiotherapy for 10 to 15 days. In the case of surgical drainage of empyema, the treatment duration is adjusted according to cultures and persistence of the pleural effusion. In the case of right-sided endocarditis, therapy is prolonged to 4 weeks according to standard recommendations for endocarditis treatment (see earlier).

Osteomyelitis

Epidemiology

Osteomyelitis has been known since antiquity. It is due to *S. aureus* in 50% to 70% of cases (Table 192-11).[166-169] There are two ways by which bacteria can infect the bones: (1) hematogenous seeding and (2) contiguous contamination.

Both the mortality and incidence of osteomyelitis have decreased markedly since the introduction of antibacterial therapy. In one pediatric case review, the mortality decreased from more than 30% before the introduction of sulfa derivatives (from 1936 to 1940) to about 13% afterward (from 1941 to 1945).[227] The mortality related to osteomyelitis continued to decline with modern antibiotics and is now close to zero. The incidence is declining as well. In children (younger

TABLE 192-11 Frequency of Osteomyelitis Caused by Various Microorganisms

	Frequency of Osteomyelitis (%)		
Reference number	167	168	169
Microorganisms			
Staphylococcus aureus	54.2	65	50
Coagulase-negative staphylococci	13.9	5	13
Streptococci, not group D	13.7	30	23
Pseudomonas aeruginosa	4.4	ND	ND
Other	13.8	0	14
Total	100	100	100
Demography			
Number of patients/episodes	454	20	62
Median age (years) (average)	6-92 (51)	0.1-12 (5.4)	0.1-13 (4)

ND, not determined.
Adapted from references 167, 168, 169.

than 13 years) resident in the area of the Greater Glasgow Board Health Center (United Kingdom), the incidence of osteomyelitis declined approximately threefold over the last 30 years and twofold during the 1990s. It was 2.9 per 100,000 population per year in 1997,[168] which is comparable to the lowest estimates for infective endocarditis.[172] This decrease was almost exclusively related to a decline in acute hematogenous forms, reflecting better handling of banal *S. aureus* skin and soft tissue infections, which are often the source of transient bacteremia.

However, the incidence of osteomyelitis varies with the presence of underlying risk factors. In one large study (454 patients), males were affected twice as often as females and 90% of cases were due to contiguous infections. Patients with diabetes had a 4.9-fold greater risk of bone infection than the population of healthy people, followed by a 2-fold greater risk in patients with vascular diseases.[167] Other risk groups include individuals with an increased risk of bacteremia such as patients receiving hemodialysis.

Pathogenesis

Bone infection requires certain predisposing circumstances. In children with hematogenous osteomyelitis, the disease is usually located at the distal end of the long bones' metaphyses, including the humerus, femur, and tibia. The nature of the blood flow close to the growing plate may be responsible. Terminal arterioles followed by stagnant blood in the venous sinusoids may facilitate the settlement of blood-borne staphylococci. A similar model may apply for vertebral osteomyelitis, in which blood flow at the vertebral interface with the intervertebral disks is somewhat similar. Microscopic (or macroscopic) bone trauma may facilitate infection as well, by affecting the local blood supply or exposing host matrix proteins to which staphylococci can adhere.[228]

On the bacterial side, *S. aureus* is equipped with several surface adhesins or MSCRAMMs (see "Pathogenesis I"), including collagen-binding protein and sialoprotein-binding protein, which were shown to promote experimental osteoarticular infection (Table 192-1). After local settlement, secreted proteases and hemolysins promote tissue destruction and invasion, as indicated by decreased virulence of *sar* and *agr* mutants that are affected in toxin secretion (see "Pathogenesis I").[229]

The combination of *S. aureus* factors and immune cell–mediated production of oxygen radicals and cytokines results in local necrosis and abscess formation. If adequate antibacterial therapy is given, the nascent abscess can heal totally. Alternatively, bone necrosis can extend and circumscribe devitalized bone fragments, or sequestra, floating in the abscess cavity. The formation of necrosis and sequestra exemplifies the evolution of acute osteomyelitis to the chronic form (see later), which requires a combination of antibiotics and surgical débridement and sequestrectomy for successful treatment.

Clinical Features

Osteomyelitis is conventionally divided into acute and chronic disease. Acute osteomyelitis is defined as a first episode that responds to medical treatment within 6 weeks.[166,230] It is usually hematogenous and predominant in children and elderly patients. Symptoms are those of an acute septic syndrome with chills, high fever, malaise, and local pain and swelling. Blood cultures are positive in about 50% of cases and blood plus tissue cultures in 65% of cases.[169]

Chronic infection is considered in all other situations, including relapse of a previously treated or untreated disease and infection arising by contiguity. The process can evolve over months or even years and is characterized by low-grade inflammation, necrosis, sequestra, pus, fistula, and recurrences.

Aside from open-wound fractures, contiguous osteomyelitis involves diabetes-related and unrelated vascular diseases as well as prosthesis-related osteomyelitis. Diabetes- and vascular disease–related osteomyelitis principally involves the feet. This form of osteomyelitis complicates chronic ulcers, which may be paradoxically painless because of associated neuritis. The ulcerative lesion should be explored gently but in depth with a surgical probe. If the probe encounters the bone surface, osteomyelitis is present.[231] Other investigations involve radiology and surgical biopsy. Cultures of deep tissues and bone biopsy are mandatory for microbiologic diagnosis. Cultures of surface swabs and fistula fluids mostly yield skin contaminants but not the responsible pathogen or pathogens.

Infection of Prostheses

Osteosynthetic prostheses become infected in about 1% to 2% of cases.[232] *S. aureus* is the second cause of infection after coagulase-negative staphylococci. Infections occurring within the first 12 weeks after implantation are considered early or acute, and infections occurring from 12 weeks to 24 months after operation are considered late or chronic. *S. aureus* are mostly responsible for early infection. As with prosthetic heart valves, the organisms usually originate from the skin and are likely to be introduced at the time of operation. Although early symptoms may be acute, patients with chronic infection may have low-grade fever and the clinical signs may focus around local pain and loosening of the prosthesis.

Blood cultures are often negative. Cultures of the fluid from the artificial joint are critical but can be negative as well. If the prosthesis is surgically removed, multiple culture samples should be taken from the contiguous bone and cement because bacteria may remain clustered in circumscribed areas.

Diagnosis

Diagnosis of osteomyelitis integrates clinical signs, radiology, and microbiology. However, clinical signs may be scarce in chronic infection. Current radiologic techniques include standard radiography, technetium 99m (^{99m}Tc) methylene diphosphonate bone scanning, computed tomography scanning, and MRI (Fig. 192-16). Less established techniques include [111]In- or ^{99m}Tc-labeled granulocytes, ^{99m}Tc-labeled antigranulocyte antibodies, ^{99m}Tc-labeled polyclonal immunoglobulins, ^{99m}Tc-labeled ciprofloxacin, and gallium-67 citrate scanning.[233,234]

Conventional radiography may be negative within the first 10 days of acute osteomyelitis because necrosis, decalcification, and peripheral sclerosis are not yet apparent. In one study it was positive in only 50% of cases of acute osteomyelitis.[169] However, it is still useful to follow the healing process. [99m]Tc bone scanning and MRI are very sensitive and were positive in more than 80% of cases in the same study. [99m]Tc bone scanning is also sensitive in chronic osteomyelitis. However, because it detects bone remodeling, it may be difficult to interpret when underlying osteosynthetic prostheses or degenerative bone lesions are present.

Cultures are indispensable to guide therapy. Whenever possible, both blood cultures and tissue cultures should be performed. Chronic infection may be associated with persistent forms of *S. aureus* such as SCVs, especially if aminoglycosides have been used in conjunction with osteosynthetic material.[30]

Treatment

Rapid institution of antibiotic therapy is mandatory to prevent bone necrosis and the passage of acute osteomyelitis to more problematic chronic disease. The duration of drug treatment in most studies is 4 and 6 weeks but varies up to 10 weeks or more in complicated situations. The classic regimens are (1) for penicillin-susceptible *S. aureus,* intravenous penicillin G, 2-3 million units every 4 hours; (2) for penicillin-resistant *S. aureus,* intravenous nafcillin, cloxacillin, or, outside the United States, flucloxacillin, 2 g every 4 hours; and (3) for MRSA, intravenous vancomycin, 1 g every 12 hours.

The question of whether there is a proven "best" antibiotic treatment for osteomyelitis was addressed in a meta-analysis of 22 trials encompassing 927 episodes.[235] The results indicated that almost any of the drugs or drug combinations tested (including β-lactams, glycopeptides, clindamycin, and quinolones) were equivalent. However, the analysis also disclosed that the comparative trials were generally of poor quality.

The addition of rifampin to ciprofloxacin appeared clearly useful in the management of selected patients with *S. aureus* prosthesis infec-

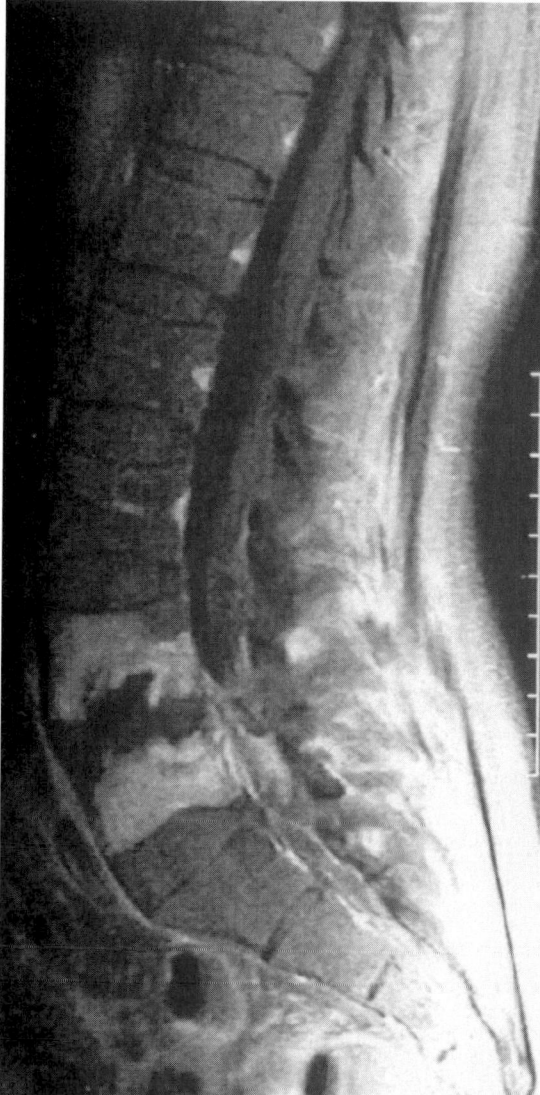

A

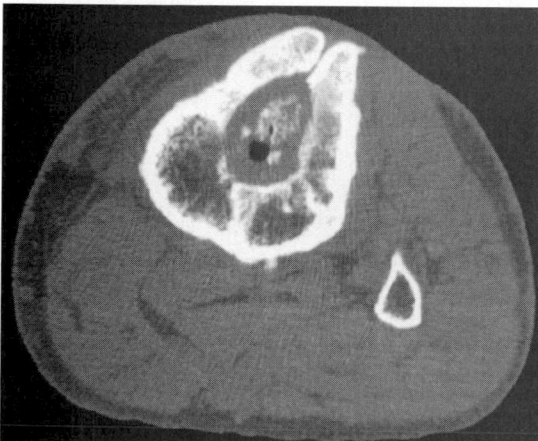

B

FIGURE 192-16. Osteomyelitis imaging. **A,** Nuclear magnetic resonance imaging of L4-L5 lumbar osteomyelitis after injection of gadolinium contrast medium (T1 view). **B,** Chronic osteomyelitis of the left tibia. A vast necrotic cavern containing a sequestrum surrounded by air can be seen. A fistula with drainage to the skin is present.

tion without loosening.[236] Combining rifampin with ciprofloxacin and probably newer anti–gram-positive quinolones as well may be considered in such situation. Otherwise, the classic two-step approach consisting of prosthesis removal followed by antibiotherapy (for 4 to 6 weeks) before the placement of a new prosthesis is mandatory. With *S. aureus* infection of a total knee prosthesis, the infected prosthesis is replaced by a spacer that is held in place with antibiotic-containing cement; antimicrobial therapy is then continued until it is considered safe to implant a new prosthesis (see Chapter 100).

In children with hematogenous *S. aureus* osteomyelitis, a relatively short course (4 to 7 days) of intravenous treatment is often followed by oral therapy with amoxicillin or penicillinase-stable β-lactams for 4 to 6 weeks, allowing outpatient therapy.[237] Oral treatment is currently not recommended in adults, although newer quinolones may be appropriate because of their high bioavailability. However, outpatient therapy is also increasingly used. Therapy may be achieved with ceftriaxone (2 g once a day), which was shown to be effective against *S. aureus* osteomyelitis in two studies.[167,238] In one of them, ceftriaxone and penicillinase-stable β-lactams performed significantly better than vancomycin.[167]

Finally, osteomyelitis related to multiresistant MRSA remains difficult to treat. No good experimental data exist to suggest whether either quinupristin-dalfopristin, linezolid, or other newer molecules would be more effective than standard alternatives (mostly vancomycin) in osteomyelitis models.

Septic Arthritis, Septic Bursitis, and Pyomyositis

Septic Arthritis

S. aureus remains the most frequent cause of septic arthritis in children and of nongonococcal arthritis of adults.[239] In adults, rheumatoid arthritis and diabetes are risk factors. Septic arthritis may follow hematogenous seeding and local trauma or may be iatrogenic in the case of joint puncture or arthroscopy. Symptoms include acute pain and joint swelling. Joint destruction within a few days is due to both bacterial and host inflammatory factors and probably also ischemic lesions because of the increased intra-articular hydrostatic pressure. Therefore, patients with underlying arthritis with acute pain in a single joint should have it aspirated immediately and the fluid examined for cell count, chemistry, and culture.

The prognosis of hematogenous arthritis in children is good. In adults, the prognosis is mostly associated with the underlying disease, that is, rheumatoid arthritis or endocarditis or other deep-seated condition responsible for the initial bacteremia. Medical treatment is identical to that for osteomyelitis. Open joint drainage is usually unnecessary except for hip infections in children, in which it may help prevent necrosis of the femoral head.[240]

Septic Bursitis

Septic bursitis is an acute infection involving the periarticular bursa. It is most often located in pressure areas such as the olecranon and the patella. It is manifest as an acute juxta-articular inflammation. The overlying skin is usually inflamed. Unlike the situation in arthritis and osteomyelitis, the underlying bone and joint are usually painless with pressure or mobilization. The portal of entry is likely to be local. More than 80% of bursitis cases are due to *S. aureus*.[241] Diagnosis is made by puncture and examination of the bursa fluid. Septic bursitis may be the origin of both local and distant septic complications. Thus, careful clinical evaluation is mandatory. The prognosis is good, but 2 to 3 weeks of appropriate antibiotherapy are required. Repeated aspiration of the bursa is preferable to incision and drainage for patients with persistent swelling and pain. Complicated cases may require hospitalization and intravenous treatment. Surgical excision of the bursa may be considered in the case of recurrences.

Pyomyositis

Primary pyomyositis, also called tropical myositis, infective myositis, pyogenic myositis, and myositis purulenta tropica, is a rare subacute infection of skeletal muscles. It does not follow contiguous contamination and is probably of hematogenous origin. The rarity of the disease is attributed to the resistance of muscles to infection. A history of prior muscle trauma is often reported.

Pyomyositis is frequently seen in Africa and the South Pacific but is rare in the Northern Hemisphere. Hence, it could be related to particular local conditions or bacterial properties. In a review of 676 cases, the disease occurred in all age groups. However, it was about twice as frequent in children and adults younger than 30 years than in older adults, and males were predominantly affected.[242] Any muscle may be involved, but the quadriceps and iliopsoas muscles were most often implicated, in 26% and 14%, respectively. *S. aureus* was the etiologic agent in about 80% of cases.

Clinical symptoms evolve in three stages. The first stage starts with the insidious onset of dull cramping and low-grade fever, general malaise, and muscle aches. Because only the aponeurosis is innervated, overt muscle pain may be delayed for 1 or 2 weeks, before frank abscess formation. In the second stage, the formation of a muscle abscess becomes symptomatic, with pain, muscle swelling, tenderness, and sepsis. Most patients are seen at this stage. If not treated, the disease evolves to the third stage, with muscle destruction, local extension with osteomyelitis or osteoarthritis, septicemia, and distant dissemination. Diagnosis involves radiographic imaging (computed tomography and MRI) and bacteriologic diagnosis by blood cultures and possibly muscle puncture. Treatment is essentially based on antibiotherapy. Treatment duration is a matter of debate. It is often recommended to start with parenteral treatment for 7 to 14 days, followed by oral treatment for up to 6 weeks. The prognosis before stage 3 is usually excellent.

Acknowledgment

This work was supported by grants 3200-47099.96 and 3200-0458.95/2 from the Swiss National Funds for Scientific Research.

REFERENCES

1. Lowy FD. *Staphylococcus aureus* infections. N Engl J Med. 1998;339:520-532.
2. Dinges MM, Orwin PM, Schlievert PM. Exotoxins of *Staphylococcus aureus*. Clin Microbiol Rev. 2000;13:16-34.
3. Ladhani S, Joannou CL, Lochrie DP, et al. Clinical, microbial, and biochemical aspects of the exfoliative toxins causing staphylococcal scalded-skin syndrome. Clin Microbiol Rev. 1999;12:224-242.
4. McCormick JK, Yarwood JM, Schlievert PM. Toxic shock syndrome and bacterial superantigens: An update. Annu Rev Microbiol. 2001;55:77-104.
5. Balaban N, Rasooly A. Staphylococcal enterotoxins. Int J Food Microbiol. 2000;61:1-10.
6. Cheung AL, Projan SJ, Gresham H. The genomic aspect of virulence, sepsis, and resistance to killing mechanisms in *Staphylococcus aureus*. Curr Infect Dis Rep. 2002;4:400-410.
7. Kloos WE, Schleifer KH, Goetz F. The genus staphylococcus. In: Balows A, Trüper HG, Dworkin M, et al, eds. The Prokaryotes. 2nd ed. New York: Springer-Verlag; 1992:1369-1420.
8. Kuroda M, Ohta T, Uchiyama I, et al. Whole genome sequencing of methicillin-resistant *Staphylococcus aureus*. Lancet. 2001;357:1225-1240.
9. Novick RP. Mobile genetic elements and bacterial toxinoses: The superantigen-encoding pathogenicity islands of *Staphylococcus aureus*. Plasmid. 2003;49:93-105.
10. Novick RP, Schlievert P, Ruzin A. Pathogenicity and resistance islands of staphylococci. Microbes Infect. 2001;3:585-594.
11. Baba T, Takeuchi F, Kuroda M, et al. Genome and virulence determinants of high virulence community-acquired MRSA. Lancet. 2002;359:1819-1827.
12. Ogston A. Micrococcus poisoning. J Anat Physiol (Lond). 1883;17:24-58.
13. Kloos WE, Bannerman TL. Staphylococcus and Micrococcus. In: Murray PR, Baron EJ, Pfaller MA, et al, eds. Manual of Clinical Microbiology. 6th ed. Washington, DC: ASM Press; 1995:282-298.
14. Rainard P, Corrales JC, Barrio MB, et al. Leucotoxic activities of *Staphylococcus aureus* strains isolated from cows, ewes, and goats with mastitis: Importance of LukM/LukF'-PV leukotoxin. Clin Diagn Lab Immunol. 2003;10:272-277.
15. Kluytmans J, van Belkum A, Verbrugh H. Nasal carriage of *Staphylococcus aureus*: Epidemiology, underlying mechanisms, and associated risks. Clin Microbiol Rev. 1997;10:505-520.
16. von Eiff C, Becker K, Machka K, et al. Nasal carriage as a source of *Staphylococcus aureus* bacteremia. Study Group. N Engl J Med. 2001;344:11-16.
17. von Eiff C, Kipp F, Becker K. Intranasal mupirocin to prevent postoperative infections. N Engl J Med. 2002;347:1207-1208; author reply 1207-1208.
18. Laupland KB, Church DL, Mucenski M, et al. Population-based study of the epidemiology of and the risk factors for invasive *Staphylococcus aureus* infections. J Infect Dis. 2003;187:1452-1459.
19. Chambers HF. The changing epidemiology of *Staphylococcus aureus*? Emerg Infect Dis. 2001;7:178-182.
20. Gorak EJ, Yamada SM, Brown JD. Community-acquired methicillin-resistant *Staphylococcus aureus* in hospitalized adults and children without known risk factors. Clin Infect Dis. 1999;29:797-800.
21. Dufour P, Gillet Y, Bes M, et al. Community-acquired methicillin-resistant *Staphylococcus aureus* infections in France: Emergence of a single clone that produces Panton-Valentine leukocidin. Clin Infect Dis. 2002;35:819-824.
22. From the Centers for Disease Control and Prevention. Public health dispatch: Outbreaks of community-associated methicillin-resistant *Staphylococcus aureus* skin infections. Los Angeles County, California, 2002-2003. JAMA. 2003;289:1377.
23. Proctor RA, Balwit JM, Vesga O. Variant subpopulations of *Staphylococcus aureus* as cause of persistent and recurrent infections. Infect Agents Dis. 1994;3:302-312.
24. Baumert N, von Eiff C, Schaaff F, et al. Physiology and antibiotic susceptibility of *Staphylococcus aureus* small colony variants. Microb Drug Resist. 2002;8:253-260.
25. Chuard C, Vaudaux PE, Proctor RA, et al. Decreased susceptibility to antibiotic killing of a stable small colony variant of *Staphylococcus aureus* in fluid phase and on fibronectin-coated surfaces. J Antimicrob Chemother. 1997;39:603-608.
26. Jonsson IM, von Eiff C, Proctor RA, et al. Virulence of a *hemB* mutant displaying the phenotype of a *Staphylococcus aureus* small colony variant in a murine model of septic arthritis. Microb Pathog. 2003;34:73-79.
27. Bates DM, von Eiff C, McNamara PJ, et al. *Staphylococcus aureus menD* and *hemB* mutants are as infective as the parent strains, but the menadione biosynthetic mutant persists within the kidney. J Infect Dis. 2003;187:1654-1661.
28. Vaudaux P, François P, Bisognano C, et al. Increased expression of clumping factor and fibronectin-binding proteins by *hemB* mutants of *Staphylococcus aureus* expressing small colony variant phenotypes. Infect Immun. 2002;70:5428-5437.
29. Vesga O, Groeschel MC, Otten MF, et al. *Staphylococcus aureus* small colony variants are induced by the endothelial cell intracellular milieu. J Infect Dis. 1996;173:739-742.
30. von Eiff C, Bettin D, Proctor RA, et al. Recovery of small colony variants of *Staphylococcus aureus* following gentamicin bead placement for osteomyelitis. Clin Infect Dis. 1997;25:1250-1251.
31. Nakatomi Y, Sugiyama J. A rapid latex agglutination assay for the detection of penicillin-binding protein 2'. Microbiol Immunol. 1998;42:739-743.
32. Anthony RM, Brown TJ, French GL. Rapid diagnosis of bacteremia by universal amplification of 23S ribosomal DNA followed by hybridization to an oligonucleotide array. J Clin Microbiol. 2000;38:781-788.
33. Brown DF. Detection of methicillin/oxacillin resistance in staphylococci. J Antimicrob Chemother. 2001;48(Suppl 1):65-70.
34. François P, Pittet D, Bento M, et al. Rapid detection of methicillin-resistant *Staphylococcus aureus* directly from sterile or nonsterile clinical samples by a new molecular assay. J Clin Microbiol. 2003;41:254-260.
35. Goldenberger D, Kunzli A, Vogt P, et al. Molecular diagnosis of bacterial endocarditis by broad-range PCR amplification and direct sequencing. J Clin Microbiol. 1997;35:2733-2739.
36. Anthony RM, Brown TJ, French GL. DNA array technology and diagnostic microbiology. Expert Rev Mol Diagn. 2001;1:30-38.
37. Bosshard PP, Kronenberg A, Zbinden R, et al. Etiologic diagnosis of infective endocarditis by broad-range polymerase chain reaction: A 3-year experience. Clin Infect Dis. 2003;37:167-172.
38. Novick RP. Autoinduction and signal transduction in the regulation of staphylococcal virulence. Mol Microbiol. 2003;48:1429-1449.
39. Novick RP, Ross HF, Projan SJ, et al. Synthesis of staphylococcal virulence factors is controlled by a regulatory RNA molecule. EMBO J. 1993;12:3967-3975.
40. Giraudo AT, Cheung AL, Nagel R. The *sae* locus of *Staphylococcus aureus* controls exoprotein synthesis at the transcriptional level. Arch Microbiol. 1997;168:53-58.
41. Fournier B, Hooper DC. A new two-component regulatory system involved in adhesion, autolysis, and extracellular proteolytic activity of *Staphylococcus aureus*. J Bacteriol. 2000;182:3955-3964.
42. Yarwood JM, McCormick JK, Schlievert PM. Identification of a novel two-component regulatory system that acts in global regulation of virulence factors of *Staphylococcus aureus*. J Bacteriol. 2001;183:1113-1123.
43. Chan PF, Foster SJ. The role of environmental factors in the regulation of virulence-determinant expression in *Staphylococcus aureus* 8325-4. Microbiology. 1998;144:2469-2479.
44. Nicholas RO, Li T, McDevitt D, et al. Isolation and characterization of a *sigB* deletion mutant of *Staphylococcus aureus*. Infect Immun. 1999;67:3667-3669.
45. Cheung AL, Koomey JM, Butler CA, et al. Regulation of exoprotein expression in *Staphylococcus aureus* by a locus (*sar*) distinct from *agr*. Proc Natl Acad Sci USA. 1992;89:6462-6466.
46. Chien Y, Cheung AL. Molecular interactions between two global regulators, *sar* and *agr*, in *Staphylococcus aureus*. J Biol Chem. 1998;273:2645-2652.
47. Balaban N, Goldkorn T, Nhan RT, et al. Autoinducer of virulence as a target for vaccine and therapy against *Staphylococcus aureus*. Science. 1998;280:438-440.
48. Balaban N, Goldkorn T, Gov Y, et al. Regulation of *Staphylococcus aureus* pathogenesis via target of RNAIII-activating protein (TRAP). J Biol Chem. 2001;276:2658-2667.
49. Garvis S, Mei JM, Ruiz-Albert J, et al. *Staphylococcus aureus svrA*: A gene required for virulence and expression of the *agr* locus. Microbiology. 2002;148:3235-3243.
50. Gov Y, Bitler A, Dell'Acqua G, et al. RNAIII inhibiting peptide (RIP), a global inhibitor of *Staphylococcus aureus* pathogenesis: Structure and function analysis. Peptides. 2001;22:1609-1620.

51. Mayville P, Ji G, Beavis R, et al. Structure-activity analysis of synthetic autoinducing thiolactone peptides from *Staphylococcus aureus* responsible for virulence. Proc Natl Acad Sci USA. 1999;96:1218-1223.

52. Cheung AL, Eberhardt KJ, Chung E, et al. Diminished virulence of a *sar*−/*agr*− mutant of *Staphylococcus aureus* in the rabbit model of endocarditis. J Clin Invest. 1994;94:1815-1822.

53. Que YA, François P, Haefliger JA, et al. Reassessing the role of *Staphylococcus aureus* clumping factor and fibronectin-binding protein by expression in *Lactococcus lactis*. Infect Immun. 2001;69:6296-6302.

54. Lyon GJ, Mayville P, Muir TW, et al. Rational design of a global inhibitor of the virulence response in *Staphylococcus aureus,* based in part on localization of the site of inhibition to the receptor-histidine kinase, AgrC. Proc Natl Acad Sci USA. 2000;97:13330-13335.

55. Ji G, Beavis R, Novick RP. Bacterial interference caused by autoinducing peptide variants. Science. 1997;276:2027-2030.

56. Goerke C, Kummel M, Dietz K, et al. Evaluation of intraspecies interference due to *agr* polymorphism in *Staphylococcus aureus* during infection and colonization. J Infect Dis. 2003;188:250-256.

57. Dufour P, Jarraud S, Vandenesch F, et al. High genetic variability of the *agr* locus in *Staphylococcus* species. J Bacteriol. 2002;184:1180-1186.

58. Gerke C, Kraft A, Sussmuth R, et al. Characterization of the *N*-acetylglucosaminyl-transferase activity involved in the biosynthesis of the *Staphylococcus epidermidis* polysaccharide intercellular adhesin. J Biol Chem. 1998;273:18586-18593.

59. Heilmann C, Schweitzer O, Gerke C, et al. Molecular basis of intercellular adhesion in the biofilm-forming *Staphylococcus epidermidis*. Mol Microbiol. 1996;20:1083-1091.

60. Cramton SE, Gerke C, Schnell NF, et al. The intercellular adhesion (*ica*) locus is present in *Staphylococcus aureus* and is required for biofilm formation. Infect Immun. 1999;67:5427-5433.

61. François P, Tu Quoc PH, Bisognano C, et al. Lack of biofilm contribution to bacterial colonisation in an experimental model of foreign body infection by *Staphylococcus aureus* and *Staphylococcus epidermidis*. FEMS Immunol Med Microbiol. 2003;35:135-140.

62. Karakawa WW, Fournier JM, Vann WF, et al. Method for the serological typing of the capsular polysaccharides of *Staphylococcus aureus*. J Clin Microbiol. 1985;22:445-447.

63. Thakker M, Park JS, Carey V, et al. *Staphylococcus aureus* serotype 5 capsular polysaccharide is antiphagocytic and enhances bacterial virulence in a murine bacteremia model. Infect Immun. 1998;66:5183-5189.

64. Shinefield H, Black S, Fattom A, et al. Use of a *Staphylococcus aureus* conjugate vaccine in patients receiving hemodialysis. N Engl J Med. 2002;346:491-496.

65. Patti JM, Allen BL, McGavin MJ, et al. MSCRAMM-mediated adherence of microorganisms to host tissues. Annu Rev Microbiol. 1994;48:585-617.

66. Fischetti VA, Pancholi V, Schneewind O. Conservation of a hexapeptide sequence in the anchor region of surface proteins from gram-positive cocci. Mol Microbiol. 1990;4:1603-1605.

67. Roche FM, Massey R, Peacock SJ, et al. Characterization of novel LPXTG-containing proteins of *Staphylococcus aureus* identified from genome sequences. Microbiology. 2003;149:643-654.

68. Mazmanian SK, Ton-That H, Schneewind O. Sortase-catalysed anchoring of surface proteins to the cell wall of *Staphylococcus aureus*. Mol Microbiol. 2001;40:1049-1057.

69. Patti JM, Bremell T, Krajewska-Pietrasik D, et al. The *Staphylococcus aureus* collagen adhesin is a virulence determinant in experimental septic arthritis. Infect Immun. 1994;62:152-161.

70. Peterson PK, Verhoef J, Sabath LD, et al. Effect of protein A on staphylococcal opsonization. Infect Immun. 1977;15:760-764.

71. Palmqvist N, Foster T, Tarkowski A, et al. Protein A is a virulence factor in *Staphylococcus aureus* arthritis and septic death. Microb Pathog. 2002;33:239-249.

72. Lee LY, Miyamoto YJ, McIntyre BW, et al. The *Staphylococcus aureus* Map protein is an immunomodulator that interferes with T cell-mediated responses. J Clin Invest. 2002;110:1461-1471.

73. Deininger S, Stadelmaier A, Von Aulock S, et al. Definition of structural prerequisites for lipoteichoic acid-inducible cytokine induction by synthetic derivatives. J Immunol. 2003;170:4134-4138.

74. Cossart P, Jonquieres R. Sortase, a universal target for therapeutic agents against gram-positive bacteria? Proc Natl Acad Sci USA. 2000;97:5013-5015.

75. Majcherczyk PA, Rubli E, Heumann D, et al. Teichoic acids are not required for *Streptococcus pneumoniae* and *Staphylococcus aureus* cell walls to trigger the release of tumor necrosis factor by peripheral blood monocytes. Infect Immun. 2003;71:3707-3713.

76. Dmitriev BA, Toukach FV, Schaper KJ, et al. Tertiary structure of bacterial murein: The scaffold model. J Bacteriol. 2003;185:3458-3468.

77. Berger-Bächi B. Expression of resistance to methicillin. Trends Microbiol. 1994;2:389-393.

78. Bayer AS, Ramos MD, Menzies BE, et al. Hyperproduction of alpha-toxin by *Staphylococcus aureus* results in paradoxically reduced virulence in experimental endocarditis: A host defense role for platelet microbicidal proteins. Infect Immun. 1997;65:4652-4660.

79. Panton P, Valentine F. Staphylococcal toxins. Lancet. 1932;222:506-508.

80. Lina G, Piemont Y, Godail-Gamot F, et al. Involvement of Panton-Valentine leukocidin-producing *Staphylococcus aureus* in primary skin infections and pneumonia. Clin Infect Dis. 1999;29:1128-1132.

81. Von Rittershain GR. Die exfoliative Dermatitis jungere Senglinge. Z Kinderheilkd. 1878;2:3-23.

82. Becker K, Friedrich AW, Lubritz G, et al. Prevalence of genes encoding pyrogenic toxin superantigens and exfoliative toxins among strains of *Staphylococcus aureus* isolated from blood and nasal specimens. J Clin Microbiol. 2003;41:1434-1439.

83. Lina G, Gillet Y, Vandenesch F, et al. Toxin involvement in staphylococcal scalded skin syndrome. Clin Infect Dis. 1997;25:1369-1373.

84. Tanabe T, Sato H, Ueda K, et al. Possible receptor for exfoliative toxins produced by *Staphylococcus hyicus* and *Staphylococcus aureus*. Infect Immun. 1995;63:1591-1594.

85. Davis MM, Bjorkman PJ. T-cell antigen receptor genes and T-cell recognition. Nature. 1988;334:395-402.

86. Williams RJ, Ward JM, Henderson B, et al. Identification of a novel gene cluster encoding staphylococcal exotoxin-like proteins: Characterization of the prototypic gene and its protein product, SET1. Infect Immun. 2000;68:4407-4415.

87. Fitzgerald JR, Reid SD, Ruotsalainen E, et al. Genome diversification in *Staphylococcus aureus*: Molecular evolution of a highly variable chromosomal region encoding the staphylococcal exotoxin-like family of proteins. Infect Immun. 2003;71:2827-2838.

88. Ulrich RG. Evolving superantigens of *Staphylococcus aureus*. FEMS Immunol Med Microbiol. 2000;27:1-7.

89. Stevens F. The occurrence of *Staphylococcus aureus* infection with a scarlatiniform rash. JAMA. 1927;88:1957-1958.

90. Shands KN, Schmid GP, Dan BB, et al. Toxic-shock syndrome in menstruating women: Association with tampon use and *Staphylococcus aureus* and clinical features in 52 cases. N Engl J Med. 1980;303:1436-1442.

91. Cone LA, Woodard DR, Byrd RG, et al. A recalcitrant, erythematous, desquamating disorder associated with toxin-producing staphylococci in patients with AIDS. J Infect Dis. 1992;165:638-643.

92. Stolz SJ, Davis JP, Vergeront JM, et al. Development of serum antibody to toxic shock toxin among individuals with toxic shock syndrome in Wisconsin. J Infect Dis. 1985;151:883-889.

93. Reingold AL, Hargrett NT, Shands KN, et al. Toxic shock syndrome surveillance in the United States, 1980 to 1981. Ann Intern Med. 1982;96:875-880.

94. Kaul R, McGeer A, Norrby-Teglund A, et al. Intravenous immunoglobulin therapy for streptococcal toxic shock syndrome—A comparative observational study. The Canadian Streptococcal Study Group. Clin Infect Dis. 1999;28:800-807.

95. Weems JJ, Beck LB. Nasal carriage of *Staphylococcus aureus* as a risk factor for skin and soft tissue infections. Curr Infect Dis Rep. 2002;4:420-425.

96. Gampfer J, Thon V, Gulle H, et al. Double mutant and formaldehyde inactivated TSST-1 as vaccine candidates for TSST-1-induced toxic shock syndrome. Vaccine. 2002;20:1354-1364.

97. Altekruse SF, Cohen ML, Swerdlow DL. Emerging foodborne diseases. Emerg Infect Dis. 1997;3:285-293.

98. Hamad AR, Marrack P, Kappler JW. Transcytosis of staphylococcal superantigen toxins. J Exp Med. 1997;185:1447-1454.

99. Petersson K, Pettersson H, Skartved NJ, et al. Staphylococcal enterotoxin H induces V alpha-specific expansion of T cells. J Immunol. 2003;170:4148-4154.

100. Yarwood JM, Leung DY, Schlievert PM. Evidence for the involvement of bacterial superantigens in psoriasis, atopic dermatitis, and Kawasaki syndrome. FEMS Microbiol Lett. 2000;192:1-7.

101. Kaneko J, Kimura T, Narita S, et al. Complete nucleotide sequence and molecular characterization of the temperate staphylococcal bacteriophage phiPVL carrying Panton-Valentine leukocidin genes. Gene. 1998;215:57-67.

102. Lindsay JA, Ruzin A, Ross HF, et al. The gene for toxic shock toxin is carried by a family of mobile pathogenicity islands in *Staphylococcus aureus*. Mol Microbiol. 1998;29:527-543.

103. Ito T, Okuma K, Ma XX, et al. Insights on antibiotic resistance of *Staphylococcus aureus* from its whole genome: Genomic island SCC. Drug Resist Updat. 2003;6:41-52.

104. Katayama Y, Ito T, Hiramatsu K. A new class of genetic element, staphylococcus cassette chromosome *mec*, encodes methicillin resistance in *Staphylococcus aureus*. Antimicrob Agents Chemother. 2000;44:1549-1555.

105. Chambers HF, Hartman BJ, Tomasz A. Increased amounts of a novel penicillin binding protein in a strain of methicillin-resistant *Staphylococcus aureus*. J Clin Invest. 1985;76:325-331.

106. Zhang HZ, Hackbarth CJ, Chansky KM, et al. A proteolytic transmembrane signaling pathway and resistance to beta-lactams in staphylococci. Nature. 2001;291:1962-1965.

107. Ito T, Katayama Y, Asada K, et al. Structural comparison of three types of staphylococcal cassette chromosome *mec* integrated in the chromosome in methicillin-resistant *Staphylococcus aureus*. Antimicrob Agents Chemother. 2001;45:1323-1336.

108. Ma XX, Ito T, Tiensasitorn C, et al. Novel type of staphylococcal cassette chromosome *mec* identified in community-acquired methicillin-resistant *Staphylococcus aureus* strains. Antimicrob Agents Chemother. 2002;46:1147-1152.

109. Couto I, de Lencastre H, Severina E, et al. Ubiquitous presence of a *mecA* homologue in natural isolates of *Staphylococcus sciuri*. Microb Drug Resist. 1996;2:377-391.

110. Nimmo GR, Bell JM, Mitchell D, et al. Antimicrobial resistance in *Staphylococcus aureus* in Australian teaching hospitals, 1989-1999. Microb Drug Resist. 2003;9:155-160.

111. Kesah C, Ben Redjeb S, Odugbemi TO, et al. Prevalence of methicillin-resistant *Staphylococcus aureus* in eight African hospitals and Malta. Clin Microbiol Infect. 2003;9:153-156.

112. Ghuysen JM. Molecular structures of penicillin-binding proteins and beta-lactamases. Trends Microbiol. 1994;2:372-380.

113. Goffin C, Ghuysen JM. Multimodular penicillin-binding proteins: An enigmatic family of orthologs and paralogs. Microbiol Mol Biol Rev. 1998;62:1079-1093.

114. Gillespie MT, May JW, Skurray RA. Antibiotic resistance in *Staphylococcus aureus* isolated at an Australian hospital between 1946 and 1981. J Med Microbiol. 1985;19:137-147.

115. Jevons MP. "Celbenin"-resistant staphylococci. Br Med J. 1961;1:124-125.

116. Voss A, Milatovic D, Wallrauch-Schwarz C, et al. Methicillin-resistant *Staphylococcus aureus* in Europe. Eur J Clin Microbiol Infect Dis. 1994;13:50-55.

117. Panlilio AL, Culver DH, Gaynes RP, et al. Methicillin-resistant *Staphylococcus aureus* in U.S. hospitals, 1975-1991. Infect Control Hosp Epidemiol. 1992;13:582-586.

118. Diekema DJ, Pfaller MA, Schmitz FJ, et al. Survey of infections due to *Staphylococcus* species: Frequency of occurrence and antimicrobial susceptibility of isolates collected in the United States, Canada, Latin America, Europe, and the Western Pacific region for the SENTRY Antimicrobial Surveillance Program, 1997-1999. Clin Infect Dis. 2001;32(Suppl 2):S114-S132.

119. Salgado CD, Farr BM, Calfee DP. Community-acquired methicillin-resistant *Staphylococcus aureus*: A meta-analysis of prevalence and risk factors. Clin Infect Dis. 2003;36:131-139.

120. McDougal LK, Thornsberry C. The role of beta-lactamase in staphylococcal resistance to penicillinase-resistant penicillins and cephalosporins. J Clin Microbiol. 1986;23:832-839.

121. de Jonge BL, Tomasz A. Abnormal peptidoglycan produced in a methicillin-resistant strain of *Staphylococcus aureus* grown in the presence of methicillin: Functional role for penicillin-binding protein 2A in cell wall synthesis. Antimicrob Agents Chemother. 1993;37:342-346.

122. de Lencastre H, Wu SW, Pinho MG, et al. Antibiotic resistance as a stress response: Complete sequencing of a large number of chromosomal loci in *Staphylococcus aureus* strain COL that impact on the expression of resistance to methicillin. Microb Drug Resist. 1999;5:163-175.

123. Pinho MG, de Lancastre H, Tomasz A. An acquired and a native penicillin-binding protein cooperate in building the cell wall of drug-resistant staphylococci. Proc Natl Acad Sci USA. 2001;98:10886-10891.

124. Lim D, Strynadka NC. Structural basis for the beta lactam resistance of PBP2a from methicillin-resistant *Staphylococcus aureus*. Nat Struct Biol. 2002;9:870-876.

125. Franciolli M, Bille J, Glauser MP, et al. Beta-lactam resistance mechanisms of methicillin-resistant *Staphylococcus aureus*. J Infect Dis. 1991;163:514-523.

126. Entenza JM, Hohl P, Heinze-Krauss I, et al. BAL9141, a novel extended-spectrum cephalosporin active against methicillin-resistant *Staphylococcus aureus* in treatment of experimental endocarditis. Antimicrob Agents Chemother. 2002;46:171-177.

127. Tomasz A. "Intelligence coup" for drug designers: Crystal structure of *Staphylococcus aureus* beta-lactam resistance protein PBP2A. Lancet. 2003;361:795-796.

128. Hiramatsu K, Hanaki H, Ino T, et al. Methicillin-resistant *Staphylococcus aureus* clinical strain with reduced vancomycin susceptibility. J Antimicrob Chemother. 1997;40:135-136.

129. Ploy MC, Grelaud C, Martin C, et al. First clinical isolate of vancomycin-intermediate *Staphylococcus aureus* in a French hospital. Lancet. 1998;351:1212.

130. Sieradzki K, Roberts RB, Haber SW, et al. The development of vancomycin resistance in a patient with methicillin-resistant *Staphylococcus aureus* infection. N Engl J Med. 1999;340:517-523.

131. Standards NCCLS. Methods for dilution antimicrobial susceptibility tests for bacteria that grow aerobically. Approved standards M7-A5. Wayne, PA: NCCLS; 2000.

132. Hiramatsu K, Aritaka N, Hanaki H, et al. Dissemination in Japanese hospitals of strains of *Staphylococcus aureus* heterogeneously resistant to vancomycin. Lancet. 1997;350:1670-1673.

133. Hanaki H, Labischinski H, Inaba Y, et al. Increase in glutamine-non-amidated muropeptides in the peptidoglycan of vancomycin-resistant *Staphylococcus aureus* strain Mu50. J Antimicrob Chemother. 1998;42:315-320.

134. Walsh TR, Bolmstrom A, Qwarnstrom A, et al. Evaluation of current methods for detection of staphylococci with reduced susceptibility to glycopeptides. J Clin Microbiol. 2001;39:2439-2444.

135. Arthur M, Courvalin P. Genetics and mechanisms of glycopeptide resistance in enterococci. Antimicrob Agents Chemother. 1993;37:1563-1571.

136. Noble Wc, Virani Z, Cree RGA. Co-transfer of vancomycin and other resistance genes from *Enterococcus faecalis* NCTC 12201 to *Staphylococcus aureus*. FEMS Microbiol Lett. 1992;93:195-198.

137. Chang S, Sievert DM, Hageman JC, et al. Infection with vancomycin-resistant *Staphylococcus aureus* containing the *vanA* resistance gene. N Engl J Med. 2003;348:1342-1347.

138. Leclercq R, Courvalin P. Intrinsic and unusual resistance to macrolide, lincosamide, and streptogramin antibiotics in bacteria. Antimicrob Agents Chemother. 1991;35:1273-1276.

139. Weisblum B. Erythromycin resistance by ribosome modification. Antimicrob Agents Chemother. 1995;39:577-585.

140. Siberry GK, Tekle T, Carroll K, Dick J. Failure of clindamycin treatment of methicillin-resistant *Staphylococcus aureus* expressing inducible clindamycin resistance in vitro. Clin Infect Dis 2003;37:1257-1260.

141. Ross JI, Eady EA, Cove JH, et al. Identification of a chromosomally encoded ABC-transport system with which the staphylococcal erythromycin exporter MsrA may interact. Gene. 1995;153:93-98.

142. Clancy J, Petitpas J, Dib-Hajj F, et al. Molecular cloning and functional analysis of a novel macrolide-resistance determinant, *mefA*, from *Streptococcus pyogenes*. Mol Microbiol. 1996;22:867-879.

143. Tait-Kamradt A, Clancy J, Cronan M, et al. *mefE* is necessary for the erythromycin-resistant M phenotype in *Streptococcus pneumoniae*. Antimicrob Agents Chemother. 1997;41:2251-2255.

144. Dholakia N, Rolston KV, Ho DH, et al. Susceptibilities of bacterial isolates from patients with cancer to levofloxacin and other quinolones. Antimicrobial Agents Chemother. 1994;38:848-852.

145. Borner K, Hoffken G, Lode H, et al. Pharmacokinetics of ciprofloxacin in healthy volunteers after oral and intravenous administration. Eur J Clin Microbiol. 1986;5:179-186.

146. Yoshida H, Bogaki M, Nakamura S, et al. Nucleotide sequence and characterization of the *Staphylococcus aureus norA* gene, which confers resistance to quinolones. J Bacteriol. 1990;172:6942-6949.

147. Fournier B, Hooper DC. Mutations in topoisomerase IV and DNA gyrase of *Staphylococcus aureus*: Novel pleiotropic effects on quinolone and coumarin activity. Antimicrob Agents Chemother. 1998;42:121-128.

148. Entenza JM, Vouillamoz J, Glauser MP, et al. Levofloxacin versus ciprofloxacin, flucloxacillin, or vancomycin for treatment of experimental endocarditis due to methicillin-susceptible or -resistant *Staphylococcus aureus*. Antimicrob Agents Chemother. 1997;41:1662-1667.

149. Craig WA. Does the dose matter? Clin Infect Dis. 2001;33(Suppl 3):S233-S237.

150. Blondeau JM, Zhao X, Hansen G, et al. Mutant prevention concentrations of fluoroquinolones for clinical isolates of *Streptococcus pneumoniae*. Antimicrob Agents Chemother. 2001;45:433-438.

151. Small PM, Chambers HF. Vancomycin for *Staphylococcus aureus* endocarditis in intravenous drug users. Antimicrob Agents Chemother. 1990;34:1227-1231.

152. Moise PA, Schentag JJ. Vancomycin treatment failures in *Staphylococcus aureus* lower respiratory tract infections. Int J Antimicrob Agents. 2000;16(Suppl 1):S31-S34.

153. Levine DP, Fromm BS, Reddy BR. Slow response to vancomycin or vancomycin plus rifampin in methicillin-resistant *Staphylococcus aureus* endocarditis. Ann Intern Med. 1991;115:674-680.

154. Cocito C, Di Giambattista M, Nyssen E, et al. Inhibition of protein synthesis by streptogramins and related antibiotics. J Antimicrob Chemother. 1997;39(Suppl A):7-13.

155. Vouillamoz J, Entenza JM, Feger C, et al. Quinupristin-dalfopristin combined with beta-lactams for treatment of experimental endocarditis due to *Staphylococcus aureus* constitutively resistant to macrolide-lincosamide-streptogramin B antibiotics. Antimicrob Agents Chemother. 2000;44:1789-1795.

156. Norrby R. Linezolid—A review of the first oxazolidinone. Expert Opin Pharmacother. 2001;2:293-302.

157. Pfaller MA, Jones RN, Doern GV, et al. Bacterial pathogens isolated from patients with bloodstream infection: Frequencies of occurrence and antimicrobial susceptibility patterns from the SENTRY antimicrobial surveillance program (United States and Canada, 1997). Antimicrob Agents Chemother. 1998;42:1762-1770.

158. Fluit AC, Schmitz FJ, Verhoef J. Frequency of isolation of pathogens from bloodstream, nosocomial pneumonia, skin and soft tissue, and urinary tract infections occurring in European patients. Eur J Clin Microbiol Infect Dis. 2001;20:188-191.

159. Rubin RJ, Harrington CA, Poon A, et al. The economic impact of *Staphylococcus aureus* infection in New York City hospitals. Emerg Infect Dis. 1999;5:9-17.

160. Mylotte JM, Tayara A. *Staphylococcus aureus* bacteremia: Predictors of 30-day mortality in a large cohort. Clin Infect Dis. 2000;31:1170-1174.

161. Jensen AG, Wachmann CH, Espersen F, et al. Treatment and outcome of *Staphylococcus aureus* bacteremia: A prospective study of 278 cases. Arch Intern Med. 2002;162:25-32.

162. Jensen AG, Wachmann CH, Poulsen KB, et al. Risk factors for hospital-acquired *Staphylococcus aureus* bacteremia. Arch Intern Med. 1999;159:1437-1444.

163. Cosgrove SE, Sakoulas G, Perencevich EN, et al. Comparison of mortality associated with methicillin-resistant and methicillin-susceptible *Staphylococcus aureus* bacteremia: A meta-analysis. Clin Infect Dis. 2003;36:53-59.

164. Giacometti A, Cirioni O, Schimizzi AM, et al. Epidemiology and microbiology of surgical wound infections. J Clin Microbiol. 2000;38:918-922.

165. Hoban DJ, Biedenbach DJ, Mutnick AH, et al. Pathogen of occurrence and susceptibility patterns associated with pneumonia in hospitalized patients in North America: Results of the SENTRY Antimicrobial Surveillance Study (2000). Diagn Microbiol Infect Dis. 2003;45:279-285.

166. Lew DP, Waldvogel FA. Osteomyelitis. N Engl J Med. 1997;336:999-1007.

167. Tice AD, Hoaglund PA, Shoultz DA. Risk factors and treatment outcomes in osteomyelitis. J Antimicrob Chemother. 2003;51:1261-1268.

168. Blyth MJ, Kincaid R, Craigen MA, et al. The changing epidemiology of acute and subacute haematogenous osteomyelitis in children. J Bone Joint Surg Br. 2001;83:99-102.

169. Bonhoeffer J, Haeberle B, Schaad UB, et al. Diagnosis of acute haematogenous osteomyelitis and septic arthritis: 20 years experience at the University Children's Hospital Basel. Swiss Med Wkly. 2001;131:575-581.

170. Lark RL, Chenoweth C, Saint S, et al. Four year prospective evaluation of nosocomial bacteremia: Epidemiology, microbiology, and patient outcome. Diagn Microbiol Infect Dis. 2000;38:131-140.

171. Valles J, Rello J, Ochagavia A, et al. Community-acquired bloodstream infection in critically ill adult patients: Impact of shock and inappropriate antibiotic therapy on survival. Chest. 2003;123:1615-1624.

172. Moreillon P, Que YA. Infective endocarditis. Lancet. 2004;363:135-149.

173. Chiang FY, Climo M. *Staphylococcus aureus* carriage and health care–acquired infection. Curr Infect Dis Rep. 2002;4:498-504.

174. Harrison LM, Morris JA, Telford DR, et al. The nasopharyngeal bacterial flora in infancy: Effects of age, gender, season, viral upper respiratory tract infection and sleeping position. FEMS Immunol Med Microbiol. 1999;25:19-28.

175. Armstrong-Esther CA. Carriage patterns of *Staphylococcus aureus* in a healthy non-hospital population of adults and children. Ann Hum Biol. 1976;3:221-227.

176. Vandenbergh MF, Verbrugh HA. Carriage of *Staphylococcus aureus*: Epidemiology and clinical relevance. J Lab Clin Med. 1999;133:525-534.

177. Zanelli G, Sansoni A, Zanchi A, et al. *Staphylococcus aureus* nasal carriage in the community: A survey from central Italy. Epidemiol Infect. 2002;129:417-420.

178. Bassetti S, Dunagan DP, D'Agostino RB Jr, et al. Nasal carriage of *Staphylococcus aureus* among patients receiving allergen-injection immunotherapy: Associated factors and quantitative nasal cultures. Infect Control Hosp Epidemiol. 2001;22:741-745.

179. Kalmeijer MD, van Nieuwland-Bollen E, Bogaers-Hofman D, et al. Nasal carriage of *Staphylococcus aureus* is a major risk factor for surgical-site infections in orthopedic surgery. Infect Control Hosp Epidemiol. 2000;21:319-323.

180. Kluytmans JA, Mouton JW, Ijzerman EP, et al. Nasal carriage of *Staphylococcus aureus* as a major risk factor for wound infections after cardiac surgery. J Infect Dis. 1995;171:216-219.

181. Turner K, Uttley L, Scrimgeour A, et al. Natural history of *Staphylococcus aureus* nasal carriage and its relationship to exit-site infection. Perit Dial Int. 1998;18:271-273.

182. Thompson RL, Cabezudo I, Wenzel RP. Epidemiology of nosocomial infections caused by methicillin-resistant *Staphylococcus aureus*. Ann Intern Med. 1982;97:309-317.

183. Boyce JM. Methicillin-resistant *Staphylococcus aureus*. Detection, epidemiology, and control measures. Infect Dis Clin North Am. 1989;3:901-913.

184. Lucet JC, Chevret S, Durand-Zaleski I, et al. Prevalence and risk factors for carriage of methicillin-resistant *Staphylococcus aureus* at admission to the intensive care unit: Results of a multicenter study. Arch Intern Med. 2003;163:181-188.

185. Pittet D, Hugonnet S, Harbarth S, et al. Effectiveness of a hospital-wide programme to improve compliance with hand hygiene. Infection Control Programme. Lancet. 2000;356:1307-1312.

186. Boyce JM. MRSA patients: Proven methods to treat colonization and infection. J Hosp Infect. 2001;48(Suppl A):S9-S14.

187. Doebbeling BN, Breneman DL, Neu HC, et al. Elimination of *Staphylococcus aureus* nasal carriage in health care workers: Analysis of six clinical trials with calcium mupirocin ointment. The Mupirocin Collaborative Study Group. Clin Infect Dis. 1993;17:466-474.

188. Doebbeling BN, Reagan DR, Pfaller MA, et al. Long-term efficacy of intranasal mupirocin ointment. A prospective cohort study of *Staphylococcus aureus* carriage. Arch Intern Med. 1994;154:1505-1508.

189. Fernandez C, Gaspar C, Torrellas A, et al. A double-blind, randomized, placebo-controlled clinical trial to evaluate the safety and efficacy of mupirocin calcium ointment for eliminating nasal carriage of *Staphylococcus aureus* among hospital personnel. J Antimicrob Chemother. 1995;35:399-408.

190. Bommer J, Vergetis W, Andrassy K, et al. Elimination of *Staphylococcus aureus* in hemodialysis patients. ASAIO J. 1995;41:127-131.

191. Perez-Fontan M, Garcia-Falcon T, Rosales M, et al. Treatment of *Staphylococcus aureus* nasal carriers in continuous ambulatory peritoneal dialysis with mupirocin: Long-term results. Am J Kidney Dis. 1993;22:708-712.

192. Vasquez JE, Walker ES, Franzus BW, et al. The epidemiology of mupirocin resistance among methicillin-resistant *Staphylococcus aureus* at a Veterans' Affairs hospital. Infect Control Hosp Epidemiol. 2000;21:459-464.

193. Walker ES, Vasquez JE, Dula R, et al. Mupirocin-resistant, methicillin-resistant *Staphylococcus aureus*: Does mupirocin remain effective? Infect Control Hosp Epidemiol. 2003;24:342-346.

194. Light IJ, Walton RL, Sutherland JM, et al. Use of bacterial interference to control a staphylococcal nursery outbreak. Deliberate colonization of all infants with the 502A strain of *Staphylococcus aureus*. Am J Dis Child. 1967;113:291-300.

195. Houck PW, Nelson JD, Kay JL. Fatal septicemia due to *Staphylococcus aureus* 502A. Report of a case and review of the infectious complications of bacterial interference programs. Am J Dis Child. 1972;123:45-48.

196. Kokai-Kun JF, Walsh SM, Chanturiya T, et al. Lysostaphin cream eradicates *Staphylococcus aureus* nasal colonization in a cotton rat model. Antimicrob Agents Chemother. 2003;47:1589-1597.

197. Fischetti VA. Novel method to control pathogenic bacteria on human mucous membranes. Ann NY Acad Sci. 2003;987:207-214.

198. Caelli M, Porteous J, Carson CF, et al. Tea tree oil as an alternative topical decolonization agent for methicillin-resistant *Staphylococcus aureus*. J Hosp Infect. 2000;46:236-237.

199. Weinstein MP, Towns ML, Quartey SM, et al. The clinical significance of positive blood cultures in the 1990s: A prospective comprehensive evaluation of the microbiology, epidemiology, and outcome of bacteremia and fungemia in adults. Clin Infect Dis. 1997;24:584-602.

200. Morin CA, Hadler JL. Population-based incidence and characteristics of community-onset *Staphylococcus aureus* infections with bacteremia in 4 metropolitan Connecticut areas, 1998. J Infect Dis. 2001;184:1029-1034.

201. Lark RL, Saint S, Chenoweth C, et al. Four-year prospective evaluation of community-acquired bacteremia: Epidemiology, microbiology, and patient outcome. Diagn Microbiol Infect Dis. 2001;41:15-22.

202. Abbott KC, Agodoa LY. Hospitalizations for bacterial endocarditis after initiation of chronic dialysis in the United States. Nephron. 2002;91:203-209.

203. Gouello JP, Asfar P, Brenet O, et al. Nosocomial endocarditis in the intensive care unit: An analysis of 22 cases. Crit Care Med. 2000;28:377-382.

204. Berrington A, Gould FK. Use of antibiotic locks to treat colonized central venous catheters. J Antimicrob Chemother. 2001;48:597-603.

205. Bouza E, Burillo A, Munoz P. Catheter-related infections: Diagnosis and intravascular treatment. Clin Microbiol Infect. 2002;8:265-274.

206. Moreillon P, Que YA, Bayer AS. Pathogenesis of streptococcal and staphylococcal endocarditis. Infect Dis Clin North Am. 2002;16:297-318.

207. Hemler ME, Elices MJ, Chan BM, et al. Multiple ligand binding functions for VLA-2 (alpha 2 beta 1) and VLA-3 (alpha 3 beta 1) in the integrin family. Cell Differ Dev. 1990;32:229-238.

208. Sinha B, François P, Que YA, et al. Heterologously expressed *Staphylococcus aureus* fibronectin-binding proteins are sufficient for invasion of host cells. Infect Immun. 2000;68:6871-6878.

209. Yeaman MR, Bayer AS, Koo SP, et al. Platelet microbicidal proteins and neutrophil defensin disrupt the *Staphylococcus aureus* cytoplasmic membrane by distinct mechanisms of action. J Clin Invest. 1998;101:178-187.

210. Fowler VG Jr, McIntyre LM, Yeaman MR, et al. *In vitro* resistance to thrombin-induced platelet microbicidal protein in isolates of *Staphylococcus aureus* from endocarditis patients correlates with an intravascular device source. J Infect Dis. 2000;182:1251-1254.

211. Sullam PM, Frank U, Yeaman MR, et al. Effect of thrombocytopenia on the early course of streptococcal endocarditis. J Infect Dis. 1993;168:910-914.

212. Kupferwasser LI, Yeaman MR, Nast CC, et al. Salicylic acid attenuates virulence in endovascular infections by targeting global regulatory pathways in *Staphylococcus aureus*. J Clin Invest. 2003;112:222-233.

213. Tornos P, Almirante B, Mirabet S, et al. Infective endocarditis due to *Staphylococcus aureus*: Deleterious effect of anticoagulant therapy. Arch Intern Med. 1999;159:473-475.

214. Durack DT, Lukes AS, Bright DK. New criteria for diagnosis of infective endocarditis: Utilization of specific echocardiographic findings. Duke Endocarditis Service. Am J Med. 1994;96:200-209.

215. Li JS, Sexton DJ, Mick N, et al. Proposed modifications to the Duke criteria for the diagnosis of infective endocarditis. Clin Infect Dis. 2000;30:633-638.

216. Brouqui P, Raoult D. Endocarditis due to rare and fastidious bacteria. Clin Microbiol Rev. 2001;14:177-207.

217. Miro JM, Moreno A, Mestres CA. Infective endocarditis in intravenous drug abusers. Curr Infect Dis Rep. 2003;5:307-316.

218. Francioli PB, Freedman LR. Streptococcal infection of endocardial and other intravascular vegetations in rabbits: Natural history and effect of dexamethasone. Infect Immun. 1979;24:483-491.

219. Heldman AW, Hartert TV, Ray SC, et al. Oral antibiotic treatment of right-sided staphylococcal endocarditis in injection drug users: Prospective randomized comparison with parenteral therapy. Am J Med. 1996;101:68-76.

220. Jensen AG, Espersen F, Skinhoj P, et al. *Staphylococcus aureus* meningitis. A review of 104 nationwide, consecutive cases. Arch Intern Med. 1993;153:1902-1908.

221. Klacsmann PG, Bulkley BH, Hutchins GM. The changed spectrum of purulent pericarditis: An 86 year autopsy experience in 200 patients. Am J Med. 1977;63:666-673.

222. Osiyemi O, Dickinson G. Gram-positive pneumonia. Curr Infect Dis Rep. 2000;2:207-214.

223. El-Solh AA, Sikka P, Ramadan F, et al. Etiology of severe pneumonia in the very elderly. Am J Respir Crit Care Med. 2001;163:645-651.

224. Sethi S. Bacterial pneumonia. Managing a deadly complication of influenza in older adults with comorbid disease. Geriatrics. 2002;57:56-61.

225. Lynch JP 3rd. Hospital-acquired pneumonia: Risk factors, microbiology, and treatment. Chest. 2001;119(2 Suppl):373S-384S.

226. Bryant RE, Salmon CJ. Pleural empyema. Clin Infect Dis. 1996;22:747-762; quiz 763-764.

227. White M, Dennison WM. Acute haematogeneous osteitis in childhood: A review of 212 cases. J Bone Joint Surg Br. 1952;34:608-623.

228. Kabak S, Tuncel M, Halici M, et al. Role of trauma on acute haematogenic osteomyelitis aetiology. Eur J Emerg Med. 1999;6:219-222.

229. Blevins JS, Elasri MO, Allmendinger SD, et al. Role of *sarA* in the pathogenesis of *Staphylococcus aureus* musculoskeletal infection. Infect Immun. 2003;71:516-523.

230. Cunha BA. Osteomyelitis in elderly patients. Clin Infect Dis. 2002;35:287-293.

231. Grayson ML, Gibbons GW, Balogh K, et al. Probing to bone in infected pedal ulcers. A clinical sign of underlying osteomyelitis in diabetic patients. JAMA. 1995;273:721-723.

232. Lentino JR. Prosthetic joint infections: Bane of orthopedists, challenge for infectious disease specialists. Clin Infect Dis. 2003;36:1157-1161.

233. Malamitsi J, Giamarellou H, Kanellakopoulou K, et al. Infecton: A 99mTc-ciprofloxacin radiopharmaceutical for the detection of bone infection. Clin Microbiol Infect. 2003;9:101-109.

234. Schiesser M, Stumpe KDM, Trentz O, et al. Detection of metallic implant–associated infections with FDG PET in patients with trauma: Correlation with microbiologic results. Radiology. 2003;226:391-398.

235. Stengel D, Bauwens K, Sehouli J, et al. Systematic review and meta-analysis of antibiotic therapy for bone and joint infections. Lancet Infect Dis. 2001;1:175-188.

236. Zimmerli W, Widmer AF, Blatter M, et al. Role of rifampin for treatment of orthopedic implant-related staphylococcal infections: A randomized controlled trial. Foreign-Body Infection (FBI) Study Group. JAMA. 1998;279:1537-1541.

237. Vinod MB, Matussek J, Curtis N, et al. Duration of antibiotics in children with osteomyelitis and septic arthritis. J Paediatr Child Health. 2002;38:363-367.

238. Guglielmo BJ, Luber AD, Paletta D Jr, et al. Ceftriaxone therapy for staphylococcal osteomyelitis: A review. Clin Infect Dis. 2000;30:205-207.

239. Shirtliff ME, Mader JT. Acute septic arthritis. Clin Microbiol Rev. 2002;15:527-544.

240. Broy SB, Schmid FR. A comparison of medical drainage (needle aspiration) and surgical drainage (arthrotomy or arthroscopy) in the initial treatment of infected joints. Clin Rheum Dis. 1986;12:501-522.

241. Zimmermann B 3rd, Mikolich DJ, Ho G Jr. Septic bursitis. Semin Arthritis Rheum. 1995;24:391-410.

242. Bickels J, Ben-Sira L, Kessler A, et al. Primary pyomyositis. J Bone Joint Surg Am. 2002;84:2277-2286.

243. Roche FM, Meehan M, Foster TJ. The *Staphylococcus aureus* surface protein SasG and its homologues promote bacterial adherence to human desquamated nasal epithelial cells. Microbiology. 2003;149:2759-2767.

244. Wilson WR, Karchmer AW, Dajani AS, et al. Antibiotic treatment of adults with infective endocarditis due to streptococci, enterococci, staphylococci, and HACEK microorganisms. JAMA. 1995;274:1706-1713.

Staphylococcus epidermidis and Other Coagulase-Negative Staphylococci

GORDON L. ARCHER

MICHAEL W. CLIMO

Staphylococcus epidermidis and other coagulase-negative staphylococci, often present in clinical specimens as culture contaminants, can also be true pathogens (Table 193-1). Infections caused by these organisms involve indwelling foreign bodies and increase as the use of catheters and artificial devices becomes more prevalent. These infections are characterized by their indolence but may necessitate the removal of the catheter or device. Resistance of infecting isolates to multiple antibiotics may further complicate therapy. The importance of coagulase-negative staphylococci as nosocomial pathogens has prompted more interest in their detailed characterization, including the determination of the complete nucleotide sequence of the genome of a clinical *S. epidermidis* isolate. A working knowledge of the biology and antimicrobial susceptibility of these organisms may be necessary to distinguish infecting from contaminating isolates and to devise appropriate therapy.

MICROBIOLOGY

Identification

All staphylococci are members of the family Micrococcaceae. They are gram-positive cocci that produce catalase and divide in irregular clusters to produce packets of cells. In the clinical microbiology laboratory, staphylococci are differentiated primarily by their capacity to produce or not produce an enzyme (coagulase) that congeals rabbit plasma. Coagulase-positive staphylococci also ferment mannitol, contain an immunoglobulin G (IgG)–binding protein (protein A) in their cell walls, and produce a cell-associated protein (clumping factor) that binds fibrinogen, characteristics not shared by most coagulase-negative staphylococci. Agglutination of latex beads coated with IgG, fibrinogen, and capsule-specific antibody is used by clinical microbi-

---

TABLE 193-1 Well-Documented Infections Caused by *Staphylococcus epidermidis* and Other Coagulase-Negative Staphylococci

Bacteremia in immunosuppressed patients
Urinary tract infections
  Hospital acquired (*S. epidermidis*)
  Outpatient women (*Staphylococcus saprophyticus*)
Osteomyelitis
  Sternal wound
  Hematogenous
Native valve endocarditis
Bacteremia in immunosuppressed patients
Endophthalmitis after ocular surgery
Infections of indwelling foreign devices
  Intravenous catheters
  Hemodialysis shunts and grafts
  Cerebrospinal fluid shunts
  Peritoneal dialysis catheters
  Pacemaker wires and electrodes
  Prosthetic joints
  Vascular grafts
  Prosthetic cardiac valves
  Breast implants
  Penile prostheses

TABLE 193-2 Human Coagulase-Negative Staphylococcal Species Groups

S. epidermidis[†]
S. capitis
S. warneri
S. haemolyticus
S. hominis
S. saccharolyticus[*]
S. caprae
S. pasteuri

S. saprophyticus[†]
S. xylosus
S. cohnii

S. simulans

S. auricularis

S. lugdunensis

S. schleiferi

[*]Formerly *Peptococcus saccharolyticus;* strict anaerobe.
[†]Species shown to be consistently pathogenic for humans.

---

ology laboratories as an alternative to coagulase testing in differentiating coagulase-positive from coagulase-negative staphylococci. However, although human coagulase-positive staphylococci comprise a fairly uniform species *(Staphylococcus aureus),* human coagulase-negative staphylococci have been subdivided into 32 species, 15 of which are indigenous to humans.[1,2] The relatedness of all staphylococci at the genus level has been confirmed by their similar deoxyribonucleic acid (DNA) content of guanine plus cytosine; their divergence into separate species has been ascertained by the examination of specific DNA sequence homology. Using restrictive criteria for DNA-DNA hybridization studies, groups of staphylococci with less than 50% DNA homology have been designated as separate species. Certain species are more related to one another than others and form species groups. The current species grouping of coagulase-negative staphylococci relevant to humans is shown in Table 193-2.

Kloos and Schleifer devised a scheme by which coagulase-negative staphylococci could be easily differentiated into species by using biochemical characteristics.[3] Biochemical characterization was further simplified by the marketing of miniaturized kits that facilitated the rapid identification of staphylococci.[4] The value of routine speciation of all staphylococci from clinical specimens is unclear, however. Speciation would be of potential clinical value if it could be used for biotyping or if there were clear associations of certain species with specific infections or antibiotic-susceptibility patterns. *S. epidermidis* and *Staphylococcus saprophyticus* have been identified as being consistently pathogenic for humans. In addition, some data suggest that of the remaining coagulase-negative staphylococcal species, *Staphylococcus haemolyticus, Staphylococcus lugdunensis,* and *Staphylococcus schleiferi* are more likely to cause infections than others.[5-7]

Ecology

Coagulase-negative staphylococci are resident bacteria, indigenous to mammalian hosts, and are natural inhabitants of human skin.[1,2] *S. epidermidis* is the most prevalent and persistent species on human glabrous skin and mucous membranes, constituting from 65% to 90% of all staphylococci recovered; *Staphylococcus hominis* is the next most frequent species recovered. *Staphylococcus saccharolyticus* (formerly *Peptococcus saccharolyticus*) is the only strictly anaerobic staphylococcus constituting resident skin flora; its prevalence has not yet been evaluated. Other staphylococcal species are either less frequent members of the resident population *(Staphylococcus haemolyticus, Staphylococcus warneri),* found only transiently on skin *(Staphylococcus xylosus, Staphylococcus simulans, S. lugdunensis, Staphylococcus cohnii),* or found only in specific niches *(Staphylococcus capitis* [head], *Staphylococcus auricularis* [ear canal], *S. saprophyticus* [genitourinary skin]). The type and location of coagulase-negative species can be altered by antibiotic therapy[8] and the presence on mucous membranes of competing *S. aureus.*[1,2]

Genetics and Virulence Factors

Plasmid DNA is abundant in all species of coagulase-negative staphylococci,[9] but only a few of the plasmid-encoded genes have been identified. Resistances to such antibiotics as penicillin, macrolides, lincosamides, streptogramins, tetracyclines, chloramphenicol, trimethoprim, and aminoglycosides have all been associated with specific plasmids. Plasmid-mediated resistance has been confirmed by the transfer of these plasmids to suitable plasmid-free recipients. Of considerable epidemiologic significance is the demonstration that certain aminoglycoside-resistance plasmids found in *S. epidermidis* can be transferred by conjugation to other *S. epidermidis* and to *S. aureus* organisms.[9,10] These conjugative plasmids also encode resistance to penicillin, trimethoprim, mupirocin, and disinfectants (quaternary ammonium compounds) and can mobilize the transfer of plasmids encoding resistance to macrolides, lincosamides, and chloramphenicol. Conjugative resistance transfer may help explain the rapid increase in resistance seen among hospital-associated *S. epidermidis* isolates.[11]

Electron microscopic studies suggest a two-step process in the association of *S. epidermidis* with plastic surfaces.[12] Cells first adhere to the surface and then form multilayered clusters that become embedded in an exopolysaccharide matrix, forming a biofilm. The first, or adherence, phase may involve both polysaccharide factors, such as PS/A,[13] and surface proteins.[14,15] The second phase, intercellular adhesion, is mediated by a polysaccharide, called PIA[16]; an extracellular protein may also be involved.[17] Biosynthesis of PIA is encoded by a gene cluster designated *ica.* The production of PIA also enables *S. epidermidis* to agglutinate erythrocytes.[18] The role of PS/A, surface proteins, and PIA in the association of *S. epidermidis* with foreign bodies is confirmed by the inability of mutants to form biofilms on plastic surfaces and the abrogation by specific antibody of catheter-related infections in animal models.[13,15-17] The biofilm that forms on surfaces of intravascular catheters and other foreign devices protects embedded organisms from host phagocytic cells and decreases the ability of some antimicrobial agents to eradicate adherent staphylococcal microcolonies.[19]

S. saprophyticus produces a number of proteins that may be responsible for the organism's propensity to cause urinary tract infections. A protein hemagglutinin may mediate the organism's attachment to uroepithelial cells,[20] surface fibrillar proteins may have a separate role in attachment,[21] and a urease has been implicated in the invasion of the organism into the urinary bladder.[22]

EPIDEMIOLOGY

With the exception of natural valve endocarditis and some infections of peritoneal dialysis catheters, virtually all *S. epidermidis* infections are hospital acquired. In contrast, *S. saprophyticus* infections (urinary tract infections) are all acquired outside the hospital.[23,24] Hospital-associated *S. epidermidis* isolates are multiply antibiotic resistant, probably reflecting the selection pressure of widespread antibiotic use in the hospital.[8] Colonization of patients and hospital staff with antibiotic-resistant *S. epidermidis* precedes infection with these organisms. Thus, patients and personnel constitute the hospital reservoir for *S. epidermidis.* The organisms probably gain access to foreign bodies by direct inoculation during the insertion of the device and subsequent handling and contamination of catheter hubs and access ports.

Epidemiologic investigations of coagulase-negative staphylococci were hampered in the past by the absence of reliable markers with which to fingerprint isolates. Antibiotic-susceptibility determinations, phage typing, and biotyping all suffer from a lack of sensitivity and specificity,[25] although they may be more helpful when they are used in concert.[26] The molecular analysis of the abundant plasmid DNA in co-

agulase-negative staphylococci has been used successfully in outbreak investigations[25,27] and in differentiating infecting from contaminating culture isolates.[28] However, the loss, gain, and rearrangement of plasmid DNA by coagulase-negative staphylococci in their native environment over time diminish the power of this technique for longitudinal studies.[25,29] Techniques that separate chromosomal DNA into different-size fragments using pulsed field gel electrophoresis or that identify chromosomal DNA fragment polymorphisms using probe hybridization or polymerase chain reaction amplification are more reliable.[30] Ultimately, however, application of techniques that involve determination of the DNA sequence of specific gene segments, such as multilocus sequence typing (MLST), offers more promise because differences are unambiguous and can be stored in easily accessible databases. Software for analysis of sequence differences and a website for displaying sequence types is currently in use for *S. aureus* and has been shown to work equally well for *S. epidermidis.*[31,32]

Antibiotic Susceptibility

Coagulase-negative staphylococci from nosocomial infections, particularly *S. epidermidis* and *S. haemolyticus,* are usually resistant to multiple antibiotics, with more than 80% resistant to methicillin.[33] Resistance to methicillin in coagulase-negative staphylococci exhibits the same heterotypic expression, altered by changes in culture or environmental conditions, as does methicillin-resistant *S. aureus.*[34] The methicillin-resistance gene *(mecA)* is identical in *S. aureus* and *S. epidermidis.* In addition, DNA hybridization studies have established that methicillin-resistant coagulase-negative staphylococci of many different species also contain *mecA.*[35]

However, the heterotypy of methicillin resistance expression for coagulase-negative staphylococci, particularly *S. epidermidis,* is much greater than that seen for *S. aureus.* This results in a low minimal inhibitory concentration for methicillin or oxacillin, often below the accepted breakpoint for resistance for *S. aureus.*[36] These isolates with low minimal inhibitory concentration values contain *mecA*[37-39] and are fully resistant to all β-lactam antibiotics when evaluated in animal models of infection.[40,41] Because of the difficulty of detecting methicillin resistance in *S. epidermidis,* the oxacillin minimal inhibitory concentration breakpoints for defining resistance are lower than those determined for *S. aureus.*[36,42] Identification of *mecA* by PCR amplification or PBP2A, the low affinity penicillin-binding protein encoded by *mecA,* by slide agglutination is the most sensitive and specific resistance-detection method.[37,39,43]

In addition to β-lactams, antimicrobials to which more than 50% of *S. epidermidis* and *S. haemolyticus* nosocomial isolates are resistant include erythromycin, clindamycin, trimethoprim/sulfamethoxazole, gentamicin and ciprofloxacin.[33,44,45] Nosocomial isolates of coagulase-negative staphylococci demonstrate varying degrees of resistance to rifampin, tetracylcines, newer fluoroquinolones and chloramphenicol Like *S. aureus,* virtually all *S. epidermidis* produce β-lactamase.

Antimicrobials to which most coagulase-negative staphylococci are susceptible in vitro include vancomycin, minocycline, linezolid, the combination streptogramin, quinupristin/dalfopristin, and daptomycin (see Chapter 29).[33,45,46] *S. haemolyticus* is the first staphylococcus to demonstrate resistance to vancomycin, but other coagulase-negative staphylococci, including *S. epidermidis,* have been described that have reduced susceptibility to glycopeptide antibiotics.[44,47,48]

Infections

Nosocomial Bacteremia

Coagulase-negative staphylococci are the most common cause of nosocomial bacteremia, particularly in areas of the hospital where the use of indwelling vascular catheters is common.[11,49] However, although the overall rate of blood culture contamination is typically 1% to 3%, approximately 25% to 74% of all coagulase-negative staphylococcal bacteremias represent contaminants.[50-52] Single positive blood cultures almost always represent contamination. It is important, therefore, to obtain multiple blood cultures from separate venipuncture or access sites and to use rigorous criteria for defining true bacteremia. Proper attention to phlebotomy technique as well as the use of more effective skin antiseptic preparations can lower the rate of blood culture contamination within hospitals.[53,54]

Endocarditis of Native and Prosthetic Valves

Infections of native cardiac valves with coagulase-negative staphylococci are relatively uncommon, accounting for 5% to 8% of all cases of infective endocarditis.[55,56] The infection presumably arises as a result of the seeding of damaged cardiac valves and endocardium with the organism after transient bacteremia, in a manner similar to that of infection with viridans streptococci. In fact, the subacute nature of the disease resembles that of infective endocarditis caused by viridans streptococci. However, in one study from the United States, 67% of 21 patients with native valve endocarditis had complicated courses (systemic embolization, congestive heart failure, or new conduction abnormalities).[57] As many as one half of the infecting isolates in this study were coagulase-negative staphylococcal species other than S. epidermidis. A study of European patients also emphasized the severity of native valve endocarditis caused by coagulase-negative staphylococci.[58] Acute presentations were reported in 26%, neurologic abnormalities in 23%, and valve replacement, often emergent, was required in 51%. The mortality of patients in this study was 36%.

More than 80% of these isolates were susceptible to penicillinase-resistant semisynthetic penicillins, but most produced inducible β-lactamase and were therefore resistant to penicillin G. Some studies report that S. lugdunensis may have a particular propensity to cause native valve endocarditis that leads to valve destruction.[59] It may be misidentified as S. aureus because it produces clumping factor.

In contrast to the low frequency with which coagulase-negative staphylococci infect native cardiac valves, they are the single most common cause of infections of prosthetic cardiac valves. S. epidermidis was implicated as the cause of approximately 40% of the cases of prosthetic valve endocarditis at two large medical centers.[60] Similarly, recent unpublished data from the International Collaboration on Endocarditis (ICE) Prospective Cohort Study[61] identified coagulase-negative staphylococci as the cause of 39% of 214 cases of prosthetic valve endocarditis that occurred in 16 countries between 2000 and 2002 (Vance Fowler, unpublished observation). Furthermore, coagulase-negative staphylococci other than S. epidermidis are rarely implicated.[62] More than 80% of patients who develop prosthetic valve endocarditis due to S. epidermidis have a complicated infection.[62] That is, there is evidence of prosthetic valve dysfunction or persistent fever during therapy. Complicated prosthetic valve endocarditis results from infection of the valve sewing ring as opposed to infection of the working components or leaflets. Complications arising from infection of the sewing ring are valve dehiscence, dysrhythmia owing to extension of an abscess into the conducting system, or obstruction of the valve orifice owing to overgrowth of vegetative material. Dehiscence and dysrhythmia are more common with aortic prostheses, whereas obstruction is the most common complication of infected mitral prostheses. Fever persists during therapy because the valve-ring abscess is relatively protected from antibiotics. The indolent nature of the infection and the extravascular location of the valve-ring abscesses characteristic of S. epidermidis prosthetic valve endocarditis also result in the absence of such classic endocarditis findings as peripheral emboli and multiple positive blood cultures. Valve dysfunction and fever are often the only findings associated with an infected valve.

All cases of prosthetic valve endocarditis caused by S. epidermidis that occur in the first year after surgery are probably caused by inoculation of organisms at the time of surgery. The usual postsurgical interval of 2 months that differentiates early (surgically acquired) from late (nonsurgically acquired) prosthetic valve endocarditis caused by other organisms is probably not appropriate for S. epidermidis infections.[60,61] This is based on several observations. First, most of the infections that occur in the first year are complicated, involving the sewing ring. Bacteremic seeding of this area after discharge from the hospital would be unlikely. Second, 87% of cases of S. epidermidis

prosthetic valve endocarditis occurring in the first year after surgery are caused by methicillin-resistant organisms.[62] This multiresistant phenotype is associated with hospital-acquired organisms; patients out of the hospital are colonized with antibiotic-susceptible staphylococci.[8] Third, two patients known to have acquired S. epidermidis prosthetic valve endocarditis during an outbreak associated with cardiopulmonary bypass pump contamination had incubation periods of 8 and 13 months before the appearance of symptoms of infection.[27] Thus, patients infected at the time of surgery with S. epidermidis can have long latency periods before their disease becomes apparent.

Diagnosis of S. epidermidis prosthetic valve endocarditis is based on a high level of suspicion. In a patient with a prosthetic cardiac valve, fever, and even a few blood cultures positive for S. epidermidis, every effort should be made to detect valve dysfunction. This should include serial electrocardiograms, two-dimensional echocardiography, and, if necessary, angiography. Multiple blood isolates can also be examined for specific markers in an attempt to differentiate contamination from infection. Repetitive blood isolates with different markers are unlikely to have arisen from a single infected focus.

Therapy of S. epidermidis prosthetic valve endocarditis is usually both medical and surgical. The mainstay of antibiotic therapy for methicillin-resistant organisms is vancomycin. However, cure rates have been improved in both animals[36,63] and humans[62,64] by the addition of gentamicin, rifampin, or both, to vancomycin. Antibiotics alone are often not adequate for cure, however, and surgical intervention may be crucial. In one series, 30 of 32 patients with complicated S. epidermidis prosthetic valve endocarditis who were cured required surgery.[62] Surgical removal of the infected valve should be attempted in any patient with valve dysfunction after stabilization on antibiotics or in any patient who is hemodynamically unstable as a result of a poorly functioning valve. Antibiotics are presumed to be important for sterilizing the perivalvular tissue around an infected prosthesis before implantation of a new valve. The relative roles of antibiotics and surgical débridement in preventing infection of the replacement prosthesis are unknown.

The role that antibiotic prophylaxis plays in preventing S. epidermidis prosthetic valve endocarditis is unclear. Antibiotic prophylaxis has been shown to increase the hospital reservoir of resistant organisms.[8] Patients then become infected with S. epidermidis resistant to the antibiotics used as prophylaxis.[8] Cephalosporins are the antibiotics most widely used and recommended for prophylaxis although they are ineffective in preventing experimental methicillin-resistant S. epidermidis endocarditis when animals are challenged with a high bacterial inoculum.[65] However, cephalosporin prophylaxis may decrease the number of infections with methicillin-sensitive S. epidermidis. Prophylaxis with vancomycin during cardiac surgery is currently recommended in institutions that have a high incidence of prosthetic valve endocarditis or sternal wound infections caused by methicillin-resistant coagulase-negative staphylococci.[66]

Intravenous Catheter Infections

S. epidermidis is reported to be the single most common organism infecting intravenous catheters as defined by semiquantitative culture techniques.[67] Studies evaluating central hyperalimentation catheters,[68,69] peripheral intravenous lines,[70,71] subclavian catheters for plasmapheresis or hemodialysis,[72] Hickman or Broviac central lines in infants[73] or cancer patients,[74,75] and Swan-Ganz catheters[76] have all reported S. epidermidis to be the most common infecting organism. From 12% to 37% of all inserted catheters have become infected; S. epidermidis accounted for 50% to 75% of organisms cultured. Along with the increase in catheter-associated infections has been an increase in the incidence of catheter-associated bacteremia due to S. epidermidis with a consequent marked increase in the number of cases of nosocomial S. epidermidis bacteremia. This increase has resulted in gram-positive bacteria supplanting gram-negative bacteria as the leading cause of hospital-acquired bacteremia.[49]

The reasons for the increase are not entirely clear, but there are various proposed explanations. These explanations include the operative insertion of central lines, resulting in a decrease in contamination with gram-negative bacteria and fungi and an increase in contamination with usual skin bacteria; the decreased use of antibiotics for long-term indwelling catheters, resulting in a decrease in candidal overgrowth; the long period of time that lines stay in place, increasing their chance of contamination with skin bacteria; the increasing resistance of *S. epidermidis* to antibiotics, prolonging the survival of the organisms on the skin of seriously ill patients receiving multiple antibiotics; and the selection of a more catheter-adherent population of colonizing organisms.

The increase in true *S. epidermidis* bacteremias due to the increasing use of long-term indwelling intravenous catheters poses new problems for the clinician faced with positive blood cultures from a patient who does not appear clinically ill. Infected catheters may be present without gross evidence of purulence or erythema, and bacteremia may occur with few symptoms.[71,75] It seems prudent to regard as significant all percutaneous blood cultures that grow *S. epidermidis* and are obtained from patients who have indwelling catheters. Repeat blood cultures and careful examination of the catheter site would then be warranted. Serious complications, including lung abscesses and death, have been attributed to catheter-related *S. epidermidis* bacteremia.[68]

The most effective strategies to decrease the incidence of catheter-related infections of central venous catheters include improved hand washing, strict aseptic technique during the insertion of central lines and subsequent manipulation, proper catheter site dressing changes, and the proper use of antiseptic skin preparations during insertion and subsequent site care.[77] Preparations that contain chlorhexidine appear to be superior for both site preparation and site care in comparison to povidone-iodine.[78] The use of antimicrobial-impregnated catheters has been shown to decrease the incidence of catheter-related infections significantly, particularly those caused by coagulase-negative staphylococci.[79,80] Catheters impregnated with minocycline and rifampin are particularly effective in this regard.[81] However, the impact of the use of these catheters on antimicrobial resistance will have to be monitored carefully. Ultimately, the decision to use antimicrobial impregnated catheters should be based on local infection rates and the need to enhance prevention of catheter-related blood stream infection after standard procedures to improve aseptic technique in catheter site insertion and maintenance have been implemented.[77] Therapy for *S. epidermidis* catheter infections would include removal of the catheter, if this is feasible. This may be accomplished by guide wire exchange or by removal and use of a new site.[82,83] The use of antibiotic lock solutions in catheter ports[84] has also been shown to be effective in some circumstances when catheter salvage is desired. If the catheter cannot be removed, antibiotic therapy alone has been successful.[85] Antibiotic infusions should be rotated among all the ports of multiport catheters. Vancomycin would be the most logical choice based on the high percentage of isolates from catheter-associated bacteremia that are reported to be methicillin resistant.

Cerebrospinal Fluid Shunt Infections (See Chapter 81)

S. epidermidis is the most common organism causing infection of cerebrospinal fluid shunts. In one series, 27% of 289 hydrocephalic patients developed shunt infections over a 10-year period; more than 50% of infections were caused by *S. epidermidis*.[86] In a more recent study confined to pediatric patients, 11% of 820 ventriculoperitoneal shunts were infected, 52% with coagulase-negative staphylococci.[87] *S. epidermidis* is also a common cause of infections of ventriculostomy tubes inserted for drainage of cerebrospinal fluid in patients with head trauma and of indwelling cerebrospinal fluid catheters in patients receiving cancer chemotherapy for neoplastic meningitis.[88,89]

Infections usually occur within 2 weeks of implantation, revision, or manipulation of the shunt. A recent study found that intraoperative use of a neuroendoscope increased the risk of infection.[87] In many cases, usual physical findings of meningitis may be absent, with low-grade temperature, shunt malfunction, or wound infection as the only finding. Cerebrospinal fluid pleocytosis is almost always present but may be modest. Lumbar cerebrospinal fluid may be more normal than ventricular cerebrospinal fluid and is often culture negative, but both

should be obtained to optimize diagnosis. The cerebrospinal fluid glucose level is often only mildly low. A rare complication of prolonged bacteremia associated with ventriculoatrial shunts is glomerulonephritis caused by deposition of immune complexes in the kidney.[90]

Because the infections are hospital acquired, infection with *S. epidermidis* should be assumed to be methicillin resistant. Therapy usually involves a combination of systemic and intraventricular administration of antibiotics, with vancomycin, rifampin, and gentamicin the drugs of choice.[91-93] Vancomycin and gentamicin can be given intraventricularly. This is the preferred route of administration.[93,94] Rifampin achieves adequate cerebrospinal fluid concentrations after systemic administration.[92] Patients with methicillin-sensitive *S. epidermidis* infections should receive a semisynthetic, penicillinase-resistant penicillin systemically. Some cerebrospinal fluid shunt infections have been successfully treated without shunt removal,[92,94] but removal is often required.[95] Although several studies have shown no benefit of using antibiotic prophylaxis during shunt insertion to prevent subsequent infections,[96] a meta-analysis of all available studies concluded that prophylaxis is efficacious.[97]

Peritoneal Dialysis Catheter-Associated Peritonitis

The development of chronic ambulatory peritoneal dialysis as an alternative to hemodialysis for patients with chronic renal failure has been a remarkable breakthrough in the management of these patients. However, as many as 40% of these patients may develop peritonitis during the first year, with the overall incidence ranging from 0.5 to 6.3 episodes per patient-year.[98,99] The criteria for diagnosis are not uniform among various studies but include some combination of abdominal pain, cloudy fluid, more than 100 white blood cells/mm³ with the majority polymorphonuclear leukocytes, and a positive culture. Gram stains of peritoneal fluid are usually negative.[100] The organism most frequently isolated from patients with peritonitis is *S. epidermidis*, which is recovered from the peritoneal fluid in 17% to 50% of patients.[99-101] However, routine culture of small volumes of fluid may not yield an organism, and more sensitive techniques may be required. These techniques include inoculation and subculture of broth and the filtration or culture of large volumes (more than 100 ml) of peritoneal fluid.[100,102,103] Because these techniques detect very small numbers of organisms, there is obviously the possibility that some episodes of *S. epidermidis* peritonitis represent procurement contamination of sterile peritoneal fluid.

Antibiotic therapy of *S. epidermidis* peritonitis in patients on chronic ambulatory peritoneal dialysis is generally successful without catheter removal. Many treatment regimens have been used with approximately equal success. These include semisynthetic penicillinase-resistant penicillins, cephalosporins, trimethoprim-sulfamethoxazole, gentamicin, or vancomycin.[100,102,104-106] Parenteral antibiotics alone, parenteral plus oral, oral alone, or intraperitoneal antibiotics have all been effective routes of administration. In contrast to most *S. epidermidis* infections, more than half of the isolates recovered from patients with peritonitis may be susceptible to methicillin.[101,107,108] This probably explains cure rates of 80% or greater with conventional therapy.[100,104,106] However, a recent survey found that the methicillin-resistant phenotype increased among coagulase-negative staphylococci, causing peritoneal dialysis-associated infections from 18.9% in 1992 to 73.9% in 1998.[99] These infections have been successfully treated with weekly injections of vancomycin.[104] Treatment failures require retreatment or catheter removal.

Urinary Tract Infections

Two distinct populations of patients develop urinary tract infections with coagulase-negative staphylococci (Table 193-3). *S. saprophyticus* is a coagulase-negative staphylococcus that is cultured infrequently from the genitourinary mucosa of young women.[24,109] This organism is readily identified by the clinical microbiology owing to its resistance to a 5-μg novobiocin disk. Novobiocin resistance is rarely found among even multiply resistant coagulase-negative staphylococci of other species that are grown from the urine.[23] *S. saprophyticus* is a

TABLE 193-3 Urinary Tract Infections Caused by Coagulase-Negative Staphylococci: Characteristics of Infections

Organism	S. epidermidis	S. saprophyticus
Age and sex of affected patients	Men and women equal Usually older than 50 years	Women 95% 16 to 35 years old
Population at risk	Hospitalized patients with urinary tract complications	Healthy outpatients
Incidence	Uncommon: 3.5% or less of all urinary tract infections in hospitalized patients	Common: 20% or more of all urinary tract infections in this age group
Presentation	90% asymptomatic	90% symptomatic; indistinguishable from *Escherichia coli* urinary tract infections
Therapy	Often resistant to multiple antibiotics	Responds readily to urinary tract antimicrobials; except nalidixic acid
Outcome	Bacteriuria often persists after therapy	Relapse rare; occasional reinfection

true urinary tract pathogen causing both upper and lower urinary tract disease.[110] Symptoms of a urinary tract infection are present in more than 90% of women from whom *S. saprophyticus* is cultured, and pyuria is present in 70% to 85% of these women; the organism is a culture contaminant only 5% of the time. Conversely, 95% of all coagulase-negative staphylococci cultured from the urine of symptomatic female outpatients are *S. saprophyticus*.[23,24] Signs, symptoms, and urinalyses of women infected with this organism are indistinguishable from those of women infected with enteric bacteria. It is clearly an organism predominantly infecting young, sexually active women. Almost 70% of women in one study gave a history of sexual intercourse within the 24 hours preceding the onset of symptoms of their urinary tract infection.[24] Older studies of female outpatients in Sweden and at the Universities of Florida and Washington found *S. saprophyticus* to be the cause of 32%, 30%, and 11%, of urinary tract infections, respectively, second only to *Escherichia coli,* the cause of 65% to 80% of infections.[24,110,111] However, a collaborative study of acute, uncomplicated, community-acquired urinary tract infections conducted in 16 European countries and Canada between 1999 and 2001 found that only 4.6% of infections in women between ages 16 and 50 were caused by *S. saprophyticus*.[112] Unlike infections with enteric bacteria, there appears to be a seasonal predilection for *S. saprophyticus* urinary tract infections, with the incidence rising in late summer and early fall.[110,111,113] Furthermore, because urine colony counts for *S. saprophyticus* are often lower than those for enteric bacteria ($<10^5$ CFU/ml) this staphylococcus has been implicated as one cause of the dysuria-pyuria syndrome (acute urethral syndrome or abacteriuric pyuria).[114]

Therapy is usually effective with most urinary tract antimicrobial agents, including norfloxacin.[113] However, therapeutic failures have been reported with sulfonamides and nitrofurantoin, and the organism is uniformly resistant to nalidixic acid.[111] Relapse is uncommon, but the infection may recur in 10% or more of patients.

In contrast, other coagulase-negative staphylococci rarely infect the urine. Of non–*S. saprophyticus* coagulase-negative staphylococci cultured from the urine in significant numbers (10^4 CFU/ml), *S. epidermidis* is the predominant species, accounting for 80% to 90% of the isolates.[23] It is cultured almost exclusively from the urine of hospitalized patients with complications of the urinary tract. Half these patients have an indwelling urinary catheter, and nearly all have such complications as recent urinary tract surgery, renal transplantation, neurogenic bladder, stone disease, or obstructive uropathy.[23,115] Coagulase-negative staphylococci are recovered from less than 5% of all of the urine specimens from hospitalized patients from whom a sig-

nificant number of bacteria are grown.[115] Furthermore, when it is present in the urine, it is associated with pyuria and a clinically significant urinary tract infection only about 10% of the time.[115,116] Men and women are equally affected, and most patients are 50 years of age or older. The causative organisms are multiply antibiotic resistant in at least 50% of the episodes.[23] When treatment is necessary, antibiotic therapy should be tailored to the susceptibility of the organism.

Bacteremia in Immunocompromised Patients

S. epidermidis was not usually considered to be an important pathogen in immunosuppressed patients until reports from two large cancer centers in the United States[75,117] identified it as the most common cause of bacteremia among patients receiving immunosuppressive therapy in their hospitals. Investigators at the Baltimore Cancer Research Center identified *S. epidermidis* as the single most common cause of bacteremia in their patients between 1977 and 1979.[117] Most patients were neutropenic and heavily colonized with the organism in their rectum. The addition of oral vancomycin to the oral regimen of antibiotics for gut sterilization decreased both gastrointestinal colonization with *S. epidermidis* and bacteremia in these patients. Thus these investigators considered the gastrointestinal tract to be the source for these *S. epidermidis* bacteremias. In contrast, investigators at the UCLA Center for the Health Sciences felt that infected Hickman or Broviac central intravenous catheters were the source of *S. epidermidis* bacteremias in their patients.[75] Between 1977 and 1980, *S. epidermidis* accounted for 26% of bacteremias in their patients, most of whom were also profoundly neutropenic.

Subsequent studies have more consistently implicated long-term indwelling catheters as the source of bacteremia in patients with hematologic malignancies and bone marrow transplants; the insertion of long-term catheters in these patients has become standard practice. As noted (see "Intravenous Catheter Infections"), gram-positive bacteria, particularly *S. epidermidis,* account for 50% to 80% of the organisms causing catheter-related bacteremia in this population.[74,85,118,119] Furthermore, *S. epidermidis* bacteremia has been documented to be a prominent source of morbidity and even mortality[120] in immunocompromised patients.

These studies illustrate several important points. First, colonization of the gut and skin with antibiotic-resistant *S. epidermidis* can follow the intensive use of oral and systemic antimicrobials.[8] Bacteremia originating from these sites can result from a compromise in both general and local defense mechanisms in severely immunocompromised patients. Second, *S. epidermidis* can be a lethal pathogen in neutropenic patients and should not be dismissed when it is grown from blood cultures that are appropriately obtained.

Osteomyelitis

Most reports that attempt to implicate *S. epidermidis* as an important cause of chronic osteomyelitis are not convincing. The organism is usually grown from sinus tracts as one of several potential pathogens. However, three infections meet valid criteria that establish *S. epidermidis* as the cause of some infections of bone. These are sternal osteomyelitis resulting from infection of the median sternotomy wound after cardiothoracic surgery,[121-123] infection of bone surrounding a prosthetic joint,[124] and hematogenous osteomyelitis resulting from infections of hemodialysis shunts.[125]

Sternal osteomyelitis is an uncommon but serious complication of cardiothoracic surgery, occurring in 1% to 4.5% of operations in several series.[121-123,126,127] *S. epidermidis* was the cause of 16% to 57% of the infections. Whenever the deep sternal wound becomes infected, osteomyelitis is assumed to be present, and surgical débridement is necessary. However, diagnosis may be difficult with fever, minimal wound erythema, and persistent costochondral pain as the only symptoms. If these symptoms occur within 30 days of surgery, aggressive diagnostic studies should be undertaken including computed axial tomography scanning of the chest, needle aspiration of the wound for Gram stain and culture, and, if necessary, exploratory surgery. One study suggested that such nuclear imaging studies as technetium 99m methylene diphosphonate bone and indium-111 white blood cell scans were more sensitive and specific than computed tomography (CT) scans.[128] Advanced infection may require multiple reoperations, delayed secondary closure, and grafting. Mortality rates for complicated infections range from 35% to 75%.[121,127] For this infection, antibiotics serve only as an adjunct to appropriate surgical débridement.

Osteomyelitis can result from infections of prosthetic joints and is discussed later. Hematogenous osteomyelitis can conceivably result from any bacteremic *S. epidermidis* infection but is surprisingly uncommon given the number of patients with bacteremia caused by this organism.

Infections of Prosthetic Joints

Infection rates for implanted hip and knee prostheses are generally less than 2.5% for primary infections but can be as high as 5% for revision procedures (see also Chapter 100).[129,130] Coagulase-negative staphylococci have been reported to cause from 19% to 37.5% of these infections.[129] In one study, 56% of the *S. epidermidis* infections were diagnosed more than a year after surgical implantation of the device and in all but two the organism was felt to be surgically acquired.[131]

The diagnosis is most often suggested by pain in the hip or knee; fever, swelling, joint dislocation, and drainage. These findings are seen in fewer than half of the patients. The erythrocyte sedimentation rate is usually elevated, and radiolucencies may be seen at the bone-cement interface in two thirds of patients. Radionuclide scans, such as indium-111–labeled leukocyte scanning, may be useful in some patients.[131] Definitive diagnosis is made by Gram stain and culture of infected material obtained by needle aspiration, bone biopsy, or at surgery.

Therapy is surgical in all cases with removal of the infected prosthesis and débridement of infected bone; osteomyelitis is invariably present. Both one- and two-stage procedures for replacement of hips and knees infected with coagulase-negative staphylococci, using antimicrobials systemically and incorporated into bone cement, have been successful in more than 80% of cases.[129,132] The disastrous consequences of infection have led to a great deal of attention being paid to its prevention. The use of laminar flow operating suites, antimicrobial prophylaxis, and antibiotic-impregnated bone cement have all been used with apparent success, markedly reducing the infection rate over the past 40 years, but their relative merits are unclear.[124,133,134]

Infection of Vascular Grafts

S. aureus and coagulase-negative staphylococci are the most common cause of intra-abdominal vascular graft infections.[135-137] However, although most of the *S. aureus* infections occur in the early postoperative period, coagulase-negative staphylococcal infections are diagnosed months to years after surgery.[135,138] In one series, *S. epidermidis* caused 18 of 30 (60%) aortofemoral graft infections diagnosed over a 10-year period; the mean interval from surgery to infection was 41 months with a range of 14 to 80 months.[138] Most of the infections are probably acquired at the time of surgery, as suggested by the multiresistant nature of infecting isolates[138] and the frequent perioperative isolation of contaminating *S. epidermidis* from the implanted graft.[139,140] The incidence of all graft infections is highest in aortofemoral and femoropopliteal grafts in which the surgical incision is made in the groin area; it is lowest in aortoiliac grafts.

Clinical findings suggesting late graft infection with *S. epidermidis* include anastomotic aneurysm and pseudoaneurysm formation, the development of inguinal sinus tracts, and vasculoenteric fistulas with gastrointestinal bleeding. Fever and leukocytosis are often absent.[138]

Surgical replacement of the graft and drainage of local abscesses are always required.[135] In situ replacement of the infected graft with antibiotic-bonded material has been effective therapy for infections caused by *S. epidermidis*.[137] Antibiotic therapy is necessary to prevent infection of the replacement graft and should be devised to treat methicillin-resistant bacteria. As with prosthetic cardiac valve infections, vancomycin, rifampin, and gentamicin are most likely to be effective against susceptible organisms. Antibiotic prophylaxis is recommended during initial graft implantation to prevent infection, and a well-designed controlled clinical trial has documented its efficacy, particularly in abdominal aortic resection and femoral–lower leg bypass surgery.[141]

Lower extremity bypass grafts and hemodialysis grafts are also commonly infected by coagulase-negative staphylococci.[142,143] Infections of lower extremity bypass grafts can lead to loss of the limb. Infections of hemodialysis grafts and tunneled catheters lead to bacteremia and sepsis.

Pediatric Infections

There has been a dramatic increase in coagulase-negative staphylococcal bacteremia in neonatal intensive care units. The incidence of bacteremia in this area alone has been a major reason for the increase in hospital-wide nosocomial coagulase-negative staphylococcal bacteremia.[11,49] One longitudinal study conducted over 2.5 years found that 73% of all nosocomial bacteremias in a neonatal intensive care unit were caused by coagulase-negative staphylococci; 22% of all low-birth-weight infants admitted to this unit became bacteremic with these organisms.[144] Bacteremia in neonates is associated with low birth weight, the presence and duration of use of indwelling peripheral or umbilical catheters, and mechanical ventilation. The administration of intravenous lipid emulsions has also been associated with coagulase-negative staphylococcal bacteremia in neonates.[145] The clinical presentation is late-onset sepsis as opposed to early-onset sepsis that is most often related to *E. coli*.[146] As with bacteremia in adults, the rate of blood culture contaminants with coagulase-negative staphylococci can be substantial, and measures to reduce the rate of false positivity can profoundly affect reported bacteremic rates.[147] The coagulase-negative staphylococcal isolates from these infants are typically *S. epidermidis* and are resistant to multiple antibiotics, but outbreaks of infections caused by *S. haemolyticus*,[7] *S. warneri*,[148] and *S. capitis*[149] have all been reported. Despite the prevalence of coagulase-negative bacteremia among neonatal intensive care units, mortality is low for these infections.[150]

An additional intriguing observation has been the association of coagulase-negative staphylococci colonizing the gut of neonates in intensive care units with necrotizing enterocolitis.[151] Whether or not gut colonization with coagulase-negative staphylococci proves to be the cause of necrotizing enterocolitis, it provides another source for the development of bacteremia.

Ocular Infections

S. epidermidis has become the most common cause of endophthalmitis after ocular surgery, especially cataract extraction or lens implantation[152,153] and is not rare after trauma.[154] This infection has also been reported in intravenous drug abusers.[155] Diagnosis of endophthalmitis is made by physical and ocular examination, often with the aid of echography. The etiologic organism is determined by needle aspiration of the vitreous with Gram stain and culture of the fluid.[152] Although the prognosis for maintaining sight in the affected eye used to be grim, new aggressive use of antibiotics has improved the outlook markedly.[156] One study reported that visual acuity was preserved in 7 of 10 cases of *S. epidermidis* endophthalmitis by using combined systemic and intravitreal antibiotic administration without vitrectomy.[152] The penicillins, cephalosporins, aminoglycosides, and vancomycin penetrate the vitreous poorly after systemic administration, but all have been injected safely into the vitreous of either rabbits with experimental endophthalmitis or infected patients and shown to produce therapeutic vitreal levels.[152] Rifampin penetrates the vitreous well after systemic administration.

Miscellaneous Infections

Additional foreign bodies that have been associated with infection by *S. epidermidis* include pacemaker wires and power packs,[157] hemodialysis shunts,[125] breast implants,[158] penile prostheses,[159] and left ventricular assist devices.[160] As the number of indwelling foreign devices that are implanted increases, the list of foreign bodies associated with *S. epidermidis* infection should also increase. More innovative strategies may have to be devised to prevent these infections in the future.

Although isolated reports of well-documented pneumonias, intra-abdominal abscesses, and wound infections caused by *S. epidermidis* have appeared, most of these infections do not meet strict criteria implicating the organism as a pathogen. The organism is usually isolated in mixed culture with other potential pathogens, is cultured only once or intermittently, and is never reported to have been seen on Gram stain or in pathologic specimens. Because the opportunity for contamination of a culture with *S. epidermidis* is present whenever intact skin is crossed, the interpretation of cultures growing the organism must be cautious. Stricter criteria for infection must be met than with traditional pathogens. However, the growing list of infections in which *S. epidermidis* has been conclusively implicated as the etiologic agent increases the difficulty with culture interpretation. Careful culture collection and Gram stain of infected material are thus more important than ever in these situations.

REFERENCES

1. Kloos WE, Bannerman TL. Update on clinical significance of coagulase-negative staphylococci. Clin Microbiol Rev. 1994;7:117-140.
2. Kloos WE. Taxonomy and systematics of staphylococci indigenous to humans. In: Crossley KB, Archer GL, eds. The Staphylococci in Human Disease. New York: Churchill Livingstone; 1997:113-137.
3. Kloos WE, Schleifer KH. Simplified scheme for routine identification of human *Staphylococcus* species. J Clin Microbiol. 1975;1:82-88.
4. Kloos WE, Wolfshohl JF. Identification of *Staphylococcus* species with the API STAPH-IDENT system. J Clin Microbiol. 1982;16:509-516.
5. Herchline TE, Ayers LW. Occurrence of *Staphylococcus lugdunensis* in consecutive clinical cultures and relationship of isolation to infection. J Clin Microbiol. 1991;29:419-421.
6. Lambe DW Jr, Ferguson KP, Keplinger JL, et al. Pathogenicity of *Staphylococcus lugdunensis, Staphylococcus schleiferi,* and three other coagulase-negative staphylococci in a mouse model and possible virulence factors. Can J Microbiol. 1990;36:455-463.
7. Low DE, Schmidt BK, Kirpalani HM, et al. An endemic strain of *Staphylococcus haemolyticus* colonizing and causing bacteremia in neonatal intensive care unit patients. Pediatrics. 1992;89(4 Pt 2): 696-700.
8. Archer GL, Armstrong BC. Alteration of staphylococcal flora in cardiac surgery patients receiving antibiotic prophylaxis. J Infect Dis. 1983;147:642-649.
9. Kloos WE, Orban BS, Walker DD. Plasmid composition of *Staphylococcus* species. Can J Microbiol. 1981;27:271-278.
10. Archer GL, Johnston JL. Self-transmissible plasmids in staphylococci that encode resistance to aminoglycosides. Antimicrob Agents Chemother. 1983;24:70-77.
11. Schaberg DR, Culver DH, Gaynes RP. Major trends in the microbial etiology of nosocomial infection. Am J Med. 1991;91(3B):72S-75S.
12. Peters G, Locci R, Pulverer G. Microbial colonization of prosthetic devices. II. Scanning electron microscopy of naturally infected intravenous catheters. Zentralbl Bakteriol Mikrobiol Hyg (B). 1981;173:293-299.
13. Goldmann DA, Pier GB. Pathogenesis of infections related to intravascular catheterization. Clin Microbiol Rev. 1993;6:176-192.
14. Timmerman CP, Fleer A, Besnier JM, et al. Characterization of a proteinaceous adhesin of *Staphylococcus epidermidis* which mediates attachment to polystyrene. Infect Immun. 1991;59:4187-4192.
15. Heilmann C, et al. Evidence for autolysin-mediated primary attachment of *Staphylococcus epidermidis* to a polystyrene surface. Mol Microbiol. 199;24: 1013-1024.
16. Heilmann C, et al. Molecular basis of intercellular adhesion in the biofilm-forming *Staphylococcus epidermidis.* Mol Microbiol. 1996;20:1083-1091.
17. Hussain M, et al. Insertional inactivation of Eap in *Staphylococcus aureus* strain Newman confers reduced staphylococcal binding to fibroblasts. Infect Immun. 2002;70:2933-2940.
18. Rupp ME, Archer GL. Hemagglutination and adherence to plastic by *Staphylococcus epidermidis.* Infect Immun. 1992;60:4322-4327.
19. Peters G, Locci R, Pulverer G. Adherence and growth of coagulase-negative staphylococci on surfaces of intravenous catheters. J Infect Dis. 1982;146:479-482.
20. Gatermann S, Meyer HG, Wanner G. *Staphylococcus saprophyticus* hemagglutinin is a 160-kilodalton surface polypeptide. Infect Immun. 1992;60:4127-4132.
21. Gatermann S, et al. Identification and characterization of a surface-associated protein (Ssp) of *Staphylococcus saprophyticus.* Infect Immun. 1992;60:1055-1060.
22. Gatermann S, John J, Marre R. *Staphylococcus saprophyticus* urease: Characterization and contribution to uropathogenicity in unobstructed urinary tract infection of rats. Infect Immun. 1989;57:110-116.
23. Nicolle LE, Hoban SA, Harding GK. Characterization of coagulase-negative staphylococci from urinary tract specimens. J Clin Microbiol. 1983:17:267-271.
24. Jordan PA, et al. Urinary tract infection caused by *Staphylococcus saprophyticus.* J Infect Dis. 1980;142:510-515.
25. Parisi JT. Coagulase-negative staphylococci and the epidemiological typing of *Staphylococcus epidermidis.* Microbiol Rev. 1985;49:126-139.
26. Christensen GD, et al. Characterization of clinically significant strains of coagulase-negative staphylococci. J Clin Microbiol. 1983;18:258-269.
27. Archer GL, Vishniavsky N, Stiver HG. Plasmid pattern analysis of *Staphylococcus epidermidis* isolates from patients with prosthetic valve endocarditis. Infect Immun. 1982;35:627-632.
28. Archer GL, et al. Plasmid-pattern analysis for the differentiation of infecting from noninfecting *Staphylococcus epidermidis.* J Infect Dis. 1984;149:913-920.
29. Archer GL, Dietrick DR, Johnston JL. Molecular epidemiology of transmissible gentamicin resistance among coagulase-negative staphylococci in a cardiac surgery unit. J Infect Dis. 1985;151:243-251.
30. Arbeit R. Laboratory procedures for epidemiologic analysis. In: Crossley KB, Archer GL, eds. The Staphylococci in Human Disease. New York: Churchill Livingstone; 1997:253-286.
31. Chan MS, Maiden MC, Spratt BG. Database-driven multilocus sequence typing (MLST) of bacterial pathogens. Bioinformatics. 2001;17:1077-1083.
32. Wisplinghoff H, Rosato AE, Enright MC, et al. Related clones containing SCCmec Type IV predominate among clinically significant *Staphlococcus epidermidis* isolates. Antimicrob Agents Chemother. 2003;47:3574-3579.
33. Archer GL, Climo MW. Antimicrobial susceptibility of coagulase-negative staphylococci. Antimicrob Agents Chemother. 1994;38:2231-2237.
34. Coudron PE, et al. Evaluation of laboratory tests for detection of methicillin-resistant *Staphylococcus aureus* and *Staphylococcus epidermidis.* J Clin Microbiol. 1986;24:764-769.
35. Archer GL, Pennell E. Detection of methicillin resistance in staphylococci by using a DNA probe. Antimicrob Agents Chemother. 1990;34:1720-1724.
36. McDonald CL, Maher WE, Fass RJ. Revised interpretation of oxacillin MICs for *Staphylococcus epidermidis* based on mecA detection. Antimicrob Agents Chemother. 1995;39:982-984.
37. Marshall SA, et al. *Staphylococcus aureus* and coagulase-negative staphylococci from blood stream infections: Frequency of occurrence, antimicrobial susceptibility, and molecular (mecA) characterization of oxacillin resistance in the SCOPE program. Diagn Microbiol Infect Dis. 1998;30:205-214.
38. Reischl U, et al. Rapid identification of methicillin-resistant *Staphylococcus aureus* and simultaneous species confirmation using real-time fluorescence PCR. J Clin Microbiol. 2000;38:2429-2433.
39. van Griethuysen A, et al. Rapid slide latex agglutination test for detection of methicillin resistance in *Staphylococcus aureus.* J Clin Microbiol. 1999;37:2789-2792.
40. Vazquez GJ, Archer GL. Antibiotic therapy of experimental *Staphylococcus epidermidis* endocarditis. Antimicrob Agents Chemother. 1980;17:280-285.
41. Berry AJ, Johnston, JL, Archer GL. Imipenem therapy of experimental *Staphylococcus epidermidis* endocarditis. Antimicrob Agents Chemother. 1986;29:748-752.
42. Tenover FC, et al. Methods for improved detection of oxacillin resistance in coagulase-negative staphylococci: Results of a multicenter study. J Clin Microbiol. 1999;37:4051-4058.
43. Cavassini M, et al. Evaluation of MRSA-screen, a simple anti-PBP 2a slide latex agglutination kit, for rapid detection of methicillin resistance in *Staphylococcus aureus.* J Clin Microbiol. 1999;37:1591-1594.
44. Froggatt JW, Johnston JL, Galetto DW, et al. Antimicrobial resistance in nosocomial isolates of *Staphylococcus haemolyticus.* Antimicrob Agents Chemother. 1989; 33:460-466.
45. Diekema DJ, et al. Survey of infections due to *Staphylococcus* species: Frequency of occurrence and antimicrobial susceptibility of isolates collected in the United States, Canada, Latin America, Europe, and the Western Pacific region for the SENTRY Antimicrobial Surveillance Program, 1997-1999. Clin Infect Dis. 2001;32(Suppl 2):S114-S132.
46. John MA, Pletch C, Hussain Z. In vitro activity of quinupristin/dalfopristin, linezolid, telithromycin and comparator antimicrobial agents against 13 species of coagulase-negative staphylococci. J Antimicrob Chemother. 2002;50:933-938.
47. Garrett DO, et al. The emergence of decreased susceptibility to vancomycin in *Staphylococcus epidermidis.* Infect Control Hosp Epidemiol. 1999;20:167-170.
48. Sieradzki K, Villari P, Tomasz A. Decreased susceptibilities to teicoplanin and vancomycin among coagulase-negative methicillin-resistant clinical isolates of staphylococci. Antimicrob Agents Chemother. 1998;42:100-107.
49. Boyce J. Epidemiology and prevention of nosocomial infections. In: Crossley KB, Archer GL, eds. Staphylococci in Human Disease. New York: Churchill Livingstone; 1997:309-329.
50. Souvenir D, et al. Blood cultures positive for coagulase-negative staphylococci: Antisepsis, pseudobacteremia, and therapy of patients. J Clin Microbiol. 1998;36: 1923-1926.
51. Weinstein MP, et al. The clinical significance of positive blood cultures in the 1990s: A prospective comprehensive evaluation of the microbiology, epidemiology, and outcome of bacteremia and fungemia in adults. Clin Infect Dis. 1997;24:584-602.
52. Herwaldt LA, et al. The positive predictive value of isolating coagulase-negative staphylococci from blood cultures. Clin Infect Dis. 1996;22:14-20.
53. Calfee DP, Farr BM. Comparison of four antiseptic preparations for skin in the prevention of contamination of percutaneously drawn blood cultures: A randomized trial. J Clin Microbiol. 2002;40:1660-1665.
54. Richter SS, et al. Minimizing the workup of blood culture contaminants: Implementation and evaluation of a laboratory-based algorithm. J Clin Microbiol. 2002;40:2437-2444.

55. Hricak V, et al. Etiology and risk factors of 180 cases of native valve endocarditis. Report from a 5-year national prospective survey in Slovak Republic. Diagn Microbiol Infect Dis. 1998;31:431-435.
56. Kaye D. Infecting microorganism. In: Kay D, ed. Infective Endocarditis. Baltimore: University Park; 1976:43-54.
57. Caputo GM, et al. Native valve endocarditis due to coagulase-negative staphylococci. Clinical and microbiologic features. Am J Med. 1987;83:619-625.
58. Etienne J, Eykyn SJ. Increase in native valve endocarditis caused by coagulase negative staphylococci: An Anglo-French clinical and microbiological study. Br Heart J. 1990;64:381-384.
59. Vandenesch F, et al. Endocarditis due to *Staphylococcus lugdunensis*: Report of 11 cases and review. Clin Infect Dis. 1993;17:871-876.
60. Calderwood SB, et al. Risk factors for the development of prosthetic valve endocarditis. Circulation. 1985;72:31-37.
61. Cabell CH, Abrutyn E. Progress toward a global understanding of infective endocarditis. Early lessons from the International Collaboration on Endocarditis investigation. Infect Dis Clin North Am. 2002;16:255-272, vii.
62. Karchmer AW, Archer GL, Dismukes WE. *Staphylococcus epidermidis* causing prosthetic valve endocarditis: Microbiologic and clinical observations as guides to therapy. Ann Intern Med. 1983;98:447-455.
63. Kobasa WD, et al. Therapy for experimental endocarditis due to *Staphylococcus epidermidis*. Rev Infect Dis. 1983;5(Suppl 3):S533-S537.
64. Massanari RM, Donta ST. The efficacy of rifampin as adjunctive therapy in selected cases of staphylococcal endocarditis. Chest. 1978;73:371-375.
65. Archer GL, Vazquez GJ, Johnston JL. Antibiotic prophylaxis of experimental endocarditis due to methicillin-resistant *Staphylococcus epidermidis*. J Infect Dis. 1980;142:725-731.
66. Antimicrobial prophylaxis in surgery. Med Lett Drugs Ther. 1997;39:97-101.
67. Maki DG, Weise CE, Sarafin HW. A semiquantitative culture method for identifying intravenous-catheter-related infection. N Engl J Med. 1977;296:1305-1309.
68. Christensen GD, et al. Nosocomial septicemia due to multiply antibiotic-resistant *Staphylococcus epidermidis*. Ann Intern Med. 1982;96:1-10.
69. Snydman DR, et al. Total parenteral nutrition-related infections. Prospective epidemiologic study using semiquantitative methods. Am J Med. 1982;73:695-699.
70. Sherertz RJ, et al. Infections associated with subclavian Uldall catheters. Arch Intern Med. 1983;143:52-56.
71. Moyer MA, Edwards LD, Farley L. Comparative culture methods on 101 intravenous catheters. Routine, semiquantitative, and blood cultures. Arch Intern Med. 1983;143:66-69.
72. Cheesbrough JS, Finch RG, Burden RP. A prospective study of the mechanisms of infection associated with hemodialysis catheters. J Infect Dis. 1986;154:579-589.
73. Raucher HS, et al. Quantitative blood cultures in the evaluation of septicemia in children with Broviac catheters. J Pediatr. 1984;104:29-33.
74. Press OW, et al. Hickman catheter infections in patients with malignancies. Medicine (Baltimore). 1984;63:189-200.
75. Winston DJ, et al. Coagulase-negative staphylococcal bacteremia in patients receiving immunosuppressive therapy. Arch Intern Med. 1983;143:32-36.
76. Cooper GL, Hopkins CC. Rapid diagnosis of intravascular catheter-associated infection by direct Gram staining of catheter segments. N Engl J Med. 1985;312:1142-1147.
77. O'Grady NP, et al. Guidelines for the prevention of intravascular catheter-related infections. Centers for Disease Control and Prevention. MMWR Recomm Rep. 2002;51(RR 10):1-29.
78. Humar A, et al. Prospective randomized trial of 10% povidone-iodine versus 0.5% tincture of chlorhexidine as cutaneous antisepsis for prevention of central venous catheter infection. Clin Infect Dis. 2000;31:1001-1007.
79. Heard SO, et al. Influence of triple-lumen central venous catheters coated with chlorhexidine and silver sulfadiazine on the incidence of catheter-related bacteremia. Arch Intern Med. 1998;158:81-87.
80. Veenstra DL, et al. Efficacy of antiseptic-impregnated central venous catheters in preventing catheter-related bloodstream infection: A meta-analysis. JAMA. 1999;281:261-267.
81. Darouiche RO, et al. A comparison of two antimicrobial-impregnated central venous catheters. Catheter Study Group. N Engl J Med. 1999;340:1-8.
82. Martinez E, et al. Central venous catheter exchange by guidewire for treatment of catheter-related bacteraemia in patients undergoing BMT or intensive chemotherapy. Bone Marrow Transplant. 1999;23:41-44.
83. Robinson D, Suhocki P, Schwab SJ. Treatment of infected tunneled venous access hemodialysis catheters with guidewire exchange. Kidney Int. 1998;53:1792-1794.
84. Krishnasami Z, et al. Management of hemodialysis catheter-related bacteremia with an adjunctive antibiotic lock solution. Kidney Int. 2002;61:1136-1142.
85. Raad II, Bodey GP. Infectious complications of indwelling vascular catheters. Clin Infect Dis. 1992;15:197-208.
86. Schoenbaum SC, Gardner P, Shillito J. Infections of cerebrospinal fluid shunts: Epidemiology, clinical manifestations, and therapy. J Infect Dis. 1975;131:543-552.
87. McGirt MJ, et al. Risk factors for pediatric ventriculoperitoneal shunt infection and predictors of infectious pathogens. Clin Infect Dis. 2003;36:858-862.
88. Mayhall CG, et al. Ventriculostomy-related infections. A prospective epidemiologic study. N Engl J Med. 1984;310:553-559.
89. Trump DL, et al. CSF infections complicating the management of neoplastic meningitis. Clinical features and results of therapy. Arch Intern Med. 1982;142:583-586.
90. Dobrin RS, et al. The role of complement, immunoglobulin and bacterial antigen in coagulase-negative staphylococcal shunt nephritis. Am J Med. 1975;59:660-673.
91. Gombert ME, et al. Vancomycin and rifampin therapy for *Staphylococcus epidermidis* meningitis associated with CSF shunts: Report of three cases. J Neurosurg. 1981;55:633-636.

92. Archer GL, Tenenbaum MJ, Haywood HB 3rd. Rifampin therapy of *Staphylococcus epidermidis*. Use in infections from indwelling artificial devices. JAMA. 1978;240:751-753.
93. Wald SL, McLaurin RL. Cerebrospinal fluid antibiotic levels during treatment of shunt infections. J Neurosurg. 1980;52:41-46.
94. Frame PT, McLaurin RL. Treatment of CSF shunt infections with intrashunt plus oral antibiotic therapy. J Neurosurg. 1984;60:354-360.
95. James HE, et al. Prospective randomized study of therapy in cerebrospinal fluid shunt infection. Neurosurgery. 1980;7:459-463.
96. Wang EE, et al. Prophylactic sulfamethoxazole and trimethoprim in ventriculoperitoneal shunt surgery. A double-blind, randomized, placebo-controlled trial. JAMA. 1984;251:1174-1177.
97. Langley JM, et al. Efficacy of antimicrobial prophylaxis in placement of cerebrospinal fluid shunts: meta-analysis. Clin Infect Dis. 1993;17:98-103.
98. Gokal R. Peritonitis in continuous ambulatory peritoneal dialysis. J Antimicrob Chemother. 1982;9:417-420.
99. Zelenitsky S. et al. Analysis of microbiological trends in peritoneal dialysis-related peritonitis from 1991 to 1998. Am J Kidney Dis. 2000;36:1009-1013.
100. Rubin J, et al. Peritonitis during continuous ambulatory peritoneal dialysis. Ann Intern Med. 1980;92:7-13.
101. West TE, et al. Staphylococcal peritonitis in patients on continuous peritoneal dialysis. J Clin Microbiol. 1986;23:809-812.
102. Knight KR, et al. Laboratory diagnosis and oral treatment of CAPD peritonitis. Lancet. 1982;2:1301-1304.
103. Dawson MS, et al. Total volume culture technique for the isolation of microorganisms from continuous ambulatory peritoneal dialysis patients with peritonitis. J Clin Microbiol. 1985;22:391-394.
104. Krothapalli RK, Senekjian HO, Ayus JC. Efficacy of intravenous vancomycin in the treatment of gram-positive peritonitis in long-term peritoneal dialysis. Am J Med. 1983;75:345-348.
105. de Paepe M, et al. Gentamicin for treatment of peritonitis in continuous ambulatory peritoneal dialysis. Lancet. 1981;2:424-425.
106. Boeschoten EW, et al. CAPD peritonitis: A prospective randomized trial of oral versus intraperitoneal treatment with cephradine. J Antimicrob Chemother. 1985;16:789-797.
107. Baddour LM, et al. Comparison of microbiologic characteristics of pathogenic and saprophytic coagulase-negative staphylococci from patients on continuous ambulatory peritoneal dialysis. Diagn Microbiol Infect Dis. 1986;5:197-205.
108. de Mattos EM, et al. Isolation of methicillin-resistant coagulase-negative staphylococci from patients undergoing continuous ambulatory peritoneal dialysis (CAPD) and comparison of different molecular techniques for discriminating isolates of *Staphylococcus epidermidis*. Diagn Microbiol Infect Dis. 2003;45:13-22.
109. Rupp ME, Soper DE, Archer GL. Colonization of the female genital tract with *Staphylococcus saprophyticus*. J Clin Microbiol. 1992;30:2975-2979.
110. Latham RH, Running K, Stamm WE. Urinary tract infections in young adult women caused by *Staphylococcus saprophyticus*. JAMA. 1983;250:3063-3066.
111. Wallmark G, Arremark I, Telander B. *Staphylococcus saprophyticus*: A frequent cause of acute urinary tract infection among female outpatients. J Infect Dis. 1978;138:791-797.
112. Kahlmeter G. An international survey of the antimicrobial susceptibility of pathogens from uncomplicated urinary tract infections: The ECO.SENS Project. J Antimicrob Chemother. 2003;51:69-76.
113. Coordinated multicenter study of norfloxacin versus trimethoprim-sulfamethoxazole treatment of symptomatic urinary tract infections. The Urinary Tract Infection Study Group. J Infect Dis. 1987;155:170-177.
114. Stamm WE, et al. Causes of the acute urethral syndrome in women. N Engl J Med. 1980;303:409-415.
115. Lewis JF, et al. Urinary tract infection due to coagulase-negative staphylococcus. Am J Clin Pathol. 1982;77:736-739.
116. Sewell CM, et al. Clinical significance of coagulase-negative staphylococci. J Clin Microbiol. 1982;16:236-239.
117. Wade JC, et al. *Staphylococcus epidermidis*: An increasing cause of infection in patients with granulocytopenia. Ann Intern Med. 1982;7:503-508.
118. Pirsch JD, Maki DG. Infectious complications in adults with bone marrow transplantation and T-cell depletion of donor marrow. Increased susceptibility to fungal infections. Ann Intern Med. 1986;104:619-631.
119. Wisplinghoff H, et al. Current trends in the epidemiology of nosocomial bloodstream infections in patients with hematological malignancies and solid neoplasms in hospitals in the United States. Clin Infect Dis. 2003;36:1103-1110.
120. Bender JW, Hughes WT. Fatal Staphylococcus epidermidis sepsis following bone marrow transplantation. Johns Hopkins Med J. 1980;146:13-15.
121. Grossi EA, et al. A survey of 77 major infectious complications of median sternotomy: A review of 7,949 consecutive operative procedures. Ann Thorac Surg. 1985;40:214-223.
122. Bor DH, et al. Mediastinitis after cardiovascular surgery. Rev Infect Dis. 1983;5:885-897.
123. Miholic J, et al. Risk factors for severe bacterial infections after valve replacement and aortocoronary bypass operations: Analysis of 246 cases by logistic regression. Ann Thorac Surg. 1985;40:224-228.
124. Fitzgerald RH Jr, et al. Deep wound sepsis following total hip arthroplasty. J Bone Joint Surg Am. 1977;59:847-855.
125. Parker MA, Tuazon CU. Cervical osteomyelitis. Infection due to *Staphylococcus epidermidis* in hemodialysis patients. JAMA. 1978;240:50-51.
126. Tegnell A, et al. Changes in the appearance and treatment of deep sternal infections. J Hosp Infect. 2002;50:298-303.

127. Farinas MC, et al. Suppurative mediastinitis after open-heart surgery: A case-control study covering a seven-year period in Santander, Spain. Clin Infect Dis. 1995;20: 272-279.
128. Bessette PR, et al. Evaluation of postoperative osteomyelitis of the sternum comparing CT and dual Tc-99m MDP bone and In-111 WBC SPECT. Clin Nucl Med. 1993;18:197-202.
129. Lentino JR. Prosthetic joint infections: Bane of orthopedists, challenge for infectious disease specialists. Clin Infect Dis. 2003;36:1157-1161.
130. Salvati EA, et al. Infection rates after 3175 total hip and total knee replacements performed with and without a horizontal unidirectional filtered air-flow system. J Bone Joint Surg Am. 1982;64:525-535.
131. Rand JA, Brown ML. The value of indium 111 leukocyte scanning in the evaluation of painful or infected total knee arthroplasties. Clin Orthop. 1990;(259):179-182.
132. Hope PG, et al. Deep infection of cemented total hip arthroplasties caused by coagulase-negative staphylococci. J Bone Joint Surg Br. 1989;71:851-855.
133. Norden CW. A critical review of antibiotic prophylaxis in orthopedic surgery. Rev Infect Dis. 1983;5:928-932.
134. Lidgren L. Joint prosthetic infections: A success story. Acta Orthop Scand. 2001; 72:553-556.
135. O'Brien T, Collin J. Prosthetic vascular graft infection. Br J Surg. 1992;79: 1262-1267.
136. Henke PK, et al. Current options in prosthetic vascular graft infection. Am Surg. 1998;64:39-45; discussion 45-46.
137. Bandyk DF, et al. Expanded application of in situ replacement for prosthetic graft infection. J Vasc Surg. 2001;34:411-419; discussion 419-420.
138. Bandyk DF, et al. Aortofemoral graft infection due to Staphylococcus epidermidis. Arch Surg. 1984;119:102-108.
139. Wooster DL, Louch RE, Krajden S. Intraoperative bacterial contamination of vascular grafts: A prospective study. Can J Surg. 1985;28:407-409.
140. Bunt TJ. Sources of Staphylococcus epidermidis at the inguinal incision during peripheral revascularization. Am Surg. 1986;52:472-473.
141. Kaiser AB, et al. Antibiotic prophylaxis in vascular surgery. Ann Surg. 1978;188: 283-289.
142. Saeed Abdulrahman I, et al. A prospective study of hemodialysis access-related bacterial infections. J Infect Chemother. 2002;8:242-246.
143. Chang JK, et al. Risk factors associated with infection of lower extremity revascularization: analysis of 365 procedures performed at a teaching hospital. Ann Vasc Surg. 2003;17:91-96.
144. Anday EK, Talbot GH. Coagulase-negative Staphylococcus bacteremia—A rising threat in the newborn infant. Ann Clin Lab Sci. 1985;15:246-251.
145. Freeman J, et al. Association of intravenous lipid emulsion and coagulase-negative staphylococcal bacteremia in neonatal intensive care units. N Engl J Med. 1990;323:301-308.
146. Stoll BJ, et al. Late-onset sepsis in very low birth weight neonates: The experience of the NICHD Neonatal Research Network. Pediatrics. 2002;110(2 Pt 1):285-291.
147. Sharek PJ, et al. Effect of an evidence-based hand washing policy on hand washing rates and false-positive coagulase negative staphylococcus blood and cerebrospinal fluid culture rates in a level III NICU. J Perinatol. 2002;22:137-143.
148. Raimundo O, et al. Molecular epidemiology of coagulase-negative staphylococcal bacteraemia in a newborn intensive care unit. J Hosp Infect. 2002;51:33-42.
149. Van Der Zwet WC, et al. Nosocomial spread of a Staphylococcus capitis strain with heteroresistance to vancomycin in a neonatal intensive care unit. J Clin Microbiol. 2002;40:2520-2525.
150. Chapman RL, Faix RG. Persistent bacteremia and outcome in late onset infection among infants in a neonatal intensive care unit. Pediatr Infect Dis J. 2003;22:17-21.
151. Gruskay JA, et al. Staphylococcus epidermidis–associated enterocolitis. J Pediatr. 1986;109:520-524.
152. Diamond JG. Intraocular management of endophthalmitis. A systematic approach. Arch Ophthalmol. 1981;99:96-99.
153. Weber DJ, et al. Endophthalmitis following intraocular lens implantation: Report of 30 cases and review of the literature. Rev Infect Dis. 1986;8:12-20.
154. Fisch A, et al. Epidemiology of infective endophthalmitis in France. The French Collaborative Study Group on Endophthalmitis. Lancet. 1991;338:1373-1376.
155. Schlossberg D, Jan AM. Endophthalmitis in intravenous drug abuse. Ann Ophthalmol. 1993;25:77-78.
156. Heaven CJ, Mann PJ, Boase DL. Endophthalmitis following extracapsular cataract surgery: A review of 32 cases. Br J Ophthalmol. 1992;76:419-423.
157. Wohl B, et al. Late unheralded pacemaker pocket infection due to Staphylococcus epidermidis: A new clinical entity. Pacing Clin Electrophysiol. 1982;5:190-195.
158. Burkhardt BR, et al. Capsules, infection, and intraluminal antibiotics. Plast Reconstr Surg. 1981;68:43-49.
159. Kabalin JN, Kessler, R. Infectious complications of penile prosthesis surgery. J Urol. 1988;139:953-955.
160. Gordon SM, et al. Nosocomial bloodstream infections in patients with implantable left ventricular assist devices. Ann Thorac Surg. 2001;72:725-730.

CHAPTER **194**

Classification of Streptococci

ALAN L. BISNO

KATHRYN L. RUOFF

Members of the genus *Streptococcus* are catalase-negative, gram-positive bacteria that form oval or coccoid cells arranged in pairs and chains. Streptococci are nutritionally fastidious and require complex media, preferably supplemented with blood, for optimal growth. They are homofermentative lactic acid bacteria, producing lactic acid without gas as the major end product of glucose metabolism. Although streptococci are referred to as facultative anaerobes, growing both aerobically and anaerobically, streptococci do not use oxygen metabolically. In addition, some strains are capnophilic whereas others grow better under anaerobic conditions. This large and heterogeneous group of parasites of humans and animals harbors relatively avirulent normal flora organisms as well as some of the most impressive human pathogens.[1]

Early attempts to classify streptococci of clinical importance centered around their action on blood-containing agars[2] and antigens contained in their cell walls.[3] Some streptococci (β-hemolytic) can lyse blood cells and cause complete clearing of blood in the vicinity of their growth (Fig. 194-1). Other strains cause no change in blood agar (γ- or nonhemolytic), while the remainder of the streptococci (α-hemolytic) reduce hemoglobin and cause a greenish discoloration of the agar (Fig. 194-2). Lancefield,[3] concentrating initially on virulent, β-hemolytic streptococci, found that they could be subdivided based on cell wall antigens. It was thought that β-hemolytic organisms with the same Lancefield antigen were closely related, but this correlation

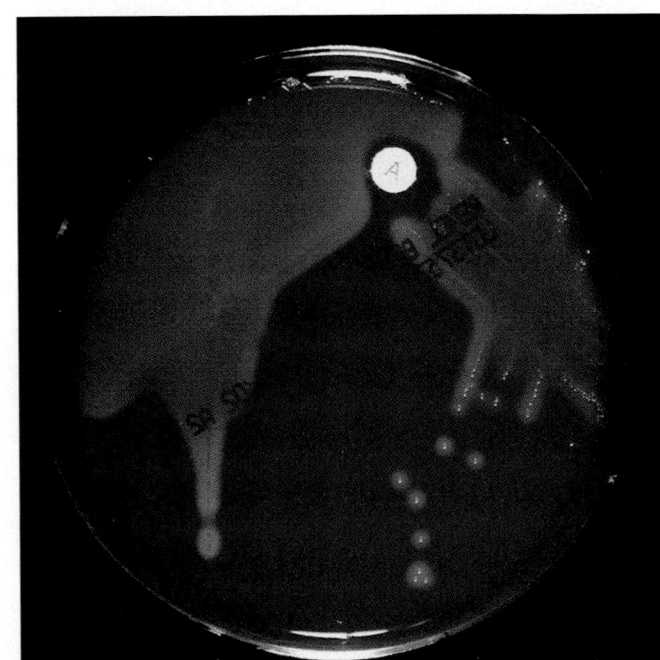

FIGURE 194-1. Group A streptococci growing in pure culture on a sheep blood-agar plate. Individual colonies are surrounded by zones of complete (β) hemolysis. Subsurface hemolysis (agar stab) is due in part to the action of streptolysin O, which is oxygen labile. The zone of inhibition around a low-potency bacitracin disk is a presumptive test for group A organisms.

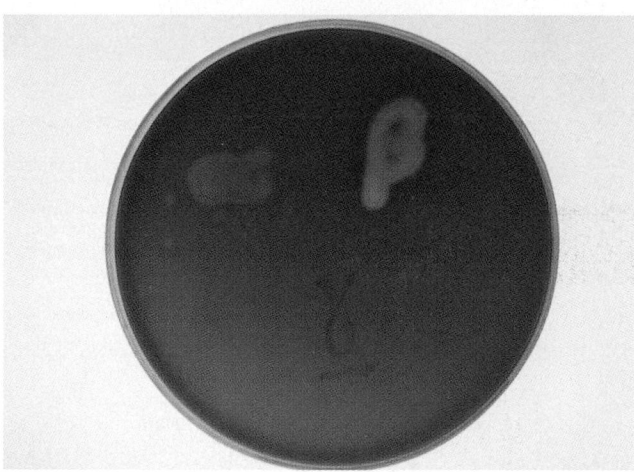

FIGURE 194-2. Sheep blood-agar plate with α, β, and γ-hemolytic streptococci.

By the mid-1980s, the enterococcal streptococci (Lancefield group D, bile esculin-positive and salt tolerant) had taken up residence in their own newly created *Enterococcus* genus and the "dairy" or "lactic" streptococci (Lancefield group N, occasionally documented in human infection) were moved to the new *Lactococcus* genus. Ensuing studies of streptococci isolated from human and animal infections gave rise to updated classification schemes based on 16S ribosomal RNA sequences and other molecular information. These investigations also aided accurate differentiation of genera of streptococcal-like catalase-negative gram-positive cocci (e.g., *Leuconostoc, Pediococcus,* and numerous others) that had previously been unrecognized in clinical specimens. Many, but not all, β-hemolytic streptococci were found to be members of the pyogenic group, while the viridans streptococci were divided into five species groups. Although the viridans strains, normal flora of the oral cavity and gastrointestinal tract, were traditionally characterized as α-hemolytic, it was realized that some members of this group also displayed β-hemolysis. Organisms considered to be nutritionally variant streptococci (also referred to as pyridoxal-dependent or satelliting streptococci) were reclassified in two new genera, *Abiotrophia* and *Granulicatella*.[6-8] It became apparent that the hemolytic reactions, Lancefield antigens, and other phenotypic characteristics relied on in the past were not always accurate predictors of genetic relatedness among strains. These characteristics are, however, still useful to clinical laboratorians for the presumptive identification of many commonly encountered streptococci. Table 194-1 summarizes currently described streptococcal species and species groups that are frequently isolated from humans. Streptococci normally associated with animals that are infrequently isolated from human infection are displayed in Table 194-2.

was not always valid for non–β-hemolytic strains. Other phenotypic traits of streptococci were also examined and catalogued throughout the 20th century, giving rise to various classification schemes. In 1937, Sherman[4] classified the streptococci into the pyogenic, viridans, enterococcal, and lactic divisions, based on phenotypic traits. Subsequent molecular studies generally upheld these basic divisions,[5] but revealed multiple genera among organisms traditionally thought to be streptococci.

TABLE 194-1 Classification of Streptococci Commonly Isolated from Humans*

Species	Lancefield Antigen(s)	Hemolytic Reaction(s)	Comments
S. pyogenes	A	β	Pyogenic; can be differentiated from β-hemolytic anginosus group strains with the group A antigen by the formation of relatively large colonies and other phenotypic traits. Agent of pharyngitis and respiratory, skin, and other infections. Can cause nonsuppurative sequelae (acute rheumatic fever, acute glomerulonephritis).
S. agalactiae	B	β, γ	Pyogenic; hemolytic reaction is weak. Agent of chorioamnionitis, puerperal sepsis, neonatal sepsis and meningitis, and infections in nonpregnant adults.
S. dysgalactiae subsp. *equisimilis*	C, G†	β	Pyogenic; formerly named *S. equisimilis*. Can be differentiated from β-hemolytic anginosus group strains with the C or G antigen by the formation of relatively large colonies and other phenotypic traits. Agent of respiratory and deep tissue infections, cellulitis, and septicemia.
S. pneumoniae	No detectable antigen	α	Closely related to members of the "viridans" streptococcal mitis species group. Agent of respiratory infections, otitis media, and meningitis.
Anginosus species group	A, C, F, G or no detectable antigen	α, β, γ	"Viridans" streptococcal group composed of three species: *S. anginosus, S. constellatus,* and *S. intermedius*. Formerly known as "*S. milleri*." β-Hemolytic strains form small colonies compared to those of pyogenic β-hemolytic group A, C, and G streptococci and also differ in other phenotypic traits. Agents of purulent infections.
Bovis species group	D	α, γ	"Viridans" streptococcal group formerly known as "group D nonenterococcal" streptococci. Species commonly isolated from humans have recently been reclassified as *S. gallolyticus* (formerly *S. bovis* biotype I), *S. pasteurianus* (formerly *S. bovis* biotype II/2), *S. infantarius* (formerly *S. bovis* biotype II/1), and *S. lutetiensis*. Some strains produce extracellular polysaccharides.‡ Agents of endocarditis; isolated from blood in patients with colonic cancer.
Mutans species group	Not useful for differentiation	α, γ, occasionally β	"Viridans" streptococcal group. *S. mutans* and *S. sobrinus* are the species commonly isolated from humans. Produce extracellular polysaccharides.‡ Agents of dental caries and endocarditis.
Salivarius species group	Not useful for differentiation	α, γ	"Viridans" streptococcal group. *S. salivarius* and *S. vestibularis* are the species commonly isolated from humans. Strains in the salivarius group may react with Lancefield's group K antiserum and may produce extracellular polysaccharides.‡ Infrequent opportunists in compromised hosts.
Mitis species group	Not useful for differentiation	α	"Viridans" streptococcal group. Species commonly isolated from humans include *S. mitis, S. oralis, S. sanguis,* and *S. gordonii*. Strains in the mitis group may react with Lancefield's group H antiserum and may produce extracellular polysaccharides.‡ Agents of endocarditis and systemic infection in neutropenic patients.

*See references 6 and 7 for additional information on streptococci mentioned in this table.
†Isolates with the group A antigen have also been described.
‡Extracellular polysaccharides (dextran, levan) are thought to aid colonization and may play a role in virulence.

TABLE 194-2 Streptococci Primarily Isolated from Animals that May Occasionally Cause Human Infection*

Species	Lancefield Antigen(s)	Hemolytic Reaction	Comments
S. dysgalactiae subsp. dysgalactiae	C, L	α, β, γ	Pathogen of domesticated animals. Participation in human infections not well documented.
S. equi subsp. equi	C	β	Agent of equine strangles. Participation in human infections not well documented.
S. equi subsp. zooepidemicus	C	β	Agent of bovine mastitis and infection in other domesticated animals. Implicated in outbreaks of nephritis in humans.
S. porcinus	E, P, U, V	β	Swine are usual hosts. Isolated from human female genital tract. May cross-react with commercially available group B streptococcal grouping reagents.
S. canis	G	β	Dogs and other animals are the usual hosts. Documented as an infrequent human pathogen.
S. suis	R, S, T	α, β[†]	Swine are the usual hosts. Isolated infrequently from cases of human meningitis.
S. iniae	No detectable antigen	β	Fish are the usual hosts. Isolated infrequently from cutaneous and systemic infection in humans.

*See references 6 and 7 for additional information on streptococci mentioned in this table.
[†]α-Hemolytic on sheep blood agar, but some strains may be β-hemolytic on horse blood agar.

REFERENCES

1. Hardie JM. *Streptococcus Rosenbach* 184,22AL. In: Sneath PHA, Mair NS, Sharpe ME, Holt JG, eds. Bergey's Manual of Systematic Bacteriology. Baltimore, MD: Williams & Wilkins; 1986:1042-1071.
2. Brown JH. The use of blood agar for the study of streptococci. New York: The Rockefeller Institute for Medical Research; 1919.
3. Lancefield RC. A serological differentiation of human and other groups of hemolytic streptococci. J Exp Med. 1933;57:571-595.
4. Sherman JM. The Streptococci. Bacteriol. Rev. 1937; 1:3-97.
5. Bentley RW, Leigh JA, Collins MD. Intrageneric structure of *Streptococcus* based on comparative analysis of small-subunit rRNA sequences. Int J Syst Bacteriol. 1991; 41:487-494.
6. Facklam R. What happened to the streptococci: Overview of taxonomic and nomenclature changes. Clin Microbiol Rev. 2002;15:613-630.
7. Ruoff KL, Whiley RA, Beighton D. *Streptococcus.* In: Murray PR, Baron EJ, Jorgensen JH, et al., eds. Manual of Clinical Microbiology. Washington, DC: American Society for Microbiology; 2003:405-421.
8. Ruoff KL. *Aerococcus, Abiotrophia,* and other infrequently isolated aerobic catalase-nagative, Gram positive cocci. In: Murray PR, Baron EJ, Jorgensen JH, et al., eds. Manual of Clinical Microbiology. Washington, DC: American Society for Microbiology; 2003:434-444.

CHAPTER **195**

Streptococcus pyogenes

ALAN L. BISNO
DENNIS L. STEVENS

Streptococcus pyogenes (group A Streptococcus) is one of the most important bacterial pathogens of humans. This ubiquitous organism is the most frequent bacterial cause of acute pharyngitis, and it also gives rise to a variety of cutaneous and systemic infections. Its unique place in medical microbiology stems from its propensity to initiate two non-suppurative sequelae: acute rheumatic fever (ARF) and poststreptococcal acute glomerulonephritis (AGN). The former malady has been responsible for suffering, disability, and mortality in all parts of the world.

HISTORY

Streptococci were demonstrated in cases of erysipelas and wound infections by Billroth in 1874 and in the blood of a patient with puerperal sepsis by Pasteur in 1879. Fehleisen, in 1883, isolated chain-forming organisms in pure culture from erysipelas lesions and then demonstrated that these organisms could induce typical erysipelas in humans. Rosenbach applied the designation *Streptococcus pyogenes* to these organisms in 1884.

Initial progress toward a rational classification of streptococci dates from the description by Schötmuller in 1903 of the blood agar technique for differentiating hemolytic from nonhemolytic streptococci. In 1919 J. H. Brown[1] made a systematic study of patterns of hemolysis and introduced the terms α-, β-, and γ-hemolysis (see Chapter 194). Lancefield's classification of β-hemolytic streptococci into distinct serogroups in 1933[2] was a major turning point in our understanding of the epidemiology of streptococcal infections. Most strains pathogenic for humans were found to belong to serogroup A *(S. pyogenes).* Systems of serotyping group A streptococci were developed on the basis of M-protein precipitin reactions (Lancefield) or T-protein agglutination reactions (Griffith). In addition, Lancefield established the critical role of M protein in streptococcal virulence and the type-specific nature of protective immunity to group A streptococcal infection. Studies by Dochez and collaborators and by George and Gladys Dick in the 1920s established the relationship of scarlet fever to hemolytic streptococcal infection. A few years later, Todd's description of the method for titration of anti–streptolysin O (ASO) in serum added still another important tool to the armamentarium available for study of the immunology and epidemiology of streptococcal disease. Such tools were used by a number of investigators, including Coburn, Collis, Rammelkamp, Stollerman, and Wannamaker, to establish the relationship of group A streptococcal infection to ARF and AGN. Much of our knowledge of the detailed epidemiology of streptococcal infections and of ARF derives from the pioneering studies performed at Warren Air Force Base, Wyoming, during the years 1949 to 1951 by Rammelkamp, Wannamaker, and Denny.[3-5]

DESCRIPTION OF THE PATHOGEN

Group A streptococci (GAS) grow as spherical or ovoid cells 0.6 to 1.0 μm in diameter and occur as pairs or as short to moderate-sized chains in clinical specimens. When growing in broth media enriched with serum or blood, long chains are frequently formed, and many strains produce capsules of hyaluronic acid. The organisms are gram positive, nonmotile, non–spore forming, catalase negative, and facultatively anaerobic. Group A streptococci are nutritionally fastidious and are usually cultivated in complex media, often supplemented with blood or serum.

When cultured on blood agar plates, *S. pyogenes* appears as white to gray colonies 1 to 2 mm in diameter surrounded by zones of complete ("β") hemolysis. (Strains that fail to produce such hemolysis occur but are rare.) Strains that produce copious amounts of the hyaluronate capsular material appear mucoid, at times resembling a water drop on the plate. Less mucoid strains assume a crinkled, so-called matte appearance. Small opaque colonies of organisms that lack capsules and detectable M protein are termed *glossy*.

The complete genome sequences from several distinct *S. pyogenes* serotypes have been reported,[6-8] and this genome information is beginning to provide insight into the subtle genetic differences between streptococcal types that arm them to produce specific syndromes. A large number of somatic constituents and extracellular products of group A streptococci have been identified. The most important of these are indicated in the following sections.

Somatic Constituents

The organism is enveloped in a hyaluronic acid capsule that serves as an accessory virulence factor in retarding phagocytosis by polymorphonuclear leukocytes and macrophages of the host.[9,10] Streptococcal strains vary greatly in their degree of encapsulation, and those with the most exuberant capsule production have a mucoid appearance when cultivated on blood agar plates. In certain heavily encapsulated GAS strains, the capsule may take precedence over M protein in mediating resistance to phagocytosis.[10] GAS capsular hyaluronate is chemically quite similar to that found in human connective tissue. For this reason, it is a poor immunogen, and antibodies to GAS hyaluronic acid have not been demonstrated in humans.

The cell wall is a complex structure containing many different antigenic substances. The group-specific carbohydrate of group A strains is a dimer of rhamnose and *N*-acetylglucosamine in a ratio of approximately 2:1. The mucopeptide (peptidoglycan) layer provides rigidity to the cell wall; it is composed of polymers of repeating subunits of *N*-acetylglucosamine and *N*-acetylmuramic acid connected by amino acid side chains.

M protein is the major somatic virulence factor of group A streptococci. Strains rich in this protein are resistant to phagocytosis by polymorphonuclear leukocytes, multiply rapidly in fresh human blood, and are capable of initiating disease. Strains that do not express M protein are avirulent.[11] GAS may be divided into serotypes on the basis of antigenic differences in M-protein molecules, and more recently into genotypes on the basis of nucleotide differences in the *emm* gene encoding the molecule. More than 120 such serotypes and/or genotypes are currently recognized.[12] Acquired human immunity to streptococcal infection is based on the development of opsonic antibodies directed against the antiphagocytic moiety of M protein. Such immunity is type specific and quite durable, lasting for many years and perhaps indefinitely.

M protein is a filamentous macromolecule that exists as a stable dimer with an α-helical coiled-coil structure.[13] The molecule, which is anchored to the cell membrane, traverses and penetrates the cell wall. The more proximal portion of the molecule contains epitopes widely conserved among group A streptococci, whereas the more distal portion contains type-specific epitopes.[14] This configuration localizes the type-specific moiety on the tips of fibrils protruding from the cell surface (Fig. 195-1). In the nonimmune host M protein exerts its antiphagocytic effect by inhibiting activation of the alternate complement pathway on the cell surface.[15,16] Such inhibition appears to be mediated by the binding to the M-protein molecule of host proteins, among which are complement control proteins (factor H, a factor H–like protein, and human C4b-binding protein)[17-19] and fibrinogen.[20-22] The antiphagocytic effect is nullified in the presence of adequate concentrations of type-specific antibody. M proteins analogous to those of group A streptococci are present in many strains of groups C[23] and G[24] streptococci.

Additional surface proteins related to M protein have now been identified. Although their structure is overall quite similar to that of M protein, they differ in the types of repeats and in their ability to interact with different human proteins. Genes encoding these proteins (*enn*, *mrp*, *fcrA*, *arp*, and *protH* and others) have been designated as members of the *emm* gene superfamily. A number of the M–like proteins bind IgG or IgA at the non–antigen binding site and appear to be cooperative with M protein in antiphagocytic effect.[25,26] Indeed, a notable

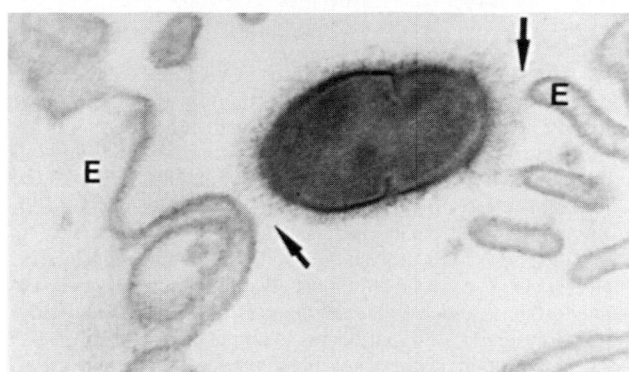

FIGURE 195-1. Electron micrograph of group A streptococci. Surface fibrils contain type-specific, antiphagocytic epitopes of M protein. Lipoteichoic acid and fibronectin binding proteins facilitate adherence of streptococci to the membrane (arrows) of a human oral epithelial cell (E). (X67,500) *(From Beachey EH, Ofek I. Epithelial cell binding of group A streptococci by lipoteichoic acid on fimbriae denuded of M protein. J Exp Med. 1976;143:759-771, with permission.)*

function of the M-protein family is its ability to bind to a wide range of host proteins, including, among others, albumin, fibrinogen, and plasminogen. Still other anti-opsonic surface proteins continue to be described.[27] For example, Mac, a secreted group A streptococcal protein with homology to a human β₂-integrin, binds to CD16 on the surface of human PML and inhibits phagocytosis and bacterial killing.[28] These observations underscore the extreme virtuosity with which the bacterium develops multiple mechanisms to evade phagocytic killing.

Another protein antigen very closely associated with the M-protein molecule of group A streptococcus is the so-called serum opacity factor (OF). This factor is an α-lipoproteinase that is detected by its ability to opacify horse serum and that also has fibronectin binding properties.[29] Strains of a minority of the currently identified M types elaborate this antigen.[30] OF itself is antigenic and type specific; that is, its ability to opacify serum can be specifically inhibited by antiserum raised against homologous but not heterologous M types. Type-specific and non–type-specific immune responses to streptococcal M protein are generally weaker after pharyngeal infection with OF-positive than with OF-negative types.[31] The former importance of this substance as an ancillary typing system for strains that could not be M serotyped has been obviated by the advent of *emm* genotyping.

A number of somatic streptococcal constituents play critical roles in the first step of colonization, namely, adherence to the surface of human epithelial cells. At least 17 adhesin candidates have been described,[32] but the most extensively studied have been lipoteichoic acid (LTA), M protein, and fibronectin binding proteins. It is believed that LTA serves by hydrophobic interactions as a "first-step" adhesin, bringing the organisms into close contact with host cells and then allowing other adhesins to promote high-affinity binding.[33] Although M protein does not appear to promote adhesion to human buccal or tonsillar epithelial cells,[34,35] it does mediate adherence to skin keratinocytes via the attachment of the C repeat region to keratinocyte membrane cofactor CD46.[36,37] Group A streptococcal surface proteins that bind fibronectin have been studied extensively and are important in adherence to both throat and skin. These include protein F1 (PrtF1),[38] also known as SfbI (streptococcal fibronectin binding protein I),[39] and related proteins known as SbfII,[40] FBP54,[41] protein F2,[42] and PFBB.[43]

Moreover, the expression of these adhesins has been reported to be environmentally regulated.[44] Expression of protein F1 is enhanced in an O2-rich environment, whereas that of M protein is greater at higher partial pressures of CO_2.[45] Thus, teliologically, it might be postulated that the organism displays protein F1 on its surface when it seeks to adhere to the cutaneous surface but expresses M protein in the deeper tissues, where it is more likely to encounter phagocytic cells.

Extracellular Products

During the course of growth in vitro or in vivo, group A streptococci elaborate numerous extracellular products, only a limited number of which have been well characterized. Two distinct hemolysins are elaborated. Streptolysin O derives its name from its oxygen lability. It is reversibly inhibited by oxygen and irreversibly inhibited by cholesterol. In addition to its effect on erythrocytes, it is toxic to a variety of cells and cell fractions including polymorphonuclear leukocytes, platelets, tissue culture cells, lysosomes, and isolated mammalian and amphibian hearts. Streptolysin O is produced by almost all strains of *S. pyogenes* (as well as many group C and G organisms) and is antigenic. Measurement of anti-streptolysin O (ASO) antibodies in human sera has proved exceedingly useful as an indicator of recent streptococcal infection.

Streptolysin S is a hemolysin produced by streptococci growing in the presence of serum (hence the "S") or in the presence of a variety of other substances such as serum albumin, α-lipoprotein, ribonucleic acid, or detergents such as Tween. Streptolysin S is nonantigenic, or at least no antibody to it has been detected that neutralizes its hemolytic activity. Streptolysin S shares with streptolysin O the capacity to damage the membranes of polymorphonuclear leukocytes, platelets, and subcellular organelles. Unlike streptolysin O, it is not inactivated by oxygen, but it is quite thermolabile. Most strains of *S. pyogenes* produce both hemolysins. Hemolysis on the surface of blood agar plates is due primarily to streptolysin S, whereas streptolysin O exerts its hemolytic effect best in subsurface colonies, in pour plates, or in anaerobic cultures. An occasional strain may produce only one of the two hemolysins. Rarely, strains are encountered that lack both hemolysins.

Several extracellular products may, theoretically, serve to facilitate the liquefaction of pus and the spreading of streptococci through tissue planes that are characteristic of streptococcal cellulitis and necrotizing fasciitis. These include (1) four antigenically distinct enzymes that participate in the degradation of deoxyribonucleic acid (DNases A, B, C, and D); (2) hyaluronidase, which enzymatically degrades hyaluronic acid found in the ground substance of connective tissue; (3) streptokinase, which promotes the dissolution of clots by catalyzing the conversion of plasminogen to plasmin; (4) streptococcal pyrogenic exotoxin B (Spe B), which is a potent protease; and (5) C5a peptidase, which specifically cleaves the human chemotaxin C5a at the PMN binding site.[46,47]

The streptococcal pyrogenic exotoxins (Spe) are a family of bacterial superantigens believed to be associated with streptococcal toxic shock syndrome (Strep TSS), necrotizing fasciitis, and other severe infections. This family includes the bacteriophage-encoded SpeA[48] and SpeC, historically known as the scarlatinal toxins due to their association with scarlet fever, as well as the cysteine protease SpeB, a number of additional pyrogenic exotoxins [e.g., mitogenic factor (MF, SpeF) and streptococcal superantigen (SSA)] have more recently been identified.[49]

Superantigens are potent immunostimulators able to simultaneously bind to the major histocompatibility complex (MHC) class II molecules and the T-cell receptor.[50] This binding results in activation of a large number of T cells expressing specific V-β subsets of the T cell repertoire. Superantigen activation of T cells leads to increased secretion of proinflammatory cytokines. This issue is discussed in more detail in the section on pathogenesis of Strep TSS.

Emerging concepts regarding the molecular biology of streptococcal virulence, colonization, and tissue invasion have been reviewed.[49,51] Control of the expression of the heretofore-mentioned virulence factors over time and under diverse environmental circumstances depends on a complex system of genetic modulation. Of the known transcriptional regulators in *S. pyogenes,* the two most intensively studied are Mga[52] (multiple gene regulator) or Mry, the regulator of M-protein expression, and a two-component regulatory system known as CsrRS[53] (capsule synthesis regulator) or, alternatively, CovRS[54] ("control of virulence genes"), which represses the synthesis of the capsule and several exotoxins.[55]

STREPTOCOCCAL PHARNYGITIS

Epidemiology

Streptococcal sore throat is among the most common bacterial infections of childhood. Group A streptococci are responsible for the great majority of such infections, but strains of other serogroups, especially groups C and G,[56] are occasionally involved. The disease occurs primarily among children 5 to 15 years of age, with the peak incidence occurring during the first few years of school. All age groups are susceptible, however, and severe epidemics are common in military training facilities. There is no sex predilection. The disease is ordinarily spread by direct person-to-person contact, most likely via droplets of saliva or nasal secretions. Crowding such as occurs in schools or barracks favors interpersonal spread of the organism (Fig. 195-2) and may also enhance its virulence by processes of natural selection analogous to those that occur during mouse passage in the laboratory. The effect of crowding in facilitating transmission may account in part for the increased incidence of streptococcal pharyngitis in northern latitudes during the colder months of the year. Explosive food-borne or waterborne outbreaks are also well documented. Contamination of dust, clothing, blankets, or other fomites does not play a significant role in contagion.

Group A streptococci frequently colonize the throats of asymptomatic persons. Pharyngeal carriage rates among normal schoolchildren vary with geographic location and season of the year. Carriage rates of 15% to 20% have been noted in several studies. The carriage rate among adults is considerably lower.

Studies of experimentally induced human infections and of transmission within military barracks have shed considerable light on the variables involved in interpersonal spread. During the acute phase of tonsillopharyngeal infection, M-typeable group A streptococci are frequently present in large numbers in both the nose and throat. In untreated infections, organisms may persist for many weeks, although the signs and symptoms of illness abate within a few days. During convalescence, the organisms decrease in numbers, and they tend to disappear from the anterior nares sooner than from the throat. In addition, the M-protein content and virulence of persisting organisms gradually decline. The result of these qualitative and quantitative changes is that convalescent carriers are much less likely to transmit the organism to close contacts than are acutely infected persons.

In patients who do not receive effective antibiotic therapy for acute streptococcal pharyngitis, type-specific antibodies are frequently detectable in the serum between 4 and 8 weeks after the infection. These opsonic antibodies protect against subsequent infection with organisms of the same M type, but the person remains susceptible to infec-

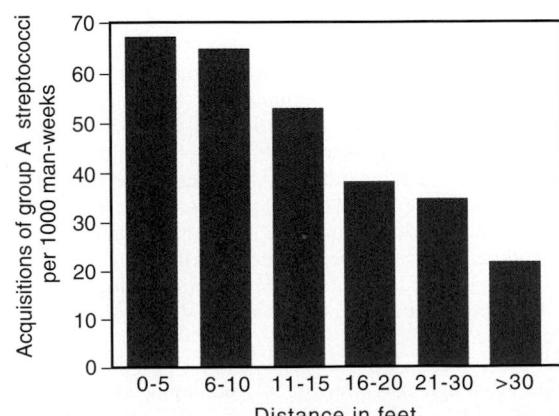

FIGURE 195-2. Transmission of group A streptococci in a military barracks according to bed distance from the nearest carrier. *(From Wannamaker LW. The epidemiology of streptococcal infection. In: McCarty M, ed. Streptococcal Infections. New York: Columbia University Press; 1953:157-175, with permission.)*

tion by heterologous types. Prompt and effective antibiotic therapy may ablate the type-specific immune response.

Clinical Manifestations

The usual incubation period of streptococcal pharyngitis is 2 to 4 days. The onset of illness is heralded by the rather abrupt onset of sore throat accompanied by malaise, feverishness, and headache. Nausea, vomiting, and abdominal pain are common in children. Prominent physical findings include redness, edema, and lymphoid hyperplasia of the posterior portion of the pharynx; enlarged, hyperemic tonsils; patchy discrete tonsillopharyngeal exudates; enlarged, tender lymph nodes at the angles of the mandibles; and a temperature of 101° F or higher. In the absence of the aforementioned symptoms and signs, simple coryza, hoarseness, cough, or conjunctivitis does not suggest the presence of streptococcal infection. Laboratory findings include a positive throat culture for β-hemolytic streptococci and a total white blood cell count usually exceeding 12,000/mm³ with increased numbers of polymorphonuclear leukocytes. The test for C-reactive protein is usually positive.[57]

Not all patients with streptococcal pharyngitis have the full-blown syndrome just described. Endemically occurring infections in open populations manifest a wide spectrum of clinical severity. For example, only approximately half such patients with sore throats and positive throat cultures have tonsillar or pharyngeal exudates. Patients who have undergone tonsillectomy tend to experience a milder clinical syndrome. In infants, the response to streptococcal infection is much less sharply focalized to the lymphoid tissue of the faucial and posterior pharyngeal area. Rhinorrhea, suppurative complications, low-grade fever, and a more protracted course tend to characterize infections at this age. Exudative pharyngitis in children less than 3 years of age is rarely streptococcal in etiology.

In the absence of suppurative complications, the disease is self-limited. Fever abates within 3 to 5 days. Virtually all acute signs and symptoms subside within 1 week, although several additional weeks may be required for tonsils and lymph nodes to return to their usual size. Penicillin shortens the period of fever, toxicity, and infectivity.[58-60] Given the rather brief time course of untreated disease, however, such shortening of the clinical syndrome may not be striking unless therapy is initiated within the first 24 hours of illness.

Scarlet Fever

Scarlet fever results from infection with a streptococcal strain that elaborates streptococcal pyrogenic exotoxins (erythrogenic toxins). Although this disease is usually associated with pharyngeal infections, it may follow streptococcal infections at other sites such as wound infections or puerperal sepsis. The clinical syndrome is similar in most respects to that associated with nontoxigenic strains, save for the scarlatinal rash. The latter must be differentiated from those of viral exanthems, drug eruptions, staphylococcal toxic shock syndrome, and Kawasaki disease.

The rash usually appears on the second day of clinical illness as a diffuse red blush with many points of deeper red that blanch on pressure. It is often first noted over the upper part of the chest and then spreads to the remainder of the trunk, neck, and extremities. The palms, soles, and usually the face are spared. Skin folds in the neck, axillae, groin, elbows, and knees appear as lines of deeper red (Pastia's lines). There are scattered petechiae, and the Rumpel-Leeds test of capillary fragility is positive. Occlusion of sweat glands imparts a sandpaper texture to the skin, a particularly helpful finding in dark-skinned patients.

The face appears flushed except for marked circumoral pallor. In addition to findings of exudative pharyngitis and tonsillitis, patients display an enanthem characterized by small, red, hemorrhagic spots on the hard and soft palate. The tongue is initially covered with a yellowish white coat through which may be seen the red papillae ("white strawberry tongue"). Later the coating disappears, and the tongue is beefy red in appearance ("red strawberry tongue"). The skin rash fades over the course of 1 week and is followed by extensive desquamation lasting for several weeks. A modest eosinophilia may be present early in the course of the illness.

Severe forms of scarlet fever, either associated with local and hematogenous spread of the organism (septic scarlet fever) or with profound toxemia (toxic scarlet fever), are characterized by high fever and marked systemic toxicity. The course may be complicated by arthritis, jaundice, and, very rarely, hydrops of the gallbladder. Such severe forms of the disease are quite infrequent in the antibiotic era. Intracutaneous administration of erythrogenic toxin in humans elicits local erythema (positive Dick test). No reaction occurs in persons with acquired immunity to the toxin. This test is not used clinically at the present time.

Suppurative Complications

Inflammation in the faucial area induced by acute streptococcal infection may affect structures that are directly contiguous to the pharynx or that drain that site. Such relatively rare complications include peritonsillar cellulitis, peritonsillar abscess, retropharyngeal abscess, suppurative cervical lymphadenitis, mastoiditis, acute sinusitis, and otitis media.[61] Peritonsillar or retropharyngeal abscesses, however, frequently contain a variety of other oral flora including anaerobes, with or without group A streptococci.[62] Group A streptococci are responsible for only a small minority of cases of otitis media or sinusitis.

Extension up the cribiform plate of the ethmoid or via the mastoid bone may cause meningitis, brain abscess, or thrombosis of the intracranial venous sinuses. Streptococcal pneumonia, another potential suppurative complication, is discussed later. Finally, bacteremic spread of the streptococci may result in a variety of metastatic foci of infection, such as, suppurative arthritis, endocarditis, meningitis, brain abscess, osteomyelitis, or liver abscess. Such complications of streptococcal pharyngitis are extremely rare since the advent of effective chemotherapy.

Nonsuppurative Complications

The nonsuppurative complications of streptococcal pharyngitis, acute rheumatic fever and acute post−streptococcal glomerulonephritis, are discussed in Chapter 196. The role of streptococci vis-à-vis other infectious and noninfectious agents in initiating certain other acute inflammatory disorders such as erythema nodosum and anaphylactoid purpura remains unresolved.

Diagnosis

Pharyngitis and tonsillitis may be due to a variety of infectious agents other than *S. pyogenes*.[56] Among these are streptococci of groups C[63,64] and G.[65-67] *Corynebacterium diphtheriae,* the other major bacterial pathogen associated with exudative pharyngitis, is now extremely rare in the United States,[68] and when it occurs in the classic form, it is differentiated by the appearance of the diphtheritic membrane, respiratory embarrassment, severe systemic toxicity, and myocardial and neurologic manifestations. Other bacterial agents such as *Neisseria gonorrheae* and perhaps *Neisseria meningitidis* occasionally cause pharyngitis, as does *Mycoplasma pneumoniae.*

Pharyngitis due to *Arcanobacterium* (formerly *Corynebacterium*) *hemolyticum,* although rare, may closely mimic that due to *S. pyogenes.*[69,70] *Arcanobacterium hemolyticum* affects primarily teenagers and young adults, and the patients may exhibit both an exudative pharyngitis and a scarlatiniform rash. The organism is more readily identified on rabbit or human blood agar than on sheep blood agar. Another rare cause of acute pharyngitis is *Yersinia enterocolitica.*[71] Patients infected with this organism may appear quite ill and may or may not have associated enteric symptoms. When *Y. enterocolitica* pharyngitis is associated with disseminated yersinosis, the mortality rate may be appreciable. Diagnosis depends on clinical clues because the organism is unlikely to be detected on routine throat cultures and antistreptococcal therapy is unavailing (see Chapter 226). The oropharyngeal form of tularemia is characterized by severe sore throat, exudative and ulcerative tonsillopharyngitis and cervical adenopathy (see Chapter 224).

Acute pharyngitis is more frequently caused by viruses than by bacteria. Infectious mononucleosis and adenovirus infections frequently give rise to exudative pharyngitis and thus may closely mimic streptococcal sore throat. Herpes simplex viruses 1 and 2,[72-74] influenza,[75] and parainfluenza viruses may also simulate streptococcal pharyngitis, as may initially the acute retroviral syndrome in human immunodeficiency virus infection. Pharyngitis associated with the acute retroviral syndrome is, however, not exudative.[76] Even when careful microbiologic techniques are used to detect bacteria, mycoplasma, and viruses, no etiologic agent can be detected in a substantial proportion of all cases of acute sore throat.[77] A more complete discussion of the differential diagnosis of acute pharyngitis may be found in Chapter 51.

Approximately one fourth to one third of all children complaining of sore throat have a positive throat culture for group A streptococci. Of these, about one half can be demonstrated to have immunologically significant infection, as judged by a significant rise in serum titer of one or more antistreptococcal antibodies. Many of the remainder are likely to be asymptomatic carriers, because the average carriage rate among school-age children in temperate climates during the winter months may approximate 15%. Such asymptomatic carriers are at no risk of developing suppurative and nonsuppurative complications and do not require antibiotic therapy. Although acutely infected individuals tend to have more strongly positive throat cultures, this distinction cannot be made with confidence in patients whose signs and symptoms are compatible with streptococcal pharyngitis.

Numerous studies have tested the precision with which physicians may differentiate between streptococcal and nonstreptococcal sore throat by clinical criteria alone. In the presence of a classic scarlatinal rash or during a documented epidemic of streptococcal infections, such differentiation is usually easy. On the other hand, in the case of endemically occurring infections the problem is much more complex. Certain clinical findings, particularly tonsillopharyngeal exudate and tender, enlarged lymph nodes at the angles of the jaws, have a statistically significant correlation with the presence of positive throat cultures for group A streptococci.[78] Such findings are not diagnostic, however. Although only approximately one half of the patients with immunologically proven streptococcal sore throat have tonsillar exudate, a substantial proportion of cases of exudative pharyngitis are nonstreptococcal in etiology.

It is possible to identify individual patients in which "strep throat" can be effectively excluded on a combination of epidemiologic (see earlier) and clinical grounds. For example, symptoms of the common cold are not due to *S. pyogenes*. Likewise, the presence of hoarseness and conjunctivitis and the absence of fever or pharyngeal erythema make streptococcal pharyngitis very unlikely. A number of investigators have developed clinical algorithms in children and adults to assist in determining the likelihood that a particular patient has group A streptococcal pharyngitis.[79-84] These algorithms are useful and accurate in identifying patients whose risk of streptococcal infection is so low as to obviate the need for further microbiologic testing. Controversy remains, however, as to whether such algorithms can replace diagnostic testing entirely, at least in adults.

A practice guideline[85,86] for the diagnosis of acute pharyngitis in adults is endorsed by the American College of Physicians—American Society of Internal Medicine, Centers for Disease Control and Prevention, and American Academy of Family Physicians. That guideline employs an algorithm, developed by Centor and co-workers,[84] using four clinical criteria: presence of tonsillar exudates, presence of swollen tender anterior cervical nodes (i.e., cervical lymphadenitis), lack of cough, and history of fever. These four characteristics have been reported to be independently associated with the likelihood of a positive throat culture for group A streptococci.[87] The algorithm provides two alternative management strategies: (1) empirical antimicrobial treatment of adults with at least three of four clinical criteria and nontreatment of all others and (2) empirical treatment of adults with all four criteria and performance of a group A streptococcal rapid antigen diagnostic test (RADT) in patients with three (or perhaps two) clinical criteria and treatment of those with positive tests.[86]

In the Centor study, however, approximately 60% of the adult pharyngitis patients with three or four clinical criteria had negative throat cultures.[88] Very similar results in adults were reported by McIsaac and co-workers.[82] Thus the empirical strategy could lead to a considerable amount of overtreatment.[89,89a] This is of concern in view of the fact that 73% of the 6.7 million adults visiting primary care providers annually in the United Sates with the complaint of sore throat receive a prescription for antibiotics.[90] Moreover, a cost-benefit analysis determined that empirical therapy was neither the most cost-effective nor the least expensive strategy at any level of group A streptococcal pharyngitis in adults.[91] Thus for both adults and children, expert panels recommend that the presence of group A streptococci in the pharynx should be documented by a throat culture or RADT.[92-94]

Throat Culture

Throat culture remains the gold standard for diagnosing streptococcal pharyngitis. Failure to isolate β-hemolytic streptococci in a carefully obtained and accurately interpreted throat culture rules out the diagnosis of streptococcal sore throat for practical purposes. In cases in which doubt exists as to the validity of a negative culture, it may be preferable to repeat the culture rather than to treat empirically with antimicrobial agents.

Although a negative culture eliminates the necessity for therapy, a positive culture does not differentiate between acute infection and asymptomatic carriage. Serum antibody titers do not rise until convalescence and thus are of no help in short-term management. Although the degree of positivity of the throat culture may assist in making this differentiation, it is best to assume that all positive cultures in patients with acute pharyngitis are significant and to treat accordingly, while recognizing that, even with the use of the throat culture, some degree of overtreatment is inevitable.

Detailed instructions for obtaining and processing a throat culture have been published by the American Heart Association.[95] Sheep blood agar is preferred because clear-cut patterns of hemolysis are obtained on this medium. In regard to isolation of group A streptococci, there is controversy in the literature as to the relative merits of plain sheep blood agar plates versus plates to which trimethoprim-sulfamethoxazole has been added to suppress competing normal pharyngeal flora. Similar controversy exists as to the optimal atmosphere of incubation: aerobic, aerobic in the presence of 5% to 10% carbon dioxide, or anaerobic. Detailed analysis of these issues has been published elsewhere.[96,97] If blood agar plates are not immediately available, the swab may be placed in a dry sterile tube for transportation to the laboratory. After overnight incubation at 35° C to 37° C, culture plates from patients with streptococcal pharyngitis show colonies surrounded by clear zones of hemolysis as well as β-hemolysis around the agar stab. Plates that are negative on first reading should be reexamined after an additional 24 hours of incubation. Serologic grouping of β-hemolytic streptococcal isolates may now be readily performed by using commercially available kits. Fluorescent antibody techniques provide excellent results and specifically identify group A organisms. No quantitative information is gained as to the degree of positivity of the culture. A less expensive screening procedure, the bacitracin sensitivity test, may be performed once the organism has been isolated in pure culture. This susceptibility procedure is based on the observation that greater than 95% of all group A streptococcal strains are inhibited by low-potency (0.04 unit) bacitracin disks, whereas 80% to 90% of non—group A strains are resistant.

Because no group A streptococci resistant to penicillin have yet been described, antibiotic testing is unnecessary if this drug is to be used. The same holds true in general for erythromycin because group A streptococci resistant to this drug are rare in the United States at this time.[98,99] Rates of erythromycin resistance in excess of 5% have, however, been reported in certain localized areas.[100-103] In areas where resistance to erythromycin is known to be prevalent, antimicrobial susceptibility testing should be performed if this agent or the newer macrolides are used to treat group A streptococcal infections.

Rapid Antigen Detection Tests

These tests allow detection of the presence of the group A carbohydrate antigen directly from throat swabs. Unlike the throat culture, which requires overnight or longer to yield a definitive result, RADT can be completed in a matter of minutes. By facilitating early diagnosis and therapy, an RADT may shorten the duration of illness, decrease secondary spread of the organism, and allow earlier return of patients and parents to school and work. Earlier tests based on latex agglutination methodology have been largely replaced by enzyme immunoassays that are easier to interpret and more sensitive. More recently, tests using optical immunoassay (OIA) and chemiluminescent DNA probes have become available.

Most currently commercially available RADTs are highly specific (≥95%), so a positive result obviates the need for a throat culture. Unfortunately, the sensitivity of these tests is lower than that of the conventional throat culture, and therefore they may be negative in patients in whom conventional culture proves to be positive. Investigators[104,105] have found newer tests such as optical immunoassay to have sensitivity equivalent to that of culture, but others have reached opposite conclusions.[106-108] At the present time, the American Academy of Pediatrics recommends that a negative RADT be confirmed with a throat culture. In view of conflicting data about sensitivity of commercially available RADTs, as well as the paucity of studies directly comparing the various tests with each other, physicians who elect to use any RADT in children and adolescents without culture backup of negative results should do so only after confirming in their own practice that the rapid test is comparable in sensitivity to the throat culture.[94]

In considering appropriate laboratory diagnostic testing for adults, certain epidemiologic distinctions from pediatric disease deserve consideration. The group A streptococcus causes 15% to 30% of cases of acute pharyngitis in pediatric patients but only 5% to 10% of such illnesses in adults.[83,109,110] (However, the risk of streptococcal pharyngitis may be higher in parents of school-aged children and adults whose occupation brings them into close association with children.) Moreover, the risk of a first attack of acute rheumatic fever is extremely low in adults, even if they experience an undiagnosed and untreated episode of streptococcal pharyngitis. These facts make performance of RADT without culture backup of negative results an acceptable alternative to throat culture.[92] The generally high specificity of RADTs should minimize overprescribing of antimicrobials in adults. This later point is of particular importance in view of national data indicating that antibiotics are prescribed for approximately three fourths of adults consulting community primary care physicians for the complaint of sore throat and that the prescription of more expensive, broader-spectrum antibiotics is frequent.[90]

Physicians who wish to ensure they are achieving maximal sensitivity in diagnosis may continue to use the conventional throat culture or to back up a negative RADT with a culture.

Treatment

Antimicrobial therapy is indicated for individuals with symptomatic pharyngitis after the presence of the organism in the throat is confirmed by culture or RADT. The goals of antimicrobial therapy are (1) prevention of acute rheumatic fever, (2) prevention of suppurative complications, (3) improvement in clinical symptoms and signs, and (4) rapid decrease in infectivity so as to reduce transmission of group A β-hemolytic streptococci to family members, classmates, and other close contacts and to allow the rapid resumption of usual activities. There is no firm evidence that post−streptococcal acute glomerulonephritis is preventable by treatment of the antecedent streptococcal infection.[111]

Treatment of group A streptococcal sore throat as long as 9 days after onset is still effective in the prevention of rheumatic fever.[112] Thus if the patient is seen early in the course of his illness, the delay in initiation of therapy occasioned by obtaining a positive throat culture is not ordinarily a matter of concern in this regard. As discussed earlier, patients with signs and symptoms of acute pharyngitis and a positive rapid test (properly performed and interpreted) for group A carbohydrate antigen should receive appropriate antimicrobial therapy.

In the minority of patients who are severely ill or toxic at presentation and in whom there is clinical and epidemiologic evidence resulting in a high index of suspicion, oral antimicrobial therapy can be initiated while awaiting the results of the throat culture (either as a primary diagnostic tool or in confirmation of a negative RADT). If oral therapy is prescribed, a positive throat culture serves as a guide to the necessity of completion of a full antimicrobial course or, alternatively, of recalling the patient for an injection of penicillin G benzathine. Early initiation of antimicrobial therapy results in faster resolution of the signs and symptoms,[58-60] but Group A streptococcal pharyngitis is usually a self-limited disease; fever and constitutional symptoms are markedly diminished within 3 or 4 days of onset even without antimicrobial therapy.[113] Thus antimicrobial therapy initiated within the first 48 hours of onset hastens symptomatic improvement by only 1 to 2 days.

The drug of choice in the treatment of streptococcal infection is penicillin, because of its efficacy in the prevention of rheumatic fever, safety, narrow spectrum, and low cost[92-94,114] (Table 195-1). Prevention of acute rheumatic fever is believed to require eradication of the infecting streptococcus from the pharynx, an effect that depends on prolonged rather than high-dose penicillin therapy. This objective may be accomplished by the administration of a single injection of 1.2 million units of penicillin G benzathine. For children weighing less than 60 pounds, the dose is reduced to 600,000 units. Most physicians in the United States, however, elect to administer oral therapy. In this case, penicillin V, in one of the regimens listed in Table 195-1, must be con-

TABLE 195-1 Antimicrobial Therapy for Group A Streptococcal Pharyngitis[*]

Drug	*Dose*	*Duration*
Oral		
Penicillin V[†]	250 mg 2-3 times daily for children	10 days
	250 mg 4 times daily or 500 mg 2 times daily for adolescents and adults	
Intramuscular		
Penicillin G benzathine	600,000 units for patients weighing ≤27 kg (60 lb)	1 dose
	1,200,000 units for patients weighing >27 kg	
Penicillin G benzathine combined with penicillin G procaine[‡]	Varies with formulation	1 dose
For Patients Allergic to Penicillin[§]		
Erythromycin estolate[ǁ]	20-40 mg/kg of body weight/day orally, divided into 2 to 4 doses (maximum, 1 g/day)	10 days
Erythromycin ethyl-succinate	40 mg/kg/day, divided into 2 to 4 oral doses (maximum 1600 mg/day)	10 days
Erythromycin stearate	1 g/day, divided into 2 or 4 oral doses for adolescents and adults	10 days
First-generation cephalosporins[¶]	Varies with agent and patient age	10 days

[*]Modified from Bisno et al.[92,110]
[†]Due to issues of palatability, amoxicillin suspension may be used in children unable to swallow tablets.
[‡]These mixtures contain less than 1.2 million units of benzathine penicillin G and are not recommended for adolescents and adults.
[§]Azithromycin and clarithromycin are acceptable alternatives to erythromycin in the penicillin-allergic patient but are much more expensive.
[ǁ]Erythromycin estolate should not be prescribed to pregnant women because of a reported increased risk of cholestatic hepatitis.
[¶]These agents should not be used to treat patients with immediate-type hypersensitivity to β-lactam antibiotics.

tinued for a full 10 days, Amoxicillin is often prescribed in preference to penicillin V in children requiring liquid medication because of poor palatability of oral suspensions of penicillin V. Preliminary investigations have demonstrated that once daily amoxicillin therapy is effective in the treatment of group A streptococcal pharyngitis.[115,116] If confirmed by additional investigations, once-daily amoxicillin therapy, because of its convenience, low cost, and relatively narrow spectrum, could become an alternative regimen for the treatment of group A β-hemolytic streptococcal pharyngitis.

A variable percentage of patients, averaging approximately 15%,[117] continue to harbor group A streptococci of the original infecting serotype in their pharynx after completion of a course of oral penicillin. Such bacteriologic treatment failures are sometimes associated with symptomatic relapse. Because penicillin is ineffective in eradicating asymptomatic streptococcal pharyngeal carriage, apparent treatment failures may actually represent persistence of such carriage in patients with superimposed viral pharyngitis.[118]

In penicillin-allergic patients, erythromycin is the therapy of choice[92,93] (see Table 195-1). The newer macrolides (azithromycin, clarithromycin) appear to be effective, but these agents are more expensive than erythromycin. There have been reports of relatively high levels of resistance to macrolide and azalide antibiotics from several countries,[119-121] but less than 5% of group A streptococci isolated in the United States have been shown to be resistant to erythromycin.[98,99] Although there have been recent isolated reports of macrolide resistance in the United States,[102,103] such resistance does not appear to be widespread at the present time. The mechanisms of this emerging problem have been studied extensively (see Chapters 17 and 28). However, given the increasing use of azalides for upper and lower respiratory tract infections, the situation may change. Physicians should therefore be cognizant of local patterns of antimicrobial resistance.

Oral cephalosporins are highly effective in the treatment of streptococcal pharyngitis, and a meta-analysis of 19 studies suggests that streptococcal eradication rates and clinical cure rates attained with these agents are slightly higher than those achieved with penicillin.[117,122] This analysis, particularly as regards cure rates, has however been strongly challenged on methodologic grounds.[123] Penicillin remains the drug of choice as recommended by expert committees of the American Heart Association,[93] American Academy of Pediatrics,[94] and Infectious Diseases Society of America.[92] First-generation oral cephalosporins are, however, acceptable alternatives in the penicillin-allergic patient whose allergy is not of the immediate type. The physician should bear in mind the possibility of an increased risk of allergic reactions to cephalosporins when treating penicillin-allergic patients.

There has been considerable recent interest in abbreviated courses of antimicrobial therapy. It has been reported that clarithromycin,[124] cefuroxime,[125] cefixime,[126] ceftibuten,[127] cefdinir,[128] cefpodoxime,[129] and azithromycin[130-133] are effective in eradication of group A streptococci from the pharynx when administered for 5 days or less, although only the latter three are approved for a 5-day course of therapy by the U.S. Food and Drug Administration (FDA) at this writing. The potential ecologic effects of using broader-spectrum agents to treat such a common bacterial infection are of concern. This is especially true in the case of macrolides, whose widespread use has been associated with development of resistance by group A streptococci.[119,120] Moreover, even when administered for short courses, these agents are considerably more expensive than penicillin.

Because tetracycline-resistant group A streptococci are prevalent in many areas, this drug is not recommended. Sulfonamides, which are effective in secondary prophylaxis of rheumatic fever (see Chapter 196), are ineffective in the eradication of pharyngeal organisms or in the prevention of rheumatic fever when used as therapy for acute pharyngeal infections.

Patients with more severe suppurative infections such as those involving the mastoid or ethmoid may require larger doses of penicillin administered parenterally. When streptococcal upper respiratory infection is complicated by the development of abscesses associated with suppurative cervical adenitis or in the peritonsillar or retropharyngeal soft tissues, aspiration or incision and drainage are usually required.

Because prevention of rheumatic fever appears to require eradication of the streptococcus from the pharynx, treatment failures are of concern. In addition to true treatment failure (i.e., reisolation of the original infecting streptococcal serotype shortly after completion of a full course of antibiotic therapy), causes of post-treatment culture positivity include failure of compliance with oral medication schedules and reinfection with the same or different streptococcal types in the home or school environment. Apparent failure may also occur when the patient is in reality a streptococcal carrier suffering from an acute viral pharyngitis. In everyday practice, it is often impossible to differentiate between these alternatives.

Nevertheless, routine reculture of the throat after a course of antistreptococcal therapy is not advised[92] because the cost-benefit ratio of such cultures continues to decline in parallel with the incidence of acute rheumatic fever in developed countries. Certainly such cultures should be undertaken in high-risk circumstances (e.g., if the patient or a family member has a history of rheumatic fever) or when symptoms compatible with streptococcal infection persist or recur. When an increased incidence of acute rheumatic fever is detected in a community, as happened in a number of U.S. cities during the 1980s, the approach to streptococcal infection must be particularly rigorous, and serious consideration should be given to routine performance of post-treatment cultures. If reculture is undertaken, only a single retreatment course is warranted for patients who still harbor group A streptococci. Retreatment with an oral cephalosporin might be considered, in view of the slightly increased eradication rates observed with these agents.

The presence of persistently but weakly positive throat cultures after repeated courses of antibiotic therapy in an otherwise asymptomatic patient is not a cause for alarm. Such persons are streptococcal carriers[118] who are neither at risk of developing rheumatic fever nor highly likely to spread their infection to others. Their most frequent problem is anxiety produced by multiple medical consultations associated with the streptococcal colonization. In the event in which, for medical or psychological reasons, eradication of chronic streptococcal carriage becomes highly desirable, clindamycin,[134] amoxicillin-clavulanate,[135] or azithromycin may be efficacious.[92,136]

Streptococcal acquisition rates of 25% or greater have been recorded in family contacts. Certainly, family contacts with symptoms of upper respiratory infection should be cultured and treated appropriately if positive. Asymptomatic family contacts should also be cultured in high-risk circumstances, such as the presence of a person in the family who has had rheumatic fever or known cases of rheumatic fever or poststreptococcal glomerulonephritis occurring in the general area. In situations of lesser risk, routine culture of asymptomatic family contacts is not recommended.[92,93] The advisability of culture and/or prophylaxis of household contacts of patients with invasive group A streptococcal infection is discussed later.[136]

There is no firm evidence to suggest that tonsillectomy reduces the incidence of rheumatic fever, either in healthy persons or in persons who have had rheumatic fever and faithfully maintained continuous antibiotic prophylaxis. In certain patients with recurrent bouts of tonsillopharyngitis, however, tonsillectomy may decrease the frequency of incapacitating acute infections.[137] Clearly, tonsillectomy should be considered in only the most severely affected patients.[138]

STREPTOCOCCAL PYODERMA

Pyoderma, impetigo, and *impetigo contagiosa* are terms used synonymously to describe discrete purulent lesions that are primary infections of the skin and that are extremely prevalent in many parts of the world. In the great majority of cases, pyoderma is caused by β-hemolytic streptococci and/or *Staphylococcus aureus*.

Epidemiology

Pyoderma occurs most frequently among economically disadvantaged children dwelling in tropical or subtropical climates. It is also prevalent

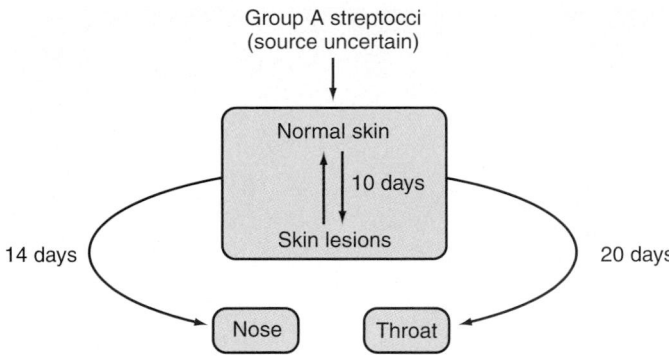

FIGURE 195-3. Representative sequence of the spread of pyoderma strains of group A streptococci among different body sites. *(From Ferrieri P, Dajani AS, Wannamaker LW, Chapman SS. Natural history of impetigo. I. Site sequence of acquisition and familial patterns of spread of cutaneous streptococci. J Clin Invest. 1972;51:2851-2862, with permission.)*

in northern climates during the summer months of the year.[139] The peak incidence of impetigo is in children aged 2 to 5 years. This disorder also occurs among older children and adults whose recreational activities or occupation results in cutaneous cuts or abrasions.[140,141] There is no sex predilection, and all races appear to be susceptible.

The prevalence of streptococcal pyoderma is markedly influenced by several factors, the most important of which appear to be climate and level of hygiene. Studies among Colombian schoolchildren[142] showed the lowest prevalence in Bogotá (8700-ft elevation, cool climate), intermediate prevalence in Medellin (5000-ft elevation, temperate climate), and highest incidence in Apartado (sea level, tropical climate). At each level of elevation, skin lesions were more frequent among persons with poor hygiene than among those with good hygiene. Among Colombian military troops in the field, those conducting operations in humid tropical rain forests experienced a considerably greater incidence of pyoderma than those operating in the dry tropical savanna.

Meticulous prospective studies of streptococcal impetigo have demonstrated that the responsible microorganisms initially colonize the unbroken skin,[139] an observation that probably explains the influence of personal hygiene on disease incidence. Development of skin colonization with a given streptococcal strain precedes the development of impetiginous lesions by an average interval of 10 days (Fig. 195-3). The mechanism of production of skin lesions is unproved, but it is most likely due to intradermal inoculation of surface organisms by abrasions, minor trauma, or insect bites. Frequently there is a transfer of the streptococcal strains from the skin and/or pyoerma lesions to the upper respiratory tract. The interval between colonization of the skin and colonization of nose and/or throat averages 2 to 3 weeks.

Bacteriology and Immunology

Streptococci isolated from pyodermal lesions are primarily group A, but occasionally representatives of other serogroups such as C and G are responsible. Group A streptococci that cause impetigo differ in several respects from those usually associated with tonsillitis and pharyngitis. "Skin strains" belong to different M serotypes or genotypes from the classic "throat strains"; because most have been identified more recently, they tend to comprise the higher-numbered M types. Throat and skin strains can also be differentiated by genetic markers.[143]

The well-known streptococcal M types that frequently give rise to exudative tonsillitis (e.g., types 1, 3, 5, 6, 12, 18, 19, 24, and others) are rarely found in pyoderma lesions. (This is not necessarily true of more deeply invasive skin and soft tissue infections, as discussed later.) On the other hand, as pointed out before, "skin strains" frequently colonize the throat. In populations in which pyoderma is highly endemic, streptococcal carriage rates of 10% to 15% are seen during the warmer months, and most of these streptococci belong to "pyoderma" serotypes. For the most part, however, "skin strains"

cause few or no symptoms when lodged in the throat. A relatively small number of serotypes seem capable of regularly initiating both pharyngitis and pyoderma.[144]

Assays of streptococcal antibodies are of no value in diagnosis and management of impetigo, but they provide helpful supporting evidence of recent streptococcal infection in patients suspected of having post–streptococcal glomerulonephritis. The ASO response is weak in patients with streptococcal impetigo,[145,146] presumably because streptolysin O response is suppressed by skin lipids,[147] whereas anti–DNase B levels are elevated.[145,146]

In uncomplicated pyoderma, type-specific opsonic antibodies are detectable 2 to 3 months after the development of infection. In one study[148] such antibodies were present in 12% of a small group of patients with pyoderma alone but in over half of the people who had concomitant pharyngeal carriage. In another study, type-specific antibodies were present in most patients convalescing from pyoderma-associated nephritis due to M type 55.[149] It is not yet known whether such antibodies play a role in the prevention of reinfection analogous to that which has been established in pharyngeal infections.

Clinical Manifestations

The lesion of streptococcal pyoderma begins as a papule that rapidly evolves into a vesicle surrounded by an area of erythema. The vesicular lesions are evanescent and rarely recognized clinically; they give rise to pustules that gradually enlarge and then break down over a period of 4 to 6 days to form characteristic thick crusts (Fig. 195-4). The lesions heal slowly and leave depigmented areas. A deeply ulcerated form of impetigo is known as *ecthyma.*

Streptococcal impetigo occurs on exposed areas of the body, most frequently on the lower extremities or face. The lesions remain well localized but are frequently multiple. Although regional lymphadenitis may occur, systemic symptoms are not ordinarily present.

In the past, the lesions described above could be rather confidently diagnosed as streptococcal. This was the predominant form of impetigo and could be distinguished from bullous impetigo due to phage group II *S. aureus.* Although bullous impetigo remains almost exclusively staphylococcal in etiology, the bacteriology of nonbullous impetigo has changed.[150] A number of studies conducted over the past decade have found *S. aureus,* either alone or in combination with *S. pyogenes,* to be the predominant etiologic agent.[151-153] Nearly all such staphylococci are penicillinase producers. Therefore, treatment with penicillin, which in the past had been highly effective in nonbullous impetigo even when both streptococci and staphylococci were isolated from the lesions, now frequently fails.[152]

Therapy and Prevention

Due to the current frequency of isolation of *S. aureus* from nonbullous impetigo lesions and concomitant reports of penicillin failures,[152,154,155]

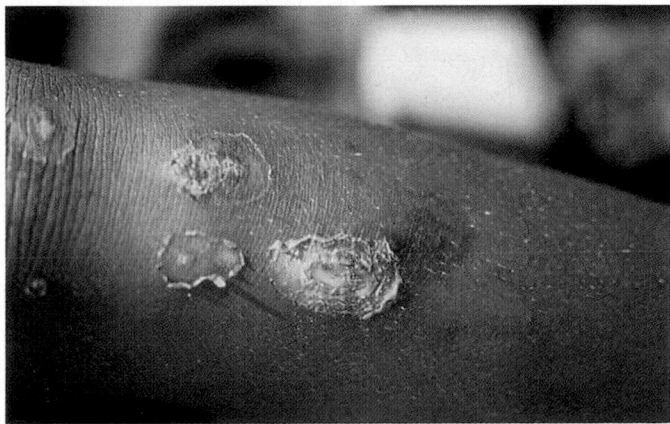

FIGURE 195-4. Multiple pyoderma lesions on the lower extremities of a child in rural Mississippi. *(Courtesy of Dr. K. Nelson, Baltimore, MD.)*

penicillinase-resistant penicillins or first-generation cephalosporins are to be preferred.[152] Erythromycin has long been a mainstay of pyoderma therapy, but its use may be lessened in areas in which erythromycin-resistant strains of *S. aureus* or, more recently, *S. pyogenes* are prevalent. Therapy is usually continued for 10 days. Topical therapy with mupirocin is equivalent to oral systemic antimicrobials[156,157] and may be used when lesions are limited in number. It is expensive, however, and some strains of staphylococci may be resistant.[158] Adherence to good regimens of personal hygiene is the most effective preventive measure currently available.

Complications

Suppurative complications are quite uncommon. For as yet unexplained reasons, rheumatic fever does not occur after streptococcal pyoderma. On the other hand, cutaneous infections with nephritogenic strains of group A streptococci are the major antecedent of poststreptococcal glomerulonephritis in many areas of the world. There are as yet no conclusive data to indicate that treatment of an individual case of pyoderma prevents the subsequent occurrence of nephritis in these patients. Such therapy is nevertheless important as an epidemiologic measure in eradicating nephritogenic strains from the environment.

INVASIVE STREPTOCOCCAL INFECTIONS OF SKIN AND SOFT TISSUES

In the mid 1980s outbreaks of acute rheumatic fever began to occur throughout the United States, concomitant with the reappearance of certain streptococcal strains exhibiting characteristics known to be associated with rheumatogenicity (see Chapter 196). Shortly thereafter, invasive streptococcal infections, of a frequency and severity not seen in the preceding decades, began to be reported both in the United States and abroad.[159-162] Although strains of a number of group A streptococcal M types have been isolated from invasive infections, there has been a definite and consistent tendency for M types 1 and 3 to be associated with life-threatening infections.[160-164] A high proportion of these cases has occurred in adults, and the portal of entry is frequently the skin or soft tissues. In some instances the infections give rise to shock and multiorgan failure, features that simulate in certain respects the staphylococcal toxic shock syndrome.[165] This entity has thus been named Strep TSS. Clinical features of serious streptococcal skin and soft tissue infections and TSS are summarized later.

Erysipelas

Erysipelas is a superficial cutaneous process, usually restricted to the dermis but with prominent lymphatic involvement. It is distinguished clinically from other forms of cutaneous infection by two features: the lesions are raised above the level of the surrounding skin, and there is a clear line of demarcation between involved and uninvolved tissue. This disorder is more common in infants, young children, and older adults. It is almost always caused by β-hemolytic streptococci. In most cases the infecting agent is the group A streptococci, but similar lesions can be caused by streptococci of group C or G. Rarely, group B streptococci or *S. aureus* may be the culprits. In older reports, erysipelas was described as characteristically involving the butterfly area of the face (Fig. 195-5), but at present the lower extremities are more frequently involved (Fig. 195-6). In patients with facial erysipelas, there is frequently a history of preceding streptococcal sore throat, although the exact mode of spread to the skin is unknown. When erysipelas involves the extremities, breaks in the cutaneous barrier serve as portals of entry; these include surgical incisions, trauma or abrasions, dermatologic diseases such as psoriasis, or local fungal infections.

The cutaneous lesion begins as a localized area of erythema and swelling and then spreads rapidly with advancing red margins, which are raised and well demarcated from adjacent normal tissue. There is marked edema, often with bleb formation, and in facial erysipelas the eyes are frequently swollen shut. The lesion may demonstrate central

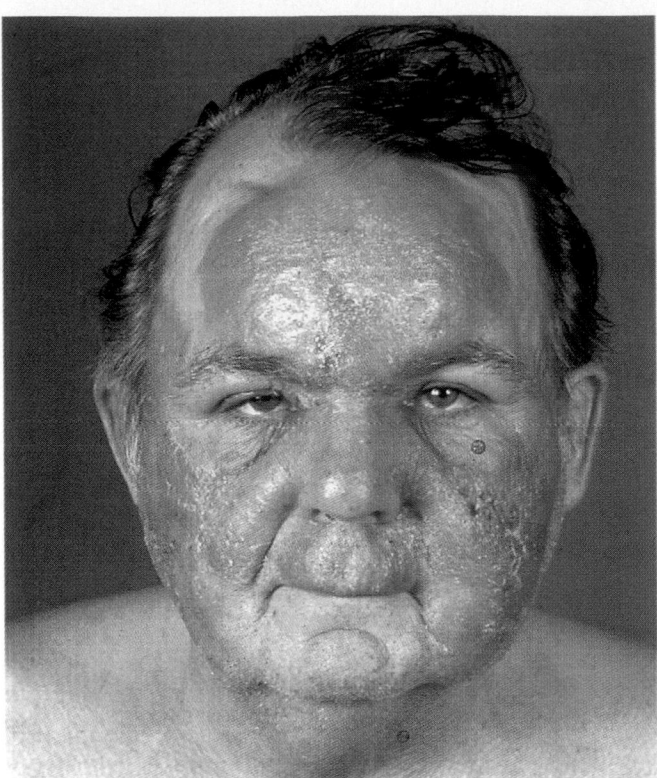

FIGURE 195-5. Facial erysipelas. The lesion is well demarcated from surrounding skin and illustrates the typical "butterfly" distribution. *(From Bisno AL. Cutaneous infections: Microbiologic and epidemiologic considerations. Am J Med. 1984;76[5A]:172-179, with permission.)*

resolution while continuing to extend on the periphery. The cutaneous inflammation is accompanied by chills, fever, and toxicity.

The differential diagnosis is limited. Early on, the lesions of facial herpes zoster, contact dermatitis or giant urticaria may be confused with erysipelas. Lesions resembling erysipelas may occur in patients with familial Mediterranean fever. Cutaneous lesions similar in appearance to those of erysipelas may occur on the hands of patients who sustain cuts or abrasions while handling fish or meats. This entity, known as erysipeloid of Rosenbach and caused by *Erysipelothrix rhusiopathiae*, is usually unaccompanied by fever or systemic symptoms.

With early diagnosis and treatment, the prognosis is excellent. Rarely, however, the process may spread to deeper levels of the skin and soft tissues. Penicillin, either parenterally or orally, depending on clinical severity, is the treatment of choice. If staphylococcal infection is suspected, a penicillin-resistant, semisynthetic penicillin or cephalosporin should be selected. In a randomized, prospective multicenter trial,[166] roxithromycin, a macrolide antimicrobial, was equivalent to penicillin. Increased levels of macrolide resistance among group A streptococci, however, have been detected in certain areas of the United States.[102,103]

Streptococcal Cellulitis

Streptococcal cellulitis, an acute, spreading inflammation of the skin and subcutaneous tissues, results from infection of burns, wounds, or surgical incisions but may also follow mild trauma. Clinical findings include local pain, tenderness, swelling, and erythema. The process may extend rapidly to involve large areas of skin. Systemic manifestations include fever, chills, and malaise, and there may be associated lymphangitis or bacteremia, or both. In contrast to erysipelas, the lesion is not raised, and the demarcation between involved and uninvolved skin is indistinct. Often, however, the clinical differentiation between these entities is not clear-cut.

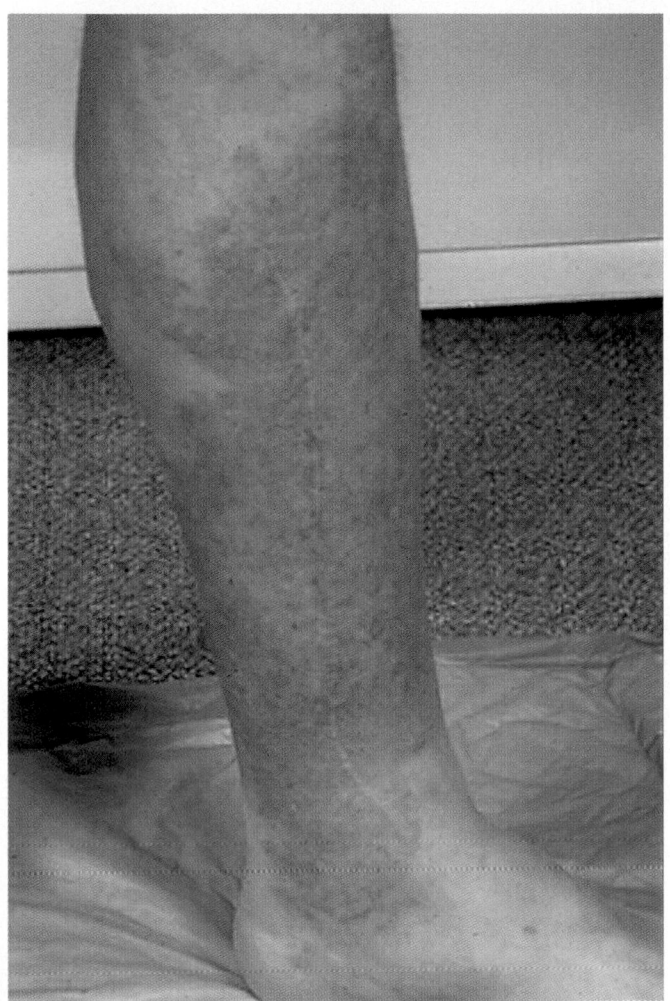

FIGURE 195-6. Erysipelas in saphenous venectomy limb of a patient who had undergone coronary artery bypass grafting.

Two predisposing causes of streptococcal cellulitis deserve special mention. One is the parenteral injection of illicit drugs.[167-169] These cases are often associated with bacteremia and deep tissue infections such as septic thrombophlebitis, suppurative arthritis, osteomyelitis, and occasionally infective endocarditis. Second, patients who have impaired lymphatic drainage from upper or lower extremities are prone to recurrent episodes of streptococcal cellulitis. Examples include individuals with filariasis and women who have undergone radical mastectomy with axillary node dissection.[170] It is speculated that repetitive infection further damages local lymphatics and worsens lymphatic stasis.[171]

Recurrent episodes of severe cellulitis have also been reported in certain patients who have undergone coronary artery bypass grafting.[172] The lesion invariably occurs in the extremity from which the saphenous vein was removed, and at times it may exhibit features of erysipelas (Fig. 195-6). Patients with tinea pedis of the venectomy limb appear to be particularly at risk.[173-175] As with other forms of cellulitis, pathogenic bacteria are difficult to recover during these episodes. The appearance of the lesions and the response to penicillin therapy suggest, however, a streptococcal etiology. The few β-hemolytic streptococci that have been recovered and characterized often belong to serogroups other than A.[176]

Disruption of the cutaneous barrier (leg ulcers, wounds, dermatophytosis) is a risk factor for development of cutaneous streptococcal infection.[177] Indeed, there is suggestive evidence that local dermatophyte infection (i.e., athlete's foot) may serve as a reservoir for β-hemolytic streptococci that initiate episodes of erysipelas or cellulitis

of the lower extremities.[173,178] Thus, care should be taken to eradicate such fungal infections in patients who experience recurrent bouts of erysipelas or cellulitis. Another potential reservoir is anal streptococcal colonization.[179] Other risk factors include venous insufficiency, edema, and obesity.[177]

Cellulitis may be caused by infection with a variety of bacterial pathogens (see Chapter 86), but most cases are due to *S. pyogenes* (or occasionally streptococci of groups B, C, and G) or to *S. aureus*. In the absence of positive blood cultures, which are present in only 5% of cases of cellulitis, a specific microbiologic diagnosis is often not possible. Aspirate or biopsy samples from sites of active cellulitis are helpful when positive on smear or culture, but unfortunately such specimens are usually negative in adult patients.[180-182]

Although intramuscular or intravenous penicillin is the drug of choice for severe forms of streptococcal cellulitis, it is often impossible to confidently differentiate streptococcal from staphylococcal cellulitis on initial presentation. In this case a semisynthetic, penicillinase-resistant penicillin should be used. In penicillin-allergic patients, a first-generation cephalosporin may be used if the hypersensitivity is not of the immediate type. Clindamycin or vancomycin may be used in patients who manifest anaphylactic hypersensitivity to β-lactam antibiotics, and the latter should be administered if there is reason to suspect infection with methicillin-resistant strains of *S. aureus*. Patients with milder cases of streptococcal cellulitis may be switched to oral medications after an initial favorable response to parenteral therapy.

The role of continuous antimicrobial prophylaxis[183-185] in patients prone to frequent recurrences remains unsettled. At present, such prophylaxis seems justified only in patients with very frequent or severe episodes, and the optimal regimen has not been established.

Necrotizing Fasciitis (Streptococcal Gangrene)

Necrotizing fasciitis is an infection of the deeper subcutaneous tissues and fascia, characterized by extensive and rapidly spreading necrosis and by gangrene of the skin and underlying structures. As detailed in Chapter 72, this entity may arise in several distinct epidemiologic settings, be caused by multiple aerobic and anaerobic microorganisms, and vary in clinical manifestations. The present discussion is limited to necrotizing fasciitis caused by the group A streptococcus[186] and described by Meleney[187] in 1924 as hemolytic streptococcal gangrene. Characteristically, streptococcal gangrene begins at a site of trivial or even inapparent trauma or in an operative incision. The initial lesion may appear only as an area of mild erythema but over the next 24 to 72 hours undergoes a rapid evolution. The inflammation becomes more pronounced and extensive, the skin becomes dusky and then purplish, and bullae containing yellow or hemorrhagic fluid appear. Bacteremia is frequently present, and metastatic abscesses may occur. By the fourth to fifth day, frank gangrenous changes are evident in the affected skin,[188] and this is followed by extensive sloughing. The process may march inexorably over large bodily areas unless measures are taken to contain it. The patient with streptococcal gangrene appears perilously ill, with high fever and extreme prostration. Mortality rates are high even with appropriate treatment.[188] Fournier's gangrene, a form of necrotizing fasciitis involving the male genital area, may rarely be due to group A streptococci.

The course of necrotizing fasciitis today appears to be much more fulminant than that described by Meleney. Specifically, ecchymoses and bullae may appear within 2 to 3 days and associated myonecrosis is more common. In addition, the mortality rate in 1924 was 20%, whereas mortality rates of 20% to 70% have been reported in the current era. This difference is even more remarkable because antibiotics, intravenous fluids, ventilators, and dialysis were not available in 1924.

Diagnosis and Differential Diagnosis

Successful management of necrotizing fasciitis is dependent on early recognition, yet early in their course, patients may present with fever and toxicity at a time when the cutaneous lesion may appear relatively benign.[189] Fever and severe pain are the first manifestations of disease. In those with a defined portal of entry such as a surgical incision, burn, insect bite or varicella lesion, there is redness of the skin, pain, and swelling. In the 50% of patients who develop necrotizing fasciitis without a defined portal of entry, the infection begins deep to the skin, frequently at the site of a hematoma, muscle strain, or traumatic joint injury. In these, crescendo pain is the most reliable clinical clue.

Routine radiographs, computed tomography (CT) scanning, and magnetic resonance imaging (MRI) may show localized swelling of the deep structures but characteristically do not show frank abscess formation or gas in the tissue and *thus are not definitive procedures.* This is particularly problematic in those patients without a portal of entry who have deep infection at the site of recent trauma such as muscle tear, hematoma, or prior surgery, in which the clinician cannot distinguish the cause of the deep swelling. Unfortunately, imaging studies often serve to delay rather than facilitate a diagnosis. Fever and increasingly severe pain are the best and earliest signs of infection. Some patients do not present with fever,[189] and others may have taken nonsteroidal anti-inflammatory drugs that mask fever and reduce pain. Unexplained tachycardia, marked left shift, and elevated creatine phosphokinase are also important clues to the diagnosis of necrotizing fasciitis, and their presence should prompt surgical inspection of the deep tissues. Gram stains of aspirated fluid reveal chains of gram-positive cocci that contain few, if any, white blood cells. Similarly, a biopsy with frozen section may aid in the diagnosis of necrotizing fasciitis.[190,190a]

Myositis and Myonecrosis

Most cases of purulent muscle infection occur in the tropics, and *S. aureus* is the predominant etiologic agent. Myositis due to the group A streptococci has been rare but occurs in many patients with necrotizing fasciitis and Strep TSS. Most of these cases occur after blunt, nonpenetrating trauma or occur spontaneously. Most likely bacteria are translocated to the deep tissue hematogenously from the throat. Systemic toxicity is common and mortality as high as 80% has been reported.[191] Destruction of tissue is poorly understood, but infection and inflammation within the confined muscle compartment space may result in pressures exceeding arterial pressure, necessitating emergent fasciotomy and débridement (Fig. 195-7). There is much overlap in the clinical features of necrotizing fasciitis and myonecrosis,[188,191] and the differentiation must be made by surgical inspection or biopsy.

Streptococcal Toxic Shock Syndrome

Strep TSS is defined as described in Table 195-2, but, simply put, it is any streptococcal infection associated with the sudden onset of shock and organ failure. Such cases were first described in the mid to late

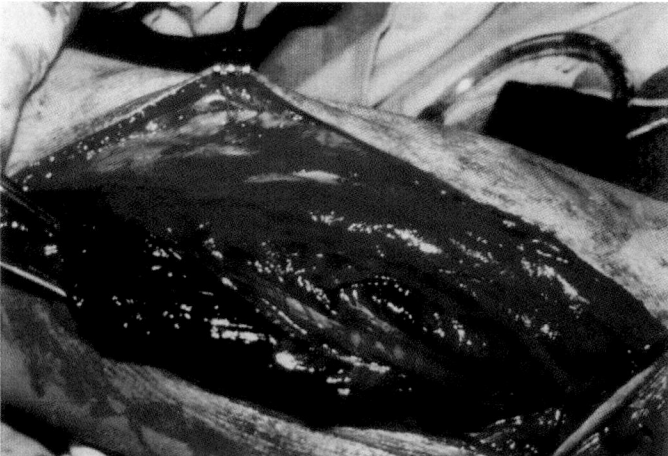

FIGURE 195-7. Surgical exploration of patient with streptococcal toxic shock syndrome with necrotizing fasciitis and myositis that occurred spontaneously with no prior injury to site. *(From Stevens D. Streptococcal toxic shock syndrome. Infect Med. 1992;9:33-39, with permission.)*

1980s, and reports of Strep TSS have subsequently emanated from North America, Europe, Australia, and Asia.[160,164,165,192-200] Most cases have occurred sporadically. The highest incidence of invasive streptococcal disease occurred recently in a small community of Minnesota where 26 cases per 100,000 population were recorded.[199] In addition, outbreaks of invasive group A streptococcal infections have occurred in closed environments such as nursing homes[201-205] and hospital environments.[206] Secondary cases of Strep TSS are unusual, but transmission to family members[206,207] or health care workers[206,208] has been well documented by demonstrating identical pulsed-field gel electrophoresis patterns from cross-infecting strains. Although many of the studies cited earlier have described Strep TSS in adults, several reports have documented that this disorder also occurs in children.[193,198,199,209,210] Thus persons of all ages are afflicted, and although some have underlying medical conditions such as diabetes and alcoholism,[193,195,211-215] many have no predisposing medical condition and are not immunocompromised. This contrasts sharply with reviews of group A streptococcal bacteremia from several decades ago[211-213] that found the disease to occur primarily among the very young, the very old, or patients with predisposing conditions such as cancer, renal failure, leukemia, severe burns, or iatrogenic immunosuppression.

The portals of entry for streptococci are the vagina, pharynx, mucosa, and skin in 50% of cases.[164] Surgical procedures such as suction lipectomy, hysterectomy, vaginal delivery, bunionectomy, reduction mammoplasty, hernia repair, bone pinning, and vasectomy have provided portals in such cases (Table 195-3). Rarely, infection occurs secondary to streptococcal pharyngitis.[216-218] Virus infections such as varicella and influenza have provided portals of entry in other cases.[164,198,216]

Additional factors that increase the risk of invasive group A streptococcal infection, including bacteremia, Strep TSS, and necrotizing fasciitis, are listed in Table 195-3. Three studies have demonstrated that a high or increasing prevalence of M-1 or M-3 strains among throat isolates may signal an increased incidence of Strep TSS in that community.[198,214,219] Nonsteroidal anti-inflammatory agents, taken for muscle strain, trauma, postpartum pain, etc., may mask the early signs and symptoms of streptococcal infection or possibly predispose to more severe infection such as necrotizing fasciitis or Strep TSS.[164,220,221]

Pathogenesis

Entry of group A streptococci into the deeper tissues and blood stream may occur as a result of breach of a barrier, or the organism itself may penetrate intact mucous membranes such as the pharyngeal mucosa. Although bacteremia is a very uncommon phenomenon in streptococcal pharyngitis, transient bacteremia must occur in those 50% of patients who develop invasive infections without a portal of entry. In either case, group A streptococci avoid phagocytosis largely due to the antiphagocytic properties of M protein.[11] Adherence of group A streptococci to pharyngeal mucosal cells is a prerequisite to colonization or infection and has been related to surface structures such as lipoteichoic acid and fibronectin binding proteins. Penetration or translocation of group A streptococci through respiratory epithelial cells has recently been demonstrated for M-1 types of group A streptococci. Some suggest that those M-1 strains possessing an invasin (*inv+*) gene penetrate more efficiently.[222] If penetration of mucosal barriers occurs commonly, it does not result in clinically detectable bacteremia in the vast majority of patients since the incidence of invasive infection is very low, that is, 3.5 cases per 100,000 population.[223] Thus, clearance of group A streptococci must be highly efficient in the vast majority of humans due to either preexisting type-specific immunity or nonspecific clearance mechanisms in the reticuloendothelial system.

Mechanisms of Shock and Organ Failure

Cytokine Induction

Within the deeper tissues and blood stream, the induction of cytokine synthesis plays a critically important role in the production of shock and organ failure. Pyrogenic exotoxins (scarlatina toxins, erythrotoxins) have the ability to cause fever, enhance susceptibility to endotoxin,

TABLE 195-2 Case Definition for the Streptococcal Toxic Shock Syndrome*

I. Isolation of group A streptococci *(Streptococcus pyogenes)*
 A. From a normally sterile site (e.g., blood, cerebrospinal, pleural, or peritoneal fluid, tissue biopsy, surgical wound, etc.)
 B. From a nonsterile site (e.g., throat, sputum, vagina, superficial skin lesion, etc.)
II. Clinical signs of severity
 A. Hypotension: systolic blood pressure ≤90 mm Hg in adults or <5th percentile for age in children
And
 B. 2 or more of the following signs
  1. Renal impairment: creatinine ≥177 μmol/L (≥2 mg/dL) for adults or greater than or equal to twice the upper limit of normal for age. In patients with preexisting renal disease, a twofold or greater elevation over the baseline level.
  2. Coagulopathy: platelets ≤100 × 10⁹/L (≤100,000/mm³) or disseminated intravascular coagulation defined by prolonged clotting times, low fibrinogen level, and the presence of fibrin degradation products.
  3. Liver involvement: alanine aminotransferase (SGOT), aspartate aminotransferase (SGPT), or total bilirubin levels greater than or equal to twice the upper limit of normal for age. In patients with preexisting liver disease, a twofold or greater elevation over the baseline level.
  4. Adult respiratory distress syndrome defined by acute onset of diffuse pulmonary infiltrates and hypoxemia in the absence of cardiac failure, or evidence of diffuse capillary leak manifested by acute onset of generalized edema, or pleural or peritoneal effusions with hypoalbuminemia.
  5. A generalized erythematous macular rash that may desquamate.
  6. Soft tissue necrosis, including necrotizing fasciitis or myositis, or gangrene.

*An illness fulfilling criteria IA and II (A and B) can be defined as a definite case. An illness fulfilling criteria IB and II (A and B) can be defined as a probable case if no other etiology for the illness is identified.
From The Working Group on Severe Streptococcal Infections. Defining the group A streptococcal toxic shock syndrome: Rationale and consensus definition. JAMA 1993;269:390-391, with permission.

suppress IgM antibody synthesis, and act as superantigens. These toxins, like the staphylococcal enterotoxins (A, B, C) and TSST-1, can stimulate T-cell responses through their ability to bind to both the MHC class II complex of antigen presenting cells and the V-β region of the T-cell receptor.[224] The net effect is the induction of monocyte cytokines (TNFα, IL-1β, and interleukin [IL]-6) as well as the lymphokines (TNFβ, IL-2, and interferon-γ).[225-228] There is evidence that M-protein fragments may also act as superantigens.[229] Pyrogenic exotoxins C and MF as well as SSA and several new Spe are also capable of inducing proinflammatory cytokines as well as lymphokines.[230]

Other streptococcal virulence factors are also capable of inducing pro-inflammatory cytokines such as TNFα and IL-1β. Specifically SpeB, a potent cysteine protease, causes release of IL-1β from preformed intracellular pools.[231] Streptolysin O also stimulates mononuclear cells to produce TNFα and IL-1β and in the presence of SpeA has synergistic effects on IL-1β production.[232] Heat-killed group A streptococci as well as peptidoglycan and lipoteichoic acid are also potent inducers of TNFα and IL-1β.[233,234] Noncytokine mechanisms of shock may also play a role. A cysteine protease produced by group A streptococci was shown to release bradykinin from a high-molecular-weight kininogen.[235] Bradykinin is a potent vasodilator of systemic as well as pulmonary vasculature and could be responsible at least in part for the early hypotension observed in Strep TSS.[235]

Thus there are likely many streptococcal and host factors that contribute to the shock and organ failure characteristic of Strep TSS. That TNF plays a central role is supported by two observations. First, high levels of TNF are observed in a baboon model of group A streptococcal bacteremia at a point in time when profound hypotension is manifest.[236] Second, in that model, a neutralizing monoclonal antibody against TNF restored normal blood pressure and reduced mortality by 50%.[236]

TABLE 195-3 Factors That Increase the Likelihood of Developing Streptococcal Toxic Shock Syndrome

Age (neonates and elderly)
Diabetes
Alcoholism
Surgical procedures
Trauma
  Penetrating (insect bites, lacerations, slivers, abrasions, burns)
  Nonpenetrating (hematoma, bruise, muscle strain, hemarthrosis)
Varicella
Contact with a case
High prevalence of invasive strains in the community
Nonsteroidal anti-inflammatory agents*

*Based on limited evidence.

Clinical Manifestations

The first phase of Strep TSS begins with an influenza-like prodrome characterized by fever, chills, myalgias, nausea, vomiting, and diarrhea that precedes hypotension by 24 to 48 hours.[164] Confusion and/or combativeness is present in 55% of patients. Where there is a defined or superficial portal of entry such as a laceration, suspicion of streptococcal infection or frank evidence of infection may be present at this phase of infection. In contrast, in patients without a portal of entry (50% of cases) and who subsequently develop necrotizing fasciitis, postpartum infection, peritonitis, or joint space infection, pain that progressively increases in severity is the most common initial symptom that prompts patients to seek medical care and, interestingly, precedes clinical evidence of localized infection by 12 to 24 hours.[164] In both children[198] and adults[164] the soft tissues are the most common primary site of infection. In the remaining cases, pneumonia, meningitis, endophthalmitis, meningitis, peritonitis, myocarditis, joint infection, and intrauterine infection have been described.[164,198]

Phase 2 of Strep TSS is characterized by tachycardia, tachypnea, persistent fever, and, in patients who subsequently have necrotizing fasciitis or myonecrosis, increasingly severe pain at the site of infection. In others, fever and severe pain are the best early clinical clues.[237] In children, toxicity during varicella or persistence of fever greater than 4 days should also prompt careful evaluation. Many patients are seen in emergency departments at this stage and frequently sent home on one or two occasions with mistaken diagnoses, which include deep vein thrombophlebitis, muscle strain, viral gastroenteritis, dehydration, and sprained ankle, as well as others.[189] High fever and excruciating pain, particularly in individuals with no risk factors for deep vein thrombosis, should arouse suspicion of a deep-seated infection. Laboratory tests described below are very helpful, and CT and MRI may be useful to define the level of tissue injury but are not specific (see discussion of necrotizing fasciitis).

Phase 3 of Strep TSS is characterized by the above symptoms and signs but with the sudden onset of shock and organ failure. Many patients are in florid shock at the time of admission, but in nearly half hypotension is apparent during the first 4 to 8 hours after admission. Clinical evidence of necrotizing fasciitis is frequently a late finding, often occurring after hypotension is present. The appearance of purple bullae and dusky-appearing skin is a bad prognostic sign and should prompt emergent surgical exploration (see discussion of necrotizing fasciitis). It should be noted that the progression of necrotizing fasciitis from red skin to purple bullae in modern times may take place within a 24-hour period of time, whereas that described by Meleney in 1924 took 7 to 10 days. In addition, the rapidity with which shock and multiorgan failure can progress is impressive, and many patients die within 24 to 48 hours of hospitalization.[164]

Laboratory tests should be obtained in patients with aggressive soft tissue infections or patients with severe pain and fever who appear toxic. The serum creatinine measurement is particularly useful because renal impairment (creatinine >2 times normal) is apparent even during phase 2, before hypotension is apparent. In addition, creatine phosphokinase levels in serum are markedly elevated in those with necrotizing fasciitis and myonecrosis. The white blood count is usually normal or elevated at admission but with a profound left shift that includes myelocytes and metamyelocytes. Finally, serum albumin and calcium are usually low on admission and drop precipitously as a diffuse capillary leak syndrome develops. Thrombocytopenia does not develop until later in the course but is the earliest sign of disseminated coagulopathy.[164] Profound metabolic acidosis develops early in phase 3, and serum bicarbonate, lactate, and blood gas pH are crucial tests to follow therapeutic progress. Because the acute respiratory distress syndrome (ARDS) develops in 55% of patients with Strep TSS, pulse oximetry and, later, blood gases are necessary to evaluate the need for intubation and ventilation.

Management

Source Control

Prompt and aggressive surgical exploration and débridement of suspected deep-seated streptococcal infection are mandatory. It is as important to establish the etiology of the infection as it is to determine the extent of necrosis. CT and MRI are helpful to locate the primary site of infection, but because the group A streptococci do not form gas or frank abscess, radiologist interpretations are frequently not definitive. Such findings in a patient with extreme pain and fever or who is toxic should prompt surgical consultation. Once necrosis is established, extensive débridement is necessary as shock and organ failure continue to progress if devitalized tissue remains.

Fluid Resuscitation

If several liters of crystalloid intravenous fluid challenge do not rapidly improve either blood pressure (mean arterial pressure, >60 mm Hg) or tissue perfusion, then invasive monitoring is indicated. The goal should be to maintain a pulmonary artery occlusion pressure of 12 to 16 mm Hg.[238] If this goal is reached but hypotension persists, serum albumin concentration and hematocrit should be checked, because profoundly low albumin levels are common and because hemolysins produced by GAS can cause dramatic drops in circulating red cell mass. Thus, transfusion with packed red blood cells with or without albumin may be useful to improve blood pressure and preserve tissue perfusion.

Because of intractable hypotension and diffuse capillary leak, massive amounts of intravenous fluids (10 to 20 L) per day in an adult may be required. Albumin replacement may be necessary as many patients' serum albumin levels drop to less than 2.0 g/dL.

Antimicrobial Treatment

Prompt antimicrobial therapy is mandatory, and empiric broad-spectrum coverage for septic shock should be instituted initially. Once the streptococcal etiology is confirmed, high-dose penicillin and clindamycin should be given. This recommendation is based on the following information: (1) all strains of group A streptococci remain sensitive to penicillin; (2) resistance to erythromycin is currently found in less than 5% of group A streptococci in the United States, but the rate is higher in certain localized areas, and there have been rare reports of resistance to clindamycin; (3) clindamycin and erythromycin are more active in experimental models of necrotizing fasciitis and myonecrosis; (4) penicillin binding proteins are not expressed during stationary-phase growth of group A streptococci, and thus penicillin is ineffective in severe deep infections where large numbers of bacteria are present; (5) clindamycin suppresses exotoxin and M-protein production by group A streptococci; (6) clindamycin has a much longer half-life; (7) combinations of penicillin and clindamycin have indifferent interaction against group A streptococci in vitro at clinically relevant concentrations of antibiotics (no antagonistic effects were found)[239]; and (8) clindamycin and azithromycin suppress cytokine production by human mononuclear cells.[240,241]

Management in the Intensive Care Unit

In patients with persistent hypotension, monitoring of cardiac outputs, pulmonary artery occlusion pressure, and mean arterial pressure is important. Intubation and ventilator support are usually required due to the high incidence of ARDS (55%) in patients with Strep TSS. Pressors such as dopamine are used frequently, although no controlled trials have been performed in Strep TSS. In patients with intractable hypotension, high doses of dopamine, epinephrine, or phenylephrine have been used, but caution should be exercised in those with evidence of disseminated intravascular coagulation and in particular in those with cold, cyanotic digits. Symmetrical gangrene involving all 20 digits and toes, the tip of the nose, and the breast areola have been described. In addition, amputation of one, two, three, and even four extremities has been observed (authors' unpublished data).

Dialysis and Hemoperfusion

Either of these methodologies may be necessary because more than 50% of patients develop acute renal failure. Both dialysis and hemoperfusion may also nonspecifically reduce the concentrations of circulating toxins. It is interesting that a study from Sweden that used hemofiltration achieved the lowest mortality rate in patients with Strep TSS ever recorded.[215] Finally, a polystyrence superantigen absorbing device (SAAD) was developed in Japan and shown to be highly efficacious in absorbing either pyrogenic exotoxin A or TSST-1 from plasma, and when used extracorporally in animals infused with TSST-1 and LPS, mortality improved from 100% to 50%.[242]

Intravenous Immune Globulin

The rationale for the use of intravenous immune globulin (IGIV) in the treatment of Strep TSS is based on the data implicating extracellular exotoxins as mediators of shock and organ failure. George and Gladys Dick in 1924 demonstrated that convalescent sera from patients with scarlet fever neutralized scarlatina toxins and that, when passively administered, attenuated the course of severe scarlet fever.[243] Just as penicillin was becoming available, anti-scarlatina toxin horse serum became commercially available in the United States, but because of the availability of penicillin and the decline in the severity of scarlet fever, it was never used. Several reports have described the successful use of IGIV in patients with Strep TSS.[244-246] The largest treatment group (15 patients) showed a significant reduction in mortality compared with matched historical controls.[247] The mortality rate of 70% in the control group was among the highest ever reported, whereas the rate was 30% in the IGIV group. This rate is similar to that of some series that did not use IGIV.[164] A double-blind clinical trail was undertaken in northern Europe comparing IGIV with albumin in patients with Strep TSS. All patients received clindamycin. The mortality rate in the IGIV group was 16%, whereas that in the albumin group was 32%.[248] Unfortunately, the study was stopped due to low enrollment and only seven or eight patients with proved GAS infections were in each group. Thus, the differences were not significant. It is hoped that further, double-blind studies with sufficient numbers of cases will resolve the continuing dilemma regarding the potential efficacy of IGIV.[249] It is clear that if IGIV were to be used, it should be given early and probably more than one dose should be given, because batches of IGIV have variable neutralizing activity against streptococcal exotoxins.[230,250]

There have been no comparative trials describing the efficacy of hyperbaric oxygen treatment in Strep TSS, although some state that such treatment reduces mortality and the need for further débridements.[251] Certainly, use of this modality should not delay or be used in preference to surgical débridement when the latter is indicated.

BACTEREMIA

Group A streptococcal bacteremia has been relatively uncommon in the antibiotic era.[252] Before the mid 1980s, bacteremia occurred predominantly at the extremes of life and was usually community acquired. Occasional cases were seen in young and middle-aged adults associated with surgical wound infections and endometritis.

During the past decade, however, there has been an increase in the number of reported cases of group A streptococcal bacteremia, reflecting the changing epidemiology and clinical patterns of invasive streptococcal infection as detailed above. Many of the patients have been previously healthy adults between the ages of 20 and 50 years. There has been an apparent increase in cases associated with parenteral injection of illicit drugs,[167-169,213] as well as nosocomial outbreaks in nursing homes.[201-205]

Bacteremia in children may emanate from an upper respiratory infection, but it is more commonly associated with cutaneous foci, including burns and varicella.[210] Elderly patients with streptococcal bacteremia present with a variety of chronic illnesses, the relation of which to their bacteremia is often unclear. Diabetes mellitus and peripheral vascular disease do appear, however, to be predisposing factors in older adults, and, as in children, the portal of entry is usually the skin. Malignancy and immunosuppression are risk factors in both age groups.[188,254] Although group A streptococcal bacteremia may at times be transient and relatively benign,[255] it is more often fulminant. The onset is abrupt, with chills, high fever, and prostration. Rarely, patients may present with acute abdominal pain.[255,256] Mortality in five modern series[211,255-258] ranged from 27% to 38%.

OTHER STREPTOCOCCAL INFECTIONS

Lymphangitis may accompany cellulitis or may occur after clinically minor or inapparent skin infection. Lymphangitis is readily recognized by the presence of red, tender, linear streaks directed toward enlarged, tender regional lymph nodes. It is accompanied by systemic symptoms such as chills, fever, malaise, and headache. Puerperal sepsis follows abortion or delivery when streptococci colonizing the patient herself or transmitted from medical personnel invade the endometrium and surrounding structures, lymphatics, and blood stream. The resulting endometritis and septicemia may be complicated by pelvic cellulitis, septic pelvic thrombophlebitis, peritonitis, or pelvic abscess. This disease was associated with high mortality in the preantibiotic era. Although endocarditis due to *S. pyogenes* was relatively common in the preantibiotic era, it is now rarely seen.[259,260] Meningitis due to *S. pyogenes* usually follows upper respiratory infection, including sinusitis or otitis,[261] or neurosurgical conditions.[262] It is indistinguishable clinically from other forms of acute pyogenic meningeal infection.[263]

Pneumonia due to *S. pyogenes* is frequently associated with preceding viral infections such as influenza, measles, or varicella or with chronic pulmonary disease. Numerous epidemics have been described in military recruit populations.[264,265] An increased number of cases has been reported over the past few years in association with the resurgence of invasive streptococcal infections. In one third or fewer of the cases, there is a history of preceding streptococcal upper respiratory infection. The onset is typically abrupt, and the disease is characterized by chills, fever, dyspnea, cough productive of blood-streaked sputum, pleuritic chest pain, and, in more severe cases, cyanosis. The pulmonary picture is that of bronchopneumonia with consolidation being uncommon. Empyema develops in 30% to 40% of the cases, tends to appear early in the disease, and typically consists of copious amounts of thin serosanguinous fluid. Bacteremia occurs in 10% to 15% of the cases. Complications include mediastinitis, pericarditis, pneumothorax, and bronchiectasis, and the clinical course of the disease is often prolonged. Mortality has generally been low with penicillin therapy and adequate drainage of empyema, perhaps reflecting its occurrence in healthy military recruits. However, in a recent Canadian report of 222 cases of community-acquired pneumonia among adults (median age, 56 years), the case-fatality ratio was 38%.[266]

Group A streptococcal perianal cellulitis and vulvovagiitis are symptomatic but benign disorders primarily affecting children.[267,268] Asymptomatic carriage of group A streptococci in the vagina, anus, scalp, or, rarely, upper respiratory tract of adults has, however, been the source of outbreaks of nosocomial streptococcal infection.[269]

Prophylaxis and the Risk of Secondary Cases of Streptococcal Toxic Shock Syndrome

Strep TSS is most commonly community acquired and sporadic in nature, yet clusters of invasive cases have been described in nursing homes,[201-205] among families,[206,207] and among hospital workers.[208,270] Recently, in San Francisco 23 hospital workers became colonized or infected with GAS as a result of contact from a single case of Strep TSS.[270] This example as well as many historical studies in schools, military posts, and nursing homes have taught us that group A streptococci are highly contagious. Luckily, mere contact or colonization is usually not sufficient to cause a secondary case of invasive GAS infection. Epidemiologic studies by the Centers for Disease Control and Prevention found one secondary case of invasive infection among more than 1500 contacts.[136] This would extrapolate to 66:100,000 population per year for secondary cases.[271] As stated previously, the current incidence of primary cases of invasive GAS infections in the United States is 3.5:100,000 population per year. Thus the risk to contacts is roughly 20 times greater than that for the general population but still very low. Given the relative infrequency of these infections and the lack of a clearly effective chemprophylactic regimen, routine screening for and prophylaxis against streptococcal infection are not recommended for household contacts of index patients. In deciding who should receive prophylaxis, the clinician needs to factor in the duration of contact, the intimacy of contact, and the underlying host factors of individual contacts. Specifically, contacts with open wounds, recent surgery, recent childbirth, concurrent viral infections such as varicella or influenza, or immune deficiency diseases should receive prophylaxis. In a multicenter study of adults aged 18 to 45 years, human immunodeficiency virus infection and injecting drug use were independently associated with an increased risk of invasive group A streptococcal disease. In individuals aged 45 years or greater, diabetes, cardiac disease, cancer, and corticosteroid use were significant risk factors.[272] Moreover, persons aged 65 years or greater are at increased risk of mortality should they contract invasive disease. Thus, it may be prudent to initiate prophylaxis in households containing elderly persons or those with the above-mentioned risk factors.

Lacking firm data on which to base antimicrobial prophylaxis, it seems reasonable to choose those agents that have achieved highest rates of pharyngeal eradication in asymptomatic individuals; among these are clindamycin and azithromycin. Specific regimens have been published elsewhere.[136]

REFERENCES

1. Brown JH. The Use of Blood Agar for the Study of Streptococci. New York: The Rockefeller Institute for Medical Research, 1919.
2. Lancefield RC. A serological differentiation of human and other groups of hemolytic streptococci. J Exp Med. 1933;57:571-595.
3. Rammelkamp CH. Epidemiology of streptococcal infections. Harvey Lect. 1955;51:113-142.
4. Wannamaker LW. The epidemiology of streptococcal infection. In: McCarty M, ed. Streptococcal Infections. New York: Columbia University Press; 1953:157-175.
5. Rammelkamp CH, Denny FW, Wannamaker LW. Studies on the epidemiology of rheumatic fever in the armed services. In: Thomas L, ed. Rheumatic Fever. Minneapolis: University of Minnesota Press; 1952:72-89.
6. Ferretti JJ, McShan WM, Ajdic D, et al. Complete genome sequence of an M1 strain of Streptococcus pyogenes 1. Proc Natl Acad Sci U S A. 2001;98:4658-4663.
7. Beres SB, Sylva GL, Barbian KD, et al. Genome sequence of a serotype M3 strain of group A Streptococcus: Phage-encoded toxins, the high-virulence phenotype, and clone emergence. Proc Natl Acad Sci U S A. 2002;99:10078-10083.
8. Smoot JC, Barbian KD, Van Gompel JJ, et al. Genome sequence and comparative microarray analysis of serotype M18 group A Streptococcus strains associated with acute rheumatic fever outbreaks. Proc Natl Acad Sci U S A. 2002;99:4668-4673.

9. Moses AE, Wessels MR, Zalcman K, et al. Relative contributions of hyaluronic acid capsule and M protein to virulence in a mucoid strain of the group A *Streptococcus.* Infect Immun. 1997;65:64-71.

10. Dale JB, Washburn RG, Marques MB, Wessels MR. Hyaluronate capsule and surface M protein in resistance to opsonization of group A streptococci. Infect Immun. 1996;64:1495-1501.

11. Lancefield RC. Current knowledge of type-specific M antigens of group A streptococci. J Immunol. 1962;89:307-313.

12. Facklam RF, Martin DR, Lovgren M, et al. Extension of the Lancefield classification for group A streptococci by addition of 22 new M protein gene sequence types from clinical isolates: emm103 to emm124. Clin Infect Dis. 2002;34:28-38.

13. Phillips GN Jr, Flicker PF, Cohen C, et al. Streptococcal M protein: Alpha-helical coiled-coil structure and arrangement on the cell surface. Proc Natl Acad Sci U S A. 1981;78:4689-4693.

14. Jones KF, Manjula BN, Johnston KH, et al. Location of variable and conserved epitopes among the multiple serotypes of streptococcal M protein. J Exp Med. 1985;161:623-628.

15. Bisno AL. Alternate complement pathway activation by group A streptococci: Role of M-protein. Infect Immun. 1979;26:1172-1176.

16. Peterson PK, Schmeling D, Cleary PP, et al. Inhibition of alternative complement pathway opsonization by group A streptococcal M protein. J Infect Dis. 1979;139:575-585.

17. Horstmann RD, Sievertsen HJ, Knobloch J, Fischetti VA. Antiphagocytic activity of streptococcal M protein: Selective binding of complement control protein factor H. Proc Natl Acad Sci U S A. 1988;85:1657-1661.

18. Kihlberg BM, Collin M, Olsen A, Bjorck L. Protein H, an antiphagocytic surface protein in Streptococcus pyogenes. Infect Immun. 1999;67:1708-1714.

19. Morfeldt E, Berggard K, Persson J, et al. Isolated hypervariable regions derived from streptococcal M proteins specifically bind human C4b-binding protein: Implications for antigenic variation. J Immunol. 2001;167:3870-3877.

20. Whitnack E, Dale JB, Beachey EH. Common protective antigens of group A streptococcal M proteins masked by fibrinogen. J Exp Med. 1984;159:1201-1212.

21. Whitnack E, Beachey EH. Biochemical and biological properties of the binding of human fibrinogen to M protein in group A streptococci. J Bacteriol. 1985;164:350-358.

22. Whitnack E, Beachey EH. Inhibition of complement-mediated opsonization and phagocytosis of *Streptococcus pyogenes* by D fragments of fibrinogen and fibrin bound to cell surface M protein. J Exp Med. 1985;162:1983-1997.

23. Bisno AL, Collins CM, Turner JC. M proteins of group C streptococci isolated from patients with acute pharyngitis. J Clin Microbiol. 1996;34:2511-2515.

24. Campo RE, Schultz DR, Bisno AL. M-proteins of group G streptococci: mechanisms of resistance to phagocytosis. J Infect Dis. 1995;171:601-606.

25. Podbielski A, Schnitzler N, Beyhs P, Boyle MDP. M-related protein (Mrp) contributes to group A streptococcal resistance to phagocytosis by human granulocytes. Mol Microbiol. 1996;19:429-441.

26. Ji Y, Schnitzler N, DeMaster E, Cleary P. Impact of M49, Mrp, Enn, and C5a peptidase proteins on colonization of the mouse oral mucosa by Streptococcus pyogenes. Infect Immun. 1998;66:5399-5405.

27. Dale JB, Chiang EY, Liu S, et al. New protective antigen of group A streptococci. J Clin Invest. 1999;103:1261-1268.

28. Lei B, DeLeo FR, Hoe NP, et al. Evasion of human innate and acquired immunity by a bacterial homolog of CD11b that inhibits opsonophagocytosis. Nat Med. 2001;7:1298-1305.

29. Rakonjac JV, Robbins JC, Fischetti VA. DNA sequence of the serum opacity factor of group A streptococci: Identification of a fibronectin-binding repeat domain. Infect Immun. 1995;63:622-631.

30. Johnson DR, Kaplan EL. A review of the correlation of T-agglutination patterns and M-protein typing and opacity factor production in the identification of group A streptococci. J Med Microbiol. 1993;38:311-315.

31. Widdowson JP, Maxted WR, Notley CM, Pinney AM. The antibody responses in man to infection with different serotypes of group A streptococci. J Med Microbiol. 1974;7:483-496.

32. Courtney HS, Hasty DL, Dale JB. Molecular mechanisms of adhesion, colonization, and invasion of group A streptococci. Ann Med. 2002;34:77-87.

33. Hasty DL, Ofek I, Courtney HS, Doyle RJ. Multiple adhesins of streptococci. Infect Immun. 1992;60:2147-2152.

34. Ofek I, Beachey EH, Jefferson W, Campbell GL. Cell membrane-binding properties of group A streptococcal lipoteichoic acid. J Exp Med. 1975;187:1161-1167.

35. Caparon MG, Stephens DS, Olsen A, Scott JR. Role of M protein in adherence of group A streptococci. Infect Immun. 1991;59:1811-1817.

36. Okada N, Pentland AP, Falk P, Caparon MG. M protein and protein F act as important determinants of cell-specific tropism of *Streptococcus pyogenes* in skin tissue. J Clin Invest. 1994;94:965-977.

37. Okada N, Liszewski MK, Atkinson JP, Caparon M. Membrane cofactor protein (CD46) is a keratinocyte receptor for the M protein of the group A streptococcus. Proc Natl Acad Sci U S A. 1995;92:2489-2493.

38. Hanski E, Caparon M. Protein F, a fibronectin-binding protein, is an adhesin of the group A streptococcus *Streptococcus pyogenes.* Proc Natl Acad Sci U S A. 1992;89:6172-6176.

39. Talay SR, Valentin-Weigand P, Jerlstrom PG, et al. Fibronectin-binding protein of *Streptococcus pyogenes:* Sequence of the binding domain involved in adherence of streptococci to epithelial cells. Infect Immun. 1992;60:3837-3844.

40. Kreikemeyer B, Talay SR, Chhatwal GS. Characterization of a novel fibronectin-binding surface protein in group A streptococci. Mol Microbiol. 1995;17:137-145.

41. Courtney HS, Dale JB, Hasty DL. Differential effects of the streptococcal fibronectin-binding protein, FBP54, on adhesion of group A streptococci to human buccal cells and HEp-2 tissue culture cells. Infect Immun. 1996;64:2415-2419.

42. Jaffe J, Natanson-Yaron S, Caparon MG, Hanski E. Protein F2, a novel fibronectin-binding protein from Streptococcus pyogenes, possesses two binding domains. Mol Microbiol. 1996;21:373-384.

43. Rocha CL, Fischetti VA. Identification and characterization of a novel fibronectin-binding protein on the surface of group A streptococci. Infect Immun. 1999;67:2720-2728.

44. Gibson C, Fogg G, Okada N, et al. Regulation of host cell recognition in *Streptococcus pyogenes.* Dev Biol Stand. 1995;85:137-144.

45. Caparon MG, Geist RT, Perez-Casal J, Scott JR. Environmental regulation of virulence in group A streptococci: Transcription of the gene encoding M protein is stimulated by carbon dioxide. J Bacteriol. 1992;174:5693-5701.

46. Yinduo J, McLandsborough L, Kondagunta A, Cleary PP. C5a peptidase alters clearance and trafficking of group A streptococci by infected mice. Infect Immun. 1996;64:503-510.

47. Wexler DE, Chenoweth DE, Cleary PP. Mechanism of action of the group A streptococcal C5a inactivator. Proc Natl Acad Sci U S A. 1985;82:8144-8148.

48. Baker M, Gutman DM, Papageorgiou AC, et al. Structural features of a zinc binding site in the superantigen streptococcal pyrogenic exotoxin A (SpeA1): Implications for MHC class II recognition. Prot Sci. 2001;10:1268-1273.

49. Bisno AL, Brito MO, Collins CM. Molecular basis of group A streptococcal virulence. Lancet Infect Dis. 2003;3:191-200.

50. Marrack P, Kappler J. The staphylococcal enterotoxins and their relatives. Science. 1990;248:705-711.

51. Cunningham MW. Pathogenesis of group A streptococcal infections. Clin Microbiol Rev. 2000;13:470-511.

52. Perez-Casal J, Caparon MG, Scott JR. Mry, a *trans*-acting positive regulator of the M protein gene of *Streptococcus pyogenes* with similarity to the receptor proteins of two-component regulatory systems. J Bacteriol. 1991;173:2617-2624.

53. Levin JC, Wessels MR. Identification of csrR/csrS, a genetic locus that regulates hyaluronic acid capsule synthesis in group A Streptococcus. Mol Microbiol. 1998;30:209-219.

54. Federle MJ, McIver KS, Scott JR. A response regulator that represses transcription of several virulence operons in the group A streptococcus. J Bacteriol. 1999;181:3649-3657.

55. Heath A, DiRita VJ, Barg NL, Engleberg NC. A two-component regulatory system, CsrR-CsrS, represses expression of three Streptococcus pyogenes virulence factors, hyaluronic acid capsule, streptolysin S, and pyrogenic exotoxin B. Infect Immun. 1999;67:5298-5305.

56. Bisno AL. Acute pharyngitis: Etiology and diagnosis. Pediatrics. 1996;97(6 Pt 2):949-954.

57. Kaplan EL, Wannamaker LW. C-reactive protein in streptococcal pharyngitis. Pediatrics. 1977;60:28-32.

58. Randolph MF, Gerber MA, DeMeo KK, Wright L. Effect of antibiotic therapy on the clinical course of streptococcal pharyngitis. J Pediatr. 1985;106:870-875.

59. Krober MS, Bass JW, Michels GN. Streptococcal pharyngitis: Placebo-controlled double-blind evaluation of clinical response to penicillin therapy. JAMA. 1985;253:1271-1274.

60. Nelson JD. The effect of penicillin therapy on the symptoms and signs of streptococcal pharyngitis. Pediatr Infect Dis J. 1984;3:10-13.

61. Shulman ST. Complications of streptococcal pharyngitis. Pediatr Infect Dis J. 1994;13:S70-S74.

62. Shoemaker M, Lampe RM, Weir MR. Peritonsillitis: Abscess of cellulitis? Pediatr Infect Dis J. 1986;5:435-439.

63. Turner JC, Fox A, Fox K, et al. Role of group C beta-hemolytic streptococci in pharyngitis: Epidemiologic study of clinical features associated with isolation of group C streptococci. J Clin Microbiol. 1993;31:808-811.

64. Meier FA, Centor RM, Graham L Jr, Dalton HP. Clinical and microbiological evidence for endemic pharyngitis among adults due to group C streptococci. Arch Intern Med. 1990;150:825-829.

65. Hill HR, Caldwell GG, Wilson E, et al. Epidemic of pharyngitis due to streptococci of Lancefield group G. Lancet. 1969;2:371-374.

66. McCue JD. Group G streptococcal pharyngitis: Analysis of an outbreak at a college. JAMA. 1982;248:1333-1336.

67. Cimolai N, Elford RW, Bryan L, et al. Do the beta-hemolytic non-group A streptococci cause pharyngitis? Rev Infect Dis. 1988;10:587-601.

68. Bisgard KM, Hardy IR, Popovic T. Respiratory diphtheria in the United States, 1980-1995. Am J Public Health. 1998;88:787-791.

69. Miller RA, Brancato F, Holmes KK. *Corynebacterium hemolyticum* as a cause of pharyngitis and scarlatiniform rash in young adults. Ann Intern Med. 1986;105:867-872.

70. Karpathios T, Drakonaki S, Zervoudaki A, et al. *Arcanobacterium haemolyticum* in children with presumed streptococcal pharyngotonsillitis or scarlet fever. J Pediatr. 1992;121:735-737.

71. Tacket CO, Davis BR, Carter GP, et al. *Yersinia enterocolitica* pharyngitis. Ann Intern Med. 1983;99:40-42.

72. Glezen WP, Fernald GW, Lohr JA. Acute respiratory disease of university students with special reference to the etiologic role of *Herpesvirus hominis.* Am J Epidemiol. 1975;101:111-121.

73. McMillan JA, Weiner LB, Higgins AM, Lamparella VJ. Pharyngitis associated with herpes simplex virus in college students. Pediatr Infect Dis J. 1993;12:280-284.

74. Young EJ, Vainrub B, Musher DM, et al. Acute pharyngotonsillitis caused by herpesvirus type 2. JAMA. 1978;239:1885-1886.

75. McMillan JA, Sandstrom C, Weiner LB, et al. Viral and bacterial organisms associated with acute pharyngitis in a school-aged population. J Pediatr. 1986;109:747-752.
76. Vanhelms P, Allard R, Cooper DA, et al. Acute human immunodeficiency virus type 1 disease as a mononucleosis-like illness: Is the diagnosis too restrictive? Clin Infect Dis. 1997;24:965-970.
77. Glezen WP, Clyde WAJ, Senior RJ, et al. Group A streptococci, mycoplasmas, and viruses associated with acute pharyngitis. JAMA. 1967;202:455-460.
78. Kaplan EL, Top FH Jr, Dudding BA, Wannamaker LW. Diagnosis of streptococcal pharyngitis: Differentiation of active infection from the carrier state in the symptomatic child. J Infect Dis. 1971;123:490-501.
79. Breese BB. A simple scorecard for the tentative diagnosis of streptococcal pharyngitis. Am J Dis Child. 1977;131:514-517.
80. Wald ER, Green MD, Schwartz B, Barbadora K. A streptococcal score card revisited. Pediatr Emerg Care. 1998;14:109-111.
81. Walsh BT, Bookheim WW, Johnson RC, Tompkins RK. Recognition of streptococcal pharyngitis in adults. Arch Intern Med. 1975;135:1493-1497.
82. McIsaac WJ, White D, Tannenbaum D, Low DE. A clinical score to reduce unnecessary antibiotic use in patients with sore throat. Can Med Assoc J. 1998;158:75-83.
83. Komaroff AL, Pass TM, Aronson MD, et al. The prediction of streptococcal pharyngitis in adults. J Gen Intern Med. 1986;1:1-7.
84. Centor RM, Witherspoon JM, Dalton HP, et al. The diagnosis of strep throat in adults in the emergency room. Med Decis Making. 1981;1:239-246.
85. Cooper JR, Hoffman JR, Bartlett JG, et al. Principles of appropriate antibiotic use for acute pharyngitis in adults: Background. Ann Intern Med. 2001;134:509-517.
86. Snow V, Mottur-Pilson C, Cooper RJ, Hoffman JR. Principles of appropriate antibiotic use of acute pharyngitis in adults. Ann Intern Med. 2001;134:506-508.
87. Ebell MH, Smith MA, Barry HC, et al. The rational clinical examination. Does this patient have strep throat? JAMA. 2000;284:2912-2918.
88. Bisno AL, Peter GS, Kaplan EL. Diagnosis of strep throat in adults: Are clinical criteria really good enough? Clin Infect Dis. 2002;35:126-129.
89. Bisno AL. Diagnosing strep throat in the adult patient: Do clinical criteria really suffice? Ann Intern Med. 2003;139:150-151.
89a. McIsaac WJ, Kellner JD, Aufricht P, et al. Empirical validation of guidelines for the management of pharyngitis in children and adults. JAMA. 2004;291:1587-1595.
90. Linder JA, Stafford RS. Antibiotic treatment of adults with sore throat by community primary care physicians: A national survey, 1989-1999. JAMA. 2001;286:1181-1186.
91. Neuner JM, Hamel MB, Phillips RS, et al. Diagnosis and management of adults with pharyngitis. A cost-effectiveness analysis. Ann Intern Med. 2003;139:113-122.
92. Bisno AL, Gerber MA, Gwaltney JM Jr, et al. Practice guidelines for the diagnosis and management of group A streptococcal pharyngitis. Infectious Diseases Society of America. Clin Infect Dis. 2002;35:113 125.
93. Dajani A, Taubert K, Ferrieri P, et al. Treatment of acute streptococcal pharyngitis and prevention of rheumatic fever: A statement for health professionals. Committee on Rheumatic Fever, Endocarditis, and Kawasaki Disease of the Council on Cardiovascular Disease in the Young, the American Heart Association. Pediatrics. 1995;96(4 Pt 1):758-764.
94. Committee on Infectious Diseases. Group A streptococcal infections. In: Pickering LK, ed. 2003 Red Book. Elk Grove Village, Ill: American Academy of Pediatrics; 2003:573-584.
95. Rheumatic Fever Committee, American Heart Association. Throat Cultures for Rational Treatment of Sore Throat. New York: New York Affiliate, American Heart Association; 1972.
96. Kellogg JA, Manzella JP. Detection of group A streptococci in the laboratory or physician's office. JAMA. 1986;255:2638-2642.
97. Kellogg JA. Suitability of throat culture procedures for detection of group A streptococci and as reference standards for evaluation of streptococcal antigen detection kits. J Clin Microbiol. 1990;28:165-169.
98. Kaplan EL, Johnson DR, Del Rosario MC, Horn DL. Susceptibility of group A beta-hemolytic streptococci to thirteen antibiotics: Examination of 301 strains isolated in the United States between. 1994 and. 1997. Pediatr Infect Dis J. 1999;18:1069-1072.
99. Freeman AF, Shulman ST. Macrolide resistance in group A Streptococcus. Pediatr Infect Dis J. 2002;21:1158-1160.
100. Coonan K, Kaplan EL. Therapeutic implications of erythromycin resistance in group A streptococci. Pediatr Infect Dis J. 1993;12:261-262.
101. Gentry JL, Burns WW. Antibiotic-resistant streptococci. Am J Dis Child. 1980;134:801.
102. Martin JM, Green M, Barbadora KA, Wald ER. Erythromycin-resistant group A streptococci in schoolchildren in Pittsburgh. N Engl J Med. 2002;346:1200-1206.
103. York MK, Gibbs L, Perdreau-Remington F, Brooks GF. Characterization of antimicrobial resistance in Streptococcus pyogenes isolates from the San Francisco Bay area of northern California. J Clin Microbiol. 1999;37:1727-1731.
104. Gerber MA, Tanz RR, Kabat W, et al. Optical immunoassay test for group A beta-hemolytic streptococcal pharyngitis. An office-based, multicenter investigation. JAMA. 1997;277:899-903.
105. Fries SM. Diagnosis of group A streptococcal pharyngitis in a private clinic: Comparative evaluation of an optical immunoassay method and culture. J Pediatr. 1995;126:933-936.
106. Schlager TA, Hayden GA, Woods WA, et al. Optical immunoassay for rapid detection of group A beta-hemolytic streptococci. Arch Pediatr Adolesc Med. 1996;150:245-248.
107. Baker DM, Cooper RM, Rhodes C, et al. Superiority of conventional culture technique over rapid detection of group A *Streptococcus* by optical immunoassay. Diagn Microbiol Infect Dis. 1995;21:61-64.
108. Gieseker KE, Mackenzie T, Roe MH, Todd JK. Comparison of two rapid Streptococcus pyogenes diagnostic tests with a rigorous culture standard. Pediatr Infect Dis J. 2002;21:922-927.
109. Poses RM, Cebul RD, Collins M, Fager SS. The accuracy of experienced physicians' probability estimates for patients with sore throats: implications for decision making. JAMA. 1985;254:925-929.
110. Bisno AL. Acute pharyngitis. N Engl J Med. 2001;344:205-211.
111. Weinstein L, Le Frock J. Does antimicrobial therapy of streptococcal pharyngitis or pyoderma alter the risk of glomerulonephritis? J Infect Dis. 1971;124:229-231.
112. Catanzaro FJ, Stetson CA, Morris AJ, et al. The role of streptococcus in the pathogenesis of rheumatic fever. Am J Med. 1954;17:749-756.
113. Brink WR, Rammelkamp CH Jr, Denny FW, Wannamaker LW. Effect of penicillin and aureomycin on the natural course of streptococcal tonsillitis and pharyngitis. Am J Med. 1951;10:300-308.
114. Shulman ST, Gerber MA, Tanz RR, Markowitz M. Streptococcal pharyngitis: The case for penicillin therapy. Pediatr Infect Dis J. 1994;13:1-7.
115. Shvartzman P, Tabenkin H, Rosentzwaig A, Dolginov F. Treatment of streptococcal pharyngitis with amoxycillin once a day. BMJ. 1993;306:1170-1172.
116. Feder HMJ, Gerber MA, Randolph MF, et al. Once-daily therapy for streptococcal pharyngitis with amoxicillin. Pediatrics. 1999;103:47-51.
117. Pichichero ME, Margolis PA. A comparison of cephalosporins and penicillins in the treatment of group A beta-hemolytic streptococcal pharyngitis: A meta-analysis supporting the concept of microbial copathogenicity. Pediatr Infect Dis J. 1991;10:275-281.
118. Kaplan EL, Gastanaduy AS, Huwe BB. The role of the carrier in treatment failures after antibiotic therapy for group A streptococci in the upper respiratory tract. J Lab Clin Med. 1981;98:326-335.
119. Cresti S, Lattanzi M, Zanchi A, et al. Resistance determinants and clonal diversity in group A streptococci collected during a period of increasing macrolide resistance. Antimicrob Agents Chemother. 2002;46:1816-1822.
120. Seppala H, Klaukka T, Vuopio-Varkila J, et al. The effect of changes in the consumption of macrolide antibiotics on erythromycin resistance in group A streptococci in Finland. N Engl J Med. 1997;337:441-446.
121. Cornaglia G, Ligozzi M, Mazzariol A, et al. Resistance of *Streptococcus pyogenes* to erythromycin and related antibiotics in Italy. Clin Infect Dis. 1998;27(suppl 1):S87-S92.
122. Pichichero ME. Cephalosporins are superior to penicillin for treatment of streptococcal tonsillopharyngitis: Is the difference worth it? Pediatr Infect Dis J. 1993;12:268-274.
123. Shulman ST, Gerber MA, Tanz RR, Markowitz M. Streptococcal pharyngitis: the case for pencillin therapy. Pediatr Infect Dis J. 1994;13:1-7.
124. McCarty J, Hedrick JA, Gooch WM. Clarithromycin suspension vs penicillin V suspension in children with streptococcal pharygitis. Adv Ther. 2000;17:14-26.
125. Mehra S, van Moerkerke M, Welck J, et al. Short course therapy with cefuroxime axetil for group A streptococcal tonsillopharyngitis in children. Pediatr Infect Dis J. 1998;17:452-457.
126. Adam D, Hostalck U, Troster K. 5-Day therapy of bacterial pharyngitis and tonsillitis with cefixime: Comparison with 10-day treatment with penicillin V. Klinische Padiatrie. 1996;208:310-313.
127. Boccazzi A, Tonelli P, DeAngelis M, et al. Short course therapy with ceftibutin versus azithromycin in pediatric streptococcal pharyngitis. Pediatr Infect Dis J. 2000;19:963-967.
128. Tack KJ, Henry DC, Gooch WM, et al. Five-day cefdinir treatment for streptococcal pharyngitis. Cefdinir Pharyngitis Study Group. Antimicrob Agents Chemother. 1998;42:1073-1075.
129. Pichichero ME, Gooch WM, Rodriguez W, et al. Effective short-course treatment of acute group A beta-hemolytic streptococcal tonsillopharyngitis: Ten days of penicillin vs 5 days or 10 days of cefpodoxime therapy in children. Arch Pediatr Adolesc Med. 1994;148:1053-1060.
130. Still JG. Management of pediatric patients with group A beta-hemolytic *Streptococcus* pharyngitis: Treatment options. Pediatr Infect Dis J. 1995;14:S57-S61.
131. Hamill J. Multicentre evaluation of azithromycin and penicillin V in the treatment of acute streptococcal pharyngitis and tonsillitis in children. J Antimicrob Chemother. 1993;31(suppl E):89-94.
132. Weippl G. Multicentre comparison of azithromycin versus erythromycin in the treatment of paediatric pharyngitis or tonsillitis caused by group A streptococci. J Antimicrob Chemother. 1993;31(suppl E):95-101.
133. Hooton TM. A comparison of azithromycin and penicillin V for the treatment of streptococcal pharyngitis. Am J Med. 1991;91(suppl 3A):3A-23A.
134. Tanz RR, Poncher JR, Corydon KE, et al. Clindamycin treatment of chronic pharyngeal carriage of group A streptococci. J Pediatr. 1991;119:123-128.
135. Kaplan EL, Johnson DR. Eradication of group A streptococci from the upper respiratory tract by amoxicillin with clavulanate after oral penicillin V treatment failure. J Pediatr. 1988;113:400-403.
136. Prevention of Invasive Group A Streptococcal Infections Workshop Participants. Prevention of invasive group A streptococcal disease among household contacts of case patients and among postpartum and postsurgical patients: Recommendations from the Centers for Disease Control and Prevention. Clin Infect Dis. 2002;35:950-959.
137. Paradise JL, Bluestone CD, Bachman RZ, et al. Efficacy of tonsillectomy for recurrent throat infection in severely affected children: Results of parallel randomized and nonrandomized clinical trials. N Engl J Med. 1984;310:674-683.
138. Paradise JL, Bluestone CD, Colborn DK, et al. Tonsillectomy and adenotonsillectomy for recurrent throat infection in moderately affected children. Pediatrics. 2002;110(1 Pt 1):7-15.
139. Ferrieri P, Dajani AS, Wannamaker LW, Chapman SS. Natural history of impetigo. I. Site sequence of acquisition and familial patterns of spread of cutaneous streptococci. J Clin Invest. 1972;51:2851-2862.
140. Adams BB. Dermatologic disorders of the athlete. Sports Med. 2002;32:309-321.
141. Fehrs LJ, Flanagan K, Kline S, et al. Group A beta-hemolytic streptococcal skin infections in a US meat-packing plant. JAMA. 1987;258:3131-3134.

142. Taplin D, Lansdell L, Allen AM, et al. Prevalence of streptococcal pyoderma in relation to climate and hygiene. Lancet. 1973;1:501-503.

143. Fiorentino TR, Beall B, Mshar P, Bessen DE. A genetic-based evaluation of the principal tissue reservoir for group A streptococci isolated from normally sterile sites. J Infect Dis. 1997;176:177-182.

144. Anthony BF, Kaplan EL, Wannamaker LW, Chapman SS. The dynamics of streptococcal infections in a defined population of children: Serotypes associated with skin and respiratory infections. Am J Epidemiol. 1976;104:652-666.

145. Kaplan EL, Anthony BF, Chapman SS, et al. The influence of the site of infection on the immune response to group A streptococci. J Clin Invest. 1970;49:1405-1414.

146. Bisno AL, Nelson KE, Waytz P, Brunt J. Factors influencing serum antibody responses in streptococcal pyoderma. J Lab Clin Med. 1973;81:410-420.

147. Kaplan EL, Wannamaker LW. Suppression of the antistreptolysin O response by cholesterol and by lipid extracts of rabbit skin. J Exp Med. 1976;144:754-767.

148. Bisno AL, Nelson KE. Type-specific opsonic antibodies in streptococcal pyoderma. Infect Immun. 1974;10:1356-1361.

149. Bergner-Rabinowitz S, Ofek I, Davies MA, Rabinowitz K. Type-specific streptococcal antibodies in pyodermal nephritis. J Infect Dis. 1971;124:488-493.

150. Barnett BO, Frieden IJ. Streptococcal skin diseases in children. Semin Dermatol. 1992;11:3-10.

151. Gonzalez A, Schachner LA, Cleary T, et al. Pyoderma in children. Adv Dermatol. 1989;4:127-142.

152. Demidovich CW, Wittler RR, Ruff ME, et al. Impetigo. Current etiology and comparison of penicillin, erythromycin, and cephalexin therapies. Am J Dis Child. 1990;144:1313-1315.

153. Rasmussen JE. The changing nature of impetigo. Patient Care. 1992;15:233-239.

154. Dagan R, Bar-David Y. Comparison of amoxicillin and clavulanic acid (augmentin) for the treatment of nonbullous impetigo. Am J Dis Child. 1989;143:916-918.

155. Barton LL, Friedman AD. Impetigo: A reassessment of etiology and therapy. Pediatr Dermatol. 1987;4:185-188.

156. Barton LL, Friedman AD, Sharkey AM, et al. Impetigo contagiosa III. Comparative efficacy of oral erythromycin and topical mupirocin. Pediatr Dermatol. 1989;6:134-138.

157. Britton JW, Fajardo JE, Krafte-Jacobs B. Comparison of mupirocin and erythromycin in the treatment of impetigo. J Pediatr. 1990;117:827-829.

158. Yun HJ, Lee SW, Yoon GM, et al. Prevalence and mechanisms of low- and high-level mupirocin resistance in staphylococci isolated from a Korean hospital. J Antimicrob Chemother. 2003;51:619-623.

159. Hoge CW, Schwartz B, Talkington DF, et al. The changing epidemiology of invasive group A streptococcal infections and the emergence of streptococcal toxic shock-like syndrome. A retrospective population-base study. JAMA. 1993;269:384-389.

160. Martin PR, Hoiby EA. Streptococcal serogroup A epidemic in Norway. 1987-1988. Scand J Infect Dis. 1990;22:421-429.

161. Stromberg A, Romanus V, Burman LG. Outbreak of group A streptococcal bacteremia in Sweden: An epidemiological and clinical study. J Infect Dis. 1991;164:595-598.

162. Demers B, Simor AE, Vellend H, et al. Severe invasive group A streptococcal infections in Ontario, Canada: 1987-1991. Clin Infect Dis. 1993;16:792-800.

163. Johnson DR, Stevens DL, Kaplan EL. Epidemiologic analysis of group A streptococcal serotypes associated with severe systemic infections, rheumatic fever, or uncomplicated pharyngitis. J Infect Dis. 1992;166:374-382.

164. Stevens DL, Tanner MH, Winship J, et al. Severe group A streptococcal infections associated with a toxic shock-like syndrome and scarlet fever toxin A. N Engl J Med. 1989;321:1-7.

165. Bartter T, Dascal A, Carroll K, Curley FJ. 'Toxic strep syndrome': A manifestation of group A streptococcal infection. Arch Intern Med. 1988;148:1421-1424.

166. Bernard P, Plantin P, Roger H, et al. Roxithromycin versus penicillin in the treatment of erysipelas in adults: A comparative study. Br J Dermatol. 1992;127:155-159.

167. Lentnek AL, Giger O, O'Rourke E. Group A beta-hemolytic streptococcal bacteremia and intravenous substance abuse: A growing clinical problem? Arch Intern Med. 1990;150:89-93.

168. Barg NL, Kish MA, Kauffman CA, Supena RB. Group A streptococcal bacteremia in intravenous drug abusers. Am J Med. 1985;78:569-574.

169. Craven DE, Rixinger AI, Bisno AL, et al. Bacteremia caused by group G streptococci in parenteral drug abusers: Epidemiological and clinical aspects. J Infect Dis. 1986;153:988-992.

170. Simon MS, Cody RL. Cellulitis after axillary lymph node dissection for carcinoma of the breast. Am J Med. 1992;93:543-548.

171. de Godoy JM, de Godoy MF, Valente A, et al. Lymphoscintigraphic evaluation in patients after erysipelas. Lymphology. 2000;33:177-180.

172. Baddour LM, Bisno AL. Recurrent cellulitis after saphenous venectomy for coronary bypass surgery. Ann Intern Med. 1982;97:493-496.

173. Semel JD, Goldin H. Association of athlete's foot with cellulitis of the lower extremities: Diagnostic value of bacterial cultures of ipsilateral interdigital space samples. Clin Infect Dis. 1996;23:1162-1164.

174. Greenberg J, DeSanctis RW, Mills RM Jr. Vein-donor-leg cellulitis after coronary artery bypass surgery. Ann Intern Med. 1982;97:565-566.

175. Baddour LM, Bisno AL. Recurrent cellulitis after coronary bypass surgery: Association with superficial fungal infection in saphenous venectomy limbs. JAMA. 1984;251:1049-1052.

176. Baddour LM, Bisno AL. Non-group A beta-hemolytic streptococcal cellulitis: Association with venous and lymphatic compromise. Am J Med. 1985;79:155-159.

177. Dupuy A, Benchikhi H, Roujeau JC, et al. Risk factors for erysipelas of the leg (cellulitis): Case-control study. BMJ. 1999;318:1591-1594.

178. Roldan YB, Mata-Essayag S, Hartung C. Erysipelas and tinea pedis. Mycoses. 2000;43:181-183.

179. Eriksson BK. Anal colonization of group G beta-hemolytic streptococci in relapsing erysipelas of the lower extremity. Clin Infect Dis. 1999;29:1319-1320.

180. Hook EWI, Hooton TM, Horton CA, et al. Microbiologic evaluation of cutaneous cellulitis in adults. Arch Intern Med. 1986;146:295-297.

181. Howe PM, Fajardo JE, Orcutt MA. Etiologic diagnosis of cellulitis: Comparison of aspirates obtained from the leading edge and the point of maximal inflammation. Pediatr Infect Dis J. 1987;6:685.

182. Newell PM, Norden CW. Value of needle aspiration in bacteriologic diagnosis of cellulitis in adults. J Clin Microbiol. 1988;26:401-404.

183. Wang JH, Liu YC, Cheng DL, et al. Role of benzathine penicillin G in prophylaxis for recurrent streptococcal cellulitis of the lower legs. Clin Infect Dis. 1997;25:685-689.

184. Sjoblom AC, Eriksson B, Jorup-Ronstrom C, et al. Antibiotic prophylaxis in recurrent erysipelas. Infection. 1993;21:390-393.

185. Kremer M, Zuckerman R, Avraham Z, Raz R. Long-term antimicrobial therapy in the prevention of recurrent soft-tissue infections. J Infect. 1991;22:37-40.

186. Bisno AL, Stevens DL. Streptococcal infections of skin and soft tissues. N Engl J Med. 1996;334:240-244.

187. Meleney FL. Hemolytic streptococcus gangrene. Arch Surg. 1924;9:317-364.

188. Stevens DL. Invasive group A streptococcus infections. Clin Infect Dis. 1991;14:2-13.

189. Bisno AL, Cockerill FR III, Bermudez CT. The initial outpatient-physician encounter in group A streptococcal necrotizing fasciitis. Clin Infect Dis. 2000;31:607-608.

190. Stamenkovic I, Lew PD. Early recognition of potentially fatal necrotizing fasciitis: The use of frozen-section biopsy. N Engl J Med. 1984;310:1689-1693.

190a. Majeski J, Majeski E. Necrotizing fasciitis: improved survival with early recognition by tissue biopsy and aggressive surgical treatment. South Med J. 1997;90:1065-1068.

191. Adams EM, Gudmundsson S, Yocum DE, et al. Streptococcal myositis. Arch Intern Med. 1985;145:1020-1023.

192. Holm SE. Invasive group A streptococcal infections (Editorial, Comment). N Engl J Med. 1996;335:590-591.

193. Wheeler MC, Roe MH, Kaplan EL, et al. Outbreak of group A streptococcus septicemia in children: Clinical, epidemiologic, and microbiological correlates. JAMA. 1991;266:533-537.

194. Gaworzewska ET, Hallas G. Group A streptococcal infections and a toxic shock-like syndrome. N Engl J Med. 1989;321:1546.

195. Schwartz B, Facklam RR, Breiman RF. Changing epidemiology of group A streptococcal infection in the USA. Lancet. 1990;336:1167-1171.

196. Hribalova V. Streptococcus pyogenes and the toxic shock syndrome. Ann Intern Med. 1988;108:772.

197. Greenberg RN, Willoughby BG, Kennedy DJ, et al. Hypocalcemia and "toxic" syndrome associated with streptococcal fasciitis. South Med J. 1983;76:916-918.

198. Kiska DL, Thiede B, Caracciolo J, et al. Invasive group A streptococcal infections in North Carolina: Epidemiology, clinical features, and genetic and serotype analysis of causative organisms. J Infect Dis. 1997;176:992-1000.

199. Cockerill FR, MacDonald KL, Thompson RL. An outbreak of invasive group A streptococcal disease associated with high carriage rates of the invasive clone among school-aged children. JAMA. 1997;277:38-43.

200. Davies HD, McGreer A, Schwartz B, et al. Invasive group A streptococcal infections in Ontario, Canada. N Engl J Med. 1996;335:547-554.

201. Auerbach SB, Schwartz B, Facklam RR, et al. Outbreak of invasive group A streptococcal (GAS) disease in a nursing home. Abstract 508. Presented at the 1990 Interscience Conference on Antimicrobial Agents and Chemotherapy, Atlanta, Ga, 1990.

202. Hohenboken JJ, Anderson F, Kaplan EL. Invasive group A streptococcal (GAS) serotype M-1 outbreak in a long-term care facility (LTCF) with mortality. Abstract J198. Presented at the 1994 Interscience Conference on Antimicrobial Agents and Chemotherapy, Orlando, Fla, 1994.

203. Schwartz B, Ussery XT. Group A streptococcal outbreaks in nursing homes. Infect Control Hosp Epidemiol. 1992;13:742-747.

204. Harkness GA, Bentley DW, Mottley M, Lee J. Streptococcus pyogenes outbreak in a long-term care facility. Am J Infect Control. 1992;20:142-148.

205. Ruben FL, Norden CW, Heisler B, Korica Y. An outbreak of Streptococcus pyogenes infections in a nursing home. Ann Intern Med. 1984;101:494-496.

206. DiPersio JR, File TM Jr, Stevens DL, et al. Spread of serious disease-producing M3 clones of group A streptococcus among family members and health care workers. Clin Infect Dis. 1996;22:490-495.

207. Gamba MA, Martinelli M, Schaad HJ. Familial transmission of a serious disease-producing group A streptococcus clone: Case reports and review. Clin Infect Dis. 1997;24:1118-1121.

208. Valenzuela TD, Hooton TM, Kaplan EL, Schlievert P. Transmission of 'toxic strep' syndrome from an infected child to a firefighter during CPR. Ann Emerg Med. 1991;20:90-92.

209. Givner LB, Abramson JS, Wasilauskas B. Apparent increase in the incidence of invasive group A beta-hemolytic streptococcal disease in children. J Pediatr. 1991;118:341-346.

210. Brogan TV, Nizet V, Waldhausen JHT, et al. Group A streptococcal necrotizing fasciitis complicating primary varicella: A series of fourteen patients. Pediatr Infect Dis J. 1995;14:588-594.

211. Francis J, Warren RE. Streptococcus pyogenes bacteraemia in Cambridge—A review of 67 episodes. Q J Med. 1988;68:603-613.

212. Barnham M. Invasive streptococcal infections in the era before the acquired immune deficiency syndrome: A 10 years' compilation of patients with streptococcal bacteraemia in North Yorkshire. J Infect. 1989;18:231-248.

213. Braunstein H. Characteristics of group A streptococcal bacteremia in patients at the San Bernardino County Medical Center [published erratum appears in Rev Infect Dis. 1991;13:533]. Rev Infect Dis. 1991;13:8-11.

214. Holm SE, Norrby A, Bergholm AM, Norgen M. Aspects of pathogenesis of serious group A streptococcal infections in Sweden, 1988-1989. J Infect Dis. 1992;166:31-37.

215. Stegmayr B, Bjorck S, Holm S, et al. Septic shock induced by group A streptococcal infection: Clinical and therapeutic aspects. Scand J Infect Dis. 1992;24:589-597.

216. Herold AH. Group A beta-hemolytic streptococcal toxic shock from a mild pharyngitis. J Fam Pract. 1990;31:549-551.

217. Bradley JS, Schlievert PM, Peterson BM. Toxic shock-like syndrome, a complication of strep throat. Pediatr Infect Dis J. 1991;10:790.

218. Chapnick EK, Gradon JD, Lutwick LI, et al. Streptococcal toxic shock syndrome due to noninvasive pharyngitis. Clin Infect Dis. 1992;14:1074-1077.

219. Sellers BJ, Woods ML, Morris SE, Saffle JR. Necrotizing group A streptococcal infections associated with streptococcal toxic shock syndrome. Am J Med. 1996;172:523-528.

220. Stevens DL. Could nonsteroidal antiinflammatory drugs (NSAIDs) enhance the progression of bacterial infections to toxic shock syndrome? Clin Infect Dis. 1995;21:977-980.

221. Barnham M. Nonsteroidal anti-inflammatory drugs: Concurrent or causative drugs in serious infection? Clin Infect Dis. 1997;25:1272-1273.

222. LaPenta D, Rubens C, Chi E, Cleary PP. Group A streptococci efficiently invade human respiratory epithelial cells. Proc Natl Acad Sci U S A. 1994;91:12115-12119.

223. O'Brien KL, Beall B, Barrett NL, et al. Epidemiology of invasive group A streptococcus disease in the United States, 1995-1999. Clin Infect Dis. 2002;35:268-276.

224. Mollick JA, Rich RR. Characterization of a superantigen from a pathogenic strain of *Streptococcus pyogenes*. Clin Res. 1991;39:213A.

225. Hackett SP, Stevens DL. Superantigens associated with staphylococcal and streptococcal toxic shock syndrome are potent inducers of tumor necrosis factor-beta synthesis. J Infect Dis. 1993;168:232-235.

226. Fast DJ, Schlievert PM, Nelson RD. Toxic shock syndrome-associated staphylococcal and streptococcal pyrogenic toxins are potent inducers of tumor necrosis factor production. Infect Immun. 1989;57:291-294.

227. Norrby-Teglund A, Newton D, Kotb M, et al. Superantigenic properties of the group A streptococcal exotoxin SpeF (MF). Infect Immun. 1994;62:5227-5233.

228. Norrby-Teglund A, Norgren M, Holm SE, et al. Similar cytokine induction profiles of a novel streptococcal exotoxin, MF, and pyrogenic exotoxins A and B. Infect Immun. 1994;62:3731-3738.

229. Kotb M, Ohnishi H, Majumdar G, et al. Temporal relationship of cytokine release by peripheral blood mononuclear cells stimulated by the streptococcal superantigen pep M5. Infect Immun. 1993;61:1194-1201.

230. Norrby-Teglund A, Basma H, Andersson J, et al. Varying titres of neutralizing antibodies to streptococcal superantigens in different preparations of normal polyspecific immunoglobulin G (IVIG): Implications for therapeutic efficacy. Clin Infect Dis. 1998;26:631-638.

231. Kapur V, Majesky MW, Li LL, et al. Cleavage of interleukin 1beta (IL-1beta) precursor to produce active IL-1beta by a conserved extracellular cysteine protease from *Streptococcus pyogenes*. Proc Natl Acad Sci U S A. 1993;90:7676-7680.

232. Hackett SP, Stevens DL. Synthesis of tumor necrosis factor and interleukin-1 by monocytes stimulated with pyrogenic exotoxin A and streptolysin O. J Infect Dis. 1992;165:885.

233. Hackett S, Ferretti J, Stevens D. Cytokine induction by viable group A streptococci: suppression by streptolysin O. Abstract B-249. Presented at the American Society for Microbiology, Las Vegas, NV, 1994.

234. Muller-Alouf H, Alouf JE, Gerlach D, et al. Comparative study of cytokine release by human peripheral blood mononuclear cells stimulated with *Streptococcus pyogenes* superantigenic erythrogenic toxins, heat-killed streptococci, and lipopolysaccharide. Infect Immun. 1994;62:4915-4921.

235. Herwald H, Collin M, Muller-Esterl W, Bjorck L. Streptococcal cysteine proteinase releases kinins: A novel virulence mechanism. J Exp Med. 1996;184:665-673.

236. Stevens DL, Bryant AE, Hackett SP, et al. Group A streptococcal bacteremia: The role of tumor necrosis factor in shock and organ failure. J Infect Dis. 1996;173:619-626.

237. Stevens DL. Streptococcal toxic-shock syndrome: Spectrum of disease, pathogenesis, and new concepts in treatment. Emerg Infect Dis. 1995;1:69-78.

238. Cruz K, Hollenberg S. Update on septic shock: The latest approaches to treatment. J Crit Illness. 2003;18:162-168.

239. Stevens DL, Madaras-Kelly KJ, Richards DM. In vitro antimicrobial effects of various combinations of penicillin and clindamycin against four strains of *Streptococcus pyogenes*. Antimicrob Agents Chemother. 1998;42:1266-1268.

240. Stevens DL, Bryant AE, Hackett SP. Antibiotic effects on bacterial viability, toxin production and host response. Clin Infect Dis. 1995;20(suppl 2):S154-S157.

241. Stevens DL, Hackett SP, Bryant AE. Suppression of monuclear cell synthesis of tumor necrosis factor by azithromycin. Abstract 181. Presented at the Infectious Disease Society of America, San Francisco, Calif, 1997.

242. Miwa K, Fukuyama M, Ida N, et al. Preparation of a superantigen-adsorbing device and its superantigen removal efficacies in vitro and in vivo. Int J Infect Dis. 2003;7:21-26.

243. Dick GF, Dick GH. Therapeutic results with concentrated scarlet fever antitoxin. JAMA. 1925;84:803.

244. Lamothe F, D'Amico P, Ghosn P, et al. Clinical usefulness of intravenous human immunoglobulins in invasive group A streptococcal infections: Case report and review. Clin Infect Dis. 1995;21:1469-1470.

245. Barry W, Hudgins L, Donta ST, Pesanti EL. Intravenous immunoglobulin therapy for toxic shock syndrome. JAMA. 1992;267:3315-3316.

246. Stevens DL. Rationale for the use of intravenous gamma globulin in the treatment of streptococcal toxic shock syndrome (Editorial Response). Clin Infect Dis. 1998;26:639-641.

247. Kaul R, McGeer A, Norrby-Teglund A, et al. Intravenous immunoglobulin therapy for streptococcal toxic shock syndrome—A comparative observational study. Clin Infect Dis. 1999;28:800-807.

248. Darenberg J, Ihendyane N, Sjolin J, et al. Intravenous immunoglobulin G therapy in streptococcal toxic shock syndrome: A European randomized, double-blind, placebo-controlled trial. Clin Infect Dis. 2003;37:333-340.

249. Stevens DL. Dilemmas in the treatment of invasive Streptococcus pyogenes infections. Clin Infect Dis. 2003;37:341-343.

250. Norrby-Teglund A, Kaul R, Low DE, et al. Evidence for the presence of streptococcal-superantigen-neutralizing antibodies in normal polyspecific immunoglobulin G. Infect Immun. 1996;64:5395-5398.

251. Riseman JA, Zamboni WA, Curtis A, et al. Hyperbaric oxygen therapy for necrotizing fasciitis reduces mortality and the need for debridements. Surgery. 1990;108:847-850.

252. Weinstein MP, Reller B, Murphy JR, Lichtenstein KA. The clinical significance of positive blood cultures: A comparative analysis of 500 episodes of bacteremia and fungemia in adults. I. Laboratory and epidemiologic observations. Rev Infect Dis. 1983;5:35-53.

253. Schwartz B, Elliott JA, Butler JC, et al. Clusters of invasive group A streptococcal infections in family, hospital, and nursing home settings. Clin Infect Dis. 1992;15:277-284.

254. Duma RJ, Weinberg AN, Medrek TF, Kunz LJ. Streptococcal infections: A bacteriological and clinical study of streptococcal bacteremia. Medicine. 1969;48:87-127.

255. Dan M, Maximova S, Siegman-Igra Y, et al. Varied presentations of sporadic group A streptococcal bacteremia: Clinical experience and attempt at classification. Rev Infect Dis. 1990;12:537-542.

256. Ispahani P, Donald FE, Aveline AJ. Streptococcus pyogenes bacteraemia: An old enemy subdued, but not defeated. J Infect. 1988;16:37-46.

257. Bucher A, Martin PR, Hoiby EA, et al. Spectrum of disease in bacteraemic patients during a *Streptococcus pyogenes* serotype M-1 epidemic in Norway in 1988. Eur J Clin Microbiol Infect Dis. 1992;11:416-426.

258. Burkert T, Watanakunakorn C. Group A streptococcal bacteremia in a community teaching hospital—1980-1989. Clin Infect Dis. 1992;14:29-37.

259. Ramirez CA, Naraqi S, McCulley DJ. Group A beta-hemolytic streptococcus endocarditis. Am Heart J. 1984;108:1383-1386.

260. Baddour LM. Infective endocarditis caused by beta-hemolytic streptococci. The Infectious Diseases Society of America's Emerging Infections Network. Clin Infect Dis. 1998;26:66-71.

261. van de Beek D, de Gans J, Spanjaard L, et al. Group A streptococcal meningitis in adults: Report of 41 cases and a review of the literature. Clin Infect Dis. 2002;34:e32-e36.

262. Sommer R, Rohner P, Garbino J, et al. Group A beta-hemolytic streptococcus meningitis: Clinical and microbiological features of nine cases. Clin Infect Dis. 1999;29:929-931.

263. Murphy DJ Jr. Group A streptococcal meningitis. Pediatrics. 1983;71:1-5.

264. Basiliere JL, Bistrong HW, Spence WF. Streptococcal pneumonia: Recent outbreaks in military recruit populations. Am J Med. 1968;44:580-589.

265. Crum NF, Hale BR, Bradshaw DA, et al. Outbreak of Group A streptococcal pneumonia among Marine Corps recruits—California, November 1-December 20, 2002. MMWR Morb Mortal Wkly Rep. 2003;52:106-109.

266. Muller MP, Low DE, Green KA, et al. Clinical and epidemiologic features of group A streptococcal pneumonia in Ontario, Canada. Arch Intern Med. 2003;163:467-472.

267. Petersen JP, Kaltoft MS, Misfeldt JC, et al. Community outbreak of perianal group A streptococcal infection in Denmark. Pediatr Infect Dis J. 2003;22:105-109.

268. Mogielnicki NP, Schwartzman JD, Elliott JA. Perineal group A streptococcal disease in a pediatric practice. Pediatrics. 2000;106(2 Pt 1):276-281.

269. Mastro TD, Farley TA, Elliott JA, et al. An outbreak of surgical wound infections due to group A *Streptococcus* carried on the scalp. N Engl J Med. 1990;323:968-972.

270. Kakis A, Gibbs L, Eguia J, et al. An outbreak of group A Streptococcal infection among health care workers. Clin Infect Dis. 2002;35:1353-1359.

271. Robinson KA, Rothrock G, Phan Q, et al. Risk for severe group A streptococcal disease among patients' household contacts. Emerg Infect Dis. 2003;9:443-447.

272. Factor SH, Levine OS, Schwartz B, et al. Invasive group A streptococcal disease: Risk factors for adults. Emerg Infect Dis. 2003;9:970-977.

CHAPTER 196

Nonsuppurative Poststreptococcal Sequelae: Rheumatic Fever and Glomerulonephritis

ALAN L. BISNO

RHEUMATIC FEVER

Acute rheumatic fever (ARF) is a disease characterized by nonsuppurative inflammatory lesions involving primarily the heart, joints, subcutaneous tissues, and central nervous system. In its classic form, ARF is acute, febrile, and largely self-limited. However, damage to heart valves may occur, and such damage may be chronic and progressive and lead to severe cardiac failure, total disability, and, not infrequently, death many years after the acute attack. The manifestations of ARF are extremely variable; the disorder remains for the most part a clinical syndrome for which no specific diagnostic test exists. All cases of ARF follow group A streptococcal upper respiratory tract infection, although the exact mechanisms mediating development of the disease remain speculative. Persons who have suffered an attack of ARF are particularly predisposed to recurrent episodes after subsequent group A streptococcal infections.

History

Guillaume de Baillou (1538-1616), also known as "Ballonius," first clearly distinguished acute arthritis from gout. Thomas Sydenham (1624-1689) described chorea but failed to associate this entity with other manifestations of ARF. Raymond Vieussens (1641-1715) published pathologic descriptions of mitral stenosis and aortic insufficiency. It remained, however, for William Charles Wells in 1812 to emphasize the association of rheumatism and carditis and to provide the first clear description of subcutaneous nodules. Jean-Baptiste Bouillard in 1836 and Walter B. Cheadle in 1889 published extensive studies of rheumatic arthritis and carditis that have come to be regarded as classic works in this field and form the basis for modern clinical concepts of ARF. In 1904, Ludwig Aschoff described the specific rheumatic lesion in the myocardium.[1]

In 1880, J. K. Fowler pointed out the association between sore throat and rheumatic fever, and shortly after the dawn of the 20th century, Bela Schick identified ARF as one of the "nachkrankheiten" of scarlet fever. The introduction of Rebecca Lancefield's grouping system for β-hemolytic streptococci allowed clarification of the epidemiology of the disease by a number of investigators in the United States and the United Kingdom, including Coburn, Collis, Rammelkamp, Wannamaker, Massell, and Stollerman. Finally, the widespread introduction of antibiotic agents after World War II resulted in the development of strategies for primary and secondary prevention of rheumatic fever.

Etiology and Pathogenesis

ARF is a delayed nonsuppurative sequela of upper respiratory infection caused by group A streptococci, a conclusion firmly supported by several lines of evidence. There is a close temporal relationship between epidemics of streptococcal sore throat and scarlet fever and epidemics of ARF. Most patients with ARF relate a history of preceding pharyngitis; even in the absence of such clear-cut evidence, elevated serum levels of antistreptococcal antibodies nearly always document recent streptococcal infection. Prospective studies of primary and recurrent ARF have shown this disease occurs only after an immunologically significant streptococcal infection. Finally, continuous antimicrobial prophylaxis, when successful in preventing intercurrent

TABLE 196-1   M Serotypes of Group A Streptococci Associated with Nonsuppurative Sequelae in the Western Hemisphere*

ARF	Pharyngitis-Associated AGN	Pyoderma-Associated AGN
1	1	2
3	4	49[†]
5	12	55[†]
6	25	57
14		59
18		60
19		61
24		

*This list represents the major serotypes known to be associated with ARF and AGN in the Western Hemisphere, but it is not all inclusive. M types of streptococcal strains isolated from various geographic areas varies widely.[6,186]

[†]M types 49 and 55 have also been reported on occasion to cause pharyngitis-associated AGN.

AGN, Acute glomerulonephritis; ARF, acute rheumatic fever.

streptococcal infections, also effectively prevents ARF recurrences in rheumatic persons.

An intriguing and as yet unexplained aspect of the host-parasite relationship is the fact that, insofar as is known, cutaneous streptococcal infections do not initiate ARF. This may indicate a requirement for the pharyngeal site, with its rich endowment of lymphoid tissue, for initiation of the disease process, or it may result from a lack of rheumatogenicity among the so-called pyoderma strains of group A streptococci.

A substantial body of evidence indicates that group A streptococci do indeed vary in their rheumatogenic potential. Studies of outbreaks of streptococcal pharyngitis reveal that strains of certain M serotypes or genotypes are strongly and repeatedly associated with ARF[2] (Table 196-1), whereas strains of other equally prevalent types fail to initiate the disease or even to reactivate it in exquisitely susceptible hosts.[3] Investigations of endemic ARF cases in Trinidad[4] and Chile[5] indicate that streptococci causing ARF belong to different serotypes than those causing acute glomerulonephritis (AGN) occurring simultaneously in the same population. Strains of group A streptococci isolated from ARF patients may, however, differ widely in different geographic locales.[6] Although the association of pyoderma strains of group A streptococci (see Chapter 195) with ARF has been postulated,[6,7] such strains have never been definitively associated with ARF[8,9] even when, as frequently occurs, they colonize the throat.

Variations in the rheumatogenicity of prevalent group A streptococci likely account for the striking temporal and geographic fluctuations in the incidence of ARF. For example, strains of mucoid group A streptococci that were genetically identical, or nearly so, were prevalent in Salt Lake City, Utah during two peak periods of rheumatic fever incidence occurring 12 years apart.[10,11]

Rheumatogenic streptococcal strains exhibit distinct biologic characteristics. Their M protein molecules share a particular surface-exposed antigenic domain[12] against which ARF patients mount a strong IgG response.[13] These strains fail to elaborate α_1-lipoproteinase (so-called streptococcal opacity factor), and they are frequently heavily encapsulated. The latter feature is manifested by the formation of mucoid colonies in blood agar plates. Whether such strains express a unique rheumatogenic antigen, however, remains unknown.

It is probable that not all strains of rheumatogenic serotypes are equally dangerous. The propensity of a given strain to cause ARF may well depend on its degree of virulence, a reflection of quantitative factors such as expression of M protein, hyaluronate, or other less well-defined biologic properties. Virulence is likely to be enhanced in epidemiologic settings that favor rapid person-to-person transmission.

Although the group A streptococcus is known to be the causative agent of rheumatic fever, the exact mechanism by which this microorganism induces the disease remains unexplained. Suggestions that the disease results from direct tissue invasion by group A streptococci or by cell wall variants of this organism have not been confirmed and are no longer considered tenable. Several theories have been advanced. These include the following: (1) toxic effects of streptococcal products, particularly streptolysins S or O, which are known to be capable of inducing tissue injury; (2) serum sickness–like reaction mediated by antigen-antibody complexes, perhaps localized to sites of tissue injury; and (3) autoimmune phenomena induced by similarity or identity of certain streptococcal antigens to a wide variety of human tissue antigens.[14]

Although none of these theories has been unequivocally proved or refuted, most attention in recent years has been focused on the concept of autoimmunity, or, more precisely, molecular mimicry.[15] Interest in this mechanism has been spurred by the identification of antibodies in the sera of patients with ARF or rheumatic heart disease that react with the human heart in a variety of test systems. These so-called heart-reactive antibodies (HRA) are also present, albeit in much lower titer, in sera of patients with uncomplicated streptococcal pharyngitis. The presence of bound immunoglobulin and complement in the myocardia of children dying of rheumatic carditis suggests that circulating HRA may have pathogenetic significance.

More recently, improved methods of purifying M protein have been developed, and molecular biology techniques have been employed in studies on the relationship between specific peptides of the M protein molecule and human tissues. Epitopes of streptococcal M proteins have been identified that share antigenic determinants with cardiac myosin,[16,17] sarcolemmal membrane proteins,[18] synovium, and articular cartilage.[19]

Goldstein and colleagues[20] described a cross-reaction between group A polysaccharide and a structural glycoprotein isolated from human and bovine heart valves. Such a cross-reaction might explain the observation that serum levels of antibodies to group A carbohydrate appear to remain elevated for many years in patients with rheumatic valvulitis, but not in rheumatic patients without valvulitis[21] and decline remarkably if valve resection is performed.

Chronic remittent nodular lesions have been observed in dermal connective tissue after injection into experimental animals of a streptococcal mucopeptide-polysaccharide cell wall complex.[22] Antibodies raised in rabbits against streptococcal hyaluronate cross react with human hyaluronate.[23] Many children with Sydenham's chorea have circulating antibodies that react both with neurons of the caudate and subthalamic nuclei and with group A streptococcal cell membranes.[24] Taken together, these cross-reactive and toxic phenomena could explain most of the individual manifestations of ARF. On the other hand, it should be emphasized that no direct proof exists that these systems play any role in the pathogenesis of rheumatic fever.

Much of the work reviewed in the preceding, particularly that related to HRA and group A carbohydrate, has focused on humoral immune responses to streptococci. Indeed, serum antibody responses to streptolysin O, non-type-specific M antigens, and virtually every other streptococcal antigen, are on the average more vigorous in patients with ARF than in persons with uncomplicated streptococcal infections. However, it is likely that delayed hypersensitivity responses to streptococcal antigens also play a critical role in the etiology of ARF.[25,26] Preparations of streptolysin S contain a nonspecific mitogen that is closely related but separable from the hemolytic activity. In rheumatic persons lymphocyte reactivity to streptococcal cell walls and membranes is heightened, but the reactivity to membranes is more striking and persists for several years after an acute attack.[27] T lymphocytes from spleens of adult guinea pigs sensitized with streptococcal cells, cell walls, or protoplast membranes are cytotoxic for cultured guinea pig heart cells.[28]

During active rheumatic carditis both the number of helper (CD4) lymphocytes and the ratio of CD4 to CD8 cells are increased in heart valves as well as in peripheral blood.[29,30] Production of interleukin-1[31] and interleukin-2[31,32] has been reported to be enhanced. The recognition that both M protein[33] and streptococcal pyrogenic exotoxins[34] function as superantigens suggests a potential mechanism mediating the unrestrained immunologic assault postulated to cause ARF.

A complete elucidation of the pathogenesis of ARF obviously requires an understanding not only of the peculiarities of the etiologic agent but also of the nature of the susceptible host. The fact that, even in severe epidemics of exudative pharyngitis, rheumatic fever affects only a small proportion of infected persons, coupled with the known familial aggregation of ARF cases, has long suggested the possibility of a genetic predisposition to rheumatic attacks. Studies of the distribution of class 1 HLA antigens in rheumatic individuals compared with controls have been inconclusive. A statistically significant association has been reported between certain of the class II HLA antigens (HLA-DR2 in blacks[35] and HLA-DR4 in whites[35,36]) and rheumatic fever. An intriguing potential link between the genetic constitution of the human host and susceptibility to ARF is the identification of certain alloantigens that are expressed in a higher proportion of circulating B lymphocytes of rheumatic subjects and their family members than of patients with AGN or normal controls.[37,38]

Pathologic Findings

Rheumatic fever is characterized pathologically by the presence of exudative and proliferative inflammatory lesions of connective tissue, most notably the heart, joints, blood vessels, and subcutaneous tissue.[39] In the early stages of the disease, there is fragmentation of collagen fibers, cellular infiltration that is predominantly lymphocytic, and fibrinoid deposition. This is followed shortly by the appearance of the myocardial Aschoff nodule. The Aschoff nodule is a perivascular focus of inflammation that consists of an area of central necrosis surrounded by a rosette of large mononuclear and giant multinuclear cells. The nuclei of these cells may contain a clear area just within the nuclear membrane ("owl-eyed nucleus") or present a serrated ("catepillar") appearance depending on their orientation in microscopic cross section. Such cells are known as Anichkov myocytes, although immunohistochemical studies demonstrate they are of macrophage/histiocyte origin.[40,41] Cardiac findings may include pericarditis, myocarditis, or endocarditis. Endocarditis involves the left side of the heart in most instances. A thickened and roughened area is frequently seen in the left atrium above the base of the posterior leaflet of the mitral valve ("MacCallum's patch"). Valvular lesions begin as edema and cellular infiltration of the leaflets and chordae with small verrucae along the line of closure. As healing progresses, the valves may become thickened and deformed, the chordae shortened, and the valve commissures fused, thereby resulting in valvular stenosis or insufficiency.

The joint lesions are characterized by fibrinous exudate over the synovial membrane and serous effusion without joint destruction. Histologic findings include cellular infiltration and fibrinoid degeneration. Subcutaneous nodules resemble Aschoff bodies in many features. They consist of a central zone of fibrinoid necrosis surrounded by histiocytes and fibroblasts; perivascular accumulations of lymphocytes and polymorphonuclear leukocytes are also apparent. Although scattered areas of arteritis and petechial hemorrhages have been found in the brain, their relationship to Sydenham's chorea remains uncertain.

Epidemiology

Acute rheumatic fever is most frequent among 5- to 15-year-old children. Indeed, its relative rarity in infants and preschool-aged children has led some observers to question whether repeated "primary" infections might be a precondition for the development of this disease. Both initial and recurrent episodes also occur in adults.[42-44] There is no clear-cut gender predilection, although a female preponderance exists in certain clinical manifestations, notably mitral stenosis and Sydenham's chorea when the latter occurs after puberty. In temperate climates rheumatic fever tends to occur less frequently during the summer.

The attack rate of rheumatic fever after untreated streptococcal exudative tonsillitis in military recruit camps has been carefully studied and has been shown to be consistently around 3%.[45] The ARF attack rate is considerably lower after endemically occurring infections among open populations of school-aged children. Siegel and colleagues[46] studied 519 untreated children with pharyngitis associated with throat cultures positive for group A streptococci. The attack rate of ARF was found to be 0.4%. Among those patients with an immunologically significant infection, as judged by a rise in the serum titer of antistreptolysin O (ASO), the attack rate was 0.9%. In that study, ARF was observed to occur only among the group of 81 patients with exudative pharyngitis, throat cultures positive for group A streptococci, ASO titer rises, and prolonged convalescent streptococcal carriage. In this group, the ARF attack rate, 2.5%, approximated that seen in military recruit camps. These and other data suggest that ARF is *more likely* to occur after more severe forms of streptococcal throat infection, as judged by clinical, bacteriologic, and immunologic criteria. Nevertheless, one third or more of ARF cases occur after asymptomatic streptococcal infection.

It may be difficult for physicians trained in North America to comprehend the magnitude of the problem of ARF in developing countries. The disease is rampant in the Middle East, the Indian subcontinent, and selected areas of Africa and South America.[47,48] For example, a World Health Organization survey conducted between 1986 and 1990 estimated the prevalence of rheumatic fever/rheumatic heart disease per 1000 schoolchildren to be 12.6 in Zambia, 10.2 in Sudan, and 7.9 in Bolivia.[47] It has been estimated that there are at least 50,000 episodes of ARF annually in India and more than one million individuals with rheumatic heart disease.[49] Extraordinarily high rates of ARF and rheumatic heart disease are seen among Aboriginal populations such as those in New Zealand and Australia. Between 1989 and 1993, the annual incidence of ARF among Aboriginal children aged 5 to 14 years in Australia's Northern Territory was 254 per 100,000, and the point prevalence of rheumatic heart disease among the Aboriginal population was 9.6 per 1000.[50]

The overall incidence of ARF in the United States cannot be ascertained precisely because of inherent difficulties in diagnosing the disease and because most states no longer maintain operational rheumatic fever registries. There is general agreement, however, that the incidence of ARF and rheumatic heart disease declined markedly over the course of the 20th century in the United States and Western Europe. The rate of decline appears to have been particularly steep during the 1960s and 1970s. Indeed, a survey in Memphis, Tennessee[51] indicated that during 1977 through 1981 the incidence of ARF among white suburban schoolchildren was only 0.5 per 100,000 per year. Similar rates have been reported from many geographic areas of the United States.[52] Traditionally, ARF in the United States has been largely a disease of lower socioeconomic groups. The incidence has been much higher among blacks than whites,[51,53] a fact that appears to relate to basic environmental conditions rather than to any genetic predisposition of the black race for the development of rheumatic fever. The major predisposing environmental condition that has been identified is crowding. The degree of crowding markedly influences the acquisition rate of group A streptococci (see Chapter 195) and hence the risk of development of ARF.[43]

In the mid 1980s, a resurgence of ARF occurred in many communities in the United States.[54] Beginning in early 1985, an epidemic of the disease occurred in Salt Lake City, Utah, and the surrounding intermountain area.[52,55] By the year 2000, more than 500 cases had been diagnosed at the Primary Children's Medical Center in Salt Lake City. Smaller clusters of ARF, ranging from 15 to 40 cases, were reported during approximately the same time period from Columbus[56]; Akron, Ohio[57]; Pittsburgh, Pennsylvania[58]; Nashville[59]; Memphis, Tennessee[60]; Kansas City, Missouri[61]; Morgantown[62]; Charleston, West Virginia[63]; Dallas, Texas[64]; and New York, New York.[65] Moreover, for the first time in many years, outbreaks occurred in army and navy training camps.[66,67]

Quite surprisingly, a number of the 1980s civilian outbreaks[52,56-58,68] involved children of middle-class families residing in suburban or rural settings. The group A streptococcal strains most strongly associated epidemiologically with these ARF outbreaks belong to the well-recognized rheumatogenic serotypes (e.g., types 1, 3, 5, 6, and 18).[69] Particularly prominent in this regard were highly mucoid strains of M18.[69]

Persons who have suffered an initial attack of rheumatic fever have a marked predilection to develop recurrences after subsequent episodes of streptococcal pharyngeal infection. The risk of recurrence after streptococcal infection is highest within the first few years after the initial attack and then declines. It is unclear whether the reason for this decline is the length of time since the preceding attack or to the older age

of the patient. Nevertheless, rheumatic patients remain at an increased risk of recurrence well into adult life. Two other factors positively correlated with a risk of rheumatic recurrences after streptococcal infection are the magnitude of the ASO response and the presence of preexisting heart disease. In the classic studies conducted at Irvington House, New York,[70] for example, 56% of streptococcal infections occurring in persons with rheumatic heart disease and accompanied by four-tube or greater ASO titer rises induced ARF recurrences.

Clinical Manifestations

Rheumatic fever manifests itself as a variety of signs and symptoms that may occur singly or in combination. The most important of these, in terms of diagnosis, have been termed the *major manifestations* and include carditis, polyarthritis, chorea, subcutaneous nodules, and erythema marginatum. Certain additional findings that are frequently present in ARF but are nonspecific in nature constitute the so-called *minor manifestations:* fever, arthralgia, heart block, and acute-phase reactants in the blood (C-reactive protein, elevation of the leukocyte count and erythrocyte sedimentation rate).

The latent period between the onset of preceding streptococcal sore throat and the onset of ARF averages 19 days.[71] The range has been difficult to establish precisely but appears to be between 1 and 5 weeks. The average latent period is the same for recurrent attacks as for initial episodes.

The mode of onset is quite variable. If acute polyarthritis is the initial complaint, the disease may have a rather abrupt onset and may be marked by fever and toxicity. On the other hand, when isolated mild carditis is the initial manifestation, the onset of ARF may be insidious or even subclinical.

Most attacks begin with polyarthritis, although occasionally this may be preceded by abdominal pain. Carditis, if it appears, usually does so early in the course of the disease. Overall, arthritis occurs in approximately 75% of first attacks of ARF, clinically evident carditis in 40% to 50%, chorea in 15%, and subcutaneous nodules and erythema marginatum in fewer than 10%.[72] These incidences vary with age: carditis occurs most frequently when ARF strikes younger children, whereas the proportion of cases with arthritis increases with the age of the patients.

Carditis is the only manifestation of ARF that has the potential to cause long-term disability or death. Heart involvement in ARF is frequently a pancarditis involving the endocardium, myocardium, and pericardium. Nevertheless, in the absence of high fever or symptoms of acute pericarditis or congestive heart failure, it may be asymptomatic. Carditis almost always manifests itself within the first 3 weeks of an attack of ARF if it is to appear at all. The clinical signs of carditis include the development of organic heart murmur(s) not previously present, cardiac enlargement, congestive heart failure, pericardial friction rubs, or signs of effusion.

Intractable heart failure may cause death in the acute phase of the disease, but fortunately, this occurrence is quite rare. Echocardiographic studies have shown that patients with rheumatic fever and congestive heart failure have preserved left ventricular systolic function and severe mitral and/or aortic regurgitation.[73-76] Serum levels of cardiac troponin I are not elevated in ARF patients with congestive failure.[73,77] Thus the etiology of heart failure appears to be acute valvular dilatation and not myocarditis.[78]

Chronic inflammatory changes involving the myocardium and endocardium may lead to the delayed development of chronic rheumatic heart disease (Fig. 196-1). Endocarditis involves the mitral valve more frequently than it does the aortic valve. There are three characteristic murmurs of acute rheumatic carditis: a high-pitched blowing holosystolic apical murmur of mitral regurgitation, a low-pitched apical middiastolic flow murmur (Carey Coombs murmur), and a high-pitched decrescendo diastolic murmur of aortic regurgitation heard at the secondary and primary aortic areas. Murmurs of mitral and aortic stenosis are associated with chronic but not with acute rheumatic valvular disease. The tricuspid valve is involved much less frequently and pulmonic valve very rarely. Delayed atrioventricular conduction, as manifested by first-degree or even greater degrees of heart block,[79] is a

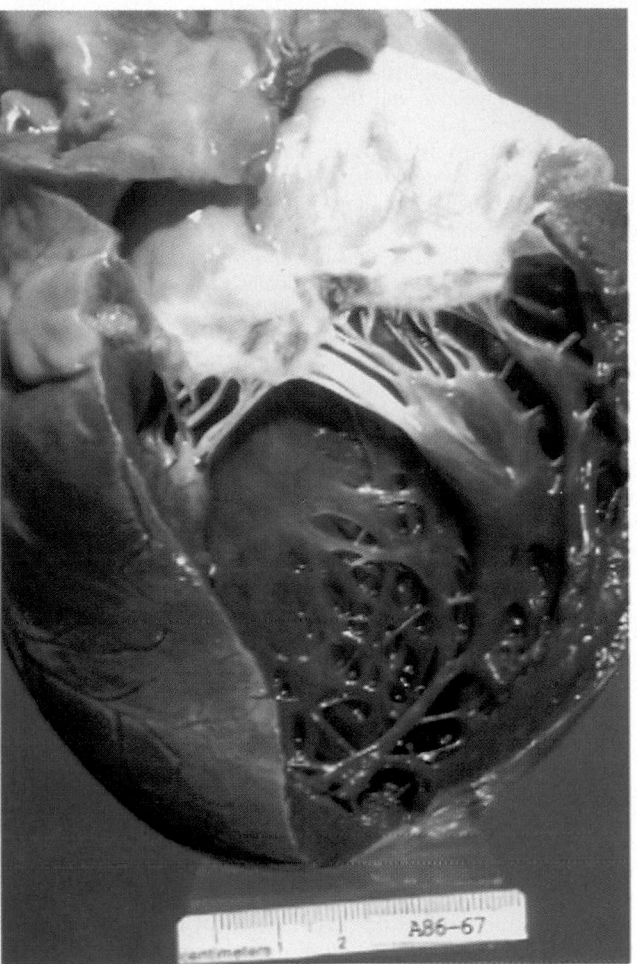

FIGURE 196-1. Chronic rheumatic valvular heart disease. The mitral valve leaflets and chordae are thickened, fibrotic, and distorted; intercommissural adhesions are present. *(Courtesy of Dr. L. Alvarez, VA Medical Center, Miami, FL.)*

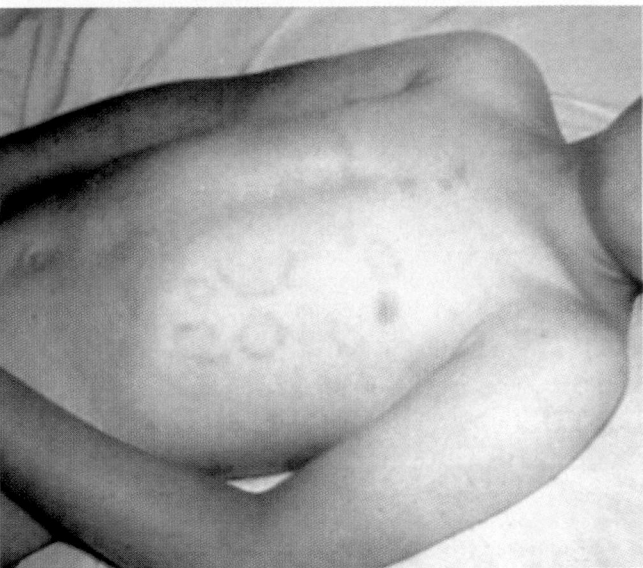

FIGURE 196-2. Annular plaques (complete rings) of varying sizes with macular centers and erythematous, raised margins. Note the serpginous borders formed by coalescence of several partial rings. *(Courtesy of Dr. M. Tyrell, Saskatoon, Canada; from Bisno AL. Noncardiac manifestations of rheumatic fever. In: Narula J, Vrmani R, Reddy KS, Tandon R, eds. Rheumatic Fever. Washington, DC: Armed Forces Institute of Pathology; 1999;245-256. Courtesy of the Armed Forces Institute of Pathology.)*

toxic phenomenon associated with ARF but not in itself diagnostic of rheumatic carditis.

Joint involvement in ARF ranges from arthralgia without objective findings to frank arthritis characterized by heat, swelling, redness, and exquisite tenderness. There is an inverse relationship between the severity of joint involvement and the risk of development of carditis.[80] The most frequently involved joints are the knees, ankles, elbows, and wrists. The small joints of the hands are less frequently affected, and the spine is only rarely involved. When the course of the illness is not suppressed by anti-inflammatory drugs, multiple joints are usually involved; approximately 50% of the patients develop arthritis in more than six joints. Arthritis in ARF is classically migratory in nature, that is, the inflammation travels from joint to joint. Once a joint becomes involved, inflammation begins to subside within a few days to a week and disappears within 2 to 3 weeks. The evolution of arthritis in individual joints tends to overlap, so multiple joints may be inflamed at the same time. The typical migratory polyarthritis pattern may not be present, however, if effective anti-inflammatory therapy is administered early in the course of the disease. Moreover, the classic migratory pattern is not invariable. In some cases the pattern may initially be additive, persisting in several joints simultaneously, or even, rarely, monoarthritic.[81]

In most instances the entire bout of polyarthritis subsides within 4 weeks, leaving no residual articular damage. One possible exception to this has been claimed by several authors, who report the very rare occurrence of the so-called Jaccoud form of periarticular fibrosis after rheumatic arthritis.

The existence of a reactive "poststreptococcal arthritis" distinct from ARF has been postulated to occur in certain patients whose arthritis is atypical in time of onset or duration,[44] is nonmigratory, is unaccompanied by other major manifestations of rheumatic fever, and fails to respond promptly to salicylate therapy.[82,83] The ultimate prognosis of such cases is unknown, but in some instances rheumatic heart disease has ensued.[84-86] Although the issue remains controversial,[87] it seems prudent to consider all cases of poststreptococcal polyarthritis that fulfill the diagnostic criteria of Jones as representing ARF,[83] providing other common causes of polyarthritis have been excluded.[88-90]

Subcutaneous nodules usually are associated with severe carditis and tend to occur several weeks after its onset. They are firm and painless and vary in size from a few millimeters to 2.0 cm. Such nodules are usually found over bony surfaces or prominences and over tendons. Common sites are adjacent to elbows, knees, wrists, or ankles and over Achilles tendons, the occiput, or spinous processes of the vertebrae. Their number varies from one to a few dozen. They usually persist for a week or two. Somewhat similar but more persistent lesions are seen in rheumatoid arthritis.

Erythema marginatum is a nonpruritic, nonpainful erythematous eruption usually seen on the trunk or proximal aspects of the extremities. The individual lesions are evanescent, moving over the skin in serpiginous patterns that change before the observer's eyes and are often likened to smoke rings, with a tendency to advance at the margins while clearing in the center (Fig. 196-2). The lesions are usually macular with raised margins and appear to be more a vasomotor phenomenon than a manifestation of cutaneous pathologic changes. Individual lesions may come and go in minutes to hours, but the process may go on intermittently for weeks to months.

Sydenham's chorea ("St. Vitus dance") is a neurologic disorder characterized by emotional lability, muscular weakness, and rapid, incoordinated, involuntary purposeless movements. The choreiform movements disappear during sleep and may be partially suppressed by sedation. The nonrhythmic movements are most notable in the face, hands, and feet. Sensation remains intact. Detailed descriptions of the nature of the choreiform movements can be found elsewhere.[1,91] Individual attacks in hospitalized patients usually last 2 to 4 months.

Chorea may occur in relatively close association with other rheumatic manifestations or in isolated form ("pure chorea"). In cases of "pure chorea," laboratory evidence of acute inflammation (C-reactive protein, elevated erythrocyte sedimentation rate) or recent streptococcal infection (elevated levels of antistreptococcal antibodies) may be lacking. This observation, which led investigators in the past to question the relationship of ARF to "pure chorea," is now known to result from the fact that Sydenham's chorea often occurs with a longer latent period than do the other manifestations of ARF. Relapses of pure chorea may occur in some patients despite faithful adherence to prophylaxis with intramuscular benzathine penicillin.[92,93] Some patients with "pure chorea" are found on follow-up to have rheumatic heart disease manifested primarily by mitral stenosis.[94]

Recent interest has focused on the possibility that certain other neurologic conditions, including tics, obsessive-compulsive disorder, and Tourette's syndrome, may be poststreptococcal sequelae.[95,96] Studies of this putative entity, known as "poststreptococcal autoimmune neuropsychiatric disorders associated with streptococci" (PANDAS), are continuing.

Several clinical manifestations of ARF occur with some frequency but are not in themselves specific enough to be considered major manifestations. These include fever, which accompanies almost all ARF attacks at their onset, arthralgia, abdominal pain, and epistaxis. The pulmonary parenchyma in ARF may be involved by a variety of pathologic processes including pulmonary edema, atelectasis, pulmonary embolism, or thromboses. Some observers feel that in addition a specific rheumatic pneumonia may occur in rare instances.[97]

The average duration of an attack, in the absence of anti-inflammatory therapy, is approximately 3 months. Fewer than 5% of the cases persist for longer than 6 months, justifying the designation of "chronic" rheumatic fever. Stollerman[1] lists the criteria for continuing clinical activity as follows: joint symptoms, new organic murmurs, changing heart size, congestive heart failure in the absence of long-standing valvular disease, subcutaneous nodules, sleeping pulse rate greater than 100 beats per minute, erythema marginatum, chorea, positive test for C-reactive protein, and a rectal temperature of 100.4° F or higher for 3 or more consecutive days.

Diagnosis

Because ARF can have such diverse manifestations (acute polyarthritis, congestive heart failure, chorea, or combinations of these) and because there is no specific diagnostic test for the disease, the differential diagnostic possibilities in an individual case may be quite broad. Among the diseases that most frequently need to be differentiated are rheumatoid arthritis, juvenile rheumatoid arthritis, systemic lupus erythematosus, serum sickness, sickle cell crisis or cardiopathy, rubella arthritis, septic arthritis (especially gonococcal arthritis in adolescent patients), Lyme disease,[98] infective endocarditis, viral myocarditis, and early stages of Henoch-Schönlein purpura. Less frequent differential diagnostic considerations include gout, sarcoidosis, Hodgkin disease, and leukemia. Choreiform movements have been described in patients with systemic lupus erythematosus,[99] neoplasms involving the basal ganglia,[100] legionnaires' disease,[101] hypoparathyroidism,[102] antiphospholipid syndrome,[103] Wilson disease, and Huntington disease. Chorea is also seen occasionally in women taking oral contraceptives,[104] and during pregnancy ("chorea gravidarum").[105]

Arriving at the correct diagnosis is particularly important in ARF, not only in terms of prescribing appropriate therapy for the acute attack and formulating an accurate prognosis but also because of the necessity for prescribing continuous antistreptococcal prophylaxis. To minimize over- and underdiagnosis, the criteria originally formulated by T. Duckett Jones[106] and most recently updated and modified by a committee of the American Heart Association,[89] have been generally accepted as the basis for reaching a diagnosis of ARF (Table 196-2). The updated criteria are to be applied most stringently to the diagnosis of an initial ARF attack. Although most patients with recurrences fulfill the criteria, the diagnosis of recurrent ARF may be less apparent. In a patient with established rheumatic heart disease, for example,

it may be difficult to diagnose confidently recurrent carditis unless a previously normal valve is affected. The updated criteria therefore allow a presumptive diagnosis of recurrent ARF to be made if clinical findings are suggestive and there is supporting evidence of recent streptococcal infection.

Echocardiograms may at times demonstrate valvular regurgitation in ARF patients who do not have clinical evidence of carditis.[52,107,108] The significance of such findings remains to be clarified,[109] and they do not per se establish the diagnosis of acute carditis in the updated Jones criteria.[110] This issue remains controversial, however.[78,111]

The criteria are not infallible, particularly when the diagnosis rests on the presence of acute polyarthritis as the sole major criterion with supporting evidence of fever plus an elevated erythrocyte sedimentation rate or a positive test result for C-reactive protein. For this reason, it is important to recognize that evidence of recent streptococcal infection must be obtained to satisfy the revised Jones criteria. Such evidence might include a recent microbiologically documented episode of streptococcal pharyngitis, a positive throat culture for group A streptococci (although here the differentiation of infection from colonization presents a problem), or the demonstration of an elevated serum titer of antistreptococcal antibodies. In most cases, physicians rely on the latter criterion.

If a serum sample is obtained within 2 months of onset, approximately 80% of patients with ARF will have an ASO titer of greater than 200 Todd units/mL. If a second streptococcal antibody test is performed on the same serum specimen, the proportion of patients with ARF with at least one elevated titer will rise to 90%.[112] Although an elevated antistreptococcal antibody titer is certainly not diagnostic of ARF, failure to demonstrate evidence of recent immunologically significant streptococcal infection using both ASO and anti-DNase B tests makes the diagnosis of ARF doubtful. An exception to this statement must be made for the patient with "pure" chorea whose antibody titers may have declined to the normal range owing to the long latent period between the antecedent streptococcal infection and the onset of this manifestation. Likewise, the onset of isolated carditis may be difficult to date; if recognition of isolated carditis is delayed, immunologic evidence of recent streptococcal infection may have disappeared.

A simple slide hemagglutination test (Streptozyme, Wampole Laboratories) has been marketed for the detection of antibodies to strep-

---

TABLE 196-2 Guidelines for the Diagnosis of Initial Attack of Rheumatic Fever (Jones Criteria, Updated 1992)*

Major manifestations
  Carditis
  Polyarthritis
  Chorea
  Erythema marginatum
  Subcutaneous nodules
Minor manifestations
  Clinical findings
    Arthralgia
    Fever
  Laboratory findings
    Elevated acute phase reactants
      Erythrocyte sedimentation rate
      C-reactive protein
    Prolonged PR interval
Supporting evidence of antecedent group A streptococcal infection
  Positive throat culture or rapid streptococcal antigen test
  Elevated or rising streptococcal antibody titer

*If supported by evidence of preceding group A streptococcal infection, the presence of two major manifestations or of one major and two minor manifestations indicates a high probability of acute rheumatic fever. Failure to fulfill the Jones Criteria should make the diagnosis doubtful except in situations in which rheumatic fever is first discovered after a long latent period from the antecedent infection (e.g., Sydenham's chorea or indolent carditis).
From Dajani AS, Ayoub E, Bierman FZ, et al. Guidelines for the diagnosis of rheumatic fever: Jones criteria, updated 1992. Circulation. 1993; 87:302-307, with permission.

tococcal extracellular antigens.[113] Unfortunately, the exact nature of the antibodies assayed by this test has not been ascertained,[114] and considerable lot-to-lot variability in the standardization of the reagent has been reported.[115] In view of these problems, the test cannot be recommended.

Treatment and Prognosis

The objectives of therapy in ARF are to quiet inflammation, decrease fever and toxicity, and control cardiac failure. The mainstays of treatment are salicylates and corticosteroids. Neither of these agents prevents or modifies the development of chronic rheumatic heart disease.[116] A suggested treatment schedule is outlined in Table 196-3. Analgesics without anti-inflammatory properties are recommended for patients with mild disease. This allows complete expression of the clinical manifestations to aid in diagnosis and also avoids post-therapeutic rebounds. Most patients require salicylates. Serum levels of 20 to 25 mg/100 mL are usually adequate to control the inflammatory response. If the high doses of salicylates required cannot be tolerated because of gastric irritation or if symptoms of salicylism develop, a reduction in the aspirin dosage or a change to corticosteroids is necessary. The more potent anti-inflammatory action of corticosteroids should be brought to bear whenever salicylates fail to control the inflammatory process or whenever carditis with congestive heart failure is present. The reader is referred elsewhere for a more detailed description of the therapeutic regimen.[1] Although the use of nonsteroidal anti-inflammatory agents seems reasonable in patients who cannot tolerate salicylates and who do not require corticosteroids,[117] there is a paucity of data on the use of these agents in ARF. Their role in the management of the disease thus remains to be defined.

Reactivation of clinical or laboratory manifestations of rheumatic inflammation may occur after cessation of anti-inflammatory therapy. This "rebound" phenomenon is more frequent after therapy with corticosteroids than with aspirin. For this reason, therapy should be tapered rather than discontinued abruptly, and aspirin administration should be continued for a month after treatment with adrenal steroids is discontinued.

Heart failure should be treated by conventional measures. The potential risk of digitalis-induced arrhythmias in the patient with active myocarditis must be kept in mind. As mentioned in the preceding, in the absence of preexistng valvular disease, congestive heart failure in ARF patients is usually attributable primarily to valvular dilatation and not to myocardial failure. Patients with chorea require a quiet, nonstimulatory environment and sedation. Agents such as phenobarbitol or diazepam may be employed. In patients with severe and debilitating hyperkinesis, haloperidol has been utilized. The potential role of plasmapheresis and intravenous immunoglobulin for the rare cases of intractable chorea is under investigation.[118]

The only long-term sequela of ARF is that of rheumatic heart disease. The prognosis in rheumatic patients has been greatly improved by our ability to prevent recurrent attacks with their concomitant threat of additional valvular damage. The ultimate prognosis of an individual attack is rather directly related to the severity of cardiac involvement during the acute phase. This was best studied in the United Kingdom–United States Collaborative Study.[119] In that study, only 6% of the patients with no carditis or with only questionable carditis during their attack of ARF were found to have heart murmurs when reexamined 10 years later. Heart disease was present at follow-up in 30% of the patients initially found to have only apical systolic murmurs, in 40% of those with basal diastolic murmurs during the acute phase, and in 68% of those who initially suffered from congestive heart failure, pericarditis, or both. Patients with "pure" chorea appear to have a relatively high incidence of late development of rheumatic heart disease, even if carditis is not recognized at the time of the initial attack. It may be, however, that the initial findings of carditis are no longer prominent by the time that chorea, which often occurs after a long latent period, becomes apparent.

Prevention

Prevention of ARF in persons without a prior history of this disease depends on an accurate diagnosis and appropriate treatment of the antecedent streptococcal infection. This approach (so-called primary prevention) is outlined in Chapter 193. It is effective[120] but suffers from the limitation that one third or more of ARF cases follow streptococcal infections that are either entirely subclinical or too mild to bring them to medical attention.

Rheumatic patients are at extremely high risk of developing recurrent ARF after immunologically significant streptococcal upper respiratory infections. These persons require continuous prophylaxis to prevent intercurrent streptococcal infections. The recommended regimen[121] for most patients in the United States and other countries in which ARF incidence is low consists of a single injection of 1.2 million units of penicillin G benzathine administered every 4 weeks (Table 196-4). In the most comprehensive study reported to date,[122] children following this regimen experienced a rheumatic fever recurrence rate of only 0.4 per 100 patient-years of observation. In areas of the world where ARF and rheumatic heart disease remain very highly prevalent, ARF recurrence rates have been found to be even lower when injections of penicillin G benzathine are administered every 3 weeks rather than every 4 weeks.[123] A similar regimen may be appropriate for high-risk individuals such as those with rheumatic heart disease. The possible benefits of the 3-week regimen must be balanced against the potential decrease in patient compliance and increase in associated costs.

Oral sulfadiazine or penicillin V are also acceptable prophylactic agents but are less effective than is penicillin G benzathine (see Table

---

TABLE 196-3 Suggested Schedule of Anti-inflammatory Therapy in Rheumatic Fever

Clinical Severity	Treatment
Arthralgia or mild arthritis; no carditis	Analgesics only, such as codeine or propoxyphene
Moderate or severe arthritis; no carditis, or carditis *with or without* cardiomegaly, but without failure	Aspirin, 90-100 mg/kg/day for 2 weeks; increased if necessary; 60-70 mg/kg/day for the subsequent 6 weeks
Carditis with failure, with or without joint manifestations	Prednisone, 40-60 mg/day; increased, if necessary; methyl prednisone sodium succinate IV in fulminating cases; after 2-3 weeks, slow withdrawal to be completed in 3 more weeks. Aspirin to be continued for a month after discontinuation of prednisone.

From Stollerman GH. Rheumatic Fever and Streptococcal Infection. New York: Grune & Stratton, 1975, with permission.

TABLE 196-4 Secondary Prevention of Rheumatic Fever (Prevention of Recurrent Attacks)

Agent	Dose	Mode
Benzathine penicillin G	1,200,000 U every 4 wks*	Intramuscular
	or	
Penicillin V	250 mg twice daily	Oral
	or	
Sulfadiazine	0.5 g once daily for patients ≤27 kg (60 lb) 1.0 g once daily for patients >27 kg (60 lb)	Oral
For individuals allergic to penicillin and sulfadiazine		
Erythromycin	250 mg twice daily	Oral

*In high-risk situations, administration every 3 weeks is justified and recommended.

From Dajani A, Taubert K, Ferrieri P, et al. Treatment of acute streptococcal pharyngitis and prevention of rheumatic fever: A statement for health professionals. Pediatrics. 1995;96(4 Pt 1):758-764, with permission.

TABLE 196-5 Duration of Secondary Rheumatic Fever Prophylaxis

Category	Duration
Rheumatic fever with carditis and residual heart disease (persistent valvar disease*)	At least 10 yr since last episode and at least until age 40 yr, sometimes lifelong prophylaxis
Rheumatic fever with carditis but no residual heart disease (no valvar disease*)	10 yr or well into adulthood, whichever is longer
Rheumatic fever without carditis	5 yr or until age 21 yr, whichever is longer

*Clinical or echocardiographic evidence.
From Dajani A, Taubert K, Ferrieri P, et al. Treatment of acute streptococcal pharyngitis and prevention of rheumatic fever: A statement for health professionals. Pediatrics. 1995;96(4 Pt 1):758-764, with permission.

196-4). The lesser efficacy of oral regimens is at least in part the result of the extreme difficulty of enforcing compliance. Patients allergic to penicillin and sulfadiazine may be given erythromycin. Patients requiring protection for many years are often begun on a regimen of penicillin G benzathine, which is changed to oral prophylaxis later in life when the risk of recurrence is deemed to be lower.

The optimal duration of continuous antimicrobial prophylaxis remains controversial. The risk of ARF recurrence is neither continuous nor uniform. It declines with the age of the patient and the number of years since the most recent attack. It is positively correlated with the number of previous attacks and with the presence and severity of pre-existing rheumatic heart disease. Thus, the risk of recurrence becomes quite low in older adults without heart disease who are not in intimate contact with school-aged children. In view of these facts, the physician must make the decision as to when and if to discontinue prophylaxis after discussion with the patient and after careful assessment of the patient's risk of acquiring a streptococcal infection, the anticipated recurrence rate per infection, and the likely consequences of such recurrence. In the author's opinion, even when all these factors are favorable, prophylaxis should never be discontinued until the patient has reached his or her early 20s, and at least 5 years have elapsed since the most recent rheumatic attack.[124] Current recommendations of the American Heart Association are set forth in Table 196-5.

In addition to preventing recurrences of ARF, it is important to protect patients with residual rheumatic valvular disease from bacterial endocarditis whenever they undergo dental or surgical procedures that consistently evoke bacteremia or are known to be associated with the development of endocarditis.[125] The antimicrobial regimens suggested for endocarditis prophylaxis are entirely distinct from those required for rheumatic fever prophylaxis. This concept is a potential source of confusion both to physicians and to dentists. Regimens for the prevention of bacterial endocarditis are discussed in Chapter 76.

Investigative efforts are currently being directed toward the development of a safe, effective M-protein vaccine for the prevention of streptococcal infection and ARF. Such a vaccine would have to provide protection against the major serotypes associated with ARF and deeply invasive infections. The considerable progress that has been made in recent years in elucidating the molecular biology of group A streptococci may well foreshadow a solution to this problem.[126,127]

GLOMERULONEPHRITIS

Poststreptococcal acute glomerulonephritis (AGN) is an acute inflammatory disorder of the renal glomerulus that is characterized pathologically by diffuse proliferative glomerular lesions and clinically by edema, hypertension, hematuria, and proteinuria. The disease is a delayed nonsuppurative sequela of pharyngeal or cutaneous infection with certain "nephritogenic" group A streptococcal strains belonging to a limited number of serotypes.

History

Richard Bright (1789-1858) clearly differentiated cardiac from renal dropsy. He also noted the association between acute diseases, particularly scarlet fever, and AGN.[128] Subsequently, many investigators confirmed the relationship between β-hemolytic streptococcal infections and AGN. Schick[129] in 1907 commented on the similarity of the latent period in serum sickness to that in AGN, thus suggesting the possibility of an immunologic basis for the latter disease. Rammelkamp and Weaver[130] explained the puzzling variations in attack rate of AGN after group A streptococcal infection by proposing that only certain serotypes of *Streptococcus pyogenes* were nephritogenic. Detailed prospective studies of the epidemiology, bacteriology, immunology, and natural history of pyoderma-associated nephritis by Wannamaker and associates[131] in Minnesota, Potter and colleagues[132] in south Trinidad, and Dillon and co-workers[133] in Alabama have added greatly to our understanding of this disease.

Etiology and Pathogenesis

Poststreptococcal AGN follows infection with a limited number of group A streptococcal serotypes (see Table 196-1). Type 12 is the most frequent M serotype causing AGN after pharyngitis or tonsillitis, whereas M-49 is the type most frequently related to pyoderma-associated nephritis. Not all streptococcal strains belonging to these serotypes are nephritogenic, however. As yet, there are no reliable biologic markers to differentiate nephritogenic from non-nephritogenic streptococci. Poststreptococcal AGN is almost always due to strains of serogroup A. Well-documented outbreaks caused by group C organisms (*Streptococcus zooepidemicus*) have, however, been reported.[134,135]

The precise mechanism by which streptococcal infection gives rise to AGN has not been delineated. The weight of evidence favors the view that the renal injury is immunologically mediated. Such evidence includes the latent period between infection and the development of AGN; the associated hypocomplementemia; and the fact that immunoglobulins, complement components, and antigens that react with streptococcal antisera are present in the renal glomerulus early in the course of the disease.[136-139] It is possible that antibodies elicited by nephritogenic streptococci react with renal tissues in such a way as to produce glomerular injury. Indeed, antigenic similarities between constituents of the streptococcus and the human kidney have been described.[140-142] On the other hand, the electron microscopic finding of nodular subepithelial "humps" in renal biopsy specimens from patients with AGN suggests that the renal injury may be due to deposition of preformed complexes consisting of streptococcal antigen and host antibody within the glomerulus. Such subepithelial nodular deposits are a characteristic feature of experimentally induced disease caused by circulating immune complexes. Several groups[143-145] have detected circulating immune complexes in AGN. The possible role of cellular immune mechanisms has as yet been inadequately explored.

The identity of the streptococcal constituent(s) involved in the pathogenesis of AGN remains unknown. M protein is an obvious candidate because of the close association of nephritogenicity and the M serotype. Indeed, monoclonal antibodies raised against human glomeruli have been found to cross react with streptococcal M protein.[142] Moreover, in an animal model of nephritis induced by nephritogenic type 12 streptococci, eluted bound glomerular antibodies were found to be directed against type 12 M protein but not against other streptococcal and renal antigens.[146] Others, however, have described cross-reactions between fragments of streptococcal cell membrane and human glomerular basement membrane[140] and produced proliferative glomerular lesions in rhesus monkeys by immunization with streptococcal membrane fragments or by intravenous injection of antibodies to these fragments.[147]

Two antigens isolated from nephritogenic streptococci are currently under investigation as regards their role in the pathogenesis of AGN. These are streptococcal pyrogenic exotoxin B and its zymogen precursor[148,149] and a nephritis-associated plasmin-receptor (NAPlr).[150] The latter demonstrates both plamin(ogen)-binding activity and glyceraldehyde phosphate dehydrogenase (GAPDH) activity. Both of these substances have affinity for the glomeruli and induce long-lasting antibody responses. Another nephritis-strain associated protein, initially identified as an extracellular product of nephritogenic streptococci, has been characterized as a streptokinase.[151] Streptokinase production has been postulated to play a role in pathogenesis of AGN[151] and, indeed, has been found essential for development of the disease in a mouse model.[152] However, there is no unique reactivity to group A streptokinase in sera of AGN patients, nor has streptokinase deposition been demonstrated in biopsy specimens obtained early in the disease.[153]

Pathologic Characteristics

In the acute phase of illness, light microscopic examination of renal biopsy specimens demonstrates a marked increase in glomerular intracapillary cellularity caused by endothelial and mesangial cell proliferation. These changes involve virtually all the glomeruli, which appear enlarged and bloodless, tending to fill the Bowman space.[154] In addition to this diffuse proliferative endocapillary process, a variable degree of polymorphonuclear leukocytic exudation is observed. Proliferation of parietal and visceral epithelial cells occurs to a modest degree only and is rarely extensive enough to give rise to well-developed crescent formation. Thin sectioning and special strains may reveal discrete deposits on the epithelial side of the basement membrane that correspond to the "humps" visible on electron microscopy. Focal degeneration, interstitial edema, and cellular infiltration also occur in the renal tubular cells, but these tubular changes are far less prominent than is the glomerulitis. Arterioles are normal or nearly so in most cases of AGN.

Immunofluorescence technique demonstrates considerable variability in the pattern of deposition of immunoglobulin and complement components. C3 is virtually always present in the glomeruli, and deposits of IgG are also frequently demonstrable. These substances are present in the form of discrete deposits similar in size and location to the subepithelial humps visualized under the electron microscope,[137,138] although deposits of C3 may also occur in an interrupted linear pattern along the basement membrane or in the mesangium.[138] Deposits of IgM, C1q, C4, and fibrin are found less commonly. The rather weak and inconsistent deposition of early complement components suggests that activation of the alternate complement pathway may play a role in the immunopathology of AGN.

Epidemiology

The epidemiologic characteristics of AGN largely reflect those of the antecedent group A streptococcal infection, that is, pharyngitis or pyoderma (Table 196-6). Thus, the classic streptococcal sore throat occurs primarily among school-age children during the cooler months of the year. Pyoderma is largely a disease of children aged 2 to 6 years and occurs, in temperate climates, during the summer and early fall. There are data to suggest that, given a skin infection with a nephritogenic strain, the attack rate of AGN is higher in children 6 or younger than in older children.[155] AGN can also follow cutaneous infections other than pyoderma.[156,157] The latent period of AGN is variable but averaged 10 days after pharyngeal infection in the studies of Stetson and colleagues[158]; prospective studies at Red Lake Indian Reservation in Minnesota indicate the usual latent period of pyoderma-associated AGN to be 3 weeks or longer.[155]

Although the attack rate of AGN after throat or skin infection with a nephritogenic strain is substantial (i.e., 10% to 15%),[155,159] the disease differs dramatically from acute rheumatic fever in that recurrences are rare. This is attributable at least in part to the relatively limited number of streptococcal strains that are nephritogenic and presumably also to the acquisition of type-specific protective immunity to the serotype that elicited the initial attack. When second attacks of AGN do occur, they are clinically and histologically indistinguishable from the initial attack.[160] A more commonly recognized phenomenon than recurrent AGN attacks is the propensity for streptococcal infections to precipitate exacerbations of chronic glomerulonephritis.[161]

TABLE 196-6 Epidemiologic Characteristics of Pharyngitis-Associated and Pyodermia-Associated Acute Glomerulonephritis

Feature	Pharyngitis-Associated AGN	Pyoderma-Associated AGN
Age	Early school age	Preschool age
Sex	M/F ratio approx. 2:1	Equally distributed
Season	Winter and spring	Late summer and early fall
Geographic distribution	North and South	Predominantly South
Familial occurrence	Common	Common
Latent period	10 days	3 wk
Attack rate*	10-15%	10-15%
Serologic types	Limited types	Also limited, but different types
Recurrences	Rare	Rare

*After infection with known nephritogenic strain.
AGN, Acute glomerulonephritis.
From Wannamaker LW. Differences between streptococcal infections of the throat and of the skin. N Engl J Med. 1970;282:23-31, with permission.

Such exacerbations often occur after a relatively brief latent period of 1 to 4 days. The coexistence of ARF and AGN in the same patient after pharyngeal infection is quite rare, but a few such cases have been reported.[162,163]

The introduction of a highly nephritogenic strain into a family unit may result in multiple cases. Where systematic screening of sibling contacts for hypertension, urinary abnormalities, and serum complement levels has been performed, the incidence of proven and suspected cases of AGN in sibling contacts has been extremely variable,[164-167] with estimates ranging as high as 20%.[168]

Clinical and Laboratory Features

The typical clinical features of AGN, as seen in children entering the hospital with this disease, include edema, hypertension, and smoky or rusty colored urine. Patients also exhibit pallor and may complain of lethargy, malaise, weakness, anorexia, headache, and dull back pain. Fever is not a prominent finding.

Facial and periorbital edema are usually present, especially on arising in the morning, but edema also involves dependent areas such as feet and legs, scrotum, and sacrum. In severe cases, ascites or pleural effusions may occur. Another manifestation of fluid overload is circulatory congestion, which may give rise to dyspnea, orthopnea, rales at the lung bases, distended neck veins, and even frank pulmonary edema. Manifestations of circulatory overload tend to be particularly prominent in the occasional cases of AGN occurring in older adults and, in such persons, may obscure the correct diagnosis if urinary findings are not properly interpreted.

Hypertension occurs in most patients but is usually of modest degree. Hypertensive retinopathy or heart failure do not ordinarily complicate the clinical picture. On the other hand, a small proportion of AGN patients, perhaps 5% to 10%, develop severe hypertension complicated by signs and symptoms of encephalopathy. These range from headache and vomiting to confusion, somnolence, and convulsions.

Although the clinical features enumerated above are typical of hospitalized patients, many cases of AGN are so mild as to escape detection unless persons at risk are tested prospectively for urinary sediment abnormalities and serum complement levels. Two studies that included renal biopsy data have concluded that, in epidemic situations, as many as 50% of cases of AGN may be subclinical.[165,168] Whatever the exact proportion might be (and chances are this varies considerably in differing epidemiologic settings), it seems clear that subclinical episodes of AGN are by no means rare.

Laboratory findings include a mild normocytic normochronic anemia, elevated erythrocyte sedimentation rate, slight hypoproteinemia, and elevations of the blood urea nitrogen and serum creatinine concentrations. Hypercholesterolemia and hyperlipemia may also be present.

Serum levels of total hemolytic complement and C3 complement are markedly reduced in the great majority of patients with clinically apparent AGN. Urine volume may be significantly diminished, and the urine itself is smoky, rusty, or brownish with a high specific gravity and positive test findings for protein and hemoglobin. Total urinary protein excretion is usually less than 3 g/day.[169] Microscopic examination of the urine reveals erythrocytes, leukocytes, and hyaline, granular, and red blood cell casts.

The urinary abnormalities in AGN must be distinguished from the mild hematuria and proteinuria that may be seen during the acute phase of acute streptococcal infection and other febrile illnesses. The relationship, if any, of these early urinary findings to the development of AGN is at present unknown.[170] Finally, diagnostic confusion is almost inevitable in the rare cases in which pronounced clinical manifestations of AGN occur in patients with minimal or no urinary sediment abnormalities.[171]

Diagnosis

The diagnosis of AGN is based on the clinical history, physical findings, and confirmatory evidence of antecedent streptococcal infection. The latter may include a recent history of scarlet fever, isolation of group A streptococci from throat or skin lesions, or demonstration of elevated serum titers of streptococcal antibodies. Even in the absence of bacteriologic isolation of streptococci, the presence of skin lesions morphologically compatible with streptococcal impetigo is highly suggestive.

It is almost always possible to demonstrate an elevated level of streptococcal antibodies in AGN,[113] although, in cases with relatively short latent periods, serial bleedings may be necessary. It must be recalled that in pyoderma-associated nephritis ASO responses are weak and it is frequently necessary to perform serum titrations of anti-DNase B. Although anti-Streptozyme titers rise in pyoderma nephritis, technical problems limit the reliability of the test (see earlier). Finally, if renal biopsy is performed, the demonstration of diffuse proliferative glomerulonephritis with subepithelial electron-dense deposits is a very helpful confirmatory finding.

Poststreptococcal acute glomerulonephritis must be differentiated from a variety of other infectious processes involving the kidney. It is, for example, often extremely difficult to differentiate an acute exacerbation of chronic glomerulonephritis, such as may be precipitated by streptococci or by a variety of other intercurrent infections, from a true attack of AGN. A short latent period of 1 to 4 days suggests that the episode is an exacerbation of preexisting renal disease. Patients with subacute bacterial endocarditis tend to develop high serum levels of circulating immune complexes and may develop either diffuse proliferative or focal glomerulonephritis, both of which may be confused clinically with poststreptococcal nephritis. A variety of other bacterial and protozoan illnesses such as pneumococcal pneumonia, typhoid fever, leptospirosis, syphilis, toxoplasmosis, and *Plasmodium falciparum* malaria have been reported on occasion to be associated with nephritis. Viral infections such as hepatitis B and C, infectious mononucleosis, measles, mumps, and togaviral and enteroviral disease have likewise been implicated as causes of viruria, transient renal dysfunction, or actual glomerulonephritis.[172] In addition to the development of focal and segmental glomerulosclerosis, patients infected with the human immunodeficiency virus may rarely develop an immune complex glomerulonephritis.[173] Other entities that may at times mimic AGN are Henoch-Schönlein disease, systemic lupus erythematosus, polyarteritis nodosa, acute tubular necrosis, focal glomerulonephritis with hematuria, hereditary nephritis, rapidly progressive glomerulonephritis, idiopathic nephrotic syndrome, and malignant hypertension.

Therapy

Because no form of treatment is known to alter the long-term prognosis of AGN, therapy is directed toward management of the acute problems. Attention is directed to what is ordinarily the most immediate problem, namely, circulatory overload. In most cases this is handled adequately by salt and fluid restriction alone, but at times diuretics are required. Digitalis is not indicated because the risk of toxicity is sub-

stantial and in most instances myocardial function is intact.[174] Specific antihypertensive therapy is usually unnecessary, but in cases of severe hypertension and hypertensive encephalopathy, potent parenteral agents are required. Patients developing acute pulmonary edema or severe and prolonged oliguria require measures conventionally used in these conditions.

All nonallergic patients should receive penicillin, preferably penicillin G benzathine (see Chapter 195 for dosage schedule), to eradicate the nephritogenic streptococcal strain. Penicillin-allergic patients should receive one of the alternative regimens listed in Chapter 195. In addition to urinalysis and serum C3 complement determination, family contacts should have cultures of throat and skin lesions. Persons with positive cultures for group A streptococci should be treated appropriately. Such treatment is for epidemiologic purposes only and will not modify the course of preexistent AGN nor, in all probability, abort the disease in persons who are within the latent period (see later).

With skillful use of the supportive measures outlined in the preceding, mortality during the acute phase of AGN is now rare. Perhaps 1% or fewer of patients develop severe and irreversible renal failure. In the remainder, signs and symptoms often begin to abate within a few days after admission. Serum complement levels return to normal within a month, but microscopic hematuria and cylinduria frequently persist for months despite the patient's general feeling of well-being.

Prevention

Although penicillin treatment of the antecedent streptococcal infection is highly efficacious in preventing acute rheumatic fever, the same does not appear to be the case in AGN. Stetson and colleagues,[158] studying in a controlled fashion an epidemic of pharyngitis-associated (type 12) AGN in a military population, found a small but not statistically significant[175] preventive effect of penicillin. Uncontrolled observations during an epidemic of nephritis in Israel[176] (both throat and skin infections due to M type 55) documented the occurrence of AGN in a number of subjects who had received prior antibiotic therapy according to a variety of different dosage regimens. Moreover, there was no difference in the clinical severity of AGN between subjects who had and those who had not received antibiotic therapy. Data available at present are not adequate to determine whether penicillin might have a small effect on the primary prevention of AGN, but such effect, at any rate, is not striking.[177]

As indicated above, penicillin is, nevertheless, effective in epidemiologic attempts to eradicate nephritogenic strains by treatment of AGN patients and their colonized family contacts. In appropriate high-risk settings during epidemics of AGN, universal penicillin prophylaxis of selected populations might be considered in a manner somewhat analogous to that used in U.S. military recruit camps for rheumatic fever control. Such universal prophylaxis is rarely indicated and should be used only after careful consideration of the specific epidemiologic parameters involved.

Because recurrent episodes of AGN are so rare, continuous antistreptococcal prophylaxis, such as is used in the secondary prevention of rheumatic fever, is unnecessary.

Prognosis

One of the most important issues relating to poststreptococcal glomerulonephritis is the frequency with which patients afflicted with the disease eventually develop chronic glomerulonephritis. In a certain group of AGN patients constituting only a small percentage of its victims, the acute attack is never resolved and the disease enters a subacute phase leading to a virtually complete loss of renal function within 6 months to 2 years. It is the ultimate fate of the remainder of the patients in whom the illness appears clinically to have resolved that remains controversial. Most observers now agree that the long-term prognosis in children is excellent. A 10-year follow-up of 61 patients involved in an epidemic at Red Lake, Minnesota,[178] revealed no cases of chronic glomerulonephritis. Moreover, in a 12- to 17-year follow-up of 534 Trinidadians convalescent from AGN,[179] only 3.5% of the subjects had persistent urine abnormalities, 3.7% were hypertensive, and none had serum creatinine values greater than 1.25 mg/dL. These figures are not in excess of what would be expected in surveys of normal populations. Almost all the Trinidadian patients had been children at the time of their attack of AGN. There was no difference in outcome of sporadic AGN cases as opposed to those associated with epidemics. A recent report from Australia, however, noted increased prevalences of albuminuria and hematuria in Aboriginal children several years convalescent from two epidemics of AGN. There were no significant differences between patients and controls in blood pressure, serum creatinine level, or calculated glomerular filtration rate.[179a]

These data stand in sharp contrast to the findings of Baldwin,[180] who followed 168 subjects for periods up to 18 years and concluded that "irreversible renal damage has ensued in 50% of these patients, as evidenced by the presence of proteinuria and/or hypertension," although clinical uremia occurred in only six patients. Renal biopsy specimens from the subjects in Baldwin's series showed that proliferative changes had decreased whereas glomerulosclerosis of marked degree was present in more than half of the specimens. Baldwin's study population contains a high proportion of adults, who are generally agreed to have a worse prognosis than do children.[181] Moreover, the results presented have been challenged because of the difficulty of sorting out exacerbations of chronic nephritis from true de novo attacks of AGN in studies of sporadically occurring disease[182] and because of the paucity of published data documenting the poststreptococcal etiology of the cases studied.[183] More recently, however, a 2-year follow-up of Brazilian adults who contracted AGN from consumption of cheese contaminated with *Streptococcus zooepidemicus* revealed a high rate of hypertension and renal abnormalities, with some patients having reached end-stage renal disease.[184]

Based on the bulk of currently available data, it seems likely that more than 90% of the children with AGN make an uneventful recovery and that this disease in the pediatric age group is not an important precursor of chronic glomerulonephritis or hypertension. The prognosis appears more guarded in adult patients,[185] but the proportion who might be left with residual renal function impairment is at present unknown.

REFERENCES

1. Stollerman GH. Rheumatic Fever and Streptococcal Infection. New York: Grune & Stratton, 1975.
2. Bisno AL. The concept of rheumatogenic and non-rheumatogenic group A streptococci. In: Read SE, Zabriskie JB, eds. Streptococcal Diseases and the Immune Response. New York: Academic Press; 1980:789-803.
3. Kuttner AG, Krumwiede E. Observations on the effect of streptococcal upper respiratory infections on rheumatic children: A three-year study. J Clin Invest. 1941;20: 273-287.
4. Potter EV, Svartman M, Mohammed I, et al. Tropical acute rheumatic fever and associated streptococcal infections compared with concurrent acute glomerulonephritis. J Pediatr. 1978;92:325-333.
5. Berrios X, Quesney F, Morales A, et al. Acute rheumatic fever and poststreptococcal glomerulonephritis in an open population: Comparative studies of epidemiology and bacteriology. J Lab Clin Med. 1986; 108:535-542.
6. Martin DR, Voss LM, Walker SJ, Lennon D. Acute rheumatic fever in Auckland, New Zealand: Spectrum of associated group A streptococci different from expected. Pediatr Infect Dis J. 1994;13:264-269.
7. McDonald M, Currie BJ, Carapetis JR. Acute rheumatic fever: a chink in the chain that links the heart to the throat? Lancet Infect Dis. 2004;4:240-245.
8. Bisno AL, Pearce IA, Wall HP, et al. Contrasting epidemiology of acute rheumatic fever and acute glomerulonephritis: Nature of the antecedent streptococcal infection. N Engl J Med. 1970;283:561-565.
9. Bisno AL, Pearce IA, Stollerman GH. Streptococcal infections that fail to cause recurrences of rheumatic fever. J Infect Dis. 1977;136:278-285.
10. Smoot JC, Barbian KD, Van Gompel JJ, et al. Genome sequence and comparative microarray analysis of serotype M18 group A Streptococcus strains associated with acute rheumatic fever outbreaks. Proc Natl Acad Sci USA. 2002;99:4668-4673.
11. Smoot JC, Korgenski EK, Daly JA, et al. Molecular analysis of group A Streptococcus type emm18 isolates temporally associated with acute rheumatic fever outbreaks in Salt Lake City, Utah. J Clin Microbiol. 2002;40:1805-1810.
12. Bessen DE, Fischetti VA. Differentiation between two biologically distinct classes of group A streptococci by limited substitutions of amino acids within the shared region of M protein-like molecules. J Exp Med. 1990;172:1757-1764.
13. Bessen DE, Veasy LG, Hill HR, et al. Serologic evidence for a class I group A streptococcal infection among rheumatic fever patients. J Infect Dis. 1995;172:1608-1611.
14. Stollerman GH. Rheumatogenic streptococci and autoimmunity. Clin Immunol Immunopathol. 1991;61:131-142.
15. Froude J, Gibofsky A, Buskirk DR, et al. Cross-reactivity between streptococcus and human tissue: A model of molecular mimicry and autoimmunity. Curr Top Microbiol Immunol. 1989;145:5-26.
16. Cunningham MW. T cell mimicry in inflammatory heart disease. Mol Immunol. 2004;40:1121-1127.
17. Dale JB, Beachey EH. Epitopes of streptococcal M proteins shared with cardiac myosin. J Exp Med. 1985;162:583-591.
18. Dale JB, Beachey EH. Protective antigenic determinant of streptococcal M protein shared with sarcolemmal membrane protein of human heart. J Exp Med. 1982;156:1165-1176.
19. Baird RW, Bronze MS, Kraus W, et al. Epitopes of group A streptococcal M protein shared with antigens of articular cartilage and synovium. J Immunol. 1991;146: 3132-3137.
20. Goldstein I, Rebeyrotte P, Parlebas J, Halpern B. Isolation from heart valves of glycopeptides which share immunological properties with *Streptococcus haemolyticus* group A polysaccharides. Nature. 1968;219:866-868.
21. Dudding BA, Ayoub EM. Persistence of streptococcal group A antibody in patients with rheumatic valvular disease. J Exp Med. 1968;128:1081-1098.
22. Schwab JH, Cromartie WJ. Immunological studies on a C polysaccharide complex of group A streptococci having a direct toxic effect on connective tissue. J Exp Med. 1960;111:295-307.
23. Fillit HM, McCarty M, Blake M. Induction of antibodies to hyaluronic acid by immunization of rabbits with encapsulated streptococci. J Exp Med. 1986;164:762-776.
24. Husby G, van de Rijn I, Zabriskie JB, et al. Antibodies reacting with cytoplasm of subthalamic and caudate nuclei neurons in chorea and rheumatic fever. J Exp Med. 1976;144:1094-1110.
25. Zabriskie JB. T-cells and T-cell clones in rheumatic fever valvulitis: Getting to the heart of the matter? Circulation. 1995;92:281-282.
26. Carreno-Manjarrez R, Visvanathan K, Zabriskie JB. Immunogenic and genetic factors in rheumatic fever. Curr Infect Dis Rep. 2000;2:302-307.
27. Read SE, Fischetti VA, Utermohlen V, et al. Cellular reactivity studies to streptococcal antigens. Migration inhibition studies in patients with streptococcal infections and rheumatic fever. J Clin Invest. 1974;54:439-450.
28. Yang LC, Soprey PR, Wittner MK, Fox EN. Streptococcal-induced cell-mediated-immune destruction of cardiac myofibers in vitro. J Exp Med. 1977;146:344-360.
29. Morris K, Mohan C, Wahi PL, et al. Increase in activated T cells and reduction in suppressor/cytotoxic T cells in acute rheumatic fever and active heart disease: A longitudinal study. J Infect Dis. 1993;167:979-983.
30. Kemeny E, Grieve T, Marcus R, et al. Identification of mononuclear cells and T cell subsets in rheumatic valvulitis. Clin Immunol Immunopathol. 1989;52:225-237.
31. Morris K, Mohan C, Wahi PL, et al. Enhancement of IL-1, IL-2 production and IL-2 receptor generation in patients with acute rheumatic fever and active rheumatic heart disease; a prospective study. Clin Exp Immunol. 1993;91:429-436.
32. Zedan MM, el-Shennawy FA, Abou-Bakr HM, Al-Basousy AM. Interleukin-2 in relation to T cell subpopulations in rheumatic heart disease. Arch Dis Child. 1992;67:1373-1375.
33. Tomai M, Kotb M, Majumdar G, Beachey EH. Superantigenicity of streptococcal M protein. J Exp Med. 1990;172:359-362.
34. Schlievert PM. Role of staphylococcal and streptococcal pyrogenic-toxin superantigens in human disease. Mediguide Infect Dis. 1993;13:1-7.
35. Ayoub EM, Barrett DJ, Maclaren NK, Krischer JP. Association of class II human histocompatibility leukocyte antigens with rheumatic fever. J Clin Invest. 1986;77: 2019-2026.
36. Anastasiou-Nana MI, Anderson JL, Carlquist JF, Nanas JN. HLA-DR typing and lymphocyte subset evaluation in rheumatic heart disease: A search for immune response factors. Am Heart J. 1986;112:992-997.
37. Khanna AK, Buskirk DR, Williams RC Jr, et al. Presence of a non-HLA B cell antigen in rheumatic fever patients and their families as defined by a monoclonal antibody. J Clin Invest. 1989;83:1710-1716.
38. Gibofsky A, Khanna A, Suh E, Zabriskie JB. The genetics of rheumatic fever: Relationship to streptococcal infection and autoimmune disease. J Rheumatol (Suppl). 1991;30:1-5.
39. Virmani R, Farb A, Burke AP, Narula J. Pathology of acute rheumatic carditis. In: Narula J, Virmani R, Reddy KS, Tandon R, eds. Rheumatic Fever. Washington, DC: Armed Forces Institute of Pathology; 1999:217-234.
40. Chopra P, Wanniang J, Kumar AS. Immunochemical and histochemical profile of Aschoff bodies in rheumatic carditis in excised left atrial appendages: an immunoperoxidase study in fresh and paraffin-embedded tissue. Int J Cardiol. 1992;34:199-207.
41. Husby GH, Arora R, Williams RC, et al. Immunofluorescent studies of florid rheumatic Aschoff lesions. Arthritis Rheum. 1986;29:207-211.
42. Ben-Dov I, Berry E. Acute rheumatic fever in adults over the age of 45 years: an analysis of 23 patients together with a review of the literature. Semin Arthritis Rheum. 1980;10:100-110.
43. Feuer J, Spiera H. Acute rheumatic fever in adults: A resurgence in the Hasidic Jewish community. J Rheumatol. 1997;24:337-340.
44. Deighton C. Beta haemolytic streptococci and reactive arthritis in adults. Ann Rheum Dis. 1993;52:475-482.

45. Rammelkamp CH, Denny FW, Wannamaker LW. Studies on the epidemiology of rheumatic fever in the armed services. In: Thomas L, ed. Rheumatic Fever. Minneapolis: University of Minnesota Press; 1952:72-89.

46. Siegel AC, Johnson EE, Stollerman GH. Controlled studies of streptococcal pharyngitis in a pediatric population. I. Factors related to the attack rate of rheumatic fever. N Engl J Med. 1961;265:559-566.

47. WHO programme for the prevention of rheumatic fever/rheumatic heart disease in 16 developing countries: Report from Phase I (1986-90). Bull WHO. 1992;70:213-218.

48. Eisenberg MJ. Rheumatic heart disease in the developing world: Prevalence, prevention, and control. Eur Heart J. 1993;14:122-128.

49. Vijaykumar M, Narula J, Reddy KS, Kaplan EL. Incidence of rheumatic fever and prevalence of rheumatic fever disease in India. Int J Cardiol. 1994;43:221-228.

50. Carapetis JR, Wolff DR, Currie BJ. Acute rheumatic fever and rheumatic heart disease in the top end of Australia's Northern Territory. Med J Aust. 1996;164:146-149.

51. Land MA, Bisno AL. Acute rheumatic fever: A vanishing disease in suburbia. JAMA. 1983;249:895-898.

52. Veasy LG, Wiedmeier SE, Orsmond GS, et al. Resurgence of acute rheumatic fever in the intermountain area of the United States. N Engl J Med. 1987;316:421-427.

53. Ferguson GW, Shultz JM, Bisno AL. Epidemiology of acute rheumatic fever in a multi-ethnic, multi-racial U.S. urban community: The Miami-Dade experience. J Infect Dis. 1991;164:720-725.

54. Bisno AL. The resurgence of acute rheumatic fever in the United States. Annu Rev Med. 1990;41:319-329.

55. Veasy LG, Tani LY, Hill HR. Persistence of acute rheumatic fever in the intermountain area of the United States. J Pediatr. 1994;124:9-16.

56. Hosier DM, Craenen JM, Teske DW, Wheller JJ. Resurgence of acute rheumatic fever. Am J Dis Child. 1987;141:730-733.

57. Congeni B, Rizzo C, Congeni J, Sreenivasan VV. Outbreak of acute rheumatic fever in northeast Ohio. J Pediatr. 1987;111:176-179.

58. Wald ER, Dashefsky B, Feidt C, et al. Acute rheumatic fever in western Pennsylvania and the tristate area. Pediatrics. 1987;80:371-374.

59. Westlake RM, Graham TP, Edwards KM. An outbreak of acute rheumatic fever in Tennessee. Pediatr Infect Dis J. 1990;9:97-100.

60. Leggiadro RJ, Birnbaum SE, Chase NA, Myers LK. A resurgence of acute rheumatic fever in a mid-South children's hospital. South Med J. 1990;83:1418-1420.

61. Jackson MA, Sotiropoulos SV, Christensen B, et al. Mucoid group A streptococcal disease in Kansas City, MO (Abstract 1024). Pediatr Res. 1988;23(Suppl):372A.

62. Mason R, Fisher M, Kujala G. Acute rheumatic fever in West Virginia: Not just a disease of children. Arch Intern Med. 1991;151:133-136.

63. Eckerd JM, McJunkin JE. Recent increase in incidence of acute rheumatic fever in southern West Virginia. WV Med J. 1989;85:323-325.

64. Burns DL, Ginsburg CM. Recrudescence of acute rheumatic fever in Dallas, Texas (Abstract 496). Pediatr Res. 1987;21:256A.

65. Griffiths SP, Gersony WM. Acute rheumatic fever in New York City (1969 to 1988): A comparative study of two decades. J Pediatr. 1990;116:882-887.

66. Wallace MR, Garst PD, Papadimos TJ, Oldfield EC. The return of acute rheumatic fever in young adults. JAMA. 1989;262:2557-2561.

67. Centers for Disease Control U. Acute rheumatic fever among Army trainees - Fort Leonard Wood, Missouri, 1987-1988. Morbid Mortal Wkly Rep. 1988;37:519-522.

68. Zangwill KM, Wald ER, Londino AV Jr. Acute rheumatic fever in western Pennsylvania: A persistent problem into the 1990s. J Pediatr. 1991;118:561-563.

69. Bisno AL. Group A streptococcal infections and acute rheumatic fever. N Engl J Med. 1991;325:783-793.

70. Taranta A, Wood HF, Feinstein AR, et al. Rheumatic fever in children and adolescents. A long-term epidemiologic study of subsequent prophylaxis, streptococcal infections, and clinical sequelae. IV. Relation of the rheumatic fever recurrence rate per streptococcal infection to the titers of streptococcal antibodies. Ann Intern Med. 1964;60(Suppl 5):47-57.

71. Rammelkamp CH, Jr, Stolzer BL. The latent period before the onset of acute rheumatic fever. Yale J Biol Med. 1961;34:386-398.

72. Sanyal SK, Thapar MK, Ahmed SH, et al. The initial attack of acute rheumatic fever during childhood in North India; a prospective study of the clinical profile. Circulation. 1974;49:7-12.

73. Kamblock J, Payot L, Iung B, et al. Does rheumatic myocarditis really exists? Systematic study with echocardiography and cardiac troponin I blood levels. Eur Heart J. 2003;24:855-862.

74. Gentles TL, Colan SD, Wilson NJ, et al. Left ventricular mechanics during and after acute rheumatic fever: Contractile dysfunction is closely related to valve regurgitation. J Am Coll Cardiol. 2001;37:201-207.

75. Vasan RS, Shrivastava S, Vijayakumar M, et al. Echocardiographic evaluation of patients with acute rheumatic fever and rheumatic carditis. Circulation. 1996;94:73-82.

76. Essop MR, Wisenbaugh T, Sareli P. Evidence against a myocardial factor as the cause of left ventricular dilation inactive rheumatic carditis. J Am Coll Cardiol. 1993;22:826-829.

77. Williams RV, Minich LL, Shaddy RE, et al. Evidence for lack of myocardial injury in children with acute rheumatic carditis. Cardiol Young. 2002;12:519-523.

78. Minich LL, Tani LY, Veasy LG. Role of echocardiography in the diagnosis and follow-up evaluation of rheumatic fever. In: Narula N, Virmani R, Reddy KS, Tandon R, eds. Rheumatic Fever. Washington, DC: Armed Forces Institute of Pathology; 1999:307-318.

79. Reddy DV, Chun LT, Yamamoto LG. Acute rheumatic fever with advanced degree AV block. Clin Pediatr. 1989;28:326-328.

80. Feinstein AR, Spagnuolo M. The clinical patterns of acute rheumatic fever: A reappraisal. Medicine. 1962;41:279-305.

81. Carapetis JR, Currie BJ. Rheumatic fever in a high incidence population: The importance of monoarthritis and low grade fever. Arch Dis Child. 2001;85:223-227.

82. Arnold MH, Tyndall A. Poststreptococcal reactive arthritis. Ann Rheum Dis. 1989;48:686-688.

83. Tutar E, Atalay S, Yilmaz E, et al. Poststreptococcal reactive arthritis in children: Is it really a different entity from rheumatic fever? Rheumatol Int. 2002;22:80-83.

84. de Cunto CL, Giannini EH, Fink CW, et al. Prognosis of children with poststreptococcal reactive arthritis. Pediatr Infect Dis J. 1988;7:683-686.

85. Shulman ST, Ayoub EM. Poststreptococcal reactive arthritis. Curr Opin Rheumatol. 2002;14:562-565.

86. Lehman TJ, Edelheit BS. Clinical trials for post-streptococcal reactive arthritis. Curr Rheumatol Rep. 2001;3:363-364.

87. Iglesias-Gamarra A, Mendez EA, Cuellar ML, et al. Poststreptococcal reactive arthritis in adults: Long-term follow-up. Am J Med Sci. 2001;321:173-177.

88. Herold BC, Shulman ST. Poststreptococcal arthritis. Pediatr Infect Dis J. 1988;4:681-682.

89. Dajani AS, Ayoub E, Bierman FZ, et al. Guidelines for the diagnosis of rheumatic fever: Jones criteria, updated 1992. Circulation. 1993;87:302-307.

90. Ayoub EM, Majeed HA. Poststreptococcal reactive arthritis. Curr Opin Rheumatol. 2000;12:306-310.

91. Taranta A. Rheumatic fever: Clinical aspects. In: Hollander JL, McCarty DJ Jr, eds. Arthritis and Allied Conditions. Philadelphia: Lea & Febiger; 1972:764-820.

92. Berrios X, Quesney F, Morales A, et al. Are all recurrences of "pure" Sydenham's chorea true recurrences of acute rheumatic fever? J Pediatr. 1985;107:867-872.

93. Terreri MT, Roja SC, Len CA, et al. Sydenham's chorea—clinical and evolutive characteristics. Sao Paulo Med J. 2002;120:16-19.

94. Bland EF. Chorea as a manifestation of rheumatic fever: A long-term perspective. Trans Am Clin Climatol Assoc. 1961;73:209-213.

95. Murphy ML, Pichichero ME. Prospective identification and treatment of children with pediatric autoimmune neuropsychiatric disorder associated with group A streptococcal infection (PANDAS). Arch Pediatr Adolesc Med. 2002;156:356-361.

96. Leonard HL, Swedo SE. Paediatric autoimmune neuropsychiatric disorders associated with streptococcal infection (PANDAS). Int J Neuropsychopharmacol. 2001;4:191-198.

97. Burgert SJ, Classen DC, Burke JP, Veasy LG. Rheumatic pneumonia: Reappearance of a previously recognized complication of acute rheumatic fever. Clin Infect Dis. 1995;21:1020-1022.

98. Dlesk A, Balian AA, Sullivan BJ, et al. Diagnostic dilemma for the 1990s: Lyme disease versus rheumatic fever. Wis Med J. 1991;90:632-634.

99. Herd JK, Medhi M, Uzendoski DM, Saldivar VA. Chorea associated with systemic lupus erythematosus: Report of two cases and review of the literature. Pediatrics. 1978;61:308-315.

100. Thompson HG Jr, Carpenter MB. Hemichorea due to metastatic lesion in the subthalamic nucleus. Arch Neurol. 1960;2:83-87.

101. Bamford JM, Hakin RN. Chorea after legionnaire's disease. Br Med J Clin Res. 1982;284:1232-1233.

102. McKinney AS. Idiopathic hypoparathyroidism presenting as chorea. Neurology. 1962;12:485-491.

103. Figueroa F, Berrios X, Gutierrez M, et al. Anticardiolipin antibodies in acute rheumatic fever. J Rheumatol. 1992;19:1175-1180.

104. Riddoch D, Jefferson M, Bickerstaff ER. Chorea and the oral contraceptives. Br Med J. 1971;4:217-218.

105. Jonas S, Spagnuolo M, Kloth HH. Chorea gravidarum and streptococcal infection. Obstet Gynecol. 1972;39:77-79.

106. Jones TD. The diagnosis of rheumatic fever. JAMA. 1944;126:481-484.

107. Veasy LG, Dajani AS, Allen HD, Taubert KA. Echocardiography for diagnosis and management of rheumatic fever. JAMA. 1993;269:2084.

108. Minich LL, Tani LY, Pagotto LT, et al. Doppler echocardiography distinguishes between physiologic and pathologic "silent" mitral regurgitation in patients with rheumatic fever. Clin Cardiol. 1997;20:924-926.

109. Figueroa FE, Fernandez MS, Valdes P, et al. Prospective comparison of clinical and echocardiographic diagnosis of rheumatic carditis: Long term follow up of patients with subclinical disease. Heart. 2001;85:407-410.

110. Ferrieri P. Proceedings of the Jones Criteria workshop. Circulation. 2002;10:2521-2523.

111. Lanna CC, Tonelli E, Barros MV, et al. Subclinical rheumatic valvitis: a long-term follow-up. Cardiol Young. 2003;13:431-438.

112. Stollerman GH, Lewis AJ, Schultz I, Taranta A. Relationship of immune response to group A streptococci to the course of acute, chronic and recurrent rheumatic fever. Am J Med. 1956;20:163-169.

113. Bisno AL, Ofek I. Serologic diagnosis of streptococcus infection. Comparison of a rapid hemagglutination technique with conventional antibody tests. Am J Dis Child. 1974;127:676-681.

114. Bisno AL, Ofek I, Beachey EH. Antigens of group A streptococci involved in passive hemagglutination reactions. Infect Immun. 1976;13:407-412.

115. Kaplan EL, Kunde C. Quantitative evaluation of variation in composition of the Streptozyme agglutination reagent for detection of antibodies to group A streptococcal extracellular antigens. J Clin Microbiol. 1981;14:678-680.

116. Cilliers AM, Manyemba J, Saloojee H. Anti-inflammatory treatment for carditis in acute rheumatic fever (Cochrane Review). Cochrane Database Syst Rev. 2003;2:CD003176.

117. Uziel Y, Hashkes PJ, Kassem E, et al. The use of naproxen in the treatment of children with rheumatic fever. J Pediatr. 2000;137:269-271.
118. Swedo SE. Sydenham's chorea: A model for childhood autoimmune neuropsychiatric disorders. JAMA. 1994;272:1788-1791.
119. United Kingdom and United States Joint Report on Rheumatic Heart Disease. The treatment of acute rheumatic fever in children. A cooperative clinical trial of ACTH, cortisone and aspirin. Circulation. 1955;11:343-377.
120. Gordis L. Effectiveness of comprehensive care programs in preventing rheumatic fever. N Engl J Med. 1973;289:331-335.
121. Dajani A, Taubert K, Ferrieri P, et al. Treatment of acute streptococcal pharyngitis and prevention of rheumatic fever: A statement for health professionals. Committee on Rheumatic Fever, Endocarditis, and Kawasaki Disease of the Council on Cardiovascular Disease in the Young, the American Heart Association. Pediatrics. 1995;96(4 Pt 1):758-764.
122. Wood HF, Feinstein AR, Taranta A, et al. Rheumatic fever in children and adolescents. A long-term epidemiologic study of subsequent prophylaxis, streptococcal infections, and clinical sequelae. III. Comparative effectiveness of three prophylaxis regimens in preventing streptococcal infections and rheumatic recurrences. Ann Intern Med. 1964;60(Suppl 5):31-46.
123. Lue HC, Wu MH, Wang JK, et al. Three- versus four-week administration of benzathine penicillin G: Effects of incidence of streptococcal infections and recurrences of rheumatic fever. Pediatrics. 1996;97(Suppl):984-988.
124. Berrios X, del Campo E, Guzman B, Bisno AL. Discontinuing rheumatic fever prophylaxis in selected adolescents and young adults: A prospective study. Ann Intern Med. 1993;118:401-406.
125. Dajani AS, Taubert KA, Wilson W, et al. Prevention of bacterial endocarditis. Recommendations by the American Heart Association. JAMA. 1997;277:1794-1801.
126. Hu MC, Walls MA, Stroop SD, et al. Immunogenicity of a 26-valent group A streptococcal vaccine. Infect Immun. 2002;70:2171-2177.
127. Fischetti VA. Vaccine approaches to protect against group A streptococcal pharyngitis. In: Fischetti VA, Novick RP, Ferretti JJ, et al, eds. Gram-Positive Pathogens. Washington, DC: American Society for Microbiology; 2000:96-104.
128. Bright R. Cases and observations, illustrative of renal disease accompanied with the secretion of albuminous urine. Guys Hosp Rep. 1936;1:338-400.
129. Schick B. Die nachkrankheiten des Schariach. Jb Kinderheilk. 1907;65:132-173.
130. Rammelkamp CH Jr, Weaver RS. Acute glomerulonephritis: The significance of the variations in the incidence of the disease. J Clin Invest. 1953;32:345-358.
131. Wannamaker LW. Differences between streptococcal infections of the throat and of the skin. N Engl J Med. 1970;282:23-31.
132. Potter EV, Ortiz JS, Sharrett R, et al. Changing types of nephritogenic streptococci in Trinidad. J Clin Invest. 1971;50:1197-1205.
133. Dillon HC, Derrick CW, Dillon MS. M-antigens common to pyoderma and acute glomerulonephritis. J Infect Dis. 1974;130:257-267.
134. Duca E, Teodorovici G, Radu C, et al. A new nephritogenic streptococcus. J Hyg. 1969;67:691-698.
135. Barnham M, Thornton TJ, Lange K. Nephritis caused by *Streptococcus zooepidemicus* (Lancefield group C). Lancet. 1983;1:945-948.
136. Seegal BC, Andres GA, Hsu KC, Zabriskie JB. Studies on the pathogenesis of acute and progressive glomerulonephritis in man by immunofluorescein and immunoferritin technique. Fed Proc. 1965;24:100-108.
137. Michael AF, Drummond KN, Good RA, et al. Acute poststreptococcal glomerulonephritis: Immune deposit disease. J Clin Invest. 1966;45:237-248.
138. Michael AF, Hoyer JR, Westberg NG, Fish AJ. Experimental models for the pathogenesis of acute poststreptococcal glomerulonephritis. In: Wannamaker LW, Masten JM, eds. Streptococci and Streptococcal Disease. New York: Academic Press; 1972:481-500.
139. Zabriskie JB. The role of streptococci in human glomerulonephritis. J Exp Med. 1971;134(Suppl):180S-192S.
140. Lange CF. Chemistry of cross-reactive fragments of streptococcal cell membrane and human glomerular basement membrane. Transplant Proc. 1969;1:959-963.
141. Bisno AL, Wood JW, Lawson J, et al. Antigens in urine of patients with glomerulonephritis and in normal human serum which cross-react with group A streptococci: Identification and partial characterization. J Lab Clin Med. 1978;91:500-513.
142. Goroncy-Bermes P, Dale JB, Beachey EH, Opferkuch W. Monoclonal antibody to human renal glomeruli cross-reacts with streptococcal M protein. Infect Immun. 1987;55:2416-2419.
143. Ooi YM, Vallota EH, West CD. Serum immune complexes in membranoproliferative and other glomerulonephritides. Kidney Int. 1977;11:275-283.
144. Tung KSK, Woodroffe AJ, Ahlin TD, et al. Application of the solid phase C1q and raji cell radioimmune assays for the detection of circulating immune complexes in glomerulonephritis. J Clin Invest. 1978;62:61-72.
145. van de Rijn I, Fillit H, Brandeis WE, et al. Serial studies on circulating immune complexes in post-streptococcal sequelae. Clin Exp Immunol. 1978;34:318-325.
146 Lindberg LH, Vosti KL. Elution of glomerular bound antibodies in experimental streptococcal glomerulonephritis. Science. 1969;166:1032-1033.
147. Markowitz AS, Horn D, Aseron C, et al. Streptococcal related glomerulonephritis. 3. Glomerulonephritis in rhesus monkeys immunologically induced both actively and passively with a soluble fraction from nephritogenic streptococcal protoplasmic membranes. J Immunol. 1971;107:504-511.
148. Cu GA, Mezzano S, Bannan JD, Zabriskie JB. Immunohistochemical and serological evidence for the role of streptococcal proteinase in acute post-streptococcal glomerulonephritis. Kidney Int. 1998; 54:819-826.
149. Parra G, Rodriguez-Iturbe B, Batsford S, et al. Antibody to streptococcal zymogen in the serum of patients with acute glomerulonephritis: A multicentric study. Kidney Int. 1998; 54:509-517.
150. Rodriguez-Iturbe B. Postinfectious glomerulonephritis. Am J Kidney Dis. 2000; 35:xlvi-xiviii.
151. Johnson KH, Zabriskie JB. Purification and partial characterization of the nephritis strain-associated protein from *Streptococcus pyogenes,* group A. J Exp Med. 1986; 163:697-712.
152. Nordstrand A, Norgren M, Ferretti JJ, Holm SE. Streptokinase as a mediator of acute post-streptococcal glomerulonephritis in an experimental mouse model. Infect Immun. 1998;66:315-321.
153. Mezzano S, Burgos E, Mahabir R, et al. Failure to detect unique reactivity to streptococcal streptokinase in either the sera or renal biopsy specimens of patients with acute poststreptococcal glomerulonephritis. Clin Nephrol. 1992;38:305-310.
154. Lewy JE, Salinas-Madrigal L, Herdson PB, et al. Clinico-pathologic correlations in acute poststreptococcal glomerulonephritis. A correlation between renal functions, morphologic damage and clinical course of 46 children with acute poststreptococcal glomerulonephritis. Medicine. 1971;50:453-501.
155. Anthony BF, Kaplan EL, Wannamaker LW, et al. Attack rates of acute nephritis after type 49 streptococcal infection of the skin and of the respiratory tract. J Clin Invest. 1969;48:1697-1704.
156. Tasic V, Polenakovic M. Acute poststreptococcal glomerulonephritis following circumcision. Pediatr Nephrol. 2000;15:274-275.
157. Nair S, Schoeneman MJ. Acute glomerulonephritis with group A streptococcal vulvovaginitis. Clin Pediatr (Philadelphia). 2000;39:721-722.
158. Stetson CA, Rammelkamp CH Jr, Krause RM, et al. Epidemic acute nephritis: Studies on etiology, natural history and prevention. Medicine. 1955;34:431-450.
159. Lange K, Ahmed U, Kleinberger H, Treser G. A hitherto unknown streptococcal antigen and its probable relation to acute poststreptococcal glomerulonephritis. Clin Nephrol. 1976;5:207-215.
160. Roy S, Wall HP, Etteldorf JN. Second attacks of acute glomerulonephritis. J Pediatr. 1969;75:758-767.
161. Seegal D, Lyttle JD, Loeb EN, et al. On the exacerbation in chronic glomerulonephritis. J Clin Invest. 1940;19:569-589.
162. Bisno AL. The coexistence of acute rheumatic fever and acute glomerulonephritis. Arthritis Rheum. 1989;32:230-232.
163. Matsell DG, Baldree LA, DiSessa TG, et al. Acute poststreptococcal glomerulonephritis and acute rheumatic fever: Occurrence in the same patient. Child Nephrol Urol. 1990;10:112-114.
164. Poon-King T, Mohammed I, Cox R, et al. Recurrent epidemic nephritis in South Trinidad. N Engl J Med. 1967;277:728-733.
165. Kaplan EL, Anthony BF, Chapman SS, Wannamaker LW. Epidemic acute glomerulonephritis associated with type 49 streptococcal pyoderma. Am J Med. 1970;48:9-27.
166. Derrick CW, Reeves MS, Dillon HC Jr. Complement in overt and asymptomatic nephritis after skin infection. J Clin Invest. 1970;49:1178-1187.
167. Sharrett AR, Poon-King T, Potter EV, et al. Subclinical nephritis in South Trinidad. Am J Epidemiol. 1971;94:231-245.
168. Dodge WF, Spargo BH, Travis LB. Occurrence of acute glomerulonephritis in sibling contacts of children with sporadic acute glomerulonephritis. Pediatrics. 1967;40:1029-1030.
169. Schwartz WB, Kassirer JP. Clinical aspects of acute poststreptococcal glomerulonephritis. In: Strauss MB, Welt LG, eds. Disease of the Kidney. Boston: Little, Brown; 1971:419-462.
170. Freedman P, Meister HP, Lee HJ, et al. The renal response to streptococcal infection. Medicine. 1970;49:433-463.
171. Berman LB, Vogelsang P. Poststreptococcal glomerulonephritis without proteinuria. N Engl J Med. 1963;268:1275-1277.
172. Smith RD, Aquino J. Viruses and the kidney. Med Clin North Am. 1971;55:89-106.
173. Humphreys MH. Renal complications of HIV infection. In: Sande MA, Volbercling PA, eds. The Medical Management of AIDS. Philadelphia: WB Saunders, 1997.
174. Balat A, Baysal K, Kocak H. Myocardial functions of children with acute poststreptococcal glomerulonephritis. Clin Nephrol. 1993;39:151-155.
175. Kassirer JP, Schwartz WB. Acute glomerulonephritis. N Engl J Med. 1961;265:686-692.
176. Lasch EE, Frankel V, Vardy PA, et al. Epidemic glomerulonephritis in Israel. J Infect Dis. 1971;124:141-147.
177. Weinstein L, Le Frock J. Does antimicrobial therapy of streptococcal pharyngitis or pyoderma alter the risk of glomerulonephritis? J Infect Dis. 1971;124:229-231.
178. Perlman LV, Herdman RC, Kleinman H. Poststreptococcal glomerulonephritis: A ten-year follow-up of an epidemic. JAMA. 1965;194:63-70.
179. Potter EV, Lipschultz SA, Abidh S, et al. Twelve to seventeen-year follow-up of patients with poststreptococcal acute glomerulonephritis in Trinidad. N Engl J Med. 1982;307:725-729.
179a. White AV, Hoy WE, McCredie DA. Childhood post-streptococcal glomerulonephritis as a risk factor for chronic renal disease in later life. Med J Aust. 2001;174:492-496.
180. Baldwin DS. Poststreptococcal glomerulonephritis. A progressive disease? Am J Med. 1977;62:1-11.
181. Jennings RB, Earle DP. Post-streptococcal glomerulonephritis: Histopathologic and clinical studies of the acute, subsiding acute and early chronic latent phases. J Clin Invest. 1961;40:1525-1595.

182. Kurtzman NA. Does acute poststreptococcal glomerulonephritis lead to chronic renal disease? N Engl J Med. 1978;298:795-796.
183. Kaplan EL, Vernier RL. Progressive nephritis after strep infection questioned. Am J Med. 1978;64:910-911.
184. Pinto SW, Sesso R, Vasconcelos E, et al. Follow-up of patients with epidemic post-streptococcal glomerulonephritis. Am J Kidney Dis. 2001;38:249-255.
185. Richmond DE, Doak PB. The prognosis of acute post infectious glomerulonephritis in adults: A long-term prospective study. Aust N Z J Med 1990;20:215-219.
186. Kaplan EL, Johnson DR, Nanthapisud P, et al. A comparison of group A streptococcal serotypes isolated from the upper respiratory tract in the USA and Thailand: Implications. Bull WHO 1992;70:433-437.

CHAPTER 197

Streptococcus pneumoniae

DANIEL M. MUSHER

Long recognized as a major cause of pneumonia, meningitis, sinusitis, and otitis media, *Streptococcus pneumoniae* is an important bacterial pathogen in humans; it is a less frequent cause of endocarditis, septic arthritis, and peritonitis and an uncommon cause of a variety of other infectious diseases.

HISTORY

A brief review of the history of *S. pneumoniae,* also known as pneumococcus, documents the important part this organism played in the history of microbiology.[1-3] In 1881, the organism was identified concurrently in the Old and New Worlds; Pasteur, in France named it *Microbe septice mique du salive,* and Sternberg, in the United States, called it *Micrococcus pasteuri.* By the late 1880s the term *pneumococcus* was generally used because this bacterium had come to be recognized as the most common cause of lobar pneumonia. The genus name *Diplococcus* was assigned in 1926 because of its appearance in Gram-stained sputum, and in 1974 the organism was renamed once again, this time as *Streptococcus pneumoniae* because of its morphology during growth in liquid medium.

S. pneumoniae was the first organism to be shown to behave as what is now regarded as a prototypic extracellular bacterial pathogen; in the absence of antibody, this bacterium resists phagocytosis and replicates extracellularly in mammalian tissues. In the early 1890s, Felix and Georg Klemperer showed that immunization with killed pneumococci protected animals against subsequent pneumococcal challenge and, further, that protection could be transferred by infusing serum (the essential "humoral" substance) from immunized mice into naive recipients. Subsequently, serum from persons who had recovered from pneumococcal pneumonia was found to confer the same degree of protection. The basis for this immunity was shown by Neufeld and Rimpau to be the presence of factor(s) in serum that facilitated ingestion by white blood cells (WBCs), a process that these investigators called *opsonization,* which is derived from the Greek word for preparing food. These observations provided the basis for what we now call humoral immunity. Serotypes were also recognized after it was observed that injection of killed organisms into a rabbit stimulated the production of serum antibody that agglutinated and caused capsular swelling of the immunizing strain, as well as some, but not all other pneumococcal isolates. Early in the 20th century, three serotypes were distinguished and called serotypes 1, 2, and 3; all other pneumococci were called group 4.

In the first decade of the 20th century, Maynard, Lister, Wright, and others began to apply the concepts of humoral immunity to the problem of epidemic lobar pneumonia that each year affected as many as 1 in 10 men who were working in African mines.[1,4] Inoculation of min-

ers with killed pneumococci caused a substantial reduction in the incidence of pneumonia. In the 1920s, Heidelberger and Avery[5] demonstrated that the antibody that conferred immunity was reactive with surface capsular polysaccharides. Felton[6] prepared the first purified pneumococcal capsular polysaccharides for immunization of human subjects, and a preparation of type 1 polysaccharide was used to abort an epidemic of pneumonia at a state hospital in Worcester, Massachusetts, in 1938.[7] Taken together, these studies supported a novel set of concepts by showing that a specific bacterial polysaccharide antigen could be used to stimulate humoral antibodies that conferred protection against epidemic human infection. Further confirmation was provided during World War II, when MacLeod and co-workers[8] found that vaccinating military recruits with capsular material from four serotypes of *S. pneumoniae* greatly reduced the incidence of pneumonia caused by serotypes in the vaccine, but not by other pneumococcal serotypes.

S. pneumoniae also played a central role in the discovery of DNA. Experiments done by Griffith[9] in the 1920s had shown that intraperitoneal injection of live, unencapsulated (mutant) pneumococci together with heat-killed encapsulated pneumococci into mice led to the emergence of viable, encapsulated bacteria; he called this process *transformation.* This observation remained unexplained until the 1940s, when Avery and co-workers[10] provided conclusive evidence that these mutants had recovered the capacity to produce capsule by taking up DNA from killed, virulent organisms—in other words, that DNA is responsible for transformation and, in fact, is the genetic material that encodes for phenotype.

MICROBIOLOGY

S. pneumoniae is a gram-positive coccus that replicates in chains in liquid medium. The organism is catalase negative, but it generates H_2O_2 via a flavoenzyme system and therefore grows better in the presence of a source of catalase such as red blood cells. Pneumococci produce pneumolysin (formerly called α-hemolysin), which breaks down hemoglobin into a green pigment; as a result, pneumococcal colonies are surrounded by a green zone during growth on blood-agar plates. This property is still termed α-hemolysis, although properly speaking it should not be, because lysis of red blood cells is not responsible. This point becomes readily apparent when one observes the greenish yellow color that appears around colonies of *S. pneumoniae* during growth on chocolate agar, a medium in which all the red blood cells have already been lysed during preparation. Growth of pneumococci is inhibited by ethyl hydrocupreine (optochin), and the organisms are lysed by bile salts. Thus, pneumococci are identified in the microbiology laboratory by four reactions: (1) α-hemolysis of blood agar, (2) catalase negativity, (3) susceptibility to optochin, and (4) solubility in bile salts. The finding that some pneumococci are optochin-resistant[11] has led to greater reliance on the use of bile solubility for definitive identification. A highly reliable probe that detects rRNA sequences unique to *S. pneumoniae* is also commercially available.

ANATOMY AND PHYSIOLOGY

Nearly every clinical isolate of *S. pneumoniae* contains an external capsule; unencapsulated isolates have mainly been implicated in outbreaks of conjunctivitis.[12] Capsules[13] (Fig. 197-1) are made up of repeating oligosaccharides that are synthesized within the cytoplasm, polymerized, and transported to the bacterial surface by cell membrane transferases. These polysaccharides are covalently bound to peptidoglycan and cell wall (C−) polysaccharide, which explains the difficulty of separating capsular from cell wall polysaccharide. Genetic control of this complex set of events has been elucidated for some serotypes; a cassette of 15 genes that function as a single transcriptional unit is responsible for serogroup 19.[14] Ninety serotypes of *S. pneumoniae* have been identified on the basis of antigenic differences in their capsular polysaccharides. Immunization of rabbits stimulates the appearance of antibodies that cause agglutination and microscopic demonstrability of the capsule; in the latter reaction, called the quellung reaction, antibody renders the capsule refractile and therefore more readily visible. Because serum antibody is the basis for identifying these types of pneumococcus, they are called serotypes. In the American numbering system, serotypes are numbered from 1 to 90 in the order in which they were identified. The more widely accepted Danish numbering system distinguishes groups of serotypes according to antigenic similarities. For example, Danish serogroup 19 includes types 19F, 19A, 19B, and 19C (the letter F indicates the first member of the group to be identified, followed by A, B, C, etc.), which in the American system would be types 19, 57, 58, and 59, respectively. Serotypes that most frequently cause human disease were the earliest to be identified and were the first to be assigned numbers, which explains why the lower-numbered serotypes are generally more likely to be implicated in human infection. Serotyping was clinically relevant in the 1930s, when antisera were administered for therapy, and is of great interest from epidemiologic and public health standpoints today, especially as new vaccines are being developed, but has little relevance for the clinician in an individual case of pneumococcal infection.

Some DNA sequences that govern capsule formation have been found in all pneumococci studied to date, whereas others are unique to a particular serotype.[15-18] As part of its quorum-sensing mechanism, *S. pneumoniae* expresses a competence-sensing protein and undergoes alterations that enable it to internalize DNA from other pneumococci or from other bacterial species.[19] Because of this property, pneumococci are able to acquire new traits in a process that is called *transformation*. Transformation of capsular types occurs under experimental conditions but, more importantly, also occurs in nature.[20] Careful study of clinical isolates with fingerprinting techniques has shown that, during colonization or infection of humans, pneumococci can acquire a cassette of DNA that encodes the production of a serotypically different capsule—in other words, pneumococci in vivo can switch capsules.

As with other streptococci, peptidoglycan and teichoic acid are the principal constituents of the pneumococcal cell wall[21] (see Fig. 197-1). Peptidoglycan consists of long chains of alternating *N*-acetyl-D-glucosamine and *N*-acetylmuramic acid, from which extend chains of four to six amino acids called stem peptides. Stem peptides are cross-linked by pentaglycine bridges, which provides substantial strength to the cell wall. Teichoic acid, a carbohydrate polymer that contains phosphorylcholine, is covalently linked to the peptidoglycan and probably also to lipoteichoic acid on the outermost surface of the bacterial wall and protrudes into the capsule. This teichoic acid, together with tightly adherent fragments of peptidoglycan makes up C-polysaccharide, a substance that is present in all pneumococci and is otherwise detected only in a few species of viridans streptococci. This region is responsible for the reaction between pneumococci and proteins that appear in the blood stream in certain illnesses (called acute-phase reactants or C-reactive proteins) or that occur in some cases of multiple myeloma. Many proteins are expressed on the cell surface. Of particular importance in pathogenesis of disease are those that bind to ("decorate") choline, also called the choline-binding proteins, including pneumococcal surface proteins A and C, pneumococcal surface adhesin (choline-binding protein) A, choline-binding protein C, and proteins involved in competence, all of which appear to have a role in virulence and will be discussed later under pathogenetic mechanisms. The characteristic three-layered cell membrane consists of lipid and teichoic acid and is called F antigen because of cross-reactivity with Forssman antigens.

EPIDEMIOLOGY

As with many other microorganisms, *S. pneumoniae* finds its ecologic niche in colonizing the nasopharynx. On a single occasion, appropriate culturing yields pneumococci in 5% to 10% of healthy adults and 20% to 40% of healthy children. With repeated attempts at culture, the percentage increases in all age groups, rising to 40% to 60% or greater[22] in toddlers and young children in daycare. For reasons that remain unclear, the rate of colonization is seasonal, with an increase in the midwinter period, although pneumococci can be recovered from healthy children and adults throughout the year, and a huge sample is required to document such seasonality. A careful prospective study in infants[23] showed that the first pneumococcus to colonize an infant is generally acquired at approximately 6 months of age and can be detected for a mean of about 4 months. In adults, an individual serotype persists for shorter periods, usually 2 to 4 weeks,[24] but sometimes much longer.

Population-based studies carried out in different parts of the world (and summarized by Fedson and colleagues[25]) show that the overall rate

FIGURE 197-1. A representation of the cell membrane, cell wall, and capsule of *Streptococcus pneumoniae*. Within the cell wall, M = *N*-acetylmuramic acid and G = *N*-acetyl-D-glucosamine. The stem peptides and the cross-linked pentaglycine bridges that extend from the long M-G-M-G chains are not shown. Cell wall (C−) polysaccharide consists of teichoic acid with peptidoglycan and phosphorylcholine (not shown). F antigen is the lipid/teichoic acid moiety in the cell membrane that extends into the cell wall.

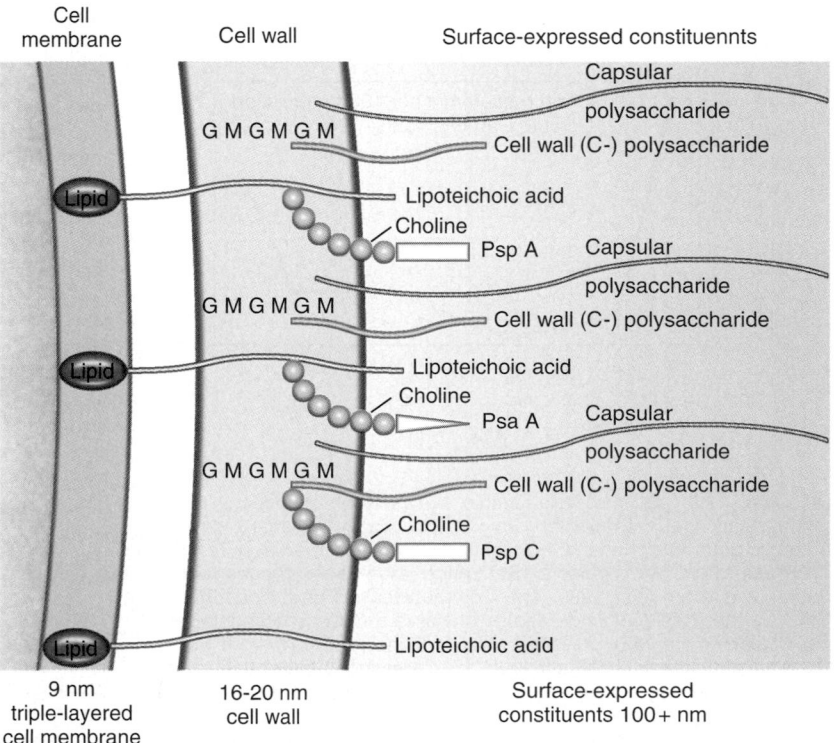

of invasive pneumococcal disease, defined as the isolation of *S. pneumoniae* from a normally sterile site such as blood, pleural fluid, or cerebrospinal fluid (CSF), is about 15 per 100,000 persons per year. In certain populations, including African-Americans,[26] Native Americans (especially Alaskans),[27] and Australian Aboriginals,[28] the incidence may be increased as much as 10-fold greater, although it is unclear to what extent genetic or environmental factors are responsible. Invasive pneumococcal infection is relatively common in newborns and infants up to 2 years of age and much less so in teenaged children and young adults, again increasing in adults older than 65 years[1,29,30] (Fig. 197-2). Data from South Carolina[30] are representative and show the incidence of pneumococcal bacteremia to be 160, 5, and 70 per 100,000 persons, respectively, in infants, young adults, and those 70 years or older. Although the overall incidence of pneumococcal infection in the population is greatly reduced when compared with the preantibiotic era, this relationship to age has not changed. Most cases of bacteremia in adults are caused by pneumonia, and probably 3 or 4 cases of nonbacteremic pneumonia occur for every bacteremic one, thus leading to estimates of 25 cases of pneumococcal pneumonia per 100,000 young adults and 280 per 100,000 elderly individuals each year. Because of lack of ascertainment, the true incidence may be several times greater. By contrast, in the preantibiotic era, about 700 cases of pneumonia occurred per 100,000 young adults.[1] Some investigators have suggested[31,32] that the incidence of pneumococcal disease is increasing; recent data from the United States[33] indicate that the incidence is decreasing, perhaps owing to widespread use of protein-conjugate pneumococcal vaccine in children.

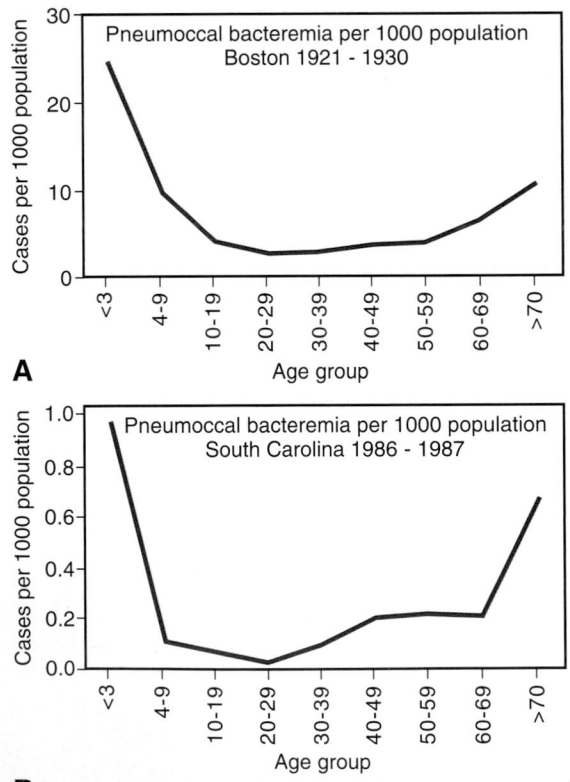

FIGURE 197-2. The relationship between pneumococcal bacteremia and age is shown for two studies, widely separated in time. **A** shows data published in the preantibiotic era. (Adapted from Heffron R. Pneumonia: With Special Reference to Pneumococcus Lobar Pneumonia. Copyright 1939. The Commonwealth Fund. Copyright © 1979 by the President and Fellows of Harvard College. Reprinted by permission of Harvard University Press.) **B** includes data from South Carolina obtained in 1986 and 1987.[30] Interestingly, the shape of the curve is remarkably similar, although the vertical axis in the lower curve shows a vastly reduced incidence when compared with that in the upper one. More recent studies continue to confirm these earlier findings.

The occurrence of infection, for example, otitis media[34,35] or bacteremia,[36,37] is related to season, perhaps because of the association with viral respiratory illnesses. A November through April clustering with a clear peak in February was apparent for otitis media in the study of Gray and Dillon.[23] In Houston, Texas (Fig. 197-3), invasive disease in children occurs mainly during September through May, thus coinciding with the school year and sparing the summer months, but with no clear midwinter peak. In contrast, invasive disease in adults clearly reaches a peak in the middle of winter, inversely related to ambient temperature and directly associated with the peak of viral respiratory disease.[36]

Pneumococci are transmitted from one individual to another as a result of extensive, close contact,[38] but infection is generally not regarded as contagious because so many factors intervene between acquisition of the organism (colonization) and disease. Daycare centers are very likely to be places for spread of these organisms in toddlers.[39-41] In adults, close, crowded living conditions such as occur in military camps,[42] prisons,[43] shelters for the homeless,[44] and nursing homes[45] are associated with epidemics, but contact in schools or in the workplace is generally not.[38]

PATHOGENETIC MECHANISMS

To cause disease, pneumococci, like other extracellular bacterial pathogens, must adhere to mammalian cells; replicate in situ; be carried to, replicate in, and fail to be cleared from anatomic areas that are normally free of them; escape phagocytosis; and damage tissue by causing inflammation and/or producing substances that directly damage cells. Many of these reactions are governed at a molecular level by bacterial and host properties.[46,47]

Adherence, Colonization, Invasion

The prevalence of pneumococcal colonization attests to the adaptational success of this organism in adhering to mammalian cells and replicating in situ in the nasopharynx. *S. pneumoniae* attaches to human pharyngeal cells through a variety of mechanisms involving the specific interaction of bacterial surface adhesins (such as pneumococcal surface adhesin A and choline-binding proteins) and epithelial cell receptors.[48] Epithelial cell glycoconjugates containing the disaccharide GlcNAcb1-4Gal[49] or asialo-GM glycolipid[50] are possible binding sites. Phase variation of pneumococci may also play a role. On culture in vitro, a mixed population of transparent and opaque colonies can be identified. Organisms from transparent colonies have greatly increased quantities of phosphorylcholine and choline binding protein A (distinct from surface adhesin A), which contribute to their capacity to adhere to mammalian cells.[51] When an opaque colony is inoculated intranasally into an experimental animal, only those organisms that make transparent colonies persist. In contrast, intraperitoneal inoculation of opaque colonies may be lethal, whereas transparent colonies are less likely to be so; increased capsule production by opaque forms may in part be responsible.

Once colonization has taken place, infection may result if the organisms are carried into cavities from which they are not readily cleared. Under normal circumstances, when organisms find their way into eustachian tubes, sinuses, or bronchi, clearance mechanisms, chiefly ciliary action, lead to their rapid removal. If allergy or coexisting viral infection, for example, has caused edema that obstructs the opening of the eustachian tube into the pharynx or the ostium of a paranasal sinus, clinically recognizable infection may result. Similarly, damage to ciliated bronchial cells or increased production of mucus, whether chronic (e.g., from cigarette smoking or occupational exposure) or acute (from influenza or some other viral infection), may prevent the clearance of inhaled or aspirated organisms and lead to infection.

In some cases, pneumococci also act as invasive organisms, penetrating mucosal barriers. This is thought to occur because choline-binding protein A interacts with polymeric immunoglobulin receptor on the surface of epithelial and mucosal cells,[52] with subsequent endocytosis, transport through the cell, and release through the inner cell membrane. If pneumococci are released into the blood stream, they may invade the central nervous system by interacting with the receptor for platelet activating factor[53] which has been upregulated by inflammatory events; it is not certain whether the site of invasion is the choroid plexus or endothelial cells.[47]

Escape from Phagocytosis

S. pneumoniae causes disease because it is able to avoid ingestion and killing by host phagocytic cells. In an immunologically naive host, specifically in the absence of anticapsular antibody, pneumococci are poorly ingested and killed by the host's professional phagocytes, polymorphonuclear leukocytes (PMNs), and macrophages. Capsule plays a central role in preventing phagocytosis. Possible contributing mechanisms include (1) the absence of receptors on phagocytic cells that recognize capsular polysaccharides, (2) the presence of electrochemical forces that repel phagocytic cells, (3) the masking of antibody to cell wall constituents and C3b that may have fixed to the cell wall but beneath the capsule, and (4) the inactivation of complement.[54] Surface-expressed proteins also contribute to the evasion of phagocytosis. PspA prevents deposition and activation of C3b by interfering with complement factor B,[55] and PspC blocks activation of the complement cascade by binding complement factor H.[56] Much of the evidence supporting the overwhelming importance of the capsule as the major determinant of virulence has been summarized earlier in the brief history of pneumococcus. To those concepts should be added that by the use of transposon mutagenesis, interruption of capsule production in *S. pneumoniae* type 3 renders the organism essentially avirulent, with the lethal dose in mice shifted from 2 to 3 colony-forming units to more than 3×10^7.[57] In addition, a close relationship has been observed between the absolute amount of anticapsular antibody infused into mice and the level of protection against challenge with each of several serotypes of *S. pneumoniae*.[58]

Noncapsular Virulence Factors

As mentioned in the preceding paragraph, noncapsular protein constituents, including pneumolysin, surface proteins, and autolysin, contribute to the pathogenesis of pneumococcal disease. Genetically engineered mutants that lack the ability to produce one or more of these substances have generally been shown to have diminished virulence, and immunization with the purified substance has stimulated the production of antibodies that confer protection in experimental animals

(Table 197-1). It needs to be emphasized, however, that despite the current interest in these and other protein constituents of *S. pneumoniae*,[59,60] at the time of this writing (May, 2004), only indirect evidence of a protective effect of antibody to any of these substances has been found in humans.

All serotypes of *S. pneumoniae* produce pneumolysin, a thiol-activated toxin that inserts into the lipid bilayer of cell membranes via its interaction with cholesterol. Pneumolysin is cytotoxic for phagocytic and respiratory epithelial cells and causes inflammation by activating complement and inducing the production of tumor necrosis factor-α and interleukin-1 (IL-1).[61,62] Injection of pneumolysin into rat lung causes all the histologic findings of pneumonia,[63] and immunization of mice with this substance before infection[64] or challenge with genetically engineered pneumococci that do not produce it[65] is associated with a significant reduction in virulence. Different regions of the pneumolysin molecule are responsible for cytotoxic and complement activity properties, and recent studies have used strains with defined point mutations to show that the cytotoxic activity is dominant in causing disease after intraperitoneal but not necessarily after intranasal challenge of mice.[66] Human antibody to pneumolysin increases after pneumococcal pneumonia; the presence of this antibody is associated with a decreased likelihood of bacteremic infection, and it protects mice against pneumococcal challenge.[67]

Proteins on the pneumococcal surface that bind to choline residues may mediate attachment to and penetration of mammalian cells, especially if these cells have been upregulated by prior cytokine exposure.[53] Pneumococcal surface protein A is present on the surface of nearly all pneumococci and exerts an antiphagocytic force, perhaps by blocking deposition of complement.[68] Despite some antigenic variability, antibody raised against pneumococcal surface protein A protects experimental animals to a greater or lesser extent against challenge with the same or different strain,[69] and genetically engineered mutants that lack it have reduced virulence for mice.[70] Human antibody to this protein protects mice against pneumococcal infection,[71] and this substance is a major constituent of a vaccine that is currently in development. Pneumococcal surface adhesin A, a surface-expressed permease, is universally present in *S. pneumoniae*. This protein shows very little antigenic variability. Antibody to it reduces pneumococcal colonization of the nasopharynx in mice,[72] perhaps by blocking attachment[73]; this antibody may also be associated with reduced risk of otitis media.[74] It may

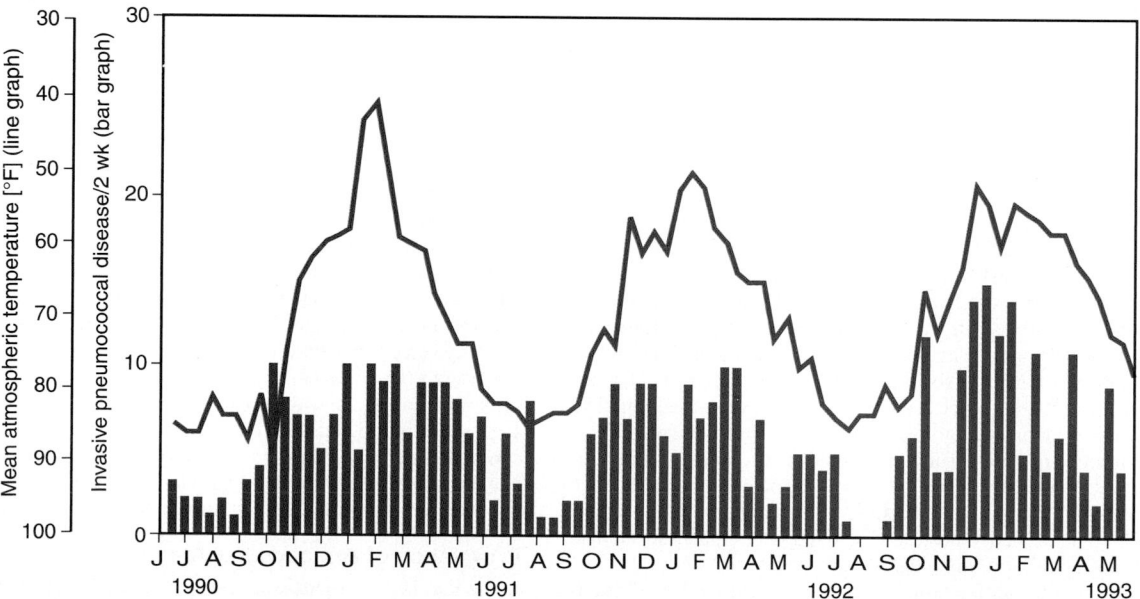

FIGURE 197-3. Each bar shows the number of cases of invasive pneumococcal disease at four tertiary care hospitals (adult and pediatric) in Houston, Texas, during a 2-week period. A fall, winter, and early spring predominance is noted. The line graph[36] is the number of specimens from patients thought to have a viral syndrome, obtained by a consortium of physicians in cooperation with the Influenza Research Center of the Baylor College of Medicine, Houston, Texas.

TABLE 197-1 Role of Pneumococcal Constituents as Virulence Factors*

Pneumococcal Constituent	Mechanism	Strength of Evidence as a Virulence Factor	
		Antibody Prevents Disease†	Mutants Lack Virulence
Capsular polysaccharide	Prevents phagocytosis; activates complement	4+	4+
Cell wall polysaccharide	Stimulates inflammation by strongly activating complement and stimulating release of cytokines	0	ND
Pneumolysin	Cytotoxic; activates complement, cytokines	2-3+	2-3+
PspA	Inhibits phagocytosis by blocking activation and deposition of complement on bacterial surface	2+	2+
PspC	Inhibits phagocytosis by binding complement factor H	1-2+	1-2+
PsaA	Mediates adherence	1-2+	1-2+
Autolysin	Causes bacterial disintegration, releases components	1+	2+
Neuraminidase	Possibly mediates adherence	0-1+	0-1+

*The grading system is subjective and indicates (on a scale of 1+ to 4+) the stringency and importance of the demonstrated effect. For discussion and references, see the text.
†Animal models only except capsular polysaccharides.
ND, Not done; Psa, pneumococcal surface adhesin; Psp, pneumococcal surface protein.

be involved in colonization of the nasopharynx, but it appears to contribute to virulence in other, as yet undetermined ways. Autolysin[65] disrupts the bacterial wall at the site of attachment of stem proteins. In nature, this enzyme contributes to cell wall remodeling. In infection, it probably contributes to disease by releasing peptidoglycan components that more vigorously activate complement, as well as substances (such as pneumolysin) to which the tissues of the infected host might otherwise not be exposed. As with other putative virulence factors, strains that lack autolysin are less virulent in experimental animals, and antibody to autolysin is modestly protective.[75] Pneumococci produce neuraminidase, which may contribute to bacterial adherence and colonization by cleaving sialic acid on mucous membrane surfaces and exposing GlcNAc-Gal, to which *S. pneumoniae* adheres more readily. Immunization of mice with neuraminidase has also provided modest protection against parenteral pneumococcal challenge, perhaps suggesting a role in virulence other than inhibition of colonization. All pneumococci also produce hyaluronidase, but a role in pathogenesis has not been clearly demonstrated.

Activation of Complement and Inflammatory Cytokines

Unlike certain other organisms such as *Streptococcus pyogenes,* which produce a variety of tissue-damaging substances, *S. pneumoniae* produces few toxins, of which pneumolysin is the principal one. Pneumococcus largely causes disease because its cell wall constituents and pneumolysin generate an intense inflammatory response; this inflammatory response is attributable to activation of complement and upregulation of leukocytes via toll-like receptors. The cell wall of *S. pneumoniae,* including both teichoic acid and peptidoglycan constituents activate complement by the alternative pathway.[76,77] Injection of either of these substances into the subarachnoid space causes an inflammatory reaction that has the characteristics of bacterial meningitis, although the kinetics vary with the substance injected.[77] C-reactive protein may also play an active part.[78] Polysaccharide capsule in addition appears to activate the alternative pathway in vitro,[79,80] albeit to a somewhat lesser extent. This type of activation is associated with the release of C5a, so that whether or not complement is fixed on the bacterial surface, C5a, a potent attractant for PMNs, is released to the surrounding medium. The classic pathway is activated by antibody to cell wall polysaccharides even in the absence of anticapsular antibody.[80] Thus, an intense inflammatory response fueled by vigorous activation of both the alternative and classic complement pathways accompanies pneumococcal infection of an immunologically naive host; as discussed later, pneumolysin also contributes substantially to this inflammatory response.

Peptidoglycan and lipoteichoic acid interact with CD14, stimulating toll-like receptor 2,[81] and pneumolysin interacts with toll-like receptor 4[82] to induce nuclear factor kappa B (NF-κB). NF-κB, in turn, upregulates production of inflammatory cytokines IL-1, IL-6, and tumor necrosis factor-α (TNF-α). Pneumolysin and bacterial DNA

(largely released by the action of autolysin) also stimulate the generation of inflammatory cytokines, apparently by other mechanisms. These observations are all consistent with the notion that pneumococcal disease is largely a result of inflammation and is severe in direct proportion to its intensity.

IMMUNOLOGICALLY SPECIFIC MECHANISMS OF HOST DEFENSE IN HUMANS

Antibody to Pneumococcal Capsule

Ample evidence shows that in humans, anticapsular antibody is protective against pneumococcal infection, with little or no evidence to date to support a role for antibody to other bacterial constituents: (1) antibody to capsule appears in the blood stream 5 to 8 days after the onset of infection, which is the time that fever spontaneously resolves in the absence of treatment; (2) in the preantibiotic era, administration of serum that contained type-specific antibody was moderately effective in treating pneumococcal pneumonia; and (3) various assays all seem to show greatly increased uptake and killing of pneumococci in vitro in the presence of anticapsular antibody.[1,83,84] In contrast, except for indirect data suggesting an association between antibody to pneumolysin[67] or pneumococcal surface adhesin a,[74] there are few data to support a protective role for antibody to other substances. It is important to note, however, that in the preantibiotic era, some proportion of patients recovered from pneumococcal pneumonia without producing measurable amounts of anticapsular antibody. Furthermore, some adults lack the capacity to make antibody to most pneumococcal capsules,[85] yet live long and healthy lives free of pneumococcal disease. Although immunoglobulin G (IgG) antibody as measured by enzyme-linked immunosorbent assay (ELISA) generally predicts protection of experimental animals and opsonophagocytosis activity in vitro, such is not uniformly the case. Elderly persons, for example, may have relatively high levels of anticapsular antibody, yet the antibody may not opsonize pneumococci for phagocytosis or protect mice against experimental challenge (see "Prevention"). The precise reason for the lack of protection is not known; perhaps the IgG antibody relatively less avid for capsular material. Thus, when present, anticapsular antibody is regarded as a generally good, but not ideal, surrogate marker of immunity. The converse—namely, that the absence of such antibody indicates a relative degree of susceptibility—is probably true, even though many other factors enter into protection against pneumococcal disease.

Prevalence of Anticapsular Antibody

In the late 1980s, a sensitive and specific ELISA technique was developed that used adsorption to remove cross-reacting antibody to cell wall polysaccharides.[86,87] This ELISA was used to show that the great majority of 19-year-old military recruits lack antibody to most pneumococcal serotypes.[88] On average, these young adults have type-specific anticapsular IgG to only 15% of commonly infecting serotypes. The rate of reactivity is 33% in working adult men or elderly men. To the extent that immunity is determined by the prevalence of measurable levels of antibody, these data suggest that healthy adults of all ages tend to be susceptible to most serotypes of *S. pneumoniae* that commonly cause infection.

Natural Emergence of Antibody

After pneumococcal infection, antibody to the infecting serotype, as measured in older studies by agglutination in vitro or mouse protection, appears in the serum of adults in about two thirds of cases, with some variability depending on the serotype.[89] In children, the rate of appearance of antibody is lower[90-92]; these studies need to be repeated with ELISA. The reason or reasons for the failure of detectable levels of antibody to develop after infection remain unclear. One explanation is a genetically mediated incapacity to recognize as foreign the relevant capsular polysaccharide and, therefore, to make antibody to it.[85] Failure to switch to IgG synthesis or to make certain IgG subclasses may also be implicated.[93]

Colonization also leads to antibody formation. Studies of families carried out in the preantibiotic era[94] and of infants and toddlers in the 1970s[23] suggested that the acquisition of antibody also follows colonization. Serotype-specific antibody developed within 30 days in about two thirds of military personnel who became colonized during an outbreak of pneumococcal pneumonia.[88] Levels of antibody appear to be at least as high as those that follow infection. Thus, colonization with *S. pneumoniae* is an immunizing event, although the cellular and subcellular events responsible for the response remain unclear.

Colonization and Immunity

These observations help explain the very low incidence of pneumococcal disease despite the relatively low prevalence of detectable antipneumococcal antibody in the adult population. In the absence of conditions that predispose to infection, antibody to the capsular polysaccharide of a colonizing organism is likely to appear before infection. However, pneumonia is more likely to develop before antibody appears in adults who aspirate pharyngeal contents or who have diminished mechanisms of lower airway clearance. Similarly, otitis media is more likely to precede antibody in children who have acute congestion of nasal mucosal membranes secondary to a viral infection. Of course, persons who have a diminished capacity to form antibody remain susceptible as long as they are colonized, which explains the high rate of pneumococcal pneumonia in patients with multiple myeloma, acquired immunodeficiency syndrome, and other such conditions. The major protective role of antibody to other constituents may be to prevent infection until antibody to capsular polysaccharide appears.

The Spleen in Defense of Pneumococcal Infection

The principal organ that clears unopsonized pneumococci from the blood stream is the spleen.[95,96] A series of experiments in human subjects has shown that highly opsonized particles are removed from the circulation by the liver but, with decreasing opsonization, the spleen increasingly assumes the role of clearance[97]; presumably, the slow passage of blood through the spleen and prolonged contact time with reticuloendothelial cells in the cords of Billroth and the splenic sinuses allow for the relatively less efficient removal of nonopsonized particles.[98] Overwhelming pneumococcal infection occurs in children and adults in whom the spleen has been removed or does not function normally. The heralding event in an outbreak of pneumococcal pneumonia in a metropolitan prison[43] was the overwhelmingly rapid, septic death of two prisoners, both of whom had previously undergone splenectomy. Pneumococcal disease progressed so rapidly in these cases that pneumonia was not initially detectable clinically or even with certainty by chest radiographs, although pneumonia was seen at autopsy. The 100-fold increase in the incidence of pneumococcal bacteremia or meningitis in children with sickle cell disease is probably due to splenic dysfunction, although other factors such as complement abnormalities may also contribute.[95,99]

TABLE 197-2 General Schema of Conditions That Predispose to Pneumococcal Infection

Defective antibody formation
  Primary
    Congenital agammaglobulinemia
    Common variable (acquired) hypogammaglobulinemia
    Selective IgG subclass deficiency
  Secondary
    Multiple myeloma
    Chronic lymphocytic leukemia
    Lymphoma
    HIV infection
Defective complement (primary or secondary)
  Decreased or absent C1, C2, C3, C4
Insufficient numbers of PMNs
  Primary
    Cyclic neutropenia
  Secondary
    Drug-induced neutropenia
    Aplastic anemia
Poorly functioning PMNs
  Alcoholism
  Cirrhosis of the liver
  Diabetes mellitus
  Glucocorticosteroid treatment
  Renal insufficiency
    Poorly avid receptors for FCγII (R131 allele)
Defective clearance of pneumococcal bacteremia
  Primary
    Congenital asplenia, hyposplenia
  Secondary
    Splenectomy
    Sickle cell disease (autosplenectomy)
Multifactorial and/or uncertain
  Infancy and aging
  Glucocorticosteroid treatment
  Malnutrition
  Cirrhosis of the liver
  Renal insufficiency
  Diabetes mellitus
  Alcoholism
  Chronic disease, hospitalization
  Fatigue
  Stress
  Cold exposure
Excess likelihood of exposure
  Daycare centers
  Military training camps
  Prisons
  Shelters for the homeless
Prior respiratory infection
  Influenza
  Other
Inflammatory condition
  Cigarette smoking
  Asthma
  COPD

COPD, Chronic obstructive pulmonary disease; HIV, human immunodeficiency virus; PMNs, polymorphonuclear leukocytes.

FACTORS THAT PREDISPOSE TO PNEUMOCOCCAL INFECTION

S. pneumoniae is a prototypic extracellular bacterial pathogen; host defenses against infection rely heavily on humoral factors such as antibody and complement, on the one hand, and phagocytic cells, specifically PMNs, on the other. A representative schema of conditions that have an impact on the immunologic capacity of the host and predispose to pneumococcal infection is shown in Table 197-2 and observed underlying conditions are listed in Table 197-3.

Defective antibody formation, whether congenital or acquired, has the greatest impact on susceptibility to pneumococcal infection. Bruton's original description of congenital agammaglobulinemia stressed the prominence of *S. pneumoniae* as an infecting agent. Pneumococcus is also a major cause of serious infection in acquired agammaglobulinemia (common variable immunodeficiency)[100] and perhaps in IgG subclass deficiency[101] as well; subtle defects may also

TABLE 197-3 Factors Predisposing Adults to Invasive Pneumococcal Disease*

Predisposing Factor	All Invasive Pneumococcal Infection (Sweden)[29]	All Community-acquired Pneumonia (Pittsburgh)[114]	Pneumococcal Bacteremia, Meningitis (Israel)[116]	Bacteremic Pneumococcal Pneumonia (Ohio)[117]	Nonbacteremic Pneumococcal Pneumonia (Houston)[115]	Bacteremic Pneumococcal Pneumonia (Houston)[115]
Alcoholism	32	33	NL	11	35	58
Cigarette smoking	40	55	NL	56	67	69
Chronic lung disease	17	31	19	28	58	42
Congestive heart failure	NL	13	35	16	17	27
Diabetes mellitus	6	13	15	18	12	11
Malignancy	12	29	NL	26	17	25
Kidney disease	1	7	13	4	4	2
Liver disease	2	5	6	NL	21	23
Immunosuppression	NL	36	36	NL	24	32
Recent hospitalization	NL	NL	NL	NL	37	35
No underlying disease	21	31	22	10	0	0

*With the exception of "no underlying disease," the finding of low numbers in some studies and much higher ones in others suggests the possibility of incomplete availability of data in the former. In the Swedish study,[29] 20% of patients with meningitis had prior head injury.
NL, Not listed.

be responsible.[93] Homozygous expression of the R131 allele of the FCγII receptor on PMNs, a receptor that binds the Fc of IgG$_2$ only poorly, or absence of the mannose-binding protein may associate with susceptibility to pneumococcal bacteremia.[102]

Pneumococcus continues to be the most common bacterial pathogen to infect persons who have multiple myeloma, lymphoma, or chronic lymphocytic leukemia, before chemotherapy and hospitalization tip the balance toward gram-negative infections.[103] Human immunodeficiency virus (HIV) infection causes defects at several points in host defense, but defective antibody production probably predominates in the predisposition to pneumococcal infection. As HIV infection progresses and CD4 lymphocyte counts fall below 500/mm^3, the ability to make antibody to pneumococcal capsular polysaccharides falls off rapidly.[104,105] The incidence of pneumococcal bacteremia in HIV-infected persons approaches 10 per 1000 per year,[106] a 200-fold increase for an age-related population; if 3 to 4 nonbacteremic cases of pneumonia occur for each bacteremic case, 1 in 25 HIV-infected persons may be expected to have pneumococcal pneumonia in a given year. Some authorities recommend that bacteremic pneumonia or unusual pneumococcal infections in young adults[107,108] trigger a search for HIV infection. The incidence of pneumococcal infection can even be used to estimate the number of HIV-infected persons in a population.[108]

Of the many possible defects in complement, only those factors required to generate C3b are associated with pneumococcal infection. Because pneumococci are not killed by serum, the host response is unaffected by defects in C6, C7, C8, or C9, which results in decreased membrane attack complexes. In contrast, deficiencies in C1, C2, and C4, whether congenital or acquired, are expected to be associated with increased susceptibility to pneumococcal infection, although cases documenting the association are reported only rarely.[109]

Neutropenia of whatever cause is associated with *S. pneumoniae* infection, although somewhat surprisingly, leukocyte adhesion deficiency syndrome (Mac-1 deficiency) is generally not.[110] One study[111] has shown that at the time of initial hospitalization for acute leukemia, patients are more likely to have infection caused by more ordinary gram-positive pathogenic bacteria, probably analogous to the pretreatment situation in multiple myeloma.[103] Defective bacterial killing by PMNs as seen in chronic granulomatous disease does not predispose to infection with *S. pneumoniae;* the absence of catalase renders this organism susceptible to the interaction between its endogenous H$_2$O$_2$ and myeloperoxidase and the halide present in PMNs.

The susceptibility of aged persons to pneumococcal pneumonia is multifactorial, reflecting, among other factors, senescence of the immune system because of diminished production of immunoglobulins (or production of poorly functional ones), impaired response to cytokines, and general debilitation caused by weakening of the gag reflex, malnutrition, and the presence of other diseases. The effect of alcoholism is also multifactorial and involves lifestyle (such as cold exposure and malnutrition), suppression of the gag reflex, and possibly deleterious ef-

fects on PMN function, although in most instances these alterations have been difficult to attribute to the effect of alcohol alone.[112,113] Heffron[1] cites studies that found 30% of patients hospitalized for pneumonia at Johns Hopkins Hospital to have a history of alcoholism and 19% and 29% of those at the Rockefeller Hospital to be heavy and moderate alcohol drinkers, respectively. More recent studies that reflect data in the population at large have found similar results, with about one third of patients being listed as alcoholic.[29,114,115] A disproportionately high number of patients who have pneumococcal infection have diabetes mellitus,[29,114-117] a condition in which PMN chemotaxis is reduced[118] and phagocytic function is defective,[119] especially if renal insufficiency is also present. Anemia (hemoglobin 10 g/dL) may be present in one third of patients with pneumococcal pneumonia.[115]

Many chronic diseases are associated with pneumococcal pneumonia by virtue of an association with pneumonia of whatever cause, which suggests that the predisposition is a general one rather than being specific for *S. pneumoniae*. Pneumococcal pneumonia follows hospitalization for all causes[120] and has even been observed as a nosocomial infection.[121] Other factors such as cold exposure, stress, and fatigue[1] may predispose to pneumococcal pneumonia by unknown mechanisms.

As mentioned earlier, prior respiratory viral infection, perhaps especially infection caused by influenza virus, appears to play a prominent role in predisposing to pneumococcal infection.[36,37,122,123] Upregulation of surface receptors during viral infection may enhance pneumococcal adherence[124] and invasion. Bacteria are certainly less well cleared from the airways because of viral-induced damage. Pneumococcal disease is greatly increased in people with altered pulmonary clearance, such as those who have chronic bronchitis, asthma, or chronic obstructive pulmonary disease. Only in the past few years has a study finally supported an association between cigarette smoking and pneumonia.[125] It is an interesting sign of the times that Heffron's classic work[1] on the pneumococcus published in 1939 had a section on inhalation of "noxious substances," yet did not mention cigarette smoking.

CLINICAL SYNDROMES

S. pneumoniae causes infection of the middle ear, sinuses, trachea, bronchi, and lungs by direct spread of organisms from the nasopharyngeal site of colonization and causes infection of the central nervous system, heart valves, bones, joints, and peritoneal cavity by hematogenous spread. A schema demonstrating the ways in which these major pathogenetic pathways interrelate is shown in Figure 197-4. Infection of the central nervous system, pleura or peritoneal cavity may occur by direct extension or by hematogenous spread; in any individual case, the route of infection can usually not be determined. Bacteremia that occurs without an apparent source or focus of infection is called primary bacteremia. In a recent population-based study of adults in

FIGURE 197-4. A schema showing the events that take place between initial response to pneumococci and the eventual development of disease.

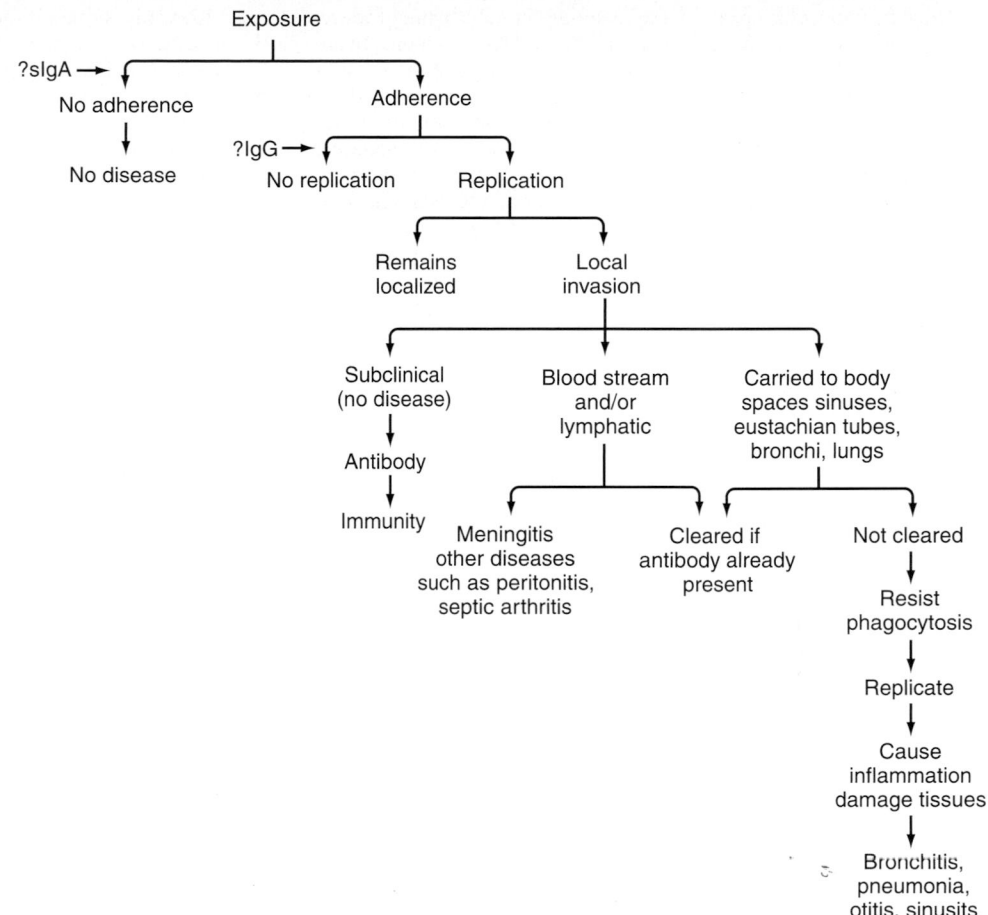

Israel,[126] pneumonia was present in 71% of cases of pneumococcal bacteremia, meningitis was present in 8%, and otitis media or sinusitis was found in 4%; bacteremia was regarded as primary in 18%. Primary bacteremia has always been more common in children than adults; when therapy has been withheld, a focus of infection has often become apparent.

Otitis Media

Virtually every study of acute otitis media in which material from the middle ear has been cultured has shown *S. pneumoniae* to be the most common isolate or second only to nontypable *Haemophilus influenzae; Moraxella (Branhamella) catarrhalis* is usually a distant third.[127] In these studies, which are usually carried out in children aged 6 months to 4 years, *S. pneumoniae* is implicated in about 40% to 50% of cases in which an etiologic agent is isolated or in 30% to 40% of all cases. Pneumococcus is the most prevalent pathogen in otitis media in adults as well.[128] Prior infection by a respiratory virus is thought to play a major contributory role by causing congestion of the opening to the eustachian tube. Prospective longitudinal studies[23,34,129] have shown that when infection occurs, in most cases it follows fairly closely after colonization by a new serotype, although, of course, most instances of colonization occur without disease. Perhaps related to more avid adherence to mammalian cells, serotypes 6, 14, 19F, and 23F predominate as both colonizing and infecting organisms; this finding explains why these serotypes are currently under the most intensive study for use in vaccines in young children.

Sinusitis

Acute infection of the sinuses is caused by the same organisms as acute otitis media; thus, *S. pneumoniae* dominates or is second to *H. influenzae.*[130] Important in the pathogenesis of this infection is congestion of the mucosal membranes caused by allergy or viral infection. The result-

ing obstruction prevents clearance of bacteria. The accumulation of fluid in the paranasal sinus cavities, even during simple colds,[131] provides a medium for bacterial proliferation and subsequent acute sinus infection.

Meningitis

Except during an epidemic of meningococcal infection, *S. pneumoniae* is the most common cause of bacterial meningitis in adults.[132] In countries that have implemented effective vaccination programs for *H. influenzae* type b, pneumococcus has become the most common sporadic cause of meningitis in children over the age of 6 months, as well. The impact of widespread pneumococcal vaccination of children is currently being elucidated.

The pathogenesis of meningitis may be by direct extension from sinuses or the middle ear or as a result of bacteremia.[47] Favoring the former possibility are the association between acute otitis media or sinusitis and infection of the central nervous system and the well-documented role of *S. pneumoniae* as the most common cause of recurrent bacterial meningitis associated with head trauma, CSF leak, or a break in the integrity of the dura.[133] Favoring the latter is the high association of pneumococcal pneumonia or bacteremia without a known focus with subsequent meningitis. In addition, an autopsy study of the temporal bones of children who died of bacterial meningitis[134] showed no evidence for extension from the middle ear, which supports the possibility that even when it follows otitis media, meningitis may develop as a result of bacteremia. Although hematogenous spread to the choroid plexus was originally thought to be the pathogenesis in most cases of pneumococcal meningitis, it is now believed that infection up-regulates platelet activating factor on vascular endothelial surfaces in the meninges, and that pneumococci adhere and are internalized by this mechanism. Communication through the cochlear aqueduct between the inner ear and the subarachnoid space[135] may explain deafness in patients with hematogenous bacterial meningitis.

Once pneumococci appear in the meninges or subarachnoid space, the capacities to escape phagocytosis and to produce inflammation are central to the disease process. As noted earlier, injection of cell wall constituents, principally peptidoglycan and, to a lesser extent, teichoic acid, intracisternally in rabbits causes the CSF abnormalities of bacterial meningitis, presumably through a variety of mediators, including C5a, tumor necrosis factor, IL-1, IL-6, and other active inflammatory peptides.[47,136] No distinctive clinical or laboratory features of pneumococcal meningitis enable the physician to suspect *S. pneumoniae* over any other causative agent. Using current laboratory techniques for centrifugation of specimens in a cytocentrifuge, examination of a Gram-stained specimen of CSF provides the correct diagnosis in nearly all cases,[137] unless 3 to 6 hours have passed since the administration of an effective antibiotic, in which case the number of bacteria may be greatly decreased. Immunologic detection of pneumococcal capsular material ("bacterial antigen") generally does not add information beyond what is determined by Gram stain.[137a]

Acute Exacerbation of Chronic Bronchitis

Careful microbiologic observation[138,139] has confirmed clinical impression that *S. pneumoniae* is a common cause of exacerbation in patients who have chronic bronchitis, with our without obstructive lung disease. In addition, a clinically recognizable exacerbation of the chronic disease is highly associated with acquisition of a new pneumococcal strain.[140]

Pneumonia

Pathogenesis

If potentially protective mechanisms fail to prevent both the access of pneumococci to the alveoli and their subsequent replication, pneumonia results. Bacteria proliferate in alveolar spaces and are carried along the alveolar septa; in these sites, they activate complement, generate cytokine production and upregulate receptors on vascular endothelial surfaces. Exudative fluid and WBCs accumulate in the septa and alveoli and extend to uninvolved areas through the pores of Kohn. This filling of alveoli with microorganisms and inflammatory exudate defines the presence of pneumonia, and a clinical diagnosis is made when fluid accumulation is great enough to allow it to be seen radiographically as a nonlucent or "consolidated" area.

Predisposing Factors

In a recent prospective study of pneumococcal pneumonia,[115] nearly all patients had two or more predisposing conditions such as cigarette smoking, chronic obstructive pulmonary disease, alcohol abuse, neurological disease (stroke, seizures, and dementia), malignancy, liver disease (hepatitis and cirrhosis), recent intravenous drug use, congestive heart failure, diabetes mellitus, or HIV infection. One third of patients had been discharged from a hospital within the preceding 6 months. A number of patients were admitted for myocardial infarction and were found to have pneumococcal pneumonia, as well; increased metabolic demands resulting from pneumonia may well have precipitated the infarction.

Symptoms and Physical Findings

Cough, fatigue, fever, chills (there may be a single shaking chill), sweats, and shortness of breath are the most frequent symptoms of pneumonia; these are all more prominent in younger than in older patients.[141,142] Patients with pneumococcal pneumonia usually appear ill and have a grayish, anxious appearance. The temperature may be elevated to 102° F to 103° F, the pulse to 90 to 110 beats per minute, and the respiratory rate to 20 to 24 per minute. Elderly patients may have only a slight temperature elevation or be afebrile but are more likely to have an increased respiratory rate.[141] The absence of fever in young or middle-aged adults is associated with increased morbidity and mortality, as, especially, is hypothermia.

Physical examination may reveal diminished respiratory excursion (splinting) on the affected side because of pain. Dullness to percussion is present in about half of cases. Crackling sounds are heard on careful auscultation in nearly all cases, but in patients who have chronic lung disease it is often difficult to be certain that such sounds signify the presence of pneumonia. Bronchial or tubular breath sounds may be heard if consolidation is present. Flatness to percussion at the lung base and an inability to detect the expected degree of diaphragmatic motion based on the patient's respiratory excursion suggest the presence of pleural fluid. Unless all the vital signs are normal, which substantially reduces the likelihood of pneumonia, no set of physical findings can reliably replace the chest x-ray in diagnosing the presence or absence of pneumonia.[143] The finding of a heart murmur raises concern about endocarditis, a rare but serious complication. Confusion, obtundation, or especially neck stiffness should lead to consideration of meningitis.

Radiographic Findings

In most cases of pneumococcal pneumonia, chest radiography reveals an area of infiltration involving one or more segments within a single lobe.[115] Air-space consolidation is detected radiographically in most cases, and is more frequent in bacteremic cases; air bronchogram, which reflects especially dense air-space consolidation highly correlates with bacteremia.[115,144] Rarely, *S. pneumoniae* infection causes a lung abscess.[145] As emphasized earlier, these organisms do not produce highly toxic, tissue-damaging substances. Thus, abscesses do not generally occur, even at a microscopic level, and if an abscess is seen, concurrent anaerobic infection or an anatomic abnormality such as bronchial obstruction, cancer, or pulmonary infarction should be suspected. Although pleural effusion may be found in 40% of patients with pneumococcal pneumonia by careful search, only 10% have sufficient amounts of fluid to aspirate, and in only a minority of these, perhaps 2% of the total, is empyema present.[146]

General Laboratory Findings

Twenty-five percent of patients with pneumococcal pneumonia have a hemoglobin of 10 mg/dL or less.[115] Although the majority have leukocytosis (WBC count >12,000/mm³), a substantial proportion may have normal WBC counts, at least at the time of admission. A WBC count less than 6000/mm³ occurs in 5% to 10% of persons hospitalized for pneumococcal pneumonia and indicates a very poor prognosis.[147] Experimental studies have suggested that this situation reflects the accumulation of all available WBCs at the infected site; more often than not, it is seen in the presence of conditions such as ethanol ingestion or malnutrition, which suppress the bone marrow.[148] The low serum albumin that often is present may result from malnutrition, and therefore indicate a predisposing condition, or reflect catabolism and fluid shifts that are part of sepsis.[115] Serum bilirubin may be increased to 3 to 4 mg/dL; the pathogenesis of this abnormality is multifactorial, with hypoxia, hepatic inflammation, and breakdown of red blood cells in the lung all thought to contribute. Levels of lactate dehydrogenase may be elevated. The likelihood that underlying disease is present must always be considered when evaluating abnormal laboratory findings. Laboratory abnormalities in empyema are reviewed in Chapter 61.

Diagnostic Microbiology

The etiologic role of the pneumococcus in a patient who has pneumonia is strongly suggested by microscopic demonstration of large numbers of PMNs, very few epithelial cells (PMN/epithelial cell ratio, approximately 10 to 20:1), and numerous, slightly elongated gram-positive cocci in pairs and chains in a Gram-stained sputum (Table 197-4). If accepted terminology is strictly followed, a presumptive diagnosis of pneumococcal pneumonia is then made if *S. pneumoniae* is identified by sputum culture and the diagnosis is proved if *S. pneumoniae* is identified by blood culture. The argument that the diagnosis is never certain unless the blood culture is also positive is overly restrictive because most patients with pneumococcal pneumonia do not have detectable bacteremia.

Attempts to make a diagnosis based on an inadequate sputum specimen[149-151] are largely responsible for studies claiming that microscopic examination and culture of sputum are not reliable. To be reliable, the sputum sample should contain material that on microscopic examination reveals areas with hundreds of WBCs and few epithelial

TABLE 197-4 Microscopic Examination and Culture of Sputum for Pneumococci

Gram Stain	Sputum Culture	Blood Culture	Comment
+	+	+	Generally regarded as conclusive diagnosis of invasive pneumococcal disease (pneumonia), but does not exclude contribution by another etiology such as influenza virus infection or lung cancer
+	+	−	Good evidence for nonbacteremic pneumococcal pneumonia if a clinical syndrome suggesting pneumonia is present, microscopic examination of Gram-stained sputum is characteristic (see Fig. 197-5), and culture shows strongly predominant growth of pneumococci with no other likely pathogenic bacteria
+ or −	−	+	With symptoms and signs of pneumonia and an infiltrate on the chest radiograph, these findings are generally taken to indicate invasive pneumococcal pneumonia even if organisms are not found in sputum
+	−	−	In the presence of the appropriate clinical syndrome, still remains suggestive of pneumococcal pneumonia because organisms can be missed on culture as a result of sampling error and overgrowth of streptococci from saliva
−	+	−	Less suggestive of pneumococcal disease. Pneumococci can be isolated by culture of sputum from persons who are colonized. However, especially in patients already treated with antibiotics, the positive culture may be the only supporting evidence for diagnosis of nonbacteremic pneumococcal pneumonia
−	−	−	Does not support a diagnosis of pneumococcal pneumonia

cells at low-power magnification (×100) and at least 10 to 20 WBCs with no epithelial cells under ×1000 magnification. At this higher magnification, pneumococci are generally present in large numbers (>25 per field) (Fig. 197-5), although occasionally as few as 1 to 2 may be seen per field. If sufficient numbers of inflammatory cells are not present, relevant material has not been obtained; if many epithelial cells are detected, the finding of bacteria cannot be trusted to reflect what is present in the bronchi or lungs. A good-quality sputum specimen is far more likely to be obtained by a physician, who best understands its central role in establishing an etiologic diagnosis and determining therapy, than by ancillary personnel, who may not.[151,152] If a patient has received effective antibiotics for more than 6 to 12 hours, the Gram stain is likely to be nonrevealing; after 12 to 24 hours the culture will also fail to disclose pneumococci.[151]

With a sputum sample of good quality, bacterial culture is expected to reliably reflect material present below the larynx,[153] especially if extra care is taken to inoculate plates with sputum rather than saliva. Although colonies of *S. pneumoniae* serotype 3 are highly mucoid and readily recognizable on a blood-agar plate, most pneumococci do not produce distinctively mucoid colonies, and identification on a culture plate depends on distinguishing pneumococcal colonies, which may have an umbilicated appearance because of autolysis, from other α-hemolytic streptococci which are the most numerous bacteria in saliva. Failure to detect pneumococci by culture even when they are plainly seen on microscopic examination results from the following factors: (1) the most prevalent organisms in saliva are other streptococci; (2) during microscopic examination, the observer focuses on the area of special interest, but the specimen itself may contain an admixture of saliva and sputum, and in that part of the specimen inoculated on the plate viridans streptococci may outnumber pneumococci; and (3) in selecting one or more α-hemolytic colonies for identification, the laboratory technologist may not be able to find the pneumococcus. This circumstance leads to the unfortunate, but all-too-common situation in which the laboratory reports "normal flora" on a specimen that really seemed to show pneumococci.

When a patient who has pneumonia cannot provide an expectorated specimen, the potential problems of empirical therapy should be balanced against the time and trouble that it may take to obtain a specimen, for example, by nasotracheal suction, hydration, or breathing humidified air or hypertonic saline mist. Undue delay should be avoided because it has been shown in large series of cases to be associated with a worse outcome; nevertheless, this author believes that many individual patients receive suboptimal care because the causative organism has not been identified which comprises initial selection and/or completion of appropriate antibiotic therapy. It is difficult to know the proportion of patients with pneumococcal pneumonia who have positive blood cultures because the denominator is so uncertain; 25% is the number that is given, but it is based on data from the preantibiotic era.

Other diagnostic techniques focus on the detection of antigen or antibody. In general, if the sputum is not of sufficiently good quality that the

Gram stain is positive, other tests, such as coagglutination, antigen detection, or polymerase chain reaction, that look for pneumococci in the sputum are not helpful because they are confounded by the same problem, namely, the amount of contaminating material relative to the number of pneumococci, as well as by the potential problem of detecting carriage rather than infection. Pneumococcal cell wall polysaccharide may be detected in urine in about two thirds of patients with pneumococcal pneumonia versus 10% to 15% of patients with nonpneumococcal pneumonia[154]; the reader may decide for him/herself if that is likely to be a

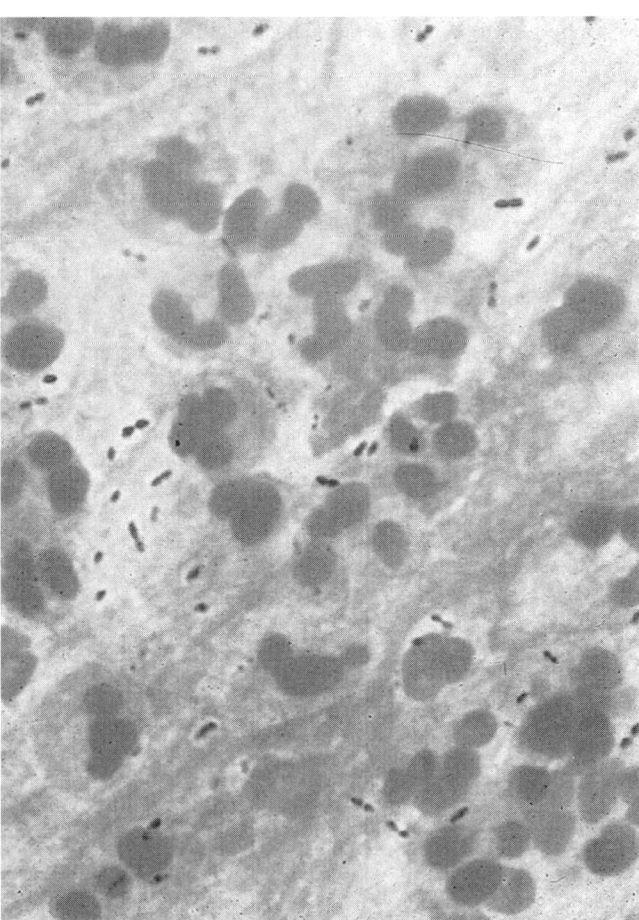

FIGURE 197-5. Gram-stained sputum from a patient with pneumococcal pneumonia at 1000× magnification. The photograph shows many polymorphonuclear neutrophils and no epithelial cells with large numbers of slightly elongated, gram-negative cocci in pairs and chains indicative of *Streptococcus pneumoniae*. A clear area surrounding bacteria indicates the capsule.

useful test. In children, the test is positive with pharyngeal colonization, and it is not useful diagnostically.[155] Polymerase chain reaction amplification may be relatively sensitive and quite specific in CSF and less sensitive in blood. Antibody to pneumococcal constituents may be present in immune complexes at the time that adult patients are hospitalized for pneumonia, but tests to detect such antibody are nonspecific because they also detect serum (i.e., noncomplexed) IgG,[156] and clinical or epidemiological studies based on this kind of diagnostic technique are not reliable. Diagnosing pneumococcal infection by antibody rises is also problematic because persons who are infected may be the very ones who do not make much antibody and, for reasons that are not understood, infected persons increase their antibody levels to other, noninfecting serotypes as well, at least as detected by ELISA.

Complications

Empyema, the most common complication of pneumococcal pneumonia in the preantibiotic era, occurred in about 5% of cases and remains the most common today, with an incidence of approximately 2%.[146] As noted earlier, pleural fluid appears in a substantial proportion of cases of pneumonia but is usually reactive. When bacteria reach the pleural space, either hematogenously or as a result of extension of the pneumonia to the visceral pleura with spread via lymphatics, empyema results. Persistence of fever, even if "low grade," and leukocytosis after 4 to 5 days of appropriate antibiotic treatment of pneumococcal pneumonia is suggestive of empyema, and this diagnosis is even more likely if the radiograph shows persistence of pleural fluid. The presence of frank pus, a positive Gram stain, or fluid with pH 7.1 or less are all indications for aggressive and complete drainage with repeated needle aspiration or prompt insertion of a chest tube. If no response is seen, immediate removal of infected material by thoracoscopy or open thoracotomy is indicated.[157] One study of medical empyema caused by all organisms found that mortality exceeded 30% in two hospitals where the therapeutic approach was not aggressive but was less than 10% in a third hospital where it was.[158]

Other Syndromes

S. pneumoniae can be implicated in a wide variety of infectious states. Isolated or epidemic conjunctivitis may occur, caused, somewhat surprisingly, by unencapsulated pneumococci (and essentially the only condition in which unencapsulated pneumococci play a role).[159,160] Peritonitis[161] may be primary, occurring in patients who have preexisting ascites without a documented source of infection elsewhere, or secondary. In secondary disease, pneumococci may reach the peritoneal cavity by migrating up the female reproductive tract, with or without clinically recognizable infection of the genital organs or as a result of bowel perforation. Pneumococcal infections of the female reproductive organs[162-164] may occur with or without peritonitis. A case of pneumococcal endocarditis[165] is seen once or twice per decade at a large tertiary care hospital in the United States. A recent study of 14 cases identified in Denmark (population of 5 million) in a 10-year period[166] showed that 3 persons were alcoholic and only 1 had known of prior valvular disease; 8 had pneumonia and 4 had meningitis.

Purulent pericarditis[167] caused by pneumococcus has also become exceedingly rare, whether it occurs as a separate entity or together with endocarditis. Septic arthritis[168] occurs spontaneously in a natural or prosthetic[168,169] joint or as a complication of rheumatoid arthritis.[170] Osteomyelitis in adults tends to involve the vertebral bones.[171] Epidural and brain abscesses are rarely described.[172] Soft tissue infections[173,174] occur, especially in persons who have connective tissue diseases or HIV infection. Finally, the appearance of unusual pneumococcal infections in a young adult might suggest that tests for HIV infection be undertaken.[107]

ANTIBIOTIC SUSCEPTIBILITY

Until the mid-1970s, pneumococci were inhibited or killed by readily achievable levels of all relevant antibiotics, with the possible exception of tetracycline, to which a variable number of strains showed resistance. This remarkable susceptibility of the major bacterial pathogen in otitis, sinusitis, and pneumonia allowed for a somewhat cavalier approach to diagnosis and antibiotic therapy, an approach that may no longer be valid because during the past two decades pneumococci have increasingly become more resistant to penicillin and other antibiotics.[175-177] The subject of antibiotic resistance of *S. pneumoniae* is reviewed in detail elsewhere.[178-180]

The susceptibility of *S. pneumoniae* to penicillin is currently defined by the National Committee for Clinical Laboratory Standards as follows. Susceptible isolates are inhibited by 0.06 μg/mL (i.e., minimal inhibitory concentration [MIC] ≤0.06 μg/mL). Isolates with reduced susceptibility (also known as intermediate resistance) are inhibited by 0.1 to 1.0 μg/mL, and resistant isolates are inhibited by 2.0 μg/mL or more. This definition was derived based on achievable concentrations of penicillin in CSF during treatment of children for meningitis. From a clinical point of view, the meaning of the MIC depends on the infection being treated.[181] A strain with reduced susceptibility (e.g., MIC of 1.0 μg/mL) behaves as a susceptible organism when it causes pneumonia, but may not when it causes otitis and does not when it causes meningitis. The recently revised definition of amoxicillin resistance (susceptible, MIC μg/mL; intermediately resistant, MIC 4 g/mL, resistant, MIC >8 g/mL) is based on serum levels, assuming that no physician would knowingly treat meningitis with this oral medication.

Penicillin inhibits the replication of *S. pneumoniae* by binding one or more enzymes needed to synthesize peptidoglycan, including higher-molecular-weight transpeptidases and a lower-molecular-weight carboxypeptidase. The binding is covalent, and a serine ester–linked, enzymatically nonactive penicilloyl complex is formed. The reaction with penicillin is used to recognize these enzymes by two general methods: incubating with radiolabeled penicillin, followed by electrophoresis and autoradiography, or incubating with nonlabeled penicillin, followed by electrophoresis and immunoblotting with antipenicilloyl antibody. Six such enzymes are identified: 1A, 1B, 2A, 2B, 2X, and 3. In fully susceptible isolates of *S. pneumoniae,* these six enzymes, which are also called penicillin-binding proteins (PBPs), are identifiable after incubation with low concentrations of penicillin. Resistant isolates have PBPs with decreased affinity for penicillin in very approximate proportion to the degree of resistance. Changes in the genes that encode these enzymes, with relatively minor alterations in the amino acids at essential loci,[182] may result in the decreased affinity. Alterations in PBP 2B are more likely to account for low-level resistance, whereas mutations in PBP 2X have been associated with high-level resistance.[183]

Pneumococci have become resistant by acquiring genetic material from other bacteria with which they coexist in close proximity—presumably viridans streptococci in the nasopharynx. In fact, the altered sequence in the gene for PBP 2B in many penicillin-resistant isolates appears to have originated in *Streptococcus mitis.*[184] The unique capacity of *S. pneumoniae* to be transformed is a major determinant of this process. Extensive diversity among isolates[185] or within the transpeptide-encoding region of the pneumococcal genome[183,186] indicates that many discrete mutational events have occurred, some of which reflect acquisition and others, rearrangement of DNA. Alterations in several PBPs may eventually appear within an individual isolate, and a mosaic array of PBPs results. Nevertheless, the major source of resistance worldwide has been the geographic spread of a few clones that seem to have special capacity to spread and to colonize.[187] One well-documented example was the importation into Iceland of a strain that was prevalent in Spain during the 1992 Olympics; this strain rapidly spread throughout that small country.[188] In the United States during the 1990s, the dominant factor in the emergence of antibiotic-resistant pneumococci has been human-to-human spread of relatively few clonal groups that harbor resistance determinants to multiple classes of antibiotics.[189] These same clones seem to have spread world wide and may be found, for example, in Korea or Thailand, as well as in Europe.[190] Geographic spread is greatly facilitated by antibiotic pressure. A prominent site for this selection is daycare centers. Point prevalence studies in the United States have shown that at any given time, a remarkably high proportion of children in daycare are receiving antibiotics. These conditions (1) suppress sus-

TABLE 197-5 The Likelihood (%) that, When Causing Non-CNS Infection Such as Pneumonia, a Pneumococcus Will Be Susceptible In Vivo to the Antibiotic Indicated (see text)*

Penicillin, ampicillin, piperacillin	90[†]
Amoxicillin	90[†]
Cefuroxime, cefpodoxime, cefdinir	90[†]
Cefotaxime, ceftriaxone, cefepime	95[†]
Imipenem, meropenem, ertapenem	95
Azithromycin, clarithromycin	85[‡]
Lincosamine (clindamycin)	91
Ketolides (telithromycin, cethromycin)	100
Trimethoprim/sulfamethoxazole	65
Doxycycline	82
Vancomycin	100
Quinolone[§]	98

*The author's estimate of the likelihood (%) of a bacteriologic response during treatment with customary doses, based on numerous approximations which are dealt with in the text as well as in Musher et al.[181] This is not the same as in vitro susceptibility, which is defined by a committee of the NCCLS, nor is it the same as the likelihood of producing a curve in vivo, which depends in part on bacterial susceptibility but also on a variety of host factors.

[†]With high doses of these drugs, nearly all pneumococci are expected to be susceptible.

[‡]This number reflects a balance between the 25% rate of resistance in vitro and clinical experience which has documented some failures but shows a generally high rate of response; at the time of this writing (August, 2003), the precise relationship between in vitro resistance and in vivo failure is still uncertain.

[§]Quinolone = levofloxacin, moxifloxacin, gatifloxacin, gemifloxacin.

TABLE 197-6 Susceptibility (μg/ml) of Pneumococci to Representative Beta-lactam Antibiotics, Distinguishing Between CNS and Non-CNS Isolates*

	Susceptible	Intermediate	Resistant
Penicillin[†]	≤.06	0.1-1	≥2
Amoxicillin[‡]			
non-CNS	≤2	4	≥8
Ceftriaxone or cefotaxime			
non-CNS	≤1	2	≥4
CNS	≤0.5	1	≥2

*Definitions of the National Committee for Clinical and Laboratory Standards (NCCLS).

[†]In the case of penicillin, no official distinction has been made between CNS and non-CNS isolates. Because the present definitions appear to be valid for CNS isolates, it seems reasonable, in the opinion of this author, to shift these numbers upwards for non-CNS isolates.

[‡]In the case of amoxicillin, no definition is made for CNS isolates under the assumption that physicians would not use an oral antibiotic to treat patients with meningitis.

ceptible flora, thereby creating a niche for resistant organisms; (2) spare antibiotic-resistant pneumococci; (3) increase the prevalence of antibiotic-resistant viridans streptococci, thus setting the stage for further transformation of pneumococci to antibiotic resistance; and (4) provide close contact among small children, which allows for the spread of organisms. Other situations characterized by close contact and excessive antibiotic use, such as nursing homes, may also serve as breeding grounds for these organisms.

Resistance to penicillin is only the tip of the proverbial iceberg. Resistance results from acquisition of a cassette of genetic elements that encode resistance to other antibiotics, as well. Many of the penicillin-resistant strains have alterations in PBPs, especially PBP 2X and 1A,[186] that render them resistant to third-generation cephalosporins such as cefotaxime or ceftriaxone. Resistance to penicillin is also associated with resistance to most other widely used antibiotics, including the macrolides, folic acid inhibitors (trimethoprim-sulfamethoxazole), tetracyclines and, to a lesser extent, the quinolones. The current state of pneumococcal susceptibility/resistance to antibiotics is summarized in Tables 197-5 and 197-6. Based on the fact that much higher drug levels are attained throughout the body than in the cerebrospinal fluid, a distinction in interpreting susceptibility to beta-lactams is now being made for treatment of meningitis (see Table 197-6).[181] Such distinctions will undoubtedly be refined during the next few years.

An understanding of macrolide resistance is important clinically. Macrolides insert into a pocket of the 23S subunit of the 50S ribosome, specifically by attaching at domain V of the peptidyl transferase loop, thereby blocking protein assembly. In doing so, these drugs exert a bactericidal effect on *Streptococcus pneumoniae*. (The mechanism for killing of pneumococci is complex; macrolides are generally regarded as bacteriostatic drugs against gram positive pathogens such as *Staphylococcus aureus,* but are bactericidal against pneumococcus.) Acquisition of genetic material, designated *ermB* or *mefA,* often together with genes that encode penicillin resistance, may lead to resistance: (1) *ermB* encodes methylation of a base in domain V of the 23S rRNA (A2058). This methylation essentially blocks the ribosomal pocket; since the macrolide no longer fits into the pocket, increasing its concentration has little effect, and high-level resistance results (≥64 μg/mL). (2) *mefA* encodes an efflux pump that excludes macrolides. High antibiotic concentrations might be expected to overcome the pump, forcing enough antibiotic into the bacterium to exert an antibacterial effect; this resistance is at a lower level (usually ≤16 μg/mL)

and, at a sufficient dosage, a macrolide might be expected to be effective. The debate about whether such resistance is clinically meaningful[179] is based on the fact that the majority of macrolide-resistant isolates in the United States have *mefA,* and that present doses of macrolides may be effective despite the in vitro finding that an isolate is resistant. Other mutations are responsible for resistance in a small percentage of isolates, causing other base substitutions in domain V or altering protein sequences within or adjacent to the macrolide binding site, especially involving ribosomal proteins L4 and L22.[191] Mechanisms of resistance in pneumococci and putative advantages of a ketolide for treating pneumococcal pneumonia are discussed in Chapter 28.

Prevalence of Resistance

As of July, 2003, in the United States, depending on the source of the isolates, about 60% of *S. pneumoniae* isolates remain fully susceptible to penicillin.[192-194] Variations occur from city to city and within segments of the population or even within institutions in a single city, so the actual likelihood that a patient will be infected with a resistant strain varies greatly. Rates of resistance are higher in most European countries, with the notable exception of The Netherlands and Germany, where accepted standards of practice strictly limit antibiotic usage,[195] especially among very young children, and are even greater in Korea, Hong Kong and Thailand.[196] Pneumococci that are not resistant to penicillin remain susceptible to most other antibiotics. As resistance to penicillin increases, organisms are progressively more likely to exhibit resistance to nearly all other commonly used antibiotics.[194] Data presented in Table 197-5 reflect the rates of susceptibility of pneumococci to various antimicrobials as of July 2003 and are likely to change. The incidence of antibiotic resistance appears to be declining somewhat, perhaps because of the widespread use of conjugate vaccine which is directed against the most highly antibiotic resistant strains. It is of great importance to note the relatively high rate of resistance of pneumococci to doxycycline, macrolides and trimethoprim-sulfamethoxazole. At present, in the United States, about 25% of all pneumococci are resistant to macrolides, ranging from 17% in the Northeast to 35% in the Southeast. One third of these strains (about 8% of all isolates), have *ermB* and are also resistant to clindamycin, ranging from 5% in the Northeast to 10% in the Southeast; two thirds of these resistant strains carry *mefA.* The level of resistance among *mefA* strains has steadily increased in the past few years; in other words, even those organisms that have had lower-level resistance are becoming less likely to respond to treatment with macrolides. In Europe, a higher proportion of pneumococci show some level of macrolide resistance, and *ermB* is responsible in the majority of isolates. Rates of resistance are lower in Canada than in the United States and higher in the Far East than in Europe. Most isolates remain susceptible to fluoroquinolones. In Canada, an increase in resistance has paralleled increased quinolone use,[197] and in high-usage locales, such as chest clinics[198] or nursing homes,[199] the rate of resistance may exceed 5%. Resistance to vancomycin and the new ketolides such as telithromycin and cethromycin has not yet been documented; an extensive experience in treating respiratory infections with ketolides has begun to accumulate.[179] Pneumococci are also susceptible in vitro to linezolid and quinupristin/dalfopristin, but the clinical efficacy of these drugs has not been reported to date.

TREATMENT

The basic principles of treatment of pneumococcal infection are similar to those for treating other infections: (1) administer an antibiotic that provides a level sufficient to inhibit or kill the infecting organism, (2) continue treatment at least until the host is able to complete the curing and healing processes on its own, (3) drain infections of closed spaces if necessary, (4) know what response to expect, and (5) be prepared to reevaluate if this response is not observed. These basic principles having been stated, the reader will discover that their application is by no means simple. A few selected factors include the following: (1) for most diseases caused by pneumococcus, when therapy is begun, the etiologic agent is unknown; (2) even if *S. pneumoniae* is presumed to be causative, antibiotic susceptibility is not known when treatment is begun; (3) for many common infections, the appropriate duration of therapy has not been established by scientific study; (4) in otitis media and sinusitis, the most common infections caused by *S. pneumoniae,* drainage is not usually done; and (5) many physicians do not clearly understand what response to expect after treatment has begun.

Otitis Media

In 1998, The Otitis Media Working Group of the Centers for Disease Control and Prevention[127] recommended amoxicillin, 30 mg/kg, three times daily, to treat children with otitis media. The group reasoned that (1) *S. pneumoniae* is the most common identifiable cause of this infection and the one associated with the greatest morbidity, (2) penicillin-susceptible and intermediately resistant pneumococci are likely to respond better to this treatment than to any other, and (3) no other oral therapy is likely to be more effective for resistant pneumococci. In a relatively small, but carefully monitored, prospective, randomized comparison of amoxicillin and cefuroxime that included tympanocentesis to monitor etiologic agents and response to therapy, Dagan and associates[200,201] showed that the bacteriologic response to treatment is closely related to the level of resistance or susceptibility of the infecting bacterium and that amoxicillin provided the best outcome. When cefuroxime, an oral cephalosporin with good activity against *S. pneumoniae,* was compared with another less active cephalosporin (cefaclor), the failure rate was closely related to the greater MIC for cefaclor and was substantially higher for this latter drug.[202] In the absence of a perforated tympanic membrane, therapy need not be given for more than 5 days.[203]

Patients whose infection does not respond in 24 to 48 hours are most likely to have infection caused by a highly penicillin-resistant pneumococcus or a β-lactamase-producing organism of another genus such as *H. influenzae* or *M. catarrhalis.* In such cases, the Otitis Media Working Group recommends amoxicillin/clavulanate, cefuroxime, cefpodoxime or cefdinir orally, or one to three parenteral doses of ceftriaxone[204] followed by a few additional days of oral cefpodoxime or cefdinir. This therapy is likely to be effective against *H. influenzae* and *M. catarrhalis,* as well as additional pneumococcal strains. Three to five daily doses of ceftriaxone are recommended for more resistant cases. The group rejected alternatives, such as azithromycin, for general use because of steadily increasing rates of resistance. At present, quinolones have not yet been approved for use in young children.

Under ideal circumstances, a specimen should be obtained (or in the case of failure of therapy, would already have been obtained) from the middle ear, and culturing can help determine the causative organism. If therapy to cover these broader possibilities fails, a drainage problem is likely to be present, and repeat tympanocentesis may be therapeutic, as well as diagnostic. In some communities, this procedure is regarded as essential to correctly diagnose and treat otitis media. In the United States, tympanocentesis is rarely done; perhaps there is greater need for this procedure in an era of increasing pneumococcal resistance.

Sinusitis

Because the pathogenesis and causative organisms of acute sinusitis are essentially identical to those of otitis media, the same therapeutic considerations apply. Once again, the physician is left with the essential problem of empirical therapy, not knowing whether *S. pneumoniae* is present or, if it is present, whether it is susceptible or resistant to the selected therapy. Amoxicillin is regarded as first-line therapy, with amoxicillin/clavulanic acid as the backup in cases of failure.[205-207] Unlike children, for whom quinolones have not been approved, adults can be treated with this class of drugs. The new ketolides also are likely to provide excellent therapy for sinusitis.[179]

Pneumonia

Outpatient Therapy

This section will generally be confined to the selection of therapy for pneumonia caused by *S. pneumoniae* because the broader question of treatment of pneumonia is covered in Chapter 60. Some redundancy is, however, necessary. The Pneumonia Outcomes Research Team[208] showed that (1) in most patients who are treated as outpatients, no attempt is made to establish an etiologic diagnosis; (2) when such attempts are made, *S. pneumoniae* is the predominant agent, accounting for more than half of cases in which a bacterium is cultured and more than one third in which a diagnosis is made (or suspected) by bacteriologic or serologic means; (3) when patients are stratified by risk groups,[209] the mortality reported (without regard to etiology) is very low among patients who do not require hospitalization; and (4) most importantly, although analyzed without regard to etiologic agent, the response appeared to be excellent and was observed irrespective of the therapy chosen. Specifically, treatment with quinolones, macrolides, penicillins or penicillins with β-lactamase inhibitors, trimethoprim-sulfamethoxazole, or doxycycline all seemed to be equally effective. Nevertheless, the study design would not have recognized an association between inappropriate therapy and failure to respond, and this study took place before such a substantial proportion of pneumococci had become resistant to macrolides, trimethoprim-sulfamethoxazole and doxycycline. Attention has increasingly been called to clinical failures when macrolides are used to treat outpatient pneumonia caused by macrolide-resistant pneumococci.[210]

To treat outpatients for pneumonia, the Infectious Disease Society of America[211] recommends, in no particular order, the use of a macrolide, doxycycline, amoxicillin (with or without clavulanic acid) or a quinolone. At present, the use of a quinolone or a ketolide would largely bypass the problem of resistance among pneumococci, but the rate of quinolone resistance has begun to increase and resistance to ketolides will surely increase in proportion to usage.

Inpatient Therapy

The importance of the decision to hospitalize or even to directly admit to intensive care cannot be overemphasized (see Chapter 60). Published guidelines[211-214] should generally be used, although not followed slavishly. Stratification in accord with recommendations by PORT[209] should be used to help decide whether hospitalization is needed although, if the physician is in doubt, he or she should hospitalize, at least for the initiation of therapy. The remainder of this section deals with selection of an antibiotic to treat pneumococcal pneumonia.

The emergence of antibiotic resistance in pneumococci has made the treatment of pneumococcal pneumonia much more difficult than could ever have been imagined two decades ago. Pneumococcal pneumonia caused by organisms that are susceptible or intermediately resistant to penicillin responds to treatment with penicillin, 1 million units intravenously every 4 hours; ampicillin, 1 g every 6 hours; or ceftriaxone, 1 g every 24 hours. The principal concern is whether pneumonia caused by resistant organisms responds to such therapy.

Retrospective studies of small numbers of cases found a similar outcome in patients who were treated with a penicillin or a cephalosporin for pneumococcal pneumonia, without regard to whether the infection was caused by a susceptible or nonsusceptible organism. In contrast, a study by the Centers for Disease Control and Prevention[215] found mortality in treated pneumococcal pneumonia to be increased threefold when caused by penicillin-resistant and sevenfold when caused by ceftriaxone-resistant pneumococci, even after adjustment for severity of the underlying illness and previous hospitalization, both of which increase the likelihood that resistant pneumococci will be present. This study was problematic for several reasons, and others are in progress. It seems unlikely that we will ultimately be able to count on penicillin or ceftriaxone to cure infection caused by *S. pneumoniae* strains that require 4 to 16 μg/mL or 2 to 8 μg/mL of these drugs, respectively, to inhibit growth. In the meantime, because such high-level resistance is very uncommon, ceftriaxone 1 g every 12 hours or cefotaxime, 1 g every 6 hours, is appropriate for resistant organisms. These considerations have led the Infectious Disease Society of America[214] to recommend, for empiric therapy of community-acquired pneumonia, a third generation cephalosporin or a β-lactam/β-lactamase inhibitor plus a macrolide or quinolone, or a quinolone as sole therapy. Although vancomycin is likely to treat pneumococcal infection effectively, the impetus to not use this drug is strong because of the fear of emergence of resistant organisms and its lack of efficacy against other organisms that commonly cause pneumonia. Studies of the new ketolides suggest that one of these drugs might also be effective and would provide coverage for other agents that are likely to cause pneumonia, as well.

Patients who are treated for pneumococcal pneumonia with an effective antibiotic generally have substantially reduced fever and feel much better within 48 hours. Based on all the foregoing considerations, if a patient has responded to treatment with a β-lactam antibiotic, this therapy should be continued even if the antibiotic-susceptibility test shows that the causative organism is resistant. If, however, a clear response is not observed and the organism is resistant, therapy should be changed in accordance with susceptibility testing results. In such a circumstance, it is likely that good treatment will require a quinolone or vancomycin.

The optimal duration of therapy for pneumococcal pneumonia is uncertain. Pneumococci are not readily detected microscopically in sputum more than 6 to 12 hours after the administration of an effective antibiotic, and are usually not detectable by culture after 24 hours.[151] A small-scale study in the 1950s showed that a single dose of procaine penicillin, which maintains an effective antimicrobial level for as long as 24 hours, could cure otherwise healthy young adults of pneumococcal pneumonia. Experience obtained early in the antibiotic era showed that 5 to 7 days of therapy sufficed. Nevertheless, the tendency of the medical profession has been to prolong therapy and, in the absence of data to prove additional benefit, most physicians now treat pneumonia for 10 to 14 days. The inclination to prolong therapy is a two-edged sword because of the risk of emergence of antibiotic-resistant organisms. Close observation for 3 to 5 days with parenteral therapy for pneumococcal pneumonia and a final few days of oral treatment, in all not exceeding 5 days after the patient has become afebrile (temperature not exceeding 99°F), may be the best approach. Failure of the patient to defervesce within 2 to 3 days should stimulate a review of the organism's antibiotic susceptibility, as well as a search for a loculated infection such as empyema.

Meningitis

Pneumococcal meningitis has been treated with 12 to 24 million units of penicillin every 24 hours or 1 to 2 g of ceftriaxone every 12 hours. Either regimen is effective against antibiotic-susceptible *S. pneumoniae* and may be effective against intermediately resistant ones; pharmacokinetic considerations and achievable CSF levels favor the third-generation cephalosporins cefotaxime or ceftriaxone. During treatment of resistant strains, β-lactam antibiotics are likely not to achieve therapeutic levels in CSF. This explains why, until susceptibility results are reported, vancomycin is recommended along with the β-lactam antibiotic, the vancomycin because of its more certain an-

timicrobial efficacy and the β-lactam because it crosses the blood-brain barrier more reliably and the organism may be susceptible. In patients who have major penicillin and cephalosporin allergies, vancomycin and/or imipenem can be used; unless the history suggests life-threatening reactions to penicillin, ceftriaxone or cefotaxime are preferred.

Some anecdotal reports have claimed a better outcome when rifampin is added to a β-lactam antibiotic in the treatment of pneumococcal meningitis. In experimental animals, the addition of rifampin to ceftriaxone[216] or vancomycin[217] has not produced synergy except in the presence of concomitant glucocorticosteroid administration, which may diminish central nervous system penetration of the antibiotics. A systematic study in vitro has shown indifference or antagonism when rifampin is added to β-lactam drugs.[218] Although some authorities[136] recommend that rifampin be added when steroids are given together with a third-generation cephalosporin, in my view, the available data do not justify this practice. A recent study in adults[219] found, as was previously shown in children, that addition of dexamethasone, 10 mg four times daily, leads to a better outcome in all-cause bacterial meningitis, one third of which were due to pneumococcus. Because of the possibility that steroids may diminish the penetration of antibiotics into the central nervous system,[220-222] when physicians add steroids to treat meningitis caused by pneumococci with reduced antibiotic susceptibility, they should observe their patients particularly closely; repeat spinal taps may be needed to document abatement of CSF abnormalities, especially if there is any suggestion of a delayed clinical response.

Miscellaneous

Pneumococcal endocarditis is associated with rapid destruction of heart valves. Initial therapy should include vancomycin and ceftriaxone until the results of minimal bactericidal concentration testing are known. An aminoglycoside may inhibit the bactericidal activity of β-lactam antibiotics[223] and should not be added unless synergy in vitro is documented to occur.

PREVENTION

The subject of vaccination to protect against pneumococcal infection has been reviewed extensively in recent years.[25] Two kinds of pneumococcal vaccine are now available in the United States. Pneumococcal capsular polysaccharide vaccine, marketed as Pneumovax, contains 25 μg of capsular polysaccharides from each of 23 common infecting serotypes of *S. pneumoniae*. Protein-conjugate pneumococcal vaccine contains lesser amounts of capsular material from seven pneumococcal serotypes that are most commonly implicated in disease of children; this vaccine is released only for pediatric use.

Antibody Levels Postvaccination

After vaccination, healthy young adults respond with antibody to an average of about three quarters of the antigens.[85] IgG and IgM become detectable within 5 to 7 days after vaccination; in persons with prior exposure, increases in antibody appear according to the same kinetics that are seen with initial exposure.[88] Although the concept is prevalent that IgM antibody appears first and then production switches to IgG, both classes of antibody appear at the same time in the blood stream, as well as in lymphocytic cultures in vitro.[88,224] IgG levels then rise to a peak in 4 to 12 weeks, after which they subside gradually and variably over several years. Protection is thought to persist only as long as antibody is detectable, but it is not known what level of antibody can be used to determine a threshold for immunity, and it is difficult to distinguish a low level of antibody from background "noise" in the ELISA.

Genetic factors govern the capacity to make antibody to capsular polysaccharides, and the inheritance is autosomal and dominant.[85] After vaccination, some individuals have high levels of IgG to all capsular polysaccharides, whereas others may fail to respond to most polysaccharides and the IgG levels to the polysaccharide antigens to which they do respond may be very low. Repeated vaccination does not elicit antibody in nonresponders, although IgG to some of the antigens may appear in some subjects after administration of a protein-conjugated vaccine.[225] Older persons may have lower antibody levels after vaccination than do younger persons.[226,227] A number of disease states suppress responses to vaccine. Antibody responses may be somewhat lower in elderly subjects who have chronic lung or heart disease.[83,87] Persons who have immunosuppressive conditions that place them at highest risk of pneumococcal infection, such as multiple myeloma, Hodgkin's disease, splenectomy, lymphoma, nephrotic syndrome, renal failure, cirrhosis, sickle cell disease, bone marrow transplantation, and HIV infection, have diminished capacity to make IgG to polysaccharide antigens. Persons with acquired immunodeficiency syndrome may lose responsiveness to some antigens while retaining relatively normal responses to others.[104,228] Unlike proteins, polysaccharides do not stimulate long-lived lymphocyte lines that respond to a rechallenge with earlier and more vigorous antibody responses. Revaccination years after an initial vaccine leads to antibody levels that approach, but do not usually even reach the original peak.

Protection Postvaccination

Field trials in the first two decades of the 20th century showed that vaccination of South African miners with whole, killed organisms was protective.[1] Vaccine efficacy with purified preparations of capsular polysaccharide was also demonstrated in civilians and in members of the armed forces in the 1930s and 1940s[229,230]; the reduction in pneumococcal disease was thought to be about 60% in these studies. In subgroups in the population who are at greatest risk of pneumococcal infection, such as elderly persons with underlying diseases, some trials have shown similar efficacy,[231,232] but others have failed to find a protective effect.[233-235] For example, in a blinded, prospective study carried out under the auspices of the Veterans Administration,[235] 2354 subjects who were at least 55 years old and had one or more underlying diseases for which vaccine is routinely recommended (principally chronic obstructive lung disease, alcoholism, chronic renal insufficiency, and congestive heart failure) were randomized to receive 14-valent pneumococcal vaccine or placebo. During nearly 3 years of follow-up, no difference in the frequency of pneumococcal pneumonia or bronchitis was noted in the two groups. More recently,[236] a placebo-controlled study of pneumococcal vaccine in persons who were discharged from the hospital (a particularly high-risk group) showed a fivefold decrease in pneumococcal bacteremia but no difference in what was called pneumococcal pneumonia, a finding based on not-well-established serologic techniques.

Other methods of investigation have been used to show the efficacy of pneumococcal vaccine. Use of an indirect cohort method showed that when organisms causing invasive pneumococcal disease were serotyped, previously vaccinated persons had a significantly lower incidence of infection by vaccine versus nonvaccine serotypes than did controls.[237] A retrospective cohort study showed an approximately 56% reduction in proven pneumococcal bacteremia, but no impact on the overall rate of pneumonia in an older population.[238] Several case-control studies have also shown efficacy.[239-241] In all these studies the efficacy of vaccine was about 60% to 70%, the same efficacy that had been recorded in prospective field trials. In one trial (Table 197-7) the protective effect of pneumococcal vaccine was shown to decline slowly with time; it persisted beyond 5 years in healthy young adults but not in the elderly.[240]

Antibody Efficiency

Recent laboratory investigations have helped explain why vaccine efficacy might be reduced in those who are in greatest need of it. First, although postvaccination IgG levels are similar in very healthy elderly and younger adults, antibody levels in elderly persons who have underlying diseases may be lower. Second, the capacity of IgG to opsonize pneumococci for phagocytosis and to protect experimental animals against pneumococcal challenge is diminished in ill and elderly persons.[227,242] Finally, about one third of adults who are hospitalized with pneumococcal pneumonia have antibody to their infecting serotype at the time of admission, but this antibody is nonopsonic in vitro and does not pro-

TABLE 197-7 Case-Control Study: Protection by Pneumococcal Vaccine*

Age (yr)	Pairs of Subjects	Years Since Vaccination		
		<3	3-5	>5
<55	125	93	89	85
55-64	149	88	82	75
65-74	213	80	71	58
75-84	188	67	53	32
≥85	133	46	33	0

*Results of a case-control study[240] that estimated the efficacy of pneumococcal vaccination by matching infected patients with uninfected controls (pairs of subjects) and examining the incidence of prior vaccination in each group. Data are shown as a percentage indicating efficacy as estimated percent protection.

tect mice against experimental challenge with that organism.[243] Thus, antibody levels may be lower and/or antibody may have lesser capacity to protect those who are in greatest need of vaccine.

Vaccine Recommendations

With data demonstrating its safety, low cost, and efficacy, failure to use pneumococcal vaccine more widely can be regarded as a missed opportunity in public health policy.[244] Since the last edition of this textbook, the Immunization Practices Advisory Committee of the Centers for Disease Control[245] has broadened its recommendations for pneumococcal vaccine to include all persons older than 2 years of age who are at substantially increased risk of developing pneumococcal infection or a serious complication of such an infection. General categories included within these recommendations are as follows: (1) persons older than 65 years of age; (2) persons with anatomic or functional asplenia, CSF leak, diabetes mellitus, alcoholism, cirrhosis, chronic renal insufficiency, chronic pulmonary disease, or advanced cardiovascular disease; (3) persons who have an immunocompromised condition that is associated with increased risk of pneumococcal disease, such as multiple myeloma, lymphoma, Hodgkin's disease, HIV infection, organ transplantation, or chronic use of glucocorticosteroids; (4) persons who are genetically at increased risk, such as Alaskan and Native Americans; and (5) persons who live in special environments where outbreaks may occur, such as nursing homes.

Recommendations regarding revaccination seem to be somewhat inconsistent because the committee advocates a single revaccination in persons older than age 65. Because antibody levels decline and there is no anamnestic response, it seems more reasonable simply to recommend revaccination at 5-year intervals, especially in adults older than age 65 years, who will have a minimal local reaction. Such a recommendation, however, may not be a worthwhile use of limited resources. Persons who are at highest risk of recurring pneumococcal infection are those who have undergone splenectomy or have a CSF leak; in my opinion, these persons should be vaccinated every 3 to 5 years. If penicillin-resistant pneumococci continue to increase in their prevalence, routine immunization of children older than age 2 years should also be considered. Pneumococcal vaccine has not been useful in children younger than 2 years old because they do not respond well to polysaccharide antigens.

Protein Conjugate Vaccines

Pneumococcal capsular polysaccharides have been covalently conjugated to carrier proteins such as tetanus or diphtheria toxoid, a genetically engineered protein that closely resembles diphtheria toxoid (CRM 197), outer-membrane proteins of *Neisseria meningitidis,* pneumolysin toxoid, and pneumococcal surface protein A. The resulting antigens are recognized as T-cell dependent; they stimulate good antibody responses in children younger than 2 years of age (who otherwise do not respond to polysaccharide antigens) and induce immunologic memory. A series of three or four injections into infants and young children stimulates reasonably good antibody levels before the age of 18 months. Remarkably, invasive disease (bacteremic infection or meningitis) is nearly eliminated by the full set of immunizations.[246] The impact on less clearly proven entities is much less striking, indicating, in my opinion, a problem with definitions of disease and diagnosis, not with the vaccine. Thus, proven pneumococcal otitis media is reduced by 65%, whereas all-cause otitis is reduced by only 8%,[247] and bacteremic pneumococcal pneumonia may be reduced by more than 90%, whereas all cause pneumonia is reduced by only 21%.[248] Conjugate pneumococcal vaccine also reduces the rate of carriage of vaccine strains among recipients, but there is a concern—with some preliminary data to support it—that vaccine strains may eventually be replaced by other strains.[249]

In adults, conjugate vaccine can induce a response in persons who do not make antibody to nonconjugated polysaccharide[225] and may possibly stimulate higher mean levels of IgG in persons who respond normally or in immunocompromised persons. Evidence supporting this last point is not at all clear; two studies [250,251] have shown no difference in IgG levels after nonconjugated versus conjugated vaccine in older adults, but another study [252] has suggested that if an initial dose of conjugate vaccine is given, a second dose of nonconjugated vaccine stimulates a better response in patients with Hodgkin's disease. Protein-conjugate vaccine appeared to be somewhat more effective than polysaccharide vaccine in stimulating HIV-infected patients to generate opsonizing antibody to *S. pneumoniae.*[253] At present, conjugate vaccine is not recommended for adults.

Other Preventive Measures

Surface proteins of pneumococcus, specifically PspA and PsaA, are currently under study for use in a vaccine. Levels of antibody have been detected post-vaccination, and serum from vaccinated persons has been shown to be protective in mice, as was noted earlier in this chapter. Other proteins, such as the highly conversed surface BVH protein may also eventually find a use in vaccines.

In the past, the prophylactic use of oral penicillin reduced the likelihood of serious pneumococcal infection in children with sickle cell disease, but it seems unlikely that such prophylaxis will continue to be of benefit because of the impact of penicillin resistance.

Regular infusion of normal human globulin protects against pneumococcal infection, as has been shown in the case of children with HIV infection[254] and adults with lymphoma.[255] Such patients are unlikely to produce antibody to pneumococcal vaccine. Whether globulin should in fact be infused each month becomes a societal issue because of the high cost.

REFERENCES

1. Heffron R. Pneumonia, with special reference to pneumococcus lobar pneumonia. A Commonwealth Fund Book. Cambridge, MA: Harvard University Press (reprinted 1979), 1938.
2. White B. The Biology of Pneumococcus. The Bacteriologic, Biochemical and Immunological Characters and Activities of *Diplococcus pneumoniae*. A Commonwealth Fund Book. Cambridge, MA: Harvard University Press (reprinted 1979), 1938.
3. Watson DA, Musher DM, Jacobson JW, Verhoef J. A brief history of the pneumococcus in biomedical research: A panoply of scientific discovery. Clin Infect Dis. 1993;17:913-924.
4. Musher DM, Watson DA, Dominguez EA. Pneumococcal vaccination: Work to date and future prospects. Am J Med Sci. 1990;300:45-52.
5. Heidelberger M, Avery OT. The soluble specific substance of pneumococcus. J Exp Med. 1923;38:73.
6. Felton LD. Studies on the immunizing substances in pneumococci. J Immunol. 1934;27:379-393.
7. Smillie WG, Wornock GH, White HJ. A study of a type I pneumococcus epidemic at the State Hospital at Worcester, Mass. Am J Publ Health. 1938;28:293-302.
8. MacLeod CM, Hodges RG, Heidelberger M, Bernhard WG. Prevention of pneumococcal pneumonia by immunization with specific capsular polysaccharides. J Exp Med. 1945;82:445-465.
9. Griffith F. The significance of pneumococcal types. J Hyg. 1928;27:113-159.
10. Avery OT, MacLeod C, McCarty M. Studies on the chemical nature of the substance inducing transformation of pneumococcal types. J Exp Med. 1944;79:137-157.
11. Munoz R, Fenoll A, Vicioso D, Casal J. Optochin-resistant variants of *Streptococcus pneumoniae*. Diagn Microbiol Infect Dis. 1990;13:63-66.
12. Ertugrul N, Rodriguez-Barradas MC, Musher DM, et al. BOX-polymerase chain reaction-based DNA analysis of nonserotypeable *Streptococcus pneumoniae* implicated in outbreaks of conjunctivitis. J Infect Dis. 1997;176:1401-1405.
13. van Dam JE, Fleer A, Snippe H. Immunogenicity and immunochemistry of *Streptococcus pneumoniae* capsular polysaccharides. Antonie Van Leeuwenhoek. 1990;58:1-47.
14. Morona JK, Morona R, Paton JC. Molecular and genetic characterization of the capsule biosynthesis locus of *Streptococcus pneumoniae* type 19B. J Bacteriol. 1997;179:4953-4958.
15. Guidolin A, Morona JK, Morona R, et al. Nucleotide sequence analysis of genes essential for capsular polysaccharide biosynthesis in *Streptococcus pneumoniae* type 19F. Infect Immun. 1994;62:5384-5396.
16. Watson DA, Kapur V, Musher DM, et al. Identification, cloning, and sequencing of DNA essential for encapsulation of *Streptococcus pneumoniae*. Curr Microbiol. 1995;31:251-259.
17. Dillard JP, Caimano M, Kelly T, Yother J. Capsules and cassettes: Genetic organization of the capsule locus of *Streptococcus pneumoniae*. Dev Biol Stand. 1995;85:261-265.
18. Caimano MJ, Hardy GG, Yother J. Capsule genetics in *Streptococcus pneumoniae* and a possible role for transposition in the generation of the type 3 locus. Microb Drug Resist. 1998;4:11-23.
19. Peterson S, Cline RT, Tettelin H, et al. Gene expression analysis of the *Streptococcus pneumoniae* competence regulons by use of DNA microarrays. J Bacteriol. 2000;182:6192-6202.
20. Nesin M, Ramirez M, Tomasz A. Capsular transformation of a multidrug-resistant *Streptococcus pneumoniae* in vivo. J Infect Dis. 1998;177:707-713.
21. Sorensen UB. Pneumococcal polysaccharide antigens: Capsules and C-polysaccharide. An immunochemical study. Dan Med Bull. 1995;42:47-53.
22. Dudley S, Ashe K, Winther B, Hendley JO. Bacterial pathogens of otitis media and sinusitis: Detection in the nasopharynx with selective agar media. J Lab Clin Med. 2001;138:338-342.
23. Gray BM, Dillon HC Jr. Epidemiological studies of *Streptococcus pneumoniae* in infants: Antibody to types 3, 6, 14, and 23 in the first two years of life. J Infect Dis. 1988;158:948-955.
24. Ekdahl K, Ahlinder I, Hansson HB, et al. Duration of nasopharyngeal carriage of penicillin-resistant *Streptococcus pneumoniae*: Experiences from the South Swedish Pneumococcal Intervention Project. Clin Infect Dis. 1997;25:1113-1117.
25. Fedson DS, Musher DM. Pneumococcal vaccine. In: Plotkin SA, Orenstein WB, eds. Vaccines. Philadelphia: WB Saunders, 2003.
26. Harrison LH, Dwyer DM, Billmann L, et al. Invasive pneumococcal infection in Baltimore, Md: Implications for immunization policy. Arch Intern Med. 2000;160:89-94.
27. Davidson M, Parkinson AJ, Bulkow LR, et al. The epidemiology of invasive pneumococcal disease in Alaska, 1986-1990—ethnic differences and opportunities for prevention. J Infect Dis. 1994;170:368-376.
28. Torzillo PJ, Hanna JN, Morey F, et al. Invasive pneumococcal disease in central Australia. Med J Aust. 1995;162:182-186.
29. Burman LA, Norrby R, Trollfors B. Invasive pneumococcal infections: Incidence, predisposing factors, and prognosis. Rev Infect Dis. 1985;7:133-142.
30. Breiman RF, Spika JS, Navarro VJ, et al. Pneumococcal bacteremia in Charleston County, South Carolina. A decade later. Arch Intern Med. 1990;150:1401-1405.
31. Baer M, Vuento R, Vesikari T. Increase in bacteraemic pneumococcal infections in children. Lancet. 1995;345:661.
32. Kyaw MH, Clarke S, Jones IG, Campbell H. Incidence of invasive pneumococcal disease in Scotland, 1988-99. Epidemiol Infect. 2002;128:139-147.
33. Whitney CG, Farley MM, Hadler J, et al. Decline in invasive pneumococcal disease after the introduction of protein-polysaccharide conjugate vaccine. N Engl J Med. 2003;348:1737-1746.
34. Gray BM, Converse GM 3rd, Dillon HC Jr. Epidemiologic studies of *Streptococcus pneumoniae* in infants: acquisition, carriage, and infection during the first 24 months of life. J Infect Dis. 1980;142:923-933.
35. Frenck RW Jr, Glezen WP. Respiratory tract infections in children in day care. Semin Pediatr Infect Dis. 1990;1:234-244.
36. Kim PE, Musher DM, Glezen WP, et al. Association of invasive pneumococcal disease with season, atmospheric conditions, air pollution, and the isolation of respiratory viruses. Clin Infect Dis. 1996;22:100-106.
37. Dowell SF, Whitney CG, Wright C, et al. Seasonal patterns of invasive pneumococcal disease. Emerg Infect Dis. 2003;9:573-579.
38. Musher DM. How contagious are common respiratory infections? N Engl J Med. 2003;348:1256-1266.
39. Henderson FW, Gilligan PH, Wait K, Goff DA. Nasopharyngeal carriage of antibiotic-resistant pneumococci by children in group day care. J Infect Dis. 1988;157:256-263.
40. Rauch AM, O'Ryan M, Van R, Pickering LK. Invasive diease due to multiply resitant *Streptococcus pneumoniae* in a Houston, Texas day care center. Am J Dis Child. 1990;144:923-927.
41. Doyle MG, Morrow AL, Van R, Pickering LK. Intermediate resistance of *Streptococcus pneumoniae* to penicillin in children in day-care centers. Pediatr Infect Dis J. 1992;11:831-835.
42. Hodges R, MacLeod C. Epidemic pneumococcal pneumonia: I. Description of the epidemic. Am J Hyg. 1946;44:183-192.
43. Hoge CW, Reichler MR, Dominguez EA, et al. An epidemic of pneumococcal disease in an overcrowded, inadequately ventilated jail. N Engl J Med. 1994;331:643-648.
44. Mercat A, Nguyen J, Dautzenberg B. An outbreak of pneumococcal pneumonia in two men's shelters. Chest. 1991;99:147-151.

45. Gleich S, Morad Y, Echague R, et al. *Streptococcus pneumoniae* serotype 4 outbreak in a home for the aged: Report and review of recent outbreaks. Infect Contr Hosp Epidemiol. 2000;21:711-717.

46. Watson DA, Musher DM, Verhoef J. Pneumococcal virulence factors and host immune responses to them. Eur J Clin Microbiol Infect Dis. 1995;14:479-490.

47. Koedel U, Scheld WM, Pfister HW. Pathogenesis and pathophysiology of pneumococcal meningitis. Lancet Infect Dis. 2002;2:721-736.

48. Cundell DR, Pearce BJ, Sandros J, et al. Peptide permeases from *Streptococcus pneumoniae* affect adherence to eucaryotic cells. Infect Immun. 1995;63:2493-2498.

49. Krivan H, Roberts D, Ginsberg V. Many pulmonary pathogenic bacteria bind specifically to the carbohydrate sequence GalNAc B1-4-Gal found in some glycolipids. Proc Natl Acad Sci USA. 1988;85.

50. Sundberg-Kovamees M, Holme T, Sjorgren A. Interaction of the C-polysaccharide of *Streptococcus pneumoniae* with the receptor asialo-GM. Microb Pathog. 1996;21.

51. Weiser JN, Markiewicz Z, Tuomanen EI, Wani JH. Relationship between phase variation in colony morphology, intrastrain variation in cell wall physiology, and nasopharyngeal colonization by *Streptococcus pneumoniae*. Infect Immun. 1996;64:2240-2245.

52. Brock SC, McGraw PA, Wright PF, Crowe JE Jr. The human polymeric immunoglobulin receptor facilitates invasion of epithelial cells by *Streptococcus pneumoniae* in a strain-specific and cell type-specific manner. Infect Immun. 2002;70:5091-5095.

53. Cundell DR, Gerard NP, Gerard C, et al. *Streptococcus pneumoniae* anchor to activated human cells by the receptor for platelet-activating factor. Nature. 1995;377:435-438.

54. Angel CS, Ruzek M, Hostetter MK. Degradation of C3 by *Streptococcus pneumoniae*. J Infect Dis. 1994;170:600-608.

55. Ren B, Szalai AJ, Thomas O, et al. Both family 1 and family 2 PspA proteins can inhibit complement deposition and confer virulence to a capsular serotype 3 strain of *Streptococcus pneumoniae*. Infect Immun. 2003;71:75-85.

56. Duthy TG, Ormsby RJ, Giannakis E, et al. The human complement regulator factor H binds pneumococcal surface protein PspC via short consensus repeats 13 to 15. Infect Immun. 2002;70:5604-5611.

57. Watson DA, Musher DM. Interruption of capsule production in *Streptococcus pneumonia* serotype 3 by insertion of transposon Tn916. Infect Immun. 1990;58:3135-3138.

58. Musher DM, Johnson B Jr, Watson DA. Quantitative relationship between anticapsular antibody measured by enzyme-linked immunosorbent assay or radioimmunoassay and protection of mice against challenge with *Streptococcus pneumoniae* serotype 4. Infect Immun. 1990;58:3871-3876.

59. Boulnois GJ. Pneumococcal proteins and the pathogenesis of disease caused by *Streptococcus pneumoniae*. J Gen Microbiol. 1992;138(Pt 2):249-259.

60. Paton JC, Berry AM, Lock RA. Molecular analysis of putative pneumococcal virulence proteins. Microb Drug Resist. 1997;3:1-10.

61. Rubins JB, Charboneau D, Paton JC, et al. Dual function of pneumolysin in the early pathogenesis of murine pneumococcal pneumonia. J Clin Invest. 1995;95:142-150.

62. Rubins JB, Janoff EN. Pneumolysin: A multifunctional pneumococcal virulence factor. J Lab Clin Med. 1998;131:21-27.

63. Feldman C, Munro NC, Jeffery PK, et al. Pneumolysin induces the salient histologic features of pneumococcal infection in the rat lung in vivo. Am J Respir Cell Mol Biol. 1991;5:416-423.

64. Alexander JE, Lock RA, Peeters CC, et al. Immunization of mice with pneumolysin toxoid confers a significant degree of protection against at least nine serotypes of *Streptococcus pneumoniae*. Infect Immun. 1994;62:5683-5688.

65. Berry AM, Paton JC, Hansman D. Effect of insertional inactivation of the genes encoding pneumolysin and autolysin on the virulence of *Streptococcus pneumoniae* type 3. Microb Pathog. 1992;12:87-93.

66. Berry AM, Alexander JE, Mitchell TJ, et al. Effect of defined point mutations in the pneumolysin gene on the virulence of *Streptococcus pneumoniae*. Infect Immun. 1995;63:1969-1974.

67. Musher DM, Phan HM, Baughn RE. Protection against bacteremic pneumococcal infection by antibody to pneumolysin. J Infect Dis. 2001;183:827-830.

68. Roche H, Hakansson A, Hollingshead SK, Briles DE. Regions of PspA/EF3296 best able to elicit protection against *Streptococcus pneumoniae* in a murine infection model. Infect Immun. 2003;71:1033-1041.

69. McDaniel LS, Sheffield JS, Delucchi P, Briles DE. PspA, a surface protein of *Streptococcus pneumoniae*, is capable of eliciting protection against pneumococci of more than one capsular type. Infect Immun. 1991;59:222-228.

70. McDaniel LS, Yother J, Vijayakumar M, et al. Use of insertional inactivation to facilitate studies of biological properties of pneumococcal surface protein A (PspA). J Exp Med. 1987;165:381-394.

71. Briles DE, Hollingshead SK, King J, et al. Immunization of humans with recombinant pneumococcal surface protein A (rPspA) elicits antibodies that passively protect mice from fatal infection with *Streptococcus pneumoniae* bearing heterologous PspA. J Infect Dis. 2000;182:1694-1701.

72. Johnson SE, Dykes JK, Jue DL, et al. Inhibition of pneumococcal carriage in mice by subcutaneous immunization with peptides from the common surface protein pneumococcal surface adhesin a. J Infect Dis. 2002;185:489-496.

73. Romero-Steiner S, Pilishvili T, Sampson JS, et al. Inhibition of pneumococcal adherence to human nasopharyngeal epithelial cells by anti-PsaA antibodies. Clin Diagn Lab Immunol. 2003;10:246-251.

74. Rapola S, Kilpi T, Lahdenkari M, et al. Do antibodies to pneumococcal surface adhesin a prevent pneumococcal involvement in acute otitis media? J Infect Dis. 2001;184:577-581.

75. Lock RA, Hansman D, Paton JC. Comparative efficacy of autolysin and pneumolysin as immunogens protecting mice against infection by *Streptococcus pneumoniae*. Microb Pathog. 1992;12:137-143.

76. Winkelstein JA, Tomasz A. Activation of the alternative complement pathway by pneumococcal cell wall teichoic acid. J Immunol. 1978;120:174-178.

77. Tuomanen EI, Liu H, Hengstler B, et al. The induction of meningeal inflammation by components of the pneumococcal cell wall. J Infect Dis. 1985;151:859-868.

78. Wolbink GJ, Bossink AW, Groeneveld AB, et al. Complement activation in patients with sepsis is in part mediated by C-reactive protein. J Infect Dis. 1998;177:81-87.

79. Winkelstein JA, Bocchini JA Jr, Schiffman G. The role of the capsular polysaccharide in the activation of the alternative pathway by the pneumococcus. J Immunol. 1976;116:367-370.

80. Rodriguez-Barradas MC, Das TS, Watson DA, Musher DM. Relative contribution of cell wall and capsular polysaccharides in activating alternative and classical complement pathways by *Streptococcus pneumoniae*. Med Microbial Letters. 1993;2:427-435.

81. Schroder NW, Morath S, Alexander C, et al. Lipoteichoic acid (LTA) of *Streptococcus pneumoniae* and Staphylococcus aureus activates immune cells via Toll-like receptor (TLR)-2, lipopolysaccharide-binding protein (LBP), and CD14, whereas TLR-4 and MD-2 are not involved. J Biol Chem. 2003;278:15587-15594.

82. Malley R, Henneke P, Morse SC, et al. Recognition of pneumolysin by Toll-like receptor 4 confers resistance to pneumococcal infection. Proc Natl Acad Sci USA. 2003;100:1966-1971.

83. Musher DM, Chapman AJ, Goree A, et al. Natural and vaccine-related immunity to *Streptococcus pneumoniae*. J Infect Dis. 1986;154:245-256.

84. Romero-Steiner S, Libutti D, Pais LB, et al. Standardization of an opsonophagocytic assay for the measurement of functional antibody activity against *Streptococcus pneumoniae* using differentiated HL-60 cells. Clin Diagn Lab Immunol. 1997;4:415-422.

85. Musher DM, Groover JE, Watson DA. Genetic regulation of the capacity to make immunoglobulin G to pneumococcal capsular polysaccharides. J Invest Med. 1997;45:57-68.

86. Siber GR, Priehs C, Madore DV. Standardization of antibody assays for measuring the response to pneumococcal infection and immunization. Pediatr Infect Dis J. 1989;8:S84-91.

87. Musher DM, Luchi MJ, Watson DA, et al. Pneumococcal polysaccharide vaccine in young adults and older bronchitics: Determination of IgG responses by ELISA and the effect of adsorption of serum with non-type-specific cell wall polysaccharide. J Infect Dis. 1990;161:728-735.

88. Musher DM, Groover JE, Rowland JM, et al. Antibody to capsular polysaccharides of *Streptococcus pneumoniae:* Prevalence, persistence, and response to revaccination. Clin Infect Dis. 1993;17:66-73.

89. Finland M, Winkler AW. Antibody response to infections with type II and with the related type VIII pneumococcus. J Clin Invest. 1934;13:97-107.

90. Finland M, Shuman HI. The type-specific agglutinin response of infants and children with pneumococcal pneumonias. J Immunol. 1942;45:215-223.

91. Sloyer JLJ, Howie VM, Ploussard JH, et al. Immune response to acute otitis media in children. I. Serotypes isolated and serum and middle ear fluid antibody in pneumococcal otitis media. Infect Immun. 1974;9:1028-1032.

92. Prober CG, Frayha H, Klein MJ. Immunologic responses of children to serious infections with *Streptococcus pneumoniae*. J Infect Dis. 1983;148:427-435.

93. Sanders LAM, Rijkers GT, Kuis W, et al. Defective antipneumococcal polysaccharide antibody response in children with recurrent respiratory tract infections. J. Allergy Clin Immunol. 1993;91:110-119.

94. Finland M, Tilghman RC. Bacteriological and immunological studies in families with pneumococci infections: The development of type-specific antibodies in healthy contact carriers. J Clin Invest. 1936;15:500-508.

95. Wara DW. Host defense against I *Streptococcus pneumoniae:* The role of the spleen. Rev Infect Dis. 1981;3:299-309.

96. Styrt B. Infection associated with asplenia: Risks, mechanisms, and prevention. Am J Med. 1990;88:33N-42N.

97. Jandl JH, Jones AR, Castle WB. The destruction of red cells by antibodies in man. I. Observations on the sequestration and lysis of red cells altered by immune mechanisms. J Clin Invest. 1957;36:1428-1459.

98. Frank MM, Hosea SW, Brown EJ, Hamburger MI. Opsonic requirements for intravascular clearance after splenectomy. N Engl J Med. 1981;304:245-250.

99. Wong WY, Overturf GD, Powars DR. Infection caused by *Streptococcus pneumoniae* in children with sickle cell disease: Epidemiology, immunologic mechanisms, prophylaxis, and vaccination. Clin Infect Dis. 1992;14:1124-1136.

100. Cunningham-Rundles C. Clinical and immunologic analyses of 103 patients with common variable immunodeficiency. J Clin Immunol. 1989;9:22-33.

101. Umetsu DT, Ambrosino DM, Quinti I, et al. Recurrent sinopulmonary infection and impaired antibody response to bacterial capsular polysaccharide antigen in children with selective IgG subclass deficiency. N Engl J Med. 1985;313:1247-1251.

102. Yee AMF, Phan HM, Zuniga R, et al. The FcyRIIa-R131 allotype increases risk for bacteremic pneumococcal infections. Clin Infect Dis. 1999;29.

103. Savage DG, Lindenbaum J, Garrett TJ. Biphasic pattern of bacterial infection in multiple myeloma. Ann Intern Med. 1982;96:47-50.

104. Rodriguez-Barradas MC, Musher DM, Lahart C, et al. Antibody to capsular polysaccharides of *Streptococcus pneumoniae* after vaccination of human immunodeficiency virus-infected subjects with 23-valent pneumococcal vaccine. J Infect Dis. 1992;165:553-556.

105. Janoff EN, O'Brien J, Thompson P, et al. *Streptococcus pneumoniae* colonization, bacteremia, and immune response amoung persons with human immunodeficiency virus infection. J Infect Dis. 1993;167:49-56.

106. Redd SC, Rutherford GWI, Sande MA, et al. The role of human immunodeficiency virus infection in pneumococcal bacteremia in San Francisco residents. J Infect Dis. 1990;162:1012-1017.

107. Rodriguez Barradas MC, Musher DM, Hamill RJ, et al. Unusual manifestations of pneumococcal infection in human immunodeficiency virus-infected individuals: the past revisited. Clin Infect Dis. 1992;14:192-199.

108. Schuchat A, Broome CV, Hightower A, et al. Use of surveillance for invasive pneumococcal disease to estimate the size of the immunosuppressed HIV-infected population. JAMA. 1991;265:3275-3279.

109. Figueroa JE, Densen P. Infectious diseases associated with complement deficiencies. Clin Microbiol Rev. 1991;4:359-395.

110. Anderson DC, Schmalstieg FC, Finegold MJ, et al. The severe and moderate phenotypes of heritable Mac-1, LFA-1 deficiency: Their quantitative definition and relation to leukocyte dysfunction and clinical features. J Infect Dis. 1985;152:668-689.

111. Beam TRJ, Allen JC. Patterns of infection in untreated acute leukemia: Impact of initial hospitalization. South Med J. 1979;72:282-286.

112. Gluckman SJ, Dvorak VC, MacGregor RR. Host defenses during prolonged alcohol consumption in a controlled environment. Arch Intern Med. 1977;137:1539-1543.

113. Young CL, MacGregor RR. Alcohol and host defenses: Infectious consequences. Infect Med. 1989;6:163-175.

114. Fang GD, Fine M, Orloff J, et al. New and emerging etiologies for community-acquired pneumonia with implications for therapy. A prospective multicenter study of 359 cases. Medicine (Baltimore). 1990;69:307-316.

115. Musher DM, Alexandraki I, Graviss EA, et al. Bacteremic and nonbacteremic pneumococcal pneumonia. A prospective study. Medicine (Baltimore). 2000;79:210-221.

116. Rahav G, Toledano Y, Engelhard D, et al. Invasive pneumococcal infections: A comparison between adults and children. Medicine (Baltimore). 1997;76:295-303.

117. Watanakunakorn C, Bailey TA. Adult bacteremic pneumococcal pneumonia in a community teaching hospital, 1992-1996. A detailed analysis of 108 cases. Arch Intern Med. 1997;157:1965-1971.

118. Mowat AG, Baum J. Chemotaxis of polymorphonuclear leukocytes from patients with diabetes mellitus. N Engl J Med. 1980;142:869-875.

119. Repine JE, Clawson CC, Goetz FC. Bactericidal function of neutrophils from patients with acute bacterial infections and from diabetics. J Infect Dis. 1980;6:869-875.

120. Lipsky BA, Boyko EJ, Inui TS, Koepsell TD. Fisk factors for acquiring pneumococcal infections. Arch Intern Med. 1986;146:2179-2185.

121. Chang JL, Mylotte JM. Pneumococcal bacteremia: Updated from an adult hospital with a high rate of nosocomial cases. J Am Geriatr Soc. 1987;35:747-754.

122. Hodges R, MacLeod C. Epidemic pneumococcal pneumonia. II. The influence of population characteristics and the environment. Am J Hyg. 1946;44:193-206.

123. Jones EE, Alford PL, Reingold AL, et al. Predisposition to invasive pneumococcal illness following parainfluenza type 3 virus infection in chimpanzees. J Am Vet Med Assoc. 1998;185:1351-1353.

124. Fainstein V, Musher DM, Cate TR. Bacterial adherence to pharyngeal cells during viral infection. J Infect Dis. 1980;141:172-176.

125. Nuorti JP, Butler JC, Farley MM, et al. Cigarette smoking and invasive pneumococcal disease. Active Bacterial Core Surveillance Team. N Engl J Med. 2000;342:681-689.

126. Raz R, Elhanan G, Shimoni Z, et al. Pneumococcal bacteremia in hospitalized Israeli adults: Epidemiology and resistance to penicillin. Clin Infect Dis. 1997;24:1164-1168.

127. Dowell SF, Butler JC, Giebink GS, et al. Acute otitis media: Management and surveillance in an era of pneumococcal resistance—a report from the drug-resistant *Streptococcus pneumoniae* Therapeutic Working Group. Pediatr Infect Dis J. 1999;18:1-9.

128. Schwartz LE, Brown RB. Purulent otitis media in adults. Arch Intern Med. 1992;152:2301-2304.

129. Faden H, Duffy L, Wasielewski R, et al. Relationship between nasopharyngeal colonization and the development of otitis media in children. J Infect Dis. 1997;175:1440-1445.

130. Gwaltney JMJ, Scheld WM, Sande MA, Sydnor A. The microbial etiology and antimicrobial therapy of adults with acute community-acquired sinusitis: A fifteen-year experience at the University of Virginia and review of other selected studies. J Allergy Clin Immunol. 1992;90:457-462.

131. Gwaltney JMJ, Phillips CD, Miller RD, Riker DK. Computed tomographic study of the common cold. N Engl J Med. 1994;330:25-30.

132. Quagliariello VJ, Scheld WM. Treatment of bacterial meningitis. N Engl J Med. 1997;336:708-716.

133. Hand WL, Sanford JP. Posttraumatic bacterial meningitis. Ann Intern Med. 1970;72:869-874.

134. Eavey RD, Gao Y, Schuknecht HF, Gonzalez-Pineda M. Otologic features of bacterial meningitis of childhood. J Pediatr. 1985;106:2025-2029.

135. Bhatt SM, Lauretano A, Cabellos C, et al. Progression of hearing loss in experimental pneumococcal meningitis: Correlation with cerebrospinal fluid cytochemistry. J Infect Dis. 1993;167:675-683.

136. Quagliariello V, Scheld WM. Bacterial meningitis: Pathogenesis, pathophysiology, and progress. N Engl J Med. 1992;327:864-72.

137. Dunbar SA, Eason RA, Musher DM, Clarridge JE 3rd. Microscopic examination and broth culture of cerebrospinal fluid in diagnosis of meningitis. J Clin Microbiol. 1998;36:1617-1620.

137a. Perkins MD, Mirrett S, Reller LB. Rapid bacterial antigen detection is not clinically useful. J Clin Microbiol. 1995;33:1486-1491.

138. Chodosh S. Acute bacterial exacerbations in bronchitis and asthma. Am J Med. 1987;82:154-163.

139. Chodosh S, McCarty J, Farkas S, et al. Randomized, double-blind study of ciprofloxacin and cefuroxime axetil for treatment of acute bacterial exacerbations of chronic bronchitis. The Bronchitis Study Group. Clin Infect Dis. 1998;27:722-729.

140. Sethi S, Evans N, Grant BJ, Murphy TF. New strains of bacteria and exacerbations of chronic obstructive pulmonary disease. N Engl J Med. 2002;347:465-471.

141. Murphy TF, Fine BC. Bacteremic pneumococcal pneumonia in the elderly. Am J Med Sci. 1984;288:114-118.

142. Metlay JP, Schulz R, Li Y-H, et al. Influence of age on symptoms at presentation in patients with community-acquired pneumonia. Arch Intern Med. 1997;157:1453-1459.

143. Metlay JP, Kapoor WN, Fine MJ. Does this patient have community-acquired pneumonia? Diagnosing pneumonia by history and physical examination. JAMA. 1997;278:1440-1445.

144. Ort S, Ryan RL, Barden G, et al. Pneumococcal pneumonia in hospitalized patients. JAMA. 1983;249:214-218.

145. Yangco BG, Deresinski SC. Necrotizing or cavitating pneumonia due to *Streptococcus pneumoniae*: Report of four cases and review of the literature. Medicine (Baltimore). 1980;59:449-457.

146. Light RW, Girard WM, Jenkinson SG, George RB. Parapneumonic effusions. Am J Med. 1980;69:507-512.

147. Hook EWI, Horton CA, Schaberg DR. Failure of intensive care unit support to influence mortality from pneumococcal bacteremia. JAMA. 1983;249:1055-1057.

148. Perlino CA, Rimland D. Alcoholism, leukopenia, and pneumococcal sepsis. Am Rev Respir Dis. 2985;132:757-760.

149. Barrett-Connor E. The nonvalue of sputum culture in the diagnosis of pneumococcal pneumonia. Am Rev Respir Dis. 1971;103:845-848.

150. Perlino CA. Laboratory diagnosis of pneumonia due to *Streptococcus pneumoniae*. J Infect Dis. 1984;150:139-144.

151. Musher DM, Montoya R, Wanahita A. Reliability of microscopic examination of gram-stained sputum and sputum culture in patients with bacteremic pneumococcal pneumonia. Clin Inf Dis. 2004. In Press.

152. Fine MJ, Orloff JJ, Rihs JD, et al. Evaluation of housestaff physicians' preparation and interpretation of sputum Gram stains for community-acquired pneumonia. J Gen Intern Med. 1991;6:189-198.

153. Thorsteinsson SB, Musher DM, Fagan T. The diagnostic value of sputum culture in acute pneumonia. JAMA. 1975;233:894-895.

154. Gutierrez F, Masia M, Rodriguez JC, et al. Evaluation of the immunochromatographic Binax NOW assay for detection of *Streptococcus pneumoniae* urinary antigen in a prospective study of community-acquired pneumonia in Spain. Clin Infect Dis. 2003;36:286-292.

155. Dowell SF, Garman RL, Liu G, et al. Evaluation of Binax NOW, an assay for the detection of pneumococcal antigen in urine samples, performed among pediatric patients. Clin Infect Dis. 2001;32:824-825.

156. Musher DM, Mediwala R, Phan HM, et al. Nonspecificity of assaying for IgG antibody to pneumolysin in circulating immune complexes as a means to diagnose pneumococcal pneumonia. Clin Infect Dis. 2001;32:534-538.

157. Anstadt MP, Guill CK, Gordon HS, et al. Surgical vs. nonsurgical treatment of empyema: an outcomes analysis. Am J Med Sci. 2003;326:9-14.

158. Franco M, Musher DM. Thoracic empyema: The impact of management on outcome (Abstract). Am Rev Respir Dis. 1982;124:82.

159. Barker JH, Musher DM, Silberman R, et al. Genetic relatedness among nontypeable pneumococci implicated in sporadic cases of conjunctivitis. J Clin Microbiol. 1999;37:4039-4041.

160. Martin M, Turco JH, Zegans ME, et al. An outbreak of conjunctivitis due to atypical *Streptococcus pneumoniae*. N Engl J Med. 2003;348:1112-1121.

161. Dugi DD 3rd, Musher DM, Clarridge JE 3rd, Kimbrough R. Intraabdominal infection due to *Streptococcus pneumoniae*. Medicine (Baltimore). 2001;80:236-244.

162. Westh H, Skibsted L, Korner B. *Streptococcus pneumoniae* infections of the female genital tract and in the newborn child. Rev Infect Dis. 1990;12:416-422.

163. Robinson ENJ. Pneumococcal endometritis and neonatal sepsis. Rev Infect Dis. 1990;12:416-422.

164. Rahav G, Ben-David L, Persitz E. Postmenopausal pneumococcal tubo-ovarian abscess. Rev Infect Dis. 1991;13:896-897.

165. Powderly WG, Stanley SL Jr, Medoff G. Pneumococcal endocarditis: Report of a series and review of the literature. Rev Infect Dis. 1986;8:786-791.

166. Lindberg J, Prag J, Schonheyder HC. Pneumococcal endocarditis is not just a disease of the past: An analysis of 16 cases diagnosed in Denmark 1986-1997. Scand J Infect Dis. 1998;30:469-472.

167. Case Records of the Massachusetts General Hospital. Weekly clinicopathological exercises. Case 49-1990. A 47-year-old Cape Verdean man with pericardial disease. N Engl J Med. 1990;323.

168. Ross JJ, Saltzman CL, Carling P, Shapiro DS. Pneumococcal septic arthritis: Review of 190 cases. Clin Infect Dis. 2003;36:319-327.

169. Ryczak M, Sands M, Brown RB, Sklar JH. Pneumococcal arthritis in a prosthetic knee. A case report and review of the literature. Clin Orthop. 1987:224-227.

170. Morley PK, Hull RG, Hall MA. Pneumococcal septic arthritis in rheumatoid arthritis. Ann Rheum Dis. 1987;46:482-484.

171. Turner DP, Weston VC, Ispahani P. *Streptococcus pneumoniae* spinal infection in Nottingham, United Kingdom: not a rare event. Clin Infect Dis. 1999;28:873-881.

172. Grigoriadis E, Gold WL. Pyogenic brain abscess caused by *Streptococcus pneumoniae*: Case report and review. Clin Infect Dis. 1997;25.

173. Peters NS, Eykyn SJ, Rudd AG. Pneumococcal cellulitis: A rare manifestation of pneumococcaemia in adults. J Infect. 1989;19:57-59.

174. DiNubile MJ, Albornoz MA, Stumacher RJ, et al. Pneumococcal soft-tissue infections: Possible association with connective tissue diseases. J Infect Dis. 1991;163:897-900.

175. Spika JS, Facklam RR, Plikaytis BD, Oxtoby MJ. Antimicrobial resistance of *Streptococcus pneumoniae* in the United States, 1979-1987. The Pneumococcal Surveillance Working Group. J Infect Dis. 1991;163:1273-1278.

176. Appelbaum PC. Antimicrobial resistance in *Streptococcus pneumoniae:* An overview. Clin Infect Dis. 1992;15.

177. Doern GV, Pfaller MA, Kugler K, et al. Prevalence of antimicrobial resistance among respiratory tract isolates of *Streptococcus pneumoniae* in North America: 1997 results from the SENTRY antimicrobial surveillance program. Clin Infect Dis. 1998;27: 764-770.

178. Musher DM. Antibiotic resistance of *Streptococcus pneumoniae:* Beta-lactam antibiotics. In: Rose BD, ed. Uptodate, 2003.

179. Musher DM. Antibiotic resistance of *Streptococcus pneumoniae:* Macrolides, lincosamines and ketolides. In: Rose BD, ed. Uptodate, 2003.

180. Musher DM. Antibiotic resistance of *Streptococcus pneumoniae:* Fluoroquinolones, doxycycline and trimethoprim/sulfamethoxazole. In: Rose BD, ed. Uptodate, 2003.

181. Musher DM, Bartlett JG, Doern GV. A fresh look at the definition of susceptibility of *Streptococcus pneumoniae* to beta-lactam antibiotics. Arch Intern Med. 2001;161:2538-2544.

182. Smith AM, Klugman KP. Alterations in penicillin-binding protein 2B from penicillin-resistant wild-type strains of *Streptococcus pneumoniae.* Antimicrob Agents Chemother. 1995;39.

183. Smith AM, Klugman KP, Coffey TJ, Spratt BG. Genetic diversity of penicillin-binding protein 2B and 2X genes from *Streptococcus pneumoniae* in South Africa. Antimicrob Agents Chemother. 1993;37:1938-1944.

184. Dowson CG, Coffey TJ, Kell C, Whiley RA. Evolution of penicillin resistance in *Streptococcus pneumoniae;*the role of Streptococcus mitis in the formation of a low affinity PBP2B in S. pneumoniae. Mol Microbiol. 1993;9:635-643.

185. Versalovic J, Kapur V, Mason EO Jr, et al. Penicillin-resistant *Streptococcus pneumoniae* strains recovered in Houston: Identification and molecular characterization of multiple clones. J Infect Dis. 1993;167:850-856.

186. McDougal LK, Rasheed JK, Biddle JW, Tenover FC. Identification of multiple clones of extended-spectrum cephalosporin-resistant *Streptococcus pneumoniae* isolates in the United States. Antimicrob Agents Chemother. 1995;39:2282-2288.

187. Tomasz A. Antibiotic resistance in *Streptococcus pneumoniae.* Clin Infect Dis. 1997;24(Suppl 1):S85-88.

188. Soares S, Kristinsson KG, Musser JM, Tomasz A. Evidence for the introduction of a multiresistant clone of serotype 6B *Streptococcus pneumoniae* from Spain to Iceland in the late l980's. J Infect Dis. 1993;168:158-163.

189. Richter SS, Heilmann KP, Coffman SL, et al. The molecular epidemiology of penicillin-resistant *Streptococcus pneumoniae* in the United States, 1994-2000. Clin Infect Dis. 2002;34:330-339.

190. Overweg K, Bogaert D, Sluijter M, et al. Molecular characteristics of penicillin-binding protein genes of penicillin-nonsusceptible *Streptococcus pneumoniae* isolated in the Netherlands. Microb Drug Resist. 2001;7:323-334.

191. Musher DM, Dowell ME, Shortridge VD, et al. Emergence of macrolide resistance during treatment of pneumococcal pneumonia. N Engl J Med. 2002;346:630-631.

192. Whitney CG, Farley MM, Hadler J, et al. Increasing prevalence of multidrug-resistant *Streptococcus pneumoniae* in the United States. N Engl J Med. 2000;343:1917-1924.

193. Thornsberry C, Sahm DF, Kelly LJ, et al. Regional trends in antimicrobial resistance among clinical isolates of *Streptococcus pneumoniae, Haemophilus influenzae,* and *Moraxella catarrhalis* in the United States: Results from the TRUST Surveillance Program, 1999-2000. Clin Infect Dis. 2002;34(Suppl 1):S4-S16.

194. Karlowsky JA, Thornsberry C, Jones ME, et al. Factors associated with relative rates of antimicrobial resistance among *Streptococcus pneumoniae* in the United States: Results from the TRUST Surveillance Program (1998-2002). Clin Infect Dis. 2003;36:963-970.

195. Harbarth S, Albrich W, Brun-Buisson C. Outpatient antibiotic use and prevalence of antibiotic-resistant pneumococci in France and Germany: A sociocultural perspective. Emerg Infect Dis. 2002;8:1460-1467.

196. Overweg K, Bogaert D, Sluijter M, et al. Genetic relatedness within serotypes of penicillin-susceptible *Streptococcus pneumoniae* isolates. J Clin Microbiol. 2000;38:4548-4553.

197. Chen DK, McGeer A, de Azavedo JC, Low DE. Decreased susceptibility of *Streptococcus pneumoniae* to fluoroquinolones in Canada. Canadian Bacterial Surveillance Network. N Engl J Med. 1999;341:233-239.

198. Weiss K, Restieri C, Gauthier R, et al. A nosocomial outbreak of fluoroquinolone-resistant *Streptococcus pneumoniae.* Clin Infect Dis. 2001;33:517-522.

199. Kupronis BA, Richards C, Whitney CG. Invasive pneumococcal disease among the elderly residing in long-term care facilities and community-living elderly. J Am Geriatr Soc. 2003;51:1520-1525.

200. Dagan R, Johnson CE, McLinn S, et al. Bacteriologic and clinical efficacy of amoxicillin/clavulanate vs. azithromycin in acute otitis media. Pediatr Infect Dis J. 2000;19:95-104.

201. Piglansky L, Leibovitz E, Raiz S, et al. Bacteriologic and clinical efficacy of high dose amoxicillin for therapy of acute otitis media in children. Pediatr Infect Dis J. 2003;22:405-413.

202. Dagan R, Abramson O, Leibovitz E, et al. Bacteriologic response to oral cephalosporins: Are established susceptibility breakpoints appropriate in the case of acute otitis media? J Infect Dis. 1997;176:1253-1259.

203. Hendrickse WA, Kusmiesz H, Shelton S, Nelson JD. Five vs. ten days of therapy for acute otitis media. Pediatr Infect Dis J. 1988;7:14-23.

204. Leibovitz E, Piglansky L, Raiz S, et al. Bacteriologic and clinical efficacy of one day vs. three day intramuscular ceftriaxone for treatment of nonresponsive acute otitis media in children. Pediatr Infect Dis J. 2000;19:1040-1045.

205. Antimicrobial treatment guidelines for acute bacterial rhinosinusitis. Otolaryngol Head Neck Surg. 2000;123:S1-S132.

206. Hickner JM, Bartlett JG, Besser RE, et al. Principles of appropriate antibiotic use for acute rhinosinusitis in adults: Background. Ann Emerg Med. 2001;37:703-710.

207. Snow V, Mottur-Pilson C, Hickner JM. Principles of appropriate antibiotic use for acute sinusitis in adults. Ann Intern Med. 2001;134:495-497.

208. Gleason PP, Kapoor WN, Stone RA, et al. Medical outcomes and antimicrobial costs with the use of the American Thoracic Society guidelines for outpatients with community-acquired pneumonia. JAMA. 1997;278:32-39.

209. Fine MJ, Auble TE, Yealy DM, et al. A prediction rule to identify low-risk patients with community-acquired pneumonia. N Engl J Med. 1997;336:243-250.

210. Lonks JR, Garau J, Gomez L, et al. Failure of macrolide antibiotic treatment in patients with bacteremia due to erythromycin-resistant *Streptococcus pneumoniae.* Clin Infect Dis. 2002;35:556-564.

211. Bartlett JG, Dowell SF, Mandell LA, et al. Practice guidelines for the management of community-acquired pneumonia in adults. Clin Infect Dis. 2000;31:347-382.

212. Niederman MS, Mandell LA, Anzueto A, et al. Guidelines for the management of adults with community-acquired pneumonia. Diagnosis, assessment of severity, antimicrobial therapy, and prevention. Am J Respir Crit Care Med. 2001;163:1730-1754.

213. Clinical policy for management and risk stratification of community-acquired pneumonia in adults in the emergency department. Ann Emerg Med. 2001;38:107-113.

214. Mandell LA, Bartlett JG, Dowell SF, et al. Update of practice guidelines for the management of community-acquired pneumonia in immunocompetent adults. Clin Infect Dis. 2003;37:1405-1433.

215. Feikin DR, Schuchat A, Kolczak M, et al. Mortality from invasive pneumococcal pneumonia in the era of antibiotic resistance, 1995-1997. Am J Publ Health. 2000;90:223-229.

216. Friedland IR, Paris M, Shelton S, McCracken GH. Time-kill studies of antibiotic combinations against penicillin-resistant and -susceptible *Streptococcus pneumoniae.* J Antimicrob Chemother. 1994;34:231-237.

217. Paris MM, Hickey SM, Uscher MI, et al. Effect of dexamethasone on therapy of experimental penicillin- and cephalosporin-resistant pneumococcal meningitis. Antimicrob Agents Chemother. 1994;38:1320-1324.

218. Giron KP, Gross ME, Musher DM, et al. In vitro antimicrobial effect against *Streptococcus pneumoniae* of adding rifampin to penicillin, ceftriaxone, or 1-ofloxacin. Antimicrob Agents Chemother. 1995;39:2798-800.

219. de Gans J, van de Beek D. Dexamethasone in adults with bacterial meningitis. N Engl J Med. 2002;347:1549-1556.

220. Scheld WM. Drug delivery to the central nervous system: General principles and relevance to therapy for infections of the central nervous system. Rev Infect Dis. 1989;11(Suppl 7):S1669-690.

221. Cabellos C, Martinez-Lacasa J, Martos A, et al. Influence of dexamethasone on efficacy of ceftriaxone and vancomycin therapy in experimental pneumococcal meningitis. Antimicrob Agents Chemother. 1995;39:2158-2160.

222. Ahmed A, Jafri H, Lutsar I, et al. Pharmacodynamics of vancomycin for the treatment of experimental penicillin- and cephalosporin-resistant pneumococcal meningitis. Antimicrob Agents Chemother. 1999;43:876-881.

223. Gross ME, Giron KP, Septimus JD, et al. Antimicrobial activities of beta-lactam antibiotics and gentamicin against penicillin-susceptible and penicillin-resistant pneumococci. Antimicrob Agents Chemother. 1995;39:1166-1168.

224. Kehrl JH, Fauci AS. Activation of human B lymphocytes after immunization with pneumococcal polysaccharides. J Clin Invest. 1983;71:1032-1040.

225. Musher DM, Groover JE, Watson DA, et al. IgG responses to protein-conjugated pneumococcal capsular polysaccharides in persons who are genetically incapable of responding to unconjugated polysaccharides. Clin Infect Dis. 1998;27:1487-1490.

226. Musher DM, Groover JE, Graviss EA, Baughn RE. The lack of association between aging and postvaccination levels of IgG antibody to capsular polysaccharides of *Streptococcus pneumoniae.* Clin Infect Dis. 1996;22:165-167.

227. Romero-Steiner S, Musher DM, Cetron MS, et al. Reduction in functional antibody activity against *Streptococcus pneumoniae* in vaccinated elderly individuals highly correlates with decreased IgG antibody avidity. Clin Infect Dis. 1999;29:281-288.

228. Janoff EN, Breiman RF, Daley CL, Hopewell PC. Pneumococcal disease during HIV infection. Epidemiologic, clinical, and immunologic perspectives. Ann Intern Med. 1992;117:314-324.

229. Austrian R, Douglas RM, Schiffman G, et al. Prevention of pneumococcal pneumonia by vaccination. Trans Assoc Am Phys. 1976;89:184-194.

230. Austrian R. Some observations on the pneumococcus and on the current status of pneumococcal disease and its prevention. Rev Infect Dis. 1981;3(Suppl).

231. Gaillat J, Zmirou D, Mallaret MR, et al. [Clinical trial of an antipneumococcal vaccine in elderly subjects living in institutions]. Rev Epidemiol Sante Publique. 1985;33:437-444.

232. Koivula I, Sten M, Leinonen M, Makela PH. Clinical efficacy of pneumococcal vaccine in the elderly: A randomized, single-blind population-based trial. Am J Med. 1997;103:281-290.

233. Bentley DW. Pneumococcal vaccine in the institutionalized elderly: Review of past and recent studies. Rev Infect Dis. 1981;3(Suppl):S61-70.

234. Bentley DW, Ha K, Mamot K, et al. Pneumococcal vaccine in the institutionalized elderly: Design of a nonrandomized trial and preliminary results. Rev Infect Dis. 1981;3(Suppl):S71-81.

235. Simberkoff MS, Cross AP, Al-Ibrahim M, et al. Efficacy of pneumococcal vaccine in high-risk patients. Results of a Veterans Administration Cooperative Study. N Engl J Med. 1986;315:1318-1327.

236. Ortqvist A, Hedlund J, Burman LA, et al. Randomised trial of 23-valent pneumococcal capsular polysaccharide vaccine in prevention of pneumonia in middle-aged and elderly people. Swedish Pneumococcal Vaccination Study Group. Lancet. 1998;351:399-403.

237. Bolan G, Broome CV, Facklam RR, et al. Pneumococcal vaccine efficacy in selected populations in the United States. Ann Intern Med. 1986;104:1-6.
238. Jackson LA, Neuzil KM, Yu O, et al. Effectiveness of pneumococcal polysaccharide vaccine in older adults. N Engl J Med. 2003;348:1747-1755.
239. Sims RV, Steinmann WC, McConville JH, et al. The clinical effectiveness of pneumococcal vaccine in the elderly. Ann Intern Med. 1988;108:653-657.
240. Shapiro ED, Berg AT, Austrian R, et al. The protective efficacy of polyvalent pneumococcal polysaccharide vaccine. N Engl J Med. 1991;325:1453-1460.
241. Farr BM, Johnston BL, Cobb DK, et al. Preventing pneumococcal bacteremia in patients at risk. Results of a matched case-control study. Arch Intern Med 1995;155:2336-2340.
242. Rubins JB, Puri AK, Loch J, et al. Magnitude, duration, quality, and function of pneumococcal vaccine responses in elderly adults. J Infect Dis. 1998;178:431-440.
243. Musher DM, Phan HM, Watson DA, Baughn RE. Antibody to capsular polysaccharide of *Streptococcus pneumoniae* at the time of hospital admission for pneumococcal pneumonia. J Infect Dis. 2000;182:158-167.
244. Fedson DS. Influenza and pneumococcal vaccination in Canada and the United States, 1980-1993: What can the two countries learn from each other? Clin Infect Dis. 1995;20:1371-1376.
245. Centers for Disease Control and Prevention. Prevention of pneumococcal disease: Recommendations of the Advisory Committee on Immunization Practices (ACIP). MMWR Morb Mortal Wkly Rep. 1997;46:1-18.
246. Black S, Shinefield H, Fireman B, et al. Efficacy, safety and immunogenicity of heptavalent pneumococcal conjugate vaccine in children. Northern California Kaiser Permanente Vaccine Study Center Group. Pediatr Infect Dis J. 2000;19:187-195.
247. Fireman B, Black SB, Shinefield HR, et al. Impact of the pneumococcal conjugate vaccine on otitis media. Pediatr Infect Dis J. 2003;22:10-16.
248. Black SB, Shinefield HR, Ling S, et al. Effectiveness of heptavalent pneumococcal conjugate vaccine in children younger than five years of age for prevention of pneumonia. Pediatr Infect Dis J. 2002;21:810-815.
249. Dagan R, Givon-Lavi N, Zamir O, et al. Reduction of nasopharyngeal carriage of *Streptococcus pneumoniae* after administration of a 9-valent pneumococcal conjugate vaccine to toddlers attending day care centers. J Infect Dis. 2002;185:927-936.
250. Powers DC, Anderson EL, Lottenbach K, Mink CM. Reactogenicity and immunogenicity of a protein-conjugated pneumococcal oligosaccharide vaccine in older adults. J Infect Dis. 1996;173:1014-1018.
251. Shelly MA, Jacoby H, Riley GJ, et al. Comparison of pneumococcal polysaccharide and CRM197-conjugated pneumococcal oligosaccharide vaccines in young and elderly adults. Infect Immun. 1997;65:242-247.
252. Chan CY, Molrine DC, George S, et al. Pneumococcal conjugate vaccine primes for antibody responses to polysaccharide pneumococcal vaccine after treatment of Hodgkin's disease. J Infect Dis. 1996;173:256-258.
253. Feikin DR, Elie CM, Goetz MB, et al. Randomized trial of the quantitative and functional antibody responses to a 7-valent pneumococcal conjugate vaccine and/or 23-valent polysaccharide vaccine among HIV-infected adults. Vaccine. 2001;20:545-553.
254. The National Institute of Child Health and Human Development Intravenous Immunoglobulin Study Group. Intravenous immune globulin for the prevention of bacterial infections in children with symptomatic human immunodeficiency virus infection. N Engl J Med. 1991;325:73-80.
255. Weeks JC, Tierney MR, Weinstein MC. Cost effectiveness of prophylactic intravenous immune globulin in chronic lymphocytic leukemia. N Engl J Med. 1991;325:81-86.

CHAPTER **198**

Enterococcus Species, *Streptococcus bovis*, and *Leuconostoc* Species

ROBERT C. MOELLERING, JR.

ENTEROCOCCUS SPECIES

General Clinical Microbiology

Enterococci are gram-positive cocci that occur in singles, pairs, and short chains. As such they are difficult to distinguish morphologically from true streptococci, and until recently they were actually classified as streptococci.[1] In the Lancefield classification scheme, enterococci were included among the group D streptococci, which contained both enterococcal and nonenterococcal species.[2] The nonenterococcal

TABLE 198-1 Enterococcal Species	
E. faecalis	*E. gallinarum*
E. faecium	*E. hirae*
E. durans	*E. mundtii*
E. avium	*E. raffinosus*
E. casseliflavus	*E. solitarius*
E. malodoratus	*E. pseudoavium*

species such as *Streptococcus bovis* and *Streptococcus equinus* remain classified as true streptococci. In the 1980s, however, it was shown that enterococci differ sufficiently from streptococci that they have been classified in their own genus, *Enterococcus,* which contains at least 12 species (Table 198-1).[3,4] This classification scheme is constantly being modified, and more recent data cast doubt on the validity of including *Enterococcus solitarius* as a major enterococcal species.[5] In addition, a number of other species have recently been proposed, including *E. cecorum, E. columbae, E. saccharolyticus, E. dispar, E. sulfureus, E. seriolicida,* and *E. flavescens.*[5]

Enterococci are facultative anaerobes that are able to grow under rather extreme conditions. Thus they are able to grow in 6.5% NaCl at pH 9.6 and at temperatures ranging from 10° C to 45° C. Many can survive 30 minutes at 60° C, and they grow in the presence of 40% bile salts. They hydrolyze esculin and L-pyrrolidonyl-β-naphthylamide (PYR).[4-6]

Most clinical isolates of enterococci are *E. faecalis,* which until recently accounted for 80% to 90% of the organisms encountered in the clinical microbiology laboratory.[7] *Enterococcus faecium* accounted for 5% to 10% of isolates. More recent evidence suggests that the prevalence of *E. faecium,* especially multiresistant strains, is increasing in a number of hospital centers. In the United States the increase in vancomycin resistance in *E. faecium* has been a major contributor to the increased prevalence of this organism; and in a recent study, *E. faecium* accounted for 37% of cases of enterococcal bacteremia.[8] Occasional isolates of *E. durans, E. avium, E. casseliflavus, E. gallinarum, E. raffinosus,* and *E. hirae* are encountered clinically.[7]

Enterococci occur in a remarkable array of environments, because of their ability to grow and survive under harsh conditions. Thus they can be found in soil, food, water, and a wide variety of living animals. The major habitat of these organisms appears to be the gastrointestinal tract of humans and of other animals, where they make up a significant portion of the normal gut flora.[4,5] Most enterococci isolated from human stools are *E. faecalis,* although *E. faecium* is also commonly found in the gastrointestinal tract of humans.[9] Small numbers of enterococci are occasionally found in oropharyngeal secretions, vaginal secretions, and on the skin, especially in the perineal area.

Pathogenicity and Virulence

Until recently, surprisingly little was known about the factors that contribute to the ability of enterococci to cause infections in humans. Studies have documented high mortality rates (42% to 68%) in patients with enterococcal bacteremia, but they have nonetheless failed to establish unequivocally the pathogenicity of the causative organism in this setting.[10] The reason is that because most of the patients in these described series have been severely debilitated, raising the possibility that the enterococcal bacteremia was merely a marker of this state and not the proximate cause of death in these patients. In many cases, enterococci are part of a polymicrobial bacteremia, and their independent contribution to morbidity and mortality is thus difficult to assess. Despite these difficulties, several epidemiologic studies have determined an attributed mortality of 31% to 37% in patients with enterococcal bacteremia and vancomycin resistance has been suggested to be an independent predictor of mortality, although this has not been shown in all studies of vancomycin-resistant enterococci (VRE) bacteremia.[8,11,12,13] What is clear is that enterococci are not as intrinsically virulent as organisms such as *Staphylococcus aureus* and *Streptococcus pyogenes.* They do not secrete exotoxins or produce superantigens.

Even though most enterococci do not have classic virulence factors, the resistance of enterococci to multiple antimicrobial agents allows them to survive and proliferate in patients receiving antimicrobial chemotherapy.[14,15] This almost certainly accounts for their ability to cause superinfections in patients receiving a number of different broad-spectrum antimicrobial agents. Although they are capable of colonizing the oropharynx, enterococci rarely cause lower respiratory tract infections. Enterococci are able to adhere to heart valves and renal epithelial cells, properties that undoubtedly contribute to their ability to cause endocarditis and urinary tract infections.[16] Several extracellular molecules likely play important roles in colonization and adherence. There is some evidence that the aggregation substance produced in pheromone-responsive strains may contribute to their ability to adhere to renal epithelial cells.[17] A second extracellular surface protein (designated the Esp protein) appears to play an important role in colonization and infection of humans with enterococci.[18] Infection-derived strains of enterococci are enriched for the *esp* genes encoding Esp protein and the expression of these genes may determine ability of enterococci from animals to colonize and cause disease in humans.[18-21]

A recently discovered quorum-sensing system encoded by the *fsr* locus in *E. faecalis* has been shown to regulate the transcription of genes responsible for the production of extracellular serine protease and gelatinase (GelE) and is associated with enhanced enterococcal virulence.[22,23] The GelE protease may enhance virulence by aiding in the dissemination of *E. faecalis* in high-density environments.[24] Biofilm production in *E. faecalis* is also regulated by the *fsr* locus and may play an important role in the ability of these organisms to colonize and infect urinary and vascular catheters and to colonize heart valves.[19] Several investigators have suggested that plasmid-mediated hemolysins secreted by some strains of *E. faecalis* may contribute to virulence in animals and humans.[25,26] However, the ultimate role of hemolysin production in enterococcal pathogenicity in humans remains to be determined. There is little evidence that antibodies play a significant role in defense against enterococcal infections in humans, but this area needs further study before definitive conclusions can be reached. Although enterococci are natural inhabitants of the gastrointestinal tract, they are not known to cause gastroenteritis in humans with the single possible exception of a strain of *E. hirae* (isolated from a patient with diarrhea) that did cause diarrhea in suckling rats.[27]

Enterococci are commonly found in cultures of intra-abdominal and pelvic infections. Despite extensive study, their role in this setting has not been fully defined, but it is clear that a complex set of interactions among various bacteria occur in this setting and that the growth of enterococci is often facilitated by the presence of other organisms or products of other organisms, such as *Bacteroides fragilis,*[27] and it has been suggested that enterococci act synergistically with other bacteria in intra-abdominal sepsis to enhance morbidity or mortality,[28] but the exact role played by enterococci in this setting remains to be fully delineated.[29,30]

Epidemiology

Because they are part of the normal gut flora of almost all humans, enterococci are capable of causing infections both in and out of the hospital setting, and it was previously thought that most infections due to these organisms were endogenously acquired from the patient's own flora.[31] Most enterococcal infections, however, occur in hospitalized patients or in patients undergoing therapy such as peritoneal or hemodialysis, and the organisms causing such infections often appear to be exogenously acquired. There is clear-cut evidence for the spread of strains of enterococci between patients and even the dissemination of such strains from one institution to another.[32-35] Strains of enterococci causing nosocomial infections have occasionally been found on the hands of medical personnel and have frequently been isolated from environmental sources in hospitals and nursing homes, and patients in nursing homes have been shown to be a significant reservoir of stool carriage of VRE.[34,36,37] The importance of these findings is difficult to assess, because the environment may simply have been passively contaminated by stool or urine from infected patients.[34] In fact, studies

suggest that with the exception of drug-addicted persons, direct cross-infection is rare.[38,39] Instead, it appears that resistant organisms from patients or hospital personnel first colonized the gastrointestinal tract, or occasionally the skin and groin or other contiguous areas, before causing infections in patients.[40] Moreover, there is evidence that hospital personnel harboring resistant enterococci in their own gastrointestinal tracts may be responsible for colonization of patients under their care.[40] Once colonized with resistant enterococci, patients may carry them in their gastrointestinal tract for months or even years.[41] In addition, devices such as electronic thermometers may also aid in the spread of resistant organisms.[42]

Currently, enterococci rank second or third in frequency as causes of nosocomial infections in the United States.[43] Risk factors for acquiring nosocomial enterococcal infections include gastrointestinal colonization; serious underlying disease; a long hospital stay; prior surgery; renal insufficiency; neutropenia; transplantation, especially liver and bone marrow; the presence of urinary or vascular catheters; and residency in an intensive care unit.[43-46] Prior antibiotic therapy, especially with vancomycin, cephalosporins, or aminoglycosides, is also a major risk factor for the acquisition of vancomycin-resistant and other multiple-drug-resistant enterococci.[31,36,44-49] Other antimicrobial agents, including aztreonam, imipenem, and ciprofloxacin, have been associated with nosocomial enterococcal infections.[44,50,52] Antimicrobials with activity against anaerobic bacteria seem to potentiate stool colonization with VRE.[53] Enterococci have caused a cluster of cases of endocarditis in Cleveland, Ohio, but the source of this infection was not defined, and there have been no subsequent reports of this phenomenon.[54] Until recently enterococcal bacteremia appeared to be a surprisingly unusual complication of cancer or hematologic malignancy, and when it did occur in this setting, it appeared to be a marker of cytotoxic drug damage to the mucosa of the gastrointestinal tract, rather than an invasive infection in the usual sense, and most cases subsided spontaneously or rapidly responded to therapy.[55] The advent of VRE appears to have changed this paradigm. In addition to a high prevalence of bacteremias and invasive infections in bone marrow transplant patients, other patients with malignancies also appear to be at significant risk of VRE infections.[56] Therapeutic and prophylactic use of vancomycin is a major risk factor of both gastrointestinal colonization and bacteremia in this setting. Indeed, extensive vancomycin use in a bone marrow transplant unit has led to an outbreak of infection with vancomycin-dependent enterococci.[57]

Clinical Infections

Urinary Tract Infections

Urinary tract infections are the most common type of clinical disease produced by enterococci, and urine cultures are the most frequent sources of enterococci in the clinical microbiology laboratory.[58] In addition to uncomplicated cystitis or pyelonephritis, or both, enterococci have also been shown to cause prostatitis and perinephric abscess.[4,59] Most enterococcal urinary tract infections are nosocomial and are associated with urinary catheterization or instrumentation, or both.[60,61] There is strong evidence to suggest that the prevalence of nosocomial enterococcal urinary tract infections is increasing in a number of hospitals.[43,60] In contrast, enterococci only rarely cause infections such as uncomplicated cystitis in nonhospitalized women. Bacteremia is a relatively rare complication of enterococcal urinary tract infections.[62]

Bacteremia and Endocarditis

Most cases of enterococcal bacteremia are not associated with endocarditis. Indeed, only about 1 out of 50 cases of enterococcal bacteremia results in endocarditis (R. C. Moellering, Jr., unpublished data). Endocarditis is much more commonly seen in patients whose bacteremia is community acquired than in those with nosocomial enterococcal bacteremia.[63] Nosocomial enterococcal bacteremias are commonly polymicrobial, and in this setting endocarditis appears even less likely.[63] As is true with enterococcal infections in general, nosocomial bacteremias due to these organisms appear to be increasing in a number of institutions.[63,64] Portals of entry for enterococcal bacteremia include the urinary tract; intra-abdominal or pelvic sepsis; wounds especially thermal burns, decubitus ulcers, or diabetic foot infections; intravenous or intra-arterial catheters; or cholangitis, in roughly that descending order.[58,63-65] The respiratory tract is an exceedingly rare portal of entry for enterococcal bacteremia.[63] Increasingly, there are reports of "primary enterococcal bacteremia" in patients with severe underlying illness, usually associated with immunosuppression. These bacteremias are usually monomicrobial and come from a presumed gastrointestinal source.[66] Although enterococcal bacteremia can be associated with septic shock or disseminated intravascular coagulation, these complications are rare in pure enterococcal bacteremia, and when they do occur, they are often the result of accompanying gram-negative bacilli in polymicrobial bacteremias.[63] Metastatic infections (other than endocarditis) are rare in enterococcal bacteremia.[67] As noted earlier, the mortality rate in patients with enterococcal bacteremia is high, but this is because enterococcal bacteremia commonly occurs in debilitated patients, and the exact role of the bacteremia in their deaths is often difficult to define. Indeed, although enterococcal bacteremias are often transient and self limited, there is evidence that treatment with appropriate regimens is associated with an improved outcome.[67,68]

Enterococci account for approximately 5% to 15% of all cases in most series of infective endocarditis.[4,69] Most are caused by *E. faecalis,* but *E. faecium, E. avium, E. casseliflavus, E. durans, E. gallinarum,* and *E. raffinosus* have also been isolated from patients with a presumed diagnosis of endocarditis.[70-72] Enterococcal endocarditis is increasingly a disease of older patients, with men outnumbering women in most series.[4,69,73,74] Most cases occur in patients with underlying valvular heart disease or prosthetic valves, but *Enterococcus* is capable of causing infections of anatomically normal valves as well.[4,73] Enterococcal prosthetic valve endocarditis is increasing in prevalence, and in one series the prevalence of enterococcal prosthetic valve endocarditis nearly approximated that of native valve endocarditis.[73] Although studies have suggested an association between enterococcal endocarditis and urinary tract infection or urinary instrumentation in older men and abortion or childbirth in younger women, the latter has not been seen in more recent series.[69,73,75-77] The gastrointestinal tract often serves as the portal of entry for enterococci, although the association between gastrointestinal malignancy and enterococcal bacteremia is not as strong as that for *S. bovis* bacteremia.[73] Enterococci usually produce left-sided endocarditis with more frequent involvement of the mitral than the aortic valve, even in drug addicted patients.[4,54,69,77] There is a suggestion that patients with aortic valve involvement require surgical intervention more frequently than those with mitral valve endocarditis.[73] Enterococci usually produce a clinical course consistent with subacute bacterial endocarditis; the clinical picture in this setting is unremarkable and basically indistinguishable from that caused by viridans streptococci or *S. bovis.*[4,69,77] Acute bacterial endocarditis due to enterococci is seen in some patients, but it is a less frequent presentation.[77] Because the disease process is an indolent one, some patients have symptoms for a prolonged time before seeking medical care. There is a suggestion that the relapse rate is higher in patients who have had symptoms of endocarditis for more than 3 months before treatment.[78] Impaired renal function occurs with relatively high frequency in the course of enterococcal endocarditis, but this is probably related to the fact that most patients with this disease are treated with nephrotoxic agents including aminoglycosides or vancomycin, or both.[73]

Intra-abdominal and Pelvic Infections

Enterococci are frequently found as part of a mixed aerobic and anaerobic flora in intra-abdominal and pelvic infections. Their role in these settings has been questioned, especially because they seem to cause bacteremia less frequently than *Escherichia coli* or *Bacteroides* spp. when present in mixed abdominal or pelvic infections.[30,79,80] It has also been noted that treatment with antimicrobial regimens devoid of activity against *Enterococcus* can cure such infections.[79,81] However, although antimicrobial combinations such as clindamycin or metronidazole plus gentamicin may lack in vitro activity against enterococci, animal studies suggest that these regimens may have in vivo bacteriostatic activity against enterococci and may contribute to the successful therapeutic outcome noted previously.[82] Moreover, perioperative treatment with agents active against enterococci in trauma patients requiring abdominal exploration has been shown to decrease subsequent enterococcal wound infection.[83]

Although the exact role of enterococci in mixed intra-abdominal and pelvic infections remains murky, it is clear that these organisms can cause spontaneous peritonitis in patients with nephrotic syndrome or cirrhosis and can cause peritonitis in patients undergoing chronic ambulatory peritoneal dialysis.[4,84] "Pure" enterococcal peritonitis is also seen occasionally as a complication of abdominal surgery or trauma. These organisms can also produce abscesses and bacteremia as a complication of endometritis, cesarean section, or acute salpingitis.[65,85] The presence of enterococci in pure culture in the latter settings is, however, distinctly unusual.

Wound and Tissue Infections

Enterococci by themselves rarely, if ever, cause cellulitis or other deep tissue infections. They are frequently isolated from mixed cultures with gram-negative bacilli and anaerobes in surgical wound infections, decubitus ulcers, and diabetic foot infections, and in these cases, as is true for intra-abdominal and pelvic sepsis, their significance is difficult to assess.[86] On rare occasions, they may cause bacteremia from such a setting, but it is clear that they are not nearly as invasive as organisms such as *S. aureus.*[86] Enterococcal wound colonization and sepsis have been described in burn patients whose wounds were covered with porcine xenografts presumably contaminated with enterococci.[87] Enterococci have also occasionally been found in diabetic and nondiabetic patients with chronic osteomyelitis. In this setting, they are often of doubtful pathogenic significance, and when they are shown to be causes of infection by direct bone biopsy, it is likely that their presence is the result of superinfection and does not represent primary enterococcal osteomyelitis. The author has seen a case of enterococcal endophthalmitis in a diabetic patient who had enterococcal bacteremia from a diabetic foot infection several months after undergoing vitrectomy for diabetic retinopathy, again emphasizing that these organisms can be opportunistic pathogens in a variety of settings.

Meningitis

Enterococci rarely, if ever, cause meningitis in normal adults. Most cases of enterococcal meningitis occur in patients with anatomic defects of the central nervous system, prior neurosurgery, or head trauma.[88,89] Meningitis is a rare complication of high-grade bacteremia in patients with enterococcal endocarditis.[88] Meningitis also occasionally complicates enterococcal bacteremia in patients with severe immunodeficiencies including acquired immunodeficiency syndrome and acute leukemias. It is also seen in neonatal sepsis.[90] Enterococcal meningitis appears to be associated with low cerebrospinal fluid leukocyte counts (usually $<200/m^3$) in most, but not all, patients.[88,91]

Respiratory Tract Infections

Respiratory tract infections due to enterococci are exceedingly unusual. Although well-documented cases of enterococcal pneumonia and even lung abscess exist, they usually occur in patients with severe and debilitating diseases.[92,93] Broad-spectrum antimicrobial therapy, especially with cephalosporins, coupled with enteric feeding in severely debilitated patients has been the setting in which some of the rare cases of enterococcal pneumonia have been described.[92]

Neonatal Sepsis

Enterococci have clearly been documented to cause neonatal sepsis characterized by fever, lethargy, and respiratory difficulty accompanied by bacteremia or meningitis, or both.[90] Although early-onset bacteremia in otherwise normal neonates is characteristic of this disease,[91,95,96] several nosocomial outbreaks of bacteremia or meningitis,

TABLE 198-2 Antimicrobial Susceptibility of Enterococci

	Enterococcus faecalis		Enterococcus faecium	
Antimicrobial	MIC_{50} ($\mu g/mL$)	MIC_{90} ($\mu g/mL$)	MIC_{50} ($\mu g/mL$)	MIC_{90} ($\mu g/mL$)
Ampicillin	1	1	8	32
Penicillin	2	4	16	64
Piperacillin	2	4	16	64
Imipenem	2	2	16	32
Vancomycin	2	2	1	2
Teicoplanin	0.5	1	0.5	1
Tetracycline	>16	>16	>16	>16
Chloramphenicol	8	>16	4	16
Erythromycin	>256	>256	>256	>256
Ciprofloxacin	1	2	4	16
Linezolid	2	4	2	4
Quinupristin/ dalfopristin	4	16	0.5	4
Daptomycin	0.5	1	2	4

MIC, Minimal inhibitory concentration.

TABLE 198-3 Antimicrobial Resistance in Enterococci

Intrinsic resistance
 Aminoglycosidic aminocyclitols (low level)
 β-Lactams (relatively high MICs)
 Lincosamides (low level)
 Trimethoprim-sulfamethoxazole (in vivo only)
 Quinupristin/dalfopristin (*E. faecalis*)

Acquired resistance
 Aminoglycosidic aminocyclitols (high level)
 β-Lactams (altered PBPs)
 Cell wall-active agents (tolerance)
 Fluoroquinolones
 Lincosamides (high level)
 Macrolides
 Penicillin and ampicillin (β-lactamase)
 Rifampin
 Tetracyclines
 Vancomycin
 Quinupristin/dalfopristin
 Linezolid

MIC, Minimal inhibitory concentration; PBP, penicillin-binding protein.

or both, due to *E. faecium* or *E. faecalis* have been described in premature or low-birth-weight neonates who had nasogastric tubes and intravascular devices.[96,97] In general, neonates with enterococcal sepsis have responded well to appropriate antimicrobial therapy.[90,95]

Antimicrobial Susceptibility and Resistance

The most striking attribute of enterococci is the relative and absolute resistance of these organisms to a variety of antimicrobial agents commonly used to treat infections due to gram-positive organisms.[4,10,15] Susceptibility of enterococci to certain commonly used antimicrobial agents is shown in Table 198-2. The picture that is provided here is the result of both intrinsic and acquired resistance determinants in enterococci (Table 198-3).[98] Not only are these organisms intrinsically resistant to a large number of antimicrobial agents, but they also show a remarkable ability to acquire new mechanisms of resistance.[15] As a result, susceptibility patterns such as those given in Table 198-2 are subject to considerable temporal and geographic variation. In many hospitals in the United States, for example, there are much higher rates of resistance to ampicillin, penicillin, and vancomycin, especially among *E. faecium*, than depicted in the table. All enterococci, including those from antibiotic-virgin populations, exhibit relative resistance to β-lactam antimicrobial agents, which is caused by a diminished affinity of the lower-weight penicillin-binding proteins, especially PBP 5, of *E. faecalis* and *E. faecium* for penicillin, ampicillin, and other β-lactams including the cephalosporins.[99,100] In general, the cephalosporins, and especially the cephamycins, are less active against enterococci than the penicillins, and none of the cephalosporins available at present have clinically useful activity against enterococci. Although there has been little change in the intrinsic resistance of *E. faecalis* to the penicillins, there has been a striking increase in intrinsic resistance to the penicillins among *E. faecium*. Many isolates of these organisms in the United States and elsewhere are currently relatively and absolutely resistant to penicillin and ampicillin because of further alterations in PBP 5.[101] Intrinsic resistance to the aminoglycosides is caused by a decreased ability of these agents to penetrate through the outer cell envelope of enterococci, a phenomenon that can be overcome with the addition of an appropriate cell wall-active agent, resulting in synergistic killing of enterococci.[102] Although enterococci are susceptible to trimethoprim-sulfamethoxazole when tested under the proper conditions in vitro,[4] these organisms are able to use exogenous folinic acid, dihydrofolate, and tetrahydrofolate, and hence in vivo they circumvent the block in folate synthesis produced by trimethoprim-sulfamethoxazole. As a result, trimethoprim-sulfamethoxazole has been shown to fail in the therapy of enterococcal infections in both animal models and patients.[103-105]

In addition to their intrinsic resistance, enterococci have acquired new mechanisms of resistance to a wide variety of antimicrobial agents. Most of these resistance mechanisms are mediated by genes encoded on plasmids or transposons.[4] As subsequently described, enterococci have evolved a number of remarkably efficient methods of transferring resistance genes among themselves, and between themselves and other organisms, and this greatly facilitates their acquisition of new resistance determinants.[106] One important form of acquired resistance that does not appear to be plasmid or transposon mediated is tolerance to cell wall-active agents. Although enterococci from antibiotic-virgin populations exhibit the same relative resistance to the inhibitory effect of penicillins and cephalosporins (manifested by relatively high minimal inhibitory concentrations [MICs]) as strains from populations previously exposed to antimicrobials, enterococci without prior antibiotic exposure are killed (and lysed) by cell wall-active agents.[107] A relatively brief exposure to penicillin or other cell wall-active agents, however, results in the rapid acquisition of *tolerance*.[107] Because of the intrinsic resistance and tolerance of enterococci to antimicrobial agents that inhibit cell wall synthesis, combination therapy with cell wall-active agents plus aminoglycosides is currently the standard treatment for enterococcal infections such as endocarditis and meningitis, which require bactericidal therapy. High-level resistance (MICs greater than 500 to 2000 $\mu g/mL$) to aminoglycosidic aminocyclitol antimicrobial agents can be caused either by ribosomal mutation (for streptomycin only) or by the production of plasmid-mediated aminoglycoside-modifying enzymes.[4,106,108] Enterococci with high-level resistance to streptomycin and kanamycin have been relatively common, but high-level resistance to gentamicin has become a clinical problem only since the 1980s.[4,10,15] The most prevalent enzyme that mediates high-level gentamicin resistance (a fused 6′-acetytransferase-2′-phosphotransferase) also produces resistance to synergism with all other clinically useful aminoglycosides except streptomycin.[106] Enterococci that contain this gene as well as a 6-adenylyltransferase that modifies streptomycin are resistant to synergy by all combinations of cell wall-active agents and aminoglycosides.[15,106] Several other gentamicin-phosphorylating enzymes have been described. One, designated APH(2″)-Id, mediates high-level resistance to gentamicin, and the other, APH(2″)-Ic, mediates intermediate levels of resistance that may not be detected by the screening tests currently employed in most clinical microbiology laboratories.[109,110] Both enzymes eliminate β-lactam-gentamicin synergism. Fortunately, both enzymes are infrequently found at present. All strains of *E. faecium* produce a chromosomally mediated 6′-acetyltransferase that inactivates tobramycin, netilmicin, kanamycin, and sisomicin but that does not produce high-level resistance to these compounds.[111,112] Thus these agents should not be used, even in combination with cell wall-active agents, against *E. faecium*, because they do not result in enhanced killing of these organisms. *Enterococcus faecalis* and *E. faecium* with high-level resistance to all aminoglycosides are being seen with increased frequency throughout the world, and clinical failures and relapses after therapy in patients with endocarditis caused by these organisms are being increasingly encountered.[15,113] All enterococci from patients with endocarditis or meningitis should be subjected to high-level aminoglycoside testing to determine whether a synergistic aminoglycoside-containing combination should be employed therapeutically. Only time-kill tests for in vitro synergism will reveal the effects of the presence of the rare isolate containing APH(2″)-Ic.

VRE were first described in the late 1980s. Initially seen in Europe, these isolates have now begun to have a major impact in the United States as well.[15,114,115] A number of phenotypes of vancomycin resistance have been discovered. Strains exhibiting the VanA phenotype show high-level resistance to vancomycin and teicoplanin, and VanB strains exhibit moderate to high-level resistance to vancomycin but remain susceptible to teicoplanin. The genes for both these resistance phenotypes have been cloned and sequenced and have been shown to be transferable.[116-120] Vancomycin resistance of the VanA phenotype is the result of the production of a ligase with altered specificity that results in the synthesis of cell wall precursors ending in the depsipeptide D-alanyl-lactate rather than the dipeptide D-alanyl-D-alanine, which is the target for vancomycin.[116] Vancomycin resistance is the result of the inability of vancomycin to bind to the altered depsipeptide, which can nonetheless be cross-linked by enterococcal transpeptidases to form a normal cell wall and thus does not result in a selective disadvantage to the enterococci. Low levels of vancomycin resistance without teicoplanin resistance are also found in *E. gallinarum* (VanC) and *E. casseliflavus.*[121] The genes responsible for this appear to be chromosomally located and are not transferable.[116] A fourth vancomycin-resistance genotype, VanD, has been described in a strain of *E. faecium* that exhibited moderate levels of resistance to vancomycin and teicoplanin.[122,123] We have subsequently identified several additional strains from Boston exhibiting the VanD genotype, which is clearly different from the VanA, VanB, and VanC genotypes.[124] A fifth genotype, VanE, has also been described in *E. faecalis.*[125] The genes encoding this type of vancomycin resistance are more closely related to VanC than the other known genotypes in enterococci, which is consistent with the fact that, similar to VanC, the terminal dipeptides of these organisms consist of D-alanine-D-serine, rather than D-alanine-D-lactate. Strains of vancomycin-dependent enterococci have also been described. These organisms have a defect in their ligase gene (*ddl*) and must rely on acquired vancomycin-resistant ligases to survive.[126] It is possible that other genotypes will be discovered, but to date the most prevalent genes are those encoding VanA and VanB vancomycin resistance. The genes responsible for VanA, VanB, and VanD resistance are on transposable genetic elements that do not appear to have originated in enterococci. Although the exact source of these genes is not clear, the discovery of a *VanB* locus homologous to that in enterococci in *E. lenta* and *C. innocuum* raises the possibility that gastrointestinal anaerobes may be a source of these genetic elements.[127]

The problem of VREs has risen to alarming proportions since the problem was first reported in 1988. The percentage of nosocomial infections caused by VREs increased more than 20-fold between 1989 and 1993, rising from 0.3% to 7.9%.[128] The trend has continued. The Surveillance Network Database-USA, which obtains data from more than 100 clinical laboratories, found that 52% of 1482 isolates of *E. faecium* collected in 1997 were vancomycin resistant.[128] Resistance to vancomycin would be less of a concern were not 83% of the 1482 isolates also ampicillin resistant. The incidence of VREs in that year among *E. faecalis* was only 1.9% of 4364 isolates, illustrating the dramatic difference between these two species. Although hospitals vary, the incidence of VREs in intensive care units in the United States now generally exceeds 30% of enterococci, including all species. Factors predisposing to VRE colonization or infection include the percentage of hospital days receiving antimicrobial therapy, the use of intravenous vancomycin, severe underlying disease, immunosuppression, and abdominal surgery.[129] Transmission of VREs within institutions has been indicated by the appearance of predominant strains.[130] Evidence strongly suggests that the vehicle is the hands of medical personnel.[128] Colonization of a patient's gastrointestinal tract appears to precede infection in a given patient.

The Centers for Disease Control and Prevention has made a series of recommendations to help control the spread of VREs within hospitals.[129]

These include rapid identification of patients who are colonized or infected with VREs and placing them in a separate room or in a room with another VRE patient. All persons entering the room should wear gloves. In addition, those who will have substantial contact with the patient or environmental surfaces in the room should wear a gown. Noncritical items such as stethoscopes, thermometers, and sphygmomanometers should remain in the room. On leaving the room, personnel should remove the gown and gloves, and wash their hands thoroughly. Criteria should be established for allowing isolation to be terminated, such as three negative weekly stool cultures or rectal swabs. Anecdotal reports have suggested that oral bacitracin may help shorten the usual long period of colonization, but success has been modest at best and combinations of bacitracin and doxycycline have not been successful in eradicating enterococcal carriage in the GI tract.[131,132] Ramoplanin is an investigational agent that is being studied for suppression of VRE in the stool. Terminal cleaning and disinfection of the room should be thorough. Among the other recommendations of the Centers for Disease Control and Prevention were control measures to limit inappropriate vancomycin usage. Although these recommendations make sense intuitively, it has been difficult to demonstrate the value of certain of the measures, especially the use of masks and gowns in caring for patients with infections or gastrointestinal colonization caused by VRE.[133-136] The definitive answer remains to be determined.[137]

A strain of β-lactamase-producing *E. faecium* was initially found in eastern Texas in the early 1980s.[138] Subsequently, β-lactamase-producing strains have been found in a number of other U.S. cities and in Buenos Aires, Argentina.[4] Although the β-lactamase in enterococci is identical to the plasmid-mediated β-lactamase from *S. aureus,* it is produced constitutively in enterococci because the genes that control the inducible production of β-lactamase in *S. aureus* have not been transferred into *Enterococcus* in toto with the β-lactamase genes.[139] β-Lactamase-producing enterococci show a marked inoculum effect and when tested under standard laboratory conditions do not appear to have MICs significantly different from those of non-β-lactamase-producing strains.[4] Accordingly, the clinical laboratory must use a test for β-lactamase production (such as nitrocefin) to effectively identify these strains.[4] Interestingly, β-lactamase-producing strains have not become widely disseminated in the United States or elsewhere, and after several initial descriptions of outbreaks of colonization and infection with these organisms, they have not caused further clinical difficulty.[40]

Several new antimicrobials have been used to treat infections caused by vancomycin-resistant enterococci. Given the track record of the enterococcus, it is not surprising that the use of both quinupristin/dalfopristin and linezolid has been associated with the emergence of resistant strains.[140,141] Whether resistance will arise to daptomycin now that it is on the market is unknown (see Chapter 29).

The transfer of resistance genes to and from enterococci can be accomplished by the conjugal exchange of plasmids or transposons.[4,106] Three separate transfer systems for conjugative transfer have been described in enterococci.[4] The first involves narrow-host-range plasmids that transfer genes at high frequency only among enterococci. This system is the result of the response of recipient cells that produce an aggregation substance on exposure to pheromones from the donor cells, resulting in visible clumping between donors and recipients.[142] Broad-host-range plasmids not under pheromone control can be transferred among *Enterococcus* spp. and between these organisms and various species of streptococci, *S. aureus,* lactobacilli, *Bacillus subtilis, Listeria monocytogenes,* and others.[106,143,144] Finally, enterococci may exchange conjugative transposons as well.[142] These systems have undoubtedly contributed to the explosive increase in multiple drug resistance among enterococci isolated worldwide.

Therapy

Treatment of enterococcal infections is complicated both by the fact that these organisms often exhibit unusual patterns of susceptibility or resistance and by the fact that it is necessary to use specialized techniques to demonstrate their true susceptibility in the clinical microbiology laboratory. For instance, standard methods of susceptibility testing will not predict resistance to penicillin-aminoglycoside synergism. Instead, the laboratory must test for high-level aminoglycoside resistance or subject the organism to testing against antimicrobial combinations in vitro by methods using time-kill curves.[4,145] Likewise, standard testing will also fail to demonstrate penicillin or ampicillin resistance in many β-lactamase-producing strains.[4] Finally, susceptibility testing may produce frankly misleading results. The clinician faced with a report suggesting that an organism is only moderately susceptible to penicillin (which is "standard" for these organisms) and susceptible to vancomycin may conclude that vancomycin is better, even though penicillin or ampicillin are the initial agents of choice for most enterococcal infections.

As noted previously, penicillin or ampicillin remain the antibiotics of choice for treating enterococcal infections such as urinary tract infections, peritonitis, and wound infections that do not require bactericidal treatment.[146] Vancomycin (or teicoplanin) is the alternative agent in patients who are allergic to penicillin or for organisms (usually *E. faecium*) with high-level penicillin resistance.[146] Most strains of enterococci (90% to 96% in most centers) remain susceptible to nitrofurantoin, and this agent has been used successfully to treat enterococcal urinary tract infections.[147] Fosfomycin also exhibits good in vitro activity against *E. faecalis* and *E. faecium* and may be useful for urinary tract infections caused by these organisms.[148,149] The fluoroquinolones such as ciprofloxacin and ofloxacin have in vitro activity against enterococci[150] and may be useful for treating some enterococcal urinary tract infections, but their effectiveness for enterococcal infections in general has not been demonstrated convincingly, and increasing resistance in some centers may further decrease their attractiveness for enterococcal infections.[151] Levofloxacin, gatifloxacin, and moxifloxacin are more active than ciprofloxacin or ofloxacin against enterococci in vitro, but their activity is diminished against ciprofloxacin-resistant strains, suggesting that their utility for treating infections caused by multi-drug-resistant enterococci will be limited, at best.[150] Although erythromycin has been used to treat enterococcal infections (with failures documented in occasional cases of endocarditis),[77] most (80% to 90%) enterococci in the United States are now resistant to erythromycin and related macrolides. Tetracycline and chloramphenicol may exhibit in vitro activities against some strains of enterococci, but they are only bacteriostatic against these organisms, and both clinical success and failure of chloramphenicol are documented.[91,116,117]

Although it appears that combination therapy is optimal for enterococcal endocarditis and probably for enterococcal meningitis as well,[4,69,154] the situation is not as clear-cut in cases of enterococcal bacteremia without endocarditis. Many such cases are transient and self-limited.[67] Nonetheless, there is evidence that appropriate therapy does improve the outcome in uncomplicated enterococcal bacteremia.[68] There is no consensus as to whether combination therapy is required in this setting, and a number of studies have suggested that combination therapy provides no advantage over monotherapy.[67,155] In the absence of a controlled trial, however, some infectious disease specialists continue to use penicillin or ampicillin plus aminoglycoside therapy, especially when enterococcal bacteremia occurs in critically ill patients. Combination therapy also appears more effective than monotherapy for therapy of bacteremia associated with indwelling intravascular catheters, but this has not been subjected to a prospective randomized trial, either.[156]

Combinations of cell wall-active agents (usually penicillin, ampicillin, or vancomycin) with aminoglycosides (usually streptomycin or gentamicin) have been the standard for treatment of enterococcal endocarditis since the first demonstration of penicillin-streptomycin synergy in 1947.[157] Before that, high relapse rates (30% to 60%) were documented in patients with enterococcal endocarditis treated with penicillin alone. Although there has never been a controlled trial of combination versus monotherapy in enterococcal endocarditis, it is generally agreed that combination therapy is necessary for enterococcal endocarditis and meningitis because most enterococci are tolerant to the killing activity of penicillins and glycopeptides.[146,155,158,159] Moreover, relapses are now being demonstrated in patients who have

TABLE 198-4 Antibiotic Therapy of Enterococcal Endocarditis

Antibiotic	Dosage	Route	Duration (wk)
Organism not highly resistant to streptomycin or gentamicin			
Pencillin G	20-30 million U/day	IV	4-6
Or			
Ampicillin	12-16 g/day	IV	4-6
Plus			
Streptomycin	15 mg/kg/day*	IM	4-6
Or			
Gentamicin	3-5 mg/kg/day	IM or IV	4-6
Organism highly resistant to streptomycin but not gentamicin			
Penicillin G	20-30 million U/day	IV	4-6
Or			
Ampicillin	12-16 g/day	IV	4-6
Plus			
Gentamicin	3-5 mg/kg/day	IM or IV	4-6
Patient allergic to penicillin; desensitization not feasible			
Vancomycin	30 mg/kg/day*	IV	4-6
Plus			
Streptomycin or gentamicin	Use above guidelines in choice of aminoglycoside	IM or IV	4-6
Organism highly resistant to streptomycin and gentamicin			
Ampicillin	12-16 g/day	IV	8-12

*Maximum dose 2 g/day.

developed enterococcal endocarditis due to organisms with high-level gentamicin resistance and who are treated with penicillin or ampicillin alone.[15] Although penicillin or ampicillin plus streptomycin was originally the regimen of choice for enterococcal endocarditis, it has been shown that penicillin plus gentamicin is equally effective, and this is now generally used for enterococcal endocarditis and enterococcal meningitis.[69,73,75-78,146,159,160] Vancomycin is substituted for penicillin or ampicillin in combination with streptomycin or gentamicin in patients who are allergic to penicillin.[146] Dosage recommendations for these regimens are given in Table 198-4. In most cases, 4 weeks of combination therapy appears to be adequate,[69,73,78] with the 6-week regimens reserved for patients who have had symptoms for more than 3 months before starting treatment, patients with prosthetic valves, or patients who have relapsed after previous shorter courses of therapy.[69,78] It is possible that a shorter course of aminoglycoside therapy (15 days) plus prolonged therapy with a cell wall-active agent (42 days) may also be effective,[161] but this requires confirmation. Similar therapeutic regimens have been used to treat patients with enterococcal meningitis, but there is not a sufficient body of experience with this disease to assess the therapeutic effectiveness or optimal length of treatment. Most patients with enterococcal meningitis seem to respond well to treatment, which is generally given for 2 to 3 weeks.[88] Because of its excellent penetration into the CSF and activity against vancomycin-resistant enterococci, linezolid may be useful for VRE meningitis despite the fact that it is usually bacteriostatic against enterococci.[162]

The emergence of multiply resistant enterococci now greatly complicates the therapeutic choices in some cases.[163] For patients who have endocarditis or meningitis caused by enterococci with high-level gentamicin resistance, it is useful to test for high-level streptomycin resistance because some highly gentamicin-resistant strains are synergistically killed by cell wall-active agents plus streptomycin.[15] For endocarditis caused by strains with high-level resistance to both streptomycin and gentamicin, no combination will produce synergism. The possible exception would be the strains containing the newly described phosphotransferase mediating high-level resistance to gentamicin without accompanying acetyltransferase activity.[110] Some of these strains are killed synergistically by combinations of cell wall-active agents and amikacin, but others are not, and clinical data to support these in vitro observations are not available. Our current recommendation for the remainder of cases of endocarditis caused by enterococci exhibiting high-level resistance to both streptomycin and gentamicin is to treat such patients for long periods (8 to 12 weeks) with intravenous ampicillin, which produces slightly greater killing of enterococci in vitro than penicillin alone, given by continuous infusion. There are not enough data to know how effective such therapy will be, but there are anecdotal examples of success. Nonetheless, this approach should be considered experimental. Surgical excision of infected valves has been required to cure some cases of enterococcal endocarditis caused by organisms with high-level streptomycin and gentamicin resistance.[15,73,164] Infections due to *E. faecium* with high-level penicillin resistance (MIC > 16 to 32 μg/mL) should be treated with vancomycin. Many vancomycin-resistant enterococci (especially *E. faecalis*) remain relatively susceptible to penicillin or ampicillin (MICs of 0.5 to 2 μg/mL), and these agents can be tried therapeutically for infections caused by such organisms. Infections caused by organisms (usually *E. faecium*) with both high-level penicillin resistance and vancomycin resistance are even more of a challenge. The combination of vancomycin plus penicillin or ampicillin has been shown to produce bacteriostatic but not bactericidal synergism against some such organisms in vitro.[164,165] However, this has not been universally true,[44,166] and, although combinations of ampicillin plus vancomycin plus gentamicin have demonstrated bactericidal activity against several enterococcal strains in animal models,[167,168] the clinical effectiveness of such therapy remains to be demonstrated. Despite the fact that vancomycin-resistant enterococci of the VanB phenotype remain susceptible to teicoplanin in vitro, therapy of infections caused by such strains with teicoplanin has not been universally successful; and in several reported cases, it has been associated with the emergence of organisms resistant to teicoplanin during therapy.[169,170] There is a report of a number of cases of enterococcal endocarditis caused by vancomycin-resistant enterococci of the VanB phenotype that were successfully treated with teicoplanin plus a second active antibiotic (usually an aminoglycoside).[171] Combination therapy seems essential in this setting to prevent the emergence of resistance.[172]

β-Lactamase-producing enterococci remain susceptible to vancomycin (and teicoplanin) and to combinations of β-lactams and β-lactamase inhibitors such as ampicillin-sulbactam and amoxicillin-clavulanate. These agents have been shown to be effective in animal models as well.[173] There are no convincing published reports of endocarditis caused by β-lactamase-producing organisms, so the clinical effectiveness of these regimens cannot be assessed.

Teicoplanin alone has been used to treat a small number of patients with enterococcal endocarditis (none of which were caused by vancomycin-resistant strains) in Europe, and preliminary results show some success in this setting, but there have also been documented failures and relapses.[174,175] There are reports of in vitro activity of other agents including novobiocin, ciprofloxacin, fosfomycin, and pristinamycin[176] in various combination regimens against enterococci, but none of these has been proven clinically useful. The treatment of infections due to multiple-drug-resistant enterococci remains a highly empirical endeavor and requires the backup of a clinical or research laboratory well versed in antimicrobial susceptibility testing.[177]

Based on their in vitro activities, quinupristin/dalfopristin and linezolid have recently been used in the therapy of enterococcal infections, especially those caused by VRE.[178,179] Quinupristin/dalfopristin is useful only for infections caused by *E. faecium*, as *E. faecalis* are intrinsically resistant to this combination.[180] It has been used extensively in the therapy of a variety of infections caused by vancomycin-resistant *E. faecium* with response rates consistently in the range of 65% to 75%.[140,181,182] Because of the possibility of emergence of resistance during therapy, some investigators advocate addition of doxycycline to quinupristin/dalfopristin for serious infections such as bacteremia and endocarditis, but controlled trials are not available.[183] Linezolid is active in vitro against both *E. faecalis* and *E. faecium*. It has proven useful for the treatment of a wide variety of infections caused by vancomycin-resistant enterococci, including patients who have failed previous therapy with quinupristin/dalfopristin.[184-186] Like quinupristin/dalfopristin, linezolid is bacteriostatic, not bactericidal,

against enterococci and for that reason, should be used with caution in patients with suspected endocarditis.

Several antimicrobial agents under clinical development are bactericidal against enterococci and may be useful for treatment of VRE infections including endocarditis. Daptomycin and oritavancin (LY333328) are both completing phase III development.[187,188]

STREPTOCOCCUS BOVIS

Streptococcus bovis organisms are gram-positive cocci that may sometimes be misidentified as enterococci or viridans streptococci (especially *Streptococcus salivarius*) unless careful testing is performed in the clinical microbiology laboratory.[189-191] They are classified as group D streptococci on the basis of their reaction with group D-specific antiserum, but this testing is no longer routinely carried out in most clinical laboratories.[190,192] In addition to their positive reaction with group D antiserum, *S. bovis* share other properties in common with true enterococci including their ability to grow in the presence of 40% bile and to hydrolyze esculin.[190,192] However, a number of simple tests, including growth in 6.5% salt broth or the pyrrolidonyl arylamidase (PYR) reaction, easily differentiate *S. bovis* from true enterococci.[190-192] The use of the API Rapid Strep system not only results in accurate identification of *S. bovis* and distinguishes these organisms from viridans streptococci and enterococci, but it also allows identification of *S. bovis* to the biotype level.[191] Several biotypes have been described including *S. bovis* biotype I (also known simply as *S. bovis*) and *S. bovis* biotypes II/1 and II/2 (also known as *S. bovis* variants).[193] This differentiation may be important because bacteremia caused by *S. bovis* I shows a much higher correlation with underlying gastrointestinal malignancy and endocarditis (71% and 94%, respectively, in one series) than *S. bovis* II or *S. salivarius*.[191] Although *S. bovis* is occasionally identified in cultures from the urinary tract and in other miscellaneous infections including very rare cases of meningitis or neonatal sepsis,[190-192] by far the most important clinical infections caused by *S. bovis* are bacteremias and endocarditis.[190-200] A variety of other less common infections including osteomyelitis and meningitis have been described.[201,202] The gastrointestinal tract is the usual portal of entry in *S. bovis* bacteremia, although the hepatobiliary tree, the urinary tract, and even dental procedures have been implicated as possible sources.[190,191,195,197] Some or all of the latter cases, however, may represent bacteremias or cases of endocarditis in which *S. salivarius* was misidentified as *S. bovis*.[189,190,197] In a high percentage of cases (25% to 50% or more), *S. bovis* bacteremia is associated with endocarditis. The endocarditis produced by these organisms usually runs a subacute course and is clinically indistinguishable from that caused by viridans streptococci with rare peripheral septic complications and excellent response to antimicrobial therapy.[190,195,197,200,203] *S. bovis* usually, but not always, produces endocarditis in patients with preexisting valvular abnormalities or prosthetic valves.[190]

There is a striking association between *S. bovis* bacteremia and underlying malignancy of the colon.[197-204] Indeed, the prevalence of malignancy exceeds 50% in some series, and all patients with *S. bovis* bacteremia should undergo a careful workup to exclude colonic neoplasms. Although some authors have suggested an association with other gastrointestinal malignancies, the most striking association is with colonic carcinoma.[205] It is not clear if *S. bovis* plays an etiologic role in carcinoma of the colon or is merely a marker for the disease, but several studies have shown a definite increase in stool carriage of *S. bovis* in patients with malignant or premalignant lesions of the colon compared with healthy people, from whom *S. bovis* is rarely isolated in stool cultures.[199,204]

Unlike enterococci, *S. bovis* is very susceptible to penicillin, with penicillin MICs ranging between 0.01 and 0.12 μg/mL. They are also susceptible to ampicillin, the antipseudomonal penicillins, cephalothin, erythromycin, clindamycin, and vancomycin.[190,191] Although penicillin-aminoglycoside combinations show synergy against *S. bovis* and have been successfully used to treat infections due to these organisms,[196] it appears that penicillin alone is equally effective when given for 4 weeks to patients with endocarditis.[190,197] It is likewise the drug of choice for *S. bovis* bacteremia. Vancomycin is a reasonable alternative in penicillin-allergic patients, but the identification of a vancomycin-resistant clinical isolate of *S. bovis* (which contained the *VanB* genome)[206] raises the possibility of more widespread glycopeptide resistance in these organisms in the future and means that it is prudent to confirm vancomycin susceptibility before using this agent therapeutically for *S. bovis* infections.[206]

LEUCONOSTOC SPECIES

Leuconostoc spp. are gram-positive cocci or coccobacilli that grow in pairs and chains and may be morphologically mistaken for streptococci.[207,208] They are one of several genera of naturally vancomycin-resistant gram-positive organisms that include *Lactobacillus* spp., *Pediococcus* spp., *Erysipelothrix* spp., and some enterococci. *Leuconostoc* are facultative anaerobes that are catalase-negative, are leucine aminopeptidase-positive, and produce gas from glucose.[207] Although several species are known,[209] they are not usually speciated in the clinical microbiology laboratory and are generally identified only as *Leuconostoc* or *Leuconostoc* spp.

Until the 1970s, these organisms were not thought to be pathogenic for humans.[209] They are commonly found on plants and vegetables and less commonly in dairy products and wine.[209,210] Although they may occasionally be isolated from human stool specimens, there are insufficient data to determine the frequency with which this occurs.[207,210] Virtually nothing is known about the way in which these organisms colonize or infect humans. Indeed, documented infections due to *Leuconostoc* are rare, in part because it is likely that these organisms are often mistaken or misidentified in the clinical laboratory. Most information on clinical infections caused by *Leuconostoc* comes from isolated reports of one or two cases.[210-214] *Leuconostoc* has been isolated from gastrostomy tube sites in the absence of obvious infection.[210,213] They have been documented to cause isolated bacteremias; intravenous-line sepsis with localized exit site infection or bacteremia, or both; meningitis (including a case of neonatal meningitis); and dental abscess with odontogenic infection of the buccal soft tissues. Many of the documented infections have occurred in severely ill or immunocompromised patients, but a few (including meningitis) have been seen in otherwise healthy persons. Nonetheless, it is clear that *Leuconostoc* is only very rarely pathogenic for humans.

All *Leuconostoc* species are resistant to vancomycin because their pentapeptide cell wall precursors end in a depsipeptide (alanine-lactate) rather than the alanine-alanine dipeptide, which is the binding site for vancomycin in vancomycin-susceptible gram-positive cocci. The ligase for assembling the depsipeptide has not been identified, but it does not appear to be related to the altered ligases responsible for vancomycin resistance in enterococci.[215] These organisms are usually cross-resistant to teicoplanin. Despite their resistance to vancomycin and teicoplanin, *Leuconostoc* remains susceptible to most agents with activity against streptococci.[216-218] Thus, these organisms are generally quite susceptible to penicillin, ampicillin, clindamycin, minocycline, erythromycin, tobramycin, and gentamicin. They are moderately susceptible to imipenem, the cephalosporins, tetracycline, doxycycline, and chloramphenicol. Strains resistant to the sulfonamides, trimethoprim-sulfamethoxazole, fusidic acid, and fosfomycin have been described.[210,216,217,219] From the limited clinical data available it appears that penicillin or ampicillin is the agent of choice for treating documented infections caused by *Leuconostoc* spp. An experimental drug, daptomycin, has also been used successfully in two cases of line-related *Leuconostoc* bacteremia.[220]

REFERENCES

1. Sherman JM. The streptococci. Bacteriol Rev. 1937;1:3-97.
2. Deibel RH. The group D streptococci. Bacteriol Rev. 1964;28:330-336.
3. Schleifer KH, Kilpper-Balz R. Molecular and chemotaxonomic approaches to the classification of streptococci, enterococci, and lactococci: A review. Syst Appl Microbiol. 1987;10:1-19.
4. Murray BE. The life and times of the enterococcus. Clin Microbiol Rev. 1990;3:46-65.
5. Facklam RR, Sahm DF, Teixeira LM. Enterococcus. In: Murray PR, Baron EJ, Pfaller MA, et al, eds. Manual of Clinical Microbiology. 7th ed. Washington, DC: American Society for Microbiology; 1999:297-305.
6. Facklam RR, Collins MD. Identification of Enterococcus species isolated from human infections by a conventional test scheme. J Clin Microbiol. 1989;27:731-734.
7. Ruoff KL, de la Maza L, Murtagh MJ, et al. Species identities of enterococci isolated from clinical specimens. J Clin Microbiol. 1990;28:435-437.
8. Vergis EN, Hayden MK, Chow JW, et al. Determinants of vancomycin resistance and mortality rates in enterococcal bacteremia. Ann Intern Med. 2001;135:484-492.
9. Mead GC. Streptococci in the intestinal flora of man and other non-ruminant animals. In: Skinner FA, Quesnel LB, eds. Streptococci. London: Academic Press; 1978:345-361.
10. Hoffmann SA, Moellering RC Jr. The enterococcus: "Putting the bug in our ears." Ann Intern Med. 1987;106:757-761.
11. Garbutt JM, Ventrapragada M, Littenberg B, et al. Association between resistance to vancomycin and death in cases of Enterococcus faecium bacteremia. Clin Infect Dis. 2000;30:466-472
12. Edmond MB, Ober JF, Weinbaum DL, et al. Vancomycin-resistant E. faecium bacteremia: Risk factors for infection. Clin Infect Dis. 1995;20:1126.
13. Edmond MB, Ober JF, Dawson JD, et al. Vancomycin-resistant enterococcal bacteremia: Natural history and attributable mortality. Clin Infect Dis. 1996;23:1234.
14. Moellering RC Jr. Emergence of Enterococcus as a significant pathogen. Clin Infect Dis. 1992;14:1173-1178.
15. Moellering RC Jr. The Garrod Lecture: The enterococcus: A classic example of the impact of antimicrobial resistance on therapeutic options. J Antimicrob Chemother. 1991;28:1-12.
16. Guzman CA, Pruzzo C, Lipira G, et al. Role of adherence in pathogenesis of Enterococcus faecalis urinary tract infection and endocarditis. Infect Immun. 1989;57:1834-1838.
17. Shankar V, Baghdayan AS, Huycke MM, et al. Infection-derived Enterococcus faecalis strains are enriched in esp, a gene encoding a novel surface protein. Infect Immun. 1999;67:193-200.
18. Pillai SK, Sakoulas G, Gold HS, et al. fsr-mediated catabolic repression of biofilm in Enterococcus faecalis. J Infect Dis. 2004 (in press).
19. Willems RJL, Homan W, Top J, et al. Variant esp gene as a marker of a distinct genetic lineage of vancomycin-resistant Enterococcus faecium spreading in hospitals. Lancet. 2001;357:853-855.
20. Coque TM, Willems R, Canton R, et al. High occurrence of esp among ampicillin-resistant and vancomycin-susceptible Enterococcus faecium clones from hospitalized patients. J Antimicrob Chemother. 2002;50:1035-1038.
21. Qin X, Singh KV, Weinstock GM, et al. Effects of Enterococcus faecalis fsr genes on production of gelatinase and a serine protease and virulence. Infect Immun. 2000;68:2579-2586.
22. Qin X, Singh KV, Weinstock GM, et al. Characterization of fsr, a regulator controlling expression of gelatinase and serine protease in Enterococcus faecalis OG1RF. J Bacteriol. 2001;183:3372-3382.
23. Waters CM, Antiporta MN, Murray BE, et al. Role of the Enterococcus faecalis GelE protease in determination of cellular chain length, supernatant pheromone levels, and degradation of fibrin and misfolded surface proteins. J Bacteriol. 2003;185:3613-3623.
24. Kreft B, Marre R, Schramm U, et al. Aggregation substance of Enterococcus faecalis mediates adhesion to cultured renal tubular cells. Infect Immun. 1992;60:25-30.
25. Ike Y, Hashimoto H, Clewell DB. Hemolysin of Streptococcus faecalis subspecies zymogenes contributes to virulence in mice. Infect Immun. 1984;45:528-530.
26. Ike Y, Hashimoto H, Clewell DB. High incidence of hemolysin production by Enterococcus (Streptococcus) faecalis strains associated with human parenteral infections. J Clin Microbiol. 1987;25:1524-1528.
27. Etheridge ME, Yolken RH, Vonderfecht SL. Enterococcus hirae implicated as a cause of diarrhea in suckling rats. J Clin Microbiol. 1988;26:1741-1744.
28. Willey SH, Hindes RG, Eliopoulos GM, et al. Effects of clindamycin and gentamicin and other antimicrobial combinations against enterococci in an experimental model of intra-abdominal abscess. Surg Gynecol Obstet. 1989;169:199-202.
29. Matlow AG, Bohnen JMA, Nohr C, et al. Pathogenicity of enterococci in a rat model of fecal peritonitis. J Infect Dis. 1989;160:142-144.
30. Nichols RL, Muzik AC. Enterococcal infections in surgical patients: The mystery continues. Clin Infect Dis. 1992;15:72-76.
31. Kaye D. Enterococci: Biologic and epidemiologic characteristics and in vitro susceptibility. Arch Intern Med. 1982;142:2006-2009.
32. Murray BE, Singh KV, Markowitz SM, et al. Evidence for clonal spread of a single strain of β-lactamase-producing Enterococcus faecalis to six hospitals in five states. J Infect Dis. 1991;163:780-785.
33. Murray BE, Lopardo HA, Rubeglio EA, et al. Intrahospital spread of a single gentamicin-resistant, β-lactamase-producing strain of Enterococcus faecalis in Argentina. Antimicrob Agents Chemother. 1992;36:230-232.
34. Zervos MJ, Terpenning MS, Schaberg DR, et al. High-level aminoglycoside-resistant enterococci. Colonization of nursing home and acute care hospital patients. Arch Intern Med. 1987;147:1591-1594.
35. Fridkin SK, Yokoe DS, Whitney CG, et al. Epidemiology of a dominant clonal strain of vancomycin-resistant Enterococcus faecium, at separate hospitals in Boston, Massachusetts. J Clin Microbiol. 1998;965-970.
36. Zervos MJ, Dembinski S, Mikesell T, et al. High-level resistance to gentamicin in Streptococcus faecalis: Risk factors and evidence for exogenous acquisition of infection. J Infect Dis. 1986;153:1075-1083.
37. Elizaga ML, Weinstein RA, Hayden MK. Patients in long-term care facilities: A reservoir for vancomycin-resistant enterococci. Clin Infect Dis. 2002;34:441-446.

38. Hall RW, Bayer AS, Mayer WP, et al. Infective endocarditis following human-to-human enterococcal transmission. Arch Intern Med. 1976;136:1173-1174.
39. Hall LMC, Duke B, Urwin G, et al. Epidemiology of *Enterococcus faecalis* urinary tract infection in a teaching hospital in London, United Kingdom. J Clin Microbiol. 1992;30:1953-1957.
40. Rhinehart E, Smith NE, Wennersten C, et al. Rapid dissemination of β-lactamase-producing, aminoglycoside-resistant *Enterococcus faecalis* among patients and staff on an infant-toddler surgical ward. N Engl J Med. 1990;323:1814-1818.
41. Schoonmaker DJ, Bopp LH, Baltch AL, et al. Genetic analysis of multiple vancomycin-resistant *Enterococcus* isolates obtained serially from two long-term-care patients. J Clin Microbiol. 1998;36:2105.
42. Livornese LL Jr, Drus S, Samel C, et al. Hospital-acquired infection with vancomycin-resistant *Enterococcus faecium* transmitted by electronic thermometers. Ann Intern Med. 1992;117:112-116.
43. Schaberg DR, Culver DH, Gaynes RP. Major trends in the microbial etiology of nosocomial infection. Am J Med. 1991;91(Suppl 3B):3B72S-3B75S.
44. Handwerger S, Raucher B, Altarac D, et al. Nosocomial outbreak due to *Enterococcus faecium* highly resistant to vancomycin, penicillin and gentamicin. Clin Infect Dis. 1993;16:750-755.
45. Wells VD, Wong ES, Murray BE, et al. Infections due to beta-lactamase producing, high-level gentamicin-resistant *Enterococcus faecalis*. Ann Intern Med. 1992;116:285-292.
46. Centers for Disease Control and Prevention. Nosocomial enterococci resistant to vancomycin-United States, 1989-1993. Morb Mortal Wkly Rep. 1993;42:597-599.
47. Moellering RC Jr, Wennersten C, Medrek T, et al. Prevalence of high-level resistance to aminoglycosides in clinical isolates of enterococci. Antimicrob Agents Chemother. 1970;335-340.
48. Moellering RC Jr. Enterococcal infections in patients treated with moxalactam. Rev Infect Dis. 1982;4(Suppl):S708-S711.
49. Fridkin SK, Edwards JR, Courval JM, et al. The effect of vancomycin and third-generation cephalosporins on prevalence of vancomycin-resistant enterococci in 126 U.S. adult intensive care units. Ann Intern Med. 2001;135:175-183.
50. Zervos MJ, Bacon AE III, Patterson JE, et al. Enterococcal superinfection in patients treated with ciprofloxacin. J Antimicrob Chemother. 1988;21:113-115.
51. Jones RN. Gram-positive superinfections following beta-lactam chemotherapy: The significance of the enterococcus. Infection. 1988;13(Suppl 1):S81-S88.
52. Harvarth S, Cosgrove S, Carmeli Y. Effects of antibiotics on nosocomial epidemiology of vancomycin-resistant enterococci. Antimicrob Agents Chemother. 2002;46:1619-1628.
53. Donskey CJ, Chowdhry TK, Hecker MT et al. Effect of antibiotic therapy on the density of vancomycin-resistant enterococci in the stool of colonized patients. N Engl J Med. 2000;343:1925-1932.
54. Reiner NE, Gopalakrishna KV, Lerner PI. Enterococcal endocarditis in heroin addicts. JAMA. 1976;235:1861-1863.
55. Venditti M, Tarasi A, Visco Comandini U, et al. Enterococcal septicemia in patients with hematological malignancies. Eur J Clin Microbiol Infect Dis. 1993;12:241-247.
56. Zaas AK, Song X, Tucker P, et al. Risk factors for development of vancomycin-resistant enterococcal bloodstream infection in patients with cancer who are colonized with vancomycin-resistant enterococci. Clin Infect Dis. 2002;35:1139-1146.
57. Kirkpatrick BD, Harrington SM, Smith D, et al. An outbreak of vancomycin-dependent *Enterococcus faecium* in a bone marrow transplant unit. Clin Infect Dis. 1999;29:1268-1273.
58. Moellering RC Jr. Infections due to group D streptococci. Infect Dis Rev. 1981;6:1-17.
59. Edelstein H, McCabe RE. Perinephric abscess. Modern diagnosis and treatment in 47 cases. Medicine. 1988;67:118-131.
60. Morrison AJ Jr, Wenzel RP. Nosocomial urinary tract infections due to enterococcus; ten years' experience at a university hospital. Arch Intern Med. 1986;146:1549-1551.
61. Warren JW, Tenney JH, Hoopes JM. A prospective microbiologic study of bacteriuria in patients with chronic indwelling urethral catheters. J Infect Dis. 1982;146:719-723.
62. Krieger JN, Kaiser DL, Wenzel RP. Urinary tract etiology of bloodstream infections in hospitalized patients. J Infect Dis. 1983;148:57-62.
63. Maki DG, Agger WA. Enterococcal bacteremia: Clinical features, the risk of endocarditis, and management. Medicine. 1988;64:248-269.
64. Graninger W, Ragette R. Nosocomial bacteremia due to *Enterococcus faecalis* without endocarditis. Clin Infect Dis. 1992;15:49-57.
65. Shlaes DM, Levy J, Wolinsky E. Enterococcal bacteremia without endocarditis. Arch Intern Med. 1981;141:578-581.
66. Linden PK, Pasculle AW, Manez R, et al. Differences in outcomes for patients with bacteremia due to vancomycin-resistant *Enterococcus faecium* or vancomycin-susceptible *E. faecium.* Clin Infect Dis. 1996;22:663.
67. Gullberg RM, Homann SR, Phair JP. Enterococcal bacteremia: Analysis of 75 episodes. Rev Infect Dis. 1989;11:74-85.
68. Hoge CW, Adams J, Buchanan B, et al. Enterococcal bacteremia: To treat or not to treat, a reappraisal. Rev Infect Dis. 1991;13:600-605.
69. Moellering RC Jr. Treatment of enterococcal endocarditis. In: Sande MA, Kaye D, Root RK, eds. Endocarditis. New York: Churchill Livingstone; 1984:113-133.
70. Facklam RR, Collins MD. Identification of *Enterococcus* species isolated from human infections by a conventional test scheme. J Clin Microbiol. 1989;27:731-734.
71. Ratanasuwan W, Iwen PC, Hinrichs SH, et al. Bacteremia due to motile *Enterococcus* species: Clinical features and outcomes. Clin Infect Dis. 1999;28:1175-1177.
72. Dargere S, Vergnaud M, Verdon R, et al. *Enterococcus gallinarum* endocarditis occurring on native heart valves. J Clin Microbiol. 2002;40:2308-2310.
73. Rice LB, Calderwood SB, Eliopoulos GM, et al. Enterococcal endocarditis: A comparison of prosthetic and native valve disease. Rev Infect Dis. 1991;13:1-7.
74. Megran DW. Enterococcal endocarditis. Clin Infect Dis. 1992;15:63-71.
75. Koenig MG, Kaye D. Enterococcal endocarditis: Report of nineteen cases with long-term follow-up data. N Engl J Med. 1961;264:257-264.
76. Mandell G, Kaye D, Levison ME, et al. Enterococcal endocarditis. An analysis of 38 patients observed at the New York Hospital-Cornell Medical Center. Arch Intern Med. 1970;125:258-264.
77. Moellering RC Jr, Watson BK, Kunz LJ. Endocarditis due to group D streptococci: Comparison of disease caused by *Streptococcus bovis* with that produced by the enterococci. Am J Med. 1974;57:239-258.
78. Wilson WR, Wilkowske CJ, Wright AJ, et al. Treatment of streptomycin-susceptible and streptomycin-resistant enterococcal endocarditis. Ann Intern Med. 1984;100:816-823.
79. Dougherty SH. Role of enterococcus in intraabdominal sepsis. Am J Surg. 1984;148:308-312.
80. Harding GKM, Buckwold FJ, Ronald AR, et al. Prospective, randomized comparative study of clindamycin, chloramphenicol, and ticarcillin, each in combination with gentamicin, in therapy for intraabdominal and female genital tract sepsis. J Infect Dis. 1980;142:384-393.
81. Bartlett JG, Onderdonk AB, Louis T, et al. A review: Lessons from an animal model of intra-abdominal sepsis. Arch Surg. 1978;113:853-857.
82. Willey SH, Hindes RG, Eliopoulos GM, et al. Effects of clindamycin-gentamicin and other antimicrobial combinations against enterococci in an experimental intraabdominal abscess model. Surg Gynecol Obstet. 1989;169:199-202.
83. Weigelt JA, Easley SM, Thal ER, et al. Abdominal surgical wound infection is lowered with improved perioperative enterococcus and bacteroides therapy. J Trauma. 1993;34:579-585.
84. Weinstein MP, Iannini PB, Stratton CW, et al. Spontaneous bacterial peritonitis: A review of 28 cases with emphasis on improved survival and factors influencing prognosis. Am J Med. 1978;64:592-598.
85. Ledger WJ, Norman M, Gee C, et al. Bacteremia on an obstetric-gynecologic service. Am J Obstet Gynecol. 1975;121:205-212.
86. Horvitz RA, von Graevenitz A. A clinical study of the role of enterococci as sole agents of wound and tissue infection. Yale J Biol Med. 1977;50:391-395.
87. Smith RF, Dayton SL. Colonization of burns by *Streptococcus faecalis* related to contaminated porcine xenografts. Tex Rep Biol Med. 1973;31:47-54.
88. Bayer AS, Seidel JS, Yoshikawa TT, et al. Group D enterococcal meningitis. Clinical and therapeutic considerations with report of three cases and review of the literature. Arch Intern Med. 1976;136:883-886.
89. Kurup A, Tee WSN, Loo LH, et al. Infection of central nervous system by motile *Enterococcus:* First case report. J Clin Microbiol. 2001;39:820-822.
90. Buchino JJ, Ciambarella E, Light E. Systemic group D streptococcal infection in newborn infants. Am J Dis Child. 1979;133:270-273.
91. Ryan JJ, Pachner A, Andriole VT, et al. Enterococcal meningitis: Combined vancomycin and rifampin therapy. Am J Med. 1980;68:449-451.
92. Berk SL, Verghese A, Holtsclaw SA, et al. Enterococcal pneumonia. Occurrence in patients receiving broad-spectrum antibiotic regimens and enteral feeding. Am J Med. 1983;74:153-154.
93. Morris JF, Okies JE. Enterococcal lung abscess: Medical and surgical therapy. Chest. 1974;65:688-691.
94. Siegel JD, McCracken GH. Group D streptococcal infections. J Pediatr. 1978;93:542-543.
95. Bavikatte K, Schreiner RL, Lemons JA, et al. Group D streptococcal septicemia in the neonate. Am J Dis Child. 1979;133:493-496.
96. Coudron PE, Mayhall CG, Facklam RR, et al. *Streptococcus faecium* outbreak in a neonatal intensive care unit. J Clin Microbiol. 1984;20:1044-1048.
97. Luginbuhl LM, Rotbart HA, Facklam RR, et al. Neonatal enterococcal sepsis: Case control study and description of an outbreak. Pediatr Infect Dis. 1987;6:1022-1030.
98. Moellering RC Jr, Krogstad DJ. Antibiotic resistance in enterococci. In: Schlessinger D, ed. Microbiology-1979. Washington, DC: American Society for Microbiology; 1979:293-298.
99. Williamson R, Calderwood SB, Moellering RC, et al. Studies on the mechanism of intrinsic resistance to beta-lactam antibiotics in enterococcal group D streptococci. J Gen Microbiol. 1983;129:813-822.
100. Williamson R, LeBouguenec C, Gutmann L, et al. One or two low affinity penicillin-binding proteins may be responsible for the range of susceptibility of *Enterococcus faecium* to benzylpenicillin. J Gen Microbiol. 1985;131:1933-1940.
101. Grayson ML, Eliopoulos GM, Wennersten CB, et al. Increasing resistance to β-lactam antibiotics among clinical isolates of *E. faecium*: A 22-year review at one institution. Antimicrob Agents Chemother. 1991;35:2180-2184.
102. Moellering RC Jr, Weinberg AN. Studies on antibiotic synergism against enterococci. II. Effect of various antibiotics on the uptake of ^{16}C-labelled streptomycin by enterococci. J Clin Invest. 1971;50:2580-2584.
103. Hamilton-Miller JMT. Reversal of activity of trimethoprim against gram-positive cocci by thymidine, thymine, and "folates." J Antimicrob Chemother. 1988;22:35-39.
104. Grayson ML, Thauvin-Eliopoulos C, Eliopoulos GM, et al. Failure of trimethoprim-sulfamethoxazole therapy in experimental enterococcal endocarditis. Antimicrob Agents Chemother. 1990;34:1792-1794.
105. Goodhart GL. In vivo v. in vitro susceptibility of *Enterococcus* to trimethoprim-sulfamethoxazole. JAMA. 1984;252:2748-2749.
106. Leclercq R, Dutka-Malen S, Brisson-Noël A, et al. Resistance of enterococci to aminoglycosides and glycopeptides. Clin Infect Dis. 1992;15:495-501.
107. Zighelboim-Daum S, Moellering RC Jr. Mechanisms and significance of antimicrobial resistance in enterococci. In: Actor P, Daneo-Moore L, Higgins ML, et al, eds. Antibiotic Inhibition of Bacterial Cell Surface Assembly and Function. Washington, DC: American Society for Microbiology; 1988:603-625.
108. Eliopoulos GM, Farber BF, Murray BE, et al. Ribosomal resistance of clinical enterococcal isolates to streptomycin. Antimicrob Agents Chemother. 1984;25:398-399.

109. Chow JW, Zervos MJ, Lerner SA, et al. A novel gentamicin resistance gene in *Enterococcus.* Antimicrob Agents Chemother. 1997;41:511.
110. Tsai SF, Zervos MJ, Clewell DB, et al. A new high-level gentamicin resistance gene, aph(2″)-Id, in *Enterococcus* spp. Antimicrob Agents Chemother. 1998;42:1229.
111. Wennersten CB, Moellering RC Jr. Mechanism of resistance to penicillin-aminoglycoside synergism in *Streptococcus faecium.* In: Nelson JD, Grassi C, eds. Current Chemotherapy and Infectious Disease. Proceedings of the 11th International Congress of Chemotherapy and the 19th Interscience Congress on Antimicrobial Agents and Chemotherapy, Boston. Washington, DC: American Society for Microbiology; 1979:710-712.
112. Costa Y, Galimand M, Leclercq R, et al. Characterization of the chromosomal *aac(6′)-Ii* gene specific for *Enterococcus faecium.* Antimicrob Agents Chemother. 1993;37:1896-1903.
113. Eliopoulos GM, Wennersten C, Zighelboim-Daum S, et al. High level resistance to gentamicin in clinical isolates of *Streptococcus (Enterococcus) faecium.* Antimicrob Agents Chemother. 1988;32:1528-1532.
114. Frieden TR, Munsiff SS, Low DE, et al. Emergence of vancomycin-resistant enterococci in New York City. Lancet. 1993;342:76-79.
115. Moellering RC Jr. Vancomycin-resistant enterococci. Clin Infect Dis. 1998;26:1196.
116. Arthur M, Courvalin P. Genetics and mechanisms of glycopeptide resistance in enterococci. Antimicrob Agents Chemother. 1993;37:1563-1571.
117. Williamson R, Al-Obeid S, Shlaes JH, et al. Inducible resistance to vancomycin in *Enterococcus faecium* D 366. J Infect Dis. 1989;159:1095-1104.
118. Handwerger S, Perlman DC, Altarac D, et al. Concomitant high-level vancomycin and penicillin resistance in clinical isolates of enterococci. Clin Infect Dis. 1992;14:655-661.
119. Quintiliani R Jr, Evers S, Courvalin P. The *vanB* gene confers various levels of self-transferable resistance to vancomycin in enterococci. J Infect Dis. 1993;167:1220-1223.
120. Gold HS, Ünal S, Cercenado E, et al. A gene conferring resistance to vancomycin but not teicoplanin in isolates of *Enterococcus faecalis* and *Enterococcus faecium* demonstrates homology with *vanB, vanA,* and *vanC* genes of enterococci. Antimicrob Agents Chemother. 1993;37:1604-1609.
121. Arias CA, Courvalin P, Reynolds PR. *vanC* cluster of vancomycin-resistant *Enterococcus gallinarum* BM4174. Antimicrob Agents Chemother. 2000;44:1660-1666.
122. Perichon B, Reynolds P, Courvalin P. VanD-type glycopeptide-resistant *E. faecium* BM 4339. Antimicrob Agents Chemother. 1997;41:2016.
123. Depardieu F, Reynolds PE, Courvalin P. VanD-type vancomycin-resistant *Enterococcus faecium* 10/96A. Antimicrob Agents Chemother. 2003;47:7-18.
124. Ostrowsky B, Clark N, Eliopoulos CT, et al. A cluster of VanD vancomycin-resistant *E. faecium:* Molecular characterization and clinical epidemiology. J Infect Dis. 1999;180:1177-1185
125. Fines M, Perichon B, Reynolds PR, et al. VanE, a new type of acquired glycopeptide resistance in *Enterococcus faecalis* BM4405. Antimicrob Agents Chemother. 1999;43:2161-2164.
126. Van Bambeke F, Chauvel M, Reynolds PR, et al. Vancomycin-dependent *Enterococcus faecalis* clinical isolates and revertant mutants. Antimicrob Agents Chemother. 1999;43:41-47.
127. Stinear TP, Olden DC, Johnson PDR, et al. Enterococcal *vanB* resistance locus in anaerobic bacteria in human faeces. Lancet. 2001;357:855-856.
128. Huycke MM, Sahm DF, Gilmore MS. Multiple-drug resistant enterococci: The nature of the problem and an agenda for the future. Emerg Infect Dis. 1998;4:239-249.
129. Recommendations for preventing the spread of vancomycin resistance. Morb Mortal Wkly Rep. 1995;44(Sept 22): No. RR12.
130. Murray BE. Diversity among multidrug-resistant enterococci. Emerg Infect Dis. 1998;4:37-47.
131. O'Donovan CA, Fan-Habard P, Tecson-Tumang FT, et al. Enteric eradication of vancomycin-resistant *Enterococcus faecium* with oral bacitracin. Diagn Microbiol Infect Dis. 1994;18:105-109.
133. Ostrowsky BE, Trick WE, Sohn AH, et al. Control of vancomycin-resistant enterococcus in health care facilities in a region. N Engl J Med. 2001;344:1427-1433.
134. Montecalvo MA, Jarvis WR, Uman J, et al. Infection-control measures reduce transmission of vancomycin-resistant enterococci in an endemic setting. Ann Intern Med. 1999;131:269-272.
135. Puzniak LA, Leet T, Mayfield J, et al. To gown or not to gown: The effect on acquisition of vancomycin-resistant enterococci. Clin Infect Dis. 2002;35:18-25.
136. Richardson LP, Wiseman SW, Malani PN, et al. Effectiveness of a vancomycin restriction policy in changing the prescribing patterns of house staff. Microb Drug Resist. 2000;6:327-330.
137. Saint S, Atherton S, Lipsky BA. Controlling the spread of vancomycin-resistant enterococci with contact precautions: Time for a randomized trial. Int J Infect Dis. 1999;3:179-180.
132. Weinstein MR, Dedier H, Brunton J, et al. Lack of efficacy of oral bacitracin plus doxycycline for the eradication of stool colonization with vancomycin-resistant *Enterococcus faecium.* Clin Infect Dis. 1999;29:361-366.
138. Murray BE, Mederski-Samoraj B. Transferable β-lactamase: A new mechanism for in vitro penicillin resistance in *Streptococcus faecalis.* J Clin Invest. 1983;72:1168-1171.
139. Zschek KK, Murray BE. Genes involved in the regulation of β-lactamase production in enterococci and staphylococci. Antimicrob Agents Chemother. 1993;37:1966-1970.
140. Winston DJ, Emmanouilides C, Kroeber A, et al. Quinupristin/dalfopristin therapy for infections due to vancomycin-resistant *Enterococcus faecium.* Clin Infect Dis. 2000;30:790-797.
141. Herrero IA, Issa NC, Patel R. Nosocomial spread of linezolid-resistant, vancomycin-resistant *Enterococcus faecium.* N Engl J Med. 2002;346:867-868.
142. Clewell DB. Conjugative transposons and the dissemination of antibiotic resistance in streptococci. Am Rev Microbiol. 1986;40:635-659.
143. Schaberg DR, Zervos MJ. Intergenic and interspecies gene exchange in gram-positive cocci. Antimicrob Agents Chemother. 1986;30:817-822.
144. Chang S, Sievert DM, Hageman JC, et al. Infection with vancomycin-resistant *Staphylococcus aureus* containing the *VanA* resistance gene. N Engl J Med. 2003;348:1342-1347.
145. Eliopoulos GM, Moellering RC Jr. Antimicrobial combinations. In: Lorian V, ed. Antibiotics in Laboratory Medicine. Baltimore: Williams & Wilkins; 1991;432:92.
146. The choice of antibiotic agents. Med Lett. 1992;34:49-56.
147. Zhanel GG, Hoban DJ, Karlowsky JA. Nitrofurantoin is active against vancomycin-resistant enterococci. Antimicrob Agents Chemother. 2001; 45:324-326.
148. Allerberger F, Klare I. In-vitro activity of fosfomycin against vancomycin-resistant enterococci. J Antimicrob Chemother. 1999;43:211-217.
149. Fuchs PC, Barry AL, Brown SD. Fosfomycin tromethamine susceptibility ofoutpatient urine isolates of *Escherichia coli* and *Enterococcus faecalis* from ten North American medical centres by three methods. J Antimicrob Chemother. 1999;43:137-140.
150. Martinez-Martinez L, Joyanas P, Pascual A, et al. Activity of eight fluoroquinolones against enterococci. Clin Microbiol Infect. 1997;3:497.
151. Schaberg DR, Dillon WI, Terpenning MS, et al. Increasing resistance of enterococci to ciprofloxacin. Antimicrob Agents Chemother. 1992;36:2523-2535.
152. Dougherty SH, Flohr AB, Simmons RL. "Breakthrough" enterococcal septicemia in surgical patients. Arch Surg. 1983;118:232-237.
153. Ricuarte JC, Boucher HW, Turett GS, et al. Chloramphenicol treatment for vancomycin-resistant *Enterococcus faecium* bacteremia. Clin Microbiol Infect. 2001;7:17-21.
154. Moellering RC Jr. *Streptococcus faecalis.* In: Magilligan DJ, Quinn EL, eds. Endocarditis. Medical and Surgical Management. New York: Marcel Dekker; 1986: 49-56.
155. Watanakunakorn C, Patel R. Comparison of patients with enterococcal bacteremia due to strains with and without high-level resistance to gentamicin. Clin Infect Dis. 1993;17:74-78.
156. Sandoe JAT, Witherden IR, Au-Yeung H-KC, et al. Enterococcal intravascular catheter-related bloodstream infection: Management and outcome in 61 consecutive cases. J Antimicrob Chemother. 2002;50:577-582.
157. Hunter TH. Use of streptomycin in treatment of bacterial endocarditis. Am J Med. 1947;2:436-442.
158. Krogstad DJ, Parquette AR. Defective killing of enterococci: A common property of antimicrobial agents acting on the cell wall. Antimicrob Agents Chemother. 1980;17: 965-968.
159. Bisno AL, Dismukes WE, Durack DT, et al. Antimicrobial treatment of infective endocarditis due to viridans streptococci, enterococci and staphylococci. JAMA. 1989;261:1471-1477.
160. Weinstein AJ, Moellering RC Jr. Penicillin and gentamicin therapy for enterococcal infections. JAMA. 1973;223:1030-1032.
161. Olaison L, Schadewitz K, Swedish Society of Infectious Diseases Quality Assurance Group for Endocarditis. Enterococcal endocarditis in Sweden, 1995-1999: Can shorter therapy with aminoglycosides be used? Clin Infect Dis. 2002;34:159-166.
162. Zeana C, Kubin CJ, Della-Latta P, et al. Vancomycin-resistant *Enterococcus faecium* meningitis successfully managed with linezolid: Case report and review of the literature. Clin Infect Dis. 2001;33:477-482.
163. Murray BE. Vancomycin-resistant enterococcal infections. N Engl J Med. 2000;342: 710-721.
164. Herman DJ, Gerding DW. Screening and treatment of infections caused by resistant enterococci. Antimicrob Agents Chemother. 1991;35:215-219.
165. Shlaes DM, Etter L, Gutmann L. Synergistic killing of vancomycin-resistant enterococci of classes A, B, and C by combinations of vancomycin, penicillin and gentamicin. Antimicrob Agents Chemother. 1991;35:776-779.
166. Cercenado E, Eliopoulos GM, Wennersten CB, et al. Absence of synergistic activity between ampicillin and vancomycin against highly vancomycin-resistant enterococci. Antimicrob Agents Chemother. 1922;36:2201-2203.
167. Caron F, Caron C, Gutmann L. Triple-combination penicillin-vancomycin-gentamicin for experimental endocarditis caused by a moderately penicillin- and highly glycopeptide-resistant isolate of *Enterococcus faecium.* J Infect Dis. 1991;164:888-893.
168. Caron F, Lemeland J-F, Humbert G, et al. Triple combination penicillin-vancomycin-gentamicin for experimental endocarditis caused by a highly penicillin- and glycopeptide-resistant isolate of *Enterococcus faecium.* J Infect Dis. 1993;168:681-686.
169. Hayden MK, Trenholme GM, Schultz JE, et al. In vivo development of teicoplanin resistance in a VanB *Enterococcus faecium* isolate. J Infect Dis. 1993;167:1224-1227.
170. Kawalec M, Gniadkowski M, Kedzierska J, et al. Selection of a teicoplanin-resistant *Enterococcus faecium* mutant during an outbreak caused by vancomycin-resistant enterococci with the vanB phenotype. J Clin Microbiol. 2001;39:4274-4282.
171. Moellering RC, Harding I, Gibbs M, et al. Compassionate use of teicoplanin in cases of vancomycin hypersensitivity, resistance and failure. Abstract LM-20b. In: Abstracts of the 37th Interscience Conference on Antimicrobial Agents and Chemotherapy (ICAAC). Washington, DC: American Society for Microbiology; 1997:367.
172. Lefort A, Baptista M, Fantin B, et al. Two-step acquisition of resistance to the teicoplanin-gentamicin combination by VanB-type *Enterococcus faecalis* in vitro and in experimental endocarditis. Antimicrob Agents Chemother. 1999;43:476-482.
173. Eliopoulos GM, Thauvin-Eliopoulos C, Moellering RC Jr. Contribution of animal models in the search for effective therapy for endocarditis due to enterococci with high-level resistance to gentamicin. Clin Infect Dis. 1992;15:58-62.
174. Presterl E, Graninger W, Georgopoulos A. The efficacy of teicoplanin in the treatment of endocarditis caused by gram-positive bacteria. J Antimicrob Chemother. 1993;31:755-766.

175. Schmitt JL. Efficiency of teicoplanin for enterococcal infections: 63 cases and review. Clin Infect Dis. 1992;15:302-306.
176. Hamilton-Millen JMT. From foreign pharmacopoeias: "New" antibiotics from old? J Antimicrob Chemother. 1991;27:702-705.
177. Eliopoulos GM. Activity of antimicrobials alone and in combination against vancomycin-resistant enterococci. In: Abstracts of 33rd Interscience Conference on Antimicrobial Agents and Chemotherapy (ICAAC), New Orleans; 1993:17.
178. Collins LA, Malanoski GJ, Eliopoulos GM, et al. In vitro activity of RP59500 an injectable streptogramin antibiotic, against vancomycin-resistant gram-positive organisms. Antimicrob Agents Chemother. 1993;37:598.
179. Singh KV, Weinstock GM, Murray BE. An *Enterococcus faecalis* ABC homologue (Lsa) is required for the resistance of this species to clindamycin and quinupristin/dalfopristin. Antimicrob Agents Chemother. 2002;46:1845-1850.
180. Bostic GD, Perri MB, Thal LA, et al. Comparative in vitro and bactericidal activity of oxazolidinone antibiotics against multidrug-resistant enterococci. Diagn Microbiol Infect Dis. 1998;30:109.
181. Moellering RC Jr, Cerwinka SL. Early clinical results with quinupristin/dalfopristin for the therapy of bacteremia due to resistant gram-positive bacteria. In: Zinner SH, Young LS, Acar JF, Neu HC, eds. Expanding Indications for the New Macrolides, Azalides, and Streptogramins. New York: Marcel Dekker; 1997:173-176.
182. Moellering RC Jr, Linden PK, Reinhardt MDJ, et al. The efficacy and safety of quinupristin/dalfopristin (Synercid) for the treatment of infections caused by vancomycin-resistant *Enterococcus faecium*. J Antimicrob Chemother. 1999;44:251-261.
183. Raad I, Hachem R, Hanna H, et al. Treatment of vancomycin-resistant enterococcal infections in the immunocompromised host: Quinupristin/dalfopristin in combination with minocycline. Antimicrob Agents Chemother. 2001;45:3202-3204.
184. Noskin GA, Siddiqui F, Stosor V, et al. Successful treatment of persistent vancomycin-resistant *Enterococcus faecium* bacteremia with linezolid and gentamicin. Clin Infect Dis. 1999;28:689-690.
185. Babcock HM, Ritchie DJ, Christiansen E, et al. Successful treatment of vancomycin-resistant *Enterococcus* endocarditis with oral linezolid. Clin Infect Dis. 2001;32:1373-1375.
186. McNeil SA, Clark NM, Chandrasekar PH, et al. Successful treatment of vancomycin-resistant *Enterococcus faecium* bacteremia with linezolid after failure of treatment with Synercid (quinupristin/dalfopristin). Clin Infect Dis. 2000;30:403-404.
187. de la Maza L, Ruoff KL, Ferraro MJ. In vitro activities of daptomycin and other antimicrobial agents against vancomycin-resistant gram-positive bacteria. Antimicrob Agents Chemother. 1989;33:1383-1384.
188. Van Teil FH, van den Bogaard TE. In vitro susceptibility to LY333328 of vancomycin-resistant enterococci isolated from humans and animals. J Antimicrob Chemother. 1997;40:733.
189. Ruoff KL, Ferraro MJ, Holden J, et al. Identification of *Streptococcus bovis* and *Streptococcus salivarius* in clinical laboratories. J Clin Microbiol. 1984;20:223-226.
190. Moellering RC Jr, Watson BK, Kunz L. Endocarditis due to group D streptococci. Comparison of disease caused by *Streptococcus bovis* with that caused by the enterococci. Am J Med. 1974;57:239-250.
191. Ruoff KL, Miller SI, Garner CV, et al. Bacteremia with *Streptococcus bovis* and *Streptococcus salivarius:* Clinical correlates of more accurate identification of isolates. J Clin Microbiol. 1989;27:305-308.
192. Facklam RR. Recognition of group D streptococcal species of human origin by biochemical and physiological tests. Appl Microbiol. 1972;23:1131-1139.
193. Coykendall AL, Gustafson KB. Deoxyribonucleic acid hybridization among strains of *Streptococcus salivarius* and *Streptococcus bovis*. Int J Syst Bacteriol. 1985;35:274-280
194. Raverby WD, Bottone EJ, Keusch GT. Group D streptococcal bacteremia, with emphasis on the incidence an presentation of infections due to *Streptococcus bovis*. N Engl J Med. 1973;289:1400-1403.
195. Hoppes WL, Lerner PI. Nonenterococcal group-D streptococcal endocarditis, caused by *Streptococcus bovis*. Ann Intern Med. 1974;81:588-593.
196. Watanakunakorn C. *Streptococcus bovis* endocarditis. Am J Med. 1974;56:256-260.
197. Murray HW, Roberts RB. *Streptococcus bovis* bacteremia and underlying gastrointestinal disease. Arch Intern Med. 1978;138:1097-1099.
198. Reynolds JG, Silva E, McCormack WM. Association of *Streptococcus bovis* bacteremia with bowel disease. J Clin Microbiol. 1983;17:696-697.
199. Klein RS, Recco RA, Catalano MT, et al. Association of *Streptococcus bovis* with carcinoma of the colon. N Engl J Med. 1977;297:800-802.
200. Klein RS, Catalano MT, Edberg SC, et al. *Streptococcus bovis* septicemia and carcinoma of the colon. Ann Intern Med. 1979;91:560-562.
201. Wittrup IH, Schaadt MLC, Arpi M, et al. Bacteremia complicated by vertebral osteomyelitis due to *Streptococcus bovis*. Eur J Clin Microbiol Infect Dis. 1999;18:365-367.
202. Grant RJ, Whitehead TR, Orr JE. *Streptococcus bovis* meningitis in an infant. J Clin Microbiol. 2000;38:462-463.
203. Duval X, Papastamopoulos V, Longuet P, et al. Definite *Streptococcus bovis* endocarditis: Characteristics in 20 patients. Clin Microbiol Infect. 2001;7:3-10.
204. Burns CA, McCaughey M, Lauter CB. The association of *Streptococcus bovis* fecal carriage and colon neoplasia: Possible relationship with polyps and their premalignant potential. Am J Gastroenterol. 1985;80:42-46.
205. Klein RS, Warman SW, Knackmuhs GG, et al. Lack of association of *Streptococcus bovis* with noncolonic gastrointestinal carcinoma. Am J Gastroenterol. 1987;82:540-543.
206. Poyart C, Pierre C, Quesne G, et al. Emergence of vancomycin resistance from the genus *Streptococcus:* Characterization of a vanB transferable determinant in *Streptococcus bovis*. Antimicrob Agents Chemother. 1997;41:24.
207. Ruoff KL. *Leuconostoc, Pediococcus, Stomatococcus* and miscellaneous gram-positive cocci that grow aerobically. In: Murray PR, Baron EJ, Pfaller MA, eds. Manual of Clinical Microbiology. 7th ed. Washington, DC: American Society for Microbiology; 1999;306-315.
208. Mackey T, Lejeune V, Janssens M, et al. Identification of vancomycin-resistant lactic bacteria isolated from humans. J Clin Microbiol. 1993;31:2499-2501.
209. Garvie EI. Genus *Leuconostoc*. In: Sneath PHA, Mair NS, Sharpe ME, et al, eds. Bergey's Manual of Systematic Bacteriology, v. 2. Baltimore: Williams & Wilkins; 1986:1071-1075.
210. Ruoff KL, Kuritzkes DR, Wolfson JS, et al. Vancomycin-resistant gram-positive bacteria isolated from human sources. J Clin Microbiol. 1988;26:2064-2068.
211. Buu-Hoi A, Branger C, Acar JF. Vancomycin-resistant streptococci or *Leuconostoc* sp. Antimicrob Agents Chemother. 1985;28:458-460.
212. Coovadia YM, Solwa Z, van den Ende J. Meningitis caused by a vancomycin-resistant *Leuconostoc* sp. J Clin Microbiol. 1987;25:1784-1785.
213. Isenberg HD, Vellozzi EM, Shaprio J, et al. Clinical laboratory challenges in the recognition of *Leuconostoc* spp. J Clin Microbiol. 1988;26:479-483.
214. Wenocur HS, Smith MA, Vellozzi EM, et al. Odontogenic infection secondary to *Leuconostoc* species. J Clin Microbiol. 1988;26:1893-1894.
215. Arthur M, Courvalin P. Genetics and mechanisms of glycopeptide resistance in enterococci. Antimicrob Agents Chemother. 1993;37:1563-1571.
216. De La Maza L, Ruoff KL, Ferraro MJ. In vitro activities of daptomycin and other antimicrobial agents against vancomycin-resistant gram-positive bacteria. Antimicrob Agents Chemother. 1989;33:1383-1384.
217. Swensen JM, Facklam RR, Thornsberry C. Antimicrobial susceptibility of vancomycin-resistant *Leuconostoc, Pediococcus,* and *Lactobacillus* species. Antimicrob Agents Chemother. 1990;34:543-549.
218. Collins LA, Malanoski GJ, Eliopoulos GM, et al. In vitro activity of RP 59500, an injectable streptogramin antibiotic against vancomycin-resistant gram-positive organisms. Antimicrob Agents Chemother. 1993;37:598-601.
219. Martinez-Martinez L, Saavedra JM, Conejo MC. Bacteremia caused by *Leuconostoc* spp. Clin Microbiol Newslett. 1992;14:102-104.
220. Golan Y, Poutsiaka DD, Tozzi S, et al. Daptomycin for line-related *Leuconostoc* bacteremia. J Antimicrob Chemother. 2001;47:357-368.

Streptococcus agalactiae (Group B Streptococcus)

MORVEN S. EDWARDS

CAROL J. BAKER

HISTORICAL PERSPECTIVE

Group B streptococci (*Streptococcus agalactiae*) were first reported as human pathogens in 1938 by Fry, who described three cases of fatal puerperal sepsis.[1] Before Fry, Lancefield and Hare[2] had identified these organisms in vaginal cultures from asymptomatic postpartum women.[2] Human group B streptococcal infection, however, was reported infrequently until the early 1960s, when several authors indicated that disease caused by these organisms might be more common than was appreciated previously.[3-5] By the 1970s, group B streptococcus had become the predominant pathogen causing septicemia and meningitis in neonates and infants younger than 3 months. Initially a concern of pediatricians, group B streptococci also cause substantial pregnancy-related morbidity. Implementation of recommendations for the use of maternal intrapartum chemoprophylaxis in the mid-1990s has been associated with a dramatic decrease in the incidence of early-onset disease in neonates and with a significant decline in the incidence of invasive disease during pregnancy.[6]

Invasive group B streptococcal infection in nonpregnant adults has recently been recognized as a major health concern. In the past 2 decades, two- to fourfold increases in the incidence of group B streptococcal disease have been reported in nonpregnant adults, most of whom have underlying medical conditions.[7,8] Active, population-based surveillance indicates that two thirds of patients with invasive group B streptococcal disease now are nonpregnant adults.[6,9] The highest case-fatality rate as a consequence of group B streptococcal infection is among nonpregnant adults older than 65 years of age. Nursing home residents have a markedly higher incidence of invasive group B streptococcal disease than do community-dwelling residents.[10] These shifts in group B streptococcal disease incidence and outcome suggest that older adults may be a target population for immunization with group B streptococcal vaccines as these become commercially available. Publication in 2002 of the complete genome sequence of serotypes III and V group B streptococci opens new avenues for the identification of novel vaccine targets as well as for further elucidating the molecular basis for virulence of the organism.[11,12]

DESCRIPTION

Classification and Morphologic Characteristics

S. agalactiae is the species designation for streptococci belonging to Lancefield group B. The serologic differentiation of hemolytic streptococci by groups was described in 1933.[13] It is based on the capillary precipitin reaction between the group-specific carbohydrate cell wall antigen and hyperimmune rabbit antisera. Group B streptococci are facultative, gram-positive diplococci that grow on a variety of bacteriologic media. Isolated colonies on sheep blood agar are 3 to 4 mm in diameter and grayish white. The flat, somewhat mucoid colonies are surrounded by a narrow zone of β–hemolysis that, for some strains, is detectable only on lifting a colony from the agar. One percent to 2% of strains are nonhemolytic. To enhance the accurate detection of low numbers of group B streptococci from sites such as the genital or gastrointestinal tract, a number of selective broth media have been employed. These usually contain Todd-Hewitt broth with or without

sheep red blood cells and antimicrobial agents such as nalidixic acid and gentamicin or colistin.[14]

Identification

Definitive identification of group B streptococci is based on detection of the group B–specific cell wall antigen common to all strains. A number of serologic methods using hyperimmune group B–specific antisera have been developed for the detection of the group B antigen. Latex agglutination is the most widely employed. When the manufacturer's instructions are followed, these products for serogrouping β-hemolytic streptococci are comparable to the Lancefield capillary precipitin method.

Biochemical methods that permit the presumptive identification of group B streptococci include resistance to bacitracin or trimethoprim-sulfamethoxazole, positive sodium hippurate hydrolysis, and the production of an orange pigment during anaerobic growth on certain media. β-Hemolytic streptococci that hydrolyze sodium hippurate belong to either group B or group D; these may be distinguished on the basis of hydrolysis of bile esculin agar. Among group D strains, 99% hydrolyze bile esculin, whereas 99% to 100% of group B strains fail to react. Production of CAMP factor, which is a thermostable extracellular protein that results in synergistic hemolysis on sheep blood agar with the β-lysin of *Staphylococcus aureus,* is observed in 98% to virtually 100% of group B streptococci. The combination of the CAMP test with bacitracin sensitivity and the bile esculin reaction is adequate for the presumptive differentiation of group B from other serogroups of β-hemolytic streptococci.[15]

Classification and Typing

Group B streptococci are currently classified serologically by capsular polysaccharide type and by cell-surface expressed proteins. Lancefield defined two cell wall carbohydrate antigens for group B streptococci, the group B–specific or C substance common to all strains of this serogroup and the type-specific or S substance that allowed classification into the serotypes I, II, and III.[16] Later, Lancefield reported distinct differences in serotype I strains, and in the early 1970s these were designated Ia, Ib, and Ic.[17] These strains possess a capsular polysaccharide antigen, Ia or Ib, and some Ia and all Ib strains also have a surface-protein antigen, now designated c protein, that is found in approximately 60% of type II strains and rarely in type III and type V strains. The nomenclature of group B streptococci was revised in 1984 to designate the capsular polysaccharides as type-specific antigens with surface proteins as additional antigenic markers.[18] Additional capsular polysaccharide types, IV, V, VI, VII, and VIII, each with unique polysaccharides alone or with protein antigens, have been defined,[19-22] and additional candidates are being evaluated. At least two distinct types of c protein, α and β, are defined, and individual strains may contain one or both components. Other proteins, designated R, X, and Rib, are found in some strains.

Each of the common polysaccharide types has a characteristic predominant protein expression pattern. For type Ia it is α, for type III it is R4, and for type V it is R1 plus R4. The expression of α protein is always mutually exclusive of the expression of R proteins.[23] Antibodies directed against the Ia, Ib, and II polysaccharide antigens, but not against III, were shown by Lancefield to provide passive protection for mice challenged with homologous—but not heterologous—antigen-containing strains.[24] Although mouse virulence for type III strains could not be achieved in the original mouse-protective assay, others subsequently modified this experimental model so that antibody to the type III capsular polysaccharide antigen also protected against challenge with strains containing the homologous but not the heterologous antigens.[25] The α and β proteins and Rib also can elicit protective antibodies in animals,[26-28] but their role in human infections is not known. Antibodies directed at the group B antigen are not protective.

The classical method for serotyping group B streptococcal isolates is by analysis of capillary precipitin or immunodiffusion in agarose reactions between acid extracts of the organism and hyperimmune rabbit antisera. Recently, genetic approaches to genotyping of group B streptococcal isolates have been developed. Analysis of *Sma*1 digests of chromosomal DNA by pulsed-field gel electrophoresis has facilitated identification of isolates in which capsular polysaccharide is not detectable by immunologic means.[29] Sequencing primers also are being designed that allow identification of capsular polysaccharide gene clusters.[30] Such polymerase chain reaction (PCR)-based methods offer the potential for widespread availability in the future of a practical alternative to conventional serotyping for identifying the serotype of group B streptococcal isolates. Molecular subtyping also provides a powerful tool to document the epidemiologic relatedness of group B streptococcal strains.[31,32] Such methods could assist in determining whether recurrent infections are caused by separate or identical strains and in tracking virulent clone families that may be disproportionate causes of invasive disease.[31-33]

EPIDEMIOLOGY AND TRANSMISSION

Asymptomatic Colonization

Group B streptococci have been isolated from genital or lower gastrointestinal tract cultures of pregnant and nonpregnant women at rates ranging from 10% to 40%. These variations in the reported prevalence of asymptomatic colonization relate not only to differences in the sites sampled and bacteriologic methods used for detection of the organism, but also to demographic differences in the populations studied (Table 199-1). When more than one appropriate site such as the lower vagina or the periurethral area and the rectum is sampled, and when the selective broth media is utilized, the rate of colonization usually exceeds 20%. Group B streptococci may be associated with asymptomatic bacteriuria during pregnancy,[34] and bacteriuria is a marker for a high genital inoculum ("heavy colonization").

Colonization with group B streptococci occurs more frequently among black women than in other racial or ethnic groups.[35,36] Diabetes mellitus is also independently associated with higher rates of group B streptococcal colonization during pregnancy.[37] Sexual activity is an important risk factor for vaginal acquisition of group B streptococci.[38,39] Multiple partners and frequent or recent sexual intercourse are associated with increased risk for vaginal group B streptococcal acquisition over time.[38] It is proposed that sexual activity alters the microenvironment of the vagina in a manner that makes it more permissive for group B streptococcal colonization. Sexual activity and particularly male-to-female oral sex also increase the risk for cocolonization with identical group B streptococcal strains among heterosexual college couples.[40] Significantly lower genital colonization rates have been reported for women who are sexually inexperienced,

older than 20 years, or multiparous.[41] Pregnancy itself does not influence the prevalence of colonization with group B streptococci.

The principal reservoir for group B streptococci is the lower gastrointestinal tract. Studies documenting a rectal or vaginal isolation ratio greater than 1 and the rectum as the site most accurately predicting chronicity of carriage support the premise that genital colonization may reflect acquisition from the rectal site.[42,43] Further, group B streptococci have been isolated from the proximal part of the small intestine of adults. The prevalence of oropharyngeal colonization is low (approximately 5%), but this may approach 20% in homosexual men. The group B streptococcal colonization rate among a group of healthy older adults with a mean age of 73 years was 22%. Among colonized women, two thirds were colonized at rectal and vaginal sites, whereas most men had rectal colonization only.[44]

Transmission to Neonates

Mucous membrane colonization of newborns results from vertical transmission of the organism from the mother, either in utero by the ascending route or at the time of delivery. Vaginally colonized pregnant women are at an increased risk for premature labor.[45] The rate of vertical transmission among neonates born to women colonized with group B streptococci at the time of delivery is approximately 50%.[46,47] Paired isolates from mothers and their neonates are usually of concordant serotypes. A high genital inoculum at delivery, as detected by semiquantitative culture methods, significantly increases the likelihood of vertical transmission.[42,47,48] Infants born to heavily colonized women are more likely to develop early-onset (younger than 7 days) disease.[42] In addition to maternal intrapartum exposure, nosocomial colonization of the neonate may occasionally occur. Infant-to-infant spread via the hands of personnel is the most likely mode of acquisition. Community acquisition of group B streptococci in young infants occurs, but infrequently.

Vertical transmission is required for the development of invasive early-onset infection.[46,47] Factors that increase the incidence of invasive early-onset infection among neonates born to colonized mothers include group B streptococcal bacteriuria; rupture of membranes or delivery at less than 37 weeks of gestation; intrapartum fever ($\geq 38°$ C) or amnionitis; and rupture of membranes for 18 or more hours before delivery.[49] Studies of maternal features associated with higher attack rates for early-onset neonatal disease have reported black race, an age younger than 20 years, and a history of previous miscarriage.[50] Although some infants who develop late-onset infection acquire the organism from nonmaternal sources,[47] the concordance of serotypes between infant and maternal genital isolates in one half to two thirds

TABLE 199-1 Factors Influencing Detection of Group B Streptococcal Colonization

| Feature | Effect on Isolation Rate | | |
	Increased	Decreased	None
Method Employed			
Culture medium	Broth media	Agar media	—
	Antibiotic-containing media	Nonselective broth media	—
Site(s)	Lower vagina and rectum	Cervical os	—
	Multiple sites	Single site	—
Interval	≥ 2 cultures in interval of 6-8 wk	Single sampling time	—
Genital Carriage in Women			
Pregnancy	—	—	+
Time during pregnancy	—	—	+
Day of menstrual cycle	First half	—	—
Age	≤ 20 yr	—	—
Sexual activity	Active	Virgin	—
Frequency of sexual intercourse or total number of partners	—	—	+
Vaginal discharge	—	—	+
Birth control method	Intrauterine device	—	Oral contraceptives
Parity	Primigravida	>3 pregnancies	—
Ethnic origin	Black	—	—
Marital status	—	—	+
Socioeconomic group	Lower income	—	—

of cases suggests that the vertical or household contact route of acquisition also is a major determinant of risk for late-onset infections.

Incidence and Serotype Distribution of Isolates

Historically, the incidence of early-onset group B streptococcal infection in neonates ranged from 1 to 3 per 1000 live births. The incidence of early-onset neonatal infections has declined significantly in association with the implementation of maternal intrapartum chemoprophylaxis guidelines.[6] Results of active, population-based surveillance in a population ranging from 12 million in 1993 to 20 million in 1998 revealed a 65% reduction in early-onset disease incidence, from 1.7 to 0.6 per 1000 live births. There was a 75% decrease in excess incidence in black infants compared with white infants. In marked contrast, the implementation of intrapartum chemoprophylaxis had no impact on the incidence of late-onset infections in infants. This incidence remains approximately 0.5 per 1000 live births.

Pregnant women are another group of patients in whom group B streptococcal disease is frequently diagnosed. These organisms are estimated to cause 15% to 25% of the cases of peripartum febrile morbidity with or without bacteremia, or an estimated 50,000 cases annually.[51-53] Intrapartum vaginal colonization with group B streptococci is an independent risk factor for chorioamnionitis.[52] Women with heavy colonization are at significantly greater risk for intra-amniotic infection than those with light vaginal colonization.[54] The incidence of invasive disease in pregnancy has also declined significantly in association with the use of intrapartum maternal chemoprophylaxis, from 0.29 per 1000 live births in 1993 to 0.23 per 1000 live births in 1998.[6] Among the women with invasive group B streptococcal disease for whom the outcome of pregnancy was known, 54% had infants who remained well, 17% had infants who survived invasive disease, and 29% had spontaneous abortions, stillborn infants, or infants who died of invasive infection.

Nonpregnant adults with underlying medical conditions such as diabetes mellitus, chronic liver or renal disease, human immunodeficiency virus (HIV) infection, malignancy, and stroke also are susceptible to group B streptococcal infections. These nonpregnant adults in a population-based study had an annual incidence of infection of 4.4 cases per 100,000 population.[9] Nonpregnant adults now account for nearly two thirds of all invasive group B streptococcal infections.[6] The incidence of invasive group B streptococcal disease among older adults has been rising for the past 2 decades and is estimated to be 18 to 20 per 100,000.[6,10] In a recent population-based surveillance report, adults 65 years of age and older represented one third of cases of invasive group B streptococcal disease. Nursing home residents had a markedly higher incidence (72 per 100,000 population) than community residents 65 years of age and older.[10] The biologic basis for the high risk among nursing home residents is not known but is likely to be related to their having a higher proportion of underlying medical conditions that predispose them to invasive infection.

In the 1970s and 1980s, type III strains of group B streptococci accounted for one third of early-onset infections, for nearly 90% of late-onset infections, and for most cases of meningitis regardless of the age at the onset of infection. Data from the 1990s indicate a shift in the serotype distribution of invasive isolates from infants and adults. Among neonates with early-onset disease, type Ia predominates and accounts for 35% to 40% of infections, followed by types III (25% to 30%) and V (about 15%).[55-57] Late-onset infant disease and meningitis is still caused predominantly by serotype III strains.[58] The emergence of serotype V has been echoed in the distribution of isolates that asymptomatically colonize and cause invasive disease in pregnant women. Taken together, serotypes Ia, III, and V comprise more than two thirds of colonizing isolates in pregnancy.[59] Serotypes Ia (34%), III (25%), and V (23%) also accounted for over 80% of strains from 53 pregnant women with invasive group B streptococcal infection.[57] Among nonpregnant adults, a population-based surveillance found that types Ia and V were the most prevalent serotypes, each accounting for one third of invasive isolates, with type III strains accounting for another 20% of cases.[60] In some reports, V is now the most com-

mon serotype causing invasive disease in nonpregnant adults, accounting for one third of the isolates.[61] In a recent seroepidemiologic assessment, serotype V accounted for almost half of the strains asymptomatically colonizing healthy older adults.[44] Types IV, VI through VIII, and nontypable isolates are rarely associated with invasive infection, but in Japan, serotypes VI and VIII are frequently isolated from pregnant women.[62]

PATHOGENETIC MECHANISMS

To cause disease, group B streptococci, like other extracellular bacterial pathogens, must colonize mucosal surfaces and then breach these surfaces to enter normally sterile sites such as the blood stream. The group B streptococcus produces a capsule that inhibits complement deposition and phagocytosis. Strains that effectively evade host phagocytes may damage tissues by inducing the release of substances that cause inflammation or by the production of substances that directly damage cells.

Adherence. Adherence of group B streptococci to epithelial cells is integral to several steps in the pathogenesis of disease, including colonization of the rectum and genital tract in pregnant women and nonpregnant adults and as a necessary condition for the invasion of respiratory epithelial cells in newborn infants. The association between maternal genital tract colonization with group B streptococci at delivery and invasive early-onset infection in neonates is well established.[46,47] Similarly, there is an increased risk for invasive infection rather than mucosal colonization in neonates when exposure to the organism is prolonged by a rupture of membranes for 18 or more hours before delivery or intensified by a high genital inoculum or maternal chorioamnionitis.[42,47,48] Heavy maternal colonization with group B streptococci is associated with an increased risk for delivering a preterm, low-birth-weight infant.[63] However, these factors do not fully explain the low frequency of invasive infection (estimated at 1% to 2%) among newborns born to colonized mothers.

The nature of the bacterial structures involved in adhering to and penetrating cellular barriers is not fully elucidated, but a role for the α protein is proposed in the interaction between the bacterium and the host cell.[64] The α protein is a prototype for a family of long, tandem repeat-containing surface proteins that are common to the serotypes of group B streptococci causing most invasive disease. In contrast, the capsular polysaccharide attenuates adherence.[65]

Invasion. Group B streptococci have been shown to invade respiratory epithelial and endothelial cells as well as brain microvascular endothelial cells in vitro.[65,66] The invasive capacity of an unencapsulated mutant appears enhanced compared with that of an encapsulated parent strain.[65] However, by use of a dynamic in vitro attachment and invasion system, Malin and Paoletti[67] have demonstrated that invasion is independent of capsular polysaccharide expression and can be regulated by growth rate. Growth rate–dependent invasion occurred when group B streptococci were grown in continuous culture under glucose-defined, thiamine-defined, and undefined nutrient limitations. Group B streptococcal hemolysin expression promotes invasion of lung epithelial cells.[68] Its expression also correlates with lung epithelial cell injury and promotes injury of lung microvascular endothelial cells, increasing cell permeability in vitro. It is proposed that this increased permeability is a factor that contributes to alveolar edema and to the hemorrhage that may be a feature of group B streptococcal pneumonia.[69] Inhibition studies suggest that the α protein and, in particular, its N-terminal region, also are involved in bacterial entry into epithelial cells.[64]

Host Factors. Baker and Kasper reported in 1976 that neonates and young infants at risk for invasive type III group B streptococcal infection were those with low concentrations of passively acquired maternal antibodies to the type III capsular antigen.[70] Because infants born prematurely acquire proportionately lower levels of maternal immunoglobulin G (IgG) than do those born at term, premature infants are less likely to acquire protective levels of type-specific antibodies. Women colonized with type III group B streptococci and delivering healthy neonates have significantly higher concentrations of type III–specific IgG than women whose infants develop early-onset type III disease.[71,72] A low concentration of maternal antibodies to capsular polysaccharides Ia, Ib, and II at delivery also is a determinant of neonatal susceptibility to infection caused by these serotypes of group B streptococci.[73-75] Antibody to the group B–specific polysaccharide, however, is not protective.[76]

The classical complement pathway and heat-stable opsonins are required for maximal opsonic activity of group B streptococcal strains of the major serotypes.[77-79] The alternative complement pathway participates in opsonophagocytosis of type III strains when specific antibody is present in a sufficient concentration. The opsonophagocytic requirements for type II strains are complex, modulated in part by the surface protein components α and β as well as the type II polysaccharide, and the integrity of the classical complement pathway appears essential for effective opsonophagocytosis in vitro.[78,80] For clinical isolates of type Ia group B streptococcus, opsonization and phagocytosis may proceed by the classical complement pathway in an antibody-independent fashion.[81] Deficient activity by a portion of neonatal sera for clinical isolates of this serotype correlated significantly with low levels of the classical pathway components C1q and C4.[82] Physiologically low levels of complement components or their receptors on phagocytes may provide a partial explanation for age-related susceptibility to group B streptococcal disease. In addition, neutrophil reserves are exhausted rapidly in newborns, so their marrow capacity to infection is limited.[83]

Neutrophil complement and Fc receptors are important in opsonic recognition of group B streptococci. Blockade of complement receptor 3 on neutrophils from adults or neonates inhibits killing of types Ia, III, and V strains of group B streptococci.[79,84] Blockade of neutrophil Fc receptor III inhibits phagocytosis of type III group B streptococci to an even greater extent.[85] In complement-inactivated serum, Fc receptor II also has a substantial role in mediating ingestion of serotype III strains.[86]

Inflammatory Mediators. Group B streptococci have been shown in vitro and in experimental models of infection to induce the release of proinflammatory cytokines, including tumor necrosis factor-α (TNF-α), interleukin-1β, interleukin-6, and interleukin-8.[87-89] In animal models, elevated levels of TNF-α correlate with the severity of disease and with mortality. Purified group-specific polysaccharide and peptidoglycan, rather than serotype-specific capsular polysaccharide, are the bacterial components that induce the inflammatory response. The molecular mechanisms responsible for group B streptococcus–induced TNF-α production have been explored. The interaction of type III group B streptococci with cord blood monocytes induces host cell transduction pathways that lead to activation of the transcription factors nuclear factor (NF)-κB and activator protein-1 through a pathway that involves phosphorylation of the p38 mitogen-activated protein kinase pathway.[90] Engagement of mammalian Toll-like receptors (TLRs) 2 and 6 as well as CD14 expression were essential for cells to respond to the presence of group B streptococci.[91] However, this recognition is due to a novel secreted or shed bacterial product. Whole group B streptococci activated macrophages independently of TLR2 and TLR6.

Bacterial Virulence Factors. In addition to host factors, bacterial virulence factors contribute to the host–parasite interaction that determines the outcome between exposure and the development of colonization or invasive group B streptococcal infection. A high quantity of cell-associated sialic acid and its elaboration in supernatant fluid are associated with virulence of type III strains.[92] Transposon mutant strains of type III group B streptococcus have been constructed that are unencapsulated or that express a capsular polysaccharide differing from the wild type in expressing a capsule lacking sialic acid.[93,94] Each of these changes in capsular expression is associated with a loss of virulence in a neonatal rat model of lethal infection, supporting the critical nature of capsular antigen as a virulence factor. The unique capsular structures of group B streptococci also might enhance the invasiveness of one serotype over another. Type III strains, for exam-ple, invade brain microvascular endothelial cells more efficiently than strains from other common serotypes (although the capsule itself does not facilitate invasion).[95] The capsular polysaccharides of types Ia, II, III, IV, and V all contain glucose, galactose, glucosamine, and sialic acid, but their structural arrangements are distinct. Sialic acid, which constitutes the exclusive terminal residue of the types Ia, Ib, and III—but not type II or V—group B streptococcal capsular polysaccharide, inhibits activation of the alternative pathway of complement.[96] Types VI and VIII lack glucosamine, and type VIII contains rhamnose.[21,22,97] A novel insertion sequence in the hyaluronidase gene has been identified predominantly in group B streptococcal strains causing endocarditis.[98] The mechanism by which this genetic alteration and the lack of hyaluronidase increases disease potential is speculative.

The capsular polysaccharide is the best defined virulence factor of group B streptococcus. β-Hemolysin expression enhances virulence by promoting invasion and cell injury.[69,70] Hyperhemolytic variants derived by transposon mutagenesis had enhanced lethality and promoted joint injury compared with a nonhemolytic group B streptococcal variant in a murine model of infection.[99] The organism expresses additional factors that allow it to resist host defenses. A recent report indicated that the surface-localized β protein binds human complement factor H and that the complexed factor H retains its ability to downregulate complement activation.[100] In addition, *cspA*, a novel gene encoding a surface-localized, serine protease–like protein has been identified.[101] It promotes group B streptococcal survival by evasion of opsonophagocytosis and is required for group B streptococcal cleavage of fibrinogen.

CLINICAL MANIFESTATIONS

Neonatal Infections

Early-Onset Infection

As the incidence of neonatal group B streptococcal infections rose during the 1970s, a bimodal distribution of cases by age at the onset of symptoms became apparent. Two distinctive clinical syndromes related to age were described by Franciosi and co-workers[102] (acute and delayed) and by Baker and colleagues[103] (early and late-onset). Early-onset infection, defined as the development of systemic infection during the first 6 days of life, has a mean age of 12 hours at its onset. Maternal obstetric complications are frequent (50% to 60%), and infants born at less than 37 weeks of gestation have significantly higher attack rates than infants born at term. The three major clinical expressions of infection are bacteremia or septicemia, pneumonia, and meningitis, and they occur at frequencies of approximately 60%, 30%, and 10%, respectively.

Clinical abnormalities are present at or within a few hours after birth in most infants. The presenting signs of early-onset group B streptococcal infection—lethargy, poor feeding, jaundice, abnormal temperature, grunting respirations, pallor, and hypotension—are indistinguishable from those in neonates with bacterial infections of other causes. Regardless of the focus of infection, signs of respiratory distress such as apnea, grunting, tachypnea, and cyanosis are observed in the majority. Pulmonary infiltrates or a radiograph consistent with respiratory distress syndrome or transient tachypnea of the newborn may suggest the diagnosis. Infants with meningitis have a clinical presentation that initially cannot be distinguished from those without meningeal invasion.

Increased awareness of the disease and improvements in supportive therapy have resulted in decreased mortality among infants with early-onset group B streptococcal infection, and present rates range from 5% to 10%.[104] Mortality rates are inversely proportional to birth weight.

Late-Onset Infection

The late-onset syndrome has an onset between 7 days and 89 days of age, with a mean of about 24 days. Maternal obstetric complications are uncommon, and the case-fatality ratio is low, estimated to be at 3%.[50,104] Occult bacteremia and meningitis are common clinical manifestations of late-onset infection, but a variety of focal infections, usually with accompanying bacteremia, are also described. The non-specific initial signs of late-onset disease, such as lethargy, poor feeding, and irritability, generally occur in association with fever. These infants can present with fulminant infection characterized by rapid progression to a moribund state with septic shock and seizures and sheets of organisms on Gram stains of cerebrospinal fluid (CSF). An increased risk for death or permanent neurologic sequelae occurs in patients with this fulminant presentation.[105] Additional clinical findings that have been associated with a fatal outcome or permanent neurologic sequelae include neutropenia at admission, prolonged seizures, and high concentrations of type III polysaccharide antigen in admission CSF specimens. Of survivors of group B streptococcal meningitis, whether early- or late-onset, 25% to 50% have permanent neurologic sequelae.[105,106]

Bone and joint infections are the other clinical forms of late-onset group B streptococcal disease that occur relatively frequently.[107] Uncommon foci of infection include cellulitis and adenitis (usually preauricular or submandibular), otitis media, conjunctivitis, pleural empyema, peritonitis, endocarditis, and deep abscesses.[108]

Infection beyond Early Infancy

Infants older than 3 months constitute 10% to 15% of the total with late-onset disease.[104,109] Many of these infections occur among very low birth weight infants who may still be hospitalized for complications of prematurity. The term *very late onset* is often used in this setting. Healthy older infants occasionally present with occult bacteremia.[109] Congenital heart disease and immune deficiency, including HIV infection, should be considered when group B streptococcal disease is diagnosed beyond early infancy.[110,111]

Infections in Adults

Invasive group B streptococcal infection causes substantial morbidity and mortality among adults. In one analysis covering 1975 to 1984, the composite attack rate for group B streptococcal bacteremia was 0.2 cases per 1000 hospital admissions, and 53% of group B streptococcal blood culture isolates were from adults.[112] In a contemporary, prospective, population-based assessment of invasive group B streptococcal disease, men and nonpregnant women accounted for 66% of the total number of cases.[6] Adults with bacteremia unrelated to pregnancy are usually older, but ages range from 18 to 99 years.[112-116] The mean age in one report was 62 years, and 57% were men.[9] The incidence increases with age, is higher in blacks than in other races or ethnicities, and is quadrupled in older adults in nursing homes compared with community-dwelling older adults.[9,10,116]

One or more medical conditions predisposing to infection can be identified in most adults with invasive disease (Table 199-2). Diabetes mellitus is the most common underlying medical condition. Of patients with soft tissue infections, one third report diabetes mellitus as a comorbid condition.[61] Neurologic abnormalities associated with infection include dementia, cerebrovascular disease resulting in alterations of mental status, and paraplegia or quadriplegia. Young adults (20 to 40 years of age) with diabetes, cancer, or HIV infection are at significantly increased risk (28- to 30-fold) for invasive group B streptococcal disease.[9] In a case-control study, diabetes, cirrhosis, stroke, breast cancer, decubitus ulcer, and neurogenic bladder significantly increased the risk for community-acquired group B streptococcal infection. Nosocomial infection was independently associated with the placement of a central venous line, diabetes, congestive heart failure, and a seizure disorder.[117]

Age 65 years or older is also a risk factor for group B streptococcal infection. The incidence doubles when 50 to 64 year olds are compared to those 65 years of age and older.[61] Among a group of community-dwelling older adults, the age-specific incidence increased steadily and was approximately threefold higher in those older than 85 years than in the 65 to 74-year-old group.

Mortality is increased in older patients, in those with polymicrobial infection, and in those with diabetes mellitus, liver disease, or malig-

TABLE 199-2 Underlying Conditions in Invasive Group B Streptococcal Infections[*]

Condition	n (%)
Diabetes mellitus	82(30)
Liver disease or history of alcohol abuse	66(24)
Neurologic impairment	58(21)
Malignancy	52(19)
Renal failure	37(14)
Cardiovascular disease or heart failure	37(14)
Pulmonary disease	21(8)
Urologic disease	11(4)
Peripheral vascular disease	9(3)
Human immunodeficiency virus infection	7(3)
Intravenous catheter-related infection	5(2)
Gastrointestinal disease	5(2)
Steroid administration	5(2)
Hypertension	4(1)
Functional or surgical splenectomy	3(1)
Other	7(3)
None	5(2)

[*]*N* = 271 adults. Streptococcal infections listed were not related to pregnancy. Some patients had more than one underlying condition.

From Farley MM. Group B streptococcal disease in nonpregnant adults. Clin Infect Dis. 2001;33:556-561; Opal SM, Cross A, Palmo M, et al. Group B streptococcal sepsis in adults and infants: Contrasts and comparisons. Arch Intern Med. 1988;148:641-645; Gallagher PG, Watanakunakorn C. Group B streptococcal bacteremia in a community teaching hospital. Am J Med. 1985;78:795-800; Verghese A, Mireault K, Arbeit RD. Group B streptococcal bacteremia in men. Rev Infect Dis. 1986;8:912-917; Lerner PI, Gopalakrishna KV, Wolinsky E, et al. Group B streptococcus (S. agalactiae) bacteremia in adults: Analysis of 32 cases and review of the literature. Medicine (Baltimore). 1977;56:457-473; Schwartz B, Schuchat A, Oxtoby MJ, et al. Invasive group B streptococcal disease in adults: A population-based study in metropolitian Atlanta. JAMA. 1991;266:1112-1114.

nancy. Case-fatality rates ranging from 8% to 70% have been reported,[112-114,118,119] but in more recent years case-fatality rates have ranged from 5% to 25% in nonpregnant adults.[6-8,10,61] Adults are more likely to die as a result of group B streptococcal infection than are infants.[6] Shock and alcoholism are associated independently with a significant risk for death.[7] Nursing home residents are significantly more likely to have a fatal outcome than are community-dwelling older adults.[10] Of 29 adults with bacteremia described by Opal and associates,[112] only 34% acquired infection in the community. Others have described rates of nosocomial infection from 38% to 70%,[114,120] but case clustering has not been observed.[112-114,118,120] The latter suggests that endogenous respiratory, genitourinary, or gastrointestinal colonization rather than the acquisition of group B streptococci in the hospital is the source of these bacteremias. Approximately one fourth of patients with group B streptococcus isolated from the blood stream have polymicrobial bacteremia. *S. aureus* is a frequently observed second isolate. The age distribution, mortality rate, and proportion of nosocomial cases does not differ among patients with bacteremia caused only by group B streptococcus and those with polymicrobial bacteremia.[117]

Postpartum bacteremia due to group B streptococci increased during the 1970s, an increase that paralleled that reported for neonatal infections. Group B streptococci account for 10% to 20% of blood culture isolates from women admitted to obstetric services.[51,121] Faro reported an incidence of group B streptococcal–associated endometritis of 1.3 per 1000 deliveries; one third of these patients had concomitant bacteremia.[51] An uncomplicated outcome after appropriate antimicrobial therapy is the rule for these patients, although complications such as meningitis or endocarditis have been described.[52,118]

Most adult group B streptococcal infections occur in association with one of several clinical expressions of infection.

Primary Bacteremia

When no clear site of active infection can be established, patients in whom group B streptococcus has been isolated from the blood stream are classified as having primary bacteremia. In several reports, primary bacteremia is the most frequent diagnosis, accounting for 20% to 40% of cases.[7,112,115,119] Approximately one half of these patients have a fatal outcome.[119] Among survivors, recurrence of infection may be associated with a focus of infection such as endocarditis or osteomyelitis,[33] or another defined ongoing focus.

Infections of the Female Genital Tract

A substantial number of adult infections due to group B streptococcus are associated with pregnancy. The female genital tract is the source of these infections. Group B streptococci alone or as a component of polymicrobial infection are among the most commonly isolated facultative aerobes from women with early postpartum endometritis. A variety of clinical manifestations may occur, but the most common of these are endometritis and wound infection, both associated with cesarean section. Most women with group B streptococcal endometritis develop focal signs and symptoms of infection within 48 hours after delivery. A striking association between abdominal delivery and endometritis has been noted.[122] Among patients who delivered abdominally, those who were colonized with group B streptococci had a significantly increased frequency of premature rupture of membranes, postpartum fever, and endometritis when compared with noncolonized women. The clinical findings of endometritis are nonspecific and include fever with or without chills, malaise, moderate uterine tenderness, and normal lochia. In the report by Gibbs and Blanco,[123] the initial lack of symptoms referable to the genital area was followed by the subsequent diagnosis of chorioamnionitis in 19% and endometritis in 81% of patients. The frequency of life-threatening sequelae of endometritis such as pelvic abscess, septic shock, or septic thrombophlebitis is less than 2%.[124] Another frequent manifestation of morbidity in pregnant women is urinary tract infection. Group B streptococcal peripartum bacteriuria may be asymptomatic or less often may be diagnosed in association with cystitis or rarely pyelonephritis.

The role of group B streptococcus as an etiologic agent causing vaginitis has not been established. It is regarded as a commensal organism in the vaginal tract and is not considered to elicit a vaginal inflammatory response. There are, however, reports suggesting the pathogenic potential of group B streptococcus in vaginitis and of resolution of the symptoms of vaginitis in association with a short course of antibiotic administration.[125,126]

Pneumonia

Group B streptococci appear to behave as opportunistic pathogens in patients whose immune function is altered. The specific mechanisms underlying the predilection for this infection have not yet been delineated. However, these patients have in common the apparent inability to limit the spread of the organism from colonizing mucous membrane sites to the blood stream. The most common underlying medical conditions among patients with group B streptococcal pneumonia include diabetes mellitus and neurologic disease. The seven patients described by Verghese and associates were older (median age, 78 years), debilitated, and bedridden.[127] All patients were febrile, had leukocytosis, and were hypoxic in room air. Chest radiographs showed bilateral or lobar infiltrates. Infection was frequently polymicrobic, although group B *Streptococcus* was the predominant organism. Pleural empyema has been described in association with the pneumonia.[128] Fatality rates in patients with pneumonia range from 30% to 85%.

Endocarditis

A major shift in the clinical expression of group B streptococcal endocarditis was documented by Lerner and colleagues.[115] In contrast to the predominance of acute mitral valve endocarditis in pregnant women during the preantibiotic era, cases reported since 1945 have had no sex predilection, have been both acute and subacute in onset, and have occurred in older patients (mean age, approximately 50 years).[115,129] The mitral valve is most frequently affected (48%); infections involving the aortic (29%), mitral and aortic (10%), and tricuspid valves (5%) have been described. Tricuspid valve involvement is reported usually in injection drug users.[111] An increasing rate of pros-

thetic valve endocarditis and endocarditis in association with injection drug use has been noted in a contemporary report.[130] Underlying heart disease is present in more than half of the cases reported since 1962, rheumatic heart disease being the most common diagnosis.[129] Valvular disease, atherosclerotic heart disease, and mitral valve prolapse also may be predisposing conditions.[129,131] Large friable vegetations are a frequent feature of endocarditis caused by group B streptococcus. These may resemble atrial myxomas, and embolization may occur early in the clinical course.[129] Rapid valve destruction may occur, necessitating early valve replacement in some patients.[132,133] The mortality rate from group B streptococcal endocarditis is approximately 35% to 50%.[115,118,129,130,134]

Arthritis

Group B streptococcal arthritis is monoarticular in two thirds of patients and involves more than one joint in the remainder.[135] Polyarticular disease with a central pattern has been described.[115] In a review of 75 adults with group B streptococcal arthritis, the mean age was 58 years and 45% were men.[135] The most commonly affected joints, in descending order of frequency, were the knee, shoulder, hip, and sternoclavicular and sacroiliac joints. One or more underlying medical conditions were present in three quarters, most commonly diabetes mellitus, malignancy, or chronic liver disease. One third had a nonjoint focus of group B streptococcal infection, such as vertebral osteomyelitis or urinary tract infection. The most common presenting features were fever and joint pain, but approximately 14% of patients did not present with fever before diagnosis. The erythrocyte sedimentation rate, when performed, was above 30 mm/hr in 95% of patients, and group B streptococci were isolated from blood cultures in two thirds. With appropriate antimicrobial therapy, repeated joint aspirations or surgical débridement, and (usually) removal of a prosthesis, if present, complete recovery was achieved in one half of patients.[136] In the remainder, disease was associated with substantial functional sequelae.[134] The overall mortality rate is approximately 10%.

Osteomyelitis

Osteomyelitis occurs as a consequence of adjacent arthritis, peripheral vascular disease, orthopedic surgery, or an adjacent focus of infection such as frontal sinusitis.[137] In a review of 39 cases of group B streptococcal osteomyelitis, half were diagnosed as acute and half as chronic episodes.[138] The mean age was 56 years, one third of patients were greater than 65 years of age, and two thirds were men. The most commonly affected bones were the vertebrae, followed in order of frequency by the foot, bones about the hip, tibia, and toes. Underlying medical conditions were almost invariably present, most commonly diabetes mellitus, previous bone surgery, prosthetic bone or joint, or peripheral vascular disease. Foot bone involvement occurred predominantly in diabetic patients. Bones about the hip were involved in association with prior surgical procedures or trauma to the hip joint.

No specific clinical signs were associated with group B streptococcal osteomyelitis. A majority of patients were afebrile and had a normal erythrocyte sedimentation rate at the time of presentation. Cultures of bone or blood yielded group B streptococci in approximately 90% and approximately 40% of patients, respectively.[138] One fourth of infections were polymicrobial, with *S. aureus* the most commonly associated microorganism. Most patients with group B streptococcal osteomyelitis require a combined medical and surgical approach. The mean duration of antibiotic therapy is 10 weeks. Fatal infections are uncommon and are a consequence of associated foci of infection such as endocarditis, but amputation may be required for resolution of infection for diabetics with vascular insufficiency.

Skin and Soft Tissue Infections

Skin and soft tissues are the most common sites of focal group B streptococcal infections in adults, accounting for more than one third of infections in some reports.[9,116,139] Cellulitis, foot ulcers, abscess, and infection of decubitus ulcers are common manifestations. Cellulitis has occurred in association with foreign bodies, such as breast or penile implants. Less common manifestations of skin and soft tissue infections are pyomyositis, blistering dactylitis, and necrotizing fasciitis, on occasion associated with toxic shock–like syndrome.[140-142] There are no features of these latter infections unique to group B streptococci except that predisposing conditions such as diabetes mellitus generally exist. In one report of 37 patients, the mean age (44 years) of the two thirds who had serious underlying conditions was significantly greater than that of otherwise normal hosts (21 years), who often acquired infection in association with minor trauma.[139] Abscess formation was observed in 46% of these infections. Group B streptococcus was the only organism isolated from 71% of patients with an abscess. Appropriate drainage and parenteral antimicrobial therapy effected complete recovery in 89% of these patients.

Meningitis

Meningitis due to group B streptococci has been reported in at least 64 adults, most of whom have had the previously mentioned underlying predisposing comorbid conditions.[5,115,118,143-148] The mean age of nonparturient adults is 52 years; almost one half are men. Several have had proven or possible disruption of the anatomic barrier protecting the brain in consequence of surgery for carcinoma or chronic sinusitis. The overall case-fatality rate is 34%. Advanced age and overwhelming illness with presenting features such as coma or septic shock are associated with a poor outcome.[147] Deafness, reported in 7% of the survivors, is the most common neurologic sequela.[143,147]

Uncommon Manifestations of Infection

Group B streptococci, alone or as a component of mixed infection, have been isolated from a number of patients with keratitis or endophthalmitis. These infections were in eyes with severely damaged surfaces; the outcome was poor, with light perception being lost in one half of the affected eyes.[149,150]

Group B streptococci are a cause of urinary tract infections in nonobstetric populations, accounting for approximately 2% of positive urine cultures in one prospective evaluation.[151] Such infections are most often community acquired, occurring in middle-aged women. Almost all the patients have an underlying disease, most commonly alterations of urinary flow or stones. Clinical manifestations are referable to the upper or lower urinary tracts in equal numbers. Despite appropriate treatment, the clinical outcome is poor in approximately one fifth of the patients. Treatment failure or relapse is most likely the result of persistent vaginal or enteric colonization. Group B streptococcus may also be a cause of nongonococcal urethritis in men.[152]

Unusual infections caused by group B streptococcus include breast abscess in a nonlactating woman,[153] epiglottic abscess,[154] mycotic aneurysm of the femoral artery,[155] liver abscess,[112,119] peritonitis,[7,115,118] and infection of a pacemaker wire after sigmoidoscopy.[156] Group B streptococcus has also been reported to cause bacteremia after traumatic splenectomy,[157] bacteremia after cardiac catheterization,[158] and fever of unknown origin.[159]

Recurrent Invasive Group B Streptococcal Infection

Approximately 4% of nonpregnant adults surviving an episode of group B streptococcal bacteremia and followed for at least 1 year have a second episode.[33] The mean interval between episodes of bacteremia is 24 weeks, but the interval is shorter when the recurrent episode is caused by the same strain (mean, 14 weeks) than when it is caused by another strain (mean, 43 weeks between episodes). Several patients in whom primary bacteremia was the diagnosis of the first episode presented with focal infection, such as endocarditis or osteomyelitis, during the second episode. Little is known regarding host factors that predispose adults to developing group B streptococcal infection. Very limited data suggest that at least some adults already have relatively high concentrations of antibodies to the infecting serotype when illness occurs.[160] Although a specific antibody may be protective in many cases, the susceptibility of some adult patients to group B streptococcal infection may be the result of defects in other aspects of the host defense.

DIAGNOSIS

Isolation of group B streptococcus from blood, CSF, another usually sterile site, or a site of focal suppuration is the only means by which the diagnosis of invasive infection can be documented. Recovery of the organism from mucous membrane sites is of no diagnostic significance.

Intrapartum detection of colonization with group B streptococcus in women presenting for delivery would allow the accurate identification of at-risk patients who might benefit from early chemoprophylaxis or empirical treatment. Reports comparing the results of cultures processed by direct plating of swabs onto nonselective agar, with Gram stains of vaginal or cervical swabs from pregnant women found a good sensitivity (90%) but a poor specificity (67%).[161,162] A method requiring approximately 6 hours for the processing of vaginal swabs detected 40% of colonized patients.[163] Employing a similar technique, Howe and associates reported a sensitivity of 100% and specificity of 92%.[164] In evaluating two enzyme immunoassays and an optical immunoassay, Baker found that none of these rapid immunoassays was sufficiently accurate for routine use in the intrapartum detection of women vaginally colonized with group B streptococcus.[165] For women with heavy colonization, a sensitivity of 100% was shown for the optical immunoassay method. Specificity for these assays was high, but there was variability in positive and negative predictive values.

Bergeron and colleagues have described a fluorogenic real-time PCR technique for rapid detection of group B streptococci in pregnant women at delivery.[166] As compared with cultures of vaginal and rectal swabs inoculated in selective broth medium, the PCR assay had a sensitivity of 97% and a specificity of 100%. The length of time required to obtain results was 45 minutes, as compared with 100 minutes for a conventional PCR assay and 36 hours or longer for the conventional culture technique. If similar results were obtained in clinical practice and if the recently approved rapid assay were comparable to cultures in sensitivity and specificity, a PCR method could augment or even replace the culture-based method currently in use for identifying women in labor who are colonized with group B streptococci.

TREATMENT

The antimicrobial regimens recommended for treatment of group B streptococcal infections in infants and adults are summarized in Table 199-3. Group B streptococci remain uniformly susceptible to penicillins and cephalosporins in vitro, and penicillin G is the drug of choice once the diagnosis is established.[167] These organisms are also susceptible to ampicillin, vancomycin, and teicoplanin.[167,168] Meropenem and imipenem also have good in vitro activity.[167,169] Ciprofloxacin and rifampin have moderate in vitro activity but have not been evaluated for efficacy.[167,170] Increasing resistance to erythromycin and clindamycin now precludes their use as empiric treatment for invasive infection or for intrapartum prophylaxis. Resistance rates for isolates colonizing the genital tract of college students or pregnant women range from 18% to 29% for erythromycin and from 5% to 21% for clindamycin.[171-173] Among isolates from patients with invasive disease, resistance rates range from 7% to 32% for erythromycin and 3% to 12% for clindamycin.[167,174,175] A majority of macrolide-resistant strains present an MLS$_B$ phenotype, mainly constitutive, due to *erm* genes.[176] Tetracycline resistance has increased to nearly 90%.[167,177] Group B streptococci are uniformly resistant to nalidixic acid, trimethoprim-sulfamethoxazole, metronidazole, and aminoglycosides.

The initial use of ampicillin and an aminoglycoside for suspected neonatal bacteremia or meningitis due to group B streptococcus is based on their in vitro synergy for these organisms and on the need for broad-spectrum antimicrobial coverage until the diagnosis is established with certainty.[178] Once the diagnosis is established and a clinical response is documented, treatment can be completed with penicillin G alone. Penicillin tolerance in vitro has been noted in 4% to 6% of strains, but the clinical importance of this in vitro phenomenon is unknown.[168]

TABLE 199-3 Treatment of Group B Streptococcal Infections

	Antibiotic (IV Dosage)			
Diagnosis	**Neonate and Infant**	**Adult**	**Alternative for Penicillin-Allergic Adults**	**Duration**
Bacteremia, soft tissue infections	Ampicillin (150 mg/kg/day) plus an aminoglycoside initially, then penicillin G (200,000 U/kg/day)	Penicillin G (10-12 million U/day)	Vancomycin	10 day
Meningitis	Ampicillin (300-400 mg/kg/day) plus gentamicin initially, then penicillin G (500,000 U/kg/day)	Penicillin G (20-30 million U/day)	Vancomycin	14-21 day (minimum)
Osteomyelitis	Penicillin G (200,000 U/kg/day)	Penicillin G (10-20 million U/day)	Vancomycin	3-4 wk
Endocarditis (see Chapter 74)	Penicillin G (400,000 U/kg/day)	Penicillin G (20-30 million U/day) with gentamicin for 2 wk	Vancomycin with an aminoglycoside	4-6 wk

Therapy of 10 days' duration is recommended for the treatment of bacteremia, pneumonia, and pyelonephritis, whereas a 14-day minimal duration is recommended for the treatment of soft tissue infections or meningitis, and a 4-week minimum for the treatment of osteomyelitis, endocarditis, or ventriculitis is recommended. In infants, oral therapy is never appropriate. In adults with endocarditis, cardiac surgery early in the course may be necessary because of rapid left-sided valvular destruction.[131] Relapses of infection have occurred in association with both an inadequate dosage and an inadequate duration of therapy. High-dose penicillin therapy does not reliably eliminate mucous membrane infection with group B streptococci, a source that may explain some recurrences.[108]

PREVENTION

Two basic approaches, chemoprophylaxis and immunoprophylaxis, have been suggested to prevent group B streptococcal infections. New insights into the potential feasibility of both approaches have been achieved. Chemoprophylaxis theoretically could be given to pregnant women antenatally or intrapartum, or to neonates at birth. The problem with antepartum prophylaxis is that oral antimicrobial therapy during pregnancy fails to eradicate group B streptococcal colonization. By contrast, successful interruption of vertical transmission by mothers colonized with group B streptococci at delivery can be achieved only through the administration of intravenous penicillin G or ampicillin during labor.[179] Because most infants with early-onset sepsis are ill at or within a few hours of birth, prophylaxis of the newborn would be too late in most circumstances.

Intrapartum Chemoprophylaxis

In the first prospective, randomized, and controlled trial of maternal chemoprophylaxis to prevent early-onset infection, Boyer and Gotoff detected colonization at 26 to 28 weeks of gestation through use of lower vaginal and rectal swabs processed in selective broth medium.[179] Women colonized with group B streptococci who also had onset of labor at less than 37 weeks of gestation or rupture of membranes for more than 12 hours before delivery received either routine care or intravenous ampicillin until delivery. All women with intrapartum fever were treated with ampicillin. Of the 79 neonates born to untreated women, five (6.3%) had group B streptococcal sepsis and one died; none of the 85 neonates born to ampicillin-treated women developed sepsis ($P = .02$).[179] Another study employed the same approach and noted that 1.8% of infants born to women given ampicillin prophylaxis and 13% of those born to untreated women developed group B streptococcal sepsis ($P = .04$).[180] When a cost-effectiveness analysis was applied to the method of selective prophylaxis (based on the detection of colonization and the presence of one or more intrapartum risk factors), efficacy was reported.[181]

The American College of Obstetricians and Gynecologists (ACOG) and the American Academy of Pediatrics (AAP) each published documents in 1992 concerning intrapartum chemoprophylaxis.[182,183] Both emphasized the need to reduce maternal and infant morbidity from group B streptococcal infection, but their approaches to the selection of women at risk differed, and neither approach was implemented fully. A consensus approach from the Centers for Disease Control and Prevention was endorsed in 1996 by the ACOG and the AAP.[184] The selection of women for chemoprophylaxis could be determined either by screening cultures of vaginal and rectal sites at 35 to 37 weeks of gestation or by recognizing one or more factors known to increase the risk for early-onset neonatal infection without screening cultures. Pregnant women are often willing to perform their own cultures, and the accuracy of culture results from patient-collected samples correlates well with that of samples collected by nurses, and it is greater than those collected by physicians.[185,186]

The impact of maternal antibiotic prophylaxis on the incidence of early-onset group B streptococcal disease was assessed by active, population-based surveillance in selected counties of eight states.[6] Over a 6-year period, the incidence of early-onset neonatal infections decreased by 65%, from 1.7 per 1000 live births in 1993 to 0.6 per 1000 in 1998. An estimated 3900 cases of early-onset disease and 200 neonatal deaths were prevented in the United States in 1998 by the intrapartum use of antibiotic prophylaxis. Among pregnant women, the incidence of invasive group B streptococcal disease declined by 21%.

A comparison of the culture-screening and the risk-based strategies for identifying at-risk pregnant women was conducted in a multistate retrospective cohort study.[187] The culture-based screening approach was more than 50% more effective than the risk-based approach in preventing early-onset group B streptococcal infection. On the basis of these findings, revised guidelines for the prevention of perinatal group B streptococcal infection have been issued by the Centers for Disease Control and Prevention, and endorsed by the ACOG and the AAP.[188] These specify that lower vaginal and rectal group B streptococcal screening cultures be performed at 35 to 37 weeks of gestation for all pregnant women with the exception of patients with documented group B streptococcal bacteriuria during the current pregnancy or with a previous infant with invasive group B streptococcal disease. The indications for intrapartum prophylaxis are shown in Table 199-4. When the culture status is not known, prophylaxis is indicated when there is a significant risk for preterm delivery, when amniotic membranes have been ruptured for 18 hours or longer, and when there is fever during labor. Prophylaxis is not indicated for planned cesarean delivery performed in the absence of labor or membrane rupture, regardless of the maternal group B streptococcal colonization status.

Penicillin G is the preferred agent for intrapartum prophylaxis because of its narrow spectrum of antimicrobial activity. The current recommendations require the administration of 5 million units of penicillin G initially and then 2.5 million units every 4 hours until delivery. Ampicillin is an alternative agent, but its use is discouraged because of its broader antimicrobial spectrum. Because of the increasing prevalence of resistance of group B streptococci to erythromycin and clindamycin, cefazolin (2 g initially, then 1 g every 8 hours) is recommended for use in women who are allergic to penicillin but are at low risk for anaphylaxis. Vancomycin (1 g every 12 hours until delivery) is

TABLE 199-4 Indications* for Intrapartum Antibiotic Prophylaxis to Prevent Perinatal Group B Streptococcal (GBS) Disease

Intrapartum Prophylaxis Indicated	Intrapartum Prophylaxis Not Indicated
Previous infant with invasive GBS disease	Previous pregnancy with a positive GBS screening culture (unless a culture was also positive during the current pregnancy)
GBS bacteriuria during the current pregnancy	Planned cesarean delivery performed in the absence of labor or membrane rupture (regardless of maternal GBS culture status)
Positive GBS screening culture during current pregnancy	Negative vaginal and rectal GBS screening culture in late gestation during the current pregnancy, regardless of intrapartum risk factors

GBS status unknown (culture not done, incomplete, or results unknown) and any of the following:
  Delivery at <37 weeks' gestation[†]
  Amniotic membrane rupture ≥18 hours
  Intrapartum temperature ≥100.4° F (≥38.0° C)[‡]	

*Indications are based on a universal prenatal screening strategy that involves obtaining combined vaginal and rectal GBS cultures from *all* pregnant women at 35 to 37 weeks' gestation. (Screening is not necessary if a woman has already been shown to have GBS bacteriuria during the current pregnancy, or if a previous infant had invasive GBS disease. In these cases, prophylaxis is indicated.)

[†]If onset of labor or rupture of amniotic membranes occurs at <37 weeks' gestation and there is a significant risk for preterm delivery (as assessed by the clinician), a suggested algorithm for GBS prophylaxis management is provided.[188]

[‡]If amnionitis is suspected, broad-spectrum antibiotic therapy that includes an agent known to be active against GBS should replace GBS prophylaxis.

the suggested alternative for penicillin-allergic women at high risk for anaphylaxis.

Guidelines from the AAP provide a detailed algorithm for management of infants born to mothers who have received intrapartum antibiotic prophylaxis.[189] These guidelines advocate a full diagnostic evaluation and empiric treatment for infants when intrapartum antimicrobials have been administered for treatment of suspected chorioamnionitis in a woman with documented group B streptococcal colonization and for infants with signs of neonatal sepsis. One key change from the former guidelines bases the decision to perform limited sepsis evaluation on a duration of intrapartum prophylaxis of less than 4 hours rather than less than 2 doses of an antibiotic. Another specifies that a healthy-appearing infant who was term gestation at delivery and whose mother received 4 or more hours of intrapartum prophylaxis before delivery may be discharged home after 24, rather than the former 48, hours of observation if other discharge criteria have been met and a person able to comply fully with instructions for home observation will be present with the neonate.

Group B Streptococcal Vaccines

Because the risk for invasive group B streptococcal disease in pregnant women and neonates is associated with low concentrations of maternal antibodies to the type-specific capsular polysaccharides of these organisms at delivery,[70] immunization to prevent these infections has been proposed. Purified capsular polysaccharides from types Ia, II, and III group B streptococci have been evaluated for safety and immunogenicity in adult volunteers.[190-192] Although the rate of immune response to these vaccines in adults with preexisting type-specific antibodies approached 100%, that in nonimmune adults ranged from 40% to 85%.[192] Vaccine-induced type III–specific antibodies were predominantly IgG$_1$ and IgG$_2$, crossed the placenta efficiently,[193] were protective in animal models of lethal infection,[194] and persisted for up to 10 years after immunization.[108] However, because some of these

polysaccharides are poorly immunogenic in nonimmune adults, type-specific polysaccharides coupled to tetanus toxoid or other carrier proteins have been developed.[195-197] The first, composed of type III polysaccharide and tetanus toxoid, was immunogenic in rabbits and mice, and the antibodies elicited were functional in vitro and protective in vivo.[195] In healthy young women, type III group B streptococcal polysaccharide–tetanus toxoid conjugate vaccine was safe and significantly more immunogenic than uncoupled capsular polysaccharide.[198] Additional conjugate vaccines have been developed for capsular types Ia, Ib, II, and V polysaccharides.[199-201] Each of these has been demonstrated to be safe and significantly more immunogenic than uncoupled capsular polysaccharide in nonpregnant adults.[202-204] A type V polysaccharide–tetanus toxoid conjugate vaccine has been shown to be safe and immunogenic in adults 65 years of age and older.[205] A type III polysaccharide–tetanus toxoid conjugate vaccine has been administered to healthy women in the third trimester of pregnancy.[206] The concentration of capsular polysaccharide–specific IgG was sufficient to provide antibodies transplacentally that were functional in vitro through the first 2 months of life for infants born to these women. The concept that two monovalent conjugated vaccines combined would elicit immune responses comparable to those of the monovalent vaccines alone has been proved feasible through the administration to healthy adults of a bivalent group B streptococcal conjugate vaccine for serotypes II and III.[207]

Administration of a multivalent group B streptococcal polysaccharide–tetanus toxoid conjugate vaccine to women during the last third of pregnancy theoretically could provide type-specific antibodies in sufficient concentrations to passively protect neonates from early- and from late-onset disease. Such a multivalent conjugate vaccine tested in a murine model provided infant protection against infection with multiple group B streptococcal serotypes.[208] This approach to prevention, in contrast to maternal intrapartum chemoprophylaxis, offers a method that is simple, cost-effective, and durable and would not promote antimicrobial resistance. The demonstration that type V group B streptococcal tetanus toxoid conjugate vaccine was well tolerated and immunogenic in a group of healthy older adults offers promise that immunization could confer protection from invasive infection in at-risk nonpregnant adults, but further studies are needed.[205] The concept that group B streptococcal conjugate vaccines are safe, immunogenic, and elicit functionally active antibodies in vitro has been amply demonstrated. The impact of an immunization program on the group B streptococcal disease burden cannot be realized until development by the pharmaceutical industry begins.

REFERENCES

1. Fry RM. Fatal infections by haemolytic streptococcus group B. Lancet. 1938;1:199-201.
2. Lancefield RC, Hare R. The serological differentiation of pathogenic and nonpathogenic strains of hemolytic streptococci from parturient women. J Exp Med. 1935;61:335-349.
3. Hood M, Janney A, Dameron G. Beta hemolytic streptococcus group B associated with problems of perinatal period. Am J Obstet Gynecol. 1961;82:809-818.
4. Eickhoff TC, Klein JO, Daly AL, et al. Neonatal sepsis and other infections due to group B beta-hemolytic streptococci. N Engl J Med. 1964;271:1221-1228.
5. Butter MNW, DeMoor CE. *Streptococcus agalactiae* as a cause of meningitis in the newborn, and of bacteremia in adults. Antonie van Leeuwenhoek. 1967;33:439-450.
6. Schrag SJ, Zywicki S, Farley MM, et al. Group B streptococcal disease in the era of intrapartum antibiotic prophylaxis. N Engl J Med. 2000;342:15-20.
7. Muñoz P, Llancaqueo A, Rodriguez-Creixems M, et al. Group B streptococcus bacteremia in nonpregnant adults. Arch Intern Med. 1997;157:213-216.
8. Farley MM. Group B streptococcal disease in nonpregnant adults. Clin Infect Dis. 2001;33:556-561.
9. Farley MM, Harvey RC, Stull T, et al. A population-based assessment of invasive disease due to group B streptococcus in nonpregnant adults. N Engl J Med. 1993;328:1807-1811.
10. Henning KJ, Hall EL, Dwyer DM, et al. Invasive group B streptococcal disease in Maryland nursing home residents. J Infect Dis. 2001;183:1138-1142.
11. Glaser P, Rusniok C, Buchrieser C, et al. Genome sequence of *Streptococcus agalactiae*, a pathogen causing invasive neonatal disease. Mol Microbiol. 2002;45:1499-1513.
12. Tettelin H, Masignani V, Cieslewicz MJ, et al. Complete genome sequence and comparative genomic analysis of an emerging human pathogen, serotype V *Streptococcus agalactiae*. Proc Natl Acad Sci USA. 2002;99:12391-12396.

13. Lancefield RC. A serological differentiation of human and other groups of hemolytic streptococci. J Exp Med. 1933;57:571-595.

14. Baker CJ, Clark DJ, Barrett FF. Selective broth medium for isolation of group B streptococci. Appl Microbiol. 1973;26:884-885.

15. Facklam RR, Padula JR, Wortham EC, et al. Presumptive identification of group A, B and D streptococci on agar plate medium. J Clin Microbiol. 1979;9:665-672.

16. Lancefield RC. A serological differentiation of specific types of bovine hemolytic streptococci (group B). J Exp Med. 1934;59:441-458.

17. Wilkinson HW, Eagon RG. Type-specific antigens of group B type Ic streptococci. Infect Immun. 1971;4:596-604.

18. Henrichsen J, Ferrieri P, Jelinkova J, et al. Nomenclature of antigens of group B streptococci. Int J Syst Bacteriol. 1984;34:500.

19. Jelinkova J, Motlova J. Worldwide distribution of two new serotypes of group B streptococci: Type IV and provisional type V. J Clin Microbiol. 1985;21:361-362.

20. Wessels MR, DiFabio JL, Benedi V-J, et al. Structural determination and immunochemical characterization of the type V group B streptococcus capsular polysaccharide. J Biol Chem. 1991;266:6714-6719.

21. Von Hunolstein C, D'Ascenzi S, Wagner B, et al. Immunochemistry of capsular type polysaccharide and virulence properties of type VI Streptococcus agalactiae (group B streptococci). Infect Immun. 1993;61:1272-1280.

22. Kogan G, Uhrin D, Brisson J-R, et al. Structure and immunochemical characterization of the type VIII group B streptococcus capsular polysaccharide. J Biol Chem. 1996;271:8786-8796.

23. Ferrieri P, Flores AE. Surface protein expression in group B streptococcal invasive isolates. Adv Exp Med Biol. 1997;418:635-637.

24. Lancefield RC, McCarty M, Everly WN. Multiple mouse-protective antibodies directed against group B streptococci. Special reference to antibodies effective against protein antigens. J Exp Med. 1975;142:165-179.

25. Baltimore RS, Kasper DL, Vecchitto JS. Mouse protection test for type III strains of group B streptococcus. J Infect Dis. 1979;140:81-88.

26. Stålhammar-Carlemalm M, Stenberg L, Lindahl G. Protein Rib: A novel group B streptococcal cell surface protein that confers protective immunity and is expressed by most strains causing invasive infections. J Exp Med. 1993;177:1593-1603.

27. Michel JL, Madoff LC, Kling DE, et al. Cloned alpha and beta C-protein antigens of group B streptococci elicit protective immunity. Infect Immun. 1991;59:2023-2028.

28. Madoff LC, Michel JL, Gong EW, et al. Protection of neonatal mice from group B streptococcal infection by maternal immunization with beta C protein. Infect Immun. 1992;60:4989.

29. Benson JA, Flores AE, Baker CJ, et al. Improved methods for typing nontypeable isolates of group B streptococci. Int J Med Microbiol. 2002;292:37-42.

30. Kong F, Gowan S, Martin D, et al. Serotype identification of group B streptococci by PCR and sequencing. J Clin Microbiol. 2002;40:216-226.

31. Quentin R, Huet H, Wang F-S, et al. Characterization of Streptococcus agalactiae strains by multilocus enzyme genotype and serotype: Identification of multiple virulent clone families that cause invasive neonatal disease. J Clin Microbiol. 1995;33:2576-2581.

32. Blumberg HM, Stephens DS, Licitra C, et al. Molecular epidemiology of group B streptococcal infections: Use of restriction endonuclease analysis of chromosomal DNA and DNA restriction fragment length polymorphisms of ribosomal RNA genes (ribotyping). J Infect Dis. 1992;166:574-579.

33. Harrison LH, Ali A, Dwyer DM, et al. Relapsing invasive group B streptococcal infection in adults. Ann Intern Med. 1995;123:421-427.

34. Persson K, Bjerre B, Elfstrom L, et al. A longitudinal study of group B streptococcal carriage during late pregnancy. Scand J Infect Dis. 1987;19:325-329.

35. Newton ER, Butler MC, Shain RN. Sexual behavior and vaginal colonization by group B streptococcus among minority women. Obstet Gynecol. 1996;88:577-582.

36. Campbell JR, Hillier SL, Krohn MA, et al. Group B streptococcal colonization and serotype-specific immunity in pregnant women at delivery. Obstet Gynecol. 2000;96:498-503.

37. Ramos E, Gaudier FL, Hearing LR, et al. Group B streptococcus colonization in pregnant diabetic women. Obstet Gynecol. 1997;89:257-260.

38. Meyn LA, Moore DM, Hillier SL, et al. Association of sexual activity with colonization and vaginal acquisition of group B streptococcus in nonpregnant women. Am J Epidemiol. 2002;155:949-957.

39. Bliss SJ, Manning SD, Tallman P, et al. Group B streptococcus colonization in male and nonpregnant female university students: A cross-sectional prevalence study. Clin Infect Dis. 2002;34:184-190.

40. Manning SD, Tallman P, Baker CJ, et al. Determinants of co-colonization with group B streptococcus among heterosexual college couples. Epidemiology. 2002;13:533-539.

41. Baker CJ, Goroff DK, Alpert S, et al. Vaginal colonization with group B streptococcus: A study in college women. J Infect Dis. 1977;135:392-397.

42. Boyer KM, Gadzala CA, Kelly PD, et al. Selective intrapartum chemoprophylaxis of neonatal group B streptococcal early-onset disease: II. Predictive value of prenatal cultures. J Infect Dis. 1983;148:802-809.

43. Dillon HC, Gray E, Pass MA, et al. Anorectal and vaginal carriage of group B streptococci during pregnancy. J Infect Dis. 1982;145:794-799.

44. Edwards MS, Rench MA, Palazzi DA, et al. Definition of factors influencing the potential for invasive group B streptococcal disease in the healthy elderly. Submitted for publication.

45. Allen U, Nimrod C, MacDonald N, et al. Relationship between antenatal group B streptococcal vaginal colonization and premature labour. Paediatr Child Health. 1999;4:465-469.

46. Baker CJ, Barrett FF. Transmission of group B streptococci among parturient women and their neonates. J Pediatr. 1973;83:919-925.

47. Pass MA, Gray BM, Khare S, et al. Prospective studies of group B streptococcal infections in infants. J Pediatr. 1979;95:437-443.

48. Ancona RJ, Ferrieri P, Williams PP. Maternal factors that enhance the acquisition of group B streptococci by newborn infants. J Med Microbiol. 1980;13:273-280.

49. Schuchat A, Deaver-Robinson K, Plikaytis BD, et al. Multistate case-control study of maternal risk factors for neonatal group B streptococcal disease. Pediatr Infect Dis J. 1994;13:623-629.

50. Schuchat A, Oxtoby M, Cochi S, et al. Population-based risk factors for neonatal group B streptococcal disease: Results of a cohort study in metropolitan Atlanta. J Infect Dis. 1990;162:672-677.

51. Faro S. Group B beta-hemolytic streptococci and puerperal infections. Am J Obstet Gynecol. 1981;139:686-689.

52. Yancey MK, Duff P, Clark P, et al. Peripartum infection associated with vaginal group B streptococcal colonization. Obstet Gynecol. 1994;84:816-819.

53. Institute of Medicine, National Academy of Sciences. Committee on Issues and Priorities for New Vaccine Developments. Appendix P: New vaccine development: Establishing priorities. In: Diseases of Importance in the United States, v. 1. Washington, DC: National Academy; 1985:242-439.

54. Krohn MA, Hillier SL, Baker CJ. Maternal peripartum complications associated with vaginal group B streptococci colonization. J Infect Dis. 1999;179:1410-1415.

55. Lin F-YC, Clemens JD, Azimi PH, et al. Capsular polysaccharide types of group B streptococcal isolates from neonates with early-onset systemic infection. J Infect Dis. 1998;177:790-792.

56. Harrison LH, Elliott JA, Dwyer DM, et al. Serotype distribution of invasive group B streptococcal isolates in Maryland: Implications for vaccine formulation. J Infect Dis. 1998;177:998-1002.

57. Zaleznik DF, Rench MA, Hillier S, et al. Invasive disease due to group B streptococcus in pregnant women and neonates from diverse population groups. Clin Infect Dis. 1999;30:276-281.

58. Davies HD, Raj S, Adair C, et al. Population-based active surveillance for neonatal group B streptococcal infections in Alberta, Canada: Implications for vaccine formulation. Pediatr Infect Dis J. 2001;20:879-884.

59. Davies HD, Adair C, McGeer A, et al. Antibodies to capsular polysaccharides of group B streptococcus in pregnant Canadian women: Relationship to colonization status and infection in the neonate. J Infect Dis. 2001;184:285-291.

60. Blumberg HM, Stephens DS, Modansky M, et al. Invasive group B streptococcal disease: The emergence of serotype V. J Infect Dis. 1996;173:365-373.

61. Tyrrell GJ, Senzilet LD, Spika JS, et al. Invasive disease due to group B streptococcal infection in adults: Results from a Canadian, population-based, active laboratory surveillance study-1996. J Infect Dis. 2000;182:168-173.

62. Lachenauer C, Kasper DL, Shimada J, et al. Serotypes VI and VIII predominate among group B streptococci isolated from pregnant Japanese women. J Infect Dis. 1999;174:1030-1033.

63. Regan JA, Klebanoff MA, Nugent RP, et al. Colonization with group B streptococci in pregnancy and adverse outcome. Am J Obstet Gynecol. 1996;174:1354-1360.

64. Bolduc GR, Baron MJ, Gravekamp C, et al. The alpha C protein mediates internalization of group B Streptococcus within human cervical epithelial cells. Cell Microbiol. 2002;4:751-758.

65. Tamura GS, Rubens CE. Host-bacterial interactions in the pathogenesis of group B streptococcal infections. Cur Opin Infect Dis. 1994;7:317-322.

66. Nizet V, Kim KS, Stins M, et al. Invasion of brain microvascular endothelial cells by group B streptococci. Infect Immun. 1997;65:5074-5081.

67. Malin G, Paoletti LC. Use of a dynamic in vitro attachment and invasion system (DI-VAS) to determine influence of growth rate on invasion of respiratory epithelial cells by group B streptococcus. Proc Natl Acad Sci U S A. 2001;98:13335-13340.

68. Doran KS, Chang JCW, Benoit VM, et al. Group B streptococcal β-hemolysin/cytolysin promotes invasion of human lung epithelial cells and the release of interleukin-8. J Infect Dis. 2002;185:196-203.

69. Gibson RL, Nizet V, Rubens CE. Group B streptococcal beta-hemolysin promotes injury of lung microvascular endothelial cells. Pediatr Res. 1999;45:626-634.

70. Baker CJ, Kasper DL. Correlation of maternal antibody deficiency with susceptibility to neonatal group B streptococcal infection. N Engl J Med. 1976;294:753-756.

71. Baker CJ, Edwards MS, Kasper DL. Role of antibody to native type III polysaccharide of group B streptococcus in infant infection. Pediatrics. 1981;68:544-549.

72. Baker CJ, Kasper DL, Tager IB, et al. Quantitative determination of antibody to capsular polysaccharide in infection with type III strains of group B streptococcus. J Clin Invest. 1977;59:810-818.

73. Lin F-YC, Philips JB II, Azimi PH, et al. Level of maternal antibody required to protect neonates against early-onset disease caused by group B streptococcus type Ia: A multicenter, seroepidemiology study. J Infect Dis. 2001;184:1022-1028.

74. Gotoff SP, Papierniak CK, Klegerman ME, et al. Quantitation of IgG antibody to the type-specific polysaccharide of group B streptococcus type Ib in pregnant women and infected infants. J Pediatr. 1984;105:628-630.

75. Gray BM, Pritchard DG, Dillon HC Jr. Seroepidemiological studies of group B streptococcus type II. J Infect Dis. 1985;151:1073-1080.

76. Anthony BF, Concepcion NF, Concepcion KF. Human antibody to the group-specific polysaccharide of group B streptococcus. J Infect Dis. 1985;151:221-226.

77. Shigeoka AO, Hall RT, Hemming VG, et al. Role of antibody and complement in opsonization of group B streptococci. Infect Immun. 1978;21:34-40.

78. Baker CJ, Webb BJ, Kasper DL, et al. The role of complement and antibody in opsonophagocytosis of type II group B streptococci. J Infect Dis. 1986;154:47-54.

79. Hall MA, Hickman ME, Baker CJ, et al. Complement and antibody in neutrophil-mediated killing of type V group B streptococcus. J Infect Dis. 1994;170:88-93.

80. Payne NR, Kim Y, Ferrieri P. Effect of differences in antibody and complement requirements on phagocytic uptake and intracellular killing of "c" protein-positive and -negative strains of type II group B streptococci. Infect Immun. 1987;55:1243-1251.
81. Baker CJ, Edwards MS, Webb BJ, et al. Antibody-independent classical pathway-mediated opsonophagocytosis of type Ia, group B streptococcus. J Clin Invest. 1982;63:394-404.
82. Edwards MS, Buffone GJ, Fuselier PA, et al. Deficient classical complement activity in newborn sera. Pediatr Res. 1983;17:685-688.
83. Christensen RD, Hill HR, Rothstein G. Granulocytic stem cell (CFUc) proliferation in experimental group B streptococcal sepsis. Pediatr Res. 1983;17:278-280.
84. Smith CL, Baker CJ, Anderson DC, et al. Role of complement receptors in opsonophagocytosis of group B streptococci by adult and neonatal neutrophils. J Infect Dis. 1990;162:489-495.
85. Yang KD, Bathras JM, Shigeoka AO, et al. Mechanisms of bacterial opsonization by immune globulin intravenous: Correlation of complement consumption with opsonic activity and protective efficacy. J Infect Dis. 1989;159:701-707.
86. Noya FJD, Baker CJ, Edwards MS. Neutrophil Fc receptor participation in phagocytosis of type III group B streptococci. Infect Immun. 1993;61:1415-1420.
87. Vallejo JG, Baker CJ, Edwards MS. Roles of the bacterial cell wall and capsule in induction of tumor necrosis factor alpha by type III group B streptococci. Infect Immun. 1996;64:5042-5046.
88. Teti G, Mancuso G, Tomasello F, et al. Production of tumor necrosis factor-α and interleukin-6 in mice infected with group B streptococci. Circ Shock. 1992;38:138-144.
89. Rowen JL, Smith CW, Edwards MS. Group B streptococci elicit leukotriene B₄ and interleukin-8 from human monocytes: Neonates exhibit a diminished response. J Infect Dis. 1995;172:420-426.
90. Vallejo JG, Knuefermann P, Mann DL, et al. Group B streptococcus induces TNF-α gene expression and activation of the transcription factors NFκB and activator protein-1 in human cord blood monocytes. J Immunol. 2000;165:419-425.
91. Henneke P, Takeuchi O, van Strijp JA, et al. Novel engagement of CD14 and multiple toll-like receptors by group B streptococci. J Immunol. 2001;167:7069-7076.
92. Takahashi S, Adderson EE, Nagano Y, et al. Identification of a highly encapsulated, genetically related group of invasive type III group B streptococci. J Infect Dis. 1998;177:1116-1119.
93. Rubens CE, Wessels MR, Heggen LM, et al. Transposon mutagenesis of group B streptococcal type III capsular polysaccharide: Correlation of capsule expression with virulence. Proc Natl Acad Sci U S A. 1987;84:7208-7212.
94. Wessels MR, Rubens CE, Benedi V-J, et al. Definition of a bacterial virulence factor: Sialylation of the group B streptococcal capsule. Proc Natl Acad Sci U S A. 1989;86:8983-8987.
95. Nizet V, Kim KS, Stins M, et al. Invasion of brain microvascular endothelial cells by group B streptococci. Infect Immun. 1997;65:5074-5081.
96. Kasper DL, Baker CJ, Edwards MS, et al. The type III group B streptococcal capsular polysaccharide: Structure, immunospecificity, immunogenicity, and relationship to virulence. In: Weinstein L, Fields BN, eds. Seminars in Infectious Disease, v. 4. Bacterial Vaccines. New York: Thieme-Stratton; 1982:275-278.
97. Kogan G, Brisson JR, Kasper DL, et al. Structural elucidation of the novel type VII group B streptococcus capsular polysaccharide by high resolution NMR spectroscopy. Carbohydr Res. 1995;277:1-9.
98. Granlund M, Oberg L, Sellin M, Norgren M. Identification of a novel insertion element, IS1548, in group B streptococci, predominantly in strains causing endocarditis. J Infect Dis. 1998;177:967-976.
99. Puliti M, Nizet V, von Hunolstein C, et al. Severity of group B streptococcal arthritis is correlated with beta-hemolysin expression. J Infect Dis. 2000;182:824-832.
100. Areschoug T, Stalhammar-Carlemalm M, Karlsson I, et al. Streptococcal beta protein has separate binding sites for human factor H and IgA-Fc. J Biol Chem. 2002;277:12642-12648.
101. Harris TO, Shelver DW, Bohnsack JF, et al. A novel streptococcal surface protease promotes virulence, resistance to opsonophagocytosis, and cleavage of human fibrinogen. J Clin Invest. 2003;111:61-70.
102. Franciosi RA, Knostman JD, Zimmerman RA. Group B streptococcal neonatal and infant infections. J Pediatr. 1973;82:707-718.
103. Baker CJ, Barrett FF, Gordon RC, et al. Suppurative meningitis due to streptococci of Lancefield group B: A study of 33 infants. J Pediatr. 1973;82:724-729.
104. Yagupsky P, Menegus MA, Powell KR. The changing spectrum of group B streptococcal disease in infants: An eleven-year experience in a tertiary care hospital. Pediatr Infect Dis J. 1991;10:801-808.
105. Edwards MS, Rench MA, Haffar AA, et al. Long-term sequelae of group B streptococcal meningitis in infants. J Pediatr. 1985;106:717-722.
106. Wald ER, Bergman I, Taylor HG, et al. Long-term outcome of group B streptococcal meningitis. Pediatrics. 1986;77:217-221.
107. Edwards MS, Baker CJ, Wagner ML, et al. An etiologic shift in infantile osteomyelitis: The emergence of the group B streptococcus. J Pediatr. 1978;93:578-583.
108. Baker CJ, Edwards MS. Group B streptococcal infections. In: Remington JS, Klein JO, eds. Infectious Diseases of the Fetus and Newborn Infant. 5th ed. Philadelphia: Saunders; 2000:1091-1156.
109. Garcia Peña BM, Harper MB, Fleisher GR. Occult bacteremia with group B streptococci in an outpatient setting. Pediatrics. 1998;102:67-72.
110. Hussain SM, Luedtke GS, Baker CJ, et al. Invasive group B streptococcal disease in children beyond early infancy. Pediatr Infect Dis J. 1995;14:278-281.
111. Alsoub H, Najma F, Robida A. Group B streptococcal endocarditis in children beyond the neonatal period. Pediatr Infect Dis J. 1997;16:418-420.
112. Opal SM, Cross A, Palmo M, et al. Group B streptococcal sepsis in adults and infants: Contrasts and comparisons. Arch Intern Med. 1988;148:641-645.
113. Gallagher PG, Watanakunakorn C. Group B streptococcal bacteremia in a community teaching hospital. Am J Med. 1985;78:795-800.
114. Verghese A, Mireault K, Arbeit RD. Group B streptococcal bacteremia in men. Rev Infect Dis. 1986;8:912-917.
115. Lerner PI, Gopalakrishna KV, Wolinsky E, et al. Group B streptococcus (S. agalactiae) bacteremia in adults: Analysis of 32 cases and review of the literature. Medicine (Baltimore). 1977;56:457-473.
116. Schwartz B, Schuchat A, Oxtoby MJ, et al. Invasive group B streptococcal disease in adults: A population-based study in metropolitan Atlanta. JAMA. 1991;266:1112-1114.
117. Jackson LA, Hilsdon R, Farley MM, et al. Risk factors for group B streptococcal disease in adults. Ann Intern Med. 1995;123:415-420.
118. Bayer AS, Chow AW, Anthony BF, et al. Serious infections in adults due to group B streptococci. Am J Med. 1976;61:498-503.
119. Colford JM Jr, Mohle-Boetani J, Vosti KL. Group B streptococcal bacteremia in adults: Five years' experience and a review of the literature. Medicine. 1995;74:176-190.
120. Roberts FJ. Group A and group B β-hemolytic streptococcal bacteremia. Rev Infect Dis. 1988;10:228-229.
121. Ledger WJ, Norman J, Gee C, et al. Bacteremia on an obstetric-gynecologic service. Am J Obstet Gynecol. 1975;121:205-212.
122. Minkoff HL, Sierra MF, Pringle GF, et al. Vaginal colonization with group B beta-hemolytic streptococcus as a risk factor for post-cesarean section febrile morbidity. Am J Obstet Gynecol. 1982;142:992-995.
123. Gibbs RS, Blanco JD. Streptococcal infections in pregnancy: A study of 48 bacteremias. Am J Obstet Gynecol. 1981;140:405-411.
124. Duff P. Pathophysiology and management of postcesarean endomyometritis. Obstet Gynecol. 1986;67:269-276.
125. Maniatis AN, Palermos J, Kantzanou M, et al. Streptococcus agalactiae: A vaginal pathogen? J Med Microbiol. 1996;44:199-202.
126. Boyle D, Smith JR. Group B streptococcal vulvovaginitis. J R Soc Med. 1997;90:298-299.
127. Verghese A, Berk SL, Boelen LJ, et al. Group B streptococcal pneumonia in the elderly. Arch Intern Med. 1982;142:1642-1645.
128. George AL Jr, Savage AM. Fatal group B streptococcal empyema in an adult. South Med J. 1987;80:1436-1438.
129. Gallagher PG, Watanakunakorn C. Group B streptococcal endocarditis: Report of seven cases and review of the literature, 1962-1985. Rev Infect Dis. 1986;8:175-188.
130. Sambola A, Miro JM, Tornos MP, et al. Streptococcus agalactiae infective endocarditis: Analysis of 30 cases and review of the literature, 1962-1998. Clin Infect Dis. 2002;34:1576-1584.
131. Watanakunakorn C, Habte-Gabr E. Group B streptococcal endocarditis of tricuspid valve. Chest. 1991;100:569-571.
132. Pringle SD, McCartney AC, Marshall DAS, et al. Infective endocarditis caused by Streptococcus agalactiae. Int J Cardiol. 1989;24:179-183.
133. Scully BE, Spriggs D, Neu HC. Streptococcus agalactiae (group B) endocarditis-a description of twelve cases and review of the literature. Infection. 1987;15:169-176.
134. Duma RJ, Weinberg AN, Merdrek RF, et al. Streptococcal infections: A bacteriologic and clinical study of streptococcal bacteremia. Medicine (Baltimore). 1969;48:87-127.
135. Nolla JM, Gómez-Vaquero C, Corbella X, et al. Group B streptococcus (Streptococcus agalactiae) pyogenic arthritis in nonpregnant adults. Medicine. 2003;82:119-128.
136. Small CB, Slater LN, Lowy FD, et al. Group B streptococcal arthritis in adults. Am J Med. 1984;76:367-375.
137. Pischel KD, Weisman MH, Cone RO. Unique features of group B streptococcal arthritis in adults. Arch Intern Med. 1985;145:97-102.
138. García-Lechuz JM, Bachiller P, Vasallo FJ, et al. Group B streptococcal osteomyelitis in adults. Medicine. 1999;78:191-199.
139. McCarty JM, Haber J. Group B streptococcal soft tissue infections beyond the neonatal period. West J Med. 1987;147:558-560.
140. Riefler J III, Molavi A, Schwartz D, et al. Necrotizing fasciitis in adults due to group B streptococcus. Arch Intern Med. 1988;148:727-729.
141. Sutton GP, Smirz LR, Clark DH, et al. Group B streptococcal necrotizing fasciitis arising from an episiotomy. Obstet Gynecol. 1985;66:733-736.
142. Tang WM, Ho PL, Yau WP, et al. Report of 2 fatal cases of adult necrotizing fasciitis and toxic shock syndrome caused by Streptococcus agalactiae. Clin Infect Dis. 2000;31:e15-17.
143. Harburg TD, Leonard HA, Kimbrough RC III, et al. Group B streptococcal meningitis appearing as acute deafness in an adult. Arch Neurol. 1984;41:214-216.
144. Sepkowitz KA, Kasemsri T, Brown AE, et al. Meningitis due to β-hemolytic non-A, non-D streptococci among adults at a cancer hospital: Report of four cases and review. Clin Infect Dis. 1992;14:92-97.
145. Vartian CV, Septimus EJ. Meningitis caused by group B streptococcus in association with cerebrospinal rhinorrhea. Clin Infect Dis. 1992;14:1261-1262.
146. Dunne DW, Quagliarello V. Group B streptococcal meningitis in adults. Medicine. 1993;72:1-10.
147. Domingo P, Barquet N, Alvarez M, et al. Group B streptococcal meningitis in adults: Report of twelve cases and review. Clin Infect Dis. 1997;25:1180-1187.
148. Guerin JM, Leibinger F, Mofredj A, et al. Streptococcus B meningitis in post-partum. J Infect. 1997;34:151-153.
149. Farber BP, Weinbaum DL, Dummer JS. Metastatic bacterial endophthalmitis. Arch Intern Med. 1985;145:62-64.
150. Ormerod LD, Paton BG. Severe group B streptococcal eye infections in adults. J Infect. 1989;18:29-34.
151. Muñoz P, Coque T, Rodriguez-Creixems M, et al. Group B streptococcus: A cause of urinary tract infection in nonpregnant adults. Clin Infect Dis. 1992;14:492-496.

152. Lefevre J-C, Lepargneur J-P, Bauriand R, et al. Clinical and microbiologic features of urethritis in men in Toulouse, France. Sex Transm Dis. 1991;18:76-79.

153. Weiss RL, Matsen JM. Group B streptococcal breast abscess. Arch Pathol Lab Med. 1987;111:74-75.

154. Ridgeway NA, Perlman PE, Verghese A. Epiglottic abscess due to group B streptococcus. Ann Otol Rhinol Laryngol. 1984;93:277-278.

155. Burnet NG, Wilkinson RC, Evans DS. Mycotic aneurysm caused by group B streptococcus: A cautionary tale of management problems and a rare organism. Br J Clin Pract. 1990;44:372-374.

156. Baddour LM, Cox JW Jr. Group B streptococcal infection of a pacemaker wire following sigmoidoscopy. Clin Infect Dis. 1992;15:1069.

157. Raz R, Raichman N, Flatau E. Group B streptococcal bacteremia in a normal splenectomized adult. Isr J Med Sci. 1987;23:920-921.

158. Stampfer MJ, Ullman RF, Sacks-Berg A, et al. Group B streptococcal bacteremia after cardiac catheterization. Crit Care Med. 1987;15:625-626.

159. O'Mahony D, Hyland CM. Group B streptococcal infection as a pyrexia of unknown origin. Isr J Med Sci. 1989;158:233.

160. Wessels MR, Kasper DL, Johnson KD, et al. Antibody responses in invasive group B streptococcal infection in adults. J Infect Dis. 1998;178:569-572.

161. Feld SM, Harrigan JT. Vaginal gram stain as an immediate detector of group B streptococci in selected obstetric patients. Am J Obstet Gynecol. 1987;156:446-448.

162. Hollis WM, Thomas J, Troyer V. Cervical gram stain for rapid detection of colonization with β-*Streptococcus*. Obstet Gynecol. 1987;69:354-357.

163. Wald ER, Dashefsky B, Green M, et al. Rapid detection of group B streptococci directly from vaginal swabs. J Clin Microbiol. 1987;25:573-574.

164. Howe RS, Voychehovski TH, Uraizee F, et al. Neonatal group B streptococcal disease. N Engl J Med. 1987;316:1163.

165. Baker CJ. Inadequacy of rapid immunoassays for intrapartum detection of group B streptococcal carriers. Obstet Gynecol. 1996;88:51-55.

166. Bergeron MG, Ke D, Ménard C, et al. Rapid detection of group B streptococci in pregnant women at delivery. N Engl J Med. 2000;343:175-179.

167. Fernandez M, Hickman ME, Baker CJ. Antimicrobial susceptibilities of group B streptococci isolated between 1992 and 1996 from patients with bacteremia or meningitis. Antimicrob Agents Chemother. 1998;42:1517-1519.

168. Kim KS. Antimicrobial susceptibility of GBS. Antibiot Chemother. 1985;35:83-89.

169. Kropp H, Gerckens L, Sundelof JG. Antibacterial activity of imipenem: The first thienamycin antibiotic. Rev Infect Dis. 1985;7(Suppl):389-410.

170. Rolston KVI. Susceptibility of group B and group G streptococci to newer antimicrobial agents. Eur J Clin Microbiol. 1986;5:534-536.

171. Manning SD, Pearlman MD, Tallman P, et al. Frequency of antibiotic resistance among group B streptococcus isolated from healthy college students. Clin Infect Dis. 2001;33:e137-139.

172. Morales WJ, Dickey SS, Bornick P, et al. Change in antibiotic resistance of group B streptococcus: Impact on intrapartum management. Am J Obstet Gynecol. 1999;181:310-314.

173. Manning SD, Foxman B, Pierson CL, et al. Correlates of antibiotic-resistant group B streptococcus isolated from pregnant women. Obstet Gynecol. 2003;101:74-79.

174. Murdoch DR, Reller LB. Antimicrobial susceptibilities of group B streptococci isolated from patients with invasive disease: 10-year perspective. Antimicrob Agents Chemother. 2001;45:3623-3624.

175. Lin F-YC, Azimi PH, Weisman LE, et al. Antibiotic susceptibility profiles for group B streptococci isolated from neonates, 1995-1998. Clin Infect Dis. 2000;31:76-79.

176. Aracil B, Miñambres M, Oteo J, et al. Susceptibility of strains of *Streptococcus agalactiae* to macrolides and lincosamides, phenotype patterns and resistance genes. Clin Microbiol Infect. 2002;8:745-748.

177. Berkowitz K, Regan JA, Greenberg E. Antibiotic resistance patterns of group B streptococci in pregnant women. J Clin Microbiol. 1990;28:5-7.

178. Schauf V, Deveikis A, Riff L, et al. Antibiotic-killing kinetics of group B streptococci. J Pediatr. 1976;89:194-198.

179. Boyer KM, Gotoff SP. Prevention of early-onset neonatal group B streptococcal disease with selective intrapartum chemoprophylaxis. N Engl J Med. 1986;314:1665-1669.

180. Teres FO, Matorras R, Perea AG, et al. Prevention of neonatal group B streptococcal sepsis. Pediatr Infect Dis J. 1987;6:874.

181. Mohle-Boetani JC, Schuchat A, Plikaytis BD, et al. Comparison of prevention strategies for neonatal group B streptococcal (GBS) infection. JAMA. 1993;270:1442-1448.

182. American College of Obstetricians and Gynecologists. Group B streptococcal infections in pregnancy. ACOG Tech Bull. 1992;170:1-5.

183. Committee on Infectious Diseases and Committee on Fetus and Newborn. Guidelines for prevention of group B streptococcal (GBS) infection by chemoprophylaxis. Pediatrics. 1992;90:775-778.

184. Centers for Disease Control. Prevention of perinatal group B streptococcal disease: A public health perspective. MMWR Morb Mortal Wkly Rep. 1996;45:1-24.

185. Molnar P, Biringer A, McGeer A, et al. Can pregnant women obtain their own specimens for group B streptococcus? A comparison of maternal versus physician screening. Fam Pract. 1997;14:403-406.

186. Mercer BM, Taylor MC, Fricke JL, et al. The accuracy and patient preference for self-collected group B streptococcus cultures. Am J Obstet Gynecol. 1995;173:1325-1328.

187. Schrag SJ, Zell ER, Lynfield R, et al. A population-based comparison of strategies to prevent early-onset group B streptococcal disease in neonates. N Engl J Med. 2002;347:233-239.

188. Centers for Disease Control and Prevention. Prevention of perinatal group B streptococcal disease. MMWR Recomm Rep. 2002;51(RR-11):1-22.

189. American Academy of Pediatrics. Group B streptococcal infections. In: Pickering LK, ed. 2003 Red Book: Report of the Committee on Infectious Diseases. 26th ed. Elk Grove Village, IL: American Academy of Pediatrics; 2003:584-591.

190. Baker CJ, Edwards MS, Kasper DL. Immunogenicity of polysaccharides from type III, group B streptococcus. J Clin Invest. 1978;61:1107-1110.

191. Eisenstein TK, DeCuenick BJ, Resavy D, et al. Quantitative determination in human sera of vaccine-induced antibody to type-specific polysaccharides of group B streptococci using an enzyme-linked immunosorbent assay. J Infect Dis. 1983;147:847-856.

192. Baker CJ, Kasper DL. Group B streptococcal vaccines. Rev Infect Dis. 1985;4:458-467.

193. Baker CJ, Rench MA, Edwards MS, et al. Immunization of pregnant women with a polysaccharide vaccine. N Engl J Med. 1988;319:1180-1185.

194. Givner LB, Baker CJ. Pooled human IgG hyperimmune for type III group B streptococci: Evaluation against multiple strains in vitro and in experimental disease. J Infect Dis. 1991;163:1141-1145.

195. Wessels MR, Paoletti LC, Kasper DL, et al. Immunogenicity in animals of a polysaccharide-protein conjugate vaccine against type III group B streptococcus. J Clin Invest. 1990;86:1428-1433.

196. Paoletti LC, Kasper DL, Michon F, et al. An oligosaccharide-tetanus toxoid conjugate vaccine against type III group B streptococcus. J Biol Chem. 1990;265:18278-18283.

197. Madoff LC, Paoletti LC, Tai JY, et al. Maternal immunization of mice with group B streptococcal type III polysaccharide-beta C protein conjugate elicits protective antibody to multiple serotypes. J Clin Invest. 1994;94:286-292.

198. Kasper DL, Paoletti LC, Wessels MR, et al. Immune response to type III group B streptococcal polysaccharide–tetanus toxoid conjugate vaccine. J Clin Invest. 1996;98:2308-2314.

199. Wessels MR, Paoletti LC, Rodewald AK, et al. Stimulation of protective antibodies against type Ia and Ib group B streptococci by a type Ia polysaccharide–tetanus toxoid conjugate vaccine. Infect Immun. 1993;61:4760-4766.

200. Paoletti LC, Wessels MR, Michon F, et al. Group B streptococcus type II polysaccharide–tetanus toxoid conjugate vaccine. Infect Immun. 1992;60:4009-4014.

201. Wessels MR, Paoletti LC, Pinel J, et al. Immunogenicity and protective activity in animals of a type V group B streptococcal polysaccharide–tetanus toxoid conjugate vaccine. J Infect Dis. 1995;171:879-884.

202. Baker CJ, Paoletti LC, Wessels MR, et al. Safety and immunogenicity of capsular polysaccharide–tetanus toxoid conjugate vaccines for group B streptococcal types Ia and Ib. J Infect Dis. 1999;179:142-150.

203. Baker CJ, Paoletti LC, Rench MA, et al. Use of capsular polysaccharide-tetanus toxoid conjugate vaccine for type II group B streptococcus in healthy women. J Infect Dis. 2000;182:1129-1138.

204. Baker CJ, Rench MA, Ward ME, et al. Immune response of healthy women to two different type V group B streptococcal capsular polysaccharide-protein conjugate vaccines. J Infect Dis. 2004;189:1103.

205. Palazzi DL, Rench MA, Paoletti LC, et al. Group B streptococcal (GBS) type V capsular polysaccharide (CPS)-tetanus toxoid (V-TT) conjugate vaccine (CV) in healthy adults 65 to 85 years of age. J Infect Dis. In Press.

206. Baker CJ, Rench MA, McInnes P. Immunization of pregnant women with group B streptococcal type III capsular polysaccharide-tetanus toxoid conjugate vaccine. Vaccine. 2003;21:3468-3472.

207. Baker CJ, Rench MA, Fernandez M, et al. Safety and immunogenicity of a bivalent group B streptococcal conjugate vaccine for serotypes II and III. J Infect Dis. 2003;188:66-73.

208. Paoletti LC, Wessels MR, Rodewald AK, et al. Neonatal mouse protection against infection with multiple group B streptococcal (GBS) serotypes by maternal immunization with a tetravalent GBS polysaccharide-tetanus toxoid conjugate vaccine. Infect Immun. 1994;62:3236-3243.

CHAPTER **200**

Viridans Streptococci, Groups C and G Streptococci, and *Gemella morbillorum*

CAROLINE C. JOHNSON

ALLAN R. TUNKEL

Viridans streptococci and the β-hemolytic streptococci constitute a diverse group of organisms with varying environmental niches and pathogenicity. Although these organisms usually reside as commensals in the respiratory and intestinal tracts of animals and humans, they may also invade sterile body sites, resulting in life-threatening diseases. This chapter reviews infections caused by the viridans streptococci, nutritionally variant (deficient) streptococci (NVS, genera

Abiotrophia and *Granulicatella*), and β-hemolytic streptococci (other than groups A, B, and D) that are associated with human disease. Although the *Streptococcus anginosus (milleri)* group (*S. anginosus, S. intermedius,* and *S. constellatus*) are viridans streptococci, they are discussed in detail elsewhere (see Chapter 201). *Stomatococcus* and *Pediococcus* are also discussed in this chapter.

VIRIDANS GROUP STREPTOCOCCI

Microbiology

Viridans streptococci possess the general characteristics common to all streptococci (see Chapter 192). They are facultatively anaerobic, gram-positive cocci that do not produce catalase or coagulase; on blood agar, their colonies are rarely β-hemolytic. The term *viridans* derives from the Latin word *viridis,* meaning "green." Many species in this group cause partial destruction of erythrocytes with resultant green discoloration on blood agar (α-hemolysis), whereas others have no effect on blood (γ-hemolysis).[1] Although some isolates react with Lancefield grouping antisera, the species do not conform to specific serogroups, and many isolates are entirely nongroupable.[2,3] Viridans streptococci can be distinguished from *Streptococcus pneumoniae,* another species producing α-hemolysis on blood agar, by resistance to optochin and lack of bile solubility. They are distinguished from enterococci by their inability to grow in broth containing 6.5% sodium chloride. *Streptococcus bovis,* one of the nonenterococcal group D streptococci, has previously been considered a member of the viridans group but has a different habitat and clinical significance (see Chapter 196).[4]

Viridans streptococci are fastidious with respect to their nutritional growth requirements; enriched agars and broths are recommended for optimal recovery from primary cultures.[5] Most strains grow well in conventional blood culture media. On solid agar, viridans streptococci are usually facultatively anaerobic, but some strains are decidedly capnophilic or microaerophilic. The colonies vary in size and appearance depending on the composition of the medium and the incubation atmosphere.[5] In broth cultures, streptococci appear as spherical or ovoid cells that form chains or pairs. The organisms are nonmotile and non–spore-forming, and they ferment carbohydrates with production of acid but not gas.

Species Identification

In the past, terminology applied to the viridans group of streptococci was confusing and inconsistent. When organisms were recovered in clinical laboratories, species designation often sidestepped identification of the isolate in favor of a generic descriptive term such as "non-hemolytic" or "α-hemolytic." In addition, terms such as *Streptococcus mutans* and *Streptococcus sanguis* were used loosely to refer to groups of organisms without denoting clear relationship. In the 1970s, two schemes for identification of viridans streptococci were proposed. Colman and Williams suggested classification of the group into five species: *S. mutans, S. milleri, S. sanguis, S. salivarius,* and *S. mitior,* which they termed "the human oral viridans streptococci."[6] The scheme of Facklam recognized 10 physiologic species: *S. sanguis* I and II, *S. mitis, S. salivarius, S. mutans, S. uberis, S. acidominimus, S. morbillorum,* and two subdivisions of the *S. milleri* group, *S. anginosus-constellatus* and *S. MG-intermedius.*[7] The various species, as defined by these two schemes, were not identical. More recently, a molecular approach has been applied to define the taxonomy of viridans streptococci based on genetic relatedness.[8] Application of 16S rRNA gene sequencing has proven especially useful in defining phylogenetic relationships between species.[9] Analyses have resulted in emended descriptions of well-recognized species (e.g., *S. mitis, S. sanguis*), the discovery and description of several new species (e.g., *S. gordonii, S. vestibularis*), and the division of the serotypes of the *S. mutans* group into distinct species. Expanded batteries of phenotypic tests combined with differences observed between genotypes have permitted laboratories to identify accurately species for correlation with clinical syndromes. The current taxonomy is shown in Table 200-1. When reviewing older literature pertaining to the viridans group of

TABLE 200-1 Classification of Viridans Other than the *S. anginosus* Group, *S. bovis,* and *S. pneumoniae*

Mitis group
   S. mitis
   S. sanguis (biotypes 1, 2, and 3)
   S. parasanguis
   S. gordonii
   S. crista
   S. peroris
   S. infantis
   S. oralis
Mutans group
   S. mutans
   S. sobrinus
   S. criceti
   S. rattus
   S. downei
   S. macacae
Salivarius group
   S. salivarius
   S. vestibularis
   S. thermophilus

streptococci, the extensive changes in taxonomy and nomenclature should be taken into consideration.

At present, clinically significant species of viridans group streptococci can be assigned to one of the following groups: the Anginosus group (*S. anginosus, S. constellatus,* and *S. intermedius*), the Mitis group (*S. sanguis, S. parasanguis, S. gordonii, S. crista, S. infantis, S. mitis, S. oralis,* and *S. peroris*), the Mutans group (*S. criceti, S. downei, S. macacae, S. mutans, S. rattus,* and *S. sobrinus*), and the Salivarius group (*S. salivarius, S. thermophilus,* and *S. vestibularis*).[9] Some of these species are newly described; others have undergone name changes to comply with rules of nomenclature since publication of prior reviews.[10] All have either been recovered from human clinical specimens or have a potential for causing human disease based on transmission from nonhuman sources.[9] Viridans streptococcal species can be distinguished phenotypically by their physiologic and biochemical characteristics, in particular their type of hemolysis on blood agar, Voges-Proskauer reaction, pattern of acid formation from carbohydrates, ability to hydrolyze esculin and arginine, and production of dextran, levan, alkaline phosphatase, hydrogen peroxide, and acetoin (Table 200-2).[1-21] A simplified scheme, consisting of 14 biochemical tests, has also been proposed.[22] Although rapid, automated systems for species identification of streptococci are commercially available, their performance is variable. For some, the databases have not been updated or expanded to include newer species; others require supplemental procedures to ensure they perform accurately. Conventional biochemical tests remain the most reliable method for identification of these organisms in clinical laboratories.[23]

S. morbillorum was once considered to be a viridans streptococcus because it failed to produce β-hemolysis on blood agar, lacked distinguishing serogroup antigens, and did not have the biochemical characteristics of enterococci or pneumococci. In Facklam's review, one half of the 46 isolates described were associated with serious infections.[7] The organism has recently been reclassified as the second species in the genus *Gemella* (*G. morbillorum*).[18] Infections associated with this organism are similar to those seen with viridans streptococci, and the principles of treatment are the same.

Although NVS were also once thought to be viridans streptococci, they have been shown to form a genetically unrelated group (genera *Abiotrophia* and *Granulicatella;* see later discussion).[24-26]

Epidemiology

Viridans streptococci are an important part of the normal microbial flora of humans and animals. They are indigenous to the upper respiratory tract, the female genital tract, and all regions of the gastrointestinal tract, but are most prevalent in the oral cavity.[1,5] On average, streptococci represent 28% of the total culturable flora from dental plaque, 29% from gingival crevices, 45% from the tongue, and 46%

TABLE 200-2 Biochemical Characteristics for Differentiation of Viridans Streptococci

Organism	Pattern of Hemolysis	Voges-Proskauer	Hydrolysis of			Acid Production from						Production of		
			Exculin	Arginine	H₂O₂	Mannitol	Sorbitol	Lactose	Trehalose	Inulin	Raffinose	Alkaline Phosphatase	Dextran	Levan
S. mutans	α, β, γ	+	+	−	−	+	+	+	+	+	+	−	+	−
S. mitis	α	−	−	−	+	−	−	+	v	−	v	v	−	−
S. oralis	α	−	−	−	+	−	−	+	v	−	v	+	v	−
S. sanguis	α	−	v	+	+	−	v	+	+	+	v	−	+	−
S. gordonii	α	−	+	+	+	−	−	+	+	+	v	+	+	−
S. crista	α	−	−	v	+	−	−	v	+	−	−	−	v	na
S. salivarius	α	+	+	−	−	−	v	v	v	v	+	v	−	+
S. vestibularis	α	v	v	−	+	−	v	v	v	−	−	v	−	−
S. parasanguis	α	−	v	+	+	−	−	+	v	−	+	+	−	−
G. morbillorum	α, γ	na	−	−	na	−	−	−	−	−	−	na	−	na

+, 85% or more of strains positive; −, 85% or more of strains negative; v, variable; na, not available.

from saliva.[27] The various species, however, are not distributed uniformly throughout the oral cavity. Studies from the early 1970s showed that strains of *S. salivarius* predominated on the tongue and those of *S. mitis* on the buccal mucosa, whereas *S. mutans* and *S. sanguis* were more often associated with dental structures.[28] Gibbons and van Houte demonstrated that this proportional distribution of viridans streptococcal species was determined by their selective adherence to the various oral tissues.[29] Using the emended descriptions of viridans species, the ecology of strains in the oral cavity and oropharynx can now be described as follows: the buccal mucosa is associated with *S. sanguis* and *S. mitis;* the dorsum of the tongue with *S. mitis* and *S. salivarius;* initial dental plaque with *S. sanguis, S. mitis,* and *S. oralis;* mature supragingival plaque with *S. gordonii;* and subgingival plaque with *S. anginosus.*[30]

In healthy persons, adherence of viridans streptococci may provide "colonization resistance" within the oral cavity to prevent establishment of more pathogenic bacteria. Fibronectin, a complex glycoprotein found on the surface of oral epithelial cells, selectively promotes attachment of *S. salivarius, S. mutans,* "*S. mitior,*" (probably now *S. mitis*) and other gram-positive cocci.[31] If fibronectin is lost or diminished, as occurs in chronically ill or hospitalized patients, adherence of organisms such as *Pseudomonas aeruginosa* to oral epithelial cells is increased.[32,33] Because oropharyngeal colonization with enteric gram-negative bacilli often precedes invasion (e.g., development of gram-negative bacillary pneumonia), selective adherence of viridans streptococci in the oral cavity can be viewed as a protective mechanism for the host.[34,35]

Pathogenicity

Viridans streptococci are considered to be bacteria of low virulence. They are not known to possess endotoxin or secrete exotoxins, and they are fully susceptible to lysis by serum and lysosomal enzymes. Although some species make proteolytic enzymes, these enzymes are not clearly related to the pathogenesis of infection.[36] Therefore, viridans streptococci do not have the traditional virulence factors that characterize more pathogenic bacteria. Some strains have been shown to invade and kill human endothelial cells in vitro.[37] This cytotoxicity is mediated by peroxidogenesis and acidogenesis but not by production of protein exotoxins.

The pathogenicity of viridans group streptococci is best exemplified by their ability to produce endocarditis. Extracellular dextran plays an important role in adherence and propagation of these organisms on cardiac valves. Clinical observations have noted that after bacteremia caused by dextran-producing streptococci there is a higher incidence of infective endocarditis than when bacteremia is caused by non–dextran-producing streptococci.[38] Investigators have also shown that the amount of dextran produced by a streptococcal strain correlates with its ability to adhere to cardiac valves in vitro and to induce infective endocarditis in experimental animal models.[39,40] Pretreatment with dextranase abolishes the differences in pathogenicity of various

strains. In addition, production of dextran by the pathogen also mediates the response to antimicrobial therapy. Endocarditis caused by dextran-producing strains is more resistant to penicillin treatment and yields larger vegetations than infection caused by dextran-negative strains.[41] Treatment of experimental endocarditis with penicillin and dextranase results in higher rates of valve sterilization than does treatment with penicillin alone.[42] Another bacterial factor that might be related to the pathogenesis of endocarditis is FimA. This surface-associated protein of *S. parasanguis* has been associated with initial colonization of damaged heart tissue in an endocarditis model. Immunization with recombinant FimA resulted in antibody-mediated inhibition of bacterial adherence and protection from endocarditis in an animal model.[43,44]

Fibronectin, which is secreted by endothelial cells, platelets, and fibroblasts in response to vascular injury, is one possible factor that mediates adherence of streptococci to cardiac valves.[45] It constitutes about 4% of the mass of a blood clot and has been found on the surfaces of traumatized rabbit valves.[46] Microorganisms more likely to cause endocarditis bind significantly better to fibronectin in vitro than do non–endocarditis-producing strains.[47] A low-fibronectin-binding mutant of *S. sanguis* was less able to induce endocarditis in an experimental animal model than its high-fibronectin-binding parent strain.[48] Lipoteichoic acid appears to be the fibronectin adhesin on streptococci. Exposure of the organism to subinhibitory concentrations of antibiotics results in loss of surface lipoteichoic acid and a subsequent decrease in ability to produce endocarditis.[49,50] Once adherent to the surface of the valve, viridans streptococci induce propagation of the infected vegetation by stimulating production of tissue factor from the underlying valvular tissue and by directly triggering further platelet aggregation.[51-53]

In addition to causing infective endocarditis, certain species of viridans streptococci, notably *S. mutans,* have a strong association with development of dental caries. The organism is acquired early in life, through horizontal and vertical transmission from mother to infant.[54] Laboratory experiments have shown that caries develop in germ-free animals after infection with *S. mutans.* However, colonization of dental surfaces and production of caries occurs only in the presence of dietary sucrose.[55,56] The organism uses sucrose to synthesize a number of extracellular polysaccharides, including glucans, that serve to bind it to dental enamel and to other bacteria. The high cariogenic potential of *S. mutans* is thought to be related to its dual ability to adhere in large masses on teeth and to produce high concentrations of acid from the fermentation of dietary sugars.[57]

Occasionally, viridans streptococci produce bacteremia and septic shock in neutropenic patients. The mechanism by which this occurs is unclear. In vitro studies have shown that clinical isolates of viridans streptococci from shock patients were able to induce tumor necrosis factor-α (TNF-α) in murine macrophages.[58] Production of TNF-α was dose dependent and followed kinetics similar to that of *Escherichia coli* isolates. In a study of patients with neutropenia and overwhelm-

TABLE 200-3 Antimicrobial Therapy for Infective Endocarditis due to Viridans and Nutritionally Variant Streptococci*

Organism (MIC)	Antibiotic	Dosage and Route[†]	Duration (week)
Penicillin-susceptible viridans streptococci (≤0.1 μg/mL)	Aqueous penicillin G	10-20 million units iv q24h continously or in 6 divided doses	4
	Aqueous penicillin G	10-20 million units iv q24h continuously or in 6 divided doses	2
	with streptomycin[‡]	7.5 mg/kg im (not to exceed 500 mg) q12h	2
	or with gentamicin	1 mg/kg im or iv (not to exceed 80 mg) q8h	2
	Aqueous penicillin G	10-20 million units iv q24h continuously or in 6 divided doses	4
	with streptomycin	7.5 mg/kg im (not to exceed 500 mg) q12h	2
	or with gentamicin	1 mg/kg im or iv (not to exceed 80 mg) q8h	2
	Ceftriaxone	2 g im or iv daily	4
Relatively resistant viridans streptococci (>0.1 μg/mL and <0.5 μg/mL) and all nutritionally variant streptococci	Aqueous penicillin G	20 million units iv q24h continuously or in 6 divided doses	4
	with streptomycin	7.5 mg/kg im (not to exceed 500 mg) q12h	2
	or with gentamicin	1 mg/kg im or iv (not to exceed 80 mg) q8h	2
Resistant viridans streptococci (≥0.5 μg/mL)	Aqueous penicillin G	20-30 million units iv q24h continuously or in 6 divided doses	4-6
	with streptomycin	7.5 mg/kg im (not to exceed 500 mg) q12h	4-6
	or with gentamicin	1 mg/kg im or iv (not to exceed 80 mg) q8h	4-6

MIC, minimum inhibitory concentration; iv, intravenously; im, intramuscularly.
*Adapted from the Committee Recommendations of the American Heart Association's Council on Cardiovascular Disease in the Young.[80]
[†]Doses should be adjusted according to renal function.
[‡]Peak streptomycin and gentamicin levels of 20 and 3 μg/ml, respectively, are desirable. Choice of a particular aminoglycoside may depend on susceptibility of the strain at high concentrations.

ing infection, serum levels of TNF-α and interleukin-6 were found to be increased, regardless of whether shock was caused by viridans streptococci or gram-negative bacilli.[59] Thus, the pathogenesis of viridans streptococcal shock appears to be not unlike that of gram-negative septic shock.

Clinical Manifestations

Endocarditis

In the preantibiotic era, viridans streptococci accounted for approximately 75% of cases of infective endocarditis.[60,61] At the present time, their relative frequency in association with infective endocarditis has declined to as low as 20%.[62] This change in epidemiology reflects an increase in the number of patients acquiring staphylococcal endocarditis in association with injection drug use or prosthetic valves rather than a decrease in the overall annual incidence of streptococcal endocarditis.[63] Many different species have been reported to cause endocarditis, including *S. sanguinis, S. mitis, S. mutans, S. salivarius, S. gordonii, S. vestibularis,* and *S. oralis.* Because of the changes in taxonomy and the number of isolates previously unspeciated, it is likely that other viridans streptococci have also been associated with infective endocarditis. The clinical manifestations and outcomes associated with the various species causing endocarditis appear to be similar.[64]

Infective endocarditis caused by viridans streptococci occurs most often in patients with underlying valvular heart disease. In the past, rheumatic and congenital heart disease were the major predisposing lesions, accounting for 37% to 76% and 6% to 24% of endocarditis cases, respectively. With the declining incidence of rheumatic fever, mitral valve prolapse (29%) and degenerative valvular lesions (21%) have assumed a more prominent role.[65] Viridans streptococci are more frequently the cause of endocarditis in patients known to have heart disease (55%) than in those not previously known to have heart disease (29%).[66] Among cases of infective endocarditis in injection drug users, viridans streptococci account for a small proportion (6%).[67] In patients with prosthetic valves, the incidence of infective endocarditis increases according to the length of time since valve surgery. In early disease (60 days since valve replacement), only 7% of infections are caused by streptococci; the frequency increases to 30% in patients in whom infection develops 1 year or longer after surgery.[68]

Viridans streptococcal endocarditis has an insidious onset followed by a subacute but progressive course. In most patients symptoms develop within 2 weeks of presumed onset; however, it is often 5 weeks or more from the time of initial symptoms until the diagnosis is established.[69] Fever, the single most common finding in endocarditis, is present in almost all patients except those who have preexisting renal

failure, congestive heart failure, or concomitant antibiotic use.[61,64] Constitutional symptoms such as fatigue, anorexia, weight loss, and malaise often accompany the fever. Cardiac murmurs are detected in more than 90% of patients with streptococcal endocarditis,[70] and splenomegaly is noted in up to half of cases.[71] Manifestations of circulating immune complexes such as Osler's nodes, petechiae, and splinter hemorrhages may also occur (28% of cases).[72]

The critical element for diagnosis of infective endocarditis is demonstration of continuous bacteremia. With viridans streptococci, the bacteremia is often low grade (1 to 30 colony-forming units per milliliter of blood). In the absence of recent antimicrobial therapy, 96% of one set of blood cultures and 98% of two sets of blood cultures yield the pathogen.[73] Echocardiography is used as a confirmatory test in patients with blood cultures positive for viridans streptococci; 39% to 72% of patients with endocarditis have vegetations identified on a two-dimensional echocardiogram.[64,74] Echocardiography can also be used to identify valvular dysfunction, hemodynamic complications, and myocardial abscesses, findings that may indicate the need for surgical intervention. Whether echocardiography provides prognostic information about the risk of systemic emboli is a controversial issue.[75]

Recommended regimens for treatment of streptococcal endocarditis are based largely on clinical observations and studies of antibiotic efficacy in experimental models of endocarditis.[76,77] In an experimental rabbit model, prolonged penicillin therapy adequately sterilized vegetations, but addition of streptomycin or gentamicin led to more rapid eradication of the pathogen.[78,79] Penicillin G remains the mainstay of therapy for viridans streptococcal endocarditis. As with other types of infective endocarditis, the antibiotic is administered in high doses for extended periods, usually 4 weeks. If given in combination with an aminoglycoside, the duration of penicillin therapy can be shortened, although the patient is exposed to the additional risk of aminoglycoside toxicity (nephrotoxicity and ototoxicity). Although most clinical experience with two-drug regimens has been with streptomycin plus penicillin, gentamicin is now considered interchangeable with streptomycin in the combination. Because of the ready availability of serum level determinations and the convenience of intravenous administration, gentamicin has become the preferred agent in clinical practice.

Antibiotic regimens that are currently recommended by the American Heart Association are summarized in Table 200-3.[80] For streptococcal strains that are highly susceptible to penicillin (minimal inhibitory concentration [MIC] ≤0.1 μg/mL), three regimens are endorsed. All can be expected to achieve very high bacteriologic cure rates. In a review of endocarditis treatment outcomes, Wilson and Geraci found a relapse rate of 0.6% (1/154) for patients receiving 4 weeks of penicillin alone, and 2.0% (6/295) for those treated with a

2-week course of penicillin plus streptomycin.[81] Ceftriaxone shows similar efficacy, with no cases of microbiologic failure or relapse reported in a noncomparative trial (although 10 of the 55 patients ultimately required valve replacement for congestive heart failure or recurrent embolization).[82] Another study compared the efficacy of a daily 2-g dose of ceftriaxone for 4 weeks with that of a regimen of 2 weeks of ceftriaxone followed by 2 weeks of oral amoxicillin (1 g four times daily) and reported relapse in only 1 of 30 patients.[83,84]

Because relapse is uncommon, selection of a specific antimicrobial regimen should be individualized for each patient. The 2-week regimen is most appropriate for uncomplicated cases of endocarditis occurring in patients at low risk for aminoglycoside toxicity. It is not indicated for patients with extracardiac foci of infection or intracardiac abscess.[80] Longer courses of treatment may also be preferred for patients with protracted illness (symptoms lasting longer than 3 months), aortic insufficiency, moderate to severe congestive heart failure, or a documented relapse.[85] In patients whose infection involves prosthetic valves or other prosthetic material, a 6-week regimen of penicillin is recommended together with gentamicin for at least the first 2 weeks.[80]

Although endocarditis caused by penicillin-resistant viridans streptococci is uncommon,[86] patients infected with such strains may be at higher risk of relapse after antimicrobial therapy.[87] For relatively resistant strains (penicillin MIC greater than 0.1 μg/mL but less than 0.5 μg/mL), gentamicin should be given for the first 2 weeks of a 4-week course of penicillin therapy (see Table 200-3). For resistant strains (those requiring 0.5 μg/mL of penicillin or more for inhibition), treatment is the same as for enterococci and consists of penicillin plus gentamicin for a full 4 to 6 weeks. Serum levels of the aminoglycoside should be monitored during therapy to avoid toxicity.

For patients who have immediate-type hypersensitivity to penicillin, 4 weeks of vancomycin is an appropriate alternate regimen. Addition of an aminoglycoside is not required, regardless of whether or not the isolate is resistant to penicillin. In patients with other types of penicillin allergy (e.g., nonurticarial skin rashes), cefazolin or another first-generation cephalosporin may be administered to treat viridans streptococcal endocarditis caused by isolates that are moderately resistant to penicillin (MICs, 0.1 to <0.5 μg/mL). The cephalosporin may be given alone for 4 weeks or, if there is no contraindication to short-course therapy, in combination with an aminoglycoside for 2 weeks. Cephalosporins are not indicated in cases where the pathogen is highly resistant to penicillin (MIC ≥0.5 μg/mL).

Bacteremia

Viridans streptococci account for 2.6% of positive blood cultures reported from clinical laboratories. Of these, only 21% are thought to be clinically significant.[88] The remainder have been attributed to contamination despite the fact that viridans streptococci are not typically part of the normal skin flora.[89] In many cases, failure to ascribe clinical significance to these organisms in blood cultures occurs because of their low virulence and the transient nature of the bacteremia.[90] In contrast, prolonged bacteremia has emerged as a genuine problem among patients undergoing cancer chemotherapy. In some centers, viridans streptococci are now a leading cause of bacteremia in febrile, neutropenic patients.[91-93] At the M. D. Anderson Cancer Center in Houston, the incidence of streptococcal bacteremia increased from 1 case per 10,000 admissions in 1972 to 47 per 10,000 in 1989.[94] In another study, viridans streptococci were recovered from the blood in 35 (17.5%) of 200 consecutive recipients of autologous stem cell transplants at a median of 6 days after the procedure.[95] S. mitis and S. oralis are the species most commonly identified in neutropenic cancer patients with streptococcal bacteremia.[96]

Viridans streptococcal bacteremia usually occurs in association with aggressive cytoreductive therapy for acute leukemia or allogeneic bone marrow transplantation, especially after high-dose cytosine arabinoside treatment.[97,98] In a study in which patients with other gram-positive bacteremias served as controls, the risk of streptococcal infection was reported to increase with profound neutropenia, prophylactic administration of trimethoprim-sulfamethoxazole or a

fluoroquinolone, and use of antacids or histamine type 2 (H$_2$) receptor antagonists.[94] Another risk factor strongly implicated is the presence of mucositis.[92,97,99] In one noncomparative study of 32 patients, 78% had oral inflammation or ulceration at the time of their infection.[99] Similarly, Bostrom and Weisdorf reported an association of viridans streptococcal bacteremia with increased radiation dose to the oral cavity,[100] and Ringden and colleagues described an association with herpes simplex infection.[101] In the latter, use of prophylactic acyclovir decreased the frequency of bacteremia after allogeneic bone marrow transplantation. The presence of an indwelling venous catheter poses an additional risk factor for streptococcal bacteremia in neutropenic patients.[92,93]

Bacteremia with viridans streptococci is more common in children than in adults,[102,103] typically developing within 15 days of chemotherapy or bone marrow transplantation, at the time of profound neutropenia. In a series of 123 patients, 73% presented with fever alone, whereas 27% also had evidence of organ dysfunction.[102] A fulminant shock syndrome characterized by hypotension, rash, palmar desquamation, and adult respiratory distress syndrome has been described in approximately one fourth of patients.[94,104] S. mitis has been the cause in most such cases.[105] Very few cases of viridans streptococcal bacteremia in immunocompromised patients have led to clinically apparent endocarditis.

Despite early initiation of broad-spectrum antibiotics, the mortality rate for viridans streptococcal bacteremia in immunocompromised patients is approximately 6% to 12%.[94,99,102] Fatal cases have been characterized by early, fulminant cardiovascular collapse or secondary central nervous system involvement. In most, the isolates were susceptible in vitro to the selected empirical antimicrobial regimen, usually a β-lactam plus an aminoglycoside. Lack of treatment efficacy is associated with the poor clinical status of patients at the time of antibiotic initiation. Because penicillin susceptibility cannot be assumed, some authorities recommend use of vancomycin for empirical treatment of neutropenic patients in whom streptococcal septicemia is suspected.[105]

Use of antimicrobial agents to prevent streptococcal bacteremia is controversial. Some studies have shown potential benefit[104,106]; others have not.[95] At one cancer institute, the incidence of streptococcal bacteremia decreased from 11.5% in 1989 to 2.5% in 1995 after penicillin was introduced for prophylaxis in neutropenic patients.[106] Similarly, in a sequential cohort study of 289 bone marrow transplant recipients, both vancomycin and β-lactam prophylaxis were shown to decrease the incidence of gram-positive bacteremia compared with controls (by 40%, 27%, and 0%, respectively); however, no differences in mortality could be demonstrated.[107] In contrast, Bilgrami and coworkers found that prophylactic use of ampicillin failed to decrease the incidence of viridans streptococcal sepsis in bone marrow transplant recipients.[95] Regardless of efficacy, a consequence of prophylactic use of β-lactam antibiotics in many of these studies was emergence of resistance. The proportion of penicillin-resistant viridans streptococcal bacteremias increased from 0% in 1989 before any prophylaxis was given to marrow transplant recipients, to 16% in 1991 when quinolones were used for prophylaxis, to 44% when penicillin was added to the quinolones.[106] Fatality rates among neutropenic patients with bacteremia caused by penicillin-resistant viridans streptococci may be higher than for penicillin-susceptible strains.[97,106,108] Concerns over hypersensitivity reactions and selection of resistant strains may preclude routine use of penicillin prophylaxis, except in centers with high infection rates.

Meningitis

Despite the frequency with which viridans streptococci cause bacteremia, they are an uncommon cause of meningitis, accounting for only 0.3% to 5% of culture-proven cases.[109,110] Although species designation was often not provided in the early literature, more recent reports suggest that S. salivarius is most commonly associated with meningitis.[111-116] Infections with S. mitis and S. sanguis have also been described.[117-119] Infections occur in patients of all ages, including neonates. Clinical manifestations are typical of acute pyogenic meningitis with signs of meningeal irritation, neurologic deficits, seizures, and altered sensorium.

The source of infection for most cases of viridans streptococcal meningitis is endogenous flora. In instances of neonatal meningitis, the infection was presumed to be acquired perinatally from the mother.[114,117-119] Portals of entry have been various and not always identifiable. In the largest review of viridans streptococcal meningitis (55 cases), ear, nose, or throat pathology was found in 31% of patients; endocarditis in 13%; primary extracranial infection in 13%; and head trauma or neurosurgery in 8%; no portal for entry was identified in 35% of patients.[109] Other predisposing factors include gastrointestinal pathology,[111,120] gastrointestinal manipulation such as endoscopy with cauterization,[110,112,121] trauma,[122] ganglionic thermocoagulation,[110] and severe immunocompromise after chemotherapy.[102,123] In a review of 60 cases of iatrogenic meningitis, streptococcal species were responsible for 33 (63%).[124] Spinal anesthesia, myelography, and diagnostic lumbar puncture were the most common predisposing events, respectively. Iatrogenic meningitis due to viridans streptococci has been reported in association with nonobservance of infection control precautions while performing lumbar puncture, especially regarding use of face masks.[125]

When α-hemolytic streptococci other than pneumococci are recovered from cerebrospinal fluid (CSF), they are more likely to be contaminants than true pathogens. In 43 patients from whom various species of α-hemolytic streptococci were isolated on culture of CSF, only eight isolates (19%) were determined to be clinically relevant.[126] The significance of isolation of α-hemolytic streptococci from CSF depends on the clinical setting and CSF laboratory parameters. CSF protein concentrations and white blood cell differential counts are clearly abnormal in patients with true infection, but CSF glucose levels may be normal.[120] A positive Gram stain is highly significant but occurs in fewer than 50% of patients with viridans streptococcal meningitis.[126] Differentiation of these streptococci from *S. pneumoniae* on the basis of a spinal fluid Gram stain is seldom possible.[113]

The finding of positive blood cultures in association with viridans streptococcal meningitis is suggestive of underlying endocarditis. Bacteremia with meningitis in the absence of cardiac involvement has also been described, especially in severely immunocompromised patients.[102] Meningitis is an uncommon complication of viridans streptococcal endocarditis.[127] Among 41 patients with infective endocarditis who also had symptoms suggestive of meningitis or encephalitis, the organism was recovered on CSF culture in only 4 cases.[128]

In the preantibiotic era, viridans streptococcal meningitis was almost uniformly fatal; only nine surviving patients were reported before 1937.[109] After introduction of antibiotic therapy, mortality rates declined significantly, with most fatalities occurring in patients who were immunocompromised. Although early reports suggested a worse prognosis in infants and children,[109] this was not substantiated in a later study.[120] Penicillin G in doses of 24 million units per day is the antibiotic of choice for treatment of viridans streptococcal meningitis. Most clinical isolates have MICs of 0.1 μg/mL or less, and thus are extremely sensitive. Meningitis caused by multiple-antibiotic–resistant viridans streptococci has also been described.[123] MICs to penicillin for these strains are 4 μg/mL or greater, similar to those seen with antibiotic-resistant *S. pneumoniae*. Although clinical data are lacking, vancomycin plus a third-generation cephalosporin is the preferred treatment of meningitis caused by such strains, pending full susceptibility test results. Whether the recent overall increase in penicillin resistance among viridans isolates is cause to modify empirical treatment regimens for meningitis is controversial (see later discussion).[124] Because of the unpredictable susceptibility patterns of viridans streptococci, in vitro susceptibility testing of all CSF isolates is mandatory.

Pneumonia

Although viridans streptococci are often isolated from respiratory tract specimens, they are rarely ascribed clinical significance. Recovery of these organisms from expectorated sputum is usually attributable to their presence as normal oral flora. However, they may also be cultured from lower respiratory tract specimens obtained by transtracheal

aspiration or protected bronchial brush. Here, viridans streptococci occur, in association with other oral organisms (e.g., anaerobes), as part of the aspiration pneumonia syndrome.[129-131] In one study of community-acquired aspiration pneumonia, cultures of transtracheal aspirates yielded streptococci in 9 of 24 patients.[132] In another review, the organism was recovered from 51% of 189 transtracheal aspirations performed on patients with suspected bacterial pneumonia.[133] The relative importance of viridans streptococci in the pathogenesis of these polymicrobial infections is unknown.

Several reports describe isolation of viridans streptococci as sole pathogens from lower respiratory tract infections.[134-138] Pratter and Irwin described two patients in whom the diagnosis was ascertained by culture of transtracheal aspirate and pleural fluid.[134] Sarkar and colleagues reported three cases of acute community-acquired viridans streptococcal pneumonia in which the diagnosis was confirmed by the presence of positive blood cultures.[135] In a series of patients described by Marrie, an association with predisposing host factors was noted. All seven patients with bacteremic community-acquired pneumonia were older (49 to 80 years) and had multiple underlying conditions, such as alcoholism, lung carcinoma, and diabetes mellitus.[139] Viridans streptococcal pneumonia has also been described in children.[136]

The prognosis for patients with primary viridans streptococcal pneumonia is good. Fatalities are rare in the absence of immunocompromise. Penicillin G has been used successfully as therapy in most cases reported in the literature.

Miscellaneous Infections

Viridans streptococci are associated with a variety of other infections. A pathogenic role in these cases has been confirmed by recovery of the organism in pure culture and often by concurrent presence of bacteremia. Excluding localized purulent collections associated with the *S. anginosus (milleri)* group (see Chapter 201), viridans strains have been identified in patients with pericarditis,[138] peritonitis,[138] acute bacterial sialadenitis,[140] orofacial odontogenic infections,[141] endophthalmitis (see Chapter 108), spondylodiscitis,[142] and various upper respiratory tract infections (otitis media, sinusitis).[136]

Therapy

Viridans group streptococci had been uniformly susceptible to most antimicrobial agents, including β-lactam antibiotics, macrolides, tetracyclines, and aminoglycosides. In recent years, however, resistance has emerged as a significant problem, especially resistance to penicillin and related β-lactam agents. Among 352 unselected blood culture isolates obtained from across the United States during 1993 and 1994, only 44% were susceptible to penicillin (using the National Committee for Clinical Laboratory Standards interpretive criterion of MIC ≤0.125 μg/mL).[143] Resistance occurs more frequently in nosocomial blood-stream isolates and in those obtained from immunocompromised patients. In a national surveillance program, 61% of 98 nosocomial blood-stream isolates were susceptible to penicillin,[144] whereas rates as low as 43% have been reported in neutropenic cancer patients.[108] Resistance in this latter group appears to be selected by use of antimicrobial prophylaxis with cancer chemotherapy. In contrast, most community isolates of viridans group streptococci remain susceptible to penicillin. For example, the susceptibility of endocarditis isolates has not changed appreciably in the last several decades.[145,146] In a 1986 review, only 2 of 31 viridans streptococcal isolates were reported to be penicillin resistant.[147] Moreover, penicillin prophylaxis given to children with rheumatic fever is rarely complicated by endocarditis caused by resistant streptococci,[87] despite increasing numbers of penicillin-resistant strains in the normal flora of the oropharynx.[148,149]

Some strains of viridans group streptococci exhibit a high level of resistance to penicillin. In a survey of South African blood culture isolates, 9% had penicillin MICs of 4.0 μg/mL or greater.[150] Note that the breakpoint for resistance as defined by National Committee for Clinical Laboratory Standards[151] differs from the MIC criterion (≥0.5 μg/mL) used in the American Heart Association guidelines for determining treatment of streptococcal endocarditis (see Table 200-3).[80] Surveys of viridans streptococci from the United States report high-level penicillin resistance in 5% to 13% of blood-stream isolates.[143,152] Rates reported from other areas of the world approach 50%, depending on the types of patients and specimens studied.[108] Like penicillin-resistant pneumococci, resistant viridans strains are non–β-lactamase-producing and possess altered penicillin-binding proteins.[153] In vitro studies suggest the presence of genes homologous to the pneumococcal PBP 1a and 2b genes.[154] Transfer of resistance determinants between these gram-positive bacteria has been accomplished in vitro and may be an important means of disseminating resistance in nature.

Whether species identity for viridans streptococci can be used to predict antimicrobial susceptibility and thus guide therapeutic selections is controversial.[9] Continuous changes in the taxonomy and nomenclature of these organisms combined with the incomplete species identification provided in many reports limits the usefulness of the historical literature. Nevertheless, there do appear to be trends in species-related differences in penicillin susceptibility among viridans group streptococci.[145,155] *S. mitis* is the least sensitive, with only 40% of isolates inhibited by 0.125 µg/mL penicillin or less.[156] *S. oralis* is the next most likely to be resistant, especially those isolates recovered from blood cultures of neutropenic cancer patients.[96] *S. sanguis*, a frequent cause of endocarditis, appears to be the least resistant to β-lactam antibiotics.

Some strains of viridans streptococci exhibit a phenomenon termed *tolerance*, in which the organism is readily inhibited by low concentrations of penicillin but 32 times that level is required for bactericidal activity. In experimental animal models of endocarditis, tolerant strains are eradicated more slowly from vegetations than nontolerant strains, although this effect may be relevant only when low doses of penicillin are used.[157-159] There are conflicting reports on the incidence of tolerance in viridans streptococci.[160] Tolerance is probably observed in most *S. sanguis* and *S. gordonii* strains, but it occurs in a minority of *S. mitis* strains and rarely, if at all, in *S. salivarius*.[161] No clinical significance has been attached to tolerance in the treatment of infective endocarditis. Relapse after a 4-week course of high-dose parenteral penicillin is rare and has not been associated with tolerance in the pathogen.[81] Addition of an aminoglycoside may enhance bactericidal activity in vitro but is not routinely recommended.[80]

Other β-lactam antibiotics have in vitro activity similar to penicillin against viridans streptococci. Generally, community-acquired endocarditis isolates tend to be highly susceptible. Ceftriaxone inhibited 100% of 20 endocarditis strains at a concentration of 2.0 µg/mL or less, and 16 strains (80%) were susceptible to 0.25 µg/mL or less.[162] In another study, 98% of 49 strains were inhibited by 0.1 µg/mL or less.[82] Among surveys of isolates collected from hospitalized or neutropenic cancer patients, ceftriaxone has been less active, with approximately 15% to 23% of isolates found to be resistant.[144,152] Most such isolates also have high-level resistance to penicillin (MIC >4 µg/mL) as well as resistance to other antimicrobial agents.[163]

Viridans streptococci are resistant to aminoglycosides when traditional breakpoint concentrations for these agents are applied. However, in vitro studies and experimental models of endocarditis have demonstrated synergistic bactericidal activity for combinations of penicillin and aminoglycosides.[78,79] In strains with a streptomycin MIC of 1000 µg/mL or greater, synergy is lost for streptomycin but not for gentamicin.[164,165] The breakpoint for predicting synergy with gentamicin is not clear. Strains with a gentamicin MIC of 16 µg/mL have shown synergy, whereas strains with MICs of 64 and 128 µg/mL have not.[150]

Antibiotics with consistently good in vitro activity against viridans streptococci are chloramphenicol and vancomycin; only rare isolates are resistant to the former, and none to the latter. The fluoroquinolones, ofloxacin and levofloxacin, also demonstrate good in vitro activity.[143,166] However, neutropenic cancer patients who receive prophylaxis with a fluoroquinolone antibiotic often develop breakthrough bacteremia with isolates expressing high-level resistance.[167] Therefore, the role of these agents in therapy is uncertain. Tetracycline, clindamycin, and erythromycin have variable activity, often with 25% to 50% of isolates reported resistant.[163] Most strains of viridans streptococci are resistant to trimethoprim-sulfamethoxazole.

NUTRITIONALLY VARIANT (DEFICIENT) STREPTOCOCCI (*ABIOTROPHIA* AND *GRANULICATELLA*)

NVS were first described in 1961 as fastidious gram-positive bacteria that grow as satellite colonies around other bacteria.[168] Originally isolated from patients with endocarditis and otitis media, these organisms were deemed to be mutant subspecies of *S. mitis* ("*S. mitior*") because of their sugar fermentation and cell wall composition.[63] They also possessed a heat-acid–extractable chromophore such as that of *S. mitis*.[169] However, despite evidence for similarity between NVS and *S. mitis*, important phenotypic differences were also evident, such as their enzymatic capabilities and patterns of penicillin-binding proteins.[170] On the basis of DNA-DNA hybridization studies, Bouvet and colleagues found that NVS fit the genus description of *Streptococcus* but were taxonomically unrelated to other viridans group organisms. The names *S. adjacens* and *S. defectivus* were proposed as new designations.[24] Subsequently, studies using 16S ribosomal RNA (rRNA) sequence analysis showed that these two species were actually not related to other members of the *Streptococcus* genus. Therefore, in 1995, Kawamura and associates proposed placing them in a new genus *Abiotrophia*, as *A. adiacens* and *A. defectiva*.[25] Subsequently, three new species were identified: *A. elegans*, *A. balaenopterae*, and *A. para-adiacens*. In 2000, the genus *Abiotrophia* was taxonomically revised, reclassifying all species except *A. defectiva* to the new genus *Granulicatella*.[26] All NVS species require pyridoxal for growth, are susceptible to vancomycin, and produce leucine aminopeptidase and arylamidase. Species can be differentiated by their patterns of carbohydrate fermentation, production of α- and β-galactosidases and β-glucuronidase, and hydrolysis of hippurate or arginine.[171] With the exception of *G. balaenopterae*, all species have been recovered from human specimens.

In the laboratory NVS are recognized by their requirement for pyridoxal or thiol group supplementation for growth. They tend to form satellite colonies around *Staphylococcus aureus* and other microbes, including some Enterobacteriaceae and other streptococci.[172] Colonies of NVS are small, measuring 0.2 to 0.5 mm in diameter, and are either nonhemolytic or α-hemolytic on blood agar. On Gram staining, cells may be pleomorphic and may exhibit variable staining characteristics. There appears to be sufficient pyridoxal in human blood to support growth of NVS in most blood culture media (with the notable exception of unsupplemented tryptic soy broth).[173,174] For subculture, however, solid media must be supplemented with 0.001% pyridoxal or 0.01% L-cysteine to sustain growth. Alternatively, the subculture plate can be cross-streaked with *S. aureus* to provide these factors and permit growth as satellite colonies. Some studies suggest that blood cultures suspected of harboring NVS should be subcultured within 48 hours, because viability of the organism may decline with continued incubation.[173,174]

NVS are found as normal flora of the upper respiratory, urogenital, and gastrointestinal tracts of humans. They cause approximately 5% of cases of bacterial endocarditis.[63] Historically, NVS also accounted for most cases of culture-negative endocarditis, but with current laboratory media and techniques, recovery of strains is no longer a significant problem. Endocarditis caused by NVS carries greater morbidity and mortality than endocarditis caused by other streptococci. A comparison between 49 patients with NVS endocarditis and 130 patients with infection caused by other oral species revealed a higher mortality rate (14% versus 5%), more frequent complications of embolization (33% versus 11%) and congestive heart failure (33% versus 18%), and an increased rate of surgical intervention (33% versus 18%).[85] Vegetations visualized by two-dimensional echocardiography are seen in a large proportion of patients (64%).[74] Several reports indicate that endocarditis caused by NVS carries a higher mortality rate than that reported for viridans streptococci (approximately 15% versus 5%).[63,175] Similarly, these infections may respond poorly to antibiotics; bacteriologic failure and relapse have been observed in 41% and 17% of the cases, respectively.[175]

NVS are less susceptible in vitro to penicillin than are other streptococci. Approximately 33% to 65% of strains are relatively resistant

(MICs, 0.2 to 2.0 µg/mL), and some isolates are highly resistant to the antibiotic (MIC >4 µg/mL).[63,176-179] Depending on the method used, many strains of NVS also exhibit tolerance to penicillin. In a study using 11 strains, tolerance was demonstrated in the presence of pyridoxal, L-cysteine, penicillinase, and a staphylococcal cross-streak in all strains, but in no strains when only pyridoxal and L-cysteine were added to the subculture medium.[180] Aminoglycosides show variable in vitro activity against NVS, with an MIC range of 0.5 to 32 µg/mL.[176,178] High-level resistance (MIC >500 µg/mL), as seen in enterococci and viridans streptococci, has not been reported in NVS. Synergy between penicillin or vancomycin in combination with an aminoglycoside is observed both in vitro and in experimental animal models of endocarditis for both tolerant and nontolerant strains of NVS.[181-183] One such study suggested that the combination of penicillin with low-dose gentamicin was superior to penicillin combined with low-dose streptomycin.[182] All strains of NVS are susceptible to vancomycin in vitro, and most are also susceptible to clindamycin, chloramphenicol, and erythromycin. The activity of the cephalosporins and tetracycline is variable. In time-kill studies rifampin, which is highly active in vitro, has been observed to produce synergistic bactericidal activity when given in combination with vancomycin.[184]

In vitro antimicrobial susceptibility testing of NVS is beyond the scope of many routine clinical laboratories. Moreover, the results of in vitro susceptibility tests do not correlate well with clinical outcome in patients treated for endocarditis. Even in the case of infections with strains highly susceptible to penicillin, relapse may occur after a course of therapy is completed.[181] Because of the difficulties in performing susceptibility tests and correlating the results with clinical outcome, it is recommended that all patients with NVS endocarditis be treated with long-term combination therapy (e.g., penicillin plus gentamicin for 4 to 6 weeks [see Table 200-3]).[80] Even with this regimen, however, the rates of bacteriologic failure and relapse are high.[175]

NVS also are a cause of primary bacteremia in patients with hematologic malignancy and neutropenic fever.[179,185] Their precise role as pathogens in other disease processes is unknown. Because the organisms grow poorly on solid media, they can easily be overlooked if broth cultures are not performed or not subcultured to appropriately supplemented media. Isolation of NVS as likely pathogens has been reported in patients with pancreatic abscess,[186] otitis media,[168] conjunctivitis,[187] infectious crystalline keratopathy,[188] total knee arthroplasty infection,[189] cirrhosis, and postpartum and postabortal sepsis.[190]

β-HEMOLYTIC STREPTOCOCCI (GROUPS C AND G)

Microbiology

Confusing and conflicting results from taxonomic studies make it impossible to recommend a practical identification scheme that would correlate with genetic descriptions of the non–group A, B, and D β-hemolytic streptococci. For convenience, these streptococci can initially be divided into groups based on colony size.[1] Small or minute colony types (<0.5 mm in diameter) have been placed into the *S. anginosus* group (see Chapter 201). β-Hemolytic streptococci of large

colony size (≥0.5 mm in diameter) can almost always be grouped with Lancefield antisera using latex agglutination or coagglutination directed against the cell wall carbohydrate of groups A, B, C, or G.[191] Although serologic typing according to cell wall components has classically been used to separate streptococci into species, DNA homology studies have shown that this method is not always valid. Nevertheless, this classification remains useful as an aid to identification of clinical isolates. In many diagnostic microbiology laboratories, bacitracin disk susceptibility is also used as a screening test to separate group A streptococci from other *pyogenes*-like organisms. Studies employing the standard 0.04-unit bacitracin disk have demonstrated that only 6% to 8% of groups C and G β-hemolytic streptococci are susceptible.[192] However, other investigators have found greater variation in the bacitracin susceptibility of these streptococcal strains (see discussion of specific microorganisms).

Large colony-forming β-hemolytic strains not containing group antigens are rarely etiologic agents of human disease. Those possessing group antigens other than A, B, C, and G have been isolated primarily from animals and environmental sources and may be carried as the normal flora of the pharynx, vagina, or skin of wild or domestic animals. Rare infections in humans have been reported to be caused by serogroups E, L, M, N, and O[2,193-195]; these types are not discussed here. The following sections review in detail the microbiologic and clinical characteristics of groups C and G β-hemolytic streptococci.

Group C Streptococci

Most group C β-hemolytic streptococci produce β-hemolysis on sheep blood agar, although all types of hemolysis have been noted.[196] All group C streptococci are common pathogens in domestic animals, birds, rabbits, and guinea pigs. Although bacitracin resistance characterizes most group C streptococcal isolates, at least one third, and in one study up to 62% of isolates were bacitracin sensitive.[196-198] Therefore, group C streptococci may be misidentified as group A streptococci if sensitivity to bacitracin is used for presumptive identification of group A strains. This indicates the importance of performing Lancefield serologic testing on all bacitracin-sensitive and -resistant β-hemolytic streptococci. Identification by antibiotic screening can be improved with the use of a trimethoprim-sulfamethoxazole disk, to which group C organisms are sensitive and group A organisms resistant.[199]

There are three species of group C streptococci; their microbiologic and biochemical characteristics are shown in Table 200-4.[200-202] *Streptococcus dysgalactiae* subsp. *dysgalactiae* is uncommon in humans but causes mastitis in cows and suppurative polyarthritis in lambs.[203] It generally produces α-hemolysis or no hemolysis on blood agar, ferments trehalose, and produces a single hemolysin that is not streptolysin O or S.[204]

Streptococcus dysgalactiae subsp. *equisimilis* is the most common group C streptococcus to colonize and cause infection in humans. It ferments trehalose but not sorbitol, and it produces streptokinase and streptolysin O but not streptolysin S.[204] The streptokinase used for human thrombolytic therapy is derived from *S. equisimilis*.[205] Because *S. dysgalactiae* subsp. *equisimilis* produces streptolysin O, infections caused by this organism may result in elevated antistreptolysin O

TABLE 200-4 Microbiologic and Biochemical Characteristics of Group C Streptococci*

| Subgroup | Hemolysis | Fermentation Pattern | | | Production of | |
		Trehalose	Lactose	Sorbitol	Streptokinase	Streptolysin O
S. dysgalactiae	α or none	+	±	±	−	−
S. equisimilis	β	+	±	−	+	+
S. zooepidemicus	β	−	±	+	−	−
S. equi	β	−	−	−	−	−

+, ferments consistently or produces streptokinase or streptolysin O; −, does not ferment or does not produce streptokinase or streptolysin O; ±, variable ability to ferment.

*All streptococcal subgroups exhibited large colony (≥0.5 mm) morphology and were Voges-Proskauer test negative (i.e., did not produce acetoin from glucose in bacterial cultures).

Data from Arditi et al.[200] Ortel et al.[201] Bradley et al.[202]

(ASO) antibody titers, which are classically used to screen patients for antecedent group A β-hemolytic streptococcal infection.[206] *S. dysgalactiae* subsp. *equisimilis* has been isolated from the throat, nose, and genital tract of asymptomatic carriers[207,208] and from the umbilicus of up to two thirds of asymptomatic newborns.[209] Domestic animals (e.g., horses, cattle, pigs, and chickens) may also be infected.

Streptococcus equi subsp. *zooepidemicus* causes significant, often epidemic, infections in domestic animals (horses, cattle, sheep, and pigs). Most cases of human infection can be traced to an animal source.[202] *S. equi* subsp. *zooepidemicus* has been isolated as the etiologic agent in cases of bovine mastitis, equine respiratory tract infections and infertility, and severe infections in poultry.[203] It ferments sorbitol but not trehalose, produces a novel hemolysin but not streptolysin O or S, does not produce streptokinase, and is not considered part of the normal human flora.[204] Human infection is uncommon and has been associated with consumption of homemade cheese and unpasteurized cow's milk.[210,211] In one study from England, *S. equi* subsp. *zooepidemicus* represented 1.4% of 214 isolates recovered from a variety of clinical specimens,[212] although it has been suggested that this organism causes a higher proportion of aggressive infections than would be expected from its rare occurrence at superficial sites.

Streptococcus equi is primarily a pathogen of young horses, in which it causes strangles, a serious and highly contagious respiratory disease.[203,213] It ferments neither trehalose nor sorbitol, produces a soluble hemolysin but not streptolysin O or S, and does not produce streptokinase.

Although large colony-size group C streptococci have traditionally been divided into the four species just described, more recent studies have shown extensive similarities between *S. equi* subsp. *equi* and *S. equi* subsp. *zooepidemicus,* suggesting that they represent a single genotype.[214-216] Because of differences in fermentation patterns of lactose and sorbitol, in fructose diphosphate aldolases,[217] and in numerical taxonomic studies,[216] it is recommended that strains previously identified as *S. zooepidemicus* be identified as *S. equi* subsp. *zooepidemicus.*[215] In addition, *S. equisimilis* has been shown to be closely related to *S. dysgalactiae* and is now named *S. dysgalactiae* subsp. *equisimilis.*[214-216,218]

Group G Streptococci

β-Hemolytic streptococcal strains carrying the group G antigen were first described by Lancefield and Hare in 1935.[219] The great majority of group G strains demonstrate β-hemolysis when incubated in 5% to 10% carbon dioxide at 35°C for 18 to 48 hours on trypticase soy agar with 5% sheep's blood.[220] One criterion used for separating group A streptococci from other β-hemolytic strains is development of a 10-mm zone of inhibition around a 6-mm disk containing 0.04 units of bacitracin.[220,221] However, with this criterion, 3% to 30% of non–group A β-hemolytic streptococcal strains are also bacitracin sensitive.[222] Of group G β-hemolytic streptococci, 8% to 67% can be sensitive to bacitracin.[192,198,221] These organisms also carry a wide variety of type antigens (i.e., protein T, M types, and polysaccharide), in addition to the Lancefield group G antigen, that are found in other streptococci. Group G β-hemolytic streptococci produce a streptolysin that is antigenically similar to the streptolysin O produced by group A β-hemolytic streptococci.[223] Therefore, patients with group G streptococcal pharyngitis may have a significant increase in serum ASO antibody titers.[224,225]

Epidemiology

Group C Streptococci

Group C β-hemolytic streptococci have been identified as part of the normal human flora of the nasopharynx, skin, and genital tract; the organism has also been cultured from umbilical specimens in newborns without signs of infection and in routine puerperal vaginal cultures.[199,207,209,226] In addition, many animal species are colonized with group C streptococci; infection in humans has been traced to animal sources. Underlying conditions have been noted in most patients with group C streptococcal infection; in one review of 31 cases, such con-

ditions included cardiopulmonary disease (26%), diabetes mellitus (20%), chronic dermatologic conditions (20%), malignancy (20%), immunosuppression (19%), alcohol abuse (13%), renal or hepatic failure (10%), and injection drug use (6%).[199] In another review of 88 cases of group C streptococcal bacteremia, 73% of the patients had a significant underlying condition (cardiovascular disease in 20%; malignancy in 20%); prior exposure to animals was documented in 24% of cases.[202]

Group G Streptococci

Group G streptococci may be found to colonize the nasopharynx, skin, and genital tract[227]; intestinal colonization has also been reported. Several investigators have noted that up to 65% of patients with group G streptococcal infections have an underlying malignancy.[2,228,229] However, a study of 57 cases of group G streptococcal infection in 11 hospitals in northeastern Ohio found that only 21% of patients had an underlying malignancy[229]; 21% were alcohol abusers and 14% had diabetes mellitus. Similar rates were found in two other studies: one found that only 2 of 15 patients with group G streptococcal infection had an underlying malignancy,[230] and in another review of 24 patients with group G streptococcal bacteremia the rate of underlying neoplastic disease was 25%.[231]

Clinical Manifestations

Numerous reports of groups C and G streptococcal suppurative infections of various organ systems have been published.[199,200,202,227,229,230,232,233] Infection can be endogenous (i.e., from organisms residing on skin or mucous membranes) or exogenous (i.e., from animal sources). Endogenous infection often occurs in hosts predisposed by age (neonate or elderly), alcoholism, injection drug abuse, diabetes mellitus, immunosuppressive therapy with corticosteroids or cytotoxic drugs, or underlying malignancy. Infections are often severe, resembling those caused by groups A and B β-hemolytic streptococci.

Pharyngitis

Non–group A β-hemolytic streptococci have been associated with outbreaks of pharyngitis,[234] although their precise role in the causation of epidemic pharyngitis has not been defined.[235] In one report of children and adolescents with sporadic pharyngitis,[206] 17% of β-hemolytic isolates were non–group A; of these, fewer than one half were groups C and G. The symptoms and signs of pharyngitis caused by group C streptococci are very similar to those caused by group A β-hemolytic streptococci[234] and include fever, mild to moderate sore throat, pharyngeal exudate, and cervical adenopathy. Group C streptococci can cause a severe pharyngitis, followed by bacteremia and metastatic infection.

Several studies comparing group C β-hemolytic streptococcal isolation rates among pharyngitis patients versus controls have reported contradictory results.[235] In five studies, group C streptococci were isolated more frequently from patients than from controls, although the results were statistically significant in only one study.[236] In this study, which used optimal laboratory techniques, the isolation rate of group C streptococci was higher among 1425 adult patients than among 284 controls (6% versus 1.4%; $P = .002$). In five other studies, group C streptococci were isolated from pharyngitis patients as often or more frequently than from controls, although the differences were not statistically significant.[235,237]

In a carefully done study of 232 college students with pharyngitis,[238] a strong epidemiologic association between group C streptococci and endemic pharyngitis was demonstrated; group C streptococci were isolated significantly more often from patients than from 198 age-matched controls (26% versus 11%; $P < .0001$). Culture-positive patients also had fever, exudative tonsillitis, and anterior cervical adenopathy more often than culture-negative patients, and quantitative colony counts were generally higher among patients compared with controls. The 11% isolation rate among controls suggested that group C streptococci may represent normal oropharyngeal flora. In another study in college students, *S. equisimilis* was isolated more frequently from patients with exudative pharyngitis than from controls (11% versus 2%; $P = .001$).[239] Rapid detection of group C streptococci from throat swabs has been attempted. Compared with culture, the rapid test had poor sensitivity (34.4%) but very high specificity (99.4%) in detection of group C β-hemolytic streptococci[240]; the sensitivity of the test improved with an increasing quantity of colonies isolated from throat cultures.

Asymptomatic pharyngeal carriage of group G β-hemolytic streptococci occurs in up to 23% of humans.[224] Symptoms and signs in patients with group G streptococcal pharyngitis range from a mild upper respiratory tract infection with coryza to an exudative pharyngitis with fever and lymphadenopathy. As with group C streptococci, the illness is indistinguishable from pharyngitis caused by group A β-hemolytic streptococci. Initial reports that suggested an etiologic role of group G streptococci in pharyngitis consisted of anecdotes, small case clusters, and investigations of predominantly food-borne outbreaks (related to consumption of eggs and chicken salad).[224,225,235,237,241,242] Few of these studies were adequately controlled, and the isolation rate of group G streptococci was too low to demonstrate a statistically significant difference between symptomatic and asymptomatic groups. More recently, in an outbreak of pharyngitis among children, throat cultures for group G β-hemolytic streptococci were positive in 56 (25%) of 222 patients; DNA fingerprinting revealed identical strains in 75% of cases.[243] In this outbreak, 67% of isolates were detected within an 8-week period. Patients with group G streptococcal pharyngitis were comparable to those with group A streptococcal pharyngitis with respect to clinical findings, ASO antibody titer response, and clinical response to antimicrobial therapy; however, patients with group G streptococci were significantly older (mean age, 11.5 versus 10.0 years; $P < .05$). In this study, antimicrobial therapy appeared to have a dramatic impact on the clinical course of group G streptococcal pharyngitis, although other investigators have found no evidence that antimicrobial therapy modifies the duration or severity of symptoms.[241]

Complications of Pharyngitis

Poststreptococcal glomerulonephritis has been associated with group C streptococcal pharyngitis.[210] In these reports infection was acquired by consumption of unpasteurized milk from cattle with mastitis; the etiologic agent was *S. zooepidemicus*. No ASO antibody titer response was detected in these outbreaks because *S. zooepidemicus* does not produce streptolysin O. In an outbreak associated with consumption of a locally produced cheese product, the outbreak was confirmed by amplification and sequence of the M-like protein gene designated Szp5058.[244] The pathogenesis of poststreptococcal glomerulonephritis from group C streptococcal infection is unclear, although certain group C streptococcal strains recovered from throat cultures were found to possess human antibody receptors that were thought to be virulence factors for these organisms.[245] In addition, endostreptosin, a cytoplasmic polypeptide antigen that plays a role in poststreptococcal glomerulonephritis associated with group A streptococcal infection, was demonstrated in the cytoplasm of infecting group C isolates, and elevated concentrations of anti-endostreptosin antibodies were detected in the patients' sera. Acute glomerulonephritis in association with group G streptococcal infection has also been reported.[246] Type 12 M-protein antigen, identical to the nephritogenic antigen of the group A streptococcus,[247] has been isolated from the group G streptococcus. However, association of group G β-hemolytic streptococci with acute glomerulonephritis is anecdotal; a causal relation is not yet established.[227,248] Group C and G streptococcal pharyngitis has also been associated with sterile reactive arthritis.[249,250] Group C streptococci, and possibly group G streptococci, can produce a class C1 M protein that may be responsible for development of streptococcal-associated sequel diseases.[251] Acute rheumatic fever has not been described in association with either group C or group G streptococcal pharyngitis.

Skin and Soft Tissue Infection

Colonization of human skin with groups C and G streptococci is common, and these organisms have been responsible for various cutaneous and subcutaneous infections including cellulitis, wound infections, pyoderma, erysipelas, impetigo, and cutaneous ulcers.[199,208,226] Breeches in skin integrity may provide a portal of entry leading to bacteremia. Group C streptococci have been isolated in patients with cellulitis after vein harvest for coronary artery bypass grafts and in conditions associated with abnormal venous or lymphatic drainage.[252] Accompanying lymphangitis may also be seen.

Group G streptococcal bacteremia often occurs as a complication of skin and soft tissue infections. In one review of 37 patients with group G streptococcal bacteremia,[229] 14 (58%) of 24 patients with an underlying malignancy were thought to have a skin or soft tissue source. Of 13 other patients without a known malignancy, 11 had cellulitis and 2 had cutaneous abscesses. Therefore, a total of 73% of patients from this series became bacteremic from a cutaneous source. This contrasts with other reviews of group G streptococcal infections, in which only 13% to 25% of bacteremic patients had an identified cutaneous focus of infection.[230,232]

Arthritis

β-Hemolytic streptococci account for 11% to 28% of cases of nongonococcal septic arthritis, with most cases in both children and adults caused by group A streptococci. Group C streptococcal arthritis most frequently occurs in joints with preexisting rheumatologic abnormalities.[201,253,254] In an extensive literature review of 18 cases of group C streptococcal septic arthritis,[255] underlying conditions, both rheumatic and nonrheumatic, were recognized in 72% of patients. The specific microorganism was identified in nine cases: *S. equisimilis* in six patients and *S. zooepidemicus* in three patients. The skin was the presumed portal of entry in five patients, although in most cases the source of infection was not identified. Almost any joint can be involved, and frequently the arthritis is polyarticular (30% of cases in one review).[201] Infective endocarditis was diagnosed in two patients. Antimicrobial therapy (primarily penicillin G) and surgical drainage were used in most cases. Three of the patients died, all of whom were bacteremic; in two cases death was related to the underlying condition (i.e., congestive heart failure and pneumonia).

Group G streptococci are the second most common of the β-hemolytic streptococci to cause septic arthritis.[256-261] In one review of 57 cases,[262] clinical features were known in 46 patients, including 13 with infected prosthetic joints. Forty-eight percent of those with group G streptococcal septic arthritis of native joints had polyarticular involvement. An extra-articular focus of infection was present in 55% of patients with native joints and 62% of those with prosthetic joints; the major foci were cellulitis and endocarditis. Underlying joint disease was present in 33% of patients with infected native joints. Only four patients had no underlying conditions or joint abnormalities. Antimicrobial therapy included penicillin, penicillin plus an aminoglycoside, and other antimicrobial agents (e.g., cefazolin, vancomycin, erythromycin); length of therapy ranged from 14 to 90 days, with the organism cleared rapidly from the joint in most instances. However, in some patients the clinical course was protracted, and bacteriologic relapse after medical therapy was common. There may be a slow response to antimicrobial therapy despite in vitro susceptibility.[257,258] Surgical drainage was required in 13 patients, including 5 with prosthetic joints. Patients with infected prosthetic joints have been noted to do well even without joint removal.[262] Coexistent osteomyelitis may be present (see next section), and recurrent sterile joint effusions may also occur.

Osteomyelitis

Isolated reports have described cases of group C streptococcal osteomyelitis.[263-265] A review of the literature described 11 patients with group G streptococcal osteomyelitis,[262] 3 of whom also had septic arthritis. Six of seven patients with group G streptococcal osteomyelitis in this review had underlying conditions (malignancy, alcoholic cirrhosis, osteoarthritis, internal fixation for fractures, and prosthesis). Three patients were treated with antibiotics, and another three patients required antimicrobial therapy plus surgery. Two cases of group G streptococcal vertebral osteomyelitis have also been reported.[266]

Respiratory Tract Infections

The group C streptococcus is an uncommon cause of pneumonia, but it is associated with significant morbidity and mortality, similar to infection caused by the group A streptococcus.[199,267-272] Development of pneumonia is often preceded by a viral upper respiratory tract infection. In one review of nine cases,[273] the pneumonia was typically lobar and often heralded by fever, chills, dyspnea, and pleuritic chest pain. Bacteremia was documented in 75% of cases. All patients had pleural effusions. Complications included metastatic infection, empyema, and cavitation. All patients received therapy with intravenous penicillin, sometimes in combination with other antimicrobial agents.

Pneumonia caused by the group G streptococcus is rare. In a literature review of eight cases of group G streptococcal pneumonia and empyema,[2,228,229,274,275] seven occurred in adults with various malignancies. In a more recent series of seven cases,[232] only two patients had an underlying malignancy.

Group C streptococcal sinusitis has also been reported.[276] Common to all cases was age younger than 18 years, the presence of central nervous system complications (perhaps secondary to inadequate medical or surgical therapy), and a delay in initiation of adequate therapy. In one review of five cases, three patients were bacteremic and two patients died.[276]

Endocarditis

Infective endocarditis caused by groups C and G streptococci is uncommon, accounting for fewer than 1% of total cases and 8.4% of cases caused by β-hemolytic streptococci.[199,229,230,232,277-281] In a review of 4705 cases of infective endocarditis,[282] 166 (3.5%) were caused by β-hemolytic streptococci, 8 were group C, and 14 were group G. The likelihood of infective endocarditis appears to be more common with groups C and G streptococcal bacteremia than with groups A and B, even though the latter more often cause bacteremia.[2,229]

In a review of 88 cases of group C streptococcal bacteremia,[202] patients with endocarditis (24 cases) usually presented subacutely (mean duration of symptoms, 17.4 days). Major emboli to the central nervous system, eye, limbs, and lungs were observed in 10 cases; one third of the patients died. Response to single-agent β-lactam therapy was poor, leading the authors to favor the use of bactericidal combinations (e.g., penicillin plus gentamicin), although no comparative data were available to make firm recommendations. Four patients required surgical valve replacement for congestive heart failure. In contrast, in another review of group C streptococcal infections in which 20 cases of infective endocarditis were identified,[199] the presentation was typically acute with a propensity for involvement of normal valves, a high mortality rate (approaching 40% to 50%), embolic complications, and a frequent need for valve replacement. More than one half of the patients developed cardiac complications, including destruction of the valve leaflets, myocardial abscesses, conduction abnormalities, and severe congestive heart failure. Major systemic emboli to the spleen, kidneys, myocardium, and central nervous system occurred in about one half of the patients. In 12 patients for whom there was information on antimicrobial therapy, there were no bacteriologic failures among those treated with penicillin with or without an aminoglycoside. However, patients who received combination therapy required valve replacement less frequently than patients treated with penicillin alone. Combination therapy may be more rapidly bactericidal, although the relation of antimicrobial therapy to surgery cannot be adequately assessed given the small number of patients reviewed.

Group G streptococcal endocarditis tends to occur in older patients with multiple underlying disorders.[230,232,283] Both native and prosthetic valves may be affected, and left-sided disease is more common. Infective endocarditis caused by group G streptococci has occurred in patients with normal cardiac valves as well as in those with preexisting congenital or acquired valvular disease. The onset is generally abrupt, with rapid valve destruction and perivalvular infection; metastatic foci are not uncommon. In a review of 40 cases of group G streptococcal endocarditis,[284] the mean age of the patients was 56 years. Underlying

conditions included malignancy (six cases), injection drug abuse (three cases), alcohol abuse (four cases), and diabetes mellitus (six cases). The presentation was acute in 26 of 40 patients. The portal of entry was the skin in almost half of the cases. In 17 cases, infective endocarditis complicated underlying valvular heart disease, whereas 16 patients had normal cardiac valves before infection; no details with regard to underlying valvular heart disease were given for the remaining 7 cases. Among the 29 patients in whom complications were reported, 25 had cardiac or embolic complications. The mortality rate was 36%, but it has ranged from 43% to 67% in other studies.[280,283] There was a trend to improved survival in patients treated with the antimicrobial combination of a β-lactam plus an aminoglycoside for at least 28 days.

Meningitis

Cases of groups C and G streptococcal meningitis have been reported and are often associated with infective endocarditis.[199,200,230,285-288] Infection may occur in healthy patients; one case occurred as a possible equine zoonosis,[286] one occurred after ingestion of unpasteurized goat's milk,[289] and another after head trauma as a result of a kick by a horse.[290] Group C streptococci were also recovered from the CSF in a preterm infant whose mother had received intrapartum antimicrobial therapy for chorioamnionitis.[291] The clinical presentation is typically acute, and the response to antimicrobial therapy slow. In a review of the literature of 18 previous cases (9 in adults) of group C streptococcal meningitis,[292] the case-fatality rate was 55%. Thirty cases of group C streptococcal meningitis have been reported in the literature.[290,293,294] *S. zooepidemicus* accounted for 13 cases, *S. equisimilis* for 5 cases, and *S. dysgalactiae* for 3 cases; the organisms were not further identified in 9 reports. Complications have included bacteremia, pneumonia, sinusitis, subdural empyema, bacterial endocarditis, brain abscess, and otitis media. The mortality rate was high (43%), and most significant at the extremes of age (neonates and the elderly).

Puerperal Infection

In their original paper, Lancefield and Hare recovered group G streptococci from 5 of 855 antepartum vaginal swabs and from the blood of a patient with puerperal sepsis who was also infected with *S. aureus*.[219] About 5% of asymptomatic women harbor group G β-hemolytic streptococci in their genital tracts. Both group C and group G streptococci have been associated with epidemic and nonepidemic puerperal sepsis and endometritis.[226,232,295,296] When endometritis occurs without bacteremia, it may be relatively mild and associated with few systemic symptoms.

Neonatal Sepsis

Neonatal sepsis caused by group G streptococci occurs in premature or low-birth-weight infants and in the setting of premature rupture of membranes.[297-300] Infection most likely complicates colonization of the birth canal with spread to the child after vaginal delivery. The onset of disease is typically within the first week of life. Infection in the child is also associated with a high incidence of maternal obstetric complications. In a review of neonatal sepsis from one institution over a 5-year period, group G streptococci accounted for 7 of 305 cases.[300] Symptoms and signs included hypothermia, irritability, seizures, apnea, bradycardia, and cardiac arrest. Complications such as progressive respiratory distress, shock, and disseminated intravascular coagulation are invariably fatal.

Bacteremia

Group C streptococci are rarely isolated from blood cultures, accounting for fewer than 1% of all bacteremias.[2,233,301-303] However, in patients with group C streptococcal infections, bacteremia is frequently detected. In one review of 31 cases of group C streptococcal infections,[199] bacteremia was observed in 23 (74%). The bacteremia was polymicrobial in eight patients, with facultative gram-negative bacteria predominating as the second microorganism; *S. aureus* and *Bacteroides fragilis* were also isolated as second organisms in some bacteremic cases. In another review of 88 cases of group C streptococcal bacteremia,[202] 27% of patients had infective endocarditis, 10% had meningitis, 9% had cutaneous infections, and 23% had primary bacteremia; 88% of cases were community acquired. Many of the patients had underlying illnesses, including cardiovascular disease (20%), malignancy (20%), and immunosuppression (15%); 23 patients (26%) had no underlying diseases. Acute illness with fever, chills, and prostration was most common, except in patients with infective endocarditis, who usually presented subacutely. Mortality rates were high (25%), especially among older patients and those with endocarditis, meningitis, or disseminated infection. In a review of 45 cases of *S. equi* subsp. *zooepidemicus* septicemia, 27% of patients had underlying cardiovascular disease; the overall mortality rate was 22%.[304] Similar epidemiologic features were observed from a survey of cases of group C streptococcal bacteremia in Israel; morbidity and mortality were high (20% to 30%) in this review, probably reflecting the patients' underlying state as well as the severity of infection.[305]

Group G streptococci account for 8% to 11% of all β-hemolytic streptococcal bacteremias[227]; an underlying malignancy is reported in 21% to 65% of patients.[2,229-232] Polymicrobial bacteremia is not uncommon, with *S. aureus* the most frequently isolated copathogen. Patients usually have another primary site of infection, such as pneumonia, septic arthritis, ophthalmitis, or meningitis. In a review of 24 cases of group G streptococcal bacteremia over a 29-month period,[231] underlying conditions included alcohol abuse (8 patients), malignancy (6 patients), diabetes mellitus (5 patients), neurologic disease (4 patients), atherosclerotic cardiovascular disease (2 patients), end-stage renal disease (2 patients), and valvular heart disease (2 patients). The rate of underlying malignancy was 25%, compared with rates as high as 65% in other series.[229] The skin was the portal of entry in 79% of cases. Infective endocarditis was uncommon in this series, documented in only one patient. In another review of 56 cases of group G streptococcal bacteremia from 11 hospitals in northeastern Ohio,[232] polymicrobial infection, including bacteremia, was an important feature. The most common copathogen was *S. aureus* (seen in seven of eight cases of polymicrobial bacteremia), probably secondary to the presence of skin and soft tissue infection, the background of surgical procedures and invasive diagnostic maneuvers, and the effects of chemotherapy and underlying malignant disease. Mortality (39% in those with only bacteremia) was usually related to the severity of the underlying disease. In a review from the Mayo Clinic,[229] group G streptococci accounted for 0.3% of all bacteremias and 10.8% of those caused by β-hemolytic streptococci; bacteremia was community-acquired in 70% of cases. Twenty-four of 37 patients had an underlying malignancy, although it was unclear whether this subset of patients was more prone to group G streptococcal colonization. The most frequent portal of entry was the skin (73% of patients), usually in cases with preexisting edema resulting from chronic venous insufficiency or from previous surgical removal, irradiation, or tumor infiltration of lymph nodes. No portal of entry was found in four patients, although all had malignant disease with severe granulocytopenia related either to the malignancy or to use of immunosuppressive drugs. In another retrospective report, group G streptococcal bacteremia was seen most often in patients older than 60 years of age with the skin as the most common portal of entry, although there was an association between age younger than 60 years and malignancy.[306] In a more recent study, group G streptococci accounted for 20% of bacteremias at a single university teaching hospital in Sheffield, UK,[307] a higher proportion than previously reported. The skin was the portal of entry in 62% of patients. Immunosenescence represented the major risk factor for group G streptococcal bacteremia in this study; comorbities, such as carcinoma, may be markers of the senescent immune system. Other studies have also confirmed an increase in the incidence of group G streptococcal bacteremia,[309] usually seen in older male patients with skin and soft tissue infections as the primary portals of entry. Mortality rates have ranged from 8% to 17%.

Miscellaneous Infections

Several other infections have been reported to be caused by groups C and G β-hemolytic streptococci. These include acute group C streptococcal pericarditis,[310,311] group G streptococcal pericarditis as the initial presentation of colon cancer,[312] group C streptococcal pyomyositis,[313,314] Henoch-Schönlein purpura associated with *S. equisimilis* upper respiratory tract infection,[315] and a group G streptococcal spinal epidural abscess.[316] A "toxic shock–like syndrome" associated with both group C and group G streptococci has also been reported,[317-319] although these organisms are not known to secrete any exotoxin. Other documented infections caused by group C streptococci include brain abscess[320] and epiglottitis[321,322] caused by *S. equi* subsp. *equisimilis,* cervical lymphadenitis caused by *S. equi* subsp. *zooepidemicus,*[323] intra-abdominal infections,[199] subdural empyema,[324,325] infected arteriovenous fistula,[199] and peritonitis in dialysis patients.[199] Group G streptococci have also been reported to cause panophthalmitis,[232] and were found in one case of a polymicrobial brain abscess in a patient infected with the human immunodeficiency virus.[326]

Therapy

Group C Streptococci

The antimicrobial agent of choice for group C β-hemolytic streptococci is penicillin G.[327,328] Other agents with good in vitro activity include cefazolin, vancomycin, erythromycin, the semisynthetic penicillins, and cefotaxime. However, aside from vancomycin, the clinical experience with antimicrobial agents other than penicillin is not extensive. Strains resistant to erythromycin have been reported[329]; in one study, 95% of isolates manifested resistance due to the presence of the *mefA* or *mefE* drug efflux gene.[330] Tetracycline sensitivity is also variable.[202] A case of pharyngitis caused by penicillin-resistant *S. equi* subsp. *equisimilis* has been reported, although the mechanism of resistance was not clear.[331] Tolerance has been reported in group C streptococci with minimal bactericidal concentrations ranging from 32- to 512-fold greater than the MIC.[332,333] The frequency of tolerance is unclear; it was reported in 2 of 25 cases in one series[328] and in 16 of 17 cases in another.[332] A marked synergy for in vitro killing of group C streptococci by penicillin plus gentamicin, independent of penicillin tolerance, has been demonstrated. The addition of gentamicin or rifampin to a β-lactam antibiotic or vancomycin has resulted in bactericidal activity against group C streptococci.[332,333] Although the clinical relevance of these findings is uncertain, retrospective reviews of group C streptococcal endocarditis noted a trend to better outcome (i.e., fewer patients requiring cardiac valve replacement) in those treated with the combination of penicillin plus gentamicin, compared with penicillin alone,[199] leading the authors to recommend combination therapy in patients with severe infections (endocarditis, meningitis, septic arthritis, or bacteremia in neutropenic hosts) caused by group C streptococci. Tolerance to cephalothin and vancomycin has also been reported for group C streptococci.

Group G Streptococci

Group G streptococci are susceptible in vitro to various antimicrobial agents, including penicillin G, the ureidopenicillins, most cephalosporins, vancomycin, and erythromycin[328]; the most active drugs are penicillin, ampicillin, and cefotaxime.[230] Clindamycin, erythromycin, and chloramphenicol have relatively poor bactericidal activity against group G streptococci.[230] In a study of erythromycin resistance mechanisms in group G streptococci, 94% of resistant isolates had the *ermTR* gene.[330] Combinations of gentamicin with either penicillin, cefotaxime, or vancomycin are synergistic against 80% to 90% of isolates.[334]

Penicillin tolerance is not a major feature of group G streptococci, and it has been demonstrated only in the presence of a high inoculum and stationary growth phase of the organism.[208] When strains were tested at high inocula (10^8 cfu/mL) of stationary-phase cells, there was a marked reduction in killing by penicillin G. This impaired bactericidal effect was not seen either at high inocula of logarithmic-phase organisms or at low inocula of stationary-phase organisms. The paradigm of this high inoculum-stationary phase in vitro situation is infective endocarditis, which may partially explain the relatively poor clinical outcome seen in group G streptococcal endocarditis caused by sensitive organisms. Vancomycin tolerance has also been reported in group G streptococci,[335] although tolerance to this agent may also depend on the growth phase and laboratory media employed.[230] In a retrospective review of patients with invasive group G streptococcal infections,[336] vancomycin tolerance (defined as a minimal bactericidal concentration 32 or more times higher than the MIC) was exhibited by 18 isolates. The clinical significance of tolerance is unclear, and does not necessarily reflect clinical efficacy. The combinations of gentamicin with a β-lactam and of gentamicin or rifampin with vancomycin are bactericidal against tolerant strains.[326] Of concern, however, are the recent reports of the emergence of high-level gentamicin resistance in group G streptococci,[337,338] which may impact the bactericidal therapy required for treatment of serious infections caused by this organism. Surveillance for high-level aminoglycoside resistance must be carefully monitored.

STREPTOCOCCUS INIAE

Streptococcus iniae, a pathogen recognized only recently in humans, is a β-hemolytic streptococcus that does not react with any Lancefield grouping sera. The organism was first reported in 1976 as a cause of subcutaneous abscesses in freshwater dolphins.[339] *Streptococcus shiloi,* a cause of meningoencephalitis in trout, is biochemically and genetically identical and is probably synonymous with *S. iniae.*[340]

In the clinical laboratory, *S. iniae* may elude identification. Few commercial laboratory systems include this species in their database. In addition, the organism's β-hemolysis may be inapparent under certain growth conditions. As a result, isolates are often misidentified as viridans group streptococci and discounted as contaminants. In 6 of the 11 patients reported by Weinstein and co-workers, *S. iniae* isolates were initially misidentified as *S. uberis,* a viridans group streptococcus not typically pathogenic in humans.[341]

To date, invasive infections caused by *S. iniae* have been confirmed by the presence of bacteremia. Almost all have had cellulitis of the hand as the presumed primary site of infection. Handling of live or killed fish, especially tilapia, was the suspected exposure source.[341] Patients have responded readily to therapy with a β-lactam antibiotic.

STOMATOCOCCUS AND PEDIOCOCCUS

Stomatococcus mucilaginosus is a gram-positive aerobic coccus that can cause oral, cutaneous, and central nervous system infections in impaired hosts as well as intravenous catheter-related sepsis. Most strains are susceptible to third-generation cephalosporins, vancomycin, and carbapenems.[342,343]

Pediococcus spp. are gram-positive aerobic cocci that have caused nosocomial infections and are often resistant to vancomycin.[344-346]

REFERENCES

1. Baron EJ, Finegold SM. Streptococci and related genera. In: Baron EJ, Finegold SM, eds. Bailey and Scott's Diagnostic Microbiology. 8th ed. St. Louis: CV Mosby; 1986:333-352.
2. Duma RJ, Weinberg AN, Medrek TF, et al. Streptococcal infections: A bacteriologic and clinical study of streptococcal bacteremia. Medicine (Baltimore). 1969;48:87-105.
3. Kilian M, Nyvad B, Mikkelson L. Taxonomic and ecological aspects of some oral streptococci. In: Hamada S, Michalek SM, Kiyono H, et al, eds. Molecular Microbiology and Immunobiology of Streptococcus mutans. Amsterdam: Elsevier; 1986:391-400.
4. Coykendall AL. Classification and identification of the viridans streptococci. Clin Microbiol Rev. 1989;2:315-328.
5. Ruoff KL, Whiley RA, Beighton D. Streptococcus. In: Murray PR, Baron EJ, Jorgensen JH, et al, eds. Manual of Clinical Microbiology. 8th ed. Washington, DC: American Society for Microbiology; 2003:405-421.
6. Colman G, Williams REO. Taxonomy of some human viridans streptococci. In: Wannamaker LW, Matsen JM, eds. Streptococci and Streptococcal Diseases: Recognition, Understanding, and Management. New York: Academic Press; 1972:281-299.
7. Facklam RR. Physiological differentiation of viridans streptococci. J Clin Microbiol. 1977;5:184-201.
8. Koneman EW, Allen SD, Janda WM, et al. The gram-positive cocci: Part II. Streptococci, enterococci, and the "streptococcus-like" bacteria. In: Color Atlas and Textbook of Diagnostic Microbiology. 5th ed. Philadelphia: JB Lippincott; 1997.
9. Facklam R. What happened to the streptococci: Overview of taxonomic and nomenclature changes. Clin Microbiol Rev. 2002;15:613-630.
10. Bruckner DA, Colonna P. Nomenclature for aerobic and facultative bacteria. Clin Infect Dis. 1997;25:1-10.
11. Handley P, Coykendall A, Beighton D, et al. Streptococcus crista sp. nov., a viridans streptococcus with tufted fibrils, isolated from the human oral cavity and throat. Int J Syst Bacteriol. 1991;41:543-547.
12. Kilian M, Mikkelson L, Henrichsen J. Taxonomic study of viridans streptococci: Description of Streptococcus gordonii sp. nov. and amended descriptions of Streptococcus sanguis (White and Niven 1946), Streptococcus oralis (Bridge and Sneath 1982), and Streptococcus mitis (Andrews and Horder 1906). Int J Syst Bacteriol. 1989;39:471-484.
13. Whiley RA, Beighton D. Emended descriptions and recognition of Streptococcus constellatus, Streptococcus intermedius, and Streptococcus anginosus as distinct species. Int J Syst Bacteriol. 1991;41:1-5.
14. Whiley RA, Hardie JM. Streptococcus vestibularis sp. nov. from the human oral cavity. Int J Syst Bacteriol. 1988;38:2623-2633.
15. Whiley RA, Fraser HY, Douglas CWI, et al. Streptococcus parasanguis sp. nov.: An atypical viridans streptococcus from human clinical specimens. FEMS Microbiol Lett. 1990;68:115-122.
16. Coykendall AL. Streptococcus sobrinus nom. rev. and Streptococcus ferus nom. rev.: Habitat of these and other mutans streptococci. Int J Syst Bacteriol. 1983;33:883-885.
17. Coykendall AL. Proposal to elevate the subspecies of Streptococcus mutans to species status, based on their molecular composition. Int J Syst Bacteriol. 1977;27:26-30.
18. Kilpper-Balz R, Schleifer KH. Transfer of Streptococcus morbillorum to the Gemella genus, Gemella morbillorum comb. nov. Int J Syst Bacteriol. 1988;38:442-443.
19. Schleifer KH, Kilpper-Balz R. Molecular and chemotaxonomic approaches to the classification of streptococci, enterococci, and lactococci: A review. Syst Appl Microbiol. 1987;10:1-19.
20. Kawamura Y, Hou XG, Todome Y, et al. Streptococcus peroris sp. nov. and Streptococcus infantis sp. nov., new members of the Streptococcus mitis group, isolated from human clinical specimens. Int J Syst Bacteriol. 1998;48:921-927.
21. Schlegel L, Grimont F, Collins MD, et al. Streptococcus infantarius sp. nov., Streptococcus infantarius subsp infantarius subsp. nov. and Streptococcus infantarius subsp. coli subsp. nov., isolated from human and food. Int J Syst Evol Microbiol. 2000;50:1425-1434.
22. Beighton D, Hardie JM, Whiley RA. A scheme for the identification of viridans streptococci. J Med Microbiol. 1991;35:367-372.
23. Hinnebusch CJ, Nikolai DM, Bruckner DA. Comparison of API Rapid Strep, Baxter Microscan Rapid Pos ID Panel, BBL Minitek Differential Identification System, IDS RapID STR System, and Vitek GPI to conventional biochemical tests for identification of viridans streptococci. Am J Clin Pathol. 1991;96:459-463.
24. Bouvet A, Grimont F, Grimont PAD. Streptococcus defectivus sp. nov. and Streptococcus adjacens sp. nov.: Nutritionally variant streptococci from human clinical specimens. Int J Syst Bacteriol. 1989;39:290-294.
25. Kawamura Y, Hou XG, Sultana F, et al. Transfer of Streptococcus adjacens and Streptococcus defectivus to Abiotrophia gen. nov. as Abiotrophia adiacens comb. nov. and Abiotrophia defectiva comb. nov., respectively. Int J Syst Bacteriol. 1995; 45:798-803.
26. Collins MD, Lawson PA. The genus Abiotrophia (Kawamura et al.) is not monophyletic: proposal of Granulicatella gen.noiv., Granulicatella adiacens comb. nov., Granulicatella elegans comb. nov. and Granulicatella balaenopterae com. nov. Int J Syst Evol Microbiol. 2000;50:365-369.
27. Marsh P, Martin M. Oral Microbiology. 2nd ed. Washington, DC: American Society for Microbiology; 1984.
28. Gibbons RJ, van Houte J. Bacterial adherence in oral microbial ecology. Annu Rev Microbiol. 1975;29:19-44.
29. Gibbons RJ, van Houte J. Selective bacterial adherence to oral epithelial surfaces and its role as an ecological determinant. Infect Immun. 1971;3:567-573.
30. Frandsen EVG, Pedrazzoli V, Kilian M. Ecology of viridans streptococci in the oral cavity and pharynx. Oral Microbiol Immunol. 1991;6:129-133.
31. Babu J, Simpson WA, Courtney HS, et al. Interaction of human plasma fibronectin with cariogenic and non-cariogenic oral streptococci. Infect Immun. 1983;41:162-168.
32. Woods DE, Straus DC, Johanson WG Jr, et al. Role of fibronectin in the prevention of adherence of Pseudomonas aeruginosa to buccal cells. J Infect Dis. 1981;143:784-790.
33. Woods DE, Straus DC, Johanson WG Jr. Role of salivary protease activity in adherence of gram-negative bacilli to mammalian buccal epithelial cells in vivo. J Clin Invest. 1981;68:1435-1440.
34. Johanson WG Jr, Pierce AK, Sanford JP. Changing pharyngeal flora of hospitalized patients: Emergence of gram-negative bacilli. N Engl J Med. 1969;281:1137-1140.
35. Johanson WG Jr, Pierce AK, Sanford JP, et al. Nosocomial respiratory infections with gram-negative bacilli: The significance of colonization of the respiratory tract. Ann Intern Med. 1972;77:701-706.
36. Straus DC. Protease production by Streptococcus sanguis associated with subacute bacterial endocarditis. Infect Immun. 1982;38:1037-1045.
37. Stinson MW, Alder S, Kumar S. Invasion and killing of human endothelial cells by viridans group streptococci. Infect Immun. 2003;71:2365-2372.
38. Parker MT, Ball LC. Streptococci and aerococci associated with systemic infections in man. J Med Microbiol. 1976;9:275-302.
39. Scheld WM, Valone JA, Sande MA. Bacterial adherence in the pathogenesis of endocarditis. J Clin Invest. 1978;61:1394-1404.
40. Ramirez-Ronda CH. Adherence of glucan-positive and glucan-negative streptococcal strains to normal and damaged heart valves. J Clin Invest. 1978;62:805-814.

41. Pulliam L, Dall L, Inokuchi S, et al. Effects of exopolysaccharide production by viridans streptococci on penicillin therapy of experimental endocarditis. J Infect Dis. 1985;151:153-156.

42. Dall L, Barnes WG, Lane JW, et al. Enzymatic modification of glycocalyx in the treatment of experimental endocarditis due to viridans streptococci. J Infect Dis. 1987;156:736-740.

43. Burnette-Curley D, Wells V, Viscount H, et al. FimA, a major virulence factor associated with *Streptococcus parasanguis* endocarditis. Infect Immun. 1995;63:4669-4674.

44. Viscount HB, Munro CL, Burnette-Curley D, et al. Immunization with FimA protects against *Streptococcus parasanguis* endocarditis in rats. Infect Immun. 1997;65:994-1002.

45. Proctor RA, Mosher DF, Olbrantz PJ. Fibronectin binding to *Staphylococcus aureus*. J Biol Chem. 1982;257:14788-14794.

46. Scheld WM, Keeley JM, Balian G, et al. Microbial adhesion to fibronectin in the pathogenesis of infective endocarditis (Abstract). Clin Res. 1983;31:542A.

47. Scheld WM, Strunk RW, Balian G, et al. Microbial adhesion to fibronectin in vitro correlates with production of endocarditis in rabbits. Proc Soc Exp Biol Med. 1985;180:474-482.

48. Lawrance JH, Baddour LM, Simpson WA. The role of fibronectin binding in the rat model of experimental endocarditis caused by *Streptococcus sanguis*. J Clin Invest. 1990;86:7-13.

49. Lowy FD, Chang DS, Neuhaus EG, et al. Effect of penicillin on the adherence of *Streptococcus sanguis* in vitro and in the rabbit model of endocarditis. J Clin Invest. 1983;71:668-675.

50. Nealon TJ, Beachey EH, Courtney HS, et al. Release of fibronectin-lipoteichoic acid complexes from group A streptococci with penicillin. Infect Immun. 1986;51:529-535.

51. Drake TA, Rodgers GM, Sande MA. Tissue factor is a major stimulus for vegetation formation in enterococcal endocarditis. J Clin Invest. 1984;73:1750-1753.

52. Drake TA, Pang M. Effects of interleukin-1, lipopolysaccharide, and streptococci on procoagulant activity of cultured human cardiac valve endothelial and stromal cells. Infect Immun. 1989;57:507-512.

53. Sullam PM, Valone FH, Mills J. Mechanisms of platelet aggregation by viridans group streptococci. Infect Immun. 1987;55:1743-1750.

54. Berkowitz RJ. Acquisition and transmission of mutans streptcococci. J Calif Dent Assoc. 2003;31:135-138.

55. Hamada S, Slade HD. Biology, immunology, and cariogenicity of *Streptococcus mutans*. Microbiol Rev. 1980;44:331-384.

56. McGhee JR, Michalek SM. Immunobiology of dental caries: Microbial aspects and local immunity. Annu Rev Microbiol. 1981;35:595-638.

57. Gibbon RJ. Microbiol ecology: Adherent interactions which may affect microbial ecology in the mouth. J Dent Res. 1984;63:378-385.

58. Orlicek SL, Branum KC, English BK, et al. Viridans streptococcal isolates from patients with septic shock induce tumor necrosis factor-alpha production from murine macrophages. J Lab Clin Med. 1997;130:515-519.

59. Engel A, Kern P, Kern WV. Levels of cytokines and cytokine inhibitors in the neutropenic patients with α-hemolytic streptococcus shock syndrome. J Infect Dis. 1996;23:785-789.

60. Kaye D, McCormick RC, Hook EW. Bacterial endocarditis: The changing pattern since the introduction of penicillin therapy. Antimicrob Agents Chemother. 1962;1:37-46.

61. Lerner PI, Weinstein L. Infective endocarditis in the antibiotic era. N Engl J Med. 1966;274:323-331.

62. Hoen B, Alla F, Selton-Suty C, et al. Changing profile of infective endocarditis: Results of a 1-year survey in France. JAMA. 2002;288:75-81.

63. Roberts RB, Kreiger AG, Schiller NI, et al. Viridans streptococcal endocarditis: The role of various species, including pyridoxal-dependent streptococci. Rev Infect Dis. 1979;1:955-965.

64. Sussman JI, Baron EJ, Tenenbaum MJ, et al. Viridans streptococcal endocarditis: Clinical, microbiological, and echocardiographic correlations. J Infect Dis. 1986;154:597-603.

65. McKinsey DS, Ratts TE, Bisno AL. Underlying cardiac lesions in adults with infective endocarditis: The changing spectrum. Am J Med. 1987;82:681-688.

66. Van der Meer JTM, Thompson J, Valkenburg HA, et al. Epidemiology of bacterial endocarditis in the Netherlands: Patient characteristics. Arch Intern Med. 1992;152:1863-1868.

67. Sande MA, Lee BL, Mills J, et al. Endocarditis in intravenous drug users. In: Kaye D, ed. Infective Endocarditis. 2nd ed. New York: Raven Press; 1992:345-360.

68. Douglas JL, Cobbs CG. Prosthetic valve endocarditis. In: Kaye D, ed. Infective Endocarditis. 2nd ed. New York: Raven Press; 1992:375-396.

69. Starkebaum M, Durack D, Beeson P. The "incubation period" of bacterial endocarditis. Yale J Biol Med. 1977;50:49-58.

70. Garvey GJ, Neu HC. Infective endocarditis: An evolving disease. A review of endocarditis at the Columbia Presbyterian Medical Center, 1968-1973. Medicine (Baltimore). 1978;57:105-127.

71. Von Reyn CF, Levy BS, Arbeit RD, et al. Infective endocarditis: An analysis based on strict case definitions. Ann Intern Med. 1981;94:505-518.

72. Bush LM, Johnson CC. Clinical syndrome and diagnosis of endocarditis. In: Donald Kaye, ed. Infective Endocarditis. 2nd ed. Philadelphia: Raven Press; 1992:99-115.

73. Werner AS, Cobbs CG, Kaye D, et al. Studies on the bacteremia of bacterial endocarditis. JAMA. 1967;202:127-131.

74. Steckelberg JM, Murphy JG, Ballard D, et al. Emboli in infective endocarditis: The prognostic value of echocardiography. Ann Intern Med. 1991;114:635-640.

75. Sokil AB. Cardiac imaging in infective endocarditis. In: Kaye D, ed. Infective Endocarditis. 2nd ed. New York: Raven Press; 1992:125-150.

76. Wolfe JC, Johnson WD. Penicillin-sensitive streptococcal endocarditis: In vitro and clinical observations on penicillin-streptomycin therapy. Ann Intern Med. 1974;81:178-181.

77. Tunkel AR, Scheld WM. Experimental models of endocarditis. In: Kaye D, ed. Infective Endocarditis. 2nd ed. New York: Raven Press; 1992:37-56.

78. Sande MA, Irvin RG. Penicillin-aminoglycoside synergy in experimental streptococcal viridans endocarditis. J Infect Dis. 1974;129:572-576.

79. Carrizosa J, Kaye D. Antibiotic concentration in serum, bactericidal activity, and results of therapy of streptococcal endocarditis in rabbits. Antimicrob Agents Chemother. 1977;12:479-483.

80. Wilson WR, Karchmer AW, Dajani AS, et al. Antimicrobial treatment of adults with infective endocarditis due to streptococci, enterococci, staphylococci, and HACEK microorganisms. JAMA. 1995;274:1706-1713.

81. Wilson WR, Geraci JE. Treatment of streptococcal endocarditis. Am J Med. 1985;78(Suppl 6B):128-137.

82. Francioli P, Etienne J, Hoigne R, et al. Treatment of streptococcal endocarditis with a single daily dose of ceftriaxone sodium for 4 weeks: Efficacy and outpatient treatment feasibility. JAMA. 1992;267:264-279.

83. Stamboulian D, Bonvehi P, Arevalo C, et al. Antibiotic management of outpatients with infectious endocarditis due to penicillin-susceptible streptococci. Rev Infect Dis. 1991;13(Suppl 2):S160-S168.

84. Francioli PB. Ceftriaxone and outpatient treatment of infective endocarditis. Infect Dis Clin North Am. 1993;7:97-115.

85. Roberts RB. Streptococcal endocarditis: The viridans and β-hemolytic streptococci. In: Kaye D, ed. Infective Endocarditis. 2nd ed. New York: Raven Press; 1992:191-208.

86. Levy CS, Kogulan P, Gill VJ, et al. Endocarditis caused by penicillin-resistant viridans streptococci: 2 cases and controversies in therapy. Clin Infect Dis. 2001;33:577-579.

87. Parillo JE, Borst GC, Mazur MH, et al. Endocarditis due to resistant viridans streptococci during oral penicillin chemoprophylaxis. N Engl J Med. 1979;300:296-300.

88. Swenson FJ, Rubin SJ. Clinical significance of viridans streptococci isolated from blood cultures. J Clin Microbiol. 1982;15:725-727.

89. Roth RR, James WD. Microbial etiology of the skin. Annu Rev Microbiol. 1988;42:441-464.

90. Faden H, Zyndol N. Significance of viridans streptococci in blood cultures from children (Letter). Pediatr Infect Dis J. 1992;11:418.

91. Henslee J, Bostrom B, Weisdorf D, et al. Streptococcal sepsis in bone marrow transplant patients. Lancet. 1984;1:393.

92. Gonzalez-Barca E, Fernandez-Sevilla A, Carratala J, et al. Prospective study of 288 episodes of bacteremia in neutropenic cancer patients in a single institution. Eur J Clin Microbiol Infect Dis. 1996;15:291-296.

93. Weisman SJ, Scoopo FJ, Johnson GM, et al. Septicemia in pediatric oncology patients: The significance of viridans streptococcal infections. J Clin Oncol. 1990;8:453-459.

94. Elting LS, Bodey GP, Keefe BH. Septicemia and shock syndrome due to viridans streptococci: A case-control study of predisposing factors. Clin Infect Dis. 1992;14:1201-1207.

95. Bilgrami S, Feingold JM, Dorsky D, et al. Streptococcus viridans bacteremia following autologous peripheral blood stem cell transplantation. Bone Marrow Transplant. 1998;21:591-595.

96. Alcaide F, Benitez MA, Carratala J, et al. In vitro activities of the new ketolide HMR 3647 (telithromycin) in comparison with those of eight other antibiotics against viridans group streptococci isolated from blood of neutropenic patients with cancer. Antimicrob Agents Chemother. 2001;45:624-626.

97. Engelhard D, Elishoov H, Or R, et al. Cytosine arabinoside as a major risk factor for *Streptococcus viridans* septicemia following bone marrow transplantation: A 5-year prospective study. Bone Marrow Transplant. 1995;16:565-570.

98. Richard P, Amador Del Valle G, Moreau P, et al. Viridans streptococcal bacteraemia in patients with neutropenia. Lancet. 1995;345:1607-1609.

99. Burden AD, Oppenheim BA, Crowther D, et al. Viridans streptococcal bacteremia in patients with haematological and solid malignancies. Eur J Cancer. 1991;27:409-411.

100. Bostrom B, Weisdorf D. Mucositis and α-streptococcal sepsis in bone marrow transplant recipients. Lancet. 1984;1:1120-1121.

101. Ringden O, Heimdahl A, Lonnqvist B, et al. Decreased incidence of viridans streptococcal septicaemia in allogeneic bone marrow transplant recipients after the introduction of acyclovir. Lancet. 1984;1:744.

102. Villablanca JG, Steiner M, Kersey J, et al. The clinical spectrum of infections with viridans streptococci in bone marrow transplant patients. Bone Marrow Transplant. 1990;6:387-393.

103. Mascret B, Maraninchi D, Gastaut JA, et al. Risk factors for streptococcal septicaemia after marrow transplantation. Lancet. 1984;1:1185-1186.

104. Martino R, Manteiga R, Sanchez I, et al. Viridans streptococcal shock syndrome during bone marrow transplantation. Acta Haematol. 1995;94:69-73.

105. Tunkel AR, Sepkowitz KA. Infections caused by viridans streptococci in patients with neutropenia. Clin Infect Dis. 2002;34:1524-1529.

106. Koren P, Kremery V Jr. Viridans streptococcal bacteremia due to penicillin-resistant and penicillin-sensitive streptococci: Analysis of risk factors and outcome in 60 patients from a single cancer centre before and after penicillin is used for prophylaxis. Scand J Infect Dis. 1997;29:245-249.

107. Arns da Cunha C, Weisdorf D, Shu XO, et al. Early gram-positive bacteremia in BMT recipients: Impact of three different approaches to antimicrobial prophylaxis. Bone Marrow Transplant. 1998;21:173-180.

108. Carratala J, Alcaide F, Fernandez-Sevilla A, et al. Bacteremia due to viridans streptococci that are highly resistant to penicillin: Increase among neutropenic patients with cancer. Clin Infect Dis. 1995;20:1169-1173.

109. Hoyne AL, Herzon H. *Streptococcus viridans* meningitis: A review of the literature and report of nine recoveries. Ann Intern Med. 1950;33:879-902.

110. Enting RH, deGans J, Blankevoort JP, Spanjaard L. Meningitis due to viridans streptococci in adults. J Neurol. 1997;244:435-438.

111. Leiger JF. *Streptococcus salivarius* meningitis and colonic carcinoma. South Med J. 1991;84:1058-1059.

112. Carley NH. *Streptococcus salivarius* bacteremia and meningitis following upper gastrointestinal endoscopy and cauterization for gastric bleeding. Clin Infect Dis. 1992;14:947-948.

113. Lerner PI. Meningitis caused by *Streptococcus* in adults. J Infect Dis. 1975;131:S9-S16.

114. Freedman RM, Baltimore R. Fatal *Streptococcus viridans* septicemia and meningitis: Relationship to fetal scalp electrode monitoring. J Perinatol. 1990;10:272-274.

115. Majka FA, Gysin WM, Zaayer RL. *Streptococcus salivarius* meningitis following lumbar puncture. Nebr State Med J. 1956;41:279-281.

116. Watanakunakorn C, Stahl C. *Streptococcus salivarius* meningitis following myelography (Letter). Infect Control Hosp Epidemiol. 1992;13:454.

117. Heath RE, Rogers JA, Cheldelin LV, et al. *Streptococcus sanguis* sepsis and meningitis: A complication of vacuum extraction. Am J Obstet Gynecol. 1980;138:343-344.

118. Hellwege HH, Ram W, Scherf H, et al. Neonatal meningitis caused by *Streptococcus mitis*. Lancet. 1984;1:743-744.

119. Bignardi GE, Isaacs D. Neonatal meningitis due to *Streptococcus mitis*. Rev Infect Dis. 1989;11:86-88.

120. Koorevaar CT, Scherpenzeel PGN, Neijens HJ, et al. Childhood meningitis caused by enterococci and viridans streptococci. Infection. 1992;20:118-121.

121. Eng RH, Mangia AJ, Smith SM, et al. Meningitis following bacteremia with *Streptococcus sanguis*. NY State J Med. 1989;98:625-626.

122. Appelbaum E. Meningitis following trauma to the head and face. JAMA. 1960;173:116-120.

123. Goldfarb J, Wormser GP, Glaser JH. Meningitis caused by multiply antibiotic-resistant viridans streptococci. J Pediatr. 1984;105:891-895.

124. Yaniv LG, Potasman I. Iatrogenic meningitis: an increasing role for resistant viridans streptococci? Case report and review of the last 20 years. Scand J Infect Dis. 2000;32:693-696.

125. Schneeberger PM, Janssen M, Voss A. α-Hemolytic streptococci: A major pathogen of iatrogenic meningitis following lumbar puncture. Infection. 1996;24:29-33.

126. Nachamkin I, Dalton HP. The clinical significance of streptococcal species isolated from cerebrospinal fluid. Am J Clin Pathol. 1983;79:195-199.

127. Smith WF. Meningitis secondary to subacute bacterial endocarditis. N Engl J Med. 1939;220:587.

128. Neal JB, Jackson HW, Appelbaum E. Neurological complications of subacute bacterial endocarditis. NY State J Med. 1936;36:1819.

129. Gonzalez-CL, Calia FM. Bacteriologic flora of aspiration-induced pulmonary infections. Arch Intern Med. 1975;135:711-714.

130. Brook I, Finegold SM. Bacteriology of aspiration pneumonia in children. Pediatrics. 1980;65:1115-1120.

131. Bartlett JG, Finegold SM. Anaerobic infections of the lung and pleural space. Am Rev Respir Dis. 1974;110:56-77.

132. Lorber B, Swenson RM. Bacteriology of aspiration pneumonia. Ann Intern Med. 1974;81:329-331.

133. Rose H. Viridans streptococcal pneumonia (Letter). JAMA. 1981;245:32.

134. Pratter MR, Irwin RS. Viridans streptococcal pulmonary parenchymal infections. JAMA. 1980;243:2515-2517.

135. Sarkar TK, Murarka RS, Gilardi GL. Primary *Streptococcus viridans* pneumonia. Chest. 1989;96:831-834.

136. Gaudreau C, Delage G, Rousseau D, et al. Bacteremia caused by viridans streptococci in 71 children. Can Med Assoc J. 1981;125:1246-1249.

137. Sattler FR, Ruskin J. Empyema due to *Streptococcus mutans*. Chest. 1977;71:229-231.

138. Catto BA, Jacobs MR, Shlaes DM. *Streptococcus mitis:* A cause of serious infection in adults. Arch Intern Med. 1987;147:885-888.

139. Marrie TJ. Bacteremic community-acquired pneumonia due to viridans group streptococci. Clin Invest Med. 1993;16:38-44.

140. Raad II, Sabbagh MF, Caranasos GJ. Acute bacterial sialadenitis: A study of 29 cases and review. Clin Infect Dis. 1990;12:591-601.

141. Gill Y, Scully C. Orofacial odontogenic infections: Review of microbiology and current treatment. Oral Surg Oral Med Oral Pathol. 1990;70:155-158.

142. Weber M, Gubler J, Fahrer H, et al. Spondylodiscitis caused by viridans streptococci: Three cases and review of the literature. Clin Rheumatol. 1999;18:417-421.

143. Doern GV, Ferraro MJ, Brueggemann AB, et al. Emergence of high rates of antimicrobial resistance among viridans group streptococci in the United States. Antimicrob Agents Chemother. 1996;40:891-894.

144. Pfaller MA, Jones RN, Marshall SA, et al. Nosocomial streptococcal blood stream infections in the SCOPE program: Species occurrence and antimicrobial susceptibility. Diagn Microbiol Infect Dis. 1997;29:259-263.

145. Bourgault AM, Wilson WR, Washington JA II. Antimicrobial susceptibilities of species of viridans streptococci. J Infect Dis. 1979;140:316-321.

146. Roberts RB, Krieger AG, Gross KC. The species of viridans streptococci associated with microbial endocarditis: Incidence and antimicrobial susceptibility. Am Clin Climat Assoc. 1977;89:36-48.

147. Tuazon CU, Gill V, Gill F. Streptococcal endocarditis: Single vs. combination antibiotic therapy and role of various species. Rev Infect Dis. 1986;8:54-60.

148. Spencer WH, Thornsberry C, Moody MD, et al. Rheumatic fever chemoprophylaxis and penicillin-resistant gingival organisms. Ann Intern Med. 1970;73:683-688.

149. Sprunt K, Redman W, Leidy G. Penicillin-resistant α-streptococci in the pharynx of patients given oral penicillin. Pediatrics. 1968;42:957-958.

150. Potgeiter E, Carmichael M, Koornhof HJ, et al. In vitro susceptibility of viridans streptococci isolated from blood cultures. Eur J Clin Microbiol Infect Dis. 1992;11:543-546.

151. National Committee for Clinical Laboratory Standards. Methods for Dilution Antimicrobial Susceptibility Tests for Bacteria that Grow Aerobically; Approved Standard. 6th ed. (M7-A6). Villanova, PA: NCCLS; 2003.

152. Pfaller MA, Marshall SA, Jones RN. In vitro activity of cefepime and ceftazidime against 197 nosocomial blood stream isolates of streptococci: A multicenter study. Diagn Microbiol Infect Dis. 1997;29:273-276.

153. Farber BF, Eliopoulos GM, Ward JI, et al. Multiple resistant viridans streptococci: Susceptibility to lactam antibiotics and comparison of penicillin-binding protein patterns. Antimicrob Agents Chemother. 1983;24:702-705.

154. Chalkley L, Schuster C, Potgeiter E, et al. Relatedness between *Streptococcus pneumoniae* and viridans streptococci: Transfer of penicillin resistance determinants and immunological similarities of penicillin-binding proteins. FEMS Microbiol Lett. 1991;69:35-42.

155. Venditti M, Baiocchi P, Santinin C, et al. Antimicrobial susceptibilities of *Streptococcus* species that cause septicemia in neutropenic patients. Antimicrob Agents Chemother. 1989;33:580-582.

156. Tuohy M, Washington JA. Antimicrobial susceptibility of viridans group streptococci. Diagn Microbiol Infect Dis. 1997;29:277-280.

157. Brennan RD, Durack DT. Therapeutic significance of penicillin tolerance in experimental streptococcal endocarditis. Antimicrob Agents Chemother. 1983;23:273.

158. Pulliman L, Inokuchi S, Hadley KW, et al. Penicillin tolerance of viridans streptococci delays sterilization of vegetations in experimental animals. Clin Res. 1980;28:45A.

159. Lowy FD, Neuhaus EG, Chang DS, et al. Penicillin therapy of experimental endocarditis induced by tolerant *Streptococcus sanguis* and non-tolerant *Streptococcus mitis*. Antimicrob Agents Chemother. 1983;28:607-611.

160. Handwerger S, Tomasz A. Antibiotic tolerance among clinical isolates of bacteria. Rev Infect Dis. 1985;7:368-386.

161. James PA, Young SEJ, White DG. Incidence of penicillin tolerance among blood culture isolates of *Streptococcus sanguis,* 1987-1988. J Clin Pathol. 1991;44:160-163.

162. Etienne J, Vandenesch F, Fauvel JP, et al. Susceptibilities to ceftriaxone of streptococcal strains associated with infective endocarditis. Chemotherapy. 1989;35:355-358.

163. Alcaide F, Carratala J, Linares J, et al. In vitro activities of eight macrolide antibiotics and RP-59500 (quinupristin-dalfopristin) against viridans group streptococci isolated from blood of neutropenic cancer patients. Antimicrob Agents Chemother. 1996;40:2117-2120.

164. Farber BF, Yee Y. High-level aminoglycoside resistance mediated by aminoglycoside-modifying enzymes among viridans streptococci: Implications for the therapy of endocarditis. J Infect Dis. 1987;155:948-953.

165. Enzler MJ, Rouse MS, Henry NK, et al. In vitro and in vivo studies of streptomycin-resistant, penicillin-susceptible streptococci from patients with infective endocarditis. J Infect Dis. 1987;155:954-958.

166. Pfaller MA, Jones RN. Comparative antistreptococcal activity of two newer fluoroquiolones, levofloxacin, and sparfloxacin. Diagn Microbiol Infect Dis. 1997;29:199-201.

167. McWhinney PHM, Patel S, Whiley RA, et al. Activities of potential therapeutic and prophylactic antibiotics against blood culture isolates of viridans group streptococci from neutropenic cancer patients receiving ciprofloxacin. Antimicrob Agents Chemother. 1993;37:2493-2495.

168. Frenkel A, Hirsch W. Spontaneous development of L forms of streptococci requiring secretions of other bacteria or sulphydryl compounds for normal growth. Nature. 1961;191:728-730.

169. Bouvet A, van de Rijn I, McCarty M. Nutritionally variant streptococci from patients with endocarditis: Growth parameters in a semisynthetic medium and demonstration of a chromophore. J Bacteriol. 1981;146:1075-1082.

170. Bouvet A, Villeroy F, Cheng F, et al. Characterization of nutritionally variant streptococci by biochemical tests and penicillin binding proteins. J Clin Microbiol. 1985;22:1030-1034.

171. Christensen JJ, Facklam RR. *Granulicatella* and *Abiotrophia* species from human clinical specimens. J Clin Microbiol. 2001;39:3520-3523.

172. Ruoff KL. Nutritionally variant streptococci. Clin Microbiol Rev. 1991;4:184-190.

173. Tillotson GS. Evaluation of ten commercial blood culture systems to isolate pyridoxal-dependent streptococci. J Clin Pathol. 1981;34:930-934.

174. Gross KC, Houghton MP, Roberts RB. Evaluation of blood culture media for isolation of pyridoxal-dependent *Streptococcus mitior (mitis)*. J Clin Microbiol. 1981;14:266-272.

175. Stein DS, Nelson KE. Endocarditis due to nutritionally deficient streptococci: Therapeutic dilemma. Rev Infect Dis. 1987;9:908-916.

176. Cooksey RC, Swenson JM. In vitro antimicrobial inhibition patterns of nutritionally variant streptococci. Antimicrob Agents Chemother. 1979;16:514-518.

177. Gephart JF, Washington JA. Antimicrobial susceptibilities of nutritionally variant streptococci. J Infect Dis. 1982;146:536-539.

178. Bosley GS, Facklam RR. Biochemical and antimicrobic testing of "nutritionally variant streptococci." Abstract. Proceedings of the 90th Annual Meeting of the American Society for Microbiology. Washington, DC: American Society for Microbiology; 1990:395.

179. Murray CK, Walter EA, Crawford S, McElmeel ML, Jorgensen JH. *Abiotrophia* bacteremia in a patient with neutropenic fever and antimicrobial susceptibility testing of *Abiotrophia* isolates. Clin Infect Dis. 2001;15:E140-142.

180. Holloway Y, Dankert J. Penicillin tolerance in nutritionally variant streptococci. Antimicrob Agents Chemother. 1982;22:1073-1075.

181. Bouvet A, Cremieux AC, Contrepois A, et al. Comparison of penicillin and vancomycin, individually and in combination with gentamicin and amikacin, in the treatment of experimental endocarditis induced by nutritionally variant streptococci. Antimicrob Agents Chemother. 1985;28:607-611.

182. Henry NK, Wilson WR, Roberts RB. Antimicrobial therapy of experimental endocarditis caused by nutritionally variant viridans group streptococci. Antimicrob Agents Chemother. 1986;30:465-467.

183. Carey RB, Brause BD, Roberts RB. Antimicrobial therapy of vitamin B$_6$-dependent streptococcal endocarditis. Ann Intern Med. 1977;87:150-154.

184. Stein DS, Libertin CR. Time kill curve analysis of vancomycin and rifampin alone and in combination against nine strains of nutritionally deficient streptococci. Diagn Microbiol Infect Dis. 1988;10:139-144.

185. Woo PC, Fung AM, Lau SK, et al. Granulicatella adiacens and Abiotrophia defectiva bacteraemia characterized by 16S rRNA gene sequencing. J Med Microbiol. 2003;52:137-140.

186. Carey RB, Gross KC, Roberts RB. Vitamin B$_6$-dependent Streptococcus mitior (mitis) isolated from patients with systemic infections. J Infect Dis. 1975;131:722-726.

187. Barrios H, Bump CM. Conjunctivitis caused by a nutritionally variant streptococcus. J Clin Microbiol. 1986;23:379-380.

188. Ormerod LD, Ruoff KL, Meisler DM, et al. Infectious crystalline keratopathy: Role of nutritionally variant streptococci and bacterial factors. Ophthalmology. 1991;98:159-169.

189. Ince A, Tiemer B, Gille J, et al. Total knee arthroplasty infection due to Abiotrophia defectiva. J Med Microbiol. 2002;51:899-902.

190. McCarthy LR, Bottone EJ. Bacteremia and endocarditis caused by satellite streptococci. Am J Clin Pathol. 1974;61:585-591.

191. Facklam RR, Cooksey RC, Wortham EC. Evaluation of commercial latex agglutination reagents for grouping streptococci. J Clin Microbiol. 1979;10:641-646.

192. Pollock HM, Dahlgren BJ. Distribution of streptococcal groups in clinical specimens with evaluation of bacitracin screening. Appl Microbiol. 1974;27:141-143.

193. Foley GE. Further observations on the occurrence of streptococci of groups other than A in human infection. N Engl J Med. 1947;237:809-811.

194. Barnham M, Neilson DJ. Group L β-hemolytic streptococcal infection in meat handlers: Another streptococcal zoonosis. Epidemiol Infect. 1987;9:257-264.

195. Broome CV, Moellering RC Jr, Watson BK. Clinical significance of Lancefield groups L-T streptococci from blood and cerebrospinal fluid. J Infect Dis. 1976;133:382-392.

196. Feingold DS, Stagg NL, Kunz LJ. Extrarespiratory streptococcal infections. N Engl J Med. 1966;275:356-361.

197. Damask LJ, Montoya O, Axelrod JL. Rapid slide agglutination test for Lancefield grouping of streptococci. Arch Pathol Lab Med. 1979;103:456-457.

198. Matthieu DE, Wasilauskas BL, Stallings RA. A rapid staphylococcal coagglutination technique to differentiate group A from other streptococcal groups. Am J Clin Pathol. 1979;72:463-465.

199. Salata RA, Lerner PI, Shlaes DM, et al. Infections due to Lancefield group C streptococci. Medicine (Baltimore). 1989;68:225-239.

200. Arditi M, Shulman ST, Davis AT, et al. Group C β-hemolytic streptococcal infections in children: Nine pediatric cases and review. Rev Infect Dis. 1989;11:34-45.

201. Ortel TL, Kallianos J, Gallis HA. Group C streptococcal arthritis: Case report and review. Rev Infect Dis. 1990;12:829-837.

202. Bradley SF, Gordon JJ, Baumgartner DD, et al. Group C streptococcal bacteremia: Analysis of 88 cases. Rev Infect Dis. 1991;13:270-280.

203. Wilson CD, Salt GFH. Streptococci in animal disease. In: Skinner FA, Quesnel LB, eds. Streptococci. New York: Academic Press; 1978:143-156.

204. Deibel RH, Seeley HW Jr. Streptococcaceae. In: Buchanan RE, Gibbons NE, eds. Bergey's Manual of Determinative Bacteriology. 8th ed. Baltimore: Williams & Wilkins; 1974:490-509.

205. Marder VJ. The use of thrombolytic agents: Choice of patients, drug administration, laboratory monitoring. Ann Intern Med. 1979;90:802-808.

206. Schwartz RH, Shulman ST. Group C and group G streptococci: In-office isolation from children and adolescents with pharyngitis. Clin Pediatr. 1986;25:496-502.

207. Christensen KK, Christensen P, Flamholg L, et al. Frequency of streptococci of groups A, B, C, D and G in urethra and cervix swab specimens from patients with suspected gonococcal infection. Acta Pathol Microbiol Scand. 1974;82:470-474.

208. Goldman DA, Breton SJ. Group C streptococcal surgical wound infections transmitted by an anorectal and nasal carrier. Pediatrics. 1978;61:235-237.

209. Drusin LM, Ribble JC, Topf B. Group C streptococcal colonization in a newborn nursery. Am J Dis Child. 1973;125:820-821.

210. Barnham M, Thorton TJ, Lange K. Nephritis caused by Streptococcus zooepidemicus (Lancefield group C). Lancet. 1983;1:945-948.

211. Centers for Disease Control and Prevention. Group C streptococcal infection associated with eating homemade cheese—New Mexico. MMWR Morb Mortal Wkly Rep. 1983;32:510-516.

212. Barnham M, Kerby J, Chandler RS, et al. Group C streptococci in human infection: A study of 308 isolates with clinical correlations. Epidemiol Infect. 1989;102:379-390.

213. Bryans JT, Moore BO. Group C streptococcal infections of the horse. In: Wannamaker LW, Matsen JM, eds. Streptococci and Streptococcal Diseases: Recognition, Understanding and Management. New York: Academic Press; 1972:327-338.

214. Kilpper-Balz R, Schleifer KH. Nucleic acid hybridization and cell wall composition studies of pyogenic streptococci. FEMS Microbiol Lett. 1984;24:355-364.

215. Farrow JAE, Collins MD. Taxonomic studies on streptococci of serological groups C, G, and L and possibly related taxa. Syst Appl Microbiol. 1984;5:483-493.

216. Feltham RKA. A taxonomic study of the genus Streptococcus. In: Parker MT, ed. Pathogenic Streptococci. Surrey, UK: Reedbooks; 1979:247-248.

217. Jones D. Composition and differentiation of the genus Streptococcus. In: Skinner FA, Quesnel LB, eds. Streptococci. New York: Academic Press; 1978:1-50.

218. Colman G, Ball LC. Identification of streptococci in a medical laboratory. J Appl Bacteriol. 1984;57:1-14.

219. Lancefield RC, Hare R. The serological differentiation of pathogenic and non-pathogenic strains of hemolytic streptococci from parturient women. J Exp Med. 1935;61:335-349.

220. Coleman DJ, McGhie D, Tebbutt GM. Further studies on the reliability of the bacitracin inhibition test for the presumptive identification of Lancefield group A streptococci. J Clin Pathol. 1977;30:421-426.

221. Stoner RA. Bacitracin and coagglutination for grouping of β-hemolytic streptococci. J Clin Microbiol. 1978;7:463-466.

222. Cudney NJC, Albers AC. Group G streptococci: A review of the literature. Am J Med Technol. 1982;48:37-42.

223. Gaunt PN, Seal DV. Group G streptococcal infections. J Infect. 1987;15:5-20.

224. Hill HR, Wilson E, Caldwell GG, et al. Epidemic of pharyngitis due to streptococci of Lancefield group G. Lancet. 1969;2:371-374.

225. Stryker WS, Fraser DW, Facklam RR. Foodborne outbreak of group G streptococcal pharyngitis. Am J Epidemiol. 1982;116:533-540.

226. Hutchinson RI. Pathogenicity of group C (Lancefield) hemolytic streptococcus. Br Med J. 1946;2:575-576.

227. Rolston KVI. Group G streptococcal infections. Arch Intern Med. 1986;146:857-858.

228. Armstrong D, Blevins A, Louria DB, et al. Groups B, C, and G streptococcal infections in a cancer hospital. Ann NY Acad Sci. 1970;174:511-522.

229. Auckenthaler R, Hermans PE, Washington JA II. Group G streptococcal bacteremia: Clinical study and review of the literature. Rev Infect Dis. 1983;5:196-204.

230. Lam K, Bayer AS. Serious infections due to group G streptococci. Am J Med. 1983;75:561-570.

231. Wasky KL, Kollisch N, Densen P. Group G streptococcal bacteremia: The clinical experience at Boston University Medical Center and a critical review of the literature. Arch Intern Med. 1985;145:58-61.

232. Vartian C, Lerner PI, Shlaes DM, et al. Infections due to Lancefield group G streptococci. Medicine (Baltimore). 1985;64:75-88.

233. Mohr DN, Feist DJ, Washington JA II, et al. Infections due to group C streptococci in man. Am J Med. 1979;66:450-456.

234. Benjamin J, Perriello VA. Pharyngitis due to group C hemolytic streptococci in children. J Pediatr. 1976;89:254-255.

235. Cimolai N, Elford RW, Bryan L, et al. Do the β-hemolytic non-group A streptococci cause pharyngitis? Rev Infect Dis. 1988;10:587-601.

236. Meier FA, Centor RM, Graham L, et al. Clinical and microbiological evidence for endemic pharyngitis among adults due to group C streptococci. Arch Intern Med. 1990;150:825-829.

237. Hayden GF, Murphy TF, Hendley JO. Non-group A β-hemolytic streptococci in the pharynx: Pathogens or innocent bystanders? Am J Dis Child. 1989;143:794-797.

238. Turner JC, Hayden GF, Kiselica D, et al. Association of group C β-hemolytic streptococci with endemic pharyngitis among college students. JAMA. 1990;264:2644-2647.

239. Turner JC, Hayden FG, Lobo M, et al. Epidemiologic evidence for Lancefield group C beta-hemolytic streptococci as a cause of exudative pharyngitis in college students. J Clin Microbiol. 1997;35:1-4.

240. Hayden GF, Turner JC, Kiselica D, et al. Latex agglutination testing directly from throat swabs for rapid detection of β-hemolytic streptococci from Lancefield serogroup C. J Clin Microbiol. 1992;30:716-718.

241. McCue JD. Group G streptococcal pharyngitis: Analysis of an outbreak at a college. JAMA. 1982;248:1333-1336.

242. Cohen D, Ferne M, Rouach T, et al. Food-borne outbreak of group G streptococcal sore throat in an Israeli military base. Epidemiol Infect. 1987;99:249-255.

243. Gerber MA, Randolph MF, Martin NJ, et al. Community-wide outbreak of group G streptococcal pharyngitis. Pediatrics. 1991;87:598-603.

244. Nicholson ML, Ferdinand L, Sampson JS, et al. Analysis of immunoreactivity to a Streptococcus equi subsp. zooepidemicus M-like protein to confirm an outbreak of poststreptococcal glomerulonephritis, and sequences of M-like proteins from isolates obtained from different host species. J Clin Microbiol. 2000;38:4126-4130.

245. Lebrun L, Guibert M, Wallet P, et al. Human Fc(g) receptors for differentiation in throat cultures of group C "Streptococcus equisimilis" and group C "Streptococcus milleri." J Clin Microbiol. 1988;24:705-707.

246. Gnann JW Jr, Gray BM, Griffin FM Jr, et al. Acute glomerulonephritis following group G streptococcal infection. J Infect Dis. 1987;156:411-412.

247. Maxted WR, Potter EV. The presence of type 12 M-protein antigen in group G streptococci. J Gen Microbiol. 1967;49:119-125.

248. Reid HF, Bassett DC, Poon-King T, et al. Group G streptococci in healthy schoolchildren and in patients with glomerulonephritis in Trinidad. J Hyg. 1985;94:61-68.

249. Young L, Deighton CM, Chuck AJ, et al. Reactive arthritis and group G streptococcal pharyngitis. Ann Rheum Dis. 1992;51:1268.

250. Jansen TL, Janssen M, de Jong AJ. Reactive arthritis associated with group C and group G beta-hemolytic streptococci. J Rheumatol. 1998;25:1126-1130.

251. Geyer A, Roth A, Vettermann S, et al. M protein of a Streptococcus dysgalactiae human wound isolate shows multiple binding to different plasma proteins and shares epitopes with keratin and human cartilage. FEMS Immunol Med Microbiol. 1999;26:11-24.

252. Baddour LM, Bisno AL. Non-group A β-hemolytic streptococcal cellulitis: Association with venous and lymphatic compromise. Am J Med. 1985;79:155-159.

253. Ike RW. Septic arthritis due to group C streptococcus: Report and review of the literature. J Rheumatol. 1990;17:1230-1236.

254. Sobrino J, Bosch X, Wennberg P, et al. Septic arthritis secondary to group C streptococcus typed as *Streptococcus equisimilis*. J Rheumatol. 1991;18:485-486.

255. Collazos J, Echevarria MJ, Ayarza R, et al. *Streptococcus zooepidemicus* septic arthritis: Case report and review of group C streptococcal arthritis. Clin Infect Dis. 1992;15:744-746.

256. Lin AM, Karaski A, Salit IE, et al. Group G streptococcal arthritis. J Rheumatol. 1982;9:424-427.

257. Fujita NK, Lam K, Bayer AS. Septic arthritis due to group G streptococcus. JAMA. 1982;247:812-813.

258. Nakata MM, Silvers JH, George WL. Group G streptococcal arthritis. Arch Intern Med. 1983;143:1328-1330.

259. Gaunt PN, Seal DV. Group G streptococcal infection of joints and joint prostheses. J Infect. 1986;13:115-123.

260. Rady M, Turner PG, Ross ERS. Group G streptococcal septic arthritis. Br J Clin Pract. 1990;44:287-289.

261. Bronze MS, Whitby S, Schaberg DR. Group G streptococcal arthritis: A case report and review of the literature. Am J Med Sci. 1997;313:239-243.

262. Burkert T, Watanakunakorn C. Group G streptococcus septic arthritis and osteomyelitis: Report and literature review. J Rheumatol. 1991;18:904-907.

263. Asciutto R, Drennan J, Fitzgerald V, et al. Group C streptococcal arthritis and osteomyelitis in an adolescent with a hereditary sensory neuropathy. Pediatr Infect Dis. 1985;4:553-554.

264. Barson WJ. Group C streptococcal osteomyelitis. J Pediatr Orthop. 1986;6:346-348.

265. Asplin CM, Beeching NJ, Slack MPE. Osteomyelitis due to *Streptococcus equisimilis* (group C). Br Med J. 1979;1:89-90.

266. Tobias JH, Lee PYC, Bruckner FE. Group G β-haemolytic streptococcal vertebral osteomyelitis. J Infect. 1992;25:115-116.

267. Stamm AM, Cobbs CG. Group C streptococcal pneumonia: Report of a fatal case and review of the literature. Rev Infect Dis. 1980;2:889-898.

268. Rose HD, Allen JR, Witte G. *Streptococcus zooepidemicus* (group C) pneumonia in a human. J Clin Microbiol. 1980;11:76-78.

269. Noble JT, McGowan K. Group C streptococcal pneumonia in an adolescent. Am J Dis Child. 1983;137:1023.

270. Rivest N, Turgeson PL, Brady JF. Rare case of streptococcal C empyema. Can Med Assoc J. 1985;133:1009-1010.

271. Siefkin AD, Peterson DL, Hansen B. *Streptococcus equisimilis* pneumonia in a compromised host. J Clin Microbiol. 1984;17:386-388.

272. Vartian C. Bacteremic pneumonia due to group C streptococci. Rev Infect Dis. 1991;13:1029-1030.

273. Dolinski SY, Jones PG, Zabransky RJ, et al. Group C streptococcal pleurisy and pneumonia: A fulminant case and review of the literature. Infection. 1990;18:239-241.

274. Ancona RJ, Thompson TR, Ferrieri P. Group G steptococcal pneumonia and sepsis in a newborn infant. J Clin Microbiol. 1979;10:758-759.

275. Vracin W, Gage K, Ortega G, et al. Bacteremic group G streptococcal pneumonia. South Med J. 1982;75:1427.

276. Gallagher PG, Hyer CM III, Crone K, et al. Group C streptococcal sinusitis. Am J Otolaryngol. 1990;11:352-354.

277. Sanders V. Bacterial endocarditis due to group C hemolytic streptococcus. Ann Intern Med. 1963;58:858-861.

278. Lawrence MS, Cobbs CG. Endocarditis due to group C streptococci. South Med J. 1972;65:487-489.

279. Finnegan P, Fitzgerald MXM, Cumming G, et al. Lancefield group C streptococcal endocarditis. Thorax. 1974;29:245-247.

280. Bouza E, Meyer RD, Busch DF. Group G streptococcal endocarditis. J Clin Pathol. 1978;70:108-111.

281. Tuazon CU. Group G streptococcus. Am J Med Sci. 1980;279:121-124.

282. Blair DC, Martin DB. β-Hemolytic streptococcal endocarditis: Predominance of non-group A organisms. Am J Med Sci. 1978;276:269-277.

283. Venezio FR, Gullberg RM, Westenfelder GO, et al. Group G streptococcal endocarditis and bacteremia. Am J Med. 1986;81:29-34.

284. Smyth EG, Pallett AP, Davidson RN. Group G streptococcal endocarditis: Two case reports, a review of the literature and recommendations for treatment. J Infect. 1988;16:169-176.

285. Mohr DN, Feist DJ, Washington JA II, et al. Meningitis due to group C streptococci in an adult. Mayo Clin Proc. 1978;53:529-532.

286. Low DE, Young MR, Harding GKM. Group C streptococcal meningitis in an adult: Probable acquisition from a horse. Arch Intern Med. 1980;140:977-978.

287. Chung SJ. Meningitis caused by *Streptococcus equisimilis* (group C). South Med J. 1982;75:769.

288. Daly MP. Group G streptococcal infection in an elderly patient. South Med J. 1992;85:43-44.

289. Edwards AT, Roulson M, Ironside MJ. A milk-borne outbreak of serious infection due to *Streptococcus zooepidemicus* (Lancefield group C). Epidemiol Infect. 1988;101:43-51.

290. Downar J, Willey BM, Sutherland JW, et al. Streptococcal meningitis resulting from contact with an infected horse. J Clin Microbiol. 2001;39:2358-2359.

291. Faix RG, Soskolne EI, Schumacher RE. Group C streptococcal infection in a term newborn infant. J Perinatol. 1997;17:79-82.

292. Mollison LC, Donaldson E. Group C streptococcal meningitis. Med J Aust. 1990;152:319-320.

293. Ural O, Tuncer I, Dikici N, Aridogan B. *Streptococcus zooepidemicus* meningitis and bacteraemia. Scand J Infect Dis. 2003;35:206-207.

294. Shah S, Matthews RP, Cohen C. Group C streptococcal meningitis: Case report and review of the literature. Pediatr Infect Dis J. 2001;20:445-448.

295. Ramsay AM, Gillespie M. Puerperal infection associated with haemolytic streptococci other than Lancefield's group A. J Obstet Gynecol Br Empire. 1941;48:569-585.

296. Filker RS, Monif GRG. Postpartum septicemia due to group G streptococci. Obstet Gynecol. 1979;53(Suppl):28-30.

297. Baker CJ. Unusual occurrence of neonatal septicemia due to group G streptococcus. Pediatrics. 1974;53:568-569.

298. Krishna Mohan VK, Tilton TC, Raye JR, et al. Fatal group G streptococcal sepsis in a preterm neonate. Am J Dis Child. 1980;134:894-895.

299. Appelbaum PC, Friedman Z, Fairbrother PF, et al. Neonatal sepsis due to group G streptococci. Acta Paediatr Scand. 1980;69:559-562.

300. Dyson AE, Read SE. Group G streptococcal colonization and sepsis in neonates. J Pediatr. 1981;99:944-947.

301. Skogberg K, Simonen H, Renkonen OV, et al. β-Hemolytic group A, B, C and G streptococcal septicemia: A clinical study. Scand J Infect Dis. 1988;20:119-125.

302. Berenguer J, Sampedro I, Cercenado E, et al. Group-C β-hemolytic streptococcal bacteremia. Diagn Microbiol Infect Dis. 1992;15:151-155.

303. Carmeli Y, Ruoff KL. Report of cases of and taxonomic considerations for large-colony-forming Lancefield group C streptococcal bacteremia. J Clin Microbiol. 1995;33:2114-2117.

304. Yuen KY, Seto WH, Choi CH, et al. *Streptococcus zooepidemicus* (Lancefield group C) septicaemia in Hong Kong. J Infect. 1990;21:241-250.

305. Carmeli Y, Schapiro JM, Neeman D, et al. Streptococcal group C bacteremia. Arch Intern Med. 1995;155:1170-1176.

306. Yang SP, You KW, Liu CY, et al. Clinical characteristics of group G streptococcal bacteremia in Taiwan. Scand J Infect Dis. 2001;33:179-181.

307. Lewthwaite P, Parsons HK, Bates CJ, et al. Group G streptococcal bacteraemia: An opportunistic infection associated with immune senescence. Scand J Infect Dis. 2002;34:83-87.

308. Sylvetsky N, Raveh D, Schlesinger Y, et al. Bacteremmia due to beta-hemolytic streptococcus group G: increasing incidence and clinical characteristics of patients. Am J Med. 2002;112:622-626.

309. Woo PCY, Fung AMY, Lau SKP, et al. Group G beta-hemolytic streptococcal bacteremia characterized by 16S ribosomal RNA gene sequencing. J Clin Microbiol. 2001;39:3147-3155.

310. Hanson G, Engel PJ. Purulent pericarditis caused by β-hemolytic group C streptococcus: A case report. Arch Intern Med. 1981;141:1351-1353.

311. Marsa RJ, Blomquist IK, Bansal RC, et al. Acute pericarditis due to group C streptococcus: Report of a medically treated case. Am J Med. 1989;86:474-476.

312. Kim NH, Park JP, Jeon SH, et al. Purulent pericarditis caused by group G streptococcus as an initial presentation of colon cancer. J Korean Med Sci. 2002;17:571-573.

313. Nitta AT, Kuritzkes DR. Pyomyositis due to group C streptococci in a patient with AIDS. Rev Infect Dis. 1991;13:1254-1255.

314. Pong A, Chartrand SA, Huurman W. Pyomyositis and septic arthritis caused by group C streptococcus. Pediatr Infect Dis J. 1998;17:1052-1054.

315. Cimolai N, Macnab A. Schönlein-Henoch purpura and *Streptococcus equisimilis*. Br J Dermatol. 1991;125:403.

316. Klygis LM, Reisberg BE. Spinal epidural abscess caused by group G streptococci. Am J Med. 1991;91:89-90.

317. Keiser P, Campbell W. "Toxic strep syndrome" associated with group C streptococcus. Arch Intern Med. 1992;152:882-883.

318. Natoli S, Fimiani C, Faglieri N, et al. Toxic shock syndrome due to group C streptococci: A case report. Intensive Care Med. 1996;22:985-989.

319. Wagner JG, Schlievert PM, Assimacopoulos AP, et al. Acute group G streptococcal myositis associated with streptococcal toxic shock syndrome: A case report and review. Clin Infect Dis. 1996;23:1159-1161.

320. Dinn JJ. Brain abscess due to *Streptococcus equisimilis* in a maltworker. J Ir Med Assoc. 1971;64:50-51.

321. Schwartz RH, Knerr RJ, Hermansen K, et al. Acute epiglottitis caused by β-hemolytic group C streptococci. Am J Dis Child. 1982;136:558-559.

322. Lee TW, Sandoe JA. Epiglottitis caused by group C streptococcus. Acta Paediatr. 2001;90:1085.

323. Kohler W, Cederberg A. *Streptococcus zooepidemicus* (group C streptococci) as a cause of human infection. Scand J Infect Dis. 1976;8:217-218.

324. Layton J, McCulley D. Subdural empyema and group C streptococcus. South Med J. 1985;78:64-66.

325. Koenigsberg RA, Roman N, Turtz A, et al. Group C streptococcal leptomeningitis and brain abscess secondary to frontal sinusitis: A case report. J Neuroimaging. 1994;4:239-240.

326. Maniglia RJ, Roth T, Blumber EA. Polymicrobial brain abscess in a patient with human immunodeficiency virus. Clin Infect Dis. 1997;24:449-451.

327. Finland M, Garner C, Wilcox C, et al. Susceptibility of β-hemolytic streptococci to 65 antibacterial agents. Antimicrob Agents Chemother. 1976;9:11-19.

328. Rolston KVI, LeFrock JL, Schell RF. Activity of nine antimicrobial agents against Lancefield group C and group G streptococci. Antimicrob Agents Chemother. 1982;22:930-932.

329. Rotta J. Pyogenic hemolytic streptococci. In: Srveath PH, Sharpe ME, Holt JG, eds. Bergey's Manual of Systemic Bacteriology. 9th ed. Baltimore: Williams & Wilkins; 1986:1047-1054.

330. Kataja J, Seppala H, Skurnik M, et al. Different erythromycin resistance mechanisms in group C and group G streptococci. Antimicrob Agents Chemother. 1998;42:1493-1494.

331. Hutchinson NA, Eltringham IL. Therapeutic failure in group C streptococcal pharyngitis (Letter). Lancet. 1995;346:1367.

332. Portnoy D, Prentis J, Richards GK. Penicillin tolerance of human isolates of group C streptococci. Antimicrob Agents Chemother. 1981;20:235-238.
333. Rolston KVI, Chandraseker PH, LeFrock JL. Antimicrobial tolerance in group C and group G streptococci. J Antimicrob Chemother. 1984;13:389-392.
334. Lam K, Bayer AS. In vitro bactericidal synergy of gentamicin combined with penicillin G, vancomycin, or cefotaxime against group G streptococci. Antimicrob Agents Chemother. 1984;26:260-262.
335. Noble JT, Tyburski MB, Berman M, et al. Antimicrobial tolerance in group G streptococci. Lancet. 1980;2:982.
336. Zaoutis T, Schneider B, Moore LS, Klein JD. Antibiotic susceptibilities of group C and group G streptococci isolated from patients with invasive infections: Evidence of vancomycin tolerance among group G serotypes. J Clin Microbiol. 1999;37:3380-3383.
337. Galimand M, Lambert T, Gerbaud G, Courvalin P. High-level aminoglycoside resistance in the beta-hemolytic group G *Streptococcus* isolate BM2721. Antimicrob Agents Chemother. 1999;43:3008-3010.
338. Faibis F, Fiacre A, Demachy MC. Emergence of high-level gentamicin resistance in group G streptococci. Eur J Clin Microbiol Infect Dis. 2001;20:901-902.
339. Pier GB, Madin SH. *Streptococcus iniae* sp. nov., a beta-hemolytic streptococcus isolated from an Amazon freshwater dolphin, *Imia geoffrensis*. Int J Syst Bacteriol. 1976;26:545-553.
340. Eldar A, Frelier PF, Assenta L, et al. *Streptococcus shiloi,* the name for an agent causing septicemic infection in fish, is a junior synonym of *Streptococcus iniae*. Int J Syst Bacteriol. 1995;45:840-842.
341. Weinstein MR, Litt M, Kert DA, et al. Invasive infections due to a fish pathogen, *Streptococcus iniae*. N Engl J Med 1997;337:589-594.
342. von Eiff C, Herrmann M, Peters G. Antimicrobial susceptibilities of *Stomatococcus mucilaginosus* and of *Micrococcus* spp. Antimicrob Agents Chemother. 1995;39:268-270.
343. Park MK, Khan J, Stock F, Lucy DR. Successful treatment of *Stomatococcus mucilaginosus* meningitis with intravenous vancomycin and intravenous ceftriaxone. Clin Infect Dis. 1997;24:278.
344. Sarma PS, Mohanty S. *Pediococcus acidilactici* pneumonitis and bacteremia in a pregnant woman (Letter). J Clin Microbiol. 1998;36:2392-2393.
345. Corocoran Gd, Gibbons N, Mulvihill TE. Septicaemia caused by *Pediococcus pentosaceus:* A new opportunistic pathogen. J Infect Dis. 1991;23:179-182.
346. Mastro TD, Spika JS, Lozano P, et al. Vancomycin-resistant *Pediococcus acidilactici:* Nine cases of bacteremia. J Infect Dis. 1990;1612:956-960.

CHAPTER **201**

Streptococcus anginosus Group

YAZDAN MIRZANEJAD
CHARLES W. STRATTON

Streptococcus intermedius, Streptococcus constellatus, and Streptococcus anginosus are three distinct species[1] that constitute the "*Streptococcus anginosus* group."[2] This group is also referred to as the "*Streptococcus milleri* group"[3] or, in the past, as the "*Streptococcus intermedius* group" or simply as "*Streptococcus anginosus*."[4] The classification, nomenclature, and identification of members of this group have been confusing, to say the least. However, the preferred name for these three streptococcal species collectively is the *S. anginosus* group.[2] Genetic and phenotypic studies[5-9] clearly demonstrate that the *S. anginosus* group consists of these three distinct streptococcal species, with *S. constellatus* having two subspecies, *S. constellatus* subsp. *constellatus* and *S. constellatus* subsp. *pharyngis*. These species and subspecies appear to be associated with a number of different body habitats as well as sites and types of clinical infections.[5,10,11]

Clinically, this group has long been characterized by a propensity for invasive pyogenic infections, which readily differentiates them from the other viridans streptococci.[3,4,9] Microbiologically, members of this group are recognized by their microaerophilic or anaerobic growth requirements, their formation of minute colonies, and the frequent presence of a characteristic caramel-like odor when cultured on agar

plates.[2,12] This chapter defines the three species currently making up the *S. anginosus* group and discusses their role in clinical infections.

BACTERIOLOGIC CHARACTERISTICS

Members of the *S. anginosus* group share the phenotypic characteristics of the members of the genus *Streptococcus* whose classification in general is based on patterns of hemolysis, Lancefield serologic antigenic reactions (i.e., groupings), growth properties, and biochemical reactions.[2] In contrast to other members of the genus, *S. anginosus* group isolates often require carbon dioxide for growth; because of this, isolates are sometimes mistaken for anaerobic streptococci. Even under microaerophilic-anaerobic growth conditions, the resulting colonies are tiny (0.5 mm in diameter), only one half to two thirds the diameter of colonies of other streptococci.[2] Some strains of *S. anginosus* isolated from genitourinary sources exhibit a spreading growth on certain types of agar, owing to increased production of extracellular glycocalyx (i.e., capsule).[13] Like other streptococci, these organisms may be β-hemolytic, α-hemolytic, or γ-hemolytic on sheep blood agar.[2] Members of the *S. anginosus* group often exhibit Lancefield antigens A, C, F, or G.[14] Strains containing the group F antigen may cross-react with the other grouping sera. Lancefield groupings therefore are of little value in identifying these organisms, because any one of a number of antigens may be exhibited. In fact, false-positive detection of group A streptococcal antigen has been reported with cross-reacting antigens from *S. intermedius*.[15]

A number of microbiologists have described a characteristic caramel-like odor associated with agar cultures of the *S. anginosus* group.[2,12] It has been suggested that this odor, when present, may be diagnostic for this group of microorganisms. The caramel-like odor has been shown to be caused by the formation of the metabolite diacetyl, and its presence indeed is of diagnostic value. However, by gas chromatography, a number of strains that appear to be devoid of an obvious caramel-like odor on agar cultures have been noted to produce the diacetyl metabolite.

The usefulness of Lancefield groupings and the distinctive caramel-like odor for presumptive identification has been examined in a prospective study of 100 consecutive streptococcal isolates from pus or blood cultures.[12] Lancefield group F alone had a specificity of 100% and a sensitivity of 47%; Lancefield group F accompanied by a caramel-like odor had a specificity of 100% and a sensitivity of only 19.5%. The study reported no significant association between species, Lancefield groupings, site of infection, severity of infection, or pathogenicity.

Gram staining of the members of the *S. intermedius* group reveals spherical or ovoid cells that form chains or pairs in broth culture and that stain gram-positive. It is possible to distinguish members of the *S. anginosus* group from other streptococci by means of selected biochemical reactions. *S. anginosus* group can be differentiated from other streptococci by a combination of three rapid tests: a positive Voges-Proskaur test for acetonin production, hydrolysis of arginine, and failure to ferment sorbitol.[2] In addition, the presence of the caramel-like odor can be helpful. The characteristics that allow the presumptive identification of members of the *S. anginosus* group, as adapted from the identification scheme of Whiley and colleagues,[5] are summarized in Table 201-1.

TAXONOMY

The diversity of hemolytic and Lancefield groupings and the disagreement regarding taxonomy and speciation of the *S. anginosus* group have contributed to a lack of recognition of these pathogens in many laboratories.[16,17] Whiley and colleagues[5] noted that almost all *S. intermedius* strains (93%) were not β-hemolytic, whereas 38% of *S. constellatus* and 12% of *S. anginosus* were β-hemolytic. These investigators also found that of those strains of *S. constellatus* and *S. anginosus* that reacted with Lancefield serologic group F antibody, virtually all of the former but almost none of the latter were β-hemolytic.

TABLE 201-1 Presumptive Identification of Members of the *Streptococcus anginosus* Group[12]

Growth of minute streptococcal colonies under microaerophilic/ anaerobic conditions
Acid from
    Insulin−
    Sorbitol−
    Salicin+
Hydrolysis of
    Hippurate−
    Esculin+
    Deoxyribonuclease−
    Arginine dihydrolysis+
    Voges-Proskauer test+[*]
    Caramel-like odor V
↓
Presumptive S. *anginosus* group

+, ≥90% of strains have a positive reaction; −, ≥90% of strains have a negative reaction; V, variable; [*], rare exceptions.
Adapted from Whiley RA, Fraser HY, Hardie JM, et al. Phenotypic differentiation of *Streptococcus constellatus, Streptococcus intermedius,* and *Streptococcus anginosus* (the *Streptococcus milleri* group): Association with different body sites and clinical infections. J Clin Microbiol. 1990;28:1497-1501.

Laboratories can readily differentiate the three members of the S. *anginosus* group using phenotypic characteristics that have correlated well with molecular taxonomic techniques,[2,5,7-10] and it is reasonable to do so.[11,18,19] Useful characteristics adapted from the identification schemes of Whiley and colleagues[5,6] are presented in Fig. 201-1. These characteristics include conventional biochemical tests, which continue to be the recommended method for identification of viridans streptococci, including the S. *anginosus* group.

A number of commercial systems are available for the identification of viridans streptococci. They include API Rapid PosID (Analytab Products, Plainview, NY); Baxter Microscan (West Sacramento, CA);

BBL Minitek Differential System (Becton-Dickinson Microbiology Systems, Cockeysville, MD); Fluo-Card Milleri (KEY Scientific, Round Rock, TX); IDS RapID STR System (Innovative Diagnostic Systems, Atlanta, GA); and Vitek GPI (bioMerieux Vitek, Hazelwood, MD). An early comparison of many of these tests with conventional methods revealed that none showed more than 74% agreement.[20] S. *constellatus* and S. *intermedius* were among those isolates most frequently misidentified. However, a more recent comparison with conventional methods for one of these tests (Fluo-Card Milleri) reported a 98% agreement for S. *anginosus* strains, 97% agreement for S. *constellatus* strains, and 88% agreement for S. *intermedius* strains.[21]

Polymerase chain reaction (PCR) assays have now been developed for the identification of clinically relevant viridans group streptococci to the species and group level. One of these assays uses PCR-amplified 23S ribosomal RNA (rRNA) gene sequences followed by species-specific hybridization probes.[22] This molecular genetic approach has already identified several strains suspected of being members of the S. *anginosus* group on the basis of biochemical testing as being more closely related to S. *parasanguis*. PCR-amplified partial 16S rRNA gene sequences followed by species-specific hybridization probes have been used in a similar manner to identify a distinct rRNA population sharing 98% sequence homology with S. *constellatus*.[23] Another PCR assay that has been used is based on amplification of specific internal gene fragments encoding D-alanine: D-alanine ligases that are species-specific are ubiquitous in microbial cells possessing peptidoglycans.[24] The availability and use of genetic-based molecular methods for classification of the viridans streptococci is now placing these microorganisms in unequivocal taxonomic positions.[7-9,22-24]

NORMAL HABITAT

Members of the S. *anginosus* group are found in the human oral cavity, where they have been considered harmless commensals.[25] These microorganisms can be isolated from gingival crevices, dental plaque, and dental root canals.[26] They can also be found in the throat and na-

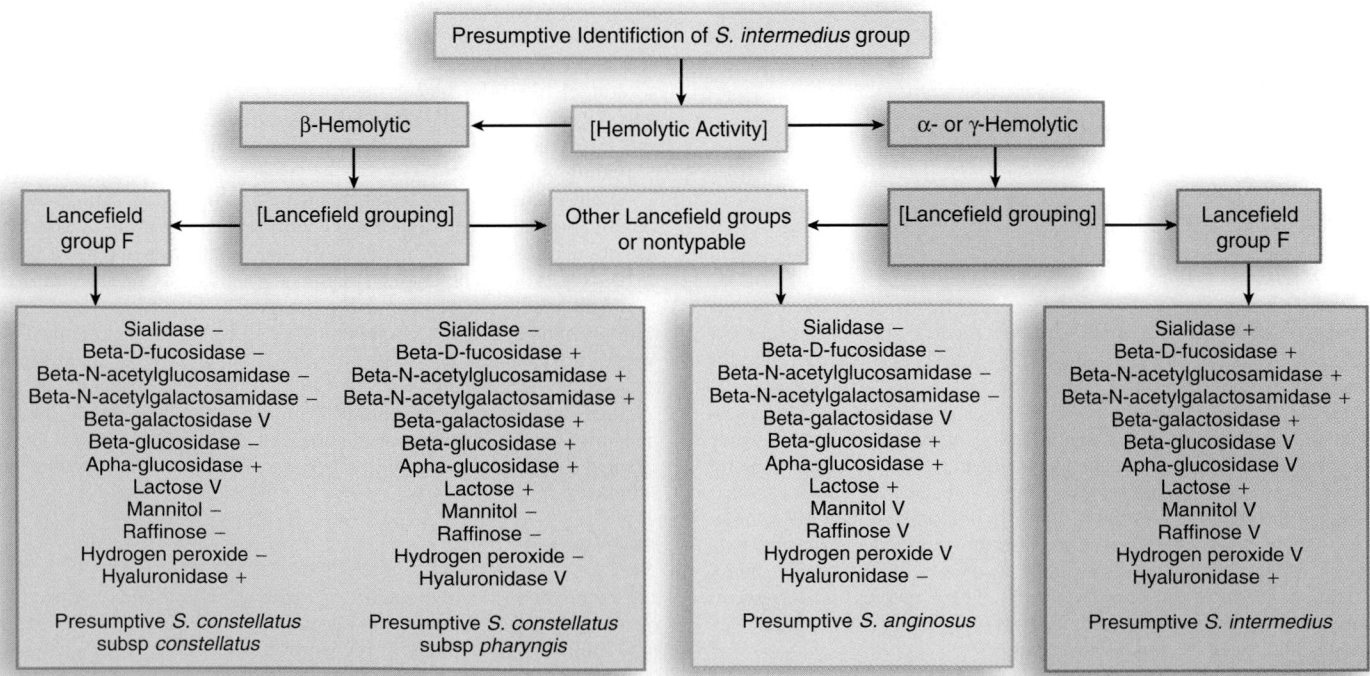

FIGURE 201-1. Phenotypic differentiation of the members of the *Streptococcus interanginosus* group. *Abbreviations:* V, Variable; +, at least 90% of strains have a positive reaction; −, at least 90% of strains have a negative reaction. *(Adapted from Whiley RA, Fraser HY, Hardie JM, et al. Phenotypic differentiation of Streptococcus constellatus, Streptococcus intermedius, and Streptococcus anginosus [the Streptococcus milleri group]: Association with different body sites and clinical infections. J Clin Microbiol. 1990;28:1497–1501 and Whiley RA, Hall LMC, Hardie JM, Beighton D. A study of small colony beta-haemolytic, Lancefield group C streptococci within the anginosus group: Description of Streptococcus constellatus subsp. pharyngis subsp. nonassociated with the human throat and pharyngitis. Int J Syst Bacteriol 1999;49:1443-1449.)*

sopharynx;[6] these latter locations might represent spread from the oral cavity. Not surprisingly, these organisms are also found in the gastrointestinal tract and have been recovered from stool[27] and from the appendix.[28] Within the *S. anginosus* group, *S. intermedius* is most commonly found in dental plaque and *S. anginosus* is most frequently found in the gastrointestinal tract.[10] Spread from the gastrointestinal tract to the vagina with subsequent vaginal colonization is common.[29] *S. anginosus* is the species most often found in the vagina; these isolates are heavily encapsulated.[13] Their presence in the birth canal can result in neonatal infection.[30] Spread from the vagina to the urinary tract appears to occur with these organisms, although infection in these sites is rare.[31]

PATHOGENICITY

The association of the *S. anginosus* group with the tendency to form abscesses has long been recognized.[31] However, the reasons for this pathogenic characteristic are not yet completely understood. Growth characteristics of the *S. anginosus* group appear to be important in their pathogenicity. Members of this group are able to grow well in acidic environments such as those found in abscesses.[32] Part of the explanation also appears to be that mixed infections involving members of the *S. anginosus* group and other microbes (e.g., *Eikenella corrodens* and anaerobes) allow more rapid replication of the streptococci.[33-35] For example, one study noted that exponential growth for *S. intermedius* and *S. constellatus* in mixed culture with *E. corrodens* occurred within 6 hours after incubation, compared with 25 hours without *E. corrodens*.[34] No growth stimulation *of S. anginosus* was observed. A possible clinical correlate of this in vitro phenomenon has been reported.[36] Another study using a murine model of pneumonia demonstrated a similar synergy between members of the *S. anginosus* group and oral anaerobes.[37] This study found that mortality was higher, abscesses or empyema were more frequently noted on histopathologic examination, and viable bacteria were more numerous in the lungs of mice with mixed infections caused by members of the *S. intermedius* group and oral anaerobes than in the lungs of mice with monomicrobial infection. In vitro studies by these investigators confirmed that anaerobes enhanced the growth of *S. anginosus* group organisms. Finally, the authors pointed out that in 45 cases of acute pneumonia and/or pulmonary abscess and 25 cases of thoracic empyema, the predominant species recovered were anaerobic bacteria and members of the *S. anginosus* group, confirming the clinical importance of this phenomenon in pulmonary infections.

In addition, members of the *S. anginosus* group have been shown to possess intrinsic factors that are likely to be involved in their pathogenesis. Streptococci, including members of the *S. anginosus* group, express a number of different adhesins on their cell surfaces that facilitate adherence to substrates found in their natural environment.[38] Many of these adhesins are cell wall–associated proteins containing repeated sequence blocks of amino acids. Sequences and function of these adhesion proteins among the streptococci have become assorted through gene duplication and horizontal transfer between microbial populations.[39] All members of the *S. anginosus* group are able to bind fibronectin via a cell-surface protein, and some strains are able to bind to platelets-fibrin, fibrin clots, and fibrinogen.[40] This property is thought to be a factor in the ability of these pathogens to cause endocarditis. Fibrinogen binding may, in turn, aid in platelet aggregation, which would also facilitate the development of endocarditis.[41]

These adhesion proteins would explain the success of streptococci in colonizing oral and epithelial surfaces and would allow these pathogens to attach to sites of tissue damage. Attachment to and colonization of sites of tissue damage may precede tissue invasion and immune modulation presaging the development of infection.[42,43] In an experimental rat endocarditis model in which all three strains of the *S. anginosus* group were studied, *S. anginosus* strains produced infective vegetations and bacteremia in almost all catheterized rats, *S. constellatus* strains did so less frequently, and *S. intermedius* strains did so only occasionally.[44] Moreover, the vegetations infected with *S. anginosus* strains harbored significantly higher numbers of microorganisms than did those infected by other strains. However, no strong correlation was found between endocardial infectivity and platelet-aggregating capacity of the strains.

Another potential virulence factor is the frequent presence in members of the *S. anginosus* group of a polysaccharide capsule[13] that hinders phagocytosis. The ability to escape phagocytosis would allow these pathogens to replicate after arriving at and adhering to a site of tissue damage. A murine model used to investigate the pathogenicity *of S. constellatus* in pulmonary infections demonstrated that virulent strains are less likely to be phagocytized and killed than avirulent strains, presumably because of capsular variation.[45]

The production of pyrogenic exotoxins by *Streptococcus* species is well known.[46] Despite this known propensity for streptococcal exotoxins, few have been reported for members of the *S. anginosus* group. A unique cytolytic toxin specific for human cells, intermedilysin, was described from a strain of *S. intermedius* isolated from a liver abscess.[47] In particular, intermedilysin was noted to have a potent hemolytic effect on human erythrocytes, suggesting that this or similar exotoxins may be responsible for β-hemolysis on blood agar plates. The intermedilysin gene has been found to exist only in *S. intermedius*.[48] Production of intermedilysin in *S. intermedius* isolates from deepseated infections such as abscesses is higher than that in strains from normal habitats, suggesting that this cytolysin is a virulence factor.[48]

In addition, members of the *S. anginosus* group produce a wide variety of hydrolytic enzymes, including hyaluronidase, deoxyribonuclease, and chondroitin sulfatase.[49] These enzymes may facilitate the spread of these pathogens through tissues, play a role in microbial nutrition, and assist in liquefaction of pus. One of the most prevalent hydrolytic enzymes is hyaluronidase.[50] Hyaluronidase has been found in pus and shown to be a growth factor.[51,52] One study used a collection of more than 500 strains of *S. intermedius* to assess the presence of hydrolytic enzymes and found that their presence was related to the clinical significance of the isolates.[18] Ribonuclease activity was equally distributed among all the strains, whereas hyaluronidase activity was linked to *S. intermedius* and *S. constellatus*. Neither enzyme was significantly associated with strains isolated from infections. However, deoxyribonuclease and chondroitin sulfatase activity was also linked to *S. intermedius* and *S. constellatus* and was associated with strains isolated from infections. Chondroitin sulfatase has been shown to be produced by *S. intermedius*.[53] In addition, a novel glycosaminoglycan depolymerase isolated from *S. intermedius* acts on both chondroitin sulfate and hyaluronic acid.[54] Another enzyme that may play a role in pathogenesis is sialidase (neuraminidase), which is produced by *S. intermedius*.[55] Sialidase production by other bacteria such as *Corynebacterium diphtheriae*, *Streptococcus pneumoniae*, *Vibrio cholerae*, and *Clostridium perfringens* is considered to be an important feature of their pathogenicity. Sialic acid is known to be a nutrient source for these microorganisms; members of the *S. anginosus* group are able to use sialic acid efficiently as a sole carbon source. Sialidase therefore may be a growth factor and may play an important role in the ability of these microorganisms to proliferate.

A number of other possible virulence factors related to the host immune response have been identified. One of these, a 90-kDa protein that suppresses lymphocyte and fibroblast proliferation, was recovered from *S. intermedius*.[56,57] This protein may have a virulence effect that is mediated by stimulation of suppressor lymphocytes. Leukocyte migration was not affected by this protein. In addition, the absence of receptors for the Fc fragment of human immunoglobulin G has been noted[58] and may be related to virulence.

However, the most important virulence factor for members of the *S. anginosus* group in relation to the host immune response may be superantigens. Superantigens are a diverse collection of molecules that share the ability to activate specific lymphocyte subsets without regard to the antigenic specificity of the T cells and without prior cellular processing.[59] The lymphocyte subsets are stimulated in a manner that is restricted to the variable regions on the β-chain (Vjb region) of the T-cell receptor; after stimulation, superantigen-responsive T cells often die through apoptosis. Reports suggest that groups B, C, F, and G streptococci and *S. sanguis* produce pyrogenic toxin superantigens that stimulate T cells to proliferate nonspecifically.[60] This is accomplished by the interaction of these superantigens with class II major histocompatibility complex products on antigen-producing B cells, which are then cross linked to T cells via the Vjb region of the T-cell receptor complex. Because superantigens are potent producers of inflammatory (Th1) cytokines, they may play a central role in determining the severity of invasive streptococcal infections. These superantigens are now thought to produce acute toxic shock syndromes, necrotizing fasciitis, and multisystem illnesses via release of these inflammatory cytokines.[43,61] Streptococcal erythrogenic exotoxins are known to have superantigen properties,[62] and it is possible that intermedilysin,[47,48] the recently recognized hemolysin of *S. intermedius*, may act as a superantigen.

The interaction of the *S. anginosus* group and human polymorphonuclear cells also has been examined because of their striking propensity to cause abscesses.[63,64] One study demonstrated that a virulent strain of *S. constellatus* was less likely to be killed by human polymophonuclear cells than the avirulent strains.[63] A second study showed that members of the *S. anginosus* group stimulated less chemotaxis than did *Staphylococcus aureus*, which may provide a head start to proliferating bacteria.[64] Moreover, members of the *S. anginosus* group survived ingestion by polymorphonuclear cells better than did *S. aureus*.[64] These characteristics help explain the capacity of members of the *S. anginosus* group to cause abscesses.

That members of *S. anginosus* group do have virulence factors, however ill-defined, can be appreciated by the fact that many times these pathogens are the sole isolate from serious infections, including those with abscess formation.[31,65,66]

CLINICAL MANIFESTATIONS

Head and Neck Infections

Most of the original *S. anginosus* group isolates were recovered from dental abscesses. These pathogens continue to be recovered from endodontic and periapical dental abscesses,[67] most often after a dental procedure such as surgery or extraction or after trauma. Although *S. anginosus* group species are often isolated in pure culture, other microorganisms such as *Bacteroides fragilis* may be recovered.[31] Bacteremia may occur with dental abscesses[31] and has been associated with metastatic abscesses.[68,69] Finally, members of the *S. anginosus* group have been isolated from dental caries and periodontal disease,[26] although their role, if any, in these processes is unclear. The periodontal location would allow transient bacteremias to occur and possibly predispose to metastatic infections.

The presence of members of the *S. anginosus* group in the oral cavity clearly predisposes to oral and maxillofacial infections,[70] as well as head and neck infections.[71] Acute pansinusitis with bacteremia caused by members of the *S. anginosus* group has been described.[72] In several series this group represented the most common microorganisms isolated in sinus-induced intracranial sepsis, being recovered from intracranial and orbital empyemas in up to 50% of the cases.[73-75] Because of the potential for metastatic spread, sinusitis caused by *S. anginosus* group isolates requires aggressive management.[73] Finally, *S. anginosus* group pathogens have been described as causing neck infections[71] as well as a fulminant fasciitis of the head and neck that also can be life threatening.[76]

Bacteremia and Endocarditis

Many reports in the medical literature have stressed the clinical significance of bacteremia caused by *S. anginosus* group isolates.[3,4,19,31,76-80] Most of these bacteremic episodes were associated with an identifiable focus of infection—usually a deep-seated abscess in a visceral organ, implicating the gastrointestinal tract as the source. Such bacteremia, therefore, should alert the clinician to initiate an appropriate investigation for the detection of a possible suppurative focus of infection. A number of reports have noted an increase in the rate of viridans streptococcal bacteremia, including isolates from the *S. anginosus* group, in patients with cancer.[81,82] In one such study, *S. anginosus* was responsi-

ble for eight episodes of bacteremia in which the upper respiratory tract was the source of infection.[82] Nosocomial bacteremias caused by streptococci represent an increasingly important problem, particularly among neutropenic cancer patients; the viridans group streptococci, including members of the *S. anginosus* group, account for up to 50% of the nosocomial blood-stream isolates.[83] Bacteremias by *S. anginosus* group isolates have also been described in neonates[30] and in the pediatric population, including pediatric oncology patients.[17,84,85]

Viridans streptococci have been recognized as an increasingly important cause of bacteremia in neutropenic cancer patients undergoing chemotherapy.[81,82,86] Viridans streptococci are associated with adult respiratory distress syndrome (ARDS) and a toxic shock–like syndrome in neutropenic patients that is not seen in non-neutropenic patients with viridans streptococci bacteremia.[86] The syndrome observed is clinically similar to the toxic shock syndrome associated with *Staphylococcus aureus* infection and includes a rash with subsequent palmar desquamation, shock, ARDS, and a high mortality rate. Of the *S. anginosus* group, *S. intermedius* and *S. constellatus* have been associated with this syndrome.[86] To date no exotoxins of viridans streptococci have been directly implicated, although streptococcal erythrogenic exotoxins are known to induce cytokines, and *S. intermedius* is known to produce a cytolysin[47,48,87] that is an erythrogenic exotoxin. Moreover, cell-free bacterial supernatants derived from viridans streptococci have been shown to induce the production of a number of cytokines from human peripheral blood mononuclear cells.[62] The cytokines included tumor necrosis factor-α (TNF-α) TNF-β, and interleukin-8. Antineoplastic regimens that denude and ulcerate the oral and gastrointestinal mucosa probably predispose to this syndrome. The situation is then complicated by selective overgrowth of microorganisms (e.g., viridans streptococci) that are resistant to trimethoprim-sulfamethoxazole or earlier fluoroquinolones such as ciprofloxacin. This overgrowth is also assisted by an alkaline gastric environment created by antacids or histamine type 2 (H$_2$) antagonists.[86] Other risk factors include profound neutropenia.

Bacteremia by *S. anginosus* group isolates may be caused by, or may cause, bacterial endocarditis.[88,89] It is estimated that members of this group represent between 3% and 15% of streptococcal isolates from patients with endocarditis.[3] The propensity for suppuration of these pathogens has resulted in the complication of myocardial abscess or metastatic abscess,[64,77,78,90,91] although these complications do not occur in all patients.[88] The endocarditis most often involves an abnormal heart valve, although the exact attachment mechanism is unknown. *S. anginosus* group strains have been shown to adhere to buccal epithelial cells and also to bind to fibronectin, which may contribute to their pathogenicity in endocarditis.[40-45]

Central Nervous System Infections

S. anginosus group organisms have a strikingly prominent association with brain abscesses and have been isolated in approximately 50% to 80% of these infections.[31,64,77,92] These organisms may be isolated in pure culture or mixed with anaerobes. Factors associated with brain abscesses caused by these isolates include congenital heart defects, sinusitis, otitis media, liver disease, and direct trauma. Members of this group have been found to have an affinity for the central nervous system of young mice.[93] Of the three members, *S. intermedius* appears to be the one most commonly isolated from brain abscesses. Although *S. intermedius* can be found in the mouth, it has been suggested that most brain abscesses caused by this pathogen originate from the intestine.[77] On rare occasions, *S. anginosus* group organisms cause meningitis; this often is preceded by trauma or purulent infection at another site.[94] Finally, these bacteria have been isolated from acute spondylodiskitis, spinal epidural abscesses, and subdural empyema.[69,75,95,96] Rapid surgical drainage is a critical prognostic factor for effective management of these spinal cord abscesses.

Abdominal Infections

Given that members of the *S. anginosus* group are considered commensal organisms of the intestinal tract, it is not surprising to find these pathogens causing infections within the abdominal cavity. Such infections include liver abscesses,[3,36,65,66,97-99] peritonitis,[3,36,65,66] pelvic abscesses,[3,66] subphrenic abscesses,[3,66] appendicitis,[100] abdominal wound infections,[3] and cholangitis.[3,65] The use of antimicrobial drugs with minimal or no activity against the *S. anginosus* group for prophylaxis or therapy involving the abdominal cavity has been associated with the development of infections by these organisms clinically[101] and experimentally.[102] Specifically, metronidazole alone or in combination with gentamicin appears to allow these bacteria to become pathogens. Infections caused by members of the *S. anginosus* group can be seen after abdominal surgery, particularly if prophylactic antibiotics do not cover these pathogens. The proclivity for liver abscess and bacteremia,[98] cholangitis,[65] and silent colonic cancer[99] must be appreciated. Finally, *S. anginosus*[10] and *S. constellatus*[11] are the species within the *S. anginosus* group most frequently recovered from infections in the abdominal cavity.

Thoracic Infections

The presence of *S. anginosus* group organisms in the oropharynx can lead to aspiration pneumonia followed by pulmonary complications such as lung abscess or pleural empyema, or both.[31,37,66,103-106] Such complications are particularly likely to occur with mixed pulmonary infections.[33-37,106] A retrospective study of lung abscesses and pleural empyemas caused by viridans streptococci revealed that the majority (68%) were caused by members of the *S. anginosus* group.[105] Predisposing factors to *S. anginosus* group pulmonary infections include male gender, previous pneumonia, alcoholism, and cancer.[103] Significant morbidity and mortality (death rates of 15% to 30%) has been associated with these infections. Management of pulmonary infections caused by the *S. anginosus* group must be aggressive.[107] Mediastinitis has also been reported.[108] *S. constellatus* and *S. anginosus* are the species of the group most frequently identified from respiratory tract infections.[10,11]

Miscellaneous Infections

A number of other infections caused by members of the *S. anginosus* group have been reported. These include osteomyelitis,[31,66] septic arthritis,[109] flexor sheath infection,[110] and subcutaneous abscess or cellulitis.[14,31,66,111] The latter condition has been described in drug addicts[31] and in patients with chronic hidradenitis suppurativa of the anogenital region.[112] Peritonsillar abscesses involving anaerobic microorganisms mixed with *S. anginosus* group members have been described.[6]

ANTIMICROBIAL THERAPY

Early studies reported that most members of the *S. anginosus* group had minimal inhibitory concentrations (MICs) to penicillin G of less than 0.06 μg/mL, with occasional strains resistant to greater than 1.0 μg/mL.[113,114] However, increasing resistance to penicillin G and other β-lactam agents attributable to altered penicillin-binding proteins has been reported.[115-119] In one study, 29% of viridans streptococci overall, including members of the *S. anginosus* group, were resistant to intermediate concentrations of penicillin G (MICs, 0.25 to 2 μg/mL) and 9% of all strains were resistant to high concentrations of penicillin G (MICs >4 μg/mL).[116] Another study noted emerging penicillin resistance among *S. anginosus* and *S. intermedius*.[117] Moreover, resistance to erythromycin and clindamycin has been described.[118,119] Other studies continue to report penicillin resistance in fewer than 2% of *S. anginosus* group isolates.[120-125] Nonetheless, the potential for penicillin and cephalosporin resistance clearly exists because of the horizontal transfer of genes among streptococci.[39,126] When penicillin resistance is seen, it is more common among *S. anginosus* and *S. intermedius* isolates. Although most strains of the *S. anginosus* group are relatively resistant to aminoglycosides, synergy with a β-lactam agent usually can be demonstrated. Therefore, the addition of an aminoglycoside to a β-lactam agent for treatment of endocarditis caused by members of the *S. anginosus* group is a reasonable practice, particularly for strains with intermediate MICs.

Clinically, infections caused by these streptococci have responded well to penicillin G and cephalosporins. Vancomycin and clindamycin have been useful in patients with β-lactam allergies. The recent increase in MICs to penicillin G suggests that initiation of penicillin G combined with gentamicin may be prudent. Alternatively, vancomycin could be used. Of the cephalosporins that are clinically available, cefepime, cefotaxime, and ceftriaxone have been noted to be superior in potency and spectrum for empirical coverage of patients at risk for streptococcal bacteremias.[127,128] Macrolides do not appear to be potent enough for such empirical therapy.[129] Newer quinolones and quinupristin-dalfopristin may prove useful; these agents have demonstrated comparable or superior bactericidal activity in comparison to penicillins against *S. anginosus* group and other viridans group streptococci tested.[130-132] Finally, it is important to remember that surgical drainage of abscesses may be needed as adjunctive therapy.

REFERENCES

1. Whiley RA, Beighton D. Emended description and recognition of *Streptococcus constellatus, Streptococcus intermedius,* and *Streptococcus anginosus* as distinct species. Int J Syst Bacteriol. 1991;41:1-5.
2. Ruoff KL, Whiley RA, Beighton D. Streptococcus. In: Murray PR, Baron EJ, Jorgenson JH, et al, eds. Manual of Clinical Microbiology. 8th ed. Washington: American Society for Microbiology Press; 2003:413-414.
3. Gossling J. Occurrence and pathogenicity of the *Streptococcus milleri* group. Rev Infect Dis. 1988;10:257-285.
4. Ruoff KL. *Streptococcus anginosus* ("*Streptococcus milleri*"): The unrecognized pathogen. Clin Microbiol Rev. 1988;1:102-108.
5. Whiley RA, Fraser HY, Hardie JM, et al. Phenotypic differentiation of *Streptococcus constellatus, Streptococcus intermedius,* and *Streptococcus anginosus* (the *Streptococcus milleri* group): Association with different body sites and clinical infections. J Clin Microbiol. 1990;28:1497-1501.
6. Whiley RA, Hall LMC, Hardie JM, Beighton D. A study of small colony beta-hemolytic, Lancefield group C streptococci within the anginosus group: Description of *Streptococcus constellatus* subsp. *pharyngis* subsp. nov associated with the human throat and pharyngitis. Int J Syst Bacteriol. 1999;49:1443-1449.
7. Clarridge JE III, Osting C, Jalali M, et al. Genotypic and phenotypic characterization of "*Streptococcus milleri*" group isolates from a Veterans Administration Hospital population. J Clin Microbiol. 1999;37:3681-3687.
8. Jacobs JA, Schot CS, Schouls LM. The *Streptococcus anginosus* group comprises five 16S rRNA ribogroups with different phenotypic characteristics and clinical relevance. Int J Syst Evol Microbiol. 2000;50:1073-1079.
9. Jacobs JA, Tjhie JH, Smeets MG, et al. Genotyping by amplified fragment length polymorphism analysis reveals persistence and recurrence of infection with *Streptococcus anginosus* group organisms. J Clin Microbiol. 2003;41:2862-2866.
10. Whiley RA, Beighton D, Winstanley TG, et al. *Streptococcus intermedius, Streptococcus constellatus,* and *Streptococcus anginosus* (the *Streptococcus milleri* group): Association with different body sites and clinical infections. J Clin Microbiol. 1992;30:243-244.
11. Clarridge JE III, Attori S, Musher DM, et al. *Streptococcus intermedius, Streptococcus constellatus,* and *Streptococcus anginosus* ("*Streptococcus milleri* group") are of different clinical importance and are not equally associated with abscess. Clin Infect Dis. 2001;32:1511-1515.
12. Brogan O, Malone J, Fox C, et al. Lancefield grouping and smell of caramel for presumptive identification and assessment of pathogenicity in the *Streptococcus milleri* group. J Clin Pathol. 1997;50:332-335.
13. Bergman S, Selig M, Collins MD, et al. "*Streptococcus milleri*" strains displaying a gliding type of motility. Int J Syst Bacteriol. 1995;45:235-239.
14. Ball LC, Parker MT. The cultural and biochemical characteristics of *Streptococcus milleri* in various body sites. J Clin Pathol. 1979;32:764-768.
15. Rubin LG, Kahn RA, Vellozzi EM, et al. False positive detection of group A *Streptococcus* antigen resulting from cross-reacting *Streptococcus intermedius* (*Streptococcus milleri* group). Pediatr Infect Dis J. 1996;15:715-717.
16. Piscitelli SC, Shwed J, Schreckenberger P, et al. *Streptococcus milleri* group: Renewed interest in an elusive pathogen. Eur J Clin Microbiol Infect Dis. 1992;11:491-498.
17. Belko J, Goldmann DA, Macone A, Zaidi AKM. Clinically significant infections with organisms of the *Streptococcus milleri* group. Pediatr Infect Dis. 2002;21:715-726.
18. Jacobs JA, Pietersen HG, Stobberingh EE, et al. *Streptococcus anginosus, Streptococcus constellatus* and *Streptococcus intermedius:* Clinical relevance, hemolytic and serologic characteristics. Am J Clin Pathol. 1995;104:547-553.
19. Jacobs JA, Schouten HC, Stobberingh EE, et al. Viridans streptococci isolated from the bloodstream: Relevance of species identification. Diagn Microbiol Infect Dis. 1995;22:267-273.
20. Hinnebusch CJ, Nikolai DM, Bruckner DA. Comparison of API Rapid Strep, Baxter Microscan Rapid Pos ID panel, BBL Minitek Differential Identification System, IDS RapID STR System and Vitek GPI to conventional biochemical tests for identification of viridans streptococci. Am J Clin Pathol. 1991;96:459-463.

21. Flynn CE, Ruoff KL. Identification of *"Streptococcus milleri"* group isolates to the species level with a commercially available rapid test system. J Clin Microbiol. 1995;33:2704-2706.

22. Sultana F, Kawamura Y, Hou XG, et al. Determination of 23S rRNA sequences from members of the genus *Streptococcus* and characterization of genetically distinct organisms previously identified as members of the *Streptococcus anginosus* group. FEMS Microbiol Lett. 1998;158:223-230.

23. Jacobs JA, Schot CS, Bunschoten AE, et al. Rapid species identification of *"Streptococcus milleri"* strains by line blot hybridization: Identification of a distinct 16S rRNA population closely related to *Streptococcus constellatus*. J Clin Microbiol. 1996;34:1717-1721.

24. Garnier F, Gerbaud G, Courvalin P, et al. Identification of clinically relevant viridans group streptococci to the species level by PCR. J Clin Microbiol. 1997;35:2337-2341.

25. Winkler KC, van Amerongen J. Bacteriologic results from 4,000 root canal cultures. Oral Surg Oral Med Oral Pathol. 1959;12:857-862.

27. Unsworth PF. The isolation of streptococci from human faeces. J Hyg Camb. 1980;85:153-164.

28. Pool PM, Wilson G. *Streptococcus milleri* in the appendix. J Clin Pathol. 1977;30:937.

29. Ahmet Z, Warren M, Houang ET. Species identification of members of the *Streptococcus milleri* group isolated from the vagina by ID 32 Strep system and differential characteristics. J Clin Microbiol. 1995;33:1592-1595.

30. Raymond J, Bergeret M, Francoual C, et al. Neonatal infection with *Streptococcus milleri*. Eur J Clin Microbiol. 1995;14:799-801.

31. Shlaes DM, Lerner PI, Wolinsky E, et al. Infection due to Lancefield group F and related streptococci (*S. milleri, S. anginosus*). Medicine (Baltimore). 1981;60:197-207.

32. Osawa R, Whiley RA. Effects of different acidulants on growth of *"Streptococcus milleri* group" strains isolated from various sites of the human body. Lett Appl Microbiol. 1995;20:263-267.

33. Shinzato T, Saito A. A mechanism of pathogenicity of *"Streptococcus milleri* group" in pulmonary infection: Synergy with an anaerobe. J Med Microbiol. 1994;40:118-123.

34. Young KA, Allaker RP, Hardie JM, et al. Interactions between *Eikenella corrodens* and *"Streptococcus milleri*-group" organisms: Possible mechanisms of pathogenicity in mixed infections. Antonie Van Leeuwenhoek. 1996;69:371-373.

35. Nagashima H, Takao A, Maeda N. Abscess forming ability of *Streptococcus milleri* group: Synergistic effect with *Fusobacterium nucleatum*. Microbiol Immunol. 1999;43:207-216.

36. Quinlivan D, Davis TM, Daly FJ, et al. Hepatic abscess due to *Eikenella corrodens* and *Streptococcus milleri:* Implications for antibiotic therapy. J Infect. 1996;33:47-48.

37. Shinzato T, Saito A. The *Streptococcus milleri* group as a cause of pulmonary infections. Clin Infect Dis. 1995;21(Suppl 3):S238-S243.

38. Jenkinson HF, Lamont RJ. Streptococcal adhesion and colonization. Crit Rev Oral Biol Med. 1997;8:175-200.

39. Dowson CG, Barcus V, King S, et al. Horizontal gene transfer and the evolution of resistance and virulence determinants in *Streptococcus*. Soc Appl Bacteriol Symp Ser. 1997;26:42-51.

40. Wilcox MD, Knox KW. Surface-associated properties of *Streptococcus milleri* group strains and their potential relation to pathogenesis. J Med Microbiol. 1990;31:259-270.

41. Wilcox MD, Oakey HJ, Harty DW, et al. Lancefield group C *Streptococcus milleri* group strains aggregate human platelets. Microb Pathog. 1994;16:451-457.

42. Wilcox MD. Potential pathogenic properties of members of the *"Streptococcus milleri"* group in relation to the production of endocarditis and abscesses. J Med Microbiol. 1995;43:405-410.

43. Kitada K, Inoue M, Kitano M. Infective endocarditis-inducing abilities of *"Streptococcus milleri"* group. Adv Exp Med Biol. 1997;418:161-163.

44. Kitada K, Inoue M, Kitano M. Experimental endocarditis induction and platelet aggregation by *Streptococcus anginosus, Streptococcus constellatus* and *Streptococcus intermedius*. FEMS Immunol Med Microbiol. 1997;19:25-32.

45. Toyoda K, Kusano N, Saito A. Pathogenicity of the *Streptococcus milleri* group in pulmonary infections. Kansenshogaku Zasshi. 1995;69:308-315.

46. Bohach GA, Stauffacher CV, Ohlendorf DH, et al. The staphylococcal and streptococcal pyrogenic toxin family. Adv Exp Med Biol. 1996;391:131-154.

47. Nagamune H, Ohnishi C, Katsuura A, et al. Intermedilysin: A cytolytic toxin specific for human cells of a *Streptococcus intermedius* isolated from human liver abscess. Adv Exp Med Biol. 1997;418:773-775.

48. Magamune H, Whiley RA, Goto T, et al. Distribution of intermedilysin gene among the anginosus group streptococci and correlation between intermedilysin production and deep-seated infection with *Streptococcus intermedius*. J Clin Microbiol. 2000;38:220-226.

49. Jacobs JA, Stobberingh EE. Hydrolytic enzymes of *Streptococcus anginosus, Streptococcus constellatus* and *Streptococcus intermedius* in relation to infection. Eur J Clin Microbiol Infect Dis. 1995;14:818-820.

50. Shain H, Homer KA, Aduse-Opoku J, et al. A conserved region of a hyaluronidase gene from *Streptococcus intermedius*. Adv Exp Med Biol. 1997;418:769-772.

51. Takao A, Nagashima H, Usui H, et al. Hyaluronidase activity in human pus for which *Streptococcus intermedius* was isolated. Mirobiol Immunol. 1997;41:795-798.

52. Homer K, Shain H, Beighton D. The role of hyaluronidase in growth of *Streptococcus intermedius* on hyaluronate. Adv Exp Med Biol. 1997;418:681-683.

53. Shain H, Homer KA, Beighton D. Degradation and utilisation of chondroitin sulphate by *Streptococcus intermedius*. J Med Microbiol. 1996;44:372-380.

54. Shain H, Homer KA, Beighton D. Purification and properties of a novel glycosaminoglycan depolymerase for *Streptococcus intermedius*. J Med Microbiol. 1996;44:381-389.

55. Byers Hl, Homer KA, Beighton D. Sialic acid utilisation by viridans streptococci. Adv Exp Med Biol. 1997;418:713-716.

56. Arala-Chaves MP, Higerd TB, Porto MT, et al. Evidence for the synthesis and release of strongly immunosuppressive noncytotoxic substances by *Streptococcus intermedius*. J Clin Invest. 1979;64:871-883.

57. Arala-Chaves MP, Ribeiro AS, Santarem MMG, et al. Strong mitogenic effect for murine B lymphocytes of an immunosuppressor substance released by *Streptococcus intermedius*. Infect Immun. 1986;54:543-548.

58. Lebrun L, Guibert M, Wallet P, et al. Human Fc(g) receptors for differentiation in throat cultures of group C *"Streptococcus equisimilis"* with group C *"Streptococcus milleri."* J Clin Microbiol. 1986;24:705-707.

59. Proft T, Fraser J. Superantigens: Just like peptides only different. J Exp Med. 1998;187:819-821.

60. Rago JV, Schlievert PM. Mechanisms of pathogenesis of staphylococcal and streptococcal superantigens. Curr Topics Microbiol Immunol. 1998;225:81-97.

61. Norrby-Teglund A, Thulin P, Gan BS, et al. Evidence for superantigen involvement in severe group A streptococcal tissue infections. J Infect Dis. 2001;184:853-860.

62. Soto A, Evans TJ, Cohen J. Proinflammatory cytokine production by human peripheral blood mononuclear cells stimulated with cell-free supernatants of viridans streptococci. Cytokine. 1996;8:300-304.

63. Toyoda K, Kusano N, Saito A. Pathogenicity of the *Steptococcus milleri* group in pulmonary infections—effect on phagocytic killing by human polymorphonuclear neutrophils. Kansenshogaku Zasshi. 1995;69:308-315.

64. Wanahita A, Goldsmith EA, Musher DM, et al. Interaction between human polymorphonuclear leukocytes and *Streptococcus milleris* group bacteria. J Infect Dis. 2002;185:85-90.

65. Murray HW, Gross KC, Masur H, et al. Serious infections caused by *Streptococcus milleri*. Am J Med. 1978;64:759-764.

66. Molina J-M, Leport C, Bure A, et al. Clinical and bacterial features of infections caused by *Streptococcus milleri*. Scand J Infect Dis. 1991;23:659-666.

67. Wickremesinghe R, Russell C. Viridans streptococci associated with periapical dental abscesses. Infection. 1976;4:196-230.

68. Feigenbaum JA, Stein WE. Infections of the cervical disc space after dental extractions. J Neurol Neurosurg Psychiatry. 1974;37:1361-1365.

69. Dhariwal DK, Patton DW, Gregory MC. Epidural spinal abscess following dental extraction—a rare and potentially fatal complication. Br J Oral Maxillofac Surg. 2003;41:56-58.

70. Bancescu G, Lofthus B, Hofstad T, et al. Isolation and characterization of *"Streptococcus milleri"* group stains from oral and maxillofacial infections. Adv Exp Med Biol. 1997;418:165-167.

71. Han JK, Kerschner JE. *Streptococcus milleri:* An organism for head and neck infections and abscess. Arch Otolaryngol Head Neck Surg. 2001;127:650-654.

72. El-Guizaoui AE, Watanakunakorn C. Acute pansinusitis with bacteremia due to a beta-hemolytic group C streptococcus: *Streptococcus milleri*. South Med J. 1997;90:1248-1249.

73. Jones RL, Vioares NS, Chavda SV, et al. Intracranial complications of sinusitis: The need for aggressive management. J Laryngol Otol. 1995;109:1061-1062.

74. Watkins LM, Pasternack MS, Banks M, et al. Bilateral cavernous sinus thromboses and intraorbital abscesses secondary to *Streptococcus milleri*. Ophthalmology. 2003;110:569-574.

75. Greenlee JE. Subdural empyema. Curr Treat Options Neurol. 2003;5:13-22.

76. Flanagan PG, Mills RG. Fulminant septicemia due to *Streptococcus milleri* infection in a previously healthy adult. Eur J Clin Microbiol Infect Dis. 1994;13:274-278.

77. Libertin CR, Hermans PE, Washington JA II. Beta hemolytic group F streptococcal bacteremia: A study and review of the literature. Rev Infect Dis. 1985;7:498-503.

78. Casariego E, Rodriguez A, Corredoira JC, et al. Prospective study of *Streptococcus milleri* bacteremia. Eur J Clin Microbiol Infect Dis. 1996;15:194-200.

79. Salavert M, Gomez L, Rodgriguez-Carballeira M, et al. Seven-year review of bacteremia caused by *Streptococcus milleri* and other viridans streptococci. Eur J Clin Microbiol Infect Dis. 1996;15:365-371.

80. Bert F, Bariou-Lancelin M, Lambert-Zechovsky N. Clinical significance of bacteremia involving the *"Streptococcus milleri"* group: 51 cases and review. Clin Infect Dis. 1998;27:385-387.

81. Cohen J, Donnelly JP, Worsley AM, et al. Septicemia caused by viridans streptococci in neutropenic patients with leukaemia. Lancet. 1983;2:1452-1454.

82. Awada A, van der Auwera P, Meunier F, et al. Streptococcal and enterococcal bacteremia in patients with cancer. Clin Infect Dis. 1992;15:33-48.

83. Pfaller MA, Jones RN, Marshall SA, et al. Nosocomial streptococcal blood stream infections in the SCOPE Program: Species occurrence and antimicrobial resistance. Diagn Microbiol Infect Dis. 1997;29:259-263.

84. Hamoudi AC, Hribar MM, Marcon MJ, et al. Clinical relevance of viridans and nonhemolytic streptococci isolated from blood and cerebrospinal fluid in a pediatric population. Am J Clin Pathol. 1990;93:270-272.

85. Weisman SJ, Scoopo FJ, Johnson GM, et al. Septicemia in pediatric oncology patients: The significance of viridans streptococcal infections. J Clin Oncol. 1990;8:453-459.

86. Elting LS, Bodey GP, Keefe BH. Septicemia and shock syndrome due to viridans streptococci: A case-control study of predisposing factors. Clin Infect Dis. 1992;14:1201-1207.

87. Nagamune H, Ohnishi C, Katsuura A, et al. Intermedilysin: A novel cytotoxin specific for human cells secreted by *Streptococcus intermedius* UNS46. Infect Immun. 1996;64:3093-3100.

88. Sussman JI, Baron EJ, Tenenbaum MJ, et al. Viridans streptococcal endocarditis: Clinical, microbiological, and echocardiographic correlations. J Infect Dis. 1986;154:597-603.

89. Lefort A, Lortholary O, Casassus P, et al. Comparison between adult endocarditis due to beta-hemolytic streptococci (serogroups A, B, C, and G) and *Streptococcus milleri:* A multicenter study in France. Arch Intern Med 2002;162:2450-2456.

90. Levandowski RA. *Streptococcus milleri* endocarditis complicated by myocardial abscess. South Med J. 1985;78:892-893.

91. Hurle A, Nistal JF, Gutierrez JA, et al. Isolated apical intracavitary left ventricular abscess in a normal heart: A rare complication of *Streptococcus milleri* endocarditis. Cardiovasc Surg. 1996;4:61-63.

92. Mathisen GE, Johnson JP. Brain abscess. Clin Infect Dis. 1997;25:763-781.

93. DeLouvois J, Gortvai P, Hurley R. Affinity of certain streptococci for the central nervous system. J Neurol Neurosurg Psychiatry. 1974;37:1281-1282.

94. Cabellos C, Viladrich PF, Corredoira J, et al. Streptococcal meningitis in adult patients: Current epidemiology and clinical spectrum. Clin Infect Dis. 1999;28:1104-1108.

95. Gelfand MS, Bakhtian BJ, Simmons BP. Spinal sepsis due to *Streptococcus milleri:* Two cases and review. Rev Infect Dis. 1991;13:559-563.

96. Balsam LB, Shepherd GM, Ruoff KL. *Streptococcus anginosus* spondylodiskitis. Clin Infect Dis. 1997;24:93-94.

97. Gelfand MS, Hodgkiss T, Simmons BP. Multiple hepatic abscesses caused by *Streptococcus milleri* in association with an intrauterine device. Rev Infect Dis. 1989;11:983-987.

98. Corredoira J, Casariego E, Moreno C, et al. Prospective study of *Streptococcus milleri* hepatic abscess. Eur J Clin Microbiol Infect Dis. 1998;17:556-560.

99. Tzur T, Liberman S, Felzenstein I, et al. Liver abscesses caused by *Streptococcus milleri:* An uncommon presenting sign of silent colonic cancer. Isr Med Assoc. 2003;5:206-207.

100. Hardwick RH, Taylor A, Thompson MH, et al. Association between *Streptococcus milleri* and abscess formation after appendicitis. Ann R Coll Surg Engl. 2000;82:24-26.

101. Tresadern JC, Farrand RJ, Irving MH. *Streptococcus milleri* and surgical sepsis. Ann R Coll Surg Engl. 1983;65:78-79.

102. Onderdonk AB, Cisneros R. Comparison of clindamycin and metronidazolefor the treatment of experimental intra-abdominal sepsis produced by *Bacteroidesfragilis* and *Streptococcus intermedius.* Curr Ther Res Clin Exp. 1985;38:893-898.

103. Wong CA, Donald F, Macfarlane JT. *Streptococcus milleri* pulmonary disease: A review and clinical description of 25 patients. Thorax. 1995;50:1093-1096.

104. Marinella MA, Harrington GD, Standiford TJ. Empyema necessitans due to *Streptococcus milleri.* Clin Infect Dis. 1996;23:203-204.

105. Jerng JS, Hsueh PR, Teng LJ, et al. Empyema thoracis and lung abscesses caused by viridans streptococci. Am J Respir Crit Care Med. 1997;156:1508-1514.

106. Porta G, Rodriguez-Carballeira M, Gomez L, et al. Thoracic infection caused by *Streptococcus milleri.* Eur Respir J. 1998;12:357-362.

107. Galea JL, De Souza A, Beggs D, et al. The surgical management of empyema thoraci. J R Coll Surg Edinb. 1997;42:15-18.

108. Shishido H, Watanabe K, Matsumoto K, et al. Primary purulent mediastinitis due to *Streptococcus milleri.* Respiration. 1997;64:313-315.

109. Houston BD, Crouch ME, Finch RG. *Streptococcus MG-intermedius (Streptococcus milleri)* septic arthritis in a patient with rheumatoid arthritis. J Rheumatol. 1980;7:89-92.

110. Lunn JV, Rahman KJ, Macey AC. *Streptococcus milleri* infection. J Hand Surg. 2001;26:56-57.

111. Jackson DS, Welch DF, Pickett DA, et al. Suppurative infections of children caused by non-beta-hemolytic members of the *Streptococcus milleri* group. Pediatr Infect Dis J. 1995;14:80-82.

112. Highet AS, Warren RE, Staughton RCD, et al. *Streptococcus milleri* causing treatable infection in perineal hidradenitis suppurativa. Br J Dermatol. 1980;103:375-382.

113. Bourgault A, Wilson WR, Washington JA. Antimicrobial susceptibilities of species of viridans streptococci. J Infect Dis. 1979;140:316-321.

114. Tillotson GS, Ganguli LA. Antibiotic susceptibilities of clinical strains of *Streptococcus milleri* and related streptococci. J Antimicrob Chemother. 1984;14:557-560.

115. Faber BF, Eliopoulos GM, Ward JI, et al. Multiply resistant viridans streptococci: Susceptibility to β-lactam antibiotics and comparison of penicillin-binding protein patterns. Antimicrob Agents Chemother. 1983;24:702-705.

116. Dorn GV, Ferraro MJ, Brueggemann AB, et al. Emergence of high rates of antimicrobial resistance among viridans group streptococci in the United States. Antimicrob Agents Chemother. 1996;34:891-894.

117. Bantar C, Canigia LF, Relloso S, et al. Species belonging to the "*Streptococcus milleri*" group: Antimicrobial susceptibility and comparative prevalence in significant clinical specimens. J Clin Microbiol. 1996;34: 2020-2022.

118. Limia A, Jimenez ML, Alarcon T, Lopez-Brea M. Five-year analysis of antimicrobial susceptibility of the *Streptococcus milleri* group. Eur J Clin Microbiol Infect Dis. 1999;18:440-444.

119. Yamamoto N, Kubota T, Tohyama M, et al. Trends in antimicrobial susceptibility of the *Streptococcus milleri* group. J Infect Chemother. 2002;8:134-137.

120. Potgieter E, Carmichael M, Kornhof HJ, et al. In vitro antimicrobial susceptibility of viridans streptococci isolated from blood cultures. Eur J Clin Microbiol Infect Dis. 1992;11:543-546.

121. Bantar C, Fernandez Canigia L, Relloso S, et al. Species belonging to the "*Streptococcus milleri*" group: Antimicrobial susceptibility and comparative prevalence in significant clinical specimens. J Clin Microbiol. 1996;34:2020-2022.

122. Renneberg J, Niemann LL, Gutschik E. Antimicrobial susceptibility of 278 streptococcal blood isolates to seven antimicrobial agents. J Antimicrob Chemother. 1997;39:135-140.

123. Tuohy M, Washington JA. Antimicrobial susceptibility of viridans group streptococci. Diagn Microbiol Infect Dis. 1997;29:277-280.

124. Aracil B, Gomez-Garces JL, Alos JL. A study of susceptibility of 100 clinical isolates belonging to the *Streptococcus milleri* group to 16 cephalosporins. J Antimicrob Chemother. 1999;43:399-402.

125. Tracy M, Wanahita A, Shuhatovich Y, et al. Antibiotic susceptibilities of genetically characterized *Streptococcus milleri* group strains. Antimicrob Agents Chemother. 2001;45:1511-1514.

126. Reichmann P, Konig A, Linares J, et al. A global gene pool for high-level cephalosporin resistance in commensal *Streptococcus* species and *Streptococcus pneumoniae.* J Infect Dis. 1997;176:1001-1012.

127. Pfaller MA, Jones RN. In vitro evaluation of contemporary beta-lactam drugs tested against viridans group and beta-haemolytic streptococci. Diagn Microbiol Infect Dis. 1997;27:151-154.

128. Pfaller MA, Marshall SA, Jones RN. In vitro activity of cefepime and ceftazidime against 197 nosocomial blood stream isolates of streptococci: A multicenter sample. Diagn Microbiol Infect Dis. 1997;29:273-276.

129. Alcaide F, Carratala J, Linares J, et al. In vitro activities of eight macrolide antibiotics and RP-59500 (quinupristin-dalforpristin) against viridans streptococci isolated from blood of neutropenic cancer patients. Antimicrob Agents Chemother. 1996;40: 2117-2120.

130. Biedenbach DJ, Jones RN. The comparative antimicrobial activity of levofloxacin tested against 350 clinical isolates of streptococci. Diagn Microbiol Infect Dis. 1996;25:47-51.

131. Pfaller MA, Jones RN. Comparative antistreptococcal activity of two newer fluoroquinolones, levofloxacin and sparfloxacin. Diagn Microbiol Infect Dis. 1997;199-201.

132. Schouten MA, Hoogkamp-Korstanje JA. Comparative in-vitro activities of quinupristin-dalfopristin against gram-positive bloodstream isolates. J Antimicrob Chemother. 1997;40:213-219.

CHAPTER **202**

Corynebacterium diphtheriae

ROB ROY MACGREGOR

The name *diphtheria* was coined by Bretonneau from the Greek root for "leather," describing the tough pharyngeal membrane that is the hallmark of the disease. The definition of diphtheria as a unique syndrome, the explanation of its pathogenesis, and its subsequent control parallel the development of the fields of pathology, bacteriology, and immunology. During the first half of the 20th century, it was a major worldwide health problem, then yielded to scientifically grounded vigorous public health control measures. Now, since 1990, it has reemerged in epidemic form in the former Soviet Union and other areas where relaxed immunization practices and social disorganization have allowed its escape from control.

HISTORY

Although clinical descriptions of sore throat, membrane production, and death by suffocation appear in Hippocratic writings, epidemics of "throat distemper" are not described until the 16th century.[1] A major epidemic occurred in New England in the early 1700s, killing an estimated 2.5% of the total population, and up to one third of all children. Thereafter, similar epidemics were reported at approximately 25-year intervals throughout the 18th and 19th centuries. Diphtheria was not clearly differentiated from other upper respiratory illnesses viewed collectively as "croup" or "distemper" until an epidemic in southern France in 1821 when the clinician-pathologist Pierre Bretonneau first described its unique clinical characteristics. However, arguments over the differentiation between diphtheria, croup, and other throat distempers continued through most of the 1800s.[2]

The first major advance occurred in 1883 when Klebs described chain-forming cocci and bacilli in microscopic sections of diphtheritic membranes. The following year, working in Koch's laboratory in Berlin, Friedrich Loeffler first isolated the diphtheria bacillus in pure culture, aided by a culture medium of his own design that is still used today. He then demonstrated that the organism could reproduce the disease in guinea pigs, thus fulfilling his mentor's postulates for proof that it was the etiologic agent for diphtheria.[3] Using his special culture medium, he demonstrated that healthy individuals could carry the organism asymptomatically in their throats, thus establishing the carrier state as an important phenomenon in the maintenance and spread of the disease. He also noted that the organisms remained in the membrane without invading the tissues of the throat or more distant sites, and theorized that the neurologic and cardiologic manifestations of the disease were caused by a toxic substance elaborated by the organism. In 1888, Roux and Yersin, working at the Pasteur Institute, proved him correct by demonstrating that bacteria-free filtrates of cultures of diphtheria bacilli were able to kill guinea pigs. Two years later, von Behring, also working in Koch's laboratory, demonstrated that antiserum against the toxin was capable of protecting infected animals from death following infection. Then in 1894, after showing that horses were the most efficient animals at producing antitoxin, Roux reported that its administration reduced mortality from diphtheria among foundlings in Paris from 51% to 24%.

In 1913, Schick reported that an individual's local reaction to injection of toxin into the skin could be used to predict susceptibility to infection (a negative reaction indicated presence of protective antitoxin antibodies). At the same time, Theobald Smith and von Behring successfully immunized children with a toxin-antitoxin mixture, and in 1923, Ramon, at the Pasteur Institute, found that exposure of toxin to formalin and heat rendered it nontoxic to recipients while retaining the ability to induce an antibody response. The following year, clinical trials showed that injection of this "toxoid" induced a high level of protection among recipients. Problems of antigenic standardization, determining optimal dosage, frequency of administration, needs for boosting, and so forth, delayed widespread immunization with toxoid, but between 1930 and 1945 most Western countries established intensive programs of childhood immunization. The result was a dramatic fall in the incidence of diphtheria, from approximately 200,000 in the United States in 1921 to zero to two cases yearly at present. During the 1950s, Freeman, Groman, Barksdale, Pappenheimer, and others demonstrated that toxin production by *Corynebacterium diphtheriae* depended on the presence of a lysogenic β-phage, and during the following decade, the mechanism by which toxin inhibited protein synthesis was elucidated.[4-6] By the 1980s diphtheria had become a rare occurrence in most countries that had effective immunization programs, but in 1990, a large epidemic of diphtheria began in the former Soviet Union and extended to eastern Europe and parts of Asia. The reestablishment of vigorous immunization policies and other public health measures after the peak of the epidemic in 1994 is again controlling this ancient scourge.[7]

THE PATHOGEN

Corynebacterium diphtheriae is a nonsporulating, unencapsulated, nonmotile, pleomorphic gram-positive bacillus. Its name is derived from the Greek *korynee*, or "club," referring to its clubbed ends, and *diphtheria*, meaning "leather hide," for the characteristic leathery pharyngeal membrane that it provokes. When inoculated on the nutritionally inadequate medium devised by Loeffler, consisting of a heat-coagulated mixture of 75% serum and 25% broth, it initially outgrows other throat flora; plates therefore should be inspected for growth at 12 to 18 hours. The characteristic metachromatic granules and "Chinese character" palisading morphology that differentiate it from other corynebacteria are displayed more prominently on smears taken from colonies grown on this medium than in direct smears from clinical specimens. Alternatively, selective media containing potassium tellurite inhibit many of the normal throat flora and identify any *C. diphtheriae* present as gray-black colonies containing reduced tellurite. The species is subdivided into three types—*gravis, intermedius,* and *mitis*—based on differing colonial morphology on tellurite agar, fermentation reactions, and hemolytic potential. Modern molecular techniques have proven to be more sensitive in recent outbreaks for tracking different strains: ribotyping, which is the use of restriction endonucleases to detect polymorphisms of rRNA genes; pulsed field gel electrophoresis analysis of genomic DNA; and multilocus enzyme electrophoresis of organism sonicates have shown that an epidemic clone of *C. diphtheriae* emerged in Russia in 1990 and became increasingly common as the epidemic progressed.[8,9] An International *C. diphtheriae* Ribotype Database has been established at the Pasteur Institute, Paris, France, curated by Prof. Patrick Grimont, and contains more than 80 distinct *Bst*EII ribotypes of toxigenic and nontoxigenic *C. diphtheriae* submitted from laboratories throughout the world.[10]

Exotoxin production by *C. diphtheriae* depends on the presence of a lysogenic β-phage, which carries the gene encoding for toxin *(tox+)*.[4,6] In its lysogenic phase, the phage's circular DNA integrates into the host bacteria's genetic material as a prophage, with the result that the host cell now can express the gene necessary for synthesis of the polypeptide toxin. When induced by stimuli such as ultraviolet light, the phage enters a lytic cycle, destroying the host cell and releasing new β-phage. Strains of *C. diphtheriae* lacking lysogenic phage do not produce toxin, but they can be converted to toxigenicity in the laboratory by infection with the lysogenic tox+ phage ("lysogenization"). Evidence has been found that such conversion also occurs in nature.[11] Even though the frequency of carriage of tox+ lysogenic *C. diphtheriae* currently is very low in the West, there is an ongoing risk that resident nontoxigenic strains could become lysogenized by introduction of a β-phage–bearing strain from another part of the world. Significant toxin production requires, in addition to the *tox+* gene, that bacterial growth be slowed by exhaustion of iron in the environment. Historically, toxigenicity of individual *C. diphtheriae* strains was demonstrated in vivo by lethality in guinea pigs, but this has been replaced by more rapid in vitro tests (see "Diagnosis").

EPIDEMIOLOGY

Humans are the only known reservoir for *C. diphtheriae*. The primary modes of spread are via airborne respiratory droplets or direct contact with either respiratory secretions or exudate from infected skin lesions. Fomites can play a role in transmission, and epidemics have been caused by contaminated milk. Most respiratory tract disease occurs in the colder months in temperate climates, associated with crowded indoor living conditions and hot dry air. Asymptomatic respiratory carriage is important in perpetuating both endemic and epidemic diphtheria, and immunization reduces an individual's likelihood of being a carrier. Current reservoirs for disease are obscure. In endemic conditions, 3% to 5% of healthy individuals may harbor the organism in their throats,[12] but in the West, where the disease has become very uncommon, isolation of the organism from healthy individuals has become extremely rare. Skin infection, once thought to be a problem primarily in tropical environments, has caused several recent epidemics in Europe and North America among people who abuse alcohol and various disadvantaged groups.[13,14] Thus skin carriage of *C. diphtheriae* can act as a silent reservoir for the organism, and it has been found that person-to-person spread from infected skin sites is more efficient than from the respiratory tract.[15,16]

The incidence and pattern of diphtheria in the Western world has changed dramatically in the last 50 to 75 years. From 1921 to 1924, it was the leading cause of death among Canadian children aged 2 to 14 years. Since then, the incidence has decreased steadily (Fig. 202-1), to the point where diphtheria is a rare event. For example, 147,991 cases were reported in the United States in 1920 (151 cases/100,000 population), and 5 or fewer since 1980 (0.002/100,000).[17] From the 1960s to 1990, similar decreases occurred in Europe,[18,19] and, less dramatically, worldwide, although the disease remained endemic in many parts of the Third World (e.g., Brazil, Nigeria, Eastern Mediterranean region, the Indian subcontinent, Indonesia, and the Philippines).[20] Moreover, pockets of skin and pharyngeal colonization and disease continue to be identified among Native American groups, destitute inner city dwellers, substance abusers, and homosexual men, giving rise to concern that

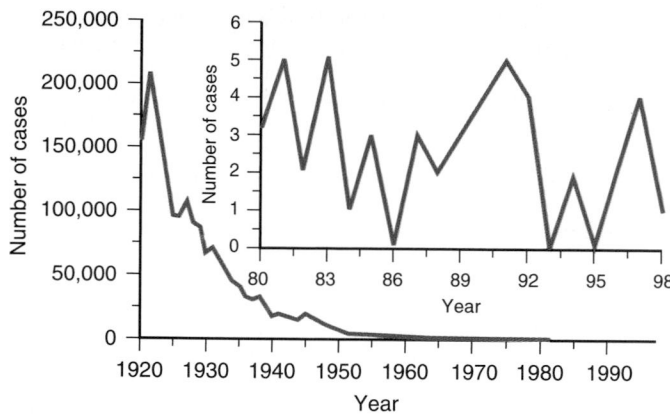

FIGURE 202-1. Annual incidence of diphtheria in the United States, 1920-1998. *(From Golaz A, Hardy IR, Strebel P, et al. Epidemic diphtheria in the Newly Independent States of the former Soviet Union: Implications for diphtheria control in the United States. J Infect Dis 2000;181[Suppl 1]:S237-S243.)*

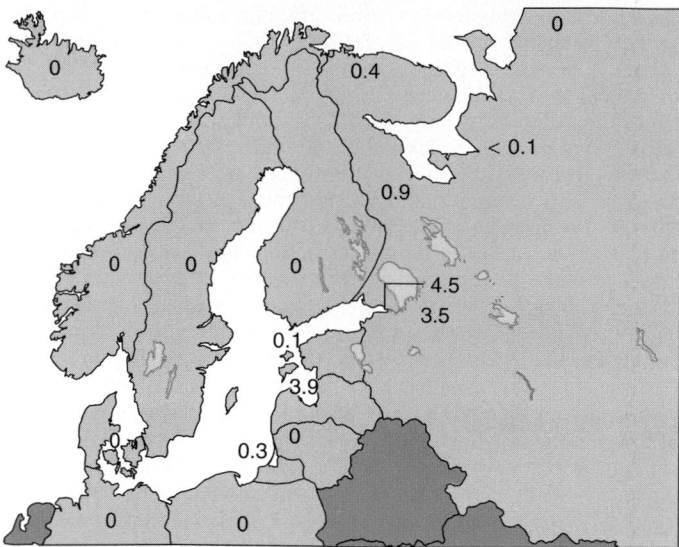

FIGURE 202-3. Incidence of diphtheria in 2001 per 100,000 population, Baltic Sea Region. Saint Petersburg (4.5/100,000) is designated by the leader line. The Leningrad Oblast is designated as 3.5/100,000, and Latvia as 3.9/100,000. *(From Blystad H, Blad J, Giesecke J. Surveillance and trends of priority infectious diseases in the Baltic Sea Region. Epinorth: Bull Network Commun Dis Contr N Eur 2002;3:62.)*

outbreaks could occur, particularly among adults in the West, where the proportion of adults with protective antibody levels is as low as 50%.[21]

Beginning in 1990, an epidemic of diphtheria began in Russia (Fig. 202-2) and swiftly spread to all countries of the Newly Independent States (NIS).[7,22] In 1995, 50,425 cases were reported in the Russian Federation, for a yearly rate of 17.3/100,000.[22] WHO and UNICEF formulated a strategic plan to control the epidemic, including (1) mass immunization with at least one dose of toxoid to the whole population, (2) early detection and proper management of cases, and (3) early identification and proper management of close contacts. In response, new cases in the Russian Federation declined from 20,215 in 1996, to 7196 in 1997, and to 1377 in 2001 (0.6/100,000 since 1999).[23] However, a surge of cases in the Baltic Region, centering in Latvia and St. Petersburg, is a warning that pockets of disease remain a risk[24] (Fig. 202-3). A defining characteristic of the epidemic has been that half or more of all cases have occurred among those 15 years of age or older, suggesting that the young remained relatively well protected by the high rates of infant immunization operative in the 1980s, but that the older population were vulnerable because they had either not been vaccinated as children, or their protective antibody levels had faded in the absence of subsequent boosting by vaccine or colonization.[7,21,25,26]

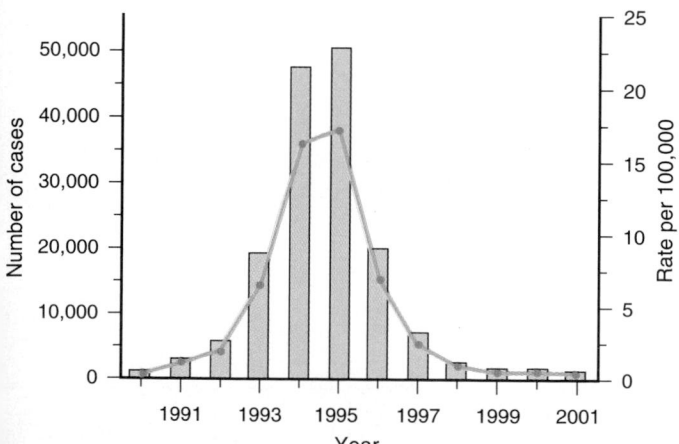

FIGURE 202-2. Number of reported cases of diphtheria and rate per 100,000 population in the Russian Federation and the Baltic states, 1990-2001. Bars represent the total yearly number of cases, and the connected dots represent the yearly rate per 100,000 people.

When it was common in the West, diphtheria affected primarily children under 15 years of age, but recent outbreaks have also involved unimmunized or poorly immunized adults, particularly the urban and rural poor. Recent reports have cited pharyngeal carriage of nontoxigenic strains in homosexual men[27] and invasive disease in intravenous drug users.[28] Minority racial groups have had attack rates 5 to 20 times higher than those of whites. Cases in the United States have been distributed primarily in the Southern and Pacific Northwest states, but sporadic cases have been reported throughout the country.[17,29] For example, in 1996, a focus of toxigenic diphtheria was discovered among Native Americans in South Dakota, which by molecular subtyping methods was found to have been endemic in the area since the 1970s. Enhanced surveillance of patients in this community with upper respiratory symptoms showed that almost 4% of them were carrying toxigenic *C. diphtheriae*.[30,31]

Although immunized individuals can still develop clinical diphtheria, prior immunization reduces the frequency and severity of disease: in the United States between 1959 and 1970, two thirds of reported cases had received no immunization, 13% more had had one to two doses of toxoid, and only 19% reported receiving three or more doses and could be considered fully immunized.[29] Among cases reported since 1980, *none* of the individuals were fully immunized.[17] Disease was considered severe in 25% of unimmunized patients, versus 6.3% of those fully immunized. Nineteen percent of unimmunized patients died, compared with 1.3% among those fully immunized; even partial immunization reduced morbidity and mortality by more than 50%. The benefit of prior immunization has also been demonstrated in the recent Russian epidemic.[32,33]

The full explanation for the dramatic decrease in diphtheria's incidence in immunized populations is not evident. Immunization with toxoid is generally thought to attenuate only the local and systemic effects of toxin without preventing local colonization with the organism. If so, carriage would be expected to remain high in the population, and epidemics should be an ongoing occurrence among the sizable proportion believed to be inadequately immunized. However, disease has become rare, and evidence points to an extremely low incidence of carrier state, despite results from the Third National Health & Nutrition Examination Survey, 1988-1994, which showed what are considered to be subprotective levels of serum antitoxin in 40% of the overall population.[34] The percentage with protective antibody decreased with increasing age, and only 30% of men aged 60 to 69 years were thought to have protective levels. In 1985, the U.S. preschool immunization rate was only 64.9% for diphtheria-pertussis-tetanus (DPT).[35] Fortunately, the 2001 National Immunization Survey showed that 82% of children 19 to 35 months of age had received at least four doses of DPT vaccine, although the state-specific coverage varied from 91.7% down to 74.1%.[36] Several factors may contribute to the current low incidence of disease: first, although unproved, historical evidence suggests that diphtheria has occurred in cycles that include gaps of 100 years or more.[1] Second, organisms isolated from immunized individuals are less likely to be toxigenic than are those from unimmunized carriers (64% versus 94%).[34] If toxin production confers no advantage to the organism in an immunized host, its metabolic cost would put toxigenic organisms at a selective disadvantage, and so loss of this attribute might be predicted.[5] Third, some experts believe that the local elaboration of toxin, in the absence of antibody, enhances an organism's ability to colonize. Immunization with toxoid could counteract this selective advantage of toxigenic strains. Fourth, some virulence factor(s) other than toxin production may exist. For example, in a recent outbreak in Sweden, investigators used genetic probes to demonstrate that all clinical cases were caused by a single strain, although several different toxigenic strains were present in the population.[37] Finally, protection may correlate with lower serum concentrations of antitoxin antibody, or other immune mechanisms may be protective that are not measured. To explain the absence of diphtheria in the West and the occurrence of the recent epidemic in the NIS, the following model has been proposed[21,22,25,33]: absence of an effective immunization program allows for high carriage rates of toxigenic strains which leads to high rates of infant disease; survivors in such populations are continually immunized by adult colonization with toxigenic strains, which explains low adult disease rates. Pediatric immunization programs reduce carriage rates of toxigenic strains because toxin production does not provide an advantage to the organism, and even nontoxigenic strain carriage falls. As a result, adults lose the opportunity for natural antibody boosting from asymptomatic carriage, and so protective antibody levels wane in the adult population immunized only in childhood. Fortunately, good pediatric immunization programs appear to be sufficient to keep toxigenic strains from circulating and causing adult disease. Ultimately, if pediatric programs lapse, the population then contains both vulnerable children and adults, a situation that promotes epidemics. Thus, the public health strategy must be to maintain pediatric programs with greater than 90% immunization rates, and to strongly promote periodic adult boosters.

PATHOGENESIS

C. diphtheriae is not a very invasive organism, ordinarily remaining in the superficial layers of the respiratory mucosa and skin lesions, where it can induce a mild inflammatory reaction in the local tissue. The major virulence of *C. diphtheriae* results from the action of its potent exotoxin, which inhibits protein synthesis in mammalian cells but not in bacteria. The 62,000-dalton polypeptide toxin is comprised of two segments: B, which binds to specific receptors on susceptible cells, and A, the active segment. Following proteolytic cleavage of the bound molecule, segment A enters the cell, where it catalyzes inactivation of the transfer RNA (tRNA) translocase, "elongation factor 2," present in eukaryotic cells but not in bacteria. Loss of this enzyme prevents the interaction of messenger RNA and tRNA, stopping further addition of amino acids to developing polypeptide chains.[38] The toxin affects all cells in the body, but the most prominent effects are on the heart (myocarditis), nerves (demyelination), and kidneys (tubular necrosis). Diphtheria toxin is extremely potent: a single molecule can stop protein synthesis in a cell within several hours, and 0.1 μg/kg will kill susceptible animals.

Within the first few days of respiratory tract infection, toxin elaborated locally induces a dense necrotic coagulum composed of fibrin, leukocytes, erythrocytes, dead respiratory epithelial cells, and organisms (Fig. 202-4). Removal of this adherent gray-brown "pseudomembrane" reveals a bleeding edematous submucosa. The membrane can be local (tonsillar, pharyngeal, nasal), or extend widely, forming a cast of the pharynx and tracheobronchial tree. The underlying soft tissue edema and cervical adenitis can be intense, and, particularly in the proportionally smaller airways of children, can cause respiratory embarrassment and a "bull neck" appearance. In both adults and children,

FIGURE 202-4. Diphtheria involving a pharyngeal tonsil. The membrane-tissue junction is clearly marked by intense cellular infiltration. *(From Moore RA. A Textbook of Pathology. Philadelphia: WB Saunders; 1944.)*

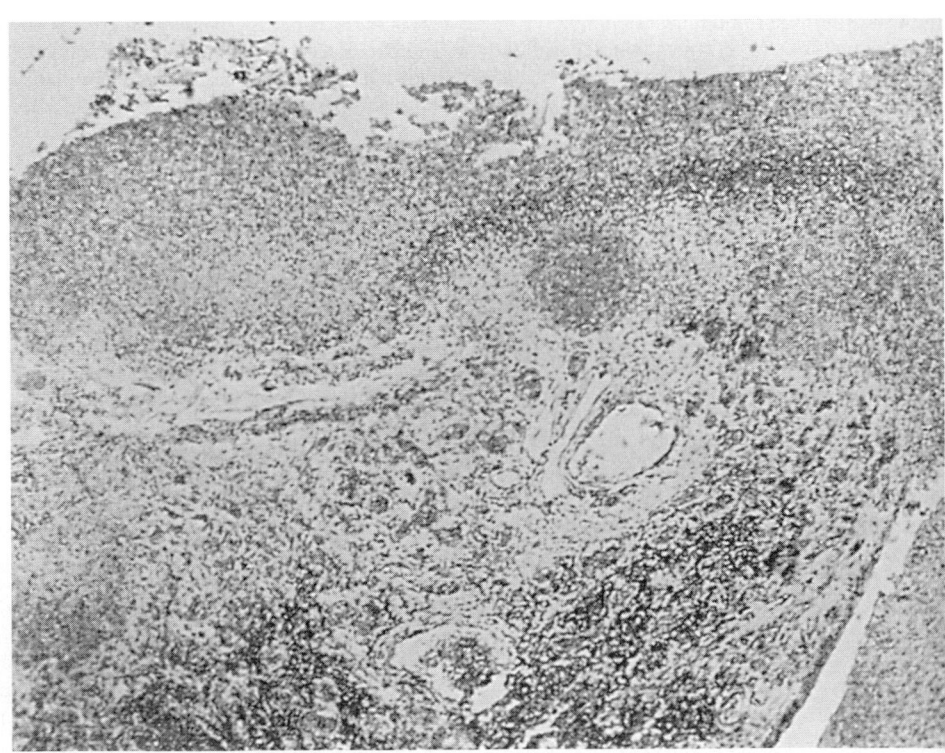

a common cause of death is suffocation following aspiration of the membrane.

CLINICAL MANIFESTATIONS

Symptoms of infection with *C. diphtheriae* occur locally in the respiratory tract and skin secondary to noninvasive infection of these two organs, and at distant sites secondary to absorption and dissemination of diphtheria toxin. Occasionally, *C. diphtheriae* disseminates from the skin or respiratory tract and causes systemic infections including bacteremia, endocarditis, and arthritis.

Respiratory Tract Diphtheria

Asymptomatic upper respiratory tract carriage of the organism occurs commonly in areas where diphtheria is endemic and is an important reservoir for maintenance and spread of the organism in a population. However, in the industrial Western world, throat colonization has become exceedingly rare except in individuals associated with pockets of infection such as the inner city (e.g., homeless people) and rural poverty areas.

Following an incubation period averaging 2 to 4 days, local signs and symptoms of inflammation can develop at various sites within the respiratory tract.

Anterior Nasal Infection

Infection limited to the anterior nares presents with a serosanguineous or seropurulent nasal discharge often associated with a subtle whitish mucosal membrane, particularly on the septum. The discharge can excite an erosive reaction on the external nares and upper lip, but symptoms generally are quite mild, and signs indicating toxin effects are rare.

Faucial Infection

Including the posterior structures of the mouth and the proximal pharynx, this area is the most common site for clinical diphtheria. Onset is usually abrupt, with low-grade fever (rarely >103° F), malaise, sore throat, mild pharyngeal injection, and development of a membrane typically on one or both tonsils, with extension variously to involve the tonsillar pillars, uvula, soft palate, oropharynx, and nasopharynx (Fig. 202-5). The membrane initially appears white and glossy, but evolves into a dirty gray color, with patches of green or black necrosis. The extent of the membrane correlates with the severity of symptoms: localized tonsillar disease is often mild, but involvement of the posterior pharynx, soft palate, and periglottal areas is associated with profound malaise, weakness, prostration, cervical adenopathy, and swelling. The latter can distort the normal contour of the submental and cervical area, creating a "bull neck" appearance and causing respiratory stridor.

Laryngeal and Tracheobronchial Infection

Pharyngeal infection may spread downward into the larynx, or occasionally the disease may begin there. Symptoms then include hoarseness, dyspnea, respiratory stridor, and a brassy cough. Edema and membrane involving the trachea and bronchi can embarrass respiration further, and a child so afflicted will appear anxious and cyanotic, use accessory muscles of respiration, and demonstrate inspiratory retractions of intercostal, supraclavicular, and substernal tissues. If this state is not relieved promptly by intubation and mechanical removal of membrane, patients become exhausted and die.

Systemic complications are due to diphtheria toxin, which, although toxic to all tissues, has its most striking effects on the heart and nervous system.

Cardiac Toxicity

Subtle evidence of myocarditis can be detected in as many as two thirds of patients, but 10% to 25% will develop clinical cardiac dysfunction, with the risk to an individual patient correlating directly with the extent and severity of local disease.[39,40] Characteristically, the first evidence of cardiac toxicity occurs after 1 to 2 weeks of illness, often when the local oropharyngeal disease is improving. Changes in electrocardiograph (ECG) pattern, particularly ST-T wave changes and first-degree heart block, can progress to more severe forms of block, atrioventricular (AV) dissociation, and other arrhythmias, which carry an ominous prognosis. Clinically, myocarditis can present acutely with congestive failure and circulatory collapse, or more insidiously with progressive dyspnea, weakness, diminished heart sounds, cardiac dilatation, and gallop rhythm. Because patients without clinical evidence of myocarditis may have significant electrical changes, it is important to monitor their cardiograms routinely. Elevations of serum AST concentration closely parallel the intensity of myocarditis, and so

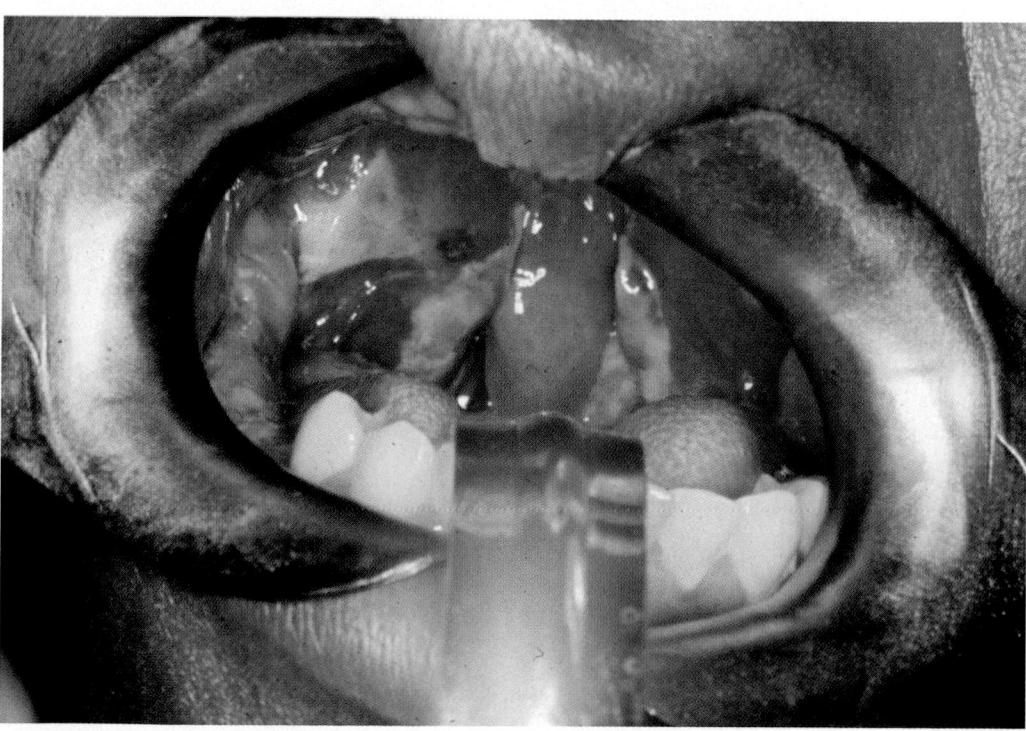

FIGURE 202-5. Pharynx of a 39-year-old woman with bacteriologically confirmed diphtheria. The photograph was taken 4 days after the onset of fever, malaise, and sore throat. Hemorrhage caused by removal of the membrane by swabbing appears as a dark area on the left.

may be used to monitor its course. From a prognostic standpoint, patients with ECG changes of myocarditis have a mortality rate three to four times higher than those with normal tracings. In particular, AV and left bundle branch blocks carry a mortality rate of 60% to 90%. Patients with prolonged P-R interval and minor T-wave changes generally do well, and these abnormalities ordinarily resolve with time. Patients with bundle-branch blocks and complete AV dissociation have a much higher incidence of death, and survivors may be left with permanent conduction defects.[41]

Neurologic Toxicity

This complication is also proportional to the severity of the primary infection: mild disease only occasionally produces neurotoxicity, but up to three fourths of patients with severe disease can develop neuropathy. Within the first few days of disease, local paralysis of the soft palate and posterior pharyngeal wall occurs commonly, manifested by regurgitation of swallowed fluids through the nose. Thereafter, cranial neuropathies causing oculomotor and ciliary paralysis are also common, and dysfunction of facial, pharyngeal, or laryngeal nerves, although rare, can contribute to the risk of aspiration. Peripheral neuritis develops later, from 10 days to 3 months after the onset of disease in the throat.[42] Principally a motor defect, it begins with proximal muscle groups in the extremities and extends distally, affecting particularly the dorsiflexors of the feet. Dysfunction varies from mild weakness with diminished tendon reflexes to total paralysis. Occasionally motor nerves of the trunk, neck, and upper extremity are involved, as are sensory nerves, resulting in a glove-and-stocking neuropathy. Microscopic examination of affected nerves shows degeneration of myelin sheaths and axon cylinders. Although slow, total resolution of all diphtheritic nerve damage is the rule.

Several excellent clinical descriptions of endemic and epidemic diphtheria in the United States indicate that both the frequency of various symptoms and the severity of disease are inversely proportional to the patient's immunization history.[42-46] Roughly one half of these reported cases were categorized as mild, often without a membrane. Mortality rates vary from 3.5% to 12%, and have not changed in the last 50 years. Rates are highest in the very young and the very old. Most deaths occur in the first 3 to 4 days, from asphyxia or myocarditis; fatal outcome is rare in a fully immunized individual. Sore throat (85% to 90%), fever (50% to 85%), and dysphagia (26% to 40%) are the most common symptoms, and membranes and cervical adenopathy are seen in approximately one half of the cases. The recent experience in Russia has been similar.[32] The frequency of complications such as myocarditis and neuritis is directly related to the time between onset of symptoms and administration of antitoxin, and to the extent of membrane formation.

Cutaneous Diphtheria

It has long been recognized that, particularly in the tropics, C. diphtheriae can cause clinical skin infections characterized by chronic nonhealing ulcers with a dirty gray membrane and often associated with Staphylococcus aureus and group A streptococci. More recently, the significance of this infection in the United States has been emphasized by several outbreaks among alcoholic homeless men and impoverished groups such as native Americans.[14-16] The presentation is indolent and nonprogressive, and is only rarely associated with signs of intoxication. Nonetheless, these infections can induce high antitoxin levels, and thus appear to act as natural immunizing events.[47,48] They also serve as a reservoir for the organism under conditions of both endemic and epidemic respiratory tract diphtheria: cutaneous sites of C. diphtheriae have been shown both to contaminate the inanimate environment and to induce throat infections more efficiently than does pharyngeal colonization, and bacterial shedding from cutaneous infections continues longer than from the respiratory tract.[15,26,49] Despite these facts, the clinical significance of isolating the organism from an individual skin lesion is often unclear. Most lesions from which C. diphtheriae is isolated are indistinguishable from other chronic dermatologic conditions (eczema, psoriasis, etc.), and only

about 15% fit the classic description of diphtheritic ulcers given above.[50] Moreover, because C. diphtheriae is usually isolated in association with other known skin pathogens, and because the ulcers do not respond to antitoxin therapy, there is debate as to whether or not the isolates are actually causing clinical disease. By 1975, cutaneous diphtheria accounted for 56% of total C. diphtheriae isolates reported in the United States, and, in 1980, the U.S. Centers for Disease Control and Prevention (CDC), in an effort to focus attention on respiratory tract diphtheria, removed nontoxigenic skin isolates from its list of reportable diseases.

Invasive Disease

Endocarditis, mycotic aneurysms, osteomyelitis, and septic arthritis have been described recently in clusters of drug addicts, alcoholics, Australian Aboriginals, and young adults,[51-54] all caused by nontoxigenic C. diphtheriae. Ribotyping has indicated that these outbreaks have been caused by unique epidemic strains, and both skin and throat colonization have been implicated as portals of entry. These illnesses have been characterized by aggressive course, a high proportion of endocarditis, arterial embolization, metastatic sites of infection (joints, spleen, CNS), and high mortality. Why these nontoxigenic strains are so virulent remains a mystery. Coincident with these outbreaks of invasive disease, examples of non-toxin-producing strains causing clinical pharyngitis[55-57] and even fatal respiratory tract diphtheria[58] have been published since 1990.

Other Sites

On rare occasions, clinical infection with C. diphtheriae can be seen in other sites such as the ear, conjunctivae, or vagina.

DIAGNOSIS

The clinical outcome in diphtheria is improved by the prompt initiation of treatment. Therefore, physicians must act on a presumptive diagnosis, based on several clinical clues: (1) mildly painful tonsillitis and/or pharyngitis with associated membrane, especially if the membrane extends to the uvula and soft palate; (2) adenopathy and cervical swelling, especially if associated with membranous pharyngitis and signs of systemic toxicity; (3) hoarseness and stridor; (4) palatal paralysis; (5) serosanguineous nasal discharge with associated mucosal membrane; and (6) temperature elevation rarely in excess of 103° F. Moderate elevation of white blood cell count and transient proteinuria are common, but nonspecific. In former times when the disease was common, skilled practitioners could often make the diagnosis on examination of methylene blue-stained smears of the membrane or of throat swabs. Currently, rapid diagnosis is sometimes possible with immunofluorescent staining of 4-hour cultures, but definitive identification of C. diphtheriae is made on the basis of colonial morphology, microscopic appearance, and fermentation reactions of isolates from bits of membrane or submembrane swabs cultured on Loeffler's or tellurite selective media such as Tinsdale agar (Fig. 202-6). Although Tinsdale medium has a short shelf life and individual batches may vary in their ability to grow C. diphtheriae, it has an advantage in that a black colony with a surrounding gray-brown halo is quite suggestive of the diagnosis. Corynebacterium diphtheriae characteristically shows metachromatic granules when stained with Loeffler stain, but these are best shown when organisms are grown in Loeffler's rather than Tinsdale medium. The combination of "Chinese characters" as seen on Gram stain, distinctive colonies with halos on Tinsdale medium, and the presence of metachromatic granules allows a presumptive identification of C. diphtheriae. Final identification requires biochemical tests. Toxin production is normally demonstrated by an in vitro test which detects the development of an immunoprecipitin band on antitoxin-impregnated filter paper that has been laid over an agar culture of the organism in question (Elek test). Recently, PCR probing of suspect organisms for DNA sequences coding for the toxin's A subunit has proven to be sensitive and accurate in rapid identification of tox+ strains.[59] In addition, an immunochromatographic strip test has been developed which has

FIGURE 202-6. Algorithm for laboratory diagnosis of diphtheria. *Abbreviations:* EIA, Enzyme immunoassay; PCR, polymerase chain reaction. *(From Efstratiou A, Engler KH, Mazurova IK, et al. Current approaches to the laboratory diagnosis of diphtheria. J Infect Dis 2000;181[Suppl 1]:S138-S145.)*

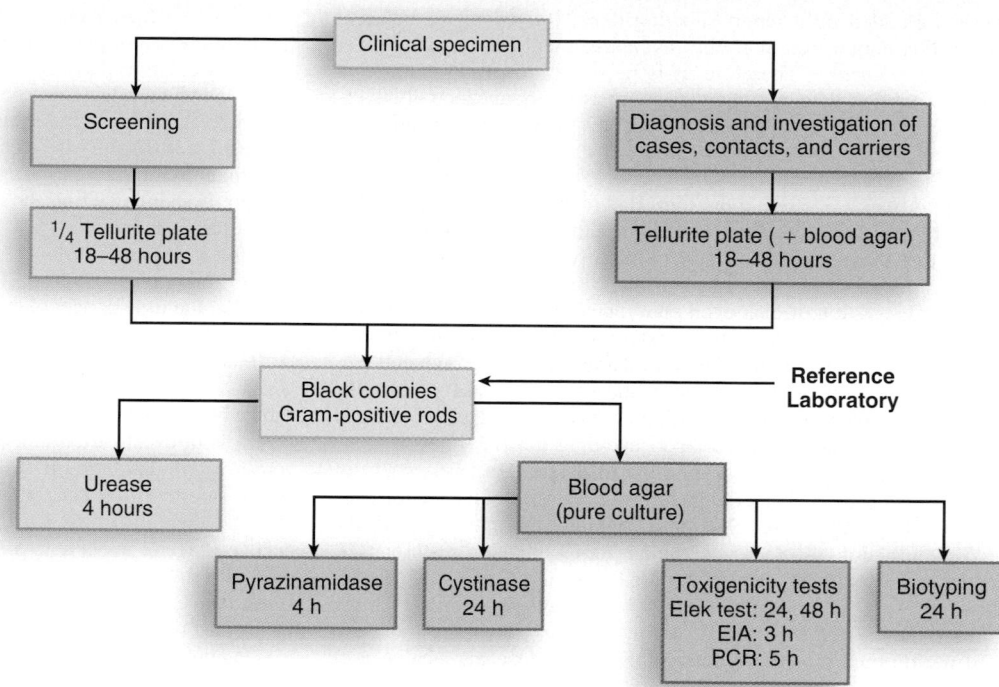

shown excellent correlation with the Elek test.[60] Because routine methods of throat culture do not promote the isolation and identification of *C. diphtheriae,* the laboratory must be alerted to use selective media when the disease is suspected.

The differential diagnosis includes infectious mononucleosis, streptococcal or viral pharyngitis and tonsillitis, Vincent's angina, and acute epiglottitis. The membrane of infectious mononucleosis characteristically remains on the tonsils, rarely loses its creamy white appearance, and does not cause bleeding when removed. Streptococcal infection usually produces a more intense local pharyngitis, higher fever, and more pronounced dysphagia. Vincent's angina often involves the gums, and Gram stain of the exudate from the necrotic ulcerative pharyngeal lesions shows characteristic fusobacteria and spirochetes. Bacterial epiglottitis secondary to *Haemophilus influenzae* often develops more acutely, and indirect laryngoscopy shows a bright red epiglottis without associated membrane.

TREATMENT

Diphtheria antitoxin (DAT), hyperimmune antiserum produced in horses, has been the cornerstone of therapy for diphtheria since it was first shown to reduce mortality from 7 to 2.5% in a controlled trial published in 1898. The antibodies only neutralize toxin before its entry into cells, and so it is critical that DAT be administered as soon as a presumptive diagnosis has been made. The degree of protection is inversely related to the duration of clinical illness preceding its administration.[43] Although the minimum therapeutic dose has never been determined, traditional (empirical) dosage recommendations assume that the duration of disease and extent of membrane formation roughly indicate the patient's toxin burden. The Committee on Infectious Diseases of the American Academy of Pediatrics recommends 20,000 to 40,000 units of antitoxin for pharyngeal or laryngeal disease of less than or equal to 48 hours' duration; 40,000 to 60,000 units for nasopharyngeal lesions; and 80,000 to 120,000 units for extensive disease of 3 or more days' duration and for anyone with brawny swelling of the neck.[61] It recommends administration by intravenous infusion over 60 minutes to inactivate toxin as rapidly as possible, but other experts suggest intramuscular injection of antitoxin for moderate disease, and combined intramuscular/intravenous administration for severe disease. Repeated injections are of no additional benefit. Because

up to 10% of individuals may show some hypersensitivity to horse protein, even very sick patients must be questioned first concerning known allergy and evaluated first with a "scratch test" (a drop of 1:1000 dilution of serum applied to a superficial scratch on the forearm), followed in 15 minutes if no wheal develops with 0.02 mL of a 1:1000 dilution injected intracutaneously, with epinephrine available for immediate administration.[61] If an immediate reaction occurs, the patient should be desensitized with progressively higher doses of antiserum. The incidence of serum sickness of approximately 10% is acceptable in light of the pronounced reduction in mortality resulting from antitoxin administration. Diphtheria antitoxin is no longer licensed in the United States, but a foreign-licensed product is available from the National Immunization Program of the CDC by calling 404-639-2889.

Antibiotic therapy, by killing the organism, has three benefits: (1) termination of toxin production; (2) amelioration of the local infection; and (3) prevention of spread of the organism to uninfected contacts. Although several antibiotics, including penicillin, erythromycin, azithromycin, clarithromycin, fluoroquinolones, clindamycin, rifampin, and tetracycline, are effective in vitro, only penicillin and erythromycin have been studied in controlled trials. Intramuscular administration of procaine penicillin G (300,000 units for patients weighing less than 20 lbs, 600,000 units for those weighing more than 20 lbs) at 12-hour intervals is recommended until the patient is able to swallow comfortably, when oral penicillin V (125 to 250 mg qid) or erythromycin estolate or succinate (125 to 500 mg qid) may be substituted for a recommended total treatment period of 14 days. Both drugs are equally effective in resolving fever and local symptoms, and in time to disappearance of membrane. Because erythromycin is marginally superior to penicillin in eradicating the carrier state, some authorities prefer it for initial treatment, despite a significant incidence of thrombophlebitis when it is given intravenously, and of gastrointestinal irritation when given orally. Patients should be maintained in strict isolation throughout therapy and, following therapy, should have two consecutive negative cultures at 24-hour intervals to document eradication of the organism.[61] The carrier state has a slow rate of spontaneous resolution (12% after 1 month in one study)[62] and so should be treated to prevent spread of infection. Erythromycin orally for 7 days is the treatment of choice because of several reports demonstrating its greater efficacy in comparison with penicillin.[45,46] However, the issue is clouded by a report showing that 21% of cultures taken 2 weeks after completion of erythromycin treatment were again positive for *C. diphtheriae*.[63] Therefore, it is necessary to obtain cultures at least 2 weeks after completing therapy to assure eradication of the organism. A single intramuscular dose of benzathine penicillin G (600,000 to 1,200,000 units) is prudent when compliance with oral therapy is uncertain.

Supportive care is also important. Bed rest is recommended during the acute phase of illness, but proof of its benefit once the patient feels able to ambulate is lacking. Early in the disease, respiratory and cardiac complications are the biggest threats: airway obstruction can result from aspiration of dislodged pharyngeal membrane, its direct extension into the larynx, or from external compression by enlarged nodes and edema. For this reason, many experts recommend tracheostomy or intubation as an early measure, particularly when the larynx is involved, thereby providing access for mechanical removal of tracheobronchial membranes and avoiding the risk of sudden asphyxia. Vigilance must be maintained to detect the development of primary or secondary bacterial pneumonia. Cardiac complications can be minimized by close electrocardiographic monitoring and the prompt initiation of electrical pacing for conduction disturbances, drugs for arrhythmias, or digitalis for heart failure. Physical therapy should preserve range of motion in paretic extremities while awaiting return of neurologic function. A recent study has shown that treatment of acute diphtheria with prednisone did not reduce the incidence of carditis or neuritis.[64]

Treatment of systemic infection such as endocarditis and arthritis has not been studied systematically, but most reports describe administration of intravenous penicillin or ampicillin, usually with an aminoglycoside, for 4 to 6 weeks.[54] Mortality rates of 30-40% occur with bacteremic disease, and valve replacement is often necessary in cases of endocarditis.[51,52]

PREVENTION

The major manifestations of diphtheria can be prevented in individual patients by immunization with formalin-inactivated toxin. Therefore, documentation of inadequate levels of antitoxin in a large proportion of the adult population in North America and Western Europe has caused great concern that a toxigenic strain introduced into these populations could cause an outbreak of disease similar to that in the former Soviet Union. Historically, the presence of immunity against diphtheria toxin was determined by the response to intradermal injection of small amounts of toxin (the Schick test). Currently, serum antitoxin levels can be measured by toxin neutralization tests in rabbit or guinea pig skin or by protection against cytopathic effect in Vero cell culture, with roughly equivalent results. Hemagglutination and ELISA assays are less sensitive at the lower levels of antitoxin. Concentrations of 0.1 to 0.01 IU (international units) generally are thought to confer protection. For example, data from a recent outbreak showed that 90% of clinical cases had antitoxin levels below 0.01 IU/mL, whereas 92% of asymptomatic carriers had titers above 0.1 IU/mL.[65] Following immunization, antitoxin levels decline slowly over time so that as many as 50% of individuals older than 60 years of age have serum titers below 0.01 IU/mL.[21,66,67] For this reason, booster doses of toxoid should be administered at 10-year intervals, to maintain antitoxin levels in the protective range.

Recommendations from the Advisory Committee on Immunization Practices were updated in 2002, and published by CDC[68]:

For children from 6 weeks to 7 years of age: Three 0.5-mL intramuscular injections of (DTaP) vaccine should be given at 4- to 8-week intervals, beginning at 6 to 8 weeks of age, followed by a fourth dose 6 to 12 months after the third.

For persons 7 years or more of age: 0.5 mL Td (toxoid-adult) is given twice at a 4-8-week interval, with a third dose 6 to 12 months later. Because the pertussis component of DPT is responsible for most of its side effects, and the risk of pertussis is much less after age 6, that component of the vaccine is omitted. Moreover, because subjects over age 7 have a higher incidence of local and systemic reactions to the concentration of diphtheria toxoid in pediatric DTaP vaccine (7 to 25 limit flocculation [Lf] units) and because a lower dose of toxoid has been shown to induce protective levels of antitoxin,[69] the Td formulation of vaccine contains a maximum concentration of 2 Lf units of diphtheria toxoid. If the recommended sequence of primary immunizations is interrupted, normal levels of immunity can be achieved simply by administering the remaining doses without need to restart the series.

Booster immunizations: Children who have completed their primary immunization before age 4 should receive a booster dose of DTaP at the time of school entry. Persons above 7 years of age should receive booster immunization with Td at 10-year intervals. As a help to memory, this should be done at decade or mid-decade intervals (e.g., ages 15, 25, 35, etc., or 20, 30, 40, etc.). Careful attention to this adult booster strategy is important to assure population protection in areas with excellent childhood immunization programs. Travelers to areas where diphtheria is still endemic should be particularly careful to be sure their immunization is current. Although the recommended booster dose of 1.5 to 2.0 Lf units will increase antitoxin levels to above 0.01 IU in 90% to 100% of previously immunized individuals,[70,71] some authorities have recommended using 5 Lf units, because antitoxin levels remain above 0.01 IU/mL for a longer period than with 2 Lf units.[70]

Patients should receive toxoid immunization in the convalescent stage of their disease because clinical infection does not always induce adequate levels of antitoxin. Close contacts whose immunization status is incomplete or unclear should promptly receive a dose of toxoid appropriate for their age, and complete the proper series of immunizations. In addition, they should receive prophylactic treatment with erythromycin or penicillin, pending the results of pretreatment cultures. Given these preventive measures, the prophylactic use of antitoxin is considered unwarranted.

REFERENCES

1. English PC. Diphtheria and theories of infectious disease: Centennial appreciation of the critical role of diphtheria in the history of medicine. Pediatrics. 1985;76:1-9.
2. Childhood's Deadly Scourge. Evelynn M. Hammonds. Baltimore: Johns Hopkins University Press; 1999.
3. Loeffler F. Untersuchugen uber die Bedeutung der Mikroorganismen fur die Entstehung der Diphtherie. Mitt Kaiserlichen Gesundheitsamt. 1884;2:421-499.
4. Groman NB. Conversion by corynephages and its role in the natural history of diphtheria. J Hyg (Cambridge). 1984;93:405-417.
5. Pappenheimer AM. Diphtheria studies on the biology of an infectious disease. Harvey Lect. 1982;76:45-73.
6. Freeman VJ. Studies on the virulence of bacteriophage-infected strains of *Corynebacterium diphtheriae*. J Bacteriol. 1951;61:675-688.
7. Golaz A, Hardy IR, Strebel P, et al. Epidemic diphtheria in the newly independent states of the former Soviet Union: Implications for diphtheria control in the United States. J Infect Dis. 2000;181(Suppl 1):S237-S243.
8. DeZoysa A, Efstratiou A, George RC, et al. Molecular epidemiology of *C. diphtheriae* from Northwestern Russia and surrounding countries studied by using ribotyping and pulsed-field gel electrophoresis. J Clin Microbiol. 1995;33:1080-1083.
9. Popovic T, Kombarova SY, Reeves MW, et al. Molecular epidemiology of diphtheria in Russia, 1985-1994. J Infect Dis. 1996;174:1064-1072.
10. Grimont F, Lelay-Collin M, Grimond PAD. Adaptation of the international *Corynebacterium diphtheriae* ribotypes database to RiboPrinter, 7th International Meeting of the European Laboratory Working Group on Diphtheria. Vienna, Austria, 2002, pp. 82-83.
11. Pappenheimer AM, Murphy JR. Studies on the molecular epidemiology of diphtheria. Lancet. 1983;2:923-926.
12. Kalapothaki V, Sapounas T, Xirouchaki E, et al. Prevalence of diphtheria carriers in a population with disappearing clinical diphtheria. Infection. 1984;12:387-389.
13. Heath CW, Zusman J. An outbreak of diphtheria among skid-row men. N Engl J Med. 1962;267:809-812.
14. Harnisch JP, Tronca E, Nolan CM, et al. Diphtheria among alcoholic urban adults. A decade of experience in Seattle. Ann Intern Med. 1989;111:71-82.
15. Koopman JS, Campbell J. The role of cutaneous diphtheria infections in a diphtheria epidemic. J Infect Dis. 1975;131:239-244.
16. Belsey MA, Sinclair M, Roder MR, et al. *Corynebacterium diphtheriae* skin infections in Alabama and Louisiana. N Engl J Med. 1969;280:135-141.
17. Bisgard KM, Hardy IRB, Popovic T, et al. Respiratory diphtheria in the United States, 1980-1995. Am J Publ Hlth 1998;88:787-791.
18. Dixon JMS. Diphtheria in North America. J Hyg (Cambridge). 1984;93:419-32.
19. Kwantes W. Diphtheria in Europe. J Hyg (Cambridge). 1984;93:433-437.

20. World Health Organization. Expanded Programme on Immunization (EPI) Information System, April 1993, Geneva.
21. Galazka AM, Robertson SE: Diphtheria: Changing patterns in the developing world and the industrialized world. Eur J Epidemiol. 1995;11:107-117.
22. Dittmann S, Wharton M, Vitek C, et al. Successful control of epidemic diphtheria in the states of the former Union of Soviet Socialist Republics: Lessons learned. J Infect Dis. 2002;181(Suppl 1):S10-S22.
23. Diphtheria Morbidity in the Russian Federation, 1999-2003. Public Health and Environment Bulletin, Issues 1-3 (2001, 2002, 2003). Federal Center of the State Sanitary and Epidemiological Surveillance of the Public Health Ministry of the Russian Federation (Moscow, RF). www.fcgsen.ru
24. Blystad H, Blad J, Giesecke J: Surveillance and trends of priority infectious diseases in the Baltic Sea Region. Epinorth Bull Netwk Commun Dis Control N Eur. 2002;3:62.
25. Hardy IRB, Dittmann S, Sutter RW. Current situation and control strategies for resurgence of diphtheria in newly independent states of the former Soviet Union. Lancet. 1996;347:1739-1744.
26. Vitek CR, Wharton M. Diphtheria in the former Soviet Union: Re-emergence of a pandemic disease. Emerg Infect Dis. 1998;4:539-550.
27. Wilson APR, Efstratiou A, Weaver E, et al. Unusual non-toxigenic *Corynebacterium diphtheriae* in homosexual men. Lancet. 1992;339:998.
28. Millar OS, Cooper ON, Kakkar VV, et al. Invasive infection with *Corynebacterium diphtheriae* among drug users. Lancet. 1992;339:1359.
29. Brooks GF, Bennett JV, Feldman RA. Diphtheria in the United States, 1959-1970. J Infect Dis. 1974;129:172-178.
30. Popovic T, Kim C, Reiss J, et al. Use of molecular subtyping to document long-term persistence of *Corynebacterium diphtheriae* in South Dakota. J Clin Microbiol. 1999;37:1092-1099.
31. Centers for Disease Control and Prevention. 1997. Toxigenic *Corynebacterium diphtheriae*—Northern Plains Indian community, August-October 1996. MMWR Morbid Mortal Wkly Rep. 46:506-510.
32. Rakhmanova AG, Lumio J, Groundstroem K, et al. Diphtheria outbreak in St. Petersburg: Clinical characteristics of 1,860 adult patients. Scand J Infect Dis 1996;28:37-40.
33. Galazka A. The changing epidemiology of diphtheria in the vaccine era. J Infect Dis. 2000;181(Suppl 1):S2-S9.
34. McQuillan GM, Kruszon-Moran D, Deforest A, et al. Serologic immunity to diphtheria and tetanus in the United States. Ann Intern Med. 2002;136:660-666.
35. Williams BC. Immunization coverage among preschool children: The United States and selected European countries. Pediatrics. 1990;86:1052-1056.
36. Estimated Vaccine Coverage of Children 19-35 Months of Age by State—US, National Immunization Survey, Q1/2001-Q4/2001. http://www.cdc.gov/nip/coverage/NIS/01/TABS-antigen_state.htm
37. Rappuoli R, Perugini M, Falsen E. Molecular epidemiology of the 1984-86 outbreak of diphtheria in Sweden. N Engl J Med. 1988;318:12-14.
38. Pappenheimer AM. The diphtheria bacillus and its toxin: A model system. J Hyg (Cambridge). 1984;93:397-440.
39. Boyer NH, Weinstein L. Diphtheritic myocarditis. N Engl J Med. 1948;239:913.
40. Morgan BC. Cardiac complications of diphtheria. Pediatrics. 1963;32:549-557.
41. Ledbetter MK, Cannon AB, Costa AF. The electrocardiogram in diphtheritic myocarditis. Am Heart J. 1964;68:599-611.
42. Dobie RA, Tobey DN. Clinical features of diphtheria in the respiratory tract. JAMA. 1979;242:2197-2201.
43. Naiditch MJ, Bower AG. Diphtheria. A study of 1433 cases observed during a ten year period at the Los Angeles County Hospital. Am J Med. 1954;17:229-245.
44. Kallick CA, Brooks GF, Dover AS, et al. A diphtheria outbreak in Chicago. Ill Med J. 1970;137:505-512.
45. Zalma VM, Older JJ, Brooks GF. The Austin, Texas, diphtheria outbreak. JAMA. 1970;211:2125-2129.
46. McCloskey RV, Eller JJ, Green M, et al. The 1970 epidemic of diphtheria in San Antonio. Ann Intern Med. 1971;75:495-503.
47. Bray JP, Burt EG, Potter EV, et al. Epidemic diphtheria and skin infections in Trinidad. J Infect Dis. 1972;126:34-40.
48. Hewlett EL. Selective primary health care: Strategies for control of disease in the developing world. XVIII. Pertussis and diphtheria. Rev Infect Dis. 1985;7:426-433.
49. Belsey MA, LeBlanc DR. Skin infections and the epidemiology of diphtheria: Acquisition and persistence of *C. diphtheriae* infections. Am J Epidemiol. 1975;102:179-184.
50. Jellard CH. Diphtheria infection in Northwest Canada, 1969, 1970, and 1971. J Hyg. 1972;70:503-510.
51. Lortholary O, Buu-Hoi A, Gutmann L, et al. *Corynebacterium diphtheriae* endocarditis in France. Clin Infect Dis. 1993;17:1072-1074.
52. Tiley SM, Kociuba KR, Heron LG, et al. Infective endocarditis due to nontoxigenic *Corynebacterium diphtheriae*: Report of seven cases and review. Clin Infect Dis. 1993;16:271-275.
53. Gruner E, Opravil M, Altwegg M, et al. Nontoxigenic *Corynebacterium diphtheriae* isolated from intravenous drug users. Clin Infect Dis. 1994;18:94-96.
54. Patey O, Bimet F, Riegel P, et al. Clinical and molecular study of *Corynebacterium diphtheriae* systemic infections in France. J Clin Microbiol. 1997;35:441-445.
55. Wilson APR. The return of *Corynebacterium diphtheriae*: The rise of non-toxigenic strains. J Hosp Infect. 1995;30(Suppl):306-312.
56. Efstratiou A, George RC, Begg NT. Non-toxigenic *Corynebacterium diphtheriae* var *gravis* in England. Lancet. 1993;341:1592-1593.
57. Reacher M, Ramsay M, White J, et al. Nontoxigenic *Corynebacterium diphtheriae*: An emerging pathogen in England and Wales? Emerg Infect Dis. 2000;6:640-645.
58. Rakhmanova AG, Lumio J, Groundstroem KWE, et al. Fatal respiratory tract diphtheria apparently caused by nontoxigenic strains of *Corynebacterium diphtheriae*. Eur J Clin Microbiol Infect Dis. 1997;16:816-820.
59. Mikhailovich VM, Melnikov VG, Mazurova IK, et al. Application of PCR for detection of toxigenic *Corynebacterium diphtheriae* strains isolated during the Russian diphtheria epidemic, 1990 through 1994. J Clin Microbiol. 1995;33:3061-3063.
60. Engler KH, Efstratiou A, Norn D, et al. Immunochromatographic strip test for rapid detection of diphtheria toxin: Description and multicenter evaluation in areas of low and high prevalence of diphtheria. J Clin Microbiol, 2002;40:80-83.
61. American Academy of Pediatrics. Diphtheria. In: Pickering LK, ed. Red Book: 2003 Report of the Committee on Infectious Diseases. 26th ed. Elk Grove Village, IL: American Academy of Pediatrics; 1997:263-266.
62. Kiselev VI. The use of various antibiotic combinations in the control of diphtheria bacilli carrier state. Antibiotiki. 1964;9:361-363.
63. Miller LW, Bickham S, Jones WL, et al. Diphtheria carriers and the effect of erythromycin therapy. Antimicrob Agents Chemother. 1974;6:166-169.
64. Thisyakorn USA, Wongvanich J, Kumpeng V. Failure of corticosteroid therapy to prevent diphtheritic myocarditis or neuritis. Pediatr Infect Dis. 1984;3:126-128.
65. Bjorkholm B, Bottiger M, Christenson B, et al. Antitoxin antibody levels and the outcome of illness during an outbreak of diphtheria among alcoholics. Scand J Infect Dis. 1986;18:235-239.
66. Millian SJ, Cherubin CE, Sherwin R, et al. A serologic survey of tetanus and diphtheria immunity in New York City. Arch Environ Hlth. 1967;15:776-781.
67. Kjeldsen K, Simonsen O, Heron I. Immunity against diphtheria 25-30 years after primary vaccination in childhood. Lancet. 1985;1:900-902.
68. Centers for Disease Control and Prevention. General Recommendations on Immunization. Recommendations of the Advisory Committee on Immunization Practices and the American Academy of Family Physicians. MMWR Morbid Mortal Wkly Rep. 2002;51:RR-2.
69. Myers MG, Beckman CW, Vosdingh RA, et al. Primary immunization with tetanus and diphtheria toxoids. JAMA. 1982;248:2478-2480.
70. Simonsen O, Klaerke M, Klaerke A, et al. Revaccination of adults against diphtheria II: Combined diphtheria and tetanus revaccination with different doses of diphtheria toxoid 20 years after primary vaccination. Acta Pathol Microbiol Immunol Scand [C]. 1986;94:219-225.
71. Ruben RL, Nagel J, Fireman P. Antitoxin responses in the elderly to tetanus-diphtheria immunization. Am J Epidemiol. 1978;108:145-149.
72. Moore RA. A Textbook of Pathology. Philadelphia: WB Saunders; 1944.
73. Efstratiou A, Engler KH, Mazurova IK, et al. Current approaches to the laboratory diagnosis of diphtheria. J Infect Dis 2000;181(Suppl 1):S138-S45.

CHAPTER 203

Other Coryneform Bacteria and *Rhodococcus*

DANIEL K. MEYER

ANNETTE C. REBOLI

CORYNEFORM BACTERIA OTHER THAN *C. DIPHTHERIAE*

Corynebacterium was proposed as a genus by Lehmann and Neumann in 1896, who derived the name from the Greek *koryne,* which means "club," and *bacterion,* meaning "little rod."[1] *Corynebacterium diphtheriae* serves as the type species, leading to the term diphtheroids to describe other bacteria sharing similar morphology. A synonym for diphtheroids is coryneform bacteria, or bacteria demonstrating morphology similar to that of Corynebacteria, and includes the genera *Corynebacterium, Arcanobacterium, Brevibacterium, Dermabacter, Microbacterium, Rothia, Turicella, Arthrobacter,* and *Oerskovia.*[2,3]

Coryneform bacteria are widely distributed in the environment as normal inhabitants of soil and water.[4] They are commensals colonizing the skin and mucous membranes of humans and other animals.[5-7] In the hospital setting coryneforms may be cultured from the hospital environment including surfaces and medical equipment.[8,9] Coryneform bacteria other than *C. diphtheriae* have been isolated frequently in clinical specimens, and were commonly considered contaminants without clinical significance. There is an increasing body of evidence of the pathogenicity of the coryneform bacteria, particularly as a cause of nosocomial infection in hospitalized and immunocompromised patients.[10-12] Several of the members of the genus *Corynebacterium* are better known as pathogens in animals, and only incidentally cause infection in humans as zoonoses.

The coryneform bacteria are pleomorphic, demonstrating different forms at various stages of the life cycle, irregularly shaped gram-positive rods that are aerobically cultured, non–spore forming, and non–partially acid-fast.[2,3] A history of misidentification of coryneform bacteria has made interpretation of the medical literature difficult.[3] Initial identification is aided by observation of colony size and appearance and the presence or absence of hemolysis on sheep blood agar. Odor production by colonies assists in identification, particularly of *Brevibacterium casei* and *Corynebacterium urealyticum*. Several of the medically relevant coryneform bacteria are lipophilic, demonstrating enhanced growth with the addition of Tween 80 to the culture medium.

True *Corynebacteria* demonstrate club-shaped gram-positive rods on Gram stain, while other coryneform bacteria may not appear distinctly club shaped. Cells demonstrate variable sizes and appearance, from coccoid to bacillary forms depending on the stage of the life cycle, and Gram stain results may be uneven. Coryneform bacteria typically form arrangements such as "Chinese letters" or picket fence configurations as a result of "snapping" after the cells divide. Lack of spore formation helps distinguish them from *Bacillus* species.[2,3]

The spectrum of human infections attributed to the coryneform bacteria is broad, but can be understood in two general categories: community-acquired infections and nosocomial infections. Community-acquired infections include pharyngitis, native valve endocarditis, genitourinary tract infections, acute and chronic prostatitis, and periodontal infections (Table 203-1).[13] Many case reports of nosocomial infections attributed to coryneform bacteria are in the medical literature and include intravascular catheter-associated septicemia, native and prosthetic valve endocarditis, device-related infections, and postoperative surgical site infections. Common nosocomial pathogens include *Corynebacterium jeikeium*, *Corynebacterium urealyticum*, *Corynebacterium amycolatum*, and *Corynebacterium striatum* (Table 203-2).[14] It is expected that nosocomial infections with the coryneform bacteria will continue to increase, reflecting the increased numbers of severely ill patients with extended stays in intensive care units and multiple antibiotic exposures.

Taxonomy

The taxonomy of the coryneform bacteria has evolved extensively over the past 20 years, and continues to be refined. Hollis and Weaver

TABLE 203-1 Community-acquired Coryneform Infections

Conjunctivitis	*Corynebacterium macginleyi*
Pharyngitis	*Arcanobacterium hemolyticum*
	Corynebacterium ulcerans
	Corynebacterium pseudodiphtheriticum
Peritonsillar and pharyngeal abscess	*A. hemolyticum*
Odontogenic infections	*A. hemolyticum*
	Rothia dentocariosa
Lymphadenitis	*Corynebacterium pseudotuberculosis*
Genitourinary tract infection	*Corynebacterium glucuronolyticum*
	Corynebacterium riegelii
Chronic prostatitis	*Corynebacterium glucuronolyticum*
Skin and soft tissue infections	*Arcanobacterium hemolyticum*
	Arcanobacterium pyogenes
	Corynebacterium minutissimum
	Corynebacterium pseudotuberculosis
	Corynebacterium confusum
Breast abscess	*Corynebacterium kroppenstedtii*
	Corynebacterium tuberculostearicum
	C. minutissimum
Native valve endocarditis	*A. hemolyticum*
	R. dentocariosa
	Corynebacterium pseudodiphtheriticum

TABLE 203-2 Nosocomial Infections Caused by Coryneform Bacteria

CSF shunt infections	*C. jeikeium*
Meningitis	*C. jeikeium*
	Brevibacterium spp
Pneumonia	*C. amycolatum* (*C. xerosis*)
	C. striatum
	C. urealyticum
Intravenous catheter–related blood-stream infection	*C. jeikeium*
	C. amycolatum
	C. striatum
	C. urealyticum
	Brevibacterium casei
	C. macginleyi
	C. minutissimum
	C. afermentans afermentans
	Arcanobacterium bernardiae
	Arcanobacterium pyogenes
	Oerskovia
	Microbacterium
Native valve endocarditis	*C. amycolatum*
	C. jeikeium
	C. striatum
	C. urealyticum
Prosthetic valve endocarditis	*C. jeikeium*
	C. amycolatum
	C. striatum
	Brevibacterium casei
Skin and soft tissue infection	*C. amycolatum*
	C. minutissimum
	C. urealyticum
Postsurgical infections	*C. jeikeium*
	C. urealyticum
	C. striatum
Prosthetic joint infections	*C. jeikeium*
Urinary tract infections and encrusted cystitis	*C. urealyticum*
CAPD-related peritonitis	*C. jeikeium*
	Brevibacterium spp.
	C. urealyticum
	Dermabacter
	Rothia dentocariosa

at the Special Bacteriology Laboratory, Centers for Disease Control and Prevention (CDC) in Atlanta, GA completed the first extensive compilation of coryneform bacteria isolated from clinical specimens.[15] They grouped the coryneforms based on colony and biochemical characteristics. Since then, further work has been done to analyze these groups and define species. Table 203-3 lists the significant coryneform bacteria and the CDC group to which they previously belonged. New species continue to be identifed yearly, not all of which appear to be clinically relevant.

Analysis of cell wall composition and cellular fatty acid patterns is performed in reference laboratories to confirm species identification.[3,16] In addition, the use of molecular genetics has resulted in continued revision of the taxonomy of the coryneform bacteria and provides useful information on the epidemiology and pathogenicity of the genera. Molecular genetic studies such as restriction analysis of 16S rDNA and repetitive extragenic palindromic polymerase chain reaction (PCR) typing are used in reference laboratories to confirm identification at the species level.[3,17,18]

Microbiology

Because the coryneforms are frequently cultured in polymicrobial infections and may be contaminants in cultures collected with poor sterile technique, clinician communication to the microbiology laboratory is essential to determine when species identification is appropriate. The decision to identify the coryneform bacteria to the species level is recommended when the bacteria are cultured from normally sterile sites such as blood or cerebrospinal fluid (CSF), if the bacteria appear in significant numbers on Gram stains of clinical material, if they are obtained in pure culture, or if they are cultured in large numbers from the specimen.[3]

TABLE 203-3 Medically Relevant Coryneform Bacteria

Classification	CDC Coryneform Group
Nonlipophilic, fermentative corynebacteria	
C. ulcerans	C. diphtheriae group
C. pseudotuberculosis	C. diphtheriae group
C. xerosis	F-2, I-2
C. striatum	I-1
C. minutissimum	
C. amycolatum	F-2, I-2
C. glucuronolyticum	
Others: C. argentoratense, C. matruchotii,	
C. riegelii, C. confusum, C. simulans,	
C. sundvallense, C. thomssensii, C. freneyi,	
C. aurimucosum	
Nonlipophilic nonfermentative Corynebacteria	
C. afermentans afermentans	ANF-1
C. auris	
C. pseudodiphtheriticum	
C. propinquum	ANF-3
Lipophilic Corynebacteria	
C. jeikeium	JK
C. urealyticum	D-2
Others: C. afermentans lipophilum, C. accolens,	
C. macginleyi, C. tuberculostearum,	
C. kroppenstedtii, C. bovis,	
CDC coryneform groups F-1 and G,	
C. lipophiloflavum	
Arcanobacteria	
A. haemolyticum	
A. pyogenes (Actinomyces pyogenes)	
A. bernardiae	
Other coryneform bacterial genera:	
Turicella, Arthrobacter, Brevibacterium,	
Dermabacter, Rothla, Oerskovla,	
Microbacterium, Leifsonia aquatica	
Rhodococcus	

Media used for initial specimen processing are standard blood agar plates for most specimens, thioglycollate broth for wound cultures, and standard blood culturing systems using continuous monitoring for CO_2 production. Special media used for species identification include tryptic soy agar with and without 1% Tween 80 to assess lipid-enhanced growth.[3]

Identification to the species level in the microbiology laboratory is confirmed by biochemical testing. Initial testing includes the catalase test with 3% H_2O_2. Additional tests include nitrate reduction; urea production; and hydrolysis patterns from glucose, maltose, sucrose, mannitol, and xylose. A frequently used system of biochemical testing for medically relevant coryneform bacteria is the API CORYNE system, which includes 20 biochemical tests and will identify many of the important *Corynebacteria* species and other coryneforms including *Arcanobacterium* species and *Brevibacterium* species, as well as *Rhodococcus equi, Listeria monocytogenes, Erysipelothrix rhusiopathiae,* and *Gardnerella vaginalis.*[19,20] An evaluation of the updated CORYNE database 2.0 gave correct identification for 90.5% of the coryneforms tested.[21] The RapID CB Plus system correctly identifies 80.9% strains to the species level and an additional 12.2% to the genus level. It has the advantage of requiring only 4 hours to perform, compared to 24 hours for the CORYNE system.[22]

In a few cases the CAMP test, named for the initial investigators Christie, Atkins, and Munch-Petersen, helps to identify the organism to the species level.[3] A streak of a β-lysin producing strain of *Staphylococcus aureus* is plated on sheep blood agar and a streak of the test strain is plated perpendicular to it. A positive CAMP reaction is noted if the CAMP factor, a cohemolysin secreted by the tested coryneform, enhances hemolysis in a synergistic fashion. Although most coryneform bacteria are CAMP negative, a few species such as *Corynebacterium auris* and *Corynebacterium gluronolyticum* have been shown to produce CAMP factor.[23]

Susceptibility testing has proven problematic in the coryneforms.[23] To date the media to be used have not been standardized and the interpretation of breakpoints has not been standardized by the National Committee for Clinical Laboratory Standards (NCCLS). Application of breakpoints for streptococci or *S. aureus* has been used by some investigators.[23,24] Isolates uniformly show susceptibility to the glycopeptides vancomycin and teicoplanin and the lipopeptide daptomycin.[24,25] The *vanA* gene has been identified in *Oerskovia turbata* and *Arcanobacterium haemolyticum,* but no documented infections with vanocmycin-resistant coryneforms have appeared in the literature.[26]

For consistency, the coryneform bacteria are reviewed here within groups identified by the presence or absence of lipid-enhanced culture (lipophilic or nonlipophilic) and fermentation activity.

Nonlipophilic Fermentative Corynebacteria

Advances made in the identification of species in the nonlipophilic fermentative group have resulted in a revision of thinking of the pathogenic role of several species, particularly for *Corynebacterium xerosis* and *Corynebacterium amycolatum.*[27] Interpretation of the literature that does not include detailed information on laboratory identification is difficult, as recent reviews have found a great deal of misidentification in the nonlipophilic fermentative group. As laboratories implement improved strategies for identification of coryneform bacteria in clinical specimens from normally sterile sites, one hopes the pathogenic role of the nonlipophilic fermentative corynebacteria will be clarified.[3]

Corynebacterium ulcerans and *Corynebacterium pseudotuberculosis*

C. ulcerans and *C. pseudotuberculosis* are members of the *C. diphtheriae* group, and are known primarily as animal pathogens, although disease in humans has been reported as a zoonotic infection. Both *C. ulcerans* and *C. pseudotuberculosis* may elaborate diphtheria toxin.[28]

C. ulcerans is known primarily as a cause of bovine mastitis, but has the potential to elaborate diphtheria toxin and cause an exudative pharyngitis in humans indistinguishable from diphtheria.[29,30] Several reported outbreaks of diphtheria have been found to be caused by *C. ulcerans* rather than *C. diphtheriae.*[31,32] This has made the identification of the causative organism important for epidemiology, and guidelines for laboratory diagnosis of diphtheria cases have been published.[33] The spectrum of illness with *C. ulcerans* is similar to *C. diphtheriae.*[34,35] Fatalities have been reported, including sudden death from toxin-induced cardiac injury and a case of fatal necrotizing sinusitis.[36,37] Skin infection by *C. ulcerans* mimics that of *C. diphtheriae.*[38] Infection of the lower respiratory tract may occur causing pneumonia and pulmonary nodules.[39] Treatment of pharyngitis caused by *C. ulcerans* is similar to treatment of diphtheria, including the use of antibiotics such as erythromycin and diphtheria antitoxin when appropriate.

C. pseudotuberculosis is a significant pathogen in animals, particularly sheep, in which it causes caseous lymphadenitis. Human disease is rare, manifesting as granulomatous lymphadenitis, found mainly in farm workers and veterinarians who have had exposure to infected animals.[40-42] It has been reported to be a cause of eosinophilic pneumonia and has also been isolated from soft tissue abscesses in a young butcher.[43,44] Management of C. *pseudotuberculosis* infection includes excision of affected lymph nodes, and treatment with β-lactam antibiotics, macrolides, or tetracyclines. A vaccine for sheep is now being used that may reduce the incidence of human disease.

Corynebacterium xerosis

C. xerosis is a colonizer of the human nasopharynx, conjunctiva, and skin.[45,46] *C. xerosis* has been described in the literature as a pathogen causing serious human disease, especially in immunocompromised hosts, including sepsis, endocarditis, pneumonia, peritonitis, ventriculoperitoneal shunt infection, and postoperative sternal wound infection.[47-52] Recent investigations have questioned the reliability of *C. xerosis* identification in the microbiology laboratory.[53,54] In one study, all isolates originally identified as *C. xerosis* were in actuality *Corynebacterium amycolatum.*[54] This calls into question preceding case reports attributing disease to *C. xerosis,* as true *C. xerosis* isolates apparently are quite rare. Recent reports have included *C. xerosis* isolated from a brain abscess and a case of sepsis in a pediatric patient with sickle cell disease.[55,56] Future case reports that include methods of identification used to identify the organism may help to clarify the role of *C. xerosis* in human disease. True *C. xerosis* strains are susceptible to most antibiotics, which helps to distinguish them from *C. amycolatum,* which demonstrates multiple antibiotic resistances.

Corynebacterium striatum

C. striatum has been one of the more commonly isolated coryneform bacteria in the clinical microbiology laboratory.[2,3,12] As in the case of other nonlipophilic fermentative *Corynebacteria,* a high degree of misidentification of *C. striatum* has occurred in the past in microbiology laboratories, and investigators have found many isolates to be *C. amycolatum* on detailed retesting.[53,57]

C. striatum is ubiquitous, and colonizes the skin and mucous membranes of normal hosts and hospitalized patients.[58,59] Although it is isolated frequently in polymicrobial infections, its degree of pathogenicity has been unclear, and differentiation of colonization from pathogen causing infection has been difficult.[10-12] In a large recent series of 150 clinical specimens from which coryneform bacteria had been isolated, *C. striatum* was identified in 11 isolates, only one of which was considered to be related to an infectious process.[10] There is evidence for patient-to-patient transmission of *C. striatum* in hospital settings, which may account for the frequency with which it is isolated in hospitalized patients.[60,61]

Reports of true infection confirmed by isolation of *C. striatum* from a sterile site are rare, and have been reported mainly for patients with indwelling devices or immunosuppression. Recent case reports in the literature include native and prosthetic valve endocarditis, pacemaker-related endocarditis, meningitis, pulmonary abscess, septic arthritis, and vertebral osteomyelitis.[62-70] There is one report of *C. striatum* isolated from a postoperative breast abscess. The finding is inconclusive because initial cultures of the breast abscess were negative and the patient received clindamycin before a second surgical specimen was obtained for culture.[71] Nosocomial endocarditis has been reported in a patient with vascular access for dialysis that was successfully treated with vancomycin and rifampicin.[72] *C. striatum* may be resistant to penicillin, but is susceptible to other β-lactams and vancomycin. Resistance has been demonstrated to ciprofloxacin, erythromycin, rifampin, and tetracyclines; there is variable susceptibility to aminoglycosides.[73,74]

Corynebacterium minutissimum

Defined in 1983 by Collins, *C. minutissimum* is a colonizer of human skin, particularly moist intertriginous areas.[75-77] As with other members of this group, *C. amycolatum* has been misidentified as *C. minutissimum* in the past.[78] Although historically *C. minutissimum* has been considered the causative agent in erythrasma, that association has been questioned because cultures tend to show polymicrobial infection.[3] Erythrasma is a superficial skin infection occurring in intertriginous areas between skin folds, axillae, groin, and between fingers and toes. It presents as reddened scaling patches that may be accompanied by pruritus. Skin patches will glow coral-red under Wood's lamp. Diagnosis is made by clinical appearance and symptoms, and by culture of skin scrapings. Colonies will also appear coral-red under ultraviolet light. Treatment includes topical and oral antibiotics. Recurrences are frequent.

Other rare infections attributed to *C. minutissimum* include septicemia and endocarditis in immunocompromised patients and patients with indwelling central venous catheters, peritonitis in patients undergoing continuous ambulatory peritoneal dialysis (CAPD), and pyelonephritis.[79-82] It has been reported to cause cutaneous granulomas

and costochondral abscess in patients with acquired immunodeficiency virus (AIDS) and been implicated as a cause of recurrent breast abscesses.[83-85] Supporting evidence for the microbiological diagnosis in several case reports is slim, and these infections may actually have been caused by other members of the nonlipophilic fermentative group.

Corynebacterium amycolatum

Defined as a new species in 1988 by Collins, *C. amycolatum* was first isolated from the skin of healthy humans.[86] Noted for its lack of mycolic acids, the species corresponds to the CDC coryneform groups F-2 and I-2. *C. amycolatum* forms small dry nonhemolytic colonies of 1 mm to 1.5 mm when cultured at 37° C.[3] The organisms are pleomorphic and vary from single organisms to an array of Chinese letters. *C. minutissimum* and C. *amycolatum* may not be correctly identified on the API CORYNE system, but can be distinguished on the basis of colony morphology.[3,27] New techniques to identify Corynebacteria to the species level have increased the reporting of isolates identified as *C. amycolatum.* By recent identification techniques, it is the non-lipophilic coryneform bacteria most frequently isolated from clinical specimens.[10,11]

Although case reports of infections attributed to *C. amycolatum* are rare, many previously reported infections by other members of the non-lipophilic fermentative group were most likely caused by *C. amycolatum.* Recent reports with reliable information on organism identification include nosocomial endocarditis following intravenous catheter–related infection, septic arthritis, and a case of native valve endocarditis with aorta-to-left atrial fistula.[87-89] Susceptibility testing has shown resistance to penicillins, cephalosporins, macrolides, fluoroquinolones, and rifampin, and susceptibility to vancomycin and teicoplanin. There is variable resistance to aminoglycosides and tetracyclines.[23-25] Reports of successful treatment include the use of vancomycin and rifampin.

C. glucuronolyticum

C. glucuronolyticum was defined in 1995, and since 2000 the species has included those isolates previously identified as *Corynebacterium seminale* that had been defined by Riegel et al. in 1996.[90,91] Although it has been isolated from the genitourinary tract of animals, in humans it may be included in the normal flora of the genitourinary tract. It is commonly isolated from males with genitourinary tract infections, and is associated with chronic prostatitis.[92] *C. glucuronolyticum* strains are susceptible to β-lactam antibiotics, gentamicin, rifampin, and vancomycin, but demonstrate resistance to fluoroquinolones, macrolides, and tetracyclines.[23]

Other Nonlipophilic Fermentative Corynebacteria

Corynebacterium argentoratense has been isolated from the throats of healthy volunteers, but to date there have been no clinical reports of human disease associated with it.[5,93] *Corynebacterium matruchotii* is identified by its characteristic "whip handle" appearance on Gram stain.[3] It was previously identified as *Bacterionema matruchotii* until 1983, when it was reclassified as a Corynebacterium by Collins. Mainly an inhabitant of the oral cavity of humans and animals, *C. matruchotii* has been rarely associated with human disease.[94,95]

In 1998 Funke et al. identified a new species of Corynebacterium isolated from female patients with symptomatic urinary tract infections. Given the name *Corynebacterium riegelii,* it is nonlipophilic, weakly fermentative, and facultatively anaerobic.[96] Similar to the lipophilic *Corynebacterium urealyticum,* it demonstrates strong urease activity. It is susceptible to penicillins, cephalosporins, gentamicin, fluoroquinolones, rifampin, and tetracyclines.

Corynebacterium confusum was defined in 1998 by Funke et al. from three human clinical specimens.[97] It is nonlipophilic and very slowly fermentative. Two of the specimen sources were from foot infections and the third from a blood-stream isolate. No further reports have been published. Additional nonlipophilic fermentative *Corynebacterium* species identified recently from human clinical specimens include *Corynebacterium simulans, Corynebacterium sundvallense, Corynebacterium thomssenii, Corynebacterium freneyi,* and

Corynebacterium aurimucosum.[98-101] Further information from case reports is needed to determine the medical relevance of these isolates.

Nonlipophilic Nonfermentative Corynebacteria

The nonlipophilic nonfermentative group of Corynebacteria do not produce acid from any sugars, and were designated as absolute nonfermenters (ANF) by Hollis and Weaver.[15] They are colonizers of the human respiratory tract and ear canal and infrequent pathogens.

Corynebacterium afermentans subsp. *afermentans*

C. afermentans subsp. *afermentans* was included in the CDC coryneform group ANF (absolute nonfermenter) -1 until 1993, when Riegel et al. defined the species as *C. afermentans* with two subspecies: *C. afermentans* subsp. *afermentans* and *C. afermentans* subsp. *lipophilum.*[102] *C. afermentans* subsp. *afermentans* is a rare human pathogen, but has been reported to cause septicemia in immunocompromised patients.[103]

Corynebacterium auris

As in the case of *Turicella otitidis*, *C. auris* was initially isolated from middle ear fluid of pediatric patients with otitis media, and was presumed to be among the pathogens causing otitis media.[104] Subsequent studies have cultured *C. auris* from the external ear canal and cerumen of healthy subjects, both children and adults, and its role as a pathogen has been discounted.[6,105] *C. auris* is resistant to penicillins, clindamycin, and erythromycin, and susceptible to fluoroquinolones, gentamicin, rifampin, tetracyclines, and vancomycin.[23]

Corynebacterium pseudodiphtheriticum

C. pseudodiphtheriticum is included in the normal bacterial flora of the human upper respiratory tract. Lehmann and Neumann described the organism in 1896, giving it the name *Bacillus pseudodiphtheriticum.*[1] Since 1925 it has been known as *Corynebacterium pseudodiphtheriticum.* Historically, *C. pseudodiptheriticum* was associated with endocarditis of native and prosthetic valves.[106,107] The first cases of infections at other sites attributable to *C. pseudodiphtheriticum* became known in 1982, and since then *C. pseudodiphtheriticum* has been associated primarily with respiratory infections, particularly in immunocompromised hosts.[107-111] It has been isolated from patients with pneumonia and advanced AIDS.[112] Other sites of infections have been the eye, interevertebral disk, and lymph nodes.[113-116] Although *C. pseudodiphtheriticum* does not elaborate toxins, it has been isolated from three patients with exudative pharyngitis with pseudomembrane formation, not unlike *C. diphtheriae.*[117,118] In one case, colonization of close contacts was demonstrated. Some isolates of *C. pseudodiphtheriticum* have demonstrated resistance to macrolide antibiotics, but have maintained susceptibility to penicillins, cephalosporins, doxycycline, and glycopeptides.

Corynebacterium propinquum

Prior to 1994, *C. propinquum* was known as CDC coryneform group ANF-3.[119] Primarily isolated from the human respiratory tract, its role as a pathogen is yet to be defined. There are reports of isolation of *C. propinquum* from blood specimens that lack clinical information necessary to interpret the finding and one case of endocarditis.[120] One report of *C. propinquum* isolated from a pulmonary pleural effusion has been published.[121]

Lipophilic Corynebacteria

Lipophilic corynebacteria are fastidious, slow-growing bacteria that form tiny nonhemolytic colonies on standard media, but demonstrate enhanced growth with the addition of lipids to the culture medium.[2,3] The group includes the significant human pathogens *Corynebacterium jeikeium* and *Corynebacterium urealyticum.*

Corynebacterium jeikeium

Overview. *C. jeikeium* was initially described in 1976 as a highly resistant coryneform bacteria causing severe sepsis in patients with hematologic malignancies and profound neutropenia and in one patient with

ventricular CSF shunt.[122] In 1979 it was designated as CDC group JK, and in 1988 the designation was revised to *Corynebacterium jeikeium.*[123] *C. jeikeium* colonizes the skin of hospitalized patients, especially those treated with multiple antibiotics, and can also be isolated from the hospital environment.[124,125] There is some evidence that patient-to-patient transmission occurs in the hospital.[9,126] It is the most frequently isolated Corynebacterium in the acute care setting, and is the most important pathogen of the lipophilic corynebacteria.[10,12]

Microbiology. *C. jeikeium* is a pleomorphic gram-positive rod, which varies in form varying from coccobacillary to bacillary; some appear club shaped. It is nonhemolytic on standard media, and forms small gray-white colonies on routine culture.[2,3] It is lipophilic, forming large colonies on sheep blood agar supplemented with 1% Tween 80. Identification is confirmed with biochemical testing. *C. jeikeium* produces urease, reduces nitrate, and ferments glucose. It has variable fermentation of galactose and maltose.[127]

Pathogenicity. *C. jeikeium* is a cause of severe infections in the hospitalized patient.[9,128] Predisposing factors for infection include immunocompromised states such as malignancy, neutropenia, and AIDS.[9,129] Other risk factors include the presence of indwelling medical devices such as central venous catheters, peritoneal dialysis catheters, prosthetic valves, and CSF shunts. Prolonged hospital stay, treatment with broad-spectrum antibiotics, and impairmed skin integrity are well-described risk factors for development of infection with *C. jeikeium.*[9,125]

Infectious processes include septicemia from infected intravascular devices, native and prosthetic valve endocarditis, CSF shunt infections, meningitis and transverse myelitis, and prosthetic joint infections.[130-134] It has been reported to cause postsurgical infections, peritonitis in patients undergoing CAPD, liver abscess, otitis media, and osteomyelitis of the foot.[135-138] Skin findings with *C. jeikeium* infection are common: Fifty percent of neutropenic patients with *C. jeikeium* septicemia have reported skin findings including rash and subcutaneous nodules.[139,140] Palpable purpura have been reported in patients with *C. jeikeium* endocarditis.[141]

Treatment. *C. jeikeium* is resistant to many antibiotics, including penicillins, cephalosporins, and aminoglycosides, and there is inducible resistance to macrolides.[142,143] It remains susceptible to vancomycin, which is the recommended treatment. Although catheter removal has been routinely recommended in the setting of intravascular catheter–related infection, recent experience has shown a high success rate in catheter salvage with appropriate antimicrobial therapy.[144]

Corynebacterium urealyticum

First described in 1974, this bacteria was designated as CDC group D2 until 1992, when the name *Corynebacterium urealyticum* was proposed.[145] *C. urealyticum* colonizes the skin of 25% to 37% of hospitalized patients.[146] Because of its ability to adhere to uroepithelial cells, it is most commonly associated with urinary tract infections, and has been implicated as the cause of encrusted cystitis and encrusted pyelitis.[147]

Microbiology. Colonies of *C. urealyticum* are slow growing, lipophilic, and appear nonhemolytic and pinpoint when cultured on sheep blood agar under CO_2 for 48 hours.[2,3] It is a strict aerobe, with no growth under anaerobic conditions. On Gram stain, organisms are palisading, non–spore-forming coccobacilli. They are catalase positive and oxidase negative, with a rapid production of urease. Laboratories should be made aware of the need for further investigation of diphtheroid bacilli from urinary tract specimens in the proper clinical setting, as *C. urealyticum* may not grow in standard urine culture.[3,146]

Pathogenicity. *C. urealyticum* is primarily a cause of chronic and recurrent urinary tract infections, occurring mainly in the elderly and those with debilitation or immunosuppression. Additional risk factors include prolonged hospitalization, the use of bladder drainage catheters, and urinary tract procedures. Clues to diagnosis of *C. urealyticum* infection include sterile pyuria, alkaline urine, and the presence of white blood cells and struvite crystals.[148] *C. urealyticum* causes encrusted cystitis, which appears as chronic inflammation of the bladder mucosa with crystal deposits on the bladder mucosa surrounded by erythema. Encrusted pyelitis may occur if there are abnormalities of the upper urinary tract. In rare cases, *C. urealyticum* has been reported as a causative agent in peritonitis, endocarditis, pneumonia, septicemia, osteomyelitis, soft tissue infections, and superinfection of wounds.[149-151]

Treatment. In general, *C. urealyticum* is resistant to β-lactams, aminoglycosides, and trimethoprim-sulfamethoxazole. There is variable susceptibility to fluoroquinolones, macrolides, and tetracycline.[10,150] The treatment of choice is vancomycin, to which it remains susceptible. For urinary tract infections, in addition to vancomycin, endoscopic removal of bladder mucosa encrustations or acidification of urine by instilling acid into the bladder in cases of encrusted cystitis may be required, and urological consultation is recommended. Percutaneous nephrostomy tube place and irrigation of upper urinary tract with Thomas' acid solution in cases of upper tract disease has been described.[152]

Other Lipophilic Corynebacteria

Corynebacterium afermentans subsp. *lipophilum* is a rarely reported human pathogen.[102] It has been reported to cause intravascular catheter–related septicemia, prosthetic valve endocarditis, and brain abscess.[153] *Corynebacterium accolens* was previously known as CDC coryneform group 6. There were discrepancies in the definition until 1991, when it was defined further by Neubauer et al. and given the name *Corynebacterium accolens*. Known to colonize the human upper respiratory tract, *C. accolens* is a rarely reported human pathogen, but has been reported to cause septicemia and endocarditis.[154] *Corynebacterium macginleyi* was initially isolated solely from the human eye as a cause of conjunctivitis.[155] There has been one report of intravascular catheter–associated blood-stream infection by *C. macginleyi,* and one report of urinary tract infection associated with a bladder drainage catheter.[156] Other lipophilic corynebacteria including *Corynebacterium tuberculostearicum* and *Corynebacterium kroppenstedtii* have been cultured from inflammatory breast tissue in cases of granulomatous mastitis.[157,158] *Corynebacterium bovis* is a cause of bovine mastitis, but in humans has been described as a cause of endocarditis, chronic otitis media, and central nervous system (CNS) infection.[159] CDC coryneform group F1 may be a cause of urinary tract infection; it is similar to *C. urealyticum* in its very rapid urease reaction and differs from the latter in its very high susceptibility on antimicrobial testing.[160] CDC coryneform group G has been a cause of endocarditis and septic arthritis, and shows multiple antibiotic resistances.[161] *Corynebacterium lipophiloflavum* has been isolated from a patient with bacterial vaginosis.[162]

Arcanobacterium

Overview

Collins defined the genus *Arcanobacterium* in 1982, from "arcane," meaning "mysterious or secret" and "bacterium."[163] For many years *Arcanobacterium haemolyticum* was the only species in this genus. However, in 1997 further investigation of several Actinomyces species resulted in the reclassification of *Actinomyces pyogenes* and *Actinomyces bernardiae* as *Arcanobacterium* species, and defined two additional new species of Arcanobacteria.[164]

Arcanobacterium haemolyticum

Arcanobacterium haemolyticum was first isolated by MacLean et al. in 1946 from American soldiers and Pacific Islanders with pharyngeal and skin infections in the South Pacific.[165] The initial classification as *Corynebacterium haemolyticum* endured until 1982, when the genus *Arcanobacterium* was defined by Collins.

Microbiology. *Arcanobacterium haemolyticum* is a catalase-negative, gram-positive to gram-variable rod that does not form spores and is nonmotile.[2,3] It is β-hemolytic, but expression can vary by culture media and conditions, with hemolysis best observed on human blood agar.[166] Growth is enhanced in the presence of CO_2. It is known for forming dark pits under the colonies. Poor growth on tellurite helps to differentiate it from *C. diphtheriae*.

Colony morphology has been described as either rough or smooth type.[167] Rough type colonies are rough appearing, nonhemolytic, β-glucuronidase positive, and do not ferment sucrose and trehalose.

Smooth type are smooth appearing colonies, β-hemolytic, β-glucuronidase negative, and ferment sucrose or trehalose. Both types ferment glucose and maltose. Rough type colonies are most frequently associated with respiratory isolates; smooth biotypes are most frequently associated with wound isolates.[167] *A. haemolyticum* does not ferment xylose, which differentiates it from *A. pyogenes*. The α-mannosidase test has been proposed as a useful tool for identification. A positive test identifies *A. haemolyticum* and differentiates it from from *Arcanobacterium (Actinomyces) pyogenes,* and other coryneform-like bacteria including *Rhodococcus equi* and *Erysipelothrix rhusiopathiae*.[168] Because of the presence of phospholipase D activity similar to *C. ulcerans* and *C. pseudotuberculosis,* the reverse CAMP test will be positive, with inhibition of the hemolytic zone of a β-lysin–producing strain of *Staphylococcus aureus*.[169] Other secreted toxins include neuraminidase and a hemolysin.

Infections in Humans. *Arcanobacterium haemolyticum* is a well recognized cause of pharyngitis in humans, with a spectrum of illness from mild to diphtheria-like.[170-172] It accounts for about 0.5% of pharyngeal infections overall, and 2.5% in individuals in the 15- to 25-year–old age range. In studies, *A. haemolyticum* has not been isolated from healthy control populations, but has been isolated from 2.5% of a symptomatic young adult population.[172-174] It is indistinguishable from streptococcal pharyngitis in clinical appearance, and about 50% of cases of pharyngitis are exudative. Cervical adenopathy is usually present.[173] *A. haemolyticum* pharyngitis is accompanied with an exanthem in approximately 50% of cases. The rash generally appears after the onset of the pharyngitis, and has a variable appearance, often described as an erythematous morbilliform or scarlatiniform rash, appearing on the trunk, neck, and extremities. It may also present as an erythematous urticarial rash with an appearance similar to that of erythema multiforme.[170-172] Complications of *A. hemolyticum* pharyngitis include peritonsillar and pharyngeal abscesses, with *A. hemolyticum* the sole pathogen in 50% of cases in adolescents and young adults, and the remaining 50% coinfected with β-hemolytic streptococci.[173,175]

A. haemolyticum has been isolated from soft tissue infections including chronic ulcers, wound infections, cellulitis, and paronychia. It is frequently a component of polymicrobial infection in this setting, but has been isolated as the sole pathogen as well. Underlying conditions in polymicobial chronic ulcers include diabetes and peripheral vascular disease. Post-traumatic wound infections have been reported, as well as coinfection or superinfection with leprosy ulcers.[176,177]

Lemierre's disease with *Fusobacterium necrophorum* and *A. haemolyticum* has been reported, accompanied by a skin rash typical for *A. haemolyticum* infection.[178] Sepsis syndrome from *A. haemolyticum* has been described, occurring in all age groups and without predisposing factors. Other infections reported include sinusitis, orbital cellulitis, brain abscess, endocarditis, cavitary pneumonia, and vertebral osteomyelitis. *A. haemolyticum* may be present in subperiosteal abscesses in periodontal disease.[176,179-182]

Treatment. Susceptibility information for *A. haemolyticum* has been reviewed extensively.[183] Although in vitro studies show most strains to be penicillin susceptible, treatment failures may occur because of tolerance and poor penetration into the intracellular space. Other β-lactams have shown in vitro activity as well. The most reliable clinical data has shown efficacy of the macrolides, and erythromycin and azithromycin have been proposed as drugs of choice.[183] Clindamicin and doxycycline are also efficacious, as are ciprofloxacin and vancomycin. Resistance to trimethoprim-sulfamethoxazole is well documented. Three vancomycin-resistant strains of *A. haemolyticum* expressing the *vanA* gene were recovered in a surveillance study, but no vancomycin-resistant infections have been reported.[184] Surgical management of wound infections and drainage of soft tissue abscesses is recommended.

Arcanobacterium (Actinomyces) pyogenes

Initially described by Glage in 1903, this organism was initially named *Bacillus pyogenes*. It was known as *Corynebacterium pyogenes* until 1982, when it was reassigned to the genus *Actinomyces*. Since

1997 it has been known as *Arcanobacterium pyogenes*.[164] *A. pyogenes* is primarily an animal pathogen causing pyogenic infections in cattle, including pneumonia, endometritis, endocarditis, wound infections, and mastitis. Abscess formation is aided by neuraminidases, which facilitate adhesion to host epithelial cells.[185] Transmission of *A. pyogenes* by flies has been proposed.[186] *A. pyogenes* has not been isolated as normal human flora. Most human cases are acquired in rural settings. Human infections include annual outbreaks of leg ulcers in Thai children, septicemia in a patient with colon carcinoma, polymicrobial infected diabetic foot ulcers, spondylodiscitis and psoas abscess, subcutaneous abscesses, and intraabdominal infections.[186-189] *A. pyogenes* is cultured on sheep blood agar under CO_2 enrichment. Colonies are weakly hemolytic at 24 hours, and become more strongly hemolytic at 48 hours.[2,3] Differentiation from *A. haemolyticum* is made by observation of the CAMP reaction, by fermentation of xylose, and the α-mannosidase test.[3,168] *A. pyogenes* is susceptible to most antibiotics, including penicillins, cephalosporins, macrolides, tetracyclines, and aminoglycosides.

Arcanobacterium bernardiae

Originally described as CDC coryneform group 2 in 1987, it was assigned the species name *Actinomyces bernardiae* in 1995. In 1997 it was transferred to the genus *Arcanobacterium* as *Arcanobacterium bernardiae*.[164] On Gram stain it appears as short gram-positive rods without branching. It is identified by the ability to ferment maltose more rapidly than glucose, which separates it from other coryneform bacteria. It is distinguished from *A. pyogenes* by the inability to ferment sucrose, mannitol, and xylose.[3] *A. bernardiae* is a rare human pathogen, with recovery of the organism from the blood stream, abscesses, urinary tract, the eye, and wounds.[190-192]

Miscellaneous Coryneforms

Turicella otitidis

Initially isolated from patients with otitis media, *Turicella otitidis* is believed to be a colonizer of the human auditory canal and not a true pathogen in this setting, as it has been isolated in the same frequency from an asymptomatic control population.[6,105,193,194] It has been reported as a cause of mastoiditis and posterior auricular abscess in immunocompetent children, and septicemia in a neutropenic child.[195-197] *T. otitidis* is resistant to clindamycin and erythromycin, but susceptible to penicillins, cephalosporins, tetracyclines, fluoroquinolones, rifampin, and vancomycin.[23]

Arthrobacter Species

An environmental coryneform found in animal sheds, schools, and day care centers, Arthrobacter has rarely been isolated from human clinical specimens.[4] Identified species include *Arthrobacter cumminsii, Arthrobacter oxydans, Arthrobacter luteolus,* and *Arthrobacter albus*.[198,199] There are reports of septicemia in immunocompromised patients, and isolation of *Arthrobacter* from human urine specimens.[200] One unusual case report was of Whipple's syndrome, in which clinical specimens were negative for *Tropheryma whippeli,* but by 16S ribosomal RNA amplification of genetic material from a surgical specimen an identification of *Arthrobacter* was made.[201]

Brevibacterium Species

Brevibacterium species are short coryneforms isolated from milk and dairy products and are known colonizers of human skin.[11] They have been identified in environmental dust in schools, day care centers, and animal sheds.[4] Brevibacteria show a biphasic morphology on culture, with young colonies demonstrating typical coryneform features. As colonies age, the organisms mature into cocci or a coccobacillary appearance.[3] Brevibacteria have been implicated in causing human foot odor when confining footwear results in a moist environment. Although seven species of *Brevibacterium* exist, only four species have been associated with human infection: *Brevibacterium casei, Brevibacterium epidermidis, Brevibacterium mcbrellneri,* and *Brevibacterium otitidis*.[202]

B. casei is the species of this genus that is most frequently isolated from human clinical specimens. On culture it forms white-gray colonies with a distinctive cheese odor. On Gram stain it is a short, club-shaped rod that is catalase positive and non–spore-forming.[3,202] Human infections with Brevibacteria have most frequently been intravascular catheter–related bloodstream infections, particularly in immunocompromised patients and patients with AIDS.[203,204] There have been additional reports of meningitis, cholangitis, salpingitis, and peritonitis in patients undergoing CAPD. In addition, there is one report each of prosthetic valve endocarditis and osteomyelitis of the sternum in a neonate following an episode of mastitis in the mother.[207,208] Susceptibility testing shows some resistance to β-lactam antibiotics, fluoroquinolones, clindamycin, and macrolides. Vancomycin is the treatment of choice for serious infections.[23,209]

Dermabacter hominis

Dermabacter species were previously identified as CDC group 3 and group 5 coryneform bacteria, and are skin colonizers of humans.[210] They have been a cause of bacteremia in patients with prolonged hospitalizations and who have immune compromise and peritonitis in patients undergoing CAPD. *Dermabacter* has been isolated from a cerebral abscess in a renal transplant recipient and from a patient with chronic osteomyelitis with *Actinomyces neuii* as co-pathogen.[211-214] *D. hominis* exhibits variable resistance to many antibiotics, including penicillins, fluoroquinolones, macrolides, chloramphenicol, and tetracyclines, and susceptibility to vancomycin and teicoplanin.[23]

Rothia dentocariosa

Rothia are found as colonizers of the human oral cavity and have been isolated from dental plaque and in cases of periodontal disease.[12,215] *Rothia dentocariosa* has the potential for misidentification as *Dermabacter* or *Actinomyces* species in the microbiology laboratory.[3]

Case reports with reliable information on identification of the organisms have found it to be a pathogen in several cases of native and prosthetic valve endocarditis, including presentations with abscesses and vertebral osteomyelitis.[216-220] It has also been isolated as a cause of bacteremia without endocarditis.[221] It has been found in cases of pneumonia in patients with leukemia and lung cancer, and has caused peritonitis in a patient undergoing CAPD.[222,223]

Oerskovia

Included in CDC group A-1 and A-2, *Oerskovia* species are rare human pathogens but have been reported to cause infection in immunocompromised hosts, patients with implanted devices, and those with indwelling central venous catheters.[3] The spectrum of infections has ranged from bacteremia, endocarditis, meningitis associated with CSF shunt infection, soft tissue infection, prosthetic joint infection, and peritonitis in a patient undergoing CAPD.[224-228] One report of endophthalmitis following eye injury with a metallic foreign body exists in the literature.[229]

Microbacterium

CDC coryneform group A-4 and A-5 bacteria have been found to be *Microbacterium* species on further investigation and since 1998, the genus *Aureobacterium* has been included in the genus *Microbacterium*.[230,231] *Microbacterium* species have been found as a cause of bacteremia in patients on an oncology ward, and in specimens from patients with endophthalmitis. Most commonly it has been a nosocomial pathogen in debilitated and immunocompromised patients.[232-235]

Leifsonia aquatica

Corynebacterium aquaticum was reclassified in 2000 as *Leifsonia aquatica*.[236] Because of inconsistencies of identification and confusion with *Aureobacterium* in previous reports, it has been difficult to determine the pathogenicity of this species.[237,238] It is expected that future case reports will help to clarify this. At this time, no case reports have been published for *Leifsonia aquatica,* although *C. aquaticum* had been reported to cause septicemia in immunocompromised hosts as well as peritonitis in patients on CAPD.[239-242] In addition, urinary tract infection in a neonate and meningitis in an infant have been reported.[243,244]

Although strains of *Exiguobacterium*, *Cellulomonas*, and *Sanguibacter* have been isolated from human clinical specimens, no reports of human disease attributed to them exist in the literature.[3,245]

RHODOCOCCUS

Rhodococcus (red coccus) belongs to the family Nocardioform, order Actinomycetes, which includes *Nocardia*, *Corynebacterium*, *Mycobacterium*, and *Gordonia* species. *Rhodococcus equi* is the most commonly isolated species causing human infection, especially among immunocompromised hosts. Other members of this genus that are human pathogens include *Rhodococcus rhodochrous*, *Rhodococcus fascians* (*Rhodococcus luteus*), and *Rhodococcus erythropolis*.

Rhodococcus equi

R. equi (formerly *Corynebacterium equi*) was first identified as a pathogen in 1923 when it was isolated from the lungs of foals with pyogranulomatous pneumonia.[246] It has subsequently been identified in a variety of animals including cattle, swine, sheep, goats, deer, bears, wild birds, seals, and dogs and cats.[247] The first case of human infection was reported in 1967 when *R. equi* was cultured from lung specimens of a young man working in a stockyard who was being treated with corticosteroids and 6-mercaptopurine for autoimmune hepatitis and presented with fever and cavitary pneumonia.[248] During the next decade, sporadic cases of infection in humans were reported.[249] Beginning in the early 1980s, the incidence of *R. equi* infection increased markedly. This increase has been attributed to the human immunodeficiency virus (HIV) infection epidemic, advances in chemotherapy for malignancies, and organ transplantation. In addition, improvements in microbiology laboratory identification techniques and increasing recognition of *R. equi* as a pathogen may also explain part of the increase in incidence.[250,251] The frequency of *R. equi* infections in HIV-infected patients seems to have decreased in recent years, largely related to highly active antiretroviral therapy (HAART) and possibly to prophylaxis with clarithromycin, azithromycin, and rifabutin. More than 175 cases of infection caused by *R. equi* have been published. *R. equi* has been isolated from soil worldwide and from the manure of herbivores.[247,250] Infection in both animals and humans is thought to be acquired through inhalation or ingestion of the organism. Inoculation into a wound can also lead to infection. Exposure to farm soil, animals, or manure has been reported in many human cases, although it is less common in HIV-positive patients.[248,250,252,253] *R. equi* has been rarely isolated from healthy persons.[254] Most infected individuals have had defective cell-mediated immunity, with or without a history of animal exposure. Nosocomial cases of *R. equi* have been reported.[255] Human-to-human transmission has been suspected in cases of *R. equi* pneumonia acquired by HIV-infected patients who were roommates of patients infected with *R. equi*.[256] Occupational acquisition of *R. equi* by a healthy laboratory worker who developed pneumonia has been reported. *Rhodococcus* species with properties very similar to those of *R. equi* have been isolated as nasal flora in adults.[257]

R. equi is a gram-positive obligate aerobe that is asporogenous and nonmotile. It may appear coccoid or bacillary depending on growth conditions. Its bacillary appearance varies from long, curved, clubbed forms to short filaments with branching. *R. equi* can grow at a variety of temperatures but grows optimally at 30° C. Colonies on solid media appear large, irregular, smooth, and mucoid. They are pale salmon-pink in color; however, this characteristic color may not appear until days 4 to 7 of incubation. Although they grow well on ordinary media, if cultured in this manner, the organism may be overlooked or discarded as a nonpathogenic coryneform. Isolation of *R. equi* from contaminated specimens is facilitated by the use of selective media such as colistin-nalidixic agar (CNA), phenyl-ethanol agar (PEA), or ceftazidime-novobiocin agar. *R. equi* is catalase, lipase, urease, and phosphatase positive. It is oxidase, elastase, DNase and protease negative. Differentiation from other pathogenic coryneforms is based on a lack of ability to ferment carbohydrates or liquefy gelatin.[2] Because it is sometimes acid fast, it may be mistaken for a *Mycobacterium*.[247,250] It

can be distinguished from some mycobacterial species by the 14-day arylsulfatase test, as Rhodococcus is negative for this reaction. Two special features of *R. equi* help distinguish it from other similar organisms: (1) When *R. equi* is cultured on sheep blood agar that is cross-streaked with other bacteria, such as *Staphylococcus aureus*, *Corynebacterium pseudotuberculosis*, or *Listeria monocytogenes*, synergistic hemolysis occurs.[250] (2) In vitro antagonism between imipenem and other β-lactams is widespread among *R. equi* isolates.[258] Generally, the identification of *Rhodococcus* species using traditional tests may be difficult. There is no simple, reproducible method for rapid identification and differentiation. Ribotyping and PCR-restriction fragment length polymorphism (RFLP) identification may prove to be rapid, useful adjuncts.[259,260]

R. equi is a facultative, intracellular pathogen. It infects macrophages and survives inside the lysosomes. Its ability to cause chronic infection may be based on its complex cell wall, which is thought to prevent phagosome-lysosome fusion, resists the oxidative burst, and causes a nonspecific degranulation of lysosomes, which permits intrahistiocytic survival.[261] Although virulence factors associated with *R. equi* infections in animals have been defined and include plasmid-associated surface proteins, they may not be important in infection in humans.[262-267] Histopathology usually reveals a necrotizing granulomatous reaction. Multiple microabscesses may be seen. Malakoplakia is a rare, chronic, granulomatous inflammatory process that is associated with an impaired ability to process microorganisms within histiocytes. It is characterized by accumulations of benign macrophages associated with intracellular and extracellular aggregates of periodic acid-Schiff–positive histiocytes that contain lamellated iron and calcium inclusions, and are termed Michaelis-Guttman bodies.[261] Lung malakoplakia is a very rare condition; most of the reported patients had *R. equi* pneumonia.[268,269]

R. equi has been cultured from a variety of human tissues and fluids including sputum, bronchial washings, lung tissue, pleural fluid, blood, CSF, brain, skin, lymph nodes, peritoneal fluid, bone, stool, pharyngeal exudates, and wounds.[252,270-295] It has been recovered from dialysate and intravenous catheters.[252] Pneumonia accounts for approximately 80% of human cases of infection reported in the literature.[251,296] Most published cases of pulmonary infection have occurred in immunocompromised hosts.[250,296] The lung was the only site of infection in over 80% of cases; a concurrent extrapulmonary site was reported in approximately 20% of cases of pulmonary infection.[252] Typically, the presentation is subacute in onset. Common symptoms include fever, productive or nonproductive cough, and fatigue.[252] Pleuritic chest pain is also common. Hemoptysis has been reported in approximately 15% of patients.[297] *R. equi* bacteremia frequently complicates pneumonia. Other complications include the development of pleural effusion, empyema, pneumothorax, endobronchial lesions, cardiac tamponade, and mediastinitis.[252,294,296] Chest radiographs reveal nodules, cavities, which may be single or multiple, infiltrates, and pleural effusions.[256,294,297] More than one type of lesion may be present. In a case series of pulmonary cavitary lesions in HIV-infected persons, *R. equi* was the fifth most common microbiologically proven cause, accounting for approximately 9% of cases.[298] It followed *Mycobacterium tuberculosis*, *Pneumocystis jirovecii*, *Pseudomonas aeruginosa*, and *Staphylococcus aureus* in frequency. The cavities have been described as thick walled and sometimes have an air fluid level.[252] Necrotizing pneumonia due to *R. equi* closely resembles tuberculosis or nocardiosis. Nodules or cavities of the upper lung lobes, or both, may be seen. Air fluid levels are seen in cavitary lesions caused by *R. equi*, but not in those seen with tuberculosis. Other radiological findings include mediastinal enlargement or pulmonary nodules. Although a good quality sputum specimen can yield a microbiological diagnosis, in many instances, invasive techniques such as bronchoscopy, thoracentesis, or surgical resection are required to make a microbiological diagnosis. Blood cultures are positive in approximately 50% of HIV-infected individuals and in 25% of solid organ transplant recipients who are infected with *R. equi*. Up to 30% of immunocompetent hosts are bacteremic.[254,272,274]

Extrapulmonary infection with *R. equi* occurs in approximately 20% of cases with pulmonary infection; infection of extrapulmonary sites occurs in approximately 25% of cases without evidence of pulmonary involvement. Most common extrapulmonary sites reported were brain and subcutaneous abscesses.[252] Extrapulmonary infection is frequently a late manifestation of the initial pulmonary infection. Abscesses in the liver, spleen, thyroid, kidney, psoas muscle, bone, prostate, intra-abdominal cavity, and paraspinous tissue have occurred.[296] Extrapulmonary infections not associated with pulmonary disease have been noted to present in three distinct patterns.[252] The first pattern includes wound infections, traumatic septic arthritis, and endophthalmitis following ocular injury. In these cases, infection remains localized at the primary site and drainage procedures appear to hasten recovery. The second group consists of cases of isolated bacteremia that manifested with fever. The majority of these patients had malignancies and were neutropenic or had recently received chemotherapy. Central venous catheters were present in most of these cases. The third pattern may have resulted from inoculation of the gastrointestinal tract with dissemination to regional lymph nodes. Conditions in this group included peritonitis, pelvic masses, and mesenteric adenitis. Other reported types of infection include otitis media with mastoiditis; colonic polyps infiltrated with *R. equi;* and osteomyelitis of the vertebrae, long bones, and mandible.[252]

More than 85% of cases of *R. equi* infection described in the literature have occurred in immunocompromised hosts, particularly those with HIV infection. HIV-infected patients account for two thirds of cases.[251] Infection of immunocompetent persons with *R. equi,* however, may be more common than previously assumed because in a recent series, immunocompetent hosts accounted for 42% of cases.[254] Clearance of *R. equi* is impaired in the immunocompromised host and relapses are common despite maintenance antibiotic therapy. In the pre-HAART era, relapses of pneumonia were described in up to 80% of HIV-infected patients. Infection occurs primarily in patients with CD4 counts of fewer than 100 cells/microliter.[251] Approximately 10% of *R. equi* infections occur in transplant recipients receiving immunosuppressive therapy and are generally a late complication.[251,276,289,290] Most of these patients were solid organ transplant recipients. The primary site of infection was the lung. Findings included both nodular lesions and infiltrates. Cavitary lesions were frequent. In approximately half of transplant recipients, extrapulmonary infection was present and included brain abscesses, paravertebral abscess, purulent pericarditis, subcutaneous nodules, and osteomyelitis of the femur. Among immunocompetent hosts, localized infections account for nearly 50%.[254] Pulmonary infection was present in more than 40%. Disseminated infection also occurred.[287,288] The mortality rate is greatest among patients with HIV and has been reported to be as high as 58%.[252,272,274] Mortality in immunocompetent hosts has been reported to be 11%; it is approximately 20% for non-HIV–infected immunocompromised hosts.[251,276]

For several reasons, including the small number of reported cases, standards for treatments of *R. equi* infection have not been established. *R. equi* is usually susceptible in vitro to vancomycin, erythromycin, fluoroquinolones, rifampin, glycopeptides, imipenem, aminoglycosides, and linezolid.[251-252,299,300] Susceptibility to clindamycin, tetracycline, chloramphenicol, and cephalosporins is variable; *R. equi* is usually resistant to penicillins, and even if susceptible in vitro, the use of penicillins is not recommended because resistance can develop.[252,254] In an animal model, the most effective agents were vancomycin, imipenem, and rifampin.[301] Rifampin-resistant isolates have been reported.[302] Monotherapy has been ineffective in a number of cases and is not recommended. Combinations of two or three antimicrobial agents have generally yielded partial or complete therapeutic responses.[303] Localized, non-CNS infections in immunocompetent hosts can usually be treated with oral agents.[254] Two-drug regimens that include a macrolide, rifampin, and/or a fluoroquinolone can be started empirically and should be adjusted based on the results of susceptibility testing.[251] Immunocompromised hosts and those with serious infections should be treated with two- or three-drug regimens that include vancomycin or a carbapenem (imipenem or meropenem),

rifampin, a fluoroquinolone, an aminoglycoside, or a macrolide. It has been suggested that intravenous antibiotics be continued until clinical improvement occurs or for a minimum of 2 to 3 weeks.[251] Oral agents should then be given until cultures are negative and signs and symptoms have resolved. A minimum of 2 to 6 months of antimicrobial therapy is advised for immunocompromised hosts and those with pulmonary, bone, and joint or CNS infections. Because the CNS is a frequent secondary site of infection, agents that penetrate this site should be administered.[252] Drainage of localized abscesses, empyemas, and large cavities may be beneficial. Lung lobectomy has been performed when poor clinical response was noted after antimicrobial therapy. It is generally recommended that after the treatment course is completed, HIV-infected individuals and persons with ongoing immunosuppression receive long-term suppressive therapy with a macrolide plus rifampin or a quinolone or doxycycline with rifampin. For HIV-positive patients, oral suppressive therapy should be continued until immune reconstitution occurs. Infection may develop or become manifest at other sites during therapy. Relapses are common. They can occur at the initial site of infection or at other sites.

Other *Rhodococcus* Species and Related Genera

Infections caused by other *Rhodococcus* species and related genera such as *Gordonia* and *Tsukamurella* have generally been associated with medical procedures or devices. *Gordonia bronchialis* (formerly *Rhodococcus bronchialis*) has been reported to cause sternal wound infection after coronary artery bypass surgery.[304] *Tsukamurella paurometabola* (formerly *Rhodococcus aurantiacus* and *Corynebacterium paurometabolum*) has caused central venous catheter–related bacteremia in patients with malignancies or who were receiving parenteral nutrition, pneumonia, meningitis, and soft tissue abscesses and necrotizing tenosynovitis.[305-309] *Rhodococcus fascians* (*Rhodococcus luteus*) and *Rhodococcus erythropolis* have been associated with chronic endopthalmitis after lens implantation.[310] *R. erythropolis* has been isolated from patients with peritonitis who were undergoing ambulatory peritoneal dialysis, from subcutaneous nodules in a patient with AIDS, and from sputum in a patient with pneumonia.[311,312] Pulmonary infection resembling tuberculosis has been reported to be caused by *Gordonia rubripertinctus* (formerly *Rhodococcus rubropertinctus*) in a patient who was not immunosuppressed.[306,313] *Rhodococcus rhodochrous* has caused pneumonia, bacteremia, pericarditis, skin lesions, meningoencephalitis, VP shunt infection, and chronic corneal ulceration.[314,315] Meningitis due to non-*equi Rhodococcus* has been reported in an immunocompetent host.[316] Antimicrobial therapy for these infections should be based on susceptibility testing. When *Rhodococcus* infection occurs in association with a medical device, the device should be removed. With regard to *R. equi,* surgical resection may play a role in certain circumstances, such as failure to respond to antimicrobial therapy and focal abscesses.

REFERENCES

1. Lehmann KB, Neumann R. Atlas und Grundriss der bakteriologie und Lehrbuch der speziellen bacteriologischen Diagnostik. 1st ed. Munich: JF Lehmann; 1896
2. Coyle MB, Lipsky BA. Coryneform bacteria in infectious diseases: Clinical and laboratory aspects. Clin Microbiol Rev. 1990;3:227-246.
3. Funke G, von Graevenitz A, Clarridge J III, et al. Clinical microbiology of coryneform bacteria. Clin Microbiol Rev. 1997;10:125-159.
4. Andersson AM, Weiss N, Rainey F, et al. Dust-borne bacteria in animal sheds, schools and children's day care centres. J Appl Microbiol. 1999;86:622-634.
5. von Graevenitz A, Punter-Streit V, Riegel P, et al. Coryneform bacteria in throat cultures of healthy individuals. J Clin Microbiol. 1998;36:2087-2088.
6. Stroman DW, Roland PS, Dohar J, et al. Microbiology of normal external auditory canal. Laryngoscope. 2001;111:2054-2059.
7. Shapiro M, Smith KJ, James WD, et al. Cutaneous microenvironment of human immunodeficiency virus (HIV)-seropositive and HIV-seronegative individuals, with special reference to *Staphylococcus aureus* colonization. J Clin Microbiol. 2000;38:3174-3178.
8. Stauffer F, Kittler H, Forstinger C, et al. The dermatoscope: A potential source of nosocomial infection? Melan Res. 2001;11:153-156.
9. Young VM, Meyers WF, Moody MR, et al. The emergence of coryneform bacteria as a cause of nosocomial infections in compromised hosts. Am J Med. 1981;70:646-650.

10. Lagrou K, Verhaegen J, Janssens M, et al. Prospective study of catalase-positive coryneform organisms in clinical specimens: Identification of clinical relevance and antibiotic susceptibility. Diagn Microbiol Infect Dis. 1998;30:7-15.

11. Bernard KA, Munro C, Wiebe D, et al. Characteristics of rare or recently described *Corynebacterium* species recovered from human clinical material in Canada. J Clin Microbiol. 2002;40:4375-4381.

12. Marshall RJ, Johnson E. *Corynebacteria:* Incidence among samples submitted to a clinical laboratory for culture. Med Lab Sci. 1990;47:36-41.

13. Kuriyama T, Karasawa T, Nakagawa K, et al. Bacteriology and antimicrobial susceptibility of gram-positive cocci isolated from pus specimens of orofacial odontogenic infections. Oral Microbiol Immunol. 2002;17:132-135.

14. Riegel P, Ruimy R, Christen R, Monteil H. Species identities and antimicrobial susceptibilities of Corynebacteria isolated from various clinical sources. Eur J Clin Micrbiol Infect Dis. 1996;15:657-662.

15. Hollis DG, Weaver RE. 1981. Gram-positive organisms: A guide to identification. Special Bacteriology Section, Centers for Disease Control and Prevention, Atlanta, Georgia.

16. Bernard, KA, Bellefeuille M, Ewan EP. Cellular fatty acid composition as an adjunct to identification of asporogenous, aerobic gram-positive rods. J Clin Microbiol. 1191;29:83-89.

17. Tang Y, von Graevenitz A, Waddington M, et al. Identification of coryneform bacterial isolates by ribosomal DNA sequence analysis. J Clin Microbiol. 2000;38:1676-1678.

18. Vaneechoutte M, Riegel P, de Briel D, et al. Evaluation of the applicability of amplified rDNA-restriction analysis (ARDRA) to identification of species of the genus *Corynebacterium*. Res Microbiol. 1995;146:633-641.

19. Gavin SE, Leonard RB, Briselden AM, Coyle MB. Evaluation of the rapid CORYNE identification system for *Corynebacterium* species and other coryneforms. J Clin Microbiol. 1992;30:1692-1695.

20. Soto A, Zapardiel J, Soriano F. Evaluation of API CORYNE system for identifying coryneform bacteria. J Clin Pathol. 1994;47:756-759.

21. Funke G, Renaud FN, Freney J, Riegel P. Multicenter evaluation of the updated and extended API (RAPID) Coryne database 2.0. J Clin Microbiol. 1997;35:3122-3126.

22. Funke G, Peters K, Aravena-Roman M. Evaluation of the RapID CB plus system for identification of coryneform bacteria in *Listeria* spp. J Clin Microbiol. 1998;36:2439-2442.

23. Funke G, Punter V, von Graevenitz A. Antimicrobial susceptibility patterns of some recently established coryneform bacteria. Antimicrob Agents Chemother. 1996;40:2874-2878

24. Balci I, Eksi F, Bayram A. Coryneform bacteria isolated from blood cultures and their antibiotic susceptibilities. J Int Med Res. 2002;30:422-427.

25. Goldstein EJ, Citron DM, Merriam CV, et al. In vitro activities of daptomycin, vancomycin, quinupristin-dalfopristin, linezolid, and five other antimicrobials against 307 gram-positive anaerobic and 31 *Corynebacterium* clinical isolates. Antimicrob Agents Chemother. 2003;47:337-341.

26. Power EG, Abdulla YH, et al. *vanA* genes in vancomycin-resistant clinical isolates of *Oerskovia turbata* and *Arcanobacterium (Corynebacterium) haemolyticum*. J Antimicrob Chemother. 1995;36:595-606.

27. Wauters G, Van Bosterhaut B, Janssens M, et al. Identification of *Corynebacterium amycolatum* and other nonlipophilic fermentative corynebacteria of human origin. J Clin Micrbiol. 1998;36:1430-1432.

28. Wong TP, Groman N. Production of diphtheria toxin by selected isolates of *Corynebacterium ulcerans* and *Corynebacterium pseudotuberculosis*. Infect Immun. 1984;43:1114-1116.

29. Efstratiou A, Engler KH, Dawes CS, et al. Comparison of phenotypic and genotypic methods for detection of diphtheria toxin among isolates of pathogenic corynebacteria. J Clin Microbiol. 1998;36:3173-3177.

30. von Hunolstein C, Alfarone G, Scopetti F, et al. Molecular epidemiology and characteristics of *Corynebacterium diphtheriae* and *Corynebacterium ulcerans* strains isolated in Italy during the 1990's. J Med Microbiol. 2003;52:181-188.

31. Anonymous. Three cases of toxigenic *Corynebacterium ulcerans* infection. CDR Wkly. 2000;10:49, 52.

32. Anonymous. Respiratory diphtheria caused by *Corynebacterium ulcerans*-Terre Haute, Indiana, 1996. MMWR Morbid Mortal Wkly Rep. 1997;46:330-332.

33. Efstratiou A, George RC. Laboratory guidelines for the diagnosis of infections caused by *Corynebacterium diphtheriae* and *C.* ulcerans. Commun Dis Publ Hlth. 1999;2:250-257.

34. Mann PG. *Corynebacterium ulcerans* infections. Lancet. 1970;1:839.

35. Kaufmann D, Ott P, Zbinden R. Laryngopharyngitis by *Corynebacterium ulcerans*. Infect. 2002;30:168-170.

36. Leek MD, Sivaloganathan S, Devaraj SK, et al. Diphtheria with a difference—a rare *Corynebacterium* fatality with associated apoptotic cell death. Histopathology. 1990;16:187-189.

37. Wellinghausen N, Sing A, Kern WV, et al. A fatal case of necrotizing sinusitis due to toxigenic *Corynebacterium ulcerans*. Int J Med Microbiol. 2002;292:59-63.

38. Wagner J, Ignatius R, Voss S, et al. Infection of the skin caused by *Corynebacterium ulcerans* and mimicking classical cutaneous diphtheria. Clin Infect Dis. 2001;33:1598-1600.

39. Dessau RB, Brandt-Christensen M, Jensen OJ, et al. Pulmonary nodules due to *Corynebacterium ulcerans*. Eur Respir J. 1995;8:651-653.

40. Henderson A. Pseudotuberculous adenitis caused by *Corynebacterium pseudotuberculosis*. J Med Microbiol. 1979;12:147-149.

41. Mills AE, Mitchell RD, Lim EK. *Corynebacterium pseudotuberculosis* is a cause of human necrotising granulomatous. Pathology. 1997;29:231-233.

42. Peel MM, Palmer GG, Stacpoole AM, et al. Human lymphadenitis due to *Corynebacterium pseudotuberculosis:* Report of ten cases from Australia and review. Clin Infect Dis. 1997;24:185-191.

43. Keslin MH, McCoy EL, McCusker JJ, et al. *Corynebacterium pseudotuberculosis*. A new cause of infectious and eosinophilic pneumonia. Am J Med. 1979;67:228-231.

44. Richards W, Hurse A. *Corynebacterium pseudotuberculosis* abscesses in a young butcher. Aust N Z J Med. 1985;15:85-86.

45. Porschen RK, Goodman Z, Rafai B. Isolation of *Corynebacterium xerosis* from clinical specimens: Infection and colonization. Am J Clin Pathol. 1977;68:290-293.

46. Bergamini M, Fabrizi P, Pagani S, et al. Evidence of increased carriage of *Corynebacterium* spp. in healthy individuals with low antibody titres against diphtheria toxoid. Epidemiol Infect. 2000;125:105-112.

47. Geraci JE, Forth RJ, Ellis FH Jr. Postoperative prosthetic valve bacterial endocarditis due to *Corynebacterium xerosis*. Mayo Clin Proc. 1967;42:736-743.

48. Roder BL, Frimodt-Moller N. *Corynebacterium xerosis* as a cause of community-acquired endocarditis. Eur J Clin Microbiol Infect Dis. 1990;9:233-234.

49. Vettese TE, Craig CP. Spontaneous bacterial peritonitis due to *Corynebacterium xerosis*. Clin Infect Dis. 1993;17:815.

50. Arisoy ES, Demmler GJ, Dunne WM Jr. *Corynebacterium xerosis* ventribuloperitoneal shunt infection in an infant: Report of a case and review of the literature. Pediatr Infect Dis J. 1993;12:536-538.

51. Malik AS, Johari MR. Pneumonia, pericarditis, and endocarditis in a child with *Corynebacterium xerosis* septicemia. Clin Infect Dis. 1995;20:191-192.

52. King CT. Sternal wound infection due to *Corynebacterium xerosis*. Clin Infect Dis. 1994;19:1171-1172.

53. Esteban J, Nieto E, Calvo R, et al. Microbiological characterization and clinical significance of *Corynebacterium amycolatum* strains. Eur J Clin Microbiol Infect Dis. 1999;18:518-521.

54. Funke G, Lawson PA, Bernard KA, et al. Most *Corynebacterium xerosis* strains identified in the routine clinical laboratory correspond to *Corynebacterium amycolatum*. J Clin Microbiol. 1996;34:1124-1128.

55. Wooster SL, Qamruddin A, Clarke R, et al. Brain abscess due to *Corynebacterium xerosis*. J Infect. 1999;38:55-56.

56. Robins E, Haile-Selassie T. *Corynebacterium xerosis* sepsis in a pediatric patient with sickle cell disease (as case report). Clin Pediatr. 2001;40:181-182.

57. Voisin S, Deruaz D, Freney J, et al. Differentiation of *Corynebacterium amycolatum, C. minutissimum, C. striatum* and related species by pyrolysis-gas-liquid chromatography with atomic emission detection. Res Microbiol. 2002;153:307-311.

58. Watkins DA, Chahine A, Creger RJ, et al. *Corynebacterium striatum:* A diphtheroid with pathogenic potential. Clin Infect Dis. 1993;17:21-25.

59. Martinez-Martinez L, Suarez AI, Winstanley J, et al. Phenotypic characteristics of 31 strains of *Corynebacterium striatum* isolated from clinical samples. J Clin Microbiol. 1995;33:2458-2461.

60. Brandenburg AH, van Belkum A, van Pelt C, et al. Patient-to-patient spread of a single strain of *Corynebacterium striatum* causing infections in a surgical intensive care unit. J Clin Microbiol. 1996;34:2089-2094.

61. Leonard RB, Nowowiejski DJ, Warren JJ, et al. Molecular evidence of person-to-person transmission of a pigmented strain of *Corynebacterium striatum* in intensive care units. J Clin Microbiol. 1994;32:164-169.

62. Melero-Bascones M, Munoz P, Rodriguez-Creixems M, et al. *Corynebacterium striatum:* An undescribed agent of pacemaker-related endocarditis. Clin Infect Dis. 1996;22:576-577.

63. Juurlink DN, Borczyk A, Simor AE. Native valve endocarditis due to *Corynebacterium striatum*. Eur J Clin Microbiol Infect Dis. 1996;15:963-965.

64. Rufael DW, Cohn SE. Native valve endocarditis due to *Corynebacterium striatum:* Case report and review. Clin Infect Dis. 1994;19:1054-1061.

65. de Arriba JJ, Blanch JJ, Mateos F, et al. *Corynebacterium striatum* first reported case of prosthetic valve endocarditis. J Infect. 2002;44:193.

66. Fernandez-Ayala M, Nan DN, Farinas MC. Vertebral osteomyelitis due to *Corynebacterium striatum*. Am J Med. 2001;111:167.

67. Bowstead TT, Santiago SM. Pleuropulmonary infection due to *Corynebacterium striatum*. Br J Dis Chest. 1980;74:198-200.

68. Cone LA, Curry N, Wuestoff MA, et al. Septic synovitis and arthritis due to *Corynebacterium striatum* following an accidental scalpel injury. Clin Infect Dis. 1998;27:1532-1533.

69. Tattevin P, Cremieux AC, Muller-Serieys C, et al. Native valve endocarditis due to *Corynebacterium striatum:* First reported case of medical treatment alone. Clin Infect Dis. 1996;23:1330-1331.

70. Weiss K, Labbe AC, Laverdiere M. *Corynebacterium striatum* meningitis: Case report and review of an increasingly important *Corynebacterium* species. Clin Infect Dis. 1996;23:1246-1248.

71. Stone N, Gillett P, Burge S. Breast abscess due to *Corynebacterium striatum*. Br J Dermatol. 1997;137:623-625.

72. Knox KL, Holmes AH. Nosocomial endocarditis caused by *Corynebacterium amycolatum* and other nondiphtheriae *Corynebacteria*. Emerg Infect Dis. 2002;8:97-99.

73. Roberts MC, Leonard RB, Briselden A, et al. Characterization of antibiotic-resistant *Corynebacterium striatum* strains. J Antimicrob Chemother. 1992;30:463-474.

74. Martinez-Martinez L, Pascual A, Bernard K, et al. Antimicrobial susceptibility pattern of *Corynebacterium striatum*. Antimicrob Agents Chemother. 1996;40:2671-2672.

75. Collins MD, Jones D. *Corynebacterium minutissimum* sp. nov., nom. rev. Int J Syst Bacteriol. 1983;33:870-871.

76. Yassin AF, Steiner U, Ludwig W. *Corynebacterium aurimucosum* sp. nov. and emended description of *Corynebacterium minutissimum* Collins and Jones (1983). Int J Systemat Evol Microbiol. 2002;52:1001-1005.

77. Kates SG, Nordstrom KM, McGinley KJ, et al. Microbial ecology of interdigital infections of toe web spaces. J Am Acad Dermatol. 1990;22:578-582.

78. Zinkernagel AS, von Graevenitz A, Funke G. Heterogeneity within *Corynebacterium minutissimum* strains is explained by misidentified *Corynebacterium amycolatum* strains. Am J Clin Pathol. 1996;106:378-383.

79. Granok AB, Benjamin P Garrett LS. *Corynebacterium minutissimum* bacteremia in an immunocompetent host with cellulitis. Clin Infect Dis. 2002;35:e40-e42.
80. Fernandez GF, Saavedra MJM, Benitez SM, et al. *Corynebacterium minutissimum* peritonitis in a CAPD patient. Periton Dialys Int. 1998;18:345-346.
81. Craig J, Grigor W, Doyle B, et al. Pyelonephritis caused by *Corynebacterium minutissimum*. Pediatr Infect Dis J. 1994;13:1151-1152.
82. Cavendish J, Cole JB, Ohl CA. Polymicrobial central venous catheter sepsis involving a multiantibiotic-resistant strain of *Corynebacterium minutissimum*. Clin Infect Dis. 1994;19:204-205.
83. Santos-Juanes J, Galache C, Martinez-Cordero A, et al. Cutaneous granulomas caused by *Corynebacterium minutissimum* in an HIV-infected man. J Eur Acad Dermatol Venereol. 2002;16:643-645.
84. Bandera A, Gori A, Rossi MC, et al. A case of costochondral abscess due to *Corynebacterium minutissimum* in an HIV-infected patient. J Infect. 2000;41:103-105.
85. Berger SA, Gorea A, Stadler J, et al. Recurrent breast abscesses caused by *Corynebacterium minutissimum*. J Clin Microbiol. 1984;20:1219-1220.
86. Collins MD, Burton RA, Jones D. *Corynebacterium amycolatum* sp. nov., a new mycolic acid-less *Corynebacterium* species from human skin. FEMS Microbiol Lett. 1988;49:349-352.
87. von Graevenitz A, Frommelt L, Punter-Streit V, et al. Diversity of coryneforms found in infections following prosthetic joint insertion and open fractures. Infection 1998;26:36-38.
88. Clarke R, Qamruddin A, Taylor M, et al. Septic arthritis caused by *Corynebacterium amycolatum* following vascular graft sepsis. J Infect. 1999;38:126-127.
89. Daniels C, Schoors D, van Camp G. Native valve endocarditis with aorta-to-left atrial fistula due to *Corynebacterium amycolatum*. Eur J Echocardiogr. 2003;4:68-70.
90. Funke G, Bernard KA, Bucher C, et al., *Corynebacterium glucuronolyticum* sp. nov., isolated from male patients with genitourinary tract infections. Med Microbiol Lett. 1995;4:204-215.
91. Devriese LA, Riegel P, Hommez J, et al. Identification of *Corynebacterium glucuronolyticum* strains from the urogenital tract of humans and pigs. J Clin Microbiol. 2000;38:4657-4659.
92. Tanner MA, Shoskes D, Shahed A, et al. Prevalence of corynebacterial 16S rRNA sequences in patients with bacterial and "nonbacterial" prostatitis. J Clin Microbiol. 1999;37:1863-1870.
93. Riegel P, Ruimy R, De Briel D, et al. *Corynebacterium argentoratense* sp. nov., from the human throat. Int J Syst Bacteriol. 1995;45:533-537.
94. Barrett SL, Cookson BT, Carlson LC. Diversity within reference strains of *Corynebacterium matruchotii* includes corynebacterium durum and a novel organism. J Clin Microbiol. 2001;39:943-948.
95. Pellat BP, Grand M. Inorganic pyrophosphatase activity in a plaque calcifying microorganism: *Bacterionema matruchotii*. J Biol Bucc. 1986;14:223-228.
96. Funke G, Lawson PA, Collins MD. *Corynebacterium riegelii* sp. nov.: An unusual species is isolated from female patients with urinary tract infections. J Clin Microbiol. 1998;36:624-627.
97. Funke G, Osorio CR, Frei R, et al. *Corynebacterium confusum* sp. nov., isolated from human clinical specimens. Int J Syst Bacteriol. 1998;48:1291-1296.
98. Wattiau P, Janssens M, Wauters G. *Corynebacterium simulans* sp. nov., a non-lipophilic, fermentative *Corynebacterium*. Int J Syst Evol Microbiol. 2000;50:347-353.
99. Collins MD, Bernard KA, Hutson RA, et al. *Corynebacterium sundsvallense* sp. nov., from human clinical specimens. Int J Syst Bacteriol. 1999;49:361-366.
100. Zimmermann O, Sproer C, Kroppenstedt RM, et al. *Corynebacterium thomssenii* sp. nov., a *Corynebacterium* with N-acetyl-beta-glucosaminidase activity from human clinical specimens. Int J Syst Bacteriol. 1998;48:489-494.
101. Renaud FN, Aubel D, Riegel P, et al. *Corynebacterium freneyi* sp. nov., alpha-glucosidase-positive strains related to *Corynebacterium xerosis*. Int J Syst Evol Microbiol. 2001;51:1723-1728.
102. Riegel P, de Briel D, Prevost G, et al. Taxonomic study of *Corynebacterium* group ANF-1 strains: Proposal of *Corynebacterium afermentans* sp. nov. containing subspecies *C. afermentans* subsp. *afermentans* subsp. nov. and *afermentans* subsp. *lipophilum* subsp. nov. Int J Syst Bacteriol. 1993;43:287-292.
103. Kumari P, Tyagi A, Marks P, et al. *Corynebacterium afermentans* spp. *afermentans* sepsis in a neurosurgical patient. J Infect. 1997;35:201-202.
104. Funke G, Lawson PA, Collins MD. Heterogeneity within human-derived centers for disease control and prevention (CDC) coryneform group ANF-1-like bacteria and description of *Corynebacterium auris* sp. nov. Int J Syst Bacteriol. 1995;45:735-739.
105. Holzmann D, Funke G, Linder T, et al. *Turicella otitidis* and *Corynebacterium auris* do not cause otitis media with effusion in children. Pediatr Infect Dis J. 2002;21:1124-1126.
106. Wilson ME, Shapiro DS. Native valve endocarditis due to *Corynebacterium pseudodiphtheriticum*. Clin Infect Dis. 1992;15:1059-1060.
107. Morris A, Guild I. Endocarditis due to *Corynebacterium pseudodiphtheriticum*: Five case reports, review, and antibiotic susceptibilities of nine strains. Rev Infect Dis. 1991;13:887-892.
108. Manzella JP, Kellogg JA, Parsey KS. *Corynebacterium pseudodiphtheriticum*: A respiratory tract pathogen in adults. Clin Infect Dis. 1995;20:37-40.
109. Ahmed K, Kawakami K, Watanabe K, et al. *Corynebacterium pseudodiphtheriticum*: A respiratory tract pathogen. Clin Infect Dis. 1995;20:41-46.
110. Freeman JD, Smith HJ, Haines HG, et al. Seven patients with respiratory infections due to *Corynebacterium pseudodiphtheriticum*. Pathology 1994;26:311-314.
111. Martaresche C, Fournier PE, Jacomo V, et al. A case of *Corynebacterium pseudodiphtheriticum* nosocomial pneumonia. Emerg Infect Dis. 1999;5:722-723.
112. Gutierrez-Rodero F, Ortiz de la Tabla V, Martinez C, et al. *Corynebacterium pseudodiphtheriticum*: An easily missed respiratory pathogen in HIV-infected patients. Diagn Microbiol Infect Dis. 1999;33:209-216.
113. Li A, Lal S. *Corynebacterium pseudodiphtheriticum* keratitis and conjunctivitis: A case report. Clin Exp Ophthalmol. 2000;28:60-61.
114. Hemsley C, Abraham S, Rowland-Jones S. *Corynebacterium pseudodiphtheriticum*—a skin pathogen. Clin Infect Dis. 1999;29:938-939.
115. Wright ED, Richards AJ, Edge AJ. Discitis caused by *Corynebacterium pseudodiphtheriticum* following, ear, nose and throat surgery. Br J Rheumatol. 1995;34:585-586.
116. LaRocco M, Robinson C, Robinson A. *Corynebacterium pseudodiphtheriticum* associated with suppurative lymphadenitis. Eur J Clin Microbiol. 1987;6:79.
117. Izurieta HS, Strebel PM, Youngblood T, et al. Exudative pharyngitis possibly due to *Corynebacterium pseudodiphtheriticum*, a new challenge in the differential diagnosis of diphtheria. Emerg Infect Dis. 1997;3:65-68.
118. Santos MR, Gandhi S, Vogler M, et al. Suspected diphtheria in an Uzbek national: Isolation of *Corynebacterium pseudodiphtheriticum* resulted in a false-positive presumptive diagnosis. Clin Infect Dis. 1996;22:735.
119. Riegel P, De Briel D, Prevost G, et al. Proposal of *Corynebacterium propinquum* sp. nov. for *Corynebacterium* group ANF-3 strains. FEMS Microbiol. 1993;113:229-234.
120. Petit PL, Bok JW, Thompson J, et al. Native-valve endocarditis due to CDC coryneform group ANF-3: Report of a case and review of corynebacterial endocarditis. Clin Infect Dis. 1994;19:897-901.
121. Babay HAH. Pleural effusion due to *Corynebacterium propinquum* in a patient with squamous cell carcinoma. Ann Saudi Med. 2001;21:337-339.
122. Hande KR, Witebsky FG, Brown MS, et al. Sepsis with a new species of *Corynebacterium*. Ann Intern Med. 1976;85:423-426.
123. Jackman PJ, Pitcher DG, Pelczynska S, Borman P. Classification of corynebacteria associated with endocarditis (group JK) as *Corynebacterium jeikeium* sp. nov. Syst Appl Microbiol. 1987;9:83-90.
124. Soriano F, Rodriguez-Tudela JL, Fernandez-Roblas R, et al. Skin colonization by *Corynebacterium* groups D2 and JK in hospitalized patients. J Clin Microbiol. 1988;26:1878-1880.
125. Telander B, Lerner R, Palmblad J, Ringertz O. *Corynebacterium* group JK in a haematological ward: Infections, colonization and environmental contamination. Scand J Infect Dis. 1988;20:55-61.
126. Pitcher D, Johnson A, Allerberger F, et al. An investigation of nosocomial infection with *Corynebacterium jeikeium* in surgical patients using a ribosomal RNA gene probe. Eur J Clin Microbiol Infect Dis. 1990;9:643-648.
127. Ersgaard H, Justesen T. Multiresistant lipophilic corynebacteria from clinical specimens. Biochemical reactions and antimicrobial agents susceptibility. Acta Pathol Microbiol Scand. 1984;92:39-43.
128. Rozdzinski E, Kern W, Schmeiser T, Kurrle E. *Corynebacterium jeikeium* bacteremia at a tertiary care center. Infection. 1991;19:201-204.
129. van der Lelie H, Leverstein-Van Hall M, Mertens M, et al. *Corynebacterium* CDC group JK (*Corynebacterium jeikeium*) sepsis in haemotologic patients: A report of three cases and a systematic literature review. Scand J Infect Dis. 1995;27:581-584.
130. Murray BE, Karchmer AW, Moellering RC Jr. Diphtheroid prosthetic valve endocarditis. A study of clinical features and infecting organisms. Am J Med. 1980;69:838-848.
131. Vanbosterhaut B, Surmont I, Vandeven J, et al. *Corynebacterium jeikeium* (group JK diphtheroid) endocarditis. A report of five cases. Diagn Microbiol Infect Dis. 1989;12:265-268.
132. Ross MJ, Sakoulas G, Manning WJ, et al. *Corynebacterium jeikeium* native valve endocarditis following femoral access for coronary angiography. Clin Infect Dis. 2001;32:e120-e121.
133. Greene KA, Clark RJ, Zabramski JM. Ventricular CSF shunt infections associated with *Corynebacterium jeikeium*: Report of three cases and review. Clin Infect Dis. 1993;16:139-141.
134. Johnson A, Hulse P, Oppenheim BA. *Corynebacterium jeikeium* meningitis and transverse myelitis in a neutropenic patient. Eur J Clin Microbiol Infect Dis. 1992;11:473-474.
135. Altwegg M, Zaruba K, von Graevenitz A. *Corynebacterium* group JK peritonitis in patients on continuous ambulatory peritoneal dialysis. Klin Wochenschr 1984;62:793-794.
136. Turett GS, Fazal BA, Johnston BE, Telzak EE. Liver abscess due to *Corynebacterium jeikeium* in a patient with AIDS. Clin Infect Dis. 1993;17:514-515.
137. de Miguel-Martinez I, Ramos-Macias A, Martin-Sanchez AM. Otitis media due to *Corynebacterium jeikeium*. Eur J Microbiol Infect Dis. 1999;18:231-232.
138. Boc SF, Martone JD. Osteomyelitis caused by *Corynebacterium jeikeium*. J Am Podiatr Med Assoc. 1995;85:338-339.
139. Dan M, Somer I, Knobel B, Gutman R. Cutaneous manifestations of infection with *Corynebacterium* group JK. Rev Infect Dis. 1988;10:1204-1207.
140. Jerdan MS, Shapiro RS, Smith MB, et al. Cutaneous manifestations of *Corynebacterium* JK sepsis. J Am Acad Dermatol. 1987;16:444-447
141. Spach DH, Celum CL, Collier AC, et al. Palpable purpura associated with *Corynebacterium jeikeium* endocarditis. Arch Dermatol. 1991;127:1071-1072.
142. Traub WH, Geipel U, Leonhard B, et al. Antibiotic susceptibility of testing (agar disk diffusion and agar dilution) of clinical isolates of *Corynebacterium jeikeium*. Chemotherapy. 1998;44:230-237.
143. Rosato AE, Lee BS, Nash KA. Inducible macrolide resistance in *Corynebacterium jeikeium*. Antimicrob Agents Chemother. 2001;45:1982-1989.
144. Wang CC, Mattson D, Wald A. *Corynebacterium jeikeium* bacteremia in bone marrow transplant patients with Hickman catheters. Bone Marrow Transplant. 2001;27:445-449.
145. Pitcher D, Soto A, Soriano F, Valero-Guillen P. Classification of coryneform bacteria associated with human urinary tract infection (group D2) as *Corynebacterium urealyticum* sp. nov. Int J Syst Bacteriol. 1992;42:178-181.

146. Van Bosterhaut B, Claeys G, Gigi J, et al. Isolation of *Corynebacterium* group D2 from clinical specimens. Eur J Clin Microbiol. 1987;6:418-419.
147. Soriano F, Ponte C, Santamaria M, et al. *Corynebacterium* group D2 as a cause of alkaline-encrusted cystitis: Report of four cases and characterizations of the organisms. J Clin Microbiol. 1985;21;788-792.
148. Soriano F, Ponte C, Santamaria M, et al. In vitro and in vivo study of stone formation by *Corynebacterium* group D2 *(Corynebacterium urealyticum)*. J Clin Microbiol. 1986;23:691-694.
149. Natal IF, Garcia FC, Laso JG, et al. Brief reports: Bacteremia caused by multiply resistant *Corynebacterium urealyticum:* Six case reports and review. Eur J Clin Microbiol Infect Dis. 2001;20:514-517.
150. Soriano F, Ponte C, Ruiz P, et al. Non-urinary tract infections caused by multiply antibiotic-resistant *Corynebacterium urealyticum*. Clin Infect Dis. 1993;17:890-891.
151. Ronci-Koenig TJ, Tan JS, File TM, et al. Infections due to *Corynebacterium* group D2. Arch Intern Med. 1990;150:1965-1966.
152. Meria P, Desgrippes A, Fournier R, et al. The conservative management of *Corynebacterium* group D2 encrusted pyelitis. BJU Int. 1999;84:270-275.
153. Sewell DL, Coyle MB, Funke G. Prosthetic valve endocarditis caused by *Corynebacterium afermentans* subsp. *lipophilum* (CDC coryneform group ANF-1). J Clin Microbiol. 1995;33:759-761.
154. Claeys G, Vanhouteghem H, Riegel P, et al. Endocarditis of native aortic and mitral valves due to *Corynebacterium accolens:* Report of a case and application of phenotypic and genotypic techniques for identification. J Clin Microbiol. 1996;34:1290-1292.
155. Funke G, Pagano-Niederer M, Bernauer W. *Corynebacterium macginleyi* has to date been isolated exclusively from conjunctival swabs. J Clin Microbiol. 1998;36:3670-3673.
156. Dobler G, Braveny I. Highly resistant *Corynebacterium macginleyi* as a cause of intravenous catheter-related infection. Eur J Clin Microbiol Infect Dis. 2003;22:72-73.
157. Taylor G, Paviour S. Musaad S, et al. A clinicopathological review of 34 cases of inflammatory breast disease showing an association between corynebacteria infection and granulomatous mastitis. Pathology 2003;34:109-119.
158. Paviour S, Musaad S, Roberts S, et al. *Corynebacterium* species isolated from patients with mastitis. Clin Infect Dis. 2002;35:1434-1440.
159. Vale JA, Scott GW. *Corynebacterium bovis* as a cause of human disease. Lancet 1977;2:682-684.
160. Soriano F, Ponte C. A case of urinary tract infection caused by *Corynebacterium urealyticum* and group F1. Eur J Clin Microbiol Infect Dis. 1992;11:626-628.
161. Losada IM, Daza RM, Mendaza MP, et al. *Corynebacterium* G-1. Enferm Infect Microbiol Clin. 1994;12:362-363.
162. Funke G, Hutson RA, Hilleringmann M, et al. *Corynebacterium lipophiloflavum* sp. nov. isolated from a patient with bacterial vaginosis. FEMS Microbiol Lett. 1997;150:219-224.
163. Collins MD, Jones D, Schofield GM. Reclassification of '*Corynebacterium haemolyticum*' (MacLean Liebow & Rosenberg) in the genus *Arcanobacterium* gen.nov. *Arcanobacterium haemolyticum* nom.rev., comb.nov. J Gen Microbiol. 1982;128:1279-1281.
164. Ramos CP, Foster G, Collins MD. Phylogentic analysis of the genus *Actinomyces* based on 16S rRNA gene sequences: description of *Arcanobacterium phocae* sp. nov., *Arcanobacterium bernardiae* comb. nov., and *Arcanobacterium pyogenes* comb. nov. Int J Syst Bacteriol. 1997;47:46-53.
165. MacLean PD, Liebow AA, Rosenberg A. Haemolytic corynebacterium resembling *Corynebacterium ovis* and *C. pyogenes* in man. J. Infect. Dis. 1946;79:69-90.
166. Cummings LA, Wu WK, Larson AM, et al. Effects of media, atmosphere, and incubation time on colonial morphology of *Arcanobacterium haemolyticum*. J Clin Microbiol. 1993;31:3223-3226.
167. Carlson P, Lounatmaa K, Kontiainen S. Biotypes of *Arcanobacterium haemolyticum*. J Clin Microbiol. 1994 ;32:1654-1657.
168. Carlson P, Kontiainen S. Alpha-mannosidase: A rapid test for identification of *Arcanobacterium haemolyticum*. J Clin Microbiol. 1994;32:854-855.
169. Cuevas WA, Songer JG. *Arcanobacterium haemolyticum* phospholipase D is genetically functionally similar to *Corynebacterium pseudotuberculosis* phospholipase D. Infect Immun. 1993;61:4310-4316.
170. Ryan WJ. Throat infection and rash associated with an unusual *Corynebacterium*. Lancet. 1972;2:1345-1347.
171. Miller RA, Brancato F, Holmes KK. *Corynebacterium hemolyticum* as a cause of pharyngitis and scarlatiniform rash in young adolescents. Ann Intern Med. 1986;105:867-872.
172. Banck G, Nyman M. Tonsillitis and rash associated with *Corynebacterium haemolyticum*. J Infect Dis. 1986;154:1037-1040.
173. Carlson P, Renkonen OV, Kontiainen S. *Arcanobacterium haemolyticum* and streptococcal pharyngitis. Scand J Infect Dis. 1994;26:283-287.
174. Mackenzie A, Fuite LA, Chan FT, et al. Incidence and pathogenicity of *Arcanobacterium haemolyticum* during a 2-year study in Ottawa. Clin Infect Dis. 1995;21:177-181.
175. Miller RA, Brancoato F. Peritonsillar abscess associated with *Corynebacterium hemolyticum*. West J Med. 1984;140:449-451.
176. Skov RL, Sanden AK, Danchell VH, et al. Note: Systemic and deep-seated infections caused by *Arcanobacterium haemolyticum*. Eur J Clin Microbiol Infect Dis. 1998;17:578-582.
177. Sturm AW, Jamil B, McAdam KP, et al. Microbial colonizers in leprosy skin ulcers and intensity of inflammation. Int J Lepr Other Mycobact Dis. 1996;64:274-281.
178. Younus F, Chua A, Tortora G, Jimenez VE. Lemierre's disease caused by co-infection of *Arcanobacterium haemolyticum* and *Fusobacterium necrophorum:* A case report. J Infect 2002;45:114-117.
179. Washington JA, Martin WJ, Spiekerman RE. Brain abscess with *Corynebacterium hemolyticum:* Report of a case. Am J Clin Pathol. 1971;56:212-215.

180. Worthington MG, Daly BD, Smith FE. *Corynebacterium hemolyticum* endocarditis on native valve. South Med J. 1985;78:1261-1262.
181. Ford JG, Yeatts RP, Givner LB. Orbital cellulitis, subperiosteal abscess, sinusitis, and septicemia caused by *Arcanobacterium haemolyticum*. Am J Ophthalmol. 1995;120:261-262.
182. Waller KS, Johnson J, Wood BP. Radiological case of the month. Cavitary pneumonia due to *Arcanobacterium hemolytic*. Am J Dis Child. 1991;145:209-210.
183. Carlson P, Kontiainen S, Renkonen OV. Antimicrobial susceptibility of *Arcanobacterium haemolyticum*. Antimicrob Agents Chemother. 1994;38:142-143.
184. French G, Abdulla Y, Heathcock R, et al. Vancomycin resistance in South London. Lancet 1992;339:818-819.
185. Jost BH, Songer JG, Billington SJ. Identification of a second *Arcanobacterium pyogenes* neuraminidase and involvement of neuraminidase activity in host cell adhesion. Infect Immun. 2002;70:1106-1112.
186. Kotrajaras R, Tagami H. *Corynebacterium pyogenes*. Its pathogenic mechanism in epidemic leg ulcers in Thailand. Int J Dermatol 1987;26:45-50.
187. Barnaham M. *Actinomyces pyogenes* bacteremia in a patient with carcinoma of the colon. J Infect. 1988;17:231-234.
188. Gahrn-Hansen B, Frederiksen W. Human infections with *Actinomyces pyogenes* (*Corynebacterium pyogenes*). Diagn Microbiol Infect Dis 1992;15:349-354.
189. Lynch M, O'Leary J, Murnaghan D, et al. *Actinomyces pyogenes* septic arthritis in a diabetic farmer. J Infect 1998;37:71-73
190. Lepargneur JP, Heller R, Soulie R, Riegel P. Urinary tract infection due to *Arcanobacterium bernardiae* in a patient with a urinary tract diversion. Eur J Clin Microbiol Infect Dis. 1998;17:399-401.
191. Adderson EE, Croft A, Leonard R, et al. Septic arthritis due to *Arcanobacterium bernardiae* in an immunocompromised patient. Clin Infect Dis. 1998;27:211-212.
192. Ieven M, Verhoeven J, Gentens P, et al. Severe infection due to *Actinomyces bernardiae:* Case report. Clin Infect Dis. 1996;22:157-158.
193. Funke G, Pfyffer GE, von Graevenitz A. A hitherto undescribed coryneform bacterium isolated from patients with otitis media. Med Microbiol Lett. 1993;2:183-190.
194. Funke G, Stubbs S, Altwegg M, et al. Turicella otitidis gen. nov., sp. nov. a coryneform bacterium isolated from patients with otitis media. Int J Syst Bacteriol. 1994;44:270-273.
195. Loiez C, Wallet F. Fruchart A, et al. *Turicella otitidis* in a bacteremic child with acute lymphoblastic leukemia. Eur Soc Clin Microbiol Infect Dis. 2002;8:758-759.
196. Dana A, Fader R, Sterken D. *Turicella otitidis* mastoiditis in a healthy child. Pediatr Infect Dis J. 2001;20:84-85.
197. Reynolds SJ, Behr M, McDonald J. *Turicella otitidis* in an unusual agent causing a posterior auricular abscess. J Clin Microbiol. 2001;39:1672-1673.
198. Funke G, Pagano-Niederer M, Sjoden B, et al. Characteristics of *Arthrobacter cumminsii*, the most frequently encountered *Arthrobacter* species in human clinical specimens. J Clin Microbiol. 1998;36:1539-1543.
199. Wauters G, Charlier J, Janssens M, et al. Identification of *Arthrobacter oxydans, Arthrobacter luteolus* sp. nov., and *Arthrobacter albus* sp. nov., isolated from human clinical specimens. J Clin Microbiol. 2000;38:2412-2415.
200. Hsu CL, Shih LY, Leu HS, et al. Septicemia due to *Arthrobacter* species in a neutropenic patient with acute lymphoblastic leukemia. Clin Infect Dis. 1998;27:1334-1335.
201. Bodaghi B, Dauga C, Cassoux N, et al. Whipple's syndrome (uveitis, B27-negative spondylarthropathy, meningitis, and lymphadenopathy) associated with *Arthrobacter* sp. infection. Ophthalmology. 1998;105:1891-1896.
202. Funke G, Carlotti A. Differentiation of *Brevibacterium* spp. encountered in clinical specimens. J Clin Microbiol. 1994;32:1729-1732.
203. Brazzola P, Zbinden R, Rudin C, et al. *Brevibacterium casei* sepsis in an 18-year-old female with AIDS. J Clin Microbiol. 2000;38:3513-3514.
204. Reinert RR, Schnitzler N, Haase G, et al. Recurrent bacteremia due to *Brevibacterium casei* in an immunocompromised patient. Eur J Clin Micriobiol Infect Dis. 1995;14:1082-1085.
205. Gruner E, Steigerwalt AG, Hollis DG, et al. Human infections caused by *Brevibacterium casei,* formerly CDC groups B-1 and B-3. J Clin Microbiol. 1994;32: 1511-1518.
206. Wauters G, Van Bosterhaut B, Avesani V, et al. Peritonitis due to *Brevibacterium otitidis* in a patient undergoing continuous ambulatory peritoneal dialysis. J Clin Microbiol. 2000;38:4292-4293.
207. Neumeister B, Mandel T, Gruner E, et al. *Brevibacterium* species as a cause of osteomyelitis in a neonate. Infect. 1993;21:177-178.
208. Dass KN, Smith MA, Gill VJ, et al. *Brevibacterium* endocarditis: A first report. Clin Infect Dis. 2002;35:e20-e21.
209. Troxler R, Funke G, von Graevenitz A, et al. Natural antibiotic susceptibility of recently established coryneform bacteria. Eur J Clin Microbiol Infect Dis. 2001;20:315-323.
210. Funke G, Stubbs S, Pfyffer GE, et al. Characteristics of CDC group 3 and group 5 coryneform bacteria isolated from clinical specimens and assignment to the genus *Dermabacter*. J Clin Microbiol. 1994;32:1223-1228.
211. Gruner E, Steigerwalt AG, Hollis DG, et al. Recognition of *Dermabacter hominis,* formerly CDC fermentative coryneform group 3 and group 5, as a potential human pathogen. J Clin Microbiol. 1994;32:1918-1922.
212. Radtke A, Bergh K, Oien CM, et al. Peritoneal dialysis-associated peritonitis caused by *Dermabacter hominis*. J Clin Microbiol. 2001;39:3420-3421.
213. Bavbek M, Caner H, Arslan H, et al. Cerebral *Dermabacter hominis* abscess. Infect. 1998;26:181-183.
214. Van Bosterhaut B, Boucquey P, Janssens M, et al. Chronic osteomyelitis due to *Actinomyces neuii* subspecies *neuii* and *Dermabacter hominis*. Eur J Clin Microbiol Infect Dis. 2002;21:486-487.
215. Lesher RJ, Gerencser VF, Morrison DJ. Presence of *Rothia dentocariosa* strain 477 serotype 2 in gingiva of patients with inflammatory periodontal disease. J Dent Res. 1977;56:189.

216. Schafer FJ, Wing EJ, Norden CW. Infectious endocarditis caused by *Rothia dentocariosa*. Ann Intern Med. 1979;91:747-748.
217. Binder D, Zbinden R, Widmer U, et al. Native and prosthetic valve endocarditis caused by *Rothia dentocariosa:* Diagnostic and therapeutic considerations. Infect. 1997;25:22-26.
218. Llopis F. Carratala J. Vertebral osteomyelitis complicating *Rothia dentocariosa* endocarditis. Eur J Clin Microbiol Infect Dis. 2000;19:562-563.
219. Sudduth EJ, Rozich JD, Farrar WE. *Rothia dentocariosa* endocarditis complicated by perivalvular abscess. Clin Infect Dis. 1993;17:772-775.
220. Anderson MD, Kennedy CA, Walsh TP, et al. Prosthetic valve endocarditis due to *Rothia dentocariosa*. Clin Infect Dis. 1994;17:945-946.
221. Salamon SA, Prag J. Three cases of *Rothia dentocariosa* bacteraemia: Frequency in Denmark and a review. Scand J Infect Dis. 2002;34:153-157.
222. Schiff MJ, Kaplan MH. *Rothia dentocariosa* pneumonia in an immunocompromised patient. Lung. 1987;165:279-282.
223. Bibashi E, Kokolina E, Mitsopoulos E, et al. Peritonitis due to *Rothia dentocariosa* in a patient receiving continuous ambulatory peritoneal dialysis. Clin Infect Dis. 1999;28:696.
224. Reller LB, Maddoux GL, Eckman MR, et al. Bacterial endocarditis caused by *Oerskovia turbata*. Ann Intern Med. 1975;83:664-666.
225. Maguire JD, McCarthy MC, Decker CF. *Oerskovia xanthineolytica* bacteremia in an immunocompromised host: Case report and review. Clin Infect Dis. 1996;22:554-556.
226. Harrington RD, Lewis CG, Aslanzadeh J, et al. *Oerskovia xanthineolytica* infection of a prosthetic joint: Case report and review. J Clin Microbiol. 1996;34:1821-1824.
227. Rihs JD, McNeil MM, Brown JM, et al. *Oerskovia xanthineolytica* implicated in peritonitis associated with peritoneal dialysis: Case report and review of *Oerskovia* infections in humans. J Clin Microbiol. 1990;28:1924-1937.
228. Kailath EJ, Goldstein E, Wagner FH. Meningitis caused by *Oerskovia xanthineolytica*. Am J Med Sci. 1988;295:216-217.
229. Hussain Z, Gonder JR, Lannigan R, et al. Endophthalmitis due to *Oerskovia xanthineolytica*. Can J Ophthalmol. 1987;22:234-236.
230. Funke G, Falsen E, Barreau C. Primary identification of *Microbacterium* spp. encountered in clinical specimens as CDC coryneform group A-4 and A-5 bacteria. J Clin Microbiol. 1995;33:188-192.
231. Takeuchi M, Hatano K. Union of the genera *Microbacterium* Orla-Jensen and *Aureobacterium* Collins *et al.* in a redefined genus *Microbacterium*. Int J Syst Bacteriol.1998;48:739-747.
232. Alonso-Echanove J, Shah SS, Valenti AJ, et al. Nosocomial outbreak of *Microbacterium* species bacteremia among cancer patients. J Infect Dis. 2001;184:754-760.
233. Lau SK, Woo PC, Woo GK, et al. Catheter-related *Microbacterium* bacteremia identified by 16S rRNA gene sequencing. J Clin Microbiol. 2002;40:2681-2685.
234. Funke G, Haase G, Schnitzler N, et al. Endophthalmitis due to *Microbacterium* species: Case report and review of *Microbacterium* infections. Clin Infect Dis. 1997;24:713-716.
235. Laffineur K, Avesani V, Cornu G, et al. Bacteremia due to a novel *Microbacterium* species in a patient with leukemia and description of *Microbacterium paraoxydans* sp. nov. J Clin Microbiol. 2003;41:2242-2246.
236. Evtushenko LI, Dorofeeva LV, Subbotin SA, et al. *Leifsonia poae* gen. nov., sp. nov., isolated from nematode galls on Poa annua, and reclassification of 'Corynebacterium aquaticum' Leifson 1962 as *Leifsonia aquatica* (ex Leifson 1962) gen. nov., nom. rev., comb. nov. and *Clavibacter xyli* Davis ct al. 1984 with two subspecies as *Leifsonia xyli* (Davis et al. 1984) gen. nov., comb. nov. Int J Syst Evol Microbiol. 2000;50:371-380.
237. Funke G, von Graevenitz A, Weiss N. Primary identification of *Aureobacterium* spp. isolated from clinical specimens as "Corynebacterium aquaticum." J Clin Microbiol. 1994;32:2686-2691.
238. Grove DI, Der-Haroutian V, Ratcliff RM. *Aureobacterium* masquerading as "Corynebacterium aquaticum" infection: Case report and review of the literature. J Med Microbiol. 1999;48:965-970.
239. Morris AJ, Henderson GK, Bremner DA, et al. Relapsing peritonitis in a patient undergoing continuous ambulatory peritoneal dialysis due to *Corynebacterium aquaticum*. J Infect. 1986;13:151-156.
240. Fischer RA, Peters G, Gehrmann J, et al. *Corynebacterium aquaticum* septicemia with acute lymphoblastic leukemia. Pediatr Infect Dis J. 1994;13:836-837.
241. Saweljew P, Kunkel J, Feddersen A, et al. Case of fatal systemic infection with an *Aureobacterium* sp.: Identification of isolate by 16S rRNA gene analysis. J Clin Microbiol. 1996;34:1540-1541.
242. Kaplan A, Israel F. *Corynebacterium aquaticum* infection in a patient with a chronic gramulomatous disease. Am J Med Sci. 1988;296:57-58.
243. Tendler C, Bottone EJ. *Corynebacterium aquaticum* urinary tract infection in a neonate, and concepts regarding the role of the organism as a neonatal pathogen. J Clin Microbiol. 1989;27:343-345.
244. Beckwith DG, Jahre JA, Haggerty S. Isolation of *Corynebacterium aquaticum* from spinal fluid of an infant with meningitis. J Clin Microbiol. 1986;23:375 376.
245. Funke G, Ramos CP, Collins MD. Identification of some clinical strains of CDC coryneform group A-3 and A-4 bacteria as *Cellulomonas* species and proposal of *Cellulomonas hominis* sp. nov. for some group A-3 strains. J Clin Microbiol. 1995;33:2091-2097.
246. Magnusson H. Spezifische infektiose pneumonie beim fohlen: Ein neuer eitererreger beim pferd [in German]. Arch Wiss Prakt Tierheilkd. 1923;50:22-38.
247. Walsh RD, Schoch PE, Cunha BA. *Rhodococcus*. Infect Contr Hosp Epidemiol. 1993;14:282-287.
248. Golub B, Falk G, Spink WW. Lung abscess due to *Corynebacterium equi:* Report of first human infection. Ann Intern Med. 1967;66:1174-1177.

249. Van Etta LL, Filice GA, Ferguson RM, Gerding DN. *Corynebacterium equi:* A review of 12 cases of human infection. Rev Infect Dis. 1983;5:1012-1018.
250. Prescott JF. *Rhodococcus equi:* An animal and human pathogen. Clin Microbiol Rev. 1991;4:20-34.
251. Weinstock DM, Brown AE. *Rhodoccus equi:* An emerging pathogen. Clin Infect Dis. 2002;34:1379-1385.
252. Verville TD, Huycke MM, Greenfield RA, et al. *Rhodococcus equi* infections in humans: 12 cases and a review of the literature. Medicine. 1994;73:119-132.
253. Takai S, Ohbushi S, Koike K, et al. Prevalence of virulent *Rhodococcus equi* in isolates from soil and feces of horses from horse-breeding farms with and without endemic infections. J Clin Microbiol. 1991;29:2887-2889.
254. Kedlaya I, Ing MB, Wong SS. *Rhodococcus equi* infections in immunocompetent hosts: Case report and review. Clin Infect Dis. 2001; 32:39-46.
255. Scotton PG, Tonon E, Giobbia M, et al. *Rhodococcus equi* nosocomial meningitis cured by levofloxacin and shunt removal. Clin Infect Dis. 2000;30:223-224.
256. Arlotti M, Zoboli G, Moscatelli GL, et al. *Rhodococcus equi* infection in HIV-positive subjects: A retrospective analysis of 24 cases. Scand J Infect Dis. 1996;28:463-467.
257. Rasmussen TT, Kirkeby LP, Poulsen K, et al. Resident aerobic microbiota of the adult human nasal cavity. APMIS. 2000;108:663-675.
258. Nordmann P, Nicolas MH, Gutmann L. Pencillin-binding proteins of *Rhodococcus equi:* potential role in resistance to imipenem. Antimicrob Agents Chemother. 1993;37:1406-1409.
259. Lasker BA, Brown JM, McNeil MM. Identification and epidemiological typing of clinical and environmental isolates of the genus *Rhodococcus* with use of a digoxigenin-labeled rDNA gene probe. Clin Infect Dis. 1992;15:223-233.
260. Steingrube VA, Wilson RW, Brown BA, et al. Rapid identification of clinically significant species and taxa of aerobic actinomycetes, including Actinomadura, Gordona, Nocardia, Rhodococcus, Streptomyces, and Tsukamurella isolates, by DNA amplification and restriction endonuclease analysis. J Clin Microbiol. 1997;35:817-822.
261. Drancourt M, Bonnet E, Gallais H, et al. *Rhodococcus equi* infection in patients with AIDS. J Infect. 1992;24:123-131.
262. Takai S, Sekizaki T, Ozawa T, et al. Association between a large plasmid and 15 to 17 kilodalton antigens in virulent *Rhodococcus equi*. Infect Immun. 1991;59:4056-4060.
263. Takai S, Fukunaga N, Ochiai S, et al. Identification of intermediately virulent *Rhodococcus equi* isolates from pigs. J Clin Microbiol. 1996;34:1034-1037.
264. Giguere S, Hondalus MK, Yager JA, et al. Role of the 85-kilobase plasmid and plasmid-encoded virulence-associated protein A in intracellular survival and virulence of *Rhodococcus equi*. Infect Immun. 1999;67:3548-3557.
265. Takai S, Sasaki Y, Ikeda T, et al. Virulence of *Rhodococcus equi* isolated from patients with and without AIDS. J Clin Microbiol. 1994;32:457-460.
266. Takai S, Imai Y, Fukunaga N, et al. Identification of virulence associated antigens and plasmids in *Rhodococcus equi* from patients with AIDS. J Infect Dis. 1995;172:1306-1311.
267. Caterino-De-Araujo A, de Los Santos-Fortuna E, Zandona-Meleiro MC, et al. Search for an antibody profile of *Rhodococcus equi* infection in AIDS patients despite the diversity of isolates and patient immune dysfunction. Microbes Infect. 1999;1:663-670.
268. Scott MA, Graham BS, Verrall R, et al. *Rhodococcus equi:* An increasingly recognized opportunistic pathogen. Am J Clin Pathol. 1995;103:649-655.
269. Guerrero MF, Ramos JM, Renedo G, et al. Pulmonary malacoplakia associated with *Rhodococcus equi* infection in patients with AIDS: Case report and review. Clin Infect Dis. 1999;28:1334-1336.
270. Thomsen VF, Henriques U, Magnusson M. *Corynebacterium equi* Magnusson isolated from a tuberculoid lesion in a child with adenitis colli. Dan Med Bull. 1968;15:135-138.
271. Egawa T, Hara H, Kawase I, et al. Human pulmonary infection with *Corynebacterium equi*. Eur Respir J. 1990;3:240-242.
272. Harvey RL, Sunstrum JC. *Rhodococcus equi* infection in patients with and without human immunodeficiency virus infection. Rev Infect Dis. 1991;13:139-145.
273. Lasky JA, Pulkingham N, Powers MA, Durack DT. *Rhodococcus equi* causing human pulmonary infection: Review of 29 cases. South Med J. 1991;84:1217-1220.
274. Donisi A, Suardi MG, Casari S, et al. *Rhodococcus equi* infection in HIV-infected patients. AIDS. 1996;10:359-362.
275. Hsueh P-R, Hung C-C, Teng L-J, et al. Report of invasive *Rhodococcus equi* infections in Taiwan, with an emphasis on the emergence of multidrug-resistant strains. Clin Infect Dis. 1998;27:370-375.
276. Munoz P, Burillo A, Palomo J, et al. *Rhodococcus equi* infection in transplant recipients: Case report and review of the literature. Transplantation. 1998;65:449-453.
277. Linder R. *Rhodococcus equi* and *Arcanobacterium haemolyticum:* Two "coryneform" bacteria increasingly recognized as agents of human infection. Emerg Infect Dis. 1997;3:145-153.
278. Emmons W, Reichwein B, Winslow DL. *Rhodococcus equi* infection in the patient with AIDS: Literature review and report of an unusual case. Rev Infect Dis. 1991;13:91-96.
279. Doig C, Gill MH, Church DL. *Rhodococcus equi:* An easily missed opportunistic pathogen. Scand J Infect Dis. 1991;23:1-6.
280. Roca V, Vinuelas J, Perez-Cecilia E, et al. Bacteremic pneumonia caused by *Rhodococcus equi* and HIV infection: Report of a new case and review of the literature. Enferm Infecc Microbiol Clin. 1991;9:627-629.
281. Cecconi L, Mazzuoli G, Busi-Rizzi E, et al. *Rhodococcus equi* pulmonitis in HIV positive patients: A review of the literature and a case report. Radiol Med (Torino). 1993;85:122-125.
282. Ferruzzi S, Mamprim F, Vailati F. *Rhodococcus equi* infection in non-HIV-infected patients: Two case reports and review. Clin Microbiol Infect. 1997;3:12-18.
283. Gray KJ, French N, Lugada E, et al. *Rhodococcus equi* and HIV-1 infection in Uganda. J Infect. 2000;41:227-231.

284. Fierer J, Wolf P, Seed L, et al. Non-pulmonary *Rhodococcus equi* infections in patients with acquired immune deficiency syndrome (AIDS). J Clin Pathol. 1987;40:556-558.

285. Mohammedi I, Vedrinne JM, Floccard B, et al. Disseminated *Rhodococcus equi* and *Nocardia farcinica* infection in a patient with sarcoidosis. J Infect. 1998;36:134-135.

286. Akan H, Akova M, Ataoglu H, et al. *Rhodococcus equi* and *Nocardia brasiliensis* infection of the brain and liver in a patient with acute nonlymphoblastic leukemia. Eur J Clin Microbiol Infect Dis. 1998;17:737-739.

287. Sigler E, Miskin A, Shtlarid M, Berrebi A. Fever of unknown origin and anemia with *Rhodococcus equi* infection in an immunocompetent patient. Am J Med. 1998;104:510.

288. Linares MJ, Lopez-Encuentra A, Perea S. Chronic pneumonia caused by *Rhodococcus equi* in a patient without impaired immunity. Eur Respir J. 1997; 10:248-250.

289. Munoz P, Palomo J, Guembe P, et al. Lung nodular lesions in heart transplant recipients. J Heart Lung Transplant. 2000;19:660-667.

290. La Rocca E, Gesu G, Caldara R, et al. Pulmonary infection caused by *Rhodococcus equi* in a kidney and pancreas transplant recipient: A case report. Transplantation. 1998;65:1524-1525.

291. Kohl O, Tillmanns HH. Cerebral infection with *Rhodococcus equi* in a heart transplant recipient. J Heart Lung Transplant. 2002;21:1147-1149.

292. Kwak EJ, Strollo DC, Kulich SM, et al. Cavitary pneumonia due to *Rhodococcus equi* in a heart transplant recipient. Transpl Infect Dis. 2003;5:43-46.

293. Yoo SJ, Sung H, Chae JD, et al. *Rhodococcus equi* pneumonia in a heart transplant recipient in Korea, with emphasis on microbial diagnosis. Clin Microbial Infect. 2003; 9:230-233.

294. Torres-Tortosa M, Arrizabalaga J, Villanueva JL, et al. Prognosis and clinical evaluation of infection caused by *Rhodococcus equi* in HIV-infected patients: A multicenter study of 67 cases. Chest. 2003;123:1970-1976.

295. Antinori S, Esposito R, Cernuschi M, et al. Disseminated *Rhodococcus equi* infection initially presenting as foot mycetoma in an HIV-positive patient. AIDS. 1992;6:740-742.

296. Cornish N, Washington JA. *Rhodococcus equi* infections: Clinical features and laboratory diagnosis. Curr Clin Top Infect Dis. 1999;19:198-215.

297. Capdevila JA, Bujan S, Gavalda J, et al. *Rhodococcus equi* pneumonia in patients infected with the human immunodeficiency virus. Report of 2 cases and review of the literature. Scand J Infect Dis. 1997;29:535-541.

298. Rodriguez Arrondo F, von Wichmann MA, Arrizabalago J, et al. Pulmonary cavitation lesions in patients with the human immunodeficiency virus: An analysis of a series of 78 cases. Med Clin (Barcelona). 1998;111:725-730.

299. Bowersock TL, Salmon SA, Portis ES, et al. MICs of oxazolidinones for *Rhodococcus equi* strains isolated from humans and animals. Antimicrob Agents Chemother. 2000;44:1367-1369.

300. Jacks SS, Giguere S, Nguyen A. In vitro susceptibilities of *Rhodococcus equi* and other common equine pathogens to azithromycin, clarithromycin, and 20 other antimicrobials. Antimicrob Agents Chemother. 2003;47:1742-1745.

301. Nordmann P, Kerestedjian JJ, Ronco E. Therapy of *Rhodococcus equi* disseminated infections in nude mice. Antimicrob Agents Chemother. 1992;36:1244-1248.

302. Asoh N, Watanabe H, Fines-Guyon M, et al. Emergence of rifampin-resistant *Rhodococcus equi* with several types of mutations in the *rpoB* gene among AIDS patients in northern Thailand. J Clin Microbiol. 2003;41:2337-2340.

303. Rouquet RM, Clove D, Massip P, et al. Imipenem/vancomycin for *Rhodococcus equi* pulmonary infection in an HIV-positive patient [Letter]. Lancet. 1991;337:375.

304. Richet HM, Craven PC, Brown JM, et al. A cluster of *Rhodococcus (Gordona) bronchialitis* sternal-wound infections after coronary-artery bypass surgery. N Engl J Med. 1991;324:104-109.

305. Shapiro CL, Haft RF, Gantz NM, et al. *Tsukamurella paurometabolum:* A novel pathogen causing catheter-related bacteremia in patients with cancer. Clin Infect Dis. 1992;14:200-203.

306. Osoagbaka OU. Evidence for the pathogenic role of *Rhodococcus* species in pulmonary disease. J Appl Bacteriol. 1989;66:497-506.

307. Tsukamura M, Kawakami K. Lung infection caused by *Gordona aurantiaca (Rhodococcus aurantiacus).* J Clin Microbiol. 1982;16:604-607.

308. Tsukamura M, Hikosaka K, Nishimura K, et al. Severe progressive subcutaneous abscesses and necrotizing tenosynovitis caused by *Rhodococcus aurantiacus.* J Clin Microbiol. 1988;26:201-205.

309. Prinz G, Ban E, Fekete S, et al. Meningitis caused by *Gordona aurantiaca (Rhodococcus aurantiacus).* J Clin Microbiol. 1985;22:472-474.

310. von Below H, Wilk CM, Schaal KP, et al. *Rhodococcus luteus* and *Rhodococcus erythropolis* chronic endophthalmitis after lens implantation. Am J Ophthalmol. 1991;112:596-597.

311. Brown E, Hendler E. *Rhodococcus* peritonitis in a patient treated with peritoneal dialysis. Am J Kidney Dis. 1989;14:417-418.

312. Vernazza PL, Bodmer T, Galeazzi RL. *Rhodococcus erythropolis* infection in HIV-associated immunodeficiency. Schweiz Med Wochenschr. 1991;121:1095-1098.

313. Hart DH, Peel MM, Andrew JH, et al. Lung infection caused by *Rhodococcus.* Aust N Z J Med. 1988;18:790-791.

314. Haburchak DR, Jeffrey B, Higbee JW, et al. Infections by *Rhodachrous.* Am J Med. 1978; 65;298-302.

315. Gopaul D, Ellis C, Maki A Jr, et al. Isolation of *Rhodococcus rhodochrous* from a chronic corneal ulcer. Diagn Microbiol Infect Dis. 1988;10:185-190.

316. DeMarais PL, Kocka FE. *Rhodococcus* meningitis in an immunocompetent host. Clin Infect Dis. 1995;20:167-169.

CHAPTER **204**

Listeria monocytogenes

BENNETT LORBER

Listeria monocytogenes is an uncommon cause of illness in the general population. However, in some groups, including neonates, pregnant women, elderly persons, immunosuppressed transplant recipients, and others with impaired cell-mediated immunity, it is an important cause of life-threatening bacteremia and meningoencephalitis.[1,2] Growing interest in this organism has resulted from foodborne outbreaks, concerns about food safety, and the realization that *L. monocytogenes* can cause acute, self-limited febrile gastroenteritis in otherwise healthy persons.

MICROBIOLOGY

L. monocytogenes is a small, facultatively anaerobic, nonsporulating, catalase-positive, oxidase-negative, gram-positive bacillus that grows readily on blood agar, producing incomplete β-hemolysis.[3] The bacterium possesses one to five polar flagellae and exhibits a characteristic tumbling motility at 25°C. Optimal growth occurs at 30 to 37°C, but *L. monocytogenes* grows better than other bacteria at refrigerator temperatures (4 to 10°C), and by so-called cold enrichment can be separated from other contaminating bacteria by long incubation in this temperature range. Selective media have been developed to isolate the organism from specimens containing multiple species (food, stool) and appear superior to cold enrichment.[4] When grown on blood-free agar and viewed with light transmitted at a 45-degree angle (Henry's illumination), colonies of *L. monocytogenes* appear blue, whereas other bacterial colonies appear yellowish or orange.

Routine media are effective for isolating *L. monocytogenes* from specimens obtained from normally sterile sites (cerebrospinal fluid [CSF], blood, joint fluid), but media typically used to isolate diarrhea-causing bacteria from stool cultures inhibit listerial growth. *Listeria monocytogenes* grows best at a neutral to slightly alkaline pH and dies at a pH below 5.5.

In clinical specimens, the organisms may be gram-variable and look like diphtheroids, cocci, or diplococci. Laboratory misidentification as diphtheroids, streptococci, or enterococci is not uncommon,[5] and the isolation of a "diphtheroid" from blood or CSF always should alert one to the possibility that the organism is really *L. monocytogenes.*

Of the six species of *Listeria, L. monocytogenes, L. seeligeri, L. welshimeri, L. innocua, L. ivanovii,* and *L. grayi* (Table 204-1), only *L. monocytogenes* is pathogenic for humans. There are at least 13 serotypes of *L. monocytogenes,* based on cellular O and flagellar H antigens, but almost all disease is due to types 4b, 1/2a, and 1/2b,[6] limiting the value of serotyping for epidemiologic investigations. Phage typing can be accomplished for 60% to 80% of clinical isolates. A number of molecular techniques including ribotyping, multilocus enzyme electrophoresis, and pulsed-field gel electrophoresis (PFGE) have been employed to separate isolates into distinct groups for epidemiologic purposes.[3] Multilocus enzyme electrophoresis and PFGE can separate *L. monocytogenes* serovars into many unique types and have proved useful in investigating outbreaks.[7,8]

EPIDEMIOLOGY

L. monocytogenes is an important cause of zoonoses, especially in herd animals. It is widespread in nature, being found commonly in soil, decaying vegetation, water, and as part of the fecal flora of many mammals.[6] The organism has been isolated from the stool of approximately 5% of healthy adults,[6,9] with higher rates of recovery reported from household contacts of patients with clinical infection.[10] Many

TABLE 204-1 Laboratory Differentiation of Species in the Genus *Listeria**

Characteristic	*L. monocytogenes*	*L. grayi*	*L. innocua*	*L. ivanovii* subsp. *ivanovii*	*L. ivanovii* subsp. *londoniensis*	*L. seeligeri*	*L. welshimeri*
β-hemolysis	+	–	–	++†	++	+	–
CAMP test reaction:							
Staphylococcus aureus	+	–	–	–	–	+	–
Rhodococcus equi	V	–	–	+	+	–	–
Acid production from:							
Mannitol	–	+	–	–	–	–	–
α-Methyl-D-mannoside	+	+	+	–	–	–	+
L-Rhamnose	+	V	V	–	–	–	V
Soluble starch	–	+	–	–	–	ND	ND
D-xylose	–	–	–	+	+	+	+
Ribose	–	V	–	+	–	–	–
N-Acetyl-β-D-mannosamine	ND	ND	V	V	+	ND	ND
Hippurate hydrolysis	+	–	+	+	+	ND	ND
Reduction of nitrate	–	V	–	–	–	ND	ND
Pathogenicity for mice	+	–	–	+	?	–	–
Serotype	1/2a, 1/2b, 1/2c, 3a, 3b, 3c, 4a, 4ab, 4b, 4c, 4d, 4e, 7	S	4ab, US, 6a, 6B	5	5	1/2a, 1/2b, 1/2c, US, 4b, 4d, 6b	1/2b, 4c, 6a, 6b, US

*+, ≥90% of strains are positive; –, ≥90% of strains are negative; ND, not determined; V, variable; US, undesignated serotype; S, specific.
†Usually a wide zone or multiple zones.
From Swaminathan B, Rocourt J, Bille J. *Listeria.* In: Murray PR, Baron EJ, eds. Manual of Clinical Microbiology. 6th ed. Washington, DC: American Society for Microbiology Press; 1995:341-348.

foods are contaminated with *L. monocytogenes,* and recovery rates of 15% to 70% are common from raw vegetables, raw milk, cheese, and meats, including fresh, frozen, and processed chicken and beef available at supermarkets or delicatessen counters.[11] Ingestion of *L. monocytogenes* must be an exceedingly common occurrence.

Listeriosis was not made a nationally reportable disease until 2000. Data from two active surveillance studies performed in 1980-1982 and 1986 by the Centers for Disease Control and Prevention (CDC) indicated annual infection rates of 7.4 per million population, accounting for approximately 1850 cases/year in the United States with 425 deaths.[7,12] By 1993, following food industry regulations instituted to minimize the risk of foodborne listeriosis, the annual incidence had declined to 4.4 cases per million, or 1092 cases with 248 deaths.[13] The highest infection rates are seen in infants younger than 1 month and adults older than 60 years.[12] Pregnant women account for about 30% of all cases and 60% of cases in the 10- to 40-year age group. Almost 70% of nonperinatal infections occur in those with hematologic malignancy, acquired immunodeficiency syndrome (AIDS), or organ transplantation, or those receiving corticosteroid therapy; but seemingly normal persons may develop invasive disease, particularly those older than 60 years.[14-17]

Subsequent to the 1983 report of a widespread outbreak of foodborne human listerial infection caused by contaminated coleslaw,[9] a number of other foodborne outbreaks have been documented[2] with vehicles including milk, soft cheeses,[18] butter,[19] pâté, ready-to-eat pork products, gravad or cold-smoked trout, hot dogs,[20] and deli-ready turkey.[21] Sporadic cases have been traced to contaminated cheese, turkey frankfurters, and alfalfa tablets.[1,2] The importance of food as a source for sporadic listeriosis is illustrated by two CDC studies in which 11% of all refrigerator food samples were contaminated and 64% of patients had at least one contaminated food, and, in 33% of instances, both the patient and the food isolates had the same multilocus enzyme electrophoresis type (much higher than would be predicted by chance).[22,23] Delicatessen ready-to-eat meats, especially chicken, had the highest rates of contamination. Patients were more likely than controls to have eaten soft cheeses or delicatessen counter meats, and 32% of sporadic cases could be attributed to these foods.

Although most human listeriosis appears to be foodborne, other modes of transmission occur including from mother to child transplacentally or through an infected birth canal, cross-infection in neonatal nurseries,[24] and one common-source outbreak traced to contaminated mineral oil used for bathing infants.[25] Localized cutaneous infections have occurred in veterinarians and farmers after direct contact with aborted calves and infected poultry.

The CDC has established PulseNet (*http://www.cdc.gov/pulsenet/*), a network of public health and food regulatory laboratories that use pulsed-field gel electrophoresis to subtype food-borne pathogens in order to quickly detect disease clusters that may have a common source.[26] *Listeria monocytogenes* was added to PulseNet in 1998; this system has proved effective in the early detection of outbreaks of listeriosis.[20,21]

PATHOGENESIS

Except for vertical transmission from mother to fetus and rare instances of cross-contamination in the delivery suite or newborn nursery, human-to-human infection has not been documented.

Infection most likely begins after ingestion of the organism in a foodborne source. The oral inoculum required to produce clinical infection is unknown; experiments in healthy mammals indicate that 10^9 organisms or more are required.[27] Alkalinization of the stomach by antacids, H_2 blockers, or ulcer surgery may promote infection.[28] The incubation period for invasive illness is not well established, but evidence from a few cases related to specific ingestions points to incubation periods ranging from 11 to 70 days, with a mean of 31 days. In one report, two pregnant women whose only common exposure was attendance at a party developed listerial bacteremia with the same uncommon enzyme type; incubation periods for illness were 19 and 23 days.[29]

Virulent *L. monocytogenes* are probably sufficient to cause disease without promoter organisms, but one outbreak that could not be traced to a particular source suggested that intercurrent gastrointestinal infection with another pathogen may enhance invasion in individuals colonized with *L. monocytogenes.*[30] Evidence for this is found in the common history of antecedent gastrointestinal symptoms in patients and household contacts, the long incubation period from ingestion to clinical illness, and two instances in which invasive listeriosis closely followed shigellosis.[31,32] Both listerial meningitis and bacteremia have occurred shortly after colonoscopy or sigmoidoscopy.[33,34]

In the intestine, *L. monocytogenes* crosses the mucosal barrier aided by active endocytosis of organisms by endothelial cells.[11,35] Once in the blood stream, hematogenous dissemination may occur to any site; *L. monocytogenes* has a particular predilection for the central nervous system (CNS) and the placenta. It is generally believed that listeriae reach the CNS through a bacteremic route, but animal experiments suggest that rhombencephalitis may develop by intraaxonal spread of bacteria from peripheral sites to the CNS.[36]

The intracellular, molecular pathogenesis of listeriosis has been reviewed in detail.[37-40] Obviously, it is advantageous for an intracellular organism such as *L. monocytogenes* to get inside mammalian cells as efficiently as possible. Listeriae possess the cell surface protein internalin, which interacts with E-cadherin, a receptor on epithelial cells, resulting in the induction of phagocytosis. A recently described lipoprotein appears to promote entry into non-macrophage cells.[41] Once phagocytosed, listeriolysin O, the major virulence factor, along with phospholipases, enables listeriae to escape from phagosomes and avoid intracellular killing. Now free in the cytoplasm, the bacteria can divide (doubling time about 1 hour) and, by inducing host cell actin polymerization, propel themselves to the cell membrane. Subsequently, by pushing against the host cell membrane, they form elongated pseudopod-like projections (filopods) that can be ingested by adjacent cells such as macrophages, enterocytes, and hepatocytes. The bacterial surface protein Act A is necessary for the induction of actin filament assembly and cell-to-cell spread and, therefore, is a major virulence factor. Thus, through this novel life cycle, *L. monocytogenes* can move from cell to cell without being exposed to antibodies, complement, or neutrophils.

Iron, essential for the life of all microorganisms, appears to be an important virulence factor for *L. monocytogenes*. *Listeria monocytogenes* siderophores enable it to take iron from transferrin.[11] In vitro, iron enhances organism growth. In animal models of listerial infection, iron overload is associated with enhanced susceptibility to infection, whereas iron depletion results in prolonged survival and iron supplementation in enhanced lethality.[42] The clinical associations of sporadic listerial infection with hemochromatosis[5] and outbreaks with transfusion-induced iron overload in dialysis patients[43] attest to the importance of iron as a virulence factor in humans.

IMMUNITY

Resistance to infection with the intracellular bacterium *L. monocytogenes* is predominantly cell mediated,[44] as evidenced by the experiments of Mackaness showing that immunity could be transferred by sensitized lymphocytes but not by serum that contained antibodies. Further evidence is provided by the overwhelming clinical association between listerial infection and conditions of impaired cellular immunity including lymphomas, pregnancy, AIDS, and corticosteroid immunosuppression, particularly, but not exclusively, in transplant recipients.[1,2,5,7,14,15] Combined treatment with fludarabine and prednisone in patients with chronic lymphocytic leukemia decreased their CD4+ T-lymphocyte counts and increased their incidence of listeriosis; fludarabine alone was not associated with listeriosis.[45] Tumor necrosis factor-α neutralizing agents (e.g., infliximab) are increasingly used to treat rheumatoid arthritis and Crohn's disease; invasive listeriosis has complicated use of these immune modulating agents.[46] The production of nitric oxide by activated macrophages may play a role in natural immunity to listeriosis independent of T-cell function.[47] The role of humoral immunity is unknown, although both immunoglobulin M (absent in newborns) and classic complement activity (low in newborns) have been shown to be necessary for efficient opsonization of *L. monocytogenes*[48]; and protein 60 specific antibodies, present in most immune-competent adults, opsonize *L. monocytogenes* and enhance their uptake by monocyte-derived dendritic cells which are active in killing the organism.[49]

Although listeriosis is 100 to 1000 times more common in patients with AIDS than in an age-matched population,[2,50] it is somewhat surprising that it is not seen more commonly given the ubiquity of the organism.[51] A partial explanation may lie in the experimental observation that resistance to listeriosis appears to be mediated by lymphocytes that do not carry CD4 or CD8 markers.[52] In addition, it is likely that many cases are prevented by routine *Pneumocystis* prophylaxis with trimethoprim-sulfamethoxazole. Most cases have occurred in those with advanced disease, that is, CD4 lymphocyte counts of less than 100/mm³.

There is no increased frequency of listeriosis in those with deficiencies in neutrophil numbers or function, splenectomy, complement deficiency, or immunoglobulin disorders, the latter not surprising given that *L. monocytogenes* can be passed from cell to cell without being exposed to antibody.

CLINICAL SYNDROMES

The species name derives from the fact that an extract of the *L. monocytogenes* cell membrane has potent monocytosis-producing activity in rabbits,[53] but monocytosis is a very uncommon feature of human infection.

Infection in Pregnancy

During gestation, there is a mild impairment of cell-mediated immunity,[54] and pregnant women are prone to develop listerial bacteremia with an estimated 17-fold increase in risk.[55] Listeriae may proliferate in the placenta in areas that appear to be unreachable by usual defense mechanisms. For unexplained reasons, CNS infection, a commonly recognized form of listeriosis in other groups, is extremely rare during pregnancy in the absence of other risk factors.[7,12,55] Bacteremia is manifested clinically as an acute febrile illness, often accompanied by myalgias, arthralgias, headache, and backache. Illness usually occurs in the third trimester, probably related to the major decline in cell-mediated immunity seen at 26 to 30 weeks of gestation.[54] Twenty-two percent of human perinatal infections result in stillbirth or neonatal death; spontaneous abortion is common. Untreated bacteremia is generally self-limited, although if there is a complicating amnionitis, fever in the mother may persist until the fetus is spontaneously or therapeutically aborted. Among women who have listeriosis during pregnancy, two thirds of surviving infants develop clinical neonatal listeriosis.[54] Early diagnosis and antimicrobial treatment of the infected woman can result in the birth of a healthy infant.

There is no convincing evidence that listeriosis is a cause of habitual abortion in humans.

Neonatal Infection

In a pregnant primate model, oral administration of *L. monocytogenes* resulted in stillbirth with isolation of the bacterium from placental and fetal tissues.[56] When human in utero infection occurs, it may precipitate spontaneous abortion and the fetus may be stillborn or die within hours of a disseminated form of listerial infection known as *granulomatosis infantiseptica* characterized by widespread microabscesses and granulomas, particularly prevalent in the liver and spleen. In this entity, abundant bacteria are often visible on Gram stain of meconium.[57]

More commonly, neonatal infection manifests like group B streptococcal disease in one of two forms[1]: (1) an early-onset sepsis syndrome usually associated with prematurity and probably acquired in utero, and (2) a late-onset meningitis occurring about 2 weeks postpartum in term babies most likely infected by organisms present in the maternal vagina at parturition, although cases have occurred after cesarean section, and nosocomial transmission has been suggested. In early-onset disease, *L. monocytogenes* can be isolated from the conjunctivae, external ear, nose, throat, meconium, amniotic fluid, placenta, blood, and sometimes CSF; Gram stain of meconium may show gram-positive rods and provide early diagnosis. Highest concentrations of bacteria are found in the neonatal lung and gut, suggesting that infection is acquired in utero by inhalation of infected amniotic fluid rather than via a hematogenous route.[58] Purulent conjunctivitis and a disseminated papular rash rarely have been described in newborns with early-onset disease, but clinical infection is otherwise similar to that due to other bacterial pathogens.

Bacteremia

Bacteremia without an evident focus has been the most common manifestation of listeriosis in compromised hosts; meningitis is second in frequency.[7] Clinical manifestations are similar to those seen in bacteremia with other causes and typically include fever and myalgias; a prodromal illness with diarrhea and nausea may occur. Because immunocompromised patients are more likely than healthy persons to have blood cultured during febrile illnesses, transient bacteremias in healthy persons may go undetected.

Central Nervous System Infection

The organisms that most frequently cause bacterial meningitis (*Streptococcus pneumoniae, Neisseria meningitidis, Haemophilus influenzae*) rarely cause parenchymal brain infections such as cerebritis and brain abscess. In contrast, *L. monocytogenes* has tropism for the brain itself, particularly the brain stem, as well as for the meninges.[1,5] Many patients with meningitis have altered consciousness, seizures, or movement disorders, or all of these, and truly have a meningoencephalitis.

Meningitis

In an active surveillance study of bacterial meningitis reported by the CDC in 1990, *L. monocytogenes* was the fifth most common cause behind *H. influenzae, S. pneumoniae, N. meningitidis,* and group B streptococcus but had the highest mortality at 22%.[59] In 1995, 5 years after the introduction of *H. influenzae* conjugate vaccines, a survey of bacterial meningitis showed that *H. influenzae* had become less common than *L. monocytogenes,* which accounted for 20% of cases in neonates and 20% in those older than 60 years.[60] Mortality is low (zero to 13%) for adults without serious underlying disease or immunosuppressive treatment.[5]

Worldwide, *L. monocytogenes* is one of the three major causes of neonatal meningitis; is second only to pneumococcus as a cause of bacterial meningitis in adults older than 50 years; and is the most common cause of bacterial meningitis in patients with lymphomas, organ transplant recipients, or those receiving corticosteroid immunosuppression for any reason.[1]

Clinically, meningitis caused by *L. monocytogenes* is usually similar to that due to more common causes[1,14]; features particular to listerial meningitis are summarized in Table 204-2. Despite the name *monocytogenes,* the CSF pleocytosis is more often neutrophilic than monocytic.

Brain Stem Encephalitis (Rhombencephalitis)

An unusual form of listerial encephalitis involves the brain stem[61] and is similar to the unique zoonotic listerial infection known as circling disease of sheep. In contrast to other listerial CNS infections, this illness usually occurs in healthy adults; neonatal cases have not been reported. The typical clinical picture is one of a biphasic illness with a prodrome of fever, headache, nausea, and vomiting lasting about 4 days followed by the abrupt onset of asymmetric cranial nerve deficits, cerebellar signs, and hemiparesis or hemisensory deficits, or both. About 40% of patients develop respiratory failure. Nuchal rigidity is

TABLE 204-2 Clinical Features Particular to Listerial Meningitis as Compared to More Common Bacterial Etiologies

Presentation is usually acute but may be subacute and may mimic tuberculous meningitis.
Nuchal rigidity less common (not present in 15% to 20% of adult cases).
Movement disorders (ataxia, tremors, myoclonus) are more common (15% to 20%).
Seizures are more common (at least 25%).
Fluctuating mental status is common.
Blood cultures are more often positive (75%).
Cerebrospinal fluid:
    Gram stain is negative in most (organisms seen in approximately 40%).
    CSF glucose is not low in most (normal >60%).
    Mononuclear cell predominance is present in about one third.

present in about one half, and CSF findings are only mildly abnormal with a positive CSF culture in about 40%. Almost two thirds of patients are bacteremic. Magnetic resonance imaging is superior to computed tomography for demonstrating encephalitis (Fig. 204-1). Mortality is high, and serious sequelae are common in survivors.

Brain Abscess

Macroscopic brain abscesses account for about 10% of CNS listerial infections. Bacteremia is almost always present, and concomitant meningitis with isolation of *L. monocytogenes* from the CSF is found in 25% to 40%; both these features are rare in other forms of bacterial brain abscess.[62] Most cases occur in known risk groups for listerial infection. Subcortical abscesses located in the thalamus, pons, and medulla are common; these sites are exceedingly rare when abscesses are caused by other bacteria. Mortality is high, and survivors usually have serious sequelae.

Endocarditis

Listerial endocarditis accounts for about 7.5% of adult listerial infections,[5] affects the population at risk for viridans streptococcal endocarditis, produces both native valve and prosthetic valve disease, and has a high rate of septic complications and a mortality of 48%.[63] Listerial endocarditis, but not bacteremia per se, may be an indicator of underlying gastrointestinal tract abnormality, including cancer.[1] Cases in the pediatric age group have not been reported.

Localized Infection

Rare reports of focal infections from which *L. monocytogenes* has been isolated include direct inoculation resulting in conjunctivitis, skin infection, and lymphadenitis. Bacteremia can lead to hepatitis and hepatic abscess, cholecystitis, peritonitis, splenic abscess, pleuropulmonary infection, joint infection, osteomyelitis, pericarditis, myocarditis, arteritis, and endophthalmitis. There is nothing clinically unique about these localized infections; many, but not all, have occurred in those known to be at risk for listeriosis.

Febrile Gastroenteritis

Many patients with listerial bacteremia or CNS infection give a history of antecedent gastrointestinal symptoms including diarrhea, nausea, and vomiting, often accompanied by fever.[5,30] Large inocula of orally administered *L. monocytogenes* produce diarrheal disease in primates.[27] Investigation of a point-source foodborne listeriosis outbreak, which resulted in bacteremia in two pregnant women, strongly suggested that ingestion of contaminated food by healthy, nonpregnant individuals produced a self-limited, febrile gastroenteritis.[29]

Convincing evidence that *L. monocytogenes* can cause foodborne noninvasive disease in healthy persons was provided by the report of an outbreak of diarrhea and fever among attendees at a Holstein cow show in Illinois traced to ingestion of contaminated chocolate milk.[64] A high illness attack rate of 75% was seen in the 60 people who consumed the chocolate milk. The most common symptoms were diarrhea (79%), fever (72%), chills (65%), and headache (65%). Also common were myalgias (59%) and abdominal cramps (55%); nausea occurred in 47% and vomiting in 26%. The median incubation period was 20 hours (range 9 to 32), and diarrhea lasted a median of 42 hours with a median of 12 stools during the 24 hours of maximal diarrhea. The contamination level in the milk was exceedingly high, and the median dose of ingested listeriae may have been as high as 2.9×10^{11} colony-forming units per person. The epidemic appeared to be caused by post-pasteurization contamination. In this outbreak serologic testing for antibodies to listeriolysin O was shown to be a useful tool for retrospectively identifying infected ill persons. Active surveillance identified three persons with invasive disease (bacteremia, brain abscess) related to ingestion of chocolate milk from the implicated dairy, providing further evidence that many cases of seemingly sporadic invasive disease are, in fact, part of foodborne outbreaks.

In a very large outbreak,[8] more than 1500 illnesses (attack rate 72%) occurred in Italian school children who ingested a catered corn

FIGURE 204-1. Magnetic resonance imaging scan of the brain of a patient with chronic lymphocytic leukemia, cerebritis, hemiparesis, *Listeria monocytogenes* in blood cultures, and a negative result on spinal fluid examination. Six weeks of ampicillin and gentamicin resulted in a complete recovery.

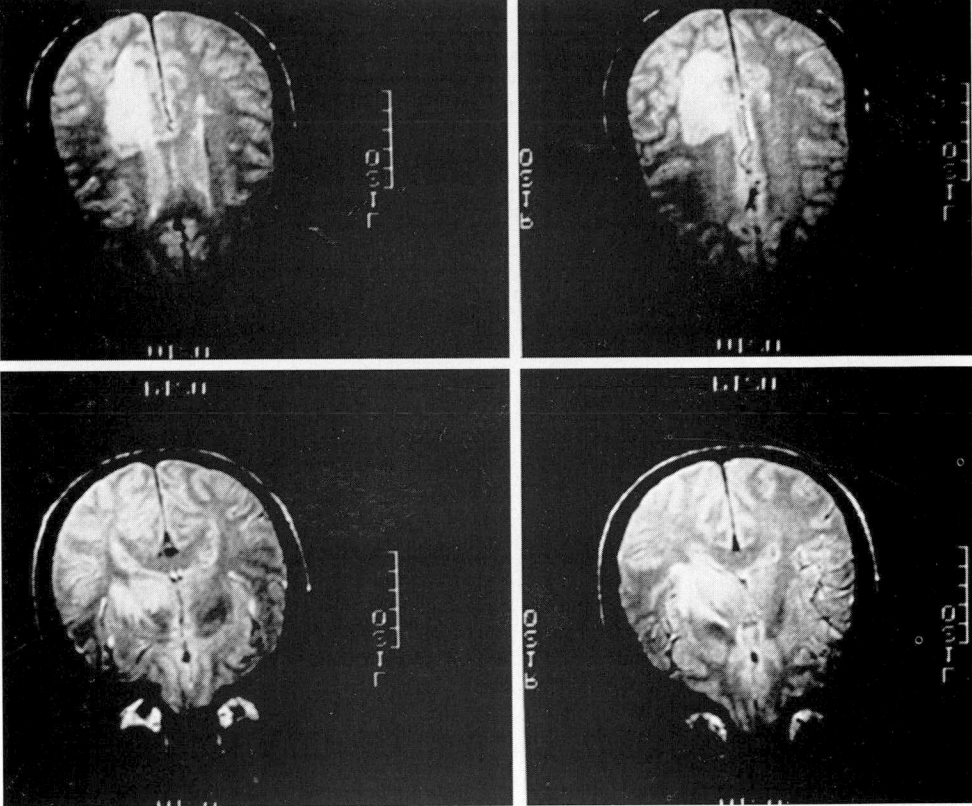

salad as part of a school lunch program; 19% were hospitalized, 87% of stool cultures were positive, and one of 40 blood cultures grew *L. monocytogenes.* In another outbreak,[65] fever and gastrointestinal symptoms developed in 16 of 44 healthy attendees of a Los Angeles county catered party who ingested precooked, sliced turkey; and in another small cluster,[66] 5 persons developed gastroenteritis after eating cold-smoked trout. *Listeria monocytogenes* should be considered as a possible cause of foodborne outbreaks of febrile gastroenteritis when routine stool cultures fail to identify a pathogen.

Complications

Complications of invasive disease including disseminated intravascular coagulation, adult respiratory distress syndrome, and rhabdomyolysis with acute renal failure have been documented. Rare episodes of reinfection have occurred.[67]

DIAGNOSIS

Clinical settings in which listeriosis should be given strong consideration as part of the differential diagnosis are listed in Table 204-3.

Diagnosis requires isolation of *L. monocytogenes* from normally sterile clinical specimens (CSF, blood, joint fluid, and so forth) and identification through standard microbiologic techniques. Antibodies to listeriolysin O have not proved useful for acute diagnosis of invasive disease; nor yet have polymerase chain reaction probes. Serodiagnosis of listeriosis employing measurement of antibodies to listeriolysin O has proved useful for identifying infected individuals with noninvasive disease (asymptomatic infection, gastroenteritis) during foodborne outbreaks.[64] A polypeptide limited to an amino-terminal residue of listeriolysin O appears to be a more specific antigen for use in serologic tests than those previously employed.[68]

Magnetic resonance imaging is superior to computerized tomography for demonstrating parenchymal brain involvement, especially in the brain stem.[61,69]

TREATMENT

There have been no controlled trials to establish a drug of choice or the duration of therapy for listerial infection. Comprehensive reviews of antimicrobial activity against *L. monocytogenes* and treatment of listeriosis have been published.[70,71] Recommendations regarding therapy are based on data obtained from in vitro susceptibility testing, animal models, and clinical experience with small numbers of patients compared with historical controls and, therefore, are subject to interpretation and individual preferences. In the absence of a positive CSF Gram stain, initial therapy for bacterial meningitis in all adults older than 50 years should include either ampicillin or trimethoprim-sulfamethoxazole, especially if there is no associated pneumonia, otitis, sinusitis, or endocarditis that would point to causes other than *L. monocytogenes.*

Ampicillin is generally considered the preferred agent, although its superiority to penicillin is questionable. The β-lactam antibiotics are often described as being bacteriostatic for listeriae. In fact, they

TABLE 204-3 Clinical Settings in Which Listeriosis Should be Considered Strongly in the Differential Diagnosis

Neonatal sepsis or meningitis
Meningitis or parenchymal brain infection in patients with hematological malignancies, AIDS, organ transplantation, or corticosteroid immuno-suppression
Meningitis or parenchymal brain infection in adults older than 50 years of age
Simultaneous infection of the meninges and brain parenchyma
Subcortical brain abscess
Fever during pregnancy, particularly in the third trimester
Blood, CSF or other normally sterile specimen reported to have "diphtheroids" on Gram stain or culture
Foodborne outbreak of febrile gastroenteritis when routine cultures fail to identify a pathogen

demonstrate delayed in vitro bactericidal activity (48 hours) at levels that are obtainable in the CSF. The same phenomenon has been shown with imipenem and vancomycin. Based on synergy in vitro and in animal models, most authorities suggest adding gentamicin to ampicillin for the treatment of bacteremia in those with severely impaired T-cell function and in all cases of meningitis and endocarditis.

For those intolerant of penicillins, trimethoprim-sulfamethoxazole as a single agent is thought to be the best alternative. Although data are limited, this combination is bactericidal for listeriae, and outcomes appear at least comparable to those achieved with ampicillin and gentamicin. In a preliminary study of patients with severe listerial meningoencephalitis, the combination of trimethoprim-sulfamethoxazole plus ampicillin was associated with a much lower failure rate and fewer neurologic sequelae than ampicillin combined with an aminoglycoside.[72] In the absence of underlying immunosuppressive illness or treatment, pregnant women virtually never develop CNS infection. Therefore, a penicillin allergic pregnant woman, at a time in the pregnancy when sulfonamides should be avoided, could reasonably be treated with a macrolide or vancomycin.

Chloramphenicol should not be used to treat listerial infection because of unacceptable failure and relapse rates. No currently available cephalosporin should be used; they have limited activity, and meningitis has developed in patients while receiving cephalosporins. Reports have documented the utility of erythromycin and tetracycline in isolated cases, but these agents are unreliable and should be avoided. One center has reported a clindamycin resistance rate of >95%.[73] Several quinolones have good in vitro activity, but clinical experience is lacking, and listerial meningitis may have developed, or at the very least progressed, during ciprofloxacin treatment.[74]

Vancomycin has been used successfully in a few penicillin-allergic patients, but others have developed listerial meningitis while receiving the drug. Rifampin is quite active in vitro and is known to penetrate into phagocytic cells; however, clinical experience is minimal, and in animal models the addition of rifampin to ampicillin was not more effective than ampicillin alone. Both imipenem and meropenem have been used successfully to treat listeriosis, but caution is advised because both drugs lower the seizure threshold, and imipenem was less effective than ampicillin in a mouse model.[75]

Meningitis doses should be used for all patients, even in the absence of CNS or CSF abnormalities, because of the high affinity of this organism for the CNS. Relapses and treatment failures are reported in those with meningitis treated for less than 2 weeks; therefore, treatment for 3 weeks is recommended for all cases of meningitis.[14] Bacteremic patients without CSF abnormalities can be treated for 2 weeks. Patients with rhombencephalitis or brain abscess should be treated for at least 6 weeks and followed with serial magnetic resonance imaging studies (or computed tomography scans). Endocarditis should be treated for 4 to 6 weeks.

No data exist concerning antimicrobial efficacy in listerial gastroenteritis; the illness is self-limited, and treatment is not warranted.

Clinically significant antimicrobial resistance has not been encountered, but vigilance is warranted because transfer of resistance from enterococci to *L. monocytogenes* has been documented.[76]

Iron is a virulence factor for *L. monocytogenes* and, clinically, iron-overload states are risk factors for listerial infection. Therefore, in patients with iron deficiency, it seems prudent to withhold iron replacement until treatment for listerial infection is completed. Corticosteroids appear to be important adjunctive agents in treating the most common forms of bacterial meningitis; their role in the treatment of listerial CNS infections is unknown.

PREVENTION

Recommendations for consumer prevention of listeriosis from a foodborne source were developed by the CDC in 1992 and are presented in Table 204-4.

In 1989, following documentation of listeriosis after the ingestion of contaminated turkey frankfurters, the US Department of Agriculture

---

TABLE 204-4   Dietary Recommendations for Preventing Foodborne Listeriosis

For all persons:
Thoroughly cook raw food from animal sources (e.g., beef, pork, and poultry).
Thoroughly wash raw vegetables before eating.
Keep uncooked meats separate from vegetables, cooked foods, and ready-to-eat foods.
Avoid consumption of raw (unpasteurized) milk or foods made from raw milk.
Wash hands, knives, and cutting boards after handling uncooked foods.

Additional recommendations for persons at high risk (those immuno-compromised by illness or medications, pregnant women, and the elderly):
Avoid soft cheeses (e.g., Mexican-style, feta, Brie, Camembert, and blue-veined cheese). (There is no need to avoid hard cheeses, cream cheese, cottage cheese, or yogurt).
Leftover foods or ready-to-eat foods (e.g., hot dogs) should be reheated until steaming hot before eating.
Although the risk for listeriosis associated with foods from delicatessen counters is relatively low, pregnant women and immunosuppressed persons may choose to avoid these foods or to thoroughly reheat cold cuts before eating.

---

began a surveillance program for *L. monocytogenes* in ready-to-eat processed meats and enforced regulations prohibiting the sale of contaminated meat (so-called zero-tolerance policy).[13] Active surveillance of listeriosis in the United States suggests that industry cleanup efforts combined with the 1992 dietary recommendations for persons at increased risk were effective measures. From 1989 through 1993 there was a 44% reduction in invasive listerial illness and a 48% reduction in deaths.[13] A similar decline in incidence of human listeriosis was seen in France following control measures to decrease food contamination.[77]

Except from infected mother to fetus, human-to-human transmission of listeriosis does not occur; patients do not need to be isolated. Second episodes of neonatal listerial infection are virtually unheard of, and intrapartum antibiotics are not recommended for mothers with a history of perinatal listeriosis. There is no vaccine.

Listerial infections are effectively prevented by trimethoprim-sulfamethoxazole given as *Pneumocystis* prophylaxis to organ transplant recipients or individuals with human immunodeficiency virus infection.[63,78] In areas with a high prevalence of AIDS, the widespread use of trimethoprim-sulfamethoxazole prophylaxis against *Pneumocystis* pneumonia appears to have resulted in a marked decline in nonperinatal listeriosis.

The utility, or even the feasibility, of eradicating gastrointestinal colonization as a means to prevent invasive disease is unknown. However, asymptomatic people at high risk for listeriosis, known to have ingested a food implicated in an outbreak, reasonably could be given several days of oral ampicillin or trimethoprim-sulfamethoxaxole.

ADDITIONAL READING

Ryser ET, Marth EH, eds. Listeria, Listeriosis and Food Safety. 2nd ed. New York: Marcel Dekker; 1999.

REFERENCES

1. Lorber B. Listeriosis. Clin Infect Dis. 1997;24:1-11.
2. Slutsker L, Schuchat A. Listeriosis in humans. In: Ryser ET, Marth EH, eds. Listeria, Listeriosis and Food Safety. 2nd ed. New York: Marcel Dekker; 1999:75-95.
3. Bille J, Rocourt J, Swaminathan B. *Listeria* and *Erysipelothrix*. In: Murray PR, Baron EJ, Jorgensen JH, et al., eds. Manual of Clinical Microbiology. 8th ed. Washington, DC: American Society for Microbiology Press; 2003:461-471.
4. Hayes PS, Graves LM, Ajello GW, et al. Comparison of cold enrichment and US Department of Agriculture methods for isolating *Listeria monocytogenes* from naturally contaminated foods. Appl Environ Microbiol. 1991;57:2109-2113.
5. Nieman RE, Lorber B. Listeriosis in adults: A changing pattern. Report of eight cases and review of the literature, 1968-1978. Rev Infect Dis. 1980;2:207-227.
6. Schuchat A, Swaminathan B, Broome CV. Epidemiology of human listeriosis. Clin Microbiol Rev. 1991;4:169-183.

7. Gellin BG, Broome CV, Bibb WF, et al. The epidemiology of listeriosis in the United States-1986. Am J Epidemiol. 1991;133:392-401.
8. Aureli P, Fiorucci GC, Caroli D, et al. An outbreak of febrile gastroenteritis associated with corn contaminated by *Listeria monocytogenes.* N Engl J Med. 2000;342:1235-1241.
9. Schlech WF III, Lavigne PM, Bortolussi RA, et al. Epidemic listeriosis-Evidence for transmission by food. N Engl J Med. 1983;308:203-206.
10. Schuchat A, Deaver K, Hayes PS, et al. Gastrointestinal carriage of *Listeria monocytogenes* in household contacts of patients with listeriosis. J Infect Dis. 1993;167:1261-1262.
11. Farber JM, Peterkin PI. *Listeria monocytogenes,* a food-borne pathogen. Microbiol Rev. 1991;55:476-511.
12. Ciesielski CA, Hightower AW, Parsons SK, et al. Listeriosis in the United States: 1980-1982. Arch Intern Med. 1988;148:1416-1419.
13. Tappero JW, Schuchat A, Deaver KA, et al. Reduction in the incidence of human listeriosis in the United States. Effectiveness of prevention efforts? JAMA. 1995;273:1118-1122.
14. Mylonakis E, Hohmann EL, Calderwood SB. Central nervous system infection with Listeria monocytogenes. 33 years' experience at a general hospital and review of 776 episodes from the literature. Medicine. 1998;77:313-336.
15. Siegman-Igra Y, Levin R, Weinberger M, et al. *Listeria monocytogenes* infection in Israel and review of cases worldwide. Emerg Infect Dis. 2002;8:305-310.
16. Buchholz U, Mascola L. Transmission, pathogenesis, and epidemiology of *Listeria monocytogenes.* Infect Dis Clin Pract. 2001;10:34-41.
17. Safdar A. Papadopoulous EB, Armstrong D. Listeriosis in recipients of allogeneic blood and marrow transplantation: Thirteen year review of disease characteristics, treatment outcomes and a new association with human cytomegalovirus infection. Bone Marrow Transplant. 2002;29:913-916.
18. Centers for Disease Control and Prevention. Outbreak of listeriosis associated with homemade Mexican-style cheese- North Carolina, October 2000-January 2001. Morbid Mortal Wkly Rep. 2001;50:560-562.
19. Lyytikainen O, Autio T, Maijala R, et al. An outbreak of *Listeria monocytogenes* serotype 3a infections from butter in Finland. J Infect Dis. 2000;181:1838-1841.
20. Centers for Disease Control and Prevention. Update: Multistate outbreak of listeriosis- United States, 1998-1999. Morbid Mortal Wkly Rep. 1999;47:1117-1118.
21. Centers for Disease Control and Prevention. Public Health Dispatch: Outbreak of Listeriosis- Northeastern United States, 2002. Morbid Mortal Wkly Rep. 2002;51:950-951.
22. Schuchat A, Deaver KA, Wenger JD, et al. Role of foods in sporadic listeriosis. 1. Case-control study of dietary risk factors. JAMA. 1992;267:2041-2045.
23. Pinner RW, Schuchat A, Swaminathan B, et al. Role of foods in sporadic listeriosis II. Microbiologic and epidemiologic investigation. JAMA. 1992;267:2046-2050.
24. Farber JM, Peterkin PI, Carter AO, et al. Neonatal listeriosis due to cross-infection confirmed by isoenzyme typing and DNA fingerprinting. J Infect Dis. 1991;163:927-928.
25. Schuchat A, Lizano C, Broome CV, et al. Outbreak of neonatal listeriosis associated with mineral oil. Pediatr Infect Dis. 1991;10:183-189.
26. Swaminathan B, Barrett TJ, Hunter SB, et al. PulseNet: The molecular subtyping network for foodborne bacterial disease surveillance, United States. Emerg Infect Dis. 2001;7:382-389.
27. Farber JM, Daley E, Coates F, et al. Feeding trials of *Listeria monocytogenes* with a nonhuman primate model. J Clin Microbiol. 1991;29:2606-2608.
28. Schlech WF III, Chase DP, Badley A. A model of food-borne *Listeria monocytogenes* infection in the Sprague-Dawley rat using gastric inoculation: Development and effect of gastric acidity on infective dose. Int J Food Microbiol. 1993;18:15-24.
29. Riedo FX, Pinner RW, Tosca ML, et al. A point-source foodborne listeriosis outbreak: Documented incubation period and possible mild illness. J Infect Dis. 1994;170: 693-696.
30. Schwartz B, Hexter D, Broome CV, et al. Investigation of an outbreak of listeriosis: New hypotheses for the etiology of epidemic *Listeria monocytogenes* infections. J Infect Dis. 1989;159:680-685.
31. Schroter GPJ, Weil R. *Listeria monocytogenes* infection after renal transplantation. Arch Intern Med. 1977;137:1395-1399.
32. Lorber B. Listeriosis following shigellosis. Rev Infect Dis. 1991;13:865-866.
33. Sheehan GJ, Galbraith JCT. Colonoscopy-associated listeriosis: Report of a case. Clin Infect Dis. 1993;17:1061-1062.
34. Witlox MA, Klinkenberg-Knol EC, Meuwissen SGM. *Listeria* sepsis as a complication of endoscopy. Gastrointest Endosc. 2000;51:235-236.
35. Lecuit M, Vandormael-Pournin S, Lefort J, et al. A transgenic model for listeriosis: Role of Internalin in crossing the intestinal barrier. Science. 2001;292:1722-1725.
36. Antal E-A, Leberg EM, Bracht P, et al. Evidence for intraaxonal spread of *Listeria monocytogenes* from the periphery to the central nervous system. Brain Pathol. 2001;11:432-438.
37. Southwick FS, Purich DL. Intracellular pathogenesis of listeriosis. N Engl J Med. 1996;334:770-776.
38. Vazquez-Boland JA, Kuhn M, Berche P, et al. *Listeria* pathogenesis and molecular virulence determinants. Clin Microbiol Rev. 2001;14:584-640.
39. Wing EJ, Gregory SH. *Listeria monocytogenes:* Clinical and experimental update. J Infect Dis. 2002;185(Suppl 1):S18-S24.
40. Portnoy DA, Auerbuch V, Glomski IJ. The cell biology of *Listeria monocytogenes* infection: The intersection of bacterial pathogenesis and cell-mediated immunity. J Cell Biol. 2002;158:409-414.
41. Reglier-Poupet H, Pellegrini E, Charbit A, et al. Identification of LpeA, a PsaA-like membrane protein that promotes cell entry by *Listeria monocytogenes.* Infect Immun. 2003;71:474-482.
42. Ampel NM, Bejarano GC, Saavedra M Jr. Deferoxamine increases the susceptibility of beta-thalassemic, iron-overloaded mice to infection with *Listeria monocytogenes.* Life Sci. 1992;50:1327-1332.
43. Mossey RT, Sondheimer J. Listeriosis in patients with long-term hemodialysis and transfusional iron overload. Am J Med. 1985;79:379-400.
44. Parham P, Unanue ER, eds. Immunity to *L. monocytogenes:* A model intracellular pathogen. Immunol Rev. 1997;158:1-169.
45. Anaissie E, Kontoyiannis DP, Kantarjian H, et al. Listeriosis in patients with chronic lymphocytic leukemia who were treated with fludarabine and prednisone. Ann Intern Med. 1992;117:466-469.
46. Slifman NR, Gershon SK, Lee JH, et al. *Listeria monocytogenes* infection as a complication of treatment with tumor necrosis factor alpha-neutralizing agents. Arthritis Rheum. 2003;48:319-324.
47. Hibbs JB Jr. Infection and nitric oxide. J Infect Dis. 2002;185(Suppl):S9-S17.
48. Bortolussi R, Issekutz A, Faulkner G. Opsonization of *Listeria monocytogenes* type 4b by human adult and newborn sera. Infect Immun. 1986;52:493-498.
49. Kolb-Maurer A, Pilgrim S, Kampgen E, et al. Antibodies against listerial protein 60 act as an opsonin for phagocytosis of *Listeria monocytogenes* by human dendritic cells. Infect Immun. 2001;69:3100-3109.
50. Ewert DP, Lieb L, Hayes PS, et al. *Listeria monocytogenes* infection and serotype distribution among HIV-infected persons in Los Angeles County, 1985-92. J Acquir Immune Defic Syndr Hum Retrovirol. 1995;8:461-465.
51. Decker CF, Simon GL, DiGioia RA, et al. *Listeria monocytogenes* infections in patients with AIDS: Report of five cases and review. Rev Infect Dis. 1991;13: 413-417.
52. Dunn PL, North RJ. Resolution of primary murine listeriosis and acquired resistance to lethal secondary infection can be mediated predominantly by Thy-1$^+$ CD$^-$ CD8$^-$ cells. J Infect Dis. 1991;164:869-877.
53. Stanley NF. Studies of *Listeria monocytogenes.* I. Isolation of a monocytosis-producing agent (MPA). Aust J Exp Biol Med Sci. 1949;27:123-131.
54. Weinberg ED. Pregnancy-associated depression of cell-mediated immunity. Rev Infect Dis. 1984;6:814-831.
55. Mylonakis E, Paliou M, Hohmann EL, et al. Listeriosis during pregnancy. A case series and review of 222 cases. Medicine. 2002;81:260-269.
56. Smith MA, Takeuchi K, Brackett RE, et al. Nonhuman primate model for *Listeria monocytogenes*-induced stillbirths. Infect Immun. 2003;71:1574-1579.
57. Larsson S, Linell F. Correlations between clinical and postmortem findings in listeriosis. Scand J Infect Dis. 1979;11:55-58.
58. Becroft DMO, Farmer K, Seddon RJ, et al. Epidemic listeriosis in the newborn. Br Med J. 1971;3:747-751.
59. Wenger JD, Hightower AW, Facklam RR, et al. Bacterial meningitis in the United States, 1986; Report of a multistate surveillance study. J Infect Dis. 1990;162:1316-1623.
60. Schuchat A, Robinson K, Wenger JD, et al. Bacterial meningitis in the United States in 1995. N Engl J Med. 1997;337:970-976.
61. Armstrong RW, Fung PC. Brainstem encephalitis (rhombencephalitis) due to *Listeria monocytogenes:* Case report and review. Clin Infect Dis. 1993;16:689-702.
62. Eckburg PB, Montoya JG, Vosti KL. Brain abscess due to *Listeria monocytogenes.* Five cases and a review of the literature. Medicine. 2001;80:223-235.
63. Carvajal A, Frederiksen W. Fatal endocarditis due to *Listeria monocytogenes.* Rev Infect Dis. 1988;10:616-623.
64. Dalton CB, Austin CC, Sobel J, et al. An outbreak of gastroenteritis and fever due to *Listeria monocytogenes* in milk. N Engl J Med. 1997;336:100-105.
65. Frye DM, Zweig R, Sturgeon J, et al. An outbreak of febrile gastroenteritis associated with delicatessen meat contaminated with *Listeria monocytogenes.* Clin Infect Dis. 2002;35:943-949.
66. Miettinen MK, Siitonen A, Heiskanen P, et al. Molecular epidemiology of an outbreak of febrile gastroenteritis caused by *Listeria monocytogenes* in cold-smoked rainbow trout. J Clin Microbiol. 1999;37:2358-2360.
67. Van J-C N, Nguyen L, Guillemam R, et al. Relapse of infection or reinfection by *Listeria monocytogenes* in a patient with heart transplant: Usefulness of pulsed-field gel electrophoresis for diagnosis. Clin Infect Dis. 1994;19:208-209.
68. Gholizadeh Y, Poyart C, Jovin M, et al. Serodiagnosis of listeriosis based on detection of antibodies against recombinant truncated forms of listeriolysis O. J Clin Microbiol. 1996;34:1391-1395.
69. Faidas A, Shepard DL, Lim J, et al. Magnetic resonance imaging in listerial brain stem encephalitis. Clin Infect Dis. 1993;16:186-187.
70. Hof H, Nichterlein T, Kretschmar M. Management of listeriosis. Clin Microbiol Rev. 1997;10:345-357.
71. Lorber B. *Listeria monocytogenes* in Antimicrobial Therapy and Vaccines. In: Yu VL, Weber R, Raoult, eds. Antimicrobial Therapy and Vaccines. 2nd ed. New York: Apple Trees Productions; 2002:429-436.
72. Merle-Melet M, Dossou-Gbete L, Meyer P, et al. Is amoxicillin-cotrimoxazole the most appropriate antibiotic regimen for *Listeria* meningoencephalitis? Review of 22 cases and the literature. J Infect. 1996;33:79-85.
73. Safdar A, Armstrong D. Antimicrobial activities against 84 *Listeria monocytogenes* isolates from patients with systemic listeriosis at a comprehensive cancer center (1955-1997). J Clin Microbiol. 2003;41:483-485.
74. Grumbach NM, Mylonakis E, Wing EJ. Development of listerial meningitis during ciprofloxacin treatment. Clin Infect Dis. 1999;29:1340-1341.
75. Kim KS. In vitro and in vivo studies of imipenem—cilastatin alone and in combination with gentamicin against *Listeria monocytogenes.* Antimicrob Agents Chemother. 1986;29:289-293.
76. Charpentier E, Courvalin P. Antibiotic resistance in *Listeria* spp. Antimicrob Agents Chemother. 1999;43:2103-2108.
77. Goulet V, de Valk H, Pierre O, et al. Effect of prevention measures on incidence of human listeriosis, France, 1987-1997. Emerg Infect Dis. 2001;7:983-989.
78. Dworkin MS, Williamson J, Jones JL, et al. Prophylaxis with trimethoprim-sulfamethoxazole for human immunodeficiency virus-infected patients: Impact on risk for infectious diseases. Clin Infect Dis. 2001;33:393-398.

CHAPTER **205**

Bacillus anthracis (Anthrax)

DANIEL LUCEY

HISTORY

The word "anthrax" derives from the Greek root for "coal," applicable to the black eschar that forms in cutaneous anthrax. Anthrax may have been the fifth plague that killed the cattle of the Egyptians as described in the Book of Exodus in the Bible. Several founders of microbiology and immunology made major contributions through their research with *Bacillus anthracis,* as exemplified by Koch, Pasteur, and Metchnikoff. In the introductory speech to his Nobel Prize in 1905 for work on tuberculosis, the presenter cited Koch's prior groundbreaking work on anthrax in 1876 as his entry into the field of microbiology research.[1] Koch's detailed work on the organism, *B. anthracis,* and the disease, anthrax, resulted in the first proof that a single bacterium caused a specific disease, and to the articulation of Koch's postulates. By 1881 Pasteur had demonstrated that his heat-attenuated anthrax vaccine protected animals from challenge with live *B. anthracis.* Therefore, he is generally given credit for the first effective vaccine against anthrax.[2]

Working in Pasteur's laboratory, Metchnikoff in 1884 demonstrated that heat-attenuated strains of *B. anthracis,* such as the one used in Pasteur's vaccines, could be phagocytosed by macrophages. In contrast, nonattenuated, virulent strains of *B. anthracis* could not be phagocytosed.[3,4] Later, the explanation for this observation was provided when it was found that heat-attenuated strains of anthrax do not have a capsule and that it is this capsule that inhibits the phagocytosis of virulent strains of *B. anthracis.* Metchniioff's early work with anthrax provided a key part of his foundation for the field of cell-mediated immunity. The contending field of humoral immunity would soon dominate the young science of immunology, however, and decades would pass before cell-mediated immunity would reemerge and recognize Metchnikoff's early contributions such as his work with anthrax.

Anthrax has been a disease of animals primarily, with a long history of animal-associated disease in humans. Terms applied to anthrax include "woolsorter's disease" and "ragpicker's disease," reflecting environmental exposures, and the clinical misnomer "malignant pustule." Although anthrax has remained endemic in many parts of the world, it is unusual in the United States, in part as a result of vaccination of animals and preventive measures in the processing of animal products such as wool and hides. Most recently, in 2001 human cutaneous and inhalational forms of anthrax were acquired in a novel manner when *B. anthracis* spores were sent in contaminated letters as an act of bioterrorism in the United States causing the death of five persons from inhalational anthrax. Anthrax as a bioterrorism weapon is described in Chapter 324. Although overlap between these two anthrax chapters occurs, it is intended to be limited, and some information appears in only one of the chapters.

MICROBIOLOGY

B. anthracis is a gram-positive rod 4 μm by 1 μm that is aerobic or facultatively anaerobic. In culture the organisms can appear as very long "boxcar" or "cigar-shaped" chains. In contrast, smears of tissue, blood, or fluid with *B. anthracis* may show only short chains or several organisms. *B. anthracis* grows readily on sheep blood agar. Colony appearance and microbiologic tests are characteristic, but not completely diagnostic. Therefore, confirmatory testing is required to distinguish *B. anthracis* from other bacillus species and other organisms. Colony appearance on sheep blood agar is typically white or gray-white, tenacious, flat, with a "Medusa's head" or a curly tail appearance at the periphery. The organism is nonmotile, nonhemolytic, catalase-positive, lysed by γ-phage, and classically sensitive to penicillin. When the anthrax endospore forms it is located centrally or subterminally, and is oval-shaped. Polymerase chain reaction (PCR) is used to confirm the organism growing in culture as *B. anthracis,* along with γ-phage lysis. The Centers for Disease Control and Prevention (CDC) have provided detailed guidance and algorithms on how to culture and perform preliminary tests for the identification of *B. anthracis.*[5] Confirmatory testing should be performed only at a reference public health laboratory, and they will coordinate obtaining samples and involving FBI and law enforcement organizations if bioterrorism is suspected.

Under anaerobic conditions, with bicarbonate present, a polypeptide capsule is secreted consisting of poly-D-glutamic acid. This capsule can be visualized with India ink stain. The negatively charged capsule is one of the major virulence factors of *B. anthracis,* along with the anthrax toxins. Synthesis of the capsule is coded for by three enzymes encoded on the pX02 plasmid: capA, capB, and capC. In addition, a fourth protein, encoded by the *dep* gene, is thought to function as a depolymerase that catalyzes formation of lower molecular weight polyglutamates by the hydrolysis of the higher molecular weight poly-D-glutamic acid.[6] These lower molecular weight capsule polyglutamates appear responsible for inhibition of phagocytosis.[7]

In addition to the capsule, the other virulence factors are the two binary toxins of anthrax termed "edema factor" (EF) and "lethal factor" (LF). Both of these factors must first bind the third toxin component, termed "protective antigen" (PA), before they can enter a target cell, such as a macrophage or dendritic cell. The cellular receptor for PA, the anthrax toxin receptor (ATR), was identified in 2001. The precise function and natural ligand for the ATR, however, are still uncertain.[8] The three toxin components are also encoded on a plasmid, termed pX-01. The crystal structures of PA, LF, and EF have been reported recently.[9-11]

The pathogenesis of fatal anthrax infection is thought to be caused by anthrax toxin, although the complete process is still not known. After PA binds to its cellular receptor (ATR), it is cleaved by a cellular protease into a 20-kDa and a 63-kDa portion. Seven copies of the 63-kDa PA combine to form a heptamer that remains bound to the cell membrane ATR. Next a maximum of three copies of either LF or EF, or a combination of the two, bind to the PA heptamer. This complex of PA and LF and/or EF is then internalized and enters the intracellular endosome. The low pH of the endosome is required for the LF and EF to cross the endosome membrane into the cytosol.[12] Once in the cytosol the LF and EF trigger their toxin effects, including immune system evasion and damage, and death can result in hours to days.

LF is a zinc-dependent metallopeptidase that has been recently shown to inhibit the mitogen-activated protein kinase ("MAP kinase") intracellular signal transduction pathways by cleaving critical enzymes in a family known as MAP kinase kinases.[12] In 2003 it was reported that lethal toxin inhibits MAP kinase pathways in dendritic cells, a critical antigen-presenting cell, and thereby impairs antigen-specific T cells and subsequent T-cell–dependent immune responses.[13] Lethal toxin blocked dendritic cell function at several levels. It prevented upregulation of costimulatory molecules CD40, CD80, and CD86 necessary for dendritic cell activation, inhibited dendritic cell production of activation cytokines such as interleukin 12 (IL-12), and blocked dendritic cells from priming naïve T cells. Previously, the effect of lethal toxin had focused primarily on the macrophage and not on dendritic cells.

Much of the pathogenesis of anthrax has previously been attributed to macrophage-mediated cytokine release, particularly tumor necrosis factor-α (TNF-α) and IL-1, on toxin-induced lysis of infected macrophages, and septic shock resulting in death.[14] This view was challenged in 2003, however, using a murine model in which lethal toxin was shown to kill through a mechanism that appeared to be cytokine independent and specifically did not require TNF-α or IL-1. Macrophage lysis was not required for anthrax-induced death. Instead, striking tissue hypoxia and liver necrosis were observed, although the exact mechanism for this damage was not defined.[15]

Edema factor functions as a calmodulin-dependent adenylate cyclase enzyme that converts ATP to cyclic adenosine monophosphate (cAMP). Intracellular increases in cAMP result in dysregulation of water and ions, including calcium, that are linked to the characteristic edema formation observed with anthrax infection. Edema toxin is also thought to impair polymorphonuclear leukocyte function. When the structure of EF was demonstrated by x-ray crystallography in 2002, the enzyme was demonstrated to be activated only after binding to calmodulin and undergoing a conformational change.[11]

EPIDEMIOLOGY

The World Health Organization (WHO) maintains a comprehensive website with data on the global epidemiology of anthrax in animals and humans.[16] This database includes a chronology of outbreaks in individual countries across each continent. One or more endemic nations exist in Asia, South America, North America, Africa, and Europe. Sporadic cases occur in Australia. Although anthrax has remained endemic in many parts of the world, it is unusual in the United States, in part as a result of vaccination of animals and preventive measures in the processing of animal products such as wool and hides. Anthrax infections in animals occasionally still occur in the Midwest and western United States, but not along the east coast, where the bioterrorism-related anthrax deaths occurred in 2001. In the United States between 1900 and 2000 only 18 cases of inhalational anthrax were reported[17] and no culture-proven cases of gastrointestinal anthrax. Only two cases of cutaneous anthrax were reported between 1992 and 2000.[18] In contrast, many cases of veterinary and human anthrax occur worldwide. The largest recent outbreak in humans, linked to disease in cattle, involved more than 10,000 persons and occurred in Zimbabwe from 1979 to 1985. Most of the cases were cutaneous anthrax, although rarely meningitis also occurred.[19,20]

The World Health Organization also provides a comprehensive online resource on guidelines for control of anthrax in animals and humans, including ecology and epidemiology issues.[21] Infection of humans with anthrax is typically linked to infection of herbivores including cattle, horses, goats, sheep, pigs, and kudu, or the soil where they graze. Animal products that can transmit anthrax infection include wool, hair, meat, bones, bone-meal or other contaminated foodstuffs, and hides. Infection occurs most frequently by exposure to the spore of anthrax, although when the vegetative form of the organism is ingested in the meat of an infected animal the clinical disease can also occur. Anthrax spores can survive for months or even decades depending on pH, temperature, and nutrients in the soil. Spores ingested from the soil by cattle or other herbivores then germinate into the vegetative form in the spleen and lymph nodes, resulting in bacteremia and hemorrhage as a terminal event. Vegetative forms are deposited in the soil and sporulation occurs, continuing the cycle of infection.

CLINICAL MANIFESTATIONS

Cutaneous Anthrax

Approximately 95% of all human anthrax is cutaneous anthrax. Two excellent sources of information for the clinician on cutaneous anthrax appeared in late 2001. The American Academy of Dermatology published online a detailed algorithm for the management of cutaneous anthrax (www.aad.org/BioInfo/anthrax.html). In addition, the Universidad Peruana Cayetano Heredia Gorgas Course in Clinical Tropical Medicine published online multiple photographs of cutaneous anthrax and contrasted them with photographs of spider bites (loxoscelism) (http://info.dom.edu/gorgas/anthrax.html).

The incubation period of cutaneous anthrax is from 1 to 12 days. The initial skin lesion is a papule that is typically pruritic, may resemble a bug or spider bite, and usually occurs on the exposed area of the neck, head, or upper extremity. The papule progresses to include a central vesicular or bullous lesion, with peripheral nonpitting edema that is often a characteristic clue to the diagnosis of anthrax. This cen-

tral vesicular or bullous lesion then becomes necrotic and hemorrhagic, and may develop satellite vesicles. Finally, the classic central black eschar appears, often with striking edema. This eschar is usually painless, in contrast to the painful lesions of a spider bite.[22] In most cases the eschar will fall off in 1 to 2 weeks unless systemic disease ensues, but total resolution may take 6 weeks.[21] This progression of cutaneous anthrax lesions from papule through to black eschar with surrounding edema is thought to be mediated by the anthrax toxins and occurs even if appropriate antibiotics are given. Nonprogressive primary pustules are very unusual for anthrax. Thus, clinicians should not be confused by the historical term "malignant pustule" that describes only one stage of cutaneous anthrax.

Cutaneous anthrax is in the differential diagnosis of ulceroglandular illnesses because tender lymphadenopathy can occur near the skin lesion. Important clinical clues to cutaneous anthrax, in addition to any history of potential exposure, include the typical progression of skin lesions beginning with a pruritic papule, the surrounding edema, and the painless black eschar. The differential diagnosis provided by the American Academy of Dermatology[22] is extensive and includes brown recluse spider bite, coumadin or heparin necrosis, orf, cutaneous leishmaniasis, melioidosis, glanders, tularemia, plague, typhus, and others.

Importantly, specimens for the laboratory diagnosis of cutaneous or any form of anthrax should be obtained whenever possible prior to giving antibiotics. These specimens may include swabs of the exudates, full-thickness punch biopsy, and blood cultures. Skin lesions often become sterile after 1 to 2 days of appropriate antibiotics. Dry Rayon or Dacron tipped swabs, rather than cotton swabs, should be used to obtain vesicular fluid, or rolled under the edge of a black eschar. A moist Dacron or Rayon swab should be applied to the base of an ulcer if no vesicle or eschar is present. When a full-thickness 4-mm punch biopsy is obtained, then the American Academy of Dermatology recommends that the edge of a vesicle and adjacent nonvesicular skin be obtained, or if an eschar is present to biopsy the erythematous area adjacent to the edge of the eschar. A second biopsy from the center of the eschar should be obtained if feasible.[22] The punch biopsy can be studied by immunohistochemical staining, histology and PCR. Current antibody tests for anthrax are not positive until after the acute illness and therefore are of diagnostic value primarily in survivors for whom a seroconversion can be demonstrated.

Mortality due to cutaneous anthrax is less than that due to inhalational, gastrointestinal, or meningeal anthrax but still approaches 20% if the anthrax is untreated. With appropriate antibiotics, and adjunctive steroid therapy for airway compression, mortality is less than 1%. Fatality is more likely in patients who develop bacteremia, meningitis, or extensive edema including that causing airway compression from cutaneous lesions of the neck and upper thorax.[23-25] One of the cases of cutaneous anthrax attributable to the bioterrorism attacks in 2001 occurred in a 7-month-old infant and was reported with imaging demonstrating the marked peripheral and soft-tissue edema present with the lesion[26,27] (Fig. 205-1).

Anthrax is not transmitted from person to person through the air, either by droplets or droplet nuclei, so respiratory isolation is not required. In theory, active skin lesions could transmit infection. Such an event is so unlikely, however, that infection control guidelines from the CDC and Association of Professional in Infection Control and epidemiology (APIC) advise standard precautions, including the use of gloves if skin lesions are present.[28] Discussion of whether full contact precautions are required for anthrax skin lesions is provided on the bioterrorism section of the IDSA website.[29]

Gastrointestinal Anthrax

Gastrointestinal anthrax, a rare disease accounting for fewer than 5% of all cases of anthrax in humans, was reviewed in 2002-2003.[30,31] When anthrax is ingested in food or liquid it can cause two syndromes: oropharyngeal and/or intestinal anthrax. The oropharyngeal form is more unusual than the intestinal form. The largest reported series, involving 24 patients from Chiang Mai, Thailand occurred after consumption of infected water buffalo meat. The clinical presentation was

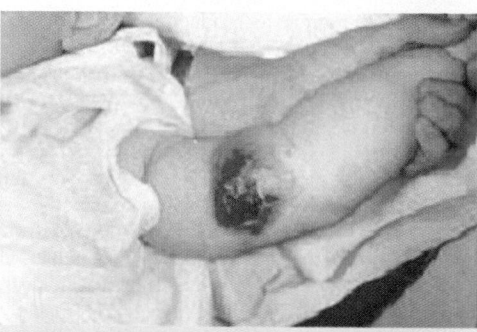

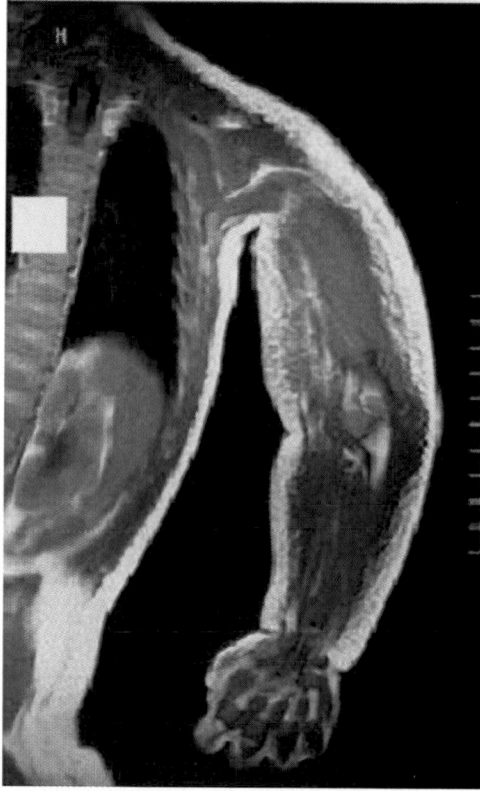

FIGURE 205-1. *Top,* Cutaneous anthrax with extensive nontender swelling and erythema in a 7-month-old infant in New York City 2001. *Bottom,* Magnetic resonance imaging demonstrates extensive subcutaneous edema from the shoulder to the hand on a coronal T1-weighted sequence. *(From Roche KJ, Chang MW, Lazarus H. Cutaneous anthrax infection. Images in Clinical Medicine. N Engl J Med. 2001;345:1611. Copyright © 2001 Massachusetts Medical Society. All rights reserved.)*

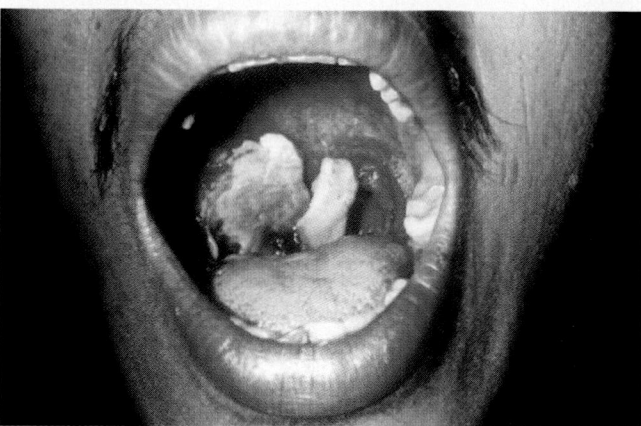

FIGURE 205-2. Oropharyngeal anthrax. Nine days after the onset of symptoms a white pseudomembrane has developed over the right tonsil, soft palate and uvula. *(From Sirisanthana T, Brown AE. Anthrax of the gastrointestinal anthrax. Emerg Infect Dis J. 2002; 8:649-651.)*

a febrile painful swelling of the neck caused by cervical adenopathy and soft tissue edema, occurring 2 to 144 hours after ingestion of the meat. Dysphagia and hoarseness were also found. Oral lesions and edema were seen on the tonsils, hard palate, or posterior pharynx initially, and then after 1 week ulceration and central necrosis occurred with development of a whitish patch which formed a pseudomembrane covering the ulcer (Fig. 205-2). The organism could be seen on Gram stain and grown in culture. Even with antibiotic therapy 3/24 (12.5%) patients died.[32]

The intestinal form of anthrax is more common. More than 100 cases were seen in the Bekka Valley of Lebanon from 1960 to 1974. The authors who reviewed this experience noted three stages to abdominal anthrax.[31] Phase I included low-grade fevers, syncope, and malaise. About 24 hours later, phase II was characterized by mild to severe abdominal pain, nausea and vomiting. Examination usually revealed abdominal distention, and an ill-defined mass in the right lower quadrant or periumbilical area. Unlike early appendicitis, patients with intestinal anthrax had evidence of ascites, intravascular depletion, and severe weakness following an initial phase of syncope and malaise. Phase III was characterized by paroxysmal abdominal pain, rapidly increasing abdominal girth, ascites, flushed face, red conjunctivae, and often shock. Exploratory laparotomy revealed thick yellow ascites, hypertrophic mesenteric lymph nodes particularly in the ileocecal area, and edema most notably involving one segment of the bowel.

Surgical resection of the involved segment of bowel, usually small intestine or cecum, was attempted in an unspecified number of patients in phase III. Two patients were described who appeared to be failing antibiotics and medical therapy, but who then underwent surgical resection of the involved sections of bowel. Based on this limited data, the authors suggested that intestinal anthrax should initially be treated with intravenous antibiotics and medical therapy, but then if improvement was not quickly evident wide surgical resection of the area of involved bowel extending into apparently uninvolved tissue should be performed. Continuous drainage of ascites should also be performed owing to its continued reaccumulation postoperatively. In general, the overall mortality of intestinal anthrax is estimated to be 25% to 60% in reported cases.[33]

In the United States there have been no culture-proven cases of gastrointestinal anthrax reported. There have been two recent events, however, in which intestinal disease caused by anthrax appears to have occurred. In August, 2000 at least five members of a family in Minnesota ate meat from a cow that was subsequently demonstrated to be infected with anthrax. The meat was reportedly well cooked, but two of the family members developed a self-limited gastrointestinal illness within 48 hours after eating the meat. Prophylaxis with ciprofloxacin was begun even though the symptoms had resolved. Several days later vaccination with the anthrax vaccine was begun [33] and antibiotic prophylaxis continued. Thus, although no clinical specimens were positive for anthrax after consumption of cooked meat taken from a cow whose carcass did grow *B. anthracis*, anthrax may have been the cause of their gastrointestinal illness. The second event involved the 2001 anthrax bioterrorism attack. One of the patients who died was reported to have had nausea, vomiting, light-headedness, and abdominal pain. Abdominal CT scan showed intramural pneumatosis consistent with a necrotizing enteritis. At autopsy he was found to have 2500 mL of ascites with necrotizing infection, hemorrhage, and abundant gram-positive bacilli in a part of the ileum.[34]

Inhalational Anthrax

The reader is referred to Chapter 324 on anthrax in the biodefense section for a detailed discussion of inhalational anthrax based on the 11 documented cases during the 2001 anthrax bioterrorism attacks. Inhalational anthrax is always a medical emergency and in our era always warrants consideration of bioterrorism. Specific points of emphasis for the clinician include: an incubation period that is often less than 1 week but sometimes much longer, the rapid disease progression over days from symptom onset to death if untreated, the typical presence of hemorrhagic mediastinal adenopathy more than multilobar pneumonia on chest imaging, the development of large and hemorrhagic pleural effusions, and frequent bacteremia with blood cultures demonstrating *B. anthracis* in less than 24 hours if no antibiotics have been given.

Importantly, the presence of bacteremia, bloody pleural effusions, and mediastinal adenopathy on chest roentgenogram or chest CT scan were not markers of a fatal outcome in 2001 in patients otherwise treated aggressively with appropriate antibiotics and pleural fluid drainage.[35-38] In fact, the case-fatality rate in 2001 was 45% (5/11 patients) whereas historically it was closer to 85%. Future additional therapeutic approaches, such as anthrax toxin inhibitors, and more rapid diagnostic tests may decrease the case-fatality rate further. Currently, there is no clinical, serologic, or PCR assay to diagnose inhalational anthrax reliably during the initial phase of illness.

The number of spores necessary to cause inhalation anthrax is uncertain, in part owing to the large numbers of animals that would be needed for such experiments. Peters and Hartley in 2002 extrapolated from studies by the US Army on cynomolgous monkeys in which the lethal dose for 50% of the animals (LD_{50}) was found to be between 4100 and 8000 spores.[39] It is important to emphasize that this number of spores is not the number required to kill one monkey, but the number that will kill 50% of the monkeys. The number of spores that would kill 10% of monkeys (LD_{10}) or 1% of monkeys (LD_1) would be much lower but would require too many animals to perform the experiment and to be able to measure an exact number of spores. By extrapolation, however, the authors estimated that the LD_{10} is 50 or 98 spores and the LD_1 is one or three spores. Such extrapolations could be of relevance when large numbers of persons are exposed to anthrax, particularly given underlying differences in immune system function and age across a population. In addition, if secondary reaerosolization of spores can occur in a contaminated environment, as was documented experimentally in the Senate Hart building after its closure in 2001, then calculations of the lethal dose of spores and the incubation period of inhalational anthrax could be impacted.[40]

Anthrax Hemorrhagic Meningoencephalitis

Chapter 324, in the section on biodefense, includes a more detailed discussion of anthrax meningoencephalitis. Points of emphasis for the clinician include: The historical case-fatality rate is approximately 95% even with treatment, meningoencephalitis is a fourth type of initial clinical presentation of anthrax, distinguishing cerebrospinal fluid findings include hemorrhage and characteristic large gram-positive bacilli, and anthrax meningoencephalitis in our era should prompt a search for inhalational anthrax and possible bioterrorism.

In addition to meningitis, anthrax can cause parenchymal brain hemorrhages, hematomas, vasculitis, subarachnoid hemorrhage, and cerebral edema.[41,42] The autopsy reports from the 1979 outbreak of anthrax in Sverdlovsk, Russia revealed that 21 of 42 patients had hemorrhagic meningitis.[43] The first recognized case of anthrax in the 2001 bioterrorist attacks was a patient who presented in Florida with meningitis and was found to have the characteristic large gram-positive bacilli in his cerebrospinal fluid.[44] Clinically, patients with anthrax can present in at least four ways. Meningitis or meningoencephalitis should be added to the three traditionally recognized anthrax presentations of cutaneous, inhalational, and gastrointestinal, which are also the three portals of entry of *B. anthracis*.

PREVENTION

Vaccination

Vaccines to prevent anthrax exist both for animals and humans. Because human anthrax is usually linked with veterinary anthrax, vaccination of animals and surveillance for infected animals, and removal of their meat, hides, skins, wool, or other products is critical to preventing human disease.

The WHO lists four nations as producing anthrax vaccines for humans: China, Russia, Britain, and the United States.[21] China and Russia use a live spore–based vaccine and vaccinate by scarification. Britain and the United States use bacteria-free filtrates of cultures adsorbed or precipitated by aluminum hydroxide (alum). The US Food and Drug administration (FDA) licensed one anthrax vaccine in 1970 for use to prevent anthrax prior to exposure. The vaccine antigen is almost exclusively the protective antigen (PA) and the adjuvant is alum, an FDA-licensed vaccine adjuvant. The PA is derived from cell-free culture filtrates of an onencapsulated and nonvirulent strain of *B. anthracis*. Thus, the vaccine can never cause anthrax. The primary series of vaccination is unlike that of any other vaccine in that it consists of six injections, given subcutaneously, over 18 months. The exact schedule is: time 0, 2, and 4 weeks, then months 6, 12, and 18. Subsequently, booster doses are required at yearly intervals.[45] The immediate next generation of human anthrax vaccines in the United States will likely focus on recombinant PA, a shorter vaccination schedule, fewer immunizations, and possibly an intramuscular route of vaccination. Other approaches to investigational anthrax vaccines in the more distant future include generating immune responses against the other components to the anthrax toxin besides PA, and against the poly-D-glutamic acid capsule virulence factor.[46] Phase 1 clinical studies of two recombinant PA vaccines are currently underway.

A precise immunologic correlate of protection in humans has not been established for the immune response elicited by the vaccine. Although antibody clearly appears important there is not a specific level above which a vaccine recipient is definitely protected, as there is for hepatitis B vaccine, for example. While antibody to PA (anti-PA IgG) clearly is important to the efficacy of the vaccine, a contributing role for cellular immunity is also possible.

The FDA-licensed anthrax vaccine is not commercially available and has been given primarily to designated US military personnel and to civilians who work with anthrax in the laboratory or are otherwise potentially exposed occupationally. Detailed information on the anthrax vaccine is available on the Department of Defense website *www.anthrax.osd/mil*.

The Advisory Committee on Immunization Practices (ACIP) to the CDC published a detailed review of the safety and efficacy of the anthrax vaccine in December 2000.[45] After the anthrax bioterrorism attacks the ACIP/CDC provided supplemental recommendations in November 2002 for licensed use of vaccination preexposure, as well as investigational use post-exposure to anthrax. These supplemental recommendations occurred after the US Department of Health and Human Services obtained a limited supply from the Department of Defense of the vaccine "BioThrax," formerly "Anthrax Vaccine Adsorbed" (AVA) manufactured by Bioport in Lansing, Michigan. The recommendation for preexposure vaccination of civilians was only for persons at risk for repeated exposures to *B. anthracis* spores. These included laboratory personnel working with environmental specimens and performing confirmatory testing for *B. anthracis* in the US Laboratory Response Network (LRN) for level B or above, workers making repeated entries to known spore-contaminated areas after a terrorist attack, and other workers in which repeated exposure to aerosolized spores may occur. In particular, vaccination preexposure was not recommended for health care workers or other emergency first responders who might have to respond to an anthrax terrorist attack, or for the general public.[47]

In 2002 the US Institute of Medicine issued a report addressing whether the current FDA-licensed anthrax vaccine is safe and efficacious. The complete report is posted online at *www.nap.edu/catalog/10310.html*. The committee concluded that "The available evidence from studies with humans and animals, coupled with reasonable assumptions of analogy, shows that AVA as licensed is an effective vaccine for the protection of humans, including inhalational anthrax, caused by any known or plausible engineered strains of *B. anthracis*."[48] In terms of vaccine safety, the Institute of Medicine report found that the licensed six-dose vaccination schedule did "appear to be associated with a higher incidence of immediate-onset, local effects than is intramuscular administration or a vaccination schedule with fewer doses of AVA," and that there are gender differences in local reactions following vaccination such that for "female service members, reactions following vaccination with AVA can have a transient adverse impact on their ability to perform their duties." Importantly, however, in contrast to the above local reactions at the vaccine site no evidence was found "that life-threatening or permanently disabling immediate-onset adverse events occur at higher rates in individuals who have received AVA than in the general population" or that persons receiving this vaccine have elevated risks of later-onset health events.[48]

Antibiotic Prophylaxis

Antibiotics for prophylaxis against anthrax were given prior to the 2001 bioterrorist attacks, although on a much smaller scale. For example, the persons who consumed meat infected with anthrax in Minnesota in 2000 were given ciprofloxacin prophylaxis. In 1997 antibiotic prophylaxis recommendations from the US Army Medical Research Institute of Infectious Diseases at Ft. Detrick included either ciprofloxacin or doxycycline twice a day for at least 4 weeks if the person had not been immunized. Vaccination immediately post-exposure was recommended while continuing on one of these two antibiotics until at least the third dose of vaccine had been given at 1 month.[49] Discussion of post-exposure vaccination as an adjunct to prolonged (60 days or more) antibiotic post-exposure prophylaxis in the setting of the 2001 bioterrorist event is discussed in Chapter 324.

Ciprofloxacin was approved by the FDA on August 30, 2000 for inhalational anthrax post-exposure.[50] This was the first antibiotic specifically requested for use as post-exposure prophylaxis against inhalational anthrax. The FDA had approved other antibiotics previously for the treatment of anthrax, such as penicillin and doxycycline, but no request for a specific indication of post-exposure prophylaxis had been made. On October 26, 2001 the FDA issued a notice in the Federal Register [51] clarifying that doxycycline and penicillin G procaine were also indicated for post-exposure prophylaxis against anthrax. FDA information on antibiotics for anthrax prophylaxis and therapy were discussed by Meyerhoff and Murphy in 2002.[52]

On October 19, 2001 the CDC provided new guidelines for post-exposure prophylaxis when inhalational exposure to anthrax may have occurred. Sixty days of either ciprofloxacin 500 mg every 12 hours, or doxycycline 100 mg orally every 12 hours were recommended as equivalent initial options.[53] Although amoxicillin was not FDA-approved for anthrax post-exposure prophylaxis the CDC recommended it as an option for prophylaxis, but not initial therapy, in children, pregnant women and breastfeeding mothers.[54]

TREATMENT

Therapy for isolated cutaneous anthrax prior to the 2001 anthrax bioterrorism events was for only 7 to 10 days[55] using intravenous penicillin 4 million units every 4 to 6 hours. Corticosteroids were sometimes added if marked edema was present, particularly if airway compression occurred as a result of lesions on the neck and upper thorax. The duration of therapy for cutaneous anthrax in 2001 was extended to 60 days given the concern that simultaneous aerosol exposure may have occurred and that risk of reactivation of latent infection may persist after the standard 7- to 10-day course of treatment for cutaneous disease.[55] Similarly, inhalational anthrax had been treated with high dose penicillin 2 million units every 2 hours.[49] Anthrax meningitis and gastrointestinal anthrax were also treated with high-dose penicillin. Given the nearly uniformly fatal outcome with anthrax meningitis additional antibiotics such as chloramphenicol, steroids, or anthrax-specific antiserum, if available, were sometimes used, although without clear benefit. All naturally occurring strains of anthrax have been sensitive to erythromycin, but the sensitivity of the isolate used in the 2001 attacks was only intermediate to erythromycin.[55]

After the bioterrorism attacks in 2001 treatment protocols for inhalational and cutaneous anthrax were provided by the CDC (Tables 205-1 and 205-2).[55] Both protocols recommended either ciprofloxacin or doxycycline as the cornerstone of initial therapy. In addition, patients with inhalational anthrax or with cutaneous anthrax and either

---

TABLE 205-1 Inhalational Anthrax Treatment Protocol[*,†] for Cases Associated with This Bioterrorism Attack

Category	Initial Therapy (intravenous)[§,¶]	Duration
Adults	Ciprofloxacin 400 mg every 12 hr **or** Doxycycline 100 mg every 12 hr[‡] **and** One or two additional antimicrobials[¶]	IV treatment initially.[**] Switch to oral antimicrobial therapy when clinically appropriate: Ciprofloxacin 500 mg PO BID **or** Doxycycline 100 mg PO BID Continue for 60 days (IV and PO combined)[§§]
Children	Ciprofloxacin 10-15 mg/kg every 12 hr[¶,***] **or** Doxycycline:[††,†††] >8 yr and >45 kg: 100 mg every 12 hr >8 yr and ≤45 kg: 2.2 mg/kg every 12 hr ≤8 yr: 2.2 mg/kg every 12 hr **and** One or two additional antimicrobials[¶]	IV treatment initially.[**] Switch to oral antimicrobial therapy when clinically appropriate: Ciprofloxacin 10-15 mg/kg PO every 12 hr[***] **or** Doxycycline:[†††] >8 yr and >45 kg: 100 mg PO BID >8 yr and ≤45 kg: 2.2 mg/kg PO BID ≤8 yr: 2.2 mg/kg PO BID Continue for 60 days (IV and PO combined)[§§]
Pregnant women[§§§]	Same for nonpregnant adults (the high death rate from the infection outweighs the risk posed by the antimicrobial agent)	IV treatment initially. Switch to oral antimicrobial therapy when clinically appropriate.[†] Oral therapy regimens same for nonpregnant adults.
Immunocompromised persons	Same for nonimmunocompromised persons and children	Same for nonimmunocompromised persons and children

[*]For gastrointestinal and oropharyngeal anthrax, use regimens recommended for inhalational anthrax.

[†]Ciprofloxacin or doxycycline should be considered an essential part of first-line therapy for inhalational anthrax.

[§]Steroids may be considered as an adjunct therapy for patients with severe edema and for meningitis based on experience with bacterial meningitis of other etiologies.

[¶]Other agents with in vitro activity include rifampin, vancomycin, penicillin, ampicillin, chloramphenicol, imipenem, clindamycin, and clarithromycin. Because of concerns of constitutive and inducible β-lactamases in *Bacillus anthracis,* penicillin and ampicillin should not be used alone. Consultation with an infectious disease specialist is advised.

[**]Initial therapy may be altered based on clinical course of the patient: one or two antimicrobial agents (e.g., ciprofloxacin or doxycycline) may be adequate as the patient improves.

[††]If meningitis is suspected, doxycycline may be less optimal because of poor central nervous system penetration.

[§§]Because of the potential persistence of spores after an aerosol exposure, antimicrobial therapy should be continued for 60 days.

[¶¶]If intravenous ciprofloxacin is not available, oral ciprofloxacin may be acceptable because it is rapidly and well absorbed from the gastrointestinal tract with no substantial loss by first-pass metabolism. Maximum serum concentrations are attained 1 to 2 hr after dosing but may not be achieved if vomiting or ileus are present.

[***]In children, ciprofloxacin dosage should not exceed 1 g/day.

[†††]The American Academy of Pediatrics recommends treatment of young children with tetracyclines for serious infections (e.g., Rocky Mountain spotted fever).

[§§§]Although tetracyclines are not recommended during pregnancy, their use may be indicated for life-threatening illness. Adverse effects on developing teeth and bones are dose related; therefore, doxycycline might be used for a short time (7 to 14 days) before 6 months of gestation.

TABLE 205-2 Cutaneous Anthrax Treatment Protocol* for Cases Associated with This Bioterrorism Attack

Category	Initial Therapy (oral)[†]	Duration
Adults*	Ciprofloxacin 500 mg BID or Doxycycline 100 mg BID	60 days[§]

Children*	Ciprofloxacin 10-15 mg/kg every 12 hr (not to exceed 1 g/day)[†]
	or
	Doxycycline:[¶]
	   >8 yr and >45 kg: 100 mg every 12 hr
	   >8 yr and ≤45 kg: 2.2 mg/kg every 12 hr
	   ≤8 yr: 2.2 mg/kg every 12 hr
		60 days[§]

Pregnant women*,**	Ciprofloxacin 500 mg BID or Doxycycline 100 mg BID	60 days[§]
Immunocompromised persons*	Same for nonimmunocompromised persons and children	60 days[§]

*Cutaneous anthrax with signs of systemic involvement, extensive edema, or lesions on the head or neck require intravenous therapy, and a multidrug approach is recommended (Table 205-1).

[†]Ciprofloxacin or doxycycline should be considered first-line therapy. Amoxicillin 500 mg PO TID for adults or 80 mg/kg/day divided every 8 hours for children is an option for completion of therapy after clinical improvement. Oral amoxicillin dose is based on the need to achieve appropriate minimum inhibitory concentration levels.

[§]Previous guidelines have suggested treating cutaneous anthrax for 7 to 10 days, but 60 days is recommended in the setting of this attack, given the likelihood of exposure to aerosolized *B. anthracis.*[6]

[¶]The American Academy of Pediatrics recommends treatment of young children with tetracyclines for serious infections (e.g., Rocky Mountain spotted fever).

**Although tetracyclines or ciprofloxacin are not recommended during pregnancy, their use may be indicated for life-threatening illness. Adverse effects on developing teeth and bones are dose related; therefore, doxycycline might be used for a short time (7 to 14 days) before 6 months of gestation.

systemic involvement, head or neck lesions, or extensive edema required intravenous therapy with at least one or two other antibiotics along with either ciprofloxacin or doxycycline. Cutaneous lesions not meeting these criteria could be treated with either oral ciprofloxacin or doxycycline alone. The duration of therapy was 60 days for both inhalational and cutaneous disease.

The only specific mention of therapy for meningitis was that adjunctive steroids could be considered and that doxycycline may be less optimal than ciprofloxacin owing to poor central nervous system penetration. Penicillin was a recommended option for all forms of anthrax, as long as it was not given alone, because of the potential induction of a β-lactamase that would result in resistance. Erythromycin, cephalosporins, and trimethoprim-sulfamethoxazole were not included as options owing to lack of susceptibility.

In the event of a multidrug-resistant *B. anthracis* infection treatment would have to be guided by antibiotic susceptibility testing. In that situation a broad range of antibiotics should be tested, including chloramphenicol, to which historical isolates have uniformly been sensitive and that penetrates into the central nervous system. In addition, an investigational form of therapy using anthrax-specific hyperimmune globulin could be considered. Several approaches to development of such anthrax neutralizing antibody are under development. These include both monoclonal and polyclonal antibody as well as plasma with anti-PA IgG antibody derived from persons who have been vaccinated with the current FDA-licensed anthrax vaccine.[56]

Other potential investigational therapies, in conjunction with antibiotics, have been discussed recently. These include potential inhibitors of anthrax toxin synthesis, toxin assembly and release, or downstream toxin-mediated pathology. This spectrum of potential therapeutics includes clindamycin, chloroquine, soluble anthrax toxin receptor (sATR), dominant negative toxin inhibitors, calcium-channel blockers, angiotensin-converting enzyme inhibitors, and tumor necrosis factor inhibitors.[12,57,58]

REFERENCES

1. Morner KAH. Presentation speech for the Nobel Prize in Physiology or Medicine 1905. *www.nobel.se/medicine/laureates/1905/press.html.*
2. Miksell P, Ivins BE, Ristroph JD, et al. Plasmids, Pasteur, and Anthrax. Am Soc Microbiol News. 1983;49:320-322.
3. LaForce FM. Anthrax. Clin Infect Dis. 1994;19:1009-1014.
4. Metchnikoff E. Concerning the relationship between phagocytes and anthrax bacilli. Rev Infect Dis. 1984;6:761-770.
5. CDC. Laboratory Response Network (LRN). Level A laboratory procedures for identification of *Bacillus anthracis.* (revised March 24, 2003). P 1-18. *www.bt.cdc.gov/agent/anthrax/LevelAProtocol/anthraxlabprotocol.pdf*
6. Ezzell JW, Welkos SL. The capsule of *bacillus anthracis,* a review. J Appl Microbiol. 1999;87:250.
7. Makino S, Watarai M, Cheun HI, et al. Effect of the lower molecular capsule released from the cell surface of *Bacillus anthracis* on the pathogenesis of anthrax. J Infect Dis. 2002;186:227-233.
8. Bradley KA, Mogridge J, Mourez M, et al. Identification of the cellular receptor for anthrax toxin. Nature. 2001;414:225-229.
9. Petosa C, Collier RJ, Klimpel KR, et al. Crystal structure of the anthrax toxin protective antigen. Nature. 1997;385:833-838.
10. Pannifer AD, Wong TY, Schwarzenbacher R, et al. Crystal structure of the anthrax lethal factor. Nature. 2001;414:229-233.
11. Drum CL, Yan S-Z, Bard J, et al. Structural basis for the activation of anthrax adenylyl cyclase exotoxin by calmodulin. Nature. 2002;415:396-402.
12. Young JAT, Collier, RJ. Attacking anthrax. Sci Am. 2002;March:48-59.
13. Agrawal A, Lingappa J, Leppla S, et al. Impairment of dendritic cells and adaptive immunity by anthrax lethal toxin. Nature. 2003;424:329-334.
14. Hanna PC, Acosta D, Collier RJ. On the role of macrophages in anthrax. Proc Natl Acad Sci USA. 1993;90:10198-10201.
15. Moayeri M, Haines D, Young HA, Leppla SH. *Bacillus anthracis* lethal toxin induces TNF-alpha-independent hypoxia-mediated toxicity in mice. J Clin Invest. 2003;112:670-682.
16. WHO. World Anthrax data site. *www.vetmed.Isu.edu/whocc/mp_world.htm*
17. Brachman PS. Inhalational anthrax. Ann NY Acad Sci. 1980;353:83-93.
18. CDC. Morbid Mortal Wkly Rep. 2000;49:814.
19. Davies JCA. A major epidemic of anthrax in Zimbabwe. Centr Afr J Med. 1982;28:291-298.
20. Myenye K, Siziya S, Peterson D. Factors associated with human anthrax outbreak in the Chikupo and Ngandu villages of Murewa district in Mashonaland East Province, Zimbabwe. Centr Afr J Med. 1996;42:312-315.
21. WHO. Guidelines for the surveillance and control of anthrax in humans and animals. *www.who.int/emc-documents/zoonoses/docs/whoemczdi986.html*
22. American Academy of Dermatology. An algorithm for the management of cutaneous anthrax 2001. *www.aad.org/BioInfo/anthrax.html*
23. Dixon TC, Meselson M, Guillemin J, Hanna PC. Anthrax. N Engl J Med. 1999; 341:815-826.
24. Garcia AG, Jimenez RR. *Bacillus anthracis* meningitis. Images in Clinical Medicine. N Engl J Med. 1999;341:814.
25. Swartz M. Recognition and management of anthrax—An update. N Engl J Med. 2001;345:1621-1626.
26. Roche KJ, Chang MW, Lazarus H. Cutaneous anthrax infection (Images in Clinical Medicine). N Engl J Med 2001;345:1611.
27. Freedman A, Afonja O, Chang MW, et al. Cutaneous anthrax associated with microangiopathic hemolytic anemia and coagulaopathy in a 7 month old infant. JAMA. 2002;287:869-874.
28. English JF, Cundiff MY, Malone JD, et al. Bioterrorism readiness plan: A template for healthcare facilities. 4/13/99. p.11-15. Association for Professionals in Infection Control and Epidemiology (APIC) and the CDC Hospital Infections Program Bioterrorism Working Group. Posted on the CDC website at: *www.bt.cdc.gov/agent/anthrax/infection-control/index.asp*

29. Infectious Disease Society of America (IDSA) website. Clinical Pathway: Inhalational anthrax. 2002. *www.idsociety.org*
30. Sirisanthana T, Brown AE. Anthrax of the gastrointestinal anthrax. Emerg Infect Dis J. 2002;8:649-651.
31. Kanafani ZA, Ghossain A, Sharara AI, et al. Endemic gastrointestinal anthrax in 1960's Lebanon: Clinical manifestations and surgical findings. Emerg Infect Dis J. 2003;9:520-525.
32. Sirisanthana T, Navachareon N, Tharavichitkul W, et al. Outbreak of oral-pharyngeal anthrax: an unusual manifestation of human infection with *Bacillus anthracis*. Am J Trop Med Hyg. 1984;33:144-150.
33. CDC. Human ingestion of *Bacillus anthracis*–contaminated meat-Minnesota, August, 2000. Morb Mort Wkly Rep. 2000;49:813-816.
34. Borio L, Frank D, Mani V, et al. Death due to bioterrorism-related inhalational anthrax. Report of 2 patients. JAMA. 2001;286:2554-2559.
35. Jernigan JA, Stephens DS, Ashford DA, et al. Bioterrorism-related inhaltional anthrax: The first 10 cases reported in the United States. Emerg Infect Dis. 2001;7:933-944.
36. Inglesby T, O'Toole T, Henderson DA, et al. Anthrax as a biological weapon, 2002: Updated recommendations for management. JAMA. 2002;287;2236-2252.
37. Bartlett JG, Inglesby TV, Borio L. Management of anthrax. Clin Infect Dis. 2002; 35:851-858.
38. Shafzand S. When bioterrorism strikes: Diagnosis and management of inhalational anthrax. Semin Resp Infect. 2003;18:134-145.
39. Peters CJ, Hartley DM. Anthrax inhalation and lethal human infection. Lancet 2002;359:710-711.
40. Weis CP, Intrepido AJ, Miller AK, et al. Secondary aerosolization of viable Bacillus anthracis spores in a contaminated US Senate office. JAMA. 2002;288:2853-2858.
41. Meyer MA. Neurologic complications of anthrax: a review of the literature. Arch Neurol. 2003;60:483-488.
42. Lanska DJ. Anthrax meningoencephalitis. Neurology. 2002;59:327-334.
43. Abramova FA, Grinberg LM, Yampolskaya OV, Walker DA. Pathology of inhalational anthrax in 42 cases from the Sverdlovsk outbreak of 1979. Proc Natl Acad Sci USA. 1993;90:2291-2294.
44. Bush LM, Abrams BH, Beall A, Johnson CC. Index case of fatal inhalational anthrax due to bioterrorism in the United States. N Engl J Med. 2001;345:1607-1610.
45. CDC. Morbid Mortal Wkly Rep. 2000;49. No.RR-15:1-20. Use of anthrax vaccine in the United States. Recommendations of the Advisory Committee on Immunization Practices (ACIP).
46. Schneerson R, Kubler-Kiel J, Liu TY, et al. Poly (gamma-D-glutamic acid) protein conjugates induce IgG antibodies in mice to the capsule of *Bacillus anthracis:* A potential addition to the anthrax vaccine. Proc Natl Acad Sci USA. 2003;100:8945-8950.
47. CDC. Morbid Mortal Wkly Rep. 2002;51;1024-1026. Notice to Readers: Use of Anthrax vaccine in response to terrorism: Supplemental recommendations of the advisory committee on immunization practices.
48. Joellenbeck LM, Zwanziger LL, Durch JS, Strom BL, eds. Washington D.C. The anthrax vaccine: Is it safe? Does it work? National Academy Press 2002. See the complete report at *http://www/nap.edu/catalog/10310.html*
49. Franz DR, Jahrling PB, Friedlander AM, et al. Clinical recognition and management of patients exposed to biological warfare agents. JAMA. 1997;278:399-411.
50. Food and Drug administration. Center for Drug Evaluation and Research. Approval Package. Aug 30, 2000. *www.fda.gov/cder/foi/nda/2000/19-537SO38_Cipro.htm*
51. Food and Drug Administration. Prescription drug products; doxycycline and Penicillin G procaine administration for inhalaitonal anthrax (post-exposure). Fed Reg. 2001;66:55679-55682.
52. Meyerhoff A, Murphy D. Guidelines for Treatment of anthrax. JAMA. 2002; 288:1848.
53. CDC. Update: Investigation of anthrax associated with intentional exposure and interim Public Health Guidelines, October 2001. Morbid Mortal Wkly Rep. 2001 (Oct 19); 50:893-896.
54. CDC. Update: Interim recommendations for antimicrobial prophylaxis for children and breastfeeding mothers and treatment of children with anthrax. Morbid Mortal Wkly Rep. 2001;50:1014-1016.
55. CDC. Update: Investigation of bioterrorism-related anthrax and interim guidelines for exposure management and antimicrobial therapy, October 2001. Morb Mort Wkly Rep. Oct 26, 2001;50:909-919.
56. Enserink M. 'Borrowed immunity' may save future victims (Letter). Science. 2002;295:777.
57. Gordon VM, Leppla SH, Hewlett EL. Inhibitors of receptor-mediated endocytosis block the entry of *Bacillus anthracis* adenylate cyclase toxin but not that of *Bordetella pertussis* adenylate cyclase toxin. Infect Immun. 1988;56:1066-1069.
58. Bell DM, Kozarsky PE, Stephens DS. Conference summary: Clinical issues in the prophylaxis, diagnosis, and treatment of anthrax. Emerg Infect Dis J. 2002;8:222-225.

Bacillus Species and Related Genera Other than *Bacillus anthracis*

THOMAS FEKETE

MICROBIOLOGY

Bacteria of the genus *Bacillus* are well adapted to their normal environment of soil. These gram-positive or gram-variable, aerobic or facultatively anaerobic rod-shaped bacilli have either rounded or squared off ends, form endospores, tolerate extremes of temperature and moisture, and are ubiquitous. They are found in superficial lake and ocean sediment, even in deep water. Their hardiness under conditions of desiccation and heat has been used to determine the efficacy of heat sterilization *(B. stearothermophilus)* and fumigation procedures *(B. subtilis).* For many members of the genus *Bacillus* an association with animals (either saprophytic or pathogenic) has also been noted. These animals range from small insects to large mammals including humans.

Recent changes in the taxonomy of *Bacillus* species include the movement of *B. alvei* into the genus *Paenibacillus* and placement of both *B. brevis* and *B. laterosporus* into the genus *Brevibacillus.*[1] *B. cereus*, *B. anthracis*, *B. thuringiensis*, and *B. mycoides* have been placed into a single group, termed the *B. cereus* group, based on their close similarity.[2] Much of this relatedness has to do with the substantial amount of genetic and enzymatic heterogeneity within *B. cereus.* On the other hand, there is a very narrow range of diversity within *B. anthracis,* whose isolates occupy a tight band within the breadth of *B. cereus,* suggesting that *B. anthracis* is a newer species derived from *B. cereus.* This similarity of DNA and various enzymes may seem surprising insofar as there are great clinical differences between *B. cereus* and *B. anthracis* disease, but it should serve as a reminder of how little need change to convert a fairly innocuous organism into a serious pathogen. Less related species of *Bacillus* that may be encountered less commonly in the human clinical microbiology laboratory are *B. subtilis*, *B. licheniformis*, *B. megaterium*, *B. pumilus*, and *B. sphaericus.* *Bacillus* species are easy to grow on the usual culture media of the clinical laboratory. Most strains grow best at environmental temperatures (25 to 37° C). All have the capacity to form spores (as this is part of the definition of the genus) but they vary widely in motility, colony morphology, and nutritional requirements. They are fairly large bacteria, with dimensions ranging from 3 by 0.4 μm to 9 by 2 μm. Although they are usually gram-positive in early growth, old cultures can be gram-variable or even gram-negative.[3] In most clinical laboratories, the first and most urgent task is to distinguish *B. anthracis* from other *Bacillus* species. *B. anthracis* is nonhemolytic on sheep or horse blood agar and nonmotile whereas most other clinical isolates are motile and β-hemolytic. Strains of *B. anthracis* that are slightly hemolytic have been reported, and some of the less frequently isolated non-*anthracis* strains are nonmotile and nonhemolytic. For the latter strains, detailed biochemical analysis and toxin testing may be required. Automated diagnostic kits for gram-positive bacteria are usually able to distinguish *B. anthracis* from other *Bacillus* species. Some species such as *B. sphaericus* and *B. badius* are biochemically unreactive and difficult to identify in commercial biochemical kits. Identification and characterization of individual strains can be made in reference laboratories with a variety of tests including flagellar antigens, phage typing, gas-liquid chromatography, and mass spectroscopy.[3]

EPIDEMIOLOGY

The widespread distribution in nature of *Bacillus* species explains its frequent isolation in the laboratory. In many cases, the isolation of *Bacillus* species from a clinical specimen raises the possibility of contamination, as environmental spores can germinate quickly on various laboratory media. *Bacillus* species is a transient but normal part of the fecal flora.[4] Children and adults were tested for the presence of *B. cereus* in the stool and rates of recovery from none to 43% were found in the absence of diarrhea. The density of *B. cereus* in stool is usually low (about 100 viable organisms per gram), but can be considerably higher. Strains of *B. cereus* in the stool are the same as those found in the food supply, and the ubiquity of *B. cereus* is reflected in a large number of different strains in fecal cultures of healthy people. However, during outbreaks it can be shown that the strain of *B. cereus* causing food poisoning is consistent by biotype, serotype, toxin production, and phage type among patients.[5]

Hospital outbreaks of *Bacillus* species infection have occasionally been reported.[6] In one medical center, *B. cereus* was an ongoing cause of positive respiratory cultures and morbidity (including two cases of true bacteremia and one fatal pneumonia) in an intensive care unit.[6] This epidemic was the consequence of inadequate sterilization of respiratory circuits. No other bacterial infections occurred at higher than usual rates during the epidemic period because the degree of sterilization was sufficient to eradicate non–spore-forming bacteria but not *B. cereus.* Other species of *Bacillus* can persist for a long period of time and then can cause intermittent medical problems such as 12 cases in 10 years of *B. sphaericus* bacteremia in a children's cancer hospital in Italy.[7]

PSEUDOINFECTION AND CONTAMINATION

More common than true outbreaks are pseudoepidemics in which a strain or strains of *Bacillus* species are recovered from patients with a common source of contamination.[8,9] In these settings, biochemical and molecular studies can show that a single strain is found even though it was not actually causing disease. Conversely, clusters of *Bacillus* spp. infection may look like point-source outbreaks when they represent a higher-than-expected rate of infection by environmental organisms. One small cluster of serious *Bacillus* spp. infections (all of which were accompanied by bacteremia) occurring over 10 days in a children's cancer ward showed that the strains recovered were different from one another and from other isolates submitted for analysis.[10]

Bacillus spp. contamination has resulted in false-positive rates of up to 0.1% to 0.9% of all blood cultures submitted.[11] Because *Bacillus* spp. is such a common contaminant and such a rare cause of disease, many laboratories do not identify *Bacillus* to the species level (except to exclude the possibility of *B. anthracis*). *Bacillus* spp. can survive in high concentrations of ethyl alcohol (up to 95%) including the sprays of 70% ethanol that are sometimes used for hand hygiene.[8] In one pseudoepidemic, construction on a hospital driveway resulted in a 13-fold increase in the number of blood cultures that tested positive for *Bacillus* species.[9] The problem was related to direct contamination of stored blood culture bottles and inadequate cleaning of the bottles before introduction of the specimen. Even in the absence of a pseudoepidemic, it can be difficult to separate true *Bacillus* spp. infection from contamination. The best indicator of true bacteremia, for instance, is the presence of multiple positive cultures or recurrent bacteremia. In one study that compared patients for whom *both* bottles were positive in a set with *Bacillus* species against patients with only a single bottle positive, 29% (5/17) of episodes with both bottles positive were associated with a subsequent positive blood culture as opposed to 3% (2/59) in patients with only a single bottle positive.[12] This suggests that skin preparation may be less important than specimen handling in false-positive blood cultures for *Bacillus* spp. In a Japanese hospital, 29 patients were noted to have *Bacillus* spp. bacteremia (more than one half of these were *B. cereus*).[13] However, these patients were not treated for *Bacillus* spp. and did well clinically. Review of infection control policies showed suboptimal approaches to handling the catheters (wrong disinfectant, pauses during infusion, and reuse of caps on stopcocks). When these shortcomings were corrected, the *Bacillus* spp. bacteremia pseudoepidemic ceased. False-positive cultures of cerebrospinal fluid (CSF) for *Bacillus* spp. have also been reported.[14]

COMMERCIAL USES OF *BACILLUS* SPECIES

The toxins of the insect pathogen *B. thuringiensis* (Bt) have been purified and are among the most widely used "natural" control agents in agriculture. Either *B. thuringiensis* organisms or their purified toxins can be applied to commercially important plants to reduce damage from insect pests, and these can be easily purchased in garden centers to spray or dust in areas of insect activity. Genetic engineering has allowed the insertion of the toxin gene from Bt into other bacteria that can live closely with plants (e.g., among their roots or even between their cells) and protect them. Bt toxin genes have been inserted into commercially farmed plants such as tobacco, tomato, and cotton, making them naturally resistant to insects. *Bacillus* spp. spores have been marketed in nonchemical drain cleaners that work when the spores germinate and enzymatically digest part of the clog.[15] *B. subtilis* has been sold as a "probiotic" for ingestion, resulting in infection of at least one immunocompromised patient.[16]

ADHERENCE PROPERTIES

Adherence of some *Bacillus* species to plastic intravascular catheters may help account for the frequency with which *Bacillus* spp. infection presents as bacteremia, accounting for 26 of 38 patients in one series.[17] Scanning electron microscopy of a Hickman catheter removed from a cancer patient with persistent *Bacillus* spp. bacteremia showed organisms embedded in a layer of glycocalyx.[18] *B. licheniformis* is often mucoid in colonial morphology and this may account in part for its ability to cause somewhat indolent but difficult to treat infections in patients with long-term indwelling vascular catheters.[19]

CLINICAL MANIFESTATIONS

Food Poisoning

Intoxication from the ingestion of *Bacillus* species derived toxins is an uncommon but well described form of food poisoning. A report from England and Wales in the mid-1980s showed that there was one food poisoning from *Bacillus* spp. for every 129 of *Campylobacter,* 95 of other bacteria (*Salmonella, Shigella,* etc.), and 5.6 of *Clostridium perfringens.*[20] Like other toxin-mediated food poisonings, *Bacillus* spp. food poisoning occurs within 24 hours of eating—often within a few hours of the offending meal. *Bacillus* spp. toxins can produce one of two distinct syndromes: diarrheal and emetic. The diarrheal syndrome is characterized by profuse diarrhea and cramping but rarely vomiting or fever. The onset is about 8 to 16 hours after the ingestion of contaminated food, and the illness is brief (median duration of 24 hours). The emetic form (similar to *Staphylococcus aureus* food enterotoxin) has an even faster onset (1 to 5 hours) and is characterized by nausea, vomiting, and cramps although diarrhea can occur in about one third of cases. It also resolves within 24 hours. The toxins responsible for these two clinical syndromes have been shown to differ in a number of ways. The diarrheal toxin is actually a mixture of two or more proteins with molecular weights of 36,000 to 45,000 daltons. The precise mode of action is unknown although in animal models the toxins disrupt cell membranes and may have sphingomyelinase activity. The diarrheal toxin is heat labile and can be reduced or eliminated by heating food enough to kill the vegetative phase of the organism. This is important because it is believed that the ingestion of toxin-producing *Bacillus* spp. can lead to diarrheal food poisoning by elaboration of toxin in the upper gastrointestinal tract. Foods most commonly associated with *Bacillus* spp. diarrheal food poisoning include meats, vegetables, and sauces.[20] While the majority of isolates of the diarrheal form of *Bacillus* spp. food poisoning are *B. cereus,* there have been outbreaks related to *B. licheniformis* and *B. pumilus.*[21]

The emetic toxin is a small peptide of about 10,000 daltons. It is heat stable and is associated with starchy foods such as rice. This problem is worsened when rice is kept at room temperature overnight (to prevent clumping during refrigeration) and reheated the next day (e.g.,

fried rice). Heating or reheating food may eliminate viable *Bacillus* spp. organisms and the diarrheal toxin but not the emetic toxin. Strains of *Bacillus* may produce one toxin or the other, but they almost never produce both. Certain strains of *B. cereus* (109/110 strains of the H-1 serovar phenotype that were tested) are associated with the production of emetic toxin whereas other strains seldom produce this toxin.[22] At least one outbreak of *B. licheniformis* food poisoning was clinically comparable with the emetic syndrome of *B. cereus* but the polypeptide toxin of *B. licheniformis* differs from that found in *B. cereus.*[23] On rare occasions, emetic toxin can lead to significant liver disease including fulminant hepatic failure.[24] This is felt to be the result of inhibition of mitochondrial fatty acid oxidation.

Both of these food poisonings can be diagnosed by culturing food, diarrheal fluid or vomitus. Although cultivation of the *Bacillus* spp. organisms is easy, it is not routinely done in the evaluation of diarrhea when stool culture are submitted. Testing for the toxins themselves is difficult because commercial assays are not widely available. Although *Bacillus* spp. food poisoning often occurs in point-source epidemics, the exact infective/toxic dose of *Bacillus* spp. in food is not known. Food screening that finds concentrations of *B. cereus* that are higher than 10^5 per gram of food are worrisome and should lead to a careful assessment of food handling and storage, even in the absence of known food poisoning.[25] In one outbreak in which *B. cereus* food poisoning was associated with mayonnaise in potato salad, only 10^3 bacteria were recovered per gram of mayonnaise.[26] The concentration of *B. cereus* in the food actually served may have been higher because the potato salad was prepared by an inexperienced caterer and left at room temperature. Some *Bacillus* spp. food poisoning epidemics have been large. In London, diarrheal *B. cereus* food poisoning involved at least 139 out of nearly 1000 people who ate together at a university field event where a barbeque meal was served.[27] Of the responders with food poisoning, one fifth had fever (low-grade) and one third developed symptoms outside the usual 6- to 24-hour window (mostly 6 hours) after exposure. Some people were ill for up to 20 days after the start of symptoms, although the median duration was 2 days. The vehicle was pork with $>10^5$ *Bacillus cereus* per gram (as determined from leftovers after the actual food poisoning; the concentration at the time of the event is unknown).

Attack rates with *Bacillus* spp. food poisoning can be high. In an outbreak from a hospital cafeteria, 160 of 249 (64%) employees reported an illness compatible with the diarrheal form of *Bacillus* spp. food poisoning related to rice or chicken (both of which cultured positive for *B. cereus*).[28]

A distinct form of food poisoning has been associated with *B. subtilis.* This syndrome is characterized by a short incubation period (median 2.5 hours), vomiting, diarrhea (in about half the cases), and various other manifestations such as flushing, sweating, and headaches in about 10% of the patients.[20] Large amounts of *B. subtilis* are required to cause this syndrome as cultures of vomitus and food show 10^7 to 10^9 organisms per gram.

Systemic Infections

The rare but definite association between *Bacillus* spp. and deep infection have been recognized for over four decades (Table 206-1). Bacteremia has been the most common presentation but distinguishing infection from contamination may be difficult.[6,13,29] In a review of positive blood cultures for *Bacillus* spp. in a North Carolina hospital in the 1980s, 5 of 78 isolates were thought to represent true infection.[30] All the definite infections were caused by *B. cereus* whereas 70% of the possible and only 45% of the nonsignificant isolates were *B. cereus.* The most common feature in true *Bacillus* spp. bacteremia is the presence of an intravascular catheter, particularly a surgically implanted catheter.[19] The largest number of the blood-stream isolates of *Bacillus* are *B. cereus,* but other species such as *B. licheniformis* are also reported.[19]

Disseminated *Bacillus* spp. infections in neonates and young children have been described. These infections can cause multisystem involvement, and in neonates they seem to be acquired perinatally.[32] A

TABLE 206-1 *Bacillus* Species and Related Genera with Their Reported Clinical Syndromes, Other than Anthrax

Bacillus cereus	Bacteremia, pneumonia, ophthalmitis, keratitis, osteomyelitis, endocarditis, soft tissue infections, nosocomial infections, meningoencephalitis, fulminant hepatitis, diarrheal food poisoning, emetic food poisoning
Bacillus circulans	Meningitis, CSF shunt infection, endocarditis, wound infection, endophthalmitis
Bacillus licheniformis	Bacteremia, catheter-related sepsis, food poisoning, CNS infections after surgery or trauma
Bacillus megaterium	Meningitis, bacteremia
Bacillus pumilus	Meningitis, bacteremia, soft tissue infection
Bacillus sphaericus	Peritonitis, pleuritis, pericarditis, pseudotumor of the lung, meningitis, bacteremia
Bacillus subtilis	Meningitis after lumbar puncture or head trauma, otitis, mastoiditis, wound infection, bacteremia, pneumonia, endocarditis, shunt infection, emetic food poisoning
Brevibacillus brevis	Keratitis, food poisoning
Brevibacillus laterosporus	Bacteremia
Paenibacillus alvei	Sepsis, meningitis, prosthetic joint infection, wound infection

case of probable maternal-fetal infection has been reported in an injection drug user.[33]

Bacillus spp. infections can be serious and even fatal especially when the patient has major immune compromise such as neutropenia.[29,34] Injection drug users also seem to be at higher than average risk of *Bacillus* spp. infection (presumably from direct injection of the organism from the drugs themselves or the injection paraphernalia),[35] although these infections are very rarely fatal. Bacteremia from *Bacillus* spp. can be disseminated to other body sites such as the bones or eyes. *Bacillus* species are rarely the cause of native valve endocarditis, and when this occurs it is almost always in injection drug users.[35,36]

Central Nervous System Infections

Bacillus spp. usually enters the neuraxis through trauma or surgery, particularly implantation of a CSF shunt.[37] Removal of the hardware is usually required to achieve a cure. Lumbar puncture for diagnostic or therapeutic purposes can also lead to *Bacillus* spp. meningitis.[38] Brain abscess or encephalitis can be found alone or in combination with meningitis.[39]

Eye Infections

Bacillus species, usually *B. cereus,* can cause a rapidly destructive endophthalmitis, resulting from ocular trauma or surgery or through hematogenous dissemination.[40-42] The latter route is most commonly in an injection drug user. In animal models the presence of toxins accounts for a significant amount of tissue ocular destruction.[43] A large case series of *Bacillus* spp. endophthalmitis (mostly but not entirely the result of trauma) from India showed that aggressive therapy (combining vitrectomy, topical and systemic antibiotics, and occasionally steroids) could result in a surprisingly good outcome.[44] A small retrospective case series from the United States showed that five patients with traumatic *B. cereus* endophthalmitis had a sustained visual acuity of 20/200 or better after aggressive management.[45] All patients had pars plana vitrectomy and intraocular antibiotics.

Bacillus spp. keratitis is an uncommon sequela to eye trauma or other conditions that affect the cornea. Scrapings of the cornea can reveal characteristic gram-positive or gram-variable rods that grow easily in culture.[46] The eye complaints usually begin soon after injury but may be delayed for weeks or even months. Conservative treatment is often successful in curing the infection with reasonable visual acuity following therapy. There have also been reports of *B. cereus* keratitis as a result of contact lens wear.[47] In this case, normal disinfection methods for the contact lens case were insufficient to eliminate *B. cereus.*

Soft Tissue and Muscle Infection

Bacillus spp. soft tissue and bone infection has been associated with injuries and wounds, notably including motor vehicle accidents.[31] In one series of Swedish orthopedic patients with postoperative or posttraumatic wounds, about one patient per month had *Bacillus* spp. obtained from wounds of which half were considered to represent moderate to severe infections.[48] *Bacillus* spp. was isolated from a fourth of the patients with wound complications following total hip arthroplasty, and these patients had a longer hospital stay than other patients. In a case series from Costa Rica, *B. cereus* was found in 14 of 18 patients with traumatic wounds acquired in the rain forest.[49] These isolates were toxin producers, and in most cases they were found in pure and heavy growth. A drug abuser with *Bacillus* sp. crepitant cellulitis had the same isolate obtained from his heroin.[50]

PREVENTION OF *BACILLUS* SPECIES INFECTION

Guidelines for the safe preparation and handling of food are available at *www.cfsan.fda.gov/list.html.* Education of commercial food vendors is of obvious importance.[25] The best way to avoid both forms of food poisoning is to cook foods adequately and to eat them immediately. Cooking will kill vegetative *Bacillus* spp. and destroy preformed diarrheal toxin although not emetic toxin. If food cannot be consumed immediately, it should be refrigerated as soon as possible, as *Bacillus* spp. metabolism and toxin production are inhibited by cold temperature. Cooked rice should not be held at room temperature for prolonged periods before preparation of fried rice. Education of contact lens wearers about proper decontamination is important in preventing keratitis.[47]

TREATMENT

There is no specific treatment for the food poisoning syndromes other than symptomatic measures. For deep tissue infections, removal of prosthetic material, including infected intravascular catheters, is vital to cure.[12] Most *Bacillus* spp. isolates are susceptible to vancomycin, clindamycin, fluoroquinolones, aminoglycosides, carbapenems, and, variably, penicillins and cephalosporins.[51-53] *B. cereus* is often resistant to all β-lactams (other than carbapenems) and serious infections are best treated with vancomycin or clindamycin, with or without an aminoglycoside.[52,53]

Ciprofloxacin was the only drug uniformly active in vitro and was effective in vivo in a series of children with *B. sphaericus* bacteremia.[11] The β-lactamase of *B. cereus* and several other species of *Bacillus* spp. is a zinc-based enzyme that is evolutionarily different from β-lactamases in other gram-positive bacteria. Imipenem and some extended spectrum β-lactams such as mezlocillin seem to be active against almost all *Bacillus* spp. despite the presence of a β-lactamase enzyme in *B. cereus* and *B. thuringiensis.* For strains other than *B. cereus,* various β-lactams are active in vitro but clindamycin is less reliably active. Vancomycin appears to be active in vitro against most *Bacillus* strains, but resistance via the *VanA* gene cluster has been reported.[54]

For native valve endocarditis, a long course of therapy has been reported to be successful[34] and clindamycin has been surprisingly effective in a few cases despite its bacteriostatic activity. For prosthetic valve disease, valve replacement is usually performed.[35] In some patients with deep infection, removal of a device can be effective without antimicrobial therapy, and in a small number of cases, no intervention was needed to achieve a good outcome.[14] Surgical drainage and removal of necrotic debris or implanted devices is important. In endophthalmitis, pars plana vitrectomy and intravitreal antibiotics have been advocated. *Bacillus* spp. keratitis is treated topically, for example, with a fluoroquinolone. A good visual outcome is most likely when the lesion is treated early and does not involve the central part of the cornea.[42]

REFERENCES

1. Logan NA, Turnbull PCB. Bacillus and other aerobic endospore-forming bacteria. In: Murray PR, Baron EJ, Jorgensen JH, et al, eds. Manual of Clinical Microbiology. Washington, DC: American Society for Microbiology Press; 2003:445-460.
2. Helgason E, Okstad OA, Caugant DA, et al. *Bacillus anthracis, Bacillus cereus,* and *Bacillus thuringiensis*—one species on the basis of genetic evidence. Appl Environm Microbiol. 2000;66:2627-2630.
3. Drobniewski FA. *Bacillus cereus* and related species. Clin Microbiol Rev. 1993; 6:324-338.
4. Turnbull PC, Kramer JM. Intestinal carriage of *Bacillus cereus:* Faecal isolation in three population groups. J Hyg. 1985;95:629-638.
5. DeBuono BA, Brondum J, Kramer JM, et al. Plasmid, serotypic and enterotoxin analysis of *Bacillus cereus* in an outbreak setting. J Clin Microbiol. 1988;26: 1571-1574.
6. Bryce EA, Smith JA, Tweeddale M, et al. Dissemination of *Bacillus cereus* in an intensive care unit. Infect Contr Hosp Epidemiol. 1993;14:459-462.
7. Castagnola E, Fioredda F, Barretta MA, et al. *Bacillus sphaericus* bacteraemia in children with cancer: Case reports and literature review. J Hosp Infect 2001;48: 142-145.
8. Hsueh PR, Teng LJ, Yang PC, et al. Nosocomial pseudoepidemic caused by *Bacillus cereus* traced to contaminated ethyl alcohol from a liquor factory. J Clin Microbiol. 1999;37:2280-2284.
9. Loeb M, Wilcox L, Thornley D, et al. *Bacillus* species pseudobacteremia following hospital construction. Can J Infect Contr. 1995;10:37-40.
10. Christenson JD, Byington C, Korgensi EK, et al. *Bacillus cereus* infections among oncology patients at a children's hospital. Am J Infect Contr. 1999;27:543-546.
11. Pearson HE. Human infections caused by organisms of the bacillus species. Am J Clinic Pathol. 1970;53:506-515.
12. Cotton DJ, Gill VJ, Marshall DJ, et al. Clinical features and therapeutic interventions in 17 cases of *Bacillus* bacteremia in an immunosuppressed patient population. J Clin Microbiol. 1987;25:672-674.
13. Matsumoto S, Suenaga H, Naito K, et al. Management of suspected nosocomial infection: An audit of 19 hospitalized patients with septicemia caused by *Bacillus* species. Jpn J Infect Dis. 2000;53:196-202.
14. Cunha BA, Schoch PE, Bonoan JT. *Bacillus* species pseudomeningitis. Heart Lung. 1997;26:249-251.
15. Hannah WN, Ender PT. Persistent *Bacillus licheniformis* bacteremia associated with an intentional injection of organic drain cleaner. Clin Infect Dis. 1999; 29:659-661.
16. Oggioni MR, Pozzi G, Valensin PE, et al. Recurrent septicemia in an immunocompromised patient due to probiotic strains of *Bacillus subtilis.* J Clin Microbiol. 1998;36:325-326.
17. Sliman R, Rehm S, Schlaes DM. Serious infections caused by *Bacillus* species. Medicine. 1987;66:218-223.
18. Banerjee C, Bustamante CI, Wharton R, et al. *Bacillus* infections in patients with cancer. Arch Intern Med. 1988;148:1769-1774.
19. Blue SR, Singh VR, Saubolle MA. *Bacillus licheniformis* bacteremia: Five cases associated with indwelling central venous catheters. Clin Infect Dis. 1995;20:629-633.
20. Lund BM. Foodborne disease due to *Bacillus* and *Clostridium* species. Lancet 1990;336:982-986.
21. Mikkola R, Kolari M, Andersson MA, et al. Toxic lactonic lipopeptide from food poisoning isolates of *Bacillus licheniformis.* Eur J Biochem. 2000;267:4068-4074.
22. Agata N, Ohta M, Mori M. Production of an emetic toxin, cereulide, is associated with a specific class of *Bacillus cereus.* Curr Microbiol. 1996;33:67-69.
23. Salkinoja-Salonen MS, Vuorio R, Andersson MA, et al. Toxigenic strains of *Bacillus licheniformis* related to food poisoning. Appl Environm Microbiol. 1999;65: 4637-4645.
24. Mahler H, Pasi A, Kramer JM, et al. Fulminant liver failure in association with the emetic toxin of *Bacillus cereus.* N Engl J Med 1997;336:1142-1148.
25. Little CL, Barnes J, Mitchell RT. Microbiological quality of take-away cooked rice and chicken sandwiches: Effectiveness of food hygiene training of the management. Commun Dis Publ Hlth 2002;5:289-298.
26. Gaulin C, Viger YB, Fillion L. An outbreak of *Bacillus cereus* implicating a part-time banquet caterer. Can J Publ Hlth 2002;93:353-355.
27. Luby S, Jones J, Dowda H, et al. A large outbreak of gastroenteritis caused by diarrheal toxin-producing *Bacillus cereus.* J Infect Dis. 1993;167:1452-1455.
28. Baddour LM, Gaia SM, Griffin R, Hudson R. A hospital cafeteria-related food-borne outbreak due to *Bacillus cereus:* Unique features. Infect Contr. 1986;7:462-465.
29. Ihde DC, Armstrong D. Clinical spectrum of infection due to *Bacillus* species. Am J Med. 1973;55:839-845.
30. Weber DJ, Saviteer SM, Rutala WA, Thomann CA. Clinical significance of *Bacillus* species isolated from blood cultures. South Med J. 1989;82:705-709.
31. Wong MT, Dolan MJ. Significant infections due to *Bacillus* species following abrasions associated with motor vehicle-related trauma. Clin Infect Dis. 1992;15:855-857.
32. Patrick CC, Langston C, Baker CJ. *Bacillus* species infections in neonates. Rev Infect Dis. 1989;4:612-615.
33. Workowski KA, Flaherty JP. Systemic *Bacillus* species infection mimicking listeriosis of pregnancy. Clin Infect Dis. 1992;14:694-696.
34. Guioit HFL, de Planque MM, Richel DJ, van't Wout JW. *Bacillus cereus:* A snake in the grass for granulocytopenic patients. J Infect Dis. 1986;153:1186.
35. Tuazon CU, Murray HW, Levy C, et al. Serious infections from *Bacillus* sp. JAMA. 1979;241:1137-1140.
36. Steen MK, Bruno-Murtha LA, Chaux G, et al. *Bacillus cereus* endocarditis: Report of a case and review. Clin Infect Dis. 1992;14:945-946.
37. Berner R, Heinen F, Pelz K, et al. Ventricular shunt infection and meningitis due to *Bacillus cereus.* Neuropediatrics. 1997;28:333-334.
38. Gaur AH, Patrick CC, McCullers JA, et al. *Bacillus cereus* bacteremia and meningitis in immunocompromised children. Clin Infect Dis. 2001;32:1456-1462.
39. Weisse ME, Bass JW, Jarrett RV, Vincent JM. Nonanthrax *Bacillus* infections of the central nervous system. Pediatr Infect Dis J. 1991;10:243-246.
40. Davey TF, Tauber WB. Posttraumatic endophthalmitis: The emerging role of *Bacillus cereus* infection. Rev Infect Dis. 1987;9:110-123.
41. Shamsuddin D, Tuazon CU, Levy C, Curtin J. *Bacillus cereus* panophthalmitis: Source of the organism. Rev Infect Dis. 1982;4:97-103.
42. Shrader SK, Band JD, Lauter CB, Murphy P. The clinical spectrum of endophthalmitis: Incidence, predisposing factors, and features influencing outcome. J Infect Dis. 1990;162:115-120.
43. Beecher DJ, Pulido JS, Barney NP, Wong AC. Extracellular virulence factors in *Bacillus cereus* endophthalmitis: Methods and implication of involvement of hemolysin BL. Infect Immun. 1995;63:632-639.
44. Das T, Choudhury K, Sharma S, et al. Clinical profile and outcome in *Bacillus* endophthalmitis. Ophthalmology. 2001;108:1819-1825.
45. Foster RE, Martinez JA, Murray TG, et al. Useful visual outcomes after treatment of *Bacillus cereus* endophthalmitis. Ophthalmology. 1996;103:390-397.
46. Choudhuri KK, Sharma S, Garg P, Rao GN. Clinical and microbiological profile of Bacillus keratitis. Cornea. 2000;19:301-306.
47. Pinna A, Sechi LA, Zanetti S, et al. *Bacillus cereus* keratitis associated with contact lens wear. Ophthalmology. 2001;108:1830-1834.
48. Akesson A, Hedstrom SA, Ripa T. *Bacillus cereus:* A significant pathogen in postoperative and post-traumatic wounds on orthopaedic wards. Scand J Infect Dis. 1991;23:71-77.
49. Dryden MS, Kramer JM. Toxigenic *Bacillus cereus* as a cause of wound infections in the tropics. J Infect. 1987;15:207-212.
50. Dancer SJ, McNair D, Finn P, Kolsto AB. *Bacillus cereus* cellulitis from contaminated heroin. J Med Microbiol. 2002;51:278-281.
51. Andrews JM, Wise R. Susceptibility testing of *Bacillus* species. J Antimicrob Chemother. 2002;49:1039-1046.
52. Krause A, Freeman R, Sisson PR, Murphy OM. Infection with *Bacillus cereus* after close-range gunshot injuries. J Trauma. 1996;41:546-548.
53. Weber DJ, Saviteer SM, Rutala WA, Thomann CA. In vitro susceptibility of *Bacillus* spp. to selected antimicrobial agents. Antimicrob Agents Chemother. 1988;32:642-645.
54. Ligozzi M, Cascio GL, Fontana R. *vanA* gene cluster in a vancomycin-resistant clinical isolate of *Bacillus circulans.* Antimicrob Agents Chemother. 1998;42:2055-2059.

CHAPTER **207**

Erysipelothrix rhusiopathiae

ANNETTE C. REBOLI

W. EDMUND FARRAR

Erysipelothrix rhusiopathiae, formerly known as *Erysipelothrix insidiosa,* is a thin, pleomorphic, nonsporulating, gram-positive rod. First isolated from mice by Robert Koch in 1878 and from swine by Louis Pasteur in 1882, it was established as the etiologic agent of swine erysipelas in 1886 by Löffler and as a human pathogen in 1909 when Rosenbach isolated it from a patient with localized cutaneous lesions.[1,2] Rosenbach coined the term *erysipeloid* to avoid confusion with *erysipelas,* a superficial cellulitis with prominent lymphatic involvement that is almost always caused by group A streptococci.[2]

MICROBIOLOGY

E. rhusiopathiae is a straight or slightly curved aerobic or facultatively anaerobic bacillary organism; it is 0.2 to 0.4 μm in diameter and 0.8 to 2.5 μm in length. It is gram-positive but may appear gram-negative because it decolorizes readily. Organisms may be arranged singly, in short chains, in pairs in a V configuration, or grouped randomly. Nonbranching filaments that can be longer than 60 μm are sometimes seen. Colonial and microscopic appearance varies with the medium, pH, and temperature of incubation.[1] After growing for 24 hours at 37°C, colonies are small and transparent with a smooth, glistening surface. On blood agar it may be α-hemolytic. *E. rhusiopathiae* is catalase-, oxidase-, indole-, Voges-Proskauer-, and methyl red-negative.[3] Acid without gas is produced from the fermentation of glucose, fructose, lactose, and galactose. Most strains produce hydrogen sulfide, a diagnostically important reaction. On triple sugar iron (TSI) agar slants, hydrogen sulfide causes a blackened butt. *E. rhusiopathiae* is sometimes confused with other gram-positive bacilli, in particular, *Listeria monocytogenes, Actinomyces (Arcanobacterium) pyogenes,* and *Arcanobacterium (Corynebacterium) haemolyticum,* but these three species are β-hemolytic on blood agar and do not produce hydrogen sulfide in the butt on TSI agar slants. Furthermore, *L. monocytogenes* is catalase-positive and motile.[4]

EPIDEMIOLOGY

E. rhusiopathiae is found worldwide. It has been reported as a commensal or a pathogen in a wide variety of vertebrate and invertebrate species, but the major reservoir is believed to be domestic swine.[3,5] It does not appear to cause disease in fish but can persist for long periods of time in the mucoid exterior slime of these animals.[6] It may live long enough in soil to cause infection weeks or months after initial contamination. The greatest commercial impact of *E. rhusiopathiae* infection is due to disease in swine, but infection of turkeys, ducks, and sheep is also important. The organism is communicable from animals to humans by direct cutaneous contact. There have been reports of bacteremia, one with endocarditis, which occurred after ingestion of undercooked pork.[1] The risk of human infection with *Erysipelothrix* is closely related to the opportunity for exposure to the organism; accordingly, most human cases are related to occupational exposure. Although infection with *Erysipelothrix* has been associated with many occupations, persons at greatest risk include fishermen, fish handlers, butchers, farmers, slaughterhouse workers, veterinarians, and homemakers.[5,7,8] Infection is especially common among persons who handle fish. Of the 329 cases of erysipeloid described by Gilchrist, 323 were associated with injuries from crabs.[9] "Whale finger" is erysipeloid seen in persons who sustain cuts to the fingers and hands while engaged in whaling.[10] Human-to-human transmission of infection has not been reported. Instances of infection that do not have an occupational link have occurred mainly in immunocompromised hosts and suggest that colonization of the oropharynx or gastrointestinal tract may occur.[11] Chronic alcoholism is a common underlying condition. There have been a few recent reports of erysipeloid following cat and dog bites.[12]

PATHOGENESIS

Abrasions or puncture wounds of the skin probably serve as the portal of entry of *Erysipelothrix* organisms in most cases of infection in humans and in animals. Virulence factors include a capsule, enzymes (neuraminidase and hyaluronidase) and surface proteins.[13] In the absence of specific antibodies, *E. rhusiopathiae* evades phagocytosis, but even if phagocytized, it is capable of intracellular replication.[13]

CLINICAL MANIFESTATIONS

Three well-defined clinical categories of human disease have been described: (1) erysipeloid, a localized skin lesion, (2) a diffuse cutaneous eruption with systemic symptoms, and (3) bacteremia, which is often associated with endocarditis.[1]

The localized cutaneous form—the "erysipeloid" of Rosenbach— is a subacute cellulitis and is the most common type of *Erysipelothrix* infection seen in humans. Because the organism is acquired through contact with infected animals or fish, or with products made from

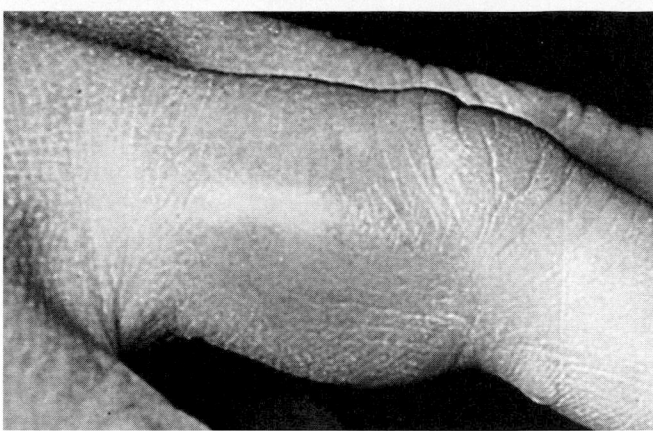

FIGURE 207-1. Lesion of erysipeloid. *(From Lambert HP, Farrar WE. Cutaneous manifestations of infection. II: Bacterial infections. In: Lambert HP, Farrar WE, eds. Infectious Diseases Illustrated. London: Gower Medical Publishing; 1982:Section 5.10. By permission of Mosby International Ltd.)*

them, gaining entrance via cuts or abrasions on the skin, most lesions are on the fingers. Following an incubation period of 2 to 7 days, pain (which is often severe and described as burning, itching, or throbbing) and swelling of the involved digit or part of the hand develop. The lesion is well defined, slightly raised, and violaceous (Fig. 207-1).[14] As it spreads peripherally, the central area fades. Vesiculation may occur. Regional lymphadenopathy and lymphangitis occur in approximately a third of cases.[15] There may be inflammation of an adjacent joint. Systemic symptoms are uncommon. Approximately 10% of the patients have low-grade fever and arthralgias.[15] Clinically, erysipeloid resembles staphylococcal or streptococcal cellulitis, but a history of occupational exposure, lesions on the hands, subacute course, absence of suppuration, lack of pitting edema, violaceous color, and the disproportionate pain should suggest the possibility of erysipeloid.[16] Because organisms are located only in deeper parts of the skin in erysipeloid, aspirates or biopsy specimens should incorporate the entire thickness of the dermis, as well as tissue from the periphery of the lesion, to maximize the chance of recovery of the organism. Erysipeloid usually resolves without treatment within 3 or 4 weeks.

The diffuse cutaneous form, which is rare, occurs when the violaceous cutaneous lesion progresses proximally from the site of inoculation or appears at remote areas.[1,14] Lesions may appear urticarial, with the rhomboid pattern characteristic of swine erysipelas.[8] Fever and arthralgias are common. Blood cultures are negative. The course is more protracted than in the localized form, and recurrence is common.

Systemic infection with *E. rhusiopathiae* is unusual. More than 70 cases of bacteremia have been reported, most complicated by endocarditis.[17-19] Although this organism has caused prosthetic valve endocarditis, most reported cases of endocarditis have involved native valves.[19,20] There was a history of an antecedent or concurrent skin lesion of erysipeloid in 36% of the patients.[18] When clinical features of *E. rhusiopathiae* endocarditis were compared with those of endocarditis caused by other bacteria, there was a higher male-to-female ratio (which probably reflects occupational exposure), a greater propensity for involvement of the aortic valve, and a much higher mortality rate among patients with *E. rhusiopathiae* endocarditis (38% versus 20% in endocarditis caused by other organisms).[16] In approximately 60% of patients, *E. rhusiopathiae* endocarditis developed in previously normal heart valves. In patients with bacteremia or endocarditis, or both, routine blood culture techniques are adequate for recovery of the organism.[4] Complications of *Erysipelothrix* endocarditis include congestive heart failure, myocardial abscess, aortic valve perforation, meningitis, brain infarctions, and glomerulonephritis.[21-23] More than one third of the patients required valve replacement.[18]

Bacteremia without endocarditis has been reported with increasing frequency. It has occurred primarily in immunocompromised hosts.[24-26] Brain abscess, peritonitis, osteomyelitis, and septic arthritis have also been reported.[1,14,27-30]

Definitive diagnosis of infection with *Erysipelothrix* requires isolation of the organism from a biopsy specimen or blood. There are no reliable serologic tests for the diagnosis of infection in humans. PCR has been used for rapid diagnosis in swine and has been applied successfully to human samples.[31,32]

TREATMENT AND PREVENTION

Susceptibility data for *E. rhusiopathiae* are limited. Most strains are highly susceptible to penicillins, cephalosporins, clindamycin, imipenem, and ciprofloxacin.[33-35] Penicillin and imipenem are the most active agents in vitro.[33] Susceptibility to chloramphenicol, erythromycin, and tetracycline is variable. Most strains are resistant to vancomycin, sulfonamides, trimethoprim-sulfamethoxazole, novobiocin, teicoplanin, and aminoglycosides. Resistance to vancomycin is important because this agent is often used empirically to treat bacteremia caused by gram-positive organisms. Because minimum inhibitory concentrations (MICs) of penicillin range from 0.0025 to 0.06 μg/mL, and minimum bactericidal concentrations (MBCs) have been reported in the range of 0.0025 to 0.75 μg/mL, penicillin G (12 million to 20 million units/day) is the drug of choice for serious infections caused by *E. rhusiopathiae*. Ampicillin and ceftriaxone have also been used successfully. Ciprofloxacin has MIC and MBC values similar to those obtained with β-lactam antibiotics.[34,35] Use of fluoroquinolones may be considered in *Erysipelothrix* infections when β-lactams are contraindicated. In cases of endocarditis, the duration of intravenous antibiotic therapy should be 4 to 6 weeks, although shorter courses (2 weeks of intravenous therapy followed by 2 to 4 weeks of oral therapy) have been successful.[8] Although erysipeloid usually resolves spontaneously, healing is hastened by antibiotic therapy. Oral therapy with amoxicillin or a quinolone can be used.

Prevention of infection for persons in high-risk occupations depends on adequate hand washing, the use of protective attire such as gloves, and disinfection of contaminated surfaces. Unprotected direct contact with animal body tissues and secretions should be avoided. Commercial vaccines are available for veterinary use. Use of vaccination along with other measures such as improved waste disposal has helped to control swine erysipelas.

REFERENCES

1. Grieco M, Sheldon C. *Erysipelothrix rhusiopathiae*. Ann NY Acad Sci. 1970;174:523-532.
2. Rosenbach FJ. Experimentelle, morphologische und klinische Studie über die krankheitserregenden Mikroorganismen des Schweinerotlauf, des Erysipeloids und der Mäsesepsis. Z Hyg Infektionskr. 1909;63:343-369.
3. Sneath PHA, Abbott JD, Cunliffe AC. The bacteriology of erysipeloid. Br Med J. 1951;2:1063-1066.
4. Reboli AC, Farrar WE. The genus *Erysipelothrix*. In: Balows A, Truper HG, Dworkin M, et al, eds. The Prokaryotes. A Handbook on the Biology of Bacteria: Ecophysiology, Isolation, Identification, Applications. New York: Springer-Verlag; 1992:1629-1642.
5. Woodbine M. *Erysipelothrix rhusiopathiae*. Bacteriol Rev. 1950;14:161-178.
6. Wood RL. *Erysipelothrix* infection. In: Hubbert WT, McCollough WF, Schnurrenburger PR, eds. Diseases Transmitted from Animals to Man. Springfield, IL: Charles C Thomas; 1975:271-281.
7. Klauder JV. Erysipeloid as an occupational disease. JAMA. 1938;111:1345-1348.
8. Reboli AC, Farrar WE. *Erysipelothrix rhusiopathiae:* An occupational pathogen. Clin Microbiol Rev. 1989;2:354-359.
9. Gilchrist TC. Erysipeloid, with a record of 329 cases, of which 323 were caused by crab bites, or lesions produced by crabs. J Cutan. Dis. 1904;22:507-519.
10. Hillenbrand FKM. Whale finger and seal finger: Their relation to erysipeloid. Lancet. 1953:1:680-681.
11. Schuster MG, Brennan PJ, Edelstein P. Persistent bacteremia with *Erysipelothrix rhusiopathiae* in a hospitalized patient. Clin Infect Dis. 1993;17:783-784.
12. Talan DA, Citron DM, Abrahamian FM, et al. Bacteriologic analysis of infected dog and cat bites. Emergency Medicine Animal Bite Infection Study Group. N Engl J Med. 1999;340:85-92.
13. Shimoji Y. Pathogenicity of *Erysipelothrix rhusiopathiae:* Virulence factors and protective immunity. Microbes Infect. 2000;2:965-972.
14. Erlich JC. *Erysipelothrix rhusiopathiae* infection in man. Arch Intern Med. 1946;78:565-577.
15. Nelson E. Five hundred cases of erysipeloid. Rocky Mtn Med J. 1955;52:40-42.
16. Robson JM, McDougall R, van der Valk S, et al. *Erysipelothrix rhusiopathiae:* An uncommon but ever present zoonosis. Pathology. 1998;30:391-394.
17. Hill DC, Ghassemian JN. *Erysipelothrix rhusiopathiae* endocarditis. Clinical features of an occupational disease. South Med J. 1997;90:1147-1148.
18. Gorby GL, Peacock JE. *Erysipelothrix rhusiopathiae* endocarditis: Microbiologic, epidemiologic and clinical features of an occupational disease. Rev Infect Dis. 1988;10:317-325.
19. Gransden WR, Eykyn SJ. *Erysipelothrix rhusiopathiae* endocarditis. Rev Infect Dis. 1988;10:1228.
20. Hayek LJ. *Erysipelothrix* endocarditis affecting a porcine heart valve. J Infect. 1993;27:203-204.
21. Artz AL, Szabo S, Zabel LT, Hoffmeister HM. Aortic valve endocarditis with paravalvular abscesses caused by *Erysipelothrix rhusiopathiae*. Eur J Clin Microbiol Infect Dis. 2001;20:587-588.
22. Nandish S, Khardori N. Valvular and myocardial abscesses due to *Erysipelothrix rhusiopathiae*. Clin Infect Dis. 1999;29:1351-1352.
23. Ko SB, Kim DE, Kwon HM, Roh JK. A case of multiple brain infarctions associated with Erysipelothrix rhusiopathiae endocarditis. Arch Neurol. 2003;60:434-436.
24. Ognibene FP, Cunnion RE, Gill V, et al. *Erysipelothrix rhusiopathiae* bacteremia presenting as septic shock. Am J Med. 1985;78:861-864.
25. Totemchokchyakarn K, Janwityanujit S, Sathapatayavongs B, Puavilai S. *Erysipelothrix rhusiopathiae* septicemia in systemic lupus erythematosus. Int J Dermatol. 1996;35:818-820.
26. Jones N, Khoosal M. *Erysipelothrix rhusiopathiae* septicemia in a neonate. Clin Infect Dis. 1997;24:511.
27. Dunbar SA, Clarridge JE 3rd. Potential errors in recognition of *Erysipelothrix rhusiopathiae*. J Clin Microbiol. 2000;38:1302-1304.
28. Ruiz ME, Richards JS, Kerr GS, Kan VL. *Erysipelothrix rhusiopathiae* septic arthritis. Arthritis Rheum. 2003;48:1156-1157.
29. Wong RC, Kong KO, Lin RV, Barkham T. Chronic monoarthritis of the knee in systemic lupus erythematosus. Lupus. 2003;12:324-326.
30. Allianatos PG, Tilentzoglou AC, Koutsoukou AD. Septic arthritis caused by Erysipelothrix rhusiopathiae infection after arthroscopically assisted anterior cruciate ligament reconstruction. Arthroscopy. 2003;19:26E.
31. Brook CJ, Riley TV. *Erysipelothrix rhusiopathiae:* Bacteriology, epidemiology and clinical manifestations of an occupational pathogen. J Med Microbiol. 1999;48:789-799.
32. Takeshi K, Makino S, Ikeda T, et al. Direct and rapid detection by PCR of *Erysipelothrix* sp. DNAs prepared from bacterial strains and animal tissues. J Clin Microbiol. 1999;37:4093-4098.
33. Takahashi T, Sawada T, Ohmae K, et al. Antibiotic resistance of *Erysipelothrix rhusiopathiae* isolated from pigs with chronic swine erysipelas. Antimicrob Agents Chemother. 1984;25:385-386.
34. Venditti M, Gelfusa V, Tarasi A, et al. Antimicrobial susceptibilities of *Erysipelothrix rhusiopathiae*. Antimicrob Agents Chemother. 1990;34:2038-2040.
35. Fidalgo SG, Longbottom CJ, Riley TV. Susceptibility of *Erysipelothrix rhusiopathiae* to antimicrobial agents and home disinfectants. Pathology. 2002;34:462-465.

CHAPTER **208**

Neisseria meningitidis

MICHAEL A. APICELLA

Epidemic cerebrospinal fever (meningococcal meningitis) was first described in Geneva by Vieusseaux in 1805.[1] Subsequent reports throughout the 19th century confirmed its episodic, epidemic nature with a propensity for afflicting young children and military recruits assembled in stationary barracks situations.[2] In 1887, Weichselbaum isolated the meningococcus from cerebrospinal fluid (CSF), and the etiologic relationship between this organism and epidemic meningitis was firmly established.[3] Kiefer in 1896[4] and Albrecht and Ghon in 1901[5] found that healthy persons could become carriers of the meningococcus. Serotypes of the meningococcus were first recognized by Dopter in 1909.[6] This finding laid the basis for serum therapy in the treatment of meningococcal infection proposed by Flexner in 1913.[7] Glover was the first to note that carrier rates in military recruit camps rose with periods of crowding, and he believed that they were associated with an increased incidence of cases.[8] Significant national and worldwide epidemics occurred in 1928 to 1930[9,10] and in 1941.[11] In 1937, sulfonamide therapy radically altered the outcome of meningococcal infection and replaced serum as its treatment.[12] Prophylaxis with sulfonamides eradicated the carrier state[13] and provided a simple and safe method for the prevention of epidemics, particularly in the crowded environments of military barracks. With the advent of antibiotic agents, treatment of meningococcal infection became more effective, and mortality declined. Increasing sulfonamide resistance among meningococci was recognized by Schoenback and Phair[14] in 1941 to 1943 but did not become a clinically significant problem until meningococcal epidemics occurred in 1963 in two military bases in California.[15,16] With the subsequent worldwide emergence of resistant strains and the absence of effective chemoprophylaxis, renewed interest in immunoprevention led to the development of safe and effective vaccines against serogroup A and C meningococcal infection.[17]

Many problems still exist in the understanding, prevention, and treatment of meningococcal infection, including the susceptibilities of certain populations to this infection, its sporadic epidemic nature, the mechanisms responsible for carrier eradication by antibiotics, the reasons for the fulminant nature of the infection, and the inability of humans to develop antibody to the group B polysaccharide vaccine. Until these and many other questions are answered, meningococcal infections will continue to be a scourge among human populations.

ETIOLOGIC AGENT AND MORPHOLOGIC, CULTURAL, AND BIOCHEMICAL CHARACTERISTICS

N. meningitidis is a gram-negative diplococcus (0.6×0.8 μm). The adjacent sides are flattened to produce the typical biscuit shape. Because the organism tends to undergo autolysis readily, considerable size and shape variation can be seen in older cultures. The organism produces a polysaccharide capsule, which is the basis of the serogroup typing system. Because the organism is considered fastidious in its growth conditions, appropriate media and growth conditions are necessary. On solid media, the meningococcus grows as a transparent, nonpigmented, nonhemolytic colony approximately 1 to 5 mm in diameter. Colonies are convex and, if large amounts of polysaccharide are present, will appear mucoid rather than smooth. Optimal growth conditions are achieved in a moist environment at 35°C to 37°C under an atmosphere of 5% to 10% carbon dioxide. The organism will grow well on a number of medium bases, including blood agar base, trypticase soy agar, supplemented chocolate agar, and Mueller-Hinton agar. Confirmation of the presence of this organism in clinical specimens is dependent on a series of carbohydrate fermentations. The meningococcus will metabolize glucose and maltose to acid without gas formation and fails to metabolize sucrose or lactose. In addition, the cell wall of the organism contains cytochrome oxidase. This enzyme will oxidize the dye tetramethylphenylenediamine from colorless to deep pink. This latter test was initially considered specific for *Neisseria*, but subsequent studies have shown that other genera also exhibit high tetramethylphenylenediamine oxidase activities, including *Pseudomonas, Aeromonas,* and *Moraxella.* Recently, the use of molecular methods based on a variety of polymerase chain reaction (PCR) techniques have supplemented culture in confirmation of patients infected with the meningococcus, particularly for individuals who had been treated with antibiotics before their specimens were cultured.

The meningococcus has a rapid autolytic rate. Hebeler and Young have demonstrated the presence of an autolysin, an amidase, that acts on the peptidoglycan layer of the gonococcus.[18] Whether the mechanism of autolysis is similar in the meningococcus is uncertain. The process appears to be enzymatic because autolysis can be stopped by the addition of potassium cyanide or formalin or by heating cultures to 65°C for 30 minutes.

The importance of iron in the survival of microbes has stimulated interest in the mechanisms that *Neisseria* organisms use for iron acquisition. It has been shown that iron-loaded animals are more susceptible to fatal meningococcal infection.[19] The meningococcus does not produce a soluble siderophore but possesses a series of membrane proteins that selectively scavenge iron from hemoglobin, transferrin, and lactoferrin.[20,21]

Antigenic Structure of the Meningococcus

Capsular Polysaccharides

Shortly after identification of the meningococcus as the etiologic agent in epidemic meningitis and after recognition of healthy nasopharyngeal carriers of the organism, investigations into the application of immunologic methods for the detection and differentiation of meningococci were performed. It became apparent that antigenically diverse meningococci existed, and spurred by the introduction of serum therapy,[7] English workers identified four antigenically distinct types of meningococci.[22] Clapp and associates established the relationship between this antigenic polysaccharide[23] and the capsule of the meningococcus via the Quellung reaction in group A strains.[24] Branham and Carlin, using group C strains, were able to demonstrate that these antigens elicited antibodies that conferred specific protection in mice.[25] Meningococci can now be segregated by seroagglutination into at least 13 serogroups: A, B, C, D[26,27]; X, Y, Z[28,29]; E, W-135[29]; H, I, K[30]; and L.[31] Table 208-1 gives the chemical composition of the capsular polysaccharide of the eight most common capsular serogroups causing human disease. Capsular polysaccharides responsible for the serogrouping specificity of groups A, B, C, X, Y, Z, W-135, and L have been purified. These polysaccharides have been isolated from the broth supernatant of overnight cultures, and a number of effective methods using either detergent precipitation or molecular sieve and ion-exchange chromatography have been used in their separation.[32-34] Group C polysaccharides can be biochemically divided into neuraminidase-sensitive and neuraminidase-resistant polysaccharides.[35,36]

After the introduction of antibiotics, interest in the development of serogroup-specific antigens for use as vaccines diminished greatly, but Watson and colleagues continued their efforts and identified the specific soluble substance from the group C meningococcus and showed its sialic acid nature.[37] A major impetus that renewed interest in meningococcal immunobiology was the emergence of sulfonamide-resistant meningococci as a clinical problem. This development made antibiotic prophylaxis ineffective, and persistent epidemics of serogroup B and C strains on military recruit reservations during the 1960s prompted reinvestigations into the feasibility of using capsular polysaccharide antigens as vaccine materials.

The immunogenicity of group A and C polysaccharide in humans appears to be a function of their molecular size.[38] In addition, studies have indicated that group C vaccine is stable and immunogenic after up to 4 years of storage. Group B polysaccharide has been purified and described immunochemically,[39,40] but it has proved to be a very poor immunogen in humans. At the present time no effective vaccine preparation exists for this serogroup.[41] With the increasing frequency of clinical cases caused by group Y meningococci, interest in capsular

TABLE 208-1 Chemical Composition of Meningococcal Capsular Polysaccharides	
Capsular Serogroup Antigen	*Chemical Composition of Capsular Polymer*
A	Partially *O*-acetylated 2-acetamido-2-deoxy-D-mannose-6-phosphate
B	$(2 \rightarrow 8)$-Linked *N*-acetylneuraminic acid
C_{1+}	*O*-acetylated $(2 \rightarrow 9)$-linked *N*-acetylneuraminic acid
C_1	$(2 \rightarrow 9)$-Linked *N*-acetylneuraminic acid
X	2-Acetamido-2-deoxy-D-glucose-4-phosphate
Y	Partially *O*-acetylated alternating sequence of D-glucose and *N*-acetylneuraminic acid
W-135	Alternating sequence of D-galactose and *N*-acetylneuraminic acid
L	*N*-acetylglucosamine phosphate

polysaccharide strains from this serogroup has renewed,[42] and studies by Griffiss and co-workers have demonstrated the safety and immunogenicity of group Y and W-135 capsular polysaccharides in humans.[43]

Noncapsular Cell Wall Antigens

The meningococcal outer membrane is similar in structure to that of other gram-negative bacteria. It contains a number of somatic antigens that are important in pathogenesis and immunobiology. The principal antigens that have been studied include lipooligosaccharide, which is analogous to the lipopolysaccharide of enteric gram-negative bacilli and the outer membrane proteins. Lipooligosaccharide is serologically diverse, and Mandrell and Zollinger have demonstrated at least 12 different serotypes.[44] The chemical structure of the oligosaccharide portion of meningococcal lipooligosaccharide from all L types has been studied by Jennings and co-workers.[45,46] Several of these structures are immunochemically similar to human glycosphingolipid antigens. An association between lipooligosaccharide immunotype expression and invasive disease has been found.[47] Ninety-seven percent of isolates from epidemics in England expressed the L3, 7, 9 immunotype. The lipooligosaccharide immunotypes of carriers were more heterogeneous. Studies have suggested that specific lipooligosaccharide epitopes of oligosaccharide may be effective vaccines.[48,49]

Interest in the meningococcal outer membrane proteins was stimulated by the work of Gold and associates, who showed that a noncapsular typing system could be derived by using bactericidal techniques.[50,51] Using similar methods, Frasch and Chapman succeeded in identifying 11 distinct serotypes of group B meningococci.[52] Frasch and Gotschlich have shown that the antigens responsible for this serotyping system are protein in nature and reside in the outer membrane as part of a lipoprotein-lipooligosaccharide complex. Serogroup B and C meningococci can be subdivided into at least 15 protein serotypes based on antigenically different outer membrane proteins.[53] Studies by Broud and co-workers indicate that endemic meningococcal disease appears to be caused by a broad, heterogeneous distribution of serotypes,[54] in contrast to epidemics that appear to be caused by a single serotype. The successful application of molecular biology techniques has resulted in the cloning of a number of important outer membrane protein antigens of the meningococcus.[55,56] Frasch and co-workers[57] suggested revising the classification system for the somatic antigen serotypes of the meningococcus. These investigators proposed a schema based on the major class 2 (41,000 kDa) and class 3 (38,000 kDa) outer membrane proteins and the lipooligosaccharides. In their example, a meningococcal strain would be identified by serogroup, protein serotype, and lipooligosaccharide serotype. Addition of the class 1 protein (46,000 kDa) characteristics could be also used to define the strain further. This system has worked well in identifying epidemic strains of serogroup B.

The lack of a serogroup B vaccine combined with the availability of the sequence of the meningococcal genome has spurred interest in using this database to identify new noncapsular vaccine targets in an approach designated "reverse vaccinology."[58]

Using analysis of multilocus enzyme genotypes, Selander and co-workers have developed a system for defining the clonal distribution of bacterial isolates.[59] Applying this method to studies of the meningococcus, Achtman and colleagues have shown that worldwide epidemics caused by a strain of serogroup A meningococcus are derived from a single clonotype.[60] Caugant and co-workers have studied 650 meningococcal strains of different capsular serogroups and have shown that over periods of many years the genetic structure of *N. meningitidis* is basically clonal as a result of low rates of recombination of chromosomal genes.[61]

Meningococci have been shown to have pili.[62,63] Meningococcal pili undergo both phase and antigenic variation. These structures can be maintained under special cultural conditions in vitro, and their role as ligands in attachment to human cells has been studied.[64] Piliated meningococci attach to human nasopharyngeal cells in greater numbers than do meningococci devoid of pili. Trypsin or mechanical shearing causes loss of pili and decreased attachment. Meningococci

appear to have wide differences in attachment capability that depend on the site of isolation of the epithelial cell.[65]

Pathogenesis of Infection

The pathogenesis of *N. meningitidis* begins on the nasopharyngeal surface. The nasopharynx is a mixed epithelial surface containing ciliated secretory and nonciliated nonsecretory cells. The airway epithelial surface is covered with a mucus layer that the organism must penetrate. How penetration occurs is not clearly understood. The meningococcus uses bacterial surface factors to adhere to nonciliated cells on the airway surface. Pili act as long-range attachment organelles and enhance attachment, but they are not necessary for the process.[65] It has been shown that purified pili bind to a human cell surface protein, CD46, that is widely distributed and involved in regulation of complement activation.[66] Transgenic mice expressing this human protein become susceptible to meningococcal disease because bacteria cross the blood-brain barrier.[67] Attachment of the bacteria to epithelial cells is blocked by polyclonal and monoclonal antibodies directed against membrane cofactor protein, which suggests that this complement regulator is a receptor for piliated *Neisseria*. Recombinant membrane cofactor protein produced in *Escherichia coli* inhibits attachment of the bacteria to target cells. As the organism draws closer to the cell, outer membrane surface proteins such as the class V proteins (Opa and Opc) play a role in attachment and may be important in defining the tissue specificity of the organism.[68]

The hydrophilic, highly charged nature of the capsular polysaccharide prevents interactions with the epithelial cell surface. Only unencapsulated meningococci enter epithelial cells, and capsular biosynthesis has been shown to stop as the meningococcus enters the epithelial cell.[69,70] This is the result of a mechanism designated slip-strand mispairing that results in the termination of translation of one of the sialyltransferases involved in capsular biosynthesis.[69] This "molecular switch" varies capsular expression at a frequency of 10^{-3}. Blood-stream encapsulated meningococcal isolates were universally found to have the "switch" in the "on" position whereas nasopharyngeal unencapsulated carrier isolates had the switch in the "off" position. This suggested that a correlation exists between capsular phase variation, bacterial invasion, and the outbreak of meningococcal disease.[69] On contact with epithelial and endothelial cells, the meningococcus initiates cytoskeletal changes within these cell types. It appears that either Opc- or OpaA-mediated adhesion can trigger cortical actin rearrangements.[71,72] These rearrangements are not triggered by nonadherent meningococcal strains, by heat-killed or chloramphenicol-treated organisms, or by *E. coli* recombinants that adhere to cells via OpaA or Opa1 fusion proteins. These observations suggest that additional neisserial components are involved. Recent studies have indicated that neisserial porin, which can translocate into eukaryotic membranes, might be the factor responsible for actin rearrangement. The bacteria are incorporated into vacuoles and are transported to the basolateral surface of the cell. Factors allowing survival of the organism within the epithelial cell are now being elucidated. So and co-workers have shown that the *Neisseria* type 2 IgA$_1$ protease cleaves LAMP1 and promotes the survival of bacteria within epithelial cells. Infection of human epithelial cells by *N. meningitidis* and *Neisseria gonorrhoeae* increases the rate of degradation of LAMP1, a major integral membrane glycoprotein of late endosomes and lysosomes.[73] Nassif and colleagues have suggested that meningococcal *pilC* is upregulated and that pilus-mediated attachment may be important in crossing of the blood-brain barrier.[74]

Human Immunologic Response to Meningococcal Antigens

Goldschneider and associates have demonstrated that the percentage of people with bactericidal activity against *N. meningitidis* in their serum is inversely proportional to the incidence of meningococcal meningitis during the first 12 years of life.[75,76] At birth, as a result of maternal transfer of antibodies, approximately 50% of infants have bactericidal antibody titers. The prevalence of bactericidal antibody decreases after birth and reaches its nadir between 6 and 24 months of age. Thereafter, a linear increase in antibody occurs until age 12. In early adulthood, the prevalence of bactericidal antibody varies with the serogroup but ranges from 67% for group A to 86% for group B. These same investigators demonstrated the protective nature of bactericidal antibody against homologous serogroups during an epidemic situation. Only 3 of 54 sera from patients contained bactericidal antibody in prebleed specimens against the ultimately infecting serogroup, whereas 444 of 550 prebleed sera from matched control subjects who did not become infected contained homologous bactericidal antibody. Goldschneider and colleagues observed that systemic meningococcal disease developed in 38.5% of persons in a military recruit environment who lacked bactericidal antibody and acquired the epidemic strain through the nasopharynx. Their conclusion was that in the presence of nasopharyngeal colonization with a disease-causing strain, deficiency of circulating antimeningococcal antibodies is firmly associated with the establishment of meningococcemia. It appears that bactericidal antibodies are directed against both the capsular polysaccharide and other cell wall antigens, which may cross-react within the family Neisseriaceae and with other bacterial genera. Goldschneider and associates demonstrated that the meningococcal carrier state is an immunizing process and that production of antibodies to meningococci can be identified within 2 weeks of colonization.[75,76] Nontypeable meningococcal strains, which are seen in carrier studies in children, contain antigens that cross-react with the encapsulated strains, and bactericidal antibody to these strains develops after nasopharyngeal colonization. Goldschneider and co-workers also showed that serogroup-specific antibodies arise during the carrier state.

Studies of Robbins and associates indicate that serologic cross-reactions occur between meningococcal group A polysaccharide and *Bacillus pumilis* and that *E. coli* K1 antigen is immunologically and chemically identical to group B capsular polysaccharide.[77,78] These unrelated yet immunologically similar antigens may play a very important role in the development of natural immunity to the meningococcus and ultimately in protection against virulent meningococci. Cross reactivity has now been clearly demonstrated between neonatal tissue and group B capsular polysaccharide. Monoclonal antibodies specific for this capsule have been used to show that cross-reactivity exists between central nervous system, cardiac, liver, and renal glycoproteins[79] in the infant rat and group B polysaccharide. As the animal matures, the cross-reacting antigens persist in the central nervous system. These studies suggest that the poor immunogenicity of this polysaccharide may be attributable to the fact that it resembles host antigens.

It should be stressed that although specific antibody is generally protective, this immunity is not absolute. Greenwood and co-workers and Kayhty and associates documented illness in individuals with preexisting antibody titers that are considered protective.[80,81]

The exact role of local IgA antibody in protection or modulation of the carrier state is unknown. Plaut and colleagues have shown that the meningococcus produces a protease that cleaves the Fc fragment of secretory and serum IgA from the Fab portion of the molecule.[82] The impact of this enzyme on carriage is not known. However, production of this enzyme in *Neisseria* organisms is confined to the pathogenic members, the meningococcus and the gonococcus.[83]

The Meningococcal Carrier State

Carriage of *N. meningitidis* in the nasopharynx in otherwise healthy humans has been recognized since 1896. Like the carrier states seen in cases of cholera, diphtheria, and typhoid, the dichotomy between the presence of these dreaded organisms and absence of the associated disease process seemed a paradox to early investigators. Before the elucidation of distinct meningococcal serogroups, Dopter found organisms in the nasopharynx that had all the characteristics of meningococci but failed to agglutinate with antimeningococcic serum prepared from strains isolated from cerebrospinal fluid. He labeled these organisms parameningococci.[6] Considerable confusion arose, but subsequent investigators demonstrated that all four of the known serotypes, including the parameningococci of Dopter, could cause meningitis.

In 1908, Bruns and Hohn noted a close relationship between the carrier rate in a population and the onset, rise, and decline of an epi-

demic.[84] Glover noted the same association in the British Army military camps of World War I and believed that when the carrier rate exceeded 20%, the community was in danger of an epidemic, usually caused by the predominant carrier serotype.[8]

Transmission of meningococci from carrier to carrier is probably via the respiratory route. The rate of spread of the carrier state through a population has been the subject of a number of studies. During epidemics in military camps, the rate of new carrier acquisition can be very rapid, whereas in nonepidemic situations, both military and civilian, the rate of new carrier acquisition can be considerably slower, and the state of carriage can exist for prolonged periods. Rake demonstrated that carriers fall into three groups—chronic, intermittent, and transient—and that chronic carriers could be constantly affected for up to 2 years.[85] He also demonstrated that such factors as coryza unassociated with concomitant rises in other bacterial flora had no effect on the population of meningococci, whereas streptococcal pharyngitis or any other condition that increases other members of the resident flora of the nasopharynx causes a concomitant decrease in the number of meningococci present. Greenfield and colleagues studied carrier rates in families not exposed to clinically important meningococcal infection during a nonepidemic period. Eighty-eight percent of the strains isolated were groupable, with group B being the most common serogroup isolated.[86] During the 32-month observation period, 18% of the population were carriers at least once. The median duration of carriage was 9.6 months, and in 38% it exceeded 16 months. Adult men had the highest incidence of carriage, from 19% to 39%. The adult male introduced the organism into the household 50% of the time, and when such a pattern occurred, the carrier rate in the children and women in the family increased to levels comparable to those for adult men. The rate of transmission in these circumstances was considered low in comparison to most communicable pathogens, and it was estimated that at this level a susceptible person would have more than a 50% chance of escaping carriage even if continually exposed to household carriers for a 5-year period.

A combination of factors is probably responsible for the transition from nasopharyngeal carriage to invasive disease. We previously have pointed out the role of the encapsulation switching. Interestingly, organisms from healthy meningococcal carriers lacked the operons necessary for the synthesis, lipid modification, and transport of capsular polysaccharide.[87] Invasive meningococcal disease occurs primarily in persons who become newly infected with the organism.[88] Edwards and co-workers found that 31 of 36 patients had negative nasopharyngeal cultures during the 2 weeks before becoming ill and that 4 of these patients were culture negative the day before the development of disease.[88] The remaining 5 of 36 patients had positive cultures less than 4 days before the onset of illness. Other studies have shown that meningococcal epidemics occur not at times of high pharyngeal carriage but when the rates of acquisition of infection are increasing.[89] Coincident viral infection may affect the acquisition of meningococcal nasopharyngeal carriage. It has been noted that in a study of household contacts, individuals who had a recent history of symptoms of upper respiratory infection had a significantly higher carriage rate than did household members without such symptoms.[90] Moore and co-workers have shown that preceding *Mycoplasma* infection may be a cofactor in meningococcal meningitis in Chad.[91]

The carrier state is an immunizing process. Indirect evidence for this phenomenon is the fact that although military recruits have a high frequency of meningococcal carriage and disease, seasoned veterans have a much lower carriage rate and a disease incidence no different from that of the civilian population. In military recruits, antimeningococcal antibodies have been shown to persist for a minimum of 4 to 6 months after exposure. These antibodies are of the three major immunoglobulin classes and combine with group-specific and cross-reactive antigens.[75,76] Reller and associates demonstrated the development of bactericidal antibodies to the meningococcus in 38 military recruits who became colonized with nongroupable meningococcal strains. Thirty-nine percent of these men had bactericidal antibody to the homologous strains, and in addition, antibodies directed against groupable strains developed in 7% to 52%.[92] These same investigators found greatly enhanced (10- to 100-fold increase) bactericidal activity to known pathogenic strains of groups A, B, C, and Y after colonization with nongroupable meningococci, which suggests that these organisms may be at least as capable of stimulating cross-reactive antibody as groupable meningococci through either an initial or anamnestic response. A review of the meningococcal carrier state has been provided by Broome.[93]

EPIDEMIOLOGY OF MENINGOCOCCAL DISEASE

Recent epidemics in Africa, New Zealand, and Singapore indicate that this infection is still a worldwide major public health problem[94-96] Children previously and presently account for the greatest percentage of these cases. Meningococcal disease is still a major worldwide health problem. Feldman estimates that during the period 1939 to 1962, almost 600,000 cases of meningococcal disease developed around the world, more than 100,000 of which were fatal.[97]

The case rate during endemic situations varies widely and has increased in the United States over a 5-year period (1991-1996) from 0.84 to 1.3 per 100,000 population. In 2001, 2333 cases were reported to the Centers for Disease Control and Prevention (CDC).[98] Serogroup Y accounted for 33% of the typed isolates. Peltola and co-workers have pointed out that shifts in this age distribution of meningococcal disease in a population can forecast an epidemic situation. Relatively more cases arise in the 5- through 19-year-old group during epidemic than during nonepidemic circumstances.[99,100] Careful surveillance of age distribution patterns may be valuable in recognizing an epidemic during its inception.

Outbreaks of meningococcal infection account for fewer than 5% of reported cases in the United States but continue to occur in semi-closed populations, such as child care centers, military recruit camps, colleges, and school.

The case-fatality rate varies depending on the prevalence of disease, the nature of the infection, and the socioeconomic conditions of the society in which the infections occur. During endemic situations in industrialized countries, case-fatality rates can be as low as 7% for meningitis and as high as 19% for septicemia without meningeal involvement.[101] During epidemic situations in some Third World countries, mortality for meningitis can vary from 2% to 10% and mortality for septicemia can be as high as 70%.[102,103] In the United States an 8% case-fatality rate has been reported from major medical centers during endemic periods.[104]

The dramatic effect of antibiotics on the case-fatality rate can be seen by comparing two epidemics. Norton and Gordon described an epidemic in Detroit from 1929 to 1931 that involved 1272 patients. The overall case-fatality rate was 50%, with the highest mortality occurring in infants (84%) and in adults older than 40 years (72%).[9] During an epidemic in Chile in 1940 to 1943,[11] the case rate in the province of Valparaiso during 1942 was 188.1 per 100,000 population. In Santiago at the peak of the same epidemic, the case rate in infants was 838.1 per 100,000 population. The meningococcal serotype responsible for this epidemic was group A. Sulfonamides were used for treatment, and the case-fatality rate was 16%.

It is clear that serogroup A, B, and C strains have different epidemic potential.[105] Serogroup B strains cause epidemics usually in developed nations with attack rates of 50 to 100 cases per 10^5 population. Serogroup C disease occurs in both developed and less developed nations and can have attack rates as high as 500 cases per 10^5 population. Serogroup A epidemics occur in less developed nations and have attack rates usually as high as 500 cases per 10^5 population. In all instances, epidemics occur among the poorest groups, where crowding and lack of sanitation are common.

Over the past decade, areas of the world that have experienced recent epidemic meningococcal disease are Australia, Norway, the Netherlands, China, Egypt, Saudi Arabia, Kenya, and eastern Canada. Epidemics have occurred in schoolchildren in northern Georgia and Los Angeles County. Several reviews about the problems of meningo-

coccal epidemics in Africa have been written.[106,107] An epidemic of meningococcal disease has been occurring in New Zealand since 1991. The case rate has gone from 1.6/100,000 population in 1990 to 16.9/100,000 population in 1997. The predominate strain has had the phenotype B:4:P1.7b.4 which accounted for 84% of the cases by year 2000.[96] The case-fatality rate has been 4.5% and the diseases has disproportionately effected Maori and Pacific Island children in the northern part of North Island New Zealand.

An international outbreak of meningococcal disease caused by *Neisseria meningitidis* W135 occurred in association with the Hajj pilgrimage in 2000 and 2001[94] with a high attack rate not only among the pilgrims but also among household contacts of returning pilgrims.[95] Although vaccination may protect the pilgrims from invasive disease, the data show that returning pilgrims represent a sizeable reservoir of a highly transmissible and persistent W135 clone, which places their unvaccinated family contacts (and possibly the community at large) at risk of invasive disease.[95] *N. meningitidis* W-135 cases related to the ET-37 clone associated with the Haji outbreak have been reported since 2000 in countries in Europe, Africa, and Asia.

Epidemic meningococcal disease occurs during the dry season in the sub-Sahara regions of Africa with regularity. Because of the poor economic conditions of the countries involved, the inaccessibility of some of the regions, the paucity of the infrastructure, and the lack of funds available to international agencies, little has been done in terms of prevention until these epidemics begin. By that time, thousands of cases with a very high mortality have occurred, primarily in small children. The currently available vaccines have been shown to provide protection for a limited period in young children (between 2 and 4 years old).[108] Recent studies in Great Britain indicate that the development of meningococcal protein-capsular conjugate vaccine can overcome this problem if costs can be kept to a level that the less-well developed countries can afford.[109]

CLINICAL MANIFESTATIONS

Studies in Boston describing a 20-year experience have shown that *N. meningitidis* is the second most common cause of community-acquired adult bacterial meningitis.[110] The successful use of *Haemophilus influenzae* type B capsular conjugate vaccine has made *N. meningitidis* the leading cause of bacterial meningitis in children and young adults in the United States, with an overall mortality rate of 13% for meningitic disease. The clinical manifestations of meningococcal disease can be quite varied and can range from transient fever and bacteremia to fulminant disease with death ensuing within hours of the onset of clinical symptoms. Wolfe and Birbara[111] have described four clinical situations:

1. *Bacteremia without sepsis.* Admission is for an upper respiratory illness or viral exanthem. After recovery and frequently after discharge without specific antimicrobial therapy, the results of blood cultures are reported as positive for *N. meningitidis.* Sullivan and LaScolea recently reported three children with such occult bacteremia who recovered from meningococcal bacteremia spontaneously without antibiotics. The serum level of bacteremia in these children was low, from 22 to 325 organisms per milliliter of blood.[112]

2. *Meningococcemia without meningitis.* In these cases the patient's condition is septic, and signs of leukocytosis, skin rash, generalized malaise, weakness, headache, and hypotension develop on admission or shortly thereafter.

3. *Meningitis with or without meningococcemia.* In these patients, headache, fever, and meningeal signs are present with a cloudy spinal fluid. The state of the sensorium may vary widely from fully alert to completely depressed. Deep tendon and superficial reflexes are present. No pathologic reflexes are seen.

4. *The meningoencephalitic manifestation.* These patients are profoundly obtunded with meningeal signs and septic spinal fluid. The deep tendon and superficial reflexes are altered (either absent or rarely hyperactive). Pathologic reflexes are frequently present.

Variations of these manifestations can occur, and the patient can progress from one to the other during the course of disease.

The wide range of clinical expression requires a high index of suspicion and a careful search for clues of disease, particularly in an endemic situation in which a sporadic case is involved. Carpenter and Petersdorf in 53 such cases of meningococcal meningitis reported that headache, confusion, and stiff neck occurred as symptoms in less than half the patients.[113] In infants and small children, fever and vomiting are often the only complaints, and children are frequently not brought to the hospital until an insidious impairment in consciousness or convulsions occur.

The signs of meningococcal disease can vary widely. Petechial lesions are a common harbinger of this infection, but occasionally if the patient is not completely undressed when examined or if examination of mucous surfaces such as the palpebral conjunctiva is omitted, important telltale lesions can be missed (Fig. 208-1). The petechial rash is manifested as discrete lesions 1 to 2 mm in diameter most frequently on the trunk and lower portions of the body (Figs. 208-2 and 208-3). These lesions are commonly seen in clusters in areas where pressure may be applied to the skin by elastic in underwear or stockings, thus demonstrating the importance of completely disrobing the patient for an adequate examination. The petechial lesions can coalesce and form larger lesions that appear ecchymotic. These lesions may actually be secondary to subcutaneous hemorrhage, can occasionally be vesicular, and frequently desquamate as the patients recover. The petechiae correlate with the degree of thrombocytopenia and are clinically important as an indicator in the evolution of bleeding complications secondary to the disseminated intravascular coagulopathy (DIC) that ensues.

A number of authors have described another type of rash associated with meningococcal infection.[97,111] This rash is a maculopapular eruption that can vary somewhat in hue and can be mistaken for a wide variety of viral exanthems, particularly rubella (Fig. 208-4). This eruption is not purpuric or pruritic and is transient; it usually does not last more than 2 days and is frequently gone hours after first observation. Generalized muscle tenderness may also be an important differential sign. Occasionally, the pain from these myalgias is quite intense and causes the patient considerable discomfort.

The neurologic problems seen with meningococcal meningitis are somewhat different from those seen with other forms of purulent meningitis. Evidence of meningeal irritation is common except in the very young and old. Feigin and Dodge showed that focal neurologic signs and seizures were less common in meningococcal meningitis than in pneumococcal meningitis or in meningitis caused by *Haemophilus,* whereas levels of unconsciousness were very similar in the three diseases.[114] This observation correlates with postmortem findings described by Thomas in which focal cerebral involvement in meningococcal meningitis was rare. The cause of death was related to toxins produced by the agent or by cerebral edema and to secondary effects on the vital centers in the midbrain region.[115] Ducker and Simmons supported these clinical findings by observing that doses of meningococcal endotoxin that produced no effect intravenously when introduced into the ventricular system of dogs produced massive hemorrhagic pulmonary edema, subendocardial hemorrhage, hemorrhage and edema of both the mitral and tricuspid valves, visceral congestion, and adrenal hemorrhage.[116] These lesions are similar to those seen outside the central nervous system in soldiers dying of meningococcal meningitis and bacteremia.[117]

Brandtzaeg and co-workers have made major contributions to our understanding of the physiologic effects of lipooligosaccharide during sepsis and meningitis caused by *N. meningitidis.* Their studies have placed a pathogenetic rationale for the clinical states of infection described by Wolfe and Birbara.[111,118-123] Brandtzaeg and colleagues have demonstrated the ability to measure lipooligosaccharide in the plasma

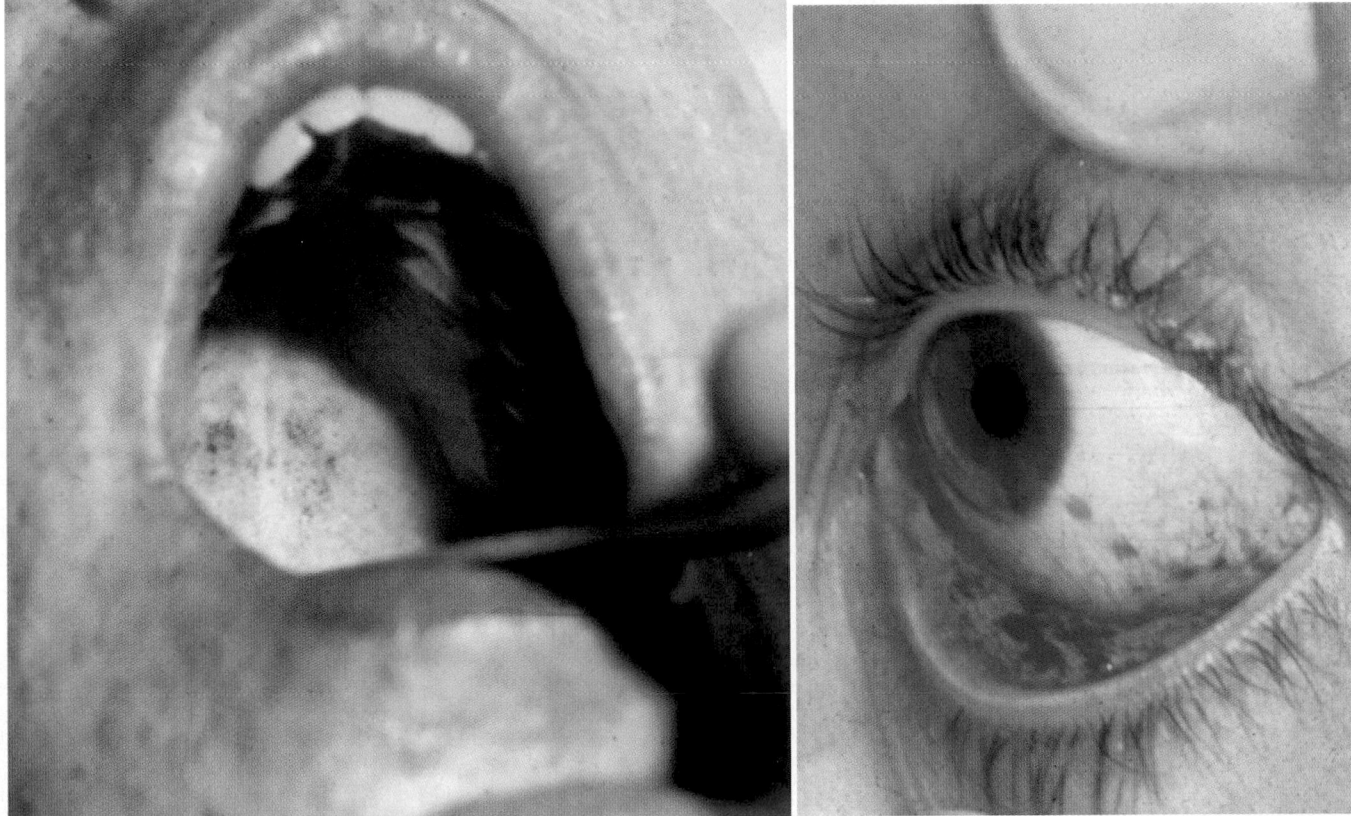

A　　　　　　　　　　　　　　**B**

FIGURE 208-1. *A,* Petechial rash on the hard palate in a patient with meningococcemia. *B,* Palpebral and conjunctival petechiae resulting from meningococcal sepsis.

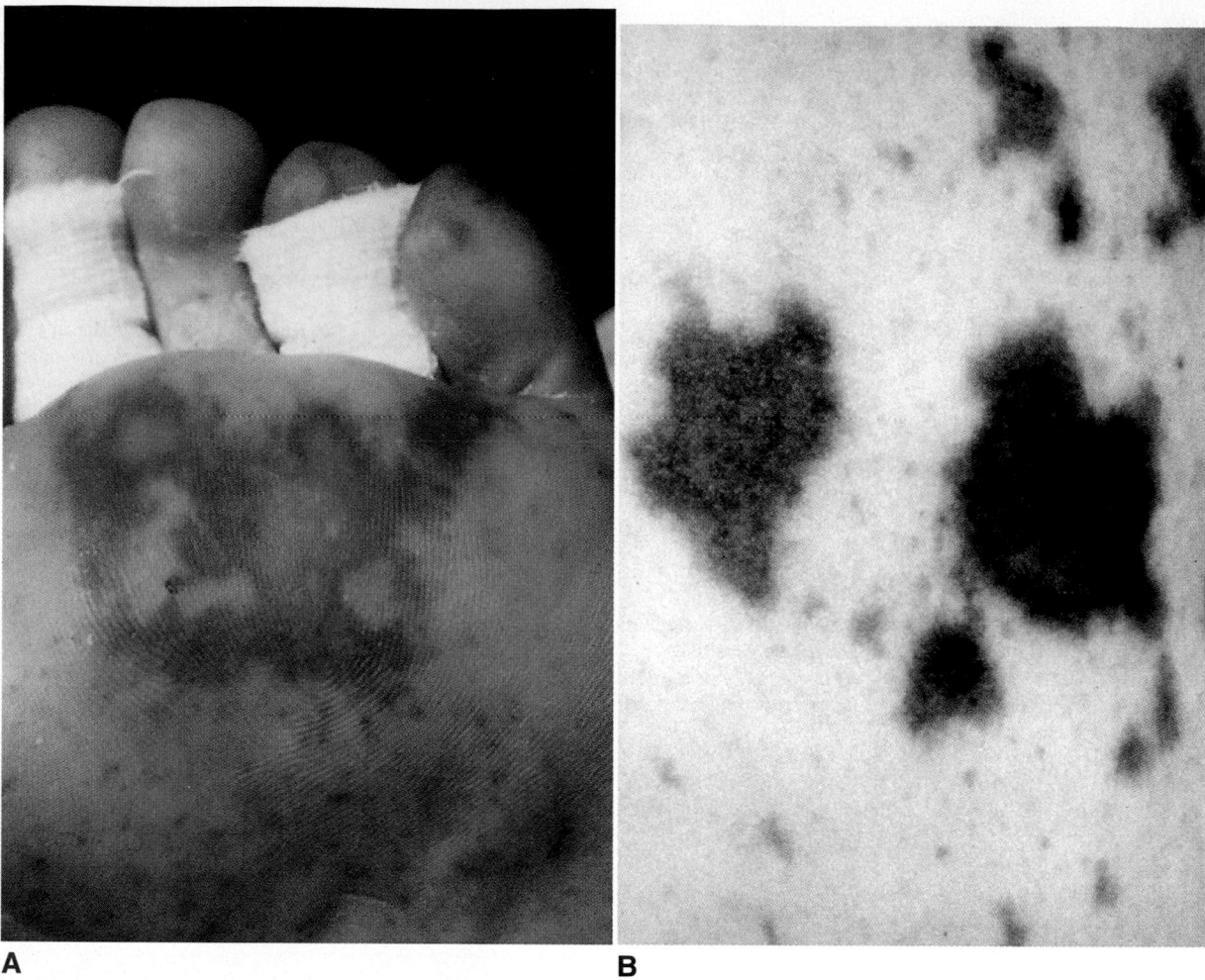

A   **B**

FIGURE 208-2. *A,* Subcutaneous ecchymoses on a sole resulting from meningococcal sepsis. *B,* Subcutaneous ecchymoses on the back resulting from meningococcal sepsis. *(Courtesy of Dr. Peter Densen.)*

and CSF of infected patients and have shown a close correlation between plasma lipooligosaccharide levels and prognosis. They have demonstrated that compartmentalization of lipooligosaccharide production correlates with the clinical findings in meningococcal infection.[120] Lipooligosaccharide levels in patients defined as having septicemia were high in plasma (median, 3500 ng/L) and low in CSF, whereas in patients with meningitis, lipooligosaccharide was detectable in the plasma of 3 of 19 patients and in the CSF of 18 of 19 patients with median levels of 2500 ng/L. Physiologic studies of meningococcal lipooligosaccharide in the plasma of infected patients revealed that it has a high sedimentation coefficient. Bacterial outer membrane fragments were found in the plasma of three patients. The plasma of one of these patients contained a bacterium covered with multiple, long membrane protrusions, thus indicating that surplus outer membrane (blebbing) does occur in vivo.[119] Mass spectrometric analysis of the endotoxin from patients with meningococcal sepsis indicated that it was of meningococcal origin rather than arising from the gastrointestinal tract as a result of increased permeability during infection.[123] Sedimentation analysis indicated that the majority of the lipooligosaccharide in these patients was not associated with high-density or low-density lipoproteins.

Outer membrane bleb formation by the group A meningococcus was first demonstrated by Cesarini and co-workers.[124] DeVoe and Gilchrist found that strains of meningococcal serogroups A, B, and C released membrane blebs in the log phase of growth but not in the lag phase.[125] The release of lipooligosaccharide from the surface of the meningococcus in the form of membrane blebs is now considered to be the principal factor associated with the high endotoxin levels in meningococcal sepsis.

The myocardial problems associated with this infection have been described.[126] Evidence of myocardial failure as manifested by a gallop rhythm, by congestive heart failure with pulmonary edema, and by high central venous pressure in the face of poor peripheral perfusion has been reported.[126] Treatment of the myocardial failure with cardiac glycosides has resulted in reversing this constellation of problems. Postmortem studies by Hardman[117] and by Gore and Saphir[127] have indicated that myocarditis of varying degrees of severity is present in over half the patients who die of meningococcal disease. More recent studies have also shown myocardial dysfunction in children with acute meningococcemia.[128] Acute meningococcemia was not fatal in children without evidence of myocardial dysfunction. In contrast, three of seven children with evidence of myocardial dysfunction died.

The shock state all too frequently dominates the clinical picture. The patient is poorly responsive, and peripheral vasoconstriction is maximal, with cyanotic, poorly perfused extremities. Arterial blood gas analysis demonstrates evidence of acidosis in the range of pH 7.25 to 7.3, and depending on the degree of shock, anoxia may be manifested by an arterial PO_2 below 70 mmHg. Probably the most dramatic consequence of this clinical problem is the presence of DIC. Clinical evidence of its occurrence can be obtained by documenting increasing petechiae within prescribed areas, gastric or gingival bleeding, or oozing at sites of venipuncture or intravenous infusions.

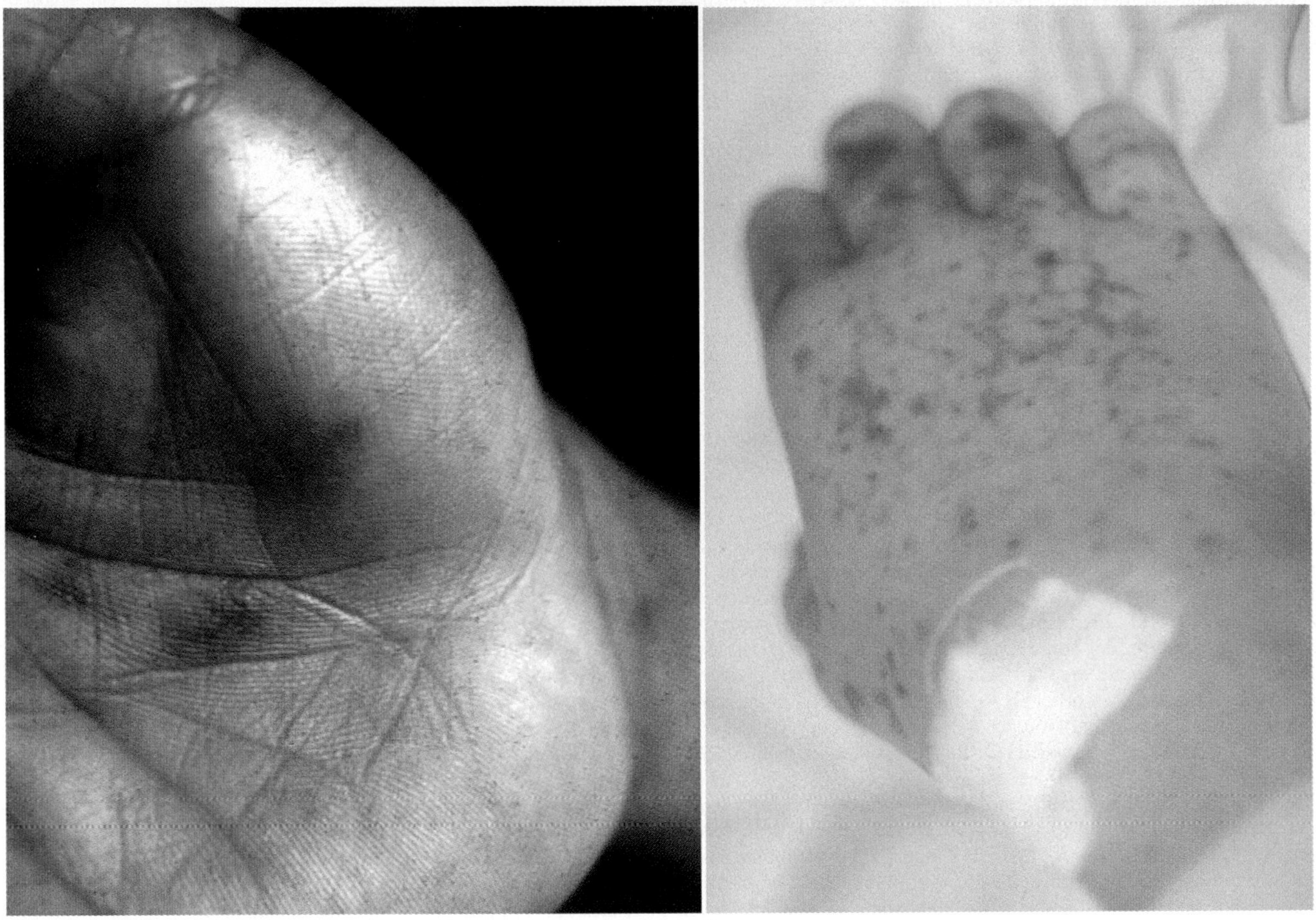

A   **B**

FIGURE 208-3. *A,* Embolic lesions on a palm secondary to meningococcal sepsis. ***B,*** Petechiae on the dorsum of a hand resulting from meningococcal sepsis. *(Courtesy of Dr. Peter Densen.)*

Either concomitant with the initial evaluation of the patient or later in the recovery phase of the illness, a number of unusual complications have been reported, including arthritis, pericarditis, conus medullaris syndrome, and cranial nerve dysfunction, particularly of the sixth, seventh, and eighth cranial nerves.[114,129-133] The pericarditis can cause massive tamponade. It is of interest that this complication may be unrelated to organism invasion of the pericardium but rather be due to an immunologic reaction or toxin. In the report of Pierce and Cooper, evidence of pericardial involvement occurred after two of the patients were in the recovery phase of their disease.[131] In one of these patients, the first symptoms of pericarditis occurred on the 20th day after the institution of therapy with penicillin. In the other patient, the first symptoms occurred 5 days after therapy began and recurred after pericardiocentesis and prednisone therapy on the 34th hospital day. This patient had a friction rub until the 49th hospital day and was not discharged until almost 3 months after admission. The incidence of this complication is approximately 19%. Cases of pericarditis occurred in the convalescent phase of the disease and in disease caused by the group C meningococcus. A recent report described serogroup W-135 in a patient with meningococcal myopericarditis.[131]

Chronic Meningococcemia

Persistent meningococcal bacteremia associated with low-grade fever, rash, and arthritis has been reported.[134-136] The distribution and appearance of the cutaneous lesions are identical to those seen in chronic gonococcemia, for which it is mistaken. Feldman has commented on

FIGURE 208-4. Rubella-like rash seen early in meningococcal sepsis.

a patient with chronic meningococcemia who appeared normal in every respect, including the ability to produce antibodies against the capsular polysaccharide of the infecting organism.[97] The frequency of meningococcus in the acute arthritis-dermatitis syndrome appears to be increasing.[135] Rompalo and co-workers compared the isolation of gonococcus and meningococcus from blood or synovial fluid from 1970 to 1972 with isolation of these organisms from 1980 to 1983.[136] The ratio of gonococcal to meningococcal isolates changed from 15 to 1 in 1970 to 1972 to 9 to 5 in 1980 to 1983. These authors believe that systemic meningococcal infection should figure more prominently in the differential diagnosis of the acute arthritis-dermatitis syndrome.

Complement Deficiency and Meningococcemia

The syndrome of chronic meningococcemia must be distinguished from the problem of recurrent episodes of meningococcal meningitis. Studies by Lim and co-workers have demonstrated an absence of the sixth complement component in such a patient.[137] In addition, at least one of the patients with recurrent meningococcal disease studied by Alper and colleagues lacked C3.[138] Studies by Petersen and associates indicated that human deficiency of C8 has been found in some persons with disseminated gonococcal infection and that this complement component is required for serum bactericidal activity against the gonococcus.[139] Ellison and co-workers have evaluated the complement system in 20 patients with first episodes of serious systemic meningococcal infection. Six of 20 had a complement deficiency. Three had deficiencies in a terminal complement protein or proteins, and three had deficiencies of multiple factors associated with underlying disease states.[140] Densen and co-workers have studied a family with properdin deficiency who had a high rate of fatal meningococcal disease.[141] These investigators demonstrated that the bactericidal defect could be corrected by vaccination of this population. Studies by Ross and co-workers suggest that vaccinating individuals deficient in late-complement components may shift the burden of host defense from serum bactericidal activity to phagocytosis.[142] These studies would stress the previously unrecognized importance of the complement system in protection against neisserial infections. The role of complement in meningococcal infection has been reviewed by Densen.[143]

Respiratory Infections with the Meningococcus

Meningococcal pneumonia has been recognized as a clinical syndrome for more than 80 years. Because of nasopharyngeal carriage of the meningococcus, establishing the diagnosis by sputum culture alone is hazardous. The incidence of sepsis associated with this type of meningococcal infection appears to be quite low.[144] Therefore, blood cultures may not be of value. Koppes and associates used transtracheal cultures to establish the diagnosis in 68 Air Force recruits with group Y meningococcal pneumonia.[144] In this series, a history of cough, chest pain, chills, and previous upper respiratory infection occurred in more than half of the patients. Rales and fever occurred in almost all patients, and evidence of pharyngitis was present in more than 80%. The disease involved more than one lobe in 40%, with the right lower and middle lobes involved most frequently. The prognosis was good, with no deaths occurring in the 68 patients with pneumonia. The association of meningococcal infection with preceding viral respiratory infection has been reported. Young and co-workers investigated an outbreak of meningococcal infection in an aged population, most of whom had serologic evidence of influenza.[145] Goldstein and associates have shown that pulmonary clearance of meningococci is diminished in animals previously exposed to an avirulent encephalomyocarditis virus.[146] In a study of the etiology of community-acquired pneumonia in Finland, N. meningitidis was implicated as the etiologic agent in 6 of 162 cases.[147]

A review of 58 cases of meningococcal pneumonia over a twenty-five year period revealed both marked changes in antibiotic therapy and variation of serogroups causing disease. Antibiotic therapy had shifted from primarily penicillin to cephalosporins over the past decade. In patients from whom organisms were isolated, serogroup Y was the most prevalent single serogroup causing disease (44%), fol-

lowed by serogroup B (18%), W-135 (16%), and C (14%). There were five fatalities (8.6%) in this study.[148]

Meningococcal upper respiratory tract infection (pharyngitis) associated with contacts of cases and as a prior symptom and sign in cases of serious meningococcal disease has been described.[149] Suggestions that pharyngeal inflammation is the predecessor to bacteremic dissemination have been made but are unsubstantiated.

Fulminant Meningococcal Epiglottitis

Fulminant meningococcal epiglottitis is a rare presentation of meningococcal infection. It was first reported as a syndrome in 1995, and since then five reports have been published. The diagnosis should be considered with the patient's clinical picture of sore throat, dysphagia, fever, muffled voice, and swollen supraglottic tissues, as seen on plain films, fiberoptic laryngoscopy, and cervical CT scan.[150]

Meningococcal Urethritis

Meningococci have been isolated from the urethra and can be the etiologic agent in urethritis. An association between orogenital sex and acquisition of the organism has been suggested.[151] In a population of homosexual males, the organism was isolated from the oropharynx (93% of isolates), rectum (6% of isolates), and urethra (1% of isolates).[151]

LABORATORY DIAGNOSIS OF MENINGOCOCCAL INFECTION

Definitive diagnosis of serious meningococcal infection has as a prerequisite the bacteriologic isolation of N. meningitidis from a usually sterile body fluid such as blood, CSF, or synovial, pleural, or pericardial fluid. CSF and blood are the most fruitful sources of positive cultures. In an analysis of 727 cases of meningococcal disease, Hoyne and Brown described the results of 400 blood cultures in which 51.4% were positive for meningococci.[152] Spinal fluid examination of 423 patients from the same series indicated that 94% were positive for gram-negative diplococci by either smear or culture for the meningococci. Carpenter and Petersdorf indicate that 46% of their cases of meningococcal meningitis were positive by CSF culture.[113] In an additional 12% of the cases, the diagnosis was made by smear of the spinal fluid and by the clinical manifestations. Levin and Painter studied 28 patients with culture-proven meningococcal disease, and in 22 of 27 patients tested the spinal fluid was positive, whereas 15 of 28 had positive blood cultures.[126] It is of interest that in 8 of 12 patients considered to have meningococcemia without clinical evidence of meningitis, spinal fluid cultures were positive. Feldman has quantitated the bacterial counts of meningococcal meningitis in CSF and reported a mean of 1.27×10^5 (1.5×10^2 to 6×10^7) organisms per milliliter.[153] The ability to see or to culture meningococci in petechial skin and mucosal lesions varies widely. Hoyne and Brown reported identification in 69.8% of the petechial smears examined.[152] Care should be taken with these specimens because of difficulty in interpretation. Studies of pericardial fluid have failed to demonstrate the organism by smear or culture.[130] Chemical and cytologic examination of spinal fluid in meningococcal infection can yield variable results. Carpenter and Petersdorf examined the spinal fluid of 58 patients with meningococcal meningitis.[113] The median leukocyte count was approximately 1200 with a range of less than 10 to 65,000/mm³. Approximately 75% had CSF glucose levels below 40 mg/dL. Unfortunately, spinal fluid/serum glucose ratios were not given. CSF protein levels ranged from 25 to more than 800 mg/dL, with the median value approximately 150 mg/dL. Although not commented on specifically by these authors, the cell type in untreated cases is almost always polymorphonuclear. Partially treated patients may have a pleomorphic spinal fluid.

Polymerase chain reaction has been used in the diagnosis of meningococcal meningitis by examination of CSF. The sensitivity and specificity of polymerase chain reaction for the diagnosis of meningococcal meningitis are greater than 90%. This technique has proven to be particularly useful in confirmation of the diagnosis in situations in which culture has little value because of prior antibiotic administration. Studies in Great Britain have shown that usefulness of multiplex

PCR in establishing the diagnosis of meningococcal disease.[154-157] PCR also has the capability of rapidly typing strains, a very useful adjunct in situations that appear to be an evolving epidemic.[154] PCR has now established itself as an important tool in the rapid diagnosis of meningococcal infection.

TREATMENT OF MENINGOCOCCAL INFECTIONS

The introduction of antibiotics has dramatically altered the prognosis of meningococcal disease. Today, the expected mortality under optimal conditions should not exceed 8% to 10%.[101,111] Random cases frequently fare poorer than those in an epidemic because medical personnel are not alerted to the diagnosis and may overlook the early signs and symptoms. The value of early diagnosis in lowering the mortality is exemplified by the results at Fort Dix, where an intense surveillance program was established between 1968 and 1969 and the mortality was less than 5%.

In addition to the use of antibiotics, the application of supportive care to treat the problems of DIC, shock, heart failure, prolonged mental obtundation, pericarditis, and pneumonia, which complicate this infection, has had a decided impact on prognosis.

Antibiotic Therapy

The era of chemotherapy for meningococcal infection began with a report of Schwentker and associates in 1937 that demonstrated that sulfonamides could be successfully used in the treatment of meningococcal meningitis and meningococcemia.[12] Feldman and co-workers confirmed these observations. A dramatic change occurred in the prognosis of epidemic meningitis.[158] As new antibiotics were introduced through the 1940s and 1950s, reports appeared that documented the efficacy of several agents used alone and in combination. Early studies of penicillin given in relatively low doses (120,000 units/day intramuscularly) indicated that it was not as effective as sulfonamides.[159] Using larger amounts of the drug (360,000 units/day intramuscularly), Kinsman and D'Alonzo demonstrated that treatment results with penicillin were identical to those with sulfonamides.[160] The efficacy of chloramphenicol as a therapeutic agent was demonstrated by McCrumb and co-workers.[161] In 15 patients treated with this drug, all survived, and only 1 patient had a complication secondary to the infection, ophthalmoplegia, which subsequently cleared.

The therapeutic efficacy of first-generation cephalosporins was studied in the 1960s. These agents produced variable results, and their use is now contraindicated in treating meningococcal infection.[162] Third-generation cephalosporins demonstrate excellent in vitro effectiveness against the meningococcus[163] and achieve central nervous system concentrations adequate to treat meningococcal meningeal infection (Table 208-2).

Sulfonamides now have a very limited role in the treatment of meningococcal infection. Studies by Schoenback and Phair[14] and by Love and Finland[167] revealed small populations of sulfonamide-resistant meningococci. In 1963, an epidemic of group B meningococcal infection occurred at Ford Ord, California, in which the infecting strain was resistant to sulfonamides.[18,168] Since that time, most isolates, primarily serogroups B and C in this country and group A from worldwide locations, have been resistant to sulfadiazine.[169-171]

Penicillin therapy for meningococcal infections is safe and effective. Almost all U.S strains remain sensitive to this antibiotic.[165] The drug can be administered intravenously or intramuscularly, but the intrathecal route is contraindicated because of the severe neurotoxicity of penicillin in high concentrations in the central nervous system. A goal of antibiotic therapy for meningitis is to establish concentrations of antibiotics in the spinal fluid that approximate 10 times the minimal inhibitory concentration of the organism for that agent.[172] A dose of 300,000 units/kg/day is recommended, with an upper limit of 24 million units/day as 2 million units every 2 hours.[173] Reports of penicillin-insensitive *N. meningitidis* have come from Great Britain, Spain, and less commonly, the United States.[174,175] In these cases, penicillin should never be used and third generation cephalosporins would be the agents of choice (care should be taken to choose an active cephalosporin[175]).

TABLE 208-2 Treatment and Prevention of Serious Meningococcal Infection

Problem	Treatment
Meningococcal meningitis and meningococcemia	Ceftriaxone, in children 25 mg/kg every 12 hours up to 1 g. Adult dose, 1 g IV every 12 hours.[164] Or penicillin G, 50,000 U/kg every 4 hours IV, up to 4 million U every 4 hours. If penicillin and cephalosporin allergic, chloramphenicol, 25 mg/kg every 6 hours IV up to 1 g every 6 hours.[173]
Antibiotic chemoprophylaxis for household or intimate contacts*	Rifampin: adults, 600 mg q12h for 2 days; children <1 mo, 5 mg/kg q12h for 2 days; children > 1 mo, 10 mg/kg q12h (maximum 600 mg) orally for 2 days. Ciprofloxacin: adults, 500 mg, single dose. Ceftriaxone: children <15 yr, 125 mg, single IM dose; adults, 250 mg, single dose[165,166]
Immunoprophylaxis	Monovalent A, monovalent C, bivalent A-C, or quadrivalent A, C, Y and W-135 vaccine is administered once by volume according to the manufacturer's instructions. The amount of polysaccharide delivered is usually 50 µg. Vaccination should be considered an adjunct to antibiotic chemoprophylaxis for household or intimate contacts of patients with meningococcal disease when appropriate serogroups are causing disease[165]

*Recommended groups for chemoprophylaxis, based on exposure to the case in the week prior to onset of illness.
- Household contacts and persons sharing the same living quarters, particularly young children
- Daycare center or child care contacts, frequent playmates of young children
- Close social contacts who were exposed to oral secretions in week prior to onset, such as by kissing, sharing eating utensils or toothbrushes

Relative resistance to penicillin is due to a reduced affinity of penicillin-binding proteins 2 and 3.[175] Spinal fluid levels of penicillin averaged 0.8 µg/mL on the first day of therapy. This concentration approximated the minimal inhibitory concentration for penicillin G for the most resistant isolate studied by this group. These strains were also relatively resistant to cefuroxime, but cefotaxime and ceftriaxone appear to be active against these strains in vitro. High-level resistance in β-lactamase–producing strains has also been reported. Although resistant meningococcal strains have been infrequently reported to date, clinicians should be alerted to the possibility of their occurrence in unexplained treatment failures or in cases of slowly resolving, documented meningococcal central nervous system infections. Chloramphenicol is an effective substitute in penicillin-allergic patients and should be administered intravenously in a dose of 100 mg/kg/day up to a maximum of 4 g/day in total dose.[173] Chloramphenicol-resistant strains have been reported but remain rare in the United States (see Chapter 80).[176] Third-generation cephalosporins, including cefotaxime, ceftriaxone, ceftizoxime, and ceftazidime, have been used successfully in the treatment of pediatric cases of meningococcal meningitis and treatment with ceftriaxone is the treatment of choice in the United States.[164] Penetration of second- and third-generation agents into spinal fluid has been studied (Table 208-3).[177] Ceftriaxone, cefotaxime, and ceftazidime achieve

TABLE 208-3 Susceptibilities of Meningococci, Kinetics, and Cerebrospinal Fluid Penetration of Selected Second- and Third-Generation Cephalosporins

Cephalosporin	Susceptibility (µg/mL)	CSF Concentration (µg/mL)	CSF Penetration (%)
Cefuroxime	<0.2-1.6	1.1-17.1	11.6-13.7
Ceftriaxone	<0.001	2.1-7.2	1.5-7.4
Cefotaxime	<0.008	1.2-83 (mean, 6.3)	4-54 (mean, 22.7)
Ceftazidime	0.007-0.5	2.5-30 (mean, 9.8)	14

Data from references 178-184.

levels in CSF several orders of magnitude greater than the susceptibility of the meningococcus to these agents. The duration of antibiotic therapy will vary somewhat with the manifestation of the disease and with the response of the patient. At present, when the meningococcus is sensitive to the agents just mentioned, 10 to 14 days of therapy is usually sufficient. A recent prospective study in 58 patients (44 confirmed and 14 probable) during an epidemic of serogroup B meningococcal disease indicated that benzyl penicillin G (8 to 12 million units/day) could be used for 3 days with an 8.6% mortality. Three of the five patients who died in this study, did so within 24 hours of admission. None of the surviving patients relapsed (mean follow-up was 23.9 months +/- 14.7 months).[178] This study was performed during an epidemic situation when awareness of the illness was high and such therapy should be reserved for epidemic situations, where cost of treatment may be a major factor and the antibiotic sensitivity is known.

Studies in England have suggested that administration of parenteral penicillin by practitioners as soon as the diagnosis was suspected led to a significantly more favorable outcome.[185,186] The doses given in the studies were not provided. Recent studies have confirmed the value of early treatment of invasive meningococcal infection to a favorable outcome.[187] Studies by Barquet and co-workers have shown that receipt of antibiotic therapy before hospital admission was associated with a reduced likelihood of death. In the patient group defined as having acute clinical infection, a single death occurred in 119 patients treated with antibiotics before admission as compared with 15 deaths in 329 similar patients ($P = .04$) who were not given prehospitalization therapy.

Supportive Care

Common complications of meningococcal disease are vascular collapse and shock, primarily caused by the effects of meningococcal lipooligosaccharide, which is a potent toxin. The cytokine tumor necrosis factor-α (TNF-α) may be a mediator of endotoxic shock because when it is injected into animals, it induces hypotension, metabolic acidosis, and death.[188-191] Studies in animals suggest that treatment or pretreatment with polyclonal[190] or monoclonal[192] antibodies against TNF-α could be beneficial in purpura fulminans. Girardin and co-workers have demonstrated that serum levels of TNF-α, interleukin-1 (IL-1), and interferon-γ correlated with the severity of meningococcemia in children.[193] At the present time, it is not known whether these cytokines play a deleterious or protective role in shock secondary to meningococcal sepsis. Brandtzaeg and co-workers have extensively studied this question during an epidemic in Norway.[118-123,189] These investigators showed that IL-6 and IL-1 are released into the serum and coexist with TNF-α and lipopolysaccharide in the systemic circulation during the initial phase of meningococcal septic shock. High levels of IL-6 and IL-1 are associated with a fatal outcome, and IL-1 was detected exclusively in patients who had high levels of IL-6, TNF-α, and lipopolysaccharide and a rapid fatal outcome. These investigators also showed that lipopolysaccharide was compartmentalized primarily in the plasma in patients with meningococcemia, whereas patients with meningitis had high levels in CSF and low or undetectable levels in plasma. In other studies, this group has shown that extensive complement activation occurs in fulminant cases of meningococcemia.[121] The results in these studies suggested that the lipopolysaccharide was an important activator of complement in systemic meningococcal disease and that complement-activating products in concert with other mediators may contribute to the multiple organ failure and death occurring in the most severe cases.[121] New therapies are emerging that may have a significant impact on the management of meningococcal sepsis. Preliminary evaluation of the administration of a recombinant protein composed of the N-terminal fragment of human bactericidal/permeability-increasing protein in children with meningococcal sepsis has been encouraging. Data from the phase III, randomized, placebo-controlled trial indicate that administration of recombinant bactericidal permeability increasing protein (rBPI 21) reduces clinically significant morbidities and improves the functional outcome of children with severe meningococcemia.[194] No statistically significant benefit in mortality was demonstrated. Because of the rare incidence of disease and the rapidity of death in this study, the trial was substantially underpowered to detect a statistically significant mortality advantage. Before the completion of the trial, the probability that the study might have been underpowered to detect a significant reduction in mortality was recognized. An attempt at selecting a previously unvalidated composite end point to increase the meaningful event rate for the primary end point proved unsuccessful. Significant improvements were seen in other prospectively defined outcome variables that suggest an overall substantial benefit of therapy with rBPI21 in children with severe meningococcemia.

Clinical studies in patients with septic shock treated with recombinant activated protein C substitution (Xigris, drotrecogin alfa) have demonstrated its safety and efficacy. The incidence of serious bleeding was increased in the drotrecogin alfa treated group.[195] A study of recombinant activated protein C substitution on imminent peripheral necroses and outcome was performed on 12 patients, five of whom had meningococcal sepsis. This study concluded that protein C limited the extent of tissue necrosis but the study was too small to make any recommendations on the use of protein C in sepsis related purpura fulminans and shock.[196] Whenever a patient with meningococcal sepsis and shock is being considered for drotrecogin alfa therapy, the exclusion criteria used in the PROWESS trial should be reviewed and applied.[195,197] Meningococcal shock patients who evidence bleeding should be excluded.

In every case of systemic meningococcal infection, the potential for shock must be always considered. Observation for shock and its therapy[198-201] are best accomplished in an intensive care unit. The use of steroids, particularly in patients with evidence of purpura fulminans and concomitant adrenal hemorrhage (Waterhouse-Friderichsen syndrome), is still controversial. In the 1950s, several investigators recommended the use of corticosteroid replacement therapy. However, the studies of Belsey and colleagues were inconclusive in demonstrating a beneficial effect of the application of low-dose steroid in meningococcal infection.[202] In a study of the clinical effect of early adjunctive dexamethasone therapy in management of adults with bacterial meningitis, Thomas and co-workers could not demonstrate differences in outcome as measured by neurologic sequellae. They did demonstrate that antibiotic penetration into the cerebrospinal fluid was impaired and cautioned about the effect this might have on outcomes in patients with borderline sensitive organisms.[203]

As pointed out earlier, the problem of DIC is ominous. Petechiae are frequent accompaniments of meningococcal sepsis. The development of increasing petechial lesions, confluent ecchymoses, persistently bleeding venipuncture sites, and bleeding gums despite adequate antimicrobial therapy and supportive care is indicative of DIC. Heparin treatment of this complication of meningococcal disease is probably not indicated.[204] As many patients can be harmed by the inappropriate treatment of DIC as by DIC itself. To complicate matters, in severe DIC the problem of plasmin activation with fibrinolysis becomes a clinical reality. It appears that impairment of the protein C anti-coagulation pathway is critical to the thrombosis associated with sepsis and to the development of purpura fulminans in meningococcemia. This occurs because protein C activation is impaired, a finding consistent with the down-regulation of the thrombomodulin-endothelial protein C receptor pathway.[205]

Other major life-threatening complications necessitating therapy include adult respiratory distress syndrome, neurologic sequelae ranging from coma to diabetes insipidus, pneumonia that is not necessarily meningococcal but may be secondary to aspiration during the obtunded state, and pericarditis. This last problem can be insidious and can appear in the convalescent stage of disease. Awareness that it can occur will readily lead to its diagnosis and treatment.

The ability to define the outcome of meningococcal sepsis based on a number of indicators has been studied extensively.[206-208] Kornelisse and co-workers have used a set of objective indicators, including the C-reactive protein level, base excess, serum potassium level, and platelet count. This system was predictive of death or survival in 86% of the patients studied.[206]

Studies have shown that children with meningococcal sepsis have higher than normal concentrations of plasminogen activator inhibitor 1 (PAI-1) in plasma. It has been found that children with the functional deletion/insertion (4G/5G) polymorphism in the promoter region of PAI-1 produce higher concentrations of PAI-1, develop more severe coagulopathy and are at greater risk of death during meningococcal sepsis.[209]

Chemoprophylaxis of the Meningococcal Carrier

Shortly after the clinical use of sulfonamides for the treatment of serious meningococcal disease, it became apparent that short courses of the sulfadiazine resulted in the disappearance of meningococcal carriage for prolonged periods.[210,211] As Feldman points out, despite the arguments about the relationship "if there are no carriers, there are no cases," the use of sulfonamides to reduce carrier rates did decrease the number of cases.[97]

Treatment of the meningococcal carrier state with sulfonamides eradicated carriage quickly and for prolonged periods.[212] The length of time was a function of the initial dose of sulfonamides, and with doses as high as 8 g the carrier rate was reduced from approximately 45% to less than 10% at 16 weeks. Cheever demonstrated that after two doses of 3 g and 2 g of sulfadiazine the carrier rate dropped from 79% to 0% in 72 hours.[213] On military bases and in closed environments such as boarding schools, institutions, and family units in which cases arose, this form of chemoprophylaxis was effective in disrupting the spread of meningococcal infection.

With the recognition of widespread sulfonamide-resistant meningococci and the failure of sulfadiazine to have an impact on the epidemic at Fort Ord,[15,16,168] these agents have been abandoned for meningococcal chemoprophylaxis except in instances in which the meningococcal case strains are known to be sulfa sensitive.

The search for new agents for chemoprophylaxis has been extensive. Penicillin has proved ineffective for several reasons: long-acting mixtures do not eradicate nasopharyngeal carriage, and although massive doses cause people to become noncarriers, the carrier state recurs promptly after discontinuation of use of the drug.[97,214] Minocycline and rifampin have been shown to eradicate the carrier state rapidly, and this eradication persists for up to 6 to 10 weeks after treatment.[215,216] Problems occur with both drugs. Minocycline has been shown to cause vertigo, probably secondary to an effect on the vestibular system.[217] Rifampin treatment can result in the emergence of rifampin-resistant meningococci in 10% to 27% of patients treated.[218] In addition, rifampin causes red urine in almost all patients, which can be quite disconcerting unless some forewarning is given. Rifampin should be avoided in pregnant women and may reduce efficacy of oral contraceptives. Studies by Pugsley and co-workers have demonstrated in 21 persistent meningococcal nasopharyngeal carriers that ciprofloxacin, 500 mg every 12 hours for 5 days, eradicated the meningococcus from the nasopharynx in 100% of individuals for up to 13 days after the completion of therapy. An untreated comparative control group had a carriage rate of 85% at that time.[219] Gilja and co-workers used a single dose of 400 mg of ofloxacin in a controlled study and showed that it can eradicate nasopharyngeal carriage for up to 33 days in 97% of subjects.[220] A single dose of ceftriaxone (250 mg intramuscularly for adults and 125 mg for children younger than 15 years) has also been shown to eradicate nasopharyngeal carriage for 14 days.[221] A single 500-mg dose of azithromycin has been found to be as effective as riafampin in eradicating meningococci from the nasopharynx of asymptomatic carriers.[222]

The recommended therapy for meningococcal prophylaxis has been expanded to include either rifampin, ciprofloxacin, or ceftriaxone[165] (see Table 208-2).

A number of other agents active against meningococci in vitro have been tested but have failed to provide prophylaxis. These agents include erythromycin, trimethoprim, cephalexin, oxytetracycline, and nalidixic acid. Hoeprich has studied a number of these drugs and speculates that the primary factor determining effectiveness as a meningococcal prophylactic agent is the ability to achieve bactericidal levels in tears and saliva.[223]

The question of who should receive prophylaxis has concerned public health officials since the advent of effective chemoprophylaxis. Initially with sulfonamides, little discrimination between high-risk and low-risk populations was attempted, and the drug was administered very widely to people without the remotest increased risk of disease. Since the clinical emergence of sulfa resistance and the problem in finding agents that are safe and effective, more attention has been paid to the populations at greatest risk who need chemoprophylaxis. During epidemics and in endemic situations in civilian populations, household contacts have been shown to be at increased risk of infection.[9,11,104] Analysis by the CDC meningococcal surveillance group showed that the attack rate in this group was 500 to 800 times greater than that determined for the general population studied.[104] Similar high-risk situations exist in closed populations such as in some college dormitories, long-term care hospitals, nursery schools,[224] and military barracks. In the community, chemoprophylaxis is recommended for household contacts, daycare center members, and anyone exposed to the patient's oral secretions, but not school, transportation, or office contacts. Secondary cases usually occur within 10 days of the primary case, but longer intervals have been described. Close surveillance of this group for at least 10 days would ensure prompt treatment of any secondary cases that might arise in the absence of effective chemoprophylaxis. Beginning chemoprophylaxis more than 2 weeks after exposure to the index case would be too late to prevent secondary cases. Hospital personnel are not at increased risk and in general should not receive chemoprophylaxis[225]; however, medical staff who have an intimate exposure such as mouth-to-mouth resuscitation or secretions aerosolized during endotracheal intubation should receive prophylaxis.[97,226]

Immunoprophylaxis of Meningococcal Infection

Subsequent to the problem of prevention of epidemic meningococcal disease on military recruit bases after the emergence of sulfa-resistant meningococci, an intense effort was directed at the development of a vaccine for prevention of meningococcal infections in this high-risk population. The result was the development of two vaccine preparations derived from the capsular polysaccharide of groups A and C meningococci. Artenstein and co-workers demonstrated the effectiveness of the group C vaccine in studies of U.S. Army recruits.[17] Only 1 case of meningococcal disease occurred among 13,763 vaccinees, whereas 38 bacteriologically proven cases occurred in a control group of 68,072. This vaccine resulted in an 87% reduction in disease, which was statistically significant. Makela and associates showed that administration of group A polysaccharide to Finnish military recruits significantly lowered the incidence of disease caused by this serogroup when compared with an unvaccinated control population.[227] Studies from Finland during a group A epidemic demonstrated the effectiveness of this vaccine in children 3 months to 5 years of age.[16] Studies from Africa by Reingold and colleagues indicate that efficacy in this population 1 year after serogroup A vaccination is less than 30% in children younger than 4 years.[108] The immunologic response of the group C vaccine in children younger than 2 years is poor, and studies from Brazil indicate that group C vaccine is not protective in children younger than 24 months.[228] Studies of the immune response to the A and C vaccine by Gold and co-workers in infants have demonstrated that detectable levels of antibody are generated but that these levels are significantly lower than the levels in older children.[229] In adults, the duration of group C antibody titer persisted for 2 to 4 years after vaccination, and in children studied in Egypt who were vaccinated with group A polysaccharide, protection lasted at least 2 years.[230,231] The vaccine is safe.[232,233] Reactions appear to be limited to local erythema at the site of injection in approximately 4% and some increased irritability in young children in about 6% of the vaccine recipients. One instance of immunologic hyporesponsiveness to group C antigen was reported in a population of young adult volunteers who had received group A vaccine contaminated with trace amounts of group C polysaccharide.[234] It is assumed that this hyporesponsiveness represents an example of low-dose tolerance in humans. Commercial vaccine materials are now carefully tested to ensure that such cross-contamination does not occur. Because the meningococcal vaccines are poorly immunogenic in children younger than 2 years and because of the lack of a vaccine to the serogroup B meningococcus, chemoprophylaxis is recommended in lieu of vaccine for the prevention of secondary cases of meningococcal disease in daycare centers.[235]

The use of these vaccines in developing countries in epidemic areas has become increasingly important. Factors such as underlying parasitic infections, the state of nutrition, and age of the vaccine recipient play a role in the response to vaccination.[236]

Current commercial vaccines include a quadrivalent product containing polysaccharides of groups A, C, Y, and W-135.[233] No vaccine is presently available for use in prevention of group B disease. Group B capsular polysaccharide is not sufficiently immunogenic to produce a reliable antibody response in humans to be effective. Several solutions to this problem are being studied, including a search for other cell wall antigens that are capable of eliciting bactericidal antibodies against B meningococci with a minimum of serious side effects.

With the increased frequency of meningococcal disease caused by serogroup C, the CDC has provided recommendations for the evaluation and management of suspected outbreaks. These recommendations include confirmation of the diagnosis, administration of chemoprophylaxis to appropriate contacts, enhancement of surveillance, investigation of linkage between cases, utilization of subtyping of organisms, determination of whether the outbreak is organizational (nursery school, university, etc.) or community based, definition of the population at risk, calculation of the attack rate, and determination of the target group for vaccination.

Vaccine Recommendations

In the United States, routine vaccination with the tetravalent vaccine is not recommended because of its relative ineffectiveness in children younger than 2 and the relatively short duration of protection.[237] The vaccine is recommended for use in control of serogroup C meningococcal outbreaks. An outbreak is defined as the occurrence of three or more confirmed or probable cases of serogroup C meningococcal disease during a period of less than 3 months with a resulting primary attack rate of at least 10 cases per 100,000 population.[237] It is recommended that these principles may be applicable to outbreaks caused by other vaccine preventable meningococcal serogroups, A, Y, and W135. College freshmen, particularly those living in dormitories are at modestly increased risk for meningococcal disease compared with persons of the same age who are not attending college. These individuals should be educated about the risks of meningococcal infection and vaccination. The vaccine should be offered to those who are interested.[238] Health care providers need not initiate discussion of the meningococcal tetravalent vaccine as part of routine medical care.[239]

New vaccines against the meningococcus are under development, as well as methods to enhance the immune response to current vaccines. The meningococcal C polysaccharide conjugate vaccine has been licensed in Europe and conjugate vaccines to the serogroups A, Y, and W135 are being developed.[240,241] The available meningococcal C conjugate vaccines are composed of the C polysaccharide conjugated with CRM-197 mutant diphtheria toxin or tetanus toxoid. A three vaccination protocol was successful in evoking high titers by 4 months of age and re-immunization at one year demonstrated a brisk memory response. Preterm and term infants also responded very well to this vaccine.[242] Studies of vaccine efficacy in toddlers and teenagers indicated an overall reduction of meningococcal C infection of 92% in the vaccinated group.[243] The vaccine has proven to be safe in the groups tested. In addition to the prevention of meningococcal diseases, there appears to have been significant reduction of nasopharyngeal carriage of the meningococcal C organism from 1999 to 2000 in the vaccinated populations.[244] The vaccine also appears to have reduced the attack rate in the unvaccinated population by 67%.[245]

REFERENCES

1. Vieusseaux M. Memoire sur le maladie qui a regne a Geneve au printemps de 1805. J Med Chir Pharmacol. 1805;11:163.
2. Hedrich AW. The movements of epidemic meningitis, 1915-1930. Publ Hlth Rep. 1931;46:2709.
3. Weichselbaum A. Ueber die Aetiologie der akuten Meningitis cerebrospinalis. Fortschr Med. 1887;5:573.
4. Kiefer F. Zur differential Diagnose des Erregers der epidemischen Cerebrospinalmeningitis und der Gonorrhoea. Berl Klin Wochenschr. 1896;33:628.
5. Albrecht H, Ghon A. Uber die Aetiologie und pathologische Anatomie der Meningitis cerebro spinalis epidemica. Wien Klin Wochenschr. 1901;14:984.
6. Dopter C. Etude de quelques germes isoles du rhino-pharynx, voisans du meningocoque (parameningocoques). C R Soc Biol (Paris). 1909;67:74.
7. Flexner S. The results of the serum treatment in thirteen hundred cases of epidemic meningitis. J Exp Med. 1913;17:553.
8. Glover JA. The cerebrospinal fever epidemic of 1917 at "X" depot. J R Army Med Corps. 1918;30:23.
9. Norton JF, Gordon JE. Meningococcus meningitis in Detroit in 1928-1929. I. Epidemiology. J Prev Med. 1930;4:207.
10. French MR. Epidemiological study of 383 cases of meningococcus meningitis in the city of Milwaukee, 1927-1928 and 1929. Am J Publ Hlth. 1931;21:130.
11. Pizzi M. A severe epidemic of meningococcus meningitis in Chile, 1941 and 1942. Am J Publ Hlth. 1944;34:231-238.
12. Schwentker FF, Gelman S, Long PH. The treatment of meningococcic meningitis with sulfonamide. Preliminary report. JAMA. 1937;108:1407.
13. Kuhns DM, Nelson CT, Feldman HA, et al. The prophylactic value of sulfadiazine in the control of meningococcic meningitis. JAMA. 1943;123:335-339.
14. Schoenback EB, Phair JJ. The sensitivity of meningococci to sulfadiazine. Am J Hyg. 1948;47:177-186.
15. Gauld JR, Nitz RE, Hunter DH, et al. Epidemiology of meningococcal meningitis at Fort Ord. Am J Epidemiol. 1965;82:56-72.
16. Bristow MW, Van Peenen PFD, Volk R. Epidemic meningitis in naval recruits. Am J Publ Hlth. 1965;55:1039-1045.
17. Artenstein MS, Gold R, Zimmerly JG, et al. Prevention of meningococcal disease by group C polysaccharide vaccine. N Engl J Med. 1970;282:417-420.
18. Hebeler BH, Young FE. Autolysis of Neisseria gonorrhoeae. J Bacteriol. 1976;122:385-392.
19. Holbein BE. Enhancement of Neisseria meningitidis infection in mice by addition of iron bound to transferrin. Infect Immun. 1981;34:120-125.
20. West WF, Sparling PF. The response of Neisseria gonorrhoeae to iron limitation: Alterations in expression of membrane proteins without apparent siderophore production. Infect Immun. 1985;47:388-394.
21. Dyer D, West EP, Sparling PF. Effects of seven carrier proteins on the growth of pathogenic Neisseria with heme-bound iron. Infect Immun. 1987;55:2171.
22. Gorden MH, Murray EG. Identification of the meningococcus. J R Army Med Corps. 1915;5:411.
23. Scherp HW, Rake GJ. Studies on the meningococcus. VIII. The type I specific substance. J Exp Med. 1935;61:753.
24. Clapp FL, Phillips SW, Stahl HJ. Quantitative use of Neufeld reaction with special reference to titration of type III anti-pneumococcic sera. Proc Soc Exp Biol Med. 1935;33:302.
25. Branham SE, Carlin SA. Comments on a newly recognized group of the meningococcus. Proc Soc Exp Biol Med. 1942;49:141-144.
26. Branham SE. Serological relationship among meningococci. Bacteriol Rev. 1953;17:175-188.
27. Branham SE. Reference strains for the serologic groups of meningococcus (Neisseria meningitidis). Int Bull Bacteriol Nomenclat Taxon. 1958;8:1-15.
28. Slaterus K. Serological typing of meningococci by means of microprecipitation. Antonie Van Leeuwenhoek. 1961;27:304-315.
29. Evans JR, Artenstein MS, Hunter DH. Prevalence of meningococcal serogroups and a description of new groups. Am J Epidemiol. 1968;87:643-646.
30. Ding S, Ye R, Zhang H. Three new serogroups of Neisseria meningitidis. J Biol Stand. 1981;9:305-315.
31. Ashton FE, Ryan A, Diena B, et al. A new serogroup (L) of Neisseria meningitidis. J Clin Microbiol. 1983;17:722-727.
32. Gotschlich EC, Liu TY, Artenstein MS. Preparation and immunochemical properties of the group A, group B, and group C meningococcal polysaccharides. J Exp Med. 1969;129:1349-1365.
33. Bundle DR, Jennings JH, Kenny CP. Studies on the group specific polysaccharide of Neisseria meningitidis serogroup X and an improved procedure for its isolation. J Biol Chem. 1974;249:4797-4801.
34. Robinson JA, Apicella MA. Isolation and characterization of Neisseria meningitidis groups A, C, X and Y polysaccharide antigens. Infect Immun. 1970;1:8-14.
35. Apicella MA. Identification of a subgroup antigen on the Neisseria meningitidis group C capsular polysaccharide. J Infect Dis. 1974;129:147-153.
36. Apicella MA. Immunological and biochemical studies of meningococcal C polysaccharide isolated by diethylaminoethyl chromatography. Infect Immun. 1976;14:106-113.
37. Watson RG, Marinetti GV, Scherp HW. The specific hapten of group C (group II) meningococcus. II. Chemical nature. J Immunol. 1958;81:337-344.
38. Brandt BL, Artenstein MS, Smith CD. Antibody response to meningococcal polysaccharide vaccines. Infect Immun. 1973;8:590-596.
39. Bhattacharjee AK, Jennings HJ, Kenny CP, et al. Structural determination of the sialic acid polysaccharide antigens of Neisseria meningitidis serogroup B and C with carbon 13 nuclear magnetic resonance. J Biol Chem. 1975;250:1926-1932.

40. Maloney PC, Schneider H, Brandt BL. Production and degrading of serogroup B *Neisseria meningitidis* polysaccharide. Infect Immun. 1972;6:657-661.

41. Wyle FA, Artenstein MS, Brandt BL, et al. Immunologic response of man to group B meningococcal polysaccharide vaccines. J Infect Dis. 1972;126:514-522.

42. Bhattacharjee AK, Jennings JH, Kenny CP. Characterization of 3-deoxy-D-manno-octulosonic acid as a component of the capsular polysaccharide antigen from *Neisseria meningitidis* serogroup 29E. Biochem Biophys Res Commun. 1974;61:489-493.

43. Griffiss JM, Brandt BL, Broud DO. Human immune response to various doses of group Y and W135 meningococcal polysaccharide vaccines. Infect Immun. 1982;37:205-208.

44. Mandrell RE, Zollinger WD. Lipopolysaccharide serotyping of *Neisseria meningitidis* by hemagglutination inhibition. Infect Immun. 1977;16:471-475.

45. Jennings HL, Johnson KG, Kenne L. The structure of the R-type oligosaccharide core obtained from some lipopolysaccharides of *Neisseria meningitidis*. Carbohydr Res. 1983;121:233-241.

46. Gamian A, Beurret M, Michon F, et al. Structure of the L2 lipopolysaccharide core oligosaccharides of *Neisseria meningitidis*. J Biol Chem. 1992;267:922-925.

47. Jones DM, Borrow R, Fox AJ, et al. The lipooligosaccharide immunotype as a virulence determinant in *Neisseria meningitidis*. Microbiol Pathol. 1992;13:219-224.

48. Verheul AFM, Snippe H, Poolman JT. Meningococcal lipopolysaccharides: Virulence factor and potential vaccine component. Microbiol Rev. 1993;57:34-49.

49. Estabrook MM, Baker CJ, Griffiss JM. The immune response of children to meningococcal lipooligosaccharides during disseminated disease is directed primarily against two monoclonal antibody-defined epitopes. J Infect Dis. 1993;167:966-970.

50. Gold R, Wyle FA. New classification of *Neisseria meningitidis* by means of bactericidal reactions. Infect Immun. 1970;1:479-484.

51. Gold R, Winklehake JL, Mars RS, et al. Identification of epidemic strain of group C *Neisseria meningitidis* by bactericidal serotyping. J Infect Dis. 1971;124:593-597.

52. Frasch CE, Chapman SS. Classification of *Neisseria meningitidis* group B into distinct serotypes. III. Application of a new bactericidal-inhibition technique to distribution of serotypes among cases and carriers. J Infect Dis. 1973;127:149-154.

53. Frasch CE, Golschlich EC. Noncapsular surface antigens of *Neisseria meningitidis*. In: Weinstein L, Fields BN, eds. Seminars in Infectious Diseases. New York: Stratton; 1979:304-337.

54. Broud DD, Griffiss JM, Baker CJ. Heterogeneity of serotypes of *Neisseria meningitidis* that cause endemic disease. J Infect Dis. 1979;140:465-470.

55. Kawula TH, Spinola SM, Klapper DG, et al. Localization of a conserved epitope and an azurin-like domain in the H.8 protein of pathogenic *Neisseria*. Mol Microbiol. 1987;1:179-185.

56. Barlow AK, Heckels JE, Clarke IN. Molecular cloning and expression of *Neisseria meningitidis* class 1 outer membrane protein in *Escherichia coli* K-12. Infect Immun. 1987;55:2734-2740.

57. Frasch CE, Zollinger WD, Poolman JT. Proposed schema for identification of serotypes of *Neisseria meningitidis*. In: Schoolnik GK, ed. The Pathogenic Neisseria. Washington, DC: American Society for Microbiology; 1985:519-524.

58. Rappuoli R. Reverse vaccinology, a genome-based approach to vaccine development. Vaccine. 2001;19:2688-2691.

59. Selander RK, Caugant DA, Ochman H, et al. Methods of multilocus enzyme electrophoresis for bacterial populations genetics and systematics. Appl Environ Microbiol. 1986;132:2855-2861.

60. Olyhoek T, Crowe B, Achtman M. Epidemiological analysis and geographic distribution of *Neisseria meningitidis* group A. In: Schoolnik GK, ed. The Pathogenic Neisseria. Washington, DC: American Society for Microbiology; 1985:530-535.

61. Caugant DA, Mocca IF, Frasch CE, et al. Genetic structure of *Neisseria meningitidis* populations in relation to serogroup, serotype, and outer membrane protein pattern. J Bacteriol. 1987;169:2781-2792.

62. Pinner R, Spellmam P, Stephens DS. Evidence for functionally distinct pili expressed by *Neisseria meningitidis*. Infect Immun. 1991;59:3169-3175.

63. DeVoe IW, Gilchrist JE. Piliation and colonial morphology among laboratory strains of meningococci. J Clin Microbiol. 1978;7:379-384.

64. DeVoe IW, Gilchrist JE. Pili on meningococci from primary culture of nasopharyngeal carriers and cerebrospinal fluid of patients with acute disease. J Exp Med. 1975;141:297-305.

65. Stephens DS, McGee ZA. Attachment of *Neisseria meningitidis* to human mucosal surfaces: Influence of pili and type of receptor cell. J Infect Dis. 1981;143:525-532.

66. Kallstrom H, Liszewski MK, Atkinson JP, et al. Membrane cofactor protein (MCP or CD46) is a cellular pilus receptor for pathogenic *Neisseria*. Mol Microbiol. 1997;25:639-647.

67. Johansson L, Rytkönen A, Bergman P, et al. CD46 in meningococcal disease. Science. 2003;301:373-375.

68. Virji M, Makepeace K, Ferguson DJ, et al. Meningococcal Opa and Opc proteins: Their role in colonization and invasion of human epithelial and endothelial cells. Mol Microbiol. 1993;10:499-510.

69. Hammerschmidt S, Muller A, Sillmann H, et al. Capsule phase variation in Neisseria meningitidis serogroup B by slipped-strand mispairing in the polysialyltransferase gene (siaD): correlation with bacterial invasion and the outbreak of meningococcal disease. Mol Microbiol. 1996;20:1211-1220.

70. Hammerschmidt S, Hilse R, van Putten JPM, et al. Modulation of cell surface sialic acid expression in *Neisseria meningitidis* via a transposable genetic element. EMBO J. 1996;15:192-198.

71. Virji M, Makepeace K, Peak IR, et al. Pathogenic mechanisms of pathogenic *Neisseria*. Ann NY Acad Sci. 1995;797:273-276.

72. Lin L, Ayala P, Larson J, et al. The *Neisseria* type 2 IgA1 protease cleaves LAMP1 and promotes survival of bacteria within epithelial cells. Mol Microbiol. 1997;24:1083-1094.

73. Lin L, Ayala P, Larson J, et al. The *Neisseria* IgA1 protease cleaves LAMP1 and promotes survival of bacteria within epithelial cells. Mol Microbiol. 1997;24:1083-1094.

74. Nassif X, Marceau M, Pujol C, et al. Type-4 pili and meningococcal adhesiveness. Gene. 1997;192:149-153.

75. Goldschneider I, Gotschlich EC, Artenstein MS. Human immunity to the meningococcus. I. The role of humoral antibody. J Exp Med. 1969;129:1307-1326.

76. Goldschneider I, Gotschlich EC, Artenstein MS. Human immunity to the meningococcus. II. Development of natural immunity. J Exp Med. 1969;129:1327-1328.

77. Robbins JB, Myerowitz RL, Whesnant JK, et al. Enteric bacteria cross-reactive with *Neisseria meningitidis* groups A and C and *Diplococcus pneumoniae* types I and II. Infect Immun. 1972;6:651-656.

78. Grados O, Ewing WH. Antigenic relationship between *Escherichia coli* and *Neisseria meningitidis*. J Infect Dis. 1970;122:100-103.

79. Finne J, Bitter-Suermann D, Goudis C, et al. An IgG monoclonal antibody to group B meningococci cross reacts with developmentally regulated polysialic acid units of glycoproteins in neural and extraneural tissue. J Immunol. 1987;138:4402-4407.

80. Greenwood BM, Greenwood AM, Bradley AK, et al. Factors influencing the susceptibility to meningococcal disease during an epidemic in The Gambia, West Africa. J Infect. 1987;14:167-184.

81. Kayhty H, Jousimies-Somer H, Peltola H, et al. Antibody response to capsular polysaccharides of groups A and C *Neisseria meningitidis* and *Haemophilus influenzae* type b during bacteremic disease. J Infect Dis. 1981;143:32-41.

82. Plaut AG, Gilbert JV, Artenstein MS, et al. *Neisseria gonorrhoeae* and *Neisseria meningitidis:* Extracellular enzyme cleaves human immunoglobulin A. Science. 1975;190:1103-1105.

83. Mulks M, Plaut AG. IgA protease production as a characteristic distinguishing pathogenic from harmless Neisseriaceae. N Engl J Med. 1978;299:973-976.

84. Bruns H, Hohn J. Meningokokken im Nasenrachenram. Klin Jahrb Jena. 1908;28:285.

85. Rake G. Studies on meningococcus infection. VI. The carrier problem. J Exp Med. 1934;59:553.

86. Greenfield S, Sheede PR, Feldman HA. Meningococcal carriage in a population of "normal" families. J Infect Dis. 1971;123:67-73.

87. Claus H, Maiden MC, Maag R, et al. Many carried meningococci lack the genes required for capsule synthesis and transport. Microbiology. 2002;148:1813-1819.

88. Edwards EA, Devine LF, Sengbusch CH, et al. Immunological investigations of meningococcal disease. III. Brevity of group c acquisition prior to disease occurrence. Scand J Infect Dis. 1987;9:105-110.

89. Wenzel RP, Davies JA, Mitzel JR, et al. Nonusefulness of meningococcal carriage rates. Lancet. 1973;2:205.

90. Olcen P, Kellander J, Danielsson D, et al. Epidemiology of *Neisseria meningitidis* prevalence and symptoms from the upper respiratory tract in family members to patients with meningococcal disease. Scand J Infect Dis. 1981;13:105-109.

91. Moore PS, Hierholzer J, DeWitt W, et al. Respiratory viruses and mycoplasma as cofactors for epidemic group A meningococcal meningitis. JAMA. 1990;264:1271-1275.

92. Reller BL, MacGregor RR, Beaty HN. Bactericidal antibody after colonization with *Neisseria meningitidis*. J Infect Dis. 1973;127:56-62.

93. Broome CV. The carrier state: *Neisseria meningitidis*. J Antimicrob Chemother. 1986;18(Suppl A):S25-S34.

94. Meningococcal disease, serogroup W135. Wkly Epidemiol Rec. 2001;76:141-142.

95. Wilder-Smith A, Barkham TM, Ravindran S, et al. Persistence of W135 *Neisseria meningitidis* carriage in returning Hajj pilgrims: Risk for early and late transmission to household contacts. Emerg Infect Dis. 2003;9:123-126.

96. Martin DR, Walker SJ, Baker MG, Lennon DR. New Zealand epidemic of meningococcal disease identified by a strain with phenotype B:4:P1.4. J Infect Dis. 1998;177:497-500.

97. Feldman HA. Meningococcal infections. Adv Intern Med. 1972;18:117-140.

98. Centers for Disease Control and Prevention. Summary of notifiable diseases, United States-2001. MMWR Morb Mortal Wkly Rep. 2003;50:1-136.

99. Peltola H. Meningococcal disease: Still with us. Rev Infect Dis. 1983;5:71-91.

100. Peltola H, Kataja JM, Makela PH. Shift in the age distribution of meningococcal disease as predictor of an epidemic. Lancet. 1982;2:595-597.

101. Andersen BM. Mortality in meningococcal infections. Scand J Infect Dis. 1978;10:277-282.

102. deMorais JS, Munford RS, Risi JB, et al. Epidemic disease due to serogroup C *Neisseria meningitidis* in Sao Paulo, Brazil. J Infect Dis. 1974;129:568-571.

103. Oberli J, Hoi NT, Caravano R, et al. Etude d'une epidemie de meningococcie au Viet Nam (provinces du Sud). Bull WHO. 1981;59:585-590.

104. The Meningococcal Disease Surveillance Group. Analysis of endemic meningococcal disease by serogroup and evaluation of chemoprophylaxis. J Infect Dis. 1976;134:201.

105. Schwartz B, Moore P, Broome CV. Global epidemiology of meningococcal disease. Clin Rev Microbiol. 1989;2(Suppl):S118-S124.

106. Greenwood BM. The epidemiology of acute bacterial meningitis in tropical Africa. In: Williams JD, Burnet J, eds. Bacterial Meningitis. New York: Academic Press; 1987:61-92.

107. Tikhomirov E, Santamaria M, Esteves K. Meningococcal disease: Public health burden and control. World Health Stat Q. 1997;50:170-177.

108. Reingold AL, Hightower AW, Bolan GA, et al. Age specific differences in duration of clinical protection after vaccination with meningococcal polysaccharide vaccine. Lancet. 1985;2:114-118.

109. Ramsay ME, Andrews N, Kaczmarski EB, Miller E. Efficacy of meningococcal serogroup C conjugate vaccine in teenagers and toddlers in England. Lancet. 2001;357:195-196.

110. Durand ML, Calderwood SB, Weber DJ, et al. Acute bacterial meningitis in adults. N Engl J Med. 1993;328:21-28.
111. Wolfe RE, Birbara CA. Meningococcal infections at an army training center. Am J Med. 1968;44:243-255.
112. Sullivan TD, LaScolea LJ. *Neisseria meningitidis* bacteremia in children: Quantitation of bacteremia and spontaneous clinical recovery without antibiotic therapy. Pediatrics. 1987;80:63-87.
113. Carpenter RR, Petersdorf RG. The clinical spectrum of bacterial meningitis. Am J Med. 1962;33:262-275.
114. Feigin RD, Dodge PR. Bacterial meningitis: Newer concepts of pathophysiology and neurologic sequelae. Pediatr Clin North Am. 1976;23:541-556.
115. Thomas HM. Meningococcic meningitis and septicemia. Report of an outbreak in the fourth service command during the winter and spring of 1942-1943. JAMA. 1943;123:264-272.
116. Ducker TB, Simmons RL. The pathogenesis of meningitis. Systemic effects of meningococcal endotoxin within the cerebrospinal fluid. Arch Neurol. 1968;18:123-128.
117. Hardman JM. Fatal meningococcal infections: The changing pathologic picture in the '60's. Mil Med. 1968;133:951-964.
118. Brandtzaeg P, Oktedalen O, Kierulf P, et al. Elevated VIP and endotoxin plasma levels in human gram-negative septic shock. Regul Pept. 1989;24:37-44.
119. Brandtzaeg P, Kierulf P, Gaustad P, et al. Plasma endotoxin as a predictor of multiple organ failure and death in systemic meningococcal disease. J Infect Dis. 1989;159:195-204.
120. Brandtzaeg P, Ovsteboo R, Kierulf P. Compartmentalization of lipopolysaccharide production correlates with clinical presentation in meningococcal disease. J Infect Dis. 1992;166:650-652.
121. Brandtzaeg P, Mollnes TE, Kierulf P. Complement activation and endotoxin levels in systemic meningococcal disease. J Infect Dis. 1989;160:58-65.
122. Brandtzaeg P, Sandset PM, Joo GB, et al. The quantitative association of plasma endotoxin, antithrombin, protein C, extrinsic pathway inhibitor and fibrinopeptide A in systemic meningococcal disease. Thromb Res. 1989;55:459-470.
123. Brandtzaeg PK, Bryn P, Kierulf P, et al. Meningococcal endotoxin in lethal septic shock plasma studied by gas chromatography, mass-spectrometry, ultracentrifugation, and electron microscopy. J Clin Invest. 1992;89:816-823.
124. Cesarini JP, Vandekerkove M, Faucon R, et al. Ultrastructure of the wall of *Neisseria meningitidis* (in French). Ann Inst Pasteur. 1967;113:833-841.
125. Devoe IW, Gilchrist JE. Release of endotoxin in the form of cell wall blebs during in vitro growth of *Neisseria meningitidis*. J Exp Med. 1973;138:1156-1167.
126. Levin S, Painter MB. The treatment of acute meningococcal infection in adults. Ann Intern Med. 1966;64:1049-1056.
127. Gore I, Saphir Q. Myocarditis, a classification of 1402 cases. Am Heart J. 1947;34:827-831.
128. Boucek MM, Boerth RC, Artman M, et al. Myocardial dysfunction in children with acute meningococcemia. J Pediatr. 1984;105:538-542.
129. Gotschall RA. Conus medullaris syndrome after meningococcal meningitis. N Engl J Med. 1972;286:882-883.
130. Herman RA, Rubin HA. Meningococcal pericarditis without meningitis presenting as tamponade. N Engl J Med. 1974;290:143-144.
131. Pierce I, Cooper E. Meningococcal pericarditis, clinical features and therapy in five patients. Arch Intern Med. 1972;129:918-922.
132. Maron BJ, Macoul KL, Benaron P. Unusual complications of meningococcal meningitis. Johns Hopkins Med J. 1972;131:64-68.
133. Brasier AR, Macklis JD, Vaughn D, et al. Myopericarditis as an initial presentation of meningococcemia. Unusual manifestations of infection with serotype W135. Am J Med. 1987;82:641-644.
134. Frank ST, Gomez RM. Chronic meningococcemia. Mil Med. 1968;133:918-920.
135. Saslaw S. Chronic meningococcemia: Report of a case. N Engl J Med. 1962;266:605-607.
136. Rompalo AM, Hood EW, Roberts PL, et al. The acute arthritis dermatitis syndrome. The changing importance of *Neisseria gonorrhoeae* and *Neisseria meningitidis*. Arch Intern Med. 1987;147:281-283.
137. Lim D, Gewurz A, Lint TF, et al. Absence of the sixth component of complement in a patient with repeated episodes of meningococcal meningitis. J Pediatr. 1976;89:42.
138. Alper CA, Abramson N, Johnston RB Jr. Increased susceptibility to infection associated with abnormalities of complement-mediated functions and of the third component of complement (C3). N Engl J Med. 1970;282:349-354.
139. Petersen BH, Graham JA, Brooks GF. Human deficiency of the eighth component of complement. The requirement of C8 for serum *Neisseria gonorrhoeae* bactericidal activity. J Clin Invest. 1976;57:283-290.
140. Ellison RT, Kohler PF, Curd JG, et al. Prevalence of congenital or acquired complement deficiency in patients with sporadic meningococcal disease. N Engl J Med. 1983;308:913-916.
141. Densen P, Weiler JM, Griffiss JM, et al. Familial properdin deficiency and fatal bacteremia. Correction of the bactericidal defect by vaccination. N Engl J Med. 1987;316:922-926.
142. Ross SC, Rosenthal PJ, Berberich HM, et al. Killing of *Neisseria meningitidis* by human neutrophils: Implications for normal and complement deficient individuals. J Infect Dis. 1987;155:1266-1275.
143. Densen P. Complement deficiencies and meningococcal disease. Clin Exp Immunol. 1991;86(Suppl 1):S57-S62.
144. Koppes GM, Ellenbogen C, Gebhart RJ. Group Y meningococcal disease in United States Air Force recruits. Am J Med. 1977;62:661-666.
145. Young LS, LaForce FM, Head JJ, et al. A simultaneous outbreak of meningococcal and influenza infections. N Engl J Med. 1972;287:5-9.

146. Goldstein E, Buhlers WC, Akers TC, et al. Murine resistance to inhaled *Neisseria meningitidis* after infection with an encephalomyocarditis virus. Infect Immun. 1972;6:398-402.
147. Kerttula Y, Leinonen M, Koskela M, et al. The etiology of pneumonia, application of bacterial serology and basic laboratory methods. J Infect. 1987;14:21-30.
148. Winstead JM, McKinsey DS, Tasker S, et al. Meningococcal pneumonia: Characterization and review of cases seen over the past 25 years. Clin Infect Dis. 2000;30:87-94
149. McCracken GH. Rapid identification of specific etiology in meningitis. J Pediatr. 1976;88:706-708.
150. Schwam E, Cox J. Fulminant meningococcal supraglottitis: An emerging infectious syndrome? Emerg Infect Dis. 1999;5:464-467.
151. Salet IE, Frasch CE. Seroepidemiologic aspects of *Neisseria meningitidis* in homosexual men. Can Med Assoc J. 1982;126:38-41.
152. Hoyne AL, Brown RH. 727 Meningococcic cases, an analysis. Ann Intern Med. 1948;28:248-259.
153. Feldman WE. Concentrations of bacteria in cerebrospinal fluid of patients with bacterial meningitis. J Pediatr. 1976;88:549-552.
154. Borrow R, Claus H, Chaudhry U, et al. siaD PCR ELISA for confirmation and identification of serogroup Y and W135 meningococcal infections. FEMS Microbiol Lett. 1998;159:209-214.
155. Seward RJ, Towner KJ. Evaluation of a PCR-immunoassay technique for detection of *Neisseria meningitidis* in cerebrospinal fluid and peripheral blood. J Med Microbiol. 2000;49:451-456.
156. Corless CE, Guiver M, Borrow R, et al. Simultaneous detection of *Neisseria meningitidis, Haemophilus influenzae,* and *Streptococcus pneumoniae* in suspected cases of meningitis and septicemia using real-time PCR. J Clin Microbiol. 2001;39:1553-1558.
157. Diggle MA, Clarke SC. Detection and genotyping of meningococci using a nested PCR approach. J Med Microbiol. 2003;52:51-57.
158. Feldman HA, Sweet LA, Dowling HF. Sulfadiazine therapy of purulent meningitis. War Med. 1942;2:995-1007.
159. Mead M, Harris W, Samper BA, et al. Treatment of meningococcal meningitis with penicillin. N Engl J Med. 1944;231:509-517.
160. Kinsman JM, D'Alonzo CA. Meningococcemia: A description of the clinical picture and a comparison of the efficacy of sulfadiazine and penicillin in the treatment of thirty cases. Ann Intern Med. 1946;24:606-617.
161. McCrumb FR, Hall HE, Meridith AM, et al. Chloramphenicol in the treatment of meningococcal meningitis. Am J Med. 1951;10:696-703.
162. Brown JD, Mathies AW, Ivler D, et al. Variable results of cephalothin therapy for meningococcal meningitis. In: Hobby G, ed. Antimicrobial Agents and Chemotherapy 1969. Bethesda, MD: American Society for Microbiology; 1970:432.
163. Schribner RK, Wedro BC, Weber AH, et al. Activities of eight new beta-lactam and seven antibiotic combinations against *Neisseria meningitidis*. Antimicrob Agents Chemother. 1982;21:678-680.
164. Neu HC. Cephalosporins in the treatment of meningitis. Drugs. 1987;34(Suppl 2):S135-S153.
165. Centers for Disease Control and Prevention. Control and prevention of meningococcal disease and control and prevention of serogroup C meningococcal diseases: Evaluation and management of suspected outbreaks. MMWR Morb Mortal Wkly Rep. 1997;46(RR-5):1-22.
166. Anonymous. Meningococcal disease prevention and control strategies for practice-based physicians. Committee on Infectious Diseases, American Academy of Pediatrics, Infectious Diseases and Immunization Committee, Canadian Paediatric Society. Pediatrics. 1996;97:404-412.
167. Love BD, Finland M. In vitro susceptibility of meningococcus to 11 antibiotics and sulfadiazine. Am J Med. 1954;228:534-539.
168. Brown JW, Condit PK. Meningococcal infections: Fort Ord and California. Calif Med. 1965;102:171-180.
169. Eickhoff TC, Finland M. Changing susceptibility of meningococci to antimicrobial agents. N Engl J Med. 1965;272:395-398.
170. Feldman HA. Sulfonamide resistant meningococci. Annu Rev Med. 1967;18:495-506.
171. Alexander CE, Sanborn WR, Cherriere G, et al. Sulfadiazine resistant group A *Neisseria meningitidis*. Science. 1968;161:1019.
172. Scheld WM, Sande M. Bactericidal versus bacteriostatic antibiotic therapy of experimental pneumococcal meningitis in rabbits. J Clin Invest. 1983;71:411-419.
173. Berkow R, ed. The Merck Manual of Diagnosis and Therapy. Rahway, NJ: Merck Sharp & Dohme; 1977:1432.
174. Sprott MS, Kearns AM, Field JM. Penicillin insensitive *Neisseria meningitidis* (Letter). Lancet. 1988;1:1167.
175. Saez-Nieto JA, Lujan R, Berron S, et al. Epidemiology and molecular basis of penicillin-resistant *Neisseria meningitidis* in Spain: A 5-year history (1985-1989). Clin Infect Dis. 1992;14:394-402.
176. Galimand M, Gerbaud G, Guibourdenche M, et al. High level chloramphenicol resistance in *Neisseria meningitidis*. N Engl J Med. 1998;339:868-874.
177. Cherubin CE, Eng RK, Noorby R, et al. Penetration of newer cephalosporins into spinal fluid. Rev Infect Dis. 1989;11:526-548.
178. Ellis-Pegler R, Galler L, Roberts S, et al. Three days of intravenous benzyl penicillin therapy for meningococcal disease in adults. Clin Infect Dis. 2003;37:658-662.
179. Humbert G, Leroy A, Nair SR, et al. Concentration of cefotaxime and the desacetyl metabolite in serum and CSF of patients with meningitis. J Antimicrob Chemother. 1984;13:487-494.
180. Latif R, Dajani AS. Ceftriaxone diffusion into cerebrospinal fluid of children with meningitis. Antimicrob Agents Chemother. 1983;23:46-48.
181. Modai J, Vittecoq D, Decazes JM, et al. Penetration of ceftazidime into cerebrospinal fluid of patients with bacterial meningitis. Antimicrob Agents Chemother. 1983;24:126-128.

182. Fu KP, Neu H. Antimicrobial activity of ceftizoxime, a beta lactamase-stable cephalosporin. Antimicrob Agents Chemother. 1980;17:583-590.
183. Jones RN, Barry AL, Thornsberry C. Ceftriaxone: A summary of in vitro antibacterial susceptibility tests with 30 μg disks. Diagn Microbiol Infect Dis. 1983;1:295-311.
184. Phillips I, Warren C, Shannon K, et al. Ceftazidime: In vitro antibacterial activity and susceptibility to beta-lactamases compared with that of cefotaxime, moxalactam and other beta-lactam antibiotics. J Antimicrob Chemother. 1981;8(Suppl B):S23-S31.
185. Cartwright K, Reilly S, White D, et al. Early treatment with parenteral penicillin in meningococcal disease. Br Med J. 1992;305:143-147.
186. Strang JR, Pugh EJ. Meningococcal infections: Reducing the case fatality rate by giving penicillin before admission to hospital. Br Med J. 1992;305:141-143.
187. Barquet N, Domingo P, Cayla JA, et al. Prognostic factors of a bedside predictive model and scoring system. JAMA. 1997;278:491-496.
188. Waage A, Brandtzaeg P, Halstensen A, et al. The complex pattern of cytokines in serum from patients with meningococcal septic shock. J Exp Med. 1989;169:333-338.
189. Beutler B, Milsark IW, Cerami AC. Passive immunization against cachectin/tumor necrosis factor protects mice from the lethal effects of endotoxin. Science. 1985;229:869-871.
190. Beutler B, Cerami A. Cachectin: More than a tumor necrosis factor. N Engl J Med. 1987;316:379-385.
191. Tracey KJ, Beutler B, Lowry SF, et al. Shock and tissue injury induced by recombinant human cachectin. Science. 1986;234:470-474.
192. Tracey KJ, Fong Y, Hesse DG, et al. Anti-cachectin/TNF monoclonal antibodies prevent septic shock during lethal bacteremia. Nature. 1987;330:662-664.
193. Girardin E, Grau GE, Dayr JM, et al. Tumor necrosis factor and interleukin-1 in the serum of children with severe infectious purpura. N Engl J Med. 1988;319:397-400.
194. Giroir BP, Scannon PJ, Levin M. Bactericidal/permeability-increasing protein—lessons learned from the phase III, randomized, clinical trial of rBPI21 for adjunctive treatment of children with severe meningococcemia. Crit Care Med. 2001;29(7 Suppl):S130-135.
195. Bernard G, Vincent JL, Laterre PF, et al. Efficacy and safety of recombinant human activated protein C for severe sepsis. N Engl J Med. 2001;344:699-709.
196. Rintala E, Kauppila M, Seppala OP, et al. Protein C substitution in sepsis-associated purpura fulminans. Crit Care Med. 2000;28:2373-2378.
197. Morris PE, Light RB, Garber GE. Identifying patients with severe sepsis who should be not be treated with drotrecogin alfa (activated). Am J Surg. 2002;184 (Suppl 1):19S-24S.
198. Monsalve F, Rucabado L, Salvador A, et al. Myocardial depression in septic shock caused by meningococcal infection. Crit Care Med. 1984;12:1021-1032.
199. de la Cal MA, Miravalles E, Pascual T, et al. Dose-related hemodynamic and renal effects of dopamine in septic shock. Crit Care Med. 1984;12:22-25.
200. Fisher CJ, Horowilx BZ, Albertson TE. Cardiorespiratory failure in toxic shock syndrome: Effect of dobutamine. Crit Care Med. 1985;13:160-165.
201. Duff P. Pathophysiology and management of septic shock. J Reprod Med. 1980;24:109-117.
202. Belsey MA, Hoffpauir CW, Smith MHD. Dexamethasone in the treatment of acute bacterial meningitis: The effect of study design on the interpretation of results. Pediatrics. 1969;44:503-513.
203. Thomas R, Le Tulzo Y, Bouget J, et al. Trial of dexamethasone treatment for severe bacterial meningitis in adults. Adult Meningitis Steroid Group. Intens Care Med. 1999;25:475-480.
204. Corrigan JJ Jr, Jordan CM. Heparin therapy in septicemia with disseminated intravascular coagulation. Effect on mortality and on correction of hemostatic defects. N Engl J Med. 1970;283:778-782.
205. Faust SN, Levin M, Harrison OB, et al. Dysfunction of endothelial protein C activation in severe meningococcal sepsis. N Engl J Med. 2001;345:408-416.
206. Kornelisse RF, Hazelzet JA, Hop WCJ, et al. Meningococcal septic shock in children: Clinical and laboratory features, outcome, and development of a prognostic score. Clin Infect Dis. 1997;25:640-646.
207. LeClerc F, Chenaud M, Delepoulle F, et al. Prognostic value of C-reactive protein level in severe infectious purpura: A comparison with eight other scores. Crit Care Med. 1991;19:430-432.
208. Pollack MM, Ruttimann UE, Getson PR. Pediatric risk of mortality (PRISM) score. Crit Care Med. 1988;16:1-25.
209. Hermans PWM, Hibbard ML, Booy R, et al., and the Meningococcal Research Group. 4G/5G promoter polymorphism in the plasminogen-activator-inhibitor-1 gene and outcome of meningococcal disease. Lancet. 1999;354:556-560.
210. Fairbrother RW. Cerebrospinal meningitis: The use of sulphonamide derivatives in prophylaxis. Br Med J. 1940;2:859-862.
211. Gray FC, Gear J. Sulphapyridine, M and B 693 as a prophylactic against cerebrospinal meningitis. S Afr Med J. 1941;15:139.
212. Aycock WL, Mueller JH. Meningococcus carrier rates and meningitis incidence. Bacteriol Rev. 1950;14:115-160.
213. Cheever FS. The control of meningococcal meningitis by mass chemoprophylaxis with sulfadiazine. Am J Med Sci. 1945;209:74-75.
214. Artenstein MS, Lamson TH, Evans JR. Attempted prophylaxis against meningococcal infection using intramuscular penicillin. Mil Med. 1967;132:1009-1011.
215. Guttler RB, Counts GW, Avent CK, et al. Effect of rifampin and minocycline on meningococcal carrier rates. J Infect Dis. 1971;124:199-205.
216. Devine LF, Johnson DP, Rhode SL, et al. Rifampin: Effect of two day treatment on meningococcal carrier state and the relationship of the levels of drug in sera and saliva. Am J Med Sci. 1971;261:79-83.
217. Jacobson JA, Daniel B. Vestibular reactions associated with minocycline. Antimicrob Agents Chemother. 1975;8:453-456.
218. Weidner CE, Dunkel TB, Pettyjohn FS, et al. Effectiveness of rifampin in eradicating the meningococcal carrier state in a relatively closed population: Emergence of resistant strains. J Infect Dis. 1971;124:172-178.
219. Pugsley MP, Dworzack DI, Horowitz EA, et al. Efficacy of ciprofloxacin in treatment of nasopharyngeal carriers of Neisseria meningitidis. J Infect Dis. 1987;156:211-213.
220. Gilja HO, Halstensen A, Digranes A, et al. Single-dose ofloxacin to eradicate tonsillopharyngeal carriage of Neisseria meningitidis. Antimicrob Agents Chemother. 1993;37:2024-2026.
221. Schwartz B. Chemoprophylaxis for bacterial infections: Principles of and application to meningococcal infection. Rev Infect Dis. 1991;13(Suppl 2):S170-S173.
222. Girgis N, Sultan Y, Frenck RW Jr, et al. Azithromycin compared with rifampin for eradication of nasopharyngeal colonization by Neisseria meningitidis. Pediatr Infect Dis J. 1998;17:816-819.
223. Hoeprich PD. Prediction of antimeningococcic chemoprophylactic efficacy. J Infect Dis. 1971;123:125-133.
224. DeWals P, Herlozhe L, Borlee-Grimee I, et al. Meningococcal disease in Belgium. Secondary attack rate among household day-care nursery and pre-elementary school contacts. J Infect. 1983;1(Suppl 1):S53-S61.
225. Artenstein MS, Ellis RE. The risk of exposure to a patient with meningococcal meningitis. Mil Med. 1968;133:474-477.
226. Centers for Disease Control and Prevention. Meningococcal infections in the United States, 1981. MMWR Morb Mortal Wkly Rep. 1981;30:113-115.
227. Makela PH, Kayhty H, Weekstrom P, et al. Effect of group A meningococcal vaccine in army recruits in Finland. Lancet. 1975;2:883-886.
228. Taunay A de E, Galvao PA, de Morais JS, et al. Disease prevention by meningococcal serogroup C polysaccharide vaccine in pre-school: Results after eleven months in Sao Paulo, Brazil (Abstract). Pediatr Res. 1974;8:429.
229. Gold R, Lepow ML, Goldschneider I, et al. Clinical evaluation of group A and group C meningococcal polysaccharide vaccines in infants. J Clin Invest. 1975;56:1536-1547.
230. Wahdan MH, Rizh F, El-Akkad AM, et al. A controlled field trial of a serogroup A meningococcal polysaccharide vaccine. Bull WHO 1973;48:667-673.
231. Brandt B, Artenstein MS. Duration of antibody responses after vaccination with group C Neisseria meningitidis polysaccharide. J Infect Dis. 1975;131:569.
232. Advisory Committee on Immunization Practices. Meningococcal polysaccharide vaccines. Ann Intern Med. 1976;84:179-180.
233. Lepow ML, Beeler J, Randolph M, et al. Reactogenicity and immunogenicity of a quadrivalent combined meningococcal vaccine in children. J Infect Dis. 1986;154:1033-1036.
234. Artenstein MS, Brandt B. Immunologic hyporesponsiveness in man to group C meningococcal polysaccharide vaccine. J Immunol. 1975;115:5-7.
235. Broome CV. Use of bacterial vaccines for prevention of pneumococcal and meningococcal disease in day care settings. Rev Infect Dis. 1986;8:584-588.
236. Greenwood BM, Bradley AK, Blakebrough IS, et al. The immune response to a meningococcal polysaccharide in an African village. Trans R Soc Trop Med Hyg. 1980;74:340-346.
237. Centers for Disease Control and Prevention. Update on adult immunizations: Recommendations of the Immunization Practices Advisory Committee (ACIP). MMWR Morbid Mortal Wkly Rep. 1991;40(No. RR-12).
238. Centers for Disease Control and Prevention. Control and prevention of meningococcal disease and control and prevention of serogroup C meningococcal disease: Evaluation and management of suspected outbreaks: Recommendations of the Advisory Committee on Immunization Practices (ACIP). MMWR Morbid Mortal Wkly Rep. 1997;46(No. RR-5).
239. Centers for Disease Control and Prevention. Notice to Readers: Recommended Adult Immunization Schedule—United States, 2002-2003. MMWR Morbid Mortal Wkly Rep. 2002;51:904-908.
240. Jodar L, Feavers IM, Salisbury D, Granoff D. Development of vaccines against meningococcal disease. Lancet, 2001;359:1499-1508.
241. Soriano-Gabarro M, Stuart JM, Rosenstein NE. Vaccines for the prevention of meningococcal disease in children. Semin Pediatr Infect Dis. 2002;13:182-189.
242. Slack MH, Schapira D, Thwaites RJ, et al. Immune response of premature infants to meningococcal serogroup C and combined diphtheria-tetanus toxoids-acellular pertussis-Haemophilus influenzae type b conjugate vaccines. J Infect Dis. 2001;184:1617-1620.
243. Ramsay ME, Andrews N, Kaczmarski EB, Miller E. Efficacy of meningococcal serogroup C conjugate vaccine in teenagers and toddlers in England. Lancet. 2001;357:195-196.
244. Maiden MC, Stuart JM. The UK Meningococcal Carraige Group. Carriage of serogroup C meningococci 1 year after meningococcal C conjugate polysaccharide vaccination. Lancet. 2002;359:1829-1831.
245. Ramsay ME, Andrews NJ, Trotter CL, Kaczmarski EB, Miller E. Herd immunity from meningococcal serogroup C conjugate vaccination in England: Database analysis. Br Med J. 2003;326:365-366.

CHAPTER 209

Neisseria gonorrhoeae

H. HUNTER HANDSFIELD
P. FREDERICK SPARLING

Gonorrhea is a common bacterial infection that is transmitted almost exclusively by sexual contact or perinatally and primarily affects the mucous membranes of the urethra and cervix and less frequently those of the rectum, oropharynx, and conjunctivae. Ascending genital infection in women leads to acute salpingitis, the predominant complication and one of the most common causes of female infertility. Other complications include acute epididymitis, ophthalmitis, and disseminated infection with arthritis, dermatitis, and sometimes endocarditis.

Gonorrhea is one of the oldest known human illnesses, and references to sexually acquired urethritis can be found in ancient Chinese writings, the biblical Old Testament (Leviticus), and other works of antiquity. Galen (AD 130) introduced the term *gonorrhea* ("flow of seed"), implying interpretation of urethral exudate as semen. The causative organism was described by Neisser in 1879 and was first cultivated in 1882 by Leistikow and Löffler. Untreated infections were understood to resolve spontaneously over several weeks or months, but reinfection was recognized to occur. Many therapies were tried, but not until advent of the sulfonamides in the 1930s and penicillin in 1943 was truly effective treatment available. Growth of fundamental knowledge about the organism and the host response to infection was slow for 80 years, but a remarkable surge of new information began in the 1970s, and currently as much is known of the molecular biology of the gonococcus and the pathogenesis of gonorrhea as for any bacterial pathogen. Public health control efforts have met with variable success, and gonorrhea remains a prime example of the influence that social, behavioral and demographic factors can have on the epidemiology of an infectious disease despite highly effective, readily available antimicrobial therapy.

THE ORGANISM

Description

Neisseria gonorrhoeae is a nonmotile, non–spore-forming, gram-negative coccus that characteristically grows in pairs (diplococci) with adjacent sides flattened. It closely resembles the related pathogen *Neisseria meningitidis,* as well as several species of nonpathogenic *Neisseria.* All *Neisseria* spp. rapidly oxidize dimethylparaphenylene diamine or tetramethylparaphenylene diamine, the basis of the diagnostic oxidase test. Traditionally, gonococci are differentiated from other *Neisseria* by their ability to grow on selective media; to use glucose but not maltose, sucrose, or lactose; to reduce nitrites; and by their inability to grow well at reduced temperature or on simple nutrient agar.[1]

Growth and Cultivation

Gonococci do not tolerate drying, and patient samples should be inoculated immediately onto appropriate agar medium. However, some non-nutrient transport media, such as Amies' modification of Stuart's medium, variations of which are used in many commercial specimen collection kits, can maintain viable gonococci for up to 6 hours before inoculation into growth media. Growth is best for most strains at 35°C to 37°C, and many freshly isolated strains have a relative or absolute requirement for atmospheric CO_2 in concentrations around 5%. All strains are strictly aerobic under usual growth conditions, but the organism grows anaerobically when nitrite is provided as an electron acceptor. Colonies appear in 24 to 48 hours, but on most media viability is rapidly lost after 48 hours because of autolysis.[1]

Gonococci are inhibited by many fatty acids, and it is necessary to incorporate starch or other substances that absorb fatty acids into most growth media. All strains have complex growth requirements, including requirements for several vitamins, amino acids, iron, and other factors. For clinical purposes, a satisfactory medium is chocolate agar enriched with glucose and other defined supplements. Isolation of gonococci from sites that normally contain high concentrations of saprophytic microorganisms, especially the pharynx, rectum, and cervix, may be difficult because of overgrowth of the hardier normal flora, a problem that is largely overcome by use of media containing antimicrobial agents that inhibit most nonpathogenic *Neisseria* and other species but permit growth of most strains of *N. gonorrhoeae* and *N. meningitidis.* Chocolate agar that contains vancomycin, colistin, nystatin and trimethoprim (modified Thayer-Martin medium) is widely used for this purpose in the United States; a similarly constituted translucent selective medium (New York City medium) also is commonly used.[1] Selective media fail to support the growth of some gonococci, in part because some strains are relatively sensitive to vancomycin; where such strains are prevalent, deleting vancomycin from the medium may significantly improve diagnostic sensitivity.[2,3] Material from sites that usually do not harbor indigenous flora (e.g., blood, synovial fluid, cerebrospinal fluid) should be cultured on antibiotic-free medium.

Surface Structures

The envelope of *N. gonorrhoeae* is similar in basic structure to that of other gram-negative bacteria. As the interface between the gonococcus and host, the cell surface has been intensively studied (Fig. 209-1), and specific surface components have been related to adherence, tissue and cellular penetration, cytotoxicity, and evasion of host defenses both systemically and at the mucosal level.

Pili

Varied colonial forms can be distinguished when *N. gonorrhoeae* is grown on translucent agar.[4] Fresh clinical isolates initially form colony types P+ and P++ (formerly called T1 and T2), and the organisms have numerous pili extending from the cell surface (Fig. 209-2); P− colonies (formerly T3 and T4) lack pili. Piliated gonococci are better able than organisms from P− colonies to attach to human mucosal surfaces and are more virulent in animal and organ culture models and in human inoculation experiments than nonpiliated variants.[4-7] Expression of pili is a function of the *pil* gene complex. A spontaneous shift between P+ or P++ colonies to P− colony types, known as phase variation, occurs after 20 to 24 hours of growth in vitro and is mediated principally by recombination between incomplete (silent) loci that contain slightly variant copies of *pil* DNA and loci with the complete *pil* structural gene, *pilE.*[8]

Pili traverse the outer membrane of the gonococcus and are composed of repeating protein subunits (pilin) with a molecular weight of 19 + 2.5 kD.[5] Pilin has regions of considerable interstrain antigenic similarity, especially near the amino terminus, but areas of extreme antigenic variability are also present.[5,8] A single strain of *N. gonorrhoeae* is capable of producing pili with differing antigenic compositions, compromising the utility of pilus-based vaccines against gonorrhea. In addition to mediating attachment, pili contribute to resistance to killing by neutrophils. In the fallopian tube mucosa model (Fig. 209-3), pili facilitate attachment to nonciliated epithelial cells, which initiates a process of entry and transport through these cells into intercellular spaces near the basement membrane or directly into the subepithelial space, while concurrently nearby ciliated mucosal cells lose their cilia and are sloughed.[6] CD46 is the main pilin receptor.[8] Other factors also mediate attachment, notably opacity proteins (Opa), discussed later.

Outer Membrane

Like all gram-negative bacteria, the gonococcus possesses a cell envelope composed of three distinct layers: an inner cytoplasmic membrane, a middle peptidoglycan cell wall, and an outer membrane. The outer membrane contains lipo-oligosaccharide (LOS), phospholipid, and a variety of proteins (see Fig. 209-1). Porin, formerly designated

FIGURE 209-1. Schematic representation of the surface structure of *Neisseria gonorrhoeae*, showing the major components that contribute to pathogenicity. Opa, Por, and Rmp are the designations of the major outer membrane proteins. (see text); LOS, lipo-oligosaccharide.

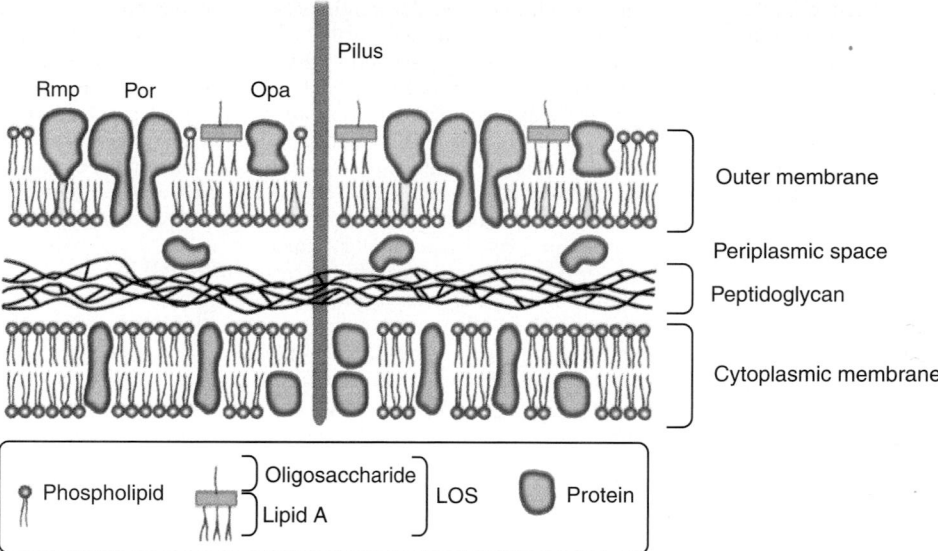

protein I, has a molecular weight of 32 to 36 kD and is closely associated in the membrane with LOS. Porin provides channels that allow aqueous solutes to pass through the otherwise hydrophobic outer membrane and is believed to play an important role in pathogenesis.[10] Porin occurs in two major antigenic classes, PorA and PorB, each of which is composed of many distinct serovars, the basis for the most commonly used gonococcal serotyping system.[11] Strains expressing PorA are associated with genotypic resistance of *N. gonorrhoeae* to the bactericidal effect of normal (nonimmune) human serum and, perhaps as a direct result, with an enhanced propensity to cause bacteremia.[11] PorA also appears to directly promote invasion of epithelial cells,[12] which also helps explain the propensity for bacteremic dissemination. Porin is the focus of extensive investigation directed toward the development of a gonococcal vaccine.[13]

Opa proteins are outer-membrane proteins with molecular weights of 20 to 28 kD. They are members of a family of proteins, each produced from its own *opa* gene. The amino acid sequence of the Opa proteins varies somewhat, primarily because of differences in two hypervariable regions in each protein.[14] Expression of Opa varies because of high-frequency variations in *opa* DNA that result in translational frame shifting. An individual strain of *N. gonorrhoeae* can express none or up to 11 Opa variants, but usually not more than 3 at a time.[14] Gonococci isolated from mucosal sites usually express Opa and their colonies are opaque, but most cervical isolates during men-

struation and isolates from normally sterile sites, such as fallopian tubes, blood, and synovial fluid apparently lack Opa and form translucent colonies.[15] Many Opa proteins increase adherence between gonococci themselves and to a variety of eukaryotic cells, including phagocytes.[15] Certain Opa variants appear to promote invasion of epithelial cells. Two classes of Opa receptor on eukaryotic cells have been identified: heparin-related compounds[16] and CD66, or carcinoembryonic antigen-related cell adhesion molecules (CEACAM).[17] Certain Opa proteins are able to bind to CEACAM receptors on B and T cells, resulting in downregulation of immune responses.[18] This may help account for the poor immune response to natural infection.[19]

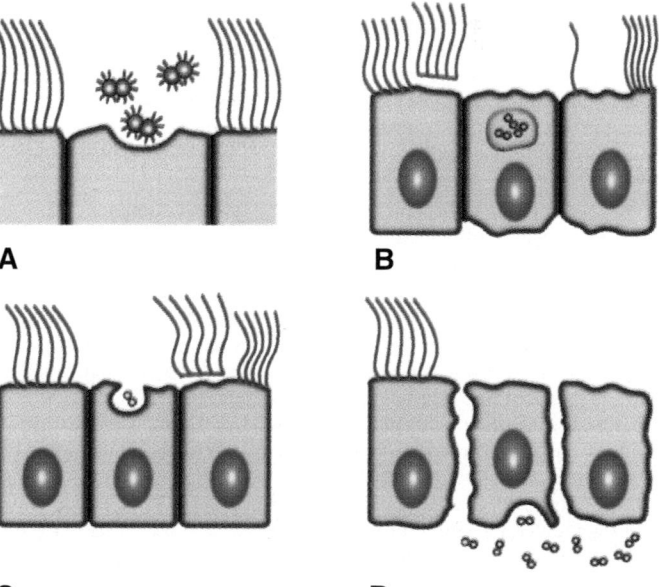

FIGURE 209-3. Schematic representation of the interaction between fallopian tube explant epithelial cells and *Neisseria gonorrhoeae*. **A,** Attachment of the piliated gonococci to the surface of a nonciliated host cell. **B,** Endocytosis of gonococci and loss of cilia on adjacent cells, mediated by lipo-oligosaccharide (LOS). **C,** Transport of gonococci through an epithelial cell in an endocytotic vacuole, in which the organism may replicate; progression of LOS-associated cytotoxicity. **D,** Release of organisms into subepithelial space. *(From Dallabetta G, Hook EW III. Gonococcal infections. Infect Dis Clin North Am 1987;1:25-54.)*

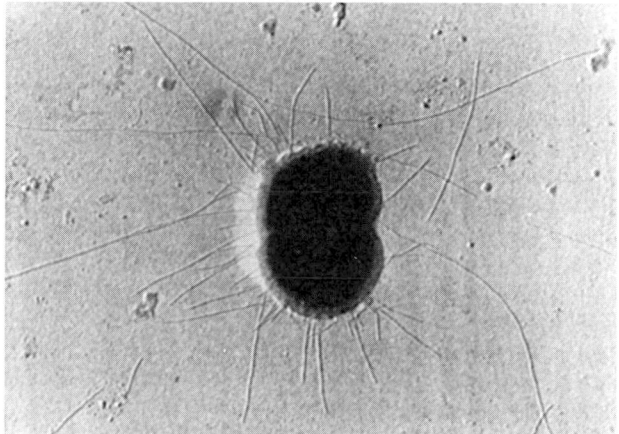

FIGURE 209-2. *Nesseria gonorrhoeae* with numerous pili extending from the cell surface. (Courtesy of Dr. Gour Biswas, Chapel Hill, NC.)

Reduction-modifiable protein (Rmp) has a molecular weight of 30 to 31 kD, is present in all gonococci in close association with porin and LOS, and shows little if any interstrain antigenic variation.[10] Rmp can stimulate blocking antibodies that reduce serum bactericidal activity against *N. gonorrhoeae,* which may potentiate infection after sexual exposure to an infected partner.[20] Several other outer-membrane proteins have been identified, including multiple iron-repressible proteins, some of which are shared with *N. meningitidis.* Two of the iron-repressible proteins (85 and 110 kD) constitute a specific receptor for transferrin,[21] and two others form a receptor for human lactoferrin.[22] The transferrin receptor is required for successful experimental urethral infection, but the role of the lactoferrin receptor is unclear; it does not influence infectivity.[23,24] Two additional proteins constitute a receptor for hemoglobin.[23] Other proteins are expressed only during anaerobic growth.[25] The ability of *N. gonorrhoeae* to grow anaerobically after removing available oxygen from the microenvironment may contribute to secondary invasion of fallopian tubes by strict anaerobes and thus to the pathogenesis of salpingitis. IgA$_1$ proteases, present in *N. gonorrhoeae* and *N. meningitidis* but not in nonpathogenic *Neisseria,* are assumed to protect the organism from secretory IgA antibody at mucosal surfaces, but this role has not been proved.

Gonococcal LOS is composed of lipid A and a core oligosaccharide that, in contrast with the polysaccharide of most gram-negative bacteria, lacks O-antigenic side chains. Sialylation of LOS core sugars in vitro or in vivo[26] masks epitopes on both LOS and porin and contributes to resistance to bactericidal antibodies.[27] LOS possesses endotoxic activity and contributes to ciliary loss and the death of mucosal cells in the fallopian tube explant model (see Fig. 209-3).[6] LOS core sugars undergo high-frequency phase and antigenic variation in vitro and in vivo,[26] which may contribute to the pathogenesis of infection, including resistance to bacterial anti-LOS antibodies present in normal serum and invasion of epithelial cells.[28]

The peptidoglycan layer of *N. gonorrhoeae* may also contribute to the inflammatory response. Peptidoglycan fragments are toxic in the fallopian tube explant system and cause complement consumption in vitro. In addition, peptidoglycan fragments have been found in the apparently sterile synovial fluid of patients with gonococcal arthritis-dermatitis syndrome.[29] Gonococci produce a surface polyphosphate that may have capsulelike functions, such as creating a hydrophilic, negatively charged cell surface. However, a carbohydrate capsule analogous to that of *N. meningitidis* or *Streptococcus pneumoniae* is not produced.

Strain Typing

Studies of the clinical manifestations and epidemiology of gonorrhea have been greatly enhanced by the development of reproducible methods for typing *N. gonorrhoeae.* Characterization of gonococcal strains is based on two primary methodologies, auxotyping and serotyping.[11,30] Auxotyping is based on the genetically stable requirements of strains for specific nutrients or cofactors, as defined by isolates' ability to grow on chemically defined media that lack selected factors.[30] Examples of common auxotypes, among more than 30 that have been identified, include prototrophic, also known as "zero" or "wild type"; proline-requiring (pro$^-$); and strains that require arginine, either hypoxanthine or proline, and uracil (AHU$^-$ and PAU$^-$).

The most widely used serotyping system is based on porin, which is antigenically classified into two groups, IA and IB.[11] (The terminology is based on the original designation of porin as protein I.) Subdivision of these groups into serovars is in turn based on patterns of coagglutination reactions with panels of monoclonal antibodies that react with various epitopes of Por IA (e.g., serovar IA-4) or IB (e.g., serovar IB-12).[11] In practice, auxotyping and porin serotyping are often used together to provide enhanced discrimination of strains. This system has been instrumental in mapping the geographic and temporal occurrence of gonorrhea in communities, in analyzing patterns of antibiotic resistance, and in studies of sexual transmission dynamics.[11,31]

Patterns of susceptibility to various antimicrobial agents, antigenic variations in LOS, and the plasmid content of isolates have also been analyzed to distinguish gonococcal strains, but with less success and reproducibility because these characteristics are not genetically stable. Analysis of DNA sequence variations, either by the method of Opa typing[32] or by automated DNA sequencing of particular genes (e.g., *por*), is also playing an important role in strain typing.[33] Pulsed-field gel electrophoresis of selected gonococcal DNA sequences can rapidly differentiate genetically distinct strains of *N. gonorrhoeae,* often within auxotype/serovar classes.[34] Multilocus sequence typing[35] is a new tool that can rapidly differentiate between strains of several organisms and likely will prove useful in future epidemiologic studies of gonorrhea.

Genetics

Plasmids

Many gonococci possess a 24.5 mD conjugative plasmid and can thereby conjugally transfer other non–self-transferable plasmids with high efficiency; chromosomal genes are not mobilized. Many gonococci carry a plasmid (Pc^r) that specifies production of a TEM-1 type of β-lactamase (penicillinase). The two most common Pc^r plasmids have molecular weights of 3.2 and 4.4 mD and are closely related to each other and to similar plasmids found in certain *Haemophilus* spp., including *Haemophilus ducreyi.*[36] In fact, it is suspected that gonococci first acquired Pc^r plasmids from *H. ducreyi.*[36] Pc^r plasmids are commonly mobilized to other gonococci by the conjugative plasmid.

Gonococci with plasmid-mediated high-level resistance to tetracycline, with minimal inhibitory concentrations (MIC) of 16 mg/L or greater, carry the 24.5 mD conjugative plasmid into which the *tetM* transposon has been inserted.[37] The *tetM* determinant also confers tetracycline resistance to a variety of other bacteria, including some *Streptococcus* and *Mycoplasma* spp. and various genital organisms such as *Gardnerella vaginalis* and *Ureaplasma urealyticum.* Because of its location on the conjugative plasmid, high-level tetracycline resistance is readily transferred among gonococci.[37] The *tetM* determinant functions by encoding a protein that protects ribosomes from the effect of tetracycline. Finally, all gonococci contain a small (2.6 mD) cryptic plasmid of unknown function.

Chromosomal Mutations and Transformation

Mutations in biosynthetic pathways are common, presumably reflecting the ready availability in vivo of essential nutrients such as amino acids, purines, and pyrimidines at infected mucosal sites. Nevertheless, *N. gonorrhoeae* is not highly mutable in that it lacks error-prone repair systems and is relatively resistant to external mutagenic stimuli such as ultraviolet light. Instead, gonococci have evolved efficient systems for phase and antigenic variation of surface components (pili, Opa, LOS) that do not depend on such mutagenic pathways.

Gonococci also use transfer of naked DNA between cells (transformation) to promote genetic variability. The piliated variants of virtually all clinical isolates of *N. gonorrhoeae* are highly competent in transformation, but loss of the ability to express pili is always accompanied by a dramatic reduction in transformation competence. Uptake of transforming DNA is limited to homologous (i.e., gonococcal) DNA, which reflects recognition of a unique nucleotide sequence by a surface receptor.[38] No bacteriophages have been found in *N. gonorrhoeae.*

Chromosomal resistance of *N. gonorrhoeae* to β-lactam antibiotics and the tetracyclines results from interactions between a series of individual mutations, some of which (e.g., the *mtr* determinant) alter the net accumulation of antimicrobials inside the cell. The *mtr* locus has been shown to be an efflux pump similar to other membrane transporters.[39] The *penA* locus alters penicillin-binding protein 2 to reduce its affinity for penicillin.[40] For epidemiologic purposes, chromosomal resistance is defined when the MIC is such that clinical failures are common with the maximum practical therapeutic dose, which corresponds to MICs of 2 mg/L or greater for both tetracycline and penicillin G.[41] Clinically significant resistance to the fluoroquinolones, indicated by MICs of ciprofloxacin of 1 mg/L or higher (up to 16 mg/L),[41] result from the additive effects of multiple chromosomal mutations involving the genes *gyrA* and *gyrB*, which code for DNA gyrases, and *parC* and *parE*, which code for topoisomerases.[42,43]

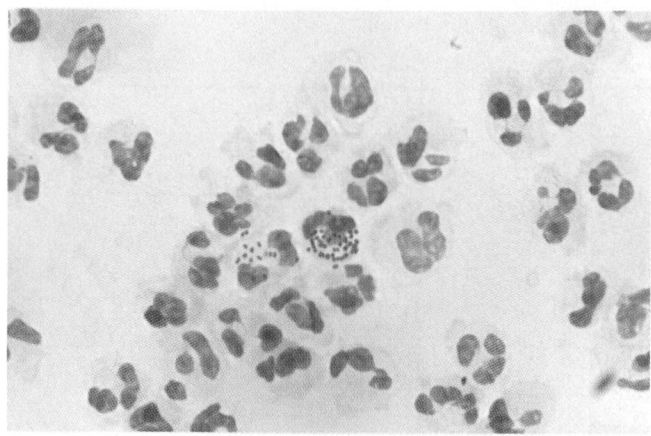

FIGURE 209-4. Gram-stained smear of urethral exudates showing intracellular gram-negative diplococci that is characteristic of gonorrhea.

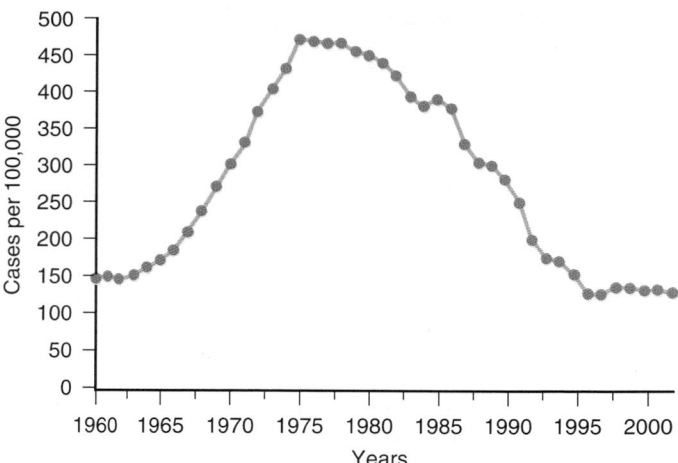

FIGURE 209-5. Incidence of reported gonorrhea per 100,000 residents, United States, 1960-2002. *(From Centers for Disease Control and Prevention. Sexually Transmitted Disease Surveillance, 2002. Atlanta, GA: U.S. Department of Health and Human Services, 2003.)*

PATHOLOGY

N. gonorrhoeae primarily infects columnar or cuboidal epithelium. The histopathology of gonorrhea is not materially different from that of most mucosal pyogenic infections. Attachment to mucosal epithelium, mediated in part by pili and Opa, is followed within 24 to 48 hours by penetration of the organism between and through epithelial cells to the submucosal tissues (see Fig. 209-3).[6] A vigorous response by neutrophils ensues, with sloughing of the epithelium, development of submucosal microabscesses, and exudation of pus. Stained smears usually reveal large numbers of gonococci within a few neutrophils, whereas most cells contain no organisms (Fig. 209-4). The explanation for this phenomenon may involve stimulation or production of cellular receptors for gonococci after initial contact with the first organism, or other alterations of the host cell cytoskeleton[44] might stimulate efficient phagocytosis of additional organisms. In addition, some gonococci may evade killing mechanisms and continue to multiply intracellularly. In untreated infections, neutrophils are gradually replaced by macrophages and lymphocytes. Lymphocytic and mononuclear infiltration persists in tissue for up to several weeks after *N. gonorrhoeae* can no longer be identified histologically or recovered by culture.

EPIDEMIOLOGY

Incidence

Many industrialized countries but few developing ones possess reporting systems that permit reasonably reliable estimates of the incidence of gonorrhea. The number of reported cases in the United States, probably about half the true number, rose from approximately 250,000 cases in the early 1960s to a high of 1.01 million cases in 1978. The peak incidence of reported infection in modern times, 468 cases per 100,000 population, occurred in 1975 (Fig. 209-5).[45] The incidence then declined rapidly, largely the result of systematic public health prevention measures implemented in the 1970s. The decline ceased in the mid-1990s, and from 1998 through 2002 the incidence was stable at 128 to 130 cases per 100,000.[45,46] The incidence is substantially lower in all countries of western Europe than in the United States, but high and rising rates have been documented in eastern Europe. The highest incidences of gonorrhea and its complications occur in developing countries. For example, the median prevalence of gonorrhea in unselected populations of pregnant women has been estimated to be 10% in Africa and 4% to 5% in most countries of Latin America and Asia.[47]

In the United States, the highest attack rates occur in 15- to 24-year-old women and men, but after adjustment for sexual experience the highest rates are seen in sexually active 15- to 19-year-old women (Fig. 209-6).[45,46,48,49] More cases are reported in men than women, which probably reflects both a greater ease of diagnosis in men and a sub-

stantially higher rate of infection in men who have sex with men (MSM) than in heterosexual men and women. Most health jurisdictions do not systematically measure or report sexually transmitted disease (STD) rates according to sexual orientation, but in Seattle, Washington, the minimum incidence of gonorrhea in MSM more than tripled from 1995, when there were at least 209 cases per 100,000 MSM in the population, to 2002 and 2003, where there were 725 and 645 cases per 100,000, respectively (Fig. 209-7).[50] During the same years, the rate of reported infection in the remainder of the Seattle population varied between 74 and 97 cases per 100,000. Similarly rising rates of gonorrhea, syphilis, and other STDs in MSM were reported throughout North America, Europe, and Australia after the late 1990s, the result of behavioral changes in response to improved therapy and survival of persons with human immunodeficiency virus (HIV) infection.[50,51]

The rate of gonorrhea in African American populations in the United States is almost 25 times higher than that in whites or persons of Asian ancestry; Latino populations and Native Americans experience intermediate rates (Table 209-1). Only a small portion of these differences can be explained by greater attendance of nonwhite populations at public clinics, where case reporting is more complete than in private health facilities.[48,49] Race and ethnicity are demographic markers of increased risk, not factors that directly denote a high risk for gonorrhea or other STDs. Other markers of gonorrhea risk in the United States include lower socioeconomic attainment, lesser education, residence in the southeastern part of the country, being unmarried, and illicit drug use. Contrary to popular perceptions, the population-based incidence of gonorrhea is as high in many rural settings in the United States as in urban ones.[52] Differing incidence rates between population subgroups are related less to variations in numbers of sex partners than to complex and poorly understood differences in sex partner networks, as well as access to health care and related societal factors.[52,53] The demographic predictors of gonorrhea around the world are qualitatively similar to those in the United States.

Transmission

The overriding risk factor for acquiring gonorrhea is sexual intercourse with an infected partner. The risk of transmission of *N. gonorrhoeae* from an infected woman to the urethra of her male partner is approximately 20% per episode of unprotected vaginal intercourse and rises to 60% to 80% after four or more exposures.[54] The risk of male-to-female transmission has been less well studied, but probably approximates 50% to 70% per contact.[55] Transmission by anal intercourse is efficient but has not been quantified. Transmission occurs

FIGURE 209-6. Distribution of reported gonorrhea incidence according to age and sex, United States, 2002. *(From Centers for Disease Control and Prevention. Sexually Transmitted Disease Surveillance, 2002. Atlanta, GA: U.S. Department of Health and Human Services, 2003.)*

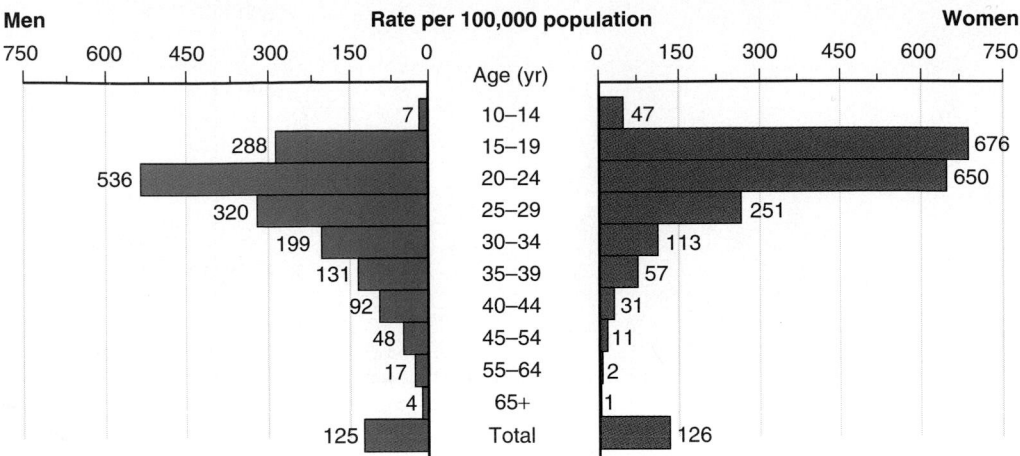

less readily by fellatio, especially from the oropharynx to the urethra, and transmission in either direction by cunnilingus is believed to be rare.[56] Data are conflicting as to whether women using hormonal contraception are at increased risk for gonorrhea; if so, the magnitude of the effect is small.[57]

The incubation period is brief and prominent symptoms often promptly bring infected persons to treatment, so that the mean duration of gonorrhea is short, typically several days in men and often less than 2 weeks in women. The approximate 50% transmission efficiency of uncomplicated gonorrhea through heterosexual intercourse[54,55] dictates that especially high rates of sex partner change—an average of 2 new partners within the 1- to 2-week interval between acquisition of infection and its resolution, equivalent to 50 or more partners per year—are required to sustain transmission in a population. People who have unprotected intercourse with new partners with sufficient frequency to maintain a stable prevalence in the community are defined as core transmitters.[58,59] Demographic and social characteristics that directly or indirectly influence the frequency with which new partners are acquired include young age, low educational and socioeconomic levels, commercial sex, illicit drug use, and similar factors.[58,59] Other characteristics of core transmitters include poorly understood psy-

chosocial determinants of partner selection, cultural factors that affect the response to symptoms, and reduced access to health care (whether real or perceived).[52,53] People who lack these characteristics often acquire infection by sexual contact with core group members, but transmission is not sustained outside the core group.

Originally developed as a mathematical model,[58] the core transmission hypothesis has been empirically confirmed by several studies,[31,48,59] and a central focus of gonorrhea control is to identify the core group and to target members for case finding, treatment, and other prevention strategies. Core groups sustain the transmission of all STDs, but the parameters that define core transmitters are different for each infection. For example, *Chlamydia trachomatis* infections are clinically milder, more often are asymptomatic, and therefore last longer than most cases of gonorrhea. Thus, lower rates of partner change are sufficient to sustain the prevalence of infection, and chlamydial infections typically affect a broader spectrum of the population than does gonorrhea.[49,53] Genital herpes simplex virus infections persist indefinitely and the duration of human papillomavirus infections is measured in months to years, so that low rates of partner change, rates that are the norm for the population as a whole, sustain these infections, partly explaining their high prevalence in all segments of society. A recent variation on the core group concept is the "risk space" hypothesis, that the locations where risk populations live and the sites where sexual exposures occur may be equally or more important determinants of STD incidence than other demographic predictors.[60]

Gonorrhea and other STDs are usually transmitted by people with asymptomatic infections or by those who have symptoms that they ignore or discount.[61] The behavioral response to symptoms is presumably determined by education and various demographic and sociocultural factors, such as substance abuse and the economic determinants of commercial sex.[48,59,60] Nevertheless, most people with new genital

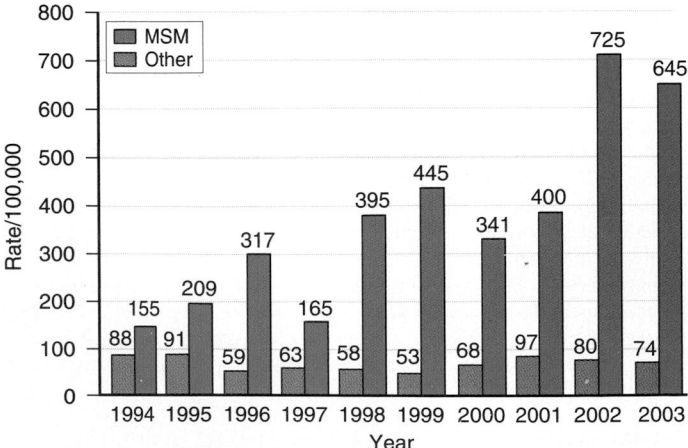

FIGURE 209-7. Estimated incidence of gonorrhea in men who have sex with men (MSM) and in the remainder of the population, King County, Washington, 1994-2003. The incidence in MSM is an underestimate, based on cases in men attending a public STD clinic who acknowledged sex with other men, plus reported cases of rectal gonococcal infection in men diagnosed in other clinical settings, and on an estimate that 42,500 MSM reside in King County. (Author's unpublished data.)

TABLE 209-1 Reported Cases and Rates of Gonorrhea According to Race and Ethnicity, United States, 2002

Racial/Ethnic Group	Reported Cases	Cases per 100,000 Population	Rate Ratio
White, non-Hispanic	61,671	31	Referent
African American, non-Hispanic	257,986	742	23.9
Hispanic	26,829	76	2.5
Native American	2,704	127	4.1
Asian/Pacific Islander	2,646	24	0.8
Total	351,836	125	

From Centers for Disease Control and Prevention. Sexually Transmitted Disease Surveillance, 2002. Atlanta, GA: U.S. Department of Health and Human Services, 2003.

symptoms cease sexual activity and seek care. It follows that many transmitters belong to a subset of infected people who lack or ignore symptoms. This concept underlies the importance of taking active steps to ensure treatment of the sex partners of infected persons, who often will not spontaneously seek health care.

Antimicrobial Resistance

As for most bacterial pathogens, the antimicrobial susceptibility of *N. gonorrhoeae* has evolved under the influence of antimicrobial therapy. Initially gonococci were almost uniformly susceptible to the sulfonamides, penicillin, tetracyclines, macrolides and fluoroquinolones, but none of these now is suitable for routine therapy of uncomplicated gonorrhea in most of the world. Declining susceptibility to penicillin, now attributed to chromosomal mutations, was documented almost immediately after the drug was introduced in the 1940s, but for almost three decades penicillin remained useful despite gradually rising relative resistance that required incrementally higher doses and co-treatment with probenecid to enhance and prolong blood levels.

Two nearly simultaneous developments rendered the penicillins unsuitable for routine gonorrhea therapy worldwide. Most dramatic was the appearance in the 1970s of β-lactamase–producing strains of *N. gonorrhoeae* bearing plasmids with the Pc[r] determinant, followed by worldwide dissemination within a decade. Several plasmid variants now carry the Pc[r] determinant, including the still dominant 4.4 mD and 3.2 mD plasmids originally associated with Asia and Africa, respectively.[31,62] Second, in the 1970s and 1980s chromosomal resistance progressed to the point that treatment failures became common with the maximum practical single-dose regimens of procaine penicillin, ampicillin, or amoxicillin. Although the proportion of gonococcal infections in the United States due to β-lactamase–producing strains declined from a peak of 11% in 1991 to only 2% of isolates in 2001, an additional 9% of infections are due to gonococci with high-level chromosomal penicillin resistance.[41]

Strains of *N. gonorrhoeae* with plasmid-mediated high-level tetracycline resistance were first documented in the United States in 1985. The location of the responsible *tetM* gene on the conjugative plasmid probably contributed to especially rapid worldwide spread of such strains, which accounted for 5% to 7% of gonococcal infections in the United States in 1999-2001.[41] Fortunately, the tetracyclines are no longer recommended and are little used as sole therapy for gonorrhea.

The mutations responsible for chromosomal resistance include *mtr*, which results in increased efflux of several antibiotics and other toxic compounds, such as fatty acids and bile salts; *penA*, which modifies the affinity of penicillin-binding proteins to β-lactam antibiotics; and *penB*, which alters the ability of antibiotics to transit the cell membrane through the porin protein.[39,40] Simultaneous mutations are common, with additive effects that result in resistance to several antibiotics and to all or most members of each affected drug class. Thus simultaneous chromosomal resistance to penicillin, the tetracyclines, and macrolides is common.[41] The cephalosporins also are affected, but MICs remain within ranges that do not typically affect treatment efficacy. For example, the MICs of ceftriaxone for strains with chromosomal resistance are many times higher (e.g., 0.015 to 0.125 mg/L) than those for fully susceptible gonococci (usually 0.0001 to 0.008 mg/L), but even these higher levels are greatly exceeded by the blood levels achieved with routinely recommended regimens, so therapeutic efficacy is not affected.[41,62,63] Infection with chromosomally resistant *N. gonorrhoeae* is especially common in MSM.[64] This occurs because rectal infection is required for propagation of gonorrhea in MSM, and fecal bile salts and fatty acids confer selection pressure for *mtr*.[65]

The most important recent development in gonorrhea therapeutics is the spread of strains resistant to the fluoroquinolones and their recent appearance in significant numbers in North America and Europe. As for penicillin and other drugs, low-level resistance to the fluoroquinolones began to appear in *N. gonorrhoeae* almost immediately after they were introduced and soon was observed sporadically around the world.[66,67] Clinically significant resistance, with ciprofloxacin MICs of 1 to 16

mg/L, began to evolve soon thereafter, due to the additive effects of multiple chromosomal mutations, particularly in the DNA gyrase complex *(gyrA, gyrB)* and topoisomerases *(parC, parE)*.[42] Ciprofloxacin MICs of 4 mg/L or greater are associated with at least 50% rates of treatment failure with the recommended regimens of ciprofloxacin or other fluoroquinolones.[68] In the Philippines the prevalence of high-level resistance to the fluoroquinolones among persons with gonorrhea increased from 12% in 1994 to more than 70% between 1996 and 1997[68] and similar prevalences now are the norm throughout Asia and the Pacific.[67-69] Such strains caused about 20% of all gonorrhea cases in Hawaii by 2001 and 10% of all gonorrhea in California in 2002, and by late 2003 they had appeared in substantial numbers in Washington State and Massachusetts and appeared to be especially frequent among MSM.[41,67,69] Gonococci with high-level fluoroquinolone resistance also have appeared in parts of Canada and are now common in India, Israel, and parts of Europe; their spread throughout North America and Europe in the near future appears certain.

CLINICAL MANIFESTATIONS

Genital Infection In Men

Uncomplicated Infection

Acute urethritis is the predominant manifestation of gonorrhea in men (see Chapter 102). The incubation period is typically 2 to 5 days but ranges from 1 to 10 days or longer (Fig. 209-8). Urethral discharge and dysuria, usually without urinary frequency or urgency, are the major symptoms. The discharge may initially be scant and mucoid, but within a day or two it becomes overtly purulent. These observations have been confirmed in studies of experimental gonococcal urethritis in humans.[7] When compared with nongonococcal urethritis, the incubation period of gonorrhea is shorter, dysuria is usually more prominent, and the discharge is generally more profuse and more purulent (Fig. 209-9), but exceptions are common and a small proportion of men with urethral gonorrhea remain asymptomatic and lack signs of urethritis.[61] These features depend in part on the infecting organism; some Por IA serovars and the AHU⁻ and related auxotypes of *N. gonorrhoeae* are more frequently associated with asymptomatic infection in men than are other gonococcal types.[11,70] The decline in the prevalence of such strains in North America probably has been accompanied by a decreasing frequency of asymptomatic gonorrhea in men. Most cases of untreated gonococcal urethritis resolve spontaneously over several weeks.

Localized Complications

Acute epididymitis is the most common complication of urethral gonorrhea but now is uncommon in industrialized countries; most cases of

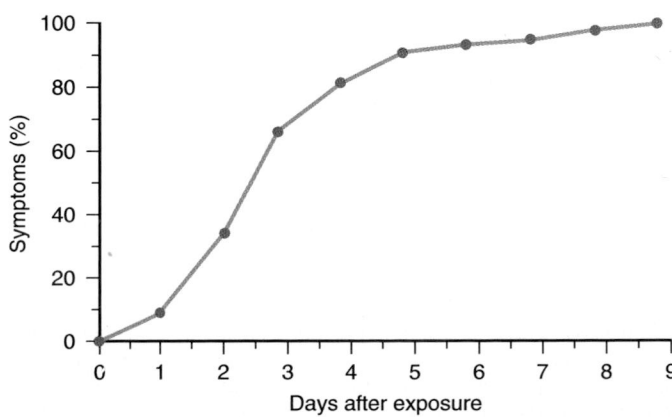

FIGURE 209-8. Incubation period in 44 men with gonococcal urethritis. *(From Harrison WO, Hooper RR, Weisner PJ, et al. A trial of minocycline given after exposure to prevent gonorrhea. N Engl J Med 1979;300:1074-1078.)*

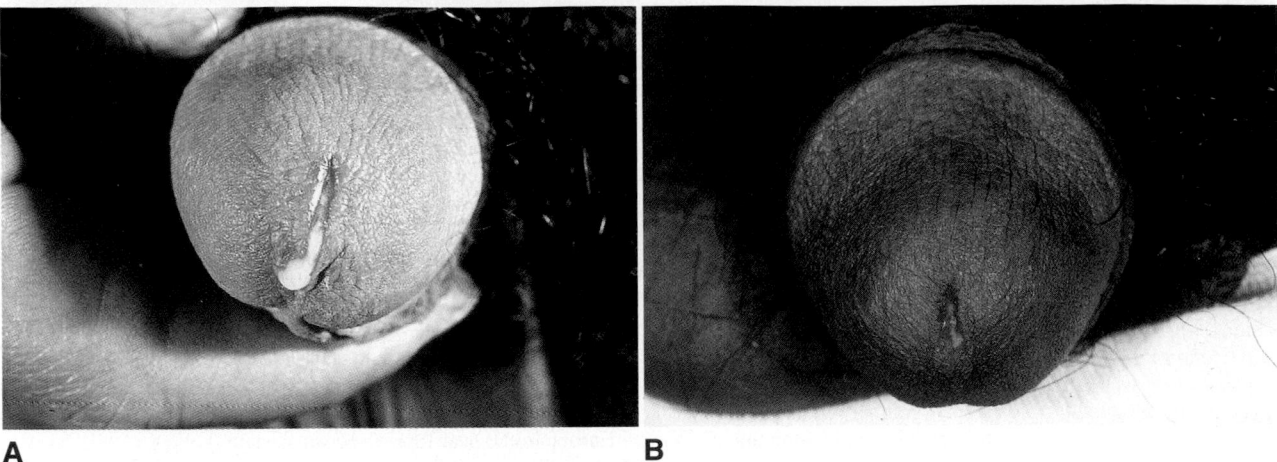

A   **B**

FIGURE 209-9. Gonococcal urethritis. **A,** Purulent exudates due to gonorrhea. **B,** Mucopurulent discharge mimicking the usual appearance of nongonococcal urethritis due to *Chlamydia trachomatis* and other pathogens.

epididymitis in young men are due to *C. trachomatis* (see Chapter 105).[71] Penile edema without other overt inflammatory signs ("bull-headed clap") is occasionally seen in gonococcal or nongonococcal urethritis. Penile lymphangitis, periurethral abscess, acute prostatitis, seminal vesiculitis, and infections of Tyson's and Cowper's glands are uncommon complications. Urethral stricture as a result of gonorrhea is also uncommon; it is likely that many strictures in the preantibiotic era resulted from treatment by urethral irrigation with caustic solutions, such as silver nitrate or potassium permanganate, rather than from gonorrhea itself.

Uncomplicated Urogenital Infection in Women

The primary locus of genital infection in women is the endocervix (see Chapter 103). *N. gonorrhoeae* often can be recovered from the urethra or rectum and occasionally from the periurethral (Skene's) glands and the ducts of Bartholin's glands, but these are rarely the sole infected sites except in women who have undergone hysterectomy. The vagina per se is not infected in sexually mature women, because under the influence of estrogen the squamous epithelium of the vaginal mucosa is not susceptible to gonococcal infection.

The natural course of gonorrhea is less well understood in women than in men, partly because of high prevalences of concurrent infection with *C. trachomatis, Trichomonas vaginalis,* and bacterial vaginosis. Symptoms probably develop in most infected women,[72] but many remain asymptomatic or have only minor symptoms and do not seek medical care.[73] Thus women with subclinical infection accumulate in the population, and in settings where sexually active women are routinely screened for subclinical infection, up to 80% of women with gonorrhea are asymptomatic.[61,73] By contrast, in settings that attract symptomatic patients, such as urgent care clinics and hospital emergency departments, most women with gonorrhea are overtly symptomatic.[73] Women infected with AHU⁻ and related auxotypes of *N. gonorrhoeae,* like men, are more likely to have asymptomatic infection and more subtle inflammatory signs.[70]

Most infected women who develop symptoms do so within 10 days.[72] The dominant symptoms are increased vaginal discharge, dysuria (often without urgency or frequency), and intermenstrual bleeding, sometimes triggered by coitus.[73,74] Abdominal or pelvic pain usually denotes ascending infection, but some women with these symptoms lack evidence of salpingitis at laparoscopy. Physical examination may show purulent or mucopurulent cervical exudate (Fig. 209-10) and other signs of mucopurulent cervicitis, such as edema in a zone of cervical ectopy or endocervical bleeding induced by gentle swabbing,[74] but the contribution of *N. gonorrhoeae* to these signs, versus that of other pathogens, remains unclear; in many infected women the examination is entirely normal. Purulent discharge can

sometimes be expressed from the urethra or the ducts of Bartholin's glands.

Rectal Gonococcal Infection

N. gonorrhoeae can be isolated from the rectum in up to 40% of women and a similar proportion of MSM with uncomplicated gonorrhea. The rectum often is the only infected site in MSM, whereas isolated rectal infection is found in about 5% of women with gonorrhea.[64,73,75] Rectal infection is acquired both through receptive anal intercourse, which accounts for virtually all cases in men, and perineal contamination with cervicovaginal secretions, which is believed to be responsible for many infections in women. Rectal gonococcal infection usually is asymptomatic, but some patients have acute proctitis manifested by anal pruritus, tenesmus, purulent discharge, or rectal bleeding.[76] The apparently higher rate of overt proctitis in men than women suggests that inoculum size or trauma during anal intercourse may influence the development of symptoms. Anoscopy sometimes reveals mucopurulent exudate and inflammatory changes in the rectal mucosa, but infection with *C. trachomatis,* herpes simplex virus, or other sexually transmitted pathogens can produce the same findings.[76]

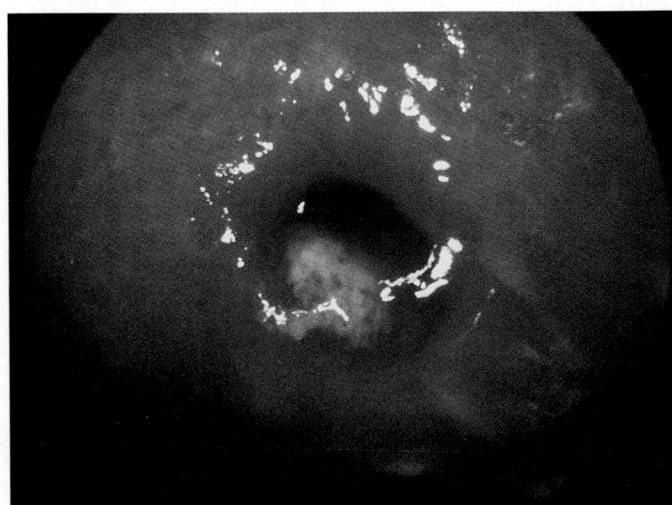

FIGURE 209-10. Purulent endocervical exudate in gonococcal cervicitis. *(From Handsfield HH. Color Atlas and Synopsis of Sexually Transmitted Diseases. 2nd ed. New York, McGraw-Hill, 2001; courtesy of King K. Holmes.)*

Pharyngeal Infection

Pharyngeal gonococcal infection is acquired by oral sexual exposure but probably rarely, if ever, by kissing. Acquired more efficiently by fellatio than by cunnilingus,[56] pharyngeal infection can be found in 10% to 20% of heterosexual women with gonorrhea and 10% to 25% of infected homosexual men, but it is present in only 3% to 7% of heterosexual men with gonorrhea.[56,64,75] Almost all pharyngeal infections are asymptomatic, but rare cases may cause overt pharyngitis.[56]

The importance of documenting pharyngeal gonorrhea is debated, and several factors argue against routine screening or diagnostic testing. Most cases are asymptomatic and resolve spontaneously, pharyngeal infection probably is less transmissible than rectal or genital gonorrhea, and the pharynx rarely is the only infected site. Further, identification of *N. gonorrhoeae* in pharyngeal cultures is more expensive than identification in anogenital cultures, nonculture diagnostic assays have not been validated, and most of the regimens recommended for treatment of genital or rectal gonorrhea will eradicate undiagnosed pharyngeal infection.[77,78] On the other hand, pharyngeal infection can be symptomatic and sometimes is the source of transmission to sex partners, especially among MSM,[79] or of systemic dissemination of *N. gonorrhoeae*.[56] Many experts routinely test MSM for pharyngeal infection but do not collect pharyngeal specimens from heterosexual men or women, unless there is clinical evidence of pharyngitis.

Other Local Manifestations

Gonococcal conjunctivitis in adults usually is seen in persons with genital gonorrhea and most cases probably result from autoinoculation, but some cases may be acquired by other routes, such as orogenital exposure. Gonococcal conjunctivitis is usually painful, with prominent photophobia and copious, purulent exudate (Fig. 209-11), and corneal ulceration can supervene rapidly in the absence of prompt antibiotic therapy. However, some infections are mild, perhaps related to specific gonococcal strains. *N. gonorrhoeae* has been isolated in cases of acute gingivitis, otherwise unexplained oral ulcerations, and intraoral abscesses. Cutaneous abscesses have been described, typically involving the finger or the penile shaft, and probably result from inoculation of preexisting lesions; for example, gonococcal abscess sometimes is the first clinical presentation of a congenitally patent median raphe duct of the penis.

Pelvic Inflammatory Disease

Pelvic inflammatory disease (PID) (see Chapter 104) is estimated to occur in 10% to 20% of women with gonorrhea and is manifested by various combinations of endometritis, salpingitis, tuboovarian ab-

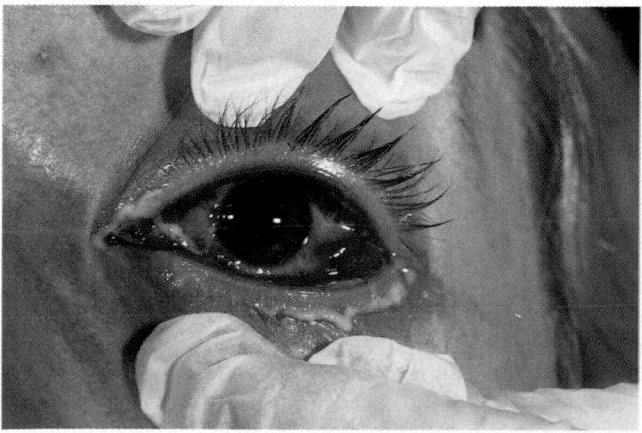

FIGURE 209-11. Acute gonococcal conjunctivitis in an adult. *(From Handsfield HH. Color Atlas and Synopsis of Sexually Transmitted Diseases, 2nd ed. New York, McGraw-Hill, 2001.)*

scess, pelvic peritonitis, and perihepatitis.[73,80,81] The immediate and long-term sequelae are a primary impetus for prevention strategies against gonorrhea and chlamydial infection. Infection with *N. gonorrhoeae, C. trachomatis,* perhaps *Mycoplasma genitalium,* and probably other sexually transmitted infections are the proximate causes of the large majority of cases of acute PID.[81] Teen girls are at higher risk than older women, probably because of both innate susceptibility, perhaps owing to a high prevalence of cervical ectopy that may facilitate ascending infection, and behavioral factors, such as choice of sex partners. Some intrauterine contraceptive devices may increase the risk, whereas women using anovulatory hormones have a lower risk of chlamydial salpingitis but apparently not of gonococcal PID.[82] Prior PID increases a woman's risk for recurrent episodes. Case-control studies have suggested that vaginal douching, whether for perceived infection or as a hygienic measure, is a potent risk factor for PID and ectopic pregnancy,[83] but a recent prospective study challenged the association of douching with PID.[84] Bacterial vaginosis, which is characterized by a marked increase in the vaginal concentration of potentially pathogenic anaerobic and facultative bacteria, is strongly associated with the occurrence of PID.

The most consistent symptom of PID is low abdominal pain, and most women also have symptoms of lower genital tract infection.[80] Gonococcal PID often follows the onset of menses by a few days.[73,80] Fever, chills, nausea, and vomiting may occur, but most patients lack these manifestations.[80] The primary finding on physical examination is pelvic adnexal tenderness, usually bilateral. Other common findings are uterine fundal tenderness, pain elicited on moving the cervix, and one or more tender adnexal masses. Abdominal examination usually elicits tenderness over the lower quadrants, and signs of peritoneal inflammation are common in severe cases. Most women with PID have bacterial vaginosis and many have signs of mucopurulent cervicitis. Fever, leukocytosis, and an elevated erythrocyte sedimentation rate or C-reactive protein level are common, but they are absent in about one third of patients with laparoscopically documented PID.[80] In practice, the clinical diagnosis of PID is imprecise; series using laparoscopy have found that the clinical diagnosis of acute PID is both insensitive and nonspecific.[52,80]

The proportion of PID cases associated with gonorrhea varies greatly across population groups and with the background rates of gonorrhea and chlamydial infection. In the 1980s, 20% to 40% of cases of PID in most urban areas of the United States were associated with gonorrhea. The presence of cervical gonococcal or chlamydial infection does not exclude fallopian tube infection with other organisms, nor does failure to isolate *N. gonorrhoeae* or *C. trachomatis* definitively exclude their contribution to salpingitis.[80] Facultative and anaerobic bacterial flora of the vagina may also contribute to acute PID, especially in patients with pelvic abscess or otherwise severe infections.[80,81]

Infertility resulting from fallopian tube obstruction is the most common serious consequence of PID and occurs in 15% to 20% of women after a single episode and 50% to 80% of those who experience three or more episodes.[81] Infertility may be more common after chlamydial than gonococcal PID, perhaps because the more acute inflammatory signs associated with gonorrhea bring women to diagnosis and treatment sooner. A nationwide epidemic of ectopic pregnancies in the United States followed the gonorrhea/chlamydia epidemic of the 1970s and 1980s, and evidence of prior salpingitis can be found in 50% to 80% of women with ectopic pregnancies. Chronic pelvic pain caused by adhesions or other poorly understood mechanisms occurs in up to 20% of women after PID, and may be difficult to differentiate from recurrent infection.

Perihepatitis

Acute perihepatitis, or Fitz-Hugh-Curtis syndrome, occurs primarily by direct extension of *N. gonorrhoeae* or *C. trachomatis* from the fallopian tube to the liver capsule and overlying peritoneum. Some cases may result from lymphangitic spread or bacteremic dissemination, which may explain rare cases of apparent perihepatitis in men. Perihepatitis results in abdominal pain, hepatic tenderness, and right upper quadrant peritoneal inflammatory signs. Most cases occur in association with overt PID, but many women lack pelvic symptoms or signs. Perihepatitis should be considered in the differential diagnosis of right upper quadrant pain in young, sexually active women; it is commonly mistaken for acute cholecystitis or viral hepatitis. Laparoscopy may show "violin string" adhesions between the liver capsule and the parietal peritoneum.

Gonorrhea in Pregnancy

Gonorrhea during pregnancy is associated with spontaneous abortion, premature labor, early rupture of fetal membranes, and perinatal infant mortality.[85] The clinical manifestations of gonorrhea are unchanged in pregnant women, except that PID and perihepatitis are uncommon after the first trimester, when the products of conception obliterate the uterine cavity. A higher prevalence of pharyngeal infection has been reported in pregnant than nonpregnant women with gonorrhea,[86] perhaps because the frequency of fellatio rises in lieu of vaginal intercourse as pregnancy progresses. However, the anatomic sites of gonococcal infection in pregnant women have not been studied in recent decades. Reports are conflicting as to whether pregnancy is a risk factor for gonococcemia.

Disseminated Gonococcal Infection

Disseminated gonococcal infection (DGI) results from bacteremic dissemination of *N. gonorrhoeae,* although immune complexes or other indirect immunologic mechanisms may contribute to pathogenesis and symptoms in some cases. Although estimated to occur in 0.5% to 3% of infected patients,[87,88] the rate undoubtedly is lower at present because of declining prevalences of gonococcal strains prone to disseminate.[89] Septic arthritis and a characteristic syndrome of polyarthritis and dermatitis are the predominant manifestations, and DGI is a relatively common cause of infective arthritis in young adults.[87,88] Gonococcal endocarditis was common in the preantibiotic era but now is rare.[90] Meningitis, osteomyelitis, septic shock, and acute respiratory distress syndrome are rare manifestations.[91-94]

Properties of *N. gonorrhoeae* classically associated with dissemination include resistance to the bactericidal action of nonimmune human serum, the AHU⁻ auxotype, specific Por IA serovars, and marked susceptibility to penicillin, characteristics also associated with asymptomatic genital gonorrhea.[11,89] However, an increasing proportion of DGI cases have been associated with other auxotype/serovar classes as the prevalence of Por IA/AHU⁻ gonococci has declined, and antibiotic-resistant strains have caused DGI.[88,89] According to one report, as the frequency of DGI has declined more apparent cases in fact are due to meningococcemia.[95]

Complement deficiency predisposes to gonococcal and meningococcal bacteremia.[96] Up to 13% of patients with DGI have a complement deficiency, and patients with repeated episodes of neisserial bacteremia should be tested with an assay for total hemolytic complement activity. Other host factors associated with dissemination include female sex, menstruation, and perhaps pharyngeal gonococcal infection and pregnancy.[87,88,96] In about half of affected women, symptoms of DGI begin within 7 days of the onset of menses.[87]

The most common presentation of DGI is the arthritis-dermatitis syndrome. During the first few days, most patients experience polyarthralgias that primarily involve the knees, elbows, and more distal joints; the axial skeleton usually is not involved. Physical examination usually shows objective signs of arthritis or tenosynovitis in at least two joints.[87,88] Asymmetrical involvement of only a few joints helps distinguish DGI from polyarthritis caused by most immune complex-mediated disorders, which typically are manifested by symmetrical involvement of many joints. A characteristic dermatitis (Fig. 209-12) is present in about 75% of patients[87,88] and consists of discrete papules and pustules, often with a hemorrhagic component. Hemorrhagic bullae or overtly necrotic lesions that mimic ecthyma gangrenosum sometimes are seen. The lesions usually number 5 to 40 and occur predominantly on the extremities. Fever, systemic toxicity, and polymorphonuclear leukocytosis are common, but they are usually mild and are often absent.[87,88]

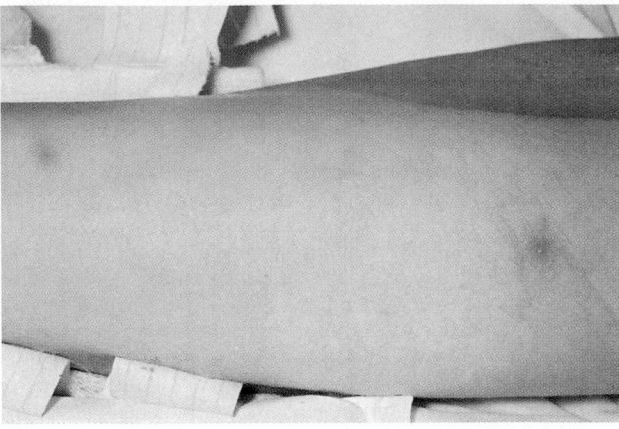

A

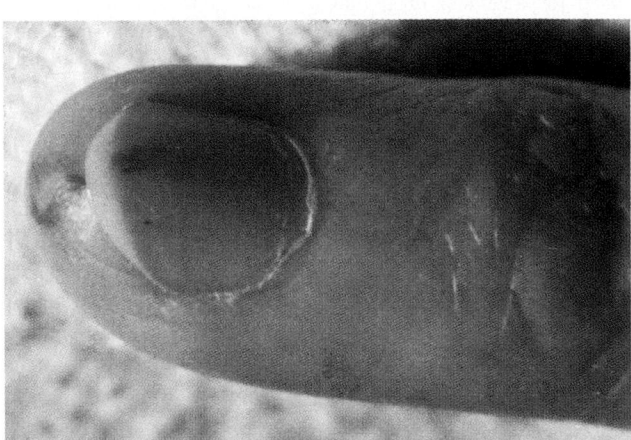

B

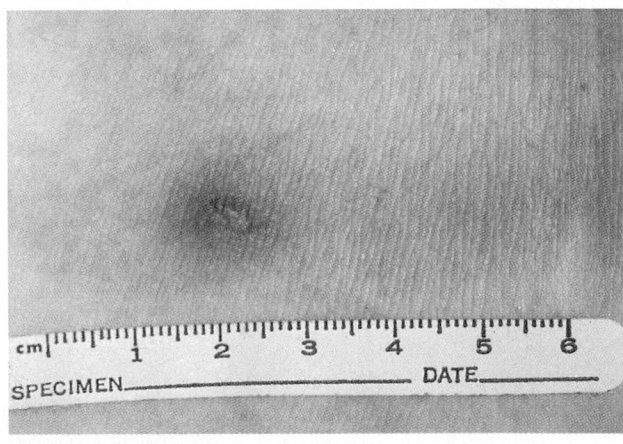

C

FIGURE 209-12. Cutaneous lesions in disseminated gonococcal infection. **A,** Early papular lesions. **B,** Pustular lesion associated with subungual hemorrhage. **C,** Ulcerated pustular lesion.

Untreated, inflammation regresses in most joints and the dermatitis resolves, but overt septic arthritis supervenes in one or two joints, most commonly the knee, ankle, elbow, or wrist, although any joint may be involved. Septic gonococcal arthritis develops in some patients without prior polyarthritis or dermatitis, and in the absence of the characteristic dermatitis or overt genital infection is clinically indistinguishable from septic arthritis of any etiology.[87,88]

During the arthritis-dermatitis stage, gonococci often can be recovered by blood culture, but synovial fluid, if it can be obtained, usually contains fewer than 20,000 leukocytes/mm³ and is sterile. Gonococci can often be seen by immunochemical methods in biopsy specimens of skin lesions, but cultures are generally sterile. In septic gonococcal arthritis, synovial fluid usually contains more than 50,000 leukocytes/mm³ and culture is often positive, but at this stage blood cultures are usually negative.[87,88]

Gonococcal bacteremia often is intermittent, so that a minimum of three blood cultures should be obtained when DGI is suspected. Synovial fluid should be cultured if a specimen can be obtained. However, only about half of patients with DGI have positive cultures of blood or synovial fluid. Although uncommonly positive, Gram-stained smears and cultures of pustular skin lesions are simple to perform and should be obtained. *N. gonorrhoeae* can be recovered from a mucosal site in at least 80% of patients,[87,88] so the urethra or endocervix, the rectum, and the pharynx should be tested regardless of symptoms or exposure history, and patients' sex partners should be examined and tested. Polymerase chain reaction (PCR) appears to be more sensitive than culture in detecting gonococci in synovial fluid[97]; it seems likely that other nucleic acid amplification tests (NAATs) would perform similarly. Fluorescent polyclonal antibody often can detect gonococci in culture-negative skin lesions, suggesting that NAATs might perform well, but no data have been reported. The diagnosis of DGI is confirmed if *N. gonorrhoeae* is identified in a nonmucosal specimen such as blood, synovial fluid, or a skin lesion, and is probable if infection is documented at a mucosal site or in a sex partner of a patient with a typical clinical syndrome.

The differential diagnosis of the gonococcal arthritis–dermatitis syndrome includes meningococcemia,[95] septic arthritis due to other pyogenic bacteria, and the entire range of inflammatory arthritis. Reiter's syndrome and other kinds of reactive arthritis are easily confused with DGI because they are common in sexually active young adults and are associated with urethritis, cervicitis, and skin lesions that sometimes have a pustular component. Usually, careful clinical and microbiologic assessment readily differentiates these disorders, but a trial of antibiotic therapy may be required.[87,88]

Gonococcal endocarditis, which usually involves the aortic valve, is a rare but serious manifestation that occurs in an estimated 1% to 2% of patients with DGI.[87,90] Although often associated with the arthritis-dermatitis syndrome, endocarditis may be the sole manifestation of DGI.[90] In the preantibiotic era, median survival was 6 to 8 weeks, reflecting a typical rate of valve destruction between that of acute staphylococcal or pneumococcal endocarditis and subacute endocarditis caused by viridans streptococci.

Neonatal and Pediatric Infections

Gonococcal conjunctivitis of the newborn (ophthalmia neonatorum) is the most common clinically recognized manifestation of neonatal infection[98-100]; it was once a common cause of blindness in the United States and may remain so in some developing countries. Prophylaxis by instillation of antibiotics or a 1% aqueous solution of silver nitrate into the conjunctivae soon after delivery is highly effective, although occasional failures occur. The most important preventive measure is routine screening and treatment of pregnant women for gonorrhea before term. The diagnosis of gonococcal ophthalmia should be suspected clinically when acute conjunctivitis develops within a few days of delivery and is confirmed by identification of gonococci in conjunctival secretions. Systemic illness with septicemia and arthritis can also develop in newborns exposed to gonorrhea, but these are rare. *N. gonorrhoeae* can often be recovered from the gastric aspirates of infants born to infected mothers, but many cases probably reflect transient colonization rather than clinically important infection.[98]

Rectal gonococcal infection is sometimes seen in newborns, but vaginal infection is uncommon, because the neonatal vaginal mucosa is well estrogenized by circulating maternal hormone. Purulent vaginitis is the primary manifestation of gonorrhea in prepubertal girls after the neonatal period,[98,100] but otherwise the clinical manifestations of gonorrhea in children are not materially different from those in adults. After the neonatal period until 1 year of age, most cases in children are probably acquired nonsexually from an infected parent, usually in a setting of poor hygiene.[100] After 1 year of age, most cases are acquired by sexual abuse, most commonly by a male relative or the mother's nonmarital sex partner, other than the child's biological father.[98,100] Nonsexual transmission of ocular infection occasionally occurs among young children in tropical settings.

DIAGNOSIS

Isolation of *N. gonorrhoeae* is the historic standard for diagnosis. Culture is inexpensive and reasonably sensitive, is the only validated diagnostic test for rectal and pharyngeal infection, and preserves an isolate for antimicrobial susceptibility testing when clinically indicated or for surveillance. Culture is widely considered the only appropriate test in forensic settings, as in testing persons who have been sexually assaulted or children with suspected gonorrhea. Nevertheless, NAATs are supplanting culture in many settings, owing to convenient specimen management and their utility in testing urine and self-obtained vaginal swabs. Nonamplified DNA probe tests remain in common use despite their lower sensitivity compared with culture or NAAT. Enzyme immunoassays for gonococcal antigen achieved modest usage in the 1980s but no longer have a significant role. Microscopy of Gram-stained smears is effective in the diagnosis of symptomatic urethritis in men but has marginal utility in other settings. There is no clinically useful serological test.

Culture

A single culture on antibiotic-containing selective medium, such as modified Thayer-Martin agar, has a sensitivity of 95% or more for urethral specimens from men with symptomatic urethritis and 80% to 90% for endocervical infection in women. Results may vary depending on the quality of the medium and the adequacy of the clinical specimen.[1,3,101] Simultaneous inoculation of both selective and nonselective media maximizes sensitivity for cervical infection[3,101] but is impractical in most settings. Normally sterile clinical specimens such as blood, synovial fluid, and cerebrospinal fluid should be inoculated onto enriched chocolate agar or another nonselective medium as well as broth medium[87] and probably should be tested by NAAT,[97] but no published studies have systematically analyzed the detection of *N. gonorrhoeae* in broth cultures with the automated techniques now used by most clinical laboratories.

Depending in part on symptoms and the anatomic sites exposed, in general the urethra should be cultured in heterosexual men and endocervical specimens should be collected from women; vaginal fluid is inadequate. Among asymptomatic MSM, the highest yield will be achieved by culturing the rectum if the patient practices receptive anal intercourse. Some experts recommend screening for urethral infection as well, although asymptomatic urethral gonorrhea is uncommon in this population.[64,75] In screening women or heterosexual men, a pharyngeal culture should be obtained if symptoms of pharyngitis are present and may be warranted if the patient has performed fellatio on a person known to have genital gonorrhea. Pharyngeal testing usually is routine when screening asymptomatic MSM.[56,64,75]

Up to 5% of gram-negative, oxidase-positive diplococci isolated from the genitals and substantially greater proportions of those from the rectum and pharynx are in fact *N. meningitidis*,[56,75,102,103] and some cases are associated with urethritis, cervicitis or proctitis that is clinically indistinguishable from gonorrhea.[75,104] Therefore, speciation of *Neisseria* isolates is desirable for positive genital cultures and should be routine for pharyngeal and rectal specimens. The NAATs for *N. gonorrhoeae* are believed to reliably exclude meningococcal infection.[105,106] Antimicrobial susceptibility testing of *N. gonorrhoeae* is not generally recommended except when conducting surveillance for antimicrobial resistance, but should be routine following treatment failure and in cases of disseminated infection.

Nucleic Acid Amplification Tests

Currently available NAATs for *N. gonorrhoeae* utilize several related technologies, including transcription mediated amplification, e.g.,

Aptima (Gen-Probe; San Diego, CA); polymerase chain reaction, e.g., Amplicor (Roche; Nutley, NJ); or the DNA strand displacement assay, e.g., Probe-Tec (Becton Dickinson; Franklin Lakes, NJ). An assay based on ligase chain reaction (LCx, Abbott; Abbott Park, IL) no longer is commercially available in the United States. The NAATs have largely replaced culture in many settings where persons are screened for asymptomatic genital infection.[105-107] These tests are not significantly more sensitive than culture for detecting *N. gonorrhoeae* in cervical or urethral specimens (unlike diagnosis of *C. trachomatis,* for which the NAATs are more sensitive than all other tests). However, the NAATs for *N. gonorrhoeae* appear to have specificities greater than 99%, offer important advantages in specimen management, and retain sensitivity when used to test voided urine or self-collected vaginal swabs, an important advantage for laboratory screening in many settings.[105,107] The transcription mediated amplification test has a positive predictive value of at least 95% in women in settings with gonorrhea prevalences as low as 0.5%, indicating that false-positive results are rare even when screening low-prevalence populations.[108] Concern has been expressed that persisting DNA may cause false-positive results when NAATs are used to test patients soon after treatment, but NAATs for *N. gonorrhoeae* become negative within 2 weeks of successful treatment.[109] Unpublished data suggest that some NAATs for *N. gonorrhoeae* and *C. trachomatis* are reliable for diagnosis of rectal and pharyngeal infection, but confirmatory data are needed.

Gram-Stained Smears

Methylene blue and other dyes have been used to identify gonococci in clinical specimens, but the Gram stain is used almost exclusively in the United States. Microscopy of Gram-stained smears is positive if gram-negative diplococci of typical morphology are observed in association with neutrophils (see Fig. 209-4), negative if no such organisms are seen, and equivocal if typical morphotypes are not associated with neutrophils or morphologically atypical organisms are seen.[101] Nonpathogenic Neisseraceae are not usually associated with leukocytes. In men with symptomatic urethritis, microscopy is at least 95% sensitive and is highly specific for diagnosis of gonorrhea, but microscopy is less useful for other anatomic sites. The sensitivity approximates 50% for asymptomatic urethral infection in men[60] and for cervical or rectal infection[101]; the specificity is said to be high, but this likely is true only for highly experienced observers. Microscopy is both insensitive and nonspecific for detection of pharyngeal gonococcal infection and is not recommended.

Other Diagnostic Methods

Nonamplified DNA probe tests are somewhat less sensitive than culture or NAATs, and they are not useful in the diagnosis of rectal or pharyngeal infection or for testing urine. However, these assays are inexpensive, are offered by many laboratories in combination with assays for *C. trachomatis,* and remain in common use in some settings. Immunochemical detection of gonococcal antigens, such as enzyme immunoassays with polyclonal antigonococcal antibodies and fluorescein-conjugated monoclonal antibodies for direct fluorescence microscopy, had modest usage in the 1980s, but these tests were relatively insensitive and had no important advantages and now are little used.

TREATMENT

The antimicrobial susceptibility of *N. gonorrhoeae* is labile, varies greatly across geographic areas and populations, and fluctuates over time. Treatment decisions almost invariably are made without knowledge of the antimicrobial susceptibility of the infecting strain. Therefore, when possible the regimens for routine treatment of gonorrhea should have efficacies that approach 100%, regardless of the distribution of sensitive and resistant strains of *N. gonorrhoeae* in the community, and treatments with efficacies less than 95% should be avoided.[78,110] Other factors that influence therapeutic decisions for gonorrhea are the pharmacokinetic characteristics of the agent, its efficacy in complicated versus uncomplicated infection, differential efficacy at

various anatomic sites of infection, toxicity, convenience of administration, and cost. An additional consideration is the potential efficacy of an agent for concurrent infection. Historically this concern focused on syphilis, but even in settings with high prevalences of both gonorrhea and syphilis, the occurrence of syphilis in persons with gonorrhea is not measurably affected by use of treatment regimens with or without activity against *Treponema pallidum.*[111] The most common coexisting pathogen in persons with gonorrhea is *C. trachomatis,* and many studies over three decades have given remarkably consistent results: 15% to 25% of heterosexual men, 10% to 15% of MSM, and 35% to 50% of women with gonorrhea also have chlamydial infections.[49,77]

Uncomplicated Gonorrhea in Adults

Initial Single-Dose Treatment

Recommendations for the treatment of uncomplicated gonorrhea, modified from those promulgated in 2002 by the Centers for Disease Control and Prevention (CDC),[77] are summarized in Table 209-2. Either a single 125-mg intramuscular dose of ceftriaxone or a single 400-mg oral dose of cefixime is effective for infection of all mucosal sites, with cure rates that exceed 98% for urethral, cervical, and rectal gonorrhea and 90% for pharyngeal infection, and both regimens are safe and effective in pregnant women.[63,77,78,112] Cefixime recently became unavailable in the United States but probably will be reintroduced. Cefpodoxime, in a single oral dose of 400 mg, has favorable pharmacokinetics, performed favorably in a dose-ranging trial,[113] and is approved for treatment of gonorrhea by the U.S. Food and Drug Administration, implying that comparative clinical trials conducted by the manufacturer support its therapeutic efficacy, but those studies have not been published. The efficacy of cefpodoxime is unknown for pharyngeal infection and for rectal infection in men. Cefuroxime, 1 g orally, appears effective in women, with a reported cure rate of 97%, but was only 93% effective against gonococcal urethritis in men.[114]

TABLE 209-2 Treatment of Uncomplicated Gonorrhea in Adults

Initial Single-Dose Treatment

Regimens of Choice
Ceftriaxone, 125 mg IM*
or
Cefixime, 400 mg PO[†]

Alternatives
Cefpodoxime axetil, 400 mg PO[†]
or
Ciprofloxacin, 500 mg PO[‡]
or
Ofloxacin, 400 mg PO[‡]
or
Levofloxacin, 250 mg PO[‡]
or
Azithromycin, 2.0 g PO[§]
or
Spectinomycin, 2.0 g IM[‖]

Follow-up Treatment for Chlamydial Infection[¶]
Azithromycin, 1.0 g PO, single dose
or
Doxycycline, 100 mg PO bid for 7 d

*May be reconstituted in 1% lidocaine solution to minimize injection pain.
[†]Cefixime is the recommended cephalosporin for oral treatment, but availability has been intermittent in the United States. Limited data support the use of cefpodoxime as an oral alernative.
[‡]Fluoroquinolone-resistant strains of *Neisseria gonorrhoeae* are spreading in the United States, and widespread resistance may preclude routine use in the near future; see text.
[§]Recommended only if both cephalosporins and fluoroquinolones are contraindicated; see text.
[‖]Not effective against pharyngeal gonococcal infection.
[¶]Unnecessary if azithromycin, 2.0 g, is used for initial single-dose treatment.
Modified from Centers for Disease Control and Prevention. Sexually Transmitted Diseases Treatment Guidelines 2002. MMWR Morb Mortal Wkly Rep 2002;51(No. RR-6).

Gonorrhea in pregnant women responds to the recommended regimens, but the fluoroquinolones should be avoided during pregnancy.[77,78,115]

The three recommended fluoroquinolone regimens are highly effective against infection due to susceptible gonococci, with cure rates at least 98% for all anatomic sites,[78,116] but must be avoided when treating persons who acquire gonorrhea in most developing countries, Asia, the Pacific (including Hawaii), California, or other geographic areas with substantial prevalences of fluoroquinolone-resistant *N. gonorrhoeae*.[67,78] These drugs also should be used with caution elsewhere in North America and Europe, and clinicians should closely monitor local and regional trends in resistance, with the expectation that their utility will end in the near future. Allergic cross-reactions between penicillin and the cephalosporins appear to be uncommon and penicillin-allergic persons often can be treated for gonorrhea with a cephalosporin, but a fluoroquinolone normally should be used if antimicrobial resistance is not an immediate concern.

Single-dose regimens with several other cephalosporins, quinolones, or other antibiotics may be used, but they have no advantages over the recommended regimens.[77,78] In small trials, a single dose of 2 g of azithromycin has been effective against both gonorrhea and chlamydial infection, but cost and gastrointestinal intolerance limit its utility, and increasing resistance is a potential concern; 1 g should not be used.[78,117,118] Spectinomycin, 2 g intramuscularly, remains effective for genital and rectal gonorrhea in the United States despite the occasional occurrence of spectinomycin-resistant gonococci, but it is ineffective for pharyngeal infection.[78] Its sole remaining indication is the treatment of pregnant women with histories of rapid-onset allergic reactions to penicillin or documented cephalosporin allergy, a rare confluence of events.

Co-treatment for Chlamydial Infection

Regardless of the single-dose regimen used, initial treatment should be followed by a regimen active against *C. trachomatis*.[49,77] In addition to treating chlamydial infection, with attendant reduction in the risk of postgonococcal urethritis and salpingitis,[119] giving a second drug with a different mechanism of action than the primary treatment may reduce selection pressure for antimicrobial resistance in *N. gonorrhoeae*. Indeed, it is possible that the worldwide spread of fluoroquinolone-resistant gonococci was slower than the dissemination of penicillinase-producing strains 25 years earlier in part because penicillin monotherapy was the rule in the 1970s, whereas antichlamydial co-therapy was the norm in the 1990s. The recommended regimens are a single oral dose of azithromycin, 1 g, or doxycycline, 100 mg orally twice daily for 7 days.[77] Erythromycin, in a divided-dose regimen totaling 2 g/day orally, is acceptable as follow-up therapy if neither azithromycin nor a tetracycline can be given,[77] and ofloxacin or levofloxacin (but not ciprofloxacin) undoubtedly would be effective.

Follow-up of Patients Treated for Uncomplicated Gonorrhea

Treatment failure is uncommon and retesting to document cure is not recommended unless therapeutic compliance is in question or symptoms persist.[77,78] However, most patients with gonorrhea remain at continuing risk, and recent studies have found recurrent gonorrhea in 10% to 15% of both women and heterosexual men retested 1 to 4 months after treatment.[52,120] Accordingly, retesting for recurrent or persistent infection, or "rescreening," should be done routinely 3 to 4 months after treatment. Rescreening also is indicated for men and women with chlamydial infection.[121,122] Testing urine or self-collected vaginal specimens by NAAT can be accomplished in asymptomatic patients without a clinical examination or, if using mailed specimens, without a clinic visit.[120]

Pelvic Inflammatory Disease

The treatment of PID is addressed in detail in Chapter 104. In individual patients, the specific pathogens responsible for ascending genital infection usually are not known, and the recommendations for initial treatment of acute PID are similar regardless of whether the initial infection is due to *N. gonorrhoeae*, *C. trachomatis*, or other

---

TABLE 209-3 Recommended Treatment of Acute Pelvic Inflammatory Disease

Hospitalized Patients
Regimen A
  Cefotetan, 2 g IV q12h, or cefoxitin, 2 g IV q6h
  plus
  Doxycycline, 100 mg IV or PO q12h
  Continue both drugs IV for 24 hr after the patient substantially improves, then continue doxycycline, 100 mg PO bid, to complete 14 days total therapy. Either clindamycin or metronidazole may be added to the oral regimen if tuboovarian abscess is suspected
  or
Regimen B
  Clindamycin, 900 mg IV q8h
  plus
  Gentamicin, 2 mg/kg IV once, followed by 1.5 mg/kg q8h*
  Continue both drugs IV for 24 hr after the patient substantially improves, then continue doxycycline, 100 mg PO twice daily, or clindamycin, 450 mg PO 4 times daily, to complete 14 days total therapy. Clindamycin may be preferable when tuboovarian abscess is suspected

Outpatients
Regimen A
  Ofloxacin, 400 mg PO bid for 14 days
  plus
  Metronidazole, 500 mg PO bid for 14 days
  or
Regimen B
  Single-dose cefoxitin, 2 g IM, plus probenecid, 1 g PO; or ceftriaxone, 250 mg IM; or other parenteral third-generation cephalosporin (e.g., ceftizoxime or cefotaxime)
  plus
  Doxycycline, 100 mg PO bid for 14 days

*Single daily dosing may be substituted.
Modified from Centers for Disease Control and Prevention. 1998 Guidelines for treatment of sexually transmitted diseases. MMWR Morb Mortal Wkly Rep. 1997;47(Suppl RR-1):S59-S69.

---

pathogens.[123-125] The CDC's 2002 treatment guidelines for PID[77] are summarized in Table 209-3.

The importance of routinely providing treatment active against anaerobic bacteria for the entire 2-week treatment period is debated. Anaerobes often can be isolated from intra-abdominal specimens obtained from women with PID, but clinical resolution appears to be equally rapid and complete for women treated only with ofloxacin[125] or doxycycline,[123] neither of which inhibits most anaerobes associated with PID. Nevertheless, because direct comparative trials have not been undertaken and no published data address long-term efficacy in preventing infertility, ectopic pregnancy, or chronic pelvic pain, the CDC and most experts recommend routine provision of anaerobic coverage.[77]

For oral therapy of outpatients, 14 days of the combination of either levofloxacin, 500 mg once daily, or ofloxacin, 400 mg twice daily, plus metronidazole, 500 mg twice daily, provides coverage of all likely pathogens, but should be avoided or used with caution if there is a possibility of gonorrhea acquired in a geographic area where fluoroquinolone-resistant gonococci are prevalent. The other main regimen for outpatient therapy is single-dose treatment with ceftriaxone or with cefoxitin plus probenecid, followed by oral therapy with doxycycline, 100 mg twice a day orally, and metronidazole, 500 mg twice a day orally. In a recent well-designed study, this regimen (without metronidazole) was equally effective as the equivalent inpatient, parenteral regimen both in short-term resolution and in preservation of fertility after 3 years' follow-up.[123] The use of azithromycin for treatment of PID has been controversial, but a recent trial showed clinical efficacy, as well as microbiologic efficacy against *N. gonorrhoeae*, *C. trachomatis*, and other bacteria (including anaerobes), of azithromycin 500 mg intravenously in a single dose, followed by 250 orally once daily to complete 7 days treatment, with or without metronidazole.[126]

Regardless of the initial treatment, close follow-up is indicated. Clinical progression or failure of the patient to improve within 3 days is an indication to hospitalize the patient and for laparoscopy to confirm the diagnosis and obtain intra-abdominal culture specimens to facilitate selection of improved, parenteral antimicrobial therapy.[77,124] The patient's sex partner(s) should be tested and treated for chlamydial infection and gonorrhea, unless both infections can be reliably excluded in the index patient.

Acute Epididymitis

The treatment of acute epididymitis is addressed in Chapter 105. Most cases in young adults are due to *C. trachomatis* or *N. gonorrhoeae,* but coliforms and other urinary tract pathogens are common causes in older men or after urinary tract instrumentation, and perhaps in men who participate in unprotected insertive anal intercourse. Most cases can be managed on an outpatient basis with ceftriaxone, 250 mg intramuscularly, plus 10 days of treatment with doxycycline, 100 mg twice daily.[77] Ofloxacin, 400 mg orally twice daily, or levofloxacin, 500 mg daily, for 10 days, provides better coverage for coliforms and nonsexually transmitted pathogens, and is effective against chlamydial infection, but should be avoided in patients at risk for fluoroquinolone-resistant gonococcal infection.

Disseminated Gonococcal Infection

Few data are available on the treatment of patients with DGI since the evolution and spread of gonococci with high levels of antibiotic resistance, and all recommendations are empirical. Antimicrobial susceptibility testing should be routinely employed to guide therapy in case the initial response to empirical treatment is suboptimal. Patients with the gonococcal arthritis–dermatitis syndrome should be treated initially with ceftriaxone, 1 g once daily, either intramuscularly or intravenously.[77,88,127] Most patients without complications can be treated as outpatients. Equivalent doses of other third-generation cephalosporins undoubtedly would be effective and are recommended as options, as is treatment with spectinomycin, 2 g intramuscularly twice daily.[77] No reported studies have systematically evaluated the fluoroquinolones, but these drugs undoubtedly are effective if the organism is susceptible. After clinical improvement begins, treatment of patients without septic arthritis or other complications may be switched to an oral cephalosporin (e.g., cefixime 400 mg twice daily) or a fluoroquinolone (e.g., levofloxacin 500 mg daily) to complete 7 to 10 days' total therapy.[77] The penicillins or tetracyclines may be used if the infecting organism is documented to be susceptible.[127] Patients with gonococcal endocarditis should receive 4 weeks of parenteral therapy, usually starting with ceftriaxone or an equivalent cephalosporin and later modifying the regimen if dictated by the results of antimicrobial susceptibility testing.[77,90] Meningitis should be treated with a 10- to 14-day course of ceftriaxone.[77]

Gonorrhea in Children

Relatively few cases of gonorrhea are seen in children, and treatment has not been well studied; most treatment recommendations are extrapolated from those for adults. Uncomplicated infections in neonates and older children should normally be treated with ceftriaxone in a single intramuscular dose of 25 to 50 mg/kg body weight, up to 125 mg.[77] Little is known about the prevalence of chlamydial infection in pediatric patients with gonorrhea, and the usual practice is to perform a test for *C. trachomatis* and withhold specific treatment unless infection is diagnosed.[100] DGI and gonococcal conjunctivitis in children are treated with 7 to 10 days of ceftriaxone, 25 to 50 mg/kg body weight per day intramuscularly or intravenously, or with an equivalent regimen of another third-generation cephalosporin. Continuous irrigation of the conjunctivae with physiologic saline solution is often used in gonococcal conjunctivitis, but topical antibiotics probably offer no additional benefit.[77]

Management of Sex Partners

Management of sex partners is an integral part of treating patients with gonorrhea and other STDs, because failure to ensure that the partner is treated risks reinfection of the patient and fosters continued transmission. Few state or local health departments in the United States provide direct assistance in contacting or managing the partners of persons with gonorrhea or chlamydial infection diagnosed outside public clinics (and often not there)[128]; the physician and patient should work together to this end.

Ideally, the sex partners of persons with gonorrhea or chlamydial infection should be examined, tested for both infections and other common STDs, and counseled on prevention. Unfortunately, success in bringing partners to clinical care is low, and in most settings treatment can be documented for less than half the partners of infected persons.[128] Recent studies suggest that this proportion can be increased and the rate of reinfection in index patients reduced by arranging for treatment without examination, i.e., by giving the index patient antibiotic for the partner or a prescription in the partner's name, a strategy termed patient-delivered partner therapy (PDPT).[129,130] Although PDPT sometimes has been condemned by public health authorities and has uncertain legal underpinnings in some states, surveys indicate that many clinicians frequently pursue the practice in managing their patients with STDs. Indeed, PDPT has been the historic norm for trichomoniasis, one of the most common STDs. Clinicians should routinely employ PDPT for the partners of persons with gonorrhea or chlamydial infection, to the extent permitted by regional laws and regulations, whenever success is not ensured in personal evaluation of the partners. PDPT for gonorrhea can be accomplished with single-dose oral therapy active against both *N. gonorrhoeae* (e.g., cefixime or ciprofloxacin) and *C. trachomatis* (azithromycin); for the partners of patients with chlamydial infection alone, azithromycin is appropriate.[130]

PREVENTION AND CONTROL

Public Health Strategies

Screening of sexually active persons is a mainstay of public health strategies to prevent gonorrhea and the other treatable bacterial STDs, and is largely responsible for the dramatic declines observed in the incidence of gonorrhea nationwide after the mid-1970s (see Fig. 209-5) and perhaps for declining rates of chlamydial infection in the 1990s. Women at risk who undergo routine pelvic examinations should be tested for *N. gonorrhoeae* and *C. trachomatis*; when pelvic examination is otherwise not indicated, urine or a self-collected vaginal swab can be tested by NAAT. Universal screening of all heterosexual men and women usually is not cost effective except in special settings, such as public STD clinics; in most settings, selective screening of those at highest risk is more practical. Unfortunately, although screening criteria are well established for chlamydial infection, few studies have systematically addressed such criteria for gonorrhea. Accordingly, clinicians should use their knowledge of local gonorrhea morbidity in the population groups represented by their patients. As multiplex NAATs that simultaneously test for *N. gonorrhoeae* and *C. trachomatis* come into increasing use, the screening criteria for chlamydial infection (see Chapter 175) can be employed. Sexually active MSM should be tested routinely for both gonococcal and chlamydial infection, depending on the anatomic sites exposed.[131]

Public health control measures for gonorrhea and chlamydial infection also include routine rescreening and treatment of patients' sex partners, both discussed above. Other elements include appropriate diagnostic testing in persons with compatible clinical syndromes, adherence to recommended treatment regimens, and periodic testing of gonococcal isolates to monitor trends in antimicrobial resistance. Reporting of cases by health care providers, preferably supplemented by direct reporting by laboratories of persons with positive test results, is important for epidemiologic monitoring and to facilitate targeted control efforts. Public education and personal counseling, in an effort to induce conservative sexual behavior and the use of barrier contraceptives, is central to the control of gonorrhea and all STDs. Finally, all persons with a newly acquired STD should routinely be tested for other common infections. For example, screening tests for gonorrhea, chlamydial infection, syphilis, and perhaps type 2 herpes simplex virus infection should be undertaken in persons diagnosed with any STD; women with STDs should have cervical cytology and diagnostic testing for vaginal infections; and anyone with a new STD diagnosis should routinely undergo serological testing for HIV infection.[77]

Condoms and Microbicides

Properly used condoms provide a high degree of protection against transmission or acquisition of gonorrhea, chlamydial infection, HIV, and other STDs transmitted by infected secretions. Less protection is conferred against infections that can be transmitted by cutaneous apposition, such as genital herpes and perhaps syphilis, and little success has been documented in preventing transmission of human papillomavirus infections by condoms.[77,132] It is likely that the female condom would provide more effective protection than the male condom against some infections, but no data are available and acceptance of the female condom has been low. Diaphragms and cervical caps probably are partly protective against secretion-borne infections, albeit less so than condoms. The spermicide nonoxynol-9 provides no significant protection against gonorrhea or chlamydial infection,[133] is associated with increased risk of vulvovaginal candidiasis and bacterial urinary tract infection, and may increase the risk of HIV infection.[134,135] Although spermicidal preparations with nonoxynol-9 enhance the contraceptive efficacy of barrier methods, they should be avoided by people at high risk for STD, as should condoms packaged with lubricant containing nonoxynol-9.[135] Research is underway to identify alternative microbicides for vaginal or rectal use. No evidence has been presented that such time-honored measures as washing, urinating, or douching after exposure materially reduce the risk of gonorrhea or any other STD.

Other Prevention Strategies

Administration of systemic antibiotics immediately before or soon after sexual exposure can reduce the risk of gonorrhea,[136] and mass treatment of populations with high rates of syphilis and other treponematoses has been effective in reducing morbidity. At best, however, such approaches have had transient, minor influences on the incidence of gonorrhea in treated populations, and they may carry a risk of fostering the spread of resistant gonococci.[136]

The development of a vaccine to prevent gonorrhea is a high research priority, but an experimental vaccine containing purified gonococcal pili conferred only partial protection against experimental infection with the homologous strain of *N. gonorrhoeae* and no protection from heterologous challenge.[137] The extraordinary degree of antigenic variability in pili, Opa, and LOS, both at the community level and during the course of each infection, presents formidable barriers to developing a gonorrhea vaccine based on these antigens.[7,13] Other more antigenically stable proteins, including porin, are under investigation as possible vaccine candidates, but success probably lies in the distant future.[13,137]

REFERENCES

1. Janda WM, Knapp JS. *Neisseria* and *Moraxella catarrhalis.* In: Murray PR, Baron EJ, Jorgensen JH, et al, eds. Manual of Clinical Microbiology. 8th ed. Washington, DC: American Society for Microbiology; 2002:585-608.
2. Minnett S, Reller LB, Knapp JS. *Neisseria gonorrhoeae* strains inhibited by vancomycin in selective media and correlation with auxotype. J Clin Microbiol. 1981;14:94-99.
3. Bonin P, Tanino TT, Handsfield HH. Isolation of *Neisseria gonorrhoeae* on selective and nonselective media in a sexually transmitted disease clinic. J Clin Microbiol. 1984;19:218-220.
4. Kellogg DS Jr, Peacock WL Sr, Deacon WE, et al. *Neisseria gonorrhoeae:* I. Virulence genetically linked to clonal variation. J Bacteriol. 1963;85:1274-1279.
5. Schoolnik GK, Fernandez R, Tai J-Y, et al. Gonococcal pili: Primary structure and receptor binding domain. J Exp Med. 1984;159:1351-1370.
6. McGee ZA, Johnson AP, Taylor-Robinson D. Pathogenic mechanisms of *Neisseria gonorrhoeae:* Observations on damage to human fallopian tubes in organ culture by gonococci of colony type 1 or type 4. J Infect Dis. 1981;143:413-422.
7. Cohen MS, Cannon JG. Human experimentation with *Neisseria gonorrhoeae:* Progress and goals. J Infect Dis. 1999;179(Suppl 2):S375-S379.
8. Forest KT, Bernstein SL, Getzoff ED, et al. Assembly and antigenicity of the *Neisseria gonorrhoeae* pilus mapped with antibodies. Infect Immun. 1996;64:644-652.
9. Kallstrom H, Liszewski MK, Atkinson JP, Jonsson AB. Membrane cofactor protein (MCP or CD46) is a cellular pilus receptor for pathogenic *Neisseria.* Mol Microbiol. 1997;25:639-647.
10. Blake MS, Gotschlich EC. Gonococcal membrane proteins: Speculation on their role in pathogenesis. Prog Allergy. 1983;33:298-313.
11. Knapp JS, Tam MR, Nowinski RC, et al. Serological classification of *Neisseria gonorrhoeae* with use of monoclonal antibodies to gonococcal outer membrane protein I. J Infect Dis. 1984;150:44-48.
12. Van Putten JPM. Gonococcal invasion of epithelial cells driven by the P.IA porin. In: Nassif X, Quentin-Millet M-J, Taha M-K, eds. Proceedings of the Eleventh International Pathogenic Neisseria Conference, Nice, France, November 1998. Paris: Editions E.D.K.; 1998:35.
13. Blake MS, Wetzler LM. Vaccines for gonorrhea: Where are we on the curve? Trends Microbiol. 1995;3:469-474.
14. Connell TD, Shaffer D, Cannon JG. Characterization of the repertoire of hypervariable regions in the protein II (opa) gene family of *Neisseria gonorrhoeae.* Mol Microbiol. 1990;4:439-449.
15. Fischer SH, Rest RF. Gonococci possessing only certain P.II outer membrane proteins interact with human neutrophils. Infect Immun. 1988;56:1574-1579.
16. Van Putten JPM, Duensing TD, Cole RL. Entry of OpaA_ gonococci into Hep-2 cells requires concerted action of glycosaminoglycans, fibronectin and integrin receptors. Mol Microbiol. 1998;29:369-379.
17. Wang J, Gray-Owen SD, Knorre A, et al. Opa binding to cellular CD66 receptors mediates the transcellular traversal of *Neisseria gonorrhoeae* across polarized T84 epithelial cell monolayers. Mol Microbiol 1998;30:657-671.
18. Boulton IC, Gray-Owen SD. Neisserial binding to CEACAM I arrests the activation and proliferation of CD4+ T lymphocytes. Nature Immunol 2002;3:229-236.
19. Hedges SR, Mayo MS, Mestecky J, et al. Limited local and systemic antibody responses to *Neisseria gonorrhoeae* during uncomplicated genital infections. Infect Immun 1999;67:3937-3946.
20. Plummer FA, Chubb H, Simonsen JN, et al. Antibody to Rmp (outer membrane protein 3) increases susceptibility to gonococcal infection. J Clin Invest. 1993;91:339-343.
21. Cornelissen C, Sparling PF. Iron piracy: Acquisition of transferrin-bound iron by bacterial pathogens. Mol Microbiol. 1994;14:843-850.
22. Biswas GD, Sparling PF. Characterization of *lbpA*, the structural gene for a lactoferrin receptor in *Neisseria gonorrhoeae.* Infect Immun. 1995;63:2958-2967.
23. Chen CJ, Sparling PF, Lewis LA, et al. Identification and purification of a hemoglobin-binding outer membrane protein from *Neisseria gonorrhoeae.* Infect Immun. 1996;64:5008-5014.
24. Cornelissen CN, Kelley M, Hobbs MM, et al. The gonococcal transferrin receptor is required for human infection. Mol Microbiol. 1998;27:611-616.
25. Clark VL, Campbell LA, Palermo DA, et al. Induction and repression of outer membrane proteins by anaerobic growth of *Neisseria gonorrhoeae.* Infect Immun. 1987;55:1359-1364.
26. Mandrell RE, Lesse AJ, Sugai JV, et al. Phenotypic variation in epitope expression of the *Neisseria gonorrhoeae* lipooligosaccharide. J Exp Med. 1990;171:1649-1664.
27. Elkins C, Carbonetti NH, Varela VA, et al. Antibodies to N-terminal peptides of gonococcal porin are bactericidal when gonococcal lipopolysaccharide is not sialylated. Mol Microbiol. 1992;6:2617-2628.
28. Van Putten JPM, Robertson BD. Molecular mechanisms and implications for infection of lipopolysaccharide variation in *Neisseria.* Mol Microbiol. 1995;16:847-853.
29. Fleming TJ, Wallsmith DE, Rosenthal RS. Arthropathic properties of gonococcal peptidoglycan fragments: Implications for the pathogenesis of disseminated gonococcal disease. Infect Immun. 1986;52:600-608.
30. Catlin BW. Nutritional profiles of *Neisseria gonorrhoeae, Neisseria meningitidis,* and *Neisseria lactamica* in chemically defined media and the use of growth requirements for gonococcal typing. J Infect Dis. 1973;128:178-194.
31. Handsfield HH, Rice RJ, Roberts MC, et al. Localized outbreak of penicillinase-producing *Neisseria gonorrhoeae:* Paradigm for introduction and spread of gonorrhea in a community. JAMA. 1989;261:2357-2360.
32. O'Rourke M, Ison CA, Renton AM, et al. Opa-typing: A high-resolution tool for studying the epidemiology of gonorrhoea. Mol Microbiol. 1995;17:865-875.
33. McKnew DL, Lynn F, Zenilman JM, Bash MC. Porin variation among clinical isolates of *Neisseria gonorrhoeae* over a 10-year period, as determined by *Por* variable region typing. J Infect Dis. 2003;187:1213-1222.
34. Unemo M, Berglund T, Olcen P, Fredlund H. Pulsed-field gel electrophoresis as an epidemiologic tool for *Neisseria gonorrhoeae:* Identification of clusters within serovars. Sex Transm Dis. 2002;29 :25-31.
35. Meats E, Feil EJ, Stringer S, et al. Characterization of encapsulated and noncapsulated *Haemophilus influenzae* and determination of phylogenetic relationships by multilocus sequence typing. J Clin Microbiol. 2003;41:1623-1636.
36. Anderson B, Albritton WL, Biddle J, et al. Common β-lactamase-specifying plasmid in *Haemophilus ducreyi* and *Neisseria gonorrhoeae.* Antimicrob Agents Chemother. 1984;25:296-297.
37. Morse SA, Johnson SR, Biddle JW, et al. High-level tetracycline resistance in *Neisseria gonorrhoeae* is result of acquisition of streptococcal *tetM* determinant. Antimicrob Agents Chemother. 1986;30:664-670.
38. Elkins C, Thomas CE, Seifert HS, et al. Species-specific uptake of DNA by gonococci is mediated by a 10-base-pair sequence. J Bacteriol. 1991;173:3911-3913.
39. Shafer WM, Balthazar JT, Hagman KE, et al. Missense mutations that alter the DNA-binding domain of the MtrR protein occur frequently in rectal isolates of *Neisseria gonorrhoeae* that are resistant to faecal lipid. Microbiology. 1995;141:907-911.
40. Spratt BG. Hybrid penicillin-binding proteins in penicillin-resistant strains of *Neisseria gonorrhoeae.* Nature. 1988;332:173-176.
41. Centers for Disease Control and Prevention. Sexually Transmitted Disease Surveillance 2001 Supplement: Gonococcal Isolate Surveillance Project (GISP) Annual Report, 2001. Atlanta, Ga: U.S. Department of Health and Human Services, 2002.

42. Deguchi T, Yasuda M, Nakano M, et al. Quinolone-resistant *Neisseria gonorrhoeae*: Correlation of alterations in the GyrA subunit of DNA gyrase and the ParC subunit of topoisomerase IV with antimicrobial susceptibility profiles. Antimicrob Agents Chemother. 1996;40:1020-1023.

43. Linback E, Rahman M, Jalal S, Wretlind B. Mutations in *gyrA, gyrB, parC,* and *parE* in quiolone-resistant strains of *Neisseria gonorrhoeae*. APMIS. 2002;110:651-657.

44. Giardina PC, Williams R, Lubaroff D, et al. *Neisseria gonorrhoeae* induces focal polymerization of actin in primary human urethral epithelium. Infect Immun. 1998;66:3416-3419.

45. Centers for Disease Control and Prevention. Sexually Transmitted Disease Surveillance, 2002. Atlanta, Ga: U.S. Department of Health and Human Services; 2003.

46. Fox KK, Whittington WL, Levine WC, et al. Gonorrhea in the United States 1981-1996: Demographic and geographic trends. Sex Transm Dis. 1998;25:386-393.

47. Brunham RC, Embree JE. Sexually transmitted diseases: Current and future dimensions of the problem in the third world. In: Germain A, Holmes KK, Piot P, et al, eds. Reproductive Tract Infections: Global Impact and Priorities for Women's Reproductive Health. New York: Plenum; 1992:35-58.

48. Rice RJ, Roberts PL, Handsfield HH, et al. Sociodemographic distribution of gonorrhea incidence: Implications for prevention and behavioral research. Am J Public Health. 1991;81:1252-1258.

49. Dicker LW, Mosure DJ, Berman SM, Levine WC. Gonorrhea prevalence and coinfection with chlamydia in women in the United States, 2000. Sex Transm Dis. 2003;30:472-476.

50. Centers for Disease Control and Prevention. Resurgent bacterial sexually transmitted disease among men who have sex with men—King County, Washington, 1997-1999. MMWR Morb Mortal Wkly Rep. 1999;48:773-777.

51. Chen SY, Gibson S, Katz MH, et al. Continuing increases in sexual risk behavior and sexually transmitted diseases among men who have sex with men: San Francisco, Calif, 1999-2001, USA. Am J Public Health. 2002;92:1387-1388.

52. Thomas JC, Schoenbach VJ, Weiner DH, et al. Rural gonorrhea in the southeastern United States: A neglected epidemic? Am J Epidemiol. 1996;143:269-277.

53. Stoner BP, Whittington WL, Hughes JP, et al. Comparative epidemiology of heterosexual gonococcal and chlamydial networks: Implications for transmission patterns. Sex Transm Dis. 2000;27:215-223.

54. Hooper RR, Reynolds GH, Jones OG, et al. Cohort study of venereal disease: I. The risk of gonorrhea transmission from infected women to men. Am J Epidemiol. 1978;108:136-144.

55. Lin J-S, Donegan SP, Heeren TC, et al. Transmission of *Chlamydia trachomatis* and *Neisseria gonorrhoeae* among men with urethritis and their female sex partners. J Infect Dis. 1998;178:1707-1712.

56. Wiesner PJ, Tronca E, Bonin P, et al. Clinical spectrum of pharyngeal gonococcal infection. N Engl J Med. 1973;288:181-185.

57. McCormack WM, Reynolds GH, Cooperative Study Group. Effect of menstrual cycle and method of contraception on recovery of *Neisseria gonorrhoeae*. JAMA. 1982;247:1292-1294.

58. Yorke JA, Hethcote HW, Nold A. Dynamics and control of the transmission of gonorrhea. Sex Transm Dis. 1978;5:51-56.

59. Wasserheit JN, Aral SO. The dynamic topology of sexually transmitted disease epidemics: Implications for prevention strategies. J Infect Dis. 1996;174(Suppl 2):S201-S213.

60. Fichtenberg CM, Ellen JM. Editorial response: Moving from core groups to risk spaces. Sex Transm Dis. 2003;30:825-827.

61. Handsfield HH, Lipman TO, Harnisch JP, et al. Asymptomatic gonorrhea in men: Diagnosis, natural course, prevalence and significance. N Engl J Med. 1973;290:117-123.

62. Dillon JR, Yeung K-H. β-Lactamase plasmids and chromosomally mediated antibiotic resistance in pathogenic *Neisseria* species. Clin Microbiol Rev. 1989;2:125-133.

63. Handsfield HH, Hook EW III. Ceftriaxone for treatment of uncomplicated gonorrhea: Routine use of a single 125-mg dose in a sexually transmitted disease clinic. Sex Transm Dis. 1987;14:227-230.

64. Handsfield HH, Knapp JS, Diehr PK, et al. Correlation of auxotype and penicillin susceptibility of *Neisseria gonorrhoeae* with sexual preference and clinical manifestations of gonorrhea. Sex Transm Dis. 1980;7:1-5.

65. Morse SA, Lysko OG, McFarland L, et al. Gonococcal strains from homosexual men have outer membranes with reduced permeability to hydrophobic molecules. Infect Immun. 1982;37:4328.

66. Fox KK, Knapp JS, Holmes KK, et al. Antimicrobial resistance in *Neisseria gonorrhoeae* in the United States 1988-1994: The emergence of resistance to the fluoroquinolones. J Infect Dis. 1997;175:1396-1403. .

67. Zenilman JA. Update on quinolone resistance in *Neisseria gonorrhoeae*. Curr Infect Dis Rep. 2002;4:144-147.

68. Aplasca de los Reyes MR, Pato-Mesola V, Klausner JD, et al. A randomized trial of ciprofloxacin versus cefixime for treatment of gonorrhea after rapid emergence of gonococcal ciprofloxacin resistance in the Philippines. Clin Infect Dis. 2001;32:1313-1318.

69. Centers for Disease Control and Prevention. Increases in fluoroquinolone-resistant *Neisseria gonorrhoeae*—Hawaii and California, 2001. MMWR Morb Mortal Wkly Rep. 2002;41:1041-1044.

70. Brunham RC, Plummer F, Slaney L, et al. Correlation of auxotype and protein I type with expression of disease due to *Neisseria gonorrhoeae*. J Infect Dis. 1985;152:339-343.

71. Berger RE, Alexander ER, Harnisch JP, et al. Etiology, manifestations and therapy of acute epididymitis: Prospective study of 50 cases. J Urol. 1979;121:750-754.

72. Platt R, Rice PA, McCormack WM. Risk of acquiring gonorrhea and prevalence of abnormal adnexal findings among women recently exposed to gonorrhea. JAMA. 1983;250:3205-3209.

73. McCormack WM, Stumacher RJ, Johnson K, et al. Clinical spectrum of gonococcal infections in women. Lancet. 1977;1:1182-1185.

74. Brunham RC, Paavonen J, Stevens CE, et al. Mucopurulent cervicitis—The ignored counterpart in women of urethritis in men. N Engl J Med. 1984;311:1-6.

75. Janda WM, Bohnhoff M, Morello JA, et al. Prevalence and site pathogen studies of *Neisseria meningitidis* and *Neisseria gonorrhoeae* in homosexual men. JAMA. 1980;244:2060-2064.

76. Quinn TC, Stamm WE, Goodell SE, et al. The polymicrobial origin of intestinal infections in homosexual men. N Engl J Med. 1983;309:576-582.

77. Centers for Disease Control and Prevention. Sexually transmitted diseases treatment guidelines 2002. MMWR Morb Mortal Wkly Rep. 2002;51(No. RR-6):36-42.

78. Moran JS, Handsfield HH. *Neisseria gonorrhoeae*. In: Yu VL, Weber R, Raoult D, et al (eds). Antimicrobial Therapy and Vaccines. Volume I: Microbes. 2nd ed. New York: Apple Tree Productions; 2002:457-469.

79. Lafferty WE, Hughes JP, Handsfield HH. Sexually transmitted diseases among men who have sex with men: Acquisition of gonorrhea and nongonococcal urethritis by fellatio and implications for STD/HIV prevention. Sex Transm Dis. 1997;24:272-278.

80. Holmes KK, Eschenbach DA, Knapp JS. Salpingitis: Overview of etiology and epidemiology. Am J Obstet Gynecol. 1980;138:893-900.

81. Ross JD. An update on pelvic inflammatory disease. Sex Transm Infect. 2002;78:18-19.

82. Wølner-Hanssen P, Eschenbach DA, Paavonen J, et al. Decreased risk of symptomatic pelvic inflammatory disease associated with oral contraceptive use. JAMA. 1990;264:2072-2074.

83. Scholes D, Daling JR, Stergachis A, et al. Vaginal douching as a risk factor for acute pelvic inflammatory disease. Obstet Gynecol. 1993;81:601-606.

84. Ness R, Richter HE, Stamm C, et al. Does douching elevate the risk for incident gonococcal/chlamydial cervicitis and pelvic inflammatory disease (PID)? International Society for Sexually Transmitted Diseases Research, Ottawa, Canada, July 27-30, 2003: Abstract 0052.

85. Wendel GD Jr. Sexually transmitted diseases in pregnancy. Semin Perinatol. 1990;14:171-178.

86. Corman LC, Levison ME, Knight R, et al. The high frequency of pharyngeal gonococcal infection in a prenatal clinic population. JAMA. 1974;230:568-570.

87. Holmes KK, Counts GW, Beaty HN. Disseminated gonococcal infection. Ann Intern Med. 1971;74:979-993.

88. Wise CN, Morris CR, Wasilauskas BL, Salzer WL. Gonococcal arthritis in an era of increasing penicillin resistance: Presentations and outcomes in 41 recent cases (1985-1991). Arch Intern Med. 1994;154:2690-2695.

89. Tapsall JW, Phillips EA, Schultz TR, et al. Strain characteristics and antibiotic susceptibility of isolates of *Neisseria gonorrhoeae* causing disseminated gonococcal infection in Australia. Int J STD AIDS. 1992;3:273-277.

90. Jackman JD Jr, Glamann DB. Gonococcal endocarditis: Twenty-five year experience. Am J Med Sci. 1991;301:221-230.

91. Billings FT III, Evans VA, Wittlinger PS, et al. "Primary" gonococcal meningitis. Sex Transm Dis. 1991;18:129-130.

92. Ingram CW, Nichole B, Martinez S, et al. Gonococcal osteomyelitis: Case report and review of the literature. Arch Intern Med. 1991;151:177-179.

93. Belding ME, Carbone J. Gonococcemia associated with adult respiratory distress syndrome. Rev Infect Dis. 1991;13:1105-1107.

94. Thiery G, Tankovic J, Brun-Buisson C, Blot F. Gonococcemia associated with fatal septic shock. Clin Infect Dis. 2001;32:E92-E93.

95. Rompalo AM, Hook EW III, Roberts PL, et al. The acute arthritis-dermatitis syndrome: The changing importance of *Neisseria gonorrhoeae* and *Neisseria meningitidis*. Arch Intern Med. 1987;147:281-283.

96. Ellison RT III, Curd JG, Kohler PF, et al. Underlying complement deficiency in patients with disseminated gonococcal infection. Sex Transm Dis. 1987;14:201-204.

97. Liebling MR, Arkfeld DG, Michelini GA, et al. Identification of *Neisseria gonorrhoeae* in synovial fluid using polymerase chain reaction. Arthritis Rheum. 1994;37:702-709.

98. Ingram DL. *Neisseria gonorrhoeae* in children. Pediatr Ann. 1994;23:341-345.

99. Desenclos JC, Garrity D, Scraggs M, et al. Gonococcal infection of the newborn in Florida, 1984-1989. Sex Transm Dis. 1992;19:105-110.

100. Rawston SA, Bromberg K, Hammerschlag MR. STD in children: Syphilis and gonorrhea. Genitourin Med. 1993;69:66-75.

101. Ison CA. Laboratory methods in genitourinary medicine: Methods of diagnosing gonorrhea. Genitourin Med. 1990;66:453-459.

102. McKenna JG, Fallon RJ, Moyes A, Young H. Anogenital non-gonococcal neisseriae: Prevalence and clinical significance. Int J STD AIDS. 1993;4:8-12.

103. Russell JM, Azidian BS, Roberts AP, Talboys CA. Pharyngeal flora in a sexually active population. Int J STD AIDS. 1995;6:211-215.

104. Maini M, French P, Prince M, Bingham JS. Urethritis due to *Neisseria meningitidis* in a London genitourinary medicine clinic population. Int J STD AIDS. 1992;3:423-425.

105. Koumans EH, Johnson RE, Knapp, JS, et al. Laboratory testing for *Neisseria gonorrhoeae* by recently introduced nonculture tests: A performance review with clinical and public health considerations. Clin Infect Dis. 1998;27:1171-1180.

106. Koumans EH, Black CM, Markowitz LE, et al. Comparison of methods for detection of *Chlamydia trachomatis* and *Neisseria gonorrhoeae* using commercially available nucleic acid amplification tests and a liquid pap smear medium. J Clin Microbiol. 2003;4:1507-1511.

107. Cosentino LA, Landers DV, Hillier SL. Detection of *Chlamydia trachomatis* and *Neisseria gonorrhoeae* by strand displacement amplification and relevance of the amplification control for use with vaginal swab specimens. J Clin Microbiol. 2003;41:3592-3596.

108. Golden MR, Cles L, Crouse K, et al. Performance of transcription mediated amplification testing for *Neisseria gonorrhoeae* in a low prevalence population of women. 2004 National STD Prevention Conference, Philadelphia, Pa. March 8-11, 2004: Abstract .

109. Bachman LH, Desmond RA, Stephens J, et al. Duration of persistence of gonococcal DNA detected by ligase chain reaction in men and women following recommended therapy for uncomplicated gonorrhea. J Clin Microbiol. 2002;40:3596-3601.

110. Handsfield HH, McCutchan JA, Corey L, et al. Evaluation of new anti-infective drugs for the treatment of uncomplicated gonorrhea in adults and adolescents. Clin Infect Dis. 1992;15(Suppl 1):S123-S130.

111. Peterman TA, Zaidi AA, Lieb S, Wroten JE. Incubating syphilis in patients treated for gonorrhea: a comparison of treatment regimens. J Infect Dis. 1994;170:689-692.

112. Handsfield HH, McCormack WM, Hook EW III, et al. A comparison of single-dose cefixime with ceftriaxone as treatment for uncomplicated gonorrhea. N Engl J Med. 1991;325:1337-1341.

113. Novak E, Paxton LM, Tubbs HJ, et al. Orally administered cefpodoxime proxetil for treatment of uncomplicated gonococcal urethritis in males: A dose-response study. Antimicrob Agents Chemother. 1992;36:1764-1765.

114. Thorpe EM, Schwebke JS, Hook EW III, et al. Comparison of single-dose cefuroxime axetil with ciprofloxacin in treatment of uncomplicated gonorrhea caused by penicillinase-producing and non-penicillinase-producing *Neisseria gonorrhoeae* strains. Antimicrob Agents Chemother. 1996;40:2775-2780.

115. Ramus RMN, Sheffield JS, Mayfield JA, Wendel GD Jr. A randomized trial that compared oral cefixime and intramuscular ceftriaxone for the treatment of gonorrhea in pregnancy. Am J Obstet Gynecol. 2001;185:629-632.

116. Stoner BP, Douglas JM Jr, Martin DH, et al. Single-dose gatifloxacin compared with ofloxacin for the treatment of uncomplicated gonorrhea: A randomized, double-blind, multicenter trial. Sex Transm Dis. 2001;28:136-142.

117. Cousin SL Jr, Whittington WL, Roberts MC. Acquired macrolide resistance genes and the 1 bp deletion in the *mtrR* promoter in *Neisseria gonorrhoeae*. J Antimicrob Chemother. 2003;51:131-133.

118. Tapsall JW, Shultz TR, Limnios EA, et al. Failure of azithromycin therapy in gonorrhea and discorrelation with laboratory test parameters. Sex Transm Dis. 1998;25:505-508.

119. Stamm WE, Guinan ME, Johnson C, et al. Effect of treatment regimens for *Neisseria gonorrhoeae* on simultaneous infection with *Chlamydia trachomatis*. N Engl J Med. 1984;310:545-549.

120. Sparks R, Helmers JR, Totten PA, et al. Rescreening for gonorrhea and chlamydial infection through the mail: A randomized trial. International Society for Sexually Transmitted Diseases Research, Ottawa, Canada, July 27-30, 2003: Abstract 0297.

121. Whittington WL, Kent C, Kissinger P, et al. Determinants of persistent and recurrent *Chlamydia trachomatis* infection in young women: Results of a multicenter cohort study. Sex Transm Dis. 2001;28:117-123.

122. Mårdh P-A, Persson K. Is there a need for rescreening of patients treated for genital chlamydial infection? Int J STD AIDS. 2002;13:363-367.

123. Ness RB, Soper DE, Holley RL, et al. Effectiveness of inpatient and outpatient treatment strategies for women with pelvic inflammatory disease: Results from the pelvic inflammatory disease evaluation and clinical health (PEACH) randomized trial. Am J Obstet Gynecol. 2002;186:929-937.

124. Ross JD. Pelvic inflammatory disease: How should it be managed? Curr Opin Infect Dis. 2003;16:37-41.

125. Peipert JF, Sweet RL, Walker CK, et al. Evaluation of ofloxacin in the treatment of laparscopically documented acute pelvic inflammatory disease (salpingitis). Infect Dis Obstet Gynecol. 1999;7:138-144.

126. Bevan CD, Ridgway GL, Rothermel CD. Efficacy and safety of azithromycin as monotherapy or combined with metronidazole compared with two standard multidrug regimens for the treatment of acute pelvic inflammatory disease. J Int Med Res. 2003;31:45-54.

127. Handsfield HH, Wiesner PJ, Holmes KK. Treatment of the gonococcal arthritis-dermatitis syndrome. Ann Intern Med. 1976;84:661-667.

128. Golden MR, Hogben M, Handsfield HH, et al. Partner notification for HIV and STD in the United States: Low coverage for gonorrhea, chlamydial infection, and HIV. Sex Transm Dis. 2003;30:490-496.

129. Schillinger JA, Kissinger P, Calvet H, et al. Patient-delivered partner treatment with azithromycin to prevent repeated *Chlamydia trachomatis* infection among women: A randomized, controlled trial. Sex Transm Dis. 2003;30:49-56.

130. Golden MR, Whittington WLH, Handsfield HH, et al. Impact of sex partner treatment without mandatory prior clinical evaluation on recurrent/persistent infection in patients with gonorrhea or chlamydial infection: A randomized trial. International Society for Sexually Transmitted Diseases Research, Ottawa, Canada, July 27-30, 2003: Abstract 0703.

131. Mayer KH, Klausner JD, Handsfield HH. Intersecting epidemics and educable moments: Sexually transmitted disease risk assessment and screening in men who have sex with men. Sex Transm Dis. 2001;28:464-467.

132. Cates W Jr. The NIH condom report: The glass is 90% full. Fam Plan Perspect. 2001;33:231-233.

133. Roddy RE, Zekeng L, Ryan KA, et al. Effect of nonoxynol-9 gel on urogenital gonorrhea and chlamydial infection: A randomized controlled trial. JAMA. 2002;287:1117-1122.

134. Richardson BA. Nonoxynol-9 as a vaginal microbicide for prevention of sexually transmitted infections: It's time to move on. JAMA. 2002;287:1171-1172.

135. Centers for Disease Control and Prevention. CDC statement on study results of products containing nonoxynol-9. MMWR Morb Mortal Wkly Rep. 2000;49:717-718.

136. Harrison WO, Hooper RR, Wiesner PH, et al. A trial of minocycline given after exposure to prevent gonorrhea. N Engl J Med. 1979;300:1074-1078.

137. Boslego JW, Tramont EC, Chung RC, et al. Efficacy trial of a parenteral gonococcal pilus vaccine in men. Vaccine. 1991;9:154-612.

Moraxella (Branhamella) catarrhalis and Other Gram-negative Cocci

TIMOTHY F. MURPHY

Over the past three decades, *Moraxella (Branhamella) catarrhalis* has emerged as an important and common human respiratory tract pathogen. Current classification schemes have the family Neisseriaceae composed of five genera: *Neisseria, Moraxella* (including two subgenera, *Moraxella* and *Branhamella*), *Kingella, Acinetobacter,* and *Oligella.* The taxonomy and the nomenclature of these bacteria are the subject of investigation and debate. Suffice it to say that the classification of these gram-negative cocci and bacilli will undoubtedly undergo changes as more is learned about the relationships among them.

In this chapter, *M. catarrhalis* is discussed. In addition, several related bacteria, including *Neisseria* other than *N. meningitidis* and *N. gonorrhoeae,* other *Moraxella,* and *Kingella,* which are less common causes of human infection, are considered. *Acinetobacter* is discussed in Chapter 219 and *Oligella* is discussed in Chapter 234. *N. meningitidis* and *N. gonorrhoeae* are discussed in Chapters 208 and 209, respectively.

MORAXELLA (BRANHAMELLA) CATARRHALIS

History

M. catarrhalis has an interesting and checkered taxonomic history. The bacterium was first described by Ghon and Pfeiffer[1] a century ago and was suspected by Sir William Osler to be the cause of his own terminal pneumonia.[2] After having been initially named *Micrococcus catarrhalis,* the organism's name was subsequently changed to *Neisseria catarrhalis* because of its similarities in phenotype and ecologic niche to *Neisseria* species. In 1970, it was transferred to the new genus *Branhamella* on the basis of differences in fatty acid content and DNA hybridization studies compared with other *Neisseriaceae.*[3] The name *Moraxella (Branhamella) catarrhalis* was subsequently proposed and this is the most widely accepted name at this time.[4]

For most of the last century, *M. catarrhalis* was regarded as an upper respiratory tract commensal. However, since the late 1970s, investigators from many centers have accumulated compelling evidence that *M. catarrhalis* is an important and common respiratory tract pathogen in humans.[2,5-9]

Microbiology

M. catarrhalis is a gram-negative diplococcus that is indistinguishable from *Neisseria* by Gram stain. Other *Moraxella, Kingella, Acinetobacter,* and *Oligella* are all gram-negative bacilli or coccobacilli. The organism grows well on blood agar, chocolate agar, and a variety of media. *M. catarrhalis* are difficult to distinguish from *Neisseria* by colony morphology, particularly after overnight growth on agar plates. After 48 hours of growth, *M. catarrhalis* colonies tend to be larger than *Neisseria* and take on a pink color. In addition, colonies display the "hockey puck sign" by sliding along the surface of the agar when pushed. Because samples from the respiratory tract frequently contain *Neisseria,* suspicious colonies should be tested for the possibility that they are *M. catarrhalis. M. catarrhalis* produce oxidase, catalase, and DNase. Several kits to speciate *M. catarrhalis* are commercially available.[10,11] For isolates of *Moraxella* and *Neisseria* that are difficult to identify by biochemical testing and test kits, sequence analysis of 16S ribosomal DNA is useful in facilitating species identification.[12,13]

Epidemiology and Respiratory Tract Colonization

M. catarrhalis has been recovered exclusively from humans. The prevalence of colonization is highly dependent on age. The upper respiratory tract of approximately 1% to 5% of healthy adults is colonized by *M. catarrhalis*.[14,15] Based on results of sputum cultures, adults with chronic lung diseases have a somewhat higher rate of colonization compared to healthy adults.[16,17]

Nasopharyngeal colonization with *M. catarrhalis* is common throughout infancy. Some published studies have shown a higher rate of colonization during winter months; this higher rate may be due to the appearance of respiratory viral illnesses during colder months. Substantial regional differences in colonization rates are observed. For example, 66% of infants in a study in Buffalo, New York, were colonized during the first year of life,[18] whereas a similar study in Goteborg, Sweden, showed a colonization rate of approximately half of that level.[19] A study of rural aboriginal infants near Darwin, Australia, revealed that 100% of infants were colonized by *M. catarrhalis* by the age of 3 months.[20] The explanation for the marked differences in rates of colonization is not yet defined. One study showed a higher rate of colonization with *M. catarrhalis* in children who attend daycare centers compared to those who do not.[21] Several factors, including living conditions, hygiene, environmental factors (e.g., household smoking), genetic characteristics of the populations, and host factors, may play a role.

Nasopharyngeal colonization with middle ear pathogens, including *M. catarrhalis,* is associated with otitis media. Early colonization is a risk factor for recurrent otitis media.[18,22] Otitis-prone children are colonized with *M. catarrhalis* at a higher rate compared to healthy children.[16,18,23-25]

In order to study the epidemiology and dynamics of colonization by *M. catarrhalis,* several methods for typing isolates have been employed.[5,26-28] Analysis of isolates recovered prospectively have shown that colonization of the human respiratory tract by *M. catarrhalis* is a dynamic process, with frequent elimination and acquisition of new strains.[16-18] This active turnover of strains has been demonstrated in both infants and in adults with chronic lung disease. Elucidating the immune response that mediates elimination of an isolate from the respiratory tract will be important in identifying potentially protective immune responses to *M. catarrhalis.*

Pathogenesis

M. catarrhalis causes mucosal infections in children and adults. The pathogenesis of infection appears to involve contiguous spread of the bacterium from its colonizing position in the respiratory tract to cause clinical signs of infection. In the case of otitis media, the isolates recovered from the middle ear are present in the nasopharynx, indicating that the middle ear isolate came from the nasopharynx via the eustachian tube. The current data suggest that colonization of the upper respiratory tract with middle ear pathogens, including *M. catarrhalis,* is a necessary first step in the pathogenesis of otitis media. However, colonization alone is not sufficient to cause disease. An inciting event in a child colonized with a middle ear pathogen is probably necessary for bacteria to move to the middle ear and cause otitis media.

Little is known about the events that lead to the transition from asymptomatic colonization to lower respiratory tract infections in adults with chronic lung disease. An alteration in the host-pathogen relationship likely accounts for the development of infection, but the mechanisms remain to be elucidated. Published studies have provided evidence that a subset of strains of *M. catarrhalis* is associated with selected virulence traits, suggesting that some strains are more virulent than others.[26,27]

A reliable animal model that parallels human infection has not yet been developed for *M. catarrhalis.* The chinchilla model of otitis media, which is used widely to study otitis media caused by other bacteria, is not useful because chinchillas readily clear *M. catarrhalis* from the middle ear. The specificity of *M. catarrhalis* for humans may preclude the development of a useful model to study pathogenesis. The most widely used model is a mouse pulmonary clearance model that measures the rate of clearance of *M. catarrhalis* from the lungs following intratracheal challenge. This model does not parallel human infection but has been used as a guide to identify and study potential vaccine antigens.

Surface Antigens

The recognition of *M. catarrhalis* as an important human pathogen has led to substantial progress in elucidating the surface antigenic structure of *M. catarrhalis.* Such work is important in understanding mechanisms of pathogenesis, elucidating the human immune response to the bacterium, and guiding vaccine development.[29]

The identification of methods for purifying the outer membrane of *M. catarrhalis* led to the observation that outer membrane protein (OMP) patterns detected by sodium dodecyl sulfate–polyacrylamide gel electrophoresis (SDS-PAGE) showed a high degree of similarity among strains from diverse geographic and clinical sources. Several major OMPs have been identified and characterized. The study of OMPs of *M. catarrhalis* is an active area of research. Several of these OMPs are being studied as potential vaccine antigens in an effort to develop a vaccine to prevent infections caused by *M. catarrhalis.*

The outer membrane of *M. catarrhalis* contains lipo-oligosaccharide (LOS). LOS consists of a lipid A core coupled to oligosaccharides. The structure of the LOS resembles that of other nonenteric gram-negative bacteria in that the molecule lacks the long polysaccharide side chains observed in enteric gram-negative bacteria. Three major antigenic types of LOS can be distinguished, accounting for 95% of all strains.[30,31] The different serotypes are based on differences in terminal sugars in the LOS molecule.[32] As in the case of other gram-negative pathogens, LOS is likely a virulence factor for *M. catarrhalis.*

Several adhesins of *M. catarrhalis* have been identified, including outer membrane proteins UspA1 and MID (Hag).[33-36] OMP CD, a highly conserved porin protein, binds human mucin.[37] Many strains of *M. catarrhalis* appear to express pili, which likely play a role in adherence to epithelial cells.

Clinical Manifestations

Otitis Media

Approximately 80% of children experience at least one episode of acute otitis media by the age of 3 years. A subset of children experiences recurrent otitis media, which is associated with a delay in speech and language development. Careful studies from many centers have defined the etiology of acute otitis media by culturing middle ear fluid obtained by tympanocentesis. Culture of middle ear fluid is the most reliable method for determining the etiology of otitis media. Figure 210-1 shows a summary of the results of nine studies that employed cultures of middle ear fluids to determine the etiology of acute otitis media and have been published since 1992.[38-46] Although some differences among studies are observed, the results from centers in the United States and Europe are remarkably consistent in showing that *Streptococcus pneumoniae,* nontypeable *Haemophilus influenzae,* and *M. catarrhalis* are the predominant bacterial causes of acute otitis media. Overall, based on cultures of middle ear fluid, approximately 15% to 20% of cases of acute otitis media are caused by *M. catarrhalis.*

Otitis media with effusion is defined as the presence of middle ear fluid in the absence of signs and symptoms of acute otitis media. Bacterial cultures are negative in a majority of middle ear fluids from children with otitis media with effusion. Analysis of middle ear fluids by polymerase chain reaction reveals that a substantial proportion contain bacterial DNA, particularly from *M. catarrhalis* and *H. influenzae,* suggesting a bacterial etiology.[47-50]

Lower Respiratory Tract Infections in Chronic Obstructive Pulmonary Disease

M. catarrhalis causes lower respiratory tract infections in adults, particularly in the setting of chronic obstructive pulmonary disease (COPD). The recognition of *M. catarrhalis* as a pathogen in this setting was delayed until the past 20 years because *M. catarrhalis* is indistin-

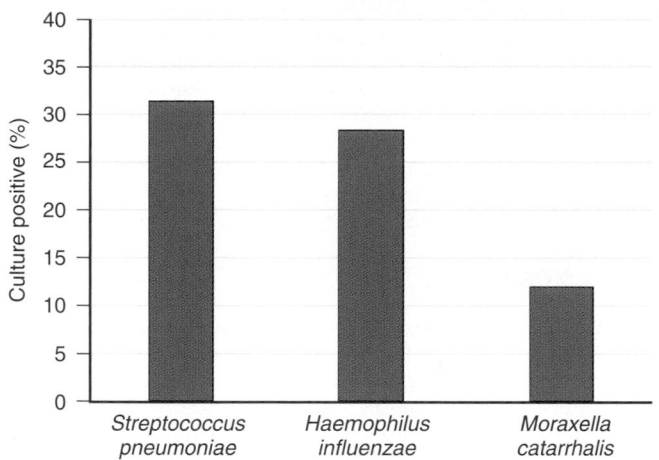

FIGURE 210-1. Results of bacterial cultures of middle ear fluids obtained from children with otitis media. Results are averages from nine studies.

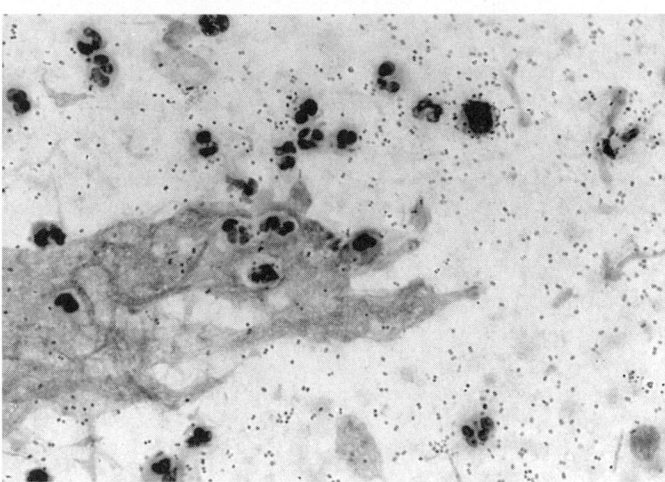

FIGURE 210-2. Photomicrograph (magnification × 1000) of a Gram-stained sputum sample from a patient with chronic bronchitis experiencing an exacerbation caused by *M. catarrhalis*. Note the abundance of leukocytes, the presence of large numbers of gram-negative diplococci as the exclusive bacterial form, and the presence of intracellular bacteria in leukocytes.

guishable from commensal *Neisseria* by Gram stain and difficult to distinguish by colony morphology. Therefore, unless clinical microbiology laboratories specifically test colonies that appear to be *Neisseria*, *M. catarrhalis* will be missed as a potential pathogen in sputum.

Several lines of evidence have established that *M. catarrhalis* causes exacerbations of COPD[5,6,51-53]:

- Analysis of sputum samples of a subset of patients with exacerbations of COPD demonstrates a predominance of gram-negative diplococci on Gram stain and nearly pure cultures of *M. catarrhalis*.
- Studies employing transtracheal aspiration and bronchoscopy with the protected specimen brush to sample the lower airways have revealed pure cultures of *M. catarrhalis* in some patients with exacerbations of COPD.[54-58]
- Clinical improvement of patients with *M. catarrhalis* as the presumed cause of exacerbations is observed following administration of antibiotics that are active against *M. catarrhalis*.
- A specific immune response has been observed following exacerbations of COPD associated with *M. catarrhalis* in the sputum.[59-61]
- Acquisition of a new strain of *M. catarrhalis* is associated with clinical exacerbation.[17]

Based on the type of evidence outlined above, *M. catarrhalis* is the second most common bacterial cause of exacerbations of COPD after nontypeable *H. influenzae*. One study estimated that 30% of exacerbations were caused by *M. catarrhalis*.[62]

The clinical manifestations of exacerbations of COPD caused by *M. catarrhalis* are similar to those of exacerbations caused by other bacteria such as nontypeable *H. influenzae*. Patients experience increased cough and sputum production, increased sputum purulence, and increased dyspnea compared to baseline symptoms. Sputum Gram stain shows intracellular and extracellular gram-negative diplococci as the exclusive or predominant bacterial form (Fig. 210-2), and cultures grow predominantly *M. catarrhalis*.

Pneumonia in the Elderly

Studies from centers in the United States and Europe indicate that *M. catarrhalis* causes a significant proportion of pneumonia in the elderly.[63-66] Because *M. catarrhalis* can colonize the respiratory tract in the absence of clinical infection, it is difficult to state the precise proportion of pneumonia in the elderly caused by *M. catarrhalis*. One prospective study estimated that *M. catarrhalis* caused 10% of community-acquired pneumonia in the elderly.[67] Most elderly patients who experience pneumonia caused by *M. catarrhalis* have underlying illnesses including COPD, congestive heart failure, and diabetes. Although *M. catarrhalis* causes a significant illness in the elderly, fulminant pneumonia is uncommon.

Nosocomial Respiratory Tract Infections

Nosocomial lower respiratory tract infections caused by *M. catarrhalis* have been observed in respiratory units in health care facilities. The presence of a susceptible population of adults with underlying cardiopulmonary disease may be important in these apparent outbreaks. Analysis of isolates by various typing methods indicate that some of these clusters involved multiple strains of *M. catarrhalis* and some were caused by a single strain, indicating person-to-person spread of the organism.

Sinusitis

The etiology of sinusitis is determined by culture of sinus aspirates, a relatively invasive procedure that is not performed routinely. Studies that have used sinus aspiration to determine the etiology of sinusitis have shown that *M. catarrhalis* is the third most common cause of sinusitis in adults and children after nontypeable *H. influenzae* and *S. pneumoniae*.

Bacteremia

Published reports have documented the occurrence of bacteremia caused by *M. catarrhalis*.[65,66,68,69] Bacteremia is an infrequent manifestation of *M. catarrhalis* infection. The severity of clinical manifestations ranges from mild to life threatening. Bacteremia has been reported in people of all ages, from neonates to the elderly. A majority of patients have clinical evidence of respiratory tract infection. Most patients with bacteremia caused by *M. catarrhalis* have underlying illnesses, including cardiopulmonary disease, malignancy, immunodeficiency, and chronic debilitation. A review of *M. catarrhalis* bacteremia notes a mortality of 21%.[70] The underlying illness is an important determinant of outcome.

Treatment

A rapid increase in the proportion of strains that produce β-lactamase occurred simultaneously in the United States and Europe beginning in the late 1970s.[71] This is one of the most dramatic examples of a rapid increase in antimicrobial resistance by a bacterial species. Currently, virtually all strains of *M. catarrhalis* produce β-lactamase. Three different β-lactamases (BRO-1, BRO-2, and BRO-3) have been identified and characterized.[72,73] The β-lactamase of *M. catarrhalis* is inducible and cell associated. Because an inoculum-dependent susceptibility to ampicillin is observed, ampicillin should not be used for β-lactamase–producing strains regardless of the results of susceptibility testing.

Many infections caused by *M. catarrhalis* can be treated with oral antibiotics. The organism is generally susceptible to amoxicillin-clavulanate, trimethoprim-sulfamethoxazole, tetracyclines, oral cephalosporins (e.g., cefixime, cefpodoxime, cefaclor, loracarbef, cefuroxime), macrolides (e.g., azithromycin, clarithromycin), and fluoroquinolones.[74-77] *M. catarrhalis* is also uniformly susceptible to ticarcillin, piperacillin, second- and third-generation cephalosporins, and aminoglycosides. *M. catarrhalis* is resistant to penicillin, ampicillin, vancomycin, and clindamycin.

OTHER *NEISSERIA*

N. meningitidis and *N. gonorrhoeae* have long been recognized as the "pathogenic *Neisseria*." Other *Neisseria* species are common components of the normal flora of the upper respiratory tract of humans and are often called "commensal *Neisseria*." Table 210-1 lists several biochemical and growth characteristics that are used to distinguish among various *Neisseria* species and *M. catarrhalis*. Commensal *Neisseria* species lack several virulence factors, including pili, Opa, and the H8 antigen, that are expressed by meningococci and gonococci.[78] However, commensal *Neisseria* express a variety of surface antigens that share homology with antigens of *N. meningitidis* and *N. gonorrhoeae*.[79,80] Immune responses to cross-reactive antigens on commensal *Neisseria*, particularly *N. lactamica*, may contribute to acquisition of natural immunity to *N. meningitidis*.[81]

Neisseria species such as *N. sicca*, *N. subflava*, *N. cinerea*, *N. lactamica*, and others occasionally cause invasive infections in humans. These infections, documented primarily by individual case reports, include meningitis, endocarditis, bacteremia, ocular infections, pericarditis, empyema, septic arthritis, bursitis, and osteomyelitis.[82-87] *N. cinerea* appears to have a propensity to cause ocular infections in young children.[88,89]

N. weaveri (formerly CDC group M5) is a component of the normal oropharyngeal flora of dogs and is an important cause of infection in dog bite wounds in humans.[90,91] These infections are occasionally associated with bacteremia.[92]

Many of these infections have been treated successfully with penicillin and ampicillin. However, isolates of *Neisseria* species have shown increased resistance to penicillin, so susceptibility testing should be performed on isolates that cause invasive infections and the results should be used to guide antimicrobial therapy.

Neisseria are naturally competent for uptake of DNA. Genetic recombination occurs among bacteria that make up the complex flora of the upper respiratory tract. Virulence determinants are exchanged with pathogenic *Neisseria*, genes encoding altered penicillin-binding proteins are passed between species, and extensive interspecies recombination of a variety of genes occurs in vivo.[93-95] These observations have important implications in the role of acquisition of antibiotic resistance and evolution of pathogens in the human respiratory tract. Indeed, interspecies transfer of *penA* genes from commensal *Neisseria* is an important mechanism of acquisition of penicillin resistance of *N. gonorrhoeae* and *N. meningitidis*.[94]

OTHER *MORAXELLA*

Bacteria of the genus *Moraxella* are normal commensals of the human upper respiratory tract and are occasionally recovered from the skin and urogenital tract. The taxonomy of *Moraxella* species is a dynamic area of research and, as a result, species classifications are continuing to change as knowledge in the area expands. Analysis of ribosomal sequences is particularly useful in elucidating phylogenetic relationships.[96] Species are generally differentiated biochemically. Table 210-2 shows biochemical reactions and growth characteristics that are used to distinguish among several *Moraxella* species.

Moraxella species other than *M. catarrhalis* are unusual pathogens in humans. Several reports have emphasized the role of other *Moraxella* as ocular pathogens. These bacteria cause conjunctivitis, keratitis, and rarely endophthalmitis.[97-101] *Moraxella* species are susceptible to all conventional topical ocular antibiotics.

Case reports have established *Moraxella* species as unusual causes of invasive infections in humans, including endocarditis, bacteremia, septic arthritis, purulent pericarditis, cellulitis, and meningitis.[102-110] Patients who experience meningitis caused by *Moraxella* species have a high frequency of inherited and acquired complement deficiencies, and these should be investigated following recovery.[111]

Antimicrobial susceptibility should be performed on isolates recovered from normally sterile sites, but *Moraxella* species are generally susceptible to penicillins and cephalosporins.

KINGELLA

History and Microbiology

In 1976, *Moraxella kingae* was transferred to the new genus *Kingella*.[112,113] *Kingella* are short gram-negative coccoids to medium-sized rod with tapered ends. Four species have been identified: *K. kingae*, *K. indologenes*, *K. denitrificans*, and the newly described *K.*

TABLE 210-1   Biochemical and Growth Characteristics of *Neisseria* and *Moraxella catarrhalis*

Species	Glucose	Maltose	Sucrose	Lactose (ONPG)	Fructose	H₂S*	Oxidase	Extra CO₂	Growth at 22° C	Polysaccharide†	Pigment‡
N. gonorrhoeae	+	−	−	−	−	−	+	VI	−	NG	−
N. meningitidis	+	+	−	−	−	−	+	I	−	NG	−
N. lactamica	+	+	−	+	−	+	+	v	v	−	+Y
N. sicca	+	+	+	−	+	+	+	−	+	+	−(slY)
N. subflava	+	+	v	−	v	+	+	−	+	v	+Y
N. mucosa	+	+	+	−	+	+	+	−	+	+	−(slY)
N. flavescens	−	−	−	−	−	+	+	−	+	+	+Y
N. cinerea	−	−	−	−	−	−	+	−	v	−	grayish
N. polysaccharea	+	+	−	−	−	−	+	−	−	+	−(slY)
N. elongata	−	−	−	−	−	−	+	−	+	−	grayish/slY
N. weaveri	−	−	−	−	−	+	+	−	+	−	−(slY)
M. catarrhalis	−	−	+	−	−	+	+	−	v	−	grayish

*With lead acetate paper.
†Synthesis of polysaccharide from 5% sucrose.
‡On Loeffler slant.
I, important for growth; NG, no growth; ONPG, O-nitrophenol-β-D-galactopyranoside; sl, slightly; VI, very important for growth; v, variable; Y, yellow.
From Gröschel DM. *Moraxella catarrhalis* and other gram-negative cocci. In: Mandell GL, Bennett JE, Dolin R, eds. Principles and Practice of Infectious Diseases. 4th ed. New York: Churchill Livingstone; 1995:1926.

oralis. Kingella species are recovered from the human respiratory tract and have previously been recognized as rare causes of human disease. However, in the past two decades, infections caused by *Kingella* have been recognized with surprising frequency in reports from the United States, Europe, and Israel.

The increase in the recognition of *Kingella* infections may be a result of several factors. Because the bacterium is slow growing and fastidious, special attention by the microbiology laboratory is often required to isolate the organism. For example, *K. kingae* in joint fluid will often fail to grow when plated directly on solid media, but will grow when the joint fluid is inoculated into blood culture bottles.[114,115] Another factor accounting for the increased recognition of *Kingella* as a human pathogen is that the bacterium has likely been misidentified as *Moraxella* and other *Neisseria* by many laboratories. Finally, in the past, *Kingella* has been unfamiliar to most personnel in clinical microbiology laboratories and was likely frequently dismissed as a contaminant.[116]

K. kingae, the most common human pathogen of the *Kingella* species, grows on blood and chocolate agar but fails to grow on MacConkey agar. The bacterium has a tendency to resist decolorization and may therefore sometimes be mistaken for a gram-positive organism. It is oxidase positive, produces acid from glucose and maltose, and lacks catalase, urease, and indole. Table 210-2 lists several characteristics that distinguish *Kingella* from related bacteria.

Epidemiology and Respiratory Tract Colonization

K. kingae frequently colonizes the throats of young children.[117] In one prospective study in which cultures were performed every 2 weeks for 11 months, 73% of all children had at least one positive throat culture for *K. kingae*.[117] The organism has not been recovered from cultures of the nasopharynx. The highest rate of colonization is observed in children ages 6 months to 4 years, which corresponds to the peak age incidence of invasive disease. Infants younger than 6 months of age are not colonized. This pattern of colonization parallels that of other respiratory tract pathogens such as *M. catarrhalis* and *S. pneumoniae*, which show low rates of colonization in the neonatal period (presumably as a result of maternal antibodies) followed by higher rates of colonization and infection in infancy and childhood, with a declining incidence of infection in adulthood.

In studies of the microbiology of the human oral cavity, a bacterium that resembled *Eikenella corrodens* was recovered frequently from dental plaque.[118] On the basis of 16S ribosomal sequences, these organisms were designated as the new species *K. oralis*.[119] *K. oralis* is present in plaque or on the tooth surface in the majority of people with or without periodontal disease.[120] The role of *K. oralis* in periodontal disease is not known at this time.

Clinical Manifestations

K. kingae is the most frequent human pathogen of the *Kingella* species. Approximately 90% of invasive disease caused by *K. kingae* occurs in children younger than the age of 4 years, with the majority occurring between the age of 6 months and 2 years. Invasive infections have not been reported in infants younger than the age of 6 months. Infection shows a seasonal distribution with the rate of cases being higher in the autumn and winter months.[115,121,122] The most common clinical manifestation of *K. kingae* disease are skeletal infections, endocarditis, and bacteremia.

Skeletal Infections

K. kingae has a remarkable propensity to cause infections of the skeletal system in young children.[116,123-127] The most common such infection is septic arthritis. The disease most frequently affects large, weight-bearing joints, especially the knee and ankle. Gram stain of the joint fluid is usually negative. The diagnosis is made by recovering the organism from culture of joint fluid. Inoculating blood culture bottles with joint fluid substantially enhances the likelihood of recovering the organism compared to direct inoculation of agar plates.[114,115] Osteomyelitis caused by *K. kingae* most frequently involves the bones of the lower extremity. The onset is insidious and the diagnosis is often delayed. Hematogenous invasion of the intervertebral disk by *K. kingae* is observed most commonly in the lumbar intervertebral spaces but can occur at any level.[128,129]

Endocarditis

In contrast to other clinical manifestations of *Kingella* infections, endocarditis can be seen at all ages, including school-age children and adults.[130-134] Endocarditis has involved both native and prosthetic valves. Although many cases of endocarditis occur in people who have preexisting valvular disease, *Kingella* can cause endocarditis on normal valves as well. Cases of endocarditis can be caused by *K. denitrificans* and *K. indologenes* as well as *K. kingae*. *Kingella* are one of the so-called HACEK group of organisms, which include fastidious bacteria capable of causing endocarditis. The HACEK group consists of *Haemophilus* species (*H. aphrophilus* and *H. parainfluenzae*), *Actinobacillus actinomycetemcomitans*, *Cardiobacterium hominis*, and *Eikenella corrodens* in addition to *K. kingae*. The difficulty in recovering and identifying *K. kingae* in blood cultures frequently results in a delay in the diagnosis, which may account for the relatively high rate of morbidity seen with *Kingella* endocarditis. Because of the serious nature of *Kingella* endocarditis, all patients with *Kingella* bacteremia should be carefully evaluated for the presence of endocarditis.

TABLE 210-2 Laboratory Procedures Useful for the Identification of *Moraxella, Oligella, Moraxella*-like Organisms, and *Kingella*

Species	Motility	Oxidase	Catalase	OF Glucose	Serum Required	Urease	Indole	Nitrate	Phenylalanine	Gelatin	Assimilation of Acetate	Growth on MacConkey Agar
M. catarrhalis	−	+	+	−	−	−	−	−	−	−	v	v
M. lacunata	−	+	+	−	+	−	−	+	v	v	−	−
M. nonliquefaciens	−	+	+	−	v	−	−	+	−	−	−	−
M. osloensis	−	+	+	−	−	−	−	v	v	−	+	v
M. phenylpyruvica	−	+	+	−	−	+	−	v	+	−	v	v
M. atlantae	−	+	+	−	+	−	−	−	−	−	v	+
O. urethralis	−	+	+	−	−	−	−	−	+	−	v	+
N. weaveri (M-5)	−	+	+	−	−	−	−	−	+	−	v	−
N. elongata (M-6)	−	+	−	−	−	−	−	+	−	−	v	v
K. kingae*	−	+	−	F†	−	−	−	−	−	−	−	v
K. indologenes	−	+	−	F	−	−	+	−	−	−	−	−
K. denitrificans	−	+	−	F	−	−	−	+	−	−	−	−

*Most strains hemolytic on blood agar.
†May take 3 or more days; some strains require serum supplement.
OF, oxidation or fermentation; v, variable.
From Gröschel DM. *Moraxella catarrhalis* and other gram-negative cocci. In: Mandell GL, Bennett JE, Dolin R, eds. Principles and Practice of Infectious Diseases. 4th ed. New York: Churchill Livingstone; 1995:1926.

Bacteremia

Approximately half of children with *K. kingae* bacteremia have a concomitant focal source such as the skeletal system. The remainder have occult bacteremia.[121,135-137] The presumed source of the bacteremia is the respiratory tract.

Other Infections

Kingella species have been documented by case reports to cause infections in a variety of sites, including pneumonia, epiglottitis, meningitis, soft tissue infections, and ocular infections.[116,138-141]

Treatment

The antimicrobial susceptibility of isolates of *Kingella* has not been well studied. *Kingella* species appear to be susceptible to a wide variety of penicillins and cephalosporins, although a single isolate of β-lactamase producing *K. kingae* has been identified.[142-144] Disease-associated isolates should be tested for antimicrobial susceptibility; if the isolate is susceptible, a penicillin or cephalosporin should be used. Other agents with in vitro activity include aminoglycosides, trimethoprim-sulfamethoxazole, tetracycline, erythromycin, and fluoroquinolones.

The drugs of choice for the treatment of endocarditis caused by *Kingella* species (and other HACEK organisms) are the third-generation cephalosporins cefotaxime or ceftriaxone.[145] The duration of treatment for native valve endocarditis should be 3 to 4 weeks and the duration of treatment for prosthetic valve endocarditis should be 6 weeks.

REFERENCES

1. Ghon A, Pfeiffer H. Der *Micrococcus catarrhalis* (R. Pfeiffer) als Krankheitserreger. Z Klin Med. 1902;44:263-281.
2. Berk SL. From *Micrococcus* to *Moraxella*—The reemergence of *Branhamella catarrhalis*. Arch Intern Med. 1990;150:2254-2257.
3. Catlin BW. Transfer of the organism named *Neisseria catarrhalis* to *Branhamella* genus. Int J Syst Bacteriol. 1970;20:155-159.
4. Bovre K. Proposal to divide the genus *Moraxella* into two subgenera, subgenus *Moraxella* and subgenus *Branhamella*. Int J Syst Bacteriol. 1979;29:403-406.
5. Murphy TF. *Branhamella catarrhalis*: Epidemiology, surface antigenic structure, and immune response. Microbiol Rev. 1996;60:267-279.
6. Enright MC, McKenzie H. *Moraxella (Branhamella) catarrhalis*—Clinical and molecular aspects of a rediscovered pathogen. J Med Microbiol. 1997;46:360-371.
7. Catlin BW. *Branhamella catarrhalis*: An organism gaining respect as a pathogen. Clin Microbiol Rev. 1990;3:293-320.
8. Karalus R, Campagnari A. *Moraxella catarrhalis*: A review of an important human mucosal pathogen. Microbes Infect. 2000;2:547-559.
9. Christensen JJ. *Moraxella (Branhamella) catarrhalis*: Clinical, microbiological and immunological features in lower respiratory tract infections. APMIS. 1999; 107(Suppl):1-36.
10. Speeleveld E, Fossepre J-M, Gordts B, Van Landuyt HW. Comparison of three rapid methods, tributyrine, 4-methylumbelliferyl butyrate, and indoxyl acetate, for rapid identification of *Moraxella catarrhalis*. J Clin Microbiol. 1994;32:1362-1363.
11. Janda WM, Montero MC, Wilcoski LM. Evaluation of the BactiCard Neisseria for Identification of pathogenic *Neisseria* species and *Moraxella catarrhalis*. Eur J Clin Microbiol Infect Dis. 2002;21:875-879.
12. Harmsen D, Singer C, Rothganger J, et al. Diagnostics of *Neisseriaceae* and *Moraxellaceae* by ribosomal DNA sequencing: Ribosomal differentiation of medical microorganisms. J Clin Microbiol. 2001;39:936-942.
13. Pettersson B, Kodjo A, Ronaghi M, et al. Phylogeny of the family *Moraxellaceae* by 16S rDNA sequence analysis, with special emphasis on differentiation of *Moraxella* species. Int J Syst Bacteriol. 1998;48(Pt 1):75-89.
14. Ejlertsen T, Thisted E, Ebbesen F, et al. *Branhamella catarrhalis* in children and adults: A study of prevalence, time of colonisation, and association with upper and lower respiratory tract infections. J Infect. 1994;29:23-31.
15. Vaneechoutte M, Verschraegen G, Claeys G, et al. Respiratory tract carrier rates of *Moraxella (Branhamella) catarrhalis* in adults and children and interpretation of the isolation of *M. catarrhalis* from sputum. J Clin Microbiol. 1990;28:2674-2680.
16. Klingman KL, Pye A, Hill S, Murphy TF. Dynamics of respiratory tract colonization by *Moraxella (Branhamella) catarrhalis* in bronchiectasis. Am J Respir Crit Care Med. 1995;152:1072-1078.
17. Sethi S, Evans N, Grant BJB, Murphy TF. New strains of bacteria and exacerbations of chronic obstructive pulmonary disease. N Engl J Med. 2002;347:465-471.
18. Faden H, Harabuchi Y, Hong JJ. Epidemiology of *Moraxella catarrhalis* in children during the first 2 years of life: Relationship to otitis media. J Infect Dis. 1994;169:1312-1317.
19. Aniansson G, Alm B, Andersson B, et al. Nasopharyngeal colonization during the first year of life. J Infect Dis. 1992;165(Suppl 1):S38-S42.
20. Leach AJ, Boswell JB, Asche V, et al. Bacterial colonization of the nasopharynx predicts very early onset and persistence of otitis media in Australian Aboriginal infants. Pediatr Infect Dis J. 1994;13:983-989.
21. Peerbooms PG, Engelen MN, Stokman DA, et al. Nasopharyngeal carriage of potential bacterial pathogens related to day care attendance, with special reference to the molecular epidemiology of *Haemophilus influenzae*. J Clin Microbiol. 2002;40:2832-2836.
22. Faden H, Duffy L, Wasielewski R, et al. Relationship between nasopharyngeal colonization and the development of otitis media in children. J Infect Dis. 1997;175:1440-1445.
23. Dhooge I, Van Damme D, Vaneechoutte M, et al. Role of nasopharyngeal bacterial flora in the evaluation of recurrent middle ear infections in children. Clin Microbiol Infect. 1999;5:530-534.
24. Karlidag T, Demirdag K, Kaygusuz I, et al. Resistant bacteria in the adenoid tissues of children with otitis media with effusion. Int J Pediatr Otorhinolaryngol. 2002;64:35-40.
25. Prellner K, Christensen P, Hovelius B, Rosen C. Nasopharyngeal carriage of bacteria in otitis-prone and non-otitis-prone children in day-care centres. Acta Otolaryngol. 1984;98:343-350.
26. Verduin CM, Kools-Sijmons M, van der Plas J, et al. Complement-resistant *Moraxella catarrhalis* forms a genetically distinct lineage with the species. FEMS Microbiol Lett. 2000;184:1-8.
27. Bootsma HJ, van der Heide HG, van de Pas S, et al. Analysis of *Moraxella catarrhalis* by DNA typing: Evidence for a distinct subpopulation associated with virulence traits. J Infect Dis. 2000;181:1376-1387.
28. Wolf B, Kools-Sijmons M, Verduin C, et al. Genetic diversity among strains of *Moraxella catarrhalis* cultured from the nasopharynx of young and healthy Brazilian, Angolan and Dutch children. Eur J Clin Microbiol Infect Dis. 2000;19:759-764.
29. McMichael JC. Vaccines for *Moraxella catarrhalis*. Vaccine. 2000;19:S101-S108.
30. Rahman M, Holme T. Antibody response in rabbits to serotype-specific determinants in lipopolysaccharides from *Moraxella catarrhalis*. J Med Microbiol. 1996;44:348-354.
31. Vaneechoutte M, Verschraegen G, Claeys G, Van Den Abeele AM. Serological typing of *Branhamella catarrhalis* strains on the basis of lipopolysaccharide antigens. J Clin Microbiol. 1990;28:182-187.
32. Edebrink P, Jansson P-E, Rahman MM, et al. Structural studies of the O-polysaccharide from the lipopolysaccharide of *Moraxella (Branhamella) catarrhalis* serotype A (strain ATCC 25238). Carbohydrate Res. 1994;257:269-284.
33. Aebi C, LaFontaine ER, Cope LD, et al. Phenotypic effect of isogenic uspA1 and uspA2 mutations on *Moraxella catarrhalis* 035E. Infect Immun. 1998;66:3113-3119.
34. Hoiczyk E, Roggenkamp A, Reichenbecher M, et al. Structure and sequence analysis of *Yersinia* YadA and *Moraxella* UspAs reveal a novel class of adhesins. EMBO J. 2000;22:5989-5999.
35. Forsgren A, Brant M, Karamehmedovic M, Riesbeck K. The immunoglobulin D-binding protein MID from *Moraxella catarrhalis* is also an adhesin. Infect Immun. 2003;71:3302-3309.
36. Pearson MM, Lafontaine ER, Wagner NJ, et al. A *hag* mutant of *Moraxella catarrhalis* strain O35E is deficient in hemagglutination, autoagglutination, and immunoglobulin D-binding activities. Infect Immun. 2002;70:4523-4533.
37. Reddy MS, Murphy TF, Faden HS, Bernstein JM. Middle ear mucin glycoprotein: Purification and interaction with nontypeable *Haemophilus influenzae* and *Moraxella catarrhalis*. Otolaryngol Head Neck Surg. 1997;116:175-189.
38. Faden H, Bernstein J, Stanievich J, et al. Effect of prior antibiotic treatment on middle ear disease in children. Ann Otol Rhinol Laryngol. 1992;101:87-91.
39. DelBeccaro MA, Mendelman PM, Inglis AF, et al. Bacteriology of acute otitis media: A new perspective. J Pediatr. 1992;120:81-84.
40. Chonmaitree T, Owen MJ, Patel JA, et al. Effect of viral respiratory tract infection on outcome of acute otitis media. J Pediatr. 1992;120:856-862.
41. Owen MJ, Anwar R, Nguyen HK, et al. Efficacy of cefixime in the treatment of acute otitis media in children. Am J Dis Child. 1993;147:81-86.
42. Aspin MM, Hoberman A, McCarty J, et al. Comparative study of the safety and efficacy of clarithromycin and amoxicillin-clavulanate in the treatment of acute otitis media in children. J Pediatr. 1994;125:135-141.
43. Gehanno P, Berche P, Boucot I, et al. Comparative efficacy and safety of cefprozil and amoxicillin-clavulanate in the treatment of acute otitis media in children. J Antimicrob Chemother. 1994;33:1209-1218.
44. Feingold M, Klein JO, Haslam GE, et al. Acute otitis media in children. Am J Dis Child. 1966;111:361-365.
45. Block SL, McCarty JM, Hedrick JA, et al. Comparative safety and efficacy of cefdinir vs amoxicillin/clavulanate for treatment of suppurative acute otitis media in children. Pediatr Infect Dis J. 2000;19:S159-S165.
46. Kilpi T, Herva E, Kaijalainen T, et al. Bacteriology of acute otitis media in a cohort of Finnish children followed for the first two years of life. Pediatr Infect Dis J. 2001;20:654-662.
47. Hendolin PH, Markkanen A, Ylikoski J, Wahlfors JJ. Use of multiplex PCR for simultaneous detection of four bacterial species in middle ear effusions. J Clin Microbiol. 1997;35:2854-2858.
48. Hendolin PH, Paulin L, Ylikoski J. Clinically applicable multiplex PCR for four middle ear pathogens. J Clin Microbiol. 2000;38:125-132.
49. Post JC, Preston RA, Aul JJ, et al. Molecular analysis of bacterial pathogens in otitis media with effusion. JAMA. 1995;273:1598-1604.
50. Post JC, Aul JJ, White GJ, et al. PCR-based detection of bacterial DNA after antimicrobial treatment is indicative of persistent, viable bacteria in the chinchilla model of otitis media. Am J Otolaryngol. 1996;17:106-111.

51. Murphy TF, Sethi S. Chronic obstructive pulmonary disease: Role of bacteria and guide to antibacterial selection in the older patient. Drugs Aging. 2002;19:761-775.
52. Murphy TF, Sethi S. Bacterial infection in chronic obstructive pulmonary disease. Am Rev Respir Dis. 1992;146:1067-1083.
53. Sethi S, Murphy TF. Bacterial infection in chronic obstructive pulmonary disease in 2000: A state of the art review. Clin Microbiol Rev. 2001;14:336-363.
54. Fagon J-Y, Chastre J, Trouillet J-L, et al. Characterization of distal bronchial microflora during acute exacerbation of chronic bronchitis. Am Rev Respir Dis. 1990;142:1004-1008.
55. Monso E, Ruiz J, Rosell A, et al. Bacterial infection in chronic obstructive pulmonary disease: A study of stable and exacerbated outpatients using the protected specimen brush. Am J Respir Crit Care Med. 1995;152:1316-1320.
56. Ninane G, Joly J, Kraytman M. Bronchopulmonary infection due to *Branhamella catarrhalis:* 11 cases assessed by transtracheal puncture. Br Med J. 1978;1:276-278.
57. Pela R, Marchesani F, Agostinelli C, et al. Airways microbial flora in COPD patients in stable clinical conditions and during exacerbations: A bronchoscopic investigation. Monaldi Arch Chest Dis. 1998;53:262-267.
58. Soler N, Torres A, Ewig S, et al. Bronchial microbial patterns in severe exacerbations of chronic obstructive pulmonary disease (COPD) requiring mechanical ventilation. Am J Respir Crit Care Med. 1998;157:1498-1505.
59. Chapman AJ, Musher DM, Jonsson S, et al. Development of bactericidal antibody during *Branhamella catarrhalis* infection. J Infect Dis. 1985;151:878-882.
60. Bakri F, Brauer AL, Sethi S, Murphy TF. Systemic and mucosal antibody response to *Moraxella catarrhalis* following exacerbations of chronic obstructive pulmonary disease. J Infect Dis. 2002;185:632-640.
61. Murphy TF, Kirkham C, Liu DF, Sethi S. Human immune response to outer membrane protein CD of *Moraxella catarrhalis* in adults with chronic obstructive pulmonary disease. Infect Immun. 2003;71:1288-1294.
62. Verghese A, Roberson D, Kalbfleisch JH, Sarubbi F. Randomized comparative study of cefixime versus cephalexin in acute bacterial exacerbations of chronic bronchitis. Antimicrob Agents Chemother. 1990;34:1041-1044.
63. Hager H, Verghese A, Alvarez S, Berk SL. *Branhamella catarrhalis* respiratory infections. Rev Infect Dis. 1987;9:1140-1149.
64. Barreiro B, Esteban L, Prats E, et al. *Branhamella catarrhalis* respiratory infections. Eur Respir J. 1992;5:675-679.
65. Collazos J, de Miguel J, Ayarza R. *Moraxella catarrhalis* bacteremic pneumonia in adults: Two cases and review of the literature. Eur J Clin Microbiol Infect Dis. 1992;11:237-240.
66. Sugiyama H, Ogata E, Shimamoto Y, et al. Bacteremic *Moraxella catarrhalis* pneumonia in a patient with immunoglobulin deficiency. J Infect Chemother. 2000;6:61-62.
67. Carr B, Walsh JB, Coakley D, et al. Prospective hospital study of community acquired lower respiratory tract infection in the elderly. Respir Med. 1991;85:185-187.
68. Meyer GA, Shope TR, Waecker NJ Jr, Lanningham FH. *Moraxella (Branhamella) catarrhalis* bacteremia in children. Clin Pediatr. 1995;34:146-150.
69. Rotta AT, Asmar BI. *Moraxella catarrhalis* bacteremia and preseptal cellulitis. South Med J. 1994;87:541-542.
70. Ioannidis JPA, Worthington M, Griffiths JK, Snydman DR. Spectrum and significance of bacteremia due to *Moraxella catarrhalis.* Clin Infect Dis. 1995;21:390-397.
71. Nissinen A, Gronroos P, Huovinen P, et al. Development of β-lactamase-mediated resistance to penicillin in middle-ear isolates of *Moraxella catarrhalis* in Finnish children, 1978-1993. Clin Infect Dis. 1995;21:1193-1196.
72. Bootsma HJ, van Dijk H, Vauterin P, et al. Genesis of β-lactamase-producing *Moraxella catarrhalis:* evidence for transformation-mediated horizontal transfer. Mol Microbiol. 2000;36:93-104.
73. Schmitz FJ, Beeck A, Perdikouli M, et al. Production of BRO beta-lactamases and resistance to complement in European *Moraxella catarrhalis* isolates. J Clin Microbiol. 2002;40:1546-1548.
74. Jones ME, Karlowsky JA, Blosser-Middleton R, et al. Apparent plateau in beta-lactamase production among clinical isolates of *Haemophilus influenzae* and *Moraxella catarrhalis* in the United States: Results from the LIBRA Surveillance initiative. Int J Antimicrob Agents. 2002;19:119-123.
75. Thornsberry C, Sahm DF, Kelly LJ, et al. Regional trends in antimicrobial resistance among clinical isolates of *Streptococcus pneumoniae, Haemophilus influenzae,* and *Moraxella catarrhalis* in the United States: Results from the TRUST Surveillance Program, 1999-2000. Clin Infect Dis. 2002;34(Suppl 1):S4-S16.
76. Turnak MR, Bandak SI, Bouchillon SK, et al. Antimicrobial susceptibilities of clinical isolates of *Haemophilus influenzae* and *Moraxella catarrhalis* collected during 1999-2000 from 13 countries. Clin Microbiol Infect. 2001;7:671-677.
77. Zhanel GG, Palatnick L, Nichol KA, et al. Antimicrobial resistance in *Haemophilus influenzae* and *Moraxella catarrhalis* respiratory tract isolates: Results of the Canadian Respiratory Organism Susceptibility Study, 1997 to 2002. Antimicrob Agents Chemother. 2003;47:1875-1881.
78. Aho EL, Murphy GL, Cannon JG. Distribution of specific DNA sequences among pathogenic and commensal *Neisseria* species. Infect Immun. 1987;55:1009-1013.
79. Serino L, Virji M. Phosphorylcholine decoration of lipopolysaccharide differentiates commensal *Neisseriae* from pathogenic strains: Identification of licA-type genes in commensal *Neisseriae.* Mol Microbiol. 2000;35:1550-1559.
80. Zhu P, Klutch MJ, Derrick JP, et al. Identification of opcA gene in *Neisseria polysaccharea:* Interspecies diversity of Opc protein family. Gene. 2003;307:31-40.
81. Troncoso G, Sanchez S, Criado MT, Ferreiros CM. Analysis of *Neisseria lactamica* antigens putatively implicated in acquisition of natural immunity to *Neisseria meningitidis.* FEMS Immunol Med Microbiol. 2002;34:9-15.
82. Apisarnthanarak A, Dunagan WC, Dunne WM. *Neisseria elongata* subsp. elongata, as a cause of human endocarditis. Diagn Microbiol Infect Dis. 2001;39:265-266.
83. Baraldes MA, Domingo P, Barrio JL, et al. Meningitis due to *Neisseria subflava:* case report and review. Clin Infect Dis. 2000;30:615-617.
84. Domingo P, Coll P, Maroto P, et al. *Neisseria subflava* bacteremia in a neutropenic patient. Arch Intern Med. 1996;156:1762-1765.
85. Amsel BJ, Moulijn AC. Nonfebrile mitral valve endocarditis due to *Neisseria subflava.* Chest. 1996;109:280-282.
86. Kirchgesner V, Plesiat P, Dupont MJ, et al. Meningitis and septicemia due to *Neisseria cinerea.* Clin Infect Dis. 1995;21:1351.
87. Obeid EMH. *Neisseria subflava* causing septic arthritis of the ankle in a child. J Infect. 1993;27:100-101.
88. Dolter J, Wong J, Janda JM. Association of *Neisseria cinerea* with ocular infections in paediatric patients. J Infect. 1998;36:49-52.
89. Bourbeau P, Holla V, Piemontese S. Ophthalmia neonatorum caused by *Neisseria cinerea.* J Clin Microbiol. 1990;28:1640-1641.
90. Andersen BM, Steigerwalt AG, O'Connor SP, et al. *Neisseria weaveri* sp. nov., formerly CDC group M-5, a gram-negative bacterium associated with dog bite wounds. J Clin Microbiol. 1993;31:2456-2466.
91. Holmes B, Costas M, On SLW, et al. *Neisseria weaveri* sp. nov. (formerly CDC group M-5), from dog bite wounds of humans. Int J System Bacteriol. 1993;43:687-693.
92. Carlson P, Kontiainen S, Anttila P, Eerola E. Septicemia caused by *Neisseria weaveri.* Clin Infect Dis. 1997;24:739.
93. Lujan R, Zhang Q-Y, Saez-Nieto JA, et al. Penicillin-resistant isolates of *Neisseria lactamica* produce altered forms of penicillin-binding protein 2 that arose by interspecies horizontal gene transfer. Antimicrob Agents Chemother. 1991;35:300-304.
94. Bowler LD, Zhang Q-Y, Riou J-Y, Spratt BG. Interspecies recombination between the *penA* genes of *Neisseria meningitidis* and commensal *Neisseria* species during the emergence of penicillin resistance of *N. meningitidis:* natural events and laboratory simulation. J Bacteriol. 1994;176:333-337.
95. Feil E, Zhou J, Smith JM, Spratt BG. A comparison of the nucleotide sequences of the *adk* and *recA* genes of pathogenic and commensal *Neisseria* species: Evidence for extensive interspecies recombination within adk. J Mol Evol. 1996;43:631-640.
96. Enright MC, Carter PE, MacLean IA, McKenzie H. Phylogenetic relationships between some members of the genera *Neisseria, Acinetobacter, Moraxella,* and *Kingella* based on partial 16S ribosomal DNA sequence analysis. Int J System Bacteriol. 1994;44:387-391.
97. Schaefer F, Bruttin O, Zografos L, Guex-Crosier Y. Bacterial keratitis: A prospective clinical and microbiological study. Br J Ophthalmol. 2001;85:842-847.
98. Berrocal AM, Scott IU, Miller D, Flynn HW Jr. Endophthalmitis caused by *Moraxella osloensis.* Graefes Arch Clin Exp Ophthalmol. 2002;240:329-330.
99. Laukeland H, Bergh K, Bevanger L. Posttrabeculectomy endophthalmitis caused by *Moraxella nonliquefaciens.* J Clin Microbiol. 2002;40:2668-2770.
100. Sherman MD, York M, Irvine AR, et al. Endophthalmitis caused by β-lactamase-positive *Moraxella nonliquefaciens.* Am J Ophthalmol. 1993;115:674-676.
101. Schmidt ME, Smith MA, Levy CS. Endophthalmitis caused by unusual gram-negative bacilli: Three case reports and review. Clin Infect Dis. 1993;17:686-690.
102. Shah SS, Ruth A, Coffin SE. Infection due to *Moraxella osloensis:* Case report and review of the literature. Clin Infect Dis. 2000;30:179-181.
103. De Baere T, Muylaert A, Everaert E, et al. Bacteremia due to *Moraxella atlantae* in a cancer patient. J Clin Microbiol. 2002;40:2693-2695.
104. Vuori-Holopainen E, Salo E, Saxen H, et al. Clinical "pneumococcal pneumonia" due to *Moraxella osloensis:* Case report and a review. Scand J Infect Dis. 2001;33:625-627.
105. Tripodi MF, Adinolfi LE, Rosario P, et al. First definite case of aortic valve endocarditis due to *Moraxella phenylpyruvica.* Eur J Clin Microbiol Infect Dis. 2002;21:480-482.
106. Guttigoli A, Zaman MM. Bacteremia and possible endocarditis caused by *Moraxella phenylpyruvica.* South Med J. 2000;93:708-709.
107. Vaneechoutte M, Claeys G, Steyaert S, et al. Isolation of *Moraxella canis* from an ulcerated metastatic lymph node. J Clin Microbiol. 2000;38:3870-3871.
108. Graham DR, Band JD, Thornsberry C, et al. Infections caused by *Moraxella, Moraxella urethralis, Moraxella*-like groups M-5 and M-6, and *Kingella kingae* in the United States, 1953-1980. Rev Infect Dis. 1990;12:423-431.
109. Johnson DW, Lum G, Nimmo G, Hawley CM. *Moraxella nonliquefaciens* septic arthritis in a patient undergoing hemodialysis. Clin Infect Dis. 1995;21:1039-1040.
110. Cox NH, Knowles MA, Porteus ID. Pre-septal cellulitis and facial erysipelas due to *Moraxella* species. Clin Exp Dermatol. 1994;19:321-323.
111. Fijen CAP, Kuijper EJ, Tjia HG, et al. Complement deficiency predisposes for meningitis due to nongroupable meningococci and *Neisseria*-related bacteria. Clin Infect Dis. 1994;18:780-784.
112. Snell JJS, Lapage SP. Transfer of some saccharolytic *Moraxella* species to *Kingella* Henriksen and Bovre 1976, with descriptions of *Kingella indologenese* sp. nov. and *Kingella dentrificans* sp. nov. Int J System Bacteriol. 1976;26:451-458.
113. Odum L, Frederiksen W. Identification and characterization of *Kingella kingae.* Acta Pathol Microbiol Scand Sect B. 1981;89:311-315.
114. Host B, Schumacher H, Prag J, Arpi M. Isolation of *Kingella kingae* from synovial fluids using four commercial blood culture bottles. Eur J Clin Microbiol Infect Dis. 2000;19:608-611.
115. Yagupsky P, Dagan R, Howard CW, et al. High prevalence of *Kingella kingae* in joint fluid from children with septic arthritis revealed by the BACTEC blood culture system. J Clin Microbiol. 1992;30:1278-1281.
116. Yagupsky P, Dagan R. *Kingella kingae* bacteremia in children. Pediatr Infect Dis J. 1994;13:1148-1149.
117. Yagupsky P, Dagan D, Prajgrod F, Merires M. Respiratory carriage of *Kingella kingae* among healthy children. Pediatr Infect Dis J. 1995;14:673-678.
118. Chen C-KC, Dunford RG, Reynolds HS, Zambon JJ. *Eikenella corrodens* in the human oral cavity. J Periodontol. 1989;60:611-616.

119. Dewhirst FE, Chen C-KC, Paster BJ, Zambon JJ. Phylogeny of species in the family *Neisseriaceae* isolated from human dental plaque and description of *Kingella oralis* sp. nov. Int J Syst Bacteriol. 1993;43:490-499.
120. Chen C. Distribution of a newly described species, *Kingella oralis,* in the human oral cavity. Oral Microbiol Immunol. 1996;11:425-427.
121. Claesson B, Falsen E, Kjellman B. *Kingella kingae* infections: A review and a presentation of data from 10 Swedish cases. Scand J Infect Dis. 1985;17:233-243.
122. Yagupsky P, Peled N, Katz O. Epidemiological features of invasive *Kingella kingae* infections and respiratory carriage of the organism. J Clin Microbiol. 2002;40:4180-4184.
123. La Scola B, Lorgulescu I, Bollini G. Five cases of *Kingella kingae* skeletal infection in a French hospital. Eur J Clin Microbiol Infect Dis. 1998;17:512-515.
124. Dodman T, Robson J, Pincus D. *Kingella kingae* infections in children. J Paediatr Child Health. 2000;36:87-90.
125. Moylett EH, Rossmann SN, Epps HR, Demmler GJ. Importance of *Kingella kingae* as a pediatric pathogen in the United States. Pediatr Infect Dis J 2000;19:263-265.
126. Luhmann JD, Luhmann SJ. Etiology of septic arthritis in children: An update for the 1990s. Pediatr Emerg Care. 1999;15:40-42.
127. Birgisson H, Steingrimsson O, Gudnason T. *Kingella kingae* infections in paediatric patients: 5 cases of septic arthritis, osteomyelitis and bacteraemia. Scand J Infect Dis. 1997;29:495-498.
128. Amir J, Schockelford PG. *Kingella kingae* intervertebral disk infection. J Clin Microbiol. 1991;29:1083-1086.
129. Woolfrey BF, Lally RT, Faville RJ. Intervertebral diskitis caused by *Kingella kingae.* Am J Clin Pathol. 1986;85:745-749.
130. Wells L, Rutter N, Donald F. *Kingella kingae* endocarditis in a sixteen-month-old-child. Pediatr Infect Dis J. 2001;20:454-455.
131. Wolak T, Abu-Shakra M, Flusser D, et al. *Kingella* endocarditis and meningitis in a patient with SLE and associated antiphospholipid syndrome. Lupus. 2000;9:393.
132. Jenny DB, Letendre PW, Iverson G. Endocarditis caused by *Kingella indologenes.* Rev Infect Dis. 1987;9:787-789.
133. Rabin RL, Wong P, Noonan JA, Plumley DD. *Kingella kingae* endocarditis in a child with a prosthetic aortic valve and bifurcation graft. Am J Dis Child. 1983;137:403-404.
134. Hassan IJ, Hayek L. Endocarditis caused by *Kingella denitrificans.* J Infect. 1993;27:291-295.
135. Yagupsky P, Dagan R. *Kingella kingae:* An emerging cause of invasive infections in young children. Clin Infect Dis. 1997;24:860-866.
136. Yagupsky P, Dagan R, Howard CB, et al. Clinical features and epidemiology of invasive *Kingella kingae* infections in southern Israel. Pediatrics. 1993;92:800-804.
137. Goutzmanis JJ, Gonis G, Gilbert GL. *Kingella kingae* infection in children: Ten cases and a review of the literature. Pediatr Infect Dis J. 1991;10:677-683.
138. Reekmans A, Noppen M, Naessens A, Vincken W. A rare manifestation of *Kingella kingae* infection. Eur J Intern Med. 2000;11:343-344.
139. Rolle U, Schille R, Hormann D, et al. Soft tissue infection caused by *Kingella kingae* in a child. J Pediatr Surg. 2001;36:946-947.
140. Kennedy CA, Rosen H. *Kingella kingae* bacteremia and adult epiglottitis in a granulocytopenic host. Am J Med. 1988;85:701-702.
141. Mollee T, Kelly P, Tilse M. Isolation of *Kingella kingae* from a corneal ulcer. J Clin Microbiol. 1992;30:2516-2517.
142. Yagupsky P, Katz O, Peled N. Antibiotic susceptibility of *Kingella kingae* isolates from respiratory carriers and patients with invasive infections. J Antimicrob Chemother. 2001;47:191-193.
143. Kugler KC, Biedenbach DJ, Jones RN. Determination of the antimicrobial activity of 29 clinically important compounds tested against fastidious HACEK group organisms. Diagn Microbiol Infect Dis. 1999;34:73-76.
144. Sordillo EM, Rendel M, Sood R, et al. Septicemia due to β-lactamase-positive *Kingella kingae.* Clin Infect Dis. 1993;17:818-819.
145. Wilson WR, Karchmer AW, Dajani AS, et al. Antibiotic treatment of adults with infective endocarditis due to streptococci, enterococci, staphylococci, and HACEK microorganisms. JAMA. 1995;274:1706-1713.

CHAPTER **211**

Vibrio cholerae

CARLOS SEAS
EDUARDO GOTUZZO

Cholera is a historically feared epidemic diarrheal disease. New epidemics continue to affect different regions of the world and impose significant economic constraint on the already impoverished developing countries. The Latin American extension of the seventh pandemic of cholera at the beginning of 1991, the epidemic of cholera in Zaire in 1994, and the epidemic of cholera caused by *Vibrio cholerae* O139

in 1992 in Asia are recent examples. These epidemics show that it is still not possible to predict when and where a new epidemic of cholera will start, that appropriate therapy may reduce the mortality to values below 1%, and that changes in the etiology of this ancient disease are still taking place.

The term *cholera* has ancient origins and is derived from Greek words meaning "a flow of bile."[1,2] Thomas Sydenham was the first to distinguish cholera the disease from cholera the state of anger.[1] He proposed the term *cholera morbus* for the disease. Because earlier descriptions of the disease confused cholera with other diarrheal diseases, the modern history of cholera began with Sydenham's description in 1817.

The modern era of cholera is characterized by seven pandemics. The first six occurred between 1817 and 1923. These pandemics were most likely caused by *V. cholerae* O1 of the classic biotype and largely originated in Asia, usually the Indian subcontinent, with subsequent extension to Europe and the Americas.[2] Filippo Pacini published his observations on the discovery of a curved bacillus in the stools of victims of cholera in Italy in 1854. He coined the name *Vibrio cholerae.*[3] In 1883 Robert Koch made the same discovery. Transmission of the disease was recognized only after the brilliant work of John Snow during the second pandemic affecting London in 1849, even before knowing the etiology of the disease. He reduced the transmission of cholera by blocking access to contaminated water in one area of London.

The seventh pandemic of cholera differed from the prior six. This pandemic was caused by the biotype El Tor of *V. cholerae* O1, a biotype that had been isolated for the first time in Egypt at the beginning of the century and was associated with sporadic cases until 1961. The pandemic originated in the Celebes Islands, Indonesia, in 1961 instead of the Indian subcontinent. This pandemic has been the longest lasting and has affected more countries and continents than the other six. The last extension of this pandemic in Latin America occurred in 1991, where it caused higher attack rates than seen during the last century but the lowest case-fatality rates.[4,5] The pandemic is still going on in many countries. Fifty-eight countries officially reported 184,311 cases to the World Health Organization in 2001, with 2728 deaths; 94% of these cases were reported from Africa.[6] Epidemic cholera is mostly restricted to Africa during 2003, with continuous outbreaks officially reported from six countries (*www.who.int/csr/don*). For instance, the Democratic Republic of the Congo reported 13,452 cases up to the second week of June 2003, with a case fatality rate of 2.8%.

Finally, in October 1992, a totally unexpected epidemic of a cholera-like disease was observed in Madras, India, with subsequent cases being reported along the Bay of Bengal.[7] *V. cholerae* of the new serogroup O139 was responsible for this epidemic, the first non-O1 *Vibrio* to do so. The epidemic was widespread in the Asiatic continent, with imported cases reported from developed countries.[8-10] Some regarded this as the eighth cholera pandemic,[11] although the epidemic has remained confined to Bangladesh and India. The O139 serogroup nowadays coexists with O1 *V. cholerae,* being responsible for continuous epidemics in Bangladesh.[12]

MICROBIOLOGY

V. cholerae is a curved gram-negative bacillus varying in size from 1 to 3 μm in length by 0.5 to 0.8 μm in diameter that belongs to the family Vibrionaceae and shares common characteristics with the family Enterobacteriaceae. The bacterium has a single polar flagellum that confers the erratic movement on microscopy. The antigenic structure of *V. cholerae* is similar to that of other members of the family Enterobacteriaceae, with a flagellar H antigen and a somatic O antigen. The O antigen is used to further classify *V. cholerae* in serogroups, O1 and non-O1. Approximately 206 serogroups of *V. cholerae* have been identified to date, but only the serogroups O1 and O139 are associated with clinical cholera and have pandemic potential.

V. cholerae O1 can be classified into three serotypes according to the presence of somatic antigens and into two biotypes according to specific phenotypic characteristics. Serotype Inaba carries the O antigens A and C, serotype Ogawa carries the antigens A and B, and serotype Hikojima carries the three antigens A, B, and C. No evidence of different clinical spectra among these three serotypes of *V. cholerae* has ever been presented. During epidemics, a shift from one serotype to another may occur.[13] This phenomenon was also reported more recently during the Latin American extension of the seventh pandemic of cholera.[14] The differences between the two biotypes of *V. cholerae* O1 are remarkable. The classic biotype, probably responsible for the first six pandemics of cholera, causes an approximately equal number of symptomatic and asymptomatic cases. In contrast, the El Tor biotype causes more asymptomatic infections, with a ratio between 20 and 100 asymptomatic infections to 1 symptomatic case.[15] The classic biotype is confined to the south of Bangladesh, whereas the El Tor biotype is responsible for the current pandemic.[16] Current evidence suggests that the El Tor and classic biotypes are not derived from each other, but rather from environmental nontoxigenic strains.[17] These two biotypes have coexisted for decades in Bangladesh, possibly interacting genetically to produce hybrids, as has been reported recently from patients with diarrhea in Matlab, Bangladesh.[18] The persistence of the classic biotype has implications for the development of vaccines. The O139 serogroup is composed of a variety of genetically diverse strains, both toxigenic and nontoxigenic, with at least nine different ribotypes identified.[12] This novel serogroup is genetically closer to El Tor *V. cholerae,* and might have been originated from it, acquiring distinctive features from a nonidentified donor, likely a non-O1 vibrio, through recombination of genetic material.[12]

Isolation and Identification

V. cholerae O1 or O139 can easily be observed under darkfield examination. The chaotic movement and the high number of bacteria seen in a stool sample from patients with clinical disease are characteristic of *V. cholerae* infection. The use of specific antisera against the serotype blocks the movement of these vibrios and allows confirmation of the diagnosis. However, under epidemic conditions, the presence of bacteria with a darting movement under darkfield microscopy in a stool sample from patients highly suspected of having cholera is sufficient to make the diagnosis, but definitive confirmation still requires isolation of the bacteria in culture. Specific medium is needed to isolate *V. cholerae* from stool. The two media most commonly used are thiosulfate citrate bile salts sucrose agar and tellurite taurocholate gelatin agar. These two media are equally sensitive to isolate either O1 or O139 *V. cholerae.* Enrichment media may be used when the number of bacteria in the stool is small or when environmental samples are evaluated for the presence of *Vibrio.* High sensitivity and specificity have been reported more recently using polymerase chain reaction (PCR) for detecting vibrio in stool and environmental samples.[19,20]

PATHOPHYSIOLOGY

V. cholerae O1 and O139 cause clinical disease by secreting an enterotoxin that promotes secretion of fluids and electrolytes by the small intestine. The infectious dose of bacteria varies with the vehicle. When water is the vehicle, more bacteria (10^3 to 10^6) are needed to cause disease, but when the vehicle is food, the amount needed is lower (10^2 to 10^4).[21] Conditions that reduce gastric acidity, such as the use of antacids or histamine receptor blockers, gastrectomy, or chronic gastritis induced by *Helicobacter pylori,* increase the risk of getting the disease and predispose the patient to more severe clinical forms. Toxin is produced, but *V. cholerae* does not invade the intestinal wall and few neutrophils are found in the stool. The incubation period varies with the infectious dose and gastric acidity and lasts 12 to 72 hours.

Both Robert Koch and John Snow suspected that a toxin was responsible for some of the disease manifestations, but it was not until 1959 that S. N. De and N. K. Dutta and colleagues, working in different laboratories, showed that *V. cholerae* promoted intestinal secretion in animal models.[22,23] The toxin was finally purified by Finkelstein and LoSpalluto in 1969.[24] The toxin has five B subunits and two A sub-

TABLE 211-1 Electrolyte Concentration of Cholera Stools and Common Solutions Used for Treatment

	Electrolyte and Glucose Concentration (mmol/L)				
	Na^+	Cl^-	K^+	HCO_3^-	Glucose
Cholera stool					
Adults	130	100	20	44	
Children	100	90	33	30	
Intravenous solutions					
Ringer's lactate	130	109	4	28*	0
Dhaka	133	98	13	48	0
Normal saline	154	154	0	0	0
Peru polyelectrolyte	90	80	20	30	111
WHO ORS	90	80	20	30†	111

*Ringer's lactate does not contain HCO_3^-; it has lactate instead.
†Bicarbonate is replaced by trisodium citrate, which persists longer than bicarbonate in sachets.
WHO ORS, World Health Organization oral rehydration solution.

units.[25] The B subunits allow binding of the toxin to a specific receptor, a ganglioside (GM_1) located on the surface of the cells lining the mucosa along the intestine of humans and certain suckling mammals. The active, or A, subunit has two components, A1 and A2, linked by a disulfide bond. Activation of the A1 component by adenylate cyclase results in a net increase in cyclic adenosine monophosphate, which blocks the absorption of sodium and chloride by microvilli and promotes the secretion of chloride and water by crypt cells. The result of these events is the production of watery diarrhea with electrolyte concentrations similar to that of plasma, as shown in Table 211-1. A few other toxins have been isolated from pathogenic *V. cholerae,*[26] but their role in genesis of the disease is less clear.

The complete genomic sequence of *V. cholerae* O1 El Tor has been published recently.[27] The genetic material consists of two circular chromosomes, the larger containing 3 megabases, and the smaller coantaining 1.07 megabases. The main virulence genes are *ctx*A; *ctx*B, which encode for cholera toxin subunits A and B, respectively; and *tcp*A, which codes for toxin coregulated pilus. The regulation of the expression of these genes is complex. Recent data suggest that environmental factors, such as sunlight and potentially other factors, may influence the expression of genes encoding for cholera toxin.[28] Genes unique to the El Tor biotype of *V. cholerae,* the agent of the seventh pandemic of cholera, have been identified.[29] These genes, VSP-I and VSP-II, might encode for specific features of these strains that allow them to survive better in the environment, as well as to be more infectious to humans, but their role is yet to be established.

EPIDEMIOLOGY

Cholera has unique epidemiologic features. Perhaps the most intriguing are the predisposition to cause epidemics with pandemic potential and the ability to remain endemic in all affected areas.[30] These two epidemiologic patterns, the epidemic and endemic patterns, are summarized in Table 211-2. Recognizing the different age groups at risk, depending on the epidemiologic pattern, is useful in designing preventive measures.

New insights into the life cycle of *V. cholerae* have allowed a better understanding of cholera transmission. *V. cholerae* lives in aquatic environments, which are their natural reservoirs.[31] Both O1 and non-O1 strains coexist in these environments, with non-O1 and nontoxigenic O1 strains predominating over toxigenic O1 strains.[32] In its natural environment, *V. cholerae* lives attached to a particular kind of algae or attached to crustacean shells and copepods (zooplankton), coexisting in a symbiotic manner, as shown in Figure 211-1.[33,34] When conditions in the environment such as temperature, salinity, and availability of nutrients are suitable, *V. cholerae* multiplies and can survive for years in a free-living cycle without the intervention of humans. Otherwise, when conditions are not suitable for its growth, *V. cholerae*

TABLE 211-2 Epidemiologic Patterns of Cholera

Epidemiologic Features	Epidemic Pattern	Endemic Pattern
Age at greatest risk	All ages	Children 2-15 yr
Modes of transmission	Single introduction with fecal-oral spread	Multiple modes of introduction: water, food, fecal-oral spread
Reservoir	None	Aquatic reservoir
Asymptomatic infections	Less common	Asymptomatic people More common
Immune status of the population	No preexisting immunity	Preexisting immunity, evidence of infection increases with age
Secondary spread	High	Variable

Modified from Glass RI, Black RE. The epidemiology of cholera. In: Barua D, Greenough WB III. eds. Cholera. New York: Plenum; 1992:129.

switches from a metabolically active state to a dormant state.[32] In this dormant state *V. cholerae* cannot be cultured from the water on either standard or enrichment media but appears to survive under difficult environmental conditions. Immunofluorescent techniques using monoclonal antibodies have been used to detect dormant *V. cholerae*.[35] Experimentally, the switch from a nonculturable to a culturable state has been attained in the laboratory, as well as in human volunteers.[36] *V. cholerae* may also persist in the environment and adopts a rugose form visible on a special agar, Luria agar.[37] Humans infected by *V. cholerae* may shed the bacteria for a long time, sometimes for months or years,[38] but their importance as reservoirs is minimal in comparison to the aquatic environment.

From its aquatic environment, *V. cholerae* is introduced to humans through contamination of water sources and contamination of food. The cycle of transmission is closed when infected humans shed the bacteria into the environment and contaminate water sources and food. Once humans are infected, incredibly high attack rates may occur, especially in previously nonexposed populations. Additional evidence of very high household transmission rates exists, as occurred during the last Latin American epidemic or more recently during the epidemic in Zaire in 1994.[39,40] Transmission via contaminated water and food has been recognized for years.[41-45] During the Latin American epidemic and more recent epidemics in Africa, acquisition of the disease by drinking contaminated water from rivers, ponds, lakes, and even tube well sources has been documented.[46-49] Contamination of municipal water was the main route of transmission of cholera in Trujillo, Peru, during the epidemic in 1991.[50] Drinking unboiled water,[45,50] introduc-

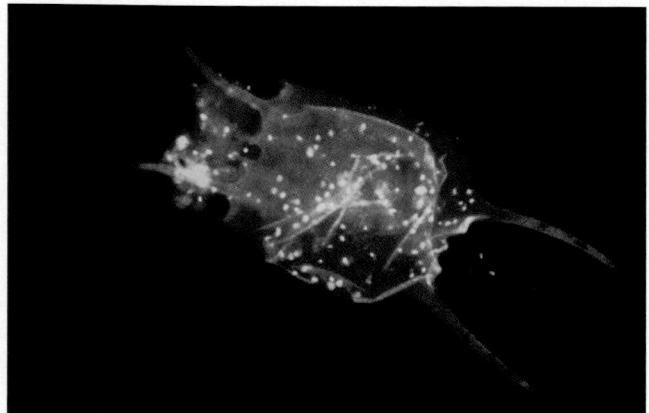

FIGURE 211–1. Vibrio cholerae *attached to a copepod stained with fluorescent techniques. (Courtesy of Dr. Rita Colwell and Dr. Anwarul Huq, University of Maryland.)*

ing hands into containers used to store drinking water,[51,52] drinking beverages from street vendors,[45,53] drinking beverages when contaminated ice had been added,[45] and drinking water outside the home were risk factors to acquire cholera.[53] On the other hand, drinking boiled water, acidic beverages, and carbonated water, as well as using narrow-necked vessels for storing water, was protective.[45,54,55] *V. cholerae* survives for up to 14 days in some foods, especially when contamination occurs after preparation of the food.[56] Cooking and heating the food eliminate the bacteria. Epidemics of cholera associated with the ingestion of leftover rice,[57] yellow rice in a restaurant,[9] raw fish,[58,59] cooked crabs,[60] seafood,[61,62] raw oysters,[63] and fresh vegetables and fruits[50] have been documented.

Transmission of cholera during funerals in Africa has been reported.[64,65] Risk factors identified included eating at the funeral with a nondisinfected corpse and touching the body.[64] Eating rice at the funeral was the main risk factor for the acquisition of cholera in one study.[65] Person-to-person transmission is less likely to occur because a large inoculum is necessary to transmit disease. Anecdotal reports exist in the literature, however.[66-68] Careful evaluation of these reports shows that other potential risk factors might have been implicated in the transmission. Other vehicles of transmission such as insects and fomites have been reported,[69,70] but are less likely to be important in epidemic situations.

Seasonality is another typical characteristic of cholera. Epidemics tend to occur during the hot seasons, and countries with more than one hot season per year may also have more than one epidemic, such as seen in Bangladesh.[71] Data from the epidemic of cholera in Peru from 1991 to 1995 also confirm that outbreaks are associated with the warmest months of the year.[72] Climate change and climate variability may affect the incidence of certain infectious diseases.[73] The El Niño–southern oscillation (ENSO), a periodic phenomenon representative of global climate variability, has been studied in relation to its effect on the transmission of cholera and vector-borne diseases. A strong association between ENSO and cholera has been observed in Bangladesh, with data suggesting that this relationship may be even more intense in future years.[74,75] ENSO causes warming of normally cool waters on the Pacific coastline of Peru, promoting phytoplankton bloom, which in turn promotes zooplankton bloom and *V. cholerae* proliferation.[73] Colwell and her associates have elegantly described the complex associations among various climatic, seasonal, bacterial, and human factors acting on cholera transmission in a hierarchical model[73] shown in Figure 211-2. Interestingly, as we mentioned before, environmental conditions may affect the expression of virulence genes of *V. cholerae*,[28,73] thus promoting the beginning of epidemics, as might have been the situation in Peru during 1991.[76] Some host factors are important in the transmission of cholera. Among them, infection by *H. pylori* and the effect of the O blood group deserve special consideration. Data from Bangladesh show that people infected by *H. pylori* are at higher risk of acquiring cholera than are people not infected by *H. pylori*.[77] Additionally, the risk of acquiring severe cholera among people infected by *H. pylori* was higher in patients without previous contact with *V. cholerae*, as measured by the absence of vibriocidal antibodies in the serum.[77] *H. pylori* causes a chronic gastritis that induces hypochlorhydria, which in turn reduces the ability of the stomach to contain the *Vibrio* invasion. The impact of the association of these two infections is particularly interesting because *H. pylori* infection is very common in persons of all ages in developing countries.[78] An unexplained predisposition toward severe disease in persons with the O blood group has been observed in Asia[79] and more recently in Latin America.[80]

Although mainly countries with poor sanitary conditions are affected by cholera, a few developed countries such as the United States, Canada, and Australia have reported indigenous cases. Two different *V. cholerae* O1 strains have been isolated from these regions, and these vibrios differ from the strain responsible for the seventh pandemic.[81-83] Sporadic cases are reported periodically from these areas. Surveillance of cholera is needed to detect future epidemics, as well as to identify current trends in serogroup predominance and susceptibil-

FIGURE 211-2. A hierarchical model for cholera transmission. *(From Colwell RR, Huq A. Environmental reservoir of vibrio cholerae. The causative agent of chlorea. Ann NY Acad Sci 1994; 740:44-54.)*

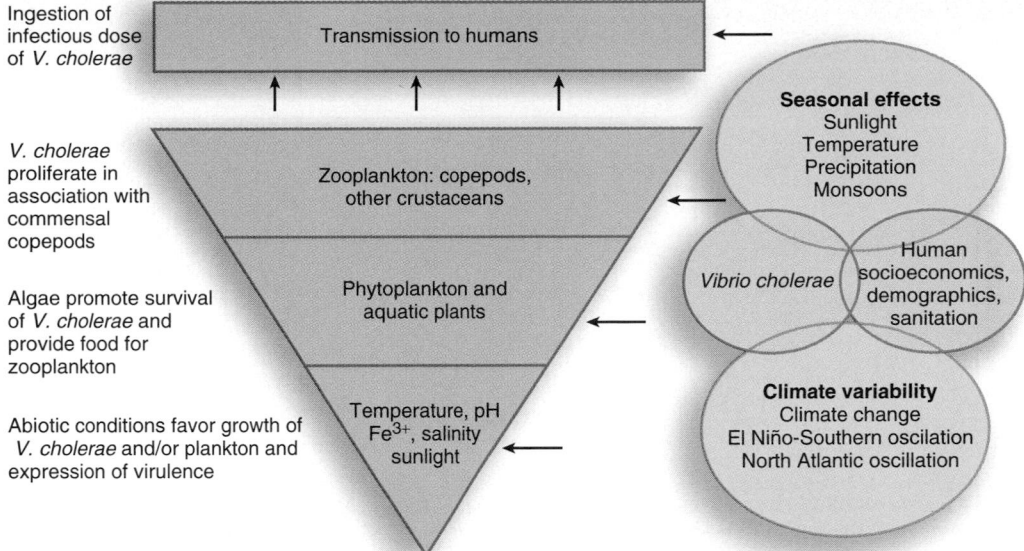

Ingestion of infectious dose of *V. cholerae*

Transmission to humans

V. cholerae proliferate in association with commensal copepods

Zooplankton: copepods, other crustaceans

Algae promote survival of *V. cholerae* and provide food for zooplankton

Phytoplankton and aquatic plants

Abiotic conditions favor growth of *V. cholerae* and/or plankton and expression of virulence

Temperature, pH Fe^{3+}, salinity sunlight

Seasonal effects
Sunlight
Temperature
Precipitation
Monsoons

Vibrio cholerae

Human socioeconomics, demographics, sanitation

Climate variability
Climate change
El Niño-Southern oscilation
North Atlantic oscillation

ity to antimicrobial agents in endemic areas. Recent data from a 4-year surveillance study in four rural areas of Bangladesh showed that non-cholera pathogens predominated as a cause of diarrhea in children younger than 2 years of age, O1 *V. cholerae* predominated in young children, and O139 *V. cholerae* was observed in people of all ages but especially in older adults, suggesting that this new serogroup is still not endemic in the area.[84] Identifying areas of high transmission is desirable to focus prevention on a more local level. Integration of socioeconomic, behavioral, and biologic factors is needed to achieve that goal, as has been described recently in a highly endemic area of Bangladesh.[85]

CLINICAL MANIFESTATIONS AND LABORATORY ABNORMALITIES

The hallmark of cholera is the production of watery diarrhea with varying degrees of dehydration ranging from none to severe and life-threatening diarrhea. Patients with mild to moderate dehydration secondary to cholera are difficult to differentiate from those infected by other enteric pathogens such as enterotoxigenic *Escherichia coli* or rotavirus. Patients with severe dehydration from cholera are easy to identify because no other clinical illness produces such severe dehydration in a matter of a few hours as cholera. Onset of the disease is abrupt and characterized by the production of watery diarrhea without strain, tenesmus, or prominent abdominal pain, rapidly followed or sometimes preceded by vomiting. As the diarrhea continues, other symptoms of severe dehydration are manifest, such as generalized cramps and oliguria. Physical examination will show an alert patient most of the time despite the fact that the pulse is nonpalpable and blood pressure cannot be measured. Fever is observed in less than 5% of cases. Patients look anxious and restless or sometimes obtunded, the eyes are very sunken, mucous membranes are dry, the skin has lost its elasticity and when pinched retracts very slowly, the voice is almost nonaudible, and the intestinal sounds are prominent. Patients in this condition are difficult to confuse with patients with other medical conditions. Figure 211-3 shows a typical patient with severe cholera. Table 211-3 shows the clinical manifestations according to the degree of dehydration as a guide to the proper administration of fluids. Although watery diarrhea is the hallmark of cholera, some patients do not have diarrhea but instead have abdominal distention and ileus, a relatively rare type of cholera called cholera "sicca."[86] Management of these patients is particularly difficult because evaluation of the degree of dehydration is overshadowed by the accumulation of fluid in the intestinal lumen.

Laboratory abnormalities reflect the isotonic dehydration characteristic of cholera. Increases in packed cell volume, serum specific gravity, and total protein are typically seen in patients with moderate to severe dehydration. Although abnormal results of these tests correlate with the degree of dehydration on arrival at a health center, they are less useful for monitoring rehydration status.[87] Biochemical and acid-base laboratory abnormalities typical of severe dehydration are prerenal azotemia, metabolic acidosis with a high anion gap, normal or low serum potassium levels, and normal or slightly low sodium and chloride levels.[39] The calcium and magnesium content in plasma is also high as a result of hemoconcentration.[88] The white blood cell count is high in patients with severe cholera. Hyperglycemia caused by high concentrations of epinephrine, glucagon, and cortisol stimulated by hypovolemia is more commonly seen than hypoglycemia,[89] but children with hypoglycemia have a higher risk of dying than do nonhypoglycemic children.[90] Acute renal failure is the most severe complication of cholera. Incidence rates of 10.6 cases per 1000 have been reported in Peru during the first months of the epidemic in 1991.[39] Patients with acute renal failure had a history of improper rehydration. All age groups were equally affected, and the mortality rate in this group of patients was extremely high (18%), particularly in the elderly.[39]

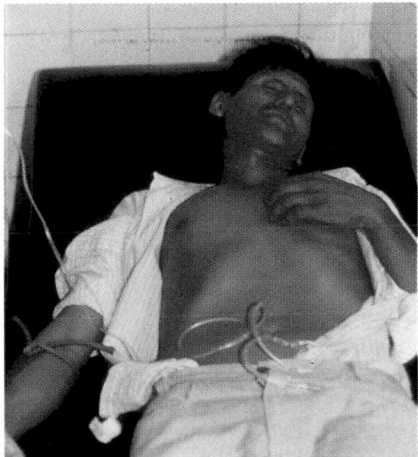

FIGURE 211-3. A Peruvian patient with severe cholera. Sunken eyes and washerwoman's hands are typical of patients with severe dehydration.

TABLE 211-3 Clinical Findings According to Degree of Dehydration

Finding	Mild Dehydration	Moderate Dehydration	Severe Dehydration
Loss of fluid*	<5%	5-10%	>10%
Mentation	Alert	Restless	Drowsy or comatose
Radial pulse			
rate	Normal	Rapid	Very rapid
intensity	Normal	Weak	Feeble or impalpable
Respiration	Normal	Deep	Deep and rapid
Systolic blood pressure	Normal	Low	Very low or unrecordable
Skin elasticity	Retracts rapidly	Retracts slowly	Retracts very slowly
Eyes	Normal	Sunken	Very sunken
Voice	Normal	Hoarse	Not audible
Urine production	Normal	Scant	Oliguria

*Percentage of body weight.
From Bennish ML. Cholera: Pathophysiology, clinical features, and treatment. In: Wachsmuth IK, Blake PA, Olsvik O, eds. *Vibrio cholerae* and Cholera: Molecular to Global Perspectives. Washington, DC: ASM Press; 1994:229.

TABLE 211-4 Practical Guidelines for the Treatment of Cholera

1. Evaluate the degree of dehydration on arrival
2. Rehydrate the patients in two phases:
   Rehydration phase: lasts 2-4 h
   Maintenance phase: lasts until diarrhea abates
3. Register output and intake volumes in predesigned charts and periodically review the data
4. Use the intravenous route only for
   Severely dehydrated patients during the rehydration phase, in whom an infusion rate of 50-100 ml/kg/h is advised
   Moderately dehydrated patients who do no tolerate the oral route
   High stool volume (>10 ml/kg/h) during the maintenance phase
5. Use ORS for patients during the maintenance phase at a rate of 800-1000 ml/h, matching ongoing losses with ORS
6. Discharge patients to the treatment center if the following conditions are fulfilled:
   Oral tolerance, ≥ 1000 ml/h
   Urine volume, ≥ 40 ml/h
   Stool volume, ≤ 400 ml/h

ORS, Oral rehydration solution.
From Seas C, Dupont HL, Valdez LM, et al. Practical guidelines for the treatment of cholera. Drugs. 1996;51:966-973.

The clinical manifestation of cholera in children is similar to that in adults. However, hypoglycemia, seizures, fever, and mental alteration are more common in children.[91] Cholera in pregnant women carries a bad prognosis and portends more severe clinical illness, especially when the disease is acquired at the end of the pregnancy.[92] Fetal loss occurs in as many as 50% of these pregnancies.[92] Cholera in the elderly also carries a bad prognosis because of more complications, particularly acute renal failure, severe metabolic acidosis, and pulmonary edema.[39] Proper hydration may correct all electrolyte and acid-base abnormalities in elderly patients.[93]

TREATMENT

The goal of therapy is to restore the fluid losses caused by diarrhea and vomiting. Although treatment of patients without severe dehydration is easy, treatment of patients with severe dehydration requires experience and proper training. Basic training in how to recognize the degree of dehydration, how to select the proper intravenous solution, and how rapidly to rehydrate the patient is crucial. Recent experience during the epidemic in Zaire, where untrained people played a negative role, cannot be emphasized more. Conversely, well-trained people provided with adequate supplies can successfully treat patients even under epidemic situations.[40,94] Guidelines to rehydrate cholera patients have been written and reviewed elsewhere.[95-98] The intravenous route should be restricted to patients with moderate dehydration who do not tolerate the oral route, to those who purge more than 10 to 20 mL/kg/hr, and to patients with severe dehydration. Rehydration should be accomplished in two phases: the rehydration phase and the maintenance phase. The purpose of the rehydration phase is to restore normal hydration status, and it should last no more than 4 hours. Intravenous fluids should be infused at a rate of 50 to 100 mL/kg/hr in severely dehydrated patients. Ringer's lactate solution is the most frequently recommended solution, but other solutions may be used as well, as shown in Table 211-1. Normal saline solution is not recommended because it does not correct the metabolic acidosis. When intravenous access proves difficult, nasogastric tubes or intraosseous catheters can be used,[99] although problems with intravenous access were not common during the recent cholera epidemic in Peru.[72]

After finishing the rehydration phase, all signs of dehydration should have abated and the patient should pass urine at a rate of 0.5 mL/kg/hr or greater. Then starts the maintenance phase. During this phase the objective is to maintain normal hydration status by replacing ongoing losses. The oral route is preferred during this phase, and the use of oral rehydration solutions at a rate of 500 to 1000 mL/hr is

highly recommended. Oral rehydration therapy uses the principle of common transportation of solutes, electrolytes, and water by the intestine not affected by the cholera toxin. People with diarrhea can undergo successful rehydration with simple solutions containing glucose and electrolytes that may be prepared at home. The standard oral rehydration solution recommended by the World Health Organization is currently used worldwide; solutions with reduced osmolarity may have some advantages, however.[100] Evaluation of rehydration status and accurate recording of intake and output volumes are essential. Patients without severe dehydration who tolerate the oral route can be rehydrated with oral rehydration solutions exclusively and discharged promptly from the health center. Practical guidelines have recently been published[98] and are summarized in Table 211-4.

Discharging patients from health centers, particularly those with severe dehydration, is a critical issue, especially during epidemics. No significant readmission of patients was observed in Peru during the epidemic in 1991 when the following criteria were used to discharge patients: urine volume higher than 40 mL/hr, diarrhea output below 400 mL/hr, and oral ingestion of rehydration solutions between 600 and 800 mL/hr.[39] Adequate organization of health centers to accommodate and properly treat hundreds of patients, and proper allocation of available resources are critical under epidemic situations. Examples of successful use of resources during the O139 cholera epidemic of 1993 in Dhaka, Bangladesh, and during the O1 epidemic in Peru during 1991 are shown in Figures 211-4 and 211-5, respectively. Case-fatality rate during epidemics may be reduced to values below 1% even in disaster situations, provided that adequate access to health care centers and proper management of patients can be ensured.[39,101] A case-fatality rate of 3.7% among hospitalized patients was reported from a specialized center in Dhaka, Bangladesh, in 1996.[102] In this setting, the overall case-fatality rate was 0.14%, and pneumonia was the leading cause of death. In contrast, figures as high as 10% have been reported in epidemic settings when patients had no access to health care or received improper treatment.[103] Treatment of cholera caused by O139 V. cholerae is the same. No significant differences in clinical manifestations of the disease caused by these two agents have been found.[104]

Antimicrobial agents play a secondary role in the treatment of cholera. Clinical trials have shown that, when patients with severe dehydration are given antibiotics, the duration of diarrhea is decreased and the volume of stool is reduced by nearly half.[105] Early discharge and lessened hydration decrease hospital expense. These benefits are critical in epidemic conditions. Oral tetracycline and doxycycline are the agents of choice in areas of the globe where sensitive strains predominate. A single dose of doxycycline (300 mg) is the preferred regimen.[106] Tetracyclines are not safe in children younger than 7 years,

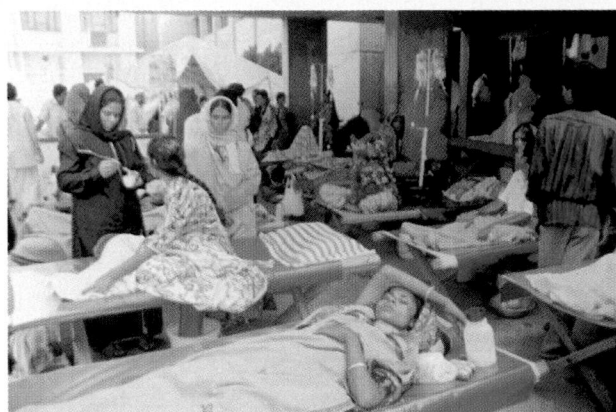

FIGURE 211-4. Patients with cholera caused by the O139 serogroup of *V. cholerae* being treated in the parking lot of the International Center for Diarrhoeal Disease Research, Dhaka, Bangladesh (ICDDR,B). Use of cholera cots, rehydration by intravenous route of severely dehydrated patients, and rehydration by the oral route with oral rehydration therapy are shown in the picture. *(Courtesy of Dr. Wasif Ali Khan, ICDDR,B.)*

and alternatives such as trimethoprim-sulfamethoxazole, erythromycin, and furazolidone are preferred over tetracyclines. Pregnant women can be treated with erythromycin or furazolidone. Currently recommended regimens are presented in Table 211-5.

Selection of an adequate antimicrobial in certain parts of the world has been complicated by the appearance of strains resistant to tetracyclines and other antimicrobial agents.[107-109] New agents have been tested in endemic and epidemic areas, with quinolones being the most effective.[110] Ciprofloxacin has been more extensively studied than other quinolones. Two regimens of ciprofloxacin have shown at least comparable if not better results than other antibiotics in randomized, double-blind clinical trials in patients with severe cholera caused by either O1 or O139 *V. cholerae*: a single dose of 1 g or once-daily regimens of 250 mg for 3 days.[111,112] However, strains resistant to quinolones have recently been reported from India.[113-116] The high cost and concern about cartilage damage in young children are drawbacks to large-scale quinolone use. Azithromycin has arisen as an alternative for the treatment of certain diarrheal diseases of bacterial origin. A single dose of azithromycin (20 mg/kg) in children with severe cholera in Bangladesh showed clinical and bacteriologic results comparable to a

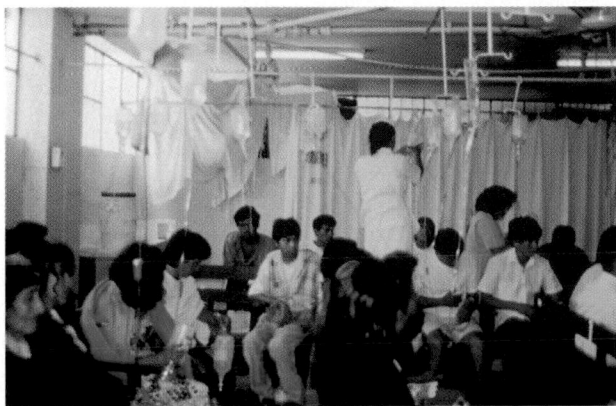

FIGURE 211-5. Patients with cholera caused by the El Tor *V. cholerae* O1 being treated in the Rehydration Unit at Hospital Nacional Cayetano Heredia in Lima, Peru. Cholera chairs instead of cholera cots were successfully used during the large epidemic of 1991. *(Courtesy of Dr. Eduardo Salazar, Department of Pediatrics, Hospital Nacional Cayetano Heredia.)*

TABLE 211-5 Antimicrobial Regimens for the Treatment of Cholera

Drug	Dose	
	Adult	*Children*
Tetracycline	500 mg qid for 3 d	50 mg/kg of body weight qid for 3 d
Doxycycline	300 mg as a single dose	Not evaluated
Furazolidone	100 mg qid for 3 d	5 mg/kg per day in 4 divided doses for 3 d or 7 mg/kg as a single dose
Cotrimoxazole	160 mg of trimethoprim/800 mg of sulfamethoxazole bid for 3 d	8 mg of trimethoprim-40 mg of sulfamethoxazole/kg divided in 2 doses for 3 d
Norfloxacin	400 mg bid for 3 d	Not recommended
Ciprofloxacin	250 mg/d for 3 d	Not recommended
	1 g as a single dose	Not recommended

From Seas C, DuPont HL, Valdez LM, et al. Practical guidelines for the treatment of cholera. Drugs. 1996;51:966-973.

3-day regimen with erythromycin.[117] Advantages of single-dose regimens like this are not only assurance of compliance, but also the potential reduction of resistance, and the appeal for using them under extreme epidemic situations. The use of other drugs, such as antimotility agents (e.g., loperamide or diphenoxylate), adsorbents, analgesics, and antiemetics is not recommended.[118] Racecadrotil, an encephalinase inhibitor that acts as an antisecretory drug, has shown promising results in children with secretory diarrhea,[119] but it is not used or recommended by experts.[118] A chemical substance (a gallate compound) that inhibits cholera toxin activity has been recently identified in a traditional herbal preparation of China and Japan called Kampo[120]; further studies with this drug are warranted. Chemoprophylaxis of household contacts of cholera cases has been proposed. However, published data do not support this concept.[121] More recently it has been shown that, when transmission of the disease is low, as occurs in endemic areas, the utility of chemoprophylaxis is not significant.[122] Prophylaxis with antibiotics might be considered in situations in which the rate of transmission of the disease is high, along with other measures to curtail transmission.

PREVENTION AND THE ROLE OF VACCINES

John Snow was the first scientist to show that transmission of cholera may be significantly reduced when uncontaminated water is provided to the population. Providing potable water and ensuring proper management of excreta to avoid contamination of other water sources are important measures to reduce cholera transmission. The limited number of indigenous cases reported from the United States and Australia despite the fact that *Vibrio* is isolated from the environment in these countries provides further evidence that hygiene and sanitation contain cholera transmission. However, the experience with continuing epidemics in developing countries shows that these simple measures are almost impossible to implement.

Alternative ways to prevent cholera transmission are necessary. Water can be made safer to drink by boiling or adding chlorine. Both methods are expensive and difficult to implement under epidemic situations. Exposing water to sunlight has also been considered, but its implementation is again not feasible in developing countries. Education of the population at risk on appropriate hygienic practices is always recommended, but the impact of massive educational campaigns on the reduction of cholera transmission is questionable. Identification of local customs that place people at risk may help in eliminating such practices. A simple preventive measure derived from better knowledge of the ecologic basis for disease transmission has been proposed by Colwell and her associates.[123] Sari cloth, a traditional cloth of India and Bangladesh made of cotton, folded eight times to retain particles above 20 μ size, including copepods to which

V. cholerae is attached, was used to filter water for drinking purposes in the field. A marked reduction in cholera incidence in rural Bangladesh was observed by using this method. Simple measures like this may be implemented in developing countries with potential impact on transmission. Predicting the onset of an epidemic may have a tremendous impact on prevention. Two recent studies conducted in Lima, Peru, showed that identification of *V. cholerae* O1 from municipal sewage and environmental samples preceded the occurrence of human cases by 1 to 3 months.[124,125] Active surveillance of vibrios in the environment and in populations at risk by the application of uniform case definitions[126] is recommended on the basis of these data. More recently, the possibility of predicting an epidemic by monitoring the movement of plankton by satellite seems attractive, but more data are needed to support this method.[127]

An inability to implement the aforementioned measures to curtail cholera transmission has necessitated a search for vaccines. An ideal vaccine against cholera should elicit a fast and long-lasting immune response with minimal side effects. Additionally, the vaccine should be locally produced and, to increase compliance, a single dose is highly desirable. The disappointing experience with parenteral vaccines and the better knowledge of the immune response to natural infection that has accumulated during recent years clearly show that an oral route for administering the vaccine is preferred. The ideal vaccine is still not available,[128] but significant progress has been made. Two oral vaccines have been studied in epidemic and endemic settings. The oral inactivated vaccine WC-BS (whole cell plus B subunit) has been more extensively evaluated. A large field trial conducted in Matlab-Bangladesh with subsequent follow-up of 3 and 5 years has shown promising results.[129,130] Two doses 2 weeks apart conferred protection similar to that of three doses. The short-term protective efficacy of this vaccine was very high. Results at 3 and 5 years were less impressive, with only about 50% of vaccines protected. Significant drawbacks were less protection against the El Tor biotype, less protection in children, and less protection in persons with blood group O. Recombinant techniques have been used to produce a B-subunit vaccine locally in Vietnam at a significantly reduced cost.[131] More recently, a killed oral whole-cell cholera vaccine (without the B-subunit component), containing both O1 and O139 serogroups (biv-WC), attained similar results in terms of safety and immunogenicity, with better response in children, than a monovalent (anti–*V. cholerae* O1) vaccine containing the B subunit.[132] Another group of promising oral vaccines are the live-attenuated oral cholera vaccines, especially the third-generation CVD 103–HgR.[133] Promising results with this vaccine even in people with O blood group[134,135] were not confirmed when a large field trial was conducted in Jakarta, Indonesia.[136] The field trial showed no benefit from receiving the vaccine. New developments in this area include the evaluation of new vaccine candidates,[137,138] combining antigens of *E. coli* with the B subunit of *V. cholerae*,[139] the evaluation of auxotrophic vaccines,[140] and adding zinc to improve vibriocidal seroconversion in children.[141] None of the vaccines tested thus far has prevented cholera transmission, and none is recommended for general usage. Clearly, more research on safe, effective vaccines is needed. Potential indications for currently available cholera vaccines include travelers, even though the risk of getting cholera in this population is very low,[142] and situations in which high attack rates of cholera are expected, such as after environmental disasters, in refugee camps, and in urban slums in highly endemic areas.[143,144] Current challenges are how to predict new epidemics, how to early detect the appearance of new strains in the environment that may cause epidemics, and how to induce lasting protective immunity, irrespective of age and blood group, with a single dose of an oral vaccine. Our understanding of this ancient scourge has improved significantly since the time of John Snow, but the solution remains the same.[145]

REFERENCES

1. Barua D. History of cholera. In: Barua D, Greenough WB, eds. Cholera. New York: Plenum; 1992:1.
2. Pollitzer R. Cholera. Geneva: World Health Organization; 1959.
3. Barua D. Cholera during the last hundred years (1884-1983). In: Takeda Y, ed. *Vibrio cholerae* and Cholera. Tokyo: KTK Scientific; 1988:9.
4. Centers for Disease Control. Cholera—Peru, 1991. MMWR Morb Mortal Wkly Rep. 1991;40:108.
5. Carpenter CJ. The treatment of cholera: Clinical science at the bedside. J Infect Dis. 1992;166:2-14.
6. World Health Organization. Cholera. Wkly Epidemiol Rec. 2002;77:257-268.
7. Cholera Working Group. International Centre for Diarrhoeal Disease Research, Bangladesh. Large epidemic of cholera-like disease in Bangladesh caused by *Vibrio cholerae* O139 synonym Bengal. Lancet. 1993;342:387-390.
8. Hoge CW, Bodhidatta L, Echeverria P, et al. Epidemiologic study of O1 and O139 in Thailand: At the advancing edge of the eighth pandemic. Am J Epidemiol. 1996;143:263.
9. Boyce TG, Mintz DE, Greene KD, et al. *Vibrio cholerae* O139 Bengal infections among tourists to Southeast Asia: An intercontinental foodborne outbreak. J Infect Dis. 1995;172:1401.
10. Cheasty R, Rowe B, Said B, et al. *Vibrio cholerae* serogroup O139 in England and Wales. Lancet. 1993;307:1007.
11. Swerdlow DL, Ries AA. *Vibrio cholerae* non-O1—the eighth pandemic? Lancet. 1993;342:382.
12. Faruque SM, Sack DA, Sack RB, et al. Emergence and evolution of *Vibrio cholerae* O139. Proc Natl Acad Sci U S A. 2003;100:1304-1309.
13. Stroeher UH, Karageogos LE, Morona R, et al. Serotype conversion in *Vibrio cholerae* O1. Proc Natl Acad Sci U S A. 1992;89:2566-2570.
14. Vugia DJ, Rodriguez M, Vargas M, et al. Epidemic cholera in Trujillo, Peru 1992: Utility of a clinical case definition and shift in *Vibrio cholerae* O1 serotype. Am J Trop Med Hyg. 1994;50:566.
15. Mujica O, Seminario L, Tauxe R, et al. Investigación epidemiológica de cólera en el Perú: Lecciones para un continente en riesgo. Rev Med Herediana. 1991;2:121.
16. Siddique AK, Baqui AH, Eusof A, et al. Survival of classic cholera in Bangladesh. Lancet. 1991;337:1125.
17. Karaolis DK, Lan R, Reeves PR. The sixth and seventh cholera pandemics are due to independent clones separately derived from environmental nontoxigenic non-O1 *Vibrio cholerae*. J Bacteriol. 1995;177:3191.
18. Nair GB, Faruque SM, Bhuiyan NA, et al. New variants of *Vibrio cholerae* O1 biotype El Tor with attributes of the classical biotype from hospitalized patients with acute diarrhea in Bangladesh. J Clin Microbiol. 2002;40:3296-3299.
19. Nandy B, Nandy RK, Mukhopadhyay S, et. al. Rapid method for species-specific identification of *Vibrio cholerae* using primers targeted to the gene of outer membrane protein Omp W. J Clin Microbiol. 2000;38:4145-4151.
20. Theron J, Cilliers J, Du Preez M, et al. Detection of toxigenic *Vibrio cholerae* from environmental water samples by an enrichment broth cultivation-pit-stop semi-nested PCR procedure. J Appl Microbiol. 2000;89:539-546.
21. Cash RA, Music SI, Libonati JP, et al. Response of man to infection with *Vibrio cholerae*. 1. Clinical, serologic, and bacteriologic responses to a known inoculum. J Infect Dis. 1974;129:45.
22. De SN. Enterotoxicity of bacteria-free culture filtrate of *Vibrio cholerae*. Nature. 1959;183:1533-1534.
23. Dutta NK, Panse MW, Kulkarni DR. Role of cholera toxin in experimental cholera. J Bacteriol. 1959;78:594.
24. Finkelstein RA, LoSpalluto JJ. Pathogenesis of experimental cholera: Preparation and isolation of choleragen and choleragenoid. J Exp Med. 1969;130:185-202.
25. Finkelstein RA. Cholera enterotoxin (choleragen): An historical perspective. In: Barua D, Greenough WB III, eds. Topics in Infectious Diseases: Cholera. New York: Plenum; 1992:155.
26. Kaper JB, Fasano A, Trucksis M. Toxins of *Vibrio cholerae*. In: Wachsmuth IK, Blake PA, Olsvik O, eds. *Vibrio cholerae* and Cholera: Molecular to Global Perspectives. Washington, DC: ASM Press; 1994:145.
27. Heidelberg JF, Eisen JA, Nelson WC, et al. DNA sequence of both chromosomes of the cholera pathogen *Vibrio cholerae*. Nature. 2000;406:477-483.
28. Faruque SM, Rahman MM, Waldor MK, et al. Sunlight-induced propagation of the lysogenic phage encoding cholera toxin. Infect Immun. 2000;68:4795-4801.
29. Dziejman M, Balon E, Boyd D, et al. Comparative genomic analysis of *Vibrio cholerae*: Genes that correlate with cholera endemic and pandemic disease. Proc Natl Acad Sci U S A. 2002;99:1556-1561.
30. Glass RI, Black RE. The epidemiology of cholera. In: Barua D, Greenough WB III, eds. Cholera. New York: Plenum; 1992:129.
31. Kaper JB, Morris JG, Levine MM. Cholera. J Clin Microbiol Rev. 1995;8:48-86.
32. Colwell RR, Huq A: Vibrios in the environment: Viable but nonculturable *Vibrio cholerae*. In: Wachsmuth IK, Blake PA, Olsvik O, eds. *Vibrio cholerae* and Cholera: Molecular to Global Perspectives. Washington DC: ASM Press; 1994:117.
33. Huq A, Small EB, West PA, et al. Ecology of *Vibrio cholerae* O1 with special reference to planktonic crustacean copepods. Appl Environ Microbiol. 1983;45:275.
34. Huq A, West PA, Small EB, et al. Influence of water temperature, salinity, and pH on survival and growth of toxigenic *Vibrio cholerae* serovar O1 associated with live copepods in laboratory microcosms. Appl Environ Microbiol. 1983;48:420.
35. Huq A, Colwell RR, Rahman R, et al. Detection of *Vibrio cholerae* O1 in the aquatic environment by fluorescent-monoclonal antibody and culture methods. Appl Environm Microbiol. 1990;56:2370.
36. Colwell RR, Tamplin ML, Brayton PR, et al. Environmental aspects of *Vibrio cholerae* in transmission of cholera. In: Sack RB, Zinnaka Y, eds. Advances in Research on Cholera and Related Diarrheas, v. 7. Tokyo: KTK Scientific; 1990:327.
37. Rice EW, Johnson CJ, Clark RM, et al. Chlorine and survival of rugose *Vibrio cholerae*. Lancet. 1992;340:740.
38. Dizon JJ. Cholera carriers. In: Barua D, Burrows W, eds. Cholera. Philadelphia: WB Saunders; 1974:367.

39. Gotuzzo E, Cieza J, Estremadoyro L, et al. Cholera: Lessons from the epidemic in Peru. Med Clin North Am. 1994;8:183.
40. Goma Epidemiology Group. Public health impact of Rwandan refugee crisis: What happened in Goma, Zaire, in July 1994. Lancet. 1995;345:339-344.
41. Hughes JM, Boyce JM, Levine RJ, et al. Epidemiology of El Tor cholera in rural Bangladesh: Importance of surface water in transmission. Bull World Health Organ. 1982;60:395.
42. Sinclair GS, Mphahlele SM, Duvenhage H, et al. Determination of the mode of transmission of cholera in Lebowa. S Afr Med J. 1982;62:753.
43. Blake PA, Rosenberg ML, Costa JB, et al. Cholera in Portugal, 1974. I. Modes of transmission. Am J Epidemiol. 1977;105:344.
44. Morris JG, West GR, Holck SE, et al. Cholera among refugees in Rangsit, Thailand. J Infect Dis. 1982;145:131.
45. Ries AA, Vugia DJ, Beingolea L, et al. Cholera in Piura, Peru: A modern urban epidemic. J Infect Dis. 1992;166:1429.
46. Tauxe RV, Holmberg SD, Dodin A, et al. Epidemic cholera in Mali: High mortality and multiple routes of transmission in a famine area. Epidemiol Infect. 1988;100:279.
47. Umoh JU, Adesiyun AA, Adekeye JO. Epidemiological features of an outbreak of gastroenteritis/cholera in Katsina, Northern Nigeria. J Hyg. 1983;91:101.
48. Birmingham ME, Lee LA, Ndayimirije N, et al. Epidemic cholera in Burundi: Patterns of transmission in the Great Rift Valley Lake region. Lancet. 1997;349:981.
49. Swerdlow DL, Malenga G, Begkoyian G, et al. Epidemic cholera among refugees in Malawi Africa: Treatment and transmission. Epidemiol Infect. 1997;118:207.
50. Swerdlow DL, Mintz ED, Rodriguez M, et al. Waterborne transmission of epidemic cholera in Trujillo, Peru: Lessons for a continent at risk. Lancet. 1992;340:28.
51. Deb B, Sirkar CBK, Sengupta PG, et al. Studies on interventions to prevent El Tor cholera transmission in urban slums. Bull World Health Organ. 1986;64:127.
52. Deb B, Sirkar CBK, Sengupta PG, et al. Intra-familial transmission of *Vibrio cholerae* biotype El Tor in Calcutta slums. India J Med Res. 1982;76:814.
53. Quick RE, Thompson BL, Zuniga A, et al. Epidemic cholera in rural El Salvador: Risk factors in a region covered by a cholera prevention campaign. Epidemiol Infect. 1995;114:249.
54. Blake PA, Rosenberg ML, Florencia J, et al. Cholera in Portugal, 1974. II. Transmission by bottled mineral water. Am J Epidemiol. 1977;105:344.
55. Deb BC, Sircar BK, Sengupta PG, et al. Studies on intervention to prevent El Tor cholera transmission in urban slums. Bull World Health Organ. 1986;64:127.
56. Kolvin JL, Roberts D. Studies on the growth of *Vibrio cholerae* biotype El Tor and biotype classical in foods. J Hyg. 1982;89:243.
57. Koo D, Aragon A, Moscoso V, et al. Epidemic cholera in Guatemala 1993: Transmission of a newly introduced epidemic strain by street vendors. Epidemiol Infect. 1996;116:121.
58. McIntyre RC, Tira CT, Flood T, et al. Modes of transmission of cholera in a newly infected population on an atoll: Implications for control measures. Lancet. 1979;1:311.
59. Merson MH, Martin WT, Craig JP, et al. Cholera in Guam 1974: Epidemiologic findings and isolation of non-toxigenic strains. Am J Epidemiol. 1977;105:349.
60. Centers for Disease Control. Cholera—New Jersey and Florida. MMWR Morb Mortal Wkly Rep. 1991;40:287.
61. Centers for Disease Control. Importation of cholera from Peru. MMWR Morb Mortal Wkly Rep. 1991;40:287.
62. Centers for Disease Control. Cholera associated with international travel, 1992. MMWR Morb Mortal Wkly Rep. 1992;41:664.
63. Centers for Disease Control. Toxigenic *Vibrio cholerae* O1 infection acquired in Colorado. MMWR Morb Mortal Wkly Rep. 1989;38:19.
64. Gunnlaugsson G, Einarsdottir J, Angulo FJ, et al. Funerals during the 1994 cholera epidemic in Guinea-Bissau, West Africa: The need for disinfection of bodies of persons dying of cholera. Epidemiol Infect. 1998;120:7.
65. St. Louis ME, Porter JD, Helal A, et al. Epidemic cholera in West Africa: The role of food handling and high-risk foods. Am J Epidemiol. 1990;131:719.
66. Mhalu FS, Mtango EDE, Msengi AE. Hospital outbreaks of cholera transmitted through close person-to-person contact. Lancet. 1984;2:82.
67. Cliff JL, Zinkin P, Martelli A. A hospital outbreak of cholera in Maputo, Mozambique. Trans R Soc Trop Med Hyg. 1986;80:473.
68. Mosley WH, Alvero MG, Joseph PR, et al. Studies of cholera El Tor in the Philippines. 4. Transmission of infection among neighborhood and community contacts of cholera patients. Bull World Health Organ. 1965;33:651.
69. Riley LW, Waterman SH, Faruque ASG, et al. Breast-feeding children in the household as a risk factor for cholera in rural Bangladesh: An hypothesis. Trop Geogr Med. 1987;39:9.
70. Fotedar R. Vector potential of houseflies (*Musca domestica*) in the transmission of *Vibrio cholerae* in India. Acta Trop. 2001;78:31-34.
71. Glass RI, Becker S, Huq MI, et al. Endemic cholera in rural Bangladesh, 1966-1980. Am J Epidemiol. 1982;116:959.
72. Seas C, Gotuzzo E. Cholera: Overview of epidemiologic, therapeutic, and preventive issues learned from recent epidemics. Int J Infect Dis. 1996;1:37.
73. Lipp EK, Huq A, Colwell RR. Effects of global climate on infectious disease: the cholera model. Clin Microbiol Rev. 2002;15:757-770.
74. Pascual M, Rodó X, Ellner SP, et al. Cholera dynamics and El Niño–southern oscillation. Science. 2000;289:1766-1769.
75. Rodó X, Pascual M, Fuchs G, Faruque ASG. ENSO and cholera: a nonstationary link related to climate change? Proc Natl Acad Sci U S A. 2002;99:12901-12906.
76. Seas C, Miranda J, Gil AI, et al. New insights on the emergence of cholera in Latin America during 1991: The Peruvian experience. Am J Trop Med Hyg. 2000;62:513-517.
77. Clemens J, Albert MJ, Rao M, et al. Impact of infection by *Helicobacter pylori* on the risk and severity of endemic cholera. J Infect Dis. 1995;171:1653.
78. Taylor DN, Blaser MJ. The epidemiology of *Helicobacter pylori* infection. Epidemiol Rev. 1991;13:42.
79. Barua D, Paguio AS: ABO blood group and cholera. Ann Hum Biol. 1977;4:489.
80. Swerdlow DL, Mintz ED, Rodriguez M, et al. Severe life-threatening cholera associated with blood group O in Peru: Implications for the Latin American epidemic. J Infect Dis. 1994;170:468.
81. Rogers RC, Cuffe RG, Cossins YM, et al. The Queensland cholera incident of 1977. 2. The epidemiological investigation. Bull World Health Organ. 1980;58:665.
82. Johnston JM, Martin DL, Perdue J, et al. Cholera on a Gulf Coast oil rig. N Engl J Med. 1983;309:523.
83. Blake PA, Allegra DT, Snyder JD, et al. Cholera—a possible endemic focus in the United States. N Engl J Med. 1980;302:305.
84. Sack RB, Siddique AK, Longini IM, et al. A 4-year study of the epidemiology of Vibrio cholerae in four rural areas of Bangladesh. J Infect Dis. 2003;187:96-101.
85. Emch M. Diarrhoeal disease risk in Matlab, Bangladesh. Soc Sci Med. 1999;49:519-530.
86. Greenough WB III. *Vibrio cholerae* and cholera. In: Mandell GL, Douglas JE, Dolin R, eds. Principles and Practice of Infectious Diseases. 4th ed. New York: Churchill Livingstone; 1995:1934.
87. Chatterjee A, Mahalanabis D, Jalan KN, et al. Plasma specific gravity and haematocrit values as indices of the degree of dehydration in infantile diarrhoea. Indian J Med Res. 1979;70:229.
88. Wang F, Butler T, Rabbani GH, et al. The acidosis of cholera: Contributions of hyperproteinemia, lactic acidemia, and hyperphosphatemia to an increased anion gap. N Engl J Med. 1986;315:1591.
89. Rahaman MM, Majid MA, Monsur KA. Evaluation of two intravenous rehydration solutions in cholera and non-cholera diarrhoea. Bull World Health Organ. 1979;57:977.
90. Bennish ML, Azad AK, Rahman O, et al. Hypoglycemia during diarrhea: Prevalence, pathophysiology and therapy in Asiatic cholera. N Engl J Med. 1990;322:1357.
91. Mahalanabis D, Wallace CK, Kallen RJ, et al. Water and electrolyte losses due to cholera in infants and small children: A recovery balance study. Pediatrics. 1970;45:374.
92. Hirschhorn N, Chowdhury AKMA, Lindenbaum J. Cholera in pregnant women. Lancet. 1969;1:1230.
93. Cieza J, Sovero Y, Estremadoyro L, et al. Electrolyte disturbances in elderly patients with severe diarrhea due to cholera. J Am Soc Nephrol. 1995;6:1463.
94. Piarroux R. Management of cholera epidemic by a humanitarian organization. Med Trop. 2002;62:361-367.
95. World Health Organization. Guidelines for Cholera Control (WHO/CDD/SER/80.4 REV.4). Geneva: World Health Organization; 1992.
96. Mahalanabis D, Molla AM, Sack DA. Clinical management of cholera. In: Barua D, Greenough WB III, eds. Cholera. New York: Plenum; 1992:253.
97. Bennish ML: Cholera: Pathophysiology, clinical features, and treatment. In: Wachsmuth IK, Blake PA, Olsvik O, eds. *Vibrio cholerae* and Cholera: Molecular to Global Perspectives. Washington, DC: ASM Press; 1994:229.
98. Seas C, DuPont HL, Valdez LM, et al. Practical guidelines for the treatment of cholera. Drugs. 1996;51:966-973.
99. Robert M, Flocard F, Adam JC, et al. Emergency intra-osseous rehydration in children during a cholera epidemic. Med Trop. 1995;55:101.
100. Alam NH, Majunder RN, Fuchs GJ. Efficacy and safety of oral rehydration solution with reduced osmolarity in adults with cholera: A randomized double blind trial. CHOICE Study Group. Lancet. 1999,354:296-299.
101. Heyman SN, Ginosar Y, Shapiro M, et al. Diarrheal epidemics among Rwandan refugees in 1994: Management and outcome in a field hospital. J Clin Gastroenterol. 1997;25:595.
102. Ryan ET, Dhar U, Khan WA, et al. Mortality, morbidity, and microbiology of endemic cholera among hospitalized patients in Dhaka, Bangladesh. Am J Trop Med Hyg. 2000;63:12-20.
103. Quick RE, Vargas R, Moreno D, et al. Epidemic cholera in the Amazon: The challenge of preventing death. Am J Trop Med Hyg. 1993;48:597.
104. Dhar U, Bennish ML, Khan WA, et al. Clinical features, antimicrobial susceptibility and toxin production in *Vibrio cholerae* O139 infection: Comparison with *Vibrio cholerae* O1 infection. Trans R Soc Trop Med Hyg. 1996;90:402.
105. Greenough WB III, Gordon RS, Rosenberg IS, et al. Tetracycline in the treatment of cholera. Lancet. 1964;1:355.
106. Alam AN, Alam NH, Ahmed T, et al. Randomized double blind trial of single dose doxycycline for treating cholera in adults. BMJ 1990;300:1619.
107. O'Grady EM, Lewis J, Pearson NJ. Global surveillance of antibiotic sensitivity of *Vibrio cholerae*. Bull World Health Organ. 1976;54:181.
108. Yamamoto Q, Nair GB, Albert MJ, et al. Survey of in-vitro susceptibilities of *Vibrio cholerae* O1 and O139 to antimicrobial agents. Antimicrob Agents Chemother. 1995;39:241.
109. Dubon JM, Palmer CJ, Ager AL, et al. Emergence of multiple drug-resistant *Vibrio cholerae* in San Pedro Sula, Honduras. Lancet. 1997;349:924.
110. Seas C, Gotuzzo E. Recent advances in the treatment and prophylaxis of cholera. Curr Opin Infect Dis. 1996;9:380.
111. Gotuzzo E, Seas C, Echevarriá J, et al. Ciprofloxacin for the treatment of cholera: A randomized, double-blind, controlled trial of a single daily dose in Peruvian adults. Clin Infect Dis. 1995;20:1485.
112. Khan WA, Bennish ML, Seas C, et al. Randomized controlled comparison of single-dose ciprofloxacin and doxycycline for cholera caused by *Vibrio cholerae* O1 or O139. Lancet. 1996;348:296.

113. Mukhopadhyay AK, Basu I, Bhattacharya SK, et al. Emergence of fluoroquinolone resistance in strains of *Vibrio cholerae* isolated from hospitalized patients with acute diarrhea in Calcutta, India. Antimicrob Agents Chemother. 1998;42:206.

114. Battacharya MK, Gosh S, Mukhopadhyay AK, et al. Outbreak of cholera caused by *Vibrio cholerae* O1 intermediately resistant to norfloxacin in Malda, west Bengal. Ind J Med Assoc. 2000;98:389-390.

115. Garg P, Sinha S, Chakraborty R, et al. Emergence of fluoroquinolone resistant strains of *Vibrio cholerae* O1 among hospitalized patients in Calcutta, India. Antimicrob Agents Chemother. 2001;45:1605-1606.

116. Jesudason MV, Balaji V, Thomson CJ. Quinolone susceptibility of *Vibrio cholerae* O1 and O139 isolates from Vellore. Indian J Med Res. 2002;116:96-98.

117. Khan WA, Saha D, Rahman A, et al. Comparison of single-dose azithromycin and 12-dose, 3-day erythromycin for childhood cholera: a randomized, double-blind trial. Lancet. 2002;360:1722-1727.

118. Bhattacharya SK. An evaluation of current cholera treatment. Expert Opin Pharmacother. 2003:4:141-146.

119. Salazar E, Santisteban J, Chea E, Gutierrez M. Racecadotril in the treatment of acute watery diarrhea in children. N Engl J Med. 2000;343:463-467.

120. Oi H, Matsuura D, Miyake M, et al. Identification in traditional herbal medications and confirmation by synthesis of factors that inhibit cholera toxin-induced fluid accumulation. Proc Natl Acad Sci U S A. 2002;99:3042-3046.

121. Ghosh S, Sengupta PG, Gupta DN, et al. Chemoprophylaxis studies in cholera: A review of selective works. J Commun Dis. 1992;24:55.

122. Echevarria J, Seas C, Carrillo C, et al. Efficacy and tolerability of ciprofloxacin prophylaxis in adult household contacts of patients with cholera. Clin Infect Dis. 1995;20:1480.

123. Colwell RR, Huq A, Islam MS, et al. Reduction of cholera in Bangladeshi villages by simple filtration. Proc Natl Acad Sci U S A. 2003;100:1051-1055.

124. Madico G, Checkley W, Gilman RH, et al. Active surveillance for *Vibrio cholerae* O1 and vibriophages in sewage water as a potential tool to predict cholera outbreaks. J Clin Microbiol. 1996;34:2968.

125. Franco AA, Fix AD, Prada A, et al. Cholera in Lima, Peru, correlates with prior isolation of *Vibrio cholerae* from the environment. Am J Epidemiol. 1997;146:1067.

126. Koo D, Traverso H, Libel M, et al. Epidemic cholera in Latin America 1991-1993: Implications of case definitions used for public health surveillance. Bull Pan Am Health Organ. 1996;30:134-143.

127. Colwell RR. Global climate and infectious disease: The cholera paradigm. Science. 1996;274:2025.

128. Finkelstein RA. Why do we not yet have a suitable vaccine against cholera? Adv Exp Med Biol. 1995;37:1633.

129. Clemens JD, Sack DA, Harris JR, et al. Field trial of oral cholera vaccines in Bangladesh: Results from three-year follow-up. Lancet. 1990;335:270.

130. Van Loon FP, Clemens JD, Chakraborty J, et al. Field trial of inactivated oral cholera vaccines in Bangladesh: Results from 5 years of follow-up. Vaccine. 1996;14:162.

131. Trach DD, Clemens JD, Ke NT, et al. Field trial of a locally produced killed oral cholera vaccine in Vietnam. Lancet. 1997;349:231.

132. Trach DD, Cam PD, Ke NT, et al. Investigations into the safety and immunogenicity of a killed oral cholera vaccine developed in Viet Nam. Bull World Health Organ. 2002;80:2-8.

133. Levine MM, Kaper JB, Herrington D, et al. Safety, immunogenicity, and efficacy of recombinant live oral cholera vaccines, CVD 103 and CVD 103–HgR. Lancet. 1988;2:468.

134. Gotuzzo E, Butron B, Seas C, et al. Safety, immunogenicity, and excretion pattern of single-dose live oral cholera vaccine CVD 103 HgR in Peruvian adults of high and low socio-economic levels. Infect Immun. 1993;61:3994.

135. Lagos R, Avendaño A, Prado V, et al. Attenuated live cholera vaccine strain CVD 103–HgR elicits significantly higher serum vibriocidal antibody titers in persons of blood group O. Infect Immun. 1995;63:707.

136. Richie EE, Punjabi NH, Sidharta YY, et al. Efficacy trial of a single-dose live oral cholera vaccine CVD 103-HgR in North Jakarta, Indonesia, a cholera-endemic area. Vaccine. 2000;18:2339-2410.

137. Ledon T, Valle E, Valmaseda T, et al. Construction and characterisation of O139 cholera vaccine candidates. Vaccine. 2003;21:1282-1291.

138. Cohen MB, Gianella RA, Bean J, et al. Randomized, controlled human challenge study of the safety, immunogenicity, and protective efficacy of a single dose of Peru-15, live attenuated oral cholera vaccine. Infect Immun. 2002;70:1965-1970.

139. Qadri F, Ahmed T, Ahmed F, et al. Safety and immunogenicity of an oral, inactivated enterotoxigenic *Escherichia coli* plus cholera toxin B subunit vaccine in Bangladeshi children 18-36 months of age. Vaccine. 2003;21:2394-2403.

140. Valle E, Ledon T, Cedre B, et al. Construction and characterization of a nonproliferative El Tor cholera vaccine candidate derived from strain 638. Infect Immun. 2000;68:6411-6418.

141. Albert MJ, Qadri F, Wahed MA, et al. Supplementation with zinc, but not vitamin A, improves seroconversion to vibriocidal antibody in children given an oral cholera vaccine. J Infect Dis. 2003;187:909-913.

142. Snyder JD, Blake PA. Is cholera a problem for US travelers? JAMA. 1982;247:2268.

143. Naficy A, Rao MR, Paquet C, et al. Treatment and vaccination strategies to control cholera in sub-Saharan refugee settings. JAMA. 1998;279:521.

144. Seas C, Gotuzzo E. *Vibrio cholerae* (Cholera). In: Yu VL, Rainer W, Raoult D, eds. Antimicrobial Therapy and Vaccines. Volume One: Microbes. New York: Apple Trees Production; 2002:763-772.

145. Miller JF. Bacteriophage and the evolution of epidemic cholera. Infect Immun. 2003;71:2981-2982.

Other Pathogenic Vibrios

MARGUERITE A. NEILL

CHARLES C. J. CARPENTER

In addition to *Vibrio cholerae* O1 and *Campylobacter fetus* (formerly known as *Vibrio fetus*), three additional major groups of vibrios have been clearly associated with human disease. These include the halophilic *V. parahaemolyticus* and *V. vulnificus,* of which the epidemiologic and clinical features are well delineated; other halophilic vibrios, including *V. alginolyticus, V. fluvialis, V. hollisae, V. damsela, V. furnissii, V. metschnikovii,* and *V. cincinnatiensis,* which are less common causes of human disease; and the nonhalophilic non-O1 *V. cholerae* and *V. mimicus,* which are worldwide in distribution and have frequently been incriminated in human illness.

In the United States, illnesses caused by the commonly isolated pathogenic vibrios have a marked seasonal peak, with more than 90% of cases occurring between April and October. This presumably reflects seasonal changes in shellfish consumption and recreational water use, and the documented increase in densities of vibrios in both the Chesapeake Bay and the Gulf Coast waters during the warmer months.

VIBRIO PARAHAEMOLYTICUS

Vibrio parahaemolyticus, a halophilic (salt-requiring) vibrio, has long been recognized as a major cause of acute diarrheal disease in Japan.[1] In the United States, *V. parahaemolyticus* was the most commonly isolated vibrio species during a year-long Gulf Coast surveillance effort[2] as well as over a 13-year period in Florida.[3] This pathogen was the most common bacterial cause of foodborne disease in Taiwan, accounting for 35% of all outbreaks.[4] *Vibrio parahaemolyticus* is a major pathogen in a number of the less-developed countries, in which it has been incriminated in up to 20% of acute diarrheal illnesses. A specific serotype, *V. parahaemolyticus* O3:K6, has emerged as an important cause of human illness in southeast Asia.[5] In 1998 this serotype first appeared in the United States,[6] causing a large multistate outbreak and prompting regulatory changes in programs for bacteriologic monitoring of shellfish.[7] Enteric illness caused by *V. parahaemolyticus* comprises a broad spectrum of clinical manifestations ranging from mild watery diarrhea to a frank dysentery-like syndrome. As suggested by the clinical disease as well as by experimental studies in animals, *V. parahaemolyticus* has the capacities both to produce an enterotoxin and to cause an inflammatory reaction in the small bowel mucosa. The enterotoxin, however, seldom causes major degrees of intestinal fluid loss, and the tissue damage caused by this halophilic vibrio is generally less extensive than that observed in shigellosis.

The genome of *V. parahaemolyticus* has been sequenced.[8] Like *V. cholerae, V. parahaemolyticus* has two circular chromosomes, but unlike *V. cholerae,* a type III secretion system has been found within a pathogenicity island on chromosome 2 of *V. parahaemolyticus.* Type III secretion systems permit direct injection of bacterial toxins or other proteins into host cells, and are a feature shared by enteropathogenic *E. coli,* shigellae, and salmonellae. This molecular finding likely underlies the inflammatory diarrhea seen in *V. parahaemolyticus,* but not *V. cholerae,* infection, and suggests that these two pathogenic vibrios have distinctively different mechanisms for causing diarrhea.

Epidemiology

Because of lack of specificity of the clinical features of the illness, the epidemiologic history usually provides the most important clue to diagnosis. The halophilic *V. parahaemolyticus* is ubiquitous in coastal waters,[1,9] although this pathogen typically is not recovered from estuarine waters during winter months in temperate zones. During periods of low temperature or nutrient deprivation, it enters a viable but nonculturable state.[10] Plankton blooms and temperature upshifting in the spring are followed by rapid outgrowth of most vibrios, including *V. parahaemolyticus*. Molluscan shellfish, which are filter feeders, acquire vibrios as part of their normal microflora during the warmer months. Shellfish contamination thus occurs as a consequence of the normal climate-associated changes in vibrio prevalence in coastal waters rather than as a result of sewage contamination of shellfish beds. In a microbiologic survey of oysters harvested from U.S. waters, the frequency of *V. parahaemolyticus* contamination was consistently greater than that for *V. vulnificus*.[11]

Consumption of raw or undercooked shellfish is the most common means of acquiring *V. parahaemolyticus* infection. In the United States, raw oysters are the most common vehicle.[12] Inadequately cooked seafood can harbor small numbers of surviving vibrios, as can food contaminated by seawater on ships. *V. parahaemolyticus* can proliferate rapidly to reach high colony counts in contaminated foods held at ambient temperature for a few hours. This presumably contributes to the high attack rate seen in common source outbreaks.

Person-to-person transmission has not been documented in the Western Hemisphere[13] or Japan, and secondary cases are rare in areas in which environmental sanitation is less adequate. This observation suggests that the infective dose for normal persons is relatively high.

Vibrio parahaemolyticus has rarely been cultured from asymptomatic people, and no carrier state has been identified. There is no known mammalian reservoir of infection.

Clinical Manifestations

Gastroenteritis is the most common clinical illness associated with *V. parahaemolyticus* infection; wound infections and septicemia may be seen but much less frequently.[2,3] Enteric illness commonly begins with the acute onset of explosive watery diarrhea, often accompanied by mild to moderately severe cramping and abdominal pain. In North America and Japan, the onset of illness is generally within 24 hours of ingestion of the contaminated seafood. The diarrhea is accompanied by low-grade fever, mild chills, and headache in less than half of the cases. The fluid loss is rarely severe enough to cause decreased skin turgor or postural hypotension. Deaths caused by *V. parahaemolyticus* are rare, usually occurring in very young children, the elderly, or persons with underlying disease.

Laboratory Findings

The diarrheal fluid is characteristically watery, sometimes mucoid, and occasionally bloody (<15%). Fecal leukocytes are often present. *Vibrio parahaemolyticus* is a pleomorphic gram-negative rod that is a facultative anaerobe. It grows poorly on the standard desoxycholate culture plates but is readily identified on the selective thiosulfate citrate bile salts sucrose (TCBS) agar, on which it appears as a distinct opaque green colony. Final identification is made by standard biochemical tests.[1] Enrichment of fecal culture specimens, especially useful for epidemiologic investigation, can be carried out in hypertonic saline containing 3% sodium chloride in 1% peptone broth, pH 7.4,[13] or in taurocholate-tellurite water.[14] Almost all clinical isolates of *V. parahaemolyticus* cause β-hemolysis of human erythrocytes (the Kanagawa reaction), which is due to production of thermostable direct hemolysin (TDH).[15] Environmental isolates of *V. parahaemolyticus* are Kanagawa negative and lack the *tdh* gene, indicating that TDH is a virulence marker. Of interest, growth in a bile salt-containing environment has been shown to enhance the expression of several virulence traits in *V. parahaemolyticus*.[16]

Recently, the immune response in patients with *V. parahaemolyticus* enteric infection has been described.[17] Both serum and coproantibody responses to lipopolysaccharide and to TDH were detected. Mucosal biopsies from the duodenum and rectum showed inflammatory changes in both, suggesting that both small and large intestine are affected. Tumor necrosis factor-α (TNF-α) levels were noted to be elevated acutely in *V. parahaemolyticus* infection, similar to what has been observed in shigellosis and in contrast to cholera infections, in which TNF-α is not elevated.

Differential Diagnosis

Because the halophilic *V. parahaemolyticus* is ubiquitous in coastal waters throughout the temperate and tropical zones of the world, this pathogen must be considered in the differential diagnosis of all acute diarrheal illnesses that follow the ingestion of seafood. There are no clinical features that, in the individual case, reliably distinguish diarrhea caused by *V. parahaemolyticus* from that caused by enterotoxigenic *Escherichia coli* or from milder cases of shigellosis or salmonellosis. Vomiting is characteristically less prominent than in disease caused by staphylococcal enterotoxin, and the cramping abdominal pain is generally less severe than that typical of food poisoning caused by *Clostridium perfringens*.

Treatment

No treatment is required by the majority of patients because the disease is usually self-limited. However, antimicrobial therapy could be considered for those patients with diarrhea lasting greater than 5 days.[18] Therapy with a tetracycline or quinolone would be expected to shorten the clinical course and duration of pathogen excretion. Antiperistaltic agents are of no clear-cut benefit. Occasional patients, usually at the extremes of age, may lose sufficient quantities of fluid to require oral or intravenous electrolyte therapy. In such cases, therapy is guided by the same principles used in the treatment of cholera.

Prevention

Because the illness usually results from the ingestion of raw or inadequately cooked seafood or food that has been rinsed with contaminated seawater, simple means of prevention are available. *Vibrio parahaemolyticus* can remain viable in shrimp or crab meat for several minutes at temperatures as high as 80° C, and it is especially important in cooking large quantities of such foods to ensure that all portions of the seafood are exposed to cooking temperatures adequate to kill the microorganism. Of only slightly less importance is the necessity of refrigerating cooked seafood if it is not to be ingested immediately after cooking. Shipboard outbreaks can obviously be prevented either by avoiding the use of untreated seawater in galleys or by adequate refrigeration of cooked seafood until it is served. The use of irradiation at a dose of 3.0 kGy can reduce *V. parahaemolyticus* levels by 6 logs without killing the oysters or adversely affecting their organoleptic qualities[19]; however, lower doses may not inactivate viruses.

Prevention of disease caused by *V. parahaemolyticus* in Japan remains a problem because of the popularity of uncooked seafood in that nation. Because there is little likelihood of changing the custom of ingesting raw seafood, *V. parahaemolyticus* will probably remain a major cause of acute diarrheal disease in Japan. Likewise, in delta areas such as Bangladesh in which people have daily contact with contaminated water, there is little likelihood of altering the incidence of *V. parahaemolyticus* infections in the foreseeable future.

It is not known whether protective immunity is conferred by clinical infection. No effective vaccine is currently available.

VIBRIO VULNIFICUS

Like other potentially pathogenic halophilic vibrios, *V. vulnificus* is part of the normal marine flora and, in the temperate zones, reaches sufficient concentrations to cause clinical illness only in the warmer months of the year. Nearly all oysters harvested in the summer from the Chesapeake Bay contain this pathogen, as do 10% of crabs. This pathogen was the second and third most common *Vibrio* species isolated from human cases in Florida[3] and the Gulf states,[2] respectively. There is some evidence suggesting that infections from *V. vulnificus* may be increasing in the United States, particularly in association with Gulf Coast oyster consumption,[20] and warmer water temperatures (>22° C) in the Gulf of Mexico may be contributing in part to the increase. The case-fatality rate of 25% is the highest among infections caused by the *Vibrio* species and *V. vulnificus* is estimated to account for 90% of all seafood-related deaths in the United States. Hippocrates may have provided the first description of a *V. vulnificus* infection in the fifth century B.C.; he described the rapid progression of a severe foot cellulitis with black blisters in Criton of Thasos, which was fatal in 48 hours.[21]

Clinical Manifestations

Vibrio vulnificus is the most virulent of the noncholera vibrios. It is primarily associated with a severe, distinctive soft tissue infection and/or septicemia rather than diarrheal illness.[22,23] In compromised hosts, especially patients with cirrhosis, *V. vulnificus* has the ability to invade the blood stream without causing gastrointestinal symptoms. The clinical picture is one of abrupt onset of chills and fever, often (in 33% of cases) followed by hypotension, usually (in 75%) followed by the development of metastatic cutaneous lesions within 36 hours after onset. These begin as erythematous lesions, and rapidly evolve to hemorrhagic bullae or vesicles and then to necrotic ulcers. *V. vulnificus* bacteremia has been fatal in over 50% of patients in whom this syndrome has been identified, including all patients in whom hypotension developed.[23] More than 90% of such patients have a history of having consumed raw oysters in the 7 days prior to illness onset; concentrations of *V. vulnificus* of 10^3 colony-forming units (cfu)/g of oysters have produced illness. Although oysters harbor genetically heterogeneous populations of *V. vulnificus,* only one strain type has been recovered from human tissues in invasive infections.[24] Besides cirrhosis, other risk factors for the septicemic form of *V. vulnificus* infection include liver disease, iron overload states such as hemochromatosis, hemolytic anemia or chronic renal failure, malignancy, human immunodeficiency virus (HIV) infection, and immunosuppressive medications.[3,25] In chronic alcoholics undergoing treatment for substance abuse, reduced levels of glutathione correlated with decreased cytokine production by peripheral blood mononuclear cells after exposure in vitro to *V. vulnificus.*[26] Such a weak cytokine response could explain the poor blood-stream clearance and resulting high frequency of bacteremia in *V. vulnificus* infections.

In both healthy persons and compromised hosts, *V. vulnificus* causes a rapidly developing, intense cellulitis, necrotizing vasculitis, and ulcer formation and is often associated with bacteremia after contamination of a superficial wound by warm seawater. In one case, *V. vulnificus* apparently survived on intact skin for more than 24 hours after handling tilapia fish, with the subsequent development of a necrotic cellulitis following a traumatic injury to the hand while the patient was working on a motor vehicle engine.[27] The cellulitis generally responds to appropriate antimicrobials, but incision and drainage or débridement or both are often necessary.[22] *Vibrio vulnificus* has also rarely been associated with acute, self-limited diarrheal illnesses in persons receiving antacid therapy.[28] This pathogen has also been noted to cause ocular infections, usually following an injury from molluscan shell fragments.[29] Rarely this infection can present as a septic arthritis.[30]

The major determinant of virulence in *V. vulnificus* is its polysaccharide capsule, which renders the bacterium resistant to serum killing and which can directly stimulate release of inflammatory cytokines such as TNF-α.[31,32] Other contributors to pathogenicity include a variety of extracellular proteins and cell wall lipopolysaccharide. Host-derived factors that contribute to the pathogen's virulence include the availability of iron and at least one inflammatory mediator. The predilection of this vibrio to cause disease in patients with iron overload states can be explained by its ability to sequester iron from hemoglobin and 100% saturated (but not 30%, or normally, saturated) transferrin. Local bradykinin generation has been shown to enhance *V. vulnificus* bacteremia in mice, and this could be inhibited by a specific antagonist.[33] Elevated levels of several proinflammatory cytokines, including TNF-α, interleukin-1β, and interleukin-6, have been noted in septicemic patients with *V. vulnificus* infection.[34]

Differential Diagnosis

Vibrio vulnificus should be suspected in any compromised host (especially with underlying cirrhosis) who develops a septicemic illness associated with necrotizing cutaneous lesions within 1 to 3 days after the ingestion of oysters. Although rare, the clinical syndrome appears to be a distinct one and should suggest this diagnosis.

Similarly, the development of cellulitis in persons occupationally or recreationally exposed to seawater should suggest *V. vulnificus* (especially in the presence of severe, necrotizing cellulitis). Other *Vibrio* species may cause soft tissue infections.

Vibrio vulnificus grows readily on MacConkey agar and the more selective TCBS medium; final identification is made by standard biochemical tests. Because *V. vulnificus* ferments lactose, it can be overlooked in cultures grown on MacConkey agar in a routine diagnostic laboratory unless the technician is advised to look specifically for this microorganism. Clinicians cannot rely on routine diagnostic practice in the laboratory as a means to microbiologically diagnose *Vibrio* infections even in endemic areas, because only a quarter of laboratories in Gulf Coast states routinely culture all stools for *Vibrio* species.[35] Thus communication between the clinician and microbiology laboratory personnel is key to ensure diagnosis.

Treatment

Soft tissue infections caused by *V. vulnificus* generally respond well to appropriate antibiotics and, when necessary, surgical drainage. Early administration of antibiotics is critical because the cellulitis can spread very rapidly. Bacteremic *V. vulnificus* infections in compromised hosts respond less well to therapy. A tetracycline is the first-choice agent, with cefotaxime or ciprofloxacin as alternatives. *V. vulnificus* is not uniformly susceptible to the aminoglycosides, which are often used in apparently septic patients. Reported mortality was lowest for bacteremic patients begun on antibiotics within 24 hours of onset of illness but was still unacceptably high at 33%.[23]

Prevention

Although patients with underlying liver disease and other chronic illnesses should be warned of the hazards of eating raw oysters, this has not been accomplished effectively in the United States even when required by law.[36] A capsular polysaccharide conjugate vaccine has been developed, but studies indicate that polyclonal immunoglobulin, either actively or passively derived, was necessary for cross-protection among capsular types of *V. vulnificus.*[37] At present, thorough cooking of seafood remains the only effective means of prevention.

VIBRIO ALGINOLYTICUS

Vibrio alginolyticus has been etiologically associated with cellulitis and acute otitis media or externa. These infections have generally occurred after local trauma in otherwise healthy seawater swimmers or fishermen and have responded well to appropriate antibiotics.[38,39] Necrotizing fasciitis has developed following a soft tissue injury from a coral reef to the leg of an apparently immune-competent individual.[40] *V. alginolyticus* occasionally causes life-threatening bacteremia in immunocompromised individuals. Isolation is similar to that for *V. vulnificus;* however, *V. alginolyticus* does not ferment lactose.

OTHER HALOPHILIC VIBRIOS

Several other *Vibrio* species have been recognized as causative agents of human disease, and their acquisition is through either ingestion of contaminated seafood or contact of traumatized skin with seawater or brackish water. Surveillance for *Vibrio* infections along the Gulf Coast in the United States has provided a useful perspective on the overall frequency and clinical illnesses associated with these microorganisms.[2,3] *V. fluvialis* and *V. hollisae* primarily cause diarrhea, whereas *V. damsela* causes wound infections. *V. hollisae* can cause severe cellulitis, mimicking the clinical picture of a *V. vulnificus* infection, but, unlike *V. vulnificus,* it grows poorly on the TCBS media typically used for vibrio isolation. *V. furnissii* has been rarely isolated in sporadic cases of diarrhea.[41] *V. metschnikovii* has caused bacteremia[42] and *V. cincinnatiensis,* bacteremia and meningitis.[43] *Vibrio carchariae* has caused a cellulitis following a shark bite.[44]

INFECTIONS CAUSED BY NONHALOPHILIC VIBRIOS: NON-O1 *VIBRIO CHOLERAE* AND *VIBRIO MIMICUS*

Vibrios that are biochemically similar to *V. cholerae* but that do not agglutinate in *V. cholerae* O1 or O139 antiserum are taxonomically included in the species *V. cholerae* and are referred to as non-O1 *V. cholerae*. *V. mimicus* is closely related to non-O1 *V. cholerae*, but differs biochemically in being sucrose negative and Voges-Proskauer reaction negative. These nonhalophilic vibrios require only trace amounts of sodium chloride for growth in culture medium; this characteristic distinguishes them from the true halophilic vibrios *V. parahaemolyticus*, *V. vulnificus*, and *V. alginolyticus*, which require larger concentrations of sodium chloride in culture media and have the remarkable ability to grow in 10% sodium chloride.

Clinical Manifestations

Non-O1 *V. cholerae* organisms produce a wide spectrum of diarrheal illness ranging from severe watery diarrhea indistinguishable from cholera to the milder traveler's diarrhea of the type commonly associated with enterotoxigenic *E. coli*. Some clinical isolates of non-O1 *V. cholerae* produce an enterotoxin, nearly identical either to cholera toxin of *V. cholerae*[45] or heat-stable enterotoxin of *E. coli*[46]; other clinical isolates have been nontoxigenic[47] or produced a cytotoxic activity demonstrable on HEP-2 cells.[48] No clinical features distinguish the severe diarrheal illnesses caused by enterotoxin-producing non-O1 *V. cholerae* from those caused by classic *V. cholerae*.[49] Non-O1 *V. cholerae* strains can rarely cause bacteremia, almost invariably in patients with liver disease[50] but occasionally in normal persons also.[48]

V. mimicus has caused sporadic outbreaks of acute diarrheal illness in healthy individuals who have ingested raw seafood, both along the American Gulf Coast[51] and in Bangladesh.[52] This marine bacterium may rarely cause acute otitis in saltwater swimmers.

Laboratory Findings

With intestinal infections caused by both non-O1 *V. cholerae* and *V. mimicus*, the diarrheal fluid varies from the watery isotonic fluid characteristic of cholera gravis to loose stools in which small numbers of leukocytes and erythrocytes may be seen. The organisms are readily identified on TCBS agar, on which *V. cholerae* appears as opaque yellow colonies and *V. mimicus* as green; final speciation is made by biochemical tests and lack of agglutination in O1 antisera.

Treatment

No treatment is required by the large majority of patients with diarrheal disease, and antimicrobials have not been shown to shorten the clinical course.[49] In occasional patients, especially those in the developing world, the intestinal fluid loss is sufficient to require oral or intravenous electrolyte therapy. In this situation, therapy is guided by the same principles used in the treatment of cholera.

Epidemiology

Non-O1 *V. cholerae* organisms are worldwide in distribution and ubiquitous in water sources. Sporadic cases result from the ingestion of very large inocula from contaminated water and, occasionally, food. The burden of disease from these strains has been in the severity of illness in individual patients. They have not been observed to cause sweeping epidemics, as have *V. cholerae* O1 and O139, although a few non-O1 strains have caused explosive outbreaks. The molecular basis for this epidemiologic behavioral difference has recently been elucidated.[53] A large (39.5-kb) vibrio pathogenicity island (VPI) has been described in *V. cholerae* that contains gene clusters responsible for cholera toxin acquisition and expression as well as sequences involved in colonization. The group of virulence genes within the VPI is strongly tied to epidemic ability. The VPI is present in epidemic and pandemic *V. cholerae* O1 strains, in Bengal O139, and in two non-O1 *V. cholerae* strains that caused outbreaks. The VPI was absent in sporadic diarrheal and nontoxigenic environmental isolates of non-O1 *V. cholerae*.[53] Horizontal gene transfer of this pathogenicity island may be an initial step for the acquisition of epidemic capability by non-O1 *V. cholerae* strains. Rather than being regarded as a heterogeneous group of lesser consequence, the non-O1 *V. cholerae* organisms are perhaps more properly viewed as strains with the underlying potential to cause epidemic disease if the appropriate complement of virulence genes is acquired.

In every carefully studied major outbreak of cholera, non-O1 vibrios have been isolated from a small proportion of patients (1% to 5%) with illnesses indistinguishable from those caused by *V. cholerae*. Possible explanations for this observation include the loss by certain classic *V. cholerae* of the relevant agglutinating surface antigens and the acquisition by non-O1 *V. cholerae* of the gene coding for the production of cholera enterotoxin.

Prevention

Because non-O1 *V. cholerae* organisms exist in a variety of water sources ranging from freshwater rivers to the oceans, purification of water sources and adequate cooking of fish and other seafood provide the only certain protection against these occasional pathogens.

REFERENCES

1. Zen-Yoji H, Sakai S, Terayama T, et al. Epidemiology, enteropathogenicity, and classification of *Vibrio parahaemolyticus*. J Infect Dis. 1965;115:436.
2. Levine WC, Griffin PM, and the Gulf Coast *Vibrio* Working Group. *Vibrio* infections on the Gulf Coast: Results of the first year of regional surveillance. J Infect Dis. 1993;167:479.
3. Hlady WG, Klontz KC. The epidemiology of *Vibrio* infections in Florida, 1981-1993. J Infect Dis. 1996;173:1176.
4. Pan T-M, Wang T-K, Lee C-L, et al. Food-borne disease outbreaks due to bacteria in Taiwan, 1986 to 1995. J Clin Microbiol. 1997;35:1260.
5. Okuda J, Ishibashi M, Hayakawa E, et al. Emergence of a unique O3:K6 clone of *Vibrio parahaemolyticus* in Calcutta, India, and isolation of strains from the same clonal group from Southeast Asian travelers arriving in Japan. J Clin Microbiol. 1997;35:3150-3155.
6. Daniels NA, Ray B, Easton A, et al. Emergence of a new *Vibrio parahaemolyticus* serotype in raw oysters. JAMA. 2000;284:1541-1545.
7. Oliver JF, Ostroff SM. Preventing *Vibrio parahaemolyticus* infection. JAMA. 2001;285:42-43.
8. Makino K, Oshima K, Kurokawa K, et al. Genome sequence of *Vibrio parahaemolyticus*: A pathogenic mechanism distinct from that of *V. cholerae*. Lancet. 2003;361:743-749.
9. Colwell RR. Human pathogens in the aquatic environment. In: Colwell RR, Foster J, eds. Aquatic Microbial Ecology. College Park, MD: University of Maryland Sea Grant Program, 1980:337-344.
10. Jiang X, Chai T-J. Survival of *Vibrio parahaemolyticus* at low temperatures under starvation conditions and subsequent resuscitation of viable, nonculturable cells. Appl Environ Microbiol. 1996;62:1300.
11. Cook DW, O'Leary P, Hunsucker JC, et al. *Vibrio vulnificus* and *Vibrio parahaemolyticus* in U.S. retail shell oysters: A national survey from June 1998 to July 1999. J Food Prot. 2002;65:79-87.
12. Daniels NA, MacKinnon L, Bishop R, et al. *Vibrio parahaemolyticus* infections in the United States, 1973-1998. J Infect Dis. 2000;181:1661-1666.
13. Dadisman TA, Nelson R, Molenda JR, et al. *Vibrio parahaemolyticus* gastroenteritis in Maryland. I. Clinical and epidemiological aspects. Am J Epidemiol. 1973;96:414.
14. Farmer JJ, Janda JM, Birkhead K. *Vibrio*. In: Murray PR, Baron EJ, Jorgensen JH, et al, eds. Manual of Clinical Microbiology. 8th ed. Washington, DC: ASM Press; 2003:706-718.
15. Nishibuchi M, Kaper JB. Thermostable direct hemolysin gene of *Vibrio parahaemolyticus*: A virulence gene acquired by a marine bacterium. Infect Immun. 1995;63:2093.
16. Pace JL, Chai T-J, Rossi HA, et al. Effect of bile on *Vibrio parahaemolyticus*. Appl Environ Microbiol. 1997;63:2372.
17. Qadri F, Alam MS, Nishibuchi M, et al. Adaptive and inflammatory immune responses in patients infected with strains of *Vibrio parahaemolyticus*. J Infect Dis. 2003;187:1085-1096.
18. Morris JG. Cholera and other types of vibriosis: A story of human pandemics and oysters on the half shell. Clin Infect Dis. 2003;37:272-280.
19. Jakabi M, Gelli DS, Torre J. Inactivation by ionizing radiation of *Salmonella enteritidis*, *Salmonella infantis*, and *Vibrio parahaemolyticus* in oysters (*Crassostrea brasiliana*). J Food Prot. 2003;66:1025-1029.
20. Shapiro RL, Altekruse S. Hutwagner L, et al. The role of Gulf Coast oysters harvested in warmer months in *Vibrio vulnificus* infections in the United States, 1988-1996. J Infect Dis. 1998;178:752-759.
21. Baethge BA, West BC. *Vibrio vulnificus*: Did Hippocrates describe a fatal case? Rev Infect Dis. 1988;10:614.
22. Tacket CO, Brenner F, Blake PA. Clinical features and an epidemiologic study of *Vibrio vulnificus* infections. J Infect Dis. 1984;149:558.

23. Klontz KC, Lieb S, Schreiber M, et al. Syndromes of *Vibrio vulnificus* infections: Clinical and epidemiologic features in Florida cases, 1981-1987. Ann Intern Med. 1988;109:318.

24. Jackson JK, Murphree RL, Tamplin ML. Evidence that mortality from V*ibrio vulnificus* infection results from single strains among heterogeneous populations in shellfish. J Clin Microbiol. 1997;35:2098.

25. Johnston JM, Becker SF, McFarland LM. *Vibrio vulnificus:* Man and the sea. JAMA. 1985;253:2850.

26. Powell JL, Strauss KA, Wiley C, et al. Inflammatory cytokine response to *Vibrio vulnificus* elicited by peripheral blood mononuclear cells from chronic alcohol users is associated with biomarkers of cellular oxidative stress. Infect Immun. 2003;71:4212-4216.

27. Colondner R, Chazan B, Kopelowitz J, et al. Unusual portal of entry of *Vibrio vulnificus:* Evidence of its prolonged survival on the skin. Clin Infect Dis. 2002;34:714-715.

28. Johnston JM, Becker SF, McFarland LM. Gastroenteritis in patients with stool isolates of *Vibrio vulnificus.* Am J Med. 1986;80:336.

29. Penland RL, Boniuk M, Wilhelmus KR. *Vibrio* ocular infections on the U.S. Gulf Coast. Cornea. 2000;19:26-29.

30. Johnson RW, Arnett FC. A fatal case of *Vibrio vulnificus* presenting as septic arthritis. Arch Intern Med. 2002;161:2616-2618.

31. Morris JG. *Vibrio vulnificus*—A new monster of the deep? Ann Intern Med. 1988;109:261.

32. Powell JL, Wright AC, Wasserman SS, et al. Release of tumor necrosis factor alpha in response to V*ibrio vulnificus* capsular polysaccharide in in vivo and in vitro models. Infect Immun. 1997;65:3713.

33. Maruo K, Akaike T, Ono T, et al. Involvement of bradykinin generation in intravascular dissemination of V*ibrio vulnificus* and prevention of invasion by a bradykinin antagonist. Infect Immun. 1998;66:866.

34. Shin SH, Shin DH, Ryu PY, et al. Proinflammatory cytokine profile in *Vibrio vulnificus* septicemic patients' sera. FEMS Immunol Med Microbiol. 2002;33:133-138.

35. Marano NN, Daniels NA, Easton AN, et al. A survey of stool culturing practices for *Vibrio* species at clinical laboratories in Gulf Coast states. J Clin Microbiol. 2000;38:2267-2270.

36. Mouzin E, Mascola L, Tormey M, et al. Prevention of *Vibrio vulnificus* infections: Assessment of regulatory educational strategies. JAMA. 1997;278:576.

37. Devi SJN, Hayat U, Powell, JL, et al. Preclinical immunoprophylactic and immunotherapeutic efficacy of antisera to capsular polysaccharide-tetanus toxoid conjugate vaccines of V*ibrio vulnificus.* Infect Immun. 1996;64:2220.

38. Schmidt U, Chmel H, Cobbs C. *Vibrio alginolyticus* infections in humans. J Clin Microbiol. 1979;10:666.

39. Opal SM, Saxon JR. Intracranial infection by *Vibrio alginolyticus* following injury in salt water. J Clin Microbiol. 1986;23:373.

40. Gomez JM, Fajardo R, Patino JF, Arias CA. Necrotizing fasciitis due to *Vibrio alginolyticus* in an immunocompetent patient. J Clin Microbiol. 2003;41:3427-3429.

41. Brenner DJ, Hickman-Brenner FW, Lee JV, et al. *Vibrio furnissii* (formerly aerogenic biogroup of *Vibrio fluvialis*), a new species isolated from human feces and the environment. J Clin Microbiol. 1983;18:816.

42. Jean-Jacques W, Rajashekaraiah KR, Farmer JJ 3rd. *Vibrio metschnikovii* bacteremia in a patient with cholecystitis. J Clin Microbiol. 1981;14:711.

43. Bode RB, Brayton PR, Colwell RR, et al. A new *Vibrio* species, *Vibrio cincinnatiensis,* causing meningitis: Successful treatment in an adult. Ann Intern Med. 1986;104:55.

44. Pavia AT, Bryan JA, Maher KL, et al. *Vibrio carchariae* infection after a shark bite. Ann Intern Med. 1989;111:85.

45. Yamamoto K, Takeda Y, Miwatani T, et al. Evidence that a non-O1 *Vibrio cholerae* produces enterotoxin that is similar but not identical to cholera enterotoxin. Infect Immun. 1983;41:896.

46. Arita M, Takeda T, Honda T, et al. Purification and characterization of *Vibrio cholerae* non-O1 heat-stable enterotoxin. Infect Immun. 1986;52:45.

47. Morris JG Jr, Picardi JL, Lieb S, et al. Isolation of nontoxigenic *Vibrio cholerae* O group 1 from a patient with severe gastrointestinal disease. J Clin Microbiol. 1984;19:296.

48. Namdari H, Klaips CR, Hughes JL. A cytotoxin-producing strain of *Vibrio cholerae* non-O1, non-O139 as a cause of cholera and bacteremia after consumption of raw clams. J Clin Microbiol. 2000;38:3518-3519.

49. Morris JG, Wilson R, Davis BR, et al. Non-O group 1 *Vibrio cholerae* gastroenteritis in the United States: Clinical, epidemiologic and laboratory characteristics of sporadic cases. Ann Intern Med. 1982;94:656.

50. Safrin S, Morris JG, Adams M, et al. Non O1 *Vibrio cholerae* bacteremia: Case report and review. Rev Infect Dis.1988;10:1012.

51. Shandera WX, Johnston JJ, David BR, et al. Disease from infection with *Vibrio mimicus:* A newly recognized *Vibrio* species. Ann Intern Med. 1983;99:169.

52. Spira WM, Fedorka-Cray PJ: Purification of enterotoxins from *Vibrio mimicus* that appear to be identical to cholera toxin. Infect Immun. 1984;45:679.

53. Karaolis DK, Johnson JA, Bailey CC, et al. A *Vibrio cholerae* pathogenicity island associated with epidemic and pandemic strains. Proc Natl Acad Sci U S A. 1998; 95:3134.

CHAPTER 213

Campylobacter jejuni and Related Species

MARTIN J. BLASER

BAN M. ALLOS

Campylobacteriosis refers to the group of infections caused by gram-negative bacteria of the genus *Campylobacter.* Among the most common bacterial infections of humans in all parts of the world, campylobacters cause both diarrheal and systemic illnesses. Infection of domesticated animals with campylobacters also is widespread. *Campylobacter* is derived from the Greek *campylos,* meaning "curved," and *baktron,* meaning "rod," and is so named to distinguish this genus from otherwise identical-appearing vibrios. Following the recognition of *Campylobacter jejuni* as a major human pathogen, numerous related *Campylobacter, Arcobacter,* and *Helicobacter* species have been identified. The solving of the *C. jejuni* genomic sequence opens new doors in our understanding of these organisms.[1]

ETIOLOGY

Campylobacter organisms are motile, non–spore-forming, comma-shaped, gram-negative rods.[2] Originally isolated from aborted sheep fetuses in 1909, these and similar organisms were considered subspecies of *Vibrio fetus.* However, because these organisms did not ferment carbohydrates and differed in their guanine plus cytosine (G + C) DNA content from true members of the genus *Vibrio,* a new genus, *Campylobacter,* was created. Fourteen species have been recognized within the genus; however, in recent years, taxonomic studies have indicated that splitting the genus is more appropriate.[3] The genus *Arcobacter* has been created, which now includes *Arcobacter butzleri* and *Arcobacter skirrowi.*[4] *Helicobacter cinaedi* and *Helicobacter fennelliae* had been named *Campylobacter cinaedi* and *Campylobacter fennelliae* when first discovered.[5] Although transfer to the genus *Helicobacter* is more appropriate on taxonomic grounds, because these two species cause intestinal rather than gastric illnesses, they are discussed in this chapter. *Helicobacter pylori,* previously named *Campylobacter pylori,* is discussed in Chapter 214. It is clear that new members of *Campylobacter* and related genera are being identified with regularity,[6-8] and that many of these will be found to be human pathogens.

Table 213-1 lists the *Campylobacter* and related species most commonly associated with human disease and indicates the differentiating characteristics. Certain species such as *Campylobacter nitrofigilis, Arcobacter cryaerophila,* and *Campylobacter concisus* have not yet been associated with human illness. In contrast, the "nitrate-negative" campylobacters are associated with diarrheal illnesses, but the appropriate nomenclature for the organisms has not been determined. Two types of illnesses are associated with *Campylobacter* spp.: enteric and extraintestinal. For each of these illnesses, one *Campylobacter* species predominates, and other species are less commonly present. The prototype for enteric infection is *C. jejuni;* for extraintestinal infection it is *Campylobacter fetus* (Table 213-2). Because the organisms causing enteric and extraintestinal illnesses are generally the same, they are considered together in the following discussion.

Campylobacters and related organisms grow best in an atmosphere containing 5% to 10% oxygen and are thus considered microaerophilic.[2,3] Although most of these organisms will not grow under aerobic or anaerobic conditions, *C. jejuni* can grow in candle jars, which permits isolation when the optimal atmosphere cannot be achieved. All campylobacters grow at 37° C; however, *C. jejuni* grows best at 42° C. Because *C. jejuni* is the most common enteric pathogen of humans, many laboratories have used incubation at 42° C for opti-

TABLE 213-1 Differential Characteristics of *Campylobacter* and Related Species Most Commonly Associated with Pathogenicity in Humans

Species	Growth 25° C	Growth 37° C	Growth 42° C	Nitrate Reduction	H$_2$S Production On TSI	H$_2$S Production On Lead Acetate Paper	Hippurate Hydrolysis	Susceptibility to 30-μg Disk Cephalothin	Susceptibility to 30-μg Disk Nalidixic Acid	C-19 Fatty Acid Reduction
Campylobacter jejuni	−	+	+	+	−	+	+*	R	S	+
Campylobacter coli	−	+	+	+	v	+	−	R	S	+
Campylobacter lari	−	+	+	+	−	+	−	R	R	−
Campylobacter fetus subsp. fetus	+	+	v	+	−	v	−	S	R	−
Campylobacter hyointestinalis	v	+	v	+	+	+	−	S	R	+
Helicobacter cinaedi	−	+	−	+	−	+	−	S	S	−
Campylobacter upsaliensis†	−	+	+‡	+	−	+	−	S	S	−
Helicobacter fennelliae	2	+	−	−	−	+	−	S	S	−

*About 5% to 10% of *C. jejuni* strains are hippurate negative.
†Catalase negative or weak.
‡Occasional isolates fail to grow at 42° C.
−, Does not have the characteristic; +, has the characteristic; R, resistant; S, susceptible; TSI, triple sugar iron agar slant; v, variable (some strains show the characteristic).

mal isolation; however, use of this temperature will not permit detection of infections by many of the related species. In particular, *C. upsaliensis* may be missed.

Campylobacters multiply more slowly than do the usual bacteria of the enteric flora and therefore cannot be isolated from fecal specimens unless selective techniques are used. The most common isolation methods use blood-based, antibiotic-containing media. Three such media—Skirrow's, Butzler's, and Campy-BAP—or variations of these have been in wide use.[3] The last two media contain cephalothin, which inhibits *C. fetus* and several other *Campylobacter* subspecies, but are best suited for isolating *C. jejuni*. Several enrichment broths have been developed, but because ill humans usually excrete 10^6 to 10^9 *C. jejuni* colony-forming units (cfu)/g of stool, enrichment usually is not necessary. Blood-free media also can be used.[9] Owing to their small size (0.3 to 0.6 μm in diameter) and motility, campylobacters and related organisms pass through 0.45- or 0.65-μm filters that retard the usual enteric flora. Filtration methods permit isolation without use of antibiotic-containing media. It is now clear that use of filtration techniques and nonselective rich media such as chocolate agar, with incubation of plates at 37° C, improves stool culture yields of both *C. jejuni* and the "atypical" enteric campylobacters.[10,11] The development of filtration techniques represents a significant advance over the use of selective media, and such techniques are now recommended for primary isolation of campylobacters from fecal specimens or swabs.

TABLE 213-2 *Campylobacter, Helicobacter,* and *Arcobacter* Species Associated with Different Clinical Manifestations of Infection

Disease Syndrome	
Enteric	Extraintestinal
Major Pathogen	
Campylobacter jejuni	*Campylobacter fetus*
Minor Pathogens	
Campylobacter coli	*Campylobacter jejuni*
Campylobacter lari	*Campylobacter coli*
Campylobacter fetus	*Campylobacter lari*
Helicobacter fennelliae	*Helicobacter fennelliae*
Helicobacter cinaedi	*Helicobacter cinaedi*
Campylobacter upsaliensis	*Campylobacter sputorum*
Arcobacter butzleri	*Campylobacter hyointestinalis*
Arcobacter skirrowi	*Helicobacter rappini*
Arcobacter cryaeophila	

Visible colonies usually appear on the plating media within 24 to 48 hours. Occasionally, growth takes place after 72 to 96 hours of incubation, especially for the "atypical" species. The campylobacters can be distinguished from other microorganisms on the basis of several standard criteria and can be distinguished from one another on the basis of biochemical testing.[3,12] Organisms from young cultures have a typical vibrioid appearance (Fig. 213-1), but after 48 hours of incubation, organisms appear coccoid. Ability to hydrolyze hippurate distinguishes *C. jejuni* from most other members of the genus, but hippurate-negative *C. jejuni* isolates also occur. State-of-the-art identification to the species level should include polymerase chain reaction (PCR) studies of 16S recombinant RNA or other targets for comparison with known species.[13,14] Isolation of campylobacters from sites without a normal flora, such as the blood stream, is not difficult, although when this organism is the suspected pathogen, incubation of cultures should be extended to 2 weeks. With radiometric detection systems, turbidity of the medium may not be present, and the increase in released radiolabel may be less than usually specified thresholds, reflecting suboptimal conditions for certain of these organisms.[15] PCR-based techniques have been developed for culture confirmation and for typing of strains.[16-18]

As with other bacteria whose ecologic niche is the gastrointestinal tract of mammals, the serotypic diversity of *C. jejuni* is enormous. More than 90 different serotypes based on somatic (O) antigens and 50 different serotypes based on heat-labile (capsular and flagellar) antigens have been identified[3]; phase variation of flagellar antigens occurs. O-antigen variation reflects the presence of differing genetic cassettes that contain the enzymes for O-antigen formation. No group somatic or flagellar antigen has been identified; however, several superficial proteins appear to have broad serotypic specificity, a factor that may aid in the development of a broadly specific vaccine.

C. jejuni cannot long withstand drying or freezing temperatures, which are characteristics that limit its transmission.[19] However, *C. jejuni* survives in milk or other foods or in water kept at 4° C for several weeks. Pasteurization effectively destroys the organism, as does chlorine at concentrations in standard use for water disinfection.

EPIDEMIOLOGY

Campylobacteriosis is a worldwide zoonosis. Campylobacters are commonly found as commensals of the gastrointestinal tract in wild or domesticated cattle, sheep, swine, goats, dogs, cats, rodents, and all varieties of fowl.[2,19] *C. jejuni* has a very varied reservoir, but *Campylobacter coli* and *Campylobacter hyointestinalis* are most commonly isolated

FIGURE 213-1. Fine curved, S-shaped, or spiral, lightly staining gram-negative appearance of *Campylobacter jejuni* in pure culture (×1000).

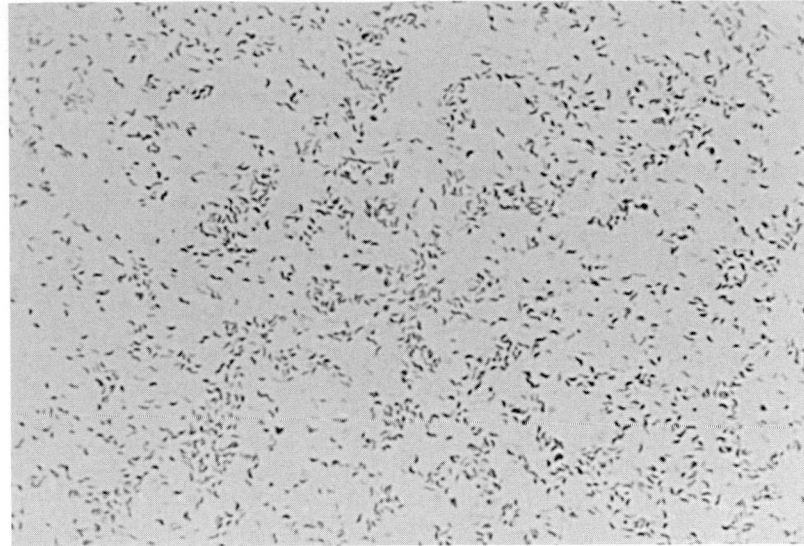

from swine, and *Campylobacter upsaliensis* from dogs.[20] *C. fetus* subsp. *fetus* has been isolated from sheep, cattle, poultry, reptiles, and swine.[2] Primary acquisition of *Campylobacter* species by animals often occurs early in life and may lead to morbidity or mortality, but in most colonized animals, a lifelong carrier state develops. The vast reservoir in animals is probably the ultimate source for most enteric *Campylobacter* infections in humans. Meats originating from infected animals frequently become contaminated with intestinal contents during the slaughtering process.[19] In particular, commercially raised poultry is nearly always colonized with *C. jejuni*, slaughterhouse procedures amplify contamination, and chicken and turkey in supermarkets, ready for consumers to take home, frequently is contaminated.[19,21] Excreta from infected animals may contaminate soil or water. Most infections in humans probably result from consumption of contaminated food and water. Investigations of more than 50 outbreaks indicate that unpasteurized (raw) milk is such a vehicle.[19] Similarly, untreated surface water has been responsible for both endemic and epidemic campylobacteriosis. Backpackers in Wyoming who drank untreated water and developed acute diarrheal illnesses had *Campylobacter* infections three times as commonly as *Giardia* infections.[22] Several large outbreaks have been traced to defects in municipal water systems.[23] Undercooked meats, especially poultry, have been associated with infection.[24] Other vehicles include raw clams, raw or undercooked beef, and unpasteurized cheeses and goat's milk. Nevertheless, consumption of undercooked poultry is estimated to be responsible for 50% to 70% of sporadic *Campylobacter* infections in developed countries. Increases in the isolation of *Campylobacter* spp. reflect both improved recognition and increased consumption of poultry in recent years.

Direct contact with infected animals may result in transmission. Household pets, especially young dogs and cats with diarrhea, have been implicated as vectors for campylobacteriosis.[17,20,25] Because healthy dogs, cats, rodents, and birds may excrete campylobacters and related organisms, it is not surprising that human infections associated with these animals also have been reported. Persons with occupational exposure to cattle, sheep, and other farm animals are at increased risk for infection, and laboratory-acquired infections have been reported.

As with other enteric pathogens, fecal-oral person-to-person transmission of *C. jejuni* has been reported. Persons in contact with the excreta of infected persons who are not feces continent (such as infants) are at risk of infection. Infected school-age children rarely may transmit *Campylobacter* infection. Transmission from infected food handlers who are asymptomatic is at best uncommon. Perinatal transmission from a mother who may not have been symptomatic may be due to exposure in utero, during passage through the birth canal, or during the first days of life.[26] Infection has been associated with blood transfusion from an infected patient.[27] Because of a variety of sexual practices, homosexual men appear to be at increased risk for infection caused by *H. cinaedi, H. fennelliae,* and other "atypical" campylobacters.[28] Human immunodeficiency virus (HIV)–infected patients are at substantially increased risk of infection.[29] The standardization of serotyping methods[30] and the development of molecular methods for identification and typing of *C. jejuni* and related organisms[13,14,16-18,31] should improve our understanding of transmission.

C. jejuni infections occur year-round in the United States and other developed countries but with a sharp peak in summer and early fall. *C. fetus* infections show the same seasonal variation, but the peak is less marked. In tropical countries, the seasonal variation of *C. jejuni* infection appears to be influenced by rainfall. Because of incomplete surveillance, the actual incidence of *Campylobacter* infections in the United States is not known. However, laboratory-based studies in the United States and other developed countries indicate that *C. jejuni* is more commonly isolated from fecal specimens obtained from diarrheal patients than either *Salmonella* or *Shigella*.[32,33] In England, the number of reported *Campylobacter* infections now exceeds those of *Salmonella* and *Shigella* infections combined, and the incidence continues to increase. Based on estimates of the number of *Salmonella* infections, there are probably more than 2 million *Campylobacter* infections annually in the United States. Population-based studies show peak incidence in children under 1 year of age and in persons 15 to 29 years of age[34]; however, cases have been reported in patients of all ages. The incidence in males may be higher. The prevalence of infection in healthy people is very low (less than 1%).

The epidemiology of infection in developing countries is markedly different. *C. jejuni* is often isolated from healthy persons, and the infection is especially common during the first 5 years of life.[35,36] During the first 2 years of life, most children have numerous *Campylobacter* infections, but those occurring early in life frequently are symptomatic, whereas later infections are mostly asymptomatic.[36] The source of these frequent infections has not been defined, but preliminary evidence suggests that human-to-human transmission may be more common than in developed countries. The substantial age-related difference in the infection-to-illness ratios in developed and developing countries appears primarily to be due to differences in age- or exposure-related immunity of the populations rather than to differences in the isolates.[37,38] *C. jejuni* and other campylobacters are important causes for the acute diarrheal illnesses suffered by travelers.[39]

PATHOGENESIS AND PATHOLOGIC CHARACTERISTICS

Not all *Campylobacter* infections produce illness. Although all factors responsible for this phenomenon are not known, three of the most important appear to be the dose of organisms reaching the small intestine, the virulence of the infecting strain, and the specific immunity of the host to the pathogen ingested. Among exposed persons who become ill, the incubation period varies from 1 to 7 days, a characteristic that is probably inversely related to the dose ingested. Most infections occur 2 to 4 days after exposure. In one study, volunteers became ill after ingesting as few as 500 organisms, but with a dose of less than 10^4 organisms, illness was infrequent.[40] *C. jejuni*, like *Salmonella typhimurium*, is susceptible to hydrochloric acid.[41] Taken together, these data suggest that the infectious dose for *C. jejuni* is similar to that for *Salmonella*. Vehicles such as milk, fatty foods, and water that favor passage through the gastric acid barrier may permit some infections to occur at relatively low doses.

C. jejuni multiplies in human bile,[41] a characteristic that aids colonization of the bile-rich upper small intestine early in infection. The sites of tissue injury include the jejunum, ileum, and colon, with similar pathologic features in each. Inspection of affected tissues may reveal a diffuse, bloody, edematous, and exudative enteritis,[42] but pathologic examinations are generally performed on specimens from patients with the most severe cases. Microscopic examination of rectal biopsy specimens has shown a nonspecific colitis with an inflammatory infiltrate of neutrophils, mononuclear cells, and eosinophils in the lamina propria; degeneration, atrophy, loss of mucus, and crypt abscesses in the epithelial glands; and ulceration of the mucosal epithelium.[43,44] Rectal biopsy samples with these nonspecific features have been interpreted as showing acute ulcerative colitis or Crohn's disease. In other cases, the appearance of the rectal biopsy sample has been similar to that of specimens obtained in *Salmonella* or *Shigella* infections. In a series of 124 patients with *C. jejuni* infection, 18 of the most severely ill patients underwent sigmoidoscopic examination or rectal biopsy; 17 of these procedures showed colonic involvement.[45] Some patients have terminal ileitis as well as colitis. Host factors also are clearly important; in volunteers, a single strain produced a wide spectrum of clinical manifestations.[40]

The presence of bacteremia in some patients and the finding of cellular infiltration in biopsy specimens from patients with *Campylobacter* colitis suggest that tissue invasion may be one pathogenetic mechanism. No animal model closely analogous to human infection has been reported except in primates.[31] Experimental challenges both in monkeys[46] and in vitro[47-50] confirm the invasiveness of *C. jejuni*. The process of *C. jejuni* invasion is multifactorial. After invasion, cellular architecture is altered. Microtubule-dependent mechanisms may be important in the organism's ability to invade the intestinal epithelium.[51] The bacteria's flagellae also are important virulence factors because they promote the motility and chemotaxis needed for *C. jejuni* to colonize the intestinal tract.[47,52] In vivo passage favors flagellated cells[53]; intact flagellar synthesis genes are required for maximal *C. jejuni* invasiveness.[54,55] A cytolethal distending toxin may affect cell cycle kinetics.[56] A high-molecular-weight plasmid also enhances the invasive capabilities of *C. jejuni* virulence.[57,58] *C. jejuni* may adhere to epithelial cells,[59] which favors gut colonization. A superficial antigen (PEB1) that appears to be the major adhesin[60] is conserved among *C. jejuni* strains, is a target of the immune response,[61] and may represent a vaccine candidate.[62,63] Chemotaxis[64] and production of fimbriae[65] also are important in virulence.

Campylobacter outer membranes contain lipopolysaccharides (LPSs) with typical endotoxic activity.[66] The structure of the LPS O antigen is highly variable.[30] Many *C. jejuni* O antigens possess sialic acid–containing structures.[67] Their close resemblance to those seen in human gangliosides such as GM_1, GD_{1a}, GD_3, and GT_{1a}, and their presence in strains isolated from patients who developed the Guillain-Barré syndrome (GBS) suggest a role in the pathogenesis of this disorder.[67-69]

Extracellular toxins with cytopathic activities have been found, and classic enterotoxins have also been demonstrated, although generally at low concentrations.[70-72] Two strains lacking detectable enterotoxin production and with low-level in vitro cytotoxin production were found to be fully virulent in volunteers.[40] Infected persons do not develop neutralizing antibodies to these toxins, casting further doubt on their in vivo significance. A protein that distends epithelial cells and is cytolethal is expressed by many *C. jejuni* strains, but its role in pathogenesis has not been fully defined.[56,73]

Patients in developed countries with *Campylobacter* infection excrete the organism in feces for an average of 2 to 3 weeks. By 3 months after infection, convalescent excretion is rare. In developing countries, the period of convalescent excretion is even briefer, probably reflecting high levels of immunity in the population.[37]

Bacteremia sometimes can be detected in patients with *Campylobacter* infections, whether or not they show signs of systemic illness. Most bacteremias reported to the Centers for Disease Control and Prevention (CDC) have been due to *C. fetus* subsp. *fetus*, whereas *C. jejuni* is by far the more common pathogen. One explanation for the apparently greater tendency of *C. fetus* to cause bacteremia is that it is usually resistant, whereas *C. jejuni* is susceptible to the bactericidal activity present in normal human serum.[74] After oral ingestion and intestinal colonization with or without acute diarrheal disease, *C. fetus* bacteremia may occur.[75]

C. fetus is covered with a surface (S)-layer protein that functions as a capsule.[76,77] Virtually all human isolates of *C. fetus* possess an S-layer protein that completely disrupts C3b binding to these organisms.[78] Lack of C3b binding explains both serum and phagocytosis resistance. In a mouse model, after oral inoculation, strains carrying the S-layer protein develop bacteremia, whereas strains without the S-layer protein do not.[79] *C. fetus* also has the ability to change the major S-layer protein expressed. This results in antigenic variation[80] and is facilitated by recombination among several highly homologous genes encoding full-length proteins.[81] The S-layer protein of *C. fetus* is the major virulence factor explaining its extraintestinal spread (Fig. 213-2).

IMMUNITY

As reported in published studies, volunteers rechallenged with the homologous *C. jejuni* organism developed infection but were protected from illness.[40,82] In developing countries, where *C. jejuni* infection is hyperendemic, the decreasing case-to-infection ratio with age suggests acquisition of immunity. Patients infected with campylobacters develop

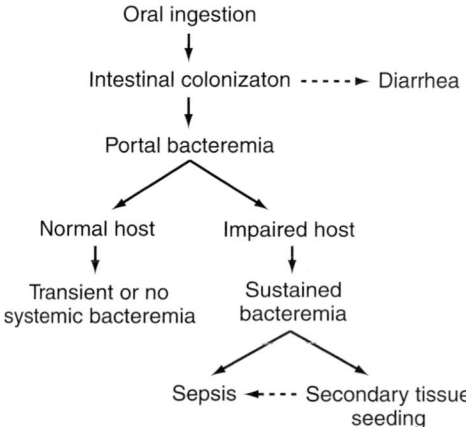

FIGURE 213-2. Pathogenesis of *Campylobacter fetus* infections. *(From Blaser MJ. Campylobacter fetus: Emerging infection and model system for bacterial pathogenesis at mucosal surfaces. Clin Infect Dis. 1998;27:256-258.)*

specific immunoglobulin (Ig)G, IgM, and IgA antibodies in serum[71,82] and IgA antibodies in intestinal secretions.[82]

In developing countries, specific serum IgA levels rise progressively with age, reflecting recurring exposure to *C. jejuni*. In volunteers, increasing levels of specific serum IgA have been correlated with increasing specific intestinal levels as well.[40,82] Supporting the notion that humoral immunity is protective against *C. jejuni* infections have been the numerous reports of severe and recurrent *C. jejuni* infection in patients with congenital or acquired hypogammaglobulinemia.[83,84] In HIV-infected patients as well, failure of *C. jejuni* infection to respond to antimicrobial therapy has been correlated with failure to produce a humoral response to infection.[85] Nevertheless, the markedly increased incidence of *C. jejuni* infection in patients with acquired immunodeficiency syndrome (AIDS)[29] suggests that cell-mediated immunity also is important in preventing and terminating infection.

Despite these exceptions, most patients who become infected with *C. jejuni* were previously healthy and recover rapidly from infection. In contrast, patients with *C. fetus* infections much more frequently have evidence of impaired immunity, including conditions such as chronic alcoholism, liver disease, old age, diabetes mellitus, and malignancies.[86,87] *C. fetus* infections may produce diarrheal illnesses in healthy people or opportunistic infections in debilitated persons.[75]

CLINICAL MANIFESTATIONS

Campylobacter jejuni Infections

The clinical manifestations of infections caused by all of the *Campylobacter* spp. that cause enteric illnesses appear identical; *C. jejuni* infection may be regarded as the prototype.[88] Acute enteritis is the most common presentation of *C. jejuni* infection. Symptoms may last from 1 day to 1 week or longer. Often there is a prodrome with fever, headache, myalgia, and malaise 12 to 24 hours before the onset of intestinal symptoms.[89] In some patients, the constitutional symptoms may coincide with the intestinal phase, or, less often, may follow it. The most common symptoms are diarrhea, malaise, fever, and abdominal pain.[88-91] Diarrhea may range in severity from loose stools to massive watery or grossly bloody stools. In any patient, the entire spectrum of diarrhea may be seen. For most patients, there are 10 or more bowel movements on the worst day of the illness. Abdominal pain is usually cramping in nature and is relieved by defecation; it may be the predominant manifestation of illness. *Campylobacter* enteritis is frequently self-limiting, with a gradual resolution of symptoms over several days; however, illness lasting longer than 1 week occurs in about 10% to 20% of patients seeking medical attention, and relapse may be seen in another 5% to 10% of patients who do not receive treatment.[31,88-90]

Infection also may be manifested as an acute colitis, with symptoms of fever, abdominal cramps, and bloody diarrhea persisting for 1 week or longer.[43,91] Fever may be low grade or consist of daily peaks above 40° C. Initially stools may be watery, but as the illness progresses they may become frankly bloody; tenesmus is a common symptom. In the severest forms patients appear very ill, and toxic megacolon has been reported.[92] Because of the propensity of *Campylobacter* infection to affect young adults and the characteristic clinical presentation, it may be readily confused with ulcerative colitis or Crohn's disease.[43,89] The pathologic findings on rectal biopsy are nonspecific, and the clinical features and radiographic findings also are nondiagnostic. Therefore, the clinician should have a high index of suspicion for *Campylobacter* infection in a patient who presents with this symptom complex. Because of the often fastidious nature of these organisms,[93,94] a single negative culture does not rule out infection, especially if optimal filtration methods are not used for primary isolation of a pathogen.

Occasionally, acute abdominal pain may be the major or only symptom of infection.[88,95] Although any quadrant of the abdomen may be affected, patients most often complain of pain in the right lower quadrant. As with *Yersinia enterocolitica* and *Salmonella enteritidis*, *C. jejuni* may cause pseudoappendicitis.[31,89] In most cases, the re-

moved appendix has shown minimal or no inflammation. Enlarged mesenteric nodes (mesenteric adenitis) and terminal ileitis[31] also may be responsible for symptoms. Diagnosis is often made during the postoperative period, when diarrhea ensues. *Campylobacter* infection occasionally may present solely as a gastrointestinal hemorrhage.[96] Among neonates, *C. jejuni* infection may be manifested as one or more grossly bloody stools and no other symptoms, with findings suggesting intussusception,[97] or with extraintestinal foci.[98] Fever also may be the sole manifestation of *C. jejuni* infection. Temperature elevation may be so severe and persistent that typhoid fever is the initial diagnosis until *C. jejuni* is isolated from stools. Febrile convulsions in young children before the onset of the enteric phase of illness also may occur.[99]

Bacteremia has been noted in less than 1% of patients with *C. jejuni* infection. In part, this low frequency reflects the fact that physicians rarely perceive diarrheal illness as an indication for blood culture, even when fever is present. Nevertheless, bacteremia appears to be more common in infections in persons at the extremes of age.[34,100] Meningitis and endocarditis are rare manifestations of *C. jejuni* infection. In general, three patterns of extraintestinal *C. jejuni* infection have been noted.[101] First, there may be a transient bacteremia in a normal host with acute *Campylobacter* enteritis. The bacteremia may be discovered several days after blood cultures are obtained, by which time the patient usually has completely recovered. The course is benign, and no specific treatment based on the positive blood culture result is usually indicated. Second, there may be a sustained bacteremia or deep focus of infection in a previously normal host; usually the patient has an acute enteritis as well. The *C. jejuni* isolates are generally relatively or absolutely serum resistant.[101] Bacteremia usually has its origin in the intestinal tract inflammation and responds to antimicrobial therapy. Third, sustained bacteremia or deep infection may occur in a compromised host; many such patients do not have an acute enteritis. *C. jejuni* isolates usually are serum sensitive.[101] Antimicrobial therapy, which may need to be prolonged, is required for elimination or suppression of this infection.

C. jejuni may cause septic abortion,[102] but sustained bacteremia in a pregnant patient does not necessarily imply fetal infection or a bad outcome.[101] There have been infrequent reports of *C. jejuni* infections manifesting as acute cholecystitis,[103] pancreatitis,[104,105] and cystitis.[105-107] These manifestations probably reflect local extension rather than hematogenous (metastatic) spread of infection. Persons with immunoglobulin deficiencies often develop prolonged, severe, and recurrent *C. jejuni* infections,[83,84] often with bacteremia and other extraintestinal manifestations such as erysipelas-like skin lesions or osteomyelitis.[108] A reactive arthritis may occur up to several weeks after infection in persons with the HLA-B27 histocompatibility antigens,[109] and prolonged rheumatic symptoms also have been reported. Hepatitis,[110] interstitial nephritis, the hemolytic uremic syndrome, and IgA nephropathy[111] are other reported complications.[31]

GBS is an uncommon consequence of *C. jejuni* infection (estimated at 1 case per 2000 infections) that usually occurs 2 to 3 weeks after the diarrheal illness.[112,113] From 20% to 50% of Guillain-Barré cases follow *C. jejuni* infections, reflecting in part the high incidence of these infections.[112-116] A particular *C. jejuni* clone marked by LPS(O) type 19 is overrepresented among persons who develop GBS.[116-118] O-type 41 also has been implicated, and other sporadic cases may be due to specific *C. jejuni* strains with sialylation of their LPS molecules.[67-69]

Campylobacter fetus Infections

In contrast to *C. jejuni*, *C. fetus* subsp. *fetus* less frequently causes diarrheal illness. As summarized in Table 213-3, the clinical, laboratory, and epidemiologic characteristics of *C. jejuni* infections differ significantly from those of *C. fetus* subsp. *fetus*, which often produce systemic manifestations. *C. fetus* infections may cause intermittent diarrhea or nonspecific abdominal pain without localizing signs. The diarrheal illness may manifest exactly like *C. jejuni* infection and is more common than was suspected several years ago. Clinical mani-

TABLE 213-3 Biologic and Clinical Characteristics of *Campylobacter Jejuni* and *Campylobacter Fetus* Subsp. *Fetus*

Feature	Campylobacter jejuni	Campylobacter fetus subsp. fetus
Epidemiologic Characteristics		
Major reservoir	Avian species, food animals	Cattle and sheep
Affected hosts	Normal hosts; all ages affected; often in clusters of cases	Opportunistic agent in debilitated hosts; clustering rare; healthy hosts may be affected
Laboratory Characteristics		
Range of growth temperatures	32-42° C	25-37° C*
Usual source of isolation	Feces	Blood stream
Clinical Characteristics		
As a cause for diarrheal illness	Common	Uncommon
Clinical manifestations	Acute gastroenteritis, colitis Usually self-limited	Systemic illness with bacteremia, meningitis, vascular infections, abscesses; gastroenteritis
Outcome of infection		May be fatal in debilitated hosts

*Occasionally grows at 42° C.

festations are similar and sequelae uncommon. Nearly all affected patients survive the infections when appropriate antibiotic treatment is given and usually do well without antibiotic treatment. *C. fetus* also may cause a prolonged relapsing illness characterized by fever, chills, and myalgias in which a source of infection cannot be demonstrated.[86,87,119] Occasionally, secondary seeding of an organ will occur, leading to a more complicated infection[119-122] and sometimes to a fulminant, fatal course.

C. fetus infections appear to have a predilection for vascular sites; vascular necrosis occurs in patients with endocarditis and pericarditis resulting from this organism.[123,124] Mycotic aneurysms of the abdominal aorta also occur. Thrombophlebitis may be associated with *C. fetus* bacteremia,[125] but whether it is the primary event or a secondary manifestation of the infection is uncertain. Those patients with a bacteremic illness without localization should be carefully evaluated for the presence of septic thrombophlebitis, because when this condition is treated with appropriate antibiotics, the response is good. Infections during pregnancy primarily have been manifested as upper respiratory symptoms, pneumonitis, fever, and bacteremia. However, four of five *C. fetus*–infected second-trimester patients delivered dead infants despite antibiotic therapy. One patient received antibiotic therapy and delivered a normal term infant. All the mothers survived their infection.[126]

Central nervous system (CNS) infections with *C. fetus* occur in neonates and adults. The prognosis is poor for premature infants, but five of six full-term neonates in one series survived infection. Infection is manifested as a meningoencephalitis with a cerebrospinal fluid polymorphonuclear pleocytosis. Subdural effusion may complicate infection. Meningoencephalitis also is the most common CNS manifestation of *C. fetus* infection in adults.[127] Cerebrovascular accidents, subarachnoid hemorrhages, and brain abscesses also occur. The prognosis is better in adults than in neonates, with a survival rate of approximately 67%, although neurologic sequelae are frequent.[119] *C. fetus* has been shown to cause a variety of other types of localized infections, including septic arthritis, spontaneous bacterial peritonitis, salpingitis, lung abscess, empyema, cellulitis, urinary tract infection, vertebral osteomyelitis, and cholecystitis.[119,128,129] Although most patients with these illnesses recovered with appropriate antibiotics and drainage procedures, the clinical course was frequently prolonged and relapsing. Antibiotic resistance to fluoroquinolones may develop in im-

munocompromised patients who receive monotherapy regimens.[130] Nevertheless, in other patients, self-limiting bacteremia without any sequelae has been observed. Hypogammaglobulinemic patients may have persistent bacteremia and local symptoms unless given chronic suppressive therapy with antibiotics.

Infection Caused by Other Enteric *Campylobacter* Species

The clinical manifestations of infection caused by other enteric campylobacters overlap substantially with those of *C. jejuni* infection.[94,131,132] On average, *Campylobacter coli* may produce more mild disease.[37] In one series of homosexual men, *H. cinaedi* and *H. fennelliae* infections were more often asymptomatic than were those caused by *C. jejuni*.[133] Among immunocompromised patients, especially those with AIDS, bacteremia from the "atypical" campylobacters appears relatively commonly.[134-136] As with *C. fetus*, *C. upsaliensis* mostly causes diarrheal diseases in previously normal persons,[20,137] and bacteremia in compromised hosts; most strains of the latter species are serum resistant.[138] Other extraintestinal manifestations such as breast abscess have been observed.[139] Cellulitis may occur in compromised hosts infected with any of a variety of these "atypical" species.[136] *C. hyointestinalis*, which resembles *C. fetus* in its biochemical characteristics,[140] also may cause bacteremia in compromised hosts. *A. butzleri* may cause abdominal cramps without diarrheal illness.[141] *Helicobacter (Flexispira) rappini* has recently been reported to cause bacteremia in compromised hosts.[142]

C. fetus subsp. *venerealis*, which had never been considered a human pathogen, was reported to have been isolated from stools from two homosexual men in Australia, and from two women with bacterial vaginosis. *C. fetus* subsp. *fetus* has been isolated from two other patients with vaginosis. *Campylobacter sputorum* subsp. *sputorum*, which is indigenous to the human mouth and intestine, has now been isolated from perianal boils and lung abscesses. *C. sputorum* subsp. *bubulus*, a commensal of sheep and cattle, has been isolated from boils and skin abscesses from humans.

DIAGNOSIS

Clinical diagnosis of enteric campylobacteriosis may be established by demonstration of the organisms by direct examination of feces, or by isolation of the organisms. The use of serologic methods for diagnosis is at present a research tool only.

Direct Examination of Feces

Examination of diarrheal fecal specimens by darkfield or phase-contrast microscopy within 2 hours of passage can permit a rapid presumptive diagnosis of *Campylobacter* enteritis if the characteristic darting motility of the *Campylobacter* organism is seen.[91,143] This test is particularly useful in the acute phase of the illness. Similarly, the presence of vibrio forms in Gram-stained stool specimens is a very specific diagnostic feature, although the sensitivity of this finding is 50% to 75% (Fig. 213-3).[144] Direct microscopy is also of value for detecting red blood cells and neutrophils, which are present in the feces of 75% of patients with *Campylobacter* enteritis.[40,89] Use of PCR techniques for direct detection of organisms has been successful in research studies but has not yet been applied to the clinical setting.

Bacteriologic Studies

Confirmation of the diagnosis of *C. jejuni* infection is based on a positive result on stool culture or, occasionally, blood culture. Because blood cultures are not often performed in the evaluation of patients presenting with diarrheal symptoms, the frequency of bacteremia is not known. Results with use of radiometric blood culture detection systems may be falsely negative for some *Campylobacter* and related species using standard procedures.[15] Campylobacters cannot be isolated from fecal specimens unless microaerobic incubation conditions and selective techniques that reduce the growth of competing microorganisms are used.[3,30] *C. fetus* is usually isolated from blood cultures 4 to 14 days after the specimen has been obtained.[87] On occasion,

FIGURE 213-3. Gram stain of fecal specimen from a patient with *Campylobacter* enteritis. *Arrows* point to typical gram-negative fine, small, spiral, and *Vibrio*-like organisms (×1024).

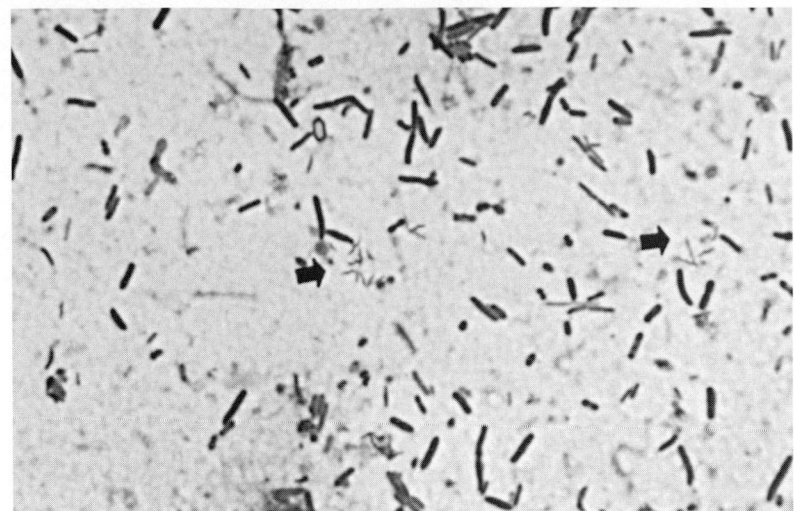

C. fetus may be isolated from feces of patients with either diarrheal or systemic infections.[75] If *C. fetus* or another of the atypical species is suspected, incubation at 37° C and use of media without cephalosporins are necessary. The use of filtration techniques will eliminate such difficulties.

THERAPY

Fluid and electrolyte replacement constitutes the cornerstone of treatment of diarrheal illnesses. Patients with *Campylobacter* infections who are severely dehydrated should undergo rapid volume expansion using intravenous solutions of electrolytes in water. For patients with less serious volume depletion, oral rehydration using glucose and electrolyte solutions is indicated. Persons infected with *C. jejuni* who are ill enough to seek medical attention and from whom a fecal culture is obtained represent only a subset of all those infected. Nevertheless, even among these patients, less than half are candidates for specific antimicrobial therapy.[88,89] Studies in children with dysentery caused by *C. jejuni* showed a clear benefit from early treatment with erythromycin.[145] In contrast, other studies in which initiation of treatment was delayed for several days until *C. jejuni* was isolated did not show a therapeutic effect.[146] Therefore, rapid presumptive diagnosis of *Campylobacter* infection by means of direct visualization of the organisms in stool is clinically relevant. On the basis of anecdotal reports,[43,88-90] wide clinical experience, and controlled trials,[145] treatment with antibiotics seems prudent in those patients with high fever, bloody diarrhea, or more than eight stools per day; in patients whose symptoms have not lessened or are worsening at the time the diagnosis is made; or in those in whom symptoms have persisted for more than 1 week.

In vitro, *C. jejuni* is susceptible to a wide variety of antimicrobial agents, including erythromycin, the tetracyclines, the aminoglycosides, chloramphenicol, the quinolones, the nitrofurans, and clindamycin.[147-151] Because of ease of administration, lack of serious toxicity, and apparent efficacy, erythromycin has been the agent of choice.[91,152,153] The recommended dosage for adults is 250 mg PO four times daily for 5 to 7 days; the recommended dosage for children is 30 to 50 mg/kg/day in divided doses for the same period. Therapy with extended-spectrum macrolides such as clarithromycin or azithromycin should be equally effective. In a trial involving U.S. military personnel in Thailand, azithromycin was effective in shortening duration of illness and *Campylobacter* excretion,[154] but macrolide resistance, based on mutations in 23S ribosomal DNA, is increasing.[155] An alternative agent is ciprofloxacin, 500 mg PO twice daily for 5 to 7 days, which has activity across a broad spectrum of bacteria causing diarrheal illness as well as against campylobacters. However, owing to the widespread usage of quinolones in both humans and food animals, resistance of *Campylobacter* to these agents is increasing in many parts of the world, including the United States.[155-158] This phenomenon now limits the utility of quinolones for empirical treatment of acute diarrheal illness.[159] Another alternative agent is tetracycline, except in children under 9 years of age; in such patients, clindamycin may be used. Most *C. jejuni* and *C. coli* isolates are not susceptible to most cephalosporins or penicillin, and these agents should not be used. However, amoxicillin or ticarcillin plus clavulanic acid (but not sulbactam or tazobactam) appears to be universally effective.[160] Susceptibility to sulfonamides and metronidazole is variable. Unlike in *Salmonella* infections, treatment with antimicrobial agents does not prolong carriage of *C. jejuni;* on the contrary, erythromycin eliminates carriage within 72 hours in most patients.[146]

H. cinaedi and those *Campylobacter* strains acquired in developing countries, especially *C. coli,* are more likely to be resistant to erythromycin and tetracycline.[161] In such cases, when treatment is indicated, alternative agents should be used until susceptibility is known. Use of an antimotility agent appears to prolong duration of symptoms and has been associated with fatalities.[162] The necessity for treating septic or bacteremic episodes with agents other than erythromycin has not been established. For those patients who appear very ill, treatment with gentamicin, imipenem, cefotaxime, or chloramphenicol is indicated, but susceptibility tests should be performed. In hypogammaglobulinemic patients with recurrent *C. jejuni* bacteremias, fresh-frozen plasma with appropriate antibiotics may eradicate the infection[108]; oral immune globulin therapy may have some value as well for recurrent diarrheal illness.[163] Systemic *C. fetus* infections should be treated parenterally, but erythromycin should not be used.[164,165] Occasionally, systemic infections diagnosed only retrospectively by positive results on blood culture resolve after empirical oral therapy. In these cases, follow-up cultures are recommended; if results are no longer positive, further treatment is not required. If necessary, ampicillin treatment has been associated with good results. Patients with endovascular infections caused by *C. fetus* require at least 4 weeks of therapy, and gentamicin or ampicillin are probably the agents of choice.[165] Treatment with imipenem or meropenem constitutes another alternative. Infections of the CNS should be treated with ampicillin, imipenem, or chloramphenicol for 2 to 3 weeks. Patients with other serious infections should also receive parenteral gentamicin or another aminoglycoside, ampicillin, or imipenem for at least 2 weeks. Because antibodies to *C. fetus* are not usually present in serum from normal persons, intravenous immune globulin is not helpful for this infection in immunodeficient patients.[122] For *C. fetus*–infected patients with diarrheal illness or other less severe infections, treatment need not be as intense or as prolonged.

PROGNOSIS

The vast majority of patients recover fully after *C. jejuni* infections, either spontaneously or after appropriate antimicrobial therapy. The "reactive arthritis," or Reiter's syndrome, occurring in HLA-B27–positive persons closely resembles that seen after *Yersinia, Salmonella,* or *Shigella* infections and should not be considered a specific consequence of *C. jejuni* infection. However, rheumatologic symptoms may persist for several months, or possibly for years in a few affected persons.[166] GBS is an uncommon sequela of *Campylobacter* enteritis, but because of their high prevalence, *Campylobacter* infections are the most important recognized antecedent of this disorder.[112,113] Occasional deaths after *C. jejuni* infections have been reported in developed countries[162]; in most cases, the victim was an elderly person or a compromised host. However, fatalities in previously healthy young adults may occur, probably as a result of volume depletion. Some of the deaths that occur in Guillain-Barré patients can be attributed to the consequences of *C. jejuni* infection. Because in the developing countries most symptomatic *Campylobacter* infections occur in children under 2 years of age[36] and frequently produce a dysenteric picture, it is reasonable to conclude that *C. jejuni* infection may play a role in the dehydration and malnutrition that often accompany infantile diarrhea in these geographic areas. The outcome of infections caused by newly discovered *Campylobacter*-like organisms[6,142] remains to be determined.

C. fetus infection may be lethal to patients with chronic compensated diseases such as cirrhosis or diabetes mellitus or may hasten the demise of seriously compromised patients. For compromised hosts with systemic *C. fetus* infections, prognosis is most dependent on the rapidity with which appropriate antimicrobial therapy is begun. Previously healthy persons infected with *C. fetus* usually survive the illness without permanent sequelae.

Because *C. jejuni* infections are "accidentally" acquired by humans, and because there is evidence for the natural development of immunity among persons in developing countries, the goal of producing a vaccine is probably achievable.

REFERENCES

1. Parkhill J, Wren BW, Mungall K, et al. The genome sequence of the food-borne pathogen *Campylobacter jejuni* reveals hypervariable sequences. Nature. 2000;403:665-668.
2. Smibert RM. Genus *Campylobacter.* In: Krieg NR, Holt HG, eds. Bergey's Manual of Systematic Bacteriology, v. 1. Baltimore: Williams & Wilkins; 1984:111-118.
3. Nachamkin I. *Campylobacter, Helicobacter,* and related spiral bacteria. In: Manual of Clinical Microbiology. 6th ed. Washington, DC: American Society for Microbiology; 1996:402-409.
4. Vandamme P, Vancanneyt M, Pot B, et al. Polyphasic taxonomic study of the emended genus *Arcobacter* with *Arcobacter butzleri* comb. nov. and *Arcobacter skirrowi* sp. nov., an aerotolerant bacterium isolated from veterinary specimens. Int J Syst Bacteriol. 1992;42:344-356.
5. Fennell CL, Totten PA, Quinn TC, et al. Characterization of *Campylobacter*-like organisms isolated from homosexual men. J Infect Dis. 1984;149:58-66.
6. Burnens AP, Stanley J, Schaad UB, et al. Novel *Campylobacter*-like organism resembling *Helicobacter fennelliae* isolated from a boy with gastroenteritis and from dogs. J Clin Microbiol. 1993;31:1916-1917.
7. Foley JE, Solnick JV, LaPointe J-M, et al. Identification of a novel enteric *Helicobacter* species in a kitten with severe diarrhea. J Clin Microbiol. 1998;36:908-912.
8. Husman M, Gries C, Jehnichen P, et al. *Helicobacter* sp. strain *Mainz* isolated from an AIDS patient with septic arthritis: Case report and nonradioactive analysis of 16S rRNA sequence. J Clin Microbiol. 1994;32:3037-3039.
9. Bolton GJ, Hutchinson DN, Coates D. Blood-free selective medium for isolation of *Campylobacter jejuni* from feces. J Clin Microbiol. 1984;19:169-171.
10. Steele TW, McDermott JN. Technical note: The use of membrane filters applied directly to the surface of agar plates for the isolation of *Campylobacter jejuni* from feces. Pathology. 1984;16:263-265.
11. Lastovica AJ, LeRoux E. Efficient isolation of *Campylobacter upsaliensis* from stools. J Clin Microbiol. 2001;39:4222-4223.
12. Burnens AP, Nicolet J. Three supplementary diagnostic tests for *Campylobacter* species and related organisms. J Clin Microbiol. 1993;31:708-710.
13. van Camp G, Fierens H, Vandamme P, et al. Identification of enteropathogenic *Campylobacter* species by oligonucleotide probes and polymerase chain reaction based on 16S rRNA genes. Syst Appl Microbiol. 1993;16:30-36.
14. Ng L-K, Kingombe CIB, Yan W, et al. Specific detection and confirmation of *Campylobacter jejuni* by DNA hybridization and PCR. Appl Environ Microbiol. 1997;63:4558-4563.
15. Wang WLL, Blaser MJ. Detection of pathogenic *Campylobacter* species in blood culture systems. J Clin Microbiol. 1986;23:709.
16. Giesendorf BAJ, Quint WGV, Henkens MHC, et al. Rapid and sensitive detection of *Campylobacter* spp. by using the polymerase chain reaction. Appl Environ Microbiol. 1992;58:3804-3808.
17. Giesendorf BAJ, van Belkum A, Koeken A, et al. Development of species-specific DNA probes for *Campylobacter jejuni, Campylobacter coli,* and *Campylobacter lari* by polymerase chain reaction fingerprinting. J Clin Microbiol. 1993;31:1541-1546.
18. Oyofo BA, Thornton SA, Burr DH, et al. Specific detection of *Campylobacter jejuni* and *Campylobacter coli* by using polymerase chain reaction. J Clin Microbiol. 1992;30:2613-2619.
19. Blaser MJ, Taylor DN, Feldman RA. Epidemiology of *Campylobacter jejuni* infections. Epidemiol Rev. 1983;5:157.
20. Labarca JA, Sturgen J, Borenstein L, et al. *Campylobacter upsaliensis:* Another pathogen for consideration in the United Status. Clin Infect Dis. 2002;34:e59-e60.
21. Atabay HI, Corry JEL. The prevalence of campylobacters and arcobacters in broiler chickens. J Appl Microbiol. 1997;83:619-626.
22. Taylor DN, McDermott KT, Little JR, et al. *Campylobacter* enteritis associated with drinking untreated water in back-country areas of the Rocky Mountains. Ann Intern Med. 1983;99:38.
23. Mentzing L-O. Waterborne outbreaks of *Campylobacter* enteritis in central Sweden. Lancet. 1981;2:352.
24. Deming MS, Tauxe RV, Blake PA, et al. *Campylobacter* enteritis at a university: Transmission from eating chicken and from cats. Am J Epidemiol. 1987;126:526-534.
25. Skirrow MB. *Campylobacter* enteritis in dogs and cats: A "new" zoonosis. Vet Res Commun. 1981;5:13.
26. Vesikari T, Huttunen L, Maki R. Perinatal *Campylobacter fetus* ss. *jejuni* enteritis. Acta Paediatr Scand. 1981;70:261.
27. Pepersack F, Prigogyne T, Butzler JP, et al. *Campylobacter jejuni* posttransfusional septicemia. Lancet. 1979;2:911.
28. Totten PA, Fennell CL, Tenover FC, et al. *Campylobacter cinaedi* (sp. nov.) and *Campylobacter fennelliae* (sp. nov.): Two new *Campylobacter* species associated with enteric disease in homosexual men. J Infect Dis. 1985;151:131.
29. Sorvillo FJ, Lieb LE, Waterman SH. Incidence of campylobacteriosis among patients with AIDS in Los Angeles County. J Acquir Immune Defic Syndr. 1991;4:598-602.
30. Penner JL. The genus *Campylobacter:* A decade of progress. Clin Microbiol Rev. 1988;1:157-172.
31. Nachamkin I, Blaser MJ, eds. *Campylobacter jejuni.* 2nd ed. Washington, DC: American Society for Microbiology; 2000.
32. Blaser MJ, Wells JF, Feldman RA, et al. *Campylobacter* enteritis in the United States: A multicenter study. Ann Intern Med. 1983;98:360.
33. Mead PS, Slutsker L, Dietz V, et al. Food-related illness and death in the United States. Emerg Infect Dis. 1999;5:607-625.
34. Tauxe RV. Epidemiology of *Campylobacter jejuni* infections in the United States and other industrialized nations. In: Nachamkin I, Blaser MJ, Tompkins LS, eds. *Campylobacter jejuni:* Current Status and Future Trends. Washington, DC: American Society for Microbiology; 1992:9-19.
35. Glass RI, Stoll BJ, Huq MI, et al. Epidemiologic and clinical features of endemic *Campylobacter jejuni* infection in Bangladesh. J Infect Dis. 1983;148:292.
36. Calva JJ, Ruiz-Pallacios GM, Lopez-Vidal AB, et al. Cohort study of intestinal infection with *Campylobacter* in Mexican children. Lancet. 1988;1:503-506.
37. Taylor DN, Echeverria P, Pitarangsi C, et al. The influence of immunity and strain characteristics on the epidemiology of campylobacteriosis. J Clin Microbiol. 1988;26:863.
38. Taylor DN, Perlman D, Echeverria PD, et al. *Campylobacter* immunity and quantitative excretion rates in Thai children. J Infect Dis. 1993;168:754-758.
39. Speelman P, Struelens MJ, Sanyal SC, et al. Detection of *Campylobacter jejuni* and other potential pathogens in traveler's diarrhea in Bangladesh. Scand J Gastroenterol. 1983;84(18 Suppl):19-23.
40. Black RE, Levine MM, Clements ML, et al. Experimental *Campylobacter jejuni* infection in humans. J Infect Dis. 1988;157:472.
41. Blaser MJ, Hardesty HL, Powers B, et al. Survival of *Campylobacter fetus* subsp. *jejuni* in biological milieus. J Clin Microbiol. 1980;11:309.
42. King EO. The laboratory recognition of *Vibrio fetus* and a closely related vibrio isolated from cases of human vibriosis. Ann N Y Acad Sci. 1962;90:700.
43. Lambert ME, Schofield PF, Ironside AG, et al. *Campylobacter* colitis. Br Med J. 1979;1:857.
44. Van Spreeuwel JP, Duursma GC, Meijer CJLM, et al. *Campylobacter* colitis: Histologic, immunohistochemical and ultrastructural findings. Gut. 1985;26:945-951.
45. Blaser MJ, Reller LB, Luechtefeld NW, et al. *Campylobacter* enteritis in Denver. West J Med. 1982;136:287.
46. Russell RG, O'Donnoghue M, Blake DC Jr, et al. Early colonic damage and invasion of *Campylobacter jejuni* in experimentally challenged infant *Macaca mulatta.* J Infect Dis. 1993;168:210-215.
47. Grant CCR, Konkel ME, Cieplak W, et al. Role of flagella in adherence, internalization, and translocation of *Campylobacter jejuni* in nonpolarized and polarized epithelial cell cultures. Infect Immun. 1993;61:1764-1771.
48. Babakhani FK, Joens LA. Primary swine intestinal cells as a model for studying *Campylobacter jejuni* invasiveness. Infect Immun 1993;61:2723-2726.
49. Konkel ME, Hays SF, Joens LA, Cieplak W. Characteristics of the internalization and intracellular survival of *Campylobacter jejuni* in human epithelial cell cultures. Microb Pathog. 1992;13:357-370.
50. Hu L, Kopecko J. *Campylobacter jejuni* 81-176 associates with microtubules and dynein during invasion of human intestinal cells. Infect Immun. 1999;67:4171-4182.

51. Kopecko DJ, Hu L, Zaal KJM. *Campylobacter jejuni*—microtubule-dependent invasion. Trends Microbiol. 2001;9:389-396.
52. Yao R, Burr DH, Doig P, et al. Isolation of motile and non-motile insertional mutants of *Campylobacter jejuni*: the role of motility in adherence and invasion of eukaryotic cells. Mol Microbiol. 1994;14:883-893.
53. Caldwell MB, Guerry P, Lee EC, et al. Reversible expression of flagella in *Campylobacter jejuni*. Infect Immun. 1985;50:941-943.
54. Rivera-Amill V, Konkel ME. Secretion of *Campylobacter jejuni* Cia proteins is contact dependent. In: Paul PS, Francis DH, eds. Mechanisms in the Pathogenesis of Enteric Diseases 2. New York: Plenum; 1999:225-229.
55. Konkel ME, Kim BJ, Rivera-Amill V, Garvis SG. Bacterial secreted proteins are required for the internalization of *Campylobacter jejuni* into cultured mammalian cells. Mol Microbiol. 1999;32:691-701.
56. Whitehouse CA, Balbo PB, Pesci EC, et al. *Campylobacter jejuni* cytolethal distending toxin causes a G_2-phase cell cycle block. Infect Immun. 1998;66:1934-1940.
57. Bacon DJ, Alm RA, Burr DH, et al. Involvement of a plasmid in virulence of *Campylobacter jejuni* 81-176. Infect Immun. 2000;68:4384-4390.
58. Bacon DJ, Alm RA, Hu L, et al. DNA sequence and mutational analyses of the pVir plasmid of *Campylobacter jejuni* 81-176. Infect Immun. 2002;70:6242-6250.
59. Fauchere JL, Rosenau A, Veron M, et al. Association with HeLa cells of *Campylobacter jejuni* and *Campylobacter coli* isolated from human feces. Infect Immun. 1986;54:283-287.
60. Kervella M, Pages J-M, Pei Z, et al. Isolation and characterization of two *Campylobacter* glycine-extracted proteins that bind to HeLa cell membranes. Infect Immun. 1993;61:3440-3448.
61. Pei Z, Ellison RT III, Blaser MJ. Identification, purification and characterization of major antigenic proteins of *Campylobacter jejuni*. J Biol Chem. 1991;266:16363-16369.
62. Pei Z, Blaser MJ. PEB1, the major cell-binding factor of *Campylobacter jejuni*, is a homolog of the binding component in gram negative nutrient transport systems. J Biol Chem. 1993;267:18717-18725.
63. Pei Z, Burucoa C, Grignon B, et al. Mutation in the *peb1A* locus of *Campylobacter jejuni* reduces interactions with epithelial cells and intestinal colonization of mice. Infect Immun. 1998;66:938-943.
64. Yao R, Burr DH, Guerry P. Che Y-mediated modulation of *Campylobacter jejuni* virulence. Mol Microbiol. 1997;23:1021-1031.
65. Doig P, Yao R, Burt DH, et al. An environmentally regulated pilus-like appendage involved in *Campylobacter* pathogenesis. Mol Microbiol. 1996;20:885-894.
66. Pérez-Pérez GI, Blaser MJ. Lipopolysaccharide characteristics of pathogenic campylobacters. Infect Immun. 1985;47:353-359.
67. Aspinall GO, Fujimoto S, McDonald AG, et al. Lipopolysaccharides from *Campylobacter jejuni* associated with Guillain-Barré syndrome patients mimic human gangliosides in structure. Infect Immun. 1994;62:2122-2125.
68. Ang CW, De Klerk MA, Endtz HP, et al. Guillain-Barre syndrome- and Miller Fisher syndrome-associated *Campylobacter jejuni* lipopolysaccharides induce anti-GM1 and GQ1b antibodies in rabbits. Infect Immun. 2001;69:2462-2469.
69. Goodyear CS, O'Hanlon GM, Plomp JJ, et al. Monoclonal antibodies raised against Guillain-Barre syndrome-associated *Campylobacter jejuni* lipopolysaccharides react with neuronal gangliosides and paralyze muscle-nerve preparations. J Clin Invest. 1999;104:697-708.
70. Johnson WM, Lior H. Cytotoxic and cytotonic factors produced by *Campylobacter jejuni*, *Campylobacter coli*, and *Campylobacter laridis*. J Clin Microbiol. 1986;24:275-281.
71. Walker RI, Caldwell MB, Lee EC, et al. Pathophysiology of *Campylobacter* enteritis. Microbiol Rev. 1985;50:81-94.
72. Wassenaar T. Toxin production by *Campylobacter* spp. Rev Clin Microbiol. 1997;10:466-476.
73. Pickett CL, Pesci EC, Cottle DL, et al. Prevalence of cytolethal distending toxin production in *Campylobacter jejuni* and relatedness of *Campylobacter* sp *cdtB* genes. Infect Immun. 1996;64:2070-2078.
74. Blaser MJ, Smith PF, Kohler PA. Susceptibility of *Campylobacter* isolates to the bactericidal activity in human serum. J Infect Dis. 1985;151:227.
75. Blaser MJ. *Campylobacter fetus*: Emerging infection and model system for bacterial pathogenesis at mucosal surfaces. Clin Infect Dis. 1998;27:256-258.
76. Blaser MJ, Smith PF, Hopkins JA, et al. Pathogenesis of *Campylobacter fetus* infections. Serum resistance associated with high molecular weight surface proteins. J Infect Dis. 1987;155:696.
77. Dworkin J, Blaser MJ. Molecular mechanisms of *Campylobacter fetus* surface layer protein expression. Mol Microbiol. 1997;26:433-440.
78. Blaser MJ, Smith PF, Repine JE, et al. Pathogenesis of *Campylobacter fetus* infections: Failure of C3b to bind explains serum and phagocytosis resistance. J Clin Invest. 1988;81:1434-1444.
79. Pei Z, Blaser MJ. Pathogenesis of *Campylobacter fetus* infections: Role of surface array proteins in virulence in a mouse model. J Clin Invest. 1990;85:1036-1043.
80. Wang E, Garcia MM, Blake MS, et al. Shift in S-layer protein expression responsible for antigenic variation in *Campylobacter fetus*. J Bacteriol. 1993;175:4979-4984.
81. Tummuru MKR, Blaser MJ. Rearrangement of *sapA* homologs with conserved and variable regions in *Campylobacter fetus*. Proc Natl Acad Sci U S A. 1993;90:7265-7269.
82. Black RF, Perlman D, Clements ML, et al. Human volunteer studies with *C. jejuni*. In: Nachamkin I, Blaser MJ, Tompkins LS, eds. *Campylobacter fetus*: Current Status and Future Trends. Washington, DC: American Society for Microbiology; 1992:207-215.
83. Johnson RJ, Wang SP, Shelton WR, et al. Persistent *Campylobacter jejuni* infection in an immunocompromised host. Ann Intern Med. 1984;100:832-834.
84. Melamed I, Bujanover Y, Igra YS, et al. *Campylobacter* enteritis in normal and immunodeficient children. Am J Dis Child. 1983;137:752-753.
85. Perlman DM, Ampel NM, Schiffman RB, et al. Persistent *Campylobacter jejuni* infections in patients infected with the human immunodeficiency virus: Association with abnormal serological response to *C. jejuni* and emergence of erythromycin resistance during therapy. Ann Intern Med. 1988;108:540-546.
86. Bokkenheuser V. *Vibrio fetus* infection in man. I. Ten new cases and some epidemiologic observations. Am J Epidemiol. 1970;91:400.
87. Guerrant RL, Lahita RG, Winn EC Jr, et al. Campylobacteriosis in man: Pathogenic mechanisms and review of 91 bloodstream infections. Am J Med. 1978;65:484.
88. Skirrow MB. Campylobacter. Lancet. 1990;336:921-923.
89. Blaser MJ, Berkowitz ID, LaForce FM, et al. *Campylobacter* enteritis; clinical and epidemiologic features. Ann Intern Med. 1979;91:179.
90. Skirrow MB. *Campylobacter* enteritis: A "new" disease. Br Med J. 1977;2:9.
91. Karmali MA, Fleming PC. *Campylobacter* enteritis in children. J Pediatr. 1979;94:527.
92. McKinley MJ, Taylor M, Sangree MH. Toxic megacolon with campylobacter colitis. Conn Med. 1980;44:496.
93. Tee W, Anderson BN, Ross BC, et al. Atypical campylobacters associated with gastroenteritis. J Clin Microbiol. 1987;25:1248-1252.
94. Steele TW, Sangster N, Lanser JA. DNA relatedness and biochemical features of *Campylobacter* spp. isolated in Central and South Australia. J Clin Microbiol. 1985;22:71-74.
95. Drake AA, Gilchrist MJR, Washington JA II, et al. Diarrhea due to *Campylobacter fetus* subspecies *jejuni*: A clinical review of 73 cases. Mayo Clin Proc. 1981;56:414.
96. Michalak DM, Perrault J, Gilchrist MJ, et al. *Campylobacter fetus* ss. *jejuni*: A cause of massive lower gastrointestinal hemorrhage. Gastroenterology. 1980;79:742.
97. Anders BJ, Lauer BA, Paisley JW. *Campylobacter* gastroenteritis in neonates. Am J Dis Child. 1981;135:900.
98. Goossens H, Henocque G, Kremp L, et al. Nosocomial outbreak of *Campylobacter jejuni* meningitis in newborn infants. Lancet. 1986;2:146-149.
99. Wright EP, Seager J. Convulsions associated with *Campylobacter* enteritis. BMJ. 1980;281:454.
100. Orlicek SL, Welch DF, Kuhls TL. Septicemia and meningitis caused by *Helicobacter cinaedi* in a neonate. J Clin Microbiol. 1993;31:569-571.
101. Blaser MJ, Perez GP, Smith PF, et al. Extraintestinal *Campylobacter jejuni* and *Campylobacter coli* infections: Host factors and strain characteristics. J Infect Dis. 1986;153:552.
102. Gilbert GL, Davoren RA, Cole ME, et al. Midtrimester abortion associated with septicaemia caused by *Campylobacter jejuni*. Med J Aust. 1981;1:585.
103. Mertens A, DeSmet M. *Campylobacter* cholecystitis. Lancet. 1979;1:1092.
104. Gallagher P, Chadwick P, Jones DM, et al. Acute pancreatitis associated with *Campylobacter* infection. Br J Surg. 1981;68:383.
105. Ezpeleta C, Rojo de Ursua P, Obregon F, et al. Acute pancreatitis associated with *Campylobacter jejuni* bacteremia. Clin Infect Dis. 1992;15:1050.
106. Davies JS, Penfold JB. *Campylobacter* urinary infection. Lancet. 1979;1:1091.
107. Feder HM, Rasoulpour M, Rodriquez AJ. *Campylobacter* urinary tract infection: Value of the urine gram stain. JAMA. 1986;256:2389.
108. Kersten PJSM, Endtz HP, Meis JFGM, et al. Erysipelas-like skin lesions associated with *Campylobacter jejuni* septicemia in patients with hypogammaglobulinemia. Eur J Clin Microbiol Infect Dis. 1992;11:842-847.
109. Kosunen TU, Kauranen O, Martio J, et al. Reactive arthritis after *Campylobacter jejuni* enteritis in patients with HLA-B27. Lancet. 1980;1:1312.
110. Humphrey KS. *Campylobacter* infection and hepatocellular injury. Lancet. 1993;341:49.
111. Carter JE, Cimolai N. IgA nephropathy associated with *Campylobacter jejuni* enteritis. Nephron. 1991;58:101-102.
112. Mishu B, Blaser MJ. The role of *Campylobacter jejuni* infection in the initiation of Guillain-Barré syndrome. Clin Infect Dis. 1993;17:104-108.
113. Rees JH, Soudain SE, Gregory NA, Hughes RAN. *Campylobacter jejuni* infection and Guillain-Barré syndrome. N Engl J Med. 1995;333:1374-1379.
114. Kaldor J, Speed BR. Guillain-Barré syndrome and *Campylobacter jejuni*: A serological study. Br Med J (Clin Res Ed). 1984;288:1867-1870.
115. Mishu B, Ilyas AA, Koski CL, et al. Serologic evidence of *Campylobacter jejuni* infection preceding Guillain-Barré syndrome. Ann Intern Med. 1993;118:947-953.
116. Kuroki S, Saida T, Nukina M, et al. *Campylobacter jejuni* strains from patients with Guillain-Barré syndrome belong mostly to Penner serogroup 19 and contain β-*N*-acetylglucosamine residues. Ann Neurol. 1993;33:243-247.
117. Fujimoto S, Allos BM, Misawa N, et al. Restriction fragment length polymorphism analysis and random amplified polymorphic DNA analysis of *Campylobacter jejuni* strains isolated from patients with Guillain-Barré syndrome. J Infect Dis. 1997;176:1105-1108.
118. Allos BM, Lippy FT, Carlsen A, et al. *Campylobacter jejuni* strains from patients with Guillain-Barré syndrome. Emerg Infect Dis. 1998;4:263-268.
119. Franklin B, Ulmer DD. Human infection with *Vibrio fetus*. West J Med. 1974;120:200.
120. Collins HS, Blevins A, Baxter E. Protracted bacteremia and meningitis due to *Vibrio fetus*. Arch Intern Med. 1964;113:361.
121. Park CH, McDonald F, Twohig AM, et al. Septicemia and gastroenteritis due to *Vibrio fetus*. South Med J. 1973;66:531.
122. Neuzil KM, Wang E, Haas D, Blaser MJ. Persistence of *Campylobacter fetus* bacteremia associated with absence of opsonizing antibodies. J Clin Microbiol. 1994;32:1718-1720.
123. Loeb H, Bettag JL, Yantz NK, et al. *Vibrio fetus* endocarditis. Am Heart J. 1966;71:381.

124. Killiam HA, Crowder JG, White AC, et al. Pericarditis due to *Vibrio fetus.* Am J Cardiol. 1966;17:723.
125. Vesely D, MacIntyre S, Ratzan KR. Bilateral deep brachial vein thrombophlebitis due to *Vibrio fetus.* Arch Intern Med. 1975;135:994.
126. Eden AH. Perinatal mortality caused by *Vibrio fetus:* Review and analysis. J Pediatr. 1966;68:297.
127. Gunderson CH, Sack GE. Neurology of *Vibrio fetus.* Neurology (NY). 1971;21:307.
128. Kilo C, Hagemann PO, Maryi J. Septic arthritis and bacteremia due to *Vibrio fetus.* Am J Med. 1965;38:962.
129. Lawrence R, Nibbe AF, Levin S. Lung abscess secondary to *Vibrio fetus* malabsorption syndrome and acquired agammaglobulinemia. Chest. 1971;60:191.
130. Meier PA, Dooley DP, Jorgensen JH, et al. Development of quinolone-resistant *Campylobacter fetus* in human immunodeficiency virus-infected patients. J Infect Dis. 1998;177:951-954.
131. Benjamin JS, Leaper S, Owen RJ, et al. Description of *Campylobacter laridis,* a new species comprising the nalidixic acid resistant thermophilic *Campylobacter* (NARTC group). Curr Microbiol. 1983;8:231-238.
132. Simor AE, Wilcox L. Enteritis associated with *Campylobacter laridis.* J Clin Microbiol. 1987;25:10-12.
133. Quinn TC, Goodell SE, Fennell C, et al. Infections with *Campylobacter jejuni* and *Campylobacter*-like organisms in homosexual men. Ann Intern Med. 1984;101:187-192.
134. Kemper CA, Mickelsen P, Morton A, et al. *Helicobacter (Campylobacter) fennelliae*–like organisms as an important but occult cause of bacteremia in a patient with AIDS. J Infect. 1993;26:97-101.
135. Fleisch F, Burnens A, Weber R, Zbinden R. *Helicobacter* species strain *Mainz* isolated from cultures of blood from two patients with AIDS. Clin Infect Dis. 1998;26:526-527.
136. Kiehlbauch JA, Tauxe RV, Baker CN, Wachsmuth IK. *Helicobacter cinaedi*–associated bacteremia and cellulitis in immunocompromised patients. Ann Intern Med. 1994;121:90-93.
137. Goosens H, Pot B, Vlaes L, et al. Characterization and description of "*Campylobacter upsaliensis*" isolated from human feces. J Clin Microbiol. 1990;28:1039-1046.
138. Patton CM, Shaffer N, Edmonds P et al. Human disease associated with "*Campylobacter upsaliensis*" (catalase-negative or weakly positive *Campylobacter* species) in the United States. J Clin Microbiol. 1989;27:66-73.
139. Gaudreau C, Lamothe F. *Campylobacter upsaliensis* isolated from a breast abscess. J Clin Microbiol. 1992;30:1354-1356.
140. Edmonds P, Patton CM, Griffin PM, et al. *Campylobacter hyointestinalis* associated with human gastrointestinal disease in the United States. J Clin Microbiol. 1987;25:685-691.
141. Vandamme P, Pugina P, Benzi G, et al. Outbreak of recurrent abdominal cramps associated with *Arcobacter butzleri* in an Italian school. J Clin Microbiol. 1992;30:2335-2337.
142. Sorlin P, vanDamme P, Nortier J, et al. Recurrent "*Flexispira rappini*" bacteremia in an adult patient undergoing hemodialysis: Case report. J Clin Microbiol. 1999;37:1319-1323.
143. Paisley JW, Mirrett S, Lauer BA, et al. Darkfield microscopy of human feces for the presumptive diagnosis of *Campylobacter* enteritis. J Clin Microbiol. 1982;15:61.
144. Sazie ESM, Titus AE. Rapid diagnosis of *Campylobacter* enteritis. Ann Intern Med. 1982;96:62.
145. Salazar-Lindo E, Sack RB, Chea-Woo E, et al. Early treatment with erythromycin of *Campylobacter jejuni*–associated dysentery in children. J Pediatr. 1986;109:355.
146. Anders BJ, Lauer BA, Paisley JW, et al. Double-blind placebo controlled trial of erythromycin for treatment of *Campylobacter* enteritis. Lancet. 1982;1:131.
147. Vanhoof R, Vanderlinden MP, Dierickx R, et al. Susceptibility of *Campylobacter fetus* subsp. *jejuni* to twenty-nine antimicrobial agents. Antimicrob Agents Chemother. 1978;14:553.
148. Walder M. Susceptibility of *Campylobacter fetus* subsp. *jejuni* to twenty antimicrobial agents. Antimicrob Agents Chemother. 1979;16:37.
149. Vanhoof R, Gordts B, Dierickx R, et al. Bacteriostatic and bactericidal activities of 24 antimicrobial agents against *Campylobacter fetus* subsp. *jejuni.* Antimicrob Agents Chemother. 1980;18:118.
150. Huang MB, Baker CN, Banerjee S, et al. Accuracy of the E test for determining antimicrobial susceptibilities of staphylococci, enterococci, *Campylobacter jejuni,* and gram-negative bacteria resistant to antimicrobial agents. J Clin Microbiol. 1992;30:3243-3248.
151. Sjögren E, Kaijser B, Werner M. Antimicrobial susceptibilities of *Campylobacter jejuni* and *Campylobacter coli* isolated in Sweden: A 10-year follow-up report. Antimicrob Agents Chemother. 1992;36:2847-2849.
152. Blaser MJ, Reller LB. *Campylobacter* enteritis. N Engl J Med. 1981;305:1444.
153. Skirrow MB, Blaser MJ. *Campylobacter jejuni.* In: Blaser MJ, Smith PD, Ravdin J, et al, eds. Infections of the Gastrointestinal Tract. 2nd ed. Philadelphia: Lippincott-Raven; 2002:825-848.
154. Kuschner RA, Trofa AF, Thomas RJ, et al. Use of azithromycin for the treatment of *Campylobacter* enteritis in travelers to Thailand, an area where ciprofloxacin resistance is prevalent. Clin Infect Dis 1995;21:536-541.
155. Engberg J, Aarestrup FM, Taylor DE, et al. Quinolone and macrolide resistance in *Campylobacter jejuni* and *C. coli:* resistance mechanisms and trends in human isolates. Emerg Infect Dis. 2001;7:24-34.
156. Segreti J, Gootz TD, Goodman LJ, et al. High-level quinolone resistance in clinical isolates of *Campylobacter jejuni.* J Infect Dis. 1992;165:667-670.
157. Reina J, Borrell N, Serra A. Emergence of resistance to erythromycin and fluoroquinolone in thermotolerant *Campylobacter* strains isolated from feces 1987-1991. Eur J Clin Microbiol Infect Dis. 1992;11:1163-1166.
158. Smith KE, Besser JM, Hedberg CW, et al. Quinolone-resistant *Campylobacter jejuni* infections in Minnesota, 1992-1998. N Engl J Med. 1999;340:1525-1532.
159. Wistrom J, Jertborn M, Ekwall E, et al. Empiric treatment of acute diarrheal disease with norfloxacin: A randomized, placebo-controlled study. Ann Intern Med. 1992;117:202-208.
160. Lachance N, Gaudreau C, Lamothe F, et al. Susceptibilities of β-lactamase–positive and –negative strains of *Campylobacter coli* to β-lactam agents. Antimicrob Agents Chemother. 1993;37:1174-1176.
161. Taylor DN, Blaser MJ, Echeverria P, et al. Erythromycin-resistant *Campylobacter* infections in Thailand. Antimicrob Agents Chemother. 1987;31:438-442.
162. Smith GS, Blaser MJ. Fatalities associated with *Campylobacter jejuni* infections. JAMA. 1985;253:2873.
163. Hammarström V, Smith CIE, Hammarström L. Oral immunoglobulin treatment in *Campylobacter jejuni* enteritis. Lancet. 1993;341:1036.
164. Francioli P, Herzstein J, Grob J-P, et al. *Campylobacter fetus* subspecies *fetus* bacteremia. Arch Intern Med. 1985;145:289-292.
165. Tremblay C, Gaudreau C, Lorange M. Epidemiology and antimicrobial susceptibilities of 111 *Campylobacter fetus* subsp. *fetus* strains isolated in Quebec, Canada from 1983 to 2000. J Clin Microbiol. 2003;41:463-466.
166. Bremell T, Bjelle A, Svedhem A. Rheumatic symptoms following an attack of campylobacter enteritis: A five year follow up. Ann Rheum Dis. 1991;50:934-948.

CHAPTER **214**

Helicobacter pylori and Other Gastric *Helicobacter* Species

MARTIN J. BLASER

Helicobacter pylori (formerly known as *Campylobacter pylori* or *pyloridis*) was first isolated from humans in 1982.[1] This highly motile, curved, gram-negative rod lives within the mucus layer overlying the gastric and occasionally the duodenal or esophageal mucosal epithelium.[2] *H. pylori* is commonly found in the human stomach; essentially all persons colonized with *H. pylori* have a cellular infiltrate in the lamina propria of the gastric antrum and fundus.[3] Of special significance is that *H. pylori* is present in most persons with "idiopathic" peptic ulcer disease. The presence of *H. pylori* increases the risk of peptic ulcer disease[4] and gastric cancer,[5,6] but may diminish the risk of esophageal reflux and its consequences.[7] With the development of effective therapies to eradicate *H. pylori,* physicians are faced with the challenge of determining which patients will benefit from therapy and which may be harmed. This view of the role of *H. pylori* in human disease represents a major departure from the previous decade's assessment of gastroduodenal pathophysiology. Other *Helicobacter* species and related organisms are increasingly being recognized in clinical materials; however, their role in disease is largely uncertain.

MICROBIOLOGY

H. pylori organisms are small (0.5 to 1.0 μm in width and 2.5 to 4.0 μm in length), curved, microaerophilic gram-negative rods.[8,9] Because they closely resemble members of the genus *Campylobacter,* they were initially considered to belong to that genus. However, multiple genotypic and phenotypic characteristics are different from those of campylobacters, and a new genus, *Helicobacter,* was established.[9] Other newly recognized organisms include *Helicobacter mustelae* in ferrets,[9,10] *Helicobacter felis* in dogs and cats,[10] *Helicobacter muridarum* in mice, *Helicobacter nemestrinae* in nonhuman primates, and *Helicobacter acinonyx* in cheetahs.[11] Essentially every mammal studied to date has gastric colonization with one or more *Helicobacter* species. These appear largely species specific and indicate that the mammalian stomach is a major niche for these organisms.

TABLE 214-1 Biochemical Characteristics of *Helicobacter pylori* and Related Bacteria

Characteristic	Helicobacter pylori	Helicobacter mustelae	Helicobacter felis	Campylobacter jejuni
Urease	+	+	+	−
Catalase	+	+	+	+
Oxidase	+	+	+	+
H₂S production	−	−	−	+
Guanosine plus cytosine content	35–38	36	42.5	33–36
Hippurate hydrolysis	−	−	−	+
Nitrate reduction	−	+	+	+
Resistance to nalidixic acid (30-μg disk)	+	−	+	−
Cephalothin (30-μg disk)	−	+	−	+
Growth at 42° C	−	+	+	+
Growth at 37° C	+	+	+	+
Growth at 25° C	−	−	−	−

Data from references 9-12.

Helicobacter heilmannii is a gastric spirochete of humans and is considered in a separate section of this chapter. *Helicobacter fennelliae* and *Helicobacter cinaedi* are intestinal organisms causing diarrheal illnesses; because the clinical features of these infections resemble those of *Campylobacter* spp., they are discussed in Chapter 213. Based on the recent and intense interest of microbiologists in gastric bacteria, it is likely that the genus *Helicobacter* will continue to expand. Nevertheless, *H. pylori* is the most important human pathogen and may be considered the prototype for these organisms. *Helicobacter* species (such as *H. hepaticus, H. bilis,* and *H. rappini*) have also been identified in the colon and biliary tract of rodents, and there is human carriage as well.[11-13] Preliminary evidence suggests that they might colonize the diseased human biliary tract,[14,15] but whether they participate in the pathophysiologic process is uncertain.[16] They have caused chronic bacteremia and indolent cellulitis in patients with X-linked hypogammaglobulinemia and common variable immunodeficiency. Thus there are both gastric and intestinal *Helicobacter* species in humans, but the role, if any, of the intestinal species in human mucosal disease has not been defined.

H. pylori cells are highly motile, with a rapid corkscrew motion, and have multiple polar sheathed flagella.[9] Although these cells are classically curved or spiral in fresh cultures, spherical (coccoid) forms are present in older cultures. The major biochemical properties of *H. pylori* and several related bacteria are shown in Table 214-1. The outstanding biochemical characteristic of helicobacters is their high production of urease. *H. pylori* urease is a hexadimer consisting of 61- and 28-kDa subunits, both of which are essential for activity.[17] Regulation of urease is complex, and at least eight other genes are currently recognized as necessary for full activity.[18] All clinical isolates are urease positive, but urease-negative strains have been derived in the laboratory.

The nucleotide sequence of the chromosome from two *H. pylori* strains (26695 and J99) has been determined.[19,20] Comparison of the two sequences has opened new avenues for the study of *H. pylori* microbiology. The two strains share most but not all genes, and even conserved genes show polymorphisms, strain-specific genes that include restriction-modification (R-M) enzymes,[21] and others concerned with cell surface structures.[22,23] *H. pylori* has few two-component regulatory proteins, but frameshifts are common, within open reading frames encoding certain *H. pylori* proteins. This suggests that *H. pylori* may use mutation to control phenotype, with the host selecting for the "most fit" organism within a particular environmental niche.[24,25]

Although *H. pylori* is highly homogeneous in the biochemical characteristics used in clinical microbiology, including urease, oxidase, and catalase positivity, wide variation is noted at a genetic level.[25-27] Humans may be simultaneously colonized with more than one strain of *H. pylori*.[28-30] Plasmids are present in most *H. pylori* isolates; they vary in size and mostly are cryptic at present. *H. pylori* strains are naturally competent, that is, able to take up heterologous DNA; studies of individual *H. pylori* isolates and of populations of strains indicate that recombination is an important characteristic.[27,30,31] Through point mutation and intergenomic and intragenomic recombination, *H. pylori* are among the most varied of all species in the human biosphere.[32-34] The strain-specific R-M systems[21] diminish recombination and may permit different strains to simultaneously colonize a host.[35]

The most important dichotomy among *H. pylori* strains is the presence of the *cag* pathogenicity island, a 35- to 40-kilobase chromosomal region encoding *cagA* and a number of type IV secretion system genes.[36-38] Both *cagA*⁺ and *cagA*⁻ strains are present in *H. pylori* populations in all parts of the world,[39] which suggests that the acquisition of this region by *H. pylori* is ancient. It now is known that the type IV secretion system injects its substrate, the CagA protein, into host epithelial cells.[40,41] The 3′ region of *cagA* contains DNA repeats flanking sites that encode tyrosine phosphorylation domains. By intragenomic recombination, *H. pylori* populations include individual cells with 0, 1, 2, or more domains in its CagA product.[42] Once injected into the epithelium, Src-kinases phosphorylate these tyrosine residues,[43] and the phospho-CagA interacts with SHP-2[44] and other regulatory molecules that affect MAP kinases and the actin cytoskeleton; these pathways affect cell shape and cycle events, and cytokine production.[45-47] Thus CagA is an important *H. pylori* molecule that signals the host. The *cag* island is metastable, and isolates in individual patients may vary in the presence of the island, specific genes or regions, or subgenic sequences,[48,49] as in the case of the 3′ region of *cagA*.[42] This instability creates a population of variants that can interact with the host in a myriad of ways. Although important in their own right, the cag polymorphisms are indicative of similar phenomena at other *H. pylori* loci.[50] The *cag* status of an *H. pylori* strain is relevant to the risk of a number of clinical outcomes (see below).

Another heterogeneous locus affects *vacA*, a conserved gene that encodes a secreted protein ("vacuolating cytotoxin") that interacts with epithelial cells.[51] Two parts of *vacA* have major polymorphisms—the *s* region (with alleles s1a, s1b, s1c, and s2) and the *m* region (with alleles m1, m2a, and m2b).[52,53] Because s1 genotypes are strongly linked to *cag* positivity, many of the same clinical associations with *cag* are also present.[54] Effects of the *vacA* product on pore formation[55,56] affect immune function.[57,58] It now is clear that *vacA* is an immunosuppressing molecule, analogous to FK-506, which downregulates T-cell activity.[59] Both *cagA* and *vacA* are human-specific adaptations that favor persistent colonization.

EPIDEMIOLOGY

H. pylori has been isolated from persons in all parts of the world[60,61] (Fig. 214-1). Similar organisms have been isolated from primates, but other animal sources for *H. pylori* have not been identified, nor have reservoirs been found in food, soil, or water. It now appears likely that humans are the major, if not sole reservoir for *H. pylori*. Genetic loci with phylogeographic affinities indicate that *H.* pylori has been present in humans for at least tens of thousands of years, if not longer; the current geographic distribution of *H.* pylori alleles reflects ancient migrations of human populations.[61,62] These data support the notion that

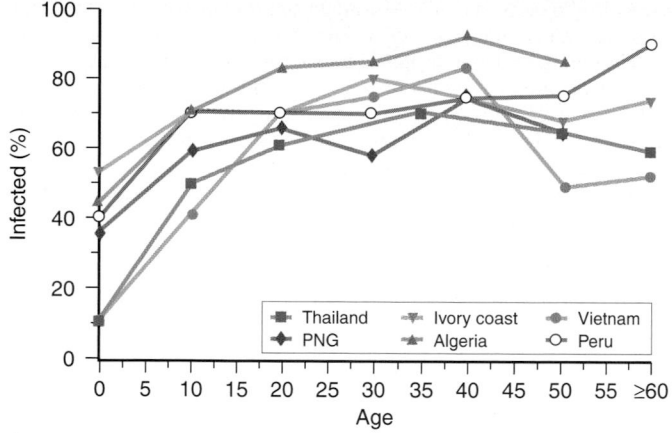

A

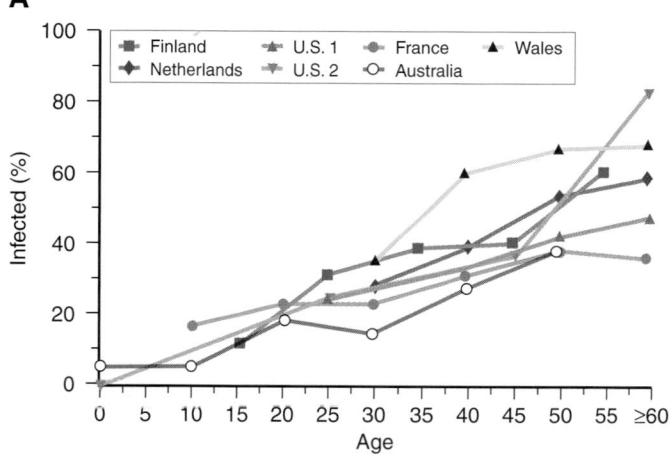

B

FIGURE 214-1. Seroprevalence of *Helicobacter pylori* colonization in populations in developing countries (**A**) and in developed countries (**B**). *H. pylori* is acquired earlier and is more common at all ages in developing countries than in developed countries. *(From Taylor DN, Blaser MJ. The epidemiology of Helicobacter pylori infections. Epidemiol Rev. 1991;13:42-59.)*

H. pylori are indigenous to humans, as their relatives are to other mammals, but that they are disappearing as a result of modernization.[63,64] On occasion, transmission occurs from person to person via improperly cleaned endoscopes.[65]

The high prevalence and incidence of colonization among persons in settings where sanitary conditions are suboptimal, including institutions for the mentally retarded, at orphanages, and in developing countries, suggests that fecal-oral transmission occurs.[60,66] *H. pylori* has occasionally been isolated from feces, especially from children.[67] *H. pylori* has been isolated from dental plaque,[28] and DNA products may be detected in saliva by polymerase chain reaction, which raises the possibility of oral-oral transmission as well. However, studies of persons attending clinics for either sexually transmitted diseases or infertility indicate that sexual transmission does not occur very frequently, if at all.[68] The relative contribution of fecal-oral or oral-oral transmission of *H. pylori* is not known. *H. pylori* infection clusters in families,[69] and the presence of a colonized child is highly associated with large family size and older siblings.[70,71]

The prevalence of *H. pylori* colonization is chiefly related to age[66,72] and geographic location. Males and females have essentially equal rates of colonization (slight male predominance). In developing countries, by age 10, 70% carry *H. pylori,* and by age 20, carriage is nearly universal. In the United States, among non-Hispanic whites little colonization occurs during childhood, and rates gradually in-

crease during adulthood and reach a prevalence of 50% among persons older than 60 years.[73] Among blacks and Hispanics, *H. pylori* is acquired earlier in life on average, and a higher prevalence is seen at all ages.[74-76] The annual incidence of infection has ranged from 0.5% among epidemiologists in the United States to 7.4% among persons at an institution for the mentally retarded in Australia.[77] In most populations, *H. pylori* appears to be mainly acquired during childhood,[60,78] but not in the first year of life.[79] The incidence of *H. pylori* has been progressively declining in the United States and other developed countries,[77,80] probably as a result of smaller family sizes, decreased crowding, and improved sanitation.[63,81,82] Thus the age-related increase in prevalence reflects both a birth cohort phenomenon (with persons born earlier having higher acquisition rates in childhood) and continuing exposure and low-level new colonization into adulthood. The birth cohort effect predominates. Being an immigrant and of lower socioeconomic status are risk factors for *H. pylori* presence.[72,74,76]

PATHOLOGY AND PATHOGENESIS

H. pylori is able to survive and multiply in the gastric environment, which is hostile to the growth of most bacteria.[24] When intraluminal acidity diminishes as a result of gastric atrophy, *H. pylori* is no longer able to colonize, possibly because of competing organisms. Outstanding *H. pylori* characteristics that permit gastric colonization include microaerophilism for survival within the mucus gel; spiral shape and flagella for motility within this viscous layer; and urease activity, which generates ammonium ions that buffer gastric acidity.[83] Numerous adaptations permit survival of *H. pylori* in the acidic milieu of the stomach.[84-88] Although most organisms appear to be free living in the mucus layer, smaller numbers appear to be adherent to the mucosal epithelial cells and form "adherence pedestals" resembling those produced by enteropathogenic *Escherichia coli*[89]; several important adhesins have been identified.[90-92]

H. pylori overlies only gastric-type but not intestinal-type epithelial cells. Affected gastric epithelial cells may be in the gastric antrum or fundus[93] or may be ectopic in the duodenum or in the esophagus.[3,94,95] In contrast, *H. pylori* does not colonize intestinal epithelium, even when present in the stomach.[3] The gastric tissue underneath *H. pylori* colonization virtually always has a cellular infiltrate. The lamina propria most commonly contains mononuclear cells, including lymphocytes, monocytes, and plasma cells. Neutrophils and, to a lesser extent, eosinophils may be present in the lamina propria and in the epithelium. The epithelial glands have a more complex architecture and less mucus than when *H. pylori* is absent.[3,96] In children, a follicular lymphoid pattern is common. The evidence is overwhelming that the presence of *H. pylori* induces these changes and the bacterium is not just a secondary colonizer.

The mechanisms of tissue injury are not clearly established, and both bacterial and host factors may be determinants of outcome.[97-101] *H. pylori* does not appear to invade tissues, except as an incidental finding. Thus the lesions are likely to reflect a response to extracellular products or to contact from the organism. Ammonia, produced by urease and by deaminases, is known to be toxic to eukaryotic cells and may potentiate neutrophil-induced mucosal injury.[102] Both the CagA and VacA proteins are important bacterial signaling molecules[103,104] (see above), and the host mounts antibody responses to both.[105,106] Strains from patients with ulcers produce higher levels of VacA in vitro than do strains from patients without ulcers.[51,52,107] Urease may be shed by *H. pylori* cells, has been observed in affected tissues, and is a chemoattractant and activator of host phagocytic cells.[108,109]

Bacterial lipopolysaccharide usually has proinflammatory activities, but *H. pylori* lipopolysaccharide has remarkably little.[110] *H. pylori* lipopolysaccharide may express the Lewis[x], Lewis[y], neither, or both of these antigens.[22,23,111] This observation is significant because these antigens are present on gastric epithelial cells and there is evidence that the host Lewis phenotype selects for the particular Lewis expression of the *H. pylori* population.[112] The presence of *H. pylori* overlying the gastric mucosa activates epithelial cells to produce proinflammatory cytokines[113-116] and activates mononuclear and polymorphonuclear cells to produce cytokines, superoxide, tumor necrosis factor-α, and other proinflammatory molecules.[109,117,118] Because *H. pylori* can persist in the stomach for many decades, these proinflammatory activities must be downregulated to permit this universally stable colonization.[24,119] Humans are polymorphic in the genetic loci involved in regulating proinflammatory cytokine production. Proinflammatory alleles regulating interleukin (IL)-1β and IL-10 affect risk of gastric cancer in *H. pylori*–positive persons.[120-122] Virtually all patients with duodenal ulceration are colonized by strains possessing *cagA* (and thus the *cag* pathogenicity island).[123] Thus *cagA*, the first gene described to not be conserved among all *H. pylori* strains, is highly associated with both peptic ulcer disease and gastric cancer.[6,61] In the Orient, most *H. pylori* strains are *cagA*+.

Persons colonized with *H. pylori* have different gastric secretory physiology than do those who are not colonized. Colonized persons on average have higher gastrin levels, which are reduced by eradication of the organism.[124,125] The mechanism for increased gastrin production appears to be related to low gastric somatostatin levels,[126,127] which may reflect cytokine production in the colonized antrum.[119,128] Increased gastrin may contribute to the increase in parietal cell mass observed in many patients with duodenal ulceration. In contrast, *H. pylori* products may directly affect parietal cells,[129] which may diminish acid production. That *H. pylori* involves gastric tissues concerned with both acid production (fundus) and its regulation (antrum) may in part be responsible for the multiplicity of potential outcomes of its colonization.[95,119,130] Differences among colonized hosts in cell-mediated immunity and cytokine responses to *H. pylori* are other possible determinants of outcome variability.[131-134] Findings similar to those observed in humans develop in nonhuman primates colonized with *H. pylori*.[135,136] The development of experimental *H. pylori* infections in conventional rodents has allowed new avenues for exploring host-microbe interactions.[137-140]

CLINICAL FEATURES OF *HELICOBACTER PYLORI* COLONIZATION

Although *H. pylori* is commonly isolated from the human stomach, colonization is associated with certain types of upper gastrointestinal pathology, appears to protect against other lesions, and is neutral for still others (Table 214-2). From a clinical standpoint, the major consequences of *H. pylori* colonization are as follows.

Acute Acquisition

Natural, volunteer, or accidental *H. pylori* acquisition may cause an acute upper gastrointestinal illness with nausea and upper abdominal pain.[65,155,156] Vomiting, burping, and fever may also be present. Symptoms last from 3 to 14 days, with most illnesses persisting less than 1 week. A diagnosis of "food poisoning" may be made in persons seeking medical attention. For many individuals, the acquisition of *H. pylori* is clinically silent.[156] Most data suggesting symptomatic acquisition relate to adults, but worldwide, most acquisition actually occurs in children; the relative proportion of symptomatic and asymptomatic acute acquisition at any age is not known. In the weeks after acquisition, intense gastritis develops; hypochlorhydria ensues and may persist for up to 1 year. In children, there is a transient increase in serum pepsinogen I levels.[79] One adult volunteer who ingested *H. pylori* appeared to have had an acute self-limited infection[155]; the frequency of this phenomenon is not known.

Persistent Colonization

It now is clear that, after acquisition, *H. pylori* persists for years, if not decades, in most persons[156,157] (Fig. 214-2). Tissue and serologic responses to colonization develop in essentially all colonized persons.[71] The acute *H. pylori*–induced upper gastrointestinal symptoms do not return in most persons; most with persistent *H. pylori* colonization are asymptomatic. However, studies of patients with nonulcer dyspepsia indicate that *H. pylori* may be slightly more common in cases than in age-matched controls[158] and that *H. pylori* colonization may be one of the causes of this common but poorly defined and probably heterogeneous group of disorders. Supporting this hypothesis are the results of some studies indicating that some patients with nonulcer dyspepsia who are colonized with *H. pylori* show better responses to antimicrobial therapy than to placebo,[159] an effect not seen in patients with nonulcer dyspepsia who do not have *H. pylori* colonization.[160] However, in other studies, no difference between *H. pylori* treatment and placebo was found.[161,162] In total, *H. pylori* is unlikely to be responsible for any more than 5-10% of cases of nonulcer dyspepsia and possibly for far fewer. Even if such an association exists, no markers are available that would indicate those patients with nonulcer dyspepsia in whom a real effect occurs. Better definition of nonulcer dyspepsia and ascertainment of both *H. pylori* and host genotypes in individual patients should permit elucidation of the question of whether *H. pylori* persistence is associated with symptoms in particular patients in the absence of ulceration or neoplasia.

Duodenal Ulceration

In the absence of medication-associated ulceration, more than 90% of patients with duodenal ulceration carry *H. pylori*,[144] an occurrence that is significantly more common than in age-matched controls.[143] Conversely, duodenal ulceration in the absence of aspirin or nonsteroidal anti-inflammatory drug (NSAID) use or the Zollinger-Ellison syndrome usually is associated with *H. pylori* colonization. *H. pylori* may colonize the duodenum but only overlies metaplastic islands of gastric-type epithelium (gastric metaplasia).[3,146] The occurrence of *H. pylori* colonization and gastric metaplasia is highly associated with active duodenitis, a precursor lesion to ulceration,[163] and the presence of *H. pylori* in the duodenum is associated with a markedly increased risk of duodenal ulceration.[146] Prior *H. pylori* colonization is associated with a threefold to fourfold increased risk of development of either

TABLE 214-2 Association of *Helicobacter pylori* with Common Pathologic Lesions of the Upper Gastrointestinal Tract

Lesion	Association with H. pylori
Chronic diffuse superficial gastritis	Nearly always associated[3,72]
Type A (pernicious anemia) gastritis	Negative association[141,143]
NSAID gastropathy	Negative or no association[142]
Acute erosive gastritis (alcohol, aspirin, etc.)	No association[3]
Gastric ulceration	Commonly observed in patients who are not ingesting NSAIDs or aspirin[4,143,144,168]
Duodenal ulceration	Usually associated with "idiopathic" lesions (non–drug induced, non–Zollinger-Ellison syndrome)[4,145,146,168]
Gastric adenocarcinoma	Positively associated with (noncardia) cancers of the body and antrum[86-88,6,7,95,147-149]
Gastric lymphoma	Strongly associated with MALT-type B-cell lymphomas[150,151]
Gastroesophageal reflux disease	Presence of *cag*+ strains has protective association[152,153]
Barrett's esophagus	May colonize distal-most gastric epithelium in patients with gastric colonization.[3] Presence of *cag*+ strains has protective association[154]
Adenocarcinoma of the esophagus	Presence of *cag*+ strains has protective association[95,154]
Non-ulcer dyspepsia	Little or no association[158-162]

MALT, mucosa-associated lymphoid tumor; NSAID, nonsteroidal anti-inflammatory drug.

FIGURE 214-2. Association of *Helicobacter pylori* colonization and disease states. After *H. pylori* acquisition, virtually all persons develop persistent colonization that lasts for life. Colonization induces tissue responses termed "chronic gastritis." This process affects gastric physiology, including glandular structure, acid secretion, and antigen processing, which in turn affect disease risk. Colonization with *H. pylori* increases the risk for certain diseases (duodenal ulcer, gastric ulcer, noncardia gastric adenocarcinoma, and B-cell lymphomas) but appears to decrease the risk for gastroesophageal reflux disease and its complications, including Barrett's esophagus, and adenocarcinoma of the esophagus or gastric cardia.

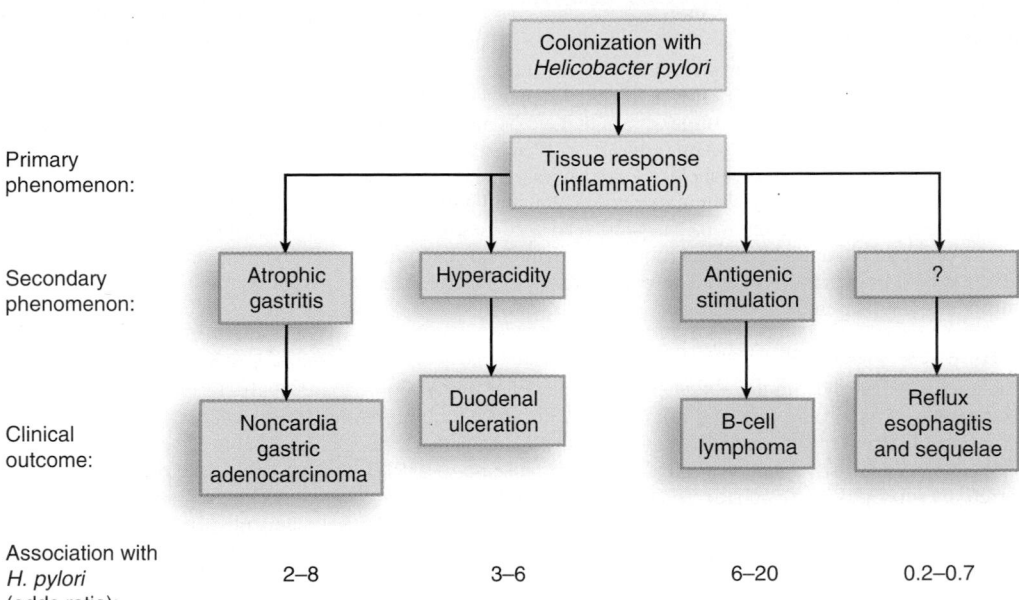

gastric or duodenal ulceration,[144] and that risk is enhanced with *cagA*⁺ strains.[4] In total, a significant body of evidence associating *H. pylori* colonization with "idiopathic" duodenal ulceration has accumulated. A causative role of *H. pylori* in ulcer disease is unproved; none of the experimental human studies have shown progression to ulceration, and why peptic ulcer disease has a remitting and relapsing course in the face of persistent colonization has never been resolved.[63] However, a large number of treatment studies using antimicrobial agents have helped define the natural history of ulcer disease. First, the use of antimicrobial agents (in the absence of acid-suppressive therapy) can heal duodenal ulcers at a rate similar to that observed with acid-suppressive therapy alone.[164,165] Second, after ulcer healing, eradication of *H. pylori* is associated with significantly lower recurrence rates than if the organism remains present.[164,165] When antimicrobial therapy that eradicates *H. pylori* is added to short-term acid-suppressive treatment, long-term ulcer relapse rates are markedly reduced,[166,167] although not completely eliminated.

Altogether, these findings implicate *H. pylori* as playing a role in ulcer pathogenesis and demonstrate that antimicrobial therapy rather than long-term acid-suppressive therapy is indicated for most patients.[168] However, recent studies have provided evidence that, after *H. pylori* eradication, the incidence of reflux esophagitis doubled in comparison to failed eradication.[169] Thus removal of *H. pylori* from the stomach of patients with duodenal ulceration has both benefits and costs. As evidence becomes available, physicians will need to optimize criteria for treatment to optimize the therapeutic-to-toxic ratio.

Gastric Ulceration

A smaller (50% to 80%) proportion of patients with benign gastric ulcers than with duodenal ulceration are colonized by *H. pylori*. The major reason is that a much higher proportion of gastric ulcers are due to NSAID or aspirin use. When such use is excluded, most of the remaining patients with benign gastric ulcers are colonized with *H. pylori*, which is significantly more common than in age-matched controls.[4,143,144] The results of treatment of gastric ulceration with antimicrobial agents parallel the results of treatment of duodenal ulceration.[170]

Gastric Carcinoma

Because *H. pylori* colonization induces a tissue response (termed "chronic gastritis") and because "chronic gastritis" is well known as a risk factor for the development of gastric carcinoma,[171] a role of this organism in carcinogenesis has been advanced.[95] The decreasing incidence of gastric carcinoma in developed countries is consistent with the later age and decreasing frequency of acquiring *H. pylori* as industrialization has proceeded.[172,173] The epidemiologic characteristics of *H. pylori* colonization, including increasing prevalence at an older age, higher prevalence in blacks, Hispanics, and Asians, association with lower socioeconomic status, and early-life crowding, are all similar to the characteristics associated with gastric cancer.[59] In addition, the development of intestinal metaplasia and atrophic gastritis, two pathologic entities that are risk factors for gastric cancer, is associated with *H. pylori*.[174,175] Thus a direct role of this organism in gastric cancer is biologically plausible, and countries with high *H. pylori* prevalence rates have high gastric cancer rates.[176,177] Prospective studies of gastric cancer conducted in Hawaii, California, and England[147-149] and several retrospective and prospective studies each indicate that *H. pylori* is a risk factor for gastric cancer.[95] This association involves adenocarcinoma of the antrum and body of the stomach of both the intestinal and diffuse histologic types.[7,147-149] Odds ratios range from about 2.7 to 6.0, and the risk of gastric cancer attributable to *H. pylori* infection is about 60% to 80%.[148,149,177] The presumed mechanism for adenocarcinoma involves the chronicity of *H. pylori*–induced tissue responses (inflammation), with progression to atrophic and subsequently metaplastic histology as important pathogenetic steps.[171] The relation between epithelial cell proliferation and apoptosis probably also is important.[178-180] However, this process probably requires decades on average, and *H. pylori* colonization is neither necessary nor sufficient for oncogenesis. No positive association has been observed with cancers at the cardia,[7,147-149] and preliminary data suggest that *H. pylori* carriage may have a protective effect.[154] Further understanding of the role of *H. pylori* in carcinogenesis could lead to reevaluation of the clinical approach to asymptomatic colonization. *H. pylori* alteration of signal transduction and cell cycle kinetics in epithelial cells also may predispose to neoplasia.[181-184] Definition of additional host and bacterial factors that increase the risk of cancer development (or protection; see later) is an important research priority. Nevertheless, in Japan treatment of high-risk persons to eradicate *H. pylori* lowered subsequent gastric cancer risk.[185]

Reflecting the decline in *H. pylori* acquisition in developed countries, the incidence of adenocarcinomas of the gastric antrum and body has fallen. In contrast, the incidence of adenocarcinoma of the gastric cardia (and lower portion of the esophagus) has risen dramatically.[186] This temporal relationship suggests that *H. pylori* loss may play a role in the rise of these cancers, and preliminary evidence supports this hypothesis.[154]

Gastric Lymphoma

Most gastric lymphomas arise from B lymphocytes and are termed mucosa-associated lymphoid tumors (MALTomas). *H. pylori* colonization is strongly associated with these tumors,[150,151] and eradication of *H. pylori* often leads to improvement in tumor histology.[187] Whether *H. pylori* eradication improves true malignancies, which are rare,[188] in contrast to the more common and more benign monoclonal lymphoid proliferation in response to *H. pylori* is unknown. The pathogenesis of these disorders may involve chronic antigenic stimulation by *H. pylori* and subsequent induction of a polyclonal lymphoid response, a single clone of which proliferates and then undergoes neoplastic transformation.

Esophageal Diseases

Much evidence has accumulated that the incidence of *H. pylori* colonization has been progressively diminishing in developed countries during the 20th century,[173] especially *cagA*+ strains.[64] During this time, three related diseases—gastroesophageal reflux disease (GERD), Barrett's esophagus, and adenocarcinoma of the esophagus—have been rising dramatically.[189] It is generally believed that Barrett's esophagus will develop in a proportion of patients with GERD and that adenocarcinoma will develop in some of these patients. An extremely important question is whether the loss of *H. pylori* from populations in developed countries may in some way predispose to this pathogenetic sequence. The presence of *cagA*+ *H. pylori* strains is inversely associated with Barrett's esophagus and esophageal adenocarcinomas.[190-192] Similarly, eradication of *H. pylori* in patients with duodenal ulceration doubled the rate of GERD development,[169] and patients with GERD are less likely to be colonized with *H. pylori* (especially *cagA* strains) than are controls.[152] The presence of diminished gastric acidity induced by long-term *H. pylori* persistence may be partially responsible.[192-195] Research is ongoing in this area, but these findings substantially alter clinical approaches to *H. pylori*.

DIAGNOSIS

Ascertainment of *H. pylori* colonization can be made either invasively by endoscopy and biopsy or noninvasively by serologic analysis, breath test, or fecal antigen analysis. Properly done, each of these methodologies has diagnostic accuracy exceeding 95%; each has advantages and disadvantages (Table 214-3).

Endoscopy with biopsy involves the most expense and invasion of the patient, but it may be used to yield a great deal of information.[196] Biopsy specimens may be cultured for *H. pylori* on antibiotic-containing media (to diminish overgrowth by any competing flora) such as Skirrow's medium, as well as with a nonselective medium such as chocolate agar.[196] Use of two media increases the yield. Plates should

be incubated for 2 to 5 days at 35° C to 37° C in a moist microaerobic atmosphere (with 5% oxygen). Comma- or S-shaped motile organisms with catalase, oxidase, and urease activity may be identified as *H. pylori*.[196] Culture enables a determination of antimicrobial susceptibilities, which may be increasingly important as antimicrobial resistance broadens. Alternatively, the organisms may be visualized on histologic sections prepared with Gram, silver, Giemsa, or acridine orange stains or by immunofluorescence or immunoperoxidase methods.[196] DNA probe and polymerase chain reaction methodologies have been developed as well, but they have no current clinical justification unless genotyping of strains becomes more clinically important.[122] For rapid detection of *H. pylori*, biopsy samples may be incubated at 37° C to examine for preformed urease activity.[120] After incubation for 1 hour, the assay has a sensitivity of about 60%, and by 24 hours, greater than 90%; bacterial overgrowth of the stomach may reduce the test's specificity, especially for longer incubations and in older patients. Endoscopy also permits assessment of structural lesions such as ulcers, masses, and strictures.

High-titer, stable serum immunoglobulin (Ig)G responses and, less frequently, IgA responses nearly universally develop in *H. pylori*–colonized persons.[196-198] Because serology in essence samples the entire stomach, whereas biopsy only samples a small region, and the inflammatory process may be patchy, serologic analysis may be more sensitive than diagnostic methods involving biopsies.[198] With successful antimicrobial therapy, antibody levels decline, although 3 to 6 months may be required for a noticeable effect; after ineffective therapy, high antibody levels persist.[199,200] Soon after the initial acquisition of *H. pylori*, IgM seroconversion is noted, but levels return to baseline; with recurrence after inadequate therapy, IgM seroconversion may again be observed.[157] A number of testing services and kits are now commercially available that allow physicians to detect *H. pylori* in individual patients; the serologic assays have generally been standardized for adults, and thus interpretation of results in children requires caution.[201] Office-based rapid diagnostic tests have lower sensitivity and specificity for both adults and children. *H. pylori*–positive persons also shed *H. pylori* antigens in their stools. Stool assay is a relatively noninvasive means to detect positivity and to monitor therapeutic responses 1 month after ending treatment.

The high urease activity of *H. pylori* has also facilitated the development of urease breath tests. Subjects fast and are then given a meal containing ^{13}C- or ^{14}C-urea; over the next hour, their breath is correspondingly examined for ^{13}CO$_2$ or ^{14}CO$_2$.[202,203] Results of these assays correlate with numbers of urease-producing *H. pylori* organisms and can be falsely negative after therapy that suppresses but does not eradicate the organism. However, negativity 1 to 3 months after therapy has ceased usually indicates eradication of the organism. Urea breath testing services are commercially available.

TABLE 214–3 Modalities for *Helicobacter pylori* Diagnosis

Modality	Advantages	Disadvantages
Endoscopy with biopsy	Permits inspection of pathology, allows detection of ulcers, neoplasms	Invasive, expensive, time consuming
Culture	Permits determination of antimicrobial susceptibilities and pathogenic features of isolates	Not optimally sensitive in most laboratories. Requires several days for results
Histology	Generally more sensitive than culture. Allows direct visualization of organism and extent and nature of tissue involvement	Gastritis may be patchy and biopsy may be performed on wrong area. Insensitivity to detect small numbers of organisms. Requires several days for results
Urease detection	Rapid; most positives seen within 2 hr	Increased sensitivity requires longer incubation. May be false positives with bacterial overgrowth
Serology	Noninvasive, rapid, quantitative, inexpensive	No determination of lesions or pathology, no antimicrobial susceptibility. Not rapidly responsive to therapy
Urea breath tests	Relatively noninvasive, relatively rapid, quantitative, rapidly responsive to therapy. Most valuable for assessing response to eradication therapy after 4–8 wk	Involves expensive instrumentation or administration of radioisotopes. More invasive and less convenient than serology. No determination of lesions or pathology, no antimicrobial susceptibility
Stool antigen tests	Relatively noninvasive, relatively rapid, rapidly responsive to therapy. Most valuable for assessing response to eradication therapy after 6-8 wk.	Not quantitative. Requires stool specimen, relatively expensive for developing countries. No determination of lesions or pathology, no antimicrobial susceptibility

TREATMENT

Indications

At present, several indications have emerged for considering therapy directed against *H. pylori*. For patients with peptic ulceration who are colonized with *H. pylori,* antimicrobial therapies that eradicate *H. pylori* are associated with substantially lower ulcer recurrence rates than are short-course therapies directed exclusively against gastric acidity.[166,167] Thus antimicrobial therapy now is included in the primary therapy for most cases of duodenal ulceration.[168] Gastric ulcers associated with *H. pylori* can be treated in the same manner as for duodenal ulceration.[170] In patients with gastric MALTomas, antimicrobial therapy directed against *H. pylori* appears to cause tumor regression in most patients.[186,187] For most cases of *H. pylori*–associated nonulcer dysplasia, data concerning the efficacy of antimicrobial therapy are not clear cut.[159,162,163] Because of the risk of developing or worsening esophageal disease, treatment is not recommended in asymptomatic persons who are *H. pylori* positive; a possible exception would be a patient with a strong family history of gastric cancer. Similarly, the persistence of antibiotic resistance of *H. pylori* and commensal bacteria after treatment argues against widespread eradication campaigns.[204] Similarly, if *H. pylori* protects against diarrheal diseases, as some evidence suggests,[205-207] eradication of *H. pylori* among children in developing countries could increase risk of morbidity and mortality in childhood.

Therapies

Virtually all *H. pylori* isolates are susceptible in vitro to a variety of antimicrobial agents, including bismuth salts, amoxicillin, macrolides, nitrofurans, tetracyclines, and aminoglycosides.[195,208,209] However, in vitro susceptibility is no guarantee of in vivo effectiveness. Primary resistance to imidazoles (such as metronidazole and tinidazole) occurs in 20% to 40% of isolates[209,210] and is most common in young women, who may have received this agent for gynecologic infections, or in persons from developing countries treated for parasitic infection. However, primary resistance is present in isolates from both men and women in all age groups[211] and is associated with prior exposure to a nitroimidazole, even decades earlier.[212] Primary resistance to macrolides is less common but increasing,[209] and resistance to amoxicillin and fluoroquinolones also has been reported.

Several principles of chemotherapy have emerged. First, treatment with a single agent has not yet resulted in apparent eradication of organisms in more than a minority of cases. As a result, all current treatments use combination therapy.[213] Second, certain agents that are effective in vitro may be ineffective in vivo even in combination with other agents. Erythromycin is a good example of this phenomenon.[214] The ineffectiveness of many antibiotics at an acidic pH may be responsible for the lack of activity in vivo. Third, acquired resistance frequently develops after therapy with certain agents but not others. To date, no confirmed resistance to bismuth salts and tetracycline has been reported. In contrast, acquired resistance to quinolones is so frequent that it appears to preclude their use. Secondary resistance to imidazoles occurs in 10% to 30% of cases, even when used in combination with other agents.[215] The development of resistance to macrolides and rifampin has also been reported. Fourth, to determine true eradication of the organism and not just temporary suppression, the patient must be shown to be free of the organism at least 1 month after the cessation of therapy if biopsy or the breath test is used and at least 6 months if serologic examination is used. Better definition of these end points is currently under investigation.

Combination therapy with a bismuth salt and two antibiotics has been widely used. Bismuth salts appear to be particularly useful against slowly growing bacteria.[216] Although bismuth salts vary in their particular minimal inhibitory concentrations toward *H. pylori* and in their pharmacokinetics, the levels achieved in the gastric lumen after oral administration are so high that no difference among the salts is apparent. "Triple therapy" with bismuth salts, metronidazole, and amoxicillin has resulted in eradication rates of 60% to 90%.

Tetracycline appears to be at least as beneficial as amoxicillin.[166,215] Both poor patient compliance[136] and primary and secondary resistance to metronidazole appear to be important factors limiting eradication. The optimal therapeutic regimen has not been defined. One regimen that can be considered is bismuth subsalicylate tablets (available in the United States as Pepto-Bismol), 1 to 2 tablets orally four times daily, tetracycline, 500 mg orally four times daily, and metronidazole, 250 mg orally three times daily for 7 to 10 days. In studies of patients with duodenal ulceration, combination therapies reduced 1-year recurrence rates from 80% to under 30%.[164-167] For ulcer healing, several excellent regimens have been described in which an acid-suppressing agent is used for 4 to 6 weeks and antimicrobial therapy for the first 10 to 14 days. One standard is ranitidine plus triple therapy[166]; similarly, ranitidine bismuth citrate plus two antibiotics is also highly effective. No evidence has shown any one histamine$_2$ (H$_2$) antagonist to be superior to the others, but patient compliance is an important variable.[217] Other useful therapies include proton pump inhibitors (PPIs) such as omeprazole or lansoprazole. These agents are directly inhibitory to *H. pylori*[218] and appear to be potent urease inhibitors,[219] in contrast to H$_2$ receptor antagonists, and are also more effective at inducing pH neutrality, which may permit better antimicrobial efficacy. One week of twice-daily therapy[220] with a PPI plus amoxicillin and clarithromycin or the combination of a PPI, amoxicillin, and metronidazole is also highly effective. Quadruple therapy with a PPI (for 10 days) and bismuth-based triple therapy (for days 4 to 10) appears to be most effective.[221] Physicians must balance the use of these particular regimens with possible adverse consequences, which include medication-induced upper gastrointestinal symptoms and uncommon complications such as antibiotic-associated colitis and candidiasis, and development of antimicrobial resistance. Determination of optimal therapy must await head-to-head clinical trials. There is preliminary evidence that eradication of *H. pylori* affects the gastric hormones leptin and ghrelin,[222-224] which affect appetite and satiety.[225-226] Weight gain after eradication may reflect disruption of this physiologic axis.[223]

In patients in whom *H. pylori* is again isolated after therapy, the organisms usually are identical to the initial isolates, thus indicating that recurrence reflects relapse rather than the acquisition of a new agent. When imidazoles or macrolides are used and fail, virtually all the recurrent organisms are resistant. After treatment failure, a second course of triple therapy (containing metronidazole) may nevertheless be effective; alternatively, a regimen not including imidazoles may be used.

OTHER GASTRIC HELICOBACTERS

In addition to *H. pylori,* other spiral organisms may occasionally be present in the human stomach. The predominant organisms, originally called *"Gastrospirillum hominis,"* are spirochetal in morphology and also are strongly urease positive.[227-229] Taxonomic study based on ribosomal RNA homologies indicates that this organism is a member of the genus *Helicobacter,* and the name *H. heilmanii* has been used.[230] *H. heilmanii* is much less commonly observed in the gastric mucosa than *H. pylori* is and occurs in perhaps 1% of persons.[229] This organism rarely has been cultivated in vitro, which limits studies of its clinical role. However, these 0.5- to 1.0-μm by 4- to 8-μm spirochetes are easily visualized in specimens from colonized persons. Both *H. pylori* and *H. heilmanii* may be present in the same person. In monkeys, these organisms appear to not be pathogens, and their role in humans is uncertain.

REFERENCES

1. Marshall BJ. History of the discovery of *Campylobacter pylori.* In: Blaser MJ, ed. *Campylobacter pylori* in Gastritis and Peptic Ulcer Disease. New York: Igaku Shoin; 1989:7-23.
2. Hazell SL, Lee A, Brady L, et al. *Campylobacter pyloridis* and gastritis: Association with intracellular spaces and adaptation to an environment of mucus as important factors in colonization of the gastric epithelium. J Infect Dis. 1986;153:658-663.
3. Tham KT, Peek RM, Atherton JC, et al. *Helicobacter pylori* genotypes, host factors, and gastric mucosal histopathology in peptic ulcer disease. Hum Pathol. 2001;32:264-273.

4. Nomura AMY, Perez-Perez GI, Lee J, et al. Relationship between *H. pylori cagA* status and risk of peptic ulcer disease. Am J Epidemiol. 2002;155:1054-1059.
5. Blaser MJ. The changing relationships of *Helicobacter pylori* and humans: Implications for health and disease. J Infect Dis. 1999;179:1523-1530.
6. Nomura AMY, Lee J, Stemmerman G, et al. *Helicobacter pylori cagA* seropositivity and gastric carcinoma risk in a Japanese American population. J Infect Dis. 2002;186:1138-1144.
7. *Helicobacter* and Cancer Collaborative Group. Gastric cancer and *Helicobacter pylori:* A combined analysis of twelve case-control studies nested within prospective cohorts. Gut. 2001;49:347-353.
8. Marshall BJ, Warren JR. Unidentified curved bacilli in the stomach of patients with gastritis and peptic ulceration. Lancet. 1984;1:1311-1313.
9. Goodwin CS, Armstrong JA, Chilvers T, et al. Transfer of *Campylobacter pylori* and *Campylobacter mustelae* to *Helicobacter* gen. nov. as *Helicobacter pylori* comb. nov. and *Helicobacter mustelae* comb. nov., respectively. Int J Syst Bacteriol. 1989;39:397-405.
10. Paster BJ, Lee A, Fox JG, et al. Phylogeny of *Helicobacter felis* sp. nov, *Helicobacter mustelae,* and related bacteria. Int J Syst Bacteriol. 1991;41:31-38.
11. Eaton KA, Dewhirst FE, Radin MJ, et al. *Helicobacter acinonyx* sp. nov., isolated from cheetahs with gastritis. Int J Syst Bacteriol. 1993;43:99-106.
12. Fox JG, Dewhirst FE, Tully JG, et al. *Helicobacter hepaticus* sp nov, a microaerophilic bacterium isolated from livers and intestinal mucosal scrapings from mice. J Clin Microbiol. 1994;32:1238-1245.
13. Fox JG, Drolet R, Higgins R, et al. *Helicobacter canis* isolated from a dog liver with multifocal necrotizing hepatitis. J Clin Microbiol. 1996;34:2479-2482.
14. Fox JG, Dewhirst FE, Shen Z, et al. Hepatic *Helicobacter* species identified in bile and gallbladder tissue from Chileans with chronic cholecystitis. Gastroenterology. 1998;114:755-763.
15. Matsukura N, Yokomuro S, Yamada S, et al. Association between *Helicobacter bilis* in bile and biliary tract malignancies: *H. bilis* in bile from Japanese and Thai patients with benign and malignant diseases in the biliary tract. J Cancer Res. 2002;93:842-847.
16. Blaser MJ. Helicobacters and biliary tract disease. Gastroenterology. 1998;114:840-842.
17. Dunn BE, Campbell GP, Pérez-Pérez GI, et al. Purification and characterization of *Helicobacter pylori* urease. J Biol Chem. 1990;265:9464-9469.
18. Cussac V, Ferrero RL, Labigne A. Expression of *Helicobacter pylori* urease genes in *Escherichia coli* grown under nitrogen-limiting conditions. J Bacteriol. 1992;174:2466-2473.
19. Tomb J-F, White O, Kerlavage AR, et al. The complete genome sequence of the gastric pathogen *Helicobacter pylori*. Nature. 1997;388:539-547.
20. Alm RA, Ling LL, Moir DT, et al. Genomic-sequence comparison of two unrelated isolates of the human gastric pathogen *Helicobacter pylori*. Nature. 1999;397:176-180.
21. Xu Q, Morgan RD, Roberts RJ, Blaser MJ. Identification of type II restriction and modification systems in *Helicobacter pylori* reveals their substantial diversity among strains. Proc Natl Acad Sci U S A. 2000;97:9671-9676.
22. Appelmelk BJ, Martino MC, Veenhof E, et al. Phase variation in H type I and Lewis a epitopes of *Helicobacter pylori* lipopolysaccharide. Infect Immun. 2000;68:5928-5932.
23. Wang G, Ge Z, Rasko DA, Taylor DE. Lewis antigens in *Helicobacter pylori:* Biosynthesis and phase variation. Mol Microbiol. 2000;36:1187-1196.
24. Blaser MJ, Atherton JC. *Helicobacter pylori* persistence: biology and disease. J Clin Invest. 2004;113:321-333.
25. Webb GF, Blaser MJ. Dynamics of bacterial phenotype selection in a colonized host. Proc Natl Acad Sci U S A. 2002;99:3135-3140.
26. Akopyanz N, Bukanov NO, Westblom TU, et al. DNA diversity among clinical isolates of *Helicobacter pylori* detected by PCR-based RAPD fingerprinting. Nucleic Acids Res. 1992;20:5137-5142.
27. Achtman M, Azuma T, Berg DE, et al. Recombination and clonal groupings within *Helicobacter pylori* from different geographical regions. Mol Microbiol. 1999;32:459-470.
28. Shames B, Krajden S, Fuksa M, et al. Evidence for the occurrence of the same strain of *Campylobacter pylori* in the stomach and dental plaque. J Clin Microbiol. 1989;27:2849-2850.
29. Kersulyte D, Chalkauskas H, Berg DE. Emergence of recombinant strains of *Helicobacter pylori* during human infection. Mol Microbiol. 1999;31:31-43.
30. Suerbaum S, Smith JM, Bapumia K, et al. Free recombination with *Helicobacter pylori*. Proc Natl Acad Sci U S A. 1998;95:12619-12624.
31. Falush D, Kraft C, Taylor NS, et al. Recombination and mutation during long-term gastric colonization by *Helicobacter pylori:* Estimates of clock rates, recombination size, and minimal age. Proc Natl Acad Sci U S A. 2001;98:15056-15061.
32. Bjorkholm B, Sjolund M, Falk PG, et al. Mutation frequency and biological cost of antibiotic resistance in *Helicobacter pylori*. Proc Natl Acad Sci U S A. 2001;98:14607-14612.
33. Israel DA, Salama N, Krishna U, et al. *Helicobacter pylori* genetic differsity within the gastric niche of a single human host. Proc Natl Acad Sci U S A. 2001;98:14625-14630.
34. Aras RA, Kang J, Tschumi A, et al. Extensive repetitive DNA facilitates prokaryotic genome plasticity. Proc Natl Acad Sci U S A. 2003;100:13579-13584.
35. Ando T, Xu Q, Torres M, et al. Restriction-modification system differences in *Helicobacter pylori* are a barrier to interstrain plasmid transfer. Mol Microbiol. 2000;7:1052-1065.
36. Censini S, Lange C, Xiang J, et al. *cag,* a pathogenicity island of *Helicobacter pylori* encodes type I–specific and disease-associated virulence factors. Proc Natl Acad Sci U S A. 1996;93:14648-14653.
37. Akopyanz NS, Clifton SW, Kersulyte D, et al. Analyses of the *cag* pathogenicity island of *Helicobacter pylori*. Mol Microbiol. 1998;28:37-53.
38. Tummuru MKR, Sharma SA, Blaser MJ. *Helicobacter pylori picB,* a homologue of the *Bordetella pertussis* toxin secretion protein, is required for induction of IL-8 in gastric epithelial cells. Mol Microbiol. 1995;18:867-876.
39. Pérez-Pérez GI, Bhat N, Gaensbauer J, et al. Country-specific constancy by age in *cagA+* proportion of *Helicobacter pylori* infections. Int J Cancer. 1997;72:453-456.
40. Odenbreit S, Puls J, Sedlmaier B, et al. Translocation of *Helicobacter pylori* CagA into gastric epithelial cells by type IV secretion. Science. 2000;287:1497-1500.
41. Segal ED, Cha J, Lo J, et al. Altered states: Involvement of phosphorylated CagA in the induction of host cellular growth changes by *Helicobacter pylori*. Proc Natl Acad Sci U S A. 1999;96:14559-14564.
42. Aras RA, Lee Y, Kim S-K, et al. Natural variation in populations of persistently colonizing bacteria affect human host cell phenotype. J Infect Dis. 2003;188:486-496.
43. Selbach M, Moese S, Hauck CR, et al. Src is the kinase of *Helicobacter pylori* CagA protein in vitro and in vivo. J Biol Chem. 2002;277:6775-6778.
44. Higashi H, Tsutsumi R, Muto S, et al. SHP-2 tyrosine phosphatase as an intracellular target of *Helicobacter pylori* CagA protein. Science. 2002;295:683-686.
45. Mimuro H, Suzuki T, Tanaka J, et al. Grb2 is a key mediator of *Helicobacter pylori* CagA protein activities. Mol Cell. 2002;10:745-755.
46. Tsutsumi R, Higashi H, Higuchi M, et al. Attenuation of *Helicobacter pylori* CagA x SHP-2 signaling by interaction between CagA and C-terminal Src kinase. J Biol Chem. 2003;278:3664-3670.
47. Selbach M, Moese S, Hurwitz R, et al. The *Helicobacter pylori* CagA protein induces cortactin dephosphorylation and actin rearrangement by c-Src inactivation. EMBO J. 2003;22:515-528.
48. Sozzi M, Crosarri M, Kim S-K, et al. Heterogeneity of *Helicobacter pylori cag* genotypes in experimentally infected mice. FEMS Microbiol Lett. 2001;203:109-114.
49. Ko JS, Seo JK. cag pathogenicity island of *Helicobacter pylori* in Korean children. Helicobacter 2002;7:232-236.
50. Aras RA, Takata T, Ando T, et al. Regulation of the HpyII restriction-modification system of *Helicobacter pylori* by gene deletion and horizontal reconstitution. Mol Microbiol. 2001;42:369-382.
51. Cover TL. The vacuolating cytotoxin of *Helicobacter pylori*. Mol Microbiol. 1996;20:241-246.
52. Atherton J, Cao P, Peek RM, et al. Mosaicism in vacuolating cytotoxin alleles of *Helicobacter pylori:* Association of specific *vacA* types with cytotoxin production and peptic ulceration. J Biol Chem. 1995;270:1771-1777.
53. van Doorn L-J, Figueiredo C, Sanna R, et al. Expanding allelic diversity of *Helicobacter pylori vacA*. J Clin Microbiol. 1998;36:2597-2603.
54. Atherton JC, Peek RM, Tham KT, et al. The clinical and pathological importance of heterogeneity in *vacA*, encoding the vacuolating cytotoxin of *Helicobacter pylori*. Gastroenterology. 1997;112:92-99.
55. Papini E, Satin B, Norais N, et al. Selective increase of the permeability of polarized epithelial cell monolayers by *Helicobacter pylori* vacuolating toxin. J Clin Invest. 1998;102:813-820.
56. Iwamoto H, Czajkowsky DM, Cover TL, et al. VacA from *Helicobacter pylori:* A hexameric chloride channel. FEBS Lett. 1999;450:101-104.
57. Molinari M, Salio M, Galli C, et al. Selective inhibition of Ii-dependent antigen presentation by *Helicobacter pylori* toxin VacA. J Exp Med. 1998;187:135-140.
58. Zheng PY, Jones NL. *Helicobacter pylori* strains expressing the vacuolating cytotoxin interrupt phagosome maturation in macrophages by recruiting and retaining TACO (coronin 1) protein. Cell Microbiol. 2003;5:25-40.
59. Gebert B, Fischer W, Weiss E, et al. Helicobacter pylori vacuolating cytotoxin inhibits T lymphocyte activation. Science. 2003;301:1099-1102.
60. Taylor DN, Blaser MJ. The epidemiology of *Helicobacter pylori* infections. Epidemiol Rev. 1991;13:42-59.
61. Falush D, Wirth T, Linz B, et al. Traces of human migration in *Helicobacter pylori* populations. Science. 2003;299:1582-1585.
62. Ghose C, Perez-Perez GI, Dominguez-Bello MG, et al. East Asian genotypes of *Helicobacter pylori:* Strains in Amerindians provide evidence for its ancient human carriage. Proc Natl Acad Sci U S A. 2002;99:15107-15111.
63. Blaser MJ. Helicobacters are indigenous to the human stomach: Duodenal ulceration is due to changes in gastric microecology in the modern era. Gut. 1998;43:721-727.
64. Perez-Perez GI, Salomaa A, Kosunen TU, et al. Evidence that *cagA+ Helicobacter pylori* strains are disappearing more rapidly than *cagA−* strains. Gut. 2002;50:295-298.
65. Graham DY, Alpert LC, Smith JL, et al. Iatrogenic *Campylobacter pylori* infection is a cause of epidemic achlorhydria. Am J Gastroenterol. 1988;83:974-980.
66. Pérez-Pérez GI, Bodhidatta L, Wongsrichanalai J, et al. Seroprevalence of *Helicobacter pylori* infections in Thailand. J Infect Dis. 1990;161:1237-1241.
67. Thomas JE, Gibson GR, Darboe MK, et al. Isolation of *Helicobacter pylori* from human faeces. Lancet. 1992;340:1194-1195.
68. Polish LB, Douglas JM, Davidson AJ, et al. Characterization of risk factors for *Helicobacter pylori* infection among men attending an STD clinic: Lack of evidence for sexual transmission. J Clin Microbiol. 1991;29:2139-2143.
69. Drumm B, Pérez-Pérez GI, Blaser MJ, et al. Intrafamilial clustering of *Helicobacter pylori* infection. N Engl J Med. 1990;322:359-363.
70. Goodman KJ, Correa P, Tengana Aux HJ, et al. *Helicobacter pylori* infection in the Colombian Andes: A population-based study of transmission pathways. Am J Epidemiol. 1996;144:290-299.
71. Goodman KJ, Correa P. Transmission of *Helicobacter pylori* among siblings. Lancet. 2000;355:358-362.
72. Dooley CP, Fitzgibbons PL, Cohen H, et al. Prevalence of *Helicobacter pylori* infection and histologic gastritis in asymptomatic persons. N Engl J Med. 1989;321:1562-1566.
73. Everhart JE, Kruszon-Moran D, Perez-Perez GI, et al. Seroprevalence and ethnic differences in *Helicobacter pylori* infection among adults in the United States. J Infect Dis. 2000;181:1359-1363.

74. Graham DY, Malaty HM, Evans DG, et al. Epidemiology of *Helicobacter pylori* in an asymptomatic population in the United States: Effect of age, race and socioeconomic status. Gastroenterology. 1991:100:1495-1501.
75. Dehesa M, Dooley CP, Cohen HA, et al. High prevalence of *Helicobacter pylori* in an asymptomatic hispanic population. J Clin Microbiol. 1991;29:1128-1131.
76. Everhart JE, Kruszon-Moran D, Perez-Perez G. Reliability of *Helicobacter pylori* and CagA serological assays. Clin Diagn Lab Immunol. 2002;9:412-416.
77. Parsonnet J. The incidence of *Helicobacter pylori* infection. Aliment Pharmacol Ther. 1995;9:45-51.
78. Mitchell HM, Li YY, Hu PJ, et al. Epidemiology of *Helicobacter pylori* in southern China: Identification of early childhood as the critical period for acquisition. J Infect Dis. 1992;166:149-153.
79. Perez-Perez GI, Sack RB, Reid R, et al. Transient and persistent *Helicobacter pylori* colonization in Native American children. J Clin Microbiol. 2003;41:2401-2407.
80. Banatvala N, Mayo K, Megraud F, et al. The cohort effect and *Helicobacter pylori*. J Infect Dis. 1993;168:219-221.
81. Mendall MA, Googin PM, Molineaux N, et al. Childhood living conditions and *Helicobacter pylori* seropositivity in adult life. Lancet. 1992;339:896.
82. Sitas F, Forman D, Yarnell JWG, et al. *Helicobacter pylori* infection rates in relation to age and social class in a Welsh male population. Gut. 1941;32:25-28.
83. Scott DR, Weeks D, Hong C, et al. The role of internal urease in acid resistance of *Helicobacter pylori*. Gastroenterology. 1998;114:58-70.
84. Amieva MR, Vogelmann R, Covacci A, et al. Disruption of the epithelial apical-junctional complex by *Helicobacter pylori* CagA. Science. 2003;300:1430-1434.
85. McGowan CC, Necheva AS, Forsyth MH, et al. Promoter analysis of *Helicobacter pylori* genes whose expression is enhanced at low pH. Mol Microbiol. 2003;48:1225-1239.
86. Wirth H-P, Yang M, Peek RM, et al. Phenotypic diversity in Lewis expression of *Helicobacter pylori* isolates from the same host. J Lab Clin Med. 1999;133:488-500.
87. Mimuro H, Suzuki T, Tanaka J, et al. Grb2 is a key mediator of *Helicobacter pylori* CagA protein activities. Mol Cell. 2002;295:683-686.
88. Selbach M, Moese S, Hurwitz R, et al. The *Helicobacter pylori* CagA protein induces cortactin dephosphorylation and actin rearrangement by c-Src inactivation. EMBO J. 2003;22:515-528.
89. Smoot DT, Resau JH, Naab T, et al. Adherence of *Helicobacter pylori* to cultured human gastric epithelial cells. Infect Immun. 1993;61:350-355.
90. Ilver D, Arnqvist A, Ogren J, et al. *Helicobacter pylori* adhesion binding fucosylated histo-blood group antigens revealed by retagging. Science. 1998;279:373-377.
91. Mahdavi J, Sonden B, Hurtig M, et al. *Helicobacter pylori* SabA adhesin in persistent infection and chronic inflammation. Science. 2002;297:573-578.
92. Pride DT, Blaser MJ. Concerted evolution between duplicated genetic elements in *Helicobacter pylori*. J Mol Biol. 2002;316:627-640.
93. Morris A, Maher K, Thomsen L, et al. Distribution of *Campylobacter pylori* in the human stomach obtained at postmortem. Scand J Gastroenterol. 1988;23:257-264.
94. Price AB. Histological aspects of *Campylobacter pylori* colonization and infection of gastric and duodenal mucosa. Scand J Gastroenterol. 1988;23:21-24.
95. Peek RM, Blaser MJ. *Helicobacter pylori* and gastrointestinal tract adenocarcinomas. Nat Rev Cancer. 2002;2:28-37.
96. Gilman RJ, Leon-Barua R, Koch J, et al. Rapid identification of pylori campylobacter in Peruvians with gastritis. Dig Dis Sci. 1986;31:1089-1094.
97. Letley DP, Rhead JL, Twells RJ, et al. Determinants of non-toxicity in the gastric pathogen *Helicobacter pylori*. J Biol Chem. 2003;278:26734-26741.
98. D'Elios MM, Manghetti M, De Carli M, et al. T helper 1 effector cells specific for *Helicobacter pylori* in the gastric antrum of patients with peptic ulcer disease. J Immunol. 1997;158:962-967.
99. Wang J, Brooks EG, Bamford KB, et al. Negative selection of T cells by *Helicobacter pylori* as a model for bacterial strain selection by immune evasion. J Immunol. 2001;167:926-934.
100. Allen LA, Schlesinger LS, Kang B. Virulent strains of *Helicobacter pylori* demonstrate delayed phagocytosis and stimulate homotypic phagosome fusion in macrophages. J Exp Med. 2000;191:115-128.
101. Mohammadi M, Nedrud J, Redline R, et al. Murine CD4 T cell response to Helicobacter infection: TH1 cells enhance gastritis and TH2 cells reduce bacterial load. Gastroenterology. 1997;113:1848-1857.
102. Suzuki M, Miura S, Suematsu M, et al. *Helicobacter pylori*–associated ammonia production enhances neutrophil-dependent gastric mucosal cell injury. Am J Physiol. 1992;263:G719-G725.
103. Yamazaki S, Yamakawa A, Yoshiuki I, et al. The CagA protein of *Helicobacter pylori* is translocated into epithelial cells and binds to SHP-2 in human gastric mucosa. J Infect Dis. 2003;187:334-337.
104. McClain MS, Cao P, Iwamoto H, et al. A 12-amino-acid segment, present in type s2 but not type s1 *Helicobacter pylori* VacA proteins, abolishes cytotoxin activity and alters membrane channel formation. J Bacteriol. 2001;183:6499-6508.
105. Cover TC, Cao P, Murthy UK, et al. Serum neutralizing antibody response to the vacuolating cytotoxin of *Helicobacter pylori*. J Clin Invest. 1992;90:913-918.
106. Aras RA, Fischer W, Perez-Perez GI, et al. Plasticity of repetitive DNA sequences within a bacterial (type IV) secretion system component. J Exp Med. 2003;198:1349-1360.
107. Figura N, Guglielmetti P, Rossolini A, et al. Cytotoxin production by *Campylobacter pylori* strains isolated from patients with peptic ulcers and from patients with chronic gastritis only. J Clin Microbiol. 1989;27:225-226.
108. Mai UE, Pérez-Pérez GI, Allen JB, et al. Surface proteins from *Helicobacter pylori* exhibit chemotactic activity for human leukocytes and are present in gastric mucosa. J Exp Med. 1992;175:517-525.
109. Mai UEH, Pérez-Pérez GI, Wahl LM, et al. Soluble surface proteins from *Helicobacter pylori* activate monocytes/macrophages by lipopolysaccharide-independent mechanism. J Clin Invest. 1991;87:894-900.
110. Pérez-Pérez GI, Shepherd VL, Morrow JD, Blaser MJ. Activation of human THP-1 and rat bone marrow–derived macrophages by *Helicobacter pylori* lipopolysaccharide. Infect Immun. 1995;63:1183-1187.
111. Aspinall GO, Monteiro MA, Pang H, et al. Lipopolysaccharide of the *Helicobacter pylori* type strain NCTC 11637 (ATCC 43504): Structure of the O antigen and core oligosaccharide regions. Biochemistry. 1996;35:2489-2497.
112. Wirth HP, Yang M, Peek RM, et al. *Helicobacter pylori* Lewis expression is related to the host Lewis phenotype. Gastroenterology. 1997;113:1091-1098.
113. Sharma SA, Tummuru MKR, Miller GG, Blaser MJ. Interleukin-8 response of gastric epithelial cell lines to *Helicobacter pylori* stimulation in vitro. Infect Immun. 1995;63:1681-1687.
114. Isomoto H, Miyazaki M, Mizuta Y, et al. Expression of nuclear factor kappa B in *Helicobacter pylori*-infected gastric mucosa detected with Southwestern histochemistry. Scand J Gastroenterol. 2000;35:247-254.
115. Su B, Ceponis PJ, Lebel S, et al. *Helicobacter pylori* activates Toll-like receptor 4 expression in gastrointestinal epithelial cells. Infect Immun. 2003;71:3496-3502.
116. Backhed F, Rokbi B, Torstensson E, et al. Gastric mucosal recognition of *Helicobacter pylori* is independent of Toll-like receptor 4. J Infect Dis. 2003;187:829-836.
117. Foryst-Ludwig A, Naumann M. p21-activated kinase 1 activates the nuclear factor kappa B (NF-kappa B)-inducing kinase-I kappa B kinases NF-kappa B pathway and proinflammatory cytokines in *Helicobacter pylori* infection. J Biol Chem. 2000;275:39779-39785.
118. Crabtree JE, Shallcross T, Wyatt JI, et al. Tumour necrosis factor alpha secretion by *Helicobacter pylori* colonized gastric mucosa. Gut. 1991;32:1473-1477.
119. Blaser MJ. Hypotheses on the pathogenesis and natural history of *Helicobacter pylori*–induced inflammation. Gastroenterology. 1992;102:720-727.
120. El-Omar EM, Carrington M, Chow WH, et al. Interleukin-1 polymorphisms associated with increased risk of gastric cancer. Nature. 2000;404:398-402.
121. El-Omar EM, Rabkin CS, Gammon MD, et al. Increased risk of noncardia gastric cancer associated with proinflammatory cytokine gene polymorphisms. Gastroenterology. 2003;124:1193-1201.
122. Figueiredo C, Machado JC, Pharoah P, et al. *Helicobacter pylori* and interleukin 1 genotyping: An opportunity to identify high-risk individuals for gastric carcinoma. J Natl Cancer Inst. 2002;94:1680-1687.
123. Blaser MJ, Crabtree JE. CagA and the outcome of *Helicobacter pylori* infection. Am J Clin Pathol. 1996;106:565-567.
124. Smith JTL, Pounder RF, Nwokolo CU, et al. Inappropriate hypergastrinaemia in asymptomatic healthy subjects with *Helicobacter pylori*. Gut. 1990;31:522-525.
125. McColl KEL, Fullarton GM, Nujumi AM, et al. Lowered gastrin and gastric activity after eradication of *Campylobacter pylori* in duodenal ulcer. Lancet. 1989;2:499-500.
126. Moss SF, Legon S, Bishop AE, et al. Effect of *Helicobacter pylori* on gastric somatostatin in duodenal ulcer disease. Lancet. 1992;340:930-932.
127. Tham TCK, Chen L, Dennison N, et al. Effect of *Helicobacter pylori* eradication on antral somatostatin cell density in humans. Eur J Gastroenterol Hepatol. 1998;10:289-291.
128. Yamamoto S, Kaneko H, Konagaya T, et al. Interactions among gastric somatostatin, interleukin-8, and mucosal inflammation in *Helicobacter pylori*-positive peptic ulcer patients. Helicobacter. 2001;6:136-145.
129. Cave DR, Vargas M. Effect of a *Campylobacter pylori* protein on acid secretion by parietal cells. Lancet. 1989;2:187-189.
130. Blaser MJ. Ecology of *Helicobacter pylori* in the human stomach. J Clin Invest. 1997;100:759-762.
131. Karttunen R. Blood lymphocyte proliferation, cytokine secretion and appearance of T cells with activation surface markers in cultures with *Helicobacter pylori:* Comparison of the responses of subjects with and without antibodies to *H. pylori*. Clin Exp Immunol. 1991;83:396-400.
132. Fox JG, Beck P, Dangler CA, et al. Concurrent enteric helminth infection modulates inflammation and gastric immune responses and reduces helicobacter-induced gastric atrophy. Nat Med. 2000;6:536-542.
133. El-Omar E, Rabkin CS, Gammon MD, et al. Pro-inflammatory genotypes of IL-1 beta, TNF-alpha and IL-10 increase risk of distal gastric cancer but not of cardia or oesopageal adenocarcinomas. Gastroenterology. 2001;120:459.
134. Machado JC, Pharoah P, Sousa S, et al. Interleukin 1B and interleukin 1RN polymorphisms are associated with increased risk of gastric carcinoma. Gastroenterology. 2001;121:823-829.
135. Hazell SL, Eichberg JW, Lee DR, et al. Selection of the chimpanzee over the baboon as a model for *Helicobacter pylori* infection. Gastroenterology. 1992;103:848-854.
136. Dubois A, Berg DE, Incecik ET, et al. Transient and persistent experimental infection of non-human primates with *Helicobacter pylori:* Implications for human disease. Infect Immun. 1996;64:2885-2891.
137. Marchetti M, Arico B, Burroni D, et al. Development of a mouse model of *Helicobacter pylori* infection that mimics human disease. Science. 1995;267:1655-1658.
138. Wirth H-P, Beins MH, Yang M, et al. Experimental infection of Mongolian gerbils with wild-type and mutant *Helicobacter pylori* strains. Infect Immun. 1998;66:4856-4866.
139. Sakagami T, Dixon M, O'Rourke J, et al. Atrophic gastric changes in both *Helicobacter felis* and *Helicobacter pylori* infected mice are host dependent and separate from antral gastritis. Gut. 1996;39:639-648.
140. Peek RM Jr, Wirth HP, Moss SF, et al. *Helicobacter pylori* alters gastric epithelial cell cycle events and gastrin secretion in Mongolian gerbils. Gastroenterology. 2000;118:48-59.
141. Fong T-L, Dooley CP, Dehesa M, et al. *Helicobacter pylori* infection in pernicious anemia: A prospective controlled study. Gastroenterology. 1991;100:328-332.
142. Inglehart LW, Edlow DW, Mills L, et al. The presence of *Campylobacter pylori* in nonsteroidal antiinflammatory drug associated gastritis. J Rheumatol. 1989;16:599-603.
143. Blaser MJ, Pérez-Pérez GI, Lindenbaum J, et al. Association of infection due to *Helicobacter pylori* with specific upper gastrointestinal pathology. Rev Infect Dis. 1991;13(Suppl):S704-S708.

144. Nomura A, Stemmerman GN, Chyou PH, et al. *Helicobacter pylori* infection and the risk for duodenal and gastric ulceration. Ann Intern Med. 1994;120:977-981.
145. Johnston BJ, Reed PI, Ali MH. *Campylobacter*-like organisms in duodenal and antral endoscopic biopsies: Relationship to inflammation. Gut. 1986;27:1132-1137.
146. Carrick J, Lee A, Hazell S, et al. *Campylobacter pylori,* duodenal ulcer and gastric metaplasia: Possible role of functional heterotrophic tissue in ulcerogenesis. Gut. 1989;30:790-797.
147. Forman D, Newell DG, Fullerton F, et al. Association between infection with *Helicobacter pylori* and risk of gastric cancer: Evidence from a prospective investigation. BMJ. 1991;302:1302-1305.
148. Nomura A, Stemmerman GN, Chyou P-H, et al. *Helicobacter pylori* infection and gastric carcinoma in a population of Japanese-Americans in Hawaii. N Engl J Med. 1991;325:1132-1136.
149. Parsonnet J, Friedman GD, Vandersteen DP, et al. *Helicobacter pylori* infection and the risk of gastric carcinoma. N Engl J Med. 1991;325:1127-1131.
150. Parsonnet J, Hansen S, Rodriguez L, et al. *Helicobacter pylori* infection and gastric lymphoma. N Engl J Med. 1994;330:1267-1271.
151. Wotherspoon AC, Ortiz Hidalgo C, Falzon MR, et al. *Helicobacter pylori*–associated gastritis and primary B-cell gastric lymphoma. Lancet. 1991;338:1175-1176.
152. Loffeld RJLF, Werdmuller BFM, Kusters JG, et al. Colonization with *cagA*-positive *H. pylori* strains inversely associated with reflux oesophagitis and Barrett's oesophagitis. Digestion. 2000;62:95-99.
153. Vicari JJ, Peek RM, Falk GW, et al. The seroprevalence of *cagA* positive *Helicobacter pylori* strains in the spectrum of gastroesophageal reflux disease. Gastroenterology. 1998;115:50-57.
154. Chow W-H, Blaser MJ, Blot WJ, et al. An inverse relation between *cagA*$^+$ strains of *Helicobacter pylori* infection and risk of esophageal and gastric cardia adenocarcinoma. Cancer Res. 1998;58:588-590.
155. Morris A, Nicholson G. Experimental and accidental *C. pylori* infection of humans. In: Blaser MJ, ed. *Campylobacter pylori* in Gastritis and Peptic Ulcer Disease. New York: Igaku Shoin; 1989:61-72.
156. Harford WV, Barnett C, Lee E, et al. Acute gastritis with hypochlorhydria: report of 35 cases with long-term follow-up. Gut. 2000;47:467-472.
157. Morris AJ, Ali MR, Nicholson GI, et al. Long term follow-up of voluntary ingestion of *Helicobacter pylori.* Ann Intern Med. 1991;114:662-663.
158. Shallcross TM, Rathbone BJ, Heatley RV. *Campylobacter pylori* and non-ulcer dyspepsia. In: Rathbone BJ, Heatley RV, eds. *Campylobacter pylori* and Gastroduodenal Disease. Oxford: Blackwell; 1989:155-166.
159. McColl K, Murray L, El-Omar E, et al. Symptomatic benefit from eradicating *Helicobacter pylori* infection in patients with nonulcer dyspepsia. N Engl J Med. 1998;339:1869-1874.
160. Kang JY, Tay HH, Wee A, et al. Effect of colloidal bismuth subcitrate on symptoms and gastric histology in non-ulcer dyspepsia: A double blind placebo controlled study. Gut. 1990;31:476-480.
161. Talley NJ, Vakil N, Ballard ED 2nd, Fennerty MB. Absence of benefit of eradicating *Helicobacter pylori* in patients with nonulcer dyspepsia. N Engl J Med. 1999;341:1106-1111.
162. Blum AL, Talley NJ, O'Moráin C, et al. Lack of effect of treating *Helicobacter pylori* infection in patients with nonulcer dyspepsia. N Engl J Med. 1998;339:1875-1881.
163. Wyatt JI, Rathbone BJ, Dixon MF, et al. *Campylobacter pyloridis* and acid-induced gastric metaplasia in the pathogenesis of duodenitis. J Clin Pathol. 1987;40:841-848.
164. Coghlan JG, Gilligan D, Humphreys H, et al. *Campylobacter pylori* and recurrence of duodenal ulcers—a 12-month follow-up study. Lancet. 1987;2:1109-1111.
165. Marshall BJ, Goodwin CS, Warren JR, et al. Prospective double-blind trial of duodenal ulcer relapse after eradication of *Campylobacter pylori.* Lancet. 1988;2:1437-1445.
166. Graham DY, Lew GM, Klein PD, et al. Effect of treatment of *Helicobacter pylori* infection on the long-term recurrence of gastric or duodenal ulcer: A randomized, controlled study. Ann Intern Med. 1992;116:705-708.
167. Hentschel E, Brandstatter G, Dragoisics B, et al. Effect of ranitidine and amoxicillin plus metronidazole on the eradication of *Helicobacter pylori* and the recurrence of duodenal ulcer. N Engl J Med. 1993;328:308-312.
168. NIH Consensus Conference. *Helicobacter pylori* in peptic ulcer disease. JAMA. 1994;272:65-69.
169. Labenz J, Blum AL, Bayerdörffer E, et al. Curing *Helicobacter pylori* infection in patients with duodenal ulcer may provoke reflux esophagitis. Gastroenterology. 1997;112:1442-1447.
170. Sung JJ, Chung SC, Ling TK, et al. Antibacterial treatment of gastric ulcers associated with *Helicobacter pylori.* N Engl J Med. 1995;332:139-142.
171. Correa P. Human gastric carcinogenesis: A multistep and multifactorial process—First American Cancer Society Award lecture on cancer epidemiology and prevention. Cancer Res. 1992;52:6735-6740.
172. Blaser MJ, Chyou PH, Nomura A. Age at establishment of *Helicobacter pylori* infection and gastric carcinoma, gastric ulcer, and duodenal ulcer risk. Cancer Res. 1995;55:562-565.
173. Kosunen TU, Aromaa A, Knekt P, et al. *Helicobacter* antibodies in 1973 and 1994 in the adult population of Vammala, Finland. Epidemiol Infect. 1997;119:29-34.
174. Craanen ME, Dekker W, Blok P, et al. Intestinal metaplasia and *Helicobacter pylori:* An endoscopic bioptic study of the gastric antrum. Gut. 1992;33:16-20.
175. Kuipers EJ, Uyterlinde AM, Pena AS, et al. Long-term sequelae to *Helicobacter pylori* gastritis. Lancet. 1995;345:1525-1528.
176. Forman D, Sitas F, Newell DG, et al. Geographic association of *Helicobacter pylori* antibody prevalence and gastric cancer mortality in rural China. Int J Cancer. 1990;46:608-611.
177. The Eurogast Study Group. An international association between *Helicobacter pylori* infection and gastric cancer. Lancet. 1993;341:1359-1362.
178. Peek RM Jr, Moss SF, Tham KT, et al. *Helicobacter pylori* cagA+ strains and dissociation of gastric epithelial cell proliferation from apoptosis. J Natl Cancer Inst. 1997;89:863-868.
179. Moss SF, Calam J, Agarwal B, et al. Induction of gastric epithelial apoptosis by *Helicobacter pylori.* Gut. 1996;38:498-501.
180. Hoshi T, Sasano H, Kato K, et al. Cell damage and proliferation in human gastric mucosa infected by *Helicobacter pylori*—a comparison before and after *H. pylori* eradication in non-atrophic gastritis. Hum Pathol. 1999;30:1412-1417.
181. Smoot DT, Wynn Z, Elliott TB, et al. Effects of *Helicobacter pylori* on proliferation of gastric epithelial cells in vitro. Am J Gastroenterol. 1999;94:1508-1511.
182. Wagner S, Beil W, Westermann J, et al. Regulation of gastric epithelial cell growth by *Helicobacter pylori:* Evidence for a major role of apoptosis. Gastroenterology. 1997;113:1836-1847.
183. Meyer-ter-Vehn T, Covacci A, Kist M, Pahl HL. *Helicobacter pylori* activates mitogen-activated protein kinase cascades and induces expression of the proto-oncogenes c-fos and c-jun. J Biol Chem. 2000;275:16064-16072.
184. Maeda S, Yoshida H, Mitsuno Y, et al. Analysis of apoptotic and antiapoptotic signaling pathways induced by *Helicobacter pylori.* Mol Pathol. 2002;55:286-293.
185. Uemura N, Okamoto S, Yamamoto S, et al. *Helicobacter pylori* infection and the development of gastric cancer. N Engl J Med. 2001;345:784-789.
186. Devesa SS, Blot WJ, Fraumeni JF Jr. Changing patterns in the incidence of esophageal and gastric carcinoma in the United States. Cancer. 1998;83:2049-2053.
187. Neubauer A, Thiede C, Morgner A, et al. Cure of *Helicobacter pylori* infection and duration of remission of low-grade gastric mucosa–associated lymphoid tissue lymphoma. J Natl Cancer Inst. 1997;89:1350-1353.
188. Pinotti G, Zucca E, Roggero E, et al. Clinical features, treatment and outcome in a series of 93 patients with low-grade gastric MALT lymphoma. Leuk Lymphoma. 1997;26:527-537.
189. El-Serag HB, Sonnenberg A. Opposing time trends of peptic ulcer and reflux disease. Gut. 1998;43:327-333.
190. Vaezi MF, Falk GW, Peek RM, et al. CagA-positive strains of *Helicobacter pylori* may protect against Barrett's esophagus. Am J Gastroenterol. 2000;95:2206-2211.
191. Warburton-Timms VJ, Charlett A, Valori RM, et al. The significance of cagA(+) *Helicobacter pylori* in reflux oesophagitis. Gut. 2001;49:341-346.
192. Roulton-Jones J, Logan R. An inverse relation between *cagA*-positive strains of *Helicobacter pylori* infection and risk of esophageal and gastric cardia adenocarcinoma. Helicobacter. 1999;4:281-283.
193. Yamaji Y, Mitsushima T, Ikuma H, et al. Inverse background of *Helicobacter pylori* antibody and pepsinogen in reflux oesophagitis compared with gastric cancer: Analysis of 5732 Japanese subjects. Gut. 2001;49:335-340.
194. Quieroz DMM, Rocha GA, de Oliveira CA, et al. Role of corpus gastritis and *cagA*-positive *Helicobacter pylori* infection in reflux esophagitis. J Clin Microbiol. 2002;40:2849-2853.
195. Koike T, Ohara S, Sekine H, et al. *Helicobacter pylori* infection prevents erosive reflux oesophagitis by decreasing gastric acid secretion. Gut. 2001;49:330-334.
196. Dunn BE, Cohen H, Blaser MJ. *Helicobacter pylori.* Clin Microbiol Rev. 1997;10:720-741.
197. Evans DJ Jr, Evans DG, Graham DY, et al. A sensitive and specific serologic test for detection of *Campylobacter pylori* infection. Gastroenterology. 1989;96:1004-1008.
198. Romero-Gallo J, Perez-Perez GI, Novick RP, et al. Responses to *Helicobacter pylori* whole cell and CagA antigens amongst Ladakh patients undergoing endoscopy. Clin Diagn Lab Immunol. 2002;9:1313-1317.
199. Kosunen TU, Seppala K, Sarna S, et al. Diagnostic value of decreased IgG, IgA, and IgM antibody titres after eradication of *Helicobacter pylori.* Lancet. 1992;339:893.
200. Pérez-Pérez GI, Cutler AF, Blaser MJ. Value of serology as a non-invasive method to evaluate the efficacy of treatment in *Helicobacter pylori* infection. Clin Infect Dis. 1997;25:1038-1043.
201. Khanna B, Cutler A, Israel NR, et al. Use caution with serologic testing for *Helicobacter pylori* infection in children. J Infect Dis. 1998;178:460-465.
202. Graham DY, Evans DJ, Alpert LC, et al. *Campylobacter pylori* detected non-invasively by the ^{13}C-urea breath test. Lancet. 1987;1:1174-1177.
203. Marshall BJ, Surveyor I. Carbon-14 urea breath test for the diagnosis of *Campylobacter pyloridis*–associated gastritis. J Nucl Med. 1988;29:11-16.
204. Sjolund M, Wreiber K, Andersson DI, et al. Long-term persistence of resistant Enterococcus species after antibiotics to eradicate *Helicobacter pylori.* Ann Intern Med. 2003;139:483-487.
205. Rothenbacher D, Blaser MJ, Bode G, Brenner H. An inverse relationship between gastric colonization by *Helicobacter pylori* and diarrheal illnesses in children: Results of a population-based cross-sectional study. Infect Dis. 2000;182:1446-1449.
206. Putsep K, Branden CI, Boman HG, Normark S. Antibacterial peptide from *H. pylori.* Nature. 1999;398:671-672.
207. Mattsson A, Lonroth H, Quiding-Jarbrink M, Svennerholm AM. Induction of B cell responses in the stomach of *Helicobacter pylori*-infected subjects after oral cholera vaccination. J Clin Invest. 1998;102:51-56.
208. Goodwin CS, Blake P, Blincow E. The minimum inhibitory and bactericidal concentrations of antibiotics and anti-ulcer agents against *Campylobacter pyloridis.* J Antimicrob Chemother. 1986;17:309-314.
209. Megraud F. Resistance of *Helicobacter pylori* to antibiotics. Aliment Pharmacol Ther. 1997;11:43-53.
210. Xia HX, Daw MA, Beattie S, et al. Prevalence of metronidazole-resistant *Helicobacter pylori* in dyspeptic patients. Ir J Med Sci. 1993;162:91-94.
211. Rautelin H, Seppala K, Renkonen OV, et al. Role of metronidazole resistance in therapy of *Helicobacter pylori* infections. Antimicrob Agents Chemother. 1992;36:163-166.
212. European Study Group on Antibiotic Susceptibility of *Helicobacter pylori.* Results of a multicentre European survey in 1991 of metronidazole in *Helicobacter pylori.* Eur J Clin Microbiol Infect Dis. 1992;11:777-781.
213. Pavicic MJ, Namavar F, Verboom T, et al. In vitro susceptibility of *Helicobacter pylori* to several antimicrobial combinations. Antimicrob Agents Chemother. 1993;37:1184-1186.

214. McNulty CAM, Gearty JC, Crump B, et al. *Campylobacter pyloridis* and associated gastritis: Investigator blind, placebo controlled trial of bismuth salicylate and erythromycin ethylsuccinate. Br Med J (Clin Res Ed). 1986;293:645-649.

215. Logan RPH, Gummett PA, Misiewicz JJ, et al. One week eradication regimen for *Helicobacter pylori.* Lancet. 1991;338:1249-1252.

216. Millar MR, Pike J. Bactericidal activity of antimicrobial agents against slowly growing *Helicobacter pylori.* Antimicrob Agents Chemother. 1992;36:185-187.

217. Graham DY, Lew GM, Malaty HM, et al. Factors influencing the eradication of *Helicobacter pylori* with triple therapy. Gastroenterology. 1992;102:493-496.

218. Iwahi T, Satoh H, Nakao M, et al. Lansoprazole, a novel benzimidazole proton pump inhibitor, and its related compounds have selective activity against *Helicobacter pylori.* Antimicrob Agents Chemother. 1991;35:490-496.

219. Nagata K, Satoh H, Iwahi T, et al. Potent inhibitory action of the gastric proton pump inhibitor lansoprazole against urease activity of *Helicobacter pylori:* Unique action selective for *H. pylori* cells. Antimicrob Agents Chemother. 1993;37: 769-774.

220. Bazzoli F, Zagari RM, Fossi S, et al. Short-term low-dose triple therapy for the eradication of *Helicobacter pylori.* Eur J Gastroenterol Hepatol. 1994;6:773-777.

221. de Boer W, Driessen W, Jansz A, Tytgat G. Effect of acid suppression on efficacy of treatment for *Helicobacter pylori* infection. Lancet. 1995;345:817-820.

222. Breidert M, Miehlke S, Glasow A, et al. Leptin and its receptor in normal human gastric mucosa and in Helicobacter pylori-associated gastritis. Scand J Gastroenterol. 1999;34:954-961.

223. Azuma T, Suto H, Ito Y, et al. Gastric leptin and *Helicobacter pylori* infection. Gut. 2001;49:324-329.

224. Nwokolo CU, Freshwater DA, O'Hare P, Randeva HS. Plasma ghrelin following cure of *Helicobacter pylori.* Gut. 2003;52:637-640.

225. Konturek JW, Konturek SJ, Kwiecien N, et al. Leptin in the control of gastric secretion and gut hormones in humans infected with *Helicobacter pylori.* Scand J Gastroenterol. 2001;36:1148-1154.

226. Sobhani I, Bado A, Vissuzaine C, et al. Leptin secretion and leptin receptor in the human stomach. Gut. 2000;47:178-183.

227. Dent JC, McNulty CAM, Ulff JS, et al. Spiral organisms in the gastric antrum. Lancet. 1987;2:96.

228. McNulty CAM, Dent JC, Curry A, et al. New spiral bacterium in gastric mucosa. J Clin Pathol. 1989;42:585-591.

229. Heilmann KL, Borchard F. Gastritis due to spiral shaped bacteria other than *Helicobacter pylori:* Clinical, histological, and ultrastructural findings. Gut. 1991;32: 137-140.

230. Solnick JV, O'Rourke J, Lee A, et al. An uncultured gastric spiral organism is a newly identified *Helicobacter* in humans. J Infect Dis. 1993;168:379-385.

TABLE 215-1   Medically Important Genera and Species of the Family Enterobacteriaceae

Genus	Species
Citrobacter	freundii
	disversis
	amalonaticus
Edwardsiella	tarda
Enterobacter	cloacae
	aerogenes
	sakasakii
Escherichia	coli
	albertii
Hafnia	alvei
Klebsiella	pneumoniae
	oxytoca
	granulomatis
Morganella	morganii
Pantoea (formerly *Enterobacter*)	agglomerans
Plesiomonas	shigelloides
Proteus	mirabilis
	vulgaris
Providencia	stuartii
	retgeri
Salmonella	enterica
Serratia	marcescens
Shigella (belongs within the *E. coli* species)	dysenterii
	flexneri
	sonnei
	boydei
Yersinia	pestis
	enterocolitica
	pseudotuberculosis

CHAPTER **215**

Enterobacteriaceae

MICHAEL S. DONNENBERG

The family Enterobacteriaceae falls within the domain Bacteria, phylum Proteobacteria, class Gammaproteobacteria, and order Enterobacteriales *(dx.doi.org/10.1007/bergeysoutline200210)* and includes the medically important genera and species listed in Table 215-1. Of these genera, *Salmonella, Shigella* (actually not a true genus, but in fact a pathotype of *Escherichia coli*),[1] and *Yersinia* have distinctive features and particular medical importance that merit separate discussions found elsewhere in this volume (see Chapters 220, 221, and 226). Members of the family Enterobacteriaceae are gram-negative, non–spore-forming, facultative anaerobes that ferment glucose and other sugars, reduce nitrate to nitrite, and produce catalase, but (with the exception of *Plesiomonas*) do not produce oxidase. Most are motile by virtue of peritrichous (as opposed to polar) flagellae. Members of the family Enterobacteriaceae are often referred to as "enterics" because the principal habitat of many of these organisms is the lower gastrointestinal tract of various vertebrates and invertebrates. However, these terms are not synonymous because several species do not typically inhabit the human gastrointestinal tract, and other intestinal pathogens that do not fall within the family, such as *Vibrio* spp., are also referred to as enteric bacteria. Furthermore, the designation belies the fact that members of the family Enterobacteriaceae are widely distributed and are commonly found in the environment. This chapter includes a dis-

cussion of the general properties of the group, including common pathogenic features, followed by sections on individual pathogens and the diseases that they cause.

GENERAL PROPERTIES

Epidemiology

Although the natural habitat of many medically important members of the family Enterobacteriaceae is the lower gastrointestinal tract of humans and other animals, these organisms are actually quite widespread in nature and may be found, for example, in water and soil. Furthermore, certain individuals, including alcoholics and those with diabetes mellitus, have high rates of oropharyngeal colonization with members of this family.[2] Moreover, enterobacterial species rapidly colonize the oropharynx of many hospitalized patients regardless of whether they receive antimicrobials.[3] In addition, women who use diaphragms and/or spermicidal agents for contraception and postmenopausal women have increased rates of vaginal colonization with *E. coli* and other members of the family.[4,5] The extended niche that Enterobacteriaceae may occupy under these circumstances is an important predisposing factor that allows subsequent extraintestinal infections to occur.

Members of the family Enterobacteriaceae cause a wide variety of infections in both the community and the hospital setting, affecting normal hosts and those with preexisting illnesses. They comprise the most common gram-negative isolates in microbiology laboratories, including the vast majority of urinary isolates and a large proportion of isolates from the blood, the peritoneal cavity, and the respiratory tract. They may be isolated from numerous other sites, including cerebrospinal fluid, synovial fluid, and abscesses. The proportion of multiple-antimicrobial-resistant isolates, including those producing extended-spectrum β-lactamases, has increased steadily so that the majority of nosocomial and many community-acquired isolates are now resistant to several important antimicrobial classes.

Infections caused by members of the family Enterobacteriaceae may be sporadic or occur in outbreaks. The recognition of community-acquired or nosocomial outbreaks of these infections is facilitated by molecular diagnostic techniques that indicate whether strains isolated from

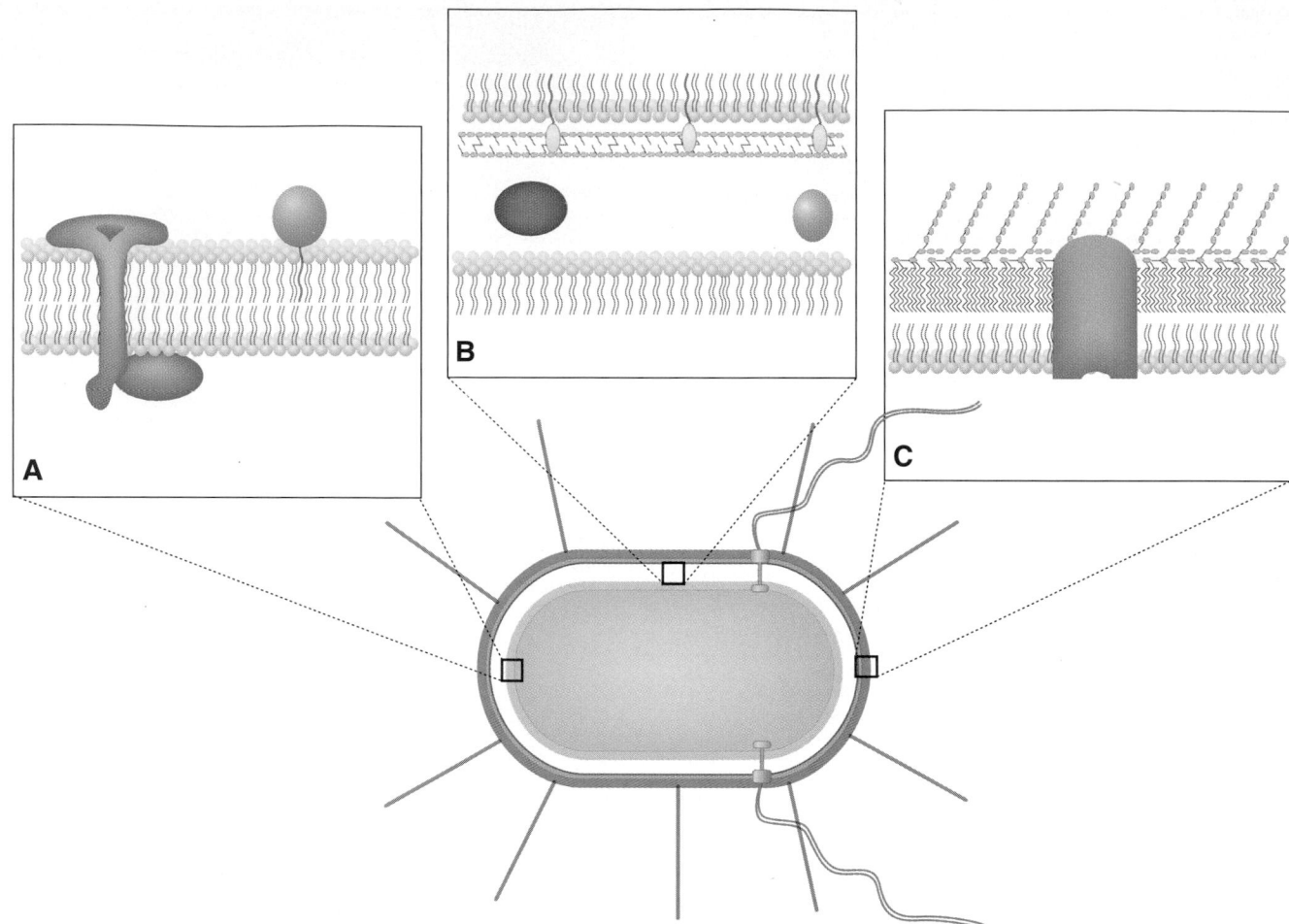

FIGURE 215-1. Cartoon of the architecture of an enterobacterial cell. The cytoplasm is depicted in blue, the inner (cytoplasmic) membrane in yellow, the periplasmic space in white, the peptidoglycan layer in purple, and the outer membrane in orange. Pili (also known as fimbriae) are depicted in black as linear organelles extending from the outer membrane, and flagellae are shown in green as hollow, flexible organelles emanating from an assembly and secretion apparatus that spans both membranes and the periplasmic space. *Inserts* show closer views of the envelope. **A,** The cytoplasmic membrane has a phospholipid bilayer, transmembrane (red) proteins, peripheral membrane (green) proteins, and lipoproteins (purple). **B,** The periplasmic space is surrounded by the inner and outer membrane and includes soluble proteins (purple and violet). The peptidoglycan layer, composed of disaccharide and peptide cross-linkages, is associated with the inner leaflet of the outer membrane through covalent attachment to lipoprotein (yellow). **C,** The outer membrane layer has an inner phospholipid leaflet and an outer lipopolysaccharide leaflet. Traversing the membrane are porin proteins that regulate the passage of molecules (green).

different patients arose from a recent common ancestor (i.e., belong to the same clone). Among these techniques are pulsed-field gel electrophoresis, ribotyping, and random-primed polymerase chain reaction. Databases containing archived electrophoresis patterns resulting from applying these techniques to previously isolated strains under standard conditions are increasingly available to facilitate outbreak recognition.[6,7]

Structural and Surface Antigenic Features

Members of the family Enterobacteriaceae are rod-shaped organisms, generally 1 to 3 μm in length and 0.5 μm in diameter. Surface appendages, including pili and flagellae, are common and may be numerous. The cytoplasm of enterobacterial organisms, like that of other bacteria, does not have membrane-enclosed organelles, as do eukaryotic cells. Therefore, there is no nucleus and the genome, which usually consists of a single circular chromosome and may include multiple plasmids of various sizes, is dispersed within the cytoplasm. Likewise, there is no endoplasmic reticulum and so ribosomes are not membrane associated, and respiration takes place at the cytoplasmic membrane rather than in mitochondria. As gram-negative organisms, enterobacteria have both an inner and an outer phospholipid membrane, which enclose a periplasmic space that contains the peptidoglycan cell wall (Fig. 215-1). Much of the specific information in the following sections comes from studies of *E. coli,* but may be assumed to apply to the entire family.

Inner Membrane

The inner or cytoplasmic membrane, impermeable to polar molecules, regulates the passage of nutrients, metabolites, macromolecules, and information in and out of the cytoplasm and maintains the proton motive force required for energy storage. More than 100 different proteins are associated with the inner membrane of *E. coli,*[8] including integral membrane proteins that have one or more transmembrane domains that traverse the phospholipid bilayer, lipoproteins inserted into the outer leaflet of the membrane, and peripheral membrane proteins that may be associated with the inner or outer leaflet or may be components of protein complexes that include integral membrane proteins. Among these inner membrane proteins are those involved in electron transfer and oxidative phosphorylation, the F_1F_0 ATPase that couples proton transport to ATP synthesis, numerous specific solute transporters, various protein translocation systems, polysaccharide export systems, and a large number of two-component histidine kinase signaling proteins that link external stimuli to changes in gene transcription.[9]

Periplasmic Space

Between the inner and outer membrane is the periplasm, an aqueous environment containing a high concentration of proteins and the peptidoglycan, which probably forms a hydrated gel.[10] In contrast to the reducing environment of the cytoplasm, the periplasm is an oxidizing environment and thus the cysteine residues of periplasmic proteins are frequently involved in disulfide bonds. A variety of functional categories of protein are found in the periplasm, including disulfide oxidoreductases, peptidyl-prolyl isomerases, chaperones, and proteases involved in protein folding and degradation; solute-binding proteins that ferry sugars, amino acids, ions, and vitamins across the space; lipoprotein sorting proteins; detoxifying enzymes; and enzymes involved in biogenesis of peptidoglycan, lipopolysaccharide (LPS), and capsule.

Peptidoglycan Cell Wall

The gram-negative cell wall is composed of a thin layer of peptidoglycan (also known as murein), which consists of alternating N-acetylglucosamine and N-acetylmuramic acid amino sugars joined by β-1,4 linkages, with a short peptide composed of L-alanine, D-glutamic acid, L-meso-diaminopalmelic acid, and D-alanine attached to the carboxyl group of the muramic acid.[11] Strands of the linear peptidoglycan molecules are covalently linked principally through an amide bond between the carboxyl group of the D-alanine residue at position 4 and the free amino group of the diaminopalmelic acid in an adjacent strand. Murein lipoprotein is also covalently attached to the peptide, which anchors the layer to the inner leaflet of the outer membrane in which the lipoprotein is embedded. The peptidoglycan layer of each bacterium is thought to comprise a single contiguous molecule enveloping the organism. In contrast to that of gram-positive organisms, this murein sacculus of gram-negative organisms is predominantly one layer thick. This thin envelope is responsible for the shape and osmotic stability of the organism, but it is constantly being remodeled as the bacterium elongates and divides.

Outer Membrane

The outer membrane of gram-negative bacteria is an asymmetrical lipid bilayer. Phospholipids occur almost exclusively in the inner leaflet, whereas the outer lipid is mostly composed of LPS. The polar nature of the LPS protruding from the outer membrane poses a significant barrier to the penetration of lipophilic molecules, and thus plays a major role in protecting the bacteria from various detergents (including bile salts), dyes (including methylene blue), and hydrophobic antibiotics.[12] These features are exploited in the microbiology lab on selective media for gram-negative organisms. In addition to containing lipoproteins, the outer membrane features porin proteins that regulate the passage of hydrophilic molecules. Porins, like other integral outer membrane proteins, have a conserved β-barrel fold that encloses a central aqueous channel.[13]

Lipopolysaccharide

The enterobacterial LPS is an extremely potent virulence factor, as discussed later. LPS has three major domains, the lipid A backbone, the core phosphorylated oligosaccharide, and the repeating oligosaccharide side chains.[14] Lipid A, also known as endotoxin, is the biologically active portion of the molecule that is recognized by the host. It is composed of a β-1,6 disaccharide of glucosamine, which is phosphorylated and substituted with saturated hydroxylated acyl chains. The acyl groups of lipid A are inserted into the outer leaflet of the outer membrane. The core oligosaccharide is composed of a pair of 8-carbon sugars known as Kdo linked to lipid A, which are in turn linked to 6 to 10 additional sugars, forming a branched chain. Core oligosaccharides are heterogeneous and differ within and between species. The repeating oligosaccharide attached to the LPS core is known as the O antigen. There may be 1 to 60 repeats of the oligosaccharide unit. The O antigen is the basis for serogroup classification. There are over 170 different O-antigen serogroups in E. coli alone.[15] The genes encoding the enzymes that synthesize the O antigen are quite variable and show evidence of interspecies lateral gene transfer. Mutants lacking the ability to synthesize O antigen, including the venerable K-12 laboratory strain of E. coli and its many derivatives, have rough colony morphologies.

Capsule and Other Surface Polysaccharides

In addition to the O-antigen component of LPS, members of the family Enterobacteriaceae produce additional surface polysaccharides including enterobacterial common antigen (ECA), colanic acid, and an envelope of surface polysaccharide known as "capsule." ECA is a repeating trisaccharide covalently linked to phosphoglyceride and, in some strains also to LPS, which is imbedded in the outer leaflet of the outer membrane.[16] The role of ECA in the biology of the bacteria is not known, but its remarkable conservation in all members of the family favors an important function. Many strains of E. coli and related organisms produce a surface layer of another polysaccharide termed *colanic acid,* which resembles in many ways a subset of capsule types. True capsules fall into several types, depending on genetic and biochemical features including whether they are linked to LPS or α-glycerol phosphate.[17] In some genera, such as *Klebsiella* and *Enterobacter,* the capsules can be quite luxuriant, imparting to the bacteria a highly mucoid colonial morphology. Early on, capsules were characterized on the basis of their ability to mask the O antigen from agglutinating antibody, in a manner that was sensitive to heating. Capsules vary widely in chemical structure and are the basis of the K-antigen serotyping scheme. There are over 80 K-antigen types in E. coli alone.[15]

Flagellae

Most members of the enterobacterial family are motile, and even those that are not often possess the genes that specify the expression of flagellae and may retain the capacity for motility under certain conditions.[18] Flagellae are flexible surface appendages that rotate and propel the bacteria through liquid environments. In most enterobacteria they emanate from all sides of the microorganisms (Fig. 215-2A). The biogenesis of flagellae is quite complex, proceeds in a specific order from the base to the tip of the organelle, and involves an intricate secretion machinery that resembles that of the type III secretion systems[19] (see later). Flagellar assembly and motility are under the control of a complex regulatory network that responds to a variety of extracellular signals. The flagellar filament is composed of a hollow helical array of a single protein, flagellin. The amino and carboxyl termini of flagellin are highly conserved within and across species of the family. However, the middle of the molecule, which is surface exposed, is highly variable in amino acid composition, apparently as a result of both recombination following horizontal gene transfer and selection for diversifying mutations.[20] This diversity is represented in the H-antigen typing scheme, the third component of O:K:H serotyping. There are currently 54 flagellin H-antigen types in E. coli alone. Despite this diversity, flagellin is one of several microbial molecules recognized by the host innate immune system pattern recognition receptors, in this case Toll-like receptor 5 (TLR5).[21] Signaling through TLR5 results in activation of nuclear factor kappa-B (NF-κB) and transcription and secretion of interleukin-6 and interleukin-8, which can lead to neutrophil recruitment and initiation of a proinflammatory response.[21-23]

Fimbriae

In addition to flagellae, most enterobacterial species produce surface appendages referred to as either *fimbriae* (from the Latin for "thread") or *pili* (from the Latin for "hair"). These appendages are thinner than flagellae, ranging in diameter from 2 to 7 nm and extending several micrometers from the surface.[24] Fimbriae serve several functions, including roles in adhesion and genetic exchange through conjugation. There are several types of fimbriae, which differ in morphology, biosynthetic pathways, and function.

The chaperone-usher group of fimbriae is widespread among the Enterobacteriaceae and includes the ubiquitous type-1 pili, produced by most members of the family (see Fig. 215-2B). Individual strains may have the genes required to produce as many as 10 different

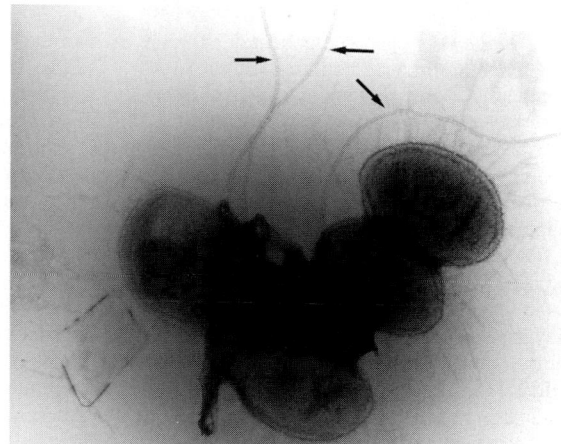

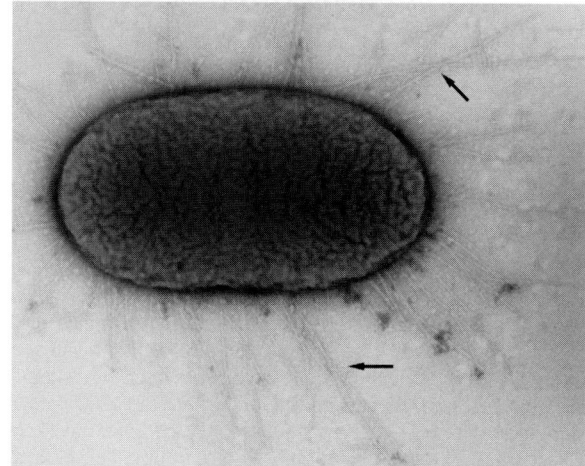

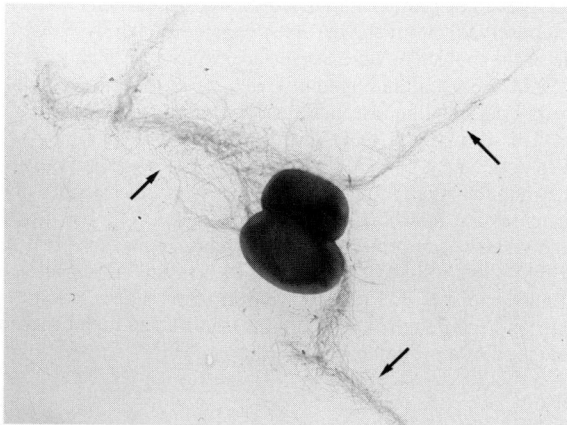

FIGURE 215-2. Transmission electron micrographs of negatively stained *E. coli* cells. **A** and **B,** An extraintestinal pathogenic *E. coli* strain grown under conditions favoring the expression of type-1 pili demonstrates both flagellae (*arrows* in **A**) and pili (*arrows* in **B**). **C,** An enteropathogenic *E. coli* strain grown under conditions favoring expression of bundle-forming type IV pili (*arrows*). (*Courtesy of Eric Buckles and Paula J. Fernandes.*)

chaperone-usher type pili.[25-27] Many of these pili are composite fibers, with a rigid rod composed of a helical array of the major structural subunit pilin protein joined end-to-end to a thinner, more flexible tip.[28,29] The adhesin may be at the distal end of the tip. Other members of the family, sometimes referred to as fibrillae, have a uniform wiry appearance that resembles that of the tip of the composite fibers. Assembly of the chaperone-usher type of fimbria proceeds by a dedicated pathway in which the subunits are exported by the general secretion machinery to the periplasm, where they bind to specific chaperones that prevent premature interactions between subunits. The pilin-chaperone complexes are delivered to an outer membrane channel protein known as the usher, which exports the subunits across the outer membrane in a specific order starting with the tip protein and to which the proximal end of the pilus remains attached.[30]

Type IV fimbriae are not as widespread as chaperone-usher pili among the Enterobacteriaceae, but are nevertheless produced by several important members of the family, including certain pathotypes of *E. coli*[31,32]; certain strains of *S. enterica*, including serovar Typhi[33]; and some strains of *Yersinia pseudotuberculosis*.[34] In many, but not all cases type IV pili are expressed exclusively at the poles of the bacteria, and they often aggregate laterally to form ropelike bundles (see Fig. 215-2C). Type IV pili are retractable, and this retraction can be harnessed for a type of bacterial locomotion called "twitching motility."[35] The ability of the fimbriae to bundle and retract is associated with bacterial aggregation and disaggregation. Type IV pili are generally formed of a single pilin protein, which is processed to its mature form by a dedicated pre-pilin peptidase that also *N*-methylates the amino-terminal residue. A complex and poorly understood molecular machine responsible for pilin export and pilus formation is composed of approximately 10 proteins localized to the cytoplasm, inner membrane, periplasm, and outer membrane.[36] Some of the components of this machine are related to components of the type II secretion apparatus (see later).

Self-transmissible plasmids, which allow DNA transfer via conjugation, are ubiquitous in the family Enterobacteriaceae. These plasmids, which often harbor virulence genes, transposons, and antibiotic resistance genes, encode pili that mediate intercellular contact and DNA transfer. Some of these plasmids are host restricted, but others are capable of transfer among distantly related species. The pili and transfer mechanisms encoded by such plasmids are related to type IV secretion systems that export virulence factors in *Helicobacter pylori* and *Bordetella pertussis*.[37]

Virulence and Virulence Factors

The capability of members of the family Enterobacteriaceae to cause disease is quite variable, encompassing rarely harmful commensal flora, opportunistic pathogens that can inflict considerable morbidity and mortality on compromised hosts, and potent pathogens capable of initiating illness in individuals in perfect health. This range of pathogenic potential is a reflection of the expression, or lack thereof, of specific virulence factors that play roles in the disease process. The precise definition of a virulence factor is often the subject of vigorous debate. Researchers do not agree as to whether or not structures or functions that are indispensable for disease, but which are not specific to pathogens or to the disease process, should be considered virulence factors. However, there is general conceptual agreement on the principle of "molecular Koch's postulates" as articulated by Stanley Falkow.[38] By this definition, a trait is considered to be a virulence factor if it is found specifically in strains of a microbe that cause disease; if mutation of a gene encoding the factor results in less severe infection in a suitable model of the disease; and if restoration of a wild-type allele of the gene to the mutant (genetic complementation, usually achieved by transforming the mutant with a plasmid that contains the gene) results in reinstatement of the original disease severity.

In considering virulence factors, it is useful to contemplate the phases of the infectious cycle implemented by most pathogenic microorganisms. These phases include entry, establishment and multiplication, avoidance of host defense mechanisms, tissue damage, and exit.[39-41] The following sections review the established and proposed virulence factors common to many members of the enterobacterial family. Specific factors are also considered during the discussions of individual microorganisms.

Adhesins

Part of the accepted dogma of microbial pathogenesis holds that initial adherence of pathogen to host cells is an absolute prerequisite for disease. Furthermore, adherence is not the result of nonspecific stickiness, but rather requires particular microbial adhesins that bind selectively and avidly to cognate receptors on host surfaces to overcome the electrostatic repulsion resulting from the net negative charge on both host and microbial cells. Enterobacterial pathogens may produce a variety of adhesins, including fimbriae and outer membrane proteins. In some cases surface carbohydrates can also have adhesive properties. The bacteria may simultaneously produce many different adhesins or produce various adhesins in sequence, as a result of random phase variation or in response to environmental cues.

Type-1 fimbriae are ubiquitous among the Enterobacteriaceae. These organelles belong to the chaperone-usher family of pili and are composed of a rigid rod formed by repeating subunits of the FimA (also known as PilA) protein arranged in a tight helical array. The tips of these pili contain a short fiber, which is composed of the FimG and FimH subunits, joined end-to-end to the FimA rod.[28] FimH, the type-1 fimbrial adhesin, binds to mannose residues found in glycoproteins and glycolipids on host cell surfaces.[42,43] The expression of type-1 fimbriae is subject to phase variation because of the presence of an invertible DNA element that flanks the promoter for the *fim* operon encoding the pili.[44] This invertible element allows the orientation of the promoter to oscillate so that it either faces toward or away from the operon, allowing or precluding pilus expression. Thus bacteria that produce the pili arise at random from populations of bacteria that do not, and vice versa. Under conditions in which type-1 pili are useful, bacteria expressing them predominate, whereas under conditions in which type-1 pili are detrimental, selection favors those lacking them. In a murine model of *E. coli* urinary tract infections (UTIs), type-1 pili have been proven to be critical for colonization and disease.[45] Type-1 pili have also been demonstrated to play an important role in transmission of bacteria from neonatal rats that have *E. coli* colonization of the intestine to the oropharynx and subsequently gastrointestinal tract and blood of littermates.[46,47]

In addition to type-1 fimbriae, individual strains may produce 10 or perhaps more additional chaperone-usher type pili and may produce one or more type IV fimbriae. Together members of the enterobacterial family undoubtedly produce a vast number of distinct fimbrial types. Characterized pili bind to a wide variety of different receptors. Thus the entire repertoire of adhesive pili and their receptors must be quite extensive. Additional pili that play roles in the pathogenesis of particular strains within the enterobacterial family are discussed in sections devoted to these bacteria.

Pili are not the only adhesins produced by bacteria. A variety of outer membrane proteins also serve as adhesins. Perhaps the best characterized of these is the invasin-intimin family of proteins. These proteins share a common structure and have detectable amino acid sequence similarities, especially in their amino-terminal and central domains. They are inserted into the outer membrane via their amino termini, which are predicted to form the β-barrel structure typical of outer membrane proteins. The membrane portion of these molecules is connected via a flexible hinge region to a rigid rod composed of repeating units, each similar in structure to portions of immunoglobulin molecules. The carboxyl-terminal adhesin domain bears similarities to calcium-binding lectin molecules.[48-50] In the case of the invasin molecule of *Y. pseudotuberculosis,* this portion of the molecule binds to β-integrins in the host cell membrane with an affinity over 100-fold greater than does their natural ligand fibronectin.[51] In the case of intimin from enteropathogenic strains of *E. coli,* the receptor is a protein produced by the bacteria and injected into the host cell membrane.[52]

Secretion Systems and Toxins

Toxins were the first and arguably remain the best studied virulence factors. Toxins are released by bacteria into the environment or directed to host cells. Toxins have physiologically relevant activity when injected in purified form into animals or applied to tissue culture cells. However, enterobacterial toxins usually do not fully reproduce the disease in the absence of the bacteria that produce them. Thus toxins often play ancillary or unknown roles in pathogenesis. Toxins are numerous and may be categorized in various schemes, such as by function, target, activity, or structural similarity.

The inner and outer membranes of gram-negative bacteria together pose a formidable barrier against the diffusion of macromolecules. Thus many toxins require specific secretion machineries for their export. The simplest of these export strategies is exemplified by the autotransported proteases produced by many gram-negative species.[53] These proteins are produced with typical signal sequences at their amino termini, which are cleaved as the proteins are exported across the inner membrane by the general secretion machinery. The proteins are then inserted into the outer membrane via the β-barrel structure of their mature amino termini. The so-called passenger domain, which possesses the enzymatic activity located at the carboxyl terminus, may then be cleaved off and released into the media, via either its own protease activity or that of other bacterial proteases. A subset of these proteins has been termed the SPATE family (serine protease autotransporters of the Enterobacteriaceae). Several SPATE family members have been characterized from various pathotypes of *E. coli* and *Shigella*. These proteins include several toxins categorized as having cytopathic effects and toxins that elicit fluid secretion from intestinal epithelia.[54-58] The precise roles of these proteins in disease and the relevant host cell targets are largely unknown.

Many members of the family Enterobacteriaceae produce toxins capable of inducing lysis of host cells. Strains that produce these factors are usually characterized because they induce zones of clearing on blood agar plates, so the toxins are often termed *hemolysins*. One of the best studied hemolysins is that of *E. coli*. This protein is secreted in a single step across both inner and outer membrane by a three-protein apparatus known as a type I secretion system (TISS). The TISS is composed of an integral inner membrane ATPase (HlyD) and another integral inner membrane protein (HlyB), both of which are able to recognize a carboxyl-terminal secretion signal and bind the hemolysin protein. The HlyD-HlyB-hemolysin complex is then able to engage a remarkable tunnel-channel protein called TolC, which spans the periplasmic space and outer membrane, opens up to allow passage of hemolysin through the outer membrane, and then disengages from the HlyD-HlyB complex.[59,60] TolC interacts with different substrate-specific inner membrane proteins to serve the same function for a variety of other substrates, including other toxins such as *E. coli* heat-stable enterotoxin,[61] and antibiotics. The precise mechanism by which hemolysin induces cell lysis is still under investigation. It is clear that hemolysin inserts into host cell membranes, but it is not clear whether it forms a transmembrane channel that leads to osmotic lysis or it inserts only into the outer leaflet of the host cell membrane and induces lysis by another mechanism.[62] Furthermore, low concentrations of hemolysin, which may be relevant in vivo, lead to oscillations in intracellular calcium concentrations and signaling through NF-κB.[63] Hemolysin is found in a higher proportion of extraintestinal pathogenic *E. coli* than in fecal strains or strains associated with diarrhea, but the potential role of hemolysin in virulence remains to be convincingly demonstrated.

E. coli, most if not all members of the enterobacterial family, and many other gram-negative organisms contain an additional secretion machine known as the main terminal branch of the general secretory pathway or the type II secretion system (T2SS).[64] A variety of enzymes, including some toxins, are exported first by the general secretion system to the periplasmic space and then by the T2SS to the external environment. For example, the *E. coli* chromosome encodes a T2SS that secretes chitinase, while the O157:H7 clone of enterohemorrhagic *E. coli* expresses an additional, plasmid-encoded T2SS that secretes a metalloprotease capable of degrading C1 esterase inhibitor.[65] T2SSs are composed of approximately 12 proteins, including an outer membrane gated channel and several inner membrane proteins.[66] It is proposed that these proteins are the components of a piston-like machine that exports the proteins across the outer membrane. T2SSs are related to systems required for the biogenesis of type IV pili and filamentous bacteriophages.

Many gram-negative organisms that interact directly with eukaryotic cells, including several important enterobacterial pathogens, have an additional dedicated type III secretion system (T3SS) that not only exports proteins through the inner and outer bacterial membranes, but also injects them into or through the host cell membrane.[67] More than 20 proteins make up this remarkably complex secretion machine, which resembles both morphologically and evolutionarily the apparatus responsible for assembly of flagella. The T3SS apparatus has been likened to a molecular syringe that spans both inner and outer membranes, with a needle that extends from the outer membrane toward the host cell. Specific "translocator" proteins secreted presumably through this needle are thought to form a pore in the host cell membrane through which other secreted "effector" proteins pass. Translocation of effector proteins requires direct contact between the bacterium and the host cell. A wide variety of such effector proteins exist, many of which subvert host cell pathways through structural mimicry to serve diverse functions for the bacterium.[68] Among these effector proteins are bacterial adhesin receptors, protein tyrosine phosphatases, serine kinases, and proteins that either activate the GTPase activity or catalyze the exchange of GTP for GDP in small regulatory G proteins. These effector proteins may be considered to be a newly discovered class of toxins, which are delivered by pathogens directly to target cells.

Iron Acquisition

Iron is an essential element, required by virtually all organisms as a cofactor for several indispensable enzymes. Microorganisms that colonize the surfaces or invade the tissues of mammals must compete with their hosts to acquire free iron, which the host maintains at extremely low concentrations ($\sim 10^{-24}$M) through the use of iron-binding proteins such as transferrin and lactoferrin. Thus enterobacterial pathogens have developed several highly efficient systems that scavenge iron. These systems are under the control of a ubiquitous regulator protein called Fur, which activates gene transcription at low iron concentrations.[69] Many members of the family Enterobacteriaceae, even commensal *E. coli* strains such as K-12 and its derivatives, produce a chromosomally encoded siderophore known as enterobactin.[70] Siderophores are low-molecular-weight iron-chelating molecules that are synthesized, secreted, and recaptured by microorganisms. Humans appear to have countered enterobactin by producing a protein that has even higher affinity for the siderophore than does the bacterial enterobactin outer membrane receptor protein. Thus enterobacterial species produce other siderophores in addition to enterobactin. For example, many strains of *E. coli* isolated from extraintestinal infections produce a plasmid-encoded siderophore called aerobactin.[71,72] Some strains are also able to bind and transport heme. Common to all of these iron uptake systems, and to systems for the transport of nutrients such as vitamin B_{12}, is a cytoplasmic membrane protein called TonB.[73] TonB spans the periplasm and contacts siderophore receptors and other gated porins in the outer membrane to allow them to open upon ligand binding.[74] Thus TonB is a point of convergence in enterobacterial iron uptake pathways and a potential drug target. The role of iron-scavenging systems in enterobacterial virulence is well established. Early studies showed that the minimum lethal dose of *E. coli* is reduced substantially when iron is delivered by vein along with the inoculum. More recently, molecular Koch's postulates were fulfilled for TonB, and evidence implicating the importance of aerobactin and heme uptake was provided using a murine model of ascending *E. coli* UTI.[73]

Lipopolysaccharide and Capsules

Lipopolysaccharide is an essential component of the outer membrane of all gram-negative bacteria. Therefore, some would argue that LPS is not a true virulence factor. However, LPS molecules from different organisms have different chemical compositions and different biologic activities and potency, and, therefore, the effects of LPS on the host differ depending on its source and chemical composition.[75] Moreover, the highly variable O-antigen component of LPS has biologic properties that may influence virulence as well. Thus it is appropriate to consider LPS in any discussion of the virulence of gram-negative organisms.

The extraordinary potency of enterobacterial LPS as an inducer of the innate immune response is due to signaling through Toll-like receptor 4 (TLR4).[76-78] Lipopolysaccharide, often in complex with LPS binding protein, binds to CD14, a glycerophosphatidylinositol-linked non-transmembrane receptor. It is believed that this complex interacts with TLR4,[79] which through a series of intermediates activates NF-κB to initiate transcription of a variety of proinflammatory mediators, including cytokines such as tumor necrosis factor, chemokines, and major histocompatibility complex receptors. The host response to LPS through TLR4 is a key factor in determining outcome to infections with gram-negative infections. Mice deficient in TLR4 are highly susceptible to bacteremia with enterobacterial organisms and fail to recruit neutrophils to clear *E. coli* UTIs.[80,81] There may also be an association between TLR4 polymorphisms and susceptibility to severe gram-negative infections in humans.[82]

In addition to the important biologic effects of lipid A, the highly variable O antigen of LPS is also important for pathogenesis and immunity to enterobacterial infections. For example, *E. coli* mutants lacking the ability to synthesize O antigen are highly sensitive to serum.[83] There also appears to be a relationship between presence of antibodies against LPS and against specific O antigens and susceptibility to disease with several enterobacterial pathogens.[84-87] However, these studies are not able to distinguish whether the anti-LPS antibodies are themselves protective or merely a marker for protective responses.

Capsules are common among members of the family Enterobacteriaceae. Some capsules appear to endow the bacteria with the ability to avoid phagocytosis and to avoid killing by human serum.[88-90] In some cases, a role of capsule in the pathogenesis of particular infections has been suggested. For example, the K1 capsule produced by many *E. coli* strains isolated from patients with neonatal sepsis and meningitis has been implicated in bacterial survival while passing through the blood-brain barrier.[91] A screen for mutants of a uropathogenic *E. coli* strain that were deficient in surviving in a murine model of ascending UTI identified three mutants with disruptions of genes required for biosynthesis of K2 capsule.[92] The capsule of *Klebsiella pneumoniae* has also been implicated in colonization of the murine urinary tract.[93] In contrast, no significant difference in ability to cause UTI could be demonstrated when a K54 capsule *E. coli* mutant was compared to its parental strain.[94]

Plasmids

Plasmids, extrachromosomal autonomously replicating DNA elements, are not virulence factors per se. However, the genes encoded on plasmids may play major roles in pathogenesis. As examples, the entire T3SS that endows enteroinvasive *E. coli* and *Shigella* strains with the ability to invade epithelial cells is encoded on similar large plasmids[95]; the type IV pilus of enteropathogenic *E. coli* strains is encoded on a large plasmid that is required for full virulence[96,97]; and the large plasmids of enterohemorrhagic *E. coli* strains encode a T2SS, a protease, and a hemolysin that are potential virulence factors.[65,98,99] In addition, plasmids may be self-transmissible, encoding elaborate systems specifying the production of pili for DNA transfer.[37] Many of these plasmids are very promiscuous with regard to their ability to transfer between disparate genera. The emergence and dissemination of broad-host-range R plasmids containing antimicrobial resistance genes has been a major factor in the global spread of bacteria resistant to multiple antibiotics. These resistance genes may be present on transposons, allowing them to jump to other plasmids or chromosomes, or they may be found on integrons, which have loci downstream of strong promoters at which resistance genes may insert by site-specific recombination to be expressed at high levels. Such mobile genetic elements are important factors contributing to the rapid evolution of highly antibiotic-resistant isolates and subsequent dissemination within the enterobacterial family.[100]

THE SPECIFIC PATHOGENS

Escherichia

E. coli is the type species of the genus *Escherichia,* which in turn is the type genus of the family Enterobacteriaceae. The genus is named for Theodore Escherich, who performed pioneering studies on the fecal flora of neonates and described the organism in 1885. *E. coli* is both the most common species of facultative anaerobe found in the human gastrointestinal tract and the most commonly encountered pathogen in the enterobacterial family. An enormous amount of information is available regarding the genetics, structure, and physiology of this organism, and an effort is underway to fully characterize the biochemistry and cell biology of the nonpathogenic K-12 strain of this species (*www.biomedcentral.com/news/20020904/04/*). *E. coli* is usually distinguished from other members of the family by the ability of most strains to ferment lactose and other sugars and to produce indole from tryptophan. In addition, most strains are motile.

While most strains of *E. coli* reside harmlessly in the lumen of the colon and appear to be poorly adapted to cause disease in healthy individuals, there exist a plethora of pathotypes that can cause specific types of illness in both normal hosts and those with compromised nonspecific defense mechanisms (Table 215-2). Pathogenic strains differ from commensal organisms in that they produce virulence factors specific for each pathotype, which may be encoded by bacteriophages, on plasmids, or on stretches of the chromosome known as pathogenicity islands. Comparisons among the fully sequenced genomes of the nonpathogenic K-12 strain and several pathogenic strains have revealed that as much as 25% of the genomes of pathogenic strains consist of genes absent from nonpathogenic strains, whereas there are many fewer genes present in the K-12 strain that are lacking in the pathogenic strains. Furthermore, most of the genes that are not found in the K-12 strain are specific to particular pathotypes. Thus, of the many genes that may be found in various *E. coli* strains, only a small minority is common to all.

Despite the vast repertoire of virulence factors that may be produced by various pathotypes, there are some common features of pathogenic *E. coli* strains. These include fimbrial adhesins, secretion systems to export proteins involved in pathogenesis, and toxins.

Extraintestinal Pathogenic *E. coli*

E. coli is the most common cause of UTIs, is a leading cause of neonatal meningitis, and can cause a wide variety of other extraintestinal infections, including nosocomial pneumonia, cholecystitis and cholangitis, peritonitis, cellulitis, osteomyelitis, and infectious arthritis. It has been appreciated for some time that strains of *E. coli* isolated from the urine or blood of patients with UTIs differ from those cultured from the feces of healthy individuals and from those that cause diarrhea.[101,102] Thus the term *uropathogenic E. coli* (UPEC) was coined to refer to such strains. Furthermore, community outbreaks and geographically widespread clones causing UTI have been reported.[103-109] UPEC strains are more likely than fecal strains to produce P fimbriae, which bind to glycolipid receptors on the surface of host cells, to be encapsulated, to produce the cytolytic toxin hemolysin, and to have multiple systems for the acquisition of iron. Similarly, strains isolated from patients with neonatal meningitis are more likely than fecal strains to produce the K1 capsule and to produce S fimbriae.[110] However, it is now appreciated that many of these same factors are found in strains isolated from a wide variety of extraintestinal infections, including those listed previously.[111] Furthermore, strains representing the same clonal group that commonly cause neonatal meningitis are frequently isolated from UTIs.[103] Therefore, there is increasing recognition that the distinction between UPEC and strains that cause other extraintestinal infections is artificial and that these strains should fall into a single pathotype termed *extraintestinal pathogenic E. coli*

TABLE 215-2 Summary of Epidemiology, Clinical Features, Pathogenesis, Diagnosis, and Therapy of *E. coli* Pathotypes That Cause Diarrhea

Pathotype*	Epidemiology	Clinical Features	Pathogenesis	Diagnosis	Adjunctive Therapy†
ETEC	Contaminated water and food. Major cause of childhood diarrhea in developing countries; leading cause of travelers' diarrhea	Acute watery diarrhea, occasionally severe	Large number of fimbrial adhesins; heat-stable and heat-labile enterotoxins	PCR or DNA probes for enterotoxins	Fluoroquinolones plus loperamide for travelers
EPEC	Person-to-person transmission. Leading cause of infantile diarrhea in developing countries	Severe acute diarrhea and vomiting, may be persistent	Localized adherence via bundle-forming pilus; attaching and effacing via intimin-Tir	PCR or DNA probes for *bfp*‡ or *eae* genes or tissue culture assay for localized adherence†	Antibiotics guided by susceptibility testing for severe or protracted cases
EHEC and other STEC	Food, water, and person-to-person spread. Major cause of bloody diarrhea in developed countries	Watery and bloody diarrhea, may be complicated by hemolytic uremic syndrome	Shiga toxins; intimin-Tir–mediated attaching and effacing in EHEC strains	Sorbitol-MacConkey agar,§ PCR or DNA probes for *stx* genes	Supportive care. Antibiotics and antimotility agents contraindicated
EAEC	Mode of transmission unknown. Important cause of chronic diarrhea in developing countries; emerging cause of travelers' diarrhea	Mucoid diarrhea, often persistent	Aggregative adherence via several fimbriae; Pet and other toxins	Tissue culture assay for aggregative adherence or PCR for *aggR* gene	Fluoroquinolones may be of benefit for travelers and HIV patients
EIEC	Contaminated food. Outbreaks in developed countries	Watery diarrhea or dysentery	Cellular invasion, intracellular motility, and cell-to-cell spread	PCR or DNA probes for *inv* genes	Unknown
DAEC	Mode of transmission unknown. Diarrhea in older children in developing countries	Poorly described	Unknown	Tissue culture assay for diffuse adherence	

*ETEC, enterotoxigenic *E. coli;* EPEC, enteropathogenic *E. coli;* EHEC, enterohemorrhagic *E. coli;* STEC, Shiga toxin–producing *E. coli;* EAEC, enteroaggregative *E. coli;* EIEC, enteroinvasive *E. coli;* DAEC, diffuse adhering *E. coli.*
†The cornerstone of therapy for all diarrheal disease is rehydration, preferably via oral route.
‡Detects typical strains only.
§Detects O157:H7 strains only
HIV, human immunodeficiency virus; PCR, polymerase chain reaction.

(ExPEC).[112] It should be noted that *E. coli* strains isolated from individuals with compromised defenses against infection are less likely to resemble ExPEC and more likely to resemble control strains isolated from the fecal flora. This observation holds both for strains that cause UTI in patients with abnormal urinary tracts (e.g., those with stones, disorders of bladder function, anatomic abnormalities, and foreign bodies)[113-115] and for infections elsewhere (e.g., cholangitis in patients with biliary tract obstruction).[116]

Efforts to elucidate the molecular pathogenesis of *E. coli* UTI have begun to bear fruit. A murine animal model of ascending infection has been useful because it distinguishes between ExPEC strains and control strains from the feces of healthy volunteers and, among ExPEC strains, between strains isolated from patients with cystitis and those from patients with pyelonephritis.[117-119] A primate model has also been extremely valuable, but at considerable cost.[120,121] Using these models, it has been firmly established that type-1 fimbriae are essential virulence determinants in *E. coli* UTI.[45,120] Type-1 fimbriae appear to be especially important in colonization of the bladder,[122] where potential mannose-containing receptors include uroplakin.[123] Apparent binding of *E. coli* to uroplakin in superficial bladder epithelial cells via type-1 pili has been observed by electron microscopy, and this binding appears to lead to exfoliation of the cells and invasion of deeper cell layers.[124] As mentioned earlier, the expression of type-1 pili is subject to phase variation under the control of an invertible DNA element that includes the promoter for the operon.[44] Thus *E. coli* can produce the pili when it is most advantageous to do so, such as early in the course of UTI, and not when it may be detrimental to the bacteria.[125,126] Despite the importance of type-1 pili in the pathogenesis of UTI, the ability to express these fimbriae does not explain the relative virulence of ExPEC strains, because essentially all *E. coli* and other members of the enterobacterial family are able to do so. Among other potential adhesins relevant to the pathogenesis of UTI, P fimbriae stand out as being particularly associated with ExPEC strains, especially those isolated from patients with pyelonephritis.[101,102] These chaperone-usher pili bind to glycosphingolipids containing the disaccharide galactose(α1-4)galactose, which are found on the surface of epithelial cells in the human kidney.[127,128] A role for P fimbriae in the pathogenesis of UTI has been substantiated by the fact that a strain with a mutation in *papG*, the gene encoding the P fimbrial tip adhesin, colonized the kidney of cynomolgus monkeys for a shorter period and did less damage than did the wild-type strain from which it was derived.[129] However, molecular Koch's postulates remain unfulfilled for P fimbriae, because complementation studies were not performed. In addition to type-1 and P fimbriae, ExPEC may express many other types of pilus and nonpilus adhesins[27,130]; the roles played by these factors in the establishment of *E. coli* UTI have not been sufficiently studied. Besides adhesion, other attributes that have been implicated in the pathogenesis of *E. coli* UTI, include the production of the toxins hemolysin[131,132] and cytotoxic necrotizing factor (CNF, discussed later);[133] the ability to sequester iron[73]; the production of O antigen, capsule, and other extracellular polysaccharides[92,94]; and the expression of regulatory genes.[134] Further details on clinical aspects of *E. coli* UTI can be found elsewhere (see Chapter 66).

E. coli is one of the leading causes of neonatal bacteremia, sepsis, and meningitis, traditionally second only to *Streptococcus agalactiae* in this regard. However, with improved strategies to prevent infections caused by the latter species, this hierarchy may soon be reversed. Studies of newborns with *E. coli* bacteremia and experiments in neonatal rats have shown that meningitis is much more likely when the level of *E. coli* bacteremia exceeds 10^3 cfu/mL of blood.[135] The *E. coli* strains that cause neonatal meningitis frequently express the K1 capsule, which may facilitate this high level of bacteremia. Although this polysialic acid capsule, indistinguishable from that of *Neisseria meningitidis* group B strains, is one of the most common types produced by *E. coli*, it is expressed by a disproportionate percentage of neonatal meningitis isolates.[110,136] In addition to its role in serum resistance and resistance to phagocytosis, it appears that K1 capsule facilitates survival of the bacteria as they traverse the blood-brain barrier.[91,135] Many strains isolated from neonates with sepsis or meningitis express S fimbriae, members of the chaperone-usher fimbrial family that bind to oligosaccharides containing sialic acid,[137] which can be found on brain endothelial cells[138] and human kidney cells.[139] P fimbrial expression is also common among these strains.[110] Strains isolated from neonatal sepsis and meningitis frequently express toxins such as hemolysin,[110] CNF, and cytolethal distending toxin.[140] CNF, which is found almost exclusively in strains that produce hemolysin and is frequently encoded adjacent to the hemolysin operon,[141,142] affects the host cell cytoskeleton by deamidating members of the Rho family of small GTPases, which regulate actin filament formation.[143] Mutants with disruptions in the *cnf* gene are less able to invade human brain endothelial cells in vitro and less able to enter the cerebrospinal fluid in vivo.[135,144] This ability to invade human brain endothelial cells has been exploited to identify other genes that may play a role in traversal of the blood-brain barrier.[144,145] Among *E. coli* strains that cause neonatal meningitis, the serotype O18:K1:H7 is particularly common, and strains belonging to this clone have been used as prototypes in research. Interestingly, strains of the same serotype are often found in cases of cystitis and belong to the same clone, a finding that supports the concept that ExPEC may cause different types of infections.[146]

Very little is known about the pathogenesis of extraintestinal *E. coli* infections other than UTI and neonatal meningitis.

Enterotoxigenic *E. coli*

E. coli can cause diarrhea by no less (and probably more) than six different mechanisms.[147] Each type of *E. coli* diarrhea is associated with a different pathotype of *E. coli*, and each pathotype has characteristic virulence determinants that contribute to its pathogenic mechanisms. Five of these pathotypes, for which at least some information on pathogenic mechanisms is available, are included in the discussion in this chapter. The first pathotype of diarrheogenic *E. coli* for which the broad outlines of pathogenesis were elucidated was enterotoxigenic *E. coli* (ETEC).

ETEC strains are a common and important cause of childhood diarrhea throughout the developing world and a leading cause of diarrhea in travelers who visit these countries.[147,148] ETEC infections are acquired through ingestion of heavily contaminated water or food and thus result from a failure of sanitation. Infections caused by ETEC range from asymptomatic carriage to severe cholera-like illness. The predominant symptom is watery diarrhea, which may be accompanied by nausea and cramps. Vomiting, severe cramps, and fever are not prominent and the stool does not contain blood, mucus, or fecal leukocytes. The incubation period ranges from a few hours to 2 days, and symptoms usually last less than 5 days.

The pathogenesis of ETEC infection as it is currently understood involves pilus-mediated adherence and toxin-mediated fluid secretion. The genes encoding the toxins and many of the genes encoding the adhesins are found on plasmids. However, recent research has focused on chromosomal loci that may be involved in pathogenesis.[149-152]

For historical reasons the pili of ETEC are known as colonization factor antigens (CFAI, CFAIII, etc.) or coli surface antigens (CS3, CS6, etc.). These appendages include classic chaperone-usher–type pili; thinner, more wiry chaperone-usher type fibrillae; and type IV pili. Some strains express afimbrial factors that are not associated with detectable organelles. More than 20 of these pilus-related factors have been described.[153] Strains of ETEC that produce several such factors at a time and strains that produce none of the known factors are common.[154] The ETEC colonization factors are presumed to mediate attachment to the small intestinal mucosa. Experiments involving strains of ETEC that naturally infect animals have demonstrated that expression of these pili is required for colonization and signs of disease. In adult volunteer experiments, immunity against ETEC disease can be demonstrated upon rechallenge with the same strain, but not with a heterologous strain.[155] The diversity of colonization factors that may be expressed by ETEC strains is thought to be a major factor that allows children in developing countries to suffer from multiple bouts of ETEC diarrhea. According to this theory, adults in developing countries are protected from illness after repeated exposure to multiple ETEC strains during their lifetime.

ETEC strains may express either or both of two enterotoxins, known as heat-labile enterotoxin (LT) and heat-stable enterotoxin (ST), that are responsible for the secretory diarrhea seen in symptomatic patients. LT is closely related to cholera toxin, has an almost identical quaternary structure,[156] and has an identical mechanism of action. Like cholera toxin, LT is composed of a single catalytic A subunit and a pentamer of identical receptor-binding B subunits, which are secreted as the holotoxin via a T2SS.[152] The B subunits bind to the glycolipid asialo-GM_1 in the apical membrane of enterocytes. After endocytosis and passage through the Golgi apparatus, the A subunit makes its way to its target in the basolateral membrane: the regulatory subunit of a heterotrimeric G protein, $G\alpha_S$. The A subunit is an ADP ribosyltransferase that cleaves NAD and attaches ADP-ribose covalently to $G\alpha_S$, thereby locking the protein in its active form so that it, in turn, constitutively activates its target, adenylyl cyclase. The elevated levels of cyclic AMP that ensue lead to activation of protein kinase A, which phosphorylates and activates the cystic fibrosis transmembrane conductance regulator (CFTR). Thus a complex cascade leads to active secretion of chloride and, when sodium and water passively follow, copious fluid secretion into the small intestinal lumen. ST is a very different molecule than LT. ST is a small peptide that contains six cysteine residues involved in three intramolecular disulfide bonds. It resembles a mammalian peptide hormone, guanylin, and binds to the guanylin receptor, a GTPase found in the apical membrane.[157] The resulting elevated cyclic GMP levels lead to activation of protein kinase G, phosphorylation of CFTR, and chloride secretion.[158]

The diagnosis of ETEC infection is not usually confirmed because it rests on detection of the genes encoding LT and ST by polymerase chain reaction (PCR) or DNA probes or on assays for the biologic activity of these toxins.

Travelers to endemic areas can reduce the risk of ETEC infection by strict adherence to advice regarding the ingestion of safe food and water.[148] Those wishing to avoid travelers' diarrhea should drink only bottled beverages, avoid ice, eschew meat and vegetables that are not served steaming hot, and shun fruit that they do not peel themselves. Dry packaged or canned foods carry no risk. The prophylactic use of bismuth subsalicylate tablets can also reduce the risk of travelers' diarrhea, but conveys some inconvenience.[159] The development of a safe and effective ETEC vaccine has been the goal of numerous laboratories for many years, but is hampered by the heterogeneity of antigenic determinants required for protective immunity.

Treatment of all diarrheal disease rests first and foremost on providing adequate fluid replacement, by the oral or if necessary parenteral routes. Further information on treatment of ETEC infections can be inferred from trials enrolling patients with travelers' diarrhea, much of which is caused by ETEC. Prompt therapy with an antimotility agent such as loperamide can reduce symptoms. Combination therapy with a fluoroquinolone and loperamide appears to provide the most rapid response.[160] These medications can be provided to travelers for use should diarrhea develop during a trip to an endemic country.

Enteropathogenic *E. coli*

Enteropathogenic *E. coli* (EPEC) strains are defined by the characteristic attaching and effacing effect that they elicit upon interaction with epithelial cells (Fig. 215-3) and by the fact that they do not produce Shiga toxins.[161] EPEC strains were first identified as the cause of devastating outbreaks of nosocomial and community-acquired neonatal diarrhea in the 1940s,[162] but now rarely cause disease in the developed world. Instead EPEC remain a leading cause of severe diarrhea among very young children in developing countries, where they cause disease principally in those less than 6 months of age.[163-169] EPEC infections appear to be acquired principally by person-to-person spread,[170,171] and hospitals continue to be a source of infection.[172] Infections caused by EPEC are difficult to differentiate from those with other causes; symptoms include watery diarrhea sometimes accompanied by low-grade fever and vomiting.[166] However, EPEC infection may be severe, vom-

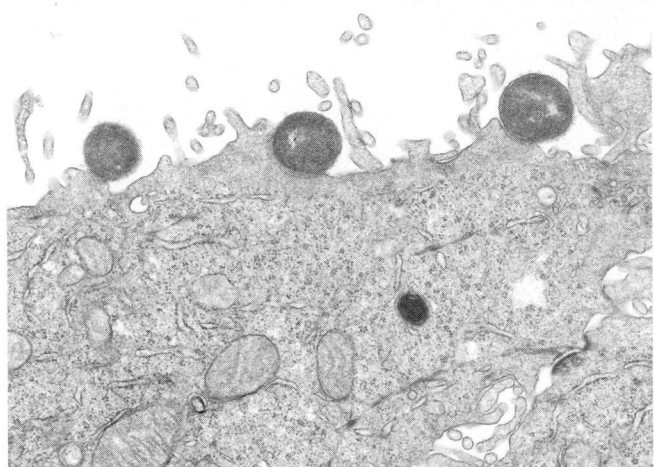

FIGURE 215-3. Transmission electron micrograph of enteropathogenic *E. coli* infecting a tissue culture cell demonstrating the attaching and effacing effect. Note the loss of microvilli, the intimate attachment of bacteria to the cell, and the cuplike pedestal composed of cytoskeletal proteins to which the bacteria are attached. Attaching and effacing effects are also seen with enterohemorrhagic *E. coli* strains and *E. albertii* strains.

iting may make oral rehydration difficult, and life-threatening dehydration may ensue.[164,173,174] Furthermore, disease caused by EPEC may be protracted resulting in weight loss, malnutrition, and death.[175]

A great deal of information has come to light in the last decade regarding the molecular pathogenesis of EPEC infection. The histopathologic hallmark of EPEC infection, the attaching and effacing effect, involves the intimate attachment of the bacteria to the apical surface of intestinal epithelial cells accompanied by the loss (effacement) of microvilli and the formation of a cuplike pedestal composed of actin and other cytoskeletal proteins upon which the bacteria rest.[176,177] The attaching and effacing effect is directed by a 41-gene pathogenicity island known as the locus of enterocyte effacement (LEE) that encodes a T3SS (see earlier section on Secretion Systems and Toxins), the outer membrane adhesin intimin, the translocated intimin receptor (Tir), and other proteins.[178-180] The EPEC T3SS has a unusual translocation protein known as EspA that forms a filamentous extension of the needle and connects the bacteria to the host cells.[181,182] Tir is believed to transit a central canal in the EspA filament, pass through a putative pore in the host cell membrane formed by the EspB and EspD proteins,[183] and then insert in the host cell membrane, where it serves as the receptor for intimin.[52] Intimin, a proven EPEC virulence factor,[184] protrudes from the surface of the bacteria and binds to Tir in a ratio of two intimin molecules to one Tir dimer.[50] When Tir binds intimin, it becomes phosphorylated by an unknown host kinase, and then a cascade of events leads to the activation of the host actin-nucleating and filament formation machinery and pedestal formation.[185-187] Thus EPEC carries around its own receptor, injects it into host cells, binds to it, and uses it to modify host cell architecture.

Many EPEC strains possess an EPEC adherence factor (EAF) plasmid that encodes a type IV fimbria called the bundle-forming pilus (BFP).[96] Such strains are referred to as typical EPEC and attach to epithelial cells in a localized adherence pattern (Fig. 215-4A).[188,189] In contrast, atypical EPEC strains do not display localized adherence, lack the EAF plasmid, and do not produce BFP. Such strains may be less pathogenic than typical EPEC strains.[190,191] Both the EAF plasmid and BFP have been demonstrated to be virulence factors.[97,192] Because BFP aggregate into ropelike bundles (see Fig. 215-2C), and expression of BFP is associated with reversible autoaggregation of the bacteria in culture and localized adherence, BFPs are believed to mediate the initial adherence to and subsequent dispersal of bacteria from the intestinal surface.[192] The relative importance of BFP, EspA, and intimin in

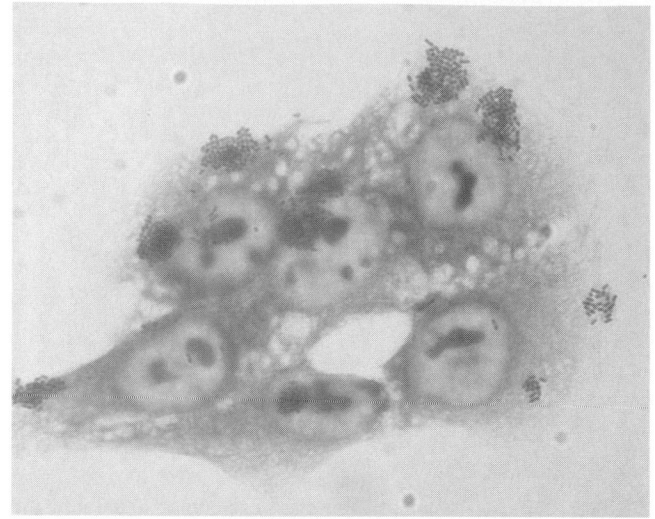

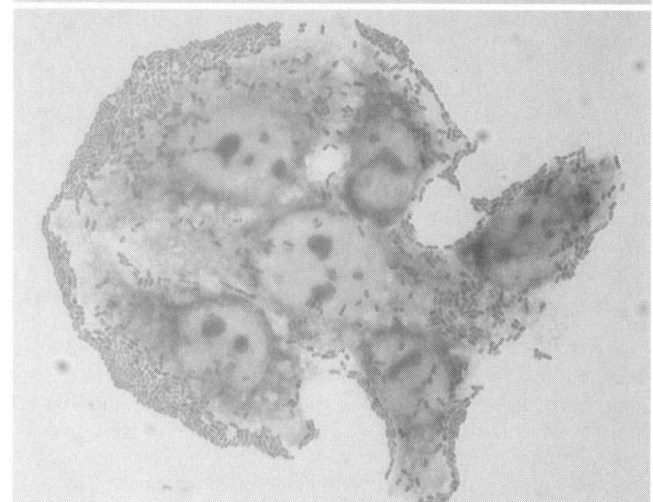

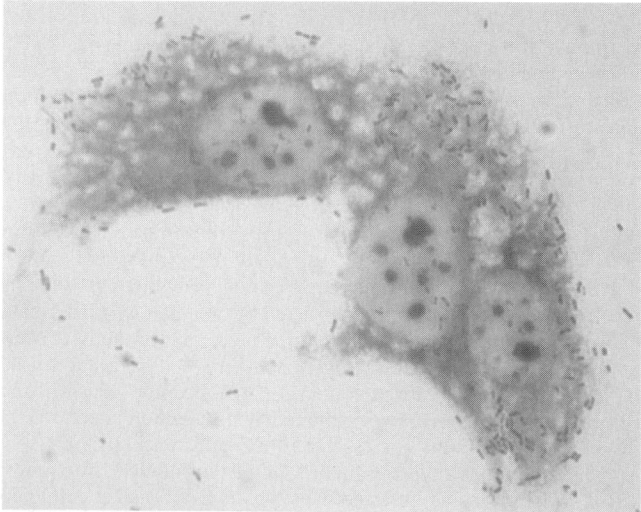

FIGURE 215-4. Patterns of cellular adherence displayed by various *E. coli* pathotypes that cause diarrhea. **A,** The localized adherence pattern exhibited by typical strains of enteropathogenic *E. coli* is characterized by discrete three-dimensional microcolonies of bacteria. **B,** The aggregative adherence pattern exhibited by enteroaggregative *E. coli* strains is characterized by two-dimensional "stacked brick" aggregates associated with both host cells and the glass or plastic substratum. **C,** Diffuse adherent *E. coli* strains adhere individually at random to tissue culture cells.

binding to the intestinal epithelium is a matter of some debate, but a triple-mutant strain unable to express any of these three adhesins does not adhere in detectable numbers to cells.[193]

The mechanism by which EPEC strains cause diarrhea is not fully understood. In fact, there is evidence that several factors may be involved, including loss of microvillous surface area, loosening of tight junctions, and direct fluid secretion.

The diagnosis of EPEC infection rests on detection of the genes encoding specific virulence factors using DNA probes or PCR with targets such as the *eae* gene that encodes intimin, the *bfpA* gene that encodes the structural subunit of BFP, and the *stx* genes that encode Shiga toxins (which are negative in EPEC strains).[194-197] Alternatively, tissue culture assays for the localized adherence pattern are highly specific for EPEC but do not detect atypical strains, which appear to be recognized with increased frequency of late.[191,198]

Since the discovery of EPEC, it has been appreciated that breast-feeding is highly protective against EPEC infection, and recent studies continue to confirm this finding.[172,199-201] Breast milk contains factors found in both the lipid and the immunoglobulin fractions that inhibit EPEC adherence, including, in women from endemic areas, antibodies against intimin, BFP, EspA, and EspB.[202-206] There is at present no vaccine to prevent EPEC. Treatment of EPEC infection rests first on fluid replacement, which may require parenteral routes of administration in children who have profuse vomiting. Mild EPEC illness does not require antimicrobial therapy, but antibiotics can shorten the duration of illness in those with more severe disease.[207,208] Unfortunately, strains of EPEC are often resistant to multiple antibiotics.[209-211]

Enterohemorrhagic *E. coli* and Other Shiga Toxin–Producing *E. coli* Strains

Shiga toxins (also called verotoxins) are related bacteriophage-encoded cytotoxins that induce host cell death by destroying the ribosomal protein synthesis machinery. Strains that produce Shiga toxins can cause disease of varying severity, including watery diarrhea, bloody diarrhea, hemorrhagic colitis, hemolytic uremic syndrome (HUS), and death.[212] Among Shiga toxin–producing *E. coli* (STEC) strains, those that share with EPEC strains the ability to induce the attaching and effacing effect encoded by the LEE pathogenicity island are known as enterohemorrhagic *E. coli* (EHEC) (Fig. 215-5). EHEC strains, especially those belonging to serotype O157:H7, have been responsible for larger outbreaks of infection, have higher rates of complications, and appear to be more pathogenic than non-EHEC STEC strains. The reservoir of EHEC strains is the gastrointestinal tract of young cattle and other large herbivorous mammals, but these strains can survive for long periods in the environment even at very low pH and can proliferate in vegetables and other foods and beverages. Outbreaks are often linked to the consumption of undercooked ground beef, but can arise from a wide variety of other food sources, contaminated drinking and recreational water, and petting zoos, and by direct person-to-person contact.[213-217] The low infectious dose of EHEC strains, estimated to be less than 100 organisms,[218] no doubt facilitates the transmission of the organism. EHEC infections are manifest by the onset of severe abdominal cramping, which may progress to watery and bloody diarrhea. The frequent absence of fever and the appearance of frank hematochezia can divert the clinician toward considering noninfectious diagnoses such as intussusception in children, inflammatory bowel disease in young adults, or ischemic bowel in the elderly.[213] EHEC infection is the primary cause of HUS and the leading cause of renal insufficiency in children, which may occur in 5% to 10% of individuals during EHEC outbreaks and is often heralded by high leukocytosis. Children under the age of 5 and the elderly are more likely than those between the age extremes to develop HUS. HUS is a microangiopathic hemolytic anemia marked by the appearance of schistocytes, thrombocytopenia, and azotemia. Although the kidneys are the most vulnerable target organs, any tissue can become ischemic from capillary and larger vessel thrombosis. The brain (strokes), eyes (blindness), and colon (ischemic bowel) are other organs commonly affected. In adults, the involvement of the brain and other organs often

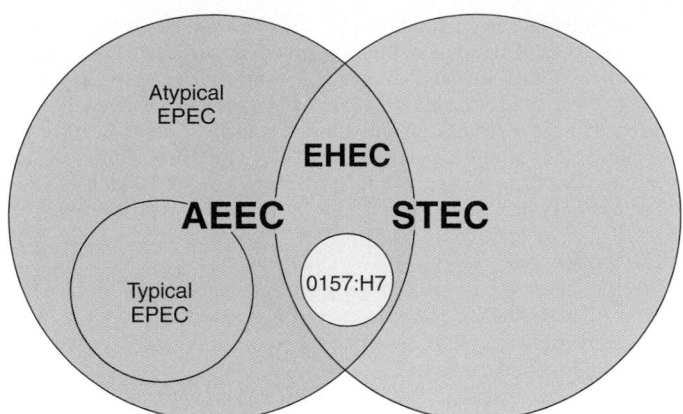

FIGURE 215-5. Venn diagram illustrating the relationship between enteropathogenic *E. coli* (EPEC) and Shiga toxin–producing *E. coli* (STEC) strains. Both the EPEC and the enterohemorrhagic *E. coli* (EHEC) subsets of STEC strains are capable of the attaching and effacing effect and are sometimes referred to as attaching and effacing *E. coli* (AEEC). The O157:H7 serotype is the most important clone of EHEC. EPEC can be divided into typical strains that produce bundle-forming pili and exhibit localized adherence and atypical strains with neither of these properties. *(Adapted from Donnenberg MS, Whittam TS. Pathogenesis and evolution of virulence in enteropathogenic and enterohemorrhagic* Escherichia coli. *J Clin Invest 2001;107:539-548.)*

leads to the diagnosis of thrombotic thrombocytopenic purpura. HUS carries a 12% risk of death or end-stage renal disease, and 25% of survivors experience long-term renal sequelae such as hypertension, proteinuria, or renal insufficiency.[219]

The principal virulence factors of STEC strains are a group of related cytotoxins called Shiga toxins. Stx1 is virtually identical to the toxin produced by *Shigella dysenteriae* type 1, and Stx2 shares a high degree of sequence similarity and identical functional features. Shiga toxins are encoded on temperate bacteriophages.[220] Importantly, these bacteriophages are induced and lyse the *E. coli* strains that harbor them when the cells are stressed by various conditions, including exposure to certain antibiotics.[221,222] As a result, high levels of Shiga toxins are released. Shiga toxins have five identical B subunits that bind to globotriaosylceramide and related glycosphingolipids (the same receptor used by P fimbriae and parvovirus B19).[223] The single catalytic A subunit, after endocytosis and retrograde transport to the endoplasmic reticulum,[224] catalyzes the depurination of a specific adenine residue in the 28S ribosomal RNA, rendering the ribosome nonfunctional. Recent reports suggest that leukocytes bind Shiga toxins and may be the primary mechanism for toxin dissemination from the gastrointestinal tract throughout the blood stream.[225] Endothelial cells are susceptible to intoxication and may be the most relevant target cells in EHEC-induced HUS.[226] Endothelial cell intoxication is believed to result in increased expression of procoagulants and subsequent microvascular thrombosis.[227]

In addition to Shiga toxins, EHEC strains (but not non-EHEC STEC strains) harbor the LEE pathogenicity island and are capable of inducing the attaching and effacing effect.[228] Mutation of the gene encoding intimin from an O157:H7 EHEC strain resulted in reduced colonization of neonatal piglets[229] but did not affect neurologic complications, which are manifestations of Shiga toxin.[230]

STEC infection should be suspected in any patient with grossly bloody diarrhea, and should be considered in any individual with diarrhea and cramps. The diagnosis of infection with STEC is extremely important because of the importance of recognizing potential outbreaks and of taking action to prevent further infections.[213] Most microbiology laboratories are able to make a presumptive diagnosis of O157:H7 EHEC infection because these strains ferment sorbitol slowly and hence form white colonies on sorbitol-MacConkey agar plates. However, it is critically important that the laboratory is notified

that STEC infection is suspected, because many laboratories do not routinely employ these plates. Furthermore, STEC strains of serotypes other than O157:H7 are not detected on these plates. Confirmatory testing consists of assays, such as PCR, to detect the genes that encode Shiga toxins. Several enzyme immunoassays for Shiga toxin are available for clinical use directly on stool specimens.

The risk of STEC infection can be reduced by following safe practices in food handling and preparation and in other areas of hygiene. Ground beef should be cooked to 155° F (68.3° C)[231] or until "the juices run clear," caution should be applied to prevent cross-contamination between uncooked meat and foods to be served without further cooking, unpasteurized juices and milk should be avoided, care should be taken to prevent infants and children who are not toilet trained from defecating in public swimming areas, and hands should be washed after touching animals in farms and petting zoos. Investigators are taking several approaches to vaccine development, including an O157 polysaccharide-protein conjugate vaccine, Shiga toxoid vaccines, and intimin vaccines.[232-235] Such vaccines and other preventative strategies may be targeted either to cattle or humans.

Treatment of EHEC infection is entirely supportive. Antibiotics are currently contraindicated because they can induce the expression and release of Shiga toxins and because some studies have indicated that their use is associated with a higher risk of HUS in children with EHEC infection.[236] Whether any antibiotics are safe is a matter not yet settled. Studies of alternative treatment modalities, including soluble toxin receptors and humanized monoclonal antitoxin antibodies, are ongoing.[237-239] In one randomized, double-blind clinical study, an oral toxin receptor analogue did not reduce mortality, extrarenal complications, or the need for dialysis in patients with HUS.[240] Whether this approach would have benefit if initiated prior to the onset of HUS is not known. More potent polyvalent receptor analogues are under development and have yielded promising results in animal studies.[241,242]

Enteroaggregative *E. coli*

Enteroaggregative *E. coli* (EAEC) may be considered a true emerging infection, both because of its recent description and because of apparent increases in its importance in some settings. EAEC strains, first recognized as a cause of diarrhea in 1987,[243] are defined by their aggregative pattern of adherence to tissue culture cells (see Fig. 215-4B). These bacteria form two-dimensional clusters when they adhere to cells in vitro, to glass slides, to plastic, or to the intestinal mucosa.[244,245] Some, but not all, case-control studies have revealed that *E. coli* strains with this pattern of adherence are isolated with increased frequency from children with diarrhea.[167,246-251] Similarly, volunteer studies have confirmed the pathogenicity of one EAEC strain, but not others.[252] This and other evidence indicates that EAEC strains are heterogeneous and some may be more pathogenic than others.[253,254] Studies have linked EAEC strains to acute diarrhea in developing countries,[247] chronic diarrhea in developing countries,[247,255-258] and acute diarrhea in developed countries.[259] Recently EAEC has been associated with travelers' diarrhea at frequencies rivaling those recorded for ETEC.[260,261] EAEC strains have also been implicated as a cause of persistent diarrhea in human immunodeficiency virus (HIV)–infected patients.[262-264] Clinical descriptions of EAEC infection are sparse, but infection has been associated with intestinal colic, hematochezia, and mucus.[252,256,259,265] Infection with EAEC, whether symptomatic or not, has also been correlated with intestinal interleukin-8 production and growth retardation.[266]

The pathogenesis of EAEC disease is not well understood. EAEC strains cause mucosal damage with loss of microvilli and cell death when they adhere to polarized colonic epithelial cells or to explanted human colonic mucosa.[245] Aggregative adherence has been linked to the expression of several related plasmid-encoded chaperone-usher–type pili known as aggregative adherence fimbria (AAF/I, AAF/II, etc.).[267,268] However, many strains that display aggregative adherence express none of these fimbrial types. AggR, a positive regulator of expression of AAF fimbrial operons, is present in a majority of EAEC strains and appears to be specific for this pathotype. Dispersin, a surface protein secreted by EAEC strains that is recognized by antibodies from volunteers after experimental infection, appears to play a role in limiting the aggregation of the strains.[269] Several toxins have been described that are expressed by some, but not all, EAEC strains. EAST is similar to heat-stable enterotoxin and appears to act by a similar mechanism, but is found in many non-EAEC E. coli strains.[270] Pet (plasmid-encoded enterotoxin) is a member of the SPATE family (see earlier section on Secretion Systems and Toxins). Pet causes cell rounding and detachment in tissue culture and crypt dilation and cell damage in human intestinal explants.[271,272]

A diagnosis of EAEC infection can be suspected in the appropriate setting (childhood diarrhea in developing countries, acute diarrhea in travelers, persistent diarrhea in children or HIV-infected patients), but confirmation requires performing tissue culture adhesion assays.[243] A simple test for identifying EAEC involving clump formation in Mueller-Hinton broth has been reported but not validated.[273] DNA probes and PCR tests currently available do not appear to have sufficient sensitivity or specificity. Because strains that display aggregative adherence are extremely heterogeneous and may vary in pathogenicity, and EAEC are often isolated from asymptomatic individuals, it is difficult to be certain that an EAEC strain isolated from an individual patient with diarrhea is the cause of his or her symptoms.

Data regarding the prevention and treatment of EAEC infections are sparse. One might assume that nonspecific methods for preventing other E. coli enteric infections would be effective for EAEC as well. There is no vaccine. There are reports that HIV-infected individuals and travelers may benefit from treatment of EAEC infections with fluoroquinolones, but neither study had a prospective randomized, placebo-controlled, non-crossover design.[265,274] Like EPEC strains, EAEC strains are often resistant to multiple antibiotics.[275]

Enteroinvasive E. coli

Because enteroinvasive E. coli (EIEC) strains are very similar to Shigella strains in terms of clinical features and pathogenesis, they are discussed only briefly here. Like Shigella, EIEC strains have a large invasion plasmid that encodes a T3SS enabling the bacteria to invade epithelial cells, escape from the phagosome, multiply in the cytoplasm, usurp the host actin-filament assembly machine, and spread directly from cell to cell. In fact, unlike most E. coli, both EIEC and Shigella strains are usually nonmotile, cannot ferment lactose, and, because of a chromosomal deletion, are lysine decarboxylase negative.[276] They are differentiated from Shigella principally by the fact that EIEC strains ferment glucose and xylose.[95] The pathophenotype of EIEC and Shigella strains appears to represent a remarkable example of convergent evolution involving gain of similar plasmids and gain and loss of chromosomal loci, because EIEC and Shigella strains each represent several distinct evolutionary lineages within the genus Escherichia.[1,277,278] Like infection with Shigella, infection with EIEC can lead to watery diarrhea, which may progress to dysentery characterized by severe abdominal cramps, fever, tenesmus, and frequent passage of small-volume stools that may contain mucus and blood. Based on a volunteer study, it has been estimated that the infectious dose of EIEC is approximately 10^8 bacteria, considerably higher than that of Shigella.[279] EIEC strains are detected in culture as lactose-negative colonies and confirmed either by DNA probes or PCR for virulence-associated genes. By analogy with Shigella infections, it is assumed that antibiotic treatment of EIEC infection may shorten the duration of illness, but care must be taken to exclude infection with STEC prior to initiating therapy.

Other Pathotypes of E. coli and Species of Escherichia

Several epidemiologic studies have provided evidence that E. coli strains that adhere to tissue culture cells in a diffuse pattern (see Fig. 215-4C) are associated with diarrhea, especially in older children.[167,249,250,280] However, Koch's postulates have not been fulfilled in volunteer studies.[281] It is clear that these strains, like EAEC, are quite heterogeneous, and perhaps some are more pathogenic than others.[253]

In addition to E. coli, the genus Escherichia contains several other species including E. blattae, E. fergusonii, and E. vulneris, but these are rarely isolated from human infections. In 1991 Albert and colleagues reported that a strain of Hafnia alvei isolated in pure culture from the feces of an infant in Bangladesh with diarrhea had pathogenic properties similar to those of EPEC.[282] Similar strains were subsequently isolated from additional patients.[283] Further DNA studies revealed that these strains, although biochemically similar to H. alvei, actually belonged to the genus Escherichia.[284] Recently it has been appreciated that these strains belong to a new species for which the name E. albertii has been proposed.[285]

Klebsiella

Three species in the genus Klebsiella are associated with illness in humans: K. pneumoniae, K. oxytoca, and K. granulomatis. Organisms previously known as K. ozaenae and K. rhinoscleromatis are considered nonfermenting subspecies of K. pneumoniae that are associated with particular diseases. With those exceptions, strains within this genus ferment lactose, most produce highly mucoid colonies on plates because of the production of a luxuriant polysaccharide capsule, and all are non-motile.

K. pneumoniae is a primary pathogen capable of causing UTIs and pneumonia in otherwise healthy people. However, most infections caused by K. pneumoniae are acquired in the hospital and/or occur in those who are debilitated by various underlying conditions.[286] In addition to pneumonia and UTIs, nosocomial infections caused by K. pneumoniae include wound infections, infections of intravascular and other invasive devices, biliary tract infections, peritonitis, and meningitis. K. pneumoniae is second in incidence only to E. coli as a cause of gram-negative bacteremia.[287,288] K. pneumoniae can cause UTIs in individuals with normal as well as abnormal urinary tracts and again is second only to E. coli as a cause of bacteremia resulting from UTI.[289] UTIs caused by K. pneumoniae do not have clinical features that distinguish them from those caused by other bacterial species. Pneumonia caused by K. pneumoniae has classically been described as having particular distinguishing features, warranting the eponym "Friedländer's disease." Among these classic features are its severity, its frequency in alcoholics, its propensity to affect the upper lobes, the production of "currant jelly" sputum resulting from hemoptysis (see Fig. 1 in Chapter 61), the "bulging fissure sign" on roentgenography caused by edematous lobar consolidation, and its tendency for abscess formation. Despite these compelling descriptions, pneumonia caused by K. pneumoniae cannot be distinguished on clinical grounds from that caused by other organisms, and many of the described features are likely the result of misdiagnosis, caused by culture of expectorated sputum, of anaerobic pulmonary infections.[290]

The principal virulence factor that has been described for K. pneumoniae is its polysaccharide capsule, which comes in over 70 antigenic varieties and is responsible for its luxuriant mucoid growth on laboratory media.[291] The mechanism by which capsule promotes virulence is thought to be due to inhibition of phagocytosis (see earlier). A role for the capsule in colonization of the urinary tract has been suggested.[93] K. pneumoniae can produce a variety of fimbrial types, including type-1 pili that are involved in adherence to host cells.[291-293] Little else is known about its pathogenetic mechanisms.

All strains of K. pneumoniae are resistant to ampicillin as a result of the presence of a chromosomal gene encoding a penicillin-specific β-lactamase.[294] In addition, nosocomial isolates are frequently resistant to numerous other antibiotics as a result of the acquisition of multidrug resistance (MDR) plasmids. For example, K. pneumoniae is one of the most common organisms to carry plasmids encoding extended-spectrum β-lactamases (ESBLs), and such strains are isolated with increasing frequency.[295] Therapeutic options for infections caused by non-MDR strains include first-generation cephalosporins, penicillin/β-lactamase inhibitor combinations, trimethoprim-sulfamethoxazole, fluoroquinolones, and aminoglycosides. For MDR strains, especially those expressing ESBLs, treatment options are often limited to fourth-generation cephalosporins or carbapenems.

K. pneumoniae subspecies rhinoscleromatis is the causative agent of respiratory scleroma, also known as rhinoscleroma, a chronic granulomatous infection of the nasal passages and other parts of the respiratory tract.[296] The disease is found primarily in impoverished areas of Central and South America, Africa, and Asia and is transmitted by close contact. Respiratory scleroma is characterized by nodules and masses that often involve the nasal passages, but may be found in the palate, the glottis, and the lower respiratory tract. The differential diagnosis includes tuberculosis, leprosy, fungal infections, Wegener's granulomatosis, malignancies, and sarcoidosis. Biopsies show granulomatous inflammation with foamy macrophages (Mikulicz cells) containing intracellular organisms.[297] The bacteria can be grown on ordinary laboratory media. Antibiotic therapy for 6 to 8 weeks is required for cure, but relapses are common. Traditionally streptomycin or tetracycline has been used, but more recent reports indicate success and perhaps less risk of adverse effects with trimethoprim-sulfamethoxazole or fluoroquinolones.[298]

K. pneumoniae subspecies *ozaenae* can colonize the nasopharynx of healthy individuals. Its association with chronic atrophic rhinitis (ozena) has been noted, but its etiologic role in this syndrome is controversial. The organism has only rarely been isolated from patients with a variety of infections, including otitis media and mastoiditis, cystitis and pyelonephritis, soft tissue infections, bacteremia associated with neutropenia, pneumonia, and meningitis.[299,300] It is usually susceptible to multiple antibiotics except when isolated from hospitalized patients who had received prior antimicrobial therapy.

K. oxytoca, like *K. pneumoniae,* can cause a variety of nosocomial infections. It is distinguished from *K. pneumoniae* on the basis of its ability to produce indole from tryptophan. It may also be resistant to multiple antibiotics.

Calymmatobacterium granulomatis is now considered by some authorities to be a species of *Klebsiella,* designated *K. granulomatis.* This organism, which causes chronic genital ulcerative disease, has been reported to be grown in cell culture (see Chapter 233). Although cultivation is difficult, taxonomic classification based on the sequences of the 16S ribosomal RNA and *phoE* genes has revealed that the organism belongs within the genus *Klebsiella.*[301,302]

Enterobacter, Pantoea, Serratia, Citrobacter, and *Hafnia*

Microorganisms belonging to the genera *Enterobacter, Pantoea, Serratia,* and *Citrobacter* rarely cause infections in normal hosts, but are common nosocomial isolates. *Hafnia* is not as common, but is included in this section because of its close phylogenic relationship to the group.

Enterobacter Species and *Pantoea (Enterobacter) agglomerans*

Three species of *Enterobacter, E. cloacae, E. aerogenes,* and *E. sakazakii,* are responsible for the vast majority of *Enterobacter* infections. *Pantoea agglomerans,* until recently known as *Enterobacter agglomerans,* is also a common isolate and, because its new nomenclature is not yet widely in use, is grouped with the *Enterobacter* spp. here. These bacteria ferment lactose, are motile, and form mucoid colonies. *Enterobacter* strains commonly arise from the endogenous intestinal flora of hospitalized patients, but can occur in common source outbreaks or are spread from patient to patient. Infections are especially common in patients who have received antimicrobial therapy and in those in intensive care units.[303] *Enterobacter* spp. may cause a wide variety of nosocomial infections, including pneumonia, UTIs, wound and burn infections, infections of intravascular and other prosthetic devices, and meningitis. There do not appear to be distinguishing characteristics among infections caused by different species within the genus, except that *E. sakazakii* is primarily found in neonates and *P. agglomerans* has more frequently been associated with exogenous sources.[303]

Little is known regarding potential virulence characteristics of these bacteria. In addition to their capsule, which may contribute to serum resistance and resistance to phagocytosis, strains of *E. cloacae* frequently produce aerobactin, adhere to tissue culture cells, and exhibit mannose-sensitive hemagglutination, possibly the result of type-1 fimbriae expression.[304] *E. cloacae, E. aerogenes,* and most strains of

E. sakazakii are intrinsically resistant to ampicillin and first- and second-generation cephalosporins as a result of an inducible *ampC* chromosomal β-lactamase that is controlled by both positive and negative regulators.[305] Furthermore, mutants that constitutively produce high levels of β-lactamase, conferring resistance to third-generation cephalosporins, arise at frequencies of 10^{-4} to 10^{-7}, usually as a result of mutations in the regulatory loci, such that resistant mutants are already present in most patients with *Enterobacter* infections prior to initiation of therapy. In addition, like other members of the family Enterobacteriaceae, members of the genus *Enterobacter* may carry plasmids encoding resistance to multiple antimicrobial agents. Therapy for *Enterobacter* infections must therefore be tailored to individual isolates and based on antimicrobial susceptibility testing. However, clinicians must be aware that emergence of stably derepressed resistant mutants may lead to treatment failure when third-generation cephalosporins are chosen, even if the isolates appear susceptible on initial testing.[306] Therefore, fourth-generation cephalosporins, carbapenems, or other agents may be better choices than other β-lactam antibiotics for serious infections involving large numbers of bacteria.

Serratia Species

Of the many species in the genus *Serratia, S. marcescens* is the one most commonly isolated from human infections, and *S. liquefaciens* is occasionally grown. *Serratia* strains are motile, rarely ferment lactose, and produce an extracellular DNase. The organism is widespread in the environment but not a common component of the human fecal flora. Thus most infections are acquired exogenously. Many environmental and some clinical strains of *S. marcescens* produce a red pigment, prodigiosin. In fact, in one of the first instances in which artificial medium was used to cultivate a microorganism, an Italian pharmacist named Bartolemeo Bizio first described the organism in 1819 as the cause of red discoloration of polenta (corn meal mush), thereby discrediting the claim that the growth was due to the miraculous appearance of blood. He gave the bacterium its genus name to honor Serafino Serrati, whom he felt had not received proper credit for invention of the steamboat, and its species name for the Latin word for "to decay," because of the tendency of the pigment to change color as the colonies age.[307] The production of prodigiosin, and the belief that the bacterium was harmless, led to its frequent use as a biologic marker to study, among other things, transmission of bacteria through speech and contact, ascending colonization of the bladder in patients with urinary catheters, and the dissemination of aerosolized bacteria after experimental release in models of biologic warfare.[308] It is now appreciated that *S. marcescens* can cause a wide variety of nosocomial infections. In addition, the bacterium has a particular association with infections in injecting drug users.

Potential virulence factors of *Serratia* have not received a great deal of attention, but strains may be capable of both mannose-sensitive (presumably as a result of type-1 fimbriae) and mannose-resistant hemagglutination, as well as adherence to uroepithelial cells, and may be cytotoxic to tissue culture cells.[293,309] The organism can survive under hostile conditions, including in a variety of disinfectants, some of which have been the sources of outbreaks.[310] Infections caused by *S. marcescens* may begin with exogenous contamination and spread within or among hospitals on the hands of personnel.[308] The most common site of infection is the urinary tract, but the organism is frequently isolated from the respiratory tract and from wounds.[311] Cases of osteomyelitis, infectious arthritis, and endophthalmitis may follow hematogenous dissemination, while meningitis may occur after neurologic procedures. As previously noted, injection drug users are at particular risk of *S. marcescens* infections, including endocarditis, which is frequently left-sided,[312] and infections at other sites after hematogenous spread.[308] *Serratia* isolates are resistant to ampicillin and first-generation cephalosporins because of an inducible, chromosomal AmpC β-lactamase similar to that of *Enterobacter.*[313] Mutants that produce high levels of these enzymes as a result of stable derepression may arise during therapy. In addition, many isolates possess plasmids encoding resistance to other cephalosporins, penicillins, carbapenems, and aminoglycosides.[310,311] Fluoroquinolone resistance and resistance to trimethoprim-sulfamethoxazole are also encountered. Thus treatment of infections caused by *S. marcescens* can be quite difficult, and every effort should be made to identify point sources of outbreaks and control spread of the organism.

Citrobacter Species

Members of the genus *Citrobacter* are named for their ability to use citrate as their sole carbon source. Of the dozen species, *C. freundii, C. diversus,* and *C. amalonaticus* are linked to human disease. They are differentiated by their ability to convert tryptophan to indole, ferment lactose, and utilize malonate.[314] *C. freundii* produces H_2S and hence can be confused with *Salmonella,* with which it was classified at one time. The urinary tract is the most frequent site from which *Citrobacter* is cultured, often in association with an indwelling catheter. These bacteria may also be cultured from the respiratory tract, a finding that more often represents colonization than symptomatic infection. *Citrobacter* strains are also involved in intra-abdominal infections and can cause soft tissue infections and osteomyelitis.[315] Invasive procedures may play a role in *Citrobacter* bacteremia.[316] *C. diversus* has caused frequent nosocomial outbreaks of neonatal meningitis. In several instances the outbreaks have been accompanied by high rates of intestinal colonization in infants by the organism and by carriage of the bacteria on the hands of health care workers.[317] *C. freundii* strains, like strains of *Enterobacter* and *Serratia,* have inducible *ampC* genes encoding resistance to ampicillin and first-generation cephalosporins that can be produced constitutively at high levels following mutations. In addition, like members of these other genera, isolates of *Citrobacter* may be resistant to multiple other antibiotics as a result of plasmid-encoded resistance genes.

Hafnia alvei

Hafnia alvei (formerly *Enterobacter hafniae*) is the sole species in the genus *Hafnia* and is most closely related to members of the genus *Serratia.*[318] These microorganisms are motile, but do not ferment lactose. Although *H. alvei* may be cultured from various sites, it is frequently isolated along with other organisms.[319] Thus in many cases the role of the organism in disease is not clear. Most infections with *H. alvei* occur in patients with severe underlying illness, including malignancies, trauma, and postoperative patients. There have been numerous reports linking diarrhea to the isolation of *H. alvei* from stool specimens. Because the organism is part of the normal fecal flora, these reports must be interpreted with caution. Furthermore, those strains initially reported to produce attaching and effacing lesions via a mechanism similar to that used by EPEC are now recognized as belonging to a new species, *Escherichia albertii.*[285] However, in a case-control study of Finnish tourists returning from Morocco, the prevalence of *H. alvei* in those with diarrhea was significantly greater than in those without diarrhea, substantiating a possible etiologic role.[320] Furthermore, these strains were all negative in PCR testing for the *eae* gene encoding intimin, which is found in EPEC and *E. albertii.* Treatment of serious *H. alvei* infections is guided by antimicrobial susceptibility testing.

Proteus, Providencia, and Morganella

The genera *Proteus, Providencia,* and *Morganella* are related members of the family Enterobacteriaceae that are lactose negative and motile and produce phenylalanine deaminase. There are several species of *Proteus,* but *P. mirabilis* and *P. vulgaris* account for the vast majority of clinical isolates in this genus. Both produce urease, and the latter is indole positive. Members of this genus also produce H_2S. These bacteria are capable of swarming motility as they differentiate from typical enterobacterial bacilli expressing fimbriae and flagellae into highly elongated rods with thousands of flagellae that translocate rapidly across the surface of agar plates. In fact the name "Proteus" was chosen from a character in Homer's Odyssey, who was capable of changing form. *Providencia stuartii* is the most common species of its

genus isolated from clinical specimens, but *P. rettgeri* is occasionally grown. These bacteria can be differentiated from *Proteus* and *Morganella* on the basis of their ability to utilize citrate and ferment D-mannitol.[321] *Morganella morganii* is at present the only member of its genus. It is citrate negative.

Proteus spp. are common causes of UTIs, occasionally in normal hosts and very commonly in those with indwelling catheters or anatomic or functional abnormalities of the urinary tract. UTIs caused by *Proteus* spp. tend to be more severe than those caused by *E. coli,* with a higher proportion representing pyelonephritis.[322] *Proteus* spp. are commonly isolated from the blood stream, the vast majority secondary to UTI, often associated with urinary catheters.[289] *P. mirabilis* may be second only to *E. coli* as a cause of bacteremia from a urinary source.[289,323] In addition to UTI, *Proteus* spp. may cause miscellaneous other infections particularly in hospitalized patients. There is some suspicion, based on anecdotal reports and case-control studies, that some strains of *P. mirabilis* can cause diarrhea.[324] The pathogenesis of UTI caused by *P. mirabilis* has received considerable attention. These microorganisms may produce several types of pili, the most important of which, known as MR/P fimbriae, is subject to phase variation as a result of an invertible element similar to that which controls type-1 pili in *E. coli.*[325,326] MR/P fimbriae have been shown to contribute to bladder colonization in a murine model of UTI.[327] The ability of *P. mirabilis* to produce a potent urease has also been confirmed to be a virulence factor in this murine model,[328] contributing to both colonization and stone formation. Indeed the enzyme, by hydrolyzing urea to form CO_2 and ammonia, alkalinizes the urine, which leads to the precipitation of struvite, formation of calculi, and obstruction of urinary catheters. The kidney stones serve as foreign bodies in which the bacteria are embedded and from which they emerge to cause recurrent infections. Treatment of infections caused by *P. mirabilis* is usually straightforward because most strains are susceptible to commonly used antibiotics except tetracycline.[321] Of course, multiply resistant strains are sometimes encountered, and strains of *P. vulgaris* are generally more resistant.

Providencia stuartii is a rather uncommon clinical isolate except from the urine of nursing home patients with long-term indwelling urinary catheters. In that setting *P. stuartii* is found as commonly as more familiar urinary tract isolates.[329] These infections are sometimes complicated by bacteremia and death.[330] *P. stuartii* and *P. rettgeri* are often resistant to multiple antibiotics, including gentamicin, first-generation cephalosporins, and ampicillin. Therapy is guided by susceptibility testing.

M. morganii is an infrequent nosocomial isolate, usually isolated from urine or wounds.[321,331] When it was initially described it was proposed to be a cause of summer diarrhea.[321] More recently it has been linked in a case-control study to diarrhea,[324] but this finding has not been confirmed.[332] In one study from Korea, *M. morganii* bacteremia was frequently associated with biliary tract disease and biliary drainage catheters, and prior surgery or procedures.[333] As with other members of this group, *M. morganii* may cause nosocomial outbreaks.[331] *M. morganii* strains possess inducible AmpC β-lactamases and therefore are intrinsically resistant to ampicillin and first-generation cephalosporins; spontaneous derepressed mutants resistant to ESBLs similar to those described previously for *Enterobacter* spp. may arise.[334]

Miscellaneous Genera

There are a number of other genera within the family Enterobacteriaceae that have been associated with human disease.

Edwardsiella tarda is found in freshwater environments. It has been associated in case-control studies with diarrhea and can cause wound infections and bacteremia with high mortality, especially in patients with liver disease and iron overload.[335]

Plesiomonas shigelloides is another organism found in water that has been associated with diarrhea and rarely with extraintestinal infections.[336] *P. shigelloides* was previously grouped with vibrios because of a number of shared features, including oxidase production and polar flagellae, but was recently assigned to the enterobacterial family on the basis of phylogeny as assessed by ribosomal DNA sequencing.[337] It is an infrequent isolate from patients with gastroenteritis, but case-control studies reveal a signification association with diarrhea. Furthermore, there have been reports of outbreaks of gastroenteritis in which the organism was the only potential pathogen cultured from patients. Patients in the United States with *P. shigelloides*–associated diarrhea frequently have gross blood in the stool and are more likely than controls to have recently ingested raw shellfish or to have traveled outside the United States.[338] Despite these compelling associations, volunteer experiments have failed to confirm the capacity of this organism to cause diarrhea.[339]

Ewingella americana, named after William Ewing, who made many contributions to our understanding of the microbiology of the Enterobacteriaceae, is an extremely rare cause of nosocomial bacteremia, peritonitis associated with peritoneal dialysis, and conjunctivitis.[340-342] Most isolates have been highly sensitive to antibiotics.

Infections caused by organisms belonging to the genus *Kluyvera,* which closely resembles *E. coli,* are rare. These bacteria have been recovered from urine, sputum, or wounds, and in many cases the pathologic significance of their presence is unclear. However, pyelonephritis, bacteremia, and soft tissue infections caused by *Kluyvera* spp. have occurred, and some infections have been fatal.[343,344]

Bacteria belonging to the genus *Photorhabdus* are fascinating bioluminescent symbionts of nematodes that are parasites of certain insect larvae. Recently there have been a few case reports from Australia and the United States of soft tissue infections and bacteremia caused by members of this genus.[345]

Most reported human infections caused by bacteria described as *Erwinia* were caused by the organism now known as *Pantoea agglomerans* (see earlier). Current members of the genus *Erwinia* are primarily pathogens of plants rather than humans.

REFERENCES

1. Pupo GM, Karaolis DKR, Lan RT, et al. Evolutionary relationships among pathogenic and nonpathogenic *Escherichia coli* strains inferred from multilocus enzyme electrophoresis and *mdh* sequence studies. Infect Immun. 1997;65:2685-2692.
2. Mackowiak PA, Martin RM, Jones SR, et al. Pharyngeal colonization by gram-negative bacilli in aspiration-prone persons. Arch Intern Med. 1978;138:1224-1227.
3. Johanson WG, Pierce AK, Sanford JP. Changing pharyngeal bacterial flora of hospitalized patients: Emergence of gram-negative bacilli. N Engl J Med. 1969;281:1137-1140.
4. Raz R, Stamm WE. A controlled trial of intravaginal estriol in postmenopausal women with recurrent urinary tract infections. N Engl J Med 1993;329:753-756.
5. Gupta K, Hillier SL, Hooton TM, et al. Effects of contraceptive method on the vaginal microbial flora: A prospective evaluation. J Infect Dis. 2000;181:595-601.
6. Banatvala N, Magnano AR, Cartter ML, et al. Meat grinders and molecular epidemiology: Two supermarket outbreaks of *Escherichia coli* O157:H7 infection. J Infect Dis. 1996;173:480-483.
7. Bender JB, Hedberg CW, Besser JM, et al. Surveillance for *Escherichia coli* O157:H7 infections in Minnesota by molecular subtyping. N Engl J Med. 1997;337:388-394.
8. Kadner RJ. Inner membrane. In: Neidhardt FC, ed. *Escherichia coli* and *Salmonella:* Cellular and Molecular Biology. Washington, DC: ASM Press; 1996:58-87.
9. Blattner FR, Plunkett G III, Bloch CA, et al. The complete genome sequence of *Escherichia coli* K-12. Science. 1997;277:1453-1462.
10. Oliver DB. Periplasm. In: Neidhardt FC, ed. *Escherichia coli* and *Salmonella:* Cellular and Molecular Biology. Washington, DC: ASM Press; 1996:88-103.
11. Park JT. The murein sacculus. In: Neidhardt FC, ed. *Escherichia coli* and *Salmonella:* Cellular and Molecular Biology. Washington, DC: ASM Press; 1996:48-57.
12. Nikaido H. Outer membrane. In: Neidhardt FC, ed. *Escherichia coli* and *Salmonella:* Cellular and Molecular Biology. Washington, DC: ASM Press; 1996:29-47.
13. Koebnik R, Locher KP, Van Gelder P. Structure and function of bacterial outer membrane proteins: Barrels in a nutshell. Mol Microbiol. 2000;37:239-253.
14. Raetz CRH. Bacterial lipopolysaccharides: A remarkable family of bioactive macroamphiphiles. In: Neidhardt FC, ed. *Escherichia coli* and *Salmonella:* Cellular and Molecular Biology. Washington, DC: ASM Press; 1996:1035-1063.
15. Ørskov F, Ørskov I. *Escherichia coli* serotyping and disease in man and animals. Can J Microbiol. 1992;38:699-674.
16. Rick PD, Silver RP. Enterobacterial common antigen and capsular polysaccharides. In: Neidhardt FC, Curtiss R III, Ingraham JL, et al, eds. *Escherichia coli* and *Salmonella:* Cellular and Molecular Biology. Washington, DC: ASM Press; 1996:104-122.
17. Whitfield C, Roberts IS. Structure, assembly and regulation of expression of capsules in *Escherichia coli*. Mol Microbiol. 1999;31:1307-1319.
18. Girón JA. Expression of flagella and motility by *Shigella*. Mol Microbiol. 1995;18:63-75.
19. Kubori T, Matsushima Y, Nakamura D, et al. Supramolecular structure of the *Salmonella typhimurium* type III protein secretion system. Science. 1998;280:602-605.
20. Wang L, Rothemund D, Curd H, et al. Species-wide variation in the *Escherichia coli* flagellin (H-antigen) gene. J Bacteriol. 2003;185:2936-2943.
21. Hayashi F, Smith KD, Ozinsky A, et al. The innate immune response to bacterial flagellin is mediated by Toll-like receptor 5. Nature. 2001;410:1099-1103.
22. Gewirtz AT, Simon PO Jr, Schmitt CK, et al. *Salmonella typhimurium* translocates flagellin across intestinal epithelia, inducing a proinflammatory response. J Clin Invest. 2001;107:99-109.
23. Steiner TS, Nataro JP, Poteet-Smith CE, et al. Enteroaggregative *Escherichia coli* expresses a novel flagellin that causes IL-8 release from intestinal epithelial cells. J Clin Invest. 2000;105:1769-1777.
24. Ottow JC. Ecology, physiology, and genetics of fimbriae and pili. Annu Rev Microbiol. 1975;29:79-108.
25. McClelland M, Sanderson KE, Spieth J, et al. Complete genome sequence of *Salmonella enterica* serovar Typhimurium LT2. Nature. 2001;413:852-856.
26. Parkhill J, Dougan G, James KD, et al. Complete genome sequence of a multiple drug resistant *Salmonella enterica* serovar Typhi CT18. Nature. 2001;413:848-852.
27. Welch RA, Burland V, Plunkett G III, et al. Extensive mosaic structure revealed by the complete genome sequence of uropathogenic *Escherichia coli*. Proc Natl Acad Sci U S A. 2002;99:17020-17024.
28. Jones CH, Pinkner JS, Roth R, et al. FimH adhesin of type 1 pili is assembled into a fibrillar tip structure in the Enterobacteriaceae. Proc Natl Acad Sci U S A. 1995;92:2081-2085.
29. Kuehn MJ, Heuser J, Normark S, et al. P pili in uropathogenic *E. coli* are composite fibres with distinct fibrillar adhesive tips. Nature. 1992;356:252-255.
30. Bann JG, Dodson KW, Frieden C, et al. Adhesive pili of the chaperone-usher family. In: Donnenberg MS, ed. *Escherichia coli:* Virulence Mechanisms of a Versatile Pathogen. San Diego: Academic Press; 2002:289-306.
31. Girón JA, Ho ASY, Schoolnik GK. An inducible bundle-forming pilus of enteropathogenic *Escherichia coli*. Science. 1991;254:710-713.
32. Girón JA, Levine MM, Kaper JB. Longus: A long pilus ultrastructure produced by human enterotoxigenic *Escherichia coli*. Mol Microbiol. 1994;12:71-82.
33. Zhang XL, Tsui IS, Yip CM, et al. *Salmonella enterica* serovar Typhi uses type IVB pili to enter human intestinal epithelial cells. Infect Immun. 2000;68:3067-3073.
34. Collyn F, Lety MA, Nair S, et al. *Yersinia pseudotuberculosis* harbors a type IV pilus gene cluster that contributes to pathogenicity. Infect Immun. 2002;70:6196-6205.
35. Merz AJ, So M, Sheetz MP. Pilus retraction powers bacterial twitching motility. Nature. 2000;107:98-102.
36. Schreiber W, Donnenberg MS. Type IV pili. In: Donnenberg MS, ed. *Escherichia coli:* Virulence Mechanisms of a Versatile Pathogen. San Diego: Academic Press; 2002:307-336.
37. Lessl M, Lanka E. Common mechanisms in bacterial conjugation and Ti-mediated T-DNA transfer to plant cells. Cell 1994;77:321-324.
38. Falkow S. Molecular Koch's postulates applied to microbial pathogenicity. Rev Infect Dis. 1988;10(Suppl 2):S274-S276.
39. Mims CA. The Pathogenesis of Infectious Disease. San Diego: Academic Press; 1987.
40. Finlay BB, Falkow S. Common themes in microbial pathogenicity. Microbiol Rev. 1989;53:210-230.
41. Finlay BB, Falkow S. Common themes in microbial pathogenicity revisited. Microbiol Rev. 1997;61:136-169.
42. Hung CS, Bouckaert J, Hung D, et al. Structural basis of tropism of *Escherichia coli* to the bladder during urinary tract infection. Mol Microbiol. 2002;44:903-915.
43. Ofek I, Mirelman D, Sharon N. Adherence of *Escherichia coli* to human mucosal cells mediated by mannose receptors. Nature. 1977;265:623-625.
44. Abraham JM, Freitag CS, Clements JR, et al. An invertible element of DNA controls phase variation of type 1 fimbriae of *Escherichia coli*. Proc Natl Acad Sci U S A. 1985;82:5724-5727.
45. Connell H, Agace W, Klemm P, et al. Type 1 fimbrial expression enhances *Escherichia coli* virulence for the urinary tract. Proc Natl Acad Sci U S A. 1996;93:9827-9832.
46. Bloch CA, Orndorff PE. Impaired colonization by and full invasiveness of *Escherichia coli* K1 bearing a site-directed mutation in the type 1 pilin gene. Infect Immun. 1990;58:275-278.
47. Bloch CA, Stocker BAD, Orndorff PE. A key role for type 1 pili in enterobacterial communicability. Mol Microbiol. 1992;6:697-701.
48. Hamburger ZA, Brown MS, Isberg RR, et al. Crystal structure of invasin: A bacterial integrin-binding protein. Science. 1999;286:291-295.
49. Kelly G, Prasannan S, Daniell S, et al. Structure of the cell-adhesion fragment of intimin from enteropathogenic *Escherichia coli*. Nat Struct Biol. 1999;6:313-318.
50. Luo Y, Frey EA, Pfuetzner RA, et al. Crystal structure of enteropathogenic *Escherichia coli* intimin-receptor complex. Nature. 2000;405:1073-1077.
51. Tran Van Nhieu G, Isberg RR. The *Yersinia pseudotuberculosis* invasin protein and human fibronectin bind to mutually exclusive sites on the a5b1 integrin receptor. J Biol Chem. 1991;266:24367-24375.
52. Kenny B, DeVinney R, Stein M, et al. Enteropathogenic *E. coli* (EPEC) transfers its receptor for intimate adherence into mammalian cells. Cell. 1997;91:511-520.
53. Henderson IR, Nataro JP. Virulence functions of autotransporter proteins. Infect Immun. 2001;69:1231-1243.
54. Eslava C, Navarro-García F, Czeczulin JR, et al. Pet, an autotransporter enterotoxin from enteroaggregative *Escherichia coli*. Infect Immun. 1998;66:3155-3163.
55. Guyer DM, Henderson IR, Nataro JP, et al. Identification of sat, an autotransporter toxin produced by uropathogenic *Escherichia coli*. Mol Microbiol. 2000;38:53-66.
56. Mellies JL, Navarro-Garcia F, Okeke I, et al. *espC* pathogenicity island of enteropathogenic *Escherichia coli* encodes an enterotoxin. Infect Immun. 2001;69:315-324.

57. Guyer DM, Radulovic S, Jones FE, et al. Sat, the secreted autotransporter toxin of uropathogenic *Escherichia coli,* is a vacuolating cytotoxin for bladder and kidney epithelial cells. Infect Immun. 2002;70:4539-4546.
58. Benjelloun-Touimi Z, Sansonetti PJ, Parsot C. SepA, the major extracellular protein of *Shigella flexneri:* Autonomous secretion and involvement in tissue invasion. Mol Microbiol. 1995;17:123-135.
59. Koronakis V, Sharff A, Koronakis E, et al. Crystal structure of the bacterial membrane protein TolC central to multidrug efflux and protein export. Nature. 2000;405:914-919.
60. Thanabalu T, Koronakis E, Hughes C, et al. Substrate-induced assembly of a contiguous channel for protein export from *E. coli:* reversible bridging of an inner-membrane translocase to an outer membrane exit pore. EMBO J. 1998;17:6487-6496.
61. Foreman DT, Martinez Y, Coombs G, et al. TolC and DsbA are needed for the secretion of ST_B, a heat-stable enterotoxin of *Escherichia coli.* Mol Microbiol. 1995;18:237-245.
62. Soloaga A, Veiga MP, García-Segura LM, et al. Insertion of *Escherichia coli* a-haemolysin in lipid bilayers as a non-transmembrane integral protein: Prediction and experiment. Mol Microbiol. 1999;31:1013-1024.
63. Uhlén P, Laestadius Å, Jahnukainen T, et al. a-Haemolysin of uropathogenic *E. coli* induces Ca^{2+} oscillations in renal epithelial cells. Nature. 2000;405:694-697.
64. Russel M. Macromolecular assembly and secretion across the bacterial cell envelope: Type II protein secretion systems. J Mol Biol. 1998;279:485-499.
65. Lathem WW, Grys TE, Witowski SE, et al. StcE, a metalloprotease secreted by *Escherichia coli* O157:H7, specifically cleaves C1 esterase inhibitor. Mol Microbiol. 2002;45:277-288.
66. Sandkvist M. Biology of type II secretion. Mol Microbiol. 2001;40:271-283.
67. Galán JE, Collmer A. Type III secretion machines: Bacterial devices for protein delivery into host cells. Science. 1999;284:1322-1328.
68. Stebbins CE, Galán JE. Structural mimicry in bacterial virulence. Nature. 2001;412:701-705.
69. Escolar L, Perez-Martin J, De Lorenzo V. Opening the iron box: Transcriptional metalloregulation by the Fur protein. J Bacteriol. 1999;181:6223-6229.
70. Raymond KN, Dertz EA, Kim SS. Enterobactin: An archetype for microbial iron transport. Proc Natl Acad Sci U S A. 2003;100:3584-3588.
71. Carbonetti NH, Boonchai S, Parry SH, et al. Aerobactin-mediated iron uptake by *Escherichia coli* isolates from human extraintestinal infections. Infect Immun. 1986;51:966-968.
72. Johnson JR, Moseley SL, Roberts PL, et al. Aerobactin and other virulence factor genes among strains of *Escherichia coli* causing urosepsis: Association with patient characteristics. Infect Immun. 1988;56:405-412.
73. Torres AG, Redford P, Welch RA, et al. TonB-dependent systems of uropathogenic *Escherichia coli:* Aerobactin and heme transport and TonB are required for virulence in the mouse. Infect Immun. 2001;69:6179-6185.
74. Jiang XQ, Payne MA, Cao ZH, et al. Ligand-specific opening of a gated-porin channel in the outer membrane of living bacteria. Science. 1997;276:1261-1264.
75. Reife RA, Shapiro RA, Bamber BA, et al. *Porphyromonas gingivalis* lipopolysaccharide is poorly recognized by molecular components of innate host defense in a mouse model of early inflammation. Infect Immun. 1995;63:4686-4694.
76. Dobrovolskaia MA, Vogel SN. Toll receptors, CD14, and macrophage activation and deactivation by LPS. Microbes Infect. 2002;4:903-914.
77. Beutler B. Tlr4: Central component of the sole mammalian LPS sensor. Curr Opin Immunol. 2000;12:20-26.
78. Chow JC, Young DW, Golenbock DT, et al. Toll-like receptor-4 mediates lipopolysaccharide-induced signal transduction. J Biol Chem. 1999;274:10689-10692.
79. Jiang Q, Akashi S, Miyake K, et al. Lipopolysaccharide induces physical proximity between CD14 and toll-like receptor 4 (TLR4) prior to nuclear translocation of NF-kappa B. J Immunol. 2000;165:3541-3544.
80. Poltorak A, He X, Smirnova I, et al. Defective LPS signaling in C3H/HeJ and C57BL/10ScCr mice: Mutations in Tlr4 gene. Science. 1998;282:2085-2088.
81. Haraoka M, Hang L, Frendéus B, et al. Neutrophil recruitment and resistance to urinary tract infection. J Infect Dis. 1999;180:1220-1229.
82. Agnese DM, Calvano JE, Hahm SJ, et al. Human toll-like receptor 4 mutations but not CD14 polymorphisms are associated with an increased risk of gram-negative infections. J Infect Dis. 2002;186:1522-1525.
83. Pluschke G, Mayden J, Achtman M, et al. Role of the capsule and the O antigen in resistance of O18:K1 *Escherichia coli* to complement-mediated killing. Infect Immun. 1983;42:907-913.
84. Zinner SH, McCabe WR. Effects of IgM and IgG antibody in patients with bacteremia due to gram-negative bacilli. J Infect Dis. 1976;133:37-45.
85. Neter E, Westphal O, Lüderitz O, et al. Demonstration of antibodies against enteropathogenic *Escherichia coli* in sera of children of various ages. Pediatrics. 1955;16:801-808.
86. Cohen D, Green MS, Block C, et al. Prospective study of the association between serum antibodies to lipopolysaccharide O-antigen and the attack rate of shigellosis. J Clin Microbiol. 1991;29:386-389.
87. Cohen D, Green MS, Block C, et al. Serum antibodies to lipopolysaccharide and natural immunity to shigellosis in an Israeli military population. J Infect Dis. 1988;157:1068-1071.
88. Horwitz MA, Silverstein SC. Influence of the *Escherichia coli* capsule on complement fixation and on phagocytosis and killing by human phagocytes. J Clin Invest. 1980;65:82-94.
89. Cross AS, Kim KS, Wright DC, et al. Role of lipopolysaccharide and capsule in the serum resistance of bacteremic strains of *Escherichia coli.* J Infect Dis. 1986;154:497-503.
90. Russo TA, Moffitt MC, Hammer CH, et al. *TnphoA*-mediated disruption of K54 capsular polysaccharide genes in *Escherichia coli* confers serum sensitivity. Infect Immun. 1993;61:3578-3582.
91. Hoffman JA, Wass C, Stins MF, et al. The capsule supports survival but not traversal of *Escherichia coli* K1 across the blood-brain barrier. Infect Immun. 1999;67:3566-3570.
92. Bahrani-Mougeot FK, Buckles EL, Lockatell CV, et al. Type-1 fimbriae and extracellular polysaccharides are preeminent uropathogenic *Escherichia coli* virulence determinants in the murine urinary tract. Mol Microbiol. 2002;45:1079-1093.
93. Struve C, Krogfelt KA. Role of capsule in *Klebsiella pneumoniae* virulence: Lack of correlation between in vitro and in vivo studies. FEMS Microbiol Lett. 2003;218:149-154.
94. Russo TA, Brown JJ, Jodush ST, et al. The O4 specific antigen moiety of lipopolysaccharide but not the K54 group 2 capsule is important for urovirulence of an extraintestinal isolate of *Escherichia coli.* Infect Immun. 1996;64:2343-2348.
95. Day WA, Maurelli AT. *Shigella* and enteroinvasive *Escherichia coli:* Paradigms for pathogen evolution and host-parasite interactions. In: Donnenberg MS, ed. *Escherichia coli:* Virulence Mechanisms of a Versatile Pathogen. San Diego: Academic Press; 2002:209-237.
96. Girón JA, Donnenberg MS, Martin WC, et al. Distribution of the bundle-forming pilus structural gene *(bfpA)* among enteropathogenic *Escherichia coli.* J Infect Dis. 1993;168:1037-1041.
97. Levine MM, Nataro JP, Karch H, et al. The diarrheal response of humans to some classic serotypes of enteropathogenic *Escherichia coli* is dependent on a plasmid encoding an enteroadhesiveness factor. J Infect Dis. 1985;152:550-559.
98. Bauer ME, Welch RA. Characterization of an RTX toxin from enterohemorrhagic *Escherichia coli* O157:H7. Infect Immun. 1996;64:167-175.
99. Schmidt H, Kernbach C, Karch H. Analysis of the EHEC *hly* operon and its location in the physical map of the large plasmid of enterohaemorrhagic *Escherichia coli* O157:H7. Microbiology. 1996;142:907-914.
100. Leverstein-van Hall MA, Blok HEM, Donders AR, et al. Multidrug resistance among Enterobacteriaceae is strongly associated with the presence of integrons and is independent of species or isolate origin. J Infect Dis. 2003;187:251-259.
101. Johnson JR. Virulence factors in *Escherichia coli* urinary tract infection. Clin Microbiol Rev. 1991;4:80-128.
102. Donnenberg MS, Welch RA. Virulence determinants of uropathogenic *Escherichia coli.* In: Mobley HLT, Warren JW, eds. Urinary Tract Infections: Molecular Pathogenesis and Clinical Management. Washington, DC: ASM Press; 1996:135-174.
103. Kunin CM, Hua TH, Krishnan C, et al. Isolation of a nicotinamide-requiring clone of *Escherichia coli* O18:K1:H7 from women with acute cystitis: Resemblance to strains found in neonatal meningitis. Clin Infect Dis. 1993;16:412-416.
104. Manges AR, Johnson JR, Foxman B, et al. Widespread distribution of urinary tract infections caused by a multidrug-resistant *Escherichia coli* clonal group. N Engl J Med. 2001;345:1007-1013.
105. Phillips I, Eykyn S, King A, et al. Epidemic multiresistant *Escherichia coli* infection in West Lambeth health district. Lancet. 1988;1:1038-1041.
106. Tullus K, Hörlin K, Svenson SB, et al. Epidemic outbreaks of acute pyelonephritis caused by nosocomial spread of P fimbriated *Escherichia coli* in children. J Infect Dis. 1984;150:728-736.
107. Johnson JR, Stapleton AE, Russo TA, et al. Characteristics and prevalence within serogroup O4 of a J96-like clonal group of uropathogenic *Escherichia coli* O4:H5 containing the class I and class III alleles of *papG*. Infect Immun. 1997;65:2153-2159.
108. Johnson JR, O'Bryan TT, Delavari P, et al. Clonal relationships and extended virulence genotypes among *Escherichia coli* isolates from women with a first or recurrent episode of cystitis. J Infect Dis. 2001;183:1508-1517.
109. Zhang LX, Foxman B, Tallman P, et al. Distribution of *drb* genes coding for Dr binding adhesins among uropathogenic and fecal *Escherichia coli* isolates and identification of new subtypes. Infect Immun. 1997;65:2011-2018.
110. Korhonen TK, Valtonen MV, Parkkinen J, et al. Serotypes, hemolysin production, and receptor recognition of *Escherichia coli* strains associated with neonatal sepsis and meningitis. Infect Immun. 1985;48:486-491.
111. Johnson JR, Russo TA. Uropathogenic *Escherichia coli* as agents of diverse non-urinary tract extraintestinal infections. J Infect Dis. 2002;186:859-864.
112. Russo TA, Johnson JR. Proposal for a new inclusive designation for extraintestinal pathogenic isolates of *Escherichia coli*: ExPEC. J Infect Dis. 2000;181:1753-1754.
113. Benton J, Chawla J, Parry S, et al. Virulence factors in *Escherichia coli* from urinary tract infections in patients with spinal injuries. J Hosp Infect. 1992;22:117-127.
114. Johnson JR, Roberts PL, Stamm WE. P fimbriae and other virulence factors in *Escherichia coli* urosepsis: Association with patients' characteristics. J Infect Dis. 1987;156:225-229.
115. Warren JW. Clinical presentations and epidemiology of urinary tract infections. In: Mobley HLT, Warren JW, eds. Urinary Tract Infections: Molecular Pathogenesis and Clinical Management. Washington, DC: ASM Press; 1996:3-27.
116. Wang MC, Tseng CC, Chen CY, et al. The role of bacterial virulence and host factors in patients with *Escherichia coli* bacteremia who have acute cholangitis or upper urinary tract infection. Clin Infect Dis. 2002;35:1161-1166.
117. Mobley HLT, Green DM, Trifillis AL, et al. Pyelonephritogenic *Escherichia coli* and killing of cultured human renal proximal tubular epithelial cells: Role of hemolysin in some strains. Infect Immun. 1990;58:1281-1289.
118. Johnson DE, Russell RG. Animal models of urinary tract infection. In: Mobley HLT, Warren JW, eds. Urinary Tract Infections: Molecular Pathogenesis and Clinical Management. Washington, DC: ASM Press; 1996:377-403.
119. Johnson DE, Lockatell CV, Russell RG, et al. Comparison of *Escherichia coli* strains recovered from human cystitis and pyelonephritis infections in transurethrally challenged mice. Infect Immun. 1998;66:3059-3065.
120. Langermann S, Mollby R, Burlein JE, et al. Vaccination with FimH adhesin protects cynomolgus monkeys from colonization and infection by uropathogenic *Escherichia coli.* J Infect Dis. 2000;181:774-778.
121. Roberts JA, Kaack B, Källenius G, et al. Receptors for pyelonephritogenic *Escherichia coli* in primates. J Urol. 1984;131:163-168.

122. Gunther NW IV, Snyder JA, Lockatell V, et al. Assessment of virulence of uropathogenic *Escherichia coli* type 1 fimbrial mutants in which the invertible element is phase-locked on or off. Infect Immun. 2002;70:3344-3354.
123. Wu XR, Sun TT, Medina JJ. *In vitro* binding of type 1-fimbriated *Escherichia coli* to uroplakins Ia and Ib: Relation to urinary tract infections. Proc Natl Acad Sci U S A. 1996;93:9630-9635.
124. Mulvey MA, Lopez-Boado YS, Wilson CL, et al. Induction and evasion of host defenses by type 1-piliated uropathogenic *Escherichia coli*. Science. 1998;282:1494-1497.
125. Gunther NW, Lockatell V, Johnson DE, et al. In vivo dynamics of type 1 fimbria regulation in uropathogenic *Escherichia coli* during experimental urinary tract infection. Infect Immun. 2001;69:2838-2846.
126. Lim JK, Gunther NW, Zhao H, et al. In vivo phase variation of *Escherichia coli* type 1 fimbrial genes in women with urinary tract infection. Infect Immun. 1998;66:3303-3310.
127. Johanson I, Lindstedt R, Svanborg C. Roles of the *pap-* and *prs*-encoded adhesins in *Escherichia coli* adherence to human uroepithelial cells. Infect Immun. 1992;60: 3416-3422.
128. Korhonen TK, Virkola R, Holthofer H. Localization of binding sites for purified *Escherichia coli* P fimbriae in the human kidney. Infect Immun. 1986;54:328-332.
129. Roberts JA, Marklund B-I, Ilver D, et al. The Gal(α1-4)Gal-specific tip adhesin of *Escherichia coli* P-fimbriae is needed for pyelonephritis to occur in the normal urinary tract. Proc Natl Acad Sci U S A. 1994;91:11889-11893.
130. Bahrani-Mougeot FK, Gunther NW IV, Donnenberg MS, et al. Uropathogenic *Escherichia coli*. In: Donnenberg MS, ed. *Escherichia coli:* Virulence Mechanisms of a Versatile Pathogen. San Diego: Academic Press; 2002:239-268.
131. O'Hanley P, Lalonde G, Ji G. Alpha-hemolysin contributes to the pathogenicity of piliated digalactoside-binding *Escherichia coli* in the kidney—Efficacy of an alpha-hemolysin vaccine in preventing renal injury in the BALB/c mouse model of pyelonephritis. Infect Immun. 1991;59:1153-1161.
132. Marre R, Hacker J, Henkel W, et al. Contribution of cloned virulence factors from uropathogenic *Escherichia coli* strains to nephropathogenicity in an experimental rat pyelonephritis model. Infect Immun. 1986;54:761-767.
133. Rippere-Lampe KE, O'Brien AD, Conran R, et al. Mutation of the gene encoding cytotoxic necrotizing factor type 1 (*cnf*$_1$) attenuates the virulence of uropathogenic *Escherichia coli*. Infect Immun. 2001;69:3954-3964.
134. Nagy G, Dobrindt U, Schneider G, et al. Loss of regulatory protein RfaH attenuates virulence of uropathogenic *Escherichia coli*. Infect Immun. 2002;70:4406-4413.
135. Kim KS. Meningitis-associated *Escherichia coli*. In: Donnenberg MS, ed. *Escherichia coli:* Virulence Mechanisms of a Versatile Pathogen. San Diego: Academic Press; 2002:269-286.
136. Siitonen A, Takala A, Ratiner YA, et al. Invasive *Escherichia coli* infections in children: Bacterial characteristics in different age groups and clinical entities. Pediatr Infect Dis J. 1993;12:606-612.
137. Parkkinen J, Rogers GN, Korhonen T, et al. Identification of the O-linked sialyloligosaccharides of glycophorin A as the erythrocyte receptors for S-fimbriated *Escherichia coli*. Infect Immun. 1986;54:37-42.
138. Parkkinen J, Korhonen TK, Pere A, et al. Binding sites in the rat brain for Escherichia coli S fimbriae associated with neonatal meningitis. J Clin Invest 1988;81:860-865.
139. Korhonen TK, Parkkinen J, Hacker J, et al. Binding of *Escherichia coli* S fimbriae to human kidney epithelium. Infect Immun. 1986;54:322-327.
140. Johnson JR, Oswald E, O'Bryan TT, et al. Phylogenetic distribution of virulence-associated genes among *Escherichia coli* isolates associated with neonatal bacterial meningitis in the Netherlands. J Infect Dis. 2002;185:774-784.
141. Blum G, Falbo V, Caprioli A, et al. Gene clusters encoding the cytotoxic necrotizing factor type 1, Prs-fimbriae and a-hemolysin form the pathogenicity island II of the uropathogenic *Escherichia coli* strain J96. FEMS Microbiol Lett. 1995;126:189-196.
142. Falbo V, Famiglietti M, Caprioli A. Gene block encoding production of cytotoxic necrotizing factor 1 and hemolysin in *Escherichia coli* isolates from extraintestinal infections. Infect Immun. 1992;60:2182-2187.
143. Schmidt G, Sehr P, Wilm M, et al. Gln 63 of Rho is deamidated by *Escherichia coli* cytotoxic necrotizing factor-1. Nature. 1997;387:725-729.
144. Badger JL, Wass CA, Weissman SJ, et al. Application of signature-tagged mutagenesis for identification of *Escherichia coli* K1 genes that contribute to invasion of human brain microvascular endothelial cells. Infect Immun. 2000;68:5056-5061.
145. Badger JL, Wass CA, Kim KS. Identification of *Escherichia coli* K1 genes contributing to human brain microvascular endothelial cell invasion by differential fluorescence induction. Mol Microbiol. 2000;36:174-182.
146. Johnson JR, Delavari P, O'Bryan TT. *Escherichia coli* O18:K1:H7 isolates from patients with acute cystitis and neonatal meningitis exhibit common phylogenetic origins and virulence factor profiles. J Infect Dis. 2001;183:425-434.
147. Nataro JP, Kaper JB. Diarrheogenic *Escherichia coli*. Clin Microbiol Rev. 1998;11:142-201.
148. Ericsson CD, DuPont HL. Travelers' diarrhea: Approaches to prevention and treatment. Clin Infect Dis. 1993;16:616-626.
149. Elsinghorst EA, Weitz JA. Epithelial cell invasion and adherence directed by the enterotoxigenic *Escherichia coli tib* locus is associated with a 104-kilodalton outer membrane protein. Infect Immun. 1994;62:3463-3471.
150. Mammarappallil JG, Elsinghorst EA. Epithelial cell adherence mediated by the enterotoxigenic *Escherichia coli* Tia protein. Infect Immun. 2000;68:6595-6601.
151. Fleckenstein JM, Lindler LE, Elsinghorst EA, et al. Identification of a gene within a pathogenicity island of enterotoxigenic *Escherichia coli* H10407 required for maximal secretion of the heat-labile enterotoxin. Infect Immun. 2000;68:2766-2774.
152. Tauschek M, Gorrell RJ, Strugnell RA, et al. Identification of a protein secretory pathway for the secretion of heat-labile enterotoxin by an enterotoxigenic strain of *Escherichia coli*. Proc Natl Acad Sci U S A. 2002;99:7066-7071.
153. Elsinghorst EA. Enterotoxigenic *Escherichia coli*. In: Donnenberg MS, ed. *Escherichia coli*: Virulence Mechanisms of a Versatile Pathogen. San Diego: Academic Press; 2002:155-187.
154. Steinsland H, Valentiner-Branth P, Perch M, et al. Enterotoxigenic *Escherichia coli* infections and diarrhea in a cohort of young children in Guinea-Bissau. J Infect Dis. 2002;186:1740-1747.
155. Levine MM, Nalin DR, Hoover DL, et al. Immunity to enterotoxigenic *Escherichia coli*. Infect Immun. 1979;23:729-736.
156. Sixma TK, Pronk SE, Kalk KH, et al. Crystal structure of a cholera toxin-related heat-labile enterotoxin from *E. coli*. Nature. 1991;351:371-377.
157. Forte LR, Eber SL, Turner JT, et al. Guanylin stimulation of Cl^- secretion in human intestinal T84 cells via cyclic guanosine monophosphate. J Clin Invest. 1993;91:2423-2428.
158. Field M. Intestinal ion transport and the pathophysiology of diarrhea. J Clin Invest 2003;111:931-943.
159. DuPont HL, Ericsson CD. Drug therapy: Prevention and treatment of traveler's diarrhea. N Engl J Med. 1993;328:1821-1827.
160. Adachi JA, Ostrosky-Zeichner L, DuPont HL, et al. Empirical antimicrobial therapy for traveler's diarrhea. Clin Infect Dis. 2000;31:1079-1083.
161. Kaper JB. Defining EPEC. Rev Microbiol (Sao Paulo). 1996;27(Suppl 1):130-133.
162. Bray J. Isolation of antigenically homogeneous strains of *Bact. coli neapolitanum* from summer diarrhoea of infants. J Pathol Bacteriol. 1945;57:239-247.
163. Kain KC, Barteluk RL, Kelly MT, et al. Etiology of childhood diarrhea in Beijing, China. J Clin Microbiol. 1991;29:90-95.
164. Gomes TAT, Rassi V, Macdonald KL, et al. Enteropathogens associated with acute diarrheal disease in urban infants in São Paulo, Brazil. J Infect Dis. 1991;164:331-337.
165. Gunzburg ST, Chang BJ, Burke V, et al. Virulence factors of enteric *Escherichia coli* in young Aboriginal children in north-west Australia. Epidemiol Infect. 1992;109:283-289.
166. Thorén A, Stintzing G, Tufvesson B, et al. Aetiology and clinical features of severe infantile diarrhoea in Addis Ababa, Ethiopia. J Trop Pediatr. 1982;28:127-131.
167. Germani Y, Begaud E, Duval P, et al. Prevalence of enteropathogenic, enteroaggregative, and diffusely adherent *Escherichia coli* among isolates from children with diarrhea in New Caledonia. J Infect Dis. 1996;174:1124-1126.
168. Rosa ACP, Mariano AT, Pereira AMS, et al. Enteropathogenicity markers in *Escherichia coli* isolated from infants with acute diarrhoea and healthy controls in Rio de Janeiro, Brazil. J Med Microbiol. 1998;47:781-790.
169. Albert MJ, Faruque SM, Faruque ASG, et al. Controlled study of *Escherichia coli* diarrheal infections in Bangladeshi children. J Clin Microbiol. 1995;33:973-977.
170. Paulozzi LJ, Johnson KE, Kamahele LM, et al. Diarrhea associated with adherent enteropathogenic *Escherichia coli* in an infant and toddler center, Seattle, Washington. Pediatrics. 1986;77:296-300.
171. Wu S-X, Peng R-Q. Studies on an outbreak of neonatal diarrhea caused by EPEC 0127:H6 with plasmid analysis restriction analysis and outer membrane protein determination. Acta Paediatr Scand. 1992;81:217-221.
172. Blake PA, Ramos S, Macdonald KL, et al. Pathogen-specific risk factors and protective factors for acute diarrheal disease in urban Brazilian infants. J Infect Dis. 1993;167:627-632.
173. Bower JR, Congeni BL, Cleary TG, et al. *Escherichia coli* O114:nonmotile as a pathogen in an outbreak of severe diarrhea associated with a day care center. J Infect Dis. 1989;160:243-247.
174. Clausen CR, Christie DL. Chronic diarrhea in infants caused by adherent enteropathogenic *Escherichia coli*. J Pediatr. 1982;100:358-361.
175. Rothbaum R, McAdams AJ, Giannella R, et al. A clinicopathological study of enterocyte-adherent *Escherichia coli:* a cause of protracted diarrhea in infants. Gastroenterology 1982;83:441-454.
176. Staley TE, Jones EW, Corley LD. Attachment and penetration of *Escherichia coli* into intestinal epithelium of the ileum in newborn pigs. Am J Pathol. 1969;56:371-392.
177. Moon HW, Whipp SC, Argenzio RA, et al. Attaching and effacing activities of rabbit and human enteropathogenic *Escherichia coli* in pig and rabbit intestines. Infect Immun. 1983;41:1340-1351.
178. Elliott SJ, Wainwright LA, McDaniel TK, et al. The complete sequence of the locus of enterocyte effacement (LEE) of enteropathogenic *E. coli* E2348/69. Mol Microbiol. 1998;28:1-4.
179. McDaniel TK, Kaper JB. A cloned pathogenicity island from enteropathogenic *Escherichia coli* confers the attaching and effacing phenotype on K-12 *E. coli*. Mol Microbiol. 1997;23:399-407.
180. McDaniel TK, Jarvis KG, Donnenberg MS, et al. A genetic locus of enterocyte effacement conserved among diverse enterobacterial pathogens. Proc Natl Acad Sci U S A. 1995;92:1664-1668.
181. Knutton S, Rosenshine I, Pallen MJ, et al. A novel EspA-associated surface organelle of enteropathogenic *Escherichia coli* involved in protein translocation into epithelial cells. EMBO J. 1998;17:2166-2176.
182. Daniell SJ, Kocsis E, Morris E, et al. 3D structure of EspA filaments from enteropathogenic *Escherichia coli*. Mol Microbiol. 2003;49:301-308.
183. Nougayrède JP, Fernandes PJ, Donnenberg MS. Adhesion of enteropathogenic *Escherichia coli* to host cells. Cell Microbiol. 2003;5:359-372.
184. Donnenberg MS, Tacket CO, James SP, et al. The role of the *eaeA* gene in experimental enteropathogenic *Escherichia coli* infection. J Clin Invest. 1993;92:1412-1417.
185. Kalman D, Weiner OD, Goosney DL, et al. Enteropathogenic *E. coli* acts through WASP and Arp2/3 complex to form actin pedestals. Nat Cell Biol. 1999;1:389-391.
186. Campellone KG, Giese A, Tipper DJ, et al. A tyrosine-phosphorylated 12-amino-acid sequence of enteropathogenic *Escherichia coli* Tir binds the host adaptor protein Nck and is required for Nck localization to actin pedestals. Mol Microbiol. 2002;43:1227-1241.
187. Gruenheid S, DeVinney R, Bladt F, et al. Enteropathogenic *E. coli* Tir binds Nck to initiate actin pedestal formation in host cells. Nat Cell Biol. 2001;3:856-859.
188. Cravioto A, Gross RJ, Scotland SM, et al. An adhesive factor found in strains of *Escherichia coli* belonging to the traditional infantile enteropathogenic serotypes. Curr Microbiol. 1979;3:95-99.

189. Scaletsky ICA, Silva MLM, Trabulsi LR. Distinctive patterns of adherence of enteropathogenic *Escherichia coli* to HeLa cells. Infect Immun. 1984;45:534-536.

190. Gomes TAT, Vieira MAM, Wachsmuth IK, et al. Serotype-specific prevalence of *Escherichia coli* strains with EPEC adherence factor genes in infants with and without diarrhea in São Paulo, Brazil. J Infect Dis. 1989;160:131-135.

191. Trabulsi LR, Keller R, Gomes TAT. Typical and atypical enteropathogenic *Escherichia coli*. Emerg Infect Dis. 2002;8:508-513.

192. Bieber D, Ramer SW, Wu CY, et al. Type IV pili, transient bacterial aggregates, and virulence of enteropathogenic *Escherichia coli*. Science. 1998;280:2114-2118.

193. Cleary J, Lai L-C, Donnenberg MS, et al. Enteropathogenic *E. coli* (EPEC) adhesion to intestinal epithelial cells: Role of bundle-forming pili (BFP), EspA filaments and intimin. Microbiology. 2004;150:527-538.

194. Adu-Bobie J, Frankel G, Bain C, et al. Detection of intimins alpha, beta, gamma, and delta, four intimin derivatives expressed by attaching and effacing microbial pathogens. J Clin Microbiol. 1998;36:662-668.

195. Gunzburg ST, Tornieporth NG, Riley LW. Identification of enteropathogenic *Escherichia coli* by PCR-based detection of the bundle-forming pilus gene. J Clin Microbiol. 1995;33:1375-1377.

196. Scaletsky IC, Fabbricotti SH, Aranda KR, et al. Comparison of DNA hybridization and PCR assays for detection of putative pathogenic enteroadherent *Escherichia coli*. J Clin Microbiol. 2002;40:1254-1258.

197. Tornieporth NG, John J, Salgado K, et al. Differentiation of pathogenic *Escherichia coli* strains in Brazilian children by PCR. J Clin Microbiol. 1995;33:1371-1374.

198. Gomes TAT, Blake PA, Trabulsi LR. Prevalence of *Escherichia coli* strains with localized, diffuse, and aggregative adherence to HeLa cells in infants with diarrhea and matched controls. J Clin Microbiol. 1989;27:266-269.

199. Giles C, Sangster G, Smith J. Epidemic gastroenteritis of infants in Aberdeen during 1947. Arch Dis Child. 1949;24:45-53.

200. Robins-Browne R, Still CS, Miliotis MD, et al. Summer diarrhoea in African infants and children. Arch Dis Child. 1980;55:923-928.

201. Taylor J, Powell BW, Wright J. Infantile diarrhea and vomiting: A clinical and bacteriological investigation. Br Med J. 1949;2:117-141.

202. Camara LM, Carbonare SB, Silva MLM, et al. Inhibition of enteropathogenic *Escherichia coli* (EPEC) adhesion to HeLa cells by human colostrum: Detection of specific sIgA related to EPEC outer-membrane proteins. Int Arch Allergy Immunol. 1994;103:307-310.

203. Cravioto A, Tello A, Villafán H, et al. Inhibition of localized adhesion of enteropathogenic *Escherichia coli* to HEp-2 cells by immunoglobulin and oligosaccharide fractions of human colostrum and breast milk. J Infect Dis. 1991;163:1247-1255.

204. Loureiro I, Frankel G, Adu-Bobie J, et al. Human colostrum contains IgA antibodies reactive to enteropathogenic *Escherichia coli* virulence-associated proteins: Intimin, BfpA, EspA, and EspB. J Pediatr Gastroenterol Nutr. 1998;27:166-171.

205. Parissi-Crivelli A, Parissi-Crivelli JM, Girón JA. Recognition of enteropathogenic *Escherichia coli* virulence determinants by human colostrum and serum antibodies. J Clin Microbiol. 2000;38:2696-2700.

206. Silva MLM, Giampaglia CMS. Colostrum and human milk inhibit localized adherence of enteropathogenic *Escherichia coli* to HeLa cells. Acta Paediatr Scand. 1992;81:266-267.

207. Senerwa D, Mutanda LN, Gathuma JM, et al. Antimicrobial resistance of enteropathogenic *Escherichia coli* strains from a nosocomial outbreak in Kenya. APMIS. 1991;99:728-734.

208. Thorén A, Wolde-Mariam T, Stintzing G, et al. Antibiotics in the treatment of gastroenteritis caused by enteropathogenic *Escherichia coli*. J Infect Dis. 1980;141:27-31.

209. Antai SP, Anozie SO. Incidence of infantile diarrhoea due to enteropathogenic *Escherichia coli* in Port Harcourt metropolis. J Appl Bacteriol. 1987;62:227-229.

210. Lim YS, Ngan CCL, Tay L. Enteropathogenic *Escherichia coli* as a cause of diarrhoea among children in Singapore. J Trop Med Hyg. 1992;95:339-342.

211. Vila J, Vargas M, Casals C, et al. Antimicrobial resistance of diarrheogenic *Escherichia coli* isolated from children under the age of 5 years from Ifakara, Tanzania. Antimicrob Agents Chemother. 1999;43:3022-3024.

212. Griffin PM, Ostroff SM, Tauxe RV, et al. Illnesses associated with *Escherichia coli* O157:H7 infections: A broad clinical spectrum. Ann Intern Med. 1988;109:705-712.

213. Griffin PM, Tauxe RV. The epidemiology of infections caused by *Escherichia coli* O157:H7, other enterohemorrhagic *E. coli*, and the associated hemolytic uremic syndrome. Epidemiol Rev. 1991;13:60-98.

214. Centers for Disease Control and Prevention. Outbreaks of *Escherichia coli* O157:H7 infections among children associated with farm visits—Pennsylvania and Washington, 2000. MMWR Morb Mortal Wkly Rep. 2001;50:293-297.

215. Hilborn ED, Mermin JH, Mshar PA, et al. A multistate outbreak of *Escherichia coli* O157:H7 infections associated with consumption of mesclun lettuce. Arch Intern Med. 1999;159:1758-1764.

216. Boyce TG, Swerdlow DL, Griffin PM. Current concepts: *Escherichia coli* O157:H7 and the hemolytic-uremic syndrome. N Engl J Med. 1995;333:364-368.

217. Tarr PI. *Escherichia coli* O157:H7: Clinical, diagnostic, and epidemiological aspects of human infection. Clin Infect Dis. 1995;20:1-10.

218. Tilden J Jr, Young W, McNamara AM, et al. A new route of transmission for *Escherichia coli*: Infection from dry fermented salami. Am J Public Health. 1996;86:1142-1145.

219. Garg AX, Suri RS, Barrowman N, et al. Long-term renal prognosis of diarrhea-associated hemolytic uremic syndrome—A systematic review, meta-analysis, and meta-regression. JAMA. 2003;290:1360-1370.

220. O'Brien AD, Newland JW, Miller SF, et al. Shiga-like toxin-converting phages from *Escherichia coli* strains that cause hemorrhagic colitis or infantile diarrhea. Science. 1984;226:694-696.

221. Matsushiro A, Sato K, Miyamoto H, et al. Induction of prophages of enterohemorrhagic *Escherichia coli* O157:H7 with norfloxacin. J Bacteriol. 1999;181:2257-2260.

222. Zhang XP, McDaniel AD, Wolf LE, et al. Quinolone antibiotics induce shiga toxin-encoding bacteriophages, toxin production, and death in mice. J Infect Dis. 2000;181:664-670.

223. Jacewicz MS, Mobassaleh M, Gross SK, et al. Pathogenesis of *Shigella* diarrhea: XVII. A mammalian cell membrane glycolipid, Gb3, is required but not sufficient to confer sensitivity to Shiga toxin. J Infect Dis. 1994;169:538-546.

224. Sandvig K, Garred O, Prydz K, et al. Retrograde transport of endocytosed Shiga toxin to the endoplasmic reticulum. Nature. 1992;358:510-512.

225. Te Loo DM, van Hinsbergh VW, van den Heuvel LP, et al. Detection of verocytotoxin bound to circulating polymorphonuclear leukocytes of patients with hemolytic uremic syndrome. J Am Soc Nephrol. 2001;12:800-806.

226. Yoshida T, Fukada M, Koide N, et al. Primary cultures of human endothelial cells are susceptible to low doses of Shiga toxins and undergo apoptosis. J Infect Dis. 1999;180:2048-2052.

227. Yamamoto T, Nagayama K, Satomura K, et al. Increased serum IL-10 and endothelin levels in hemolytic uremic syndrome caused by *Escherichia coli* O157. Nephron. 2000;84:326-332.

228. Perna NT, Mayhew GF, Pósfai G, et al. Molecular evolution of a pathogenicity island from enterohemorrhagic *Escherichia coli* O157:H7. Infect Immun. 1998;66:3810-3817.

229. Donnenberg MS, Tzipori S, McKee M, et al. The role of the *eae* gene of enterohemorrhagic *Escherichia coli* in intimate attachment in vitro and in a porcine model. J Clin Invest. 1993;92:1418-1424.

230. Tzipori S, Gunzer F, Donnenberg MS, et al. The role of the *eaeA* gene in diarrhea and neurological complications in a gnotobiotic piglet model of enterohemorrhagic *Escherichia coli* infection. Infect Immun. 1995;63:3621-3627.

231. Bell BP, Goldoft M, Griffin PM, et al. A multistate outbreak of *Escherichia coli* O157:H7-associated bloody diarrhea and hemolytic uremic syndrome from hamburgers: The Washington experience. JAMA. 1994;272:1349-1353.

232. Konadu EY, Parke JC Jr, Tran HT, et al. Investigational vaccine for *Escherichia coli* O157: Phase I study of O157 O-specific polysaccharide *Pseudomonas aeruginosa* recombinant exoprotein A conjugates in adults. J Infect Dis. 1998;177:383-387.

233. Ghaem-Maghami M, Simmons CP, Daniell S, et al. Intimin-specific immune responses prevent bacterial colonization by the attaching-effacing pathogen *Citrobacter rodentium*. Infect Immun. 2001;69:5597-5605.

234. Dean-Nystrom EA, Gansheroff LJ, Mills M, et al. Vaccination of pregnant dams with intimin^O157 protects suckling piglets from *Escherichia coli* O157:H7 infection. Infect Immun. 2002;70:2414-2418.

235. Konadu E, Donohue-Rolfe A, Calderwood SB, et al. Syntheses and immunologic properties of *Escherichia coli* O157 O-specific polysaccharide and Shiga toxin 1 B subunit conjugates in mice. Infect Immun. 1999;67:6191-6193.

236. Wong CS, Jelacic S, Habeeb RL, et al. The risk of the hemolytic-uremic syndrome after antibiotic treatment of *Escherichia coli* O157:H7 infections. N Engl J Med. 2000;342:1930-1936.

237. Armstrong GD, Rowe PC, Goodyer P, et al. A Phase I study of chemically synthesized verotoxin (Shiga-like toxin) Pk-trisaccharide receptors attached to Chromosorb for preventing hemolytic-uremic syndrome. J Infect Dis. 1995;171:1042-1045.

238. Mukherjee J, Chios K, Fishwild D, et al. Human Stx2-specific monoclonal antibodies prevent systemic complications of *Escherichia coli* O157:H7 infection. Infect Immun. 2002;70:612-619.

239. Mukherjee J, Chios K, Fishwild D, et al. Production and characterization of protective human antibodies against Shiga toxin 1. Infect Immun. 2002;70:5896-5899.

240. Trachtman H, Cnaan A, Christen E, et al. Effect of an oral Shiga toxin-binding agent on diarrhea-associated hemolytic uremic syndrome in children—A randomized controlled trial. JAMA. 2003;290:1337-1344.

241. Nishikawa K, Matsuoka K, Kita E, et al. A therapeutic agent with oriented carbohydrates for treatment of infections by Shiga toxin-producing *Escherichia coli* O157:H7. Proc Natl Acad Sci U S A. 2002;99:7669-7674.

242. Mulvey GL, Marcato P, Kitov PI, et al. Assessment in mice of the therapeutic potential of tailored, multivalent Shiga toxin carbohydrate ligands. J Infect Dis. 2003;187:640-649.

243. Nataro JP, Kaper JB, Robins-Browne R, et al. Patterns of adherence of diarrheogenic *Escherichia coli* to HEp-2 cells. Pediatr Infect Dis J. 1987;6:829-831.

244. Yamamoto T, Koyama Y, Matsumoto M, et al. Localized, aggregative, and diffuse adherence to HeLa cells, plastic, and human small intestines by *Escherichia coli* isolated from patients with diarrhea. J Infect Dis. 1992;166:1295-1310.

245. Nataro JP, Hicks S, Phillips AD, et al. T84 cells in culture as a model for enteroaggregative *Escherichia coli* pathogenesis. Infect Immun. 1996;64:4761-4768.

246. González R, Diaz C, Mariño M, et al. Age-specific prevalence of *Escherichia coli* with localized and aggregative adherence in Venezuelan infants with acute diarrhea. J Clin Microbiol. 1997;35:1103-1107.

247. Bhatnagar S, Bhan MK, Sommerfelt H, et al. Enteroaggregative *Escherichia coli* may be a new pathogen causing acute and persistent diarrhea. Scand J Infect Dis. 1993;25:579-583.

248. Echeverria P, Serichantalerg O, Changchawalit S, et al. Tissue culture-adherent *Escherichia coli* in infantile diarrhea. J Infect Dis. 1992;165:141-143.

249. Gunzburg ST, Chang BJ, Elliott SJ, et al. Diffuse and enteroaggregative patterns of adherence of enteric *Escherichia coli* isolated from aboriginal children from the Kimberley region of Western Australia. J Infect Dis. 1993;167:755-758.

250. Levine MM, Ferreccio C, Prado V, et al. Epidemiologic studies of *Escherichia coli* diarrheal infections in a low socioeconomic level peri-urban community in Santiago, Chile. Am J Epidemiol. 1993;138:849-869.

251. Ming ZF, Xi ZD, Dong CS, et al. Diarrhoeal disease in children less than one year of age at a children's hospital in Guangzhou, People's Republic of China. Trans R Soc Trop Med Hyg. 1991;85:667-669.

252. Nataro JP, Yikang D, Cookson S, et al. Heterogeneity of enteroaggregative *Escherichia coli* virulence demonstrated in volunteers. J Infect Dis. 1995;171:465-468.

253. Czeczulin JR, Whittam TS, Henderson IR, et al. Phylogenetic analysis of enteroaggregative and diffusely adherent *Escherichia coli*. Infect Immun. 1999;67:2692-2699.

254. Okeke IN, Lamikanra A, Czeczulin J, et al. Heterogeneous virulence of enteroaggregative *Escherichia coli* strains isolated from children in southwest Nigeria. J Infect Dis. 2000;181:252-260.

255. Wanke CA, Schorling JB, Barrett LJ, et al. Potential role of adherence traits of *Escherichia coli* in persistent diarrhea in an urban Brazilian slum. Pediatr Infect Dis J. 1991;10:746-751.

256. Cravioto A, Tello A, Navarro A, et al. Association of *Escherichia coli* HEp-2 adherence patterns with type and duration of diarrhoea. Lancet. 1991;337:262-264.

257. Bhan MK, Raj P, Levine MM, et al. Enteroaggregative *Escherichia coli* associated with persistent diarrhea in a cohort of rural children in India. J Infect Dis. 1989;159:1061-1064.

258. Lima AA, Fang G, Schorling JB, et al. Persistent diarrhea in northeast Brazil: Etiologies and interactions with malnutrition. Acta Paediatr Scand Suppl. 1992; 381:39-44.

259. Huppertz HI, Rutkowski S, Aleksic S, et al. Acute and chronic diarrhoea and abdominal colic associated with enteroaggregative *Escherichia coli* in young children living in western Europe. Lancet. 1997;349:1660-1662.

260. Adachi JA, Jiang ZD, Mathewson JJ, et al. Enteroaggregative *Escherichia coli* as a major etiologic agent in traveler's diarrhea in 3 regions of the world. Clin Infect Dis. 2001;32:1706-1709.

261. Adachi JA, Ericsson CD, Jiang ZD, et al. Natural history of enteroaggregative and enterotoxigenic *Escherichia coli* infection among US travelers to Guadalajara, Mexico. J Infect Dis. 2002;185:1681-1683.

262. Mayer HB, Wanke CA. Enteroaggregative *Escherichia coli* as a possible cause of diarrhea in an HIV-infected patient. N Engl J Med. 1995;332:273-274.

263. Kotler DP, Giang TT, Thiim M, et al. Chronic bacterial enteropathy in patients with AIDS. J Infect Dis. 1995;171:552-558.

264. Polotsky Y, Nataro JP, Kotler D, et al. HEp-2 cell adherence patterns, serotyping, and DNA analysis of *Escherichia coli* isolates from eight patients with AIDS and chronic diarrhea. J Clin Microbiol. 1997;35:1952-1958.

265. Glandt M, Adachi JA, Mathewson JJ, et al. Enteroaggregative *Escherichia coli* as a cause of traveler's diarrhea: Clinical response to ciprofloxacin. Clin Infect Dis. 1999;29:335-338.

266. Steiner TS, Lima AAM, Nataro JP, et al. Enteroaggregative *Escherichia coli* produce intestinal inflammation and growth impairment and cause interleukin-8 release from intestinal epithelial cells. J Infect Dis. 1998;177:88-96.

267. Nataro JP, Deng Y, Maneval DR, et al. Aggregative adherence fimbriae I of enteroaggregative *Escherichia coli* mediate adherence to HEp-2 cells and hemagglutination of human erythrocytes. Infect Immun. 1992;60:2297-2304.

268. Nataro JP, Steiner T. Enteroaggregative and diffusely adherent *Escherichia coli*. In: Donnenberg MS, ed. *Escherichia coli*: Virulence Mechanisms of a Versatile Pathogen. San Diego: Academic Press; 2002:189-207.

269. Sheikh J, Czeczulin JR, Harrington S, et al. A novel dispersin protein in enteroaggregative *Escherichia coli*. J Clin Invest. 2002;110:1329-1337.

270. Savarino SJ, Fasano A, Watson J, et al. Enteroaggregative *Escherichia coli* heat-stable enterotoxin 1 represents another subfamily of *E. coli* heat-stable toxin. Proc Natl Acad Sci U S A. 1993;90:3093-3097.

271. Navarro-García F, Sears C, Eslava C, et al. Cytoskeletal effects induced by Pet, the serine protease enterotoxin of enteroaggregative *Escherichia coli*. Infect Immun. 1999;67:2184-2192.

272. Henderson IR, Hicks S, Navarro-Garcia F, et al. Involvement of the enteroaggregative *Escherichia coli* plasmid-encoded toxin in causing human intestinal damage. Infect Immun. 1999;67:5338-5344.

273. Albert MJ, Qadri F, Haque A, et al. Bacterial clump formation at the surface of liquid culture as a rapid test for identification of enteroaggregative *Escherichia coli*. J Clin Microbiol. 1993;31:1397-1399.

274. Wanke CA, Gerrior J, Blais V, et al. Successful treatment of diarrheal disease associated with enteroaggregative *Escherichia coli* in adults infected with human immunodeficiency virus. J Infect Dis. 1998;178:1369-1372.

275. Yamamoto T, Echeverria P, Yokota T. Drug resistance and adherence to human intestines of enteroaggregative *Escherichia coli*. J Infect Dis. 1992;165:744-749.

276. Maurelli AT, Fernandez RE, Bloch CA, et al. "Black holes" and bacterial pathogenicity: A large genomic deletion that enhances the virulence of *Shigella* spp. and enteroinvasive *Escherichia coli*. Proc Natl Acad Sci U S A. 1998;95:3943-3948.

277. Martinez MB, Whittam TS, McGraw EA, et al. Clonal relationship among invasive and non-invasive strains of enteroinvasive *Escherichia coli* serogroups. FEMS Microbiol Lett. 1999;172:145-151.

278. Ochman H, Whittam TS, Caugant DA, et al. Enzyme polymorphism and genetic population structure in Escherichia coli and Shigella. J Gen Microbiol. 1983;129:2715-2726.

279. DuPont HL, Formal SB, Hornick RB, et al. Pathogenesis of *Escherichia coli* diarrhea. N Engl J Med. 1971;285:1-9.

280. Girón JA, Jones T, Millán-Velasco F, et al. Diffuse-adhering *Escherichia coli* (DAEC) as a putative cause of diarrhea in Mayan children in Mexico. J Infect Dis. 1991;163:507-513.

281. Tacket CO, Moseley SL, Kay B, et al. Challenge studies in volunteers using *Escherichia coli* strains with diffuse adherence to HEp-2 cells. J Infect Dis. 1990;162:550-552.

282. Albert MJ, Alam K, Islam M, et al. *Hafnia alvei*, a probable cause of diarrhea in humans. Infect Immun. 1991;59:1507-1513.

283. Albert MJ, Faruque SM, Ansaruzzaman M, et al. Sharing of virulence-associated properties at the phenotypic and genetic levels between enteropathogenic *Escherichia coli* and *Hafnia alvei*. J Med Microbiol. 1992;37:310-314.

284. Janda JM, Abbott SL, Albert MJ. Prototypal diarrheogenic strains of *Hafnia alvei* are actually members of the genus *Escherichia*. J Clin Microbiol. 1999;37: 2399-2401.

285. Huys G, Cnockaert M, Janda JM, et al. *Escherichia albertii* sp. nov., a diarrhoeogenic species isolated from stool specimens of Bangladeshi children. Int J Syst Evol Microbiol. 2003;53:807-810.

286. Jarvis WR, Munn VP, Highsmith AK, et al. The epidemiology of nosocomial infections caused by *Klebsiella pneumoniae*. Infect Control. 1985;6:68-74.

287. Geerdes HF, Ziegler D, Lode H, et al. Septicemia in 980 patients at a university hospital in Berlin: Prospective studies during 4 selected years between 1979 and 1989. Clin Infect Dis. 1992;15:991-1002.

288. Garcia de la Torre M, Romero-Vivas J, Martinez-Beltrán J, et al. Klebsiella bacteremia: An analysis of 100 episodes. Rev Infect Dis. 1985;7:143-150.

289. Bishara J, Leibovici L, Huminer D, et al. Five-year prospective study of bacteraemic urinary tract infection in a single institution. Eur J Clin Microbiol Infect Dis. 1997;16:563-567.

290. Carpenter JL. Klebsiella pulmonary infections: Occurrence at one medical center and review. Rev Infect Dis. 1990;12:672-682.

291. Sahly H, Podschun R, Ullmann U. *Klebsiella* infections in the immunocompromised host. Adv Exp Med Biol. 2000;479:237-249.

292. Sahly H, Podschun R, Oelschlaeger TA, et al. Capsule impedes adhesion to and invasion of epithelial cells by *Klebsiella pneumoniae*. Infect Immun. 2000;68:6744-6749.

293. Livrelli V, De Champs C, Di Martino P, et al. Adhesive properties and antibiotic resistance of *Klebsiella, Enterobacter,* and *Serratia* clinical isolates involved in nosocomial infections. J Clin Microbiol. 1996;34:1963-1969.

294. Haeggman S, Lofdahl S, Burman LG. An allelic variant of the chromosomal gene for class A beta-lactamase K2, specific for Klebsiella pneumoniae, is the ancestor of SHV-1. Antimicrob Agents Chemother. 1997;41:2705-2709.

295. Burwen DR, Banerjee SN, Gaynes RP. Ceftazidime resistance among selected nosocomial gram-negative bacilli in the United States. J Infect Dis. 1994;170:1622-1625.

296. Andraca R, Edson RS, Kern EB. Rhinoscleroma: A growing concern in the United States? Mayo Clinic experience. Mayo Clin Proc. 1993;68:1151-1157.

297. Lenis A, Ruff T, Diaz JA, et al. Rhinoscleroma. South Med J. 1988;81:1580-1582.

298. Badia L, Lund VJ. A case of rhinoscleroma treated with ciprofloxacin. J Laryngol Otol. 2001;115:220-222.

299. Goldstein EJ, Lewis RP, Martin WJ, et al. Infections caused by *Klebsiella ozaenae*: A changing disease spectrum. J Clin Microbiol. 1978;8:413-418.

300. Tang LM, Chen ST. *Klebsiella ozaenae* meningitis: Report of two cases and review of the literature. Infection. 1994;22:58-61.

301. Carter JS, Bowden FJ, Bastian I, et al. Phylogenetic evidence for reclassification of *Calymmatobacterium granulomatis* as *Klebsiella granulomatis* comb. nov. Int J Syst Bacteriol. 1999;49(Pt 4):1695-1700.

302. Boye K, Hansen DS. Sequencing of 16S rDNA of *Klebsiella*: Taxonomic relations within the genus and to other Enterobacteriaceae. Int J Med Microbiol. 2003;292:495-503.

303. Sanders WE Jr, Sanders CC. *Enterobacter* spp.: Pathogens poised to flourish at the turn of the century. Clin Microbiol Rev. 1997;10:220-241.

304. Keller R, Pedroso MZ, Ritchmann R, et al. Occurrence of virulence-associated properties in *Enterobacter cloacae*. Infect Immun. 1998;66:645-649.

305. Korfmann G, Wiedemann B. Genetic control of beta-lactamase production in *Enterobacter cloacae*. Rev Infect Dis. 1988;10:793-799.

306. Chow JW, Fine MJ, Shlaes DM, et al. Enterobacter bacteremia: Clinical features and emergence of antibiotic resistance during therapy (see comments). Ann Intern Med. 1991;115:585-590.

307. Sehdev PS, Donnenberg MS. Arcanum: The 19th-century Italian pharmacist pictured here was the first to characterize what are now known to be bacteria of the genus *Serratia*. Clin Infect Dis. 1999;29:770-925.

308. Yu VL. *Serratia marcescens*: Historical perspective and clinical review. N Engl J Med. 1979;300:887-893.

309. Parment PA, Svanborg-Edén C, Chaknis MJ, et al. Hemagglutination (fimbriae) and hydrophobicity in adherence of *Serratia marcescens* to urinary tract epithelium and contact lenses. Curr Microbiol. 1992;25:113-118.

310. Hejazi A, Falkiner FR. *Serratia marcescens*. J Med Microbiol. 1997;46:903-912.

311. Acar JF. *Serratia marcescens* infections. Infect Control 1986;7:273-278.

312. Mills J, Drew D. *Serratia marcescens* endocarditis: A regional illness associated with intravenous drug abuse. Ann Intern Med. 1976;84:29-35.

313. Mahlen SD, Morrow SS, Abdalhamid B, et al. Analyses of *ampC* gene expression in *Serratia marcescens* reveal new regulatory properties. J Antimicrob Chemother. 2003;51:791-802.

314. Lipsky BA, Hook EW III, Smith AA, et al. Citrobacter infections in humans: Experience at the Seattle Veterans Administration Medical Center and a review of the literature. Rev Infect Dis. 1980;2:746-760.

315. Shih CC, Chen YC, Chang SC, et al. Bacteremia due to *Citrobacter* species: Significance of primary intraabdominal infection. Clin Infect Dis. 1996;23:543-549.

316. Drelichman V, Band JD. Bacteremias due to Citrobacter diversus and Citrobacter freundii: Incidence, risk factors, and clinical outcome. Arch Intern Med. 1985;145: 1808-1810.

317. Williams WW, Mariano J, Spurrier M, et al. Nosocomial meningitis due to *Citrobacter diversus* in neonates: New aspects of the epidemiology. J Infect Dis. 1984;150:229-235.

318. Spröer C, Mendrock U, Swiderski J, et al. The phylogenetic position of *Serratia, Buttiauxella* and some other genera of the family Enterobacteriaceae. Int J Syst Bacteriol. 1999;49(Pt 4):1433-1438.

319. Gunthard H, Pennekamp A. Clinical significance of extraintestinal Hafnia alvei isolates from 61 patients and review of the literature. Clin Infect Dis. 1996;22:1040-1045.

320. Ridell J, Siitonen A, Paulin L, et al. *Hafnia alvei* in stool specimens from patients with diarrhea and healthy controls. J Clin Microbiol. 1994;32:2335-2337.

321. O'Hara CM, Brenner FW, Miller JM. Classification, identification, and clinical significance of *Proteus, Providencia*, and *Morganella*. Clin Microbiol Rev. 2000;13:534-546.

322. Fairley KF, Carson NE, Gutch RC, et al. Site of infection in acute urinary-tract infection in general practice. Lancet. 1971;2:615-618.

323. Bryan CS, Reynolds KL. Community-acquired bacteremic urinary tract infection: Epidemiology and outcome. J Urol. 1984;132:490-493.

324. Müller HE. Occurrence and pathogenic role of *Morganella-Proteus-Providencia* group bacteria in human feces. J Clin Microbiol. 1986;23:404-405.

325. Zhao H, Li X, Johnson DE, et al. *In vivo* phase variation of MR/P fimbrial gene expression in *Proteus mirabilis* infecting the urinary tract. Mol Microbiol. 1997;23:1009-1019.

326. Li X, Lockatell CV, Johnson DE, et al. Identification of MrpI as the sole recombinase that regulates the phase variation of MR/P fimbria, a bladder colonization factor of uropathogenic *Proteus mirabilis*. Mol Microbiol. 2002;45:865-874.

327. Bahrani FK, Massad G, Lockatell CV, et al. Construction of an MR/P fimbrial mutant of *Proteus mirabilis:* Role in virulence in a mouse model of ascending urinary tract infection. Infect Immun. 1994;62:3363-3371.

328. Johnson DE, Russell RG, Lockatell CV, et al. Contribution of *Proteus mirabilis* urease to persistence, urolithiasis, and acute pyelonephritis in a mouse model of ascending urinary tract infection. Infect Immun. 1993;61:2748-2754.

329. Warren JW. *Providencia stuartii:* A common cause of antibiotic-resistant bacteriuria in patients with long-term indwelling catheters. Rev Infect Dis. 1986;8:61-67.

330. Muder RR, Brennen C, Wagener MM, et al. Bacteremia in a long-term-care facility: A five-year prospective study of 163 consecutive episodes. Clin Infect Dis. 1992;14:647-654.

331. McDermott C, Mylotte JM. *Morganella morganii:* Epidemiology of bacteremic disease. Infect Control. 1984;5:131-137.

332. Ikeobi CC, Ogunsanya TO, Rotimi VO. Prevalence of pathogenic role of *Morganella-Proteus Providencia*-group of bacteria in human faeces. Afr J Med Sci. 1996;25:7-12.

333. Kim BN, Kim NJ, Kim MN, et al. Bacteraemia due to tribe Proteeae: A review of 132 cases during a decade (1991-2000). Scand J Infect Dis. 2003;35:98-103.

334. Poirel L, Guibert M, Girlich D, et al. Cloning, sequence analyses, expression, and distribution of *ampC-ampR* from *Morganella morganii* clinical isolates. Antimicrob Agents Chemother. 1999;43:769-776.

335. Janda JM, Abbott SL. Infections associated with the genus *Edwardsiella:* The role of *Edwardsiella tarda* in human disease. Clin Infect Dis. 1993;17:742-748.

336. Brenden RA, Miller MA, Janda JM. Clinical disease spectrum and pathogenic factors associated with *Plesiomonas shigelloides* infections in humans. Rev Infect Dis. 1988;10:303-316.

337. Ruimy R, Breittmayer V, Elbaze P, et al. Phylogenetic analysis and assessment of the genera *Vibrio, Photobacterium, Aeromonas,* and *Plesiomonas* deduced from small-subunit rRNA sequences. Int J Syst Bacteriol. 1994;44:416-426.

338. Holmberg SD, Wachsmuth IK, Hickman-Brenner FW, et al. Plesiomonas enteric infections in the United States. Ann Intern Med. 1986;105:690-694.

339. Herrington DA, Tzipori S, Robins-Browne RM, et al. In vitro and in vivo pathogenicity of *Plesiomonas shigelloides*. Infect Immun. 1987;55:979-985.

340. Devreese K, Claeys G, Verschraegen G. Septicemia with *Ewingella americana*. J Clin Microbiol. 1992;30:2746-2747.

341. Kati C, Bibashi E, Kokolina E, et al. Case of peritonitis caused by *Ewingella americana* in a patient undergoing continuous ambulatory peritoneal dialysis. J Clin Microbiol. 1999;37:3733-3734.

342. Pien FD, Bruce AE. Nosocomial *Ewingella americana* bacteremia in an intensive care unit. Arch Intern Med. 1986;146:111-112.

343. Luttrell RE, Rannick GA, Soto-Hernandez JL, et al. *Kluyvera* species soft tissue infection: Case report and review. J Clin Microbiol. 1988;26:2650-2651.

344. Sarria JC, Vidal AM, Kimbrough RC III. Infections caused by *Kluyvera* species in humans. Clin Infect Dis. 2001;33:E69-E74.

345. Gerrard JG, McNevin S, Alfredson D, et al. *Photorhabdus* species: Bioluminescent bacteria as emerging human pathogens? Emerg Infect Dis. 2003;9:251-254.

Pseudomonas aeruginosa

GERALD B. PIER
REUBEN RAMPHAL

MICROBIOLOGY

Pseudomonas aeruginosa is the major pathogenic species in the family Pseudomonadaceae and is readily identified as a gram-negative straight or slightly curved rod with a length ranging from 1 to 3 μm and a width of 0.5 to 1.0 μm. Major morphologic characteristics on laboratory media include production of pigments, notably a soluble blue-colored phenazine pigment called pyocyanin. Some strains produce red or black colonies because of synthesis of pigments termed pyorubin and pyomelanin, respectively. Another diffusible yellow-green to yellow-brown pigment produced by *P. aeruginosa* is pyoverdin, which, when produced along with pyocyanin, gives rise to a typical green to green-blue colony on solid media. The name *aeruginosa* stems from the green-blue hue seen within colonies of many clinical isolates. Colonies of *P. aeruginosa* can have a highly varied morphology, with typical colonies appearing to spread over the plate, lie flat with a metallic sheen, and frequently produce a gelatinous or "slimy" appearance, particularly in areas of heavy growth. However, colonial variants including dwarf, coliform, and mucoid morphotypes are seen, the last morphology particularly frequent when cultures from the respiratory tract and secretions of patients with cystic fibrosis (CF) are observed (Fig. 216-1). A characteristic "grapelike" or "corn taco-like" odor is produced by most strains as well.

P. aeruginosa is able to grow on a wide variety of media, ranging from minimal to complex, and can metabolize a large array of carbon sources. It grows best aerobically but can be grown anaerobically in the presence of nitrate as a terminal electron acceptor. *P. aeruginosa*

does not ferment carbohydrates but produces acid from sugars such as glucose, fructose, and xylose but not lactose or sucrose. It is strongly positive in an indophenol oxidase test and can grow at 42° C, which differentiates this species from the rarely pathogenic *Pseudomonas fluorescens* and *Pseudomonas putida*. A commonly used selective medium is cetrimide agar, which contains a detergent that inhibits growth of many other organisms, although with some exceptions. On triple sugar iron agar the organism has a reaction of alkaline over no change in growth, and it is Simmons' citrate positive and L-arginine dehydrolase positive. *P. aeruginosa* gives negative reactions for L-lysine decarboxylase and L-ornithine decarboxylase, and it does not produce hydrogen sulfide.

At the ultrastructural level, *P. aeruginosa* produces a single or monotrichous polar flagellum and many cell surface fimbriae or pili (Fig. 216-2). Almost all strains carry the biosynthetic genes to produce an extracellular polysaccharide known as alginate because of its chemical similarity to seaweed alginate. This material has also been referred to as mucoid exopolysaccharide in the literature,[1] and its overproduction is the basis for the mucoid colony phenotype associated with isolates from CF patients as well as occasional isolates from other patients with chronic *P. aeruginosa* infections, such as chronic obstructive pulmonary disease, or chronic infections in patients with indwelling urinary catheters. In general, strains of *P. aeruginosa* isolated from the environment and nosocomial infections are considered nonmucoid, but in

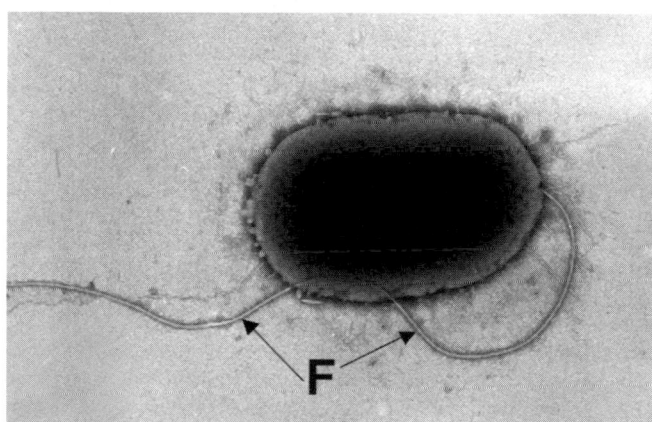

A

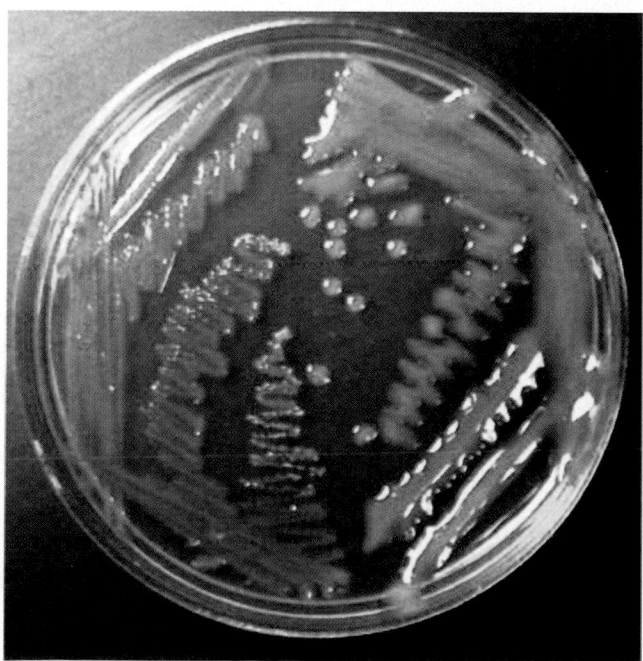

FIGURE 216-1. Phenotypic appearance of nonmucoid, generally lipopolysaccharide (LPS)-smooth (left) and mucoid, LPS-rough (right) colonies of *Pseudomonas aeruginosa*.

B

FIGURE 216-2. Electron micrographs of *Pseudomonas aeruginosa* cell showing ultrastructural features. **A,** Single cell with polar flagellum (F) with part of the flagellum running under the cell body. **B,** Two cells showing thin, hairlike pili (P). (**A,** Courtesy of Dr. Steven Lory; **B,** from Pier GB. Molecular mechanisms of bacterial pathogenesis. In: Isselbacher KJ, Braunwald E, Wilson JD, et al, eds. Harrison's Principles of Internal Medicine. 16th ed. New York: McGraw-Hill; in press.)

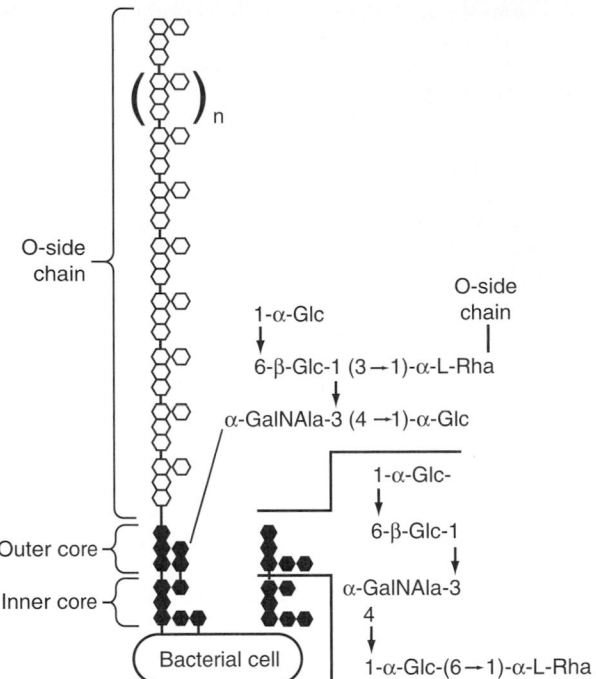

FIGURE 216-3. Structure of the two isoforms (glycoforms) of the *Pseudomonas aeruginosa* lipopolysaccharide. Left, Structure of the glycoform that accepts the long O side chains. Right, Structure of the glycoform that is not substituted with O side chains. GalNala, *N*-alanyl-galactosamine; Glc, glucose; Rha, rhamnose.

reality most nonmucoid strains can express low levels of the alginate polysaccharide when grown in vitro.[2,3] Environmental and nosocomial isolates also produce a smooth lipopolysaccharide (LPS) substituted with long (5 to 100 kDa) polysaccharide O side chains, but only about 10% to 30% of the LPS molecules contain O side chains. The rest of the LPS molecules are in the form of LPS rough molecules containing lipid A, inner- and outer-core regions (Fig. 216-3) but lacking O side chains. Studies have shown that the outer-core region of the LPS containing O side chains differs structurally from that of molecules lacking O side chains (see Fig. 216-3). The outer membrane is typical of those for gram-negative bacteria and contains a large array of outer membrane proteins (OMPs) with a variety of functions critical for cellular growth and metabolism. From the sequence of the *P. aeruginosa* genome that was completed in 2000,[4] it is estimated that there may be more than 300 potential OMPs and it is clear that their expression varies dramatically depending on growth conditions or phenotype of strains used for analysis of the OMPs.[5-7]

HISTORY

Before the advent of modern medical microbiology there was evidence that *P. aeruginosa* was a cause of serious wound and surgical infections, as elaborated by Doggett.[8] In 1850 it was noted by Sédillot that there were sometimes blue-green discharges on surgical dressings that were associated with infection, and in 1862 Luke noted rod-shaped microscopic entities within the blue-green pus. In 1882 Gessard isolated the organisms and originally designated them as *Bacillus pyocyaneus,* and other early microbiologists also isolated the organism from infected sites. Osler in 1925 thought the organism to be more of a secondary or opportunistic invader of damaged tissues as opposed to a primary cause of infection in healthy tissues, an observation well borne out since his time. *P. aeruginosa* emerged as a major human pathogen in the 1960s because of its ability to cause infections in immunocompromised and burned hosts as well as CF patients, all of whom were surviving much longer with modern medical treat-

ments. Since that time, *P. aeruginosa* has become one of the most serious causes of nosocomial bacterial infections, notably in the lung, blood, and urinary tract. Furthermore, as a result of its considerable potential to become resistant to many antibiotics, more and more multiply antibiotic-resistant strains are being encountered as clinical isolates, leaving physicians with a decreasing armamentarium of effective drugs for treatment.

EPIDEMIOLOGY

In adult clinical medicine, *P. aeruginosa* is primarily encountered as a nosocomial pathogen, which reflects its great propensity to grow in a variety of environments with minimal nutritional components.[9] However, as CF patients survive longer and their medical care as adults is increasingly shifted away from pediatric providers, treatment of CF lung disease by adult practitioners is becoming more common.[10] Outside the hospital *P. aeruginosa* is commonly found in soil, water, and plants and can on occasion be associated with colonization of otherwise healthy humans and animals. The organism is tolerant to temperatures as high as 45° C to 50° C and can grow in distilled water using dissolved carbon dioxide and residual sulfur, phosphorus, iron, and divalent cations as carbon and essential nutritional substrates. However, water buffered to a pH of 4.5 or lower does not support survival of *P. aeruginosa*. Within the hospital *P. aeruginosa* can colonize moist surfaces of patients on the axilla, ear, and perineum and is also isolated from other moist, inanimate environments including water in sinks and drains, toilets, and showers. Pathogenic strains have also been isolated from the water used for flowers in patients' rooms. Hospital equipment that comes in contact with water such as mops, respiratory ventilators, cleaning solutions, and food and food processing machines can be sources of *P. aeruginosa*.

Although much less a problem than nosocomial infection, community-acquired *P. aeruginosa* infection does occur in certain settings,[11] and infection is often associated with exposure to moist environments. *P. aeruginosa* skin infections related to use of hot tubs, whirlpools, swimming pools, and other types of baths are well-recognized clinical presentations of community-acquired infection.[12] Individuals who use contact lenses, particularly of the extended-wear variety that can be kept in the eyes for several weeks, have a greatly increased risk of *P. aeruginosa* ulcerative keratitis associated with the presence of the bacteria in their contact lens solutions.[13-15] Otitis externa is frequently caused by *P. aeruginosa*.[16] Puncture wounds through tennis shoes can give rise to serious *P. aeruginosa* infection,[17] although this condition is found primarily in children. Infected toes associated with use of topical antibiotics and nail infections associated with constant exposure to water, detergents, or mechanical stress are well-recognized clinical presentations of *P. aeruginosa* infection. *P. aeruginosa* endophthalmitis after surgery or eye trauma can result in serious compromise of vision,[18] and *P. aeruginosa* endocarditis is often found in injection drug users.[19]

P. aeruginosa nosocomial infections are usually attributed to acquisition of the organism in the hospital, particularly in patients undergoing mechanical ventilation, antibiotic treatment, chemotherapy, or surgery. However, *P. aeruginosa* can be found among normal microorganisms carried by a small proportion of humans, and it has been suggested that endogenous *P. aeruginosa* brought into intensive care units (ICUs) by patients from the community can serve as sources of serious infection.[20,21] Patients with significant burn wounds are at high risk for *P. aeruginosa* infection, but in the most modern burn-trauma centers, effective topical antimicrobial therapy and burn wound excision have greatly reduced the incidence of *P. aeruginosa* infection.[22,23] Up to 7% of healthy humans carry *P. aeruginosa* in the throat, nasal mucosa, or on the skin,[24] and carriage rates as high as 24% in the stool have been reported.[21,24]

Frequently associated with invasive *P. aeruginosa* infection is a prior period of colonization, which can be as high as 50% in patients with an underlying risk factor for infection. Yet it has still been difficult to identify precisely which patients with colonization will go on to have invasive disease or identify with any assurance what the initial source or mode of transmission of the infecting strain was. In the absence of an identifiable hospital outbreak, usually associated with a particular source, *P. aeruginosa* infection can start from any of the moist reservoirs patients come in contact with: showers, sinks, flower vases, uncooked vegetables, and so forth. Many patients, particularly those receiving mechanical ventilation, become colonized with *P. aeruginosa* in the upper airways, but only a minority go on to develop serious invasive infection.[25-27] Gastrointestinal (GI) colonization with *P. aeruginosa,* usually secondary to antibiotic use that disrupts the normal microbial populations of the GI tract, can lead to aspiration, respiratory tract colonization, and sometimes lung infection. Selective decontamination of the GI tract with orally nonabsorbable antibiotics along with a course of intravenous antibiotics for prevention of infection and associated mortality in the ICU has strong advocates, and several studies show efficacy in reducing mortality, including that from *P. aeruginosa* ventilator-associated pneumonia, with use of this treatment.[28-30] The practice has not gained widespread acceptance, however, particularly in North America, and significant questions about its efficacy remain.

Determining the source and prevalence of *P. aeruginosa* in the hospital environment is essential for effective epidemiologic control of infection, and many newer techniques are available to carry out effective investigations using modern molecular typing techniques.[31] Typing by colonial morphology or phenotype, antibiogram, serology of variant LPS antigens, bacteriophages, bacteriocins known as pyocins, or biochemical profiles using standard clinical microbiologic analysis is fairly limited and generally has insufficient discriminatory power. Preferred techniques target genomic sequences and include DNA size analysis by pulsed-field gel electrophoresis (PFGE), analysis of DNA restriction enzyme-based fragment polymorphisms (RFLPs), use of randomly amplified pieces of DNA showing a high degree of polymorphism among strains (termed RAPD for randomly amplified polymorphic DNA or AFLP for amplified fragment length polymorphism), use of multilocus sequence typing (MLST) wherein short DNA sequences in defined genes known to be variable among strains are determined and used for strain classification, and use of polymerase chain reaction (PCR)-RFLP to discriminate strains on the basis of DNA sequence variations found in the small subunit ribosomal RNA genes (ribotyping or riboprinting). Each of these techniques has strengths and some weaknesses in regard to its discriminatory power, with one common limitation being their availability primarily in specialty or research laboratories. However, automated systems for such techniques as riboprinting are commercially available[32] and PFGE systems that are generally more affordable with methods sufficiently standardized for this technique now have routine applications in many clinical microbiology laboratories.

Changes in the epidemiology and incidence of various nosocomial infections are frequent, and many of the problems seem to occur in local environments or as sporadic, epidemic outbreaks. However, infections with *P. aeruginosa* have remained relatively constant in terms of incidence and tissue sites of occurrence over the past 30 years, as tracked by the National Nosocomial Infections Surveillance System. Data from medical ICUs during the surveillance period 1992 to 1997 indicated that *P. aeruginosa* caused about 3% of blood-stream infections; 21% of pneumonias (making it the nosocomial pathogen most frequently isolated from the lungs); 10% of urinary tract infections (fourth most common pathogen); 13% of eye, ear, nose, and throat infections (third most common); and 5% of cardiovascular infections.[33] With increasing problems from strains of *P. aeruginosa* resistant to multiple antibiotics, it can be anticipated that infections with this organism will remain a major cause of morbidity and mortality for some time to come.

PATHOGENESIS

The bacterial virulence factors brought to bear on the pathologic process associated with *P. aeruginosa* infection are large and varied in both form and function. Multiple pathogenic factors with redundant functions are expressed by *P. aeruginosa* clinical isolates, often mak-

ing it difficult to determine experimentally whether a specific factor plays a significant role in pathogenesis. The role and importance of different virulence factors are affected by the host in significant ways; innate and acquired immune function, site of infection, and comorbid conditions, to name a few, determine whether a given bacterial virulence factor plays a major or minor role in pathogenesis. There is a fine balance between effective, innate immunity that controls the spread of the organism and pathologic inflammation associated with bacterial growth and poor control of the organism. As both of these states rely on the same general host effector and signaling molecules for their manifestations, tipping the balance one way or the other could be the difference between benign and serious *P. aeruginosa* infection. Nonetheless, over the past several decades a number of specific factors involved in various aspects of *P. aeruginosa* virulence have been identified through molecular, cellular, and animal studies that give us some important insights into the basis for *P. aeruginosa* disease.

Host Factors in Pathogenesis

As the major manifestations of *P. aeruginosa* infection are nosocomial infection, chronic lung infection in CF, and contact lens-associated ulcerative keratitis, it is clear that the primary determinant of the pathogenic potential of *P. aeruginosa* virulence factors is the health status of the human host . As healthy humans are generally highly resistant to *P. aeruginosa* infection, some compromise in host health status underlies most of the serious problems with *P. aeruginosa* infection. Innate immune resistance to infection starts with the anatomic barrier functions of the skin and mucosal surfaces, and any disruption to the integrity of these barriers establishes a situation wherein *P. aeruginosa* can become pathogenic. Typical problems are associated with burns and somewhat less frequently with other types of wounds to the skin, use of intravenous or urinary catheters, and particularly use of endotracheal tubes. Because of its ubiquity in the environment *P. aeruginosa* is the preeminent opportunistic pathogen taking advantage of compromises to the integrity of physical and mucosal barriers to infection.

Molecular and Cellular Basis for Loss of Host Resistance to *Pseudomonas aeruginosa* Infection

Anatomic and Physiologic Barriers. In regard to the specific molecular and cellular events that ensue when a patient enters a state of increased risk for *P. aeruginosa* infection, many of what are thought to be critical factors have come from studies in animals as well as studies focusing on *P. aeruginosa* and CF lung disease. In the simplest sense, for burn and wound infections, *P. aeruginosa* is able to take advantage of the dead or poorly perfused tissue, grow in this site, and eventually achieve a density in the wound sufficient to allow it to seed the blood at levels that overwhelm the host's innate immunity. Usually, infection of intact skin with *P. aeruginosa* is uncommon[34] and, when seen, is generally confined to localized epidermal infections of the nail beds (green nail syndrome) or web-space infection and sometimes somewhat more serious cutaneous folliculitis and otitis externa.

In burned or wounded skin, the situation is different. In the development of the burned mouse model used extensively in research on *P. aeruginosa* pathogenesis, Stieritz and Holder[35] showed that *P. aeruginosa* grew to high levels in burned skin after inoculation of as few as 10 organisms, after which there was systemic dissemination and lethality. Healthy skin required five to six logs more organisms to achieve a comparable effect. However, by 3 days after the burn, the mouse skin had recovered sufficiently that it was actually more resistant than normal skin to *P. aeruginosa* growth. In wounded tissue it appears *P. aeruginosa* can find a haven safe from host immune effectors and grow to sufficient levels to elaborate a multitude of toxins that break down such host factors as complement, fibrin, and antiproteinases. One of the major bacterial factors implicated in pathogenesis is elastase.[36] The healthy eye is highly resistant to *P. aeruginosa* infection,[13] but when the physical integrity of the corneal mucosa and epithelial surface is breached, *P. aeruginosa* becomes a major pathogen.[18,37-40] In these situations, it is likely that the major underlying cellular mechanism related to increased host susceptibility to infection is loss of tissue integrity.

Loss of mucosal barrier function is another host condition that allows *P. aeruginosa* to be a major pathogen. Mucous membranes protect against pathogens by a variety of mechanisms that, when compromised, give rise to dramatically increased susceptibility to infection. In the GI tract and oropharynx, the normal bacterial flora provides stiff competition for pathogens to colonize and grow. Mucus entraps foreign organisms, which are cleared by peristalsis in the GI tract, mucociliary clearance in the respiratory tract, and urination in the genitourinary tract, Within the mucus are antimicrobial factors such as lysozyme, lactoferrin, and defensins,[41-43] the last being small peptides that insert themselves into bacterial membranes and disrupt their integrity, leading to microbial death. The propensity of this organism to colonize the GI tract in the setting of cancer chemotherapy and antibiotic use[44] and the frequent colonization of the upper respiratory tract in patients with endotracheal tubes result from disruption of the normal resistance mechanisms present on these surfaces.

Soluble Factors on Mucosal Surfaces and in Blood: Complement. Other soluble host factors present on mucosal surfaces that have been implicated in high-level resistance to *P. aeruginosa* infection include complement proteins, lung surfactants and similar members of the collectin family, and a variety of cytokines and chemokines. Complement has two major roles in modulating *P. aeruginosa* infection; the major opsonins derived from complement component 3 (C3), C3b and iC3b, effectively promote phagocytosis and killing of *P. aeruginosa*,[45,46] and the so-called anaphylatoxins, derived from C3 and C5, C3a and C5a, promote the neutrophil recruitment and activation needed for effective phagocytosis. Complement-deficient mice are more susceptible to *P. aeruginosa* infection,[47] and failure to produce C3a in C3-deficient mice and C5a in C5-deficient mice resulted in increased *P. aeruginosa* lung burdens and mortality. Interestingly, the functions of C3a and C5a were not in polymorphonuclear neutrophil (PMN) recruitment, as both C3- and C5-deficient mice infected with *P. aeruginosa* had higher levels of these inflammatory cells in the lungs than wild-type animals,[47,48] but the ability of the neutrophils to phagocytose and kill *P. aeruginosa* was clearly compromised in complement-deficient animals. However, *P. aeruginosa* infection is not reported to be a complication of congenital complement deficiency in humans, suggesting that in this setting other effectors of immunity can compensate for loss of complement function.

Soluble Factors on Mucosal Surfaces and in Blood: Collectins. The collectins are soluble molecules involved in innate resistance to *P. aeruginosa* infection and include the surfactant proteins A (SP-A) and D (SP-D) and mannose (or mannan) binding lectin (MBL).[49] Collectins are composed of multiple subunits and include a carbohydrate recognition domain that binds to conserved pattern recognition molecules on the bacterial surface attached to a collagen-like stalk that can bind to the collectin receptor on phagocytes. In addition, the collectins activate complement through the lectin-binding pathway, a pathway that leads to generation of complement opsonins and anaphylatoxins. Mice deficient in SP-A are more susceptible to the mucoid *P. aeruginosa* strains that cause chronic lung infections in CF patients.[50] SP-D promotes opsonization of *P. aeruginosa* by alveolar macrophages,[51,52] which may be important in the early handling of *P. aeruginosa* lung infection. Variant alleles of MBL different from the most common one found in humans have been associated with more severe lung disease in *P. aeruginosa*-infected CF patients,[53] and at least one CF patient with this condition has been treated with MBL purified from human plasma with some improvement in clinical condition.[54] However, others were unable to find evidence of MBL binding to *P. aeruginosa*,[55] raising questions about the mechanisms whereby MBL deficiency led to enhanced CF lung disease during *P. aeruginosa* infection.

Soluble Factors on Mucosal Surfaces and in Blood: Cytokines, Chemokines, and Related Factors of Innate Immunity. The panoply of cytokines and chemokines humans can produce in response to infection, with their additive, synergistic, and complementary as well as antagonistic effects, makes it difficult to ascribe a role in re-

sistance to *P. aeruginosa* infection to a single cytokine. Even more problematic is the likelihood that a particular cytokine or set of cytokines may be protective at one point in the infectious cycle and contribute to inflammation-induced pathology at a later time point. As pointed out by Alexander and Rietschel,[56] the same cytokine or chemokine mediators of inflammation that provide effective antimicrobial immunity when produced in a controlled, physiologic fashion also mediate the pathology associated with highly consequential inflammation including tissue destruction, the sepsis syndrome, and death. Consistent with these observations are the numerous reports, mostly from studies in transgenic mice, implicating some cytokines and chemokines as key elements in both resistance and enhancement of pathology related to *P. aeruginosa* infection.

Interleukin-1 (IL-1) is a factor involved in both resistance to infection and succumbing to the pathologic effects of overwhelming infection. Early studies showed that pretreatment of mice with IL-1 protected against infection with *P. aeruginosa* and other gram-negative pathogens.[57-61] Proposed mechanisms for the protective effects of IL-1 against *P. aeruginosa* infection include activation of antibacterial T cells,[62] inhibition of bacterial growth,[63,64] induction of defensins,[65] and activation and modulation of phagocytic cell activity.[66,67] However, severe *P. aeruginosa* infections were associated with highly elevated levels of IL-1 in both local issues and blood[68,69] and levels of IL-1β was a marker for alveolar inflammation in mechanically ventilated patients with community-acquired pneumonia.[70] In mice given a sufficient dose of *P. aeruginosa* to cause a lethal infection, IL-1 contributed significantly to pathology, as there was a better outcome in animals after neutralization of IL-1 or in mice unable to respond to IL-1 because of loss of the IL-1 receptor.[71,72] It appears that pretreatment with IL-1 or the levels of IL-1 produced in response to low infectious doses of *P. aeruginosa* augment host resistance to infection, whereas when high infectious doses are given or *P. aeruginosa* grows to high levels in compromised hosts, the continued production of IL-1 and signaling through the IL-1 receptor increase inflammation to the point at which it contributes to pathology.

Tumor necrosis factor-α (TNF-α) has also been implicated as a cytokine affecting *P. aeruginosa* infection in both a positive and a pathologic manner. BALB/c mice, reported by some to be more resistant to *P. aeruginosa* pulmonary infection, had higher levels of TNF-α gene expression and protein secretion in the alveoli in response to this organism,[73] and malnourished mice were more susceptible to *P. aeruginosa* pulmonary infection, in part because of diminished TNF-α production.[74] TNF-α knockout mice had a diminished capacity to clear *P. aeruginosa*.[74] TNF-α modulation of inflammation has been associated with differences in outcome in experimental *P. aeruginosa* pulmonary infection,[75] with protection associated with enhanced alveolar macrophage presence and activity and pathology associated with sustained PMN infiltration in the lungs. TNF-α levels are well known to be elevated in the blood of patients with a variety of bacteremic agents, and TNF-α is thought to be a major mediator of the pathogenesis of sepsis, but attempts to blockade its activity in a therapeutic manner have all been unsuccessful.[76] Indeed, in some clinical trials, patients treated with high doses of anti-TNF molecules had a worse outcome.[77] TNF-α levels in the lungs and serum of chronically infected CF patients are elevated in comparison with those in healthy individuals, but they do not generally appear to change during exacerbation of infection.[78-81] Similarly to IL-1, TNF-α probably augments innate immunity in situations of low-level exposure to *P. aeruginosa*, but if innate immunity fails, continued attempts to reestablish tissue sterility by production of TNF-α lead to inflammation-associated pathology.

Other cytokines, chemokines, and small molecular effectors of innate immunity found in experimental studies to affect *P. aeruginosa* infection include IL-4,[82] IL-6,[39,83,84] IL-9,[85] IL-10,[69,86-88] IL-18,[89,90] transforming growth factor-β,[91] and nitric oxide.[74,75,92] As is often found in such studies, both positive and negative effects of these factors have been noted. Again, context is probably highly important, with positive effects of inflammatory cytokines such as IL-4, IL-6, and IL-18 important in innate immunity at low doses of *P. aeruginosa*, whereas high levels of these factors exacerbate illness when *P. aeruginosa* levels become elevated in infected tissues. Similarly, anti-inflammatory factors such as IL-9, IL-10, and nitric oxide are found to be deficient during *P. aeruginosa*-induced disease because of high levels of bacteria, and increasing the anti-inflammatory activity in this situation brings about salutary effects. However, the potential of any of these factors, or inducers of their production, to be clinically efficacious remains low at present because of many problems including pharmacokinetics; costs; ability to induce or inhibit the factor at the correct time during infection in the correct tissue at a therapeutic, nontoxic dose; and the complexity of the interactions among cytokines, chemokines, and related molecules that cannot be readily controlled to bring about a clinical benefit.

Immunoglobulin Deficiency. As a rule, neither agammaglobulinemia, hypogammaglobulinemia, nor hypergammaglobulinemia is commonly associated with *P. aeruginosa* infection, although antibody-mediated immunity to this pathogen is a well-established parameter of immune resistance to infection. Case reports associating certain congenital or acquired immunoglobulin pathologies with *P. aeruginosa* infection have been published,[93-96] including infections in immunoglobulin deficiency with hyperimmunoglobulin M syndrome, severe combined immunodeficiency plus leukopenia, and hyperimmunoglobulin E syndrome. It is likely that other mediators of innate immunity, particularly complement-dependent phagocytosis, play a major role in maintaining resistance to *P. aeruginosa* infection in immunoglobulinopathies. Interestingly, in some cases of X-linked agammaglobulinemia related to mutations in the *btk* gene encoding a cytoplasmic tyrosine kinase (Bruton's tyrosine kinase) that is needed for proper B-cell development, there is an associated neutropenia, the basis for which is not clear. About 20% of male infants in the first year of life with this genetic immunodeficiency plus neutropenia present with ecthyma gangrenosum and often have concomitant *P. aeruginosa* sepsis.[97,98]

Cellular Mediators of Resistance to *Pseudomonas aeruginosa* Infection

Leukocytes. Although all known monocytic, granulocytic, and lymphocytic cell types have shown some effect on *P. aeruginosa* infections in both humans and experimental animals, it is overwhelmingly clear that the major cellular mediator of resistance to *P. aeruginosa* infection is the PMN. Although the incidence of serious nosocomial *P. aeruginosa* infections seems to have declined in some hospitals in the past decade compared with that in the 1970s,[99] neutropenia in humans is still a major risk factor for *P. aeruginosa* infection.[100-102] Also, even though it is appreciated that advanced acquired immunodeficiency syndrome (AIDS) predisposes to *P. aeruginosa* infection, these patients usually have neutropenia as a complication of their disease, which contributes, along with other factors such as indwelling urinary or vascular catheters, to severe *P. aeruginosa* infection.[103] Animal studies completely confirm that neutropenia dramatically increases susceptibility to *P. aeruginosa* infection.[104-106] For example, a minimal dose of *P. aeruginosa* lethal to nearly 100% of mice when delivered to the lungs usually ranges from 10^7 to 5×10^8 colony-forming units (CFU) per animal, whereas after three doses of cyclophosphamide of 150 mg/kg, which results in absolute neutrophil counts close to zero, most wild-type *P. aeruginosa* strains are lethal to the animals after inoculation with as few as 1 to 50 CFU per animal. Indeed, it could be persuasively argued that the PMNs are the only critical mediators of innate immunity to *P. aeruginosa* infection, as their absence so dramatically affects susceptibility to infection.

As for non-PMN leukocytes, numerous papers have reported the ability of blood and alveolar macrophages to phagocytose *P. aeruginosa,* suggesting a role in resistance to infection.[107,108] However, in animal studies, depletion of alveolar macrophages in mice with liposome-encapsulated clodronate disodium[109] or liposome-encapsulated dichloromethylene diphosphonate[110] failed to alter the outcome of *P. aeruginosa* infection although changes in production of some cytokines were noted. These studies suggest no essential role for macrophages in innate immunity to *P. aeruginosa* infection, but local macrophages may affect production of soluble factors that contribute to host resistance because of effects, for example, on PMN recruitment and activation. However, these soluble factors are probably produced by multiple cell types in addition to macrophages, making the loss of the macrophage overshadowed by compensatory production of soluble factors from other cell types. Similarly, eosinophils do not appear to play a role in host resistance to *P. aeruginosa* infection, but either the cells themselves or released granule contents such as major basic protein may contribute to the atopic-like pathology found in chronically infected CF patients.[111-113] Basophils, and particularly tissue mast cells, are important producers of mediators of inflammation in response to infection, and several studies have shown the importance of mast cell mediator release in recruitment of PMNs to sites of *P. aeruginosa* infection.[114-117] Again, the major effector called into play is the PMN.

Numerous studies have indicated a role of T cell-mediated immunity in development of resistance to *P. aeruginosa* infection after vaccination with a variety of immunogens,[117-122] and some have suggested that differences in susceptibility to experimental infection in mice correlate with innate delayed-type hypersensitivity responses to *P. aeruginosa.*[123,124] The occurrence of *P. aeruginosa* infection in severely ill AIDS patients also suggests a role for CD4[+] T cells in resistance to infection,[103,125,126] but there are other associated risk factors for infection in this population. An established paradigm of modern immunology indicates that T cells can be divided into at least two populations, known as helper T 1 (Th1) and Th2 subsets, that differ in their ability to activate cell-mediated or antibody-mediated immune responses through production of IL-12 and interferon-γ (IFN-γ) (Th1 cells activate cell-mediated immunity) or production of IL-4, IL-5, and IL-10 (leading to antibody production). Some studies have suggested that a Th1 response results in better outcomes in mice chronically infected with *P. aeruginosa,*[127,128] but these studies found opposite results in regard to mouse strains producing Th1 versus Th2 responses to *P. aeruginosa.* This immunologic paradigm probably does not readily apply to most *P. aeruginosa* infections because the organism produces so many factors capable of eliciting either Th1 or Th2 responses that both subsets are activated in infected patients. Other lymphocytic subsets such as CD1-restricted T cells[129] have been reported to contribute to murine clearance of *P. aeruginosa* lung infection, and γδ T cells[130] from CF patients and healthy humans have been shown to produce cytokines in response to *P. aeruginosa.* However, the significance of these findings for the overall contribution of host factors to *P. aeruginosa* pathogenesis is unclear.

Epithelial Cells. Epithelial cells are among the first cell types to encounter *P. aeruginosa* after exposure. Principally through studies directed at elucidating why CF patients are so commonly infected with *P. aeruginosa* (more than 80% of patients infected by 15 to 20 years of age), a great deal has been learned about the role of epithelial cells in orchestrating innate immunity to *P. aeruginosa* infection. The major challenge has been to correlate the genetic defect leading to synthesis of either no cystic fibrosis transmembrane conductance regulator (CFTR) protein or dysfunctional CFTR to the pathogenesis of *P. aeruginosa* infection. CFTR is known principally as a channel conducting chloride and bicarbonate across cell membranes[131,132] but how this is related to hypersusceptibility to *P. aeruginosa* infection is not fully understood.

Four major hypotheses have been proposed for the basis for the susceptibility of CF patients to *P. aeruginosa* (listed in Table 1 of reference 133). A long-standing proposal has been that epithelial cells in the lung in CF express higher levels of a receptor for *P. aeruginosa,* asialo GM1,[134,135] and the bacteria have higher binding to epithelial cells, increasing their ability to withstand host clearance. Although several investigators have confirmed the observations of increased bacterial adherence to epithelial cells in culture,[136,137] the hypothesis has been challenged by other investigators.[138] The basis for the challenge includes inconsistent findings of increased adherence of *P. aeruginosa* to CF airway epithelial cells,[139] findings of increased adherence only to epithelial cells from the subset of CF patients homozygous for the ΔF508 allele of *CFTR* (50% of patients)[140] whereas many patients with other *CFTR* genotypes contract a comparable lung disease from *P. aeruginosa*, and the use of only a few laboratory strains to study adherence in most of the studies,[135,137,141] whereas studies with clinical isolates failed to show that asialo GM1 was a significant receptor for *P. aeruginosa*.[138] In addition, although an antiserum raised to asialo GM1 has been shown in several studies to reduce *P. aeruginosa* binding to epithelial cells,[135-137] this antiserum was found to have high titers of antibodies to *P. aeruginosa* because of use of complete Freund's adjuvant, which contains mycobacteria expressing cross-antigens cross-reactive with those of *P. aeruginosa*. It is likely that apparent reductions in bacterial binding observed in the presence of this antiserum are, in fact, due to agglutination of *P. aeruginosa* cells in the experimental tubes, which leads to reduced colony counts when agglutinated organisms are plated on agar media. More important, in none of the studies could inhibition of binding of *P. aeruginosa* to asialo GM1 on cell surfaces be ascribed to the anti-asialo GM1 activity of the serum.

It has also been proposed that the chloride ion conductance defect of CFTR leads to increased salt concentrations in the thin airway surface liquid (ASL) that overlies the bronchial epithelium between the apical surface of the cell and the more viscous mucous layer.[142,143] This high salt concentration has been proposed to interfere with the activity of antimicrobial peptides.[142,143] However, most studies failed to find a difference in salt concentration between normal and CF ASL,[144,145] and this hypothesis fails to account for the high frequency of *P. aeruginosa* in the setting of CF. A third hypothesis is that lack of functional CFTR also leads to dehydration of the ASL, producing a more viscous pericellular ASL layer that cannot be readily cleared by mucociliary activity of the respiratory epithelium.[146,147] This leads to formation of mucus plugs, which harbor mucin receptors for *P. aeruginosa*,[148,149] and also produces an anaerobic environment that has been proposed to augment synthesis of the bacterial alginate associated with infection.[150,151] Although mucus plugs loaded with *P. aeruginosa* can be clearly seen in lung sections obtained at autopsy or at transplantation from CF patients, the depleted ASL hypothesis also fails to account for the specificity of CF lung disease for *P. aeruginosa*, and there is no evidence that the initial *P. aeruginosa* infection relies on mucus plugs for bacterial adherence.

The fourth proposed hypothesis directly addresses the issue of the role of epithelial cells in susceptibility to *P. aeruginosa* lung infection, makes a direct link to CFTR, and involves the PMN, which is critically important in innate immunity to this pathogen.[152] It has been shown that cells lacking functional CFTR are less able to internalize *P. aeruginosa* and high levels of bacterial internalization correlate with host resistance to infection.[153] CFTR was shown to be an epithelial cell receptor for binding and internalization of *P. aeruginosa*[154] (Fig. 216-4), and the bacterial ligand is the outer-core oligosaccharide of the LPS.[153] Inhibiting the ability of epithelial cells to interact with *P. aeruginosa* by adding to an infectious inoculum of *P. aeruginosa* either purified outer-core oligosaccharide or a CFTR peptide that blocks bacterial binding to this protein resulted in decreased epithelial cell uptake and increased bacterial levels in the lungs.[153,154] Transgenic CF mice lacking functional CFTR also had lowered epithelial cell uptake of *P. aeruginosa* and higher total lung burdens after experimental challenge in an acute infection model.[155]

Perhaps more important than epithelial cell ingestion of *P. aeruginosa* is the CFTR-dependent activation of inflammatory gene transcription related to nuclear translocation of the nuclear factor κB (NF-κB) transcription factor that centrally orchestrates cellular responses to many pathogens.[156] In this regard, it was shown that CFTR recognition of *P. aeruginosa* leads to actual extraction of the LPS from the bacterial outer membrane and this is essential for NF-κB nuclear translocation in both cultured human airway epithelial cells and lungs of infected normal mice (see Fig. 216-4). NF-κB translocation causes increases in transcription of genes involved in PMN recruitment and activation: IL-6, IL-8, GRO1, and intercellular adhesion molecule 1 (ICAM-1). CFTR-mediated recognition of *P. aeruginosa* also facilities apoptosis of epithelial cells,[157] a process critical for resolution of

the inflammatory response. Delay in this response could underlie the expanded inflammatory state observed in CF lungs, and proper apoptosis of epithelial cells in *P. aeruginosa*-infected mice has been shown to be critical for resistance to infection.[158,159]

In addition, *P. aeruginosa* infection activates tyrosine kinase signaling molecules in infected epithelial cells, which is dependent on bacterial binding to CFTR,[160] and such signaling is clearly important in orchestrating effective host resistance to infection. Interestingly, CFTR-*P. aeruginosa* interactions have been shown to be critical components of the pathogenesis of experimental corneal keratitis in a wounded-cornea model of infection.[161,162] However, in this model the injury allows *P. aeruginosa* to penetrate through a layer of corneal epithelium that is five or six cells thick to the underlying stroma, where the bacteria use CFTR to enter the epithelial cells and avoid the host's PMN-based defenses. Thus, in contrast to the lung, where the infected epithelial cells are on the airway surface and can desquamate into the lumen to remove ingested *P. aeruginosa*, in the wounded eye the subsurface epithelial cells provide a safe haven for the microbe. Overall, there are now considerable data from numerous studies and independent groups to conclude that *P. aeruginosa*-CFTR interactions at the epithelial surface of the lung are a key molecular component of host resistance to pulmonary infection, and loss of this component of innate immunity dramatically increases susceptibility to *P. aeruginosa* infection, as seen in CF.

Bacterial Factors in Pathogenesis

P. aeruginosa is a fascinating bacterial pathogen to study and a formidable pathogen for humans because of the multitude, diversity, and complexity of its virulence factors. The organism has a large genome more than 6 megabases in size[4] that is highly plastic in terms of ability to incorporate and modify DNA. Virtually all major classes of bacterial virulence systems are found in this organism (Table 216-1), including exotoxins, endotoxins, type III secreted toxins, pili, flagella, proteases, phospholipases, iron-binding proteins, exopolysaccharides, the ability to form biofilms, and elaboration of pyocyanins. The potential of *P. aeruginosa* to cause infection in virtually any body site is probably due to the array of factors it can call upon from its large genome to establish itself at a specific site and utilize a wide variety of nutrients for growth along with the ability to produce a panoply of factors to counteract host defenses. The organism can grow anaerobically if a source of nitrate is present. *P. aeruginosa* is a significant pathogen in part because of modern medical practices that utilize an extensive array of implanted medical devices ranging from venous catheters to orthopedic implants on which the organism can colonize and form a biofilm and then disseminate systemically.

Understanding of the array of *P. aeruginosa* pathogenic factors and how they affect infection, growth, and disease has grown dramatically, but because of the redundancy of these factors in terms of their effects on the host, along with other issues such as tissue-specific sites of expression of virulence factors, there is no straightforward picture of *P. aeruginosa* pathogenesis at the molecular level. Indeed, although many of the factors demonstrated in laboratory studies to affect pathogenesis are well-accepted contributors to the pathogenic process, laboratory studies are always limited by use of a few, often highly selected, strains for studies. Thus, when investigators look at large sets of clinical isolates they can usually recover strains from patients that lack some of the factors demonstrated in laboratory studies to be important contributors to virulence.[163,164] Nonetheless, some general features of *P. aeruginosa* pathogenesis shared by the majority of strains are now very well studied and these studies have contributed greatly to our understanding of the molecular basis for virulence of *P. aeruginosa*.

Entry, Colonization, and Avoidance of Innate Clearance Mechanisms

It is often written that bacteria must first adhere to a host tissue in order to initiate infection, and although this basically obvious statement must hold true, otherwise the organism would be expelled from a mucosal surface, it is naive to consider that bacterial adherence to host tis-

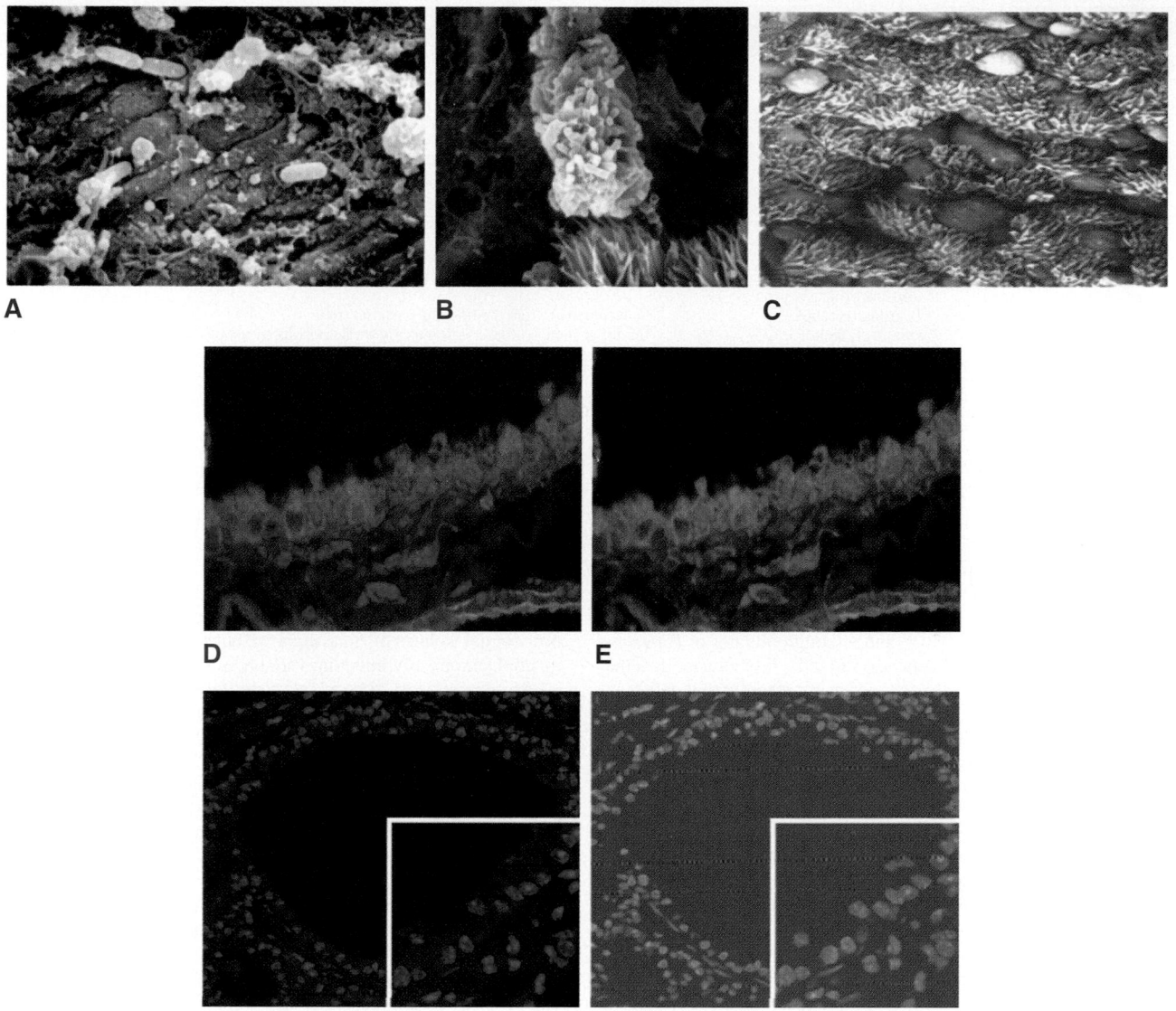

FIGURE 216-4. Entry of *Pseudomonas aeruginosa* into airway epithelial cells and activation of nuclear factor κB (NF-κB) nuclear translocation in wild-type and transgenic cystic fibrosis (CF) mice. **A,** Scanning electron micrograph (SEM) of *P. aeruginosa* entering mouse tracheal epithelial cells 4 hours after intranasal infection with bacteria. **B,** SEM of desquamating tracheal epithelial cell with internalized and attached *P. aeruginosa* cells. **C,** SEM of tracheal epithelium of a transgenic CF mouse 4 hours after intranasal infection with bacteria showing intact epithelium and no bacterial binding or entry to the cystic fibrosis transmembrane conductance regulator (CFTR)-deficient cells. **D** through **G,** Confocal laser scanning micrographs of NF-κB nuclear translocation in bronchial epithelial cells of a wild-type mouse (D and E) or transgenic CF mouse (F and G). Sections were stained for NF-κB (red), CFTR (green), and DNA in the nucleus (blue). Colocalization of NF-κB and CFTR in the cytoplasm of the cells from the wild-type mouse (D) appears as an orange-red color. Nuclear translocation of NF-κB is represented by pseudocolored magenta (colocalization of red and blue colors) in E and G. No CFTR is present in the transgenic CF mouse bronchial epithelium (F, only the red NF-κB is seen) and no NF-κB migrates to the nucleus in the transgenic CF mouse (G). D through G, ×400; insets in F and G, ×800. *(B, From Schroeder TH, Reiniger N, Meluleni G, et al. Transgenic cystic fibrosis mice exhibit reduced early clearance of Pseudomonas aeruginosa from the respiratory tract. J Immunol. 2001;166:7410-7418, copyright 2001, The American Association of Immunologists, Inc. and used with permission; D through G, from Schroeder TH, Lee MM, Yacono PW, et al. CFTR is a pattern recognition molecule that extracts Pseudomonas aeruginosa LPS from the outer membrane into epithelial cells and activates NF-kappa B translocation. Proc Natl Acad Sci USA. 2002;99:6907-6912.)*

sues is necessarily going to promote establishment of colonization. Adherence of many pathogens, including *P. aeruginosa*, to epithelial cells initiates vigorous host innate immune responses that much more often than not promote bacterial clearance. Thus, establishing early colonization is a combination of use of bacterial factors that allow the organism to find a niche in which to grow and factors that overcome innate immune clearance.

Entry of *P. aeruginosa* into most humans occurs by the oral or respiratory route. *P. aeruginosa* has virtually no pathogenic capacity in the normal GI tract, although there are occasional reports of isolation

of *P. aeruginosa* from fecal or stool cultures in patients with severe diarrhea, but no clear basis for *P. aeruginosa* contributing to this has been established. In the respiratory tract, however, establishment of *P. aeruginosa* infection can have serious consequences, particularly for those with underlying comorbidities or a genetic predisposition such as in CF. Generally the two major adhesins considered to play a role here are pili and flagella (see Fig. 216-2), which have several functions including both motility and binding to receptors.

Pili. *P. aeruginosa* pili are formed from a 15-kDa pilin monomer encoded by the *pilA* gene and are located at the poles of the rod, forming

TABLE 216-1 Virulence Factors of *Pseudomonas aeruginosa*

Location or Class	Example(s)	Activity/Effects on Host
Cell surface	Alginate	Antiphagocytic/resist opsonic killing
	LPS*	Endotoxic/antiphagocytic/avoid preformed antibody to previously encountered O antigens
	Pili	Twitching motility; biofilm formation; adherence to host tissues
	Flagella	Motility; biofilm formation; adherence to host tissues and mucin components
	Injection of type III secretion factors	PcrG, PcrV, PcrH, PopB, and PopD proteins form injection bridge for type III effectors
Outer membrane	Siderophore receptors	Provides iron for microbial growth and survival
	Efflux pumps	Remove antibiotics
Type III secretion	ExoS; ExoT; ExoU; ExoY	Intoxicates cells (ExoS/ExoT); cytotoxic (ExoU); disrupts actin cytoskeleton
Secreted proteases	LasA protease; LasB elastase; alkaline protease; protease IV	Degrades host immune effectors (antibody, complement, etc.); degrades matrix proteins
Iron acquisition	Pyoverdin; pyochelin	Scavenge iron from the host for bacterial use
Secreted toxins	Exotoxin A; leukocidin phospholipases; hemolysins; rhamnolipid	Inhibit protein synthesis; kill leukocytes; hemolysis of red blood cells; degrade host cell surface glycolipids.
Secreted oxidative factors	Pyocyanin; ferripyochelin	Produces reactive oxygen species: H_2O_2; O_2^- inflammatory; disrupts epithelial cell function
Quorum sensing	LasR/LasI;RhlR/RhlI PQS*	Biofilm formation; regulation of virulence factor secretion

*LPS, lipopolysaccharide; PQS, *Pseudomonas* quinolone system.

typical polar pili. More than 40 genetic loci have been identified that control pilin synthesis and pili production.[165] Transcription is regulated by the alternative RNA polymerase sigma factor known as RpoN or σ^{54} and by classic bacterial two-component regulators encoded by the *pilS* and *pilR* genes. Functionally, pili have been proposed as mediators of local adherence to host tissues,[140,166,167] and although mutants of *P. aeruginosa* unable to make pili have been reported to be less virulent in some animal models of infection,[168] this cannot be ascribed to any defect in binding to host tissues as this specific function of pili has never been investigated in vivo. Also, in the corneal scratch-injured eye model, lack of pili on strain PAK did not compromise virulence.[169] Pili have also been proposed to bind to asialo GM1 and GM1 on target tissues, but again this conclusion is mostly derived from in vitro studies with little in the way of in vivo correlates. Surprisingly, and problematically, the portion of the pilus that has been identified as binding to these glycolipid receptors, formed by a critical disulfide bond in the carboxyl-terminal loop of the pilin monomer, has been shown by x-ray crystallographic studies to be buried within the pilus and not surface exposed at the pilus tip, where it could mediate adhesion to host cells.[170,171] Although it is possible that the receptor-binding disulfide loop becomes exposed upon bacterial contact with glycolipid receptors on host tissues, this idea is speculative. Pilin sequences, and hence serologic relatedness, vary among *P. aeruginosa* strains, although it has been proposed that a consensus peptide can be identified in all *P. aeruginosa* pili that binds to the target glycolipid receptors. Whether this is accurate remains to be demonstrated, but there is currently significant interest in using such a peptide as the basis for an antiadherence vaccine for *P. aeruginosa*.[170,172]

Pili also mediate twitching motility of *P. aeruginosa*, a factor found to be important in formation of in vitro biofilms on abiotic surfaces.[173] Twitching motility may also be important in avoidance of host phagocytes. Pili have other roles that may be important in helping the organism to survive in vivo, such as natural DNA uptake, autoaggregation of cells, and development of microbial communities. Because studies with mutants of *P. aeruginosa* unable to make pili compromise all of the functions of this structure, one can never know which of the pili-mediated functions are essential to virulence until such times as mutants producing pili with compromises only in specific functions can be made and tested.

Flagella. The flagella of *P. aeruginosa* are one of its more prominent virulence factors as assessed by laboratory studies going back over 20 years.[174-176] *P. aeruginosa* makes a single polar flagellum that imparts a number of properties to the cell including motility and ability to bind to host tissues. Synthesis of the flagella is quite complex, with more than 40 known genes involved in regulation of transcription and production of the complex structure that makes up the entire flagellar unit, including the flagellar basal body, circular structures designated as the MS and P rings, and a motor switch complex. The key structural components of

the flagella are the flagellin subunit protein, encoded by the *fliC* gene, and a protein that caps off the flagella, FliD, encoded by the *fliD* gene. There are two major types of flagella in *P. aeruginosa*, the a type and the b type, each produced by allelic variants in the *fliC* and *fliD* genes that are coinherited.[148,177] Flagella are produced by most environmental and nosocomial isolates of *P. aeruginosa*, but production is often lost by the mucoid, chronically infecting variants isolated from CF patients.

Motility appears to be a key property of *P. aeruginosa* virulence, as flagella-minus strains are almost avirulent in animal models of infection. However, it is now appreciated that flagella also promote adherence to host tissues, another property lost when the ability to produce flagella is eliminated in mutant strains. Flagella, like pili, have been reported to bind to asialo GM1 as well as glycolipids GM1 and GD1a, but flagella-mediated binding to epithelial cells is apparently a rare event.[175] The FliD cap protein binds avidly to the carbohydrate portion of mucins, including a variety of neutral and acidic oligosaccharides.[178] Increased mucin production occurs in response to infection, and normally this would promote removal of the organism from the host tissue and prevent bacterial access to more vulnerable epithelial surfaces. However, in pulmonary and ocular infections, *P. aeruginosa* can take advantage of mucin binding to anchor itself to host tissues, which, when combined with such factors as reduced mucociliary clearance in the lung or entrapment of mucus under an extended-wear contact lens, results in an enhanced ability to cause disease.

Other Adhesins Potentially Involved in Colonization

A number of other *P. aeruginosa* molecules have been reported to mediate adherence of the organism to host tissues and cells. As noted previously, the outer-core oligosaccharide of *P. aeruginosa* binds to CFTR,[153,154,162] a process important in resistance to infection in humans with normal CFTR, and LPS has also been reported to bind to asialo GM1[179] and the galectin-3 protein on epithelial cell surfaces.[180] *P. aeruginosa* produces some lectin-like molecules known as PA-IL and PA-IIL that appear to promote binding to sugar molecules on tissues,[181] and *P. aeruginosa* OMPs, notably ompF,[182] have been shown to mediate adherence to mammalian cells as well, with one proposal that the targets on host tissues are cell surface heparin proteoglycans.[183] Overall, the adherence of *P. aeruginosa* to mucins, tissues, cells, and so forth is clearly complex and a variety of microbial products and host targets are involved, with the different interactions probably contributing to pathogenesis, but no one interaction is dominant in the context of establishing early colonization in and on host tissues.

Avoidance of Host Defenses

P. aeruginosa, like every other pathogen, encounters a rich array of innate and acquired immune factors that usually mediate high-level resistance to infection. Thus, in the settings in which colonization succeeds, it must be due to avoidance of host defenses. Host factors involved in resistance to infection were noted earlier. Counteracting these are a variety of bacterial factors.

Lipopolysaccharide. *P. aeruginosa* LPS plays a key role in resisting host innate defenses. Expression of long O side chains by environmental and nosocomial strains prevents lysis by complement.[184] The LPS O side chain structure in *P. aeruginosa* can have significant variation that affects resistance to antimicrobial peptides.[185] In CF, the lipid A portion of *P. aeruginosa* is structurally altered, leading to changes in host inflammatory responses[186] that promote pathogenesis.

Proteases. *P. aeruginosa* produces a variety of proteases that can inactivate host immune effectors, are cytotoxic to cells, and can degrade tissue components, allowing the organism to advance the infectious process. The best-studied proteases of *P. aeruginosa* are elastolytic proteases encoded by the *lasA* (LasA protease) and *lasB* (elastase) genes, alkaline protease, and protease IV. These proteins have a broad range of substrate specificities and are thought to contribute to pathogenesis by their diverse ability to degrade host proteins. However, it is not always easy to show that the various proteases produced by *P. aeruginosa* play a role in pathogenesis because of redundancy and overlap in production of related but distinct proteases. LasA enhances the elastolytic activity of elastase and can also degrade cell walls of *Staphylococcus aureus* by digesting the pentaglycine peptidoglycan bridge.[187] Elastase is well studied, has been crystallized, and has a variety of substrates, but loss of elastase activity generally does not always affect virulence in animal models.[188] Nonetheless, it is of considerable interest that the LasA protease causes shedding of the ectodomain of syndecan-1, a heparin sulfate proteoglycan produced abundantly on respiratory mucosal surfaces.[189] Although it was initially hypothesized that syndecans function in host defense, it was found that shedding of syndecan-1 enhanced *P. aeruginosa* infection in newborn mice[190] and mice genetically deficient in syndecan-1 had increased resistance to infection. Treating the syndecan-1-deficient mice with syndecan-1 at the time of infection restored their level of susceptibility to *P. aeruginosa* infection.[190] This surprising finding indicates that *P. aeruginosa* utilizes the shed ectodomain of syndecan-1 to protect itself from host defenses, possibly by interfering with the ingestion or killing capability of local phagocytes or by interfering with the activity of antimicrobial peptides.

Another major *P. aeruginosa* protease, alkaline protease, has high proteolytic activity but no clear role in virulence. A different protease, protease IV, has been reported to contribute significantly to experimental ulcerative keratitis in mice[191] and also degrades a variety of substrates, but these studies have been conducted using only one strain of *P. aeruginosa* and complementation studies wherein the mutant phenotype is changed back to the wild-type phenotype have not been reported. Numerous other proteases and potential proteases have been identified both phenotypically by activity assays and genomically by homology searches of the *P. aeruginosa* genome with those of other microbes, but to date no one protease stands out as a major contributor to pathogenesis.

The Role of Iron Acquisition, Intoxication, and Local Pathologic Effects in Virulence

For infection to proceed, *P. aeruginosa* must grow initially at the local site of infection and exert pathologic effects while still avoiding host defenses. Mammalian tissues provide a stressed environment for most microbes, with reduced availability of nutrients, oxygen, and other essential factors making growth suboptimal. Microbes counteract by producing factors for acquiring limited nutrients or using alternative metabolic pathways to survive in the stressed environment. The host environment triggers a plethora of transcriptional and regulatory responses in the microbe, and these often lead to intoxication of host antibacterial effector cells that reduces bacterial killing and also probably leads to liberation of nutrients. The balance between the microbe's ability to respond to the in vivo environment and the host's antimicrobial responses determines to a large degree the progression from colonization to infection and disease-defining pathology.

Iron Acquisition and Role in Virulence. As a nutritionally versatile organism, *P. aeruginosa* can usually grow well with a minimal amount of basic inorganic and organic nutrients. Simple sources of carbon, nitrogen, phosphorous, sulfate, and magnesium appear to be all the organism needs for growth, along with a further essential requirement for iron. Obtaining iron within an infected mammal is difficult because of sequestration in hemoglobin, transferrin, and so forth, and *P. aeruginosa,* like all microbes, has evolved sophisticated means to acquire iron and to respond to the level of iron it encounters. Iron acquisition affect a number of important *P. aeruginosa* functions, including transcription of genes involved in regulating other systems, genes that affect basic metabolic processes such as the Krebs cycle, genes required to survive oxidative stress, genes necessary for scavenging iron, and genes that contribute to virulence. Notably, iron levels regulate *P. aeruginosa*'s ability to produce exotoxin A, one of the bacterial exoproteins that probably plays an important role in pathogenesis.

P. aeruginosa uses typical siderophore systems to acquire iron. There are two well-studied iron acquisition systems in *P. aeruginosa* involving the pigments pyoverdin and pyochelin. Pyoverdin synthesis depends on genes located in the *pvc* and *pvd* loci, whereas pyochelin is produced as a nonribosomal peptide from a number of precursor biosynthetic proteins. When iron is high, the master regulator of the system, a repressor protein called Fur, negatively regulates transcription of the genes encoding proteins needed for iron acquisition, including a second-tier regulatory gene, *pvdS*. When iron is low, Fur inhibition is relieved and PvdS protein is produced, which directs transcription of the *pvd* genes and also induces synthesis of the PtxR protein, which is needed for transcription of the *pvc* genes. Pyoverdin is secreted, scavenges iron from mammalian sources, and brings it back to the cell in the form of ferripyoverdin by binding to the FpvA membrane receptor. Production of FpvA is regulated by the signaling protein FpvR and an alternative sigma factor, FpvI. The FpvR protein also affects the activity of the PvdS regulatory factor. Pyochelin binds to the ferric pyochelin receptor encoded by the *fptA* gene.

There is evidence suggesting that *P. aeruginosa* can also use siderophores produced by a variety of organisms to acquire iron,[192] and, interestingly, human neutrophils can bind *P. aeruginosa* siderophores and thus sequester iron from the microbe.[193] Limited virulence studies using only a few *P. aeruginosa* strains indicate that disruption of either the pyoverdin or pyochelin system reduces pathogenicity of *P. aeruginosa,* but, in general, because of the redundancy of these systems along with the availability of other potential means to acquire iron,[192] an essential role in virulence for either pyoverdin or pyochelin has not been demonstrated. Nonetheless, acquiring iron is indispensable for the organism's survival and growth, and hence iron acquisition is a vital virulence factor.

In addition to its role in iron acquisition, ferripyochelin damages pulmonary artery endothelial cells by catalyzing hydroxyl radical formation that enhances oxidant-mediated injury to the cells and also damages respiratory epithelial cells.[194] It has also been reported that ferripyochelin can use superoxide (O_2^-) and hydrogen peroxide (H_2O_2) generated by neutrophils to enhance damage of endothelial cells.[195] Pyochelin in the absence of bound iron does not appear to be toxic to mammalian cells. Thus, the iron-bound *P. aeruginosa* siderophore ferripyochelin contributes to local pathology by being toxic to cells.

Toxin Production: Exotoxin A, Leukocidin, Phospholipases, and Hemolysins. The major cellular toxin produced by *P. aeruginosa* is exotoxin A, an adenosine diphosphate (ADP)-ribosylating toxin with activity very similar to that of diphtheria toxin. Purified exotoxin A is lethal to experimental animals in small doses, its production is affected by iron levels, and it has been used in a variety of settings as a chimeric protein fused to growth factors or targeting antibodies to effect potential clinical benefits in settings such as autoimmune disease and cancer.[196] Exotoxin A inhibits protein synthesis by ADP-ribosylating and thus inactivating elongation factor-2 involved in moving the nascent growing peptide produced on the ribosome. Although exotoxin A has been widely studied for its part in pathogenesis, it has been difficult to define a clear role for it in *P. aeruginosa* virulence. Animal studies with a limited number of strains showed some loss of virulence when the *toxA* gene encoding exotoxin A was interrupted, but this has not been a generally applicable finding for a majority of strains. Along the same lines, immunization studies with exotoxin A toxoids have shown only a limited effect, either when used against specific strains or in combination with other immunogens.[197] Thus, although a primary or critical role for exotoxin A in virulence has not been established, its high toxicity for cells, particularly in the liver, and production by the majority of clinical isolates suggest that it certainly contributes to both local and systemic pathology.

Another *P. aeruginosa* toxin-like factor is referred to as a cytotoxin or leukocidin and is produced from the genome of a temperate phage integrated into the chromosome of *P. aeruginosa* strain 158.[198] In spite of extensive study of this toxin,[199,200] it appears to be found in only a few *P. aeruginosa* strains, although one cannot totally discount the potential of the phage genome encoding this toxin to be introduced into other strains.

Strains of *P. aeruginosa* can induce hemolysis of red blood cells by production of a hemolytic phospholipase C, PlcHR. A second, non-hemolytic phospholipase C is also made by *P. aeruginosa* strains-PlcN. PlcHR hydrolyzes phosphatidylcholine and sphingomyelin, and PlcN hydrolyzes phosphatidylcholine and phosphatidylserine.[201] PlcHR also has an unusual property for a bacterial protein in that it can synthesize sphingomyelin[202] by transferring the phosphoryl choline moiety from phosphatidylcholine onto the primary hydroxyl of ceramide, which results in sphingomyelin and diacylglycerol production. Plc-HR has been shown to modulate virulence in several animal models and in vitro systems,[203-205] whereas a contribution to virulence from PlcN has not been demonstrated.

An additional hemolysin made by *P. aeruginosa* is a rhamnolipid molecule that has multiple properties in addition to being hemolytic. Rhamnolipids function as surfactants, making them able to disrupt cell membranes,[206] and studies in nonmammalian model hosts indicate a role for rhamnolipids in virulence.[207] Rhamnolipid synthesis is controlled by the quorum-sensing systems of *P. aeruginosa*,[208] and inhibition of rhamnolipid production has effects on multiple *P. aeruginosa* virulence factors, making it difficult to ascribe a singular role in virulence to rhamnolipids.

Intoxication by Type III Secretion Factors. Type III secretion systems are highly conserved features of bacterial pathogens, including *P. aeruginosa*.[209,210] This system allows direct injection of bacterial toxins into eukaryotic cells, causing disruptions in cellular trafficking by inhibiting the actin cytoskeleton and also by affecting protein synthesis.[209] For *P. aeruginosa*, expression of type III toxins is significantly associated with poor clinical outcomes, including increased mortality in acutely infected patients.[163,211] Four major effector proteins are known: exoenzyme (Exo) S, ExoT, ExoU, and ExoY. The apparatus for injection is formed as a complex structure on the bacterial surface composed of five proteins, PcrG, PcrV, PcrH, PopB, and PopD, encoded in the chromosomal pcrGVH-popBD operon.[212] The PcrV protein, in conjunction with the PopB and PopD proteins, form the pore bridging the bacterial and eukaryotic cells through which the effector proteins are injected. PcrG and PcrH appear to be involved in regulating this apparatus, and it has been found that PcrG binds to PcrV and PcrH binds to PopB and PopD. PcrV expression by clinical isolates has been associated with enhanced mortality of patients.[163]

ExoS and ExoT have multiple enzymatic and chemical functions. Both can ADP-ribosylate target proteins, although the activity of the ExoT protein is much lower than that of ExoS. ExoS has an amino-terminal Rho guanosine triphosphatase (GTPase)-activating protein (GAP) activity and a carboxyl-terminal ADP-ribosyltransferase domain and requires the eukaryotic cellular protein known as factor-activating ExoS (FAS) for its ADP-ribosyltransferase activity. ExoS inactivates low-molecular-weight G proteins in the Ras family,[213,214] which leads to cytoskeletal changes, changes in cellular morphology and adherence, and inhibition of DNA synthesis, thus affecting target cell growth. ExoS is also required for cellular apoptosis[215] and can

ADP ribosylate itself, leading to decreases in the Rho GTPase activity of the protein.

ExoT is composed of an amino-terminal RhoGAP domain and a carboxyl-terminal ADP-ribosyltransferase domain.[216] ExoT interferes with internalization of *P. aeruginosa* by epithelial cells and macrophages,[217-219] two processes of importance in the innate immune resistance to infection. The RhoGAP domain of ExoT inactivates proteins that regulate the cytoskeleton, including Rho, Rac, and Cdc42, and the ADP-ribosylation domain targets the eukaryotic cellular proteins Crk-I and Crk-II, two Src homology adaptor proteins that affect signal transduction important for cellular adhesion and phagocytosis. Definitive evidence for an essential role of ExoT in pathogenesis has not yet been produced, although in a mouse model of *P. aeruginosa* keratitis, deletion of both ExoT and another type III effector, ExoU, reduced virulence of a strain with cytotoxic properties and virulence was recovered with restoration of production of either ExoT or ExoU proteins.[220]

ExoU is a potent cytotoxin, described as a phospholipase with phospholipase A_2-like activity,[221,222] that readily lysis a variety of target cells.[223] ExoU was first identified among *P. aeruginosa* strains shown to be cytotoxic to cultured mammalian cells,[224,225] and, interestingly, carriage of the *exoS* and *exoU* genes by *P. aeruginosa* strains is virtually a mutually exclusive phenomenon.[224] About 20% to 30% of *P. aeruginosa* strains produce ExoU, mostly isolates from eye infections and acute pneumonia. Interestingly, isolates from patients with CF rarely produce ExoU.[163] ExoU is a clear virulence factor in animal studies for the strains of *P. aeruginosa* that produce this toxin,[226,227] and ExoU appears to be a marker for highly virulent clinical isolates.[164] Strains secreting ExoU are almost always more virulent in a variety of animal models, and loss of ExoU production is associated with significant decreases in virulence in animal studies.[211] ExoU has been shown to modulate gene expression in airway epithelial cells[228] and to increase the release of Ca^{2+} from the endoplasmic reticulum, leading to the activation of Ca channels in membranes of epithelial cells.[229] Strains carrying *exoU* appear to be clonally derived, with evidence that the *exoU* gene and associated genetic material have been obtained through horizontal gene transfer and expansion of an original clone.[230]

ExoY is the fourth known type III effector protein of *P. aeruginosa*, and it has adenyl cyclase activity[231] similar to that of the extracellular adenyl cyclases of *Bordetella pertussis* and *Bacillus anthracis*. Results from animal virulence studies with mutants lacking ExoY have not been published.

Numerous environmental and genetic factors regulating expression of type III secreted toxins have been found. Expression is regulated by contact with eukaryotic cells along with the presence of serum and low calcium levels.[232] These conditions lead to transcription of four operons (*exsD-pscL*, *pscG-popD*, *pcrD-pcrR*, *pscN-pscU*) needed to produce the type III proteins and translocate them. Control of transcription is by a master regulator encoded by the *exsA* gene.[233,234] In addition, a membrane-bound adenyl cyclase distinct from ExoY regulates transcription of type III secretion genes,[235] and a global regulator of virulence in *P. aeruginosa*, Vfr, is also involved in regulation as it is a receptor for cyclic adenosine monophosphate (AMP). Insight into the regulators of type III secretion provides opportunities for development of possible therapeutic agents, given the clear role these molecules have in the pathogenesis of *P. aeruginosa* infection.

Toxic Effects of Pyocyanin and Role of Reactive Oxygen Species in Virulence. Extensive cellular injury occurs during *P. aeruginosa* infection, particularly in the lung, involving both epithelial and endothelial cells.[236] Some of this damage is mediated by pyocyanin, the blue phenazine pigment partly responsible for the color of *P. aeruginosa* on agar plates, which is also detectable in the sputum of CF patients, indicating in vivo production. Pyocyanin damages cells by producing reactive oxygen species such as hydrogen peroxide and superoxide, much as ferripyochelin does.[236] Numerous effects of pyocyanin on host cells and tissue responses have been reported, including disruption of nasal ciliary function, induction of proinflammatory effects by augmenting IL-8 production,[237] inactivating α_1-proteinase inhibitor,[238] and inhibiting prostacyclin release.[239] Mammalian cells counteract the reactive oxygen species generated by pyocyanin by producing superoxide dismutases and catalase enzymes. Pyocyanin has been reported to decrease the activity of catalase, but not the superoxide dismutases, by both transcriptional inhibition and inactivation of the enzyme.[240] In a rat model of infection, oxidant-induced stress correlated directly with the degree of pathology from *P. aeruginosa* infection.[241]

Because reactive oxygen species (also called reactive oxygen intermediates) are also deleterious to *P. aeruginosa,* the organism must protect itself from the effects of pyocyanin along with reactive oxygen species produced by aerobic respiration and by host phagocytic cells. *P. aeruginosa* accomplishes this, in part, by limiting the redox cycling of pyocyanin and producing three catalases (KatA, KatB, and KatC) and two superoxide dismutases-one using manganese as a cofactor and the other using iron.[242] Production of these detoxifying enzymes requires the Fur protein that regulates *P. aeruginosa* responses to iron.[243] Additional factors modulating the effects of reactive oxygen species include iron sequestration, agents that scavenge free radicals, DNA-binding proteins, and DNA repair enzymes.[244] *P. aeruginosa* also synthesizes four alkyl hydroperoxide reductases.[244] Sensing of O_2^- by the SoxR protein leads to changes in this protein that activate its ability to function as a transcription factor for genes involved in modulating potential oxidative stress. An additional regulator is the OxyR protein, which modulates transcriptional responses to H_2O_2.

Growth, Establishment of Infectious Foci, Local Tissue Spread, and Systemic Dissemination

For most *P. aeruginosa* infections, a period of growth at a local site of infection precedes dissemination or translocation either to additional areas of the initially infected tissue, to another tissue, or systemically through the blood, wherein clear manifestations and clinical presentations of severe infection occur. The establishment of these local foci of infection may or may not result in clinically significant disease, and the local foci of infection often present a diagnostic challenge related to the likelihood of more significant disease occurring. Examples include GI colonization that can lead to bacteremia or to aspiration to the respiratory tract, catheter colonization that can lead to local or systemic infection, growth in burned or wounded skin, and colonization of endobronchial or endotracheal tubes that can lead to serious pneumonia. All of the microbial factors noted previously continue to play important roles in maintaining the colonization phase of the pathogenic process, with additional virulence factors coming into play at the stage at which further infection occurs, resulting in disease progression.

Quorum Sensing and Virulence Factor Production. As bacterial counts increase in a tissue, the organisms reach a critical mass that is thought to allow them to communicate effectively with each other through the system of quorum sensing (QS). At critical bacterial masses, low-molecular-weight mediators of the QS response are synthesized and secreted, diffusing through the cells of the bacterial community to influence gene transcription and virulence factor production. For *P. aeruginosa* three major, interrelated QS systems are known, designated the las, rhl, and *Pseudomonas* quinolone system (PQS). The molecular mediators of the QS are known as autoinducers (AIs) because of their self-regulatory effects on bacterial responses to the environment. The AI mediator of the las QS system is an acyl-homoserine lactone known as *N*-(3-oxododecanoyl)-L-homoserine lactone (C12-HSL); for the rhl system the AI mediator is *N*-butyryl-L-homoserine lactone (C4-HSL). The PQS system uses 2-heptyl-3-hydroxy-4-quinolone for signaling. These three systems, along with some other regulatory factors, have a complex interaction in the context of regulation of gene transcription and virulence factor production.

For the las and rhl QS systems the synthetic enzymes for producing the AIs are encoded by the *lasI* and *rhlI* genes, respectively. The AIs act on a second component, the LasR or RhlR proteins, which are transcriptional regulators of the genes affected by the QS systems. When LasR complexes with C12-HSL, it forms multimers that bind to transcriptional activation sites on QS-regulated genes.[245] Similarly, when RhlR is complexed with C4-HSL it can act as a transcriptional regulator, but whether this involves multimers is not known. A regula-

tor of the transcription of the AI synthetic genes is QscR, which appears to inhibit the transcription of *lasI* and production of the C12-HSL, and it appears to act to ensure that QS responses are made under proper environmental conditions of high bacterial density. The PQS system also controls transcription of the *rhlI* gene, providing an additional level of regulation. Finally, another regulator of this system is the cyclic AMP receptor protein encoded by *vfr,* which binds to the promoter region or *lasR*.[246]

The genes whose transcription is regulated by the QS molecule are large in number, but the exact ones are not clearly known in spite of three published reports addressing this question using modern DNA microarray analysis.[247-249] Because of differences in strains used, conditions of analysis and methodologies used to identify QS-regulated genes, the three studies agreed only on 97 QS-regulated genes being present in the *P. aeruginosa* PAO1 chromosome, but each study found between 163 and 388 genes so affected. Many of these genes did not have promoter binding sites for LasR or RhlR, indicating secondary regulation through QS intermediates. The actual number probably varies from strain to strain but overall can be considered large. Notably, the majority of QS-regulated genes identified in the microarray studies have an unknown function. Genes that could be identified as being regulated by QS include membrane proteins, secreted enzymes with a variety of functions, transcription factors for regulating other genes, genes that are parts of two-component regulatory systems, genes for energy metabolism, and genes involved in movement of small molecules in and out of the cell.

Our knowledge about the importance of the QS response in the pathogenesis of *P. aeruginosa* infection is currently limited by lack of clear data concerning the extent to which it is important among clinical isolates. Virtually all of the studies of *P. aeruginosa* QS have used the PAO1 strain to identify the factors, the regulated genetic targets, and the effect of loss of QS on virulence. Dual *las* and *rhl* system mutants of strain PAO1 have reduced virulence in animal models of burn wound infection[250] and acute[251] and chronic[252] lung infection, but studies with other strains are lacking. Of note, Cabrol and colleagues studied the QS response of 35 clinical and environmental isolates and found that only one half showed a correlation between transcription of the *lasR* gene and the transcription of two QS-controlled genes, *lasB* and *aprA*.[253] Whether this indicates that only about 50% of *P. aeruginosa* clinical isolates regulate virulence factor production through the las QS system or whether the analysis of these systems by transcriptional responses is too limited to determine the extent of use of QS among *P. aeruginosa* clinical isolates is not known. However, the study of Cabrol and colleagues[253] does raise the issue that the las and rhl QS systems may not be critical for the virulence of many clinical isolates. Thus, calls for development of inhibitors of QS as potential therapeutic agents for *P. aeruginosa* infections[254] need to be tempered by the current lack of knowledge of the extent of the use of these systems by clinical isolates.

There are, however, data that indicate that the AIs are made during infection, although these findings have all come from studies of sputum samples from CF patients. Notably, the animal models for which there are the most robust data showing an important role for QS in *P. aeruginosa* virulence are models of acute, not chronic infection, whereas one might predict that it is in chronic infection that the effects of QS might be more pronounced. Nonetheless, correlations between levels of transcripts for the QS genes and the QS-regulated genes in CF sputum have been found,[255] and AIs have also been detected in CF sputum samples.[256-258] These results must be interpreted with caution, as the presence of AIs and correlations with transcription do not establish that QS-mediated virulence factor production is a critical component of the pathogenesis of CF lung infection. Notably, some patients did not have detectable AIs in sputum[256,257] and, as the progression of CF lung disease is slow, a case could be made that AI production and QS regulation of virulence factors could actually be beneficial to the patient, preventing a more acute, rapid, and life-threatening infection from occurring in the CF lung. Overall, it is still far from clear whether AI production and QS control of virulence are common among clinical isolates and contribute to the pathogenesis of either acute or chronic *P. aeruginosa* infection.

Quorum Sensing and Biofilm Formation. Another major bacterial phenotype regulated by the QS system is the formation of *P. aeruginosa* biofilms, a well-studied area but with some important limitations in terms of applicability to clinical infection and disease. The extensive use of implantable devices in modern medicine has led to the appreciation that structured bacterial communities known as biofilms can form on these devices and contribute to infection.[259] In addition, in chronic infections such as osteomyelitis or CF lung infection it is thought that biofilms play an important role in pathogenesis.[260] *P. aeruginosa* is the most studied pathogen in terms of the molecular aspects of biofilm formation,[260,261] but almost all of these studies have been done in vitro using abiotic surfaces such as polycarbonate plastic or plastic or glass flow cells. The major components of a biofilm reside in an extracellular matrix sometimes called a glycocalyx, which is thought to be heavily composed of polysaccharide for most bacterial species studied.[262] In *P. aeruginosa* a major component of the glycocalyx is actually extracellular DNA,[263] perhaps because *P. aeruginosa* does not produce an extracellular nuclease. Although impressive microscopic and artistic renditions of *P. aeruginosa* biofilms have been published[264] these structured communities are not really observed in infected tissues, notably the CF lung.[256,264] Rather, microcolonies of aggregates of bacteria are present, and these microcolonies contain not only bacterial factors but also host factors, including host DNA, mucus, actin, and probably other products from dead and dying bacterial and host cells. How these in vivo microcolonies are related to the QS-controlled biofilms studied in vitro on abiotic surfaces is still unclear, and the relationship is doubtful in many investigators' minds.

Using the in vitro systems, it has been shown that QS molecules are needed for the production of structured *P. aeruginosa* biofilms.[261,265] These structures are also produced under conditions of flow of nutrient media over a solid surface where the biofilm is forming, but such conditions are unlikely to be present in the lung or bone but may be present in vascular tissues. *P. aeruginosa* endocarditis and arterial graft infections are not uncommon, but no studies of the role of QS or biofilms in these diseases have been published. Within the chronically infected CF lung, where the biofilm mode of growth is most often invoked as representative of the importance of this bacterial lifestyle in pathogenesis, the establishment of chronic infection, the onset of accelerated deterioration in lung function, and the worsening of the patient's clinical condition are clearly associated with the emergence of the alginate-overproducing, mucoid phenotype of *P. aeruginosa*.[266-268] Yet alginate is not a component of the QS-dependent biofilms formed on abiotic surfaces under conditions of media flow,[262] further raising questions about the role of QS in biofilm formation in the CF lung. Overall, it will be a while before definitive studies linking QS, biofilm formation, and virulence in the multitude of infections *P. aeruginosa* is capable of causing will emerge. Until then, caution in ascribing a critical role for QS in virulence of *P. aeruginosa* disease, and in particular in virulence-related biofilm formation, is needed.

Local Tissue Spread. The most serious consequences of *P. aeruginosa* infection are spread throughout a susceptible tissue and vascular dissemination. Serious pneumonia is the most common manifestation of *P. aeruginosa* infection, with an attributable mortality approaching 40%.[269,270] No specific bacterial virulence factors in addition to those noted previously have been implicated in development of *P. aeruginosa* pneumonia, but it is of note that this clinical presentation is rarely accompanied by systemic spread. For *P. aeruginosa* bacteremia to occur, the organism needs to produce a smooth LPS substituted with O side chains, otherwise the bactericidal activity of serum complement would readily kill the organism in the blood.[184] Interestingly, isolates from chronically infected CF patients do not produce a smooth LPS,[271,272] indicating that in the infected lung complement levels are insufficient to be bactericidal. In addition, respiratory isolates from *P. aeruginosa* pneumonia are less likely to produce a smooth LPS than blood-stream isolates,[273] suggesting that even in acute pneumonia a smooth LPS is not a requirement.

As more and more CF patients live into adulthood, their care is being assumed by specialists in adult medicine and they are increasingly managed in nonpediatric settings. Thus, the understanding of the pathogenesis of this disease is now relevant to adult infectious disease practices. As most CF patients are chronically colonized by their 18th birthday with mucoid strains of *P. aeruginosa,* they usually have significant progression of their lung disease in adulthood. The major factors considered to be relevant to pathogenesis in this setting are overproduction of alginate[274] and the host inflammatory response,[78] the former protecting the organism from host defenses and the latter causing significant tissue damage. The molecular genetic basis for increased alginate production is well understood,[274] although whether there is a common or unifying genetic or environmental event that initiates or sustains alginate overproduction by CF isolates of *P. aeruginosa* is not clear. Alginate clearly protects the organism from phagocytosis, and it appears that the *O*-acetyl substituents on the alginate molecule are critical for manifestation of this phenotype.[275] In addition, alginate has been shown to be a key bacterial factor needed for establishing chronic *P. aeruginosa* oropharyngeal colonization in transgenic CF mice.[276]

Interestingly, CF patients produce high titers of antibodies to alginate and other *P. aeruginosa* antigens during infection, but these antibodies obviously fail to mediate protection from infection.[267,274] It has been proposed that the antibodies to alginate are deficient in opsonic killing activity,[277] a clear in vitro correlate of protective antibody activity, because of an inability to deposit the critical complement opsonin iC3b onto the bacterial surface.[45] In animal models, alginate-specific opsonic antibodies mediate protection against infection.[278] Of interest, as *P. aeruginosa* is thought to grow as some sort of biofilm in the CF lung, Meluleni and colleagues[279] showed that the antibodies CF patients make to *P. aeruginosa* are able to mediate opsonic killing of suspended or planktonic *P. aeruginosa* but not of bacterial cells growing in a biofilm. Opsonic antibodies to alginate did, however, promote killing of biofilm cells of *P. aeruginosa*. As the bacteria in the CF lung spread and fail to be cleared, the associated inflammatory response contributes significantly to tissue destruction, with the neutrophil-dominated infiltrate causing damage by a variety of molecular mechanisms emanating mostly from contents in spilled neutrophil granules.[280] However, it is important to keep in mind that CF is a chronic, progressive disease associated with high bacterial burdens for many years; probably the immune-inflammatory response in this setting is mediating important, positive outcomes that limit the kinetics and magnitude of bacterial spread and turn what otherwise would be an acute, potentially lethal situation into one in which the patient's survival is much longer.

Spread of *P. aeruginosa* throughout the cornea can cause severe tissue damage, with loss of sight a distinct possibility. In this tissue, ExoU and ExoT are also clear virulence factors for cytotoxic strains of *P. aeruginosa* (i.e., those able to kill eukaryotic cells readily in vitro) as determined in experimental models of ulcerative keratitis[220] and *exoU*-positive strains of *P. aeruginosa* are also frequently isolated from contact lens-associated keratitis.[13,224] Concurrent with tissue spread is a vigorous host inflammatory response in the eye, in spite of the fact that the cornea is avascular. It appears that the inflammation that ensues is the primary cause of corneal damage as pathology seems to continue to develop long after bacterial numbers subside in the tissue.[224] The ongoing inflammation may be due to residual bacterial factors known to activate inflammation including LPS, flagella, and toxins.

Aside from the lung and the eye, *P. aeruginosa* spread in other tissues resulting in damage and physiologic compromise is much less studied although this highly versatile organism is capable of causing serious disease in any otherwise sterile tissue that it infects. It is likely that the same factors involved in lung and eye infections dictate the magnitude and kinetics of spread of *P. aeruginosa* in other tissues.

Blood-Stream Dissemination. *P. aeruginosa* is among the top five causes of nosocomial bacteremia, and severe infection can lead to sepsis. Because of the multitude of virulence factors the organism elaborates, coupled with increasing antibiotic resistance, *P. aerugi-*

nosa continues to be a problematic pathogen in this setting. When *P. aeruginosa* spreads from a tissue source, it probably does so by breaking down epithelial and endothelial barriers to gain access to the blood.[281] Breakdown of the epithelial barrier of the lung in an experimental model of *P. aeruginosa* sepsis in rabbits was associated with release of proinflammatory mediators into the blood leading to sepsis.[281] Provision of antibodies to TNF-α or of the counterinflammatory cytokine IL-10 improved both the signs of septic shock and the levels of bacteremia in the experimental animals. Thus, the bacterial factors that promote release of TNF-α and probably IL-1, which also contributes to cytokine-mediated sepsis and death in experimental animals,[71,72] represent major virulence traits promoting pathology in *P. aeruginosa* blood-stream infection.

VACCINES AND IMMUNOTHERAPIES

A variety of antigenic targets expressed by *P. aeruginosa* are being evaluated for development of active and passive immunotherapies (Table 216-2). Active vaccination would be indicated in young CF patients, although they represent a small target population. Potential additional targets include police, firefighters, soldiers, and similar individuals at risk for burn or wound infection. Whether individuals undergoing elective surgery would be a reasonable target for immunization will probably depend on future trends in infection rates, antimicrobial resistance, cost-benefit analysis, and so forth. An effective passive immunotherapy, consisting of either immunoglobulin G derived from donors given a vaccine or an individual or set of human monoclonal antibodies, can be reasonably envisioned as a useful adjunct to antibiotic therapy or perhaps as a prophylactic measure in an ICU or similar setting of high risk for *P. aeruginosa* infection.

The highly variable O-antigen component of the LPS is clearly the most effective target for preventing *P. aeruginosa* infection, but with 20 to 30 potential O-antigen variants that need to be incorporated into an effective vaccine or passive immunotherapeutic, producing an effective vaccine or immunotherapy using these antigens is daunting. OMPs have shown success as candidate vaccines in animal models[282] and some OMPs are already in clinical trials.[283] The bacterial flagella has shown excellent promise as a vaccine in animal models,[284] and a clinical trial in European CF patients[285] has suggested some efficacy. Pili have been promoted as potential vaccines,[172] but preclinical data from animals are limited and there is significant variability in pilin monomers, which may form some of the antigenic targets in a vaccine. A promising approach has been to target the PcrV protein that is part of the type III secretion complex,[286,287] but to date this approach has been demonstrated only in one strain using a pneumonia model and three additional strains using a burn wound infection model, and protection against death by one of the three strains used in the burn wound model required additional immunization against exotoxin A.[197] Alginate has shown efficacy in animal models of chronic *P. aeruginosa* infection[278] and may also be effective against nonmucoid strains

that make small, but not zero, amounts of alginate. Antitoxic immunity to such factors as exotoxin A and proteases seems to be effective only in limited situations or with special strains and does not appear to be a generally useful strategy.

Live, attenuated vaccine strains of *P. aeruginosa* have shown efficacy in animal models of pneumonia after intranasal immunization[288,289] and could potentially deliver a variety of antigens to the immune system resulting in broad-based immunity. Of note, the finding that *P. aeruginosa* enters epithelial cells by CFTR-based endocytosis[152,156] indicates that a portion of the organisms have an intracellular phase and thus cell-mediated immunity may be an important component of host resistance to *P. aeruginosa* infection. The live, attenuated vaccine has the potential to elicit cell-mediated immune effectors, and a combination of both humoral and cellular immunity may be needed for full-fledged host resistance to infection. Overall, a *P. aeruginosa* vaccine or passive immunotherapeutic could be of tremendous benefit in a variety of infectious situations caused by this pathogen if the proper immune factors, benefits to patients, and costs appropriate to the situation are identified and evaluated.

CLINICAL CHARACTERISTICS OF PSEUDOMONAS AERUGINOSA INFECTIONS

P. aeruginosa has been reported to cause infections at almost all sites of the body or to colonize almost any site subjected to injury. Thus, this organism has a wide potential for disease causation that is determined by development of host susceptibility leading to predisposition to infection and by the possession of a wide range of virulence factors as already described. That *P. aeruginosa* is particularly adapted to the respiratory tract of humans is suggested by the fact that it is the most prominent cause of lung disease in patients with CF[133] and ranks as number one or two as a cause of ventilator-associated pneumonias.[269] It also has potential as a chronic airway colonizer of individuals with chronic lung diseases such as bronchiectasis[290] and panbronchiolitis, a disease that is seen in Japan.[291] Thus, the role of this organism as measured in both disease and the potential for disease by colonizing and infecting the airways is unmatched by most other bacteria except those traditionally associated with lung disease such as the *Streptococcus pneumoniae* and *Haemophilus influenzae*. However, the disease-producing potential of *P. aeruginosa* goes far beyond this primary site of tropism, resulting in a number of different clinical syndromes that are often manifestations of its opportunism.

Site-Specific Pseudomonas Infections

Bacteremia

P. aeruginosa remains one of the most feared organisms that cause bacteremia. In older studies of this infection there were reports of mortality rates exceeding 50%[292-294] when crude mortality was used as the end point. In neutropenic patients, mortality was as high as 70%[295] in

---

TABLE 216-2 Antigenic Targets for Vaccines

Antigen	*Mechanism of Immunity, Utility, and Problems*
LPS O side chain	Opsonic killing by phagocytes; most effective vaccine target but extensive serologic variation and problems with immunodominance of protective epitopes
Outer membrane proteins	Opsonic killing by phagocytes (not clear); antigenically conserved; effective in animals; produce recombinant forms; no effective human vaccine based on these antigens produced to date; opsonins binding to OMPs can be masked by LPS O side chains or alginate
PcrV antigen	Mechanism not clear; produced by many strains; antigenically conserved; utility for many strains not demonstrated; some strains do not produce PcrV
Alginate	Opsonic killing by phagocytes; antigenically conserved; utility for mucoid strains demonstrated, not clear if useful for nonmucoid strains; problems with immunodominance of protective epitopes
Exotoxins	Neutralization; antigenically conserved; utility in animal models is minimal and mostly effective against purified toxin, not against whole bacterial infections
Live, attenuated bacteria	Opsonization and other effects; immunity to variety of antigens induced; both humoral and cellular immunity can be induced; number of strains needed unknown; safety unknown; antigenic specificity of immunity not known.

LPS, lipopolysaccharide; OMP, outer membrane protein.

an era when aminoglycosides and polymyxins were the primary antimicrobial therapies. Consequently, *P. aeruginosa* bacteremia became a dreaded clinical syndrome, resulting in attempts to manage this disease by the administration of multiple antibiotics. However, since the introduction of β-lactam antibiotics with efficacy for *P. aeruginosa,* there have been no populations of patients in which such high mortality is now seen as a direct consequence of *P. aeruginosa* infection.[296] Examination of published mortality figures over an 8-year period showed widely different rates,[296] but even more recent publications show attributable mortality rates of 28% to 44%[297] depending on the adequacy of treatment and the seriousness of the underlying diseases. However, in a matched cohort of non-neutropenic patients, mortality attributable to *P. aeruginosa* infection has been reported to be as low 15%.[298] Whether such low rates are a reflection of early appropriate therapy or differences in the populations examined is not known. Undoubtedly, the population most at risk for *P. aeruginosa* bacteremia includes the sickest and most compromised group of hospitalized individuals. Thus, their risk for death during bacteremia is likely to remain high.

It is difficult to obtain up-to-date estimates of the true incidence of *P. aeruginosa* bacteremia in North America or for that matter anywhere else. However, cross-sectional studies, which tend to be concentrated in academic centers, were published by the SENTRY Antimicrobial Surveillance Program. Between 1997 and 1999, 4.4% of bacteremias in the United States were due to *P. aeruginosa,* with higher rates in Europe and Latin America.[299] Therefore, the occurrence of *P. aeruginosa* bacteremia may be influenced by national or regional factors or may even be related to climatic conditions. The sources of *P. aeruginosa* bacteremia have also undergone changes. The classic patient with *P. aeruginosa* bacteremia was considered to be the neutropenic or burned patient, implicating the gut and skin as the portals of entry. A minority of patients with burn wounds now suffer from bacteremic *P. aeruginosa* infections,[300] although it still remains a common organism isolated from the burn wound itself.[301] *P. aeruginosa* bacteremia is still seen in neutropenic patients, but this organism plays a much smaller role in infections in these patients, occurring on average in less than 10% of severely neutropenic patients who have documented bacterial infections.[296] The most frequently documented sources are now the respiratory and urinary tracts, probably because of changes in the management of patients in hospitals related to more prolonged supportive care utilizing ventilators and urinary catheters.

Clinical Presentation. The clinical presentation of *P. aeruginosa* bacteremia is rarely different from that of sepsis in general. Patients are usually febrile, but more severely ill patients in shock may be hypothermic. The only point differentiating this entity from other causes of gram-negative sepsis may be the occurrence of distinctive infarcted skin lesions known as ecthyma gangrenosum, which occur almost exclusively in markedly neutropenic patients. The source may be hematogenous or inoculation at the site of minor trauma, such as a vascular catheter access site or even a shaving nick. These are small, painful, reddish, maculopapular, well-circumscribed lesions that have a geographic margin and begin pink, darken to purple, and finally become black and necrotic (Fig. 216-5). Histopathology indicates that the lesions are due to vascular invasion after bacteremia and are teeming with bacteria. These lesions rarely occur with other infections,[302,303] particularly aspergillosis and mucormycosis, but their presence should suggest *P. aeruginosa* bacteremia as the most likely cause, requiring the appropriate empirical antibiotic therapy.

Treatment of Bacteremia. Removal of an infected vascular catheter may be needed to control device-related bacteremia. Antimicrobial treatment of *P. aeruginosa* bacteremia has been controversial since the introduction of carbenicillin, the first antipseudomonal penicillin. A brief description of this saga is included because this issue continues to be raised and it is especially important to discuss at a time when multidrug-resistant *P. aeruginosa* are increasingly being isolated[299,304,305] with no new antipseudomonal agents in sight. Before 1971, the outcome of *Pseudomonas* bacteremia in febrile neutropenic patients was dismal when they were treated with the available agents,

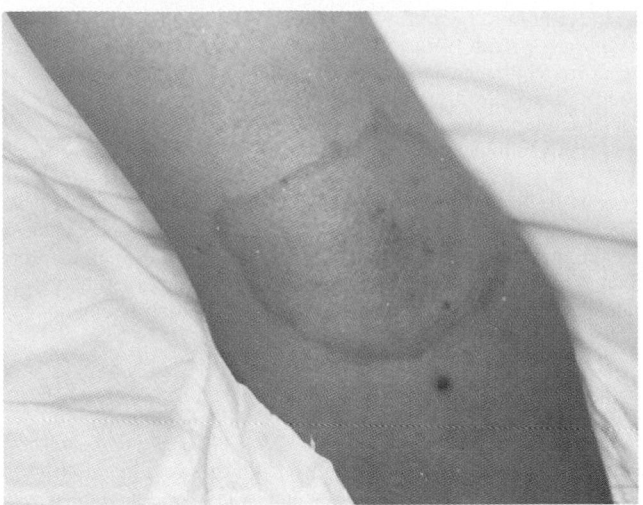

A

B

FIGURE 216-5. Ecthyma gangrenosa from *Pseudomonas aeruginosa* bacteremia in neutropenic patients. **A,** Lesion 72 hours after onset. **B,** Lesion late in the course with typical well-defined area of necrosis.

gentamicin and polymyxins.[295] At approximately the same time, two studies of the treatment of *P. aeruginosa* bacteremia in febrile neutropenic patients indicated that carbenicillin therapy with or without an aminoglycoside significantly improved the outcome in this infection.[306,307] Several animal studies to answer the question of the use of single or combination therapy showed that high doses of carbenicillin as a single agent were as efficacious as combination therapy.[308-310] However, in vitro studies demonstrated that carbenicillin resistance developed readily, and the occasional failure of this agent when used alone was reported.[311,312] Such observations also appeared at a time when the concept of antibacterial synergy in vivo began to attract considerable interest. Several retrospective analyses suggested that the use of two agents that were synergistic in vitro against gram-negative pathogens resulted in better outcomes in neutropenic patients.[313,314] Thus, the standard of care for febrile, neutropenic patients became combination therapy, and by association this also became the standard approach to the treatment of all *P. aeruginosa* infections.

In 1985, investigators at the M. D. Anderson Cancer Center published a review of that institution's experience with 410 cases of *P. aeruginosa* bacteremia, the largest number of such cases ever published, the majority occurring in neutropenic patients.[295] Monotherapy with a single antipseudomonal β-lactam yielded outcomes similar to those obtained when it was combined with an aminoglycoside.

Monotherapy with an aminoglycoside resulted in very poor outcomes. These data were largely ignored and were perhaps not convincing because the study was retrospective. The use of ceftazidime in febrile neutropenic patients presented another opportunity to examine this question because it was arguably the best antipseudomonal agent when it was introduced into clinical practice. In 1986, it was reported that 94% of 37 patients with *Pseudomonas* bacteremia were successfully treated with ceftazidime monotherapy.[315] Admittedly, none of the studies espousing monotherapy were controlled clinical trials; rather, these were retrospective analyses.

In 1989, a nonrandomized, prospective, observational study of 200 patients treated for *P. aeruginosa* bacteremia was published[316] with the conclusion that combination therapy was superior to monotherapy. On further analysis of these data, the conclusion was mostly based on a comparison of combination therapy with mainly single-drug therapy with a poorly effective aminoglycoside. Fewer than 10% of the patients in the monotherapy arm had received a modern antipseudomonal β-lactam antibiotic available at that time (e.g., ceftazidime, imipenem, or piperacillin). Thus, an alternative conclusion, that combination therapy is superior to an aminoglycoside, can be drawn from this study, an observation that was made nearly two decades earlier in neutropenic patients.[292,295]

Since the 1989 study, there have been at least four studies, none of them prospective, double-blind studies, which indicate that *P. aeruginosa* bacteremia has the same outcome when treated with a single antipseudomonal β-lactam or such an agent combined with an aminoglycoside.[99,317-319] Although the issue may seem clearer today, the latest study on this subject suggests that there is marginally higher mortality after 30 days when patients are treated with adequate empirical monotherapy compared with adequate empirical combination therapy, but no difference in mortality was found when patients were treated with an adequate, definitive monotherapy or an adequate combination therapy.[320] Thus, none of the dogmas concerning the appropriate therapy for *P. aeruginosa* bacteremia can be considered to be established by blinded, controlled clinical studies. One firm conclusion appears to be that monotherapy with an aminoglycoside dosed in the approved way should not be the primary choice for antibiotic treatment. Unquestionably, the majority of infectious disease experts still favor the use of combination therapy for *P. aeruginosa* bacteremia. However, it is difficult to indict the use of a single modern antipseudomonal β-lactam antibiotic as being inadequate therapy. Even in the patients most at risk for dying rapidly from *P. aeruginosa* bacteremia (i.e., high-risk patients with fever and neutropenia), empirical monotherapy designed to treat *P. aeruginosa* is considered to be as efficacious as empirical combination therapy in the Practice Guidelines of the Infectious Diseases Society of America (IDSA).[321]

P. aeruginosa bacteremia is almost never treated with specific antibiotics before laboratory results are available. Hence, initial therapy is most likely to be what is typically given as empirical therapy for bacteremia or sepsis. Adequate empirical therapy to cover this organism should therefore include the agents against which there are the lowest levels of antibiotic resistance within an institution and which are predictably most stably effective against *P. aeruginosa*. Depending on the antibiotic susceptibility of *P. aeruginosa* isolates in the institution, one of the following regimens would be appropriate for *P. aeruginosa* bacteremia, pending return of susceptibility results: Adult, non-azotemic patients may be given ceftazidime 2 g intravenously every 8 hours, cefepime 2 g intravenously every 12 hours, meropenem 0.5 g every 8 hours, or imipenem 0.5 g every 6 hours. Aztreonam 1.5 g every 6 hours has been used for patients with serious β-lactam allergy. If piperacillin-tazobactam is used empirically, the lack of contribution by tazobactam to the antipseudomonal activity of piperacillin may make the usual dose of 3.375 g every 6 hours inadequate, and 3.375 g every 4 hours or the addition of amikacin 15 mg/kg every 24 hours may be preferred. Addition of an aminoglycoside to the other regimens is perhaps less critical and probably depends on the level of resistance to β-lactam antibiotics in any given institution. At present, the highest levels of susceptibilities are to amikacin in most regions of the world.[299]

The pharmacodynamics and pharmacokinetics of β-lactam antibiotics have attained more importance than previously in considering the proper choice of therapy for *P. aeruginosa* bacteremia.[322] β-Lactam efficacy is best correlated with the percentage of time that the active drug is above the minimal inhibitory concentration (MIC) of the pathogen in regard to the dosing interval. For *P. aeruginosa,* enough antibiotic, dosed at intervals to achieve serum levels that exceed the MIC of *P. aeruginosa* for about 60% to 70% of the dosing interval, should be given.[116] This is achieved with 2-g doses of cefepime or ceftazidime given every 12 hours. The dosing interval and doses for piperacillin-tazobactam for the treatment of *P. aeruginosa* bacteremia have also been evaluated on the basis of pharmacodynamic behaviors.[323] It is suggested that these agents be given by continuous infusion to achieve the pharmacokinetic and pharmacodynamic parameters that predict efficacy, although there is no clinical confirmation of this recommendation. Indications for aminoglycoside dosing have also undergone changes in the past decade. Because their ability to kill is concentration dependent, a single total daily dose of an aminoglycoside is predicted to achieve better results.[324] In addition, this approach has not increased toxicity.[325] Whether aminoglycosides, when given as a single daily dose, would result in better outcomes in *P. aeruginosa* bacteremia has not been examined prospectively.

Besides the issue of outcomes, combination therapy for *P. aeruginosa* bacteremia utilizing a β-lactam antibiotic plus an aminoglycoside has been espoused to prevent the development of resistance that was seen with the use of carbenicillin alone. Development of resistance is a legitimate concern and was demonstrated in in vitro and animal studies. However, clinical data from human studies have not definitely substantiated this assumption.[326] In addition, it has been convincingly demonstrated that the addition of an aminoglycoside to a carbapenem for *P. aeruginosa* infection of the respiratory tract does not prevent the development of resistance to the carbapenem.[327]

As the issue of antibiotic monotherapy versus combination therapy remains a subject of discussion, the use of combination therapy is likely to continue for the foreseeable future. Also, there are institutions and countries where the susceptibilities of *P. aeruginosa* to the first-line antibiotic agents are less than 80%. In such settings, combination empirical therapy for a patient with bacteremia or sepsis having a significant chance of a *P. aeruginosa* infection should be started until pathogen identification and antibiotic susceptibilities are available. Whether one or two agents should be continued is usually left to individual preferences. The length of therapy for *P. aeruginosa* bacteremia has not undergone careful scrutiny. It is generally recommended that neutropenic patients be treated until recovery of their neutrophil levels. Relatively simple bacteremias in non-neutropenic patients may be treated with shorter courses of therapy, assuming that any devices that may have predisposed to the bacteremia have been removed. On the other hand, the management of some other forms of *P. aeruginosa* bacteremia is not so straightforward. Complex bacteremias that also involve infections in tissues such as the lung, kidney, and skin may be more difficult to treat, especially in neutropenic patients.[328] It is therefore recommended that such patients receive longer courses of therapy.

Acute Pneumonia

The respiratory tract remains the most frequent site of infection caused by *P. aeruginosa*. This organism ranks either first or second in most lists as the causative pathogen in ventilator-associated pneumonia.[269,329] However, much debate centers on the actual role of the organism in ventilator-associated pneumonia because the conclusion that *P. aeruginosa* plays a major role is based on results of cultures of endotracheal tube aspirates, which can frequently represent nothing more than nonpathogenic colonization of the tracheobronchial tree, formation of an innocuous biofilm on the endotracheal tube, or simple tracheobronchitis. In the absence of radiologic evidence of pneumonia, the question remains whether *P. aeruginosa* is causing purulence in the tracheobronchial secretions (i.e., tracheobronchitis).[330,331]

Although the incidence of *P. aeruginosa* pneumonia may not be as high as has been assumed on the basis of results of cultures from the upper respiratory tract, many studies using bronchoscopic techniques have supported the important role that *P. aeruginosa* plays in acute lung infections in the hospitalized patient with a ventilator.[329] *P. aeruginosa* was once thought to have a significant role in pneumonia in febrile neutropenic patients,[332] but its occurrence at this site in these patients is now relatively uncommon. There have been increasing reports of community-acquired *P. aeruginosa* pneumonia at opposite ends of the spectrum of host compromise, including the AIDS patient with low CD4 counts[330,331] and the relatively healthy patient with or without underlying lung disease.[333] Reports of community-acquired pneumonia related to *P. aeruginosa* have been rare in the past, and more recent reports that 7% of patients admitted for community-acquired pneumonia have *P. aeruginosa* are troubling.[334]

Older reports of *P. aeruginosa* pneumonia describe patients with an acute clinical syndrome of fever, chills, cough, and a necrotizing pneumonia not very different from acute staphylococcal pneumonia.[335] The pathogenesis of this disease is believed to be direct inoculation of large numbers of the organism into the lungs by aspiration or inhalation. Most of these cases occurred in hospitalized patients who had received antibiotics. The traditional accounts describe a fulminant infection, with cyanosis, tachypnea, copious sputum, and systemic toxicity. Chest radiographs demonstrated bilateral pneumonia, often with nodular densities. This picture is now remarkably rare. Today, the typical patient is receiving ventilation, has a slowly progressive lung infiltrate, and has been colonized with *P. aeruginosa* for days. Although some cases may progress rapidly over a 48- to 72-hour period, this is the exception and nodular densities are generally not seen. However, the infiltrates may go on to necrosis. This form of the disease has also been seen in the community, for example, after the inhalation of hot tub water contaminated by *P. aeruginosa*.[336] The patient is typically febrile, has a leukocytosis and purulent sputum, and the chest radiograph shows a new infiltrate or an increase in a preexisting infiltrate. Chest examination generally demonstrates rales or dullness. However, such findings are also quite common in ventilated ICU patients, making the diagnosis somewhat difficult without an invasive procedure.

There is an emerging consensus that an invasive procedure such as bronchoalveolar lavage or protective brush sampling of the distal airways should be used to obtain quantitative cultures of the lung in order to substantiate the occurrence of *P. aeruginosa* pneumonia.[329] Therapy for *P. aeruginosa* pneumonia has been unsatisfactory. The disease has an appreciable mortality rate when the organism remains confined to the lungs. Reports suggest up to 70% to 80% mortality,[329] but the question remains how much of this mortality is attributable to the underlying lung disease. Some studies suggest a mortality attributable to *P. aeruginosa* infection of about 40%.[337] However, when complicated by bacteremia, *P. aeruginosa* pneumonia in neutropenic patients or in the ventilated patient has a considerably worse prognosis with higher mortality rates.[297,338]

Treatment of Pneumonia. The therapy for *P. aeruginosa* pneumonia has not been determined by rigorous studies. Some of the issues involve the differentiation of colonization from infection and the question of attributable mortality. High failure rates were seen when aminoglycosides were used as single agents. The failure was subsequently attributed to several factors, including low antibiotic levels achieved in the airways,[339] inactivation of aminoglycosides in the acidic environment of the lungs,[340] and binding of drugs to human mucus.[341] Another factor may be the lack of an appreciation of the concentration-dependent killing mediated by aminoglycosides, which suggests that single high doses may be more effective than twice- or thrice-daily dosing at low levels. The drugs of choice for *P. aeruginosa* pneumonia appear to be similar to those given earlier for bacteremia. A strong case cannot be made for the inclusion of the aminoglycoside component for fully susceptible organisms, given the evidence that aminoglycosides are not optimally active in the lungs at concentrations normally used with intravenous administration. Aerosolized aminoglycoside might provide adequate drug levels in the tracheobronchial tree, but there is no reason to believe that drug would penetrate into the consolidated lung.[342] Densities of *P. aeruginosa* are reduced[343,344] and inflammatory markers are diminished with inhaled aminoglycosides, but efficacy in the treatment of acute *P. aeruginosa* pneumonia has not been demonstrated to date in a controlled trial. The usually recommended drug is tobramycin, 300 mg inhaled daily. Patients with nosocomial pneumonia may have *P. aeruginosa* isolates resistant to many of the usual drugs, a problem that appears to be becoming progressively worse.[345,346]

Chronic Respiratory Tract Infections

P. aeruginosa is responsible for chronic infections of the airways associated with a number of underlying or predisposing conditions, the most prevalent being CF, found mostly in white populations. The description and management of *P. aeruginosa* infection in this entity can be found in Chapter 65. A somewhat similar state of chronic colonization beginning early in childhood is seen in some Asian populations in a disease of unknown etiology called chronic or diffuse panbronchiolitis.[291] The disease is most often described in Japan but is not restricted to that country. In that disease, not unlike CF, there is a chronic relapsing infection by *P. aeruginosa*, characterized by increased sputum production, fever, and focal lung infiltrates. Strains of *P. aeruginosa* isolated from these patients undergo the same type of mucoid conversion as strains from patients with CF.[347] Patients with diffuse panbronchiolitis respond clinically to antipseudomonal therapy but the organism is not eradicated. Significant advances have, however, been made in its management with the long-term use of macrolides,[348] a class of drugs that have no antibacterial activity against *P. aeruginosa* but are thought to suppress the inflammatory response[349] and perhaps suppress production of *P. aeruginosa* virulence factors.[350] The most commonly used agents have been clarithromycin and azithromycin,

P. aeruginosa might be one of the organisms colonizing damaged bronchi and leading to bronchiectasis, a disease secondary to multiple causes in which there are profound structural abnormalities of the airways resulting in the stasis of mucus. The issues concerning the management of *P. aeruginosa* in this setting are less clear. The organism establishes a state of chronic colonization and is not eradicated by antibiotics. The behavior of the organism is not unlike that in CF. Treatment is given during exacerbations, but its role has not been examined objectively in terms of the effect of treatment on decline of lung function. Aerosolized tobramycin results in a reduction of the bacterial load.[344] Patients may also be given an injectable antipseudomonal β-lactam antibiotic.

Bone and Joint Infections

P. aeruginosa is not a frequent cause of bone or joint infections. These infections result from at least three different mechanisms: bacteremia, direct inoculation into bone, and spread from contiguous infection. Bacteremia caused either by the injection of contaminated illicit drugs or as a result of infective endocarditis in the addict population has been well documented to cause vertebral osteomyelitis[351] and sternoclavicular joint arthritis.[352] However *P. aeruginosa* bacteremia from the lungs or other tissues rarely leads to seeding of bone sites, such as the vertebral disks or the axial skeleton, compared with the frequency noted for *S. aureus*.

The clinical presentation of vertebral *P. aeruginosa* osteomyelitis is more indolent than that of staphylococcal osteomyelitis. The duration of symptoms in the addict population with vertebral osteomyelitis is weeks to months. Fever is not uniformly present and, when present, tends to be low grade.[351] There may be mild tenderness at the site of involvement. Leucocytosis may or may not be present, but the erythrocyte sedimentation rate (ESR) is invariably elevated. Blood cultures are usually negative unless there is concomitant endocarditis. Plain radiographs have been reported to be normal on admission. Therefore, when radiographs are negative, a bone scan should be obtained for possible drug addicts with symptoms suggesting osteomyelitis. A further workup including magnetic resonance imaging (MRI) helps to initiate the appropriate diagnostic procedure, which is initially a needle biopsy or aspiration in cases in which blood cultures are negative.

Open biopsy may be needed in some cases because other causes of osteomyelitis must be considered in indolent disease in addicts whose blood cultures and needle aspirates are culture negative. Vertebral osteomyelitis caused by *P. aeruginosa* has also been reported in elderly persons, originating from urinary tract infections.[353] The infection generally involves the lumbosacral area because of a shared venous drainage (Batson's plexus) between the lumbosacral spine and pelvis.

Sternoclavicular septic arthritis caused by *P. aeruginosa* is seen almost exclusively in intravenous drug addicts.[352] It may occur with or without endocarditis, but a primary site of infection is often not found. The disease is most often monoarticular. Sometimes there is sternochondral joint involvement. Patients generally complain of anterior chest pain over the involved joint and restriction of movement of the homolateral shoulder. There is often swelling over the affected joint. Laboratory findings are usually mild, but the ESR is almost always elevated. Plain radiographs show joint or bone involvement. Biopsies may be needed for diagnosis, at which time drainage and débridement may be done because there may be abscess formation and necrotic cartilage.

P. aeruginosa may also involve the pubic symphysis in addicts, but involvement at that site is not limited to this population.[354] It has been seen after pelvic surgery and as a complication of femoral artery catheterization. Patients present with a variety of ill-defined painful syndromes that may involve the lower abdomen, hips, groin, or thighs, and symptoms are exacerbated by walking. There is generally exquisite tenderness of the pubic symphysis, radiographs may be normal or abnormal, but bone scans are usually diagnostic. If there is no concomitant bacteremia, needle aspiration or biopsy should be done in these cases.

Pseudomonas osteomyelitis of the foot most often follows puncture wounds through sneakers. The organism has been found between the layers of the rubber soles of sneakers in many cases.[355,356] Most of these cases are reported in children, but it is also seen in adults.[357] The main manifestation is pain in the foot, and there may be a superficial cellulitis around the puncture wound and tenderness on deep palpation of the wound. Multiple joints or bones of the foot may be involved. Systemic symptoms are generally absent, blood cultures are usually negative, but the ESR tends to be elevated. Radiographs may or may not be abnormal but the bone scan is usually positive, as are MRI studies.[358] Needle aspiration usually yields a diagnosis. Prompt surgery, with exploration of the nail puncture tract and débridement of the involved bones and cartilage, is generally recommended for the treatment of this disease, in addition to antibiotic therapy. This entity is perhaps the only form of *P. aeruginosa* osteomyelitis wherein short courses of therapy for 2 weeks have been successful.[359] It is, however, advisable to monitor therapy with ESR or C-reactive protein measurements, which may predict treatment failure.

Another form of *P. aeruginosa* osteomyelitis, often referred to as chronic contiguous osteomyelitis, is probably a mixture of different entities that have in common infection of bone extending from an infected, contiguous area.[351] It may involve infection of an open fracture or even a closed fracture after a surgical procedure contiguous to the site of the fracture. Some of the more frequent occurrences are in the setting of decubitus ulcers, the diabetic foot, and ischemic ulcers secondary to peripheral vascular disease. In the latter situations in which the ulcer has been chronic, there is often a mixed flora, making it difficult to ascertain the role of *P. aeruginosa*. Deep bone biopsies considered the "gold standard" for making a microbiologic diagnosis[360] have been recommended to ascertain the cause of osteomyelitis but are not routinely done. A pure culture of *P. aeruginosa* would be indicative of a true *P. aeruginosa* infection given its ability to infect bone, but that is uncommon from wound cultures. Bone and gallium scans to implicate bone rather than simple soft tissue involvement followed by a bone biopsy, histology studies, and culture may be a means of making a more certain diagnosis. ESR determinations are of considerable help in diagnosis and therapy of most acute bone infections; however, in chronic contiguous osteomyelitis these measurements have been less reliable. If the ESR is elevated, it may be useful to observe the patient for bone involvement, but that is not seen in the majority of

cases. Therapy of contiguous osteomyelitis almost always requires or involves surgery to débride overlying infected or colonized tissue and to remove dead bone.

Treatment of Bone Infections. With the exception of the osteomyelitis after puncture wounds that occurs mainly in children, antibiotic therapy of *P. aeruginosa* osteomyelitis is difficult. The choices are single-drug therapy with an antipseudomonal β-lactam antibiotic[361] or ciprofloxacin.[362-365] The success of ciprofloxacin in many forms of *P. aeruginosa* osteomyelitis, despite relatively low peak serum levels with the usual doses used to treat osteomyelitis (500 or 750 mg) and low ratios of the area under the curve to the MIC, suggests that there may be specific factors that allow effective therapy. Some reasons may be a low density of organisms in osteomyelitis and perhaps slow multiplication rates allowing less selection of resistant mutants, but most important may be the good penetration of this agent into bone.[366] Vertebral disease in drug addicts has been treated with single-drug therapy, including aminoglycosides.[351] However, it is suggested that nonaminoglycosides in maximal recommended doses be used as first-line agents for at least 4 weeks of therapy, as long as the isolate is sensitive to the antibiotic. Whether *P. aeruginosa* bone infections require combination therapy has not been evaluated in clinical trials in humans. If, however, there is accompanying endocarditis, therapy should be directed to that disease, and this may change the management approach in terms of length of therapy and whether a single agent should be used. Most other acute forms of *P. aeruginosa* osteomyelitis may be managed similarly. There are no guidelines that have been subjected to scrutiny. Therapy with single β-lactam antibiotics may be started and the clinical response followed by ESR. If the patient is not responding, a second agent such as an aminoglycoside may be added. Alternatively, therapy may be started with ciprofloxacin at the higher end of the dosing range. Therapy is generally for 4 to 6 weeks, but foot infections have been treated successfully with 750 mg of ciprofloxacin taken orally for 14 days. Most of the published information for significant bone infection recommends up to 6 months of ciprofloxacin if this agent is being used.

The antibiotic therapy for chronic osteomyelitis related to *P. aeruginosa* is difficult, not unlike therapy for all forms of chronic osteomyelitis. The suggestions for acute therapy may not be appropriate in this setting. Surgery plays a much greater role in chronic osteomyelitis in order to remove dead and scarred areas where antibiotic penetration may be poor. The history of treatment of this entity is one of relapsing infection. The success of fluoroquinolones in managing a number of acute and chronic *P. aeruginosa* bone infections suggests that they may be useful alone or in conjunction with other agents. One approach, therefore, may be to begin therapy in cases of chronic osteomyelitis with a β-lactam antibiotic that is given for 4 weeks followed by 4 to 6 months of ciprofloxacin if the organism is sensitive. However, it should be noted that *Pseudomonas* resistance to ciprofloxacin has increased dramatically worldwide, which may preclude its use in many cases. In such cases, more aggressive initial therapy with 2 weeks of a combination of a β-lactam and an aminoglycoside antibiotic followed by 2 months of the β-lactam alone is suggested. If an elevated ESR is present after débridement, it may be a useful measurement for following the patient in order to determine the approximate length of therapy. It should be noted, however, that regardless of whether injectable or oral antibiotics are given, there is a high failure rate in chronic bone infections and many require retreatment.

Central Nervous System Infections

Primary central nervous system infections with *P. aeruginosa* are a relative rarity. Involvement is almost always secondary to a surgical procedure or head trauma and occasionally bacteremia.[367] The entities seen most often are postoperative or post-traumatic meningitis and occasionally subdural or epidural infections that result from contamination of these areas. Embolic disease from endocarditis in intravenous drug addicts leading to brain abscesses has also been described. The cerebrospinal fluid (CSF) profile of *P. aeruginosa* meningitis is no different from that of a pyogenic meningitis. Treatment of this entity is difficult; little published information is available[368-370] and no controlled trials in humans have been undertaken as they have for other forms of meningitis. However, the general principles involved in the treatment of meningitis apply, that is, the need for high doses of bactericidal agents in order to attain high levels within the CSF.

The agent with which there is some published experience for *P. aeruginosa* meningitis is ceftazidime,[368-370] but other antipseudomonal β-lactam agents that achieve high CSF concentrations such as cefepime and meropenem have also been used successfully. The tendency for easy development of resistance to imipenem and its neurotoxicity at high doses would preclude the use of this agent as first-line therapy. Aztreonam, which has been used successfully in the treatment of gram-negative meningitis, could also be considered if the isolate is sensitive. Ciprofloxacin has also been used in isolated cases,[371] but there is little clinical experience to suggest that it can be used as a first-line agent considering the limited CSF penetration and possible development of resistance. Some reports have used aminoglycosides in combination with β-lactam agents but their necessity is unproved unless one is dealing with a β-lactam-resistant organism, in which case intrathecal or intraventricular administration of aminoglycosides may be required for optimal activity (see Chapter 80).

The length of therapy for *Pseudomonas* meningitis has been described as a minimum of 2 weeks. Relapse even after 2 weeks of maximal doses of ceftazidime has been seen. The best guide to length of therapy may be an early trend to normalization of the CSF profile. Removal of any foreign bodies such as ventriculostomy tubes and dural grafts is mandatory for successful treatment. Even apparently successfully treated cases may relapse, requiring retreatment. It is also mandatory in such cases that the isolates be reexamined by the microbiology laboratory to ascertain that they remain susceptible to the antibiotic being used because relapse may be due to the development of drug resistance.

Other forms of *P. aeruginosa* central nervous system infection, such as brain abscesses and epidural and subdural empyema, generally require surgical drainage in addition to antibiotics. The length of therapy for these closed space infections depends on a variety of factors including adequacy of drainage. The time is left to clinical judgment, but they require at least 2 weeks of therapy.

Eye Infections

Eye infections with *P. aeruginosa* result from direct inoculation into the tissue related to trauma or surface injury caused by contact lenses. Bacteremia is also a rare cause of endophthalmitis. *P. aeruginosa* eye infections may be extremely devastating, rapidly leading to loss of sight. Keratitis is the most frequent type of disease seen, and its association with contact lens wear, especially extended-wear lenses, is well established (see Chapter 107).[372,373] However, any form of trauma may predispose to this type of infection, including surgery and burns. Cases have also occurred in intubated patients,[374] whose eyes were probably dried out and ulcerated and then contaminated by *P. aeruginosa* from the environment. The requirement for injury to the surface of the cornea leading to adhesion of the organism appears to be absolute because the disease cannot be produced in animals without injury to the cornea[13] and human cases always occur in the setting of injury to the cornea. Keratitis can be slowly or rapidly progressive, but the classic description is that of disease progressing over 48 hours leading to involvement of the entire cornea with opacification and sometimes perforation. *P. aeruginosa* keratitis should be considered a medical emergency because of the rapidity with which it can progress, leading to loss of sight. The eye lesions should be scraped and the scrapings Gram stained and cultured. If gram-negative rods are seen, the patient should be treated as though *P. aeruginosa* is present until culture results are reported. The usual therapy for keratitis is topical antibiotics. Fortified aminoglycoside preparations or fluoroquinolones are recommended. In cases in which the involvement is extensive, ceftazidime or gentamicin may be given by subconjunctival injection.

P. aeruginosa endophthalmitis is one of the most feared *P. aeruginosa* infections. Loss of sight and very much reduced visual acuity are the most common outcomes of these infections.[18] This entity may result from penetrating injuries, surgery, perforation of a corneal ulcer, or seeding from bacteremia. The disease is fulminant, with severe pain, chemosis, decreased visual acuity, anterior uveitis, vitreous involvement, and panophthalmitis. Therapy for such infections includes systemic antibiotics at high doses to achieve better concentrations in the eye as well as intravitreal antibiotics. Ceftazidime has been the most frequently used antibiotic for this entity, but little is written about outcomes. Its penetration into the vitreous is excellent.[375] Aminoglycosides are also injected subconjunctivally and by the intraocular route and sometimes given intravenously. Adjunctive surgery is generally done to remove infected vitreous.

P. aeruginosa also causes a number of uncommon eye infections, including orbital cellulitis in neutropenic patients[376] and gangrene necrosis of the eyelids,[377] both of which result from bacteremia.

Ear Infections

P. aeruginosa infections of the ears vary from the mild swimmer's ear that is seen in children, to chronic persistent draining ears, to serious life-threatening infections that lead to neurologic sequelae or even death. Swimmer's ear is commonly seen in children and results from infection of moist macerated skin of the external ear canal. The source of the organism is likely to be the swimming pool if underchlorinated.[378] The natural history of most of these cases is resolution without sequelae, but in some patients chronic drainage occurs. The pinna may be tender when pulled and the ear canal may be tender with an exudate present. The management of this entity utilizes topical antibiotic agents (otic solutions). Aminoglycoside-containing solutions are most frequently used. Recurrences are frequent and may lead to chronically draining ears that can require more intensive topical therapy. The management of such cases is described in Chapter 54.

The most dreaded form of *Pseudomonas* infection involving the ear has been given various names, two of which, malignant otitis externa and necrotizing otitis externa, are now used for the same entity. This disease was originally described in elderly diabetic patients,[379] in whom the majority of cases still occur. However, the disease is not restricted to this population and has been described in AIDS patients[380,381] and elderly patients without underlying diabetes or immunocompromise.[330] The pathogenesis is believed to start with infection of the ear canal with penetration to the cartilage surrounding the external auditory canal and eventual extension to middle ear, mastoid air cells, and temporal bone.[382] Facial paralysis occurs when the seventh cranial nerve is involved as it courses through the medial wall of the middle ear. Temporomandibular joint extension can cause pain on mastication. Extension to the petrous pyramid can cause Gradenigo's syndrome, with fifth- and sixth-nerve cranial palsies. The most serious complications occur with further extension of the infection, resulting in thrombosis of the venous sinuses of the brain, including the sigmoid (transverse) sinus, contiguous to the mastoid air cells, and the cavernous sinus, contiguous to the petrous pyramid. It may also result in thrombosis of the carotid artery with subsequent brain infarction. The infection may cross to the other side of the skull and even involve the contralateral cranial nerves.

The clinical presentation is usually decreased hearing and ear pain, which may be severe and lancinating without drainage.[382] Some patients have an exudate. These symptoms in an elderly diabetic patient must raise the specter of malignant external otitis until proved otherwise. Facial palsy may appear early. The pinna is usually painful when pulled on and the external canal may be tender on pressure. The ear canal almost always shows signs of inflammation with erythema, granulation tissue, and exudate. The tympanic membrane, if visualized, may be normal or ruptured. There may also be tenderness on pressure anterior to the tragus, extending even to the temporomandibular joint and mastoid process. Systemic symptoms such as fever occur in a small minority of patients.

Diagnosis is made easily as long as there is a high index of suspicion in diabetic patients and patients with AIDS. In less severe cases in noncompromised individuals, the distinction between ordinary otitis externa and malignant otitis externa needs to be made as the former is much more frequent. *P. aeruginosa* is often found in the ear canal if patients have not received prolonged topical or parenteral therapy. For practical purposes, this disease can be considered specific to *P. aeruginosa,* but it has been described as rarely caused by fungi[383] and *S. aureus.*[384] The ESR is invariably elevated in the range of 100 mm/hour or greater. The diagnosis is easily made on clinical grounds in the more severe cases, but the gold standard may be a positive technetium 99 bone scan[385] in a patient with otitis externa along with *P. aeruginosa* grown from the ear exudate. Even in diabetic patients who fail to grow *P. aeruginosa,* a positive technetium 99 bone scan would be presumptive evidence for the existence of this condition and for a biopsy or empirical therapy to be initiated. MRI may demonstrate inflammation of the temporal bone. Both MRI and computed tomography scans may show fluid in the middle ear and mastoid cells.[386]

Another poorly understood form of *P. aeruginosa* ear infection is chronic middle ear drainage, called chronic suppurative otitis media. *P. aeruginosa* is isolated from a large percentage of these draining middle ears. Often it is in mixed culture, but in about 30% of cases it is the sole organism isolated from aerobic cultures. The pathogenesis of this condition is unclear. It is possible that it begins with external otitis similar to swimmer's ear and then there is middle ear involvement followed by chronic mastoiditis. Topical antibiotics[387-389] have been used with success early in the disease course. Very high success rates have also been reported with intravenous ceftazidime.[389] The management is now mainly medical in the absence of cholesteatomas.

Treatment of Ear Infections. The treatment of malignant external otitis has undergone significant changes since it was first described by Chandler in 1968.[379] Extensive surgery was deemed necessary. At present, the approach appears to be débridement of the ear canal including any necrotic tissue cartilage and adjacent bone rather than extensive bone débridement or facial nerve decompression. This change may be due to earlier recognition of this disease before there is more extensive involvement.[389] Treatment with a single agent, usually ceftazidime[391] or ciprofloxacin,[391] has been successful. However, cefepime may also be used in place of ceftazidime. The generally recommended length of therapy is 6 weeks when β-lactams are used. Oral ciprofloxacin has been used for varying periods of time from 8 weeks to 6 months. There are no comparative data on relapse rates between treatment with β-lactams and ciprofloxacin, but relapses can occur up to a year after completion of therapy, typically heralded by the return of pain. Serial ESR measurements have been used to follow the progress of treatment, and gallium 67 computed tomography scans have been extremely useful in assessing the activity of disease and may be useful in selecting an end point for the length of therapy.[392] One caveat is the increasing resistance to ciprofloxacin, which suggests that empirical ciprofloxacin may lose its efficacy.[393] Some authors have suggested that hyperbaric oxygen can be used for cases that have not responded to therapy,[394] but this has not been subjected to a clinical trial.

Urinary Tract Infections

P. aeruginosa urinary tract infections generally occur as a complication of the presence of a foreign body such as a stone, stent, or catheter in the urinary tract or the presence of an obstruction within the genitourinary system or after instrumentation or surgery on the urinary tract. Paraplegic patients are at high risk[395] for *P. aeruginosa* urinary tract infections (see Chapter 313), and frequent use of antibiotics in this setting may select for *P. aeruginosa.* Notwithstanding the relationship between obstructive lesions and *P. aeruginosa* urinary tract infections, there have been descriptions of *P. aeruginosa* urinary tract infections in outpatient children[396] without stones or evident obstruction. One of the most important aspects of *P. aeruginosa* urinary tract infections is that they frequently serve as the nidus for *P. aeruginosa* bacteremia by ascending infection.

Most *P. aeruginosa* urinary tract infections fit into the category of complicated urinary tract infections, in which therapy is more prolonged than the usual course recommended for cystitis. There are no

real comparative data on proper therapies because such cases are lumped in with other cases of complicated urinary tract infections in clinical trials. Certain guidelines to prevent relapses may, however, be inferred from clinical experience. Foley catheters, stents, or stones should be removed if possible to prevent relapse. Intermittent catheterization is preferred to retaining a Foley catheter. Generally, 7 to 10 days of antibiotic treatment suffice, with up to 2 weeks for pyelonephritis. Renal abscess or bacteremia caused by *P. aeruginosa* requires a longer course of therapy. Antipseudomonal β-lactams, ciprofloxacin, levofloxacin and gatifloxacin, and aminoglycosides given once daily are all equally acceptable, given their normally high levels of urinary excretion. Alternative antibiotics that may be used for oral treatment of *P. aeruginosa* urinary tract infections include doxycycline, to which many strains are sensitive, and in cases of multiple antibiotic resistance or in patients with very low urinary output, bladder irrigation with 0.25% acetic acid may be useful. Relapse is common and may be due not to antibiotic resistance but to host factors.

Skin and Soft Tissue Infections, Including Burns

P. aeruginosa causes ecthyma gangrenosa in neutropenic patients, an entity described earlier in this chapter.[397,398] Secondary infection of chronic skin ulcers or burns (see later) can also occur. Maceration of normal skin, such as from soaking in a hot tub, can lead to superficial infection.[34,399]

Folliculitis and other papular or vesicular lesions related to *P. aeruginosa,* collectively called dermatitis, have now been extensively described.[400,401] Multiple outbreaks have been linked to whirlpools, spas, and swimming pools. One nosocomial outbreak was linked to a contaminated hydrotherapy pool in a hospital and another to a contaminated water supply in a hospital. Thus, control of growth of this organism in the home or recreational environment by proper chlorination of water is essential, comparable to the control commonly practiced in hospitals. Besides the dermatitis syndromes, contaminated water has resulted in necrotizing pneumonia[336] and even ecthyma gangrenosum in neutropenic patients[402] and in two ostensibly healthy children.[403] However, it should be noted that most cases of hot tub folliculitis are self-limited, requiring no specific form of therapy besides avoidance of exposure to the contaminated source of water.

Burn wound infections with *P. aeruginosa* constituted one of the most significant problems caused by this organism during the 1960s and 1970s. A specific clinical picture of sepsis, with high colony counts of *P. aeruginosa* exceeding 10^5 organisms per gram of tissue, was the defining feature. Patients generally had progressive formation of a black necrotic eschar, with a sepsis picture, with or without bacteremia. The occurrence of *P. aeruginosa* burn wound sepsis does not appear to be as frequent as reported in the past,[404] when as many as 10% of burn patients had *P. aeruginosa* sepsis. In a more recent large study of more than 1400 burn patients, *P. aeruginosa* sepsis occurred in only about 1% of patients.[300] However the organism still remains a prominent isolate from burn wounds.[301] Early surgical treatment and the recognition that hydrotherapy[301,405] can commonly be a source of infection may have contributed to reductions in the occurrence of burn wound sepsis, at least in developed nations. Typically, burn wound sepsis caused by *P. aeruginosa* followed invasion of the burn eschar,[406] with bacterial growth achieving high densities followed by invasion into subcutaneous tissues. From here the bacteria spread along fibrous septa into the lymphatics and also invaded blood vessels, resulting in bacteremia. Patients show all the typical manifestations of sepsis, which must be recognized as such and differentiated from the "systemic inflammatory response syndrome" that occurs as a result of thermal injury.[407] Diagnosis may be made by blood cultures or by the pathognomonic clinical picture of an expanding burn lesion related to infection by *P. aeruginosa.* Systemic manifestations of sepsis related most likely to liberated cytokines may be present before bacteremia. Quantitative wound cultures showing more than 10^5 *P. aeruginosa* organisms per gram of burn tissue[301] had been reported to be correlated with the presence of burn wound sepsis, but the imprecision of such cultures has led to less reliance on quantitative cultures as a means of diagnosis. Clinicians now rely on the isolation of *P. aeruginosa* from wounds or blood in the presence of a sepsis picture in diagnosing burn wound sepsis caused by *P. aeruginosa*.

Treatment of *Pseudomonas aeruginosa*-Infected Burn Wounds. The management of *P. aeruginosa*-infected burn wounds is both surgical and medical. Extensive débridement of colonized eschar or necrotic tissue is required. The general principle is to reduce the organism count, which would probably diminish the sepsis response but would also reduce the risk of resistance developing during therapy given the extremely high microbial burden of such wounds. At present, true burn wound sepsis related to *P. aeruginosa* is probably best managed with a combination of antibiotics.[408] There is scant literature on ceftazidime monotherapy, but the recommended dose is 6 g/day.[409] The same dose might apply to cefepime. The use of imipenem as monotherapy may not be advisable on the basis of a single study in burns in which rapid development of resistance occurred[410] and what is known about resistance developing against this agent in areas where there is a high count of *P. aeruginosa*.[345] Early *P. aeruginosa* colonization of burn wounds has been managed by the application of topical agents such as silver sulfadiazine and mafenide acetate.[411] This is done to attempt to reduce the organism count in the burn eschar and to treat local infection.

Endovascular Infections

P. aeruginosa may cause endovascular infections, including infective endocarditis.[19,412] In intravenous drug addicts, the source is usually contaminated paraphernalia or the illicit drugs.[413] This organism has also been reported to cause prosthetic valve endocarditis. *P. aeruginosa* endocarditis on native heart valves has been described in particular cities, probably resulting from local contamination of illicit drugs. One specific outbreak caused by serotype O11 among pentazocine[414] and tripelennamine abusers was probably due to a common source of contamination either in the agents or their preparation for injection. There have not been reported outbreaks since the 1980s, although they undoubtedly occur. The pathogenesis of this disease is not thought to be different from that of other forms of endocarditis. Prior injury to native valves caused by the injection of foreign material such as talc or fibers probably serves as a nidus for bacterial attachment to the heart valve. This organism appears to have strong affinity for the endocardium, and the affinity is augmented after injury.

The manifestations of *P. aeruginosa* endocarditis resemble those of other forms of acute endocarditis in addicts except that they appear to be more indolent than those of *S. aureus*. Most cases occur as right-sided disease as would be expected from the postulated etiology of injury of the right side of the heart caused by inoculation of the venous circulation, followed by bacterial adhesion. Although most disease involves the right side of the heart, left-sided involvement is not rare and multivalvular disease is common. Fever is a frequent manifestation, and pulmonary involvement occurs with septic embolization to the lungs. Hence, patients may also complain of chest pain and have hemoptysis. Involvement of the left side of the heart may lead to signs of cardiac failure, systemic embolization, and local cardiac involvement with sinus of Valsalva abscesses and conduction defects. Skin manifestations are rare in this disease, and ecthyma gangrenosum is not seen in *P. aeruginosa* endocarditis.

There are no pathognomonic symptoms or signs of endocarditis caused by *P. aeruginosa*. The diagnosis is made by blood cultures along with clinical signs of endocarditis. Other causes of *P. aeruginosa* bacteremia must be excluded; rarely, an infected prosthesis or indwelling vascular catheter leading to endocarditis may be found. *P. aeruginosa* bacteremia or osteomyelitis in an addict or healthy individual in the absence of surgery, trauma, or a chronic ulcer should trigger a search for an endovascular focus. It has been unusual to find *P. aeruginosa* endocarditis as a complication of nosocomial bacteremia despite the reported predilection of this organism for the heart valves.

Treatment of Endovascular Infections. The therapy for *P. aeruginosa* endocarditis has never been subjected to a controlled trial. It has been customary to use synergistic combinations of antibiotics against *P. aeruginosa* for a number of reasons, including the role that synergy has been shown to play in the treatment of some forms of endocarditis and the development of resistance during therapy with a single antipseudomonal β-lactam agent during therapy of *P. aeruginosa* endocarditis. In animal models resistance developed to both aminoglycosides and ceftazidime,[415] but nevertheless this is the standard of care.

Which combination therapy is best is unclear as all combinations have resulted in failures with rare exceptions.[416-418] A triple-drug combination of a β-lactam, aminoglycoside, and rifampin[419] was reported to salvage some of the failures that occurred with combination therapy, but no further studies have been published. A combination of meropenem and tobramycin[420] was successful in treating a case of left-sided *P. aeruginosa* endocarditis and is worthy of consideration because meropenem is not susceptible to the chromosomal β-lactamase of *P. aeruginosa* and does not enter through the same porin protein that results in the rapid development of resistance to imipenem. There is no published information about the efficacy of the antipseudomonal cephalosporin cefepime in endovascular infections. A possible difference between this agent and older cephalosporin drugs may be the lack of selection of *P. aeruginosa* ampC mutants. However, given the high density of this organism in vegetations, other mutants may still arise leading to drug resistance. Other antibacterial agents that have shown promise in animal models include ciprofloxacin,[421] but human data are lacking. Ciprofloxacin has been used successfully for long-term suppression of *P. aeruginosa* infection of a prosthetic heart valve.[422] The one common theme of all antibiotic therapy for *P. aeruginosa* endocarditis is the likelihood of the patient's organism becoming resistant to therapy even if there is initially blood-stream sterilization. Resistance occurs for a variety of reasons that are specific to this organism and to the nature of the disease, with very high microbial densities in vegetations that allow the selection of naturally occurring resistant mutants from this large population of bacteria.

Cases of *P. aeruginosa* endocarditis may relapse, often with resistant organisms, suggesting the need for adjunctive surgical therapy. The timing of surgical therapy is probably governed by the location of the involved cardiac valves. The average young male with right-sided endocarditis is able to survive an incompetent tricuspid valve in cases of failure of therapy or valve destruction; therefore, the case for very early surgery is not strong unless complications such as embolic disease to the lungs continue during therapy. When surgery is done the choice of surgical procedure is critical, as prosthetic valve insertion has not been successful. For tricuspid endocarditis, valvectomy may be the surgery of choice.[423] Disease on the left side of the heart,[424] either primary or relapsed, may require early surgery because of the threat of cardiac decompensation, particularly given the high failure rate of antibiotic therapy. Guidelines for the timing of surgery for the latter group are based on the behavior of other forms of endocarditis. Failure to sterilize the blood stream after 1 to 2 weeks of antibiotics, the continuing occurrence of major emboli, and increasing cardiac failure, as with other forms of endocarditis, would be some of the considerations. Patients whose primary therapy was apparently successful but who have relapses of infection should also have a valve replacement because of the high likelihood of bacterial resistance to the antibiotics used.

Pseudomonas aeruginosa Infections in Febrile Neutropenia

P. aeruginosa occupies a historical place in febrile neutropenia as the organism against which empirical coverage must always be included. This dogma results from observations in the 1960s and early 1970s that showed high mortality caused by this organism as well as its common occurrence in these patients. Currently, the organism does not appear to be as common in neutropenic patients as it once was. However, the importance of *P. aeruginosa* infection in neutropenic patients has not diminished because when it causes bacteremia mortality is likely to be high if it is not appropriately treated by empirical therapy. In some parts of the world, *P. aeruginosa* continues to be a significant problem in neutropenic patients, being responsible for the largest proportion of infections caused by a single organism. For example, in studies from the Indian subcontinent, *P. aeruginosa* was responsible for 28% of documented infections in 499 neutropenic patients[425] and constituted 31% of pathogens in another study.[426] In a large study from Japan of infections in leukemia patients, *P. aeruginosa* was the most frequently documented cause of bacterial infection.[427] In studies in North America, northern Europe, and Australia, the occurrence of *P. aeruginosa* bacteremia in the setting of febrile neutropenia is quite variable. In a review of 97 reports from 1987 to 1994, the incidence was reported to be 1% to 2.5% among febrile neutropenic patients given empirical therapy and 5% to 12% among microbiologically documented infections. Thus, the occurrence of *P. aeruginosa* bacteremia may be influenced by geography and perhaps climate and certainly by whether antibiotic prophylaxis is used.

The historical clinical syndromes in febrile neutropenic patients were bacteremia, pneumonia, and soft tissue infections that were mainly manifest as ecthyma gangrenosum. For reasons that are unclear, the occurrence of *P. aeruginosa* pneumonia in these patients has greatly diminished. Whether this is due to the use of antibiotic prophylaxis or to better methods of infection control in hematology units has not been studied. *P. aeruginosa* is still believed to cause the greatest mortality among bacterial infections in febrile neutropenic patients, but the mortality data reported show wide variability, as low as 5% in single-agent bacteremia[328] and up to 50% as part of a polymicrobial bacteremia.[328] Improvements in the response rate to antibiotic therapy have been reported in many studies. Studies from the M. D. Anderson Cancer Center involving a large number of cases of *P. aeruginosa* bacteremia showed an improvement from a historical response rate of 60% to 80%.[99] Another study of 127 patients demonstrated a reduction in mortality from 71% to 25% with the introduction of ceftazidime and imipenem.[101]

Treatment of *Pseudomonas aeruginosa* Infections in Febrile, Neutropenic Patients. The IDSA guidelines on the management of fever and neutropenia[321] recommend that modern antipseudomonal β-lactams such as cefepime, ceftazidime, or a carbapenem be used either alone or in combination with an aminoglycoside. Alternatively, an antipseudomonal penicillin, such as piperacillin, in combination with an aminoglycoside can be used if preferred. The length of therapy required has not been rigorously examined; therefore, therapy is recommended for the duration of the neutropenic episode. Maximal doses of antipseudomonal β-lactam antibiotics should be used for the management of *P. aeruginosa* bacteremia in febrile neutropenia because the normal host defenses against this organism, neutrophils, are absent. Whether the relatively low incidence of *P. aeruginosa* bacteremia in the developed world will continue is likely to depend at least in part on the extent and choice of prophylactic antibiotics.

Pseudomonas aeruginosa Infections in Acquired Immunodeficiency Syndrome

P. aeruginosa infections in AIDS were noted before the introduction of highly active antiretroviral therapy (HAART). These infections are both community and nosocomially acquired, but since the advent of HAART the majority appear to be community acquired. Since the introduction of protease inhibitors, *P. aeruginosa* infections in AIDS patients have been seen infrequently, but they still do occur, particularly sinusitis. They are most likely to occur in patients whose disease is not under control by antiretroviral agents or whose therapy has failed and can even be the initial presentation of human immunodeficiency virus infection. It was originally thought that the occurrence of *P. aeruginosa* infections in AIDS patients was due to neutropenia, but many of these patients were not quantitatively neutropenic,[428] suggesting a role of T cells in defense against this organism. This observation also suggests that qualitative defects may be present in neutrophils from AIDS patients. The risk factors for these infections in the nosocomial setting are no different from those for other patients, but low CD4 counts play a role in the ability of AIDS patients to contain *P. aeruginosa* infections. Bacteremia,[429] generally complicating pneumonia or sinusitis, is seen. A variety of other *P. aeruginosa* infections have also been seen in AIDS patients, including catheter-associated infections in the noso-

comial setting, skin infections including ecthyma gangrenosum,[430] unusual abscesses in different locations,[431] otitis externa including malignant external otitis,[380,381] and orbital cellulitis.[432]

The clinical presentation of the AIDS patient with *Pseudomonas* infection is remarkable for its "nonseverity," although infection may nonetheless be fatal. This is particularly true for pneumonia and bacteremia. Patients with bacteremia may have only a low-grade fever and rarely present with ecthyma gangrenosum. The occurrence of bacteremia may be a herald of underlying disease elsewhere, often pneumonia or sinusitis.[433] Isolated bacteremia may occur and its origin has been surmised to be the skin, with folliculitis or cellulitis possibly related to exposure to contaminated water sources such as a hot tub. Pneumonia with or without bacteremia is perhaps the most common type of *P. aeruginosa* infection seen in AIDS patients.[429,433] Patients with pneumonia may present with classic clinical signs and symptoms of pneumonia such as fever, productive cough, and chest pain. The infections may be lobar or multilobar without predisposition for any particular location. The most striking feature, however, is the frequency with which cavitary disease occurs. *P. aeruginosa, Nocardia asteroides,* and *Rhodococcus equi* are among the most frequent bacterial causes of cavitary lung disease in AIDS.[434]

Therapy of such infections is plagued by a relatively high incidence of relapse. Most patients with pulmonary disease have relapses after therapy unless suppressive antibiotic therapy is administered. The same holds for *P. aeruginosa* bacteremia and sinusitis. Although this relapsing behavior has been described commonly in the North American literature,[330,428] a European study indicates that it is being seen less frequently.[429] Therapy for any of these conditions in AIDS is no different from that in other patients except that relapse can be considered a rule unless the patient's CD4 count rises above 50 cells/μL or suppressive antibiotic therapy is given. In attempts to achieve cures and prevent relapses, therapy tends to be more prolonged that in other patients.

Uncommon *Pseudomonas aeruginosa* Infections

In addition to the entities that have been described in greater detail, *P. aeruginosa* can cause a number of infrequently seen syndromes, including noma neonatorum,[435] a necrotizing mucosal and perianal infection of newborns; toe web infections, especially in the tropics; and the "green nail syndrome" caused by *P. aeruginosa* paronychia,[34,436] which results from frequent submersion of the hands in water. In the last entity, the green discoloration results from diffusion of pyocyanin into the nail bed.

Antibiotic Resistance and Antibiotic Therapy of Multiresistant *Pseudomonas* Infections

After the introduction of carbenicillin, there were continuous improvements in the development of antipseudomonal agents that more or less ceased after the release of the fourth-generation agent cefepime and the carbapenem meropenem. Although the availability of these agents and a variety of other older agents provided the medical community with a certain degree of security, the situation has changed because of the selection of strains of *P. aeruginosa,* literally occurring worldwide, carrying multiple resistance determinants that mediate β-lactam multiresistance along with fluoroquinolone and aminoglycoside resistance.[437-440] The medical community is now turning to drugs such as colistin and polymyxin, which were discarded decades ago but are now being considered as "antimicrobials for the 21st century" (see Chapter 30).[441]

P. aeruginosa now carries multiple genetically based resistance determinants, which may act independently or in concert with others.[442] Among those of greatest concern are the chromosomal β-lactamases belonging to the Bush group 1 class of β-lactamases and extended-spectrum β-lactamases belonging to the OXA, PER, IMP, GES, and VIM families, some of which actually degrade carbapenems. The possession of such enzymes, combined with mutations that increase the levels of a number of efflux systems that pump out β-lactam antibiotics, may result in even higher MICs against β-lactam drugs, resulting in the inability to use such drugs even if only minimally degraded by β-lactamases.[443] Mutations leading to lack of expression of OprD or its decreased production may further compromise the efficacy of drugs such as imipenem by limiting the amount that enters the bacterial periplasmic space. Thus, multiresistance to β-lactam antibiotics has become a reality.

The reason why high-level antibiotic resistance in *P. aeruginosa* is occurring worldwide is of considerable importance, but the problem has not reached such levels that serious debate has begun to take place. There is some evidence that the emergence of resistance may be driven by use of carbapenems[444,445] as there is substantial resistance to all β-lactam antibiotics whenever there is imipenem resistance, but this does not explain why resistance to all β-lactam drugs, including those not degraded by the Bush group 1 chromosomal β-lactamases, also occurs. Unfortunately, such *P. aeruginosa* strains also show resistance to many aminoglycosides because of impermeability and possibly efflux. Some aminoglycoside resistance may also be encoded by genes that modify these agents,[442] especially in the case of gentamicin and tobramycin. Thus, multiple mechanisms of bacteria resistance also exist for these agents.

The last class of antibiotics with reasonable antipseudomonal activity consists of the fluoroquinolones, but the utility of these agents is now also compromised by mutational events in *P. aeruginosa* that result in loss of their activity combined with the increased production of one or more efflux pumps. That there should be a convergence of all these mechanisms on a global basis may be more than mere coincidence.

Alternative approaches to the management of multiresistant *P. aeruginosa* began some time ago because of the complexity of the management of such organisms in CF.[446,447] Colistin (polymyxin E) is used intravenously, notwithstanding its toxicity. This agent, or a related peptide antibiotic, polymyxin B, is now rapidly becoming the therapeutic agent of last resort in non-CF patients infected with multiresistant *P. aeruginosa*.[305,448-451] Recommended doses are in the range of 2.5 to 5.0 mg/kg/day in two to three divided doses for colistin and 2.5 to 3.0 mg/kg/day in four divided doses for polymyxin B. Polymyxin B is considered to be more nephrotoxic and is therefore not generally the first choice. The dose of either agent needs to be adjusted for renal insufficiency. One recommended schedule for colistin is as follows.[452] For patients with creatinine clearance greater than 20 mL/min, 75% to 100% of the daily dose given in two divided doses; creatinine clearance 5 to 20 mL/min, 50% of the daily dose given in two divided doses; creatinine clearance less than 5 mL/min, 30% of the daily dose in two divided doses every 12 to 18 hours.

The clinical outcome of multidrug-resistant *P. aeruginosa* infections treated with colistin is difficult to judge from the scant case reports and multiple drugs used in these complicated patients. Whereas the older literature found marginal efficacy and serious nephrotoxicity and neurotoxicity, more recent reports have been more encouraging, particularly considering the limited alternative choices of drugs. Colistin does show synergy with other antimicrobials in vitro,[453,454] and it may be possible to reduce the dosage of colistin when combined with another agent if there is unacceptable toxicity from the colistin, but there are no human or animal studies to support this approach at this time. Another approach to the management of multidrug-resistant *P. aeruginosa* strains may be to use combinations of antibiotics to which the strain is resistant, such as aztreonam with amikacin[455,456] or other combinations. The need for new antimicrobials is urgent. Considering the 7- to 10-year time frame required for clinical development, multidrug-resistant *P. aeruginosa* are likely to be major pathogens of the 21st century.

REFERENCES

1. Theilacker C, Coleman F, Mueschenborn S, et al. Construction and characterization of a *Pseudomonas aeruginosa* mucoid exopolysaccharide/alginate conjugate vaccine. Infect Immun. 2003;71:3875-3884.
2. Pier GB, DesJardins D, Aguilar T, et al. Polysaccharide surface antigens expressed by non-mucoid isolates of *Pseudomonas aeruginosa* from cystic fibrosis patients. J Clin Microbiol. 1986;24:189-196.
3. Anastassiou ED, Mintzas AS, Kounavis C, et al. Alginate production by clinical non-mucoid *Pseudomonas aeruginosa*. J Clin Microbiol. 1987;25:656-659.
4. Stover CK, Pham XQ, Erwin AL, et al. Complete genome sequence of *Pseudomonas aeruginosa* PA01, an opportunistic pathogen. Nature. 2000;406:959-964.
5. Poole K, Hancock RE. Phosphate-starvation-induced outer membrane proteins of members of the families Enterobacteriaceae and Pseudomonadaceae: Demonstration of immunological cross-reactivity with an antiserum specific for porin protein P of *Pseudomonas aeruginosa*. J Bacteriol. 1986;165:987-993.
6. Anwar H, Brown MRW, Day A, et al. Outer membrane antigens of mucoid *Pseudomonas aeruginosa* isolated directly from the sputum of a cystic fibrosis patient. FEMS Microbiol Lett. 1984;24:235-239.
7. Kelly NM, Macdonald MH, Martin N, et al. Comparison of the outer membrane protein and lipopolysaccharide profiles of mucoid and nonmucoid *Pseudomonas aeruginosa*. J Clin Microbiol. 1990;28:2017-2021.
8. Doggett RG. Microbiology of *Pseudomonas aeruginosa*. In: Doggett RG, ed. *Pseudomonas aeruginosa*: Clinical Manifestations of Infection and Current Therapy. New York: Academic Press; 1979:1-8.
9. Surveillance NNI. National Nosocomial Infections Surveillance (NNIS) System Report, data summary from January 1992 to June 2002, issued August 2002. Am J Infect Control. 2002;30:458-475.
10. Wilmoth D, Walters PE, Tomlin R, et al. Caring for adults with cystic fibrosis. Crit Care Nurse. 2001;21:34-44.
11. Molina DN, Colon M, Bermudez RH, et al. Unusual presentation of *Pseudomonas aeruginosa* infections: A review. Bol Asoc Med P R. 1991;83:160-163.
12. *Pseudomonas* dermatitis/folliculitis associated with pools and hot tubs—Colorado and Maine, 1999-2000. MMWR Morb Mortal Wkly Rep. 2000;49:1087-1091.
13. Fleiszig SM, Evans DJ. The pathogenesis of bacterial keratitis: Studies with *Pseudomonas aeruginosa*. Clin Exp Optom. 2002;85:271-278.
14. Koch JM, Refojo MF, Hanninen LA, et al. Experimental *Pseudomonas aeruginosa* keratitis from extended wear of soft contact lenses. Arch Ophthalmol. 1990;108:1453-1459.
15. Willcox MD, Holden BA. Contact lens related corneal infections. Biosci Rep. 2001;21:445-461.
16. Matar GM, Harakeh HS, Ramlawi F, et al. Comparative analysis between *Pseudomonas aeruginosa* genotypes and severity of symptoms in patients with unilateral or bilateral otitis externa. Curr Microbiol. 2001;42:190-193.
17. Niall DM, Murphy PG, Fogarty EE, et al. Puncture wound related pseudomonas infections of the foot in children. Ir J Med Sci. 1997;166:98-101.
18. Eifrig CW, Scott IU, Flynn HW Jr, et al. Endophthalmitis caused by *Pseudomonas aeruginosa*. Ophthalmology. 2003;110:1714-1717.
19. Rajashekaraiah KR, Dhawan VK, Rice TW, et al. Increasing incidence of *Pseudomonas* endocarditis among parenteral drug abusers. Drug Alcohol Depend. 1980;6:227-230.
20. Kropec A, Huebner J, Riffel M, et al. Exogenous or endogenous reservoirs of nosocomial *Pseudomonas aeruginosa* and *Staphylococcus aureus* infections in a surgical intensive care unit. Intensive Care Med. 1993;19:161-165.
21. Berthelot P, Grattard F, Mahul P, et al. Prospective study of nosocomial colonization and infection due to *Pseudomonas aeruginosa* in mechanically ventilated patients. Intensive Care Med. 2001;27:503-512.
22. Edwards-Jones V, Greenwood JE. What's new in burn microbiology? James Laing Memorial Prize Essay 2000. Burns. 2003;29:15-24.
23. Pruitt BA Jr, McManus AT, Kim SH, et al. Burn wound infections: Current status. World J Surg. 1998;22:135-145.
24. Morrison AJ, Wenzel RP. Epidemiology of infections due to *Pseudomonas aeruginosa*. Rev Infect Dis. 1984;6:S627-640.
25. Cardenosa Cendrero JA, Sole-Violan J, Bordes Benitez A, et al. Role of different routes of tracheal colonization in the development of pneumonia in patients receiving mechanical ventilation. Chest. 1999;116:462-470.
26. Craven DE, Steger KA. Ventilator-associated bacterial pneumonia: Challenges in diagnosis, treatment, and prevention. New Horiz. 1998;6:S30-45.
27. Ewig S, Torres A, El-Ebiary M, et al. Bacterial colonization patterns in mechanically ventilated patients with traumatic and medical head injury. Incidence, risk factors, and association with ventilator-associated pneumonia. Am J Respir Crit Care Med. 1999;159:188-198.
28. Krueger WA, Lenhart FP, Neeser G, et al. Influence of combined intravenous and topical antibiotic prophylaxis on the incidence of infections, organ dysfunctions, and mortality in critically ill surgical patients: A prospective, stratified, randomized, double-blind, placebo-controlled clinical trial. Am J Respir Crit Care Med. 2002;166:1029-1037.
29. Krueger WA, Unertl KE. Selective decontamination of the digestive tract. Curr Opin Crit Care. 2002;8:139-144.
30. de Jonge E, Schultz MJ, Spanjaard L, et al. Effects of selective decontamination of digestive tract on mortality and acquisition of resistant bacteria in intensive care: A randomised controlled trial. Lancet. 2003;362:1011-1016.
31. Speert DP. Molecular epidemiology of *Pseudomonas aeruginosa*. Front Biosci. 2002;7:e354-e361.
32. Pfaller MA, Wendt C, Hollis RJ, et al. Comparative evaluation of an automated ribotyping system versus pulsed-field gel electrophoresis for epidemiological typing of clinical isolates of *Escherichia coli* and *Pseudomonas aeruginosa* from patients with recurrent gram-negative bacteremia. Diagn Microbiol Infect Dis. 1996;25:1-8.
33. Richards MJ, Edwards JR, Culver DH, et al. Nosocomial infections in medical intensive care units in the United States. National Nosocomial Infections Surveillance System. Crit Care Med. 1999;27:887-892.
34. Agger WA, Mardan A. *Pseudomonas aeruginosa* infections of intact skin. Clin Infect Dis. 1995;20:302-308.

35. Stieritz DD, Holder IA. Experimental studies of the pathogenesis of infections due to *Pseudomonas aeruginosa*: Description of a burned mouse model. J Infect Dis. 1975;131:688-691.

36. Schmidtchen A, Holst E, Tapper H, et al. Elastase-producing *Pseudomonas aeruginosa* degrade plasma proteins and extracellular products of human skin and fibroblasts, and inhibit fibroblast growth. Microb Pathog. 2003;34:47-55.

37. Lawin-Brussel CA, Refojo MF, Leong FL, et al. Effect of *Pseudomonas aeruginosa* concentration in experimental contact lens–related microbial keratitis. Cornea. 1993;12:10-18.

38. Lawin-Brussel CA, Refojo MF, Leong FL, et al. Scanning electron microscopy of the early host inflammatory response in experimental *Pseudomonas* keratitis and contact lens wear. Cornea. 1995;14:355-359.

39. Cole N, Krockenberger M, Bao S, et al. Effects of exogenous interleukin-6 during *Pseudomonas aeruginosa* corneal infection. Infect Immun. 2001;69:4116-4119.

40. Cohen EJ, Gonzalez C, Leavitt KG, et al. Corneal ulcers associated with contact lenses including experience with disposable lenses. CLAO J. 1991;17:173-176.

41. Widdicombe J. Relationships among the composition of mucus, epithelial lining liquid, and adhesion of microorganisms. Am J Respir Crit Care Med. 1995;151:2088-2092.

42. Travis SM, Conway BA, Zabner J, et al. Activity of abundant antimicrobials of the human airway. Am J Respir Cell Mol Biol. 1999;20:872-879.

43. Cole AM, Liao HI, Stuchlik O, et al. Cationic polypeptides are required for antibacterial activity of human airway fluid. J Immunol. 2002;169:6985-6991.

44. Andremont A, Marang B, Tancrede C, et al. Antibiotic treatment and intestinal colonization by *Pseudomonas aeruginosa* in cancer patients. Antimicrob Agents Chemother. 1989;33:1400-1402.

45. Pier GB, Grout M, DesJardins D. Complement deposition by antibodies to *Pseudomonas aeruginosa* mucoid exopolysaccharide (MEP) and by non-MEP specific opsonins. J Immunol. 1991;147:1869-1876.

46. Pollack M, Koles NL, Preston MJ, et al. Functional properties of isotype-switched immunoglobulin M (IgM) and IgG monoclonal antibodies to *Pseudomonas aeruginosa* lipopolysaccharide. Infect Immun. 1995;63:4481-4488.

47. Younger JG, Shankar-Sinha S, Mickiewicz M, et al. Murine complement interactions with *Pseudomonas aeruginosa* and their consequences during pneumonia. Am J Respir Cell Mol Biol. 2003;29:432-438.

48. Hopken UE, Lu B, Gerard NP, et al. The C5a chemoattractant receptor mediates mucosal defence to infection. Nature. 1996;383:86-89.

49. Holmskov U, Thiel S, Jensenius JC. Collections and ficolins: Humoral lectins of the innate immune defense. Annu Rev Immunol. 2003;21:547-578.

50. LeVine AM, Kurak KE, Bruno MD, et al. Surfactant protein-A-deficient mice are susceptible to *Pseudomonas aeruginosa* infection. Am J Respir Cell Mol Biol. 1998;19:700-708.

51. Restrepo CI, Dong Q, Savov J, et al. Surfactant protein D stimulates phagocytosis of *Pseudomonas aeruginosa* by alveolar macrophages. Am J Respir Cell Mol Biol. 1999;21:576-585.

52. Bufler P, Schmidt B, Schikor D, et al. Surfactant protein A and D differently regulate the immune response to nonmucoid *Pseudomonas aeruginosa* and its lipopolysaccharide. Am J Respir Cell Mol Biol. 2003;28:249-256.

53. Garred P, Pressler T, Madsen HO, et al. Association of mannose-binding lectin gene heterogeneity with severity of lung disease and survival in cystic fibrosis. J Clin Invest. 1999;104:431-437.

54. Garred P, Pressler T, Lanng S, et al. Mannose-binding lectin (MBL) therapy in an MBL-deficient patient with severe cystic fibrosis lung disease. Pediatr Pulmonol. 2002;33:201-207.

55. Davies J, Neth O, Alton E, et al. Differential binding of mannose-binding lectin to respiratory pathogens in cystic fibrosis. Lancet. 2000;355:1885-1886.

56. Alexander C, Rietschel ET. Bacterial lipopolysaccharides and innate immunity. J Endotoxin Res. 2001;7:167-202.

57. van der Meer JW, Barza M, Wolff SM, et al. A low dose of recombinant interleukin 1 protects granulocytopenic mice from lethal gram-negative infection. Proc Natl Acad Sci USA. 1988;85:1620-1623.

58. Vogels MT, Eling WM, Otten A, et al. Interleukin-1 (IL-1)-induced resistance to bacterial infection: Role of the type I IL-1 receptor. Antimicrob Agents Chemother. 1995;39:1744-1747.

59. Vogels MT, Mensink EJ, Ye K, et al. Differential gene expression for IL-1 receptor antagonist, IL-1, and TNF receptors and IL-1 and TNF synthesis may explain IL-1–induced resistance to infection. J Immunol. 1994;153:5772-5780.

60. Amura CR, Fontan PA, Sanjuan N, et al. The effect of treatment with interleukin-1 and tumor necrosis factor on *Pseudomonas aeruginosa* lung infection in a granulocytopenic mouse model. Clin Immunol Immunopathol. 1994;73:261-266.

61. Ozaki Y, Ohashi T, Minami A, et al. Enhanced resistance of mice to bacterial infection induced by recombinant human interleukin-1a. Infect Immun. 1987;55:1436-1440.

62. Markham RB, Pier GB, Goellner JJ, et al. In vitro T cell–mediated killing of *Pseudomonas aeruginosa*. II. The role of macrophages and T cell subsets in T cell killing. J Immunol. 1985;134:4112-4117.

63. Meduri GU. Clinical review: A paradigm shift: The bidirectional effect of inflammation on bacterial growth. Clinical implications for patients with acute respiratory distress syndrome. Crit Care. 2002;6:24-29.

64. Meduri GU, Kanangat S, Stefan J, et al. Cytokines IL-1beta, IL-6, and TNF-alpha enhance in vitro growth of bacteria. Am J Respir Crit Care Med. 1999;160:961-967.

65. Harder J, Meyer-Hoffert U, Teran LM, et al. Mucoid *Pseudomonas aeruginosa*, TNF-alpha, and IL-1beta, but not IL-6, induce human beta-defensin-2 in respiratory epithelia. Am J Respir Cell Mol Biol. 2000;22:714-721.

66. Fontan PA, Amura CR, Buzzola FR, et al. Modulation of human polymorphonuclear leukocyte chemotaxis and superoxide anion production by *Pseudomonas aeruginosa* exoproducts, IL-1 beta and piroxicam. FEMS Immunol Med Microbiol. 1995;10:139-144.

67. Lin TJ, Garduno R, Boudreau RT, et al. *Pseudomonas aeruginosa* activates human mast cells to induce neutrophil transendothelial migration via mast cell-derived IL-1 alpha and beta. J Immunol. 2002;169:4522-4530.

68. van Heeckeren A, Walenga R, Konstan MW, et al. Excessive inflammatory response of cystic fibrosis mice to bronchopulmonary infection with *Pseudomonas aeruginosa*. J Clin Invest. 1997;100:2810-2815.

69. Bonfield TL, Panuska JR, Konstan MW, et al. Inflammatory cytokines in cystic fibrosis lungs. Am J Respir Crit Care Med. 1995;152:2111-2118.

70. Wu CL, Lee YL, Chang KM, et al. Bronchoalveolar interleukin-1 beta: A marker of bacterial burden in mechanically ventilated patients with community-acquired pneumonia. Crit Care Med. 2003;31:812-817.

71. Schultz MJ, Rijneveld AW, Florquin S, et al. Role of interleukin-1 in the pulmonary immune response during *Pseudomonas aeruginosa* pneumonia. Am J Physiol. 2002;282:L285-L290.

72. Grassme H, Jendrossek V, Riehle A, et al. Host defense against *Pseudomonas aeruginosa* requires ceramide-rich membrane rafts. Nat Med. 2003;9:322-330.

73. Gosselin D, DeSanctis J, Boule M, et al. Role of tumor necrosis factor alpha in innate resistance to mouse pulmonary infection with *Pseudomonas aeruginosa*. Infect Immun. 1995;63:3272-3278.

74. Yu H, Nasr SZ, Deretic V. Innate lung defenses and compromised *Pseudomonas aeruginosa* clearance in the malnourished mouse model of respiratory infections in cystic fibrosis. Infect Immun. 2000;68:2142-2147.

75. Sapru K, Stotland PK, Stevenson MM. Quantitative and qualitative differences in bronchoalveolar inflammatory cells in *Pseudomonas aeruginosa*–resistant and –susceptible mice. Clin Exp Immunol. 1999;115:103-109.

76. Remick DG. Cytokine therapeutics for the treatment of sepsis: Why has nothing worked? Curr Pharm Des. 2003;9:75-82.

77. Fisher CJ Jr, Agosti JM, Opal SM, et al. Treatment of septic shock with the tumor necrosis factor receptor:Fc fusion protein. The Soluble TNF Receptor Sepsis Study Group. N Engl J Med. 1996;334:1697-1702.

78. Kronborg G, Hansen MB, Svenson M, et al. Cytokines in sputum and serum from patients with cystic fibrosis and chronic *Pseudomonas aeruginosa* infection as markers of destructive inflammation in the lungs. Pediatr Pulmonol. 1993;15:292-297.

79. Wilmott RW, Frenzke M, Kociela V, et al. Plasma interleukin-1 alpha and beta, tumor necrosis factor-alpha, and lipopolysaccharide concentrations during pulmonary exacerbations of cystic fibrosis. Pediatr Pulmonol. 1994;18:21-27.

80. Wolter JM, Rodwell RL, Bowler SD, et al. Cytokines and inflammatory mediators do not indicate acute infection in cystic fibrosis. Clin Diagn Lab Immunol. 1999;6:260-265.

81. Jones AM, Martin L, Bright-Thomas RJ, et al. Inflammatory markers in cystic fibrosis patients with transmissible *Pseudomonas aeruginosa*. Eur Respir J. 2003;22:503-506.

82. Jain-Vora S, LeVine AM, Chroneos Z, et al. Interleukin-4 enhances pulmonary clearance of *Pseudomonas aeruginosa*. Infect Immun. 1998;66:4229-4236.

83. Cole N, Bao S, Willcox M, et al. Expression of interleukin-6 in the cornea in response to infection with different strains of *Pseudomonas aeruginosa*. Infect Immun. 1999;67:2497-2502.

84. Cole N, Bao S, Stapleton F, et al. *Pseudomonas aeruginosa* keratitis in IL-6–deficient mice. Int Arch Allergy Immunol. 2003;130:165-172.

85. Grohmann U, Van Snick J, Campanile F, et al. IL-9 protects mice from gram-negative bacterial shock: Suppression of TNF-alpha, IL-12, and IFN-gamma, and induction of IL-10. J Immunol. 2000;164:4197-4203.

86. Sawa T, Corry DB, Gropper MA, et al. IL-10 improves lung injury and survival in *Pseudomonas aeruginosa* pneumonia. J Immunol. 1997;159:2858-2866.

87. Yu H, Hanes M, Chrisp CE, et al. Microbial pathogenesis in cystic fibrosis: Pulmonary clearance of mucoid *Pseudomonas aeruginosa* and inflammation in a mouse model of repeated respiratory challenge. Infect Immun. 1998;66:280-288.

88. Chmiel JF, Konstan MW, Knesebeck JE, et al. IL-10 attenuates excessive inflammation in chronic *Pseudomonas* infection in mice. Am J Respir Crit Care Med. 1999;160:2040-2047.

89. Huang X, McClellan SA, Barrett RP, et al. IL-18 contributes to host resistance against infection with *Pseudomonas aeruginosa* through induction of IFN-gamma production. J Immunol. 2002;168:5756-5763.

90. Schultz MJ, Knapp S, Florquin S, et al. Interleukin-18 impairs the pulmonary host response to *Pseudomonas aeruginosa*. Infect Immun. 2003;71:1630-1634.

91. Shenkar R, Coulson WF, Abraham E. Anti–transforming growth factor-beta monoclonal antibodies prevent lung injury in hemorrhaged mice. Am J Respir Cell Mol Biol. 1994;11:351-357.

92. Davies JC. *Pseudomonas aeruginosa* in cystic fibrosis: Pathogenesis and persistence. Paediatr Respir Rev. 2002;3:128-134.

93. Mahdi OZ, Mathelier LL, Al-Bardeisi NH. Hyperimmunoglobulin-E syndrome. Saudi Med J. 2002;23:461-463.

94. Noh LM, Low SM, Lajin I, et al. Antibody deficiency with hyper IgM—A case report. Malays J Pathol. 1992;14:121-123.

95. Ownby DR, Pizzo S, Blackmon L, et al. Severe combined immunodeficiency with leukopenia (reticular dysgenesis) in siblings: Immunologic and histopathologic findings. J Pediatr. 1976;89:382-387.

96. Lim DT, Reddi C, Freel B, et al. Antibody deficiency, P. *aeruginosa* septicemia and ecthyma gangrenosa. Ann Allergy. 1978;41:30-36.

97. Farrar JE, Rohrer J, Conley ME. Neutropenia in X-linked agammaglobulinemia. Clin Immunol Immunopathol. 1996;81:271-276.

98. Baro M, Marin MA, Ruiz-Contreras J, et al. *Pseudomonas aeruginosa* sepsis and ecthyma gangrenosum as initial manifestations of primary immunodeficiency. Eur J Pediatr. 2004;163:173-174.

99. Chatzinikolaou I, Abi-Said D, Bodey GP, et al. Recent experience with *Pseudomonas aeruginosa* bacteremia in patients with cancer: Retrospective analysis of 245 episodes. Arch Intern Med. 2000;160:501-509.

100. Bodey GP. *Pseudomonas aeruginosa* infections in cancer patients: Have they gone away? Curr Opin Infect Dis. 2001;14:403-407.

101. Todeschini G, Franchini M, Tecchio C, et al. Improved prognosis of *Pseudomonas aeruginosa* bacteremia in 127 consecutive neutropenic patients with hematologic malignancies. Int J Infect Dis. 1998;3:99-104.

102. Gransden WR, Leibovici L, Eykyn SJ, et al. Risk factors and a clinical index for diagnosis of *Pseudomonas aeruginosa* bacteremia. Clin Microbiol Infect. 1995;1:119-123.

103. Vidal F, Mensa J, Martinez JA, et al. *Pseudomonas aeruginosa* bacteremia in patients infected with human immunodeficiency virus type 1. Eur J Clin Microbiol Infect Dis. 1999;18:473-477.

104. Hobden JA, Engel LS, Callegan MC, et al. *Pseudomonas aeruginosa* keratitis in leukopenic rabbits. Curr Eye Res. 1993;12:461-467.

105. Opal SM, Cross AS, Sadoff JC, et al. Efficacy of antilipopolysaccharide and anti-tumor necrosis factor monoclonal antibodies in a neutropenic rat model of *Pseudomonas* sepsis. J Clin Invest. 1991;88:885-890.

106. Cryz SJ Jr, Furer E, Germanier R. Simple model for the study of *Pseudomonas aeruginosa* infections in leukopenic mice. Infect Immun. 1983;39:1067-1071.

107. Barghouthi S, Everett KDE, Speert DP. Nonopsonic phagocytosis of *Pseudomonas aeruginosa* requires facilitated transport of D-glucose by macrophages. J Immunol. 1995;154:3420-3428.

108. Mahenthiralingam E, Speert DP. Nonopsonic phagocytosis of *Pseudomonas aeruginosa* by macrophages and polymorphonuclear leukocytes requires the presence of the bacterial flagellum. Infect Immun. 1995;63:4519-4523.

109. Kooguchi K, Hashimoto S, Kobayashi A, et al. Role of alveolar macrophages in initiation and regulation of inflammation in *Pseudomonas aeruginosa* pneumonia. Infect Immun. 1998;66:3164-3169.

110. Cheung DO, Halsey K, Speert DP. Role of pulmonary alveolar macrophages in defense of the lung against *Pseudomonas aeruginosa*. Infect Immun. 2000;68:4585-4592.

111. Koller DY, Halmerbauer G, Muller J, et al. Major basic protein, but not eosinophil cationic protein or eosinophil protein X, is related to atopy in cystic fibrosis. Allergy. 1999;54:1094-1099.

112. Warner JO, Kilburn SA. Cystic fibrosis and allergy. Pediatr Allergy Immunol. 1996;7:67-69.

113. Koller DY, Gotz M, Eichler I, et al. Eosinophilic activation in cystic fibrosis. Thorax. 1994;49:496-499.

114. Lin TJ, Maher LH, Gomi K, et al. Selective early production of CCL20, or macrophage inflammatory protein 3alpha, by human mast cells in response to *Pseudomonas aeruginosa*. Infect Immun. 2003;71:365-373.

115. Boudreau RT, Garduno R, Lin TJ. Protein phosphatase 2A and protein kinase C-alpha are physically associated and are involved in *Pseudomonas aeruginosa*–induced interleukin 6 production by mast cells. J Biol Chem. 2002;277:5322-5329.

116. Ambrose PG, Owens RC Jr, Garvey MJ, et al. Pharmacodynamic considerations in the treatment of moderate to severe pseudomonal infections with cefepime. J Antimicrob Chemother. 2002;49:445-453.

117. Bergmann U, Scheffer J, Koller M, et al. Induction of inflammatory mediators (histamine and leukotrienes) from rat peritoneal mast cells and human granulocytes by *Pseudomonas aeruginosa* strains from burn patients. Infect Immun. 1989;57:2187-2195.

118. Dunkley ML, Clancy RL, Cripps AW. A role for CD4$^+$ T cells from orally immunized rats in enhanced clearance of *Pseudomonas aeruginosa* from the lung. Immunology. 1994;83:362-369.

119. Cripps AW, Dunkley ML, Clancy RL, et al. Pulmonary immunity to *Pseudomonas aeruginosa*. Immunol Cell Biol. 1995;73:418-424.

120. Dunkley ML, Cripps AW, Reinbott PW, et al. Immunity to respiratory *Pseudomonas aeruginosa* infection: The role of gut-derived T helper cells and immune serum. Adv Exp Med Biol. 1995:771-775.

121. Powderly WG, Pier GB, Markham RB. In vitro T cell-mediated killing of *Pseudomonas aeruginosa*. V. Generation of bactericidal T cells in nonresponder mice. J Immunol. 1987;138:2272-2277.

122. Markham RB, Powderly WG. Exposure of mice to live *Pseudomonas aeruginosa* generates protective cell-mediated immunity in the absence of an antibody response. J Immunol. 1988;140:2039-2045.

123. Tam M, Jackson-Snipes G, Stevenson MM. Characterization of chronic bronchopulmonary *Pseudomonas aeruginosa* infection in resistant and susceptible inbred mouse strains. Am J Respir Cell Mol Biol. 1999;20:710-719.

124. Stevenson MM, Kondratieva TK, Apt AS, et al. In vitro and in vivo T cell responses in mice during bronchopulmonary infection with mucoid *Pseudomonas aeruginosa*. Clin Exp Immunol. 1995;99:98-105.

125. Meynard JL, Barbut F, Guiguet M, et al. *Pseudomonas aeruginosa* infection in human immunodeficiency virus infected patients. J Infect Dis. 1999;38:176-181.

126. Sorvillo F, Beall G, Turner PA, et al. Incidence and determinants of *Pseudomonas aeruginosa* infection among persons with HIV: Association with hospital exposure. Am J Infect Control. 2001;29:79-84.

127. Gosselin D, Stevenson MM, Cowley EA, et al. Impaired ability of Cftr knockout mice to control lung infection with *Pseudomonas aeruginosa*. Am J Respir Crit Care Med. 1998;157:1253-1262.

128. Moser C, Hougen HP, Song Z, et al. Early immune response in susceptible and resistant mice strains with chronic *Pseudomonas aeruginosa* lung infection determines the type of T-helper cell response. APMIS. 1999;107:1093-1100.

129. Nieuwenhuis EE, Matsumoto T, Exley M, et al. CD1d-dependent macrophage-mediated clearance of *Pseudomonas aeruginosa* from lung. Nat Med. 2002;8:588-593.

130. Raga S, Julia MR, Crespi C, et al. gammadelta T lymphocytes from cystic fibrosis patients and healthy donors are high TNF-alpha and IFN-gamma-producers in response to *Pseudomonas aeruginosa*. Respir Res. 2003;4:1-9.

131. Pitt BR. CFTR trafficking and signaling in respiratory epithelium. Am J Physiol. 2001;281:L13-L15.

132. Peters KW, Qi J, Watkins SC, et al. Mechanisms underlying regulated CFTR trafficking. Med Clin North Am. 2000;84:633-640.

133. Lyczak JB, Cannon CL, Pier GB. Lung infections associated with cystic fibrosis. Clin Microbiol Rev. 2002;15:194-222.

134. Prince A. The CFTR advantage—Capitalizing on a quirk of fate. Nat Med. 1998;4:663-664.

135. Imundo L, Barasch J, Prince A, et al. Cystic fibrosis epithelial cells have a receptor for pathogenic bacteria on their apical surface. Proc Natl Acad Sci USA. 1995;92:3019-3023.

136. Davies J, Dewar A, Bush A, et al. Reduction in the adherence of *Pseudomonas aeruginosa* to native cystic fibrosis epithelium with anti-asialoGM1 antibody and neuraminidase inhibition. Eur Respir J. 1999;13:565-570.

137. Poschet JF, Boucher JC, Tatterson L, et al. Molecular basis for defective glycosylation and *Pseudomonas* pathogenesis in cystic fibrosis lung. Proc Natl Acad Sci USA. 2001;98:13972-13977.

138. Schroeder TH, Zaidi TS, Pier GB. Lack of adherence of clinical isolates of *Pseudomonas aeruginosa* to asialo GM$_1$ on epithelial cells. Infect Immun. 2001;69:719-729.

139. Cervin MA, Simpson DA, Smith AL, et al. Differences in eukaryotic cell binding of *Pseudomonas*. Microb Pathog. 1994;17:291-299.

140. Zar H, Saiman L, Quittell L, et al. Binding of *Pseudomonas aeruginosa* to respiratory epithelial cells from patients with various mutations in the cystic fibrosis transmembrane regulator. J Pediatr. 1995;126:230-233.

141. Comolli JC, Waite LL, Mostov KE, et al. Pili binding to asialo-GM1 on epithelial cells can mediate cytotoxicity or bacterial internalization by *Pseudomonas aeruginosa*. Infect Immun. 1999;67:3207-3214.

142. Smith JJ, Travis SM, Greenberg EP, et al. Cystic fibrosis airway epithelia fail to kill bacteria because of abnormal airway surface fluid. Cell. 1996;85:229-236.

143. Travis SM, Singh PK, Welsh MJ. Antimicrobial peptides and proteins in the innate defense of the airway surface. Curr Opin Immunol. 2001;13:89-95.

144. Zhang Y, Engelhardt JF. Airway surface fluid volume and Cl content in cystic fibrosis and normal bronchial xenografts. Am J Physiol. 1999;276:C469-C476.

145. Knowles MR, Robinson JM, Wood RE, et al. Ion composition of airway surface liquid of patients with cystic fibrosis as compared with normal and disease-control subjects. J Clin Invest. 1997;100:2588-2595.

146. Boucher RC. An overview of the pathogenesis of cystic fibrosis lung disease. Adv Drug Deliv Rev. 2002;54:1359-1371.

147. Matsui H, Grubb BR, Tarran R, et al. Evidence for periciliary liquid layer depletion, not abnormal ion composition, in the pathogenesis of cystic fibrosis airways disease. Cell. 1998;95:1005-1015.

148. Arora SK, Ritchings BW, Almira EC, et al. The *Pseudomonas aeruginosa* flagellar cap protein, FliD, is responsible for mucin adhesion. Infect Immun. 1998;66:1000-1007.

149. Carnoy C, Ramphal R, Scharfman A, et al. Altered carbohydrate composition of salivary mucins from patients with cystic fibrosis and the adhesion of *Pseudomonas aeruginosa*. Am J Respir Cell Mol Biol. 1993;9:323-334.

150. Yoon SS, Hennigan RF, Hilliard GM, et al. *Pseudomonas aeruginosa* anaerobic respiration in biofilms: Relationships to cystic fibrosis pathogenesis. Dev Cell. 2002;3:593-603.

151. Worlitzsch D, Tarran R, Ulrich M, et al. Effects of reduced mucus oxygen concentration in airway *Pseudomonas infections* of cystic fibrosis patients. J Clin Invest. 2002;109:317-325.

152. Pier GB. CFTR mutations and host susceptibility to *Pseudomonas aeruginosa* lung infection. Curr Opin Microbiol. 2002;5:81-86.

153. Pier GB, Grout M, Zaidi TS, et al. Role of mutant CFTR in hypersusceptibility of cystic fibrosis patients to lung infections. Science. 1996;271:64-67.

154. Pier GB, Grout M, Zaidi TS. Cystic fibrosis transmembrane conductance regulator is an epithelial cell receptor for clearance of *Pseudomonas aeruginosa* from the lung. Proc Natl Acad Sci USA. 1997;94:12088-12093.

155. Schroeder TH, Reiniger N, Meluleni G, et al. Transgenic cystic fibrosis mice exhibit reduced early clearance of *Pseudomonas aeruginosa* from the respiratory tract. J Immunol. 2001;166:7410-7418.

156. Schroeder TH, Lee MM, Yacono PW, et al. CFTR is a pattern recognition molecule that extracts *Pseudomonas aeruginosa* LPS from the outer membrane into epithelial cells and activates NF-kappa B translocation. Proc Natl Acad Sci USA. 2002;99:6907-6912.

157. Cannon CL, Kowalski MP, Stopak KS, Pier GB. *Pseudomonas aeruginosa*–induced apoptosis is defective in respiratory epithelial cells expressing mutant cystic fibrosis transmembrane conductance regulator. Am J Respir Cell Mol Biol. 2003;29:188-197.

158. Grassme H, Kirschnek S, Riethmueller J, et al. CD95/CD95 ligand interactions on epithelial cells in host defense to *Pseudomonas aeruginosa*. Science. 2000;290:527-530.

159. Hotchkiss RS, Dunne WM, Swanson PE, et al. Role of apoptosis in *Pseudomonas aeruginosa* pneumonia. Science. 2001;294:1783.

160. Esen M, Grassme H, Riethmuller J, et al. Invasion of human epithelial cells by *Pseudomonas aeruginosa* involves src-like tyrosine kinases p60Src and p59Fyn. Infect Immun. 2001;69:281-287.

161. Zaidi TS, Lyczak J, Preston M, et al. Cystic fibrosis transmembrane conductance regulator–mediated corneal epithelial cell ingestion of *Pseudomonas aeruginosa* is a key component in the pathogenesis of experimental murine keratitis. Infect Immun. 1999;67:1481-1492.

162. Zaidi TS, Preston MJ, Pier GB. Inhibition of bacterial adherence to host tissue does not markedly affect disease in the murine model of *Pseudomonas aeruginosa* corneal infection. Infect Immun. 1997;65:1370-1376.

163. Roy-Burman A, Savel RH, Racine S, et al. Type III protein secretion is associated with death in lower respiratory and systemic *Pseudomonas aeruginosa* infections. J Infect Dis. 2001;183:1767-1774.

164. Schulert GS, Feltman H, Rabin SD, et al. Secretion of the toxin ExoU is a marker for highly virulent *Pseudomonas aeruginosa* isolates obtained from patients with hospital-acquired pneumonia. J Infect Dis. 2003;188:1695-1706.

165. Mattick JS. Type IV pili and twitching motility. Annu Rev Microbiol. 2002;56:289-314.

166. Yu L, Lee KK, Hodges RS, et al. Adherence of *Pseudomonas aeruginosa* and *Candida albicans* to glycosphingolipid (Asialo-GM1) receptors is achieved by a conserved receptor-binding domain present on their adhesins. Infect Immun. 1994;62:5213-5219.

167. Sheth HB, Lee KK, Wong WY, et al. The pili of *Pseudomonas aeruginosa* strains PAK and PAO bind specifically to the carbohydrate sequence beta GalNAc¹⁻⁴eta Gal found in glycosphingolipids asialo-GM1 and asialo-GM2. Mol Microbiol. 1994;11:715-723.

168. Hahn HP. The type-4 pilus is the major virulence-associated adhesin of *Pseudomonas aeruginosa*—A review. Gene. 1997;192:99-108.

169. Hazlett LD, Moon MM, Singh A, et al. Analysis of adhesion, piliation, protease production and ocular infectivity of several *P. aeruginosa* strains. Curr Eye Res. 1991;10:351-362.

170. Keizer DW, Slupsky CM, Kalisiak M, et al. Structure of a pilin monomer from *Pseudomonas aeruginosa:* Implications for the assembly of pili. J Biol Chem. 2001;276:24186-24193.

171. Hazes B, Sastry PA, Hayakawa K, et al. Crystal structure of *Pseudomonas aeruginosa* PAK pilin suggests a main-chain-dominated mode of receptor binding. J Mol Biol. 2000;299:1005-1017.

172. Cachia PJ, Glasier LM, Hodgins RR, et al. The use of synthetic peptides in the design of a consensus sequence vaccine for *Pseudomonas aeruginosa*. J Pept Res. 1998;52:289-299.

173. O'Toole GA, Kolter R. Flagellar and twitching motility are necessary for *Pseudomonas aeruginosa* biofilm development. Mol Microbiol. 1998;30:295-304.

174. Montie TC, Doyle-Huntzinger D, Craven RC, et al. Loss of virulence associated with absence of flagellum in an isogenic mutant of *Pseudomonas aeruginosa* in the burned-mouse model. Infect Immun. 1982;38:1296-1298.

175. Feldman M, Bryan R, Rajan S, et al. Role of flagella in pathogenesis of *Pseudomonas aeruginosa* pulmonary infection. Infect Immun. 1998;66:43-51.

176. Montie TC, Drake D, Sellin H, et al. Motility, virulence, and protection with a flagella vaccine against *Pseudomonas aeruginosa* infection. Antibiot Chemother. 1987;39:233-248.

177. Arora SK, Dasgupta N, Lory S, et al. Identification of two distinct types of flagellar cap proteins, FliD, in *Pseudomonas aeruginosa*. Infect Immun. 2000;68:1474-1479.

178. Ramphal R, Arora SK. Recognition of mucin components by *Pseudomonas aeruginosa*. Glycoconj J. 2001;18:709-713.

179. Gupta SK, Berk RS, Masinick S, et al. Pili and lipopolysaccharide of *Pseudomonas aeruginosa* bind to the glycolipid asialo GM1. Infect Immun. 1994;62:4572-4579.

180. Gupta SK, Masinick S, Garrett M, et al. *Pseudomonas aeruginosa* lipopolysaccharide binds galectin-3 and other human corneal epithelial proteins. Infect Immun. 1997;65:2747-2753.

181. Mitchell E, Houles C, Sudakevitz D, et al. Structural basis for oligosaccharide-mediated adhesion of *Pseudomonas aeruginosa* in the lungs of cystic fibrosis patients. Nat Struct Biol. 2002;9:918-921.

182. Azghani AO, Idell S, Bains M, et al. *Pseudomonas aeruginosa* outer membrane protein F is an adhesin in bacterial binding to lung epithelial cells in culture. Microb Pathog. 2002;33:109-114.

183. Plotkowski MC, Costa AO, Morandi V, et al. Role of heparan sulphate proteoglycans as potential receptors for non-piliated *Pseudomonas aeruginosa* adherence to non-polarised airway epithelial cells. J Med Microbiol. 2001;50:183-190.

184. Pier GB, Ames P. Mediation of the killing of rough, mucoid isolates of *Pseudomonas aeruginosa* from patients with cystic fibrosis by the alternative pathway of complement. J Infect Dis. 1984;150:223-228.

185. Conrad RS, Galanos C. Fatty acid alterations and polymyxin B binding by lipopolysaccharides from *Pseudomonas aeruginosa* adapted to polymyxin B resistance. Antimicrob Agents Chemother. 1989;33:1724-1728.

186. Ernst RK, Yi EC, Guo L, et al. Specific lipopolysaccharide found in cystic fibrosis airway *Pseudomonas aeruginosa*. Science. 1999;286:1561-1565.

187. Kessler E, Safrin M, Abrams WR, et al. Inhibitors and specificity of *Pseudomonas aeruginosa* LasA. J Biol Chem. 1997;272:9884-9889.

188. Preston MJ, Seed PC, Toder DS, et al. Contribution of proteases and LasR to the virulence of *Pseudomonas aeruginosa* during corneal infections. Infect Immun. 1997;65:3086-3090.

189. Park PW, Pier GB, Preston MJ, et al. Syndecan-1 shedding is enhanced by LasA, a secreted virulence factor of *Pseudomonas aeruginosa*. J Biol Chem. 2000;275:3057-3062.

190. Park PW, Pier GB, Hinkes MT, et al. Exploitation of syndecan-1 shedding by *Pseudomonas aeruginosa* enhances virulence. Nature. 2001;411:98-102.

191. Engel LS, Hill JM, Caballero AR, et al. Protease IV, a unique extracellular protease and virulence factor from *Pseudomonas aeruginosa*. J Biol Chem. 1998;273:16792-16797.

192. Poole K, McKay GA. Iron acquisition and its control in *Pseudomonas aeruginosa*: Many roads lead to Rome. Front Biosci. 2003;8:d661-686.

193. Britigan BE, Rasmussen GT, Olakanmi O, et al. Iron acquisition from *Pseudomonas aeruginosa* siderophores by human phagocytes: An additional mechanism of host defense through iron sequestration? Infect Immun. 2000;68:1271-1275.

194. DeWitte JJ, Cox CD, Rasmussen GT, et al. Assessment of structural features of the *Pseudomonas* siderophore pyochelin required for its ability to promote oxidant-mediated endothelial cell injury. Arch Biochem Biophys. 2001;393:236-244.

195. Britigan BE, Rasmussen GT, Cox CD. *Pseudomonas* siderophore pyochelin enhances neutrophil-mediated endothelial cell injury. Am J Physiol. 1994;266:L192-L198.

196. Pastan I. Immunotoxins containing *Pseudomonas* exotoxin A: A short history. Cancer Immunol Immunother. 2003;52:338-341.

197. Holder IA, Neely AN, Frank DW. PcrV immunization enhances survival of burned *Pseudomonas aeruginosa*–infected mice. Infect Immun. 2001;69:5908-5910.

198. Hayashi T, Baba T, Matsumoto H, et al. Phage-conversion of cytotoxin production in *Pseudomonas aeruginosa*. Mol Microbiol. 1990;4:1703-1709.

199. Xiong G, Struckmeier M, Lutz F. Pore-forming *Pseudomonas aeruginosa* cytotoxin. Toxicology. 1994;87:69-83.

200. Sliwinski-Korell A, Engelhardt H, Kampka M, et al. Oligomerization and structural changes of the pore-forming *Pseudomonas aeruginosa* cytotoxin. Eur J Biochem. 1999;265:221-230.

201. Terada LS, Johansen KA, Nowbar S, et al. *Pseudomonas aeruginosa* hemolytic phospholipase C suppresses neutrophil respiratory burst activity. Infect Immun. 1999;67:2371-2376.

202. Luberto C, Stonehouse MJ, Collins EA, et al. Purification, characterization, and identification of a sphingomyelin synthase from *Pseudomonas aeruginosa*. PlcH is a multifunctional enzyme. J Biol Chem. 2003;278:32733-32743.

203. Wieland CW, Siegmund B, Senaldi G, et al. Pulmonary inflammation induced by *Pseudomonas aeruginosa* lipopolysaccharide, phospholipase C, and exotoxin A: Role of interferon regulatory factor 1. Infect Immun. 2002;70:1352-1358.

204. Ochsner UA, Snyder A, Vasil AI, et al. Effects of the twin-arginine translocase on secretion of virulence factors, stress response, and pathogenesis. Proc Natl Acad Sci USA. 2002;99:8312-8317.

205. Woods DE, Lam JS, Paranchych W, et al. Correlation of *Pseudomonas aeruginosa* virulence factors from clinical and environmental isolates with pathogenicity in the neutropenic mouse. Can J Microbiol. 1997;43.541-551.

206. McClure CD, Schiller NL. Effects of *Pseudomonas aeruginosa* rhamnolipids on human monocyte-derived macrophages. J Leukoc Biol. 1992;51:97-102.

207. Cosson P, Zulianello L, Join-Lambert O, et al. *Pseudomonas aeruginosa* virulence analyzed in a *Dictyostelium discoideum* host system. J Bacteriol. 2002;184:3027-3033.

208. Pearson JP, Pesci EC, Iglewski BH. Roles of *Pseudomonas aeruginosa* las and rhl quorum-sensing systems in control of elastase and rhamnolipid biosynthesis genes. J Bacteriol. 1997;179:5756-5767.

209. Frithz-Lindsten E, Holmstrom A, Jacobsson L, et al. Functional conservation of the effector protein translocators PopB/YopB and PopD/YopD of *Pseudomonas aeruginosa* and *Yersinia pseudotuberculosis*. Mol Microbiol. 1998;29:1155-1165.

210. Galan JE, Collmer A. Type III secretion machines: Bacterial devices for protein delivery into host cells. Science. 1999;284:1322-1328.

211. Hauser AR, Cobb E, Bodi M, et al. Type III protein secretion is associated with poor clinical outcomes in patients with ventilator-associated pneumonia caused by *Pseudomonas aeruginosa*. Crit Care Med. 2002;30:521-528.

212. Allmond LR, Karaca TJ, Nguyen VN, et al. Protein binding between PcrG-PcrV and PcrH-PopB/PopD encoded by the pcrGVH-popBD operon of the *Pseudomonas aeruginosa* type III secretion system. Infect Immun. 2003;71:2230-2233.

213. Fraylick JE, Riese MJ, Vincent TS, et al. ADP-ribosylation and functional effects of *Pseudomonas* exoenzyme S on cellular RalA. Biochemistry. 2002;41:9680-9687.

214. Rucks EA, Fraylick JE, Brandt LM, et al. Cell line differences in bacterially translocated ExoS ADP-ribosyltransferase substrate specificity. Microbiology. 2003;149:319-331.

215. Kaufman MR, Jia J, Zeng L, et al. *Pseudomonas aeruginosa* mediated apoptosis requires the ADP-ribosylating activity of exoS. Microbiology. 2000;146:2531-2541.

216. Krall R, Schmidt G, Aktories K, et al. *Pseudomonas aeruginosa* ExoT is a Rho GTPase-activating protein. Infect Immun. 2000;68:6066-6068.

217. Kazmierczak BI, Engel JN. *Pseudomonas aeruginosa* ExoT acts in vivo as a GTPase-activating protein for RhoA, Rac1, and Cdc42. Infect Immun. 2002;70:2198-2205.

218. Geiser TK, Kazmierczak BI, Garrity-Ryan LK, et al. *Pseudomonas aeruginosa* ExoT inhibits in vitro lung epithelial wound repair. Cell Microbiol. 2001;3:223-236.

219. Garrity-Ryan L, Kazmierczak B, Kowal R, et al. The arginine finger domain of ExoT contributes to actin cytoskeleton disruption and inhibition of internalization of *Pseudomonas aeruginosa* by epithelial cells and macrophages. Infect Immun. 2000;68:7100-7113.

220. Lee EJ, Cowell BA, Evans DJ, et al. Contribution of ExsA-regulated factors to corneal infection by cytotoxic and invasive *Pseudomonas aeruginosa* in a murine scarification model. Invest Ophthalmol Vis Sci. 2003;44:3892-3898.

221. Sato H, Frank DW, Hillard CJ, et al. The mechanism of action of the *Pseudomonas aeruginosa*-encoded type III cytotoxin, ExoU. EMBO J. 2003;22:2959-2969.

222. Phillips RM, Six DA, Dennis EA, et al. In vivo phospholipase activity of the *Pseudomonas aeruginosa* cytotoxin ExoU and protection of mammalian cells with phospholipase A2 inhibitors. J Biol Chem. 2003;278:41326-41332.

223. Finck-Barbancon V, Goranson J, Zhu L, et al. *ExoU* expression by *Pseudomonas aeruginosa* correlates with acute cytotoxicity and epithelial injury. Mol Microbiol. 1997;25:547-557.

224. Fleiszig SMJ, Wiener-Kronish JP, Miyazaki H, et al. *Pseudomonas aeruginosa*–mediated cytotoxicity and invasion correlate with distinct genotypes at the loci encoding exoenzyme S. Infect Immun. 1997;65:579-586.

225. Evans DJ, Frank DW, Finck-Barbançon V, et al. *Pseudomonas aeruginosa* invasion and cytotoxicity are independent events, both of which involve protein tyrosine kinase activity. Infect Immun. 1998;66:1453-1459.

226. Allewelt M, Coleman FT, Grout M, et al. Acquisition of expression of the *Pseudomonas aeruginosa* ExoU cytotoxin leads to increased bacterial virulence in a murine model of acute pneumonia and systemic spread. Infect Immun. 2000;68:3998-4004.

227. Sawa T, Ohara M, Kurahashi K, et al. In vitro cellular toxicity predicts *Pseudomonas aeruginosa* virulence in lung infections. Infect Immun. 1998;66:3242-3249.

228. McMorran B, Town L, Costelloe E, et al. Effector ExoU from the type III secretion system is an important modulator of gene expression in lung epithelial cells in response to *Pseudomonas aeruginosa* infection. Infect Immun. 2003;71:6035-6044.

229. Jacob T, Lee RJ, Engel JN, et al. Modulation of cytosolic Ca^{2+} concentration in airway epithelial cells by *Pseudomonas aeruginosa*. Infect Immun. 2002;70:6399-6408.

230. Wolfgang MC, Kulasekara BR, Liang X, et al. Conservation of genome content and virulence determinants among clinical and environmental isolates of *Pseudomonas aeruginosa*. Proc Natl Acad Sci USA. 2003;100:8484-8489.

231. Yahr TL, Vallis AJ, Hancock MK, et al. ExoY, an adenylate cyclase secreted by the *Pseudomonas aeruginosa* type III system. Proc Natl Acad Sci USA. 1998;95:13899-13904.

232. Vallis AJ, Yahr TL, Barbieri JT, et al. Regulation of ExoS production and secretion by *Pseudomonas aeruginosa* in response to tissue culture conditions. Infect Immun. 1999;67:914-920.

233. Yahr TL, Hovey AK, Kulich SM, et al. Transcriptional analysis of the *Pseudomonas aeruginosa* exoenzyme S structural gene. J Bacteriol. 1995;177:1169-1178.

234. Hovey AK, Frank DW. Analyses of the DNA-binding and transcriptional activation properties of ExsA, the transcriptional activator of the *Pseudomonas aeruginosa* exoenzyme S regulon. J Bacteriol. 1995;177:4427-4436.

235. Wolfgang MC, Lee VT, Gilmore ME, et al. Coordinate regulation of bacterial virulence genes by a novel adenylate cyclase–dependent signaling pathway. Dev Cell. 2003;4:253-263.

236. Britigan BE, Roeder TL, Rasmussen GT, et al. Interaction of the *Pseudomonas aeruginosa* secretory products pyocyanin and pyochelin generates hydroxyl radical and causes synergistic damage to endothelial cells—Implications for *Pseudomonas*-associated tissue injury. J Clin Invest. 1992;90:2187-2196.

237. Denning GM, Wollenweber LA, Railsback MA, et al. *Pseudomonas* pyocyanin increases interleukin-8 expression by human airway epithelial cells. Infect Immun. 1998;66:5777-5784.

238. Britigan BE, Railsback MA, Cox CD. The *Pseudomonas aeruginosa* secretory product pyocyanin inactivates alpha1 protease inhibitor: Implications for the pathogenesis of cystic fibrosis lung disease. Infect Immun. 1999;67:1207-1212.

239. Kamath JM, Britigan BE, Cox CD, et al. Pyocyanin from *Pseudomonas aeruginosa* inhibits prostacyclin release from endothelial cells. Infect Immun. 1995;63:4921-4923.

240. O'Malley YQ, Reszka KJ, Rasmussen GT, et al. The *Pseudomonas* secretory product pyocyanin inhibits catalase activity in human lung epithelial cells. Am J Physiol. 2003;285:L1077-L1086.

241. Suntres ZE, Omri A, Shek PN. *Pseudomonas aeruginosa*–induced lung injury: Role of oxidative stress. Microb Pathog. 2002;32:27-34.

242. Hassett DJ, Charniga L, Bean K, et al. Response of *Pseudomonas aeruginosa* to pyocyanin: Mechanisms of resistance, antioxidant defenses, and demonstration of a manganese-cofactored superoxide dismutase. Infect Immun. 1992;60:328-336.

243. Hassett DJ, Sokol PA, Howell ML, et al. Ferric uptake regulator (Fur) mutants of *Pseudomonas aeruginosa* demonstrate defective siderophore-mediated iron uptake, altered aerobic growth, and decreased superoxide dismutase and catalase activities. J Bacteriol. 1996;178:3996-4003.

244. Ochsner UA, Vasil ML, Alsabbagh E, et al. Role of the *Pseudomonas aeruginosa* oxyR-recG operon in oxidative stress defense and DNA repair: OxyR-dependent regulation of katB-ankB, ahpB, and ahpC-ahpF. J Bacteriol. 2000;182:4533-4544.

245. Kiratisin P, Tucker KD, Passador L. LasR, a transcriptional activator of *Pseudomonas aeruginosa* virulence genes, functions as a multimer. J Bacteriol. 2002;184:4912-4919.

246. Albus AM, Pesci EC, Runyen-Janecky LJ, et al. Vfr controls quorum sensing in *Pseudomonas aeruginosa*. J Bacteriol. 1997;179:3928-3935.

247. Wagner VE, Bushnell D, Passador L, et al. Microarray analysis of *Pseudomonas aeruginosa* quorum-sensing regulons: Effects of growth phase and environment. J Bacteriol. 2003;185:2080-2095.

248. Schuster M, Lostroh CP, Ogi T, et al. Identification, timing, and signal specificity of *Pseudomonas aeruginosa* quorum-controlled genes: A transcriptome analysis. J Bacteriol. 2003;185:2066-2079.

249. Hentzer M, Wu H, Andersen JB, et al. Attenuation of *Pseudomonas aeruginosa* virulence by quorum sensing inhibitors. EMBO J. 2003;22:3803-3815.

250. Rumbaugh KP, Griswold JA, Iglewski BH, et al. Contribution of quorum sensing to the virulence of *Pseudomonas aeruginosa* in burn wound infections. Infect Immun. 1999;67:5854-5862.

251. Pearson JP, Feldman M, Iglewski BH, et al. *Pseudomonas aeruginosa* cell-to-cell signaling is required for virulence in a model of acute pulmonary infection. Infect Immun. 2000;68:4331-4334.

252. Wu H, Song Z, Givskov M, et al. *Pseudomonas aeruginosa* mutations in lasI and rhlI quorum sensing systems result in milder chronic lung infection. Microbiology. 2001;147:1105-1113.

253. Cabrol S, Olliver A, Pier G, et al. Transcription of quorum-sensing system genes in clinical and environmental isolates of *Pseudomonas aeruginosa*. J Bacteriol. 2003;185:7222-7230.

254. Smith R, Iglewski B. *Pseudomonas aeruginosa* quorum sensing as a potential antimicrobial target. J Clin Invest. 2003;112:1460-1465.

255. Storey DG, Ujack EE, Rabin HR, et al. *Pseudomonas aeruginosa* lasR transcription correlates with the transcription of lasA, lasB, and toxA in chronic lung infections associated with cystic fibrosis. Infect Immun. 1998;66:2521-2528.

256. Singh PK, Schaefer AL, Parsek MR, et al. Quorum-sensing signals indicate that cystic fibrosis lungs are infected with bacterial biofilms. Nature. 2000;407:762-764.

257. Geisenberger O, Givskov M, Riedel K, et al. Production of *N*-acyl-L-homoserine lactones by *P. aeruginosa* isolates from chronic lung infections associated with cystic fibrosis. FEMS Microbiol Lett. 2000;184:273-278.

258. Erickson DL, Endersby R, Kirkham A, et al. *Pseudomonas aeruginosa* quorum-sensing systems may control virulence factor expression in the lungs of patients with cystic fibrosis. Infect Immun. 2002;70:1783-1790.

259. Donlan RM, Costerton JW. Biofilms: survival mechanisms of clinically relevant microorganisms. Clin Microbiol Rev. 2002;15:167-193.

260. Parsek MR, Singh PK. Bacterial biofilms: An emerging link to disease pathogenesis. Annu Rev Microbiol. 2003;57:677-701.

261. Davies DG, Parsek MR, Pearson JP, et al. The involvement of cell-to-cell signals in the development of a bacterial biofilm. Science. 1998;280:295-298.

262. Wozniak DJ, Wyckoff TJ, Starkey M, et al. Alginate is not a significant component of the extracellular polysaccharide matrix of PA14 and PAO1 *Pseudomonas aeruginosa* biofilms. Proc Natl Acad Sci USA. 2003;100:7907-7912.

263. Whitchurch CB, Tolker-Nielsen T, Ragas PC, et al. Extracellular DNA required for bacterial biofilm formation. Science. 2002;295:1487.

264. Costerton W, Veeh R, Shirtliff M, et al. The application of biofilm science to the study and control of chronic bacterial infections. J Clin Invest. 2003;112:1466-1477.

265. De Kievit TR, Iglewski BH. Quorum sensing, gene expression, and *Pseudomonas* biofilms. Methods Enzymol. 1999;310:117-128.

266. Parad RB, Gerard CJ, Zurakowski D, et al. Pulmonary outcome in cystic fibrosis is influenced primarily by mucoid *Pseudomonas aeruginosa* infection and immune status and only modestly by genotype. Infect Immun. 1999;67:4744-4750.

267. Pedersen SS, Hoiby N, Espersen F, et al. Role of alginate in infection with mucoid *Pseudomonas aeruginosa* in cystic fibrosis. Thorax. 1992;47:6-13.

268. Demko CA, Byard PJ, Davis PB. Gender differences in cystic fibrosis: *Pseudomonas aeruginosa* infection. J Clin Epidemiol. 1995;48:1041-1049.

269. Garau J, Gomez L. *Pseudomonas aeruginosa* pneumonia. Curr Opin Infect Dis. 2003;16:135-143.

270. Valles J, Mesalles E, Mariscal D, et al. A 7-year study of severe hospital-acquired pneumonia requiring ICU admission. Intensive Care Med. 2003;29:1981-1988.

271. Pitt PL, MacDougall J, Penketh ARL, et al. Polyagglutinating and non-typable strains of *Pseudomonas aeruginosa* in cystic fibrosis. J Med Microbiol. 1986;21:179-186.

272. Hancock REW, Mutharia LM, Chan L, et al. *Pseudomonas aeruginosa* isolates from patients with cystic fibrosis: A class of serum-sensitive, nontypable strains deficient in lipopolysaccharide O side-chains. Infect Immun. 1983;42:170-177.

273. Hirakata Y, Finlay BB, Simpson DA, et al. Penetration of clinical isolates of *Pseudomonas aeruginosa* through MDCK epithelial cell monolayers. J Infect Dis. 2000;181:765-769.

274. Govan JRW, Deretic V. Microbial pathogenesis in cystic fibrosis: mucoid *Pseudomonas aeruginosa* and *Burkholderia cepacia*. Microbiol Rev. 1996;60:539-574.

275. Pier GB, Coleman F, Grout M, et al. Role of alginate O acetylation in resistance of mucoid *Pseudomonas aeruginosa* to opsonic phagocytosis. Infect Immun. 2001;69:1895-1901.

276. Coleman FT, Mueschenborn S, Meluleni G, et al. Hypersusceptibility of cystic fibrosis mice to chronic *Pseudomonas aeruginosa* oropharyngeal colonization and lung infection. Proc Natl Acad Sci USA. 2003;100:1949-1954.

277. Pier GB, Saunders JM, Ames P, et al. Opsonophagocytic killing antibody to *Pseudomonas aeruginosa* mucoid exopolysaccharide in older, non-colonized cystic fibrosis patients. N Engl J Med. 1987;317:793-798.

278. Pier GB, Small GJ, Warren HB. Protection against mucoid *Pseudomonas aeruginosa* in rodent models of endobronchial infection. Science. 1990;249:537-540.

279. Meluleni GJ, Grout M, Evans DJ, et al. Mucoid *Pseudomonas aeruginosa* growing in a biofilm in vitro are killed by opsonic antibodies to the mucoid exopolysaccharide capsule but not by antibodies produced during chronic lung infection in cystic fibrosis patients. J Immunol. 1995;155:2029-2038.

280. Johnson C, Butler SM, Konstan MW, et al. Factors influencing outcomes in cystic fibrosis: A center-based analysis. Chest. 2003;123:20-27.

281. Kurahashi K, Kajikawa O, Sawa T, et al. Pathogenesis of septic shock in *Pseudomonas aeruginosa* pneumonia. J Clin Invest. 1999;104:743-750.

282. Price BM, Barten Legutki J, Galloway DR, et al. Enhancement of the protective efficacy of an oprF DNA vaccine against *Pseudomonas aeruginosa*. FEMS Immunol Med Microbiol. 2002;33:89-99.

283. von Specht BU, Lucking HC, Blum B, et al. Safety and immunogenicity of a *Pseudomonas aeruginosa* outer membrane protein I vaccine in human volunteers. Vaccine. 1996;14:1111-1117.

284. Rotering H, Dorner F. Studies on a *Pseudomonas aeruginosa* flagella vaccine. Antibiot Chemother. 1989;42:218-228.

285. Doring G, Dorner F. A multicenter vaccine trial using the *Pseudomonas aeruginosa* flagella vaccine IMMUNO in patients with cystic fibrosis. Behring Inst Mitt. 1997:338-344.
286. Frank DW, Vallis A, Wiener-Kronish JP, et al. Generation and characterization of a protective monoclonal antibody to *Pseudomonas aeruginosa* PcrV. J Infect Dis. 2002;186:64-73.
287. Sawa T, Yahr TL, Ohara M, et al. Active and passive immunization with the *Pseudomonas* V antigen protects against type III intoxication and lung injury. Nat Med. 1999;5:392-398.
288. Priebe GP, Meluleni GJ, Coleman FT, et al. Protection against fatal *Pseudomonas aeruginosa* pneumonia in mice after nasal immunization with a live, attenuated *aroA* deletion mutant. Infect Immun. 2003;71:1453-1461.
289. Priebe GP, Brinig MM, Hatano K, et al. Construction and characterization of a live, attenuated *aroA* deletion mutant of *Pseudomonas aeruginosa* as a candidate intranasal vaccine. Infect Immun. 2002;70:1507-1517.
290. Nicotra MB, Rivera M, Dale AM, et al. Clinical, pathophysiologic, and microbiologic characterization of bronchiectasis in an aging cohort. Chest. 1995;108:955-961.
291. Yanagihara K, Kadoto J, Kohno S. Diffuse panbronchiolitis—Pathophysiology and treatment mechanisms. Int J Antimicrob Agents. 2001;18(Suppl 1):S83-S87.
292. Whitecar JP Jr, Luna M, Bodey GP. *Pseudomonas* bacteremia in patients with malignant diseases. Am J Med Sci. 1970;60:216-223.
293. Fishman LS, Armstrong D. *Pseudomonas aeruginosa* bacteremia in patients with neoplastic disease. Cancer. 1972;30:764-773.
294. Gallagher PG, Watanakunakorn C. *Pseudomonas* bacteremia in a community teaching hospital, 1980-1984. Rev Infect Dis. 1989;11:846-852.
295. Bodey GP, Jadeja L, Elting L. Pseudomonas bacteremia. Retrospective analysis of 410 episodes. Arch Intern Med. 1985;145:1621-1629.
296. Maschmeyer G, Braveny I. Review of the incidence and prognosis of *Pseudomonas aeruginosa* infections in cancer patients in the 1990s. Eur J Clin Microbiol Infect Dis. 2000;19:915-925.
297. Kang CI, Kim SH, Kim HB, et al. *Pseudomonas aeruginosa* bacteremia: Risk factors for mortality and influence of delayed receipt of effective antimicrobial therapy on clinical outcome. Clin Infect Dis. 2003;37:745-751.
298. Blot S, Vandewoude K, Hoste E, et al. Reappraisal of attributable mortality in critically ill patients with nosocomial bacteraemia involving *Pseudomonas aeruginosa.* J Hosp Infect. 2003;53:18-24.
299. Gales AC, Jones RN, Turnidge J, et al. Characterization of *Pseudomonas aeruginosa* isolates: Occurrence rates, antimicrobial susceptibility patterns, and molecular typing in the global SENTRY Antimicrobial Surveillance Program, 1997-1999. Clin Infect Dis. 2001;32 Suppl 2:S146-155.
300. Gang RK, Bang RL, Sanyal SC, et al. *Pseudomonas* septicaemia in burns. Burns. 1999;25:611-616.
301. Mayhall CG. The epidemiology of burn wound infections: Then and now. Clin Infect Dis. 2003;37:543-550.
302. Fine JD, Miller JA, Harrist TJ, et al. Cutaneous lesions in disseminated candidiasis mimicking ecthyma gangrenosum. Am J Med. 1981;70:1133-1135.
303. Prins C, Chavaz P, Tamm K, et al. Ecthyma gangrenosum-like lesions: A sign of disseminated *Fusarium* infection in the neutropenic patient. Clin Exp Dermatol. 1995;20:428-430.
304. Tacconelli E, Tumbarello M, Bertagnolio S, et al. Multidrug-resistant *Pseudomonas aeruginosa* bloodstream infections: Analysis of trends in prevalence and epidemiology. Emerg Infect Dis. 2002;8:220-221.
305. Linden PK, Kusne S, Coley K, et al. Use of parenteral colistin for the treatment of serious infection due to antimicrobial-resistant *Pseudomonas aeruginosa.* Clin Infect Dis. 2003;37:e154-160.
306. Bodey GP, Whitecar JP Jr, Middleman E, et al. Carbenicillin therapy for pseudomonas infections. JAMA. 1971;218:62-66.
307. Schimpff S, Satterlee W, Young VM, et al. Empiric therapy with carbenicillin and gentamicin for febrile patients with cancer and granulocytopenia. N Engl J Med. 1971;284:1061-1065.
308. Andriole VT. Synergy of carbenicillin and gentamicin in experimental infection with *Pseudomonas,* J Infect Dis. 1971;124(Suppl 124):146-125.
309. Saslaw S, Carlisle HN, Moheimani M. Comparison of gentamicin, carbenicillin and gentamicin, and carbenicillin in *Pseudomonas* sepsis in monkeys. Antimicrob Agents Chemother. 1973;3:274-278.
310. Scott RE, Robson HG. Synergistic activity of carbenicillin and gentamicin in experimental *Pseudomonas* bacteremia in neutropenic rats. Antimicrob Agents Chemother. 1976;10:646-651.
311. Holmes KK, Clark H, Silverblatt F, et al. Emergence of resistance in *Pseudomonas* during carbenicillin therapy. Antimicrobial Agents Chemother. 1969;9:391-397.
312. Darrell JH, Waterworth PM. Carbenicillin resistance in *Pseudomonas aeruginosa* from clinical material. Br Med J. 1969;3:141-143.
313. Klastersky J, Zinner SH. Synergistic combinations of antibiotics in gram-negative bacillary infections. Rev Infect Dis. 1982;4:294-301.
314. De Jongh CA, Joshi JH, Newman KA, et al. Antibiotic synergism and response in gram-negative bacteremia in granulocytopenic cancer patients. Am J Med. 1986;80:96-100.
315. Verhagen C, de Pauw BE, Donnelly JP, et al. Ceftazidime alone for treating *Pseudomonas aeruginosa* septicaemia in neutropenic patients. J Infect. 1986;13:125-131.
316. Hilf M, Yu VL, Sharp J, et al. Antibiotic therapy for *Pseudomonas aeruginosa* bacteremia: Outcome correlations in a prospective study of 200 patients. Am J Med. 1989;87:540-546.
317. Vidal F, Mensa J, Almela M, et al. Epidemiology and outcome of *Pseudomonas aeruginosa* bacteremia, with special emphasis on the influence of antibiotic treatment. Analysis of 189 episodes. Arch Intern Med. 1996;156:2121-2126.
318. Kuikka A, Valtonen VV. Factors associated with improved outcome of *Pseudomonas aeruginosa* bacteremia in a Finnish university hospital. Eur J Clin Microbiol Infect Dis. 1998;17:701-708.
319. Siegman-Igra Y, Ravona R, Primerman H, et al. *Pseudomonas aeruginosa* bacteremia: An analysis of 123 episodes, with particular emphasis on the effect of antibiotic therapy. Int J Infect Dis. 1998;2:211-215.
320. Chamot E, Boffi El Amari E, Rohner P, et al. Effectiveness of combination antimicrobial therapy for *Pseudomonas aeruginosa* bacteremia. Antimicrob Agents Chemother. 2003;47:2756-2764.
321. Hughes WT, Armstrong D, Bodey GP, et al. 2002 guidelines for the use of antimicrobial agents in neutropenic patients with cancer. Clin Infect Dis. 2002;34:730-751.
322. Craig W. Pharmacodynamics of antimicrobial agents as a basis for determining dosage regimens. Eur J Clin Microbiol Infect Dis. 1993;12(Suppl 1):S6-S8.
323. Kim MK, Capitano B, Mattoes HM, et al. Pharmacokinetic and pharmacodynamic evaluation of two dosing regimens for piperacillin-tazobactam. Pharmacotherapy. 2002;22:569-577.
324. Dudley MN, Zinner SH. Single daily dosing of amikacin in an in-vitro model. J Antimicrob Chemother. 1991;27(Suppl C):15-19.
325. Hansen M, Christrup LL, Jarlov JO, et al. Gentamicin dosing in critically ill patients. Acta Anaesthesiol Scand. 2001;45:734-740.
326. Barriere SL. Bacterial resistance to beta-lactams, and its prevention with combination antimicrobial therapy. Pharmacotherapy. 1992;12:397-402.
327. Cometta A, Baumgartner JD, Lew D, et al. Prospective randomized comparison of imipenem monotherapy with imipenem plus netilmicin for treatment of severe infections in nonneutropenic patients. Antimicrob Agents Chemother. 1994;38:1309-1313.
328. Elting LS, Rubenstein EB, Rolston KV, et al. Outcomes of bacteremia in patients with cancer and neutropenia: Observations from two decades of epidemiological and clinical trials. Clin Infect Dis. 1997;25:247-259.
329. Chastre J, Fagon JY. Ventilator-associated pneumonia. Am J Respir Crit Care Med. 2002;165:867-903.
330. Shepp DH, Tang IT, Ramundo MB, et al. Serious *Pseudomonas aeruginosa* infection in AIDS. J Acquir Immune Defic Syndr. 1994;7:823-831.
331. Schuster MG, Norris AH. Community-acquired *Pseudomonas aeruginosa* pneumonia in patients with HIV infection. AIDS. 1994;8:1437-1441.
332. Valdivieso M, Gil-extremera B, Zornoza J, et al. Gram-negative bacillary pneumonia in the compromised host. Medicine (Baltimore). 1977;56:241-254.
333. Hatchette TF, Gupta R, Marrie TJ. *Pseudomonas aeruginosa* community-acquired pneumonia in previously healthy adults: Case report and review of the literature. Clin Infect Dis. 2000;31:1349-1356.
334. Arancibia F, Bauer TT, Ewig S, et al. Community-acquired pneumonia due to gram-negative bacteria and *Pseudomonas aeruginosa:* Incidence, risk, and prognosis. Arch Intern Med. 2002;162:1849-1858.
335. Tillotson JR, Lerner AM. Characteristics of nonbacteremic *Pseudomonas* pneumonia. Ann Intern Med. 1968;68:295-307.
336. Crnich CJ, Gordon B, Andes D. Hot tub–associated necrotizing pneumonia due to *Pseudomonas aeruginosa.* Clin Infect Dis. 2003;36:e55-e57.
337. Fagon JY, Chastre J, Hance AJ, et al. Nosocomial pneumonia in ventilated patients: A cohort study evaluating attributable mortality and hospital stay. Am J Med. 1993;94:281-288.
338. Carratala J, Roson B, Fernandez-Sevilla A, et al. Bacteremic pneumonia in neutropenic patients with cancer: Causes, empirical antibiotic therapy, and outcome. Arch Intern Med. 1998;158:868-872.
339. Odio W, Van Laer E, Klastersky J. Concentrations of gentamicin in bronchial secretions after intramuscular and endotracheal administration. J Clin Pharmacol. 1975;15:518-524.
340. Bryant RE, Hammond D. Interaction of purulent material with antibiotics used to treat *Pseudomonas* infections. Antimicrob Agents Chemother. 1974;6:702-707.
341. Ramphal R, Lhermitte M, Filliat M, et al. The binding of anti-pseudomonal antibiotics to macromolecules from cystic fibrosis sputum. J Antimicrob Chemother. 1988;22:483-490.
342. Le Conte P, Potel G, Peltier P, et al. Lung distribution and pharmacokinetics of aerosolized tobramycin. Am Rev Respir Dis. 1993;147:1279-1282.
343. Palmer LB, Smaldone GC, Simon SR, et al. Aerosolized antibiotics in mechanically ventilated patients: Delivery and response. Crit Care Med. 1998;26:31-39.
344. Barker AF, Couch L, Fiel SB, et al. Tobramycin solution for inhalation reduces sputum *Pseudomonas aeruginosa* density in bronchiectasis. Am J Respir Crit Care Med. 2000;162:481-485.
345. Fink MP, Snydman DR, Niederman MS, et al. Treatment of severe pneumonia in hospitalized patients: Results of a multicenter, randomized, double-blind trial comparing intravenous ciprofloxacin with imipenem-cilastatin. The Severe Pneumonia Study Group. Antimicrob Agents Chemother. 1994;38:547-557.
346. Torres A, Bauer TT, Leon-Gil C, et al. Treatment of severe nosocomial pneumonia: A prospective randomised comparison of intravenous ciprofloxacin with imipenem/cilastatin. Thorax. 2000;55:1033-1039.
347. Ohno A, Miyazaki S, Tateda K, et al. [The study of pathogenic mechanisms of chronic *Pseudomonas aeruginosa* lung infections by mucoid strains]. Kansenshogaku Zasshi. 1992;66:407-415.
348. Kadota J, Mukae H, Ishii H, et al. Long-term efficacy and safety of clarithromycin treatment in patients with diffuse panbronchiolitis. Respir Med. 2003;97:844-850.
349. Jaffe A, Bush A. Anti-inflammatory effects of macrolides in lung disease. Pediatr Pulmonol. 2001;31:464-473.

350. Pechere JC. Azithromycin reduces the production of virulence factors in *Pseudomonas aeruginosa* by inhibiting quorum sensing. Jpn J Antibiot. 2001; 54(Suppl C):87-89.

351. Sapico FL, Montgomerie JZ. Vertebral osteomyelitis in intravenous drug abusers: Report of three cases and review of the literature. Rev Infect Dis. 1980;2:196-206.

352. Bayer AS, Chow AW, Louie JS, et al. Sternoarticular pyoarthrosis due to gram-negative bacilli. Report of eight cases. Arch Intern Med. 1977;137:1036-1040.

353. Sapico FL. Microbiology and antimicrobial therapy of spinal infections. Orthop Clin North Am. 1996;27:9-13.

354. Ross JJ, Hu LT. Septic arthritis of the pubic symphysis: Review of 100 cases. Medicine (Baltimore). 2003;82:340-345.

355. Lang AG, Peterson HA. Osteomyelitis following puncture wounds of the foot in children. J Trauma. 1976;16:993-999.

356. Fisher MC, Goldsmith JF, Gilligan PH. Sneakers as a source of *Pseudomonas aeruginosa* in children with osteomyelitis following puncture wounds. J Pediatr. 1985;106:607-609.

357. Siebert WT, Dewan S, Williams TW Jr. Case report. *Pseudomonas* puncture wound osteomyelitis in adults. Am J Med Sci. 1982;283:83-88.

358. Lau LS, Bin G, Jaovisidua S, et al. Cost effectiveness of magnetic resonance imaging in diagnosing *Pseudomonas aeruginosa* infection after puncture wound. J Foot Ankle Surg. 1997;36:36-43.

359. Crosby LA, Powell DA. The potential value of the sedimentation rate in monitoring treatment outcome in puncture-wound-related *Pseudomonas* osteomyelitis. Clin Orthop. 1984;September:168-172.

360. Livesley NJ, Chow AW. Infected pressure ulcers in elderly individuals. Clin Infect Dis. 2002;35:1390-1396.

361. Bach MC, Cocchetto DM. Ceftazidime as single-agent therapy for gram-negative aerobic bacillary osteomyelitis. Antimicrob Agents Chemother. 1987;31:1605-1608.

362. Hessen MT, Ingerman MJ, Kaufman DH, et al. Clinical efficacy of ciprofloxacin therapy for gram-negative bacillary osteomyelitis. Am J Med. 1987;82:262-265.

363. Norrby SR. Ciprofloxacin in the treatment of acute and chronic osteomyelitis: A review. Scand J Infect Dis Suppl. 1986;60:74-78.

364. Gentry LO, Rodriguez GG. Oral ciprofloxacin compared with parenteral antibiotics in the treatment of osteomyelitis. Antimicrob Agents Chemother. 1990;34:40-43.

365. Galanakis N, Giamarellou H, Moussas T, et al. Chronic osteomyelitis caused by multi-resistant gram-negative bacilli: Evaluation of treatment with newer quinolones after prolonged follow-up. J Antimicrob Chemother. 1997;39:241-246.

366. Fong IW, Ledbetter WH, Vandenbroucke AC, et al. Ciprofloxacin concentrations in bone and muscle after oral dosing. Antimicrob Agents Chemother. 1986;29:405-408.

367. Wise BL, Mathis JL, Jawetz E. Infections of the central nervous system due to *Pseudomonas aeruginosa*. J Neurosurg. 1969;31:432-434.

368. Marone P, Concia E, Maserati R, et al. Ceftazidime in the therapy of pseudomonal meningitis. Chemioterapia. 1985;4:289-292.

369. Fong IW, Tomkins KB. Review of *Pseudomonas aeruginosa* meningitis with special emphasis on treatment with ceftazidime. Rev Infect Dis. 1985;7:604-612.

370. Rodriguez WJ, Khan WN, Cocchetto DM, et al. Treatment of *Pseudomonas* meningitis with ceftazidime with or without concurrent therapy. Pediatr Infect Dis J. 1990;9:83-87.

371. Wong-Beringer A, Beringer P, Lovett MA. Successful treatment of multidrug-resistant *Pseudomonas aeruginosa* meningitis with high-dose ciprofloxacin. Clin Infect Dis. 1997;25:936-937.

372. Baum J, Barza M. *Pseudomonas* keratitis and extended-wear soft contact lenses. Arch Ophthalmol. 1990;108:663-664.

373. Wang AG, Wu CC, Liu JH. Bacterial corneal ulcer: A multivariate study. Ophthalmologica. 1998;212:126-132.

374. Smulders C, Brink H, Wanten G, et al. Conjunctival and corneal colonization by *Pseudomonas aeruginosa* in mechanically ventilated patients. A prospective study. Neth J Med. 1999;55:106-109.

375. Aguilar HE, Meredith TA, Shaarawy A, et al. Vitreous cavity penetration of ceftazidime after intravenous administration. Retina. 1995;15:154-159.

376. Atkins MC, Harrison GA, Lucas GS. *Pseudomonas aeruginosa* orbital cellulitis in four neutropenic patients. J Hosp Infect. 1990;16:343-349.

377. Lattman J, Massry GG, Hornblass A. Pseudomonal eyelid necrosis: Clinical characteristics and review of the literature. Ophthal Plast Reconstr Surg. 1998;14:290-294.

378. Reid TM, Porter IA. An outbreak of otitis externa in competitive swimmers due to *Pseudomonas aeruginosa*. J Hyg (Lond). 1981;86:357-362.

379. Chandler JR. Malignant external otitis. Laryngoscope. 1968;78:1257-1294.

380. Hern JD, Almeyda J, Thomas DM, et al. Malignant otitis externa in HIV and AIDS. J Laryngol Otol. 1996;110:770-775.

381. Ress BD, Luntz M, Telischi FF, et al. Necrotizing external otitis in patients with AIDS. Laryngoscope. 1997;107:456-460.

382. Rubin J, Yu VL. Malignant external otitis: Insights into pathogenesis, clinical manifestations, diagnosis, and therapy. Am J Med. 1988;85:391-398.

383. Bellini C, Antonini P, Ermanni S, et al. Malignant otitis externa due to *Aspergillus niger*. Scand J Infect Dis. 2003;35:284-288.

384. Keay DG, Murray JA. Malignant otitis externa due to *Staphylococcus* infection. J Laryngol Otol. 1988;102:926-927.

385. Parisier SC, Lucente FE, Som PM, et al. Nuclear scanning in necrotizing progressive "malignant" external otitis. Laryngoscope. 1982;92:1016-1019.

386. Lang R, Goshen S, Kitzes-Cohen R, et al. Successful treatment of malignant external otitis with oral ciprofloxacin: Report of experience with 23 patients. J Infect Dis. 1990;161:537-540.

387. Fradis M, Brodsky A, Ben-David J, et al. Chronic otitis media treated topically with ciprofloxacin or tobramycin. Arch Otolaryngol Head Neck Surg. 1997;123:1057-1060.

388. Alper CM, Dohar JE, Gulhan M, et al. Treatment of chronic suppurative otitis media with topical tobramycin and dexamethasone. Arch Otolaryngol Head Neck Surg. 2000;126:165-173.

389. Miro N. Controlled multicenter study on chronic suppurative otitis media treated with topical applications of ciprofloxacin 0.2% solution in single-dose containers or combination of polymyxin B, neomycin, and hydrocortisone suspension. Otolaryngol Head Neck Surg. 2000;123:617-623.

390. Somekh E, Cordova Z. Ceftazidime versus aztreonam in the treatment of pseudomonal chronic suppurative otitis media in children. Scand J Infect Dis. 2000;32:197-199.

391. Johnson MP, Ramphal R. Malignant external otitis: Report on therapy with ceftazidime and review of therapy and prognosis. Rev Infect Dis. 1990;12:173-180.

392. Stokkel MP, Boot CN, van Eck-Smit BL. SPECT gallium scintigraphy in malignant external otitis: Initial staging and follow-up. Case reports. Laryngoscope. 1996;106:338-340.

393. Berenholz L, Katzenell U, Harell M. Evolving resistant pseudomonas to ciprofloxacin in malignant otitis externa. Laryngoscope. 2002;112:1619-1622.

394. Davis JC, Gates GA, Lerner C, et al. Adjuvant hyperbaric oxygen in malignant external otitis. Arch Otolaryngol Head Neck Surg. 1992;118:89-93.

395. Montgomerie JZ, Guerra DA, Schick DG, et al. *Pseudomonas* urinary tract infection in patients with spinal cord injury. J Am Paraplegia Soc. 1989;12:8-10.

396. Mocan H, Karaguzel G. Community-acquired *Pseudomonas aeruginosa* urinary tract infection in young children. Pediatr Nephrol. 1997;11:784-785.

397. Greene SL, Su WP, Muller SA. Ecthyma gangrenosum: Report of clinical, histopathologic, and bacteriologic aspects of eight cases. J Am Acad Dermatol. 1984;11:781-787.

398. Huminer D, Siegman-Igra Y, Morduchowicz G, et al. Ecthyma gangrenosum without bacteremia. Report of six cases and review of the literature. Arch Intern Med. 1987;147:299-301.

399. Greene SL, Su WP, Muller SA. *Pseudomonas aeruginosa* infections of the skin. Am Fam Physician. 1984;29:193-200.

400. Alomar A, Ausina V, Vernis J, et al. *Pseudomonas* folliculitis. Cutis. 1982;30:405-409.

401. Berger RS, Seifert MR. Whirlpool folliculitis: A review of its cause, treatment, and prevention. Cutis. 1990;45:97-98.

402. el Baze P, Thyss A, Caldani C, et al. *Pseudomonas aeruginosa* O-11 folliculitis. Development into ecthyma gangrenosum in immunosuppressed patients. Arch Dermatol. 1985;121:873-876.

403. Meislich D, Long SS. Invasive *Pseudomonas* infection in two healthy children following prolonged bathing. Am J Dis Child. 1993;147:18-20.

404. McManus AT, Mason AD Jr, McManus WF, et al. Twenty-five year review of *Pseudomonas aeruginosa* bacteremia in a burn center. Eur J Clin Microbiol. 1985;4:219-223.

405. Shankowsky HA, Callioux LS, Tredget EE. North American survey of hydrotherapy in modern burn care. J Burn Care Rehabil. 1994;15:143-146.

406. Vistnes LM, Hogg GR. The burn eschar. A histopathological study. Plast Reconstr Surg. 1971;48:56-60.

407. Chen J, Zhou YP, Rong XZ. An experimental study on systemic inflammatory response syndrome induced by subeschar tissue fluid. Burns. 2000;26:149-155.

408. Dhennin C, Vesin L, Feauveaux JF, et al. [Ceftazidime in severe infections in burnt patients]. Presse Med. 1988;17:1940-1943.

409. Richard P, Le Floch R, Chamoux C, et al. *Pseudomonas aeruginosa* outbreak in a burn unit: role of antimicrobials in the emergence of multiply resistant strains. J Infect Dis. 1994;170:377-383.

410. Culbertson GR, McManus AT, Conarro PA, et al. Clinical trial of imipenem/cilastatin in severely burned and infected patients. Surg Gynecol Obstet. 1987;165:25-28.

411. Monafo WW, West MA. Current treatment recommendations for topical burn therapy. Drugs. 1990;40:364-373.

412. Reyes MP, Lerner AM. *Pseudomonas* endocarditis. JAMA. 1979;241:1576.

413. Rajashekaraiah KR, Rice TW, Kallick CA. Recovery of *Pseudomonas aeruginosa* from syringes of drug addicts with endocarditis. J Infect Dis. 1981;144:482.

414. Shekar R, Rice TW, Zierdt CH, et al. Outbreak of endocarditis caused by *Pseudomonas aeruginosa* serotype O11 among pentazocine and tripelennamine abusers in Chicago. J Infect Dis. 1985;151:203-208.

415. Bayer AS, Norman D, Kim KS. Efficacy of amikacin and ceftazidime in experimental aortic valve endocarditis due to *Pseudomonas aeruginosa*. Antimicrob Agents Chemother. 1985;28:781-785.

416. Cabinian AE, Kaatz GW. Successful therapy of *Pseudomonas aeruginosa* endocarditis with ceftazidime and tobramycin. Am J Med. 1987;83:366-367.

417. Letendre ED, Mantha R, Turgeon PL. Selection of resistance by piperacillin during *Pseudomonas aeruginosa* endocarditis. J Antimicrob Chemother. 1988;22:557-562.

418. Jimenez-Lucho VE, Saravolatz LD, Medeiros AA, et al. Failure of therapy in pseudomonas endocarditis: Selection of resistant mutants. J Infect Dis. 1986;154:64-68.

419. Yu VL, Zuravleff JJ, Peacock JE, et al. Addition of rifampin to carboxypenicillin-aminoglycoside combination for the treatment of *Pseudomonas aeruginosa* infection: Clinical experience with four patients. Antimicrob Agents Chemother. 1984;26:575-577.

420. Gavin PJ, Suseno MT, Cook FV, et al. Left-sided endocarditis caused by *Pseudomonas aeruginosa*: Successful treatment with meropenem and tobramycin. Diagn Microbiol Infect Dis. 2003;47:427-430.

421. Thauvin C, Lecomte F, Le Boete I, et al. Efficacy of ciprofloxacin alone and in combination with azlocillin in experimental endocarditis due to *Pseudomonas aeruginosa*. Infection. 1989;17:31-34.

422. Uzun O, Akalin HE, Unal S, et al. Long-term oral ciprofloxacin in the treatment of prosthetic valve endocarditis due to *Pseudomonas aeruginosa*. Scand J Infect Dis. 1992;24:797-800.

423. Arbulu A, Holmes RJ, Asfaw I. Surgical treatment of intractable right-sided infective endocarditis in drug addicts: 25 years experience. J Heart Valve Dis. 1993;2:129-137; discussion 138-129.

424. Komshian SV, Tablan OC, Palutke W, et al. Characteristics of left-sided endocarditis due to *Pseudomonas aeruginosa* in the Detroit Medical Center. Rev Infect Dis. 1990;12:693-702.

425. Raje NS, Rao SR, Iyer RS, et al. Infection analysis in acute lymphoblastic leukemia: A report of 499 consecutive episodes in India. Pediatr Hematol Oncol. 1994;11:271-280.

426. Karim M, Khan W, Farooqi B, et al. Bacterial isolates in neutropenic febrile patients. J Pak Med Assoc. 1991;41:35-37.

427. Yoshida M, Tsubaki K, Kobayashi T, et al. Infectious complications during remission induction therapy in 577 patients with acute myeloid leukemia in the Japan Adult Leukemia Study Group studies between 1987 and 1991. Int J Hematol. 1999; 70:261-267.

428. Mendelson MH, Gurtman A, Szabo S, et al. *Pseudomonas aeruginosa* bacteremia in patients with AIDS. Clin Infect Dis. 1994;18:886-895.

429. Manfredi R, Nanetti A, Ferri M, et al. *Pseudomonas* spp. complications in patients with HIV disease: An eight-year clinical and microbiological survey. Eur J Epidemiol. 2000;16:111-118.

430. el Baze P, Thyss A, Vinti H, et al. A study of nineteen immunocompromised patients with extensive skin lesions caused by *Pseudomonas aeruginosa* with and without bacteremia. Acta Derm Venereol. 1991;71:411-415.

431. Mevio E, Calabro P, De Paoli F, et al. Unusual extracranial complications of otitis media in a young HIV patient: Retropharyngeal and Mouret's abscess. Rev Laryngol Otol Rhinol (Bord). 1998;119:199-201.

432. Cano-Parra J, Espana E, Esteban M, et al. *Pseudomonas* conjunctival ulcer and secondary orbital cellulitis in a patient with AIDS. Br J Ophthalmol. 1994;78:72-73.

433. Dropulic LK, Leslie JM, Eldred LJ, et al. Clinical manifestations and risk factors of *Pseudomonas aeruginosa* infection in patients with AIDS. J Infect Dis. 1995;171:930-937.

434. Gallant JE, Ko AH. Cavitary pulmonary lesions in patients infected with human immunodeficiency virus. Clin Infect Dis. 1996;22:671-682.

435. Freeman AF, Mancini AJ, Yogev R. Is noma neonatorum a presentation of ecthyma gangrenosum in the newborn? Pediatr Infect Dis J. 2002;21:83-85.

436. Bisno AL. Cutaneous infections: Microbiologic and epidemiologic considerations. Am J Med. 1984;76:172-179.

437. Fluit AC, Verhoef J, Schmitz FJ. Antimicrobial resistance in European isolates of *Pseudomonas aeruginosa*. European SENTRY Participants. Eur J Clin Microbiol Infect Dis. 2000;19:370-374.

438. Jones RN, Kirby JT, Beach ML, et al. Geographic variations in activity of broad-spectrum beta-lactams against *Pseudomonas aeruginosa*: Summary of the worldwide SENTRY Antimicrobial Surveillance Program (1997-2000). Diagn Microbiol Infect Dis. 2002;43:239-243.

439. Goossens H. Susceptibility of multi-drug-resistant *Pseudomonas aeruginosa* in intensive care units: Results from the European MYSTIC study group. Clin Microbiol Infect. 2003;9:980-983.

440. Andrade SS, Jones RN, Gales AC, et al. Increasing prevalence of antimicrobial resistance among *Pseudomonas aeruginosa* isolates in Latin American medical centres: 5 year report of the SENTRY Antimicrobial Surveillance Program (1997-2001) J Antimicrob Chemother. 2003;52:140-141.

441. Stein A, Raoult D. Colistin: An antimicrobial for the 21st century? Clin Infect Dis. 2002;35:901-902.

442. Livermore DM. Multiple mechanisms of antimicrobial resistance in *Pseudomonas aeruginosa*: Our worst nightmare? Clin Infect Dis. 2002;34:634-640.

443. Livermore DM. Of *Pseudomonas*, porins, pumps and carbapenems. J Antimicrob Chemother. 2001;47:247-250.

444. Higgins PG, Fluit AC, Milatovic D, et al. Antimicrobial susceptibility of imipenem-resistant *Pseudomonas aeruginosa*. J Antimicrob Chemother. 2002;50:299-301.

445. Lepper PM, Grusa E, Reichl H, et al. Consumption of imipenem correlates with beta-lactam resistance in *Pseudomonas aeruginosa*. Antimicrob Agents Chemother. 2002;46:2920-2925.

446. Conway SP, Pond MN, Watson A, et al. Intravenous colistin sulphomethate in acute respiratory exacerbations in adult patients with cystic fibrosis. Thorax. 1997;52:987-993.

447. Beringer P. The clinical use of colistin in patients with cystic fibrosis. Curr Opin Pulm Med. 2001;7:434-440.

448. Evans ME, Feola DJ, Rapp RP. Polymyxin B sulfate and colistin: Old antibiotics for emerging multiresistant gram-negative bacteria. Ann Pharmacother. 1999;33:960-967.

449. Levin AS, Barone AA, Penco J, et al. Intravenous colistin as therapy for nosocomial infections caused by multidrug-resistant *Pseudomonas aeruginosa* and *Acinetobacter baumannii*. Clin Infect Dis. 1999;28:1008-1011.

450. Gunderson BW, Ibrahim KH, Hovde LB, et al. Synergistic activity of colistin and ceftazidime against multiantibiotic-resistant *Pseudomonas aeruginosa* in an in vitro pharmacodynamic model. Antimicrob Agents Chemother. 2003;47:905-909.

451. Markou N, Apostolakos H, Koumoudiou C, et al. Intravenous colistin in the treatment of sepsis from multiresistant gram-negative bacilli in critically ill patients. Crit Care. 2003;7:R78-R83.

452. Goodwin NJ, Friedman EA. The effects of renal impairment, peritoneal dialysis, and hemodialysis on serum sodium colistimethate levels. Ann Intern Med. 1968;68:984-994.

453. Rynn C, Wootton M, Bowker KE, et al. In vitro assessment of colistin's antipseudomonal antimicrobial interactions with other antibiotics. Clin Microbiol Infect. 1999;5:32-36.

454. Giamarellos-Bourboulis EJ, Sambatakou H, Galani I, et al. In vitro interaction of colistin and rifampin on multiresistant *Pseudomonas aeruginosa*. J Chemother. 2003;15:235-238.

455. Song W, Woo HJ, Kim JS, et al. In vitro activity of beta-lactams in combination with other antimicrobial agents against resistant strains of *Pseudomonas aeruginosa*. Int J Antimicrob Agents. 2003;21:8-12.

456. Oie S, Uematsu T, Sawa A, et al. In vitro effects of combinations of antipseudomonal agents against seven strains of multidrug-resistant *Pseudomonas aeruginosa*. J Antimicrob Chemother. 2003;52:911-914.

CHAPTER **217**

Stenotrophomonas maltophilia and *Burkholderia cepacia*

GEORG MASCHMEYER

ULF B. GÖBEL

Stenotrophomonas maltophilia and *Burkholderia cepacia* are important nosocomial pathogens in hospitalized patients, particularly those with prior broad-spectrum antibacterial therapy, including patients with cystic fibrosis (CF) (see Chapter 65). Both species are intrinsically resistant to most antimicrobial or disinfectant agents, are phenotypically unremarkable, and exhibit an extensive diversity of genotypes.

MICROBIOLOGY, TAXONOMY, AND IDENTIFICATION

S. maltophilia, formerly named *Pseudomonas* and then *Xanthomonas maltophilia*, is the only species in the genus. *B. cepacia*, most recently called *Pseudomonas cepacia*, was previously named *P. multivorans* and *P. kingii*, and is now placed in the large and diverse genus *Burkholderia*. Both *S. maltophilia* and *B. cepacia* are motile, free-living, glucose-nonfermentative, gram-negative aerobic bacilli with multitrichous polar flagella. *S. maltophilia* grows readily on most bacteriologic media, typically appearing pale yellow, grayish, or lavender-green when grown on blood agar. Preliminary identification may be facilitated by its ammonia-like odor. Most clinical isolates are oxidase negative and use maltose and usually dextrose and xylose.[1] *S. maltophilia* may produce extracellular deoxyribonuclease on selected media, can hydrolyze esculin and orthonitrophenyl-β-D-galactopyranoside, and produces catalase and a strong acid reaction in oxidation-fermentation in maltose medium. Most strains require methionine for growth.[2] In vitro resistance patterns differ markedly between institutions, and testing results may not correctly predict clinical treatment response.

The appearance of *B. cepacia* colonies is variable, depending on the strain and the culture medium used. Identification of highly treatment-resistant small-colony variants of *B. cepacia* on selective media may be of clinical importance.[3]

Based upon phenotypic and genotypic analyses, *B. cepacia* has been divided into currently nine genomic species (genomovars) representing the so-called *Burkholderia cepacia* complex (BCC): *B. cepacia* (genomovar I); *Burkholderia multivorans* (genomovar II); genomovar III, with two *recA* clusters, IIIA and IIIB; *Burkholderia stabilis* (genomovar IV); *Burkholderia vietnamiensis* (genomovar V); genomovar VI; *Burkholderia ambifaria* (genomovar VII); *Burkholderia anthina* (genomovar VIII); and *Burkholderia pyrrocinia* (genomovar IX) (Fig. 217-1).[4,5] This rather tedious way of delineating new species within the BCC may be simplified by the use of DNA macro- or microarrays as proposed by Ramisse and colleagues.[6] A representative panel of each genomovar has recently been assembled to assist with identification, epidemiologic analysis, and virulence studies.[7,8]

To isolate BCC organisms, selective media have been developed that usually contain sucrose and/or lactose and antibiotics, such as

FIGURE 217-1. A phylogenetic tree of *recA* gene sequences indicating the presence of nine *B. cepacia* complex genomovars. *(From Mahenthiralingam E, Baldwin A, Vandamme P. Burkholderia cepacia complex infection in cystic fibrosis. J Med Microbiol. 2002;51:533-538.)*

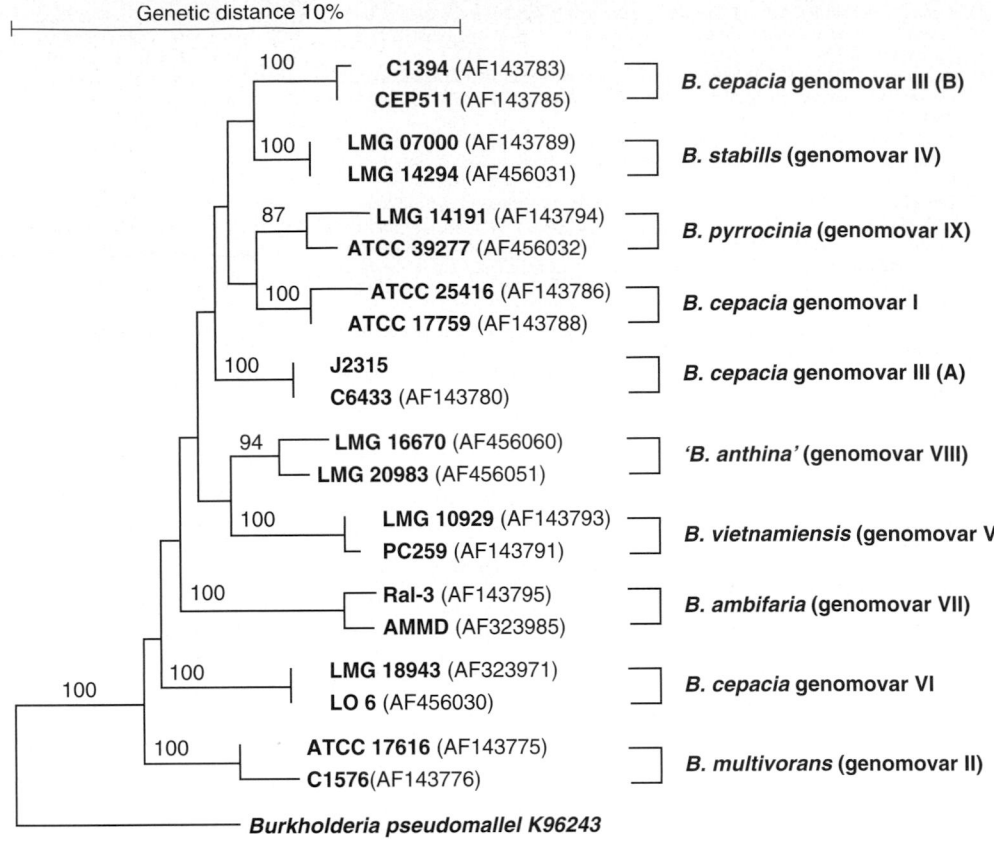

polymyxin, gentamicin, or vancomycin. Three media are in use: the *Pseudomonas cepacia* agar (PCA), the oxidation-fermentation polymyxin bacitracin lactose agar (OFBL), and recently the *B. cepacia* selective agar (BCSA). The latter is more selective by suppressing growth of non-BCC bacteria, while BCC members form visible pinpoint colonies within 24 hours. Colonies are smooth and slightly elevated. A comparison of all three media revealed a superior performance of the BCSA, achieving 43%, 93%, and 100% growth of BCC organisms at 24, 48, and 72 hours, respectively.[9] Members of the BCC can be identified by available commercial tests, such as API 20NE, Phoenix, MicroScan, or Vitek. However, misidentification occurs in a number of cases, and care should be taken to correctly differentiate *Burkholderia* species from *Achromobacter, Ralstonia,* and other nonfermenting gram-negative rods. A large polyphasic analysis of 1051 isolates from 115 CF treatment centers in 91 U.S. cities revealed a overall misidentification rate of 11% for isolates identified as *B. cepacia* by referring laboratories. This rate was even higher (36%) for isolates not specifically identified or identified as a species other than *B. cepacia.*[10] A recent comparative evaluation of two automated commercial systems (BD Phoenix, bioMérieux Vitek-2) showed that the identification rate was similar (50% and 53%, respectively) when all BCC isolates were considered. However, rates of misidentification for the BD Phoenix and Vitek-2 systems were 9% and 17% for genomovar III, 22% and 7% for *B. multivorans,* and 36% and 13% for other BCC members, respectively.[11] Exact identification may thus require genotypic methods. Several assays based upon in vitro amplification by polymerase chain reaction (PCR) of various genes (e.g., ribosomal RNA or *recA* genes) have been developed. A recent study including 114 geographically diverse bacterial isolates and 27 clinical isolates from Dutch CF patients compared four systems for biochemical identification and three PCR-based assays.[12] Many authors recommend parallel cultures on blood agar medium and selective agar plates, and subsequent phenotypic identification with the API 20NE test and PCR

amplification of the small-subunit ribosomal RNA gene followed by restriction fragment length polymorphism (RFLP) analysis. Direct amplification from clinical specimens (e.g., sputum) is still lacking sufficient sensitivity. Depending upon the target sequence, the primer pairs, and the amplification format (single round vs. semi-nested or nested assays) used, the detection limit varies between 10^1 and 10^6 colony-forming units (cfu)/g of sputum.[13-15]

VIRULENCE FACTORS AND PATHOGENESIS

Both *S. maltophilia* and *B. cepacia* uncommonly cause community-acquired infections in previously normal patients. Their resistance to most antimicrobial agents selects them in the hospital environment. Resistance in *B. cepacia* is mediated by an immunodominant drug efflux pump (bcrA).[16] This species also adheres to plastic materials, and secretes elastase and gelatinase. *B. cepacia* also displays a protein that binds respiratory mucin. It resists nonoxidative neutrophil killing and produces siderophores, hemolysin, and exopolysaccharide. One epidemic strain of *B. cepacia*, ET12, was shown to have giant cable pili, which mediate attachment to respiratory epithelia.[17,18] This strain contains a hybrid of two insertion sequences as well as a 1.4-kilobase open reading frame, which have been demonstrated in transmissible genomovar III species only. Transmissibility is genetically related to *esmR* and *cblA* genes, and *esmR* (or the *B. cepacia* epidemic strain marker [BCESM]) is detected only among genomovar III. Flagellum-mediated motility appears to facilitate penetration of epithelial barriers by *B. cepacia.*[19] Biofilm formation followed by invasion and destruction of epithelial cells has been identified as a major pattern of invasiveness in genomovar III.[20]

S. maltophilia is a nosocomial pathogen that occurs in many of the same types of hospitalized patients as *B. cepacia.* Among CF patients, long-term colonization with *S. maltophilia* has been reported but has not been found to adversely influence their prognosis. In the majority of clinical situations, however, isolation of *S. maltophilia* may represent colonization or contamination rather than true infection, and it has been difficult to substantiate the causative role of *S. maltophilia* because of its rather limited pathogenicity and the lack of obvious virulence factors.[21] One candidate virulence factor may be a recently described alkaline serine protease, the StmPr1 protease, enabling *S. maltophilia* to degrade human serum and tissue proteins (e.g., the immunoglobulin G heavy chain).[22] A most remarkable property was its resistance against pan-protease inhibitors such as α_1-antitrypsin and α_2-macroglobulin.

Patients with CF and those with chronic granulomatous disease are predisposed to infection by *B. cepacia.* Here, colonization by *B. cepacia* genomovar III of the respiratory tract is associated with significantly higher morbidity and mortality,[23] particularly after lung transplantation, increasing the mortality within the first 6 months post-transplant from 12%-14% to 33%-40%.[24,25] Whether this is strictly attributable to the virulence of *B. cepacia* or rather represents the poor disease status of CF patients affected by *B. cepacia* colonization is controversial.[26,27] Lipopolysaccharide from *B. cepacia* induces a strong proinflammatory response in lung tissue, so that *B. cepacia* infection may show a rapidly necrotizing course. *B. cepacia* has the potential to be highly invasive and can migrate across the epithelial barrier to invade lung parenchyma and capillaries.[20,28] This invasiveness may be due to inhibition of natural pulmonary defense mechanisms such as human β-defensins.[29] Moreover, invasive clinical *B. cepacia* isolates have shown their ability to survive in macrophages and pulmonary epithelial cells, whereas environmental strains may lack this ability.[30]

Current knowledge about *B. cepacia* virulence determinants contributing to colonization, invasion, and intracellular survival has been summarized in a recent review.[31] One factor affecting the early stages of colonization is the scavenging of iron. *B. cepacia* possesses at least four iron-binding siderophores: salicylic acid, ornibactin, pyochelin, and cepabactin.[31] *B. cepacia* lipopolysaccharide induces release of proinflammatory cytokines (tumor necrosis factor-α, interleukin-6, and interleukin-8) from blood monocytes and whole blood,[32,33] thus contributing to the severe inflammatory response observed in CF patients. It further induces increased surface expression of CR3 on neutrophils as well as the priming of respiratory burst activity.[34] Adherence in genomovar III bacteria is conferred by the presence of long, flexible type II pili exhibiting cable morphology. The first four genes of the *cbl* operon—*cblA, cblB, cblC,* and *cblD*—were shown to be sufficient for pilus assembly.[35] Deletion of *cblB* abrogated pilus assembly and reduced the periplasmic stability of the CblA pilin, suggesting that the CblB protein acts as a chaperone. No pili were produced after deletion of *cblD,* indicating that its gene product initiates pilus biogenesis. Recombinant *E. coli* cells expressing cable pili or *B. cepacia* cells lacking Cbl pili still bound to cytokeratin 13, a 55-kDa protein expressed on the surface of buccal and normal human bronchial epithelial cells,[18,35] indicating that other bacterial proteins (e.g., a 22-kDa protein) mediate adherence. Other fimbrial structures such as mesh (Msh), filamentous (Fil), spine (Spn), and spike (Spk) have been identified, but their pathogenetic relevance has yet to be determined.[31,36] Nonfimbrial adhesins, a 37-kDa protein corresponding to the *B. cepacia* porin C, and an unidentified 66-kDa outer membrane protein have also been described, but detailed knowledge is still lacking.[37] Martin and Mohr[30] studied the capacity of two *B. cepacia* strains, one clinical and one environmental isolate, to invade cultured macrophages and pulmonary epithelial cells. Intracellular bacteria could be detected in membrane-bound vacuoles. While both strains showed similar invasion frequencies for macrophages, the clinical strain was more invasive in epithelial cells, and able to survive and replicate both in macrophages and in epithelial cells. Invasiveness was impaired when two genes (i.e., *fliG,* encoding a component of the motor-switch complex, and *fliI,* encoding an ATPase required for protein translocation) were disrupted.[19] However, reduced invasion was not due to defective adherence. Invasion was inhibited by cytochalasin D, suggesting that the host-cell cytoskeleton may play a role in facilitating bacterial entry.[38] This is consistent with the observation that *B. cepacia* mutants lacking the *bscN* gene, encoding an ATP-binding protein possibly representing part of a type III secretion system, exhibited attenuated virulence in a murine model.[39]

Several mechanisms seem to be involved to enable intracellular survival. Reactive oxygen and nitrogen intermediates possess critical roles in the host defense against *B. cepacia,* as shown in p47$^{phox-/-}$ mice and in mice with a targeted disruption of the inducible nitric oxide synthase (iNOS) gene.[40] *B. cepacia*-infected macrophages primed with interferon-γ produced less nitric oxide than interferon-γ–primed, noninfected cells.[41] Recently it could be shown that an overexpressed azurin homologue, normally involved in electron transfer during denitrification, induced apoptosis in macrophages in a caspase-dependent manner.[42] A quorum-sensing system may be involved in the regulation of several *B. cepacia* virulence factors.[43-45]

EPIDEMIOLOGY

BCC organisms are distributed ubiquitously and found most commonly on plant roots, the rhizosphere, soil, and moist environments. They are of increasing importance for agriculture and bioremediation because of their antinematodal and antifungal properties, as well as their capability to degrade a wide range of toxic compounds.[46,47] They are infrequently isolated from hospital environments, but outbreaks have been reported originating from diverse sources such as contaminated faucets, nebulizers, chlorhexidine-cetrimide solution, alcohol-free mouthwash, multidose albuterol vials used among multiple patients, indigo-carmine dye used in enteral feeding, tap water, and bottled water. Patients may acquire BCC either from the environment or via patient-to-patient transmission. Recent progress in molecular typing methods enabled hospital epidemiologists to correctly identify outbreak strains and, hence, to identify the source and trace transmission routes. Ribotype RFLP profiles and pulsed-field gel electrophoresis (PFGE)-resolved RFLPs were used to identify a single dominant and highly transmissible clone in a hospital outbreak involving CF and non-CF patients. Their risk of acquisition was linked to hospitalization, and thus infection control policies must consider the transmission between non-CF and CF patients.[48] A comprehensive study evaluating multiple genomic typing systems including random amplified polymorphic DNA (RAPD) typing, PFGE, and BOX-PCR fingerprinting compared the results obtained by these different methods with each other as well as to data from previous studies with multilocus restriction typing (MLRT). The authors concluded that PFGE and RAPD fingerprinting were most suitable for small-scale studies (i.e., local outbreaks), whereas BOX-PCR fingerprinting appeared more appropriate for large-scale studies aimed at analyzing global epidemiology.[49] In the same study, BOX-PCR fingerprinting was considered a rapid and easy alternative to MLRT.

The availability of rapid and accurate tests for genomovar identification allowed for a comprehensive analysis of the prevalence of different BCC species. By the age of 18, about 3.5% of CF patients harbor BCC.[50] Data from the United States, Canada, and Italy show that genomovar III strains and *B. multivorans* (genomovar II) are the most prevalent genomovars among CF patients, accounting for 95% of all infections. Genomovar III strains are predominant, ranging from 80% to 50% (mean, 67.5%) among different CF populations studied so far. Further analysis of the different *recA* lineages revealed significant geographic differences. Whereas type IIIB strains represented 75% of all U.S. genomovar III isolates, type IIIA strains are more prevalent in Canada and Europe, accounting for about 70% of all genomovar III isolates.[5,51-53] A similar genomovar distribution (90% type IIIA) has recently been found in CF patients from the Czech Republic.[54] There was, however, a striking difference among CF patients from the Slovak Republic, where type IIIA accounted for only 29% of strains, while *B. stabilis* (genomovar IV) represented 54% of all isolates. The unique distribution of selected BCC genomovars indicates the presence of epidemic strains exhibiting particular virulence and transmissibility. So far, two genetic elements have been identified that are associated with epidemic spread: *cblA,* a gene encoding a protein for cable pilus production, and *esmR,* also called BCESM, representing a 1.4-kb putative open reading frame with homology to negative transcriptional regulators. Analyzing all genomovar III strains isolated from Canadian CF patients of different geographic origin, Speert and co-workers[53] identified four genetic lineages defined by random amplified polymorphic DNA (RAPD) and PFGE. Only strains from RAPD type 02, representing the ET12 clonal lineage, harbored both BCESM and *cblA.* The predominance of this RAPD type in Ontario, Canada, was correlated with a significantly higher prevalence, accounting for 22% of patients in Ontario versus 5% in Quebec.

A recent population structure analysis of *B. cepacia* genomovar III[8] revealed that 86.7% of all restriction types clustered into three major clonal complexes, comprising epidemic clones ET12 (RT-6 complex), PHDC (RT-46 complex), and Midwest (RT-88 complex). These clones have a wide geographic distribution and exhibit varying degrees of genetic recombination. Infection with clone ET12 has been associated with increased mortality and the so-called cepacia syndrome, characterized by rapid, often fatal respiratory failure and septicemia.[55] PDHC is the clone responsible for almost all BCC infections in the mid-Atlantic region of the United States.[56] A strain belonging to this clonal lineage has been isolated from organic soils in four agricultural fields that had been planted with onions for several years. This indicates that environmental strains may play a pivotal role in the epidemiology of BCC infections and could explain the ongoing human acquisition despite infection control measures.[57] The third clone described is most prevalent in CF patients from the Midwestern region of the United States.[58] In contrast to some reports advocating the identification of the *cblA* gene as a means of influencing patient segregation and infection control strategies,[59] several authors[8,56] provided evidence that the presence of putative transmissibility factors *cblA* or *esmR* varied significantly among established epidemic clones, leading to the conclusion that infection control measures should not be based upon the presence or absence of these markers. An attempt to identify other genetic elements that may be specific for epidemic BCC strains led to the identification of a novel insertion sequence, designated *IS1363,* in clone PHDC.[60] *IS1363* was also found in most isolates of clone ET12, but not in other BCC species except *B. ambifaria* (genomovar VII). At present it remains unclear, whether this IS element contributes to the increased capacity of both clones to infect CF patients. However, together with other IS elements it may contribute to the genomic plasticity of BCC species. Considering the acquisition of environmental strains by CF patients, the observation of frequent genetic recombination in genomovar III populations may have important implications for the biotechnical use of BCC species.[8,61]

CLINICAL MANIFESTATIONS

Stenotrophomonas maltophilia

The most frequent clinical manifestation of *S. maltophilia* infection is pneumonia.[21,62,63] However, the majority of *S. maltophilia* isolates from respiratory secretions represent colonization rather than infection. True *S. maltophilia* pneumonia is more likely to occur among intensive care or cancer patients and is associated with extensive use of broad-spectrum antibiotics, advanced age, mechanical ventilation, and a higher Acute Physiology and Chronic Health Evaluation II (APACHE II) score.[62] Nosocomial *S. maltophilia* pneumonia is associated with a high mortality, particularly when associated with bacteremia or obstruction. It may be complicated by septic shock and multiple organ dysfunction syndrome. Chest radiographs may show lobar, nodular, or bronchopneumonic infiltrates. The respiratory flora is often mixed, even in cases in which *S. maltophilia* is considered to be a significant pathogen. However, *S. maltophilia* may represent indirect pathogenicity through the production of at least two inducible β-lactamases, L1 and L2, hydrolyzing almost all classes of β-lactam antimicrobials and thus supporting the growth of pathogens such as *Serratia marcescens* and *Pseudomonas aeruginosa* even in the presence of imipenem or ceftazidime.[64]

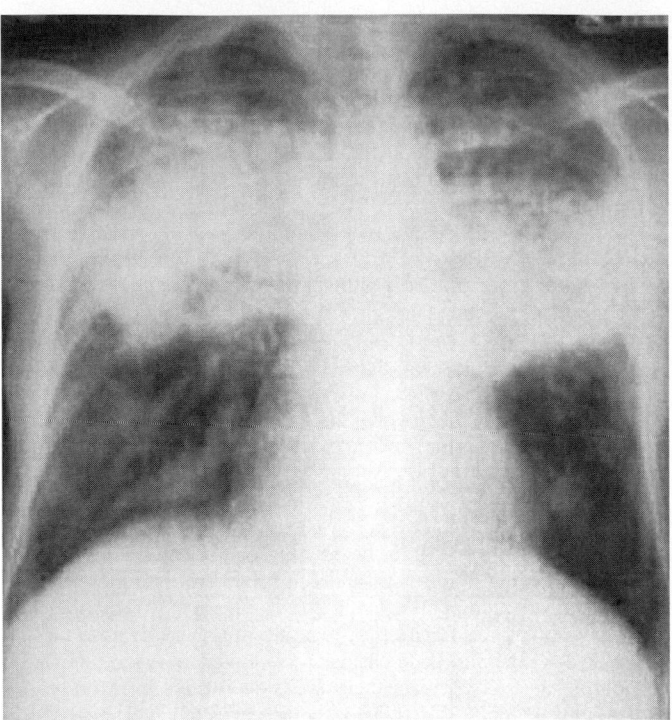

FIGURE 217-2. Chest radiograph showing typical appearances of the "cepacia syndrome." *(From Jones AM, Dodd ME, Webb AK. Burkholderia cepacia: Current clinical issues, environmental controversies and ethical dilemmas. Eur Respir J. 2001;17:295-301.)*

The second most frequent clinical manifestation of *S. maltophilia* infection is central venous catheter–related bacteremia.[21,65-67] A substantial proportion of these infections are polymicrobial.[68] In cancer patients, antimicrobial prophylaxis with oral fluoroquinolones may predispose for *S. maltophilia* bacteremia.[69] Single cases of other clinical manifestations of *S. maltophilia* infection, such as endocarditis on both native and prosthetic valves,[70] endophthalmitis,[71] sinusitis,[72] cellulitis, and myositis, have been described. Cellulitis develops around catheter insertion sites or arises hematogenously.[73,74] Liver abscesses[75,76] and meningitis[77,78] have been described as well. Ecthyma gangrenosum may be a rare cutaneous complication of both *B. cepacia* and *S. maltophilia* bacteremia.[79,80] In contrast, hematogenous skin lesions of *S. maltophilia* present as firm, tender, erythematous nodules. *S. maltophilia* isolated from the urinary tract often represent colonization in the presence of a Foley catheter rather than true infection.[21,81-83] However, the urinary tract may be the focus of severe sepsis, particularly after instrumentation or surgery.[81,83,84]

Burkholderia cepacia

Patients with CF and those with chronic granulomatous disease are predisposed to *B. cepacia* pneumonia.[5,53,85-88] Apart from chronic asymptomatic carriage, rapid and fatal clinical deterioration with necrotizing granulomatous pneumonia, called "cepacia syndrome" (Fig. 217-2),[89,90] and bacteremia may occur.[91]

Increased mortality has been observed in CF patients after colonization with *B. cepacia.*[23,55,92,93] CF patients colonized with *B. cepacia* genomovar III who are undergoing lung transplantation have been reported to carry an up to 50% risk for fatal post-transplant complications (Fig. 217-3),[24,25,94] which has led several centers to avoid lung transplantation in CF patients colonized with this organism.[95] The majority of CF patients colonized with *B. cepacia,* however, show little change in their clinical picture, and those who do may be effectively treated with adequate antimicrobial agents.[27]

B. cepacia bacteremia, most often catheter-related and polymicrobial, has been reported in cancer patients[96] and in patients undergoing he-

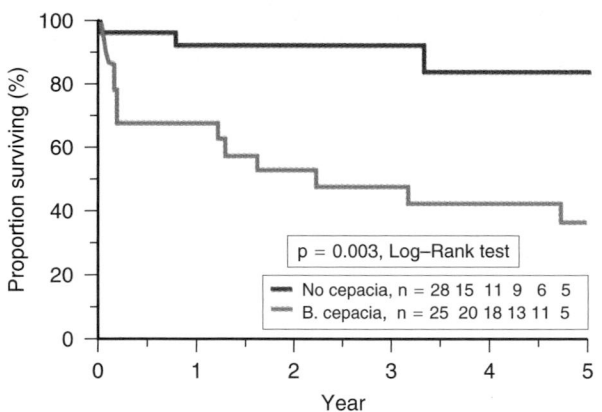

FIGURE 217-3. Kaplan-Meier survival curves of CF lung transplant recipients classified by *B. cepacia* infection status. The data show the number of subjects at each time point according to infection category. *(From Chaparro C, Maurer J, Gutierrez C, et al. Infection with Burkholderia cepacia in cystic fibrosis: Outcome following lung transplantation. Am J Respir Crit Care Med. 2001;163:43-48.)*

modialysis,[97] and nosocomial pneumonia was observed in intensive care patients who were mechanically ventilated and pretreated with broad-spectrum antibiotics such as fluoroquinolones and ceftazidime.[98-100]

B. cepacia skin and soft tissue infection may occur in patients with burns[101] or surgical wounds[102] and in soldiers with prolonged foot immersion in water.[103] Genitourinary tract infection caused by *B. cepacia* has been reported after urethral instrumentation, after transrectal prostate biopsy, or through exposure to contaminated solutions.[104]

TREATMENT

Stenotrophomonas maltophilia

Treatment recommendations for both *S. maltophilia* and *B. cepacia* infections vary profoundly, and an ideal treatment standard has not been established. It is essential to distinguish between a clinically significant *S. maltophilia* infection and colonization or polymicrobial infection with other, potentially more pathogenic microorganisms involved.[21,62,68] For treatment considerations, it should be kept in mind that prior use of fluoroquinolones[69] or cefepime[105] represents a major risk factor for the development of *S. maltophilia* bacteremia.

In patients other than those with CF, who have bacteremia caused by *S. maltophilia* alone, an indwelling venous catheter is likely to be the source of infection.[65,68] Removal of this foreign body hastens cure.[96] Some authors have found that the attributable mortality in non-CF patients with *S. maltophilia* or *B. cepacia* bacteremia may be similar to that observed in other bacteremias caused by gram-negative bacilli.[21,67,106]

Trimethoprim-sulfamethoxazole (TMP-SMZ) and ticarcillin–clavulanic acid, given alone or in combination, are the only agents with consistent therapeutic activity against *S. maltophilia* isolates.[62,65,105,107-109] Levofloxacin and ciprofloxacin appear to be less suitable.[110,111] For ticarcillin-clavulanate, very high rates of in vitro resistance among *S. maltophilia* have been reported from single centers with extensive use of β-lactam antibiotics.[108] Of note, as a result of much higher resistance rates, piperacillin-tazobactam does not represent a reliable treatment alternative in institutions where ticarcillin-clavulanate is not available.[63,112] Minocycline has excellent in vitro activity[79]; however, clinical experience with this agent is limited.[113] Most importantly, the in vitro sensitivity testing of *S. maltophilia* against antimicrobial drugs may show results that are in contrast to the clinical outcome in patients treated with these antibiotics.[71,114] This is particularly relevant for TMP-SMZ, for which in vitro resistance rates among *S. maltophilia* of up to 81% have been reported.[115] Predominantly in intensive care units, the in vitro resistance rate to TMP-SMZ among *S. maltophilia* is expected to be as high as 30%.[116-118]

Antimicrobial therapy of *S. maltophilia* infection, pending in vitro susceptibility testing, usually begins with a combination of trimethoprim-sulfamethoxazole and ticarcillin-clavulanate at high dosages (15 to 20 mg/kg/day of trimethoprim for TMP-SMZ and 3.1 g every 4 hours of ticarcillin-clavulanate). Surgical removal of prosthetic material or necrotic tissue is a valuable adjunct to medical therapy.[84,119,120]

Multivariate analysis has shown that the presence of septic shock at onset of infection, profound neutropenia, and delay in appropriate antimicrobial therapy are significant predictors of poor outcome in patients with *S. maltophilia* bacteremia.[62,65,67,96,109]

Burkholderia cepacia

B. cepacia infection in CF patients can be treated successfully, so that the prognosis is not inevitably worsened if these infections emerge after lung transplantation.[24] A high severity-of-illness score, poor nutritional status, and possibly female gender and older age may indicate an adverse clinical outcome in intensive-care patients with *B. cepacia* infection.[121]

Antimicrobial agents that are effective against *B. cepacia* in vitro include meropenem, TMP-SMZ, chloramphenicol, and minocycline. The glycylcycline tigecycline has shown lower in vitro activity as compared with minocycline.[122] Other potentially active agents include the ureidopenicillins, third-generation cephalosporins, and fluoroquinolones.[123] Rates of in vitro resistance of *B. cepacia* to TMP-SMZ range from 5% in Quebec, Canada,[53] and Latin America to 10% in Europe.[63] Although formal studies are not available, combination antimicrobial treatment is recommended for patients with pulmonary *B. cepacia* infection.[124] Successful treatment with combinations of meropenem with ciprofloxacin and tobramycin has been reported,[125] as has been for the in vitro activity of piperacillin and ciprofloxacin, whereas the combination of TMP-SMZ with a β-lactam may result in antagonism.[126] Whether combination therapy may help to minimize the likelihood of resistance has not yet been elucidated. In *B. cepacia*–infected patients with hypersensitivity against β-lactam antibiotics, meropenem monotherapy in a dosage of 2 g every 8 hours has been demonstrated to be effective.[127]

In individual CF patients with life-threatening *B. cepacia* infection, short-term adjunctive treatment with methylprednisolone may be beneficial.[128]

PREVENTION AND CONTROL

Because both *B. cepacia* and *S. maltophilia* are commonly found in the environment, and patient-to-patient transmission, though repeatedly reported,[46,51,129-132] is much less frequent than acquisition from other sources, strategies aiming at prevention of infections caused by these multidrug-resistant pathogens are difficult to design.[53] Accepted prophylactic measures include (1) an appropriate antibiotic policy, particularly a critical use of ciprofloxacin, cefepime, and imipenem; (2) strict hand hygiene and institution of barrier techniques for colonized or infected patients; and (3) surveillance among CF patients and identification of potential nosocomial reservoirs such as the water system,[74,133] drinking water,[134] sink drains,[135] faucet aerators,[136] contaminated handwash or mouthwash solutions,[99,137] and medical equipment.[138,139] Education of patients and health care workers is a cornerstone of such preventive measures. For CF patients, living with a person colonized by BCC, contact with a BCC-colonized patient, hospitalization, and attending a summer CF camp have been shown to be associated with an increased risk of becoming colonized or infected with these organisms.[140] Because of the current lack of accurate predictors for virulence and transmissibility, patient segregation and rigorous infection control measures should be reinforced to reduce or prevent transmission of BCC. Patients infected with transmissible genomovar strains should not be cohorted with patients infected with *B. multivorans* or other *B. cepacia* genomovars.[141] However, continued efforts will be required to implement CF sputum surveillance with improved species and strain identification, and to elucidate bacterial or host factors contributing to patient-to-patient transmission.[57]

A double-blind, placebo-controlled trial in adult CF patients infected with *B. cepacia* genomovar III has not shown any benefit from nebulized taurolidine.[142] In cases in which control measures did not prevent the infection of CF patients, acquisition from natural environments should be considered.[143] The widespread use of *B. cepacia* in agriculture and bioremediation of contaminated environmental sites causes a conflict about its commercial use in light of its potentially life-threatening impact on CF patients.[90,144]

REFERENCES

1. Clark WA, Hollis DG, Weaver RE, et al. Identification of unusual pathogenic gram negative aerobic and facultative aerobic bacteria. Atlanta, GA: Centers for Disease Control, 1985.
2. Burdge DR, Noble MA, Campbell ME, et al. *Xanthomonas maltophilia* misidentified as *Pseudomonas cepacia* in cultures of sputum from patients with cystic fibrosis: A diagnostic pitfall with major clinical implications. Clin Infect Dis. 1995;20:445-448.
3. Haussler S, Lehmann C, Breselge C, et al. Fatal outcome of lung transplantation in cystic fibrosis patients due to small-colony variants of the *Burkholderia cepacia* complex. Eur J Clin Microbiol Infect Dis. 2003;22:249-253.
4. Vandamme P, Holmes B, Vancanneyt M, et al. Occurrence of multiple genomovars of *Burkholderia cepacia* in cystic fibrosis patients and proposal of *Burkholderia multivorans* sp. nov. Int J Syst Bacteriol. 1997;47:1188-1200.
5. Mahenthiralingam E, Baldwin A, Vandamme P. *Burkholderia cepacia* complex infection in cystic fibrosis. J Med Microbiol. 2002;51:533-538.
6. Ramisse V, Balandreau J, Thibault F, et al. DNA-DNA hybridization study of *Burkholderia* species using genomic DNA macro-array analysis coupled to reverse genome probing. Int J Syst Evol Microbiol. 2003;53:739-746.
7. Mahenthiralingam E, Coenye T, Chung JW, et al. Diagnostically and experimentally useful panel of strains from the *Burkholderia cepacia* complex. J Clin Microbiol. 2000;38:910-913.
8. Coenye T, LiPuma JJ. Population structure analysis of *Burkholderia cepacia* genomovar III: Varying degrees of genetic recombination characterize major clonal complexes. Microbiology. 2003;149:77-88.
9. Henry D, Campbell M, McGimpsey C, et al. Comparison of isolation media for recovery of *Burkholderia cepacia* complex from respiratory secretions of patients with cystic fibrosis. J Microbiol. 1999;37:1004-1007.
10. McMenamin JD, Zaccone TM, Coenye T, et al. Misidentification of *B. cepacia* in US Cystic Fibrosis treatment centers. Chest. 2000;117:1161-1165.
11. Brisse S, Stefani, Verhoef J, et al. Comparative evaluation of the BD Phoenix and VITEK 2 automated instruments for identification of isolates of the *Burkholderia cepacia* complex. J Clin Microbiol. 2002;40:1743-1748.
12. van Pelt C, Verduin CM, Goessens WHF, et al. Identification of *Burkholderia* spp. in the clinical microbiology laboratory: Comparison of conventional and molecular methods. J Clin Microbiol. 1999;37:2158-2164.
13. McDowell A, Mahenthiralingam E, Moore JE, et al. PCR-based detection and identification of *Burkholderia cepacia* complex pathogens in sputum from cystic fibrosis patients. J Clin Microbiol. 2001;39:4247-4255.
14. Drvinek P, Hrbackova H, Cinek O, et al. Direct PCR detection of *Burkholderia cepacia* complex and identification of its genomovars by using sputum as a source of DNA. J Clin Microbiol. 2002;40:3485-3488.
15. Moore JE, Xu J, Millar BC, et al. Improved molecular detection of *Burkholderia cepacia* genomovar III and *Burkholderia multivorans* directly from sputum of patients with cystic fibrosis. J Microbiol Methods. 2002;49:183-191.
16. Wigfield SM, Rigg GP, Kavari M, et al. Identification of an immunodominant drug efflux pump in *Burkholderia cepacia*. J Antimicrob Chemother. 2002;49:619-624.
17. Sajjan US, Forstner JF. Role of a 22-kilodalton pilin protein in binding of *Pseudomonas cepacia* to buccal epithelial cells. Infect Immun. 1993;61:3157-3163.
18. Sajjan US, Sylvester FA, Forstner JF. Cable-piliated *Burkholderia cepacia* binds to cytokeratin 13 of epithelial cells. Infect Immun. 2000;68:1787-1795.
19. Tomich M, Herfst CA, Golden JW, et al. Role of flagella in host cell invasion by *Burkholderia cepacia*. Infect Immun. 2002;70:1799-1806.
20. Schwab U, Leigh M, Ribeiro C, et al. Patterns of epithelial cell invasion by different species of the *Burkholderia cepacia* complex in well-differentiated human airway epithelia. Infect Immun. 2002;70:4547-4555.
21. Denton M, Kerr KG. Microbiological and clinical aspects of infection associated with *Stenotrophomonas maltophilia*. Clin Microbiol Rev. 1998;11:57-80.
22. Windhorst S, Frank E, Georgieva DN, et al. The major extracellular protease of the nosocomial pathogen *Stenotrophomonas maltophilia*. J Biol Chem. 2002;277:11042-11049.
23. Liou TG, Adler FR, Fitzsimmons SC, et al. Predictive 5-year survivorship model of cystic fibrosis. Am J Epidemiol. 2001;153:345-352.
24. Aris RM, Routh JC, LiPuma JJ, et al. Lung transplantation for cystic fibrosis patients with *Burkholderia cepacia* complex: Survival linked to genomovar type. Am J Respir Crit Care Med. 2001;164:2102-2106.
25. Chaparro C, Maurer J, Gutierrez C, et al. Infection with *Burkholderia cepacia* in cystic fibrosis: Outcome following lung transplantation. Am J Respir Crit Care Med. 2001;163:43-48.
26. Frangolias DD, Mahenthiralingam E, Rae S, et al. *Burkholderia cepacia* in cystic fibrosis: Variable disease course. Am J Respir Crit Care Med. 1999;160:1572-1577.
27. McManus TE, Moore JE, Crowe M, et al. A comparison of pulmonary exacerbations with single and multiple organisms in patients with cystic fibrosis and chronic *Burkholderia cepacia* infection. J Infect. 2003;46:56-59.
28. Sajjan U, Corey M, Humar A, et al. Immunolocalisation of *Burkholderia cepacia* in the lungs of cystic fibrosis patients. J Med Microbiol. 2001;50:535-546.
29. Baird RM, Brown H, Smith AW, et al. *Burkholderia cepacia* is resistant to the antimicrobial activity of airway epithelial cells. Immunopharmacology. 1999;44:267-272.
30. Martin DW, Mohr CD. Invasion and intracellular survival of *Burkholderia cepacia*. Infect Immun. 2000;8:24-29.
31. Mohr CD, Tomich M, Herfst CA. Cellular aspects of *Burkholderia cepacia* infection. Microbes Infect. 2001;3:425-435.
32. Shaw D, Poxton IR, Govan JR. Biological activity of *Burkholderia (Pseudomonas) cepacia* lipopolysaccharide. FEMS Immunol Med Microbiol. 1995;11:99-106.
33. Hutchison ML, Bonell EC, Poxton IR, et al. Endotoxic activity of lipopolysaccharides isolated from emergent potential cystic fibrosis pathogens. FEMS Immunol Med Microbiol. 2000;27:73-77.
34. Hughes JE, Stewart J, Barclay GR, et al. Priming of neutrophil respiratory burst activity by lipopolysaccharide from *Burkholderia cepacia*. Infect Immun. 1997;65:4281-4287.
35. Sajjan US, Xie H, Lefebre MD, et al. Identification and molecular analysis of cable pilus biosynthesis genes in *Burkholderia cepacia*. Microbiology. 2003;149:961-971.
36. Goldstein R, Sun L, Jiang RZ. Structurally variant classes of pilus appendage fibers coexpressed from *Burkholderia (Pseudomonas) cepacia*. J Bacteriol. 1995;177:1039-1052.
37. Saiman L, Cacalano G, Prince A. *Pseudomonas cepacia* adherence to respiratory epithelial cells is enhanced by *Pseudomonas aeruginosa*. Infect Immun. 1990;58:2578-2584.
38. Burns JL, Jonas M, Chi EY, et al. Invasion of respiratory epithelial cells by *Burkholderia (Pseudomonas) cepacia*. Infect Immun. 1996;64:4054-4059.
39. Tomich M, Griffith A, Herfst CA, et al. Attenuated virulence of a *Burkholderia cepacia* type III secretion mutant in a murine model of infection. Infect Immun. 2003;71:1405-1415.
40. Segal BH, Ding L, Holland SM. Phagocyte NADPH oxidase, but not inducible nitric oxide synthase, is essential for early control of *Burkholderia cepacia* and *Chromobacterium violaceum* infection in mice. Infect Immun. 2003;71:205-210.
41. Saini LS, Galsworthy SB, John MA, et al. Intracellular survival of *Burkholderia cepacia* complex isolates in the presence of macrophage cell activation. Microbiology. 1999;145:3465-3475.
42. Punj V, Sharma R, Zaborina O, et al. Energy-generating enzymes of *Burkholderia cepacia* and their interactions with macrophages. J Bacteriol. 2003;185:3167-3178.
43. Lewenza S, Conway B, Greenberg EP, et al. Quorum sensing in *Burkholderia cepacia*: Identification of the LuxRI homologs CepRI. J Bacteriol. 1999;181:748-756.
44. Lewenza S, Sokol PA. Regulation of ornibactin biosynthesis and N-acyl-L-homoserine lactone production by CepR in *Burkholderia cepacia*. J Bacteriol. 2001;183:2212-2218.
45. Lutter E, Lewenza S, Dennis JJ, et al. Distribution of quorum-sensing genes in the *Burkholderia cepacia* complex. Infect Immun. 2001;69:4661-4666.
46. Holmes A, Govan J, Goldstein R. Agricultural use of *Burkholderia (Pseudomonas) cepacia*: a threat to human health? Emerg Infect Dis. 1998;4:221-227.
47. LiPuma JJ, Mahenthiralingam M. Commercial use of *Burkholderia cepacia*. Emerg Infect Dis. 1999;5:305-306.
48. Holmes A, Nolan R, Taylor R, et al. An epidemic of *Burkholderia cepacia* transmitted between patients with and without cystic fibrosis. J Infect Dis. 1999;179:1197-1205.
49. Coenye T, Spilker T, Martin A, et al. Comparative assessment of genotyping methods for epidemiologic study of *Burkholderia cepacia* genomovar III. J Clin Microbiol. 2002;40:3300-3307.
50. Rajan S, Saiman L. Pulmonary infections in patients with cystic fibrosis. Semin Respir Infect. 2002;17:47-56.
51. Agodi A, Mahenthiralingam E, Barchitta M, et al. *Burkholderia cepacia* complex infection in Italian patients with cystic fibrosis: Prevalence, epidemiology, and genomovar status. J Clin Microbiol. 2001;39:2891-2896.
52. LiPuma JJ, Spilker T, Gill LH, et al. Disproportionate distribution of *Burkholderia cepacia* complex species and transmissibility markers in cystic fibrosis. Am J Respir Crit Care Med. 2001;164:92-96.
53. Speert DP, Henry D, Vandamme P, et al. Epidemiology of *Burkholderia cepacia* complex in patients with cystic fibrosis, Canada. Emerg Infect Dis. 2002;8:181-187.
54. Drvinek P, Cinek O, Melter J, et al. Genomovar distribution of the *Burkholderia cepacia* complex differs significantly between Czech and Slovak patients with cystic fibrosis. J Med Microbiol. 2003;52:603-604.
55. Ledson MJ, Gallagher MJ, Jackson M, et al. Outcome of *Burkholderia cepacia* colonisation in an adult cystic fibrosis centre. Thorax. 2002;57:142-145.
56. Chen JS, Witzmann KA, Spilker T, et al. Endemicity and inter-city spread of *Burkholderia cepacia* genomovar III in cystic fibrosis. J Pediatr. 2001;139:643-649.
57. LiPuma JJ. Preventing *Burkholderia cepacia* complex infection in cystic fibrosis: Is there a middle ground? J Pediatr. 2002;141:467-469.
58. Kumar A, Dietrich S, Schneider W, et al. Genetic relatedness of *Burkholderia (Pseudomonas) cepacia* isolates from five cystic fibrosis centers in Michigan. Respir Med. 1997;91:485-492.
59. Clode FE, Kaufmann ME, Malnick H, et al. Distribution of genes encoding putative transmissibility factors among epidemic and nonepidemic strains of *Burkholderia cepacia* from cystic fibrosis patients in the United Kingdom. J Clin Microbiol. 2000;38:1763-1766.
60. Liu L, Spilker T, Coenye T, et al. Identification by subtractive hybridization of a novel insertion element specific for two widespread *Burkholderia cepacia* genomovar III strains. J Clin Microbiol. 2003;41:2471-2476.
61. Parke JL, Gurian-Sherman D. Diversity of the *Burkholderia cepacia* complex and implications for risk assessment of biological control strains. Annu Rev Phytopathol. 2001;39:225-258.

62. Gopalakrishnan R, Hawley HB, Czachor JS, et al. *Stenotrophomonas maltophilia* infection and colonization in the intensive care units of two community hospitals: A study of 143 patients. Heart Lung. 1999;28:134-141.
63. Gales AC, Jones RN, Forward KR, et al. Emerging importance of multidrug-resistant *Acinetobacter* species and *Stenotrophomonas maltophilia* as pathogens in seriously ill patients: Geographic patterns, epidemiological features, and trends in the SENTRY Antimicrobial Surveillance Program (1997-1999). Clin Infect Dis. 2001;32(Suppl 2):S104-S113.
64. Kataoka D, Fujiwara H, Kawakami T, et al. The indirect pathogenicity of *Stenotrophomonas maltophilia*. Int J Antimicrob Agents. 2003;22:601-606.
65. Friedman ND, Korman TM, Fairley CK, et al. Bacteraemia due to *Stenotrophomonas maltophilia*: An analysis of 45 episodes. J Infect. 2002;45:47-53.
66. Ladhani S, Gransden W. Septicaemia due to glucose non-fermenting, gram-negative bacilli other than *Pseudomonas aeruginosa* in children. Acta Paediatr. 2002;91:303-306.
67. Senol E, DesJardin J, Stark PC, et al. Attributable mortality of *Stenotrophomonas maltophilia* bacteremia. Clin Infect Dis. 2002;34:1653-1656.
68. Sattler CA, Mason EO Jr, Kaplan SL. Nonrespiratory *Stenotrophomonas maltophilia* infection at a children's hospital. Clin Infect Dis. 2000;31:1321-1330.
69. Krupova Y, Novotny J, Sabo A, et al. Aetiology, cost of antimicrobial therapy and outcome in neutropenic patients who developed bacteraemia during antimicrobial prophylaxis: A case-control study. Int J Antimicrob Agents. 1998;10:313-316.
70. Khan IA, Mehta NJ. *Stenotrophomonas maltophilia* endocarditis: A systematic review. Angiology. 2002;53:49-55.
71. Benian O, Alimgil L, Erda N. Two cases of *Stenotrophomonas maltophilia* endophthalmitis. Ophthalmic Surg Lasers. 2002;33:253-256.
72. Gunnarsson G, Steinsson K. Sinusitis due to *Stenotrophomonas maltophilia*. Scand J Infect Dis. 2002;34:136-137.
73. Downhour NP, Petersen EA, Krueger TS, et al. Severe cellulitis/myositis caused by *Stenotrophomonas maltophilia*. Ann Pharmacother. 2002;36:63-66.
74. Sakhnini E, Weissmann A, Oren I. Fulminant *Stenotrophomonas maltophilia* soft tissue infection in immunocompromised patients: An outbreak transmitted via tap water. Am J Med Sci. 2002;323:269-272.
75. Calza L, Manfredi R, Marinacci G, et al. Liver abscess caused by *Stenotrophomonas (Xanthomonas) maltophilia* in a patient with AIDS. AIDS. 2001;15:2465-2467.
76. Petri A, Tiszlavicz L, Nagy E, et al. Liver abscess caused by *Stenotrophomonas maltophilia*: Report of a case. Surg Today. 2003;33:224-228.
77. Lo WT, Wang CC, Lee CM, et al. Successful treatment of multi-resistant *Stenotrophomonas maltophilia* meningitis with ciprofloxacin in a pre term infant. Eur J Pediatr. 2002;161:680-682.
78. Platsouka E, Routsi C, Chalkis A, et al. *Stenotrophomonas maltophilia* meningitis, bacteremia and respiratory infection. Scand J Infect Dis. 2002;34:391-392.
79. Vartivarian SE, Papadakis KA, Palacios JA, et al. Mucocutaneous and soft tissue infections caused by *Xanthomonas maltophilia*: A new spectrum. Ann Intern Med. 1994;121:969-973.
80. Mandell IN, Feiner HD, Price NM, et al. *Pseudomonas cepacia* endocarditis and ecthyma gangrenosum. Arch Dermatol. 1977;113:199-202.
81. Khardori N, Elting L, Wong E, et al. Nosocomial infections due to *Xanthomonas maltophilia* (*Pseudomonas maltophilia*) in patients with cancer. Rev Infect Dis. 1990;12:997-1003.
82. Holmes B, Lapage SP, Easterling BG. Distribution in clinical material and identification of *Pseudomonas maltophilia*. J Clin Pathol. 1979;32:66-72.
83. Morrison AJ, Hoffman KK, Wenzel RP. Associated mortality and clinical characteristics of nosocomial *Pseudomonas maltophilia* in a university hospital. J Clin Microbiol. 1986;24:52-55.
84. Vartivarian SE, Papadakis KA, Anaissie EJ. *Stenotrophomonas (Xanthomonas) maltophilia* urinary tract infection: A disease that is usually severe and complicated. Arch Intern Med. 1996;156:433-435.
85. Burdge DR, Nakielna EM, Noble MA. Case-control and vector studies of nosocomial acquisition of *Pseudomonas cepacia* in adult patients with cystic fibrosis. Infect Control Hosp Epidemiol. 1993;14:127-130.
86. Taccetti G, Campana S, Marianelli L. Multiresistant non-fermentative gram-negative bacteria in cystic fibrosis patients: The results of an Italian multicenter study. Italian Group for Cystic Fibrosis Microbiology. Eur J Epidemiol. 1999;15:85-88.
87. Bevivino A, Dalmastri C, Tabacchioni S, et al. *Burkholderia cepacia* complex bacteria from clinical and environmental sources in Italy: Genomovar status and distribution of traits related to virulence and transmissibility. J Clin Microbiol. 2002;40:846-851.
88. Winkelstein JA, Marino MC, Johnston RB Jr, et al. Chronic granulomatous disease: Report on a national registry of 368 patients. Medicine (Baltimore). 2000;79:155-169.
89. Belchis DA, Simpson E, Colby T. Histopathologic features of *Burkholderia cepacia* pneumonia in patients without cystic fibrosis. Mod Pathol. 2000;13:369-372.
90. Jones AM, Dodd ME, Webb AK. *Burkholderia cepacia*: Current clinical issues, environmental controversies and ethical dilemmas. Eur Respir J. 2001;17:295-301.
91. Tablan OC, Chorba TL, Schidlow DV, et al. *Pseudomonas cepacia* colonization in patients with cystic fibrosis: Risk factors and clinical outcome. J Pediatr. 1985;107:382-387.
92. Beringer PM, Appleman MD. Unusual respiratory bacterial flora in cystic fibrosis: Microbiologic and clinical features. Curr Opin Pulm Med. 2000;6:545-550.
93. Soni R, Marks G, Henry DA, et al. Effect of *Burkholderia cepacia* infection in the clinical course of patients with cystic fibrosis: A pilot study in a Sydney clinic. Respirology. 2002;7:241-245.
94. De Soyza A, McDowell A, Archer L, et al. *Burkholderia cepacia* complex genomovars and pulmonary transplantation outcomes in patients with cystic fibrosis. Lancet. 2001;358:1780-1781.
95. LiPuma JJ. *Burkholderia cepacia* complex: A contraindication to lung transplantation in cystic fibrosis? Transpl Infect Dis. 2001;3:149-160.
96. Martino R, Gomez L, Pericas R, et al. Bacteraemia caused by non-glucose-fermenting gram-negative bacilli and *Aeromonas* species in patients with haematological malignancies and solid tumours. Eur J Clin Microbiol Infect Dis. 2000;19:320-323.
97. Kaitwatcharachai C, Silpapojakul K, Jitsurong S, et al. An outbreak of *Burkholderia cepacia* bacteremia in hemodialysis patients: An epidemiologic and molecular study. Am J Kidney Dis. 2000;36:199-204.
98. Gruson D, Hilbert G, Vargas F, et al. Rotation and restricted use of antibiotics in a medical intensive care unit: Impact on the incidence of ventilator-associated pneumonia caused by antibiotic-resistant gram-negative bacteria. Am J Respir Crit Care Med. 2000;162:837-843.
99. Matrician L, Ange G, Burns S, et al. Outbreak of nosocomial *Burkholderia cepacia* infection and colonization associated with intrinsically contaminated mouthwash. Infect Control Hosp Epidemiol. 2000;21:739-741.
100. Siddiqui AH, Mulligan ME, Mahenthiralingam E, et al. An episodic outbreak of genetically related *Burkholderia cepacia* among non-cystic fibrosis patients at a university hospital. Infect Control Hosp Epidemiol. 2001;22:419-422.
101. Brauner A, Hfiby N, Kjartansson J, et al. *Pseudomonas cepacia* septicemia in patients with burns: Report of two cases. Scand J Infect Dis. 1985;17:63-66.
102. Sobel JD, Hashman N, Reinherz G, et al. Nosocomial *Pseudomonas cepacia* infection associated with chlorhexidine contamination. Am J Med. 1982;73:183-186.
103. Taplin D, Bassett DCJ, Mertz PM. Foot lesions associated with *Pseudomonas cepacia*. Lancet. 1971;2:568-571.
104. Keizur JJ, Lavin B, Leidich RB. Iatrogenic urinary tract infection with *Pseudomonas cepacia* after transrectal ultrasound guided biopsy of the prostate. J Urol. 1993;149:523-526.
105. Hanes SD, Demirkan K, Tolley E, et al. Risk factors for late-onset nosocomial pneumonia caused by *Stenotrophomonas maltophilia* in critically ill trauma patients. Clin Infect Dis. 2002;35:228-235.
106. Yu WL, Wang DY, Lin CW, et al. Endemic *Burkholderia cepacia* bacteraemia: Clinical features and antimicrobial susceptibilities of isolates. Scand J Infect Dis. 1999;31:293-298.
107. Betriu C, Sanchez A, Palau ML, et al. Antibiotic resistance surveillance of *Stenotrophomonas maltophilia*, 1993-1999. J Antimicrob Chemother. 2001;48:152-154.
108. Barbier-Frebour N, Boutiba-Boubake I, Nouvello M, et al. Molecular investigation of *Stenotrophomonas maltophilia* isolates exhibiting rapid emergence of ticarcillin-clavulanate resistance. J Hosp Infect. 2000;45:35-41.
109. Micozzi A, Venditti M, Monaco M, et al. Bacteremia due to *Stenotrophomonas maltophilia* in patients with hematologic malignancies. Clin Infect Dis. 2000;31:705-711.
110. Schmitz FJ, Verhoef J, Fluit AC. Comparative activities of six different fluoroquinolones against 9,682 clinical bacterial isolates from 20 European university hospitals participating in the European SENTRY surveillance programme. The SENTRY participants group. Int J Antimicrob Agents. 1999;12:311-317.
111. Weiss K, Restieri C, De Carolis E, et al. Comparative activity of new quinolones against 326 clinical isolates of *Stenotrophomonas maltophilia*. J Antimicrob Chemother. 2000;45:363-365.
112. Blondeau JM, Laskowski R, Borsos S. In-vitro activity of cefepime and seven other antimicrobial agents against 1518 non-fermentative gram-negative bacilli collected from 48 Canadian health care facilities. Canadian Afermenter Study Group. J Antimicrob Chemother. 1999;44:545-548.
113. Fujita J, Yamadori I, Xu G, et al. Clinical features of *Stenotrophomonas maltophilia* pneumonia in immunocompromised patients. Respir Med. 1996;90:35-38.
114. Carroll KC, Cohen S, Nelson R, et al. Comparison of various in vitro susceptibility methods for testing *Stenotrophomonas maltophilia*. Diagn Microbiol Infect Dis. 1998;32:229-235.
115. Crispino M, Boccia MC, Bagattini M, et al. Molecular epidemiology of *Stenotrophomonas maltophilia* in a university hospital. J Hosp Infect. 2002;52:88-92.
116. Giamarellos-Bourboulis EJ, Karnesis L, Giamarellou H. Synergy of colistin with rifampin and trimethoprim/sulfamethoxazole on multidrug-resistant *Stenotrophomonas maltophilia*. Diagn Microbiol Infect Dis. 2002;44:259-263.
117. Hanberger H, Diekema D, Fluit A, et al. Surveillance of antibiotic resistance in European ICUs. J Hosp Infect. 2001;48:161-176.
118. Tsiodras S, Pittet D, Carmeli Y, et al. Clinical implications of *Stenotrophomonas maltophilia* resistant to trimethoprim-sulfamethoxazole: A study of 69 patients at 2 university hospitals. Scand J Infect Dis. 2000;32:651-656.
119. Papadakis KA, Vartivarian SE, Vassilaki ME, et al. *Stenotrophomonas maltophilia* meningitis: Report of two cases and review of the literature. J Neurosurg. 1997;87:106-108.
120. Papadakis KA, Vartivarian SE, Vassilaki ME, et al. *Stenotrophomonas maltophilia*: An unusual cause of biliary sepsis. Clin Infect Dis. 1995;21:1032-1034.
121. Maningo E, Watanakunakorn C. *Xanthomonas maltophilia* and *Pseudomonas cepacia* in lower respiratory tracts of patients in critical care units. J Infect. 1995;31:89-92.
122. Milatovic D, Schmitz FJ, Verhoef J, et al. Activities of the glycylcycline tigecycline (GAR-936) against 1,924 recent European clinical bacterial isolates. Antimicrob Agents Chemother. 2003;47:400-404.
123. Bhakta DR, Leader I, Jacobson R, et al. Antibacterial properties of investigational, new, and commonly used antibiotics against isolates of *Pseudomonas cepacia* isolates in Michigan. Chemotherapy. 1992;33:319-323.
124. Husain S, Singh N. *Burkholderia cepacia* infection and lung transplantation. Semin Respir Infect. 2002;17:284-290.
125. Bonacorsi S, Fitoussi F, Lhopital S, et al. Comparative in vitro activities of meropenem, imipenem, temocillin, piperacillin, and ceftazidime in combination with tobramycin, rifampin, or ciprofloxacin against *Burkholderia cepacia* isolates from patients with cystic fibrosis. Antimicrob Agents Chemother. 1999;43:213-217.

126. Manno G, Ugolotti E, Belli ML, et al. Use of the E test to assess synergy of antibiotic combinations against isolates of *Burkholderia cepacia*-complex from patients with cystic fibrosis. Eur J Clin Microbiol Infect Dis. 2003;22:28-34.
127. Ciofu O, Jensen T, Pressler T, et al. Meropenem in cystic fibrosis patients infected with resistant *Pseudomonas aeruginosa* or *Burkholderia cepacia* and with hypersensitivity to beta-lactam antibiotics. Clin Microbiol Infect. 1996;2:91-98.
128. Okano M, Yamada M, Ohtsu M, et al. Successful treatment with methylprednisolone pulse therapy for a life-threatening pulmonary insufficiency in a patient with chronic granulomatous disease following pulmonary invasive aspergillosis and *Burkholderia cepacia* infection. Respiration. 1999;66:551-554.
129. Agodi A, Barchitta M, Giannino V, et al. *Burkholderia cepacia* complex in cystic fibrosis and non-cystic fibrosis patients: Identification of a cluster of epidemic lineages. J Hosp Infect. 2002;50:188-195.
130. Heath DG, Hohneker K, Carriker C, et al. Six-year molecular analysis of *Burkholderia cepacia* complex isolates among cystic fibrosis patients at a referral center for lung transplantation. J Clin Microbiol. 2002;40:1188-1193.
131. Labarca JA, Leber AL, Kern VL, et al. Outbreak of *Stenotrophomonas maltophilia* bacteremia in allogenic bone marrow transplant patients: Role of severe neutropenia and mucositis. Clin Infect Dis. 2000;30:195-197.
132. Garcia de Viedma D, Marin M, Cercenado E, et al. Evidence of nosocomial *Stenotrophomonas maltophilia* cross-infection in a neonatology unit analyzed by three molecular typing methods. Infect Control Hosp Epidemiol. 1999;20:816-820.
133. Zanetti F, De Luca G, Stampi S. Recovery of *Burkholderia pseudomallei* and *B. cepacia* from drinking water. Int J Food Microbiol. 2000;59:67-72.
134. Mary P, Defives C, Hornez JP. Occurrence and multiple antibiotic resistance profiles of non-fermentative gram-negative microflora in five brands of non-carbonated French bottled spring water. Microb Ecol. 2000;39:322-329.
135. Moore JE, Thompson I, Crowe M, et al. *Burkholderia cepacia* from a sink drain. J Hosp Infect. 2002;50:235-237.
136. Weber DJ, Rutala WA, Blanchet CN, et al. Faucet aerators: A source of patient colonization with *Stenotrophomonas maltophilia*. Am J Infect Control. 1999;27:59-63.
137. Klausner JD, Zukerman C, Limaye AP, et al. Outbreak of *Stenotrophomonas maltophilia* bacteremia among patients undergoing bone marrow transplantation: Association with faulty replacement of handwashing soap. Infect Control Hosp Epidemiol. 1999;20:756-758.
138. Rogues AM, Maugein J, Allery A, et al. Electronic ventilator temperature sensors as a potential source of respiratory tract colonization with *Stenotrophomonas maltophilia*. J Hosp Infect. 2001;49:289-292.
139. Ramsey AH, Skonieczny P, Coolidge DT, et al. *Burkholderia cepacia* lower respiratory tract infection associated with exposure to a respiratory therapist. Infect Control Hosp Epidemiol. 2001;22:423-426.
140. Walsh NM, Casano AA, Manangan LP, et al. Risk factors for *Burkholderia cepacia* complex colonization and infection among patients with cystic fibrosis. J Pediatr. 2002;141:512-517.
141. Mahenthiralingam E, Vandamme P, Campbell ME, et al. Infection with *Burkholderia cepacia* complex genomovars in patients with cystic fibrosis: Virulent transmissible strains of genomovar III can replace *Burkholderia multivorans*. Clin Infect Dis. 2001;33:1469-1475.
142. Ledson MJ, Gallagher MJ, Robinson M, et al. A randomized double-blinded placebo-controlled crossover trial of nebulized taurolidine in adult cystic fibrosis patients infected with *Burkholderia cepacia*. J Aerosol Med. 2002;15:51-57.
143. LiPuma JJ, Spilker T, Coenye T, et al. An epidemic *Burkholderia cepacia* complex strain identified in soil. Lancet. 2002;359:2002-2003.
144. LiPuma JJ. *Burkholderia cepacia* epidemiology and pathogenesis: Implications for infection control. Curr Opin Pulm Med. 1998;4:337-341.

CHAPTER **218**

Burkholderia pseudomallei and *Burkholderia mallei*: Melioidosis and Glanders

BART J. CURRIE

The genus *Burkholderia* is currently composed of more than 40 species, but only three are notable pathogens for humans or animals: the former *cepacia* complex (described in Chapter 217), *pseudomallei* (the agent of melioidosis), and *mallei* (the agent of equine glanders). All three are aerobic, nonsporulating, straight or slightly curved gram-negative bacilli that were formerly placed in the genus *Pseudomonas*.

MELIOIDOSIS

Melioidosis is a disease of humans and animals; it has enormous clinical diversity, spanning asymptomatic infection, localized skin ulcers or abscesses, chronic pneumonia mimicking tuberculosis, and fulminant septic shock with abscesses in multiple internal organs. Most disease is from recent infection, but latency with reactivation is described up to 29 years after exposure. Most cases are reported from Southeast Asia and northern Australia, but melioidosis is increasingly being recognized in people infected in the endemic region who return or travel to Europe and the United States. The causative bacterium, *Burkholderia pseudomallei*, is also considered a potential biological warfare agent.

History

In 1912, Whitmore and Krishnaswamy described cases of a newly recognized septicemic disease in morphine addicts in Rangoon, Burma.[1] Fatal cases were characterized by widespread caseous consolidation of the lung and abscesses in liver, spleen, kidney, and subcutaneous tissues. The bacillus isolated from tissues was similar to that causing glanders *(Burkholderia mallei)* but was motile. Whitmore noted the clinical similarity to glanders, and Stanton and Fletcher subsequently proposed the name *melioidosis,* derived from the Greek *melis* ("distemper of asses"). Various names were used for the causative bacterium, including *Bacillus whitmori* and for many years *Pseudomonas pseudomallei.*[2] In 1992, seven *Pseudomonas* species were moved to a new genus, *Burkholderia. B. cepacia* is the type species in the genus, which includes the organisms causing melioidosis *(B. pseudomallei)* and glanders *(B. mallei).*

Etiology

B. pseudomallei is a small, gram-negative, oxidase-positive, motile, aerobic bacillus with occasional polar flagella. On staining, a bipolar "safety pin" pattern is seen. The organism is easily recovered on standard culture medium but may be misidentified as *B. cepacia, Pseudomonas stutzeri,* or other *Pseudomonas* species.

The organism is present in soil and surface water in endemic regions. Humans and animals are infected by percutaneous inoculation, inhalation, or ingestion. Occasional laboratory-acquired infections are described, but person-to-person spread and zoonotic infection are very uncommon.

Epidemiology

Following the initial account in Burma, melioidosis was documented in humans and animals in Malaysia and Singapore from 1913 and then Vietnam from 1925 and Indonesia from 1929.[3-5] Thailand reports the largest number of cases,[6-8] with an estimated 2000 to 3000 cases of melioidosis each year.[9] Melioidosis is also common in Malaysia[10] and Singapore.[11,12] Other countries in the region where melioidosis is recognized in humans and animals include China (especially Hong Kong), Taiwan, Brunei, and Vietnam.[13-16] Melioidosis is also likely to occur in Cambodia, Laos, and the Philippines.[4,9] Melioidosis has been increasingly recognized in India, although reports that some of the "plague" scares of 1994 may have been cases of melioidosis have been disproved.[17,18] Cases are reported from Sri Lanka, Bangladesh, and Pakistan. Surprisingly, despite the early documentation of melioidosis in Burma and Indonesia, it appears that it is not currently being recognized and diagnosed in those countries. Cases of melioidosis have also been documented from Papua New Guinea and Fiji, but the extent of endemicity in the Pacific islands remains to be defined.

The two locations where melioidosis is arguably the most important single bacterial pathogen for humans are some northeast provinces in Thailand and the Top End of the Northern Territory of Australia. In northeast Thailand, 20% of community-acquired septicemic cases are caused by melioidosis, which accounts for 39% of fatal septicemias[7] and 36% of fatal community-acquired pneumonias.[19] In the Top End of the Northern Territory, melioidosis has been the commonest cause of fatal community-acquired bacteremic pneumonia.[20]

Occasional cases of melioidosis have been documented from outside the classical endemic region of Southeast Asia, Australasia, the Indian subcontinent, and China. These include sporadic human or animal cases or environmental isolates of *B. pseudomallei* from the Middle East, Africa, the Caribbean, and Central and South America. Although some of these reports are from incorrect species diagnosis, others are confirmed, making the endemic limitations of melioidosis very unclear.[4,13] Global warming may well result in expansion of the endemic boundaries of melioidosis.

In addition to endemic melioidosis, there are several documented situations where melioidosis became established in nontropical locations. In France in the 1970s, cases of melioidosis occurred in animals in a Paris zoo, with spread to other zoos and equestrian clubs.[4] In addition to fatal animal and human cases, there was extensive soil contamination persisting for some years. *B. pseudomallei* was considered likely to have been introduced by importation of infected animals. A cluster of cases occurred over a 25-year period in southwestern Western Australia (31° S), involving animal cases and one human infection in a farmer. Ribotyping of the farm animal and human isolates and one isolate from the soil showed identical patterns.[21] This supports the suggestion of clonal introduction of *B. pseudomallei* into this temperate region, probably via an infected animal, with environmental contamination, local dissemination, and persistence over 25 years.

Melioidosis was an important cause of morbidity and mortality in foreign troops fighting in Southeast Asia. Dance noted that at least 100 cases occurred among French forces in Indochina between 1948 and 1954.[4] By 1973, 343 cases had been reported in American troops fighting in Vietnam. Concerns of reactivation of latent infection in soldiers returned from Vietnam, with estimates from serology studies of around 225,000 potential cases, resulted in melioidosis being called the "Vietnamese time bomb."[22] However, although occasional cases of reactivation of *B. pseudomallei* still occur in Vietnam veterans, it is rare in comparison to the numbers exposed.

Transmission

Figure 218-1 summarizes the natural history of infection with *B. pseudomallei.* Studies from Malaysia and more recently from Thailand[23] have found the organism more commonly in cleared, irrigated sites such as rice paddies. It has been suggested that the increase in melioidosis cases in Thailand may be in part the consequence of the increased number of bacteria in such environments and in part the consequence of increased exposure to bacteria resulting from changes in behaviors such as farming techniques.[13] In Australia, *B. pseudomallei* has been found most commonly in clay soils to a depth of 25 to 45 cm, and it has been proposed that the bacteria move to the surface with the rising water table during the wet season.[24] An alternative explanation for the variable bacterial presence found is that during times of stress such as in prolonged dry seasons, *B. pseudomallei* may persist in soil in a viable but nonculturable state.[25] Differential gene activation may allow such environmental bacteria to respond and adapt to different environmental conditions. This possibility is also relevant to pathogenicity, latency, and reactivation of infection with *B. pseudomallei* in humans. The role of biofilms in the persistence of *B. pseudomallei* in the environment as well as in animal and human hosts requires study.[26] There is increasing interest in the intracellular survival of *B. pseudomallei,* and it has been proposed that an ecologic niche for the bacteria in the environment may be within environmental protozoa or fungi.[25]

In most endemic regions there is a close association between melioidosis and rainfall. In northeast Thailand[27] and northern Australia,[28] 75% and 85% of cases, respectively, occur in the wet season. Although early animal studies showed infection with *B. pseudomallei* through oral or nasal exposure and from ingestion, recent reviews consider that the majority of human cases are from percutaneous inoculation of *B. pseudomallei* following exposure to muddy soils or surface water in endemic locations.[2,3,20] Ingestion and sexual transmission have been suggested as unusual modes of transmission of *B. pseudomallei.* Presentations of melioidosis pneumonia following presumptive inoculating skin injuries have been documented in patients with soil-contaminated burns and are also common in tropical Australia.[20] This suggests hematogenous spread to the lung rather than inhalation or spread from the upper respiratory tract. Under certain epidemiologic conditions, the inhalation route may predominate, as suggested for soldiers exposed to dusts raised by helicopter rotor blades in Vietnam.[29] Melioidosis following near drowning is well documented, with the probable infecting event being aspiration.[14] Intensity of rainfall is an independent predictor of melioidosis exhibiting as pneumonia and of a fatal outcome,[30] suggesting that heavy monsoonal rainfall and winds may result in a shift toward inhalation as the mode of infection with *B. pseudomallei.* Several outbreaks of melioidosis in Australia have been linked to contamination of potable water with *B. pseudomallei.*[31,32] The water supplies involved were unchlorinated or the chlorination was below standard. The contamination of the water supply has been attributed to soil disturbance during excavations.

The incubation period for melioidosis is influenced by inoculating dose, mode of infection, host risk factors, and probably differential virulence of infecting *B. pseudomallei* strains. Onset of melioidosis within 24 hours has been seen in presumed aspiration following near drowning and in some cases following severe weather events. In 25 cases where a clear incubation period could be determined between the inoculating injury and the onset of symptoms, the incubation period was 1 to 21 days (mean, 9 days),[33] which is consistent with a series of nosocomial cases from Thailand, where the incubation period was 3 to 16 days (mean, 9.5 days).[34]

Pathogenesis

Serology studies show that most infection with *B. pseudomallei* is asymptomatic.[35,36] In northeast Thailand, a majority of the rural population is seropositive by indirect hemagglutination (IHA),[27] with most seroconversion occurring between 6 months and 4 years of age.[36] Although melioidosis occurs in all age groups, severe clinical disease such as septicemic pneumonia is seen mostly in those with risk factors such as diabetes, renal disease, and alcoholism.

In addition to infection by inhalation, bacterial load on exposure (inoculating dose) and virulence of the infecting strain of *B. pseudomallei* are also likely to influence severity of disease. However, it has been noted that, despite the large bacterial load in severely ill patients with septicemic pulmonary melioidosis, person-to-person transmission is extremely unusual. This, together with the rarity of fulminant melioidosis in healthy people, supports the primary importance of host

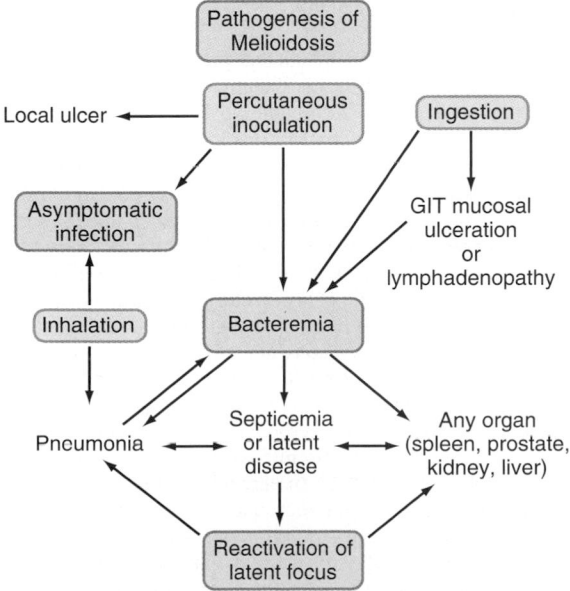

FIGURE 218-1. Natural history of infection with *Burkholderia pseudomallei.* GIT, gastrointestinal tract.

risk factors for development of melioidosis. Furthermore, although it is clear from laboratory studies of isolates of *B. pseudomallei* from animals, humans, and the environment that virulence differs among *B. pseudomallei* isolates,[37] the importance of this variation in virulence in determining clinical aspects of melioidosis remains uncertain. Molecular typing that shows clonality of isolates in animal and human clusters has revealed that the same outbreak strain can cause different clinical presentations, with host factors being most important in determining severity of disease.[32]

To date, there is no definitive evidence for development of immunity from melioidosis with natural exposure to *B. pseudomallei,* and reinfection has occurred with a different strain of *B. pseudomallei* following successful treatment of melioidosis.[38]

B. pseudomallei is a facultative intracellular pathogen. It can invade and replicate inside various cells, including polymorphonuclear leukocytes and macrophages and some epithelial cell lines.[39] The bacteria can be found intracellularly in membrane-bound vacuoles and can produce a capsular polysaccharide (exopolysaccharide) in response to low pH challenge.[40] To date, animal models have been unable to confirm a clinically relevant exotoxin for *B. pseudomallei.*[41] However, resistance to human serum (conferred by lipopolysaccharide [LPS])[40,42] and the ability of *B. pseudomallei* to survive intracellularly (conferred in part by capsular polysaccharide) appear critical in the pathogenesis of melioidosis.[43-45] Type III secretion systems in *B. pseudomallei* have also been found to be important in cell invasion and intracellular survival.[46,47]

Intracellular survival of *B. pseudomallei* in human and animal hosts is likely to explain the ability for latency. Additional factors are the ability of *B. pseudomallei* to form antibiotic-resistant small-colony variants,[48] and the ability of mucoid variants with large extracellular polysaccharide glycocalyx structures to form biofilm-encased microcolonies that are also relatively antibiotic resistant.

There have been a number of studies showing elevated levels of various endogenous inflammatory mediators and cytokines to be associated with severity and outcomes of melioidosis. However, whether these elevated cytokines are a cause or a result of severe disease is not established. In Thailand, there was an association of severe melioidosis with tumor necrosis factor (TNF)-α gene allele 2, which is linked to higher constitutive and inducible production of TNF-α.[49] However, in a mouse model of melioidosis, neutralization of TNF-α or interleukin (IL)-12 increased susceptibility to infection in vivo, and interferon-γ (INF-γ) was found to be important for survival, with mice treated with monoclonal anti-IFN-γ dying more quickly.[50] There are therefore important host protective mechanisms against *B. pseudomallei* in cytokine responses as well as potentially detrimental ones, with the timing of cytokine release and the balance between pro- and anti-inflammatory responses likely to be determining the severity of disease and outcome of infection. The extent to which host polymorphisms in immune response contribute in comparison to differences in organism virulence, infecting dose of *B. pseudomallei,* and defined host risk factors such as diabetes remains to be clarified. Nevertheless, the predominant association with fatal melioidosis is the presence of defined patient risk factors.

Table 218-1 summarizes the risk factors for melioidosis. The most important risk factors are diabetes, alcohol excess, and renal disease.[2,28,51] In Thailand, the adjusted odds ratios for diabetes and renal disease (chronic renal impairment or renal or ureteric calculi) in cases of melioidosis versus controls were 12.9 (95% confidence interval, 5.1-37.2) and 2.9 (95% CI, 1.7-5.0), respectively.[51] Other risk factors for melioidosis include chronic lung disease (including cystic fibrosis), thalassemia (odds ratio in Thailand, 10.2; 95% CI, 3.5-30.8), malignancies, steroid therapy, iron overload, and tuberculosis.[51] Severe disease and fatalities are uncommon in those without risk factors who are diagnosed and treated early, with only one death in 51 patients without risk factors in one study.[28] Risk factors are less commonly present in children than in adults.[52,53]

It has been suggested that the predisposition to melioidosis in those with diabetes, alcohol excess, or chronic renal disease may reflect impairment of their neutrophil functions, such as mobilization, delivery, adherence, and ingestion.[28] Melioidosis has also been described in chronic granulomatous disease.[54] The possible primary role of neutrophil function in containing *B. pseudomallei* led to empirical use of granulocyte colony-stimulating factor (G-CSF) in patients with strictly defined septic shock, with observational data showing a significant improvement in survival with G-CSF.[55]

Clinical Manifestations

The earliest descriptions of melioidosis documented the fulminant end of the clinical spectrum, with abscesses throughout both lungs and in many organs.[1] At the other end of the spectrum are asymptomatic infections and localized skin ulcers or abscesses without systemic illness. Howe and colleagues classified melioidosis as acute, subacute, and chronic.[29] The Infectious Disease Association of Thailand summarized 345 cases in these categories:

1. Disseminated septicemia (45% of cases, 87% mortality)
2. Nondisseminated septicemia (12% of cases, 17% mortality)
3. Localized septicemia (42% of cases, 9% mortality)
4. Transient bacteremia (0.3%).[2,6]

Recent bacteremia and overall mortality rates have been, respectively, 60% and 44% in Thailand,[27] 46% and 19% in Australia,[28] and 52% and 46% in Singapore.[12]

Table 218-2 summarizes the clinical presentations of patients with melioidosis in northern Australia. Pneumonia is the commonest clinical presentation of patients with melioidosis in all studies, accounting for around half of cases. Secondary pneumonia after another primary presentation occurs in around 10% of cases. Acute melioidosis pneumonia has a spectrum from fulminant septic shock (mortality up to 90%) (Figs. 218-2 to 218-5) to mild undifferentiated pneumonia, which can be acute or subacute in nature, with little mortality. Septicemic patients present acutely unwell with high fevers and prostration and often little initial cough or pleuritic pain. On chest radiographs, diffuse nodular infiltrates often develop throughout both lungs, and they coalesce, cavitate, and progress rapidly, consistent with the caseous necrosis and multiple metastatic abscess formation seen at autopsy. Nonsepticemic patients with pneumonia and some with septicemic pneumonia have a more predominant cough with productive sputum and dyspnea, and their chest radiographs show discrete but progressive consolidation in one or more lobes (Fig. 218-6). In endemic regions, acute pneumonia with upper lobe consolidation warrants consideration of melioidosis, although lower lobe infiltrates are also common.

In 12% of cases in northern Australia, patients present with chronic melioidosis, defined as illness with symptoms for longer than 2 months duration on presentation. Many of these patients have features mimicking tuberculosis, with fevers, weight loss, productive cough

TABLE 218-1   Risk Factors for Melioidosis

Risk Factor*	Thailand (% of cases)	Australia (% of cases)
Diabetes	23%-60%	37%
Alcohol excess	12%	39%
Renal disease	20%-27%	10%
Chronic lung disease	ND	27%
Thalassemia	7%	Nil
No risk factors	36%	20%

*Not listed: malignancy, steroid therapy, iron overload, cardiac failure.

Thailand data from Punyagupta S. Melioidosis: Review of 686 cases and presentation of a new clinical classification. In: Punyagupta S, Sirisanthana T, Stapatayavong B, eds: Melioidosis. Bangkok: Bangkok Medical; 1989:217-229; Chaowagul W, White NJ, Dance DA, et al. Melioidosis: A major cause of community-acquired septicemia in northeastern Thailand. J Infect Dis. 1989;159:890-899; and Suputtamongkol Y, Chaowagul W, Chetchotisakd P, et al. Risk factors for melioidosis and bacteremic melioidosis. Clin Infect Dis. 1999;29:408-413.

Australia data from Currie BJ, Fisher DA, Howard DM, et al. Endemic melioidosis in tropical northern Australia: A 10-year prospective study and review of the literature. Clin Infect Dis. 2000;31:981-986.

TABLE 218-2 Clinical Presentations of Melioidosis in Northern Australia

Bacteremic (*n* = 184)

	Total Cases	Deaths (Mortality)
Pneumonia		
+ ⎫ Septic shock	55	36 (65%)
− ⎭	50	2 (4%)
Genitourinary		
+ ⎫ Septic shock	8	6 (75%)
− ⎭	25	0 (0%)
Osteomyelitis/septic arthritis		
+ ⎫ Septic shock	1	1 (100%)
− ⎭	6	0 (0%)
Other		
+ ⎫ Septic shock	13	9 (69%)
− ⎭	26	0 (0%)

Nonbacteremic (*n* = 179)

Presentation	Total Cases	Deaths (Mortality)
Pneumonia	81	4 (5%)
Genitourinary	21	0 (0%)
Skin abscess(es)	45	0 (0%)
Soft tissue abscess(es)	11	0 (0%)
Neurologic	12	3 (25%)
Osteomyelitis/septic arthritis	5	0 (0%)
Other	4	0 (0%)
Total	**363**	**61 (17%)**

Updated from Currie BJ, Fisher DA, Howard DM, et al. Endemic melioidosis in tropical northern Australia: A 10-year prospective study and review of the literature. Clin Infect Dis. 2000;31:981-986.

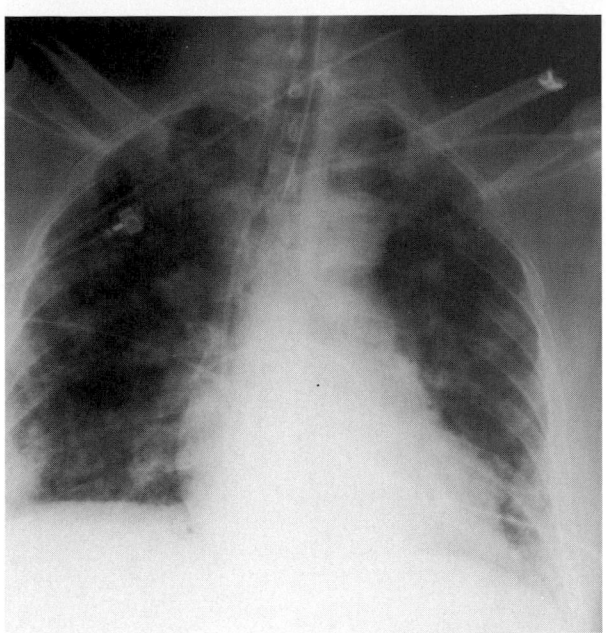

FIGURE 218-3. Chest radiograph of patient in Figure 218-2, showing multiple pulmonary abscesses.

(sometimes with hemoptysis), and classically upper lobe infiltrates with or without cavitation on chest radiographs (Fig. 218-7). In these patients, disease can be remitting and relapsing over many years, sometimes with an initial misdiagnosis of tuberculosis. Although acute deterioration with septicemia may occur, mortality in this group is low.

Until recently it was thought that a colonization state did not exist for *B. pseudomallei,* with presence in sputum or throat always reflecting disease. However, it has recently become evident that *B. pseudomallei* can both colonize airways and cause disease in patients with cystic fibrosis (CF) and bronchiectasis. The similarity to infection with *B. cepacia* in CF is of concern, given the association of *B. cepacia* with more rapid deterioration in lung function. Furthermore, likely transmission of *B. pseudomallei* between two siblings with CF has been reported.[56] Patients with CF traveling to melioidosis-endemic lo-

cations should be warned of the risk of melioidosis, and this should be considered if they become sick after returning.

It is common for patients to present with skin ulcers or abscesses (Figs. 218-8 and 218-9). Occasionally they present with septic arthritis or osteomyelitis, or one of these can develop after the patient has presented with another primary diagnosis, usually pneumonia (Fig. 218-10). Also well recognized, whatever the clinical presentation, are abscesses in internal organs, especially spleen, kidney, prostate, and liver (Figs. 218-11 to 218-15). Where available, an abdominopelvic computed tomograph (CT) is useful in all melioidosis patients to detect internal abscesses.

Three differences have been noted between Thailand and tropical Australia. First, suppurative parotitis accounts for up to 40% of melioidosis in children in Thailand,[52,57] but it is very rare in Australia. Second, prostatic melioidosis is well recognized but uncommon except in Australia, where routine abdominopelvic CT scanning of all melioidosis cases showed prostatic abscesses to be present in 18% of all male patients with melioidosis (Fig. 218-16).[28] Some were incidental in patients

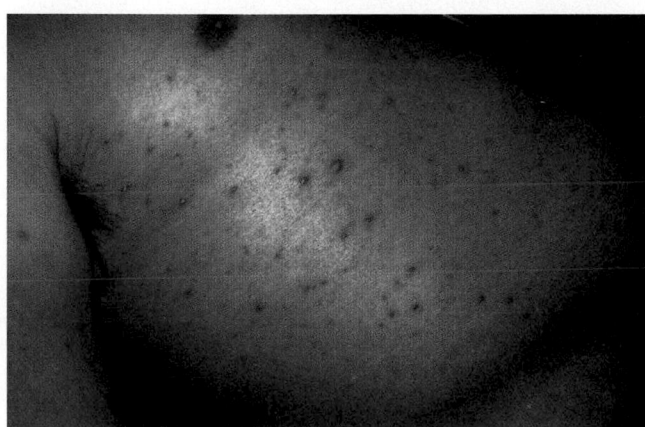

FIGURE 218-2. Multiple pustules in 46-year-old diabetic man with fatal septicemic melioidosis.

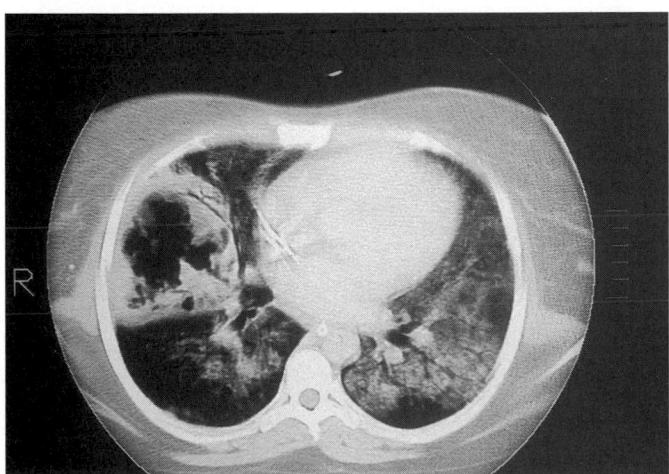

FIGURE 218-4. Computed tomographic scan of the chest of a 26-year-old woman with fatal melioidosis, showing large pulmonary abscess.

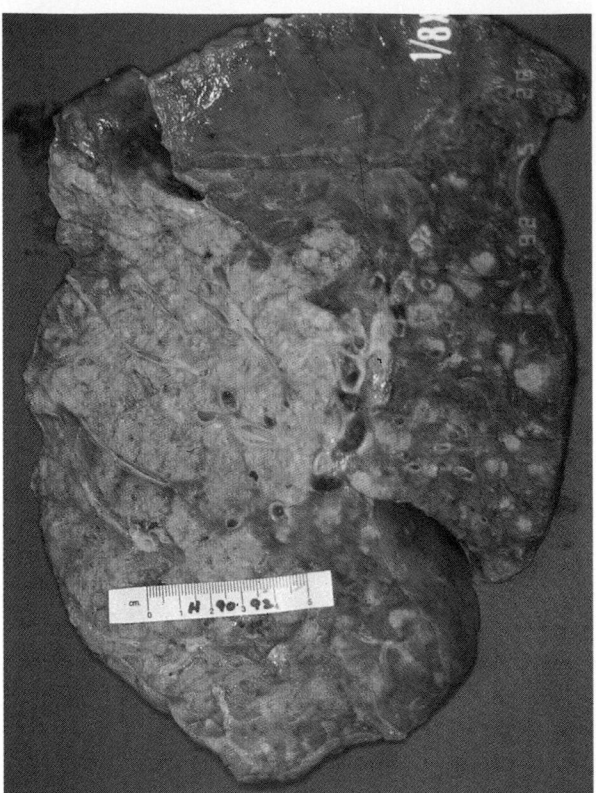

FIGURE 218-5. Multiple lung abscesses seen at autopsy of patient with acute melioidosis pneumonia.

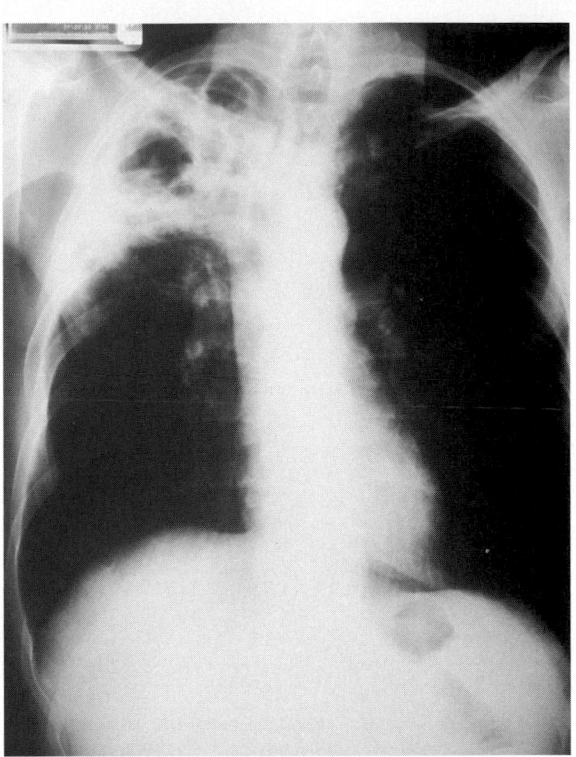

FIGURE 218-7. Radiograph showing right upper lobe cavitation of a 62-year-old man with nonfatal chronic melioidosis.

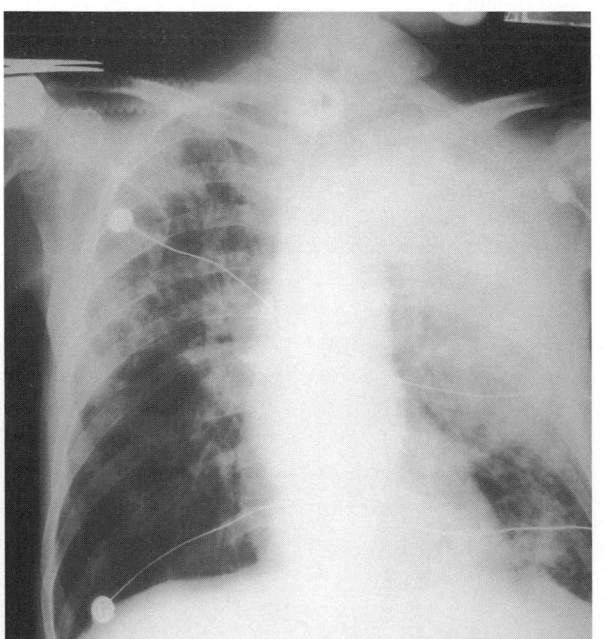

FIGURE 218-6. Extensive left upper lobe consolidation in 54-year-old man with fatal melioidosis pneumonia.

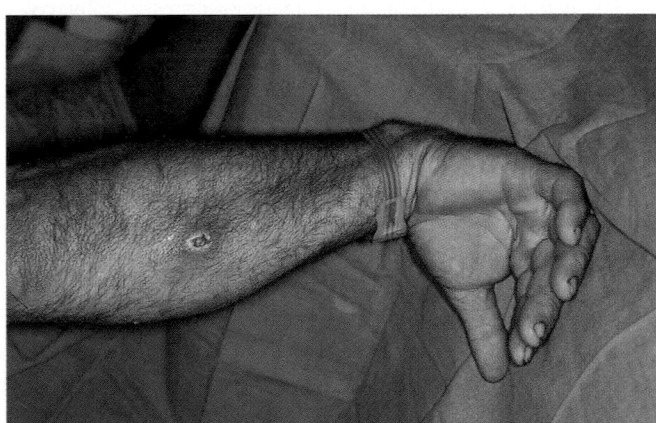

FIGURE 218-8. Cutaneous melioidosis seen on the right forearm of this 50-year-old man.

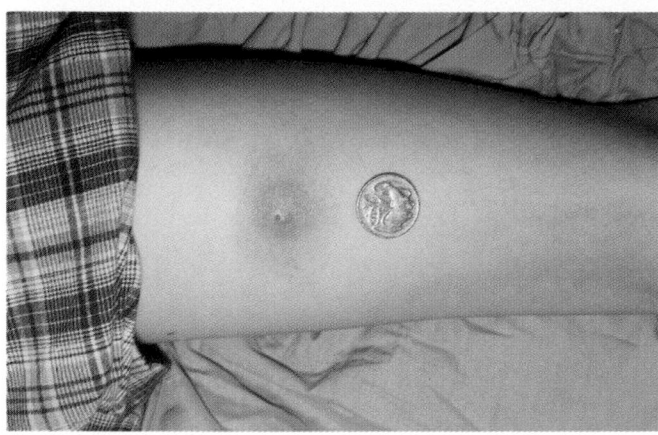

FIGURE 218-9. An 11-year-old boy with cutaneous melioidosis of the right thigh.

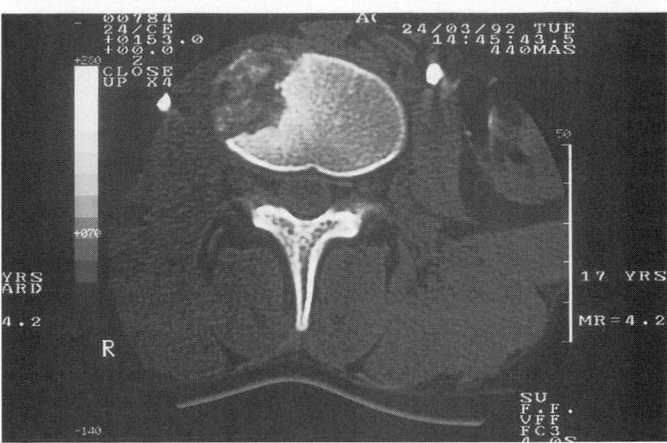

FIGURE 218-12. The patient in Figure 218-11 developed an L3 osteomyelitis 6 weeks later.

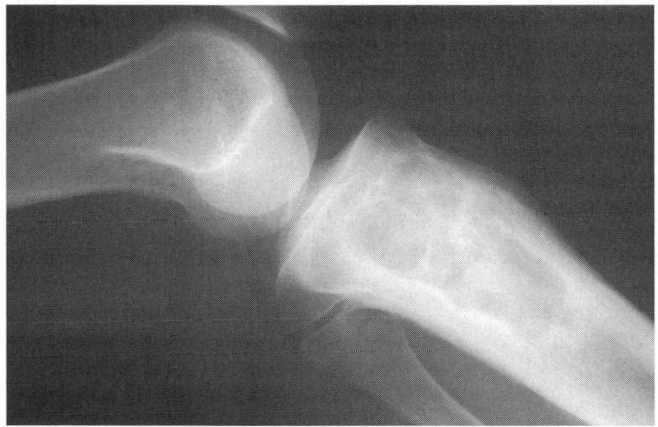

FIGURE 218-10. Radiograph shows large lucent areas in proximal tibia of a 43-year-old man.

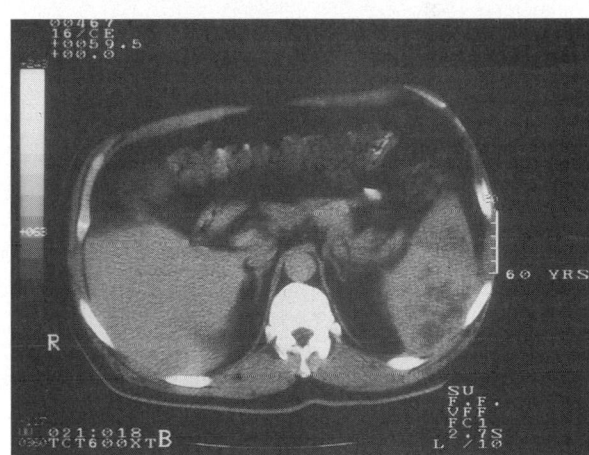

FIGURE 218-13. CT scan showing splenic abscesses in a 60-year-old diabetic.

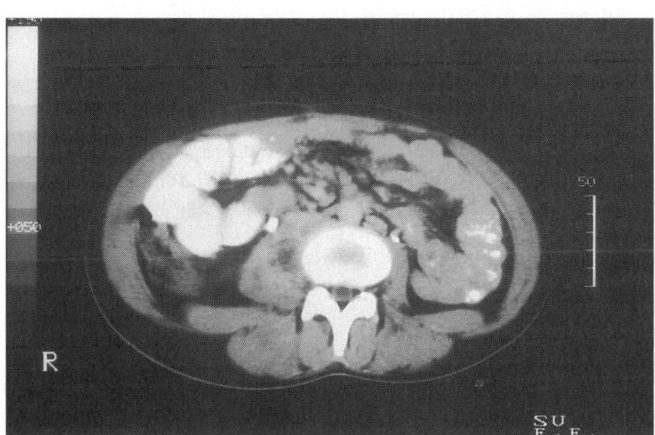

FIGURE 218-11. A right psoas abscess in a 17-year-old girl with melioidosis.

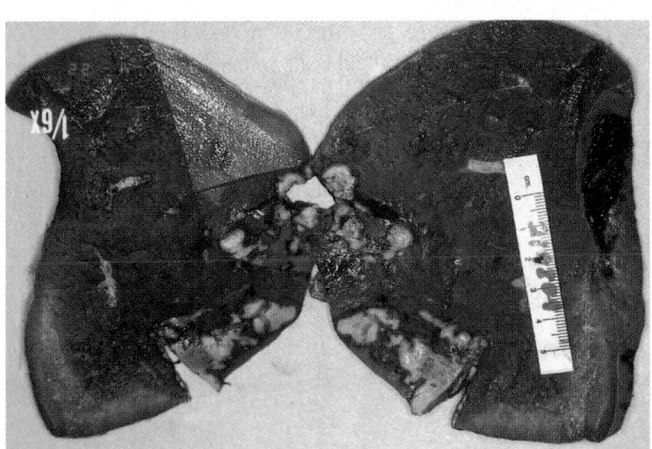

FIGURE 218-14. Abscesses seen at splenectomy performed on the patient in Figure 218-13.

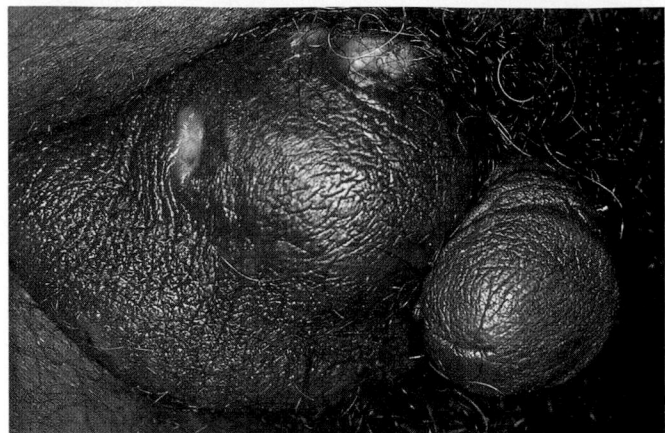

FIGURE 218-15. Melioidosis orchitis and scrotal ulcer in a 49-year-old man.

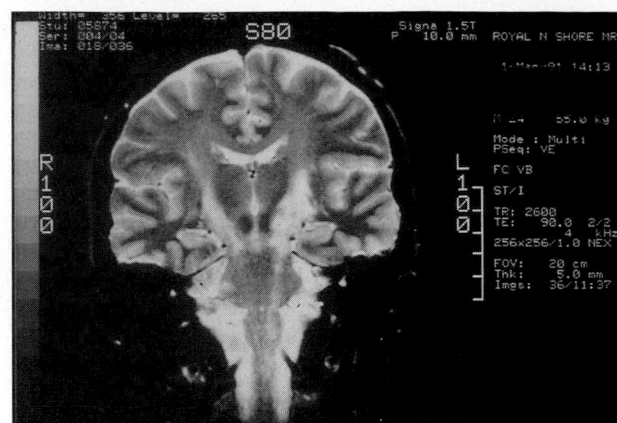

FIGURE 218-17. Melioidosis encephalomyelitis in a 24-year-old man. MRI shows increased T_2 signal extending through brain stem and into spinal cord.

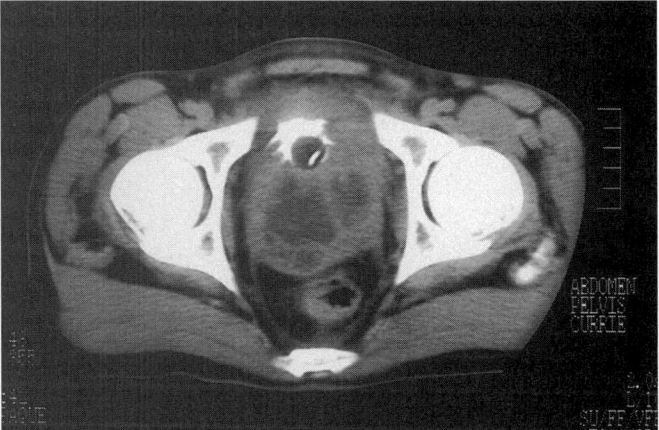

FIGURE 218-16. Melioidosis prostatic abscesses in a 31-year-old man who presented with fever and urinary retention.

presenting with pneumonia or septicemia, but a primary genitourinary presentation was common with fevers, abdominal discomfort, dysuria, and sometimes diarrhea and urinary retention. Third, neurologic melioidosis accounts for around 4% of cases in northern Australia, with the distinctive clinical features being brain stem encephalitis, often with cranial nerve palsies (especially the seventh nerve), together with peripheral motor weakness, or occasionally just flaccid paraparesis alone. The CT scan is often normal, but dramatic changes are seen on magnetic resonance imaging (MRI), most notably diffusely increased T_2 signal in midbrain, brain stem, and spinal cord (Fig. 218-17).[58] Direct bacterial invasion of the brain and spinal cord occurs with this melioidosis encephalomyelitis. Neurologic melioidosis is occasionally seen outside Australia, although mostly as macroscopic brain abscesses.[6,59]

Unusual foci of melioidosis infection described in case reports or case series include mycotic aneurysms, lymphadenitis resembling tuberculosis, mediastinal masses, pericardial collections, and adrenal abscesses.

It has long been recognized that *B. pseudomallei*, like tuberculosis, has the potential for reactivation from a latent focus, usually in the lung-hence the concern of the "Vietnamese time bomb" in returned soldiers. Latent periods from exposure to *B. pseudomallei* in an endemic region to onset of melioidosis in a nonendemic region have been documented as being as long as 29 years.[60] However, cases of reactivated *B. pseudomallei* appear to be very uncommon, accounting for only 3% of cases in northern Australia. The vast majority of cases of melioidosis occur in the monsoonal wet seasons of the various en-

demic regions, supporting the concept that in endemic areas, most patients with melioidosis have recent infections that appear with acute illness. Reactivation of melioidosis has been associated with influenza, other bacterial sepses, and development of known melioidosis risk factors such as diabetes. It remains unknown what proportion of asymptomatic seropositive people actually have latent infection with the potential for reactivation.

Laboratory Diagnosis

Definitive diagnosis of melioidosis requires a positive culture of *B. pseudomallei*. Melioidosis must be considered in febrile patients in or returning from endemic regions to enable appropriate samples and laboratory awareness. *B. pseudomallei* readily grows in commercially available blood culture media, but it is not unusual for laboratories in nonendemic locations to misidentify the bacteria as a *Pseudomonas* species, especially as some commercial identification systems are poor at identifying *B. pseudomallei*.[61] Culture from nonsterile sites increases the likelihood of diagnosis but can be problematic. The rate of successful culture is increased if sputum, throat swabs, ulcer/skin lesion swabs, and rectal swabs are placed into Ashdown's medium, a gentamicin-containing liquid transport broth that results in selective growth of *B. pseudomallei*.[62] Identification of *B. pseudomallei* can be made by combining the commercial API 20NE or 20E biochemical kit with a simple screening system involving the Gram stain, the oxidase reaction, typical growth characteristics, and resistance to certain antibiotics.[63]

There are a variety of antigen- and DNA-detection techniques used in endemic regions for early identification of *B. pseudomallei* in culture media and patient blood or urine, but these are not yet widely available.[63-66] Some polymerase chain reaction (PCR) tests developed have been found to lack specificity when tested on patient blood samples. An indirect hemagglutination test (IHA), an enzyme-linked immunosorbent assay (ELISA), and other serologic assays are available. In endemic areas, their usefulness is limited by high rates of background antibody positivity. In acute septicemic melioidosis, IHA and ELISA are often initially negative, but repeat testing may show seroconversion. A positive IHA or ELISA in a tourist returning from a melioidosis-endemic region is useful in supporting the possibility of melioidosis, but definitive diagnosis still requires a positive culture.

Treatment

B. pseudomallei is characteristically resistant to penicillin, ampicillin, first- and second-generation cephalosporins, gentamicin, tobramycin, and streptomycin. Before 1989, "conventional therapy" for melioidosis consisted of a combination of chloramphenicol, sulfamethoxazole-trimethoprim, doxycycline, and sometimes kanamycin, given for 6 weeks to 6 months.[2,67] However, there were also reports of successful use of sulfamethoxazole-trimethoprim alone and tetracycline or doxy-

TABLE 218-3 Antibiotic Therapy for Melioidosis

Initial intensive therapy-minimum of 10-14 days
Ceftazidime (50 mg/kg, up to 2 g) every 6 hours
or
meropenem (25 mg/kg, up to 1 g) every 8 hours
or
imipenem (25 mg/kg, up to 1 g) every 6 hours
+/-
sulfamethoxazole/trimethoprim (40/8 mg/kg, up to 1600/320 mg) every 12 hours

Eradication therapy-minimum of 3 months
Sulfamethoxazole/trimethoprim (40/8 mg/kg, up to 1600/320 mg) every 12 hours
+/-
doxycycline (2 mg/kg, up to 100 mg) every 12 hours

cycline alone. These "conventional antibiotics" are bacteriostatic rather than bactericidal, and in vitro studies have shown various combinations to be antagonistic.

Subsequent studies showed *B. pseudomallei* to be susceptible to various newer β-lactam antibiotics, especially ceftazidime, imipenem, meropenem, piperacillin, amoxicillin-clavulanate, ceftriaxone, and cefotaxime, with various degrees of bactericidal activity. Table 218-3 summarizes recommended antibiotic treatment.

Initial Intensive Therapy for Melioidosis

The most important therapeutic study for melioidosis was an open-label randomized trial in Thailand comparing ceftazidime (120 mg/kg/day) with conventional therapy, which showed that ceftazidime was associated with a 50% lower overall mortality in severe melioidosis.[67] Ceftazidime then became the drug of choice for initial intensive therapy for melioidosis. Another study from Thailand showed similar results when ceftazidime was used in combination with sulfamethoxazole-trimethoprim.[68] Whether sulfamethoxazole-trimethoprim added to ceftazidime is superior to ceftazidime alone is currently being studied in Thailand.

After initial favorable reports of use of amoxicillin-clavulanate, another randomized comparative trial in Thailand showed that initial therapy with high-dose intravenous amoxicillin-clavulanate was as effective as ceftazidime in preventing deaths in severe melioidosis.[69] However, when amoxicillin/clavulanate was continued as eradication therapy (see later), treatment failure was more common.

The carbapenems imipenem and meropenem have the lowest minimum inhibitory concentrations against *B. pseudomallei.* Furthermore, in vitro time-kill studies to measure the rate of bacterial killing showed the carbapenems to perform better against *B. pseudomallei* than ceftazidime.[70,71] High-dose imipenem has been shown in another comparative trial from Thailand to be at least as effective as ceftazidime for severe melioidosis, with no differences in mortality between the groups and with fewer treatment failures in those given imipenem.[72]

The duration of initial intensive therapy should be 10 to 14 days, with longer treatment required for critically ill patients, or for extensive pulmonary disease, deep-seated collections or organ abscesses, osteomyelitis, septic arthritis, and neurologic melioidosis. Even with the newer regimens, the therapeutic response can be slow, with median time to defervescence up to 9 days, and longer times seen in those with deep-seated abscesses.

Ceftazidime infusions (6 g over 24 hours, adult dose) through a peripherally inserted central catheter (PICC line) using an elastomeric infusion device (Baxter, Sydney) have enabled early discharge for hospital-in-the-home therapy. The absence of any postantibiotic effect with ceftazidime gives such a continuous infusion a theoretical advantage over intermittent dosing.

Subsequent Eradication Therapy for Melioidosis

Following initial intensive therapy, using ceftazidime or imipenem or meropenem, possibly in combination with sulfamethoxazole-trimethoprim, subsequent eradication therapy is considered necessary

for preventing recrudescence or later relapse of melioidosis. Both duration of eradication therapy and the best antibiotics to use remain uncertain. Molecular typing of isolates from patients with recurrent melioidosis has confirmed that by far the majority of cases are true relapses from failed eradication rather than new infection.

There are a number of reasons for failure of eradication therapy:

1. The most important factor responsible for most recrudescences or relapses of melioidosis is poor compliance with eradication therapy.
2. Relapses have been found to be 4.7 times (95% CI, 1.6-14.1) more common in patients with severe disease than in those with localized melioidosis.[73]
3. Use of ceftazidime in the initial intensive therapy was also associated with a halving of relapses.[73]
4. Duration of eradication therapy is also critical, with relapses following oral therapy of 8 weeks or less more likely than if eradication therapy is given for longer than 12 weeks.[73]
5. The choice of agents for the eradication therapy is important. Both amoxicillin-clavulanate[74] and oral quinolones (ciprofloxacin or ofloxacin)[75] have been found to be less effective in preventing relapse than "conventional" eradication with chloramphenicol (given usually only for the first 4 to 8 weeks), sulfamethoxazole-trimethoprim, and doxycycline. Amoxicillin-clavulanate is recommended for eradication therapy in pregnancy and is an alternative to sulfamethoxazole-trimethoprim in children. Quinolones should not be considered as first-line agents for melioidosis, with in vitro susceptibility testing generally showing resistance or intermediate results. A recent trial of eradication therapy involved a comparison of doxycycline alone versus "conventional" chloramphenicol (first 4 weeks only), sulfamethoxazole-trimethoprim, and doxycycline combination therapy.[76] Relapses were significantly commoner in the doxycycline-alone group, resulting in a recommendation that doxycycline not be used alone as first-line eradication therapy.

It has been suggested that sulfamethoxazole-trimethoprim is the critical component in the "conventional" combination therapy, and prospective studies in Australia using sulfamethoxazole-trimethoprim alone for eradication therapy support this, with relapses being almost exclusively in noncompliant patients. Interpretation of disk diffusion sensitivity testing has been problematic for sulfamethoxazole-trimethoprim, and agar dilution methods have confirmed that the majority of *B. pseudomallei* isolates are sensitive to sulfamethoxazole-trimethoprim. Further studies should ascertain whether it is still beneficial to have combination therapy for the eradication phase of melioidosis treatment or whether sulfamethoxazole-trimethoprim alone is adequate.

Adjunctive Therapy

Surgical drainage of large abscesses is indicated, but this is usually not necessary or possible for multiple small abscesses in the spleen and liver. Parotid abscesses require careful incision and drainage. Prostatic abscesses can often be drained under ultrasound guidance using a rectal probe, with transurethral resection reserved for failures of the simpler procedure.

State-of-the-art intensive care management has resulted in decreased mortality in patients with melioidosis septic shock, and preliminary data suggest addition of G-CSF may increase survival further in these patients.[55]

Prevention

Primary prevention involves education in endemic areas about minimizing exposure to wet-season soils and surface water, especially for diabetics. Footwear and gloves while gardening are recommended in northern Australia, but preventing occupational exposure in rice farmers may be unrealistic in Southeast Asia. Cystic fibrosis patients should consider avoiding travel to high-risk areas.

Laboratory-acquired infections, person-to-person spread, and zoonotic infection are all very uncommon, but secondary prophylaxis with sulfamethoxazole-trimethoprim, doxycycline, or amoxicillin-clavulanate could be considered for exceptional circumstances, especially if the exposed person is diabetic or has other risk factors for melioidosis. Isolation of patients is recommended only for those with severe suppurative pneumonia with productive sputum.

Concerns of possible bioterrorism using the bacterium or its virulence components in genetically engineered constructs and of exposure of military personnel to *B. pseudomallei* have driven funding for recent work.[77] Development of a melioidosis vaccine could also have substantial benefits for those living in the endemic regions and for commercial livestock, although cost will be a major impediment to availability. Preliminary studies in a mouse model of an exopolysaccharide-based vaccine against melioidosis have been encouraging,[78] and recently a lipopolysaccharide and capsular polysaccharide combination conjugated to *Pseudomonas aeruginosa* exotoxin A has been proposed.[79]

GLANDERS

Glanders is a highly communicable disease of solipeds (horses, donkeys, and mules) that is caused by *Burkholderia mallei*. It can be transmitted to other animals and to humans.

History

Glanders was described by Hippocrates and has long been recognized as an occupational risk for horse handlers, veterinarians, equine butchers, and laboratory workers. Together with anthrax, glanders was involved in the first modern use of microbes as weapons when German agents targeted horses in the United States, Romania, Spain, Norway, and Argentina between 1915 and 1918.[80]

Etiology

Burkholderia mallei is a small, gram-negative, oxidase-positive, aerobic bacillus. Unlike *B. pseudomallei*, it is nonmotile. It is a host-adapted pathogen that, unlike *B. pseudomallei,* does not persist in the environment outside its equine host. The *Burkholderia* genome project and multilocus sequence typing support the idea that *B. mallei* evolved in animals from the environmental pathogen *B. pseudomallei*.[81]

Epidemiology, Transmission, and Pathogenesis

With quarantine and other control measures, glanders has been eradicated from most countries, but enzootic foci continue in the Middle East, Asia, Africa, and South America. In addition to disease in equines, glanders has occurred in cats and other carnivores eating infected horse meat. Inhalation and percutaneous inoculation also occur. Discharges from the horse respiratory tract and skin are highly infectious. *B. mallei* has much greater potential for zoonotic transmission than does *B. pseudomallei,* and the risk of laboratory-acquired infection also appears to be greater for *B. mallei*.[82,83] The incubation period is from as short as 1 to 2 days (e.g., with inhalation) to many months, and, as occurs with melioidosis, reactivation from a latent focus after many years is described.

There are many parallels with the pathogenesis of *B. pseudomallei,* with recent studies showing the *B. mallei* extracellular polysaccharide capsule to be a critical determinant of virulence.[45,79,84,85] There is differential susceptibility among animals, and although it is likely that diabetics are more susceptible to infection and disease progression with *B. mallei,*[83] the human host risk factors are less well defined than for melioidosis.

Clinical Manifestations

Knowledge of the disease in horses is useful for understanding the potential for zoonotic transmission to humans. In acute glanders in horses, fever is accompanied by necrotic ulcers and nodules in the nasal passages that result in copious infectious sticky yellow discharges. Neck and mediastinal lymph nodes are enlarged, and pneumonia with nodular abscesses and dissemination to internal organs can accompany the progressive deterioration. In cutaneous glanders ("farcy"), nodular lymphatic/skin abscesses (0.5 to 2.5 cm) occur and ulcerate, discharging infectious oily yellow pus.[79]

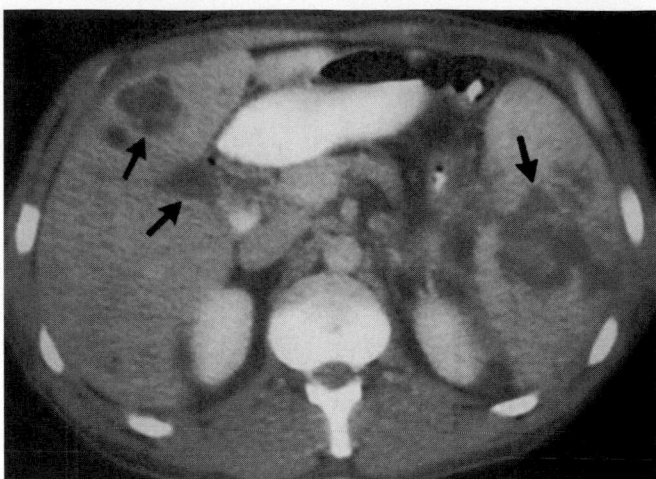

FIGURE 218-18. CT scan showing abscesses *(arrows)* in liver and spleen of a patient with laboratory-acquired glanders. *(From Srinivasan A, Kraus CN, DeShazer D, et al. Glanders in a military research microbiologist. N Engl J Med. 2001;345:256-258, with permission.)*

Human glanders, like melioidosis, can be acute or chronic, with mode of infection, inoculating dose, and host risk factors determining the clinical course. With inhaled organisms (respiratory inoculation), acute febrile illness with ulcerative necrosis of the tracheobronchial tree can occur, with mucopurulent discharge involving the nose, lips, and eyes. Lobar or bronchopneumonia, neck and mediastinal lymphadenopathy, pustular skin lesions, and septicemia with dissemination to internal organs can follow.[86] Historically, without antibiotics, death within 10 days usually occurred, but a more chronic pneumonic illness was also recognized after inhalation of *B. mallei*.[82]

Following percutaneous inoculation, local skin nodules that can suppurate and regional lymphadenopathy occur, often accompanied by fever, rigors, and malaise.[83,86] Regional lymphadenopathy is much more common than with melioidosis. Lymphatic tract nodules and suppurating abscesses in the lymph nodes are common after several weeks in untreated cases. Dissemination at 1 to 4 weeks can result in infection in almost any tissue, with spleen and liver abscesses, pneumonia, lung abscesses, pleural nodules, and multiple subcutaneous and muscle abscesses all quite common (Fig. 218-18). Central nervous system infection can also occur.

Laboratory Diagnosis

Definitive diagnosis of glanders requires a positive culture of *B. mallei*. Blood, exudates, and pus from abscesses should be cultured on standard media. Organisms are often very scanty in exudates and pus and are morphologically indistinguishable from *B. pseudomallei*. As happens with *B. pseudomallei,* some commercial identification systems may misidentify *B. mallei* as a *Pseudomonas* species, and 16S ribosomal RNA gene-sequenced analysis may be required for confirmation.[83] Serologic assays cannot distinguish *B. mallei* from *B. pseudomallei,* and the mallein skin test used extensively in animal control programs and modified for human diagnosis has poor specificity.[82]

Treatment

The antibiotic susceptibility profile of *B. mallei* resembles that of *B. pseudomallei,* except that gentamicin and newer macrolides (e.g., clarithromycin, azithromycin) are active against *B. mallei* but not *B. pseudomallei*.[87] Although response to treatment with older regimens was often slow, rapid improvement occurred in the recent U.S. military researcher with laboratory-acquired infection who was treated with imipenem and doxycycline.[83] This was the first reported case of glanders in the United States in more than 50 years. Recommended treatment and duration are the same as for melioidosis.

Prevention

Prevention depends on control of glanders in the equine species and strict precautions to prevent laboratory-acquired infection.[82,83] Unlike with melioidosis, isolation of all infected individuals is recommended to prevent person-to-person spread. Experimental infections suggest doxycycline may be useful in postexposure prophylaxis.[88] As with melioidosis, there is much current work toward a vaccine to prevent disease in humans, with encouraging data on a lipopolysaccharide and capsular polysaccharide combination conjugated to *Pseudomonas aeruginosa* exotoxin A.[79]

REFERENCES

1. Whitmore A, Krishnaswami CS. An account of the discovery of a hitherto undescribed infective disease occurring among the population of Rangoon. Indian Med Gaz. 1912;47:262-267.
2. Leelarasamee A, Bovornkitti S. Melioidosis: Review and update. Rev Infect Dis. 1989;11:413-425.
3. Dance DAB. Melioidosis. Rev Med Microbiol. 1990;1:143-150.
4. Dance DA. Melioidosis: The tip of the iceberg? Clin Microbiol Rev. 1991;4:52-60.
5. White NJ. Melioidosis. Lancet. 2003;361:1715-1722.
6. Punyagupta S. Melioidosis: Review of 686 cases and presentation of a new clinical classification. In: Punyagupta S, Sirisanthana T, Stapatayavong B, eds: Melioidosis. Bangkok: Bangkok Medical; 1989:217-229.
7. Chaowagul W, White NJ, Dance DA, et al. Melioidosis: A major cause of community-acquired septicemia in northeastern Thailand. J Infect Dis. 1989;159:890-899.
8. Vuddhakul V, Tharavichitkul P, Na-Ngam N, et al. Epidemiology of *Burkholderia pseudomallei* in Thailand. Am J Trop Med Hyg. 1999;60:458-461.
9. Leelarasamee A. Melioidosis in Southeast Asia. Acta Trop. 2000;74:129-132.
10. Puthucheary SD, Parasakthi N, Lee MK. Septicaemic melioidosis: A review of 50 cases from Malaysia. Trans R Soc Trop Med Hyg. 1992;86:683-685.
11. Yap EH, Chan YC, Goh KT, et al. Sudden unexplained death syndrome-a new manifestation in melioidosis? Epidemiol Infect. 1991;107:577-584.
12. Singapore Committee on Epidemic Diseases. Melioidosis in Singapore. Epidemiol News Bull. 1995;21:69-72.
13. Dance DA. Melioidosis as an emerging global problem. Acta Trop. 2000;74:115-119.
14. Lee N, Wu JL, Lee CH, Tsai WC. *Pseudomonas pseudomallei* infection from drowning: The first reported case in Taiwan. J Clin Microbiol. 1985;22:352-354.
15. Hsueh PR, Teng LJ, Lee LN, et al. Melioidosis: An emerging infection in Taiwan? Emerg Infect Dis. 2001;7:428-433.
16. Parry CM, Wuthiekanun V, Hoa NT, et al. Melioidosis in Southern Vietnam: Clinical surveillance and environmental sampling. Clin Infect Dis. 1999;29:1323-1326.
17. Cherian T, Raghupathy P, John TJ. Plague in India. Lancet. 1995;345:258-259.
18. Dance DA, Sanders D, Pitt TL, Speller DC. *Burkholderia pseudomallei* and Indian plague-like illness. Lancet. 1995;346:904-905.
19. Boonsawat W, Boonma P, Tangdajahiran T, et al. Community-acquired pneumonia in adults at Srinagarind Hospital. J Med Assoc Thai. 1990;73:345-352.
20. Currie BJ, Fisher DA, Howard DM, et al. The epidemiology of melioidosis in Australia and Papua New Guinea. Acta Trop. 2000;74:121-127.
21. Currie B, Smith Vaughan H, Golledge C, et al. *Pseudomonas pseudomallei* isolates collected over 25 years from a non-tropical endemic focus show clonality on the basis of ribotyping. Epidemiol Infect. 1994;113:307-312.
22. Clayton AJ, Lisella RS, Martin DG. Melioidosis: A serological survey in military personnel. Mil Med. 1973;138:24-26.
23. Wuthiekanun V, Smith MD, Dance DA, White NJ. Isolation of *Pseudomonas pseudomallei* from soil in north-eastern Thailand. Trans R Soc Trop Med Hyg. 1995;89:41-43.
24. Thomas AD, Forbes Faulkner J, Parker M. Isolation of *Pseudomonas pseudomallei* from clay layers at defined depths. Am J Epidemiol. 1979;110:515-521.
25. Inglis TJ, Mee B, Chang B. The environmental microbiology of melioidosis. Rev Med Microbiol. 2001;12:13-20.
26. Vorachit M, Lam K, Jayanetra P, Costerton JW. Resistance of *Pseudomonas pseudomallei* growing as a biofilm on silastic discs to ceftazidime and co-trimoxazole. Antimicrob Agents Chemother. 1993;37:2000-2002.
27. Suputtamongkol Y, Hall AJ, Dance DA, et al. The epidemiology of melioidosis in Ubon Ratchatani, northeast Thailand. Int J Epidemiol. 1994;23:1082-1090.
28. Currie BJ, Fisher DA, Howard DM, et al. Endemic melioidosis in tropical northern Australia: A 10-year prospective study and review of the literature. Clin Infect Dis. 2000;31:981-986.
29. Howe C, Sampath A, Spotnitz M. The pseudomallei group: A review. J Infect Dis. 1971;124:598-606.
30. Currie BJ, Jacups SP. Intensity of rainfall and severity of melioidosis, Australia. Emerg Infect Dis. 2003;9:1538-1542.
31. Inglis TJ, Garrow SC, Henderson M, et al. *Burkholderia pseudomallei* traced to water treatment plant in Australia. Emerg Infect Dis. 2000;6:56-59.
32. Currie BJ, Mayo M, Anstey NM, et al. A cluster of melioidosis cases from an endemic region is clonal and is linked to the water supply using molecular typing of *Burkholderia pseudomallei* isolates. Am J Trop Med Hyg. 2001;65:177-179.
33. Currie BJ, Fisher DA, Anstey NM, Jacups SP. Melioidosis: Acute and chronic disease, relapse and re-activation. Trans R Soc Trop Med Hyg. 2000;94:301-304.
34. Sookpranee M, Lumbiganon P, Boonma P. Nosocomial contamination of *Pseudomonas pseudomallei* in the patients at Srinagarind Hospital. In: Punyagupta S, Sirisanthana T, Stapatayavong B, eds: Melioidosis. Bangkok: Bangkok Medical; 1989:204-210.
35. Ashdown LR, Guard RW. The prevalence of human melioidosis in Northern Queensland. Am J Trop Med Hyg. 1984;33:474-478.
36. Kanaphun P, Thirawattanasuk N, Suputtamongkol Y, et al. Serology and carriage of *Pseudomonas pseudomallei*: A prospective study in 1000 hospitalized children in northeast Thailand. J Infect Dis. 1993;167:230-233.
37. Ulett GC, Currie BJ, Clair TW, et al. *Burkholderia pseudomallei* virulence: Definition, stability and association with clonality. Microbes Infect. 2001;3:621-631.
38. Desmarchelier PM, Dance DA, Chaowagul W, et al. Relationships among *Pseudomonas pseudomallei* isolates from patients with recurrent melioidosis. J Clin Microbiol. 1993;31:1592-1596.
39. Egan AM, Gordon DL. *Burkholderia pseudomallei* activates complement and is ingested but not killed by polymorphonuclear leukocytes. Infect Immun. 1996;64:4952-4959.
40. Woods DE, DeShazer D, Moore RA, et al. Current studies on the pathogenesis of melioidosis. Microbes Infect. 1999;1:157-162.
41. Brett PJ, Woods DE. Pathogenesis of and immunity to melioidosis. Acta Trop. 2000;74:201-210.
42. DeShazer D, Brett PJ, Woods DE. The type II O-antigenic polysaccharide moiety of *Burkholderia pseudomallei* lipopolysaccharide is required for serum resistance and virulence. Mol Microbiol. 1998;30:1081-1100.
43. Reckseidler SL, DeShazer D, Sokol PA, Woods DE. Detection of bacterial virulence genes by subtractive hybridization: identification of capsular polysaccharide of *Burkholderia pseudomallei* as a major virulence determinant. Infect Immun. 2001;69:34-44.
44. Woods DE. The use of animal infection models to study the pathogenesis of melioidosis and glanders. Trends Microbiol. 2002;11:483-484.
45. DeShazer D, Waag DM, Fritz DL, Woods DE. Identification of a *Burkholderia mallei* polysaccharide gene cluster by subtractive hybridization and demonstration that the encoded capsule is an essential virulence determinant. Microb Pathog. 2001;30:253-269.
46. Winstanley C, Hart CA. Presence of type III secretion genes in *Burkholderia pseudomallei* correlates with Ara⁻ phenotypes. J Clin Microbiol. 2000;38:883-885.
47. Stevens MP, Wood MW, Taylor LA, et al. An Inv/Mxi-Spa-like type III protein secretion system in *Burkholderia pseudomallei* modulates intracellular behaviour of the pathogen. Mol Microbiol. 2002;46:649-659.
48. Haussler S, Rohde M, Steinmetz I. Highly resistant *Burkholderia pseudomallei* small colony variants isolated in vitro and in experimental melioidosis. Med Microbiol Immunol (Berl). 1999;188:91-97.
49. Nuntayanuwat S, Dharakul T, Chaowagul W, Songsivilai S. Polymorphism in the promoter region of tumor necrosis factor-alpha gene is associated with severe melioidosis. Hum Immunol. 1999;60:979-983.
50. Santanirand P, Harley VS, Dance DA, et al. Obligatory role of gamma interferon for host survival in a murine model of infection with *Burkholderia pseudomallei*. Infect Immun. 1999;67:3593-3600.
51. Suputtamongkol Y, Chaowagul W, Chetchotisakd P, et al. Risk factors for melioidosis and bacteremic melioidosis. Clin Infect Dis. 1999;29:408-413.
52. Lumbiganon P, Viengnondha S. Clinical manifestations of melioidosis in children. Pediatr Infect Dis J. 1995;14:136-140.
53. Edmond K, Bauert P, Currie B. Paediatric melioidosis in the Northern Territory of Australia: An expanding clinical spectrum. J Paediatr Child Health. 2001;37:337-341.
54. Tarlow MJ, Lloyd J. Melioidosis and chronic granulomatous disease. Proc R Soc Med. 1971;64:19-20.
55. Stephens DP, Fisher DA, Currie BJ. An audit of the use of granulocyte colony-stimulating factor in septic shock. Intern Med J. 2002;32:143-148.
56. Holland DJ, Wesley A, Drinkovic D, Currie BJ. Cystic fibrosis and *Burkholderia pseudomallei*: An emerging problem? Clin Infect Dis. 2002;35:e138-140.
57. Dance DA, Davis TM, Wattanagoon Y, et al. Acute suppurative parotitis caused by *Pseudomonas pseudomallei* in children. J Infect Dis. 1989;159:654-660.
58. Currie BJ, Fisher DA, Howard DM, Burrow JN. Neurological melioidosis. Acta Trop. 2000;74:145-151.
59. Chadwick DR, Ang B, Sitoh YY, Lee CC. Cerebral melioidosis in Singapore: A review of five cases. Trans R Soc Trop Med Hyg. 2002;96:72-76.
60. Chodimella U, Hoppes WL, Whalen S, et al. Septicemia and suppuration in a Vietnam veteran. Hosp Pract. 1997;32:219-221.
61. Lowe P, Engler C, Norton R. Comparison of automated and nonautomated systems for identification of *Burkholderia pseudomallei*. J Clin Microbiol. 2002;40:4625-4627.
62. Ashdown LR. An improved screening technique for isolation of *Pseudomonas pseudomallei* from clinical specimens. Pathology. 1979;11:293-297.
63. Dance DA, Wuthiekanun V, Naigowit P, White NJ. Identification of *Pseudomonas pseudomallei* in clinical practice: Use of simple screening tests and API 20NE. J Clin Pathol. 1989;42:645-648.
64. Smith MD, Wuthiekanun V, Walsh AL, et al. Latex agglutination for rapid detection of *Pseudomonas pseudomallei* antigen in urine of patients with melioidosis. J Clin Pathol. 1995;48:174-176.
65. Steinmetz I, Reganzerowski A, Brenneke B, et al. Rapid identification of *Burkholderia pseudomallei* by latex agglutination based on an exopolysaccharide-specific monoclonal antibody. J Clin Microbiol. 1999;37:225-228.
66. Sirisinha S, Anuntagool N, Dharakul T, et al. Recent developments in laboratory diagnosis of melioidosis. Acta Trop. 2000;74:235-245.
67. White NJ, Dance DA, Chaowagul W, et al. Halving of mortality of severe melioidosis by ceftazidime. Lancet. 1989;2:697-701.
68. Sookpranee M, Boonma P, Susaengrat W, et al. Multicenter prospective randomized trial comparing ceftazidime plus co-trimoxazole with chloramphenicol plus doxycycline and co-trimoxazole for treatment of severe melioidosis. Antimicrob Agents Chemother. 1992;36:158-162.

69. Suputtamongkol Y, Rajchanuwong A, Chaowagul W, et al. Ceftazidime vs. amoxicillin/clavulanate in the treatment of severe melioidosis. Clin Infect Dis. 1994;19:846-853.

70. Smith MD, Wuthiekanun V, Walsh AL, White NJ. Susceptibility of *Pseudomonas pseudomallei* to some newer beta-lactam antibiotics and antibiotic combinations using time-kill studies. J Antimicrob Chemother. 1994;33:145-149.

71. Smith MD, Wuthiekanun V, Walsh AL, White NJ. In-vitro activity of carbapenem antibiotics against beta-lactam susceptible and resistant strains of *Burkholderia pseudomallei.* J Antimicrob Chemother. 1996;37:611-615.

72. Simpson AJ, Suputtamongkol Y, Smith MD, et al. Comparison of imipenem and ceftazidime as therapy for severe melioidosis. Clin Infect Dis. 1999;29:381-387.

73. Chaowagul W, Dance DA, et al. Relapse in melioidosis: Incidence and risk factors. J Infect Dis. 1993;168:1181-1185.

74. Rajchanuvong A, Chaowagul W, Suputtamongkol Y, et al. A prospective comparison of co-amoxiclav and the combination of chloramphenicol, doxycycline, and co-trimoxazole for the oral maintenance treatment of melioidosis. Trans R Soc Trop Med Hyg. 1995;89:546-549.

75. Chaowagul W, Suputtamongkol Y, Smith MD, White NJ. Oral fluoroquinolones in the maintenance treatment of melioidosis. Trans R Soc Trop Med Hyg. 1997;91:599-601.

76. Chaowagul W, Simpson AJ, Suputtamongkol Y, et al. A comparison of chloramphenicol, trimethoprim-sulfamethoxazole, and doxycycline with doxycycline alone as maintenance therapy for melioidosis. Clin Infect Dis. 1999;29:375-380.

77. Jeddeloh JA, Fritz DL, Waag DM, et al. Biodefense-driven murine model of pneumonic melioidosis. Infect Immun. 2003;71:584-587.

78. Steinmetz I, Nimtz M, Wray V, et al. Exopolysaccharides of *Burkholderia pseudomallei.* Acta Trop. 2000;74:211-214.

79. Lopez J, Copps J, Wilhelmsen C, et al. Characterization of experimental equine glanders. Microb Infect. 2003;5:1125-1131.

80. Wheelis M. First shots fired in biological warfare. Nature. 1998;395:213.

81. Godoy D, Randle G, Simpson AJ, et al. Multilocus sequence typing and evolutionary relationships among the causative agents of melioidosis and glanders, *Burkholderia pseudomallei* and *Burkholderia mallei.* J Clin Microbiol. 2003;41:2068-2079.

82. Howe C, Miller WR. Human glanders: Report of six cases. Ann Intern Med. 1947;26:93-115.

83. Srinivasan A, Kraus CN, DeShazer D, et al. Glanders in a military research microbiologist. N Engl J Med 2001;345:256-258.

84. Fritz DL, Vogel P, Brown DR, et al. Mouse model of sublethal and lethal intraperitoneal glanders (*Burkholderia mallei*). Vet Pathol. 2000;37:626-636.

85. Burtnick MN, Brett PJ, Woods DE. Molecular and physical characterization of *Burkholderia mallei* O antigens. J Bacteriol. 2002;184:849-852.

86. Robins GD. A study of chronic glanders in man with report of a case: Analysis of 156 cases collected from the literature. Stud R Victoria Hosp Montreal. 1906;2:1-98.

87. Heine HS, England MJ, Waag DM, Byrne WR. In vitro antibiotic susceptibilities of *Burkholderia mallei* (causative agent of glanders) determined by broth microdilution and E-test. Antimicrob Agents Chemother. 2001;45:2119-2121.

88. Russell P, Eley SM, Ellis J, et al. Comparison of efficacy of ciprofloxacin and doxycycline against experimental melioidosis and glanders. J Antimicrob Chemother. 2000;45:813-818.

CHAPTER 219

Acinetobacter Species

DAVID M. ALLEN

BARRY J. HARTMAN

Bacteria that constitute the genus *Acinetobacter* were originally identified in the first decade of the 20th century. However, it was not until the advent of modern infection control that its role as a ubiquitous opportunistic pathogen was appreciated. During the past two decades an improved understanding of the microbiology, taxonomy, and ecology of *Acinetobacter* has emerged. Issues of continuing clinical relevance include *Acinetobacter* speciation, evolving antimicrobial resistance, and appropriate therapy.

HISTORY AND MICROBIOLOGY

The genus *Acinetobacter* has had a colorful taxonomic history. Before the 1970s, *Acinetobacter* was frequently misidentified owing to an absence of distinguishing features. Subsequent use of transformation and nutritional studies defined the genus *Acinetobacter* and placed it within the family Neisseriaceae.

Historically, rediscoveries of this ubiquitous organism led to the creation of numerous genera with resultant taxonomic chaos. Probably first described in 1908 as *Diplococcus mucosus*, *Acinetobacter* was initially identified by the absence of common characteristics: no color, nonmotile, unable to reduce nitrates, and nonfermenting.[1] The lack of distinctive characteristics was a driving force in the evolving nomenclature of the day: *Micrococcus* (small), *Mima* (mimics), *Achromobacter* (colorless), *Acinetobacter* (motionless), and *anitratus* (nitrate nonreducing). In the 1930s and 1940s, while attempting to organize *Neisseria*-like organisms morphologically, De Bord proposed a new tribe, Mimeae, to encompass these organisms.[3] Later, Brisou and Prévot proposed the genus *Acinetobacter* to include colorless, nonmotile, saprophytic gram-negative bacilli regardless of oxidase activity.[4] Ultimately two of the three genera (*Mima* and *Herellea*) in the now-obsolete tribe Mimeae came to be included under the genus *Acinetobacter*. Further refinement emerged when oxidase activity was used to distinguish *Moraxella* (oxidase positive) from *Acinetobacter* (oxidase negative).

Although genus clarification was clearly established by 1971,[5] current efforts are directed toward species delineation. References published before the mid-1980s recognized one species, *Acinetobacter calcoaceticus*, with two subspecies (var. *anitratus* and var. *lwoffi*) or two species,[6] *A. calcoaceticus* and *A. lwoffi*. The two subspecies/species were distinguished by the ability of *A. calcoaceticus* var. *anitratus* to produce acid from glucose and the inability of var. *lwoffi* to do so. Efforts to further speciate the genus subsequently included bacteriocin typing, phage typing, characterization of outer membrane proteins, serotyping, phenotyping, ribotyping, transfer ribonucleic acid (tRNA) and genomic fingerprinting,[8] and DNA homology.[9] As one might anticipate, nucleic acid fingerprinting and DNA homology remain the most reliable methods for distinguishing species. Due to the practical limitations of the above-mentioned procedures efforts continue toward development of more pragmatic clinical laboratory methods for species identification.

Based on DNA-DNA hybridization studies, at least 21 different *Acinetobacter* strains (genomic species or "genospecies") have been identified. Seven of the numbered strains and two phenons (phenotypically distinct) have been given species names (Table 219-1).[10,11] Despite moderate success in applying simple, reproducible phenotypic studies to speciate *Acinetobacter* without resorting to more cumbersome studies, some clusters remain; for example, phenotypically similar genospecies 1, 2, 3, and 13 make up the *A. calcoaceticus-Acinetobacter baumannii* complex. In routine clinical practice, precise species identification is not necessary and compromises in terminology (e.g., *A. calcoaceticus-A. baumannii* complex) meet clinicians' as well as microbiologists' needs. However, for epidemiologic purposes, additional investigations such as pulsed field gel electrophoresis, amplified fragment length polymorphisms (AFLP), randomly amplified polymorphic DNA-polymerase chain reaction (PCR) (RAPD-PCR), or ribotyping may still be required for exact strain identification.

Acinetobacter are rod shaped during rapid growth and coccobacillary in the stationary phase. They are generally encapsulated, nonmotile (occasionally exhibiting twitching motility), aerobic, gram-negative organisms with a tendency to retain crystal violet and therefore to be incorrectly identified as gram-positive cocci. Versatility in exploiting a variety of carbon and energy sources allows *Acinetobacter* to grow on routine laboratory media and accounts for its prevalence in nature. Colonies are 1 to 2 mm, nonpigmented, domed, and mucoid, with smooth to pitted surfaces. Frequent misidentification of *Acinetobacter* as *Neisseria* or *Moraxella* on Gram staining is readily clarified by the negative oxidase reaction of *Acinetobacter*. The inability of *Acinetobacter* spp. to reduce nitrate or to grow anaerobically distinguishes these organisms from Enterobacteriaceae. Additionally, *Acinetobacter* are indole negative and catalase positive. Hemolysis of red blood cells, acidification of glucose, growth at 44° C, and variability in carbon source utilization are a few of the phenotypic characteristics applied to distinguish *Acinetobacter* strains (Table 219-2).

TABLE 219-1 Chronologic Nomenclature

1986-Present
  Acinetobacter calcoaceticus (genomic species 1)
  A. baumannii (genomic species 2)
  A. haemolyticus (genomic species 4)
  A. junii (genomic species 5)
  A. johnsonii (genomic species 7)
  A. lwoffi (genomic species 8/9)
  A. radioresistens (genomic species 12)
  A. ursingii (phenon 1)
  A. schindleri (phenon 2)
  A. venetianus
  Acinetobacter spp. unnamed (≥11 other genomic species)
Before 1986
  Acinetobacter calcoaceticus var. *anitratus* (1968)
    Achromobacter hemolyticus var. *glucidolytica* (1963)
    Achromobacter conjunctivae (1963)
    Acinetobacter anitratum (1957)
    Moraxella glucidolytica (1956)
    Achromobacter anitratum (1954)
    Neisseria winogradsky (1952)
    B5W (1949)
    Bacterium anitratum (1948)
    Herellea vaginicola (1942)
    Micrococcus calco-aceticus (1911)
    ?Diplococcus mucosus (1908)
  Acinetobacter calcoaceticus var. *lwoffi* (1968)
    Achromobacter citroalcaligenes (1963)
    Achromobacter hemolyticus var. *alcaligenes* (1963)
    Alcaligenes metalcaligenes (1963)
    Acinetobacter lwoffi (1957)
    Acinetobacter polymorpha (1957)
    Achromobacter lwoffi (1953)
    Moraxella lwoffi (1940)
    Mima polymorpha (1939)
    Alcaligenes haemolysis (1937)

EPIDEMIOLOGY

Acinetobacter differs from other members of the family Neisseriaceae by the simplicity of its growth requirements. The ability to use a variety of carbon sources via diverse metabolic pathways expands its habitat. Related genera *(Moraxella, Neisseria,* and *Kingella)* are parasitic in warm-blooded animals, whereas free-living *Acinetobacter* can be found on both animate and inanimate objects. Virtually 100% of soil and water samples yield *Acinetobacter. Acinetobacter* has been isolated from pasteurized milk, frozen foods, chilled poultry, foundry and hospital air, vaporizer mist, tapwater faucets, peritoneal dialysate baths, bedside urinals, washcloths, angiography catheters, ventilators, laryngoscopes, contaminated gloves, duodenoscopes, reused needles, multidose medication, plasma protein fraction, hospital pillows, soap dispensers, etc.[12] Some strains recovered from sink basins have been found to be tolerant of soap. *Acinetobacter* may survive on dry inanimate objects for days, comparable to *Staphylococcus aureus.*[13,14]

Acinetobacter has been grown from numerous human sources, including skin, sputum, urine, feces, and vaginal secretions. Up to 25% of healthy ambulatory adults exhibit cutaneous colonization,[15] and 7% of adults and infants have transient pharyngeal colonization.[16] It is the most common gram-negative organism persistently carried on the skin of hospital personnel,[17] and it has been found to frequently colonize inpatient tracheostomy sites.

The prevalence of *Acinetobacter* clinical isolates varies somewhat by country and by specimen site but has generally increased worldwide in the past two decades. Data reported to the Centers for Disease Control and Prevention (CDC) National Nosocomial Infection Surveillance (NNIS) indicated that *Acinetobacter* was the cause of 1% of all nosocomial blood-stream infections and 3% of nosocomial pneumonia in sentinel U.S. hospitals compared with 5% and 10%, respectively for Latin American hospitals.[18,19]

Risk factors associated with community-acquired *Acinetobacter* infection include alcoholism, cigarette smoking, chronic lung disease, diabetes mellitus, and residence in a tropical developing community.[20] Risk factors specific for nosocomial infection include length of hospital stay, surgery, wounds, previous infection (independent of previous antibiotic use),[21] fecal colonization with *Acinetobacter,*[22] treatment with broad-spectrum antibiotics, indwelling central intravenous or urinary catheters,[23] admission to a burn unit or intensive care unit (ICU), parenteral nutrition, and mechanical ventilation.[21,23]

PATHOGENESIS

A limited number of virulence factors reduce this bacterium to the role of an opportunist. Although growth in an acidic pH at lower temperatures may enhance its ability to invade devitalized tissue, no known cytotoxins are produced. Lipopolysaccharide is present in the cell wall, but little is known of its endotoxigenic potential in humans. Additional features that may enhance the survival of *Acinetobacter* include bacteriocin production,[7] presence of a capsule, and prolonged viability under dry conditions.[13] The capsule that surrounds most strains may inhibit phagocytosis and has been speculated to predispose persons with selective complement component deficiencies to infection.[20] In summary, without disruption of normal host defense mechanisms, the role of *Acinetobacter* in human infection remains limited.

CLINICAL MANIFESTATIONS

Acinetobacter spp. can cause suppurative infections in virtually every organ system.[24] Although *Acinetobacter* is acknowledged to be an opportunist in hospitalized patients, community-acquired infections are reported. Interpreting the significance of isolates from clinical specimens is often difficult because of the wide distribution of *Acinetobacter* in nature and its ability to colonize healthy or damaged tissues. Additionally, *Acinetobacter* are often misinterpreted on Gram staining to be other gram-negative organisms more commonly associated with particular clinical syndromes (e.g., in cerebrospinal fluid, *Neisseria meningitidis;* in sputum, *Haemophilus influenzae*). The *A. calcoaceticus-A. baumannii* complex makes up 80% of total *Acinetobacter* clinical isolates, whereas nonclinical items (e.g., food) are more likely to harbor non-*A. baumannii* species. However, repeated isolation of non-*A. baumannii* genospecies from appropriate clinical specimens should not be dismissed as contaminant.

TABLE 216-2 Characteristics of the Family *Neisseriaceae*

Characteristic	*Acinetobacter*	*Neisseria*	*Moraxella*	*Kingella*
Shape	Paired cocci to medium rods	Paired cocci	Paired cocci to short rods	Paired rods
Oxidase	−	+	+	+
Catalase	+	+	+	−
Nitrate reduction	−	+	+/−	+
Metabolism	Active, varied	Limited, simple	Limited, simple	Limited, simple
Acid from glucose	+/−	−	−	+

+, present; −, absent.

Respiratory Tract

The respiratory system is the most common site for *Acinetobacter* infection because of its transient pharyngeal colonization of healthy persons and a high rate of tracheostomy colonization.[24]

Acinetobacter has been reported to cause community-acquired bronchiolitis and tracheobronchitis in healthy children.[25] Tracheobronchitis can also occur in compromised adults. Pulmonary toilet often eradicates the organism without the use of systemic antibiotics in these latter hosts.

Adult community-acquired *Acinetobacter* pneumonia generally occurs in patients with diminished host defenses (e.g., alcoholism, tobacco use, diabetes mellitus, renal failure, underlying pulmonary disease).[26-28] Reports from developing tropical regions document a higher local prevalence of community-acquired *Acinetobacter* pneumonia compared with temperate climates.[20,29] One series from tropical northern Australia found community-acquired *Acinetobacter* pneumonia to account for 10% of all community-acquired bacteremic pneumonias and 21% of gram-negative pneumonias.[20] Mortality in various published series has been 40% to 64%. The prevalence of community-acquired *Acinetobacter* pneumonia was speculated to be a consequence of the generally poor health of persons in the communities under study, frequent use of penicillins, and/or genetic predisposition.

The greatest impact of *Acinetobacter* has been as a causative agent of nosocomial pneumonia, particularly ventilator-associated cases. Predisposing factors for nosocomial *Acinetobacter* pneumonia include endotracheal intubation, tracheostomy, previous antibiotic therapy, ICU residence, recent surgery, and underlying pulmonary disease. Nosocomial spread in the ICU setting has been attributed to ventilator equipment, gloves, colonized nursing and respiratory therapy personnel, contaminated parenteral nutrition solution, and computer keyboards[30] among others. Nosocomial *Acinetobacter* pneumonias are frequently multilobar. Cavitation, pleural effusion, and bronchopleural fistula formation have been observed. Nosocomial pneumonia reports from France found the mortality rate from *Pseudomonas* and *Acinetobacter* to be greater than 70%.[31] Mortality decreases once appropriate antibiotic therapy has been instituted for more than 3 days. Secondary bacteremia and septic shock are associated with a poor prognosis.[24] When attempting to determine the contribution of *Acinetobacter* to the morbidity and death of critically ill patients it is important to note that either colonization or infection with *A. baumannii* in ICU patients has been independently associated with excess length of stay and excess mortality. Therefore, the presence of *Acinetobacter* is attributable more to the ICU patient's poor condition rather than the virulence of *Acinetobacter*.[21]

Bacteremia

True *Acinetobacter* bacteremia should be distinguished from pseudobacteremia resulting from improper blood culture technique.[15] Nosocomial *Acinetobacter* bacteremia is frequently associated with respiratory tract infections and use of intravenous catheters; urinary tract, wound, skin, and abdominal infections are less frequent sources.[24] Although descriptions of well-appearing patients with bacteremia are recorded (generally in patients with indwelling catheters),[32] septic shock may be seen in up to 30% of bacteremic patients.[32a] The mortality rate from *Acinetobacter* bacteremia has been reported to be 17% to 46% with an inconsistent impact on increasing mortality when associated with polymicrobial bacteremia.[24,32a] *Acinetobacter* bacteremia with species other than *A. baumannii* tends to be less severe.[32a]

Genitourinary

Studies isolating *Acinetobacter* from patients with a penicillin-resistant "gonorrhea-like" urethritis led to the erroneous implication of *Acinetobacter* as a cause of this illness.[33] Despite colonization of the lower urinary tract with *Acinetobacter,* it is only rarely invasive. However, cases of cystitis and pyelonephritis have been documented in the setting of an indwelling bladder catheter or nephrolithiasis.[24]

Intracranial Infection

Initially described by Cowan in 1938,[1] *Acinetobacter* meningitis occurs infrequently.[2] Although it is generally identified following head trauma or neurosurgical procedures,[34] there are reports of *Acinetobacter* meningitis occurring in healthy hosts. Meningitis can manifest abruptly or follow a more indolent course. A petechial rash has been noted in up to 30% of patients with *Acinetobacter* meningitis.[25] *Acinetobacter* may be morphologically confused with *N. meningitidis* on Gram stain of spinal fluid. The Waterhouse-Friderichsen syndrome has also been noted in association with *Acinetobacter* meningitis.

Soft Tissue

Acinetobacter can cause cellulitis in association with an indwelling venous catheter. Resolution of catheter-induced cellulitis may occur with catheter removal alone.

Traumatic wounds, burns, and postoperative incisions become colonized by *Acinetobacter* as a result of the organism's ability to thrive on compromised tissue and foreign bodies. During the Vietnam conflict, it was the most common gram-negative bacillus to contaminate traumatic extremity injuries.[35] Serial observations of traumatic wounds in Vietnam revealed *Acinetobacter* to be present early on wounded extremities, with bacteremia occurring 3 to 5 days later. Similar findings have been reported during the 2003 Iraq conflict except that the *Acinetobacter* strains identified were multidrug resistant.[36] Synergistic necrotizing fasciitis in conjunction with *Streptococcus pyogenes* has been described.[24,35,37]

Miscellaneous

Acinetobacter infection can occur in any body site. Reported ocular cases include conjunctivitis, endophthalmitis,[38] corneal ulceration due to soft contact lens contamination, and corneal perforation.[39] Native and prosthetic valve endocarditis has been described.[40] Osteomyelitis, septic arthritis, and pancreatic and liver abscesses have also been reported.

THERAPY

Acinetobacter may colonize the skin, pharynx, gastrointestinal tract, urethra, conjunctiva, and vagina. Interpretation of culture results must take into consideration colonization and potential environmental contamination. Isolation of *Acinetobacter* from colonized patients requires no specific therapy. Appropriate isolation precautions should be instituted upon identification of *Acinetobacter* resistant to multiple antibiotic classes. In patients who present with localized cellulitis or phlebitis associated with a foreign body (e.g., intravenous cannula or suture), removal of the foreign body combined with local care is generally sufficient. The same recommendation can be made for urethritis and cystitis associated with an indwelling urinary catheter that can be removed. Tracheobronchitis after endotracheal intubation may resolve with pulmonary toilet alone. Infections involving the eyes and facial structures require systemic and local antibiotic therapy. Patients with more extensive tissue involvement, including wound dehiscence, fasciitis, or abscess formation, require débridement, drainage, and systemic antibiotic therapy. Those with sepsis syndrome, meningitis, endocarditis, osteomyelitis, or bacteremia require intensive systemic antibiotic therapy.

As with other opportunistic gram-negative organisms (e.g., *Stenotrophomonas maltophilia*), increasing antibiotic resistance has hindered therapeutic management. Although there are significant differences in *Acinetobacter* antimicrobial resistance patterns according to species, country of isolation, and region,[41] the overall trend is one of increasing resistance. Documented mechanisms of resistance include aminoglycoside-modifying enzymes, broad-spectrum β-lactamases, carbapenemases, quantitative and/or qualitative changes in outer membrane porins, and altered penicillin-binding proteins.[42,43] Resistance has been tracked to plasmids, transposons, and chromosomes.

In the 1970s, *Acinetobacter* infections were treated with ampicillin, second-generation cephalosporins, minocycline, colistin, carbenicillin, and gentamicin. For several genospecies of *Acinetobacter* many of these options may no longer exist. Most *A. baumannii* are now resistant to ampicillin, carbenicillin, cefotaxime, and chloramphenicol, with some centers reporting up to 91% of nosocomial *Acinetobacter* resistant to gentamicin.[20] Resistance to tobramycin and amikacin is increasing. Fluoroquinolones, ceftazidime, trimethoprim-sulfamethoxazole, doxycycline, polymyxin B, colistin, imipenem, and meropenem[44] may retain activity against nosocomial *Acinetobacter.* Ertapenem, the newest of the carbapenems, has little intrinsic activity against *Acinetobacter* and should not be used.[47] However, the rapid development of significant quinolone resistance in France, aminoglycoside resistance in Germany, and carbapenem resistance in selected regions worldwide[45,46] are examples of how broad therapeutic generalizations may not accurately consider local resistance patterns. As such, therapy must be individualized with observed antimicrobial resistance principles in mind.

Sulbactam has intrinsic bactericidal activity via penicillin binding protein 2 separate from its inhibition of β-lactamases against many multidrug-resistant *Acinetobacter* strains.[48] Tazobactam and clavulanic acid activities are less than that of sulbactam, and their clinical relevance is less well documented.[49] Sulbactam's efficacy is borne out by several reports documenting successful treatment of serious *Acinetobacter* infections including meningitis and ventriculitis[34,50-52]; however, resistance to sulbactam is rising.[45] In vitro data on more than 200 *A. baumannii* isolates found imipenem (and meropenem) to have the lowest minimal inhibitory concentration (MIC) of available antimicrobial agents, with ampicillin-sulbactam being the most active of the remaining β-lactams.[56] Although imipenem and meropenem remain reliable agents, outbreaks of carbapenem-resistant *Acinetobacter* (up to 80% of isolates in Spain) are an ongoing concern and have been reported in the Americas, Europe, Africa, Asia, and the Middle East.[53] Intravenous colistin (polymyxin B) has been used successfully against carbapenem-resistant *Acinetobacter,* despite concerns raised by animal model data.[54,55] Resistance has been identified to polymyxin B.[57] Bactericidal synergy has been demonstrated when carbenicillin and an aminoglycoside are combined, even when moderate aminoglycoside resistance exists.[58] Imipenem or meropenem with an aminoglycoside and β-lactam/β-lactamase inhibitor with an aminoglycoside were found to be synergistic in vitro against multidrug-resistant nosocomial *A. baumannii* isolates.[59] Additionally, quinolone and amikacin synergy was noted for *A. baumannii* isolates with a low quinolone minimal inhibitory concentration.[60] Species other than *A. baumannii* exhibit less overall antimicrobial resistance.

Limited comparative human clinical trials, supplemented by in vitro data and clinical observation provide some therapeutic guidance. Many mild to moderately severe infections respond to monotherapy with an active agent. The current approach to treating a serious, deep-seated infection involving *Acinetobacter* should be based on sensitivities of the specific isolate and the use of combination therapy.[43] The clinician using β-lactams should be aware of therapeutic failures and relapses resulting from the emergence of resistance during therapy. The induction of broad-spectrum β-lactamases during cephalosporin therapy has led some to urge avoidance of this class of drugs altogether.[61] Imipenem or meropenem has been used successfully alone and in combination with a 4-fluoroquinolone, rifampin, colistin (polymyxin B) or an aminoglycoside. Intravenous colistin compared favorably to imipenem in one small study treating multidrug-resistant *Acinetobacter* ventilator-associated pneumonia.[54] Should 4-fluoroquinolones, β-lactams, or sulbactam be used, the addition of an active aminoglycoside (and/or rifampin) may provide a more rapidly bactericidal regimen and possibly prevent the development of resistance during therapy.

A hospital outbreak involving multidrug-resistant *Acinetobacter* strains with a similar antibiogram should prompt a review of infection control procedures involving hand washing, patient isolation,[62] ventilator care, and housekeeping. In addition, a case-control study and a review of local antimicrobial prescribing habits may be in order.[43] The use of nonabsorbable antibiotics for selective decontamination of the digestive tract has been suggested.[63]

REFERENCES

1. Cowan ST. Unusual infections following cerebral operations: With a description of *Diplococcus mucosus* (von Lingelsheim). Lancet. 1938;2:1052-1054.
2. Chang WN, Lu CH, Huang CR, et al. Community-acquired *Acinetobacter* meningitis in adults. Infection. 2000;28:395-397.
3. De Bord GG. Description of *Mimaeae* Trib. nov. with three genera and three species and two new species of *Neisseria* from conjunctivitis and vaginitis. Iowa State College J Sci. 1942;16:471-480.
4. Brisou J, Prévot A-R. Etudes de systématique bactérienne: Revision des espèces réunies dans le genre Achromobacter. Ann Inst Pasteur. 1954;86:722-728.
5. Juni E. Interspecies transformation of *Acinetobacter,* genetic evidence for a ubiquitous genus. J Bacteriol. 1972;112:917-931.
6. Skerman VBD, McGowan V, Sneath PHA. Approved lists of bacterial names. Int J Syst Bacteriol. 1980;30:225-420.
7. Andrews HJ. *Acinetobacter* bacteriocin typing. J Hosp Infect. 1986;7:169-175.
8. Dijkshoorn L, Aucken H, Gerner-Smidt P, et al. Comparison of outbreak and nonoutbreak *Acinetobacter baumannii* strains by genotype and phenotypic methods. J Clin Microbiol. 1996;34:1519-1525.
9. Bouvet PJ, Grimont PAD. Taxonomy of the genus *Acinetobacter* with the recognition of *Acinetobacter baumannii* sp. nov., *Acinetobacter haemolyticus* sp. nov., *Acinetobacter johnsonii* sp. nov., and *Acinetobacter junii* sp. nov. and emended descriptions of *Acinetobacter calcoaceticus* and *Acinetobacter lwoffi.* Int J Syst Bacteriol. 1986;36:228-240.
10. Dijkshoorn L, van der Toorn J. *Acinetobacter* species: Which do we mean? Clin Infect Dis. 1992;15:748-749.
11. Nemec A, De Baere T, Tjernberg I, et al. *Acinetobacter ursingii* sp. nov. and *Acinetobacter schindleri* sp. nov., isolated from human clinical specimens. Int J Syst Evol Microbiol. 2001;51:1891-1899.
12. Villegas MV, Hartstein AI. Acinetobacter outbreaks, 1977-2000. Infect Control Hosp Epidemiol. 2003;24:284-295.
13. Wendt C, Dietze B, Dietz E, et al. Survival of *Acinetobacter baumannii* on dry surfaces. J Clin Microbiol. 1997;35:1394-1397.
14. Wagenvoort JHT, Joosten EJAJ. An outbreak of *Acinetobacter baumannii* that mimics MRSA in its environmental longevity. J Hosp Infect. 2002;52:226-227.
15. Al-Khoja MS, Darrell JH. The skin as the source of *Acinetobacter* and *Moraxella* species occurring in blood cultures. J Clin Pathol. 1979;32:497-499.
16. Baltimore RS, Duncan RL, Shapiro ED, et al. Epidemiology of pharyngeal colonization of infants with aerobic gram-negative rod bacteria. J Clin Microbiol. 1989;27:91-95.
17. Larson EL. Persistent carriage of gram-negative bacteria on hands. Am J Infect Control. 1981;9:112-119.
18. National Nosocomial Infections Surveillance (NNIS) System report: Data summary from October 1986-April 1998, issued June 1998. Am J Infect Control. 1998;26:522-533.
19. Gales AC, Jones RN, Forward KR, et al. Emerging importance of multidrug-resistant *Acinetobacter* species and *Stenotrophomonas maltophilia* as pathogens in seriously ill patients: geographic patterns, epidemiological features, and trends in the SENTRY antimicrobial surveillance program (1997-1999). Clin Infect Dis. 2001;32(Suppl 2): 104-113.
20. Anstey NM, Currie BJ, Withnall KM. Community-acquired *Acinetobacter* pneumonia in the northern territory of Australia. Clin Infect Dis. 1992;14:83-91.
21. Lortholary O, Fagon J-Y, Hoi AB, et al. Nosocomial acquisition of multi-resistant *Acinetobacter baumannii:* Risk factors and prognosis. Clin Infect Dis. 1995;20:790-796.
22. Carbella X, Piyol M, Ayats J, et al. Relevance of digestive tract colonization in the epidemiology of nosocomial infections due to multiresistant *Acinetobacter baumannii.* Clin Infect Dis. 1996;23:329-334.
23. Scerpella EG, Wanger AR, Armitige L, et al. Nosocomial outbreak caused by a multiresistant clone of *Acinetobacter baumannii:* Results of the case-control and molecular epidemiologic investigations. Infect Control Hosp Epidemiol. 1995;16:92-97.
24. Glew RH, Moellering RC Jr, Kunz LJ. Infections with *Acinetobacter calcoaceticus* (*Herellea vaginicola*): Clinical and laboratory studies. Medicine (Baltimore). 1977;56:79-97.
25. O'Connell CJ, Hamilton R. Gram negative rod infections: II. *Acinetobacter* infections in general hospital. NY State J Med. 1981;81:750-753.
26. Goodhart GL, Abrutyn E, Watson R, et al. Community acquired *Acinetobacter calcoaceticus* var *anitratus* pneumonia. JAMA. 1977;238:1516-1518.
27. Anstey NM, Currie BJ, Hassell M, et al. Community-acquired bacteremic *Acinetobacter* pneumonia in tropical Australia is caused by diverse strains of *Acinetobacter baumannii,* with carriage in the throat of at-risk groups. J Clin Microbiol. 2002;40:685-686.
28. Chen MZ, Hsueh PR, Lee LN, et al. Severe community-acquired pneumonia due to *Acinetobacter baumannii.* Chest 2001;120:1072-1077.
29. Barnes DJ, Naraqi S, Igo JD. Community-acquired *Acinetobacter* pneumonia in adults in Papua New Guinea. Rev Infect Dis. 1988;10:636-639.
30. Neely AN, Maley MP, Warden GD. Computer keyboards as reservoirs for *Acinetobacter baumannii* in a burn hospital. Clin Infect Dis 1999;29:1358-1360.
31. Fagon J-Y, Chastre J, Domart Y, et al. Mortality due to ventilator-associated pneumonia or colonization with *Pseudomonas* or *Acinetobacter* species: Assessment by quantitative culture of samples obtained by protected specimen brush. Clin Infect Dis. 1996;23:538-542.
32. Robinson RG, Garrison RG, Brown BW. Evaluation of the clinical significance of the genus *Herellea.* Ann Intern Med. 1964;60:19-25.
32a. Seifert H, Strate A, Pulverer G. Nosocomial bacteremia due to *Acinetobacter baumannii.* Clinical features, epidemiology, and predictors of mortality. Medicine (Baltimore). 1995;74:340-349.

33. Kozub WR, Bucolo S, Sami AW, et al. Gonorrhea-like urethritis due to *Mima polymorpha* var. *oxidans:* Patient summary and bacteriological study. Arch Intern Med. 1968;122:514-516.
34. Allen DM, Wong SY. *Acinetobacter:* A perspective. Singapore Med J. 1990;31:511-514.
35. Tong MJ. Septic complications of war wounds. JAMA. 1972;219:1044-1047.
36. Peterson K. Acinetobacter, drug resistant-Iraq: request for information. ProMED-mail. 2003;17 April: 20030417. 0934. <http://www.promedmail.org>.
37. Amsel MB, Horrilleno E. Synergistic necrotizing fasciitis: A case of polymicrobial infection with *Acinetobacter calcoaceticus*. Curr Surg. 1985;42:370-372.
38. Peyman GA, Vastine DW, Diamond JG. Vitrectomy and intraocular gentamicin management of *Herellea* endophthalmitis after incomplete phacoemulsification. Am J Ophthalmol. 1975;80:764-765.
39. Wand M, Olive GM, Mangiaracine AB. Corneal perforation and iris prolapse due to *Mima polymorpha*. Arch Ophthalmol. 1975;93:239-241.
40. Gradon JD, Chapnick EK, Lutwick LI. Infective endocarditis of a native valve due to *Acinetobacter:* Case report and review. Clin Infect Dis. 1992;14:1145-1148.
41. Landman D, Quale JM, Mayorga D, et al. Citywide clonal outbreak of multiresistant *Acinetobacter baumannii* and *Pseudomonas aeruginosa* in Brooklyn, NY: The pre-antibiotic era has returned. Arch Intern Med. 2002;162:1515-1520.
42. Amyes SGB, Young H-K. Mechanisms of antibiotic resistance in *Acinetobacter* spp. In: Bergogne-Bérézin E, Joly-Guillou M-L, Towner KJ, eds. *Acinetobacter:* Microbiology, Epidemiology, Infections and Management. New York: CRC Press, 1996;185-223.
43. Urban C, Segal-Maurer S, Rahal JJ. Considerations in control and treatment of nosocomial infections due to multidrug-resistant *Acinetobacter baumannii*. Clin Infect Dis. 2003;36:1268-1274.
44. Seifert H, Baginski R, Schulze A, et al. Antimicrobial susceptibility of *Acinetobacter* species. Antimicrob Agents Chemother. 1993;37:750-753.
45. Manikal VM, Landman D, Saurina G, et al. Endemic carbapenem-resistant *Acinetobacter* species in Brooklyn, New York: Citywide prevalence, interinstitutional spread, and relation to antibiotic use. Clin Infect Dis. 2000;31:101-106.
46. Corbella X, Montero A, Pujol M, et al. Emergence and rapid spread of carbapenem resistance during a large and sustained hospital outbreak of multiresistant *Acinetobacter baumannii*. J Clin Microbiol 2000;38:4086-4095.
47. Fuchs PC, Barry AL, Brown SD. In vitro activities of ertapenem (MK-0826) against clinical isolates from eleven North American medical centers. Antimicrob Agents Chemother. 2001;45:1915-1918.
48. Urban C, Go E, Mariano N, et al. Effect of sulbactam on infections caused by imipenem-resistant *Acinetobacter calcoaceticus* biotype *anitratus*. J Infect Dis. 1993;167:448-451.
49. Amyes SGB. β-lactam resistance and the use of inhibitor combinations. J Med Microbiol. 1997;46:728-731.
50. Jiménez-Mejías ME, Pachón J, Becerril B, et al. Treatment of multi-drug resistant *Acinetobacter baumannii* meningitis with ampicillin/sulbactam. Clin Infect Dis. 1997;24:932-935.
51. Jellison TK, Mkinnon PS, Rybak MJ. Epidemiology, resistance, and outcomes of *Acinetobacter baumannii* bacteremia treated with imipenem-cilastatin or ampicillin-sulbactam. Pharmacotherapy. 2001;21:142-148.
52. Wood GC, Hanes SD, Croce MA, et al. Comparison of ampicillin-sulbactam and imipenem-cilastatin for the treatment of *Acinetobacter* ventilator-associated pneumonia. Clin Infect Dis. 2002;34:1425-1430.
53. Tankovic J, Legrand P, De Gatines G, et al. Characterization of a hospital outbreak of imipenem-resistant *Acinetobacter baumannii* by phenotypic and genotypic typing methods. J Clin Microbiol. 1994;32:2677-2681.
54. Garnacho-Montero J, Ortiz-Leyba C, Jiménez-Jiménez FJ, et al. Treatment of multi-drug resistant *Acinetobacter baumannii* ventilator-associated pneumonia (VAP) with intravenous colistin: A comparison with imipenem-susceptible VAP. Clin Infect Dis. 2003;36:1111-1118.
55. Montero A, Ariza J, Corbella X, et al. Efficacy of colistin versus β-lactams, aminoglycosides, and rifampin as monotherapy in a mouse model of pneumonia caused by multiresistant *Acinetobacter baumannii*. Antimicrob Agents Chemother. 2002;46:1946-1952.
56. Visalli MA, Jacobs MR, Moore TD, et al. Activities of β-lactams against *Acinetobacter* genospecies as determined by agar dilution and e-test MIC methods. Antimicrob Agents Chemother. 1997;41:767-770.
57. Urban C, Mariano N, Rahal JJ, et al. Polymyxin B resistant *Acinetobacter baumannii* clinical isolates susceptible to recombinant BPI21 and cecropin P1. Antimicrob Agents Chemother. 2001;45:994-995.
58. Ramphal R, Kluge RM. *Acinetobacter calcoaceticus* variety *anitratus:* An increasing nosocomial problem. Am J Med Sci. 1979;277:57-66.
59. Marques MB, Brookings ES, Moser SA, et al. Comparative in vitro antimicrobial susceptibilities of nosocomial isolates of *Acinetobacter baumannii* and synergistic activities of nine antimicrobial combinations. Antimicrob Agents Chemother. 1997;41:881-885.
60. Bajaksouzian S, Visalli MA, Jacobs MR, et al. Activities of levofloxacin, ofloxacin, ciprofloxacin, alone and in combination with amikacin, against acinetobacters as determined by checkerboard and time-kill studies. Antimicrob Agents Chemother. 1997;41:1073-1076.
61. Anstey NM. Use of cefotaxime for treatment of *Acinetobacter* infections (Letter). Clin Infect Dis. 1992;15:374.
62. Brooks SE, Walczak MA, Hameed R. Are we doing enough to contain *Acinetobacter* infections? Infect Control Hosp Epidemiol. 2000;21:304.
63. Agusti C, Pujol M, Argerich MJ, et al. Short-term effect of the application of selective decontamination of the digestive tract on different body site reservoir ICU patients colonized by multi-resistant *Acinetobacter baumannii*. J Antimicrob Chemother. 2002;49:205-208.

Salmonella Species, Including *Salmonella* Typhi

DAVID A. PEGUES

MICHAEL E. OHL

SAMUEL I. MILLER

Salmonellae are named for the pathologist Salmon, who first isolated *S. choleraesuis* from porcine intestine.[1] *Salmonella* are effective commensals and pathogens that cause a spectrum of diseases in humans and animals, including domesticated and wild mammals, reptiles, birds, and insects. Some *Salmonella* serotypes, such as *S.* Typhi, *S.* Paratyphi, and *S.* Sendai, are highly adapted to humans and have no other known natural hosts, whereas others, such as *S.* Typhimurium, have a broad host range and can infect a wide variety of animal hosts and humans. Some *Salmonella* serotypes, such as Dublin (cattle) and Arizonae (reptiles), are most adapted to an animal species and only occasionally infect humans. The widespread distribution of *Salmonella* in the environment, their increasing prevalence in the global food chain, and their virulence and adaptability result in enormous medical, public health, and economic impact worldwide.

HISTORY

Before the 19th century, typhus and typhoid fever were confused. Though various clinical distinctions were proposed, none reliably distinguished these syndromes. In 1829 in Paris, P. Ch. A. Louis separated typhoid from other fevers on the basis of intestinal lymph node and spleen pathology.[2] He also described the clinical phenomena of rose spots, intestinal perforation, and hemorrhage. In the English literature, William Jenner in 1850 settled the question of whether typhus and typhoid were different diseases.[3] He distinguished typhoid based on the pathologic evidence of enlargement of the Peyer's patches and mesenteric lymph nodes. Jenner also noted that prior attacks of typhoid protected against subsequent attacks; this was not the case for typhus. In 1869, Wilson proposed the term *enteric fever* as an alternative to typhoid fever, given the anatomic site of infection.[4] Though enteric fever remains a more accurate term, the use of the term *typhoid* persists today.

In 1873 Budd demonstrated that food, water, and fomites could transmit typhoid fever.[5] Gaffkey in Germany isolated the typhoid bacillus in 1884 from the spleens of infected patients.[6] In 1896 Pfeiffer and Kalle made the first typhoid vaccine with heat-killed organisms.[7] In the same year Widal and others demonstrated that convalescent sera from typhoid patients caused the organisms to "stick together in large balls and loose their motility."[8] Widal coined the term *agglutinin* to describe this observation. The antigenic classification or serotyping of *Salmonella* used today is a result of years of study of antibody interactions with bacterial surface antigens by Kauffman and White during the 1920s to 1940s.[9] In 1948, Theodore Woodward and colleagues reported the successful treatment of Malaysian typhoid patients with chloromycetin,[10] and the modern age of antimicrobial therapy for typhoid fever began. In 1952 Zinder and Lederberg, using *Salmonella* Typhimurium, discovered genetic transduction, the transfer of genetic information from one cell to another by a virus particle (bacteriophage P22).[11] Ames and co-workers in 1973 reported the development of the Ames test that uses *S.* Typhimurium auxotrophic mutants to test the mutagenic activity of chemical compounds.[12] At present *Salmonella* pathogenesis is studied widely in animal and tissue culture models of mammalian infection as an important model of host-parasite interactions.

CLASSIFICATION AND TAXONOMY

Salmonella is a genus of the family of Enterobacteriaceae. Before 1983 the existence of multiple *Salmonella* species was taxonomically accepted. Currently, as a result of experiments indicating a high degree of DNA similarity, the genus *Salmonella* is divided into two species, each with multiple subspecies and serotypes. The two species are *S. choleraesuis,* which contains six subspecies (I, II, IIIa, IIIb, IV, and VI), and *S. bongori,* which was formerly subspecies V.[13] *S. choleraesuis* subspecies I contains almost all the serotypes pathogenic for humans, except for rare human infections with subspecies IIIa and IIIb that were formerly designated by the genus *Arizonae.* Because *S. choleraesuis* refers to both a species and a serotype, the species designation *S. enterica* has been recommended and widely adopted.

Members of the seven *Salmonella* subspecies can be serotyped into one of over 2400 serotypes (serovars) according to somatic (O), surface (Vi), and flagellar (H) antigens, and habitats (Table 220-1).[13,14] The name usually refers to the location where the *Salmonella* serotype was first isolated. According to the current *Salmonella* nomenclature system in use at the U.S. Centers for Disease Control and Prevention and World Health Organization laboratories, the full taxonomic designation *Salmonella enterica* subspecies *enterica* serotype Typhimurium can be shortened to *Salmonella* serotype Typhimurium or *Salmonella* Typhimurium.[14]

THE GENOME

Recently, the genome sequences of multidrug-resistant *S.* Typhi strain CT18 and *S.* Typhimurium strain LT2 were determined.[15,16] The CT18 genome contains 4,809,037 base pairs with 4430 open reading frames and that of LT2 4,857,432 base pairs and 5599 coding sequences, including 204 pseudogenes. The two genomes share 98% coding sequence homology and are closely related to those of other *Salmonella* subspecies as well as *Escherichia coli* and *Klebsiella pneumoniae.* Similar environmental requirements likely underlie this coevolution.[16] The 8% of genes unique to subtype 1 *Salmonella* may be involved in adaptation to warm-blooded hosts, and the 204 inactivated pseudogenes in *S.* Typhi strain CT18 may explain its host restriction to humans.[15,16]

MICROBIOLOGY

Salmonellae are gram-negative, non–spore-forming, facultatively anaerobic bacilli that measure 2 to 3 by 0.4 to 0.6 μ in size. Like other Enterobacteriaceae, they produce acid on glucose fermentation, reduce nitrates, and do not produce cytochrome oxidase.[17] All organisms except *S.* Gallinarium-Pullorum are motile as a result of peritrichous flagella, and most do not ferment lactose. However, approximately 1% of organisms are able to ferment lactose and therefore may not be detected if only MacConkey agar or other semiselective media are used to identify *Salmonella* based on colorimetric assay for fermentation of lactose. The differential metabolism of sugars can be used to distinguish many *Salmonella* serotypes; serotype Typhi is the only organism that does not produce gas on sugar fermentation.[17]

Freshly passed stool is preferred for the isolation of *Salmonella* and should be plated directly onto agar plates. Low-selective media, such as MacConkey agar and deoxycholate agar, and intermediate-selective media, such as Salmonella-Shigella, xylose-lysine-deoxycholate, or Hektoen agar, are widely used to screen for both *Salmonella* and *Shigella* species. New selective chromogenic media, such as CHROMagar and COMPASS agar, are more specific than other selective media, reduce the need for confirmatory testing and time to identification, and increasingly are used for the primary isolation and presumptive identification of *Salmonella* from clinical stool specimens.[18]

In addition to plating stool onto primary media, tetrathionate- and selenite-based enrichment broths are often used to facilitate the recovery of low numbers of organisms.[18] Highly *Salmonella*-selective medium, such as selenite with brilliant green, should be reserved for use in stool cultures of suspected carriers and for use during special circumstances, such as outbreaks. Bismuth sulfite agar, which contains an indicator of hydrogen sulfite production and does not contain lactose, is preferred for the isolation of *S.* Typhi and can be used for the detection of the 1% of *Salmonella* strains (including most *Salmonella* serogroup C strains) that ferment lactose.[19] After primary isolation, possible *Salmonella* isolates can be tested in commercial identification systems or inoculated into screening media such as triple-sugar–iron and lysine-iron agar. Methods of direct detection of *Salmonella* from stool specimens by latex agglutination and polymerase chain reaction (PCR)–based assays, including detection of virulence genes, are under development and may be most useful for detection of *Salmonella* in food samples.[20] Rapid, immunoglobulin M antibody–based serologic tests recently have been developed and may supplement stool culture for the diagnosis of acute *Salmonella* infection.[21]

Isolates with typical biochemical profiles for *Salmonella* should be serogrouped with commercially available polyvalent antisera or sent to a reference or public health laboratory for complete serogrouping. Salmonellae are serogrouped according to their polysaccharide O (somatic) antigens, Vi (capsular) antigens, and H (flagellar) antigens according to the Kauffman-White scheme.[22] The Vi antigen is a heat-labile capsular homopolymer of *N*-acetylgalactosaminouronic acid that is used for the identification of *S.* Typhi strains and occasionally other *Salmonella* serotypes by slide agglutination.[23] In *S.* Typhi and *S.* Paratyphi C, the polysaccharide Vi antigen can inhibit O antigen agglutination because it is so abundant, and boiling is required to inactive Vi antigen and to detect O antigen. Most antigenic variability occurs in the O antigen, which is composed of chains of oligosaccharide attached to a core oligosaccharide linked covalently to lipid A.

Although serotyping of all surface antigens can be used for formal identification, most laboratories perform a few simple agglutination reactions that define specific O antigens into serogroups, designated as groups A, B, C$_1$, C$_2$, D, and E *Salmonella.*[24] Strains in these six serogroups cause approximately 99% of *Salmonella* infections in humans and warm-blooded animals. Although this grouping is useful in epidemiologic studies and can be used to confirm genus identification, it cannot identify whether the organism is likely to cause enteric fever, because considerable cross-reactivity occurs among serogroups. For example, *S.* Enteritidis, which typically causes gastroenteritis, and *S.* Typhi, which causes enteric fever, are both group D. Similarly, an-

TABLE 220-1 *Salmonella* Species, Subspecies, and Serotypes and Their Usual Habitats

Salmonella *Species and Subspecies*	*No. of Serotypes within Subspecies*	*Usual Habitat*
S. enterica subsp. *enterica* (I)	1454	Warm-blooded animals
S. enterica subsp. *salmae* (II)	489	Cold-blooded animals and the environment*
S. enterica subsp. *arizonae* (IIIa)	84	Cold-blooded animals and the environment*
S. enterica subsp. *diarizonae* (IIIb)	324	Cold-blooded animals and the environment*
S. enterica subsp. *houtenae* (IV)	70	Cold-blooded animals and the environment*
S. enterica subsp. *indica* (VI)	12	Cold-blooded animals and the environment*
S. bongori (V)	20	Cold-blooded animals and the environment*
Total	2463	

*Isolates of all species and subspecies have occurred in humans.
Adapted from Brenner FW, Villar RG, Angulo FJ, et al. *Salmonella* nomenclature. J Clin Microbiol. 2000;38:2465-2467.

other frequent cause of gastroenteritis, *S.* Typhimurium, and some *S.* Paratyphi, another cause of enteric fever, are both group B.

Subtyping methods frequently are used for epidemiologic purposes to differentiate strains of common *Salmonella* serotypes. Phenotyping methods may be useful for characterizing outbreak-associated strains and sporadic multidrug-resistant isolates, and include bacteriophage typing, plasmid profile analysis, antimicrobial susceptibility, and biotyping. More discriminative genotyping techniques, including ribotyping, pulsed-field gel electrophoresis, insertion sequences analysis, PCR-based fingerprinting, and multilocus sequence typing have been used in epidemiologic studies to differentiate strains within a given serotype. Genomic DNA analysis using microarrays may complement the other genotyping methods.[25] However, a lack of standardization and time requirement limit the widespread use of these genotyping techniques.

EPIDEMIOLOGY

Salmonella Typhi and Salmonella Paratyphi

S. Typhi and *S.* Paratyphi only colonize humans, and therefore, disease can only be acquired through close contact with a person who has had typhoid fever or is a chronic carrier. Most often, acquisition of infection occurs by ingestion of fecally contaminated food or water. Usually, waterborne transmission involves the ingestion of fewer microorganisms and, as a result, has a longer incubation period and lower attack rate compared with foodborne transmission. Although direct person-to-person transmission is uncommon, person-to-person transmission of *S.* Typhi, including anal-oral transmission, has been reported.[26] Occasionally, health care workers can acquire the disease from infected patients as a result of poor hand hygiene or handling laboratory specimens.[27]

Typhoid fever continues to be a global health problem, with an estimated 16 million cases worldwide and 600,000 deaths each year.[28] The disease is endemic in many developing countries, particularly in the Indian subcontinent, Southeast Asia, South and Central America, and Africa, with annual incidence rates estimated to be greater than 900 per 100,000 population in India.[28,29] These countries share several characteristics, including rapid population growth, increased urbanization, inadequate human waste treatment, limited water supply, and overburdened health care systems. Recent outbreaks of typhoid fever in Eastern Europe and the Confederation of Independent States have followed political and social collapse.[30]

Outbreaks of typhoid fever in developing countries can result in high morbidity and mortality, especially when caused by antimicrobial-resistant strains.[31] Antimicrobial resistance in developing countries may be promoted by the widespread use of "over-the-counter" antibiotics, immigrant workers, and international travel. In the 1970s, epidemic typhoid fever caused by chloramphenicol-resistant strains emerged in Mexico and the Indian subcontinent.[32-34] Beginning in 1989, multidrug-resistant strains of *S.* Typhi, with plasmid-encoded resistance to chloramphenicol, ampicillin, and trimethoprim, emerged in the Indian subcontinent, Southeast Asia, the Middle East, and Africa, and resulted in numerous outbreaks with substantial morbidity and mortality.[35] Although these multidrug-resistant strains belonged to different Vi phage types, they typically contain a self-transferable 120-MDa plasmid of the H1 incompatibility type that often also encodes resistance to streptomycin, sulfonamides, and tetracyclines.[35] Spread results from transfer of the resistance plasmid to multiple different *S.* Typhi strains.[36]

More recently, chromosomal and plasmid encoded resistance to ciprofloxacin has appeared among *S.* Typhi isolates from the Indian subcontinent, Vietnam, and Tajikistan, associated with the widespread use of ciprofloxacin to control outbreaks of multidrug-resistant *S.* Typhi infection.[30,37] In 1999, 23% of *S.* Typhi isolates in patients in the United Kingdom had decreased susceptibility to ciprofloxacin (minimum inhibitory concentration [MIC] 0.25 to 1.0 µg/mL) and were associated with a history of travel to the Indian subcontinent.[38] High-level resistance to third-generation cephalosporins has been reported

but remains rare.[39] Although multidrug-resistant strains remain common in many areas of Asia, in some areas antimicrobial-susceptible strains have reemerged.[40]

In the United States, substantial progress has been made in the eradication of *S.* Typhi. Since 1985, an average of 245 cases of typhoid fever have been reported each year, with an annual incidence of less than 0.2 per 100,000 population, compared with 35,994 cases of typhoid fever in 1920.[41] This progress clearly is related to improved food handling practices and water treatment. Although foodborne outbreaks of typhoid fever are rare today in developed countries, the potential still exists for outbreaks related to food contamination by a chronic carrier such as "Typhoid Mary" Mallon. In the United States, although *S.* Typhi outbreaks generally are small (median, 10 cases), from 1960 to 1999, 16 (62%) of 26 foodborne outbreaks were associated with an asymptomatic food handler.[42] In 1998-1999, 16 culture-confirmed cases of typhoid fever occurred in Florida associated with a frozen tropical fruit product.[43] This was the first outbreak in the United States associated with a commercially imported food and, in contrast to previous outbreaks, cases were scattered over several counties and not concentrated in the same community. The financial costs of typhoid compared with nontyphoidal *Salmonella* outbreaks are considerable. Estimates vary from approximately $2500 to $4500/person for typhoid illness compared with $645/person for nontyphoidal salmonellosis.[44]

In the United States, typhoid fever increasingly is associated with international travel, especially to developing countries.[41,45] Between 1985 and 1994, 72% of the 2445 reported typhoid cases in the United States were associated with recent international travel, including to the Indian subcontinent (India, 25%; and Pakistan, 8%), Mexico (28%), the Philippines (10%), El Salvador (5%), and Haiti (4%).[41] The proportion of *S.* Typhi isolates resistant to chloramphenicol, ampicillin, and trimethoprim-sulfamethoxazole has increased dramatically— 0.6% during 1985 to 1989, 12% during 1990 to 1994, and 17% during 1996 to 1997 before declining to 9% in 2000 (Table 220-2).[41,45,46] From 1996 to 2000, although no fully ciprofloxacin-resistant isolates were detected in the United States, the proportion of *S.* Typhi isolates that were resistant to nalidixic acid increased from 7% to 23%.[45,46] This phenotype is associated with an increased risk of fluoroquinolone treatment failure.[38]

Nontyphoidal Salmonellae

In many countries the incidence of human *Salmonella* infections has increased markedly, although good population-based surveillance data are mostly lacking. In the United States, the incidence rate of nontyphoidal *Salmonella* infection has doubled in the last two decades, with an estimated 1.4 million cases occurring annually.[45,47] In 2002, the in-

TABLE 220-2 Antimicrobial Resistance of *Salmonella* Isolates, United States, 2000

	Salmonella Typhi (N = 177) N (%)	Non-Typhi Salmonella (N = 1378) N (%)
Amikacin	2 (1.1)	0 (0)
Amoxicillin–clavulanic acid	0 (0)	54 (4)
Ampicillin	16 (9)	219 (16)
Cefoxitin	3 (1.7)	43 (3)
Ceftriaxone	0 (0)	18 (1.3)
Cephalothin	2 (1.1)	54 (4)
Chloramphenicol	19 (11)	138 (10)
Ciprofloxacin	0 (0)	5 (0.4)
Gentamicin	1 (0.6)	37 (3)
Nalidixic acid	41 (23)	34 (2)
Streptomycin	18 (11)	223 (16)
Sulfamethoxazole	21 (12)	235 (17)
Tetracycline	19 (11)	256 (19)
Trimethoprim-sulfamethoxazole	16 (9)	29 (2)

Adapted from Centers for Disease Control and Prevention. NARMS 2000 Annual Report. Available at *www.cdc.gov/narms/annuals.htm*

FIGURE 220-1. Incidence rate per 100,000 population of laboratory-confirmed *Salmonella, Campylobacter, Shigella,* and *E. coli* O157:H7 infections by selected sites in the United States (Foodborne Diseases Active Surveillance Network, 2002). *(From Centers for Disease Control and Prevention. Preliminary FoodNet data on the incidence of foodborne illnesses-selected sites, United States, 2002. MMWR Morb Mortal Wkly Rep. 2003; 52:340-343.)*

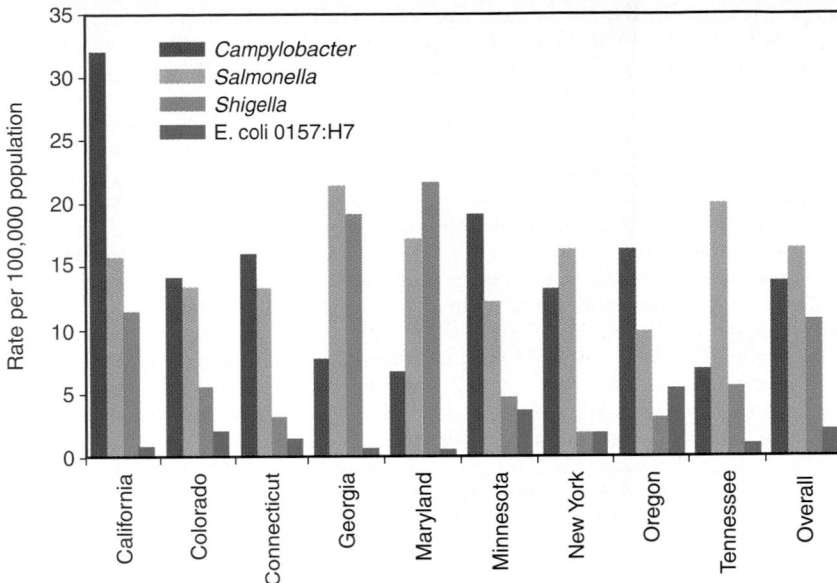

cidence rate of salmonellosis (17.7 per 100,000 population) was highest among 10 potentially foodborne diseases under active surveillance and varied little by geographic region (Fig. 220-1).[48] In 2000, *S.* Typhimurium and *S.* Enteritidis were the most common serotypes, together accounting for 42% of all laboratory-confirmed cases of human salmonellosis.[49] Nontyphoidal *Salmonella* cause a small but significant proportion of diarrhea among travelers[50] and among young children in developing countries.[51] The incidence of salmonellosis is highest during the rainy season in tropical climates and during May through October in temperate climates, coinciding with the peak in foodborne outbreaks.

In humans, nontyphoidal *Salmonella* infections are most often associated with food products and are the most frequently identified agent of foodborne disease outbreaks.[52] Food of animal origin, including meat, poultry, eggs, or dairy products, can become contaminated with *Salmonella*. Eating uncooked or inadequately cooked food or foods cross-contaminated with these products may lead to human infection. In the developed world, acquisition of nontyphoidal salmonellosis most often is associated with consumption of poultry and eggs,[52,53] but a wide range of vehicles have been implicated in transmission to humans.[52,54] Although foodborne outbreaks predominate, waterborne outbreaks of salmonellosis also have been reported.[55]

Salmonellosis associated with exotic pets is a resurgent public health problem, with an estimated 3% to 5% of all cases of salmonellosis in humans associated with exposure to exotic pets, especially reptiles.[54] As many as 90% of reptiles may be carriers of *Salmonella*.[56] The recognition of pet turtle–associated salmonellosis led to the banning of shipment of pet turtles in several countries but not to an elimination of the problem.[54] Exposure to iguanas has been associated with infection with *Salmonella*, including *S.* Marina and *S.* Chameleon, especially among infants,[57] and exposure to snakes with *S.* Arizona infection and platelet transfusion–associated *S.* Enteritidis sepsis.[58] Exposure to pet birds, pet rodents, dogs, and cats also is a potential source of salmonellosis, and outbreaks of multidrug-resistant *S.* Typhimurium infection associated with small animal veterinary facilities have been reported.[59]

During the 1980s and 1990s, *S.* Enteritidis associated with shell eggs emerged as the predominant *Salmonella* serotype and source of foodborne disease in the United States and some other countries.[53,60] In the United States, the rate of reported *S.* Enteritidis isolates increased from 0.6 per 100,000 population in 1976 to a high of 3.8 per 100,000 in 1995 before declining to 1.9 per 100,000 in 1999.[61] During 1985 to 1998, *S.* Enteritidis accounted for 796 reported outbreaks, 28,689 cases of illness, 2839 hospitalizations, and 79 deaths.[62] The recent de-

cline in incidence of *Salmonella* in the United States cases may reflect improved food safety practices, including use of traceback investigations, diversion of infected eggs into pasteurization, and industry sponsored quality-assurance programs (Fig. 220-2).[61]

Infection of egg-laying and broiler poultry flocks with *S.* Enteritidis is widespread. Transmission of *S. enteritidis* from farm to farm may be facilitated by ingestion of feed contaminated with mouse droppings, because *S.* Enteritidis strains cultured from the spleens of mice caught on farms have enhanced ability to contaminate eggs.[63] The loss of cross-immunity resulting from culling *S.* Gallinarum– and *S.* Pullorum–infected chickens in the United States and United Kingdom also may have contributed to the emergence of *S.* Enteritidis.[64] Infection localizes to the ovaries and upper oviduct tis-

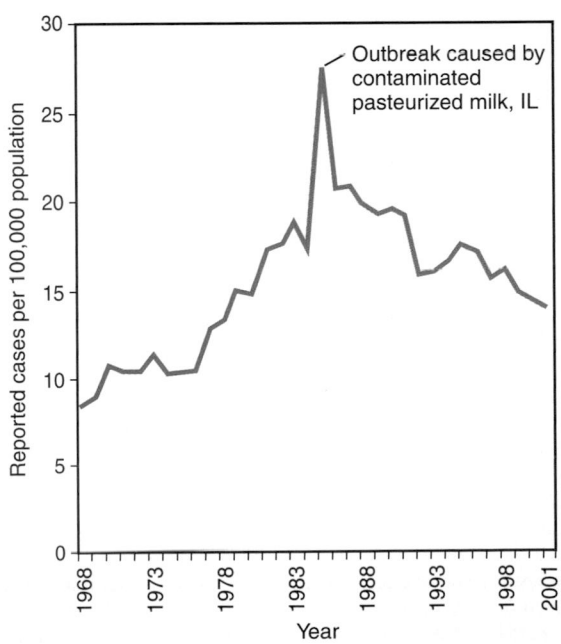

FIGURE 220-2. Incidence rate per 100,000 population of nontyphoidal salmonellosis by year, United States, 1968 through 2001. *(From Centers for Disease Control and Prevention. Summary of notifiable diseases, United States, 2001. MMWR Morb Mortal Wkly Rep. 2003;50:96.)*

sue and is transmitted to the forming egg before shell deposition. An estimated 2.3 million of 69 billion shell eggs produced annually in the United States contain *S.* Enteritidis.[65] Phage types 8 and 13a predominate in the United States[53] and phage type 4 in Europe.[60] Outbreaks of *S.* Enteritidis infection have been associated with ingestion of uncooked or lightly cooked eggs (e.g., sunny-side up), egg-containing food products, and inadequately cooked poultry.[53,62] Although cooking of eggs until all liquid yolk is solidified kills *S.* Enteritidis, the use of pasteurized egg products remains the safest alternative for institutions and the general public.

Poultry and meat are potential reservoirs of human *Salmonella* infection, and contamination of raw animal products can occur during slaughter and processing. From 1998 to 2002, the overall prevalence of *Salmonella* in raw poultry and meat decreased approximately two fold in the United States but remained highest for ground chicken (29.1%) and ground turkey (17.9%).[66] A 1998 survey found that 41 (21%) of 200 retail ground meat specimens (chicken, turkey, beef, and pork) contained *Salmonella,* and resistance was common, including to ceftriaxone (16%).[67] Although raw chicken carcasses are less commonly contaminated with *Salmonella* than is ground chicken, cross-contamination of food items when handling raw chicken and inadequate hand hygiene are risks for sporadic salmonellosis in the home.[68] There is considerable mismatch between animal and human *Salmonella* serotypes, suggesting that the risk of transmission is not equal for all food products and serotypes.[69]

Changes in food consumption and the rapid growth of international trade in agricultural food products have facilitated the dissemination of new *Salmonella* serotypes associated with fresh fruits and vegetables. Human or animal feces may contaminate the surface of fruits and vegetables and may not be removed by washing. Recent foodborne outbreaks of salmonellosis associated with fresh produce include cantaloupe, tomatoes, unpasteurized orange juice, cilantro, and raw seed sprouts. Seeds can become contaminated before sprouting, and soaking seeds with 20,000 ppm calcium hypochlorite or other disinfectant can reduce, but does not eliminate, the risk of sprout-associated illness.[70] Persons at high risk for systemic infection should not eat sprouts.

Manufactured food items pose an enormous potential hazard of foodborne salmonellosis in developed countries because of their centralized production and wide-scale distribution. In 1994 an estimated 224,000 cases of *S.* Enteritidis gastroenteritis developed among persons in the United States who ate a nationally distributed ice cream product. The source of the *S.* Enteritidis was most likely pasteurized ice cream premix that was contaminated during transport in tanker trailers that previously carried nonpasteurized liquid eggs. Other recent outbreaks associated with manufactured food products include pasteurized milk (United States; *S.* Typhimurium), powdered milk products and infant formula (Canada and United States; *S.* Tennessee), and unpasteurized goat milk cheese (France; *S.* Paratyphi).

Antimicrobial resistance among human nontyphoidal *Salmonella* isolates is increasing worldwide and is likely due, in part, to the widespread use of antimicrobial agents for the empirical treatment of febrile syndromes and as growth promoters in animal production.[71] High rates of resistance (>50% to 100%) to chloramphenicol, trimethoprim-sulfamethoxazole, and ampicillin have been reported from Africa, Asia, and South America. Multidrug-resistant nontyphoidal *Salmonella* have now emerged in developed countries, including the United States (Fig. 220-3; see also Table 220-2).[72] In 2000, 18% of isolates from over 27,000 cases of salmonellosis in Europe were multidrug resistant.[73] Persons with resistant salmonella isolates are more likely than those with susceptible ones to have been treated with an antimicrobial agent recently, to have systemic infections, to be hospitalized, and to die from their infection.[72,74] A diversity of transferable resistance plasmids have been identified from multidrug-resistant nontyphoidal *Salmonella* strains and contribute to the conjugative transfer of resistance between enteric bacterial species.[75]

Of particular concern is the worldwide emergence of a distinct strain of multidrug-resistant *S.* Typhimurium, characterized as definitive phage type 104 (DT104) that is resistant to at least five antimicrobials—ampicillin, chloramphenicol, streptomycin, sulfonamides, and tetracy-

clines.[76] All DT104 strains contain a chromosome- and integron-encoded β-lactamase (PSE-1) that appears to have been acquired from plasmids in *Pseudomonas* species.[77] The DT104 strain has broad host reservoirs and is difficult to control in domestic livestock, leading to its widespread clonal dissemination among food animals, especially cattle, and humans in Europe, the United States, Canada, and the Middle and Far East.[76-79] In the United Kingdom, *S.* Typhimurium DT104 is now the second most prevalent strain of *Salmonella* isolated from humans after *S.* Enteritidis PT4,[80] and in 2000 caused a large national outbreak associated with lettuce consumption.[81] In the United States, the prevalence of *S.* Typhimurium isolates with at least the five-drug pattern of resistance increased from fewer than 1% during 1979-1980 to 35.6% in 2000, and most were a single clone of DT104.[46,78] Acquisition of DT104 strains has been associated with contact with ill farm animals and with consumption of a variety of meat products. Although no more virulent than susceptible *S.* Typhimurium strains, infection with DT104 may be associated with greater morbidity and mortality, likely reflecting inadequate empirical antimicrobial therapy.[82]

Recently, outbreaks and sporadic cases of nontyphoidal *Salmonella* resistant to third-generation cephalosporins have been reported in both developed and developing countries.[83] Resistance to third-generation cephalosporins is conferred by conjugative plasmid-encoded β-lactamases from functional groups 1 (AmpC) and 2 (TEM).[83,84] In 1998, the first reported case of ceftriaxone-resistant *Salmonella* infection acquired in the United States occurred in a child in Nebraska and was associated with exposure to cattle on his family's ranch that harbored *S.* Typhimurium with a 160-kb plasmid encoding CMY-2 AmpC β-lactamase.[85] Recent U.S. surveys found that 5.1% of *Salmonella* isolates from cattle and pigs and 1.6% of isolates from humans were ceftriaxone resistant (MIC >16 μg/mL).[46] Carbapenem-resistant strains have been reported rarely.[86]

Quinolone-resistant *Salmonella* strains have been emerging among humans and animals, and resistance is due to mutations of the intracellular targets DNA gyrase (*gyrA* or *gyrB*) or topoisomerase IV, or to overproduction of efflux pumps that also result in increased resistance to multiple antibiotics and disinfectants.[87-89] In 2000, 1.4% of *Salmonella* isolates in the United States were resistant to the quinolone nalidixic acid and 0.4% were ciprofloxacin (fluoroquinolone) resistant.[46] In comparison, in the United Kingdom, the incidence of ciprofloxacin resistance increased from 0% in 1993 to 14% in 1996 and was highest among *S.* Hadar, *S.* Virchow, and *S.* Newport isolates.[90] This increase was concurrent with the licensing of the enrofloxacin for veterinary use in that country in 1993.[80] In Taiwan, where over half of feed-mill operators add enrofloxacin to pig feed as a growth promoter, hospital-based surveillance detected a rapid and substantial increase in ciprofloxacin resistance in *S.* Choleraesuis beginning in 2000.[91] Transmission from swine to humans of a DT104 strain that was resistant to nalidixic acid and had reduced susceptibility to ciprofloxacin has been reported from Denmark.[92] These studies raise substantial concern that the ongoing use of the fluoroquinolones as growth promoters in livestock may select for ciprofloxacin-resistant *Salmonella* among food animals and humans.

The prevalence of fluoroquinolone-resistant *Salmonella* serotypes is increasing, especially in Southeast Asia. Recent travel to Southeast Asia, especially Thailand, was associated with an increased risk of fluoroquinolone-resistant *Salmonella* infection in a Finnish study.[93] Hospitalization in the Philippines was the likely source of fluoroquinolone-resistant *S.* Schwarzengrund in the index patient in a prolonged U.S. nursing home and hospital outbreak.[94] Illness was associated with fluoroquinolone use in the prior 6 months.

Although health care–associated salmonellosis is infrequent, such infections have been associated with substantial morbidity and mortality.[27] Recurrent outbreaks of *Salmonella* wound infection among immunocompromised burn ward patients were associated with a high rate of secondary bacteremia.[95] *Salmonella* resistance to silver may emerge in a clinical setting, such as burn units, where silver is used as a biocide and is mediated by a plasmid-encoded silver-specific binding protein and efflux pumps.[96]

Nosocomial transmission of *Salmonella* from patients to health care workers has been associated with handling soiled linen, non-

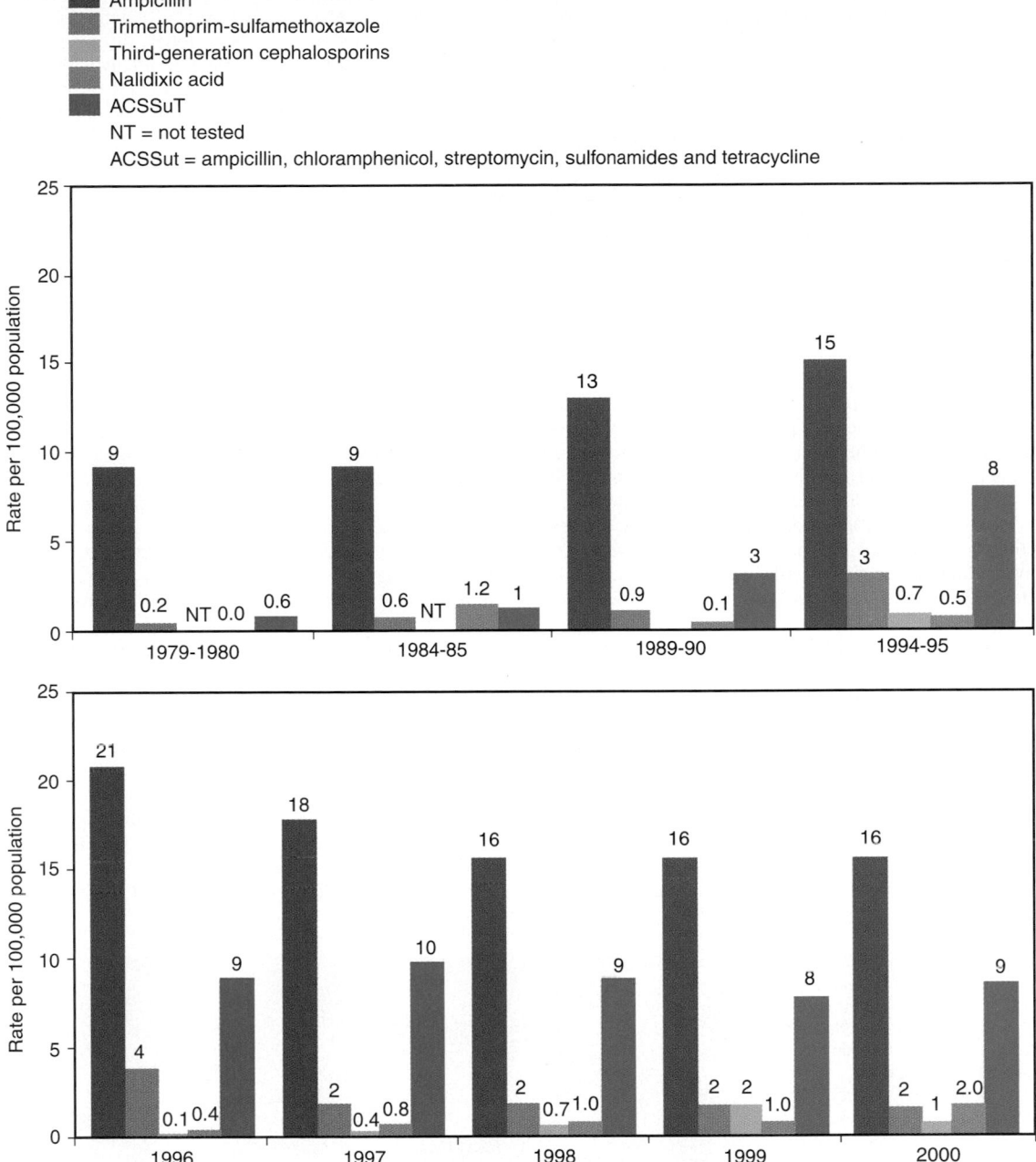

FIGURE 220-3. Summary of long-term trends in antimicrobial resistance in non-Typhi *Salmonella* isolates, United States, 1979 through 2000. *(From Centers for Disease Control and Prevention. NARMS 2000 Annual Report. Available at: www.cdc.gov/narms/annuals.htm)*

compliance with barrier precautions, and fecally incontinent residents.[97] However, the risk of transmission from health care workers to patients appears to be low if infection control measures are observed carefully.[98] In contrast, the risk of nosocomial transmission to neonates and infants from acutely or chronically infected family members is high.[99] Neonates are at high risk for fecal-oral transmission of *Salmonella* because of relative gastric achlorhydria and the buffering capacity of ingested breast milk and formula. High-iron infant formula may further increase the risk of infant salmonellosis compared with breast-feeding.[100] Contaminated enteral feeding and crowding also have been associated with nosocomial transmission among pediatric patients.[101] Control of outbreaks in daycare centers may be difficult because of the need for frequent diaper changing and the higher rate and longer duration of convalescent carriage seen in the preschool age group.[102]

The elderly are at increased risk for *Salmonella* bacteremia and extraintestinal infection as a result of debility, underlying illnesses, and waning immunity. Residents of nursing homes may be at particular risk of salmonellosis because many of these institutions have only limited infection control programs.[103] From 1975 through 1987, nontyphoidal *Salmonella* was the most common etiology of foodborne outbreaks reported from United States nursing homes, accounted for 52% of outbreaks and 81% of outbreak-associated deaths.[103]

PATHOGENESIS

Salmonella infections begin with the ingestion of bacteria in contaminated food or water. Estimates of the infectious dose vary substantially and depend on the method of determination. In studies involving administration of laboratory *Salmonella* strains to healthy human volunteers, the median dose required to produce disease was approximately 10^6 bacteria.[104] In contrast, investigations of point source outbreaks suggest that as few as 200 bacteria may produce nontyphoidal gastroenteritis in many of those exposed, and that the ingested dose is an important determinant of incubation period and disease severity.[104,105] Discrepancies in these results may stem from use of attenuated strains in the challenge experiments and from variation in disease susceptibility in the general population. Gastric acidity represents the initial barrier to *Salmonella* colonization, and conditions that increase gastric pH significantly increase susceptibility to infection. On exposure to acid in vitro, salmonellae display an adaptive acid tolerance response that probably facilitates bacterial survival in the stomach and passage to the small intestine.[106]

Interactions with Intestinal Epithelium and Induction of Enteritis

Salmonellae must evade host antimicrobial factors secreted into the intestinal lumen, including antimicrobial peptides, bile salts, and secretory immunoglobulin A, and traverse a protective mucous barrier before encountering intestinal epithelial cells.[107,108] Salmonellae express an array of distinct fimbriae that contribute to tight adherence to intestinal epithelial cells in culture. It is necessary to delete multiple fimbriae synthesis genes to prevent infection in animal models, suggesting that functional redundancy exists.[109] Microscopy reveals that salmonellae invade intestinal epithelial cells by a morphologically distinct process termed *bacteria-mediated endocytosis* (Fig. 220-4).[110] Shortly after bacteria adhere to the apical epithelial surface, profound cytoskeletal rearrangements occur in the host cell, disrupting the normal epithelial brush border and inducing formation of membrane ruffles that reach out and enclose adherent bacteria in large vesicles. This process resembles the membrane ruffling and macropinocytosis induced in many cell types by growth factors and is functionally distinct from receptor-mediated endocytosis, the mechanism by which many other pathogens enter nonphagocytic cells. Following bacteria internalization, a fraction of the *Salmonella*-containing vesicles transcytose to the basolateral membrane, and the apical epithelial brush border reconstitutes. The epithelial cell type that serves as the principal portal for *Salmonella* invasion remains uncertain. In the mouse enteric fever model, salmonellae preferentially adhere to and enter the specialized microfold cells (M cells) that overlie lymphoid tissue within Peyer's patches.[111] In bovine and rabbit models of enteritis, however, salmonellae do not appear to interact preferentially with M cells, but instead adhere to and invade intestinal enterocytes diffusely.[112] It is possible that M cells are the principal portal of entry in the enteric fever syndrome, and that generalized invasion of enterocytes plays a greater role in the enteritis induced by nontyphoidal *Salmonella* serotypes.

Salmonellae encode a type III secretion system (T3SS) within *Salmonella* pathogenicity island 1 (the SPI-1 T3SS) that is required for bacteria-mediated endocytosis and intestinal epithelial invasion. T3SSs are complex macromolecular machines that have evolved to subvert host cell function through the translocation of virulence proteins directly from the bacterial cytoplasm into the host cell (see Chapters 1 and 3 for overview). *Salmonella* mutants lacking a functional SPI-1 T3SS do not invade epithelial cells in tissue culture and are severely attenuated in animal models of infection following oral administration.[112] In the past decade considerable attention has focused on identifying the virulence proteins translocated into epithelial cells by the SPI-1 T3SS and delineating the host cell processes these proteins target.

Two SPI-1 translocated proteins, SipC and SipA, promote membrane ruffling and *Salmonella* invasion through direct interactions with the actin cytoskeleton. The SipC protein inserts into the host cell plasma membrane and forms part of a protein complex that allows translocation of additional SPI-1 virulence proteins directly into the host cell cytoplasm.[113] SipC also directly nucleates actin polymerization at the site of *Salmonella* attachment and stimulates actin filament bundling.[114] The SipA protein further enhances actin polymerization through stabilization of actin filaments and reduction of the critical concentration for polymerization.[115] *SipA* mutants invade epithelial cells less efficiently than wild-type bacteria and induce disorganized, diffuse ruffling in host cells, in contrast to the localized ruffling induced around wild-type bacteria.

Additional SPI-1 translocated proteins contribute to *Salmonella* invasion by targeting members of the Rho family of monomeric GTP binding proteins (G proteins). Rho family members, including cdc42, rac, and rho, regulate the structure and dynamics of the actin cy-

FIGURE 220-4. Scanning electron micrograph showing *Salmonella* Typhimurium entering a HEp-2 cell through bacteria-mediated endocytosis. Membrane ruffles extend from the cell surface, enclosing and internalizing adherent bacteria. *(From Ohl ME, Miller SI. Salmonella: A model for bacterial pathogenesis. Annu Rev Med. 2001;52. Available from Annual Reviews: www.annualreviews.org).*

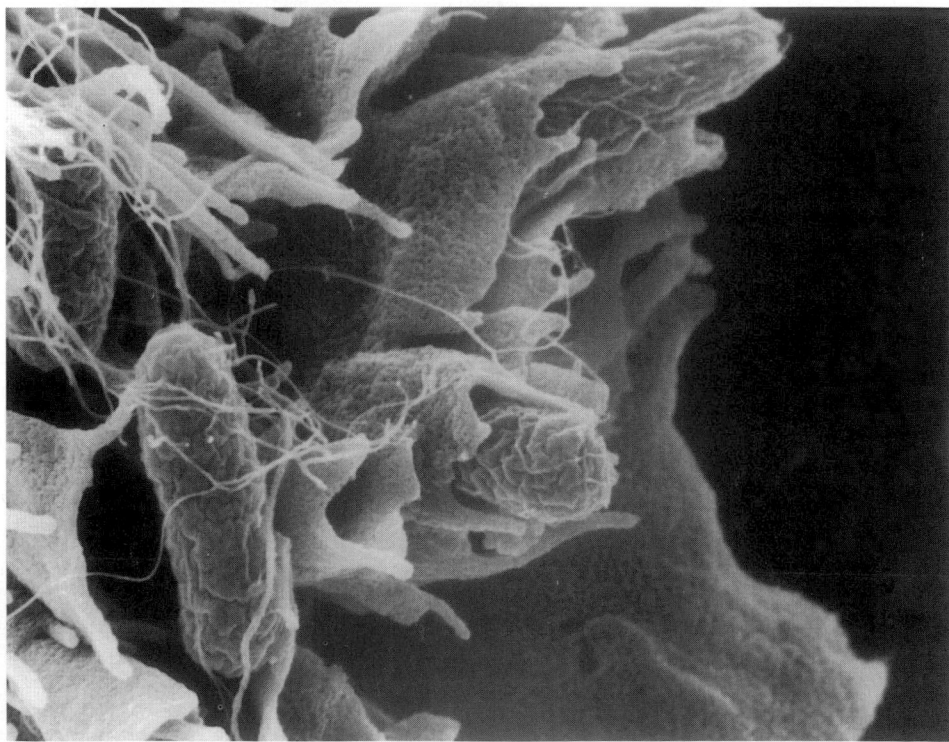

toskeleton and are required for formation of the membrane ruffles that mediate *Salmonella* internalization. The SPI-1 translocated proteins SopE and SopE2 directly activate rac1 and cdc42 in vitro by acting as GDP/GTP exchange factors (GEFs), and induce membrane ruffling and macropinocytosis following microinjection into epithelial cells.[116] SopB is an additional SPI-1 translocated protein that targets inositol phosphate signaling within the host cell by acting as an inositol polyphosphatase.[117] Among other effects, this activity indirectly stimulates Rho GTPases and promotes membrane ruffling.[118] Although mutation of *sopB*, *sopE*, or *sopE2* alone does not impact invasion, combined deletion of these three genes leads to a severe reduction in epithelial cell invasion.[118] Such functional redundancy among translocated proteins is an emerging theme in a variety of T3SSs. Overall, available data indicate that SipA and SipC act in concert with downstream cellular effectors of activated Rho GTPases to initiate and spatially direct the actin rearrangements that lead to *Salmonella* internalization.

Recent studies in mice indicate that salmonellae may also cross the intestinal epithelial border by a SPI-1–independent process involving host dendritic cells.[119,120] These cells express tight junction proteins and can intercalate between intestinal epithelial cells and access the intestinal lumen without disrupting epithelial integrity. In this manner dendritic cells may internalize bacteria in the intestinal lumen, and subsequently carry these bacteria to distant sites as they undergo their physiologic migration to lymphoid tissues.

In addition to invasion of intestinal epithelial cells, *Salmonella* serotypes clinically associated with gastroenteritis induce a secretory response in intestinal epithelium and initiate recruitment and transmigration of neutrophils into the intestinal lumen. The SPI-1 T3SS is also required for these responses in tissue culture and animal models of enteritis. Specifically, *Salmonella* strains unable to deliver any SPI-1 virulence proteins as a result of mutations in the secretion apparatus fail to induce fluid secretion or neutrophil accumulation in ligated bovine ileal loops, and do not cause gastroenteritis in calves.[121] In tissue culture models of enteritis, translocation of SPI-1 proteins into intestinal epithelial cells leads to synthesis and polarized secretion of inflammatory mediators and neutrophil chemoattractants, including interleukin (IL)-8.[122]

Several SPI-1 translocated proteins that contribute to intestinal inflammation and fluid secretion have been identified. Stimulation of Rho GTPase signaling by SopE and SopE2 also leads to activation of microtubule-associated protein kinase pathways and movement of the proinflammatory transcription factor nuclear factor-κB (NF-κB) to its site of action in the nucleus.[116] In addition to its role in invasion, the inositol polyphosphatase activity of SopB leads to accumulation of D-myo-inositol-1,4,5,6-tetrakisphosphate in epithelial cells.[123] The increased concentration of this compound ultimately leads to an increase in cellular basal chloride secretion, with associated fluid flux. The SPI-1 translocated proteins SopA and SopD also contribute to intestinal secretory and inflammatory responses in ligated ileal loops, but the molecular basis of these effects remains unclear.

Following *Salmonella* invasion, intestinal inflammation may also result from activation of the innate immune system through stimulation of proinflammatory receptors present on phagocytes and the basolateral surface of intestinal epithelia. This includes activation of Toll-like receptor 4 (Tlr4) by lipopolysaccharide and Toll-like receptor 5 (Tlr5) by bacterial flagellin.[124] Intestinal inflammation probably contributes to fluid secretion and diarrhea through disruption of the epithelial barrier and increased water flux by an exudative mechanism. In contrast to the neutrophilic inflammation and gastroenteritis induced by nontyphoidal *Salmonella* strains, *S.* Typhi induces monocytic inflammation in the human intestine and produces significantly less, if any, diarrhea.[125] The molecular basis of this difference in the host response remains unknown.

Several studies demonstrate that salmonellae also utilize the SPI-1 T3SS to deliver proteins that downregulate the host inflammatory response associated with *Salmonella* invasion. The SptP protein inactivates Rho GTPase signaling by acting as a GTPase-activating protein (Rho GAP).[126] This directly opposes the activity of SopE and SopE2 and reduces membrane ruffling and proinflammatory signaling following bacterial invasion. In addition, the SspH1 and AvrA proteins inhibit NF-κB activation and related host cell cytokine synthesis.[127,128] These SPI-1 translocated proteins may promote bacterial persistence in the host by maintaining host cell integrity and allowing evasion of the host immune response. The presence of SPI-1 translocated proteins with opposing molecular actions (e.g., SopE and SptP) suggests that there may be temporal ordering of protein function, with initial activity of SPI-1 proteins associated with invasion and proinflammatory signaling and subsequent activity of anti-inflammatory proteins. To date there are no data supporting this hypothesis.

Interactions with Macrophages and Systemic Infection

After crossing the epithelial barrier, salmonellae encounter and enter macrophages present in the submucosal space and Peyer's patches. Macrophage invasion may occur through bacteria-mediated macropinocytosis, or through phagocytosis directed by several receptors present on the macrophage. Available data in both human infection and animal models of disease indicate that the ability of *Salmonella* to survive and replicate within macrophages is essential for dissemination within the host and induction of systemic disease. In persons with enteric fever and positive blood cultures, the majority of organisms are contained within the mononuclear fraction.[129] Furthermore, the ability of *Salmonella* mutants to replicate within macrophages in tissue culture correlates with ability to produce systemic disease in the mouse typhoid model, and microscopic examination of infected mouse liver and spleen demonstrates that the majority of organisms are located within macrophages.[130,131] Although residence within the macrophage shields the bacterium from effectors of humoral immunity, it also exposes the bacterium to the microbicidal and nutrient-poor environment of the phagosome. Within the host, salmonellae induce the expression of numerous genes that allow evasion of these antimicrobial defenses.

Several regulatory proteins are required for *Salmonella* adaptation to the intracellular environment and replication within macrophages. The best studied of these is the PhoP/PhoQ two-component regulatory system. The PhoP/PhoQ system senses the intracellular environment and induces transcription of over 40 genes required for survival within macrophages. Activation of the PhoP/PhoQ regulon leads to widespread modifications in the protein and lipopolysaccharide components of the bacterial inner and outer membranes.[132] These surface modifications confer resistance to antimicrobial factors within the phagosome, including antimicrobial peptides. PhoP/PhoQ-regulated lipopolysaccharide modifications include addition of aminoarabinose, ethanolamine, palmitate, and 2-hydroxymryistate to lipid A, thus altering the charge density and fluidity of the outer membrane and discouraging antimicrobial peptide insertion in the membrane.[132] In addition, PhoP/PhoQ-regulated modifications in lipid A structure produce a lipopolysaccharide molecule with significantly less proinflammatory signaling activity, which may facilitate bacterial survival within host tissues.[132] PhoP/PhoQ mutants of *S.* Typhi are avirulent in humans and are promising new live typhoid vaccine candidates.[133] *Salmonella* Typhi also modifies its surface through synthesis of the Vi capsule, a polysaccharide structure that confers resistance to phagocytosis by neutrophils and killing by complement, and promotes survival within human macrophages.[134]

Salmonellae express several enzymes that inactivate microbicidal reactive oxygen and nitrogen species produced within the macrophage. Resistance to nitric oxide (NO) and related reactive nitrogen compounds results in part from bacterial synthesis of homocysteine, a NO antagonist.[135] *Salmonella* mutants unable to synthesize homocysteine as a result of inactivation of the *metL* gene are hypersensitive to NO and are less virulent. In addition, salmonellae produce at least one superoxide dismutase that inactivates reactive oxygen species. Repair of nucleic acid damage induced by reactive oxygen species also appears to be important for *Salmonella* replication within macrophages. This concept is supported by the finding that *recA* and *recBC* mutants, which are defective in recombination and DNA repair, are attenuated in mice and survive only in macrophages with a defective oxidative burst.[136]

Recently several laboratories have described a second *Salmonella* T3SS that is necessary for survival in the macrophage and establishment of systemic infection.[137] Encoded in *Salmonella* pathogenicity island 2 (SPI-2), this system is expressed by intracellular bacteria and translocates proteins across the membrane of the *Salmonella*-containing vacuole (SCV) into the macrophage cytosol. SPI-2 translocated proteins appear to prevent the maturation of the SCV into a mature phagolysosome, thus creating an intracellular compartment favorable for bacterial replication. Several SPI-2 translocated proteins, including SifA, SifB, SseJ, SopD2, PipB, and PipB2, localize to the surface of the SCV and may alter its fusion with other membranous compartments within the macrophage. Two additional SPI-2 translocated proteins, SspH2 and SseI, interact with the actin cytoskeleton surrounding the SCV and probably contribute to remodeling of vacuole-associated actin networks.[138,139] SpvB is a *Salmonella* virulence protein that is secreted into the macrophage cytoplasm, possibly by the SPI-2 T3SS, and ADP-ribosylates monomeric actin (G-actin), thus promoting disassembly of actin networks around the vacuole.[139,140] Work in several laboratories indicates that SPI-2–mediated modifications in the SCV lead to exclusion of the NADPH oxidase and inducible nitric oxide synthase from the vacuolar membrane, allowing the bacterium to evade the reactive oxygen and nitrogen species produced by these enzymes.[141,142]

Other bacterial factors, including incompletely characterized cytotoxin genes, genes required for synthesis of essential nutrients and iron acquisition, and the virulence plasmids found in many non-typhoidal *Salmonella* serotypes, also are important in systemic pathogenesis. The virulence plasmids of *S.* Typhimurium, *S.* Dublin, *S.* Choleraesuis, and *S.* Enteritidis all contain an 8-kb region that promotes dissemination beyond the intestine in animal models and bacteremia in humans.[143] This region encodes the SpvB protein, as well as several other proteins of unknown function.

Host Response and Immunity

The innate immune system senses invasive *Salmonella* infections using receptors that recognize conserved elements of bacterial structure. This includes recognition of lipopolysaccharide by Tlr4, bacterial lipoproteins by Toll-like receptor 2 (Tlr2), and flagellin by Tlr5.[124] Activation of these receptors on phagocytes and epithelia leads to synthesis of cytokines that orchestrate the inflammatory response and instruct the subsequent antigen-specific immune response. Mice lacking a functional Tlr4 response are highly susceptible to *Salmonella* infection, confirming the importance of this initial response to infection.[144] Studies in mice demonstrate that the initial control of *S.* Typhimurium replication in host tissue requires recruitment and activation of macrophages. In both mice and humans, macrophage activation and efficient killing of *Salmonella* is associated with production of interferon-γ, IL-12, and tumor necrosis factor-α.[145-147] Mice with targeted disruptions in these genes are highly susceptible to infection. In addition, humans with mutations in the interferon-γ and IL-12 receptor genes develop severe infections with nontyphoidal *Salmonella* serotypes.[148]

Although the innate immune system is able to suppress initial *Salmonella* replication, final clearance of infection and immunity to rechallenge requires a Th1-type CD4 T-cell response and production of specific antibodies by B cells.[147] This is supported by the observation that mice lacking mature CD4 cells (H2I;AB⁻ mice) or B cells (Igh-6⁻ mice) are unable to control *Salmonella* infection.[147,149,150] The importance of cellular immunity in controlling *Salmonella* infection in humans is made apparent by the extreme susceptibility of individuals with human immunodeficiency virus (HIV) infection, lymphoproliferative diseases, or immune suppression following transplant.[151-154] Furthermore, vaccine studies in humans demonstrate that protection against *S.* Typhi infection correlates with development of cell-mediated immunity.[155] In accord with the importance of CD4 T cell–mediated immunity, recent population based studies in humans have found an association between specific major histocompatibility complex class II alleles and susceptibility to typhoid fever.[156] CD8 T cells with cytolytic activity against *Salmonella*-infected host cells are also present in infected mice, but the importance of this activity in immunity remains unclear. Little is known about the antigen specificity of protective immune responses to *Salmonella* infection in humans, though antibodies against the Vi polysaccharide, lipopolysaccharide O antigen, and flagella are present in previously vaccinated or infected individuals.

CLINICAL MANIFESTATIONS

Specific *Salmonella* serotypes most often produce characteristic clinical manifestations that have been given the syndrome designations gastroenteritis, enteric fever, bacteremia and vascular infection, localized infections, and chronic carrier state. Although dividing salmonellosis into these syndromes is clinically useful, these designations have neither pathogenic nor prognostic significance.

Gastroenteritis

Infection with nontyphoidal *Salmonella* most often results in self-limited acute gastroenteritis that is indistinguishable from that caused by many other enteric bacterial pathogens. Within 6 to 48 hours after ingestion of contaminated food or water, nausea, vomiting, and diarrhea occur.[157] In most cases, stools are loose, of moderate volume, and without blood. In rare cases, stool may be watery and of large volume ("cholera-like") or of small volume associated with tenesmus ("dysentery-like"). Fevers (38° to 39° C), abdominal cramping, nausea, vomiting, and chills frequently are reported. Headache, myalgias, and other systemic symptoms also can occur. Microscopic examination of stools shows neutrophils and, less frequently, red blood cells. Infrequently, *Salmonella* can cause a syndrome of pseudoappendicitis or can mimic the intestinal changes of inflammatory bowel disease.[157] Toxic megacolon is a rare but potentially life-threatening complication.[158]

Diarrhea is usually self-limited, typically lasting for 3 to 7 days.[157] Diarrhea that persists for more than 10 days should suggest another diagnosis. If fever is present, it usually resolves within 48 to 72 hours. Occasionally, patients require hospitalization because of dehydration, and death occurs infrequently. In the United States, nontyphoidal *Salmonella* infections result in an estimated rate of hospitalization of 2.2 per 1 million population, and 582 deaths per year.[47] A disproportionate number of these deaths occur among the elderly, especially those residing in long-term care facilities, and among immunocompromised patients, including those with lupus or acquired immunodeficiency syndrome (AIDS).[53,103,153,159]

After resolution of gastroenteritis, the mean duration of carriage of nontyphoidal *Salmonella* in the stool is 4 to 5 weeks and varies by *Salmonella* serotype.[102] Antimicrobial therapy may increase the duration of carriage.[102] In addition, a higher proportion of neonates have prolonged carriage; in one study, 50% of neonates were still excreting *Salmonella* at 6 months.[160] However, the delayed clearance of infection in neonates does not result in permanent carriage, because almost all chronic carriers are adults.[102,160]

Enteric Fever

Human typhoid and paratyphoid fever are severe systemic illnesses characterized by fever and abdominal symptoms. In endemic areas, most patients presenting to hospitals with enteric fever are between 5 and 25 years of age.[161] Those younger than 4 years of age are more likely to have a nonspecific febrile illness not recognized as typhoid.[29] When children younger than 1 year of age acquire typhoid, the disease is often more severe and is associated with a higher rate of complications.[161] In addition, patients with immunosuppression, biliary and urinary tract abnormalities, and reticuloendothelial system defects, such as hemoglobinopathies, malaria, schistosomiasis, bartonellosis, and histoplasmosis, are at increased risk of severe disease.[125,162-164] Recently, an association between typhoid fever and the presence of serum anti–*Helicobacter pylori* antibody was described in a slum community in Delhi, India, warranting further investigation.[165]

In the preantibiotic era, approximately 15% of patients with typhoid fever died.[10,166] Although the average case-fatality rate is less than 1%, mortality rates of up to 30% to 50% have been reported from developing countries in Asia and Africa, where infection with a multidrug-resistant strain and delayed antimicrobial therapy increase the risk of death.[31,167] Currently in the United States, approximately 0.4% of persons with typhoid fever die.[41]

The syndrome of enteric fever is most often caused by *S.* Typhi. A similar but less severe syndrome is caused by *S.* Paratyphi A, *S.* Paratyphi B (*S.* Schottmuelleri), and *S.* Typhi C (*S.* Hirschfeldii).[166] When enteric fever is caused by *S.* Typhi, it is often referred to as typhoid fever and when caused by *S.* Paratyphi it is referred to as paratyphoid fever. Although enteric fever classically is described as an acute illness with fever and abdominal tenderness, the symptoms are nonspecific and may be insidious in onset. The diagnosis of enteric fever should be considered strongly in the evaluation of any traveler who returns from tropical and subtropical areas with fever. The differential diagnosis of gradual onset of fever and abdominal pain with hepatosplenomegaly also includes malaria, amebic liver abscess, visceral leishmaniasis, and viral syndromes, such as dengue fever.

The incubation period of *S.* Typhi is typically 7 to 14 days, but ranges from 5 to 21 days depending on the inoculum ingested and the health and immune status of the person. Following ingestion of the organism, persons may develop enterocolitis with diarrhea lasting several days; these symptoms usually resolve before the onset of fever. Diarrhea is more common in certain geographic areas, among patients with AIDS, and among children under 1 year of age.[161] Typically, fecal leukocytes are detected and stool protein is increased.[161] Constipation is present in 10% to 38% of patients.[161] Although fever is a classic sign of typhoid fever, it does not always develop, and the pattern of fever is not clinically useful. In addition, only 20% to 40% of patients will have abdominal pain at presentation; the frequency of other abdominal symptoms varies widely.[166]

Nonspecific symptoms, such as chills, diaphoresis, dull frontal headache, anorexia, cough, weakness, sore throat, dizziness, and muscle pains, are frequently present before the onset of fever in typhoid.[168] Neuropsychiatric manifestations, including apathy, psychosis, and confusion, occur in 5% to 10% of patients and may be related to cytokine release from *S.* Typhi–infected macrophages.[166,169,170] This so-called typhoid state has been described as "muttering delirium" and "coma vigil."[169] Picking at the bedclothes and at imaginary objects and muscle twitching are characteristic. Seizures and coma are reported in fewer than 1% of persons, and seizures may represent febrile seizures of childhood. The cerebrospinal fluid usually is normal, and abnormal CSF studies or recurrent seizures should suggest another diagnosis.

Initially, fever is low grade and rises by the second week of illness to 39° to 40° C. Patients with typhoid fever usually appear acutely ill, although those previously exposed to *S.* Typhi or who seek early medical attention can present with a milder illness. Relative bradycardia is neither a sensitive nor a specific sign of typhoid fever, occurring in fewer than 50% of patients.[166,171] Approximately 30% of patients will have rose spots—a faint salmon-colored maculopapular rash on the trunk.[171] Organisms can be cultured from punch biopsies of these lesions, and the pathology is characterized by a perivascular mononuclear cell infiltrate. The rash can be very subtle, especially in highly pigmented individuals, and frequently fades to small macules that appear to be resolving skin hemorrhages. Some patients develop cervical lymphadenopathy. Crackles on auscultation are uncommon, and chest radiographs are almost always normal.[161,169] Frequently, abdominal examination reveals pain on deep palpation and increased peristalsis. Approximately 50% of patients have hepatosplenomegaly. Approximately 3% of adults develop necrotizing cholecystitis with localized right upper quadrant pain.[166] Pancreatitis has been described rarely.[172]

Among survivors, most symptoms resolve by the fourth week of infection without antimicrobial therapy. However, weakness, weight loss, and debilitation may persist for months, and 10% of patients will relapse.[166,168] In the preantibiotic era, two thirds of pregnancies complicated by typhoid fever resulted in fetal demise and miscarriage.[173]

Several sex-specific differences in the clinical manifestations, laboratory abnormalities, and complications of typhoid fever were found in one small retrospective study from South Africa, but prospective studies are needed to determine if differences in immune response underlie these findings.[174]

Many of the complications of untreated enteric fever occur in the third or fourth week of infection.[125] As many as 3% to 10% of patients develop intestinal perforation from hyperplasia, ulceration, and necrosis of the ileocecal lymphoid tissue, with mortality rates of 10% to 32% reported.[161,170,175] Perforation may be manifested by shock or by worsening abdominal pain. In such cases, the patient's blood should be recultured and antimicrobial therapy broadened to cover aerobic and anaerobic enteric organisms. Fluid resuscitation should be administered and the abdomen emergently explored, with examination of the ileum, cecum, and proximal colon for perforations. Surgical repair may include resection and primary anastomosis; débridement, resection, or oversewing of the ulcer; or ostomy. Other infectious complications include endocarditis and localized infections such as pericarditis, pneumonitis, orchitis, and focal abscesses.

Hematologic abnormalities associated with typhoid include leukopenia, anemia, and subclinical disseminated intravascular coagulopathy.[176] Leukocytosis is seen most often in children and within the first 10 days of illness. Some patients develop thrombocytopenia and clotting abnormalities that usually resolve spontaneously. Moderately elevated liver function tests (e.g., aspartate transaminase and alanine transaminase 300 to 500 U/dL) and muscle enzymes are common[177]; liver biopsies demonstrate focal Kupffer cell hyperplasia and mononuclear cell infiltration of the portal space.[178] Creatinine clearance is usually normal. Patients rarely develop proteinuria and immune complex glomerulonephritis, and irreversible loss of renal function has not been reported. Nonspecific ST- and T-wave electrocardiographic abnormalities are seen infrequently. Up to 10% of patients develop mild relapse, usually within 2 to 3 weeks of fever resolution and associated with the same strain type and susceptibility profile. Reinfection may be distinguished from relapse using molecular typing.[179]

Enteric Fever Diagnosis

The definitive diagnosis of enteric fever requires the isolation of *S.* Typhi or *S.* Paratyphi from blood, bone marrow, other sterile site, rose spots, stool, or intestinal secretions. The sensitivity of blood culture is only 50% to 70%, probably because small quantities of *S.* Typhi (i.e., < 15 organisms/mL) are typically present in the blood of patients with typhoid fever.[129,180] Oxgall media cultures may increase sensitivity from blood but not bone marrow cultures.[170] Because almost all *S.* Typhi in blood are associated with the mononuclear cell–platelet fraction, centrifugation of blood and culture the buffy-coat fraction or the lysis direct plating–lysis centrifugation method can substantially reduce the time to isolation of the organism but does not increase sensitivity.[181]

Enteric fever is the only bacterial infection of humans for which bone marrow examination is recommended routinely and has sensitivity of up to 90%. Higher colony counts are present in the bone marrow compared to blood and, unlike blood culture, are not reduced by up to 5 days of prior antimicrobial therapy.[182] The duodenal string test is a useful noninvasive technique to sample duodenal secretions, with a sensitivity of up to 58%, but some patients may be too ill to swallow the capsule.[183] In some patients with negative bone marrow cultures, duodenal string cultures have been positive. One study found that in children the combination of blood and duodenal string culture was as sensitive as bone marrow culture.[183] Children also have a higher incidence of positive stool cultures compared with adults (60% vs. 27%).[170] Thus the optimal diagnostic approach in both children and adults is to culture blood, bone marrow, and intestinal secretions. Using this approach, the diagnosis can be established in more than 90% of patients.[184]

A number of serologic tests, including the classic Widal test, have been developed to detect *S.* Typhi antigen or antibody. None of these tests are sufficiently sensitive or specific to replace culture-based methods for the diagnosis of enteric fever in developed countries.

However, in countries where resources are limited, rapid and simple tests to detect anti–*S.* Typhi antibody against lipopolysaccharide or outer membrane protein may replace the less accurate Widal test.[185] DNA probes and PCR for detection of *S.* Typhi in blood have been developed and appear to be more rapid and sensitive than standard culture but are not yet commercially available and are impractical in many areas where typhoid is endemic.[186]

Bacteremia and Vascular Infection

Classically, *S.* Choleraesuis and *S.* Dublin produce a syndrome of sustained bacteremia with fever, but any *Salmonella* serotype can cause bacteremia.[157] From 1% to 4% of immunocompetent individuals with *Salmonella* gastroenteritis have positive blood cultures.[102] The risk of bacteremia is greater for infants, the elderly, and the immunocompromised.[151-153,162,163,187] Among children, nontyphoidal *Salmonella* bacteremia usually is associated with gastroenteritis and prolonged fever, infrequently causes focal infections, and is fatal in less than 10% of cases.[188] In contrast, adults are more likely to have primary bacteremia and have a high incidence of secondary focal infections and death.[188]

Salmonella have a propensity for infection of vascular sites, and high-grade or persistent bacteremia suggests an endovascular infection.[189] The risk of endovascular infection complicating *Salmonella* bacteremia is estimated to be 10% to 25% in persons over 50 years of age, usually involves the aorta, and most commonly results from seeding atherosclerotic plaques or aneurysms.[173,190] Mortality rates range from 14% to 60% and are lower with prompt diagnosis and combined medical and surgical therapy.[188,191] Venous septic thrombophlebitis also has been reported.[192]

Salmonellosis and HIV Infection

HIV-infected persons have up to a 20- to 100-fold increased risk of salmonellosis compared with the general population.[153] *Salmonella* is more likely to cause severe invasive disease in persons with AIDS compared with infection in immunocompetent persons and those with AIDS-related complex or asymptomatic HIV infection, including fulminate diarrhea, acute enterocolitis, rectal ulceration, recurrent bacteremia, meningitis, and death despite antimicrobial therapy.[154,193] Among HIV-infected persons in Africa, *Salmonella* species are one of the most common causes of bacteremia, are often multidrug resistant, and are associated with high mortality (24% to 80%) and recurrence (43%) rates.[194,195] Focal infections caused by nontyphoidal *Salmonella* are infrequent among HIV-infected persons, most often occurring among those with CD4 counts of less than 100/mm³.[193]

Recurrent nontyphoidal *Salmonella* bacteremia is an AIDS-defining illness that apparently results from incomplete clearance of the primary infection because of impaired cell-mediated immunity. Without maintenance antimicrobial therapy up to 45% of persons with HIV infection will have recurrent bacteremia.[154] Among persons with HIV, the incidence of recurrent nontyphoidal *Salmonella* bacteremia has declined, likely as a result of the direct bactericidal activity of antiretrovirals on *Salmonella* species, the impact of highly active antiretroviral therapy on immune reconstitution, and the use of trimethoprim-sulfamethoxazole for the prevention of *Pneumocystis* pneumonia.[154,196,197]

Localized Infections

Localized infections develop in approximately 5% to 10% of persons with *Salmonella* bacteremia, and the presentation may be delayed.[198] Extraintestinal complications of salmonellosis and their management are summarized in Table 220-3.

Chronic Carrier State

The chronic carrier state is defined as the persistence of *Salmonella* in stool or urine for periods greater than 1 year. From 0.2% to 0.6% of patients with nontyphoidal salmonellosis develop chronic carriage.[199] Up to 10% of untreated patients with typhoid excrete *S.* Typhi in the feces for up to 3 months, and 1% to 4% develop chronic carriage.[166,168,173] The frequency of chronic carriage is higher in women, in persons with biliary abnormalities or concurrent bladder infection with *Schistosoma haematobium,* and in infants.[163,200] Chronic carriage of *S.* Typhi and *S.* Paratyphi A has been associated with an increased incidence of carcinoma of the gallbladder and of other gastrointestinal malignancies.[201] Serology for the Vi antigen can be useful in distinguishing chronic carriage from acute infection with *S.* Typhi, because chronic carriers will often have a high antibody titer to this antigen.[202]

IMMUNIZATION AGAINST *S.* TYPHI

Enteric fever can be prevented by immunization, and three commercially prepared vaccines are currently available for use in the United States: an oral live-attenuated vaccine manufactured from the Ty21a strain of *S.* Typhi; a parenteral heat-phenol–inactivated vaccine that has been widely used for many years; and a parenteral capsular polysaccharide vaccine (ViCPS).[203] These vaccines have been most extensively evaluated in endemic populations, achieve approximately 50% to 80% efficacy depending on prior exposure, and confer protection that lasts only for several years.[203]

Typhoid vaccine is not required for international travel, but it is recommended for travelers to areas where there is a risk of exposure to *S.* Typhi, especially those traveling to the Indian subcontinent and other developing countries who will have prolonged exposure to potentially contaminated food and drink.[203] Vaccination is particularly recommended for those traveling to smaller cities, villages, and destinations off the usual tourist itineraries. In addition, laboratory workers who work with *S.* Typhi and household contacts of known *S.* Typhi carriers should be vaccinated. Because vaccine protective efficacy can be overcome by high inoculums that are common in food-borne exposure—the most frequent exposure among travelers[203,204]—it is controversial whether all travelers to areas with high rates of typhoid fever should be immunized. Immunization is an adjunct and not a substitute for avoiding high-risk foods and beverages or utilizing good laboratory technique. Despite all the currently available vaccines, documented cases of typhoid fever in vaccinated travelers have occurred. Immunization is not recommended for adults residing in typhoid-endemic areas or in the management of persons potentially exposed to a common-source outbreak. However, immunization of school-age children should be considered in areas where typhoid is a public health problem and antimicrobial-resistant *S.* Typhi strains are prevalent.

Since the 19th century, the heat-killed whole-organism *S.* Typhi vaccine has been the mainstay of immunization against typhoid fever. The heat-phenol–inactivated *S.* Typhi vaccine manufactured by Wyeth is from 51% to 77% effective compared with tetanus placebo in studies in endemic populations.[205] An acetone-inactivated vaccine provided greater protection (range, 79% to 94%) in endemic populations[206,207]; the higher efficacy was attributed to the preservation of Vi antigen in this preparation. However, the acetone-inactivated vaccine is associated with more frequent side effects, costs more than the heat-phenol–inactivated vaccine,[203] and in the United States is only available to the military. Both preparations appear to result in equal protection in immunologically naive persons.

Local and systemic adverse reactions occur frequently with the parenteral heat-phenol–inactivated vaccine, including fever (17% to 29%), severe headache (10%), and significant local pain at the site of administration (35% to 60%).[205,206] Reactions occur within hours after vaccination, can persist for up to 72 hours, and result in approximately 25% of individuals missing work or school. In general, reactions are milder with subsequent vaccine doses. Severe reactions to immunization can include anaphylaxis, chest pain, liver damage, neurologic problems, and reactive arthropathy.[208]

Primary vaccination with heat-phenol–inactivated vaccine consists of two 0.5-mL subcutaneous injections separated by more than 4 weeks.[203] For children older than 6 months to 10 years of age, two 0.25-mL doses should be administered separated by more than 4 weeks. The manufacturer does not recommend the vaccine for use among children younger than 6 months of age. Booster doses should

TABLE 220-3 Extraintestinal Infectious Complications of Salmonellosis

Site	Incidence	Risk Factors	Manifestations	Complications	Mortality	Diagnosis	Therapy*
Endocarditis[173,245]	0.2%-0.4%	Preexisting valvular heart disease	Valvular vegetation, infected mural thrombus	Valve perforation, relapse (20%-25%), pericarditis	~70%	Blood culture, echocardiography	Early valve surgery + 6 wk P ceph 3, P amp, or P/PO quinolone
Arteritis[188,246,247]	Rare	Atherosclerosis, aortic aneurysm, endocarditis, prosthetic graft, myelodysplasia	Prolonged fever, pain—back, chest, or abdomen	Mycotic aneurysm, aneurysm rupture, aortoenteric fistula, vertebral osteomyelitis	14%-60%	Blood culture, sonogram, MRI or CT	Early surgical intervention + 6 wk P ceph 3, P amp, or P/PO quinolone
Central nervous system[248-250]	0.1%-0.9%	Infants (esp. neonates)	Meningitis, ventriculitis, brain abscess, subdural empyema, encephalopathy	Seizures, mental retardation, hydrocephalus, brain infarction, relapse	~20%-60%	CSF culture, CT or MRI	≥3 wk P ceph 3, P amp, or a carbapenem
Pulmonary[198]	Rare	Lung malignancy, structural lung disease, sickle cell anemia	Pneumonia	Lung abscess, empyema, bronchopleural fistula	~25%-60%	Respiratory culture, chest radiograph	≥2 wk P/PO abx
Bone[251,252]	<1%	Sickle cell anemia, male gender, connective tissue disease, immunosuppression	Femur, tibia, humerus, lumbar vertebrae	Relapse, chronic osteomyelitis	Very low	Bone radiograph	≥4 wk P ceph 3, P amp, or P/PO quinolone + surgery for sequestra
Joint—reactive[253,254]	0.6%	HLA-B27, antibiotic therapy	≥3 joints involved (esp. knee, ankle, wrist, and sacroiliac)	Prolonged symptoms (mean duration, 5.5 mo)	Negligible	Joint fluid exam and culture	Nonsteroidal anti-inflammatory agent
Joint—septic[255]	0.1%-0.2%	Osteoarthritis, connective tissue disease, sickle cell disease, prosthetic joint	Knee, hip, shoulder	Joint destruction, osteomyelitis	Very low	Joint fluid exam and culture	Repeated needle aspiration + ≥4 wk P/PO abx
Muscle/soft tissue[256]	Rare	Local trauma, male gender, diabetes, HIV infection	Abscess, pyomyositis	Osteomyelitis, endovascular infection, frequent relapse	~33%	Ultrasonography, aspiration	Drainage + ≥2 wk P abx
Hepatobiliary[257]	Rare	Cholelithiasis, cirrhosis, amebic abscess, echinococcal cyst, hepatocellular carcinoma	Hepatomegaly, cholecystitis, hepatic abscess	Rupture w/ secondary peritonitis, subphrenic abscess, spontaneous bacterial peritonitis	~10%	Ultrasonography, aspiration	Drainage + ≥2 wk P abx
Splenic[258]	Rare	Sickle cell anemia, splenic cyst, splenic hematoma	Splenomegaly	Left-sided empyema, subphrenic abscess, rupture w/ secondary peritonitis	<10%	Ultrasonography, aspiration	≥2 wk P abx, ± percutaneous drainage or splenectomy
Urinary[152,259]	0.6%	Urolithiasis, malignancy, renal transplant	Cystitis, pyelonephritis	Renal abscess, interstitial nephritis, relapse	~20%	Urine culture, ultrasonography	Removal of structural abnormality + 1-2 wk P abx + ≥6 wk PO quinolone or TMP-SMX
Genital[173]	Rare	Pregnancy, renal transplant	Ovarian abscess, testicular abscess, prostatitis, epididymitis	Abscess	Very low	Ultrasonography, aspiration	Drainage of collection + 1-2 wk P abx + ≥6 wk PO quinolone or TMP-SMX
Soft tissue[260]	<1%	Local trauma, immunosuppression	Pustular dermatitis, SQ abscess, wound infection	Septic thrombophlebitis, endophthalmitis	~15%	Drainage culture	≥2 wk P abx + drainage of collection

*P ceph 3, parenteral third-generation cephalosporin; P amp, parenteral ampicillin; P/PO quinolone, parenteral or oral fluoroquinolone; P/PO abx, parenteral or oral antimicrobial (e.g., quinolone, ampicillin, TMP-SMX, chloramphenicol, or third-generation cephalosporin); TMP-SMX, trimethoprim-sulfamethoxazole.

CSF, cerebrospinal fluid; CT, computed tomography; HIV, human immunodeficiency virus; MRI, magnetic resonance imaging; PO, oral; SQ, subcutaneous.

be administered every 3 years, and can be given subcutaneously (0.5 mL for those older than 10 years and 0.25 mL for those ages 6 months to 10 years) or intradermally (0.1 mL for those older than 6 months).[203]

A live-attenuated oral vaccine, Ty21a (Vivotif Berna vaccine, Swiss Serum and Vaccine Institute) has been licensed in the United States since 1989, but has recently become difficult to obtain. The molecular basis of attenuation of Ty21a is unknown and is not related to the *galE* mutation present in the vaccine strain.[209] The oral Ty21a vaccine has a markedly reduced incidence of side effects compared with parenteral vaccines.[170,203] No serious adverse reactions have been observed in large-scale field trials or during postmarketing surveillance in Switzerland. Following administration of three doses of Ty21a vaccine containing 109 organisms on alternate days, the protective efficacy ranged from 43% to 96% in endemic populations.[210]

Primary vaccination consists of four oral doses of Ty21a in an enteric-coated capsule taken 1 hour before a meal with cool liquid on alternate days. The stored capsules must be refrigerated.[203] Noncompliance with the multidose administration schedule and the requirement for home refrigeration has been reported.[210] A booster series of four capsules is recommended every 5 years, although few data are available on the persistence of antibody titers against *S.* Typhi.

There is limited evidence for the efficacy of Ty21a in immunologically naive individuals; in some studies in travelers no efficacy was demonstrated.[211] Nevertheless, based on studies in endemic populations, it is likely that Ty21a is as effective as the heat-phenol–inactivated vaccine if compliance is adequate. Because of the possibility of illness associated with administration of a live-attenuated vaccine, Ty21a is not recommended for children under 6 years of age, the immunosuppressed, and those on antibiotic therapy.[203] Ty21a can be administered simultaneously with immunoglobulin or viral vaccines. Some antimicrobial agents, including mefloquine but not chloroquine, may inhibit growth of Ty21a in vitro, and vaccination with Ty21a should be delayed for more than 24 hours after the administration of any antibacterial agent or mefloquine. In addition, administration of proguanil may diminish anti–*S.* Typhi lipopolysaccharide antibody production.

A capsular polysaccharide vaccine, ViCPS (Typhim Vi, Pasteur-Merieux) is also licensed for use. Primary vaccination with ViCPS consists of one 0.5-mL (25-µg) dose administered intramuscularly.[203] It has fewer side effects than heat-phenol–inactivated vaccine, including fever (0% to 1%), headache (1.5% to 3%), and local erythema or induration at the injection site (7%).[212] In South African children ViCPS was 55% effective and high Vi antibody levels persisted over a 3-year period.[213] ViCPS is not recommended for use among children younger than 2 years of age. A single booster dose can be given every 2 years.

Recently a conjugate Vi vaccine formed by fusion of the Vi polysaccharide to a nontoxic recombinant *Pseudomonas aeruginosa* exotoxin A (Vi-rEPA) was tested in a typhoid-endemic area of Vietnam.[214] A two-dose regimen in children ages 2 to 5 was highly immunogenic and was 91% effective in preventing disease. This vaccine also has the potential to be immunogenic in children younger than 2 years of age, and if so could be incorporated in the World Health Organization's Expanded Programme on Immunization in typhoid-endemic areas.

In summary, none of the currently available typhoid vaccines has been demonstrated to have sufficient efficacy in travelers to recommend their widespread use. Because of the low frequency of side effects, either oral Ty21a or parenteral ViCPS can be administered to travelers who will be spending a prolonged period in a high-risk area. Use of the parenteral heat-phenol–inactivated vaccine is limited by the high incidence of serious side effects and its failure to protect against high inoculums. However, heat-phenol–inactivated vaccine is the only currently available option for persons under 2 years old or those with immunosuppression in whom prolonged exposure to *S.* Typhi is anticipated.[203] In light of the emergence of quinolone-resistant strains of *S.* Typhi in developing countries, mass immunization may be useful for the control of prolonged multidrug-resistant typhoid fever epidemics.[215]

THERAPY FOR SALMONELLOSIS

Typhoid Fever

Fluoroquinolones appear to be the most effective drugs for the treatment of typhoid, especially in areas where quinolone resistance is uncommon.[216] Fluoroquinolones are highly active against *S.* Typhi in vitro and achieve high concentrations in macrophages and in bile.[217] Data from randomized controlled clinical trials in typhoid-endemic areas have demonstrated that fluoroquinolones are more rapidly effective and are associated with lower rates of relapse and stool carriage than chloramphenicol, ampicillin, and trimethoprim-sulfamethoxazole. They are rapidly effective, with cure rates of up to 98% and fever resolution in an average of 4 days.[216] Although not compared head-to-head, fluoroquinolones also appear more effective than third-generation cephalosporins for the treatment of typhoid. Fluoroquinolones have proven to be safe for the treatment of multidrug-resistant typhoid in children and pregnant women.[218,219] Standard therapy for uncomplicated typhoid consists of 15 mg/kg/day of a fluoroquinolone, such as ciprofloxacin or ofloxacin, administered orally for 5 to 7 days. A 3-day course of oral fluoroquinolone therapy for uncomplicated multidrug-resistant typhoid fever can be used when the strain is susceptible to nalidixic acid[37] and may be especially useful for management of typhoid epidemics.

When *S.* Typhi strains are relatively quinolone resistant (resistant to nalidixic acid and with an MIC of ciprofloxacin of 0.125 to 1 µg/mL), patients treated with short-course fluoroquinolone therapy (i.e., < 5 days) had prolonged fever and 33% required re-treatment in a small study from Vietnam.[37] All *S.* Typhi isolates should be screened for nalidixic acid resistance and tested against a clinically appropriate fluoroquinolone. Patients with nalidixic acid–resistant strains should be treated with higher doses of ciprofloxacin or ofloxacin (10 mg/kg twice daily) for 10 to 14 days. Patients with *S.* Typhi strains with MIC values of ciprofloxacin of 2 µg/mL or greater should be treated with a third-generation cephalosporin or azithromycin.[220]

Third-generation cephalosporins, including ceftriaxone, cefotaxime, cefoperazone, and cefixime, and azithromycin (500 mg once daily for 7 days) also are effective in the treatment of typhoid fever,[221,222] including cases of ciprofloxacin treatment failure.[223] Ceftriaxone (1 to 2 g daily in adults or 60 mg/kg daily in children) administered either intravenously or intramuscularly for 10 to 14 days or oral cefixime (10 to 15 mg/kg twice daily for 14 days) results in cure rates of 95% and resolves fever in an average of 4 days.[221,224] Imipenem and aztreonam are alternative agents, but a prospective clinical trial in children in Malaysia was discontinued because of a high failure rate with aztreonam.[225] First- and second-generation cephalosporins are clinically ineffective and should not be used to treat typhoid fever or nontyphoidal salmonellosis, despite adequate in vitro killing activity.[226] Aminoglycosides also are clinically ineffective, perhaps because they lack activity against intracellular *Salmonella*.[227]

Chloramphenicol (500 mg four times a day), ampicillin, or amoxicillin (1 g four times a day), and trimethoprim-sulfamethoxazole (1 double-strength tablet twice a day) formerly were widely used for treatment of typhoid.[228] However, emergence of plasmid-encoded resistance to chloramphenicol in the 1970s and then to chloramphenicol, ampicillin, and trimethoprim beginning in 1989 has limited the usefulness of these agents in many developing countries, except in Latin America and sub-Saharan Africa where resistance remains relatively uncommon. The agents are inexpensive, are widely available, and remain effective for the treatment of susceptible strains, resolving fever in 5 to 7 days. However, they require 14 to 21 days of divided daily therapy, and adherence may be low.

Most patients with uncomplicated typhoid can be managed at home with oral antibiotics. The preferred agent for treatment of uncomplicated typhoid, including infection associated with a multidrug-resistant strain, is an oral fluoroquinolone (15 mg/kg daily) for 5 to 7 days (Table 220-4). The optimal oral treatment for fully fluoroquinolone-resistant typhoid fever (ciprofloxacin, MIC > 2 µg/mL) is incompletely defined, but cefixime or azithromycin appear effective.[220]

TABLE 220-4 Antimicrobial Agents of Choice for Treatment of Typhoid Fever

Susceptibility	Uncomplicated Typhoid				Complicated Typhoid			
	Agent	*Route*	*Dose*	*Days*	*Agent*	*Route*	*Dose*	*Days*
Fully susceptible								
First line	Ciprofloxacin or ofloxcain	PO	7.5 mg/kg bid	5-7	Ciprofloxacin or ofloxacin	IV	7.5 mg/kg q12h	10-14
Second line	Chloramphenicol	PO	12.5 mg/kg qid	14-21	Chloramphenicol	IV	25 mg/kg q6h	14-21
	Amoxicillin	PO	25 mg/kg tid	10-14	Ampicillin	IV	25 mg/kg q6h	10-14
	Trimethoprim-sulfamethoxazole	PO	4/20 mg/kg bid	10-14	Trimethoprim-sulfamethoxazole	IV	4/20 mg/kg q12h	14
Multidrug resistant								
First line	Ciprofloxacin or ofloxacin	PO	7.5 mg/kg bid	5-7	Ciprofloxacin or ofloxacin	IV	7.5 mg/kg q12h	10-14
Second line	Cefixime	PO	5 mg/kg bid	7-14	Ceftriaxone	IV	30 mg/kg q12h or 60 mg/kg q24h	10-14
	Azithromycin	PO	10 mg/kg daily	7				

Adapted from White NJ. *Salmonella typhi* (typhoid fever) and *S. paratyphi* (paratyphoid fever). In: Yu VL, Yu V, Weber R, Raoult D, eds. Antimicrobial Therapy and Vaccines, 2nd ed. New York, Apple Tree Productions; 2002:583-603.

Patients with complicated typhoid who require hospitalization initially should receive parenteral therapy with a fluoroquinolone or third-generation cephalosporin, fluid and electrolyte replacement, and prompt diagnosis and management of life-threatening complications. After initial control of the symptoms of typhoid fever with a parenteral agent, a total of 10 to 14 days of therapy can be completed with an oral fluoroquinolone, cefixime, or azithromycin.

The use of glucocorticosteroids has been advocated in the treatment of severe typhoid fever based upon a study in Jakarta that showed a significant reduction in mortality among patients with severe typhoid fever (i.e., associated delirium, obtundation, stupor, coma, or shock) treated with chloramphenicol and dexamethasone compared with chloramphenicol-treated control patients (case-fatality rate: 10% vs. 56%).[161] Although the case-fatality rate in the control group was high and the study has never been repeated, dexamethasone 3 mg/kg intravenously followed by eight doses of 1 mg/kg every 6 hours should be considered in the treatment of severe typhoid with altered mental status or shock. Steroid treatment beyond 48 hours may increase the relapse rate.[229]

Nontyphoidal *Salmonella*

Salmonella gastroenteritis is usually a self-limited disease, and therapy primarily should be directed to the replacement of fluid and electrolyte losses. In a large meta-analysis, antimicrobial therapy for uncomplicated nontyphoidal *Salmonella* gastroenteritis, including short-course or single-dose regimens with oral fluoroquinolones, amoxicillin, or trimethoprim-sulfamethoxazole, did not significantly decrease the length of illness, including duration of fever or diarrhea, and was associated with an increased risk of relapse, positive culture after 3 weeks, and adverse drug reactions.[230] Therefore, antimicrobials should not be used routinely to treat uncomplicated nontyphoidal *Salmonella* gastroenteritis or to reduce convalescent stool excretion.

Although fewer than 5% of all patients with *Salmonella* gastroenteritis develop bacteremia, certain patients are at increased risk for invasive infection and may benefit from preemptive antimicrobial therapy. Antimicrobial therapy should be considered for neonates, those older than 50 years, and for persons with immunosuppression or cardiac valvular or endovascular abnormalities, including prosthetic vascular grafts. Treatment should consist of an oral or intravenous antimicrobial administered for 48 to 72 hours or until the patient becomes afebrile. Longer treatment may result in a higher rate of chronic carriage and relapse. For susceptible organisms, treatment with an oral fluoroquinolone, trimethoprim-sulfamethoxazole, or amoxicillin is adequate. Occasionally, antimicrobial prophylaxis has been required to control institutional outbreaks, especially in long-term care facilities or pediatric wards, where compliance with infection control measures may be difficult.[231]

Although fluoroquinolones are not recommended for administration to children younger than 10 years of age, they may have a role in treating severe nontyphoidal salmonellosis in this age group. In one small study, seven children with severe typhoidal or nontyphoidal salmonellosis who failed conventional therapy improved rapidly when treated with oral pefloxacin (12 mg/kg daily for 7 days).[232] In addition, a double-blind, placebo-controlled trial from Turkey demonstrated that intravenous immunoglobulin (500 mg/kg on days 1, 2, 3, and 8) in combination with cefoperazone, when administered to preterm neonates with *S.* Typhimurium infection, reduced the rate of mortality, complications, and duration of antimicrobial therapy compared to treatment with cefoperazone alone, a finding that merits further study.[233]

Bacteremia

Because of the increasing prevalence of antimicrobial resistance, empirical therapy for life-threatening bacteremia or focal infection suspected to be caused by nontyphoidal *Salmonella* should include a third-generation cephalosporin and a fluoroquinolone until susceptibilities are known. It is also important to document whether the bacteremia is high grade (i.e., > 50% of three or more blood cultures positive) and, if so, to search for endovascular abnormalities by echocardiogram or other imaging techniques, such as computerized tomography or indium-labeled white blood cell scan. Low-grade bacteremia not involving vascular structures should be treated with 7 to 14 days of intravenous antimicrobial therapy. Six weeks of intravenous therapy with a β-lactam antibiotic such as ampicillin or ceftriaxone is recommended to treat documented or suspected endovascular infection. Intravenous ciprofloxacin followed by prolonged oral therapy may be an option, but published clinical experience is limited.[191] Chloramphenicol should not be used to treat endovascular infection because of high failure rates.[189,234] In addition, early surgical resection of infected aneurysms or other infected endovascular sites is recommended.[188,191] Patients with infected prosthetic vascular grafts that could not be resected have been maintained successfully on chronic suppressive oral therapy.[235]

Recurrent *Salmonella* Bacteremia in Persons with AIDS

In persons with AIDS and a first episode of *Salmonella* bacteremia, 1 to 2 weeks of intravenous antimicrobial therapy followed by 4 weeks of oral fluoroquinolone therapy (e.g., ciprofloxacin 500 to 750 mg twice daily) should be administered to attempt eradication of the organism and to decrease the risk of recurrent bacteremia.[236] Persons who relapse following 6 weeks of antimicrobial therapy should receive long-term suppressive therapy with an oral fluoroquinolone or trimethoprim-sulfamethoxazole. Fluoroquinolones and zidovudine have a synergistic antibacterial effect against *Salmonella;* administration of both drugs may dramatically decrease the risk of recurrent infection.[237] Although data are lacking, trimethoprim-sulfamethoxazole may be a good choice for long-term suppressive therapy of salmonellosis if the organism is susceptible, because of its efficacy in prevention of other opportunistic infections, including *Pneumocystis* pneumonia.

Focal Infections

Treatment recommendations for the management of focal salmonella infections are summarized in Table 220-3. Of note, treatment failure with fluoroquinolones has been associated low-dose oral therapy or with administration to patients with undrained abscesses or osteomyelitis, in which antimicrobial penetration may be poor.

Chronic Carrier State

Chronic carriage of nontyphoidal *Salmonella* is managed similar to typhoid carriage. Amoxicillin (3 g in adults or 100 mg/kg in children divided three times a day for 3 months), trimethoprim-sulfamethoxazole (one double-strength tablet twice a day for 3 months), and ciprofloxacin (750 mg twice daily for 4 weeks) are effective in eradication of chronic carriage associated with susceptible strains, with cure rates of more than 80%.[238,239] The high concentration of amoxicillin and fluoroquinolones in bile and the superior intracellular penetration of fluoroquinolones are theoretical advantages compared with trimethoprim-sulfamethoxazole. Cost considerations favor the use of amoxicillin for treating carriage of susceptible organisms. Antimicrobial agents are infrequently effective in eradicating the carrier state if anatomic abnormalities, such as biliary or kidney stones, are present. In such cases, surgery combined with antimicrobial therapy is often required for eradication.[199] Patients with urinary carriage associated with *S.* Haematobium should be treated with praziquantel before attempting eradication of *S.* Typhi. Chronic suppressive antimicrobial therapy should be considered for those patients with persistent carriage in whom no anatomic abnormality can be identified or who relapse after cholecystectomy.

PREVENTION AND CONTROL

The prevention and control of salmonellosis require both an understanding of the complex cycles of transmission and ongoing surveillance to characterize trends in *Salmonella* occurrence and to identify outbreaks. Safe drinking water and effective sewage treatment can reduce the burden of typhoid fever in developing countries, but substantial economic and social barriers hinder progress on this front. The emergence of multidrug-resistant *S.* Typhi in developing countries may shift emphasis from treatment to vaccination. In developed countries, control of foodborne salmonellosis requires barriers to the introduction and multiplication of *Salmonella* from the farm to the table.[240] Recognition of foodborne outbreaks requires that clinicians have a high index of suspicion, order the appropriate laboratory test, and promptly report positive culture results to local public health departments. Vaccination of feed animals, limiting the use of antimicrobials as growth promoters, and improved food safety practices should further reduce the burden of foodborne salmonellosis. In the United States, active population-based surveillance for foodborne diseases has improved estimates of disease burden,[48] and use of algorithms and rapid molecular subtyping have improved the ability to detect clusters and outbreaks of salmonellosis.[241] Establishment of cooperative international surveillance systems has facilitated rapid data exchange for the prevention of human salmonellosis associated with widely distributed agricultural and manufactured foods.[242,243]

Although most cases of *Salmonella* infection occur sporadically, large numbers of persons potentially may become infected when commercial kitchens serve *Salmonella*-contaminated foods that have not been sufficiently cooked or that have been mishandled. Commercial food service establishments can reduce the risk of foodborne *Salmonella* illness if they do not serve food containing raw or undercooked eggs, use pasteurized eggs whenever possible, and avoid cross-contamination of food items. Use of pasteurized eggs for all recipes calling for bulk-pooled eggs is recommended for all nursing homes and hospitals.[103]

The most cost-effective approach to the control of salmonellosis in food handlers is attention to good personal hygiene and maintenance of time-temperature standards for food handling. Routine screening of food handlers for carriage after gastroenteritis is common before allowing individuals to return to work. However, there seems to be little justification for this approach because few outbreaks are related to specific food handlers, prolonged carriage in food handlers after gastroenteritis is rare, and the number of organisms present is small. Therefore, it is reasonable to allow individuals to return to work after diarrhea is resolved. Two consecutive negative stool samples should be required only for food handlers whose work involves touching unwrapped foods that are consumed raw or served without further cooking. Routine surveillance of food handlers for asymptomatic stool carriage of *Salmonella* is not recommended.

To limit the risk of nosocomial transmission to patients and health care workers, patients excreting *Salmonella* should be managed with Standard Precautions, including the use of barrier precautions, including gloves, when performing direct patient care or handling soiled articles. Control of *Salmonella* outbreaks in long-term care facilities or neonatal care areas may be difficult because of poor compliance with isolation precautions and the increased susceptibility of these patients.[244] Although *Salmonella* infection in newborns, the elderly, or the immunocompromised can be severe, the risk of transmission of *Salmonella* from health care workers to patients appears to be very small.[98] Once the health care worker is asymptomatic and passing formed stool, the individual should be allowed to return to work if Standard Precautions are observed. However, local and state regulations should be followed, because some require work exclusion for health care workers who have salmonellosis until two or more stool cultures obtained at least 24 hours apart are negative.

REFERENCES

1. Smith T. The hog-cholera group of bacteria. US Bur Anim Ind Bull. 1894;6:6-40.
2. Louis PCA. Recherches Anatomiques, Pathologiques et Therapeutiques sur la Maladie Connue sous le Noms de Gastroenterite, Fievre Putride, Adymanique, Thiphoide, Comparee avec les Maladies Aigues les Plus Ordinaires. Paris: J-B Balliere; 1829.
3. Jenner W. On the Identity of Typhoid and Typhus Fevers. London: C. & J. Adlard; 1850.
4. Wilson JC. A Treatise on the Continued Fevers. New York: Wood; 1881.
5. Budd W. Typhoid Fever: Its Nature, Mode of Spreading, and Prevention. London: Longmans; 1873.
6. Schroeter J. Kryptogamenflora von Schlesien, bd 3. Breslau: JU Kern; 1885.
7. Pfeiffer R, Kalle W. Experimentelle untersuchunger zur Frage der Schitzimphung des Menschen geger thypus addominalis. Dtsch Med Wochenschr. 1896;22:735.
8. Widal F. Serodiagnostic de la fievre typhoide. Bull Med Hop Paris. 1896;13:561-566.
9. Kauffman F. The Diagnosis of *Salmonella* Types. Springfield, IL: Charles C Thomas, 1950.
10. Woodward TE, Smadel JE, Ley HL, et al. Preliminary report on the beneficial effect of Chloromycetin in the treatment of typhoid fever. Ann Intern Med. 1948;29:131-134.
11. Zinder ND, Lederberg J. Genetic exchange in *Salmonella*. J Bacteriol. 1952; 64:679-699.
12. Ames BN, Lee FD, Durston W. An improved bacterial test system for detection and classification of mutagens and carcinogens. Proc Natl Acad Sci U S A. 1973;70:782-786.
13. Popoff MY, Bockemühl J, Brenner FW. Supplement 1998 (no. 42) to the Kauffmann-White scheme. Res Microbiol. 2000;151:63-65.
14. Brenner FW, Villar RG, Angulo FJ, et al. Salmonella nomenclature. J Clin Microbiol. 2000;38:2465-2467.
15. Parkhill J, Dougan G, James KD, et al. Complete genome sequence of a multiple drug resistant *Salmonella enterica* serovar Typhi CT18. Nature. 2001;413:848-852.
16. McClelland M, Sanderson KE, Spieth J, et al. Complete genome sequence of *Salmonella enterica* serovar Typhimurium LT2. Nature. 2001;413:852-856.
17. Farmer JJ. Enterobacteriaceae: Introduction and identification. In: Murray PR, Baron EJ, Pfaller M, et al, eds. Manual of Clinical Microbiology, 7th ed. Washington, DC: American Society for Microbiology; 1999:442-458.
18. Perez JM, Cavalli P, Roure C, et al. Comparison of four chromogenic media and Hektoen agar for detection and presumptive identification of Salmonella strains in human stools. J Clin Microbiol. 2003;41:1130-1134.
19. Ruiz J, Nunez ML, Diaz J, et al. Comparison of five plating media for isolation of Salmonella species from human stools. J Clin Microbiol. 1996;34:686-688.
20. Malorny B, Hoorfar J, Bunge C, Helmuth R. Multicenter validation of the analytical accuracy of Salmonella PCR: Towards an international standard. Appl Environ Microbiol. 2003;69:290-296.
21. Oracz G, Feleszko W, Golicka D, et al. Rapid diagnosis of acute Salmonella gastrointestinal infection. Clin Infect Dis. 2003;36:112-115.
22. Boop CA, Brenner FW, Wells JG, Strockbine NA. *Escherichia, Shigella,* and *Salmonella*. In: Murray PR, Baron EJ, Pfaller MA, et al, eds. Manual of Clinical Microbiology. Washington, DC: American Society for Microbiology; 1999:467-471.

23. Daniels EM, Schneerson R, Egan WE, et al. Characterization of the *Salmonella paratyphi* C Vi polysaccharide. Infect Immun. 1989;57:3159-3164.

24. Gray PW, Flaggs G, Leong SR, et al. Cloning of a human neutrophil bactericidal protein: Structural and functional correlations. J Biol Chem. 1989;264:9505-9509.

25. Garaizar J, Porwollik S, Echeita A, et al. DNA microarray-based typing of an atypical monophasic Salmonella enterica serovar. J Clin Microbiol. 2002;40:2074-2078.

26. Dritz SK, Braff EH. Sexually transmitted typhoid fever. N Engl J Med. 1977;296:1359.

27. Weikel CS, Guerrant RL. Nosocomial salmonellosis. Infect Control. 1985;6:218-220.

28. Ivanoff B. Typhoid fever: Global situation and WHO recommendations. In: Proceedings of the 2nd Asia-Pacific Symposium on Typhoid Fever and Other Salmonellosis. Bangkok: Infectious Diseases Association of Thailand; 1994.

29. Sinha A, Sazawal S, Kumar R, et al. Typhoid fever in children aged less than 5 years. Lancet. 1999;354:734-737.

30. Mermin JH, Villar R, Carpenter J, et al. A massive epidemic of multidrug-resistant typhoid fever in Tajikistan associated with consumption of municipal water. J Infect Dis. 1999;179:1416-1422.

31. Bhutta ZA, Naqvi SH, Razzaq RA, Farooqui BJ. Multidrug-resistant typhoid in children: Presentation and clinical features. Rev Infect Dis. 1991;13:832-836.

32. Threlfall EJ, Rowe B, Ward LR. Occurrence and treatment of multi-resistant *Salmonella typhi*. Public Health Lab Serv Microbiol Dig. 1991;8:56-59.

33. Paniker CK, Vimala KN. Transferable chloramphenicol resistance in Salmonella typhi. Nature. 1972;239:109-110.

34. Anderson ES. The problem and implication of chloramphenicol resistance in the typhoid bacillus. J Hyg. 1975;74:289-299.

35. Rowe B, Ward LR, Threlfall EJ. Multidrug-resistant Salmonella typhi: A worldwide epidemic. Clin Infect Dis. 1997;24(Suppl 1):S106-S109.

36. Mirza S, Kariuki S, Mamun KZ, et al. Analysis of plasmid and chromosomal DNA of multidrug-resistant Salmonella enterica serovar Typhi from Asia. J Clin Microbiol. 2000;38:1449-1452.

37. Wain J, Hoa NT, Chinh NT, et al. Quinolone-resistant Salmonella typhi in Viet Nam: Molecular basis of resistance and clinical response to treatment. Clin Infect Dis. 1997;25:1404-1410.

38. Threlfall EJ, Ward LR. Decreased susceptibility to ciprofloxacin in Salmonella enterica serotype Typhi, United Kingdom. Emerg Infect Dis. 2001;7:448-450.

39. Saha SK, Talukder SY, Islam M, Saha S. A highly ceftriaxone-resistant Salmonella typhi in Bangladesh. Pediatr Infect Dis J. 1999;18:387.

40. Rahman M, Ahmad A, Shoma S. Decline in epidemic of multidrug resistant Salmonella typhi is not associated with increased incidence of antibiotic-susceptible strain in Bangladesh. Epidemiol Infect. 2002;129:29-34.

41. Mermin JH, Townes JM, Gerber M, et al. Typhoid fever in the United States, 1985-1994: Changing risks of international travel and increasing antimicrobial resistance. Arch Intern Med. 1998;158:633-638.

42. Olsen SJ, Bleasdale SC, Magnano AR, et al. Outbreaks of typhoid fever in the United States, 1960-99. Epidemiol Infect. 2003;130:13-21.

43. Katz DJ, Cruz MA, Trepka MJ, et al. An outbreak of typhoid fever in Florida associated with an imported frozen fruit. J Infect Dis. 2002;186:234-239.

44. Shandera WX, Taylor JP, Betz TG, Blake PA. An analysis of economic costs associated with an outbreak of typhoid fever. Am J Public Health. 1985;75:71-73.

45. Ackers ML, Puhr ND, Tauxe RV, Mintz ED. Laboratory-based surveillance of Salmonella serotype Typhi infections in the United States: Antimicrobial resistance on the rise. JAMA. 2000;283:2668-2673.

46. Centers for Disease Control and Prevention. NARMS 2000 Annual Report. Available at: *www.cdc.gov/narms/annuals.htm*.

47. Mead PS, Slutsker L, Dietz V, et al. Food-related illness and death in the United States. Emerg Infect Dis. 1999;5:607-625.

48. Centers for Disease Control and Prevention. Preliminary FoodNet data on the incidence of foodborne illnesses—selected sites, United States, 2002. MMWR Morb Mortal Wkly Rep. 2003;52:340-343.

49. Kohl KS, Rietberg K, Wilson S, Farley TA. Relationship between home food-handling practices and sporadic salmonellosis in adults in Louisiana, United States. Epidemiol Infect. 2002;129:267-276.

50. Gorbach SL, Kean BH, Evans DG, et al. Travelers' diarrhea and toxigenic *Escherichia coli*. N Engl J Med. 1975;292:933-936.

51. Saidi SM, Iijima Y, Sang WK, et al. Epidemiological study on infectious diarrheal diseases in children in a coastal rural area of Kenya. Microbiol Immunol. 1997;41:773-778.

52. Todd EC. Epidemiology of foodborne diseases: A worldwide review. World Health Stat Q. 1997;50:30-50.

53. Mishu B, Koehler J, Lee LA, et al. Outbreaks of *Salmonella enteritidis* infections in the United States, 1985-1991. J Infect Dis. 1994;169:547-552.

54. Woodward DL, Khakhria R, Johnson WM. Human salmonellosis associated with exotic pets. J Clin Microbiol. 1997;35:2786-2790.

55. Angulo FJ, Tippen S, Sharp DJ, et al. A community waterborne outbreak of salmonellosis and the effectiveness of a boil water order. Am J Public Health. 1997;87:580-584.

56. Chiodini RJ, Sundberg JP. Salmonellosis in reptiles: A review. Am J Epidemiol. 1981;113:494-499.

57. Mermin J, Hoar B, Angulo FJ. Iguanas and *Salmonella marina* infection in children: A reflection of the increasing incidence of reptile-associated salmonellosis in the United States. Pediatrics. 1997;99:399-402.

58. Jafari M, Forsberg J, Gilcher RO, et al. Salmonella sepsis caused by a platelet transfusion from a donor with a pet snake. N Engl J Med. 2002;347:1075-1078.

59. Centers for Disease Control and Prevention. Outbreaks of multidrug-resistant Salmonella typhimurium associated with veterinary facilities—Idaho, Minnesota, and Washington, 1999. MMWR Morb Mortal Wkly Rep. 2001;50:701-704.

60. Rodrigue DC, Tauxe RV, Rowe B. International increase in *Salmonella enteritidis:* A new pandemic? Epidemiol Infect. 1990;105:21-27.

61. Centers for Disease Control and Prevention. Outbreaks of Salmonella serotype Enteritidis infection associated with eating shell eggs—United States, 1999-2001. MMWR Morb Mortal Wkly Rep. 2003;51:1149-1152.

62. Centers for Disease Control and Prevention. Outbreaks of Salmonella serotype Enteritidis infection associated with eating raw or undercooked shell eggs—United States, 1996-1998. MMWR Morb Mortal Wkly Rep. 2000;49:73-79.

63. Guard-Petter J, Henzler DJ, Rahman MM, Carlson RW. On-farm monitoring of mouse-invasive Salmonella enterica serovar Enteritidis and a model for its association with the production of contaminated eggs. Appl Environ Microbiol. 1997;63:1588-1593.

64. Baumler AJ, Hargis BM, Tsolis RM. Tracing the origins of Salmonella outbreaks. Science. 2000;287:50-52.

65. Hope BK, Baker R, Edel ED, et al. An overview of the Salmonella enteritidis risk assessment for shell eggs and egg products. Risk Anal. 2002;22:203-218.

66. U.S. Department of Agriculture. Progress Report on Salmonella Testing of Raw Meat and Poultry Products, 1998-2002. Available at: *www.fsis.usda.gov/OPHS/haccp/salm5year.htm*

67. White DG, Zhao S, Sudler R, et al. The isolation of antibiotic-resistant salmonella from retail ground meats. N Engl J Med 2001; 345:1147-54.

68. Parry SM, Palmer SR, Slader J, Humphrey T. Risk factors for salmonella food poisoning in the domestic kitchen—A case control study. Epidemiol Infect. 2002;129:277-285.

69. Sarwari AR, Magder LS, Levine P, et al. Serotype distribution of Salmonella isolates from food animals after slaughter differs from that of isolates found in humans. J Infect Dis. 2001;183:1295-1299.

70. Brooks JT, Rowe SY, Shillam P, et al. Salmonella typhimurium infections transmitted by chlorine-pretreated clover sprout seeds. Am J Epidemiol. 2001;154:1020-1028.

71. Spika JS, Waterman SH, Hoo GW, et al. Chloramphenicol-resistant *Salmonella newport* traced through hamburger to dairy farms: A major persisting source of human salmonellosis in California. N Engl J Med. 1987;316:565-570.

72. Lee LA, Puhr ND, Maloney EK, et al. Increase in antimicrobial-resistant Salmonella infections in the United States, 1989-1990. J Infect Dis. 1994;170:128-134.

73. Threlfall EJ, Fisher IS, Berghold C, et al. Antimicrobial drug resistance in isolates of Salmonella enterica from cases of salmonellosis in humans in Europe in 2000: Results of international multi-centre surveillance. Euro Surveill. 2003;8:41-45.

74. Helms M, Vastrup P, Gerner-Smidt P, Molbak K. Excess mortality associated with antimicrobial drug-resistant Salmonella typhimurium. Emerg Infect Dis. 2002;8:490-495.

75. Boyd EF, Hartl DL. Recent horizontal transmission of plasmids between natural populations of *Escherichia coli* and *Salmonella enterica*. J Bacteriol. 1997;179:1622-1627.

76. Humphrey T. Salmonella typhimurium definitive type 104: A multi-resistant Salmonella. Int J Food Microbiol. 2001;67:173-186.

77. Casin I, Breuil J, Brisabois A, et al. Multidrug-resistant human and animal Salmonella typhimurium isolates in France belong predominantly to a DT104 clone with the chromosome- and integron-encoded beta-lactamase PSE-1. J Infect Dis. 1999;179:1173-1182.

78. Glynn MK, Bopp C, Dewitt W, et al. Emergence of multidrug-resistant *Salmonella enterica* serotype Typhimurium DT104 infections in the United States. N Engl J Med. 1998;338:1333-1338.

79. Beaudin BA, Brosnikoff CA, Grimsrud KM, et al. Susceptibility of human isolates of Salmonella typhimurium DT 104 to antimicrobial agents used in human and veterinary medicine. Diagn Microbiol Infect Dis. 2002;42:17-20.

80. Threlfall EJ, Frost JA, Ward LR, Rowe B. Increasing spectrum of resistance in multiresistant *Salmonella typhimurium* (Letter). Lancet. 1996;347:1053-1054.

81. Horby PW, O'Brien SJ, Adak GK, et al. A national outbreak of multi-resistant Salmonella enterica serovar Typhimurium definitive phage type (DT) 104 associated with consumption of lettuce. Epidemiol Infect. 2003;130:169-178.

82. Allen CA, Fedorka-Cray PJ, Vazquez-Torres A, et al. In vitro and in vivo assessment of Salmonella enterica serovar Typhimurium DT104 virulence. Infect Immun. 2001;69:4673-4677.

83. Barguellil F, Burucoa C, Amor A, et al. In vivo acquisition of extended-spectrum beta-lactamase in Salmonella enteritidis during antimicrobial therapy. Eur J Clin Microbiol Infect Dis. 1995;14:703-706.

84. Winokur PL, Vonstein DL, Hoffman LJ, et al. Evidence for transfer of CMY-2 AmpC beta-lactamase plasmids between Escherichia coli and Salmonella isolates from food animals and humans. Antimicrob Agents Chemother. 2001;45:2716-2722.

85. Fey PD, Safranek TJ, Rupp ME, et al. Ceftriaxone-resistant Salmonella infection acquired by a child from cattle (see comments). N Engl J Med. 2000;342:1242-1249.

86. Digranes A, Solberg CO, Sjursen H, et al. Antibiotic susceptibility of blood culture isolates of Enterobacteriaceae from six Norwegian hospitals 1991-1992. APMIS. 1997;105:854-860.

87. Giraud E, Cloeckaert A, Kerboeuf D, Chaslus-Dancla E. Evidence for active efflux as the primary mechanism of resistance to ciprofloxacin in Salmonella enterica serovar Typhimurium. Antimicrob Agents Chemother. 2000;44:1223-1228.

88. Heisig P. High-level fluoroquinolone resistance in a Salmonella typhimurium isolate due to alterations in both gyrA and gyrB genes. J Antimicrob Chemother. 1993;32:367-377.

89. Randall LP, Cooles SW, Sayers AR, Woodward MJ. Association between cyclohexane resistance in Salmonella of different serovars and increased resistance to multiple antibiotics, disinfectants and dyes. J Med Microbiol. 2001;50:919-924.

90. Frost JA, Kelleher A, Rowe B. Increasing ciprofloxacin resistance in salmonellas in England and Wales 1991-1994. J Antimicrob Chemother. 1996;37:85-91.

91. Chiu CH, Wu TL, Su LH, et al. The emergence in Taiwan of fluoroquinolone resistance in Salmonella enterica serotype Choleraesuis. N Engl J Med. 2002;346:413-419.

92. Mølbak K, Baggesen DL, Aarestrup FM, et al. An outbreak of multidrug-resistant, quinolone-resistant Salmonella enterica serotype Typhimurium DT104. N Engl J Med. 1999;341:1420-1425.

93. Hakanen A, Kotilainen P, Huovinen P, et al. Reduced fluoroquinolone susceptibility in Salmonella enterica serotypes in travelers returning from Southeast Asia. Emerg Infect Dis. 2001;7:996-1003.

94. Olsen SJ, DeBess EE, McGivern TE, et al. A nosocomial outbreak of fluoro-quinolone-resistant salmonella infection. N Engl J Med. 2001;344:1572-1579.

95. Nair D, Gupta N, Kabra S, et al. Salmonella senftenberg: A new pathogen in the burns ward. Burns. 1999;25:723-727.

96. Gupta A, Matsui K, Lo JF, Silver S. Molecular basis for resistance to silver cations in Salmonella. Nat Med. 1999;5:183-188.

97. Wall PG, Ryan MJ. Faecal incontinence in hospitals and residential and nursing homes for elderly people. BMJ. 1996;312:378.

98. Tauxe RV, Hassan LF, Findeisen KO, et al. Salmonellosis in nurses: Lack of transmission to patients. J Infect Dis. 1988;157:370-373.

99. Wilson R, Feldman RA, Davis J, LaVenture M. Salmonellosis in infants: The importance of intrafamilial transmission. Pediatrics. 1982;69:436-438.

100. Haddock RL, Cousens SN, Guzman CC. Infant diet and salmonellosis. Am J Public Health. 1991;81:997-1000.

101. Bornemann R, Zerr DM, Heath J, et al. An outbreak of Salmonella serotype Saintpaul in a children's hospital. Infect Control Hosp Epidemiol. 2002;23:671-676.

102. Buchwald DS, Blaser MJ. A review of human salmonellosis: II. Duration of excretion following infection with nontyphi Salmonella. Rev Infect Dis. 1984;6:345-356.

103. Levine WC, Smart JF, Archer DL, et al. Foodborne disease outbreaks in nursing homes, 1975 through 1987. JAMA. 1991;266:2105-2109.

104. Blaser MJ, Neuman LS. A review of human salmonellosis: I. Infective dose. Rev Infect Dis. 1982;4:1096.

105. Mintz ED, Cartter ML, Hadler JL, et al. Dose-response effects in an outbreak of Salmonella enteritidis. Epidemiol Infect. 1994;112:13-23.

106. Foster JW, Hall HK. Adaptive acidification tolerance response of Salmonella typhimurium. J Bacteriol. 1990;172:771-778.

107. Michetti P, Mahan MJ, Slauch JM, et al. Monoclonal secretory immunoglobulin A protects mice against oral challenge with the invasive pathogen Salmonella typhimurium. Infect Immun. 1992;60:1786-1792.

108. Selsted ME, Miller SI, Henschen AH, Ouellette AJ. Enteric defensins: Antibiotic peptide components of intestinal host defense. J Cell Biol. 1992;118:929-936.

109. van der Velden AW, Baumler AJ, Tsolis RM, Heffron F. Multiple fimbrial adhesins are required for full virulence of Salmonella typhimurium in mice. Infect Immun. 1998;66:2803-2808.

110. Francis CL, Starnbach MN, Falkow S. Morphological and cytoskeletal changes in epithelial cells occur immediately upon interaction with Salmonella typhimurium grown under low-oxygen conditions. Mol Microbiol. 1992;6:3077-3087.

111. Jones BD, Ghori N, Falkow S. Salmonella typhimurium initiates murine infection by penetrating and destroying the specialized epithelial M cells of the Peyer's patches. J Exp Med. 1994;180:15-23.

112. Watson PR, Paulin SM, Bland AP, et al. Characterization of intestinal invasion by Salmonella typhimurium and Salmonella dublin and effect of a mutation in the invH gene. Infect Immun. 1995;63:2743-2754.

113. Scherer CA, Cooper E, Miller SI. The Salmonella type III secretion translocon protein SspC is inserted into the epithelial cell plasma membrane upon infection. Mol Microbiol. 2000;37:1133-1145.

114. Hayward RD, Koronakis V. Direct nucleation and bundling of actin by the SipC protein of invasive Salmonella. EMBO J. 1999;18:4926-4934.

115. Zhou D, Mooseker MS, Galan JE. Role of the S. typhimurium actin-binding protein SipA in bacterial internalization. Science. 1999;283:2092-2095.

116. Hardt W-D, Chen L-M, Schuebel KE, et al. S. typhimurium encodes an activator of Rho GTPases that induces membrane ruffling and nuclear responses in host cells. Cell. 1998;93:815-826.

117. Norris FA, Wilson MP, Wallis TS, et al. SopB, a protein required for virulence of Salmonella dublin, is an inositol phosphate phosphatase. Proc Natl Acad Sci U S A. 1998;95:14057-14059.

118. Zhou D, Chen LM, Hernandez L, et al. A Salmonella inositol polyphosphatase acts in conjunction with other bacterial effectors to promote host cell actin cytoskeleton rearrangements and bacterial internalization. Mol Microbiol. 2001;39:248-259.

119. Rescigno M, Urbano M, Valzasina B, et al. Dendritic cells express tight junction proteins and penetrate gut epithelial monolayers to sample bacteria. Nat Immunol. 2001;2:361-367.

120. Vazquez-Torres A, Jones-Carson J, Baumler AJ, et al. Extraintestinal dissemination of Salmonella by CD18-expressing phagocytes. Nature. 1999;401:804-808.

121. Watson PR, Galyov EE, Paulin SM, et al. Mutation of invH, but not stn, reduces Salmonella-induced enteritis in cattle. Infect Immun. 1998;66:1432-1438.

122. McCormick BA, Colgan SP, Delp-Archer C, et al. Salmonella typhimurium attachment to human intestinal epithelial monolayers: Transcellular signaling to subepithelial neutrophils. J Cell Biol. 1993;123:895-907.

123. Eckmann L, Rudolf MT, Ptasznik A, et al. D-myo-Inositol 1,4,5,6-tetrakisphosphate produced in human intestinal epithelial cells in response to Salmonella invasion inhibits phosphoinositide 3-kinase signaling pathways. Proc Natl Acad Sci U S A. 1997;94:14456-14460.

124. Akira S. Mammalian Toll-like receptors. Curr Opin Immunol. 2003;15:5-11.

125. Rubin RH, Weinstein L. Salmonellosis: Microbiologic, Pathologic, and Clinical Features. New York: Stratton Intercontinental; 1977.

126. Fu Y, Galan JE. A salmonella protein antagonizes Rac-1 and Cdc42 to mediate host-cell recovery after bacterial invasion. Nature. 1999;401:293-297.

127. Collier-Hyams LS, Zeng H, Sun J, et al. Cutting edge: Salmonella AvrA effector inhibits the key proinflammatory, anti-apoptotic NF-kappa B pathway. J Immunol. 2002;169:2846-2850.

128. Haraga A, Miller SI. A Salmonella enterica serovar Typhimurium translocated leucine-rich repeat effector protein inhibits NF-kappa B-dependent gene expression. Infect Immun. 2003;71:4052-4058.

129. Rubin FA, McWhirter PD, Burr D, et al. Rapid diagnosis of typhoid fever through identification of Salmonella typhi within 18 hours of specimen acquisition by culture of the mononuclear cell-platelet fraction of blood. J Clin Microbiol. 1990;28:825-827.

130. Fields PI, Swanson RV, Haidaris CG, Heffron F. Mutants of Salmonella typhimurium that cannot survive within the macrophage are avirulent. Proc Natl Acad Sci U S A. 1986;83:5189-5193.

131. Richter-Dahlfors A, Buchan AMJ, Finlay BB. Murine Salmonellosis studied by confocal microscopy: Salmonella typhimurium resides intracellularly inside macrophages and exerts a cytotoxic effect on phagocytes in vivo. J Exp Med. 1997;186:569-580.

132. Guo L, Lim K, Gunn JS, et al. Regulation of lipid A modifications by Salmonella typhimurium virulence genes phoP-phoQ. Science. 1997;276:250-253.

133. Hohmann EL, Oletta CA, Killeen KP, Miller SI. phoP/phoQ-deleted Salmonella typhi (TY800) is a safe and immunogenic single dose typhoid fever vaccine in volunteers. J Infect Dis. 1996;173:1408-1414.

134. Looney RJ, Steigbigel RT. Role of the Vi antigen of Salmonella typhi in resistance to host defense in vitro. J Lab Clin Med. 1986;108:506-516.

135. De Groote MA, Testerman T, Xu Y, et al. Homocysteine antagonism of nitric oxide-related cytostasis in Salmonella typhimurium. Science. 1996;272:414-417.

136. Buchmeier NA, Lipps CJ, So MYH, Heffron F. Recombination-deficient mutants of Salmonella typhimurium are avirulent and sensitive to the oxidative burst of macrophages. Mol Microbiol. 1993;7:933-936.

137. Shea JE, Hensel M, Gleeson C, Holden DW. Identification of a virulence locus encoding a second type III secretion system in Salmonella typhimurium. Proc Natl Acad Sci U S A. 1996;93:2593-2597.

138. Meresse S, Unsworth KE, Habermann A, et al. Remodelling of the actin cytoskeleton is essential for replication of intravacuolar Salmonella. Cell Microbiol. 2001;3:567-577.

139. Miao EA, Brittnacher M, Haraga A, et al. Salmonella effectors translocated across the vacuolar membrane interact with the actin cytoskeleton. Mol Microbiol. 2003;48:401-415.

140. Lesnick ML, Reiner NE, Fierer J, Guiney DG. The Salmonella spvB virulence gene encodes an enzyme that ADP-ribosylates actin and destabilizes the cytoskeleton of eukaryotic cells. Mol Microbiol. 2001;39:1464-1470.

141. Chakravortty D, Hansen-Wester I, Hensel M. Salmonella pathogenicity island 2 mediates protection of intracellular Salmonella from reactive nitrogen intermediates. J Exp Med. 2002;195:1155-1166.

142. Vazquez-Torres A, Xu Y, Jones-Carson J, et al. Salmonella pathogenicity island 2-dependent evasion of the phagocyte NADPH oxidase. Science. 2000;287:1655-1658.

143. Fierer J, Krause M, Tauxe R, Guiney D. Salmonella typhimurium bacteremia: Association with the virulence plasmid. J Infect Dis. 1992;166:639-642.

144. Bernheiden M, Heinrich JM, Minigo G, et al. LBP, CD14, TLR4 and the murine innate immune response to a peritoneal Salmonella infection. J Endotoxin Res. 2001;7:447-450.

145. Mastroeni P, Harrison JA, Robinson JH, et al. Interleukin-12 is required for control of the growth of attenuated aromatic-compound-dependent salmonellae in BALB/c mice: Role of gamma interferon and macrophage activation. Infect Immun. 1998;66:4767-4776.

146. Everest P, Roberts M, Dougan G. Susceptibility to Salmonella typhimurium infection and effectiveness of vaccination in mice deficient in the tumor necrosis factor alpha p55 receptor. Infect Immun. 1998;66:3355-3364.

147. Hess J, Ladel C, Miko D, Kaufmann SH. Salmonella typhimurium aroA- infection in gene-targeted immunodeficient mice: Major role of CD4+ TCR-alpha beta cells and IFN-gamma in bacterial clearance independent of intracellular location. J Immunol. 1996;156:3321-3326.

148. Jouanguy E, Doffinger R, Dupuis S, et al. IL-12 and IFN-gamma in host defense against mycobacteria and salmonella in mice and men. Curr Opin Immunol. 1999;11:346-351.

149. Mastroeni P, Simmons C, Fowler R, et al. Igh-6 −/− (B-cell-deficient) mice fail to mount solid acquired resistance to oral challenge with virulent Salmonella enterica serovar Typhimurium and show impaired Th1 T-cell responses to Salmonella antigens. Infect Immun. 2000;68:46-53.

150. Nauciel C. Role of CD4+ T cells and T-independent mechanisms in acquired resistance to Salmonella typhimurium infection. J Immunol. 1990;145:1265-1269.

151. Han T, Sokal JE, Neter E. Salmonellosis in disseminated malignant diseases: A seven-year review (1959-1965). N Engl J Med. 1967;276:1045-1052.

152. Mussche MM, Lameire NH, Ringoir SM. Salmonella typhimurium infections in renal transplant patients: Report of five cases. Nephron. 1975;15:143-150.

153. Celum CL, Chaisson RE, Rutherford GW, et al. Incidence of salmonellosis in patients with AIDS. J Infect Dis. 1987;156:998-1002.

154. Angulo FJ, Swerdlow DL. Bacterial enteric infections in persons infected with human immunodeficiency virus. Clin Infect Dis. 1995;21(Suppl 1):S84-S93.

155. Nencioni L, Villa L, De Magistris MT, et al. Cellular immunity against Salmonella typhi after live oral vaccine. Adv Exp Med Biol. 1987;216B:1669-1675.

156. Dunstan SJ, Stephens HA, Blackwell JM, et al. Genes of the class II and class III major histocompatibility complex are associated with typhoid fever in Vietnam. J Infect Dis. 2001;183:261-268.

157. Saphra I, Winter JW. Clinical manifestations of salmonellosis in man: An evaluation of 7779 human infections identified at the New York Salmonella Center. N Engl J Med. 1957;256:1128.

158. Chaudhuri A, Bekdash BA. Toxic megacolon due to Salmonella: A case report and review of the literature. Int J Colorectal Dis. 2002;17:275-279.

159. Lim E, Koh WH, Loh SF, et al. Non-typhoidal salmonellosis in patients with systemic lupus erythematosus: A study of fifty patients and a review of the literature. Lupus. 2001;10:87-92.

160. Szanton VL. Epidemic salmonellosis. Pediatrics. 1957;20:794-808.
161. Butler T, Islam A, Kabir I, Jones PK. Patterns of morbidity and mortality in typhoid fever dependent on age and gender: Review of 552 hospitalized patients with diarrhea. Rev Infect Dis. 1991;13:85-90.
162. Barrett-Connor E. Bacterial infection and sickle cell anemia: An analysis of 250 infections in 166 patients and a review of the literature. Medicine. 1971;50:97-112.
163. Neves J, Raso P, Marinko PP. Prolonged septicemic salmonellosis intercurrent with *Schistosomiasis mansoni* infection. J Trop Med Hyg. 1971;74:9.
164. Wheat LJ, Rubin RH, Harris NL, et al. Systemic salmonellosis in patients with disseminated histoplasmosis: Case for 'macrophage blockade' caused by Histoplasma capsulatum. Arch Intern Med. 1987;147:561-564.
165. Bhan MK, Bahl R, Sazawal S, et al. Association between Helicobacter pylori infection and increased risk of typhoid fever. J Infect Dis. 2002;186:1857-1860.
166. Stuart BM, Pullen RL. Typhoid: Clinical analysis of three hundred and sixty cases. Arch Intern Med. 1946;78:629-661.
167. Arand AC, Kataria VK, Singh W, Chatterjee SK. Epidemic multiresistant enteric fever in Eastern India. Lancet. 1990;335:352.
168. Roland HAK. The complications of typhoid fever. J Trop Med Hyg. 1961;64:143.
169. Verghese A. The "typhoid state" revisited. Am J Med. 1985;79:370-372.
170. Edelman R, Levine MM. Summary of an international workshop on typhoid fever. Rev Infect Dis. 1986;8:329-349.
171. Hoffman SL, Punjabi NH, Kumala S, et al. Reduction of mortality in chloramphenicol-treated severe typhoid fever by high-dose dexamethasone. N Engl J Med. 1984;310:82-88.
172. Hearne SE, Whigham TE, Brady CEI. Pancreatitis and typhoid fever. Am J Med. 1989;86:471-473.
173. Cohen JI, Bartlett JA, Corey GR. Extra-intestinal manifestations of *Salmonella* infections. Medicine (Baltimore). 1987;66:349-388.
174. Khan M, Coovadia YM, Connolly C, Sturm AW. Influence of sex on clinical features, laboratory findings, and complications of typhoid fever. Am J Trop Med Hyg. 1999;61:41-46.
175. van Basten JP, Stockenbrugger R. Typhoid perforation: A review of the literature since 1960. Trop Geogr Med. 1994;46:336-339.
176. Khan M, Coovadia YM, Connoly C, Sturm AW. The early diagnosis of typhoid fever prior to the Widal test and bacteriological culture results. Acta Trop. 1998;69:165-173.
177. El-Newihi HM, Alamy ME, Reynolds TB. *Salmonella* hepatitis: Analysis of 27 cases and comparison with acute viral hepatitis. Hepatology. 1996;24:516-519.
178. Calva JJ, Ruiz-Palacios GM. Salmonella hepatitis: Detection of Salmonella antigens in the liver of patients with typhoid fever. J Infect Dis. 1986;154:373-374.
179. Wain J, Hien TT, Connerton P, et al. Molecular typing of multiple-antibiotic-resistant Salmonella enterica serovar Typhi from Vietnam: Application to acute and relapse cases of typhoid fever. J Clin Microbiol. 1999;37:2466-2472.
180. Farooqui BJ, Khurshid M, Ashfaq MK, Khan MA. Comparative yield of *Salmonella typhi* from blood and bone marrow cultures in patients with fever of unknown origin. J Clin Pathol. 1991;44:258-259.
181. Wain J, Diep TS, Ho VA, et al. Quantitation of bacteria in blood of typhoid fever patients and relationship between counts and clinical features, transmissibility, and antibiotic resistance. J Clin Microbiol. 1998;36:1683-1687.
182. Wain J, Pham VB, Ha V, et al. Quantitation of bacteria in bone marrow from patients with typhoid fever: Relationship between counts and clinical features. J Clin Microbiol. 2001;39:1571-1576.
183. Benavente L, Gotuzzo E, Guerra J, et al. Diagnosis of typhoid fever using a string capsule device. Trans R Soc Trop Med Hyg. 1984;78:564-565.
184. Gilman RH, Terminel M, Levine MM, et al. Relative efficacy of blood, urine, rectal swab, bone-marrow, and rose-spot cultures for recovery of *Salmonella typhi* in typhoid fever. Lancet. 1975;1:1211-1213.
185. Bhutta ZA, Mansurali N. Rapid serologic diagnosis of pediatric typhoid fever in an endemic area: A prospective comparative evaluation of two dot-enzyme immunoassays and the Widal test. Am J Trop Med Hyg. 1999;61:654-657.
186. Chaudhry R, Laxmi BV, Nisar N, et al. Standardisation of polymerase chain reaction for the detection of *Salmonella typhi* in typhoid fever. J Clin Pathol. 1997;50:437-439.
187. Sperber SJ, Schleupner CJ. Salmonellosis during infection with human immunodeficiency virus. Rev Infect Dis. 1987;9:925-934.
188. Shimoni Z, Pitlik S, Leibovici L, et al. Nontyphoid Salmonella bacteremia: Age-related differences in clinical presentation, bacteriology, and outcome. Clin Infect Dis. 1999;28:822-827.
189. Parsons R, Gregory J, Palmer DL. *Salmonella* infections of the abdominal aorta. Rev Infect Dis. 1983;5:227-231.
190. Benenson S, Raveh D, Schlesinger Y, et al. The risk of vascular infection in adult patients with nontyphi Salmonella bacteremia. Am J Med. 2001;110:60-63.
191. Hsu RB, Tsay YG, Chen RJ, Chu SH. Risk factors for primary bacteremia and endovascular infection in patients without acquired immunodeficiency syndrome who have nontyphoid salmonellosis. Clin Infect Dis. 2003;36:829-834.
192. Carey J, Buchstein S, Shah S. Septic deep vein thrombosis due to Salmonella johannesburg. J Infect. 2001;42:79-80.
193. Fernández Guerrero ML, Ramos JM, Núñez A, de Górgolas M. Focal infections due to non-typhi Salmonella in patients with AIDS: Report of 10 cases and review. Clin Infect Dis. 1997;25:690-697.
194. Wolday D, Erge W. Antimicrobial sensitivity pattern of Salmonella: Comparison of isolates from HIV-infected and HIV-uninfected patients. Trop Doctor. 1998;28:139-141.
195. Gordon MA, Banda HT, Gondwe M, et al. Non-typhoidal salmonella bacteraemia among HIV-infected Malawian adults: High mortality and frequent recrudescence. AIDS. 2002;16:1633-1641.
196. Casado JL, Valdezate S, Calderon C, et al. Zidovudine therapy protects against Salmonella bacteremia recurrence in human immunodeficiency virus-infected patients. J Infect Dis. 1999;179:1553-1556.
197. Hung CC, Hsieh SM, Hsiao CF, et al. Risk of recurrent non-typhoid Salmonella bacteraemia after early discontinuation of ciprofloxacin as secondary prophylaxis in AIDS patients in the era of highly active antiretroviral therapy. AIDS. 2001;15:645-647.
198. Aguado JM, Ramos JM, Garcia-Corbeira P, et al. The clinical spectrum of focal infection due to nontyphoid *Salmonella:* 32 years' experience (in Spanish). Med Clin (Barc). 1994;103:293-298.
199. Musher DM, Rubenstein AD. Permanent carriers of nontyphosal salmonellae. Public Health Rep. 1973;132:869.
200. Balfour AE, Lewis R, Ahmed S. Convalescent excretion of Salmonella enteritidis in infants. J Infect. 1999;38:24-25.
201. Nath G, Singh H, Shukla VK. Chronic typhoid carriage and carcinoma of the gallbladder. Eur J Cancer Prev. 1997;6:557-559.
202. Lanata CF, Levine MM, Ristori C, et al. Vi serology in detection of chronic Salmonella typhi carriers in an endemic area. Lancet. 1983;2:441-443.
203. Centers for Disease Control and Prevention. Health Information for International Travel, 2003-2004: Atlanta: Centers for Disease Control and Prevention; 2003.
204. Hornick RB, Greisman SE, Woodward TE, et al. Typhoid fever: pathogenesis and immunologic control. N Engl J Med. 1970;283:686-691.
205. Yugoslavian Typhoid Commission. A controlled field trial of the effectiveness of phenol and alcohol typhoid vaccines: Final report. Bull World Health Organ. 1962;26:357-369.
206. Ashcroft MT, Morrision RJ, Nicholson CC. Controlled field trial in British Guiana school children of heat-killed-phenolized and acetone-killed lyophilized typhoid vaccines. Am J Hyg. 1964;79:196-206.
207. Ashcroft MT, Singh B, Nicholson CC, et al. A seven-year field trial of two typhoid vaccines in Guyana. Lancet. 1967;2:1056-1059.
208. Edwards EA, Johnson DP, Pierce WE, Peckinpaugh RO. Reactions and serologic responses to monovalent acetone-inactivated typhoid vaccine and heat-killed TAB when given by jet injection. Bull World Health Organ. 1974;51:501-505.
209. Hone DM, Attridge SR, Forrest B, et al. A *galA* via (Vi-antigen negative) mutant of *Salmonella typhi* Ty2 retains virulence in humans. Infect Immun. 1988;56:1326-1333.
210. Levine MM, Ferreccio C, Black RE, Germanier R. Large-scale field trial of Ty21a live oral typhoid vaccine in enteric-coated capsule formulation. Lancet. 1987;1:1049-1052.
211. Simanjuntak CH, Paleologo FP, Punjabi NH, et al. Oral immunisation against typhoid fever in Indonesia with Ty21a vaccine. Lancet. 1991;338:1055-1059.
212. Hessel L, Debois H, Fletcher M, Dumas R. Experience with Salmonella typhi Vi capsular polysaccharide vaccine. Eur J Clin Microbiol Infect Dis. 1999;18:609-620.
213. Klugman KP, Koornhof HJ, Robbins JB, Le Cam NN. Immunogenicity, efficacy and serological correlate of protection of Salmonella typhi Vi capsular polysaccharide vaccine three years after immunization. Vaccine. 1996;14:435-438.
214. Lin FY, Ho VA, Khiem HB, et al. The efficacy of a Salmonella typhi Vi conjugate vaccine in two-to-five-year-old children. N Engl J Med. 2001;344:1263-1269.
215. Tarr PE, Kuppens L, Jones TC, et al. Considerations regarding mass vaccination against typhoid fever as an adjunct to sanitation and public health measures: Potential use in an epidemic in Tajikistan. Am J Trop Med Hyg. 1999;61:163-170.
216. Parry CM, Hien TT, Dougan G, et al. Typhoid fever. N Engl J Med. 2002;347:1770-1782.
217. Easmon CSF, Crane JP, Blowers A. Effect of ciprofloxacin on intracellular organisms: In-vitro and in-vivo studies. J Antimicrob Chemother. 1986;18:43-48.
218. Seçmeer G, Kanra G, Figen G, et al. Ofloxacin versus co-trimoxazole in the treatment of typhoid fever in children. Acta Paediatr Jpn. 1997;39:218-221.
219. Thomsen LL, Paerregaard A. Treatment with ciprofloxacin in children with typhoid fever. Scand J Infect Dis. 1998;30:355-357.
220. Threlfall EJ, Ward LR, Skinner JA, et al. Ciprofloxacin-resistant Salmonella typhi and treatment failure. Lancet. 1999;353:1590-1591.
221. Soe GB, Overturf GD. Treatment of typhoid fever and other systemic salmonelloses with cefotaxime, ceftriaxone, cefoperazone, and other newer cephalosporins. Rev Infect Dis. 1987;9:719.
222. Butler T, Frenck RW, Johnson RB, Khakhria R. In vitro effects of azithromycin on Salmonella typhi: Early inhibition by concentrations less than the MIC and reduction of MIC by alkaline pH and small inocula. J Antimicrob Chemother. 2001;47:455-458.
223. Dutta P, Mitra U, Dutta S, et al. Ceftriaxone therapy in ciprofloxacin treatment failure typhoid fever in children. Indian J Med Res. 2001;113:210-213.
224. Girgis NI, Tribble DR, Sultan Y, Farid Z. Short course chemotherapy with cefixime in children with multidrug-resistant Salmonella typhi septicaemia. J Trop Pediatr. 1995;41:364-365.
225. Choo KE, Ariffin WA, Ong KH, Sivakumaran S. Aztreonam failure in typhoid fever. Lancet. 1991;337:498.
226. Preblud SR, Gill CJ, Campos JM. Bactericidal activities of chloramphenicol and eleven other antibiotics against *Salmonella* spp. Antimicrob Agents Chemother. 1984;3:327-330.
227. Vaudaux P, Waldvogel FA. Gentamicin antibacterial activity in the presence of human polymorphonuclear leukocytes. Antimicrob Agents Chemother. 1979;16:743-749.
228. Herzog C. Chemotherapy of typhoid fever. Infection. 1976;4:166-173.
229. Cooles P. Adjuvant steroids and relapse of typhoid fever. J Trop Med Hyg. 1986;89:229-231.
230. Sirinavin S, Garner P. Antibiotics for treating Salmonella gut infections. Cochrane Database Syst Rev. 2000;93:CD001167.
231. Lightfoot NF, Ahmad F, Cowden J. Management of institutional outbreaks of *Salmonella* gastroenteritis. J Antimicrob Chemother. 1990;26:37-46.
232. Gendrel D, Raymond J, Legall MA, et al. Use of pefloxacin after failure of initial antibiotic treatment in children with severe salmonellosis. Eur J Clin Microbiol Infect Dis. 1993;12:209-211.
233. Gokalp AS, Toksoy HB, Turkay S, et al. Intravenous immunoglobulin in the treatment of *Salmonella typhimurium* infections in preterm neonates. Clin Pediatr (Phila). 1994;33:349-352.

234. Cohen PS, O'Brien TF, Schoenbaum SC, Medieiros AA. The risk of endothelial infection in adults with *Salmonella* bacteremia. Ann Intern Med. 1978;89:931-932.

235. Donabedian H. Long-term suppression of *Salmonella* aortitis with an oral antibiotic. Arch Intern Med. 1989;149:1452-1453.

236. Jacobson MA, Hahn SM, Gerberding JL, et al. Ciprofloxacin for *Salmonella* bacteremia in the acquired immunodeficiency syndrome (AIDS). Ann Intern Med. 1989;110:1027-1029.

237. Lewin CS, Allen RA, Amyes SG. Antibacterial activity of fluoroquinolones in combination with zidovudine. J Med Microbiol. 1990;33:127-131.

238. Freerksen E, Rosenfield M, Freerksen R, et al. Treatment of chronic *Salmonella* carriers. Chemotherapy. 1977;23:192.

239. Ferreccio C, Morris JG Jr, Valdivieso C, et al. Efficacy of ciprofloxacin in the treatment of chronic typhoid carriers. J Infect Dis. 1988;157:1235.

240. Hogue A, White P, Guard-Petter J, et al. Epidemiology and control of egg-associated Salmonella enteritidis in the United States of America. Rev Sci Tech. 1997;16:542-553.

241. Bender JB, Hedberg CW, Boxrud DJ, et al. Use of molecular subtyping in surveillance for Salmonella enterica serotype Typhimurium. N Engl J Med. 2001;344:189-195.

242. Fisher IST, Rowe B, Bartlett CLR, O'Noel G. 'Salm-Net'-laboratory-based surveillance of human *Salmonella* infections in Europe. PHLS Microbiol Dig. 1994;11:181.

243. Hastings L, Burnens A, de Jong B, et al. Salm-Net facilitates collaborative investigation of an outbreak of *Salmonella tosamanga* infection in Europe. Commun Dis Rep CDR Rev. 1996;6:R100-R102.

244. Standaert SM, Hutcheson RH, Schaffner W. Nosocomial transmission of Salmonella gastroenteritis to laundry workers in a nursing home. Infect Control Hosp Epidemiol. 1994;15:22-26.

245. Pace F, Fanfarillo F, Giorgino F, Baratta L. Salmonella enteritidis pericarditis: Case report and review of the literature. Ann Ital Med Int. 2002;17:189-192.

246. Soravia-Dunand VA, Loo VG, Salit IE. Aortitis due to Salmonella: Report of 10 cases and comprehensive review of the literature. Clin Infect Dis. 1999;29:862-868.

247. Chiu CH, Ou JT. Risk factors for endovascular infection due to nontyphoid salmonellae. Clin Infect Dis. 2003;36:835-836.

248. Huang LT, Ko SF, Lui CC. Salmonella meningitis: Clinical experience of third-generation cephalosporins. Acta Paediatr. 1997;86:1056-1058.

249. Lee WS, Puthucheary SD, Omar A. Salmonella meningitis and its complications in infants. J Paediatr Child Health. 1999;35:379-382.

250. Karim M, Islam N. Salmonella meningitis: Report of three cases in adults and literature review. Infection. 2002;30:104-108.

251. Santos EM, Sapico FL. Vertebral osteomyelitis due to salmonellae: Report of two cases and review. Clin Infect Dis. 1998;27:287-295.

252. Banky JP, Ostergaard L, Spelman D. Chronic relapsing salmonella osteomyelitis in an immunocompetent patient: Case report and literature review. J Infect. 2002;44:44-47.

253. Ekman P, Kirveskari J, Granfors K. Modification of disease outcome in Salmonella-infected patients by HLA-B27. Arthritis Rheum. 2000;43:1527-1534.

254. Buxton JA, Fyfe M, Berger S, et al. Reactive arthritis and other sequelae following sporadic Salmonella typhimurium infection in British Columbia, Canada: A case control study. J Rheumatol. 2002;29:2154-2158.

255. Chen JY, Luo SF, Wu YJ, et al. Salmonella septic arthritis in systemic lupus erythematosus and other systemic diseases. Clin Rheumatol. 1998;17:282-287.

256. Collazos J, Mayo J, Martínez E, Blanco MS. Muscle infections caused by Salmonella species: Case report and review. Clin Infect Dis. 1999;29:673-677.

257. Lee CC, Poon SK, Chen GH. Spontaneous gas-forming liver abscess caused by Salmonella within hepatocellular carcinoma: A case report and review of the literature. Dig Dis Sci. 2002;47:586-589.

258. Torres JR, Gatuzzo E, Isturiz R, et al. *Salmonella* splenic abscess in the antibiotic era: A Latin American perspective. Clin Infect Dis. 1994;19:871.

259. Ramos JM, Aguado JM, García-Corbeira P, et al. Clinical spectrum of urinary tract infections due to nontyphoidal Salmonella species. Clin Infect Dis. 1996;23:388-390.

260. Behr MA, McDonald J. Salmonella neck abscess in a patient with beta-thalassemia major: Case report and review. Clin Infect Dis. 1996;23:404-405.

Shigella Species (Bacillary Dysentery)

HERBERT L. DUPONT

The term *dysentery* was used by Hippocrates to indicate a condition characterized by the frequent passage of stool containing blood and mucus, accompanied by straining and painful defecation. It was not until the end of the 19th century, when the causes of amebiasis and bacillary dysentery were determined, that the two great forms of dysentery could be accurately separated. In view of the absence of liver complications, much of the dysentery in the older historical writings is considered to be of bacillary origin (shigellosis). After the causative agents of the two types of dysentery were determined, the different epidemiologic settings were described. In 1859 in Prague, Lambl and then later Osler[1] and Councilman and Lafleur[2] helped verify the pathogenicity of *Entamoeba histolytica*. In 1906, Shiga conclusively demonstrated that a bacterium was present in the stool of many patients with dysentery, and that agglutinins could be demonstrated in the serum of the infected patients.[3] At about the same time, Flexner found a similar but serologically different organism in the stools of other patients with dysentery acquired in the Philippines.[4] Rogers stated in 1913 that "epidemic dysentery in asylums, jails, or in long-occupied and unsanitary military camps during the war is nearly certain to be bacillary, while sporadic cases in a warm climate are more frequently amebic."[5]

Medical writings since the beginning of recorded history have dealt with the common problems of dysentery in civilian and military populations; perhaps the greatest historical consideration is the influence that bacillary dysentery has had on military campaigns. Nearly every long campaign and extended siege has produced epidemics of bacillary dysentery, particularly when sanitation and food sources could not be adequately controlled. In many battles described during the Peloponnesian War, the British campaigns in the 18th century, Napoleon's campaigns, the Crimean War, the American Civil War, the Franco-Prussian War, and the Sino-Japanese War, a heavier toll was ascribed to bacillary dysentery than to war-related injuries.[6]

MICROBIOLOGY

Shigella organisms are small gram-negative rods that are members of the family Enterobacteriaceae, tribe Escherichieae, and genus *Shigella*. They are nonmotile and nonencapsulated.

Isolation Techniques

The infecting strain of *Shigella* is generally present in stools in concentrations between 10^3 and 10^9 viable cells per gram of stool, depending on the stage of illness. During the first several days of illness, the counts are higher; they drop off to lower levels after several days of clinical disease. During the postconvalescent shedding period, counts fall to 10^2 to 10^3 viable cells per gram of stool. Recovery of the agent microbiologically is not usually difficult in the early stages of disease because of the higher counts present; it is more difficult during later stages of illness because of the lower counts of viable bacteria. Having negative stool cultures in patients with shigellosis at the height of their illness is actually quite common.[7] Careful selection of material and processing on appropriate media give a higher yield of organisms. The sooner after passage the specimen is processed, the higher is the yield. Stools that stand at room temperature for more than 24 hours have a profound drop in the number of viable cells, and recovery is less likely. A rectal swab obtained and seeded immediately at the bedside is the optimal way to perform a stool culture.

For bacteriologic identification of *Shigella*, a bit of blood or mucus is seeded onto at least two different media. Generally, stool is plated lightly on a medium with only mild inhibiting factors for gram-negative growth, such as MacConkey's agar, xylose-lysine-deoxycholate agar, Tergitol-7, or eosin-methylene blue (EMB) agar, whereas a separate specimen is plated heavily on a more inhibitory medium such as *Shigella-Salmonella* medium. The more plates used, the greater the recovery yield. After overnight incubation at 37° C, lactose-negative colonies are transferred to triple-sugar iron agar and lysine-iron agar slants and reincubated. Those giving a characteristic reaction (alkaline slant, acid butt, and no gas) are tested biochemically and then serologically identified with *Shigella* grouping and typing antisera.

Group and Type Identification

The 47 serotypes of *Shigella* are divided into four groups depending on serologic similarity and fermentation reactions: group A (*Shigella dysenteriae*), group B (*Shigella flexneri*), group C (*Shigella boydii*), and group D (*Shigella sonnei*). Commercial antiserum is available for determining group- and type-specific antigenicity. *S. sonnei* accounts for between 60% and 80% of the cases currently reported in the United States and other industrialized areas.

Invasive *Escherichia coli*

Certain strains of *Escherichia coli* can cause a clinical illness indistinguishable from shigellosis and should be considered as causative agents of bacillary dysentery. Nearly all the *Shigella*-like *E. coli* strains have been shown to possess somatic antigens related to *Shigella* serotypes, further demonstrating the similarity of these two groups of organisms. Invasive *E. coli* (IEC) strains that cause bacillary dysentery have been shown to serologically belong to the following *E. coli* O groups: 28, 29, 112, 115, 124, 136, 143, 144, 147, 152, 164, and 167. Serotyping may ultimately prove to be useful in detecting these strains. The classical laboratory test for determining the virulence of a bacterial isolate (*Shigella* or IEC strain) was the Sereny test.[8] Keratoconjunctivitis develops after 1 to 7 days in guinea pigs (or rabbits) when an invasive bacterial strain (*E. coli* or *Shigella*) is dropped into the conjunctival sac of the animal (Fig. 221-1).

A different form of bacillary dysentery has been shown to be caused by an O157:H7 strain of *E. coli* and other Shiga-toxin producing *E. coli* strains.[9] The source of *E. coli* O157:H7 infection has characteristically been contaminated hamburgers obtained at a fast-food chain. Other non-O157:H7 serotypes of *E. coli* have also been implicated as causative agents of the syndrome. Dysentery (bloody diarrhea) develops in affected patients, and colitis can be documented by endoscopy. The illness differs from that associated with invasive *E. coli* in that high fever is not a feature of this so-called hemorrhagic colitis.

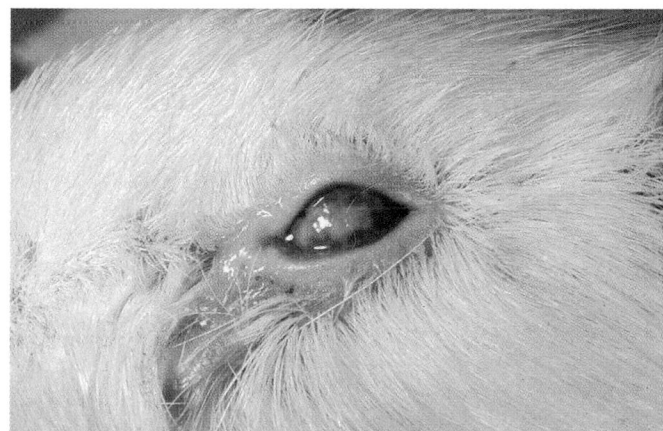

FIGURE 221-1. Guinea pig with keratoconjunctivitis after conjunctival inoculation of invasive *Escherichia coli*. This is a positive Sereny test result.

PATHOGENESIS

Communicability and Infectivity

Bacillary dysentery is one of the most, if not *the* most, communicable of the bacterial diarrheas. Experiments in volunteers have demonstrated that shigellosis is unique among bacterial enteropathogens in that fewer than 200 viable cells can readily produce the disease in healthy adults.[10] Dose-response data obtained in volunteers for virulent strains from three species of *Shigella* is given in Table 221-1. When volunteers ingested 500 or fewer viable cells of *S. flexneri, S. sonnei,* or *S. dysenteriae* 1 (the Shiga bacillus), essentially the same rate of clinical illness resulted, 27% to 45%.[10] This low dose of organisms probably explains how the illness can be transferred from person to person, why the secondary attack rate is so high when an index case is introduced into a family, and why recurrent bacillary dysentery is an important problem in institutionalized or crowded populations.

The reasons for this low-dose response are not completely clear. One possible explanation is that virulent shigellae can withstand the low pH of gastric juice. In a study of adult Bangladeshi men admitted to the hospital with diarrhea, normal gastric acid levels were seen in subjects with shigellosis, amebiasis, and pathogen-negative diarrhea, whereas patients with secretory diarrhea due to *Vibrio cholerae* and enterotoxigenic *E. coli* had low gastric acid levels, offering evidence that *Shigella* did not require reduced gastric acidity to produce enteric disease.[11] In another study, *Shigella* isolates were able to survive at pH of 2.5 for at least 2 hours, whereas *Salmonella* was not.[12] *Shigella* strains were also shown to be able to survive in acidic apple juice and tomato juice stored at 7° C and 22° C for up to 14 days, showing its resistance to acid.[13] IEC and *Shigella* possess the same virulence determinates but IEC require a dose 1000 times higher.[14] IEC strains have not been compared with *Shigella* to determine if relative acid susceptibility might explain the different dose response. Nonpathogenic *E. coli* appear to have similar acid susceptibility to strains of *Shigella*, suggesting that this is not the reason for the difference in dose response.[12]

Mucosal Invasion and Inflammation

Virulent *Shigella* and other nontoxigenic invasive *E. coli* strains produce disease after invading the intestinal mucosa.[15] Genes required for bacterial entry into epithelial cells are present on a 30-kilobase entry region of a 220-kb virulence plasmid.[16] *Shigella* infection is superficial, and only rarely does the organism penetrate beyond the mucosa, which explains the rarity of obtaining positive blood cultures in patients with shigellosis despite the common occurrence of hyperpyrexia and toxemia. *Shigella* and IEC invade colonic and rectal cells, including M cells of the follicle-associated epithelium, macrophages, and epithelial cells; invasion is followed by intracellular multiplication, spread of infection to adjacent cells, severe inflammation, and destruction of colonic mucosa.[17] Apoptotic destruction of macrophages in subepithelial tissue allows survival of the invading shigellae, and inflammation facilitates further bacterial entry.[18] Once the organisms are intracellular, they multiply within the cytoplasm and move from cell to cell by an actin-dependent process.

TABLE 221-1 Response of Adult Volunteers to Experimental Challenge with Viable Virulent Strains of *Shigella* Species

Shigella Species	Inoculum (Organisms)	N	Cases of Clinical Shigellosis n (%)
S. flexneri (strain 2467T)	≤180	72	23 (32)
	≥5 × 10³	211	124 (59)
S. sonnei (53G)	500	58	26 (45)
S. dysenteriae 1	≤200	22	6 (27)
(A-1 and M-131)	≥2 × 10³	22	14 (64)

Adapted from DuPont HL, Levine MM, Hornick RB, et al. Inoculum size in shigellosis and implications for expected mode of transmission. J Infect Dis. 1989;159:1126.

Pathogenic strains of *Shigella* have the same virulence apparatus as that used by a number of other bacterial enteropathogens. These invasive pathogens have evolved a complex type III secretion mechanism that enables them to invade the intestinal mucosa. Bacterial proteins (including toxins) are injected from the bacterial cytoplasm into the cytosol of host cells (e.g., mucosal cells), where they modulate the functions of the host cells and dictate the way the host and pathogen relate.[19-21] Each type III system consists of the secretion apparatus, secreted effector proteins, cytoplasmic chaperones (specialized for transporting the specific effector proteins), and specific transcriptional regulators.[22-24] The secreted proteins-there are approximately 20, including VirA, OspB to OspG, IpaA-D, and IpgD-stimulate bacterial entry into nonphagocytic cells and induce apoptosis.[21]

Pathogenic strains of bacterial pathogens belonging to the type III secretion system can be detected by screening for virulence genes directly.[25] DNA probes and polymerase chain reaction techniques have been developed to detect *Shigella* and invasive *E. coli* and can be used in epidemiologic studies.

Toxigenicity

The Shiga bacillus (*S. dysenteriae* 1) was shown in the early part of the 20th century to produce a neurotoxin that caused paralysis and death in mice and rabbits. Since then, it has been suspected that the toxin played an important role in the pathogenesis of clinical illness. Later, an exotoxin in the Shiga bacillus was shown to have enterotoxin activity in the ligated ileal loop model[26] and also to have cytotoxic properties when intestinal mucosa was examined.[27] Undoubtedly, invasiveness is the primary virulence characteristic of *Shigella* strains, but toxin elaboration may play a role in the evolution of the local destructive mucosal lesion once the organisms have invaded the colonic mucosa. It is possible that toxin might also help explain the watery small bowel type of diarrhea that is characteristically seen during the first or second day of illness. Shiga toxin production does appear to be the important virulence property of hemorrhagic colitis and hemolytic uremic syndrome caused by *E. coli* (O157:H7).[28]

Anatomic Location of Infection

Studies in volunteers have helped establish the intestinal localization of bacteria in experimental shigellosis. Within 12 hours after subjects swallow virulent shigellae, the bacteria transiently multiply in the small bowel to concentrations of 10⁷ to 10⁹ viable cells per milliliter of luminal contents. Abdominal pain, cramping, and fever occur while the bacteria are localized in the small bowel. Within a few days, the infecting strain is no longer detectable in small bowel fluid, the patient's temperature becomes lower, and pain and tenderness become more severe and are generally confined to the lower abdominal quadrants. Urgency, tenesmus, and passage of bloody mucoid stools (dysentery) often occur in the later stages of infection and correlate with a diffuse colonic localization of the bacteria. Although strains of *Shigella* appear to be resistant to acid (as discussed earlier), acid exposure may transiently inhibit the virulence properties of the organism, which may encourage transit through the small bowel to the colon, where virulence characteristics are once more produced.[29] The density of intramucosal bacteria is greatest at the luminal surface and extends in decreasing concentrations to reach the lamina propria and submucosa. Microabscesses form and coalesce, becoming large abscesses that slough and produce mucosal ulcerations. In shigellosis, both humoral and cellular immune mechanisms are stimulated. Cytokine levels correlate with disease severity,[30] and a number of fecal cytokines, including IL-8 and IL-1β, are higher than those seen with other enteric bacterial pathogens.[31]

EPIDEMIOLOGY

Hippocrates indicated that when a dry winter was followed by a rainy spring, an increase in the number of dysentery cases would follow in the summer. Generally, bacillary dysentery is a summertime illness. Shigellosis is characteristically seen in children living in crowded areas with inadequate sanitation and limited water. Because of the characteristic clinical picture of bacillary dysentery, it is one of the most accurately diagnosed and reported classes of infectious diarrhea. The greatest frequency of illness is reported in infants and younger or preschool children. Disease rates and also complications and severity parallel the degree of malnutrition. Flies may be important in the transmission of bacillary dysentery,[32,33] especially in tropical climates. Dysentery in warm countries is most prevalent when the fly population is at its highest. Bacteriologic surveys of fly populations indicate that flies can occasionally be shown to be positive for *Shigella* bacteria.[32] The low dose required for infection at least partially explains the potential for fly-transmission of shigellosis.

Cyclic Patterns of Disease

Since the description of bacteriologic isolation procedures, cyclic epidemics of bacillary dysentery have been described, each cycle lasting 20 to 30 years.[34] In Europe during the first 25 years of the 20th century, dysentery was generally caused by *S. dysenteriae* 1 (the Shiga bacillus), and mortality was higher than subsequently seen when other serotypes became prevalent. Between 1926 and 1938, *S. flexneri* strains became more important than the Shiga bacillus in the developing world, and *S. flexneri* remains the major *Shigella* type in these parts of the world. *S. sonnei* has become the major cause of bacillary dysentery in European countries and the United States. Widespread epidemics in the developing world may be seen for the more virulent *S. dysenteriae* 1, resulting in deaths without proper antimicrobial therapy. Shiga dysentery remains a special problem in parts in Africa and in the Indian subcontinent and Bangladesh.

Incidence of Shigellosis by Geography and Host

The annual number of *Shigella* episodes worldwide is estimated to be 165 million, of which more than 100 million occur in the developing world with more than 1 million deaths.[35] The highest rate of *Shigella* infection (69%) and the highest death rate (61%) occur in the age group of less than 5 years.[35] In the United Kingdom, shigellosis has been reported commonly in school-aged children where fecal contamination of lavatory seats in nursery and primary schools has been shown to occur from children with diarrhea and that infection is transmitted to the hands of the younger children.[36] Shigellosis has become an important problem in daycare centers for preschool children in the United States. Between 20,000 and 50,000 cases are reported each year in the United Kingdom and approximately 13,000 to 19,000 cases each year in the United States. The actual number of cases is clearly far greater than those reported.

In numerous published studies, an etiologic agent has been identified in 10% to 40% of diarrhea cases, depending on geographic location and the severity of illness reported.[37-39] Bacillary dysentery is primarily a disease of children 6 months to 10 years of age; adults often acquire the illness from their children. Bacillary dysentery does not commonly develop in children younger than 6 months. However, in industrialized countries, *Shigella* strains may (rarely) cause severe illness in newborns,[40] but in developing countries, where breast-feeding is more common, infants are highly resistant to shigellosis,[41] probably because of exclusion from contaminated food or drink, changes in the intestinal flora of breast-fed children, or the presence of specific antibody in breast milk. *Campylobacter* has been shown to be an important cause of diarrhea in all regions of the world.

Modes of Spread and Reservoirs in Nature

Most cases of bacillary dysentery are a result of person-to-person transmission. However, in a number of instances, widespread epidemics have occurred in military or civilian populations and among persons on board cruise ships who have ingested contaminated food or water. Water and food appear to be particularly important vectors of *Shigella* transmission in developing countries, where they may be the most important sources of infection.[42,43] Epidemics of waterborne shigellosis generally appear to be the result of wells contaminated with fecal material. Felsen[44] found that dysentery strains could be re-

covered for up to 6 months from water samples maintained at room temperature. Wells are often located close to cesspools and privies in developing countries where sanitation principles are not followed. In other areas, septic tank discharge may empty into lakes, ponds, or other bodies of water close to intake lines for camp water supplies or adjacent to bathing beaches. Chlorination of water, if appropriately maintained, will remove the threat of such infections. Foodborne transmission of disease is not common in industrialized countries when compared with spread by direct contact, but when it occurs, it is associated with large outbreaks. During a 5-year period (1964-1968), the Centers for Disease Control and Prevention in Atlanta reported 21 foodborne or waterborne outbreaks of shigellosis in the United States, thus indicating the relative rarity of documenting common-source epidemics.[45] In 1999 and 2000, none of 39 drinking water outbreaks were caused by *Shigella* species. In those same years, 3 of 36 recreational water outbreaks were attributed to *Shigella* species.[46] An epidemiologic observation has been made that when water sanitation improvements are implemented in a community, the incidence of typhoid fever falls but the prevalence of bacillary dysentery remains unchanged.[44] In contrast to shigellosis, diseases caused by *Salmonella, Vibrio cholerae,* and *E. coli* appear to be epidemiologically associated in almost all cases with foodborne or waterborne transmission. Such a vehicle of transmission is probably necessary with the latter agents because a larger inoculum is necessary to produce illness.[47]

Hand transmission is likely to be a common means of acquiring infection. At a custodial institution, mentally retarded persons were studied for the prevalence of hand transmission of bacteria.[32] Finger and simultaneous fecal cultures were obtained from 268 institutionalized patients. A *Shigella* strain was isolated from the stool of 39 persons, and the fingers were positive in 4 (10% of those with a positive stool culture). In addition, fecal cultures were found to be negative in an additional 229 patients, whereas a *Shigella* strain was isolated from the hands and fingers of two of these patients with negative stool cultures. *E. coli* was recovered from the fingers of 82% of those studied, which demonstrates the common occurrence of fecal organisms on the hands of institutionalized persons. These institutionalized patients had adequate washroom and showering facilities and did not show evidence of decreased personal hygiene.

Secondary cases during outbreaks of shigellosis are common. One study demonstrated that bacillary dysentery develops in 61% of the children younger than 1 year once an index case occurs in a household.[32] The attack rate was approximately 40% for those aged 1 to 4 years and 20% for all ages once an index case was identified. Secondary attack rates are increased in houses having privies and are reduced in families once sanitary toilet facilities are installed. Transmission rates also correlated with poverty and overcrowding. After a bout of shigellosis without antimicrobial therapy, fecal excretion of the infecting strain generally lasts 1 to 4 weeks. Long-term *Shigella* carriage has been well documented in a small percentage of cases and does not appear to correlate with any underlying intestinal dysfunction.[6,48] In contrast to typhoid and cholera carriers, the organisms in dysentery carriage are confined to a colonic site. In the absence of coexistent parasitic infestation of the intestine, these carriers generally respond to antimicrobial therapy. Long-term carriers may be important to the epidemiology of foodborne or waterborne illness. The number of organisms excreted by these persons is generally less than that seen in acute dysentery, and thus the disease in such individuals is less communicable than that in active cases.

DIAGNOSIS

History

Bacillary dysentery should be considered in any patient with acute diarrheal illness associated with toxemia and systemic symptoms, particularly when the illness lasts longer than 48 hours, if intrafamily spread occurs with an interval of 1 to 3 days between cases, if fever is present, and if blood or mucus is seen in stools. The occurrence of hyperpyrexia and seizures in infants and children with shigellosis has led some to the conclusion that a neurotoxin is important in the pathogenesis of clinical illness, although there is little to support this notion. In patients able to give a careful history, a descending intestinal tract infection is often described. The first symptoms may be fever and abdominal cramping, followed by voluminous watery stool (these findings correlate with a small bowel site of infection), a decrease in fever, and an increase in the number of stools with smaller volume ("fractional stools"). In a day or two, bloody mucoid stools with fecal urgency and tenesmus may develop. These latter findings reflect a colonic site of infection. It is this evolution in disease symptoms, as the infecting strain descends the intestinal tract, that often leads to a clinical diagnosis of bacillary dysentery and may indicate the need for performing stool culture. Abdominal pain and diarrhea occur in nearly all patients with shigellosis, fever can be documented in approximately one third of cases, and mucus is seen in the stools of half and gross blood in 40% of cases.[7]

Physical Examination

Findings on physical examination are nonspecific and include a variable degree of systemic toxemia, fever (which may be as high as 106° F), abdominal tenderness (especially over the lower abdominal quadrants), and hyperactive bowel sounds. Rectal examination or proctoscopy is generally painful, and an abnormally friable, hyperemic rectal mucosa, increased mucus secretion, and areas of ecchymosis are generally found. Ulcerations of rectal mucosa are seen after several days of illness.

Laboratory Findings

During the acute illness, the infecting strain is present in large enough numbers that stool cultures are generally positive. In the later stages of the disease, it may be necessary to culture material first in enrichment broth before plating. Culture of colonic or rectal biopsy does not improve the efficiency of stool culture in shigellosis.[49] The key to establishing the diagnosis of shigellosis is isolation of the organism from diarrheal stools. Laboratory identification of *Shigella* was discussed previously under "Isolation Techniques." In research centers where the service is available, direct fluorescent antibody microscopy may be useful in detecting the organism when present in small numbers,[50] but because of the numerous serotypes potentially responsible for the infection, this procedure does not have widespread application.

The total white blood cell count demonstrates no consistent findings, although leukopenia and brisk leukocytosis are seen on occasion. A "shift to the left" (an increased number of band cells in comparison to segmented neutrophils) when a leukocyte differential count is performed in a patient with diarrhea suggests bacillary dysentery. The single most important laboratory test other than stool culture is direct microscopic examination of a stained fecal smear, which will show prevalent polymorphonuclear leukocytes.[51] A wet mount preparation is made by adding stool (mucus if it is present) to an equal amount of methylene blue dye. The preparation is then covered with a coverslip and examined microscopically under the high dry objective. Alternatively, the specimen can be heat fixed before staining with dilute methylene blue. The specimen can then be examined under oil after drying. This dry preparation can be stored for later review. Numerous sheets of polymorphonuclear leukocytes are normally found in shigellosis and invasive *E. coli* diarrhea (Fig. 221-2). Prevalent leukocytes indicate a colitis in which the colonic mucosa is diffusely involved, or proctitis. The leukocyte test, when positive, indicates a pathologic process, not an etiologic one, and white cells are usually also seen in salmonellosis, *Campylobacter* enteritis, Shiga toxin-producing *E. coli* colitis, and idiopathic ulcerative colitis.

Serologic evaluation of a patient with bacillary dysentery is not generally helpful in establishing the diagnosis because humoral antibodies do not develop before recovery. Serologic procedures are helpful as an epidemiologic tool in defining the extent of an epidemic in a population known to be infected by a known *Shigella* serotype (especially the Shiga bacillus). The humoral antibody response correlates with the severity of clinical disease.[7]

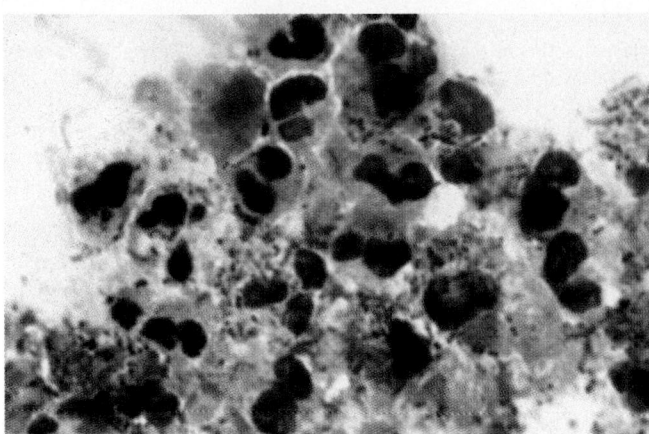

FIGURE 221-2. Methylene blue stain of fecal leukocytes taken from patient with colitis. This exudative response may be seen in shigellosis, salmonellosis, *Campylobacter* infection, and colitis due to invasive *Escherichia coli*.

TREATMENT AND CLINICAL COURSE

In certain patients with bacillary dysentery (particularly infants and older adult patients), significant dehydration may result from excessive fluid loss through diarrhea and vomiting. The fluid losses can generally be replaced by oral intake because the diarrhea associated with bacillary dysentery is not normally associated with profound fluid and electrolyte depletion. If vomiting or extreme toxemia is a prominent feature of the illness, especially in the very young or the very old, intravenous fluid replacement may be necessary.

Antibiotics are useful in the management of shigellosis and may be lifesaving. Because the infection is normally self-limited and because antibiotic resistance commonly develops in populations after prolonged use of drugs, some believe that antimicrobial therapy should be reserved for the most severely ill patients.[52] However, because the infection is generally transmitted from person to person and the infected or colonized person represents the major reservoir of infection, for public health reasons each patient with a positive stool culture or with known bacillary dysentery should be treated. The treatment of choice for shigellosis when susceptibility is unknown is a fluoroquinolone for adults. The specific drugs and doses are indicated in Table 221-2. Trimethoprim-sulfamethoxazole had been the treatment of choice for this enteric infection, but resistance has become widespread for strains of *Shigella*.[53-55] Antibiotic resistance is a growing problem for enteric bacterial pathogens. It has occurred as a result of plasmid or transposon transmission or in epidemic spread by chromosome-mediated mobile genetic elements (integrons) in horizontal transfer of antibacterial resistance.[56] Although 3-day therapy is generally recommended in shigellosis, single-dose fluoroquinolones may be given for milder forms of shigellosis.[57] For children, a variety of drugs may be used. Cephalosporins have become a common form of treatment of pediatric shigellosis.[58-60] Although not approved for use in children, short-course fluoroquinolones can be safely used.[61] Amdinocillin, an unlicensed drug, has been used in Bangladesh for shigellosis.[61,64] Azithromycin has been used successfully for treatment of multidrug-resistant *Shigella* infection in adults.[62,63] and should be useful in the management of pediatric shigellosis. The poorly absorbed rifamycin derivative rifaximin has been shown to be effective in treating other forms of bacterial diarrhea[64] and is likely to be effective in the treatment of milder forms of shigellosis. Nalidixic acid may be helpful in the management of pediatric shigellosis.[65] Although most of the drugs listed in Table 221-2 for treating shigellosis in adults and children are not approved for use in this disease, short-course therapy should be effective and safe.

Intestinal motility patterns may be important in recovery from infection, as well as in preventing mucosal invasion by a bacterial agent. In such cases, diarrhea might be viewed as a protective mechanism,

TABLE 221-2 Antibacterial Therapy for Patients with Shigellosis

Adults		Children	
Agent	**Dosage**	**Agent**	**Dose**
Levofloxacin	500 mg qd × 3 day	Ceftriaxone*	50 mg/kg IV once a day (maximum, 2 g/day) × 5 day
Ciprofloxacin	500 mg bid × 3 day	Cefixime*	8 mg/kg/day as single daily dose or divided q 12 hr × 5 day
Norfloxacin	400 mg bid × 3 day	Azithromycin*	10 mg/kg/day once a day × 3 day
Azithromycin	500 mg qd × 3 day	Rifaximin*,†	100 mg tid × 3 day
Rifaximin†	200 mg tid × 3 day	Ciprofloxacin*	25 mg/kg/day divided q 12 hr × 3-5 day

*Not approved for use in children.
†Currently unlicensed in the United States; available in countries of Europe and in Mexico; probably not effective for dysenteric disease.

and its inhibition by motility-active drugs may not be wise. Paregoric has occasionally been shown to worsen clinical salmonellosis,[66] and in occasional patients, antidiarrheal drugs such as diphenoxylate (Lomotil) worsen bacillary dysentery and could play a role in the development of toxic dilatation of the colon.[67] In dysenteric diarrhea, the antimotility drugs may be safely given if effective antimicrobial drugs are also administered.[68]

Clinical illness, if left untreated, generally lasts between 1 day and 1 month, with an average of 7 days. Although mortality is unusual in shigellosis except in malnourished children and older adults, the clinical illness is more striking and more likely to lead to hospitalization than are most other forms of infectious diarrhea. Complications, which are unusual, generally consist of severe dehydration, febrile seizures, septicemia or pneumonia from coliform organisms (and less commonly the infecting *Shigella* strain), keratoconjunctivitis, immune complex acute glomerulonephritis, and hemolytic uremic syndrome. A post-*Shigella* reactive arthritis (Reiter's syndrome) may develop in patients with HLA-B27 histocompatibility antigen and infection by group B *Shigella* (*S. flexneri*). *S. dysenteriae* 1 (the Shiga bacillus) characteristically produces a more serious form of diarrhea, and the mortality associated with untreated disease during epidemics may be as high as 20%. Bacterial strains that produce Shiga toxin (*S. dysenteriae* 1 and *E. coli* in hemorrhagic colitis) may produce the hemolytic-uremic syndrome as a complication of illness. Now that oral rehydration therapy has reduced the incidence of most cases of dehydration-associated deaths from diarrhea, shigellosis represents the most important form of fatal enteric illness in areas of high endemicity.[69] A rare fulminating form of bacillary dysentery secondary to massive small intestine invasion by the infecting bacteria is seen in children, and death early in infection is common (the "Ikari" syndrome).[69a]

CONTROL

Environmental Control

A safe water supply is important for the control of shigellosis and is probably the single most important factor in areas with substandard sanitation facilities.[70] Chlorination is another factor important in decreasing the incidence of all enteric bacterial infections. Of critical importance to the establishment of a safe water supply system are the general level of sanitation in the area and the establishment of an effective sewage disposal system. Insecticides are useful in decreasing the vector population during peak seasons, and a decrease in the incidence of shigellosis, but not salmonellosis, may be seen after their use.[33] At other times of the year, it may be helpful to attack breeding places of insects. Garbage collection and disposal of excreta and sewage may also be useful in controlling the vectors.

In many areas of the developing world, it is necessary to examine the techniques of home preparation and storage of food. Important features may be improved, such as personal and food hygienic facilities, or refrigeration may be necessary. A major prerequisite in transmission in most cases of bacillary dysentery is the degree of contact and the level of personal hygiene between patients with disease and susceptible persons. Other factors are frequent and effective hand washing, voluntary removal of persons with diarrhea from roles as food handlers, and appropriate refrigeration and proper cooking of potentially infected foods. Breast-feeding is an important means of decreasing the incidence of bacillary dysentery in developing countries and in communities with substandard hygienic practices. Also, mothers should be taught how to prepare foods to supplement breast-feeding and to constitute the diet after weaning to improve both sanitation and nutrition. Finally, cases of diarrhea should be adequately diagnosed and patients isolated, and antimicrobial therapy should be instituted in cases of bacillary dysentery to decrease the reservoir of virulent strains. The degree of symptomatology, personal hygiene, and education about ways that enteric bacteria can be spread are important factors that may determine the rate of transmission of the agent, and these factors should influence the decision for antimicrobial therapy.

Immunologic Control

Epidemiologic studies have indicated that a degree of homologous immunity can be demonstrated in those who have recovered from bacillary dysentery.[71-73] These observations have supported the idea that a protective vaccine might be developed. It was shown that killed parenteral vaccines fail to protect animals against experimentally produced shigellosis[74] and to protect humans against naturally occurring illness.[75,76] Besredka[76] suggested that the immunity against bacillary dysentery conferred by one attack of the disease was essentially the result of sensitization of the intestinal mucosa to dysentery bacilli and that the antibodies circulating in serum had a small role or none at all in protection. After more than 80 years, Besredka's concept of intestinal immunity is still held as the primary mode through which immunologic control might be feasible. The nature of the intestinal immune response has not been completely characterized. In natural shigellosis, IgA concentrations in stool increase, as do anti-*Shigella* secretory IgA antibodies directed to homologous lipopolysaccharide.[77] Also, lymphocytes, monocytes, and granulocytes, in the absence of complement but in the presence of antibody, may serve an anti-*Shigella* function through cell-mediated mechanisms.[78] Formal and co-workers worked with both spontaneously derived avirulent *Shigella* mutants and hybrid strains (*Shigella-E. coli*) in monkeys.[79-81]

The most successful outcome in the area of *Shigella* vaccine development was achieved by Mel and colleagues, who used streptomycin-dependent mutant strains of *Shigella* as orally administered immunizing agents in Yugoslavian army soldiers and in children living in areas of hyperendemicity.[82,83] These workers demonstrated that immunization with a live-attenuated bacterial strain given orally in multiple (at least four) doses would prevent clinical disease but would not alter the carrier status, provided that gastric acidity was first decreased by sodium bicarbonate swallowed just before the vaccine. Serotype-specific protection followed vaccination and lasted for at least 6 months, and the immunizing agent remained protective when combined as a bivalent preparation. Experiments in volunteers demonstrated that the protective immunity imparted by oral immunization approximated that after recovery from disease.[84]

In the future, immunologic control may be possible against a limited number of serotypes of shigellae when attack rates are shown to be particularly high. Further research is being directed toward developing an immunizing strain that multiplies in the intestinal tract so that fewer doses need to be administered. It may be possible to create such a strain by intergeneric hybridization.[85] Attenuated bacteria can be constructed that are better adapted to host intestinal proliferation and that combine multiple serotypes. Avirulent mutants and bioengineered strains may produce anti-*Shigella* immunity. Conjugate *Shigella* vaccines are also being evaluated. It is possible that antitoxin immunity might be important to susceptibility and that a successful immunizing agent should also include a toxoid component.

REFERENCES

1. Osler W. On the amebae coli in dysentery and in dysentery liver abscess. Johns Hopkins Hosp Bull. 1890;1:736.
2. Councilman WT, Lafleur HA. Amebic dysentery. Johns Hopkins Hosp Rep. 1891;2:395.
3. Shiga K. Observations on the epidemiology of dysentery in Japan. Philippine J Sci. 1906;1:485.
4. Flexner S. On the etiology of tropical dysentery. Philadelphia Med J. 1900;6:417.
5. Rogers L. Bacillary dysentery. In: Dysenteries, Their Differentiation and Treatment. London: Oxford University Press; 1913:268.
6. Davison WC. A bacteriological and clinical consideration of bacillary dysentery in adults and children. Medicine (Baltimore). 1922;1:389.
7. DuPont H, Hornick R, Dawkins A, et al. The response of man to virulent *Shigella flexneri* 2a. J Infect Dis. 1969;119:396.
8. Sereny B. Experimental shigella keratoconjunctivitis: A preliminary report. Acta Microbiol Acad Sci Hung. 1955;2:293.
9. Riley LW, Remis RS, Helgerson SD, et al. Hemorrhagic colitis associated with a rare *Escherichia coli* serotype. N Engl J Med. 1983;308:681.
10. DuPont HL, Levine MM, Hornick RB, et al. Inoculum size in shigellosis and implications for expected mode of transmission. J Infect Dis. 1989;159:1126.
11. Evans CAW, Gilman RH, Rabbani GH, et al. Gastric acid secretion and enteric infection in Bangladesh. Trans R Soc Trop Med Hyg. 1997;91:681-685.
12. Gorden J, Small PLC. Acid resistance in enteric bacteria. Infect Immun. 1993;61:364-367.
13. Bagamboula CF, Uyttendaele M, Debevere J. Acid tolerance of *Shigella sonnei* and *Shigella flexneri*. J Appl Microbiol. 2002;93:479-486.
14. DuPont HL, Formal SB, Hornick RB, et al. Pathogenesis of *Escherichia coli* diarrhea. N Engl J Med 1971;285:1-9.
15. LaBrec E, Schneider H, Magnani T, et al. Epithelial cell penetration as an essential step in the pathogenesis of bacillary dysentery. J Bacteriol. 1964;88:1503.
16. Sasakawa C, Kamata K, Sakai T, et al. Virulence-associated genetic regions comprising 31 kilobases of the 230-kilobase plasmid in *Shigella flexneri* 2a. J Bacteriol. 1988;170:2480-2484.
17. Sansonetti PJ. Rupture, invasion and inflammatory destruction of the intestinal barrier by *Shigella*, making sense of prokaryote-eukaryote cross-talk. FEMS Microbiol Rev. 2001;25:3-14.
18. Sansonetti PJ, Van Nhieu GT, Egile C. Rupture of the intestinal barrier and mucosal invasion by *Shigella flexneri*. Clin Infect Dis. 1999;28:466-475.
19. Hueck CJ. Type III protein secretion systems in bacterial pathogens of animals and plants. Microbiol Mol Biol Rev. 1998;62:379-433.
20. Cheng LW, Schneewind O. Type III machines of gram-negative bacteria: Delivering the goods. Trends Microbiol. 2000;8:214-220.
21. Galan JE, Collmer A. Type III secretion machines: Bacterial devices for protein delivery into host cells. Science. 1999;284:1322-1328.
22. Tran Van Nhieu G, Bourdet-Sicard R, Dumenil G, et al. Bacterial signals and cell responses during *Shigella* entry into epithelial cells. Cell Microbiol. 2000;2:187-193.
23. Mavris M, Sansonetti PJ, Parsot C. Identification of the *cis*-acting site involved in activation of promoters regulated by the type III secretion apparatus in *Shigella flexneri*. J Bacteriol. 2002;184:6751-6759.
24. Page AL, Sansonetti P, Parsot C. Spa15 of *Shigella flexneri*, a third type of chaperone in the type III secretion pathway. Mol Microbiol. 2002;43:1533-1542.
25. Stuber K, Frey J, Burnens AP, Kuhnert P. Detection of type III secretion genes as a general indicator of bacterial virulence. Mol Cell Probes. 2003;17:25-32
26. Keusch GT, Grady GF, Mata LJ, et al. Pathogenesis of shigella diarrhea: I. Enterotoxin production by *Shigella dysenteriae* 1. J Clin Invest. 1972;51:1212.
27. Keusch GT, Grady GF, Takeuchi A, et al. Pathogenesis of shigella diarrhea: II. Enterotoxin-induced acute enteritis in the rabbit ileum. J Infect Dis. 1972;126:92.
28. O'Brien AD, Newland JW, Miller RK, et al. Shiga-like toxin-converting phages from *Escherichia coli* strains that cause hemorrhagic colitis or infantile diarrhea. Science. 1984;226:694.
29. Speelman P, Kabir I, Islam M. Distribution and spread of shigellosis: A colonic study. J Infect Dis. 1984;150:899-903.
30. Raqib R, Wretlind B, Anderson J, et al. Cytokine secretion in acute shigellosis is correlated to disease activity and directed more to stool than to plasma. J Infect Dis. 1995;171:376.
31. Greenberg DE, Jiang ZD, Steffen R, et al. Markers of inflammation in bacterial diarrhea among travelers, with a focus on enteroaggregative *Escherichia coli* pathogenicity. J Infect Dis. 2002;185:944-949.
32. Hardy A, Watt J. Studies of the acute diarrheal diseases: XVIII. Epidemiology. Public Health Rep. 1948;63:363.
33. Watt J, Lindsay D. Diarrheal disease control studies: I. Effect of fly control in a high morbidity area. Public Health Rep. 1948;63:1319.
34. Kostrzewski J, Stypulkowska-Misiurewicz H. Changes in the epidemiology of dysentery in Poland and the situation in Europe. Arch Immunol Ther Exp. 1968;16:429.
35. Kotloff KL, Winickoff JP, Ivanoff B, et al. Global burden of *Shigella* infections: Implications for vaccine development an implementation of control strategies. Bull WHO. 1999;77:651-666.
36. Cruickshank R. Diarrheal diseases in the United Kingdom. In: Pemberton J, ed. Epidemiology Reports on Research and Teaching. London: Oxford University Press; 1963:60.
37. Gordon J, Behar M, Scrimshaw N. Acute diarrheal disease in less developed countries: I. An epidemiological basis for control. In: Control of Gastrointestinal Diseases. Pan-American Health Organization, Technical Discussion, Science Publication. 1963;100:26.
38. Ingram V, Rights F, Khan H, et al. Diarrhea in children of West Pakistan: Occurrence of bacterial and parasitic agents. Am J Trop Med Hyg. 1966;15:743.
39. Ramos-Alvarez M, Olarte J. Diarrheal diseases of children: The occurrence of enteropathogenic viruses and bacteria. Am J Dis Child. 1964;107:218.
40. Haltalin K. Neonatal shigellosis: Report of 16 cases and review of the literature. Am J Dis Child. 1967;114:603.
41. Mata L, Urrutia J, Garcia B, et al. *Shigella* infection in breast-fed Guatemalan Indian neonates. Am J Dis Child. 1969;117:142.
42. Boyce JM, Hughes JM, Alim AR, et al. Patterns of *Shigella* infection in families in rural Bangladesh. Am J Trop Med Hyg. 1982;31:1015.
43. Tjoa WS, DuPont HL, Sullivan P, et al. Location of food consumption and travelers' diarrhea. Am J Epidemiol. 1977;106:61.
44. Felson J. Bacillary Dysentery Colitis and Enteritis. Philadelphia: WB Saunders; 1945.
45. Donadio J, Gangarosa E. Foodborne shigellosis. J Infect Dis. 1969;119:666.
46. Lee SH, Levy DA, Craun GF, et al. Surveillance for waterborne-disease outbreaks—United States, 1999-2000. Morb Mortal Wkly Rep MMWR. 2002;51(SS08):1-47.
47. DuPont H, Hornick R. Clinical approach to infectious diarrheas. Medicine (Baltimore). 1973;52:265.
48. Levine M, DuPont H, Khodabandelou M, et al. Long-term shigella-carrier state. N Engl J Med. 1973;288:1169.
49. Barbut F, Beaugerie L, Dalas N, et al. Comparative value of colonic biopsy and intraluminal fluid culture for diagnosis of bacterial acute colitis in immunocompetent patients. Clin Infect Dis. 1999;29:356-360.
50. Thomason B, Cowart G, Cherry W. Current status of immunofluorescence techniques for rapid detection of shigellae in fecal specimens. Appl Microbiol. 1965;13:605.
51. Harris J, DuPont H, Hornick R. Fecal leukocytes in diarrheal illness. Ann Intern Med. 1972;76:697.
52. Weissman J, Gangarosa E, DuPont H, et al. Changing needs in the antimicrobial therapy of shigellosis. J Infect Dis. 1973;127:611.
53. Murray BE. Resistance of *Shigella, Salmonella*, and other selected enteric pathogens to antimicrobial agents. Rev Infect Dis. 1986;8(Suppl):S172.
54. Replogle ML, Fleming DW, Cieslak PR. Emergence of antimicrobial-resistant shigellosis in Oregon. Clin Infect Dis. 2000;30:515-519.
55. Flores A, Araque M, Vizcaya L. Multiresistant *Shigella* species isolated from pediatric patients with acute diarrheal disease. Am J Med Sci. 1998;316:379-384.
56. McIver CJ, White PA, Jones LA, et al. Epidemic strains of *Shigella sonnei* biotype g carrying integrons. J Clin Microbiol. 2002;40:1538-1540.
57. Bennish ML, Salam MA, Khan WA, et al. Treatment of shigellosis: III. Comparison of one- or two-dose ciprofloxacin with standard 5-day therapy: A randomized, blinded trial. Ann Intern Med. 1992;117:727.
58. Kabir I, Butler T, Khanam A. Comparative efficacies of single intravenous doses of ceftriaxone and ampicillin for shigellosis in a placebo-controlled trial. Antimicrob Agents Chemother. 1986;29:645-648.
59. Ashkenazi S, Amir J, Waisman Y, et al. A randomized, double-blind study comparing cefixime and trimethoprim-sulfamethoxazole in the treatment of childhood shigellosis. J Pediatr. 1993;123:817-821.
60. Varsano I, Eidlitz-Marcus T, Nussinovitch M, Elian I. Comparative efficacy of ceftriaxone and ampicillin for treatment of severe shigellosis in children. J Pediatr. 1991; 118:627-632.
61. Salam MA, Dhar U, Khan WA, Bennish ML. Randomized comparison of ciprofloxacin suspension and pivmecillinam for childhood shigellosis. Lancet. 1998;352:522-527.
62. Khan WA, Seas C, Dhar U, et al. Treatment of shigellosis: V. Comparison of azithromycin and ciprofloxacin: A double-blind, randomized, controlled trial. Ann Intern Med. 1997;126:697.
63. Shanks GD, Smoak BL, Aleman GM, et al. Single dose azithromycin or three-day course of ciprofloxacin as therapy for epidemic dysentery in Kenya. Clin Infect Dis. 1999;29:942-943.
64. DuPont HL, Jiang Z-D, Ericsson CD, et al. Rifaximin versus ciprofloxacin for the treatment of traveler's diarrhea: A randomized, double-blind clinical trial. Clin Infect Dis. 2001;33:1807-1815.
65. Salam MA, Bennish ML. Therapy for shigellosis. I. Randomized, double-blind trial of nalidixic acid in childhood shigellosis. J Pediatr. 1988;113:901-907.
66. Sprinz H. Pathogenesis of intestinal infections. Arch Pathol. 1969;87:556.
67. DuPont H, Hornick R. Adverse effects of Lomotil therapy in shigellosis. JAMA. 1973;226:1525.
68. Murphy GS, Bodhidatta L, Echeverria P, et al. Ciprofloxacin and loperamide in the treatment of bacillary dysentery. Ann Intern Med. 1993;118:582-586.
69. Butler T, Islam M, Azad AK, et al. Causes of death in diarrhoeal diseases after rehydration therapy: An autopsy study of 140 patients in Bangladesh. Bull World Health Organ. 1987;65:317.
69a.Shiga K. The trend of prevention, therapy and epidemiology of dysentery since the discovery of its causative organism. N Engl J Med. 1936;215:1205-1211.
70. Nyerges V, Eng N. Plan for the control of gastrointestinal diseases: Environmental sanitation, epidemiology, health education and early diagnosis and treatment. In: Control of Gastrointestinal Diseases. Pan-American Health Organization, Technical Discussion, Science Publication. 1963;100:36.
71. Cruickshank R. Acquired immunity: Bacterial infections. In: Cruickshank R, ed. Modern Trends in Immunology. Washington, DC: Butterworth; 1963:119.

72. DuPont H, Gangarosa E, Reller L, et al. Shigellosis in custodial institutions. Am J Epidemiol. 1970;92:172.

73. Hardy A, Watt J. The acute diarrheal diseases. JAMA. 1944;124:1173.

74. Formal S, Maenza R, Austin S, et al. Failure of parenteral vaccines to protect monkeys against experimental shigellosis. Proc Soc Exp Biol Med. 1967;125:347.

75. Hardy A, DeCapito T, Halbert S. Studies of acute diarrheal diseases: XIX. Immunization in shigellosis. Public Health Rep. 1948;63:685.

76. Besredka A. On the mechanism of dysenteric infection, antidysenteric vaccination per os, and the nature of antidysenteric immunity. Ann Inst Pasteur Paris. 1919;33:301.

77. Winsor DK Jr, Mathewson JJ, DuPont HL. Comparison of serum and fecal antibody responses of patients with naturally acquired *Shigella sonnei* infection. J Infect Dis. 1988;158:1108.

78. Lowell GH, MacDermott RP, Summers PL, et al. Antibody-dependent cell-mediated antibacterial activity: K lymphocytes, monocytes, and granulocytes are effective against shigella. J Immunol. 1980;125:2778.

79. Formal S, LaBrec E, Palmer A, et al. Protection of monkeys against experimental shigellosis with attenuated vaccines. J Bacteriol. 1965;90:63.

80. Formal S, Kent T, Austin S, et al. Fluorescent-antibody and histological study of vaccinated and control monkeys challenged with *Shigella flexneri.* J Bacteriol. 1966;91:2368.

81. Formal S, Kent T, May H, et al. Protection of monkeys against experimental shigellosis with a living attenuated oral polyvalent dysentery vaccine. J Bacteriol. 1966; 92:17.

82. Mel D, Arsic B, Nikolic B, et al. Studies on vaccination against bacillary dysentery: 4. Oral immunization with live monotypic and combined vaccines. Bull World Health Organ. 1968;39:375.

83. Mel D, Gangarosa E, Radovanovic M, et al. Studies on vaccination against bacillary dysentery: 6. Protection of children by oral immunization with streptomycin-dependent *Shigella* strains. Bull World Health Organ. 1971;45:457.

84. DuPont HL, Hornick RB, Snyder MJ, et al. Immunity in shigellosis: II. Protection induced by oral live vaccine or primary infection. J Infect Dis. 1972;125:12-16.

85. Baron LS, Kopecko DJ, Formal SB, et al. Introduction of *Shigella flexneri* 2a type and group antigen genes into oral typhoid vaccine strain *Salmonella typhi* Ty21A. Infect Immun. 1987;55:2797.

Haemophilus Infections

TIMOTHY F. MURPHY

HAEMOPHILUS INFLUENZAE

Description of the Pathogen

Haemophilus influenzae is a small, nonmotile, non–spore-forming bacterium and a pathogen of humans found principally in the upper respiratory tract, first reported by Pfeiffer in 1892. The sensational claim that it was the primary agent of epidemic influenza proved fallacious; nonetheless, it has a wide range of pathogenic potential. Its requirement for growth factors, which can be supplied by erythrocytes, accounts for the generic name *Haemophilus* (blood-loving). In microscopic appearance, it is a small (1×0.3 μm) gram-negative bacterium. Stained organisms obtained from clinical specimens vary microscopically from small coccobacilli to long filaments. This variable morphologic appearance (pleomorphism) and inconsistent uptake of dyes (e.g., safranin) may result in erroneous interpretations of stained smears.

Aerobic growth of *H. influenzae* requires two supplements known as X factor and V factor, although neither refers to a single substance. X factor can be supplied by heat-stable iron-containing pigments that supply protoporphyrins essential for catalases, peroxidases, and cytochromes of the electron transport chain. The requirement for X factor is used to distinguish *H. influenzae* from *Haemophilus parainfluenzae* (requires only V factor). Porphyrin-based assays represent the most reliable methods for identifying *Haemophilus* species.[1] Because X factor is not required for anaerobic growth of *H. influenzae*, confusion may arise if *H. influenzae* is grown anaerobically (e.g., after stab inoculation). The heat-labile V factor, a coenzyme, may be supplied by nicotinamide adenine dinucleotide, by nicotinamide adenine dinucleotide phosphate, or by nicotinamide nucleoside. Although present in erythrocytes, V factor must be released from the cell to sustain optimal growth, and thus standard blood agar is an unsatisfactory medium. *H. influenzae* exhibits satellitism around colonies of hemolytic *Staphylococcus aureus* (a source of V factor), and this technique may be used to identify *H. influenzae*. Superior culture results are obtained using media enriched with red blood cells that have been disrupted by heating (e.g., chocolate agar) or by peptide digestion (Fildes medium). Because excessive heat destroys V factor, commercial media must undergo quality control before use. Although it is not a strict requirement, some *H. influenzae* strains grow best in 5% to 10% carbon dioxide. Viability of *H. influenzae* is lost rapidly, so clinical specimens should be inoculated onto appropriate media without delay. A biotyping scheme devised by Kilian (based on indole production, urease, and ornithine decarboxylase activity) may be used to characterize individual isolates.[2] Biotype III includes *Haemophilus aegyptius*, the "Koch-Weeks bacillus." A clone of biotype IV strains is associated with neonatal and postpartum infections.

Colonies of *H. influenzae* are usually granular, transparent (or slightly opaque), circular, and dome-shaped. On chocolate agar, most colonies attain a size of about 0.5 to 0.8 mm during the first 24 hours of growth at 37° C, enlarging to 1.0 to 1.5 mm by 48 hours. Six serotypes, designated a to f, are based on antigenically distinct capsular polysaccharide types. Colonies of encapsulated strains are mucoid (iridescent when grown on transparent media and examined using an indirect source of light) and may attain a size of 3 to 4 mm. Capsular type b strains are important invasive pathogens in humans. Strains of *H. influenzae* that lack a polysaccharide capsule are generally referred to as nontypeable because they are nonreactive with typing antisera raised against each of the six capsules. The population structure of *H. influenzae* type b is clonal whereas nontypeable strains demonstrate substantial genetic diversity. Most unencapsulated isolates are not capsule-deficient variants of extant capsule clones; they are genetically distinct from encapsulated strains *H. influenzae*.

Epidemiology and Respiratory Tract Colonization

H. influenzae is recovered exclusively from humans; no other natural host is known. It is recovered from the upper airway and, rarely, the genital tract. Spread from one individual to another occurs by airborne droplets or by direct contact with secretions.

Exposure to nontypeable *H. influenzae* begins after birth so that from infancy onward carriage of one or more strains for periods of days to months is common; these organisms are often not eliminated by antibiotic therapy. Colonization of the respiratory tract is a dynamic process with new strains of nontypeable *H. influenzae* being acquired and cleared from the respiratory tract frequently.[3,4] Up to 80% of healthy persons are carriers of nontypeable *H. influenzae*. Children who attend daycare centers are colonized at a higher rate than control children.[5] Nasopharyngeal colonization by *H. influenzae* in the first year of life is associated with an increased risk of recurrent otitis media compared with children who remain free of colonization.[6,7]

Nontypeable *H. influenzae* frequently colonizes the lower respiratory tract in the setting of chronic obstructive pulmonary disease (COPD) and cystic fibrosis; multiple strains colonize the respiratory tract of these patients simultaneously.[8,9] Acquisition of new strains of nontypeable *H. influenzae* is associated with an increased risk of exacerbations of COPD.[10] Using selective media improves the recovery rate of *H. influenzae* from the sputum of patients with cystic fibrosis.[11]

Based on its binding to mucin and adherence to epithelial cells, *H. influenzae* has long been considered an extracellular pathogen. Several lines of evidence, however, now establish that *H. influenzae* has both an extracellular and an intracellular niche in the human respiratory tract.[12-15] Therefore, *H. influenzae* is present in the airway lumen, bound to mucin, adherent to respiratory cells, within the interstitium of the submucosa, and within cells of the respiratory tract. This observation has important implications for understanding the dynamics of colonization of the human respiratory tract and the human immune response to the bacterium.

TABLE 222-1 Comparison of Selected Features of Nontypeable and Type b Strains of *Haemophilus influenzae*

Feature	Nontypeable strains	Type b strains
Colonization rate in upper respiratory tract	30-80%	<1% in vaccinated populations; 2-4% in unvaccinated populations
Capsule	Unencapsulated	PRP capsule
Pathogenesis	Mucosal infections	Invasive infections
Clinical manifestations	Otitis media, exacerbations of COPD, sinusitis	Meningitis, epiglottitis, and other invasive infections in infants and children
Evolutionary history	Genetically diverse	Clonal
Vaccine	None available; under development	Highly effective PRP-conjugate vaccines

Before the widespread use of conjugate vaccines, type b strains colonized the nasopharynx of children at a rate of 2% to 4%. The rate of nasopharyngeal colonization by type b strains has decreased substantially with the use of conjugate vaccines to prevent invasive infections caused by *H. influenzae* type b. Table 222-1 summarizes several features of nontypeable and type b strains.

Pathogenesis

Otitis Media

The first step in the pathogenesis of infection is colonization of the upper respiratory tract. *H. influenzae* expresses a variety of adhesin molecules (Table 222-2), each of which has its own specificity for host receptors.[16] The prevalence and distribution of adhesins varies among nontypeable strains, suggesting that the pathogenic potential differs among strains.[17,18] In contrast to type b strains, which gain access to the blood stream, nontypeable strains cause disease by local invasion of mucosal surfaces. The pathogenesis of otitis media involves direct extension of bacteria from the nasopharynx to the middle ear via the eustachian tube.[19] Release of lipooligosaccharide, peptidoglycan fragments, and other antigens induces host inflammation.

Nontypeable *H. influenzae* is the second most common cause of acute otitis media, after *Streptococcus pneumoniae,* based on results of cultures of middle ear fluid obtained by tympanocentesis. Strains that cause otitis media are 3.7 times more likely than nasopharyngeal and throat strains isolated from healthy children to have the lipooligosaccharide biosynthesis gene *lic*2B, suggesting that lipooligosaccharide is a virulence factor in otitis media.[20] Nontypeable *H. influenzae* has also

TABLE 222-2 Adhesins of Haemophilus influenzae

Adhesin	Molecular Mass	Observation
Pili (fimbriae)	20–25 kDa	*hif*A-*hif*E gene cluster
HMW1 and HMW2	120–125 kDa	Homologous with filamentous hemagglutinin of *Bordetella pertussis.*
Hap	155 kDa	Homologous with IgA protease.
Hsf	~ 240 kDa	Surface fibrils. Present in type b strains. Homolog of Hia.
Hia	115 kDa	Hia is absent from strains that express HMW1 HMW2. Present in nontypeable strains.
OMP P5	~ 35 kDa	Binds mucin. Also called fimbrin. Homologous with OMP A of *Escherichia coli.*
OMP P2	36–42 kDa	Binds mucin.
PE binding adhesin	46 kDa	Binds phosphatidyl ethanolamine.
Lipooligosaccharide	2.5–3.3 kDa	Adhesin for respiratory epithelial cells.

been implicated as a cause of otitis media with effusion that refers to the presence of middle ear fluid in the absence of clinical signs of acute otitis media. In addition to positive cultures of some middle ear fluids, analysis by the PCR reveals the presence of microbial DNA and mRNA, suggesting that *H. influenzae* is present in a viable but nonculturable form in some cases of otitis media with effusion.[21-23] One hypothesis, supported by preliminary observations, is that *H. influenzae* may be present in the form of biofilms in the middle ear space.[24,25]

Exacerbations of COPD

The lower respiratory tract of adults with COPD is chronically colonized by nontypeable *H. influenzae.* The course of COPD is characterized by intermittent exacerbations of the disease. Several lines of evidence implicate *H. influenzae* as the most common bacterial cause of exacerbations, including bronchoscopic sampling of the lower respiratory tract during exacerbations, analysis of immune responses to *H. influenzae* isolated from patients experiencing exacerbations, correlation of airway inflammation with sputum bacteriology, and molecular analysis of prospectively collected isolates.[26,27] A complex host-pathogen interaction most likely determines the outcome of the acquisition of a new strain of nontypeable *H. influenzae;* the determinants include virulence of the strain, the host inflammatory response, preexisting immunity, the perception of symptoms, and other factors.

Invasive Infections Caused by *H. influenzae* Type b

The importance of the type b capsule as a critical virulence factor in the pathogenesis of invasive disease has been well established by the use of genetic techniques and an infant rat model of bacteremia and meningitis.[28] Mutants lacking the polyribitol ribose phosphate (PRP) capsule do not cause invasive disease whereas the isogenic parent strains are highly virulent in the infant rat model. The type b capsular polysaccharide is composed of PRP. The capsule enables the organism to invade the blood stream following colonization of the respiratory tract and is discussed below.

Immunity

Nontypeable *Haemophilus influenzae*

Immunity to infection by nontypeable *H. influenzae* is complex and not completely understood. A hallmark of infections caused by nontypeable *H. influenzae* is their propensity for recurrence. The immune response to surface antigens of nontypeable strains is intimately involved in the pathogenesis of recurrent infection. Studies in animal models, in adults with COPD, and in children with otitis media all demonstrate that the most prominent antibody response is directed at strain-specific determinants.[29-32] The clinical observation of recurrent infections in immunocompetent hosts (recurrent otitis media in children and recurrent exacerbations in COPD) suggests that strain-specific immune responses leave the host susceptible to recurrent infections by different strains of *H. influenzae.* A variety of membrane-associated, surface-exposed determinants are immunogenic and potential targets of protective host immune responses. For example, outer membrane protein P2, the major porin protein, contains immunodominant, strain-specific determinants on the bacterial surface. Adults with COPD make potentially protective antibodies to strain-specific determinants on P2 following infection. Patients remain susceptible to recurrent infections by other strains. Furthermore, the P2 genes of strains that colonize adults with COPD undergo point mutations in the human respiratory tract.[33,34] The mutations result in amino acid changes in the surface-exposed loops of the P2 molecule. A similar phenomenon has been observed with outer membrane protein P5.[35] These variants have a selective advantage and are able to evade the host response and cause recurrent or persistent infection.

The presence of serum bactericidal antibody is associated with protection from otitis media caused by nontypeable *H. influenzae.*[29,36] Because nontypeable *H. influenzae* causes mucosal infection, mucosal immunity likely plays a role in host defense; however, the mucosal immune response to *H. influenzae* is poorly understood. Finally, recent observations suggest that cell-mediated immune responses play a role in protection against infection.[37-39]

Haemophilus influenzae Type b

Protection against invasive *H. influenzae* type b infections is mediated by antibodies to the type b capsular polysaccharide PRP. Serum anti-PRP antibodies activate complement-mediated bactericidal and opsonic activity in vitro and mediate protective immunity against systemic infections in humans. The level of maternally acquired serum antibody to PRP declines after birth and reaches a nadir at approximately 18 to 24 months of age, the peak age incidence of meningitis caused by *H. influenzae* type b in an unimmunized child. The level of antibody to PRP then gradually rises, apparently as a result of exposure to *H. influenzae* type b or cross reacting antigens. Systemic disease is unusual after the age of 6 years even in the absence of immunization because of, at least in part, naturally acquired antibody to PRP.

Calculations of the minimal serum concentrations of anti-PRP antibody associated with protection against *H. influenzae* type b disease have been estimated to range from 0.04 to 1.00 μg/mL. These estimates must be interpreted cautiously, taking into account the functional variations (e.g., persistence, avidity of binding) of the different subclasses of anti-PRP antibodies. There is much individual variation in levels of anti-PRP antibodies; many adults lack detectable serum anti-PRP antibody but possess substantial serum bactericidal and opsonizing activity against type b organisms that is not directed at PRP. Thus, it has been evident for many years that naturally acquired protective immunity to type b disease is mediated by the eclectic activities of antibodies directed against both capsular and membrane antigens. Natural infection with type b organisms results in antibody responses to lipooligosaccharide and outer membrane proteins, and the protective potential of these antibodies has been shown in experimental infections.

Immunization with vaccines that are composed of PRP conjugated to carrier proteins afford protection by inducing antibodies to PRP. These vaccines are now used widely and are highly effective in preventing invasive disease caused by *H. influenzae* type b in infants and children.

Clinical Manifestations of Nontypeable *Haemophilus influenzae*

Otitis Media

Nontypeable *H. influenzae* accounts for about one quarter of all cases of acute otitis media.[40,41] Approximately 25 million episodes of otitis media occur annually in the United States. Although such episodes occur at any age, they are most common in children aged 6 months to 5 years. The typical clinical presentation of acute otitis media in infants is fever and irritability, whereas older children also complain of ear pain. A prior viral respiratory tract infection is commonly the antecedent of an episode of otitis media. The diagnosis is made by pneumatic otoscopy. A precise etiologic diagnosis requires tympanocentesis, but this is not performed routinely.

Exacerbations of Chronic Obstructive Pulmonary Disease

The course of COPD is characterized by intermittent exacerbations of the disease. It is estimated that approximately half of exacerbations are caused by bacteria and nontypeable *H. influenzae* is the most common bacterial cause.[26,27] The three cardinal signs of an exacerbation are an increase from baseline of sputum production, sputum purulence (change in sputum color), and dyspnea. Fever is generally absent or low grade and infiltrates are not present on chest radiography. A sputum Gram strain often reveals abundant gram-negative coccobacilli.

Community-Acquired Pneumonia

Nontypeable *H. influenzae* is an important cause of pneumonia in adults, particularly in the elderly and those with COPD and acquired immunodeficiency syndrome.[42-45] The clinical features are indistinguishable from those of pneumonia caused by other bacteria and in-

clude fever, cough, and purulent sputum, usually of several days' duration. The chest film reveals infiltrates that may be patchy or show lobar distribution. A Gram-stained smear of the sputum shows a predominance of small, gram-negative coccobacilli.

Acute Respiratory Tract Infections in Children in Developing Countries

In many countries in which adverse socioeconomic circumstances are prevalent, acute pneumonia in infants caused by nontypeable *H. influenzae* is a major cause of morbidity and mortality.[46-49] Carefully performed studies in several developing countries have established that nontypeable *H. influenzae* accounts for a significant proportion of pneumonia. The importance of acute respiratory tract infections as a major global health problem has led to the establishment of international programs (e.g., through the World Health Organization), with the aim of enhancing the recognition, appropriate management, and prevention of respiratory tract infections.

Sinusitis

Studies that have used cultures of direct sinus aspirates show that nontypeable *H. influenzae* is a common cause of acute maxillary sinusitis.[50-52] Patients experience nasal obstruction, purulent nasal discharge, headache, and facial pain. As in the case of otitis media, an invasive procedure (sinus aspiration) is required to establish an etiologic diagnosis.

Neonatal and Maternal Sepsis

Neonatal sepsis caused by nontypeable *H. influenzae* has been recognized with increasing frequency since the 1980s.[53] The infection is associated with 50% mortality and 90% mortality in premature infants. Many strains that cause neonatal sepsis are biotype IV and share several genotypic and phenotypic characteristics with one another. Indeed, studies of the genetic relationships of these potentially invasive strains and other nontypeable strains suggest that the invasive biotype IV strains represent a new species.

These same biotype IV strains also cause postpartum sepsis associated with endometritis. Nontypeable *H. influenzae* is a well-documented cause of tuboovarian abscess or chronic salpingitis. Diagnosis is established by tubal cultures at laparoscopy or cultures of peritoneal fluid by culdocentesis.

Bacteremia and Invasive Infections

Although the most common clinical manifestations of infections by nontypeable *H. influenzae* are otitis media and nonbacteremic respiratory tract infections in adults, the organism also occasionally causes bacteremia. Population-based studies estimate an incidence of 1.7 cases of invasive disease caused by *H. influenzae* per 100,000 adults and, overall, the incidence is highest among the elderly.[54] The majority of adults with bacteremia have underlying conditions such as alcoholism, cardiopulmonary disease, or cancer. The respiratory tract is the usual source of infection when bacteremia is present. Bacteremic infections caused by nontypeable *H. influenzae* are associated with significant mortality.

Nontypeable *H. influenzae* is also an unusual cause of a variety of invasive infections that are documented by case reports and small series. Indeed, all the invasive diseases that are commonly caused by type b *H. influenzae* are, on occasion, caused by nontypeable strains as well as types a, c, d, e, and f. These infections include adult epiglottitis, empyema, septic arthritis, cellulitis, osteomyelitis, pericarditis, cholecystitis, intra-abdominal infection, and vascular graft infection.

Conjunctivitis

Nontypeable *H. influenzae* is an important cause of purulent conjunctivitis and, in contrast to the sporadic nature of other *Haemophilus* infections, can occur in outbreaks, particularly in daycare centers. Clinical features include conjunctival hyperemia and purulent discharge. Occasionally, nontypeable *H. influenzae* causes severe conjunctivitis that is characterized by copious, purulent discharge, lid edema, chemoses, and keratitis.

Clinical Manifestations of *Haemophilus influenzae* Type B

Meningitis

Meningitis is the most serious acute manifestation of systemic infection caused by *H. influenzae*. Antecedent symptoms of upper respiratory infection are common. Specific questioning concerning the occurrence of disease in contacts (household, daycare centers) is prudent. None of the clinical features of meningitis caused by *H. influenzae* distinguishes it from other forms of purulent meningitis. The peak age incidence varies somewhat among populations depending in part on vaccine use, but this infection now occurs most often in incompletely immunized individuals. Adult cases are infrequent and often have a background of recent or remote head trauma, prior neurosurgery, paranasal sinusitis, otitis, or cerebrospinal fluid leak. *H. influenzae* meningitis in neonates is also rare, but such cases can resemble early-onset group B streptococcal infection. The most common signs are fever and altered central nervous system function, but the young child may have few specific signs, and nuchal rigidity is often absent. More obvious manifestations, such as seizures or coma, commonly develop as the disease progresses. The disease may be fulminating in onset, with death occurring in a few hours, usually in a child younger than 1 year. However, the more usual pattern consists of several days of mild illness (e.g., upper respiratory tract infection) followed by an ominous deterioration. Subdural effusions are a common complication. Clinical suspicion should be greatest when after 2 or 3 days of adequate therapy, there is a tense anterior fontanelle, seizures (particularly if focal), hemiparesis, or neurologic deterioration. In older children, one looks for papilledema and altered mental status.

With appropriate management, the overall mortality rate from *H. influenzae* meningitis is less than 5%, but apparently permanent sequelae occur in many of the survivors.

Epiglottitis

Acute respiratory obstruction caused by a cellulitis of the supraglottic tissues is a potentially lethal disease with a characteristically fulminating onset. Swelling of the epiglottis and aryepiglottic folds with complete obliteration of the vallecular and piriform sinuses is typical. Usually, the patient is a child (aged 2 to 7 years), but occurrence in adults is also well known. The onset is often explosive, initial features being sore throat, fever, and dyspnea progressing rapidly to dysphagia, pooling of oral secretions, and drooling of saliva from the mouth. The child is restless, anxious, and adopts a sitting position, with neck extended and chin protruding to reduce airway obstruction. Abrupt deterioration commonly occurs within a few hours, resulting in death in the absence of adequate treatment. Although these sudden deaths are the result in many instances of airway obstruction, fatal collapse may also result from less well defined mechanisms associated with acute sepsis. In some cases, the course may be less dramatic, with a prodromal illness of sore throat and hoarseness for 24 hours to 7 days preceding the onset of acute symptoms. The characteristic findings are seen above the larynx. The epiglottis is red and swollen and bears a striking resemblance to a bright red cherry obstructing the pharynx at the base of the tongue. This disorder can produce considerable local edema as a result of the loose texture of the submucosa on the lingual aspect of the epiglottis. The trachea appears normal. Examination of the larynx should be performed only in a setting in which an airway can be placed, because this examination, if injudiciously performed, may lead to fatal respiratory obstruction.

Pneumonia and Empyema

The true frequency of primary lung infections caused by *H. influenzae* b in children is difficult to determine with accuracy. Typically, the patient is between 4 months and 4 years of age and becomes ill in winter or spring, presenting with a consolidative pneumonia (often with pleural involvement) that is severe enough to require hospitalization. The only clinical feature that tends to distinguish *H. influenzae* pneumonia from bacterial pneumonias caused by *S. aureus* or *Streptococcus pneumoniae* is a more insidious onset. The development of severe dyspnea, tachycardia, and evidence of cardiovascular failure suggests pericarditis, an uncommon but important complication. Many have stressed the frequency with which primary pneumonia is accompanied by evidence of infection elsewhere (e.g., meningitis, epiglottitis, otitis).

Cellulitis

Cellulitis is predominantly seen in young children. The clinical features are fever and a raised, warm, tender area of distinctive reddish blue hue, most often located on one cheek or in the periorbital region. The distinctive color, its location, and age of the child should suggest the cause. The soft tissue involvement progresses rapidly over a few hours. Some of these children have, or develop, evidence of other septic foci (e.g., meningitis), because an accompanying bacteremia is extremely common.

Bacteremia Without Localized Disease

Children, particularly those 6 to 36 months of age, may acquire bacteremia without evidence of local disease; *S. pneumoniae* is the most common cause of this syndrome. Typically, fever, anorexia, and lethargy prompt the visit to a physician; the examination is nondiagnostic. This condition is appreciated most often in those with a temperature higher than 102° F (39° C) and an increased peripheral neutrophil count. Children with sickle cell disease or with a previous splenectomy are particularly susceptible. Early diagnosis and therapy are critical because these individuals may worsen rapidly and experience septic shock or a localized purulent focus.

SEPTIC ARTHRITIS

H. influenzae is a common cause of septic arthritis in children younger than 2 years of age. Typically, there is involvement of a single large, weight-bearing joint (without osteomyelitis), displaying decreased mobility, pain on movement, and swelling. Positive cultures of blood and joint fluid are usual. However, the signs and symptoms may be more subtle; for example, septic arthritis is an important cause of prolonged fever and irritability (or prolonged antigenemia) during the treatment of other systemic *H. influenzae* diseases (e.g., meningitis). In this context, culture-negative, antigen-positive joint fluid is common.

Response to systemic antibiotics is dramatic and often curative, but long-term follow-up is important because residual joint dysfunction occurs in a significant percentage of children.

H. influenzae septic arthritis also occurs in adults. A review of 29 adults with *H. influenzae* arthritis found that 14 had multiarticular disease and 15 monoarticular disease, with 6 being in the knee only.[55] Nineteen had extra-articular infection as well, including meningitis, pneumonia, sinusitis, and cellulitis. Twenty-two had predisposing factors such as alcohol abuse, trauma, rheumatoid arthritis, systemic lupus erythematosus, diabetes mellitus, splenectomy, multiple myeloma, lymphoma, or common variable hypogammaglobulinemia.

Diagnosis
Nontypeable *Haemophilus influenzae*

Because nontypeable *H. influenzae* is often present in the human upper airway in the absence of clinical disease, determining the etiologic pathogen in individual patients is challenging. A diagnosis of otitis media is made by pneumatic otoscopy. Culture of middle ear fluid obtained by tympanocentesis would be required to determine the microbial etiology. However, because tympanocentesis is a relatively invasive procedure, empirical therapy with antibiotics is initiated based on predictions of the likely pathogens, which are known to be *Streptococcus pneumoniae*, nontypeable *H. influenzae*, and *Moraxella catarrhalis* determined by studies that have used cultures of middle ear fluid obtained by tympanocentesis. Judicious use of tympanocentesis in children with recurrent or refractory otitis media may be indicated to identify precisely the pathogen in difficult cases but this procedure is not used routinely.[41,56]

The etiology of exacerbations of COPD and community-acquired pneumonia in individual patients is difficult to determine. The presence of nontypeable *H. influenzae* in the sputum of patients experiencing an exacerbation of COPD or pneumonia is suggestive of the diagnosis but does not establish the organism as the pathogen because it may be present in the airways in the absence of disease. In selected clinical circumstances, bronchoscopy with the protected specimen brush may be indicated to determine an etiological diagnosis. However, empiric antibiotic therapy is often administered, the choice of antibiotic being guided by the results of studies employing invasive procedures to identify etiology. Nontypeable *H. influenzae* is the most common bacterial cause of exacerbations of COPD and causes a smaller proportion of cases of community-acquired pneumonia.

Isolating the organism from a blood culture unequivocally establishes the organism as etiologic. Although blood cultures are invaluable when positive, the majority of infections caused by nontypeable *H. influenzae* are not associated bacteremia so blood cultures are relatively insensitive.

Haemophilus influenzae Type b

A provisional diagnosis of meningitis, epiglottitis, facial cellulitis, or septic arthritis is usually prompted by the history and clinical findings. Confirmation requires microbiologic studies. A positive nasopharyngeal culture for *H. influenzae* is not helpful because of the high carriage rate among healthy persons. Cultures of blood, cerebrospinal fluid (CSF), and other normally sterile fluids (e.g., from joints or pleural, subdural, or pericardial spaces) are diagnostic and therefore—under the appropriate circumstances—mandatory. Even if antibiotic therapy has been started, the yield is sufficiently great to recommend that they be taken. Cultures of the inflamed epiglottis are generally positive but should be taken only when a functional airway can be guaranteed. Whenever feasible, specimens obtained for culture should also be Gram-stained, in about 70% of cases of meningitis, CSF smears reveal typical organisms. Detection of capsular antigen in serum, CSF, or concentrated urine using immunoelectrophoresis, latex agglutination, or enzyme-linked immunosorbent assay may be diagnostic and can be made in up to 90% of culture-proven cases of meningitis. Despite the widespread distribution of immunologically cross-reactive antigens among bacteria in nature, false-positive reactions are uncommon. Antigen is also often detected in infected pleural, pericardial, or joint fluid and can facilitate diagnosis because it persists after antibiotic therapy. The concentration of PRP in serum or spinal fluid and the duration of antigenemia also provide prognostic information on the clinical outcome and course of the disease.

Treatment

Nontypeable Haemophilus influenzae

Many infections caused by nontypeable *H. influenzae,* such as otitis media and exacerbations of COPD, can be treated with oral antimicrobial agents. Overall, approximately 30% of nontypeable strains produce β-lactamase but substantial geographic variability in this rate is observed. Therefore, ampicillin and amoxicillin should be used only if the susceptibility of the infecting isolate is known. The clinician who manages patients with otitis media and exacerbations of COPD frequently chooses an antimicrobial agent empirically. In this circumstance, the antimicrobial agent should be active against *S. pneumoniae* and *Moraxella catarrhalis* as well as *H. influenzae.*

Oral antimicrobial agents that are active against nontypeable *H. influenzae* (and also *S. pneumoniae* and *M. catarrhalis*) include amoxicillin-clavulanic acid, fluoroquinolones, macrolides (e.g., azithromycin, clarithromycin), and various extended spectrum cephalosporins (e.g., cefixime, cefpodoxime, cefaclor, loracarbef, cefuroxime).

Parenteral antibiotic therapy is indicated for more serious infections caused by nontypeable *H. influenzae.* Parenteral antimicrobial agents that are active include cephalosporins (e.g., ceftriaxone, cefuroxime, ceftazidime, cefotaxime), ampicillin-sulbactam, fluoroquinolones, and azithromycin.

Individuals with certain immunodeficiencies, especially those with primary deficiency of antibody synthesis, have increased susceptibility to infection, especially with nontypeable *H. influenzae.* These persons may benefit from passive infusion of immunoglobulin preparations administered either intramuscularly or intravenously. This form of immunoglobulin replacement decreases the incidence of both systemic infections in these individuals and the number of episodes of both upper and lower respiratory tract infections caused by nontypeable *H. influenzae.*

Haemophilus influenzae Type b

Without treatment, infection caused by *H. influenzae* type b can be rapidly fatal. This is particularly true of meningitis and epiglottitis. The most favored regimen is cefotaxime or ceftriaxone. For children, cefotaxime is given as 200 mg/kg/day divided into six hourly doses. The pediatric dose of ceftriaxone is 75 to 100 mg/kg divided into 12 hourly doses. Adult doses are ceftriaxone 2 g every 12 hours or cefotaxime 2 g every 4 to 6 hours. Treatment is continued until the patient is afebrile and without clinical or laboratory signs of infection for 3 to 5 days. The usual duration of therapy is 7 to 10 days. Repeat CSF culture to confirm sterility is ordinarily not indicated. Patients with complications such as endophthalmitis, endocarditis, pericarditis, or osteomyelitis may require 3 to 6 weeks of therapy. Because approximately 30% of strains of *H. influenzae* produce β-lactamase, ampicillin as sole therapy should be used only after susceptibility of the isolate has been determined.

Administration of corticosteroids to patients with *H. influenzae* type b meningitis reduces the incidence of neurologic sequelae [57] (see Chapter 80 for a review of this subject). The presumed mechanism is the reduction of inflammation that results from release of bacterial cell wall fragments when bacteria are killed by antibiotics. Dexamethasone therapy (0.6 mg/kg/day intravenously in four divided doses for 4 days) should be administered to children older than 2 months of age.

Antibiotic therapy is only one facet of the management of the child with *H. influenzae* infection; critical attention must also be given to supportive therapy. In the management of meningitis, optimal ventilation must be ensured by maintaining an adequate airway. Fluid administration must be judiciously managed so as to obtain adequate perfusion of tissues because hypotension and acidosis may accompany severe infection. Conversely, some degree of cerebral edema and inappropriate secretion of antidiuretic hormone may complicate the course and require fluid restriction. Seizures may complicate *H. influenzae* meningitis and should bring to mind the possibility of electrolyte imbalance or subdural effusion.

Chemoprophylaxis for *Haemophilus influenzae* Type b. In the absence of prior immunization, household contacts younger than 4 years of age with individuals with invasive *H. influenzae* type b infection have a substantial incidence of disease. In the month following onset of disease in the index case, the attack rate is estimated to be 3.8% among children younger than 2 years of age, 1.5% among children 2 to 3 years of age, 0.1% among those 4 to 5 years of age, and 0% among those older than 6 years of age. Rifampin prophylaxis as 20 mg/kg once daily (600 mg maximum) for 4 days has eradicated the carrier state in approximately 95% of carriers and significantly reduced the incidence of secondary cases in household members. Rifampin comes in 150- and 300-mg capsules. The dose can be conveniently given to young children in applesauce.

Rifampin prophylaxis is recommended for all household members, including adults (except pregnant women), a contact younger than 48 months of age whose immunization status with the conjugate vaccine is incomplete, or an immunocompromised child of any age. [58] A contact is defined as a child who is either a household member or who has spent 4 or more hours each day with the index case for at least 5 of the 7 days preceding the day the index case was hospitalized. Based on efficacy of the *H. influenzae* type b vaccine, chemoprophylaxis is not recommended when all household contacts younger than 48 months of age have completed their immunization series. Children who were immunosuppressed at the time of vaccination may not have responded and for this reason should be considered unvaccinated. If rifampin is to be effective in preventing secondary cases, it should be given within 7 days after the index patient is hospitalized. The index patient should also be given rifampin if treated with regimens other than cefotaxime or ceftriaxone. Chemoprophylaxis is usually provided just before discharge from the hospital.

Rifampin prophylaxis is indicated for all attendees and personnel at a daycare center or nursery when two or more cases of invasive *H. influenzae* type b disease have occurred within 60 days if incompletely immunized children attend the facility. Duration and dose of rifampin are the same as for household contacts. Chemoprophylaxis is not indicated for a single case at a daycare center or nursery.[58]

Active Immunization Against *Haemophilus influenzae* Type b. Conjugate vaccines for invasive *H. influenzae* type b infections in infants and children are highly effective. The vaccines induce serum antibody to the PRP capsule and this antibody is bactericidal for the organism. The protective level of serum antibody to PRP has been estimated to be approximately 0.15 µg/mL, although this estimate must be interpreted cautiously, as noted previously. An unexpected finding from studies that assessed the effect of vaccination on nasopharyngeal colonization was that vaccination reduces or eliminates carriage of *H. influenzae* type b strains; this has played an important role in the effectiveness of the vaccine. With widespread use of conjugate vaccines the incidence of reported invasive disease in children under the age of 5 years has declined from an estimated 100 cases per 100,000 population to 0.3 in the United States.[59] These vaccines represent a dramatic success in disease prevention and healthcare cost savings.[60]

Certain populations, including native American and native Alaskan children, show a persistently elevated rate of infection even with widespread vaccination. Furthermore, localized populations with low vaccination rates contribute to the continued circulation of *H. influenzae* type b strains despite a national vaccination rate of greater than 90%. Therefore, continued surveillance, particularly in these high-risk populations, will be important. Determination of the serotypes of disease isolates will distinguish disease that results from lack of vaccination or vaccine failure from invasive disease caused by non–type b strains. A striking reduction in the incidence of invasive infections caused by *H. influenzae* type b has been seen in countries in which conjugate vaccines have been used widely. However, the global impact has been less impressive because the vaccines are used primarily in affluent countries. It is estimated that, currently, worldwide approximately 2% of cases of invasive *H. influenzae* type b infections are prevented by the vaccines.[61]

Three conjugate vaccines are currently licensed and available in the United States (Table 222-3). All children should be immunized with a conjugate vaccine beginning at 2 months of age.[58] A primary series consisting of 3 doses at 2, 4, and 6 months of age (HbOC or PRP-T) or 2 doses given at 2 and 4 months (PRP-OMPC), depending on the vaccine product, is recommended. After administration of the primary series, antibody titers decline, so an additional booster dose of any of the 3 licensed vaccines should be given between 12 and 15 months of age. Vaccines may be administered during visits when other vaccines are given. Adverse reactions are few; the most common are pain, redness, and swelling at the injection site.

Haemophilus influenzae Biogroup Aegyptius

H. influenzae biogroup aegyptius was formerly called *H. aegyptius*. However, recent genetic studies have established that *H. influenzae* and *H. aegyptius* are members of the same species; hence, the organism is now referred to as *H. influenzae* biogroup aegyptius.

H. influenzae biogroup aegyptius has long been known to cause conjunctivitis. In 1984, a fulminant systemic illness was described in a small Brazilian town. Following an episode of purulent conjunctivitis, children experienced high fever, vomiting, and abdominal pain. These symptoms were followed by petechiae, purpura, peripheral necrosis, and vascular collapse. Blood cultures were positive for *H. influenzae* biogroup aegyptius.[62,63] The mortality was 70%, but subsequent reports have described milder forms of the illness. The illness was called Brazilian purpuric fever and has now been described in several rural Brazilian towns in addition to two cases in Australia. Brazilian purpuric fever has occurred sporadically and as outbreaks. The peak age incidence is 1 to 4 years.

H. influenzae biogroup aegyptius is remarkable in that the organism has acquired the capacity to cause a fulminant, invasive disease in spite of lacking a capsule, which is often associated with invasive infections. Strains of *H. influenzae* biogroup aegyptius are of a clonal origin. Case clone strains share several characteristics, including a unique plasmid, identical electrophoretic type in multilocus enzyme typing, typical ribosomal DNA restriction patterns, a conserved surface epitope on outer membrane protein P1, and others.[64,65] Case clone strains contain 16 chromosomal elements and a mobile genetic element that are unique to the clonal group.[66]

Identifying the virulence factors that give case clone strains the ability to cause invasive disease will be important in understanding Brazilian purpuric fever. From a broader perspective, characterizing the molecular mechanisms that account for the invasive potential in an otherwise noninvasive bacterium (nontypeable *H. influenzae*) is of great interest in understanding the pathogenesis of invasive bacterial infections.

HAEMOPHILUS DUCREYI

Description of the Pathogen

H. ducreyi is the etiologic agent of chancroid, an infection characterized by genital ulcer and inguinal lymphadenitis. *H. ducreyi* is a highly fastidious gram-negative coccobacillus. Its microscopic appearance and its nutritional requirement for hemin account for the classification of the bacterium in the genus *Haemophilus*. However, studies of DNA homology and chemotaxonomy demonstrate substantial differences between *H. ducreyi* and other *Haemophilus* species. *H. ducreyi* will likely be reclassified in the future, but this issue awaits further study. The organism is a strict human pathogen and there are no known animal or environmental reservoirs.

Epidemiology

Chancroid is a common cause of genital ulcers in developing countries. Like other genital ulcer disease, chancroid facilitates the transmission of human immunodeficiency virus (HIV). This association between HIV and chancroid has generated increased interest in understanding the pathogenesis of *H. ducreyi* infection and in improving diagnostic tests for genital ulcer disease. In view of the limited resources in developing countries where *H. ducreyi* infection is endemic,

---

TABLE 222-3 *Haemophilus influenzae* Type b Conjugate Vaccines

Scientific Name	Commercial Name	Carbohydrate	Protein Carrier	Polysaccharide/ Protein Ratio	Recommended Dose Carbohydrate (µg)
PRP-T	Act HIB (Aventis Pasteur)	Native PRP	Tetanus toxoid	0.33	10
HbOC	HibTITER (Wyeth)	Oligosaccharide	CRM$_{197}$*	0.40	10
PRP-OMPC‡	PedvaxHIB (Merck)	Native PRP	OMPC†	0.05-0.10	15

*Mutant diphtheria toxin protein.
†Outer membrane protein complex derived from *Neisseria meningitides* serogroup B.
‡PRP-OMPC is also marketed as Comvax in combination with hepatitis B vaccine (Recombivax 5 mg) for administration at 2, 4, 12, and 15 months.

the true prevalence of chancroid is not known. The development of PCR-based diagnostic assays holds promise that the epidemiology of infection will be better understood. Initial application of these tests indicates that an increasing number of patients with genital ulcer disease have multiple agents simultaneously.[67]

Several epidemiological features of *H. ducreyi* infection are apparent. While the bacterium is a common cause of genital ulcers in developing countries, the disease occurs primarily in sporadic outbreaks in industrialized countries. Transmission is primarily heterosexual and males have outnumbered females in most studies. A high proportion of infected males report sexual contact with commercial sex workers. Chancroid has been strongly associated with illicit drug use. The transmission dynamics of the organism suggest that the disease is likely to be perpetuated in highly sexually active populations, such as commercial sex workers. [67,68]

Pathogenesis and Immune Response

Infection occurs as a result of inoculation of bacteria through breaks in the epithelium during sexual contact with an infected individual. A human model of experimental infection has been developed for studying the pathogenesis and immune response to *H. ducreyi* infection.[69-71] The bacterium colocalizes with neutrophils and macrophages but is not phagocytosed, suggesting that evasion of phagocytic killing is important in pathogenesis.[72] Ulcers contain predominantly T cells with low numbers of B cells. Patients who have had chancroid may have repeated infections indicating that natural infection does not confer protective immunity. Whether infection with *H. ducreyi* confers strain specific or partial immunity to subsequent infection is unclear.

Clinical Manifestations

The hallmark of chancroid is genital ulceration. The lesion often begins as a papule and evolves into an ulcer. Typical ulcers are painful, well circumscribed with ragged edges, and are not indurated. The base of the ulcer is covered with necrotic material and bleeds easily when scraped. Little or no inflammation of the surrounding skin is present. Approximately half of patients with chancroid have inguinal lymphadenopathy. These lymph nodes sometimes become fluctuant and rupture spontaneously.

Chancroid can present in atypical ways. Multiple ulcers may coalesce to form a giant ulcer. Ulceration may resolve before the appearance of inguinal adenopathy and suppuration, resulting in presentation as suppurative inguinal adenitis in the absence of an active genital ulcer. Multiple small ulcers may resemble folliculitis. The main differential diagnostic considerations include primary syphilis (chancre), genital herpes, lymphogranuloma venereum, donovanosis, and condyloma latum of secondary syphilis. In the presence of HIV infection, the number of ulcers at initial presentation may be greater and the duration of ulceration may be longer.

Diagnosis

Because a clinical diagnosis of chancroid is often inaccurate, laboratory confirmation of the diagnosis should be sought. Gram stain of a swab of the ulcer may reveal a predominance of gram-negative coccobacilli but these smears are difficult to interpret owing to the presence of other bacteria. Isolation of *H. ducreyi* from a swab of the lesion or from an aspirate of suppurative lymph nodes confirms the diagnosis. Because the organism is difficult to grow, use of selective and supplemented media is required. The most promising approach to the diagnosis of chancroid is a PCR-based assay. This sensitive and specific multiplex assay amplifies targets from *H. ducreyi, Treponema pallidum,* and herpes simplex virus type 1 and 2, the most common causes of genital ulcer disease.[73] When this assay becomes commercially available, it will be a useful method to establish the etiology of genital ulcers.

Treatment

The recommendation by the Centers for Disease Control and Prevention is a single 1-gram dose of azithromycin orally. Alternative regimens include ceftriaxone (250 mg intramuscularly in a single dose),

ciprofloxacin (500 mg orally twice a day for 3 days), or erythromycin base (500 mg orally three times a day for 7 days). Azithromycin and ceftriaxone have the distinct advantage of single-dose treatment.

Ulcers usually improve symptomatically by 3 days and by objective evaluation by 7 days following initiation of treatment. Lack of improvement should raise several considerations, including coinfection with another pathogen (especially genital herpes or primary syphilis), coexisting HIV infection which is associated with a delayed response to treatment of chancroid, lack of adherence to the treatment regimen, and finally, resistance of the *H. ducreyi* isolate to the antimicrobial agent prescribed. Isolates from patients who do not respond promptly to treatment should be tested for antimicrobial susceptibility.

Contacts of patients with chancroid should be identified and treated if they had sexual contact with the patient during the 10 days prior to the onset of symptoms in the patient, even in the absence of clinical symptoms in the contact.

OTHER *HAEMOPHILUS* SPECIES

Description of the Pathogen

Haemophilus species, other than *H. influenzae* and *H. ducreyi,* are unusual causes of disease in humans. However, as a result of increased awareness of these bacteria as potential pathogens and as a result of improvements in isolating the bacteria in culture, it is now apparent that other *Haemophilus* species more commonly cause human infection than previously believed, particularly in the case of infective endocarditis. *Haemophilus* are present as part of the normal bacterial flora of the human upper respiratory tract. *H. parainfluenzae* is the predominant species accounting for approximately three fourths of the *Haemophilus* flora of the human airway.

Members of the genus, *Haemophilus,* are small gram-negative coccobacilli with fastidious growth requirements. The growth requirements are used to distinguish among the species. *Haemophilus* require X factor (hemin), V factor (nicotinamide adenine dinucleotide), or both for growth. These are supplied by erythrocytes but the erythrocytes must be lysed to release V factor. This growth requirement is supplied in the clinical microbiology laboratory by growing *Haemophilus* species on chocolate agar. Table 222-4 shows differential characteristics of five *Haemophilus* species that have been documented to cause infection in humans. Species are distinguished based on their different growth requirements for X and V factor, enhancement of growth by CO_2, expression of catalase, and ability to cause hemolysis. Species designated *paraphrophilus, parainfluenzae* and *parahaemolyticus* require V factor but not X factor for growth whereas *H. aphrophilus* and *H. haemolyticus* require X and V or X only.

Clinical Manifestations

Haemophilus species, particularly *H. parainfluenzae, H. aphrophilus,* and *H. paraphrophilus,* are now recognized increasingly as a cause of infective endocarditis, causing up to 5% of cases of endocarditis.

TABLE 222-4 Differential Characteristics of *Haemophilus* Species

Organism	Growth Factor Requirement X	Growth Factor Requirement V	CO₂ Dependence	Hemolysis	Catalase
H. aphrophilus	+	−	+	−	−
H. paraphrophilus	−	+	+	−	±
H. parainfluenzae	−	+	−	−	+
H. haemolyticus	+	+	−	+	+
H. parahaemolyticus	−	+	−	+	+
H. ducreyi	+	−	±	±	−

+, present; −, absent.

Haemophilus species are included in the so-called HACEK (*Haemophilus* species, *Actinobacillus* species, *Cardiobacterium* species, *Eikenella* species, and *Kingella* species) group of bacteria, which are slow growing bacteria known to cause endocarditis. *Haemophilus* species (and others in the HACEK group) should be suspected in patients with a strong clinical suspicion of endocarditis and negative blood cultures. Blood cultures should be incubated for 2 weeks when endocarditis is suspected. Most patients with endocarditis caused by *Haemophilus* species have underlying valvular heart disease. Echocardiography, particularly transesophageal echocardiography, is useful in identifying vegetations and characterizing underlying valvular disease. The clinical course of *Haemophilus* endocarditis tends to be subacute and embolization is common.[74]

Other *Haemophilus* species are relatively rare human pathogens, presumably because of their low pathogenic potential. They have been documented as rare causes of a variety of local upper respiratory and systemic infections, including sinusitis, otitis media, conjunctivitis, dental abscess, lower respiratory tract infection, peritonitis, biliary tract infection, brain abscess, osteomyelitis, wound infections, and others. Most of these are documented by small series and case reports.

Treatment

Treatment should be guided by the antimicrobial susceptibility of the etiologic isolate. The antimicrobial susceptibility characteristics of other *Haemophilus* species are similar to those of *H. influenzae,* although fewer data on other *Haemophilus* species are available. Some strains produce β-lactamase and are thus resistant to ampicillin. Agents with generally good activity include trimethoprim-sulfamethoxasole, third-generation cephalosporins, fluoroquinolones, and aztreonam.

In view of the increasing incidence of β-lactamase production among strains of *Haemophilus,* the treatment of choice for *Haemophilus* species endocarditis is now third-generation cephalosporins (ceftriaxone or cefotaxime).[75] Treatment of native valve endocarditis should be given for 4 weeks and treatment for prosthetic valve endocarditis should continue for 6 weeks.

ACKNOWLEDGMENT

The author acknowledges the contributions of Dr. E. Richard Moxon to the chapter on this subject in the earlier edition.

REFERENCES

1. Munson E, Pfaller M, Koontz F, Doern G. Comparison of porphyrin-based, growth factor-based, and biochemical-based testing methods for identification of *Haemophilus influenzae*. Eur J Clin Microbiol Infect Dis. 2002;21:196-203.
2. Kilian M. A taxonomic study of the genus *Haemophilus,* with the proposal of a new species. J Gen Microbiol. 1976;93:9-62.
3. Samuelson A, Freijd A, Jonasson J, Lindberg AA. Turnover of nonencapsulated *Haemophilus influenzae* in the nasopharynges of otitis-prone children. J Clin Microbiol. 1995;33:2027-2031.
4. Faden H, Duffy L, Williams A, et al. Epidemiology of nasopharyngeal colonization with nontypeable *Haemophilus influenzae* in the first 2 years of life. J Infect Dis. 1995;172:132-135.
5. Peerbooms PG, Engelen MN, Stokman DA, et al. Nasopharyngeal carriage of potential bacterial pathogens related to day care attendance, with special reference to the molecular epidemiology of *Haemophilus influenzae.* J Clin Microbiol. 2002;40:2832-2836.
6. Faden H, Duffy L, Wasielewski R, et al. Relationship between nasopharyngeal colonization and the development of otitis media in children. J Infect Dis. 1997;175:1440-1445.
7. Leach AJ, Boswell JB, Asche V, et al. Bacterial colonization of the nasopharynx predicts very early onset and persistence of otitis media in Australian Aboriginal infants. Pediatr Infect Dis J. 1994;13:983-989.
8. Murphy TF, Sethi S, Klingman KL, et al. Simultaneous respiratory tract colonization by multiple strains of nontypeable *Haemophilus influenzae* in chronic obstructive pulmonary disease: Implications for antibiotic therapy. J Infect Dis. 1999;180:404-409.
9. Moller LVM, Regelink AG, Grasselier H, et al. Multiple *Haemophilus influenzae* strains and strain variants coexist in the respiratory tract of patients with cystic fibrosis. J Infect Dis. 1995;172:1388-1392.
10. Sethi S, Evans N, Grant BJB, Murphy TF. New strains of bacteria and exacerbations of chronic obstructive pulmonary disease. N Engl J Med. 2002;347:465-471.
11. Smith A, Baker M. Cefsulodin chocolate blood agar: A selective medium for the recovery of *Haemophilus influenzae* from the respiratory secretions of patients with cystic fibrosis. J Med Microbiol. 1997;46:883-885.
12. Ketterer MR, Shao JQ, Hornick DB, et al. Infection of primary human bronchial epithelial cells by *Haemophilus influenzae:* macropinocytosis as a mechanism of airway epithelial cell entry. Infect Immun. 1999; 67:4161-4170.
13. van Schilfgaarde M, Eijk P, Regelink A, et al. *Haemophilus influenzae* localized in epithelial cell layers is shielded from antibiotics and antibody-mediated bactericidal activity. Microb Pathogen. 1999;26:249-262.
14. Bandi V, Apicella MA, Mason E, et al. Nontypeable *Haemophilus influenzae* in the lower respiratory tract of patients with chronic bronchitis. Am J Respir Crit Care Med. 2001;164:2114-2119.
15. Forsgren J, Samuelson A, Ahlin A, et al. *Haemophilus influenzae* resides and multiplies intracellularly in human adenoid tissue as demonstrated by in situ hybridization and bacterial viability assay. Infect Immun. 1994;62:673-679.
16. Rao VK, Krasan GP, Hendrixson DR, et al. Molecular determinants of the pathogenesis of disease due to non-typable *Haemophilus influenzae.* FEMS Microbiol Rev. 1999;23:99-129.
17. Krasan GP, Cutter D, Block SL, St.Geme JW III. Adhesin expression in matched nasopharyngeal and middle ear isolates of nontypeable *Haemophilus influenzae* from children with acute otitis media. Infect Immun. 1999;67:449-454.
18. St.Geme JW III, Kumar VV, Cutter D, Barenkamp SJ. Prevalence and distribution of the *hmw* and *hia* genes and the HMW and Hia adhesins among genetically diverse strains of nontypeable *Haemophilus influenzae.* Infect Immun. 1998; 66:364-368.
19. Murphy TF, Bernstein JM, Dryja DD, et al. Outer membrane protein and lipooligosaccharide analysis of paired nasopharyngeal and middle ear isolates in otitis media due to nontypable *Haemophilus influenzae:* Pathogenetic and epidemiological observations. J Infect Dis. 1987;156:723-731.
20. Pettigrew MM, Foxman B, Marrs CF, Gilsdorf JR. Identification of the lipooligosaccharide biosynthesis gene *lic*2B as a putative virulence factor in strains of nontypeable *Haemophilus influenzae* that cause otitis media. Infect Immun. 2002;70:3551-3556.
21. Post JC, Preston RA, Aul JJ, et al. Molecular analysis of bacterial pathogens in otitis media with effusion. JAMA. 1995;273:1598-1604.
22. Hendolin PH, Markkanen A, Ylikoski J, Wahlfors JJ. Use of multiplex PCR for simultaneous detection of four bacterial species in middle ear effusions. J Clin Microbiol. 1997;35:2854-2858.
23. Hendolin PH, Paulin L, Ylikoski J. Clinically applicable multiplex PCR for four middle ear pathogens. J Clin Microbiol. 2000;38:125-132.
24. Ehrlich GD, Veeh R, Wang X, et al. Mucosal biofilm formation on middle-ear mucosa in the chinchilla model of otitis media. JAMA. 2002;287:1710-1715.
25. Post JC. Direct evidence of bacterial biofilms in otitis media. Laryngoscope. 2001;111:2083-2094.
26. Sethi S, Murphy TF. Bacterial infection in chronic obstructive pulmonary disease in 2000. A state of the art review. Clin Microbiol Rev. 2001;14:336-363.
27. Murphy TF, Sethi S. Chronic obstructive pulmonary disease: Role of bacteria and guide to antibacterial selection in the older patient. Drugs Aging. 2002;19:761-775.
28. Moxon ER, Deich RA, Connelly C. Cloning of chromosomal DNA from *Haemophilus influenzae.* J Clin Invest. 1984;73:298-306.
29. Faden H, Bernstein J, Brodsky L, et al. Otitis media in children. I. The systemic immune response to nontypable *Haemophilus influenzae.* J Infect Dis. 1989;160:999-1004.
30. Yi K, Sethi S, Murphy TF. Human immune response to nontypeable *Haemophilus influenzae* in chronic bronchitis. J Infect Dis. 1997;176:1247-1252.
31. Yi K, Murphy TF. Importance of an immunodominant surface-exposed loop on outer membrane protein P2 of nontypeable *Haemophilus influenzae.* Infect Immun. 1997;65:150-155.
32. Troelstra A, Vogel L, van Alphen L, et al. Opsonic antibodies to outer membrane protein P2 of nonencapsulated *Haemophilus influenzae* are strain specific. Infect Immun. 1994;62:779-784.
33. Duim B, Vogel L, Puijk W, et al. Fine mapping of outer membrane protein P2 antigenic sites which vary during persistent infection by *Haemophilus influenzae.* Infect Immun 1996;64:4673-4679.
34. Duim B, van Alphen L, Eijk P, et al. Antigenic drift of non-encapsulated *Haemophilus influenzae* major outer membrane protein P2 in patients with chronic bronchitis is caused by point mutations. Mol Microbiol. 1994;11:1181-1189.
35. Duim B, Bowler LD, Eijk PP, et al. Molecular variation in the major outer membrane protein P5 gene of nonencapsulated *Haemophilus influenzae* during chronic infections. Infect Immun. 1997; 65:1351-1356.
36. Shurin PA, Pelton SI, Tazer IB, Kasper DL. Bactericidal antibody and susceptibility to otitis media caused by nontypeable strains of *Haemophilus influenzae.* J Pediatr. 1980;97:364-369.
37. Abe Y, Murphy TF, Sethi S, et al. Lymphocyte proliferative response to P6 of *Haemophilus influenzae* is associated with relative protection from exacerbations of chronic obstructive pulmonary disease. Am J Respir Crit Care Med. 2002; 165:967-971.
38. Murphy TF. Immunity to nontypeable *Haemophilus influenzae:* Elucidating protective responses. Am J Respir Crit Care Med. 2003;167:486-487.
39. King PT, Hutchinson PE, Johnson PD, et al. Adaptive immunity to nontypeable *Haemophilus influenzae.* Am J Respir Crit Care Med. 2002;14.
40. Klein JO. Otitis media. Clin Infect Dis. 1994;19:823-833.
41. Pelton SI. Acute otitis media in an era of increasing antimicrobial resistance and universal administration of pneumococcal conjugate vaccine. Pediatr Infect Dis J. 2002;281:599-604; discussion 613-614.
42. Bartlett JG, Breiman RF, Mandell LA, et al. Community-acquired pneumonia in adults: Guidelines for management. Clin Infect Dis. 1998;26:811-838.
43. Polsky B, Gold JWM, Whimbey E, et al. Bacterial pneumonia in patients with acquired immunodeficiency syndrome. Ann Intern Med. 1986;104:38-41.

44. Nicholson SC, Webb CD, Andriole VT, et al. *Haemophilus influenzae* in respiratory tract infections in community-based clinical practice: therapy with gatifloxacin. Diagn Microbiol Infect Dis. 2002;44:101-107.
45. Rello J, Bodi M, Mariscal D, et al. Microbiological testing and outcome of patients with severe community-acquired pneumonia. Chest. 2003;123:174-180.
46. Lehmann D. Epidemiology of acute respiratory tract infections, especially those due to *Haemophilus influenzae,* in Papua New Guinean children. J Infect Dis. 1992;165:S20-S25.
47. Weinberg GA, Ghafoor A, Ishaq Z, et al. Clonal analysis of *Haemophilus influenzae* isolated from children from Pakistan with lower respiratory tract infections. J Infect Dis. 1989;160:634-643.
48. Wall RA, Corrah PT, Mabey DCW, Greenwood BM. The etiology of lobar pneumonia in the Gambia. Bull WHO. 1986;64:553-558.
49. Klein JO. Role of nontypeable *Haemophilus influenzae* in pediatric respiratory tract infections. Pediatr Infect Dis J. 1997;16:S5-S8.
50. Finegold SM, Flynn MJ, Rose FV, et al. Bacteriologic findings associated with chronic bacterial maxillary sinusitis in adults. Clin Infect Dis. 2002;35:428-433.
51. Brook I. Bacteriology of acute and chronic frontal sinusitis. Arch Otolaryngol Head Neck Surg. 2002;128:583-585.
52. Talbot GH, Kennedy DW, Scheld WM, Granito K. Rigid nasal endoscopy versus sinus puncture and aspiration for microbiologic documentation of acute bacterial maxillary sinusitis. Clin Infect Dis. 2001;33:1668-1675.
53. Quentin R, Goudeau A, Wallace RJ Jr, et al. Urogenital, maternal and neonatal isolates of *Haemophilus influenzae:* Identification of unusually virulent serologically non-typeable clone families and evidence for a new *Haemophilus* species. J Gen Microbiol. 1990;136:1203-1209.
54. Farley MM, Stephens DS, Brachman PS Jr, et al. Invasive *Haemophilus influenzae* disease in adults. Ann Intern Med. 1992;116:806-812.
55. Borenstein DG, Simon GL. *Hemophilus influenzae* septic arthritis in adults. A report of four cases and a review of the literature. Medicine. 1986;65:191-201.
56. Hoberman A, Marchant CD, Kaplan SL, Feldman S. Treatment of acute otitis media consensus recommendations. Clin Pediatr (Philadelphia). 2002;41:373-390.
57. Lebel MH, Freij BJ, Syrogiannopoulos GA, et al. Dexamethasone therapy for bacteria meningitis. Results of two double-blind, placebo-controlled trials. N Engl J Med. 1988;319:964-971.
58. American Academy of Pediatrics. *Haemophilus influenzae* infections. In: Pickering LK, ed. Red Book: 2003 Report of the Committee on Infectious Diseases. 26th ed. Elk Grove Village, IL: American Academy of Pediatrics; 2003:296.
59. Bath S, Biskard K, Murphy T, et al. Progress toward elimination of *Haemophilus influenzae* type b invasive disease among infants and children—United States, 1998-2000. Morbid Mortal Wkly Rep. 2002;51:234-237.
60. Zhou F, Bisgard KM, Yusuf HR, et al. Impact of universal *Haemophilus influenzae* type b vaccination starting at 2 months of age in the United States: an economic analysis. Pediatrics. 2002;110:653-661.
61. Peltola H. Worldwide *Haemophilus influenzae* type b disease at the beginning of the 21st century: Global analysis of the disease burden 25 years after the use of the polysaccharide vaccine and a decade after the advent of conjugates. Clin Microbiol Rev. 2000;13:302-317.
62. Brazilian Purpuric Fever Study Group . Brazilian purpuric fever: Epidemic purpura fulminans associated with antecedent purulent conjunctivitis. Lancet. 1987;2:757-761.
63. Brazilian Purpuric Fever Study Group. *Haemophilus aegyptius* bacteremia in Brazilian purpuric fever. Lancet. 1987;2:761-763.
64. Brenner DJ, Mayer LW, Carlone GM, et al. Biochemical, genetic, and epidemiologic characterization of *Haemophilus influenzae* biogroup aegyptius *(Haemophilus aegyptius)* strains associated with Brazilian purpuric fever. J Clin Microbiol. 1988;26:1524-1534.
65. Lesse AJ, Gheesling LL, Bittner WE, et al. Stable, conserved outer membrane epitope of strains of *Haemophilus influenzae* biogroup aegyptius associated with Brazilian purpuric fever. Infect Immun. 1992;60:1351-1357.
66. Li MS, Farrant JL, Langford PR, Kroll JS. Identification and characterization of genomic loci unique to the Brazilian purpuric fever clonal group of *H. influenzae* biogroup aegyptius: Functionality explored using meningococcal homology. Mol Microbiol. 2003;47:1101-1111.
67. Bong CT, Bauer ME, Spinola SM. *Haemophilus ducreyi:* Clinical features, epidemiology, and prospects for disease control. Microbes Infect. 2002;4:1141-1148.
68. DiCarlo RP, Armentor BS, Martin DH. Chancroid epidemiology in New Orleans men. J Infect Dis. 1995;172:446-452.
69. Spinola SM, Bauer ME, Munson RS Jr. Immunopathogenesis of *Haemophilus ducreyi* infection (chancroid). Infect Immun. 2002;70:1667-1676.
70. Bong CT, Throm RE, Fortney KR, et al. DsrA-deficient mutant of *Haemophilus ducreyi* is impaired in its ability to infect human volunteers. Infect Immun. 2001;69:1488-1491.
71. Fortney KR, Young RS, Bauer ME, et al. Expression of peptidoglycan-associated lipoprotein is required for virulence in the human model of *Haemophilus ducreyi* infection. Infect Immun 2000; 68:6441-6448.
72. Bauer ME, Goheen MP, Townsent CA, Spinola SM. *Haemophilus ducreyi* associates with phagocytes, collagen, and fibrin and remains extracellular throughout infection of human volunteers. Infect Immun. 2001;69:2549-2557.
73. Orle KA, Gates CA, Martin DH, et al. Simultaneous PCR detection of *Haemophilus ducreyi, Treponema pallidum,* and herpes simplex virus types 1 and 2 from genital ulcers. J Clin Microbiol. 1996;34:49-54.
74. Darras-Joly C, Lortholary O, Mainardi JL, et al. *Haemophilus* endocarditis: Report of 42 cases in adults and review. *Haemophilus* Endocarditis Study Group. Clin Infect Dis. 1997;24:1087-1094.
75. Wilson WR, Karchmer AW, Dajani AS, et al. Antibiotic treatment of adults with infective endocarditis due to streptococci, enterococci, staphylococci, and HACEK microorganisms. JAMA. 1995;274:1706-1713.

CHAPTER **223**

Brucella Species

EDWARD J. YOUNG

Brucellosis is a disease of animals (zoonosis) that under certain circumstances can be transmitted to humans.[1] Because the signs and symptoms are nonspecific, and the causative organism can be difficult to isolate, the diagnosis often depends on serologic techniques.[2]

HISTORY

The early history of brucellosis is linked to the British military and their presence on the island of Malta.[3] It was there that Marston, in 1861, first differentiated brucellosis from other clinical fevers, and where 25 years later, Bruce first isolated *Brucella melitensis,* the causative agent of Malta fever. Between 1904 and 1907, the Mediterranean Fever Commission concluded that on Malta, native goats were the reservoir of infection, and raw goat's milk was the vehicle of transmission from animal to human.[4] In Denmark, in 1895, Bang identified *B. abortus* as a cause of contagious abortion in cattle, and in 1914, in the United States, Traum recovered *B. suis* from aborted swine. However, it was not until the 1920s that the relatedness of these organisms was recognized, and the genus was named to honor Bruce. In the 1950s, *B. ovis* from sheep and *B. neotomae* from desert wood rats were added to the genus, but to date they have not been shown to cause human disease. In 1966, *Brucella canis* was isolated from kennel-bred dogs, but it is an infrequent cause of human infection.[5]

Since 1994, *Brucella* spp. with phenotypic and phylogenetic characteristics different than those of previously recognized nomen species were reported from a variety of marine mammals and presumptively termed *B. maris.*[6] Recent studies based on DNA polymorphisms and host preferences indicate the existence of at least two distinct new species.[7] The names *B. pinnipediae* and *B. ceteceae* have been proposed for the seal and cetecian isolates, respectively.[8] Two cases of human infection with the marine *Brucella spp.* have recently been reported.[9]

THE PATHOGEN

Brucellae are small Gram-negative coccobacilli that are nonmotile and do not form spores. They grow aerobically, although some species require supplemental CO_2 for primary isolation. All strains are catalase positive, but oxidase and urease activities and the production of H_2S are variable. The major nomen species of *Brucella* and their biovars are differentiated on the basis of oxidative metabolism tests, growth on media containing dyes, and lysis by brucella-phages.[10] The genus *Brucella* is divided into seven nomen species on the basis of preferred natural hosts and cultural, metabolic, and antigenic characteristics. However, DNA-DNA hybridization studies have shown a remarkable degree (greater than 95%) of homology between strains, indicating that it is a monospecific genus with subspecies corresponding to evolutionary lineages adapted to specific hosts.[11,12] Based on rRNA sequences, *Brucella* spp. belong to the α_2 group of proteobacteria having a close phylogenetic relationship with *Bartonella* spp., and plant pathogens such as *A. tumefaciens* and *S. meliloti.*[13,14] The *Brucella* genome contains two chromosomes of 2.1 Mb and 1.5 Mb except *B. suis* biovar 3, which has a single chromosome of 3.1 Mb.[15] The major cell wall antigen is the lipopolysaccharide of smooth strains (S-LPS) containing the A and M antigens first described by Wilson and Miles. The O-side chain is composed of about 100 residues of 4-formamide-4,6-dideoxymannose, which is linked $\alpha_{1,2}$ in A-dominant strains, but with every fifth residue linked $\alpha_{1,3}$ in M-dominant strains. Numerous outer and inner membrane, cytoplasmic, and periplasmic proteins have also been characterized,[16,17] some of which appear to play a role in virulence and intracellular survival.[18]

EPIDEMIOLOGY

Brucellosis is a zoonosis, and virtually all infections derive directly or indirectly from exposure to animals.[19] The disease exists worldwide, but is especially prevalent in the Mediterranean basin; the Arabian peninsula; the Indian subcontinent; and in parts of Mexico, Central, and South America. *B. abortus* is found principally in cattle, but buffalo, camels, and yaks can be of local importance. *B. melitensis* occurs primarily in goats and sheep, although camels are an important reservoir in some countries. *B. suis* biovars 1-3 occur in domestic and feral swine, and have been a cause of abattoir-associated infection.[20] *B. suis* biovar 4 is confined to reindeer and caribou or their predators in the subarctic tundra. *B. canis* is found primarily in kennel-bred dogs and is the least common cause of human brucellosis.

Routes of transmission from animals to humans include direct contact with infected animals or their secretions through cuts or abrasions in the skin, by way of infectious aerosols inhaled or inoculated into the conjunctiva, or by ingestion of unpasteurized dairy products. Consequently, brucellosis is an occupational risk for ranchers, veterinarians, abattoir workers, and laboratory personnel.[21] Meat products are rarely the source of infection because they are not usually eaten raw and the number of organisms in muscle tissue is low. Human-to-human transmission is unusual; however, rare cases in which sexual transmission was suspected have been reported.[22] Although persons infected with human immunodeficiency virus are at risk of a number of zoonotic agents,[23] very few cases of brucellosis have been reported.[24] Brucellosis is not rare in children, especially in areas where *B. melitensis* is endemic, and manifestations are similar to those in adults.[25] The role of wildlife in the epidemiology of brucellosis remains controversial. Wild hares in Europe are reservoirs for *B. suis* biovar 2 and can sporadically transmit the disease to domestic or feral

swine. Both elk and bison in Yellowstone National Park are infected with *B. abortus,* but the risk to domestic cattle sharing common grazing land is speculative.[26]

Although human brucellosis was once common in the United States, the eradication of bovine brucellosis has reduced the incidence of human infection to fewer than 0.5 cases per 100,000 population (Fig. 223-1). The epidemiology of brucellosis in Texas and California has changed from a disease associated with exposure to cattle to one linked to the ingestion of unpasteurized goat milk products imported from Mexico.[27,28] On the border with Mexico, brucellosis is eight times more prevalent than elsewhere in the United States.[29,30]

PATHOGENESIS

Infection with any *Brucella* nomen species, including naturally rough species and attenuated vaccine strains, can result in serious human illness. The nutritional and immune status of the host, as well as the size of the infectious inoculum, and possibly the route of transmission, can be determinants of disease. For example, the low pH of gastric juice appears to be more effective in preventing oral infection with *B. abortus* than *B. melitensis*[31] and the use of antacids has been implicated in food-borne infection.[32]

The brucellae are facultative intracellular pathogens that have the capacity to survive and multiply within phagocytic cells of the host. The mechanisms by which brucellae evade intracellular killing by polymorphonuclear leukocytes is incompletely understood; however, some factors include inhibition of degranulation of primary and secondary granules and of the myeloperoxidase-H_2O_2 system,[33] plus a Cu-Zn superoxide dismutase that eliminates reactive O_2 intermediates. Soon after infection, brucellae become localized within organs of the reticuloendothelial system, such as lymph nodes, liver, spleen, and bone marrow. Survival within mononuclear phagocytes is facilitated by inhibition of phagosome-lysosome fusion[34] and inhibition of apoptosis.[35] Eventual elimination of virulent brucellae depends on the activation of macrophages with the development of Th 1-type cell-mediated immunity. The principal cytokines involved in antibrucella activity of macrophages include tumor necrosis factor-α (TNF-α), TNF-γ, interleukin-1 (IL-1), and IL-12.[36] The major determinant of virulence and the immunodominant antigen of brucellae is S-LPS. Nonsmooth strains have reduced virulence and are more susceptible to lysis by normal serum. Naturally rough species (*B. canis* and *B. ovis*) have a greatly restricted host range and a limited capacity to infect other species.[10]

HOST IMMUNITY

Natural resistance to *Brucella* infection has been reported in swine and cattle, and macrophages from innately resistant cattle were better able to control the intracellular replication of *B. abortus.*[37] These data support the hypothesis that a bovine homolog of the murine *Nramp1* (natural resistance–associated macrophage protein 1) gene is a major candidate gene for determining resistance to brucellosis.[38] The acquired immune response in brucellosis is characterized by the appearance of immunoglobulin M (IgM) antibodies within the first week of infection, followed by a switch to IgG synthesis after the second week.[39] With recovery, titers of IgM and IgG antibodies decline slowly. Persistent elevation of IgG antibodies is prognostic of chronic infection or relapse.[40,41]

CLINICAL MANIFESTATIONS

The symptoms of brucellosis are nonspecific (e.g., fever, sweats, malaise, anorexia, headache, back pain). The onset can be insidious or acute, generally beginning within 2 to 4 weeks after inoculation. An "undulant" fever pattern is apparent in patients who are untreated for long periods of time. Some patients complain of malodorous sweat and a peculiar taste in the mouth. Depression is common and often out of proportion to the severity of other symptoms. Compared to the plethora of somatic complaints, physical abnormalities may be few. Mild lymphadenopathy is reported in 10% to 20%, and splenomegaly or he-

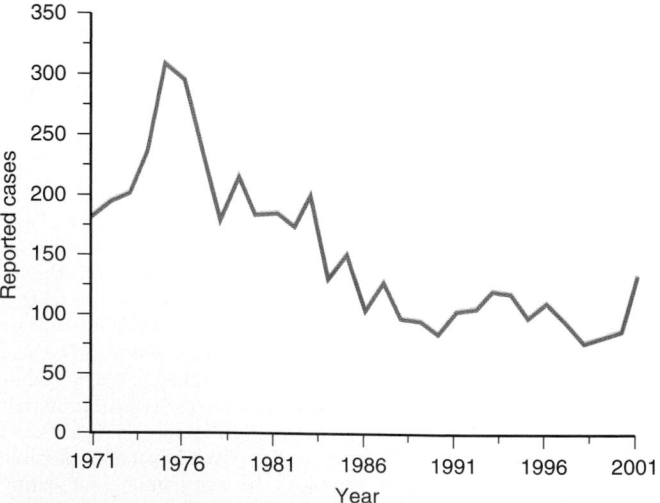

FIGURE 223-1. *Cases of human brucellosis reported annually (1971-2001) to the Centers for Disease Control and Prevention. After peaking at more than 300 cases in 1975, the number of brucellosis cases has declined and, for the last 10 years, has remained relatively stable at approximately 100 cases per year. (From Centers for Disease Control and Prevention. Summary of notifiable diseases, United States, 2001. MMWR Morb Mortal Wkly Rep. 2001;50:53.)*

patomegaly in 20% to 30% of cases.[42] Brucellosis is a systemic infection in which any organ or system of the body can be involved. Attempts to categorize the disease into acute, subacute, and chronic according to the length or severity of symptoms are purely arbitrary.[43] When involvement of a specific organ predominates, the disease is often termed focal or localized; however, there is little compelling evidence that such complications necessarily represent a distinct subset of patients.

Recurrence of symptoms following therapy may or may not be associated with relapse of the disease.[44] Bacteriologic relapse generally occurs within 3 to 6 months after discontinuing therapy and is usually not caused by antibiotic resistance.[45] Chronic brucellosis is usually caused by persistent foci of infection in tissues, such as bone, spleen, liver, and other organs.[46] In chronic brucellosis, symptoms can recur over long periods of time and are associated with objective signs, such as fever. An important laboratory finding is the persistence of high titers of IgG antibodies.[2,41] In contrast, some patients experience delayed convalescence, with persistent nonspecific complaints, but without objective signs of illness or elevated titers of antibodies. The cause of delayed convalescence is poorly understood, but some authorities believe that it may represent preexisting psychoneurosis exacerbated by the infection.[47,48]

COMPLICATIONS

Gastrointestinal Tract

Alimentary tract complaints, such as anorexia, nausea, vomiting, pain, diarrhea, or constipation, are elicited in up to 70% of patients with brucellosis. Pathologic lesions include hyperemia of the intestinal mucosa with inflammation of Peyer's patches. Acute ileitis has been documented radiographically and histologically in patients with colitis caused by *B. melitensis*.[49,50]

Hepatobiliary System

Hepatic involvement is common in brucellosis; however, transaminase levels can be normal or only mildly elevated. The histologic findings are often subtle, and can be overlooked entirely. The spectrum of hepatic pathology is quite variable, depending in part on the etiologic agent. Infection with *B. abortus* is characterized by granuloma indistinguishable from sarcoidosis.[51] In contrast, infection with *B. melitensis* yields lesions varying from small, almost insignificant aggregates of mononuclear cells surrounding foci of necrosis to a diffuse nonspecific inflammation resembling viral hepatitis.[52] In other cases, epithelioid granuloma have also been reported.[53] Hepatitis resolves with antimicrobial therapy, and in the absence of other causes (e.g., hepatitis C or alcoholism), cirrhosis does not occur despite the severity of the inflammation. Chronic suppurative abscess of the liver and spleen have been reported with *B. suis* and *B. melitensis* infections that may require surgical intervention.[54,55] *Brucella* can also be a rare cause of pancreatitis, spontaneous peritonitis, and acute cholecystitis.[56]

Skeletal System

Osteoarticular complications have been reported in 10% to 80% of cases depending on the series, the ages of the patients, and the infecting *Brucella* spp.[42] Sacroiliitis[57] and spondylitis[58] are the most frequent sites involved. Radiographic abnormalities are generally late findings, whereas bone scans may detect inflammation earlier in the disease. Computed tomography is especially useful for detecting joint destruction, vertebral osteomyelitis, and paraspinal abscess.[59] Large weight-bearing joints (e.g., hips, knees, ankles) are involved more often than small joints, and when effusions are present, they contain a preponderance of lymphocytes, but brucellae are isolated in fewer than half the cases.[60] A post-infectious spondyloarthritis, bursitis, tenosynovitis, and infection of joint prostheses have also been reported.[61]

Nervous System

Depression and mental inattention are common complaints in brucellosis; however, direct invasion of the central nervous system (CNS) occurs in fewer than 5% of cases. Neurobrucellosis includes meningitis, encephalitis, myelitis-radiculoneuronitis, brain abscess, epidural abscess, granuloma, and demyelinating and meningovascular syndromes. Acute or chronic meningitis is the most frequent nervous system complication,[62,63] and clinically it can resemble multiple sclerosis.[64] Cerebrospinal fluid (CSF) analysis reveals a lymphocytic pleocytosis, elevated protein, and low to normal glucose. Gram stains are usually negative and cultures are positive in fewer than one quarter of cases; however, the diagnosis can be made by finding specific antibodies in the CSF.[65] The prognosis of treated neurobrucellosis is generally favorable; however, cases with severe neurologic sequelae have been reported.[66]

Cardiovascular System

Endocarditis occurs in fewer than 2% of cases, but accounts for the majority of brucellosis-related deaths.[67] Before effective therapy, including valve replacement surgery, *Brucella* endocarditis was nearly always fatal.[68] The aortic valve is most often involved and both native and prosthetic valve infections have been reported. Pericarditis and mycotic aneurysms involving the brain, aorta, and other vessels are secondary complications. Deep venous thrombosis is a rare complication of acute brucellosis.[69] Newer blood culture techniques and echocardiography have improved the ability to make an early diagnosis, reducing the need for surgery.[70]

Respiratory System

Airborne transmission of brucellosis is especially common in abattoirs. Respiratory tract involvement ranges from flu-like symptoms with normal radiographic appearance to bronchitis, bronchopneumonia, lung nodules, abscess, military lesions, hilar adenopathy, and pleural effusion/empyema.[71] Rarely are brucellae identified by stain or culture of expectorated sputum.

Genitourinary Tract

Although brucellae can be recovered from the urine, renal complications of brucellosis are rare. Interstitial nephritis, pyelonephritis, glomerulonephritis, and IgA nephropathy have been reported. Very rarely, chronic renal abscess can present with calcium deposits resembling tuberculosis.[72] Epididymoorchitis occurs in up to 20% of men with brucellosis. It is usually unilateral with a normal urine sediment.[73]

Pregnancy

The principal manifestation of brucellosis in animals is spontaneous abortion, and the presence of erythritol in the tissues of susceptible animals is thought to play a role in the localization of brucellae in the genital tract. Brucellosis can also result in human abortion; however, it has been debated whether it is any more frequent than with other bacteremic infections. Reports from areas where *B. melitensis* is endemic suggest that the incidence of abortion among pregnant women is high, and that prompt therapy can be lifesaving for the fetus.[74]

Hematologic Complications

Hematologic manifestations of brucellosis include anemia, leukopenia, thrombocytopenia, and clotting disorders. Such abnormalities are generally mild and resolve with therapy.[75] Granulomas are found in the bone marrow in up to 75% of cases. Rarely, severe thrombocytopenia with cutaneous purpura and/or bleeding from mucosal sites can occur. The etiology may include hypersplenism, reactive hemophagocytosis, or immune destruction of platelets.[76]

Cutaneous Lesions

Skin lesions occur in about 5% of patients with brucellosis. Many nonspecific, often transient, lesions have been reported, including rashes, papules, ulcers, abscess, erythema nodosum, petechiae, purpura, and vasculitis.[77] Contact dermatitis was once a common finding among veterinarians exposed to infected animals.[78]

Ocular Lesions

A variety of ocular lesions have been reported in patients with brucellosis. Uveitis is generally a late complication, consisting variably of chronic iridocyclitis, nummular keratitis, multifocal choroiditis, and optic neuritis.[79] *Brucella* uveitis is considered a noninfectious immune response that responds to topical and systemic corticosteroid therapy. Rare cases of endogenous endophthalmitis have been reported in which brucellae have been isolated from vitreous humor.[80]

DIAGNOSIS

Because the symptoms of brucellosis are nonspecific, it is important to obtain a detailed history that includes occupation, avocations, travel to enzootic areas, and ingestion of high-risk foods, such as unpasteurized dairy products. The white blood cell count is often normal or low and the erythrocyte sedimentation rate is variable. The diagnosis is made with certainty when brucellae are recovered from blood, bone marrow, or other tissues. The rate of isolation ranges from 15% to more than 90% depending on the methods used.[81] Most laboratories now use continuous-monitoring automated blood culture systems (e.g., BACTEC or BacT/Alert) that have improved the time to isolation and have obviated the need for biphasic media techniques. Nevertheless, the handling of brucellae is a risk to laboratory personnel, and appropriate precautions should be taken.[82] Brucellae are isolated most often from blood and bone marrow; however, in selected cases, urine, CSF, synovial fluid, and biopsies of liver, lymph nodes, and other tissues can be successful.[83] Rapid automated bacterial identification systems should be interpreted with caution, as not all contain the appropriate profiles, and brucellae have been misidentified as *Moraxella phenylpyruvica*.[94] Molecular techniques, such as polymerase chain reaction (PCR), employing random or selected primers have been used widely in veterinary medicine and to differentiate *Brucella* spp.[85] PCR appears to be highly sensitive and specific when used on peripheral blood or other tissues[86,87]; however, additional studies are needed to establish its role in brucella diagnostics.

In the absence of bacteriologic confirmation, a presumptive diagnosis can be made by demonstrating high or rising titers of specific antibodies in the serum. A variety of tests have been applied to the serologic diagnosis of brucellosis, of which the serum agglutination test (SAT) is the most widely used.[2] Rose Bengal and a new dipstick test[88] are useful for screening; however, positive results should be confirmed by SAT. The brucella enzyme-linked immunosorbent assay (ELISA) is the most sensitive and specific serologic assay, and it may be positive when other tests are negative.[89] Regardless of the assay used, no single titer is *always* diagnostic; however, most cases of active infection have titers of 1:160 or higher. Most assays measure antibodies directed against LPS; however, an ELISA to detect *Brucella* cytoplasmic proteins has been reported to differentiate between active and inactive infection.[90]

TREATMENT

Antimicrobial therapy relieves symptoms, shortens the duration of illness, and reduces the incidence of complications and relapse. A variety of drugs have activity against brucellae; however, the results of in vitro susceptibility tests do not always predict clinical efficacy.[91] Intracellular localization of the brucellae is believed to offer some protection against antimicrobials, and drugs with good penetration into cells are thought to be necessary for cure.[92]

Tetracyclines are among the most active drugs for treating brucellosis; however, the rate of relapse with single-drug therapy is unacceptably high, and combinations of drugs are generally used. The World Health Organization (WHO) recommended regimen of doxycycline (200 mg/day) plus rifampin (600 to 900 mg/day) given for 6 weeks has the advantage of oral administration.[93] However, the regimen of doxycycline (200 mg/day oral) given for 6 weeks plus streptomycin (1 g/day intramuscular) for 2 to 3 weeks is the most effective therapy.[91,94] It appears that gentamicin can be substituted for streptomycin; however, no prospective study has compared aminoglycosides, and the optimal dose and duration of gentamicin therapy remain to be determined.[95]

Although there was initial enthusiasm for trimethoprim-sulfamethoxazole (cotrimoxazole) in the treatment of human brucellosis,

subsequent comparative studies revealed an unacceptably high rate of relapse.[96] Nevertheless, when used in combination with other drugs, such as rifampin, a quinolone, or an aminoglycoside, cotrimoxazole has found use in treating brucellosis in children younger than 8 years of age where tetracycline is contraindicated owing to the potential for staining teeth.[97] Both cotrimoxazole and rifampin appear to be safe agents for treating brucellosis in pregnancy.[74] The quinolones vary widely in activity against brucellae, but their concentration within phagocytic cells would appear to make them ideal for treating brucellosis. However, monotherapy with ciprofloxacin, for example, has been disappointing, and as a class, quinolones should be used only in combination with other drugs.[98]

The treatment of complications such as meningitis and endocarditis poses special problems, and the ideal drugs, doses, or duration of therapy have not been determined. Most authorities recommend the use of doxycycline in combination with two or more other drugs, with treatment continued for several months depending on the response. Doxycycline crosses the blood-brain barrier better than generic tetracycline, and it has been used successfully with cotrimoxazole and refampin in treatment of brucella meningitis[63] and endocarditis.[68] Some third-generation cephalosporins also reach high concentrations in CSF, but susceptibility of *Brucella* spp. is highly variable, and in vitro sensitivity should be assured.[99] Although cases of endocarditis have been cured with antibiotics alone,[100] many cases require a combined medical-surgical approach. Corticosteroids are often recommended for neurobrucellosis; however, in the absence of controlled studies, their efficacy is unproven.

PREVENTION

The prevention of human brucellosis depends on the control and elimination of the disease in domestic animals. Effective attenuated live bacterial vaccines exist for *B. abortus* (strain 19) and *B. melitensis* (strain Rev-1), but as yet, none exist for *B. suis* or *B. canis*. On rare occasions, accidents with these vaccines have resulted in human infection. A stable rough mutant of *B. abortus* (strain RB51) has largely replaced strain 19 in the United States, and it appears to be less pathogenic for humans. No safe, effective vaccine exists to immunize humans against brucellosis. The need for such a vaccine is obvious when one considers the potential use of *Brucella* spp. as agents of biologic warfare.

REFERENCES

1. Spink WW. *The Nature of Brucellosis.* Minneapolis: University of Minnesota Press, 1956.
2. Young EJ. Serologic diagnosis of human brucellosis: Analysis of 214 cases by agglutination tests and review of the literature. Rev Infect Dis. 1991;13:359-372.
3. Vassallo DJ. The Corps disease: Brucellosis and its historical association with the Royal Army Medical Corps. J R Army Med Corps. 1992;138:140-150.
4. Williams E. The Mediterranean Fever Commission: Its origin and achievements. In: Young EJ, Corbel MJ, eds. *Brucellosis: Clinical and Laboratory Aspects.* Boca Raton, FL: CRC Press; 1989:11-23.
5. Carmichael LE. *Brucella canis.* In: Nielsen K, Duncan JR, eds. *Animal Brucellosis.* Boca Raton, FL: CRC Press; 1990:335-350.
6. Van Bressem M-F, Van Waerebeck K, Raga JA, et al. Serological evidence of *Brucella* species infection in odontocetes from the south Pacific and the Mediterranean. Vet Rec. 2001;148:657-661.
7. Bricker BJ, Ewalt DR, MacMillan AP, et al. Molecular characterization of *Brucella* strains isolated from marine mammals. J Clin Microbiol. 2000;38:1258-1262.
8. González L, Patterson IA, Reid RJ, et al. Chronic meningoencephalitis associated with *Brucella* sp. infection in live-stranded striped dolphins (*Stenella coeruleoalba*). J Comp Pathol. 2002; 126:147-152.
9. Sohn AH, Probert WS, Glaser CA, et al. Human neurobrucellosis with intracerebral granuloma caused by a marine mammal *Brucella* spp. Emerg Infect Dis. 2003;9:485-488.
10. Corbel MJ. Microbiological aspects. In: Madkour MM. *Madkour's Brucellosis.* New York: Springer-Verlag; 2001:51-64.
11. Michaux-Charachon S, Bourg G, Jumas-Bilak E, et al. Genome structure and phylogeny in the genus *Brucella.* J Bacteriol. 1997;179:3244-3249.
12. Gándara B, López Merino A, Rogel MA, et al. Limited genetic diversity of *Brucella* spp. J Clin Microbiol. 2001;39:235-240.

13. Paulsen IT, Seshadri R, Nelson KE, et al. The *Brucella suis* genome reveals fundamental similarities between animal and plant pathogens and symbionts. Proc Natl Acad Sci USA. 2002; 99:13148-13153.

14. Del Vecchio VG, Kapatral V, Redkar RJ, et al. The genome sequence of the facultative intracellular pathogen *Brucella melitensis.* Proc Natl Acad Sci USA. 2002;99:443-448.

15. Jumas-Bilak E, Michaux-Charachon S, Bourg G, et al. Differences in chromosome number and genome rearrangements in the genus *Brucella.* Mol Microbiol. 1998;27:99-106.

16. Corbel MJ. Recent advances in brucellosis. J Med Microbiol. 1997;46:101-103.

17. Moriyón I, López-Goñi I. Structure and properties of the outer membranes of *Brucella abortus* and *Brucella melitensis.* Int Microbiol. 1998;1:19-26.

18. Guzmán-Verri C, Manterola L, Sola-Landa A, et al. The two-component system BvrR/BvrS essential for *Brucella abortus* virulence regulates the expression of outer membrane proteins with counterparts in members of the *Rhizobiaceae.* Proc Natl Acad Sci USA. 2002;99:12375-12380.

19. Corbel MJ. Brucellosis: Epidemiology and prevalence worldwide. In: Young EJ, Corbel MJ, eds. *Brucellosis: Clinical and Laboratory Aspects.* Boca Raton, FL: CRC Press; 1989:76-80.

20. Trout D, Gomez TM, Bernard BP, et al. Outbreak of brucellosis at a United States pork packing plant. J Occup Environ Med. 1995;37:697-703.

21. Young EJ. Human brucellosis. Rev Infect Dis. 1983;5:321-342.

22. Rubin B, Band JD, Wong P, et al. Person-to-person transmission of *Brucella melitensis.* Lancet. 1991;1:14-15.

23. Glaser CA, Angulo FJ, Rooney JA. Animal-associated opportunistic infections among persons infected with the human immunodeficiency virus. Clin Infect Dis. 1994;18:14-24.

24. Moreno S, Ariza J, Espinosa FJ, et al. Brucellosis in patients infected with the human immunodeficiency virus. Eur J Clin Microbiol Infect Dis. 1998;17:319-326.

25. Young EJ. *Brucella* species (Brucellosis). In: Long SS, Pickering LK, Prober CG, eds. *Principle and Practice of Pediatric Infectious Diseases.* 2nd ed. New York: Churchill Livingstone; 2003: 876-880.

26. Cheville NF, McCullough DR, Paulson LR, eds. *Brucellosis in the Greater Yellowstone Area.* Washington, DC: National Academy Press, 1998.

27. Taylor JP, Perdue JN. The changing epidemiology of human brucellosis in Texas, 1977-1986. Am J Epidemiol. 1989;130:160-165.

28. Chomel BB, DeBess EE, Mangiamele DM, et al. Changing trends in the epidemiology of human brucellosis in California from 1973 to 1992: A shift toward foodborne transmission. J Infect Dis. 1994;170:1216-1223.

29. Doyle TJ, Bryan RT. Infectious disease morbidity in the US region bordering Mexico, 1990-1998. J Infect Dis. 2000;182:1503-1510.

30. Fosgate GT, Carpenter TE, Chomel BB, et al. Time-space clustering of human brucellosis, California, 1973-1992. Emerg Infect Dis. 2002;8:672-678.

31. Morales-Otero P. Further attempts in experimental infection of man with a bovine strain of *Brucella abortus.* J Infect Dis. 1933;52:54-59.

32. Arnow PM, Smaron M, Ormistc V. Brucellosis in a group of travelers to Spain. JAMA. 1984;251:505-507.

33. Orduña A, Orduña C, Eiros M, et al. Inhibition of the degranulation and myeloperoxidase activity of human polymorphonuclear neutrophils by *Brucella melitensis.* Microbiologia. 1991;7:113-119.

34. Porte F, Naroeni A, Ouahrani-Bettache S, et al. Role of the *Brucella suis* lipopolysaccharide O antigen in phagosomal genesis and in inhibition of phagosome-lysosome fusion in murine macrophages. Infect Immun. 2003;71:1481-1490.

35. Fernandez-Prada CM, Zelazowska EB, Nikolich M, et al. Interactions between *Brucella melitensis* and human phagocytes: Bacterial surface O-polysaccharide inhibits phagocytosis, bacterial killing, and subsequent host cell apoptosis. Infect Immun. 2003;71:2110-2119.

36. Golding B, Scott DE, Scharf O, et al. Immunity and protection against *Brucella abortus.* Microbes Infect. 2001;3:43-48.

37. Adams LG, Templeton JW. Genetic resistance to bacterial diseases in animals. Rev Sci Tech Off Int Epizoot. 1998;17:200-219.

38. Feng J, Li Y, Hashad M, et al. Bovine natural resistance associated macrophage protein 1 (*Nramp1*) gene. Genome Res. 1996;6:956-964.

39. Ariza J, Pellicer T, Pallares RN, et al. Specific antibody profile in human brucellosis. Clin Infect Dis. 1992;14:131-140.

40. Pellicer T, Ariza J, Foz A, et al. Specific antibodies detected during relapse of human brucellosis. J Infect Dis. 1988;157:918-924.

41. Gazapo E, Lahoz JG, Subiza JL, et al. Changes in IgM and IgG antibody concentrations in brucellosis over time: Importance for diagnosis and follow-up. J Infect Dis. 1989;159:219-225.

42. Colmenero JD, Reguera JM, Martos F, et al. Complications associated with *Brucella melitensis* infection: A study of 530 cases. Medicine. 1996;75:195-211.

43. Young EJ. Overview of brucellosis. Clin Infect Dis. 1995;21:283-289.

44. Ariza J, Corredoira J, Pallares R, et al. Characteristics of and risk factors for relapse of brucellosis in humans. Clin Infect Dis. 1995;20:1241-1249.

45. Ariza J, Bosch J, Gudiol F, et al. Relevance of in vitro antimicrobial susceptibility of *Brucella melitensis* to relapse rate in human brucellosis. Antimicrob Agents Chemother. 1986;30:958-960.

46. Spink WW. What is chronic brucellosis? Ann Intern Med. 1951;35:258-274.

47. Imboden JB, Canter A, Cluff LE, et al. Brucellosis: III. Psychologic aspects of delayed convalescence. Arch Intern Med. 1959;103:404-414.

48. Cluff LE. Medical aspects of delayed convalescence. Rev Infect Dis. 1991;13(Suppl):138-140.

49. Petrella R, Young EJ. Acute brucella ileitis. Am J Gastroenterol. 1988;83:80-82.

50. Jorens PG, Michielsen PP, Van den Ender EJ, et al. A rare cause of colitis: *Brucella melitensis.* Dis Colon Rectum. 1991;34:194-196.

51. Spink WW, Hoffbauer FW, Walker WW, et al. Histopathology of the liver in human brucellosis. J Lab Clin Med. 1949;34:40-58.

52. Young EJ. *Brucella melitensis* hepatitis: The absence of granulomas. Ann Intern Med. 1979; 91:414-415.

53. Young EJ. Brucellosis. In: Connor DH, Chandler FW, Manz HJ, eds. *Pathology of Infectious Diseases.* Stamford, CT: Appleton & Lange; 1997:447-451.

54. Ariza J, Pigrau C, Cañas C, et al. Current understanding and management of chronic hepatosplenic suppurative brucellosis. Clin Infect Dis. 2001;32:1024-1033.

55. Colmenero J, Lozano E, Queipo-Ortuño MI, Reguera JM, et al. Chronic hepatosplenic abscesses in brucellosis. Clinico-therapeutic features and molecular diagnostic approach. Diagn Microbiol Infect Dis. 2002;42:159-167.

56. Terado Miranda R, Espinosa Gimeno A, Fernandez Rodriguez T, et al. Acute cholecystitis caused by *Brucella melitensis:* Case report and review. J Infect. 2001;42:77-78.

57. Ariza J, Pujol M, Valverde J, et al. Brucellar sacroiliitis: Findings in 63 episodes and current relevance. Clin Infect Dis. 1993;16:761-765.

58. Solera J, Lozano E, Martínez-Alfaro E, et al. Brucellar spondylitis: Review of 35 cases and literature survey. Clin Infect Dis. 1999;29:1440-1449.

59. Bahar RH, Al-Subaili AR, Mousa AM, et al. Brucellosis: Appearance on skeletal imaging. Clin Nucl Med. 1988;13:102-106.

60. Khateeb MI, Araj GF, Majeed SA, et al. Brucella arthritis: A study of 96 cases in Kuwait. Ann Rheum Dis. 1990;49:994-998.

61. Weil Y, Mattan Y, Liebergall M, et al. *Brucella* prosthetic joint infection: A report of 3 cases and a review of the literature. Clin Infect Dis. 2003;36:e81-86.

62. Bouza E, García de la Torre M, Parras F, et al. Brucellar meningitis. Rev Infect Dis. 1987; 9:810-822.

63. McLean DR, Russell N, Khan MY. Neurobrucellosis: Clinical and therapeutic features. Clin Infect Dis. 1992;15:582-590.

64. Murrell TGC, Matthews BJ. Multiple sclerosis – One manifestation of neurobrucellosis? Med Hypoth. 1990;33:43-48.

65. Sanchez-Sousa A, Torre C, Campello MG, et al. Serological diagnosis of neurobrucellosis. J Clin Pathol. 1990;43:79-81.

66. Bucher A, Gaustad P, Pape E. Chronic neurobrucellosis due to *Brucella melitensis.* Scand J Infect Dis. 1990;22:223-226.

67. Al-Harthi SS. The morbidity and mortality patterns of *Brucella* endocarditis. Int J Cardiol. 1989;25:321-324.

68. Jacobs F, Abramowicz D, Vereerstraeten P, et al. *Brucella* endocarditis: The role of combined medical and surgical treatment. Rev Infect Dis. 1990;12:740-744.

69. Odeh M, Pick N, Oliven A. Deep venous thrombosis associated with acute brucellosis. Angiology. 2000;51:253-256.

70. Cohen N, Golik A, Alon I, et al. Conservative treatment for *Brucella* endocarditis. Clin Cardiol. 1997;20:294-296.

71. García-Rodriguez JA, García-Sánchez JE, Muñoz Bellido JI, et al. Review of pulmonary brucellosis: A case report on brucellar pulmonary empyema. Diag Microbiol Infect Dis. 1989;11:53-60.

72. Zinneman HH, Glenchur H, Hall WH. Chronic renal brucellosis. N Engl J Med. 1961;265:872-875.

73. Navarro-Martínez A, Solera J, Corredoira J, et al. Epididymoorchitis due to *Brucella melitensis:* A retrospective study of 59 patients. Clin Infect Dis. 2001;33:2017-2022.

74. Khan MY, Mah MW, Memish ZA. Brucellosis in pregnant women. Clin Infect Dis. 2001;32:1172-1177.

75. Crosby E, Llosa L, Quesada M, et al. Hematologic changes in brucellosis. J Infect Dis. 1984;150:419-424.

76. Young EJ, Tarry A, Genta RM, et al. Thrombocytopenic purpura associated with brucellosis: Report of 2 cases and literature review. Clin Infect Dis. 2000;31:904-909.

77. Ariza J, Servitje O, Pallarés R, et al. Characteristic cutaneous lesions in patients with brucellosis. Arch Dermatol. 1989;125:380-383.

78. Milionis H, Christou L, Elisaf M. Cutaneous manifestations in brucellosis: Case report and review of the literature. Infection. 2000;28:124-126.

79. Walker J, Sharma OP, Rao NA. Brucellosis and uveitis. Am J Ophthalmol. 1992;114:374-375.

80. Al Faran MF. *Brucella melitensis* endogenous endophthalmitis. Ophthalmologica. 1990;201:19-22.

81. Yagupsky P. Detection of brucellae in blood cultures. J Clin Microbiol. 1999;37:3437-3442.

82. Yagupsky P, Peled N, Riesenberg K, et al. Exposure of hospital personnel to *Brucella melitensis* and occurrence of laboratory-acquired disease in an endemic area. Scand J Infect Dis. 2000;32:31-35.

83. Gottuzo E, Carrillo C, Guerra J, et al. An evaluation of diagnostic methods for brucellosis—the value of bone marrow culture. J Infect Dis. 1986;153:122-125.

84. Roiz MP, Peralta FG, Valle R, et al. Microbiological diagnosis of brucellosis. J Clin Microbiol 1998;36:1819.

85. Fox KE, Fox A, Nagpal M, et al. Identification of *Brucella* by ribosomal-spacer-region PCR and differentiation of *Brucella canis* from other *Brucella* spp. pathogenic for humans by carbohydrate profiles. J Clin Microbiol. 1998;36:3217-3222.

86. Queipo-Ortuño MI, Morata P, Ocón P, et al. Rapid diagnosis of human brucellosis by peripheral-blood PCR assay. J Clin Microbiol. 1997;35:2927-2930.

87. Morata P, Queipo-Ortuño MI, Reguera JM, et al. Diagnostic yield of a PCR assay in focal complications of brucellosis. J Clin Microbiol. 2001;39:3743-3746.

88. Altuglu I, Zeytinoğlu A, Bilgic A, et al. Evaluation of *Brucella* dipstick assay for the diagnosis of acute brucellosis. Diagn Microbiol Infect Dis. 2002;44:241-243.

89. Young EJ. Immunology of brucellosis. In: Madkour MM. *Madkour's Brucellosis.* 2nd ed. New York: Springer-Verlag; 2001:39-50.

90. Goldbaum FA, Velikovsky CA, Baldi PC, et al. The 18-kDA cytoplasmic protein of *Brucella* species—an antigen useful for diagnosis—is a lumazine synthase. J Med Microbiol. 1999;48:833-839.
91. Young EJ. *Brucella* species (Brucellosis). In: Yu V, Weber R, Raoult D, eds. *Antimicrobial Therapy and Vaccines*, Vol. I: *Microbes*. 2nd ed. New York: Apple Trees Productions; 2002:121-140.
92. Hall WH. Modern chemotherapy of brucellosis. Rev Infect Dis. 1990;12:1060-1099.
93. Joint FAO/WHO Expert Committee on Brucellosis (Sixth Report). Geneva: World Health Organization, 1986.
94. Solera J, Rodríguez-Zapata M, Geijo P, et al. Doxycycline-rifampin versus doxycycline-streptomycin in treatment of human brucellosis due to *Brucella melitensis*. Antimicrob Agents Chemother. 1995;39:2061-2067.
95. Solera J, Espinoza A, Martínez-Alfaro E, et al. Treatment of human brucellosis with doxycycline and gentamicin. Antimicrob Agents Chemother. 1997; 41:80-84.
96. Ariza J, Gudiol F, Pallares R, et al. Comparative trial of co-trimoxazole versus tetracycline-streptomycin in treating human brucellosis. J Infect Dis. 1985;152:1358-1359.
97. Solera J, Martínez-Alfaro E, Espinoza A. Recognition and optimum treatment of brucellosis. Drugs. 1997;53:245-256.
98. Akova M, Uzun D, Akalin HE, et al. Quinolones in treatment of human brucellosis: Comparative trial of ofloxacin-rifampin versus doxycycline-rifampin. Antimicrob Agents Chemother. 1993;37:1831-1834.
99. Lang R, Dagan R, Potasman I, et al. Failure of ceftriaxone in the treatment of acute brucellosis. Clin Infect Dis. 1992;14:506-509.
100. Cohen N, Golik A, Alon I, et al. Conservative treatment for *Brucella* endocarditis. Clin Cardiol. 1997;20:291-294.

CHAPTER **224**

Francisella tularensis (Tularemia)

ROBERT L. PENN

*F*rancisella tularensis is a gram-negative pathogen primarily of animals and occasionally of humans. The disease it causes is now recognized as tularemia in most parts of the world, but it has been called rabbit fever, deer-fly fever, and market men's disease in the United States; wild hare disease (yato-byo) and Ohara's disease in Japan; and water-rat trappers' disease in Russia.[1] Tularemia continues to be responsible for significant morbidity and mortality, despite the availability of numerous antibiotics active against the organism.[2,3]

F. tularensis infections have become a public health issue, with rising concerns regarding military or terrorist uses of the organism in biological warfare (see Chapter 322). Because of this tularemia was returned to the list of reportable diseases in the United States in 2000, after being excluded in 1995. With this heightened surveillance has come an appreciation of the continued occurrence, often in outbreaks, of natural *F. tularensis* infections throughout the world.[4,5]

HISTORY

Tularemia has been so intimately linked to investigators in the United States that it has been referred to as an "American achievement."[6] However, its history includes important contributions from many other areas of the world, including Japan and the former Soviet Union. Hare-associated illness compatible with tularemia has been known in Japan since 1818, and perhaps the earliest written description of a patient with unmistakable tularemia was provided by Homma-Soken in 1837.[2,7]

Credit for identifying the organism and recognizing the important clinical syndromes belongs to American workers. In 1911, while evaluating possible plague outbreaks after the San Francisco earthquake, McCoy[8] described a plague-like illness common in the California ground squirrel, and with Chapin he successfully cultured the causative agent in 1912.[9] They named it *Bacterium tularense* because this work took place in Tulare county, which "was once covered with extensive marshy beds of the reed tule, a large variety of bulrush."[10]

The first human case to have bacteriologic confirmation was an ocular infection reported in 1914 by Vail[11] and by Wherry and Lamb.[12,13] Wherry and Lamb also found the organism in wild rabbits near the home of another patient with proven conjunctival tularemia.[10,13] Although the cause was unknown at the time, tularemia was transmitted by contact with biting flies in Utah and was termed deer-fly fever. Dr. Edward Francis, working for the U.S. Public Health Service, established the true cause of deer-fly fever as *B. tularense* (a full decade after the organism was discovered in squirrels), proved the deer fly was the vector, and named the human disease *tularemia* to emphasize the frequent accompanying bacteremia. Francis also contributed to work that improved methods for cultivating *B. tularense* and making a serologic diagnosis, identified tick and other reservoirs for its transmission, clarified the clinical syndromes associated with tularemia, and emphasized the risk to laboratory workers and consumers from infected sources.[10,14,15] For this lifetime of achievements, the genus in which the organism is classified was renamed *Francisella* in his honor.

In Japan, Ohara had described a rabbit-associated febrile disease, transmitted the illness to his wife by rubbing rabbit hearts over her hand, and recovered an organism from her lymph nodes; Francis later showed that this Japanese organism was identical to *B. tularense*.[14] Tularemia was recognized in Astrakhan, Russia, in 1926, and over the subsequent decades scattered serious outbreaks occurred throughout the country. Scientists in the former Soviet Union also have intensively studied the disease and its causative organism.[6,7]

DESCRIPTION OF THE PATHOGEN

Francisella are small, aerobic, catalase-positive, pleomorphic, gram-negative coccobacilli. They are more uniformly rod-shaped during logarithmic growth, during which they tend to exhibit bipolar staining with Gram or Giemsa methods; this staining pattern accentuates a coccoidal appearance. The cell wall of *F. tularensis* has an unusually high level of fatty acids that have a profile unique to the genus, and wild strains possess an electron-transparent lipid-rich capsule. Loss of the capsule may lead to loss of serum resistance and virulence, but may not diminish viability or survival within neutrophils[16]; however, the capsule is neither toxic nor immunogenic.[17]

Francisella spp. belong to the γ-proteobacteria and may be categorized on the basis of growth characteristics, biochemical reactions, and virulence properties (Table 224-1). The family *Francisellaceae* includes two species in the genus *Francisella* and four subspecies of *F. tularensis*.[18] Although all have been associated with human disease, only the *tularensis* and *holarctica* subspecies of *F. tularensis* are relatively common.[19] *F. tularensis* subsp. *tularensis,* also referred to as type A, is found almost exclusively in North America and is the most virulent species. Although previously thought to be restricted to North America, it recently was isolated in Europe and its identity subsequently verified using molecular techniques.[19-21] *F. tularensis* subsp. *holarctica*, also referred to as type B, is found predominantly in Asia and Europe, but also in North America; it is less virulent in humans and of low virulence in rabbits. The *F. tularensis* live vaccine strains (LVS) are derived from *F. tularensis* subsp. *holarctica*.[21] Synonyms used in the past have included *F. tularensis nearctica* for *F. tularensis* subsp. *tularensis* and *F. tularensis palearctica* for *F. tularensis* subsp. *holarctica. Francisella novicida* was previously classified as a separate species but it is now known to be a subspecies of *F. tularensis*.[18,22] *F. tularensis* subsp. *novicida* is of low virulence. Strains isolated from a restricted area in central Asia have been designated *F. tularensis* subsp. *mediaasiatica*, are of low virulence, and produce acid from glycerol but not glucose.[18] Strains isolated in Japan have been designated *F. tularensis* subsp. *holarctica* biovar *japonica*.[17,23,24] However, like subsp. *tularensis* strains, these strains produce acid from both glucose and glycerol.[24]

The taxonomy of *Francisella* has been complicated because biochemical reactions may be variable, weak, or delayed and also in part because of the different terms given to organisms isolated in different parts of the world. A study of a small number of representative

TABLE 224-1 Characterization of *Francisella* Species

Features	*F. tularensis* Subspecies*			*F. philomiragia*
	tularensis	*holarctica*	*novicida*	
Cysteine growth requirement	+	+	−	−
Growth in broth plus 6% NaCl	−	−	+†	+†
Motility	−	−	−	−
Oxidase	−	−	−	+‡
Nitrate reduction	−	−	−	−
Acid from				
glucose	+†	+†	+†	+†
glycerol	+	−	+	+
Gelatin hydrolysis	−	−	−	+†
Relative virulence				
Humans	High	Intermediate	Low	Low
Rabbits	High	Low	Low	NA§

*The fourth *F. tularensis* subspecies, *mediaasiatica*, and the *japonica* biovar of *F. tularensis* subsp. *holarctica* are described in the text.
†Variable or delayed.
‡Using Kovacs test; negative using cytochrome-oxidase test.
§NA, not available.
Data from Eigelsbach and McGann,[17] Hollis et al.,[22] Koneman et al.,[34] and Chu and Weyant.[18]

Francisella strains found that the traditional biochemical methods for differentiating between subsp. *tularensis* and *holarctica*, testing for fermentation of glycerol and glucose and the presence of citrulline ureidase activity, were imprecise; this was true despite the fact that *holarctica* strains had the expected low virulence for rabbits.[23] The few central Asian and Japanese strains tested also had low virulence in rabbits, but analysis of their 16S rRNA showed them to be genotypically related to *F. tularensis* subsp. *tularensis* and not subsp. *holarctica*.[23] Classification of *Francisella* is being advanced by the development of molecular typing methods, including microarray analysis of the genome. Reports on relatively small collections of organisms have supported the currently accepted taxonomy as outlined earlier and in Table 224-1, and demonstrated the utility of these methods for species and subspecies typing.[19,21,25-28] However, further work is needed to identify optimal methods for discriminating individual strains. Completion of sequencing of the genome from a representative *F. tularensis* subsp. *tularensis* (strain Schu 4) will aid these efforts as well as proteomic analysis.[29,30] Preliminary analysis of the genome has revealed a high proportion of unique genes and fewer genes of certain known functions when compared to 20 other diverse organisms with completely sequenced genomes.[30]

F. tularensis requires cysteine or cystine (or another sulfhydryl source) for growth, and therefore will not grow on most routine solid media or on gram-negative selective media such as MacConkey or eosin methylene blue (EMB) agars. It may be recovered with the use of glucose cysteine blood agar, thioglycolate broth, chocolate agar suitable for gonococcal growth, modified Thayer-Martin medium, buffered charcoal-yeast agar, or cysteine heart agar with 9% chocolatized sheep blood.[17,18,24] Some strains of *F. tularensis* lack an overt requirement for cysteine or enriched medium for growth, leading the microbiology laboratory to suspect *Haemophilus* or *Actinobacillus* species because of the growth of an aerobic, small gram-negative coccobacillus.[31] In addition, clinically significant strains of *Francisella* have been reported that do not show typical fastidious growth characteristics of previous strains.[32] Differentiation of *Francisella* from other bacteria can be accomplished using direct fluorescent antibody staining, slide agglutination, polymerase chain reaction (PCR), or cellular fatty acid composition analysis.[18] It is important to note that automated laboratory identification systems should not be used for the identifica-

tion of *Francisella* because they are unreliable and may generate aerosols.[33] Federal regulations rigorously control transport of *F. tularensis* cultures, should the isolate be sent to a referral laboratory for identification.

Visible colonies take 2 to 5 days to appear.[34] Incubation at 35° C is optimal, with or without an atmosphere of increased CO_2. The recovery of *F. tularensis* from contaminated specimens may be facilitated by the addition of penicillin, cycloheximide, or polymyxin B to the media.[17,18] Virtually all *F. tularensis* strains are positive for β-lactamase.

Antisera can distinguish between *F. tularensis* subsp. *tularensis* and *novicida* but not between subsp. *tularensis* and *holarctica*; strains within subspecies do not have antigenic differences detectable by antisera. *F. tularensis* produces no known exotoxins. Whole radiation-killed organisms exhibit endotoxin-like activity in rabbits.[2] The lipopolysaccharide (LPS) from the live vaccine strain of *F. tularensis*, however, possesses at least 1000-fold less endotoxin activity than LPS from *Escherichia coli*.[35] Nonetheless, mice immunized with intact LPS purified from this strain are protected from subsequent intraperitoneal challenge with the vaccine strain but not from challenge with a fully virulent *F. tularensis* strain.[36] Furthermore, protection against the vaccine strain is not elicited by immunization with vaccine strain lipid A or O-side chain.[37] However, when mice are immunized with the vaccine strain O-side chain conjugated to bovine serum albumin they are protected against an intradermal challenge with the LVS strain and another type B *F. tularensis* strain, only partially protected against an aerosol challenge with the type B organisms, only partially protected against an intradermal challenge with a type A *F. tularensis* strain, and offered no protection against aerosol challenge against the type A strain.[38] Cowley and associates[39] demonstrated that the live vaccine strain of *F. tularensis* is capable of phase variation in LPS that alters the ability of the organism to induce rat-macrophage nitric oxide (NO) production, and consequently permits growth in the rat macrophage. This phase variation is related to the expression of two forms of LPS: one induces NO production by rat macrophages and the other does not. These two LPS forms differ both antigenically (at the O-antigen level) and functionally (at the lipid A level). Mutants of *F. novicida* with altered LPS O-side chains exhibit varying degrees of serum sensitivity and ability to grow in macrophages.[40]

Host immune responses are directed against numerous cell wall antigens, including membrane proteins, LPS, and carbohydrates, but no dominant antigens have been found.[41-43] Virulence traditionally has been associated with the capsule and citrulline ureidase activity. Wild encapsulated strains of *F. tularensis* are resistant to the bactericidal activity of normal serum, but a capsule-deficient mutant is serum sensitive.[16,43] The contribution of citrulline ureidase to virulence is unclear, and there are pathogenic isolates that do not possess this activity.[23] Virulence studies in mice have shown that the acriflavine agglutination (acf) test can be useful in determining virulence of *F. tularensis*. The acf test–positive (acf⁺) variants were exclusively low virulent and the negative (acf⁻) variants were either high or low virulent.[44] The acf⁻ variants had a larger amount of polysaccharide antigens than the acf⁺ variants, and one antigen fraction correlated with virulence.[45] Plasmids that have been found in isolates of *F. tularensis* subsp. *holarctica* and *novicida*, and in *F. philomiragia*, have not been found in the more virulent *F. tularensis* subsp. *tularensis* and thus are not essential for virulence.[18,30] Unlike other intracellular pathogens, the nonspecific tartrate-resistant acid phosphatase of *F. tularensis* is not required for growth within macrophages.[46] During growth in macrophages the vaccine strain of *F. tularensis* upregulates expression of several proteins. One of these, a 23-kDa protein, is also expressed after exposure of the organism to hydrogen peroxide.[47] Molecular studies of virulence using *F. novicida*, which is more amenable to genetic manipulation than *F. tularensis*, have identified several loci associated with growth in macrophages, including *mglAB* and *iglABCD*.[48,49] The operon *mglAB* encodes for presumed transcriptional regulatory proteins that are similar to stringent starvation proteins (SspA and B) of *E. coli* and *Haemophilus* species.[48] Interestingly, mutation in the *iglC* locus impairs *F. novicida* intracellular growth, and the protein encoded by this region is 99% homologous to the previously described *F. tularensis* 23-kDa protein.[47,49] Methods for gene replacement in *F. tularensis* recently have been developed, and used to delete both *iglC* alleles in the vaccine strain.[50] The resulting mutant did not produce the 23-kDa protein, exhibited impaired intracellular growth, and was attenuated in vivo for mice.[50] Unlike the parent strain, this mutant did not inhibit Toll-like receptor mediated signaling, through nuclear factor-kappa B (NF-κβ) and mitogen-activated protein kinase pathways, and secretion of tumor necrosis factor-α (TNF-α) and interleukin-1β (IL-β).[51] These findings suggest that intracellular survival of *Francisella* is mediated at least in part by blocking Toll-like receptor signaling and impairing production of TNF-α and IL-1β, and support an important role for the 23-kDa protein in this process.

Francisella philomiragia was previously called *Yersinia philomiragia*. It was reclassified because it shares the unique fatty-acid profile of the *Francisella* and substantial DNA relatedness to this genus, although it has some unique biochemical features (see Table 224-1) and DNA hybridization patterns that distinguish it from *F. tularensis*.[52] *F. philomiragia* is of low virulence for humans and has been isolated from muskrats and water. All strains originally tested produced β-lactamase and were most susceptible to aminoglycosides, cefoxitin, cefotaxime, fluoroquinolones, tetracycline, and chloramphenicol.[22,53] However, a more recent report documented infection caused by *F. philomiragia* resistant to cefazolin and cefotaxime.[52]

Several endosymbiotic bacteria of ticks have been classified within the *Francisellaceae* family on the basis of 16S ribosomal gene sequence data. These include *Wolbachia persica,* an endosymbiont found in Rocky Mountain wood ticks termed *Dermacentor andersoni* symbiont, and symbiont B of *Ornithodorous moubata*.[18,24,54] Similar organisms can be found in other hard and soft ticks, suggesting that they may be more widely distributed than previously observed.[54] However, at present no evolutionary relationships among these organisms and *Francisella* have been established.

EPIDEMIOLOGY

Tularemia is widely distributed, but it is primarily a disease of the Northern Hemisphere and is most common between 30° and 71° north latitude. It has been remarkably absent from the United Kingdom, Africa, South America, and Australia.[2] Tularemia was very common in the United States before World War II. However, its incidence has declined steadily since the 1950s, and has remained at fewer than 0.15 cases per 100,000 population since 1965 (Fig. 224-1).[55,56] Because of its stable and low incidence tularemia was removed from the list of nationally reportable diseases in 1995, but was added back in 2000 in part because of the concern about its use for bioterrorism. During 2000 and 2001 the case rates were 0.06 and 0.05 per 100,000 population, respectively.[57] Arkansas, Missouri, South Dakota, and Oklahoma reported 56% of the total U.S. cases from 1990 through 2000, with counties in Montana, Kansas, and Massachusetts also reporting high numbers of cases during this decade (Fig. 224-2).[55] Between 1992 and 1999 states in the West Central and Mountain regions accounted for 78% of all reported cases of tularemia (see Fig. 224-2).[56] Groups with high incidence rates include American Indians and Alaska Natives.[55,56]

Historically, in the United States tularemia incidence has been most frequent in June through August and in December. The summer peak corresponds to a greater number of tick-acquired cases, whereas the smaller peak in late winter reflects an increased number of hunting-associated cases. However, only the peak in the late spring and summer has been observed in more recent years.[55,56] Males account for the majority of cases, perhaps because of greater exposure opportunities, and tularemia can occur in individuals of any age (Fig. 224-3). Although 58% of the cases reported in the United States between 1992 and 1999 were in adults aged 25 years and older, 33% were in children between 1 and 14 years of age.[56] During the last decade incidence rates in the United States were highest in persons aged 5 to 9 years and in those 75 years and older (see Fig. 224-3).[55] Occupations that have been associated with an increased risk of tularemia are laboratory

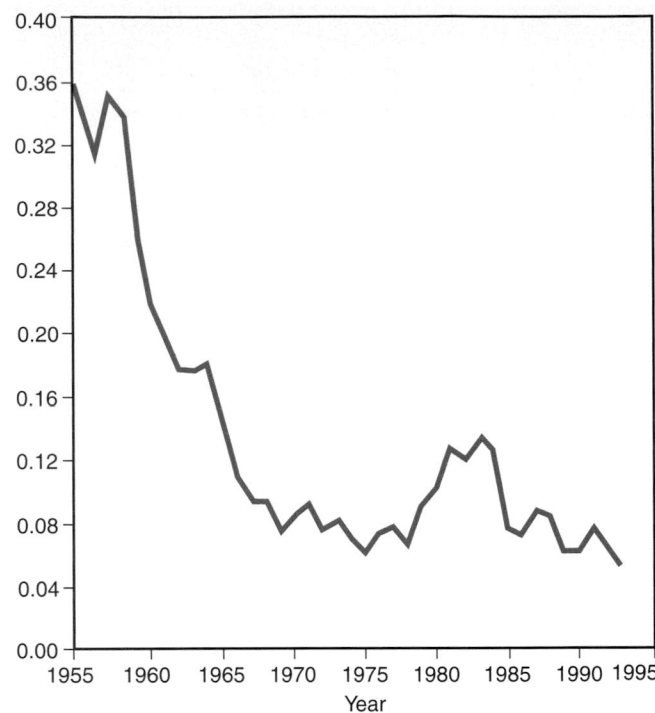

FIGURE 224-1. The incidence of tularemia in the United States from 1955 through 1993. *(From Centers for Disease Control and Prevention. Summary of notifiable diseases, United States, 1993. MMWR Morbid Mortal Wkly Rep. 1993;42:61.)*

worker, farmer, landscaper, veterinarian, sheep worker, hunter or trapper, and cook or meat handler.

F. tularensis is capable of infecting hundreds of different vertebrates and invertebrates, but no more than a dozen mammalian species are important to its ecology in any geographic region.[7] These include lagomorphs, particularly *Sylvilagus* and *Lepus* spp., and rodents such as voles, squirrels, muskrats, and beavers in North America; included in the former Soviet Union are voles, hamsters, mice, and hares. Transmission of *F. tularensis* to humans occurs most often through the bite of an insect or contact with contaminated animal products. Other routes of transmission include aerosol droplets, contact with contaminated water or mud, and animal bites. Illness may occur in families or friends because of shared activities and exposures. Nonetheless, human-to-human spread does not occur.

Bloodfeeding arthropods and flies are the most important vectors for tularemia in the United States. Ticks predominate in the Rocky Mountain states and eastward, whereas biting flies predominate in California, Nevada, and Utah.[24] In contrast, mosquitoes are the most frequent insect vector in Sweden and Finland, and they also are important in the former Soviet Union. At least 13 species of ticks have been found to be naturally infected with *F. tularensis,* and transovarial passage may occur. The dog tick *(Dermacentor variabilis),* wood tick *(D. andersoni),* and Lone Star tick *(Amblyomma americanum)* are commonly involved in North America. The organism may be present in tick saliva or feces and may be inoculated either directly or indirectly into the bite wound. Several outbreaks of tickborne tularemia have involved *F. tularensis* subsp. *holarctica* (type B), although this organism is more often linked to water, rodents, and aquatic animals; tick transmission traditionally has been associated with subsp. *tularensis* (type A). Tularemia in children in endemic areas of the United States is now most often associated with tick exposure in the summer.

Animal contact is another important mode of acquiring tularemia. Skinning, dressing, and eating infected animals, including rabbits, muskrats, beavers, squirrels, and birds, have transmitted tularemia, occasionally resulting in large outbreaks in hunters. For example, hamster hunting was responsible for an epidemic in Eastern Europe.[58] Wild

FIGURE 224-2. The total number of tularemia cases reported in the lower continental United States by county of residence from 1990 through 2000. Alaska reported 10 cases in four counties during this time. [†]Circle size is proportional to the number of cases, ranging from 1 to 39. *(From Centers for Disease Control and Prevention. Tularemia—United States, 1990-2000. MMWR Morbid Mortal Wkly Rep. 2002;51:181-184.)*

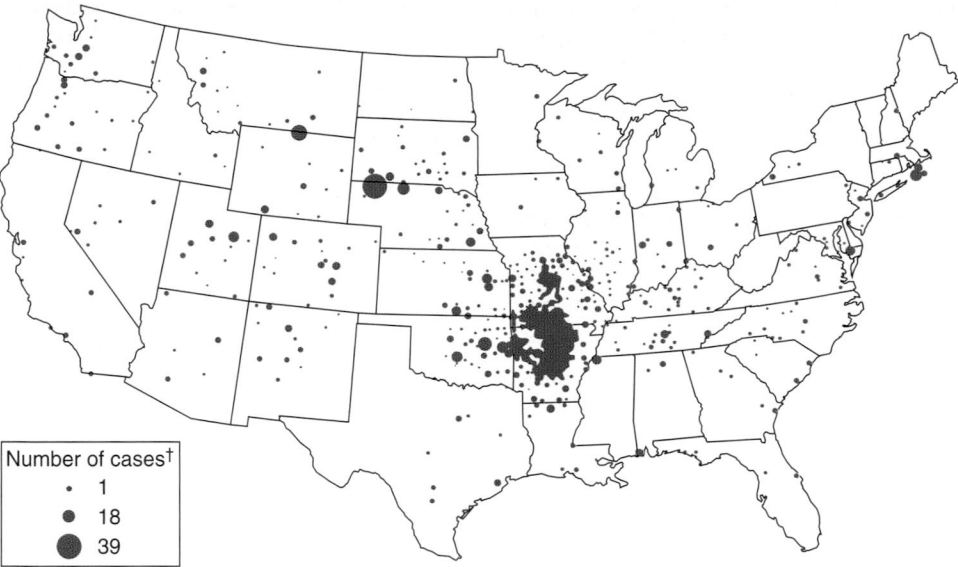

Number of cases[†]
- • 1
- ● 18
- ⬤ 39

animals sold as pets also are potential vectors, as occurred in 2002 when infected prairie dogs were widely commercially distributed.[59] The first outbreak in Spain was associated with processing hare carcasses and hare meat, and was notable for a preponderance of women patients.[60] Airborne transmission has occurred during these activities, as well as from contact with water, contaminated dust, and hay. Running over a rabbit with a lawnmower has caused pulmonary tularemia.[61] An outbreak in 2000 of pneumonic tularemia on Martha's Vineyard was associated with mowing lawns and using a brush cutter.[4] It was postulated that the environment was contaminated with viable *F. tularensis* from animals and that infective aerosols were generated by these jobs.[4] Three sporadic cases of tularemia pneumonia occurred on Martha's Vineyard during 2001; two were in landscapers and one in a farmer who was involved in mowing his fields.[62] A seroprevalence survey that year found that 9.1% of tested landscapers had anti-*F. tularensis* antibodies as compared to fewer than 1% of nonlandscaper residents, and seropositivity was highest in those who mowed more lawns and spent the most time mowing and weed-whacking.[62] Carnivorous animals may transiently carry *F. tularensis* in the mouth or on claws after killing or feeding on infected prey, whether or not they become infected. This is thought to be the mechanism by which domestic cats occasionally transmit tularemia.[63,64] *F. tularensis* may survive for prolonged periods in water, mud, and animal carcasses

even if frozen; however, cooking game meats thoroughly to the proper temperatures should minimize risk from ingestion. Contaminated water continues to be an important environmental source of tularemia.[5,14,65] In postwar Kosovo multiple factors resulted in a large tularemia outbreak that lasted several years and often presented with fever, pharyngitis, and cervical lymphadenopathy.[5] The oropharyngeal disease and results of subsequent investigations indicated that the war led to an epizootic in increased rodent populations that contaminated ransacked homes and food with *F. tularensis,* and in turn this led to a food- and waterborne outbreak among refugees returning to disrupted housing and sanitation.[5] It recently has been demonstrated that *F. tularensis* LVS strain will multiply intracellularly in *Acanthamoeba castellanii,* amoebal cysts may become infected, and that coculture of the organisms enhances the growth of *F. tularensis.*[66] Such a relationship may prove relevant to natural aquatic reservoirs for tularemia.

PATHOGENESIS

F. tularensis is a virulent organism for susceptible species, including the accidental human host. Although the organism is reported to penetrate intact skin, most investigators believe that penetration occurs through sites of inapparent skin disruption.[67] The infectious dose in humans depends on the portal of entry: 10 to 50 organisms when injected

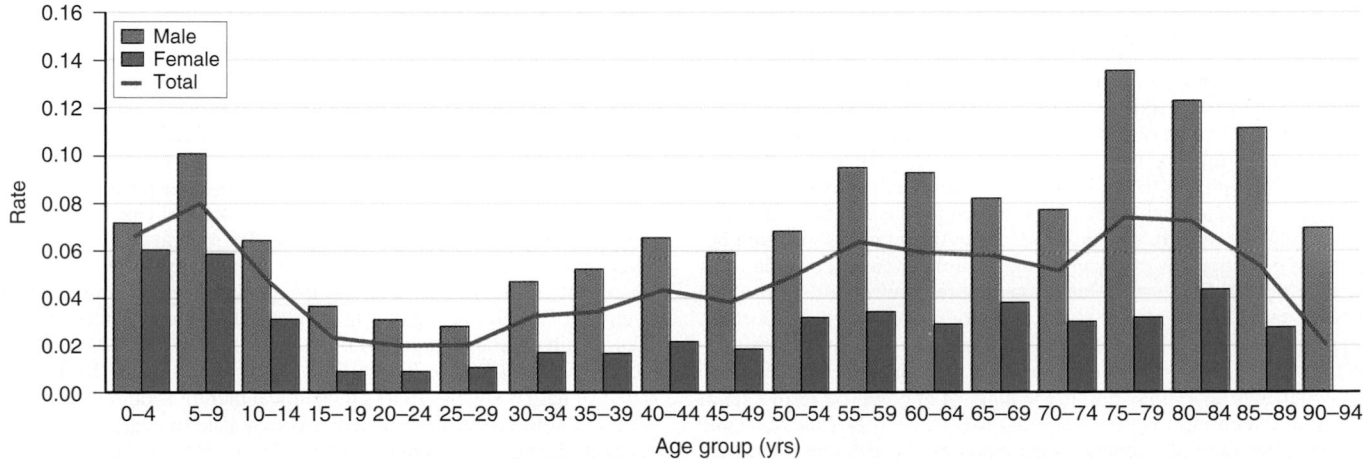

FIGURE 224-3. Ages and gender of tularemia cases reported in the United States from 1990 through 2000. *(From Centers for Disease Control and Prevention. Tularemia—United States, 1990-2000. MMWR Morbid Mortal Wkly Rep. 2002;51:181-184.)*

intradermally or when inhaled, and 10^8 organisms when ingested. That low numbers of bacteria can cause infection through the skin, mucous membranes, and airways helps to explain in part the extreme risk that *F. tularensis* poses to laboratory workers.[68] In general, *F. tularensis* subsp. *tularensis* causes more severe disease than subsp. *holarctica* and *novicida*. The molecular reasons underlying these differences in virulence are unknown at present.

Over the first 3 to 5 days after cutaneous inoculation, *F. tularensis* multiplies locally and produces a papule; ulceration occurs 2 to 4 days later. Organisms spread from the site of entry to regional lymph nodes and may disseminate via a lymphohematogenous route to involve multiple organs. Bacteremia is probably common in this early phase, although it is only occasionally detected. An elegant description of the pathogenesis is offered by Geyer and colleagues.[69] Infection with *F. tularensis* is characterized by an acute inflammatory response that involves fibrin, neutrophils, macrophages, and T lymphocytes. Neutrophils and macrophages surround earlier inflammatory cells, stimulated by the initial inoculum, that have become necrotic and degenerated. Eventually lymphocytes, epithelioid cells, and giant cells migrate into the necrotic tissue. This extensive necrosis is noted in both lung tissue and lymph nodes. As the necrotic tissue expands, adjacent veins and arteries may thrombose. The organisms usually are present at the site of the necrotic tissue but are difficult to demonstrate on routine stains. Silver impregnation techniques (Steiner, Dieterle, Warthin-Starry) enhance the visibility of the organisms, which are usually found in macrophages and epithelioid cells. Granulomas develop that occasionally may caseate; for this reason, specimens may be mistaken for tuberculosis. These changes can occur in any infected site and have been found at autopsy in lung, liver, spleen, lymph nodes, and bone marrow. Coalescence of necrotic foci may yield abscess formation. *F. tularensis* may remain viable in tissues for prolonged periods.

Humoral immunity, directed against carbohydrate antigens, develops between the second and third week after infection, with the almost simultaneous appearance of immunoglobulin M (IgM), IgG, and IgA agglutinating antibodies.[70] However, antibodies alone are insufficient to protect against virulent *F. tularensis* infection.[41] Opsonizing IgG and IgM antibodies also are produced, with the most efficient opsonization involving both immune serum and complement (C3). Nonetheless, oxygen-dependent neutrophil killing of wild virulent strains is poor; intracellular killing of the attenuated vaccine strain is mediated by hypochlorous acid, but wild strains are resistant to this compound.[41]

Complete recovery from tularemia requires cell-mediated immunity, which is demonstrable about 1 week earlier than antibody responses and is directed against protein antigens.[6,41] This cell-mediated immunity is α/β T-cell dependent but may involve either CD4+ or CD8+ T cells.[71] Attempts are being made to define the critical molecular determinants that induce protective immunity. *F. tularensis* is a facultative intracellular parasite that is capable of growing within several different cell types, including macrophages, hepatocytes, and endothelial cells.[6,41] The vaccine strain of *F. tularensis* induces apoptosis in murine macrophage-like cells, and this requires proliferating intracellular organisms.[72] Bacterial survival in rodent macrophages is associated with failure of phagosome-lysosome fusion, phagosome acidification, and utilization of host iron.[73] Interferon-γ (IFN-γ) and TNF-α activate macrophages to kill *F. tularensis* through the production of nitric oxide (NO) and other reactive nitrogen products.[74] Several mechanisms are involved in the innate response that controls infection before the development of conventional cellular immunity. Initial host defense against *F. tularensis* infection requires neutrophils, TNF-α and IFN-γ, but these are not sufficient to overcome the infection. Neutrophils and IFN-γ are not essential to defense against aerosol infection in mice, however, suggesting that other host mechanisms also may control primary infection in the lung.[75] For complete resolution of systemic infection, it is necessary that α/β+ T cells be functional and present after the initial defenses provided by the cytokines and neutrophils.[71] Some of the early responses to primary *F. tularensis* infec-

tion in mice, including cytokine production, are at least in part under genetic control and involve the *Bcg* locus.[76,77] Specific immunity that is α/β T-cell independent appears in mice within 2 days of intradermal inoculation of the attenuated vaccine strain, requires IFN-γ and TNF-α production, and involves B cells.[78] B-cell–deficient mice have impaired clearance of organisms following a primary infection with the vaccine strain (LVS), and are 100-fold less protected against secondary challenge.[79] Immunity to subsequent challenge is restored by B cells but not by passive transfer of anti-LVS antibodies.[79] Mice injected with small amounts of LPS from strain LVS are protected from subsequent LVS challenge within 2 days, and this is dependent on B cells and IFN-γ but not anti-LPS antibodies.[80] A similar early protection against murine LVS infection is induced by DNA containing CpG motifs, either in bacterial DNA or in synthetic oligonucleotides.[81] This is dependent on lymphocytes, predominantly B cells but also T cells; involves the production of IFN-γ and IL-12; and may contribute to the generation of specific memory cells.[81] IL-12, IFN-γ, and TNF-α are quickly expressed locally in the skin of immune mice challenged intradermally with the vaccine strain, with IL-12 appearing within the first 24 hours.[82] Full clearance of *F. tularensis* LVS infection in mice is dependent on the presence of IL-12 as either the intact IL-12 p70 protein or the IL-12 p40 protein.[83]

Expansion of circulating γ/δ T cells has been documented in patients with acute tularemia. These cells respond to phosphoantigens from many different pathogens, including *F. tularensis*. Poquet and coworkers[84] showed in 13 tularemia patients that a large increase in Vγ9Vδ2 cells is a characteristic of infection with *F. tularensis* but is not prominent after immunization with the LVS strain; this is true despite similar amounts and activities of phosphoantigens in the LVS and two clinical strains assayed. The observed increase in the levels of Vγ9Vδ2 cells occurs after the first week of illness and may persist for longer than 1 year after infection.[85] However, 10 to 30 years after infection long-lived memory cells responsive to *F. tularensis* heat shock proteins are α/β T cells and not γ/δ T cells.[86]

The organism's intracellular residence in the liver and other sites may help to protect it from these defenses and permit its early growth. Neutrophils and mononuclear cells accumulate at infected liver foci in mice and lyse hepatocytes harboring *F. tularensis,* thereby releasing organisms from this sequestered environment.[87]

CLINICAL MANIFESTATIONS

The clinical consequences of *F. tularensis* infection depend on the virulence of the particular organism, the portal of entry, the extent of systemic involvement, and the immune status of the host. The result can range from asymptomatic or inconsequential illness to acute sepsis and rapid death. Patients who seek medical attention usually present with at least one of six classic forms of tularemia: ulceroglandular, glandular, oculoglandular, pharyngeal, typhoidal, and pneumonic. This somewhat artificial classification emphasizes only the predominant manifestations commonly encountered, and there is overlap in many patients.

The incubation period averages 3 to 5 days, but ranges from fewer than 1 to 21 days.[88] Tularemia usually starts abruptly, with the onset of fever, chills, headache, malaise, anorexia, and fatigue. Other prominent symptoms may include cough, myalgias, chest discomfort, vomiting, sore throat, abdominal pain, and diarrhea. A pulse-temperature deficit has been noted in up to 42% of evaluable patients.[2] Fever (usually greater than 101° F) classically lasts for several days, remits for a short interval, and then recurs along with other symptoms.[14] Without treatment fever lasts an average of 32 days, and chronic debility, weight loss, and adenopathy may persist for many months longer.[89] Less virulent strains cause a milder, self-limited illness that may resolve without therapy. Systemic symptoms may abate by the time medical help is sought, so that the clinical picture is dominated by one or more of the six patterns listed; this may lead to confusion as to the correct diagnosis, particularly in the 25% to 50% of patients without an evident source of infection.[2,89]

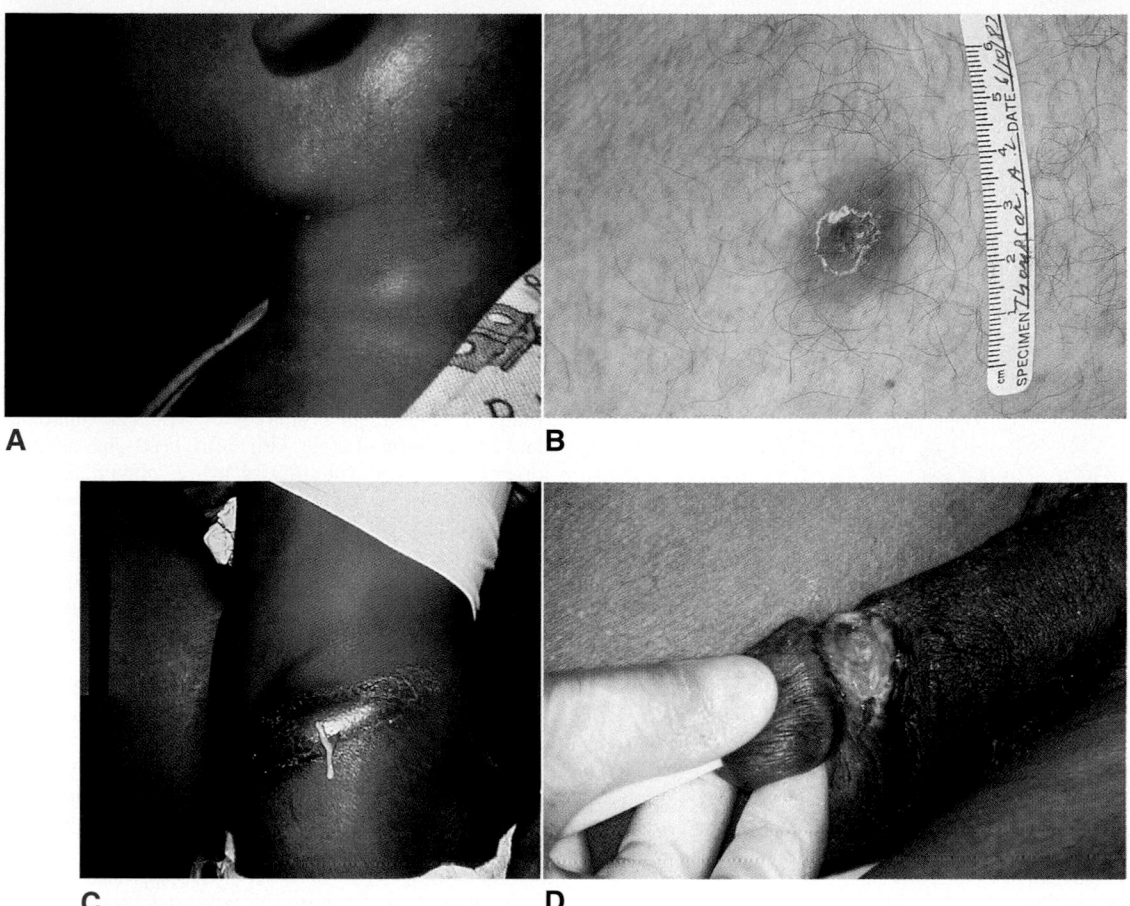

FIGURE 224-4. Examples of primary lesions seen in ulceroglandular tularemia. **A,** Large cervical and submandibular lymph nodes in a young child; an ulcer was found under the hairline on her forehead at the site of a tick bite. *(Courtesy of Dr. Joseph A. Bocchini, Louisiana State University Health Sciences Center, Shreveport, LA.)* **B,** Papule undergoing central necrosis with desquamation on the thigh of a middle-aged man. **C,** Inguinal adenopathy and suppurative mass in a young hunter who had carried a dead hare at his side. *(Courtesy of Dr. Joseph A. Bocchini, Louisiana State University Health Sciences Center, Shreveport, LA.)* **D,** Penile ulcer that was suspected of being syphilis or another sexually transmitted disease until the history of a recent tick bite was obtained by the infectious diseases consultant. *(Courtesy of Dr. John W. King, Louisiana State University Health Sciences Center, Shreveport, LA.)*

Ulceroglandular tularemia has been the presentation in 21% to 87% of cases[90-92]; tick bites and animal contacts are the usually recalled exposures. This is the form that is most quickly recognized as tularemia. The initial specific complaint is often of enlarged and tender localized lymphadenopathy (Fig. 224-4). The inciting skin lesion may appear either before, simultaneously with, or from one to several days after the adenopathy. It starts as a red, painful papule in a region draining into the involved lymph nodes. During a waterborne outbreak secondary to crayfish fishing, skin lesions were initially thought to be caused by *Mycobacterim marinum.*[65] The papule then undergoes necrosis, leaving a tender ulcer with a raised border (see Fig. 224-4). If untreated, the ulcer may take weeks to heal and leave a residual scar. Multiple lesions may occur, particularly in those with animal sources.[2] The location of the ulcer generally reflects the mode of acquisition; animal contacts tend to yield ulcers on the hands and forearms, and tick bites tend to yield ulcers on the trunk, the perineum, the lower extremities, and the head and neck. The distribution of lymphadenopathy also reflects the exposure history, as illustrated in Figure 224-5; overall, cervical and occipital adenopathy is most common in children, and inguinal adenopathy is most common in adults.[93] Skin changes over the involved nodes should suggest underlying suppuration. Some patients have a sporotrichoid presentation with ascending subcutaneous nodules.[14,94] Lymphangitis is rare unless there is bacterial superinfection of the ulcer.

Glandular tularemia occurs when patients present with tender regional lymphadenopathy but without an evident cutaneous lesion. This form accounts for 3% to 20% of cases in the United States, although 62% of cases in Japan have been of this type.[90,92] Glandular tularemia represents essentially the same process as ulceroglandular disease, except that a skin lesion either healed before presentation or was minimal or atypical and overlooked. Enlarged lymph nodes may persist for prolonged periods, and in some patients an exposure or prior febrile illness will be forgotten. For this reason, tularemia may not be considered in the initial differential diagnosis of some patients whose primary presentation is lymphadenopathy.[2] In either ulceroglandular or glandular tularemia the lymph nodes may suppurate (see Fig. 224-4). More than 20% will suppurate if left untreated or if treatment is delayed longer than 2 weeks.[6] When fluctuant, they should be needle-aspirated or surgically drained. The differential diagnosis of ulceroglandular and glandular tularemia includes pyogenic bacterial infections, cat-scratch disease, syphilis, chancroid, lymphogranuloma venereum, tuberculosis, nontuberculous mycobacterial infection, toxoplasmosis, sporotrichosis, rat-bite fever, anthrax, plague, and herpes simplex virus infection.

Oculoglandular tularemia represents only 0% to 5% of cases.[90] In this form, organisms have gained entry through the conjunctiva, either from contaminated fingers or from contaminated splashes and aerosols. Disease is bilateral in fewer than 12% of patients.[14] Early

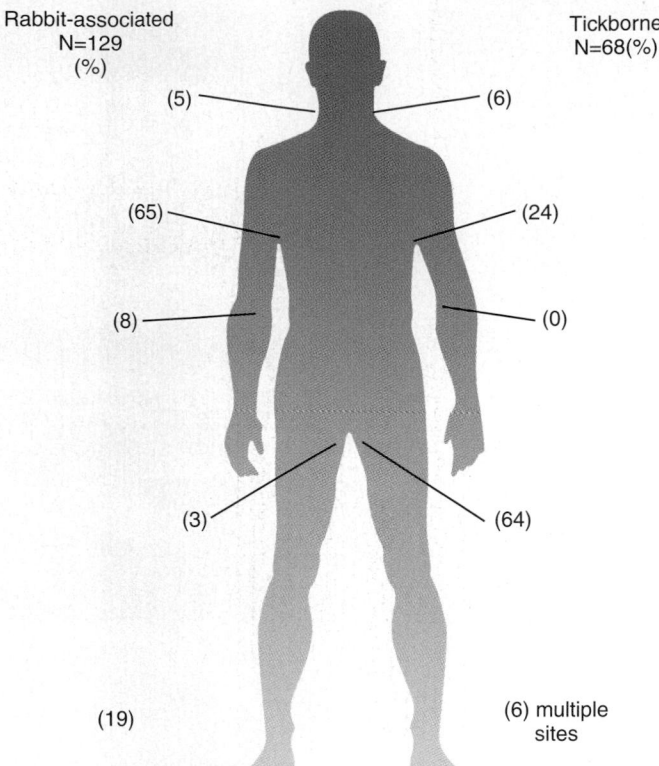

Rabbit-associated
N=129
(%)

Tickborne
N=68(%)

(5)

(6)

(65)

(24)

(8)

(0)

(3)

(64)

(19)

(6) multiple
sites

FIGURE 224-5. Distribution of lymphadenopathy in rabbit-associated and tick-borne tularemia.

complaints may include photophobia and excessive lacrimation. Examination shows lid edema and a painful conjunctivitis, with injection, chemosis, and small, yellowish conjunctival ulcers or papules in some patients. Associated tender lymphadenopathy may occur in the preauricular, submandibular, and cervical regions. If the adenopathy is extensive and more prominent than the eye findings, then this syndrome may be mistaken for mumps.[2] Visual loss is rare, but complications include corneal ulceration, dacrocystitis, and nodal suppuration.[89] The differential diagnosis of oculoglandular tularemia includes pyogenic bacterial infections, adenoviral infection, syphilis, cat-scratch disease, and herpes simplex virus infection.

Pharyngeal tularemia, another variant of ulceroglandular disease, is the result of primary invasion through the oropharynx. The source may be contaminated foods or water or contaminated droplets. This form, which represents 0% to 12% of cases overall, has been seen with increasing frequency in Japan, and may predominate in outbreaks[5,90,92,95] Children have been involved more often than adults, and several family members may be affected simultaneously.[2] It must be distinguished from the sore throat that may accompany any of the other major clinical forms of tularemia. In pharyngeal tularemia, the patient's predominant complaint typically is of fever and severe throat pain. Exudative pharyngitis or tonsillitis is the rule, and one or more ulcers may be seen. A pharyngeal membrane has been described in some patients that is similar to a diphtheritic membrane.[89] Cervical, preparotid, and retropharyngeal adenopathy may be present, occasionally with bilateral involvement or abscess formation.[95] When there is a delay in seeking care the dominant manifestation may be cervical adenopathy without prominent fever or pharyngotonsillitis.[95] The differential diagnosis includes streptococcal pharyngitis, infectious mononucleosis, adenoviral infection, and diphtheria. Tularemia should be suspected in an endemic area whenever a severe sore throat is unresponsive to penicillin therapy and routine diagnostic tests have been unrewarding.

Typhoidal tularemia refers to a febrile illness caused by *F. tularensis* that is not associated with prominent lymphadenopathy and does not fit into any of the other major forms. From 5% to 30% of cases are typhoidal, and they are the most difficult to diagnose.[90,92] This form of tularemia may result from any mode of acquisition. Because the portal of entry is usually inapparent clinically, a history of outdoor activities with tick or animal exposure should be sought. Many patients have serious underlying chronic medical disorders and their presentation can be quite dramatic, with acute prostration and rapid death, or a protracted illness.[3,68,96,97] For example, an adolescent boy with human immunodeficiency virus infection was diagnosed with typhoidal tularemia only after blood cultures grew the organism. His only possible exposure was a history of being licked by a diseased fawn with a cleft palate. The patient had a lengthy course with several relapses requiring prolonged antibiotic therapy with gentamicin and tetracycline. He never developed a positive serology, and this was thought to be a consequence of his severe immunocompromise (CD4 count of 0/mm³).[98] Prominent symptoms of typhoidal tularemia may include any combination of fever with chills, headache, myalgias, sore throat, anorexia, nausea, vomiting, diarrhea, abdominal pain, and cough. Examination may reveal dehydration, hypotension, mild pharyngitis and cervical adenopathy, meningismus, and diffuse abdominal tenderness. Hepatomegaly and splenomegaly are found uncommonly in the acute stages and become more likely the longer the duration of illness. Severe disease may be accompanied by cholestasis with jaundice.[99] Diarrhea, a major manifestation only in typhoidal tularemia, is loose and watery but only rarely bloody. Children may have more severe intestinal involvement, including focal areas of bowel necrosis.[89] Rare gastrointestinal manifestations include cholangitis, granulomatous hepatitis, and liver abscess.[99] Secondary pleuropulmonary involvement is common in this form, with pulmonary infiltrates or pleural effusions being found in up to 45% of typhoidal cases; it is even more frequent in laboratory-acquired infections. Additional findings in severely ill patients may include hyponatremia, elevated creatine phosphokinase, myoglobinuria, pyuria, renal failure, and positive blood cultures.[2,3,68,96] The differential diagnosis of typhoidal tularemia includes typhoid fever caused by *Salmonella* spp., brucellosis, *Legionella* infection, Q fever, disseminated mycobacterial or fungal infection, rickettsioses, malaria, endocarditis, and any other cause of prolonged fever without localizing signs.

Pneumonic tularemia refers to an illness whose initial presentation is dominated by pulmonary infection. This is found in 7% to 20% of all tularemia cases and may occur at any age.[90,93] It may result from direct inhalation of the organism or from secondary hematogenous spread to the lung. Primary pneumonic tularemia is a risk for certain occupations, including sheep shearers, farmers, landscapers, and laboratory workers.[4,62,100,101] Cases also have been described as resulting from common exposure in a more casual setting.[102] Secondary pneumonia may occur early or after a delay of weeks to months in the course of tularemia.[6] Although secondary pneumonia may complicate any of the syndromes already discussed, Evans and colleagues[2] found pneumonia to be most frequent in typhoidal (83%) and ulceroglandular (31%) diseases. Scofield and associates[103] reported that patients with pneumonic involvement were more likely to be older, to recall no exposure, to present with typhoidal illness, to have positive cultures, to stay hospitalized longer, and to have a higher mortality rate. From 25% to 30% of patients have infiltrates on radiographic examination without any clinical findings of pneumonia.[2] Pneumonia from *F. tularensis* subsp. *tularensis* (type A) is a significantly more severe disease than that caused by subspecies *holarctica* (type B), but illness may be prolonged with either subspecies.[6,104] Common symptoms include fever, cough, no or minimal sputum production, substernal tightness, and pleuritic chest pain. Hemoptysis may occur but is uncommon.[2] Physical examination may be nonspecific or may reveal rales, consolidation, and a friction rub or signs of effusion. Some patients need mechanical ventilation, and adult respiratory distress syndrome may complicate the course of any form of tularemia. Routine examination of sputum does not help to suggest the diagnosis. However, a false-positive direct fluorescent antibody stain for *Legionella* on bronchoscopy specimens has been reported.[105] Infected pleural fluid is ex-

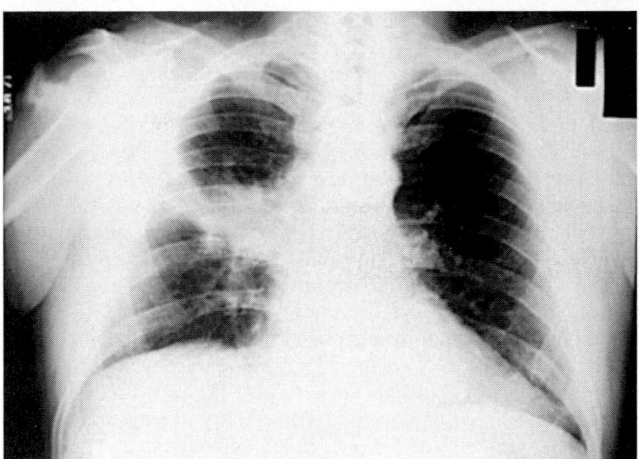

FIGURE 224-6. Chest radiograph of untreated tularemia pneumonia. This patient remained symptomatic for more than 3 months. The diagnosis was established serologically when poorly developed granulomas were found in a transbronchial biopsy, other causes were excluded, and the exposure history was finally obtained. *(From Penn RL, Kinasewitz GT. Factors associated with a poor outcome in tularemia. Arch Intern Med. 1987;147:265–268. Copyright 1987, American Medical Association.)*

udative, negative on Gram stain, and usually contains more than 1000 leukocytes/mm³; cells are predominantly lymphocytes, but neutrophilic effusions may occur.[2,100] Pleural effusions seen with tularemia frequently mimic those seen with tuberculosis. Similar findings for both include a lymphocyte-rich exudative pleural effusion and a high adenosine deaminase concentration.[106] Granulomas may be found on pleural biopsy and may be confused with tuberculosis.[100] Acute radiographic changes may include subsegmental or lobar infiltrates (Fig. 224-6), hilar adenopathy, pleural effusion, and apical or miliary infiltrates; less common changes include ovoid densities, cavitation, and bronchopleural fistula.[107] However, in some patients the initial chest films are normal.[6,107] Secondary pneumonias are more likely to involve the lower lobes and be bilateral, perhaps because of their hematogenous origin.[103] Healing usually occurs without residual changes, but fibrosis and calcifications may result. Therefore, tularemia may manifest as an enigmatic community-acquired pneumonia that does not respond to routine therapies. The differential diagnosis of pneumonic tularemia includes *Mycoplasma* pneumonia, *Legionella* infection, *Chlamydophila (Chlamydia) pneumoniae* infection, Q fever, psittacosis, tuberculosis, the deep mycoses, and many other causes of atypical or chronic pneumonias (see Chapter 64).

Secondary skin rashes are an underappreciated part of tularemia and may be found in up to 35% of cases.[108] They usually appear within the first 2 weeks of symptoms, but in a minority are delayed. Rash is more common in women than in men. Cutaneous changes may include diffuse maculopapular and vesiculopapular eruptions, erythema nodosum, erythema multiforme, acneiform lesions, and urticaria. Sweet's syndrome also has been reported in association with tularemia.[109] Although any type of secondary rash may be part of any form of tularemia, erythema nodosum has been found to occur most commonly with pneumonic tularemia.[108]

A review of tularemia in Sweden focused on reports of oropharyngeal tularemia, bacteremia, and meningitis. Tularemia was not in the initial differential diagnosis of these infections but was considered only after patients failed to respond to standard therapy for more common causes.[110] This suggests that even in endemic regions tularemia may not be detected or may be diagnosed only after a prolonged delay.

The clinical manifestations of infections caused by *F. tularensis* subsp. *novicida* are less well characterized than for the other subspecies, but are similar to those previously described.[22] *F. philomiragia* infection has caused a skin vesicle, pneumonia, empyema, sepsis,

peritonitis, splenic microabscesses, and meningitis.[52,53,111] This organism predominantly infects patients with host defenses impaired by chronic granulomatous disease, near-drowning in salt water or estuaries, or myeloproliferative disorders.[53] Recurrent *F. philomiragia* infection caused by two distinct strains has been documented in a patient with chronic granulomatous disease who had repeated occupational exposure to brackish water.[52,111]

COMPLICATIONS AND OUTCOME

Suppuration of involved lymph nodes is currently the most common complication of tularemia (see Fig. 224-4), and this may occur even after specific antibiotic therapy.[93] Nodes that suppurate after appropriate therapy are often sterile but benefit from drainage. Patients with severe disease may manifest disseminated intravascular coagulation, renal failure, rhabdomyolysis, jaundice, and hepatitis. Meningitis, encephalitis, pericarditis, peritonitis, osteomyelitis, splenic rupture, and thrombophlebitis have become very rare since antibiotic therapy has become available. Single cases of endocarditis[112] and prosthetic joint infection with bacteremia[113] caused by *F. tularensis* have been reported. The cerebrospinal fluid (CSF) in meningitis patients almost always shows a mononuclear cell pleocytosis, with a high protein concentration and hypoglycorrhachia.[114] LeDoux[115] described a 61-year-old man with bacteremic tularemia pneumonia who had a 1-week history of fevers and malaise but presented for care only after he developed cerebellar ataxia. Laboratory studies showed elevated transaminases, elevated creatine kinase, thrombocytopenia, a negative non-contrast brain magnetic resonance imaging (MRI), and normal CSF except for a protein concentration of 76 mg/dL.[115]

Tularemia may lead to months of debility in some patients, usually associated with late lymph node suppuration or persistent fatigue. Features that are associated with a worse prognosis include increasing age, serious coexisting medical conditions, symptoms lasting a month or longer before treatment, significant pleuropulmonary disease, typhoidal illness, renal failure, a delay in the diagnosis, and inappropriate antibiotic therapy.[3,103,116] Overall death rates in the antibiotic era have been 4% or less, but were as high as 33% before the introduction of streptomycin as treatment.[2,117]

DIAGNOSIS

The diagnosis of tularemia ultimately rests on clinical suspicion. Results of routine laboratory testing are nonspecific. The leukocyte count and sedimentation rate may be normal or elevated. Thrombocytopenia, hyponatremia, elevated serum transaminases, increased creatine phosphokinase, myoglobinuria, and sterile pyuria are occasionally found.[3] The organism is rarely seen on Gram-stained smears or in tissue biopsies and does not grow in routinely plated cultures. However, *F. tularensis* may be recovered from blood, pleural fluid, lymph nodes, wounds, sputum, and gastric aspirates when processed on supportive media. Because of this and its potential danger to laboratory personnel, individuals working in the area or who may come in contact with the specimens should be notified if tularemia is suspected. *F. tularensis* subsp. *holarctica* was isolated from an eschar biopsy centrifuged onto human embryonic lung cells in shell vials because a rickettsiosis was suspected.[118] Isolations by blood culture using more sensitive radiometric techniques have included the less virulent *holarctica* (type B) strains as well as the more virulent *tularensis* (type A) strains.[68,96,97,119,120] The nonradiometric culture medium also supports the growth of *F. tularensis*.[121] Animal inoculation is rarely performed at present, in part because this requires Biosafety Level 3 facilities. Biosafety Level 2 is sufficient for laboratory handling of routine clinical specimens, but Biosafety Level 3 should be used to process isolates suspected of being *F. tularensis*.[18]

The rapid diagnosis of *F. tularensis* infection has become a more urgent goal as a result of its potential use as an agent of bioterrorism (see Chapter 322). Methods for rapid diagnosis that have been reported include direct fluorescent antibody staining of smears and tissues, antigen detection in urine, detection of LPS using specific monoclonal antibodies, RNA hybridization with a 16S ribosomal probe, and PCR.[18,122] However, except for PCR they have not been accepted for widespread use.

The use of PCR is appealing in that smears and cultures are usually negative, standard microbiologic isolation may be hazardous to laboratory personnel, serologic diagnosis may take several weeks to confirm, and the methodology is widely available. Although very sensitive in artificial media, PCR assays are less sensitive when applied to biological specimens and false-negatives may occur. Nonetheless, initial studies done in murine and other animal models showed that PCR was an effective modality for diagnosing infection with *Francisella*.[122-125] Sjostedt and colleagues[126] tested wound swabs from infected patients and found a 73% sensitivity with PCR using primers for the 17-kDa lipoprotein *F. tularensis* gene and 50% sensitivity with primers for the 16S rDNA gene. A subsequent study on wound swabs from 40 patients with ulceroglandular tularemia found that PCR using the 17-kDa primers was 75% sensitive and culture was 62% sensitive.[127] In this cohort, in four of eight patients with negative serologies and cultures, *F. tularensis* DNA was detected by PCR in their wound swabs.[127] Dolan and associates[128] were able to show that PCR on lymph node aspirates was positive even after antibiotic therapy was initiated. Therefore, PCR may prove useful for diagnosing tularemia in patients already receiving suppressive empiric antibiotic therapy. Diagnostic applications of PCR and other assays for field use[122] are discussed further in Chapters 15 and 322.

Serologic studies are the most common way that the diagnosis of tularemia is confirmed. Antibodies to *F. tularensis* may be demonstrated by tube agglutination, microagglutination, hemagglutination, and enzyme-linked immunosorbent assay (ELISA).[18] Standard serologies detect infections with *F. tularensis* subsp. *tularensis* and *holarctica* equally well, and usually are negative with subspecies *novicida* and with *F. philomiragia*.[18] Standard tube agglutination titers are usually negative in the first week of illness, are positive in most patients by the end of 2 weeks, and peak after 4 to 5 weeks. The microagglutination assay is up to 100-fold more sensitive than tube agglutination. IgM and IgG antibodies appear together and high titers of both may persist for longer than a decade after infection,[6,41] limiting the value of a single positive result. A presumptive diagnosis is supported by an acute tube agglutination titer of 1:160 or more, or an acute microagglutination titer of 1:128 or more, in the face of compatible disease but this may also reflect remote infection.[18] Definitive serologic diagnosis requires a fourfold or greater rise in titer between acute and convalescent specimens; serologies may need to be repeated at 7- to 10-day intervals before a rise is demonstrated. Antibodies may cross-react with *Brucella* spp., *Proteus* OX19, and *Yersinia* spp., but titers to *F. tularensis* are almost always higher, and dithiothreitol treatment of the serum eliminates most of these other reactions.[18,41] False-positive heterophile agglutinins also rarely occur during tularemia.[89,117] Tests for cell-mediated immunity such as lymphocyte blastogenesis and delayed hypersensitivity skin test reactivity may be positive earlier than serologies, but standardized antigen preparations are not commercially available.[41,127]

THERAPY

The drug of first choice for the treatment of all forms of tularemia except meningitis is streptomycin, although gentamicin is an acceptable substitute. The minimum dosage of streptomycin that is effective therapy for tularemia is 7.5 to 10 mg/kg intramuscularly every 12 hours for 7 to 14 days. An alternative regimen is 15 mg/kg intramuscularly every 12 hours for the first 3 days, followed by half this dose to complete treatment. For patients who are very ill, 15 mg/kg every 12 hours may be given throughout a 7- to 10-day course. Doses greater than 2 g/day of streptomycin in adults do not increase efficacy.[88] The pediatric weight-based regimens for streptomycin are similar (up to a maximum of the adult dose): 30 to 40 mg/kg/day intramuscularly in two divided doses for a total of 7 days; or 40 mg/kg/day intramuscularly in two di-

vided doses for the first 3 days, followed by 20 mg/kg/day intramuscularly in two divided doses for the next 4 days. The first few days of streptomycin rarely may induce a Jarish-Herxheimer–like reaction, with an increase in symptoms and a transient drop of the serum agglutination titer.[2,89] Gentamicin has proved to be effective therapy.[2,3] A review of the literature revealed that gentamicin was effective for treatment except that the relapse and failure rates were higher with gentamicin, compared with historical rates for streptomycin.[129] A patient with tularemia endocarditis responded well to a 4-week course of gentamicin but did not return for follow-up visits, so no conclusion can be made about the long-term outcome.[112] Doxycycline has a higher relapse rate compared with the aminoglycosides. In pediatric patients, gentamicin was shown to be effective for treatment of tularemia without relapse or failure.[130] Gentamicin is given intravenously at a dose of 3 to 5 mg/kg/day in divided doses for 7 to 14 days, with desired peak serum levels of at least 5.0 μg/mL. The efficacy of single-daily dosing has not been studied. The doses of both streptomycin and gentamicin need to be adjusted for renal insufficiency. Penetration of these drugs into the CSF is poor and erratic and may be inadequate in tularemic meningitis. Pittman and colleagues[131] reported a central nervous system shunt infection caused by *F. tularensis* that was successfully treated with intrathecal gentamicin. An additional 13 cases of tularemic meningitis have been documented.[114] Successful treatment generally included combinations of streptomycin and chloramphenicol, and the more recent case was successfully treated with a combination of intravenous gentamicin and oral doxycycline.[114]

Tetracycline and chloramphenicol are bacteriostatic for *F. tularensis,* and this accounts in part for the high rate of relapse after treatment with these agents.[2] Tetracycline should not be used in children younger than 8 years of age, during pregnancy, or during lactation. Tetracycline is most effective in adults when given as 2 g/day in divided oral doses for at least 14 days[132]; a suggested oral regimen in children is 30 mg/kg/day, to a maximum of 2 g/day, in divided doses for the same duration. Doxycycline may also be used and provides the convenience of twice-daily dosing. In general, chloramphenicol should not be chosen to treat tularemia because of its potentially serious toxicity and the availability of more effective alternatives with less dangerous potential side effects. However, chloramphenicol, 50 to 100 mg/kg/day intravenously in divided doses, may be added to streptomycin to treat meningitis. When used in the past for other forms of tularemia, the oral dose of chloramphenicol has been 30 to 50 mg/kg/day in three or four divided doses for at least 14 days. The oral preparation is no longer available in the United States.

Drugs with well-established clinical efficacy have exhibited achievable minimal inhibitory concentrations (MIC) against *F. tularensis* on in vitro susceptibility tests.[133] Other agents with relatively low MICs have included erythromycin, rifampin, cefoxitin, cefotaxime, ceftriaxone, ceftazidime, most aminoglycosides, and several flouroquinolones except cinoxacin.[133-135] The effectiveness of these drugs in treating tularemia is not fully established, and ceftriaxone has failed in several patients treated as outpatients.[136] A study of 38 human and animal *F. tularensis* isolates from Finland found that all were resistant to third-generation cephalosporins, but that resistance was not present in two American Type Culture Collection (ATCC) control strains.[137] Ceftriaxone exhibited poor intracellular inhibitory activity against a strain of *F. tularensis* subsp. *holarctica* grown in macrophage-like cell monolayers, while aminoglycosides, doxycycline, telithromycin, fluoroquinolones, and rifampin were active in this assay.[138] Erythromycin has been used successfully in a few patients who were thought to have *Legionella* infections.[105,139] However, resistance to erythromycin has been described in *F. tularensis* strains from outside of North America.[135,137,139] Although imipenem was effective in a reported case,[140] Ikaheimo and associates[137] found that all 38 type B clinical isolates they tested were resistant to imipenem in vitro.

Recent in vitro susceptibility studies have found that the fluoroquinolones are active against *F. tularensis* subsp. *tularensis* as well as subsp. *holarctica*.[135,137] In mice, liposome-encapsulated ciprofloxacin delivered by aerosol inhalation was highly effective in the treatment of respiratory *F. tularensis* infection.[141] Clinical experience with the fluoroquinolones as therapy for tularemia caused by *F. tularensis* subsp. *holarctica* is growing and has been favorable even in immunocompromised hosts.[135,142] A patient with a knee prosthesis chronically infected by *F. tularensis* subsp. *holarctica* was cured following a prolonged course of ciprofloxacin plus rifampin.[113] However, the outcome with fluoroquinolone therapy may be suboptimal and there is minimal experience using these agents for infections caused by the more virulent *F. tularensis* subsp. *tularensis*.[135,142,143] During the initial Spanish tularemia outbreak, therapy with ciprofloxacin overall was statistically equivalent to that with streptomycin and superior to doxycycline.[60] However, relapses occurred in 7 of 14 patients at one Spanish hospital following ciprofloxacin given as either primary or secondary treatment.[144] Ciprofloxacin also has been effective therapy in children with tularemia.[145,146] Johansson and colleagues[145] described 12 children, ranging in age from 1 to 10 years, with tularemia given ciprofloxacin 15 to 20 mg/kg daily in two divided doses. The two patients who completed only 3½ and 7 days of treatment relapsed but all 12 patients were cured after completing 10 to 14 days of uninterrupted therapy.[145]

A monoclonal antibody to the LPS of *F. tularensis* and serum from vaccinated people are effective passive therapies for murine infection, offering the future hope of immunotherapeutic agents for tularemia.[147,148] Surgical therapies are limited to drainage of abscessed lymph nodes and chest tube drainage of empyemas.

Treatment of tularemia in the setting of a bioterrorist event is discussed in Chapter 322.

PREVENTION

Avoiding exposure to the organism is the best prevention of tularemia. Wild animals should not be skinned or dressed using bare hands, or when the animal appeared ill. Gloves, masks, and protective eye covers should be worn when performing such tasks and when disposing of dead animals brought home by household pets. Wild game should be cooked thoroughly before ingestion. Wells or other waters that are contaminated by dead animals should not be used. Treatment of community water supplies with standard chlorination protects against waterborne tularemia.[149] The most important measure to avoid tick bites in infested areas is wearing clothing that is tight at the wrists and ankles and that covers most of the body. Chemical tick repellants also may be of benefit. Frequent checks should be made for attached ticks so that they may be removed promptly; this must not be done with bare hands, and care should be taken not to crush the tick.

Hospitalized patients with tularemia do not need special isolation because person-to-person spread does not occur, and even in the preantibiotic era secondary cases were not found. Standard universal precautions for contaminated secretions are adequate when handling drainage from wounds or eyes.

Vaccines prepared from killed *F. tularensis* are ineffective, in part because they only induce an antibody response.[41] A live vaccine based on an attenuated strain of *F. tularensis* (LVS), originally obtained from the former Soviet Union, has been developed in the United States.[150] The LVS vaccine is an attenuated, live *F. tularensis* strain that occurs in two colony phenotypes, one of which is immunogenic and has major importance for the induction of protective immunity.[151] A newer vaccine lot has been used and has shown to be immunogenic in humans.[152] Live vaccine strains require constant control of their immunologic properties, because the nonimmunologic phenotype has a tendency to accumulate during storage, reducing the efficacy of the vaccine. In addition, the live vaccine strain of *F. tularensis* cannot provide high immune response in the presence of antimicrobial agents such as doxycycline.[153] This vaccine induces cell-mediated and humoral immunity, is effective in preventing typhoidal disease, and reduces the severity of ulceroglandular disease but does not prevent it.[152,154] Vaccination may be considered for persons who will be working with *F. tularensis* and for anyone else with repeated occupational exposures. Recently, use of the vaccine was suspended while the Food and Drug Administration reviewed past clinical experience. A new

Investigational New Drug protocol pending approval would permit use of the LVS tularemia vaccine only through a cooperative research agreement with the United States Army Medical Research Institute of Infectious Diseases (USAMRIID). Inquiries should be directed to the Chief, Medical Division, USAMRIID, Fort Detrick, Frederick, MD 21702, USA.

Antibiotic prophylaxis after potential exposures of unknown risk, such as tick bites, is not recommended. In the past, intramuscular streptomycin was given for preemptive treatment of documented exposures from laboratory accidents because streptomycin successfully aborts illness when given in the incubation period after experimental inoculation.[2,132] Gentamicin should be effective for this purpose as well but this has not been confirmed. Doxycycline and ciprofloxacin also were examined in the murine tularemia model, and both can be effective as preemptive therapy in mice after intraperitoneal challenge.[155] Thus, currently either doxycycline or ciprofloxacin given orally for 14 days is recommended for adults with suspected or proven high-risk exposure to *F. tularensis*.[59,149] Individuals with lower-risk exposures may be observed for fever or other signs of illness without antibiotics. Observation without antibiotics also is appropriate for exposures in vaccinated individuals. No therapy is needed for someone whose only exposure is to a patient with tularemia, human-to-human transmission does not occur. Post-exposure treatment is discussed more fully in Chapter 322.

Recovery from tularemia is thought to confer protective immunity for life, although a few recurrent infections have been documented.[154] Most recurrences have been clinically mild ulceroglandular disease, and systemic symptoms have been uncommon. Therefore, previously infected individuals are not candidates for vaccination or preemptive antibiotic therapy after a known exposure.

REFERENCES

1. Jellison WL. Tularemia: Dr. Edward Francis and his first 23 isolates of *Francisella tularensis*. Bull Hist Med. 1972;46:477-485.
2. Evans ME, Gregory DW, Schaffner W, et al. Tularemia: a 30-year experience with 88 cases. Medicine (Baltimore). 1985;64:251-269.
3. Penn RL, Kinasewitz GT. Factors associated with a poor outcome in tularemia. Arch Intern Med. 1987;147:265-268.
4. Feldman KA, Enscore RE, Lathrop SL, et al. An outbreak of primary pneumonic tularemia on Martha's Vineyard. N Engl J Med. 2001;345:1601-1606.
5. Reintjes R, Dedushaj I, Gjini A, et al. Tularemia outbreak investigation in Kosovo: Case control and environmental studies. Emerg Infect Dis. 2002;8:69-73.
6. Tarnvik A, Berglund L. Tularaemia. Eur Respir J. 2003;21:361-373.
7. Hopla CE. The ecology of tularemia. Adv Vet Sci Comp Med. 1974;18:25-53.
8. McCoy GW. A plague-like disease of rodents. Publ Hlth Bull. 1911;43:53-71.
9. McCoy GW, Chapin CW. Further observations on a plaguelike disease of rodents with a preliminary note on the causative agent *Bacterium tularense*. J Infect Dis. 1912;10:61-72.
10. Francis E. Tularemia. JAMA. 1925;84:1243-1250.
11. Vail DT. *Bacillus tularense* infection of the eye. Ophthalmol Rec. 1914;23:487.
12. Wherry WB, Lamb BH. Infection of man with *Bacterium tularense*. J Infect Dis. 1914;15:331-340.
13. Wherry WB, Lamb BH. Discovery of *Bacterium tularense* in wild rabbits, and the danger of its transmission to man. JAMA. 1914;63:2041.
14. Francis E. A summary of the present knowledge of tularemia. Medicine (Baltimore). 1928;7:411-432.
15. Sanford JP. Landmark perspective: Tularemia. JAMA. 1983;250:3225-3226.
16. Sandstrom G, Lofgren S, Tarnvik A. A capsule-deficient mutant of *Francisella tularensis* LVS exhibits enhanced sensitivity to killing by serum but diminished sensitivity to killing by polymorphonuclear leukocytes. Infect Immun. 1988;56:1194-1202.
17. Eigelsbach HT, McGann VG. Genus *Francisella* Dorofeev 1947, 176^AL. In: Krieg NR, Holt JG, eds. Bergey's Manual of Systematic Bacteriology. Baltimore: Williams & Wilkins; 1984:394-399.
18. Chu MC, Weyant RS. *Francisella* and *Brucella*. In: Murray PR, Baron EJ, Jorgensen JH, et al, eds. Manual of Clinical Microbiology, 8th ed. Vol. 1. Washington, DC: American Society for Microbiology Press; 2003:789-808.
19. Johansson A, Ibrahim A, Goransson I, et al. Evaluation of PCR-based methods for discrimination of *Francisella* species and subspecies and development of a specific PCR that distinguishes the two major subspecies of *Francisella tularensis*. J Clin Microbiol. 2000;38:4180-4185.
20. Gurycova D. First isolation of *Francisella tularensis* subsp. *tularensis* in Europe. Eur J Epidemiol. 1998;14:797-802.
21. Thomas R, Johansson A, Neeson B, et al. Discrimination of human pathogenic subspecies of *Francisella tularensis* by using restriction fragment length polymorphism. J Clin Microbiol. 2003;41:50-57.

22. Hollis DG, Weaver RE, Steigerwalt AG, et al. *Francisella philomiragia* comb. nov. (formerly *Yersinia philomiragia*) and *Francisella tularensis* biogroup novicida (formerly *Francisella novicida*) associated with human disease. J Clin Microbiol. 1989;27:1601-1608.

23. Sandstrom G, Sjostedt A, Forsman M, et al. Characterization and classification of strains of *Francisella tularensis* isolated in the central Asian focus of the Soviet Union and in Japan. J Clin Microbiol. 1992;30:172-175.

24. Ellis J, Oyston PC, Green M, et al. Tularemia. Clin Microbiol Rev. 2002;15:631-646.

25. Johansson A, Goransson I, Larsson P, et al. Extensive allelic variation among *Francisella tularensis* strains in a short-sequence tandem repeat region. J Clin Microbiol. 2001;39:3140-3146.

26. Farlow J, Smith KL, Wong J, et al. *Francisella tularensis* strain typing using multiple-locus, variable-number tandem repeat analysis. J Clin Microbiol. 2001;39:3186-3192.

27. Garcia Del Blanco N, Dobson ME, Vela AI, et al. Genotyping of *Francisella tularensis* strains by pulsed-field gel electrophoresis, amplified fragment length polymorphism fingerprinting, and 16S rRNA gene sequencing. J Clin Microbiol. 2002;40:2964-2972.

28. Broekhuijsen M, Larsson P, Johansson A, et al. Genome-wide DNA microarray analysis of *Francisella tularensis* strains demonstrates extensive genetic conservation within the species but identifies regions that are unique to the highly virulent *F. tularensis* subsp. *tularensis*. J Clin Microbiol. 2003;41:2924-2931.

29. Hernychova L, Stulik J, Halada P, et al. Construction of a *Francisella tularensis* two-dimensional electrophoresis protein database. Proteomics. 2001;1:508-515.

30. Prior RG, Klasson L, Larsson P, et al. Preliminary analysis and annotation of the partial genome sequence of *Francisella tularensis* strain Schu 4. J Appl Microbiol. 2001;91:614-620.

31. Bernard K, Tessier S, Winstanley J, et al. Early recognition of atypical *Francisella tularensis* strains lacking a cysteine requirement. J Clin Microbiol. 1994;32:551-553.

32. Clarridge JE 3rd, Raich TJ, Sjosted A, et al. Characterization of two unusual clinically significant *Francisella* strains. J Clin Microbiol. 1996;34:1995-2000.

33. Centers for Disease Control. Laboratory Response Network (LRN): Level A laboratory procedures for identification of *Francisella tularensis*. www.bt.cdc.gov/Agent/Tularemia/ftu_la_cp_121301.pdf, December 13, 2001. Accessed June 1, 2003.

34. Koneman EW, Allen SD, Janda WM, et al. Miscellaneous fastidious gram-negative bacilli. In: Koneman EW, Allen SD, Janda WM, et al., eds. Color Atlas and Textbook of Diagnostic Microbiology. 5th ed. Philadelphia: Lippincott Williams & Wilkins; 1997:436-440.

35. Ancuta P, Pedron T, Girard R, et al. Inability of the *Francisella tularensis* lipopolysaccharide to mimic or to antagonize the induction of cell activation by endotoxins. Infect Immun. 1996;64:2041-2046.

36. Fulop M, Mastroeni P, Green M, et al. Role of antibody to lipopolysaccharide in protection against low- and high-virulence strains of *Francisella tularensis*. Vaccine. 2001;19:4465-4472.

37. Conlan JW, Vinogradov E, Monteiro MA, et al. Mice intradermally-inoculated with the intact lipopolysaccharide, but not the lipid A or O-chain, from *Francisella tularensis* LVS rapidly acquire varying degrees of enhanced resistance against systemic or aerogenic challenge with virulent strains of the pathogen. Microb Pathog. 2003;34:39-45.

38. Conlan JW, Shen H, Webb A, et al. Mice vaccinated with the O-antigen of *Francisella tularensis* LVS lipopolysaccharide conjugated to bovine serum albumin develop varying degrees of protective immunity against systemic or aerosol challenge with virulent type A and type B strains of the pathogen. Vaccine. 2002;20:3465-3471.

39. Cowley SC, Myltseva SV, Nano FE. Phase variation in *Francisella tularensis* affecting intracellular growth, lipopolysaccharide antigenicity and nitric oxide production. Mol Microbiol. 1996;20:867-874.

40. Cowley SC, Gray CJ, Nano FE. Isolation and characterization of *Francisella novicida* mutants defective in lipopolysaccharide biosynthesis. FEMS Microbiol Lett. 2000;182:63-67.

41. Tarnvik A. Nature of protective immunity to *Francisella tularensis*. Rev Infect Dis. 1989;11:440-451.

42. Waag DM, McKee KT Jr, Sandstrom G, et al. Cell-mediated and humoral immune responses after vaccination of human volunteers with the live vaccine strain of *Francisella tularensis*. Clin Diagn Lab Immunol. 1995;2:143-148.

43. Sjostedt A. Virulence determinants and protective antigens of *Francisella tularensis*. Curr Opin Microbiol. 2003;6:66-71.

44. Sato T, Fujita H, Ohara Y, et al. Correlation between the virulence of *Francisella tularensis* in experimental mice and its acriflavine reaction. Curr Microbiol. 1992;25:95-97.

45. Fujita H, Sato T, Watanabe Y, et al. Correlation of the polysaccharide antigens of *Francisella tularensis* with virulence in experimental mice. Microbiol Immunol. 1995;39:1007-1009.

46. Baron GS, Reilly TJ, Nano FE. The respiratory burst-inhibiting acid phosphatase AcpA is not essential for the intramacrophage growth or virulence of *Francisella novicida*. FEMS Microbiol Lett. 1999;176:85-90.

47. Golovliov I, Ericsson M, Sandstrom G, et al. Identification of proteins of *Francisella tularensis* induced during growth in macrophages and cloning of the gene encoding a prominently induced 23-kilodalton protein. Infect Immun. 1997;65:2183-2189.

48. Baron GS, Nano FE. MglA and MglB are required for the intramacrophage growth of *Francisella novicida*. Mol Microbiol. 1998;29:247-259.

49. Gray CG, Cowley SC, Cheung KK, et al. The identification of five genetic loci of *Francisella novicida* associated with intracellular growth. FEMS Microbiol Lett. 2002;215:53-56.

50. Golovliov I, Sjostedt A, Mokrievich A, et al. A method for allelic replacement in *Francisella tularensis*. FEMS Microbiol Lett. 2003;222:273-280.

51. Telepnev M, Golovliov I, Grundstrom T, et al. *Francisella tularensis* inhibits Toll-like receptor-mediated activation of intracellular signalling and secretion of TNF-alpha and IL-1 from murine macrophages. Cell Microbiol. 2003;5:41-51.

52. Sicherer SH, Asturias EJ, Winkelstein JA, et al. *Francisella philomiragia* sepsis in chronic granulomatous disease. Pediatr Infect Dis J. 1997;16:420-422.

53. Wenger JD, Hollis DG, Weaver RE, et al. Infection caused by *Francisella philomiragia* (formerly *Yersinia philomiragia*). A newly recognized human pathogen. Ann Intern Med. 1989;110:888-892.

54. Sun LV, Scoles GA, Fish D, et al. Francisella-like endosymbionts of ticks. J Invertebr Pathol. 2000;76:301-303.

55. Tularemia—United States, 1990-2000. Morbid Mortal Wkly Rep. 2002;51:181-184.

56. Chang MH, Glynn MK, Groseclose SL. Endemic, notifiable bioterrorism-related diseases, United States, 1992-1999. Emerg Infect Dis. 2003;9:556-564.

57. Centers for Disease Control and Prevention. Summary of notifiable diseases, United States, 2001. Morbid Mortal Wkly Rep. 2001;50:1-108.

58. Munnich D, Lakatos M. Clinical, epidemiological and therapeutical experience with human tularaemia: The role of hamster hunters. Infection. 1979;7:61-63.

59. Outbreak of tularemia among commercially distributed prairie dogs, 2002. Morbid Mortal Wkly Rep. 2002;51:688, 699.

60. Perez-Castrillon JL, Bachiller-Luque P, Martin-Luquero M, et al. Tularemia epidemic in northwestern Spain: Clinical description and therapeutic response. Clin Infect Dis. 2001;33:573-576.

61. McCarthy VP, Murphy MD. Lawnmower tularemia. Pediatr Infect Dis J 1990;9:298-299.

62. Feldman KA, Stiles-Enos D, Julian K, et al. Tularemia on Martha's Vineyard: Seroprevalence and occupational risk. Emerg Infect Dis. 2003;9:350-354.

63. Capellan J, Fong IW. Tularemia from a cat bite: Case report and review of feline-associated tularemia. Clin Infect Dis. 1993;16:472-475.

64. Eliasson H, Lindback J, Nuorti JP, et al. The 2000 tularemia outbreak: A case-control study of risk factors in disease-endemic and emergent areas, Sweden. Emerg Infect Dis. 2002;8:956-960.

65. Anda P, Segura del Pozo J, Diaz Garcia JM, et al. Waterborne outbreak of tularemia associated with crayfish fishing. Emerg Infect Dis. 2001;7:575-582.

66. Abd H, Johansson T, Golovliov I, et al. Survival and growth of *Francisella tularensis* in *Acanthamoeba castellanii*. Appl Environ Microbiol. 2003;69:600-606.

67. Quan SF, McManus AG, von Fintel H. Infectivity of tularemia applied to intact skin and ingested drinking water. Science. 1956;123:942-943.

68. Tularemia—Oklahoma, 2000. Morbid Mortal Wkly Rep. 2001;50:704-706.

69. Geyer SJ, Burkey A, Chandler FW. Tularemia. In: Connor DH, ed. Pathology of Infectious Diseases. Stamford, Connecticut: Appleton & Lange; 1997:869-873.

70. Koskela P, Salminen A. Humoral immunity against *Francisella tularensis* after natural infection. J Clin Microbiol. 1985;22:973-979.

71. Yee D, Rhinehart-Jones TR, Elkins KL. Loss of either CD4+ or CD8+ T cells does not affect the magnitude of protective immunity to an intracellular pathogen, *Francisella tularensis* strain LVS. J Immunol. 1996;157:5042-5048.

72. Lai XH, Golovliov I, Sjostedt A. *Francisella tularensis* induces cytopathogenicity and apoptosis in murine macrophages via a mechanism that requires intracellular bacterial multiplication. Infect Immun. 2001;69:4691-4694.

73. Fortier AH, Leiby DA, Narayanan RB, et al. Growth of *Francisella tularensis* LVS in macrophages: The acidic intracellular compartment provides essential iron required for growth. Infect Immun. 1995;63:1478-1483.

74. Green SJ, Nacy CA, Schreiber RD, et al. Neutralization of gamma interferon and tumor necrosis factor alpha blocks in vivo synthesis of nitrogen oxides from L-arginine and protection against *Francisella tularensis* infection in *Mycobacterium bovis* BCG-treated mice. Infect Immun. 1993;61:689-698.

75. Conlan JW, KuoLee R, Shen H, et al. Different host defences are required to protect mice from primary systemic vs pulmonary infection with the facultative intracellular bacterial pathogen, *Francisella tularensis* LVS. Microb Pathog. 2002;32:127-134.

76. Hernychova L, Kovarova H, Macela A, et al. Early consequences of macrophage-*Francisella tularensis* interaction under the influence of different genetic background in mice. Immunol Lett. 1997;57:75-81.

77. Kovarova H, Hernychova L, Hajduch M, et al. Influence of the *bcg* locus on natural resistance to primary infection with the facultative intracellular bacterium *Francisella tularensis* in mice. Infect Immun. 2000;68:1480-1484.

78. Culkin SJ, Rhinehart-Jones T, Elkins KL. A novel role for B cells in early protective immunity to an intracellular pathogen, *Francisella tularensis* strain LVS. J Immunol. 1997;158:3277-3284.

79. Elkins KL, Bosio CM, Rhinehart-Jones TR. Importance of B cells, but not specific antibodies, in primary and secondary protective immunity to the intracellular bacterium *Francisella tularensis* live vaccine strain. Infect Immun. 1999;67:6002-6007.

80. Dreisbach VC, Cowley S, Elkins KL. Purified lipopolysaccharide from *Francisella tularensis* live vaccine strain (LVS) induces protective immunity against LVS infection that requires B cells and gamma interferon. Infect Immun. 2000;68:1988-1996.

81. Elkins KL, Rhinehart-Jones TR, Stibitz S, et al. Bacterial DNA containing CpG motifs stimulates lymphocyte-dependent protection of mice against lethal infection with intracellular bacteria. J Immunol. 1999;162:2291-2298.

82. Stenmark S, Sunnemark D, Bucht A, et al. Rapid local expression of interleukin-12, tumor necrosis factor alpha, and gamma interferon after cutaneous *Francisella tularensis* infection in tularemia-immune mice. Infect Immun. 1999;67:1789-1797.

83. Elkins KL, Cooper A, Colombini SM, et al. In vivo clearance of an intracellular bacterium, *Francisella tularensis* LVS, is dependent on the p40 subunit of interleukin-12 (IL-12) but not on IL-12 p70. Infect Immun. 2002;70:1936-1948.

84. Poquet Y, Kroca M, Halary F, et al. Expansion of Vg9Vd2 T cells is triggered by *Francisella tularensis*-derived phosphoantigens in tularemia but not after tularemia vaccination. Infect Immun. 1998;66:2107-2114.

85. Kroca M, Tarnvik A, Sjostedt A. The proportion of circulating gammadelta T cells increases after the first week of onset of tularaemia and remains elevated for more than a year. Clin Exp Immunol. 2000;120:280-284.
86. Ericsson M, Kroca M, Johansson T, et al. Long-lasting recall response of CD4+ and CD8+ alphabeta T cells, but not gammadelta T cells, to heat shock proteins of *Francisella tularensis*. Scand J Infect Dis. 2001;33:145-152.
87. Conlan JW, North RJ. Early pathogenesis of infection in the liver with the facultative intracellular bacteria *Listeria monocytogenes, Francisella tularensis,* and *Salmonella typhimurium* involves lysis of infected hepatocytes by leukocytes. Infect Immun. 1992;60:5164-5171.
88. Sanders CV, Hahn R. Analysis of 106 cases of tularemia. J La State Med Soc. 1968;120:391-393.
89. Dienst FT Jr. Tularemia: A perusal of three hundred thirty-nine cases. J La State Med Soc. 1963;115:114-124.
90. Cox SK, Everett ED. Tularemia, an analysis of 25 cases. Mo Med. 1981;78:70-74.
91. Foshay L. Tularemia: A summary of certain aspects of the disease including methods for early diagnosis and the results of serum treatment in 600 patients. Medicine (Baltimore). 1940;19:1-83.
92. Ohara Y, Sato T, Fujita H, et al. Clinical manifestations of tularemia in Japan—analysis of 1,355 cases observed between 1924 and 1987. Infection. 1991;19:14-17.
93. Jacobs RF, Condrey YM, Yamauchi T. Tularemia in adults and children: A changing presentation. Pediatrics. 1985;76:818-822.
94. Smego RA Jr, Castiglia M, Asperilla MO. Lymphocutaneous syndrome. A review of non-sporothrix causes. Medicine (Baltimore). 1999;78:38-63.
95. Helvaci S, Gedikoglu S, Akalin H, et al. Tularemia in Bursa, Turkey: 205 cases in ten years. Eur J Epidemiol. 2000;16:271-276.
96. Provenza JM, Klotz SA, Penn RL. Isolation of *Francisella tularensis* from blood. J Clin Microbiol. 1986;24:453-455.
97. Sarria JC, Vidal AM, Kimbrough RC, et al. Fatal infection caused by *Francisella tularensis* in a neutropenic bone marrow transplant recipient. Ann Hematol. 2003;82:41-43.
98. Gries DM, Fairchok MP. Typhoidal tularemia in a human immunodeficiency virus-infected adolescent. Pediatr Infect Dis J. 1996;15:838-840.
99. Zaidi SA, Singer C. Gastrointestinal and hepatic manifestations of tickborne diseases in the United States. Clin Infect Dis. 2002;34:1206-1212.
100. Schmid GP, Catino D, Suffin SC, et al. Granulomatous pleuritis caused by *Francisella tularensis:* Possible confusion with tuberculous pleuritis. Am Rev Respir Dis. 1983;128:314-316.
101. Syrjälä H, Kujala P, Myllylä V, et al. Airborne transmission of tularemia in farmers. Scand J Infect Dis. 1985;17:371-375.
102. Teutsch SM, Martone WJ, Brink EW, et al. Pneumonic tularemia on Martha's Vineyard. N Engl J Med. 1979;301:826-828.
103. Scofield RH, Lopez EJ, McNabb SJ. Tularemia pneumonia in Oklahoma, 1982-1987. J Okla State Med Assoc. 1992;85:165-170.
104. Bellido-Casado J, Perez-Castrillon JL, Bachiller-Luque P, et al. Report on five cases of tularaemic pneumonia in a tularaemia outbreak in Spain. Eur J Clin Microbiol Infect Dis. 2000;19:218-220.
105. Roy TM, Fleming D, Anderson WH. Tularemic pneumonia mimicking Legionnaires' disease with false-positive direct fluorescent antibody stains for *Legionella*. South Med J. 1989;82:1429-1431.
106. Pettersson T, Nyberg P, Nordstrom D, et al. Similar pleural fluid findings in pleuropulmonary tularemia and tuberculous pleurisy. Chest. 1996;109:572-575.
107. Ketai L, Alrahji AA, Hart B, et al. Radiologic manifestations of potential bioterrorist agents of infection. AJR Am J Roentgenol. 2003;180:565-575.
108. Syrjälä H, Karvonen J, Salminen A. Skin manifestations of tularemia: A study of 88 cases in northern Finland during 16 years (1967-1983). Acta Dermatol Venereol. 1984;64:513-516.
109. Ruiz AI, Gonzalez A, Miranda A, et al. Sweet's syndrome associated with *Francisella tularensis* infection. Int J Dermatol. 2001;40:791-793.
110. Tarnvik A, Sandstrom G, Sjostedt A. Infrequent manifestations of tularaemia in Sweden. Scand J Infect Dis. 1997;29:443-446.
111. Polack FP, Harrington SM, Winkelstein JA, et al. Recurrent *Francisella philomiragia* sepsis in chronic granulomatous disease. Pediatr Infect Dis J. 1998;17:442-443.
112. Tancik CA, Dillaha JA. *Francisella tularensis* endocarditis. Clin Infect Dis. 2000;30:399-400.
113. Cooper CL, Van Caeseele P, Canvin J, et al. Chronic prosthetic device infection with *Francisella tularensis*. Clin Infect Dis. 1999;29:1589-1591.
114. Rodgers BL, Duffield RP, Taylor T, et al. Tularemic meningitis. Pediatr Infect Dis J. 1998;17:439-441.
115. LeDoux MS. Tularemia presenting with ataxia. Clin Infect Dis. 2000;30:211-212.
116. Taylor JP, Istre GR, McChesney TC, et al. Epidemiologic characteristics of human tularemia in the southwest-central states, 1981-1987. Am J Epidemiol. 1991;133:1032-1038.
117. Giddens WR, Wilson JW, Dienst FT Jr, et al. Tularemia: An analysis of one hundred forty-seven cases. J La State Med Soc. 1957;109:93-98.
118. Fournier PE, Bernabeu L, Schubert B, et al. Isolation of *Francisella tularensis* by centrifugation of shell vial cell culture from an inoculation eschar. J Clin Microbiol. 1998;36:2782-2783.
119. Reary BW, Klotz SA. Enhancing recovery of *Francisella tularensis* from blood. Diagn Microbiol Infect Dis. 1988;11:117-119.
120. Hoel T, Scheel O, Nordahl SH, et al. Water- and airborne *Francisella tularensis* biovar *palaearctica* isolated from human blood. Infection. 1991;19:348-350.
121. Brion JP, Recule C, Croize J, et al. Isolation of *Francisella tularensis* from lymph node aspirate inoculated into a non-radiometric blood culture system. Eur J Clin Microbiol Infect Dis. 1996;15:180-181.
122. Grunow R, Splettstoesser W, McDonald S, et al. Detection of *Francisella tularensis* in biological specimens using a capture enzyme-linked immunosorbent assay, an immunochromatographic handheld assay, and a PCR. Clin Diagn Lab Immunol. 2000;7:86-90.
123. Long GW, Oprandy JJ, Narayanan RB, et al. Detection of *Francisella tularensis* in blood by polymerase chain reaction. J Clin Microbiol. 1993;31:152-154.
124. Junhui Z, Ruifu Y, Jianchun L, et al. Detection of *Francisella tularensis* by the polymerase chain reaction. J Med Microbiol. 1996;45:477-482.
125. Fulop M, Leslie D, Titball R. A rapid, highly sensitive method for the detection of *Francisella tularensis* in clinical samples using the polymerase chain reaction. Am J Trop Med Hyg. 1996;54:364-366.
126. Sjostedt A, Eriksson U, Berglund L, et al. Detection of *Francisella tularensis* in ulcers of patients with tularemia by PCR. J Clin Microbiol. 1997;35:1045-1048.
127. Johansson A, Berglund L, Eriksson U, et al. Comparative analysis of PCR versus culture for diagnosis of ulceroglandular tularemia. J Clin Microbiol. 2000;38:22-26.
128. Dolan SA, Dommaraju CB, DeGuzman GB. Detection of *Francisella tularensis* in clinical specimens by use of polymerase chain reaction. Clin Infect Dis. 1998;26:764-765.
129. Enderlin G, Morales L, Jacobs RF, et al. Streptomycin and alternative agents for the treatment of tularemia: review of the literature. Clin Infect Dis. 1994;19:42-47.
130. Cross JT, Jr., Schutze GE, Jacobs RF. Treatment of tularemia with gentamicin in pediatric patients. Pediatr Infect Dis J. 1995;14:151-152.
131. Pittman T, Williams D, Friedman AD. A shunt infection caused by *Francisella tularensis*. Pediatr Neurosurg. 1996;24:50-51.
132. Sawyer WD, Dangerfield HG, Hogge AL, et al. Antibiotic prophylaxis and therapy of airborne tularemia. Bacteriol Rev. 1966;30:542-550.
133. Baker CN, Hollis DG, Thornsberry C. Antimicrobial susceptibility testing of *Francisella tularensis* with a modified Mueller-Hinton broth. J Clin Microbiol. 1985;22:212-215.
134. Syrjala H, Schildt R, Raisainen S. In vitro susceptibility of *Francisella tularensis* to fluoroquinolones and treatment of tularemia with norfloxacin and ciprofloxacin. Eur J Clin Microbiol Infect Dis. 1991;10:68-70.
135. Johansson A, Urich SK, Chu MC, et al. In vitro susceptibility to quinolones of *Francisella tularensis* subspecies *tularensis*. Scand J Infect Dis. 2002;34:327-330.
136. Cross JT, Jacobs RF. Tularemia: treatment failures with outpatient use of ceftriaxone. Clin Infect Dis. 1993;17:976-980.
137. Ikaheimo I, Syrjala H, Karhukorpi J, et al. In vitro antibiotic susceptibility of *Francisella tularensis* isolated from humans and animals. J Antimicrob Chemother. 2000;46:287-290.
138. Maurin M, Mersali NF, Raoult D. Bactericidal activities of antibiotics against intracellular *Francisella tularensis*. Antimicrob Agents Chemother. 2000;44:3428-3431.
139. Harrell RE Jr, Simmons HF. Pleuropulmonary tularemia: Successful treatment with erythromycin. South Med J. 1990;83:1363-1364.
140. Lee HC, Horowitz E, Linder W. Treatment of tularemia with imipenem/cilastatin sodium. South Med J. 1991;84:1277-1278.
141. Conley J, Yang H, Wilson T, et al. Aerosol delivery of liposome-encapsulated ciprofloxacin: Aerosol characterization and efficacy against *Francisella tularensis* infection in mice. Antimicrob Agents Chemother. 1997;41:1288-1292.
142. Limaye AP, Hooper CJ. Treatment of tularemia with fluoroquinolones: Two cases and review. Clin Infect Dis. 1999;29:922-924.
143. Johansson A, Berglund L, Sjostedt A, et al. Ciprofloxacin for treatment of tularemia. Clin Infect Dis. 2001;33:267-268.
144. Chocarro A, Gonzalez A, Garcia I. Treatment of tularemia with ciprofloxacin. Clin Infect Dis. 2000;31:623.
145. Johansson A, Berglund L, Gothefors L, et al. Ciprofloxacin for treatment of tularemia in children. Pediatr Infect Dis J. 2000;19:449-453.
146. Arav-Boger R. Cat-bite tularemia in a seventeen-year-old girl treated with ciprofloxacin. Pediatr Infect Dis J. 2000;19:583-584.
147. Narayanan RB, Drabick JJ, Williams JC, et al. Immunotherapy of tularemia: characterization of a monoclonal antibody reactive with *Francisella tularensis*. J Leukoc Biol. 1993;53:112-116.
148. Drabick JJ, Narayanan RB, Williams JC, et al. Passive protection of mice against lethal *Francisella tularensis* (live tularemia vaccine strain) infection by the sera of human recipients of the live tularemia vaccine. Am J Med Sci. 1994;308:83-87.
149. Dennis DT, Inglesby TV, Henderson DA, et al. Tularemia as a biological weapon: Medical and public health management. JAMA. 2001;285:2763-2773.
150. Waag DM, Galloway A, Sandstrom G, et al. Cell-mediated and humoral immune responses induced by scarification vaccination of human volunteers with a new lot of the live vaccine strain of *Francisella tularensis*. J Clin Microbiol. 1992;30:2256-2264.
151. Sandstrom G. The tularaemia vaccine. J Chem Technol Biotechnol. 1994;59:315-320.
152. Waag DM, Sandstrom G, England MJ, et al. Immunogenicity of a new lot of *Francisella tularensis* live vaccine strain in human volunteers. FEMS Immunol Med Microbiol. 1996;13:205-209.
153. Kormilitsyna MI, Meshcheryakova IS. The new vaccine strains (or variants) of *Francisella tularensis*. FEMS Immunol Med Microbiol. 1996;13:215-219.
154. Burke DS. Immunization against tularemia: Analysis of the effectiveness of live *Francisella tularensis* vaccine in prevention of laboratory-acquired tularemia. J Infect Dis. 1977;135:55-60.
155. Russell P, Eley SM, Fulop MJ, et al. The efficacy of ciprofloxacin and doxycycline against experimental tularaemia. J Antimicrob Chemother. 1998;41:461-465.

Pasteurella Species

JOHN J. ZURLO

Pasteurella are gram-negative coccobacilli that inhabit the oral cavity and gastrointestinal tract of many animals and cause various infectious problems including septicemia and pneumonia. In humans infection is most often caused by dog and cat bites resulting in cellulitis, subcutaneous abscesses, and a number of other syndromes. Bacteria belonging to the genus *Pasteurella* were first isolated from birds with cholera in 1878; they were characterized two years later by Pasteur.[1] In 1886 Hueppe speciated the organism, *Bacterium septicemia haemorrhagica,* as the cause of hemorrhagic septicemia in animals. The first human case of *Pasteurella* infection, a case of puerperal sepsis, was described by Brugnatelli in 1913.[2] The isolation of *Pasteurella multocida* from an infection occurring after a cat bite was first described in 1930.[3] Subsequently, as additional isolates were recovered and characterized, related species were grouped together, first as *Pasteurella septica,* then by the late 1930s as the *P. multocida* group.

DESCRIPTION OF THE PATHOGEN

Species of the genus *Pasteurella* are nonmotile, facultatively anaerobic, gram-negative coccobacilli measuring 1 to 2 μm in length.[4] Deoxyribonucleic acid (DNA) hybridization studies have determined that they are closely related to *Actinobacillus* spp.[5] The majority of strains are fermentative and test indole, catalase, oxidase, and sucrose positive.[4] Many pathogenic isolates are encapsulated. Organisms grow in culture on a variety of commercial media, including sheep blood and chocolate agar media. It has been reported that the oxidase reaction is most reliable when tested on strains grown on chocolate agar.[6] The most common human isolates belong to the *P. multocida* group and appear as smooth, iridescent, blue, watery mucoid colonies on growth media.[7] Problems with misidentification of *Pasteurella* isolates using commercial test systems have been described.[8,9] In particular, *Pasteurella* spp. and *Haemophilus* spp. have been confused when the API system (Analytab Products, Plainview, NY) was used.[9]

Table 225-1 lists the most recent classification of the *Pasteurella* species that cause human disease.[10] *Pasteurella pneumotropica,* usually found in rodents but occasionally in cats and dogs, may be reclassified outside the genus *Pasteurella.* Holst and associates characterized and speciated 159 strains of *Pasteurella* recovered from

TABLE 225-1 Nomenclature for *Pasteurella* Species

Current Name	Synonym
P. aerogenes	
P. bettyae	Centers for Disease Control and Prevention (CDC) group HB-5
P. canis	P. multocida biotype 6
P. dagmatis	Pasteurella new species 1 Pasteurella "gas"
P. gallinarum	
P. haemolytica	
Pasteurella-like	CDC group EF-4
P. multocida ssp. gallicida	P. septica
P. multocida ssp. multocida	
P. multocida ssp. septica	
P. pneumotropica	
P. stomatis	

Data from Bruckner DA, Colonna P, Bearson BL. Nomenclature for aerobic and facultative bacteria. Clin Infect Dis. 1999;29:713-723.

TABLE 225-2 Clinical Characteristics of 159 Strains of *Pasteurella* Species Isolated from 146 Infected Humans over a 3-Year Period

Species	N	Wound Infections or Abscesses*	Blood	Cerebrospinal Fluid	Other
P. multocida ssp. multocida	95	85	5	1	4[†]
P. multocida ssp. septica	21	20		1	
P. canis	28	28			
P. stomatis	10	10[‡]			
P. dagmatis	5	2[§]			3[¶]

*Caused by dog or cat bites, or wounds licked by dogs or cats.
[†]Includes three cases of infection from cut wounds unassociated with any known animal contact.
[‡]In eight cases of wound infection P. multocida ssp. multocida was also recovered.
[§]In cases of wound abscesses, P. multocida ssp. multocida and P. canis were also recovered.
[¶]One case each of severe cellulitis, groin abscess, and throat abscess.
Adapted from Holst E, Rollof J, Larsson, et al. Characterization and distribution of *Pasteurella* species recovered from infected humans. J Clin Microbiol. 1992;30:2984-2987.

clinical specimens from 146 patients over 3 years.[11] The majority of infections were caused by five different species or subspecies: *P. multocida* ssp. *multocida,* *P. multocida* ssp. *septica, Pasteurella canis, Pasteurella stomatis,* and *Pasteurella dagmatis* (Table 225-2).

EPIDEMIOLOGY

Based on case reports and case series of infected patients, *Pasteurella* spp., particularly *P. multocida,* appear to have a worldwide distribution.[12] For the majority of *Pasteurella* spp., the principal reservoir is in animals. *P. multocida* has been isolated from the upper respiratory tracts of a variety of animals including dogs, cats, pigs, Norway rats, and buffalos.[13-16] Dogs and cats have particularly high colonization rates. In most cases, carriage is asymptomatic, although both upper and lower respiratory tract infections and septicemia are well known to occur in animals.[17] Although the reservoirs of some of the non-*multocida* species *(P. canis, P. stomatis, P. dagmatis,*[11] *Pasteurella aerogenes,*[18] and *Pasteurella pneumotropica*[19]) are probably animal, other non-*multocida* species *(Pasteurella ureae* [now *Actinobacillus ureae*][20] and *Pasteurella bettyae*[21]) appear to have nonanimal reservoirs that are not well defined. Respiratory tract colonization by *P. multocida* in humans is well known to occur. In most cases colonized patients have underlying upper or lower respiratory tract diseases including chronic sinusitis and bronchiectasis.[12,22,23] Most colonized patients have a history of household or domesticated animal contact.[12,24,25]

Broadly speaking human infection with *Pasteurella* can be divided into three types: infection occurring after animal bites, usually from dogs or cats; infection occurring after other animal exposures; and infection with no known animal contact. Infection after animal bites is the most commonly reported clinical setting for the organism.[11,12,25-31]

In general dog bites are most common, followed by cat bites. Approximately 15% to 20% of dog bite wounds and more than 50% of cat bite wounds become infected.[25,29] The higher incidence of infection after cat bites probably results from the fact that cat teeth are thinner and more commonly result in puncture wounds, which are known to carry a higher risk of infection. For dog bite infections, *Staphylococcus aureus* and streptococcal species are the most commonly isolated pathogens, with *Pasteurella* and other organisms next in frequency.[27,30] For cat bite infections, *Pasteurella* spp. are the most common pathogens.[30] Francis and associates, studying bite-related *P. multocida* infections in Oregon between 1962 and 1972, noted that 76% were the result of cat bites and the remaining 24% were from dog bites.[28] The difference in incidence of *Pasteurella* infections in dog and cat bites may reflect the higher rate of upper respiratory colonization in cats. *Pasteurella* infections also have been reported after bites from a variety of other animals, including pigs, rats, lions, opossums, and rabbits.[25,31] In addition to bites, *Pasteurella* infections also have been reported after dog and cat scratches and from the licking of open wounds by these animals.[11,25]

Pasteurella infections are well known to develop in patients exposed to animals but without a history of bites or scratches. These include skin and soft tissue infections, bone and joint infections, pneumonia, meningitis, endocarditis, and septicemia[25,32] (see later discussion). Persons at risk for infection from animal exposure include veterinarians, farmers, livestock handlers, pet owners, and food handlers. Although the mode of infection in most reported cases is not clear, most have been presumed to result from inadvertent direct inoculation of organisms or from upper respiratory tract colonization with subsequent dissemination to the target organ or organs.

In a significant proportion of *Pasteurella* cases, no known animal exposure or contact can be identified. Hubbert and associates[32] reviewed in 1970 what was then the world's literature, identified 72 reported cases of *P. multocida* infection unrelated to bites, and described 136 additional cases. In 16% of the reviewed cases and 31% of their additional cases, no animal exposure or contact could be identified.[32] Once again the spectrum of infectious complications was wide, similar to what was described for patients with nonbite animal exposures. Vertical transmission of *P. multocida* has been described rarely.[33] Of the non-*multocida Pasteurella* species *P. bettyae* does not appear to have an animal reservoir and has been isolated only from humans. This species may be removed from the genus *Pasteurella*. It has been recovered from genital ulcers and may be a cause of genitourinary infections.[34,35]

PATHOGENESIS

The specific mechanisms of pathogenesis of *Pasteurella* spp. have been best studied in animals. In these hosts virulent *P. multocida* strains adhere to mucosal epithelial cells in the upper respiratory tract, particularly in the tonsils. In some cases adherence is mediated by fimbriae. In any case, adherence has been best demonstrated among toxigenic strains. The tonsils may be the major site of respiratory colonization by the organism in animals.[36]

Several virulence factors have been described in *Pasteurella* spp. Toxin production has been demonstrated in some *Pasteurella* isolates from animals. Specifically, leukotoxin has been isolated from *Pasteurella haemolytica*. Leukotoxin is toxic to ruminant leukocytes and is thought to impair cellular response in lung tissue and to stimulate the inflammatory response.[37] The ToxA protein, produced by *P. multocida,* is a cause of progressive atrophic rhinitis in pigs and is detectable by polymerase chain reaction (PCR) analysis.[38] In addition, most virulent *Pasteurella* strains produce polysaccharide capsules. *P. multocida* can be grouped according to capsular antigenicity into five subgroups, A, B, D, E, and F, with subgroup strains related to specific diseases in animals. The capsule confers many possible mechanisms of pathogenicity including resistance to desiccation, promotion of adherence, and resistance to both phagocytosis and complement-mediated killing.[39] Finally, binding of transferrin by some pathogenic *Pasteurella* strains has been demonstrated and may be a mechanism used by the bacteria to ensure an iron supply necessary for growth.[40]

The humoral response to *P. multocida* infection has been characterized. Antibodies to both somatic and capsular antigenic determinants develop within 2 weeks after clinical infection. Capsular antibodies are more long lasting than somatic antibodies.[41] The precise role for such antibodies in host defense in humans is not clear.

CLINICAL MANIFESTATIONS

Most reported *Pasteurella* infections in humans are caused by *P. multocida* and involve skin and soft tissues. Other species have been described much less commonly (see Table 225-2). Beyond skin and soft tissues, other sites of infection are uncommon and have been the subject of individual case reports or small case series.

Skin and Soft Tissue Infections

Infections of skin and soft tissues most commonly develop after a bite or scratch. Less commonly, infections develop after a dog or cat has licked an open wound. Inflammation, swelling, and tenderness develop at the site of injury, usually within 24 hours from the time of exposure.[25,26,28] Regional lymphadenopathy occurs in 30% to 40% of cases.[28] Wound discharge ranging from serosanguineous to frankly purulent has been noted in 21% to 39% of cases; fever develops in approximately 20%.[25,28] Anatomically, more than 50% of cases of infection from both dog and cat bites occur in the upper extremities, followed by the lower extremities, head, face, and neck; multiple sites of infection are sometimes evident.[28,31] Abscesses and tenosynovitis are the most frequent complications of *Pasteurella* soft tissue infection, with septic arthritis and osteomyelitis being less common. Bacteremia is rare. Weber and associates[25] noted an overall complication rate of 39% among 23 patients studied. In a large study analyzing bacterial species isolated from wounds inflicted by dog and cat bites, *P. canis* was the most common isolate from dog bites, whereas *P. multocida* ssp. *multocida* and ssp. *septicum* were the most common from cat bites.[42] *P. aerogenes,* a commensal organism found in pig digestive tracts, is known to cause wound infections and soft tissue abscesses following pig bites.[43]

Bone and Joint Infections

Bone and joint infections with *Pasteurella* species have been reported uncommonly. These infections take three different forms: septic arthritis, osteomyelitis, and combined arthritis and osteomyelitis. Ewing and associates reported 2 cases each of septic arthritis and osteomyelitis caused by *P. multocida* and reviewed the literature.[44] Among 14 cases of septic arthritis reported and reviewed, 7 (50%) involved dog or cat bites or scratches, 5 (36%) involved animal exposure without recent or known bites or scratches, and in the remaining 2 cases there were no reported animal exposures. The knee was the most common joint involved (11 cases), often in the setting of rheumatoid arthritis, osteoarthritis, or joint prosthesis. Five of the 14 patients were receiving prednisone. Osteomyelitis developed either as the result of direct extension of soft tissue inflammation or by direct inoculation of the periosteum at the time of the bite. Among 13 cases of osteomyelitis reported by this group, 9 (69%) involved animal bites or scratches, 1 (8%) involved animal exposure, and in 3 cases there was no reported exposure. In contrast with septic arthritis, most cases (69%) of osteomyelitis developed in an upper extremity bone, usually the hand or wrist. Also unlike septic arthritis, chronic medical conditions and corticosteroid therapy were not common antecedents. Finally, among 7 cases of combined septic arthritis and osteomyelitis, 6 involved bones and joints of the upper extremities, usually a phalanx and interphalangeal joint infected after a cat bite.[44] Prosthetic joint infections caused by *P. multocida* have been reported infrequently, often in patients with rheumatoid arthritis receiving corticosteroids.[45]

Central Nervous System Infections

Central nervous system infections with *P. multocida* have been reported infrequently. Meningitis is most common; there have been rare cases of focal lesions such as brain abscess and subdural empyema.[25] Of 29 cases of meningitis reported in the English language literature through 1999, most patients had animal contact, usually licking of mucosa or nonintact skin. Bacteremia was seen in nearly two thirds of patients. Mortality was 25% overall, with decreasing mortality among later cases.[46]

Septicemia and Endocarditis

Septicemia is another uncommon complication of *Pasteurella* infection. Raffi and associates reported the clinical features of 13 cases of *P. multocida* bacteremia over a 12-year period and reviewed the literature of 82 previously reported cases.[47] Most patients were men (69%), and most had a localized site of infection (pneumonia, meningitis, arthritis, peritonitis). Many had a serious underlying medical condition, with cirrhosis being most common (34% of reported and reviewed cases). Thirty-two percent had associated animal-related trauma.[47] Infective endocarditis has been reported much less frequently than septicemia. Saleh and associates reported a case of *Pasteurella gallinarum* infectious endocarditis in an adolescent 10 years after surgery to correct a truncus arteriosus.[48] They found 17 other cases of *Pasteurella* infectious endocarditis in the medical literature caused by many different *Pasteurella* spp. In almost half of the cases, no preexisting heart disease was evident. Also, no animal contact was evident in 11 cases.[48] A single case of prosthetic valve endocarditis caused by *P. multocida* involving a prosthetic aortic valve has been reported. The patient was apparently cured with antibiotic therapy alone.[49]

Respiratory Tract Infections

Respiratory tract infections with *Pasteurella* spp. involve the upper respiratory tract, causing sinusitis and bronchitis, and the lower respiratory tract, causing both pneumonia and empyema. The respiratory tract is second only to skin and soft tissue in frequency of clinical isolation of *Pasteurella*.[25] *P. multocida* ssp. *multocida* has been reported to be the most common *Pasteurella* species to cause respiratory tract infections.[50] As previously discussed, asymptomatic *Pasteurella* colonization of the upper respiratory tract has been reported in patients with underlying respiratory tract disease, including chronic obstructive pulmonary disease and bronchiectasis. Presumably for a subset of this patient group the organism invades and causes disease.[20] There is nothing clinically distinguishing about upper respiratory tract infections. Pneumonia usually occurs in patients with underlying lung disease and is usually lobar with a short prodrome. Cases of multilobar and diffuse pulmonary involvement have been described.[25] *Pasteurella* empyema was the subject of a case report and review of the literature by Nelson and Hammer.[51] Most of the 14 patients were adults with a mean age of 70 years, and most had underlying pulmonary disease, either chronic obstructive pulmonary disease or bronchiectasis. Although respiratory and constitutional complaints were the dominant presenting symptoms, fever was surprisingly uncommon. Pleural fluid was described as purulent in all cases in which a sample was obtained.[51]

Intra-abdominal Infections

Of the few reported cases of *Pasteurella* intra-abdominal infections, spontaneous bacterial peritonitis and appendicitis with or without associated peritonitis have been the most frequent clinical syndromes. Among the reported cases of spontaneous bacterial peritonitis, virtually all have had cirrhosis (usually alcoholic) and preexisting ascites.[52,53] Raffi and associates reported three cases of *P. multocida* appendiceal peritonitis and identified eight additional well-documented cases of appendicitis in the literature.[54] Accompanying peritonitis was variably present. It was postulated that the source of the organism was most likely from oropharyngeal colonization.[54] Eight cases of peritonitis have been reported in association with peritoneal dialysis. Cats were the presumed source in all eight patients. Recovery with antimicrobial treatment was complete in all described cases.[55]

Other *Pasteurella* Infections

Infections of other sites with *Pasteurella* species have been reported rarely and include the genitourinary tract,[32,56,57] epiglottitis,[58] and endophthalmitis.[25,59] *Pasteurella* infections also have been reported in patients with a variety of immune deficiencies including bronchitis in a patient with Sweet's syndrome,[60] fatal sepsis in a patient with hairy cell leukemia,[61] cellulitis with bacteremia in a neutropenic host,[62] and pneumonia and malacoplakia in acquired immunodeficiency syndrome (AIDS) patients.[63,64]

TREATMENT, PREVENTION, AND PROGNOSIS

Several decades of clinical experience with *Pasteurella* and numerous in vitro studies indicate that penicillin is the best antimicrobial agent for the treatment of virtually all forms of infection.[12,25,28,65,66] Minimal inhibitory concentrations (MICs) of various strains of *P. multocida* to

penicillin G have ranged from 0.049 to 0.39 μg/mL[65] and from 0.19 to 0.78 μg/mL.[66] Other penicillins with good in vitro activity include penicillin VK, ampicillin, and amoxicillin.[65-67] Antistaphylococcal penicillins including oxacillin, nafcillin, dicloxacillin, and cloxacillin are not as active and are not recommended for treatment of documented *Pasteurella* infections.[65,66,68] Amoxicillin-clavulanic acid has excellent in vitro activity.[67] Many cephalosporins demonstrate in vitro activity against *P. multocida*. In general, activity increases with later-generation cephalosporins.[65,68] Goldstein and associates reported high minimal inhibitory concentrations for cephalexin, cefaclor, and cefadroxil and recommended that they not be used for the treatment of documented infections.[68] The oral cephalosporins, cefuroxime and cefixime, along with parenteral agents including ceftriaxone and cefoperazone, demonstrate excellent in vitro activity and are probably good substitutes for penicillin.[65]

Plasmid-mediated β-lactamase production has been described in *P. multocida* strains isolated from animals. The first β-lactamase–producing *P. multocida* strain isolated from a human source (respiratory tract) was reported in the late 1980s and characterized as an ROB-1 β-lactamase by Rosenau and associates.[69] The isolate was resistant to amoxicillin, ticarcillin, cephalothin, sulfonamides, and tetracyclines. Addition of the β-lactamase inhibitors, clavulanic acid, sulbactam, and tazobactam, reduced the minimal inhibitory concentrations of the isolate by at least 64-fold.[69]

Among non–β-lactam antibiotics, agents with in vitro activity include tetracyclines, fluoroquinolones, chloramphenicol, and trimethoprim-sulfamethoxazole.[66,67,68,70,71,72] In comparison with penicillin, limited clinical data on the usefulness of these agents are available. Doxycycline, a fluoroquinolone or trimethoprim-sulfamethoxazole should be considered as alternatives for patients with intolerance to β-lactams. Aminoglycosides have moderate to poor activity in vitro and probably should not be used, particularly given the paucity of clinical experience.[66,70] Clindamycin and erythromycin consistently demonstrate high minimal inhibitory concentrations in vitro and are not recommended. The newer long-acting macrolides (azithromycin, clarithromycin, roxithromycin, dirithromycin) appear to have better activity including postantibiotic effect but also should not be used because clinical experience with these agents is limited.[70,73]

Because animal bite wound infections are frequently polymicrobial and may include *S. aureus,* streptococcal species, and anaerobes in addition to *Pasteurella,* empirical antibiotic therapy should be directed at such organisms until or unless wound cultures define the specific bacteriology of the infection.[30] Outpatient treatment of documented, uncomplicated *Pasteurella* cellulitis can be undertaken with penicillin VK, amoxicillin, or ampicillin, with close follow-up.[25] Duration of therapy is not well defined, but 10 to 14 days is probably a reasonable time course. Patients with evidence of involvement of deeper structures (e.g., tenosynovitis, arthritis) should be hospitalized and treated parenterally. Drainage and débridement may be necessary for patients who have progressive infection with extensive suppuration.

Treatment of septic arthritis should consist of antimicrobial therapy along with frequent drainage of the involved joints.[44] Most patients recover fully.[44] Similarly, the outcome for osteomyelitis appears to be good, although débridement in addition to antimicrobial therapy is often needed.[44] The outcome of septic arthritis with osteomyelitis is not as good, with residual deformity and loss of function being common.[44] For all bone and joint *Pasteurella* infections, antimicrobial therapy should be continued for 4 to 6 weeks.

Patients with the other end-organ forms of *Pasteurella* infection do poorly overall. High mortality has been reported for most of these conditions. The high mortality rate for meningitis is probably a consequence of the frail nature of its target population: young children and the elderly. For patients with bacteremia without endovascular infection, the mortality rate also is high probably as a result of the infection itself combined with the underlying medical problem, usually alcoholic cirrhosis. For endocarditis, among 17 reported patients, 5 died and 4 required valve replacement.[48] For patients with pneumonia, both morbidity and mortality are high, almost certainly as a result of severe underlying pulmonary disease. Finally, patients with spontaneous bacterial peritonitis have an extremely high mortality rate, whereas those with appendicitis with or without peritonitis generally do well.[53,54]

Antimicrobial prophylaxis after animal bites has remained a controversial subject. Although a few small trials have been completed, none has been large enough or seen enough patients reach significant end points to unequivocally speak to the efficacy of such therapy. Nonetheless, because the rate of culture positivity of fresh animal bite wounds is high, most experts recommend a short course (3-5 days) of oral antimicrobial therapy. Amoxicillin 875 mg with clavulanic acid 125 mg, given twice daily, is a commonly used agent that has activity against *S. aureus,* streptococci, anaerobes, and *Pasteurella*. The combination of cefuroxime or doxycycline or fluoroquinolone or trimethoprim-sulfamethoxazole plus either metronidazole or clindamycin should be alternatives for patients with penicillin allergy (see Chapter 318).

REFERENCES

1. Pasteur L. Sur les maladies virulentes et en particulier sur la maladie appelee vulgairement cholera des poules. CR Acad Sci (Paris). 1880;90:239-248.
2. Brugnatelli E. Puerperal fieber durch einen Bacillus aus der Gruppe, "Hamorrhagische Septikamie" *(Pasteurella).* Centr Bakteriol Parasitenk I Abt Orig. 1913;70:337-345.
3. Kapel O, Holm J. *Pasteurella* infektion biem menschen nach katzenbiss. Zbl Chir. 1930;57:2906.
4. Holmes B, Pickett MJ, Hollis DG. *Pasteurella*. In: Murray PR, ed. Manual of Clinical Microbiology. Washington, DC: ASM Press; 1999:632-637.
5. Dewhirst FE, Paster BJ, Olsen I, et al. Phylogeny of 54 representative strains of species in the family Pasteurellaceae as determined by comparison of 16S rRNA sequences. J Bacteriol. 1992;174:2002-2013.
6. Grehn M, Muller F. The oxidase reaction of *Pasteurella multocida* strains cultured on Mueller-Hinton medium. J Microbiol Methods. 1989;9:333-336.
7. Heddleston KL, Wessman G. Characteristics of *Pasteurella multocida* of human origin. J Clin Microbiol. 1975;1:377-383.
8. Oberhofer TR. Characteristics and biotypes of *Pasteurella multocida* isolated from humans. J Clin Microbiol. 1981;13:566-571.
9. Hamilton-Miller JM. A possible pitfall in the identification of *Pasteurella* spp. with the API system. J Med Microbiol. 1993;39:78-79.
10. Bruckner DA, Colonna P, Bearson BL. Nomenclature for aerobic and facultative bacteria. Clin Infect Dis. 1999;29:713-723.
11. Holst E, Rollof J, Larsson L, et al. Characterization and distribution of *Pasteurella* species recovered from infected humans. J Clin Microbiol. 1992;30:2984-2987.
12. Jones FL, Smull CE. Infections in man due to *Pasteurella multocida*. Penn Med J. 1973;76:41-44.
13. Bailie WE, Stowe EC, Schmitt AM. Aerobic bacterial flora of oral and nasal fluids of canines with reference to bacteria associated with bites. J Clin Microbiol. 1978;7:223-231.
14. Owen CR, Buker EO, Be JF, et al. *Pasteurella multocida* in animal mouths. Rocky Mt Med J. 1968;65:45-46.
15. Schipper GJ. Unusual pathogenicity of *Pasteurella multocida* isolated from the throats of common wild rats. Johns Hopkins Hosp Bull. 1947;81:333.
16. Smith JE. Studies on *Pasteurella septica:* II. Some cultural and biochemical properties of strains from different host species. J Comp Pathol. 1958;68:315.
17. Carter GR. Pasteurellosis: *Pasteurella multocida* and *Pasteurella hemolytica*. Adv Vet Sci. 1967;11:321-379.
18. Ejlertsen T, Gahrn-Hansen B, Sogaard P, et al. *Pasteurella aeragenes* isolated from ulcers or wounds in humans with occupational exposure to pigs: A report of 7 Danish cases. Scand J Infect Dis. 1996;28:567-570.
19. Gadberry JL, Zipper R, Taylor JA, et al. *Pasteurella pneumotropica* isolated from bone and joint infections. J Clin Microbiol. 1984;19:926-927.
20. Starkebaum GA, Plorde JJ. *Pasteurella* pneumonia: Report of a case and review of the literature. J Clin Microbiol. 1977;5:332-335.
21. Moritz F, Martin E, Lemeland JF, et al. Fatal *Pasteurella bettyae* pleuropneumonia in a patient infected with human immunodeficiency virus. Clin Infect Dis. 1996;22:591-592.
22. Bartley EO. *Pasteurella septica* in chronic nasal sinusitis. Lancet. 1960;2:581-582.
23. Cawson RA, Talbot JM. The occurrence of *Pasteurella septica* (syn. *multocida*) in bronchiectasis. J Clin Pathol. 1955;8:49-51.
24. Avril J-L, Donnio P-Y, Pouedras P. Selective medium for *Pasteurella multocida* and its use to detect oropharyngeal carriage in pig breeders. J Clin Microbiol. 1990;28:1438-1440.
25. Weber DJ, Wolfson JS, Swartz MN, et al. *Pasteurella multocida* infections: Report of 34 cases and review of the literature. Medicine (Baltimore). 1984;63:133-154.
26. Arons MS, Fernando L, Polayes IM. *Pasteurella multocida:* The major cause of hand infections following domestic animal bites. J Hand Surg [Am]. 1982;7:47-52.
27. Brook I. Microbiology of human and animal bite wounds in children. Pediatr Infect Dis J. 1987;6:29-32.
28. Francis DP, Holmes MA, Brandon G. *Pasteurella multocida:* Infections after domestic animal bites and scratches. JAMA. 1975;233:42-45.
29. Goldstein EJC. Bite wounds and infection. Clin Infect Dis. 1992;14:633-640.
30. Goldstein EJC, Citron DM, Wield B, et al. Bacteriology of human and animal bite wounds. J Clin Microbiol. 1978;8:667-672.
31. Hubbert WT, Rosen MN. *Pasteurella multocida* infection due to animal bite. Am J Public Health. 1970;60:1103-1108.
32. Hubbert WT, Rosen MN. *Pasteurella multocida* infection in man unrelated to animal bites. Am J Public Health. 1970;60:1109-1117.
33. Zaramella P, Zamorani E, Freato F, et al. Neonatal meningitis due to a vertical transmission of *Pasteurella* multocida. Pediatrics International. 1999;41:307-310.
34. Baddour LM, Gelfand MS, Weaver RE, et al. CDC Group HB-5 as a cause of genitourinary infections in adults. J Clin Microbiol. 1989;27:801-805.
35. Bogaerts J, Verhaegen J, Martinez Tello W, et al. Characterization, in vitro susceptibility, and clinical significance of CDC group HB-5 from Rwanda. J Clin Microbiol. 1990;10:2196-2199.
36. Pijoan C, Trigo F. Bacterial adhesion to mucosal surfaces with special reference to *Pasteurella multocida* isolates from atrophic rhinitis. Can J Vet Res. 1990;54:S16-S21.
37. Lo RYC. Molecular characterization of cytotoxins produced by *Haemophilus, Actinobacillus, Pasteurella*. Can J Vet Res. 1990;54:S33-S35.
38. Lichtensteiger CA, Steenbergen SM, Lee RM, et al. Direct PCR analysis for toxigenic *Pasteurella* multocida. J Clin Microbiol. 1996;34:3035-3039.
39. Boyce JD, Chung JY, Adler B. *Pasteurella multocida* capsule: Composition, function and genetics. J Biotechnol. 2000;83:153-160.
40. Schryvers AB, Gonzalez GC. Receptors for transferrin in pathogenic bacteria are specific for the host's protein. Can J Microbiol. 1990;36:145-147.
41. Choudat D, Paul G, Legoff C, et al. Specific antibody responses to *Pasteurella multocida*. Scand J Infect Dis. 1987;19:453-457.
42. Talan DA, Citron DM, Abrahamian FM, et al. Bacteriologic analysis of infected dog and cat bites. Emergency Medicine Animal Bite Infection Study Group. N Engl J Med. 1999;340:85-92.
43. Ejlertsen T, Gahrn-Hansen B, Sogaard P, et al. *Pasteurella aerogenes* isolated from ulcers or wounds in humans with occupational exposure to pigs: A report of 7 Danish cases. Scand J Infect Dis. 1996;28:567-570.
44. Ewing R, Fainstein V, Musher DM, et al. Articular and skeletal infections caused by *Pasteurella multocida*. South Med J. 1980;73:1349-1352.
45. Maradona JA, Asensi V, Carton JA, et al. Prosthetic joint infection by *Pasteurella multocida*. Eur J Clin Microbiol Infect Dis. 1997;16:623-625.
46. Green BT, Ramsey KM, Nolan PE. *Pasteurella multocida* meningitis: Case report and review of the last 11 years. Scand J Infect Dis. 2002;34:213-217.
47. Raffi F, Barrier J, Baron D, et al. *Pasteurella multocida* bacteremia: Report of thirteen cases over twelve years and review of the literature. Scand J Infect Dis. 1987;19:385-393.
48. Saleh MAF, Al-Madan MS, Erwa HH, et al. First case of human infection caused by *Pasteurella gallinarum* causing infective endocarditis in an adolescent 10 years after surgical correction for truncus arteriosus. Pediatrics. 1995;95:944-948.
49. Nettles RE, Sexton DJ. *Pasteurella multocida* prosthetic valve endocarditis: Case report and review. Clin Infect Dis. 1997;25:920-921.
50. Chen HI, Hulten K, Clarridge JE 3rd. Taxonomic subgroups of *Pasteurella multocida* correlate with clinical presentation. J Clin Microbiol. 2002;40:3438-3441.
51. Nelson SC, Hammer GS. *Pasteurella multocida* empyema: Case report and review of the literature. Am J Med Sci. 1981;281:43-49.
52. Gerding DN, Khan MY, Ewing JW, et al. *Pasteurella multocida* peritonitis in hepatic cirrhosis with ascites. Gastroenterology. 1976;70:413-415.
53. Szpak CA, Woodard BH, White JO, et al. Bacterial peritonitis and bacteremia associated with *Pasteurella multocida*. South Med J. 1980;73:801-803.
54. Raffi F, David A, Mouzard A, et al. *Pasteurella multocida* appendiceal peritonitis: Report of three cases and review of the literature. Pediatr Infect Dis. 1986;5:695-698.
55. Van Langenhove G, Daelemans R, Zachee P, et al. *Pasteurella multocida* as a rare cause of peritonitis in peritoneal dialysis. Nephron. 2000;85:283-284.
56. Liu W, Chemaly RF, Tuohy MJ, et al. *Pasteurella multocida* urinary tract infection with molecular evidence of zoonotic transmission. Clin Infect Dis. 2003;36:E58-60.
57. Loiez C, Wallet F, Husson MO, et al. *Pasteurella multocida* and intrauterine device: A woman and her pets. Scand J Infect Dis. 2002;34:473.
58. Wine N, Lim Y, Fierer J. *Pasteurella multocida* epiglottitis. Arch Otolaryngol Head Neck Surg. 1997;123:759-761.
59. Baskar B, Desai SP, Parsons MA. Postoperative endophthalmitis due to *Pasteurella multocida*. Br J Ophthalmol. 1997;81:172-173.
60. Boivin S, Segard M, Piette F, et al. Sweet syndrome associated with *Pasteurella multocida* bronchitis. Arch Intern Med. 2000;160:1869.
61. Athar MK, Karim MS, Mannam S, et al. Fatal *Pasteurella* sepsis and hairy-cell leukemia. Am J Hematol. 2003;72:285.
62. Gowda RV, Stout R. *Pasteurella multocida* infection in a post-chemotherapy neutropenic host following cat exposure. Clin Oncol. 2002;14:497-498.
63. Moritz F, Martin E, Lemeland JF, et al. Fatal *Pasteurella bettyae* pleuropneumonia in a patient infected with human immunodeficiency virus. Clin Infect Dis. 1996;22:591-592.
64. Bastas A, Markou N, Botsi C, et al. Malakoplakia of the lung caused by *Pasteurella multocida* in a patient with AIDS. Scand J Infect Dis. 2002;34:536-538.
65. Noel GJ, Teele DW. In vitro activities of selected new and long-acting cephalosporins against *Pasteurella multocida*. Antimicrob Agents Chemother. 1986;29:344-345.
66. Stevens DL, Higbee JW, Oberhofer TR, et al. Antibiotic susceptibilities of human isolates of *Pasteurella multocida*. Antimicrob Agents Chemother. 1979;16:322-324.
67. Goldstein EJC, Citron DM. Comparative activities of cefuroxime, amoxicillin-clavulanic acid, ciprofloxacin, enoxacin, ofloxacin against aerobic and anaerobic bacteria isolated from bite wounds. Antimicrob Agents Chemother. 1988;32:1143-1148.
68. Goldstein EJC, Citron DM, Richwald GA. Lack of in vitro efficacy of oral forms of certain cephalosporins, erythromycin, and oxacillin against *Pasteurella multocida*. Antimicrob Agents Chemother. 1988;32:213-215.

69. Rosenau A, Labigne A, Escande F, et al. Plasmid-mediated ROB-1 β-lactamase in *Pasteurella multocida* from a human specimen. Antimicrob Agents Chemother. 1991;35:2419-2422.
70. Gaillot O, Guilbert L, Maruejouls C, et al. In-vitro susceptibility to thirteen antibiotics of *Pasteurella* spp. and related bacteria isolated from humans (Letter). J Antimicrob Chemother. 1995;36:878-880.
71. Goldstein EJC, Citron DM, Merriam CV, et al. Activity of gatifloxacin compared to those of five other quinolones versus aerobic and anaerobic isolates from skin and soft tissue samples of human and animal bite wound infections. Antimicrob Agents Chemother. 1999;43:1475-1479.
72. Mortensen JE, Giger O, Rodgers GL. In vitro activity of oral antimicrobial agents against clinical isolates of *Pasteurella multocida*. Diagn Microbiol Infect Dis. 1998;30:99-102.
73. Lim J, Yun H. Postantibiotic effects and postantibiotic sub-MIC effects of erythromycin, roxithromycin, tilmicosin, and tylosin on *Pasteurella multocida*. Int J Antimicrob Agents. 2001;17:471-476.

CHAPTER **226**

Yersinia
Species, Including Plague

THOMAS BUTLER

DAVID T. DENNIS

The genus *Yersinia* includes the pathogens *Yersinia pestis, Yersinia enterocolitica,* and *Yersinia pseudotuberculosis.* The yersinioses are zoonotic infections of rodents, pigs, birds, and various other domestic and wild animals; humans are incidental hosts for infection. *Y. pestis* is the cause of plague, whose most common clinical form is acute febrile lymphadenitis, called bubonic plague. Less common forms include septicemic, pneumonic, pharyngeal, and meningeal plague. Untreated, plague has a high fatality; treatment in the early course of illness greatly reduces the occurrence of complications and death. *Y. enterocolitica* and *Y. pseudotuberculosis* typically produce an enteric infection with fever, diarrhea, and abdominal pain that can mimic acute appendicitis. Common pathologic lesions of the enteric yersinioses are acute enteritis and mesenteric lymphadenitis.

YERSINIA PESTIS

History

Plague is a disease of antiquity that poses a diminished but present threat. Over the past two millennia, three catastrophic pandemics occurred whose effects were vividly recorded.[1] Most notable was the medieval Black Death, which was estimated to have killed one fourth of Europe's population and changed the course of history. The latest (modern) pandemic began in China in the 1860s and spread to Hong Kong in the 1890s. There, in 1894, Alexandre Yersin first isolated the causative agent. Over the ensuing 20 years, this last pandemic was spread by rats on ships to port cities on all inhabited continents, including several in the United States. Urban rat-borne plague was soon brought under control in most places using modern sanitation practices, but the infection was transferred to various species of wild rodents, becoming entrenched in newly invaded rural areas of the Americas, Africa, and Asia. In the first half of the 20th century, India was most severely affected by plague epidemics, with more than 20 million cases and 10 million deaths. In the 1960s and 1970s, war-torn Vietnam became the country most affected by plague, reporting thousands of cases annually.[2] Plague has recently resurged in sub-Saharan Africa, especially in East Africa and the adjacent island nation of Madagascar.[3,4]

Y. pestis was developed as an aerosol weapon during the Cold War, and its potential for misuse by terrorists is considered an important national security threat requiring special measures for medical and pub-

lic health preparedness[5] (see Chapter 321). The plague bacillus is a designated category A select biologic agent whose handling is regulated by federal law.[6]

Description of the Pathogen

Y. pestis is a gram-negative, bipolar-staining bacillus that belongs to the family Enterobacteriaceae.[1] It grows aerobically on most culture media, including blood agar and MacConkey agar. It grows well also in nutrient broths, such as brain-heart infusion broth. Cultures grow more slowly than most bacteria and optimally at 28° C. Small colonies are visible on MacConkey agar after 24 to 48 hours of incubation at 35° C. On triple-sugar–iron agar, *Y. pestis* produces an alkaline slant and an acid butt. It is nonmotile and non–spore forming, does not ferment lactose, and is citrate, urease, and indole negative.

Molecular genetic studies of various strains of the pathogenic yersiniae show that *Y. pestis,* a blood-borne organism, only recently (1500 to 20,000 years ago) evolved from *Y. pseudotuberculosis,* an enteric pathogen.[7] Decoding of the entire genome of *Y. pestis* (consisting of a 4.65-Mb chromosome and three plasmids) shows that the evolution of *Y. pestis* was made possible by the acquisition of virulence determinants suitable for systemic invasion and by the inactivation of genes expressing factors required for survival in the mammalian gut.[8] Three classic biovars of *Y. pestis* have been identified, including biovar Antiqua, Medievalis, and Orientalis, linked to respective pandemics and having distinct geographic distributions. Results of typing by restriction fragment length polymorphism (RFLP) analysis of ribosomal RNA genes (ribotyping) support these distinctions and identify minor chromosomal rearrangements in the Orientalis biotype following its pandemic spread about 100 years ago.[9] Further studies have shown continuing genome plasticity, even within strains from one geographic area.[10,11]

As with the other yersiniae, the plague bacillus produces V and W antigens that confer a calcium requirement for growth at 37° C.[1] The expression of these antigens, mediated by the 45-mDa plasmid (~70 kb), is essential for virulence and plays a role in adapting the organism for intracellular survival and multiplication. Other important virulence factors include an anti-phagocytic fraction I (F1) envelope antigen mediated by the approximately 110-kb (pFRA) plasmid, and a plasminogen activator protein (Pla protease) that is responsible for temperature-dependent coagulase and fibrinolysin activities and is mediated by the 9.5-kb plasmid. Chromosome-mediated factors include a potent lipopolysaccharide endotoxin and a pigmentation factor that plays a role in complex systems that regulate iron uptake and storage.[1]

Epidemiology

Plague occurs worldwide, and most human cases are reported from rural underdeveloped areas of the Third World (Fig. 226-1). In the 15-year period from 1987 to 2001, twenty-five countries reported a total of 36,876 cases (mean of about 2500 cases per year) and 2847 deaths (8% fatality ratio).[12] The countries that reported more than 1000 cases (from most to least) were Madagascar, Tanzania, Democratic Republic of Congo, Vietnam, Mozambique, Namibia, and Peru. Plague's continuing potential for emergence is demonstrated by reports of recent outbreaks by several southeastern Africa countries and by India. In Madagascar, repeated outbreaks of rat-borne plague have occurred since 1990 in the port city of Mahajanga, and in endemic foci in the highlands.[13] In the United States, more than 400 cases of plague have been reported since 1950; in 1987 to 2001 there were 125 plague cases and 12 deaths. Although wild rodent plague occurs in 17 of the contiguous western United States extending from the Pacific Coast to the Great Plains, approximately 80% of human cases occur in New Mexico, Arizona, and Colorado, and about 10% in California (Fig. 226-2).[14,15] Since the early part of the 20th century, plague in the United States has shown clear patterns of spread from California eastward to the Great Plains states, and persons are increasingly exposed around their homes as development extends into natural settings.[3] Plague arising in travelers (peripatetic plague) can present a diagnostic challenge and trigger concern about possible terrorist exposures.[16]

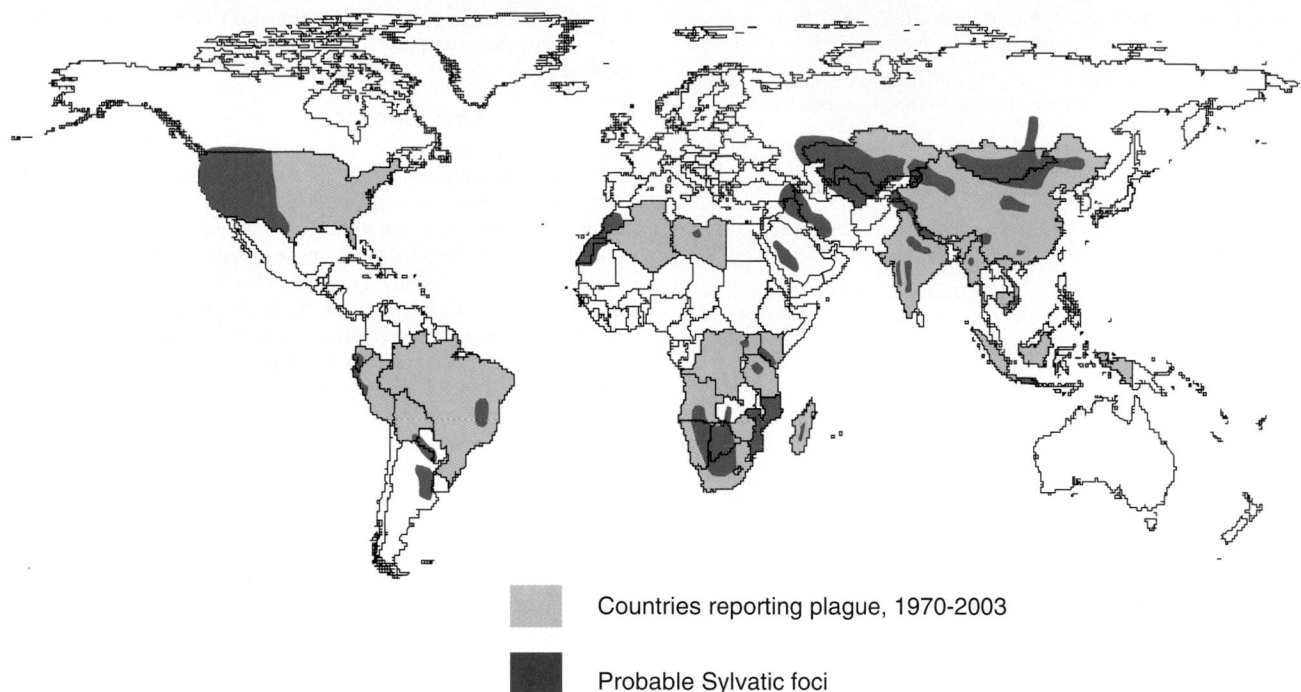

□ Countries reporting plague, 1970-2003

■ Probable Sylvatic foci

FIGURE 226-1. Worldwide distribution of plague in humans and animals. *(Data compiled from the World Health Organization, Centers for Disease Control and Prevention, and other sources. From Centers for Disease Control and Prevention. Prevention of plague. Recommendations of the Advisory Committee on Immunization Practices (ACIP). MMWR Morb Mortal Wkly Rep. 1996;45[RR-14]:1-15.)*

Plague is primarily an infection of animals. It is transmitted among its animal hosts by flea bites, and less commonly by cannibalism or predation (Fig. 226-3). Throughout the world, the domestic rats *Rattus rattus* and *Rattus norvegicus* are the most dangerous reservoirs of plague. The most efficient vector of infection to humans is the orien-

tal rat flea, *Xenopsylla cheopis*. Risk of spread of plague from rats to humans is positively correlated with the density of rats, the number of fleas per animal (flea index), and the *Y. pestis* infection rates in sampled rats and rat fleas.[17] In sylvatic plague foci, such as those in the western United States and the deserts, savannah, and steppes in other

FIGURE 226-2. Cases of plague in the western United States, 1970-2003. Each dot represents one case, with the dot placed randomly in the county of exposure. *(Map courtesy of the Centers for Disease Control and Prevention, Fort Collins, CO.)*

Plague Cases in the Western U.S., 1970-2003

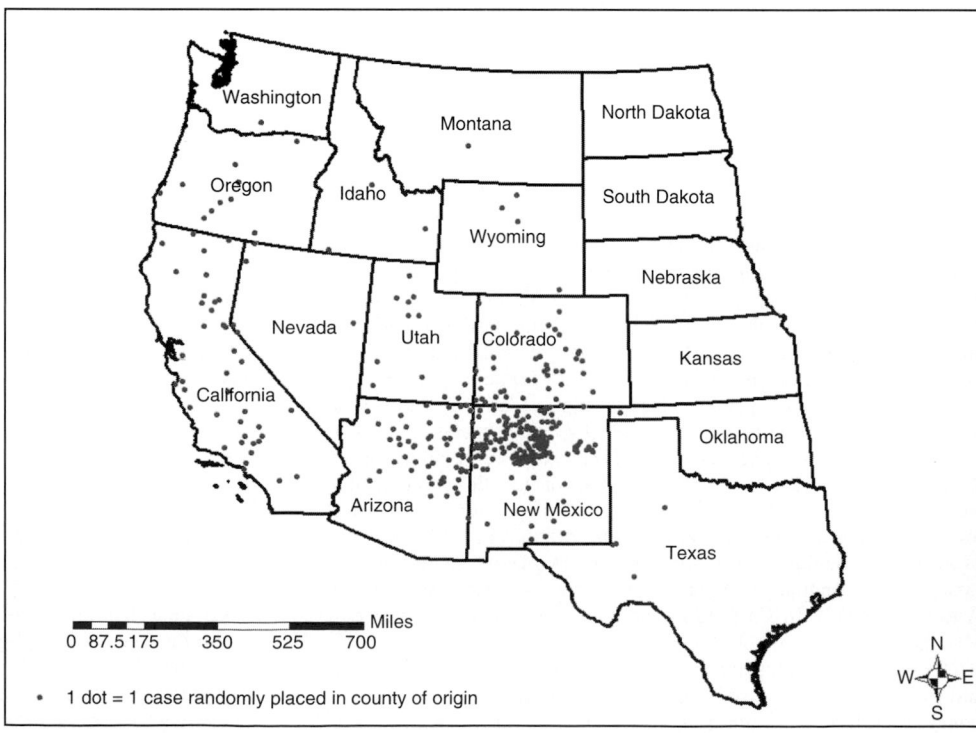

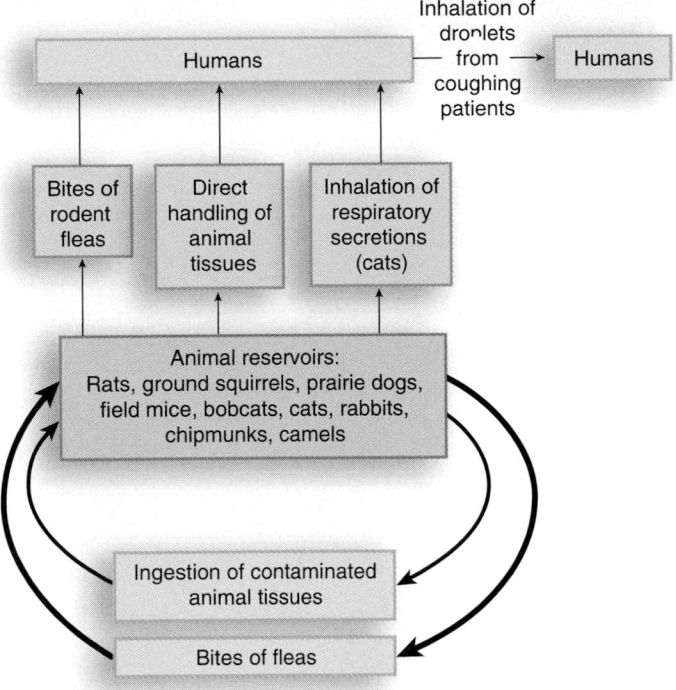

FIGURE 226-3. Transmission of plague. The *wide arrows* indicate common modes of transmission, the *medium arrows* indicate occasional transmission, and the *thin arrows* indicate rare kinds of transmission.

endemic regions, the important reservoirs are various burrowing rodents.[18] Humans become incidentally infected by the bites of rodent fleas or by direct contact with infectious materials. Because humans do not contribute to the natural cycle of plague, they are considered "dead-end" hosts. Only when there are cases of pneumonic plague is the infection passed directly from person to person. Rarely, humans develop primary pneumonic plague following exposure to cats with respiratory infection.[19]

In the United States, males and females are about equally affected by plague. More than half of cases occur in persons younger than 20 years of age. Although a majority of cases occur in whites, the incidence rate in endemic southwestern states is highest among Native Americans and Hispanic Americans.[20] Within endemic areas, elevated plague risk is associated with close contact with rodents and their feline and canine predators, the presence of harborage and food sources for wild rodents in the near vicinity of homes, and possibly a failure to control fleas on pet dogs and cats.[21] Most cases arise in the period from May to October, when plague-bearing rodents and their fleas are most numerous and active, and when people are more likely to be outdoors and exposed to natural cycles of infection.

Pathogenesis

Plasmid DNA is essential for survival of *Y. pestis* in its mammalian hosts and flea vectors and for transmission between them.[22,23] Several factors are selectively expressed at temperatures and in environments encountered in fleas or mammals, respectively. For example, hemin storage locus (*hms*) products are expressed in the low-temperature (28° C or less) environment of the flea, enabling the bacteria to form blockages of the flea gut necessary for efficient transmission.[23] When a flea ingests an infective blood meal, the coagulase expressed by *Y. pestis* causes the blood to clot in the foregut, leading to blockage of the flea's swallowing. The organism multiplies in the clotted blood. During further attempts to ingest a blood meal, a blocked flea may regurgitate many thousands of organisms into its host's skin. In the ambient temperature in the flea, very little F1 antigen is expressed, and when inoculated into mammals the unprotected bacilli are readily

phagocytized by polymorphonuclear leukocytes and mononuclear cells. *Y. pestis* resists destruction within mononuclear phagocytes, multiplies, and now at 37° C elaborates the F1 envelope antigen. If lysis of the mononuclear cells occurs, the released F1-producing bacilli are relatively resistant to further phagocytosis.[1] The invading organisms are carried via lymphatics to the regional lymph nodes, where they initiate an intense inflammatory reaction. Microscopic examination of the involved nodes reveals invasion by polymorphonuclear leukocytes, hemorrhagic necrosis with destruction of normal architecture, and dense concentrations of extracellular bacilli. Bacteremia is common in bubonic plague, and in the absence of specific therapy can lead variously to sepsis, pneumonia, and purulent, necrotic, and hemorrhagic lesions in various organs. Elaboration of endotoxin can lead to hypotension, oliguria, altered mental status, disseminated intravascular coagulation, and other manifestations of the systemic inflammatory response syndrome.[24]

Clinical Manifestations

Bubonic Plague

The most common form of infection is bubonic plague, which presents a distinctive clinical picture (Table 226-1).[24-27] During a typical incubation period of 2 to 7 days following the bite of an infected flea, bacteria proliferate in the regional lymph nodes. Onset of illness is characterized by the sudden occurrence of fever, chills, weakness, and headache. Simultaneously, or within hours, patients notice the bubo, which is signaled by intense pain in one anatomic region of lymph nodes, usually the groin, axilla, or neck. A swelling evolves in this area that is so tender that the patient typically avoids any motion that would provoke discomfort. For example, if the bubo is in a femoral area, the patient characteristically flexes, abducts, and externally rotates the hip to relieve pressure on the area and walks with a limp.

The buboes of patients with plague are oval swellings that vary from 1 to 10 cm in length and elevate the overlying skin, which may be stretched, warm, and erythematous. Palpation typically elicits extreme tenderness, and the examiner feels either smooth, uniform, egg-shaped masses or an irregular cluster of several nodes with intervening and surrounding edema. The developing mass is typically firm and nonfluctuant, and the perinodal edema can be either gelatinous or pitting in nature. Although infections other than plague can produce acute lymphadenitis, plague is unique for the suddenness of onset of the fever and bubo, the intensity of inflammation in the bubo, and the absence in the majority of cases of an obvious sentinel infected skin lesion or associated ascending lymphangitis (Fig. 226-4). On careful examination, however, skin lesions are detectable in as many as one fourth of patients with bubonic plague.[24-26] Papules, vesicles, or pustules are most common, and are found distal to the affected lymph nodes, presumably representing sites of the infective flea bites. Rarely, these lesions progress to extensive cellulitis or abscesses. Ulcerations may result from the breakdown of furuncles and be covered by eschars (Fig. 226-5). Examination of swabs or scrapings from skin lesions usually demonstrates collections of polymorphonuclear leukocytes and plague bacilli.

Buboes are most commonly located in the groin, femoral nodes being more frequently affected than the inguinal nodes. The axillary and cervical regions are other commonly involved sites. The distribution of buboes is determined by the site of entry of infection. In adults, the

TABLE 226-1	Plague Syndromes
Syndrome	*Features*
Bubonic	Fever, painful lymphadenopathy (bubo)
Septicemic	Fever, hypotension complications of inflammatory response syndrome
Pneumonic	Cough, hemoptysis with or without bubo
Pharyngeal	Painful, inflamed pharynx, local lymphadenopathy
Meningitis	Fever, nuchal rigidity usually with bubo

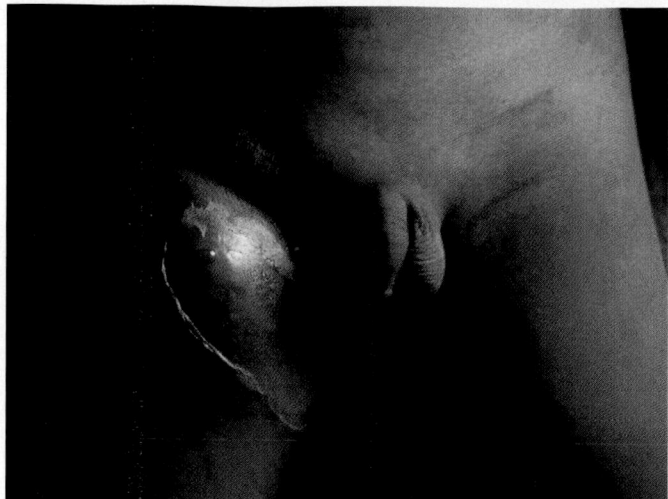

FIGURE 226-4. Femoral and inguinal buboes in young male showing marked edematous swelling, erythema, and overlying desquamation. *(Courtesy of the Centers for Disease Control and Prevention, Fort Collins, CO.)*

large majority of infective fleabites occur on the lower extremities; relatively greater numbers of bites occur on the upper body in children.

Patients often do not seek care on the first days of illness. By the time of examination, they are typically prostrate and lethargic but may exhibit restlessness or agitation. Temperatures are usually elevated in the range of 38.5° C to 40.0° C. Occasionally, patients are delirious with high fever, and seizures are common in children. Pulse rates are increased to 110 to 140 beats per minute. Blood pressure is characteristically low, in the range of 100/60 mm Hg, owing to vasodilation. The liver and spleen are often palpable and tender. Without appropriate intervention, shock may ensue, and a cascading clinical course can produce death as quickly as 2 to 3 days after the onset of symptoms.

Septicemic Plague

A distinctive feature of plague, in addition to the bubo, is a propensity for rapid multiplication of the bacillus in the blood. In the early acute states of bubonic plague, intermittent seeding of the blood stream is probably universal. In one series, single blood cultures obtained at the time of hospital admission were positive in 27% of cases.[26] A hallmark of moribund patients with plague is high-density bacteremia, and the finding of characteristic bacilli in a stained peripheral blood smear has been used as a prognostic indicator in this disease (Fig. 226-6). Occasionally, bacteria proliferate in the body without producing a bubo. Patients may become ill with fever and die with sepsis but without detectable lymphadenitis. This syndrome has been termed *primary* septicemic plague to denote systemic plague without an antecedent bubo or plague pneumonia. In New Mexico, 25% of plague cases in 1980-1984 were of the primary septicemic form, and the case-fatality ratio in these cases (33%) was three times higher than in bubonic plague, in part because of delays in diagnosis and treatment.[28,29]

If not treated quickly, plague sepsis and attendant endotoxemia lead to profound pathophysiologic effects, including complement cascade and excessive release of proinflammatory mediators, such as tumor necrosis factor-α and other kinins. The resulting systemic inflammatory response syndrome may lead to disseminated intravascular coagulation, bleeding, organ failure, and irreversible shock.[24,25] Affected tissues contain inflamed microvasculature occluded by fibrin thrombi, resulting in necrosis and hemorrhage. Purpuric skin lesions are the most obvious manifestation of a bleeding diathesis; they are usually found scattered across the extremities and trunk, are at first red but change to a dark purple, and, in the patients who survive, eventually slough (Fig. 226-7). Blockage of vessels in acral sites, such as tips of fingers, toes, ears, and nose, can lead to gangrene of these parts.[30]

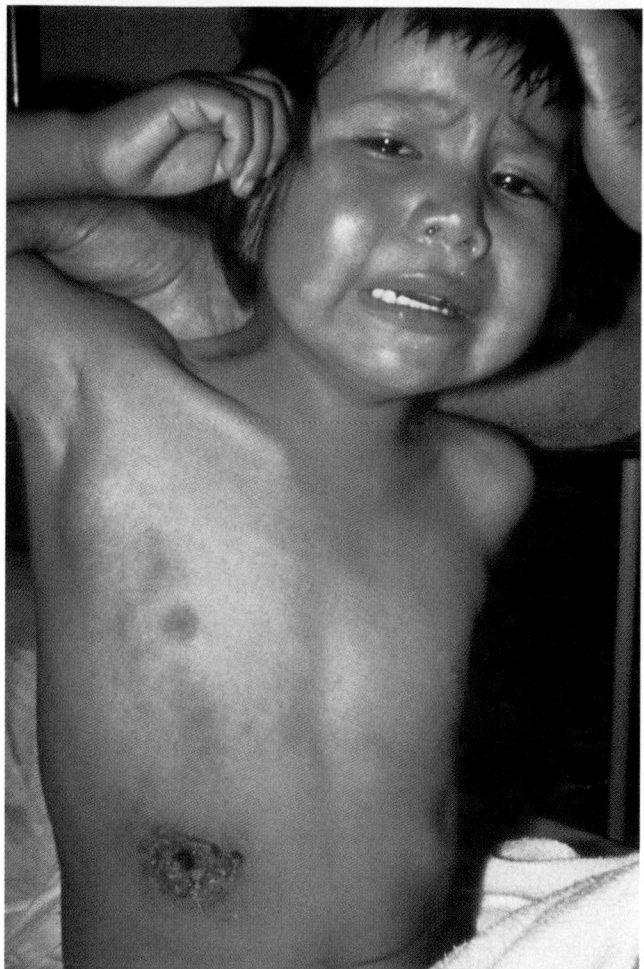

FIGURE 226-5. Axillary bubo with ulceration and small eschar at site of infective flea bite. *(Courtesy of the Centers for Disease Control and Prevention, Fort Collins, CO.)*

These startling cutaneous signs may be the origin of "Black Death," an eponym for severe plague in the Middle Ages.

Pneumonic Plague

One of the most feared complications of bubonic plague is secondary pneumonia. The infection reaches the lungs by hematogenous spread of bacteria from the bubo. It is a malignant pneumonia with rapid advance and is often complicated by sepsis and its consequences. Further, plague pneumonia is contagious to close contacts by respiratory droplet spread, and pneumonic outbreaks may ensue unless precautions are taken. Unprotected family members and care providers are especially at risk. Patients with plague pneumonia experience rapidly advancing tachypnea, dyspnea, hypoxia, chest pain, cough, hemoptysis, and general signs of endotoxemia. The sputum is often purulent but may be watery, frothy, and copious, and may be blood-tinged or grossly hemorrhagic, and it usually contains large numbers of plague bacilli.[31] Radiographs show patchy bronchopneumonia, cavities, or confluent consolidation,[32] and the radiologic findings may be more impressive than indicated by physical examination.

Primary inhalation pneumonia is a rare but serious threat to unprotected persons in direct and close respiratory contact with the symptomatic patient. Because of this, patients with suspected pneumonic plague should be managed in isolation under respiratory droplet precautions.[5,33] Strict isolation under negative pressure and filtered exhausting is not necessary because infectious dispersal by fine aerosol or dried droplet nuclei does not occur. In the United States, the last

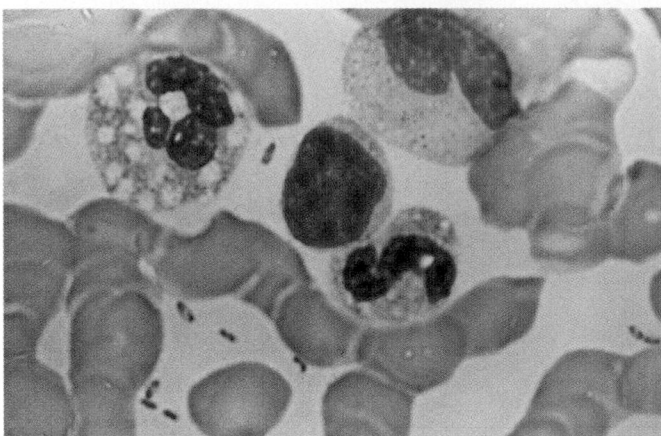

FIGURE 226-6. Peripheral blood smear of septicemic plague patient showing large numbers of bipolar-staining bacilli. *(Courtesy of the Centers for Disease Control and Prevention, Fort Collins, CO.)*

case of person-to-person respiratory spread occurred in Los Angeles during an outbreak in 1924. There have been nine subsequent cases of primary pneumonic plague, two resulting from laboratory exposures and others from exposures to domestic cats with respiratory plague.[19] Secondary plague pneumonia occurs in about 10% of all plague patients in the United States, partly as a result of delayed treatment of bubonic plague cases. Untreated pneumonic plague is almost always fatal, and mortality is very high in persons whose treatment is delayed beyond 18 to 24 hours after symptom onset. The case-fatality rate for pneumonic plague in the United States since 1950 approaches 50%.

Other Syndromes

Plague meningitis is a rare complication. It may occur as a delayed manifestation of inadequately treated bubonic plague or as a manifestation of acute early disease. Plague meningitis is characterized by fever, headache, sensorial changes, meningismus, and cerebrospinal fluid pleocytosis with a predominance of polymorphonuclear leukocytes. Bacteria are frequently demonstrable with a Gram or Wayson stain of spinal fluid sediment, and endotoxin has been demonstrated in spinal fluid with the limulus test.[34]

Plague can produce pharyngitis resembling acute tonsillitis. The anterior cervical lymph nodes are usually inflamed, and *Y. pestis* may be recovered from a throat culture or by aspiration of a cervical bubo. This is a rare clinical form of plague that follows the inhalation or ingestion of plague bacilli. Asymptomatic pharyngeal colonization with *Y. pestis* has been reported in close contacts of pneumonic plague cases.

Plague manifests sometimes with prominent gastrointestinal symptoms of nausea, vomiting, diarrhea, and abdominal pain. These symptoms may precede the bubo. In septicemic plague, they may occur without a bubo and commonly result in diagnostic confusion, delays in correct treatment, and a consequent elevated mortality.[35]

Laboratory Findings

The peripheral blood leukocyte count is typically elevated, in the range of 10,000 to 20,000 cells/mm³, with a predominance of neutrophils. Severely ill patients tend to have the higher leukocyte counts. Occasional patients develop myelocytic leukemoid reactions with leukocyte counts as high as 100,000/mm³. Examination of the leukocytes in the peripheral blood smear typically reveals cytoplasmic vacuolations, toxic granulations, and Döhle bodies that are characteristic of acute bacterial infections. Blood eosinophils are usually diminished or absent in the acute stage of infection but return to normal or show elevated levels during convalescence. Blood platelet levels may be normal or low in the early stages of bubonic plague. Although patients with plague rarely develop a generalized bleeding tendency from profound thrombocytopenia, dis-

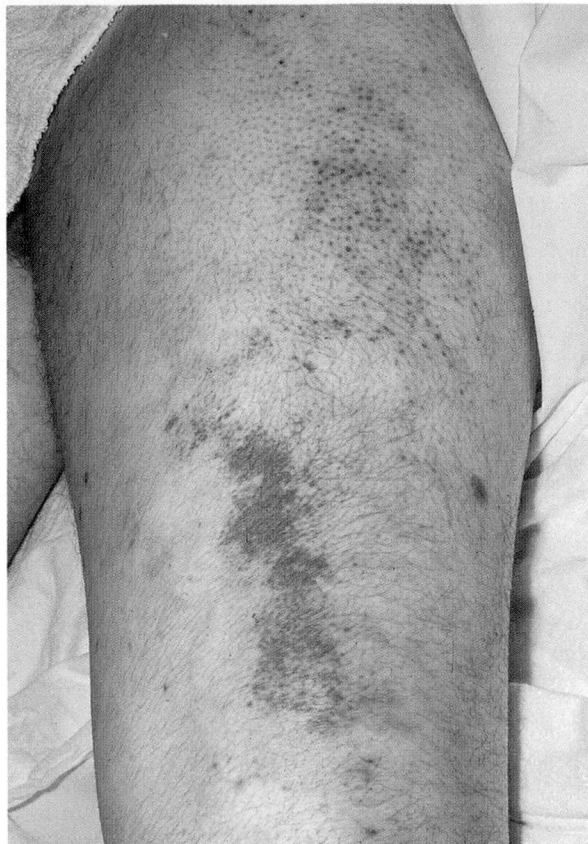

FIGURE 226-7. Ecchymoses and petechiae on lateral thigh of a patient with septicemic plague complicated by disseminated intravascular coagulation. *(Courtesy of the Centers for Disease Control and Prevention, Fort Collins, CO.)*

seminated intravascular coagulation is common in advanced illness. Fibrinogen-fibrin degradation products in the sera are usual in patients in advanced stages of illness.[25] Liver function test results, including serum aminotransferases and bilirubin, are frequently abnormal. As expected, hypotensive patients may develop impaired renal function.

Diagnosis

Plague should be included in the differential diagnosis of an acute febrile illness in a patient who was recently in a plague-endemic zone and at risk of exposure to infected animals and their fleas. Most human cases occur in the context of an obvious plague outbreak or epizootic. When plague is suspected, clinical specimens, including blood for culture, should be obtained promptly for microbiologic studies[36-38] and antimicrobial therapy initiated. Chest radiographs should be taken to rule out pneumonia. Blood and other clinical materials as indicated, such as bubo aspirates, sputum, tracheal-bronchial washes, swabs of skin lesions or pharyngeal mucosal, and cerebrospinal fluid, should be inoculated onto suitable media (e.g. brain-heart infusion [BHI] broth, sheep blood agar, chocolate agar, or MacConkey agar). Culture counts from blood typically range from fewer than 10 to 4 × 10⁷ colony-forming units/mL. In bubonic plague, a bacteriologic diagnosis can usually be made by smear and culture of a bubo aspirate. The aspirate is obtained by inserting a 20-gauge needle on a 10-mL syringe containing 2 mL of sterile saline into the bubo and withdrawing the plunger several times until the saline becomes blood tinged. Because the typical acute bubo does not contain liquid pus, it may be necessary to inject the saline into the bubo and immediately reaspirate it. Drops of the aspirate should be placed onto microscopic slides and air dried for both Gram and Wayson stains. The Gram stain reveals polymorphonuclear leukocytes and plump gram-negative coccobacilli ranging from 1 to 2 μm in length. Wayson stain is prepared by mixing 0.2 g of basic fuchsin (90%

dye content) with 0.75 g of methylene blue (90% dye content) in 20 mL of 95% ethyl alcohol. This mixture is then poured slowly into 200 mL of 5% phenol. A smear, after being fixed for 2 minutes in absolute methanol, is stained for 10 to 20 seconds in Wayson stain, washed with water, and dried. *Y. pestis* appear as light blue bacilli with dark blue polar bodies, giving the organisms a closed safety-pin appearance that is characteristic of but not pathognomonic for *Y. pestis.* The remainder of the slide has a contrasting pink counterstain. Smears of blood, sputum, or spinal fluid can be handled similarly. For more specific staining, a direct immunofluorescence test can be applied to smears of fluids or cultures.

A serologic test, the passive hemagglutination test using fraction I of *Y. pestis,* can be performed on acute- or convalescent-phase serum. In patients with negative cultures, a fourfold or greater increase in titer or a single titer of 1:16 or higher is presumptive evidence for plague infection. A single titer of 1:128 may be considered as diagnostic. A few plague patients will develop detectable antibodies as soon as 5 days after the onset of illness, most seroconvert 1 to 2 weeks after onset, a few seroconvert 3 or more weeks after onset, and a few (<5%) fail to seroconvert.[39] Early specific antibiotic treatment may delay seroconversion by several weeks. Positive serologic titers diminish gradually over months to years. Enzyme-linked immunosorbent assays (ELISAs) for detecting immunoglobulin (Ig) M and IgG antibodies to *Y. pestis* can be used to identify antibodies in early infection, and to differentiate them from antibodies developed in response to previous vaccination. Presumptive identification of *Y. pestis* can be made by polymerase chain reaction (PCR) or antigen-capture ELISA.[37,40-42] A recently developed rapid, handheld chromatographic assay designed to detect *Y. pestis* antigens in patient samples also appears highly promising for rapid presumptive diagnosis at the bedside, even when performed under primitive field conditions.[43] Protocols and algorithms have been developed for clinical laboratories to follow in diagnosing plague and other select agent diseases in the event of a bioterrorist attack.[36,37,44]

Laboratory tests for plague are highly reliable when conducted by persons trained and experienced in the microbiology of *Y. pestis.* In response to concerns regarding biologic terrorism, a national Laboratory Response Network has been established in the United States to provide upgraded, standardized diagnostic testing for *Y. pestis* and other select agents.[6,45] This network links state and local public health laboratories with other advanced-capacity laboratories, including those at the Centers for Disease Control and Prevention (CDC). Member laboratories operate either as sentinel laboratories (Level A) or as reference levels B through D, representing progressively stringent safety, containment, and technical proficiency capabilities. Sentinel (Level A) laboratories include hospital and other community clinical laboratories that practice Biosafety Level 2 (BSL-2) safety procedures and perform initial tests to presumptively identify or rule out *Y. pestis* infection, using such procedures as direct staining, bacterial culture, and biochemical screening tests. Suspicious isolates and source materials are to be forwarded to Level B and C laboratories (federal, state, and local public health laboratories with BSL-2 and BSL-3 capabilities), which are prepared to perform advanced rapid diagnostic tests, to confirm the identification of *Y. pestis,* and to characterize strain attributes. Level B and C laboratories are also prepared to carry out standardized antimicrobial susceptibility studies, and Level C laboratories routinely perform molecular subtyping tests, such as multiple locus variable number tandem-repeat assay (MLVA), RFLP, and pulsed-field gel electrophoresis (PFGE).[37,45]

For diagnosis in fatal cases, tissues, including samples of lymph nodes, liver, spleen, lungs, and bone marrow, should be collected at necropsy for culture, direct fluorescent antibody testing, and histologic studies, including immunohistochemical staining.[46]

Treatment and Prevention

Antibiotics

Untreated plague can evolve into an illness with a fulminating course, and has a case-fatality rate of more than 50%. Therefore, effective antibiotic therapy must be given as soon as possible after obtaining appropriate material for cultures. In 1948, streptomycin was identified as

the drug of choice for the treatment of plague when it reduced the mortality in bubonic plague to less than 5%. No other drug has been demonstrated to be more efficacious, although controlled comparative trials of safety and efficacy have not been reported. Streptomycin should be administered intramuscularly in two divided doses daily, in a dosage for adults of 30 mg/kg of body weight per day for 7 days, or for at least 3 days after remission of fever and other symptoms. Most patients improve rapidly and become afebrile after about 3 days of therapy.[24] Streptomycin is ototoxic and nephrotoxic. Although the risk of severe vestibular damage and hearing loss is considered to be small in the short courses required for treating plague, systematic measurements of these effects have not been made on plague patients, and streptomycin damage to the eighth cranial nerve, if it occurs, is permanent. Bilateral deafness and vestibular damage have been reported in children born of women given streptomycin during pregnancy for conditions other than plague. Therefore, streptomycin should be used cautiously in pregnant women, in older patients who are more prone to streptomycin damage, and in patients with hearing difficulty. The risk of kidney damage as a result of short courses of streptomycin therapy is also small, but renal function should be monitored as a precaution. If the serum creatinine rises above 1.5 mg/dL, consideration should be given to adjusting the streptomycin dosage. In mild renal impairment, the recommended dose is about 20 mg/kg/day, and in advanced impairment, it is 8 mg/kg every 3 days.

In the United States, there are no manufacturers of streptomycin, and the drug is no longer widely available for immediate use. Because gentamicin is readily available and commonly selected for treating other serious gram-negative infections, it is now used increasingly in the United States in place of streptomycin in the treatment of plague. The results of vitro antimicrobial susceptibility studies of *Y. pestis* strains isolated from humans and studies of treating plague in animals do not suggest that gentamicin would be inferior to streptomycin in treating human plague.[46-49] There are several anecdotal reports of its satisfactory use in treating plague patients in the United States,[50,51] and a recent retrospective analysis of 50 plague patients treated in New Mexico between 1985 and 1999 suggests that gentamicin, or a combination of gentamicin and doxycycline, is at least as efficacious as streptomycin.[52] All 36 gentamicin-treated patients survived without complications. Further, this study revealed that physicians in New Mexico selected gentamicin twice as often as streptomycin for the treatment of plague. Studies in treating patients with other diseases indicate that gentamicin is less ototoxic but more nephrotoxic than streptomycin. Damage to the kidneys caused by gentamicin is usually mild and is reversible, so the drug is considered to be safer than streptomycin for use in pregnant women and children. As well, gentamicin is approved for use by intravenous administration, and single daily doses in adults are thought to provide more favorable blood levels and be less toxic than multiple daily doses. Because of these and other considerations, gentamicin has been recommended as an alternative in first-line treatment of plague in the event of a bioterrorist attack,[5] and is included in the national pharmaceutical emergency stockpile for this purpose.

For patients with contraindications to the use of aminoglycosides, tetracycline and its congeners are satisfactory alternatives. Doxycycline is the tetracycline of choice in treating plague because of the convenience of its twice-daily dose schedule; its rapid absorption, allowing oral administration; and its superior ability to achieve peak serum concentrations. Doxycycline treatment should be initiated with a loading dose, either intravenously or orally depending on the severity of illness. In adults, a loading dose of 200 mg every 12 hours on the first day rapidly achieves a peak serum concentration of approximately 8 μg/mL,[53] and is followed by a daily dosage of 100 mg every 12 hours. Tetracycline is administered to adults in an initial loading dose of 2 g, followed by a usual dose of 2 g/day in four divided doses. Doxycycline or tetracycline can also be used to complete a course of treatment begun with an aminoglycoside. When used as principal treatment, a tetracycline should be given for 7 to 10 days, or for at least 3 days after fever and other symptoms have subsided.

Chloramphenicol is indicated for conditions in which high tissue penetration is important, such as plague meningitis, pleuritis, or myocarditis. It may be used separately or in combination with an aminoglycoside. Chloramphenicol is given as a loading dose of 25 to 30 mg/kg of body weight, followed by 50 to 60 mg/kg/day in four divided doses. As indicated by clinical response, chloramphenicol dosage may be reduced to a daily dose of 25 to 30 mg/kg/day to lessen the magnitude of bone marrow suppression, which is reversible. The irreversible marrow aplasia associated with chloramphenicol is so rare (estimated to occur in 1 in 40,000 patients) that its consideration should not deter its use in patients who are seriously ill with plague infection. Trimethoprim-sulfamethoxazole (co-trimoxazole) has been used successfully to treat bubonic plague, but responses may be delayed and incomplete, and it is not considered a first-line choice. Penicillins, cephalosporins, and macrolides have a suboptimal clinical effect and are not recommended for use in treating plague. Ciprofloxacin, ofloxacin, and some other fluoroquinolones are active in vitro and in experimental mouse infections but have not been evaluated in treating plague patients.[47-49]

Strains of *Y. pestis* that are resistant to antimicrobials have only rarely been isolated from humans. Usually these strains have shown partial resistance to a single agent only and have not been associated with treatment failures. Recently, however, several strains isolated from patients in Madagascar showed plasmid-mediated resistance to streptomycin, including one that was multiply resistant to other main drugs used to treat plague.[54] Antimicrobial resistance is not known to have emerged during treatment of plague in humans, and relapses following recommended courses of treatment are virtually unknown.

Supportive Therapy

Most patients are febrile and have constitutional symptoms, including nausea and vomiting. Hypotension and dehydration are common. Therefore, intravenous 0.9% saline solution should be given to most patients for the first few days of their illness or until improvement occurs. The patient's hemodynamic status should be monitored closely and shock managed according to general principles used to combat endotoxic shock.[55] Investigational agents to counter effects of sepsis from other gram-negative bacteria, such as recombinant activated protein C,[56] have not been evaluated in plague patients. There is no evidence that corticosteroids are beneficial in treating plague.

Buboes usually recede during the first week of antibiotic treatment, but it may be several weeks before they completely resolve; occasionally, they enlarge or become fluctuant, requiring incision and drainage. The aspirate is usually sterile, but persistence of viable *Y. pestis* in buboes after apparent clinical cure has been reported. This persistence has not been associated with relapse of systemic plague.

Precautions

All suspected plague patients should be reported promptly to state health department authorities for assistance with confirmation of microbiologic diagnosis, epidemiologic investigation, and protection of the public's health. Patients with uncomplicated infections who are promptly treated present no health hazards to other persons. Those with cough or other signs of pneumonia should be placed in isolation and managed under respiratory droplet precautions for at least 48 hours after the institution of antibiotic therapy or until the sputum culture is negative. Respiratory droplet precautions include the use of fitted masks, gowns, gloves, and protective eyewear when providing direct patient care.[33,57] Cultures of clinical materials are usually negative after 24 hours of treatment. Patients without respiratory plague can be managed under standard precautions. Potentially infective clinical fluids should be handled with gloves and with care to avoid aerosolization (such as could result from dropping a specimen or by breakage of a container during centrifugation). Routine clinical specimens are managed in the laboratory under BSL-2 precautions, but manipulation of cultures should be performed in a negative pressure hood using BSL-3 procedures.

Prevention

A formalin-killed vaccine, Plague Vaccine U.S.P., was available for use by persons who worked with *Y. pestis* in the laboratory and a few other categories of persons at high risk of exposure. It was given routinely to military personnel serving in Vietnam. However, its manufacture has been discontinued and there is now only one source worldwide (Commonwealth Serum Laboratories Ltd., 45 Poplar Road, Parkville, 3052, Australia). The killed vaccine does not protect against respiratory exposures, requires multiple doses over time, and has no utility in combating epidemic disease in a setting of modern sanitation and hygiene and availability of prophylactic antibiotics.[58] Research is underway to develop improved plague vaccines that are likely to be protective against airborne infection.[59] At present, the most promising candidates are recombinant subunit vaccines that express both the F1 and V antigens of *Y. pestis*. These recombinant vaccines have been prepared both as combination and fusion products, and appear to protect animals against infective aerosol exposures. Vaccine formulations are being developed to be delivered as inhalants.[60] Interest in developing improved plague vaccines has increased greatly in recent years because of concerns with protection against biologic weapons.

Antibiotics can be used for chemoprophylaxis against plague in persons thought to have had an infective exposure within the prior 7 days, such as family members, care providers, and others with a close and direct contact with a patient having pneumonic plague, or a laboratory worker exposed to an accident that may have created an infective aerosol.[58] Doxycycline is the prophylactic agent of first choice, given in an adult dosage of 100 mg twice daily for 7 days. Postexposure prophylaxis may be an important control measure in circumstances of intentional use of *Y. pestis* in a terrorist event. Persons potentially exposed either to an aerosol release or to persons with symptoms of plague pneumonia should be placed under surveillance for 7 days and be considered for prophylactic treatment. National guidelines for antimicrobial prophylaxis in the event of bioterrorism recommend doxycycline or ciprofloxacin for this purpose.[5]

Persons living in endemic areas should use personal protective measures against rodents and fleas, including living and working in rat-proofed dwellings, removing food and harborage for rodents, using repellents, and applying insecticides on their pets.[14]

Reservoir and Vector Control

The control of plague by health departments requires knowledge of the epidemiology of infected reservoir hosts, vectors, and the contact of humans with these animals in any particular area. In the United States, the CDC branch in Fort Collins, Colorado, fields a team of entomologists, mammalogists, and epidemiologists to investigate cases of plague. The approach to prevent further cases is specific to each circumstance, and usually consists of using insecticides around rodent runs, nests, or burrows; removing rodent harborage; and educating people on environmental sanitation, early detection and treatment of suspected plague, and avoidance of sick or dead rodents and cats. If killing of rodents is considered, flea control should be carried out before or at the time of killing to reduce the chances that infective fleas will feed on humans.[18]

Urban plague has been successfully controlled in cities around the world by modern sanitation and specific rat control programs. Sylvatic plague, however, defies definitive control because of the huge areas involved and the ecologic complexities.

YERSINIA ENTEROCOLITICA AND *YERSINIA PSEUDOTUBERCULOSIS*

History

The enteropathogenic yersiniae are relatively recently recognized causes of disease, and an understanding of their microbiology, epidemiology, and pathogenesis is evolving.[61-64] Sharing many of the virulence factors with *Y. pestis,* the enteropathogenic *Yersinia* spp. rely further on adaptive gene expressions that favor intestinal colonization, epithelial invasion, and survival in natural environments outside animal hosts. The major clinical syndromes associated with these organisms are enterocolitis, mesenteric adenitis, terminal ileitis, septicemia, and various immunoreactive conditions, especially reactive arthritis. Different disease expressions predominate in different age groups. Modes of transmission are principally fecal-oral, by hand-to-mouth transfer of organisms following handling of contaminated animals and animal carcasses, by ingestion of contaminated food or water, and rarely by transfusion of contaminated blood. Genomic studies recently established that *Y. pseudotuberculosis* is the progenitor of *Y. pestis*.[7]

Description of the Pathogens

Y. enterocolitica and *Y. pseudotuberculosis* are pleomorphic gram-negative bacilli in the family Enterobacteriaceae. They are non–lactose-fermenting, urease-positive organisms that grow at a wide range of temperature; they are motile at 25° C but not at 37° C. Both grow on BHI, MacConkey, and SS agars at room temperature and at 37° C, and in buffered saline at 4° C. Colonies are difficult to detect after incubation for 24 hours but are readily apparent at 48 hours. They can be distinguished from other enteric pathogens and from *Y. pestis* by biochemical profiles; however, rapid tests may be a cause of misidentification if not properly coded. More than 60 serotypes and six biotypes of *Y. enterocolitica* have been described. Most strains from patients belong to serotypes O:3, O:5.27, O:8, and O:9 and to biotypes 2, 3, and 4. There is a separate system for serotyping *Y. pseudotuberculosis,* also based on somatic antigens. Six serotypes (I through VI) and four subtypes of *Y. pseudotuberculosis* have been identified, with O-group I accounting for approximately 80% of human cases.

Pathogenic strains are resistant to serum complement, penetrate human epithelial cells (HeLa cells) and guinea pig conjunctivae, are lethal to mice, and demonstrate cytotoxicity. Some of these characteristics are mediated by plasmids with weights of 41 to 82 kDa.[65-68] The 70-kb plasmid, which expresses V and W antigens, encodes for at least six proteins called Yops that confer various pathogenic properties, including resistance to phagocytosis by polymorphonuclear leukocytes, cytotoxicity, ability to initiate apoptosis of monocytes, suppression of tumor necrosis factor-α, and interference with platelet aggregation and complement activation.[68] The plasmid also encodes a secreted protein kinase[69] and an outer membrane protein with tyrosine phosphatase activity.[70] *Y. enterocolitica* does not produce a siderophore for iron transport and therefore grows better in the presence of other bacteria that do produce siderophores.[71] However, it can utilize host-chelated iron

stores and chelating agents, such as desferrioxamine. Many strains of *Y. enterocolitica* produce a heat-stable enterotoxin that is similar to the heat-stable enterotoxin produced by *Escherichia coli*. This enterotoxin, which is produced at 22° C but not at 37° C, is not proven to be important in the pathogenesis of diarrhea associated with the yersinioses. Both *Y. enterocolitica* and *Y. pseudotuberculosis* produce a lipopolysaccharide endotoxin that has biologic properties similar to those of other gram-negative bacteria.

Epidemiology

Y. enterocolitica is distributed widely throughout the world, and can be isolated from multiple environmental sources, including fresh water, contaminated foods, and a wide range of wild and domestic animals. It is an infrequent cause of diarrhea and abdominal pain in the United States but is relatively common in northern Europe. Infections have been documented in other parts of the world, including South America, Africa, and Asia, but *Y. enterocolitica* is not considered an important cause of tropical diarrhea.[72] Most isolates from Europe are serotypes O:3 and O:9, whereas most of the isolates from Canada and the United States are serotypes O:3 and O:8, respectively.

Children and adults of both sexes are susceptible, but children are more often affected than are adults. The majority of cases of the enterocolitis syndrome occur in the age group 1 to 4 years, while mesenteric adenitis and terminal ileitis are more common among older children and young adults. Transmission of infection occurs by ingestion of contaminated food or water and, less commonly, by direct contact with infected animals or patients (Fig. 226-8). The zoonotic reservoirs of *Y. enterocolitica* are diverse, including rodents, rabbits, pigs, sheep, cattle, horses, dogs, and cats. Transmission of infection to humans from contact with pet dogs and cats or their feces has been suggested. In northern Europe, *Y. enterocolitica* is frequently isolated from the mouth and alimentary tract of pigs at slaughterhouses, and transmission of infection can occur by ingestion of incompletely cooked pork and contamination of other foods by pork.[73] In Finland, butchers were shown to be at increased risk of infection.[74] The ability of this organism to grow at 4° C means that refrigerated meats can be sources of infection. Outbreaks of foodborne disease have occurred in the United States, including outbreaks caused by contaminated milk, bean sprouts, and consumption of raw pork intestines (chitterlings) during holiday festivities.[63,75] In one instance, an outbreak affected infants living in households where chitterlings were being prepared but who did not eat the chitterlings.[76] Fecal-oral transmission may account for re-

FIGURE 226-8. Transmission routes of *Yersinia enterocolitica. Wide arrows* indicate common routes, *medium arrows* indicate occasional routes, and *thin arrows* indicate rare routes.

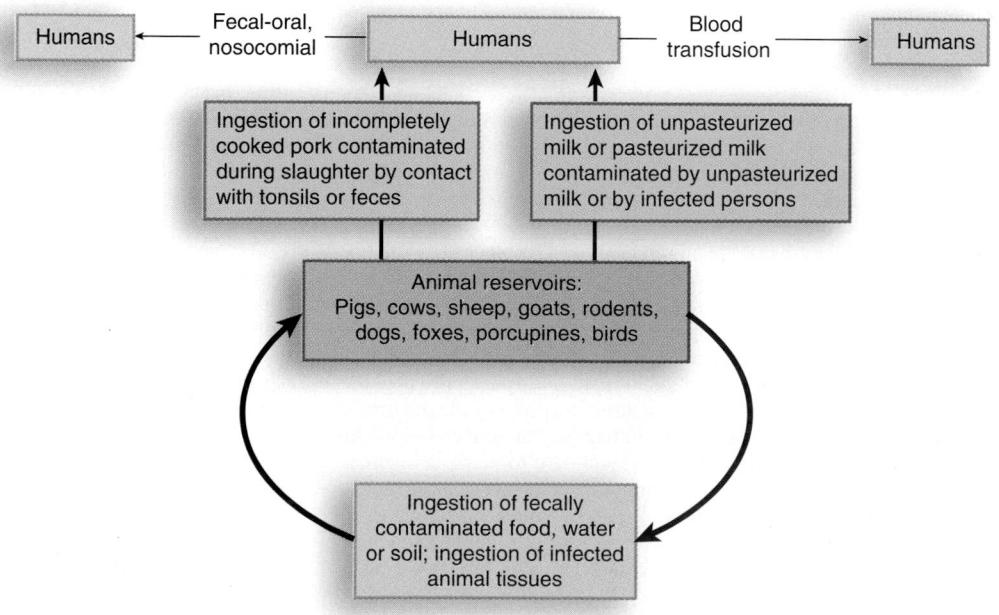

ports of secondary infections in households; studies in children with *Y. enterocolitica* enterocolitis have shown that excretion of the organism in the stool usually persists for weeks.[77] Chronic carrier states have not been reported. The organism has been isolated from lakes, streams, and drinking water, but only a few cases have been linked to ingestion of natural water sources.

Persons with impaired immune defenses are at higher risk of septicemia and localized metastatic infections; recognized predisposing factors include diabetes, malignancy, immunosuppressive therapy, chronic liver disease, alcoholism, malnutrition, old age, and iron overload caused by hemolytic anemia, such as the thalassemias and other disorders requiring multiple transfusions.[78] The treatment of iron-overloaded patients with deferoxamine has been particularly associated with *Yersinia* sepsis because this iron chelator enhances the growth of the organism and also appears to inhibit polymorphonuclear leukocyte defenses against the infection.[79] *Y. enterocolitica* can multiply in stored blood, and banked blood has been a source of sepsis, resulting in shock and death in 50% of cases.[80]

Infection caused by *Y. pseudotuberculosis* is the rarest of the yersinioses. It has its reservoirs in various rodents, rabbits, deer, farm animals, and birds, including turkeys, ducks, geese, pigeons, pheasants, and canaries. Although this infection has a worldwide distribution, most cases have been reported from Europe. Most patients have been children 5 to 14 years old. Males are affected three times as often as females. Illness occurs most frequently in the winter. The principal route of transmission is thought to be fecal-oral from handling infected animals or the environment contaminated by them, or through contamination in the household of food or water.

Pathogenesis

The alimentary tract is the portal of entry in most cases. An inoculum of 10^9 organisms may be required to cause infection. After an incubation period of 4 to 7 days, infection may result in mucosal ulcerations in the terminal ileum (rarely in the ascending colon), necrotic lesions in Peyer's patches, and enlargement of mesenteric lymph nodes.[81] In severe cases, thrombosis of mesenteric blood vessels, intestinal necrosis, and hemorrhage may occur. The appendix has a normal histologic appearance or shows mild inflammation. Septicemia may lead to focal abscesses in various organs (e.g., lung, liver, meninges). A reactive polyarthritis is not uncommon and has a predilection for patients with histocompatibility antigen HLA-B27, possibly as a result of a molecular mimicry between HLA-B27 antigen and *Yersinia* antigens.[63,82] Superantigenic activity has been found in cultures of *Y. enterocolitica* and could contribute to reactive arthritis.[83] The pathogenesis of yersiniosis-associated erythema nodosum is unknown.

Clinical Manifestations

Enterocolitis accounts for two thirds of reported cases of symptomatic *Y. enterocolitica* infections and is characterized by fever, diarrhea, and abdominal pain lasting 1 to 3 weeks. Nausea and vomiting occur in 15% to 40% of cases. Leukocytes, blood, or mucus may be present in the stool. In serious cases, perforation of the ileum and rectal bleeding may occur. Patients with mesenteric adenitis and/or terminal ileitis have fever, right lower quadrant pain and tenderness, and leukocytosis. This syndrome is most common in older children and adolescents and may be clinically indistinguishable from acute appendicitis.[84] Analysis of several common-source outbreaks in the United States disclosed that 10% of 444 patients with symptomatic undiagnosed *Y. enterocolitica* infections underwent laparotomy for suspected appendicitis.

A reactive polyarthritis, as described in 10% to 30% of adults with *Y. enterocolitica* infection in Scandinavia, begins a few days to a month after onset of acute diarrhea and may involve the knees, ankles, toes, fingers, and wrists. In most cases, two to four joints become inflamed in rapid succession over a period of 2 to 14 days. Symptoms persist for more than 1 month in two thirds of cases and for more than 4 months in one third. After 12 months, most patients are asymptomatic, but a few have persistent low back pain, including sacroiliitis, which has been specifically related to the presence of HLA-B27.[82]

Ankylosing spondylitis rarely occurs. Synovial fluid examination typically reveals a polymorphonuclear pleocytosis, usually with fewer than 25,000 leukocytes/mm³ of fluid. Cultures are usually negative. Reiter's syndrome, with arthritis, urethritis, and conjunctivitis, has also been reported. Like arthritis, this complication is much more likely to develop in persons with the HLA-B27 antigen.[85,86]

Erythema nodosum occurs in up to 30% of cases in Scandinavia. Skin lesions typically appear on the legs and trunk 2 to 20 days after onset of fever and abdominal pain and resolve spontaneously within a month in most cases. Women with this condition outnumber men by 2 to 1.

Exudative pharyngitis is a part of the spectrum of illness caused by *Y. enterocolitica*. In one large *Y. enterocolitica* enteritis outbreak in the United States, 8% of patients presented with acute pharyngitis and fever, without accompanying diarrhea.[87] Rare cases of pneumonia, empyema, and lung abscess have been reported.[88]

Y. enterocolitica septicemia is uncommon but severe and often fatal. It is most often reported in patients with underlying immunocompromising conditions, the elderly, and patients with iron overload. Septicemic patients may develop hepatic or splenic abscesses, peritonitis, septic arthritis, osteomyelitis, wound infections, or meningitis. Endocarditis and mycotic aneurysms caused by *Y. enterocolitica* have been reported.

By far the most common manifestation of *Y. pseudotuberculosis* infection in humans is mesenteric adenitis, which causes an acute appendicitis-like syndrome with fever and right lower quadrant abdominal pain.[89] Surgical exploration usually reveals a normal appendix and enlarged mesenteric lymph nodes, and sometimes an inflammation of the terminal ileum. The infection is usually self-limited, and computed tomographic scanning of the abdomen may help avoid exploratory laparotomy. Erythema nodosum and polyarthritis have also been described in patients with *Y. pseudotuberculosis* infection. *Y. pseudotuberculosis* septicemia is infrequently reported; about 50% of septicemic patients have underlying chronic disease.[67]

Diagnosis

Results of routine laboratory tests are nonspecific; leukocyte counts are usually normal or slightly elevated, with a modest shift to the left. *Yersinia* may be isolated from stool, mesenteric lymph nodes, pharyngeal exudates, peritoneal fluid, or blood, and from abscesses, depending on the clinical syndrome. Recovery of organisms from otherwise sterile materials, such as blood, cerebrospinal fluid, or mesenteric lymph node tissue, is not difficult, but isolation from feces is hampered by slow growth and by overgrowth of normal fecal flora. Yield can be increased by using cold enrichment, alkali treatment, or selective CIN agar, but these methods are unnecessarily costly because usual enteric culturing methods detect most clinically significant infections.[90]

Serologic tests are useful in diagnosing *Yersinia* infections provided sera are appropriately absorbed. Agglutination tests, ELISAs, and immunoblotting tests are used; testing against multiple serogroups is time consuming and costly and not usually performed for routine clinical diagnosis. *Y. enterocolitica* and *Y. pseudotuberculosis* cross-react with one another and with other organisms, such as *Brucella, Vibrio,* and *E. coli. Y. pseudotuberculosis* types II and IV cross-react with *Salmonella* groups B and D. Agglutinating antibodies appear soon after onset of illness, peak during the second week, and generally disappear within 2 to 6 months. Documentation of a fourfold or greater rise in antibodies is often not possible because the specimens collected early in the acute illness are already elevated. PCR and immunohistochemical staining procedures are experimental.

Patients experiencing reactive arthritis syndromes have elevated erythrocyte sedimentation rates, but rheumatoid factor and antinuclear antibodies are usually absent. Synovial fluid from affected joints is sterile.

Prevention and Therapy

Public health measures to control *Yersinia* infection should focus on safe food handling, processing, and preparation practices, especially involving pork and pork products; limiting storage times of refrigerated but unfrozen foods before consumption; and preventing cross-contamination. Special attention should be given to protecting milk. The consumption of raw or undercooked meats, especially pork and pork products such as chitterlings, should be avoided. Hand washing and the control of environmental cross-contamination are the principal measures to reduce the spread of enteric pathogens in daycare, health care, and pet care situations, and within households. The methods of slaughtering and butchering pigs can be modified to reduce contamination of meat and exposures of workers. In blood banks, donors should be asked about recent fever, abdominal pain, and diarrhea and be requested to notify the blood bank if these symptoms develop after donation.

Y. enterocolitica is usually susceptible in vitro to aminoglycosides, chloramphenicol, tetracycline, trimethoprim-sulfamethoxazole, piperacillin, ciprofloxacin, and the third-generation cephalosporins.[91] Because they produce β-lactamases, isolates are often resistant to penicillin, ampicillin, and first-generation cephalosporins. The value of antimicrobial therapy in cases of enterocolitis and mesenteric adenitis is unclear, because these infections are usually self-limited. Treatment of enterocolitis with antibiotics shortens the persistence of IgG anti-*Yersinia* antibodies to about 3 months. Patients with *Y. enterocolitica*–induced septicemia, which has a mortality rate of 50% despite treatment, should receive antibiotic therapy. The drug of choice has not yet been identified, but good responses have been reported with the aminoglycosides, trimethoprim-sulfamethoxazole, doxycycline, and ciprofloxacin,[87] whereas failures have occurred with cefuroxime, ceftazidime, and cefoperazone.[92]

Y. pseudotuberculosis is usually sensitive in vitro to ampicillin, tetracycline, chloramphenicol, cephalosporins, and aminoglycosides. Although antibiotic therapy is probably not warranted in most patients with mesenteric adenitis, patients with septicemia should receive ampicillin (100 to 200 mg/kg/day intravenously) or tetracycline, doxycycline, or a suitable aminoglycoside administered in standard doses for treating severe infections. The mortality in *Y. pseudotuberculosis* septicemia is 75% despite antibiotic therapy.

Patients with reactive arthritis may benefit from treatment with nonsteroidal anti-inflammatory agents, intra-articular steroid injections, and physical therapy.

OTHER *YERSINIA* SPECIES

Strains that were formerly considered biochemically atypical isolates of *Y. enterocolitica* have been reclassified as *Yersinia intermedia, Yersinia frederiksenii,* and *Yersinia kristensenii. Y. intermedia* and *Y. frederiksenii* have been recovered rarely from patients with enterocolitis and in a few instances have been reported to be associated with soft tissue infections. The pathogenic potential of these organisms remains unclear.

REFERENCES

1. Perry RD, Fetherston JD. *Yersinia pestis*—Etiologic agent of plague. Clin Microbiol Rev. 1997;10:35-66.
2. Butler T. Plague and Other *Yersinia* Infections. New York: Plenum; 1983.
3. Dennis DT. Plague as an emerging disease. In: Scheld WM, Craig WA, Hughes JM, eds. Emerging Infections 2. Washington, DC: ASM Press; 1998:169-183.
4. Chanteau S, Ratsifasoamanana L, Rasoamanana B, et al. Plague, a reemerging disease in Madagascar. Emerg Infect Dis. 1998;4:101-104.
5. Inglesby TV, Dennis, DT, Henderson DA, et al. Plague as a biological weapon: Medical and public health management. JAMA. 2000;283:2281-2290.
6. Centers for Disease Control and Prevention. Biological and chemical terrorism: Strategic plan for preparedness and response. Recommendations of the CDC Strategic Planning Workgroup. MMWR Morb Mortal Wkly Rep. 2000;49(RR-4):1-14.
7. Achtman M, Zurth K, Morelli G, et al. *Yersinia pestis,* the cause of plague, is a recently emerged clone of *Yersinia pseudotuberculosis.* Proc Natl Acad Sci U S A. 1999;24:14043-14048.
8. Parkhill J, Wren BW, Thompson NR, et al. Genome sequence of *Yersinia pestis,* the causative agent of plague. Nature. 2001;413:523-527.
9. Guiyoule A, Grimont F, Iteman I, et al. Plague pandemics investigated by ribotyping of *Yersinia pestis* strains. J Clin Microbiol. 1994;32:634-641.
10. Guiyoule A, Rasoamanana B, Buchrieser C, et al. Recent emergence of new variants of *Yersinia pestis* in Madagascar. J Clin Microbiol. 1997;35:2826-2833.
11. Radnedge L, Agron PG, Worsham PL, et al. Genome plasticity in *Yersinia pestis.* Microbiology. 2002;148:1687-1698.
12. World Health Organization. Human plague in 2000 and 2001. Wkly Epidemiol Rec. 2003;78:130-135.
13. Boisier P, Rahalison L, Rasolomaharo M, et al. Epidemiological features of four successive annual outbreaks of bubonic plague in Mahajanga, Madagascar. Emerg Infect Dis. 2002;8:311-316.
14. Centers for Disease Control and Prevention. Fatal human plague—Arizona and Colorado, 1996. MMWR Morb Mortal Wkly Rep. 1997;46:617-620.
15. Poland JD, Dennis DT. Plague. In: Evans AS, Brachman PS, eds. Bacterial Infections of Humans: Epidemiology and Control. New York: Plenum; 1998:545-558.
16. Centers for Disease Control and Prevention. Imported plague—New York City, 2002. MMWR Morb Mortal Wkly Rep. 2003;52[31]:725.
17. Gage KL. Plague surveillance. In: Plague Manual: Epidemiology, Distribution, Surveillance and Control. Geneva: World Health Organization; 1999:135-166.
18. Gage KL. Plague. In: Collier L, Balows A, Sussman M, Hausler WJ, eds. Topley and Wilson's Microbiology and Microbial Infections, v. 3, 9th ed. London: Arnold Publications; 1998:885-903.
19. Gage KL, Dennis DT, Orloski KA, et al. Cases of cat-associated plague in the western U.S., 1977-1998. Clin Infect Dis. 2000;30:893-900.
20. Kaufmann AF, Boyce JM, Martone WJ. Trends in human plague in the United States. J Infect Dis. 1980;141:522-524.
21. Mann JM, Martone WJ, Boyce JM, et al. Endemic human plague in New Mexico: Risk factors associated with infection. J Infect Dis. 1979;140:397-401.
22. Hinnebusch BJ. Bubonic plague: A molecular genetic case history of the emergence of an infectious disease. J Mol Med. 1997;75:645-652.
23. Hinnebusch BJ, Rudolph AE, Cherepanov P, et al. Role of murine toxin in survival of *Yersinia pestis* in the midgut of the vector flea. Science. 2002;296:733-735.
24. Butler T. *Yersinia* infections: Centennial of the discovery of the plague bacillus. Clin Infect Dis. 1994;19:655-663.
25. Butler T. A clinical study of bubonic plague: Observations on the 1970 Vietnam epidemic with emphasis on coagulation studies, skin histology and electrocardiograms. Am J Med. 1972;53:268-276.
26. Butler T, Bell WR, Nguyen NL, et al. *Yersinia pestis* infection in Vietnam. I. Clinical and hematological aspects. J Infect Dis. 1974;129(Suppl):S78-S84.
27. Pollitzer R. Plague. Geneva, World Health Organization; 1954.
28. Hull HF, Montes JM, Mann JM. Septicemic plague in New Mexico. J Infect Dis. 1987;155:113-118.
29. Crook LD, Tempest B. Plague: A clinical review of 27 cases. Arch Intern Med. 1992;152:1253-1256.
30. Dennis D, Meier F. Plague. In: Horsburgh CR, Nelson AM, eds. Pathology of Emerging Infections. Washington, DC: ASM Press; 1997:21-47.
31. Wu L-T. A Treatise on Pneumonic Plague. Geneva: League of Nations Health Organization; 1926.
32. Alsofrom DJ, Mettler FA Jr, Mann JM. Radiographic manifestations of plague in New Mexico, 1975-1980: A review of 42 proved cases. Radiology. 1981;139:561-565.
33. Garner JS. Guidelines for isolation precautions in hospitals. Hospital Infection Control Practices Advisory Committee. Infect Control Hosp Epidemiol. 1996;17:53-80.
34. Butler T, Levin J, Nguyen NL, et al. *Yersinia pestis* infection in Vietnam. II. Quantitative blood cultures and detection of endotoxin in the cerebrospinal fluid of patients with meningitis. J Infect Dis. 1976;133:493-499.
35. Hull HF, Montes JM, Mann JM. Plague masquerading as gastrointestinal illness. West J Med. 1986;145:485-487.
36. Centers for Disease Control and Prevention. Level A laboratory procedures for identification of *Yersinia pestis* (full text). 2001. Available at: *www.bt.cdc.gov/Agent/ Plague/ype_la_cp/123010.pdf*
37. Henchal EA, Teska JD, Ludwig GV, et al. Current laboratory methods for biological threat agent identification. Clin Lab Med. 2001;21:661-678.
38. Miller JM. Agents of bioterrorism: Preparing for bioterrorism at the community health care level. Infect Dis Clin North Am. 2001;15:1127-1155.
39. Butler T, Hudson BW. The serological response to *Yersinia pestis* infection. Bull World Health Organ. 1977;55:39-42.
40. Loiez C, Herwegh S, Wallet F, et al. Detection of *Yersinia pestis* in sputum by real-time PCR. J Clin Microbiol. 2003;41:4873-4875.
41. Radnedge L, Gamez-Chin S, McCready PM, et al. Identification of nucleotide sequences for the specific and rapid detection of *Yersinia pestis.* Appl Environ Microbiol. 2001;67:3759-3762.
42. Rahalison L, Vololonirina E, Ratsitorahina M, Chanteau S. Diagnosis of bubonic plague by PCR in Madagascar under field conditions. J Clin Microbiol. 2000;38:260-263.
43. Chanteau S, Rahalison L, Ralafiarisoa L, et al. Development and testing of a rapid diagnostic test for bubonic and pneumonic plague. Lancet. 2003;361:211-216.
44. American Society of Microbiology, Biological Weapons Resources Center. Detection and treatment—Sentinel (level A) laboratory. 2003. Available at: *www.asm.org*
45. Morse SA, Kellogg RB, Perry S. Detecting biothreat agents: The Laboratory Response Network. ASM News. 2003;69:433-437.
46. Gabastou JM, Proano J, Vimos A, et al. An outbreak of plague including cases with probable pneumonic infection, Ecuador, 1998. Trans R Soc Trop Med Hyg. 2000;94:387-391.
47. Wong JD, Barash JR, Sandfort RF, Janda JM. Susceptibilities of *Yersinia pestis* strains to 12 antimicrobial agents. Antimicrob Agents Chemother. 2000;44:1995-1996.
48. Frean JA, Arntzen L, Capper T, et al. In vitro activities of 14 antibiotics against 100 human isolates of *Yersinia pestis* from a Southern African plague focus. Antimicrob Agents Chemother. 1996;40:2646-2647.
49. Russell P, Eley SM, Bell DL, et al. Doxycycline or ciprofloxacin prophylaxis and therapy against experimental *Yersinia pestis* infection in mice. J Antimicrob Chemother. 1996;37:769-774.
50. Crook LD, Tempest B. Plague—a clinical review of 27 cases. Arch Intern Med. 1992;152:1253-1256.

51. Welty TK, Grabman J, Kompare E, et al. Nineteen cases of plague in Arizona: A spectrum including ecthyma gangrenosum due to plague and plague in pregnancy. West J Med. 1985;142:641-646.
52. Boulanger L, Ettestad P, Fogarty J, et al. Gentamicin and tetracyclines for the treatment of human plague: A review of 75 cases in New Mexico from 1985-1999. Clin Infect Dis. 2004;38:663-669.
53. Cunha BA. Doxycycline for community-acquired pneumonia. Clin Infect Dis. 2003;37:870.
54. Galimand M, Guiyoule A, Gerbaud G, et al. Multidrug resistance in *Yersinia pestis* mediated by a transferable plasmid. N Engl J Med. 1997;337:677-680.
55. Wheeler AP, Gordon RB. Treating patients with severe sepsis. N Engl J Med. 1999;340:207-214.
56. Dellinger PR. Inflammation and coagulation: Implications for the septic patient. Clin Infect Dis. 2003;36:1259-1265.
57. Centers for Disease Control and Prevention. Guideline for isolation precautions in hospitals. Part II. Recommendations for isolation precautions in hospitals. Hospital Infection Control Practices Advisory Committee. 1997. Available at: *www.cdc.gov/ncidod/hip/ISOLAT/isopart2.htm*
58. Centers for Disease Control and Prevention. Prevention of plague. Recommendations of the Advisory Committee on Immunization Practices (ACIP). MMWR Morb Mortal Wkly Rep. 1996;45(RR-14):1-15.
59. Titball RW, Williamson ED. Second and third generation plague vaccines. Adv Exp Med Biol. 2003;529:397-406.
60. Eyles JE, Williamson ED, Spiers ID, et al. Generation of protective immune responses to plague by mucosal administration of microspore coencapsulated recombinant subunits. J Controlled Release. 2000;63:191-200.
61. Prpic JK, Davey RB, eds. The Genus Yersinia: Epidemiology, Molecular Biology and Pathogenesis. Basel: Karger; 1987.
62. Brubacker RR. Factors promoting acute and chronic diseases caused by yersiniae. Clin Microbiol Rev. 1991;4:309-324.
63. Bottone EJ. *Yersinia enterocolitica:* The charisma continues. Clin Microbiol Rev. 1997;10:257-276.
64. Cover TL, Aber RC. *Yersinia enterocolitica.* N Engl J Med. 1989;321:16-24.
65. Cornelis G, Laroche Y, Balligand G, et al. *Yersinia enterocolitica,* a primary model for bacterial invasiveness. Rev Infect Dis. 1987;9:64-87.
66. Smego RA, Frean J, Koornhof HJ. Yersiniosis I: Microbiological and clinicoepidemiological aspects of plague and non-plague *Yersinia* infections. Eur J Clin Microbiol Infect Dis. 1999;18:1-15.
67. Bottone EJ. *Yersinia enterocolitica:* Overview and epidemiologic correlates. Microbes Infect. 1999;1:323.
68. Cornelis GR, Boland A, Boyd AP, et al. The virulence plasmid of *Yersinia,* an anti-host genome. Microbiol Mol Biol Rev. 1998;62:1315-1352.
69. Gaylov EE, Hakansson S, Forsberg A, et al. A secreted protein kinase of *Yersinia pseudotuberculosis* is an indispensable virulence determinant. Nature. 1993;361:730-732.
70. Guan K, Dixon JE. Protein tyrosine phosphatase activity of an essential virulence determinant in *Yersinia.* Science. 1990;249:553-556.
71. Cantineaux B, Boelaert J, Hariga C, et al: Impaired neutrophil defense against *Yersinia enterocolitica* in patients with iron overload who are undergoing dialysis. J Lab Clin Med. 1988;111:524-528.
72. Carniel E, Butler T, Hossain S, et al. Infrequent detection of *Yersinia enterocolitica* in childhood diarrhea in Bangladesh. Am J Trop Med Hyg. 1986;35:370-371.
73. Tauxe RV, Vandepitte J, Wauters G, et al. *Yersinia enterocolitica* infections and pork: The missing link. Lancet. 1987;1:1129-1132.
74. Merilahti-Palo R, Lahesmaa R, Granfors K, et al. Risk of *Yersinia* infection among butchers. Scand J Infect Dis. 1991;23:55-61.
75. Lee LA, Taylor J, Carter GP, et al. *Yersinia enterocolitica* 0:3: An emerging cause of pediatric gastroenteritis in the United States. J Infect Dis. 1991;163:660-663.
76. Jones TF, Buckingham SC, Bopp CA, et al. From pig to pacifier: Chitterling-associated yersiniosis outbreak among black infants. Emerg Infect Dis. 2003;9:1007-1009.
77. Abdel-Haq NM, Asmar BI, Abuhammour WM, Brown WJ. *Yersinia enterocolitica* infection in children. Pediatr Infect Dis J. 2000;19:945-948.
78. Adamkiewicz TV, Berkovitch M, Krishnan C, et al. Infection due to *Yersinia enterocolitica* in a series of patients with beta-thalassemia: Incidence and predisposing factors. Clin Infect Dis. 1998;27:1362-1366.
79. Robins-Browne RM, Prpic JK. Desferrioxamine and systemic yersiniosis. Lancet. 1983;2:1372.
80. Centers for Disease Control and Prevention. Red blood cell transfusions contaminated with *Yersinia enterocolitica*—United States, 1991-1996, and initiation of a national study to detect bacteria-associated transfusion reactions. MMWR Morb Mortal Wkly Rep. 1997;46:553-555.
81. Bradford WD, Noce PS, Gutman LT. Pathologic features of enteric infection with *Yersinia enterocolitica.* Arch Pathol. 1974;98:17-22.
82. van der Heijden IM, Res PCM, Wilbrink B, et al. *Yersinia enterocolitica:* A cause of chronic polyarthritis. Clin Infect Dis. 1997;25:831-837.
83. Stuart PM, Woodward JG. *Yersinia enterocolitica* produces superantigenic activity. J Immunol. 1992;148:225-233.
84. Strom H, Johansson C. Appendicitis followed by reactive arthritis in an HLA B27-positive man after infection with *Yersinia enterocolitica,* diagnosed by serotype specific antibodies and antibodies to *Yersinia* outer membrane proteins. Infection. 1997;25:317-319.
85. Borg AA, Gray J, Dawes PT. *Yersinia*-related arthritis in the United Kingdom: A report of 12 cases and review of the literature. Q J Med. 1992;304:575-582.
86. Granfors K, Jalkanen S, von Essen R, et al. *Yersinia* antigens in synovial-fluid cells from patients with reactive arthritis. N Engl J Med. 1989;320:216-221.
87. Rose FB, Camp CJ, Antes EJ. Family outbreak of fatal *Yersinia enterocolitica* pharyngitis. Am J Med. 1987;82:636-637.
88. Greene JN, Herndon P, Nadler JP, et al. Case report: *Yersinia enterocolitica* necrotizing pneumonia in an immunocompromised patient. Am J Med Sci. 1993;305:171-173.
89. Weber J, Finlayson NB, Mark JBD. Mesenteric lymphadenitis and terminal ileitis due to *Yersinia pseudotuberculosis.* N Engl J Med. 1970;283:172-174.
90. Kachoris M, Ruoff KL, Welch K, et al. Routine culture of stool specimens for *Yersinia enterocolitica* is not a cost-effective procedure. J Clin Microbiol. 1988;26:582-583.
91. Gayraud M, Scavizzi MR, Mollaret HH, et al. Antibiotic treatment of *Yersinia enterocolitica* septicemia: A retrospective review of 43 cases. Clin Infect Dis. 1993;17:405-410.
92. Crowe M, Ashford K, Ispahani P. Clinical features and antibiotic treatment of septic arthritis and osteomyelitis due to *Yersinia enterocolitica.* J Med Microbiol. 1996;45:302-309.

CHAPTER **227**

Bordetella Species

ERIK L. HEWLETT

Whooping cough as a clinical entity is recognized in writings from the 14th century, but Baillou, the first modern epidemiologist, is credited with providing the "earliest clear account" of the disease in 1640.[1] The name *pertussis,* meaning "violent cough," was first used by Sydenham in 1679.[2] In China, the illness is known as "the cough of 100 days," and there are specific terms for this illness in different languages, such as *tos ferina* in Spanish and *coqueluche* in French. The etiologic organism, initially named *Haemophilus pertussis,* was described by Bordet and Gengou in 1906 and subsequently isolated with the use of a medium that bears their names.[3] A detailed history of the clinical syndrome of pertussis is provided in the classic monograph by Lapin.[2]

DESCRIPTION OF THE PATHOGENS

The genus *Bordetella* now includes at least eight species—*pertussis, parapertussis, bronchiseptica,* and *avium;* the more recently added *hinzii, holmesii,* and *trematum;* plus a new environmental isolate, *petrii.* The relatedness of these *Bordetella* species and those of the genera *Alcaligenes* and *Achromobacter* has been determined by a variety of methods, and together they have been designated as a subclass of the Proteobacteria.[4] *B. pertussis* and *B. parapertussis* account for the majority of human respiratory infections with bordetellae, and most of the other species have been recognized to cause human infection (often nonpulmonary) under special circumstances.[5] For example, *B. pertussis* can cause otitis media,[6] a *B. avium*–like agent was cultured from a patient with chronic otitis,[7] *B. hinzii* was isolated from a symptomatic patient with cystic fibrosis,[8] *B. holmesii* has been associated with septicemia and isolated from a patient with sickle cell disease,[9] *B. trematum* has been recovered from wounds,[10] and a new organism in the *Bordetella-Alcaligenes* complex has been associated with septic arthritis.[11] *B. bronchiseptica,* which is primarily an animal pathogen causing kennel cough in dogs, snuffles in rabbits, and atrophic rhinitis in swine, can cause chronic, difficult-to-treat respiratory infections in humans, especially immunocompromised hosts and persons who have contact with animals.[12,13]

The bordetellae are minute coccobacillary organisms that appear singly or in pairs. The principal human pathogens (*B. pertussis* and *B. parapertussis*) are nonmotile. *B. bronchiseptica* and *B. avium* possess peritrichous flagellae that are expressed in the avirulent phase and provide motility. The original *Bordetella* species are piliated and aerobic, and oxidize amino acids, but do not ferment carbohydrates. The organisms require nicotinamide (or nicotinic acid) for growth at an optimal temperature of 35° to 37° C. Although the starch-blood-agar medium originally described by Bordet and Gengou is still used in some places, it is clear that the organisms can grow in totally synthetic medium consisting of buffers, minerals, an amino acid energy source, and growth factors such as nicotinamide.[14] Growth is enhanced by, if not dependent on, additives such as starch or β-methyl cyclodextrin to absorb and neutralize inhibitory compounds. Growth rates and colony sizes differ among the species, with *B. pertussis* often requiring 3 or more days for the pinpoint colonies to appear in cultures of clinical specimens. *B. parapertussis* grows slightly faster (and grows on sheep blood agar), produces large colonies, is oxidase negative, and in peptone agar or in liquid medium produces a characteristic brownish pigment.

Dobrogosz and colleagues[15] determined by DNA hybridization that *B. pertussis*, *B. parapertussis,* and *B. bronchiseptica* are not sufficiently diverse to be classified as distinct species, and their conclusion is supported by the work of Musser and colleagues[16] and Arico and associates.[17] As a result, von Wintzingerode and co-workers proposed that the three species be referred to as the *B. bronchiseptica* cluster.[4] Recently, Parkhill and colleagues published genome sequences from the three organisms and concluded that *B. pertussis* and *B. parapertussis* are independent derivatives of a *B. bronchiseptica*–like ancestor.[18] The conclusion from these data was that *B. pertussis* and *B. parapertussis,* which have more narrow host ranges, developed through gene loss, not acquisition.

Speciation of clinical isolates has been dependent on phenotypic characterization, including serotyping based on detection of heat-labile K agglutinogens, but bordetellae have the capacity to change serotypes in vitro or in vivo, thereby limiting the utility of this approach. As a result, more emphasis is now being placed on strain classification based on genotype, using techniques such as pulsed-field gel electrophoresis, restriction fragment length polymorphism, and polymerase chain reaction, using species-specific primers.[19]

B. pertussis produces a number of biologically active substances that are postulated to play a role in disease (reviewed by Hewlett,[20] Locht and colleagues,[21] and Mattoo and co-workers[22]). These include surface components, such as filamentous hemagglutinin (FHA), pertactin (PRN), and fimbriae; toxins such as pertussis toxin (PT), adenylate cyclase toxin (ACT), tracheal cytotoxin (TCT), and dermonecrotic toxin (DNT); and other products, including tracheal colonization factor and an autotransporter/serum resistance factor, BrkA (bordetella resistance to killing). FHA, which derives its name from the ability to agglutinate erythrocytes, is synthesized as a high-molecular-weight protein but processed to a mature form of 220 kDa. It appears to be involved in the attachment of *B. pertussis* to ciliated respiratory epithelia and other types of cells, perhaps by its RGD (arginine-glycine-aspartate) motif interacting with host integrins.[23] In addition, FHA has been demonstrated to be essential for *B. pertussis* to enter epithelial cells[24] and to elicit cytokine release and apoptotic death of several cell types.[25,26] Genome data from other gram-negative organisms has revealed widespread distribution of FHA-like sequences, thus far of unknown significance and function.[18]

Several of the agglutinogens have been isolated and characterized biochemically. Although the fimbrial nature of agglutinogens 2 and 3/6 suggests a role in attachment to target cells, strains lacking those components do adhere to nonciliated cells and can cause infection.[21,22] The contribution of adhesins to infection, whether from the bacterial surface or after release into the medium, remains an issue of interest,[27] and several adhesins are included in the acellular pertussis vaccines now in use.[28]

ACT contains an adenylate cyclase enzymatic domain that is able to enter mammalian cells, where it is activated by endogenous calmodulin to catalyze the production of cyclic adenosine monophosphate (cAMP) from adenosine triphosphate.[29,30] The resulting accumulation of cAMP to supraphysiologic levels results in impaired leukocyte functions.[31] The toxin, a protein of 1706 amino acids, is a member of the RTX family of bacterial toxins (including *Escherichia coli* hemolysin and *Pasteurella haemolytica* leukotoxin) and is itself hemolytic, responsible for the zone of hemolysis associated with virulent

B. pertussis on blood agar plates. Strains of *B. pertussis* that are defective in ACT production are avirulent in suckling mice, and antibodies against the toxin enhance bacterial uptake by phagocytes.[32,33]

DNT, also known as mouse lethal toxin or heat-labile toxin, was first discovered by Bordet and Gengou when necrotic lesions developed after intradermal injection of *B. pertussis* into suckling mice. The molecule is now known to be a deamidase, which, like the related cytotoxic necrotizing factor from *E. coli,* acts by modification of Rho proteins.[34] Because dermonecrotic lesions are not part of clinical pertussis, it is possible that DNT exerts a non-necrotizing effect on cells of the immune system and thereby alters the host immune response.

TCT is a component of *Bordetella* spp. discovered by virtue of its ability to cause ciliostasis, inhibit DNA synthesis, and ultimately kill tracheal epithelial cells in vitro.[35] The toxin is a tetrapeptide disaccharide derived from bacterial peptidoglycan. A TCT-like molecule is produced by *Neisseria gonorrhoeae* as a result of the action of a lytic transglycosylase and has similar effects on ciliated cells of the fallopian tube.[36] The biologic effects of TCT on respiratory epithelial cells involve production of interleukin-1 and nitric oxide.[37]

PT is one of the best known products of *B. pertussis* and is responsible for a number of the biologic activities recognized before its purification.[38,39] These include induction of lymphocytosis, sensitization to the lethal effects of histamine, enhancement of insulin secretion, and adjuvanticity. The active subunit possesses adenosine diphosphate-ribosyl (ADP-R) transferase activity for covalent modification of certain members of the G protein family of signal transduction molecules, resulting in inhibition of their ability to couple extracellular receptors to intracellular effector pathways involving adenylate cyclase, phospholipase, ion channels, and others. Despite the enormous literature on the molecular and cellular actions of PT, its target tissue(s) in clinical pertussis remain to be elucidated. It certainly does affect the ability of phagocytes to clear *B. pertussis,* but what it does in contributing to symptoms is not known.[40] The PT gene is present in *B. parapertussis* and *B. bronchiseptica,* but expression by those species has not been detected. The apparent absence was attributed previously to alterations in the promotor region. More recently, data from the Genome Project has revealed that the PT promotors are conserved in the two nonproducing species, suggesting that mutations in *B. pertussis* may be responsible for an increase in regulated expression that may contribute to the differential virulence.[18]

B. pertussis does not enter the circulation and become disseminated, and is considered to be sensitive to serum complement. BrkA is an autotransporter molecule that protects against antibody-dependent killing by the classical complement pathway. When compared with that from other gram-negative organisms, *Bordetella* lipopolysaccharide (LPS) has several notable features, and a detailed structure has recently been elucidated.[41] It is heterogeneous, with two major forms differing in the phosphate content of the 3-deoxy-2-octulosonic acid portions.[42] Although the unfractionated material possesses the usual effects of LPS (induction of interleukin-1 production, fever, hypotension, and the Schwartzman reaction), the distribution of those activities among the fractions is unusual. Lipid X, but not lipid A, is pyrogenic, and the polysaccharide region is very active as an adjuvant.[43] Furthermore, LPS from *B. pertussis* is more potent in the limulus amebocyte lysate assay but less potent in pyrogen release from monocytes than LPS from *E. coli.*[44] This means that extrapolation to LPS from other gram-negative organisms for biologic effects and toxicity of *B. pertussis* LPS is not appropriate. In addition, monoclonal antibodies to LPS from *B. pertussis* have protective activity in animals, suggesting that this molecule may actually serve as a protective antigen in the whole-cell vaccine.[45] Harvill and colleagues have shown that the LPS of *B. pertussis* is important in the early stages of infection and not just through interaction with the innate immune system.[46]

The production of virulence factors by *B. pertussis* is regulated in several ways. First, the organisms can undergo a genetic event, originally termed *phase variation,* that results in loss of most known virulence factors. Phase variation, which has been shown to occur at a frequency of 1 in 10^4 to 10^6 generations, results from a specific DNA frameshift caused by insertion of a single nucleotide into the bvg (also known as vir) operon.[47] A similar phenomenon, known as *phenotypic modulation,* occurs in response to environmental changes such as temperature or chemical content of the medium and is reversible. This adaptive process is mediated by protein products of the bvg operon. A two-component regulatory system that controls expression of relevant virulence factors upon entry into a host induces components required for survival and production of disease.[48,49] There are, in addition, genes that are expressed during "intermediate phase," a short interval between the Bvg$^+$ and Bvg$^-$ states, and others (*bvgR*) that are repressed by the bvg operon.[50,51] Genetic manipulation resulting in expression of BvgR proteins during infection is detrimental to lung colonization.[52] There is a Bvg-coordinated sequence of events that involves expression of adherence factors such as FHA and PRN first, followed later in time by toxins such as PT and ACT; this regulation appears to be explained by molecular events at the promoter level.[53,54]

Roles for these multiple factors in the pathophysiology of pertussis can be considered in the context of a generic sequence of events for an infectious disease: entry and attachment to a specific target tissue, production of local damage, and development of systemic disease, all dependent on an ongoing evasion and disruption of host defense mechanisms.[22] FHA, pertactin, other surface molecules, and possibly PT participate in the attachment of *B. pertussis* to the respiratory epithelium. Ciliostasis and damage to the epithelium by TCT disturb mucociliary clearance, the first line of defense. The inhibition of the routine functions of phagocytes (chemotaxis, phagocytosis, oxidative burst, and bactericidal activity) by ACT represents an acute but reversible disruption of the protection conferred by immune effector cells. PT and DNT, by covalent modification of proteins, also impair the function of phagocytes and other immune effector cells, but in a more sustained manner. TCT, DNT, and/or ACT may contribute to local damage at the respiratory mucosa. At present, PT is the leading candidate to account for systemic manifestations of disease, because it certainly produces lymphocytosis in experimental animals infected with *B. pertussis.* Although proposed to be so in the past, pertussis is not a single-toxin disease like tetanus, diphtheria, and botulism.[55] *B. parapertussis,* although unable to produce any detectable amount of PT, can cause clinical disease, which is frequently milder than but can be of comparable severity to that of *B. pertussis.*[56,57] In addition, PT has been administered intravenously to humans in doses of 0.5 or 1 μg/kg without causing clinical pertussis or any significant adverse effect.[58] It appears likely, therefore, that in the context of infection with *B. pertussis,* PT can exacerbate the disease process associated with a localized infection of the respiratory tract, but is not solely responsible.[20] This issue is particularly important in the context of the efficacy of component pertussis vaccines (see "Prevention").

Although a variety of rodent models, including one that consists of coughing in rats, have been employed to study infection with *B. pertussis,* there is none that fully mimics human disease. There is general consensus that better understanding of the pathogenesis of this illness can best be obtained from investigation of humans infected with *B. pertussis.* Intracellular *B. pertussis* organisms have been demonstrated in vitro and in clinical specimens, but the organism is not systemically invasive and does not disseminate beyond the respiratory tract. The significance of intracellular organisms in pathophysiology and transmission, if any, remains unknown.

EPIDEMIOLOGY

Pertussis continues to be a disease of worldwide importance, with an estimated 285,000 deaths in 2001, but this figure does represent progress in that it reflects a decrease over earlier mortality.[59] Conversely, in the United States during 2002, there were 8296 reported cases, the highest number for more than 40 years.[60] This increase is due in large part to disease diagnosed in adolescents and adults, but it is unclear if this is a true increase or rather an enhanced recognition of the illness in these age groups.

In most populations, the disease is endemic, with regular epidemic cycles superimposed on a background rate. Although the mechanism of the periodic pattern with 3- to 5-year cycles is not known, one explanation for the epidemics is accumulation of susceptible persons in a population between cycles. The number of organisms required for infection is not known, but *B. pertussis* is clearly very contagious. Attack rates among susceptibles range from 50% to 100%, depending on the nature of exposure.[61] Because the organism is localized to the respiratory tract, it is believed that transmission occurs predominantly by aerosol droplet, with highest attack rates for persons exposed to a coughing patient.

Although pertussis is classically described as novel among childhood infections in that higher attack, morbidity, and mortality rates occur in girls, recent mortality data from cases reported to the World Health Organization (WHO) do not show that previously observed difference.[59] Although it is possible to infect experimental animals with *B. pertussis,* there are no known natural infections of animals or animal reservoirs, and this organism is unable to survive for prolonged periods in the environment. For these reasons, it appears that transmission must occur from infected individual to susceptible host. No long-term carrier state has been identified, but asymptomatic culture-positive persons can be detected following known exposure and during outbreaks. These transient "carriers" are unlikely to be a significant source of infection because they are not coughing, but there are no clear data on this question or on the duration of time that such individuals are culture positive.

In the prevaccine era, pertussis was primarily an affliction of young children, but less so infants, at least in part because of passive protection during the first year of life through maternal antibody. For example, in a study from 1916, 60.2% of pertussis patients were 1 to 5 years of age, and only 19.4% younger than 1 year of age.[62] Under those circumstances, with most adults having had pertussis as children and being repeatedly exposed during the course of periodic outbreaks, there was a high level of residual immunity. Whole-cell pertussis vaccine has clearly been responsible for a major reduction in the incidence of disease, but it also caused a shift in the peak age of disease. Because immunity elicited by whole-cell vaccine was of limited duration (generally less than 12 years), fully immunized children were well protected, but adults had little or no immunity that could be passively transferred to infants. As a result, infants, who had not yet received the initial series of immunizations, were at the greatest risk for morbidity and mortality from pertussis and the least protected. In 1982-1983, for example, 53.1% of pertussis cases reported in the United States occurred in children younger than 1 year of age, and in 1980-1989 that group had the highest annual incidence of disease (62.8 per 100,000).[63,64] Because no booster for pertussis is given beyond childhood, virtually all adolescents and adults are susceptible, and it is clear that this group accounts for a higher proportion of the cases of pertussis. Among the 29,134 cases of pertussis in the United States reported to the Centers for Disease Control and Prevention from 1997 through 2000, 49% occurred in patients age 10 years and above, and that group represented a major source of transmission.[65]

A number of studies have addressed the incidence of pertussis in these older age groups, often focusing on individuals presenting with cough lasting 1 week or longer. Using serologies and other techniques for detection of recent exposure to *B. pertussis,* it appears that as many as 20% to 30% of adults with prolonged cough may have pertussis.[66] An outbreak in Vermont illustrates this point, in that the highest number of cases and the highest infection rate were in adolescents ages 10 to 14 years, with a secondary peak in the 40- to 49-year-old age group.[67] Given the level of protection of the pediatric population and the underreporting of pertussis in older groups, it seems likely that the majority of pertussis cases in the United States at the present time occur in adolescents and adults. Transmission and outbreaks in groups of adults, such as pilgrims participating in the Hajj in Saudi Arabia and workers at an oil refinery in Illinois, illustrate the need for booster doses in adulthood in order for control of pertussis to be a reality.[60,66,68]

CLINICAL MANIFESTATIONS

After an incubation period ranging from less than 1 week up to 3 weeks, signs and symptoms of the catarrhal phase begin.[2] Early clinical findings, such as rhinorrhea, lacrimation, mild conjunctival injection, malaise, and sometimes low-grade fever, are indistinguishable from those of many other upper respiratory tract or systemic infectious diseases. Thus, at the onset of symptoms, there is often no reason to suspect pertussis, except in the setting of known exposure to an active case. Later during this phase, which can be abbreviated to a few days or last as long as 1 week, a dry, nonproductive cough develops. Evolution of the cough to that which is characteristic of the disease heralds onset of the paroxysmal phase.

Pertussis is generally most severe in infants, but presentation and symptoms may be atypical in that age group, as well as in partially immunized children and previously immunized adolescents and adults. In those with partial immunity, the catarrhal phase can be shortened or unrecognized, and whoop and leukocytosis can be absent. Prodromal symptoms in adults can include complaints such as pharyngeal discomfort, and, as a result, correct diagnosis in this age group can be further delayed or missed.[69,70] The cough paroxysm consists of a series of short expiratory bursts, followed by an inspiratory gasp, which can result in the typical whoop. Not all children with pertussis exhibit the characteristic whoop, and it is relatively uncommon among infants, who may have apneic episodes. Whooping is variable among adults, with that symptom present in 8% to 82% of cases in different studies.[66] Paroxysms, which may number more than 30 per 24 hours and be more frequent at night, occur spontaneously or are precipitated by external stimuli such as noises or cold air. They may be sufficiently severe to cause cyanosis and classically end with an episode of vomiting. In adults, paroxysms may be associated with sweating attacks, facial flushing, and even cough syncope. The cough and vomiting may yield thick mucus plugs and watery secretions. Between paroxysms the patient appears relatively well and often sleeps. Although often not presenting with typical pertussis, adolescents and adults do have paroxysmal cough that can last a month or more and be associated with whooping and post-tussive vomiting.[66]

During the late catarrhal and early paroxysmal phases, patients may exhibit a characteristic hematologic feature of the disease, namely leukocytosis with lymphocyte predominance. The total white blood cell count, which may sometimes exceed 50,000 cells/mm[3], consists of a relative lymphocytosis with T and B cells and a less striking increase in neutrophils. Recently, leukocytosis has been suggested to be associated with increased mortality in infants with pertussis, perhaps via formation of cellular aggregates that can cause pulmonary hypertension.[71] A slight hyperinsulinemia and reduced glycemic response to epinephrine have been demonstrated during the disease. Neither was associated with hypoglycemia, but abnormally low blood glucose has been reported in pediatric pertussis patients.[2] All of these manifestations, such as leukolymphocytosis, are less common or less severe in persons who have been immunized previously.

The convalescent phase begins with a decrease in the intensity of the cough and the frequency of paroxysms, but it can still be weeks in duration. For individuals who have been severely ill, it is not uncommon for an intercurrent illness such as a viral upper respiratory infection, or even transient exposure to a pulmonary irritant, to cause recurrence of the paroxysmal cough. This occurs in the absence of detectable B. pertussis organisms and does not represent reinfection. Despite concerns over this issue, there is no agreement on whether pertussis can cause long-term impairment of pulmonary function.[72,73]

COMPLICATIONS

The principal complications of pertussis are secondary infections, such as otitis media and pneumonia, and physical sequelae of paroxysmal cough. Pneumonia can be caused by B. pertussis or secondary infection with other organisms and is a leading cause of death in pertussis. It can result from aspiration during whooping and vomiting and/or from secondary infection resulting from impaired clearance mechanisms caused by the actions of virulence factors such as TCT, ACT, and PT. Presence of these infectious complications is suggested by the onset of fever or a change in the status of the patient between paroxysms.

The increased intrathoracic and intra-abdominal pressures during coughing can result in subconjunctival and scleral hemorrhages, facial and truncal petechiae, epistaxis, hemorrhages in the central nervous system (CNS), subcutaneous emphysema, pneumothorax, umbilical and inguinal hernias, and rectal prolapse. Laceration of the lingual frenulum also occurs with severe cough episodes. B. pertussis has been isolated from the middle ear of a patient with pertussis and otitis media[6] and, in a predisposed patient, has been implicated in hemolytic uremic syndrome.[74] Recently, an association was demonstrated between childhood pertussis and subsequent development of type 1 diabetes mellitus.[75] With increasing recognition of pertussis in adolescents and adults, there are additional complications that have been identified in these age groups, including urinary incontinence, rib fracture, unilateral hearing loss, herniated disk, precipitation of angina pectoris, and possibly even carotid artery dissection.[69,76] The illness can be severe and prolonged in adults, with a mean duration of symptoms of 5 to 7 weeks.[66]

CNS abnormalities occur in patients with pertussis at a relatively high frequency. In children 6 months of age or younger with pertussis in the United States (1997-2000), 63% were hospitalized, convulsions occurred in 1.4%, encephalopathy in 0.2%, and death in 0.8%.[65] Encephalopathy and seizures even occur infrequently in adults with pertussis.[77] The convulsions may be febrile, in conjunction with secondary infection, or afebrile. There are several mechanisms postulated for these CNS sequelae, such as secondary infection with neurotropic viruses, hypoxia, hypoglycemia, and direct effects of pertussis toxin, but the only one documented pathologically is parenchymal hemorrhage in the brain, which has been attributed to venous congestion and increased pressure during cough. At the peak of the paroxysmal phase, frequent vomiting can lead, especially in infants and young children in the developing world, to dehydration and nutritional compromise.

DIAGNOSIS

With new polymerase chain reaction (PCR) technologies, the ability to detect a few Bordetella organisms has been greatly enhanced and often the issue is not sensitivity of the diagnostic test, but rather whether the primary care physician seriously considers the possibility of pertussis.[78,79] A variety of methods have been developed for detection of B. pertussis, its products, or the immune response to them.[80-82] None, however, is without its limitations in sensitivity, specificity, or practicality. Isolation of B. pertussis by culture in the setting of clinical illness is highly specific, but is clearly limited in sensitivity, and for that reason is being replaced in many labs by PCR. The starch-based medium developed by Bordet and Gengou (BG medium) is still in use, and, when supplemented with cephalexin to impair growth of normal flora and used at the bedside immediately after preparation, BG medium is equivalent to any medium available. Other media that have been developed, however, have longer shelf lives and enable recovery of B. pertussis from transported specimens.[83] The material to be used for culture, PCR, or both is obtained by calcium alginate nasopharyngeal swab (cotton inhibits growth of the organism) or by aspiration from the nasopharynx. The advantage of aspiration is that a specimen of larger volume is obtained and can be used for several diagnostic modalities.[84]

PCR has been applied to pertussis diagnosis in both investigational and routine clinical care settings and has been demonstrated to be both sensitive and specific.[66,85,86] The virtue of a PCR-based diagnosis is that the organisms do not have to be viable, as illustrated by the work of Edelman and colleagues.[87] By observing unvaccinated patients with culture-proven pertussis, they found that, on the seventh day of erythromycin treatment, all cultures were negative but 56% of the samples were still PCR positive. Several sets of primers have been used for pertussis PCR, including those derived from the ACT gene, the PT gene or its promoter, a region upstream from the porin gene, and insertion sequences, which are present in multiple copies.[88-91] Use of a combination of primers and treatment of the product with restriction enzymes allows for simultaneous detection of, but discrimination between, *B. pertussis* and *B. parapertussis* in the same assay.[88,92-94] Although there are significant advantages to the use of PCR for identification of *Bordetella* organisms, it is important that efforts to culture the organism also continue, because strain variation, rare antibiotic resistance, and other phenotypic and genotypic features in the population will be missed by a single PCR-based detection system.[95]

Serologic tests for detection of antibodies in serum are useful epidemiologically, but less so during the acute illness.[96,97] Because the ability to isolate *B. pertussis* by culture decreases progressively during the disease, the use of a combination of culture and an assay for antipertussis antibodies in serum or nasopharyngeal secretions may provide increased diagnostic sensitivity throughout the course of the illness.[98,99] Comparison of serum from mother and infant has been shown to complement the use of acute and convalescent serology in the diagnosis of pertussis in infants.[100]

In light of the limitations of all laboratory procedures for pertussis diagnosis, a clinical case definition has been developed to identify persons with the disease, for both epidemiologic and outbreak control purposes. A cough of 2 weeks' duration was found to be a sensitive and specific marker of pertussis in community outbreaks but has been shown to have limitations in determination of efficacy in clinical field trials.[101,102] The case definition established by a WHO panel and used in the clinical trials was 21 or more days of paroxysmal cough with laboratory confirmation or epidemiologic linkage.[103] It is clear in retrospect, however, that this definition resulted in omission from the case roll of culture-positive, symptomatic persons with a shorter duration of cough.[104,105]

PREVENTION

With recognition of pertussis as a contagious illness, but before the availability of effective immunoprophylaxis, isolation of infected patients was the only reasonable control measure applied to the prevention of this illness. The nonspecific nature of the symptoms early in the clinical course, however, limited the effective use of this approach to recognized community outbreaks. Attempts to use serum from immune persons for passive protection or treatment during the incubation period were intermittently popular, and one report suggested that pertussis immunoglobulin might provide some benefit in reducing severity and duration of symptoms.[106] A pilot evaluation of pertussis immune globulin has been conducted with promising results, but follow-up investigation has not occurred.[107] Antibiotic (erythromycin) prophylaxis is recommended for prevention of disease in contacts of active cases; although not fully efficacious, this has been shown to be a major factor in controlling household transmission and outbreaks.[108] Caution should be used, however, in prescribing erythromycin preparations for postexposure prophylaxis in neonates because of an observed association between the drug and development of hypertrophic pyloric stenosis.[109]

Whole-Cell Vaccine

Soon after the original isolation of *B. pertussis,* work was begun on preparation of a vaccine. Merthiolate-killed, whole-cell vaccines were found to be protective, and in the early 1950s a British Medical Research Council trial documented a correlation between protection in a mouse intracerebral potency test and vaccine protection in children.[110] One of the vaccines currently recommended by the WHO and used in much of the world is killed, whole-cell vaccine combined with diphtheria and tetanus toxoids and aluminum-containing adjuvants (DTP vaccine). Although whole-cell vaccine was believed to be more than 80% efficacious, most preparations had never been tested directly in prospective clinical efficacy trials, and calculations of efficacy from a variety of sources ranged from 0% to 100% depending on the vac-

cine preparation used, the type of study, and the case definition.[111] The Phase III trials of acellular vaccines also provided an opportunity for evaluation of several whole-cell products, which were found to differ substantially in their efficacies despite the fact that each passed the standard Kendrick mouse potency test required for lot release. This observation should not be interpreted as an indictment of all whole-cell pertussis products but should serve as a warning to heighten awareness of the need for continual assessment of the effectiveness of whole-cell vaccines in general use.

A major limitation to whole-cell vaccine use has been the associated reactogenicity. When compared with diphtheria and tetanus toxins (DT), DTP vaccine produces significantly more local and systemic reactions such as pain, swelling, fever, anorexia, fretfulness, and vomiting.[112,113] Encephalopathy and permanent neurologic sequelae, but not infantile spasms or sudden infant death syndrome, have been associated temporally with DTP vaccine administration, but it appears that few if any of these effects are caused by the vaccine.[112,114] Considerations of the benefits and risks of whole-cell vaccine have repeatedly concluded in favor of its continued use in the general population. In the past, whole-cell pertussis vaccine was used in adults only under special circumstances for control of hospital outbreaks, but immunization of adults in this and other settings is changing as more data are acquired about acellular vaccine in this segment of the population.[66]

Acellular Vaccines

At present there are five acellular pertussis vaccines licensed for use in the United States. Their development has been driven primarily by concerns about the reactogenicity and efficacy of whole-cell vaccines. This represents yet another step forward in a process that started as early as the 1930s, with efforts to prepare non–whole-cell pertussis vaccines. An early product (Eli Lilly's TriSolgen) was available on the market through the mid-1970s, but antigen contents of such vaccines were not well characterized, and controlled trials to determine their efficacies were never done.[28] The discoveries by Sato and colleagues that PT was one of two hemagglutinins on the surface of *B. pertussis* and that both PT and FHA can contribute to protection in an animal model of pertussis represented major breakthroughs toward introduction of the acellular vaccine era for pertussis.[115] Clinical interest in acellular vaccines was stimulated by the development and extensive use of such products in Japan during the early 1980s.[28,115] Because the Japanese products were initially used in children 2 years of age and older, it was deemed necessary for efficacy to be evaluated in infants (beginning at 2 months of age, as in the U.S. immunization schedule) before consideration of licensure in the United States and elsewhere. To address this aspect, PT, alone or in combination with FHA, was tested during 1986 and 1987 in Swedish children beginning at 6 months of age.[116] Although both preparations showed protection, they exceeded 70% efficacy only when the case definition included 28 or more days of cough (severe disease). No whole-cell vaccines were included in that trial, and efficacies of such products remained subject to speculation. The low efficacies of the two acellular vaccines in Sweden precluded their being licensed there or in the United States and led to additional developmental efforts for acellular pertussis vaccines.

Despite the demonstrated efficacies of most whole-cell and acellular vaccines, the mechanisms by which they produce immunity remain unknown. In the early days of studying pertussis immunity, several investigators recognized a correlation between acquisition of pertussis agglutinating antibodies and apparent resistance to infection.[117] It was not clear whether that relation represented a mechanism of protection, a significant marker of immunity, or merely an epiphenomenon. During the first Swedish trials, an effort was made to compare levels of anti-PT and/or anti-FHA antibodies with protection in individual patients, but no meaningful relation was identified, owing in part to the time between collection of serum samples and exposure to the organism. In more recent trials, several groups took a similar approach and conducted retrospective evaluations of the serologic data, using curves of antibody kinetics to determine the level of antibody at the time of exposure. With different data sets, two groups observed that antibodies to pertactin, fimbriae (type 2 or types 2 and 3), and PT were associated with reduced likelihood of pertussis.[118,119]

Another element of immunity, namely the cell-mediated immunity (CMI) response, has been implicated as relevant to acquisition and elimination of infection with *B. pertussis*. Several laboratories have demonstrated that animals challenged with *B. pertussis* and patients with pertussis acquire a cell-mediated response to *Bordetella* antigens.[120-122] More recently, however, Mills and colleagues described an animal model in which both the humoral and cellular arms of immunity are involved in the clearance of and resistance to *B. pertussis*.[123] Specimens for evaluation of cellular responses to pertussis antigens reveal that, following pertussis vaccine administration, subjects have persistence of anti-PT CMI and humoral responses that seem to be sustained for years.[124]

At present there are several acellular pertussis vaccines licensed in the United States, some as diphtheria and tetanus toxoids and acellular pertussis (DTaP) alone and others with DTaP in combination with other vaccine products such as hepatitis B, inactivated poliovirus, and *Haemophilus* B conjugate.[125] There is no product yet approved for general use as an adult booster, but consideration is being given to that possibility for the future. Because morbidity and mortality of infants from pertussis continues to be a problem, at least in part as a result of the time required to achieve protection from the primary series of immunizations over the first 5 to 6 months of life, there is also consideration of booster doses of acellular vaccine for women of childbearing age.[126] As yet, there are no recommendations for immunization of adults with acellular pertussis vaccine.

TREATMENT

Supportive Care

Despite considerable efforts to understand the pathogenesis of pertussis, for the purposes of prevention and treatment, there have been strikingly few new developments in therapy for this illness. Infants with pertussis are at greatest risk of complications with permanent sequelae, and hospitalization occurs frequently for patients younger than 1 year of age.[65] Appropriate measures for such patients with moderate to severe disease include close monitoring of vital signs; quantitation of cough paroxysms and associated vomiting, cyanosis, and apnea; frequent nasotracheal suctioning; and provision of oxygen and parenteral hydration and nutrition.

Specific Therapy

Despite earlier conflicting data, preliminary evidence has suggested that pertussis immune globulin, specifically those preparations containing anti-PT antibodies, may be useful in reducing the severity of disease, especially in infants and young children who are at high risk of complications or death. An efficacy trial of this material has been proposed but not yet conducted, leaving a void in treatment alternatives to simple support and antibiotics for early intervention.

In order to be effective against *B. pertussis,* an antibiotic must achieve therapeutic levels at the respiratory tract mucosa. Although several antibiotics, including erythromycin, tetracycline, trimethoprim-sulfamethoxazole, and chloramphenicol, have been shown to be effective in elimination of *B. pertussis,* erythromycin, especially the estolate ester, appears to be the most reliable, probably because of its higher serum levels and its ability to enter the respiratory tract.[127-129] With data on both sides, there continues to be debate about the ability of erythromycin treatment to reduce severity and duration of disease, even when it is started during the paroxysmal phase.[128,130] The recommended dose, 40 to 50 mg/kg/day (maximum 500 mg four times daily) should be given for a full 14 days to prevent bacteriologic relapse, which may occur as a result of inadequate duration of therapy rather than development of drug resistance by the organism. Trimethoprim-sulfamethoxazole is an acceptable alternative for patients who cannot tolerate erythromycin, but there is less clinical experience with this preparation. The newer macrolides such as azithromycin and clarithromycin have good in vitro activity against *B. pertussis,* and clinical data support their use in this setting. Expressed as adult doses, clarithromycin 500 mg twice daily for 7 days has been studied.[131,132] A noncomparative trial of a 5-day course of azithromycin (10 mg/kg/day on day 1, then 5 mg/kg/day for the next 4 days) has been conducted with encouraging results: 33 of 34 culture- or PCR-positive patients were negative by the second or third day of treatment.[133] Ampicillin is clinically ineffective and should not be used.

Other therapeutic agents have been evaluated for symptomatic relief during the paroxysmal phase. Corticosteroids (betamethasone, 0.075 mg/kg/day orally, or hydrocortisone succinate, 30 mg/kg/day intramuscularly) may reduce the number, severity, and duration of cough paroxysms, but at present consideration of systemic use of these agents should be limited to infants with life-threatening pertussis.[134] There are anecdotal reports of success with aerosolized corticosteroids in reducing the frequency and severity of paroxysmal cough, but this option has not been evaluated in a controlled manner.[135] Salbutamol, a β_2-adrenergic agonist, has also been proposed for use in clinical pertussis, but there are conflicting data about its efficacy.[136-138] Standard cough suppressants and antihistamines are not effective, and their administration can be detrimental by inducing cough paroxysms. It is hoped that future research on the mechanisms of disease will identify therapeutic targets, which can ameliorate symptoms in patients who are already into the paroxysmal phase.

REFERENCES

1. Major RH. A History of Medicine. Springfield, IL: Charles C Thomas; 1954.
2. Lapin JH. Whooping Cough. Springfield, IL: Charles C Thomas; 1943.
3. Bordet J, Gengou O. Le microbe de la coqueluche. Ann Inst Pasteur. 1906;20:731-741.
4. von Wintzingerode F, Gerlach G, Schneider B, Gross R. Phylogenetic relationships and virulence evolution in the genus *Bordetella.* In: Hacker J, Kaper JB, eds. Pathogenicity Islands and the Evolution of Pathogenic Microbes, v. 1. Berlin: Springer-Verlag; 2002:177-199.
5. Parton R. New perspectives on *Bordetella* pathogenicity. J Med Microbiol. 1996;44:233-235.
6. Decherd ME, Deskin RW, Rowen JL, Brindley MB. Bordetella pertussis causing otitis media: A case report. Laryngoscope. 2003;113:226-227.
7. Dorittke C, Vandamme P, Hinz KH, et al. Isolation of a *Bordetella avium*-like organism from a human specimen. Eur J Clin Microbiol Infect Dis. 1995;14:451-454.
8. Funke G, Hess T, Vandamme P. Characteristics of *Bordetella hinzii* strains isolated from a cystic fibrosis patient over a 3-year period. J Clin Microbiol. 1996;34:966-969.
9. Njamkepo E, Delisle F, Hagege I, et al. *Bordetella holmesii* isolated from a patient with sickle cell anemia: Analysis and comparison with other *Bordetella holmesii* isolates. Clin Microbiol Infect Dis. 2000;6:131-136.
10. Vandamme P, Heyndrickx M, Vancanneyt M, et al. *Bordetella trematum* sp. nov., isolated from wounds and ear infections in humans, and reassessment of *Alcaligenes denitrificans* Ruger and Tan 1983. Int J Syst Bacteriol. 1996;46:849-858.
11. Kronvall G, Hanson HS, von Stedingk LV, et al. Septic arthritis caused by a gram-negative bacterium representing a new species related to the Bordetella-Alcaligenes complex. APMIS. 2000;108:187-194.
12. Bauwens JE, Spach DH, Schacker TW, et al. *Bordetella bronchiseptica* pneumonia and bacteremia following bone marrow transplantation. J Clin Microbiol. 1992;30:2474-2475.
13. Gueirard P, Weber C, Coustumier AL, Guiso N. Human *Bordetella bronchiseptica* infection related to contact with infected animals: Persistence of bacteria in host. J Clin Microbiol. 1995;33:2002-2006.
14. Stainer DW. Growth of *Bordetella pertussis.* In: Wardlaw AC, Parton R, eds. Pathogenesis and Immunity in Pertussis. Chichester, England: Wiley; 1988:19-37.
15. Dobrogosz WJ, Ezzell JW, Kloos WE, Manclark CR. Physiology of *Bordetella pertussis.* In: Manclark CR, Hill JC, eds. International Symposium on Pertussis, 3rd ed. Bethesda, MD: National Institutes of Health; 1978.
16. Musser JM, Hewlett EL, Peppler MS, Selander RK. Genetic diversity and relationships in populations of *Bordetella* spp. J Bacteriol. 1986;166:230-237.
17. Arico B, Gross R, Smida J, Rappuoli R. Evolutionary relationships in the genus Bordetella. Mol Microbiol. 1987;1:301-308.
18. Parkhill J, Sebaihia M, Preston A, et al. Comparative analysis of the genome sequences of Bordetella pertussis, Bordetella parapertussis and Bordetella bronchiseptica. Nat Genet. 2003;35:32-40.
19. Mooi FR, Hallander H, von Konig CH, et al. Epidemiological typing of *Bordetella pertussis* isolates: Recommendations for a standard methodology. Eur J Clin Microbiol Infect Dis. 2000;19:174-181.
20. Hewlett EL. Pertussis: Current concepts of pathogenesis and prevention. Pediatr Infect Dis J. 1997;16:S78-S84.
21. Locht C, Antoine R, Jacob-Dubuisson F. *Bordetella pertussis,* molecular pathogenesis under multiple aspects. Curr Opin Microbiol. 2001;4:82-89.
22. Mattoo S, Foreman-Wykert AK, Cotter PA, Miller JF . Mechanisms of Bordetella pathogenesis. Front Biosci. 2001;6:E168-E186.
23. Alonso S, Reveneau N, Pethe K, Locht C. Eighty-kilodalton N-terminal moiety of *Bordetella pertussis* filamentous hemagglutinin: Adherence, immunogenicity, and protective role. Infect Immun. 2002;70:4142-4147.

24. Ishibashi Y, Relman DA, Nishikawa A. Invasion of human respiratory epithelial cells by *Bordetella pertussis:* Possible role for a filamentous hemagglutinin Arg-Gly-Asp sequence and α5β1 integrin. Microb Pathog. 2001;30:279-288.

25. Abramson T, Kedem H, Relman D. Proinflammatory and proapoptotic activities associated with *Bordetella pertussis* filamentous hemagglutinin. Infect Immun. 2003;69:2650-2658.

26. McGuirk P, Mills KH. Direct anti-inflammatory effect of a bacterial virulence factor: IL-10-dependent suppression of IL-12 production by filamentous hemagglutinin from *Bordetella pertussis.* Eur J Immunol. 2000;30:415-422.

27. Coutte L, Alonso S, Reveneau N, et al. Role of adhesin release for mucosal colonization by a bacterial pathogen. J Exp Med. 2003;197:735-742.

28. Hewlett EL, Cherry JD. New and improved vaccines against pertussis. In: Cobon GS, Kaper JB, Woodrow GC, Levine MM, eds. New Generation Vaccines, 2nd ed. New York: Marcel Dekker; 1997:387-416.

29. Ladant D, Ullmann A. *Bordetella pertussis* adenylate cyclase: A toxin with multiple talents. Trends Microbiol. 1999;7:172-176.

30. Zaretzky FR, Gray MC, Hewlett EL. Direct penetration of bacterial toxins across the plasma membrane. In: Burns D, et al., eds. Bacterial Protein Toxins. Washington, DC: ASM Press; 2003:149-156.

31. Harvill ET, Cotter PA, Yuk MH, Miller JF. Probing the function of *Bordetella bronchiseptica* adenylate cyclase toxin by manipulating host immunity. Infect Immun. 1999;67:1493-1500.

32. Weiss AA, Hewlett EL, Myers GA, Falkow S. Pertussis toxin and extracytoplasmic adenylate cyclase as virulence factors of *Bordetella pertussis.* J Infect Dis. 1984;150:219-222.

33. Weingart CL, Mobberley-Schuman PS, Hewlett EL, et al. Neutralizing antibodies to adenylate cyclase toxin promote phagocytosis of *Bordetella pertussis* by human neutrophils. Infect Immun. 2000;68:7152-7155.

34. Horiguchi Y. *Escherichia coli* cytotoxic necrotizing factors and Bordetella dermonecrotic toxin: The dermonecrosis-inducing toxins activating Rho small GTPases. Toxicon. 2001;39:1619-1627.

35. Flak TA, Goldman WE. Signalling and cellular specificity of airway nitric oxide production in pertussis. Cell Microbiol. 1999;1:51-60.

36. Cloud KA, Dillard JP. A lytic transglycosylase of *Neisseria gonorrhoeae* is involved in peptidoglycan-derived cytotoxin production. Infect Immun. 2002;70:2752-2757.

37. Flak TA, Goldman WE. Autotoxicity of nitric oxide in airway disease. Am J Respir Crit Care Med. 1996;154(4 Pt 2):S202-S206.

38. Ui M. Pertussis toxin as a valuable probe for G-protein involvement in signal transduction. In: Moss J, Vaughan M, eds. ADP-Ribosylating Toxins and G Proteins. Washington, DC: American Society for Microbiology; 1990:45-78.

39. Locht C, Antoine R. *Bordetella pertussis* protein toxins. In: Alouf JE, Freer JH, eds. The Comprehensive Sourcebook of Bacterial Protein Toxins. London: Academic Press; 1999:130-146.

40. Schaeffer LM, Weiss AA. Pertussis toxin and lipopolysaccharide influence phagocytosis of *Bordetella pertussis* by human monocytes. Infect Immun. 2001;69:7635-7641.

41. Caroff M, Brisson J, Martin A, Karibian D. Structure of the *Bordetella pertussis* 1414 endotoxin. FEBS Lett. 2000;477:8-14.

42. Peppler MS. Two physically and serologically distinct lipopolysaccharide profiles in strains of *Bordetella pertussis* and their phenotype variants. Infect Immun. 1984;43:224-232.

43. Ayme G, Caroff M, Chaby R, et al. Biological activities of fragments derived from *Bordetella pertussis* endotoxin: Isolation of a nontoxic, Shwartzman-negative lipid A possessing high adjuvant properties. Infect Immun. 1980;27:739-745.

44. Ray A, Redhead K, Selkirk S, Poole S. Variability in LPS composition, antigenicity and reactogenicity of phase variants of *Bordetella pertussis.* FEMS Microbiol Lett. 1991;63:211-217.

45. Shahin RD, Hamel J, Leef MF, Brodeur BR. Analysis of protective and nonprotective monoclonal antibodies specific for *Bordetella pertussis* lipooligosaccharide. Infect Immun. 1994;62:722-725.

46. Harvill ET, Preston A, Cotter PA, et al. Multiple roles for *Bordetella* lipopolysaccharide molecules during respiratory tract infection. Infect Immun. 2000;68:6720-6728.

47. Stibitz S, Aaronson W, Monack D, Falkow S. Phase variation in *Bordetella pertussis* by frameshift mutation in a gene for a novel two-component system. Nature. 1989;338:266-269.

48. Melton AR, Weiss AA. Environmental regulation of expression of virulence determinants in *Bordetella pertussis.* J Bacteriol. 1989;171:6206-6212.

49. Cotter PA, DiRita VJ. Bacterial virulence gene regulation: An evolutionary perspective. Annu Rev Microbiol. 2000;54:519-565.

50. Stockbauer KE, Fuchslocher B, Miller JF, Cotter PA. Identification and characterization of BipA, a Bordetella Bvg-intermediate phase protein. Mol Microbiol. 2001;39:65-78.

51. Merkel TJ, Stibitz S, Keith JM, et al. Contribution of regulation by the *bvg* locus to respiratory infection of mice by *Bordetella pertussis.* Infect Immun. 1998;66:4367-4373.

52. Martinez dTG, Cotter PA, Heininger U, et al. Neither the Bvg- phase nor the vrg6 locus of *Bordetella pertussis* is required for respiratory infection in mice. Infect Immun. 1998;66:2762-2768.

53. Boucher PE, Maris AE, Yang MS, Stibitz S. The response regulator BvgA and RNA polymerase alpha subunit C-terminal domain bind simultaneously to different faces of the same segment of promoter DNA. Mol Cell. 2003;11:163-173.

54. Hot D, Antoine R, Renauld-Mongenie G, et al. Differential modulation of *Bordetella pertussis* virulence genes as evidenced by DNA microarray analysis. Mol Genet Genom MGG. 2003;269:475-486.

55. Pittman M. Pertussis toxin: The cause of the harmful effects and prolonged immunity of whooping cough. A hypothesis. Rev Infect Dis. 1979;1:401-412.

56. Wirsing von Konig CH, Finger H. Role of pertussis toxin in causing symptoms of *Bordetella parapertussis* infection. Eur J Clin Microbiol Infect Dis. 1994;13:455-458.

57. Liese JG, Renner C, Stojanov S, Belohradsky BH. Clinical and epidemiological picture of *B. pertussis* and *B. parapertussis* infections after introduction of acellular pertussis vaccines. Arch Dis Child. 2003;88:684-687.

58. Toyota T, Kai Y, Kakizaki M, et al. Effects of islet-activating protein (IAP) on blood glucose and plasma insulin in healthy volunteers (Phase 1 studies). Tohoku J Exp Med. 1980;130:105-116.

59. WHO Statistical Information System. Statistics by country or region. 2004. Available at: www3.who.int/whosis/menu

60. Centers for Disease Control and Prevention. Pertussis outbreak among adults at an oil refinery—Illinois, August-October 2002. MMWR Morb Mortal Wkly Rep. 2003;52:1-4.

61. Lambert HJ. Epidemiology of a small pertussis outbreak in Kent County, Michigan. Public Health Rep. 1965;80:365-369.

62. Luttinger P. The epidemiology of pertussis. Am J Dis Child. 1916:290-315.

63. Centers for Disease Control. Pertussis—United States, 1982 and 1983. MMWR Morb Mortal Wkly Rep. 1984;33:573-575.

64. Farizo KM, Cochi SL, Zell ER, et al. Epidemiological features of pertussis in the United States, 1980-1989. Clin Infect Dis. 1992;14:708-719.

65. Centers for Disease Control and Prevention. Pertussis—United States, 1997-2000. MMWR Morb Mortal Wkly Rep. 2002;51:73-76.

66. von Konig CH, Halperin S, Riffelmann M, Guiso N. Pertussis of adults and infants. Lancet Infect Dis. 2002;2:744-750.

67. Centers for Disease Control and Prevention. Pertussis outbreak—Vermont, 1996. MMWR Morb Mortal Wkly Rep. 1997;46:822-826.

68. Wilder-Smith A, Earnest A, Ravindran S, Paton NI. High incidence of pertussis among Hajj pilgrims. Clin Infect Dis. 2003;37:1270-1272.

69. Postels-Multani S, Schmitt HJ, Wirsing von Konig CH, et al. Symptoms and complications of pertussis in adults. Infection. 1995;23:139-142.

70. Mayaud C, Bassinet L, Terrioux P, Parrot A. Clinical presentations of whooping cough in the adult: When should they be considered? Med Mal Infect. 2001;31:63S-74S.

71. Pierce C, Klein N, Peters M. Is leukocytosis a predictor of mortality in severe pertussis infection? Intensive Care Med. 2000;26:1512-1514.

72. Britten N, Wadsworth J. Long term respiratory sequelae of whooping cough in a nationally representative sample. Br Med J (Clin Res Ed). 1986;292:441-444.

73. Howenstine M, Eigen H, Tepper R. Pulmonary function in infants after pertussis. J Pediatr. 1991;118:563-566.

74. Berner R, Krause MF, Gordjani N, et al. Hemolytic uremic syndrome due to an altered factor H triggered by neonatal pertussis. Pediatr Nephrol. 2002;17:190-192.

75. Montgomery SM, Ehlin AG, Ekbom A, Wakefield AJ. Pertussis infection in childhood and subsequent type 1 diabetes mellitus. Diabet Med. 2002;19:986-993.

76. Skowronski DM, Buxton JA, Hestrin M, et al. Carotid artery dissection as a possible severe complication of pertussis in an adult: Clinical case report and review. Clin Infect Dis. 2003;36:e1-e4.

77. Halperin SA, Marrie TJ. Pertussis encephalopathy in an adult: Case report and review. Rev Infect Dis. 1991;13:1043-1047.

78. Deeks S, De Serres G, Boulianne N, et al. Failure of physicians to consider the diagnosis of pertussis in children. Clin Infect Dis. 1999;28:840-846.

79. Crowcroft NS, Booy R, Harrison T, et al. Severe and unrecognised: Pertussis in UK infants. Arch Dis Child. 2003;88:802-806.

80. Onorato IM, Wassilak SGF. Laboratory diagnosis of pertussis: The state of the art. Pediatr Infect Dis J. 1987;6:145-151.

81. Friedman RL. Pertussis: The disease and new diagnostic methods. Clin Microbiol Rev. 1988;1:365-376.

82. Halperin SA, Bortolussi R, Wort AJ. Evaluation of culture, immunofluorescence, and serology for the diagnosis of pertussis. J Clin Microbiol. 1989;27:752-757.

83. Aoyama T, Murase Y, Iwata T, et al. Comparison of blood-free medium (cyclodextrin solid medium) with Bordet-Gengou medium for clinical isolation of *Bordetella pertussis.* J Clin Microbiol. 1986;23:1046-1048.

84. Hallander HO, Reizenstein E, Renemar B, et al. Comparison of nasopharyngeal aspirates with swabs for culture of *Bordetella pertussis.* J Clin Microbiol. 1993;31:50-52.

85. Loeffelholz MJ, Thompson CJ, Long KS, Gilchrist MJR. Comparison of PCR, culture and direct fluorescent antibody testing for detection of *Bordetella pertussis.* J Clin Microbiol. 1999;37:2872-2876.

86. Lingappa JR, Lawrence W, West-Keefe S, et al. Diagnosis of community-acquired pertussis infection: Comparison of both culture and fluorescent-antibody assays with PCR detection using electrophoresis or dot blot hybridization. J Clin Microbiol. 2002;40:2908-2912.

87. Edelman K, Nikkari S, Ruuskanen O, et al. Detection of *Bordetella pertussis* by polymerase chain reaction and culture in the nasopharynx of erythromycin-treated infants with pertussis. Pediatr Infect Dis J. 1996;15:54-57.

88. Reizenstein E, Johansson B, Mardin L, et al. Diagnostic evaluation of polymerase chain reaction discriminative for *Bordetella pertussis, B. parapertussis,* and *B. bronchiseptica.* Diagn Microbiol Infect Dis. 1993;17:185-191.

89. Douglas E, Coote JG, Parton R, McPheat W. Identification of *Bordetella pertussis* in nasopharyngeal swabs by PCR amplification of a region of the adenylate cyclase gene. J Med Microbiol. 1993;38:140-144.

90. Birkebaek NH, Heron I, Skjodt K. *Bordetella pertussis* diagnosed by polymerase chain reaction. APMIS. 1994;102:291-294.

91. Li Z, Jansen DL, Finn TM, et al. Identification of *Bordetella pertussis* infection by shared-primer PCR. J Clin Microbiol. 1994;32:783-789.

92. Teunis PF, van der Heijden OG, de Melker HE, et al. Kinetics of the IgG antibody response to pertussis toxin after infection with *B. pertussis.* Epidemiol Infect. 2002;129:479-489.

93. Qin X, Turgeon DK, Ingersoll BP, et al. *Bordetella pertussis* PCR: Simultaneous targeting of signature sequences. Diagn Microbiol Infect Dis. 2002;43:269-275.

94. Cloud JL, Hymas WC, Turlak A, et al. Description of a multiplex Bordetella pertussis and *Bordetella parapertussis* LightCycler PCR assay with inhibition control. Diagn Microbiol Infect Dis. 2003;46:189-195.
95. Mooi FR, van Oirschot H, Heuvelman K, et al. Polymorphism in the *Bordetella pertussis* virulence factors P.69/pertactin and pertussis toxin in the Netherlands: Temporal trends and evidence for vaccine-driven evolution. Infect Immun. 1998;66:670-675.
96. Meade BD, Deforest A, Edwards KM, et al. Description and evaluation of serologic assays used in a multicenter trial of acellular pertussis vaccines. Pediatrics 1995;96 (3 Pt 2):570-575.
97. Halperin SA. Interpretation of pertussis serologic tests. Pediatr Infect Dis J. 1991; 10:791-792.
98. Goodman YE, Wort AJ, Jackson FL. Enzyme-linked immunosorbent assay for detection of pertussis immunoglobulin A in nasopharyngeal secretions as an indicator of recent infection. J Clin Microbiol. 1981;13:286-292.
99. Poynten M, Hanlon M, Irwig L, Gilbert GL. Serological diagnosis of pertussis: Evaluation of IgA against whole cell and specific *Bordetella pertussis* antigens as markers of recent infection. Epidemiol Infect. 2002;128:161-167.
100. Grimprel E, Njamkepo E, Begue P, Guiso N. Rapid diagnosis of pertussis in young infants: Comparison of culture, PCR, and infant's and mother's serology. Clin Diagn Lab Immunol. 1997;4:723-726.
101. Patriarca PA, Biellik RJ, Sanden G, et al. Sensitivity and specificity of clinical case definitions for pertussis. Am J Public Health. 1988;78:833-836.
102. Blackwelder WC, Storsaeter J, Olin P, Hallander HO. Acellular pertussis vaccines: Efficacy and evaluation of clinical case definitions. Am J Dis Child. 1991;145:1285-1289.
103. World Health Organization. Meeting on Case Definition of Pertussis. Geneva: World Health Organization; 1991.
104. Greco D, Salmaso S, Mastrantonio P, et al. A controlled trial of two acellular vaccines and one whole-cell vaccine against pertussis. N Engl J Med. 1996;334:341-348.
105. Cherry JD, Olin P. The science and fiction of pertussis vaccines. Pediatrics. 1999;104:1381-1383.
106. Granstrom M, Olinder-Nielsen AM, Holmblad P, et al. Specific immunoglobulin for treatment of whooping cough. Lancet. 1991;338:1230-1233.
107. Bruss JB, Malley R, Halperin S, et al. Treatment of severe pertussis: A study of the safety and pharmacology of intravenous pertussis immunoglobulin. Pediatr Infect Dis J. 1999;18:505-511.
108. Dodhia H, Miller E. Review of the evidence for the use of erythromycin in the management of persons exposed to pertussis. Epidemiol Infect. 1998;120:143-149.
109. Centers for Disease Control and Prevention. Hypertrophic pyloric stenosis in infants following pertussis prophylaxis with erythromycin—Knoxville, Tennessee, 1999. MMWR Morb Mortal Wkly Rep. 1999;48:1117-1120.
110. Anonymous. Vaccination against whooping cough. Br Med J. 1959;1:994.
111. Fine PEM, Clarkson JA. Reflections on the efficacy of pertussis vaccines. Rev Infect Dis. 1987;9:866-883.
112. Howson CP, Howe CH, Fineberg HV, eds. Adverse Effects of Pertussis and Rubella Vaccines. Washington, DC: National Academy Press; 1991.
113. Hodder SL, Mortimer EA Jr. Epidemiology of pertussis and reactions to pertussis vaccine. Epidemiol Rev. 1992;14:243-267.
114. Peter G, Easton JG, Halsey NA, for the Committee on Infectious Diseases. The relationship between pertussis vaccine and brain damage: Reassessment. Pediatrics. 1991;88:397.
115. Sato Y, Kimura M, Fukumi H. Development of a pertussis component vaccine in Japan. Lancet. 1984;1:122-126.
116. Anonymous. Placebo-controlled trial of two acellular pertussis vaccines in Sweden—Protective efficacy and adverse events. Lancet. 1988;1:955-960.
117. Miller JJ Jr, Silverberg RJ, Saito TM, Humber JB. An agglutinative reaction for *Haemophilus pertussis*. I. Persistence of agglutinins after vaccine. J Pediatr. 1943;22:637-651.
118. Storsaeter J, Hallander HO, Gustafsson L, Olin P. Levels of anti-pertussis antibodies related to protection after household exposure to *Bordetella pertussis*. Vaccine. 1998;16:1907-1914.
119. Cherry JD, Gornbein J, Heininger U, Stehr K. A search for serologic correlates of immunity to *Bordetella pertussis* cough illnesses. Vaccine. 1998;16:1901-1906.
120. De Magistris MT, Romano M, Nuti S, et al. Dissecting human T cell responses against *Bordetella* species. J Exp Med. 1988;168:1351-1362.
121. Mills KHG, Redhead K. Cellular immunity in pertussis. J Med Microbiol. 1993;39:163-164.
122. Cassone A, Ausiello CM, Urbani F, et al. Cell-mediated and antibody responses to *Bordetella pertussis* antigens in children vaccinated with acellular or whole-cell pertussis vaccines. The Progetto Pertosse-CMI Working Group. Arch Pediatr Adolesc Med. 1997;151:283-289.
123. Mills KHG, Ryan M, Ryan E, Mahon BP. A murine model in which protection correlates with pertussis vaccine efficacy in children reveals complementary roles for humoral and cell-mediated immunity in protection against *Bordetella pertussis*. Infect Immun. 1998;66:594-602.
124. Ausiello CM, Lande R, Urbani F, et al. Cell-mediated immunity and antibody responses to *Bordetella pertussis* antigens in children with a history of pertussis infection and in recipients of an acellular pertussis vaccine. J Infect Dis. 2000;181:1989-1995.
125. U.S. Food and Drug Administration, Center for Biologics Evaluation and Research. Vaccines licensed for immunization and distribution in the U.S. 2004. Available at: *www.fda.gov/cber/vaccine/licvacc.htm*
126. Edwards KM. Pertussis: An important target for maternal immunization. Vaccine. 2003;21:3483-3486.

127. Steketee RW, Wassilak SGF, Adkins WN Jr, et al. Evidence for a high attack rate and efficacy of erythromycin prophylaxis in a pertussis outbreak in a facility for the developmentally disabled. J Infect Dis. 1988;157:434-440.
128. Hoppe JE, for the Erythromycin Study Group. Comparison of erythromycin estolate and erythromycin ethylsuccinate for treatment of pertussis. Pediatr Infect Dis J. 1992;11:189-193.
129. Dodhia H, Crowcroft NS, Bramley JC, Miller E. UK guidelines for use of erythromycin chemoprophylaxis in persons exposed to pertussis. J Public Health Med. 2002;24:200-206.
130. Guris D. Treatment and chemoprophylaxis. In: National Immunization Program. Guidelines for the Control of Pertussis Outbreaks. Atlanta: Centers for Disease Control and Prevention; 2003.
131. Klein JO. Clarithromycin and azithromycin. Pediatr Infect Dis J. 1998;17:516-517.
132. Aoyama T, Sunakawa K, Iwata S, et al. Efficacy of short-term treatment of pertussis with clarithromycin and azithromycin. J Pediatr. 1996;129:761-764.
133. Pichichero ME, Hoeger WJ, Casey JR. Azithromycin for the treatment of pertussis. Pediatr Infect Dis J. 2003;22:847-849.
134. Roberts I, Gavin R, Lennon D. Randomized controlled trial of steroids in pertussis. Pediatr Infect Dis J. 1992;11:982-983.
135. Hewlett EL. Reemerging infections: Recent developments in pertussis. In: Scheld WM, Craig WA, Hughes JM, eds. Emerging Infections 2. Washington, DC: ASM Press; 1998:145-158.
136. Pavesio D, Ponzone A. Salbutamol and pertussis. Lancet. 1977;1:150-151.
137. Krantz I, Norrby SR, Trollfors B. Salbutamol vs. placebo for treatment of pertussis. Pediatr Infect Dis. 1985;4:638-640.
138. Mertsola J, Viljanen MK, Ruuskanen O. Salbutamol in the treatment of whooping cough. Scand J Infect Dis. 1986;18:593-594.

CHAPTER **228**

Streptobacillus moniliformis (Rat-Bite Fever)

RONALD G. WASHBURN

Rat-bite fever is a rare systemic febrile illness typically transmitted by the bite of a rat or other small rodent. The infection has a worldwide distribution and can be caused by either *Streptobacillus moniliformis* or *Spirillum minus,* bacteria commonly found in the oropharyngeal flora of rodents. Streptobacillary disease accounts for the vast majority of cases of rat-bite fever in the United States,[1] whereas *S. minus* (see Chapter 240) infections occur mainly in Asia. Table 228-1 compares the two different forms of rat-bite fever.

Illness following rat bites has been known in India for more than 2000 years,[2] and the characteristic syndrome of rat-bite fever was recorded in the United States as early as 1839.[3] The causative gram-negative bacillus, initially named *Streptothrix muris ratti,* was recovered from an infected individual in 1916.[4] In 1925, a blood culture isolate from a laboratory worker with fever, rash, and arthritis was called *S. moniliformis,* based on its morphologic resemblance to a beaded necklace.[5] In 1926, a similar organism, *Haverhillia multiformis,* was grown from the blood of patients during an epidemic illness resembling rat-bite fever in Haverhill, Massachusetts.[6] Both *H. multiformis* and *S. muris ratti* were subsequently shown to be identical to *S. moniliformis,* the causative agent of streptobacillary rat-bite fever.[2]

BACTERIOLOGY

S. moniliformis is a pleomorphic, nonmotile, nonsporulating, nonencapsulated gram-negative bacillus measuring 0.3 to 0.7 μm wide by 1 to 5 μm long. Filaments and beadlike chains up to 150 μm long may contain 1- to 3-μm-wide fusiform swellings.[7] The organism is microaerophilic, requiring a partial pressure of CO_2 between 8% and 10% for primary isolation. Trypticase soy agar or broth must be supplemented with 10% to 20% rabbit or horse serum, defibrinated blood, or ascites to support optimal growth. Alternatively, media may be sup-

TABLE 228-1 Comparison of Two Different Types of Rat-Bite Fever

	Streptobacillus moniliformis	*Spirillum minus*
Organism	Gram-negative bacillus	Gram-negative coiled rod
Geographic distribution	North America, Europe	Asia
Mode of transmission	Rat bite, ingestion	Rat bite
Clinical syndrome		
Ulceration of initial bite wound	No	Yes
Arthritis	Yes	No
Regional lymphadenopathy	No	Yes
Rash	Yes	Yes
Relapsing fever	Yes	Yes
Diagnosis	Culture, PCR	Direct visualization, xenodiagnosis
Therapy	Penicillin G	Penicillin G

PCR, polymerase chain reaction.

plemented with a papain digest of ox liver.[8] Sodium polyanethol sulfonate, a substance sometimes added to trypticase soy broth or thioglycollate broth to inhibit the antibacterial activity of human blood, impedes growth of *S. moniliformis* in concentrations of at least 0.0125%.[8,9]

On blood-agar plates, nonhemolytic cotton-like colonies, 1 to 2.5 mm in diameter appear after approximately 3 days of incubation at 37° C. In broth media, characteristic flocculent puffballs are seen at the bottom of the broth after 2 to 10 days. Penicillin-resistant L-phase variants may form either spontaneously or in the presence of penicillin both in vivo and in vitro.[10] Low muramic acid content in the cell envelope may contribute to propensity of *S. moniliformis* to produce L-forms,[11] which impart a slightly turbid appearance to broth media. Sugar fermentation is variable but often includes galactose, glucose, maltose, and salicin. Fatty acid analysis by gas-liquid chromatography is useful for rapid identification of *S. moniliformis* isolates.[12-15] In addition, sodium dodecyl sulfate-polyacrylamide gel electrophoresis patterns of cellular proteins may be useful for epidemiologic studies of Haverhill fever.[16]

EPIDEMIOLOGY

In the United States, persons who are at risk for percutaneous inoculation with *S. moniliformis* include animal laboratory personnel and individuals (especially children) inhabiting crowded urban dwellings or rural areas infested with wild rats.[1,17-23] Rat-bite fever is typically transmitted by the bite or scratch of rats, mice, squirrels, or carnivores that prey on those rodents, including cats, dogs, pigs, ferrets, and weasels.[17,24] One reported case followed the bite of a gerbil.[25] The infection may also be acquired by handling rats, with no apparent breach of intact skin,[18,26] or with a portal of entry such as varicella lesions.[27] From 50% to 100% of both wild and laboratory rats harbor *S. moniliformis* in their nasopharyngeal flora,[18,28-30] and they may develop otitis media.[31] Although healthy laboratory mice are generally not colonized with streptobacilli, they do share with rats the susceptibility to epizootic infections characterized by polyarthritis, septicemia, pneumonia, otitis media, and high rates of abortion.[2,29,32-34] *S. moniliformis* has also been reported to cause pleuritis in a koala,[35] cervical abscesses and pneumonia in guinea pigs,[36] and arthritis in turkeys, with positive cultures from sternal bursa and tendon sheath.

Pathophysiologically, the clinical disease is probably the consequence of failed local cutaneous defenses and bacterial dissemination. The few available published pathology reports described lymphocytic vasculitis and intravascular thrombi.[37]

Oral ingestion of organisms caused several epidemics of Haverhill fever (erythema arthriticum epidemicum), an illness clinically resembling rat-bite fever. Potential sources of such outbreaks include foods such as turkey, or milk or water contaminated with rat excrement.[5,6,8,18,38,40] Presumably, once ingested, *S. moniliformis* organisms gain access to the peripheral circulation by penetrating the gastrointestinal mucosa.

CLINICAL MANIFESTATIONS

A brief incubation period usually less than 10 days in duration (range 1 to 22 days) follows the bite of the rat. An abrupt onset of fever, chills, headache, vomiting, and severe migratory arthralgias and myalgias marks the beginning of clinical disease; by that time, the wound itself has usually already healed. Indeed, the diagnosis is often initially obscured by the patient's incognizance of a bite that probably occurred during sleep. Regional lymphadenopathy is minimal or absent, in contrast to *S. minus* infection. The peripheral white blood cell count may range as high as 30,000/mm³ with a leftward shift. Up to 25% of patients have false-positive serologic tests for syphilis.

Within 2 to 4 days after the onset of fever, a nonpruritic maculopapular, morbilliform, petechial, vesicular[39] or pustular[41] rash erupts over the palms, soles, and extremities. Skin lesions may become purpuric[37] or confluent, and they may eventually desquamate.[17] Approximately 50% of patients develop asymmetric polyarthritis or true septic arthritis concurrently with the rash or within a few days thereafter.[19,42-44,47] The knees are most commonly involved, followed by the ankles, elbows, wrists, shoulders, and hips.[38,45,46] Typically, fever subsides spontaneously after 3 to 5 days without specific antibiotic therapy, and the remaining symptoms gradually resolve within 2 weeks. However, fever may occasionally relapse in an irregular pattern for weeks or months,[10] producing a clinical picture of fever of undetermined origin, or arthritis may persist for as long as 2 years. Haverhill fever differs clinically from percutaneously acquired rat-bite fever chiefly in the heightened severity of vomiting and in the high incidence of pharyngitis.[8,17]

Reported complications of *S. moniliformis* infection include endocarditis,[18,38,44,48-51] myocarditis,[18,28] pericarditis,[2,48] meningitis,[51] pneumonia,[18,51] amnionitis,[52] and anemia.[2,28] Abscesses have been observed in virtually all organs, including brain,[53] liver, spleen, kidney, skin,[7,54] and the female genital tract.[15] In infants and young children, diarrhea and weight loss may be prominent.[18,22,51] Mortality of untreated cases ranges as high as 13%,[51] and endocarditis in the preantibiotic era was uniformly lethal. The majority of those intravascular infections involved valves previously damaged by rheumatic valvulitis or calcification.[38]

DIAGNOSIS

In a febrile patient with rash and recent rat exposure, the diagnosis can usually be narrowed to rat-bite fever or leptospirosis. However, the physician caring for a laboratory worker may step into the trap of ascribing a seemingly benign febrile illness to viral infection. Furthermore, without a positive exposure history, the proper diagnosis may be even more elusive, and diagnoses such as meningococcemia, enteric fever, drug reaction, and viral exanthem enter into consideration. When the rash involves the palms and soles, rat-bite fever may mimic Rocky Mountain spotted fever[55] or secondary syphilis. The presence of oligoarticular or migratory polyarthritis heightens concerns about disseminated gonococcal infection, Lyme disease, brucellosis, septic arthritis, infective endocarditis, collagen vascular disease, and acute rheumatic fever.

Direct visualization of pleomorphic bacillary organisms in Giemsa-, Wayson-, or Gram-stained smears of blood, joint fluid, and pus may provide an early clue to the diagnosis. However, laboratory diagnosis rests ultimately on culturing *S. moniliformis* using enriched media.[56] An enzyme-linked immunosorbent assay has been developed for detection of specific antibody against *S. moniliformis*.[57] More recently, polymerase chain reaction (PCR) techniques that amplify bacterial 16S ribosomal RNA were used to detect *S. moniliformis* infection in rodents[58] and a pediatric patient.[39]

THERAPY AND PREVENTION

Both agents of rat-bite fever, *S. moniliformis* and *Spirillum minus,* are susceptible to penicillin. In the past, procaine penicillin G was given as 600,000 units intramuscularly every 12 hours for 10 to 14 days.[2,17,42] Currently, intravenous penicillin G appears more appropriate. The Jarisch-Herxheimer reaction may complicate initial therapy of *S. minus* infections. Oral tetracycline, 500 mg every 6 hours, is preferred for penicillin-allergic patients.[2,12] Streptomycin, 7.5 mg/kg, can be given intramuscularly every 12 hours, although potential ototoxicity makes this less desirable. Limited experience indicates that erythromycin,[59] chloramphenicol,[14,55] clindamycin,[18,28] or ceftriaxone[37,41,47] might also be effective.

Most patients respond promptly to therapy. For individuals who appear well after 5 to 7 days, therapy can be completed with an additional week of oral penicillin V or ampicillin, 500 mg every 6 hours. Patients with mild disease can probably be treated orally for the entire course.

Endocarditis is so rare that optimal therapy is uncertain. Probably, 4 weeks of intravenous penicillin, with or without streptomycin, is adequate. A total daily dose of 20 million units has been advocated for patients whose isolates are resistant to 0.1 μg/mL.[49]

After a rodent bite, the wound should be thoroughly cleaned, and tetanus prophylaxis should be administered if warranted by the patient's immunization history. A 3-day course of oral penicillin, 2 g/day, would seem reasonable, although the prophylactic efficacy of penicillin in this setting is unknown, and the patient should be advised to report any subsequent symptoms. Measures to limit the incidence of rat-bite fever include eradication of rats in urban areas, avoidance of nonpasteurized milk and potentially contaminated water, and the use of gloves by laboratory workers when handling rodents.

REFERENCES

1. Anderson LC, Leary SL, Manning PJ. Rat-bite fever in animal research laboratory personnel. Lab Anim Sci. 1983;33:292-294.
2. Roughgarden JW. Antimicrobial therapy of rat-bite fever. Arch Intern Med. 1965;116:39-54.
3. Wilcox W. Violent symptoms from bite of rat. Am J Med Sci. 1839;26:245.
4. Blake FC. Etiology of rat-bite fever. J Exp Med. 1916;23:39.
5. Levaditi C, Nicolau S, Poincloux P. Sur le rôle étiologique de *Streptobacillus moniliformis* (nov spec) dans 1-erythème polymorphe aigu septicémique. C R Acad Sci. 1925;180:1188.
6. Parker F Jr, Hudson NP. The etiology of Haverhill fever (erythema arthriticum epidemicum). Am J Pathol. 1926;2:357-379.
7. Torres A, Cuende E, De Pablos M, et al. Remitting seronegative symmetrical synovitis with pitting edema associated with subcutaneous *Streptobacillus moniliformis* abscess. J Rheumatol. 2001;28:1696-1698.
8. Shanson DC, Pratt J, Greene P. Comparison of media with and without "panmede" for the isolation of *Streptobacillus moniliformis* from blood cultures and observations on the inhibitory effect of sodium polyanethol sulphonate. J Med Microbiol. 1985;19:181-186.
9. Lambe DW Jr, McPhedran AM, Mertz JA, et al. *Streptobacillus moniliformis* isolated from a case of Haverhill fever: Biochemical characterization and inhibitory effect of sodium polyanethol sulfonate. Am J Clin Pathol. 1973;60:854-860.
10. Dolman CE, Kerr De, Chang H, et al. Two cases of rat-bite fever due to *Streptobacillus moniliformis*. Can J Public Health. 1951;42:228-241.
11. Knipp LH, Sokatch JR. The chemical composition of the cell envelope of *Streptobacillus moniliformis*. Can J Microbiol. 1969;15:665-669.
12. Edwards R, Finch RG. Characterisation and antibiotic susceptibilities of *Streptobacillus moniliformis*. J Med Microbiol. 1986;21:39-42.
13. Rowbotham TJ. Rapid identification of *Streptobacillus moniliformis*. Lancet. 1983;2:567.
14. Rygg M, Brunn CF. Rat bite fever *(Streptobacillus moniliformis)* with septicemia in a child. Scand J Infect Dis. 1992;24:535-540.
15. Pins MR, Holden JM, Yang JM, et al. Isolation of presumptive *Streptobacillus moniliformis* from abscesses associated with the female genital tract. Clin Inf Dis. 1996;22:471-476.
16. Costas M, Owen RJ. Numerical analysis of electrophoretic protein patterns of *Streptobacillus moniliformis* strains from human, murine, and avian infections. J Med Microbiol. 1987;23:303-311.
17. Taber LH, Feigin RD. Spirochetal infections. Pediatr Clin North Am. 1979;26:410-411.
18. McHugh TP, Bartlett RL, Raymond JI. Rat bite fever: Report of a fatal case. Ann Emerg Med. 1985;14:1116-1118.
19. Anderson D, Marrie TJ. Septic arthritis due to *Streptobacillus moniliformis*. Arthritis Rheum. 1987;30:229-230.
20. Cole JS, Stoll RW, Bulger RJ. Rat-bite fever: Report of three cases. Ann Intern Med. 1969;71:979-981.
21. Collins CH. Laboratory-Acquired Infections: History, Incidence, Causes, and Prevention. London: Butterworths; 1983:7-13.
22. Raffin BJ, Freemark M. Streptobacillary rat-bite fever: A pediatric problem. Pediatrics. 1979;64:214-217.
23. Wullenweber M. *Streptobacillus moniliformis*—A zoonotic pathogen. Lab Anim. 1995;29:1-15.
24. Peel MM. Dog-associated bacterial infections in humans: Isolates submitted to an Australian reference laboratory, 1981-1992. Pathology. 1993;25:379-384.
25. Wilkins EGL, Millar JGB, Cockcroft PM, et al. Rat-bite fever in a gerbil breeder. J Infect. 1988;16:177-180.
26. Fordham JN, McKay-Ferguson E, Davies A, Blyth T. Rat bite fever without the bite. Ann Rheum Dis. 1992;51:411-412.
27. Prager L, Frenck RW Jr. *Streptobacillus moniliformis* infection in a child with chickenpox. Pediatr Infect Dis J. 1994;13:417-418.
28. Taylor AF, Stephenson TG, Giese HA, et al. Rat-bite fever in a college student—California. MMWR Morb Mortal Wkly Rep. 1984;33:318-320.
29. Strangeways WI. Rats as carriers of *Streptobacillus moniliformis*. J Pathol. 1933;37:45-51.
30. Koopman JP, van den Brink ME, Vennix PPCA, et al. Isolation of *Streptobacillus moniliformis* from the middle ear of rats. Lab Anim. 1991;25:35-39.
31. Wullenweber M, Jonas C, Kunstyr I. *Streptobacillus moniliformis* isolated from otitis media of conventionally kept laboratory rats. J Exp Anim Sci. 1992;35:49-57.
32. Wullenweber M, Kaspareit-Rittinghausen J, Faroug M. *Streptobacillus moniliformis* epizootic in barrier-maintained C57BL/6J mice and susceptibility to infection of different strains of mice. Lab Anim Sci. 1990;40:608-612.
33. Glastonbury JR, Morton JG, Matthews LM. *Streptobacillus moniliformis* infection in Swiss white mice. J Vet Diagn Invest. 1996;8:202-209.
34. Taylor JD, Stephens CP, Duncan RG, Singleton GR. Polyarthritis in wild mice *(Mus musculus)* caused by *Streptobacillus moniliformis*. Aust Vet J. 1994;71:143-145.
35. Russell EG, Straube EF. Streptobacillary pleuritis in a koala. J Wild Dis. 1979;15:391-394.
36. Kirchner BK, Lake SG, Wightman SR. Isolation of *Streptobacillus moniliformis* from a guinea pig with granulomatous pneumonia. Lab Anim Sci. 1992;42:519-521.
37. Ojukwu IC, Christy C. Rat-bite fever in children: case report and review. Scan J Infect Dis. 2002; 34:474-477.
38. McEvoy MB, Noah ND, Pilsworth R. Outbreak of fever caused by *Streptobacillus moniliformis*. Lancet. 1987;2:1361-1363.
39. Berger C, Altwegg M, Meyer A, et al. Broad range polymerase chain reaction for diagnosis of rat-bite fever caused by *Streptobacillus moniliformis*. Pediatr Infect Dis J. 2001; 20:1181-1182.
40. Place EH, Sutton LE. Infection with *Streptobacillus moniliformis*. Arch Intern Med. 1934;5:659.
41. Cunningham BB, Paller AS, Katz BZ. Rat bite fever in a pet lover. J Am Acad Dermatol. 1998;38:330-332.
42. Mandel DR. Streptobacillary fever: An unusual cause of infectious arthritis. Clev Clin Q. 1985;52:203-205.
43. Rumley RL, Patrone NA, White L. Rat-bite fever as a cause of septic arthritis: A diagnostic dilemma. Ann Rheum Dis. 1987;46:793-795.
44. Rupp ME. *Streptobacillus moniliformis* endocarditis: Case report and review. Clin Infect Dis. 1992;14:769-772.
45. Azimi P. Pets can be dangerous. Pediatr Infect Dis J. 1990;9:670.
46. Holroyd KJ, Reiner AP, Dick JD. *Streptobacillus moniliformis* polyarthritis mimicking rheumatoid arthritis: An urban case of rat bite fever. Am J Med. 1988;85:711-714.
47. Hockman DE, Pence CD, Whittler RR, et al. Septic arthritis of the hip secondary to rat bite fever. Clin Orthop 2000;380:173-176.
48. Carbeck RB, Murphy JF, Britt EM. Streptobacillary rat-bite fever with massive pericardial effusion. JAMA. 1967;201:703-704.
49. McCormack RC, Kaye D, Hook EW. Endocarditis due to *Streptobacillus moniliformis:* A report of two cases and review of the literature. JAMA. 1967;200:77-79.
50. Simon MW, Wilson D. *Streptobacillus moniliformis* endocarditis: A case report. Clin Pediatr. 1986;25:110-111.
51. Sens MA, Brown EW, Wilson LR, et al. Fatal *Streptobacillus moniliformis* infection in a two month old infant. Am J Clin Pathol. 1989;91:612-616.
52. Faro S, Walker C, Pierson RL. Amnionitis with intact amniotic membranes involving *Streptobacillus moniliformis*. Obstet Gynecol. 1980;55S:9S-11S.
53. Dijkmans BAC, Thomeer RTWM, Vielvoye GJ, et al. Brain abscess due to *Streptobacillus moniliformis* and *Actinobacterium meyerii*. Infection. 1984;12:34-36.
54. Vasseur E, Joly P, Nouvellon M, et al. Cutaneous abscess: a rare complication of *Streptobacillus moniliformis* infection. Br J Dermatol. 1993;129:95-96.
55. Portnoy BL, Satterwhite TK, Dyckman JD. Rat bite fever misdiagnosed as Rocky Mountain spotted fever. South Med J. 1979;72:607-609.
56. Anonymous. Rat-bite fever-New Mexico, 1996. MMWR Morb Mortal Wkly Rep. 1998;47:89-91.
57. Boot R, Bakker RH, Thuis H, et al. An enzyme-linked immunosorbent assay (ELISA) for monitoring rodent colonies for *Streptobacillus moniliformis* antibodies. Lab Anim. 1993;27:350-357.
58. Boot R, Oosterhuis A, Thuis HCW. PCR for the detection of *Streptobacillus moniliformis*. Lab Anim. 2002;36:200-208.
59. Konstantopoulos K, Skarpas P, Hitjazis F, et al. Rat-bite fever in a Greek child. Scand J Infect Dis. 1992;24:531-533.

CHAPTER **229**

Legionella

PAUL H. EDELSTEIN

NICHOLAS P. CIANCIOTTO

HISTORY

Legionnaires' disease is an acute pneumonic illness caused by gram-negative bacilli of the genus *Legionella,* the most common of which is *Legionella pneumophila.* Pontiac fever is a febrile, nonpneumonic, systemic illness closely associated with, if not caused by, *Legionella* species. *Legionellosis* is the term that encompasses all diseases caused by, or presumed to be caused by, the *Legionella* bacteria, including legionnaires' disease, focal nonpulmonary infections, and Pontiac fever.

Legionnaires' disease was first recognized when it caused an epidemic of pneumonia at a Pennsylvania State American Legion convention in Philadelphia in 1976; 221 people were affected, and 34 died. Despite intensive laboratory investigation, the cause of the outbreak went undetected for many months. An epidemiologic investigation determined that the disease was most likely airborne and focused primarily at one convention hotel, which closed because of adverse publicity.[1] About 6 months later, two investigators at the United States Centers for Disease Control and Prevention, Joseph McDade and Charles Shepard, announced that they had discovered the etiologic agent, a fastidious gram-negative bacillus.[2] Because of the historical association with the American Legion convention, this disease is now called legionnaires' disease, and the etiologic agents belong to the family *Legionellaceae,* with *L. pneumophila* being the agent responsible for the 1976 Philadelphia epidemic. Use of an antibody test for the disease showed that several prior unsolved outbreaks of pneumonia had been legionnaires' disease, including epidemics investigated in the 1950s and 1960s.[3,4] The availability of diagnostic tests uncovered a 6-year-long epidemic of legionnaires' disease amongst British tourists staying at one hotel in Spain.[5] An unsolved epidemic of a nonpneumonic febrile illness was also found to have resulted from exposure to *Legionella* bacteria; this illness was termed Pontiac fever, after Pontiac, Michigan, where this had occurred.[6,7] As with legionnaires' disease, prior epidemics of Pontiac fever had occurred as early as 1949 without determination of an etiology.[8] Bacterial culture isolates from the 1940s through the 1960s were found to be *Legionella* bacteria, although at the time they had been thought to be rickettsial agents.[9-14] Thus, both the organism and the disease had been studied decades before, but major advances in technology and epidemiology were required to properly classify the disease and determine its cause.

Even with identification of *L. pneumophila* in 1977 as the cause of legionnaires' disease, the source of the bacterium, factors promoting its multiplication and spread, and ways to abort epidemics of legionnaires' disease remained uncertain for several years. Epidemics of the disease, especially nosocomial ones, commonly lasted for years even though the cause of the disease was recognized.[15-21] Eventually it was discovered that *L. pneumophila* and other *Legionella* species were naturally occurring aquatic bacteria that had a propensity for growing in warm water, most particularly in cooling towers, water heaters, and potable-water plumbing. These discoveries led to the end of several multiyear outbreaks of the disease, and to methods for preventing the disease.[22] Now, because of improved diagnostic, environmental detection, and remediation methods, it is unusual for outbreaks of legionnaires' disease to last more than a week or two.

Legionnaires' disease still occurs, both in sporadic and in epidemic form, sometimes involving many hundreds of victims.[23,24] The disease, although a relatively rare cause of community-acquired pneumonia,

can cause high morbidity and mortality if treated improperly. Our current knowledge about the disease has resulted in the ability to abort epidemics in days, to effectively treat affected patients, and to reduce the frequency of the disease by making modifications in building design and maintenance. From a scientific basis, discovery of the disease led to major advances in the study of intracellular pathogens and their interactions with host cells.

THE ETIOLOGIC AGENT

The *Legionella* species are small gram-negative bacilli with fastidious growth requirements. Proteins rather than carbohydrates are used as an energy source. Obligate aerobes, the bacteria grow at temperatures ranging from 20° to 42° C. The *Legionella* bacteria are in the taxonomic order *Legionellales,* which includes the families *Coxiellaceae* and *Legionellaceae. Coxiella burnetii,* an obligate intracellular parasite and the etiologic agent of Q fever, is a member of the *Coxiellaceae,* and the closest relative of the *Legionellaceae.* Three different genera have been proposed for the *Legionellaceae: Legionella, Fluoribacter,* and *Tatlockia;* however, the latter two generic names have never been widely used or accepted, and the single genus *Legionella* is almost universally used to describe all species. L-Cysteine is required for the growth of all but one of the clinically important *Legionella* species, and this amino acid is needed for the initial growth of all described *Legionella* species from environmental or clinical sources. Soluble iron is required for optimal growth and for the initial isolation of the bacterium from both clinical and environmental sources. Iron, L-cysteine, α-ketoglutarate, and charcoal-containing yeast extract agar buffered with an organic buffer (BCYEα agar) is the preferred growth medium for clinical isolation. Clinically important *Legionella* species grow best at 35° C in humidified air on BCYEα medium, usually in 2 to 5 days after inoculation of plates. An incubation of up to 14 days may very rarely be required for the isolation of unusual *Legionella* species.

More than 49 different *Legionella* species have been described, 20 of which have been reported to infect humans.[25,26] *L. pneumophila* contains at least 16 different serogroups; seven other species contain two different serogroups, with the remaining species containing only one serogroup each. *L. pneumophila* serogroup 1 caused the 1976 Philadelphia outbreak and is the cause of 70% to 90% of all cases of legionnaires' disease for which there has been a bacterial isolate.[27,28] *L. pneumophila* serogroup 1 can be further divided into multiple subtypes using a variety of serologic, other phenotypic, and genetic methods. One particular subtype of *L. pneumophila* serogroup 1 causes 67% to 90% of cases of legionnaires' disease due to *L. pneumophila,* and 85% of cases due to *L. pneumophila* serogroup 1; this subtype is distinguished by its reactivity with a particular monoclonal antibody, and it is variously termed the Pontiac, the Joly monoclonal type 2 (MAb2), or the Dresden monoclonal type 3/1 (MAb 3/1) monoclonal subtype.[29] The predominance of the Pontiac subtype has implications for diagnosis (see later).

Most clinical microbiology laboratories should be able to identify *Legionella* bacteria to the genus level by detection of their typical colony morphology and Gram stain appearance, by determination of L-cysteine growth dependence, and by excluding possible mimics by using standard microbiology identification techniques (Fig. 229-1). Identification of *L. pneumophila* serogroup 1, the most common clinical isolate, can be accomplished by sophisticated clinical microbiology laboratories using relatively simple serologic testing. Identification of other *L. pneumophila* serogroups, and other *Legionella* species, is often much more difficult and is best left to specialized reference laboratories.[26] This is because these bacteria are relatively inert in the use of commonly tested biochemical substrates, and they require sophisticated phenotypic, serologic, and molecular testing. Reference laboratory-based phenotypic testing of bacteria, including determination of cellular fatty acids and ubiquinones and protein electrophoresis, can often be used to identify the bacteria. Definitive identification is based on both immunologic detection of surface antigens and bacterial DNA sequencing.

FIGURE 229-1. A, Typical opal-like colony of *L. pneumophila* grown on BCYEα agar. **B,** Gram stain of *L. pneumophila* taken from culture plate. Basic fuchsin should be used as the counterstain, as safranin stains the bacterium poorly.

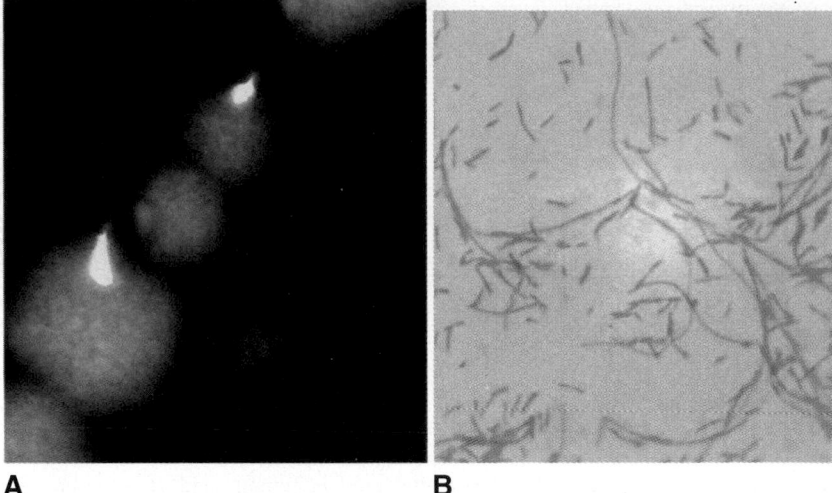

A   B

MICROBIAL ECOLOGY

The *Legionella* bacteria are found in our aqueous environment in a large variety of habitats (lakes, streams, and even coastal oceans), at temperatures ranging from 5° to greater than 50° C.[26] Warm water (25° to 40° C) supports the highest concentration of these bacteria, and warm water is the major bacterial reservoir leading to legionnaires' disease. Free-living amebas (*Naegleria, Acanthamoeba, Hartmannella,* and others) in the same waters support the intracellular growth and survival of the *Legionella* bacteria.

The interaction between amebas and *Legionella* bacteria has been studied most comprehensively for *L. pneumophila,* which is a facultative intracellular parasite of several different amebas.[30,31] The bacteria multiply many thousand-fold within the amebas (Fig. 229-2). When faced with inimical environmental factors, such as pH changes, absence of nutrients, or temperature alteration, the *Legionella*-infected amebas encyst, guaranteeing the survival of both the host and parasite until more favorable conditions allow excystment. In both natural and manmade waters, *Legionella*-infected amebas are found in consortia of many different microorganisms, all of which exist in a biofilm.

In addition to surviving within amebas, freely living *Legionella* bacteria can enter a low metabolic state termed viable but not cultivatable, which makes them difficult to recover from the environment and probably more resistant to biocides.[32] The *Legionella* bacteria, amebas, and other microorganisms constantly escape from the biofilm (the sessile phase) because of water flow and pressure fluxes into a freely

moving phase (or planktonic phase) and then return to the sessile phase. Environmental changes that disrupt the biofilm can result in the sudden and massive release of *Legionella* bacteria into the surrounding water. If this water is then aerosolized or aspirated, the bacteria can cause illness in a susceptible host. Almost all cases of legionnaires' disease result from *Legionella* contamination of warm manmade waters, such as water heaters, air conditioning and other types of cooling towers, warm-water baths, warm-water plumbing systems, and recirculating water systems. *Legionella* bacteria are present in very low concentrations in disinfectant-treated cold potable water, usually at levels of less than one bacterium per liter; up to 50 L of such water may need to be sampled to detect a single *Legionella* bacterium. However, within water distribution pipes, especially older pipes with low or no water flow, the bacterial density can be amplified by growth in biofilm. The bacteria can be further amplified in the presence of warm conditions, such as those found in many buildings or heat rejection devices. *Legionella* bacteria concentrations in air conditioning cooling towers range from 10^2 to 10^8 colony-forming units (cfu)/L. Up to 80% of air conditioning cooling towers tested contain the bacterium, as do 5% to 30% of home and industrial water heaters and hot water plumbing.[26] Contaminated water that is then aerosolized serves as a disseminator of the bacteria into the environment. The concentration of *Legionella* bacteria in a particular environmental site may spontaneously fluctuate over a wide range, presumably because of extrabacterial factors such as temperature, the presence of biofilm-disruptive forces, the type and concentration of other microorganisms in the biofilm consortium, and the concentrations of a variety of organic and inorganic compounds.

PATHOGENESIS

Legionnaires' disease is initiated by inhalation, and probably microaspiration, of *Legionella* bacteria into the lungs. Although *Legionella* bacteria are ubiquitous in our environment, they rarely cause disease. A number of factors must occur simultaneously before legionnaires' disease is possible. These factors include the presence of virulent strains in an environmental site; a means for dissemination of the bacteria, such as by aerosolization; and proper environmental conditions allowing the survival and inhalation of an infectious dose of the bacteria by a susceptible host. Strains of different virulences, at least for guinea pigs, exist in the same species, and some species and serogroups are more virulent than others.[33-36] The reasons for different virulences of strains even within the same species are not known with certainty, but they may include aerosol stability, ability to grow within amebas, and surface hydrophobicity.

The infectious form of the bacterium is not known, but in all cases the bacteria originate from water. Several possibilities exist for the in-

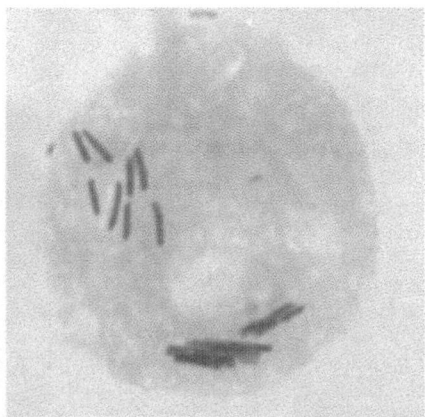

FIGURE 229-2. Gimenez stain of *L. pneumophila* growing in an ameba. The bacteria are much smaller and more uniform in morphology than when they are taken from a culture plate (see Fig. 229-1B).

fectious particle causing disease, including *Legionella* bacteria contained within an amebal cyst, a particle of biofilm containing *Legionella* bacteria and other microorganisms, and freely dispersed extracellular planktonic *Legionella* bacteria. The physiologic state of the *Legionella* bacteria causing infection is also unknown, but it may involve the stationary or logarithmic growth phase, or the newly described sporelike form of the bacterium.[37] The physiologic state of *Legionella* bacteria may be important for its virulence, as virulence increases when the bacterium is grown in amebas, in the late stationary phase in vitro, or as the sporelike form.[37-39] Because aerosolization of dispersed logarithmic phase bacteria rapidly kills most bacteria within seconds to minutes, it makes sense that the infectious form of the organism would be protected by biofilm, within an amebal cyst, or as the spore-like form; all of these infectious forms protect the bacteria from heat, cold, and disinfectants. The bacterial inoculum required to cause legionnaires' disease is unknown. Guinea pigs, which appear to be quite susceptible to experimentally introduced *L. pneumophila* pneumonia, develop asymptomatic infection with inocula as low as 10 to 100 bacteria when delivered by aerosol, disease with an inoculum of about 1000 bacteria, and death after infection with 10,000 bacteria. A packet of bacteria in amebal cysts or in a biofilm fragment easily contains more than 1000 bacteria, making it possible that inhalation of a single infected amebal cyst or biofilm fragment could cause disease. Survival of extracellular *L. pneumophila* in an aerosol depends on relative humidity, with different relative humidity optima for each strain, meaning that the disease-causing critical concentration of bacteria in the environment may differ even for the same strain, depending on environmental conditions.[40]

Water contaminated with a sufficient concentration of virulent *Legionella* bacteria can be aerosolized by water-cooled heat-rejection devices such as air conditioning cooling towers, whirlpool spas, shower heads, water misters, and some respiratory equipment. In addition, microaspiration of the contaminated water can also produce disease. Once the bacteria enter the lung, they are phagocytosed by alveolar macrophages, and perhaps also internalized by respiratory epithelial cells.[41] The *Legionella* bacteria produce virulence factors that enhance phagocytosis and then allow intracellular survival and growth (see later). After sufficient intracellular growth, the bacteria kill the macrophage, escape into the extracellular environment, and are then rephagocytosed by other macrophages. The bacterial concentration in the lung increases considerably as a result of this amplification mechanism; for example, the number of *L. pneumophila* in guinea pig lungs increases by about 1,000,000-fold over the 3-day period after initial infection.

Following this intracellular multiplication, neutrophils, additional macrophages, and erythrocytes infiltrate the alveoli, and capillary leakage results in edema.[42] Chemokines and cytokines released by infected macrophages help trigger the severe inflammatory response.[43] In the A/J mouse model of legionnaires' disease,[44] the relevant proinflammatory chemokines and cytokines include cytokine-induced neutrophil chemoattractant (KC), macrophage inflammatory protein (MIP)-2, tumor necrosis factor (TNF)-α, interleukin (IL)-12, IL-18, and interferon (IFN)-γ.[45-47] A variety of known and unknown bacterial factors prevent killing of the bacterium by neutrophils or serum complement. Systemic spread of the bacteria may be accomplished by infection of circulating monocytes. The mechanisms for systemic toxicity of the disease are unclear, but may be related to cytokine production during infection. Immune control of the infection is mediated by the cellular immune system.[48]

The helper T-cell 1 (Th1) T-cell response and its associated cytokines are particularly crucial for the clearance of *Legionella* organisms.[46] IFN-γ activation renders macrophages nonpermissive for *L. pneumophila* growth.[49] This change in host permissiveness involves, among other things, a reduction in intracellular iron, a factor that is necessary for *L. pneumophila* replication.[50] Antibodies develop during the course of *L. pneumophila* infection, but the humoral immune response does not appear to be critical for host defense. The ability of *L. pneumophila* to grow within macrophages is central to pathogenesis.[26] Indeed, the majority of legionellae seen in lung samples are associated

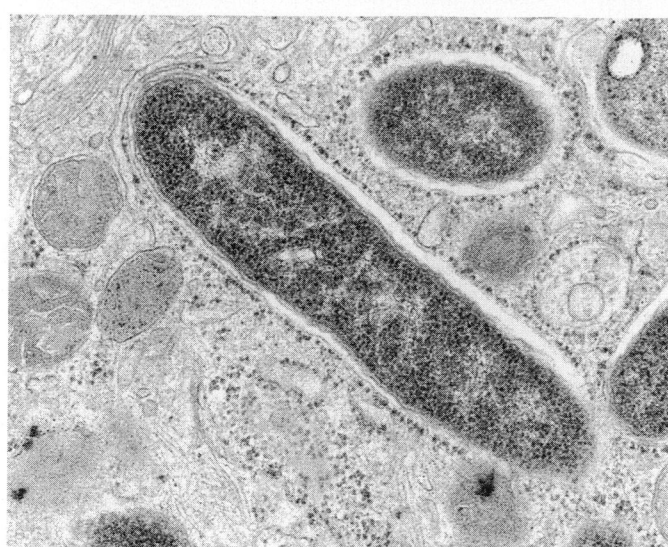

FIGURE 229-3. Electron micrograph of *L. pneumophila* growing within a phagosome of an alveolar macrophage. Note the characteristic ribosomal studding of the phagosome.

with alveolar macrophages. Furthermore, the susceptibility of an animal species correlates with the ability of *L. pneumophila* to infect its macrophages, and bacterial mutants that are impaired for in vitro infection of macrophages have reduced virulence. It is widely believed that the adaptation of *L. pneumophila* to protozoan niches in nature engendered in it the ability to infect mammalian phagocytes.[51] *L. pneumophila* enters the macrophage by conventional or by coiling phagocytosis[52-54]; both are processes that utilize the host cell actin cytoskeleton.[55] Opsonization with the C3 component of complement can promote phagocytosis,[56] but entry by this pathway dampens the oxidative burst and thereby may enhance bacterial intracellular survival. However, opsonin-independent phagocytosis also appears to be important.[39] Even in the event that the oxidative burst is triggered, *L. pneumophila* strains may be resistant to hydrogen peroxide, superoxide anion, and hydroxyl radicals. After entry, legionellae reside within a nascent phagosome (Fig. 229-3) that does not fuse with endosomes or lysosomes,[57-59] thereby avoiding acidification and degradative enzymes. The phagosome soon associates with smooth vesicles, mitochondria, and rough endoplasmic reticulum.[60-62] Later in the intracellular cycle, the *L. pneumophila* phagosome fuses with acidic lysosomal compartments, but bacterial growth continues.[63] Ultimately, the *L. pneumophila* phagosome fills the host cell. Upon nutrient depletion (e.g., amino acid depletion), *L. pneumophila* is believed to convert to a flagellated form that is primed to seek out and infect new host cells.[37,64] Macrophage death involves an early induction of apoptosis and a late necrosis that appears to be triggered by a pore-forming activity.[65,66] Drawing on the differences in susceptibility of mouse strains, investigators are determining the genetic loci that control the permissiveness of macrophages to *L. pneumophila* infection.[67]

Processes in addition to macrophage infection probably contribute to disease by *L. pneumophila*. The bacterium may replicate or, at a minimum, must temporarily survive within the extracellular spaces of the alveoli.[68] The ability of *L. pneumophila* strains to resist complement and cationic peptides may be especially relevant for extracellular survival, particularly following the onset of inflammation.[69-71] The examination of infected lung tissue suggests that *L. pneumophila* may also grow within the alveolar epithelium.[72] On the basis of in vitro models, the microbe grows within both alveolar type I and type II cells.[73,74] The importance of extramacrophage processes is also implied by the fact that mutants can be isolated that are not defective for macrophage infection but are impaired for virulence in animals.[75]

Neither the pathogenesis nor the etiology of Pontiac fever is known with certainty. Pontiac fever is caused by inhalation of a disease-causing environmental aerosol derived from water containing microorganisms including *Legionella* bacteria. Most patients with this disease have serum anti-*Legionella* antibody in higher concentrations than that found in the normally healthy population.[7,76] The prevalent assumption is that the illness is due to inhalation of the *Legionella* bacteria. However, because the aerosols contain a vast array of other microorganisms and toxins, including endotoxin, it is unclear whether the disease is due to inhalation of endotoxin, to inhalation of a number of microorganisms, to inhalation of *Legionella* bacteria alone, or to a combination of all these agents.[7,77,78] Infections with non-*Legionella* bacteria can produce *Legionella* antibodies, so the presence of such antibodies does not prove that Pontiac fever is due solely to *Legionella* infection or intoxication. Bath water fever, a clinical syndrome thought to be due to endotoxin inhalation, is very similar to Pontiac fever, suggesting that Pontiac fever may also be caused by endotoxin inhalation.[79-82] Several cases of Pontiac fever have been reported to have occurred in people exposed to environmental contamination that in some others caused legionnaires' disease; whether this is really Pontiac fever or mild legionnaires' disease is open to question and does not help answer the question of etiology and pathogenesis.[83-85] Perhaps the strongest evidence implicating systemic infection with *Legionella* bacteria as the cause of Pontiac fever has been the very rare reports of positive *L. pneumophila* urinary antigen tests or positive cultures in patients with Pontiac fever.[83-87] The rarity of such cases and the rapid recovery without antibiotic therapy argue against systemic infection as the main cause of Pontiac fever.

L. pneumophila Virulence Factors

A variety of surface structures have been implicated in *L. pneumophila* pathogenesis. Type IV pili modestly promote bacterial attachment to macrophages and epithelial cells,[88] and flagella promote invasion independent of adherence.[89] The major outer membrane protein is a porin that also serves as a binding site for complement components and thus mediates opsonophagocytosis.[90] The macrophage infectivity potentiator (Mip) protein is a surface-exposed peptidylprolyl isomerase that is required for the early stages of intracellular infection and for full virulence in animals,[91,92] whereas the heat shock protein Hsp60 has been shown to enhance epithelial cell invasion.[93] The *rtxA* gene promotes adherence and virulence, although the structure and localization of its protein product are unclear.[94] Legionella lipopolysaccharide (LPS) contains some endotoxic activity, and changes in LPS have correlated with increases in serum resistance, intracellular growth, and virulence.[95] Finally, the *rcp* gene, which appears to encode a lipid A modifying enzyme, confers resistance to cationic peptides and promotes macrophage and lung infection.[70]

L. pneumophila secretes a variety of proteins, degradative enzymes and putative toxins.[96-98] The release of proteins by *L. pneumophila* into the extracellular milieu is dependent on two different protein secretion systems–the so-called types II and IV protein secretion systems. Acid phosphatases, an RNAse, a zinc metalloprotease, mono-, di- and triacylglycerol lipases, a phospholipase A, a lysophospholipase A, and a phospholipase C are all secreted via the type II system.[99-101] Mutations within the genes encoding the type II secretion system diminish infectivity for macrophages, protozoa, and animals.[101-104] Although not essential for intracellular growth, the secreted zinc protease is produced during infection and promotes pathology in the guinea pig model of disease.[105] The *Legionella* type IV secretion system, known as Dot/Icm, promotes intracellular infection in multiple ways. First, it enhances *L. pneumophila* entry into host cells.[106,107] Second, it is essential for the ability of the *Legionella* parasite to inhibit phagosome–endo/lysosomal fusions and to establish its replicative niche.[58,108,109] Finally, the Dot/Icm system is important for apoptosis and bacterial egress from its spent host cell.[66,110] Effector proteins secreted by the type IV system are most likely responsible for altering host cell function. One such effector is the so-called RalF protein, which acts on a host protein (ARF1) that is involved in vesicular trafficking from the endoplasmic reticulum (ER) and the Golgi.[111] Mutations in *dot/icm* loci lead to loss of virulence.[75,112]

Several infectivity factors have been localized to the *L. pneumophila* periplasm or cytoplasm. A Cu-Zn superoxide dismutase re-

sides in the periplasm, affording resistance to toxic superoxide anions, and the KatB catalase-peroxidase is needed for optimal intracellular infection.[113,114] The *Legionella* phosphoenolpyruvate phosphotransferase and HtrA protein promote intracellular growth and virulence.[115,116] *L. pneumophila* iron acquisition, important for intra- and extracellular replication, involves, among other things, a secreted ferric iron chelator (the siderophore legiobactin), a periplasmic ferric reductase, and an inner membrane ferrous iron transporter (FeoB).[117-119]

EPIDEMIOLOGY

Incubation Period and Contagiousness

The incubation period during most outbreaks of legionnaires' disease has been reported to be between 2 and 10 days, with median values of 4 to 6 days, and some outliers of 1 up to 28 days.[1,120] Recent data show that the incubation period may be slightly longer. In the West Frisian Flower Show epidemic in 1999, the incubation period ranged from 2 to 19 days, with a median of 7 days; 16% of patients had an incubation period greater than 10 days. A 2-month incubation period was reported for one nosocomial case.[121] The incubation period of Pontiac fever is generally 4 hours to 3 days, with a median of 2 days, although incubation periods of up to 9 days have been reported.[6,87,122]

Person-to-person transmission of either legionnaires' disease or Pontiac fever does not occur. Apocryphal reports of legionnaires' disease being acquired from manipulation of *L. pneumophila*–infected human lung specimens exist. Disease transmission from experimentally infected animals to other animals does not occur, nor does it occur from the animals to man. Finally, laboratory transmission from bacterial cultures to man has not been documented. The lack of contagiousness and the apparent low infectivity of laboratory cultures for man, support experimental studies showing that the infectiousness of the bacterium is enhanced by intra-amebal growth and by special growth conditions; and that a sporelike bacterial form, made only under special conditions, is highly virulent.[37-39]

Patterns and Rates of Disease, and Mortality

Legionnaires' disease occurs in both sporadic and epidemic form. About 65% to 75% of reported cases are not associated with known epidemics of the disease.[27,123] Underreporting of the disease is common because many sporadic cases are treated empirically without diagnostic studies being performed, because of falsely negative diagnostic tests, because of underreporting of diagnosed cases, and because only passive surveillance systems are in place to detect disease occurrence. Thus, only about 1100 cases of legionnaires' disease are reported annually (0.4/100,000 population) to the U.S. Centers for Disease Control and Prevention (CDC). This rate is similar to that reported from France, 1.3 cases/100,000 population per year in 2001, and England and Wales in 1998, 0.4/100,000.[123,124] In contrast, prospective studies of both sporadic community-acquired and nosocomial legionnaires' disease have reported far more cases in the United States than would be expected on the basis of the number of cases reported to the CDC. One prospective community-based study in Ohio of adult patients with community-acquired pneumonia requiring hospitalization found that 2.4% of such patients had legionnaires' disease, and that the disease incidence was about 8/100,000 population per year.[125] When extrapolated to the entire population of the United States, the authors estimated that between 8000 to 18,000 cases of legionnaires' disease occur annually among adults requiring hospitalization for pneumonia. The incidence of legionnaires' disease causing community-acquired pneumonia not requiring hospitalization is not known with certainty. One small regional U.S. study estimated that the incidence of legionnaires' disease among outpatients treated for pneumonia was 4 to 28/100,000 population/year.[126] Thus, somewhere between 18,000 to 88,000 cases of legionnaires' disease are estimated to occur per year in the United States, the majority of which are not epidemic related. Some geographic regions appear to have more legionnaires' disease than others, such as western Pennsylvania and Ohio in the United States and Catalonia in Spain; whether this results from true differences in disease incidence or better case ascertainment is uncertain. Regardless, the estimates of legionnaires' disease as a cause of community-acquired pneumonia requiring hospitalization in adults ranges from 0.5% to 10% of all admitted pneumonia cases; an average value is probably about 2%, even in geographic regions with excellent diagnostic capabilities.[127-131]

Legionnaires' disease of children is thought to be uncommon, representing 1% or less of causes of pneumonia in this age group, and generally occurs as a nosocomial disease of immunosuppressed children.[132] Neonates may be at relatively high risk of legionnaires' disease because of the immaturity of their immune systems. Both nosocomially and domestically acquired cases of the disease have been reported in apparently immunologically normal newborns exposed to *Legionella*-contaminated water in incubators or bath tubs, and during birth.

Shortly after the Philadelphia outbreak, nosocomial legionnaires' disease outbreaks were reported in several cities throughout the United States and Europe. Because relatively little was known about the environmental ecology of *L. pneumophila,* or about optimal diagnostic methods, these outbreaks were characterized by long durations, often years in length, and high numbers of cases and fatalities. For example, the legionnaires' disease outbreak at the Wadsworth Veterans Administration Hospital in Los Angeles, California, resulted in more than 250 cases of disease in both patients and visitors over an 8-year period.[15,22,133] A 17-year-long outbreak of unrecognized nosocomial legionnaires' disease occurred at another U.S. hospital and involved many fewer patients.[134] Nosocomial legionnaires' disease epidemics continue to occur worldwide, albeit with durations measured in weeks rather than years.[135,136] Nosocomial pneumonia usually only affects a relatively small number of hospitalized patients, with attack rates of less than 1% of patients.[15,137] During nosocomial outbreaks of legionnaires' disease, the minority (5% to 11%) of patients with nosocomial pneumonia of all etiologies have been reported to have legionnaires' disease,[15,138-140] although in some explosive outbreaks involving a single ward the attack rates may be much higher.

Community-based legionnaires' disease epidemics continue to occur more than 25 years after the 1976 Philadelphia outbreak, some of them quite serious in terms of the number of people affected. Recent outbreaks include one in Murcia, Spain, in 2001, involving up to 700 people, with six deaths; in Barrow-in-Furness, England, in 2002, involving more than 130 people with six deaths; and in Bovenkarspel, The Netherlands, in 1999, involving 188 people, with 21 deaths.[23] Of note, two of these recent outbreaks involved people visiting a town center rather than being events inside a certain building.

Legionnaires' disease affecting travelers constitutes up to half of reported cases in some countries. In many cases, a common source outbreak has been found, but for others the cases appear to be sporadic. Multiple common source outbreaks have been uncovered in travelers by a cooperative European reporting system that collects and analyzes legionnaires' disease cases in travelers.[141-145] Such a traveler's health monitoring and analysis system does not exist in the United States, and as a result many small epidemics of the disease are likely to be undetected in this country.

Despite the immense publicity usually generated by epidemics of legionnaires' disease, sporadic cases of the disease are about fourfold more common than linked cases of the disease. Some sporadic cases are undoubtedly the result of common-source outbreaks involving just a few people. This is especially true of travelers who return to their homes during the incubation period, or while they are ill but still well enough to travel. Other evidence for common-source links for apparently unrelated cases comes from an observation in Glasgow, Scotland, showing that proximity of residence to an air conditioning cooling tower was a risk factor for legionnaires' disease.[146]

Pontiac fever often involves explosive outbreaks of disease with high attack rates. Attack rates of 70% to 90% have been reported from several epidemics.[6,86,122,147,148]

Legionnaires' disease mortality rates are highly variable, ranging from less than 1% to as high as 80%, depending on the underlying health of the patient, the promptness of specific therapy, and whether the disease is sporadic, nosocomial, or part of a large outbreak.[27,149-151] The lowest mortality rates, around 1%, have been observed in recent large outbreaks of the disease, whereas the highest mortality rates have been reported in untreated nosocomial disease in patients with severe underlying diseases. The average fatality rate for sporadic disease is estimated to be about 10% to 15%. Fatality rates of nosocomial disease have declined by more than 50% in the United States over the past 20 years; a similar but less dramatic decrease in death rates of community-acquired cases has also been observed.[27] The declines in mortality rates appear to result from better and faster disease recognition, especially through use of the urine antigen test, and more widespread use of empiric therapy for pneumonia that includes drugs active against *L. pneumophila.*[27] More detail on mortality rates and response to therapy is given under Therapy and Response to Therapy, later in this chapter.

Risk Factors

Host risk factors for legionnaires' disease are those that result in decreased local or systemic cellular immunity, and those that increase the chances of exposure to an infectious aerosol or microaspiration of contaminated water. Also important in determining if legionnaires' disease occurs are the relative virulence of the bacterium, its aerosol stability, probably the growth phase of the organism, and environmental factors that facilitate the spread of the bacterium from contaminated water to the host, such as wind direction, relative humidity, and aerosol formation.

Male sex, cigarette smoking, chronic heart or lung disease, diabetes, end-stage renal failure, organ transplantation, immunosuppression, some forms of cancer, and age older than 50 years have all been found to be host risk factors for legionnaires' disease.[23,137,152,153] The approximately twofold greater risk with male sex may be due to the greater prevalence of cigarette smoking and its complications in men. Cigarette smoking increases risk by about twofold to sevenfold, probably because of the adverse effects of cigarette use on local pulmonary defense mechanisms. Immunosuppression that decreases local or systemic cellular immunity, and particularly glucocorticoid administration, increases the risk by about twofold to sixfold; cytotoxic chemotherapy was shown to be a risk factor in one study. Lung, but not gastrointestinal tract, cancer has been shown to be a risk factor for legionnaires' disease.[152] A variety of hematologic malignancies have also been shown to be important risk factors, especially hairy cell leukemia.[138,152] Recent surgery has been an important risk factor for nosocomial disease, probably because of general anesthetic-caused defects in local lung defense, because *Legionella*-contaminated water is introduced into the respiratory tract in the perioperative or postoperative periods, or because of both factors combined.[154,155] Alcoholism has been shown to be a predisposing condition in only some studies, and it has never been shown to be a risk factor in multivariate analyses.[137,138,153,156] There appear to be no predisposing host factors for Pontiac fever.

Because legionnaires' disease cannot occur without exposure to the bacterium, activities that increase the chances of exposure to *Legionella* bacteria in water increase the risks of disease acquisition. Recent overnight travel, use of well water in the home, recent plumbing work inside the home, disruptions of water supply resulting in "brown" water at the water tap, and possibly living in a water distribution network with older plumbing or using an electric water heater, all increase the acquisition risk of community-acquired legionnaires' disease.[153,157] Other community, recreational, or travel-related activities increasing the chances of acquiring the disease include the use of, or proximity to, whirlpool spas or hot water spring spas; living in close proximity to a cooling tower; or being near decorative fountains.[23,146,158-160] Rarely reported risks are near-drowning,[9,160,161] and delivery by water birth.[162]

A wide range of nosocomial exposures can result in legionnaires' disease. Almost all involve delivery of *Legionella*-contaminated water into the respiratory tract after filling or rinsing the following apparatuses with tap water: nebulizers, humidifiers, oxygen humidifiers, ventilator tubing, and nasogastric feeding or lavage equipment.[163-166] Consumption of *Legionella*-contaminated ice can also be a risk factor for nosocomial legionnaires' disease.[167] These risk factors are in addition to exposure to *Legionella*-contaminated air originating from a cooling tower.[136,168,169] Rare cases of nosocomial *Legionella* wound infection have resulted from irrigation or bathing of wounds in *Legionella*-contaminated water.[170,171]

Modes of Transmission

Legionnaires' disease is transmitted from the environment to man by inhalation of an infectious aerosol.[172] In an unknown fraction of cases, microaspiration of contaminated water into the lungs is the mode of transmission, rather than inhalation of an aerosol.[166,173] Finally, massive aspiration of contaminated water into the lungs during near-drownings is a very unusual but reported mode of transmission of the disease.[160,161]

Multiple examples of exclusive aerosol transmission of legionnaires' disease exist, especially in epidemics having a cooling tower, water spa, water fountain, or water mister as the source of disease.[1,136,158,159,169,174-178] In these cases, proximity to the aerosol generator, duration of exposure, and presence in an area downstream of the contaminated device have all been found to be risk factors for disease acquisition. Of note, when reported, either consumption of water at the epidemic site has not occurred in the majority of disease victims, or the drinking water of the outbreak site has been culture negative for *L. pneumophila.*

The data supporting microaspiration of water as a major mode of transmission are less convincing, but in some specific reports the evidence is compelling. These data include examples of nosocomial disease in patients whose major risk factor was nasogastric tube irrigation with tap water, and interruption of nosocomial outbreaks by substituting sterile water for tap water for drinking and nasogastric tube irrigation.[166,173,179,180] Whether microaspiration is the major transmission mode for nosocomial disease is controversial and unproven.[181] Experimental animal data are unhelpful in this regard, as both aerosol delivery and tracheal instillation produce disease.[182,183]

Rare reports of peritonitis or bowel abscesses caused by *L. pneumophila* have led to speculation that oral ingestion may be a mode of disease transmission.[184-186] In all these cases, *L. pneumophila* pneumonia or empyema occurred concurrently, making it unclear which organs were the ones primarily infected. In contrast to the relative ease of producing lethal guinea pig pneumonia by the aerosol or intratracheal route, huge amounts of *L. pneumophila* delivered by oral gavage are cleared rapidly without causing severe pneumonia,[187] although another experimental study gave somewhat different results.[188] Overall it is very unlikely that oral ingestion of *Legionella*-contaminated water is more than a very minor mode of transmission of the disease.

Outbreak Investigation

Prompt notification of public health authorities of any strongly suspected or confirmed community-acquired case of legionnaires' disease is critically important for detecting epidemics of the disease, and in many regions it is legally required. What appears to be only a single case of the disease may be part of an epidemic or the index case. Alert physicians have sometimes detected pneumonia clusters that led to discovery of both emerging and long-standing epidemics of legionnaires' disease.[1,158]

In addition to reporting nosocomial legionnaires' disease to public health authorities, the medical institution should embark on extensive investigation of even a single case of nosocomial legionnaires' disease.[189] This is because more cases may have occurred previously or will appear subsequently. Retrospective review of the frequency and causes of nosocomial pneumonia for a 3- to 6-month period may yield more cases, especially if combined with testing of saved lung tissues from biopsies or necropsies. Prospective laboratory testing of all patients with nosocomial pneumonia for legionnaires' disease can also be useful in finding more cases, for a 3- to 6-month period. Hospital physicians should be notified to consider legionnaires' disease when making diagnostic and therapeutic decisions in patients with nosocomial pneumonia.

Investigation of both community-acquired and nosocomial outbreaks of legionnaires' disease requires a thorough epidemiologic in-vestigation. The epidemiologic investigation will help generate hypotheses concerning the source of the outbreak, and will demonstrate risk factors using controlled studies. Environmental testing without concurrent epidemiologic investigation can lead to misleading findings, even when molecular fingerprinting is used to compare clinical and environmental isolates.[190,191] If at all possible, it is crucial to obtain as many clinical isolates as possible of *Legionella* bacteria from affected patients; this affords the ability to compare the strain identity of environmental and clinical isolates. Detailed protocols for environmental sampling are available.[145,192,193]

Some rough clues to an environmental source of a legionnaires' disease epidemic can be found in the pace of the outbreak and its geographic distribution. Explosive outbreaks involving tens to hundreds of people over a several-day period often result from a contaminated massive aerosol generator, usually a cooling tower, but sometimes also a whirlpool spa or misting device. Potable water-associated outbreaks may produce as many cases but generally over a much longer period of time, such as many weeks or months. Potable water-related outbreaks are confined to a single building, or a building complex if the plumbing is common among buildings. In contrast, cooling tower-related epidemics often affect both building visitors and those within several hundred meters of the tower. Interior aerosol-generating devices, such as recreational spas and misters, cause disease only in building visitors.

Environmental Decontamination for Outbreaks

All aerosol-generating sources implicated as, or highly suspected of being, a source of epidemic legionnaires' disease should be taken out of operation as soon as possible; this generally includes cooling towers, hot tubs, and other such devices. Implicated potable water sources such as plumbing systems should be shut down if possible. A number of guidelines exist for emergency disinfection of such sources, and these may differ according to local regulations.[189,193,194] The emergency disinfection process usually includes hyperchlorination or other oxidant applications, or heating. Long-term remediation can be complex and can require expert engineering and public health advice.[193,194]

CLINICAL PRESENTATION

Legionnaires' Disease

Legionnaires' disease causes acute consolidating pneumonia that cannot be accurately differentiated on initial presentation from pneumococcal pneumonia. Several prospective studies have shown that the two diseases have nearly identical clinical and roentgenographic findings, and that nonspecific laboratory test results cannot differentiate between the two diseases.[195-197] However, initial clinical findings of both community-acquired and nosocomial epidemic legionnaires' disease seemed to show that a distinct clinical syndrome was observed.[198] This syndrome was characterized by fever with pulse-temperature dissociation, myalgia, nonproductive cough, few pulmonary symptoms, diarrhea, confusion, hyponatremia, hypophosphatemia, and elevated liver-associated enzymes. Although this symptom complex does occur in legionnaires' disease, it is not specific or frequent enough to allow differentiation of this disease from other common causes of community-acquired pneumonia. A clinical scoring system that was devised to help increase diagnostic accuracy is neither specific nor sensitive.[151,199]

A prodromal illness may occur, lasting for hours to several days, with symptoms of headache, myalgia, asthenia, and anorexia. Fever accompanies this prodrome, except in severely immunocompromised patients. Multiple rigors may occur, as well as diarrhea and abdominal pain. Cough, with or without chest pain, often develops hours to days after onset of the prodrome; the cough produces purulent sputum in only about 50% of patients with legionnaires' disease. The initial clinical picture may be confusing as the systemic symptoms can be more impressive than ones referable to the lower respiratory tract, leading some physicians to diagnose "influenza," a gastrointestinal illness, and in some cases an acute abdomen syndrome. However, careful physical examination of the chest, and chest roentgenography, almost always demonstrates findings of pneumonia, including focal rales and alveolar filling pulmonary infiltrates that vary from patchy infiltrates to multiple areas of consolidation.[200,201] Pleuritic chest pain, sometimes in concert with hemoptysis, may occur and can mislead the clinician into considering pulmonary infarction. Headache, which can be the most prominent feature, may be so severe as to suggest subarachnoid hemorrhage. Mental confusion is commonly reported in some series; obtundation, seizures, and focal neurologic findings also occur, but less frequently. Some patients may have negative chest x-ray films on presentation, which show within a day focal or diffuse pulmonary infiltrates. Cavitation of consolidated lung is seen in about 10% of immunosuppressed patients. Pleural effusion without pulmonary infiltrates may rarely be observed as the sole radiographic abnormality. Bronchoscopic findings in patients with consolidating pneumonia are often remarkable for the absence of inflammation or purulent secretions in the large airways. Abdominal examination may reveal generalized or local tenderness and, in rare cases, evidence of peritonitis. Splenomegaly is uncommon. Findings of pericarditis, myocarditis, and focal abscesses are rare. No rash is associated with this disease, except that caused by other factors such as drug therapy. Symptoms of rhinorrhea, chronic afebrile fatigue, and fever without pneumonia lasting for many weeks are either not seen are so rare that their presence makes the diagnosis of legionnaires' disease unlikely.

A number of nonspecific laboratory test abnormalities may occur in legionnaires' disease.[48] These include hyponatremia, hypophosphatemia, increased liver-associated enzymes (aspartate transaminase [AST], alanine transaminase [ALT], alkaline phosphatase), hyperbilirubinemia, leukopenia, thrombocytopenia, disseminated intravascular coagulation, leukocytosis, pyuria, elevated creatine kinase (MM fraction), and elevated lactate dehydrogenase (LDH). A few studies have shown that patients with legionnaires' disease are more likely to have hyponatremia than are those with other causes of pneumonia, but the range of serum sodium values is too broad for this abnormality to be diagnostic in an individual patient.[202] Laboratory markers of pancreatitis are detected if this is a complication of legionnaires' disease. Renal disease caused by legionnaires' disease may result in the presence of urine casts and white cells, elevated serum creatinine levels, or both types of abnormalities. Myoglobinuria is a relatively common finding, usually indicated by a positive dipstick test for "blood" in the absence of significant numbers of red cells in the urine. Hypoxemia occurs in proportion to the severity of the pneumonia and underlying cardiopulmonary disease.

Clinical diagnosis may be more specific if the patient's clinical course after treatment is taken into account, and if epidemiologic and immunologic risk factors are considered. The chances of a patient having legionnaires' disease are increased if an acute consolidating pneumonia fails to respond to several days of β-lactam antimicrobial therapy, or if the pneumonia is severe enough to require intensive care unit hospitalization. Important epidemiologic clues include use of a hot tub or recreational spa; travel outside the home for a day or more; recent pneumonia of a co-worker, fellow conference attendee, or fellow traveler; and recent plumbing work done at home or work (as indicated by air in the pipes or brown discoloration of the water). Patients with suppression of the cellular immune system are at high risk for getting legionnaires' disease (e.g., patients treated with glucocorticoids or with antirejection drugs after organ transplantation). Administration of very high dosage methylprednisolone or muromonabCD3 for acute organ rejection is an especially high risk factor for legionnaires' disease. It is likely that administration of the tumor necrosis factor-α antagonist etanercept is also a major risk factor for the disease, as tumor necrosis factor-α is a key host defense against the disease.

The nonspecific presentation of legionnaires' disease makes clinical diagnosis very difficult and mandates empiric therapy for this disease in most patients with community-acquired pneumonia of uncertain etiology. Diagnosis of the index or sporadic case of nosocomial legionnaires' disease can be quite difficult, especially as this disease is a very uncommon cause of nosocomial pneumonia in most hospitals.

Extrapulmonary Infections

Extrapulmonary infections are very rare and usually occur as metastatic complications of pneumonia in immunocompromised patients. Metastatic infection has been reported almost exclusively in immunocompromised patients, or in patients with fatal legionnaires' disease, who may develop abscesses and other infections of the brain, spleen or extrathoracic lymph nodes, and skeletal and cardiac muscles.[203-207] Other reported sites of metastatic infection have been the intestines and liver, the kidneys, the peritoneum, the pericardium, vascular shunts and grafts, bone marrow, surgical wounds, the perirectal area, and the skin and subcutaneous tissues.[184,208-215] In some of these cases, the onset of symptoms of the metastatic infection preceded the recognition of pneumonia by several days, and in other cases the metastatic infection presented days to weeks subsequent to onset of the pneumonia. In some cases, the metastatic infection site was the only evidence of relapse of infection. Two cases of metastatic infection have been reported in apparently previously healthy patients,[205,216] but otherwise immunosuppression has been reported in such patients. Metastatic infection complicating fatal legionnaires' disease has not generally been recognized premortem. Nonmetastatic direct extension of a thoracic empyema into the soft tissues of the chest has been reported after thoracentesis.[217]

Very rare cases of primary infection not preceded by legionnaires' disease have also been reported. These appear to be the result of direct inoculation of *Legionella*-contaminated water into various tissues, usually in hosts with compromise of local, if not systemic, immunity. Culture-proven sites of such infections have been surgical or other wounds, prosthetic heart valves, the mediastinum, and the respiratory sinuses.[170,171,218-221] Some infections were introduced by bathing postoperative patients with contaminated tap water, by the use of therapeutic baths, and by inadvertent tap water irrigation of the mediastinum after esophageal perforation.

Pontiac Fever

Pontiac fever is a self-limited short-duration febrile illness, usually diagnosed only during an outbreak of the disease.[6,87,122,148] The usual story is onset of symptoms 12 to 36 hours after exposure to a bacteria-contaminated aerosol, either in a workplace or in some other group setting. Attack rates are very high, with more than 80% to 90% of such exposed people becoming ill. The sources of contaminated aerosol have included industrial processes using sprayed water (lathes, artificial fiber plants, building humidification), recreational spas, decorative water fountains, and cooling towers. Fever, myalgia, headache, and asthenia are the dominant symptoms. Cough, dyspnea, anorexia, arthralgia, and abdominal pain occur less frequently. Most patients are not ill enough to seek medical attention, recovering without specific therapy 3 to 5 days after disease onset. There is little information about physical examination findings in the first day of illness; examination 2 to 5 days after onset may show fever and tachypnea but little else. Pneumonia does not occur. Fatigue and nonfocal neurologic complaints have been reported to persist for up to several months in a minority of affected patients. Because the clinical findings are nonspecific, it is very difficult, if not impossible, to accurately diagnose this disease in the absence of similar illnesses in co-workers or others with a common source exposure. Inquiries regarding the health of co-workers and acquaintances, and a history of known water exposure may help to confirm the diagnosis, but even these findings may be nonspecific and lack sensitivity.

LABORATORY DIAGNOSIS

Specific but relatively insensitive tests are available for the diagnosis of legionnaires' disease (Table 229-1). These include culture of lower respiratory tract secretions, tissues, and fluids; detection of *L. pneumophila* serogroup 1 antigenuria by use of immune assays; detection of *L. pneumophila* bacteria in lower respiratory tract secretions, tissues, and fluids by use of immunofluorescent microscopy; detection of *L. pneumophila*–specific antibodies by immunoassay; and detection of

TABLE 229-1 Specific Diagnostic Tests for Legionnaires' Disease Caused by *Legionella pneumophila

Test	Specimen Types	Sensitivity	Specificity	Notes
Culture	Sputum, other lower respiratory tract secretions; lung; pleural fluid; blood; extrapulmonary tissues, fluids	20%-95%	100%	May be positive up to several days after treatment; requires special media and expertise
Antigenuria	Urine	60%-95%	>99%	Highest sensitivity for *L. pneumophila* serogroup 1, Pontiac type
Immunofluorescent microscopy	Same as culture	20%-50%	99%	Highest specificity with monoclonal antibody; requires very high level of technical expertise
Antibody	Paired sera	20%-70%	95%-99%	Highest specificity for *L. pneumophila* serogroup 1
Molecular amplification	Sputum, other lower respiratory tract secretions; urine	20%-75%	90%-95%	Not well standardized; not commercially available

*Pertains only to *L. pneumophila* infections. The yield of diagnostic tests is lower for infection caused by other species, especially those tests based on immunoassay.

L. pneumophila DNA through use of molecular amplification and detection techniques.

Culture yield depends on the severity of illness, with the lowest yield (15% to 25%) for mild pneumonia and the highest yield (>90%) for severe pneumonia causing respiratory failure.[26,222] Prior specific antimicrobial therapy affects yield adversely, although some patients have positive sputum cultures for days to weeks after initiation of specific therapy. Expectorated sputum or, even better, endotracheal aspirates are good specimens for culture; neither bronchoscopy nor lung biopsy is required for good culture yield, assuming a good-quality sputum specimen. Sputum cultures may be positive despite the presence of epithelial cells and lack of leukocytes, making suspicion of legionnaires' disease an exception to the usual sputum adequacy screening criteria. The major advantage of culture diagnosis is that the yield is not dependent on *L. pneumophila* serotype, a fault of all of antibody and urine testing. Culture is also often the only test positive in cases of legionnaires' disease caused by other *Legionella* species. Complete investigation of the source of an outbreak requires a clinical isolate, another reason to perform culture. Proper culture technique requires the inoculation of multiple special selective and nonselective media, preplating decontamination of specimens, and laboratory technologists skilled in the recognition and identification of *Legionella* bacteria. Unfortunately, many clinical laboratories have neither the expertise nor the ability to properly perform this test.

Urine antigen testing has revolutionized the laboratory diagnosis of legionnaires' disease, making it the most common laboratory test ordered for diagnosis of this disease.[27,223] This is because the test can be easily performed by those without special skills, especially the card-based immunoassay, because the test is often positive when other tests are negative, and because it is highly specific. The test is not perfect, however, as it is most sensitive for the detection of the Pontiac (MAB 2+) monoclonal antibody type of *L. pneumophila* serogroup 1 (up to 90%), less sensitive for other monoclonal antibody types of *L. pneumophila* serogroup 1 (60%), and very poorly sensitive (5%) for other *L. pneumophila* serogroups and other species.[224-226] Because the majority (about 90%) of cases of community-acquired legionnaires' disease are caused by the Pontiac subtype of *L. pneumophila* serogroup 1, the average sensitivity of this test is in the range of 70% to 80%. Immunocompromised patients, patients with nosocomial legionnaires' disease, and some Australian patients are more likely to have legionnaires' disease caused by other serogroups and species, and hence a negative urine antigen test.[224] Yield can be increased by urine concentration.[227] Rare false-positive tests may be the result of rheumatoid-like factors, which are easy to inactivate although most laboratories do not perform this inactivation step. A potential clinical error is to order only urine antigen testing and to stop therapy for legionnaires' disease if the urine test is negative, as the urine test is not 100% sensitive and for some patient groups may be poorly sensitive. Positive tests are associated with more severe disease.[156] Patients with extensive bilateral legionnaires' disease may excrete urinary antigen for weeks to months after recovery; this should not cause confusion over whether a positive test is the result of new or old pneumonia in the absence of a history of recent hospitalization for severe pneumonia.

Antibody detection is insensitive and of low specificity unless paired acute and convalescent sera are tested.[228] For optimal yield, convalescent sera should be collected at 4, 6, and 12 weeks after disease onset. About 80% to 90% of seroconversions occur by 4 weeks, with the remaining seroconversions requiring an additional 2 to 8 weeks. Still, only about 75% of patients with culture-proven legionnaires' disease will seroconvert at all, even with optimally timed and tested sera. Test specificity is affected by the type of antigen used, by its fixation method, and by other details of testing methodology. Few commercially available serologic tests are of optimal specificity, because of the use of polyvalent antigen preparations and because of deviations from the standardized test methods. Only seroconversion to *L. pneumophila* serogroup 1 is of high enough specificity for clinical use; measurement of antibodies to other serogroups and species is plagued by low specificity and cannot be recommended. Serologic testing is more useful for epidemiologic investigations than for clinical use in a single patient.

Detection of *L. pneumophila* in respiratory tract tissues and fluids using immunofluorescent microscopy is very specific if a monoclonal antibody to this species is used and the test is performed by experts.[229] Use of other reagents, or testing by nonexperts, usually results in many false-positive test results. The test is insensitive, even in experienced hands, except in cases of severe pneumonia where the organism load is high.

Molecular amplification and detection of *L. pneumophila* is available only as a research test. Most, but not all, evaluations have shown that the molecular methods are about as sensitive as culture. Some studies have reported nonspecific results, but whether this results from the low sensitivity of culture or the nonspecificity of the molecular tests is uncertain. Use of this test methodology for clinical purposes should only be undertaken for very well validated and controlled assays.[222]

Optimal test yield requires performing more than one type of test; sputum culture and urine antigen testing are the two preferred tests. If both of these are negative, and there are clinical or epidemiologic reasons for making a retrospective diagnosis weeks to months later, then antibody testing should be ordered. If a very well validated molecular assay is available, then this option could be added to the other tests.

The yield of all tests but perhaps antibody determination is diminished by specific therapy, requiring testing before, or within a few days of, the start of antimicrobial therapy. However, therapy should not be withheld for an inordinate time pending collection or testing of specimens, and it should not be stopped solely on the basis of the result of a negative laboratory test.

THERAPY AND RESPONSE TO THERAPY

Legionella bacteria are intracellular parasites of monocytic phagocytes and probably some other human cells. This means that all antimicrobial agents efficacious for legionnaires' disease must be concentrated, and bioactive, within these cells. In addition, the intracellular drugs must be distributed in the same subcellular location as the bacteria. The macrolides, quinolones, and tetracyclines all meet these criteria. In contrast, none of the β-lactams, monobactams, aminoglycosides, or phenicols are active for this disease, because of their low or poorly active intracellular activity against the *Legionella* bacteria.[150]

TABLE 229-2 Preferred Therapy for Legionnaires' Disease

Clinical Condition	1st Choices	Dosage*	2nd Choices	Dosage*
Mild pneumonia, not immunocompromised, outpatient	Erythromycin -or-	500 mg PO 4×/day for 14-21 days		
	Doxycycline -or-	200 mg PO load, then 100 mg 2×/day for 14-21 days		
	Azithromycin -or-	500 mg PO 1×/day for 3-5 days		
	Telithromycin -or-	800 mg PO 1×/day for 7-10 days		
	Levofloxacin -or-	500 mg PO 1×/day for 7-10 days		
	Ciprofloxacin -or-	500 mg PO 2×/day for 7-10 days		
	Gatifloxacin -or-	400 mg PO 1×/day for 7-10 days		
	Moxifloxacin -or-	400 mg PO 1×/day for 7-10 days		
	Clarithromycin	500 mg PO 2×/day for 14-21 days		
Hospitalized with pneumonia or immunocompromised	Azithromycin	500 mg IV 1×/day for 7-10 days	Ciprofloxacin -or-	750 mg 2×/day for 14 days
			Moxifloxacin	400 mg IV 1×/day for 14 days
	-or-			
	Levofloxacin	500 mg IV 1×/day for 10-14 days	Erythromycin	1000 mg IV 4×/day for 3-7 days, then 500 mg 4×/day for a total course of 21 days
			-plus-	
			Rifampin	300-600 mg 2×/day for 5 days

*With some of these drugs, dosage adjustments have to be made for renal insufficiency. Therapy duration may need to be considerably longer for patients with lung abscesses, empyema, endocarditis, or extrathoracic infection. Oral therapy can be used in patients after response to IV antibiotic therapy.

Prospective, adequate-size clinical trials of antimicrobial therapy for legionnaires' disease have not been performed.[150,151,230] The only comparative clinical data available are retrospective data from community-acquired or nosocomial outbreaks of the disease. Patients treated with an erythromycin or a tetracycline drug had significantly lower fatality rates than did those treated with β-lactam or aminoglycoside agents; in the 1976 Philadelphia epidemic, the fatality rates for those treated with erythromycin or a tetracycline were 10%, versus 20% to 40% for those treated with other drugs.[1] Similarly, in one outbreak of nosocomial disease, immunosuppressed patients treated with erythromycin had a 24% fatality rate, compared with an 80% rate for otherwise-treated patients, and erythromycin-treated nonimmunocompromised patients had a 7% fatality rate compared with 25% for those otherwise treated.[198] A number of small uncontrolled, or underpowered prospective controlled studies of the treatment of legionnaires' disease exist. Because in most studies the expected outcome is good, with overall fatality rates of less than 10% and cure rates in excess of 80%, it is difficult to interpret the existing studies as anything but anecdotal. These studies have shown that small numbers of patients with legionnaires' disease have responded adequately to erythromycin, tetracycline, azithromycin, dirithromycin, clarithromycin, telithromycin, pefloxacin, ciprofloxacin, gatifloxacin, grepafloxacin, sparfloxacin, trovafloxacin, and levofloxacin. One retrospective study appears to show that pefloxacin therapy may be superior to erythromycin therapy for very severe legionnaires' disease, which would correlate with the superior activity of pefloxacin in animal and cell models of infection.[231] Another retrospective study of legionnaires' disease with severe pneumonia showed that patients treated with a fluoroquinolone antimicrobial agent within 8 hours of admission to an intensive care unit had significantly better outcomes than those treated later, or with other drugs, including erythromycin.[232]

In the absence of adequate-size human studies, decisions about potential antimicrobial efficacy for legionnaires' disease must be made on the basis of experimental animal and cell culture studies. The ability of a drug to inhibit or kill intracellular *L. pneumophila* usually correlates well with its clinical effectiveness for legionnaires' disease. Similarly, therapy studies using a guinea pig model of legionnaires' disease correlate quite well with drug effectiveness for the treatment of the disease in humans. The guinea pig model is generally a severe test of drug effectiveness, giving results similar to those expected for immunosuppressed or severely ill patients. These studies show that the β-lactam drugs, aminoglycosides, and chloramphenicol neither inhibit intracellular *L. pneumophila* nor effect cure in the guinea pig model.[150,230] In contrast, erythromycin, clarithromycin, and tetracyclines are able to inhibit the intracellular growth of the bacterium, and they cure guinea pigs with experimental legionnaires' disease. However, these drugs are unable either to kill intracellular *L. pneumophila* or to effectively clear the bacterium from experimentally infected guinea pigs, despite clinical cure of the animals. Many quinolone antimicrobial agents, azithromycin, and some ketolide compounds are much more active against intracellular *L. pneumophila* than erythromycin, clarithromycin, or the tetracyclines. In addition, these more active drugs have superior activity in the guinea pig model for parameters such as bacterial clearance, length of therapy and dose required for cure, and the amount of residual lung inflammation. The superior intracellular and animal model activity of the quinolones, azithromycin, and ketolides appears to result from their greater ability to kill intracellular *L. pneumophila*, from their residual antibacterial activity after drug cessation, and in some cases from their direct or indirect anti-inflammatory activities-especially for azithromycin.[150,151,230,233-236]

The decision regarding which antimicrobial agent to administer for legionnaires' disease should be guided by severity of illness, degree of immunocompromise, drug cost, drug toxicity, and drug availability. Nonimmunocompromised outpatients with mild legionnaires' disease can be treated with any of the drugs listed in Table 229-2, with drug cost, availability, and toxicity being the main deciding factors. Hospitalized or immunocompromised patients with legionnaires' disease should be treated with one of the listed quinolones or azithromycin, unless drug unavailability or cost prevents their use. Initial intravenous antimicrobial therapy may be required in severely ill patients. Even in such patients, oral antimicrobial therapy can be used as soon as there is clinical improvement and intestinal drug absorption is adequate. Very few patients can tolerate the administration of oral erythromycin in high dosage, making the maximum oral dosage lower than the intravenous dosage. Immunocompromised patients treated with erythromycin, with or without rifampin (which has good in vitro and intracellular activity), may suffer relapse days to months after cessation of therapy, especially if the level of immunosuppression subsequently increases. Co-administration of rifampin with drugs other than erythromycin or doxycycline is of questionable benefit and should not be done.

The majority of legionnaires' disease patients treated with one of the recommended antimicrobial agents respond promptly to the therapy, sometimes within hours. Within 12 to 24 hours, most patients have improvement or complete clearance of myalgia, confusion, headache, abdominal pain, diarrhea, nausea, vomiting, and anorexia. Four to 7 days may be required for complete resolution of fever, but there should be a steady decrease in fever over that period, with the most improvement being seen in the first day or two. Cough, sputum production, shortness of breath, and pleuritic chest pain respond more slowly to therapy, but major improvements usually occur within the first several days. Evidence of chest consolidation on physical examination, and especially by roentgenography, may take considerably longer to resolve. It is common to observe apparent increases in the sizes of the original pulmonary infiltrates despite substantial clinical improvement over the first several days of therapy; this is not a cause for alarm as long as by other measures the patient is improving.[237] Complete clearing of the chest roentgenograph may not occur for up to 4 months after initiation of specific antimicrobial therapy, although the majority of patients have complete clearing after 2 months.[200,238,239] Severely immunocompromised patients, or those with severe pneumonia requiring artificial ventilation, may take longer to improve after initiation of specific therapy, or they may not respond at all because of irreversible acute respiratory distress syndrome (ARDS); even in such patients, many of the systemic signs of infection, such as fever, improve, although the respiratory failure itself may worsen.

Failure to respond to specific therapy for legionnaires' disease should bring into question the validity of the diagnosis, the possibility of coinfection or superinfection, and the possibility of extrapulmonary disease complicating the legionnaires' disease. Up to 10% of patients with legionnaires' disease have coinfections or superinfections with other respiratory pathogens or other pathogens, such as pneumococcus, *Haemophilus influenzae, Staphylococcus aureus,* enteric gram-negative bacilli, *Listeria, Nocardia,* pneumocystis, *Aspergillus,* tuberculosis, *Cryptococcus,* and a variety of viruses.[151,240,241] Superinfection with opportunistic pathogens is generally seen in severely immunocompromised patients and in those with nosocomial legionnaires' disease, whereas coinfection with common respiratory pathogens may be seen in patients with community-acquired legionnaires' disease. Drug fever, pancreatitis, myocarditis, hepatitis, pericarditis, metastatic infection, and pleural empyema may rarely be complications of legionnaires' disease, or its treatment, and causes of prolonged fever or poor response to therapy.

Ancillary therapy of legionnaires' disease has not been studied systematically. Excessive oxygen therapy should be avoided, both for the purpose of preventing oxygen toxicity of the lung and to prevent progression of infection. Experiments in mice with *L. pneumophila* pneumonia show that hyperoxia mediates lung damage and progression of infection, a finding that may or may not be applicable to humans.[242] Corticosteroid therapy for treatment of ARDS caused by legionnaires' disease has been advocated by some,[151] but this therapy is of unproven benefit and could be detrimental to control of the infection[243,244]; a clinical response to administration of bactericidal quinolones is mandated before the administration of such immunosuppressive therapy, as is continuation of the antimicrobials during and after steroid therapy. Corticosteroid therapy may be indicated for postpneumonic lung diseases such as bronchiolitis obliterans organizing pneumonia and perhaps pulmonary fibrosis.[245-247]

PREVENTION

Immunization and Chemoprophylaxis

No human vaccine for legionnaires' disease exists, and prior infection does not necessarily prevent reinfection.[241] Experiments in guinea pigs have shown that vaccinations with several different *L. pneumophila* antigens are effective in preventing death from otherwise lethal bacterial challenges.[248,249] Whether such vaccines would prove useful in man is unknown.

Chemoprophylaxis with a macrolide antibiotic has been effective at preventing legionnaires' disease in immunocompromised patients during nosocomial epidemics of the disease.[250] This is a reasonable step to take for high-risk populations prior to control of an epidemic.

Engineering Modifications and Maintenance

Proper building and plumbing design and construction can reduce the frequency and intensity of *L. pneumophila* contamination of potable water systems. Design features should include properly insulating hot water pipes to prevent the warming of water in adjacent cold water pipes, eliminating blind pipe runs, eliminating stagnation, reducing or eliminating water holding tanks, eliminating the use of plumbing materials that support the growth of *L. pneumophila,* and maintaining hot water temperature above 50° C and cold water temperature below 20° C.[145,193,251] In older buildings, these modifications can be difficult and expensive for a variety of reasons. Maintaining hot water temperature above 50° C in hospitals, homes, and nursing homes can result in severe scalding burns, as immersion for only a few seconds in such water can result in third-degree burns.[252] Installation of thermostatically controlled mixing valves is then required to prevent scalding injuries. Whether any of these modifications can prevent legionnaires' disease outbreaks has not been studied.

Use of monochloroamine, rather than chlorine, to treat public drinking water may reduce the risk of nosocomial legionnaires' disease.[253] More study is required on this issue.

The risk of heavy *L. pneumophila* colonization of air conditioning cooling towers, and transmission of the biocontaminated aerosol into buildings, can be reduced by siting of the cooling towers well away from and downwind of building air intakes, by installation of drift eliminators, and by proper and regular cooling tower maintenance.[193,251] Cooling tower–related outbreaks sometimes occur despite what appears to be proper design, maintenance, and operation, highlighting the technical difficulty of maintaining cooling towers completely free of the bacterium.[169,178] Determination of the effectiveness of cooling tower maintenance for preventing colonization by *L. pneumophila* is difficult without performing quantitative cultures for the bacteria.

Recreational spas must be properly constructed, regularly maintained, and closely monitored to prevent high levels of bacterial growth, which sometimes includes *Legionella.* Guidelines for such maintenance include hourly monitoring of biocide levels during use, limiting the number of users in the spa, daily hyperhalogenation, and periodic complete spa drainage and filter cleaning.[254,255] Proper construction of recreational spas includes access to interior pipes for inspection and cleaning. Preventing *Legionella* colonization of natural hot spring spas can be very difficult, if not impossible, because elevated water temperatures and high levels of inorganic compounds can inactivate biocides.

Environmental Cultures for Legionella Bacteria

There is little national or international consensus regarding the utility of routinely obtaining environmental cultures to help prevent legionnaires' disease. The *Legionella* bacteria that are ubiquitous in our aqueous environment almost never cause disease, so simply finding the bacteria in the environment does not mean that disease will occur. That, combined with natural fluctuations and the extreme heterogeneity in environmental concentrations of *Legionella,* makes it very difficult to accurately use a specific bacterial concentration as a trigger point for action. Finally, the methods used for determining *Legionella* concentrations are imprecise. The low predictive value of positive cultures for disease occurrence is a major reason why many government and other organizations recommend against the routine use of environmental cultures in risk assessment. Included in this list are the CDC, the United Kingdom, the American Society of Heating, Refrigerating and Air-Conditioning Engineers (ASHRAE), several Australian states, France, and many other organizations. The cost and risk to the environment of remediation, without certain benefit, also add to the reluctance to perform environmental cultures.[145,189,256-258]

Some government agencies and private organizations advocate routine culturing for *Legionella,* arguing that knowledge of environmental presence of the bacterium can direct monitoring for disease, and that remediation may prevent disease. Apart from these reasons, some organizations recommend or require the use of cooling tower cultures for *Legionella* to monitor maintenance effectiveness but not directly for risk assessment.[193]

In contrast to routine culturing, many bodies recommend that hospital water systems supplying wards housing immunocompromised patients be cultured for *L. pneumophila,* and that remediation be carried out if positive cultures are found in these areas. Other organizations suggest that all hospital water supplies be checked.[189,193,256,257]

A reasonable approach is to routinely perform cultures of hospital potable water supplying wards containing severely immunocompromised patients, perhaps on a monthly basis. Negative cultures do not exclude the possibility of nosocomial legionnaires' disease, but they make it less likely. Otherwise, environmental cultures for *Legionella* should be done only if needed to monitor cooling tower treatment effectiveness or for outbreak investigation.

REFERENCES

1. Fraser DW, Tsai TR, Orenstein W, et al. Legionnaires' disease: Description of an epidemic of pneumonia. N Engl J Med. 1977; 297:1189-1197.
2. McDade JE, Shepard CC, Fraser DW, et al. Legionnaires' disease: isolation of a bacterium and demonstration of its role in other respiratory disease. N Engl J Med. 1977;297:1197-1203.
3. Osterholm MT, Chin TD, Osborne DO, et al. A 1957 outbreak of Legionnaires' disease associated with a meat packing plant. Am J Epidemiol. 1983;117:60-67.
4. Thacker SB, Bennett JV, Tsai TF, et al. An outbreak in 1965 of severe respiratory illness caused by the Legionnaires' disease bacterium. J Infect Dis. 1978;138: 512-519.
5. Grist NR, Reid D, Najera R. Legionnaires' disease and the traveller. Ann Intern Med. 1979;90:563-564.
6. Glick TH, Gregg MB, Berman B, et al. Pontiac fever. An epidemic of unknown etiology in a health department: I. Clinical and epidemiologic aspects. Am J Epidemiol. 1978;107:149-160.
7. Kaufmann AF, McDade JE, Patton CM, et al. Pontiac fever: isolation of the etiologic agent (Legionella pneumophila) and demonstration of its mode of transmission. Am J Epidemiol. 1981;114:337-347.
8. Armstrong CW, Miller GB Jr. A 1949 outbreak of Pontiac fever–like illness in steam condenser cleaners. Arch Environ Health. 1985;40:26-29.
9. Bozeman FM, Humphries JW, Campbell JM. A new group of rickettsia-like agents recovered from guinea pigs. Acta Virol. 1968;12:87-93.
10. Hébert GA, Moss CW, McDougal LK, et al. The rickettsia-like organisms TATLOCK (1943) and HEBA (1959): Bacteria phenotypically similar to but genetically distinct from *Legionella pneumophila* and the WIGA bacterium. Ann Intern Med. 1980;92:45-52.
11. Thomason BM, Harris PP, Hicklin MD, et al. A *Legionella*-like bacterium related to WIGA in a fatal case of pneumonia. Ann Intern Med. 1979;91:673-676.
12. Tatlock H. A rickettsia-like organism recovered from guinea pigs. Proc Soc Exp Biol Med. 1944;57:95-99.
13. Tatlock H. Studies on a virus from a patient with Fort Bragg fever (pretibial fever). J Clin Invest. 1947;26:287-297.
14. Tatlock H. Clarification of the cause of Fort Bragg fever (pretibial fever)—January 1982. Rev Infect Dis. 1982;4:157-158.
15. Haley CE, Cohen ML, Halter J, Meyer RD. Nosocomial Legionnaires' disease: A continuing common-source epidemic at Wadsworth Medical Center. Ann Intern Med. 1979;90:583-586.
16. Fisher-Hoch SP, Bartlett CL, Tobin JO, et al. Investigation and control of an outbreaks of Legionnaires' disease in a district general hospital. Lancet. 1981;1:932-936.
17. Broome CV, Goings SAJ, Thacker SB, et al. The Vermont epidemic of Legionnaires' disease. Ann Intern Med. 1979;90:573-577.
18. Gerber JE, Casey CA, Martin P, Winn WC Jr. Legionnaires' disease in Vermont. 1972-1976. Am J Clin Pathol. 1981;76:816-818.
19. Klaucke DN, Vogt RL, LaRue D, et al. Legionnaires' disease: The epidemiology of two outbreaks in Burlington, Vermont, 1980. Am J Epidemiol. 1984;119:382-391.
20. Brown A, Yu VL, Elder EM, et al. Nosocomial outbreak of Legionnaire's disease at the Pittsburgh Veterans Administration Medical Center. Trans Assoc Am Phys. 1980;93:52-59.
21. Best M, Yu VL, Stout J, et al. Legionellaceae in the hospital water-supply: Epidemiological link with disease and evaluation of a method for control of nosocomial Legionnaires' disease and Pittsburgh pneumonia. Lancet. 1983;2:307-310.
22. Shands KN, Ho JL, Meyer RD, et al. Potable water as a source of Legionnaires' disease. JAMA. 1985;253:1412-1416.
23. den Boer JW, Yzerman EP, Schellekens J, et al. A large outbreak of Legionnaires' disease at a flower show, the Netherlands, 1999. Emerg Infect Dis. 2002;8:37-43.
24. Barratt H. Legionnaires' disease hits north west England. BMJ. 2002;325:295
25. Park MY, Ko KS, Lee HK, et al. *Legionella busanensis* sp nov., isolated from cooling tower water in Korea. Int J Syst Evol Microbiol. 2003;53:77-80.
26. Fields BS, Benson RF, Besser RE. Legionella and Legionnaires' disease: 25 years of investigation. Clin Microbiol Rev. 2002;15:506-526.
27. Benin AL, Benson RF, Besser RE. Trends in Legionnaires disease, 1980-1998: Declining mortality and new patterns of diagnosis. Clin Infect Dis. 2002;35:1039-1046.
28. Yu VL, Plouffe JF, Pastoris MC, et al. Distribution of Legionella species and serogroups isolated by culture in patients with sporadic community-acquired legionellosis: An international collaborative survey. J Infect Dis. 2002;186:127-128.
29. Helbig JH, Bernander S, Castellani PM, et al. Pan-European study on culture-proven legionnaires' disease: Distribution of *Legionella pneumophila* serogroups and monoclonal subgroups. Euro J Clin Microbiol Infect Dis. 2002;21:710-716.
30. Rowbotham TJ. Current views on the relationships between amoebae, legionellae and man. Isr J Med Sci. 1986;22:678-689.
31. Harb OS, Gao LY, Abu-Kwaik Y. From protozoa to mammalian cells: A new paradigm in the life cycle of intracellular bacterial pathogens. Environ Microbiol. 2000;2:251-265.
32. Steinert M, Emody L, Amann R, Hacker J. Resuscitation of viable but nonculturable *Legionella pneumophila* Philadelphia JR32 by *Acanthamoeba castellanii.* Appl Environ Microbiol. 1997;63:2047-2053.
33. Samrakandi MM, Cirillo SL, Ridenour DA, et al. Genetic and phenotypic differences between *Legionella pneumophila* strains. J Clin Microbiol. 2002;40:1352-1362.
34. Dennis PJ, Lee JV. Differences in aerosol survival between pathogenic and non-pathogenic strains of *Legionella pneumophila* serogroup 1. J Appl Bacteriol. 1988;65:135-141.
35. Bezanson G, Fernandez R, Haldane D, et al. Virulence of patient and water isolates of *Legionella pneumophila* in guinea pigs and mouse L929 cells varies with bacterial genotype. Can J Microbiol. 1994;40:426-431.
36. Bollin GE, Plouffe JF, Para MF, Prior RB. Difference in virulence of environmental isolates of *Legionella pneumophila.* J Clin Microbiol. 1985;21:674-677.
37. Garduño RA, Garduño E, Hiltz M, Hoffman PS. Intracellular growth of *Legionella pneumophila* gives rise to a differentiated form dissimilar to stationary-phase forms. Infect Immun. 2002;70:6273-6283.
38. Byrne B, Swanson MS. Expression of *Legionella pneumophila* virulence traits in response to growth conditions. Infect Immun. 1998;66:3029-3034.
39. Cirillo JD, Cirillo SL, Yan L, et al. Intracellular growth in *Acanthamoeba castellanii* affects monocyte entry mechanisms and enhances virulence of *Legionella pneumophila.* Infect Immun. 1999;67:4427-4434.
40. Hambleton P, Broster MG, Dennis PJ, et al. Survival of virulent *Legionella pneumophila* in aerosols. J Hyg (Lond). 1983;90:451-460.
41. Cianciotto NP. Pathogenicity of *Legionella pneumophila.* Int J Med Microbiol. 2001;291:331-343.
42. Winn WC Jr, Myerowitz RL. The pathology of the Legionella pneumonias: A review of 74 cases and the literature. Hum Pathol. 1981;12:401-422.
43. Salins S, Newton C, Widen R, et al. Differential induction of gamma interferon in *Legionella pneumophila*–infected macrophages from BALB/c and A/J mice. Infect Immun. 2001;69:3605-3610.
44. Brieland J, Freeman P, Kunkel R, et al. Replicative *Legionella pneumophila* lung infection in intratracheally inoculated A/J mice: A murine model of human legionnaires' disease. Am J Pathol. 1994;145:1537-1546.
45. Brieland JK, Jackson C, Hurst S, et al. Immunomodulatory role of endogenous interleukin-18 in gamma interferon-mediated resolution of replicative *Legionella pneumophila* lung infection. Infect Immun. 2000;68:6567-6573.
46. Deng JC, Tateda K, Zeng X, Standiford TJ. Transient transgenic expression of gamma interferon promotes *Legionella pneumophila* clearance in immunocompetent hosts. Infect Immun. 2001;69:6382-6390.
47. Tateda K, Moore TA, Newstead MW, et al. Chemokine-dependent neutrophil recruitment in a murine model of *Legionella pneumonia:* Potential role of neutrophils as immunoregulatory cells. Infect Immun. 2001;69:2017-2024.
48. Edelstein PH, Meyer RD. Legionella. In: Weinstein RS, Graham AR, Anderson RE, et al, eds. Advances in Pathology and Laboratory Medicine. St Louis: Mosby-Year Book; 1995:149-167.
49. Nash TW, Libby DM, Horwitz MA. IFN-gamma-activated human alveolar macrophages inhibit the intracellular multiplication of *Legionella pneumophila.* J Immunol. 1988;140:3978-3981.
50. Byrd TF, Horwitz MA. Interferon gamma-activated human monocytes downregulate transferrin receptors and inhibit the intracellular multiplication of *Legionella pneumophila* by limiting the availability of iron. J Clin Invest. 1989;83:1457-1465.
51. Swanson MS, Hammer BK. *Legionella pneumophila* pathogenesis: A fateful journey from amoebae to macrophages. Annu Rev Microbiol. 2000;54:567-613.
52. Horwitz MA. Phagocytosis of the Legionnaires' disease bacterium (*Legionella pneumophila*) occurs by a novel mechanism: Engulfment within a pseudopod coil. Cell. 1984;36:27-33.
53. Rechnitzer C, Blom J. Engulfment of the Philadelphia strain of *Legionella pneumophila* within pseudopod coils in human phagocytes: Comparison with other *Legionella* strains and species. APMIS. 1989;97:105-114.
54. Khelef N, Shuman HA, Maxfield FR. Phagocytosis of wild-type *Legionella pneumophila* occurs through a wortmannin-insensitive pathway. Infect Immun. 2001;69:5157-5161.
55. Elliott JA, Winn WC Jr. Treatment of alveolar macrophages with cytochalasin D inhibits uptake and subsequent growth of *Legionella pneumophila.* Infect Immun. 1986;51:31-36.
56. Payne NR, Horwitz MA. Phagocytosis of *Legionella pneumophila* is mediated by human monocyte complement receptors. J Exp Med. 1987;166:1377-1389.
57. Clemens DL, Lee BY, Horwitz MA. *Mycobacterium tuberculosis* and *Legionella pneumophila* phagosomes exhibit arrested maturation despite acquisition of Rab7. Infect Immun. 2000;68:5154-5166.

58. Joshi AD, Sturgill-Koszycki S, Swanson MS. Evidence that Dot-dependent and -independent factors isolate the *Legionella pneumophila* phagosome from the endocytic network in mouse macrophages. Cell Microbiol. 2001;3:99-114.

59. Wiater LA, Dunn K, Maxfield FR, Shuman HA. Early events in phagosome establishment are required for intracellular survival of *Legionella pneumophila*. Infect Immun. 1998;66:4450-4460.

60. Kagan JC, Roy CR. *Legionella* phagosomes intercept vesicular traffic from endoplasmic reticulum exit sites. Nat Cell Biol. 2002;4:945-954.

61. Swanson MS, Isberg RR. Association of *Legionella pneumophila* with the macrophage endoplasmic reticulum. Infect Immun. 1995;63:3609-3620.

62. Tilney LG, Harb OS, Connelly PS, et al. How the parasitic bacterium *Legionella pneumophila* modifies its phagosome and transforms it into rough ER: Implications for conversion of plasma membrane to the ER membrane. J Cell Sci. 2001;114:24-50.

63. Sturgill-Koszycki S, Swanson MS. *Legionella pneumophila* replication vacuoles mature into acidic, endocytic organelles. J Exp Med. 2000;192:1261-1272.

64. Hammer BK, Tateda ES, Swanson MS. A two-component regulator induces the transmission phenotype of stationary-phase *Legionella pneumophila*. Molec Microbiol. 2002;44:107-118.

65. Alli OA, Gao LY, Pedersen LL, et al. Temporal pore formation-mediated egress from macrophages and alveolar epithelial cells by *Legionella pneumophila*. Infect Immun. 2000;68:6431-6440.

66. Zink SD, Pedersen L, Cianciotto NP, Abu-Kwaik Y. The Dot/Icm type IV secretion system of *Legionella pneumophila* is essential for the induction of apoptosis in human macrophages. Infect Immun. 2002;70:1657-1663.

67. Wright EK, Goodart SA, Growney JD, et al. Naip5 affects host susceptibility to the intracellular pathogen *Legionella pneumophila*. Curr Biol. 2003;13:27-36.

68. Chandler FW, Blackmon JA, Hicklin MD, et al. Ultrastructure of the agent of Legionnaires' disease in the human lung. Am J Clin Pathol. 1979;71:43-50.

69. Lüneberg E, Zähringer U, Knirel YA, Steinmetz I, et al. Phase-variable expression of lipopolysaccharide contributes to the virulence of *Legionella pneumophila*. J Exp Med. 1998;188:49-60.

70. Robey M, O'Connell W, Cianciotto NP. Identification of *Legionella pneumophila rcp*, a *pagP*-like gene that confers resistance to cationic antimicrobial peptides and promotes intracellular infection. Infect Immun. 2001;69:4276-4286.

71. Edelstein PH, Hu B, Higa F, Edelstein MA. lvgA, a novel *Legionella pneumophila* virulence factor. Infect Immun. 2003;71:2394-2403.

72. Rodgers FG. Ultrastructure of *Legionella pneumophila*. J Clin Pathol. 1979;32:1195-1202.

73. Cianciotto NP, Stamos JK, Kamp DW. Infectivity of *Legionella pneumophila mip* mutant for alveolar epithelial cells. Curr Microbiol. 1995;30:247-250.

74. Mody CH, Paine R, Shahrabadi MS, et al. *Legionella pneumophila* replicates within rat alveolar epithelial cells. J Infect Dis. 1993;167:1138-1145.

75. Edelstein PH, Edelstein MA, Higa F, Falkow S. Discovery of virulence genes of *Legionella pneumophila* by using signature tagged mutagenesis in a guinea pig pneumonia model. Proc Natl Acad Sci U S A. 1999;96:8190-8195.

76. Fraser DW, Deubner DC, Hill DL, Gilliam DK. Nonpneumonic, short-incubation-period legionellosis (Pontiac fever) in men who cleaned a steam turbine condenser. Science. 1979;205:690-691.

77. Rylander R, Haglind P, Lundholm M, et al. Humidifier fever and endotoxin exposure. Clin Allergy. 1978;8:511-516.

78. Burge HA, Solomon WR, Boise JR. Microbial prevalence in domestic humidifiers. Appl Environ Microbiol. 1980;840-844.

79. Blaser M. Hot-bath syndrome, Pontiac fever, and Legionnaires' disease (Letter). Lancet. 1977;2:1226

80. Muittari A, Kuusisto P, Sovijärvi A. An epidemic of bath water fever: Endotoxin alveolitis? Eur J Respir Dis. 1982;63:108-116.

81. Rylander R, Haglind P. Airborne endotoxins and humidifier disease. Clin Allergy. 1984;14:109-112.

82. Fields BS, Haupt T, Davis JP, et al. Pontiac fever due to *Legionella micdadei* from a whirlpool spa: Possible role of bacterial endotoxin. J Infect Dis. 2001;184:1289-1292.

83. Girod JC, Reichman RC, Winn WC Jr, et al. Pneumonic and nonpneumonic forms of legionellosis: The result of a common-source exposure to *Legionella pneumophila*. Arch Intern Med. 1982;142:545-547.

84. Hunt DA, Cartwright KA, Smith MC, et al. An outbreak of Legionnaires' disease in Gloucester. Epidemiol Infect. 1991;107:133-141.

85. Thomas DL, Mundy LM, Tucker PC. Hot tub legionellosis: Legionnaires' disease and Pontiac fever after a point-source exposure to *Legionella pneumophila*. Arch Intern Med. 1993;153:2597-2599.

86. Friedman S, Spitalny K, Barbaree J, et al. Pontiac fever outbreak associated with a cooling tower. Am J Public Health 1987;77:568-572.

87. Luttichau HR, Vinther C, Uldum SA, et al. An outbreak of Pontiac fever among children following use of a whirlpool. Clin Infect Dis. 1998;26:1374-1378.

88. Stone BJ, Abu Kwaik Y. Expression of multiple pili by *Legionella pneumophila*: identification and characterization of a type IV pilin gene and its role in adherence to mammalian and protozoan cells. Infect Immun. 1998;66:1768-1775.

89. Dietrich C, Heuner K, Brand BC, et al. Flagellum of *Legionella pneumophila* positively affects the early phase of infection of eukaryotic host cells. Infect Immun. 2001;69:2116-2122.

90. Hoffman PS, Ripley M, Weeratna R. Cloning and nucleotide sequence of a gene (*ompS*) encoding the major outer membrane protein of *Legionella pneumophila*. J Bacteriol. 1992;174:914-920.

91. Cianciotto NP, Eisenstein BI, Mody CH, Engleberg NC. A mutation in the *mip* gene results in an attenuation of *Legionella pneumophila* virulence. J Infect Dis. 1990;162:121-126.

92. Fischer G, Bang H, Ludwig B, et al. Mip protein of *Legionella pneumophila* exhibits peptidyl-prolyl-cis/trans isomerase (PPIase) activity. Molec Microbiol. 1992;6:1375-1383.

93. Garduño RA, Garduño E, Hoffman PS. Surface-associated hsp60 chaperonin of *Legionella pneumophila* mediates invasion in a HeLa cell model. Infect Immun. 1998;66:4602-4610.

94. Cirillo SL, Lum J, Cirillo JD. Identification of novel loci involved in entry by *Legionella pneumophila*. Microbiology. 2000;146:1345-1359.

95. Luneberg E, Mayer B, Daryab N, et al. Chromosomal insertion and excision of a 30 kb unstable genetic element is responsible for phase variation of lipopolysaccharide and other virulence determinants in *Legionella pneumophila*. Molec Microbiol. 2001;39:1259-1271.

96. Aragon V, Kurtz S, Flieger A, et al. Secreted enzymatic activities of wild-type and pilD-deficient *Legionella pneumophila*. Infect Immun. 2000;68:1855-1863.

97. Dowling JN, Saha AK, Glew RH. Virulence factors of the family Legionellaceae. Microbiol Rev. 1992;56:32-60.

98. Nagai H, Roy CR. The DotA protein from *Legionella pneumophila* is secreted by a novel process that requires the Dot/Icm transporter. EMBO J. 2001;20:5962-5970.

99. Aragon V, Rossier O, Cianciotto NP. *Legionella pneumophila* genes that encode lipase and phospholipase C activities. Microbiology. 2002;148:7-31.

100. Flieger A, Gong S, Faigle M, et al. Novel lysophospholipase A secreted by *Legionella pneumophila*. J Bacteriol. 2001;183:2121-2124.

101. Hales LM, Shuman HA. *Legionella pneumophila* contains a type II general secretion pathway required for growth in amoebae as well as for secretion of the Msp protease. Infect Immun. 1999;67:3662-3666.

102. Liles MR, Edelstein PH, Cianciotto NP. The prepilin peptidase is required for protein secretion by and the virulence of the intracellular pathogen *Legionella pneumophila*. Molec Microbiol. 1999;31:959-970.

103. Rossier O, Cianciotto NP. Type II protein secretion is a subset of the PilD-dependent processes that facilitate intracellular infection by *Legionella pneumophila*. Infect Immun. 2001;69:2092-2098.

104. Polesky AH, Ross JT, Falkow S, Tompkins LS. Identification of *Legionella pneumophila* genes important for infection of amoebas by signature-tagged mutagenesis. Infect Immun. 2001;69:977-987.

105. Moffat JF, Edelstein PH, Regula DP Jr, et al. Effects of an isogenic Zn-metalloprotease-deficient mutant of *Legionella pneumophila* in a guinea-pig pneumonia model. Molec Microbiol. 1994;12:693-705.

106. Hilbi H, Segal G, Shuman HA. Icm/dot-dependent upregulation of phagocytosis by *Legionella pneumophila*. Molec Microbiol. 2001;42:603-617.

107. Watarai M, Derre I, Kirby J, et al. *Legionella pneumophila* is internalized by a macropinocytotic uptake pathway controlled by the Dot/Icm system and the mouse Lgn1 locus. J Exp Med. 2001;194:1081-1096.

108. Coers J, Kagan JC, Matthews M, et al. Identification of Icm protein complexes that play distinct roles in the biogenesis of an organelle permissive for *Legionella pneumophila* intracellular growth. Mol Microbiol. 2000;38:719-736.

109. Dumenil G, Isberg RR. The *Legionella pneumophila* IcmR protein exhibits chaperone activity for IcmQ by preventing its participation in high-molecular-weight complexes. Molec Microbiol. 2001;40:1113-1127.

110. Molmeret M, Alli OA, Zink S, et al. IcmT is essential for pore formation-mediated egress of *Legionella pneumophila* from mammalian and protozoan cells. Infect Immun. 2002;70:69-78.

111. Nagai H, Kagan JC, Zhu X, et al. A bacterial guanine nucleotide exchange factor activates ARF on *Legionella* phagosomes. Science. 2002;295:679-682.

112. Marra A, Blander SJ, Horwitz MA, Shuman HA. Identification of a *Legionella pneumophila* locus required for intracellular multiplication in human macrophages. Proc Natl Acad Sci U S A. 1992;89:9607-9611.

113. Bandyopadhyay P, Steinman HM. *Legionella pneumophila* catalase-peroxidases: Cloning of the *katB* gene and studies of KatB function. J Bacteriol. 1998;180:5369-5374.

114. St. John G, Steinman HM. Periplasmic copper-zinc superoxide dismutase of *Legionella pneumophila*: Role in stationary-phase survival. J Bacteriol. 1996;178:1578-1584.

115. Higa F, Edelstein PH. Potential virulence role of the *Legionella pneumophila ptsP* ortholog. Infect Immun. 2001;69:4782-4789.

116. Pedersen LL, Radulic M, Doric M, Abu K. HtrA homologue of *Legionella pneumophila*: An indispensable element for intracellular infection of mammalian but not protozoan cells. Infect Immun. 2001;69:2569-2579.

117. Liles MR, Scheel TA, Cianciotto NP. Discovery of a nonclassical siderophore, legiobactin, produced by strains of *Legionella pneumophila*. J Bacteriol. 2000;182:749-757.

118. Robey M, Cianciotto NP. *Legionella pneumophila* feoAB promotes ferrous iron uptake and intracellular infection. Infect Immun. 2002;70:5659-5669.

119. James BW, Mauchline WS, Dennis PJ, Keevil CW. A study of iron acquisition mechanisms of *Legionella pneumophila* grown in chemostat culture. Curr Microbiol. 1997;34:238-243.

120. Hindersson P, Høiby N, Bangsborg J. Sequence analysis of the *Legionella micdadei* groELS operon. FEMS Microbiol Lett. 1990;61:31-38.

121. Marrie TJ, Bezanson G, Haldane DJ, Burbidge S. Colonisation of the respiratory tract with *Legionella pneumophila* for 63 days before the onset of pneumonia. J Infect. 1992;24:81-86.

122. Goldberg DJ, Wrench JG, Collier PW, et al. Lochgoilhead fever: Outbreak of non-pneumonic legionellosis due to *Legionella micdadei*. Lancet. 1989;1:316-318.

123. Joseph CA, Harrison TG, Ilijic-Car D, Bartlett CL. Legionnaires' disease in residents of England and Wales: 1998. Commun Dis Public Health. 1999;2:280-284.

124. Campese C, Decludt B. Notified cases of Legionnaires' disease in France in 2001. Euro Surveill. 2002;7:121-128.

125. Marston BJ, Plouffe JF, File TM Jr, et al. Incidence of community-acquired pneumonia requiring hospitalization: Results of a population-based active surveillance study in Ohio. The Community-Based Pneumonia Incidence Study Group. Arch Intern Med. 1997;157:1709-1718.

126. Foy HM, Broome CV, Hayes PS, et al. Legionnaires' disease in a prepaid medical-care group in Seattle 1963-75. Lancet. 1979;1:767-770.

127. Plouffe J, Schwartz DB, Kolokathis A, et al. Clinical efficacy of intravenous followed by oral azithromycin monotherapy in hospitalized patients with community-acquired pneumonia. Antimicrob Agents Chemother. 2000;44:1796-1802.

128. Plouffe JF, Herbert MT, File TM Jr, et al. Ofloxacin versus standard therapy in treatment of community-acquired pneumonia requiring hospitalization. Pneumonia Study Group. Antimicrob Agents Chemother. 1996;40:1175-1179.

129. File TM Jr, Segreti J, Dunbar L, et al. A multicenter, randomized study comparing the efficacy and safety of intravenous and/or oral levofloxacin versus ceftriaxone and/or cefuroxime axetil in treatment of adults with community-acquired pneumonia. Antimicrob Agents Chemother. 1997;41:1965-1972.

130. Trémolières F, de Kock F, Pluck N, Daniel R. Trovafloxacin versus high-dose amoxicillin (1 g three times daily) in the treatment of community-acquired bacterial pneumonia. Euro J Clin Microbiol Infect Dis. 1998;17:447-453.

131. Breiman RF, Butler JC. Legionnaires' disease: Clinical, epidemiological, and public health perspectives. Semin Resp Infect. 1998;13:84-89.

132. Edelstein PH. Legionnaires disease, Pontiac fever, and related illnesses. In: Feigen RD, Cherry JD, eds. Pediatric Infectious Diseases. 5th ed. Philadelphia: WB Saunders; 2004:1676-1686.

133. Edelstein PH, Nakahama C, Tobin JO, et al. Paleoepidemiologic investigation of Legionnaires disease at Wadsworth Veterans Administration Hospital by using three typing methods for comparison of legionellae from clinical and environmental sources. J Clin Microbiol. 1986;23:1121-1126.

134. Kool JL, Fiore AE, Kioski CM, et al. More than 10 years of unrecognized nosocomial transmission of Legionnaires' disease among transplant patients. Infect Control Hosp Epidemiol. 1998;19:898-904.

135. Knirsch CA, Jakob K, Schoonmaker D, et al. An outbreak of *Legionella micdadei* pneumonia in transplant patients: Evaluation, molecular epidemiology, and control. Am J Med. 2000;108:290-295.

136. Fiore AE, Nuorti JP, Levine OS, et al. Epidemic Legionnaires' disease two decades later: Old sources, new diagnostic methods. Clin Infect Dis. 1998;26:426-433.

137. Broome CV, Fraser DW. Epidemiologic aspects of legionellosis. Epidemiol Rev. 1979;1:1-16.

138. Carratala J, Gudiol F, Pallares R, et al. Risk factors for nosocomial *Legionella pneumophila* pneumonia. Am J Resp Crit Care Med. 1994;149:625-629.

139. Marrie TJ, MacDonald S, Clarke K, Haldane D. Nosocomial Legionnaires' disease: Lessons from a four-year prospective study. Am J Infect Control. 1991;19:79-85.

140. Prodinger WM, Bonatti H, Allerberger F, et al. *Legionella pneumonia* in transplant recipients: A cluster of cases of eight years' duration. J Hosp Infect. 1994;26:191-202.

141. Joseph C, Morgan D, Birtles R, et al. An international investigation of an outbreak of Legionnaires disease among UK and French tourists. Eur J Epidemiol. 1996;12:215-219.

142. Lee JV, Joseph C, PHLS Atypical Pneumonia Working Group. Guidelines for investigating single cases of Legionnaires' disease. Commun Dis Public Health. 2002;5:157-162.

143. Lever F, Joseph CA. Travel-associated Legionnaires' disease in Europe in 2000 and 2001. Euro Surveill 2003;8:65-72.

144. The European working group for *Legionella* infections. Retrieved 5/30/2003 from *http://www.ewgli.org/*.

145. Lever F, Joseph CA, Lee JV, et al. European guidelines for control and prevention of travel associated Legionnaires' disease. Retrieved 6/18/2003 from *http://www.ewgli.org/pdf_files/Guidelines_June_2003.pdf*.

146. Bhopal RS, Fallon RJ, Buist EC, et al. Proximity of the home to a cooling tower and risk of non-outbreak Legionnaires' disease. BMJ. 1991;302:378-383.

147. Herwaldt LA, Gorman GW, McGrath T, et al. A new *Legionella* species, *Legionella feeleii* species nova, causes Pontiac fever in an automobile plant. Ann Intern Med. 1984;100:333-338.

148. Mangione EJ, Remis RS, Tait KA, et al. An outbreak of Pontiac fever related to whirlpool use, Michigan 1982. JAMA. 1985;253:535-539.

149. Joseph C. New outbreak of Legionnaires' disease in the United Kingdom. BMJ. 2002;325:347-348.

150. Edelstein PH. Antimicrobial chemotherapy for Legionnaires' disease: A review. Clin Infect Dis. 1995;21:S265-S276

151. Roig J, Rello J. Legionnaires' disease: A rational approach to therapy. J Antimicrob Chemother 2003;51:1119-1129.

152. Marston BJ, Lipman HB, Breiman RF. Surveillance for Legionnaires' disease: Risk factors for morbidity and mortality. Arch Intern Med. 1994;154:2417-2422.

153. Straus WL, Plouffe JF, File TM Jr, et al. Risk factors for domestic acquisition of Legionnaires disease. Ohio legionnaires Disease Group. Arch Intern Med. 1996;156:1685-1692.

154. Serota AI, Meyer RD, Wilson SE, et al. Legionnaires' disease in the postoperative patient. J Surg Res. 1981;30:417-427.

155. Korvick JA, Yu VL. Legionnaires' disease: An emerging surgical problem. Ann Thorac Surg. 1987;43:341-347.

156. Lettinga KD, Verbon A, Weverling GJ, et al. Legionnaires' disease at a Dutch flower show: Prognostic factors and impact of therapy. Emerg Infect Dis. 2002;8:1448-1454.

157. Alary M, Joly JR. Risk factors for contamination of domestic hot water systems by legionellae. Appl Environ Microbiol. 1991;57:2360-2367.

158. Jernigan DB, Hofmann J, Cetron MS, et al. Outbreak of Legionnaires' disease among cruise ship passengers exposed to a contaminated whirlpool spa. Lancet. 1996;347:494-499.

159. Hlady WG, Mullen RC, Mintz CS, et al. Outbreak of Legionnaire's disease linked to a decorative fountain by molecular epidemiology. Am J Epidemiol. 1993;138:555-562.

160. Miyamoto H, Jitsurong S, Shiota R, et al. Molecular determination of infection source of a sporadic *Legionella pneumonia* case associated with a hot spring bath. Microbiol Immunol. 1997;41:197-202.

161. Lavocat MP, Berthier JC, Rousson A, et al. *Légionellose pulmonaire* chez un enfant après noyade en eau douce. Presse Med. 1987;16:780.

162. Franzin L, Scolfaro C, Cabodi D, et al. *Legionella pneumophila* pneumonia in a newborn after water birth: A new mode of transmission. Clin Infect Dis. 2001;33:e103-e104.

163. Arnow PM, Chou T, Weil D, et al. Nosocomial Legionnaires' disease caused by aerosolized tap water from respiratory devices. J Infect Dis. 1982;146:460-467.

164. Joly JR, Déry P, Gauvreau L, et al. Legionnaires' disease caused by *Legionella dumoffii* in distilled water. Can Med Assoc J. 1986;135:1274-1277.

165. Mastro TD, Fields BS, Breiman RF, et al. Nosocomial Legionnaires' disease and use of medication nebulizers. J Infect Dis. 1991;163:667-671.

166. Marrie TJ, Haldane D, MacDonald S, et al. Control of endemic nosocomial Legionnaires' disease by using sterile potable water for high risk patients. Epidemiol Infect. 1991;107:591-605.

167. Bangsborg JM, Uldum S, Jensen JS, Bruun BG. Nosocomial legionellosis in three heart-lung transplant patients: case reports and environmental observations. Euro J Clin Microbiol Infect Dis. 1995;14:99-104.

168. Brown CM, Nuorti PJ, Breiman RF, et al. A community outbreak of Legionnaires' disease linked to hospital cooling towers: An epidemiological method to calculate dose of exposure. Int J Epidemiol. 1999;28:353-359.

169. Badenoch J. First report of the committee of inquiry into the outbreak of Legionnaires' disease in Stafford in April 1985. London: Her Majesty's Stationery Office; 1986.

170. Lowry PW, Blankenship RJ, Gridley W, et al. A cluster of Legionella sternal-wound infections due to postoperative topical exposure to contaminated tap water. N Engl J Med. 1991;324:109-113.

171. Brabender W, Hinthorn DR, Asher M, et al. *Legionella pneumophila* wound infection. JAMA. 1983;250:3091-3092.

172. Fraser DW. Legionellosis: Evidence of airborne transmission. Ann N Y Acad Sci. 1980;353:61-66.

173. Johnson JT, Yu VL, Best MG, et al. Nosocomial Legionellosis in surgical patients with head-and-neck cancer: Implications for epidemiological reservoir and mode of transmission. Lancet. 1985;2:298-300.

174. Addiss DG, Davis JP, LaVenture M, et al. Community-acquired Legionnaires' disease associated with a cooling tower: Evidence for longer-distance transport of *Legionella pneumophila*. Am J Epidemiol. 1989;130:557-568.

175. Kool JL, Warwick MC, Pruckler JM, et al. Outbreak of Legionnaires' disease at a bar after basement flooding. Lancet. 1998;351:1030.

176. Brown CM, Nuorti PJ, Breiman RF, et al. A community outbreak of Legionnaires' disease linked to hospital cooling towers: An epidemiological method to calculate dose of exposure. Int J Epidemiol. 1999;28:353-359.

177. Mahoney FJ, Hoge CW, Farley TA, et al. Communitywide outbreak of Legionnaires' disease associated with a grocery store mist machine. J Infect Dis. 1992;165:736-739.

178. Gabbay J. Broadcasting House Legionnaires' disease. Report of the Westminster Action Committee convened to co-ordinate the investigation and control of the outbreak of Legionnaires' disease associated with Portland Place, London W1 in April/May 1988. London: Department of Public Health, Parkside District Health Authority; 1988.

179. Blatt SP, Parkinson MD, Pace E, et al. Nosocomial Legionnaires' disease: Aspiration as a primary mode of disease acquisition. Am J Med. 1993;95:16-22.

180. Dournon E, Bure A, Desplaces N, et al. Legionnaires' disease related to gastric lavage with tap water. Lancet. 1982;1:797-798.

181. Yu VL. Could aspiration be the major mode of transmission for Legionella? Am J Med. 1993;95:13-15.

182. Davis GS, Winn CW Jr, Gump DW, et al. Legionnaires' pneumonia in guinea pigs and rats produced by aerosol exposure. Chest. 1983;83:15S-16S.

183. Winn WC Jr, Davis GS, Gump DW, et al. Legionnaires' pneumonia after intratracheal inoculation of guinea pigs and rats. Lab Invest. 1982;47:568-578.

184. Schmidt T, Pfeiffer A, Ehret W, et al. *Legionella* infection of the colon presenting as acute attack of ulcerative colitis. Gastroenterology. 1989;97:751-755.

185. Dournon E, Bure A, Kemeny JL, et al. *Legionella pneumophila* peritonitis. Lancet. 1982;1:1363

186. Grangeon V, Vincent L, Pacheco Y. Troubles digestifs et pneumopathie à légionelles: Signes d'accompagnement ou localisation viscérale? Rev Mal Respir. 2000;17:489-492.

187. Plouffe JF, Para MF, Fuller KA, Bollin GE. Oral ingestion of *Legionella pneumophila*. J Clin Lab Immunol. 1986;20:113-117.

188. Katz SM, Hammel JM, Matus JP, et al. A self-limited febrile illness produced in guinea pigs associated with oral administration of *Legionella pneumophila*. Gastroenterology. 1988;95:1575-1581.

189. Tablan OC, Anderson LJ, Arden NH, et al. Guideline for prevention of nosocomial pneumonia. The Hospital Infection Control Practices Advisory Committee. Am J Infect Control. 1994;22:247-292.

190. Kool JL, Buchholz U, Peterson C, et al. Strengths and limitations of molecular subtyping in a community outbreak of Legionnaires' disease. Epidemiol Infect. 2000;125:599-608.

191. Lawrence C, Reyrolle M, Dubrou S, et al. Single clonal origin of a high proportion of *Legionella pneumophila* serogroup 1 isolates from patients and the environment in the area of Paris, France, over a 10-year period. J Clin Microbiol. 1999;37:2652-2655.

192. Barbaree JM, Gorman GW, Martin WT, et al. Protocol for sampling environmental sites for legionellae. Appl Environ Microbiol. 1987;53:1454-1458.
193. Freije MR. Legionellae Control in Health Care Facilities: A Guide for Minimizing Risk. Indianapolis, Ind: HC Information Resources; 1996.
194. Lin YS, Stout JE, Yu VL, Vidic RD. Disinfection of water distribution systems for *Legionella*. Semin Resp Infect. 1998;13:147-159.
195. Roig J, Aguilar X, Ruiz J, et al. Comparative study of *Legionella pneumophila* and other nosocomial-acquired pneumonias. Chest. 1991;99:344-350.
196. Granados A, Podzamczer D, Gudiol F, Manresa F. Pneumonia due to *Legionella pneumophila* and pneumococcal pneumonia: Similarities and differences on presentation. Eur Respir J. 1989;2:130-134.
197. Woodhead MA, Macfarlane JT. Comparative clinical and laboratory features of legionella with pneumococcal and mycoplasma pneumonias. Br J Dis Chest. 1987;81:133-139.
198. Kirby BD, Snyder KM, Meyer RD, Finegold SM. Legionnaires' disease: Report of sixty-five nosocomially acquired cases and review of the literature. Medicine (Baltimore). 1980;59:188-205.
199. Gupta SK, Imperiale TF, Sarosi GA. Evaluation of the Winthrop-University Hospital criteria to identify *Legionella* pneumonia. Chest. 2001;120:1064-1071.
200. Muder RR, Yu VL, Parry MF. The radiologic manifestations of *Legionella* pneumonia. Semin Resp Infect. 1987;2:242-254.
201. Domingo C, Roig J, Planas F, et al. Radiographic appearance of nosocomial Legionnaires' disease after erythromycin treatment. Thorax. 1991;46:663-666.
202. Fernandez JA, Lopez P, Orozco D, Merino J. Clinical study of an outbreak of Legionnaire's disease in Alcoy, Southeastern Spain. Euro J Clin Microbiol Infect Dis. 2002;21:729-735.
203. Watts JC, Hicklin MD, Thomason BM, et al. Fatal pneumonia caused by *Legionella pneumophila*, serogroup 3: Demonstration of the bacilli in extrathoracic organs. Ann Intern Med. 1980;92:186-188.
204. White HJ, Felton WW, Sun CN. Extrapulmonary histopathologic manifestations of Legionnaires' disease: Evidence for myocarditis and bacteremia. Arch Pathol Lab Med. 1980;104:287-289.
205. Weisenburger DD, Rappaport H, Ahluwalia MS, et al. Legionnaires' disease. Am J Med. 1980;69:476-482.
206. Evans CP, Winn WC Jr. Extrathoracic localization of *Legionella pneumophila* in legionnaires' pneumonia. Am J Clin Pathol. 1981;76:813-815.
207. Warner CL, Fayad PB, Heffner RR Jr. Legionella myositis. Neurology. 1991;41:750-752.
208. Ferrer A, Lloveras J, Codina G, Martín N. Aislamiento de *Legionella pneumophila* en medula osea. Med Clin (Barc). 1987;88:346-347.
209. Kalweit WH, Winn WC Jr, Rocco TA Jr, Girod JC. Hemodialysis fistula infections caused by *Legionella pneumophila*. Ann Intern Med. 1982;96:173-175.
210. Arnow PM, Boyko EJ, Friedman EL. Perirectal abscess caused by *Legionella pneumophila* and mixed anaerobic bacteria. Ann Intern Med. 1983;98:184-185.
211. Ampel NM, Ruben FL, Norden CW. Cutaneous abscess caused by *Legionella micdadei* in an immunosuppressed patient. Ann Intern Med. 1985;102:630-632.
212. Reyes RR, Noble RC. Legionnaires' pericarditis. J Ky Med Assoc. 1983;81:757-758.
213. Mayock R, Skale B, Kohler RB. *Legionella pneumophila* pericarditis proved by culture of pericardial fluid. Am J Med. 1983;75:534-536.
214. Fogliani J, Domenget JF, Hohn B, et al. Maladie des légionnaires avec localisation digestive: Une observation. Nouv Presse Med. 1982;11:2699-2702.
215. Nomura S, Hatta K, Iwata T, Aihara M. *Legionella pneumophila* isolated in pure culture from the ascites of a patient with systemic lupus erythematosus. Am J Med. 1989;86:833-834.
216. Monforte R, Marco F, Estruch R, Campo E. Multiple organ involvement by *Legionella pneumophila* in a fatal case of legionnaires' disease. J Infect Dis. 1989;159:809
217. Waldor MK, Wilson B, Swartz M. Cellulitis caused by *Legionella pneumophila*. Clin Infect Dis. 1993;16:51-53.
218. Tompkins LS, Roessler BJ, Redd SC, et al. *Legionella* prosthetic-valve endocarditis. N Engl J Med. 1988;318:530-535.
219. McCabe RE, Baldwin JC, McGregor CA, et al. Prosthetic valve endocarditis caused by *Legionella pneumophila*. Ann Intern Med. 1984;100:525-527.
220. Schlanger G, Lutwick LI, Kurzman M, et al. Sinusitis caused by *Legionella pneumophila* in a patient with the acquired immune deficiency syndrome. Am J Med. 1984;77:957-960.
221. Muder RR, Stout JE, Yee YC. Isolation of *Legionella pneumophila* serogroup 5 from empyema following esophageal perforation: Source of the organism and mode of transmission. Chest. 1992;102:1601-1603.
222. Murdoch DR. Diagnosis of *Legionella* infection. Clin Infect Dis. 2003;36:64-69.
223. Formica N, Yates M, Beers M, et al. The impact of diagnosis by legionella urinary antigen test on the epidemiology and outcomes of legionellosis. Epidemiol Infect. 2001;127:275-280.
224. Helbig JH, Uldum SA, Bernander S, et al. Clinical utility of urinary antigen detection for diagnosis of community-acquired, travel-associated, and nosocomial Legionnaires' disease. J Clin Microbiol. 2003;41:838-840.
225. Okada C, Kura F, Wada A, et al. Cross-reactivity and sensitivity of two *Legionella* urinary antigen kits, Biotest EIA and Binax NOW, to extracted antigens from various serogroups of *L. pneumophila* and other *Legionella* species. Microbiol Immunol. 2002;46:51-54.
226. Edelstein PH. Urinary antigen detection for *Legionella* spp. In: Isenberg HD, ed. Clinical Microbiology Procedures Manual. 2nd ed. Washington: ASM Press; 2004:11.4.1-11.4.6.
227. Domínguez J, Gali N, Blanco S, et al. Assessment of a new test to detect *Legionella* urinary antigen for the diagnosis of Legionnaires' disease. Diagn Microbiol Infect Dis. 2001;41:199-203.
228. Edelstein PH. Detection of antibodies to *Legionella* spp. In: Rose NR, Hamilton RG, Detrick B, eds. Manual of Clinical Laboratory Immunology. 6th ed. Washington, DC: American Society for Microbiology; 2002:468-476.
229. Edelstein PH. Detection of *Legionella* antigen by direct immunofluorescence. In: Isenberg HD, ed. Clinical Microbiology Procedures Manual. 2 ed. Washington: ASM Press; 2004:11.3.1-11.3.7.
230. Edelstein PH. Chemotherapy of Legionnaires' disease with macrolide or quinolone antimicrobial agents. In: Marre R, Abu Kwaik Y, Bartlett C, et al, eds. Legionella. Washington: ASM Press; 2002:183-188.
231. Dournon E, Mayaud C, Wolff M, et al. Comparison of the activity of three antibiotic regimens in severe Legionnaires' disease. J Antimicrob Chemother. 1990;26(Suppl B): 129-139.
232. Gacouin A, Le Tulzo Y, Lavoue S, et al. Severe pneumonia due to *Legionella pneumophila:* Prognostic factors, impact of delayed appropriate antimicrobial therapy. Intensive Care Med. 2002;28:686-691.
233. Edelstein PH, Shinzato T, Doyle E, Edelstein MA. In vitro activity of gemifloxacin (SB-265805, LB20304a) against *Legionella pneumophila* and its pharmacokinetics in guinea pigs with *L. pneumophila* pneumonia. Antimicrob Agents Chemother. 2001;45:2204-2209.
234. Edelstein PH, Weiss WJ, Edelstein MA. Activities of tigecycline (GAR-936) against *Legionella pneumophila* in vitro and in guinea pigs with *L. pneumophila* pneumonia. Antimicrob Agents Chemother. 2003;47:533-540.
235. Edelstein PH, Shinzato T, Edelstein MA. BMS-284756 (T-3811ME) a new fluoroquinolone: In vitro activity against *Legionella*, efficacy in a guinea pig model of *L. pneumophila* pneumonia and pharmacokinetics in guinea pigs. J Antimicrob Chemother. 2001;48:667-675.
236. Edelstein PH, Higa F, Edelstein MA. In vitro activity of ABT-773 against *Legionella pneumophila*, its pharmacokinetics in guinea pigs, and its use to treat guinea pigs with *L. pneumophila* pneumonia. Antimicrob Agents Chemother. 2001;45:2685-2690.
237. Tan MJ, Tan JS, Hamor RH, et al. The radiologic manifestations of Legionnaire's disease. The Ohio Community-Based Pneumonia Incidence Study Group. Chest. 2000;117:398-403.
238. Fairbank JT, Mamourian AC, Dietrich PA, Girod JC. The chest radiograph in Legionnaires' disease: Further observations. Radiology. 1983;147:33-34.
239. Kirby BD, Peck H, Meyer RD. Radiographic features of Legionnaires' disease. Chest. 1979;76:562-565.
240. Marrie TJ, Haldane D, Bezanson G. Nosocomial Legionnaires' disease: Clinical and radiographic patterns. Can J Infect Dis. 1992;3:253-260.
241. Meyer RD, Edelstein PH, Kirby BD, et al. Legionnaires' disease: Unusual clinical and laboratory features. Ann Intern Med. 1980;93:240-243.
242. Tateda K, Deng JC, Moore TA, et al. Hyperoxia mediates acute lung injury and increased lethality in murine *Legionella* pneumonia: The role of apoptosis. J Immunol. 2003;170:4209-4216.
243. Skerrett SJ, Schmidt RA, Martin TR. Impaired clearance of aerosolized *Legionella pneumophila* in corticosteroid-treated rats: A model of Legionnaires' disease in the compromised host. J Infect Dis. 1989;160:261-273.
244. Amundson DE, Murray KM, Brodine S, Oldfield EC. High-dose corticosteroid therapy for *Pneumocystis carinii* pneumonia in patients with acquired immunodeficiency syndrome. South Med J. 1989;82:711-718.
245. Shankar PS, Anderson CL, Scott JH. Legionnaires' disease with severe hypoxemia and saddleback fever. Postgrad Med. 1981;69:87-92.
246. Sato P, Madtes DK, Thorning D, Albert RK. Bronchiolitis obliterans caused by *Legionella pneumophila*. Chest. 1985;87:840-842.
247. Hürter T, Rumpelt HJ, Ferlinz R. Fibrosing alveolitis responsive to corticosteroids following Legionnaires' disease pneumonia. Chest. 1992;101:281-283.
248. Blander SJ, Horwitz MA. Major cytoplasmic membrane protein of *Legionella pneumophila*, a genus common antigen and member of the hsp 60 family of heat shock proteins, induces protective immunity in a guinea pig model of Legionnaires' disease. J Clin Invest. 1993;91:717-723.
249. Weeratna R, Stamler DA, Edelstein PH, et al. Human and guinea pig immune responses to *Legionella pneumophila* protein antigens OmpS and Hsp60. Infect Immun. 1994;62:3454-3462.
250. Vereerstraeten P, Stolear JC, Schoutens-Serruys E, et al. Erythromycin prophylaxis for Legionnaire's disease in immunosuppressed patients in a contaminated hospital environment. Transplantation. 1986;41:52-54.
251. Chartered Institution of Building Services Engineers. Technical Memoranda TM13: Minimising the risk of Legionnaires' disease. London: Chartered Institution of Building Services Engineers; 2002.
252. Huyer DW, Corkum SH. Reducing the incidence of tap-water scalds: Strategies for physicians. CMAJ. 1997;156:841-844.
253. Kool JL, Carpenter JC, Fields BS. Effect of monochloramine disinfection of municipal drinking water on risk of nosocomial Legionnaires' disease. Lancet. 1999;353: 272-277.
254. Anonymous. Suggested health and safety guidelines for public spas and hot tubs. Atlanta, Ga: U.S. Dept. Health Human Services, Centers for Disease Control; 1985.
255. PHLS Spa Pools Working Party. Hygiene for spa pools. London: Public Health Laboratory Service; 1994.
256. Texas Department of Health. Report of the Texas Legionnaires' Disease Task Force. Retrieved 5/30/2003 from http://www.tdh.state.tx.us/ideas/factsht/legion/Docs/Full_report.htm.
257. Morris JG Jr, Davis C, Perl TM, Wallace MA. Report of the Maryland scientific working group to study *Legionella* in water systems in healthcare institutions. Retrieved 5/30/2003 from http://www.dhmh.state.md.us/html/legionella.htm, 2000.
258. Sehulster L, Chinn RY. Guidelines for environmental infection control in health-care facilities: Recommendations of CDC and the Healthcare Infection Control Practices Advisory Committee (HICPAC). MMWR Recomm Rep. 2003;52(RR-10):1-42.

Other *Legionella* Species

ROBERT R. MUDER

Since the discovery of *Legionella pneumophila* in 1977, the family Legionellaceae has expanded to include over 40 named species.[1] Like *L. pneumophila,* these other species are found in aquatic environments and soil. The vast majority of human infections are pneumonic, occurring after exposure to an environmental source of *Legionella.*[2] Nineteen species have been documented to cause human infection based on isolation from clinical material (Table 230-1). Isolates of the other species are limited to water and soil, although several have been implicated in human infection based on seroconversion in the absence of isolation.

In addition to the described species, there are other organisms that are in all probability members of the genus *Legionella,* based on analysis of 16S ribosomal RNA sequences.[3,4] These organisms, known as "*Legionella*-like amebal pathogens" (LLAPs), infect freshwater amebas, and are found in aquatic environments capable of supporting the growth of *Legionella.* LLAPs grow very poorly or not at all on media supporting the growth of *Legionella.* However, there is serologic evidence implicating LLAPs as occasional causes of community-acquired pneumonia.[5]

In 1977 workers from the University of Pittsburgh and the University of Virginia visualized gram-negative, weakly acid-fast organisms from lung tissue of immunosuppressed patients with acute pneumonitis.[6,7] Almost all of the patients were receiving steroids or cytotoxic chemotherapy; renal transplant recipients were a prominent group. Although organisms could be seen on biopsy and autopsy lung specimens by various stains, they could not be grown on standard bacteriologic culture media. A *Legionella*-like organism was isolated after the clinical specimens were inoculated into guinea pigs and embryonated eggs. Sera from these patients contained high titers of antibodies against this organism, confirming its etiologic role in pneumonia.

This new organism, originally called Pittsburgh Pneumonia Agent, was serologically and genetically distinct from *L. pneumophila,* although it phenotypically resembled *L. pneumophila* in growth requirements and the presence of branched-chain fatty acids in the cell wall. The organism proved to be identical to organisms isolated in 1943 ("TATLOCK") and 1959 ("HEBA") from guinea pigs injected with the blood of two patients with nonpneumonic illnesses.[8,9] The first documented isolation of *L. bozemanii* was in 1959 from the lung tissue of a patient dying of pneumonia after immersion in fresh water.[9,10]

DESCRIPTION OF THE PATHOGENS

Legionella species are gram-negative aerobic bacilli that share a number of common phenotypic features, including growth on buffered charcoal–yeast extract agar, lack of growth on blood agar, catalase activity, and requirement for cysteine. Tests for urease, nitrate reduction, and fermentative activity are uniformly negative.[11] Although individual species differ in several phenotypic characteristics, such as gelatin liquification, hippurate hydrolysis, and oxidase activity, these tests are of limited utility in differentiation. When grown on yeast extract agar, *Legionella* species produce a water-soluble, extracellular compound that fluoresces yellow-green on exposure to long-wave ultraviolet light. Several species exhibit a blue-white or red autofluorescence under ultraviolet light. Most species produce β-lactamase; *L. micdadei, L. maceachernii,* and *L. feeleii* do not. Cell wall fatty acid profiles and ubiquinone content are sufficiently distinctive to permit species identification on the basis of gas-liquid chromatography.[12] Differentiation of the common species is most conveniently made in the laboratory by

TABLE 230-1 Legionella Species Other Than *L. pneumophila* Causing Human Disease

Species	References
L. micdadei	89, 90
L. bozemannii	10, 57
L. dumoffii	10, 91
L. longbeachae	92
L. wadsworthii	93
L. hackeliae	94
L. maceachernii	95
L. feeleii	96
L. birminghamensis	62
L. cincinnatiensis	97
L. jordanis	98
L. gormanii	99
L. anisa	100
L. tusconensis	101
L. sainthelensis	102
L. lansingensis	103
L. parisiensis	104
L. oakridgensis	105

direct fluorescent antibody staining of the isolates. Slide agglutination can also be used for selected isolates.[2] Determination of DNA homology is the definitive method, especially for the less common strains. Other biochemical and immunologic methods for species classification of *Legionella* are described in Chapter 229.

L. micdadei is unique in that it retains the modified acid-fast stain.[6,7] *L. micdadei* can appear as weakly or partially acid-fast bacilli in clinical specimens. The acid-fast property is not usually present in organisms grown on solid media, but may be retained in liquid culture. The modified acid-fast stain substitutes 1% sulfuric acid (a less potent decolorizing agent) for the traditional 3% hydrochloric acid. This characteristic has occasionally led to misidentification of *L. micdadei* infection as mycobacterial infection, with initiation of antituberculous agents.[7,13,14]

Like *L. pneumophila,* other *Legionella* species are pathogenic for freshwater amebas,[15,16] and a number of species are capable of vigorous intracellular growth within human macrophages.[17] All *Legionella* species tested contain the *dot/icm* loci, composed of 24 genes essential for pathogenesis, mediating uptake of *Legionella* by macrophages, evasion of lysosomal fusion, intracellular replication, and host cell lysis. However, in vitro cytopathogenicity for macrophages varies among species, with *L. pneumophila, L. micdadei,* and *L. dumoffii* being the most cytopathogenic.[17]

EPIDEMIOLOGY

Like *L. pneumophila,* other *Legionella* species are widely distributed in aquatic habitats and soil.[18,19] Several species associated with human disease have only been isolated from clinical specimens. In addition to *L. pneumophila,* water distribution systems may be colonized with any of a number of *Legionella* species, including *L. micdadei, L. bozemanii, L. dumoffii, L. anisa,* and *L. feeleii.*[20-25] Recovery of these species is generally less frequent and technically more demanding than is recovery of *L. pneumophila.* Commensal microflora and sediment known to promote proliferation of *L. pneumophila* in water distribution systems do not support the growth of *L. micdadei.*[26] Thus the growth kinetics of *L. micdadei* may explain its infrequent presence in the water supply, such that only patients with prolonged hospitalization or immunosuppression are susceptible. Like *L. pneumophila,* other species multiply within aquatic protozoa.[15,16]

The role of non-*pneumophila Legionella* species in community-acquired pneumonia is gradually emerging. Investigators in Ohio reported seven culture-confirmed cases of community-acquired *L. bozemanii* pneumonia from a single institution over a 5-year period.[27] In a subsequent study, 14% of patients with community-acquired pneumonia showed seroconversion to *Legionella* species, including *L. bozemanii*

(8%) and *L. anisa* (4%).[28] An international study of 509 cases of culture-confirmed, community-acquired *Legionella* infection[29] found that 91% were caused by *L. pneumophila*. Of the remainder, *L. longbeachae* (3.9%) and *L. bozemanii* (2.4%) were next in frequency, followed by *L. micdadei*, *L. feeleii*, *L. dumoffii*, *L. wadsworthii*, and *L. anisa*. Other species appear to be very rare causes of human infection; for several, only a single instance of isolation from a human has been described.

Most reported patients with non-*pneumophila Legionella* infections have been immunocompromised as a result of corticosteroid therapy, organ transplantation, or malignancy.[30] Patients with *L. micdadei* pneumonia are more likely to be immunosuppressed than those with *L. pneumophila* infection.[31] *Legionella* species are frequent opportunistic pathogens in patients undergoing organ transplantation.[6,14,32-35] After *L. pneumophila*, *L. micdadei*, *L. bozemanii*, and *L. dumoffii* are the most frequent causes of *Legionella* infection in transplant patients.[35]

As with *L. pneumophila*, infection with *L. longbeachae* and *L. dumoffii* has occurred in patients with hairy cell leukemia.[36,37] Human immunodeficiency virus (HIV) infection is associated with some increased risk of infection caused by *L. pneumophila*; cases of *L. bozemanii*,[38] *L. feeleii*,[39] and *L. micdadei*[40] infection occurring in the setting of HIV infection have also been reported

Most reported clusters of infection caused by non-*pneumophila* species have been nosocomial, and have included *L. micdadei*,[6,7,20,41-43] *L. bozemanii*,[21] and *L. dumoffii*.[44] Two outbreaks of pneumonia resulting from *L. sainthelensis* occurred in Canadian nursing homes.[45] As is typically the case with *L. pneumophila* infection, the source of these outbreaks has been the facility's water system. One reported outbreak among solid-organ transplant recipients in a single center involved 12 patients over a 6-month period; the attack rate was 19%.[43] *L. micdadei* was widespread in the hospital water system, and pulsed-field gel electrophoresis of bacterial DNA showed the clinical and environmental strains to be identical. Colonization of a water system with two *Legionella* species may result in outbreaks of infection in which pneumonia may be caused by either or both species simultaneously. A simultaneous outbreak of *L. pneumophila* and *L. micdadei* infection, for example, included patients with both pathogens isolated from respiratory secretions.[46] A cluster of prosthetic valve endocarditis and a cluster of sternal wound infections caused by *L. pneumophila* and *L. dumoffii*, singly and in combination, occurred in a single hospital.[25,47] Sternal wound infection was the result of contamination of wounds by tap water during bathing.

In contrast to *L. pneumophila*, reports of community-acquired outbreaks of other *Legionella* species are rare. However, cases may be overlooked because cultures for *Legionella* are not obtained in most cases of community-acquired pneumonia, and the urinary antigen test only detects infection with *L. pneumophila* serogroup 1. In Australia and the United States there have been multiple cases of community-acquired *L. longbeachae* pneumonia[48-51] associated with exposure to potting soil. Australian investigators isolated *L. longbeachae* from the soil and commercial potting mixes from many of the patient's homes. Potting mixes made in Australia contained the organism, but not mixes made in Europe.[49] Restriction fragment length polymorphism showed that organisms isolated from the patients and soils were closely related.[50]

There are reports of outbreaks of nonpneumonic legionellosis ("Pontiac fever") associated with exposures to contaminated aerosols. One such outbreak involved 317 workers in an automobile plant in which machinery produced aerosols of water-based coolant containing *L. feeleii*.[52] A whirlpool spa contaminated with *L. micdadei* ("Lochgoilhead fever")[53] and a decorative fountain contaminated with *L. anisa*[54] have also been implicated in outbreaks of nonpneumonic disease. An outbreak of Pontiac fever with seroconversion to both *L. pneumophila* and *L. micdadei* occurred in a group of children and adults exposed to a poorly maintained whirlpool spa.[55]

Many reported cases of pneumonia resulting from *Legionella* species are sporadic infections. In such cases, it has generally not been possible to identify an environmental source of the organism. The mode of transmission of the organism from the environment to hu-

mans is uncertain except in a limited number of outbreak situations as cited earlier. There are no reports of outbreaks of pneumonic infection caused by non-*pneumophila Legionella* species associated with large aerosol-generating devices such as cooling towers. The occurrence of simultaneous infection by *L. pneumophila* and other species[25,46,47,56] suggests these other species share common modes of transmission with *L. pneumophila*. Reports of pneumonia following immersion in fresh water[9,57,58] and aspiration[59] suggest that aspiration is a mechanism of transmission to the patient, as has been documented for *L. pneumophila*.[60] Human-to-human transmission does not occur.

CLINICAL MANIFESTATIONS

The vast majority of human *Legionella* infections present as pneumonia. Clinically and radiographically, pneumonia caused by other *Legionella* species resembles that caused by *L. pneumophila*.[2,30] Fever is present in over 90% of patients, exceeding 103° F (39.4° C) in half. Cough is often nonproductive or minimally productive, although most patients produce some sputum. The majority of patients complain of dyspnea. Sixty percent have some alteration in mental status, ranging from lethargy to obtundation. In immunosuppressed patients, pleuritic chest pain is a frequent complaint,[6,7] and the presentation may mimic that of pulmonary embolism. Immunosuppressed patients may have fever without any other symptoms of pneumonia despite the radiographic presence of pulmonary infiltrates.[31,61,62] Occasionally, *Legionella* infections in these patients present as incidental radiographic abnormalities in the absence of fever.[31,61,62] Documented extrapulmonic infection is rare. Four cases of prosthetic valve endocarditis resulting from *L. dumoffii* (including one with simultaneous *L. pneumophila* infection) occurred at a single hospital.[47] The patients presented with a chronic syndrome of persistent fever, night sweats, malaise, and weight loss without embolic phenomena. All four patients responded to prolonged therapy with erythromycin and rifampin, although three required valve replacement. Sternal wound infection following cardiac surgery presented as serosanguinous wound drainage in the early postoperative period.[25] Gram stain failed to demonstrate organisms, but cultures yielded *L. dumoffii* and *L. pneumophila*. Isolated cases of pericarditis resulting from *L. bozemanii* and *L. dumoffii* have been reported in cardiac transplant patients.[63,64]

Cutaneous infection caused by *L. micdadei* has occurred following pneumonia, presumably by bacteremic seeding,[65] and in the absence of pulmonary infection.[66] Multiple recurrent soft tissue abscesses resulting from *L. cincinnatiensis* occurred in a patient with nephrotic syndrome and monoclonal gammopathy.[67] The patient did not have pneumonia, and the route of infection was not determined.

Laboratory data are not distinctive. The majority of patients show a neutrophilic leukocytosis unless receiving cytotoxic agents as immunosuppressive therapy. Elevations of hepatic transaminases or alkaline phosphatase are common. Hyponatremia, reportedly more frequent in *L. pneumophila* infection than in other pneumonias, occurs in one third of cases of *L. micdadei* infection.[68]

Radiographic manifestations are similar to those of *L. pneumophila* infection.[69] In nonimmunosuppressed patients, segmental to lobar infiltrates similar to those occurring in other bacterial pneumonias are typical.[70] An expanding pulmonary nodule has been a dramatic finding in some immunosuppressed patients.[6,61,71] Cavitation of nodules or infiltrates may occur in immunosuppressed patients (Figs. 230-1 and 230-2).[41,69] The cavities often enlarge during treatment and clinical improvement, and rarely require intervention. Small pleural effusions are common; these usually resolve without drainage, but empyema may occur.

Nonpneumonic disease caused by non-*pneumophila* species closely resembles Pontiac fever, the syndrome associated with *L. pneumophila*.[52-54] Following a brief incubation period averaging 36 to 48 hours after exposure to a *Legionella*-containing aerosol, patients experience the abrupt onset of a "flulike" syndrome of fever, chills, headache, myalgias, and malaise. Attack rates may exceed 80% among those exposed. Clinical and radiologic evidence of pneumonia

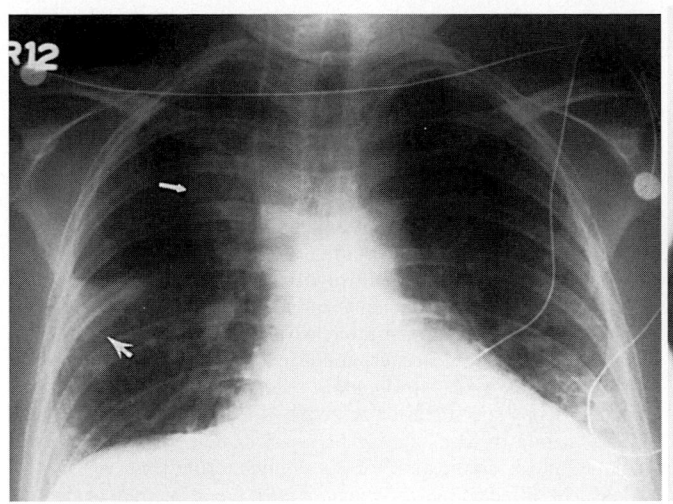

A

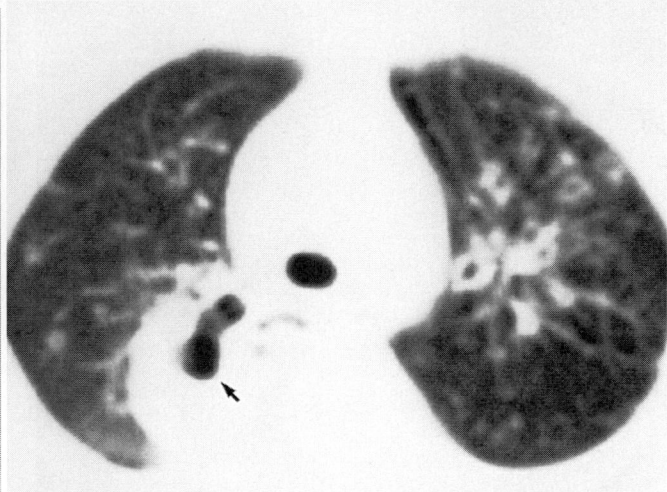

B

FIGURE 230-1. Nosocomial *L. micdadei* in a young female receiving steroids for systemic lupus erythematosus. On day 3 she experienced abrupt onset of fever, dyspnea, and pleuritic chest pain. **A,** Poorly marginated densities (*small arrow*) and a wedge-shaped density (*large arrow*) were seen on chest x-ray films, suggesting pulmonary embolus, although pulmonary angiography was nonconfirmatory. Direct fluorescent antibody stain and culture of sputum yielded *L. micdadei.* Cavitation in the right upper lobe was seen on day 7 and day 10. **B,** Computed tomography shows the cavity (*arrow*). **C,** A residual thin-walled cavity was still visible on day 15 (*arrow*). The patient ultimately made a full recovery. *(From Muder RR, Yu VL, Parry M. Radiology of Legionella pneumonia. Semin Resp Infect. 1987;2:242-254.)*

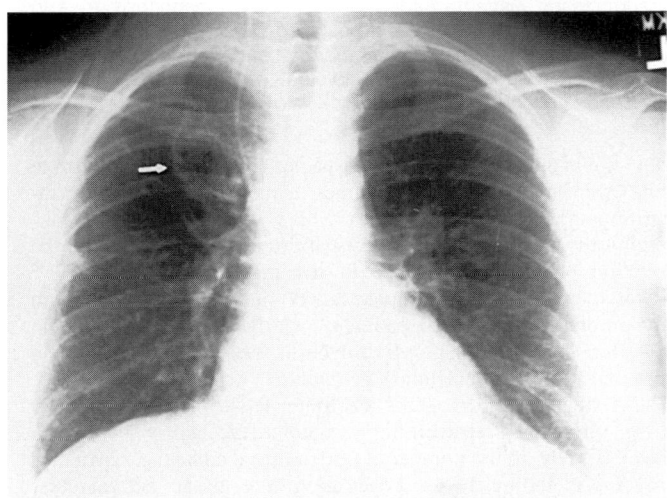

C

are absent; spontaneous recovery after 2 to 7 days is the rule. Diagnosis is made by recognition of the clinical and epidemiologic features, isolation of a *Legionella* species from an aerosol generation source, and demonstration of seroconversion to the suspected agent on the part of the patients affected. *Legionella* species are generally not detected in clinical material from these patients. There is evidence that the clinical manifestations of Pontiac fever may be the result of an immunologic reaction to high levels of endotoxin in aerosolized water containing *Legionella* rather than the result of infection.[72]

DIAGNOSIS

Isolation of the infecting agent from clinical material (such as sputum or bronchoalveolar lavage fluid) on selective media is the most reliable means of diagnosis. Buffered charcoal–yeast extract (BCYE) agars with added antibiotics to suppress commensal flora are available commercially,[73] but these media often have decreased sensitivity for isolation of non-*pneumophila* strains[74]; cefamandole is especially inhibitory. *Legionella* species lacking β-lactamase, such as *L. micdadei* and *L. bozemanii,* will not grow on BCYE formulations containing cephalosporins. A more sensitive medium consists of BCYE with added vancomycin, anisomycin, and polymyxin B. The non-*pneumophila* strains are easily missed in clinical and environmental specimens if dye-containing media are not used. Colonies of *L. micdadei* and *L. maceachernii* are blue on culture media containing bromocre-

sol purple and bromthymol blue dyes, whereas the colonies of other species are yellow-green to apple green[2,75]; the dyes color the organism, making detection easier.

Direct fluorescent antibody (DFA) stains for the visualization of *Legionella* species in clinical specimens are commercially available for a limited number of species. The sensitivity and specificity of DFA staining for species other than *L. pneumophila* is not precisely known. A *Legionella* DNA probe can detect the presence of multiple *Legionella* species, but does not differentiate among species. The DNA probe appears to have fewer false-positive reactions than does DFA staining[76]; it is no longer commercially available. The commercially available test for *Legionella* urinary antigen detects only *L. pneumophila* serogroup 1; it is not useful for other *Legionella* species. Detection of *Legionella* spp. in clinical specimens by DNA amplification is a promising technique that has been applied in a limited number of cases.[77]

Antibody seroconversion in diagnosing infection caused by non-*pneumophila* species is of uncertain specificity. Reports of infection based on seroconversion alone should be viewed with skepticism.

TREATMENT

There are no randomized trials of therapy for *Legionella* infection; the majority of reported clinical experience concerns infection with *L. pneumophila.* In vitro susceptibility data and more limited clinical experience indicate that response to the therapy of infection with other

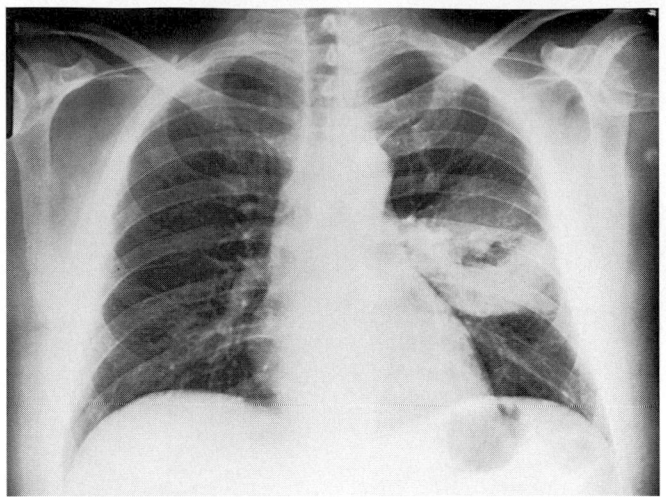

FIGURE 230-2. Nosocomial *L. bozemanii* pneumonia in an immunosuppressed patient. Although the patient responded to erythromycin and rifampin, cavitation occurred within the left lower lobe infiltrate. The infiltrate decreased by month 3 and resolved by month 6. *(From Muder RR, Yu VL, Parry M. Radiology of Legionella pneumonia. Semin Resp Infect. 1987;2:242-254.)*

species should be similar. *Legionella* species are susceptible in vitro to erythromycin, macrolides, tetracyclines, trimethoprim-sulfamethoxazole, rifampin, and fluoroquinolones.[78,79]

Erythromycin has been the historical drug of choice based on the observation of clinical response in the majority of patients.[2,37,80] However, there are a number of case reports of erythromycin failure in highly immunocompromised patients.[33,81-83] Failure of erythromycin may be due to the fact that erythromycin is bacteriostatic rather than bactericidal against intracellular *Legionella*.

The newer macrolide agents are more active than erythromycin both in vitro and intracellularly against the non-*pneumophila* species.[84-86] They offer a number of other clinical advantages over erythromycin, including better penetration into tissue and alveolar macrophages, and improved pharmacokinetics permitting once daily dosing. The fluoroquinolones are considerably more active than erythromycin.[86] Based on these factors, the newer macrolides or quinolones are the therapy of choice for infection caused by *Legionella* species. Patients who are immunocompromised or who are hospitalized with potentially life-threatening infection should receive intravenous therapy with either azithromycin or a fluoroquinolone.[87] Quinolones are preferable when treating transplant patients receiving cyclosporine or tacrolimus, because macrolides interfere with the metabolism of these antirejection agents.

The optimal duration of therapy with these agents is uncertain. Data from clinical trials of community-acquired pneumonia suggest that, in immunocompetent patients, 5 to 10 days of therapy with azithromycin or 10 to 14 days of therapy with a fluoroquinolone constitutes adequate therapy.[85] Immunocompromised patients should receive longer courses of therapy (14 to 21 days) in order to prevent relapse. Oral therapy may be used as initial treatment in immunocompetent patients who are not seriously ill. Patients receiving initial parenteral therapy may be switched to oral therapy once a clinical response is apparent.

PREVENTION

Many cases of infection caused by non-*pneumophila Legionella* species are sporadic, and the source undetermined. When identified, the source is nearly always aquatic; soil is an occasional reservoir. As with *L. pneumophila*, cases of nosocomial disease caused by *L. micdadei*, *L. bozemanii*, and *L. dumoffii* have been linked to *Legionella* colonization of hospital water systems. Although the occurrence of *L.*

pneumophila in a hospital water system is associated with a high risk of nosocomial legionellosis, the risk posed by the presence of other species in a facility's water system is less well defined.

An increasing number of state and local public health departments recommend that hospitals conduct periodic surveillance of their water systems for *Legionella* (see Chapter 229). Although this surveillance is primarily directed at prevention of disease caused by *L. pneumophila*, surveillance may reveal the presence of other species. If surveillance demonstrates the presence of *L. micdadei*, *L. bozemanii*, or *L. dumoffii*, one approach would be to investigate all cases of nosocomial pneumonia occurring in highly immunocompromised patients, including transplant recipients and patients treated with high-dose corticosteroids or immunosuppressive agents, for the occurrence of *Legionella* infection. Because the urinary antigen test detects only infection caused by *L. pneumophila* serogroup 1, culture of sputum or bronchoscopy specimens on selective media is required for diagnosis. Identification of cases among high-risk patients should prompt consideration of eradication of *Legionella* from the water system. Measures directed at *L. pneumophila* are effective against other *Legionella* species. Water disinfection using copper-silver ion generators has good long-term efficacy.[88]

REFERENCES

1. Benson RF, Fields BS. Classification of the genus *Legionella*. Semin Respir Infect. 1998;13:90-99.
2. Fang GD, Yu VL, Vickers RM. Disease due to *Legionellaceae* (other than *Legionella pneumophila*): Historical, microbiological, clinical and epidemiological review. Medicine. 1989;68:116-139.
3. Birtles RJ, Rowbotham TJ, Raoult D, Harrison TG. Phylogenetic diversity of intra-amoebal legionellae as revealed by 16s rRNA gene sequence comparison. Microbiology. 1996;142:3525-3530.
4. Adeleke A, Pruckler J, Benson R, et al. *Legionella*-like amebal pathogens—phylogenetic status and possible role in respiratory diseases. Emerg Infect Dis. 1996;2:225-230.
5. Marrie TJ, Raoult D, La Scola B, et al. *Legionella*-like and other amoebal pathogens as agents of community-acquired pneumonia. Emerg Infect Dis. 2001;7:1026-1029.
6. Myerowitz RC, Pasculle AW, Dowling J, et al. Opportunistic lung infection due to "Pittsburgh pneumonia agent." N Engl J Med. 1979;301:953-958.
7. Rogers BH, Donowitz GR, Walker GK, et al. A clinicopathological study of five cases caused by an unidentified acid-fast bacterium. N Engl J Med. 1979;301:959-961.
8. Tatlock H. Studies on a virus from a patient with Fort Bragg fever (pretibial fever). Clin Invest. 1947;26:87-93.
9. Bozeman FM, Humphries JW, Campbell JM. A new group of Rickettsia-like agents recovered from guinea pigs. Acta Virol. 1968;12:87-93.
10. Brenner DJ, Steigerwalt A, Gorman GW. *Legionella bozemanii*, sp nov and *Legionella dumoffii* sp nov: Classification of two additional species of *Legionella* associated with human pneumonia. Curr Microbiol. 1980;4:111-116.
11. Brenner DJ, Steigerwalt AG, Gorman GW, et al. Ten new species of *Legionella*. Int J Syst Bacteriol. 1985;35:50-59.
12. Lambert MA, Moss CW. Cellular fatty acid compositions and isoprenoid quinone contents of 23 *Legionella* species. J Clin Microbiol. 1989;27:465-473.
13. Hilton E, Freedman RA, Cintron F, et al. Acid-fast bacilli in sputum: A case of *Legionella micdadei* pneumonia. J Clin Microbiol. 1986;24:1102-1103.
14. Schwebke JR, Hackman R, Bowden R. Pneumonia due to Legionella micdadei in bone marrow transplant recipients. Rev Infect Dis. 1990;12:824-828.
15. Wadowsky RM, Wilson TM, Kapp NJ, et al. Multiselection of *Legionella* spp. in tap water containing *Hartmanella oerniformis*. Appl Environ Microbiol. 1991;57:1950-1955.
16. Fields BS, Barbaree JM, Sanden GN, Morrill WE. Virulence of *Legionella anisa* strain associated with Pontiac fever: An evaluation using protozoan, cell culture, and guinea pig models. Infect Immun. 1990;58:3139-3142.
17. Alli OAT, Zink S, von Lackum NK, Abu-Kwaik Y. Comparative virulence traits in *Legionella* spp. Microbiology. 2003;149:631-641.
18. Tison DL, Baross JA, Seidler RJ. Legionella in aquatic habitats in the Mount Saint Helens blast zone. Curr Microbiol. 1983;9:345-348.
19. Joly JR, Boissiot M, Duchaine J, et al. Ecological distribution of Legionellaceae in the Quebec City area. Can J Microbiol. 1984;30:63-67.
20. Best M, Yu VL, Stout J, et al. Legionellaceae in the hospital water supply—epidemiological link with disease and evaluation of a method of control of nosocomial Legionnaires' disease and Pittsburgh pneumonia. Lancet. 1983;2:307-310.
21. Parry MF, Stampleman L, Hutchinson J, et al. Waterborne Legionella bozemanii and nosocomial pneumonia in immunosuppressed patients. Ann Intern Med. 1985;103:205-210.
22. Barbaree JM. Selecting a subtyping technique for use in investigations of legionellosis epidemics. In: Barbaree JM, Brieman RF, Dufour AP, eds. *Legionella:* Current Status and Emerging Perspectives. Washington, DC: American Society for Microbiology, 1993:169-172.
23. Bornstein N, Veilly C, Marmet D, et al. Isolation of Legionella anisa from a hospital hot water system. Eur J Clin Microbiol. 1985;4:327-330.

24. Palutke WA, Crane LR, Wentworth BB, et al. *Legionella feeleii*-associated pneumonia in humans. N Engl J Med. 1986;86:348-351.
25. Lowry PW, Blankenship RJ, Gridley W, et al. A cluster of *Legionella* sternal wound infections due to postoperative topical exposure to contaminated tap water. N Engl J Med. 1991;324:109-112.
26. Best MG, Stout J, Yu VL, et al. Tatlockia micdadei growth kinetics may explain its infrequent isolation from water and the low prevalence of Pittsburgh pneumonia. Appl Environ Microbiol. 1985;49:1521-1522.
27. McNally C, Plouffe J. *Legionella bozemanii*—an important etiological agent in community-acquired pneumonia (Abstract 519). In: Program and Abstracts of the 36th Annual Meeting of the Infectious Diseases Society of America, Denver, CO; 1998.
28. McNally C, Hackman B, Fields BS, Plouffe JF. Potential importance of *Legionella* species as etiologies in community acquired pneumonia (CAP). Diagn Microbiol Infect Dis. 2000;38:79-82.
29. Yu VL, Plouffe JF, Castellani-Pastoris M, et al. Distribution of *Legionella* species and serogroups isolated by culture in consecutive patients with community acquired pneumonia: An international collaborative survey. J Infect Dis. 2002;186:127-128.
30. Muder RR, Yu VL. Infection due to *Legionella* species other than *L. pneumophila.* Clin Infect Dis. 2002;35:990-998.
31. Muder RR, Yu VL, Zuravleff JJ. Pneumonia due to the Pittsburgh pneumonia agent: New clinical perspective with a review of the literature. Medicine. 1983;62:120-128.
32. Singh N, Muder RR, Yu VL, Gayowski T. Legionella infection in liver transplant recipients: Implications for management. Transplantation. 1993;56:1549-1551.
33. Harrington RD, Woolfrey AE, Bowden R, et al. Legionellosis in a bone marrow transplant center. Clin Infect Dis. 1996;18:361-368.
34. Ernst A, Gordon FD, Hayek J, et al. Lung abscess complication: *Legionella micdadei* pneumonia in an adult liver transplant recipient. Transplantation. 1998;65:130-133.
35. Chow J, Yu VL. *Legionella:* A major opportunistic pathogen in transplant recipients. Semin Respir Infect. 1998;13:132-139.
36. Lang R, Miller I, Manon J, et al. *Legionella longbeachae* in a splenectomized hairy-cell leukemia patient. Infection. 1990;18:31-32.
37. Fang GD, Stout JE, Yu VL, et al. Community-acquired pneumonia caused by Legionella dumoffii in a patient with hairy cell leukemia. Infection. 1990;18:383-385.
38. Harris A, Lally M, Albrecht M. *Legionella bozemanii* pneumonia in three patients with AIDS. Clin Infect Dis. 1998;27:97-99.
39. Lo Presti F, Riffard S, Neyret C, et al. First isolation in Europe of *Legionella feeleii* from two cases of pneumonia. Eur J Clin Microbiol Infect Dis. 1998;17:64-66.
40. Johnson KM, Huseby JS. Lung abscess caused by Legionella micdadei (see comments). Chest. 1997;111:252-253.
41. Rudin JE, Wing EJ. A comparative study of *Legionella micdadei* and other nosocomial acquired pneumonia. Chest. 1984;86:875-880.
42. Doebbeling BN, Ishak MA, Wade BH, et al. Nosocomial *Legionella micdadei* pneumonia: 10 years experience and a case-control study. J Hosp Infect. 1989;13:289-298.
43. Knirsch CA, Jakob K, Schoonmaker D, et al. An outbreak of *Legionella micdadei* pneumonia in transplant patients: Education, molecular epidemiology, and control. Am J Med. 2000;108:290-295.
44. Brooks RG, Hofflin JM, Jamieson SW, et al. Infectious complications in heart-lung transplant recipients. Am J Med. 1985;79:412-422.
45. Loeb M, Simor AE, Mandell L, et al. Two nursing home outbreaks of respiratory infections with *Legionella sainthelensis.* J Am Geriatr Soc. 1999;47:547-552.
46. Muder RR, Yu VL, Vickers R, et al. Simultaneous infection with Legionella pneumophila and Pittsburgh pneumonia agent—Clinical features and epidemiological implications. Am J Med. 1983;74:609-614.
47. Tompkins LS, Roessler BJ, Redd SC, et al. Legionella prosthetic-valve endocarditis. N Engl J Med. 1988;318:530-535.
48. Camerson S, Walker C, Roden D, Feldheim J. Epidemiological characteristics of Legionella infection in South Australia: Implications for disease control. Aust N Z Med. 1991;21:65-70.
49. Steele TW, Moore CY, Sangster N. Distribution of *Legionella longbeachae* serogroup 1 and other legionellae in potting soil in Australia. Appl Env Microbiol. 1990;56:2984-2988.
50. Lanser JA, Adams M, Doyle R, et al. Genetic relatedness of *Legionella longbeachae* isolates from human and environmental sources in Australia. Appl Environ Microbiol. 1990;56:2784-2790.
51. Centers for Disease Control and Prevention. Legionnaires' disease associated with potting soil—California, Oregon, and Washington, May-June 2000. MMWR Morb Mortal Wkly Rep. 2000;49:777-778.
52. Herwaldt LA, Gorman GW, McGrath T, et al. A new legionella species, Legionella feeleii species nova, causes Pontiac fever in an automobile plant. Ann Intern Med. 1984;100:333-338.
53. Goldberg DJ, Wrench JG, Collier PW, et al. Lochgoilhead fever: Outbreak of non-pneumonic legionellosis due to Legionella micdadei. Lancet. 1989;1:316-318.
54. Fenstersheib M, Miller M, Diggins C, et al. Outbreak of Pontiac fever due to Legionella anisa. Lancet. 1990;336:35-37.
55. Luttichau HR, Vinther C, Uldum SA, et al. An outbreak of Pontiac fever among children following use of a whirlpool. Clin Infect Dis. 1998;26:1374-1378.
56. Tompkins LS, Trout N, Wood ST, et al. Molecular epidemiology of Legionella species by restriction endonuclease and alloenzyme analysis. J Clin Microbiol. 1987;25:1875-1880.
57. Cordes LG, Gorman GW, Wilkinson HW, et al. Atypical Legionella-like organisms: Fastidious water-associated bacteria pathogenic for man. Lancet. 1979;2:927-930.
58. Thompson BM, Harris PP, Hicklin MD, et al. A Legionella-like bacterium related to WIGA in a fatal case of pneumonia. Ann Intern Med. 1979;91:673-676.
59. Donegan EA, Deal MM, Melanephy MC, et al. Primary isolation of a new strain of the TATLOCK/Pittsburgh pneumonia agent (*Legionella micdadei*). West J Med. 1981;134:384-389.
60. Yu VL. Could aspiration be the major mode of transmission for *Legionella*? Am J Med. 1993;95:13-15.
61. Ellis AR, Mayers DL, Martone WJ, et al. Rapid expanding pulmonary nodule caused by Pittsburgh pneumonia agent. JAMA. 1981;245:1558-1559.
62. Wilkinson HW, Thacker LW, Benson RF, et al. Legionella birminghamensis sp. nov. isolated from a cardiac transplant recipient. J Clin Microbiol. 1987;25:2120-2122.
63. Swinburn CR, Gould FK, Corris PA, et al. Opportunist pulmonary infection with *Legionella bozemanii.* Thorax. 1989;44:434-435.
64. Valentine HA, Hunt SA, Gibbons R, et al. Increasing pericardial effusion in cardiac transplant recipients. Circulation. 1989;79:603-609.
65. Ampel NM, Ruben FL, Norden CW. Cutaneous abscess caused by *Legionella micdadei* in an immunosuppressed patient. Ann Intern Med. 1985;102:630-632.
66. Kilborn JA, Manz LA, O'Brien M, et al. Necrotizing cellulitis caused by Legionella micdadei. Am J Med. 1992;92:104-106.
67. Gubler JGH, Schorr M, Gaia V, et al. Recurrent soft tissue abscess caused by *Legionella cincinnatiensis.* J Clin Microbiol. 2001;39:4568-4570.
68. Fang GD, Yu VL, Vickers RM. Infections caused by the Pittsburgh pneumonia agent. Semin Respir Infect. 1987;2:262-266.
69. Muder RR, Yu VL, Parry M. Radiology of Legionella pneumonia. Semin Respir Infect. 1987;2:242-254.
70. Muder RR, Reddy S, Yu VL, et al. Pneumonia caused by Pittsburgh pneumonia agent: Radiologic manifestations. Radiology. 1984;150:633-637.
71. Pope TL, Armstrong P, Thompson R, et al. Pittsburgh pneumonia agent: Chest film manifestations. AJR Am J Roentgenol. 1982;138:237-241.
72. Fields BS, Haupt T, Davis JP, et al. Pontiac fever due to *Legionella micdadei* from a whirlpool spa: Possible role of bacterial endotoxin. J Infect Dis. 2001;15:1289-1292.
73. Vickers RM, Stout JE, Yu VL, Rihs JD. Culture methodology for the isolation of *Legionella pneumophila* and other Legionellaceae from clinical and environmental specimens. Semin Respir Infect. 1987;2:274-279.
74. Lee TC, Vickers RM, Yu VL, Wagener MM. Growth of 28 *Legionella* species on selective culture media: A comparative study. J Clin Microbiol. 1993;31:2761-2768.
75. Vickers RM, Brown A, Garrity GM. Dye-containing buffered charcoal yeast extract medium for the differentiation of members of the family Legionellaceae. J Clin Microbiol. 1981;13:380-382.
76. Finkelstein R, Brown P, Palutke WA, et al. Diagnostic efficacy of a DNA probe in pneumonia caused by *Legionella* species. J Med Microbiol. 1993;38:183-186.
77. Jaulhac B, Reinthaler FF, Pschaid A, et al. Detection of *Legionella* species in bronchoalveolar lavage fluids by DNA amplification. J Clin Microbiol. 1992;30:920-924.
78. Pasculle AW, Dowling JW, Weyent RS, et al. Susceptibility of Pittsburgh pneumonia agent (*Legionella micdadei*) and other newly recognized members of the genus Legionella to nineteen antimicrobial agents. Antimicrob Agents Chemother. 1981;20:793-799.
79. Saito A, Koga H, Shigeno H, et al. The antimicrobial activity of ciprofloxacin against Legionella species and the treatment of experimental legionella pneumonia in guinea pigs. J Antimicrob Chemother. 1986;18:251-260.
80. Wing EJ, Schafer FJ, Pasculle AW. Successful treatment of *Legionella micdadei* (Pittsburgh pneumonia agent) pneumonia with erythromycin. Am J Med. 1981;21:836-839.
81. Taylor TH, Albrecht MA. Legionella bozemanii cavitary pneumonia poorly responsive to erythromycin: Case report and review. Clin Infect Dis. 1995;20:329-334.
82. Koch CA, Robyn JA, Coccia MR. Systemic lupus erythematosus: A risk factor for pneumonia caused by *Legionella micdadei*? Arch Intern Med. 1997;157:2670-2671.
83. Rudin JE, Evans TL, Wing EJ. Failure of erythromycin in treatment of Legionella micdadei pneumonia. Am J Med. 1984;76:318-320.
84. Stout JE, Arnold B, Yu VL. Comparative activity of azithromycin, clarithromycin, roxithromycin, dirithromycin, quinupristin/dalfopristin, and erythromycin against Legionella species by broth microdilution and intracellular susceptibility testing in HL-60 cells. J Antimicrob Chemother. 1998;41:289-291.
85. Vergis EN, Yu VL. *Legionella* species. In: Yu VL, Merigan TC, Barriere SL, et al. Antimicrobial Therapy and Vaccines. Baltimore, Williams & Wilkins; 1998:257-272.
86. Stout JE, Arnold B, Yu VL. Comparative activity of ciprofloxacin, ofloxacin, levofloxacin, and erythromycin against Legionella species by broth microdilution and intracellular susceptibility testing in HL-60 cells. Diagn Microbiol Infect Dis. 1998;30:37-43.
87. Stout JE, Yu VL. Current concepts: Legionellosis. N Engl J Med. 1997;337:682-687.
88. Stout JE, Yu VL. Experience of the first 16 hospitals using copper-silver ionization for *Legionella* control: Implications for the evaluation of other disinfection modalities. Infect Control Hosp Epidemiol. 2003;24:563-568.
89. Pasculle A, Myerowitz R, Rinaldo C. New bacterial agent of pneumonia isolated from renal transplant recipients. Lancet. 1979;2:58-61.
90. Hebert GA, Steigerwalt AG, Brenner DJ. *Legionella micdadei* species nova: Classification of a third species of *Legionella* associated with human pneumonia. Curr Microbiol. 1980;3:257.
91. Lewallen KS, McKinney RM, Brenner DJ, et al. A newly identified bacterium phenotypically resembling, not genetically distinct from, *Legionella pneumophila:* An isolate in a case of pneumonia. Ann Intern Med. 1979;91:831-834.
92. McKinney RM, Porschen RK, Edelstein PH, et al. *Legionella longbeachae* species nova, another etiologic agent of human pneumonia. Ann Intern Med. 1981;94:739-743.
93. Edelstein PH, Brenner DJ, Moss CW, et al. *Legionella wadsworthii* species nova: A cause of human pneumonia. Ann Intern Med. 1982;97:809-813.
94. Wilkinson HW, Thacker WL, Steigerwalt AG, et al. Second serogroup of *Legionella hackeliae* isolated from a patient with pneumonia. J Clin Microbiol. 1985;22:488-489.
95. Wilkinson HW, Thacker WL, Brenner DJ, Ryan KH. Fatal *Legionella maceachernii* pneumonia. J Clin Microbiol. 1985;22:1055.

96. Thacker WL, Wilkinson HW, Plikaytis BB, et al. Second serogroup of *Legionella feeleii* strains isolated from humans. J Clin Microbiol. 1985;22:1-4.
97. Thacker WL, Benson RF, Staneck JL, et al. Legionella cincinnatiensis sp. nov. isolated from a patient with pneumonia. J Clin Microbiol. 1988;26:418-1834.
98. Thacker WL, Wilkinson HW, Benson RF, et al. *Legionella jordanis* isolated from a patient with fatal pneumonia. J Clin Microbiol. 1988;28:1400-1401.
99. Griffith ME, Lindsay DS, Benson RF, et al. First isolation of *Legionella gormanii* from a patient with fatal pneumonia. J Clin Microbiol. 1988;26:380-381.
100. Bornstein N, Mercatello A, Marmet D, et al. Pleural infection caused by Legionella anisa. J Clin Microbiol. 1989;27:2100-2101.
101. Thacker WL, Benson RF, Staneck JL, et al. Legionella tucsonesis sp. nov. isolated from a renal transplant recipient. J Clin Microbiol. 1989;27:1831-1834.
102. Benson RF, Thacker WL, Fang FC, et al. Legionella sainthelensis serogroup 2 isolated from patients with pneumonia. Res Microbiol. 1990;141:453-463.
103. Thacker WL, Dyke JW, Benson RF, et al. Legionella lansingensis sp. nov. isolated from a patient with pneumonia and underlying chronic lymphocytic leukemia. J Clin Microbiol. 1992;30:2398-2401.
104. Lo Presti F, Riffard S, Jarraud S, et al. The first clinical isolate of *Legionella parisiensis*. J Clin Microbiol. 1997;35:1706-1709.
105. Lo Presti F, Reffard S, Jarraud S, et al. Isolation of *Legionella oakridgenesis* from two patients with pleural effusion living in the same geographical area. J Clin Microbiol. 2000;38:3128-3130.

CHAPTER 231

Capnocytophaga

VEE J. GILL

Capnocytophaga is a genus in the family Flavobacteriaceae, and in the *Flavobacterium-Cytophaga* ribosomal RNA homology group.[1] These organisms are thin, gram-negative bacilli with tapered ends and can be grouped into (1) those species found primarily in the human oral cavity—*C. ochracea, C. gingivalis, C. sputigena, C. haemolytica, C. granulosa*—and (2) those species found in the canine oral cavity, or, less commonly, in that of other animals, and associated primarily with dog-bite infections—*C. canimorsus* and *C. cynodegmi. Capnocytophaga* species of either human or canine origin cause significant infections in normal as well as in immunocompromised hosts.

TAXONOMY

Capnocytophaga ("eater of carbon dioxide") species isolated from the human oral cavity were originally described by Prevot in 1956. The most recent edition of the Taxonomic Outline of the Procaryotes (a preparation for the next edition of *Bergey's Manual of Systematic Bacteriology*) accepts the seven aforementioned species as members of this genus.[2] Older nomenclature for these *Capnocytophaga* species has included *Fusobacterium nucleatum* var. *ochraceus* (Prevot), *Ristella ochracea* (Seball), *Bacteroides oralis* var. *elongatus* (Loesche), *Bacteroides ochraceus* (Holdeman and Moore), and Centers for Disease Control and Prevention (CDC) group DF1 (dysgonic fermenter).[3,4] The work of Newman and associates[3] and of Williams and colleagues[4] demonstrated that *B. ochraceus* and CDC group DF1 should be considered synonymous with human oral *Capnocytophaga* species. Most of the strains examined by Williams and co-workers showed highest DNA homology with *C. ochracea*, although one strain showed homology with *C. gingivalis*. Two new species described in 1994, *C. haemolytica* and *C. granulosa*, have been isolated from supra- and subgingival dental plaque of adults but have not yet been significant in human infections.[5,6]

A previously undescribed gram-negative rod was first isolated in 1976 from the blood and spinal fluid of a patient after a dog bite.[7] This organism and similar isolates were later designated by the CDC as group DF2 and were often referred to as the "dog-bite" organism, since most of the isolates were associated with infections following dog bites or exposure to dogs. In 1989, Brenner and colleagues pro-

posed the name *Capnocytophaga canimorsus* (Latin for "dog bite") for this group of organisms.[8] Their investigation also revealed a second group of nine similar organisms, designated as DF2-like, that were biochemically different from DF2 and had been isolated either from dogs or from localized infections following a dog bite. For this latter group of organisms, they proposed the name *Capnocytophaga cynodegmi* (Greek for "dog bite").

MICROBIOLOGIC CHARACTERISTICS

Capnocytophaga organisms are long, thin, gram-negative rods that are typically fusiform. They may be straight or slightly curved, but when stained from older cultures, they show pleomorphism in both size and shape. The optimal temperature for growth is 35° to 37° C, and blood or chocolate agar generally supports growth of these organisms. *Capnocytophaga* organisms are facultatively anaerobic bacteria, but for optimal growth, either aerobically or anaerobically, an atmosphere enriched with 5% to 10% CO_2 is required, particularly for initial isolation. When colonies reach sufficient size, generally in 2 to 4 days, they usually show a yellow pigmentation, although both tan and pink colonies have also been described. Colonies are flat, with a shiny but mottled spreading edge that often shows finger-like projections that result from the gliding motility that is characteristic of the genus. *Capnocytophaga* flagella are difficult to demonstrate, and traditional motility tests may be negative. Colonies of most species are nonhemolytic, with the exception of *C. cynodegmi*, which may produce β-like hemolysis in rabbit blood agar, and *C. haemolytica*, in sheep blood agar. Both the spreading edge and the color of the colony depend on the medium, and thus the appearance of the colony may vary on different media. Additional characteristics that are uniform for the genus include no growth on MacConkey's agar and a lack of indole production.

Although the morphology of the colonies, the morphology on Gram stains, and the optimal growth conditions are similar for both the human oral species and the canine species of *Capnocytophaga, C. canimorsus* is more fastidious than the other species. For example, difficulties have been encountered in subculturing this organism out of blood culture bottles, even when many organisms were seen on smear. Growth of *C. canimorsus* requires enriched agar, such as heart infusion agar with rabbit or sheep blood; in addition, blood culture subcultures should be incubated for at least 5 to 7 days in 5% to 10% CO_2 to obtain visible colonies.

Capnocytophaga species can initially be distinguished from other fastidious gram-negative bacilli by their microscopic appearance. The long, delicate, fusiform appearance of *Capnocytophaga* species is distinctive and differs from the coccobacillary appearance of *Moraxella, Kingella, Haemophilus,* and *Actinobacillus* species and from the straight, narrow, rod forms of *Eikenella* species. When stained from a blood culture bottle, the fusiform appearance of *Capnocytophaga* species may be mistaken for that of the strict anaerobe *Fusobacterium nucleatum*. Distinguishing between the two is aided by determining whether the organism is a strict anaerobe or microaerophilic. In addition, all *Capnocytophaga* species are indole negative, whereas *F. nucleatum* is indole positive.

Identification of the individual species of *Capnocytophaga* by conventional biochemical tests is difficult because phenotypic differences are few, and poor growth of the organism may result in falsely negative reactions. Commercial identification panels are unreliable for accurate species identification. The five human oral species are oxidase negative and catalase negative, which differentiates them from the two canine species, *C. canimorsus* and *C. cynodegmi*, both of which are oxidase positive and catalase positive.[9] Although conventional biochemical reactions can be used to help identify the individual species, the most accurate identification will more likely be obtained using molecular-based testing, such as 16S rRNA sequence analysis[1,10] or specific probes.[11] If such methods are available to the laboratory, identification will be both faster and more accurate than that obtained by conventional biochemical testing, because of the slow and unreliable growth of these organisms.

DISEASES AND TREATMENT

C. ochracea, C. sputigena, C. gingivalis, C. granulosa, and C. haemolytica

Capnocytophaga ochracea, C. sputigena, and *C. gingivalis* colonize the subgingival sulcus and other areas within the oral cavity of healthy adults and are thought to play a role in the pathogenesis of localized juvenile periodontitis as well as other forms of periodontal disease.[12] They possess a wide variety of enzymes, including aminopeptidases, acid and alkaline phosphatases, immunoglobulin A (IgA) protease, and trypsin-like enzymes, which may aid in invading periodontal tissues.[13] In addition, extracts and sonicates of *Capnocytophaga* species have been shown to inhibit motility and to induce morphologic abnormalities in neutrophils. Resistance to serum bactericidal activity has also been described.[14] The oral cavity is the most common site of origin of disease,[14,15] although these organisms have also been isolated from the female genital tract and have been associated with intrauterine infections, amnionitis, and neonatal infections in premature infants. Isolates have been obtained from a wide variety of clinical sources, including blood; spinal, pleural, and amniotic fluids; nose, throat, sputum, tracheal, and bronchial specimens; wounds; abscesses; bone; ocular infections; and vaginal specimens. Most reports of infections caused by the human oral strains of *Capnocytophaga* do not specify the particular species involved. Of the isolates identified to the species level, however, most have been called *C. ochracea,*[16,17] although occasional case reports of infections caused by *C. sputigena* and *C. gingivalis* can be found. The two newer species, *C. granulosa* and *C. haemolytica,* have been isolated from supragingival dental plaque of healthy adults[5] and from subgingival plaque in cases of chronic adult periodontitis.[6] There has been only one reported infection with either of these species; in this case, *C. granulosa* was isolated along with *Staphylococcus aureus* from an abscess in a 14-year-old immunocompetent boy.[18]

Sepsis is the most common presentation in immunocompromised patients, particularly in the setting of granulocytopenia and oral mucositis or ulceration.[15-17] Parenti and Snydman found that of 15 immunocompromised patients infected with *Capnocytophaga* species, including both children and adults, all had bacteremia.[15] In a review of *Capnocytophaga* sepsis in immunocompromised patients, most patients had either acute myelogenous leukemia or acute lymphocytic leukemia as their underlying illness, followed by solid tumors and a variety of other diseases such as multiple myeloma, systemic lupus erythematosus, and acute myelofibrosis.[14] In a review of patients younger than 18 years and excluding those with solely periodontal infections, Campbell and Edwards found that of 16 immunocompromised children with *Capnocytophaga* infections, all had bacteremia.[16] The majority of these children had either acute lymphocytic leukemia or acute myelogenous leukemia.

In contrast, nonimmunocompromised patients tend to present less frequently with sepsis but instead with a variety of other infections. The role of these *Capnocytophaga* species in periodontal infections such as juvenile periodontitis has already been mentioned, but, in addition, reported infections include bacteremia, endocarditis, keratitis, conjunctivitis, corneal ulcer, pericardial abscess, mediastinitis, lung and subphrenic abscess, empyema, septic arthritis, cervical and inguinal lymphadenitis, sinusitis, thyroiditis, osteomyelitis, peritonitis, abdominal abscess, wound infection, and peripartum infection. Many infections are polymicrobic, with other oral bacteria isolated concomitantly. In nonimmunocompromised children, as in adults, sepsis is uncommon, but these *Capnocytophaga* species have been isolated from kidney, cervical node, conjunctiva, thyroid abscess, bone, joint aspirate, tracheal aspirate, and pleural fluid. The reported infections are diverse and frequently without known predisposing factors. Three premature neonates with early-onset sepsis have also been described.[16]

In vitro susceptibility testing of these *Capnocytophaga* species is hampered by the slow growth and fastidious nature of the organisms. Because the organisms need enriched media to grow, most will not grow in unsupplemented susceptibility-test media. As a result of the length of time required to initially grow the organism and then to perform the susceptibility test, antibiotic therapy is most often started empirically before the receipt of in vitro results.

C. ochracea, C. sputigena, and *C. gingivalis* are generally sensitive to clindamycin, erythromycin, tetracycline, chloramphenicol, and imipenem, whereas susceptibilities are variable for penicillin, cephalosporins (including expanded-spectrum cephalosporins), aztreonam, metronidazole, and quinolones. They are generally resistant to trimethoprim and aminoglycosides.[19-21] Resistance to β-lactam antibiotics caused by production of β-lactamase has been reported to occur in these organisms. In at least one strain of *C. ochracea,* the resistance was shown to result from a plasmid-encoded extended-spectrum TEM-17 β-lactamase.[22] In 1986, Rummens and colleagues showed that 3 of 118 strains (2.5%) produced β-lactamase,[19] whereas in 1992, Roscoe and associates found 32% (6 of 19 of their strains, obtained from Canadian hospitals) to be positive.[21] Two French studies, reported in 1999 and 2000, showed, respectively, 18 of 24 strains (75%) and 34 of 43 strains (79%) to be resistant due to β-lactamase production,[23,24] whereas only 1 of 28 (3.5%) strains recovered in Spain were β-lactamase producers.[17] These results suggest that β-lactamase production in these species may be increasing rapidly in certain geographic locales. Maury and colleagues found higher β-lactamase production in strains recovered from patients with prior β-lactam treatment.[23] The β-lactamase-producing strains remained susceptible to β-lactam/β-lactam inhibitor combinations. On the basis of reported antibiotic susceptibility spectrums for these organisms, both clindamycin and amoxicillin-clavulanate have been recommended as first-line agents for therapy. Reports of fluoroquinolone resistance caution the empiric use of these agents. In addition to three case reports of fluoroquinolone-resistant strains that were also multidrug resistant (including β-lactam resistance),[25-27] Martino and colleagues found 56% of isolates (9/16) from cases of bacteremia in Spain to be resistant to ciprofloxacin. This is an inexplicably high rate of resistance, particularly as only 1 of 28 strains tested in the same series showed β-lactam resistance.[17] Imipenem has shown good in vitro activity and was used successfully to treat disease caused by 13 β-lactamase-producing strains.[23]

Infection with human oral strains of *Capnocytophaga* should be considered in the evaluation of leukemic patients with fever and neutropenia, especially if oral mucositis or ulceration is present. Difficulty in growing these fastidious organisms may delay laboratory isolation and identification. Prognosis is generally good for patients who are appropriately treated, although mortality is higher in immunocompromised patients.

C. canimorsus and C. cynodegmi

Both *C. canimorsus* and *C. cynodegmi* compose part of the normal oral flora of canines, although occasional infections associated with exposure to other animals (cats and rabbits) have also been described. Among isolates submitted to the CDC for identification, *C. canimorsus* has occurred much more commonly and has caused more serious infections than *C. cynodegmi*. Of the 150 strains of *C. canimorsus* reviewed by the CDC, 88% were from blood, 5% from spinal fluid, 2% from wounds, and 2% from dog mouths, whereas in contrast, the eight *C. cynodegmi* strains were isolated from either dog mouths or localized wound infections caused by dog bites.[8] In 2001, Sarma and Mohanty reported a case of cellulitis, bacteremia, and pneumonitis caused by *C. cynodegmi* in a diabetic man, following a dog bite.[28] The isolate was susceptible to all antibiotics tested, and the patient was successfully treated using multiple antibiotics. Interesting studies by Fischer and colleagues demonstrated destruction of cultured macrophages by culture supernates from *C. canimorsus* but not from *C. cynodegmi,* suggesting that the production of a potent cytotoxin by the former species may contribute to its greater virulence.[29]

Clinical data on 72 *C. canimorsus* strains submitted to the CDC for identification showed that infections occurred predominantly in men (74%), most frequently those in the 50- to 70-year age group. Forty-three percent of the patients had been either bitten or scratched by dogs (or by cats in two cases), whereas 10 patients (12%) had reported only exposure to dogs.[8] In a review of 60 cases of *C. canimorsus* sepsis by Kullberg and co-workers, 47% involved a history of dog bite, whereas 27% involved exposure to dogs, without bites or scratches.[30] Thirty-three percent of these patients were asplenic, 22% had a history of alcoholic abuse, and 5% were receiving corticosteroid therapy. Twenty-three patients (38%) had no known underlying condition that might have predisposed them to infection. The interval between bite and hospital admission ranged from 1 to 30 days, with an average of 5.5 days. The case-fatality rate was 28%, including the deaths of 12 of 40 patients who had intact spleens. These characteristics of *C. canimorsus* infection have been substantiated by an additional review of 39 cases of septicemia in Denmark, spanning the years 1982 through 1995.[31]

C. canimorsus can cause a wide spectrum of disease, ranging from mild to fulminant. A more rapid and severe progression occurs particularly in asplenic individuals, alcoholic persons, and patients on corticosteroids. In splenectomized patients, the infection is characterized by shock, disseminated purpuric lesions, and disseminated intravascular coagulation. In addition, renal failure, gangrene of the bite site, and pulmonary infiltrates may occur. In one review, 35% of patients presented with disseminated purpuric lesions and 38% had disseminated intravascular coagulation, often with hypotension and renal insufficiency. Blood cultures became positive after incubation for 1 to 14 days, with a mean of 6 days. In 10 cases, the organism was seen in Gram stains of buffy coats, and of these, eight were in asplenic patients.[30] Fulminant infection may occur even in healthy people, although these patients generally have a milder course. Cases of meningitis, endocarditis, pneumonia, cellulitis, corneal ulcer, and septic arthritis have been reported.[32] A review of 18 cases of *C. canimorsus* meningitis was provided by Le Moal and colleagues and showed a remarkably low mortality rate of 5%.[33] The possibility of *C. canimorsus* infection should be considered early in all infections following a dog bite, but particularly in asplenic patients, in whom the clinical course may be fulminant and the outcome fatal.

For initial treatment or prophylaxis of *C. canimorsus* infections, amoxicillin-clavulanate may be the preferred drug, rather than amoxicillin alone, because β-lactamase-producing strains occur in other *Capnocytophaga* species and may eventually arise in *C. canimorsus*. Therapy should be initiated promptly, because isolation, identification, and in vitro susceptibility testing of *C. canimorsus* will not be available for days after the cultures are taken, if at all. In vitro susceptibility testing of either species is difficult to do by any standardized procedure, because there is often slow or insufficient growth. In the published studies using either broth or agar dilution techniques, *C. canimorsus* is reported to be susceptible to penicillins, imipenem, erythromycin, vancomycin, clindamycin, third-generation cephalosporins, chloramphenicol, rifampin, doxycycline, and quinolones, but resistant to aztreonam.[20,34] There is disagreement on results for trimethoprim-sulfamethoxazole and aminoglycosides. Results for aminoglycosides may depend on the method used, with disk diffusion and agar dilution testing more likely to show resistance, and broth dilution more likely to show susceptibility.

REFERENCES

1. Vandamme P, Vancanneyt M, Van Belkum A, et al. Polyphasic analysis of strains of the genus *Capnocytophaga* and Centers for Disease Control group DF-3. Int J System Bacteriol. 1996;46:782-791.
2. Garrity GM, Bell JA, Lilburn TG, et al. Taxonomic Outline of the Procaryotes. Bergey's Manual of Systematic Bacteriology. 2nd ed, release 4.0. New York: Springer-Verlag; 2003, available at http://dx.doi.org/10.1007/bergeysoutline200310.
3. Newman MG, Sutter VL, Pickett MJ, et al. Detection, identification and comparison of *Capnocytophaga*, *Bacteroides ochraceus*, and DF1. J Clin Microbiol. 1979;10:557-562.
4. Williams BL, Hollis D, Holdeman LV. Synonymy of strains of Centers for Disease Control group DF1 with species of *Capnocytophaga*. J Clin Microbiol. 1979;10:550-556.
5. Yamamoto T, Kajiura S, Hirai Y, Watanabe T. *Capnocytophaga haemolytica* sp. nov. and *Capnocytophaga granulosa* sp. nov., from human dental plaque. Int J System Bacteriol. 1994;44:324-329.
6. Ciantar M, Spratt DA, Newman HN, et al. *Capnocytophaga granulosa* and *Capnocytophaga haemolytica*: Novel species in subgingival plaque. J Clin Periodont. 2001;28:701-705.
7. Bobo RA, Newton SJ. A previously undescribed gram-negative bacillus causing septicemia and meningitis. Am J Clin Pathol. 1976;65:564-569.
8. Brenner DJ, Hollis DG, Fanning R, et al. *Capnocytophaga canimorsus* sp. nov. (formerly CDC group DF2), a cause of septicemia following dog bite, and *C. cynodegmi* sp. nov., a cause of localized wound infection following dog bite. J Clin Microbiol. 1989;27:231-235.
9. von Graevenitz A, Zbinden R, Mutters R. *Actinobacillus, Capnocytophaga, Eikenella, Kingella, Pasteurella,* and other fastidious or rarely encountered gram-negative rods. In Murray PR, ed. in chief. Manual of Clinical Microbiology. 8th ed. Washington, DC: ASM Press; 2003:609-622.
10. Wilson MJ, Wade WG, Weightman AJ. Restriction fragment length polymorphism analysis of PCR-amplified 16s ribosomal DNA of *Capnocytophaga*. J Appl Bacteriol. 1995;78:394-401.
11. Conrads G, Mutters R, Seyfarth I, et al. DNA-probes for the differentiation of *Capnocytophaga* species. Mol Cell Probes. 1997;11:323-328.
12. Newman MG, Socransky SS, Savitt ED, et al. Studies of the microbiology of periodontosis. J Periodontol. 1976;47:373-379.
13. Soderling E, Makinen PL, Syed S, et al. Biochemical comparison of proteolytic enzymes present in rough and smooth-surfaced capnocytophagas isolated from the subgingival plaque of periodontitis patients. J Periodontol Res. 1991;26:17-23.
14. Bilgrami S, Bergstrom SK, Peterson DE, et al. *Capnocytophaga* bacteremia in a patient with Hodgkin's disease following bone marrow transplantation: Case report and review. Clin Infect Dis. 1992;14:1045-1049.
15. Parenti DM, Snydman DR. *Capnocytophaga* species: Infections in nonimmunocompromised and immunocompromised hosts. J Infect Dis. 1985;151:140-147.
16. Campbell JR, Edwards MS. *Capnocytophaga* species infections in children. Pediatr Infect Dis J. 1991;10:944-948.
17. Martino R, Ramila E, Capdevila JA, et al. Bacteremia caused by *Capnocytophaga* species in patients with neutropenia and cancer: Results of a multicenter study. Clin Infect Dis. 2001;33:e20-e22.
18. Spell DW, Szurgot JG, Greer RW, et al. Isolation of *Capnocytophaga granulosa* from an abscess in an immunocompetent adolescent. Clin Infect Dis. 2000;30:606.
19. Rummens JL, Gordts B, van Landuyt HW. In vitro susceptibility of *Capnocytophaga* species to 29 antimicrobial agents. Antimicrob Agents Chemother. 1986;30:739-742.
20. Bremmelgaard A, Pers C, Kristiansen JE, et al. Susceptibility testing of Danish isolates of *Capnocytophaga* and CDC group DF2 bacteria. Acta Pathol Microbiol Immunol Scand. 1989;97:43-48.
21. Roscoe DL, Zemcov SJV, Thornber D, et al. Antimicrobial susceptibilities and β-lactamase characterization of *Capnocytophaga* species. Antimicrob Agents Chemother. 1992;36:2197-2200.
22. Rosenau A, Cattier B, Gousset N, et al. *Capnocytophaga ochracea*: Characterization of a plasmid-encoded extended-spectrum TEM-17 in the phylum Flavobacter-Bacteroides. Antimicrob Agents Chemother. 2000;44:760-762.
23. Maury S, Leblanc T, Rousselot P, et al. Bacteremia due to *Capnocytophaga* species in patients with neutropenia: High frequency of β-lactamase-producing strains. Clin Infect Dis. 1999;28:1172-1173.
24. Jolivet-Gougeon A, Buffet A, Dupuy C, et al. In vitro susceptibilities of *Capnocytophaga* isolates to β-lactam antibiotics and β-lactamase inhibitors. Antimicrob Agents Chemother. 2000;44:3186-3188.
25. Baquero F, Fernandez J, Dronda F, et al. Capnophilic and anaerobic bacteremia in neutropenic patients: An oral source. Rev Infect Dis. 1990;12:S157-S160.
26. Gomez-Garces JL, Alos JI, Sanchez J, Cogollos R. Bacteremia by multidrug-resistant *Capnocytophaga sputigena*. J Clin Microbiol. 1994;32:167-169.
27. Geisler WM, Malhotra U, Stamm WE. Pneumonia and sepsis due to fluoroquinolone-resistant *Capnocytophaga gingivalis* after autologous stem cell transplantation. 2001;28:1171-1173.
28. Sarma PS, Mohanty S. *Capnocytophaga cynodegmi* cellulitis, bacteremia, and pneumonitis in a diabetic man. J Clin Microbiol. 2001;39:2028-2029.
29. Fischer LJ, Weyant RS, White EH, et al. Intracellular multiplication and toxic destruction of cultured macrophages by *Capnocytophaga canimorsus*. Infect Immun. 1995;63:3484-3490.
30. Kullberg BJ, Westendorp RGJ, van't Wout JW, et al. Purpura fulminans and symmetrical peripheral gangrene caused by *Capnocytophaga canimorsus* (formerly DF2) septicemia: A complication of dog bite. Medicine. 1991;70:287-292.
31. Pers C, Gahrn-Hansen B, Frederiksen W. *Capnocytophaga canimorsus* septicemia in Denmark, 1982-1995: Review of 39 cases. Clin Infect Dis. 1996;23:71-75.
32. Vanhonsebrouck AY, Gordts B, Wauters G, et al. Fatal septicemia with *Capnocytophaga* in a compromised host: A case report with review of the literature. Acta Clin Belg. 1991;46:364-370.
33. Le Moal G, Landron C, Grollier G, et al. Meningitis due to *Capnocytophaga canimorsus* after receipt of a dog bite: Case report and review of the literature. Clin Infect Dis. 2003;36:e42-e46.
34. Verghese A, Hamati F, Berk S, et al. Susceptibility of dysgonic fermenter 2 to antimicrobial agents in vitro. Antimicrob Agents Chemother. 1988;32:78-80.

Bartonella, Including Cat-Scratch Disease

LEONARD N. SLATER

DAVID F. WELCH

BACKGROUND AND CLASSIFICATION

Members of the class Alphaproteobacteria, *Bartonella* spp. are closely related to the genera *Brucella* and *Agrobacterium* on the basis of 16S ribosomal RNA (rRNA) similarity; members of the family Rickettsiaceae are more distantly related. On the basis of genetic similarity,[1,2] unification of the genera *Bartonella* and *Rochalimaea* as a single genus, and the removal of the family Bartonellaceae from the order Rickettsiales, were put forth in 1993.[2]

The genus *Bartonella,* synonymous with *Bartonia,* was described in 1913, and referred to the erythrocyte-adherent organisms originally described by Dr. A. L. Barton in 1909.[3,4] The type species (and sole member of the genus until 1993) is *Bartonella bacilliformis.* Limited to the Andes mountain regions of South America, *B. bacilliformis* infection had received little attention outside its endemic zone in recent years until related bacteria, originally classified in the genus *Rochalimaea,* were found to be pathogens in acquired immunodeficiency syndrome (AIDS) and then in other circumstances.

The former genus *Rochalimaea,* previously grouped with *Bartonella* in the order Rickettsiales, had long contained only two member species, *Rochalimaea vinsonii,* the "Canadian vole agent," and *Rochalimaea quintana* (other synonyms: *Rickettsia quintana, Rickettsia pediculi, Rickettsia wolhynica, Rickettsia weigl, Burnetia [Rocha-limae] wolhynica, Wolhynia quintanae*),[5,6] the agent of trench fever, a debilitating but self-limited human illness so named after it affected many military personnel in World War I.[7] Except for sporadic outbreaks, trench fever had all but disappeared from the clinical scene in recent decades. However, *R. quintana* reemerged in the 1990s as a pathogen of considerable interest[8-12] coincident with the discovery of two related species pathogenic to humans, originally named *Rochalimaea henselae* and *Rochalimaea elizabethae.*[13-16]

In 1995, a further merger of a number of species of the genus *Grahamella,* which are intraerythrocytic pathogens of rodents, birds, fish, and other animals, into the genus *Bartonella* took place.[17] Several additional species have been identified since then,[18-21] and there are two newly recognized subspecies of *B. vinsonii.*[22-24]

A list of presently validated members of the genus *Bartonella* is provided in Table 232-1. New species continue to be added, as phylogenetically derived trees reveal distinct but defined additional members of the genus *Bartonella.*[25,26]

EPIDEMIOLOGY OF THE COMMON HUMAN-PATHOGENIC SPECIES

Presumably as a result of the limited distribution of it sandfly vectors (genus *Lutzomyia* [formerly *Phlebotomus*]), natural transmission of *B. bacilliformis* infections occurs only at altitudes of 1 to 3 km in the Andes mountains. Even in the modern antibiotic era, focal outbreaks continue. *Bartonella quintana* is globally distributed. Outbreaks of trench fever (also known as Wolhynia fever, Meuse fever, His-Werner disease, shin bone fever, shank fever, and quintan or five-day fever), have been focal and widely separated, often associated with conditions of poor sanitation and personal hygiene, which may predispose to exposure to *Pediculus humanus,* the human body louse, *B. quintana*'s only identified vector. No nonhuman vertebrate reservoirs have been identified as yet for *B. bacilliformis* or *B. quintana.*

TABLE 232-1 *Bartonella* Species as Currently Recognized for Potential as Human Pathogens

Common as Human Pathogens	*Not Recognized as Human Pathogens*
Bartonella bacilliformis	
Bartonella henselae	*Bartonella alsatica*
Bartonella quintana	*Bartonella birtelsii*
	Bartonella bovis
Uncommon or Suspected as Human Pathogens	*Bartonella capreoli*
	Bartonella doshiae
Bartonella clarridgeiae	*Bartonella koehlerae*
Bartonella elizabethae	*Bartonella peromysci*
Bartonella grahamii	*Bartonella schoenbuchii*
Bartonella vinsonii subsp. *arupensis*	*Bartonella talpae*
Bartonella vinsonii subsp. *berkhoffii*	*Bartonella taylorii*
Bartonella washoensis	*Bartonella tribocorum*
	Bartonella vinsonii subsp. *vinsonii*

B. henselae is globally endemic; serologic studies indicate that infection of domestic cats is worldwide, with the prevalence of antibodies being higher in warm, humid climates. Free-ranging and captive wild felids in California also have a substantial prevalence of antibodies reactive with *B. henselae,*[27] although infection with other *Bartonella* species could result in cross-reactive antibodies. Rates of bacteremia in cats can vary, even between geographically close locales,[28-31] but generally tend to be higher among feral animals in any particular locale. *Bartonella henselae* bacteremia has been documented in healthy domestic cats that have been specifically associated with bacillary angiomatosis (BA)[29] or typical cat-scratch disease (CSD)[30,32] in their human contacts.

Transmission of *B. henselae* to humans has been linked to cats by serologic and epidemiologic studies,[33-36] its culture recovery from the lymphadenitis of CSD,[30,37] and its identification by polymerase chain reaction (PCR)-based DNA identification in further cases of CSD lymphadenitis[38-40] and conjunctival disease,[41] as well as in CSD skin test antigen.[42,43]

The major arthropod vector of *B. henselae* is the cat flea, *Ctenocephalides felis,* as evidenced by epidemiologic associations,[30,34,36] identification of *B. henselae* by culture and DNA amplification from such fleas,[28,30] and transmission of *B. henselae* among cats by such fleas under controlled experimental conditions.[44] Cat fleas appear to serve primarily as vectors for cat-to-cat transmission; their contribution to human infection is not as yet defined. Additional *Bartonella* species also have been identified in cat fleas.[45] Other types of fleas, as well as ixodid and *Dermacentor* ticks, have now been found to harbor various *Bartonella* species.[46-48]

B. clarridgeiae is also recognized to be an agent of asymptomatic infection of cats,[18,19,21] which may be capable of occasional transmission to humans and the uncommon induction of human illness.[20] While *B. koehlerae* is also now recognized as an agent of feline bacteremia, it has not been clearly implicated in human disease. Both agents are widespread in their distribution. Because there has been only a single human isolate of *B. elizabethae,* little is known of its epidemiology. Recent amplification of *B. elizabethae* DNA from the blood of dogs may be a lead to a better understanding.[49]

As more are discovered, it becomes evident that most *Bartonella* species are primarily infectious agents of nonhuman animals. It is reasonable to speculate that humans may be incidental hosts in most cases (even though animal hosts of *B. bacilliformis* and *B. quintana* are not yet identified), with transmission to humans occurring via arthropod vectors or direct inoculation.

CLINICAL MANIFESTATIONS OF THE COMMON HUMAN-PATHOGENIC SPECIES

Oroya Fever and Verruga Peruana: *B. bacilliformis*

The long-suspected link between Oroya fever and verruga peruana was confirmed tragically in 1885 by Daniel Carrión, a medical student who injected himself with blood from a verruga peruana lesion and subsequently died of "Oroya fever."[50] The eponym "Carrión's disease" has since denoted the full spectrum of *B. bacilliformis* infection.

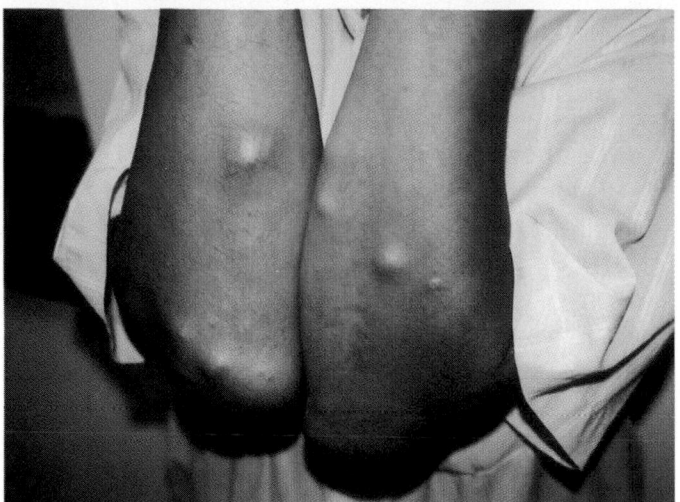

FIGURE 232-1. Multiple nodular subcutaneous lesions of verruga peruana in an inhabitant of the Peruvian Andes. Localization of such nodular eruptions about the flexures of the elbows and knees, as well as on the thighs and legs, is especially common. *(Courtesy of Dr. J.M. Crutcher, Oklahoma State Department of Health, Oklahoma City.)*

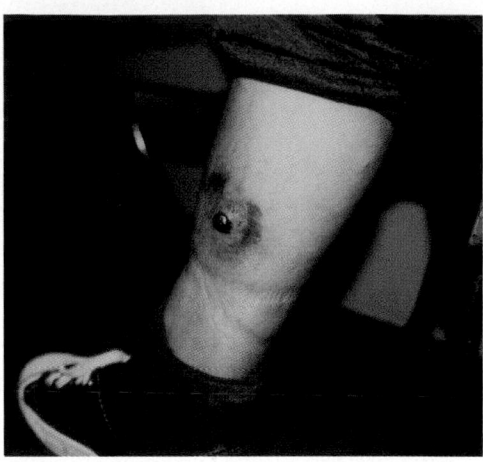

FIGURE 232-2. A single large mulaire lesion of verruga peruana on the leg of an inhabitant of the Peruvian Andes. Such lesions are prone to superficial ulceration, and copious bleeding may occur as a result of their vascular nature. Ecchymosis of the skin surrounding the lesion is also evident. *(Courtesy of Dr. J.M. Crutcher, Oklahoma State Department of Health, Oklahoma City.)*

Oroya fever, an acute hematic disease resulting from primary bacteremia, develops 3 to 12 weeks after inoculation.[51] In its mildest, insidiously developing form, a febrile illness can last less than a week, and may go unrecognized (giving rise to subsequent cutaneous manifestations that are the first recognized clinical findings).[52-54] When illness is abrupt in onset, high fever, chills, diaphoresis, anorexia, prostration, headache, and mental status changes are associated with rapidly developing, profound anemia resulting from bacterial invasion, causing shortened life span and destruction of erythrocytes.[54-57] Intense myalgias and arthralgias, abdominal pain and emesis, jaundice, lymphadenopathy, thrombocytopenia, and complications such as seizures, delirium, meningoencephalitis, obtundation, dyspnea, hepatic/gastrointestinal dysfunction, and angina pectoris can occur during this stage,[54,58,59] most believed to be a consequence of the anemia and of microvascular thrombosis, resulting in end-organ ischemia.

Without antimicrobial therapy, fatalities are high for the severe, abrupt form of hematic illness.[58] With appropriate treatment in the modern era, mortality is reported to be less than 10%.[54] For survivors, convalescence is associated with a decline of fever and disappearance of bacteria on blood smears, but also a temporarily increased susceptibility to subsequent (opportunistic) infections such as salmonellosis[54,59,60] or toxoplasmosis.[54,61,62] Asymptomatic persistent bacteremia with *B. bacilliformis* infection can occur in up to 15% of survivors of acute infection.[63] They may serve as the organism's reservoir. Whereas some modern era reports paint a picture of similar patterns of *recognized* disease,[54] others suggest that initial infection may more often be asymptomatic or mild than was previously believed.[53,64]

The eruptive phase of *B. bacilliformis* infection, "verruga peruana" lesions, usually become evident within weeks to months of resolution of acute infection if it was not treated with antibiotics. This late-stage manifestation is characterized by crops of skin lesions marked by an evolution of stages[54,55]: miliary, then nodular (Fig. 232-1), then mulaire (Fig. 232-2). Mulaire lesions are the most superficial and obviously blood filled of the eruptive manifestations, oftentimes bulbous, engorged with blood, and prone to ulceration and bleeding. Mucosal and internal lesions also can occur. Healing at a particular skin site, often punctuated by recurrences, usually takes place over several weeks to 3 or 4 months subsequently, and fibrosis of mulaire lesions may occur. The nodules may develop at one site while receding at another. Histology of active lesions demonstrates neovascular proliferation with occasional bacteria evident in interstitial spaces.

Bacterial invasion of/replication within endothelial cells (long believed the cause of cytoplasmic inclusions first described by Rocha-Lima) is actually rare.[65]

Bacteremic Illness and Endocarditis: *B. quintana, B. henselae,* Other Species

Acute mortality resulting from bacteremia with non-*bacilliformis Bartonella* species, even when persistent, is apparently uncommon. In recent years, *B. quintana* bacteremic infection outside of the context of human immunodeficiency virus (HIV) infection has been identified sporadically and in small clusters, mainly in homeless persons in North America and Europe.[66,67] "Trench fever" is characterized by a spectrum of self-limited clinical patterns.[6,7] Incubation may span 3 to 38 days before the usually sudden onset of chills and fevers. In the shortest form, a single bout of fever lasts 4 to 5 days. In the more typical periodic form, there are three to five and sometimes up to eight febrile paroxysms, each lasting about 5 days. The continuous form is manifested by 2 to 3 weeks, and up to 6 weeks, of uninterrupted fever. Afebrile infection is the least common form. Other nonspecific symptoms and signs such as headache, vertigo, retro-orbital pain, conjunctival injection, nystagmus, myalgias, arthralgias, hepatosplenomegaly, rash, leukocytosis, and albuminuria may accompany the illness.

B. quintana or *B. henselae* bacteremia in HIV-infected persons is often characterized by insidious development of malaise, body aches, fatigue, weight loss, progressively higher and longer recurring fevers, and sometimes headache. Hepatomegaly may occur, but localizing symptoms or physical findings are often lacking. By way of contrast, *B. henselae* bacteremia in HIV-uninfected persons more often may present with abrupt onset of fever, which may persist or become relapsing. Localizing symptoms or physical findings remain unusual.[13,15,68,69] Aseptic meningitis concurrent with bacteremia has been documented.[69,70] Both *B. henselae* and *B. quintana* bacteremia can evolve into long-term persistence if not treated appropriately.[67,69]

B. elizabethae has been isolated only once, as the cause of bacteremia and endocarditis.[16] *B. quintana* and *B. henselae* have been reported increasingly to cause endocarditis, especially of the "blood culture negative" variety.[9,11,71-78] Persons with *B. quintana* endocarditis often have been alcoholic and/or homeless, whereas persons with *B. henselae* endocarditis more commonly have had cat exposure. In a retrospective study of 101 patients with *Bartonella* endocarditis,[78] presentation was usually subacute, but with a significant proportion

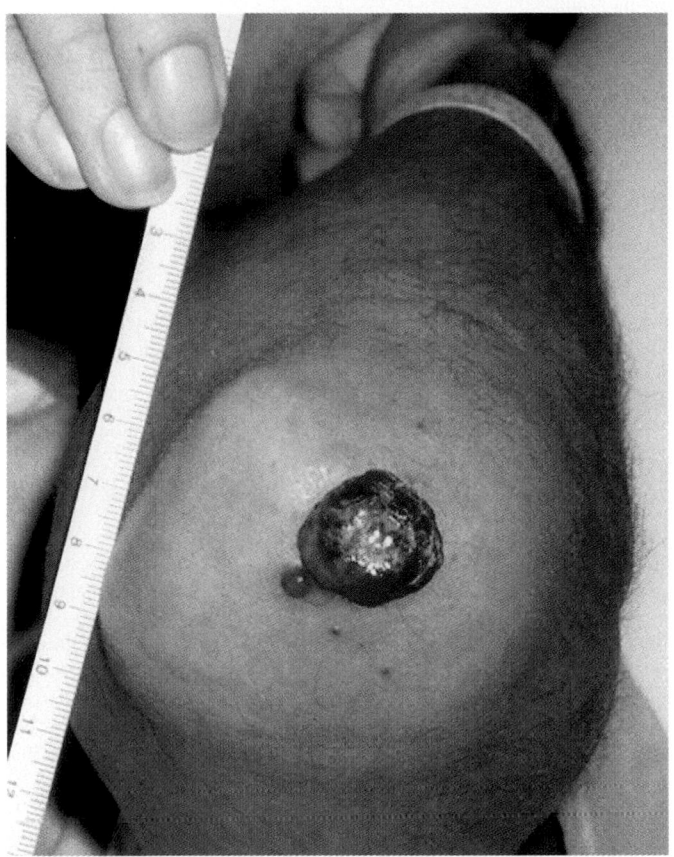

FIGURE 232-3. A crop of cutaneous bacillary angiomatosis lesions on the elbow of an AIDS patient. The largest lesion, resembling a mulaire lesion of verruga peruana, was of variegated purple color and had an ulcerated surface that wept serous fluid. It began a month earlier as a small cherry angioma-like lesion, much like the three adjacent smaller lesions that had all since erupted within the preceding week. All lesions involuted with doxycycline therapy.

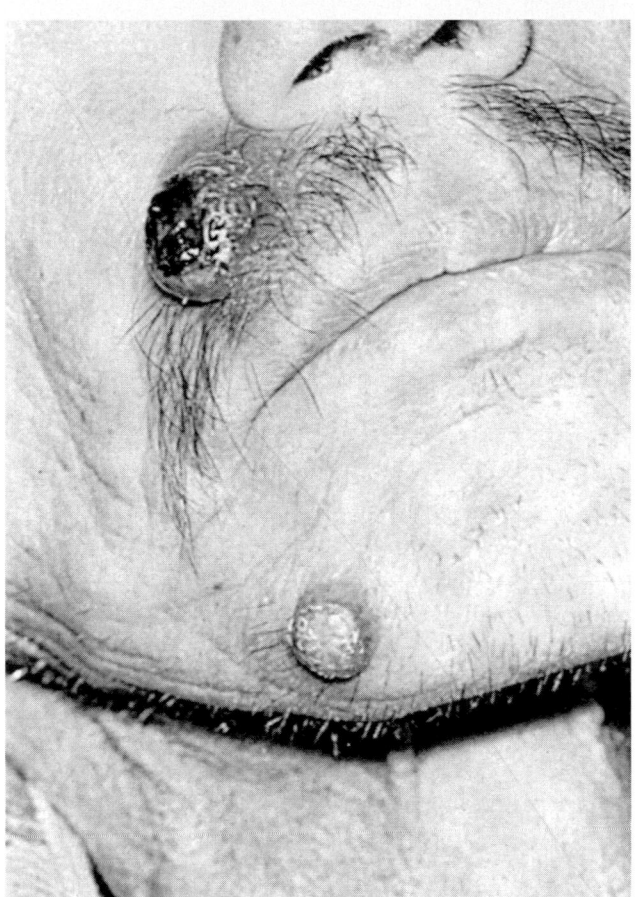

FIGURE 232-4. Cutaneous bacillary angiomatosis: friable, exophytic nodular lesion with serous crusting and surrounding erythema on upper lip; firm papular lesion with collarette of scale on chin. *(Courtesy of Drs. Jordan W. Tappero, Centers for Disease Control and Prevention, Atlanta; and Jane E. Koehler, University of California at San Francisco.)*

(17%) of patients afebrile at the time of presentation. Embolic phenomena were reported in 44 (43%) of the patients on presentation. Fifty-eight patients (57%) had previously known valvular heart disease; irrespective of antimicrobial therapy, 76 patients required valvular surgery because of severe valvular damage. Twelve patients ultimately died; two were cured only after a relapse, and the remaining 87% were cured with first therapy. Despite the pediatric predominance of CSD, pediatric *B. henselae* endocarditis has been recognized only rarely.[77] Many cases have required valve resection irrespective of antimicrobial use. Diagnoses in blood culture–negative cases have been established with serology, DNA amplification from valve tissue, and/or immunohistochemistry.

B. vinsonii, generally not considered a human pathogen, has been isolated once causing bacteremia and fever in an apparently otherwise healthy rancher from the western United States. *Bartonella vinsonii* subsp. *berkhoffii* is now known to be a cause of bacteremia and endocarditis in dogs.[22,23]

Bacillary Angiomatosis/Peliosis: *B. quintana* and *B. henselae*

BA (also referred to as epithelioid angiomatosis or bacillary epithelioid angiomatosis) is a disorder of neovascular proliferation originally described involving skin and regional lymph nodes of HIV-infected persons.[79-81] It has been demonstrated since to be able to involve a variety of internal organs, including liver, spleen, bone, brain, lung, bowel, and uterine cervix,[68,82-90] and to occur in other immunocompro-

mised[68,84,91] as well as immunocompetent hosts.[92,93] *B. henselae* and *B. quintana* have been found to be a cause of BA both by direct culture[8,15,28,68,94] and by PCR amplification from tissue of specific DNA sequences.[28,34,91,93,95,96] Either species can cause cutaneous lesions, but subcutaneous and osseous lesions are more often associated with *B. quintana* and hepatosplenic lesions only with *B. henselae*.[96]

Cutaneous BA lesions often arise in crops, but both the temporal pattern of development and the gross morphologic characteristics can vary. They can be remarkably similar to lesions of verruga peruana, but the major clinical differential diagnoses are usually Kaposi's sarcoma[97] and pyogenic granuloma. In gross appearance, BA skin lesions[98] can be subcutaneous or dermal nodules, and/or single or multiple dome-shaped, skin-colored or red to purple papules, any of which may display ulceration, serous or bloody drainage, and crusting (Figs. 232-3 and 232-4). Lesions can range in diameter from millimeters to centimeters, number from a few to hundreds, be fixed or freely mobile, be associated with enlargement of regional lymph nodes, involve mucosal surfaces or deeper soft tissues, occur in a variety of distributions, and bleed copiously when incised. Visceral lesions can be quite dramatic as well, in both their number and heterogeneity of gross appearance (Fig. 232-5). When cutaneous lesions are absent, diagnosis is often delayed because the features associated with visceral involvement (fever, lymphadenopathy, hepatomegaly, splenomegaly, CD4 lymphopenia, anemia, serum alkaline phosphatase elevation) are nonspecific.[88]

BA is distinguished from other neovascular tumors histologically.[98,99] It consists of lobular proliferations of small blood vessels

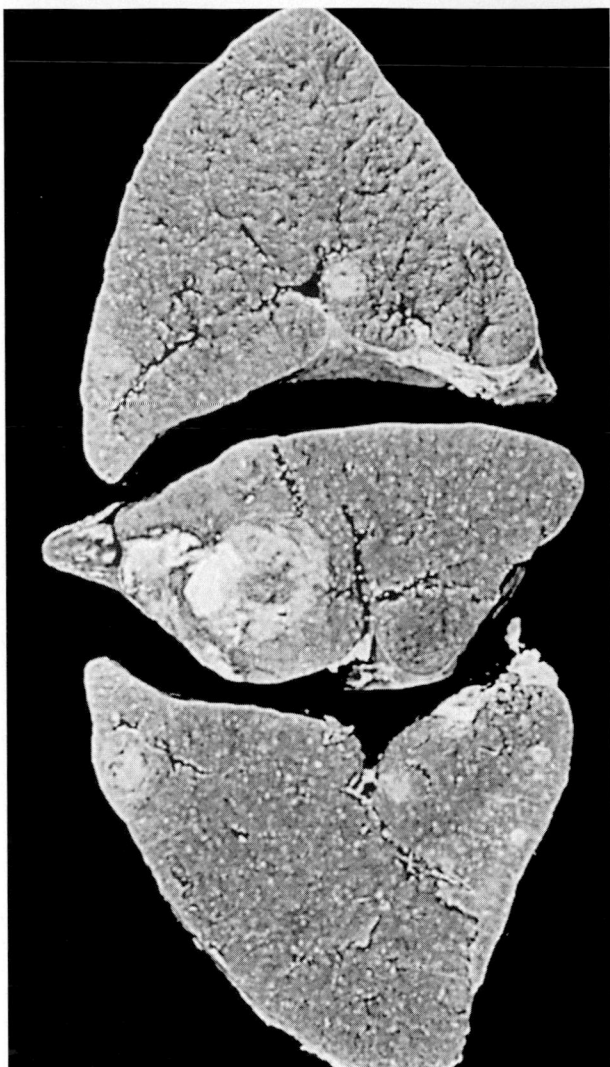

FIGURE 232-5. Cut surfaces of the spleen of a pharmacologically immunosuppressed renal transplant recipient revealed numerous *B. henselae*–induced miliary-appearing nodular lesions ranging in size from millimeters to centimeters, some of the larger of which were necrotic, while others contained hemorrhage. Histologic findings included bacillary angiomatosis, bacillary peliosis, and pyogranulomatous changes. *(From Slater LN, Welch DF, Min K-W.* Rochalimaea henselae *causes bacillary angiomatosis and peliosis hepatis.* Arch Intern Med. *1992;152:602-606.)*

containing plump, cuboidal endothelial cells interspersed with mixed inflammatory cell infiltrates having neutrophil predominance (Fig. 232-6A and B). Endothelial cell atypia, mitoses, and necrosis may be present. Fibrillar- or granular-appearing amphophilic material is often present in interstitial areas when stained by hematoxylin and eosin (H&E). Warthin-Starry staining or electron microscopy demonstrates these to be clusters of bacilli (Fig. 232-6C).

Bacillary peliosis (BP), originally described involving the liver and sometimes spleen in HIV-infected persons,[100] has since been identified in other immunosuppressed persons and found to involve lymph nodes as well.[68,101] Involved organs contain numerous blood-filled cystic structures that can range from microscopic to several millimeters in size. H&E-stained tissue reveals partially endothelial cell-lined peliotic spaces often separated from surrounding parenchymal cells by fibromyxoid stroma containing a mixture of inflammatory cells, dilated capillaries, and clumps of granular material. Such clumps are filled with Warthin-Starry–staining bacilli.[100] Molecular epidemiologic in-

vestigation has revealed that only *B. henselae* appears to be culpable in this process.[96]

Inflammatory reactions in immunocompromised hosts caused by *B. henselae* infection without associated angiomatosis or peliosis have been reported involving liver, spleen, lymph nodes, heart, lung, and bone marrow.[102,103] They are characterized by nodular collections of lymphocytes and nonepithelioid histiocytes that may become centrally necrotic, containing aggregates of neutrophils and karyorrhexic debris suggestive of microscopic abscess formation.[102,103] These may represent a clinical-pathologic link with CSD.[104]

Cat-Scratch Disease: *B. henselae,* Possibly *Afipia felis, B. clarridgeiae*

Among the *Bartonella* species, CSD has been associated nearly exclusively with *B. henselae.* Evidence indicating its cardinal role includes the serologic responses of persons with CSD[33,35,36,105]; the identification of *B. henselae* in CSD lymphadenitis by culture,[37] PCR-based DNA amplification,[38-40,106-109] and immunocytochemistry[110]; detection of *B. henselae* in CSD skin test antigens by PCR[42,43]; and the recovery of *B. henselae* from the blood of healthy cats (which can be persistently bacteremic)[28,30,111] and from cat fleas.[28]

The various manifestations comprising CSD have been recognized for over a century, but "la maladie des griffes de chat" was not defined as a syndrome until 1950.[112] CSD remained an infection in search of an agent for more than 40 years after that. Thus most cases have been identified by clinical/pathologic criteria, supplemented by reactions to unstandardized skin test antigens in some. It is reasonable to ascribe the majority of CSD cases to *B. henselae* based upon the numerous lines of evidence developed in recent years. Yet it remains likely that other agents can cause occasional "typical" CSD cases, such as has been reported with *Afipia felis*[113,114] and *B. clarridgeiae.*[20] (Non-*felis Afipia* spp. have been isolated from only skeletal and/or pleuropulmonary sites of one patient each and not in the setting of CSD; their roles as pathogens remain speculative.[113])

CSD is the most commonly recognized manifestation of human infection with *Bartonella.* In the United States, estimated CSD cases approach 25,000 annually.[115] Interestingly, veterinary care personnel do not have evidence of notably higher levels of infection than the general population.[116]

"Typical CSD" represents 88% to 89% of cases overall. A primary cutaneous papule or pustule develops about 3 to 10 days after an animal contact (most commonly a kitten or feral cat) at a site of inoculation (usually a scratch or bite) (Fig. 232-7),[117-119] and may last for 1 to 3 weeks. Regional lymphadenopathy ipsilateral to the inoculation site (mainly head, neck, or upper extremity), which develops in 1 to 7 weeks (Figs. 232-8 to 232-10), is the most prominent and common manifestation (>90% of typical cases), and the one that usually precipitates medical evaluation. Even at the time of such presentation, an inoculation site (scratch, bite, primary papule or pustule) may be detected in over two thirds of patients when actively sought. One third to 60% of patients may have low-grade fever lasting several days. One quarter may report malaise or fatigue, and about 10% report headache or sore throat. Transient rash may occur in about 5% of patients. Transient mild leukocytosis, with increased neutrophils and sometimes eosinophils, and elevated erythrocyte sedimentation rate may occur.

Nearly half of "typical" CSD patients have single lymph node involvement, and another 20% multiple node involvement at one site, and the remaining third have node involvement at multiple sites. Up to one sixth of patients with typical CSD develop lymph node suppuration. Ultrasonography may assist in the assessment of lymph node size and suppuration,[30,120] and may be used to direct needle aspiration of pus (usually done to relieve discomfort). Node enlargement usually persists for 2 to 4 months but may last considerably longer; spontaneous resolution is the rule. The histopathology of nodes includes a mixture of nonspecific inflammatory reactions including granulomata and stellate necrosis. Bacilli are best demonstrated by Dieterle, Warthin-Starry, or Steiner staining. Hypercalcemia uncommonly may

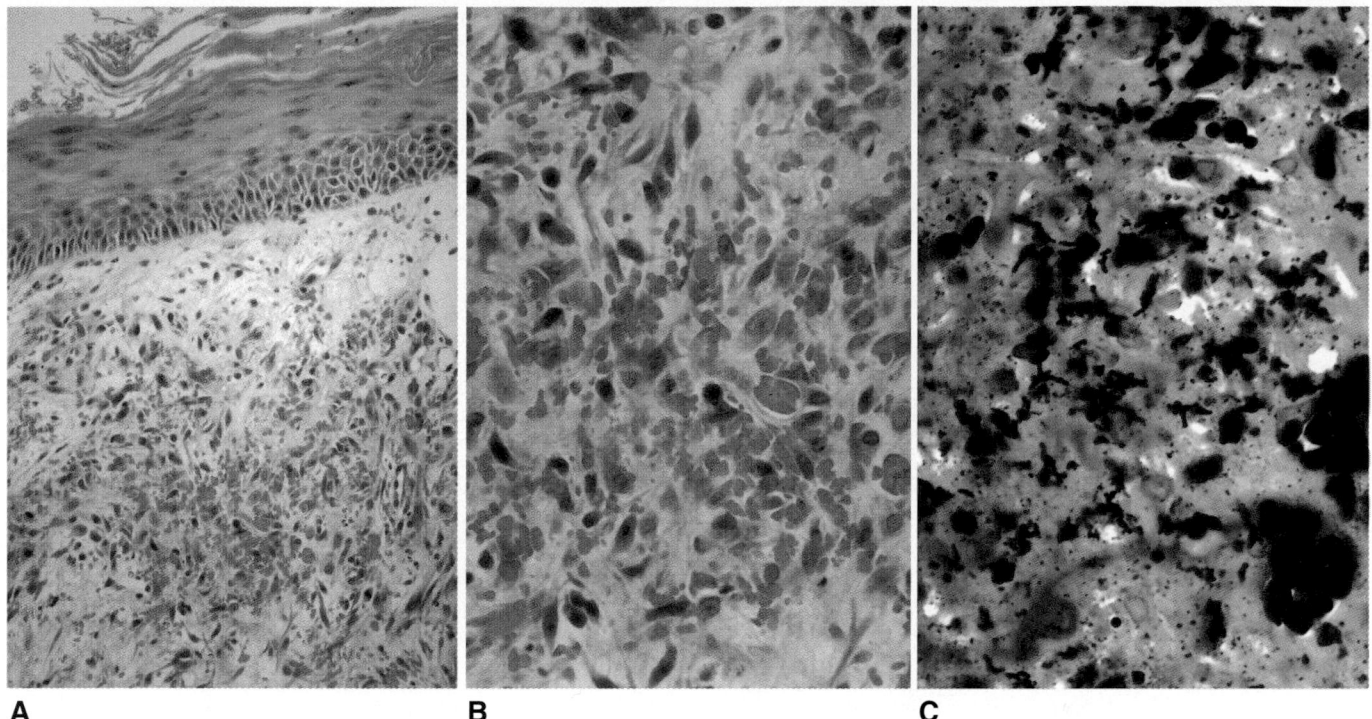

A   **B**   **C**

FIGURE 232-6. Histology of a cutaneous lesion of bacillary angiomatosis: **A,** Increased presence of erythrocytes in the dermis as a result of new capillary formation (hematoxylin and eosin stain, original magnification ×40). **B,** Typical cuboidal endothelial cells among the increased number of erythrocytes (hematoxylin and eosin stain, original magnification ×200). **C,** Dark-staining bacilli among the dark-staining erythrocytes (Warthin-Starry silver stain, original magnification ×1000).

complicate CSD lymphadenopathy as a result of endogenous overproduction of active vitamin D associated with granuloma formation.[121]

Up to half of the overall 11% to 12% of CSD cases that are atypical represent Parinaud's oculoglandular syndrome, a self-limited granulomatous conjunctivitis and ipsilateral, usually preauricular, lymphadenitis (Fig. 232-11).[122,123] Various other "atypical" manifestations[124] include self-limited granulomatous hepatitis/splenitis, atypical pneumonitis,[125] osteitis,[126] and neurologic syndromes (mainly encephalopathy and neurorctinitis). A syndrome of prolonged fever of unknown origin (FUO) in children has been described as well.[127]

Because of the insidious and nonspecific nature of the fever and abdominal pain of CSD hepatitis/splenitis, diagnosis may be delayed until a history of cat exposure prompts ultrasonographic or computed tomographic abdominal imaging, which usually demonstrates multiple hypodense lesions (Fig. 232-12), and serologic testing.[104,128-130] Similarly, the nonspecific nature and rarity of many of the other atypical manifestations beside Parinaud's syndrome may result in delay in their accurate diagnosis until a history of cat exposure or suggestive findings on histopathology prompt specific evaluation directed at *B. henselae.*[117]

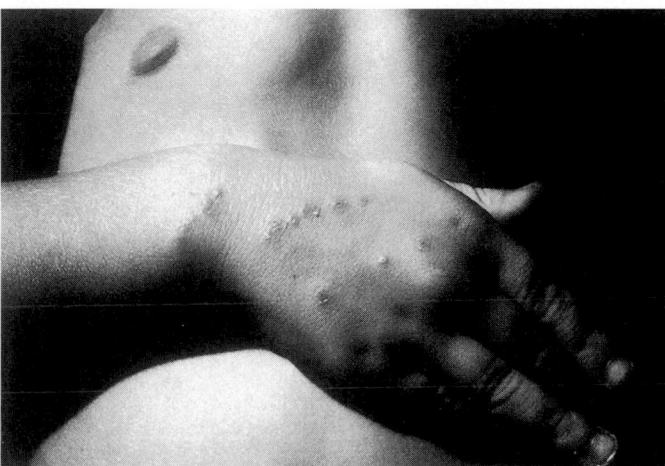

FIGURE 232-7. A child with typical cat-scratch disease demonstrating the original scratch injuries and the primary papule that soon thereafter developed proximal to the middle finger. *(Courtesy of Dr. V. H. San Joaquin, University of Oklahoma Health Sciences Center, Oklahoma City.)*

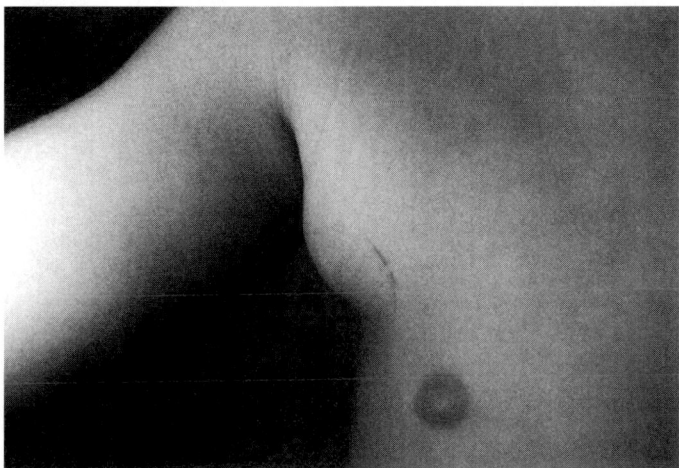

FIGURE 232-8. Right axillary lymphadenopathy followed the scratches and development of a primary papule in this child with typical cat-scratch disease, also illustrated in Figure 232-7. *(Courtesy of Dr. V. H. San Joaquin, University of Oklahoma Health Sciences Center, Oklahoma City.)*

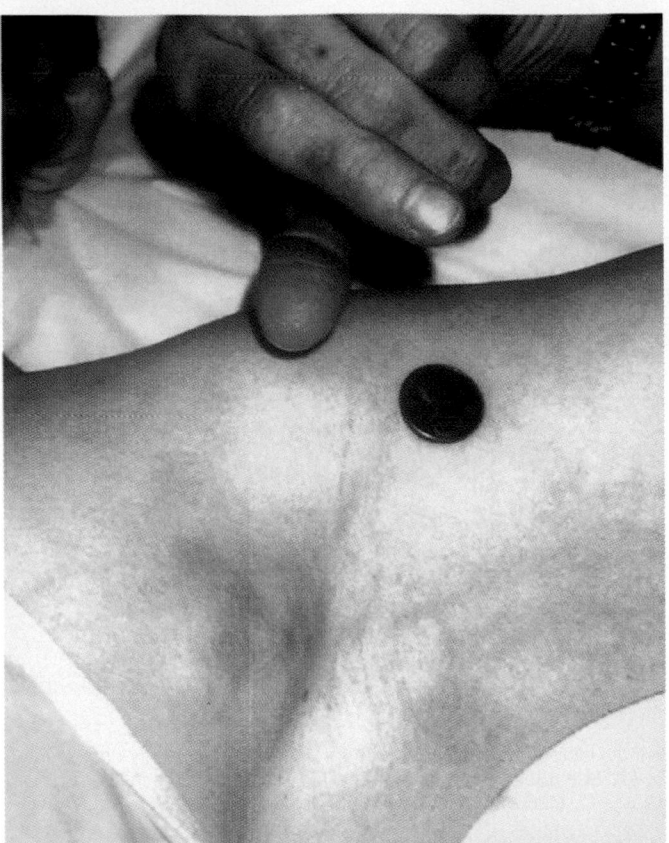

FIGURE 232-9. A 45-year-old woman with left axillary CSD lymphadenitis that developed approximately 3 weeks after sustaining a cat scratch on the left index finger, on which the primary papule is still evident. The U.S. penny was place in the image for size comparison.

A dramatic if infrequent manifestation, encephalopathy, was first reported within a few years of the description and naming of CSD.[131-134] Encephalopathy probably occurs in 2% to 4% of all CSD cases recognized, although estimates range as widely as 1% to 7%.[135] Extrapolating from the estimated U.S. CSD case rate,[115] 500 to 1000 annual CSD encephalopathy cases occur in the United States. Recognition of this phenomenon may increase with the availability of serologic testing and improved blood culture techniques. It remains predominantly a clinical diagnosis, now subject to laboratory confirmation by techniques described below (predominantly antibody testing). Adolescents and adults may represent a greater proportion of cases of CSD encephalopathy than they do of CSD overall.[136] Although encephalopathy usually follows the development of lymphadenopathy, it has also been reported to precede lymph node involvement or to occur in its absence. Persistent, generalized headache is a common part of the history, but fever is an inconsistent finding. Patients may become very restless, and combativeness is often described. Nearly half of patients can develop seizures that may range from focal to generalized, and from brief and self-limited to status epilepticus. Short-term anticonvulsant therapy may be required, as may be supportive therapy in the face of obtundation or coma. Concurrent acute neurologic manifestations may be present transiently (e.g., nuchal rigidity, pathologic reflexes, pupillary dilatation). When they occur, neurologic deficits such as aphasia, cranial nerve palsy, paresis, hemiplegia, and ataxia are also usually self-limited, although time to resolution may span weeks to months to as long as a year. However, persistence of intellectual impairment and of seizures has been reported uncommonly.[137-139]

Laboratory studies, such as cerebrospinal fluid (CSF) analysis and culture, generally do not add specific positive diagnostic findings to the clinical picture of CSD encephalopathy, but rather serve to exclude other processes. Elevations of CSF protein concentration and leukocytes occur in only about one third of patients (but do not necessarily coincide in the same patients); lymphocytes predominate. Hypoglycorrhachia is rare. CSF cultures have been consistently negative, even since the recognition of the CSD-*B. henselae* association. Studies of the brain with

FIGURE 232-10. Magnetic resonance imaging of a 25-year-old man who developed a tender, inflamed right groin mass (seen medial to the right sartorius muscle) that ultimately was proven to represent lymph node swelling of CSD lymphadenitis. He had recently acquired previously feral kittens, which frequently scratched him on the lower extremities as he played with them.

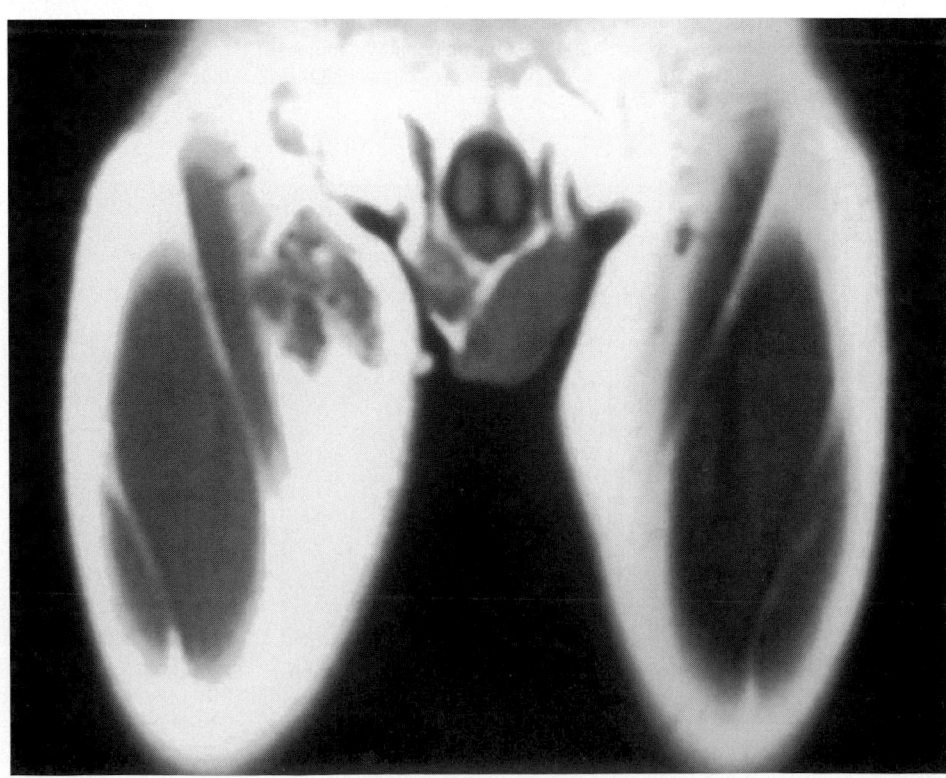

FIGURE 232-11. The granulomatous conjunctivitis of Parinaud's oculoglandular syndrome is associated with ipsilateral local lymphadenopathy, usually preauricular and less commonly submandibular.

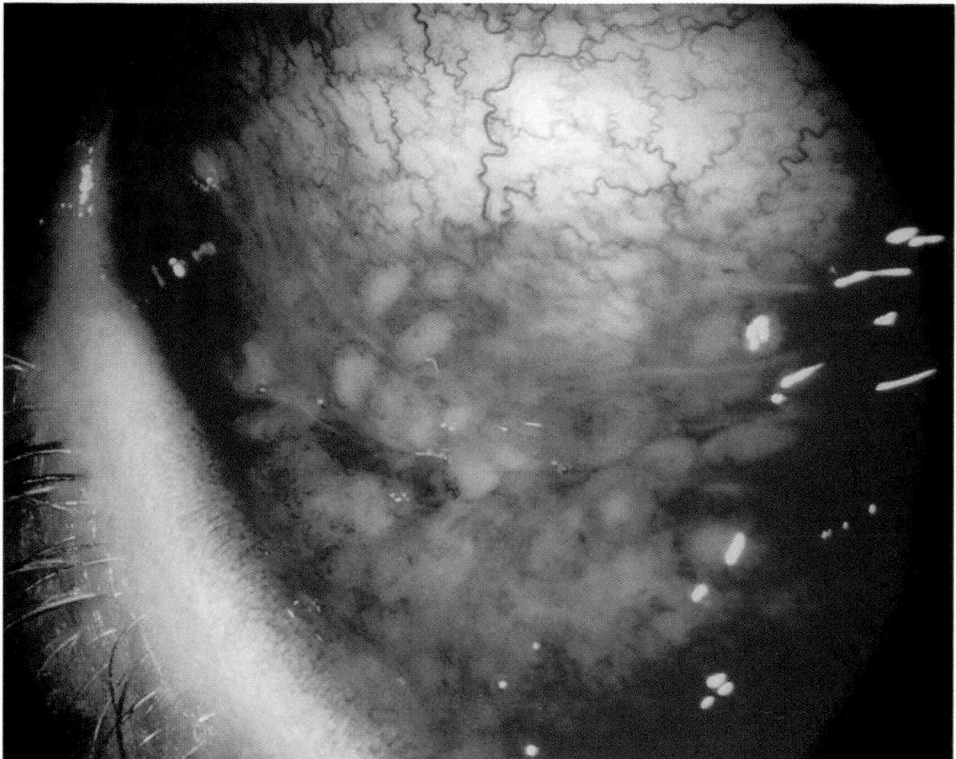

computed tomography and/or magnetic resonance imaging are usually normal, but a few cases of persistent structural abnormalities have been reported.[138,139] Electroencephalography during the acute phase of CSD encephalopathy commonly reveals diffuse slowing, yet another nonspecific feature that resolves with clinical recovery.

The pathogenesis of CSD encephalopathy and other central nervous system (CNS) manifestations associated with CSD remains unclear. It is unknown whether these rare complications are attributable to direct invasion of the CNS by *B. henselae* or to other mechanisms such as vasculitis or immune response. *B. henselae* has been shown to infect feline microglial cells in vitro and to survive intracellularly for up to 4 weeks; however, no ultrastructural abnormalities were identified by electron microscopy within the infected brain cells.[140] At autopsy of a rare fatality resulting from CSD meningoencephalitis, there was marked cerebral edema with no gross evidence of acute meningitis. Microscopic examination revealed multiple granulomatous lesions as well as a meningitis and encephalitis. Warthin-Starry silver stain of the brain and liver revealed pleomorphic rod-shaped bacilli consistent with *B. henselae*. Analysis of brain tissue with PCR confirmed the presence of *B. henselae* DNA.[141]

Unrelated to CSD encephalopathy is a newly described phenomenon of apparently tick-transmitted coinfection of humans with *Borrelia burgdorferi* and *B. henselae*, resulting in concurrent CNS infection manifestations. In each of four cases reported, patients residing in a Lyme disease–endemic area had ongoing CNS symptoms ascribed to chronic Lyme disease. When further evaluated, DNA of both *B. burgdorferi* and *B. henselae* was recovered from these patients' CSF specimens. *B. henselae*–specific DNA was subsequently amplified from deer ticks recovered from the households of two of these patients.[142]

Neuroretinitis associated with CSD[70,136,143-145] only recently has been confirmed by serologic and culture evidence to be related to *B. henselae*.[70,146] CSD neuroretinitis, like other CSD manifestations, has been primarily a clinical diagnosis since its first description in 1970,[143] but with the refinement of techniques for culture and nonculture identification of *B. henselae* infection, diagnostic accuracy should improve. *B. grahamii* has been identified once by PCR amplification and sequence analysis in the intraocular fluid of a HIV-seronegative

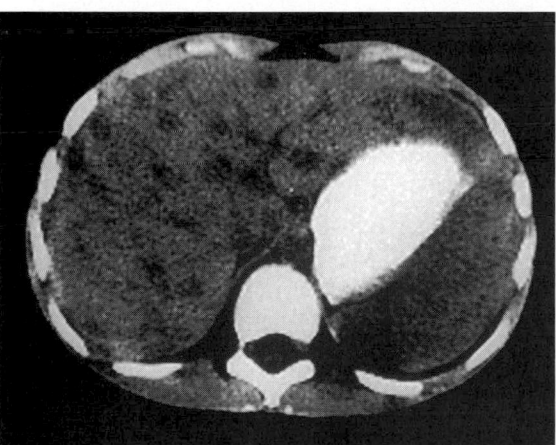

FIGURE 232-12. In this computed tomographic image of a patient with hepatic involvement of cat-scratch disease, the absence of enhancement of the multiple lesions after contrast infusion is consistent with the granulomatous inflammation of this entity. Treated empirically with various antibiotics without improvement before establishment of this diagnosis, the patient subsequently recovered fully with no further antimicrobial therapy. *(Courtesy of Dr. V. H. San Joaquin, University of Oklahoma Health Sciences Center, Oklahoma City.)*

patient with bilateral neuroretinitis and behavioral changes; *B. elizabethae* has been implicated as the pathogen in another patient with neuroretinitis by serologic antibody studies exclusively.[147,148]

Neuroretinitis manifests as fairly sudden loss of visual acuity, usually unilaterally, sometimes preceded by an influenza-like syndrome or development of unilateral lymphadenopathy. The most striking, if not most common, retinal manifestation is papilledema associated with macular exudates in a star formation (Fig. 232-13), first associated with CSD in 1984.[144] Although this manifestation is characteristic of CSD neuroretinitis, it is not pathognomonic; other types of inflammation

FIGURE 232-13. Among the most common manifestations of the neuroretinitis of cat-scratch disease, and certainly among the most striking in appearance, is papilledema associated with stellate macular exudates.

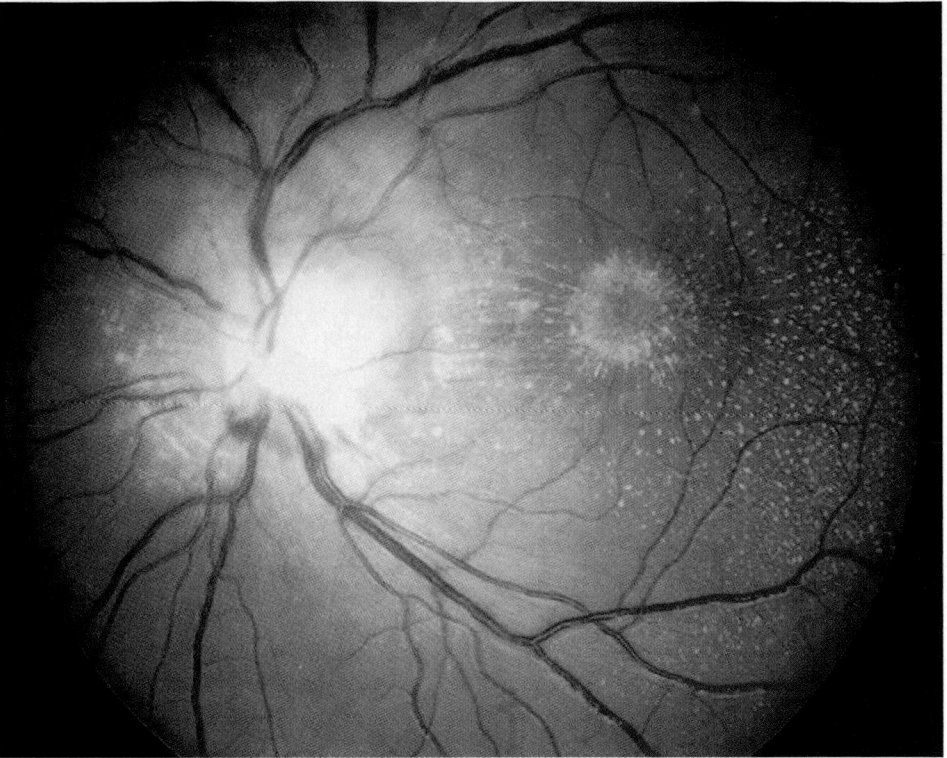

also have been reported. In a retrospective study among 24 CSD patients with 35 affected eyes, isolated foci of retinitis or choroiditis were the most common ocular manifestation, identified in 83% of eyes and 83% of patients. Optic disk swelling was the second most common finding (46% of eyes, 63% of patients), followed by a macular star (43% of eyes, 63% of patients) and vascular-occlusive events (14% of eyes, 21% of patients). Final visual acuity was 20/25 or better in 26 (74%) of 35 eyes and was similar in both treated and untreated patients.[149] Neuroretinitis usually has a favorable spontaneous course, and the utility of antimicrobial and/or corticosteroid therapy remains debated. Prospective follow-up of recently well-documented cases reveals that some have mild residual visual deficits.[70,150]

Historically, the diagnosis of a case of typical CSD required fulfillment of three of the four following criteria, whereas all four were necessary in an atypical case: (1) history of an animal (usually cat or dog) contact with the presence of a scratch or primary skin or eye lesion; (2) aspiration of "sterile" pus from the lymph node, or culture and other laboratory testing that excluded other etiologic possibilities; (3) a positive CSD skin test; and (4) a lymph node biopsy revealing pathology consistent with CSD. Skin test antigen, originally described by Hanger and Rose, is prepared by 56° C heating for 72 hours of saline-diluted "sterile" pus derived from CSD lymphadenitis. It has never been standardized or produced commercially. It is of historic interest because of its confirmatory role in diagnosis of CSD in the past. However, its potential for transmission of hepatitis viruses, HIV, and prions is a major contemporary concern, even if its sources are well screened. Its use in the era of other avenues of diagnosis is no longer warranted.

The differential diagnosis of typical CSD includes many causes of (unilateral) lymphadenopathy, among which are typical or atypical mycobacterial infection, tularemia, plague, brucellosis, syphilis, sporotrichosis, histoplasmosis, toxoplasmosis, infectious mononucleosis syndromes, lymphoma, and other neoplasms. In the inguinal area, tender adenopathy in the absence of a genital lesion suggests *Staphylococcus aureus*, CSD, lymphogranuloma venereum, and, in the febrile patient with a tick exposure, tularemia. The diagnosis of CSD easily can be overlooked if the clinician fails to obtain an adequate history, especially in the case of the atypical syndromes, and not uncommonly in the case of adults with the typical syndrome whose clinicians are inexperienced with CSD. With domestic cats representing the single largest category of companion animals in the United States, the importance of accurate history regarding animal exposure cannot be emphasized enough when evaluating a patient with findings consistent with CSD. Fortunately, in most cases, whether typical or atypical, spontaneous resolution occurs.

HIV-Associated Neurologic Syndromes

B. henselae and/or *quintana* have been implicated in a small proportion of cases of HIV-associated brain lesions, meningoencephalitis, encephalopathy, and neuropsychiatric disease[70,85,151-154] that cannot be ascribed to other causes.

A case of intracerebral BA has been described.[85] *Bartonella* infection associated with neurologic manifestations complicating HIV infection has been demonstrated by serum and CSF antibodies and CSF DNA amplification,[151] although technical limitations prevented accurate species implication in these cases. A study of autopsy brain tissue reported evidence of *B. henselae* by immunofluorescence staining and by PCR amplification in three AIDS dementia patients with elevated CSF:serum indices of *B. henselae*–reactive antibody.[153] A nested case-control study has since confirmed an association between the presence of serum anti-*Bartonella* immunoglobulin M (IgM) (implying recent infection) and increased risk of development of neuropsychological decline or dementia.[154] At least 4% of new cases of HIV-associated dementia or neuropsychological decline were estimated to result from *Bartonella* infections, and therefore to be potentially treatable with antibiotics. Additional case reports have added anecdotal evidence of the utility of antimicrobials in reversing *Bartonella*-associated neuropsychiatric abnormalities in HIV-infected persons.[152]

PATHOGENESIS

In cats, *B. henselae* appears to be a nearly perfectly adapted parasite, capable of causing long-term and/or cyclic, high-grade bacteremia largely in the absence of illness in its hosts.[28,32,44,155-157] Elucidation of mechanisms of this host-parasite relationship is in its infancy. As yet, only a small body of fundamental knowledge about the pathogenic mechanisms of *Bartonella* species in humans has been developed, primarily focused on interactions with erythrocytes and endothelial cells, induction of neoangiogenesis, and mechanisms of survival. These have been reviewed in greater detail elsewhere.[158]

B. bacilliformis cells have polar flagella that confer motility and may participate in adhesion to erythrocytes.[159,160] Aggregative fimbriae also may play a role in such adhesion.[161] Erythrocyte invasion involves an extracellular deformin protein, the flagellum, and proteins encoded by the invasion-associated locus (*ialAB*).[160,162-164] Even though *B. henselae* does not bind to human erythrocytes in vitro in a fashion similar to *B. bacilliformis,* supernatants of in vitro growth of *B. henselae* contain a protein very similar to the deformin of *B. bacilliformis.* Also in a fashion similar to *B. bacilliformis, B. henselae* outer membrane proteins bind with a number of erythrocyte ghost membrane proteins.[165] The 31-kDa outer membrane protein of *B. henselae* is involved in heme acquisition and may therefore be a virulence factor.[166]

After entry into erythrocytes, *B. bacilliformis* can replicate within and, occasionally, escape from the endosomal vacuoles.[167] Studies from the high-grade feline bacteremia of *B. henselae* have not yet resolved whether it is truly intra- or extraerythrocytic in cats.[168,169] In humans, the enhanced efficiency of recovery of these pathogens with lysis-type blood cultures suggests some degree of intracellular localization. Through use of confocal microscopy and monoclonal antibody labeling, *B. quintana* has been shown to be able to invade human erythrocytes, both in vivo and in vitro.[170,171]

B. bacilliformis has been demonstrated to stimulate endothelial cell proliferation both in vitro and in vivo, likely through a sheddable stimulatory factor.[172-174] In situ hybridization of clinical specimens of verruga peruana suggests *B. bacilliformis* stimulation of endothelial production of angiopoetin-2 and epidermal production of vascular endothelial growth factor.[175] Similar in vitro proliferative effects can be induced by *B. henselae* and *B. quintana. B. henselae* also can induce endothelial cell migration in vitro. These effects of *B. henselae* are mediated by a factor inactivated by trypsin, and therefore likely a protein.[174]

In the process of endothelial cell invasion by *B. bacilliformis*, the host cell appears to be an active participant through the pathogen's induction of rearrangement of the host's cytoskeleton.[176] *B. quintana* has been demonstrated to invade and multiply within endothelial cells in vitro and in vivo and form intracellular blebs in the process.[177] *B. henselae* interaction with the endothelial cell in vitro results in bacterial aggregation on the cell surface and subsequent engulfment and internalization of the bacterial aggregate by a unique structure, the invasome.[178]

Intracellular survival of *Bartonella* spp. may be facilitated by production of superoxide dismutases[179] and possibly production of stress-response-processing proteases.[180] Also, *B. henselae* and *B. quintana* produce heat shock proteins of the *groEL* genes, which share signature sequences with genes of other gram-negative bacteria known to invade eukaryotic cells.

LABORATORY DIAGNOSIS

Presumptive diagnosis can be made by direct examination of clinical materials in the context of a *Bartonella*-associated syndrome. Definitive diagnosis of *Bartonella*-associated diseases can be achieved through modified conventional bacteriologic culture methods, coculture with endothelial cells, immunoserologic or immunocytochemical means, and/or DNA amplification. Detailed discussion of these techniques is available in other reference sources.[181,182] Approaches that are currently practical for the majority of clinical laboratories are direct examination, culture, and serology. Serologic testing is becoming a mainstay of diagnosis, particularly for that part of the clinical spectrum of diseases occupied by CSD and CNS infection.

Direct Examination

Giemsa-stained blood films are commonly used in endemic locales to detect *B. bacilliformis* in patients with Oroya fever. A wide morphologic range is seen in such smears, with the organisms appearing as red-violet rods or rounded forms, occurring singly or in groups and associated with erythrocytes. Bacilli are the most typical, measuring 0.25 to 0.5 by 1.0 to 3.0 μm. The cells are often curved and may show uni- or bipolar enlargement and granules. Rounded organisms measure approximately 0.75 μm in diameter, and a ringlike variety is sometimes abundant.[183] Although appearing adherent to erythrocytes by light microscopy, bacteria also have been observed within erythrocytes when viewed by electron microscopy.[184] The magnitude of human bacteremia associated with *B. henselae/B. quintana* does not typically afford direct observation of bacteria in blood smears.

Bartonella spp. are gram-negative, are not acid fast, and stain poorly or not at all in tissue other than by silver impregnation techniques (e.g., Warthin-Starry, Steiner, Dieterle). *B. henselae* and *B. quintana* are demonstrable by Warthin-Starry staining in BA/BP; *B. henselae* may be silver stained during the early stages of lymphadenopathy in CSD, but typically not during the later granulomatous stage of inflammation. Species-specific direct detection of organisms in tissue by immunocytochemical labeling also has been described,[77,102,110,185] but reagents for such labeling are not widely available.

Specimen Collection and Handling for Culture

The sources from which isolation is attempted most commonly are blood and tissue. The time interval from collection to processing should be minimized. If storage of specimens is necessary, they should be frozen. A controlled study of the effects of blood collection and handling methods has shown that blood specimens from *B. henselae*-infected cats that were collected in either ethylenediaminetetraacetic acid (EDTA) or Isolator (Wampole, Cranbury, NJ.) blood-lysis tubes yielded good recovery, and that blood collected in tubes containing EDTA could be plated after 26 days at −65° C with no loss of sensitivity.[186] Whenever possible, specimens should be collected prior to antimicrobial therapy, especially with the tetracyclines and macrolides. Growth of *B. henselae* is also inhibited by concentrations of sodium polyanethol sulfonate (SPS) that are used in blood culture media.[181] The precaution of adding agents to neutralize SPS toxicity or using resin-containing media (primarily to lyse erythrocytes) should be taken if blood is cultured in commercial systems. Lytic blood culture systems (e.g., Isolator) combine the advantageous effect of neutralizing SPS toxicity by hemoglobin freed from erythrocytes with the potential release of intracellular organisms.

Culture

All *Bartonella* spp. can be cultured on cell-free media, unlike members of the order Rickettsiales. Recovery of *Bartonella* spp. is optimized using freshly prepared rabbit-heart infusion agar plates.[187] However, various formulations of blood or chocolate agar will support their growth, with the best results dependent on media freshness. Approaches used for recovery of other fastidious pathogens are generally suitable, except that most isolates require more than 7 days of incubation before they can be detected. Therefore, routine bacterial culture protocols rarely allow *Bartonella* spp. to be detected. Protocols designed to yield other slowly growing organisms (e.g., *Histoplasma capsulatum* or *Mycobacterium avium* complex on noninhibitory media) can also result in recovery of *Bartonella* spp. Cultures are not recommended to diagnose most cases of CSD, and in fact the sensitivity is at best only 20% compared to PCR assays.[188] Attempted isolation of *Bartonella* spp. may be useful in the settings of (1) FUO or neuroretinitis after cat exposure; (2) fever, lymphadenitis, neuroretinitis, or encephalitis of unknown origin in the immunocompromised patient; (3) endocarditis without recovery of typical pathogens; and (4) bacillary angiomatosis/peliosis.

Inoculated media should be incubated at 35° to 37° C under conditions of 5% to 10% CO_2 and greater than 40% humidity. (*B. bacilliformis* and possibly some strains of *B. clarridgeiae* spp. have a lower [25° to 30° C] optimal temperature for growth.) The medium should be as freshly prepared as possible. Plates sealed after 24 hours of incubation with plastic film or shrink wrap to preserve moisture content of the media usually can be incubated up to 30 days without notable deterioration.

Alternative approaches to use of the Isolator for blood cultures include use of a broth-based culture system. *B. henselae* has been isolated in the biphasic Septi-Chek system (Roche Diagnostics, Nutley, NJ) after incubation in excess of 40 days. Evidence of growth, if any, in the broth phase is a pellicle or adherent film on the glass surface. *Bartonella* spp. usually grow best on solid or semisolid media. In broth, *Bartonella* spp. rarely produce turbidity or convert enough oxidizable substrate for CO_2 detection–based systems to indicate growth. However, several isolates have been detected initially using BACTEC (Becton Dickinson, Sparks, MD) and resin-containing media combined with acridine orange staining at the termination of a 7-day incubation period, with recovery subsequently achieved by subculture to solid media.[9,10,73] Another CO_2 detection blood culture system, BacT/Alert (bioMérieux, Durham, NC), has been reported to yield positive growth algorithms in 5 cases of *B. henselae* bacteremia. Although Gram stains of the broth and routine 72-hour subcultures proved negative, acridine orange and Warthin-Starry staining demonstrated bacilli, and phase-contrast microscopy of wet mounts revealed bacilli with "rachety motility." Specific immunofluorescent labeling of organisms obtained directly from the broth or subsequently subcultured on semisolid media identified *B. henselae*.[189]

A defined cell-free medium (modified from RPMI 1640) also has been described that permits recovery of *Bartonella* spp. from primary clinical specimens.[145] Improved growth in brucella broth when supplemented with hemin (250 mg/mL) and peptic digest of blood (8% Fildes reagent) has been reported, but this technique has been applied mainly to propagation rather than primary isolation.[190] Similarly, isolates can be propagated on buffered charcoal–yeast extract medium,[13] but this is not recommended for primary isolation.

Bartonella spp. have been isolated from liver, spleen, lymph node, and skin after homogenization either by direct plating of tissue homogenate or aspirate[15,30,37,70,75] or by cocultivation with various cell lines.[8,11] *B. henselae/B. quintana* grow in endothelial cell cultures as elongated pleomorphic organisms visible in Gimenez-stained preparations 72 hours after inoculation of the cell cultures. The cocultivation method is not practical for most microbiology laboratories, although it may result in recovering occasional isolates missed with cell-free media. In the absence of coculture, more than a month of incubation often has been necessary to yield evident colonies from some tissue specimens.[30,37] Because selective culture techniques have not been developed, recovery of isolates from specimens such as skin may be more difficult if indigenous or contaminating flora are present.

Identification

Colonies of *Bartonella* spp. are of two morphologic types: (1) irregular, raised, whitish, rough, and dry in appearance (variously characterized as "cauliflower" or "molar tooth" or "verrucous") or (2) smaller, circular, tan, and moist in appearance, tending to pit and adhere to the agar. Both types are usually present in the same culture (Fig. 232-14). The degree of colonial heterogeneity varies by species and by strain, with *B. henselae* typically displaying a greater proportion of rough colonies than *B. quintana*, which may even appear as uniformly smooth in primary cultures. Repeated subcultures of *B. henselae* tend to have increasing proportions of smooth colonies. Cultures of *B. henselae* on blood agar produce an odor similar to the caramel odor (diacetyl) of *Streptococcus milleri*. Colonies contain small, gram-negative, slightly curved rods resembling *Campylobacter*, *Helicobacter*, or *Haemophilus*. Cells, especially of *B. henselae*, are very autoadherent, as demonstrable when attempting to scrape colonies from agar with a loop. Twitching motility of cells is evident in wet mounts, presumably interrelated with adherence, both features being mediated by fine fimbriae (pili) visible in negatively stained electron microscopy. Cells of *B. bacilliformis* and *B. clarridgeiae* possess polar flagella.

The features of incubation for more than 7 days before the appearance of colonies, small curved gram-negative bacilli, and negative catalase and oxidase reactions are sufficient for presumptive identification of *B. henselae* or *B. quintana*.[182,187] Additional methods to confirm the identity of isolates may be employed, or isolates may be referred to a

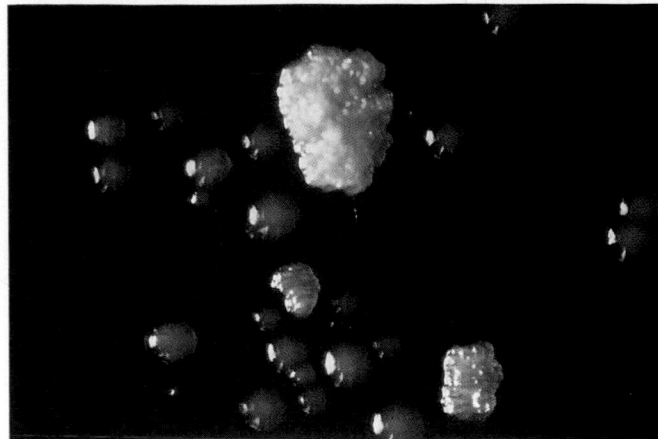

FIGURE 232-14. Smooth and verrucous colony types growing concurrently in a chocolate agar culture of *B. henselae* (magnification approximately ×40).

laboratory experienced with *Bartonella* spp. for confirmatory identification. Although the reagents are not widely available, a reliable means to distinguish *B. henselae* from *B. quintana* isolates quickly is immunofluorescence with antisera monospecific for each of these two species.[187,189,191] Characterization using conventional tests produces results that identify the *Bartonella* spp. (Table 232-2). (For comparison, the characteristics of *Afipia felis* are included in this table.)

Commercial identification kits do not contain *Bartonella* spp. in their databases, but the MicroScan (Dade Behring, Deerfield, IL) rapid anaerobe panel distinguishes *Bartonella* spp. from species that are in its database. Using this panel with careful adjustment of inoculum size to a McFarland no. 3 standard, it is also possible to distinguish *Bartonella* species on the basis of biotype codes[181,187] (10077640 = *B. henselae*, 10073640 = *B. quintana*, 10077240 = *B. bacilliformis*). Heavier inocula blur the distinctions. In other systems, the biochemical reactivity of *B. quintana* and *B. henselae* has been enhanced by addition of hemin to test media.[192]

Determination of the cellular fatty acid composition by gas-liquid chromatography is useful in identifying and distinguishing *Bartonella* spp. from other genera.[13,187] The Bartonellaceae have relatively simple gas-liquid chromatography profiles consisting mainly of $C_{18:1}$, $C_{18:0}$, and $C_{16:0}$ acids. *B. elizabethae* contains a greater amount of $C_{17:0}$ than the other species. An unusual branched-chain fatty acid (11-methyloctadec-12-enoic acid) distinguishes *Afipia* spp. from *Bartonella* spp. and other organisms.[113,193]

Antimicrobial Susceptibility Testing

Clinical correlation studies of susceptibility testing results with *Bartonella* spp. have not been performed to the extent necessary to ensure that meaningful data can be generated. If required, antimicrobial susceptibility testing can be performed by incorporation of antimicrobial agents into either blood or chocolate agar and testing by the agar dilution technique.[13,194] *Haemophilus* test medium with a broth microdilution technique has also been described, but the Etest (AB Biodisk, Solna, Sweden) may be the most practical means to assess susceptibility.[195] Testing in other types of systems has also been reported.[196-199] Because of the slow growth and fastidious nature of the organisms, some test methods may be inappropriate. Testing of isolates is problematic in any system for those strains displaying the most fastidious growth characteristics.

Generally, *B. henselae* isolates are susceptible in vitro to most antibacterial agents tested, including β-lactams, tetracyclines, macrolides, aminoglycosides, fluoroquinolones, vancomycin, rifampin, chloramphenicol, and co-trimoxazole, but resistant to nalidixic acid. In vitro resistance to penicillin and ampicillin, tetracycline, or vancomycin has been noted. *B. quintana* is similar in its in vitro susceptibility pattern. Some investigators argue that aminoglyco-

TABLE 232-2 **Differential Characteristics of Commonly Pathogenic *Bartonella* spp. and *Afipia felis***

Characteristic	Bartonella bacilliformis	Bartonella quintana	Bartonella henselae	Bartonella elizabethae	Bartonella clarridgeiae	Afipia felis
Gram reaction	−	−	−	−	−	−
Catalase	+	−	±	−	−	−
Oxidase	−	±	−	−	−	+
Nitrate reduction	−	−	−	−	−	+
Indole	−	−	−	−	−	−
Urease	−	−	−	−	−	+
Acid from carbohydrates†	−	−	−	−	−	−
Optimal temperature (° C)	25-30	35-37	35-37	35-37	35-37	25-30
Growth in nutrient broth	−	−	−	−	−	+
Hemolysis	−	−	−	−	−	−
Flagella	+	−‡	−‡	−	+	+
Cellular fatty acids constituting >90% of total	$C_{18:1\omega7C}$, $C_{16:0}$, $C_{16:1\omega7C}$	$C_{18:1\omega7C}$, $C_{16:0}$, $C_{18:0}$	$C_{18:1\omega7C}$, $C_{18:0}$, $C_{16:0}$	$C_{18:1\omega7C}$, $C_{17:0}$, $C_{16:0}$	$C_{18:1\omega7C}$, $C_{18:0}$, $C_{16:0}$	$C_{18:1\omega7C}$, $C_{BR19:1}$, $C_{19:0CYC}$

*+, positive reaction; −, negative reaction; ±, negative or weakly positive.
†Glucose, lactose, maltose, mannitol, and sucrose.
‡May demonstrate twitching motility in wet mounts.

sides most reliably demonstrate in vitro bactericidal activity, mandating their use for therapy of bacteremia and endocarditis.[67,78,200,201]

Molecular Methods

PCR-based and DNA hybridization techniques can also be used to speciate isolates.[2,14,15,18,39] Molecular subtyping of strains can also be performed using PCR-based restriction fragment length polymorphisms (RFLP),[12,202,203] repetitive extragenic palindromic PCR (REP-PCR),[18,204] and enterobacterial repetitive intergenic consensus (ERIC)-PCR with sodium dodecyl sulfate-polyacrylamide gel electrophoresis.[31] Some studies suggest a greater diversity of RFLP types in the blood of bacteremic HIV-infected persons than in the CSD lesions of immunocompetent hosts.[202,205]

Numerous PCR assays have been developed for direct detection of *Bartonella* spp. in pus, skin lesions, or tissue. A gene fragment specific for either citrate synthase or a heat shock protein of *B. henselae* is demonstrable by PCR in the majority of patients with CSD.[40,107,109] Amplification of rRNA gene segments with universal primers followed by direct nucleotide sequence analysis of the amplification product or hybridization with specific probes is another, more sensitive but more laborious approach.[91,109,206] More recently, LightCycler (Roche Diagnostics) assays have been developed.[207] Depending upon the method and the source of specimen (freshly aspirated pus, fresh tissue, fixed and paraffin-embedded tissue), the success of identification has ranged from 50% to nearly 100%.[38,39,106-109,208] Improved detection of *Bartonella* DNA in histologic material has been reported using a semi-nested PCR amplification.[209] PCR amplification has also enabled identification of *B. henselae* in CSF and brain tissue of patients with HIV-related neurologic processes in the absence of culture recovery.[151,153]

Serologic Testing

Useful *B. bacilliformis* serologic testing has been under development only in recent years. Using a simple sonic lysate antigen, an immunoglobulin G (IgG) immunoblot assay has been reported to have 70% and 94% sensitivity in persons with acute and chronic infection, respectively, but with suboptimal specificity.[210] An alternative approach has been an immunofluorescence assay detecting IgG, reported to have 82% and 93% sensitivity in persons with acute and chronic infection, respectively, but at the expense of substantial cross-reaction with other *Bartonella* species.[211] It can also detect IgM in patients with early acute disease. When used in the endemic region to assess patients with syndromes compatible with *B. bacilliformis* disease, the low specificity of these tests may be relatively less important than for geographically widespread *Bartonella* species.

Enzyme immunoassay (EIA) and radioimmunoprecipitation have been found comparably more sensitive than hemagglutination and immunofluorescence assays in older studies of human antibodies to *B. quintana*.[212] With the EIA, all cases in a small series of acute primary

or relapsed trench fever were found to have measurable, although often low, levels of anti-*B. quintana* antibodies.[213]

Immunofluorescence assay (IFA)[33,36,214-216] and several EIAs[35,105,187,208,217] have been described for *B. henselae* and *B. quintana*. To date, they have been used most commonly to demonstrate anti-*Bartonella* antibodies in persons with CSD,[33,35,36,105,146,208,214,216,217] endocarditis,[11,74-78,215] and in some cases of HIV-associated aseptic meningitis, encephalopathy, or neuropsychiatric disease.[70,151,154] Human antibody responses often have been substantially cross-reactive between *B. quintana* and *B. henselae* in assays so far reported.[105,214] Furthermore, in some of these assays there may be serologic cross-reaction with *Chlamydia* species and *Coxiella burnetii*, other potential agents of "culture-negative endocarditis" in humans.[11,76,215,218]

The IFA and one EIA for antibodies to *B. henselae* and *B. quintana*, both using bacterial whole-cell antigens, have been compared with one another, with an EIA for antibodies to *A. felis*, and with findings of cat scratch antigen skin testing in evaluating patients with the clinical diagnosis of CSD.[105,214] CSD patients had no higher levels of antibodies to *A. felis* than did control persons, although most CSD patients had evidence of elevated anti-*Bartonella* antibodies by IFA and of anti-*Bartonella* IgM by EIA compared with controls. Detection of anti-*Bartonella* antibodies was a better marker of CSD than was a reaction to skin test antigen, even though neither the IFA nor EIA could discriminate between anti-*B. henselae* and anti-*B. quintana* antibodies.

Modifications and variations of IFA and EIA assays using whole bacterial cell antigens have generally corroborated that such assays, especially if performed at only one time for a particular subject, appear to be variably and sometimes suboptimally sensitive and specific.[208,216,217] Alternative EIA methodology, using partially[77,187,219] or highly purified[220] antigen components, ultimately may prove more species sensitive and specific.

Most such studies to date have compared serologic measurements with clinical diagnoses rather than proven infection. Thus they have been flawed by the absence of definitive proof of infection by a particular agent by which to calibrate the serologic response, by token of the difficult nature of culture recovery.

Nevertheless, such assays have appropriately supplanted skin testing as a means of confirming a diagnosis of CSD[30,120] and corroborating other manifestations of *B. henselae* and *B. quintana* infections. The indirect fluorescent antibody method using *B. henselae* cells fixed on slides, as developed by the Centers for Disease Control and Prevention (CDC), is probably the most widely utilized. Reported sensitivity for its detection of anti–*B. henselae* IgG is 85% to 94%. However, this method has a high rate of cross-reaction with *B. quintana* antigens from contemporary isolates. Whereas the CDC's testing does not routinely measure IgM, commercially developed kits using the same nature of antigen preparation for immunofluorescence slides have attempted to do so with some success.

As diagnostic techniques utilizing DNA amplification for definitive microbiologic diagnosis have become more widely used, definitive comparators for serologic findings have become available. An EIA using as antigen partially purified proteins presumed to be of outer membrane origin has been reported in its application to a large population of CSD patients meeting stringent clinical criteria and having culture or PCR proof, or both, of *B. henselae* infection. With an assay specificity greater than 98%, the assay detected anti–*B. henselae* IgG in 75% of the patients and anti–*B. henselae* IgM in 44%. The assay's detection of IgG, IgM, or both was 85%, a sensitivity for detection of antibodies in the face of disease comparable to that reported for the IFA methodology.[221]

TREATMENT AND PREVENTION

The standard therapy for acute *B. bacilliformis* infection in South America has been oral chloramphenicol in a dose of 2 g/day for at least 1 week. Oral chloramphenicol is no longer available in the United States and would not be appropriate if it were available. Alternatives such as oral ciprofloxacin, doxycycline, other tetracyclines, ampicillin, or trimethoprim-sulfamethoxazole can be given for a comparable duration. Parenteral therapy can be substituted if oral intake or bowel absorption is impaired. In modern-era Peru, the agent of primary choice in the treatment of eruptive phase lesions has become rifampin.[54]

In vitro susceptibility of *B. henselae* and *B. quintana* does not necessarily predict in vivo response to therapy. Indeed, BA/BP can develop and organisms be recovered in the face of therapy with co-trimoxazole, β-lactam antibiotics, and fluoroquinolone antibiotics.[96,222] In contrast, therapy with rifampin, tetracyclines, or macrolides dramatically reduces culture recovery from BA/BP lesions, and macrolide administration appears to protect against *Bartonella* infections.[96] The routine use of rifabutin, clarithromycin, and azithromycin for the prevention of *M. avium* complex infections in persons with AIDS appears to have reduced the incidence of *Bartonella* infections in that population. Yet when appropriate care has not been accessed, *Bartonella* infection rates can rival those of *M. avium* complex in persons with advanced HIV infection. A recent study in an area of high HIV prevalence found that 18% of persons evaluated for acute or persistent unexplained fever had evidence of infection with *B. henselae* or *B. quintana* through the combined use of culture, serologic, and DNA amplification techniques. The HIV-infected majority (97%) of these had a median CD4 lymphocyte count of 35/μL and none had ever received viral load testing or antiretroviral therapy.[223]

Ease of administration, low cost, and observed clinical effectiveness make oral erythromycin (500 mg PO four times daily) or doxycycline (100 mg PO twice daily) the initial agents of choice to treat uncomplicated bacteremia and processes such as BA and BP caused by non-*bacilliformis Bartonella* spp.[96,222,224] Azithromycin (250 mg PO daily) is useful but more expensive. As long as it is of adequate duration, such therapy appears effective for most manifestations. Exceptions may include bony or parenchymal involvement and endocarditis, for which initial parenteral therapy may be advantageous. In endocarditis, addition of an aminoglycoside for the first 2 weeks appears to be beneficial.[78] Hemodynamic considerations may require valve replacement irrespective of the effect of antimicrobials upon bacterial proliferation. For bacteremia, at least 4 weeks of therapy is indicated.[69] Longer duration treatment (8 to 12 weeks) is appropriate in the HIV-infected patient, if fever or bacteremia is persistent or recurrent in the HIV-uninfected patient,[70] and in the setting of endocarditis. Some investigators argue for the addition of gentamicin to doxycycline in the treatment of all cases of *B. quintana* bacteremia.[67] For BA involving only the skin, experienced clinicians recommend 8 to 12 weeks of oral therapy.[222] Relapsing disease has been seen in both immunocompromised and immunocompetent hosts, especially, but not only, if therapy is terminated prematurely. For relapses occurring after adequately long initial treatment, chronic suppressive therapy with doxycycline or erythromycin should be considered.

There have been anecdotal reports of the utility of various agents (rifampin, gentamicin, trimethoprim-sulfamethoxazole, fluoroquinolones, azithromycin[225-229]) in the treatment of CSD. However, only azithromycin has been demonstrated to accelerate the resolution of typical CSD lymphadenopathy in a placebo-controlled, double-blinded study.[120] Although the value of antibiotic therapy of CSD remains debatable in light of the usually benign outcome of most manifestations,[228] azithromycin should be the agent of first choice for treating "typical" CSD lymphadenitis if antimicrobial administration is contemplated. Utility in treatment of "atypical" manifestations of CSD remains undefined.

Although there is no definite evidence of the utility of antibiotic therapy in altering the course of neurologic manifestations of CSD, recent case reports of neuroretinitis associated with persistent *B. henselae* bacteremia, and of *Bartonella*-associated antibiotic-responsive neuropsychiatric manifestations in the setting of HIV infection, probably support the inclination to treat with antimicrobials. One report has suggested that two-agent therapy for neuroretinitis accelerates resolution in comparison to untreated historical control cases. The agents used in such cases have usually been erythromycin or doxycycline (with or without combined rifampin), or alternatively azithromycin, clarithromycin, or fluoroquinolones.[70,150,152] Systemic corticosteroid therapy is often administered by ophthalmologists as an adjunct or alternative to antimicrobials; no definitive advantage or disadvantage to such an approach has been demonstrated. Recommendations for treatment of *Bartonella* species have recently been published.[230]

Prevention of *B. bacilliformis* and *B. quintana* infections is probably best achieved by avoiding the locales or circumstances in which exposure to their arthropod vectors occurs. In contrast, prevention of *B. henselae* (and possible *B. clarridgeiae*) infection entails avoidance of interactions with cats that might result in scratches, bites, or licks. Feral cats, cats which are allowed outdoors, cats with fleas, and kittens (<12 months old) all have a higher chance of being *B. henselae* infected.[231] Although the role of cat fleas in the transmission of *B. henselae* to humans remains inadequately defined, treatment of pet cats for such infestation may be prudent, especially if human owners or contacts are immunosuppressed. Antibiotic therapy of cats implicated in CSD transmission or otherwise demonstrated to be *B. henselae* or *B. clarridgeiae* infected does not durably eliminate bacteremia[232-234] and is not warranted, except perhaps in the setting of immunosuppressed human contacts. In general, removal of cats from the household of immunocompetent or immunosuppressed humans is unnecessary as long as the contact precautions defined above are maintained. Although certainly not recommended, direct contact with cat feces or urine does not appear to present a risk for human *B. henselae* infection.

REFERENCES

1. Relman DA, Lepp PW, Sadler KN, Schmidt TM. Phylogenetic relationships among the agent of bacillary angiomatosis, *Bartonella bacilliformis,* and other alphaproteobacteria. Mol Microbiol. 1992;6:1801-1807.
2. Brenner DJ, O'Connor SP, Winkler HH, Steigerwalt AG. Proposals to unify the genera *Bartonella* and *Rochalimaea,* with descriptions of *Bartonella quintana* comb. nov., *Bartonella vinsonii* comb. nov., *Bartonella henselae* comb. nov., and *Bartonella elizabethae* comb. nov., and to remove the family Bartonellaceae from the order Rickettsiales. Int J Syst Bacteriol. 1993;43:777-786.
3. Strong RP, Tyzzer EE, Brues CT, et al. Verruga peruviana, Oroya fever and uta: Preliminary report of the first expedition to South America from the Department of Tropical Medicine of Harvard University. J Am Med Assoc. 1913;61:1713-1716.
4. Strong RP, Sellards AW. Oroya fever: Second report. J Am Med Assoc. 1915;64:806-808.
5. Mooser H, Wyer F. Experimental infection of *Macacus rhesus* with *Rickettsia quintana* (trench fever). Proc Soc Exp Biol Med. 1953;83:699-701.
6. Liu W-T. Trench fever: A resumé of literature and a note on some obscure phases of the disease. Chinese Med J. 1984;97:179-190.
7. McNee JW, Renshaw A. "Trench fever": A relapsing fever occurring with the British forces in France. Br Med J. 1916;1:225-234.
8. Koehler JE, Quinn FD, Berger TG, et al. Isolation of *Rochalimaea* species from cutaneous and osseous lesions of bacillary angiomatosis. N Engl J Med. 1992;327:1625-1632.
9. Spach DH, Callis KP, Paauw DS, et al. Endocarditis caused by *Rochalimaea quintana* in a patient infected with human immunodeficiency virus. J Clin Microbiol. 1993;31:692-694.
10. Larson AM, Dougherty MJ, Nowowiejski DJ, et al. Detection of *Bartonella* (*Rochalimaea*) *quintana* by routine acridine orange staining of broth blood cultures. J Clin Microbiol. 1994;32:1492-1496.

11. Drancourt M, Mainardi JL, Brouqui P, et al. *Bartonella (Rochalimaea) quintana* endocarditis in three homeless men. N Engl J Med. 1995;332:419-423.

12. Spach DH, Kanter AS, Dougherty MJ, et al. *Bartonella (Rochalimaea) quintana* bacteremia in inner-city patients with chronic alcoholism. N Engl J Med. 1995;332: 424-428.

13. Slater LN, Welch DF, Hensel D, Coody DW. A newly recognized fastidious gram-negative pathogen as a cause of fever and bacteremia. N Engl J Med. 1990;323: 1587-1593.

14. Regnery RL, Anderson BE, Clarridge JE III, et al. Characterization of a novel *Rochalimaea* species, *R. henselae* sp. nov., isolated from blood of a febrile, human immunodeficiency virus-positive patient. J Clin Microbiol. 1992;30:265-274.

15. Welch DF, Pickett DA, Slater LN, et al. *Rochalimaea henselae* sp. nov., a cause of septicemia, bacillary angiomatosis, and parenchymal bacillary peliosis. J Clin Microbiol. 1992;30:275-280.

16. Daly JS, Worthington MG, Brenner DJ, et al. *Rochalimaea elizabethae* sp. nov. isolated from a patient with endocarditis. J Clin Microbiol. 1993;31:872-881.

17. Birtles RJ, Harrison TG, Saunders NA, Molyneux DH. Proposals to unify the genera *Grahamella* and *Bartonella,* with descriptions of *Bartonella talpae* comb. nov., *Bartonella peromysci* sp. nov., *Bartonella taylorii* sp. nov., and *Bartonella doshiae* sp. nov. Int J Syst Bacteriol. 1995;45:1-8.

18. Clarridge JE III, Raich TJ, Pirwani D, et al. Strategy to detect and identify *Bartonella* species in a routine clinical laboratory yields *Bartonella henselae* from human immunodeficiency virus-infected patient and unique *Bartonella* strain from his cat. J Clin Microbiol. 1995;33:2107-2113.

19. Heller R, Artois M, Xemar V, et al. Prevalence of *Bartonella henselae* and *Bartonella clarridgeiae* in stray cats. J Clin Microbiol. 1997;35:1327-1331.

20. Kordick DL, Hilyard EJ, Hadfield TL, et al. *Bartonella clarridgeiae,* a newly recognized zoonotic pathogen causing inoculation papules, fever and lymphadenopathy (cat scratch disease). J Clin Microbiol. 1997;35:1813-1818.

21. Gurfield AN, Boulouis H-J, Chomel BB, et al. Coinfection with *Bartonella clarridgeiae* and *Bartonella henselae* and with different *Bartonella henselae* strains in domestic cats. J Clin Microbiol. 1997;35:2120-2123.

22. Breitschwerdt EB, Kordick DL, Malarkey DE, et al. Endocarditis in a dog due to infection with a novel *Bartonella* subspecies. J Clin Microbiol. 1995;33:154-160.

23. Kordick DL, Swaminathan B, Greene CE, et al. *Bartonella vinsonii* subsp. *berkhoffii* subsp. nov., isolated from dogs; *Bartonella vinsonii* subsp. *vinsonii;* and emended description of *Bartonella vinsonii.* Int J Syst Bacteriol. 1996;46:704-709.

24. Welch, DF, Carroll KC, Hofmeister EK, et al. Isolation of a new subspecies, *Bartonella vinsonii* subsp. *arupensis,* from a cattle rancher: Identity with isolates found in conjunction with *Borrelia burgdorferi* and *Babesia microti* among naturally infected mice. J Clin Microbiol. 1999;37:2598-2601.

25. Zeaiter Z, Liang Z, Raoult D. Genetic classification and differentiation of *Bartonella* species based on comparison of partial ftsZ gene sequences. J Clin Microbiol. 2002;40:3641-3647.

26. Pitulle C, Strehse C, Brown JW, Breitschwerdt EB. Investigation of the phylogenetic relationships within the genus *Bartonella* based on comparative sequence analysis of the rnpB gene, 16S rDNA and 23S rDNA. Int J Syst Evol Microbiol. 2002;52: 2075-2080.

27. Yamamoto K, Chomel B, Lowenstine L, et al. *Bartonella henselae* antibody prevalence in free-ranging and captive wild felids from California. J Wildlife Dis. 1998;34:56-63.

28. Koehler JE, Glaser CA, Tappero JW. *Rochalimaea henselae* infection: A new zoonosis with the domestic cat as reservoir. JAMA. 1994;271:531-535.

29. Chomel BB, Abbot RC, Kasten RW, et al. *Bartonella henselae* prevalence in domestic cats in California: Risk factors and association between bacteremia and antibody titers. J Clin Microbiol. 1995;33:2445-2450.

30. Demers DM, Bass JW, Vincent JM, et al. Cat scratch disease in Hawaii: Etiology and seroepidemiology. J Pediatr. 1995;127:23-26.

31. Sander A, Büler C, Pelz K, et al. Detection and identification of two *Bartonella henselae* variants in domestic cats in Germany. J Clin Microbiol. 1997;35:584-587.

32. Kordick DL, Wilson KH, Sexton DJ, et al. Prolonged *Bartonella* bacteremia in cats associated with cat-scratch disease patients. J Clin Microbiol. 1995;33:3245-3251.

33. Regnery RL, Olson JG, Perkins BA, Bibb W. Serologic response to "*Rochalimaea henselae*" antigen in suspected cat-scratch disease. Lancet. 1992;339:1443-1445.

34. Tappero JW, Mohle-Boetani J, Koehler J, et al. The epidemiology of bacillary angiomatosis and bacillary peliosis. JAMA. 1993;269:770-775.

35. Barka NR, Hadfield T, Patnaik M, et al. EIA for detection of *Rochalimaea henselae*-reactive IgG, IgM, and IgA antibodies in patients with suspected cat scratch disease (letter). J Infect Dis. 1993;167:1503-1504.

36. Zangwill KM, Hamilton DH, Perkins BA, et al. Cat scratch disease in Connecticut: Epidemiology, risk factors, and evaluation of a new diagnostic test. N Engl J Med. 1993;329:8-13.

37. Dolan MJ, Wong MT, Regnery RL, et al. Syndrome of *Rochalimaea henselae* adenitis suggesting cat scratch disease. Ann Intern Med. 1993;118:331-336.

38. Waldvogel K, Regnery RL, Anderson BE, et al. Disseminated cat-scratch disease: Detection of *Rochalimaea henselae* in affected tissue. Eur J Pediatr. 1994;153:23-27.

39. Anderson B, Sims K, Regnery R, et al. Detection of *Rochalimaea henselae* DNA in specimens from cat-scratch disease patients by PCR. J Clin Microbiol. 1994;32:942-948.

40. Goral S, Anderson B, Hager C, Edwards K. Detection of *Rochalimaea henselae* DNA by polymerase chain reaction from suppurative nodes of children with cat-scratch disease. Pediatr Infect Dis J. 1994;13:994-997.

41. Le HH, Palay DA, Anderson B, Steinberg JP. Conjunctival swab to diagnose ocular cat scratch disease. Am J Ophthalmol. 1994;118:249-250.

42. Perkins BA, Swaminathan B, Jackson LA, et al. Case 22-1992. Pathogenesis of cat scratch disease (letter). N Engl J Med. 1992;327:1599-1600.

43. Anderson B, Kelly C, Threlkel R, Edwards K. Detection of *Rochalimaea henselae* in cat-scratch disease skin test antigens. J Infect Dis. 1993;168:1034-1036.

44. Chomel BB, Kasten RW, Floyd-Hawkins K, et al. Experimental transmission of *Bartonella henselae* by the cat flea. J Clin Microbiol. 1996;34:1952-1956.

45. Rolain JM, Franc M, Davoust B, Raoult D. Molecular detection of *Bartonella quintana, B. koehlerae, B. henselae, B. clarridgeiae, Rickettsia felis,* and *Wolbachia pipientis* in cat fleas, France. Emerg Infect Dis. 2003;9:338-342.

46. Chang CC, Hayashidani H, Pusterla N, et al. Investigation of *Bartonella* infection in ixodid ticks from California. Comp Immunol Microbiol Infect Dis. 2002;25:229-236.

47. Sanogo YO, Zeaiter Z, Caruso G, et al. *Bartonella henselae* in *Ixodes ricinus* ticks (Acari: Ixodida) removed from humans, Belluno province, Italy. Emerg Infect Dis. 2003;9:329-332.

48. Stevenson HL, Bai Y, Kosoy MY, et al. Detection of novel *Bartonella* strains and *Yersinia pestis* in prairie dogs and their fleas (Siphonaptera: Ceratophyllidae and Pulicidae) using multiplex polymerase chain reaction. J Med Entomol. 2003;40:329-337.

49. Mexas AM, Hancock SI, Breitschwerdt EB. *Bartonella henselae* and *Bartonella elizabethae* as potential canine pathogens. J Clin Microbiol. 2002;40:4670-4674.

50. Anonymous. La Verruga Peruana y Daniel A. Carrion, Estudiante de la Facultad de Medicina, Muerto el 5 de Octobre de 1885 Lima: Imprenta del Estado; 1886.

51. Ricketts WE. Carrion's disease: A study of the incubation period in thirteen cases. Am J Trop Med. 1947;27:657-659.

52. Amano Y, Rumbea J, Knobloch J, et al. Bartonellosis in Ecuador: Serosurvey and current status of cutaneous verrucous disease. Am J Trop Med Hyg. 1997;57:174-179.

53. Kosek M, Lavarello R, Gilman RH, et al. Natural history of infection with *Bartonella bacilliformis* in a nonendemic population. J Infect Dis. 2000;182:865-872.

54. Maguina C, Garcia PJ, Gotuzzo E, et al. Bartonellosis (Carrión's disease) in the modern era. Clin Infect Dis. 2001;33:772-779.

55. Strong RP, Tyzzer EE, Brues CT, et al. Report of the First Expedition to South America, 1913. Cambridge, MA: Harvard University Press; 1915.

56. Ricketts WE. *Bartonella bacilliformis* anemia (Oroya fever). Blood. 1948;3:1025-1049.

57. Reynafarje C, Ramos J. The hemolytic anemia of human bartonellosis. Blood. 1961;17:562-578.

58. Ricketts WE. Clinical manifestations of Carrión's disease. Arch Intern Med. 1949;84:751-781.

59. Maguiña C, Gotuzzo E, Carcelén A, et al. Compromiso gastrointestinal bartonellosis o enfermedad de Carrión. Rev Gastroenterol Peru. 1997;17:31-43.

60. Cuadra M. Salmonellosis complication in human bartonellosis. Texas Rep Biol Med. 1956;14:97-113.

61. Pinkerton H, Weinman D. Toxoplasma infection in man. Arch Pathol. 1940;30: 374-392.

62. Garcia-Caceres U, Garcia FU. Bartonellosis: An immunosuppressive disease and the life of Daniel Alcides Carrion. Am J Clin Pathol. 1991;95(Suppl 1):S56-S66.

63. Dooley JR. Bartonellosis. In: Binford CH, Connor DH, eds. Pathology of Tropical and Extraordinary Diseases. Washington, DC: Armed Forces Institute of Pathology; 1976:190-193.

64. Chamberlin J, Laughlin LW, Romero S, et al. Epidemiology of endemic *Bartonella bacilliformis:* A prospective cohort study in a Peruvian mountain valley community. J Infect Dis. 2002; 186:983-990.

65. Arias-Stella J, Lieberman PH, Erlandson RA, Arias-Stella J Jr. Histology, immunohistochemistry, and ultrastructure of the verruga in Carrion's disease. Am J Surg Pathol. 1986;10:595-610.

66. Jackson LA, Spach DH. Emergence of *Bartonella quintana* infection among homeless persons. Emerg Infect Dis. 1996;2:141-144.

67. Foucault C, Raoult D, Brouqui P. Randomized open trial of gentamicin and doxycycline for eradication of *Bartonella quintana* from blood in patients with chronic bacteremia. Antimicrob Agents Chemother. 2002;47:2204-2207.

68. Slater LN, Welch DF, Min K-W. *Rochalimaea henselae* causes bacillary angiomatosis and peliosis hepatis. Arch Intern Med. 1992;152:602-606.

69. Lucey D, Dolan MJ, Moss CW, et al. Relapsing illness due to *Rochalimaea henselae* in normal hosts: Implication for therapy and new epidemiologic associations. Clin Infect Dis. 1992;14:683-688.

70. Wong MT, Dolan MJ, Lattuada CP Jr, et al. Neuroretinitis, aseptic meningitis, and lymphadenitis associated with *Bartonella (Rochalimaea) henselae* infection in immunocompetent patients and patients infected with human immunodeficiency virus type 1. Clin Infect Dis. 1995;21:352-360.

71. Hadfield TL, Warren R, Kass M, Levy C. Endocarditis caused by *Rochalimaea henselae.* Hum Pathol. 1993;24:1140-1141.

72. Holmes AH, Greeough TC, Balady GJ, et al. *Bartonella henselae* endocarditis in an immunocompetent adult. Clin Infect Dis. 1995;21:1004-1007.

73. Spach DH, Kanter AS, Daniels NA, et al. Bartonella (Rochalimaea) species as a cause of apparent "culture-negative" endocarditis. Clin Infect Dis. 1995;20:1044-1047.

74. Jalava J, Kotilainen P, Nikkari S, et al. Use of polymerase chain reaction and DNA sequencing for detection of *Bartonella quintana* in the aortic valve of a patient with culture-negative infective endocarditis. Clin Infect Dis. 1995;21:891-896.

75. Drancourt M, Birtles R, Chaumentin G, et al. New serotype of *Bartonella henselae* in endocarditis and cat-scratch disease. Lancet. 1996;347:441-443.

76. Raoult D, Fournier P, Drancourt M, et al. Diagnosis of 22 new cases of *Bartonella* endocarditis. Ann Intern Med. 1996;125:646-652.

77. Baorto E, Payne RM, Slater LN, et al. Culture-negative endocarditis due to *Bartonella henselae.* J Pediatr. 1998;132:1052-1054.

78. Raoult D, Fournier PE, Vandenesch F, et al. Outcome and treatment of *Bartonella* endocarditis. Arch Intern Med. 2003;163:226-230.

79. Stoler MH, Bonfiglio TA, Steigbigel RT, Pereira M. An atypical subcutaneous infection associated with acquired immune deficiency syndrome. Am J Clin Pathol. 1983;80:714-718.

80. Cockerell CJ, Webster GF, Whitlow MA, Friedman-Kien AE. Epithelioid angiomatosis: A distinct vascular disorder in patients with the acquired immunodeficiency syndrome or AIDS-related complex. Lancet. 1987;2:6544-6546.

81. LeBoit PE, Egbert BM, Stoler MH, et al. Epithelioid haemangioma-like vascular proliferation in AIDS: Manifestation of cat scratch disease bacillus infection? Lancet. 1988;1:960-963.

82. Koehler JE, LeBoit PE, Egbert BM, Berger TG. Cutaneous vascular lesions and disseminated cat-scratch disease in patients with the acquired immunodeficiency syndrome (AIDS) and AIDS-related complex. Ann Intern Med. 1988;109:449-455.

83. Milam MW, Balerdi MJ, Toney JF, et al. Epithelioid angiomatosis secondary to disseminated cat scratch disease involving the bone marrow and skin in a patient with acquired immune deficiency syndrome: A case report. Am J Med. 1990;88:180-183.

84. Kemper CA, Lombard CM, Deresinski SC, Tompkins LS. Visceral bacillary epithelioid angiomatosis. Possible manifestations of disseminated cat scratch disease in the immunocompromised host: A report of two cases. Am J Med. 1990;89:216-222.

85. Spach DH, Panther LA, Thorning DR, et al. Intracerebral bacillary angiomatosis in a patient infected with the human immunodeficiency virus. Ann Intern Med. 1992;116:740-742.

86. Koehler JE, Cederberg L. Intraabdominal mass associated with gastrointestinal hemorrhage: A new manifestation of bacillary angiomatosis. Gastroenterology. 1995;109:2011-2014.

87. Coche E, Beigelman C, Lucidarme O, et al. Thoracic bacillary angiomatosis in a patient with AIDS. AJR Am J Roentgenol. 1995;165:56-58.

88. Mohle-Boetani JC, Koehler JE, Berger TG, et al. Bacillary angiomatosis and bacillary peliosis in patients infected with the human immunodeficiency virus: Clinical characteristics in a case control study. Clin Infect Dis. 1996;22:794-800.

89. Huh YB, Rose S, Schoen RE, et al. Colonic bacillary angiomatosis. Ann Intern Med. 1996;124:735-737.

90. Long SR, Whitfield MJ, Eades C, et al. Bacillary angiomatosis of the cervix and vulva in a patient with AIDS. Obstet Gynecol. 1996;881:709-711.

91. Relman DA, Loutit JS, Schmidt TM, et al. The agent of bacillary angiomatosis: An approach to the identification of uncultured pathogens. N Engl J Med. 1990;323:1573-1580.

92. Cockerell CJ, Bergstresser PR, Myrie-Williams C, Tierno PM. Bacillary epithelioid angiomatosis occurring in an immunocompetent individual. Arch Dermatol. 1990;126:787-790.

93. Tappero JW, Koehler JE, Berger TG, et al. Bacillary angiomatosis and bacillary splenitis in immunocompetent adults. Ann Intern Med. 1993;118:363-365.

94. Cockerell CJ, Tierno PM, Friedman-Kien AE, Kim KS. Clinical, histologic, microbiologic, and biochemical characterization of the causative agent of bacillary (epithelioid) angiomatosis: A rickettsial illness with features of bartonellosis. J Invest Dermatol. 1991;97:812-817.

95. Relman DA, Falkow S, LeBoit PE, et al. The organism causing bacillary angiomatosis, peliosis hepatis, and fever and bacteremia in immunocompromised patients (letter). N Engl J Med. 1991;324:1514.

96. Koehler JE, Sanchez MA, Garrido CS, et al. Molecular epidemiology of *Bartonella* infections in patients with bacillary angiomatosis-peliosis. N Engl J Med. 1997;337:1876-1883.

97. Tappero JW, Koehler JE. Bacillary angiomatosis or Kaposi's sarcoma? N Engl J Med. 1997;337:1888.

98. Cockerell CJ, LeBoit PE. Bacillary angiomatosis: A newly characterized, pseudoneoplastic, infectious, cutaneous vascular disorder. J Am Acad Dermatol. 1990;22:501-512.

99. LeBoit PE, Berger TG, Egbert BM, et al. Bacillary angiomatosis: The histology and differential diagnosis of a pseudoneoplastic infection in patients with human immunodeficiency virus disease. Am J Surg Pathol. 1989;13:909-920.

100. Perkocha LA, Geaghan SM, Yen TSB, et al. Clinical and pathological features of bacillary peliosis hepatis in association with human immunodeficiency virus infection. N Engl J Med. 1990;323:1581-1586.

101. Leong SS, Cazen RA, Yu GSM, et al. Abdominal visceral peliosis associated with bacillary angiomatosis: Ultrastructural evidence of endothelial cell destruction by bacilli. Arch Pathol Lab Med. 1992;116:866-871.

102. Slater LN, Pitha JV, Herrera L, et al. *Rochalimaea henselae* infection in AIDS causing inflammatory disease without angiomatosis or peliosis: Demonstration by immunocytochemistry and corroboration by DNA amplification. Arch Pathol Lab Med. 1994;118:33-38.

103. Caniza MA, Granger DL, Wilson KH, et al. *Bartonella henselae:* Etiology of pulmonary nodules in a patient with depressed cell-mediated immunity. Clin Infect Dis. 1995;20:1505-1511.

104. Liston TE, Koehler JE. Granulomatous hepatitis and necrotizing splenitis due to Bartonella henselae in a patient with cancer: Case report and review of hepatosplenic manifestations of Bartonella infection. Clin Infect Dis. 1996;22:951-957.

105. Szelc-Kelly CM, Goral S, Perez-Perez GI, et al. Serologic responses to *Bartonella* and *Afipia* antigens in patients with cat scratch disease. Pediatrics. 1995;96:1137-1142.

106. Dauga C, Mira I, Grimont PAD. Identification of *Bartonella henselae* and B. *quintana* 16S rDNA sequences by branch-, genus-, and species-specific amplification. J Med Microbiol. 1996;45:192-199.

107. Scott MA, McCurley TL, Vnencak-Jones CL, et al. Cat scratch disease: Detection of *Bartonella henselae* DNA in archival biopsies from patients with clinically, serologically and histologically defined disease. Am J Pathol. 1996;149:2161-2167.

108. Mouritsen CL, Litwin CM, Maiese RL, et al. Rapid polymerase chain reaction-based detection of the causative agent of cat scratch disease (*Bartonella henselae*) in formalin-fixed, paraffin-embedded samples. Hum Pathol. 1997;28:820-826.

109. Avidor B, Kletter Y, Abulafia S, et al. Molecular diagnosis of cat scratch disease: A two-step approach. J Clin Microbiol. 1997;35:1924-1930.

110. Min K-W, Reed JA, Welch DF, Slater LN. Morphologically variable bacilli of cat scratch disease are identified by immunocytochemical labeling with antibodies to *Rochalimaea henselae.* Am J Clin Pathol. 1994;101:607-610.

111. Regnery R, Martin M, Olson J. Naturally occurring *"Rochalimaea henselae"* infection in domestic cat (letter). Lancet. 1992;340:557-558.

112. Debré R, Lamy M, Jammet ML, et al. La maladie des griffes de chat. Semin Hop Paris. 1950;26:1895-1904.

113. Brenner DJ, Hollis DG, Moss CW, et al. Proposal of *Afipia* gen. nov., with *Afipia felis* sp nov. (formerly the cat scratch disease bacillus), *Afipia clevelandensis* sp. nov. (formerly the Cleveland Clinic Foundation strain), *Afipia broomeae* sp. nov., and three unnamed genospecies. J Clin Microbiol. 1991;29:2450-2460.

114. Alkan S, Morgan MB, Sandin RL, et al. Dual role for *Afipia felis* and *Rochalimaea henselae* in cat-scratch disease (letter). Lancet. 1995;345:385.

115. Jackson LA, Perkins BA, Wenger JD. Cat scratch disease in the United States: An analysis of three national databases. Am J Public Health. 1993;83:1707-1711.

116. Noah DL, Kramer CM, Verbsky MP, et al. Survey of veterinary professionals and other veterinary conference attendees for antibodies to *Bartonella henselae* and B. *quintana.* J Am Vet Med Assoc. 1997;210:342-344.

117. Carithers HA. Cat-scratch disease: An overview based on a study of 1,200 patients. Am J Dis Child. 1985;139:1124-1133.

118. Moriarty R, Margileth A. Cat scratch disease. Infect Dis Clin North Am. 1987;1:575-590.

119. Margileth AM. Cat scratch disease. Adv Pediatr Infect Dis. 1993;8:1-21.

120. Bass JW, Freitas BD, Sisier CL, et al. Prospective randomized double-blind placebo-controlled evaluation of azithromycin for treatment of cat scratch disease. Pediatr Infect Dis J. 1998;17:447-452.

121. Bosch X. Hypercalcemia due to endogenous overproduction of active vitamin D in identical twins with cat-scratch disease. JAMA. 1998;279:532-534.

122. Parinaud H. Conjontivite infectieuse par les animaux. Ann Ocul. 1889;101:252-253.

123. Cassady JV, Culbertson CS. Cat-scratch disease and Parinaud's oculoglandular syndrome. Arch Ophthalmol. 1953;50:68-74.

124. Margileth AM, Wear DJ, English CK. Systemic cat-scratch disease: Report of 23 patients with prolonged or recurrent severe bacterial infection. J Infect Dis. 1987;155:390-402.

125. Abbasi S, Chesney PJ. Pulmonary manifestations of cat-scratch disease: A case report and review of the literature. Pediatr Infect Dis J. 1995;14:547-548.

126. Muszynski M, Eppes J, Riley H. Granulomatous osteolytic lesion of the skull associated with cat scratch disease. Pediatr Infect Dis J. 1987;6:199-201.

127. Jacobs RF, Schultze GE. Bartonella henselae as a cause of prolonged fever of unknown origin in children. Clin Infect Dis. 1998;26:80-84.

128. Lenoir AA, Storch GA, DeSchryver-Kecskemeti K, et al. Granulomatous hepatitis associated with cat scratch disease. Lancet. 1988;1:1132-1136.

129. Delahoussaye PM, Osborne BM. Cat-scratch disease presenting as abdominal visceral granulomas. J Infect Dis. 1990;161:71-78.

130. Dunn MW, Berkowitz FE, Miller JJ, Snitzer JA. Hepatosplenic cat-scratch disease and abdominal pain. Pediatr Infect Dis J. 1997;16:269-272.

131. Stevens H. Cat-scratch fever encephalitis. Am J Dis Child. 1952;84:218-222.

132. Jambor J, Emura E. Benign inoculation lymphoreticulosis (cat scratch disease). Arch Dermatol Syph. 1953;67:439-442.

133. Thompson TE Jr, Miller KF. Cat scratch encephalitis. Ann Intern Med. 1953;39:146-151.

134. Weinstein L, Meade RH. Neurological manifestations of cat-scratch disease. Am J Med Sci. 1955;229:500-505.

135. Centers for Disease Control and Prevention. Encephalitis associated with cat scratch disease—Broward and Palm Beach Counties, Florida, 1994. MMWR Morb Mortal Wkly Rep. 1994;43:915-916.

136. Carithers H, Margileth A. Cat scratch disease: Acute encephalopathy and other neurologic manifestations. Am J Dis Child. 1991;145:98-101.

137. Selby G, Walker GL. Cerebral arteritis in cat-scratch disease. Neurology. 1979;29:1413-1418.

138. Revol A, Vighetto A, Jouvet A, et al. Encephalitis in cat scratch disease with persistent dementia. J Neurol Neurosurg Psychiatry. 1992;55:133-135.

139. Hahn J, Sum J, Lee K. Unusual MRI findings after status epilepticus due to cat-scratch disease. Pediatr Neurol. 1994;10:255-258.

140. Munana KR, Vitek SM, Hegarty BC, et al. Infection of fetal feline brain cells in culture with *Bartonella henselae.* Infect Immun. 2001;69:564-569.

141. Gerber JE, Johnson JE, Scott MA, Madhusudhan KT. Fatal meningitis and encephalitis due to *Bartonella henselae* bacteria. J Forensic Sci. 2002;47:640-644.

142. Eskow E, Rao R-VS, Mordechai E. Concurrent infection of the central nervous system by *Borrelia burgdorferi* and *Bartonella henselae.* Arch Neurol. 2001;58:1357-1363.

143. Sweeney VP, Drance SM. Optic neuritis and compressive neuropathy associated with cat scratch disease. Can Med Assoc J. 1970;103:1380-1381.

144. Dreyer RF, Hopen G, Gass DM, Smith JL. Leber's idiopathic stellate neuroretinitis. Arch Ophthalmol. 1984;102:1140-1145.

145. Wong MT, Thornton DC, Kennedy RC, Dolan MJ. A chemically defined medium that supports primary isolation of *Rochalimaea (Bartonella) henselae* from blood and tissue specimens. J Clin Microbiol. 1995;33:742-744.

146. Golnik KC, Marotto ME, Fanous MM, et al. Ophthalmic manifestations of *Rochalimaea* species. Am J Ophthalmol. 1994;118:145-151.

147. Kerkhoff FT, Bergmans AM, van Der Zee A, Rothova A. Demonstration of *Bartonella grahamii* DNA in ocular fluids of a patient with neuroretinitis. J Clin Microbiol. 1999;37:4034-4038.

148. O'Halloran HS, Draud K, Minix M, et al. Leber's neuroretinitis in a patient with serologic evidence of *Bartonella elizabethae.* Retina. 1998;18:276-278.

149. Solley WA, Martin DF, Newman NJ, et al. Cat scratch disease: Posterior segment manifestations. Ophthalmology. 1999;106:1546-1553.

150. Reed JB, Scales JK, Wong MT, et al. Bartonella henselae neuroretinitis in cat scratch disease. Ophthalmology. 1998;105:459-466.

151. Schwartzman WA, Patnaik M, Barka NE, Peter JB. *Rochalimaea* antibodies in HIV-associated neurologic disease. Neurology. 1994;44:1312-1316.

152. Baker J, Ruiz-Rodriguez R, Whitfield M, et al. Bacillary angiomatosis: A treatable cause of acute psychiatric symptoms in human immunodeficiency virus infection. J Clin Psychiatry. 1995;56:161-166.

153. Patnaik M, Schwartzman WA, Peter JB. *Bartonella henselae*: Detection in brain tissue of patients with AIDS-associated neurological disease (abstract). J Invest Med. 1995;43(2 Suppl 2):368A.

154. Schwartzman WA, Patnaik M, Angulo FJ, et al. *Bartonella (Rochalimaea)* antibodies, dementia, and cat ownership in human immunodeficiency virus-infected men. Clin Infect Dis. 1995;21:954-959.

155. Abbot R, Chomel B, Kasten R, et al. Experimental and natural infection with *Bartonella henselae* in domestic cats. Comp Immunol Microbiol Infect Dis. 1997;20:41-51.

156. Guptill L, Slater L, Wu C-C, et al. Experimental infection of young specific pathogen-free cats with *Bartonella henselae*. J Infect Dis. 1997;176:206-216.

157. Kordick DL, Breitschwerdt EB. Relapsing bacteremia after blood transmission of Bartonella henselae to cats. Am J Vet Res. 1997;58:492-497.

158. Greub G, Raoult D. *Bartonella*: New explanations for old diseases. J Med Microbiol. 2002;51:915-923.

159. Walker TS, Winkler HH. *Bartonella bacilliformis*: Colonial types and erythrocyte adherence. Infect Immun. 1981;31:480-486.

160. Scherer DC, DeBuron-Conners I, Minnick MF. Characterization of *Bartonella bacilliformis* flagella and effect of antiflagellin antibodies on invasion of human erythrocytes. Infect Immun. 1993;61:4962-4971.

161. Minnick MF. Virulence determinants of *Bartonella bacilliformis*. In: Anderson B, Friedman H, Bendinelli M, eds. Rickettsial Infection and Immunity. New York: Plenum Press; 1997:197-211.

162. Mernaugh G, Ihler GM. Deformation factor: An extracellular protein synthesized by *Bartonella bacilliformis* that deforms erythrocyte membranes. Infect Immun. 1992;60:937-943.

163. Xu Y-H, Lu Z-Y, Ihler GM. Purification of deformin, an extracellular protein synthesized by *Bartonella bacilliformis* which cause deformation of erythrocyte membranes. Biochem Biophys Acta. 1995;1234:173-183.

164. Mitchell SJ, Minnick MF. Characterization of a two-gene locus from *Bartonella bacilliformis* associated with the ability to invade human erythrocytes. Infect Immun. 1995;63:1552-1562.

165. Iwaki-Egawa S, Ihler GM. Comparison of the abilities of proteins from Bartonella bacilliformis and Bartonella henselae to deform red cell membranes and to bind to red cell ghost proteins. FEMS Microbiol Lett. 1997;157:207-217.

166. Zimmermann R, Kempf VA, Schiltz E, et al. Hemin binding, functional expression, and complementation analysis of Pap 31 from *Bartonella henselae*. J Bacteriol. 2003;185:1739-1744.

167. Benson LA, Kar S, McLaughlin G, Ihler GM. Entry of *Bartonella bacilliformis* into erythrocytes. Infect Immun. 1986;54:347-353.

168. Kordick DL, Breitschwerdt E. Intraerythrocytic presence of *Bartonella henselae*. J Clin Microbiol. 1995;33:1655-1656.

169. Guptill L, Wu C-C, Glickman L, et al. Extracellular *Bartonella henselae* and artifactual intraerythrocytic pseudoinclusions in experimentally infected cats. Vet Microbiol. 2000;76:283-290.

170. Rolain JM, Foucault C, Guieu R, et al. *Bartonella quintana* in human erythrocytes. Lancet. 2002;360:226-228.

171. Rolain JM, Arnoux D, Parzy D, et al. Experimental infection of human erythrocytes from alcoholic patients with *Bartonella quintana*. Ann N Y Acad Sci. 2003;990:605-611.

172. Garcia FU, Wojta J, Broadley KN, et al. *Bartonella bacilliformis* stimulates endothelial cells *in vitro* and is angiogenic *in vivo*. Am J Pathol. 1990;136:1125-1135.

173. Garcia FU, Wojta J, Hoover RL. Interactions between live *Bartonella bacilliformis* and endothelial cells. J Infect Dis. 1992;165:1138-1141.

174. Conley T, Slater L, Hamilton K. *Rochalimaea* spp. stimulate endothelial cell proliferation and migration *in vitro*. J Lab Clin Med. 1994;124:521-528.

175. Cerimele F, Brown LF, Bravo F, et al. Infectious angiogenesis: *Bartonella bacilliformis* infection results in endothelial production of angiopoietin-2 and epidermal production of vascular endothelial growth factor. Am J Pathol. 2003;163:1321-1327.

176. McGinnis-Hill E, Raji A, Valenzuela MS, et al. Adhesion to and invasion of cultured human cells by *Bartonella bacilliformis*. Infect Immun. 1992;60:4051-4058.

177. Brouqui P, Raoult D. *Bartonella quintana* invades and multiplies within endothelial cells *in vitro* and *in vivo* and forms intracellular blebs. Res Microbiol. 1996;147:719-731.

178. Dehio C, Meyer M, Berger J, et al. Interaction of *Bartonella henselae* with endothelial cells results in bacterial aggregation on the cell surface and the subsequent engulfment and internalisation of the bacterial aggregate by a unique structure, the invasome. J Cell Sci. 1997;110:2141-2154.

179. Conley TD, Wack MF, Hamilton KK, Slater LN. Stimulation of angiogenesis and protection from oxidative damage: Two potential mechanisms involved in pathogenesis by *Bartonella henselae* and other *Bartonella* species. In: Anderson B, Friedman H, Bendinelli M, eds. Rickettsial Infection and Immunity. New York: Plenum Press; 1997:213-232.

180. Mitchell SJ, Minnick MF. A carboxy terminal processing gene is located immediately upstream of the invasion-associated locus from *Bartonella bacilliformis*. Microbiology. 1997;143:1221-1233.

181. Agan BK, Dolan MJ. Laboratory diagnosis of *Bartonella* infections. Clin Lab Med. 2002;22:937-962.

182. Welch DF, Slater LN. *Bartonella* and *Afipia*. In: Murray PR, Barron JE, Jorgensen JH, et al, eds. Manual of Clinical Microbiology, 8th ed. Washington, DC: American Society for Microbiology; 2003:824-834.

183. Peters D, Wigand R. Bartonellaceae. Bacteriol Rev. 1955;19:150-159.

184. Cuadra M, Takano J. The relationship of *Bartonella bacilliformis* to the red blood cell as revealed by electron microscopy. Blood. 1969;33:708-716.

185. Reed J, Brigati DJ, Flynn SD, et al. Immunocytochemical identification of *Rochalimaea henselae* in bacillary (epithelioid) angiomatosis, parenchymal bacillary peliosis, and persistent fever with bacteremia. Am J Surg Pathol. 1992;16:650-657.

186. Brenner SA, Rooney JA, Manzewitsch P, Regnery RL. Isolation of *Bartonella (Rochalimaea) henselae*: Effects of methods of blood collection and handling. J Clin Microbiol. 1997;35:544-547.

187. Welch DF, Hensel DM, Pickett DA, et al. Bacteremia due to *Rochalimaea henselae* in a child: Practical identification of isolates in the clinical laboratory. J Clin Microbiol. 1993;31:2381-2386.

188. Fournier PE, Robson J, Zeaiter Z, et al. Improved culture from lymph nodes of patients with cat scratch disease and genotypic characterization of *Bartonella henselae* isolates in Australia. J Clin Microbiol. 2002;40:3620-3624.

189. Tierno PM Jr, Inglima K, Parisi MT. Detection of Bartonella (Rochalimaea) henselae bacteremia using BacT/Alert blood culture system. Am J Clin Pathol. 1995;104:530-536.

190. Schwartzman WA, Nesbit CA, Baron EJ. Development and evaluation of a blood-free medium for determining growth curves and optimizing growth of *Rochalimaea henselae*. J Clin Microbiol. 1993;31:1882-1885.

191. Slater LN, Coody DW, Woolridge LK, Welch DF. Murine antibody responses distinguish *Rochalimaea henselae* from *Rochalimaea quintana*. J Clin Microbiol. 1992;30:1722-1727.

192. Drancourt M, Raoult D. Proposed tests for the routine identification of *Rochalimaea* species. Eur J Clin Microbiol Infect Dis. 1993;12:710-713.

193. Moss CW, Holzer G, Wallace PL, Hollis DG. Cellular fatty acid compositions of an unidentified organism and a bacterium associated with cat scratch disease. J Clin Microbiol. 1990;28:1071-1074.

194. Myers WF, Grossman DM, Wisseman CL Jr. Antibiotic susceptibility patterns in *Rochalimaea quintana*, the agent of trench fever. Antimicrob Agents Chemother. 1984;25:690-693.

195. Wolfson C, Branley J, Gottlieb T. The Etest for antimicrobial susceptibility testing of *Bartonella henselae*. J Antimicrob Chemother. 1996;38:963-968.

196. Maurin M, Raoult D. Antimicrobial susceptibility of *Rochalimaea quintana, Rochalimaea vinsonii*, and the newly recognised *Rochalimaea henselae*. J. Antimicrob Chemother. 1993;32:587-594.

197. Maurin M, Gasquet S, Caroline D, Raoult D. MICs of 28 antibiotic compounds for 14 *Bartonella* (formerly *Rochalimaea*) isolates. Antimicrob Agents Chemother. 1995;39:2387-2391.

198. Musso D, Drancourt M, Raoult D. Lack of bactericidal effect of antibiotics except aminoglycosides on Bartonella (Rochalimaea) henselae. J Antimicrob Chemother. 1995;36:101-108.

199. Ives TJ, Manzewitsch P, Regnery RL, et al. *In vitro* susceptibilities of *Bartonella henselae, B. quintana, B. elizabethae, Rickettsia rickettsii, R. conorii, R. akari*, and *R. prowazekii* to macrolide antibiotics as determined by immunofluorescent-antibody analysis of infected Vero cell monolayers. Antimicrob Agent Chemother. 1997;44:578-582.

200. Rolain JM, Maurin M, Raoult D. Bactericidal effect of antibiotics on *Bartonella* and *Brucella* spp.: Clinical implications. J Antimicrob Chemother. 2000;46:811-814.

201. Rolain JM, Maurin M, Mallet MN, et al. Culture and antibiotic susceptibility of *Bartonella quintana* in human erythrocytes. Antimicrob Agents Chemother. 2003;47:614-619.

202. Matar GM, Swaminathan B, Hunter SB, et al. Polymerase chain reaction-based restriction fragment length polymorphism analysis of a fragment of the ribosomal operon from *Rochalimaea* species for subtyping. J Clin Microbiol. 1993;31:1730-1734.

203. Roux V, Raoult D. Inter- and intraspecies identification of *Bartonella (Rochalimaea)* species. J Clin Microbiol. 1995;33:1573-1576.

204. Rodriguez-Barradas MC, Hamill RJ, Houston ED, et al. Genomic fingerprints of *Bartonella* species by repetitive element PCR for distinguishing species and isolates. J Clin Microbiol. 1995;33:1089-1093.

205. Bergmans AM, Schellekens JFP, van Embden JDA, Schouls LM. Predominance of two *Bartonella henselae* variants among cat-scratch disease patients in the Netherlands. J Clin Microbiol. 1996;34:254-260.

206. Ritzler M, Altwegg M. Sensitivity and specificity of a commercially available enzyme-linked immunoassay for the detection of polymerase chain reaction amplified DNA. J Microbiol Methods. 1996;27:233-238.

207. Zeaiter Z, Fournier PE, Greub G, Raoult D. Diagnosis of *Bartonella* endocarditis by a real-time nested PCR assay using serum. J Clin Microbiol. 2003;41:919-925.

208. Bergmans AMC, Groothedde J-W, Schellekens JFP, et al. Etiology of cat scratch disease: Comparison of polymerase chain reaction detection of *Bartonella* (formerly *Rochalimaea*) and *Afipia felis* DNA with serology and skin tests. J Infect Dis. 1995;171:916-923.

209. Margolis B, Kuzu I, Herrmann M, et al. Rapid polymerase chain reaction-based confirmation of cat scratch disease and *Bartonella henselae* infection. Arch Pathol Lab Med. 2003;127:706-710.

210. Mallqui V, Speelmon EC, Verástegui C, et al. Sonicated diagnostic immunoblot for bartonellosis. Clin Diagn Lab Immunol. 2000;7:1-5.

211. Chamberlin J, Laughlin L, Gordon S, et al. Serodiagnosis of *Bartonella bacilliformis* by indirect immunofluorescence assay: Test development and application to a population in an area of bartonellosis endemicity. J Clin Microbiol. 2000;38:4269-4271.

212. Herrmann JE, Hollingdale MR, Collins MF, Vinson JW. Enzyme immunoassay and radioimmunoprecipitation tests for the detection of antibodies to *Rochalimaea (Rickettsia) quintana* (39655). Proc Soc Exp Biol Med. 1977;154:285-288.

213. Hollingdale MR, Herrmann JE, Vinson JW. Enzyme immunoassay of antibody to *Rochalimaea quintana*: Diagnosis of trench fever and serologic cross-reactions among other rickettsiae. J Infect Dis. 1978;137:578-582.

214. Dalton MJ, Robinson LE, Cooper J, et al. Use of *Bartonella* antigens for the serologic diagnosis of cat-scratch disease at a national referral center. Arch Intern Med. 1995;155:1670-1676.
215. La Scola B, Raoult D. Serological cross-reactions between *Bartonella quintana, Bartonella henselae,* and *Coxiella burnetii.* J Clin Microbiol. 1996;34:2270-2274.
216. Dupon M, Savin de Larclause A-M, Brouqui P, et al. Evaluation of serological response to *Bartonella henselae, Bartonella quintana,* and *Afipia felis* antigens in 64 patients with suspected cat-scratch disease. Scand J Infect Dis. 1996;28:361-366.
217. Bergmans AMC, Peeters MF, Schellekens JFP, et al. Pitfalls and fallacies of cat scratch disease serology: Evaluation of *Bartonella henselae*-based indirect fluorescence assay and enzyme-linked immunoassay. J Clin Microbiol. 1997;35:1931-1937.
218. Maurin M, Eb F, Etienne J, Raoult D. Serological cross-reactions between Bartonella and Chlamydia. J Clin Microbiol. 1997;35:2283-2287.
219. Litwin CM, Martins TB, Hill HR. Immunologic response to *Bartonella henselae* as determined by enzyme immunoassay and Western blot analysis. Am J Clin Pathol. 1997;108:202-209.
220. Anderson B, Lu E, Jones D, Regnery R. Characterization of 17-kilodalton antigen of *Bartonella henselae* reactive with sera from patients with cat scratch disease. J Clin Microbiol. 1995;33:2358-2365.
221. Giladi M, Kletter Y, Avidor B, et al. Enzyme immunoassay for the diagnosis of cat-scratch disease defined by polymerase chain reaction. Clin Infect Dis. 2001;33:1852-1858.
222. Koehler JE, Tappero JW. Bacillary angiomatosis and bacillary peliosis in patients infected with human immunodeficiency virus. Clin Infect Dis. 1993;17:612-624.
223. Koehler JE, Sanchez MA, Tye S, et al. Prevalence of *Bartonella* infection among human immunodeficiency virus-infected patients with fever. Clin Infect Dis. 2003;37:559-566.
224. Regnery RL, Childs JE, Koehler JE. Infections associated with *Bartonella* species in persons infected with the human immunodeficiency virus. Clin Infect Dis. 1995;21(Suppl 1):S94-S98.
225. Bogue C, Wise JD, Gray GF, Edwards KM. Antibiotic therapy for cat-scratch disease? JAMA. 1989;262:813-816.
226. Holley HP Jr. Successful treatment of cat-scratch disease with ciprofloxacin. JAMA. 1991;265:1563-1565.
227. Collipp PJ. Cat-scratch disease: Therapy with trimethoprim-sulfamethoxazole. Am J Dis Child. 1992;146:397-399.
228. Margileth AM. Antibiotic therapy for cat-scratch disease: Clinical study of therapeutic outcome in 268 patients and a review of the literature. Pediatr Infect Dis J. 1992;11:474-478.
229. Chia JK, Nakata MM, Lami JL, et al. Azithromycin for the treatment of cat-scratch disease. Clin Infect Dis. 1998;26:193-194.
230. Rolain JM, Brouqui P, Koehler JE, et al. Recommendations for treatment of human infections caused by *Bartonella* species. Antimicrob Agents Chemother. 2004;48:1921-1933.
231. Foley JE, Chomel B, Kikuchi Y, et al. Seroprevalence of *Bartonella henselae* in cattery cats: Association with cattery hygiene and flea infestation. Vet Q. 1998;20:1-5.
232. Greene CE, McDermott M, Jameson PH, et al. *Bartonella henselae* infection in cats: Evaluation during primary infection, treatment, and rechallenge infection. J Clin Microbiol. 1996;34:1682-1685.
233. Regnery RL, Rooney A, Johnson AM, et al. Experimentally induced *Bartonella henselae* infections followed by challenge exposure and antimicrobial therapy in cats. Am J Vet Res. 1996;57:1714-1719.
234. Kordick DL, Papich MG, Breitschwerdt EB. Efficacy of enrofloxacin or doxycycline for treatment of *Bartonella henselae* or *Bartonella clarridgeiae* infection in cats. Antimicrob Agents Chemother. 1997;41:2448-2455.

CHAPTER 233

Calymmatobacterium granulomatis (Donovanosis, Granuloma Inguinale)

RONALD C. BALLARD

Donovanosis is a chronic, progressive ulcerative disease, usually of the genital region, that is caused by an encapsulated gram-negative bacterium, *Calymmatobacterium granulomatis.* The infection has previously been known by other names including granuloma inguinale tropicum, granuloma pudenda, granuloma venereum, and, most recently, granuloma inguinale. Because these names can easily be confused with that of a completely different tropical sexually transmitted disease, lymphogranuloma venereum, caused by the invasive L-serovars of *Chlamydia trachomatis,* the term donovanosis has been adopted as the preferred name for the disease. The first description of the disease has been attributed to McLeod working in India in 1881[1] and the discovery of the causative organism to Donovan in 1905.[2]

BIOLOGY OF THE CAUSATIVE ORGANISM

Calymmatobacterium granulomatis, formerly known as *Donovania granulomatis,* is an encapsulated, pleomorphic gram-negative bacillus measuring 1 to 2×0.5 to 0.7 μm that can be found in vacuoles in the cytoplasm of large mononuclear cells.[3] The bacteria are frequently described as having bipolar densities that give Donovan bodies the appearance of closed safety pins. The bacteria appear to multiply within these cells and are subsequently released to infect others after the rupture of mature intracytoplasmic vacuoles. Ultrastructurally, the organisms have been described as characteristically gram negative with a clearly defined capsule and no flagella. However, small surface projections resembling pili or fimbriae have been observed together with electron-dense granules 35 to 45 μm in diameter in the cell periphery.[4] In the past it was thought that these granules provided evidence of bacteriophage infection; however, this remains contentious.[5]

Although culture of the organisms in chick embryo yolk sacs was reported in the early 1940s[6] in egg yolk–based media[7] and in defined liquid media, no pure isolates were stored and therefore none were available for study for a period of approximately 50 years. As a result, the organisms were poorly characterized, although a relationship with *Klebsiella* had previously been suggested owing to common morphologic characteristics. Renewed efforts to isolate *C. granulomatis* from clinical material have been successful using human monocyte cultures[8] and Hep-2 cell monolayers,[9] and therefore progress has been made in further characterizing the causative organisms. A detailed description of the phylogeny of *C. granulomatis* based on the results of molecular studies has been published, resulting in the name *Klebsiella granulomatis* comb. nov. being formally proposed.[10] However, this proposal remains controversial.[11]

GEOGRAPHIC DISTRIBUTION AND EPIDEMIOLOGY

Donovanosis is a relatively rare disease in the United States, with fewer than 100 cases reported annually, although previously it was encountered more frequently in the southern states. It is recognized as a major cause of genital ulceration in southeast India, Papua New Guinea, the Caribbean, and parts of South America (particularly Brazil) and has been recorded in Zambia, Zimbabwe, South Africa, Southeast Asia, and among Aboriginals in Australia.[3,12] Cases of donovanosis may be encountered in centers remote from endemic regions as a result of immigration and increased holiday and business travel to these predominantly tropical areas. The disease is usually assumed to be a sexually transmitted infection, and the possibility that it may be transmitted nonsexually remains a controversial issue. Goldberg[13] postulated that the causative organism is a commensal of the gastrointestinal tract and that the vagina may become infected by autoinoculation. Extragenital lesions and lesions in young children all indicate alternative modes of spread; however, the age distribution of the disease in endemic areas, the frequent coexistence of other sexually transmitted diseases, and the finding that the genital area is the most frequent anatomic site of donovanosis lesions all indicate that it is primarily a sexually transmitted infection, albeit of low infectivity.

CLINICAL MANIFESTATIONS

The primary lesion of donovanosis begins as a small painless papule or indurated nodule that occurs after an incubation period of between 8 and 80 days. The lesion soon ulcerates to form an exuberant, beefy red, granulomatous ulcer with rolled edges and with a characteristic velvet-like surface that bleeds easily on contact (Fig. 233-1). Multiple lesions may coalesce to form large ulcers, and new lesions may also form as a result of autoinoculation. Characteristically, even large ul-

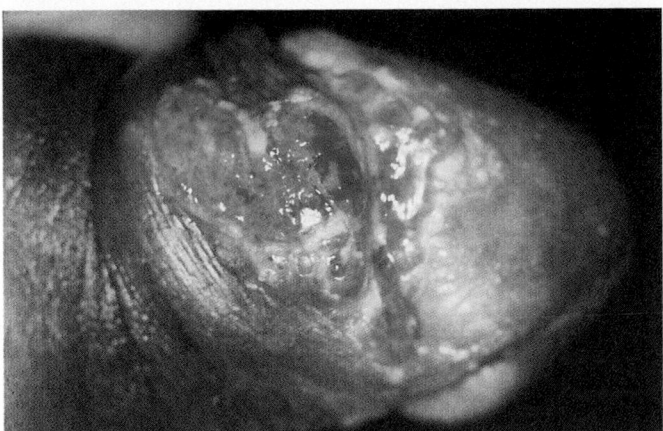

FIGURE 233-1. Early lesion of donovanosis.

FIGURE 233-3. Late lesions of donovanosis showing extensive scarring and subcutaneous spread.

cerative lesions are painless unless there is severe secondary infection. The disease spreads subcutaneously and may become progressively more destructive (Fig. 233-2). Spontaneous healing is accompanied by scar formation, which can also produce gross deformities (Fig. 233-3). Lymphedema with consequent elephantiasis of the external genitalia may occur in severe cases as a result of the blockage of the lymphatics by keloid scars. In men, the most common sites of infection are the prepuce, coronal sulcus, and penile shaft. In women, the labia and the fourchette are most commonly involved, but lesions of the vaginal wall and cervix may be an uncommon cause of vaginal bleeding. Donovanosis is frequently diagnosed during pregnancy, and it has been postulated that pregnancy causes exacerbation of the disease.[14] However, the diagnosis during pregnancy may just be a reflection of the asymptomatic nature of cervical infection and its detection on routine examination during pregnancy. Subcutaneous spread of granulomas into the inguinal region may result in the formation of groin swellings (pseudobubos), which are not a true adenitis.

Rectal lesions have been found to be associated with receptive anal intercourse among male homosexuals,[15] whereas penile lesions are often detected among their sexual partners. Systemic disease is rare but is more common in women with primary lesions of the cervix.[16]

Hematogenous spread of infection to form pelvic granulomas and to involve bones and joints has been documented, together with rare cases of lymphadenitis possibly associated with lymphatic spread.[17] Constitutional symptoms are conspicuously absent except in cases in which coinfection with other sexually transmitted diseases has been demonstrated, secondary bacterial infection is evident, or extensive spread has occurred. Donovanosis has to be distinguished from other causes of genital ulcer disease, regional lymphadenopathy, and genital elephantiasis. The lesions most likely to provide diagnostic problems

on clinical grounds include cases of "pseudogranulomatous" chancroid, ulcerating genital warts, both primary and secondary syphilis, and squamous carcinoma. Early papers suggested a link between donovanosis and squamous carcinoma of the external genitalia[18]; however, this hypothesis remains unproved, and the possible coexistence of donovanosis and human papillomavirus infection, which has proven oncogenic potential, cannot be ruled out.

DIAGNOSIS

Most cases of donovanosis are diagnosed on the basis of the characteristic clinical manifestations. However, confirmation of the diagnosis can be obtained on the basis of histologic examination of punch biopsy specimens taken from the edges of active lesions, scrapings taken from the edges of lesions, or a crush preparation made from granulation tissue obtained with a thin scalpel. In all cases, active lesions should be selected and cleansed with physiologic saline before sampling.

Although biopsy specimens are mandatory when malignancy has to be excluded, smear or crush preparations are usually adequate for the diagnosis of acute, active disease of short duration.

Ideally, smear preparations for microscopy should be made immediately with fresh, moist tissue and should be fixed and stained with Giemsa, Leishman, or Wright stain.[3,19] Although the application of newer, rapid Giemsa techniques can provide an immediate, definitive diagnosis even in resource-poor settings,[20] the standard Giemsa and silver stains are preferred when fixed, embedded tissue specimens are prepared for histologic examination.[3] The demonstration of typical intracellular Donovan bodies in stained smears obtained from lesions (Fig. 233-4) has remained the "gold standard" for the diagnosis of donovanosis since they were first described by Donovan. Subsequently, Donovan bodies have also been detected in Papanicolaou-stained smears obtained from women with cervical lesions.[21,22] Earlier, isolation of *C. granulomatis* led to the development of an intradermal skin test and also a complement fixation test for the serologic diagnosis of the disease. However, these tests are no longer performed. An indirect immunofluorescence test has been devised that employs tissue sections from proven cases of donovanosis as the antigen. This test has proved both sensitive and specific[23] but is unlikely to become routine owing to a lack of suitable clinical material that can be used as the antigen. The successful culture of *C. granulomatis* in monocytes[8,24] and Hep-2 cells[9] may provide an appropriate source of antigen for such a serologic test and offers possibilities for testing in vitro antimicrobial susceptibilities of isolates to provide a more rational basis for treatment of the disease. In particular, isolation of *C. granulomatis* in Hep-2 cell monolayers using techniques similar to those previously used for chlamydial isolation could, for the first time, provide a routine diagnostic test for donovanosis based on culture.[9]

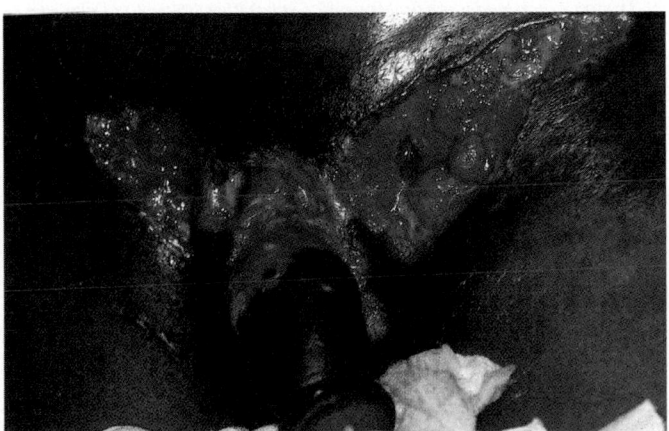

FIGURE 233-2. Extensive, active lesions of donovanosis.

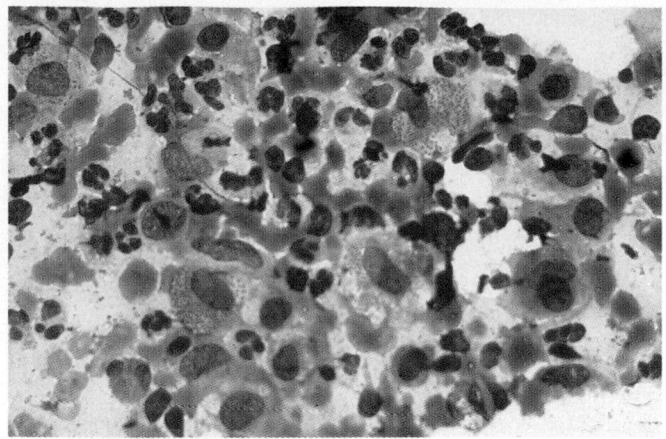

FIGURE 233-4. Scraping from an active lesion of donovanosis showing typical "Donovan" bodies in large mononuclear cells (Giemsa stain).

The same Australian workers have also demonstrated a high degree of molecular homology between *C. granulomatis* and other *Klebsiella* spp. by sequencing a region of the *pho*E (phosphatase porin) gene of *C. granulomatis* from DNA extracted from biopsy material. Although there appears to be a high degree of homology between *C. granulomatis* genes and other *Klebsiella* spp.–specific genes,[25] they found that certain primers targeting genes of the sucrose region of *Klebsiella* did not yield polymerase chain reaction (PCR) products with DNA derived from *C. granulomatis*. They therefore claim to be able to distinguish between donovanosis-associated organisms and other *Klebsiella* spp. on the basis of two PCR tests, one positive and the other negative.[26] Although these molecular approaches undoubtedly need to be refined, they represent a significant step forward in the diagnosis of the disease and may ultimately provide a viable alternative to culture or microscopy.

TREATMENT

There appears to be no consensus about the ideal treatment for donovanosis because most antibiotics have been evaluated in open trials with few data available from comparative, microbiologically controlled studies. In addition, the optimal duration of treatment for an individual case cannot be stated categorically because larger lesions appear to require longer periods of therapy.

After successful therapy, lesions begin to heal from the edges toward the center. It is our experience that treatment should be continued until complete epithelialization has taken place, which can take several weeks; otherwise relapse may occur. Tetracycline (500 mg four times daily by mouth) or doxycycline (100 mg twice daily by mouth) have, historically, been the treatments of choice for the disease, although many treatment failures or relapses have been recorded. Trimethoprim-sulfamethoxazole (two tablets twice daily by mouth) has also proved effective, but also with some failures.[3,12] Erythromycin (500 mg four times daily by mouth) has also been used extensively, especially in pregnancy with considerable success.[3,14] However, at this dosage, gastrointestinal side effects are common.

The antibiotic that exhibits the most promise in the treatment of donovanosis is azithromycin.[27] Preliminary studies indicate that 1 g taken weekly for 4 to 6 weeks is effective.[28] It is thought that this antibiotic is particularly appropriate for the treatment of the disease because it concentrates within macrophages and is released slowly from the tissues, giving it a long tissue half-life. An added advantage of this antibiotic is that it is also active against other sexually transmitted bacteria—notably *Haemophilus ducreyi, Treponema pallidum,* and

C. trachomatis. Other antibiotics that have proved effective include the quinolones; chloramphenicol and thiamphenicol[3]; ceftriaxone[29]; and the aminoglycosides, gentamicin (1 mg/kg twice daily intramuscularly) and streptomycin (1 g twice daily intramuscularly), which have often been used to supplement tetracycline therapy in severe cases. In contrast, penicillin appears to be ineffective in the treatment of the disease. Anecdotal evidence suggests that lesions may be more extensive and that prolonged periods of therapy may be required in patients with donovanosis who are coinfected with human immunodeficiency virus.

REFERENCES

1. McLeod K. Precis of operations performed in the wards of the first surgeon, Medical College O Hospital (Rio), during the year 1881. Indian Med Gaz. 1882;17:113.
2. Donovan C. Ulcerating granuloma of the pudenda. Indian Med Gaz. 1905;40:414.
3. Richens J. The diagnosis and treatment of donovanosis (granuloma inguinale). Genitourin Med. 1991;67:441-452.
4. Kuberski T, Papadimitriou JM, Phillips P. Ultrastructure of *Calymmatobacterium granulomatis* in lesions in granuloma inguinale. J Infect Dis. 1980;142:744-749.
5. Kharsany ABM, Hoosen AA, Naicker T, et al. Ultrastructure of *Calymmatobacterium granulomatis:* Comparison of culture with tissue biopsy specimens. J Med Microbiol. 1998;47:1069-1073.
6. Anderson K. The cultivation from granuloma inguinale of a microorganism having the characteristics of Donovan bodies in the yolk sac of chick embryos. Science. 1943;97:560.
7. Dulaney AD, Guo K, Packer H. Donovania granulomatis: Cultivation, antigen preparation, and immunological tests. J Immunol. 1948;59:335.
8. Kharsany ABM, Hoosen AA, Kiepiela P, et al. Culture of *Calymmatobacterium granulomatis* (Letter). Clin Infect Dis. 1996;22:391.
9. Carter J, Hutton S, Sriprakash KS, et al. Culture of the causative organism of donovanosis *(Calymmatobacterium granulomatis)* in Hep-2 cells. J Clin Microbiol. 1997;35:2915-2917.
10. Carter JS, Bowden FJ, Bastian I, et al. Phylogenetic evidence for reclassification of *Calymmatobacterium granulomatis* as *Klebsiella granulomatis* comb. nov. Int J Syst Bacteriol. 1999;49:1695-1700.
11. Kharsany ABM, Hoosen AA, Kiepiela P, et al. Phylogenetic analysis of *Calymmatobacterium granulomatis* based on 16S rRNA gene sequences. J Med Microbiol. 1999;48:841-847.
12. O'Farrell N. Clinico-epidemiological study of donovanosis in Durban, South Africa. Genotourin Med. 1993;69:108-111.
13. Goldberg J. Studies on granuloma inguinale. VII. Some epidemiological considerations of the disease. Br J Vener Dis. 1964;40:140-145.
14. O'Farrell N. Donovanosis (granuloma inguinale) in pregnancy. Int J STD AIDS. 1991;2:447-448.
15. Marmell M. Donovanosis of the anus in the male. An epidemiologic consideration. Br J Vener Dis. 1958;34:213-218.
16. Brigden MB, Guard R. Extragenital granuloma inguinale in North Queensland. Med J Aust. 1980;2:565-567.
17. Freinkel AL. Granuloma inguinale of cervical lymph nodes simulating tuberculosis lymphadenitis: Two case reports and review of published reports. Genitourin Med. 1988;64:339-343.
18. Alexander LJ, Shields TL. Squamous cell carcinoma of the vulva secondary to granuloma inguinale. Arch Dermatol Syphilol. 1953;67:395.
19. Van Dyck E, Piot P. Laboratory techniques in the investigation of chancroid, lymphogranuloma venereum and donovanosis. Genitourin Med. 1992;68:130-133.
20. O'Farrell N, Hoosen A, Coetzee K, et al. A rapid stain for the diagnosis of granuloma inguinale. Genitourin Med. 1990;66:200201.
21. De Boer AL, de Boer F, van der Merwe JV. Cytologic identification of Donovan bodies in granuloma inguinale. Acta Cytol. 1984;28:126-128.
22. Leiman G, Markowitz S, Margolius KA. Cytologic detection of cervical granuloma inguinale. Diagn Cytopathol. 1986;2:138-143.
23. Freinkel AL, Dangor Y, Koomhof HJ, et al. A serological test for granuloma inguinale. Genitourin Med. 1992;68:269-272.
24. Kharsany ABM, Hoosen AA, Kiepiela P, et al. Growth and cultural characteristics of *Calymmatobacterium granulomatis*—The aetiological agent of granuloma inguinale (donovanosis). J Med Microbiol. 1997;46:579-585.
25. Bastian I, Bowden FJ. Amplification of *Klebsiella*-like sequences from biopsy samples from patients with donovanosis. Clin Infect Dis. 1996;23:1328-1330.
26. Carter JS, Bowden FJ, Sriprakash KS, et al. Diagnostic polymerase chain reaction for donovanosis. Clin Infect Dis. 1999;28:1168-1169.
27. Bowden FJ, Mein J, Plunkett C, et al. Pilot study of azithromycin in the treatment of genital donovanosis. Genitourin Med. 1996;72:17-19.
28. Bowden FJ. Azithromycin for the treatment of donovanosis. Sex Transm Infect. 1998;74:78-79.
29. Merianos A, Gilles M, Chuah J. Ceftriaxone in the treatment of chronic donovanosis in central Australia. Genitourin Med. 1994;70:84-89.

Other Gram-Negative and Gram-Variable Bacilli

JAMES P. STEINBERG
CARLOS DEL RIO

A large number of gram-negative aerobic bacilli have been reported to cause human infection. This chapter considers selected gram-negative organisms that have not been described in other chapters and are important in certain clinical or epidemiologic circumstances (nosocomial infection, etc.), are newly described, or present special problems of diagnosis or therapy. Many of these organisms are saprophytic, and

their clinical role is uncertain. For some of the bacteria considered here, taxonomy is in a state of flux as classifications based on phenotypic characteristics are replaced by contemporary measures of genetic relationship including 16S rRNA sequencing studies. Current nomenclature and previous designations are listed in Table 234-1. Unless otherwise specified, the organisms are discussed in their order of appearance in Table 234-1. The gram-variable organisms *Gardnerella vaginalis* and *Mobiluncus* spp. are discussed at the end of the chapter.

The initial suspicion of a particular organism from the group considered here often arises after recovery of a gram-negative bacillus that is not *Pseudomonas aeruginosa* or a member of the Enterobacteriaceae. Identification of some of these organisms is difficult; the automated systems used by many microbiology laboratories cannot identify some of these bacteria and can misidentify others. Consequently, clinical laboratories sometimes use a general description (e.g., *gram-negative nonfermenter*) rather than the genus and species name. The clinical site of infection, as shown in Table 234-2, colony morphology, and the ability of the organism to metabolize carbohydrates by fermentation provide clues that can suggest a particular organism or group of organisms. This

TABLE 234-1 Current Nomenclature and Previous Names of Gram-Negative Bacteria Discussed in Chapter 234

Current Designation	Previous Names
Glucose Fermenters	
Actinobacillus spp.	
A. actinomycetemcomitans	*Bacterium actinomycetem comitans*
A. ureae	*Pasteurella ureae*
Aeromonas	
A. hydrophila	
A. caviae	
A. veronii biotype *sobria*	*A. sobria*
Cardiobacterium hominis	
Chromobacterium violaceum	
Dysgonomonas capnocytophagoides	CDC DF-3
CDC EF-4	
Plesiomonas shigelloides	*Aeromonas shigelloides, Pseudomonas shigelloides*
Glucose Nonfermenters (or Weak Fermenters)	
Achromobacter	
A. xylosoxidans subsp. *xylosoxidans*	*Alcaligenes xylosoxicans* subsp. *xylosoxicans, Achromobacter xylosoxidans, A. denitrificans*
A. xylosoxidans subsp. *dendrificans*	*A. denitrificans, A. denitrificans* subsp. *denitrificans*
Alcaligenes faecalis	*A. odorans,* CDC VI
Bergeyella zoohelcum*	*Weeksella zoohelcum,* CDC IIj
Chryseobacterium	
C. meningosepticum	*Flavobacterium meningosepticum*
C. indolenogenes	*Flavobacterium indologenes*
Chryseomonas luteola	*Pseudomonas luteola, Chryseomonas polytrichia,* CDC Ve-1
Eikenella corrodens	*Bacteroides corrodens*
Methyobacterium mesophilicum and *M. extorquens†*	*Pseudomonas mesophilica, Protomonas extorquens, Vibrio extorquens, Protaminobacter rubra,* "the pink phantom"
Myroides	
M. odoratus	*Flavobacterium odoratum*
M. odoratimimus	
Ochrobactrum	
O. anthropi	CDC Vd, *Achromobacter* groups A and D
O. intermedium	*Achromobacter* group C
Oligella	
O. ureolytica	CDC Ive
O. urethralis	*Moraxella urethralis,* CDC M4
Pseudomonas spp.	
P. fluorescens	
P. putida	
P. stutzeri	
P. oryzihabitans	*Flavimonas oryzihabitans, Chromobacterium typhiflavum,* CDC Ve-2
P. luteola	*Chryseomonas luteola,* CDC group Ve-1
Ralstonia	
R. pickettii	*Pseudomonas pickettii, Burkholderia pickettii*
R. paucula	CDC group IVc-2
Rhizobium radiobacter	*Agrobacterium radiobacter, A. tumefaciens,* A. biovar 1, CDC Vd-3
Roseomonas spp.	CDC pink coccoid group I through IV
Shewanella putrefaciens	*Pseudomonas putrefaciens,* CDC Ib-1, Ib-2
Sphingobacterium	
S. multivorum	*Flavobacterium multivorum,* CDC IIk-2
S. spiritivorum	*Flavobacterium spiritivorum,* CDC IIk-3
Sphingomonas paucimobilis	*Pseudomonas paucimobilis,* CDC IIk-1
Weeksella virosa	*Flavobacterium genitale,* CDC II-f

*See *Weeksella* in text.
†See *Roseomonas* in text.

TABLE 234-2 Classification of Selected Gram-Negative Aerobic Bacilli by Likely Site of Infection

Organism	Most Likely Clinical Settings and Sites of Infection							
	Bloodstream	Device-associated	Intestine	Soft Tissue	Bite Wound	Urine	CSF	Nosocomial Clusters
Glucose Fermenters								
Actinobacillus	X			X	X		X	
Aeromonas	X		X	X				
Cardiobacterium	X							
Chromobacterium	X			X				
Dysgonomonas			X					
CDC group EF-4					X			
Plesiomonas			X					
Glucose Nonfermenters (or Weak Fermenters)								
Achromobacter	X	X						X
Bergeyella					X			
Chryseobacterium	X						X	X
Eikenella	X			X	X			
Methylobacterium	X	X						
Ochrobactrum	X	X						X
Oligella						X		
Pseudomonas spp.	X	X						X
Ralstonia	X							X
Rhizobium	X	X						
Roseomonas	X	X						
Shewanella	X			X				
Sphingobacterium	X							
Sphingomonas	X	X						X
Weeksella						X		

information can help select the most effective way to provide definitive identification, because for some of these organisms special procedures for recovery, characterization, or antimicrobial susceptibility testing are required.[1,2] The decision to use alternative diagnostic methods is often based on the perceived clinical significance of the isolate, economic considerations, and available expertise. Because species identification is often not pursued, infections caused by some of these uncommon pathogens may go unrecognized.

GLUCOSE FERMENTERS

Actinobacillus

Actinobacillus actinomycetemcomitans, the major pathogen of this genus, is a cause of endocarditis, severe forms of periodontal disease, and soft tissue infection, the last of these usually in association with *Actinomyces israelii.* Five other species (*Actinobacillus lignieresii, equuli, suis, hominis,* and *ureae*) are rare causes of human disease. The first three are commensals and opportunistic pathogens in animals,[3] whereas the latter two are commensals of the human upper respiratory tract. *A. ureae* was previously known as *Pasteurella ureae.*

Actinobacillus actinomycetemcomitans, formerly *Bacterium actinomycetem comitans,* was first described as a human pathogen in 1912. Initial isolates were recovered only in conjunction with *A. israelii* (hence the species designation), leading to speculation that *A. actinomycetemcomitans* was not itself capable of causing disease. *A. actinomycetemcomitans* is present in at least 30% of actinomycotic lesions.[3] After the introduction of penicillin, it was observed that *A. actinomycetemcomitans* sometimes could be recovered from persistent lesions of actinomycosis after *A. israelii* was eradicated.[4] By the early 1960s, recovery of this organism in pure culture from blood and other normally sterile body fluids was reported widely.[5] The organism also has been isolated in pure culture from patients with meningitis, brain abscess, endophthalmitis (with and without concomitant endocarditis) soft tissue infections, parotitis, septic arthritis, osteomyelitis, urinary tract infection, pneumonia, empyema, and pericarditis.[3,6-9] Soft tissue infections most commonly involve the cervicofacial area, although they can occur elsewhere including the chest and abdomen. There are reports of *A. actinomycetemcomitans* mimicking actinomycosis (*A. israelii* or mixed infection) and causing pneumonia with chest wall invasion.[8,10]

Although the organism is part of the endogenous flora of the mouth and can be recovered from about 20% of teenagers and adults, it

(along with *Porphyromonas gingivalis*) is one of the major pathogens in adult and juvenile forms of periodontitis.[11] *A. actinomycetemcomitans* is present in the periodontal pockets of more than 50% of adults with refractory periodontitis and 90% of patients with localized aggressive periodontitis (formerly called localized juvenile periodontitis), a destructive form of periodontitis characterized by loss of the alveolar bone of the molars and incisors.[12,13] Clonal spread of the organism within families has been demonstrated using polymerase chain reaction (PCR)–based typing systems.[14] *A. actinomycetemcomitans* elaborates numerous substances that appear to contribute to periodontal disease. Some of the putative virulence factors, including a leukotoxin whose cellular receptor is a β-2 integrin, modulate the host inflammatory response.[13,15] Other candidate virulence factors contribute to tissue destruction and resorption of alveolar bone.

Actinobacillus actinomycetemcomitans is one of the HACEK organisms, along with *Haemophilus aphrophilus, Haemophilus paraphrophilis, Cardiobacterium hominis, Eikenella corrodens,* and *Kingella kingae,* which have in common slow growth in culture, the need for incubation in an atmosphere enhanced with CO_2 for recovery in culture, and a predilection for causing endocarditis.[2] Although often considered together, these organisms are distinct based on 16S rRNA sequencing. About 100 cases of endocarditis caused by *A. actinomycetemcomitans* have been reported, which is more than those caused by other HACEK organisms.[16] The onset of endocarditis is usually insidious, with a mean time to diagnosis of about 3 months. In a comprehensive review of 57 cases of *A. actinomycetemcomitans* endocarditis, 46% had periodontal disease or recent dental work, and 60% had underlying valvular disease, including 25% with prosthetic valves.[3] Fever was present in fewer than 50%; peripheral manifestations and splenomegaly each occurred in about a third. Therapy was successful in almost 80%, but significant embolization was common (39%), and 23% (13 of 57) required valve replacement. Prosthetic valve endocarditis with *A. actinomycetemcomitans* was usually recognized earlier than native valve endocarditis (42 versus 106 days), which probably was attributable to a higher index of suspicion. This earlier diagnosis may account for the high cure rate achieved with antibiotics alone and a relative low rate of embolization reported with prosthetic valve infection.[17,18]

Human disease caused by other species of *Actinobacillus* is rare. *Actinobacillus lignieresii, A. suis,* and *A. equuli* rarely can cause infections after bite wounds from farm animals.[19] These infections can be polymicrobial. One report has described a boar hunter who developed endocarditis caused by an *Actinobacillus* organism that resembled *A. suis* and *A. hominis* biochemically.[20] A recent report described 46 clinical *A. hominis* isolates acquired over a 22-year period, mostly from Copenhagen, Denmark.[21] Prior to this report, there were only a few case reports of human infections caused by this organism. Most of the isolates were from the respiratory tract; 18 of 33 respiratory isolates were reported to be pure cultures of *A. hominis*. The remaining respiratory cultures contained at least one other common respiratory pathogen. All of the patients in this series had underlying diseases including alcoholism, cardiovascular disease, drug addiction, chronic obstructive lung disease, and cancer. Most patients had fever and pulmonary infiltrates and 9 of 36 patients for whom clinical information was available died, including one of the two patients with bacteremia. The identification of the *A. hominis* isolates was confirmed by ribotyping and DNA hybridization. In this and other reports, automated systems had difficulty identifying *Actinobacillus* species. Fatal *A. hominis* bacteremia has also been reported in two patients with severe underlying liver disease.[22] *Actinobacillus ureae* is a rare cause of bacteremia and meningitis. Of *A. ureae* meningitis cases reported in 12 patients, 8 were post-traumatic and another occurred after neurosurgery.[23,24] Several patients had underlying chronic illnesses including alcoholism and human immunodeficiency virus (HIV) infection.

Culture isolation of *A. actinomycetemcomitans* is the usual means of diagnosis, and the fastidious, slow-growing nature of the organism makes this difficult. Material obtained from soft tissue lesions should be inoculated on blood and chocolate agar because the organism grows poorly in MacConkey's agar. The cultures must be incubated in an enhanced (5% to 10%) CO_2 atmosphere. By 18 to 24 hours, a few colonies (punctate, nonhemolytic) may be apparent, but the organism grows slowly, and incubation for at least 48 hours is needed. After colonies are seen, the organism continues to grow slowly, sometimes forming a star structure as part of the center of the mature colony. In broth or blood cultures, the organism often grows only in small "granules" adherent to the sides, with the medium remaining clear. In 13 patients with endocarditis, blood cultures required incubation for a mean of 5.6 days (range, 2 to 9 days) before growth was detected.[17] This finding underscores the need to hold blood culture bottles for a prolonged time if endocarditis caused by a fastidious organism is suspected. The appearance of the organism on Gram stain is coccoid to coccobacillary, similar to the appearance of *Haemophilus* spp. *Actinobacillus actinomycetemcomitans* is urease-negative and indole-negative, reduces nitrate, and usually is oxidase-negative. It is catalase positive, which helps differentiate it from *H. aphrophilus*. Identification of the other *Actinobacillus* species is problematic. At the genus level, these organisms are biochemically similar to *Pasteurella*. Species identification can be difficult without DNA hybridization studies.[25]

A. actinomycetemcomitans usually is susceptible to cephalosporins (especially third-generation cephalosporins), mezlocillin, rifampin, trimethoprim-sulfamethoxazole, aminoglycosides, fluoroquinolones including ciprofloxacin and moxifloxacin, tetracycline, azithromycin, and chloramphenicol.[3,26,27] In vitro susceptibility to penicillin and ampicillin is variable, but test results do not necessarily correlate with the clinical outcome.[17] In general, treatment of actinomycosis with penicillin and surgical drainage (when necessary) is sufficient, even when mixed infection is present. Vancomycin, erythromycin, and clindamycin have little activity against *A. actinomycetemcomitans*. The organisms display variable susceptibility to metronidazole, and in vitro synergy between metronidazole and both β-lactams and ciprofloxacin has been reported.[28] Because of strain-to-strain variability, testing of clinical isolates is recommended. Unfortunately, susceptibility testing is sometimes technically difficult because of the slow growth and fastidious nature of the organism. In the past, penicillin or ampicillin combined with an aminoglycoside was the usual treatment for endocarditis caused by this organism. Because of the potential for β-lactamase production, reports of failures with penicillin therapy, and difficulties with susceptibility testing, third-generation cephalosporins are now considered the drugs of choice. For endocarditis caused by

HACEK organisms, the American Heart Association recommends ceftriaxone 2 g daily for 4 weeks (6 weeks for prosthetic valve endocarditis).[29] Successful treatment of prosthetic valve endocarditis with oral ciprofloxacin has been reported.[30] *A. actinomycetemcomitans* endocarditis has developed after dental procedures despite the prophylactic use of penicillin, erythromycin, or vancomycin. Severe *A. actinomycetemcomitans*-associated periodontitis is usually treated with mechanical débridement in combination with oral tetracycline therapy. Tetracycline failures occur, however, and a report suggests that the combination of metronidazole and amoxicillin is very effective in suppressing subgingival infection.[31] *A. ureae* meningitis has been treated successfully with penicillin and third-generation cephalosporins.[24]

Aeromonas

Aeromonads are ubiquitous inhabitants of fresh and brackish water. They have also been recovered from chlorinated tap water including hospital water supplies. They occasionally cause soft tissue infections and sepsis in immunocompromised hosts and increasingly have been associated with diarrheal disease. Because of recent phylogenetic studies, *Aeromonas* spp. have been moved from the family *Vibrionaceae* to a new family, the *Areomonadaceae*.[32,33] Taxonomy of the aeromonads is in transition. In 1984, four species of *Aeromonas* (*hydrophila, sobria, caviae,* and *salmonicida*) were recognized.[34] These biochemically distinct species (phenospecies) have now been subdivided into DNA hybridization groups (genospecies), and new genospecies have been recognized. The complexity caused by the abundance of new species is compounded by attempts to reconcile genetic relatedness with the established phenospecies. For example, clinical isolates of *A. sobria* reside in the DNA hybridization group of *A. veronii* and should technically be designated *A. veronii* biovar *sobria.* There are currently 14 named species, but only 3, *A. hydrophila, A. caviae,* and *A. veronii* biovar *sobria,* are of major clinical importance.[35]

Aeromonas was first isolated more than 60 years ago, but evidence implicating this genus as a cause of gastrointestinal disease has been amassed only since the early 1980s. Reports from diverse geographic locations have associated *Aeromonas* spp. with diarrheal disease in humans; in some locales they are recovered as commonly as *Shigella* or *Campylobacter.*[36-39] Many laboratories do not routinely culture stool for *Aeromonas,* so the incidence of *Aeromonas*-associated diarrhea may be underestimated. Evidence supporting a causative role in diarrheal disease includes (1) a higher carriage rate in symptomatic compared with asymptomatic individuals; (2) an absence of other enteric pathogens in most symptomatic patients harboring *Aeromonas* spp.; (3) identification of *Aeromonas* enterotoxins[40] (although the absence of an animal model has hampered efforts to directly link toxin production with disease); (4) improvement of diarrhea with antibiotics active against *Aeromonas* spp. and clinical worsening with antibiotics ineffective against the organism; and (5) evidence of a specific secretory immune response coincident with diarrheal disease.[41]

Aeromonas caviae is the predominant isolate from diarrheal stools, but in some geographic areas, *A. hydrophila* and *A. veronii* biovar *sobria* are frequently isolated as well.[36,38,42,43] Other *Aeromonas* species appear to cause asymptomatic carriage only.[35] *Aeromonas*-associated diarrhea usually occurs during the summer, when the concentrations of aeromonads in water are the highest. Most cases are sporadic. A recent study was unable to implicate the drinking water supply as the source of diarrheal isolates; *Aeromonas* isolates from diarrheal stool were genetically unrelated to those from water supplies.[44] *Aeromonas* is increasingly being recognized as a cause of diarrhea in travelers returning from Asia, Africa, and Latin America.[42,45,46] Daycare center outbreaks have been reported, although in one study molecular typing did not suggest clonal spread.[47] The clinical manifestations of *Aeromonas*-associated diarrhea are varied. Diarrhea is usually watery and self-limited, but some persons develop fever, abdominal pain, and bloody stools. Fecal leukocytes may be present. Occasionally, diarrhea may be severe or protracted, and hospitalization may be necessary. Chronic colitis following acute *Aeromonas*-associated diarrhea has been reported in adults.[48] Although no controlled trials have validated antimicrobial therapy for *Aeromonas*-associated diarrhea, clinical improvement has occurred with antibiotics active against the organism. Hemolytic uremic syndrome associated with *Aeromonas* enterocolitis occurred in a 23-month-old infant.[49]

Most *Aeromonas* soft tissue infections are caused by *A. hydrophila*. Trauma followed by exposure to fresh water (and not salt water, even though aeromonad density in seawater is similar to that in fresh water[35]) usually, but not invariably, precedes infection. Cellulitis develops within 8 to 48 hours, and systemic signs are common.[50,51] Suppuration and necrosis around the wound are frequent, and surgical débridement is often necessary. Fasciitis, myonecrosis (occasionally associated with gas formation), and osteomyelitis may develop. In the setting of a rapidly progressive cellulitis after an injury related to water exposure, *Aeromonas* and *Vibrio* spp. infections should be considered in the differential diagnosis. *Aeromonas* soft tissue infections can develop after exposure to soil, in association with crush injuries, and as a complication of burns, typically when initial management of the burn included immersion in natural water sources.[51] There is one reported outbreak of *A. hydrophila* wound infections in participants of a mud football competition in Australia. The field was "prepared" with water from an adjacent river.[52] *Aeromonas* soft tissue infection is a recognized complication of the use of medicinal leeches in conjunction with reimplantation or flap surgery.[53] *Aeromonas hydrophila* and other *Aeromonas* spp. are normal inhabitants of the foregut of leeches. Leeches lack the requisite proteolytic enzymes and are dependent on the symbiotic *Aeromonas* to digest the blood meal.[54] *Aeromonas* infection has developed in 7% to 20% of patients treated with leeches. Prophylactic antibiotics now have been recommended at the time of leech application.[53,54] The onset of infection after the application of medicinal leeches ranges from 1 to more than 10 days.[55] Mild wound infection, loss of flap, myonecrosis, and sepsis may ensue.

Aeromonas bacteremia and sepsis are uncommon, but in the largest series reported to date, 143 *Aeromonas* bacteremias, including 104 that were monomicrobial, occurred in one institution in Taiwan over a 10-year period.[56] *Aeromonas hydrophila* caused 60% of the bacteremias; most of the other isolates that were identified by species were *A. veronii* subtype *sobria* and *A. caviae*.[57] The majority of patients in this series were immunocompromised, including 54% who were cirrhotic and 21% who had an underlying malignancy. Spontaneous bacterial peritonitis was common in cirrhotic patients with abdominal pain. There was a similar distribution of *Aeromonas* species in a study of 53 *Aeromonas* blood isolates collected from 27 medical centers in the United States over a 10-year period.[58] Most patients were immunocompromised, and underlying malignancy was much more common than liver disease in this series. Most patients with *Aeromonas* sepsis do not present with diarrhea. Interestingly, approximately one third of *Aeromonas* bacteremias are nosocomial.[57,59] In some series, the nosocomial cases were not epidemiologically linked and endogenous gut flora was the presumed source.[59] *Aeromonas* has been recovered from hospital water supplies, and clusters of nosocomial *Aeromonas* bacteremia have been described.[60] However, in one study in which molecular typing was performed, many different genotypes were found. The mortality rate for *Aeromonas* sepsis is 30% to 50%.[45,57-59] Two other species, *Aeromonas jandaei* and *A. schubertii*, have rarely been isolated from the blood.[61,62] A variety of other infections caused by *Aeromonas* spp. have been reported, including intra-abdominal abscess, hepatobiliary infection,[63] spontaneous bacterial peritonitis in patients with cirrhosis,[57] meningitis,[64] endocarditis,[65] suppurative thrombophlebitis, osteomyelitis, urinary tract infection, pneumonia including near-drowning-associated pneumonia,[66] empyema, lung abscess, tonsillitis, keratitis, and otitis media. *A. hydrophila* epididymitis and bacteremia developed in a healthy man 24 hours after he had sexual intercourse with his wife in their swimming pool. Cultures obtained from the pool grew *A. hydrophila*.[67]

Aeromonas organisms are gram-negative, nonsporulating facultative anaerobic rods that usually are β-hemolytic on blood agar and ferment carbohydrates with acid and gas production. The organisms grow well on MacConkey's agar (some strains are lactose fermenters, and some are not), but growth on thiosulfate citrate bile sucrose medium is variable. Selective techniques are often necessary for the isolation of *Aeromonas* spp. from mixed cultures. The organisms are more difficult to identify in stool cultures because enteric media may be inhibitory for some *Aeromonas* spp. Either blood agar that contains ampicillin (10 or 30 µg/mL) or cefsulodin-irgasan-novobiocin agar can be used as a selective medium.[68] Growth of colonies on plates usually occurs within 24 hours. *Aeromonas* spp. are oxidase-positive, and this test distinguishes these organisms from the oxidase-negative Enterobacteriaceae. *Aeromonas hydrophila* is catalase-positive and motile, converts nitrate to nitrite, and is urease-negative. Identification of *Aeromonas* to the genus level is not difficult; many automated systems (and consequently many clinical laboratories) proceed no further, reporting an *Aeromonas* isolate as "*Aeromonas* species" or "*Aeromonas hydrophila* complex."

The clinically relevant *Aeromonas* spp. are uniformly resistant to penicillin and ampicillin, are often resistant to cefazolin and ticarcillin, and are usually but not invariably susceptible to third-generation cephalosporins, aztreonam, and carbapenems.[69,70] Resistance to cefotaxime has developed on therapy.[56] Sensitivity to piperacillin and ticarcillin-clavulanate is variable. *Aeromonas* spp. produce as many as three β-lactamases including a Bush group 2d penicillinase, a group 1 cephalosporinase, and a metallocarbapenemase.[71] Some isolates exhibit coordinated expression of these β-lactamases after both induction and selection of derepressed mutants.[72] Despite the presence of a carbapenemase, minimal inhibitory concentrations to imipenem typically remain low, although *A. jandaei* and *A. veronii* subtype *veronii* can display imipenem resistance.[73] Unlike most carbapenemases, the *Aeromonas* metallocarbapenemases have narrow substrate profiles and specifically hydrolyze carbapenems.[74] There are reports of increasing resistance to tetracycline and trimethoprim-sulfamethoxazole.[75] Aminoglycosides are usually active, with resistance to tobramycin being more common than resistance to gentamicin or amikacin.[69] Fluoroquinolones are highly active against *Aeromonas* spp. although the existence of nalidixic acid–resistant strains containing mutations in the *gyrA* gene raise concern that fluoroquinolone resistance could easily develop.[69] *Aeromonas* spp. harboring a conjugative plasmid that confers multiple antibiotic resistance have been identified.[76]

Cardiobacterium

Cardiobacterium hominis, unlike the other HACEK organisms considered in this chapter, rarely causes disease other than endocarditis. *Cardiobacterium hominis* is the only species in the genus. It was originally called group IID and described as a *Pasteurella*-like organism. It is part of the endogenous flora in the nose, mouth, and throat and is present occasionally on other mucous membranes as well as in the gastrointestinal tract.[77]

There are more than 75 reported cases of *C. hominis* infection, and all but a few have involved the heart valves. Most patients have had underlying anatomic defects (rheumatic heart disease, ventricular septal defect, congenital bicuspid valve, etc.); prosthetic cardiac valves have been involved in about 10% of reported cases.[78,79] Many patients with endocarditis have had severe periodontitis or prior dental procedures without antimicrobial prophylaxis. *Cardiobacterium hominis* endocarditis following upper gastrointestinal endoscopy has been reported.[80] A subacute presentation, with an insidious onset (mean of 2 to 5 months before diagnosis) and an absence of fever at the time of diagnosis, is common.[81] Some of the patients have splenomegaly, anemia, immune-mediated glomerulonephritis, and hematuria, consistent with a long period between infection and diagnosis. Large vegetations, and large vessel emboli, are characteristic. The mortality rate is about 10% and valve replacement is needed in about 30% of cases.[16] Septic arthritis,[79] vertebral osteomyelitis, and mycotic aneurysms (intracranial and mesenteric) are reported complications of *C. hominis* endocarditis. Almost all clinical isolates come from blood, although meningitis associated with endocarditis has been described.[82] In one of the very rare cases of infection without endocarditis, a patient with adenocarcinoma of the kidney invading the cecum developed an abdominal abscess and bacteremia; abscess and blood cultures grew *C. hominis* and *Clostridium bifermentans*.[83] There is also a case report of *C. hominis* pacemaker lead infection without valvular involvement.[84]

The organism is gram-negative but has a pleomorphic appearance, often has swelling of one or both ends, and may be difficult to decolorize during the Gram stain procedure.[2] Under the microscope, the organisms sometimes form rosettes, but short chains, teardrops, pairs, and clusters are also common. Supplementation of the medium with yeast extract results in a loss of the pleomorphism, and most organisms become stick-like, gram-negative rods with rounded ends.[77] Incubation in high humidity and 3% to 5% CO_2 maximizes recovery of the organism. In such conditions, *C. hominis* grows well on sheep blood agar, chocolate agar, Mueller-Hinton agar, or trypticase soy agar without blood but grows poorly on MacConkey's agar or similar selective media. Colonies of 1 to 2 mm in diameter form on sheep blood agar, usually by 48 to 72 hours after incubation at 37° C under increased CO_2. However, with some systems, incubation for 5 to 7 days before growth can be confirmed is not unusual, and cultures should be held for this period or longer if *C. hominis* is suspected.[77] The colonies produce slight β-hemolysis and develop a rough appearance, with a serpentine pattern of growth from the edge to adjacent colonies.[77] The organism is oxidase-positive, is catalase-negative, and produces indole (although positivity is weak in many strains). Indole production is important for distinguishing *C. hominis* from other HACEK organisms. PCR amplification of 16S ribosomal DNA from heart valve tissue and arterio-embolic tissue has detected *C. hominis* sequences in cases of culture-negative endocarditis.

Susceptibility tests are difficult to perform because of the organism's slow growth and nutritional requirements, although a recent report suggests that the E-test appears to be a useful method.[85] When tested, the organism is usually broadly susceptible to β-lactam drugs, fluoroquinolones, chloramphenicol, rifampin, and tetracycline.[77,85] Susceptibility to aminoglycosides, erythromycin, and clindamycin is variable. Penicillin G, with or without the addition of an aminoglycoside, has been the regimen most often employed for therapy. The first β-lactamase–producing clinical isolate was reported in 1994.[86] This isolate was also resistant to cefotaxime and piperacillin but susceptible to β-lactamase inhibitor combinations. Consequently, it is unclear whether the current recommendation to administer third-generation cephalosporins for endocarditis caused by HACEK organisms enhances coverage for *C. hominis*. The role of an aminoglycoside as part of combination therapy is unknown. Although microbiologic cure is usually achieved, complications frequently arise during the course of therapy. Systemic embolization, mycotic aneurysm, or progressive cardiac failure have necessitated replacement of the damaged valve in a number of cases.

Chromobacterium

Chromobacterium violaceum is a rare human pathogen but can cause life-threatening sepsis with metastatic abscesses. The organism is a common soil and water inhabitant in tropical and subtropical areas. Fewer than 100 cases have been reported worldwide, with most recent reports coming from Southeast Asia. More than 20 cases have been reported in the United States, almost all from the Southeast, primarily Florida.[87] Cases have also been reported from Australia and South America.[88,89] *C. violaceum* is the only species of this genus that causes human disease. Although not considered a normal inhabitant of the human gastrointestinal tract, *C. violaceum* was present in the feces of 3 of 65 children whose stool was cultured at the time of admission to a hospital in Atlanta.[90]

C. violaceum infection occurs in infants, children, and adults, almost always in the summer months and usually following exposure of nonintact skin to contaminated water (often stagnant) or soil. Two cases followed near-drownings. Symptoms include pain at a local site of infection, fever, nausea, vomiting, abdominal pain, and diarrhea. Local cellulitis, pustules, ulcers with necrotic base, or lymphadenitis commonly precedes evidence of systemic infection. Septic shock develops rapidly, as can pneumonia and visceral abscesses involving the liver, spleen, and lung. This presentation can be confused with septicemic melioidosis, which is more common than *C. violaceum* infection in Southeast Asia, where both diseases are endemic.[91] The mortality rate for reported cases in the United States is approximately 60%. Urinary tract infection, conjunctivitis, orbital cellulitis, retropharyngeal infection

with prevertebral abscess,[92] osteomyelitis, brain abscess,[93] and meningitis have been reported. There are also a few case reports in the pediatric literature of *C. violaceum*-associated diarrhea.[94] *C. violaceum* infection is more common in patients with chronic granulomatous disease,[95] but cases occur in the apparently normal host. Five of six patients with chronic granulomatous disease (CGD) survived their infection, a higher survival rate compared with patients without known neutrophil dysfunction. This may reflect a selection bias because *C. violaceum* infection can be the initial manifestation of CGD, with the diagnosis of CGD being established only after recovery from the infection. Deficiency of polymorphonuclear leukocyte glucose-6-phosphate dehydrogenase and neutrophil dysfunction also were present in a 3-year-old patient who died with *C. violaceum* sepsis.[96] The pertinent virulence factors are unknown. Preliminary data from the study of only one clinical and one environmental isolate showed greater endotoxin activity and enhanced resistance to phagocytosis in the virulent strain.[97] Diagnosis is made by culture of blood, abscess fluid, or skin exudate.

C. violaceum organisms are long gram-negative bacilli; occasionally, the organisms are slightly curved and can be confused with vibrios. The organisms are facultatively anaerobic, growing readily in 18 to 24 hours on media containing tryptophan, which include common laboratory media such as sheep blood agar, chocolate agar, Mueller-Hinton agar, trypticase soy broth, and MacConkey's agar. Incubation at 37° C usually is effective, although growth is enhanced if incubation occurs at 25° C. Most strains of this organism produce violacein, a pigment insoluble in water (as opposed to the water-soluble pyocyanin of *Pseudomonas* spp.), which imparts a violet-black color to the colonies on solid media, hence the species' name. There are a few reports of infection caused by nonpigmented strains.[98] Violacein can induce apoptosis in tumor cell lines and is being investigated as a potential chemotherapeutic agent.[99] The color may be lost on subculture or after therapy is begun. The organisms produce hydrogen cyanide, so a faint cyanide smell may be present. The oxidase reaction is usually positive but hard to detect in pigmented strains; sometimes, demonstration of oxidase can be enhanced by incubating the culture anaerobically, which inhibits pigment formation.[89]

C. violaceum isolates are generally susceptible to fluoroquinolones, chloramphenicol, tetracycline, trimethoprim-sulfamethoxazole, imipenem, and gentamicin.[100] The ureidopenicillins are often active, but resistance to cephalosporins is common. Although aztreonam is a natural product of some strains of *C. violaceum*,[101] most clinical isolates are susceptible to this agent. Because of the rarity of infection, the often fulminant course, and the high mortality rate, the optimal antibiotic therapy is unknown. Ciprofloxacin is the most active antibiotic in vitro and there are recent case reports of successful treatment with fluoroquinolones, often in combination with other agents.[93] Most survivors of this infection were treated with chloramphenicol or a penicillin (carboxy or ureidopenicillin) in combination with an aminoglycoside. Relapse has occurred more than 2 weeks after the completion of therapy and apparent cure, presumably because of a residual suppurative focus.[89] Oral trimethoprim-sulfamethoxazole, doxycycline, or ciprofloxacin has been used after intravenous therapy with other antibiotics, with the oral regimen continued for several weeks to a few months to prevent relapse.

Dysgonomonas (Formerly Centers for Disease Control and Prevention Group DF-3)

DF-3, a fastidious gram-negative coccobacillus first associated with human disease in 1988, has recently been classified in the new genus *Dysgonomonas* with the species designation *D. capnocytophagoides*.[102,103] *DF* stands for *dysgonic fermenter*, indicating a fermentative organism that has difficulty growing on routine media. DF-1 and DF-2 are now *Capnocytophaga* spp. (see Chapter 231), but comparative 16S ribosomal-RNA sequence analysis showed that DF-3 is not closely related to *Capnocytophaga*.[104]

D. capnocytophagoides has been isolated from diarrheal stools of patients with immune deficiencies including common variable hypogammaglobulinemia, human immunodeficiency virus infection, diabetes with chronic renal failure, lymphoreticular and other malignancies, and from patients receiving immunosuppressive agents.[102,105-107] With the use of selective media, this organism was isolated from 11 of 690 (1.6%) stools submitted for bacterial culture at the National Cancer Institute.[105] In another prospective study of the role of DF-3 in diarrheal disease, DF-3 was recovered from 2 of 178 specimens (1.1%) submitted for *Clostridium difficile* toxin assay and from 3 of 129 (2.3%) stool specimens from patients with human immunodeficiency virus (HIV) infection. These data suggest that the paucity of reports of recovering DF-3 from stool specimens may not be attributable to its rarity (as a colonizer or pathogen) but to the inability to recover the organism on conventional media. Antibiotic therapy directed at DF-3 produced a therapeutic response in some of these patients, including 4 of 11 in the first study. Some of the responders had diarrhea of several months' duration with prompt resolution after antibiotic therapy was initiated. In other patients, the clinical significance of DF-3 was unclear; eradication of the organism from the stool was not accompanied by resolution of diarrhea or the diarrhea resolved without specific therapy. DF-3 has also been isolated from the urine of an elderly woman with rectal fissures,[108] from a polymicrobial thigh abscess in a patient with insulin-dependent diabetes,[109] and from the patients with neutropenia.[110] In one patient with acute myelocytic leukemia, a blood isolate and stool isolate of *D. capnocytophagoides* had the identical ribotype.[111] The genus *Dysgonomonas* now includes other closely related clinical isolates including *D. gadei,* which has been isolated from the gall bladder of a patient with cholecystitis.[103]

D. capnocytophagoides can be distinguished from DF-2 (*Capnocytophaga canimorsus*) by negative catalase and oxidase tests, the production of indole by most strains, and the fermentation of sucrose and xylose. It produces small gray-white colonies with a sweetish odor on blood agar after 1 to 3 days of incubation. *D. capnocytophagoides* does not grow on MacConkey's agar or routine enteric media. It grows on selective *Campylobacter* media when incubated at 37° C, but not 42° C, the routine incubation temperature for *Campylobacter.*[106] Selective media such as cefoperazone-vancomycin-amphotericin B blood agar inhibit normal flora and allow recovery of *D. capnocytophagoides* from stool specimens.

Despite a lack of established breakpoints, the Kirby-Bauer disk agar-diffusion method has been used for antimicrobial susceptibility testing. DF-3 appears to be resistant to most β-lactam drugs, ciprofloxacin, metronidazole, vancomycin, and gentamicin. Many strains are susceptible to chloramphenicol, trimethoprim-sulfamethoxazole, clindamycin, and tetracycline. Tetracycline or clindamycin was used in the few reported cases of diarrheal disease that responded promptly to antibiotic administration. Despite a Kirby-Bauer zone size suggesting susceptibility, imipenem failed to clear DF-3 from the blood stream in the one reported bacteremic patient; the bacteremia resolved after therapy with trimethoprim-sulfamethoxazole was initiated.[110]

Centers for Disease Control and Prevention Group EF-4

EF-4 is known by its CDC letter and number designation based on growth characteristics. *EF,* or *eugonic fermenter,* refers to an organism that grows well through the fermentation of glucose. Group EF-4 bacteria are normal inhabitants of the oral cavity of dogs. Most human infections follow dog bites, although infections associated with cat bites or scratches occur as well. The organism can be isolated from bite wounds that do not demonstrate signs of inflammation, but cellulitis, abscess formation, and fever may develop. Systemic infection or infection not involving skin or skin structures is extremely rare. Endophthalmitis caused by *Pasteurella multocida* and EF-4 occurred after a cat scratch in an 8-year-old girl.[112] There is one report of blood-stream infection occurring in a patient with hepatic carcinoid who denied being bitten by a dog or cat.[113] An otherwise healthy man whose dogs often licked him in the ears developed chronic EF-4 otitis media requiring mastoidectomy.[114]

EF-4 bacteria usually appear as short rods on Gram stain, but small coccoid forms or long chains may also be present. The organisms grow well on blood-agar plates, on which colonies usually form within 24 hours, but grow poorly or not at all on MacConkey's and similar agars. The colonies are small, may be slightly yellow-orange, and are smooth; some strains have a "popcorn-like" odor.[2] The organisms are oxidase-positive, are catalase-positive, and reduce nitrate. Biovar EF-4a ferments glucose only and has arginine hydroxylase activity; biovar EF-4b does neither (and is actually a nonfermenter). Initially, EF-4 was thought to resemble the Pasturellaceae family, but recent ribosomal-RNA cistron analysis places EF-4 in the Neisseriaceae family.[115]

Penicillin G, ampicillin, tetracycline, ciprofloxacin, ofloxacin, and newer fluoroquinolones are all active against EF-4 at concentrations attainable with oral administration.[116] Cephalosporins, particularly first-generation agents, are less active in vitro. Chloramphenicol and aminoglycosides also have activity against EF-4.[112]

Plesiomonas

Plesiomonas shigelloides, a ubiquitous freshwater inhabitant, has been implicated as a cause of acute diarrhea and, rarely, serious extraintestinal disease.[117,118] The name *Plesiomonas,* from the Greek word for "neighbor," was chosen because the organism was thought to be closely related to *Aeromonas.* It is, in fact, more closely related to *Proteus,*[119] although it is currently classified in the family Vibrionaceae. *P. shigelloides* is the only species in the genus. The organism was originally isolated in 1947 and given the name C27. It has also been named *Pseudomonas shigelloides, Aeromonas shigelloides,* or *Vibrio shigelloides.*

P. shigelloides is a water- and soil-associated organism that replicates at temperatures above 8° C. It is found primarily in freshwater or estuary environments within temperate and tropical climates but can exist in seawater during the warm-weather months. Asymptomatic carriage of *P. shigelloides* is very rare among healthy persons. The usual vehicles of transmission of plesiomonads to humans are water, food such as oysters, shrimp, or chicken,[117,118] and a variety of animals that may be colonized with the organism. The organism has been acquired during foreign travel.[117,120,121] *P. shigelloides* is associated with gastroenteritis, but the failure to identify an enteropathogenic mechanism, the lack of an animal model, and unsuccessful studies to induce disease in volunteers make it impossible to firmly establish a causal relationship.[122] Potential virulence factors including a β-hemolysin have been identified, but their significance is unknown.[123]

The clinical presentation of *P. shigelloides*–associated diarrhea varies from a mild self-limited illness to mucoid, bloody diarrhea with fecal leukocytes. A predominance of a secretory-type diarrhea has been reported,[118] but other series have found a high percentage with a clinical illness compatible with enteroinvasive disease featuring abdominal pain, fever, bloody diarrhea, and fecal leukocytes.[121] The majority of symptomatic patients have either traveled abroad or been exposed to potentially contaminated water or food. Outbreaks have been reported, particularly from Japan. The role of antibiotics for *Plesiomonas*-associated diarrhea is uncertain. Antimicrobial therapy did not shorten the duration of fever or diarrhea in Thai children with *Plesiomonas*-associated diarrhea.[124] On the other hand, in a small nonrandomized Canadian study in patients who developed *Plesiomonas*-associated diarrhea after travel abroad, 8 of 9 treated patients were asymptomatic within 2 weeks compared with 6 of 15 controls ($P < 0.05$).[121]

Most descriptions of extraintestinal disease come from individual case reports. These reports include cases of osteomyelitis, septic arthritis, endophthalmitis, spontaneous bacterial peritonitis,[125] pancreatic abscess, splenic abscess, cholecystitis, cellulites, pyosalpinx,[126] and epididymoorchitis. About 10 cases of neonatal sepsis with meningitis have been described.[127] Bacteremia is rare and usually occurs in immunocompromised hosts,[128] but bacteremia accompanying gastroenteritis has been reported in a healthy 15-year-old girl.[129]

P. shigelloides is a motile, facultatively anaerobic, gram-negative, oxidase-positive bacillus. It is readily isolated from some enteric agars such as MacConkey's agar but does not grow well on thiosulfate citrate bile sucrose medium. Selective techniques may be necessary for isolation of the organism from mixed cultures, such as the use of bile peptone broth or trypticase soy broth with ampicillin.[130] The organism grows well at 35° C and produces visible colonies (nonhemolytic) within 24 hours.

P. shigelloides is usually susceptible to chloramphenicol, trimethoprim-sulfamethoxazole, quinolones, cephalosporins, and imipenem.[124,131,132]

Because of β-lactamase production, most isolates are now resistant to penicillins including ureidopenicillins, although the β-lactamase inhibitor combinations appear to be active. Susceptibilities to aminoglycosides and tetracycline are variable.

GLUCOSE NONFERMENTERS (OR WEAK FERMENTERS)

Achromobacter and Alcaligenes

The taxonomic designations for *Achromobacter* and *Alcaligenes* species have been particularly confusing. *Achromobacter xylosoxidans* was renamed *Alcaligenes xylosoxidans* subsp. *xylosoxidans*[133] but recent 16S rRNA sequence analysis and GC content studies support placement of this organism back in the genus *Achromobacter* (the species and subspecies designation have been maintained).[134] Other *Alcaligenes species, A. ruhlandii, A. piechaudii,* and *A. denitrificans,* have also been transferred to *Achromobacter.* Organisms formerly considered *Achromobacter* groups A, C, and D (and before that CDC groups Vd-1 and Vd-2) are now named *Ochrobactrum anthropi* and are considered separately. The *Achromobacter* species are nonfermenting gram-negative bacilli found in soil and water. They can occasionally be recovered from the respiratory tract and gastrointestinal tract, primarily in persons with health care contact. Infection results when they are introduced into wounds or colonize those with compromised host defenses. Clinically relevant species include the asaccharolytic species *A. xylosoxidans* subsp. *dentrificans, A. piechaudi,* and *Alcaligenes faecalis* (this organism remains in the genus *Alcaligenes*)[135]; the saccharolytic species *A. xylosoxidans* subsp. *xylosoxidans;* and the unnamed Achromobacter groups B, E, and F.[136] Although sometimes considered a contaminant, *Achromobacter* group B has been recovered from the blood of patients with clinical sepsis and endocarditis.[137-139]

A. xylosoxidans subsp. *xylosoxidans* is the most clinically important of these organisms. It probably is part of the endogenous flora of the ear and gastrointestinal tract and is a common contaminant of fluids.[140] The organism has been implicated in outbreaks of nosocomial infection associated with contaminated solutions (intravenous fluids, hemodialysis fluid, irrigation fluids, mouthwash, etc.), pressure transducers, incubators and humidifiers, and contaminated soaps and disinfectants.[141-143] Contamination of well water was the source of infection in one case of bacteremia.[144]

Clinical illness that is caused by *A. xylosoxidans* subsp. *xylosoxidans* has involved isolates from blood, peritoneal and pleural fluids, urine, respiratory secretions, and wound exudates. Bacteremia, often related to intravascular catheters, is the most commonly reported infection.[145,146] Biliary tract sepsis, meningitis (sometimes with lymphocytic predominance in cerebrospinal fluid), pneumonia (nosocomial and community-acquired), peritonitis (including spontaneous bacterial peritonitis and peritonitis in patients on continuous ambulatory peritoneal dialysis), urinary tract infection, osteomyelitis, prosthetic knee infection, and prosthetic valve endocarditis have been reported.[140,144-150] Patients often have an immunosuppressed state such as cancer[151] and HIV infection,[152] but this is not always the case, especially in nosocomial outbreaks. This organism has been recovered with increasing frequency from respiratory secretions of persons with cystic fibrosis[153] and colonization has been associated with exacerbation of respiratory symptoms.[154] However, a recent case-control study failed to show increased deterioration in clinical or pulmonary function status among cystic fibrosis patients colonized with *Achromobacter* or *Alcaligenes* spp.[153] Recovery in neonatal infection may result from perinatal transfer from the mother.[155]

Phylogenetically and biochemically, *Alcaligenes* and *Achromobacter* are closely related to the genus *Brucella.* Strains of *A. xylosoxidans* subsp. *xylosoxidans* grow well on blood agar and MacConkey's agar plates; they produce flat, spreading and rough colonies and have peritrichous flagellae, features that help distinguish them from pseudomonads. The organisms are oxidase-positive, are catalase-positive, oxidize glucose to produce acid, and (as the species name indicates) oxidize xylose readily.[2] An isolate of *A. xylosoxidans* subsp. *xylosoxidans* can easily be mistaken for a non-*aeruginosa* strain of *Pseudomonas* or with a strain of the *Burkholderia cepacia* complex, but the unusual susceptibility pattern suggests the correct identity.

Usually, strains of *A. xylosoxidans* subsp. *xylosoxidans* are susceptible to trimethoprim-sulfamethoxazole, ureidopenicillins, imipenem, ceftazidime, cefoperazone, and β-lactamase inhibitor combinations.[145] Generally, they are resistant to narrow-spectrum penicillins, other cephalosporins (including cefotaxime and ceftriaxone), aztreonam, and aminoglycosides.[151,156,157] Susceptibility to the fluoroquinolones is variable.[151] High concentrations of colistin inhibit most strains.[158] Hyperproduction of β-lactamases has been implicated in resistance.[159]

Alcaligenes faecalis can be recovered in a variety of clinical settings. Most isolates of *A. faecalis* from blood or respiratory secretions are related to the contamination of hospital equipment or fluids with the organism, with resulting human colonization or infection. The urine is the other common site of recovery, although it infrequently causes symptomatic urinary tract infection. It also has been recovered from corneal ulcers, ear discharges, wound drainage, and feces.[160,161] It is rarely recovered in pure culture from any of these sites. By contrast, *A. xylosoxidans* subsp. *denitrificans* has been recovered as a single pathogen from blood, cerebrospinal fluid, and other normally sterile body fluids as well as in mixed culture from sites usually containing normal flora. Few recent publications have addressed the pathogenic role of these organisms. *A. piechaudii* was thought to cause chronic otitis in a diabetic patient,[162] and has also been recovered from blood in a patient with a hematologic malignancy and an infected Hickman catheter who had recurrent bacteremia.[163]

Identification of *Achromobacter* spp. is made by recovery of oxidase-positive, catalase-positive, indole-negative, and urease-negative organisms that produce flat colonies with spreading edges on blood-agar plates. Aerobic incubation is crucial for recovery in culture, and the organisms grow well at 35° C. The organisms also grow on MacConkey's agar. Distinguishing the organisms and confirming identification is made difficult by their lack of reactivity in many biochemical or assimilation tests.[164] *A. faecalis* produces a distinctive sweet odor resembling that of green apples.[2]

Laboratory testing often shows *A. faecalis* strains to be susceptible to trimethoprim-sulfamethoxazole, ureidopenicillins, ticarcillin-clavulanate, carbapenems, and, unlike *Achromobacter* spp., most cephalosporins.[165] Results vary for aztreonam, aminoglycosides, and fluoroquinolones, whereas *A. faecalis* strains are often resistant to amoxicillin, ticarcillin, and gentamicin.[161] Extended-spectrum β-lactamase production has also been described in *A. faecalis.*[166]

Chryseobacterium

Many species of the genus *Flavobacterium* have been reclassified into other genera. Two of the species most commonly isolated from clinical specimens, *Flavobacterium meningosepticum* and *Flavobacterium indologenes,* now reside in the genus *Chryseobacterium. Chryseobacterium* spp. are inhabitants of soil and water and can be recovered from a variety of foods. They can live in municipal water supplies despite adequate chlorination and have been recovered from the hospital environment, often in conjunction with clusters of clinical isolates. *Chryseobacterium* spp. are organisms of low virulence, and their presence in clinical specimens usually represents colonization and not infection. The exception is *C. meningosepticum,* which is clinically significant in up to half of the adults and in about two thirds of the neonates from whom it is recovered.[167] *Chryseobacterium* spp. produce proteases and gelatinase, which may contribute to virulence; these are responsible for the greenish discoloration around the colonies on blood agar.

C. meningosepticum is a cause of neonatal meningitis, especially in premature infants during the first 2 weeks of life. Clusters of neonatal meningitis have been linked to many sources including contaminated saline solution for flushing eyes, respiratory equipment, and sink drains.[167,168] Neonatal meningitis is fatal in more than half the cases and brain abscesses, and other severe sequelae are common. Most *C. meningosepticum* infections in adults are hospital acquired and occur in immunocompromised hosts. The respiratory tract is the most common site of infection, and outbreaks have been linked to contaminated ventilator tubing and aerosols.[169,170] In outbreaks, respiratory tract colonization occurs more often than infection. Bacteremia is the second most common presentation of *C. meningosepticum* infection. In one cluster of blood-stream infections related to a contaminated anesthetic, the bacteremia was transient and systemic signs of infection resolved without specific antibiotic therapy, attesting to the low virulence of this organism in adults.[171] *C. meningosepticum* has also caused endocarditis (including prosthetic valve), cellulitis, wound infection, sepsis following extensive burns, abdominal abscess, dialysis-associated peritonitis, and endophthalmitis.[167,172] Other contaminated sources include contaminated syringes in ice chests, vials, sink drains, sink taps, tube feedings, flush solutions for arterial catheters, pressure transducers, and antiseptic solutions.[167,173,174] Infections including cellulitis, septic arthritis, community-acquired respiratory tract infection, keratitis, and bacteremia have been reported in the absence of underlying diseases.[175-179] *C. indologenes* is a rare cause of human disease. Intravascular catheter–related bacteremia and bacteremia associated with malignancy and neutropenia have been reported.[180] *Chryseobacterium* spp. may be long, thin, slightly curved, and occasionally filamentous on Gram stain. *C. indologenes* colonies usually form a dark yellow pigment in culture as a result of the production of the pigment flexirubin, whereas *C. meningosepticum* colonies are smooth, large, and pale yellow (Fig. 234-1). They grow well and form colonies within 24 hours on blood or chocolate agar and grow at a much slower rate, if at all, on MacConkey's agar.[181] They are not motile and produce positive catalase and oxidase reactions.

Chryseobacterium spp. are resistant to most antibiotics, and the use of inactive drugs as empirical therapy may contribute to the poor outcome in many infections. In addition, MIC breakpoints have not been established by the National Committee for Clinical Laboratory Standards (NCCLS) for chryseobacteria. Results of susceptibility testing vary when different methods are used; disk diffusion methods especially are unreliable and broth microdilution should be employed, if possible.[182] The E-test has been also suggested as a possible alternative for testing certain antibiotics.[183] *Chryseobacterium* organisms produce β-lactamases and are resistant to most β-lactam drugs, including the carbapenems and aztreonam.[182] Cefepime has poor activity against *C. meningosepticum* and cefepime has only modest activity against *C. indolgenes.*[184] They are usually resistant to aminoglycosides, chloramphenicol, and erythromycin. Fluoroquinolones are usually active in vitro, and sparfloxacin, cinafloxacin, and levofloxacin are somewhat more active than ciprofloxacin.[185] In two 1997 reports, minocycline was the only agent active against all *C. meningosepticum* strains.[167,182] Doxycycline and trimethoprim-sulfamethoxazole susceptibility was variable. Rifampin is active against most strains and has been used as part of combination therapy to clear persistent infection.[186] Vancomycin, alone or in combination with other agents including rifampin, has been successful in the treatment of meningitis in infants.[187,188] In some reported cases of meningitis treated successfully with vancomycin, the minimal inhibitory concentrations of vancomycin were 8 to 12 μg/mL.[189] However, two groups reported that

vancomycin was inactive in vitro (minimal inhibitory concentrations of 16 to more than 64 μg/mL) and called into question the usefulness of vancomycin against *Chryseobacterium.*[167,182] Thus, there is no optimal regimen for *C. meningosepticum* meningitis, and therapy should be based on properly performed susceptibility testing. Possible regimens include rifampin in combination with trimethoprim-sulfamethoxazole, vancomycin, a fluoroquinolone, or minocycline.

Eikenella

Eikenella corrodens is a fastidious facultative anaerobic gram-negative bacillus that is part of the normal human oral flora. In 1948 Henriksen identified a gram-negative anaerobic organism that had the peculiar characteristic of creating a depression in the growth medium and referred to this organism as the *corroding bacillus.* In 1958, Eiken described and characterized a gram-negative obligate or facultative anaerobic organism for which he proposed the name *Bacteroides corrodens.* Subsequently, the strictly anaerobic organisms were renamed *Bacteroides corrodens* (and now are called *Bacteroides ureolyticus*), whereas the facultative anaerobes were reclassified in the new genus *Eikenella.*[190]

E. corrodens is present as endogenous flora in the mouth and upper respiratory tract as well as on other mucous surfaces of the body. Although it is recovered most often as a component of mixed infection,[191] commonly coexisting with streptococci,[192] it has been recovered from sterile sites in pure culture.[193] Characteristic of *Eikenella* infection is an indolent course, generally taking more than 1 week from the time of injury to clinical manifestation of disease.[194] Many patients with *Eikenella* infection have underlying diseases, especially head and neck malignancies.[195,196] In recent case series and literature reviews, the head and neck were the most common sites of *Eikenella* infections in both adults and children.[193,196] Other common clinical manifestations include respiratory tract infections[191] and human bite wounds.[197] The organism is often present in "clenched fist injuries," the most serious of human bite infections,[197] infections among chronic finger or nail biters,[198] and has been reported as a cause of "genital ulceration" after a human bite to the penis.[199] Because of the proximity of bone and joint spaces, these infections may lead to osteomyelitis and septic arthritis. It has also caused infection in insulin-requiring diabetic patients and drug-abusing "skin poppers" who lick their needles.[200] Severe soft tissue infection, with or without underlying osteomyelitis, may be slow to resolve.[201,202] Suppuration due to *Eikenella* infections is foul-smelling, mimicking an anaerobic process. Pulmonary infections, including empyema, pneumonia, and septic emboli in conjunction with internal jugular vein thrombosis (postanginal sepsis), can occur, typically in patients with underlying chronic illnesses or intrathoracic malignancies.[192] Gynecologic infections have been reported; some are associated with intrauterine contraceptive devices.[203,204] *Eikenella* has also been recovered in pure culture from synovial fluid, bone, cerebrospinal fluid, brain, subdural and visceral abscesses, pleuropulmonary infection, and blood.[191,192,205] *E. corrodens* is another of the so-called HACEK organisms, which, as mentioned, have in common the need for incubation in an atmosphere enhanced with CO_2 for recovery in culture, and a predilection for infecting the heart valves. Endocarditis caused by *E. corrodens* typically has an indolent course, but acute presentations are reported.[190] Endocarditis usually occurs after intravenous drug use or in patients with abnormal heart valves including prosthetic valves,[16,206] but infection on structurally normal heart valve in a patient without predisposing risk factors has been reported.[207]

E. corrodens is a gram-negative, small straight rod that at times can appear pleomorphic or coccobacillary. It grows in either aerobic or anaerobic environments. It is nonmotile and non–spore-forming and does not have a capsule. Cell surface components vary from strain to strain, and these differences may relate to virulence.[208] On blood or chocolate agar, even aided by the presence of 3% to 10% CO_2, the organism grows slowly, and it often requires 2 days or more to recognize the typical pinpoint colonies. Colonies are small and grayish (older colonies may become light yellow), produce a slight greenish discoloration on the blood agar, and elaborate an odor resembling that of

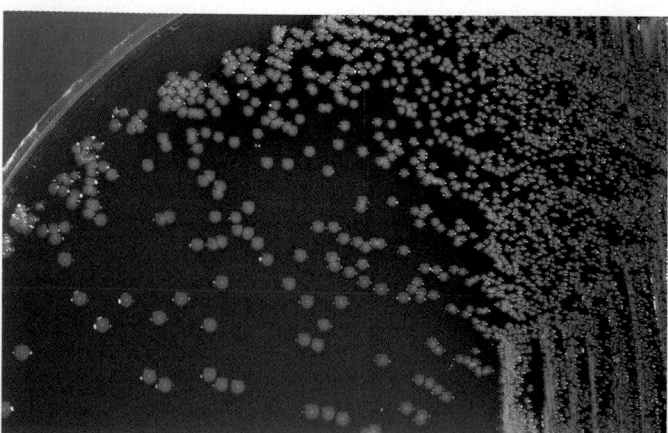

FIGURE 234-1. Yellow colonies of *Chryseobacterium meningosepticum* on blood agar plate.

bleach (hypochlorite). About half produce the pitting ("corroding") of the agar that is considered characteristic. The organism grows poorly on MacConkey's agar. Strains do not form acid from carbohydrates, are oxidase-positive, catalase-negative (a few strains are weakly catalase-positive), urease-negative, and indole-negative and reduce nitrate to nitrite. Ampicillin, ureidopenicillins, second- and third-generation cephalosporins, and tetracyclines have been reported effective against *E. corrodens* both in vitro and in producing clinical cure.[116,209] The organism is susceptible to fluoroquinolones in vitro.[116] However, the organism is uniformly resistant to clindamycin, erythromycin, and metronidazole and often resistant in vitro to aminoglycosides. β-Lactamase production is uncommon at present; some of the β-lactamases produced by *Eikenella* are inhibited by clavulanate and sulbactam.[210]

Flavobacterium and Myroides

The genus *Flavobacterium* consisted of a heterogeneous group of yellow-pigmented bacteria that did not prove to be closely related when subjected to genotypic analysis.[211] Consequently, many *Flavobacterium* species, including the clinically important species, have been reclassified to other genera and are discussed elsewhere. *Flavobacterium meningosepticum,* the most important species, and *Flavobacterium indologenes* are now members of the genus *Chryseobacterium. Flavobacterium multivorum* and *Flavobacterium spiritivorum* now reside in the genus *Sphingobacterium. Flavobacterium odoratum,* an uncommon clinical isolate, has been placed in a new genus, *Myroides,* and divided into two species, *M. odoratus* and *M. odoratimimus.*[212] Although common in soil and water, *Myrodies* spp. are rare clinical isolates and are often not considered pathogenic. However, the organism has been isolated from urine, blood, wounds, and respiratory secretions. There are case reports of catheter-associated bacteremia and soft tissue infections with secondary bacteremia occurring in both compromised and normal hosts.[213-215]

Myrodies spp. grow on most media including MacConkey agar. Colonies are yellow and produce a fruity odor similar to that of *A. faecalis.* The organisms are oxidase-, catalase-, urease-, and gelatinase-positive. They reduce nitrite and do not produce indole. *Myroides* are reportedly resistant to β-lactams including carbapenems and aminoglycosides.[214]

Ochrobactrum

Organisms formerly called CDC group Vd and *Achromobacter* groups A, C, and D were renamed *Ochrobactrum anthropi* (from the Greek *ochros* meaning "pale yellow").[133] Recent studies suggest that *Achromobacter* group C and some group A strains belong to a distinct species now designated as *O. intermedium.*[216] However, no biochemical tests currently available in clinical laboratories can separate *O. anthropi* from *O. intermedium. O. anthropi* is related to *Brucella* spp. and has been recovered from the environment and clinical sources. Published reports suggest that this organism is an emerging pathogen in immunocompromised patients and infections caused by this organism may be increasing in frequency.[217 219]

Intravascular catheter–related bacteremia is the most common infection associated with *O. anthropi.*[217,220,221] This organism has contaminated biologic products, which have been the source of small outbreaks. Five blood stream infections occurred in organ transplant recipients who received contaminated rabbit antithymocyte globulin.[222] Consistent with this organism's being of low virulence, bacteremia resolved in four of five immunosuppressed patients in this series without antibiotic administration. Three cases of postoperative meningitis in neurosurgical patients were traced to cadaveric pericardial patches possibly contaminated during processing.[223] *O. anthropi* has been cultured from tap water at a hematology unit in association with a small outbreak.[224] It has been reported to cause bacteremia in patients on hemodialysis and in patients with acquired immunodeficiency syndrome (AIDS),[225,226] peritonitis in patients undergoing continous ambulatory peritoneal dialysis,[227] and endophthalmitis, both postoperative and secondary to hematogenous spread.[228] Other reported infections include infection of pacemaker leads, pancreatic abscess, necrotizing fasciitis, and osteochondritis following a puncture wound.[218,229-231] It has also been recovered from bile, urine, wounds, stool, throat, and vagina.[232]

O. anthropi is an oxidase-positive, non–lactose-fermenting gram-negative bacillus that grows readily on MacConkey's agar. The organism oxidizes glucose and xylose, but 72 hours or more of incubation may be required before this is apparent. *O. anthropi* is motile by means of peritrichous flagella, which helps to differentiate it from pseudomonads and *Chryseobacterium.* The organism is similar to *A. xylosoxidans* subsp. *xylosoxidans* in biochemical characteristics, but it can hydrolyze urea and grows poorly on cetrimide agar.[141] As previously mentioned, *O. anthropi* and *O. intermedium* are closely related to *Brucella* spp., and misidentification can occur with some of the automated systems.[233]

O. anthropi is usually susceptible to trimethoprim-sulfamethoxazole and fluoroquinolones; they are variably susceptible to gentamicin, amikacin, netilmicin, imipenem, and tetracycline and are generally resistant to β-lactams including most cephalosporins and penicillins, at least in part as a result of the presence of an ampC β-lactamase.[220,234] Failures with imipenem therapy have been reported.

Oligella

The genus *Oligella* was named for the small size of the bacilli on Gram stain and contains two species, *Oligella urethralis* (formerly *Moraxella urethralis* and CDC group M-4) and *Oligella ureolytica* (formerly known as CDC group IVe). *O. urethralis* is a commensal of the genitourinary tract, and most clinical isolates are from the urine, predominantly from men.[25] Although symptomatic infections are rare, bacteremia, septic arthritis mimicking gonococcal arthritis,[235] and peritonitis in two patients receiving chronic ambulatory peritoneal dialysis[236] have been described. *O. ureolytica* is also primarily found in the urine, usually from patients with long-term indwelling urinary catheters or other urinary drainage systems. These patients have a propensity to develop urinary stones that may be related to the organism's ability to hydrolyze urea and alkalinize the urine, leading to precipitation of phosphates. Bacteremia has been reported in a patient with obstructive uropathy.[237] *O. ureolytica* bacteremia has been reported in a patient with acquired immunodeficiency syndrome and infected decubitus ulcers.[238]

Oligella spp., especially *O. urethralis,* resemble *Moraxella* and appear coccobacillary on Gram stain. Most strains will grow on blood or MacConkey's agar but require extended incubation (2 to 4 days) before growth can be detected. *O. urethralis* is nonmotile, while most strains of *O. ureolytica* are motile by peritrichous flagella. The rapidity of the urease reaction (within 5 minutes on a Christensen urea agar slant) is a distinctive feature of *O. ureolytica.* These organisms are oxidase-positive and catalase-positive and reduce NO_3 to NO_2. Contemporary data on antimicrobial susceptibilities are sparse. Strains of *O. urethralis* are usually susceptible to β-lactam antibiotics, but β-lactamase-producing strains as well as strains resistant to ciprofloxacin have been reported.[236] An *O. urethralis* urinary tract isolate resistant to penicillins and some cephalosporins was demonstrated to have acquired an AmpC β-lactamase from *Acinetobacter baumannii.*[239] In the past, *O. ureolytica* was susceptible to most antibiotics.

Pseudomonas spp.

The genus *Pseudomonas* has been modified considerably and now contains the organisms previously known as *Flavimonas oryzihabitans* and *Chryseomonas luteola.*[240,241] These organisms are now included in the nonfluorescent group of pseudomonads that includes *P. stutzeri* and other rarely encountered species. The fluorescent group contains *P. fluorescens, P. putida,* and *P. aeruginosa. P. aeruginosa* is the only member of the genus that possesses significant virulence factors and is an important human pathogen; it is discussed in Chapter 216. Members of the fluorescent group produce pyoverdin, a yellow-green pigment that fluoresces under UV light. Pseudomonads are environmental organisms and have a predilection for moist environments. They can contaminate solutions such as distilled water, disinfectants, and intravenous solutions. Not surprisingly, many of the infections caused by these organisms are healthcare-associated.

P. fluorescens is an uncommon cause of catheter-associated bacteremia[241] and pseudobacteremia due to contaminated blood collection tubes.[242] This organism can grow at 4° C, allowing it to proliferate in contaminated blood products and occasionally cause transfusion related sepsis.[243] *P. fluorescens* can be misidentified by commercial laboratory systems.[241] Because isolation of this organism can reflect pseudobacteremia, proper identification is important to avoid unnecessary antimicrobial therapy. *P. putida* is also an occasional cause of nosocomial bacteremia, bacteremia in patients with cancer, pneumonia, urinary tract infections, and neonatal sepsis.[244-246] Isolation of this organism from clinical specimens can reflect contamination; it has also been described as a cause of a pseudo-outbreak.[247]

P. stutzeri is another uncommon clinical isolate but has been reported to cause bacteremia and meningitis in immunocompromised hosts.[248] Rare cases of community-acquired osteomyelitis and pneumonia have also been reported.[249,250] *P. stutzeri* has also been implicated as a cause of pseudobacteremia and of delayed onset endophthalmitis after cataract surgery. *Pseudomonas oryzihabitans* (the species name means "inhabiting rice") is the current name for the organism that at various times has been called *Chromobacterium typhiflavum, Flavimonas oryzihabitans,* and CDC group Ve-2.[251] It is an infrequent cause of infection with characteristics similar to those of *P. luteola. P. oryzihabitans* is normally found in soil, water, and damp environments such as rice paddies. In the hospital setting, it has been recovered from sink drains and respiratory therapy equipment.[251] Central venous catheter-associated blood-stream infection is the most commonly reported infection. In an 8-year study from a major cancer center, 21 of 22 episodes of *P. oryzihabitans* bacteremia were catheter related.[252] In this series, most infections were non–hospital-acquired, polymicrobial infections were common, and the majority of bacteremias could be treated without catheter removal. In contrast, in another recent series, all *P. oryzihabitans* bacteremias were hospital acquired and the implicated intravascular devices were removed in the majority of cases.[253] The organism has also been associated with other foreign bodies such as peritoneal dialysis catheters, ventriculostomy tubes, vascular grafts, prosthetic joints, and intraocular lens.[254-256] Soft tissue infections, postoperative wound infections, splenic abscesses, and meningitis have been reported.[257,258] Although most patients with *P. oryzihabitans* infection are immunocompromised, the infections are indolent and recovery is the rule.

Pseudomonas luteola is another uncommon opportunistic pathogen. It was previously known as CDC group Ve-1 and *Chryseomonas luteola. P. luteola* infections are often associated with foreign bodies such as central venous and peritoneal dialysis catheters. Reported infections include bacteremia, peritonitis (associated with appendicitis and colon cancer as well as catheters), osteomyelitis, endocarditis, leg ulcers, cellulitis, and meningitis.[254,257,259,260]

Pseudomonas spp. are aerobic, non–spore-forming, gram-negative rods. They are motile owing to the presence of one or more polar flagella. They are lactose nonfermenters and grow well on MacConkey agar. Most clinical isolates (except *P. luteola* and *P. oryzihabitans*) are oxidase-positive. In addition to the negative oxidase reaction, these two species produce yellow-pigmented colonies on MacConkey's agar that help distinguish them from other pseudomonads. Unlike other fluorescent pseudomonads including *P. aeruginosa, P. fluorescens* and *P. putida* do not reduce nitrate and oxidize xylose. *P. stutzeri* colonies are brown, dry, and wrinkled on primary isolation media.

There are limited antimicrobial susceptibility data for these pseudomonads. *P. putida* can show broad resistance to β-lactam antibiotics and some isolates of this organism produce a metallo-β-lactamase that can readily hydrolyze carbapenems.[261] *P. oryzihabitans* is usually susceptible in vitro to ureidopenicillins, third-generation cephalosporins, aztreonam, imipenem, aminoglycosides, fluoroquinolones, and trimethoprim-sulfamethoxazole, but shows resistance to earlier-generation cephalosporins.[252,262] Clinical isolates of *P. luteola* are often resistant to first- and second-generation cephalosporins, tetracyclines, ampicillin, and trimethoprim-sulfamethoxazole but are susceptible to third-generation cephalosporins, mezlocillin, imipenem, aminoglycosides, and quinolones.[254]

Ralstonia

The genus *Ralstonia* was established in 1995 and initially contained one recognized pathogen, *R. pickettii* (formerly *Pseudomonas,* then *Burkholderia pickettii*).[263] Subsequently several other clinically relevant species have been added to the genus including *R. paucula* (formerly designated as CDC group IVc-2), *R. gilardii,* and, most recently, *R. mannitolilytica.* These environmental gram-negative nonfermentative bacilli are of low virulence but can cause infection related to contaminated infusates or in immunocompromised hosts including transplant recipients and patients with HIV infection or leukemia.[264-267]

R. pickettii can grow in saline and other fluids and has been the cause of many outbreaks related to contaminated infusates and pseudo-outbreaks related to contaminated solutions used in laboratory diagnosis.[268,269] The contamination of solutions has occurred during the manufacturing process and by extrinsic manipulation. In addition to bacteremia from contaminated intravenous products, airway colonization has been caused by contaminated respiratory therapy solutions.[269] In one outbreak due to a contaminated saline solutions, only 1 of 19 patients with *R. pickettii* airway colonization received antimicrobial therapy, consistent with the low virulence of the organism.[269] Clinical isolates of other *Ralstonia* species are less common. Most of the reported human infections of *R. paucula* are intravascular catheter–related blood-stream infections, either nosocomial or community acquired.[270] Peritoneal dialysis-associated peritonitis[271] and tenosynovitis following a cat bite[272] have also been reported. Most patients have responded well to antibiotic therapy.

Ralstonia spp. grow on routine media although growth may be slow and require more than 72 hours of incubation to visualize colonies. They are motile, catalase-positive and oxidase-positive, except for *R. gilardii.* Urease production, nitrate reduction, and ability to produce acid from substrates including mannitol and D-arabitol are helpful in differentiating the *Ralstonia* species. There are no validated in vitro susceptibility testing methods for *Ralstonia* spp. Isolates of *R. pickettii* have been reportedly susceptible to piperacillin, ceftazidime, imipenem, aminoglycosides, and trimethoprim-sulfamethozaxole. *R. paucula* is reportedly susceptible to these β-lactams along with ciprofloxacin and tetracycline; it is often resistant to aminoglycosides.[264,270]

Rhizobium (Formerly *Agrobacterium*)

Based on 16S rDNA analysis, organisms previously known as *Agrobacterium* have been redesignated as *Rhizobium.*[273] These organisms are well-known plant pathogens; most contain a large tumor-inducing plasmid, and infection produces neoplastic growth in many plant species. They are present in soil and plants and have a worldwide distribution. Although most clinical isolates appear nonpathogenic, there are about 50 reported cases of human disease caused by *Rhizobium* spp., primarily *R. radiobacter.* The literature contains a few reports of disease caused by another species, *Agrobacterium tumifaciens.* However, *A. tumifaciens* and *A. radiobacter* differ only by the presence or absence of the tumor-inducing plasmid, and they are now combined into the new species *Rhizobium radiobacter.*[273]

More than half the reported cases of *R. radiobacter* infection are intravascular catheter–related blood-stream infections in compromised hosts, primarily patients with malignancies.[274,275] Most of these infections were non–hospital acquired. Peritonitis in patients receiving ambulatory peritoneal dialysis is the other common presentation of *R. radiobacter* infection.[276] Urinary tract infections caused by this organism have been observed in patients with nephrostomy tubes. Thus, the majority of infections involve a device, the removal of which has been necessary in some cases to effect a cure. Other case reports include cellulitis in a patient with multiple myeloma, prosthetic valve endocarditis, bacteremias in patients with advanced AIDS, and neutropenia and bacteremic pneumonia in a patient with HIV infection.[277,278] A patient who worked in his garden the evening of cataract surgery developed *R. radiobacter* endophthalmitis 4 days later.[279] This is one of the few cases in which soil contact is mentioned. Thus, the source of the infecting organisms is for the most part unknown. Consistent with this organism's being an opportunistic pathogen of low virulence, all patients have survived. *R. radiobacter* has also caused pseudobacteremia resulting from contaminated citrated tubes used for clotting-factor studies.[280]

The organism readily grows on blood agar and MacConkey's media when incubated aerobically. Colony appearance varies for the different species. Flagellar stains show peritrichous distribution. Organisms are oxidase-positive, are catalase-positive, and produce gas from a variety of carbohydrates, including lactose. Rapid hydrolysis of urea and slower hydrolysis of esculin are key features that help to distinguish this organism from *Alcaligenes* spp. and *Pseudomonas* spp., which it otherwise closely resembles.

Clinical isolates have been variably susceptible to antibiotics and display variations in susceptibility patterns within classes of antibiotics, so in vitro testing of each isolate is important. For example, most isolates are susceptible to gentamicin but resistant to tobramycin.[274] Many strains are susceptible to third-generation cephalosporins, ciprofloxacin, and trimethoprim-sulfamethoxazole. *R. radiobacter* can produce an inducible cephalosporinase as well as an aminoglycoside acetyltransferase. Monobactams are produced by some soil strains[281]; not surprisingly, clinical isolates are often resistant to aztreonam.

Roseomonas and Other "Pink-Pigmented" Gram-Negative Bacilli

The group of organisms previously known as CDC "pink coccoid" groups I through IV have been placed in the new genus *Roseomonas* (*roseus* + *monas*, a rose-colored or pink bacterium).[25,282] There are currently three named species (*R. gilardii*, *R. cervicalis*, and *R. fauriae*) and three unnamed genospecies. Based on a limited number of reports in the literature, *Roseomonas* appears to cause more clinical disease than the related pink-pigmented bacterium *Methylobacterium*.[2,283] *Methylobacterium* spp., which are so named because of their ability to facultatively utilize methane, have been classified in the past under such names as *Pseudomonas mesophilica*, *Protomonas extorquens*, *Protaminobacter rubra*, "the pink phantom," and *Vibrio extorquens*.[281] The two most clinically relevant species, *M. mesophilicum* and *M. zatmanii*, are very similar phenotypically, and some reference laboratories limit identification to the genus level only.[25]

R. gilardii, the most commonly isolated species, is usually recovered in pure culture and, in one retrospective series, appeared to cause clinical illness more often than not.[283] Infections are usually community acquired. Blood stream infection is the most common presentation and may be related to the presence of intravascular catheters[285,286] or secondary to processes at other sites including intra-abdominal abscesses, respiratory tract or urinary tract infections. These infections usually, but not invariably, occur in patients with underlying medical illnesses such as malignancies, AIDS, chronic renal disease, or diabetes. Device removal may be necessary to clear intravascular catheter-related bacteremia.[287] Peritoneal dialysis–associated peritonitis, vertebral osteomyelitis, septic bursitis, soft tissue infections, and epiglottitis have also been reported.[283,288,289] *Roseomonas fauriae* is rarely isolated from clinical specimens but has been reported to cause peritonitis in a patient undergoing continuous ambulatory peritoneal dialysis.[290] *Methylobacterium* has also caused intravascular catheter–related bacteremia and peritonitis in patients receiving continuous ambulatory peritoneal dialysis and soft tissue infections.[291] A pseudo-outbreak of *Methylobacterium* respiratory tract infections was traced to contaminated tap water in the bronchoscopy suite.[292]

Roseomonas spp. are plump gram-negative rods or coccobacilli. In contrast, *Methylobacterium* spp. do not stain well and can appear gram-variable and also have intracellular vacuoles. Colonies are pink pigmented and are sometimes mucoid. Both these organisms can appear weakly oxidase-positive and are catalase-positive and urease-positive. *Roseomonas* can be distinguished from *Methylobacterium* by the inability to oxidize methanol, the inability to assimilate acetamide, and the absence of long-wave ultraviolet light absorption.[282] *Methylobacterium* has been isolated after 1 week of incubation on medium ordinarily used for the isolation of mycobacteria.[288]

Imipenem, aminoglycosides, and tetracycline are the most active antibiotics against *Roseomonas* spp. They are usually resistant to penicillins and cephalosporins with the exception of penicillin β-lactamase inhibitor combinations, which are frequently but not invariably active. *Roseomonas* spp. are often susceptible to fluoroquinolones but resistant to trimethoprim-sulfamethoxazole. *Methylobacterium* grows slowly, and susceptibility testing is not always possible.[284] Many *Methylobacterium* isolates produce a β-lactamase, and the organisms are resistant to penicillins and many cephalosporins. Aminoglycosides, ciprofloxacin, and trimethoprim-sulfamethoxazole are active.

Shewanella

Shewanella putrefaciens (formerly *Pseudomonas putrefaciens*, *Alteromonas putrefaciens*, or CDC group Ib) is widely distributed in the environment and has infrequently been implicated as a cause of human disease. *Shewanella* can be recovered from a variety of water sources, natural gas and petroleum reserves, dairy products, meat, and fish. *S. putrefaciens* is genetically heterogeneous, and three distinct biovars have been described. Biovar 1 (CDC group Ib-1) is a major cause of spoilage of refrigerated protein-rich foods. Clinical isolates are usually biovar 2 (CDC group Ib-2), but recent data suggest that most of these isolates should be classified as the genetically distinct species *Shewanella algae* (previously *S. alga*).[293,294] However, the typing systems currently in use by most clinical microbiology laboratories identify both species as *S. putrefaciens*.[294] Thus, in all likelihood, the use of this species name will continue.

Shewanella is frequently isolated as part of a polymicrobial infection, and its pathogenic role is often unclear. Lower extremity cellulitis in association with chronic ulcers or after burns is one of the more commonly described presentations.[295] *Shewanella* bacteremia, which also is frequently polymicrobial, can accompany soft tissue infection or biliary tract disease or occur in compromised hosts including persons with underlying liver disease or malignancy.[296,297] Compromised hosts are more likely to have accompanying signs of sepsis and have a poor outcome. Bacteremia and respiratory distress have been described in neonates and premature infants.[296] Less commonly reported infections include peritonitis, pneumonia, empyema, meningitis, osteomyelitis, otitis, urinary tract infection, endophthalmitis and an infected aortic aneurysm.[295,297,298]

On Gram stain, *Shewanella* is a short to long rod and can be filamentous. It is oxidase-positive and is the only nonfermenter that produces hydrogen sulfide on triple sugar iron agar, a key feature that allows easy identification in the laboratory. *Shewanella algae* can be distinguished from *S. putrefaciens* by growth at 42° C in 6.5% NaCl, the production of hemolysis on sheep blood agar and by the inability to produce acid from sucrose, maltose, and L-arabinose.[294] *Shewanella* is resistant to penicillin and cefazolin but susceptible to most second- and third-generation cephalosporins and piperacillin.[295] The organisms are also usually susceptible to aminoglycosides, chloramphenicol, and ciprofloxacin but less predictably susceptible to tetracycline and trimethoprim-sulfamethoxazole.[295,296] A report from South Africa found the majority of isolates resistant to imipenem.[296]

Sphingobacterium

The genus *Sphingobacterium* includes organisms previously classified as *Flavobacterium* species. The organisms that were transferred to this new genus contain large amounts of sphingophospholipid compounds in their cell membranes and have other taxonomic features that distinguish them from flavobacteria.[299] Most isolates from humans are *S. multivorum* (formerly *Flavobacterium multivorum* or CDC group IIk-2) and *Sphingobacterium spiritivorum* (formerly *Flavobacterium spiritivorum* or CDC group IIk-3).

There are reported cases of *S. multivorum* causing peritonitis, septicemia in a dialysis patient, bacteremia in a patient with lymphoma as well as in a patient with diabetes, and respiratory disease in a patient with cystic fibrosis.[300-303] Most cases of *S. multivorum* infection are nosocomial, but the natural habitat of the organism is not well defined. *S. spiritivorum* has been rarely recovered from clinical specimens, primarily urine and blood[25,304]; cellulitis presumably from soil contact with secondary bacteremia has been reported.[305]

S. multivorum and *S. spiritivorum* grow on blood agar, are oxidase- and catalase-positive, indole-negative, and produce light yellow colonies. They are biochemically similar to *Sphingomonas paucimobilis* (CDC group IIk-1).

Sphingobacterium spp. are intrinsically resistant to many commonly employed antibiotics and can grow in some antiseptics and disinfectants.[301,306] *S. multivorum* can produce an extended-spectrum β-lactamase and a metallo-β-lactamase conferring resistance to third-generation cephalosporins and carbapenems, respectively.[307] The combination of trimethoprim-sulfamethoxazole and perfloxacin produced cure in a bacteremic patient.[301] A bacteremic patient receiving hemodialysis improved clinically after receiving ampicillin and one dose of tobramycin, despite in vitro testing showing ampicillin resistance.[300]

Sphingomonas

The genus *Sphingomonas* contains at least 12 species of which only one, *S. paucimobilus,* is an occasional human pathogen.[308] This organism, formerly known as *Pseudomonas paucimobilis* and CDC group IIk-1, is widely distributed in soil and water, including water sources in the hospital environment. It has been implicated in nosocomial outbreaks associated with contaminated water[309,310] and contaminated ventilator temperature probes.[311]

S. paucimobilis infections typically occur in immunocompromised persons and can be community as well as nosocomially acquired. This is an organism of low virulence, and recovery from infection is the rule, even in debilitated hosts. There are several reports of *S. paucimobilis* intravascular catheter–associated blood-stream infection, and catheter removal was necessary in some cases for cure.[312,313] Blood-stream infection has also been reported in hemodialysis patients and after infusion of contaminated autologous bone marrow.[314] Although ventilator-associated pneumonia has been described,[313] airway colonization was much more common than infection in intensive care unit outbreaks.[309,311] Peritoneal catheter–associated peritonitis, meningitis, ventriculoperitoneal shunt infection, brain abscess, soft tissue infection, wound infection, adenitis, urinary tract infection, and a variety of visceral abscesses have been reported.[313,315,316]

S. paucimobilis is strictly aerobic, weakly oxidase-positive, and catalase-positive. Colonies grow on blood agar but not MacConkey's agar, produce a yellow pigment, and can be misidentified as *Flavobacterium* spp. Despite the presence of a single polar flagellum, a low percentage of cells are actively motile, and motility can be difficult to demonstrate in the laboratory (thus the name paucimobilis).[317]

Most isolates are susceptible to trimethoprim-sulfamethoxazole, imipenem, aminoglycosides, tetracyclines, and chloramphenicol.[313,317] Third-generation cephalosporins are usually active but not predictably so, and resistance to penicillins and first-generation cephalosporins is common. Although fluoroquinolones were active in some reports, many isolates were resistant to ciprofloxacin in one series.[313]

Weeksella and Bergeyella

The genus *Weeksella,* when proposed in 1986, contained two species, *W. zoohelcum* (CDC group IIj) and *W. virosa* (CDC group IIf), that differed from most nonfermentative gram-negative bacilli in being susceptible to penicillin. Recently, *W. zoohelcum* has been moved to the new genus *Bergeyella.*[211] *Bergeyella zoohelcum* (from the Greek "animal" + "wound") is part of the normal oral flora of dogs and other animals, and most clinical isolates come from bite wounds.[318,319] Two case reports, one of meningitis and one of bacteremia following dog bites, are the only reports of an invasive infection caused by this organism.[320,321] *W. virosa* has been isolated predominantly from the genital tract and urine of women[322,323] and is usually not a pathogen. There are case reports of dialysis-associated peritonitis and spontaneous bacterial peritonitis.[324,325] Both organisms grow well on blood agar, but most strains do not grow on MacConkey's agar. They are oxidase-positive, catalase-positive, indole-positive, and nonpigmented. In contrast to *W. virosa, B. zoohelcum* produces urease. *W. virosa* (from the Latin "slimy") forms coccoid colonies that stick tenaciously to agar surfaces.[322] Both species are susceptible to β-lactam antibiotics including

penicillin, chloramphenicol, and fluoroquinolones and are variable in susceptibility to tetracycline and trimethoprim-sulfamethoxazole. *W. virosa* is usually resistant to one or more aminoglycosides. The combination of penicillin susceptibility and aminoglycoside resistance is a clue to the identification of this organism.

New Centers for Disease Control and Prevention Groups

The CDC's Special Bacteriology Reference Laboratory receives unusual isolates from state laboratories and other reference laboratories. Some of these isolates are unnamed and are grouped by growth characteristics. Each of these groups represents one or more species. Although many of the isolates are from sterile sites, clinical information is often limited, and the pathogenic role of these organisms is uncertain. Some of the recently described CDC groups of gram-negative rods or coccobacillary organisms include the following:

1. CDC group NO-1 (NO for nonoxidizer) consists of at least 22 strains of fastidious gram-negative bacilli isolated from human wounds, most of which were related to dog or cat bites.[25,326,327] These organisms are similar to asaccharolytic strains of *Acinetobacter* but have a negative *Acinetobacter* transformation assay, have different cellular fatty acid profiles, and, unlike most *Acinetobacter* organisms, reduce nitrate. They are susceptible to many antimicrobial agents, including β-lactams, aminoglycosides, fluoroquinolones, and tetracycline.

2. CDC Group WO-1 (WO for weak oxidizer) includes 96 oxidase-positive, motile gram-negative rods, most of which were isolated from clinical specimens.[328] One third of the clinical isolates were from blood, and 10% were from cerebrospinal fluid.[328] Signs of sepsis were present in some of the patients, but the clinical significance of this group of organisms remains unclear.

3. CDC Group WO-2 isolates now reside in the genus *Pandoraea,* which has five named and at least three unnamed species. These organisms can colonize the airways of patients with cystic fibrosis and rarely can cause clinical disease including bacteremia.[329,330] *Pandoraea* spp. are often resistant to ampicillin, extended-spectrum cephalosporins, and aminoglycosides, and are variably susceptible to fluoroquinolones.[330]

4. CDC groups O-1, O-2, and O-3 are phenotypically similar, they are oxidase-positive curved gram-negative rods that do not grow on MacConkey's agar but grow on *Campylobacter*-selective media. One case of group O-1 pneumonia complicated by bronchopulmonary fistula and bacteremia has been reported.[331] One group O3 isolate that was submitted to the CDC had been identified as a *Campylobacter* spp., indicating the potential for misidentification of the O-3 group.[332] The CDC collection of group O3 includes isolates from a variety of clinical sources including blood, lymph nodes, joint fluid, bone, and lung. They were resistant to most β-lactam antibiotics except imipenem; all were susceptible to aminoglycosides and trimethoprim-sulfamethoxazole but not ciprofloxacin.

5. Fifteen strains of an oxidase-positive gram-negative rod biochemically resembling *Neisseria weaveri* (CDC group M5) are currently designated *Gilardi* rod group 1 by the CDC.[333] Most of the strains were isolated from human wounds of the extremities or blood cultures.

GARDNERELLA AND *MOBILUNCUS*

Gardnerella vaginalis is difficult to characterize in terms of its microbiologic designation and its clinical relevance. By 16S rRNA sequence analysis, it is sufficiently distinct to merit its own genus but is somewhat closely related to *Bifidobacterium* species which are anaerobic gram-positive rods.[334] It is a facultatively anaerobic, oxidase- and catalase-negative, nonsporing, nonencapsulated, nonmotile, pleomorphic, gram-variable rod. (See the excellent review by Carlin.[335]) *G. vaginalis* has a thin cell wall which does not retain the crystal violet-iodine complex upon decolorization, accounting for the gram-variable or gram-negative appearance of the organism. However, the preponderance of evidence suggests that *G. vaginalis* has a gram-positive heritage. The natural habitat for *G. vaginalis* is the human vagina, where it has been found in 15% to 69% of women without signs or symptoms of vaginal infection[336] and 13.5% of girls. *G. vaginalis* is almost universally present in the vagina of women with bacterial vaginosis (BV), where it is found with a mixed anaerobic flora (see Chapter 103).[337] Bacteremia is seen almost exclusively in women and is usually associated with postpartum endometritis, postpartum fever, chorioamnionitis, septic abortion, or infection after cesarean section.[338] It is a relatively infrequent ($< 0.5\%$) urinary tract isolate and its clinical significance can be difficult to ascertain. However, it has been recovered from suprapubic bladder aspirates from pregnant women.[339] *G. vaginalis* has also been recovered from the male urogenital tract and has occasionally been associated with disease.[335] Oral metronidazole, intravaginal metronidazole gel, or intravaginal clindamycin cream are the recommended treatments for BV.[340] The use of these agents reflects the importance of the mixed anaerobic flora in BV. Treatment of the sexual partner does not influence a woman's response to therapy or relapse rate and the routine treatment of sexual partners is not recommended.[340] β-lactams have been used to treat extravaginal infections caused by *G. vaginalis*. Screening and treatment of BV in pregnant women at high risk of preterm labor and prior to surgical abortion or hysterectomy has been recommended.[340]

Mobiluncus spp. are slowly growing, curved, gram-variable, motile, anaerobic bacteria predominantly found in the human vagina in association with BV. *Mobiluncus* has been isolated from the vagina of as many as 97% of women with BV[341] but in a minority of healthy controls.[342] The role of *Mobiluncus* in the pathogenesis of BV is unclear. *Mobiluncus* spp., more commonly *M. curtisii*, are associated with upper genitourinary tract infections and adverse pregnancy outcome. Extragenitourinary tract infections have included nonpuerperal breast abscesses as well as umbilical and mastectomy wounds.[343] There are four reported cases of *Mobiluncus* bacteremia, all in women, including one previously healthy woman who developed septic shock with coagulopathy, adult respiratory distress syndrome and renal failure.[344] *Mobiluncus* spp. are usually susceptible to penicillins, ampicillin, cefoxitin, clindamycin, erythromycin, imipenem, and vancomycin.[345] They are, however, typically resistant to metronidazole; the efficacy of metronidazole in the treatment of BV despite the presence of antibiotic resistant *Mobiluncus* underscores the uncertainty of the role of this organism in the pathogenesis of the disease.

REFERENCES

1. von Graevenitz A, Zbinden R, Zmutters R. *Actinobacillus, Capnocytophaga, Eikenella, Kingella, Pasteurella,* and other fastidious or rarely encountered Gram-negative rods. In: Murray PR, Baron EJ, Jorgensen JH, et al, eds. Manual of Clinical Microbiology. 8th ed. Washington, DC: American Society for Microbiology Press; 2003:609-622.
2. Koneman EW, Allen SD, Janda WM, et al. Color Atlas and Textbook of Diagnostic Microbiology. 5th ed. Philadelphia: JB Lippincott; 1997.
3. Kaplan AH, Weber DJ, Oddone EZ, et al. Infection due to *Actinobacillus actinomycetemcomitans:* 15 cases and review. Rev Infect Dis. 1989;11:46-63.
4. Holm P. Studies on the aetiology of human actinomycosis. II. Do the "other microbes" of actinomycosis possess virulence? Acta Pathol Microbiol Scand. 1951;28:391-406.
5. Page MI, King EO. Infection due to *Actinobacillus actinomycetemcomitans* and *Haemophilus aphrophilus*. N Engl J Med. 1966;275:181-188.
6. Horowitz EA, Pugsley MP, Turbes PG, et al. Pericarditis caused by *Actinobacillus actinomycetemcomitans*. J Infect Dis. 1987;155:152-153.
7. Ellner JJ, Rosenthal MS, Lerner PI, et al. Infective endocarditis caused by slow-growing, fastidious, gram-negative bacteria. Medicine. 1979;58:145-158.
8. Yuan A, Yang PC, Lee LN, et al. *Actinobacillus actinomycetemcomitans* pneumonia with chest wall involvement and rib destruction. Chest. 1992;101:1450-1452.
9. Binder MI, Chua J, Kaiser PK, et al. *Actinobacillus actinomycetemcomitans* endogenous endophthalmitis: report of two cases and review of the literature. Scand J Infect Dis. 2003;35:133-136.
10. Bowker CM, Connellan SJ, Freeth MG. A case of thoracic *Actinobacillus* infection. Respir Med. 1992;86:53-54.
11. Asikainen S, Chen C, Alaluusua S, et al. Can one acquire periodontal bacteria and periodontitis from a family member? J Am Dent Assoc. 1997;128:1263-1271.
12. Aass AM, Preus HR, Gjermo P. Association between detection of oral *Actinobacillus actinomycetemcomitans* and radiographic bone loss in teenagers. J Periodontol. 1992;63:682-685.
13. Henderson B, Wilson M, Sharp L, et al. *Actinobacillus actinomycetemcomitans*. J Med Microbiol. 2002;51:1013-1020.
14. Asikainen S, Chen C, Slots J. Likelihood of transmitting *Actinobacillus actinomycetemcomitans* and *Porphyromonas gingivalis* in families with periodontitis. Oral Microbiol Immunol. 1996;11:387-394.
15. Meyer DH, Fives-Taylor PM. The role of *Actinobacillus actinomycetemcomitans* in the pathogenesis of periodontal disease. Trends Microbiol. 1997;5:224-228.
16. Brouqui P, Raoult D. Endocarditis due to rare and fastidious bacteria. Clin Microbiol Rev. 2001;14:177-207.
17. Grace CJ, Levitz RE, Katz Pollak H, et al. *Actinobacillus actinomycetemcomitans* prosthetic valve endocarditis. Rev Infect Dis. 1988;10:922-929.
18. Wilson ME. Prosthetic valve endocarditis and paravalvular abscess caused by *Actinobacillus actinomycetemcomitans*. Rev Infect Dis. 1989;11:665-667.
19. Peel MM, Hornidge KA, Luppino M, et al. *Actinobacillus* spp and related bacteria in infected wounds of humans bitten by horses and sheep. J Clin Microbiol. 1991;29:2535-2538.
20. Arana-Domondon LC, Chen SH, Mann L, et al. Boar hunter's endocarditis. JAMA. 1998;279:198.
21. Friis-Moller A, Christensen JJ, Fussing V, et al. Clinical significance and taxonomy of *Actinobacillus hominis*. J Clin Microbiol. 2001;39:930-935.
22. Wust J, Gubler J, Mannheim W, et al. *Actinobacillus hominis* as a causative agent of septicemia in hepatic failure. Eur J Clin Microbiol Infect Dis. 1991;10:693-694.
23. Kingsland RC, Guss DA. *Actinobacillus ureae* meningitis: Case report and review of the literature. J Emerg Med. 1995;13:623-627.
24. Verhaegen J, Verbraeken H, Cabuy A, et al. *Actinobacillus* (formerly *Pasteurella*) *ureae* meningitis and bacteraemia: Report of a case and review of the literature. J Infect. 1988;17:249-253.
25. Weyant RS, Moss CW, Weaver RE, et al. Identification of Unusual Pathogenic Gram-Negative Aerobic and Facultatively Anaerobic Bacteria. 2nd ed. Baltimore: Williams & Wilkins; 1996.
26. Yogev R, Shulman D, Shulman ST, et al. In vitro activity of antibiotics alone and in combination against *Actinobacillus actinomycetemcomitans*. Antimicrob Agents Chemother. 1986;29:179-181.
27. Muller HP, Holderrieth S, Burkhardt U, et al. In vitro antimicrobial susceptibility of oral strains of *Actinobacillus actinomycetemcomitans* to seven antibiotics. J Clin Periodontol. 2002;29:736-742.
28. Pavicic MJ, van Winkelhoff AJ, de Graaff J. In vitro susceptibilities of *Actinobacillus actinomycetemcomitans* to a number of antimicrobial combinations. Antimicrob Agents Chemother. 1992;36:2634-2638.
29. Wilson WR, Karchmer AW, Dajani AS, et al. Antibiotic treatment of adults with infective endocarditis due to streptococci, enterococci, staphylococci, and HACEK microorganisms. JAMA. 1995;274:1706-1713.
30. Babinchak TJ. Oral ciprofloxacin therapy for prosthetic valve endocarditis due to *Actinobacillus actinomycetemcomitans*. Clin Infect Dis. 1995;21:1517-1518.
31. Van Winkelhoff AJ, Tijhof CJ, de Graaff J. Microbiological and clinical results of metronidazole plus amoxicillin therapy in *Actinobacillus actinomycetemcomitans*-associated periodontitis. J Periodontol. 1992;63:52-57.
32. Colwell RR, MacDonell MT, De Ley J. Proposal to recognize the family *Aeromonadaceae* fam nov. Int J Syst Bacteriol. 1986;36:473-477.
33. Abbott SL, Cheung WKW, Janda JM. The genus *Aeromonas*: Biochemical characteristics, atypical reactions, and phenotypic identification schemes. J Clin Microbiol. 2003;41:2348-2357.
34. Krieg NR, Holt JG, eds. Bergey's Manual of Systematic Bacteriology, v. 1. Baltimore: Williams & Wilkins; 1984.
35. Janda JM, Abbott SL. Evolving concepts regarding the genus *Aeromonas*: An expanding panorama of species, disease presentations and unanswered questions. Clin Infect Dis. 1998;27:332-344.
36. Challapalli M, Tess BR, Cunningham DG, et al. *Aeromonas*-associated diarrhea in children. Pediatr Infect Dis J. 1988;7:693-698.
37. Gluskin I, Batash D, Shoseyov D, et al. A 15-year study of the role of *Aeromonas* spp in gastroenteritis in hospitalised children. J Med Microbiol. 1992;37:315-318.
38. Rautelin H, Sivonen A, Kuikka A, et al. Role of *Aeromonas* isolated from feces of Finnish patients. Scand J Infect Dis. 1995;27:207-210.
39. King GE, Werner SB, Kizer KW. Epidemiology of *Aeromonas* infections in California. Clin Infect Dis. 1992;15:449-452.
40. Namdari H, Bottone EJ. Microbiologic and clinical evidence supporting the role of *Aeromonas caviae* as a pediatric enteric pathogen. J Clin Microbiol. 1990;28:837-840.
41. Jiang ZD, Nelson AC, Mathewson JJ, et al. Intestinal secretory immune response to infection with *Aeromonas* species and *Plesiomonas shigelloides* among students from the United States in Mexico. J Infect Dis. 1991;164:979-982.
42. Hanninen ML, Salmi S, Mattila L, et al. Association of *Aeromonas* spp with travellers' diarrhoea in Finland. J Med Microbiol. 1995;42:26-31.
43. Holmberg SD, Schell WL, Fanning GR, et al. *Aeromonas* intestinal infections in the United States. Ann Intern Med. 1986;105:683-689.
44. Borchardt MA, Semper ME, Standridge JH. *Aeromonas* isolates from human diarrheic stool and groundwater compared by pulsed-field gel electrophoresis. Emerg Infect Dis. 2003;9:224-228.
45. Jones BL, Wilcox MH. *Aeromonas* infections and their treatment. J Antimicrob Chemother. 1995;35:453-461.
46. Vila J, Ruiz J, Gallardo F, et al. *Aeromonas* spp. and traveler's diarrhea: Clinical features and antimicrobial resistance. Emerg Infect. Dis. 2003;9:552-555.
47. De la Morena ML, Van R, Singh K, et al. Diarrhea associated with *Aeromonas* species in children in day care centers. J Infect Dis. 1993;168:215-218.
48. Willoughby JM, Rahman AF, Gregory MM. Chronic colitis after *Aeromonas* infection. Gut. 1989;30:686-690.

49. Bogdanovic R, Cobeljic M, Markovic M, et al. Haemolytic-uraemic syndrome associated with *Aeromonas hydrophila* enterocolitis. Pediatr Nephrol. 1991;5:293-295.

50. Gold WL, Salit IE. *Aeromonas hydrophila* infections of skin and soft tissue: Report of 11 cases and review. Clin Infect Dis. 1993;16:69-74.

51. Kienzle N, Muller M, Pegg S. *Aeromonas* wound infection in burns. Burns. 2000;26:478-482.

52. Vally H, Whittle A, Cameron S, et al. Outbreak of *Aeromonas hydrophila* wound infections associated with mud football. Clin Infect Dis. 2004;38:1084-1089.

53. Lineaweaver WC, Hill MK, Buncke GM, et al. *Aeromonas hydrophilia* infections following use of medicinal leeches in replantation and flap surgery. Ann Plast Surg. 1992;29:238-244.

54. Mackay DR, Manders EK, Saggers GC, et al. *Aeromonas* species isolated from medicinal leeches. Ann Plast Surg. 1999;42:275-279.

55. Sartor C, Limouzin-Perotti F, Legre R, et al. Nosocomial infections with *Aeromonas hydrophila* from leeches. Clin Infect Dis. 2002;35:E1-E5.

56. Ko WC, Lee HC, Chuang YC, et al. Clinical features and therapeutic implications of 104 episodes of monomicrobial *Aeromonas* bacteraemia. J Infect. 2000;40:267-273.

57. Ko WC, Chuang YC. *Aeromonas* bacteremia: Review of 59 episodes. Clin Infect Dis. 1995;20:1298-1304.

58. Janda JM, Guthertz LS, Kokka RP, et al. *Aeromonas* species in septicemia: Laboratory characteristics and clinical observations. Clin Infect Dis. 1994;19:77-83.

59. Dryden M, Munro R. *Aeromonas* septicemia: Relationship of species and clinical features. Pathology. 1989;21:111-114.

60. Cookson BD, Houang ET, Lee JV. The use of a biotyping system to investigate an unusual clustering of bacteraemias caused by *Aeromonas* species. J Hosp Infect. 1984;5:205-209.

61. Hickman-Brenner FW, Fanning GR, Arduino MJ, et al. *Aeromonas schubertii,* a new mannitol-negative species found in human clinical specimens. J Clin Microbiol. 1988;26:1561-1564.

62. Carnahan A, Fanning GR, Joseph SW. *Aeromonas jandaei* (formerly genospecies DNA group 9 *A. sobria*), a new sucrose-negative species isolated from clinical specimens. J Clin Microbiol. 1991;29:560-564.

63. DeFronzo RA, Murray GF, Maddrey WC. *Aeromonas* septicemia from hepatobiliary disease. Am J Dig Dis. 1973;18:323-331.

64. Parras F, Diaz MD, Reina J, et al. Meningitis due to *Aeromonas* species: Case report and review. Clin Infect Dis. 1993;17:1058-1060.

65. Ong KR, Sordillo E, Frankel E. Unusual case of *Aeromonas hydrophila* endocarditis. J Clin Microbiol. 1991;29:1056-1057.

66. Ender PT, Dolan MJ, Dolan D, et al. Near-drowning-associated *Aeromonas* pneumonia. J Emerg Med. 1996;14:737-741.

67. Blair JE, Woo-Ming MA, McGuire PK. *Aeromonas hydrophila* bacteremia acquired from an infected swimming pool. Clin Infect Dis. 1999;28:1336-1337.

68. Janda JM, Abbott SL, Carnahan AM. *Aeromonas* and *Plesiomonas.* In: Murray PR, Baron EJ, Pfaller MA, et al, eds. Manual of Clinical Microbiology. Washington, DC: American Society for Microbiology Press; 1995:477-482.

69. Vila J, Marco F, Soler L, et al. In vitro antimicrobial susceptibility of clinical isolates of *Aeromonas caviae, Aeromonas hydrophila* and *Aeromonas veronii* biotype sobria. J Antimicrob Chemother. 2002;49:701-702.

70. Motyl MR, McKinley G, Janda JM. In vitro susceptibilities of *Aeromonas hydrophila, Aeromonas sobria,* and *Aeromonas caviae* to 22 antimicrobial agents. Antimicrob Agents Chemother. 1985;28:151-153.

71. Walsh TR, Stunt RA, Nabi JA, et al. Distribution and expression of beta-lactamase genes among *Aeromonas* spp. J Antimicrob Chemother. 1997;40:171-178.

72. Walsh TR, Payne DJ, MacGowan AP, et al. A clinical isolate of *Aeromonas sobria* with three chromosomally mediated inducible beta-lactamases: A cephalosporinase, a penicillinase and a third enzyme, displaying carbapenemase activity. J Antimicrob Chemother. 1995;35:271-279.

73. Overman TL, Janda JM. Antimicrobial susceptibility patterns of *Aeromonas jandaei, A. schubertii, A. trota,* and *A. veronii* biotype *veronii.* J Clin Microbiol. 1999;37:706-708.

74. Rossolini GM, Walsh T, Amicosante G. The *Aeromonas* metallo-beta-lactamases: Genetics, enzymology, and contribution to drug resistance. Microb Drug Resist. 1996;2:245-252.

75. Ko WC, Yu KW, Liu CY, et al. Increasing antibiotic resistance in clinical isolates of *Aeromonas* strains in Taiwan. Antimicrob Agents Chemother. 1996;40:1260-1262.

76. Chang BJ, Bolton SM. Plasmids and resistance to antimicrobial agents in *Aeromonas sobria* and *Aeromonas hydrophila* clinical isolates. Antimicrob Agents Chemother. 1987;31:1281-1282.

77. Wormser GP, Bottone EJ. *Cardiobacterium hominis:* Review of microbiologic and clinical features. Rev Infect Dis. 1983;5:680-691.

78. Taveras JM 3rd, Campo R, Segal N, et al. Apparent culture-negative endocarditis of the prosthetic valve caused by *Cardiobacterium hominis.* South Med J. 1993;86:1439-1440.

79. Apisarnthanarak A, Johnson RM, Braverman AC, et al. *Cardiobacterium hominis* bioprosthetic mitral valve endocarditis presenting as septic arthritis. Diagn Microbiol Infect Dis. 2002;42:79-81.

80. Pritchard TM, Foust RT, Cantely JR, et al. Prosthetic valve endocarditis due to *Cardiobacterium hominis* occurring after upper gastrointestinal endoscopy. Am J Med. 1991;90:516-518.

81. Robison WJ, Vitelli AS. Infectious endocarditis caused by *Cardiobacterium hominis.* South Med J. 1985;78:1020-1021.

82. Francioli PB, Roussianos D, Glauser MP. *Cardiobacterium hominis* endocarditis manifesting as bacterial meningitis. Arch Intern Med. 1983;143:1483-1484.

83. Rechtman DJ, Nadler JP. Abdominal abscess due to *Cardiobacterium hominis* and *Clostridium bifermentans.* Rev Infect Dis. 1991;13:418-419.

84. Nurnberger M, Treadwell T, Lin B, et al. Pacemaker lead infection and vertebral osteomyelitis presumed due to *Cardiobacterium hominis.* Clin Infect Dis. 1998;27:890-891.

85. Kugler KC, Biedenbach DJ, Jones RN. Determination of the antimicrobial activity of 29 clinically important compounds tested against fastidious HACEK group organisms. Diagn Microbiol Infect Dis. 1999;34:73-76.

86. Le Quellec A, Bessis D, Perez C, et al. Endocarditis due to beta-lactamase-producing *Cardiobacterium hominis.* Clin Infect Dis. 1994;19:994-995.

87. Ponte R, Jenkins SG. Fatal *Chromobacterium violaceum* infections associated with exposure to stagnant waters. Pediatr Infect Dis J. 1992;11:583-586.

88. Huffam SE, Nowotny MJ, Currie BJ. *Chromobacterium violaceum* in tropical northern Australia. Med J Aust. 1998;168:335-337.

89. Kaufman SC, Ceraso D, Schugurensky A. First case report from Argentina of fatal septicemia caused by *Chromobacterium violaceum.* J Clin Microbiol. 1986;23:956-958.

90. Berkowitz FE, Metchock B. Third generation cephalosporin-resistant gram-negative bacilli in the feces of hospitalized children. Pediatr Infect Dis J. 1995;14:97-100.

91. Ti TY, Tan WC, Chong AP, et al. Nonfatal and fatal infections caused by *Chromobacterium violaceum.* Clin Infect Dis. 1993;17:505-507.

92. Roberts SA, Morris AJ, McIvor N, et al. *Chromobacterium violaceum* infection of the deep neck tissues in a traveler to Thailand. Clin Infect Dis. 1997;25:334-335.

93. Moore CC, Lane JE, Stephens JL. Successful treatment of an infant with *Chromobacterium violaceum* sepsis. Clin Infect Dis. 2001;32:E107-E110.

94. Dromigny JA, Fall AL, Diouf S, et al. *Chromobacterium violaceum:* A case of diarrhea in Senegal. Pediatr Infect Dis J. 2002;21:573-574.

95. Macher AM, Casale TB, Fauci AS. Chronic granulomatous disease of childhood and *Chromobacterium violaceum* infections in the Southeastern United States. Ann Intern Med. 1982;97:51-55.

96. Mamlok RJ, Mamlok V, Mills GC, et al. Glucose-6-phosphate dehydrogenase deficiency, neutrophil dysfunction and *Chromobacterium violaceum* sepsis. J Pediatr. 1987;111:852-854.

97. Miller DP, Blevins WT, Steele DB, et al. A comparative study of virulent and avirulent strains of *Chromobacterium violaceum.* Can J Microbiol. 1988;34:249-255.

98. Lee J, Kim JS, Nahm CH, et al. Two cases of *Chromobacterium violaceum* infection after injury in a subtropical region. J Clin Microbiol. 1999;37:2068-2070

99. Melo PS, Justo GZ, de Azevedo MB, et al. Violacein and its beta-cyclodextrin complexes induce apoptosis and differentiation in HL60 cells. Toxicology. 2003;186:217-225.

100. Aldridge KE, Valainis GT, Sanders CV. Comparison of the in vitro activity of ciprofloxacin and 24 other antimicrobial agents against clinical strains of *Chromobacterium violaceum.* Diagn Microbiol Infect Dis. 1988;10:31-39.

101. Duma RJ. Aztreonam, the first monobactam. Ann Intern Med. 1987;106:766-767.

102. Wagner DK, Wright JJ, Ansher AF, et al. Dysgonic fermenter 3-associated gastrointestinal disease in a patient with common variable hypogammaglobulinemia. Am J Med. 1988;84:315-318.

103. Hofstad T, Olsen I, Eribe ER, et al. *Dysgonomonas* gen. nov. to accommodate *Dysgonomonas gadei* sp. nov., an organism isolated from a human gall bladder, and *Dysgonomonas capnocytophagoides* (formerly CDC group DF-3). Int J Syst Evol Microbiol. 2000;50:2189-2195.

104. Vandamme P, Vancanneyt M, van Belkum A, et al. Polyphasic analysis of strains of the genus *Capnocytophaga* and Centers for Disease Control group DF-3. Int J Syst Bacteriol. 1996;46:782-791.

105. Gill VJ, Travis LB, Williams DY. Clinical and microbiological observations on CDC group DF-3, a gram-negative coccobacillus. J Clin Microbiol. 1991;29:1589-1592.

106. Heiner AM, DiSario JA, Carroll K, et al. Dysgonic fermenter-3: A bacterium associated with diarrhea in immunocompromised hosts. Am J Gastroenterol. 1992;87:1629-1630.

107. Blum RN, Berry CD, Phillips MG, et al. Clinical illnesses associated with isolation of dysgonic fermenter 3 from stool samples. J Clin Microbiol. 1992;30:396-400.

108. Schonheyder H, Ejlertsen T, Frederiksen W. Isolation of a dysgonic fermenter (DF-3) from urine of a patient. Eur J Clin Microbiol Infect Dis. 1991;10:530-531.

109. Bangsborg JM, Frederiksen W, Bruun B. Dysgonic fermenter 3-associated abscess in a diabetic patient. J Infect. 1990;20:237-240.

110. Aronson NE, Zbick CJ. Dysgonic fermenter 3 bacteremia in a neutropenic patient with acute lymphocytic leukemia. J Clin Microbiol. 1988;26:2213-2215.

111. Grob R, Zbinden R, Ruef C, et al. Septicemia caused by dysgonic fermenter 3 in a severely immunocompromised patient and isolation of the same microorganism from a stool specimen. J Clin Microbiol. 1999;37:1617-1618.

112. Vartian CV, Septimus EJ. Endophthalmitis due to *Pasteurella multocida* and CDC EF-4. J Infect Dis. 1989;160:733.

113. Dul MJ, Shlaes DM, Lerner PI. EF-4 bacteremia in a patient with hepatic carcinoid. J Clin Microbiol. 1983;18:1260-1261.

114. Roebuck JD, Morris JT. Chronic otitis media due to EF-4 bacteria. Clin Infect Dis. 1999;29:1343-1344.

115. Holmes B, Costas M, Wood AC. Numerical analysis of electrophoretic protein patterns of group EF-4 bacteria, predominantly from dog-bite wounds of humans. J Appl Bacteriol. 1990;68:81-91.

116. Goldstein EJ, Citron DM. Comparative activities of cefuroxime, amoxicillin-clavulanic acid, ciprofloxacin, enoxacin, and ofloxacin against aerobic and anaerobic bacteria isolated from bite wounds. Antimicrob Agents Chemother. 1988;32:1143-1148.

117. Holmberg SD, Wachsmuth K, Hickman-Brenner FW, et al. *Plesiomonas* enteric infections in the United States. Ann Intern Med. 1986;105:690-694.

118. Brenden RA, Miller MA, Janda JM. Clinical disease spectrum and pathogenic factors associated with *Plesiomonas shigelloides* infections in humans. Rev Infect Dis. 1988;10:303-316.

119. MacDonnell MT, Colwell RR. Phylogeny of the *Vibrionaceae*, and recommendation for two new genera, *Listonella* and *Shewanella*. Syst Appl Microbiol. 1985;6:171-182.

120. Rautelin H, Sivonen A, Kuikka A, et al. Enteric *Plesiomonas shigelloides* infections in Finnish patients. Scand J Infect Dis. 1995;27:495-498.

121. Kain KC, Kelly MT. Clinical features, epidemiology, and treatment of *Plesiomonas shigelloides* diarrhea. J Clin Microbiol. 1989;27:998-1001.

122. Olsvik O, Wachsmuth K, Kay B, et al. Laboratory observations on *Plesiomonas shigelloides* strains isolated from children with diarrhea in Peru. J Clin Microbiol. 1990;28:886-889.

123. Janda JM, Abbott SL. Expression of hemolytic activity by *Plesiomonas shigelloides*. J Clin Microbiol. 1993;31:1206-1208.

124. Visitsunthorn N, Komolpis P. Antimicrobial therapy in *Plesiomonas shigelloides*-associated diarrhea in Thai children. Southeast Asian J Trop Med Publ Hlth. 1995; 26:86-90.

125. Alcaniz JP, de Cuenca Moron B, Gomez Rubio M, et al. Spontaneous bacterial peritonitis due to *Plesiomonas shigelloides*. Am J Gastroenterol. 1995;90:1529-1530.

126. Roth T, Hentsch C, Erard P, et al. Pyosalpinx: Not always a sexual transmitted disease? Pyosalpinx caused by *Plesiomonas shigelloides* in an immunocompetent host. Clin Microbiol Infect. 2002;8:803-805.

127. Fujita K, Shirai M, Ishioka T, et al. Neonatal *Plesiomonas shigelloides* septicemia and meningitis: A case and review. Acta Paediatr Jpn. 1994;36:450-452.

128. Clark RB, Westby GR, Spector H, et al. Fatal *Plesiomonas shigelloides* septicaemia in a splenectomised patient. J Infect. 1991;23:89-92.

129. Paul R, Siitonen A, Karkkainen P. *Plesiomonas shigelloides* bacteremia in a healthy girl with mild gastroenteritis. J Clin Microbiol. 1990;28:1445-1446.

130. Rahim Z, Kay BA. Enrichment for *Plesiomonas shigelloides* from stools. J Clin Microbiol. 1988;26:789-790.

131. Kain KC, Kelly MT. Antimicrobial susceptibility of *Plesiomonas shigelloides* from patients with diarrhea. Antimicrob Agents Chemother. 1989;33:1609-1610.

132. Stock I, Wiedemann B. Natural antimicrobial susceptibilities of *Plesiomonas shigelloides* strains. J Antimicrob Chemother. 2001;48:803-811.

133. Bruckner DA, Colonna P. Nomenclature for aerobic and facultative bacteria. Clin Infect Dis. 1993;16:598-605.

134. Yabuuchi E, Kawamura Y, Kosako Y, et al. Emendation of genus *Achromobacter* and *Achromobacter xylosoxidans* (Yabuuchi and Yano) and proposal of *Achromobacter ruhlandii* (Packer and Vishniac) comb. nov., *Achromobacter piechaudii* (Kiredjian et al.) comb. nov., and *Achromobacter xylosoxidans* subsp. *denitrificans* (Ruger and Tan) comb. nov. Microbiol Immunol. 1998;42:429-438.

135. Schreckenberg PC, Daneshvar MI, Weyant RS, et al. *Acinetobacter, Achromobacter, Chryseobacterium, Moraxella,* and other nonfermentative gram-negative rods. In: Murray PR, Daron EJ, Jorgensen JH, et al, eds. Manual of Clinical Microbiology. 8th ed. Washington, DC: American Society for Microbiology Press; 2003:749-779.

136. Holmes B, Moss CW, Daneshvar MI. Cellular fatty acid compositions of "*Achromobacter* groups B and E." J Clin Microbiol. 1993;31:1007-1008.

137. Jenks PJ, Shaw EJ. Recurrent septicaemia due to "*Achromobacter* group B." J Infect. 1997;34:143-145.

138. Holmes B, Lewis R, Trevett A. Septicaemia due to *Achromobacter* group B: A report of two cases. Med Microbiol Lett. 1992;1:177-184.

139. McKinley KP, Laundy TJ, Masterton RG. *Achromobacter* group B replacement valve endocarditis. J Infect. 1990;20:262-263.

140. Mandell WF, Garvey GJ, Neu HC. *Achromobacter xylosoxidans* bacteremia. Rev Infect Dis. 1987;9:1001-1005.

141. Cieslak TJ, Robb ML, Drabick CJ, et al. Catheter-associated sepsis caused by *Ochrobactrum anthropi:* Report of a case and review of related nonfermentative bacteria. Clin Infect Dis. 1992;14:902-907.

142. Cieslak TJ, Raszka WV. Catheter-associated sepsis due to *Alcaligenes xylosoxidans* in a child with AIDS. Clin Infect Dis. 1993;16:592-593.

143. Schoch PE, Cunha BA. Nosocomial *Achromobacter xylosoxidans* infections. Infect Contr Hosp Epidemiol. 1988;9:84-87.

144. Spear JB, Fuhrer J, Kirby BD. *Achromobacter xylosoxidans* (*Alcaligenes xylosoxidans* subsp *xylosoxidans*) bacteremia associated with a well-water source: Case report and review of the literature. J Clin Microbiol. 1988;26:598-599.

145. Duggan JM, Goldstein SJ, Chenoweth CE, et al. *Achromobacter xylosoxidans* bacteremia: Report of four cases and review of the literature. Clin Infect Dis. 1996;23:569-576.

146. Gomez-Cerezo J, Suarez I, Rios JJ, et al. *Achromobacter xylosoxidans* bacteremia: A 10-year analysis of 54 cases. Eur J Clin Microbiol Infect Dis. 2003;22:360-363.

147. Walsh RD, Klein NC, Cunha BA. *Achromobacter xylosoxidans* osteomyelitis. Clin Infect Dis. 1993;16:176-178.

148. Taylor P, Fischbein L. Prosthetic knee infection due to *Achromobacter xylosoxidans*. J Rheumatol. 1992;19:992-993.

149. Tang S, Cheng CC, Tse KC, et al. CAPD-associated peritonitis caused by *Alcaligenes xylosoxidans* sp. *xylosoxidans*. Am J Nephrol. 2001;21:502-506.

150. Castellote J, Tremosa G, Ben SL, Vazquez S. Spontaneous bacterial peritonitis due to *Alcaligenes xylosoxidans*. Am J Gastroenterol. 2001;96:1650-1651.

151. Legrand C, Anaissie E. Bacteremia due to *Achromobacter xylosoxidans* in patients with cancer. Clin Infect Dis. 1992;14:479-484.

152. Manfredi R, Nanetti A, Ferri M, et al. Bacteremia and respiratory involvement by *Alcaligenes xylosoxidans* in patients infected with the human immunodeficiency virus. Eur J Clin Microbiol Infect Dis. 1997;16:933-938.

153. Tan K, Conway SP, Brownlee KG, et al. *Alcaligenes* infection in cystic fibrosis. Pediatr Pulmonol. 2002;34:101-104.

154. Dunne WM Jr, Maisch S. Epidemiological investigation of infections due to *Alcaligenes* species in children and patients with cystic fibrosis: Use of repetitive-element-sequence polymerase chain reaction. Clin Infect Dis. 1995;20:836-841.

155. Hearn YR, Gander RM. *Achromobacter xylosoxidans*. An unusual neonatal pathogen. Am J Clin Pathol. 1991;96:211-214.

156. Mensah K, Philippon A, Richard C, et al. Susceptibility of *Alcaligenes denitrificans* subspecies *xylosoxydans* to beta-lactam antibiotics. Eur J Clin Microbiol Infect Dis. 1990;9:405-409.

157. Cormican MG, Jones RN. Antimicrobial activity of cefotaxime tested against infrequently isolated pathogenic species (unusual pathogens). Diagn Microbiol Infect Dis. 1995;22:43-48.

158. Saiman L, Chen Y, Tabibi S, et al. Identification and antimicrobial susceptibility of *Alcaligenes xylosoxidans* isolated from patients with cystic fibrosis. J Clin Microbiol. 2001;39:3942-3945.

159. Decre D, Arlet G, Danglot C, et al. A beta-lactamase-overproducing strain of *Alcaligenes denitrificans* subsp *xylosoxidans* isolated from a case of meningitis. J Antimicrob Chemother. 1992;30:769-779.

160. Tayeri T, Kelly LD. *Alcaligenes faecalis* corneal ulcer in a patient with cicatricial pemphigoid. Am J Ophthalmol. 1993;115:255-256.

161. Bizet J, Bizet C. Strains of *Alcaligenes faecalis* from clinical material. J Infect. 1997;35:167-169.

162. Peel MM, Hibberd AJ, King BM, et al. *Alcaligenes piechaudii* from chronic ear discharge. J Clin Microbiol. 1988;26:1580-1581.

163. Kay SE, Clark RA, White KL, Peel MM. Recurrent *Achromobacter piechaudii* bacteremia in a patient with hematological malignancy. J Clin Microbiol. 2001;39:808-810.

164. Pickett MJ, Greenwood JR. Identification of oxidase-positive, glucose-negative motile species of nonfermentative bacilli. J Clin Microbiol. 1986;23:920-923.

165. Bizet C, Tekaia F, Philippon A. In-vitro susceptibility of *Alcaligenes faecalis* compared with those of other *Alcaligenes* spp to antimicrobial agents including seven beta-lactams. J Antimicrob Chemother. 1993;32:907-910.

166. Pereira M, Perilli M, Mantengoli E, et al. PER-1 extended-spectrum beta-lactamase production in an *Alcaligenes faecalis* clinical isolate resistant to expanded-spectrum cephalosporins and monobactams from a hospital in Northern Italy. Microb Drug Resist. 2000;6:85-90.

167. Bloch KC, Nadarajah R, Jacobs R. *Chryseobacterium meningosepticum:* An emerging pathogen among immunocompromised adults. Report of 6 cases and literature review. Medicine. 1997;76:30-41.

168. Hoque SN, Graham J, Kaufmann ME, Tabaqchali S. *Chryseobacterium (Flavobacterium) meningosepticum* outbreak associated with colonization of water taps in a neonatal intensive care unit. J Hosp Infect. 2001;47:188-192.

169. Pokrywka M, Viazanko K, Medvick J, et al. A *Flavobacterium meningosepticum* outbreak among intensive care patients. Am J Infect Control. 1993;21:139-145.

170. Brown RB, Phillips D, Barker MJ, et al. Outbreak of nosocomial *Flavobacterium meningosepticum* respiratory infections associated with use of aerosolized polymixin B. Am J Infect Control. 1989;17:121-125.

171. Olsen H, Frederiksen WC, Siboni KE. *Flavobacterium meningosepticum*. Lancet. 1965;1:1294-1296.

172. Sheridan RL, Ryan CM, Pasternack MS, et al. Flavobacterial sepsis in massively burned pediatric patients. Clin Infect Dis. 1993;17:185-187.

173. Hoque SN, Graham J, Kaufmann ME, et al. *Chryseobacterium (Flavobacterium) meningosepticum* outbreak associated with colonization of water taps in a neonatal intensive care unit. J Hosp Infect. 2001;47:188-192.

174. Coyle-Gilchrist MM, Crewe P, Roberts G. *Flavobacterium meningosepticum* in the hospital environment. J Clin Pathol. 1976;29:824-826.

175. Bolivar R, Abramovits W. Cutaneous infection caused by *Flavobacterium meningosepticum*. J Infect Dis. 1989;159:150-151.

176. Sundin D, Gold BD, Berkowitz FE, et al. Community-acquired *Flavobacterium meningosepticum* meningitis, pneumonia, and septicemia in a normal infant. Pediatr Infect Dis J. 1991;10:73-76.

177. Ashdown LR, Previtera S. Community acquired *Flavobacterium meningosepticum* pneumonia and septicaemia. Med J Aust. 1992;156:69-70.

178. Bloom AH, Perry HD, Donnenfeld ED, Davis RG. *Chryseobacterium meningosepticum* keratitis. Am J Ophthalmol. 2003;136:356-357.

179. Gunnarsson G, Baldursson H, Hilmarsdottir I. Septic arthritis caused by *Chryseobacterium meningosepticum* in an immunocompetent male. Scand J Infect Dis. 2002;34:299-300.

180. Hsueh PR, Teng U, Ho SW, et al. Clinical and microbiological characteristics of *Flavobacterium indologenes* infections associated with indwelling devices. J Clin Microbiol. 1996;34:1908-1913.

181. Von Graevenitz A. *Acinetobacter, Alcaligenes, Moraxella,* and other nonfermentative gram-negative bacteria. In: Murray PR, Baron EJ, Pfaller MA, et al, eds. Manual of Clinical Microbiology. 6th ed. Washington, DC: American Society for Microbiology Press; 1995:520-532.

182. Fraser SL, Jorgensen JH. Reappraisal of the antimicrobial susceptibilities of *Chryseobacterium* and *Flavobacterium* species and methods for reliable susceptibility testing. Antimicrob Agents Chemother. 1997;41:2738-2741.

183. Hsueh PR, Chang JC, Teng LJ, et al. Comparison of Etest and agar dilution method for antimicrobial susceptibility testing of *Flavobacterium* isolates. J Clin Microbiol. 1997;35:1021-1023.

184. Hsueh PR, Teng LJ, Yang PC, et al. Susceptibilities of *Chryseobacterium indologenes* and *Chryseobacterium meningosepticum* to cefepime and cefpirome. J Clin Microbiol. 1997;35:3323-3324.

185. Visalli MA, Bajaksouzian S, Jacobs MR, et al. Comparative activity of trovafloxacin, alone and in combination with other agents, against gram-negative nonfermentative rods. Antimicrob Agents Chemother. 1997;41:1475-1481.

186. Hirsh BE, Wong B, Kiehn TE, et al. *Flavobacterium meningosepticum* bacteremia in an adult with acute leukemia. Use of rifampin to clear persistent infection. Diagn Microbiol Infect Dis. 1986;4:65-69.

187. Ratner H. *Flavobacterium meningosepticum.* Infect Control. 1984;5:237-239.
188. Di Pentima MC, Mason EO Jr, Kaplan SL. In vitro antibiotic synergy against *Flavobacterium meningosepticum:* Implications for therapeutic options. Clin Infect Dis. 1998;26:1169-1176.
189. Hawley HB, Gump DW. Vancomycin therapy of bacterial meningitis. Am J Dis Child. 1973;126:261-264.
190. Patrick WD, Brown WD, Bowmer MI, et al. Infective endocarditis due to *Eikenella corrodens:* Case report and review of the literature. Can J Infect Dis. 1990;1:139-142.
191. Suwanagool S, Rothkopf MM, Smith SM, et al. Pathogenicity of *Eikenella corrodens* in humans. Arch Intern Med. 1983;143:2265-2268.
192. Joshi N, O'Bryan T, Appelbaum PC. Pleuropulmonary infections caused by *Eikenella corrodens.* Rev Infect Dis. 1991;13:1207-1212.
193. Paul K, Patel SS. *Eikenella corrodens* infections in children and adolescents: Case reports and review of the literature. Clin Infect Dis. 2001;33:54-61.
194. Brooks GF, O'Donoghue JM, Rissing JP. *Eikenella corrodens:* A recently recognized pathogen: Infections in medical-surgical patients and in association with methylphenidate abuse. Medicine. 1974;53:325-342.
195. Tveteras K, Kristensten S, Bach V, et al. *Eikenella corrodens:* A recently recognized pathogen in head and neck infections. J Laryngol Otol. 1987;101:592-594.
196. Sheng WS, Hsueh PR, Hung CC, et al. Clinical features of patients with invasive *Eikenella corrodens* infections and microbiological characteristics of the causative isolates. Eur J Clin Microbiol Infect Dis. 2001;20:231-236.
197. Goldstein EJC. Bite wounds and infections. Clin Infect Dis. 1992;14:633-640.
198. Sagerman SD, Lourie GM. *Eikenella* osteomyelitis in a chronic nail biter: A case report. Hand Surg Am. 1995;20:71-72.
199. Rosen T, Conrad N. Genital ulcer caused by human bite to the penis. Sex Transm Dis. 1999;26:527-530.
200. Swisher LA, Roberts JR, Glynn MJ. Needle licker's osteomyelitis. Am J Emerg Med. 1994;12:343-346.
201. Pollner JH, Khan A, Tuazon CU. Severe soft-tissue infection caused by *Eikenella corrodens.* Clin Infect Dis. 1992;15:740-741.
202. Raab MG, Lutz RA, Stauffer ES. *Eikenella corrodens* vertebral osteomyelitis. A case report and literature review. Clin Orthop. 1993:144-147.
203. Jeppson KG, Reimer LG. *Eikenella corrodens* chorioamnionitis. Obstet Gynecol. 1991;78:503-505.
204. Drouet E, De Montclos H, Boude M, et al. *Eikenella corrodens* and intrauterine contraceptive device. Lancet. 1987;2:1089.
205. Stein A, Teysseire N, Capobianco C, et al. *Eikenella corrodens,* a rare cause of pancreatic abscess: Two case reports and review. Clin Infect Dis. 1993;17:273-275.
206. Decker MD, Graham BS, Hunter EB, et al. Endocarditis and infections of intravascular devices due to *Eikenella corrodens.* Am J Med Sci. 1986;292:209-212.
207. Watkin RW, Baker N, Lang S, et al. *Eikenella corrodens* infective endocarditis in a previously healthy non-drug user. Eur J Clin Morcobiol Infect Dis. 2002;21:890-891.
208. Chen C-K, Wilson ME. Outer membrane protein and lipopolysaccharide heterogeneity among *Eikenella corrodens* isolates. J Infect Dis. 1990;162:664-671.
209. Sofianou D, Kolokotronis A. Susceptibility of *Eikenella corrodens* to antimicrobial agents. J Chemother. 1990;2:156-158.
210. Goldstein EJ, Citron DM, Merriam CV, et al. In vitro activities of a new des-fluoroquinolone, BMS 284756, and seven other antimicrobial agents against 151 isolates of *Eikenella corrodens.* Antimicrob Agents Chemother. 2002;46:1141-1143.
211. Vandamme P, Bernardet J-F, Segers P, et al. New perspectives in the classification of the flavobacteria: Description of *Chryseobacterium* gen nov, *Bergeyella* gen nov and *Empedobacter* nom rev. Int J Syst Bacteriol. 1994;44:827-831.
212. Vancanneyt M, Segers P, Torck U, et al. Reclassification of *Flavobacterium odoratum* (Stutzer 1929) strains to a new genus, *Myroides,* as *Myroides odoratus* comb. Nov. and *Myroides odoratimimus* sp. Nov. Int J Syst Bacteriol. 1996;46:926-932.
213. Hsueh PR, Wu JJ, Hsiue TR, et al. Bacteremic necrotizing fasciitis due to *Flavobacterium odoratum.* Clin Infect Dis. 1995;21:1337-1338.
214. Green BT, Green K, Nolan PE. *Myroides odoratus* cellulitis and bacteremia: Case report and review. Scand J Infect Dis. 2001;33:932-934.
215. Bachman KH, Sewell DL, Strausbaugh JL. Recurrent cellulitis and bacteremia caused by *Flavobacterium odoratum.* J Clin Microbiol. 1996;22:1112-1113.
216. Velasco J, Romero C, Lopez-Goni I, et al. Evolution of the relatedness of *Brucella* spp. and *Ochrobactrum anthropi* and description of *Ochrobactrum intermedium sp.* Nov., a new species with a closer relationship to *Brucella* spp. Int J Syst Bacteriol. 1998;48:759-768.
217. Kern WV, Oethinger M, Kaufhold A, et al. *Ochrobactrum anthropi* bacteremia: Report of four cases and short review. Infection. 1993;21:306-310.
218. Cieslak TJ, Drabick CJ, Robb ML. Pyogenic infections due to *Ochrobactrum anthropi.* Clin Infect Dis. 1996;22:845-847.
219. Galanakis E, Bitsori M, Samonis G, et al. *Ochrobactrum anthropi* bacteraemia in immunocompetent children. Scand J Infect Dis. 2002;34:800-803.
220. Gransden WR, Eykyn SJ. Seven cases of bacteremia due to *Ochrobactrum anthropi.* Clin Infect Dis. 1992;15:1068-1069.
221. Stiakaki E, Galanakis E, Samonis G, et al. *Ochrobactrum anthropi* bacteremia in pediatric oncology patients. Pediatr Infect Dis J. 2002;21:72-74.
222. Ezzedine H, Mourad M, Van Ossel C, et al. An outbreak of *Ochrobactrum anthropi* bacteraemia in five organ transplant patients. J Hosp Infect. 1994;27:35-42.
223. Chang HJ, Christenson JC, Pavia AT, et al. *Ochrobactrum anthropi* meningitis in pediatric pericardial allograft transplant recipients. J Infect Dis. 1996;173:656-660.
224. Deliere E, Vu-Thien H, Levy V, et al. Epidemiological investigation of *Ochrobactrum anthropi* strains isolated from a haematology unit. J Hosp Infect. 2000;44:173-178.
225. Daxboeck F, Zitta S, Assadian O, et al. *Ochrobactrum anthropi* bloodstream infection complicating hemodialysis. Am J Kid Dis. 2002;40:E17.
226. Manfredi R, Nanetti A, Ferri M, et al. *Ochrobactrum anthropi* as an agent of nosocomial septicemia in the setting of AIDS. Clin Infect Dis. 1999;28:692-694.
227. Esteban J, Ortiz A, Rollan E, et al. Peritonitis due to *Ochrobactrum anthropi* in a patient undergoing continuous ambulatory peritoneal dialysis. J Infect. 2000;40:205-206.
228. Berman AJ, Del Priore LV, Fischer CK. Endogenous *Ochrobactrum anthropi* endophthalmitis. Am J Ophthalmol. 1997;123:560-562.
229. Barson WJ, Cromer BA, Marcon MJ. Puncture wound osteochondritis of the foot caused by CDC group Vd. J Clin Microbiol. 1987;25:2014-2016.
230. Brivet F, Guibert M, Kiredjian M, et al. Necrotizing fasciitis, bacteremia, and multiorgan failure caused by *Ochrobactrum anthropi.* Clin Infect Dis. 1993;17:516-518.
231. Earhart KC, Boyce K, Bone WD, et al. *Ochrobactrum anthropi* infection of retained pacemaker leads. Clin Infect Dis. 1997;24:281-282.
232. Alnor D, Frimodt-Moller N, Espersen F, et al. Infections with the unusual human pathogens *Agrobacterium* species and *Ochrobactrum anthropi.* Clin Infect Dis. 1994;18:914-920.
233. Elsaghir AA, James EA. Misidentification of *Brucella melitensis* as *Ochrobactrum anthropi* by API 20NE. J Med Microbiol. 2003;52(Pt 5):441-442.
234. Higgins CS, Avison MB, Jamieson L, et al. Characterization, cloning and sequence analysis of the inducible *Ochrobactrum anthropi* AmpC beta-lactamase. J Antimicrob Chemother. 2001;47:745-754.
235. Mesnard R, Sire JM, Donnio PY, et al. Septic arthritis due to *Oligella urethralis.* Eur J Clin Microbiol Infect Dis. 1992;11:195-196.
236. Riley UBG, Bignardi G, Goldberg L, et al. Quinolone resistance in *Oligella urethralis*-associated chronic ambulatory peritoneal dialysis. J Infect. 1996;32:155-156.
237. Rockhill RC, Lutwick LI. Group IVe-like gram-negative bacillemia in a patient with obstructive uropathy. J Clin Microbiol. 1978;8:108-109.
238. Manian FA. Bloodstream infection with *Oligella ureolytica, Candida krusei,* and *Bacteroides* species in a patient with AIDS. Clin Infect Dis. 1993;17:290-291.
239. Mammeri H, Poirel L, Mangeney N, et al. Chromosomal integration of a cephalosporinase gene from *Acinetobacter baumannii* into *Oligella urethralis* as a source of acquired resistance to beta-lactams. Antimicrob Agents Chemother. 2003;47:1536-1542.
240. Anzai Y, Kudo Y, Oyaizu H. The phylogeny of the genera *Chryseomonas, Flavimonas,* and *Pseudomonas* supports synonymy of these three genera. Int J Syst Bacteriol. 1997;47:249-251.
241. Hsueh PR, Teng LJ, Pan HJ, et al. Outbreak of *Pseudomonas fluorescens* bacteremia among oncology patients. J Clin Microbiol. 1998;36:2914-2917.
242. Namnyak S, Hussain S, Davalle J, et al. Contaminated lithium heparin bottles as a source of pseudobacteraemia due to *Pseudomonas fluorescens.* J Hosp Infect. 1999;4:23-28.
243. Scott JF, Boulton E, Govan JRW, et al. A fatal transfusion reaction associated with blood contaminated with *Pseudomonas fluorescens.* Vox Sang. 1988;54:201-204.
244. Anaissie E, Fainstein V, Miller P, et al. *Pseudomonas putrida:* neuwly recognized pathogen in patients with cancer. Am J Med. 1987;82:1191-1194.
245. Yang CH, Young T, Peng MY, et al. Clinical spectrum of *Pseudomonas putida* infection. J Formos Med Assoc. 1996;95:754-761.
246. Ladhani S, Bhutta ZA. Neonatal *Pseudomonas putida* infection presenting as staphylococcal scalded skin syndrome. Eur J Clin Microbiol Infect Dis. 1998;17:642-644.
247. Romney M, Sherlock C, Stephens G, Clarke A. Pseudo-outbreak of *Pseudomonas putida* in a hospital outpatient clinic originating from a contaminated commercial anti-fog solution—Vancouver, British Columbia. Can Commun Dis Rep. 2000;26:183-184.
248. Roig P, Orti A, Navarro V. Meningitis due to *Pseudomonas stutzeri* in a patient infected with human immunodeficiency virus. Clin Infect Dis. 1996;22:587-588.
249. Reisler RB, Blumberg HB. Community-acquired *Pseudomonas stutzeri* vertebral osteomyelitis in a previously health patient: Case report and review. Clin Infect Dis. 1999;29:667-669.
250. Campos-Herrero MI, Bordes A, Rodriguez H, et al. *Pseudomonas stutzeri* community-acquired pneumonia associated with empyema: Case report and review. Clin Infect Dis. 1997;25:325-326.
251. Chaudhry HJ, Schoch PE, Cunha BA. *Flavimonas oryzihabitans* (CD Group Ve-2). Infect Control Hosp Epidemiol. 1992;13:485-488.
252. Lucas KG, Kiehn TE, Sobeck KA, et al. Sepsis caused by *Flavimonas oryzihabitans.* Medicine. 1994;73:209-214.
253. Lin RD, Hsueh PR, Chang JC, et al. *Flavimonas oryzihabitans* bacteremia: Clinical features and microbiological characteristics of isolates. Clin Infect Dis. 1997;24:867-873.
254. Rahav G, Simhon A, Mattan Y, et al. Infections with *Chryseomonas luteola* (CDC group Ve-1) and *Flavimonas oryzihabitans* (CDC group Ve-2). Medicine. 1995;74:83-88.
255. Hawkins RE, Moriarty RA, Lewis DE, et al. Serious infections involving the CDC group Ve bacteria *Chryseomonas luteola* and *Flavimonas oryzihabitans.* Rev Infect Dis. 1991;13:257-260.
256. Yu EN, Foster CS. Chronic postoperative endophthalmitis due to *Pseudomonas oryzihabitans.* Am J Ophthalmol. 2002;134:613-614.
257. Kostman JR, Solomon F, Fekete T. Infections with *Chryseomonas luteola* (CDC group Ve-1) and *flavimonas oryzihabitans* (CDC group Ve-2) in neurosurgical patients. Rev Infect Dis. 1991;13:233-236.
258. Lam S, Isenberg HD, Edwards B, et al. Community-acquired soft-tissue infections caused by *Flavimonas oryzihabitans.* Clin Infect Dis. 1994;18:808-809.
259. Tsakris A, Hassapopoulou H, Skoura L, et al. Leg ulcer due to *Pseudomonas luteola* in a patient with sickle cell disease. Diagn Microbiol Infect Dis. 2002;42:141-143.
260. Rastogi S, Sperber SJ. Facial cellulitis and *Pseudomonas luteola* bacteremia in an otherwise healthy patient. Diagn Microbiol Infect Dis. 1998;32:303-305.
261. Docquier JD, Riccio ML, Mugnaioli C, et al. IMP-12, a new plasmid-encoded metallo-beta-lactamase from a *Pseudomonas putida* clinical isolate. Antimicrob Agents Chemother. 2003;47:1522-1528.

262. Rolston KV, Ho DH, LeBlanc B, et al. In vitro activities of antimicrobial agents against clinical isolates of *Flavimonas oryzihabitans* obtained from patients with cancer. Antimicrob Agents Chemother. 1993;37:2504-2505.

263. Yabuuchi E, Kosako Y, Yano I, et al. Transfer of two *Burkholderia* and an *Alcaligenes* species to *Ralstonia* gen. Nov.: Proposal of *Ralstonia pickettii* (Ralston, Palleroni and Doudoroff 1973) comb. Nov., *Ralstonia solanacearum* (Smith 1896) comb. Nov. and *Ralstonia eutropha* (Davis 1969) comb. Nov. Microbiol Immunol. 1995;39:897-904.

264. Anderson RR, Warnick P, Schreckenberger PC. Recurrent CDC group IVc-2 bacteremia in a human with AIDS. J Clin Microbiol. 1997;35:780-782.

265. Thayu M, Baltimore RS, Sleight BJ, et al. CDC group IV c-2 bacteremia in a child with recurrent acute monoblastic leukemia. Pediatr Infect Dis J. 1999;18:397-398.

266. Vandamme P, Goris J, Coenye T, et al. Assignment of Centers for Disease Control group IVc-2 to the genus *Ralstonia* as *Ralstonia paucula* sp. nov. Int J Syst Bacteriol. 1999;49 Pt 2:663-669.

267. Osterhout GJ, Valentine JL, Dick JD. Phenotypic and genotypic characterization of clinical strains of CDC group IVc-2. J Clin Microbiol. 1998;36:2618-2622.

268. Maki DG, Klein BS, McCormick RD, et al. Nosocomial *Pseudomonas pickettii* bacteremias traced to narcotic tampering. A case for selective drug screening of health care personnel. JAMA. 1991;265:981-986.

269. Labarca JA, Trick WE, Peterson CL, et al. A multistate nosocomial outbreak of *Ralstonia pickettii* colonization associated with an intrinsically contaminated respiratory care solution. Clin Infect Dis. 1999;29:1281-1286.

270. Moissenet D, Tabone M-D, Girardet J-P, et al. Nosocomial CDC Group IVc-2 bacteremia: Epidemiological investigation by randomly amplified polymorphic DNA analysis. J Clin Microbiol. 1996;34:1264-1266.

271. Zapardiel J, Blum G, Caramelo C, et al. Peritonitis with CDC group IVc-2 bacteria in a patient on continuous ambulatory peritoneal dialysis. Eur J Clin Microbiol Infect Dis. 1991;10:509-511.

272. Musso D, Drancourt M, Bardot J, et al. Human infection due to the CDC Group IVc-2 bacterium: Case report and review. Clin Infect Dis. 1994;18:482-484.

273. Young JM, Kuykendall LD, Martinez-Romero E, et al. A revision of *Rhizobium* Frank 1889, with an emended description of the genus, and the inclusion of all species of *Agrobacterium* Conn 1942 and *Allorhizobium undicola* de Lajudie et al. 1998 as new combinations: *Rhizobium radiobacter, R. rhizogenes, R. rubi, R. undicola* and *R. vitis.* Int J Syst Evol Bacteriol. 2001;51:89-103.

274. Edmond MB, Riddler SA, Baxter CM, et al. *Agrobacterium radiobacter:* A recently recognized opportunistic pathogen. Clin Infect Dis. 1993;16:388-391.

275. Amaya RA, Edwards MS. *Agrobacterium radiobacter* bacteremia in pediatric patients: Case report and review. Pediatr Infect Dis J. 2003;22:183-186.

276. Hulse M, Johnson S, Ferrieri P. *Agrobacterium* infections in humans: Experience at one hospital and review. Clin Infect Dis. 1993;16:112-117.

277. Mastroianni A, Coronado O, Nanetti A, et al. *Agrobacterium radiobacter* pneumonia in a patient with HIV infection. Eur J Clin Microbiol Infect Dis. 1996;15:960-963.

278. Manfredi R, Nanetti A, Ferri M, et al. Emerging gram-negative pathogens in the immunocompromised host: *Agrobacterium radiobacter* septicemia durig HIV disease. New Microbiol. 1999;22:375-382.

279. Miller JM, Novy C, Hiott M. Case of bactcrial cndophthalmitis caused by an *Agrobacterium radiobacter*-like organism. J Clin Microbiol. 1996;34:3212-3213.

280. Rogues AM, Sarlangue J, de Barbeyrac B, et al. *Agrobacterium radiobacter* as a cause of pseudobacteremia. Infect Control Hosp Epidemiol. 1999;20:345-347.

281. Sykes RB, Cimarusti CM, Bonner DP, et al. Monocyclic β-lactam antibiotics produced by bacteria. Nature. 1981;291:489-491.

282. Rihs JD, Brenner DJ, Weaver RE, et al. *Roseomonas,* a new genus associated with bacteremia and human infections. J Clin Microbiol. 1993;31:3275-3283.

283. Struthers M, Wong J, Janda JM. An initial appraisal of the clinical significance of *Roseomonas* species associated with human infections. Clin Infect Dis. 1996;23:729-733.

284. Kaye KM, Macone A, Kazanjian PH. Catheter infection caused by *Methylobacterium* in immunocompromised hosts: Report of three cases and review of the literature. Clin Infect Dis. 1992;14:1010-1014.

285. Marin ME, Marco Del Pont J, Dibar E, et al. Catheter-related bacteremia caused by *Roseomonas gilardii* in an immunocompromised patient. Int J Infect Dis. 2001;5:170-171.

286. Lewis L, Stock F, Williams D, et al. Infections with *Roseomonas gilardii* and review of characteristics used for biochemical identification and molecular typing. Am J Clin Pathol. 1997;108:210-216.

287. Richardson JD. Failure to clear a *Roseomonas* line infection with antibiotic therapy. Clin Infect Dis. 1997;25:155.

288. Shokar NK, Shokar GS, Islam J, et al. *Roseomonas gilardii* infection: Case report and review. J Clin Microbiol. 2002;40:4789-791.

289. Nahass RG, Wisneski R, Herman DJ, et al. Vertebral osteomyelitis due to *Roseomonas* species: Case report and review of the evaluation of vertebral osteomyelitis. Clin Infect Dis. 1995;21:1474-1476.

290. Bibashi E, Sofianou D, Kontopoulou K, et al. Peritonitis due to *Roseomonas fauriae* in a patient undergoing continuous ambulatory peritoneal dialysis. J Clin Microbiol. 2000;38:456-457.

291. Hornei B, Luneberg E, Schmidt-Rotte H, et al. Systemic infection of an immunocompromised patient with *Methylobacterium zatmanii.* J Clin Microbiol. 1999;37:248-250.

292. Flournoy DJ, Petrone RL, Voth DW. A pseudo-outbreak of *Methylobacterium mesophilica* isolated from patients undergoing bronchoscopy. Eur J Clin Microbiol Infect Dis. 1992;11:240-243.

293. Nozue H, Hayashi T, Hashimoto Y, et al. Isolation and characterization of *Shewanella alga* from human clinical specimens and emendation of the description of *S. alga.* Int J Syst Bacteriol. 1992;42:628-634.

294. Khashe S, Janda JM. Biochemical and pathogenic properties of *Shewanella alga* and *Shewanella putrefaciens.* J Clin Microbiol. 1998;36:783-787.

295. Chen YS, Liu YC, Yen MY, et al. Skin and soft-tissue manifestations of *Shewanella putrefaciens* infection. Clin Infect Dis. 1997;25:225-229.

296. Brink AJ, van Straten A, van Rensburg AJ. *Shewanella (Pseudomonas) putrefaciens* bacteremia. Clin Infect Dis. 1995;20:1327-1332.

297. Paccalin M, Grollier G, le Moal G, et al. Rupture of a primary aortic aneurysm infected with *Shewanella alga.* Scand J Infect Dis. 2001;33:774-775.

298. Butt AA, Figueroa J, Martin DH. Ocular infection caused by three unusual marine organisms. Clin Infect Dis. 1997;24:740.

299. Dees SB, Moss CW, Hollis DG, et al. Chemical characterization of *Flavobacterium odoratum, Flavobacterium breve,* and *Flavobacterium*-like groups IIe, IIh, and IIf. J Clin Microbiol. 1986;23:267-273.

300. Potvliege C, Dejaegher-Bauduin C, Hansen W, et al. *Flavobacterium multivorum* septicemia in a hemodialysis patient. J Clin Microbiol. 1984;19:568-569.

301. Freney J, Hansen W, Ploton C, et al. Septicemia caused by *Sphingobacterium multivorum.* J Clin Microbiol. 1987;25:1126-1128.

302. Reina J, Borrell N, Figuerola J. *Sphingobacterium multivorum* isolated from a patient with cystic fibrosis. Eur J Clin Microbiol Infect Dis. 1992;11:81-82.

303. Areekul S, Vongsthongsri U, Mookto T, et al. *Sphingobacterium multivorum* septicemia: A case report. J Med Assoc Thai. 1996;79:395-398.

304. Holmes B, Owen RJ, Hollis DG. *Flavobacterium spiritivorum,* a new species isolated from human clinical specimens. Int J Syst Bacteriol. 1982;32:157-165.

305. Marinella MA. Cellulitis and sepsis due to *Sphingobacterium.* JAMA. 2002;288:1985.

306. Fass RJ, Barnishan J. In vitro susceptibilities of nonfermentative gram-negative bacilli other than *Pseudomonas aeruginosa* to 32 antimicrobial agents. Rev Infect Dis. 1980;2:841-853.

307. Blahova J, Kralikova K, Krcmery V Sr, et al. Hydrolysis of imipenem, meropenem, ceftazidime, and cefepime by multiresistant nosocomial strains of *Sphingobacterium multivorum.* Eur J Clin Microbiol Infect Dis. 1997;16:178-180.

308. Yabuuchi E, Yano I, Oyaizu H, et al. Proposals of *Sphingomonas paucimobilis* gen nov and comb nov, *Sphingomonas parapaucimobilis* sp nov, *Sphingomonas yanoikuyae* sp nov, *Sphingomonas adhaesiva* sp nov, *Sphingomonas capsulata* comb nov, and two genospecies of the genus *Sphingomonas.* Microbiol Immunol. 1990;34:99-119.

309. Crane LR, Tagle LC, Palutke WA. Outbreak of *Pseudomonas paucimobilis* in an intensive care facility. JAMA. 1981;246:985-987.

310. Perola O, Nousiainen T, Suomalainen S, et al. Recurrent *Sphingomonas paucimobilis*-bacteraemia associated with a multi-bacterial water-borne epidemic among neutropenic patients. J Hosp Infect. 2002;50:196-201.

311. Lemaitre D, Elaichouni A, Hundhausen M, et al. Tracheal colonization with *Sphingomonas paucimobilis* in mechanically ventilated neonates due to contaminated ventilator temperature probes. J Hosp Infect. 1996;32:199-206.

312. Salazar R, Martino R, Sureda A, et al. Catheter-related bacteremia due to *Pseudomonas paucimobilis* in neutropenic cancer patients: Report of two cases. Clin Infect Dis. 1995;20:1573-1574.

313. Hsueh PR, Teng LJ, Yang PC, et al. Nosocomial infections caused by *Sphingomonas paucimobilis:* Clinical features and microbiological characteristics. Clin Infect Dis. 1998;26:676-681.

314. Lazarus HM, Magalhaes-Silverman M, Fox RM, et al. Contamination during *in vitro* procession of bone marrow for transplantation: Clinical significance. Bone Marrow Transplant. 1991;7:241-246.

315. Boken DJ, Romero JR, Cavalieri SJ. *Sphingomonas paucimobilis* bacteremia: Four cases and review of the literature. Infect Dis Clin Pract. 1988;7:286-291.

316. Reina J, Bassa A, Llompart I, et al. Infections with *Pseudomonas paucimobilis:* Report of four cases and review. Rev Infect Dis. 1991;13:1072-1076.

317. Holmes B, Owen RJ, Evans A, et al. *Pseudomonas paucimobilis,* a new species isolated from human clinical specimens, the hospital environment and other sources. Int J Syst Bacteriol. 1977;27:133-146.

318. Holmes B, Steigerwalt AG, Weaver RE, et al. *Weeksella zoohelcum* sp nov (formerly group IIj), from human clinical specimens. Syst Appl Microbiol. 1986;8:191-196.

319. Reina J, Borrell N. Leg abscess caused by *Weeksella zoohelcum* following a dog bite. Clin Infect Dis. 1992;14:1162-1163.

320. Bracis R, Seibers K, Julien RM. Meningitis caused by Group IIj following a dog bite. West J Med. 1979;131:438-440.

321. Montejo M, Aguirrebengoa K, Ugalde J, et al. *Bergeyella zoohelcum* bacteremia after a dog bite. Clin Infect Dis. 2001;33:1608-1609.

322. Holmes B, Steigerwalt AG, Weaver RE, et al. *Weeksella virosa* gen nov sp nov (formerly group IIf), found in human clinical specimens. Syst Appl Microbiol. 1986;8:185-190.

323. Reina J, Gil J, Alomar P. Isolation of *Weeksella virosa* (formerly CDC group IIf) from a vaginal sample. Eur J Clin Microbiol Infect Dis. 1989;8:569-570.

324. Faber MD, delBusto R, Cruz C, et al. Response of *Weeksella virosa* peritonitis to imipenem/cilasatain. Adv Perit Dial. 1991;7:133-134.

325. Boixeda D, de Luis DA, Meseguer MA, et al. A case of spontaneous peritonitis caused by *Weeksella virosa.* Eur J Gastroenterol Hepatol. 1998;10:897-898.

326. Hollis DG, Moss CW, Daneshvar MI, et al. Characterization of Centers for Disease Control Group NO-1, a fastidious, nonoxidative, gram-negative organism associated with dog and cat bites. J Clin Microbiol. 1993;31:746-748.

327. Kaiser RM, Garman RL, Bruce MG, et al. Clinical significance and epidemiology of NO-1, an unusual bacterium associated with dog and cat bites. Emerg Infect Dis. 2002;8:171-174.

328. Hollis DG, Weaver RE, Moss CW, et al. Chemical and cultural characterization of CDC group WO-1, a weakly oxidative gram-negative group of organisms isolated from clinical sources. J Clin Microbiol. 1992;30:291-295.

329. Coenye T, Liu L, Vandamme P, et al. Identification of *Pandoraea* species by 16S ribosomal DNA-based PCR assays. J. Clin Microbiol. 2001;39:4452-4455.

330. Daneshvar MI, Hollis DG, Steigerwalt AG, et al. Assignment of CDC weak oxidizer group 2 (WO-2) to the genus *Pandoraea* and characterization of three new *Pandoraea* genomospecies. J Clin Microbiol. 2001;39:1819-1826.

331. Purcell BK, Dooley DP. Centers for Disease Control and Prevention Group O1 bacterium associated pneumonia complicated by bronchopulmonary fistula and bacteremia. Clin Infect Dis. 1999;29:945-946.

332. Daneshvar MI, Hill B, Hollis DG, et al. CDC group O-3: Phenotypic characteristics, fatty acid composition, isoprenoid quinone content, and in vitro antimicrobic susceptibilities of an unusual gram negative bacterium isolated from clinical specimens. J Clin Microbiol. 1998;36:1674-1678.

333. Moss CW, Daneshvar MI, Hollis DG. Biochemical characteristics and fatty acid composition of *Gilardi* rod group 1 bacteria. J Clin Microbiol. 1993;31:689-691.

334. Van Esbroeck M, Vandamme P, Falsen E, et al. Polyphasic approach to the classification and identification of *Gardnerella vaginalis* and unidentified *Gardnerella vaginalis*-like coryneforms present in bacterial vaginosis. Int J Syst Bacteriol. 1996;46:675-682.

335. Catlin BW. *Gardnerella vaginalis:* Characteristics, clinical considerations, and controversies. Clin Microbiol Rev. 1992;5:213-237.

336. Aroutcheva AA, Simoes JA, Behbakht K, et al. *Gardnerella vaginalis* isolated from patients with bacterial vaginosis and from patients with healthy vaginal ecosystems. Clin Infect Dis. 2001;33:1022-1027.

337. Spiegel CA, Amsel R, Eschenbach D, et al. Anaerobic bacteria in nonspecific vaginitis. N Engl J Med. 1980;303:601-607.

338. Reimer LG, Reller LB. *Gardnerella vaginalis* bacteremia: A review of thirty cases. Obstet Gynecol. 1984;64:170-174.

339. McFadyen IR, Eykyn SJ. Suprapubic aspiration of urine in pregnancy. Lancet. 1968:1:1112-1114.

340. CDC. Sexually Transmitted Diseases Treatment Guidelines. MMWR. 2002;51 (No. RR-6).

341. Hoist E. Reservoir of four organisms associated with bacterial vaginosis suggests lack of sexual transmission. J Clin Microbiol. 1990;28:2035-2039.

342. Schwebke JR, Lawing LF. Prevalence of *Mobiluncus* spp among women with and without bacterial vaginosis is detected by polymerase chain reaction. Sex Transm Dis. 2001;28;195-199.

343. Spiegel CA. The genus *Mobiluncus*. In: Balows A, Trüper HG, Dworkin M, et al, eds. Prokaryotes. 2nd ed. New York: Springer-Verlag; 1992.

344. Hill DA, Seaton RA, Cameron ML, et al. Severe sepsis caused by *Mobiluncus curtisii* subsp. *ciirtisii* in a previously healthy female: case report and review. J Infect. 1998;37:194-196.

345. Spiegel CA. Susceptibility of *Mobiluncus* species to 23 antimicrobial agents and 15 other compounds. Antimicrob Agents Chemother. 1987:31:249-252.

CHAPTER **235**

Treponema pallidum (Syphilis)

EDMUND C. TRAMONT

Syphilis is a complex systemic illness with protean clinical manifestations caused by the spirochete *Treponema pallidum*. It holds a special place in the history of Western medicine because of its earlier prevalence and its variable clinical presentations, for which it earned the epigram "the great imitator" or "the great impostor."[1-3] The first medical specialists treating this disease were called syphiliologists and they established special clinics. In addition, one of the first specialized medical journals appeared, the *American Journal of Syphilis, Gonorrhea and Venereal Disease*. Syphilis is most often transmitted by sexual contact, and, unlike most other infectious diseases, it is rarely if ever diagnosed by isolation and characterization of the causative organism. Instead, indirect methods of diagnosis are used: darkfield microscopy, silver staining, immunofluorescent antibody or immunoperoxidase antibody staining, polymerase chain reaction (PCR), epidemiologic data, and clinical findings. Its natural course is classically divided into the following phases: (1) an incubation period lasting about 3 weeks; (2) a primary stage characterized by a non-

painful skin lesion known as a *chancre* that is usually associated with regional lymphadenopathy and always with early bacteremia; (3) a florid secondary bacteremic or disseminated stage accompanied by generalized skin rash, mucocutaneous lesions, lymphadenopathy, and/or protean clinical findings; (4) a period of subclinical infection (latent syphilis) detected only by reactive serologic tests; and (5) in a small number of patients, a late or tertiary stage characterized by progressive disease involving principally the ascending aorta and/or the central nervous system (CNS), including ophthalmic or auditory abnormalities or the development of a characteristic granulomatous-like lesion known as a gumma that can involve virtually any organ.

HISTORY

The historical aspects of syphilis make for absorbing reading,[4] and the impact of the disease on folklore appears destined to continue.[5] Few modern clinicians are aware of the prevalence of syphilis in Western countries through the middle of the 20th century, the prominent historical figures who were infected, or the pervasiveness of this disease in medical practice.[6] For example, syphilis was the leading cause of neurological and cardiovascular disease among middle-aged persons at the turn of the 20th century.[2,6]

The origins of syphilis are still debated to this day and essentially come down to whether the disease was imported into the Old World from the New World by shipmates of Christopher Columbus or was an established disease that spread throughout Europe as a consequence of urbanization. The two theories have not yet been reconciled.[7] A pandemic known as the Great Pox (as distinguished from the small pox) ravaged Europe and Asia at the time of the return of Columbus from America and during mass movements of armies and populations in Europe. It cannot be proved with certainty that *T. pallidum* was the cause of this scourge. Nevertheless, the first clear descriptions of this illness, including the sexual mode of transmission, were recorded in the 16th century. As noted in the *Breviary of Helthe*, published in 1547[8]:

> *In englyshe Morbus Gallicus (syphilis) is named the french pockes, whan that I was yonge they were named the spanyshe pockes the which be of many kyndes of the pockes, some be moyst, some be waterashe, some be drye, and some be skorvie, some be lyke skabbes, some be lyke ring wormes, some be fistuled, some be festered, some be cankarus, some be lyke wennes, some be lyke biles, some be lyke knobbles or burres, and some be ulcerous havyinge a lytle drye skabbe in the middle of the ulcerous skabbe, some hath ache in the jioyntes and no singe of the pockes and yet it may be the pockes. . . . The cause of these impediments or infyrmytes doth come many wayes, it maye come by lyenge in the shetes or bedde there where a pocky person hath the night before lyenin, it maye come with lyenge with a pocky person, it maye come by syttenge on a draught or sege where as a pocky person did lately syt, it may come by drynkynge oft with a pocky person, but specially it is taken when one pocky person doth synne in lechery the one with another.*

During this period, syphilis, or a disease similar to syphilis, was often accompanied by high morbidity and mortality, which attests to the extraordinarily virulent nature of the causative organism of that pestilence. It is not known whether the relatively mild nature of present-day syphilis reflects a change in the virulence of the organism, an adaptation of the human host, or the disappearance of a concomitantly occurring but unknown illness. The proponents of the "New World" or "Columbian" theory based their argument on the absence of syphilitic bone lesions in old skeletons despite the fact that the pathologic distinction between old bone lesions attributable to leprosy, endemic treponematosis, and those of syphilis is not precise. Indeed, examination of medieval skeletons with modern techniques suggests that treponemal disease existed prior to 1492,[7,9] although the exact pathogenic treponeme could not be determined because of the extreme genetic relatedness that exists between species.

One of the difficulties in sorting through older writings is that distinctions among syphilis, gonorrhea, and other venereal diseases did not emerge until the late 18th century. John Hunter's unfortunate self-inoculation with urethral pus containing both *Neisseria gonorrhoeae* and *T. pallidum* only served to prolong misconceptions, as the two diseases were considered the same for some time thereafter. However, by the mid-19th century, the cause, epidemiology, and clinical manifestations of syphilis were well known,[10] and syphilis became a frequent literary subject[4,5] as evidenced by the following anonymous poem, which can be dated from the 1920s:

There was a young man from Back Bay
Who thought syphilis just went away
He believed that a chancre
Was only a canker
That healed in a week and a day.
But now he has "acne vulgaris"-
(Or whatever they call it in Paris);
On his skin it has spread
From his feet to his head,
And his friends want to know where his hair is.
There's more to his terrible plight:
His pupils won't close in the light
His heart is cavorting,
His wife is aborting,
And he squints through his gunbarrel sight.
Arthralgia cuts into his slumber;
His aorta is in need of a plumber;
But now he has tabes,
And sabershinned babies,
While of gummas he has quite a number.
He's been treated in every known way,
But his spirochetes grow day by day;
He's developed paresis,
Has long talks with Jesus,
And thinks he's the Queen of the May.

The nickname "lues" came from the Latin *lues venereum*, which means "disease," "sickness," or "pestilence" and originally was loosely applied to any venereal disease. It became a synonym for syphilis at the turn of the 20th century.

Metchnikoff successfully transferred *T. pallidum* to chimpanzees in 1903. Two years later, the organism was described in the primary lesion and adjacent lymph nodes of syphilitic patients and given the name *Spirochaeta pallida.* By 1906, Wassermann developed the complement fixation test for the diagnosis of syphilis, first using an extract from the liver of a syphilitic stillborn baby, and soon thereafter, extracts of uninfected beef livers and hearts were shown to be equally sensitive (the forerunner of the present-day nontreponemal tests, discussed later in this chapter).

With the advent of serologic testing, the prevalence of the disease was determined: between 8% and 14% of adults living in such cities as Paris, Berlin, and New York had positive serologic test results. It was this high prevalence that led to the practice of screening blood donations and hospital admissions,[6] a practice that is no longer followed except in high-prevalence areas. During this same period, Ehrlich introduced an arsenic derivative, arsphenamine or salvarsan, as therapy. Mercury and bismuth preparations were added later. Induced-fever therapy (malaria, heat box, hot baths) was also efficacious, and its benefits were known for more than 300 years. Dr. Julius Wagner von Jauregg was awarded the Nobel Prize in 1927 for describing the use of malaria injections with its subsequent fevers to treat "paralytica dementia" (neurosyphilis).[11] But these primarily palliative therapies were quickly forgotten: No other disease was as dramatically affected by the discovery of penicillin as syphilis.

Syphilis continues to have an impact on the practice of modern medicine. From 1932 until 1962, 431 black men with syphilis were prospectively followed untreated to better establish the natural history of the disease despite the proven efficacy of penicillin by the late 1940s. The abuse of trust in the medical profession exemplified by this U.S. government-sponsored study was a major impetus for developing a legal basis for the principles of informed consent by patients.[12,13] It appears to be a major impediment today for African Americans participating in clinical trials.[13]

ETIOLOGY

The causal agent of syphilis is *T. pallidum* subsp. *pallidum,* which belongs to the order Spirochaetales, the family Spirochaetaceae, and the genus *Treponema.* Other members of the genus *Treponema* that can infect humans are *Treponema pallidum* subsp. *pertenue* (yaws), *Treponema pallidum* subsp. *endemicum* (bejel, nonvenereal, or endemic syphilis) and *Treponema carateum* (pinta). Clinically *T. pallidum* subsp. *pallidum* is at the most pathogenic extreme, pinta is at the least, and yaws and bejel are in between. The pathogenic treponemes are closely related morphologically, antigenically, by DNA homology, and by their ability to adhere to mammalian cells. No metabolic, structural, immunologic, or virulence marker differences among the pathogenic treponemes have been found, and this antigenic relatedness results in seropositive outcomes among patients infected with all pathogenic treponemes.[14]

Despite the fact that all of the species are closely related genetically and antigenically, they are immunologically distinct, as evidenced by studies in rabbit models in which experimental treponematosis infection by one species will induce complete protection against reinfection by the homologous species, but at best, only partial protection against heterologous species. Furthermore, for unknown reasons, they cause distinctly different diseases.[14,15] A number of nonpathogenic treponemes have also been isolated from humans, particularly from the oral cavity and from the prepuce of uncircumcised males. Other organisms pathogenic for humans of the family Spirochaetaceae belong to the genera *Borrelia* and *Leptospira.*

The organisms are slender, tightly coiled, unicellular, helical cells 5 to 15 nm long and 0.09 to 0.18 nm wide. The cytoplasm is surrounded by a trilaminar membrane, a peptidoglycan layer, a delicate inner mucopeptide layer known as the *periplast,* an outer lipoprotein membrane containing lipopolysaccharide, and a phospholipid-rich outer membrane containing relatively few surface-exposed proteins.[16,17] This has led to the hypothesis that this microorganism acts as a "stealth" organism by minimizing the number of surface membrane-bound targets for the host's immune system to recognize.[17] The ends of the cells are tapered, and three fibrils are inserted into each end. The organism moves with a drifting rotary motion and usually has a characteristic flexuose or undulating movement about its center, a distinctive feature used by experienced syphilologists to distinguish *T. pallidum* from other nonpathogenic treponemes on darkfield microscopy.

Unlike many nonpathogenic treponemes, the virulent treponemes, including *T. pallidum,* cannot be cultivated in vitro, although limited multiplication can be obtained in tissue cultures,[18] and they have remained motile in highly enriched and specifically defined media for up to 7 days at 35° C and up to 48 hours at 37° C in a carbon dioxide–enriched environment. They can be maintained viable in liquid nitrogen, less so at −70° C, and in many mammals. Rabbits are the laboratory animals most commonly used for maintaining virulent organisms.[18]

Because *T. pallidum* cannot be grown in vitro, it is difficult to study and determine its metabolic, physical, and pathogenic features. However, genomic sequencing has provided some insights by predicting functional activities when its sequences are compared with those of other organisms for which the function is known.[19] The genome consists of a single circular chromosome of approximately 1,138,006 basepairs, which places it close to the lowest end of the range for bacteria.[15,19] Unlike most pathogenic bacteria, its genome lacks apparent transposable elements, suggesting that the genome is extremely conserved. This is the likely explanation of why *T. pallidum* has remained exquisitely sensitive to penicillin for more than 60 years and that there are few differences in DNA sequences between subspecies. Another striking feature is the relative paucity of genes involved in biosynthesis of required nutrients or energy production. Hence, the spirochete apparently scavenges these necessary compounds from the host by transport proteins and utilizes only the glycolytic pathway for energy. Five putative proteins that resemble hemolysins and cytotoxins have been identified but have not been proven.[15,16,19]

EPIDEMIOLOGY

Syphilis can be acquired by sexual contact, by passage through the placenta (congenital syphilis), by kissing or other close contact with an active lesion, by transfusion of fresh human blood, or by accidental direct inoculation.[1-3] The overwhelming majority of cases of syphilis are transmitted by sexual intercourse. A patient is most infectious early in the disease, especially when a chancre, mucous patch, or condyloma latum is present, and gradually becomes less so over time. For all practical purposes, an immunologically intact person cannot spread syphilis by sexual contact after 4 years have passed since he or she acquired the illness.

Syphilis can be spread by kissing or touching a person who has active lesions on the lips, oral cavity, breasts, or genitals. Conversely, an infected patient may inoculate *T. pallidum* to the area on the body that is kissed. (Wet nurses occasionally spread the disease to infants, especially infants in upper-class European families, for whom the employment of a wet nurse was a socially coveted status symbol.)

Congenital syphilis occurs most frequently when the fetus becomes infected in utero, although it is possible for the neonate to acquire the infection while passing through the birth canal.

The acquisition of syphilis through transfused blood or blood products is now very rare because of the low incidence of disease, because of the requirement that all blood donors have a nonreactive nontreponemal blood test (see later discussion) before their blood can be used, and because *T. pallidum* cannot survive longer than 24 to 48 hours under the conditions of present-day blood bank storage.

Accidental direct inoculation can occur by a needlestick or during handling of infected clinical material. Indeed, syphilis of the fingers is most common in medical personnel. The number of reported new cases of syphilis in the United States has waxed and waned since the 1940s, reaching a peak during World War II and a nadir in the mid-1980s. The incidence rose again, dramatically, in the late 1980s and early 1990s before falling back to 1960 levels (Fig. 235-1). However, for reasons that remain obscure, the highest incidence persists in the southeastern United States, from Maryland to Florida to Louisiana. Syphilis nevertheless remains a global health problem,

with more than 12 million cases occurring worldwide, especially in underdeveloped countries and Eastern Europe.[20] Theoretically, syphilis can be eliminated by aggressive diagnostic, treatment, and follow-up measures.[21]

A disproportionate number of cases occurred in homosexual men from the mid-1960s until the mid-1980s, when the incidence of new cases began to decrease coincident with the adoption of safer sex practices by this group in response to the acquired immunodeficiency syndrome (AIDS) epidemic. This was followed, however, by a rapid increase in new cases occurring primarily among heterosexuals, as reflected by the dramatic increase of syphilis cases among women and neonates (congenital syphilis) between 1986 and 1994. This resurgence in the United States was primarily related to the exchange of sex for drugs, especially crack cocaine, and therefore, screening arrestees is prudent.[22,23] Concomitant infection with human immunodeficiency virus (HIV) may also have played a role (see later discussion).

Most cases occur in the most sexually active age group (15 to 30 years). Because contacts may "incubate" syphilis and have no evidence of active disease, aggressive contact tracing and "epidemiologic treatment" of all recently exposed persons are important aspects of syphilis control. Indeed, all contacts should be sought and treated unless follow-up examinations can be guaranteed.

PATHOGENESIS

Within hours to days after *T. pallidum* penetrates the intact mucous membrane or gains access through abraded skin, it enters the lymphatics or the blood stream and disseminates throughout the body. This occurs soon after contact, as evidenced by the fact that patients who received blood transfusions from syphilitic donors in the seronegative incubation period have become infected. Virtually any organ in the body can be invaded, especially the CNS.[1-3,24] The number of organisms that will establish an infection varies from patient to patient, but in rabbits an inoculum containing as few as four to eight spirochetes can result in infectivity. The organism divides every 30 to 33 hours. Clinical lesions appear when a concentration of approximately 10^7 organisms per milligram of tissue is reached. The incubation period is directly proportional to the size of the inoculum.[25]

Clinically, syphilis traditionally has been divided into the following stages: incubating, primary, secondary, latent, and late or tertiary syphilis. The median incubation period is 3 weeks, but it may vary from 3 to 90 days. Most patients control their infection and do not progress to late disease. The spirochetal and host determinants of the eventual outcome are at least partially understood.[26] The host develops

FIGURE 235-1. Reported cases of syphilis, the United States, 1941-2002. *(Adapted from Centers for Disease Control and Prevention. STD Surveillance, September 2002.)*

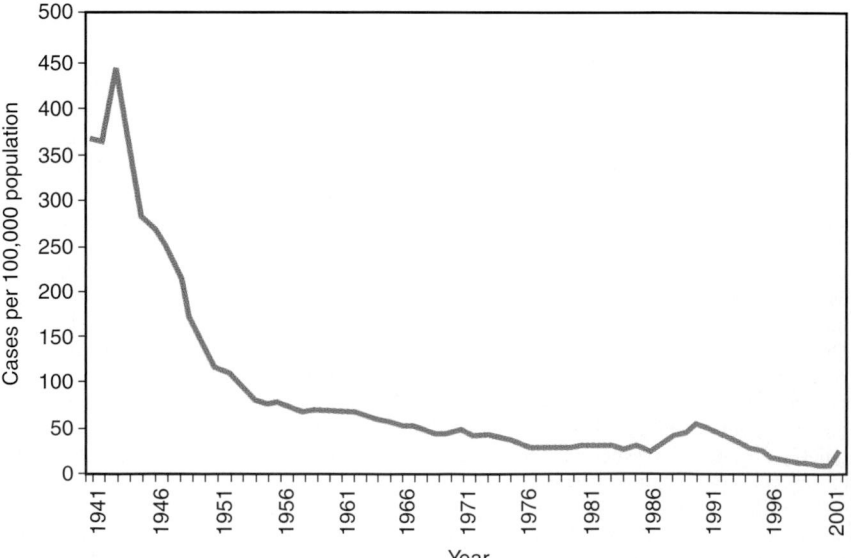

an intense immune response and the resulting inflammation is responsible for most of the subsequent clinical manifestations. It has been postulated that, as in the case of many other chronic infections, the switch from a predominant Th1 (cellular) response to a Th2 (humoral) response is a critical event in favor of the parasite and development of a chronic infection.[27,28] It has also been proposed that the paucity of proteins and lipoproteins on the outer membrane of the organism ("stealth organism") contributes in a substantial manner to the organism's evasion of an effective host response[16,17,26] and that antigenic variation may result in a subpopulation of spirochetes that are resistant to macrophage phagocytosis.[29]

The primary stage encompasses the development of the primary lesion, the chancre, which occurs at the site of inoculation. This lesion does not develop in every case, or it may be so inconspicuous as to go unnoticed. Multiple chancres can occur, especially in persons coinfected with HIV. Spirochetes are easily demonstrated in the lesions, especially early ones. Chancres usually heal spontaneously in 2 to 8 weeks but may persist for longer periods, especially in immunocompromised hosts, for example, HIV-infected persons (see below).

The secondary or disseminated stage becomes evident 2 to 12 weeks (mean, 6 weeks) after contact. This generalized condition with parenchymal, constitutional, and mucocutaneous manifestations occurs when the greatest number of treponemes (high antigen load) is present in the body, particularly in the blood stream. Treponemes can also be demonstrated in many other tissues, especially in the skin and lymph nodes. Abnormal laboratory findings or treponemes can be detected in the CNS, including the aqueous humor of the eye, in up to 40% of these patients.[1-3,24] The immune response of the host at this time becomes quite intense and is responsible for the more florid clinical signs and symptoms and pathological consequences such as an immune-complex glomerulonephritis.[30]

After the secondary stage subsides, the patient enters a latent period during which the diagnosis can be made only by obtaining a positive serologic test response for syphilis. Because relapses of secondary syphilis in non-HIV co-infected persons can occur up to 4 years after contact, this period is divided into early latent (relapses possible) and late latent (relapses very unlikely) stages. Seventy-five percent of relapses occur within the first year and are likely a consequence of dysfunction in cellular immunity.[26,27] The term *late syphilis* refers both to the clinically apparent or inapparent tertiary disease that develops in up to one third of untreated patients. Most of these lesions involve the vaso vasorum of the aorta or the small arteries of the CNS, or both; the rest consist principally of gummas, a unique granulomatous-like lesion with a coagulated or amorphous center and small vessel endarteritis. The skin, liver, bones, and spleen are the most common sites at which gummas develop.

PATHOLOGIC CHARACTERISTICS

Obliterative endarteritis consisting of concentric endothelial and fibroblastic proliferative thickening is highly suggestive of syphilis (Fig. 235-2).[2] These pathologic changes are found in all stages of syphilis. In the primary chancre, polymorphonuclear leukocytes and macrophages can often be demonstrated ingesting treponemes. Hyperkeratosis is frequently found in the skin lesions of secondary syphilis and is especially marked in condylomata. Treponemal antigen, immunoglobulin, and complement deposition in the glomeruli typical of immune-complex glomerulonephritis can be demonstrated in patients who develop a nephrotic syndrome.[30] Obliterative endarteritis of the vaso vasorum and small blood vessels is the principal histopathologic finding in cardiovascular syphilis and meningovascular neurosyphilis. Appropriate staining (i.e., direct immunofluorescent antibody, immunoperoxidase antibody, or silver stains) can be used to demonstrate *T. pallidum*.

THE NATURAL COURSE OF UNTREATED SYPHILIS

The natural course of untreated syphilis was studied in a retrospective fashion in 1404 patients who were diagnosed clinically as having early syphilis (the Oslo study, 1891-1951).[31] There were obviously many

FIGURE 235-2. Characteristic obliterative endarteritis (×150).

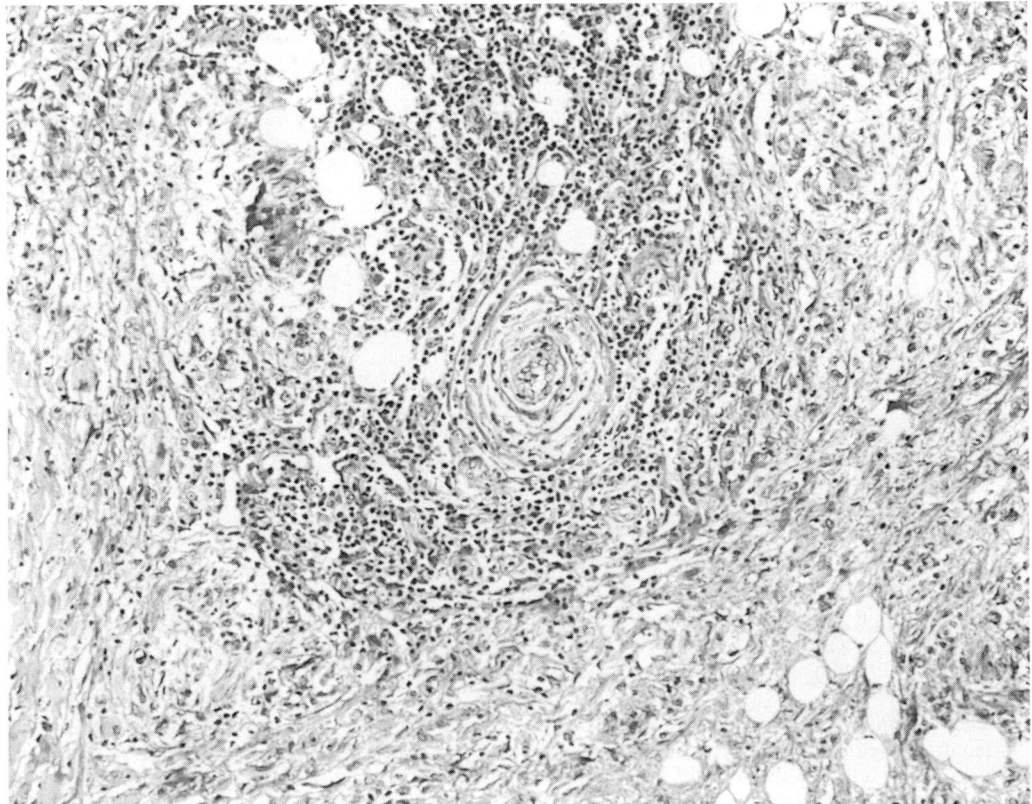

shortcomings to this observational study, the most significant being the lack of laboratory confirmation of syphilis and the method of patient selection. (The darkfield and Wassermann tests were not available at the time the study was initiated.) However, because a similar study will never be done again, a brief review is warranted.

From 1890 to 1910, Professor Boeck of the University of Oslo, Norway, monitored patients diagnosed as having primary or secondary syphilis. Because he believed that the mercury-containing compounds used at that time for treatment were more harmful to the patient than the disease itself, all of his patients were simply observed. Twenty-four percent of these untreated patients developed relapsing secondary lesions within 4 years, leading to the arbitrary designation of early latent, late latent, and late syphilis. Twenty-eight percent eventually developed clinical complications of late syphilis; 10% developed cardiovascular syphilis, but this occurred only in patients who had acquired syphilis after 15 years of age; 6.5% developed symptomatic neurosyphilis; and 16% developed the late benign syphilis or gummas. Many of these patients had one or more "late" complications. Of those in whom autopsy was performed, 35% of the men and 22% of the women had evidence of cardiovascular involvement, especially aortitis. Syphilis was considered the primary cause of death in 15% of the men and 8% of the women.

A prospective study involving 431 African American men with seropositive latent syphilis of 3 or more years' duration was undertaken in 1932; this was the infamous Tuskegee study of 1932-1962.[32] This study suggested that hypertension in syphilitic black men 25 to 50 years of age was 17% more common than in black nonsyphilitic individuals. Cardiovascular complications including hypertension were more common than neurological complications, and both were increased compared with control populations. Anatomic evidence of aortitis was found to be 25% to 35% more common in syphilitic patients on autopsy, and evidence of CNS syphilis was found in 4% of the patients. Other autopsy studies found higher rates of neurosyphilis.[2] A third large study, the Rosahn study, from 1917 to 1941, involving 382 autopsies of adults, revealed similar overall results.[33] Late syphilis was reported in 39%, and about 20% were thought to have died because of these late complications. Of the late anatomic lesions at autopsy attributable to syphilis, 83% were cardiovascular, 8% neurologic, and 9% gummas.

These studies documented the variable, waxing and waning course and unpredictable progression of late syphilis. There was an increased overall mortality in syphilitic compared with nonsyphilitic populations. The development of late complications was shown to occur about twice as often in men than in women, and a racial difference was suggested: black patients were more likely to develop cardiovascular syphilis, whereas white patients were more likely to develop neurosyphilis.

CLINICAL MANIFESTATIONS

There was once an adage that "He who knows syphilis knows medicine." Penicillin therapy changed this, but one of its legacies is the frequency of delayed and erroneous diagnoses that occurs today because of the low incidence and subsequent unfamiliarity with the disease.[34,35] Traditionally, the clinical manifestations are divided into early infectious primary and secondary stages lasting up to 4 to 5 years, often marked with periods of symptoms and signs, and latency progressing to a late or tertiary stage of tissue destruction in up to 22% of patients.

Incubating Syphilis

The median incubation period before clinical manifestations is 21 days (range: 3 to 90 days). An early spirochetemia develops during this phase, which sets the stage for secondary invasion of virtually every bodily organ.[1,2,6]

Primary Syphilis

The classic primary chancre begins at the site of inoculation as a single painless papule. It appears after the incubation period, quickly erodes, and becomes indurated (Figs. 235-3 and 235-4). The base is usually smooth; the borders are raised and firm and have a character-

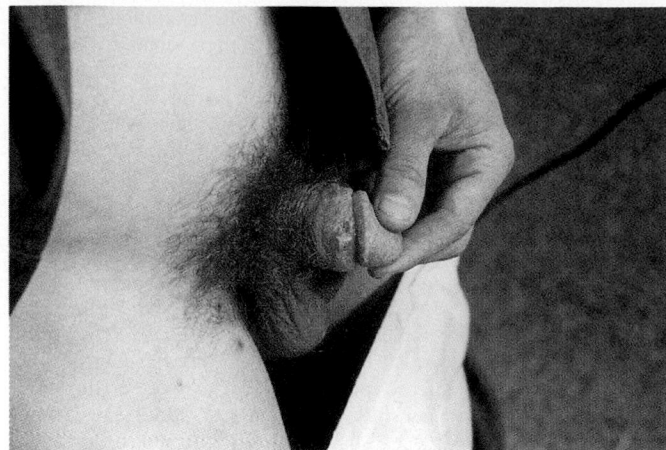

FIGURE 235-3. Primary syphilitic chancre of the penis.

istic cartilaginous consistency. Unless secondarily infected, the ulcer has a clean appearance and no exudates; it is painless but slightly tender to the touch, a conspicuous aspect of the clinical lesion, and there is little pain or bleeding when the ulcer is scraped, such as when a specimen is obtained for a darkfield examination. Multiple chancres can occur, especially in persons coinfected with HIV.[36,37] Atypical lesions occur in up to 60% of cases, and the absence of a primary skin lesion is also common. The variations in presentation depend on the number of treponemes inoculated, the immune status of the patient, intercurrent antibiotic therapy, and whether the lesion becomes secondarily infected. In human volunteers with no evidence of a previous infection, a small inoculum produces only a papular lesion and a large inoculum produces an ulcerative lesion (chancre) in which treponemes can easily be identified. Persons with a history of a previous syphilitic infection may fail to develop any lesions or develop only a small, darkfield-negative papule, depending on how long their natural infection went untreated.[25] Therefore, any genital lesion should raise the suspicion of syphilis, and appropriate studies to establish the diagnosis should be undertaken.

The chancre is located wherever the inoculation occurred. The external genitalia are most frequently involved. Other common sites include the cervix, mouth, perianal area, and anal canal in the female and the perianal area, anal canal, and mouth in homosexual men. A secondary infection of the primary lesion is more common with oral and anal lesions. Regional lymphadenopathy consisting of moderately enlarged, firm, nonsuppurative, painless lymph nodes or satellite buboes accompanies the primary lesion.

The chancre heals on its own within 3 to 6 weeks (range, 1 to 12 weeks), leaving either no trace or a thin atrophic scar. The lymphadenopathy usually persists for a longer period. The manifestations of secondary syphilis often develop while the chancre is still present,[1-3] especially in HIV-infected patients.[37]

Pathologically, the chancre is characterized by an intense infiltration of plasma cells and scattered histiocytes, a concentric endothelial and fibroblastic proliferative thickening of small blood vessels, and, eventually, the omnipresent and almost diagnostic obliterative endarteritis.[2] Spirochetes can be identified by silver, immunofluorescent, or other specific antibody staining methods (see later discussion).

Primary syphilis must be differentiated principally from herpes virus infections, chancroid, and traumatic suprainfected genital lesions. Primary genital herpes usually begins as a painful erythematous rash that develops into clusters of vesicles accompanied by regional lymphadenopathy and systemic symptoms. It runs a 10- to 14-day course. Recurrent genital herpes is less florid and is characterized by mild to moderately painful vesicles and no lymphadenopathy. A syphilitic rash is never vesicular except in congenital syphilis.[38] Chancroid is characterized by one or more painful, exudative, in-

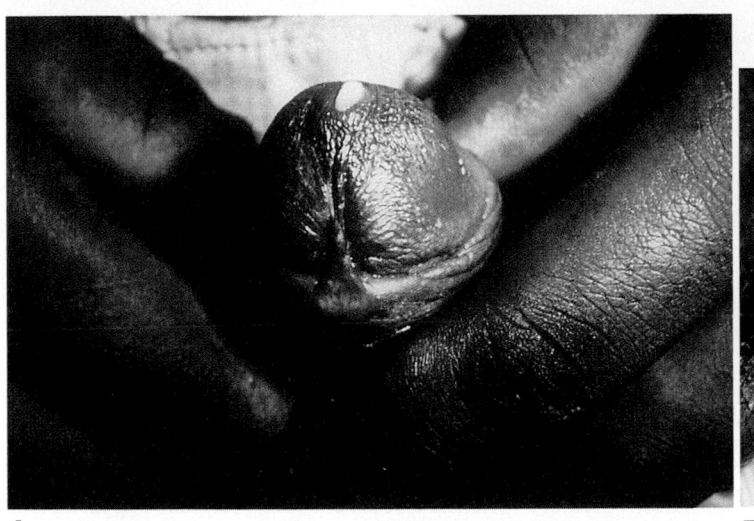

A

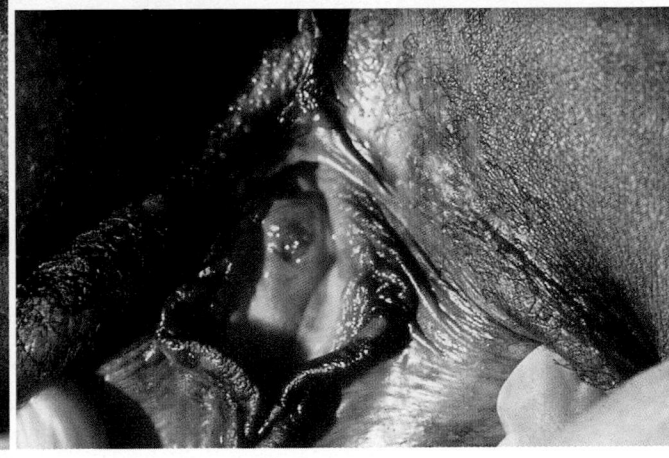

B

FIGURE 235-4. A, Primary syphilitic chancre coinfection with a pustular urethritis. **B,** Primary syphilitic chancre of the perineum.

durated ulcers associated with tender lymphadenopathy that eventually suppurate if left untreated. The ulcer has overhanging edges and bleeds easily (e.g., when scrapings are collected for a darkfield examination). Early venereal warts, granuloma inguinale, lymphogranuloma venereum, tuberculosis, atypical mycobacterial infections, tularemia, sporotrichosis, anthrax, rat bite fever, or any genital ulcer may resemble early primary syphilis.

Secondary Syphilis

Secondary (disseminated) syphilis is the term used to describe the clinically most florid stage of the infection; it results from multiplication and dissemination of the spirochete and lasts until a sufficient host response develops to exert some immune control over the spirochete. It usually begins 2 to 8 weeks after the appearance of a chancre, but this period is quite variable. The primary chancre may still be present.[1-3,39] At a time when the host's local immune process appears to be bringing the primary lesions under control, the spirochete disseminates widely and achieves its greatest numbers or antigenic load. Serological tests are always positive and it is during this stage that the pro-zone phenomenon is most likely (see below).

The manifestations of secondary syphilis are widespread and protean (Table 235-1). The classic and most commonly recognized lesions involve the skin. Nonpruritic macular, maculopapular, papular, or pustular lesions, and combinations and variations thereof, all occur.[1-3,39] Vesicular lesions are conspicuously absent except in congenital syphilis.[2,38] These skin lesions usually begin on the trunk and proximal extremities as bilateral, pink to red, discrete macular lesions 3 to 10 mm in diameter. Any surface area of the body can become involved. These lesions usually persist from a few days to 8 weeks and often evolve from macules into red papules (hence the designation *maculopapular*); in a few patients, they finally progress to pustular lesions known as *pustular syphilids*. The degree of endarteritis and perivascular mononuclear infiltration progresses in the same manner. All of the different rashes may be present at one time and may become widely distributed to involve the entire body, especially on the palms and soles, locations that strongly suggest the diagnosis (Fig. 235-5). When the hair follicles are involved (follicular syphilids), temporary patchy alopecia or thinning and a loss of eyebrows and beard may develop.[1-3,39] Sometimes a superficial scaling occurs (papulosquamous syphilids). In warm, moist intertriginous areas (i.e., perianal area, vulva, scrotum, inner aspects of the thighs, the skin under pendulous breasts, nasolabial folds, cleft of the chin, axillary and antecubital folds, webs of the fingers and toes), the papules enlarge, coalesce, and erode to produce painless, broad, moist, gray-white to erythematous, highly infectious plaques called

condylomata lata. These highly infectious lesions teeming with spirochetes may also develop on mucous membranes (i.e., lips, mouth, pharynx, tonsils, vulva, vagina, glans penis, inner prepuce cervix, anal canal). These lesions, referred to as *mucous patches,*

TABLE 235-1 The Clinical Manifestations of Secondary Syphilis

Manifestation	Percentage of Cases
Skin	90
Rash*	
Macular	
Maculopapular	
Papular	
Pustular	
Condyloma latum	
Generalized lymphadenopathy	
Mouth and throat	35
Mucous patches	
Erosions	
Ulcer (aphthous)	
Genital lesion	20
Chancre	
Chondyloma latum	
Mucous patch	
Constitutional symptoms	70
Fever of unknown origin	
Malaise	
Pharyngitis, laryngitis	
Anorexia, weight loss	
Arthralgias	
Central nervous system	8-40
Asymptomatic	
Symptomatic	1-2
Headache	
Meningismus	
Meningitis	
Ocular	
Diplopia	
Impaired vision	
Otitic	
Tinnitus	
Vertigo	
Cranial nerve involvement (II-VIII)	
Renal	Unusual
Glomerulonephritis	
Nephrotic syndrome	
Gastrointestinal	Unusual
Hepatitis	Unusual
Intestinal wall invasion	Unusual
Arthritis, osteitis, and periostitis	Unusual

*Commonly involves the palms and soles.

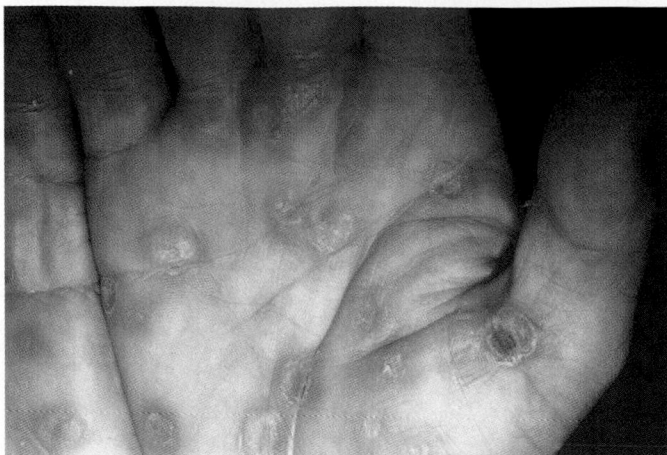

FIGURE 235-5. Palmar lesions of secondary syphilis.

typically manifest as a silvery gray, superficial erosion with a red periphery (Fig. 235-6). None of these lesions is painful unless it is infected secondarily.

During relapses of secondary syphilis, the skin lesions tend to be less florid, asymmetrically distributed, and more infiltrated, suggesting a more effective host immune response. Condylomata lata, however, are common.

Constitutional symptomatology is also commonly present in secondary syphilis. These manifestations include low-grade fever, malaise, pharyngitis, laryngitis, anorexia, weight loss, arthralgias, and generalized painless lymphadenopathy. Enlargement of the epitrochlear lymph nodes is a unique finding that should always suggest the diagnosis.

The CNS becomes involved in up to 40% of patients[1-3,24] as a result of seeding during the inevitable spirochetemia. Headache and meningismus are common, increased cerebrospinal fluid (CSF) protein levels and lymphocyte counts are found in 8% to 40% of the patients,[40] and acute symptomatic aseptic meningitis occurs in 1% to 2% of the patients. Importantly, spirochetes have also been isolated from the CSF of patients with no CSF abnormalities.[24,40,41] Individual cranial nerves, especially II through VIII, can be involved.[40] Visual disturbances, hearing loss, tinnitus, and facial weakness are the most common manifestations. Syphilitic paraplegia (Erb's paralysis) and amyotrophic meningomyelitis characterized by the insidious onset of asymmetrical paraparesis, hyperreflexia, Babinski's sign, sphincter disturbances, spastic neurogenic bladder and minimal back pain may occur. Intermittent periods of clinical manifestations, a classical clinical hallmark of secondary and early latent syphilis, may occur.[41,42] A significant portion of untreated patients (8% to 10%) will progress to late neurosyphilis. The advent of

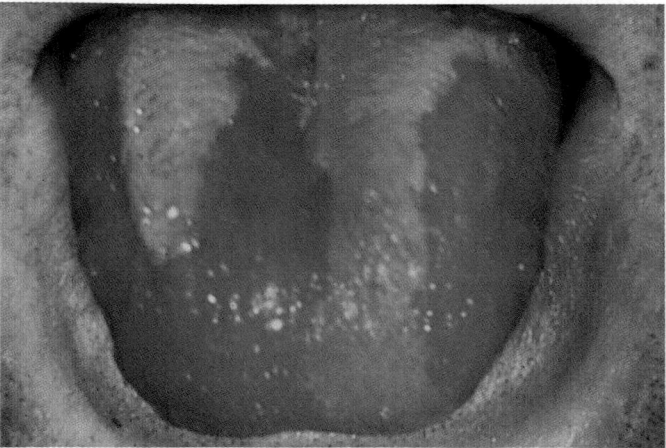

FIGURE 235-6. Mucous patch lesion of secondary syphilis.

computed tomography (CT) scanning and magnetic resonance imaging (MRI) has improved our ability to diagnose and follow patients at all stages of neurosyphilis.[42,43,43a]

Because of the omnipresent spirochetemia, virtually any organ of the body can be involved. Renal involvement may be in the form of an immune-complex glomerulonephritis (subepithelial electron-dense deposits). Proteinuria is common; an acute nephrotic syndrome may develop; and rarely, hemorrhagic glomerulonephritis can occur.[30]

Syphilitic hepatitis is characterized by a disproportionately high serum alkaline phosphatase level, a normal or moderately elevated serum bilirubin content, and a histologic picture that includes moderate inflammation with polymorphonuclear cells and lymphocytes, some hepatocellular damage, but no cholestasis. It occurs most often in conjunction with syphilitic proctitis and is seen most frequently in persons who engage in anal intercourse.

The gastrointestinal tract may also become extensively infiltrated or ulcerated, or both,[44] and this can be misdiagnosed as a lymphoma or other cancer.[35] Anterior or pan-uveitis, usually mild and asymptomatic, occurs in 5% to 10% of patients with secondary syphilis, especially in HIV-infected persons, and the diagnosis is suggested whenever the uveitis is made worse by steroid treatment.[45-47]

Synovitis, osteitis, and periosteitis can also occur. These cases are often characterized by nocturnal pain that is conspicuously increased by heat.[48] Unusual manifestations such as bone resorption of the hands and feet (acro-osteolysis) can also occur.

The differential diagnosis of secondary syphilis is extensive, and the appellation "the great imitator" or "great impostor" is appropriate.

Latent Syphilis

Latent syphilis is by definition the stage of the disease during which the fluorescent treponemal antibody absorption (FTA-abs), which is a specific treponemal antibody test; T. pallidum particle agglutination (TP-PA) tests, for example, T. pallidum hemagglutination (TPHA) or microhemagglutination for T. pallidum (MHA-TP); an enzyme-linked immunosorbent assay (ELISA), or T. pallidum immobilization (TPI) test, is positive but during which there are no clinical manifestations of syphilis; the cerebrospinal cell count and protein and glucose levels are normal; and the chest radiograph is normal. It does not imply a lack of progression of disease. A history compatible with primary or secondary syphilis, exposure to a syphilitic person, or delivery of an infant with congenital syphilis should be sought. Early latent syphilis distinguishes this period of time (first 4 years) during which a relapse may occur and, therefore, the patient is "infectious." Ninety percent of the relapses occur in the first year, and each recurring episode is less florid. Mucocutaneous relapses are the most common.

Late latent syphilis is associated with host resistance to reinfection and to infectious relapse.[1,2,25] However, a pregnant woman with late latent syphilis can infect her fetus in utero, and an infection can be transmitted via transfused contaminated blood.

Late Syphilis

Late syphilis (tertiary syphilis) is a slowly progressive, inflammatory disease that can affect any organ in the body to produce clinical illness years after the initial infection. It is generally subdivided into neurosyphilis, cardiovascular syphilis, gummatous syphilis, and sometimes leuetic osteitis ("moth eaten" appearance of involved bone on radiographic studies).[1-3,49]

Late Neurosyphilis

Because the CNS is often invaded during the septicemic phase, neurological manifestations can occur during any phase or stage of the disease. Therefore, neurosyphilis needs to be divided into acute neurosyphilis[40] and late (chronic) neurosyphilis (Fig. 235-7). Late neurosyphilis is usually divided into asymptomatic and symptomatic phases; the latter is further distinguished as meningovascular or parenchymatous neurosyphilis (Table 235-2).[50] Although this classification recognizes the existence of distinctive forms of neurosyphilis that correlate with pathological findings, there is almost always clinical overlap with combinations of meningovascular and parenchyma-

FIGURE 235-7. Chronology of neurosyphilis.

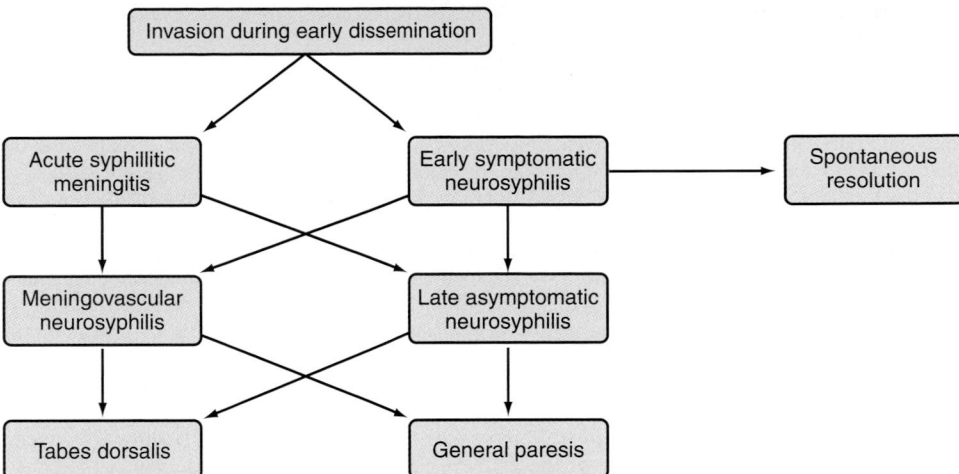

tous features. This is not surprising because neurosyphilis is fundamentally a chronic meningitis involving every portion of the CNS. The diagnosis of asymptomatic neurosyphilis is given to patients who have no clinical manifestation of neurologic involvement but who have one or more CSF abnormalities: pleocytosis, an elevated protein concentration, a decreased glucose concentration, or a positive nontreponemal or reaginic test (e.g., venereal disease research laboratory [VDRL], rapid plasma reagin [RPR]). Local CNS production of antibodies to *T. pallidum*,[51-53] a positive PCR[41,54] and a serum RPR of $\geq$ 1:32[54a] are highly suggestive of an active case of neurosyphilis. Asymptomatic neurosyphilis is the most common presentation of neurosyphilis.

The incidence of asymptomatic *acute* neurosyphilis in untreated patients ranges from 8% to as high as 40%.[1,2,24,55,56] How many of these cases progress to symptomatic *late* neurosyphilis is problematic. With the exception of the presentation of the highly suggestive Argyll Robertson pupil or tabes dorsalis, the symptoms and signs of neurosyphilis are nonspecific (Table 235-3), and there is evidence to suggest that symptomatic neurosyphilis may be present in as many as 4% of patients with normal CSF findings. Because asymptomatic neurosyphilis is curable, because a lumbar puncture is necessary to make the diagnosis of asymptomatic neurosyphilis, and because asymptomatic neurosyphilis occurs in up to 40% of patients,[1-3,24,41] a lumbar puncture should be considered as part of the follow-up care for anyone who may not have been adequately treated for neurosyphilis, especially patients treated with benzathine penicillin alone (see later discussion).

Late symptomatic neurosyphilis is divided into two major clinical categories that have been correlated with pathologic findings: meningovascular neurosyphilis and parenchymatous neurosyphilis (see Table 235-3), but a great deal of clinical overlap occurs. (As noted previously, syphilitic meningitis clinically resembling "aseptic" meningitis may occur during early syphilis, especially during the secondary stage.) The term *meningovascular neurosyphilis* refers to the development of typical endarteritis obliterans, which affects the small blood vessels of the meninges, brain, and spinal cord and leads to multiple small areas of infarction. *Parenchymatous neurosyphilis* refers to the actual destruction of nerve cells, principally in the cerebral cortex. The former condition represents an inflammatory process and the latter a degenerative one, but a mixture of the two pathologic processes is always present.

Vascular involvement (meningovascular neurosyphilis) may lead to a wide spectrum of diseases, ranging from focal ischemia and stroke to progressive neurologic deficits, as a result of the gradual destruction of nerve tissue by small-vessel endarteritis. Hemiparesis, aphasia, and either focal or generalized seizures may occur and appear to be more frequent now than in previous reports.[50,56]

Parenchymatous neurosyphilis includes general paresis (cortical involvement) and tabes dorsalis (spinal cord involvement). It is the result of widespread parenchymal damage and represents a combination of psychiatric manifestations and neurologic findings. Abnormalities correspond to the mnemonic *PARESIS: P*ersonality (emotional lability,

TABLE 235-2 Classification of Neurosyphilis

Manifestation	Percentage of Cases (N = 676)
Syphilitic meningitis as a complication of secondary syphilis	8-40
Asymptomatic	7-38
Symptomatic	1-2
Asymptomatic late neurosyphilis	31
Symptomatic late neurosyphilis	69
Meningovascular	
Cerebromeningeal	6
Diffuse	
Focal	
Cerebrovascular	10
Spinal	3
Parenchymatous	
Tabetic	30
Paretic	12
Taboparetic	3
Ocular	3
Miscellaneous	2

Modified with permission from Merritt HH, Moore M. Acute neurosyphilitic meningitis. Medicine (Baltimore). 1935;14:119.

TABLE 235-3 Clinical Manifestations of Neurosyphilis

Meningovascular
  Hemiplegia or hemiparesis
  Seizures
    Generalized
    Focal
  Aphasia
Parenchymatous
  General paresis
    Changes in personality, affect, sensorium, intellect, insight, and judgment
    Hyperactive reflexes
    Speech disturbances (slurring)
    Pupillary disturbances (Argyll Robertson, pupils)
    Optic atrophy tremors (face, tongue, hands, legs)
  Tables dorsalis
    Shooting or lightning pains into lower back or lower legs
    Ataxia
    Pupillary disturbances (Argyll Robertson pupils)
    Impotence
    Bladder disturbances
    Fecal incontinence
    Peripheral neuropathy
    Romberg sign
    Cranial nerve involvement (II-VII)

Modified with permission from Merritt HH, Moore M. Acute neurosyphilitic meningitis. Medicine (Baltimore). 1935;14:119.

paranoia); *A*ffect (carelessness in appearance); *R*eflexes (hyperactive); *E*ye (Argyll Robertson pupils); *S*ensorium (illusions, delusions, especially megalomania, hallucinations); *I*ntellect (decreased recent memory, judgment, insight); and *S*peech (slurred). Spinal cord damage involves principally demyelinization of the posterior column, dorsal roots, and dorsal root ganglia, which eventually results in the development of an ataxic, wide-based gait and footslap, paresthesias, "shooting" or "lightning" pains (sudden onset, rapid radiation, and disappearance), bladder disturbances, fecal incontinence, impotence, loss of position and vibratory sense, absent ankle and knee jerk reflexes, and loss of deep pain and temperature sensation. The Romberg sign (inability to stand with feet together and eyes closed without falling over) is classically present in patients with tabes dorsalis because of damage to the posterior columns. Trophic degenerative joint disease, known as Charcot's joints, and traumatic ulcers or sores on the lower extremities and feet resulting from the loss of sensation were prominently featured in textbooks of physical diagnosis published before the antibiotic era.

Ocular disturbances are common whenever the CNS is invaded. The Argyll Robertson pupil is a small, irregular pupil that accommodates to near vision but does not react to light or painful stimuli. Optic atrophy occurs over a period of months to years, beginning peripherally and proceeding to the center of the nerve, producing progressive concentric constriction of the visual fields with retention of normal vision. This is referred to as *gun barrel sight*.

Any inflammatory disease of the eye can be caused by syphilitic involvement. Anterior or posterior uveitis or pan-uveitis is the most common abnormal finding and appears to be increased in HIV-coinfected persons[45-47]; other ocular findings are episcleritis, vitreitis, retinitis, papillitis, interstital keratitis, acute retinal necrosis, and retinal detachment. They may occur during any stage such as an accompanying manifestation of acute syphilitic meningitis or an isolated manifestation of secondary syphilis[40] or latent syphilis.[57] Unless scarring has occurred, improvement with treatment can be dramatic. The differential diagnosis of other systemic diseases includes tuberculosis, rheumatoid arthritis, sarcoidosis, toxoplasmosis, histoplasmosis, and ocular *Toxocara canis* infections.

Although any cranial nerve can be affected, those most commonly involved are the seventh and eighth cranial nerves (40%). Involvement results in the gradual development of a loss of facial expression; tremors of the lips, tongue, and facial muscles; and difficulty enunciating multisyllable words (e.g., "Methodist," "Episcopal"). The second, third, and fourth cranial nerves are the next most commonly affected (25%).

Meningovascular syphilis usually occurs 5 to 10 years after the onset of disease, general paresis 15 to 20 years after, and tabes dorsalis 25 to 30 years after.

Another distinct variant of neurosyphilis is syphilitic otitis (asymmetric deafness, tinnitus). The ear may be involved during any stage of the disease, including congenital syphilis. This may be the only clinically apparent symptom at presentation, and it usually presents diagnostic dilemmas, especially because the CSF parameters are usually normal. In early stages syphilitic otitis is curable[58]; if untreated it causes irreversible damage. A positive treponemal antibody test (e.g., TPHA, MHA-TP, FTA-abs) is found in approximately 7% of patients with otherwise unexplained sensorineural hearing loss that is usually unilateral and in 7% of patients with cochleovestibular dysfunction (Ménière's disease), making neurosyphilis a significant cause of these disorders. Congenital otic syphilis is usually bilateral and more severe than otic involvement caused by acquired syphilis. Specialized diagnostic procedures may be required,[59] but any patient with unexplained hearing loss or vestibular disturbances who has a positive treponemal antibody test should be treated for syphilitic otitis.

The conditions from which neurosyphilis must be differentiated are numerous. They include any degenerative neurologic process, disorders that cause chronic inflammation (e.g., tuberculosis; fungal, parasitic, or sarcoid meningitis; tumors; subdural hematoma; Alzheimer's disease; multiple sclerosis; chronic alcoholism, etc.), and any chronic disorder that affects the vasculature of the CNS (e.g. cerebral vascular

disease, etc.). The axiom that syphilis can mimic any disease is particularly apropos with regard to CNS involvement.

Given the vagaries of neurosyphilis (e.g., no routinely available single sensitive or specific test and no diagnostic clinical presentation), the clinician must use a combination of clinical and laboratory data to make the diagnosis. In modern medicine, one is loath to label a patient with a specific etiologic infectious diagnosis without isolation of the infecting organism from the patient (by culture, antigen capture, or pathologic demonstration). But because *T. pallidum* cannot be cultured in vitro and isolation in animals is restricted to research laboratories, serologic or antibody tests alone are relied on to diagnose and monitor these patients. However, the demonstration of specific treponemal immunoglobulin G (IgG) and IgM antibody production in the CNS is very helpful,[41,51-53] and the PCR test establishes the presence of the etiologic agent (but not necessarily live or replicating organisms).[41,54,60]

The aim of treatment has been to develop a rational and safe therapeutic approach so that the patient has a reasonable expectation that the disease will be cured or will not progress to a severe neurologic disability. When choosing treatment approaches, several considerations must be taken into account. First, a spirochetemia always occurs in patients with syphilis before invasion of the CNS. Therefore, except in patients with immune dysfunction (e.g., HIV infection, etc.), the diagnosis of neurosyphilis cannot be made without a positive serum treponemal antibody response (e.g., TPHA, FTA-abs, MHA-TP). Second, a positive CSF VDRL or CSF RPR test always indicates active neurosyphilis. Third, a positive PCR test in the CSF establishes that CNS invasion has occurred but does not necessarily establish that the infection is active and the spirochetes are replicating.[60] Fourth, any CSF abnormality in the appropriate clinical setting and without an alternative explanation strongly suggests active neurosyphilis. Fifth, local CNS production of anti-treponemal antibody is highly suggestive of neurosyphilis. Therefore, any patient with a positive specific serum treponemal antibody test, a positive CSF VDRL, a positive CSF PCR, or evidence of local CNS antibody production with or without otherwise explained neurologic findings warrants therapy for neurosyphilis (see later discussion).

Cardiovascular Syphilis

The underlying pathologic lesion of cardiovascular syphilis is the omnipresent endarteritis obliterans, in this case involving the vaso vasorum of the aorta. This results in a medial necrosis with destruction of elastic tissue and subsequent aortitis with a saccular (or occasionally a fusiform) aneurysm. There is a predilection to involve the ascending aorta, which leads to weakness of the aortic valve ring and distortion of the cups and results in aortic regurgitation and coronary artery stenosis. The transverse segment of the aortic arch is the next most frequently involved area; the aorta below the renal arteries is seldom involved.[1-3,61] Symptomatic syphilitic aortitis occurs in approximately 10% of untreated cases, but the pathologic lesions can be demonstrated on postmortem examination in up to 83% of cases of untreated neurosyphilis.[33] A symptomatic syphilitic aortitis should be suspected whenever linear calcifications are noted on chest radiographs of the ascending aorta, a finding seldom seen in arteriosclerotic disease. Syphilitic aneurysms rarely dissect. Neurological involvement is common in patients with syphilitic aortitis. Other large arteries (e.g., temporal artery) may also be involved. Because of the success of antibiotic treatment, cardiovascular syphilis is now a medical curiosity in the United States.

Late Benign Syphilis (Gumma)

The gumma is a nonspecific, granulomatous-like lesion that occurs in late syphilis[1,2] but is rarely seen today. These indolent lesions are most commonly found in the skeletal system, skin, and mucocutaneous tissues but can develop in any organ. They may be single or multiple and vary in size from microscopic defects to large, tumor-like masses. They are of clinical importance principally as a cause of local destruction. The cutaneous manifestations range from superficial nodules to deep granulomatous lesions, which may break down to form punched-out ulcers. Involution is followed by the development of a thin, atrophic, noncontractile scar arranged in arciform patterns.[1-3] Gummatous hepatitis may cause low-grade fever, epigastric pain and tenderness, and eventually cirrhosis (hepar lobatum). Gummas of the bone may result in fractures or joint destruction, whereas those in the upper respiratory tract can lead to perforation of the nasal system or palate. Trauma may predispose to involvement of a specific site. Gummas must be distinguished from other granulomatous lesions (e.g., tuberculosis, sarcoidosis, deep fungal infections) and from neoplasms. The spirochetes in these lesions are difficult to visualize on microscopic examination. A therapeutic trial of penicillin or other effective antibiotics results in a rapid and dramatic response. Gummas were the most common late complication seen in the Oslo study described previously (approximately 15%).

Congenital Syphilis

Infection of the fetus in utero can occur at any stage of infection in any untreated or inadequately treated mother but is most likely to occur during early syphilis. The risk of fetal infection decreases progressively thereafter. Infection of the fetus before the fourth month of gestation is unusual; therefore, early abortion is unlikely to be a result of syphilis. Adequate treatment of the mother usually but not always ensures that the fetus will not be infected. A serum VDRL greater than 1:16 and primary, secondary, and early latent syphilis in the mother during pregnancy or more than 30 days since treatment are associated with a congenitally infected neonate.[41,62] Depending on the severity of the infection, late abortion, stillbirth, neonatal death, neonatal disease, or latent infection may be seen[1,2,62]; these manifestations appear to be caused largely by dysfunction of the maternal-fetal endocrine axis, which results in decreased levels of dehydroepiandrosterone produced by the fetal adrenal glands.[63] Six to seven percent of neonates with congenital syphilis will be stillborn, especially in untreated or inadequately treated mothers.[64]

The clinical pattern is variable, but often there are no abnormal physical findings (Table 235-4).[1,2,65] In the perinatal period (infantile form), the most striking lesions affect the mucocutaneous tissues, liver,

TABLE 235-4 Clinical Signs of Congenital Syphilis

Manifestation	Percentage of Cases
Early	55
Osteochondritis	
Snuffles	40
Rash	40
Anemia	30
Hepatosplenomegaly	20
Jaundice	20
Neurologic signs	20
Lymphadenopathy	5
Mucous patches	5
Late	
Frontal bosses	
Short maxillas	
Saddle nose	
Protruding mandible	
Interstitial keratitis	
Eight-nerve deafness	
High palatal arch	
Hutchinson's incisors	
Mulberry molars	
Sternoclavicular thickening (Higoumenaki's sign)	
Clutton's joints (bilateral painless swelling of knees)	
Saber shins	
Flaring scapulas	

Data from Kampmeier RH. Essentials of Syphilogy. 3rd ed. Philadelphia: JB Lippincott; 1943; and Stokes JH, Beerman H, Ingraham NR. Modern Clinical Syphilology: Diagnosis, Treatment: Case Study. 3rd ed. Philadelphia: WB Saunders; 1945.

and bones. The earliest sign of congenital syphilis is usually a rhinitis (snuffles), which is soon followed by a diffuse, maculopapular, desquamative rash with extensive sloughing of the epithelium, particularly on the palms, on the soles, and about the mouth and anus. In contrast to acquired syphilis in the adult, a vesicular rash and bullae may develop. These lesions are teeming with spirochetes and have the characteristic obliterative endarteritis and perivascular mononuclear cuffing on microscopic examination that are found in other syphilitic lesions.

The liver is often heavily infected, with associated splenomegaly, anemia, thrombocytopenia, and jaundice. The generalized spirochetemia may lead to diffuse inflammatory changes of virtually any organ of the body. Neonatal death is usually the result of liver failure, severe pneumonia, hypopituitism, or pulmonary hemorrhage. Renal involvement with an immune-complex glomerulonephritis may develop and usually occurs at about the fourth month of life.[30] A generalized osteochondritis and perichondritis or periostitis may affect the architecture of all bones of the skeletal system, but are most prominent of the long bones and can be easily discerned on radiographs.[41,59] As in adults, central nervous system involvement is common, occurring in at least 22% of neonates; the CSF-VDRL, cell count, protein and glucose determinations are of low sensitivity.[41] Importantly, although CNS involvement is most often associated with an abnormal physical examination, conventional laboratory tests, and radiologic studies, some infants can be identified only by IgM immunoblotting on the serum or CSF or PCR.[41,66] Neonatal congenital syphilis must be differentiated from other generalized congenital infections such as rubella, cytomegalovirus infection, and toxoplasmosis.

With a few notable exceptions, the untreated child who survives the first 6 to 12 months of life enters a latent period. The generalized osteochondritis, perichondritis, and periostitis may result in deformities of the nose (saddle nose) and the metaphyses of the lower extremities (anterior bowing or "saber shin"). The late development of cardiovascular syphilis is rare, but interstitial keratitis is common. Photophobia, pain, circumcorneal inflammation, and superficial and deep vascularization of the cornea may occur any time between the ages of 5 and 30 years. Asymptomatic or symptomatic neurosyphilis is also common in these patients and resembles the disease in adults. Eighth-nerve deafness is particularly common. Necrotizing funisitis, an inflammatory process involving the matrix of the umbilical cord and characterized by perivascular inflammation and obliterative endarteritis, is for all practical purposes pathognomonic of congenital syphilis. This disease should be suspected clinically whenever the umbilical cord is swollen and discolored red, white, and blue to resemble a barber's pole[67] or has a positive cord-blood VDRL/RPR.[41,66]

Other late characteristic stigmata include recurrent arthropathy and bilateral knee effusions (Clutton's joints); centrally notched, widely spread, peg-shaped upper central incisors (Hutchinson's teeth); frontal bossing; and poorly developed maxillas.[1,2] Because at least one third of the mothers who give birth to syphilitic children have not had prenatal care and about half have had a nonreactive serologic test during the first trimester of pregnancy, serologic testing of the mother is always warranted at the time of delivery, especially in high-risk patients,[2,41,62,65] and a full evaluation of the neonate to include physical examination, routine conventional blood tests, bone radiographs, VDRL/RPR, and IgM immunoblotting on serum and CSF.[68] The best means is to combine IgM antibody determination (IgM immunoblotting) with PCR antigen detection (see later discussion).[41] Because giving penicillin to the neonate is virtually risk free, all neonates born to syphilitic mothers should be treated, regardless of whether the mother was treated during her pregnancy.

So-Called Atypical Presentations of Syphilis

As noted previously, the clinical presentation and course of syphilis are quite varied, and the clinical diagnosis can sometimes elude the clinician even under the best of circumstances. Because some patients may have been treated with antibiotics that are suboptimal (e.g., oral penicillin, and in some cases, benzathine penicillin) or inadequate (e.g., spectinomycin) and because of the larger pool of immunocompromised patients and the relative inexperience of today's clinician with syphilitic patients, there is a sense that unusual patterns and atypical presentations have become more common. However, protean manifestations are the hallmark of syphilis. Older clinicians were never surprised by unusual or atypical findings, and today's clinician should not be either.

LABORATORY DIAGNOSIS

Direct Examination for Spirochetes

In primary, secondary, and early congenital syphilis, the darkfield examination or immunofluorescent staining of mucocutaneous lesions is the quickest and most direct laboratory method of establishing the diagnosis.[1-3,69] Examination of a serous transudate from moist lesions such as a primary chancre, condyloma latum, or mucous patch is most productive, because these lesions have the largest numbers of treponemes. However, *T. pallidum* can be demonstrated at times from dry skin lesions and from lymph nodes by saline aspiration (the saline must be free of bactericidal additives). For a darkfield examination, the surface of the suspected lesion should be cleaned with saline and gently abraded with dry gauze so as not to produce gross bleeding. The serous exudate can then be squeezed onto a glass slide, covered with a cover slip, and examined with darkfield or phase-contrast microscopy. A drop of nonbactericidal saline may be added if the preparation is too thick. *T. pallidum* has a corkscrew appearance and moves in a spiraling motion with a characteristic 90° undulation about its midpoint (Fig. 235-8). A lesion should be considered nonsyphilitic only after three negative examinations have been made. Specimens from mouth lesions are useless because *T. pallidum* cannot be distinguished with certainty from nonpathogenic treponemes. A scattering of a few red blood cells indicates that the specimen is adequate. Cleaning of the lesion with a topical antiseptic, soap, or bactericidal saline obscures the diagnosis because dead and nonmotile organisms are difficult to identify. However, if this is inadvertently done, direct or indirect immunofluorescent or immunoperoxidase antibody staining can be used to establish the presence of *T. pallidum*.

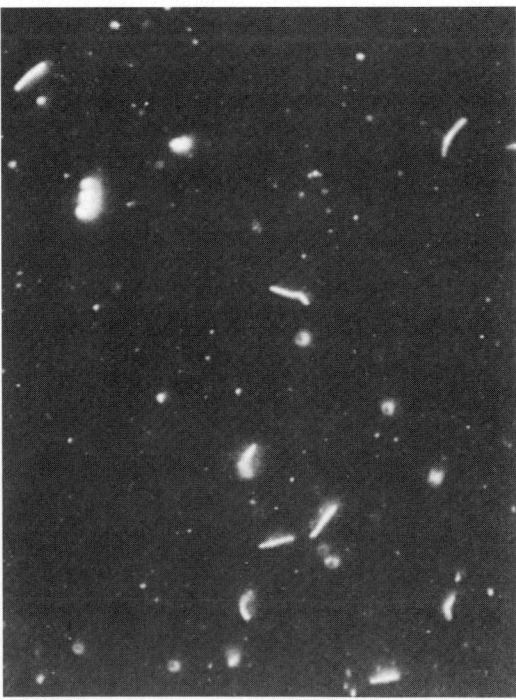

FIGURE 235-8. Darkfield examination. The morphologic characteristics of the spirochetes and the characteristic flexous motion about their centers can be appreciated.

Biopsy Specimen

The spirochete can sometimes be demonstrated in biopsy materials. A silver stain is most commonly used, but confusion with elastic tissues can occur. Specific immunofluorescent or immunoperoxidase antibody staining of nonfrozen pathologic specimens is now preferred to silver staining to establish a more precise diagnosis.

Serologic Tests

Confusion surrounds interpretation of the serologic tests for syphilis, principally because two different types of antibodies are measured: the *nonspecific* nontreponemal reaginic antibody and the *specific* anti-treponemal antibody. The test for the former is inexpensive, rapid, and convenient for screening large numbers of sera (e.g., donated blood) and as an indication of disease activity. Specific antibody tests establish the high likelihood of a treponemal infection, either currently or at some time in the past (Table 235-5). To establish a diagnosis of syphilis, the two types of serologic tests are most often used together, although attempts to improve the single tests are ongoing.[70] It should be emphasized that serologic test results for syphilis on rare occasions may be negative in active cases, especially in older patients.

Nontreponemal Reaginic Tests

Much of the confusion about these tests arises from the term *reagin*. This is the result of an unfortunate quirk in the evolution of medical terminology, because it has nothing to do with the reagin IgE that is involved in allergic reactions. "Syphilis reaginic" antibodies are IgG and IgM antibodies directed against a lipoidal antigen resulting from the interaction of host tissues with *T. pallidum* or from *T. pallidum* itself. The earliest cardiolipin antigens used to measure reaginic antibody were crude extracts made from beef livers or beef hearts. False-positive reactions were common. The cardiolipin-cholesterol-lecithin used today is a much purer preparation and gives fewer false-positive reactions. The relationship of these tests to *T. pallidum* infection is fortuitous.

The standard nontreponemal test is the VDRL slide test, in which heated serum (56° C) is tested for its ability to flocculate or agglutinate a suspension of a cardiolipin-cholesterol-lecithin antigen. It is now most often used to monitor a patient's response to therapy. Most laboratories and blood banks have adapted a modification for routine screening for syphilis: the rapid plasma reagin (RPR) card test, the automated reagin test (ART), or the toluidine red unheated syphilis test (TRUST). A prozone phenomenon occurs in up to 2% of infected persons, especially in secondary syphilis and pregnancy,[71] and appropriate dilutions should be performed whenever the index of suspicion is high (e.g., patients with another sexually transmitted disease, pregnant women, drug abusers, co-HIV–infected individuals). A fourfold change in titer using the same test method, either VDRL or RPR, is necessary to demonstrate a clinically significant difference, preferably being performed in the same laboratory at the same time. Nontreponemal antibody tests vary during the course of untreated disease.[72] They reach their highest prevalence and titer during the sec-

TABLE 235-5 Percentage of Untreated Patients with Positive Responses to Commonly Used Serologic Tests

Type of Test	Early (Primary and Secondary)	Late (Late Latent and Tertiary)
Nontreponemal (reagenic) tests VDRL, RPR, ART TRUST	70-100	60-98
Specific treponemal tests FTA-abs, TP-PA (TPHA, MHA-TP)	50-85	97-100

The nonspecific nontreponemal tests should revert to a less than 1:2 titer or negative (nonreactive) when effective treatment is given except in unusual circumstances (see text). Specific treponemal tests may also revert to negative if effective treatment is given early.

ondary and early latent stages and decline thereafter, usually to less than 1:4. Over time, at least 25% of untreated persons become VDRL or RPR negative.

One of the more difficult situations to interpret is the patient with a persistently positive VDRL test after apparently adequate therapy ("chronic persistor"). This may be attributable to a biologically false reaction, a persistent active infection, or reinfection, especially when the titer is greater than 1:4. A persistently high-titered RPR or VDRL result is more common in HIV-infected persons because of the polyclonal antibody stimulation, a manifestation of immune dysfunction often seen in these patients, especially in early HIV disease.[37,73]

The quantitative VDRL/RPR test should become nonreactive 1 year after successful therapy in primary syphilis and 2 years after successful therapy in secondary syphilis.[74,75] Most patients with late syphilis should be nonreactive by the fifth year after treatment.[76] The time required for the test to become negative correlates with the interval between contact and institution of therapy and with the severity of illness, especially with the type of skin lesions manifested in the secondary stage (i.e., a patient with a macular rash reverts to a negative titer sooner than does a patient with a papular rash).[77] Therefore, a positive VRDL or RPR response after 1 year in a patient treated for primary syphilis or after 2 years in a patient treated for secondary syphilis suggests persistent infection, reinfection, or a biologically false-positive reaction. A patient with adequately treated late syphilis should have a negative response after 5 years.[77] As with all quantitative serologic tests, only a fourfold or greater change in titer is meaningful.

In summary, these tests are inexpensive, reliable, and easy to perform. They have utility for screening sera and in areas of high prevalence (e.g., southeastern United States) should still be used to screen hospital admissions.[78] Also, they have great utility as a gauge of the success of treatment.[70,74-76]

Specific Treponemal Tests

These tests measure antibodies against specific *T. pallidum* antigens. The principal specific anti-treponemal antibody tests performed today are the FTA-abs and *T. pallidum* agglutination tests (TPHA and MHA-TP), although attempts to improve the specificity continue.[70,79] The FTA-abs is a standard indirect immunofluorescent antibody test that uses *T. pallidum* harvested from rabbit testes as the antigen. The patient's serum is first absorbed with nonpathogenic treponemal antigen (referred to as "sorbent") to remove "natural" cross-reacting antibody that may have been raised against saprophytic treponemes of the oral cavity or genital tract. The test has the disadvantage of being standardized at one serum dilution (1:5), and, as with most immunofluorescent tests, its interpretation can be quite subjective. Therefore, it requires a great attention to detail, is difficult to standardize from one laboratory to the next, and is difficult to quantify. Particle agglutination tests, the TPHA and MHA-TP, are also used to measure specific treponemal antibody. The TPHA has the advantage of being easier to perform than the FTA-abs. It uses a "sorbent" to increase specificity. Although it is as specific as the FTA-abs, it is less sensitive in early disease. For practical purposes, it is interchangeable with the FTA-abs test. The MHA-TP test is an adaptation of the TPHA that uses a microtiter plate.

These tests would be relatively expensive as screening tests, and if they were applied to a low-risk population, the number of false-positive reactions would increase proportionately. Therefore, their principal use is to verify a positive nontreponemal reaginic test result. Once positive, the patient usually remains positive for life. However, reversion to a nonreactive status may occur in up to 10% of patients, especially in those who are treated early.

The TPI test is primarily of historical interest and rarely used today, but it was the standard against which all specific treponemal tests were compared. It determines the ability of antibody plus complement to immobilize live *T. pallidum* as visualized under a darkfield microscope (i.e., it is a bactericidal test). Because it requires maintenance of replicating *T. pallidum* in rabbits, it is expensive, time consuming, and difficult to perform, and its utility in today's setting has been ques-

tioned. Only a few research laboratories have maintained the capability to perform the TPI test.

Western immunoblotting can also be used as a confirmatory test for syphilis[80,81] and is particularly important in congenital syphilis.[41,59]

The comparative reactivities of the most widely used tests are shown in Table 235-5. When the diagnosis of syphilis is being seriously considered in an individual patient, the TPHA, MHA-TP, or FTA-abs test should be done. Once these have become positive and the diagnosis is established, the usefulness of these tests is limited because they can remain positive for life. A nontreponemal antibody test is very helpful for monitoring the efficacy of therapy. The failure to fall more than fourfold or become negative suggests a persistent infection, reinfection, or a false-positive test.

In congenital syphilis, the combination of a IgM immunoblotting (Western blot for *T. pallidum*-specific IgM) and immunofluorescent spirochetal antigen detection on nasopharyngeal and umbilical cord specimens is the most effective means to establish the diagnosis.[41] The best way to monitor these infants is with serial quantitative nontreponemal tests performed over several months. As with all serial serologic determinations, the most credible results are those performed simultaneously on appropriately stored serum samples. In contrast to IgM immunoblotting. the use of the IgM FTA-abs test on cord blood to diagnose congenital syphilis has been disappointing. Serum is the specimen of choice for all of the serological tests[82]; however, EDTA, sodium citrate, and heparin plasma may be used when serum cannot be obtained.

Tests for Neurosyphilis

Serologic tests for neurosyphilis have evolved over time. The CSF-VDRL, the oldest test, is insensitive but highly specific. A positive CSF-VDRL result in the appropriate clinical setting, especially in early syphilis,[82] establishes the diagnosis of neurosyphilis although serum antibody contamination is possible. (Note: although the sensitivity or specificity of the CSF-RPR has never been determined, based on deductive reasoning, a positive CSF-RPR would be highly significant.) A negative CSF-FTA unabsorbed, CSF-abs, CSF MHA-TP or CSF-TPHA test in essence rules out neurosyphilis in patients with late disease but not in patients with early disease.[24]

A CSF serologic diagnosis based on the production of local anti-treponemal antibodies as a discriminator of CNS invasion has improved sensitivity and specificity.[51-54,83-85] The most experience has been with the intrathecal *T. pallidum* antibody (ITPA) index and the TPHA index. The ITPA index is determined as follows:

$$\text{ITPA index} = \text{TPHA-CSF IgG titer/total CSF IgG/TPHA} - \text{serum IgG titer/total serum IgG}$$

The total IgG measurements are in milligrams. As long as the albumin serum-to-CSF ratio is greater than 144, indicating an undamaged blood-brain barrier, then a ratio of 3.0 or greater indicates active production of local anti-treponemal antibodies.

The TPHA index is determined as follows:

$$\text{TPHA index} = \text{MHATP-CSF titer/CSF albumin} \times 10^3/\text{serum albumin}$$

The albumin measurements are in milligrams per deciliter. A TPHA index greater than 100 is indicative of local CNS antibody production.

If the patient is treated early these indices are likely to return to normal, but if the patient is treated late (i.e., after 2 years) they are likely to remain abnormal for a prolonged period of time.[85]

Detection of specific oligoclonal immunoglobulins by immunofixation (enzyme-labeled antibodies) electrophoresis can also be used to detect locally produced CSF antibodies.[86] The PCR test for *T. pallidum* in the CSF and IgM immunoblotting are both specific and sensitive. A negative CSF-FTA unabsorbed, CSF MHA-TP, or CSF-TPHA test in essence rules out neurosyphilis in patients with late disease but not in patients with early disease.[87]

The finding of more than five mononuclear cells per cubic millimeter of CSF in the appropriate clinical setting is also suggestive of active neurosyphilis.

In summary, the diagnosis of active neurosyphilis is dependent on the various combinations of reactive serological tests, abnormalities in the CSF cell count or protein, a reactive CSF-VDRL, local CNS production of anti-treponemal antibodies, or PCR with or without clinical neurological symptoms.

False-Positive Serologic Test for Syphilis

The likelihood of a biological false-positive (BFP) reaction depends on the population being studied. Acute or transient false-positive nontreponemal reaginic test reactions may occur whenever there is a strong immunologic stimulus (e.g., acute bacterial or viral infection, vaccination, intravenous drug abuse, HIV infection). Positive reactions persisting for months occur in the presence of continued parenteral drug abuse; with autoimmune or connective tissue diseases, especially systemic lupus erythematosus; with aging (in up to 10% of those older than 70 years of age); in hypergammaglobulinemic states; and in HIV coinfection (Table 235-6). A false-positive nontreponemal reaginic test in this setting tends to be associated with other serum factors frequently associated with autoimmune diseases, such as antinuclear, antithyroid, or antimitochondrial antibodies, rheumatoid factor, and cryoglobulins.

A false-positive nontreponemal reaginic test can usually be verified (and syphilis excluded) by obtaining a negative specific treponemal antibody test (FTA-abs, TPHA, MHA-TP). However, at times the same illnesses that produce a false-positive nontreponemal reaginic test (e.g., systemic lupus erythematosus) also result in a positive or borderline-positive FTA-abs test reaction. Also, the FTA-abs may be positive when the VDRL is negative and vice versa. This false reaction can often be suggested by noting a beaded pattern of immunofluorescence on the treponemes, but the best definitive way to make the distinction is to obtain the functional but rarely available TPI test, PCR or immunoblotting using specific T. pallidum antigens such as 17-kDa, and so forth.[88] Other spirochetal illnesses, such as relapsing fever (Borrelia spp.), yaws, bejel, pinta, leptospirosis, or rat-bite fever (Spirillum minor), also yield positive nontreponemal and treponemal tests. Infection with Borrelia burgdorferi (Lyme disease) results in a positive FTA-abs test but does not cause a positive nontreponemal reaginic reaction (VDRL or RPR).

Occasionally, an infected patient, especially with an underlying immune dysfunctional state, for example, co-HIV infection, will have a true positive nonspecific test with a false-negative specific treponemal test.[87]

In summary, the reaginic antibody tests (RPR, VDRL, ART) are used for screening large numbers of sera, the specific treponemal tests (TPHA, MHA-TP, FTA-abs) for confirming the diagnosis, and the quantitative nontreponemal antibody tests (RPR, VDRL) for assessing the adequacy of therapy.

PCR Test

PCR tests have been developed using a variety of syphilitic antigens. They are quite specific but do not distinguish live from dead organisms.[41,60] (The specimen should be shipped immediately on ice to arrive frozen to CDC; DASTLER-STD, CDC, 1600 Clifton Rd. MCS D-13, Atlanta, GA 3033.)

Isolation of *Treponema pallidum*

Because T. pallidum cannot be cultivated on artificial media, inoculation of laboratory animals (primates, rabbit testes) is the only means available at present for isolating the organism. The most experience has been with isolation in rabbits. The number of organisms that must be obtained from a human lesion to ensure a positive transfer appears to be as low as 4 to 10 spirochetes.

The lower portion of the rabbit testis is inoculated with 0.5 to 3.0 mL of the test material. The rabbits should be kept in a cool room (17° C /65° F). They must be serologically prescreened to exclude concurrent or previous infection with T. cuniculi, and they must be fed antibiotic-free chow. The rabbit testes or regional lymph nodes (or both) may be harvested after 3 weeks by mincing and then shaking

TABLE 235-6 Causes of Biological False-Positive (BFP) Serologic Test Reactions for Syphilis

Infectious diseases	*Mycoplasma* pneumonia
Lyme disease*	Measles
Leptospirosis	Chickenpox
Relapsing fever	Lymphogranuloma venereum
Ratbite fever (*Spirillum minor*)	Hepatitis (especially hepatitis C)
Leprosy	Infectious mononucleosis
Tuberculosis	Early HIV infectious
Pneumonococcal pneumonia	Noninfectious diseases
Subacute bacterial endocarditis	Drug addiction
Chancroid	Any connective disease disorder
Scarlet fever	Rheumatoid heart disease
Rickettsial disease	Blood transfusions (multiple)
Malaria	Pregnancy
Trypanosomiasis	"Old age"
Vaccinia (vaccination)	Chronic liver disease (noninfectious)

*Only specific treponemal tests, VDRL (RPR) negative.

them in a suitable buffer, usually phosphate-buffered saline, in an atmosphere of 5% to 10% carbon dioxide for 30 minutes. This material can be examined by darkfield or fluorescence antibody examination for treponemes, but if the result is negative, it should be injected into another set of test rabbits through at least two passages (because the sensitivity of a microscopic examination is approximately 10^5 organisms). Syphilitic infection in the rabbits should also be verified by serologic testing of the rabbit sera.

There has been limited success maintaining T. pallidum in tissue culture.[18]

Congenital Syphilis

The most reliable means to diagnose congenital syphilis is to test the mother at the time of birth. Most infants with congenital syphilis can be identified by physical examination and radiographic and ultrasonographic studies.[41,88] Delayed-onset syphilis (greater than 2 days) is best diagnosed by combining tests for IgM-specific antibodies (ELISA, Relispot, FTA-abs, or immunoblotting/Western blot) with antigen detection (darkfield, immunofluorescence or immunoperoxidase-labeled antibody staining, or PCR). Immunofluorescent labeled antibody staining with specifically tagged antibody is superior to darkfield examination. A calcium alginate swab is inserted into the posterior nasopharynx and rolled immediately onto slides for examination. A positive result on any test warrants a diagnosis of congenital syphilis.

TREATMENT

Although the efficacy of penicillin in the treatment of syphilis is well established, there has never been a well-controlled, carefully planned, prospective study to determine the optimal dose or duration of therapy.[88,89] Furthermore, the penicillin preparations used earlier are no longer available. Therefore, the following recommendations are based on extrapolation of older data and limited clinical experience and must be tempered with this knowledge. Furthermore, it should not be surprising that there are patients who have a persistent infection despite having received so-called "adequate therapy."[24,41,90]

Penicillin G, administered parenterally, is the preferred treatment for syphilis. The current CDC recommendation for the use of benzathine penicillin was obtained by extrapolation from the pharmacokinetics of penicillin therapy, the effect of the drug on T. pallidum under experimental conditions, and the available clinical data, and is adequate for the great majority of immunocompetent patients (Table 235-7).[91] For example, it has been shown in experimental infections that T. pallidum regenerates if penicillin blood levels are allowed to fall to subinhibitory levels after 18 to 24 hours.[89] Furthermore, it has been found from a variety of clinical and experimental data that a level equivalent to more than 0.03 μg/mL of penicillin is needed to ensure killing of T. pallidum, that maintenance of an effective blood level for at least 7 days is necessary to cure early syphilis, and that increasing the dose to more

TABLE 235-7 Recommended Therapy for Syphilis*

Stage	Patients Not Allergic to Penicillin	Patients Allergic to Penicillin
Early syphilis (primary, secondary, early latent)—adults	Benzathine penicillin G[†] 2.4 million units IM in a single dose Procaine penicillin, 2.4 million units IM daily, *plus* Probenecid 500 mg PO qid for 14 days *or* Ceftriaxone,[§] 250 mg IM qd or IV for 5 days or 1 g IM qd for 14 days *or* Azithromycin 2.0 g PO then 1g PO qd for 8 days	Doxycycline[*] 100 mg PO bid for 15 days, *or* tetracycline hydrochloride,[*] 500 mg PO qid for 15 days; *or* Azithromycin 2.0 g single dose[‡] or desensitization to penicillin in pregnant women[*] Doxycycline 100 mg PO bid for 28 days
Late latent or latent syphilis of unknown duration-adults, or tertiary syphilis or syphilis with HIV[**] or neurosyphilis-adults	Benzathine penicillin G[†] 2.4 million units IM given at weekly intervals × 3, Aqueous crystalline penicillin[†] G, 3.0-4.0 million units by IV infusion q4h for 10-14 days, *or* Ceftriaxone,[¶] 1 g IM or IV for 14 days, *or* Procaine penicillin G,[†] 2.4 million units IM, plus Probenecid, 0.5 g PO daily for 10 days or Amoxicillin 3g PO bid with 500 mg Probenecid PO bid for 10-14 days	
Pregnancy	Same regimen as for nonpregnant patient; only penicillin therapy reliably treats the infant.[‡]	
Congenital syphilis	Aqueous crystalline penicillin G, 100-150,000 units/kg IV daily in two or three divided doses for a minimum of 10 days, *or* Procaine penicillin G, 50,000 U/kg IM daily for a minimum of 10 days	
Children	Benzathine penicillin G[†] 50,000 units/kg/day IM in a single dose up to 2.4 million units	

[*]Therapeutic regimens other than penicillin have not been well studied, especially in patients with syphilis of longer than 1 year's duration; therefore, careful follow-up is mandatory.

[†]CDC recommendation; however, treatment failures with benzathine penicillin have been documented. Patients treated with benzathine penicillin should be reevaluated at 6-month intervals for neurosyphilis (see the text), HIV-positive patients should be evaluated at 3-month intervals

[‡]Because of the large number of well-documented treatment failures and corroborating laboratory studies, erythromycin is no longer recommended for the treatment of syphilis.

[§]Efficacy unknown, serologic follow-up useful, Ceftriaxone should be diluted in 1% lidocaine solution (1 g/3.6 mL) for IM injection.

[¶]Treatment failures have been reported. Chloramphenicol is theoretically beneficial treatment for neurosyphilis.

[**]Some authorities treat syphilis with HIV infection in the same manner as syphilis without HIV infection. However, treatment failures with ceftriaxone, procaine penicillin and azithromycin have been reported.

than 0.6 mg/kg over a period of 9 hours does not clear treponemes from primary chancres at an increased rate.[89,92] Therefore, it can be inferred that the most effective antibiotic treatment would be one that ensures an adequate blood level over a prolonged period (8 days or longer). The most convenient way to achieve this goal in the blood and avoid the issue of patient compliance is to treat with benzathine penicillin, despite the recognized potential inadequacies of this treatment for neurosyphilis, congenital syphilis, and during pregnancy.[24,41,90,91] *T. pallidum* has been isolated from the CSF of patients with only a chancre[24] and no other evidence of congenital neurosyphilis,[41] reflecting the early spirochetemia that always occurs and the consequent propensity to invade the CNS. Therefore, to reliably cure this readily and easily curable disease, one must adequately treat treponemes in the CNS (neurosyphilis) even in patients with primary or secondary infection. But treponemicidal levels of benzathine penicillin are not reliably achieved in the CSF of neonates, children or adults,[93] and numerous treatment failures have been recorded.[24,90,94-100] Nevertheless, the recommendation that benzathine penicillin be considered the treatment of choice was adopted despite the fact that retreatment was required in as many as 1 of 33 cases in the original study, and by extrapolation, fails to cure CNS invasion between 1 in 333 and 1 in 1000 patients.[101] On the other hand, there is ample clinical experience to suggest that, when an early diagnosis is made, fewer treponemes exist and the likelihood of a complete cure with relatively low doses of penicillin is increased.[89,92] Therefore, treatment with benzathine penicillin, which at least provides circulating penicillin, albeit at low levels, for 14 days and does not rely on patient compliance to take an antibiotic on a daily basis, is adequate for the majority of patients. However, because of the high probability of CNS invasion, an increasing number of clinicians do not accept the risk of their patients later developing neurosyphilis (between 1:333 and 1:1000) and now treat syphilis with combination or prolonged therapy. This is especially true when there is evidence to suggest that the host may be immunocompromised, particularly when the patient is infected with HIV (see later discussion).

Early incubating syphilis is probably aborted when gonorrhea is treated with the currently recommended regimens such as azithromycin,[102] spectinomycin excepted.

Because of the high risk of infection, preventive or "epidemiologic" antibiotic treatment should be given to anyone who has been exposed to infectious syphilis within the preceding 3 months. Serologic studies must also be done to establish the diagnosis and to monitor the adequacy of the response to therapy. As noted previously, adequately treated non–HIV-infected patients should have a predictable fall in their nontreponemal reaginic antibody titer. These patients should be considered to have early syphilis.

Pregnant patients should receive penicillin, following dosage schedules appropriate for the stage of syphilis as recommended for nonpregnant patients. If the patient has a well-documented penicillin allergy, the choice is more difficult, because the efficacy of treatment for the fetus in these cases is not well established. Hence, penicillin desensitization is strongly recommended (see Chapter 22).[103] The patient is given gradually increasing doses of oral or intravenous penicillin over a period of 3 to 4 hours, until full tolerance is achieved. Erythromycin was used in the past, but because of well documented unacceptable failure rates it should be used only as a last recourse. Pharmacological characteristics, studies in rabbit models, and limited studies in humans suggest that ceftriaxone and azithromycin is adequate therapy. However, conflicting clinical experience has been reported in patients who are infected with HIV.[104,105] Tetracycline, doxycycline, erythromycin, and chloramphenicol are *not* recommended because of potential adverse effects on the mother or fetus, or both. The mother should be monitored closely during and after the pregnancy, and if an increase in a nontreponemal reagin titer or a positive PCR test occurs, she and her infant must be retreated.

The risk of infection for the infant is minimal if the mother has received adequate penicillin treatment during pregnancy. Nevertheless, the child must be examined monthly after delivery and until the nontreponemal reaginic antibody test or PCR becomes negative. Penicillin treatment should never be withheld to "prove the diagnosis," and every neonate born to a syphilitic mother should be treated promptly unless adequate, serologically effective treatment with penicillin can be documented more than 1 month before delivery.[41,62] There is no evidence that the efficacy of penicillin treatment of syphilis has diminished over 60 years,[89,92] probably because of the genetic fidelity of *T. pallidum*.[15] However, there is evidence that *T. pallidum* can accept resistant plasmids, and the possibility exists that penicillin treatment may become inadequate in the future.

Tetracycline, doxycycline, chloramphenicol, ceftriaxone, and other cephalosporins and azithromycin have all been shown to be effective alternative antibiotics in animal models and in small clinical trials for treatment of early syphilis, although failures with doxycycline have been reported. Patients who are also infected with HIV, like any other immunosuppressed group, present special problems (see later discussions). An intact cellular immune system is an important determinant of the severity of syphilitic disease. Therefore, most authorities feel that these patients should be treated as if they had late latent syphilis regardless of their clinical findings, especially when they are in the later stages of their HIV infection.

Late Syphilis, Asymptomatic and Symptomatic Neurosyphilis

Because the CNS is invaded during the spirochetemia in up to 40% of patients[2,24,41] and because spirochetemia occurs soon after the infection is contracted, all patients with syphilis are at risk for neurosyphilis, and therefore a CSF examination should be considered. Specific indications for CSF examination include neurologic or ophthalmologic pathology, latent syphilis, HIV infection, and failure to respond to therapy with titers that fail to fall appropriately. Patients with manifestations of tertiary syphilis should also have a CSF examination. The finding of an elevated mononuclear cell count in the CSF, a positive reactive nontreponemal antibody test (VDRL), production of local CNS anti-treponemal antibody, or a positive PCR test establishes the diagnosis.[41,51-54]

Because benzathine penicillin G does not reliably produce detectable levels of penicillin in the CSF, this drug cannot be relied on as a treatment of neurosyphilis (failure rate: 1:333 to 1:1000).[24,91,106-108] To better ensure adequate antibiotic levels in the CNS, 12 to 24 million units of aqueous penicillin G should be given intravenously for 8 to 10 days[90]; some have used amoxicillin (3.0 g twice daily) plus probenecid (0.5 to 1.0 g orally) for 14 days,[109,110] or doxycycline (200 mg orally twice daily) for 21 days but these regimens are not recommended by the CDC.[111] Procaine benzyl penicillin (1 g intramuscularly) plus probenecid (1 g orally daily) and ceftriaxone (1 g intramuscularly daily) for 14 days has been used successfully,[105] but treatment failures have been suggested.[104] Follow-up CSF examinations should be done in every case—every 3 to 6 months for at least 3 years or until serum nontreponemal antibodies disappear, local CNS treponemal antibodies disappear, or CSF oligoclonal bands disappear. Positron emission tomography (PET), MRI, and single photon emission computed tomography (SPECT) have allowed more precise investigation of CNS invasion and have demonstrated dramatic radiographic and clinical improvement with treatment.[43a,112] Malignancy of the CNS has been associated with false-positive results on nontreponemal and treponemal tests, but this has almost always been associated with a negative serum TPHA, MHA-TP, or FTA-abs reaction.

Treatment of Syphilitic Otitis

Although the evidence is not incontrovertible that hearing loss will be reversed, patients with possible syphilitic hearing loss should be treated.[112] Treatment should be prolonged (6 weeks to 3 months) and, unless contraindicated, should include prednisone, 30 to 60 mg every day or every other day, at least for the first 7 to 8 days. Other antibiotic treatments for neurosyphilis would be an alternative choice to parenteral penicillin.

Treatment of Ocular Syphilis

Anterior and/or pan-uveitis is a frequent complication of acute and chronic neurosyphilis, and thus should be treated with antibiotic regimens appropriate for neurosyphilis. It appears to be an increased manifestation of co-HIV infection.[45-47]

Treatment of HIV-Coinfected Persons

Because of the concurrent immune dysfunction and the propensity for developing more severe disease, most authorities feel that coinfected persons should be treated with a course of antibiotics similar to those used for late latent syphilis.[54a,60,73,105,113-124] However, treatment failures with ceftriaxone, procaine penicillin[124a] and azithromycin have been reported.[124b]

Persistent Infection

The question of persistent infection despite adequate therapy has been a controversial subject for many years. Although the efficacy of treating *T. pallidum* with adequate doses of penicillin is unquestioned, in some patients in whom the spirochetes become sequestered in areas where adequate levels of penicillin are not easily achieved, such as the anterior chamber of the eye,[125] the CNS,[24,90] and the labyrinth of the inner ear.[126] Whether these persistent organisms can cause a clinically evident illness at some later date remains speculative. However, there are a number of reports of unusual neurologic, optic, and otic findings for which there was little or no explanation except a positive serologic test for syphilis. In the past, attempts at isolation of these persistent organisms have met with variable success, and their validity has been questioned. However, there is now little doubt that *T. pallidum* can persist after inadequate treatment, particularly in the CNS, and that these organisms can be isolated by inoculation of appropriate human materials into laboratory animals or by PCR.[24,41] The challenge facing clinicians is to identify and treat these few patients. Anyone with neurologic, optic, or otic abnormalities who has or has had syphilis should be considered for CSF examination, and if there are any abnormalities (see previous discussion) or unexplained neurologic signs or symptoms, the patient should be treated for neurosyphilis.

Follow-up and Retreatment

All patients with early or congenital syphilis should have repeat quantitative nontreponemal tests at 3, 6, and 12 months (see previous discussion). All patients with secondary syphilis or syphilis of more than 1 year's duration should also have a repeat nontreponemal serologic test 24 months after treatment. Examination of the CSF is also warranted in all patients, especially if they were treated with benzathine penicillin. All patients with documented neurosyphilis must be monitored carefully with serologic testing and CSF examinations including MRI, PET, or SPECT imaging scans until all abnormal parameters including local CNS production of antibodies normalize.

Retreatment should be considered whenever clinical signs and symptoms of syphilis persist or recur or there is a sustained level or an increase in the titer of a nontreponemal test after 6 months, or a positive VDRL/RPR reaction persists beyond 12 months in primary syphilis, 24 months in secondary or latent syphilis, or 5 years in late syphilis; or there is a positive PCR test result.[74-77]

Defining the Adequacy of Treatment

As noted previously, a quantitative decrease in nontreponemal reaginic tests is quite reliable as a measure of the adequacy of treatment. The time required for the tests to become nonreactive depends on the length of time the patient was infected before adequate treatment was instituted, but all patients should have a titer of less than 1:2 by year 5. Exceptions to this rule occur in persons with a chronic antigenic stimulation or immune dysfunction (e.g., HIV-infected persons).[74-77] Specific treponemal antibody tests can also revert to negative, especially when treatment is instituted early.

Management of Patients with a History of Penicillin Allergy

Because penicillin G is the most reliable treatment for all stages of syphilis, desensitization of patient should be considered.[91] This can be done orally or intravenously (see Chapter 22).

Jarisch-Herxheimer Reaction

The Jarisch-Herxheimer (JH) reaction is a systemic reaction resembling gram-negative sepsis that usually begins 1 to 2 hours after the initial treatment of syphilis with effective antibiotics, especially penicillin. It consists of the abrupt onset of fever, chills, myalgias, headache, tachycardia, hyperventilation, vasodilation with flushing, varying degrees of obtundation, and mild hypotension. It is particularly common when secondary syphilis is treated (70% to 90%) but can occur in any stage (10% to 25%).[127] It lasts from 12 to 24 hours and has been well correlated with the release from the spirochetes of heat-stable pyrogen. Patients should be warned of the reaction before treatment. Varying degrees of severity occur. The reaction is self limited but can result in acute deleterious effects. It can be prevented or treated with an anti-inflammatory agent such as aspirin every 4 hours for a period of 24 to 48 hours. Prednisone can also abort the reaction, and one dose of 60 mg PO or IV should be given as adjunctive therapy to JH patients with cardiovascular or symptomatic neurosyphilis and to pregnant patients[128] to avoid catastrophic consequences.

Immunity

Magnuson and associates[25] were able to demonstrate in human volunteers that immunity developed to reinfection. This immunity appeared not to be absolute but became more solid the longer the infection remained untreated. Humoral antibodies are only partially protective, because experimental infection in humans and rabbits can be produced when they are present. On the other hand, the granulomatous lesion (gumma), a presumed correlate of cell-mediated immunity, is produced at a time when syphilitic reinfection is resisted. HIV-infected persons have a propensity to develop more severe disease. Likewise, malnourished patients, who also have a deficit of cellular immune function, are prone to develop more severe syphilitic disease. *T. pallidum* has evolved mechanisms to evade host immune defenses and establish a chronic infection.[17,26] Suggested reasons for this include (1) a waxy, nonimmunogenic coat through which very few protein antigens protrude; (2) residence in nonimmunogenic privileged sites, such as the inner ear, in the eye, or in the CNS; (3) induction of markedly increased levels of prostaglandin E_2; and (4) a subpopulation of spirochetes that are resistant to phagocytosis. In contrast to those from uninfected rabbits, macrophages from infected rabbits respond to lipopolysaccharide but not to *T. pallidum*. This treponeme-induced macrophage downregulation is primarily caused by decreased production of interleukin-2 secondary to increased levels of prostaglandin E_2.

The likelihood of development of syphilis in a susceptible person who has unprotected sexual intercourse with a patient with infectious syphilis is estimated to be about 50%. However, in controlled volunteer experiments, all volunteers without a history of serologic evidence of previous contact with *T. pallidum* developed syphilis. Obviously, the relative importance of variations in sexual and hygienic practices, immune status, inoculum size, and other factors play an important role in the transmissibility of *T. pallidum*.

Congenital syphilis appears not to confer immunity to syphilis.[129]

SYPHILIS IN PERSONS INFECTED WITH HIV

Because HIV disease and syphilis are sexually transmitted diseases, coinfection is common. The two diseases can affect each other in a number of ways. As with other ulcer causing conditions, they may enhance the acquisition and transmission of each other[130] but also upregulate the CCR5 co-receptor expression, thereby increasing the likelihood of transmission.[131] The natural course of syphilis may be affected, usually resulting in a high antigen load and a more malignant course.[132,133] The serologic tests for syphilis may be modified, usually resulting in extremely high titers and a failure to decrease in response to adequate treatment[73]; in other cases, a serologic response may fail to develop.[134,135] Finally, high-dose or prolonged therapy may be required to effect a cure in coinfected persons.[60,114-124,136]

Although patients with syphilis and HIV coinfection have shown no distinctive or unique clinical presentation or pathological manifestations from those without concurrent HIV infection, they are at an increased risk to manifest a more protracted and malignant course, greater constitutional symptoms, greater organ involvement, atypical and florid skin rashes, multiple genital ulcers, concomitant chancre during the secondary stage, and a significant predisposition to develop symptomatic neurosyphilis, especially uveitis.[16,17] However, the failure of benzathine penicillin to cure coinfected patients has been frequently reported,[114,124,136] although the actual failure rate is not known. Given the known failure rate, which may be as high as 3% in non-HIV-

infected persons[101] and the critical role that an intact cellular arm of the immune system plays in clearing the infection, this occurrence should not be surprising. Furthermore, the most conspicuous manifestations of these treatment failures are neurological or ocular. Therefore, a more vigorous or more prolonged course of antibiotics, sufficient to cure late latent or neurosyphilis, is prudent (see Table 235-7).[59] There is also a theoretical possibility that bacteriostatic drugs such as doxycycline may be less effective because of the immune impairment.

HIV-infected patients are also more likely to develop aberrant serologic responses.[72,132,133] They may have false-positive or increasing reaginic titers despite adequate therapy, especially during the earlier phases of HIV infection, when polyclonal B-cell stimulation is most prevalent. Also, they may fail to develop a response because of an overwhelming antigen load or severe immune dysfunction occurring late in the disease. Finally, as many as 11% of HIV-infected persons have a biologic false-positive serologic test. Therefore, a high index of suspicion and extraordinary means to establish the diagnosis (e.g., special stains of biopsy specimens, PCR tests) may be required.[134,135]

After treatment, aggressive serologic follow-up is recommended (at 1, 2, 3, 6, 9, and 12 months). Failure of a serologic response should usually lead to retreatment, but clinical judgment must be used because HIV coinfection may lead to an aberrant response. HIV-2 infection appears not to impact on the clinical course of syphilis.[137]

REFERENCES

1. Kampmeier RH. Essentials of Syphilology. 3rd ed. Philadelphia: JB Lippincott; 1943.
2. Stokes JH, Beerman H, Ingraham NR. Modern Clinical Syphilology, Diagnosis, Treatment: Case Study. 3rd ed. Philadelphia: WB Saunders; 1945.
3. Hook EW 3rd, Marra CM. Acquired syphilis in adults. N Engl J Med. 1992;326:1060-1069.
4. Tramont EC. The impact of syphilis on humankind. Med Clin N Am. 2004;18:101-110.
5. Hall V, Waisbren BA. Syphilis as a major theme of James Joyce's *Ulysses*. Arch Intern Med. 1980;140:963-965.
6. Parran T. Shadow on the Land: Syphilis. New York: Reynal & Hitchcock; 1937.
7. Zimmer C. Can genes solve the syphilis mystery? Science 2001;292:291.
8. Waugh MA. Venereal disease in sixteenth century England. Med Hist. 1973;17:152-161.
9. Mays S, Crane-Kramer G, Bayliss A. Two probable cases of treponemal disease of medieval date form England. Am J Phys Antropol. 2003;120:133-134.
10. Ricord PH. A Treatise on Venereal Diseases. New York: P. Gordon; 1842.
11. Austin SC, Stolley PD, Lasky T. The history of malario-therapy for neurosyphilis. JAMA. 1992;268:516-519.
12. Katz RV, Kegeles SS, Green BL, et al. The Tuskegee Legacy Project: History, preliminary scientific findings, and unanticipated societal benefits. Dent Clin North Am. 2003;47:1-19.
13. Fairchild AL, Bayer R. Uses and abuses of Tuskegee. Science. 1999;284:219-221.
14. Antal MG, Lukehart SA, Meheus AZ. The endemic treponematoses. Microbes Infect. 2002;4:83-94.
15. Norris SJ, Weinstock GM. The genome sequence of *Treponema pallidum*, the syphilis spirochete: Will clinicians benefit? Curr Opin Infect Dis. 2000;13:29-36.
16. Blanco DR, Miller JN, Lovett MA. Surface antigens of the syphilis spirochete and their potential as virulence determinants. Emerg Infect Dis. 1997;3:11-20.
17. Radolf JD. Role of outer membrane architecture in immune evasion by *Treponema pallidum* and *Borrelia burgdorpheri*. Trends Microbiol. 1994;2:307-311.
18. Cox DL. Culture of *Treponema pallidum*. Methods Enzymol. 1994;236:390-405.
19. Norris SJ, Cox DL, Weinstock GM. Biology of *Treponema pallidum*: Correlation of functional activities with genome sequences. J. Mol Microbiol Biotechnol. 2001;3:37-62.
20. Agacfidan A, Kohl P. Sexually transmitted disease (STD's) in the world. FEMS Immunol Med Microbiol. 1999;24:431-435.
21. Rampalo AM. Can syphilis be eradicated from the world? Curr Opin Infect Dis. 2001;14:41-44.
22. Jones DL, Irwin K, Inciardi J, et al. The high-risk sexual practices of crack-smoking sex workers recruited from the streets of three American cities. Sex Transm Dis. 1998;25:187-193.
23. Kahn RH, Scholl DT, Shane SM, et al. Screening for syphilis in arrestees; usefulness for community-wide syphilis surveillance and control. Sex Transm Dis. 2002;29:150-156.
24. Lukehart S, Hook EW, Baker-Zander SH, et al. Invasion of the central nervous system by *Treponema pallidum*: Implications for diagnosis and therapy. Ann Intern Med. 1988;109:855-862.
25. Magnuson HJ, Thomas EW, Olansky S, et al. Inoculation syphilis in human volunteers. Medicine (Baltimore). 1956;35:33-42.
26. Salazar JC, Karsten ROH, Radolf JD. The immune response to infection with *Treponema pallidum*, the stealth pathogen. Microb Infect. 2002;1133-1140.
27. Fitzgerald TJ. The Th₁/Th₂ switch in syphilitic infection: Is it detrimental? Infect Immun. 1992;60:3475-3479.

28. Lusiak M, Podwinska J. Interleukin 10 and its role in the regulation of the cell-mediated immune response in syphilis. Arch Immunol Ther Exp. 2001;49:417-421.

29. Lukehart SA, Shaffer JM, Baker Zander SA. A subpopulation of *Treponema pallidum* is resistant to phagocytosis: Possible mechanism of persistence. J Infect Dis. 1992;166:1449-1453.

30. O'Regan S, Fong JSC, de Chadarevian JP, et al. Treponemal antigens in congenital and acquired syphilitic nephritis. Ann Intern Med. 1976;85:325-327.

31. Clark EG, Danbolt N. The Oslo study of the natural course of untreated syphilis. Med Clin North Am. 1964;48:613-621.

32. Rockwell DH, Yobs AR, Moore MB. The Tuskeegee study of untreated syphilis: The 30th year of observation. Arch Intern Med. 1964;114:792.

33. Rosahn PD. Autopsy studies in syphilis. J Vener Dis. 1947;649(Suppl 21).

34. Drusin LM, Topf-Olstein B, Levy-Zombeck E. Epidemiology of infectious syphilis at a tertiary hospital. Arch Intern Med. 1979;135:901-904.

35. Long BW, Johnston JH, Wetzel W, et al. Gastric syphilis: Endoscopic and histologic features mimicking lymphoma. Am J Gastroenterol. 1995;90:1504-1507.

36. Chapel TA. The variability of syphilitic chancres. Sex Transm Dis. 1978;5:68-72.

37. Rompalo AM, Lawlor J, Seaman P, et al. Modification of syphilitic genital ulcer manifestations by coexistent HIV infection. Sex Transm Dis. 200;8:448-454.

38. Vural M, Ilikkan B, Polat E, et al. A premature newborn with vesiculobullous skin lesions. Eur J Pediatr. 2003;162:197-199.

39. Chapel TA. The signs and symptoms of secondary syphilis. Sex Transm Dis. 1980;7:161-167.

40. Merritt HH, Moore M. Acute neurosyphilitic meningitis. Medicine (Baltimore). 1935;14:119.

41. Michelow IC, Wendel GD, Norgard MV, et al. Central nervous system infection in congenital syphilis. N Engl J Med 2002;346:1792-1798.

42. Lauria G, Erbetta A, Pareyson D, et al. Parenchymatous neurosyphilis. Neurol Sci. 2001;22:281-282.

43. Lauria G, Kikuchi S, Shinpo K, et al. Subacute syphilitic meningomyelitis with characteristic spinal MRI findings. J Neurol. 2003;250:106-107.

43a. Berbel-Garcia A, Porta-Esstemann J, Martinex-Salio A, et al. Magnetic resonance image, reversible lesions in a patient with general paresis. Sex Transm Dis. 2004;31:350-352.

44. Atten MJ, Attar BM, Teopengo E, et al. Gastric syphilis: A disease with multiple manifestations. Am J Gastroenterol. 1994;89:2227-2229.

45. Gurvinder PT, Kaur S, Gupta R, et al. Syphilitic panuveitis and asymptomatic neurosyphilis: A marker of HIV infection. Int J STD AIDS. 2001;12:754-756.

46. Aldave AJ, King JA, Cunningham ET. Ocular syphilis. Curr Opin Ophthalmol. 2001;12:433-441.

47. Omerod LD, Pukin JE, Sobel JD. Syphilitic posterior uveitis: Correlative findings and significance. Clin Infect Dis. 2001;32:1661-1673.

48. Hansen K, Hvid-Jacobson H, Lindewald PS, et al. Bone lesions in early syphilis detected by bone scintigraphy. Br J Vener Dis. 1984;60:256-258.

49. Sonne JE, ZieferB, Linstrom C. Manifestations of otosyphilis as visualized with computed tomography. Otol Neurotol. 2002;23:806-807.

50. Merritt HH, Adams RD, Solomon HC. Neurosyphilis. New York: Oxford University Press; 1946.

51. VanEijk RVW, Wolters EC, Tutuarima JA, et al. Effect of early and late syphilis on central nervous system: Cerebrospinal fluid changes and neurologic deficit. Genitourin Med. 1987;63:77-82.

52. Lugar A, Schmidt BL, Steyer K, et al. Diagnosis of neurosyphilis by examination of the cerebrospinal fluid. Br J Vener Dis. 1981;57:232-237.

53. Muller F, Moskophidis M. Estimation of the local production of antibodies to *Treponema pallidum* in the central nervous system of patients with neurosyphilis. Br J Vener Dis. 1983;59:80-84.

54. Inagaki H, Kawai T, Miyata M, et al. Polymerase chain reaction detection of treponemal DNA in pseudolymphomatous lesions. Hum Pathol. 1996;27:761-765.

54a. Marra CM, Maxwell CL, Smith SL, et al. Cerebrospinal fluid abnormalities in patients with syphilis: association with clinical and laboratory features. J Infect Dis. 2004;189:369-376.

55. Chesney AM, Kemp I. Incidence of *Spirochetea pallida* in cerebrospinal fluid during early stages of syphilis. JAMA. 1924;83:1725-1733.

56. Kelley RE, Bell L, Kelley SE, et al. Syphilis detection in cerebrovascular disease. Stroke. 1989;20:230-234.

57. Da Gama, RD, Cidade M. Interstital keratitis as the initial expression of syphilitic reactivation (Images in Clinical Medicine). N Engl J Med. 2002;346:1799.

58. Balkany TJ, Dans PE. Reversible sudden deafness in early acquired syphilis. Arch Otolaryngol. 1978;104:60.

59. Sanchez PJ, Wendel GD, Grimprel E, et al. Evaluation of molecular methodologies and rabbit infectivity testing for the diagnosis of congenital syphilis and neonatal central nervous system invasion by *Treponema pallidum*. J Infect Dis. 1993;167:168-177.

60. Tramont EC. Neurosyphilis in patients with human immunodeficiency virus infection. N Engl J Med. 1994;332:1169-1170.

61. Pugh PJ, Grech EV. Syphilitic aortitis (Images in Clinical Medicine. N Engl J Med; 2002;346:676.

62. Sheffield JS, Sanchez PJ, Morris F, et al. Congential syphilis after maternal treatment for syphilis during pregnancy. Am J Obstet Gynecol. 2002;186:569-573.

63. Parker CR, Wendel GD. The effects of syphilis on endocrine function of the fetoplacental unit. Am J Dis Gynecol. 1988;159:1327-1331.

64. Gust DA, Levine WC, St. Louis ME, et al. Mortality associated with congenital syphilis in the United States, 1992-1998. Pediatrics. 2002;109:79-88.

65. Dorfman DH, Glaser JH. Congenital syphilis presenting in infants after the newborn period. N Engl J Med. 1990;323:1299-1301.

66. Beeram MR, Chopde N, Dawood Y, et al. Lumbar puncture in the evaluation of possible congenital syphilis in neonates. J. Pediatr 1996;128:125-129.

67. Fojaco RM, Hensley GT, Moskowitz L. Congenital syphilis and necrotizing funisitis. JAMA. 1989;261:788-790.

68. Syphilis. In: Pickering LK, ed. Red Book: Report of the Committee on Infectious Disease. 24th ed. Elk Grove Village, IL: American Academy of Pediatrics; 2000: 547-549.

69. Program Operations, Guidelines for STD Prevention. Atlanta, GA: CDC, DHHS; 2000.

70. Zarakolu P, Buchanan I, Tam M, et al. Preliminary evaluation of an immunochromatic strip test fpr specific *Treponema pallidum* antibodies. J Clin Mirobiol. 2002;40: 3064-3065.

71. Berkowitz K, Baxi L, Fox HE. False-negative syphilis screening: The prozone phenomenon, nonimmune hydrops, and diagnosis of syphilis during pregnancy. Am J Obstet Gynecol. 1990;163:975-977.

72. Muic V, Ljubicic M, Vodopija I. Bayes' theorem-based assessment of VDRL syphilis screening miss rates. Sex Transm Dis. 1999;26:12-15.

73. Hutchinson CM, Rompalo AM, Reochart CA, et al. Characteristics of syphilis in patients attending Baltimore STD clinics: Multiple risk sub groups and interactions with HIV infection. Arch Intern Med. 1991;151:511-516.

74. Brown ST, Akbar Z, Larsen SA, et al. Serological response to syphilis treatment. JAMA. 1985;253:1296-1299.

75. Fiumara NJ. Treatment of primary and secondary syphilis: Serological response. JAMA. 1980;243:2500-2503.

76. Fiumara NJ. Serologic responses to treatment of 128 patients with late latent syphilis. Sex Transm Dis. 1979;6:243-246.

77. Fiumara NJ. Reinfection primary, secondary, and latent syphilis. Sex Transm Dis. 1980;7:111-114.

78. Burton AA, Flynn JA, Neumann TM, et al. Routine serologic screening for syphilis in hospitalized patients: High prevalence of unsuspected infection in the elderly. Sex Transm Dis. 1994;21:133-136.

79. Castro R, Rrieto MS, Santo I, et al. Evaluation of an enzyme immunoassay technique for detection of antibodies against *Treponema pallidum*. J Clin Microb. 2003;41:250-253.

80. George RW, Pope V, Larson SA. Use of Western blot for the diagnosis of syphilis. Clin Immunol Newsl. 1991;8:124-133.

81. Sambri V, Marangoni A, Eyer C, et al. Westernblotting with five *Treponema pallidum* recombinant antigens for serologic diagnosis of syphilis. Clin Diag Lab Immunol. 2001;8:534-539.

82. Larson SA, Hunter EF, Kraus SJ. Manual of tests for syphilis. Public Hlth Serv Pub 411. Washington, DC: US Government Printing Office; 1976.

83. Marra CM, Critchlow CW, Hook EW, et al. Cerebral fluid treponemal antibodies in untreated early syphilis. Arch Neurol. 1995;52:68-72.

84. Tomberlin MG, Holtom PD, Owens JL, et al. Evaluation of neurosyphilis in human immunodeficiency virus-infected individuals. Clin Infect Dis. 1994;18:288-294.

85. Prange HW, Moskophidis M, Schipper HI, et al. Relationship between neurological features and intrathecal synthesis of IgG antibodies to *Treponema pallidum* in untreated and treated human neurosyphilis. J Neurol. 1983;230:241-252.

86. Shen X, Tan Y. Detection of oiligoclonal immunoglobulins in the cerebralspinal fluid by immunofixation electrophoesis. Clin Chem Lab Med. 2001;39:1209-1210.

87. Erbelding EJ, Vladov D, Nelson KE, et al. Syphilis serology in human immunodeficiency virus infection: Evidence for false-negative flouresecent testing. J Infect Dis. 1997;176:1397-1400.

88. Wendel GD, Sheffield JS, Hollier LM, et al. Treatment of syphilis in pregnancy and prevention of congenital syphilis. Clin Infect Dis. 2002;35:S200-S209.

89. Syphilotherapyn, 1976. Sex Transm Dis. 1976;3:98.

90. Tramont EC. Persistence of *Treponema pallidum* following penicillin G therapy. JAMA. 1976;236:2206-2209.

91. Centers for Disease Control and Prevention. Sexually Transmitted Disease Treatment Guidelines 2002. Morbid Mortal Wkly Rep. 2002;51:26-29.

92. Idsoe O, Guthe T, Wilcox RR. Penicillin in the treatment of syphilis: The experience of three decades. Bull WHO. 1972;47(Suppl):1.

93. Mohr JA, Griffiths W, Jackson R, et al. Neurosyphilis and penicillin levels in cerebrospinal fluid. JAMA. 1976;236:2208-2210.

94. Mascola L, Pelosi R, Alexander CE. Inadequate treatment of syphilis in pregnancy. Am J Obstet Gynecol. 1984;150:945-947.

95. Moskovitz BL, Klimek JJ, Goldman RL, et al. Meningovascular syphilis after "appropriate" treatment of primary syphilis. Arch Intern Med. 1982;142:139-141.

96. Markovitz PM, Bentner KR, Maggio RP, et al. Failure of recommended treatment for secondary syphilis. JAMA. 1986;255:1767-1768.

97. Short DH, Knox JM, Glicksman J. Neurosyphilis: The search for adequate treatment. Arch Dermatol. 1966;93:87-91.

98. Gordon SM, Eaton ME, George R. The response of symptomatic neurosyphilis to high-dose intravenous penicillin G in patients with human immunodeficiency virus infection. N Engl J Med. 1994;331:1469-1473.

99. Savall R, Valls F, Cabre M. Syphilis and HIV infection. Genitourin Med. 1991;67:353-355.

100. Donders GG, Desmyter J, Hoft P, et al. Apparent failure of one injection of benzathine penicillin G for syphilis during pregnancy in human immunodeficiency virus-seronegative African women. Sex Transm Dis. 1997;24:94-101.

101. Schroeter AL, Lucas JB, Price EV, et al. Treatment for early syphilis and reactivity of serologic tests. JAMA. 1972;221:471-476.

102. Hook EW, Martin DH, Stephens J, et al. A randomized, comparative pilot study of azithromycin versus penicillin G for the treatment of early syphilis. Sex Transm Dis. 2002;29:468-490.

103. Saxon A, Beall GN, Rohr RS, et al. Immediate hypersensitivity reactions to beta-lactam antibiotics. Ann Intern Med. 1987;107;204-215.

104. Dowell ME, Ross PG, Musler DM, et al. Response of latent syphilis or neurosyphilis to ceftriaxone therapy in persons infected with HIV. Am J Med. 1992;93:481-488.

105. Marra CM, Boutin P, McArthur JC, et al. A pilot study evaluating ceftriaxone and penicillin G as treatment agents for neurosyphilis in human immunodeficiency virus-infected individuals. Clin Infect Dis. 2000;30:540-544.
106. Goorney B, Leahy M. Relapse of early syphilis on first line treatment. Int J STD AIDS. 2002;13:722-723.
107. Speer ME, Taber LH, Clark DB, et al. Cerebrospinal fluid levels of benzathine penicillin G in the neonate. J Pediatr. 1977;91:996-997.
108. Giles AJH. Tabes dorsalis progressing to general paresis after 20 years despite routine penicillin therapy. Br J Vener Dis. 1980;56:368.
109. Morrison E, Harrison S, Tramont EC. Oral amoxicillin, an alternative treatment of neurosyphilis. Genitourin Med. 1985;61:359-362.
110. Rolfs RT, Joesorf MR, Hendershot EF, et al. A randomized trial of enhanced therapy for early syphilis in patients with and without human immunodeficiency virus infection. N Engl J Med. 1997;337:307-314.
111. Yim CW, Flynn NM, Fitzgerald FT. Penetration of oral doxycycline into the cerebrospinal fluid of patients with latent or neurosyphilis. Antimicrob Agents Chemother. 1985;28:347-348.
112. Zoller M, Wilson WR, Nodal JB. Treatment of syphilitic hearing loss. Ann Otol. 1979;88:160.
113. Hutchinson CM, Hook EW, Sheperd M, et al. Altered clinical presentation of early syphilis in patients with human immunodeficiency virus infection. Ann Intern Med. 1994;121:94-99.
114. Flood JM, Weinstock HS, Guroy ME. Neurosyphilis during the AIDS epidemic, San Francisco, 1985-1992. J Infect Dis. 1998;177:931-940.
115. Holtom PD, Larsen RA, Leal MA. Prevalence of neurosyphilis in immunodeficiency virus infection. J Infect Dis. 1992;165:1020-1025.
116. Kastner RJ, Malone JL, Decker CF. Syphilitic osteitis in a patient with secondary syphilis and concurrent human immunodeficiency virus infection. Clin Infect Dis. 1994;18:250-252.
117. Johns DR, Tierney M, Felsenstein D. Alternation in the natural history of neurosyphilis by concurrent infections with human immunodeficiency virus. N Engl J Med. 1987;316:1569-1572.
118. Horowitz HW, Valsamis MP, Wicher V, et al. Brief report: Cerebral syphilitic gumma confirmed by the polymerase chain reaction in man with human immunodeficiency virus infection. N Engl J Med. 1994;331:1488-1491.
119. Berger JR. Spinal cord syphilis associated with human immunodeficiency virus infection: A treatable myelopathy. Am J Med. 1992;92:101-103.
120. Tramont EC. Syphilis in adults: From Christopher Columbus to Sir Alexander Fleming to AIDS. Clin Infect Dis. 1995;21:1361-1371.
121. Zaidman GW. Neurosyphilis and retrobulbar neuritis in a patient with AIDS. Ann Ophthalmol. 1986;18:260.
122. Kamling RT, Villaobos R, Latina M. Recurrent syphilitic uveitis. N Engl J Med. 1989;320:62.
123. Tomberlin MG, Holton PD, Owens JL, et al. Evaluation of neurosyphilis in human immunodeficiency virus-infected individuals. Clin Infect Dis. 1994;18:288-294.
124. Berry CD, Hooton TM, Collier AC, et al. Neurologic relapse after benzathine penicillin therapy for secondary syphilis in a patient with HIV infection. N Engl J Med. 1987;316:1587-1589.
124a. Smith NH, Musher DM, Huang DB, et al. Response of HIV-infected patients with asymptomatic syphilis to intensive intramuscular therapy with ceftriaxone or procaine penicillin. Int J STD AIDS. 2004;15:328-332.
124b. Klausner JD, Engelman J, Lukehart SA, et al. Brief report: azithromycin treatment failures in syphilis infections—San Francisco, Calif. MMWR. 2004;53:197-198.
125. Smith JL. Spirochetes in Late Seronegative Syphilis, Penicillin Notwithstanding. Springfield, IL: Charles C Thomas; 1969.
126. Mack LW, Smith JL, Walter ER, et al. Temporal bone treponemes. Arch Otolaryngol. 1969;90:11.
127. Silberstein P, Lawrence R, Pryor D, et al. A case of neurosyphilis with florid Jarisch-Herheimer reaction. J Clin Neurosci. 2002;9:689-690.
128. Klein VR, Cox SM, Mitchell MD, et al. The Jerisch-Herxheimer reaction complicating syphilotheapy in pregnancy. Obstet Gynecol. 1990;75:375-380.
129. Fiumara NJ. Acquired syphilis in three patients with congenital syphilis. N Engl J Med. 1974;290:1119.
130. Theus SA, Harrich DA, Gaynor R, et al. Treponema pallidum, lipoproteins, and synthetic lipoprotein analogues induce human immunodeficiency virus type 1 gene expression in monocytes via NFkB activation. J Infect Dis. 1998;177:941-950.
131. Sellati TJ, Wilkinson DA, Sheffield JS, et al. Virulent Treponema pallidum, lipoprotein, and synthetic lipopeptides induce CCR5 on human monocytres and enhance the susceptibility to infection of human immunodeficiency virus type 1. J Infect Dis. 2000;181:288-293.
132. Rompalo AM, Joesef MR, O'Donnell JA, et al. Clinical manifestations of early syphilis by HIV status and gender. Sex Transm Dis. 2001;28:158-165.
133. Don PC, Rubinstein R, Christie S. Malignant syphilis (lues maligna) and concurrent infection with HIV. Int J Dermatol. 1995;34:403-407.
134. Hicks CB, Benson PM, Lupton GP, et al. Seronegative secondary syphilis in a patient infected with the human immunodeficiency virus (HIV) with Kaposi sarcoma. Ann Intern Med. 1987;107:492-495.
135. Tikjob G, Russel M, Petersen CS, et al. Seronegative secondary syphilis in a patient with AIDS: Identification of Treponema pallidum in biopsy specimen. J Am Acad Dermatol. 1991;24:506-508.
136. Omerod CM, Gurvinder, Fowler VG, et al. Failure of benzathine penicillin in a case of seronegative secondary syphilis in a patient with acquired immunodeficiency syndrome: Case report and review of the literature. Arch Dermatol. 2001;1374-1376.
137. Labbe AC, Mendoca AP, Alves AC, et al. The impact of syphilis, HIV-1, and HIV-2 on pregnancy outcome in BISSAU, Guinea-Bissau. Sex Transm Dis. 2002;29:157-167.

Endemic Treponematoses

EDWARD W. HOOK III

Collectively, the endemic treponematoses include yaws, endemic syphilis, and pinta, and are caused by *Treponema pallidum,* subsp. *pertenue, T. pallidum* subsp. *endemicum,* and *T. careteum,* respectively. These diseases are most common in developing nations, and are seen in developed nations primarily as a result of immigration. The bacteria causing the endemic treponematoses are morphologically and serologically indistinguishable from *Treponema pallidum* subsp. *pallidum,* the causative agent of venereal syphilis, and there are important parallels between the natural history of these diseases and syphilis. Similarly, the tools for their management are adapted almost entirely from tools used as part of syphilis control efforts. Nonetheless the endemic treponematoses differ from syphilis in terms of their clinical manifestations as well as at the level of the genome.[1,2] Targeted for elimination in the mid-20th century, the endemic treponematoses were uncommon in the 1970s; however, more recently rates have once again begun to increase and it is currently estimated that more than 2.5 million persons are affected.[1,3]

THE ORGANISMS

Within the genus *Treponema,* four bacteria presently recognized as human pathogens: *T. pallidum* subsp. *pallidum, T. pallidum* subsp. *pertenue, T. pallidum* subsp. *endemicum,* and *T. careteum.* Much remains to be learned about these organisms. They cannot be readily cultured in vitro, they are indistinguishable from one another morphologically and immunologically, and current understanding of their biology is based on the careful study of relatively few clinical isolates, most often used in animal models.[4,5] With the sequencing of the *T. pallidum* genome,[6] however, several genetic loci have been identified that may permit differentiation of *T. pallidum* from the treponemes causing the endemic treponematoses.[1,2] In addition, application of evolving molecular biological methods to the study of human treponemes promises to provide new insights into the biology of these organisms in the future.

T. pallidum and the treponemes that cause the endemic treponematoses are long, thin (8 to 13 × 0.15 μm), motile bacteria that cannot be seen with the Gram stain and are best demonstrated in clinical specimens using darkfield microscopic examination of lesion exudate or fluorescent antibody techniques. Their regular, spiral morphology and characteristic "corkscrew" motility are helpful for their recognition in clinical specimens. Based on clinical and serological response to therapy, as well as studies performed in experimental animals, these treponemes are all sensitive to penicillins and the tetracyclines. Because the organisms cannot be propagated in vitro, data on minimal inhibitory and bactericidal concentrations on multiple clinical isolates are not available. Clinical and laboratory resistance to erythromycin and other macrolide antibiotics has been demonstrated for at least one isolate of *T. pallidum* subsp. *pallidum,* and there appears to be no activity of sulfa drugs or fluroquinolone antimicrobials against the *T. pallidum* subsp. or *T. careteum.*

EPIDEMIOLOGY

The endemic treponematoses are spread primarily through direct contact or, in the case of endemic syphilis, possibly as fomites (see later discussion). Unlike in syphilis, however, there is little evidence of transmission by blood or blood products (although this is theoretically possible) or transplacentally in pregnant women to their unborn children.

The endemic treponematoses are diseases of developing countries with varied geographic distribution, although the diseases are rare above or below the 30th parallels.[7] Yaws appears to have worldwide distribution, while endemic syphilis is most common in more arid regions of North Africa and the Arabic peninsula. Pinta has been reported only from the Caribbean islands and Central and South America. Within these regions, each of the endemic treponematoses disproportionately impacts persons living on the margins of society. Limited access to hygienic facilities has been associated with increased infection rates.

CLINICAL MANIFESTATIONS

The endemic treponematoses can be characterized by a number of common clinical characteristics as well as those characteristics that distinguish them from one another.[7] Each is a chronic bacterial infection acquired through contact with infectious material. Initial lesions occur at the site of inoculation after an incubation period of 9 to 50 (mean 21) days. Early in the course of infection, perhaps even before primary lesions develop, the treponemes causing these infections spread hematogenously throughout the body, and without treatment will subsequently give rise to secondary and late manifestations of infection. These diseases predictably progress from an early, localized stage to a later, more widespread stage. A minority of patients with untreated infection develop late complications of their infections. Early infection with the endemic treponematoses is characterized by the appearance of epithelial lesions at the site of inoculation. Soon after primary lesion development, regional lymphadenopathy occurs. In the case of venereal syphilis, primary lesions of yaws and pinta will resolve spontaneously without treatment and then recur over as long as 5 years, with the frequency of these recurrences declining with time. Recurrent manifestations of early endemic treponematoses are primarily dermatologic; however, on occasion bony or cartilaginous lesions occur as well.

In a minority of untreated patients with yaws and endemic syphilis, late infection will occur. The lesions of late infections arise from hematogenously spread organisms, tend to be more destructive than the early lesions, and are most commonly manifest as either ulcerative or hyperkeratotic cutaneous lesions or bone and joint involvement.

Another distinguishing common element of the endemic treponematoses is that unlike the situation in syphilis (*T. pallidum* subsp. *pallidum* infection), there is little if any evidence of cardiovascular involvement in late infection, neurologic sequelae of untreated infection, or transmission to children born to infected mothers who have not been treated.

YAWS

Yaws is a chronic infection caused by *T. pallidum* subsp. *pertenue* and is the most common of the endemic treponematoses. After years of relatively low levels (see discussion on control efforts), the disease apparently is once again becoming more common.[3,8] The disease is most common in children, with the majority of cases occurring in children 2 to 15 years of age. Most transmission occurs as the result of direct (nonsexual) contact resulting in the transfer of infectious exudate from lesions to uninfected individuals. Transmission is thought to be facilitated by disruption of epithelial surfaces (lacerations, insect bites, etc.) as well as by crowding and a relative lack of hygienic practices. These circumstances are, in general, more common in children than in adults and may help to explain why most initial infections occur in youth.

After inoculation of *T. pallidum* subsp. *pertenue,* and following an incubation period of 9 to 90 days (mean approximately 21 days) a primary papular lesion forms at the site of inoculation. Over a period of several months, the primary papule of yaws may increase in size and then heal spontaneously. Primary lesions are typically puritic, facilitating autoinoculation, and tender regional lymphadenopathy may develop. Fever and constitutional symptoms are uncommon. At about the time the primary papule heals, secondary lesions near or distant from

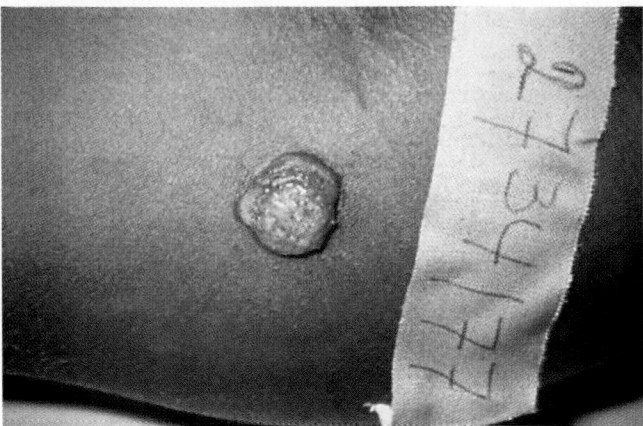

FIGURE 236-1. Initial papillomatous yaws lesion on the upper thigh (also called primary framboesioma, mother yaw, *chancre pia nique*). The initial lesion usually commences as a papule on the lower extremities and slowly enlarges to form a raspberry-like lesion. *(From Perine PL, Hopkins DR, Niemel PLA, et al. Handbook of Endemic Treponematoses. Geneva: World Health Organization, 1984.)*

the initial lesion may occur. These lesions may also be papular in nature and are thought to be a consequence of both local (autoinoculation) and hemotogenous spread of infection (Fig. 236-1). Secondary lesions of yaws predominately involve the skin, bone, and cartilage and if untreated in patients again will heal without scarring (Fig. 236-2). Occasionally secondary infection or ulceration of cutaneous lesions of yaws does occur, resulting in more pronounced lesions and scarring. Like the primary lesions of yaws, secondary lesions will resolve spontaneously without therapy and patients enter a latent stage. The differential diagnosis of early yaws includes impetigo, scabies, molluscum contagiosum, lichen planus, and cutaneous leishmaniasis.

In a small proportion (estimated to be about 10%) of untreated patients, late lesions of yaws may occur. Late lesions are characterized by hyperkeratotic plaques and lesions, destructive bony destructive lesions, or gummata. *Gangosa* is the term used to describe these disfiguring chronic manifestations as they destroy bone, cartilage, and soft

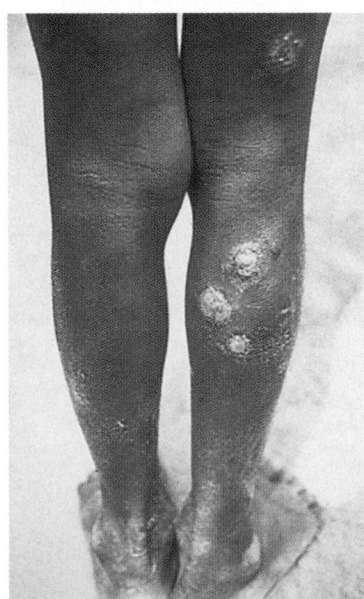

FIGURE 236-2. Early ulceropapillomatous yaws on the leg (also called *ulcére post-chancreux*). *(From Perine PL, Hopkins DR, Niemel PLA, et al. Handbook of Endemic Treponematoses. Geneva: World Health Organization, 1984.)*

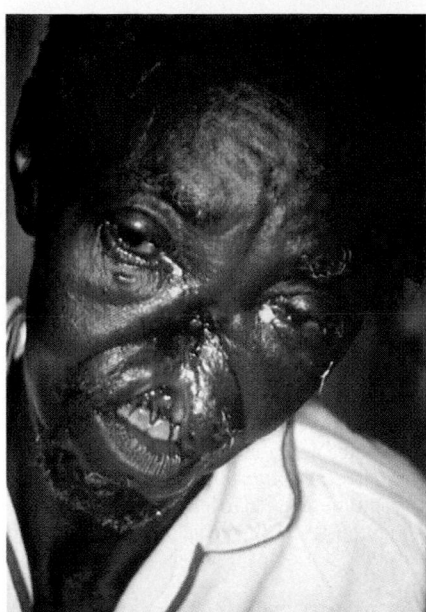

FIGURE 236-3. Gangosa. *(From Perine PL, Hopkins DR, Niemel PLA, et al. Handbook of Endemic Treponematoses. Geneva: World Health Organization, 1984.)*

tissue of the mouth and nose (Fig. 236-3). Bowing of the anterior tibiae (saber shins) may likewise be a late manifestation of yaws, arising from infectious periostitis.

Yaws infections may be aborted by prophylactic administration of penicillin in exposed patients; healing is promoted by therapeutic administration of penicillin and in early patients may occur without problems. Despite appropriate therapy, serological tests for syphilis may continue to be reactive for years.

ENDEMIC SYPHILIS (BEJEL)

Endemic syphilis is the epidemic treponematosis caused by *T. pallidum* subsp. *edemicum.* This infection is somewhat less common than yaws and occurs primarily in dry, arid areas among nomadic and seminomadic rural populations. The disease has been most common in North Africa, Southwest Asia, and the eastern Mediterranean region.

Endemic syphilis, like yaws, is a disease of childhood, with most cases occurring in individuals ages 2 to 15 years. Transmission of endemic syphilis is thought to occur by both direct contact and, because early lesions are often mucosal, also as fomites on shared eating or drinking utensils. The primary lesions of endemic syphilis occur as mucous patches on oral pharyngeal mucosa or as lesions at the angles of the lips (angular stomatitis). These painless lesions may resolve without therapy. Subsequently, as in other endemic treponematoses, secondary lesions may become apparent. Secondary lesions of endemic syphilis may appear as rashes, mucosal lesions, or bony and cartilaginous involvement. Secondary manifestations of endemic syphilis may occur as disseminated papular rashes similar to those of secondary syphilis, or as condylomata occurring predominately in moist areas of the skin. The secondary lesions of endemic syphilis may display a wide variety of morphologies comparable to those seen in secondary syphilis.

Following a period of latency, complications of endemic syphilis are relatively common. These manifestations may present as gummatous lesions or chronic ulcerative skin lesions in 25% to 50% of patients. Unlike the lesions of early endemic syphilis, late lesions tend to be destructive, chronic progressive lesions, some of which go on to cause deforming boney and cartilaginous facial lesions referred to as gangosa. In addition to the ulcerative lesions of endemic syphilis, bony involvement may occur as well, and is manifested as osteoperiostitis causing disability and deformity.

PINTA

Pinta is the endemic treponematosis caused by a unique treponemal species, *T. carateum.* Pinta, unlike yaws and endemic syphilis, which have a global distribution, is a disease limited to the New World. The disease has been described in numerous South American and Caribbean countries including Cuba.[9,10] At the current time the disease is quite rare, although recently substantial numbers of cases including a case series of more than 200 patients are described as having occurred in rural Brazil. The peak age prevalence for pinta is somewhat older than for yaws or endemic syphilis, occurring in individuals ages 15 to 30 years. Like other endemic treponematoses, pinta is thought to be spread through direct lesion contact. An important difference between pinta and the other endemic treponematoses is that without treatment the lesions tend to persist. The classic initial lesion of pinta is a papule or erythematous epithelial plaque. These lesions tend to occur on parts of the body that are not typically clothed, most often the leg, foot, forearm, or back of the hands. Typically these lesions then slowly enlarge through local extension to form hyperkeratotic pigmented lesions. The lesions of pinta are accompanied by regional lymphadenopathy. In the interval of 3 to 9 months following infection, disseminated lesions may occur distal to the initial lesion and also slowly enlarge. Over time the lesions of pinta become pigmented, initially becoming somewhat hyperpigmented and taking on a darker color described as slate blue. Late pinta is characterized further by additional pigmentary cutaneous changes; lesions may include dischromic treponeme-containing lesions and achromic treponeme-free lesions. The depigmentation process of pinta occurs at different rates in the same lesion, giving the lesions a somewhat mottled appearance. No other disability or late complications of pinta have currently been described.

DIAGNOSIS

The diagnosis of individual cases of the endemic treponematoses is in large part dependent on clinical recognition of appropriate clinical findings, confirmed by serological testing using serological tests for syphilis.[11] Although not widely available, visual demonstration of characteristic treponemes using darkfield microscopy of lesion exudates can provide immediate and highly specific diagnosis of the endemic treponematoses. Immunofluorescent antibody stains for treponemes are also available in some settings and would likewise provide specific diagnosis of infection. In settings in which the endemic treponematoses are common, however, facilities for darkfield or immunofluorescence microscopy are rare, and therefore these methods are, in practice, rarely used for diagnosis. No serological tests have been specifically developed for diagnosis of endemic treponematoses; however, because the humoral antibody response to these diseases is indistinguishable from the response to syphilis infection, serological tests for syphilis are important for confirming clinically suspected infections. In addition, serological testing is useful for estimation of population prevalence of the endemic treponematoses to guide control efforts.[7,8]

Serological tests for syphilis (and the endemic treponematoses) are divided into nontreponemal and treponemal tests.[11] The nontreponemal tests are based on the cross-reactivity of cardiolipin-cholesterol-lecithin antigens with antibodies to *T. pallidum* and are represented by tests such as the rapid plasma reagin (RPR) and venereal disease research laboratory (VDRL) tests. These tests provide quantifiable results that are useful not only for screening for infection but also for evaluation of response to therapy following treatment. In contrast, the treponemal tests are based on the reactivity of antibodies to *T. pallidum* to antigens produced from *T. pallidum* propagated in laboratory animals, or, increasingly, cloned treponemal antigens. The treponemal tests are available in a variety of formats including fluorescent treponemal antibody absorption (FTA-Abs), *T. pallidum* hemagglutination (TPHA), or enzyme-linked immunosorbent assays (ELISA). False-positive results sometimes occur with both nontreponemal and treponemal tests; however, because the tests are unrelated, use of an unrelated test to confirm an initial test result (i.e., confirmatory testing of reactive RPR or VDRL test results using a treponemal test) greatly increases the specificity of test results. The vast majority of false-positive serological tests for syphilis are positive at a dilution of 1:4 or less. Partially based on this fact, in many resource-limited settings where the prevalence of such infections is relatively high and treponemal tests are not readily available, nontreponemal test titers with a titer of greater than 1:4 are considered to represent active infection and thus to guide management decisions.

Following effective treatment, most patients with active endemic treponematoses will have a twofold (four dilutions) or greater decline in serological test result titer, although for many patients the serological test result titers will not revert to nonreactive following successful therapy. Reinfection or relapse may be indicated by a serological titer that rises two or more dilutions. Reversion of treponemal serological tests to nonreactive is considerably less common than for nontreponemal tests.

TREATMENT

Penicillin is the preferred drug for treatment of the endemic treponematoses.[1,7] The drug is relatively inexpensive, available as a long-acting preparation (benzathine penicillin G) that provides treponemicidal serum levels for several weeks following administration, and is highly effective. At present the World Health Organization recommends treatment of each of the endemic treponematoses with single intramuscular doses of benzathine penicillin G, 600,000 units for children under age 10 and 1.2 million units for persons 10 years of age or older. Treatment of all household members and close personal contacts is recommended to prevent development of infection in exposed persons. Cure rates with recommended doses of benzathine penicillin are about 97%, with treatment failure being attributed to improper administration, use of out-of-date or inactive medication, or reinfection as a result of exposure to an untreated person. More recently there have been reports of cure rates equivalent to those reported for benzathine penicillin using oral penicillin regimens[12]; however, because of potential problems relating to medication adherence, benzathine penicillin remains the preferred treatment. There are no data to suggest that any of the *T. pallidum* subspecies or *T. careteum* have clinically significant resistance to penicillin. There are no formal studies of alternative therapies for persons with penicillin allergy; however, extrapolating from experience with venereal syphilis, tetracycline or doxycycline given for 14 days is likely to be effective

Response to therapy may be determined through resolution of early lesions or, in persons with late infection, arrest of progression. Serological response to therapy may also be demonstrable as declines in nontreponemal tests for syphilis (i.e., RPR or VDRL) titers of two or more dilutions. Following treatment, however, serological test titers may not revert to seronegativity.

PUBLIC HEALTH MANAGEMENT AND CONTROL STRATEGIES

The endemic treponematoses are readily transmitted through direct contact between infected and uninfected persons. As a result, as diseases of children that do not cause systemic complaints or limit activity, it is not surprising that these infections increase in prevalence within susceptible populations. In the 1950s the World Health Organization embarked on an ambitious global control program utilizing active serologically screening and staged treatment approaches for entire communities.[1,7] In this program communities were categorized based on seroprevalence as high prevalence (greater than 10%), medium prevalence (5% to 10%), or low prevalence (less than 5%). In high-prevalence communities, the entire community was administered mass penicillin therapy; for medium-prevalence communities all identified infected individuals, as well as all children under 15 years and all contacts of infected individuals were treated; and in low-prevalence settings only individuals with active infections and their contacts were treated. In this effort, more than 450 million examinations were performed and more than 50 million persons in 46 countries were treated. This effort was quite successful, reducing global prevalence of the endemic treponematoses by 95%; however, as the disease waned so did resources for continuing surveillance.[8] Over the past two decades infection rates have once again increased, with global prevalence of infection now estimated at about 50 million cases.[2] Community-based control efforts continue to be carried out, although no longer on the scale or with the intensity of the initial eradication effort.

REFERENCES

1. Antal GM, Lukehart SA, Meheus AZ. The endemic treponematoses. Microbes Infect. 2002;4:83-94.
2. Noordhoek GT, Wieles B, van der Sluis JJ, et al. Polymerase chain reaction and synthetic DNA probes: A means of distinguishing the causative agents of syphilis and yaws? Infect Immun. 1990;58:2011-2013.
3. World Health Report. Life in the 21st Century; a vision for all. Geneva: World Health Organization; 1998.
4. Wicher K, Wicher V, Abbruscato F, et al. *Treponema pallidum* subsp. *pertenue* displays pathogenic properties different from those of *T. pallidum* subsp. *pallidum*. Infect Immun. 2000;68:3219-3225.
5. Engelkens HJ, ten Kate FJ, Judanarso J, et al. The localization of treponemes and characterization of the inflammatory infiltrate in skin biopsies from patients with primary or secondary syphilis, or early infectious yaws. Genitourin Med. 1993;69:102-107.
6. Fraser CM, Norris SJ, Weinstock GM. Complete genome sequence of *Treponema pallidum*, the syphilis spirochete. Science. 1998;281:375-387.
7. Perine PL, Hopkins DR, Niemel PLA, et al. Handbook of Endemic Treponematoses. Geneva: World Health Organization, 1984.
8. Antal GM, Causse G. The control of endemic treponematoses. Rev Infect Dis. 1985;7(Suppl 2):S220-S226.
9. Castro LG. Nonvenereal treponematosis (letter). J Am Acad Dermatol. 1994; 31:1075-1076.
10. Woltsche-Kahr I, Schmidt B, Aberer W, et al. Pinta in Austria (or Cuba?): Import of an extinct disease? Arch Dermatol. 1999;135:685-688.
11. Larsen SA, Pope V, Johnson RE, et al, eds. A Manual of Tests for Syphilis. 9th ed. Washington: American Public Health Association; 1998.
12. Scolnik D, Aronson L, Lovinsky R, et al. Efficacy of a targeted, oral penicillin-based yaws control program among children living in rural South America. Clin Infect Dis. 2003;36:1232-1238.

Leptospirosis

PAUL N. LEVETT

Leptospirosis is a zoonosis of global distribution, caused by infection with pathogenic spirochetes of the genus *Leptospira*. The disease is greatly under-reported, particularly in tropical regions, but recent attempts at surveillance suggest that it may be the most common zoonosis.[1] The disease is maintained in nature by chronic renal infection of carrier animals, which excrete the organism in their urine, contaminating the environment. Human infection occurs either by direct contact with infected urine or tissues, or more commonly by indirect exposure to the organisms in damp soil or water. Most human infections are probably asymptomatic; the spectrum of illness is extremely wide, ranging from undifferentiated febrile illness to severe multisystem disease with high mortality rates. The extreme variation in clinical presentation is partly responsible for the significant degree of under-diagnosis.

HISTORY

A syndrome of severe multisystem disease, presenting with profound jaundice and renal function impairment, was described by Weil in Heidelberg in 1886. Other descriptions of disease that probably represent leptospirosis were made earlier, but the etiology cannot be definitively ascribed to leptospiral infection.[2] Leptospires were first visualized in autopsy specimens from a patient thought to have had yellow fever,[3] but were not isolated until several years later, almost simultaneously in Germany and Japan.[4] Diagnostic confusion between severe icteric leptospirosis and yellow fever continued, with prominent researchers such as Stokes and Noguchi dying in their attempts to discover the etiologic agent.[4] Several authoritative reviews have been published.[2,4-7]

ETIOLOGY

Leptospires are thin, tightly coiled spirochetes, usually 0.1 μ by 6 to 20 μm in length. The cells have pointed ends, one or both of which is usually bent into a characteristic hook (Fig. 237-1). Motility is conferred by the rotation of two axial flagella underlying the membrane sheath, which are inserted at opposite ends of the cell and overlap in the central region.[8] Because of their small diameter, leptospires are visualized by darkfield microscopy (Fig. 237-2). Leptospires are readily cultured in polysorbate-albumin media.[9]

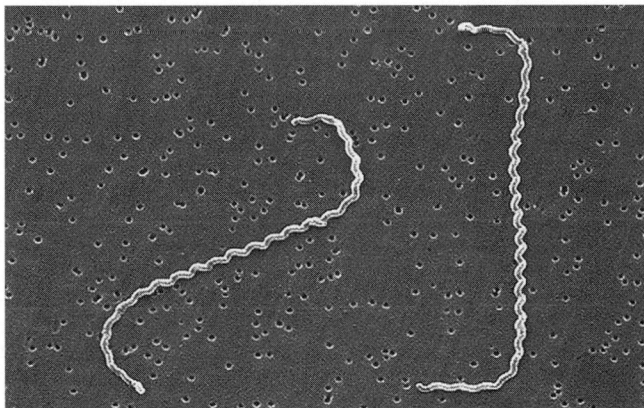

FIGURE 237-1. Scanning electron micrograph of cells *Leptospira interrogans* showing helical structure and curved (hooked) ends (original magnification × 60,000). *(Courtesy of Rob Weyant, Centers for Disease Control and Prevention).*

FIGURE 237-2. Leptospires viewed by dark-field microscopy (original magnification × 100). *(Courtesy of Mildred Galton, Public Health Image Library, CDC).*

Historically, the genus *Leptospira* was classified into two species, *L. interrogans* and *L. biflexa,* comprised of pathogenic and nonpathogenic strains, respectively. Within each species, large numbers of serovars were differentiated using polyclonal agglutinating antibodies. Serovar specificity is conferred by lipopolysaccharide (LPS) O-antigens.[10] More than 250 serovars of pathogenic leptospires have been described; because of the large number of serovars, antigenically related serovars were grouped into serogroups, for convenience in serologic testing.

Leptospires are now classified into a number of species defined by their degree of genetic relatedness, determined by DNA reassociation.[11-14] There are currently 13 named species and four unnamed genomospecies (Table 237-1). These include both pathogenic and nonpathogenic strains, and some species contain both pathogens and nonpathogens. This classification is supported by 16S RNA gene sequencing (Fig. 237-3), but is quite distinct from the former serologic classification.[5]

The system of serogroup nomenclature has no taxonomic standing, but is retained because presumptive serogroup determined by serologic testing has some epidemiological value, although it is doubtful whether this can be extrapolated to identification of the infecting serovar in an individual patient.[15]

TABLE 237-1 Species of *Leptospira* and Some Pathogenic Serovars

Species	Selected Pathogenic Serovars
L. interrogans	Icterohaemorrhagiae, Copenhageni, Canicola, Pomona, Australis, Autumnalis, Pyrogenes, Bratislava, Lai
L. noguchii	Panama, Pomona
L. borgpetersenii	Ballum, Hardjo, Javanica
L. santarosai	Bataviae
L. kirschneri	Bim, Bulgarica, Grippotyphosa, Cynopteri
L. weilii	Celledoni, Sarmin
L. alexanderi	Manhao 3
Leptospira genomospecies 1	Sichuan
L. fainei	Hurtsbridge
L. meyeri	Sofia
L. inadai	indeterminate
L. wolbachii	non-pathogens
L. biflexa	non-pathogens
Leptospira genomospecies 3	non-pathogens
Leptospira genomospecies 4	non-pathogens
Leptospira genomospecies 5	non-pathogens
L. parva	non-pathogens

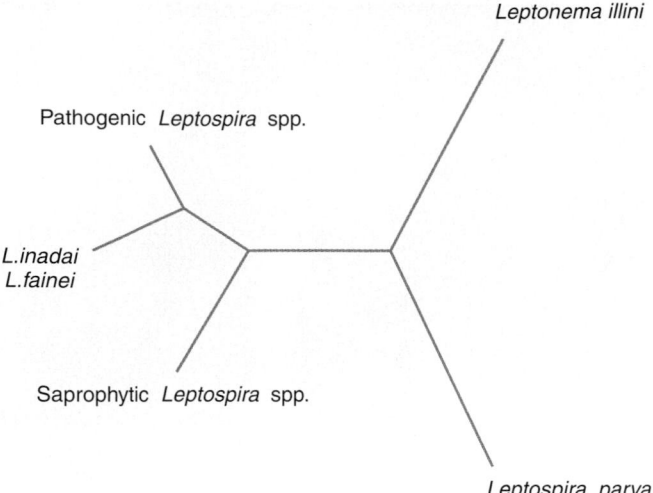

FIGURE 237-3. Unrooted phylogenetic tree based on 16s RNA gene sequences of the *Leptospiraceae* obtained from GenBank. Species comprised of pathogenic serovars (see Table 237-1) cluster separately from non-pathogenic species. *Leptospira inadai* and *L. fainei* are intermediate between pathogens and non-pathogens.

The genome sequence of one strain, *L. interrogans* serovar Lai, has been determined[16] and sequencing of other strains is underway. The availability of the genome sequence has already led to better understanding of leptospiral pathogenesis.

EPIDEMIOLOGY AND TRANSMISSION

Leptospirosis is endemic throughout the world. Human infections are endemic in most regions and the peak incidence occurs in the rainy season in tropical regions and the late summer to early fall in temperate regions. Outbreaks may follow periods of excess rainfall.[17] The incidence of leptospirosis is probably grossly underestimated, because of limited diagnostic capacity in the regions where the burden of disease is greatest.[1] In the United States, the highest incidence is found in Hawaii; active surveillance in 1992 detected an annual incidence of approximately 128 per 100,000.[18] Leptospirosis is no longer a nationally notifiable disease in the United States, although it remains notifiable in more than 20 states.

Leptospirosis is maintained in nature by chronic renal infection of carrier animals. The most important reservoirs are rodents and other small mammals, but livestock and companion animals are also significant sources of human infection. Infection of carrier animals usually occurs during infancy, and once infected, animals may excrete leptospires in their urine intermittently or continuously throughout life.

Infection occurs through direct or indirect contact with urine or tissues of infected animals. Direct contact is important in transmission to veterinarians, workers in milking sheds on dairy farms, abattoir works, butchers, hunters, and animal handlers (transmission has been reported to children handling puppies and to dog handlers). Indirect contact is more common, and is responsible for disease following exposure to wet soil or water. The great majority of cases are acquired by this route in the tropics, either through occupational exposure to water as in rice or taro farming, or through exposure to damp soil and water during avocational activities.

Recreational exposures have become relatively more important, often in association with adventure tourism to tropical endemic areas. Several large point-source water-borne outbreaks have occurred recently following athletic events.[19,20] In recent years there has been an increase in leptospirosis cases among dogs in the eastern regions of North America and in the Midwest,[21] associated with a reported change in the predominant serovars causing disease.[22,23]

PATHOGENESIS

Leptospires enter the body through cuts and abrasions; mucous membranes or conjunctivae; and aerosol inhalation of microscopic droplets; ingestion is probably not an important route of entry, but provides access to oral mucosae. Leptospires are carried in the blood throughout the body. A systemic vasculitis occurs, facilitating migration of spirochetes into organs and tissues and accounting for a broad spectrum of clinical illness. Severe vascular injury can ensue, leading to pulmonary hemorrhage, ischemia of the renal cortex and tubular-epithelial cell necrosis, and destruction of the hepatic architecture resulting in jaundice and liver cell injury with or without necrosis.[24]

The mechanisms by which leptospires cause disease are not clearly understood. Potential virulence factors include attachment,[25] toxin production, immune mechanisms, and surface proteins. Leptospiral lipopolysaccharide exhibits weak endotoxic activity but a number of serovars produce hemolysins, which may act as sphingomyelinases, phospholipases or pore-forming proteins.[26]

Immune-mediated mechanisms have been postulated as one factor influencing the severity of symptoms.[27] In humans, the significance of circulating immune complexes, anticardiolipin antibodies, and antiplatelet antibodies is unproven. However, in horses recurrent uveitis (moon blindness) results from the production of antibodies against an epitope that is shared by common equine pathogenic serovars.[28]

Much recent work has focused on the role of surface lipoproteins,[29] many of which are thermoregulated, with expression occurring in vivo at mammalian body temperatures.[30] The major surface lipoprotein, LipL32, is highly conserved among pathogenic serovars.[31] LipL32 is a major target of the human immune response[32] and appears to be involved in pathogenesis of tubulointerstitial nephritis.[33]

CLINICAL MANIFESTATIONS

Leptospiral infection is associated with a very broad spectrum of severity, ranging from subclinical illness followed by seroconversion to two clinically recognizable syndromes: a self-limited, systemic illness seen in roughly 90% of infections, and a severe, potentially fatal illness accompanied by any combination of renal failure, liver failure, and pneumonitis with hemorrhagic diathesis.[2,6,7] The disease may have two distinct phases, an initial septicemic stage that is followed by a temporary decline in fever that is followed by an immune phase in which the severe symptoms occur. In many severe cases the distinction between these two phases is not apparent; in addition many patients present only with the onset of the second phase of the illness.

The mean incubation period is 10 days, ranging from 5 to 14 days; determination of precise exposures may be difficult, leading to significant imprecision in estimated incubation times. The acute, septicemic phase of illness begins abruptly with high, remittent fever (38° to 40° C) and headache, chills, rigors, and myalgias; conjunctival suffusion without purulent discharge; abdominal pain; anorexia, nausea, and vomiting; diarrhea; cough and pharyngitis; a pretibial maculopapular cutaneous eruption occurs rarely (Table 237-2). Conjunctival suffusion and muscle tenderness, most notable in the calf and lumbar areas, are the most characteristic physical findings, but may occur in a minority of cases (see Table 237-2). Other less common signs include lymphadenopathy, splenomegaly, and hepatomegaly. The acute phase lasts from 5 to 7 days. Routine laboratory tests are nonspecific but indicative of a bacterial infection. Leptospires can be recovered from blood and CSF during the acute phase of illness, but meningeal signs are not prominent in this phase. Leptospires may also be recovered from urine, beginning about 5 to 7 days after the onset of symptoms (Fig. 237-4). Urinalysis reveals mild proteinuria and pyuria, with or without hematuria and hyaline or granular casts. Death is exceedingly rare in the acute phase of illness.

Defervescence is followed by the immune phase of illness, which generally lasts from 4 to 30 days (see Fig. 237-4). The disappearance of leptospires from the blood and cerebrospinal fluid (CSF) coincides with the appearance of IgM antibodies.[7,42] The organisms can be de-

TABLE 237-2 Signs and Symptoms on Admission in Patients with Leptospirosis in Large Case Series

	Puerto Rico, 1963[34] n = 208	China, 1965[35] n = 168	Vietnam, 1973[36] n = 150	Korea, 1987[37] n = 93	Barbados, 1990[44] n = 88	Seychelles, 1998[38] n = 75	Brazil 1999[39] n = 193	Hawaii, 2001[40] n = 353	India, 2002[41] n = 74
Percent with:									
Jaundice	49	0	1.5	16	95	27	93	39	34
Anorexia	—	46	—	80	85	—	75	82	—
Headache	91	90	98	70	76	80	75	89	92
Conjunctival suffusion	99	57	42	58	54	—	28.5	28	35
Vomiting	69	18	33	32	50	40	—	73	—
Myalgia	97	64	79	40	49	63	94	91	68
Arthralgia	—	36	—	—	—	31	—	59	12
Abdominal pain	—	26	28	40	43	41	—	51	—
Nausea	75	29	41	46	37	—	—	77	—
Dehydration	—	—	—	—	37	—	—	—	—
Cough	24	57	20	45	32	39	—	—	—
Hemoptysis	9	51	—	40	—	13	20	—	35
Hepatomegaly	69	28	15	17	27	—	—	16	—
Lymphadenopathy	24	49	21	—	21	—	—	—	15
Diarrhea	27	20	29	36	14	11	—	53	—
Rash	6	—	7	—	2	—	—	8	12

tected in almost all tissues and organs, and in urine for several weeks, depending on the severity of the disease. In addition to the acute phase symptoms described in the preceding paragraph, the immune phase may be characterized by any or all of the following signs and symptoms: jaundice, renal failure, cardiac arrhythmias, pulmonary symptoms, aseptic meningitis, conjunctival suffusion with or without hem-

orrhage; photophobia; eye pain; muscle tenderness; adenopathy; and hepatosplenomegaly (see Table 237-2).

Aseptic meningitis, with or without symptoms, is characteristic of the immune phase of illness, occurring in up to 80% of cases. In endemic populations a significant proportion of all aseptic meningitis cases may be caused by leptospiral infection.[43] Symptomatic patients

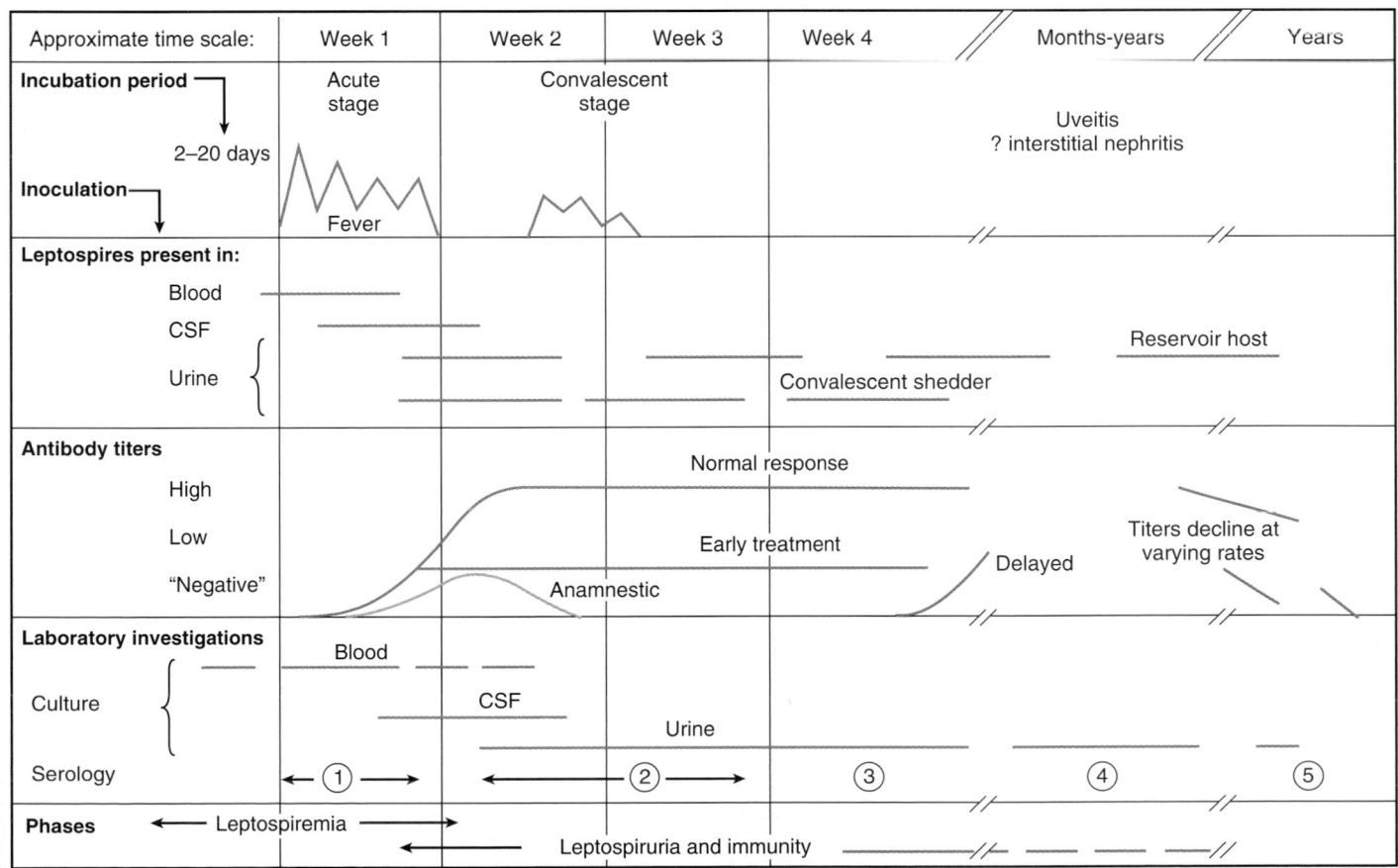

FIGURE 237-4. Biphasic nature of leptospirosis and relevant investigations at different stages of disease. Specimens 1 and 2 for serology are acute-phase specimens, 3 is a convalescent-phase sample which may facilitate detection of a delayed immune response, and 4 and 5 are follow-up samples that can provide epidemiological information, such as the presumptive infecting serogroup. (Adapted from Turner LH. Leptospirosis. British Medical Journal 1969;1:231-235, with permission of the publisher, and reproduced from Levett PN. Leptospirosis. Clin Microbiol Rev. 2001;14:296-326, with permission of ASM Press).

present with an intense, bitemporal and frontal throbbing headache with or without delirium. A lymphocytic pleocytosis occurs, with total cell counts generally below 500/mm³. CSF protein levels are modestly elevated between 50 and 100 mg/mL; the CSF glucose concentration is normal. Severe neurologic complications such as coma, meningoencephalitis, hemiplegia, transverse myelitis, or Guillain-Barré syndrome occur only rarely.[5]

The most distinctive form of severe illness that may develop after the acute phase of illness is Weil's disease, characterized by impaired hepatic and renal function. More severe cases may progress directly from the acute phase without the characteristic brief improvement in symptoms to a fulminant illness, with fever greater than 40° C and the rapid onset of liver failure, acute renal failure, hemorrhagic pneumonitis, cardiac arrhythmia, or circulatory collapse.[7] Mortality rates in patients developing severe disease have range from 5% to 40%.[2,5,6,44]

In jaundiced patients, disturbance of liver function is disproportional to the rather mild and nonspecific pathological findings. Conjugated serum bilirubin levels may rise to 80 mg/dL, accompanied by more modest elevations of serum transaminases, alanine aminotransferase, and aspartate aminotransferase, which rarely exceed 200 U/L.[45] This is in marked contrast to viral hepatitis. Jaundice is slow to resolve, but death due to liver failure almost never occurs in the absence of renal failure. At autopsy, degenerative changes are seen in hepatocytes, Kupffer cells may be hypertrophied, cholestasis is evident, and erythrophagocytosis and mononuclear cell infiltrates are observed.[46] Hepatocellular necrosis is absent.

Acute renal failure is characterized by a rapid onset of uremia and oliguria during the second week of illness, frequently accompanied by jaundice. The blood urea nitrogen level is usually below 100 mg/dL, and the serum creatinine level is usually below 2 to 8 mg/dL during the acute phase of illness.[47] Thrombocytopenia occurs in the absence of disseminated intravascular coagulation and may accompany progressive renal dysfunction.[48] Renal biopsy reveals acute interstitial nephritis; immune-complex glomerulonephritis may also be present.[49] Renal injury is compounded by concomitant dehydration, causing hypovolemia and hypotension; the development of anuria is a poor prognostic sign. In fatal cases, the kidneys are swollen and yellow, with prominent cortical blood vessels.[24] Histological findings include a diffuse, mixed tubulointerstitial inflammatory cell infiltrate of lymphocytes, plasma cells, macrophages, and polymorphonuclear leukocytes, accompanied by focal areas of tubular necrosis.[46]

Severe hemorrhagic pneumonitis and acute pulmonary distress syndrome can be prominent manifestations of infection and may occur in the absence of hepatic and renal failure.[50] Frank hemoptysis can arise simultaneously with the onset of cough during the acute phase of illness[51]; auscultatory examination may be normal. With progressive pulmonary involvement, radiographic abnormalities seen most frequently in the lower lobes evolve from small nodular densities ("snowflake-like") to patchy alveolar infiltrates; confluent consolidation is uncommon.[52] Bibasilar rales may be present when radiographic involvement is extensive. At autopsy, the lungs appear grossly congested and demonstrate focal areas of hemorrhage.[46] Histologically, damage to the capillary endothelium leads to congestion with foci of interstitial and intra-alveolar hemorrhage, diffuse alveolar damage, and severe airspace disorganization.[53] Inflammatory infiltrates are usually absent.

Congestive heart failure occurs rarely. However, nonspecific electrocardiographic changes are common.[54] In more than half of patients receiving continuous cardiac monitoring, cardiac arrhythmias may occur, including atrial fibrillation; flutter and tachycardia; and cardiac irritability, including premature ventricular contractions and ventricular tachycardia.[54] Atrial fibrillation is associated with more severe disease.[55] Cardiovascular collapse with shock can develop abruptly and in the absence of aggressive supportive care can be fatal. At autopsy, interstitial myocarditis with inflammatory involvement of the conduction system is seen[56]; acute coronary arteritis and aortitis are also common at postmortem examination.[57]

LABORATORY DIAGNOSIS

Direct Detection Methods

Direct visualization of leptospires in blood or urine by darkfield microscopic examination has been used for diagnosis. However, artefacts are commonly mistaken for leptospires, and the method has both low sensitivity (40.2%) and specificity (61.5%).[58] A range of staining methods has been applied to direct detection, including immunofluorescence staining, immunoperoxidase staining, and silver staining. These methods are not widely used, because of the lack of commercially available reagents and their relatively low sensitivity.

A monoclonal antibody-based dot-enzyme-linked immunosorbent assay (ELISA) for detection of leptospiral antigen in urine assay has been developed[59] and was positive in 75% of patients on the day of admission to the hospital. However, this assay has not been evaluated widely and is not available commercially.

Several polymerase chain reaction (PCR) assays have been developed for the detection of leptospires.[5] However, only two have been evaluated in clinical studies.[60,61] Both methods were more sensitive than culture, but did not detect all cases. The chief advantage of PCR is the prospect of confirming the diagnosis during the early acute (leptospiremic) stage of the illness, before the appearance of immunoglobulin M (IgM) antibodies, when treatment is likely to have the greatest benefit. In fulminating cases, in which death occurs before seroconversion, PCR may be of great value.[60] Leptospiral DNA has been amplified from serum, urine, aqueous humor, and a number of tissues obtained at autopsy. For early diagnosis, serum is the optimal specimen. Urine from severely ill patients is often highly concentrated and contains significant inhibitory activity. Real-time PCR assays have been developed recently[62] but have yet to be widely applied.

Histological diagnosis (Fig. 237-5) has traditionally relied on silver impregnation staining,[3] but immunohistochemical staining offers greater sensitivity and specificity.[63,64]

Isolation and Identification

Leptospires can be isolated from blood, CSF, and peritoneal dialysate fluids during the first 10 days of illness. Specimens should be collected while the patient is febrile and before antibiotic therapy is initiated. One or two drops of blood should be inoculated directly into culture medium at the bedside. Survival of leptospires in commercial blood culture media for several days has been reported.[65] Urine can be cultured after the first week of illness. Specimens should be collected aseptically into sterile containers without preservatives, and must be processed within a short time of collection; best results are obtained when the delay is less than 1 hour, as leptospires do not survive well in acidic environments.[9]

Cultures are performed in albumin-polysorbate media such as EMJH or PLM-5, which are available commercially. Older media contained serum.[5] Primary cultures are performed in semisolid medium, to which 5-fluorouracil is usually added as a selective agent. Cultures are incubated at 30° C for several weeks, as initial growth may be very slow.

Isolated leptospires are identified to serovar level either by traditional serologic methods or by molecular methods such as pulse field gel electrophoresis.[9] These techniques are limited in availability to a few reference laboratories.

Indirect Detection Methods

The majority of leptospirosis cases are diagnosed by serology. The reference standard assay is the microscopic agglutination test (MAT), in which live antigens representing different serogroups of leptospires are reacted with serum samples and then examined by darkfield microscopy for agglutination.[9] This is a complex test to maintain, perform, and interpret, and its use is restricted to a few reference laboratories.

A serologically confirmed case of leptospirosis is defined by a fourfold rise in MAT titer to one or more serovars between acute-phase and convalescent serum specimens run in parallel. A titer of at least 1:800 in the presence of compatible symptoms is strong evidence of recent or current infection.[66] Suggestive evidence for recent or cur-

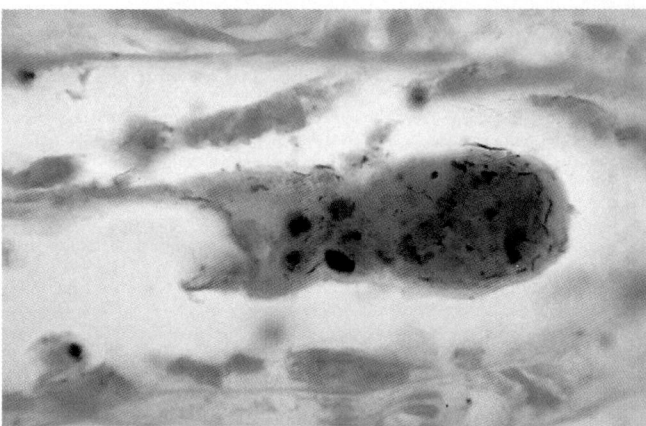

A

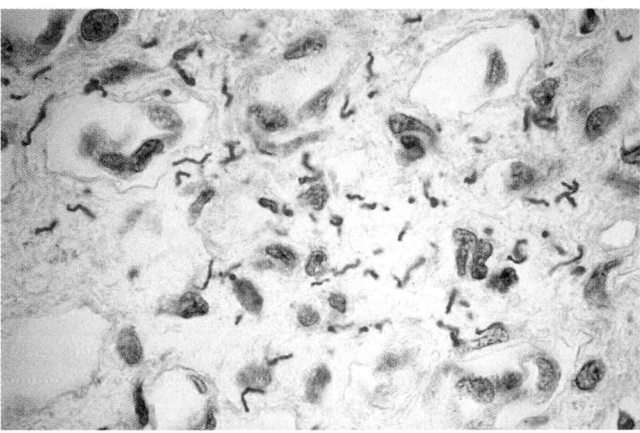

B

FIGURE 237-5. Kidney sections stained by silver staining (**A**) and immunohistochemical staining (**B**), showing presence of multiple leptospires in tubules. *(A Courtesy of Dr. Martin Hicklin, Public Health Image Library, CDC; B courtesy of Juanne Layne, University of the West Indies, Barbados).*

rent infection includes a single titer of at least 1:200 obtained after the onset of symptoms.[67] Delayed seroconversions are common, with up to 10% of patients failing to seroconvert within 30 days of the clinical onset. Cross-reactive antibodies may be associated with syphilis, relapsing fever, Lyme disease, viral hepatitis, human immunodeficiency virus (HIV) infection, legionellosis, and autoimmune diseases.[68]

The interpretation of the MAT is complicated by cross-reaction between different serogroups, especially in acute-phase samples.[5] Cross-reactivity in acute samples is attributable to IgM antibodies, which may persist for several years.[69] The MAT is a serogroup-specific assay, and cannot be used to interpret the identity of the infecting serovar.[15] However, knowledge of the presumptive serogroup may be of epidemiological value in determining potential exposures to animal reservoirs.

Diagnostic application of the MAT is limited by the relatively low sensitivity when acute serum samples are tested.[70] Other agglutination assays that detect total immunoglobulins, such as the indirect hemagglutination assay, suffer from similarly low sensitivities on acute specimens, but have high case sensitivities when acute and convalescent specimens are tested.[71] IgM antibodies are detectable after about the fifth day of illness, and IgM-detection assays are available in several formats.[71-74] Use of these assays as screening tests offers the potential to enhance the diagnostic capacity of many laboratories, particularly in developing countries, where most cases of leptospirosis occur.

TABLE 237-3 Antimicrobial Agents Recommended for Treatment and Chemoprophylaxis of Leptospirosis

Indication	Compound	Dosage
Chemoprophylaxis	Doxycycline	200 mg PO orally once per week
Treatment of mild leptospirosis	Doxycycline	100 mg bid PO
	Ampicillin	500-750 mg q6h PO
	Amoxicillin	500 mg q6h PO
Treatment of moderate to severe leptospirosis	Penicillin G	1.5 MU IV q6h
	Ceftriaxone	1 g IV q24h
	Ampicillin	0.5-1 g IV q6h

TREATMENT

Antibiotics have been used to treat leptospirosis since penicillin first became available. There have been few randomized or placebo-controlled trials[75-78] and these have produced conflicting results. However, antibiotic therapy consistently prevents or reduces the duration of leptospiruria. A recent meta-analysis concluded that there was insufficient evidence to provide clear guidelines for practice.[79] Nevertheless, severe disease is usually treated with intravenous penicillin and mild disease with oral doxycycline (Table 237-3). Once-daily ceftriaxone has been shown to be as effective as penicillin.[80]

Antibiotic therapy should be initiated as early in the course of the disease as suspicion allows. Supportive therapy is essential for hospitalized patients. Jarisch-Herxheimer reactions have been reported in patients treated with penicillin.[81] Patients receiving penicillin should be monitored because of the increased morbidity and mortality of such reactions.

PREVENTION

Prevention of leptospirosis may be achieved by avoidance of high-risk exposures, adoption of protective measures, immunization and use of chemoprophylaxis, in varying combinations depending on the environmental circumstances and the degree of human activity.

High-risk exposures include immersion in fresh water, as in swimming, and contact with animals and their body fluids.[2] Removal of leptospires from the environment is impractical, but reducing direct contact with potentially infected animals and indirect contact with urine-contaminated soil and water remains the most effective preventive strategy available. Consistent application of rodent control measures is important in limiting the extent of contamination. Appropriate protective measures depend on the activity, but include wearing boots, goggles, overalls, and rubber gloves. In tropical environments, walking barefoot is a common risk-factor.[82]

Immunization of animals with killed vaccines is widely practiced, but is short-lived and animals require periodic (usually annual) boosters.[83] Moreover, although these vaccines prevent against disease, they do not prevent infection and renal colonization; thus they have little effect on the maintenance and transmission of the disease within the animal population in which they are applied. Current bovine and porcine vaccines used in the United States contain serovars Icterohaemorrhagiae, Canciola, Grippotyphosa, Pomona, and Hardjo, while canine vaccines contain all except serovar Hardjo. A new vaccine for bovine use stimulates a type 1 cell-mediated immune response against serovar Hardjo[84] and appears to protect against renal colonization and urinary shedding.[85]

Human immunization is not widely practiced. A vaccine containing serovar Icterohaemorrhagiae is available in France for workers in high-risk occupations, and a vaccine has been developed recently for human use in Cuba.[86] Immunization has been more widely employed in Asian countries, to prevent large-scale epidemics in agricultural laborers.

For individuals who will be unavoidably exposed to leptospires in endemic environments, chemoprophylaxis with doxycycline is recommended (see Table 237-3). This approach has been shown to be effective in military personnel without previous exposure who underwent jungle training.[87] The use of doxycycline prophylaxis after excess rainfall in local populations in endemic areas has been studied.[88,89] Symptomatic disease was significantly reduced in one study, but serologic evidence of infection was found equally in subjects and controls.[88]

REFERENCES

1. World Health Organization. Leptospirosis worldwide, 1999. Wkly Epidemiol Rec. 1999;74:237-242.
2. Faine S, Adler B, Bolin C, Perolat P. *Leptospira* and leptospirosis. 2nd ed. Melbourne: MedSci; 1999.
3. Stimson AM. Note on an organism found in yellow-fever tissue. Publ Hlth Rep. 1907;22:541.
4. Everard JD. Leptospirosis. In: Cox FEG, ed. The Wellcome Trust Illustrated History of Tropical Diseases. London: The Wellcome Trust; 1996:111-119, 416-418.
5. Levett PN. Leptospirosis. Clin Microbiol Rev. 2001;14:296-326.
6. Edwards GA, Domm BM. Human leptospirosis. Medicine. 1960;39:117-156.
7. Feigin RD, Anderson DC. Human leptospirosis. CRC Crit Rev Clin Lab Sci. 1975;5:413-467.
8. Goldstein SF, Charon NW. Motility of the spirochete *Leptospira*. Cell Motil Cytoskelet. 1988;9:101-110.
9. Levett PN. *Leptospira* and *Leptonema*. In: Murray PR, Baron EJ, Jorgensen JH, et al, eds. Manual of Clinical Microbiology. 8th ed. Washington, DC: American Society for Microbiology Press; 2003:929-936.
10. Bulach DM, Kalambaheti T, de La Peña-Moctezuma A, Adler B. Lipopolysaccharide biosynthesis in *Leptospira*. J Mol Microbiol Biotechnol. 2000;2:375-380.
11. Yasuda PH, Steigerwalt AG, Sulzer KR, et al. Deoxyribonucleic acid relatedness between serogroups and serovars in the family *Leptospiraceae* with proposals for seven new *Leptospira* species. Int J Syst Bacteriol. 1987;37:407-415.
12. Brenner DJ, Kaufmann AF, Sulzer KR, et al. Further determination of DNA relatedness between serogroups and serovars in the family Leptospiraceae with a proposal for *Leptospira alexanderi* sp. nov. and four new *Leptospira* genomospecies. Int J Syst Bacteriol. 1999;49:839-858.
13. Ramadass P, Jarvis BDW, Corner RJ, et al. Genetic characterization of pathogenic *Leptospira* species by DNA hybridization. Int J Syst Bacteriol. 1992;42:215-219.
14. Pérolat P, Chappel RJ, Adler B, et al. *Leptospira fainei* sp. nov., isolated from pigs in Australia. Int J Syst Bacteriol. 1998;48:851-858.
15. Levett PN. Usefulness of serologic analysis as a predictor of the infecting serovar in patients with severe leptospirosis. Clin Infect Dis. 2003;36:447-452.
16. Ren SX, Fu G, Jiang XG, et al. Unique physiological and pathogenic features of *Leptospira interrogans* revealed by whole-genome sequencing. Nature. 2003;422:888-893.
17. Trevejo RT, Rigau-Perez JG, Ashford DA, et al. Epidemic leptospirosis associated with pulmonary hemorrhage-Nicaragua, 1995. J Infect Dis. 1998;178:1457-1463.
18. Sasaki DM, Pang L, Minette HP, et al. Active surveillance and risk factors for leptospirosis in Hawaii. Am J Trop Med Hyg. 1993;48:35-43.
19. Morgan J, Bornstein SL, Karpati AM, et al. Outbreak of Leptospirosis among Triathlon participants and community residents in Springfield, Illinois, 1998. Clin Infect Dis. 2002;34:1593-1599.
20. Sejvar J, Bancroft E, Winthrop K, et al. Leptospirosis in "Eco-Challenge" athletes, Malaysian Borneo, 2000. Emerg Infect Dis. 2003;9:702-707.
21. Ward MP, Glickman LT, Guptill LF. Prevalence of and risk factors for leptospirosis among dogs in the United States and Canada: 677 cases (1970-1998). J Am Vet Med Assoc. 2002;220:53-58.
22. Prescott JF, McEwen B, Taylor J, et al. Resurgence of leptospirosis in dogs in Ontario: Recent findings. Can Vet J. 2002;43:955-961.
23. Brown CA, Roberts AW, Miller MA, et al. *Leptospira interrogans* serovar *grippotyphosa* infection in dogs. J Am Vet Med Assoc. 1996;209:1265-1267.
24. Areán VM. The pathologic anatomy and pathogenesis of fatal human leptospirosis (Weil's disease). Am J Pathol. 1962;40:393-423.
25. Cinco M, Cini B, Perticarari S, Presani G. *Leptospira interrogans* binds to the CR3 receptor on mammalian cells. Microb Pathogen. 2002;33:299-305.
26. Lee SH, Kim S, Park SC, Kim MJ. Cytotoxic activities of *Leptospira interrogans* hemolysin SphH as a pore-forming protein on mammalian cells. Infect Immun. 2002;70:315-322.
27. Abdulkader RC, Daher EF, Camargo ED, et al. Leptospirosis severity may be associated with the intensity of humoral immune response. Revis Inst Med Trop São Paulo. 2002;44:79-83.
28. Lucchesi PM, Parma AE, Arroyo GH. Serovar distribution of a DNA sequence involved in the antigenic relationship between *Leptospira* and equine cornea. BMC Microbiol. 2002;2:3.
29. Haake DA. Spirochaetal lipoproteins and pathogenesis. Microbiology. 2000;146:1491-1504.
30. Nally JE, Timoney JF, Stevenson B. Temperature-regulated protein synthesis by *Leptospira interrogans*. Infect Immun. 2001;69:400-404.
31. Haake DA, Chao G, Zuerner RL, et al. The leptospiral major outer membrane protein LipL32 is a lipoprotein expressed during mammalian infection. Infect Immun. 2000;68:2276-2285.
32. Guerreiro H, Croda J, Flannery B, et al. Leptospiral proteins recognized during the humoral immune response to leptospirosis in humans. Infect Immun. 2001;69:4958-4968.
33. Yang CW, Wu MS, Pan MJ, et al. The *Leptospira* outer membrane protein LipL32 induces tubulointerstitial nephritis-mediated gene expression in mouse proximal tubule cells. J Am Soc Nephrol. 2002;13:2037-2045.
34. Alexander AD, Benenson AS, Byrne RJ, et al. Leptospirosis in Puerto Rico. Zoon Res. 1963;2:152-227.
35. Wang C, John L, Chang T, et al. Studies on anicteric leptospirosis. I. Clinical manifestations and antibiotic therapy. Chin Med J. 1965;84:283-291.
36. Berman SJ, Tsai CC, Holmes KK, et al. Sporadic anicteric leptospirosis in South Vietnam. Ann Intern Med. 1973;79:167-173.
37. Park S-K, Lee S-H, Rhee Y-K, et al. Leptospirosis in Chonbuk province of Korea in 1987: A study of 93 patients. Am J Trop Med Hyg. 1989;41:345-351.
38. Yersin C, Bovet P, Mérien F, et al. Human leptospirosis in the Seychelles (Indian Ocean): A population-based study. Am J Trop Med Hyg. 1998;59:933-940.
39. Ko AI, Galvao Reis M, Ribeiro Dourado CM, et al and Salvador Leptospirosis Study Group. Urban epidemic of severe leptospirosis in Brazil. Lancet. 1999;354:820-825.
40. Katz AR, Ansdell VE, Effler PV, et al. Assessment of the clinical presentation and treatment of 353 cases of laboratory-confirmed leptospirosis in Hawaii, 1974-1998. Clin Infect Dis. 2001;33:1834-1841.
41. Bharadwaj R, Bal AM, Joshi SA, et al. An urban outbreak of leptospirosis in Mumbai, India. Jpn J Infect Dis. 2002;55:194-196.
42. Turner LH. Leptospirosis I. Trans R Soc Trop Med Hyg. 1967;61:842-855.
43. Silva HR, Tanajura GM, Tavares-Neto J, et al. Aseptic meningitis syndrome due to enterovirus and *Leptospira* sp in children of Salvador, Bahia. Revis Soc Brasil Med Trop. 2002;35:159-165.
44. Edwards CN, Nicholson GD, Hassell TA, et al. Leptospirosis in Barbados: A clinical study. W Indian Med J. 1990;39:27-34.
45. Edwards GA, Domm BM. Leptospirosis. II. Med Times. 1966;94:1086-1095.
46. Zaki SR, Spiegel RA. Leptospirosis. In: Nelson AM, Horsburgh CR, eds. Pathology of Emerging Infections, vol 2. Washington, DC: American Society for Microbiology Press; 1998:73-92.
47. Abdulkader RCRM, Seguro AC, Malheiro PS, et al. Peculiar electrolytic and hormonal abnormalities in acute renal failure due to leptospirosis. Am J Trop Med Hyg 1996;54:1-6.
48. Edwards CN, Nicholson GD, Hassell TA, et al. Thrombocytopenia in leptospirosis: The absence of evidence for disseminated intravascular coagulation. Am J Trop Med Hyg. 1986;35:352-354.
49. Lai KN, Aarons I, Woodroffe AJ, Clarkson AR. Renal lesions in leptospirosis. Aust N Z J Med. 1982;12:276-279.
50. Zaki SR, Shieh W-J and The Epidemic Working Group. Leptospirosis associated with outbreak of acute febrile illness and pulmonary haemorrhage, Nicaragua, 1995. Lancet. 1996;347:535.
51. Yersin C, Bovet P, Mérien F, et al. Pulmonary haemorrhage as a predominant cause of death in leptospirosis in Seychelles. Trans R Soc Trop Med Hyg. 2000;94:71-76.
52. Im J-G, Yeon KM, Han MC, et al. Leptospirosis of the lung: Radiographic findings in 58 patients. Am J Roentgenol. 1989;152:955-959.
53. Nicodemo AC, Duarte MIS, Alves VAF, et al. Lung lesions in human leptospirosis: Microscopic, immunohistochemical, and ultrastructural features related to thrombocytopenia. Am J Trop Med Hyg. 1997;56:181-187.
54. Parsons M. Electrocardiographic changes in leptospirosis. Br Med J. 1965;2:201-203.
55. Sacramento E, Lopes AA, Costa E, et al. Electrocardiographic alterations in patients hospitalized with leptospirosis in the Brazilian city of Salvador. Arquiv Brasil Cardiol. 2002;78:267-270.
56. Areán VM. Leptospiral myocarditis. Lab Invest. 1957;6:462-471.
57. de Brito T, Morais CF, Yasuda PH, et al. Cardiovascular involvement in human and experimental leptospirosis: Pathologic findings and immunohistochemical detection of leptospiral antigen. Ann Trop Med Parasitol. 1987;81:207-214.
58. Vijayachari P, Sugunan AP, Umapathi T, Sehgal SC. Evaluation of darkground microscopy as a rapid diagnostic procedure in leptospirosis. Indian J Med Res. 2001;114:54-58.
59. Saengjaruk P, Chaicumpa W, Watt G, et al. Diagnosis of human leptospirosis by monoclonal antibody-based antigen detection in urine. J Clin Microbiol. 2002;40:480-489.
60. Brown PD, Gravekamp C, Carrington DG, et al. Evaluation of the polymerase chain reaction for early diagnosis of leptospirosis. J Med Microbiol. 1995;43:110-114.
61. Mérien F, Baranton G, Pérolat P. Comparison of polymerase chain reaction with microagglutination test and culture for diagnosis of leptospirosis. J Infect Dis. 1995;172:281-285.
62. Smythe LD, Smith IL, Smith GA, et al. A quantitative PCR (TaqMan) assay for pathogenic *Leptospira* spp. BMC Infect Dis. 2002;2:13.
63. Alves VAF, Vianna MR, Yasuda PH, de Brito T. Detection of leptospiral antigen in the human liver and kidney using an immunoperoxidase staining procedure. J Pathol. 1987;151:125-131.
64. Guarner J, Shieh W-J, Morgan J, et al. Leptospirosis mimicking acute cholecystitis among athletes participating in a triathlon. Hum Pathol. 2001;32:750-752.
65. Palmer MF, Zochowski WJ. Survival of leptospires in commercial blood culture systems revisited. J Clin Pathol. 2000;53:713-714.
66. Faine S. Guidelines for the control of leptospirosis. Geneva: World Health Organization, 1982 (Offset Publication No. 67).
67. Centers for Disease Control and Prevention. Case definitions for infectious conditions under public health surveillance. Morbid Mortal Wkly Rep. 1997;46(RR-10):49.
68. Bajani MD, Ashford DA, Bragg SL, et al. Evaluation of four commercially available rapid serologic tests for diagnosis of leptospirosis. J Clin Microbiol. 2003;41:803-809.

69. Cumberland PC, Everard COR, Wheeler JG, Levett PN. Persistence of anti-leptospiral IgM, IgG and agglutinating antibodies in patients presenting with acute febrile illness in Barbados 1979-1989. Eur J Epidemiol. 2001;17:601-608.

70. Cumberland PC, Everard COR, Levett PN. Assessment of the efficacy of the IgM enzyme-linked immunosorbent assay (ELISA) and microscopic agglutination test (MAT) in the diagnosis of acute leptospirosis. Am J Trop Med Hyg. 1999;61:731-734.

71. Levett PN, Branch SL, Whittington CU, et al. Two methods for rapid serological diagnosis of acute leptospirosis. Clin Diagn Lab Immunol. 2001;8:349-351.

72. Levett PN, Branch SL. Evaluation of two enzyme-linked immunosorbent assay methods for detection of immunoglobulin M antibodies in acute leptospirosis. Am J Trop Med Hyg. 2002;66:745-748.

73. Smits HL, Ananyina YV, Chereshsky A, et al. International multicenter evaluation of the clinical utility of a dipstick assay for detection of *Leptospira*-specific immunoglobulin M antibodies in human serum specimens. J Clin Microbiol. 1999;37:2904-2909.

74. Smits HL, van Der Hoorn MA, Goris MG, et al. Simple latex agglutination assay for rapid serodiagnosis of human leptospirosis. J Clin Microbiol. 2000;38:1272-1275.

75. McClain JBL, Ballou WR, Harrison SM, Steinweg DL. Doxycycline therapy for leptospirosis. Ann Intern Med. 1984;100:696-698.

76. Edwards CN, Nicholson GD, Hassell TA, et al. Penicillin therapy in icteric leptospirosis. Am J Trop Med Hyg. 1988;39:388-390.

77. Watt G, Padre LP, Tuazon ML, et al. Placebo-controlled trial of intravenous penicillin for severe and late leptospirosis. Lancet. 1988;i:433-435.

78. Costa E, Lopes AA, Sacramento E, et al. Penicillin at the late stage of leptospirosis: A randomized controlled trial. Revis Inst Med Trop São Paulo. 2003;45:141-145.

79. Guidugli F, Castro AA, Atallah AN. Antibiotics for treating leptospirosis (Cochrane Review). Cochrane Library, Issue 3. Oxford: Update Software; 2003.

80. Panaphut T, Domrongkitchaiporn S, Vibhagool A, et al. Ceftriaxone compared with sodium penicillin G for treatment of severe leptospirosis. Clin Infect Dis 2003;36:1507-1513.

81. Friedland JS, Warrell DA. The Jarisch-Herxheimer reaction in leptospirosis: Possible pathogenesis and review. Rev Infect Dis. 1991;13:207-210.

82. Douglin CP, Jordan C, Rock R, et al. Risk factors for severe leptospirosis in the parish of St. Andrew, Barbados. Emerg Infect Dis. 1997;3:78-80.

83. Bey RF, Johnson RC. Current status of leptospiral vaccines. Prog Vet Microbiol Immunol. 1986;2:175-197.

84. Naiman BM, Alt D, Bolin CA, et al. Protective killed *Leptospira borgpetersenii* vaccine induces potent Th1 immunity comprising responses by CD4 and gammadelta T lymphocytes. Infect Immun. 2001;69:7550-7558.

85. Bolin CA, Alt DP. Use of a monovalent leptospiral vaccine to prevent renal colonization and urinary shedding in cattle exposed to *Leptospira borgpetersenii* serovar *hardjo*. Am J Vet Res. 2001;62:995-1000.

86. Martínez Sánchez R, Pérez Sierra A, Baró Suárez M, et al. Evaluación de la efectividad de una nueva vacuna contra la leptospirosis human en grupos en riesgo. Revis Panamer Salud Publ. 2000;8:385-392.

87. Takafuji ET, Kirkpatrick JW, Miller RN, et al. An efficacy trial of doxycycline chemoprophylaxis against leptospirosis. N Engl J Med. 1984;310:497-500.

88. Sehgal SC, Sugunan AP, Murhekar MV, et al. Randomized controlled trial of doxycycline prophylaxis against leptospirosis in an endemic area. Int J Antimicrob Agents. 2000;13:249-255.

89. Gonsalez CR, Casseb J, Monteiro FG, et al. Use of doxycycline for leptospirosis after high-risk exposure in Sao Paulo, Brazil. Revis Inst Med Trop São Paulo. 1998;41:59-61.

CHAPTER **238**

Borrelia Species (Relapsing Fever)

KYU Y. RHEE

WARREN D. JOHNSON, JR.

Relapsing fever is an arthropod-borne zoonosis caused by spirochetes of the genus *Borrelia*. It is clinically characterized by cyclical fevers and nonspecific symptoms, caused by recurrent bouts of spirochetemia, which alternate with periods of relative well-being. Borrelial species associated with soft ticks of the genus *Ornithodoros* cause endemic or tick-borne relapsing fever (TBRF). Relapsing fever caused by *B. recurrentis* is transmitted by the human body louse *(Pediculus humanus)* and causes epidemic or louse-borne relapsing fever (LBRF).[1-4]

ETIOLOGY

The genus *Borrelia* belongs to the family Spirochaetaceae, which also includes the genus *Treponema*.[5] Borreliae are helical, 8 to 30 μm long, and 0.2 to 0.5 μm wide, have 3 to 10 loose spirals, are actively motile, and divide by transverse fission.[1,6] They are readily stained with aniline or acid dyes, but strains cannot be distinguished by morphologic characteristics. The ultrastructure of borreliae consists of an outer slimelike layer, a cell wall, and both an outer and cytoplasmic membrane between which are anchored numerous protoplasmic filaments and flagella that wind around the cytoplasmic body.[4] Borreliae are promptly killed by desiccation and ultraviolet rays but survive and retain their virulence when frozen at $-73°$ C for many months.[1]

Borrelia strains have been cultivated in artificial media with generation times ranging from 18 hours (*Borrelia hermsii*)[7,8] to 8 to 9 hours (*B. recurrentis*).[9] Tick-borne borreliae remain viable in their natural tick vectors for up to 12 years, and this represents the optimal method for maintaining organisms.[6] Rodents (rats, hamsters, guinea pigs) injected with some strains develop latent brain infections.[1] In mice, *B. hermsii* reversibly changes its major outer surface protein when it is transmitted by the tick to the mammalian host and back to the tick.[10] There is also tick-spirochete specificity, and this has been used to identify *Borrelia* spp.[11,12]

EPIDEMIOLOGY AND TRANSMISSION

Relapsing fever occurs throughout the world, with the exception of a few areas in the Southwest Pacific.[11,12] The distribution and occurrence of endemic relapsing fever (TBRF) is governed by the presence of enzootic cycles of the transmitting tick vector. The distribution of epidemic relapsing fever (LBRF) is determined by socioeconomic and ecologic factors.

Louse-borne relapsing fever is caused only by *B. recurrentis* and is transmitted from person to person by the human body louse (*Pediculus humanus*).[2] Following the ingestion of infective human blood by the louse, spirochetes penetrate the midgut and multiply in the hemolymph. Tissues of the louse are not invaded by spirochetes, so disease cannot be transmitted to humans by louse saliva or excrement, or transovarially to the progeny of the louse. Epidemic relapsing fever therefore results from crushing lice, with the release of infective organisms capable of penetrating intact skin or mucous membranes.[12] Lice are infective for their lifetime (10 to 60 days) and humans are the only hosts for this organism.

Louse-borne relapsing fever usually occurs in epidemics that are associated with catastrophic events, such as war or famine, that result in overcrowding and dissemination of body lice. The last great epidemic occurred during World War II in North Africa and Europe and caused an estimated 50,000 deaths.[1,2] Louse-borne relapsing fever remains endemic in the highlands of Central and East Africa (Ethiopia, Sudan, Somalia, Chad) and in the South American Andes (Bolivia, Peru).[13]

Tick-borne relapsing fever is caused by at least 15 *Borrelia* spp. Each is associated with a distinct member of the transmitting argasid soft tick genus *Ornithodoros,* from which many derive their respective species name. Members of the genus *Ornithodoros* possess distinct hosts and habitats but are all obligate blood feeders at every developmental stage and orient to the presence of exhaled breath. Typically, these ticks inhabit caves, decaying wood, rodent burrows, and animal shelters. Their range of movement is limited (less than 50 yards), although rodents may carry them passively into human dwellings. Their presence often passes unnoticed because they are night feeders and lack a painful bite. In contrast to hard ticks of the genus *Ixodes,* *Ornithidoros* ticks feed quickly (5 to 20 minutes) and females lay clutches of eggs following each blood meal.[14] Perpetuation of *Borrelial* spirochetes is maintained via the ability of adult ticks to fast for up to 15 years while living in protected environments, and in some cases, transovarial passage to tick progeny. The specific mode of transmission appears to vary with both the species and stage of tick development.

Animal reservoirs for these borreliae include rodents and small animals (chipmunks, squirrels, rabbits, rats, mice, owls, lizards).[11,12]

In TBRF, borreliae contained in the blood meal of the tick multiply rapidly and within hours invade all tissues, including salivary glands, excretory organs, and the genital system. Persistent infection of the salivary glands is thought to facilitate rapid transmission during a relatively short feeding period.[14,15] Infection of humans occurs when saliva or excrement is released by the tick while feeding.

The intrusion of humans into the tick's environment creates the opportunity for disease transmission. The largest outbreak of tick-borne relapsing fever in the Western Hemisphere occurred in 62 campers residing in log cabins in Arizona in 1973.[16] The magnitude of this outbreak may have been related to a concurrent epizootic plague that killed many of the natural rodent hosts of the tick.[12] TBRF has been reported worldwide, with the exception of a few areas in the Southwest Pacific, although infected ticks have been identified in regions where no cases of TBRF have been reported.

PATHOPHYSIOLOGY

The clinical manifestations of relapsing fever mirror closely the pathophysiology of infection. During the febrile illness, borreliae multiply in the blood stream and are often present at levels in excess of 100,000 organsism/mm³ of blood.[2] With immune recognition, these spirochetes are cleared from the blood stream and sequestered in internal organs, giving rise to intercurrent afebrile periods. Under immune pressure, borreliae undergo antigenic modification of its outer surface proteins and reemerge in the blood stream both microbiologically and clinically.[17] The mechanism for this antigenic variation is mediated by both nonreciprocal *intermolecular* recombination mechanisms similar to gene conversion and *intramolecular* recombination events similar to those occurring during immunoglobulin gene rearrangements. Each of these mechanisms allows for the placement of different surface protein (variable major protein-*vmp*) genes into a single active expression site.[18] This cyclic process of antigenic variation followed by specific antibody production is responsible for the relapsing course of this disease and can give rise to as many as 30 antigenic variants.[19] With successive relapses, borreliae revert to antigenic types similar to those present in earlier relapses. The ultimate termination of clinical disease has been attributed primarily to the development of specific borreliacidal antibody rather than to the activity of phagocytic cells.[1,20]

At autopsy, hepatitis and hepatic necrosis; miliary splenic abscesses; central nervous system lesions (hemorrhages, perivascular infiltrates, degenerative lesions); myocarditis; and hemorrhagic, gastrointestinal, and renal lesions have been described.[2,3,21]

CLINICAL MANIFESTATIONS

The clinical manifestations of louse-borne and tick-borne relapsing fever are similar.[1-4] The variations that occur may be related to differences in spirochete strains, inoculating dose, host immunity, and general condition of the patients. The clinical features of relapsing fever are summarized in Table 238-1.

The incubation period of both forms of relapsing fever is often difficult to establish, because louse exposure is often long-term, and the tick bite may not be recognized. Generally, louse-borne disease has a longer incubation period, longer febrile periods and afebrile intervals, and fewer relapses than tick-borne disease. Characteristically, both types of relapsing fever have an acute onset of high fever with rigors, severe headache, myalgias, arthralgias, and lethargy. Prodromal symptoms are rare. Initial physical findings are variable but may include altered sensorium, conjunctival suffusion, petechiae, and diffuse abdominal tenderness with hepatomegaly and splenomegaly. Less common findings include nuchal rigidity, cough, pulmonary rales and rhonchi, lymphadenopathy, and jaundice. During the course of the illness the fever is remittent and accompanied by tachycardia and tachypnea. Hemorrhage is common, and more so with LBRF, but rarely severe (petechiae, epistaxis, hemoptysis, hematuria, hemateme-

TABLE 238-1 Summary of Clinical Features of Relapsing Fever

Manifestation	Mean Value or Incidence	
	Louse-Borne Disease	Tick-Borne Disease
Case-fatality rate (%)	4-40	2-5
Incubation period (days)	8 (4-18)*	7 (4-18)
Duration of first febrile attack (days)	5.5	3
Duration of afebrile interval (days)	9	7
Duration of relapses	2	2-3
Number of relapses	1-2 (1-5)*	3 (0-13)*
Maximal temperature (°F)	101-102	105
Splenomegaly (%)	77	41
Hepatomegaly (%)	66	17
Jaundice (%)	6	7
Rash (%)	8	28
Respiratory symptoms (%)	34 (cough)	16
Central nervous system involvement (%)	30	9

*Range.

Adapted from Southern PM, Sanford JP. Relapsing fever: A clinical and microbiological review. Medicine. 1969;48:129-149.

sis). Iritis and iridocyclitis may result in permanent impairment of vision. Pneumonia, bronchitis, and otitis media may occur. A truncal skin rash of 1 to 2 days' duration is common at the end of the primary febrile episode.[3] The rash can be petechial, macular, or papular. Neurologic findings are reported in up to 30% of patients and include coma, cranial nerve palsies, hemiplegia, meningitis, and seizures.[3,21] Myocarditis with associated arrhythmias, cerebral hemorrhage, and hepatic failure are the most common causes of death.

The primary febrile episode characteristically terminates abruptly in 3 to 6 days. This crisis may be associated with fatal hypotension and shock. After 7 to 10 days, fever and symptoms suddenly recur. The duration and the intensity of the symptoms progressively decrease with each relapse. Louse-borne relapsing fever is usually associated with a single relapse, whereas multiple relapses are the rule in tick-borne disease. Relapsing fever during pregnancy is associated with increased maternal and infant morbidity and mortality.[22-24]

DIAGNOSIS

The definitive diagnosis of relapsing fever is established by the demonstration of borreliae in the peripheral blood of febrile patients (Fig. 238-1). Spirochetes are found in 70% of cases when wet blood smears are examined by darkfield microscopy or in Giemsa- or Wright-stained thick and thin smears.[3,25] Organisms are rarely found during afebrile periods. The diagnostic yield can be increased by the examination of acridine orange–stained smears by fluorescence microscopy or buffy coat smears.[26,27]

Agglutinating, complement-fixing, borreliacidal, and immobilizing antibodies are detectable in serum. However, these tests are not generally available and, if performed, are of limited diagnostic value owing to antigenic variation of strains and the complexity of the relapse phenomenon.[16,25] *Proteus* OXK agglutinin titers are elevated in relapsing fever, with the highest titers being found in patients with louse-borne disease (1:80 or greater). Antibodies to OX-19 and OX-2 are rare. The serologic tests for syphilis are positive in 5% to 10% of patients. Serologic tests for Lyme disease may also be positive.[28] Recent data suggest both louse- and tick-borne relapsing fever associated Borreliae may be discriminated from syphilis- and Lyme disease–associated treponemes based on the presence of detectable titers against the surface protein, glycerophosphodiester phosphodiesterase (GlpQ).[29] Leukocytosis (to 25,000 cells/mm³) and an increased erythrocyte sedimentation rate (to 110 mm/hour) are common. The cerebrospinal fluid pressure is usually elevated in patients with central nervous system involvement and is associ-

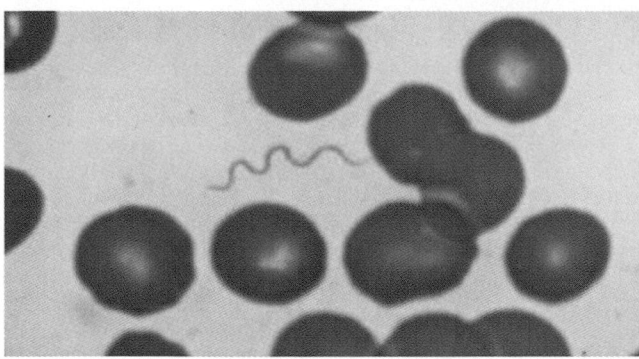

FIGURE 238-1. Peripheral blood smear from a patient with tick-borne relapsing fever acquired in Idaho. Wright stain.

ated with a pleocytosis (15 to 2200 cells/mm^3) and with an elevated protein concentration (to 160 mg/100 mL).[3] The spinal fluid glucose level is normal. Spirochetes have been detected in cerebrospinal fluid by smear or by animal inoculation in up to 12% of the patients with central nervous system signs.

An early clinical diagnosis of louse-borne relapsing fever is not difficult during epidemics unless there is coexisting epidemic typhus, a disease also transmitted by the body louse. During the initial febrile episode of an isolated case of relapsing fever, the differential diagnosis can include malaria, typhoid fever, hepatitis, leptospirosis, rat-bite fever, Colorado tick fever, and dengue.[30] Epidemiologic considerations, the occurrence of relapses, and the demonstration of spirochetemia will exclude these diagnoses. The diagnosis of tick-borne relapsing fever may be complicated in regions where Lyme disease is endemic owing to the similar neurologic manifestations of the diseases and cross-reactive serologic assays.[28,31]

TREATMENT AND PREVENTION

Relapsing fever has been treated successfully with tetracycline, chloramphenicol, penicillin, and erythromycin.[32-35] Tetracycline, in a single oral dose (0.5 g), is the preferred therapy in louse-borne relapsing fever except in pregnant women and children younger than 8 years (teeth and bone staining).[35] Erythromycin, 0.5 g in a single oral dose, is an equally effective alternative therapy.[34] Tick-borne relapsing fever is often treated with either tetracycline or erythromycin, 0.5 g every 6 hours for 5 to 10 days, because of the higher rate of treatment failures and relapses in these patients.[3,32,33] Meningitis or encephalitis should be treated with parenteral antibiotics, such as penicillin G, cefotaxime, or ceftriaxone, for 14 days or more.[21] The mortality of treated relapsing fever is less than 5%.[3] Untreated epidemic louse-borne disease has a mortality of up to 40%.[1,2]

Antibiotic treatment typically induces a Jarisch-Herxheimer reaction with severe rigors, leukopenia, an increase in temperature, and a decrease in blood pressure. The onset of the reaction occurs within 2 hours of initiating therapy and coincides with clearing of the spirochetemia. The reaction appears to be an exaggeration of the crisis observed in untreated patients and is most severe in louse-borne disease treated with penicillin. A significant percentage of patients with tick-borne relapsing fever, however, also develop the reaction. Recent studies suggest that the lipid component of the variable major protein possesses potent, although variable, tumor necrosis-α–inducing activity.[36] Because the reaction may be life-threatening, it has been recommended that patients be kept under observation for approximately 2 hours after the initiation of treatment.[28] Release of borrelial cell contents with the induction of cytokines and activation of kinins and fibrinolytic factors may have a major role in both the acute illness and the development of this reaction.[37] The Jarisch-Herxheimer reaction is associated with transient elevations of levels of plasma tumor necrosis factor, interleukin-6, and interleukin-8 concentrations.[38] It is prevented by prior administration of antibodies against tumor necrosis factor-α.[39-41] The prior administration of hydrocortisone is ineffective.[32,35]

Prevention of relapsing fever requires avoidance or elimination of the arthropod vectors. The varied habitats and the vast geographic areas populated by *Ornithodoros* ticks make their eradication impossible. Insecticides can be used in dwellings and surrounding areas, and insect repellents applied to clothing and persons may further decrease exposure opportunities. Prevention of louse-borne disease is accomplished by good personal hygiene and, if necessary, delousing procedures. DDT-resistant louse strains have developed since World War II, and other insecticides may be required, for example, dimethyl dithiophosphate (malathion).[32]

REFERENCES

1. Felsenfeld O. *Borrelia:* Strains, Vectors, Human and Animal Borreliosis. St Louis: Warren H Green; 1971:180.
2. Bryceson ADM, Parry EHO, Perine PL, et al. Louseborne relapsing fever. A clinical and laboratory study of 62 cases in Ethiopia and a reconsideration of the literature. Q J Med. 1970;39:129-170.
3. Southern PM Jr, Sanford JP. Relapsing fever: A clinical and microbiological review. Medicine. 1969;48:129-149.
4. Barbour AG, Hayes SF. Biology of *Borrelia* species. Microbiol Rev. 1986;50:381-400.
5. Garrity GM, ed. Bergey's Manual of Systematic Bacteriology. 2nd ed. New York: Springer Verlag; 2001.
6. Felsenfeld O. Borreliae, Human relapsing fever, and parasite vector host relationships. Bacteriol Rev. 1965;29:46.
7. Kelly RT. Cultivation and physiology of relapsing fever borreliae. In: Johnson RC, ed. The Biology of Parasitic Spirochetes. New York: Academic Press; 1976:87.
8. Kelly R. Cultivation of *Borrelia hermsii.* Science. 1971;173:443-444.
9. Cutler SJ, Fekade D, Hussein K, et al. Successful in-vitro cultivation of *Borrelia recurrentis.* Lancet. 1994;343:242.
10. Schwan TG, Hinnebusch BJ. Bloodstream- versus tick-associated variants of a relapsing fever bacterium. Science. 1998;280:1938.
11. Burgdorfer W. The enlarging spectrum of tickborne spirochetoses: R R Parker Memorial Address. Rev Infect Dis. 1986;8:932-940.
12. Burgdorfer W. The epidemiology of relapsing fevers. In: Johnson RC, ed. The Biology of Parasitic Spirochetes. New York: Academic Press; 1976:191.
13. Felsenfeld O. The problem of relapsing fever in the Americas. Indiana Med. 1973; 42:7.
14. Dworkin MS, Schwan TG, Anderson DE. Tick-borne relapsing fever in North America. Med Clin NA. 2002; 86:417-433.
15. Davis GE. The endemic relapsing fevers. In: Hull TG, ed. Diseases transmitted from Animal to Man. Springfield, IL: Charles C Thomas; 1955:552-565.
16. Centers for Disease Control and Prevention. Relapsing fever. Morb Mortal Wkly Rep. 1973;22:242-246.
17. Barbour AG. Antigenic variation of a relapsing fever *Borrelia* species. Annu Rev Microbiol. 1990;44:155-171.
18. Barbour AG. Relapsing fevers and other Borrelia infections. In: Guerrant RL, Walker DH, Weller PF, eds. Tropical Infectious Diseases. Philapdelphia: WB Saunders; 1999:535-546.
19. Schwann TG, Piesman J. Vector interactions and molecular adaptations of Lyme disease and relapsing fever spirochetes associated with transmission by ticks. Emerg Infect Dis. 2002;8:115-121.
20. Felsenfeld O. Immunity in relapsing fever. In: Johnson RC, ed. The Biology of Parasitic Spirochetes. New York: Academic Press; 1976:351-358.
21. Cadavid D, Barbour AG. Neuroborreliosis during relapsing fever: Review of the clinical manifestations, pathology, and treatment of infections in human and experimental animals. Clin Infect Dis. 1998;26:151.
22. Jongen VHWM, van Roosmalen J, Tiems J, et al. Tick-borne relapsing fever and pregnancey outcome in rural Tanzania. Acta Obstet Gynecol Scand. 1997;76:834.
23. Dupont HT, La Scola B, Williams R, Raoult D. A focus of tick-borne relapsing fever in southern Zaire. Clin Infect Dis. 1997;25:139.
24. Borgnolo G, Hailu B, Ciancarelli A, et al. Louse-borne relapsing fever: A clinical and an epidemiological study of 389 patients in Asella Hospital, Ethiopia. Trop Geogr Med. 1993;45:66.
25. Burgdorfer W. The diagnosis of relapsing fever. In: Johnson RC, ed. The Biology of Parasitic Spirochetes. New York: Academic Press; 1976:225.
26. Sciotto CG, Lauer BA, White WL, et al. Detection of *Borrelia* in acridine orange–stained blood smears by fluorescence microscopy. Arch Pathol Lab Med. 1983;107:384-386.
27. Cobey FC, Goldberg SH, Levian RA et al. Short report: Detection of borrelia (relapsing fever) in rural Ethiopia by means of the quantitative buffy coat technique. Am J Trop Med Hyg. 2001;65:164-165.
28. Dworkin MS, Anderson DE Jr, Schwan TG, et al. Tick-borne relapsing fever in the northwestern United States and southwestern Canada. Clin Infect Dis. 1998;26:122.
29. Porcella SF, Raffel SJ, Schrumpf ME, et al. Serodiagnosis of louse-borne relapsing fever with glycerophosphodiester phosphodiesterase (GlpQ) from *Borrelia recurrentis.* J Clin Microbiol. 2000;38:3561-3571.
30. Le CT. Tickborne relapsing fever in children. Pediatrics. 1980;66:963-966.
31. Rawlings JA. An overview of tick-borne relapsing fever with emphasis on outbreaks in Texas. Tex Med. 1995;91:56.

32. Sanford JP. Relapsing fever—treatment and control. In: Johnson RC, ed. The Biology of Parasitic Spirochetes. New York: Academic Press; 1976:389-394.
33. Horton JM, Blaser MJ. The spectrum of relapsing fever in the Rocky Mountains. Arch Intern Med. 1985;145:871-875.
34. Perine PL, Teklu B. Antibiotic treatment of louseborne relapsing fever in Ethiopia: A report of 377 cases. Am J Trop Med Hyg. 1983;32:1096-1100.
35. Butler T. Relapsing fever: New lessons about antibiotic action. Ann Intern Med. 1985;102:397.
36. Vidal, Scragg IG, Cutler SJ et al. Variable major lipoprotein is a principal TNF-inducing factor of louse-borne relapsing fever. Nat Med. 1998. 4:1416-1420.
37. Galloway RE, Levin J, Butler T, et al. Activation of protein mediators of inflammation and evidence for endotoxemia in Borrelia recurrentis infection. Am J Med. 1977;63:933-938.
38. Negussie Y, Remick DG, DeForge LE, et al. Detection of plasma tumor necrosis factor, interleukins 6 and 8 during the Jarisch-Herxheimer reaction of relapsing fever. J Exp Med. 1992;175:1207-1212.
39. Fekade D, Knox K, Hussein K, et al. Prevention of Jarisch-Herxheimer reactions by treatment with antibodies against tumor necrosis factor α. N Engl J Med. 1996;335:311.
40. Beutler B, Munford RS. Tumor necrosis factor and the Jarisch-Herxheimer reaction. N Engl J Med. 1996;335:347.
41. Coxon RE, Fekade D, Knox K, et al. The effect of antibody against TNF α on cytokine response in Jarisch-Herxheimer reactions of louse-borne relapsing fever. Q J Med. 1997;90:213.

CHAPTER **239**

Borrelia burgdorferi (Lyme Disease, Lyme Borreliosis)

ALLEN C. STEERE

Lyme disease or Lyme borreliosis, which is caused by the tick-borne spirochete *Borrelia burgdorferi (sensu lato),* occurs in temperate regions of North America, Europe, and Asia.[1] It is now the most common vector-borne disease in the United States and Europe.[2] The illness usually begins in summer (stage 1) with a characteristic expanding skin lesion, called erythema migrans (EM), which occurs at the site of the tick bite. Within several days to weeks (stage 2), the spirochete may spread to many other sites, particularly to other skin sites, the nervous system, the heart, or the joints. After months to years (stage 3), sometimes following long periods of latent infection, the spirochete may cause persistent disease, most commonly affecting the joints, nervous system, or skin. Serologic testing is the most practical laboratory aid in diagnosis. All stages of the disorder are usually curable by appropriate antibiotic therapy.

Lyme disease was recognized as a separate entity in 1976 because of close geographic clustering of affected children in Lyme, Connecticut, who were thought to have juvenile rheumatoid arthritis.[3] However, parts of the illness were recognized previously in Europe and were given different names, including erythema chronicum migrans,[4] Bannwarth's syndrome,[5] or acrodermatitis chronica atrophicans.[6] These syndromes were linked conclusively in 1982 and 1983 with the recovery of a previously unrecognized spirochete from the tick vector and from infected patients.[7-9] The basic outlines of the disease are similar worldwide, but there are regional variations, primarily between the illness found in America[9] and that in Europe and Asia.

CAUSATIVE ORGANISM

The structure of borrelia species, including *B. burgdorferi,* is similar to that of all spirochetes: a protoplasmic cylinder that is surrounded first by a cytoplasmic membrane, then by the periplasm, which contains the flagella, and finally by an outer membrane that is only loosely associated with the underlying structures (Fig. 239-1).[10] Of the

Borrelia spp., *B. burgdorferi* is the longest (20 to 30 μm) and narrowest (0.2 to 0.3 μm), and it has fewer flagella (7 to 11).[11] The complete genome of a prototypic *B. burgdorferi* strain (B31) has now been sequenced.[12] The total genome is quite small (approximately 1.5 megabases) and consists of a linear chromosome of 950 kilobases along with 9 circular and 12 linear plasmids.

The remarkable aspect of the *B. burgdorferi* genome is the large number of sequences for predicted and known lipoproteins,[12] including the plasmid-encoded outer-surface proteins (Osp) A through F. These and other differentially expressed outer-surface proteins presumably help the spirochete adapt to and survive in markedly different arthropod and mammalian environments.[13] In addition, during the disseminated phase of the infection, another surface-exposed lipoprotein, called VlsE, undergoes extensive antigenic variation.[14] The organism has few proteins with biosynthetic activity, and apparently depends on the host for much of its nutritional requirements. The genome contains no homologues for systems that specialize in the secretion of toxins or other virulence factors. The only known virulence factors of *B. burgdorferi* are surface-exposed lipoproteins that allow the spirochete to attach to mammalian cells.

Three pathogenic groups of the *B. burgdorferi (sensu lato)* complex have now been identified.[15,16] To date, all North American strains have belonged to the first group, *B. burgdorferi (sensu stricto).*[15] All three groups have been found in Europe, but most isolates there have been group 2 *(Borrelia garinii)* and 3 *(Borrelia afzelii)* strains.[15,16] Only the latter two groups have been found in Asia. These differences may well account for regional variations in the clinical picture of Lyme borreliosis. Several apparently nonpathogenic *Borrelia* groups have been described, including *B. andersoni, B. bisettii, B. japonica, B. lusitaniae,* and *B. valaisiana.*[17] *B. burgdorferi* grows best at 33° C in a complex liquid medium called Barbour-Stoenner-Kelly medium[18] and less well on various solid media.[19]

VECTOR OF TRANSMISSION AND ANIMAL HOSTS

The vectors of Lyme borreliosis are several closely related ixodid ticks that are part of the *Ixodes ricinus* complex.[20,21] In the northeastern and midwestern United States, *Ixodes scapularis* (also called *Ixodes dammini*) is the vector, and *Ixodes pacificus* is the vector in the West. In Europe, *Ixodes ricinus* is the primary vector, and in Asia it is *Ixodes persulcatus.*[21] In field studies in Connecticut and New York, the spirochetal pathogen has been found in 10% to 50% of nymphal and adult *I. scapularis.*[22] Although *B. burgdorferi* has been demonstrated in mosquitoes and deer flies,[23] only ticks of the *I. ricinus* complex seem to be important in the transmission of the spirochete to humans (Fig. 239-2).

Ixodid ticks have larval, nymphal, and adult stages; they require a blood meal at each stage. The peak questing periods for adult *I. scapularis* are spring and fall; for nymphs, May through July; and for larvae, August and September.[24] The nymphal stage is primarily responsible for transmission of the disease. The risk of infection in a given area depends largely on the density of these ticks as well as their feeding habits and animal hosts, which have evolved differently in different locations. In the northeastern and mid-Atlantic states, immature *I. scapularis* (larvae and nymphs) feed primarily on rodents, particularly on white-footed mice *(Peromyscus leucopus),*[25] and adults usually feed on larger mammals, especially deer *(Odocoileus virginianus).*[26] Infection with *B. burgdorferi* in these areas is maintained by horizontal transmission of the organism from infected nymphal *I. scapularis* to *P. leucopus* (white footed mouse) to larval *I. scapularis,* which then molt to infected nymphs to complete the cycle.[27] Deer, which are not involved in the life cycle of the spirochete, are quite important for the life cycle of *I. scapularis.*[26] The proliferation of deer was a major factor in the emergence of epidemic Lyme disease in the northeastern United States during the late 20th century.[27]

The vector ecology of *B. burgdorferi* is different on the West Coast, where the frequency of Lyme disease is low. There, two intersecting cycles are necessary for the transmission of the disease.[28] The spirochete is maintained in nature by the dusky-footed woodrat and *Ixodes spini-*

FIGURE 239-1. Electron micrographs of *Borrelia burgdorferi.* The spirochetes have a transverse diameter of about 0.2 mm and 7 to 11 flagella, which are shown **(left panel)** in cross-section in the upper and middle pictures and in tangential section in the lower picture. In longitudinal section **(right panel)**, the organism has an apparent slime layer, an outer membrane, flagellae, a cell wall, and cytoplasmic constituents; its length is 11 to 39 mm. (×40,000, except upper left [×60,000]). *(From Steere AC, Grodzicki RL, Kornblatt AN, et al. The spirochetal etiology of Lyme disease. N Engl J Med. 1983;308:733, with permission. Copyright © 1983 Massachusetts Medical Society. All rights reserved.)*

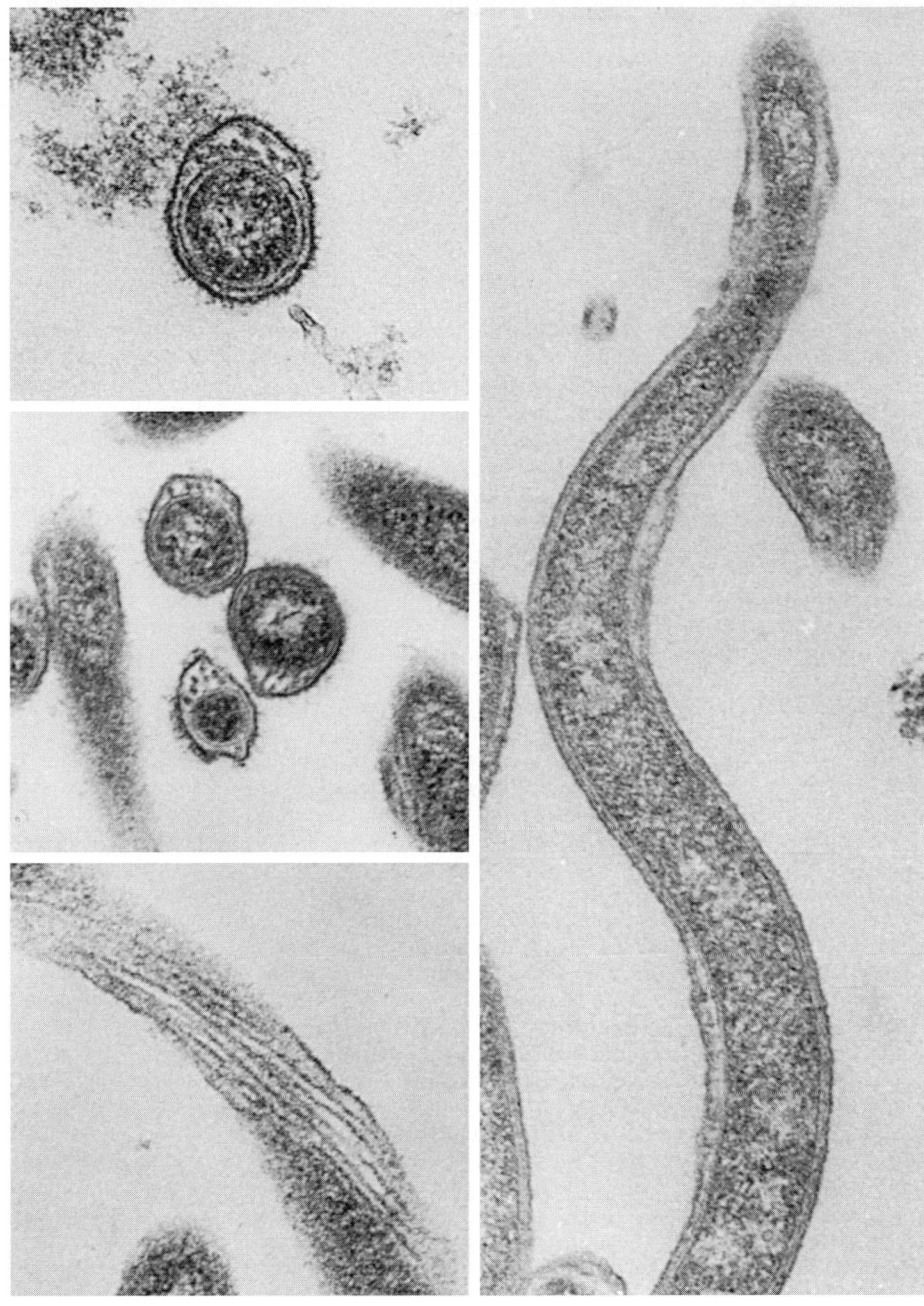

palpis (also called *Ixodes neotomae*) ticks, which do not bite humans. Although nymphal *I. pacificus* do bite humans, these ticks are usually not infected because they prefer to feed on lizards rather than rodents, and lizards are not susceptible to infection with *B. burgdorferi.* Only the relatively few *I. pacificus* ticks that fed on infected woodrats in the larval stage are responsible in the nymphal stage for transmitting the spirochete to humans. Similarly, in the southeastern United States, *I. scapularis* ticks feed primarily on lizards rather than rodents, and *B. burgdorferi* infection occurs rarely in that part of the country. There, a rash resembling erythema migrans but not caused by *B. burgdorferi* has been associated with the bite of the Lone Star tick (*Amblyomma americanum*).[29]

The tick has been found on and cultured from many other wild and domestic animals,[30] including birds,[31] which may be responsible for the spread of the tick over wide areas. Although zoonotic infection with *B. burgdorferi* is widespread within endemic foci, illness is not known to develop in wild animals. In contrast, clinical Lyme disease does occur in domestic animals, including dogs,[32] horses,[33] and cattle.[34]

EPIDEMIOLOGY

Since surveillance was begun by the Centers for Disease Control and Prevention in 1982, the number of reported cases has increased dramatically. Currently about 20,000 cases have been noted yearly, making Lyme disease the most common vector-borne infection in the United States.[2] The disorder occurs primarily in three distinct foci: in the Northeast from Massachusetts to Maryland, in the Midwest in Wisconsin and Minnesota, and in the West in northern California.[2,35] However, sporadic cases have been reported in many states. Lyme borreliosis also occurs in temperate regions of the Northern Hemisphere in Europe,[36] Scandinavia,[37] Russia,[38] China,[39] and Japan.[40]

Even though the occurrence of Lyme disease is highly focal, certain locations, primarily in the northeastern United States, have been greatly affected. Such areas have included suburban locations near Boston, New York, and Philadelphia, which are some of the most heavily populated parts of the country. In addition, *I. scapularis* ticks

FIGURE 239-2. The deer tick, *Ixodes scapularis,* is the primary vector of Lyme disease in the United States. The nymph stage is most frequently implicated. For comparison, the dog tick, *Dermacentor variabilis,* is shown, but this tick does not transmit Lyme disease. Shown actual size. *(Courtesy of the Massachusetts Department of Public Health Division and the Cape Cod Cooperative Extension.)*

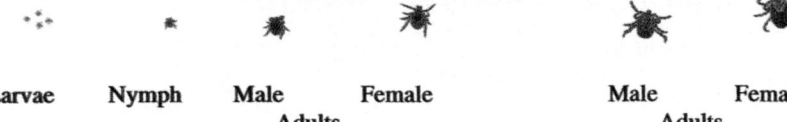

Larvae	Nymph	Male	Female		Male	Female
		Adults			**Adults**	

DEER TICK
Ixodes scapularis

AMERICAN DOG TICK
Dermacentor variabilis

continue to spread. For example, in 1985, these ticks and Lyme disease were found in only 4 counties in New York State. By 2002, the ticks had spread to all but one of 62 counties in the state.[41]

The ages of patients range from 2 to 88 years (median, 28 years), and the sex ratio is nearly 1:1.[2] Age-adjusted attack rates show a bimodal distribution, with children and middle-aged adults at the greatest risk of acquiring the illness. In the northeastern and midwestern United States, the onset of the illness is generally between May 1 and October 30; most onsets occur in June and July.

PATHOGENESIS

To maintain its complex enzootic cycle, *B. burgdorferi* must adapt to two markedly different environments, the tick and the mammalian host. For example, in the midgut of the tick, the spirochete expresses OspA.[42] When the blood meal is taken, OspC is upregulated as the organism traverses to the tick salivary gland and to the mammalian host.[43] Later, during mammalian infection, other proteins are expressed that are essential for disease pathogenesis.[44]

After injection of *B. burgdorferi* by the tick and an incubation period of 3 to 32 days, the spirochete usually first multiplies locally in the skin at the site of the tick bite. In most patients, immune cells first encounter *B. burgdorferi* at this site. Dendritic cells isolated from the dermis readily engulf *B. burgdorferi in vitro.*[45] During the initial infection, *B. burgdorferi* induces primarily pro-inflammatory responses in inflammatory cells in EM lesions,[46] and *B. burgdorferi*-stimulated peripheral blood mononuclear cells (PBMCs) produce primarily pro-inflammatory cytokines.[47] Thus, both innate and adaptive cellular elements are mobilized to fight the infection.

Within days to weeks, *B. burgdorferi* often disseminates to many sites. During this period, the spirochete has been recovered from blood and cerebrospinal fluid,[8,9,48] and it has been seen in small numbers in specimens of myocardium, retina, muscle, bone, spleen, liver, meninges, and brain.[49] A number of mechanisms may aid in the dissemination of spirochetes. For example, the sequences of OspC vary considerably among strains, and only a few groups of sequences are associated with disseminated disease.[50] Spreading though the skin and other tissue matrixes may be facilitated by the binding of plasminogen and its activators to the surface of the spirochete.[51] During dissemination and homing to specific sites, spirochetes bind to a number of host receptors. Receptor-ligands that have been identified include a 66-kDa spirochetal protein that binds the platelet-specific integrin $\alpha_{IIb}\beta_3$,[52] which may be important in hematogenous dissemination. A 26-kDa glycosaminoglycan binding protein binds heparan sulfate and dermatin sulfate,[53] which are expressed on endothelial cells. A 47-kDa fibronectin-binding protein (BBK32) binds fibronectin,[54] a ubiquitous extracellular matrix protein. Finally, decorin-binding proteins A and B (DbpA and DbpB) of the spirochete bind decorin,[55] a proteoglycan on the surface or collagen, which may explain the alignment of spirochetes with collagen fibrils in the extracellular matrix in the heart, nervous system, or joints.[49] All affected tissues show an infiltration of lymphocytes and plasma cells. Some degree of vascular damage, including mild vasculitis or hypervascular occlusion, may be seen in multiple sites, suggesting that spirochetes may have been in or around blood vessels.

B. burgdorferi seems to cross a cell monolayer at intracellular junctions, although it can penetrate through the cytoplasm of a cell.[56] In *in vitro* systems, intracellular localization of a few *B. burgdorferi* has been demonstrated within human endothelial cells,[57] macrophages,[58] and fibroblasts.[59] However, in a three-dimensional in vitro model of Lyme arthritis, synovial fibroblasts disintegrated after engulfing *B. burgdorferi* or its fragments.[60] Moreover, spirochetes have not been seen in intracellular locations in histologic sections of infected tissues from patients with Lyme disease.[49]

During disseminated infection, adaptive T- and B-cell responses in lymph nodes lead to the production of antibody against many components of the organism.[61,62] In addition, membrane lipoproteins are mitogenic for B cells.[63] The specific immunoglobulin M (IgM) response is often associated with polyclonal activation of B cells, including elevated total serum IgM levels,[64] circulating immune complexes,[65] and cryoglobulins.[64] The specific IgG response develops gradually over weeks to months to an increasing array of spirochetal polypeptides[62] and nonprotein antigens.[66] Spirochetal killing seems to be accomplished primarily by bactericidal B cell responses,[67] which utilize the classical complement pathway.[68]

Despite an active immune response, *B. burgdorferi* may survive for several years within the joints, nervous system, or skin, presumably by downregulation of outer-surface proteins, including OspC,[69] and antigenic variation of the VlsE lipoprotein.[14] During persistent infection, CD4$^+$ T helper (Th) cells from patients with Lyme arthritis or neuroborreliosis again produce preferentially the proinflammatory cytokine, interferon-γ (IFN-γ).[70,71] In patients with Lyme arthritis, *B. burgdorferi*-specific CD8$^+$ T cells are found as well,[72] which may be an important source of IFN-γ. Within the joint, *B. burgdorferi*-specific $\gamma\delta$ T cells of the Vδ1 subset may aid in the regulation of these inflammatory responses.[73] In one study of patients with acrodermatitis, the infiltrates of T cells and macrophages in these skin lesions had a restricted cytokine profile, with little or no production of IFN-γ, which may be a factor in explaining why the immune response was ineffective in eradicating the spirochete from this site.[46]

ANIMAL MODEL

Animal models of Lyme disease have been developed in mice,[74] hamsters,[75] dogs,[76] and nonhuman primates.[77] Each animal model is imperfect in that it does not induce all features of human Lyme disease. For example, inbred C3H/He mice develop acute arthritis and carditis 2 to 4 weeks after inoculation with *B. burgdorferi,* but they do not develop EM or neurologic abnormalities.[74] However, the ability to manipulate animal models has allowed important insights into pathogenetic mechanisms in Lyme disease.

Studies in inbred strains of mice have delineated immune mechanisms that are important in susceptibility to and control of *B. burgdorferi* infection. At the mild end of the spectrum, anti-inflammatory components of the innate immune response seem to protect C57BL/6 mice from the development of arthritis despite joint infection with the spirochete.[78] In the middle of the spectrum, *B. burgdorferi*-infected BALB/c mice develop mild to moderate arthritis, depending on the challenge dose, and they require adaptive immune responses for control of the spirochete and resolution of arthritis.[74] At the far end of the spectrum, C3H/He mice, which seem to have inadequate innate and adaptive immune responses, develop severe arthritis and carditis at all challenge doses, including fewer than 100 spirochetes.[74] In these mice, macrophages are the primary infiltrating cell in cardiac lesions, and cellular immunity is critical for the control of carditis.[79] In contrast, polymorphonuclear leukocytes and then lymphocytes are the prominent infiltrating cells in synovial tissue, and antibody to a 37-kDa arthritis-related protein of the spirochete lessens the severity of arthritis.[80] Despite the resolution of acute lesions, spirochetes persist throughout the life of this inbred mouse strain, primarily in the skin. Recurrent waves of spirochetemia from that site may lead to recurrent attacks of arthritis. However, no currently known mouse strain develops the equivalent of human, chronic Lyme arthritis.

The spread of *B. burgdorferi* in the nervous system has been documented in nonhuman primates,[81] one of the few animals that is susceptible to neuroborreliosis. In immunosuppressed monkeys, which had a larger spirochetal burden than did immunocompetent animals, *B. burgdorferi* infiltrated the leptomeninges, motor and sensory nerve roots, and dorsal ganglia, but not the brain parenchyma.[82] In the peripheral nervous system, spirochetes were seen in the perineurium, the connective tissue sheath surrounding each bundle of peripheral-nerve fibers.

CLINICAL CHARACTERISTICS

As with other spirochetal infections, human Lyme borreliosis generally occurs in stages, with remissions and exacerbations and different clinical manifestations at each stage.[83] Early infection consists of stage 1 (localized EM), followed within days or weeks by stage 2 (disseminated infection). Late infection, or stage 3 (persistent infection), usually begins months to years after the disease onset, sometimes following long periods of latent infection. In an individual patient, however, the infection is highly variable, ranging from brief involvement in only one system to chronic, multisystem involvement of the skin, nerves, or joints.

Early Infection: Stage 1 (Localized Infection)

In about 70% to 80% of patients, EM develops at the site of the tick bite (Fig. 239-3*A* and Table 239-1).[84,85] However, because of the small size of nymphal *I. scapularis,* most patients do not remember the tick bite. During the first several days, the lesion often has a homogeneous red appearance.[86] In addition, the centers of early lesions sometimes become intensely erythematous and indurated, vesicular, or necrotic. As the area of redness around the center expands, most lesions continue to have bright red outer borders (usually flat, but occasionally raised) and partial central clearing. In some instances, migrating lesions remain an even intense red, several red rings are found within the outside one, or the central area turns blue before it clears. Although the lesion can be located anywhere, the thigh, groin, and axilla are particularly common sites. If EM is on the head, only a linear streak might be seen to emerge from the hairline. The lesion is hot to the touch, and patients often describe it as burning, or occasionally itching or painful. In Europe, EM is often an indolent, localized infection, whereas in the United States, the lesion is associated with more intense inflammation and signs and symptoms that suggest dissemination of the spirochete.[87] In one study in the United States, spirochetes were cultured from plasma samples in 50% of patients with EM.[88]

Early Infection: Stage 2 (Disseminated Infection)

Within several days to weeks of the onset of the initial EM lesion, patients in the United States may develop multiple annular secondary skin lesions (see Fig. 239-3*B* and Table 239-1),[83,85] a sign of hematogenous dissemination. Although their appearance is similar to that of the initial lesions, they are generally smaller, migrate less, and lack indurated centers; they are not associated with previous tick bites. Individual lesions sometimes appear and fade at different times, and their borders sometimes merge. During this period, some patients develop malar rash, conjunctivitis, or, rarely, diffuse urticaria. EM and

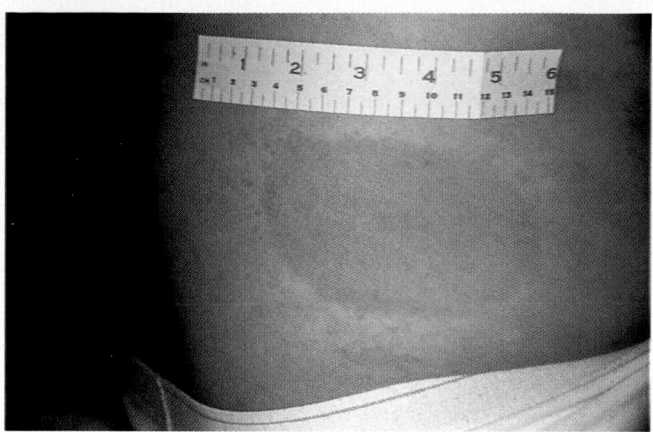

A

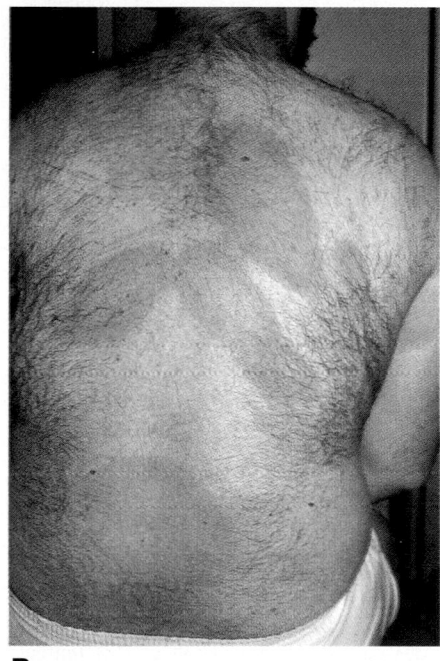

B

FIGURE 239-3. *A,* An early erythema migrans skin lesion is seen 4 days after detection. *B,* Four days after the onset of the initial skin lesion, secondary lesions have appeared, and several of their borders have merged. *(From Steere AC, Bartenhagen NH, Cratt JE, et al. The early clinical manifestations of Lyme disease. Ann Intern Med. 1983;99:76, with permission.)*

secondary lesions usually fade within 3 to 4 weeks (range, 1 day to 14 months).

EM is often accompanied by malaise and fatigue, headache, fever and chills, generalized achiness, and regional lymphadenopathy.[83,85] In about 18% of patients,[84] these symptoms are the presenting picture of the infection.[89] In addition, patients sometimes have evidence of meningeal irritation with episodic attacks of excruciating headache and neck pain, mild encephalopathy with difficulty with mentation, migratory musculoskeletal pain, hepatitis, generalized lymphadenopathy or splenomegaly, sore throat, nonproductive cough, or testicular swelling.[85] A few patients have had microscopic hematuria, sometimes with mild proteinuria (dipstick). During the first days of illness, headache and neck stiffness are not associated with a spinal fluid pleocytosis or objective neurologic deficit. Except for fatigue and lethargy, which are often constant, the early signs and symptoms are typically intermittent and changing. For example, a patient might experience

TABLE 239-1 Manifestations of Lyme Disease by Stage*

	Early Infection		Late Infection
System[†]	Localized Stage 1	Disseminated Stage 2	Persistent Stage 3
Skin	Erythema migrans (EM)	Secondary annular lesions Malar rash Diffuse erythema or urticaria Evanescent lesions Lymphocytoma	Acrodermatitis chronica atrophicans Localized scleroderma-like lesions
Musculoskeletal		Migratory pain in joints, tendons, bursae, muscle, bone Brief arthritis attacks Myositis[‡] Osteomyelitis[‡] Panniculitis[‡]	Prolonged arthritis attacks Chronic arthritis Peripheral enthesopathy Periostitis or joint subluxations below acrodermatitis
Neurologic		Meningitis Cranial neuritis, facial palsy Motor or sensory radiculoneuritis Subtle encephalitis Mononeuritis multiplex Pseudotumor cerebri Myelitis[‡] Cerebellar ataxia[‡]	Chronic encephalomyelitis Spastic parapareses Ataxic gait Subtle mental disorders Chronic axonal polyradiculopathy
Lymphatic	Regional lymphadenopathy	Regional or generalized lymphadenopathy Splenomegaly	
Heart		Atrioventricular nodal block Myopericarditis Pancarditis	
Eyes		Conjunctivitis Iritis[‡] Choroiditis[‡] Retinal hemorrhage or detachment[‡] Panophthalmitis[‡]	Keratitis
Liver		Mild or recurrent hepatitis	
Respiratory		Nonexudative sore throat Nonproductive cough	
Kidney		Microscopic hematuria or proteinuria	
Genitourinary		Orchitis[‡]	
Constitutional systems	Minor	Severe malaise and fatigue	Fatigue

*The staging system provides a guideline for the expected timing of the different manifestations of the illness, but this may vary in an individual case.
[†]The systems are listed from the most to the least commonly affected.
[‡]Because the inclusion of these manifestations is based on one or a few cases, they should be considered possible but not proven manifestations of Lyme disease.
From Steere AC. Lyme disease. N Engl J Med. 1989; 321:586. Copyright © 1989 Massachusetts Medical Society. All rights reserved.

predominantly headache and a stiff neck for several days. After a few days of improvement, musculoskeletal pain might begin.

After several weeks to months, about 15% of untreated patients in the United States develop frank neurologic abnormalities, including meningitis, encephalitis, cranial neuritis (including bilateral facial palsy), motor and sensory radiculoneuritis, mononeuritis multiplex, cerebellar ataxia or myelitis—alone or in various combinations.[90] The usual pattern consists of fluctuating symptoms of meningitis with superimposed cranial (particularly facial palsy) or peripheral radiculoneuropathy. On examination, such patients usually have neck stiffness only on extreme flexion; Kernig's and Brudzinski's signs are not present. Facial palsy may occur alone,[91] and in rare instances, it may be the presenting manifestation of the disease. In children, the optic nerve may be affected by inflammation or increased intracranial pressure, which may lead to blindness.[92] In Europe, the most common neurologic manifestation is Bannwarth's syndrome, which consists of neuritic pain, lymphocytic pleocytosis without headache, and sometimes cranial neuritis.[93]

In patients with meningitis, cerebrospinal fluid (CSF) typically has a lymphocytic pleocytosis of about 100 cells/mm³, often with an elevated protein but a normal glucose level.[90] Specific IgG, IgM, or IgA antibody to the spirochete is produced intrathecally,[94] and B. burgdorferi–specific oligoclonal bands may be present.[95] Antibodies to the flagellar antigen of B. burgdorferi have been shown to bind to a component of normal human axons identified as chaperonin-HSP60.[96] However, it is not known whether autoreactivity causes tissue damage or is a secondary epiphenomenon. Electrophysiologic studies of affected extremities suggest primarily axonal nerve involvement.[97] Histologically, the lesions show axonal nerve injury with perivascular infiltration of lymphocytes and plasmocytes around epineural blood vessels.[98] Stage 2 neurologic abnormalities usually last for weeks or months, but they may recur or become chronic.

Within several weeks after the onset of illness, about 5% of untreated patients develop cardiac involvement.[99] The most common abnormality is fluctuating degrees of atrioventricular block (first-degree, Wenckebach, or complete heart block). However, some patients have evidence of more diffuse cardiac involvement, including electrocardiographic changes or a gallium scan[100] compatible with acute myopericarditis, radionuclide evidence of mild left ventricular dysfunction, or, rarely, cardiomegaly.[99] No patients have had heart murmurs. The duration of cardiac involvement is usually brief (3 days to 6 weeks), and the insertion of a permanent pacemaker is unnecessary.[101] One patient is known to have died of cardiac involvement of Lyme disease.[102] At autopsy, that patient had a lymphoplasmacellular infiltrate in the epicardium, myocardium, and endocardium, and a few spirochetes were seen in the myocardium. In Europe, B. burgdorferi has been isolated from endomyocardial biopsy samples from several patients with chronic dilated cardiomyopathy.[103] However, this complication has not been observed in the United States.[104]

During this stage, migratory musculoskeletal pain is common in joints, tendons, bursae, muscle, or bones.[83] In addition, a few patients have been described with osteomyelitis, myositis, panniculitis, or eosinophilic fasciitis.[83,105] Conjunctivitis is the most common eye abnormality in Lyme disease, but deeper tissues in the eye may be affected as well.[85,106] There are case reports of iritis followed by panophthalmitis, choroiditis with exudative retinal detachments, or interstitial keratitis, similar to that seen in syphilis.

Late Infection: Stage 3 (Persistent Infection)

Months after the onset of the illness, within the context of strong cellular and humoral immune responses to *B. burgdorferi,* about 60% of patients begin to experience intermittent attacks of joint swelling and pain, primarily in large joints, especially the knee, usually one or two joints at a time (see Table 239-1).[85,107] Affected knees are commonly more swollen than painful and are often hot but rarely red. Baker cysts may form and rupture early. However, both large and small joints may be affected. Attacks of arthritis generally last from a few weeks to months separated by periods of complete remission. Joint fluid white blood cell counts range from 500 to 110,000 cells/mm³, most of which, in patients with high white blood cell counts, are polymorphonuclear leukocytes. The total number of patients who continue to have recurrent attacks of arthritis decreases by about 10% to 20% each year. However, attacks of knee swelling sometimes become longer during the second or third year of illness. It is usually during this period that approximately 10% of untreated patients develop chronic arthritis, defined as 1 year or more of continuous joint inflammation. However, even in untreated patients, intermittent or chronic arthritis usually resolves completely within several years.

Although most patients with either acute or chronic arthritis respond to antibiotic treatment, about 10% of patients have persistent joint inflammation for months or even several years after 2 or 3 months of antibiotic therapy.[108] Although *B. burgdorferi* DNA can often be detected in joint fluid prior to antibiotic treatment, in my experience, the results of polymerase chain reaction (PCR) testing are usually negative in synovial tissue or joint fluid after antibiotic therapy,[109,110] suggesting that joint inflammation may continue in some patients after the eradication of the spirochete from the joint with antibiotic therapy. The synovial lesion, which is similar to that seen in other forms of chronic inflammatory arthritis, shows synovial cell hyperplasia, vascular proliferation, a heavy infiltration of mononuclear cells, and upregulation of adhesion molecules.[111,112]

Chronic, antibiotic-treatment-resistant Lyme arthritis is associated with certain immunogenetic and immune markers, including HLA-DRB1*0401, DRB1*0101 and other related alleles[113] and cellular and humoral immune responses to OspA of *B. burgdorferi.*[114,115] According to a computer algorithm, the immunodominant epitope of OspA presented by the DRB1*0401 molecule was predicted to be OspA$_{165-173}$.[116] In an epitope mapping study, 15 of 16 patients with treatment-resistant Lyme arthritis had T cell reactivity with OspA$_{154-173}$ compared with 1 of 5 patients with treatment-responsive arthritis ($P = 0.004$).[115] Thus, it has been hypothesized that treatment-resistant Lyme arthritis may result from the development of autoimmunity within the pro-inflammatory milieu of the joint in genetically susceptible individuals because of molecular mimicry between this T cell epitope of OspA and a host protein. In an initial study, partial sequence homology was found between this OspA epitope and human lymphocyte function-associated antigen 1 (LFA-1$\alpha_{L332-340}$), an adhesion molecule on leukocytes. However, LFA-1$\alpha_{L332-340}$ was found to act as only a weak, partial agonist for OspA$_{165-173}$-reactive T cells from DRB1*0401-positive patients.[117] Furthermore, in direct binding assays, LFA-1$\alpha_{L332-340}$ bound the 0401 molecule well, but it did not bind the 0101 molecule, suggesting that LFA-1α would be unlikely to serve as an autoantigen in treatment-resistant Lyme arthritis.[113] Although the pathogenesis of this syndrome is incompletely delineated, future technologies may allow the identification of spirochetal components or a relevant autoantigen, or both, in the synovia of these patients.

From months to years after disease onset, sometimes following long periods of latent infection, about 5% of untreated patients develop chronic neurologic manifestations of the disorder.[83,118] In both the United States and Europe, a chronic axonal polyneuropathy may develop, manifested primarily as spinal radicular pain or distal paresthesias. Even though sensory symptoms are often localized, electrophysiologic testing frequently shows a diffuse axonal polyneuropathy affecting both proximal and distal nerve segments.[97] In Europe, *B. garinii* may cause chronic encephalomyelitis, characterized by spastic parapareses, ataxia, cognitive impairment, bladder dysfunction, and cranial neuropathy, particularly of the seventh or eighth cranial nerve, accompanied by intrathecal antibody production of IgG antibody to *B. burgdorferi.*[119] In the United States, a mild, late neurologic syndrome has been reported, called Lyme encephalopathy, manifested primarily by subtle cognitive disturbances.[118] Although there are no inflammatory changes in CSF, intrathecal antibody production to the spirochete can often be demonstrated. Neither neuropsychological tests of memory,[120] nor single photon emission computed tomography (SPECT) scanning of the brain[121] has sufficient specificity to be helpful in diagnosis. Post-infectious phenomena may also play a role in the pathogenesis of this syndrome. One unusual case of *B. burgdorferi*–induced meningoencephalitis and cerebral vasculitis has been reported that was unresponsive to antibiotics.[122] In this case, a T-cell clone recovered from the CSF responded to both spirochetal epitopes and autoantigens.

Acrodermatitis chronica atrophicans, which sometimes follows years after EM, has been observed primarily in Europe in association with *B. afzelii* infection.[123] Acrodermatitis chronica atrophicans begins with red violaceous lesions that become sclerotic or atrophic. These lesions, which may be the presenting manifestation of the disease, may last for many years, and *B. burgdorferi* has been cultured from such lesions as much as 10 years after their onset.[124]

CONGENITAL INFECTION

In the mid-1980s, the transplacental transmission of *B. burgdorferi* was reported in two infants whose mothers had Lyme borreliosis during the first trimester of pregnancy.[83] Both infants died during the first week of life. In both, spirochetes were seen in various fetal tissues stained with the Dieterle silver stain, but cultures and serologic testing were not performed. In a retrospective review of 19 patients with Lyme disease during pregnancy, 5 cases were associated with adverse fetal outcomes.[125] Because all of the outcomes differed, they could not be linked conclusively to maternal Lyme disease. In subsequent prospective studies, no cases of congenital infection have been linked to the Lyme disease spirochete.[126] In a study of pregnant white-footed mice *(P. leucopus),* all of whom were infected with *B. burgdorferi,* there was an absence of transplacental transmission of the spirochete to their offspring.[127] Although it is still possible that *B. burgdorferi* may cause an adverse fetal outcome in humans, it has not been documented conclusively.

COINFECTION

I. scapularis ticks transmit not only *B. burgdorferi,* the Lyme disease agent, but also other infectious agents, including *Babesia microti* (a red-blood cell parasite) and *Anaplasma phagocytophilum* (formerly referred to as "the agent of human granulocytic ehrlichiosis"). Each of these pathogens may cause nonspecific systemic symptoms during summer, and coinfection with these tick-borne agents may lead to more severe, acute illness.[128] However, neither *A. phagocytophilum* nor *B. microti* is known to cause chronic infection, as with untreated *B. burgdorferi* infection.

The frequency of coinfection has been quite variable, depending on geographic location and study methodology. One problem is that anaplasmosis by itself may cause a false-positive IgM Western blot for Lyme disease.[129] In one study of 93 patients with culture-proven EM, 2 patients (2%) had coinfection with *A. phagocytophilum* and 2 (2%) had coinfection with *B. microti,* demonstrated by PCR testing or IgG seroconversion.[130] At the other end of the spectrum, 75 of 192 patients (39%) in another study had evidence of coinfection, most commonly with Lyme disease and babesiosis.[131]

In Europe and Asia, *I. ricinus* and *I. persulcatus* ticks, the vectors of *B. burgdorferi (sensu lato),* also transmit tick-borne encephalitis virus.

LABORATORY DIAGNOSIS

Culture of *B. burgdorferi* from patient specimens in Barbour-Stoenner-Kelly (BSK) medium permits definitive diagnosis. However, positive cultures have been obtained mainly early in the illness, primarily from biopsies of EM lesions,[132] less often from plasma sam-

FIGURE 239-4. Antibody titers to *Borrelia burgdorferi* by enzyme-linked immunosorbent assay (ELISA) in patients with various manifestations of Lyme disease and in control subjects. Horizontal bars = mean; vertical bars = range; hatched bars = normal range. Normal range was derived from sera from 50 healthy control subjects. ALS, Amyotrophic lateral sclerosis; Con V, convalescent phase; ECM, erythema chronicum migrans; acute neuro, meningitis; chronic neuro, encephalopathy or polyneuropathy; MS, multiple sclerosis; RA, rheumatoid arthritis; SLE, systemic lupus erythematosus. *(From Dressler F, Whalen JA, Reinhardt BN, et al. Western blotting in the serodiagnosis of Lyme disease. J Infect Dis. 1993;167:392, with permission.)*

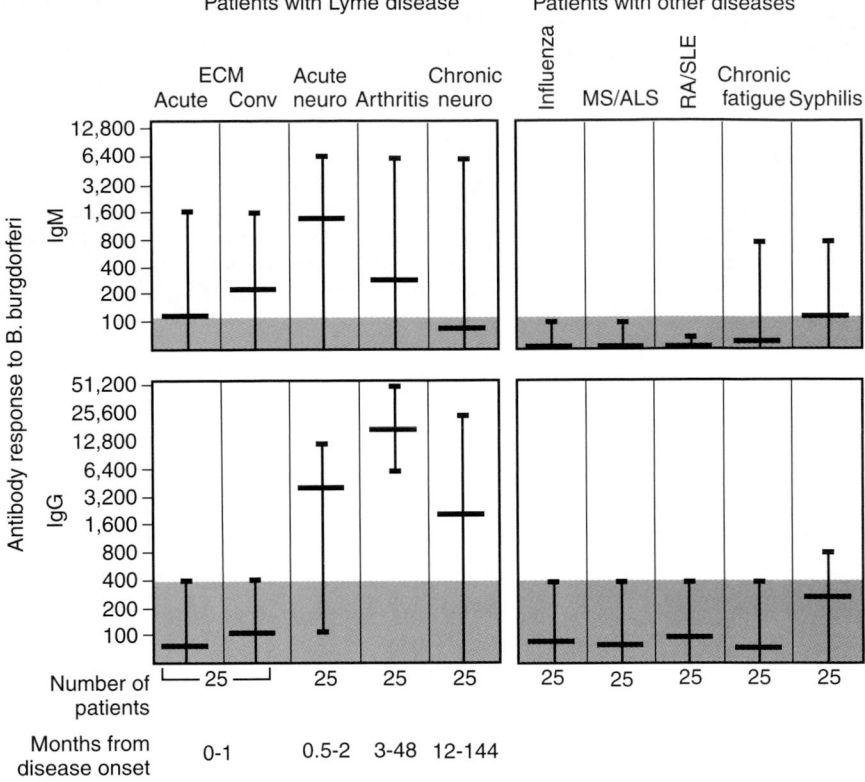

ples,[88] and only occasionally from CSF samples in patients with meningitis. Later in the infection, PCR testing is greatly superior to culture in the detection of *B. burgdorferi* in joint fluid.[109] *B. burgdorferi* has not been isolated from the CSF of patients with chronic neuroborreliosis, and *B. burgdorferi* DNA has been detected in CSF samples in only a small number of such patients.[133] The Lyme urine antigen test (LUAT), which has given grossly unreliable results,[134] should not be used to support the diagnosis of Lyme disease.

In patients in the United States, diagnosis is usually based on the recognition of a characteristic clinical picture, exposure in an endemic area, and except in those with EM, a positive antibody response to *B. burgdorferi*.[135] For serologic testing in the United States, the Centers for Disease Control and Prevention currently recommends a two-test approach in which samples are first tested by enzyme-linked immunosorbent assay (ELISA) and those with equivocal or positive results are tested by Western blotting (Fig. 239-4).[136] According to the CDC criteria, an IgM Western blot is considered positive if two of the following three bands are present: 23, 39, and 41 kDa; however, the combination of the 23- and 41-kDa bands may still be a false-positive result. An IgG blot is considered positive if 5 of the following 10 bands are present: 18, 23, 28, 30, 39, 41, 45, 58, 66, and 93 kDa (Fig. 239-5). Approximately half of the normal population has IgG reactivity with the 41-kDa flagellar antigen of the spirochete, and this response, by itself, has no diagnostic significance. In Europe, where there is less expansion of the antibody response, no single set of criteria for immunoblot interpretation give high levels of sensitivity and specificity in all countries.[137]

Serodiagnosis is insensitive during the first one or two weeks of infection. During this period, approximately 20% to 30% of patients in the United States have positive responses in acute phase samples, usually of the IgM isotype,[138,139] but by convalescence 2 to 4 weeks later, about 70% to 80% have seroreactivity, even after antibiotic treatment. After 1 month, almost all patients with active infection have positive IgG antibody responses.[139] In persons with illness for longer than 1 month, a positive IgM test alone is likely to be a false-positive result, and thus a positive IgM response should not be used to support the diagnosis after the first month of infection. In patients with acute neu-

roborreliosis, especially those with meningitis, intrathecal production of IgM, IgG, or IgA antibody to *B. burgdorferi* may often be demonstrated by antibody capture enzyme immunoassay,[94] but this test is less often positive in those with chronic neuroborreliosis.

After antibiotic treatment, antibody titers decline slowly, but IgG and even IgM responses may persist for many years after treatment.[140] Thus, even a positive IgM response cannot be interpreted as showing recent infection or reinfection unless the appropriate clinical picture is present. *B. burgdorferi* may also cause asymptomatic infection. In a Lyme disease vaccine trial in the United States in which subjects were followed prospectively for 20 months, 7% of those who met criteria for definite Lyme disease had IgG seroconversion by Western blot without symptoms of the infection.[84,141] In seroprevalence surveys in Europe, more than half of the subjects who were seropositive by ELISA did not remember symptoms of Lyme borreliosis.[142,143] If patients with past or asymptomatic infection have symptoms caused by another illness, the danger is that the symptoms may be attributed incorrectly to Lyme disease.

Several second-generation serologic tests that employ recombinant spirochetal proteins or synthetic peptides have shown promising results.[144,145] Compared with the standard two-test approach of sonicate ELISA and Western blot, similar results were obtained using an IgG ELISA that employed a peptide of the sixth invariant region of the VlsE lipoprotein of *B. burgdorferi*.[145] However, as with the sonicate tests, the response to the VlsE peptide may persist for months or years after successful antibiotic treatment; and therefore persistence of the anti-VlsE antibody response cannot be equated with spirochetal persistence in Lyme disease.[146]

DIFFERENTIAL DIAGNOSIS

Early in its course, a small, homogeneous EM lesion may resemble the red papule of an uninfected tick bite. If an erythema expands rapidly following a tick bite, it is more likely an allergic reaction to tick saliva than an EM lesion, which expands slowly (1 cm/day). Patients with secondary annular EM lesions may be thought to have erythema mul-

FIGURE 239-5. Western blots of *A,* acutephase sera from 25 patients with erythema migrans; *B,* 25 patients with Lyme meningitis or facial palsy; *C,* 25 patients with Lyme arthritis; and *D,* 24 representative patients (controls) who had influenza vaccinations, rheumatoid arthritis (RA), systemic lupus erythematosus (SLE), amyotrophic lateral sclerosis (ALS), multiple sclerosis (MS), or secondary or tertiary syphilis. Molecular masses (kDa) are at left. *(From Dressler F, Whalen JA, Reinhardt BN, et al. Western Blotting in the serodiagnosis of Lyme disease. J Infect Dis. 1993; 167:392, with permission.)*

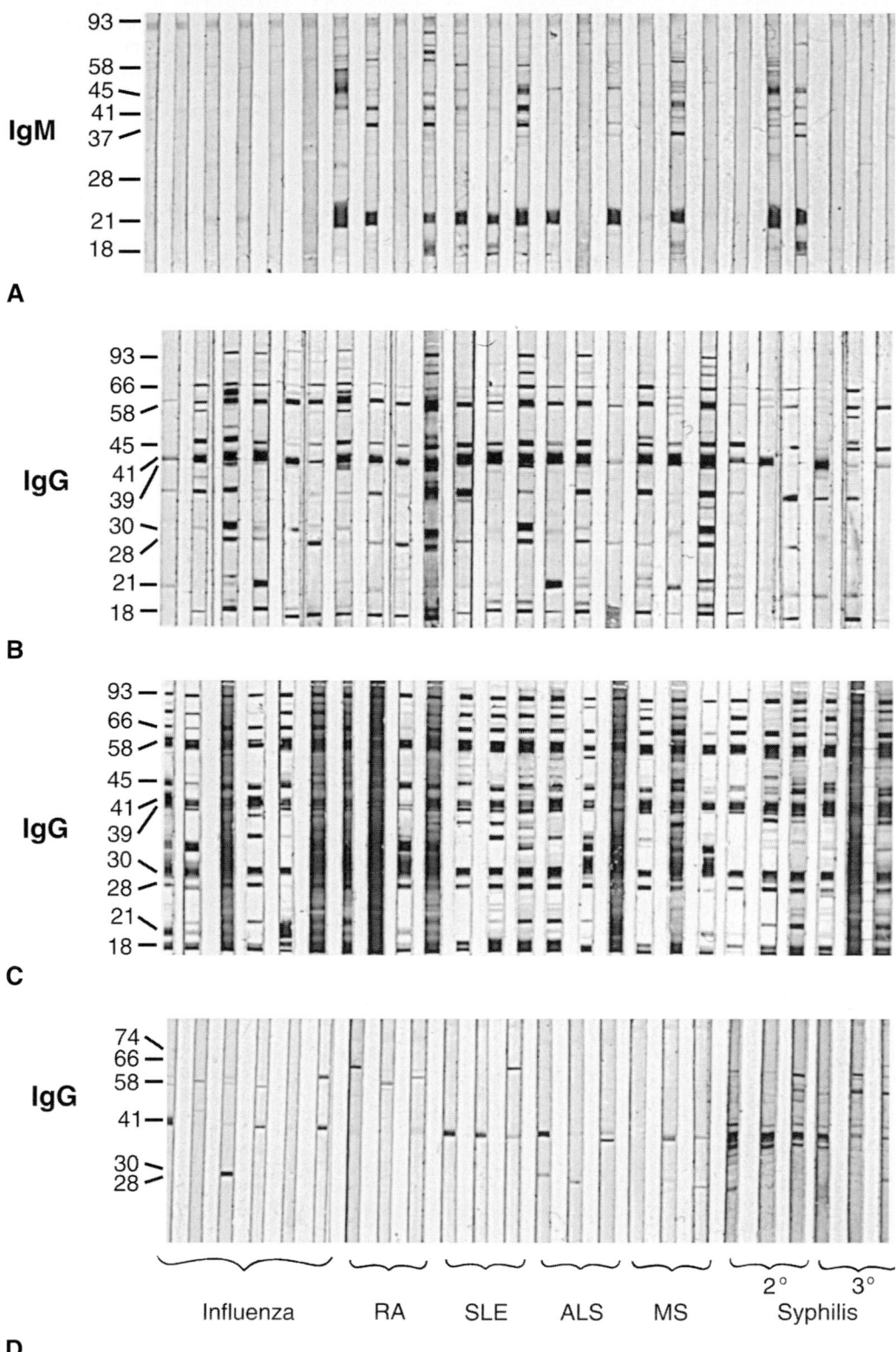

tiforme, but Lyme disease is not associated with blistering, mucosal lesions, or involvement of the palms and soles. Facial palsy caused by *B. burgdorferi* differs from that associated with herpes simplex I virus (Bell's palsy) or varicella-zoster virus (Ramsey-Hunt syndrome) by its seasonal onset (usually June through September), frequent association with EM, and positive IgM and IgG antibody responses to *B. burgdorferi.* Lyme arthritis is most like reactive arthritis in an adult or the pau-

ciarticular form of juvenile rheumatoid arthritis in a child. Patients with Lyme arthritis usually have very high borrelia-specific IgG antibody titers by ELISA with responses to many spirochetal proteins by Western blot.

The most common problem is to mistake Lyme disease for chronic fatigue syndrome or fibromyalgia.[147,148] This problem is compounded by the fact that a small percentage of patients develop pain or fatigue symptoms in association with or soon after Lyme disease.[149] This clinical picture is sometimes referred to as post-Lyme disease syndrome or chronic Lyme disease. Compared with active Lyme disease, chronic fatigue syndrome or fibromyalgia tends to produce more generalized and disabling symptoms. They include marked fatigue, severe headache, diffuse musculoskeletal pain, multiple symmetric tender points in characteristic locations, pain and stiffness in many joints, diffuse dysesthesias, difficulty with concentration, or sleep disturbance. Patients with these conditions lack evidence of joint inflammation; they have normal neurologic test results; and they usually have a greater degree of anxiety and depression.[150]

TREATMENT

Evidence-based treatment recommendations for Lyme disease have been presented by the Infectious Diseases Society of America.[151] In brief, the various manifestations of Lyme disease can usually be treated with oral antibiotic therapy, except for objective neurologic abnormalities, which seem to require intravenous therapy (Table 239-2). For early localized or disseminated infection, doxycycline for 14 to 21 days is recommended in persons age 8 or older, except for pregnant women. An advantage of doxycycline is its efficacy against *A. phagocytophilum,* a possible coinfecting agent. Amoxicillin, the second choice alternative, should be used in children or pregnant women. In case of allergy, cefuroxime axetil is a third-choice alternative. Erythromycin or its cogeners, which are fourth-choice alternatives, are recommended only for patients who are unable to take doxycycline, amoxicillin, or cefuroxime axetil. Approximately 15% of patients with disseminated infection experience a Jarisch-Herxheimer–like reaction during the first 24 hours of therapy.[152] In vitro, *B. burgdorferi* is sensitive to tetracycline, penicillin, erythromycin, and their cogeners and to third-generation cephalosporins, but it is resistant to rifampin, ciprofloxacin, and the aminoglycoside antibiotics.[153-156]

In multicenter studies of patients with EM, similar results were obtained with doxycycline, amoxicillin, and cefuroxime axetil, and more than 90% of patients had satisfactory outcomes.[157,158] Although some patients had subjective symptoms after treatment, objective evidence of persistent infection or relapse was rare, and retreatment was usually not needed. In a recent study, extending treatment with doxycycline from 10 to 20 days or adding one dose of parenteral ceftriaxone to the be-

ginning of a 10-day course of doxycycline did not enhance therapeutic efficacy in patients with EM.[159] Intravenous ceftriaxone, although effective, was not superior to oral agents in the absence of objective neurological involvement.[160] In contrast with second- and third-generation cephalosporin antibiotics, first-generation cephalosporins, such as cephalexin, were ineffective.[161]

For patients with objective neurologic abnormalities, 2- to 4-week courses of intravenous ceftriaxone are most commonly given.[118,162,163] Parenteral therapy with cefotaxime or penicillin G may be a satisfactory alternative.[164] In Europe, oral doxycycline may be adequate therapy for acute neuroborreliosis.[165] Although this medication may be used successfully in patients who have only facial palsy in the United States, it is important to assess whether such patients have more diffuse involvement of the nervous system, which is best treated with intravenous therapy. The signs and symptoms of acute neuroborreliosis usually resolve within weeks, but those of chronic neuroborreliosis improve slowly over a period of months. Objective evidence of relapse is rare after a 4-week course of therapy. In patients with high-degree atrioventricular nodal block, intravenous therapy for at least part of the course and cardiac monitoring are recommended, but insertion of a permanent pacemaker is not necessary.

Either oral or intravenous regimens are usually effective for the treatment of Lyme arthritis.[108,162] Oral therapy is easier to administer; it is associated with fewer side effects, and it is considerably less expensive.[166] Its disadvantage is that some patients treated with oral agents have subsequently manifested overt neuroborreliosis, which may require intravenous therapy for successful treatment.[108] Despite treatment with either oral or intravenous antibiotic therapy, about 10% of patients in the United States have persistent joint inflammation for months or even several years after 2 months or longer of oral antibiotics or 1 month or longer of intravenous antibiotics.[108] If patients have persistent arthritis despite this treatment and if the results of PCR testing of joint fluid are negative, such patients may be treated with anti-inflammatory agents or arthroscopic synovectomy.[167]

Following appropriately treated Lyme disease, a small percentage of patients continue to have subjective symptoms, primarily musculoskeletal pain, neurocognitive difficulties, or fatigue, in some instances, for years. This post-infectious syndrome, which is similar to chronic fatigue syndrome or fibromyalgia, occurs more frequently in patients with symptoms suggestive of early dissemination of the spiro-

---

TABLE 239-2 Treatment Regimens for Lyme Disease*

Early infection (local or disseminated)	
Adults	Doxycycline, 100 mg orally two times/day for 14-21 days
	Amoxicillin, 500 mg orally three times/day for 14-21 days
	Alternatives in case of doxycycline or amoxicillin allergy:
	Cefuroxime axetil, 500 mg orally twice daily for 14-21 days
	Erythromycin, 250 mg orally four times/day for 14-21 days
Children (age 8 or younger)	Amoxicillin, 250 mg orally three times/day or 20 mg/kg/day in divided doses for 14-21 days
	Alternatives in case of penicillin allergy:
	Cefuroxime axetil, 125 mg orally twice daily for 14-21 days
	Erythromycin, 250 mg orally three times/day or 30 mg/kg/day in divided doses for 14-21 days
Arthritis (intermittent or chronic)	Doxycycline, 100 mg orally two times/day for 30-60 days
	Amoxicillin, 500 mg orally four times/day for 30-60 days
	or
	Ceftriaxone, 2 g IV once a day for 14-28 days
	Penicillin G, 20 million U IV in four divided doses daily for 14-28 days
Neurologic abnormalities (early or late)	Ceftriaxone, 2 g IV once/day for 14-28 days
	Penicillin G, 20 million U IV in four divided doses daily for 14-28 days
	Alternative in case of ceftriaxone or penicillin allergy:
	Doxycycline, 100 mg orally three times/day for 14-28 days†
Facial palsy alone	Oral regimens may be adequate
Cardiac abnormalities	
First-degree AV block (P-R interval > 0.3 sec)	Oral regimens, as for early infection
High-degree AV block	Ceftriaxone, 2 g IV once/day for 14-21 days‡
	Penicillin G, 20 million U IV in four divided doses daily for 28 days‡

*Treatment failures have occurred with any of the regimens given, and a second course of therapy may be necessary.
†In my experience, this regimen is ineffective for the treatment of late neurologic abnormalities of Lyme disease.
‡Once the patient has stabilized, the course may be completed with oral therapy.
AV, atrioventricular.

chete to the nervous system, particularly if treatment is delayed.[168,169] However, in a large study, the frequency of pain and fatigue symptoms was no greater in patients who had had Lyme disease than in age-matched subjects who had not had this infection.[170] In a study of patients with post-Lyme disease syndrome who received intravenous ceftriaxone for 30 days followed by oral doxycycline for 60 days or intravenous and oral placebo preparations for the same duration, there were no significant differences between the groups in the percentage of patients who felt that their symptoms had improved, worsened, or remained the same.[171] Such patients are best treated symptomatically rather than with prolonged courses of antibiotic therapy. Prolonged ceftriaxone therapy for unsubstantiated Lyme disease has resulted in biliary complications[172]; and in one reported case, prolonged cefotaxime administration resulted in death.[173]

Although it has not been studied systematically, patients with asymptomatic infection are often given a course of oral antibiotics. Because the risk of maternal-fetal transmission seems to be very low, standard therapy for the stage and manifestation of the illness may be sufficient for pregnant patients, except that doxycycline should be avoided. Reinfection may occur in patients who are treated with antibiotics early in the illness,[86] but I have not observed reinfection in a patient with the expanded immune response associated with Lyme arthritis.

PREVENTION

When possible, people should avoid tick-infested areas.[174] If not, insecticides containing DEET (*N,N*-diethylmetatoluamide) or permethrin effectively deter ticks,[175] but permethrin can be applied only on clothing, and DEET may cause serious side effects when excessive amounts are applied directly to the skin.[176] Therefore, insecticides may be valuable for the occasional hike in the woods, but are less helpful for people living in endemic areas who have daily tick exposures. After exposure in tick-infested areas, tick checks are important. Immature *I. scapularis* usually stay within a few inches of the ground; they often transfer to the lower extremities of the host and attach to moist parts of the body, such as the groin or axillae. In small children, they may also be found on the head and neck, which are unusual sites for tick attachment in adults. Because 24 to 72 hours of tick attachment is necessary before transmission of the spirochete occurs,[177] removal of a tick within 24 hours of attachment is usually sufficient to prevent Lyme disease. However, if an engorged nymphal *I. scapularis* tick is found, a single, 200-mg dose of doxycycline usually prevents Lyme disease when given within 72 hours after the tick bite occurs.[178]

Environmental control of ticks over widespread areas is difficult.[174] Methods that may be helpful include application of acaracides,[179] landscaping to provide desiccating barriers between tick-infested areas and lawns, and in some settings, removal or exclusion of deer.[180] New methods of tick control, including host-targeted acaricides against rodents and deer, are being developed, and may provide help in the future.[174] A commercial Lyme disease vaccine consisting of recombinant OspA with adjuvant was marketed in 1999,[181] but it was withdrawn in 2002 because of poor sales. Although the vaccine is not available now, the experience proved that vaccination is feasible for the prevention of Lyme disease.

REFERENCES

1. Steere AC. Lyme disease. N Engl J Med. 2001;345:115.
2. Dennis DT, Hayes EB. Epidemiology of Lyme borreliosis. In: Kahl O, Gray JS, Lane RS, Stanek G, eds. Lyme Borreliosis: Biology, Epidemiology and Control. Oxford: CABI; 2002:251.
3. Steere AC, Malawista SE, Snydman DR, et al. Lyme arthritis: An epidemic of oligoarticular arthritis in children and adults in three Connecticut communities. Arthritis Rheum. 1977;20:7.
4. Afzelius A. Report to Verhandlungen der dermatologischen Gesellschaft zu Stockholm on December 16, 1909. Arch Dermatol Syph. 1910;101:405.
5. Bannwarth A. Chronische lymphocytare Meningitis, entzundliche Polyneuritis und "Rheumatismus." Arch Psychiatr Nervenkr. 1941;113:284.
6. Herxheimer K, Hartmann K, Ueber Acrodermatitis chronica atrophicans. Arch Dermatol Syph. 1923;143:365.
7. Burgdorfer W, Barbour AG, Hayes SF, et al. Lyme disease: A tick-borne spirochetosis? Science. 1982;216:1317.
8. Steere AC, Grodzicki RL, Kornblatt AN, et al. The spirochetal etiology of Lyme disease. N Engl J Med. 1983;308:733.
9. Benach JL, Bosler EM, Hanrahan JP, et al. Spirochetes isolated from the blood of two patients with Lyme disease. N Engl J Med. 1983;308:740.
10. Barbour AG, Hayes SF. Biology of *Borrelia* species. Microbiol Rev. 1986;50:381.
11. Hovind-Hougen K, Asbrink E, Stiernstedt G, et al. Ultrastructural differences among spirochetes isolated from patients with Lyme disease and related disorders, and from *Ixodes ricinus*. Zentralbl Bakteriol Hyg. 1986;263:103.
12. Fraser CM, Casjens S, Huang WM, et al. Genomic sequence of a Lyme disease spirochete, *Borrelia burgdorferi*. Nature. 1997;390:580.
13. de Silva AM, Fikrig E. Arthropod- and host-specific gene expression of *Borrelia burgdorferi*. J Clin Invest. 1997;99:377.
14. Zhang J-R, Hardham JM, Barbour AG, Norris SJ. Antigenic variation in Lyme disease Borreliae by promiscuous recombination of VMP-like sequence cassettes. Cell. 1997;39:275.
15. Baranton G, Postic D, Saint Girons I, et al. Delineation of *Borrelia burgdorferi* sensu stricto, *Borrelia garinii* sp. nov., and group VS461 associated with Lyme borreliosis. Int J Syst Bacteriol. 1992;42:378.
16. Canica MM, Nato F, du Merle L, et al. Monoclonal antibodies for identification of *Borrelia burgdorferi* sp. nov. associated with late cutaneous manifestations of Lyme borreliosis. Scand J Infect Dis. 1993;25:441.
17. Bergstrom S, Nappa L, Gylfe A, Ostberg Y. Molecular and cellular biology of *Borrelia burgdorferi* sensu lato. In: Gray JS, Kahl O, Lane RS, Stanek G, eds. Lyme Borreliosis: Biology, Epidemiology and Control. New York: CABI; 2002:47.
18. Barbour AG. Isolation and cultivation of Lyme disease spirochetes. Yale J Biol Med. 1984;57:521.
19. Preac-Mursic V, Wilske B, Reinhardt S. Culture of *Borrelia burgdorferi* on six solid media. Eur J Clin Microbiol Infect Dis. 1991;10:1076.
20. Steere AC, Broderick TE, Malawista SE. Erythema chronicum migrans and Lyme arthritis: Epidemiologic evidence for a tick vector. Am J Epidemiol. 1978;108:312.
21. Xu G, Fang QQ, Keirans JE, Durden LA. Molecular phylogenetic analyses indicate that the *Ixodes ricinus* complex is a paraphyletic group. J Parasitol. 2003;89:452.
22. Bosler EM, Coleman JL, Benach JL, et al. Natural distribution of the *Ixodes dammini* spirochetes. Science. 1983;220:321.
23. Magnarelli LA, Anderson JF. Ticks and biting insects infected with the etiologic agent of Lyme disease, *Borrelia burgdorferi*. J Clin Microbiol. 1988;26:1482.
24. Wilson ML, Spielman A. Seasonal activity of immature *Ixodes dammini* (Acari: Ixodidae). J Med Entomol. 1985;22:408.
25. Levine JF, Wilson ML, Spielman A. Mice as reservoirs of the Lyme disease spirochete. Am J Trop Med Hyg. 1985;34:355.
26. Wilson ML, Adler GH, Spielman A. Correlation between abundance of deer and that of the deer tick, *Ixodes dammini* (Acari: Ixodidae). Ann Entomol Soc Am. 1985;78:172.
27. Spielman A. The emergence of Lyme disease and human babesiosis in a changing environment. Ann NY Acad Sci. 1994;740:146.
28. Brown RN, Lane RS. Lyme disease in California: A novel enzootic transmission cycle of *Borrelia burgdorferi*. Science. 1992;256:1439.
29. Campbell GL, Paul WS, Schriefer ME, et al. Epidemiologic and diagnostic studies of patients with suspected early Lyme disease, Missouri, 1990-1993. J Infect Dis. 1995;172:470.
30. Anderson JF, Magnarelli LA, Burgdorfer W, et al. Spirochetes in *Ixodes dammini* and mammals from Connecticut. Am J Trop Med Hyg. 1983;32:818.
31. Anderson JF, Johnson RC, Magnarelli LA, et al. Involvement of birds in the epidemiology of the Lyme disease agent *Borrelia burgdorferi*. Infect Immun. 1986; 51:394.
32. Kornblatt AN, Urband PH, Steere AC. Arthritis caused by *Borrelia burgdorferi* in dogs. J Am Vet Med Assoc. 1985;186:960.
33. Marcus LC, Patterson MM, Gilfillan RE, et al. Antibodies to *Borrelia burgdorferi* in New England horses: Serologic survey. Am J Vet Res. 1985;46:2570.
34. Burgess EC. *Borrelia burgdorferi* infection in Wisconsin horses and cows. Ann NY Acad Sci. 1988;539:235.
35. Steere AC, Malawista SE. Cases of Lyme disease in the United States: Locations correlated with distribution of *Ixodes dammini*. Ann Intern Med. 1989;91:730.
36. Stanek G, Satz N, Strle F, Wilske B. Epidemiology of Lyme borreliosis. In: Weber K, Burgdorfer W, eds. Aspects of Lyme Borreliosis. Berlin, Germany: Springer-Verlag, 1993;358.
37. Berglund J, Eitrem R, Ornstein K, et al. An epidemiologic study of Lyme disease in southern Sweden. N Engl J Med. 1995;333:1319.
38. Korenberg EI, Kryuchechnikov VN, Kovalevsky YV. Advances in investigations of Lyme borreliosis in the territory of former USSR. Eur J Epidemiol. 1993;9:86.
39. Ai C, Hu R, Hyland KE, et al. Epidemiological and aetiological evidence for transmission of Lyme disease by adult *Ixodes persulcatus* in an endemic area in China. Int J Epidemiol. 1990;19:1061.
40. Kawabata M, Baba S, Iguchi K, et al. Lyme disease in Japan and its possible incriminated tick vector, *Ixodes persulcatus*. J Infect Dis. 1987;156:854.
41. Glavanakov S, White DJ, Caraco T, et al. Lyme disease in New York State: spatial pattern at a regional scale. Am J Trop Med Hyg. 2001;65:538.
42. Montgomery RR, Malawista SE, Bockenstedt LK. Direct demonstration of antigenic substitution of *Borrelia burgdorferi* ex vivo: Exploration of the paradox of the early immune response to outer surface proteins A and C in Lyme disease. J Exp Med. 1996;183:261.
43. Schwan TG, Piesman J. Temporal changes in outer surface proteins A and C of the Lyme disease-associated spirochete, *Borrelia burgdorferi*, during the chain of infection in ticks and mice. J Clin Microbiol. 2000;38:382.
44. Akin DR, Bourell KW, Caimaro MJ, et al. A new animal model for studying Lyme disease spirochetes in a mammalian host-adapted state. J Clin Invest. 1998;101:2240.

45. Filgueira L, Nestle FO, Rittig M, et al. Human dendritic cells phagocytose and process *Borrelia burgdorferi*. J Immunol. 1996;157:2998.

46. Muellegger RR, McHugh G, Ruthazer R, et al. Differential expression of cytokine mRNA in skin specimens from patients with erythema migrans or acrodermatitis chronica atrophicans. J Invest Dermatol 2000;115:1115.

47. Glickstein L, Moore B, Bledsoe T, et al. Inflammatory cytokine production predominates in early Lyme disease in patients with erythema migrans. Infect Immun. 2003;71:6051.

48. Karlsson M, Hovind-Hougen K, Svenungsson B, Stiernstedt G. Cultivation and characterization of spirochetes from cerebrospinal fluid of patients with Lyme borreliosis. J Clin Microbiol. 1990;28:473.

49. Duray PH, Steere AC. Clinical pathologic correlations of Lyme disease by stage. Ann NY Acad Sci. 1988;539:65.

50. Seinost G, Dykhuizen DE, Dattwyler RJ, et al. Four clones of *Borrelia burgdorferi* sensu stricto cause invasive infection in humans. Infect Immun. 1999;67:3518.

51. Coleman JL, Gebbia JA, Piesman J, et al. Plasminogen is required for efficient dissemination of *B. burgdorferi* in ticks and for enhancement of spirochetemia in mice. Cell. 1997;89:1111.

52. Coburn J, Chege W, Magoun L, et al. Characterization of a candidate *Borrelia burgdorferi* β3-chain integrin ligand using a phage display library. Mol Microbiol. 1999;34:926.

53. Parveen N, Leong JM. Identification of a candidate glycosaminoglycan-binding adhesin of the Lyme disease spirochete *Borrelia burgdorferi*. Mol Microbiol. 2000;35:1220.

54. Probert WS, Johnson BJB. Identification of a 47 kDa fibronectin-binding protein expressed by *Borrelia burgdorferi* isolate B31. Mol Microbiol. 1998;30:1003.

55. Guo BP, Brown EL, Dorward DW, et al. Decorin, binding adhesins from *Borrelia burgdorferi*. Mol Microbiol 1998;30:711.

56. Comstock LE, Thomas DD. Characterization of *Borrelia burgdorferi* invasion of cultured endothelial cells. Microb Pathogen. 1991;10:137.

57. Ma Y, Sturrock A, Weis J. Intracellular localization of *Borrelia burgdorferi* within human endothelial cells. Infect Immun. 1991;59:671.

58. Montgomery RR, Nathanson MH, Malawista SE. The fate of *Borrelia burgdorferi*, the agent for Lyme disease, in mouse macrophages. Destruction, survival, recovery. J Immunol. 1993;150:909.

59. Georgilis K, Peacocke M, Klempner MS. Fibroblasts protect the Lyme disease spirochete, *Borrelia burgdorferi*, from ceftriaxone in vitro. J Infect Dis. 1992;166:440.

60. Franz JK, Frize O, Rittig M, et al. Insights from a novle three-dimensional in vitro model of Lyme arthritis. Arthritis Rheum. 2001;44:151.

61. Yoshinari NH, Reinhardt BN, Steere AC. T cell responses to polypeptide fractions of *Borrelia burgdorferi* in patients with Lyme arthritis. Arthritis Rheum. 1991;34:707.

62. Akin E, McHugh GL, Flavell RA, et al. The immunoglobulin (IgG) antibody response to OspA and OspB correlates with severe and prolonged arthritis and the IgG response to P35 with mild and brief arthritis. Infect Immun. 1999;67:173.

63. Ma Y, Weis JJ. *Borrelia burgdorferi* outer surface lipoproteins OspA and OspB possess B cell mitogenic and cytokine stimulatory properties. Infect Immun. 1993;61:3843.

64. Steere AC, Hardin JA, Ruddy S, et al. Lyme arthritis: Correlation of serum and cryoglobulin IgM with activity and serum IgG with remission. Arthritis Rheum. 1979;22:471.

65. Hardin JA, Steere AC, Malawista SE. Immune complexes and the evolution of Lyme arthritis: Dissemination and localization of abnormal Clq binding activity. N Engl J Med. 1979;301:1358.

66. Wheeler CM, Garcia-Monco JC, Benach JL, et al. Nonprotein antigens of *Borrelia burgdorferi*. J Infect Dis. 1993;167:665.

67. Rousselle JC, Callister SM, Schell RF, et al. Borreliacidal antibody production against outer surface protein C of *Borrelia burgdorferi*. J Infect Dis. 1998;178:733.

68. Kochi SK, Johnson RC. Role of immunoglobulin G in killing of *Borrelia burgdorferi* in the classical complement pathway. Infect Immun. 1988;56:314.

69. Hefty PS, Jolliff SE, Caimano MJ, et al. Changes in temporal and spatial patterns of outer surface lipoprotein expression generate population heterogeneity and antigenic diversity in the Lyme disease spirochete, *Borrelia burgdorferi*. Infect Immun. 2002;70:3468.

70. Oksi J, Savolainen J, Pene J, et al. Decreased interleukin-4 and increased gamma interferon production by peripheral blood mononuclear cells of patients with Lyme borreliosis. Infect Immun. 1996;64:3620.

71. Gross DM, Steere AC, Huber BT. Dominant T helper 1 response is antigen specific and localized to synovial fluid in patients with Lyme arthritis. J Immunol. 1998;160:1022.

72. Busch DH, Jassoy C, Brinkmann U, et al. Detection of *Borrelia burgdorferi*-specific CD8⁺ cytotoxic T cells in patients with Lyme arthritis. J Immunol. 1996;157:3534.

73. Glazel A, Entschladen F, Zollner TM, et al. The responsiveness of human V delta 1 gamma delta T cells to *Borrelia burgdorferi* is largely restricted to synovial-fluid cells from patients with Lyme arthritis. J Infect Dis. 2002;186:1043.

74. Barthold SW, DeSouza MS, Janotka JL, et al. Chronic Lyme borreliosis in the laboratory mouse. Am J Pathol. 1993;143:959.

75. Lim LCL, England DM, DuChateau BK, et al. Development of destructive arthritis in vaccinated hamsters challenged with *Borrelia burgdorferi*. Infect Immun. 1994;62:2825.

76. Appel MJ, Allan S, Jacobson RH, et al. Experimental Lyme disease in dogs produces arthritis and persistent infection. J Infect Dis. 1993;167:651.

77. Philipp MT, Aydintug MK, Bohm RP Jr, et al. Early and early disseminated phases of Lyme disease in the Rhesus monkey: A model for infections in humans. Infect Immun. 1993;61:3047.

78. Ma Y, Seiler KP, Eichwals EJ, et al. Distinct characteristics of resistance to *Borrelia burgdorferi*-induced arthritis in C57BL/6N mice. Infect Immun. 1998;66:161.

79. Ruderman EM, Kerr JS, Telford SR III, et al. Early murine Lyme carditis has a macrophage predominance and is independent of major histocompatibility complex class II-CD4⁺ T cell interactions. J Infect Dis. 1995;171:362.

80. Feng S, Hodzic E, Barthold SW. Lyme arthritis resolution with antiserum to a 37-kilodalton *Borrelia burgdorferi* protein. Infect Immun. 2000;68:4169.

81. Roberts ED, Bohm RP Jr, Lowrie RC Jr, et al. Pathogeneis of Lyme neuroborreliosis in the rhesus monkey: The early disseminated and chronic phases of disease in the peripheral nervous system. J Infect Dis. 1998;178:722.

82. Cadavid D, O'Neill T Schaefer H, et al. Localization of *Borrelia burgdorferi* in the nervous system and other organs in a nonhuman primate model of Lyme disease. Lab Invest. 2000;80:1043.

83. Steere AC. Lyme disease. N Engl J Med. 1989;321:586.

84. Steere AC, Sikand VK. The presenting manifestations of Lyme disease and the outcomes of treatment (Letter). N Engl J Med. 2003;384:2472.

85. Steere AC, Bartenhagen NH, Craft JE, et al. The early clinical manifestations of Lyme disease. Ann Intern Med. 1983;99:76.

86. Smith RP, Schoen RT, Rahn DW, et al. Clinical characteristics and treatment outcomes of early Lyme disease in patients with microbiologically confirmed erythema migrans. Ann Intern Med. 2002;136:421.

87. Strle F, Nadelman RB, Cimperman J, et al. Comparison of culture-confirmed erythema migrans caused by *Borrelia burgdorferi* sensu stricto in New York state and by *Borrelia afzelii* in Slovenia. Ann Intern Med. 1999;130:32.

88. Wormser GP, Bittker S, Cooper D, Nowakowski J, et al. Comparison of the yields of blood cultures using serum or plasma from patients with early Lyme disease. J Clin Microbiol. 2000;38:1648.

89. Steere AC, Dhar A, Hernandez J, et al. Systemic symptoms without erythema migrans as the presenting picture of early Lyme disease. Am J Med. 2003;114:58.

90. Pachner AR, Steere AC. The triad of neurologic manifestations of Lyme disease: Meningitis, cranial neuritis, and radiculoneuritis. Neurology. 1985;35:47.

91. Clark JR, Carlson RD, Sasaki CT, et al. Facial paralysis in Lyme disease. Laryngoscope. 1985;95:1341.

92. Rothermel H, Hedges TR III, Steere AC. Optic neuropathy in children with Lyme disease. Pediatrics. 2001;108:477.

93. Ackermann R, Horstrup P, Schmidt R. Tick-borne meningopolyneuritis (Garin-Bujadoux, Bannwarth). Yale J Biol Med. 1984;57:281.

94. Steere AC, Berardi VP, Weeks KE, et al. Evaluation of the intrathecal antibody response to *Borrelia burgdorferi* as a diagnostic test for Lyme neuroborreliosis. J Infect Dis. 1990;161:1203.

95. Hansen K, Cruz M, Link H. Oligoclonal *Borrelia burgdorferi*-specific IgG antibodies in cerebrospinal fluid in Lyme neuroborreliosis. J Infect Dis. 1990;161:1194.

96. Dai Z, Lackland H, Stein S, et al. Molecular mimicry in Lyme disease: Monoclonal antibody H9724 to *B. burgdorferi* flagellin specifically detects chaperonin-HSP60. Biochim Biophys Acta. 1993;1181:97.

97. Logigian EL, Steere AC. Clinical and electrophysiological findings in chronic neuropathy of Lyme disease. Neurology. 1992;42:303.

98. Vallat JM, Leboutet MJ, Loubet A, et al. Tick bite neuropathy: An analysis of nerve biopsies from seven cases. Neurology. 1984;34:180.

99. Steere AC, Batsford WP, Weinberg M, et al. Lyme carditis: Cardiac abnormalities of Lyme disease. Ann Intern Med. 1980;93:8.

100. Alpert LI, Welch P, Fisher N. Gallium-positive Lyme disease myocarditis. Clin Nucl Med. 1985;10:617.

101. McAlister HF, Klementowicz PT, Andrews C, et al. Lyme carditis: An important cause of reversible heart block. Ann Intern Med. 1989;110:339.

102. Marcus LC, Steere AC, Duray PH, et al. Fatal pancarditis in a patient with coexistent Lyme disease and babesiosis: Demonstration of spirochetes in the heart. Ann Intern Med. 1985;103:374.

103. Landieri G, Salvi A, Camerini F, et al. Isolation of *Borrelia burgdorferi* from myocardium. Lancet. 1993;342:490.

104. Sonnesyn SW, Diehl SC, Johnson RC, et al. A prospective study of the seroprevalence of *Borrelia burgdorferi* infection in patients with severe heart failure. Am J Cardiol. 1995;76:97.

105. Granter SR, Barnhill RL, Hewins ME, Duray PH. Identification of *Borrelia burgdorferi* in diffuse fasciitis with peripheral eosinophilia: Borrelial fasciitis. JAMA. 1994;272:1283.

106. Karma A, Seppala I, Mikkila H, et al. Diagnosis and clinical characteristics of ocular Lyme borreliosis. Am J Ophthalmol. 1994;119:127.

107. Steere AC, Schoen RT, Taylor E. The clinical evolution of Lyme arthritis. Ann Intern Med. 1987;107:725.

108. Steere AC, Levin R, Molloy P, et al. Treatment of Lyme arthritis. Arthritis Rheum. 1994;37:878.

109. Nocton JJ, Dressler F, Rutledge BJ, et al. Detection of *Borrelia burgdorferi* DNA by polymerase chain reaction in synovial fluid in Lyme arthritis. N Engl J Med. 1994;330:229.

110. Carlson D, Hernandez J, Bloom BJ, et al. Lack of *Borrelia burgdorferi* DNA in synovial samples from patients with antibiotic treatment-resistant Lyme arthritis. Arthritis Rheum. 1999;42:2705.

111. Johnston YE, Duray PH, Steere AC, et al. Lyme arthritis: Spirochetes found in synovial microangiopathic lesions. Am J Pathol. 1985;118:26.

112. Akin E, Aversa J, Steere AC. Expression of adhesion molecules in synovia in patients with treatment-resistant Lyme arthritis. Infect Immun. 2001;63:1774.

113. Steere AC, Falk B, Drouin EE, et al. Binding of outer surface protein A and human lymphocyte function-associated 1 antigen to HLA-DR molecules associated with antibiotic treatment-resistant Lyme arthritis. Arthritis Rheum. 2003;48:534.

114. Kalish RA, Leong JM, Steere AC. Association of treatment resistant chronic Lyme arthritis with HLA-DR4 and antibody reactivity to OspA and OspB of *Borrelia burgdorferi*. Infect Immun. 1993;61:2774.

115. Chen J, Field JA, Glickstein L, et al. Association of antibiotic treatment-resistant Lyme arthritis with T cell responses to dominant epitopes of outer-surface protein A (OspA) of *Borrelia burgdorferi*. Arthritis Rheum. 1999;42:1813.

116. Gross DM, Forsthuber T, Tary-Lehman M, et al. Identification of LFA-1 as a candidate autoantigen in treatment-resistant Lyme arthritis. Science. 1998;281:703.

117. Trollmo C, Meyer AL, Steere AC, et al. Molecular mimicry in Lyme arthritis demonstrated at the single cell level: LFA-1α_L is a partial agonist for OspA-reasctive T cells. J Immunol. 2001;166:5286.

118. Logigian EL, Kaplan RF, Steere AC. Chronic neurologic manifestations of Lyme disease. N Engl J Med. 1990;323:1438.

119. Ackermann R, Rehse-Kupper B, Gollmer E, et al. Chronic neurologic manifestations of erythema migrans borreliosis. Ann NY Acad Sci. 1988;539:16.

120. Kaplan RF, Jones-Woodward L, Workman K, et al. Neuropsychological deficits in Lyme disease with or without other evidence of central nervous system pathology. Appl Neuropsychol 1999;6:3.

121. Logigian EL, Johnson KA, Kijewski MF, et al. Reversible cerebral hypoperfusion in Lyme encephalopathy. Neurology. 1997;49:1661.

122. Hemmer B, Gran B, Zhao Y, et al. Identification of candidate T-cell epitopes and molecular mimics in chronic Lyme disease. Nat Med. 1999;5:1375.

123. Asbrink E, Brehmer-Andersson E, Hovmark A. Acrodermatitis chronica atrophicans—a spirochetosis: Clinical and histopathologic picture based on 32 patients; course and relationship to erythema chronicum migrans Afzelius. Am J Dermatopathol. 1986;8:209.

124. Asbrink E, Hovmark A. Successful cultivation of spirochetes from skin lesions of patients with erythema chronica migrans afzelius and acrodermatitis chronica atrophicans. Acta Pathol Microbiol Immunol Scand. 1985;93:161.

125. Markowitz LE, Steere AC, Benach JL, et al. Lyme disease in pregnancy. JAMA. 1986;256:3394.

126. Williams CL, Stobino B, Weinstein A, et al. Maternal Lyme disease and congenital malformations: A cord blood serosurvey in endemic and control areas. Paediatr Perinat Epidemiol. 1995;9:320.

127. Mather TN, Telford SR III, Adler GH. Absence of transplacental transmission of Lyme disease spirochetes from reservoir mice *(Peromyscus leucopus)* to their offspring. J Infect Dis. 1991;164:564.

128. Krause PJ, Telford SR III, Spielman A, et al. Concurrent Lyme disease and babesiosis: Evidence for increased severity and duration of illness. JAMA. 1996;275:1657.

129. Wormser GP, Horowitz HW, Nowakowski J, et al. Positive Lyme disease serology in patients with clinical and laboratory evidence of human granulocytic ehrlichiosis. Am J Clin Pathol. 1997;107:142.

130. Steere AC, McHugh G, Suarez C, et al. Prospective study of co-infection in patients with erythema migrans. Clin Infect Dis. 2003;36:1078.

131. Krause, PJ, McKay K, Thompson CA, et al. Disease-specific diagnosis of coinfecting tickborne zoonoses: Babesiosis, human granulocytic ehrlichiosis, and Lyme disease. Clin Infect Dis. 2002;34:1184.

132. Berger BW, Johnson RC, Kodner C, et al. Cultivation of *Borrelia burgdorferi* from erythema migrans lesions and perilesional skin. J Clin Microbiol. 1992;30:359.

133. Nocton JJ, Bloom BJ, Rutledge BJ, et al. Detection of *Borrelia burgdorferi* DNA by polymerase chain reaction in cerebrospinal fluid in patients with Lyme neuroborreliosis. J Infect Dis. 1996;174:623.

134. Klempner MS, Schmid C, Hu L, et al. Intralaboratory reliability of serologic and urine testing for Lyme disease. Am J Med. 2001;110:217.

135. Centers for Disease Control. Case definitions for public health surveillance. Morb Mortal Wkly Rep. 1990;39:1.

136. Centers for Disease Control. Recommendations for test performance and interpretation from the Second International Conference on serologic diagnosis of Lyme disease. Morb Mortal Wkly Rep. 1995;44:1.

137. Robertson J, Guy E, Andrews N, et al. A European multicenter study of immunoblotting in the serodiagnosis of Lyme borreliosis. J Clin Microbiol. 2000;38:2097.

138. Engstrom SM, Shoop E, Johnson RC. Immunoblot interpretation criteria for serodiagnosis of early Lyme disease. J Clin Microbiol. 1995;33:419.

139. Dressler F, Whalen JA, Reinhardt BN, et al. Western blotting in the serodiagnosis of Lyme disease. J Infect Dis. 1993;167:392.

140. Kalish RA, McHugh G, Granquist J, et al. Persistence of immunoglobulin M and immunoglobulin G antibody responses to *Borrelia burgdorferi* 10-20 years after active Lyme disease. Clin Infect Dis. 2001;33:780.

141. Steere AC, Sikand VJ, Schoen RT, Nowakowski J. Asymptomatic infection with *Borrelia burgdorferi*. Clin Infect Dis. 2003;37:528.

142. Gustafson R, Svenungsson B, Forsgren M, et al. Two-year survey of the incidence of Lyme borreliosis and tick-borne encephalitis in a high-risk population in Sweden. Eur J Clin Microbiol Infect Dis. 1992;11:894.

143. Fahrer H, van der Linden S, Sauvain MJ, et al. The prevalence and incidence of clinical and asymptomatic Lyme borreliosis in a population at risk. J Infect Dis. 1991;163:305.

144. Gomes-Silecki MJ, Dunn JJ, Luft BJ, et al. Recombinant chimeric Borrelia proteins for the diagnosis of Lyme disease. J Clin Microbiol. 2000;38:2530.

145. Bacon RM, Biggerstaff BJ, Schriefer ME, et al. Serodiagnosis of Lyme disease by kinetic enzyme-linked immunosorbent assay using recombinant VlsE1 or peptide antigens of *Borrelia burgdorferi* compared with 2-tiered testing using whole-cell lysates. J Infect Dis. 2003;187:1187.

146. Peltomma M, McHugh G, Steere AC. Persistence of the antibody response to the VlsE sixth invariant region (IR$_6$) peptide of *Borrelia burgdorferi* after successful antibiotic treatment for Lyme disease. J Infect Dis. 2003;187:1178.

147. Steere AC, Taylor E, McHugh GL, et al. The overdiagnosis of Lyme disease. JAMA. 1993;269:1812.

148. Sigal LH. Summary of the first 100 patients seen at a Lyme disease referral center. Am J Med. 1990;88:577.

149. Dinerman H, Steere AC. Lyme disease associated with fibromyalgia. Ann Intern Med. 1992;117:281.

150. Kaplan RF, Meadows ME, Vincent LC, et al. Memory impairment and depression in patients with Lyme encephalopathy: Comparison with fibromyalgia and nonpsychotically depressed patients. Neurology 1992;42:1263.

151. Wormser GP, Nadelman RB, Dattwyler RJ, et al. Practice guidelines for the treatment of Lyme disease. Clin Infect Dis. 2000;31(Suppl 1):S1-S14.

152. Steere AC, Hutchinson GJ, Rahn DW, et al. Treatment of the early manifestations of Lyme disease. Ann Intern Med. 1983;99:22.

153. Johnson RC, Kodner C, Russell M. In vitro and in vivo susceptibility of the Lyme disease spirochete, *Borrelia burgdorferi*, to four antimicrobial agents. Antimicrob Agents Chemother. 1987;31:164.

154. Preac-Mursic V, Wilske B, Schierz G, et al. Comparative antimicrobial activity of the new macrolides against *Borrelia burgdorferi*. Eur J Clin Microbiol Infect Dis. 1989;8:651.

155. Agger WA, Callister SM, Jobe DA. In vitro susceptibilities of *Borrelia burgdorferi* to five oral cephalosporins and ceftriaxone. Antimicrob Agents Chemother. 1992; 36:1788.

156. Dever LL, Jorgensen JH, Barbour AG. In vitro antimicrobial susceptibility testing of *Borrelia burgdorferi:* A microdilution MIC method and timekill studies. J Clin Microbiol. 1992;30:2692.

157. Dattwyler RJ, Volkman DJ, Conaty SM, et al. Amoxicillin plus probenecid versus doxycycline for treatment of erythema migrans borreliosis. Lancet. 1990;336:1404.

158. Nadelman RB, Luger SW, Frank E, et al. Comparison of cefuroxime axetil and doxycycline in the treatment of early Lyme disease. Ann Intern Med. 1992;117:273.

159. Wormser GP, Ramanathan R, Nowakowski J, et al. Duration of antibiotic therapy for early Lyme disease. Ann Intern Med. 2003;138:697.

160. Dattwyler RJ, Luft BJ, Kunkel MJ, et al. Ceftriaxone compared with doxycycline for the treatment of acute disseminated Lyme disease. N Engl J Med. 1997;337:289.

161. Nowakowski J, McKenna D, Nadelman RB, et al. Failure of treatment with cephalexin for Lyme disease. Arch Fam Med. 2000;9:563.

162. Dattwyler RJ, Halperin JJ, Volkman DJ, Luft BJ. Treatment of late Lyme borreliosis—randomized comparison of ceftriaxone and penicillin. Lancet. 1988;1:1191.

163. Logigian EL, Kaplan RF, Steere AC. Successful treatment of Lyme encephalopathy with intravenous ceftriaxone. J Infect Dis. 1999;180:377.

164. Pfister HW, Preac-Mursic V, Wilske B, Einhaupl KM. Cefotaxime vs. pencillin G for acute neurologic manifestations of Lyme borreliosis; a prospective randomized study. Arch Neurol. 1989;46:1190.

165. Karlsson M, Hammers-Berggren S, Lindquist L, et al. Comparison of intravenous penicillin G and oral doxycycline for treatment of Lyme neuroborreliosis. Neurology. 1994;44:1203.

166. Eckman MH, Steere AC, Kalish RA, Pauker SG. Cost effectiveness of oral as compared with intravenous antibiotic therapy for patients with early Lyme disease or Lyme arthritis. N Engl J Med. 1997;337:357.

167. Schoen RT, Aversa JM, Rahn DW, et al. Treatment of refractory chronic Lyme arthritis with arthroscopic synovectomy. Arthritis Rheum. 1991;34:1056.

168. Shaddick NA, Phillipis CB, Sangha O, et al. Musculoskeltal and neurologic outcomes in patients with previously treated Lyme disease. Ann Intern Med. 1999;117:281.

169. Kalish RA, Kaplan RF, Taylor E, et al. Evaluation of study patients with Lyme disease, 10-20-year follow-up. J Infect Dis. 2001;183:453.

170. Seltzer EG, Gerber MA, Cartter ML, et al. Long-term outcomes of persons with Lyme disease. JAMA. 2000;283:609.

171. Klempner MS, Hu LT, Evans J, et al. Two controlled trials of antibiotic treatment in patients with persistent symptoms and a history of Lyme disease. N Engl J Med. 2001;345:85.

172. Ettestad PJ, Campbell GL, Welbel SF, et al. Biliary complications in the treatment of unsubstantiated Lyme disease. J Infect Dis. 1995;171:356.

173. Patel R, Grogg KL, Edwards WD, et al. Death from inappropriate therapy for Lyme disease. Clin Infect Dis. 2000;31:1107.

174. Hayes EB, Piesman J. How can we prevent Lyme disease? N Engl J Med. 2003; 348:2424.

175. Schreck CE, Snoddy EL, Spielman A. Pressurized sprays of permethrin or DEET on military clothing for personal protection against *Ixodes dammini* (Acari: Ixodidae). J Med Entomol. 1986;23:396.

176. Oransky S, Roseman B, Fish D, et al. Seizures temporarily associated with the use of DEET insect repellent—New York and Connecticut. Morb Mortal Wkly Rep. 1989;38:678.

177. Piesman J, Mather TN, Sinsky RJ. Duration of tick attachment and *Borrelia burgdorferi* transmission. J Clin Microbiol. 1987;25:557.

178. Nadelman RB, Nowakowski J, Fish D, et al. Prophylaxis with single-dose doxycycline for the prevention of Lyme disease after an *Ixodes scapularis* tick bite. N Engl J Med. 2001;345:79.

179. Curran KL, Fish D, Piesman J. Reduction of nymphal *Ixodes dammini* (Acari: Ixodidae) in a residential suburban landscape by area application of insecticides. J Med Entomol. 1993;30:107.

180. Wilson ML, Telford SR III, Piesman J, et al. Reduced abundance of immature *Ixodes dammini* (Acari: Ixodidae) following elimination of deer. J Med Entomol. 1988; 25:224.

181. Steere AC, Sikand VK, Meurice F, et al. Vaccination against Lyme disease with recombinant *Borrelia burgdorferi* outer surface lipoprotein A with adjuvant. N Engl J Med. 1998;339:209.

CHAPTER 240

Spirillum minus (Rat-Bite Fever)

RONALD G. WASHBURN

Spirillum minus is one of the two etiologic agents of rat-bite fever. The other causative bacterium, *Streptobacillus moniliformis,* is discussed in Chapter 228. *Spirillum minus* causes a significant portion of the cases of rat-bite fever in Asia but rarely produces infection in the United States.[1,2] In Japan, the infection is called *sodoku* (*so:* rat; *doku:* poison).

The causative organism was discovered by Carter during the 19th century.[3] In the early years of the 20th century, specimens from patients with *sodoku* were shown to contain spirochetes capable of infecting guinea pigs. Those bacteria were initially called *Spirocheta morsus muris* or *Sporozoa muris.*[4] The organism was renamed *Spirillum minus* in 1924.[5]

BACTERIOLOGY

Spirillum minus is a short, thick, gram-negative, tightly coiled spiral rod measuring 0.2 to 0.5 μm × 3 to 5 μm.[6,7] The organism has two to six regular helical turns.[7] Terminal polytrichous flagella confer darting motility, which can be demonstrated with darkfield examination. The flagella can be stained with silver impregnation methods (e.g., Fontana-Tribondeau). *Spirillum minus* cannot be cultured on artificial media.

EPIDEMIOLOGY, PATHOGENESIS, AND PATHOLOGY

The epidemiology of *S. minus* infections is similar to that of streptobacillary rat-bite fever, with the exception that oral ingestion has not been shown to cause spirillary disease. The major route of transmission is through rat bites. Approximately 25% of tested rats are positive for *S. minus* in conjunctival and nasopharyngeal secretions, pulmonary lesions, and blood.[6] Human-to-human transmission has not been documented.

Relapses of spirillary rat-bite fever have been postulated to be caused by seeding of blood and distant foci during periodic reactivation of the primary bite lesion. The available recorded autopsies show granulomatous inflammation at the original site of inoculation, with epithelial necrosis and mononuclear infiltration of the dermis. Regional lymph nodes are hyperplastic. Deep tissue specimens from distant areas of skin rash contain dilated blood vessels and round cell infiltrates. Liver, spleen, renal tubules, myocardium, and meninges may be hemorrhagic, with areas of necrosis in liver and kidney.

CLINICAL MANIFESTATIONS

The initial bite wound heals promptly but then becomes painful, swollen, and purple approximately 1 to 4 weeks later; it is associated with regional lymphangitis and lymphadenitis. This local inflammatory lesion ushers in a systemic illness characterized by fever, chills, headache, and malaise. In contrast with streptobacillary rat-bite fever, arthritis and myalgias are rare in *Spirillum minus* infection. Next, the bite wound commonly progresses to chancre-like ulceration and induration with eschar formation. During the first week of fever, a blotchy violaceous or reddish-brown macular rash erupts over the extremities, face, scalp, and trunk, and then fades during subsequent afebrile intervals. Occasionally, the rash may be urticarial.[7] Leukocytosis with peripheral white blood cell counts in the range of 10,000 to 20,000/mm³ may be observed, and up to 50% of patients have false-positive syphilis serologies.

Without specific antibiotic therapy, fevers lasting 3 to 4 days recur at regular intervals between afebrile periods of 3 to 9 days.

Spontaneous cure usually occurs within 1 to 2 months, but in selected instances fevers have relapsed for years.[7]

The most serious complication of untreated spirillary rat-bite fever is endocarditis. Most of these rare intravascular infections have been observed in patients with preexisting valvular disease, but one reported case occurred on a normal aortic valve.[8] The spectrum of reported complications also includes myocarditis, pleural effusions, hepatitis, splenomegaly, meningitis, epididymitis, conjunctivitis, and anemia.[7,9] Overall mortality of untreated *S. minus* infections in the preantibiotic era was 6% to 10%.

DIAGNOSIS

In the absence of a history of rat bite or typical clinical features, other diagnoses that might enter into the differential diagnosis of relapsing fever would include *Borrelia,* malaria, and lymphoma. Because *S. minus* cannot be grown on synthetic media, initial diagnosis relies on direct visualization of characteristic spirochetes in blood, exudate, or lymph node tissue using Giemsa stain, Wright stain, or darkfield microscopy. Organisms can also be recovered from mice or guinea pigs 1 to 3 weeks after intraperitoneal inoculation,[7,10] with the precaution that the animals must be prescreened to rule out the presence of preexisting spirochete infections. No specific serologic test is available for *S. minus* infection.

TREATMENT

The usual treatment is penicillin for 10 to 14 days. Further details are given in Chapter 228.

REFERENCES

1. Anderson LC, Leary SL, Manning PJ. Ratbite fever in animal research laboratory personnel. Lab Anim Sci. 1983;33:292-294.
2. Cole JS, Stoll RW, Bulger RJ. Ratbite fever: Report of three cases. Ann Intern Med. 1969;71:979-981.
3. Hiatt JR, Hiatt N. The forgotten first career of Doctor Henry Van Dyke Carter. J Am Coll Surg. 1995;181:464-486.
4. Roughgarden JW. Antimicrobial therapy of ratbite fever. Arch Intern Med. 1965;116:39-54.
5. Robertson A. Causal organism of ratbite fever in man. Ann Trop Med. 1924;18:157.
6. McHugh TP, Bartlett RL, Raymond JI. Rat bite fever: Report of a fatal case. Ann Emerg Med. 1985;14:1116-1118.
7. Taber LH, Feigin RD. Spirochetal infections. Pediatr Clin North Am. 1979;26:410-411.
8. McIntosh CS, Vickers PJ, Isaacs AJ. Spirillum endocarditis. Postgrad Med J. 1975;51:645-648.
9. Raffin BJ, Freemark M. Streptobacillary ratbite fever: A pediatric problem. Pediatrics. 1979;64:214-217.
10. Dow GR, Rankin RJ, Saunders BW. Ratbite fever. N Z Med J. 1992;105:133.

Anaerobic Infections: General Concepts

ARTHUR O. TZIANABOS

DENNIS L. KASPER

INTRODUCTION

Anaerobic bacteria are a major component of human microflora residing on mucous membranes and predominate in many infectious processes, particularly those arising from mucosal sites. These organisms generally cause disease subsequent to the breakdown of mucosal barriers and the leakage of indigenous flora into normally sterile sites.

The predominance of anaerobes in certain clinical syndromes can be attributed to the large numbers of these organisms residing on mucous membranes, the elaboration of a variety of virulence factors, the ability of some anaerobic species to resist oxygenated microenvironments, synergy with other bacteria, and resistance to certain antibiotics.

Clinicians have become more aware in the last few decades of the types of infections caused by anaerobic bacteria. However, difficulty in handling specimens in which anaerobes may be important and technical difficulties in cultivating and identifying these organisms in clinical microbiology laboratories still lead to many cases in which the anaerobic etiology of an infectious process remains unproven. The importance of anaerobes in certain infections is further enhanced by the failure to provide appropriate antibiotic coverage for anaerobes in mixed aerobic-anaerobic infections and an increase in the number of anaerobes that have become resistant to antimicrobial agents. These various factors combine to make it crucial to understand the types of infections in which anaerobes can have a role, to use appropriate microbiologic tools to identify the organisms in clinical specimens, and to use the most appropriate treatment. Frequently, treatment includes surgical drainage or débridement of the infected site.

DEFINITION OF AN ANAEROBE

The generally accepted definition of an *anaerobe* is an organism that requires reduced oxygen for growth. Practically, this means that an anaerobe fails to grow on the surface of solid media in 10% CO_2 in air. In contrast, *facultative* organisms can grow in the presence or absence of air, and *microaerophilic* bacteria can grow in 10% CO_2 in air or under aerobic or anaerobic conditions. As opposed to the strict requirement for survival only under anaerobic conditions of several anaerobic species inhabiting our bodily surfaces, anaerobes that commonly cause human infections are generally aerotolerant and can survive for as long as 72 hours in the presence of an oxygenated atmosphere, although they will not grow. Most anaerobes do not possess catalase, but those that cause human disease often have superoxide dismutase. In general, the degree to which this enzyme is expressed dictates the aerotolerance of the organism in question.[1]

ROLE OF ANAEROBES IN NORMAL FLORA

Several hundred species of anaerobic organisms have been identified in the human microflora. Mucosal surfaces such as the oral cavity, gastrointestinal tract, and female genital tract are the major reservoirs for this group of organisms. It is interesting to note that anaerobes inhabit areas of the body that are exposed to air: the skin, nose, mouth, and throat. It has been hypothesized that anaerobes can withstand oxygen at these sites, in part owing to the presence of aerobes and facultative organisms, which consume oxygen and reduce oxidation-reduction potential. They are also believed to reside in the areas of these sites that are more protected from oxygen, such as gingival crevices.

Despite the number of anaerobic species found in the normal flora, relatively few are involved in human infections. Table 241-1 shows the most common gram-negative and gram-positive anaerobes isolated. Infections involving anaerobes are polymicrobial in nature and usually result from the disruption of mucosal surfaces and the subsequent infiltration of resident flora. However, certain gram-negative anaerobic bacilli belonging to the genera *Bacteroides, Fusobacterium,*

TABLE 241-1 Anaerobes Commonly Found in Human Infections

Gram-negative	Gram-positive
Bacteroides spp.*	*Peptostreptococcus* spp.
Porphyromonas spp.	*Clostridium* spp.
Prevotella spp.	*Actinomyces* spp.
Fusobacterium spp.	

*B. fragilis predominates in these infections.

Porphyromonas, and *Prevotella* are the anaerobes most commonly isolated from clinical infections.[2]

Anaerobes normally reside in abundance as part of the oral flora, with concentrations ranging from 10^9/mL in saliva to 10^{12}/mL in gingival scrapings. At this site, the ratio of anaerobic to aerobic bacteria ranges from 1:1 on teeth to 1000:1 in the gingival crevice. The indigenous oral anaerobic flora primarily comprises *Prevotella* and *Porphyromonas* species, with *Fusobacterium* and *Bacteroides* (non-*Bacteroides fragilis* group; see below) present in fewer numbers.

Low numbers of anaerobic bacteria are present in the normally acidic conditions in the stomach and upper intestine. In people with decreased gastric acidity, the microflora of the stomach resembles that of the oral cavity. The upper intestine contains relatively few organisms until the distal ileum, where the flora begins to resemble that of the colon. In the colon, there are up to 10^{12} organisms per gram of stool, with anaerobes outnumbering aerobes by approximately 1000:1. *Bacteroides* and *Fusobacterium* are the predominant gram-negative genera in the colonic flora. The various *Bacteroides* species that inhabit the colon are commonly referred to as the *B. fragilis* group. This is based on their earlier designation as subspecies of *B. fragilis.* This group encompasses several species, including *B. fragilis, B. thetaiotaomicron, B. ovatus, B. vulgatus, B. uniformis,* and *B. distasonis* (although the last organism is likely to be reclassified as a *Porphyromonas* species).[3]

The normal vaginal flora is colonized by *Prevotella, Bacteroides, Fusobacterium,* and *Clostridium* species. The concentration of anaerobes at this site is approximately 10^6 organisms per gram of secretions. The most common isolates from clinical specimens are *Prevotella bivia* and *P. disiens,* although *B. fragilis* is also frequently isolated from this site. *Bacteroides* species are found in approximately 50% of women's genital tracts, with *B. fragilis* making up less than 15% of this population.

The occupation of distinct ecological niches within the intestinal environment that would otherwise be filled with potentially pathogenic organisms is among the most important roles that anaerobes serve as normal colonic microflora. This process, termed colonization resistance, effectively interferes with colonization by potentially pathogenic bacterial species through the depletion of oxygen and nutrients and the production of enzymes and toxic end products.[2] The anaerobic component of the intestinal microflora is also responsible for the production of secreted products that are helpful in human health. Production of vitamin K by anaerobes in the intestine is beneficial to the host, while the production of bile by these organisms is useful in fat absorption and cholesterol regulation.[4]

ETIOLOGY OF ANAEROBES IN CLINICAL INFECTIONS

Infections caused by anaerobes generally occur on disruption of the commensal relationship with the host. For example, anaerobic gram-negative bacilli that reside in the intestine can cause infection following contamination of normally sterile sites such as the peritoneal cavity.[5] Cecal contents are the source for microorganisms in the case of intraabdominal infections following intestinal rupture and contamination of the peritoneal cavity. Severe infections of the head and neck may arise from an abscessed tooth infected with commensal microflora of the mouth. However, it is remarkable that, despite the identification of hundreds of anaerobic species in normal flora, relatively few species seem to play a major role in infection.

After contamination of previously sterile sites by mucosal microflora, the relatively few anaerobic bacteria that survive in the infected site are those that have resisted changes in oxidation-reduction potential and host defense mechanisms. The hallmark of infection caused by these gram-negative anaerobic bacteria is abscess formation, although some sepsis syndromes have been described. Typically, abscesses form at sites of direct bacterial contamination, although distant abscesses resulting from hematogenous spread are not uncommon with the more virulent anaerobes.

The *B. fragilis* group consists of gram-negative bacilli that are among the anaerobes most commonly isolated from human infections (see Table 241-1). From this group, *B. fragilis* is the species most commonly isolated from clinical cases, particularly in infections emanating from the lower intestine, although the other members of this family are also isolated from infectious sites. Other gram-negative organisms that cause human infections are *Fusobacterium, Prevotella,* and *Porphyromonas. Bilophila wadsworthia* has also been isolated from clinical infections; however, its pathogenic role in anaerobic infections is still under investigation.[6]

The major gram-positive cocci that cause disease are the *Peptostreptococcus* spp., while clostridia are the major pathogens among the gram-positive rods. These latter organisms are commonly isolated from wounds, abscesses, and blood.

In the oral cavity, the pigmented anaerobes *Prevotella* and *Porphyromonas* are recognized as pathogenic species. *Prevotella bivia* and *Prevotella disiens* colonize the vagina and are the organisms most frequently isolated from infections arising at this site.

The fusobacteria *Fusobacterium nucleatum, F. necrophorum,* and *F. varium,* which normally reside in the oral cavity and intestinal tract, are often isolated from necrotizing pneumonia and abscesses.

CLINICAL SYNDROMES CAUSED BY ANAEROBES

Anaerobes are remarkable in their ability to cause a variety of infections at a number of different anatomical sites. Table 241-2 summarizes the types of infections that these organisms cause. It is important to note that, because anaerobes colonize sites that are home to aerobes and facultative organisms, many of the infections from which they are isolated involve both aerobic and anaerobic species. Figure 241-1 shows a Gram-stained specimen of mixed infection isolated from a patient with Melaney's gangrene. This is a form of cellulitis involving *Staphylococcus aureus* and anaerobic streptococci. The *B. fragilis* group is the most common of all anaerobic species isolated from clinical infections, with *B. fragilis* as the predominant isolate from this group.[7]

Anaerobic Infections of the Mouth, Head, and Neck

Anaerobes contribute to infection associated with periodontal disease and to disseminated infection arising from the oral cavity (see Chapter 56). Infection of the periodontal area may extend into the mandible, causing osteomyelitis of the maxillary sinuses or infection of submandibular spaces. Formation of dental plaque, which is influenced by oral hygiene and other host factors, leads to the acquisition of pathogenic bacteria and the development of gingivitis and periodontal disease. Necrotizing gingivitis is characterized by the sudden onset of a necrotizing infection with bleeding gums and ulcerated gingival mucosal tissue. A strong odor and foul taste are common in this infection. The anaerobes that predominate in this process are *Porphyromonas gingivalis* and *P. melaninogenica.*

Infections of the pharynx occur in association with ulcerative gingivitis and are accompanied by a sore throat, fever, swollen tonsils, and a foul taste. The disease can persist for long periods if not treated with antibiotics. Lymphadenopathy and leukocytosis are common outcomes of these infections.

Anaerobic infections that cause abscess formation in the pharynx can lead to suppurative thrombophlebitis of the jugular vein and the development of a sometimes fatal syndrome known as Lemierre's syndrome, characterized by bacteremia and septic emboli to the lungs, brain, and heart. *Fusobacterium necrophorum* is a common cause of these infections, which are rare in the era of antimicrobial therapy.

Anaerobic bacteria have been isolated in a large percentage of cases of suppurative otitis media, although their role in acute otitis media is less clear. These organisms also have a role in chronic sinusitis, which is most often a mixed infection where the *Bacteroides* group predominates as the anaerobic component along with facultative species.

Pleuropulmonary Infections

These infections are most commonly associated with the aspiration of oropharyngeal material or occur as a complication of periodontal disease (see Chapters 60 and 61). The anaerobes most common in these infections are indigenous to the upper airways and include *Bacteroides, Prevotella, Fusobacterium,* and *Peptostreptococcus.* Four major clinical syndromes can develop: aspiration pneumonia, necrotizing pneumonia, lung abscess, and empyema. Aspiration pneumonia develops slowly and presents with a mixed flora in sputum that is not foul-smelling initially but can become malodorous with prolonged infection. Sputum samples are not reliable for culture, as they contain normal oral flora, but cultures of samples obtained by lung biopsy may be useful. The lobes of the lung that are affected depend most often on the position of the patient during aspiration.

Necrotizing pneumonia is characterized by the development of many small abscesses within the pulmonary segments. Lung abscesses most often arise secondary to the development of periodontal disease, and, not surprisingly, oral anaerobes predominate. Empyemas are a result of long-term anaerobic pulmonary infections and present with foul-smelling sputum and pleuritic chest pain.

Intra-abdominal Infections

Infections originating from colonic sites, such as intra-abdominal abscesses, most frequently involve *Bacteroides* species, with *B. fragilis* as the most common isolate (see Chapters 68-73).[8] In these infections, anaerobes greatly outnumber aerobes; *E. coli* is the predominant aer-

---

TABLE 241-2 Infections Commonly Caused by Anaerobes

Abdominal Cavity	***Pelvic Cavity/Vagina***
Peritonitis	Pelvic inflammatory disease
Intra-abdominal abscess	Vaginal abscess
Appendicitis	
Liver abscess	***Skin and Soft Tissue Infections***
Wound infection	Diabetic foot ulcers
Biliary tract infections	Cutaneous abscess
	Gas gangrene
Mouth, Head, and Neck	Bite wound infections
Sinusitis	
Otitis media	***Central Nervous System***
Periodontitis	Brain abscess
Root canal infection	Subdural empyema
Periodontal abscess	Epidural abscess
Ocular infections	
Thoracic Cavity	
Empyema	
Lung abscess	
Aspiration pneumonia	

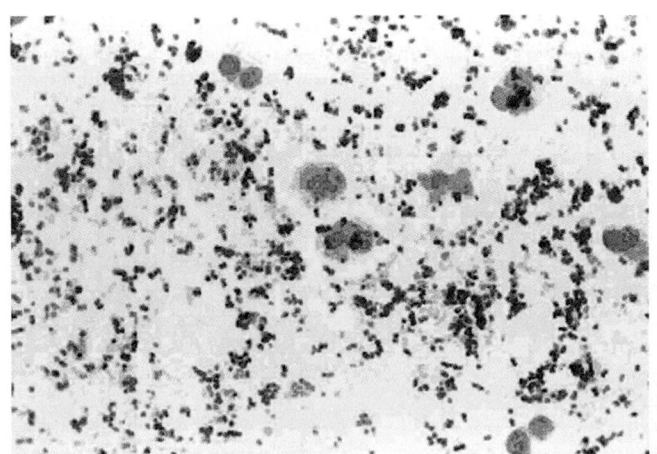

FIGURE 241-1. Gram-stained specimen from a patient with Melaney's gangrene. This is a mixed infection involving *S. aureus* and anaerobic streptococci that usually occurs around surgical wounds, stomas, and cutaneous fistulae. The infection spreads slowly and often results in skin ulceration, but lacks the severe systemic toxicity observed with necrotizing fasciitis. *(With permission from Dr. Andrew Onderdonk.)*

obic or facultative organism. Figure 241-2 shows the development of a pericolonic abscess in a patient with multiple diverticula. Other anaerobes that are commonly isolated from this type of infection include *Peptostreptococcus micros, Prevotella intermedia,* and *Fusobacterium* spp. The involvement of *Clostridium* spp. can lead to severe infections. Secondary bacterial peritonitis arises when organisms from the intestine contaminate the peritoneum. The terminal ileum and colon are the most common sites of origin because of the high numbers of organisms they contain. Patients typically develop acute peritonitis following contamination, and intraperitoneal abscess may result as a later sequela.[7]

It should be noted that there is a strong correlation between the development of carcinoma of the bowel and intra-abdominal infection. In addition, other diseases of the bowel, such as Crohn's disease or ulcerative colitis, often lead to anaerobic infection of the peritoneal cavity.

B. fragilis has also been associated with watery diarrhea in case-control studies of children with undiagnosed diarrheal disease.[9] Enterotoxin-producing strains are more prevalent in patients with diarrhea than in control groups. However, a firm etiologic relationship between enterotoxin-producing *B. fragilis* strains and diarrhea has not been established.

Pelvic Infections

The female genital tract is a major reservoir for anaerobes, which outnumber aerobes by a ratio of 10:1. Anaerobes are encountered in pelvic abscesses, septic abortion, endometritis, tuboovarian abscess, pelvic inflammatory disease, and postoperative infections (see Chapters 65 and 104). The major isolates from these infections are *B. fragilis, P. bivia, P. disiens, P. melaninogenica,* peptostreptococci, and *Clostridium* spp. As in intra-abdominal infections, most infections of the female genital tract are mixed, involving both anaerobes and aerobes. However, infections where anaerobes are isolated in pure culture occur more frequently in the pelvis than in the abdominal cavity.

Bacterial vaginosis is a disease process in which anaerobes predominate and is characterized by malodorous discharge and inflammation. The etiology of this disease is not clear, but *Gardnerella vaginalis, Prevotella* spp., *Mobiluncus* spp., and the peptostreptococci have been implicated. The development of pelvic inflammatory disease has been associated with bacterial vaginosis and in some cases may result from infection by anaerobic bacteria.[10]

Central Nervous System Infections

Either a single anaerobic species or a mixture of anaerobic and/or aerobic bacteria may be found in brain abscesses; prominent among the anaerobes are *Fusobacterium, Bacteroides,* and anaerobic gram-positive cocci. Anaerobic brain abscesses may arise by hematogenous dissemination from an infected distant site or by direct extension from otitis, sinusitis, or tooth infection. Figure 241-3 shows a computed tomography scan of a left parietal brain abscess.

Skin and Soft Tissue Infections

Anaerobic infections in the skin and soft tissue are most often caused by contamination with fecal or oral flora. In addition, anaerobes are commonly isolated from diabetic foot ulcers. Skin and soft tissue infections are usually mixed, with a 3:2 ratio of anaerobes to aerobes. *Bacteroides* spp., *Peptostreptococcus* spp., enterococci, and *Clostridium* spp., are the most common isolates. Anaerobes can also be found in necrotizing fasciitis, usually as part of a mixed anaerobic/aerobic infection. This type of infection usually occurs at sites that can be contaminated from oral secretions or feces; the disease can spread rapidly and be very destructive. Gas may be found in the infected tissues. *Peptostreptococcus* and *Bacteroides* spp. usually predominate. Fournier's gangrene is a form of cellulitis that involves the scrotum, perineum, or anterior abdominal wall and results in the extensive loss of skin.

Bone and Joint Infections

Infections such as osteomyelitis of bone and septic arthritis typically arise from infected adjacent soft tissue sites. *Fusobacterium* species are the most common gram-negative anaerobes isolated from infected joints, whereas infected bone may yield a wider variety of isolates.

Bacteremia

Approximately 5% of cases of bacteremia include anaerobic isolates. *B. fragilis* is the anaerobe most commonly isolated from these infections.[11] Anaerobic bacteremia is usually secondary to an infectious process that has emanated from the bowel, female genital tract, respiratory tract, or soft tissue. Thrombophlebitis has been reported as complicating as many as 15% of anaerobic bacteremias.

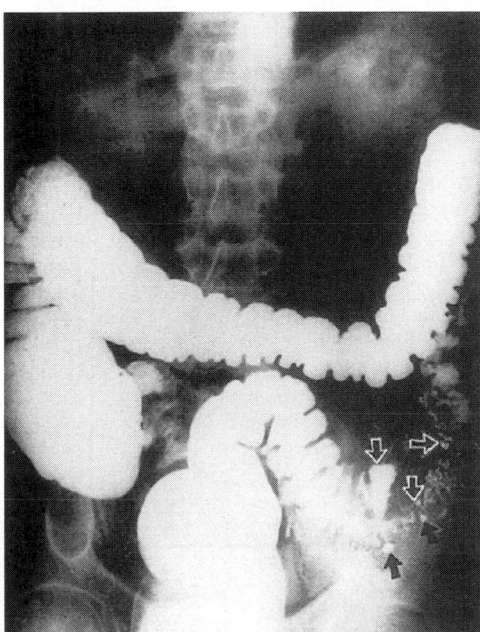

FIGURE 241-2. Development of a pericolonic abscess following a ruptured diverticulum. Barium enema reveals the abscesses *(arrows).* (From Mandell G, ed. *Atlas of Infectious Diseases.* Philadelphia, Churchill Livingstone; 1995.)

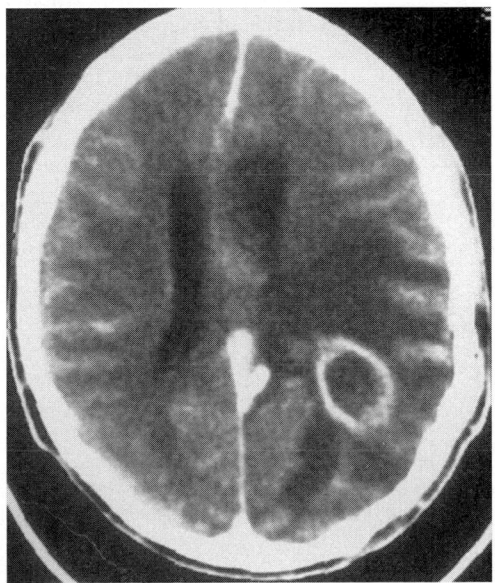

FIGURE 241-3. Patient with left parietal brain abscess. Area outlined in *white* demarcates the walled-off abscess. *(From Mandell G, ed. Atlas of Infectious Diseases. Philadelphia: Churchill Livingstone; 1995.)*

PATHOGENESIS OF ANAEROBIC INFECTIONS

Infections caused by anaerobes are generally a result of the breakdown of a mucosal barrier and subsequent leakage of indigenous polymicrobial flora into previously sterile closed spaces or tissue. The introduction of many species of bacteria into otherwise-sterile sites leads to a polymicrobial infection in which certain organisms predominate. The predominant gram-negative anaerobes in these infections include *B. fragilis*, *Prevotella* species, *Fusobacterium* species, and *Porphyromonas* species. Although some of these organisms are numerically dominant in the normal flora, others (such as *B. fragilis*) make up a much smaller proportion, indicating that they possess one or more virulence factors that contribute to their ability to cause disease. Virulence factors associated with anaerobes typically: (1) confer the ability to evade host defenses, (2) adhere to cell surfaces, (3) produce toxins and/or enzymes, or (4) display surface structures that contribute to pathogenic potential. Table 241-3 lists some of the virulence factors associated with anaerobic organisms commonly isolated from clinical infections.

The ability of different anaerobic bacteria to act synergistically during polymicrobial infection contributes to the pathogenesis of anaerobic infections. The phenomenon of microbial synergy has been described in these infections but remains poorly characterized. It has been postulated that facultative organisms function in part to lower the oxidation-reduction potential in the microenvironment and that this change allows for the propagation of obligate anaerobes. Additional studies indicate that anaerobes can produce compounds such as succinic acid and short-chain fatty acids that inhibit the ability of phagocytes to clear facultative organisms. It has also been demonstrated in experimental models that facultative and obligate anaerobes synergistically potentiate abscess formation.[5]

B. fragilis is the anaerobe most commonly isolated from clinical infections.[12] The high frequency of abscess formation associated with *B. fragilis* led to studies of this organism's pathogenic potential in relevant animal models of disease. As shown in an animal model of intra-abdominal sepsis, the *B. fragilis* capsular polysaccharide has been identified as its major virulence factor and has a specific central role in the induction of abscesses.[13]

A series of detailed biologic and molecular studies of this virulence factor show that *B. fragilis* produces at least eight distinct capsular polysaccharides,[14] far more than previously reported for any encapsulated bacterium. *B. fragilis* can exhibit a wide array of distinct surface polysaccharide combinations by regulating the expression of these different capsules in an on-off manner through the reversible inversion of DNA segments containing the promoters for their expression.

Structural analysis of two of these polysaccharides, termed PS A and PS B, revealed that each polymer consists of repeating units with positively charged free amino groups and negatively charged groups.

This structural feature is rare among bacterial polysaccharides, and the ability of PS A and PS B to induce abscesses in animals depends on this zwitterionic charge motif.[15] Numerous fecal and clinical isolates of *B. fragilis* have been examined, and this dual polysaccharide motif has been found in every strain.

Mechanistic studies of the pathogenesis of intra-abdominal abscess formation by *B. fragilis* revealed a multifunctional role for its capsular polysaccharides in this process. These polymers activate host CD4+ T cells and promote the release of interleukin-17 (IL-17) and chemokines.[16] In addition, the capsule induces the release of the proinflammatory cytokines tumor necrosis factor-α (TNF-α) and IL-1β from peritoneal macrophages. These cytokines potentiate the increase of cell adhesion molecules such as intracellular adhesion molecule-1 (ICAM-1) on mesothelial cell surfaces, which in turn leads to an increase in the binding of neutrophils to these cells and initiates abscess formation.[17] The capsules of *B. fragilis* also facilitate binding of the organism to mesothelial cells lining the surface of the peritoneal cavity.

B. fragilis produces other virulence factors that allow it to predominate in disease. Although the lipopolysaccharide (LPS) of *B. fragilis* possesses little biologic activity, this organism synthesizes pili, fimbriae, and hemagglutinins that aid in attachment to host cell surfaces. In addition, *Bacteroides* species produce many enzymes and toxins that contribute to pathogenicity. Enzymes such as neuraminidase, protease, glycoside hydrolases, and superoxide dismutases are all produced by *B. fragilis*. Recent work has shown that this organism produces an enterotoxin with specific effects on host cells in vitro. This toxin, termed BFT, is a metalloprotease that is cytopathic for intestinal epithelial cells and induces fluid secretion and tissue damage in ligated intestinal loops of experimental animals. Strains of *B. fragilis* associated with diarrhea in children (termed enterotoxigenic *B. fragilis*, or ETBF) produce a heat-labile 20-kDa protein toxin. The BFT specifically cleaves the extracellular domain of E-cadherin, a glycoprotein found on the surface of eukaryotic cells.[18] However, clear epidemiologic associations of BFT-positive *B. fragilis* and clinical episodes of diarrhea are lacking.

P. gingivalis relies on a broad range of virulence factors to cause disease. This organism is a prominent etiologic agent in adult periodontitis. The progression of this disease is hypothesized to be related to the production by *P. gingivalis* of a variety of enzymes (particularly proteolytic enzymes such as gingipains), fimbriae, capsular polysaccharide, LPS, hemagglutinin, and hemolytic activity.[19] Recently, *P. gingivalis* has been shown to invade and replicate within host cells, a mechanism that may facilitate its spread. A class of trypsin-like cysteine proteases, termed gingipains, is a major virulence factor contributing to the tissue destruction that is the hallmark of periodontal disease.

The capsular polysaccharide of *P. gingivalis* is a potent virulence factor facilitating a spreading infection in mice greater than that seen with unencapsulated strains.[20] The LPS of *P. gingivalis* has potent proinflammatory activity and has been implicated in the initiation and development of periodontal disease.[21]

F. necrophorum causes numerous necrotic conditions (necrobacillosis) and human oral infections. Toxins such as leukotoxin, endotoxin, and hemolysin all have been implicated as virulence factors, with leukotoxin and endotoxin playing an important role in the pathogenesis of disease. *F. nucleatum* has been isolated frequently from cases of periodontitis and is a major contributor to gingival inflammation.[22] This organism coaggregates with other oral bacteria to promote attachment to plaque; in addition, it produces several adhesins that facilitate attachment. Both *F. nucleatum* and *F. necrophorum* produce a potent LPS that is responsible for the release of numerous proinflammatory cytokines and other inflammatory mediators.

Virulence factors associated with *Prevotella* species are poorly defined. The organisms' ability to interact with other anaerobes has been reported.[23] Among their prominent virulence traits is the production of proteases and metabolic products such as volatile fatty acids and amines. This group of organisms is particularly noted for secretion of IgA proteases. The degradation of IgA produced by mucosal surfaces

---

TABLE 241-3 Virulence Factors Associated with Pathogenic Anaerobes

B. fragilis	*Fusobacterium nucleatum*
Capsular polysaccharides	LPSs
Neuraminidase	Adhesins
Proteases	Proteases
Enterotoxin	Leukotoxin
Hemagglutinin	
	Prevotella spp.
Porphyromonas gingivalis	LPSs
Proteases (gingipains)	Proteases
LPSs	
Capsule	
Hemolysin	
Fusobacterium necrophorum	
Leukotoxin	
Hemolysin	
LPSs	
Phospholipase	
Proteases	

allows *Prevotella* to evade this first line of host defense. A recent study demonstrated that *P. intermedia* can invade oral epithelial cells and that antibody specific for fimbriae from this organism inhibits invasion.[24]

DIAGNOSIS OF ANAEROBIC INFECTIONS

Many anaerobic infections are diagnosed because it is suspected that these organisms are present. Anaerobes can be difficult to culture, and identification of these organisms can be expensive or even misleading in some cases. Certain factors can lead the clinician to surmise that an anaerobic infection exists. Infection at particular sites, such as those proximal to mucosal surfaces with indigenous anaerobic flora, is indicative, particularly in the gastrointestinal tract, the female genital tract, or the oral cavity. The presence of foul odor or gas is highly suggestive as well, although the absence of these factors does not rule out anaerobic infection. A patient's failure to respond to a particular course of antibiotics should raise the issue of whether untreated anaerobes are persisting at the infectious site.

Diagnosis of many anaerobic infections is usually done clinically and not by culture, particularly when the culture is expected to reveal a mixed infection that includes normal flora. However, when bacteremia is suspected or specimens are collected surgically from normally sterile sites, the culture can be very helpful.[25] In addition, culture may be useful for determining whether antimicrobial-resistant organisms such as the *B. fragilis* group are present.

When samples are cultured, it is imperative that they are properly collected and transported. Samples should be collected so as to avoid contamination by indigenous flora, particularly if the infected site is proximal to mucosal tissue rich in normal flora. Pus or infected tissue is preferable to swab specimens. Suitable commercially available anaerobic transport media should be employed at all times. Although many anaerobes are aerotolerant, exposure to oxygen, even for the briefest period, can interfere with culture of some organisms. Specimens should be processed as quickly as possible and handled appropriately in the clinical microbiology laboratory. Gram stains should be performed on specimens and compared with culture results. It is not uncommon for specimens to yield no growth on culture, but to show numerous organisms (both gram-positive and -negative) on Gram staining, which suggests that anaerobic organisms are present. Sterile pus may indicate anaerobic infection with failed collection or identification methods.

Selective and nonselective media should be used for culture. Nonselective media can include agar supplemented with blood, vitamin K_1, and hemin such as brain-heart infusion (BHI) or CDC anaerobe agar. *Brucella* agar, trypticase soy agar, or Schaedler agar can also be used. Selective media such as kanamycin-vancomycin laked blood agar or *Bacteroides* bile-esculin agar (which inhibits most other anaerobes and aerobes while allowing the *B. fragilis* group to grow) are useful in the primary isolation of pathogenic anaerobes.

TREATMENT OF ANAEROBIC INFECTIONS

The two major approaches to the treatment of anaerobic infections generally involve appropriate antimicrobial therapy and/or surgical management. Because anaerobic infections can cause severe tissue damage or result in abscess formation, surgery is often required for débridement of necrotic tissue, drainage, restoration of airspaces, resection, or maintenance of blood supply. Previously, surgery was uniformly required to achieve these goals. However, with the advent of computed tomography, magnetic resonance imaging, and ultrasound, some of these procedures can be performed percutaneously.

The antibiotics used to treat anaerobic infections should have activity against both aerobic and anaerobic organisms, as many of these infections are of mixed etiology. The selection of antibiotic regimens can usually be made empirically because the patterns of antimicrobial resistance are predictable (Tables 241-4 and 241-5). Antibiotics with the greatest activity against nearly all anaerobic bacteria include the carbapenems, β-lactam/β-lactamase inhibitor combinations, metronida-

TABLE 241-4 Antimicrobial Agents Effective Against Medically Important Gram-Negative Anaerobic Rods

<2% Resistance	<15% Resistance
Imipenem	Cefoxitin
Meropenem	Clindamycin
Metronidazole	High-dose antipseudomonal penicillins
Ticarcillin/clavulanic acid	
Piperacillin/tazobactam	
Chloramphenicol	
Ampicillin/sulbactam	

zole, and chloramphenicol (see Table 241-4). Some of the quinolones have shown good activity against anaerobes in the clinic; however, resistant strains have developed quickly against these agents.[26]

Selection of antibiotics for the treatment of suspected anaerobic infections is also influenced by the type of infection, the species of organisms usually present in such cases, and Gram-stain results. In many cases, such as intra-abdominal surgery, prophylactic antimicrobial therapy is given in order to prevent infection by facultative and anaerobic organisms present in the colon. Other selection factors include the need for bactericidal activity, penetration into compartmentalized organs (such as the brain), toxicity, and impact on normal flora.

Antibiotic susceptibility testing of anaerobic bacteria is a point of contention for clinicians and clinical microbiology laboratories. It is accepted that testing is important for patients with serious or prolonged infections or in cases in which antibiotics have not had an impact. Testing is also helpful in monitoring the activity of new drugs and recording current resistance patterns among anaerobic pathogens. Snydman and colleagues[27] showed that in vitro testing of antibiotics with activity against the *B. fragilis* group was predictive of clinical outcome in cases of anaerobic bacteria. However, this report notwithstanding, the selection of antibiotic regimens is still often done empirically with good results. Clinicians should make therapeutic decisions that cover the possibility that anaerobes are present at a given site when the type of infection (e.g., abscesses) or the location (e.g., contiguous colonized mucosa) is suggestive.

Antimicrobial agents that are effective against the medically important gram-negative anaerobes are shown in Table 241-4. Antibiotics that are active against the *B. fragilis* group, *Porphyromonas* spp., *Prevotella* spp., and *Fusobacterium* spp. can be divided into two major categories based on the degree of resistance they elicit in organisms.

The medically important *Bacteroides* spp. are typically resistant to penicillin. Treatment failure with penicillin or first-generation cephalosporins is common for infections that involve *B. fragilis;* however, several options exist (see Table 241-4) for treatment of these infections. Metronidazole is a drug of choice for the treatment of *Bacteroides* infections, as resistance is rarely reported. This antibiotic is well tolerated, reaches significant levels in serum, and achieves good penetration in abscesses. Metronidazole should be used in combination with other appropriate antibiotics to treat mixed infections because it is inactive against aerobic and facultative bacteria. Metronidizole is also not effective against *Actinomyces* spp. or

TABLE 241-5 Antimicrobial Agents to Which Medically Important Gram-Negative Anaerobic Rods Are Resistant

Variable Resistance	Resistance
Penicillin	Aminoglycosides
Cephalosporins	Quinolones
Tetracycline	Monobactams
Vancomycin	
Erythromycin	

Propionibacterium spp. Truly anaerobic peptostreptococci are usually susceptible to β-lactam/β-lactamase inhibitor antibiotics and metronidazole. Those that are resistant to metronidazole are usually microaerophilic.

Intra-abdominal infections caused by anaerobes should be treated with antibiotics with activity against the *Bacteroides* group. Antibiotics with activity against penicillin-resistant anaerobes have been used successfully to reduce serious complications of these infections in recent years. Treatment should include coverage for aerobic and facultative organisms that often complicate these infections. In addition, if the clinician suspects that gram-positive facultative organisms, such as enterococci, are present in an infection, therapeutic regimens should include ampicillin or vancomycin.

Antimicrobial agents that are variably or completely ineffective in the treatment of medically important gram-negative anaerobic infections are shown in Table 241-5. The failure of antibiotic therapy against an anaerobic infection should prompt consideration of surgical drainage or débridement of the infected site. In addition, the possibility of coinfection with a drug-resistant aerobic organism(s) should be considered. In these situations, an attempt to isolate the organisms should be made in order to determine antibiotic susceptibility.

ANTIBIOTIC RESISTANCE

Resistance to antibiotics by anaerobic bacteria has increased significantly in recent years.[27] Resistance has been observed for numerous antimicrobial agents, including clindamycin, cefotetan, cefoxitin, cefotaxime, and piperacillin. Recently, increased resistance has been seen even to agents that have traditionally been effective: drugs such as metronidazole, carbapenems, and the β-lactam/β-lactamase inhibitor combinations, in some cases, are reportedly less effective.[26]

β-Lactamase production is a mechanism of resistance for the *B. fragilis* group, some non-*B. fragilis* group *Bacteroides* spp., *Prevotella* spp., *Porphyromonas* spp., and *Fusobacterium* spp. Two distinct classes of β-lactamases have been described in *B. fragilis:* the active-site serine enzymes encoded by the *cepA* gene and the metallo-β-lactamases encoded by the *cfiA* gene. Any given *B. fragilis* strain contains only one of these β-lactamase-encoding genes, and taxonomic investigations have revealed that *cfiA*+ strains and *cepA*+ strains form two genotypically distinct groups. Although these groups cannot be differentiated phenotypically, *cfiA*+ strains exhibit a distinctive and homogeneous ribotype. It is now well accepted that the anaerobic flora of the gut is a major reservoir for genetic elements carrying antibiotic-resistance genes.[28]

REFERENCES

1. Tally FP, Stewart PR, Sutter VL, Rosenblatt JE. Oxygen tolerance of fresh clinical anaerobic bacteria. J Clin Microbiol. 1975;1:161-164.
2. Hentges DJ. The anaerobic microflora of the human body. Clin Infect Dis. 1993;16 (Suppl 4):S175-180.
3. Holdeman LV, Good IJ, Moore WE. Human fecal flora: variation in bacterial composition within individuals and a possible effect of emotional stress. Appl Environ Microbiol. 1976;31:359-375.
4. Shimada K, Bricknell KS, Finegold SM. Deconjugation of bile acids by intestinal bacteria: Review of literature and additional studies. J Infect Dis. 1969;119:73-81.
5. Onderdonk AB, Bartlett JG, Louie T, et al. Microbial synergy in experimental intra-abdominal abscess. Infect Immun. 1976;13:22-26.
6. Summanen PH, Jousimies-Somer H, Manley S, et al. *Bilophila wadsworthia* isolates from clinical specimens. Clin Infect Dis. 1995;20(Suppl 2):S210-S211.
7. Gorbach SL, Thadepalli H, Norsen J. Anaerobic microorganisms in intraabdominal infections. Springfield, IL: Charles C Thomas; 1974.
8. Polk BJ, Kasper DL. *Bacteroides fragilis* subspecies in clinical isolates. Ann Intern Med. 1977;86:567-571.
9. Sears CL, Myers LL, Lazenby A, Van Tassell RL. Enterotoxigenic *Bacteroides fragilis.* Clin Infect Dis. 1995;20(Suppl 2):S142-S148.
10. Sweet RL. Role of bacterial vaginosis in pelvic inflammatory disease. Clin Infect Dis. 1995;20(Suppl 2):S271-S275.
11. Aldridge KE, Ashcraft D, O'Brien M, Sanders CV. Bacteremia due to *Bacteroides fragilis* group: Distribution of species, beta-lactamase production, and antimicrobial susceptibility patterns. Antimicrob Agents Chemother. 2003;47:148-153.
12. Nichols RL. Intraabdominal infections: an overview. Rev Infect Dis. 1985;7:S709-S715.
13. Onderdonk AB, Kasper DL, Cisneros RL, Bartlett JG. The capsular polysaccharide of *Bacteroides fragilis* as a virulence factor: comparison of the pathogenic potential of encapsulated and unencapsulated strains. J Infect Dis. 1977;136:82-89.
14. Krinos CM, Coyne MJ, Weinacht KG, et al. Extensive surface diversity of a commensal microorganism by multiple DNA inversions. Nature. 2001;414:555-558.
15. Tzianabos AO, Onderdonk AB, Rosner B, et al. Structural features of polysaccharides that induce intra-abdominal abscesses. Science. 1993;262:416-419.
16. Chung DR, Kasper DL, Panzo RJ, et al. CD4+ T cells mediate abscess formation in intra-abdominal sepsis by an IL-17-dependent mechanism. J Immunol. 2003;170:1958-1963.
17. Gibson FC 3rd, Onderdonk AB, Kasper DL, Tzianabos AO. Cellular mechanism of intraabdominal abscess formation by *Bacteroides fragilis.* J Immunol. 1998;160:5000-5006.
18. Chambers FG, Koshy SS, Saidi RF, et al. *Bacteroides fragilis* toxin exhibits polar activity on monolayers of human intestinal epithelial cells (T84 cells) in vitro. Infect Immun. 1997;65:3561-3570.
19. Kantarci A, Van Dyke TE. Neutrophil-mediated host response to *Porphyromonas gingivalis.* J Int Acad Periodontol. 2002;4:119-125.
20. Laine ML, van Winkelhoff AJ. Virulence of six capsular serotypes of *Porphyromonas gingivalis* in a mouse model. Oral Microbiol Immunol. 1998;13:322-325.
21. Ogawa T, Asai Y, Hashimoto M, et al. Cell activation by *Porphyromonas gingivalis* lipid A molecule through Toll-like receptor 4- and myeloid differentiation factor 88-dependent signaling pathway. Int Immunol. 2002;14:1325-1332.
22. Roberts GL. Fusobacterial infections: an underestimated threat. Br J Biomed Sci. 2000;57:156-162.
23. Sugita N, Kimura A, Matsuki Y, et al. Activation of transcription factors and IL-8 expression in neutrophils stimulated with lipopolysaccharide from *Porphyromonas gingivalis.* Inflammation. 1998;22:253-267.
24. Dorn BR, Leung KL, Progulske-Fox A. Invasion of human oral epithelial cells by *Prevotella intermedia.* Infect Immun. 1998;66:6054-6057.
25. Nguyen MH, Yu VL, Morris AJ, et al. Antimicrobial resistance and clinical outcome of *Bacteroides* bacteremia: Findings of a multicenter prospective observational trial. Clin Infect Dis. 2000;30:870-876.
26. Vedantam G, Hecht DW. Antibiotics and anaerobes of gut origin. Curr Opin Microbiol. 2003;6:457-461.
27. Snydman DR, Jacobus NV, McDermott LA, et al. National survey on the susceptibility of *Bacteroides fragilis* group: report and analysis of trends for 1997-2000. Clin Infect Dis. 2002;35:S126-S134.
28. Whittle G, Shoemaker NB, Salyers AA. The role of *Bacteroides* conjugative transposons in the dissemination of antibiotic resistance genes. Cell Mol Life Sci. 2002;59:2044-2054.

Clostridium tetani (Tetanus)

THOMAS P. BLECK

HISTORY

Tetanus was well known to the ancients; descriptions by Egyptian and Greek physicians survive to the present. They recognized the frequent relationship between injuries and the subsequent development of fatal spasms. Gowers provided the quintessential description of tetanus in 1888:

> *Tetanus is a disease of the nervous system characterized by persistent tonic spasm, with violent brief exacerbations. The spasm almost always commences in the muscles of the neck and jaw, causing closure of the jaws (trismus, lockjaw), and involves the muscles of the trunk more than those of the limbs. It is always acute in onset, and a very large proportion of those affected die.[1]*

Nicolaier isolated a strychnine-like toxin from anaerobic soil bacteria in 1884[2]; 6 years later, Behring and Kitasato described active immunization with tetanus toxoid.[3] This latter discovery should have reduced tetanus to an historical curiosity, but we still fail to fulfill this promise.

EPIDEMIOLOGY

The global incidence of tetanus is thought to be about 1 million cases annually, or about 18 per 100,000 population. The U.S. Centers for Disease Control and Prevention receive reports of about 35 to 70 domestic cases per year[4,5]; this represents under-reporting of about 60%.[6] Data through 2000 are summarized in Figure 242-1. The majority of reported cases are in patients older than 60 years[7]; this is one of several indicators that waning immunity is an important risk factor,[8] and may be a particularly serious problem in older women.[9,10] Changes in patterns of immigration may increase the number of unimmunized or inadequately immunized patients presenting for care in developed countries.[11] Injection drug abuse places patients at risk for tetanus,[12] as do other potentially unsterile practices that allow inoculation of spores.[13]

In developing countries, mortality rates are as high as 28 per 100,000, while in North America the rate is less than 0.1 per 100,000.

Neonatal tetanus accounts for about half of the tetanus deaths in developing nations. In a study of neonatal mortality in Bangladesh, 112 of 330 deaths were attributed to tetanus.[14] The World Health Organization reported that Somalia had the highest rate in 1999, with 16.5 neonatal tetanus deaths per thousand live births.[15] Up to one third of infants with neonatal tetanus are born to mothers of a previously afflicted child, highlighting failure to immunize as a major cause of tetanus.[16] Immunization programs clearly decrease neonatal tetanus deaths,[17] and some recent evidence suggests progress in prevention.[18] Neonatal tetanus still occurs rarely in developed countries, usually in individuals who avoid standard practices of immunization and obstetric care.[19]

Acute injuries account for about 70% of U.S. cases, evenly divided between punctures and lacerations.[20] Other identifiable conditions are noted in 23%, leaving about 7% of cases without an apparent source. Other studies cite rates of cryptogenic tetanus as high as 23%.

CHARACTERISTICS OF *CLOSTRIDIUM TETANI*

Clostridium tetani is an obligately anaerobic bacillus that is gram positive in fresh cultures but that may have variable staining in older cultures or tissue samples.[21] The complete genome of the organism has been sequenced, and its products recently compared with other

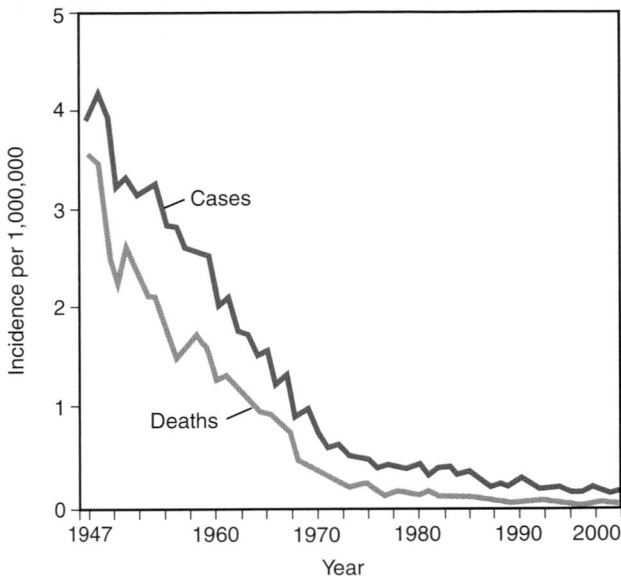

FIGURE 242-1. Reported cases and deaths from tetanus in the United States, 1947-2000. *(Data from Pascual FB, McGinley EL, Zanardi LR, et al. Tetanus surveillance—United States, 1998-2000. Centers for Disease Control and Prevention. Surveillance Summaries, June 20, 2003. MMWR Morb Mortal Wkly Rep. 2003:52.)*

Clostridia.[22] During growth, the bacilli possess abundant flagellae and are sluggishly motile. Two toxins, *tetanospasmin* (commonly called *tetanus toxin*) and tetanolysin, are produced during this phase. Tetanospasmin is encoded on a plasmid that is present in all toxigenic strains.[23] Tetanolysin is of uncertain importance in the pathogenesis of tetanus. Mature organisms lose their flagellae and develop a terminal spore, and begin to resemble a squash racquet (Fig. 242-2).[24] The spores are extremely stable in the environment, retaining the ability to germinate and cause disease indefinitely. They withstand exposure to

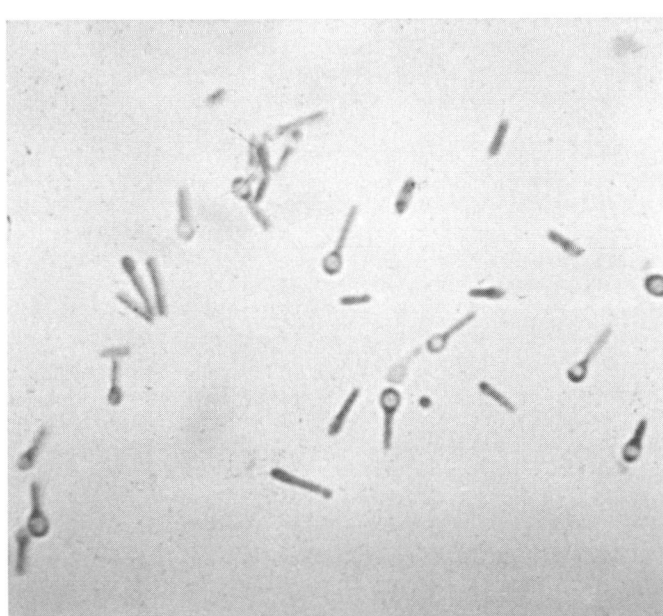

FIGURE 242-2. Gram stain of a culture of *C. tetani*. *(From Bleck TP. Tetanus. In: Scheld WM, Whitley RJ, Durack DT, eds. Infections of the Central Nervous System. New York: Raven Press; 1991:603-624, with permission. Courtesy of Paul C. Schrechenberger, PhD and Alex Kuritza, PhD.)*

ethanol, phenol, or formalin, but can be rendered noninfectious by iodine, glutaraldehyde, hydrogen peroxide, or autoclaving at 121° C and 103 kPa (15 psi) for 15 minutes. Growth in culture is optimal at 37° C under strictly anaerobic conditions, but culture results are of no diagnostic value. Antibiotic sensitivity is discussed later.

PATHOGENESIS

The clostridial toxins that produce both tetanus and botulism are very similar in structure and function despite the almost diametrically opposed clinical manifestations of the diseases. These toxins are zinc-dependent matrix metalloproteinases, a category encompassing a diverse group of enzymes ranging from normal human cellular constituents necessary for cellular remodeling,[25] through determinants of neoplastic cell function,[26] to exotoxins of other microorganisms such as *Bacteroides fragilis*.[27] *Tetanospasmin* is synthesized as a single 151-kDa chain that is cleaved extracellularly by a bacterial protease into a 100-kDa heavy chain and a 50-kDa light chain (fragment A), which remain connected by a disulfide bridge.[28] The heavy chain can be further divided into fragments B and C by pepsin. The heavy chain appears to mediate binding to cell surface receptors and transport proteins, while the light chain produces the presynaptic inhibition of transmitter release that produces clinical tetanus. The nature of the receptor to which tetanospasmin binds, previously thought to be a ganglioside, remains debated.[29] The toxin enters the nervous system primarily via the presynaptic terminals of lower motor neurons, where it can produce local failure of neuromuscular transmission. It then exploits the retrograde axonal transport system, and is carried to the cell bodies of these neurons in the brain stem and spinal cord, where it expresses its major pathogenic action.[30]

Once the toxin enters the central nervous system, it diffuses to the terminals of inhibitory cells, including both local glycinergic interneurons and descending γ-aminobutyric acid-ergic (GABAergic) neurons from the brain stem. The toxin degrades synaptobrevin, a protein required for docking of neurotransmitter vesicles with their release site on the presynaptic membrane.[31] By preventing transmitter release from these cells, tetanospasmin leaves the motor neurons without inhibition. This produces muscular rigidity by raising the resting firing rate of motor neurons, and also generates spasms by failing to limit reflex responses to afferent stimuli. Excitatory transmitter release in the spinal cord can also be impaired, but the toxin appears to have greater affinity for the inhibitory systems. The autonomic nervous system is affected as well; this is predominantly manifested as a hypersympathetic state induced by failure to inhibit adrenal release of catecholamines.

Toxin binding appears to be an irreversible event. At the neuromuscular junction, initial recovery from botulism depends on sprouting a new axon terminal; this is probably the case at other affected synapses as well. Later, the new synapses are removed when the original ones reestablish their connections.[32]

CLINICAL MANIFESTATIONS

Tetanus is classically divided into four clinical types: *generalized, localized, cephalic,* and *neonatal*. These are valuable diagnostic and prognostic distinctions, but reflect host factors and the site of inoculation rather than differences in toxin action. Terms describing the initial stages of tetanus include the *incubation period* (time from inoculation to the first symptom) and the *period of onset* (time from the first symptom to the first generalized spasm). The shorter these periods are, the worse the prognosis is.[33] Various rating scales are available.[34] Certain portals of entry (e.g., compound fractures) are associated with poorer prognoses. Tetanus may be particularly severe in narcotics addicts, for unknown reasons.[35]

Generalized tetanus is the most commonly recognized form, and often begins with *trismus* ("lockjaw"; masseter rigidity) and a *risus sardonicus* (increased tone in the orbicularis oris) (Fig. 242-3). Abdominal rigidity may also be present. The *generalized spasm* resembles decorticate posturing, and consists of opisthotonic posturing

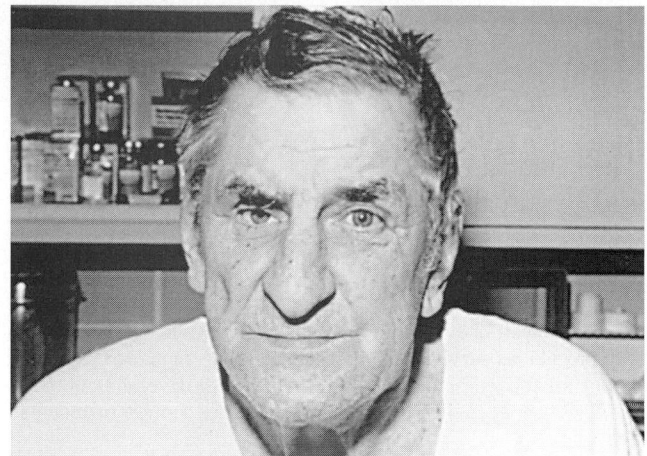

A

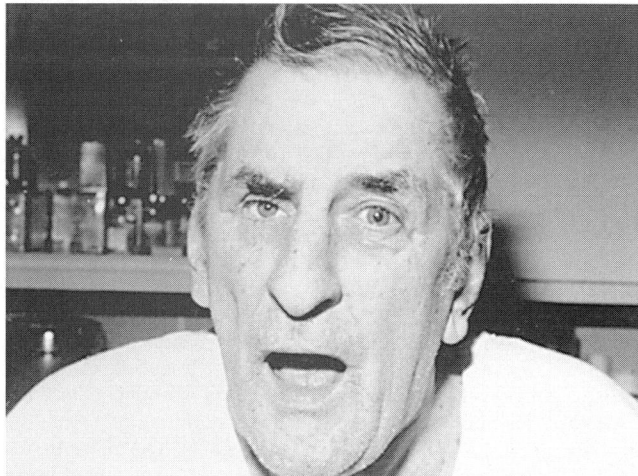

B

FIGURE 242-3. A, *Risus sardonicus. Note the straightened upper lip at rest.* **B,** *Trismus. The patient is opening his mouth as fully as possible. (From Bleck TP. Tetanus. In: Scheld WM, Whitley RJ, Durack DT, eds. Infections of the Central Nervous System. New York: Raven Press; 1991:603-624, with permission.)*

with flexion of the arms and extension of the legs (Fig. 242-4). The patient does not lose consciousness, and experiences severe pain during each spasm. The spasms are often triggered by sensory stimuli. During the spasm, the upper airway can be obstructed, or the diaphragm may participate in the general muscular contraction. Either of these compromise respiration, and even the first such spasm may be fatal. In the modern era of intensive care, however, the respiratory problems are easily managed, and autonomic dysfunction, usually occurring after several days of symptoms, has emerged as the leading cause of death.[36]

The illness can progress for about 2 weeks, reflecting the time required to complete the transport of toxin, which is already intra-axonal when antitoxin treatment is given. The severity of illness may be decreased by partial immunity.[37] Recovery takes an additional month, and is complete unless complications supervene. Lower motor neuron dysfunction may not be apparent until spasms remit, and recovery from this deficit in neuromuscular transmission may take additional weeks.[38] Recurrent tetanus may occur if the patient does not receive active immunization, as the amount of toxin produced is inadequate to induce immunity.[39]

Localized tetanus involves rigidity of the muscles associated with the site of spore inoculation. This may be mild and persistent, and often resolves spontaneously. Lower motor neuron dysfunction (weak

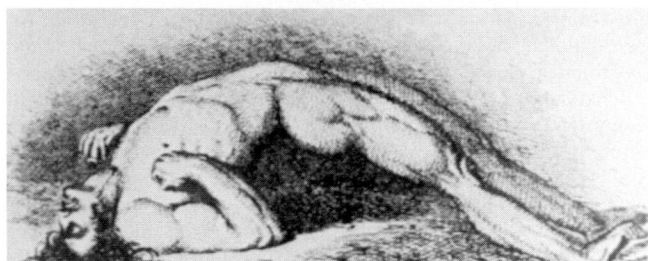

FIGURE 242-4. Opisthotonus. *(From Bell C. Essays on the Anatomy and Physiology of Expression. 2nd ed. London: J. Murray; 1824.)*

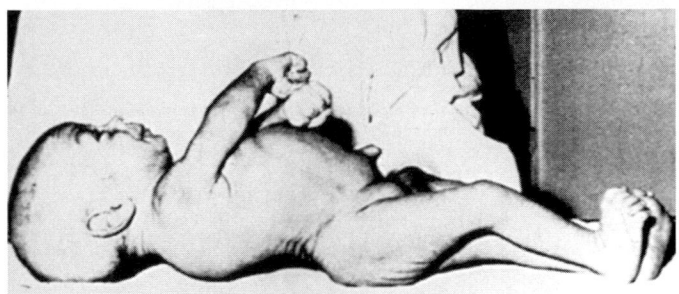

FIGURE 242-6. Neonatal tetanus. *(From Veronesi R, Focaccia R. The clinical picture. In: Veronesi R, ed. Tetanus: Important New Concepts. Amsterdam: Excerpta Medica; 1981:183-206, with permission.)*

ness and diminished muscle tone) is often present in the most involved muscle. This chronic form of the disease probably reflects partial immunity to tetanospasmin.[40] However, localized tetanus is more commonly a prodrome of generalized tetanus, which occurs when enough toxin gains access to the central nervous system.

Cephalic tetanus is a special form of localized disease affecting the cranial nerve musculature, almost always following an apparent head wound (Fig. 242-5). Although earlier reports linked cephalic tetanus to a poor prognosis, more recent studies have revealed many milder cases. A lower motor neuron lesion, frequently producing facial nerve weakness, is often apparent.[41] Extraocular muscle involvement is occasionally noted.

Neonatal tetanus (Fig. 242-6) follows infection of the umbilical stump, most commonly caused by a failure of aseptic technique if mothers are inadequately immunized.[42] Cultural practices may also contribute.[43] The condition usually presents with generalized weak-

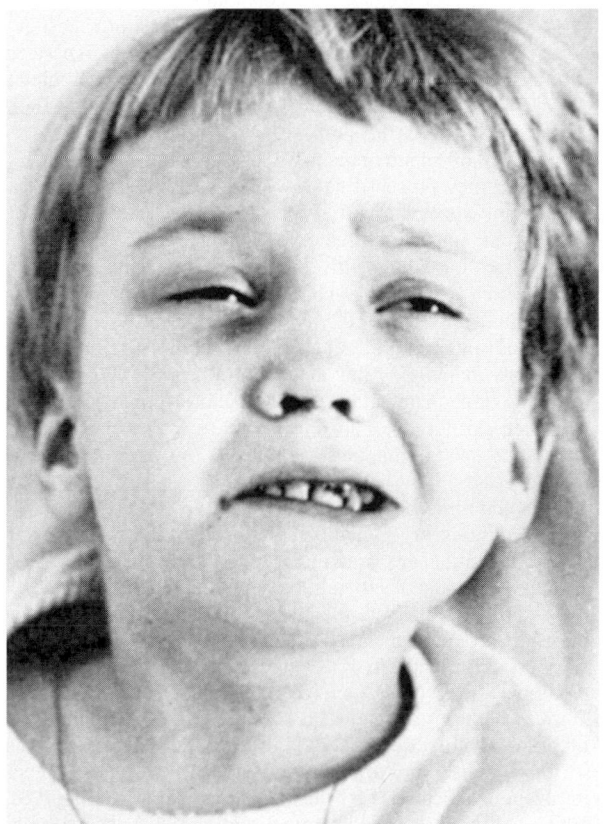

FIGURE 242-5. Cephalic tetanus. Right facial paresis is present in addition to the grimace. *(From Veronesi R, Focaccia R. The clinical picture. In: Veronesi R, ed. Tetanus: Important New Concepts. Amsterdam: Excerpta Medica; 1981:183-206, with permission.)*

ness and failure to nurse; rigidity and spasms occur later. The mortality rate exceeds 90%, and developmental delays are common among survivors.[44] Poor prognostic factors include age less than 10 days, symptoms for fewer than 5 days before presentation to hospital, and the presence of risus sardonicus or fever.[45] Apnea is the leading cause of death among neonatal tetanus patients in the first week of life, and sepsis in the second week.[46] Bacterial infection of the umbilical stump leads to sepsis in almost half of infants with neonatal tetanus, which contributes to the substantial mortality despite treatment.[47]

DIAGNOSIS

Tetanus is diagnosed by clinical observation, and has a limited differential diagnosis. Laboratory testing cannot confirm or exclude the condition, and is primarily useful for excluding intoxications that may mimic tetanus. Electromyographic studies are occasionally useful in questionable cases. Such testing becomes more important when no portal of entry is apparent. Antitetanus antibodies are undetectable in the majority of tetanus patients, but many reports document the disease in patients with antibody levels above the commonly cited "protective" concentration of 0.01 IU/L.[48] Rare patients apparently develop antibodies that are not protective.[49]

Attempts to culture *C. tetani* from wounds are not useful in diagnosis, as (1) even carefully performed anaerobic cultures are frequently negative; (2) a positive culture does not indicate whether the organism contains the toxin-producing plasmid; and (3) a positive culture may be present without disease in patients with adequate immunity.[50]

Strychnine poisoning, in which glycine is antagonized, is the only condition that truly mimics tetanus; toxicologic studies of serum and urine should be performed when tetanus is suspected, and tetanus should be considered even if strychnine poisoning appears likely. Because the initial treatment of tetanus and strychnine intoxication are similar, therapy is instituted before the assay results are available. Dystonic reactions to neuroleptic drugs or other central dopamine antagonists may be confused with the neck stiffness of tetanus, but the posture of patients with dystonic reactions almost always involves lateral head turning, which is rare in tetanus. Treatment with anticholinergic agents (benztropine or diphenhydramine) is rapidly effective against dystonic reactions. Dental infections may produce trismus, and should be sought, but do not cause the other manifestations of tetanus.

TREATMENT

The patient with tetanus requires simultaneous attention to several concerns. Attention to the airway and to ventilation is paramount at the time of presentation, but the other aspects of care, especially passive immunization, must be pursued as soon as the respiratory system is secure. Table 242-1 presents a suggested management protocol.

Tetanic spasms sometimes demand that the airway be secured before other lines of therapy are possible. An orotracheal tube can be

TABLE 242-1 Suggested Management Protocol for Generalized Tetanus

I. Diagnosis and Stabilization: First Hour After Presentation
   A. Assess airway and ventilation. If necessary, perform endotracheal intubation using benzodiazepine sedation and neuromuscular blockade (e.g., vecuronium 0.1 mg/kg).
   B. Obtain samples for antitoxin level, strychnine and dopamine antagonist assays, electrolytes, blood urea nitrogen, creatinine, creatine kinase, and urinary myoglobin determination.
   C. Determine the portal of entry, incubation period, period of onset, and immunization history.
   D. Administer benztropine (1 to 2 mg, intravenously) or diphenhydramine (50 mg, intravenously) to rule out a dystonic reaction to a dopamine blocking agent.
   E. Administer a benzodiazepine intravenously (diazepam in 5-mg increments, or lorazepam in 2-mg increments) to control spasm and decrease rigidity. Initially, employ a dose that is adequate to produce sedation and minimize reflex spasms. If this dose compromises the airway or ventilation, intubate using a short-acting neuromuscular blocking agent. Transfer the patient to a quiet, darkened area of the intensive care unit.

II. Early Management Phase: First 24 Hours
   A. Administer human tetanus immunoglobulin (HTIG), 500 units, intramuscularly; as an alternative, consider intravenous pooled immune globulin (see text).
   B. At a different site, administer adsorbed tetanus toxoid such as tetanus-diphtheria vaccine (0.5 mL) or diphtheria-pertussis-tetanus vaccine (0.5 mL), as appropriate for age, intramuscularly. Adsorbed tetanus toxoid without diphtheria toxoid is available for patients with a history of reaction to diphtheria toxoid; otherwise, the correct combination for the patient's age should be employed.
   C. Begin metronidazole 500 mg, intravenously, every 6 hr, for 7-10 days.
   D. Perform a tracheostomy after placement of an endotracheal tube and under neuromuscular blockade if spasms produce any degree of airway compromise.
   E. Débride any wounds as indicated for their own management.
   F. Place a soft, small-bore nasal feeding tube or a central venous hyperalimentation catheter, and begin feeding. Patients receiving total parental nutrition should also be given parenteral H_2 blockade or other gastric protection.
   G. Administer benzodiazepines as required to control spasms and produce sedation. If adequate control is not achieved, institute long-term neuromuscular blockade (e.g., vecuronium 6-8 mg/hr); continue benzodiazepines for sedation with intermittent electroencephalographic monitoring to ensure somnolence. Neuromuscular junction blockade should be discontinued daily to assess the patient's physical examination and to decrease the possibility of excessive accumulation of the blocking agent.

III. Intermediate Management Phase: The Next 2-3 Weeks
   A. Treat sympathetic hyperactivity with labetalol (0.25-1.0 mg/min as needed for blood pressure control) or morphine (0.5-1.0 mg/kg/hr by continuous infusion; see text for other recommendations). Consider epidural blockade with a local anesthetic. Avoid diuretics for blood pressure control, because volume depletion will worsen autonomic instability.
   B. If hypotension is present, initiate saline resuscitation. Place a pulmonary artery catheter and an arterial line, and administer fluids, dopamine, or norepinephrine as indicated.
   C. Sustained bradycardia usually requires a pacemaker. Atropine or isoproterenol may be useful during pacemaker placement.
   D. Begin prophylactic heparin.
   E. Use a flotation bed, if possible, to prevent skin breakdown and peroneal nerve palsies. Otherwise, ensure frequent turning and employ antirotation boots.
   F. Maintain benzodiazepines until neuromuscular blockade, if employed, has been terminated, and the severity of spasms has diminished substantially. Then taper the benzodiazepine dose over 14-21 days.
   G. Begin rehabilitation planning.

IV. Convalescent Stage: 2-6 Weeks
   A. When spasms are no longer present, begin physical therapy. Many patients require supportive psychotherapy.
   B. Before discharge, administer another dose of tetanus-diphtheria vaccine or diphtheria-pertussis-tetanus vaccine.
   C. Schedule a third dose of toxoid to be given 4 weeks after the second.

Adapted from Bleck TP. Tetanus. In: Scheld WM, Whitley RJ, Durack DT, eds. Infections of the Central Nervous System. New York: Raven Press; 1991:603-624.

passed under sedation and neuromuscular junction blockade; a feeding tube should be placed at the same time. Because the endotracheal tube may stimulate spasms, an early tracheostomy may be beneficial.[51]

Benzodiazepines have emerged as the mainstay of symptomatic therapy for tetanus.[52] These drugs are $GABA_A$ agonists, and thereby indirectly antagonize the effect of the toxin. They do not restore glycinergic inhibition. The patient should be kept free of spasms, and may benefit from the amnestic effects of the drugs as well. Diazepam has been studied most intensively, but lorazepam or midazolam appear equally effective. Tetanus patients have unusually high tolerance for the sedating effect of these agents, and commonly remain alert at doses normally expected to produce anesthesia.[53]

The intravenous formulations of both diazepam and lorazepam contain propylene glycol; at the doses required to control generalized tetanus, this vehicle may produce lactic acidosis.[54] Nasogastric delivery of these agents is often possible, but some tetanus patients develop gastrointestinal motility disorders and do not absorb drugs well. Intravenous midazolam (5 to 15 mg/hour or more) is effective and does not contain propylene glycol, but must be given as a continuous infusion because of its brief half-time.[55] Propofol infusion is also effective,[56] but is currently very expensive, and the amount necessary to control symptoms may exceed the patient's tolerance of the lipid vehicle. When the symptoms of tetanus subside, these agents must be tapered over at least 2 weeks to prevent withdrawal. Intrathecal baclofen is also effective in controlling tetanus, but has no clear advantage over benzodiazepines. Neuroleptic agents and barbiturates, previously used for tetanus, are inferior for this indication and should not be used. Magnesium infusion may emerge as a useful therapeutic technique in generalized tetanus.[57]

Rare patients cannot be adequately controlled with benzodiazepines alone; neuromuscular junction blockade is then indicated, with the caveat that sedation is still required for psychologic reasons. All of the available drugs have side effects, including the potential for prolonged effect after the drug is discontinued. Vecuronium (by continuous infusion) or pancuronium (by intermittent injection) are adequate choices. These agents should be stopped at least once daily to assess the patient's progress, and to observe for possible complications. Electroencephalographic monitoring is a useful adjunct for this purpose.[58]

The majority of tetanus patients will still have the portal of entry apparent when they present. If the wound itself requires surgical attention, this may be performed after spasms are controlled. However, the course of tetanus is not affected by wound débridement.

Passive immunization with human tetanus immune globulin (HTIG) shortens the course of tetanus and may lessen its severity. A dose of 500 units appears as effective as larger doses.[59] There had been no apparent advantage to intrathecal HTIG administration,[60] although recent data are challenging this idea.[61] Intrathecal HTIG was ineffective in a study of neonatal tetanus.[62] Pooled intravenous immune globulin has been proposed as an alternative to HTIG,[63] although this should be approached with caution.[64] Active immunization must also be initiated.

The role of antimicrobial therapy in tetanus remains debated. The in vitro susceptibilities of *C. tetani* include metronidazole, penicillins, cephalosporins, imipenem, macrolides, and tetracycline. A study comparing oral metronidazole to intramuscular penicillin showed better survival, shorter hospitalization, and less progression of disease in the metronidazole group.[65] This may reflect a true advantage of metronidazole over penicillin, but it more likely corresponds to a negative effect of penicillin, a known GABA antagonist. Topical antibiotic application to the umbilical stump appears to reduce the risk of neonatal tetanus.[8]

Autonomic dysfunction generally reflects excessive catecholamine release, and may respond to combined α- and β-adrenergic blockade with intravenous labetalol.[66] β-Blockade alone is rarely employed, because the resulting unopposed α effect may produce severe hypertension. If β-blockade is chosen, the short-acting agent esmolol should be employed.[67] Other approaches to hypertension include morphine infusion,[68] magnesium sulfate infusion,[69] and epidural blockade of the renal nerves.[70] Hypotension is less common, but if present may require norepinephrine infusion. Myocardial dysfunction is also common,[71] and may represent a further reflection of catecholamine excess.[72]

Nutritional support should be started as soon as the patient is stable. The volume of enteral feeding needed to meet the exceptionally high caloric and protein requirements of these patients may exceed the capacity of the gastrointestinal system.

The mortality rate in mild and moderate tetanus at present is about 6%; for severe tetanus, it may reach as high as 60%, even in expert centers.[73] A well-designed protocol for the critical care of tetanus patients can substantially reduce morbidity and mortality.[74] Among adults, age has very little effect on mortality, with octogenarians and nonagenarians faring as well as middle-aged patients.[75] Tetanus survivors often have serious psychologic problems related to the disease and its treatment that persist after recovery, and that may require psychotherapy.[76]

PROPHYLAXIS

Tetanus is preventable in almost all patients, leading to its description as the "inexcusable disease."[77] A series of three monthly intramuscular injections of alum-adsorbed tetanus toxoid provides almost complete immunity for at least 5 years (see Chapter 319). Patients younger than 7 years of age should receive combined diphtheria-tetanus-pertussis vaccine, and other patients combined diphtheria-tetanus vaccine. Routine booster injections are indicated every 10 years; more frequent administration may increase the risk of a reaction. The Advisory Committee on Immunization Practices in the United States recommends visits at age 11 to 12 years and age 50 years for health care providers to review vaccination histories and administer any needed vaccine.[78] Toxoid vaccination remains the standard; DNA-based vaccination is less efficacious.[79]

Older people may have waning tetanus immunity, related to either changes in immune function due to age or to a longer period since initial immunization.[80,81]

Some patients with humoral immune deficiencies may not respond adequately to toxoid injection[82]; such patients should receive passive immunization for tetanus-prone injuries regardless of the period since the last booster. Approximately half of patients lose tetanus immunity after chemotherapy for leukemia or lymphoma.[83] Patients who have undergone bone marrow or stem cell transplantation require revaccination after the procedure[84]; two doses (given at 12 and 24 months post-transplant) are probably sufficient.[85] Antibody production by the transplanted immune cells may play a minor role in subsequent host immunity.[86] Most young patients with human immunodeficiency virus (HIV) infection appear to retain antitetanus antibody production if their primary immunization series was completed before they acquired HIV[87]; however, only a minority will respond adequately to booster immunization.[88] Vitamin A deficiency interferes with the response to tetanus toxoid.[89]

Although a full series of maternal immunizations is ideal, even one or two doses of tetanus toxoid confers substantial protection against neonatal tetanus.[90] Tetanus occurred in infants of women immunized with toxoid later shown to be devoid of potency; this disconcerting report underscores the need for quality control in toxoid production.[5] Application of topical antimicrobial agents to the umbilical cord stump markedly decreases the incidence of neonatal tetanus when maternal immunization is insufficient.[91]

Although any wound may be inoculated with tetanus spores, some types of injury are more frequently associated with tetanus and are therefore deemed *tetanus-prone*. These include wounds that are contaminated with dirt, saliva, or feces; puncture wounds, including unsterile injections; missile injuries; burns; frostbite; avulsions; and crush injuries. Patients with these wounds who have not received adequate active immunization in the past 5 years, or in whom immunodeficiency is suspected, should receive passive immunization with HTIG (250 to 500 IU, intramuscularly) in addition to active immunization.[92]

Mild reactions to tetanus toxoid (e.g., local tenderness, edema, low-grade fever) are common. More severe reactions are rare; some

are actually caused by hypersensitivity to the preservative thiomersal.[93] Although there have been reports suggesting a connection of tetanus immunization with the Guillain-Barré syndrome, a careful epidemiologic analysis did not confirm such an association.[94]

REFERENCES

1. Gowers WR. A manual of diseases of the nervous system. Philadelphia: Blackiston, 1888.
2. Nicolaier A. Üeber infectiösen tetanus. Dtsch Med Wochenschr. 1884;10:842-844.
3. Behring E, Kitasato S. Üeber das zustandekommen der diphtherie-immunität und der tetanus-immunität bei thieren. Dtsch Med Wochenschr. 1890;16:1113-1114.
4. Pascual FB, McGinley EL, Zanardi LR, et al. Tetanus surveillance—United States, 1998-2000. Centers for Disease Control and Prevention. Surveillance Summaries, June 20, 2003. MMWR Morb Mortal Wkly Rep. 2003;52.
5. Centers for Disease Control. Summary of notifiable disease, 2001. MMWR Morb Mortal Wkly Rep. 2003;50:80.
6. Sutter RW, Cochi SL, Brink EW, Sirotkin BI. Assessment of vital statistics and surveillance data for monitoring tetanus mortality, United States, 1979-1984. Am J Epidemiol. 1990;131:132-142.
7. Gergen PJ, McQuillan GM, Kiely M, et al. A population-based serologic survey of immunity to tetanus in the United States. N Engl J Med. 1995;332:761-766.
8. Richardson JP, Knight AL. The prevention of tetanus in the elderly. Arch Intern Med. 1991;151:1712-1717.
9. Horton E, Singer C, Kozarsky P, et al. Status of immunity to tetanus, measles, mumps, rubella, and polio among U.S. travelers. Ann Intern Med. 1991;115:32-33.
10. Böttiger M, Gustavsson O, Svensson Å. Immunity to tetanus, diphtheria and poliomyelitis in the adult population of Sweden in 1991. Int J Epidemiol. 1998;27:916-925.
11. Henderson SO, Mody T, Groth DE, et al. The presentation of tetanus in an emergency department. J Emerg Med. 1998;16:705-708.
12. Talan DA, Moran GJ. Tetanus among injecting-drug users—California, 1997. Ann Emerg Med. 1998;32:385-386.
13. O'Malley CD, Smith N, Braun R, Prevots DR. Tetanus associated with body piercing. Clin Infect Dis. 1998;27:1343-1344.
14. Hlady WG, Bennett JV, Samadi AR, et al. Neonatal tetanus in Rural Bangladesh: Risk factors and toxoid efficacy. Am J Publ Hlth. 1992;82:1365-1369.
15. *www.who.int/vaccines-documents/DocsPDF02/www692.pdf*
16. Traverso HP, Kamil S, Rahim H, et al. A reassessment of risk factors for neonatal tetanus. Bull WHO. 1991;69:573-579.
17. Bjerregaard P, Steinglass R, Mutie DM, et al. Neonatal tetanus mortality in coastal Kenya: A community survey. Int J Epidemiol. 1993;22:163-169.
18. Hodges M, Williams RA. Registered infant and under-five deaths in Freetown, Sierra Leone from 1987-1991 and a comparison with 1969-1979. West Afr J Med. 1998;17:95-98.
19. Neonatal tetanus—Montana, 1998. MMWR Morb Mortal Wkly Rep. 1998;47:928-930.
20. Bleck TP. Tetanus: Dealing with the continuing clinical challenge. J Crit Illness. 1987;2:41-52.
21. Cato EP, George WL, Finegold SM. Genus Clostridium praemozski 1880, 23AL. In: Smeath PHA, Mair NS, Sharpe ME, Holt JG, eds. Bergey's Manual of Systematic Bacteriology, v. 2. Baltimore: Williams & Wilkins; 1986:1141-1200.
22. Bruggemann H, Baumer S, Fricke WF, et al. The genome sequence of *Clostridium tetani*, the causative agent of tetanus disease. Proc Natl Acad Sci USA. 2003;100:1316-1321.
23. Eisel U, Jarausch W, Goretzki K, et al. Tetanus toxin: Primary structure, expression in E. coli, and homology with botulinum toxins. EMBO J. 1986;5:2495-2502.
24. Hoeniger JFM, Tauschel HD. Sequence of structural changes in cultures of *Clostridium tetani* grown on a solid medium. J Med Microbiol. 1974;7:425-432.
25. Geisler R, Lichtinghagen R, Boker KH, Veh RW. Differential distribution of five members of the matrix metalloproteinase family and one inhibitor (TIMP-1) in human liver and skin. Cell Tissue Res. 1997;289:173-183.
26. Rooprai HK, Van Meter T, Rucklidge GJ, et al. Comparative analysis of matrix metalloproteinases by immunocytochemistry, immunohistochemistry and zymography in human primary brain tumours. Int J Oncol. 1998;13:1153-1157.
27. Wu S, Lim KC, Huang J, et al. Bacteroides fragilis enterotoxin cleaves the zonula adherens protein, E-cadherin. Proc Natl Acad Sci USA. 1998;95:14979-14984.
28. Matsuda M. The structure of tetanus toxin. In: Simpson LL, ed. Botulinum Neurotoxin and Tetanus Toxin. San Diego: Academic Press; 1989:69-92.
29. Middlebrook JL. Cell surface receptors for protein toxins. In: Simpson LL, ed. Botulinum Neurotoxin and Tetanus Toxin. San Diego: Academic Press; 1989:95-119.
30. Bleck TP, Brauner JS. Tetanus. In Scheld WM, Whitley RJ, Durack DT, eds. Infections of the Central Nervous System. 2nd ed. New York: Raven Press; 1997:629-653.
31. Cornille F, Martin L, Lenoir C, et al. Cooperative exosite-dependent cleavage of synaptobrevin by tetanus toxin light chain. J Biol Chem. 1997;272:3459-3464.
32. Meunier FA, Schiavo G, Molgo J. Botulinum neurotoxins: From paralysis to recovery of functional neuromuscular transmission. J Physiol Paris. 2002;96:105-113.
33. Veronesi R Focaccia R. The clinical picture. In: Veronesi R, ed. Tetanus: Important New Concepts. Amsterdam: Excerpta Medica; 1981:183-206.
34. Habermann E. Tetanus. In: Vinken PJ, Bruyn GW, eds. Handbook of Clinical Neurology, v. 33. Amsterdam: North-Holland; 1978:491-547.
35. Cherubin CE. Clinical severity of tetanus in narcotic addicts in New York City. Arch Intern Med. 1968;121:156-158.
36. Edmondson RS, Flowers MWW. Intensive care in tetanus: Management, complications, and mortality in 100 patients. Br Med J. 1979;1401-1404.

37. Luisto M, Iivanainen M. Tetanus of immunized children. Dev Med Child Neurol. 1993;35:351-355.
38. Bleck TP, Calderelli DD. Vocal cord paralysis complicating tetanus. Neurology. 1983;33 (Suppl 2):140.
39. Spenney J, Lamb RN, Cobbs CG. Recurrent tetanus. South Med J. 1971;64:859.
40. Risk WS, Bosch EP, Kimura J, et al. Chronic tetanus: Clinical report and histochemistry of muscle. Muscle Nerve. 1981;4:363-366.
41. Mayo J, Berciano J. Cephalic tetanus presenting with Bell's palsy. J Neurol Neurosurg Psychiatry. 1985;48:290.
42. Schofield FD, Tucker VM, Westbrook GR. Neonatal tetanus in New Guinea: Effect of active immunization in pregnancy. Br Med J. 1961:2:785-789.
43. Traverso H, Bennett JV, Kahn AJ, et al. Ghee application to the umbilical cord: A risk factor for neonatal tetanus. Lancet. 1989;1:486-488.
44. Anlar B, Yalaz K, Dizmen R. Long-term prognosis after neonatal tetanus. Dev Med Child Neurol. 1989;31:76-80.
45. Gürses N, Aydin M. Factors affecting prognosis of neonatal tetanus. Scand J Infect Dis. 1993;25:353-355.
46. Kurtoglu S, Caksen H, Ozturk A, et al. A review of 207 newborns with tetanus. JPMA J Pak Med Assoc. 1998;48:93-98.
47. Egri-Okwaji MT, Iroha EO, Kesah CN, Odugbemi TO. Bacteria causing septicaemia in neonates with tetanus. West Afr J Med. 1998;17:136-139.
48. Goulon M, Girard O, Grosbuis S, et al. Les corps antitétaniques. Nouv Presse Med. 1972;1:3049-3050.
49. Crone NE, Reder AT. Severe tetanus in immunized patients with high anti-tetanus titers. Neurology 1992;42:761-764.
50. Bleck TP. Clinical aspects of tetanus. In: Simpson LL, ed. Botulinum Neurotoxin and Tetanus Toxin. New York: Academic Press, 1989;379-398.
51. Mukherjee DK. Tetanus and tracheostomy. Ann Otol. 1977;86:67-72.
52. Vassa T, Yajnik VH, Joshi KR, et al. Comparative clinical trial of diazepam with other conventional drugs in tetanus. Postgrad Med J. 1874;50:755-758.
53. Bleck TP. Tetanus. Dis Month. 1991;37:547-603.
54. Kapoor W, Carey P, Karpf M. Induction of lactic acidosis with intravenous diazepam in a patient with tetanus. Arch Intern Med. 1981;141:944-945.
55. Orko R, Rosenberg PH, Himberg JJ. Intravenous infusion of midazolam, propofol and vecuronium in a patient with sever tetanus. Acta Anaesthiol Scand. 1988;32:590-592.
56. Borgeat A, Dessibourg C, Rochani M, Suter PM. Sedation by propofol in tetanus—is it a muscular relaxant? Intens Care Med. 1991;17:427-429.
57. Attygalle D, Rodrigo N. Magnesium sulphate for control of spasms in severe tetanus. Can we avoid sedation and artificial ventilation? Anaesthesia. 1997;52:956-962.
58. Luisto M, Seppäläinen A-M. Electroencephalography in tetanus. Acta Neurol Scand. 1989;80:157-161.
59. Blake PA, Feldman RA, Buchanan TM, et al. Serologic therapy of tetanus in the United States. JAMA. 1976;235:42-44.
60. Abrutyn E, Berlin JA. Intrathecal therapy in tetanus: A meta-analysis. JAMA. 1991;266:2262-2267.
61. Menon J, Mathews L. Intrathecal immunoglobulin in the treatment of tetanus. Indian Pediatr. 2002;39:654-657.
62. Begue RE, Lindo-Soriano I. Failure of intrathecal antitoxin in the treatment of neonatal tetanus. J Infect Dis. 1991;164:619-620.
63. Lee DC, Lederman HM. Anti-tetanus toxoid antibodies in intravenous gamma globulin: An alternative to tetanus immune globulin. J Infect Dis. 1992;166:642-645.
64. Bleck TP. Anti-tetanus toxoid antibodies in intravenous gamma globulin: An alternative to tetanus immune globulin. J Infect Dis. 1993;167:498-499.
65. Ahmadsyah I, Salim A. Treatment of tetanus: An open study to compare the efficacy of procaine penicillin and metronidazole. Br Med J. 1985;291:648-650.
66. Domenghetti GM, Savary S, Striker H. Hyperadrenergic syndrome in severe tetanus responsive to labetalol. Br Med J. 1984;288:1483-1484.
67. King WW, Cave DR. Use of esmolol to control autonomic instability of tetanus. Am J Med. 1991;91:425-428.
68. Rocke DA, Wasley AG, Pather M, et al. Morphine in tetanus: The management of sympathetic nervous system overactivity. S Afr Med J. 1986;70:666-668.
69. Lipman J, James MFM, Erskine J, et al. Autonomic dysfunction in severe tetanus: Magnesium sulfate as an adjunct to deep sedation. Crit Care Med. 1987;15:987-988.
70. Southorn PA, Blaise GA. Treatment of tetanus-induced autonomic dysfunction with continuous epidural blockade. Crit Care Med. 1986;14:251-252.
71. Udwadia FE, Sunavala JD, Jain MC, et al. Haemodynamic studies during the management of severe tetanus. Quart J Med. 1992;83:449-460.
72. Tseuda K, Oliver PB, Richter RW. Cardiovascular manifestations of tetanus. Anesthesiology. 1974;40:588-592.
73. Nolla-Salas M, Garcés-Brusés J. Severity of tetanus in patients older than 80 years: comparative study with younger patients. Clin Infect Dis. 1993;16:591-592.
74. Brauner JS, Vieira SR, Bleck TP. Changes in severe accidental tetanus mortality in the ICU during two decades in Brazil. Intens Care Med. 2002;28:930-935.
75. Jolliet P, Magnenat JL, Kobel T, Chevrolet JC. Aggressive intensive care treatment of very elderly patients with tetanus is justified. Chest. 1990;97:702-705.
76. Edwards RA, James B. Tetanus and psychiatry: Unexpected bedfellows. Med J Aust. 1979;1:483-484.
77. Edsall G. The inexcusable disease. JAMA. 1876;235:62-63.
78. Bardenheier B, Prevots DR, Khetsuriani N, Wharton M. Tetanus surveillance—United States, 1995-1997. Centers for Disease Control and Prevention. Surveillance Summaries. MMWR Morb Mortal Wkly Rep. 1998;47:1-13.
79. Saikh KU, Sesno J, Brandler P, Ulrich RG. Are DNA-based vaccines useful for protection against secreted bacterial toxins? Tetanus toxin test case. Vaccine. 1998;16:1029-1038.
80. Gergen PJ, McQuillan GM, Kiely M, et al. A population-based serologic survey of immunity to tetanus in the United States. N Engl J Med. 1995;332:761-766.
81. Redwan el-RM, Al-Awady MK. Prevalence of tetanus immunity in the Egyptian population. Hum Antibod. 2002;11:55-59.
82. Webster ADB, Latif AAA, Brenner MK, Bird D. Evaluation of test immunization in the assessment of antibody deficiency syndromes. Br Med J. 1984;288:1864-1866.
83. Hamarstrom V, Pauksen K, Svensson H, et al. Tetanus immunity in patients with hematological malignancies. Support Care Cancer. 1998;6:469-472.
84. Hammarström V, Pauksen K, Simmonsson B, et al. Tetanus immunity in autologous bone marrow and blood stem cell transplant recipients. Bone Marrow Transplant. 1998;22:67-71.
85. Vance E, George S, Guinan EC, et al. Comparison of multiple immunization schedules for Haemophilus influenzae type b-conjugate and tetanus toxoid vaccines following bone marrow transplantation. Bone Marrow Transplant. 1998;22:735-741.
86. Storek J, Viganego F, Dawson MA, et al. Factors affecting antibody levels after allogeneic hematopoietic cell transplantation. Blood. 2003;101:3319-3324.
87. Kurtzhals JAL, Kjeldsen K, Heron I, Skinhøj P. Immunity against diphtheria and tetanus in human immunodeficiency virus-infected Danish men born 1950-1959. APMIS. 1992;100:803-808.
88. Talesnik E, Vial PA, Labarca J, et al. Time course of antibody response to tetanus toxoid and pneumococcal capsular polysaccharides in patients infected with HIV. J Acquir Immune Defic Syndr Hum Retrovirol. 1998;19:471-477.
89. Semba RD, Muhilal, Scott AL, et al. Depressed immune response to tetanus in children with vitamin A deficiency. J Nutr. 1992;122:101-107.
90. Koenig MA, Roy NC, McElrath T, et al. Duration of protective immunity conferred by maternal tetanus toxoid immunization: Further evidence from Matlab, Bangladesh. Am J Publ Hlth 1998;88:903-907.
91. Parashar UD, Bennett JV, Boring JR, Hlady WG. Topical antimicrobials applied to the umbilical cord stump: A new intervention against neonatal tetanus. Int J Epidemiol. 1998;27:904-908.
92. Brand DA, Acampora D, Gottlieb AD, et al. Adequacy of antitetanus prophylaxis in six hospital emergency rooms. N Engl J Med. 1983;309:636-639.
93. Jacobs RL, Lowe RS, Lanier BQ. Adverse reactions to tetanus toxoid. JAMA. 1982;247:40-42.
94. Tuttle J, Chen RT, Rantala H, et al. The risk of Guillain-Barre syndrome after tetanus-toxoid-containing vaccines in adults and children in the United States. Am J Publ Hlth. 1997;87:2045-2048.

CHAPTER **243**

Clostridium botulinum (Botulism)

THOMAS P. BLECK

Botulism and tetanus result from intoxication with the protein neurotoxins elaborated by two related species of *Clostridium*. The toxins are very similar in structure and function, but differ dramatically in their clinical effects because they target different cells in the nervous system. Botulinum neurotoxins predominantly affect the peripheral neuromuscular junction and autonomic synapses, and primarily manifest as weakness. In contrast, although tetanus toxin can affect the same systems, its effects reflect tropism for inhibitory cells of the central nervous system (CNS), and primarily manifest as rigidity and spasm. Both conditions have potentially high fatality rates, and both are preventable through education and public health measures. The cost of care per botulism patient in Canada and the United States was estimated to be $340,000 in 1989.[1]

Clostridium botulinum produces most cases of botulism, with a few other clostridial strains accounting for the remainder. Botulinum toxins are designated types A through G based on antigenic differences.[2] Types A, B, E, and F produce human disease, whereas types C and D are almost exclusively confined to animals.[3] Type G toxin has not been associated with naturally acquired disease. The clinical forms of botulism include *foodborne botulism, infant botulism, wound botu-*

lism, and *botulism of undetermined etiology.* In the past decade, botulinum A toxin has achieved prominence as a therapeutic modality in conditions that result from excessive muscle activity, such as torticollis. Botulinum toxin has also been developed as a weapon, which could be used to contaminate food or beverage supplies, or be aerosolized (see Chapter 325).

HISTORY OF BOTULISM

The term *botulism* derives from the Latin word *botulus,* or sausage. Outbreaks of poisoning related to sausages and other prepared foods occurred in Europe in the 19th century. Justinus Kerner, a district health officer in southern Germany, recognized the connection between sausage and the paralytic illnesses of 230 patients in 1820, and made sausage poisoning a reportable disease.[4] At about the same time, physicians in Russia recognized a disease with similar symptoms, which they termed *fish poisoning.*[5] In 1897, van Ermengen published the first description of *C. botulinum* and showed that the organism elaborated a toxin that could induce weakness in animals.[6] This was subsequently shown to be type A toxin; type B was discovered in 1904.[7] Wound botulism was described in 1943,[8] and infant botulism in 1976.[9] The occurrence of sporadic cases without an apparent etiology, many related to gastrointestinal colonization, was first reported in 1986.[10] Type A toxin was isolated and purified in 1946.[11]

EPIDEMIOLOGY

In the United States, type A botulism is found most commonly in the west, and type B is more common in the east. This distribution mirrors that of the spore type found in those regions.[12] Type E is frequently associated with fish products.[13] Type F has a less defined geographic distribution. Wound botulism may be caused by either type A or type B organisms; infant botulism occurs with type A, B, or F. The infant form is often attributed to honey ingestion,[14] but other sources have emerged as feeding honey to infants has been discouraged.[15] Two infants without other exposures are believed to have contracted botulism via soil contamination.[16] Rare cases of infant botulism have been associated with *C. baratii*[17] or *C. butyricum.*[18] Adult botulism of unknown etiology usually involves type A toxin, but types B and F have also been implicated.[19] One adult case of type F botulism was caused by *C. baratii.*[20]

Foodborne botulism is most frequently recognized in outbreaks, whereas the other forms are sporadic. Although commercially canned foods were commonly the source of toxin in the early part of this century, home-canned vegetables, fruits, and fish products are now the most common sources. In some cultures, such as among Alaskan Natives, preferred food preparation practices involving fish fermentation, commonly lead to botulism.[21] In China, homemade fermented beans are the leading cause.[22] Commercial foods and restaurants are still occasional sources.[23-25] Consumption of peyote for religious reasons has resulted in botulism.[26] The pH of the implicated products is usually greater than 4.6.[27]

One hundred twenty-four outbreaks of foodborne botulism were reported to the Centers for Disease Control and Prevention (CDC) between 1976 and 1984.[18] The mean number of cases in an outbreak was 2.7, and single cases or small outbreaks were usually related to home-prepared foods. Large outbreaks were associated with restaurants, and accounted for over 40% of cases. Since 1973, the median number of reported cases per type is infant, 71; foodborne, 24; and wound, 3.[28] Prior to the advent of critical care, the case-fatality rate exceeded 60%; in the early 1970s, it was 23.1%.[29] The case-fatality rate for the 1976-1984 period was 7.5%. For patients older than 60 years, however, the fatality rate is 30%. The first (or only) patient in an outbreak has a 25% risk of death, whereas subsequent cases, who are diagnosed and treated more quickly, carry only a 4% risk.[30]

Inhalational botulism does not occur in nature, but is one of the potential routes of an attack with botulinum toxin.

CHARACTERISTICS OF *C. BOTULINUM*

C. botulinum is a large, usually gram-positive, strictly anaerobic bacillus that forms a subterminal spore.[31] The species is divided into four physiologic groups. Group I organisms are proteolytic in culture, and can produce toxin types A, B, and F. Group II organisms are nonproteolytic, and can produce toxin types B, E, and F. Group III organisms produce toxin types C and D, and Group IV produces type G. A single strain almost always produces only one toxin type. Group II organisms grow optimally between 25° and 30° C, and the other groups grow best between 30° and 37° C. Although each strain of the organism typically contains several plasmids, only type G toxin is encoded on one (c.f. *C. tetani,* in which the toxin is encoded on a plasmid).[32]

C. botulinum spores are found throughout the world in soil samples and marine sediments.[33] These spores are able to tolerate 100° C at 1 atm for several hours; because boiling renders solutions more anaerobic, it may actually favor the growth of *C. botulinum.*[34] Proper preparation of food in a pressure cooker will kill spores.

PATHOGENESIS

In foodborne botulism, toxin is ingested with the food in which it was produced. It is absorbed primarily in the duodenum and jejunum, and passes into the blood stream, by which it reaches peripheral cholinergic synapses (including the neuromuscular junction). In cases of wound botulism, spores are introduced into a wound, where they germinate and produce toxin. Wound botulism is increasingly associated with the intramuscular or subcutaneous injection of black tar heroin.[35] Infant botulism, and probably adult botulism of unknown etiology, follow ingestion of spores. Achlorhydria and antibiotic use may predispose to gastrointestinal colonization with *C. botulinum.* After inhalation, the toxin crosses through the pulmonary alveolar epithelium to gain access to the blood stream.[36] The clinical manifestations of botulism depend on the type of toxin produced, rather than the site of its production.

Botulinum toxin is synthesized as a single polypeptide chain of low potency; the molecular weight varies from 150 to 165 kDa, depending on the toxin type. The botulinum toxins are zinc-dependent metalloproteinases,[37] as is tetanospasmin. The toxin is then nicked by a bacterial protease to produce two chains, with the light chain constituting approximately one third of the total mass. As with tetanospasmin, the chains remain connected by a disulfide bond. The nicked toxin type A becomes, on a molecular weight basis, the most potent toxin found in nature. In contrast to the spores, the toxin is heat labile. Different toxin types may undergo different postsynthetic processing.[38]

Once present at the synapse, the toxin prevents the release of acetylcholine (ACh). This appears to result from a three-stage process.[39] The heavy chain of the toxin mediates binding to presynaptic receptors. The nature of these receptors is uncertain; different toxin types bind to different receptors, with type B receptors outnumbering type A receptors by a factor of 4.[40] The toxin enters the cell by receptor-mediated endocytosis.[41] Once inside the neuron, the toxin types differ in the mechanisms by which they inhibit ACh release.[42] The release of synaptic vesicles by an action potential is initiated by an abrupt rise in the intracellular free Ca^{2+} concentration, mediated by voltage-dependent calcium channels (Fig. 243-1).[43] This increase in free calcium triggers an interaction between synaptotagmin (in the vesicle membrane) and syntaxin (on the presynaptic cell membrane), clamping the vesicle to the presynaptic membrane. Synaptobrevin (also referred to as vesicle-associated membrane protein[44]) also binds to syntaxin, and appears to dock the vesicle to the membrane at the proper location for fusion. There are different isoforms of synaptobrevin within neurons; a protein termed *cellubrevin* performs a similar function in non-neuronal secretory cells.[45] Synaptophysin, the third major component of this mechanism, probably forms the fusion pore that allows release of the vesicle contents into the synaptic cleft.[46]

Clostridial neurotoxins inhibit vesicle release by cleaving peptide bonds in these proteins.[47] Each toxin has a specific locus of activity.

FIGURE 243-1. Components of the transmitter release mechanism. *(From Bleck TP, Brauner JS. Tetanus. In: Scheld WM, Whitley RJ, Durack DT, eds. Infections of the Central Nervous System. 2nd ed. New York: Raven Press; 1997:629-653.)*

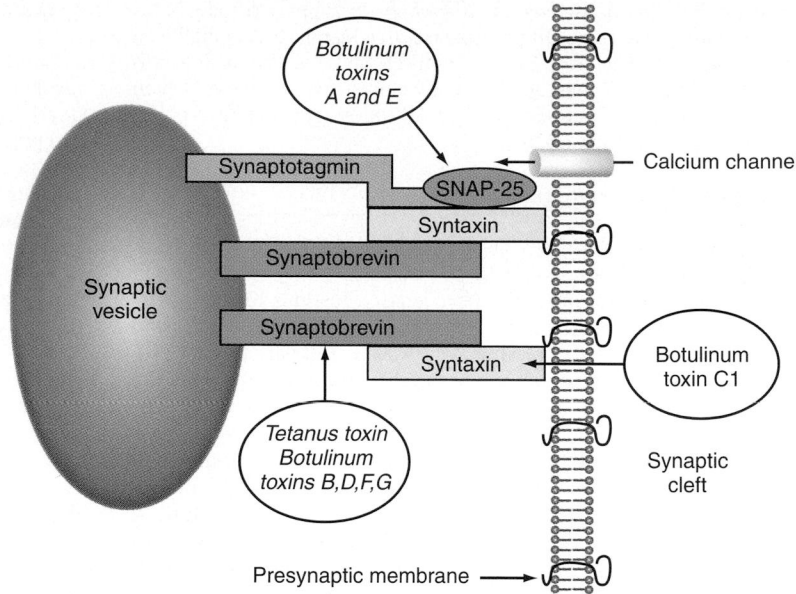

Tetanospasmin, along with botulinum neurotoxins B, D, F, and G, cleaves synaptobrevin.[48,49] Tetanospasmin and botulinum neurotoxin B appear to share the same cleavage site on synaptobrevin.[50] In contrast, botulinum toxins A[51] and E act on a 25-kDa synaptosomal-associated protein (SNAP-25),[52] and botulinum toxin C1 affects syntaxin. The toxins only affect the free proteins; once they have complexed to cause transmitter release, they are not subject to attack.[53] Synaptobrevin and synaptotagmin cleavage also occurs normally, as an effect of an endogenous protease, and these proteins are probably involved in organelle recycling.[54] The endogenous protease does not appear homologous to the clostridial toxins. However, the result is that stimulation of the presynaptic cell (e.g., the alpha motor neuron) fails to produce transmitter release, thus producing paralysis in the motor system, or autonomic dysfunction when parasympathetic nerve terminals or autonomic ganglia are involved.

Once damaged, the synapse was originally thought to be rendered useless. Because of the widespread interest in the therapeutic use of botulinum toxin, substantial research into the mechanisms of recovery is underway. The initial recovery of function in type A botulism requires sprouting of the presynaptic axon and the subsequent formation of a new synapse. Later, the original synapse recovers and the newer ones are pruned away.[55] With type F botulism, recovery is substantially faster, suggesting that the original synapse regains function more rapidly.[56]

Botulinum toxin is transported within nerves in a manner analogous to tetanospasmin, and can thereby gain access to the CNS. However, symptomatic CNS involvement is rare.[57]

CLINICAL MANIFESTATIONS

The classic presentation of botulism is that of a patient who develops acute, bilateral cranial neuropathies associated with symmetrical descending weakness. The CDC suggests attention to these cardinal features: (1) fever is absent (unless a complicating infection occurs); (2) the neurologic manifestations are symmetrical; (3) the patient remains responsive; (4) the heart rate is normal or slow in the absence of hypotension; and (5) sensory deficits do not occur (except for blurred vision).[20] The first two features were important for the exclusion of poliomyelitis; rare exceptions have been noted to most of these generalizations.

Foodborne botulism usually develops between 12 and 36 hours after toxin ingestion. The patient initially complains of nausea and a dry mouth, and diarrhea may occur at this stage. Evidence of cranial nerve dysfunction most commonly starts with the eyes, reflecting parasympathetic involvement (blurred vision as a result of pupillary dilatation) or involvement of cranial nerves III, IV, or VI.[58] Pupillary reactions may remain abnormal for months after motor recovery.[59] Nystagmus is occasionally noted, usually in type A disease. Lower cranial nerve dysfunction manifests as dysphagia, dysarthria, and hypoglossal weakness. Weakness then spreads to the upper extremities, the trunk, and the lower extremities. Respiratory dysfunction may result from either upper airway obstruction (the weakened glottis tending to close during attempted inspiration) or diaphragmatic weakness. Patients requiring mechanical ventilation require mean periods of 58 days (type A) and 26 days (type B) for ventilatory weaning.[60] Recovery may not begin for up to 100 days.[61] Autonomic problems may include gastrointestinal dysfunction, alterations in resting heart rate, loss of responsiveness to hypotension or postural change, hypothermia, and urinary retention.[62]

Hughes summarized published reports to analyze differences in the clinical findings of intoxication with different toxin types (Table 243-1).[27] Type A is significantly more commonly associated with dysarthria, blurred vision, dyspnea, diarrhea, sore throat, dizziness, ptosis, ophthalmoplegia, facial paresis, and upper extremity weakness. Types B and E appear to produce more autonomic dysfunction. None of these differences is diagnostic of the toxin type, however. It is important to note that the pupils are either dilated or unreactive in less than 50% of patients; although these are very useful signs when present, their absence in no way diminishes the likelihood of botulism.

Patients with infant botulism present with constipation, which may be followed by feeding difficulties, hypotonia, increased drooling, and a weak cry.[63] Upper airway obstruction may be the initial sign,[64] and is the major indication for intubation.[65] In severe cases, the condition progresses to include cranial neuropathies and respiratory weakness, with ventilatory failure occurring in about 50% of diagnosed patients. The condition progresses for 1 to 2 weeks, and then stabilizes for another 2 to 3 weeks before recovery starts.[25] Relapses of infant botulism may occur.[66]

Infant botulism has a somewhat different pathogenesis in that it is acquired through the ingestion of spores rather than preformed toxin. The infant's intestinal flora is thought to be particularly permissive for the germination of spores, which leads to the production of toxin. The spores are acquired from environmental sources associated with areas of soil in which botulinum spore counts are high.[65]

Wound botulism lacks the prodromal gastrointestinal disorder of the foodborne form, but is otherwise similar in presentation. Fever, if present, reflects wound infection rather than botulism. The wound it-

TABLE 243-1 Symptoms and Signs in Patients with the Common Types of Human Botulism

	Type A (%)	Type B (%)	Type E (%)
Neurologic signs and symptoms			
Dysphagia	96	97	82
Dry mouth	83	100	93
Diplopia	90	92	39
Dysarthria	100	69	50
Upper extremity weakness	86	64	NA
Lower extremity weakness	76	64	NA
Blurred vision	100	42	91
Dyspnea	91	34	88
Paresthesias	20	12	NA
Gastrointestinal signs and symptoms			
Constipation	73	73	52
Nausea	73	57	84
Vomiting	70	50	96
Abdominal cramps	33	46	NA
Diarrhea	35	8	39
Miscellaneous symptoms			
Fatigue	92	69	84
Sore throat	75	39	38
Dizziness	86	30	63
Neurologic findings			
Ptosis	96	55	46
Diminished gag reflex	81	54	NA
Ophthalmoparesis	87	46	NA
Facial paresis	84	48	NA
Tongue weakness	91	31	66
Pupils fixed or dilated	33	56	75
Nystagmus	44	4	NA
Upper extremity weakness	91	62	NA
Lower extremity weakness	82	59	NA
Ataxia	24	13	NA
DTRs diminished or absent	54	29	NA
DTRs hyperactive	12	0	NA
Initial mental status			
Alert	88	93	27
Lethargic	4	4	73
Obtunded	8	4	0

DTR, deep tendon reflex; NA, not available.
Data from references 13, 27, 34.

self may rarely appear to be healing well while neurologic manifestations are occurring. Conversely, *C. botulinum* infection may produce abscesses[67]; botulism has also been reported as a result of sinusitis with this organism after cocaine inhalation.[68] The reported incubation period varies from 4 to 14 days.

The signs and symptoms exhibited by victims of inhalational botulism are the same as those seen with ingestion. The latency between exposure and clinical disease after inhalation appears to be between 12 hours and 3 days, with maximal disease by about 5 days.[69]

Botulinum toxin has achieved widespread notoriety for its use in cosmetic procedures. It has also been used to treat a variety of chronic pain syndromes, achalasia, and anal fissures.[70] Dysphagia and other symptoms of neuromuscular impairment have been reported rarely after the therapeutic use of botulinum A toxin.[71]

DIAGNOSIS

A history appropriate to the type of botulism suspected is the most important diagnostic test. If others are already affected, the condition is easily recognized. However, because the toxin may not be evenly distributed in foodstuffs, the absence of other patients does not eliminate the diagnosis.

Botulism has a limited differential diagnosis. Myasthenia gravis and the Eaton-Lambert myasthenic syndrome (LEMS) each share some of the characteristics of botulism, but are rarely fulminant and lack autonomic features. An edrophonium test may be considered, but an improvement in strength is not pathognomonic of myasthenia

gravis and has been reported in botulism.[72] Tick paralysis is excluded by a careful physical examination, because the *Dermacentor* tick will still be attached. Classic acute inflammatory demyelinating polyneuropathy (AIPN; Guillain-Barré syndrome) frequently begins with sensory complaints, rapidly becomes areflexic, rarely begins with cranial nerve dysfunction, and does not alter pupillary reactivity. Patients with botulism do not become areflexic until the affected muscle group is completely paralyzed. The Miller Fisher variant of AIPN presents with oculomotor dysfunction and may produce other cranial neuropathies, but includes a prominent ataxia that is lacking in botulism. Patients with polio are febrile on presentation, and have asymmetrical weakness. Magnesium intoxication may mimic botulism.[73] Rarely, botulism may be confused with diphtheria, organophosphate poisoning, or brainstem infarction.[74]

Laboratory evaluation includes anaerobic cultures and toxin assays of serum, stool, and the implicated food if available. Confirmation and toxin typing is obtained in almost 75% of cases.[75] Early cases are more likely to be diagnosed by the toxin assay, whereas those studied later in the disease are more likely to have a positive culture than a positive toxin assay.[76] Specimens should be obtained and sent in consultation with the appropriate epidemiologic officials (in the United States, the state epidemiologist and the CDC). The most sensitive test for toxin remains the mouse bioassay.[77] Serum from patients with AIDP can produce paralysis in mice, however, so the test is not completely specific.[78] Alternatively, the toxin may be detected by gel hydrolysis or enzyme-linked immunosorbent assay. Toxin excretion may continue up to 1 month after the onset of illness, and stool cultures may remain positive for a similar period.

Electrophysiologic studies reveals normal nerve conduction velocities; the amplitude of compound muscle action potentials is reduced in 85% of cases, although not all motor units may demonstrate this abnormality.[79] Repetitive nerve stimulation at high rates (20 Hz or greater, compared with the 4-Hz rate employed in the diagnosis of myasthenia gravis) may reveal a small increment in the motor response (Fig. 243-2). This test is very uncomfortable, and should not be requested unless botulism or LEMS is a serious consideration.[80] In infant botulism, the increments may be very dramatic. In questionable cases, single-fiber electromyography studies may be useful. There is currently some debate regarding the sensitivity of electrodiagnostic techniques in cases of infant botulism.[81] The therapeutic use of botulinum A toxin for dystonic disorders can produce electrophysiologic evidence of toxin dissemination to distant sites.[82]

If botulinum toxin is used as a biologic weapon, the diagnosis would depend on the route of exposure. Contaminated food or beverages would result in an epidemic resembling that of a natural foodborne outbreak. The diagnosis of inhalational botulism would depend on the recognition of cases whose common exposure was presence in a particular geographic area at a particular time, rather than having ingested the same food. The amount of inhaled toxin producing disease would probably not produce measurable toxin in blood or other patient samples, except perhaps for nasopharyngeal secretions. More detailed information about weaponized botulinum toxin is available at *www.usamriid.army.mil/education/bluebook.html* and *ccc.apgea.army.mil/sara/products/textbook/Web_Version/index.htm* (the latter site requires registration).

TREATMENT

The importance of supportive therapy for botulism is underlined by the progressive improvement in mortality rates with advances in critical care, especially ventilatory support. The decision to intubate should be based on (1) bedside assessment of upper airway competency, and (2) changes in vital capacity (in general, an appropriately performed vital capacity measurement below 12 mL/kg frequently indicates intubation). One should not wait for the Paco$_2$ to rise or the oxygen saturation to fall before intubating the patient. In contrast to tetanus, the autonomic dysfunction of botulism is rarely life threatening, and patients who receive appropriate airway and ventilator management should recover unless

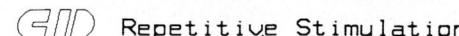

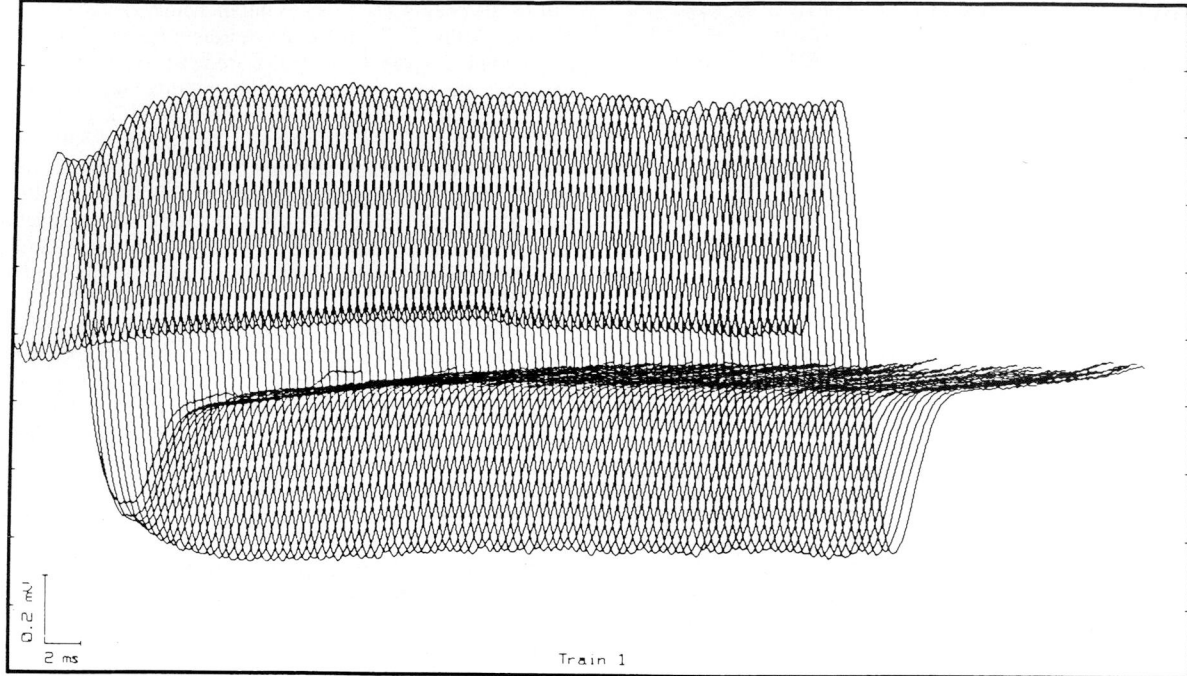

FIGURE 243-2. Repetitive nerve stimulation in infant botulism. Note the increment in response amplitude during the initial stimulations. *(Courtesy of Vern Juel, M.D., Department of Neurology and Laboratory of Electromyography, University of Virginia, Charlottesville.)*

complications supervene. Patients intubated with high-volume, low-pressure endotracheal tubes should not automatically undergo tracheostomy, regardless of the duration of intubation, unless required for mechanical reasons.[83] If contaminated food may still reside in the gastrointestinal tract, purgatives may be useful unless ileus has occurred. The detailed critical care management of botulism patients is beyond the scope of this text; Tacket and Rogawski have presented a useful approach.[34]

Antitoxin therapy is usually carried out with a trivalent (types A, B, and E) equine serum; in the United States it is obtained through state health departments; the state health department is responsible for contacting the CDC (770-488-7100). Its use is supported by inferential studies[30]; controlled clinical trials are lacking. Reported hypersensitivity rates vary between 9% and 20%.[84] Skin testing is performed prior to administering the antitoxin; a regimen for desensitization is included in the package. The standard antitoxin dose is one vial intravenously and one vial intramuscularly; although the package insert recommends repeating the dose in 4 hours in severe or progressive cases, this is not necessary.[85] A pentavalent antitoxin is available within the Department of Defense but is not available for public use. Human bolulinum immune globulin was approved by the FDA in 2003 for the treatment of infant botulism. The recommended dose is 50 mg/kg as an intravenous infusion. For more information, contact the Infant Botulism Treatment and Prevention Program, California State Department of Health Services, *http://www.dhs.cahwnet.gov/ps/dcdc/html/ibtindex.htm;* 510-231-7600.

Patients with wound botulism should also undergo débridement, even if the would appears to be healing well. Anaerobic cultures should be obtained at the time of surgery. The value of local instillation of antitoxin is unknown. The role of antibiotic treatment is untested, but penicillin G (10 to 20 MU daily) is frequently recommended. Metronidazole may be an effective alternative. Aminoglycosides and tetracyclines, which can impair neuron calcium entry, worsen infant botulism.[87] Lysis of *C. botulinum* in the gut by antibiotics may also increase the toxin available in infant botulism.[85] This effect has not been reported in adult cases, but should be considered when gastrointestinal infection is suspected.

Agents that may improve ACh release at the neuromuscular junction have been tried in botulism without success. Guanidine has received the greatest attention.[88] Other drugs are under study.

Although the greatest improvement in muscle strength occurs in the first 3 months of recovery from botulism, patients still show improvements in strength and endurance for up to 1 year after disease onset.[89] Recovery from botulism may also be followed by persistent psychological dysfunction, which may require mental health intervention.[90]

PREVENTION

The most important aspect of botulism prevention is proper food handling and preparation. It is impractical or undesirable to treat many foods in a manner to eliminate *C. botulinum* spores; hence, methods for the control of botulism focus on the inhibition of bacterial growth and toxin production.[85] Because the toxin is heat labile, terminal boiling or similarly intense heating of contaminated food will inactivate it. Food containers that appear to bulge may contain gas produced by *C. botulinum,* and should not be opened. Other foods that appear to be spoiled should not be tasted.

Immunity to botulinum toxin does not develop even with severe disease, and the repeated occurrence of botulism has been reported.[91] An experimental vaccine is available for laboratory workers. A recombinant vaccine expressing the type A binding domain,[92] or vaccination with the carboxy-terminal fragment,[93] promises to make vaccination less expensive and painful. Recent work suggests that inhalation of the toxin heavy chain would be immunogenic.[36]

REFERENCES

1. Todd ECD. Costs of acute bacterial foodborne disease in Canada and the United States. Int J Food Microbiol. 1989;9:313-326.
2. Hatheway CL. Bacterial sources of clostridial neurotoxins. In: Simpson LL, ed. Botulinum Neurotoxin and Tetanus Toxin. San Diego, CA: Academic Press; 1989:4-25.
3. Oguma K, Yokota K, Hayashi S, et al. Infant botulism due to *Clostridium botulinum* type C toxin. Lancet. 1990;336:1449-1450.

4. Kerner J. Neue Beobachtungen über die in Würtemburg so haüfig vorfallen Vergiftung durch den Genuss gerauchter Würst. Tubingen, 1820. (Quoted in Damon SR. Food Infections and Food Intoxications. Baltimore: Williams & Wilkins; 1928:67.)

5. Young JH. Botulism and the ripe olive scare of 191-1920. Bull Hist Med. 1976;50:372-391.

6. van Ermengen E. Ueber einen neuen anaëroben Bacillus und seine Beziehungen zum Botulismus. Z Hyg Infektionskrankh. 1897;26:1-56.

7. Landman G. Ueber die Ursache der Darmstadter Bohnen Vergiftung. Hyg Rundsch. 1904;14:449-452.

8. Davis JB, Mattman LH, Wiley M. *Clostridium botulinum* in a fatal wound infection. JAMA. 1951;146:646-648.

9. Midura TF, Arnon SS. Infant botulism: Identification of *Clostridium botulinum* and its toxin in faeces. Lancet. 1976;2:934-936.

10. Chia JK, Clark JB, Ryan CA, Pollack M. Botulism in an adult associated with food-borne intestinal infection with *Clostridium botulinum*. N Engl J Med. 1986;315:239-241.

11. Lamanna C, McElroy OE, Eklund HW. The purification and crystallization of *Clostridium botulinum* type A toxin. Science. 1946;103:613-614.

12. Smith LDS. The occurrence of *Clostridium botulinum* and *Clostridium tetani* in the soil of the United States. Health Lab Sci. 1978;15:74-80.

13. Weber JT, Hibbs RG, Darwish A, et al. A massive outbreak of type E botulism associated with traditional salted fish in Cairo. J Infect Dis. 1993;167:451-454.

14. Midura TF, Snowden S, Wood RM, et al. Isolation of *Clostridium botulinum* from honey. J Clin Microbiol. 1979;9:282-283.

15. Spika JS, Shaffer N, Hargrett-Bean N, et al. Infant botulism in the United States: An epidemiologic study of cases occurring outside of California. Am J Public Health. 1983;73:1385-1388.

16. Hurst DL, Marsh WW. Early severe infantile botulism. J Pediatr. 1993;122:909-911.

17. Gimenez JA, Gimenez MA, DasGupta BR. Characterization of the neurotoxin isolated from a *Clostridium baratii* strain implicated in infant botulism. Infect Immun. 1992;60:518-522.

18. Suen JC, Hatheway CL, Steigerwalt AG, et al. Genetic confirmation of the identities of neurotoxigenic *Clostridium baratii* and *Clostridium butyricum* implicated as agents of human botulism. J Clin Microbiol. 1988;26:2191-2192.

19. MacDonald KL, Cohen ML, Blake PA. The changing epidemiology of adult botulism in the United States. Am J Epidemiol. 1986;124:794-799.

20. McCroskey LM, Hatheway CL, Woodruff BA, et al. Type F botulism due to neurotoxigenic *Clostridium baratii* from an unknown source in an adult. J Clin Microbiol. 1991;29:2618-2620.

21. Shaffer N, Wainwright RB, Middaugh JP, Tauxe RV. Botulism among Alaska Natives: The role of changing food preparation and consumption practices. West J Med. 1990;153:390-393.

22. Gao QY, Huang YF, Wu JG, et al. A review of botulism in China. Biomed Environ Sci. 1990;3:326-336.

23. Centers for Disease Control. Botulism and commercial pot pie—California. MMWR Morb Mortal Wkly Rep. 1983;32:39-40,45.

24. Pourshafie MR, Saifie M, Shafiee A, et al. An outbreak of food-borne botulism associated with contaminated locally made cheese in Iran. Scand J Infect Dis. 1998;30:92-94.

25. Angulo FJ, Getz J, Taylor JP, et al. A large outbreak of botulism: The hazardous baked potato. J Infect Dis. 1998;178:172-177.

26. Hashimoto H, Clyde VJ, Parko KL. Botulism from peyote. N Engl J Med. 1998;339:203-204.

27. Hughes JM. Botulism. In: Scheld WM, Whitley RJ, Durack DT, eds. Infections of the Central Nervous System. New York: Raven Press; 1991:589-602.

28. Shapiro RL, Hatheway C, Swerdlow DL. Botulism in the United States: A clinical and epidemiologic review. Ann Intern Med. 1998;129:221-228.

29. Centers for Disease Control. Botulism in the United States, 1899-1973: Handbook for Epidemiologists, Clinicians, and Laboratory Workers. Atlanta: Centers for Disease Control; 1974.

30. Tacket CO, Shandera WX, Mann JM, et al. Equine antitoxin use and other factors that predict outcome in type A foodborne botulism. Am J Med. 1984;76:794-798.

31. Cato EP, George WL, Finegold SM. Genus *Clostridium praemozski* 1880, 23^AL. In: Smeath PHA, Mair NS, Sharpe ME, Holt JG, eds. Bergey's Manual of Systematic Bacteriology, v. 2. Baltimore: Williams & Wilkins; 1986:1141-1200.

32. Eklund MW, Poysky FT, Habig WH. Bacteriophages and plasmids in *Clostridium botulinum* and *Clostridium tetani* and their relationship to the production of toxin. In: Simpson LL, ed. Botulinum Neurotoxin and Tetanus Toxin. San Diego, CA: Academic Press; 1989:25-51.

33. Hauschild AHW. *Clostridium botulinum.* In: Doyle MP, ed. Foodborne Bacterial Pathogens. New York: Marcel Dekker; 1989:112-189.

34. Tacket CO, Rogawski MA. Botulism. In: Simpson LL, ed. Botulinum Neurotoxin and Tetanus Toxin. San Diego, CA: Academic Press; 1989:351-378.

35. Passaro DJ, Werner SB, McGee J, et al. Wound botulism associated with black tar heroin among injecting drug users. JAMA. 1998;279:859-863.

36. Park JB, Simpson LL. Inhalational poisoning by botulinum toxin and inhalation vaccination with its heavy-chain component. Infect Immun. 2003;71:1147-1154.

37. Fu FN, Lomneth RB, Cai S, Singh BR. Role of zinc in the structure and toxic activity of botulinum neurotoxin. Biochemistry. 1998;37:5267-5278.

38. Critchley EMR, Mitchell JD. Human botulism. Br J Hosp Med. 1992;43:290-292.

39. Simpson LL. Kinetic studies on the interaction between botulinum toxin type A and the cholinergic neuromuscular junction. J Pharmacol Exp Ther. 1980;212:16-21.

40. Black JD, Dolly JO. Interaction of ^{125}I-labeled botulinum neurotoxins with nerve terminals. I. Ultrastructural autoradiographic localization and quantitation of distinct membrane acceptors for types A and B on motor nerves. J Cell Biol. 1986;103:521-534.

41. Black JD, Dolly JO. Interaction of ^{125}I-labeled botulinum neurotoxins with nerve terminals. II. Autoradiographic evidence for its uptake into motor nerves by receptor-mediated endocytosis. J Cell Biol. 1986;103:535-544.

42. Simpson LL. Peripheral actions of the botulinum toxins. In: Simpson LL, ed. Botulinum Neurotoxin and Tetanus Toxin. San Diego: Academic Press; 1989:153-178.

43. Bleck TP, Brauner JS. Tetanus. In: Scheld WM, Whitley RJ, Durack DT, eds. Infections of the Central Nervous System. 2nd ed. New York: Raven Press; 1997:629-653.

44. Trimble WS, Cowan D, Scheller RH. VAMP-1: A synaptic vesicle associated integral membrane protein. Proc Natl Acad Sci U S A. 1988;85:4538-4542.

45. McMahon HT, Ushkaryov YA, Edelmann L, et al. Cellubrevin is a ubiquitous tetanus-toxin substrate homologous to a putative synaptic vesicle fusion protein. Nature. 1993;364:346-349.

46. Buckley KM, Floor E, Kelly RB. Cloning and sequence analysis of cDNA encoding p38, a major synaptic vesicle protein. J Cell Biol. 1987;105:2447-2456.

47. Blasi J, Binz T, Yamasaki S, et al. Inhibition of neurotransmitter release by clostridial neurotoxins correlates with specific proteolysis of synaptosomal proteins. J Physiol (Paris). 1994;88:235-241.

48. Schiavo G, Benfenati F, Poulain B, et al. Tetanus and botulinum-B neurotoxins block neurotransmitter release by proteolytic cleavage of synaptobrevin. Nature. 1992;359:832-835.

49. Nowakowski JL, Courtney BC, Bing QA, Adler M. Production of an expression system for a synaptobrevin fragment to monitor cleavage by botulinum neurotoxin B. J Protein Chem. 1998;17:453-462.

50. Foran P, Shone CC, Dolly JO. Differences in the protease activities of tetanus and botulinum B toxins revealed by the cleavage of vesicle-associated membrane protein and various sized fragments. Biochemistry. 1994;33:15365-15374.

51. Lacy DB, Tepp W, Cohen AC, et al. Crystal structure of botulinum neurotoxin type A and implications for toxicity. Nat Struct Biol. 1998;5:898-902.

52. Sciavo G, Santussi A, Dasgupta BR, et al. Botulinum neurotoxins serotypes A and E cleave SNAP-25 at distinct COOH-terminal peptide bonds. FEBS Lett. 1993;335:99-103.

53. Hayashi T, McMahon H, Yamasaki S, et al. Synaptic vesicle membrane fusion complex: Action of clostridial neurotoxins on assembly. EMBO J. 1994;13:5051-5061.

54. Hausinger A, Volknandt W, Zimmerman H. Calcium-dependent endogenous proteolysis of the vesicle proteins synaptobrevin and synaptotagmin. Neuroreport. 1995;6:637-641.

55. Meunier FA, Schiavo G, Molgo J. Botulinum neurotoxins: From paralysis to recovery of functional neuromuscular transmission. J Physiol (Paris). 2002;96:1015-1013.

56. Billante CR, Zealear DL, Billante M, et al. Comparison of neuromuscular blockade and recovery with botulinum toxins A and F. Muscle Nerve. 2002;26:395-403.

57. Jones S, Huma Z, Haugh C, et al. Central nervous system involvement in infantile botulism. Lancet. 1990;335:228.

58. Terranova W, Palumbo JN, Berman JG. Ocular findings in botulism type B. JAMA. 1979;241:475-477.

59. Friedman DI, Fortanasce VN, Sadun AA. Tonic pupils as a result of botulism. Am J Ophthalmol. 1990;109:236-237.

60. Hughes JM, Blumenthal JR, Merson MH, et al. Clinical features of types A and B foodborne botulism. Ann Intern Med. 1981;95:442-445.

61. Colerbatch JG, Wolff AH, Gilbert RJ, et al. Slow recovery from severe foodborne botulism. Lancet. 1989;2:1216-1217.

62. Vita G, Girlanda P, Puglisi RM, et al. Cardiovascular-reflex testing and single-fiber electromyography in botulism: A longitudinal study. Arch Neurol. 1987;44:202-206.

63. Cornblath DR, Sladky JT, Sumner AJ. Clinical electrophysiology of infantile botulism. Muscle Nerve. 1983;6:448-452.

64. Oken A, Barnes S, Rock P, Maxwell L. Upper airway obstruction and infant botulism. Anesth Analg. 1992;75:136-138.

65. Schreiner MS, Field E, Ruddy R. Infant botulism: A review of 12 years experience at the Children's Hospital of Philadelphia. Pediatrics. 1991;87:159-165.

66. Glauser TA, Maquire HC, Sladky JT. Relapse of infant botulism. Ann Neurol. 1990;28:187-189.

67. Elston HR, Wang M, Loo LK. Arm abscesses caused by *Clostridium botulinum*. J Clin Microbiol. 1991;29:2678-2379.

68. Kudrow DB, Henry DA, Haake DA, et al. Botulism associated with *Clostridium botulinum* sinusitis after intranasal cocaine abuse. Ann Intern Med. 1988;109:984-985.

69. Arnon SS, Schechter R, Inglesby TV, et al. Botulinum toxin as a biological weapon: Medical and public health management. JAMA. 2001;285:1059-1070.

70. Schantz EJ, Johnson EA. Botulinum toxin: The story of its development for the treatment of human disease. Perspect Biol Med. 1997;40:317.

71. Comella CL, Tanner CM, DeFoor-Hill L, Smith C. Dysphagia after botulinum toxin injections for spasmodic torticollis: Clinical and radiologic findings. Neurology. 1992;42:1307-1310.

72. Edell TA, Sullivan CP, Osborn KM, et al. Wound botulism associated with a positive Tensilon test. West J Med. 1983;139:218-219.

73. Cherington M. Botulism. Semin Neurol. 1990;10:27-31.

74. Dunbar EM. Botulism. J Infect. 1990;20:1-3.

75. Dowell VR, McCroskey LM, Hatheway CL, et al. Coproexamination for botulinal toxin and *Clostridium botulinum:* A new procedure for laboratory diagnosis of botulism. JAMA. 1977;238:1829-1832.

76. Woodruff BA, Griffin PM, McCroskey LM, et al. Clinical and laboratory comparison of botulism from toxin type A, B, and E in the United States, 1975-1988. J Infect Dis. 1992;166:1281-1286.

77. Notermans S, Nagel J. Assays for botulinum and tetanus toxins. In: Simpson LL, ed. Botulinum Neurotoxin and Tetanus Toxin. San Diego, CA: Academic Press; 1989, pp 319-331.

78. Notermans SHW, Wokke JHJ, van den Berg LH. Botulism and Guillain-Barré syndrome. Lancet. 1992;340:303.

79. Cherington M. Electrophysiologic methods as an aid in diagnosis of botulism: A review. Muscle Nerve. 1982;6:528-529.

80. Gutmann L, Pratt L. Pathophysiologic aspects of human botulism. Arch Neurol. 1976;33:175-179.
81. Graf W, Hays RM, Astley SJ, Mendelman PM. Electrodiagnosis reliability in the diagnosis of infant botulism. J Pediatr. 1992;120:747-749.
82. Buchman AS, Comella CL, Stebbins GT, et al. Quantitative electromyographic analysis of changes in muscle activity following botulinum toxin therapy for cervical dystonia. Clin Neuropharmacol. 1993;16:205-210.
83. Barrett DH. Endemic food-borne botulism: Clinical experience, 1973-1986. Alaska Med. 1991;33:101-108.
84. Black RE, Gunn RA. Hypersensitivity reactions associated with botulinal antitoxin. Am J Med. 1980;69:567-570.
85. Centers for Disease Control and Prevention. Botulism in the United States 1899-1996: Handbook for Epidemiologists, Clinicians, and Laboratory Workers (draft). Atlanta: Centers for Disease Control and Prevention; 1998.
86. Frankovich TL, Arnon SS. Clinical trial of botulism immune globulin for infant botulism. West J Med. 1991;154:103.
87. Wilson R, Morris JG, Snyder JD, Feldman RA. Clinical characteristics of infant botulism in the United States: A study of the non-California cases. Pediatr Infect Dis. 1982;1:148-150.
88. Kaplan JE, Davis LE, Narayan V, et al. Botulism, type A, and treatment with guanidine. Ann Neurol. 1979;6:69-71.
89. Wilcox PG, Morrison NJ, Pardy RL. Recovery of the ventilatory and upper airway muscles and exercise performance after type A botulism. Chest. 1990;98:620-626.
90. Cohen FL, Hardin SB, Nehring SB, et al. Physical and psychosocial health status 3 years after catastrophic illness—botulism. Issues Mental Health Nurs. 1988;9:387-398.
91. Beller M, Middaugh JP. Repeated type E botulism in an Alaskan Eskimo. N Engl J Med. 1990;322:855.
92. Byrne MP, Smith TJ, Montgomery VA, Smith LA. Purification, potency, and efficacy of the botulinum neurotoxin type A binding domain from Pichia pastoris as a recombinant vaccine candidate. Infect Immun. 1998;66:4817-4822.
93. Oshima M, Hayakari M, Middlebrook JL, Atassi MZ. Immune recognition of botulinum neurotoxin type A: Regions recognized by T cells and antibodies against the protective H(C) fragment (residues 855-1296) of the toxin. Mol Immunol. 1997;34:1031-1040.

CHAPTER **244**

Gas Gangrene and Other *Clostridium-* Associated Diseases

BENNETT LORBER

The genus *Clostridium* includes all anaerobic, gram-positive, spore-forming bacilli. Species can be readily isolated from soil and the intestinal tract of humans and many animals. Some produce potent exotoxins that are responsible for clinically distinctive syndromes.

MICROBIOLOGY

More than 150 species of *Clostridium* are recognized.[1] Fewer than 20 of these species are associated with clinical illness in humans.[2] Cell wall structure, as seen by electron microscopy, indicates that clostridia are gram-positive bacteria. Many strains, however, appear gram-negative or gram-variable. Loss of gram-positive appearance occurs most frequently in direct stains of clinical material, in cultures after incubation for extended periods, and in species showing terminal spores. These straight or slightly curved rods may vary in length and width, and the ends may be rounded, blunt, or tapered. Cells may occur singly, in pairs, or in short or long chains. Clostridial species vary in oxygen tolerance, motility, nutritional requirements, and limiting or optimal temperatures for growth. Some organisms, such as *Clostridium histolyticum* and *Clostridium tertium,* are relatively aerotolerant and may actually replicate, but not sporulate, with aerobic incubation. Other species, such as *Clostridium novyi* and *Clostridium haemolyticum,* are strict anaerobes and will not replicate when oxygen concentrations exceed 0.05%. Aerotolerant clostridia may be confused with *Bacillus* spp. Distinction is usually made easily by showing that

Bacillus spp. produce catalase and fail to produce spores when grown anaerobically, whereas clostridia infrequently produce catalase and rarely produce spores when grown aerobically.

Endospores are oval or spherical and usually distend the cell. Some strains, such as *Clostridium perfringens,* the most common clinical isolate, and *Clostridium ramosum,* do not readily form spores. Most clostridia, however, will sporulate at incubation temperatures below those required for optimal growth, usually 30° C. Spore formation is optimally stimulated by heating starch-broth cultures to 70° to 80° C for 10 minutes (heat shock) or by ethanol shock using an equal volume of 95% ethanol for 45 minutes, with subsequent demonstration of survival by incubation at conventional temperatures. Speciation is largely based on morphology; location of spores as central, terminal, or subterminal; biochemical reactions; and gas-liquid chromatography to distinguish products of fermentation (Table 244-1). The production of lecithinase (α-toxin, phospholipase C) may be demonstrated by growth on agar plates containing egg yolk. When α-toxin is present, a zone of opaque precipitate surrounds colonial growth and is due to lysis of the lecithin in the medium. The reaction may be inhibited by the addition of polyvalent gas gangrene antitoxin to the medium (Nagler reaction). The Nagler reaction cannot be used to identify *C. perfringens* definitively, but *C. perfringens* is clearly the most common lecithinase-producing *Clostridium* species found in clinical specimens. Egg-yolk agar may also be used to demonstrate lipase production. Lipase-producing organisms such as *Clostridium botulinum, Clostridium sporogenes,* and *C. novyi* type A break down free fats in the egg yolk to liberate free fatty acids, which appear as an oily, iridescent sheen. Other characteristics commonly used to distinguish species include the ability to ferment various carbohydrates, hydrolyze gelatin, and digest the casein in milk.[1] Microbiology laboratories should be able to speciate *C. perfringens* because of its importance in clinical medicine, frequency of recovery, and ease of identification. *Clostridium septicum* should also be identifiable because its growth from blood or untraumatized tissue often indicates underlying bowel pathology. The need to speciate other clostridia is controversial.

Clostridia are ubiquitous and found in soil, decaying vegetation, marine sediment, and the intestinal tract of humans, other vertebrates, and insects. They are also commonly recovered from infected sites but usually as a component of a polymicrobial flora, which makes their role in pathogenesis difficult to establish. The most characteristic and well-documented clostridial diseases are the histotoxic syndromes, in which specific clostridial toxins appear to be responsible for the pathophysiology of the disease process (Table 244-2). Diagnosis in these cases requires recovery of the putative agent or demonstration of the implicated toxin.

Industrially, clostridia are used to produce acids and alcohols and serve as markers for adequate sterilization of canned foods and medical equipment.

Clostridium perfringens

Clostridium perfringens (formerly *Clostridium welchii*) is the most frequent clinical isolate of *Clostridium.* It may be found in various clinical sources and is responsible for three distinctive histotoxic clostridial syndromes (see Table 244-2). Its major habitats are soil and the intestines of humans and animals. Virtually every soil sample ever examined, with the exception of the sands of the Sahara, has been shown to contain *C. perfringens.*[3] This organism has also been found in stool specimens from virtually every vertebrate animal investigated, including pets, wild and domesticated herd animals, carnivores, rodents, birds, marine mammals, and humans. Studies of human fecal flora by Finegold and colleagues showed that *C. perfringens* was recovered from 28 of 40 adult subjects in mean concentrations of approximately 10^9/g.[4]

C. perfringens is nonmotile and generally has a distinctive "boxcar" appearance on Gram stain of clinical material or subcultures. The oval, central spores are rarely seen in clinical specimens or in cultures grown in the usual laboratory media. All types produce lecithinase (α-toxin), which can be demonstrated with the Nagler reaction. *C. per-*

TABLE 244-1 Differential Features of Clinically Important Clostridia

Species	Lecithinase*	Spores	Motility	β-Hemolysis	Ferment Lactose	Ferment Glucose	H₂S	Urease	Indole	Nitrate Reduction
C. perfringens	+	C	0	+	+	+	+	0	0	+
C. septicum	0	ST	+	+	+	+	+	0	0	+
C. novyi	+	ST	+	+	0	+	+	0	0	+
C. sordellii	+	C	+	+	0	+	+	+	+	+
C. histolyticum	0	ST	+	+	0	0	+	0	0	0
C. difficile	0	ST	+	0	0	+	0	0	0	0
C. tetani	0	T	+	+	0	0	0	0	+	0
C. botulinum	0	ST	+	+	0	+	+	0	0	0

*Determined by Nagler reaction.
C, central; ST, subterminal; T, terminal.

fringens, one of the easiest of all obligate anaerobes to grow, replicates rapidly under anaerobic conditions with a generation time as short as 8 minutes at 43° to 45° C. The organism is relatively aerotolerant and shows "stormy fermentation" in milk. On blood agar, the colonies are typically surrounded by a "double zone of hemolysis": an inner zone of complete hemolysis that is due to θ-toxin and a larger outer zone of incomplete hemolysis that is due to α-toxin. Virtually all large series indicate that *C. perfringens* is the most common clinical isolate among clostridia, including blood cultures and cultures from infected sites such as intra-abdominal sepsis, genital tract infections, and soft tissue infections.[5]

With regard to the genus *Clostridium,* the term *toxin* refers to biologically active proteins that are antigenic and capable of neutralization by specific antisera. Many are lethal to animals.[2] Among the 12 toxins produced by *C. perfringens* are 4 major lethal toxins that are used to divide the species into five serologic types classified A to E. Additional virulence factors include enterotoxin, neuraminidase (sialidase), non–α-δ-θ-hemolysins, and the organism's vigorous metabolic activity.[2,5] Only type A strains are found in the microflora of both soil and the intestine. Because these strains are found in the soil as vegetative cells, it is assumed that soil is a natural habitat. When types B to E are added to soil, they are gradually eliminated over a period of months, thus indicating an inability to compete with the native type A strains.

INFECTIONS

Clostridial species may be recovered from a wide variety of commonly encountered infections, usually as a component of a polymicrobial flora. In most instances, no distinctive features are noted, and the role of *Clostridium* spp. in the pathogenesis of infection is problematic. The common denominator of these infections is that they are endogenous and reflect the normal habitat of clostridia on the skin and mucous membranes of the host. Unique features of clostridial infection that characterize a minority of cases are the production of gas at the infected site and histotoxic clostridial syndromes that reflect the activity of specific toxins; rarely, massive intravascular hemolysis may be seen.[6] Most *Clostridium* spp. produce large amounts of volatile

fatty acids in vitro. Production of hydrogen and nitrogen gas in vivo presumably accounts for the finding in some patients of gas at the infected site that may be detected by palpation, radiograph, or scans. Examples include crepitant cellulitis, emphysematous cholecystitis, and emphysematous cystitis. In each instance, other pathogens have also been implicated as causes of these conditions. At least 30 clostridial species have been isolated from infected sites; *C. perfringens,* the dominant species, accounts for about 20% to 30% of all isolates. The histotoxic clostridial syndromes (see Table 244-2) are discussed later in this chapter and in Chapters 242 and 243.

Bacteremia

The frequency of anaerobic bacteremia appears to be declining.[7] *Clostridium* spp., second only to *Bacteroides* spp. as clinically significant anaerobic isolates, account for less than 3% of all blood cultures; higher rates are seen in cancer hospitals, reflecting the importance of underlying intestinal carcinoma and leukemia.[8] *C. perfringens* is the most common isolate, followed by *C. septicum.* Clostridial endocarditis is rare but has been reported to occur on native valves as well as on vascular prostheses. In many instances, no obvious association can be found between the underlying illness and clostridial bacteremia, and one has the impression that the bacteremia often represents either contamination, presumably from the skin, or transient bacteremia of no clinical consequence. As many as 50% of clostridial isolates are judged to be contaminants. Gorbach and Thadepalli reviewed their experience with positive blood culture of 65 strains of clostridia from 49 patients.[9] They found that clostridial bacteremia was usually unrelated to the clinical syndrome and occurred in such settings as pulmonary tuberculosis, aspiration pneumonia, and meningococcemia. Their interpretation was that the organism either was a contaminant or simply caused transient bacteremia of no clinical importance. Other investigators have made similar observations, but some more recent studies have suggested a much higher percentage of clinically significant isolates.[10,11] In some clinical settings, such as intra-abdominal and soft tissue infections, decubitus ulcers, or gynecologic infections, clostridial isolates from the blood may be associated with the microbial flora of the infected site without the devastating consequences of

TABLE 244-2 Histotoxic Clostridial Syndromes

Clinical Illness	Organism	Toxin	Mouse LD₅₀ (ng)*
Soft tissue infection			
Gas gangrene	*C. perfringens*	α-Toxin (others)	50
Enteric diseases			
Food poisoning	*C. perfringens* type A	Enterotoxin	1400
Enteritis necroticans	*C. perfringens* type C	β-Toxin	8
Antibiotic-associated colitis	*C. difficile*	Toxin A	26 (ip)
Neutropenic enterocolitis	*C. septicum* (others)	Unknown, β-toxin?	
Neurologic syndromes			
Tetanus	*C. tetani*	Tetanospasmin	0.015 (ip)
Botulism	*C. botulinum*	Botulinal toxins A-G	0.00625 (type A, ip)

*Lethal dose for 50% of animals (LD₅₀) after intravenous challenge unless otherwise noted.
ip, intraperitoneal.

clostridial toxins. A clear-cut clinical relevance is found in a minority of conditions, such as infections associated with gas production, massive intravascular hemolysis, clostridial myonecrosis (gas gangrene), and *C. septicum* bacteremia in association with colon carcinoma or leukemia. An underlying bowel or female genital tract source is found in most clinically significant bacteremias.[6,10-12] In children younger than age 1, clostridial bacteremia is commonly associated with necrotizing enterocolitis,[6] although the role of clostridia species in the pathogenesis of this condition remains unclear. The dominant clostridial species isolated from blood culture, regardless of clinical significance, is *C. perfringens,* which accounts for 25% to 50% of infections.[9,11] Polymicrobial bacteremia reflecting an intestinal source is seen in about one third, with other isolates usually being *Bacteroides* spp. and Enterobacteriaceae.[10]

C. septicum bacteremia appears to be a unique syndrome associated with specific underlying diseases and a devastating clinical course.[13-15] Toxins produced in vivo by this organism include lecithinase, deoxyribonuclease, hyaluronidase, and a hemolysin. *C. septicum* is a relatively rare cause of gas gangrene and has been infrequently encountered in positive blood cultures for clostridia. When *C. septicum* bacteremia occurs, 70% to 80% of cases are associated with malignancies, most frequently leukemia in relapse or colon carcinoma. In some instances, isolation of *C. septicum* from blood culture preceded the identification of malignancy; the finding of *C. septicum* bacteremia mandates imaging of the lower intestine to rule out a carcinoma.[13,14,16] An association is also seen with cyclic neutropenia, but not other forms of congenital severe neutropenia, as well as neutropenia secondary to leukemia and cytotoxic drugs.[17,18] As many as 25% of patients with *C. septicum* bacteremia will have myonecrosis at metastatic sites,[14,15] and others may have unusual manifestations, including meningitis, osteomyelitis, septic arthritis, panophthalmitis, facial cellulitis, splenic abscess, and endocarditis. Rare cases of fatal *C. septicum* bacteremia have complicated the hemolytic uremic syndrome caused by *Escherichia coli* O157:H7.[19] *C. septicum* is a less common isolate in normal flora studies than is *C. perfringens;* it is recovered in stool in only about 2% of cases, although carriage rates in the appendix are reported at 10% to 63%.[20]

C. tertium is second to *C. septicum* as a cause of bacteremia in the setting of neutropenic enterocolitis.[21,22] Clostridial bacteremia has been reported in association with acquired immunodeficiency syndrome[10]; and, on rare occasions, *Clostridium sordellii,* has caused bacteremic illness with a high mortality.[23]

Intra-abdominal Infections

Clostridia are constant inhabitants of the intestine and are commonly encountered in endogenous infections involving bowel flora, including secondary peritonitis, intra-abdominal abscess, and wound infections after intestinal surgery. Isolation rates from intra-abdominal infections range from approximately 10% to 50% when appropriate anaerobic culture techniques are used[24,25]; in polymicrobial infections, many isolates are species other than *C. perfringens.* The great majority of these infections are polymicrobial, and the pathogenic significance of the clostridial isolates is unknown. Exceptions are the association of colon carcinoma with *C. septicum* bacteremia, as reviewed in the previous section, along with emphysematous cholecystitis and neutropenic enterocolitis (see earlier).

Biliary Tract Infections

Clostridia have been isolated from 10% to 20% of all diseased gallbladders at surgery.[26] Usually, the organism can be visualized by Gram stain of bile obtained at surgery. Cholecystitis involving clostridial species is similar to that caused by other organisms with two exceptions. First, clostridia in bile are the presumed source for gas gangrene of the abdominal wall, a rare but catastrophic complication of biliary tract surgery. The second exception is emphysematous cholecystitis, in which radiographs show gas in the gallbladder lumen, pericholecystic tissue, or biliary ducts.[27] Clostridia, particularly *C. perfringens,* are implicated in more than 50% of cases. At surgery the gallbladder is usually tense, gas is present under pressure in the lumen, the mucosa is gangrenous and often separated from the muscularis, pericholecystic abscess formation is common, and the gallbladder luminal contents are putrid and purulent. This severe form of biliary tract infection is most frequent in patients with diabetes and in men. The finding of gas in the biliary tract on radiography or computed tomography is a clear indication for early surgical intervention and antimicrobial treatment directed against clostridia, along with other enteric bacteria.

Female Genital Tract Infections

Clostridia are isolated from 4% to 20% of women with genital tract infections not involving sexually transmitted pathogens.[28,29] The most frequent conditions are tuboovarian and pelvic abscesses. These organisms have been recovered as part of normal vaginal flora in approximately 5% to 10% of women, and when present, the mean concentration was 10^8/mL of vaginal secretion.[30] In the postabortion period, the isolation frequency has been reported to be 19% to 29%.[31] Consequently, cultures or stains of specimens that are subject to contamination with vaginal flora, as well as most clostridia isolated from deep infected sites or even blood, cannot be meaningfully interpreted. Some authors have considered clostridia to be "benign saprophytes" in blood cultures of women with septic abortion. A notable exception, in which clostridia clearly play a major pathogenic role, is uterine gas gangrene, which is now a rare complication that was previously seen in the setting of septic abortion. Rarely, uterine gas gangrene has followed vaginal delivery or cesarean section or has complicated a uterine tumor or amniocentesis.[32,33] Debate continues about the role of hysterectomy in the management of clostridial uterine infection.[32]

Pleuropulmonary Infections

Clostridia have been recovered from 8% to 10% of anaerobic pulmonary infections, with *C. perfringens* accounting for half of the isolates.[34] These organisms have been reported primarily in empyema fluid but also from transtracheal aspirates. In many cases the clostridia are part of a polymicrobial flora.[9] In fewer than 20 English literature reports, clostridia have been recovered as the only isolates; the species is usually *C. perfringens.*[35] Aspiration of oropharyngeal flora has been considered to be the likely pathophysiologic mechanism in some cases, although clostridia are uncommonly isolated from typical aspiration pneumonia cases and never in pure culture.[36] Occasional cases have occurred after penetrating chest injury or thoracotomy for lung resection, and several patients have had antecedent thoracentesis or pleural biopsy, thus suggesting an iatrogenic cause. Less often, a hematogenous source has been suggested by cases complicating pulmonary infarction. The clinical features of these infections are similar to those involving other anaerobic bacteria, although an occasional case is characterized by extensive gas production in the pleural space or extensive necrosis of tissue and a rapidly progressive course.[35] Patients may be afebrile when first examined and without cough; pleuritic pain and pleural effusion are common. The mortality rate is similar to that for pleuropulmonary infections involving other anaerobic bacteria.[34]

Central Nervous System Infections

Intracranial infections involving *Clostridium* spp. are rare.[37] The great majority are manifested as cerebral abscess, with or without meningitis. Most cases involve penetrating trauma, such as lawn dart injuries[38]; additional cases are associated with infections of the middle ear. A characteristic feature is rapid evolution of symptoms after the traumatic event, often within 24 to 48 hours. Radiographs or computed tomographic scans typically show focal collections of gas. Although these cases are occasionally reported as "gas gangrene of the brain," the tendency for spread and systemic toxicity as seen with myonecrosis is minimal.

Soft Tissue Infections

Clostridial contamination of wounds is common, with isolation rates of 30% to 80% from traumatic open wounds. Clostridia may play a role in various infections of the skin, subcutaneous tissue, and muscle.

Such infections include (1) common soft tissue infections, in which clostridia are often a component of polymicrobial flora; (2) crepitant cellulitis; (3) suppurative myositis; and (4) clostridial myonecrosis (gas gangrene).

Included in the first category are a heterogeneous group of commonly encountered polymicrobial infections such as wound infections after abdominal surgery, perirectal cellulitis, perirectal abscesses, diabetic foot ulcers, decubitus ulcers, infections associated with vascular insufficiency, and stump infections after amputation. The pathogenic role of clostridia in these polymicrobial infections is unclear; clinically, they are similar to infections in which clostridia are not isolated. Numerous clostridial species may be involved, but the predominant isolates are *C. perfringens* and *C. ramosum.* The accompanying organisms are those that are commonly encountered in intra-abdominal infections, and the presumed source is the colonic flora. Monomicrobial osteomyelitis secondary to traumatic inoculation of soft tissue has been reported rarely.

Crepitant cellulitis is characterized by clinically detectable gas formation in the soft tissue.[39] These infections usually occur after trauma, the incubation period from the time of wounding to clinical evaluation is usually 3 days or longer, and systemic toxicity is generally minimal. Findings at the infected site include crepitance on palpation resulting from gas formation, which is usually far more abundant than that seen in myonecrosis. Pain is minimal, the site shows edema with little skin discoloration, and a thin, dark discharge is present, often with a characteristic foul odor, that on Gram stain shows neutrophils and typical bacteria. Clostridia, particularly *C. perfringens,* are the most common cause, although other bacteria such as Enterobacteriaceae and *Staphylococcus aureus* may be implicated. Rarely, patients have a more fulminant course, with rapid spread through fascial planes and evidence of clostridial toxemia.

Suppurative myositis that is due to clostridia is similar to tropical pyomyositis caused by *S. aureus.* It is seen most often in misusers of parenteral drugs and usually involves the thigh or forearm and not necessarily the area of trauma or drug injection.[9] In distinction from gas gangrene, which also involves muscle, clostridial myositis is characterized by a suppurative collection without myonecrosis and lack of the severe systemic complications associated with gas gangrene. These infections generally respond well to drainage and antimicrobials. Operative findings may include abscess formation, localized myositis, and dissecting fasciitis.[9]

In an unusual outbreak,[40] almost 90 injectable heroin users in the United Kingdom and Ireland developed injection site inflammation, sustained hypotension, and marked leukocytosis leading to a high mortality; *C. novyi* was implicated.

Clostridial Myonecrosis (Gas Gangrene)

Few infections are as critical as clostridial myonecrosis (gas gangrene), a rare, rapidly progressive, and devastating infection characterized by muscle necrosis and systemic toxicity caused by potent clostridial exotoxins.

History. In 1892, Welch and Nuttall characterized a gram-positive, gas-producing, anaerobic bacillus that reproduced rapidly in blood vessels post mortem. Four years later, Welch and Flexner associated this organism with a variety of clinical syndromes, including gas gangrene. The organism was known as *Bacillus aerogenes capsulatus,* later as *Bacillus perfringens,* still later as *C. welchii,* and now as *C. perfringens.* The history of the clinical entity, gas gangrene, is largely the history of wars of the 20th century.[41] Although scattered reports go back to antiquity, before World War I the disease was curiously rare, even in times of conflict, including the American Civil War. During World War I, the clostridial infections gas gangrene and tetanus were both common and due to severe trauma, gross soil contamination, and delayed surgical intervention.

The incidence of gas gangrene complicating battlefield trauma in World War I was 5% and dropped to 0.3% to 0.7% in World War II, 0.2% in the Korean War, and 0.0002% during the war in Vietnam.[42-44] These declining rates reflect improving management of battlefield

trauma with prompt wound cleansing and débridement and, in Vietnam, rapid transport of casualties to sites of high-quality trauma surgery.

Pathogens. *C. perfringens* is the major causative species and accounts for approximately 80% of cases with positive cultures. Other clostridial causative species include *C. septicum, C. novyi, C. sordellii, C. histolyticum, C. fallax,* and *C. bifermentans.* During World War I, *C. septicum* was second only to *C. perfringens* in causing gas gangrene, and it ranked third in World War II. Some patients have more than one species of clostridia at the infected site, as well as other species of bacteria at the infected site. Implicated clostridial species produce at least 12 exotoxins, including 7 that are lethal when injected intraperitoneally into mice (Table 244-3). In gas gangrene, the most important toxins are thought to be phospholipase C (α-toxin), which has a molecular weight of about 43,000 Da and is responsible for splitting lecithin, the major phospholipid in eukaryotic cell membranes, to phosphoryl choline and diacylglycerol; and a thiol-activated hemolysin (θ-toxin or perfringolysin O).[2,5] The role of other extracellular enzymes such as collagenase (κ-toxin), hyaluronidase (μ-toxin), DNase (ν-toxin), and neuraminidase (sialidase) is unclear. The structural genes for α-toxin (*plc*) and θ-toxin (*pfoA*) have been cloned and mapped. Expression of these genes in *E. coli* has permitted the production of pure toxin products, allowing for the elucidation of structure-function relationships. Intravenous administration of α-toxin in experimental animals results in massive hemolysis, platelet destruction, capillary damage, and death.

Studies using recombinant α-toxin and θ-toxin in rabbits have shown that α-toxin is the major lethal factor in *C. perfringens* infections and induces cardiovascular collapse by direct inhibition of myocardial contractility; hypotension resulting from θ-toxin is not associated with direct cardiotoxicity and is probably due to induction of endogenous mediators.[45]

Immunocompetent survivors of *C. septicum* myonecrosis, but not bacteremia alone, form antibodies to α-toxin.[46]

Epidemiology. Gas gangrene usually complicates wounds associated with trauma or surgery. Routine cultures from traumatic open wounds indicate that 20% to 80% percent are contaminated by clostridia, although gas gangrene remains rare. MacLennan reported

TABLE 244-3   *Clostridium perfringens* **Toxins**

Toxin	Biologic Activity*	Strain Type
Major lethal		
α	Lethal, lecithinase, necrotizing, hemolytic	A-E
β	Lethal, necrotizing, transmural necrosis with small bowel inoculation; trypsin labile	B, C
ϵ	Lethal, permease, trypsin activatable	B, D
ι	Lethal, dermonecrotic, binary, ADP ribosylating, trypsin activatable	E
Minor		
δ	Hemolysin, lethal	B, C
θ	Hemolysin (O$_2$ labile), cytolysin, lethal	A-E
κ	Collagenase, gelatinase, necrotizing, lethal	A-E
λ	Protease	B, D, E
μ	Hyaluronidase	A-E
ν	Deoxyribonuclease, leukocidin, hemolytic, necrotizing, lethal	A-E
Neuraminidase	*N*-acetylneuraminic acid, glycohydrolase	A-E
Other		
Enterotoxin	Enterotoxic, cytotoxic	A, C, D (B, E not tested)

*Lethality tested in mice with intravenous or intraperitoneal injection.
ADP, adenosine diphosphate.

that, in the Western Desert Campaign of World War II, 20% to 30% of all battlefield wounds were contaminated by clostridia, but gas gangrene developed in only 0.32% of these wounds.[42] A review of 187,936 major open wounds of violence by Altemeier and Furste found the incidence of gas gangrene to be 1.7%.[43] Interestingly, no difference was seen between the bacteriology of wounds in which gas gangrene later developed and that of wounds in which it did not. These observations emphasize the importance of local wound conditions in the pathogenesis of infection. Factors that promote the replication of vegetative forms and elaboration of toxins in the setting of hypoxic tissue include the presence of foreign bodies, vascular insufficiency, and concurrent infection with other microbes. The minimum dose of bacteria required to produce gas gangrene in guinea pigs was reduced by 10^3 by injection into devitalized tissue and reduced by 10^6 by contamination of muscle with sterile soil.[47]

In the civilian population, approximately half of gas gangrene cases follow trauma, and most others occur postoperatively. The most frequent traumatic injuries are vehicular or agricultural accidents with open fractures, followed by crush injuries, industrial accidents, and gunshot wounds.[44] In the surgical setting, the most frequent antecedent procedures are intestinal surgery, especially colon resection and biliary tract surgery. Occasional cases of gas gangrene are associated with vascular insufficiency in the lower extremities occurring in association with vascular gangrene, diabetic foot ulcers, and decubitus ulcers, or they are seen as a complication of burns or amputation. Case clusters have occurred among injection drug users[48]; other cases have occurred after intramuscular or even subcutaneous injection of epinephrine.[49] Uterine gas gangrene usually occurs in the setting of a septic, usually criminal abortion and less commonly with other gynecologic procedures or after delivery.[32,33] Spontaneous or nontraumatic gas gangrene is a rare form of the infection without any associated traumatic or surgical wounding. Recent data suggest that most cases of spontaneous gas gangrene are due to *C. septicum*.[15]

Unlike typical cases of gas gangrene, which follow trauma, in most of those caused by *C. septicum,* no obvious external portal of entry can be found. In this more recently recognized syndrome, often referred to as nontraumatic or spontaneous gas gangrene, the presumed source is the colon.[14,15] Typical symptoms include a sudden onset of fever, abdominal pain, vomiting, and diarrhea, and rapid progression to shock is common. The patient may initially appear to have appendicitis, but the fulminant course is clearly atypical. Intravascular hemolysis is rarely encountered. Up to 25% of patients have myonecrosis at metastatic sites,[14] and nearly all patients have evidence of altered integrity of the bowel mucosa that is due to leukemic infiltrates, tumor, or "neutropenic enterocolitis." In one instance, *C. septicum* gas gangrene developed in temporal relation to surveillance colonoscopy with biopsies in a man with ulcerative colitis; 10 days later a cecal carcinoma was found.[50]

The source of the organism has been controversial. Clostridia are ubiquitous and found in soil and air samples, including operating room air, dust, food, and clothing.[51] Concentrations vary, but fertile soil typically contains 10^8/g. The highest concentrations are in the intestinal tract; intestinal strains are also believed to be more virulent, and an endogenous source is suspected even in cases associated with gross soil contamination. Person-to-person transmission is rare, although occasional "outbreaks" have been reported.[51] Altemeier and Furste showed that *C. perfringens* strains recovered from an infected wound were 10^3 to 10^6 times more virulent in guinea pigs than were soil strains.[47]

Clinical Manifestations. Gas gangrene is a fulminant infection with prominent findings at the infection site and severe systemic toxicity.[42,44,52] Typical clinical settings are (1) traumatic injury or a penetrating wound, usually of an extremity; (2) surgery, primarily of the intestine or biliary tract; (3) septic criminal abortion or delivery; (4) soft tissue lesions associated with vascular insufficiency or burns; and (5) underlying colorectal or pelvic cancer or neutropenia complicating leukemia or cytotoxic therapy.

The usual incubation period from the time of injury to the onset of symptoms is 1 to 4 days (range, 6 hours to 3 weeks). The earliest symptom noted by the patient is the sudden onset of unrelenting and severe pain at the site of the wound; less commonly, the sensation is described as heaviness or pressure. Initial physical examination of the site may be normal, and a sudden onset of severe pain in the proper clinical setting, even in the absence of local findings, should alert the practitioner to the possibility of gas gangrene. The disease process progresses rapidly, and within minutes to hours localized tense edema, pallor, and tenderness are seen. Gas may be noted in the soft tissues by palpation, radiographs, or scans, but crepitance is a late finding and should not be considered a sine qua non; it is neither a sensitive nor a specific feature. The skin initially appears pale and then progresses to a magenta or bronze discoloration, often followed by the appearance of hemorrhagic bullae and gross subcutaneous emphysema (Fig. 244-1). As the lesion progresses, a thin, dirty brown, serosanguineous discharge may be present along with a characteristic offensive odor described as sweetish or "mousey" and different from the putrid odor of other more common anaerobic infections. Gram stain of the discharge often shows a large number of typical gram-positive or gram-variable rods with sparse or no white blood cells (Fig. 244-1). When *C. perfringens* is involved, the organism shows the typical boxcar appearance without spores. The absence of white cells locally is ascribed to the lecithinase, θ-toxin, or other toxins that lyse neutrophils. Stevens and colleagues examined bulla fluid from a patient with nontraumatic gas gangrene caused by *C. septicum* and demonstrated the typical finding of numerous gram-positive bacilli with an absence of neutrophils.[15] Using standard assays, they were unable to demonstrate α-toxin or θ-toxin in the blister fluid; however, they were able to show, in vitro, that minute amounts of fluid had adverse effects on neutrophil viability, morphology, and function, including chemotaxis and phagocytosis.

In a mouse model of gas gangrene, Stevens and associates used isogenic, toxin-deficient mutants of *C. perfringens* and toxin-neutralizing monoclonal antibodies to show that both α-toxin and θ-toxin attenuate the inflammatory response by impeding directed migration of neutrophils and destroying neutrophils at the site of infection. Furthermore, toxins induce dysregulation of neutrophil–endothelial cell adhesion, thereby contributing to vascular leukostasis, impaired tissue perfusion, and the rapid invasion of viable tissue.[53]

The host response to infection of soft tissue with most bacterial pathogens results in increased blood flow, as evidenced by the classic findings of inflammation: *rubor, calor,* and *tumor.* In contrast, tissues involved with gas gangrene do not bleed. Experimental studies have shown that myonecrosis in gas gangrene results from ischemia caused by profound obstruction to blood flow produced by intravascular aggregation of platelets, fibrin, and neutrophils.[54] These platelet activation responses are precipitated by phospholipase C and mediated by platelet gpIIb/IIIa.[55]

Profound systemic findings accompany these changes at the wound site, including diaphoresis, tachycardia disproportionate to temperature, and extreme anxiety on the part of the patient, who often remains exceedingly alert until the very terminal stages. Fever may be deceptively low or absent in the early stages. Bacteremia occurs in about 15% of cases. Late complications include intravascular hemolysis (the hematocrit may fall by one-half in a matter of hours), hemoglobinuria, hypotension, renal failure, and metabolic acidosis. Terminally, coma develops and the patient's entire body may become swollen and crepitant, with a typical magenta or bronze color.

Diagnosis. Early diagnosis is critical. The diagnosis of gas gangrene is based on the clinical findings, demonstration of myonecrosis at surgery, and supporting microbiologic data. Early clinical clues to this infection include the recognized settings of infection, severe pain disproportionate to the physical findings, and systemic toxicity with tachycardia. Typical findings at the site of injury include tense edema, discoloration, and hemorrhagic bullae; evidence of gas in soft tissue; Gram stains of exudate showing typical rods with sparse or absent white blood cells; the typical discharge with an offensive odor; and computed tomography or magnetic resonance imaging showing muscle compartment involvement with gas in the muscle and fascial planes.

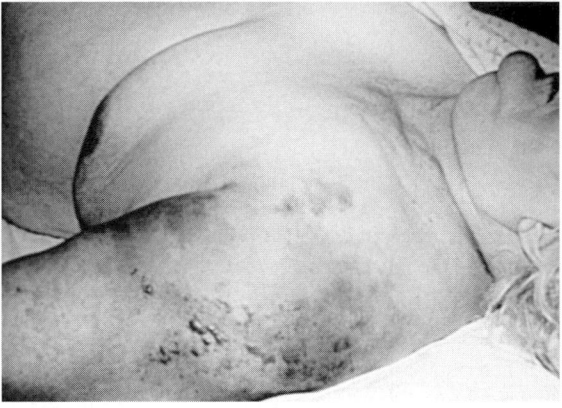

A

B

C

FIGURE 244-1. A 77-year-old woman with endometrial carcinoma and poorly controlled diabetes mellitus suddenly and spontaneously developed severe shoulder pain followed by discoloration, blister formation, and crepitance. A surgical specimen of devitalized deltoid muscle grew *Clostridium septicum*, as did premortem blood cultures. **A,** Appearance of the shoulder a few hours after the onset of pain showing edema, mottled discoloration, and bullae. **B,** Gram stain of a watery blister aspirate showing gram-positive rods and an absence of inflammatory cells. **C,** Gram stain of deltoid muscle obtained at surgery showing myonecrosis, numerous gram-positive rods, and an absence of inflammatory cells (× 1000). *(Courtesy of Dr. Steven Pancoast, Scranton, PA.)*

Bacteriologic studies support the diagnosis when clostridia are seen in the Gram stain of exudate and when the species implicated in gas gangrene (primarily *C. perfringens*) are recovered in cultured exudate or blood. Only 10% to 15% of patients with clostridial myonecrosis will have documented bacteremia.

In the differential diagnosis, the major considerations are other severe soft tissue infections, among which are crepitant cellulitis, streptococcal fasciitis, necrotizing fasciitis resulting from a mixed aerobic-anaerobic infection, and necrotizing infections caused by *Vibrio vulnificus*. Ultimately, gas gangrene is a surgical diagnosis made when involved muscle is visualized. Affected muscle has a pale or darkened, "cooked" appearance and fails to contract when incised or electrically stimulated; the cut surface does not bleed. The extent of myonecrosis is often greater than the skin changes indicate.

Therapy. Current treatment practice has been derived from many retrospective human studies and a number of animal model experiments (Fig. 244-2). The most important component of treatment is prompt and extensive surgical débridement, with wide excision of involved muscle when the abdominal wall is involved, aggressive débridement or amputation of an involved extremity, and hysterectomy in most cases of uterine gas gangrene. All necrotic muscle must be débrided, which often requires daily reoperation. Some authors argue that antecedent hyperbaric oxygen therapy (see later) facilitates surgery by clearly demarcating viable tissue and permitting less radical tissue excision.[52,56] Patients with evidence of a compartment syndrome should have prompt fasciotomy without delay for hyperbaric oxygen, even if it is immediately at hand.

Demello and colleagues used a dog model of gas gangrene to evaluate the roles of antibiotics, surgery, and hyperbaric oxygen in varied combinations.[56] These studies showed that only antibiotics consistently enhanced survival and that, without antibiotics, regardless of alternative treatment, no dogs survived. Treatment of human infection solely with surgery and hyperbaric oxygen in the antibiotic era has been reported, but the weight of evidence is that early antimicrobial therapy is essential for an optimal outcome.

Penicillin G in dosages of 10 to 24 million units daily is generally considered to be the drug of choice for patients with gas gangrene.[57] Data indicate increasing resistance of *C. perfringens* and more profound resistance in other species.[58] Nevertheless, most authorities continue to regard penicillin as the preferred agent because most strains are still susceptible at easily obtained drug levels. Alternatives for patients who have contraindications to penicillin or when resistance is a concern include chloramphenicol, metronidazole, and imipenem. In vitro, these drugs are active against virtually all strains of clostridia, but extensive clinical experience is lacking. Other agents with good in vitro activity are erythromycin, rifampin, clindamycin, and tetracycline.[58,59] Cefoxitin is less active against clostridia than are most other cephalosporins and should be avoided. Gas gangrene has been reported to develop during and in spite of surgical prophylaxis with cephalothin.[60]

Concerns about the efficacy of penicillin G arise not only from in vitro susceptibility data showing increasing resistance but also from experimental animal studies. Studying gas gangrene in guinea pigs, Altemeier and co-workers showed that tetracycline and chloramphenicol were superior to penicillin.[43,61] More recently, Stevens and associates evaluated antimicrobials in a mouse model of gas gangrene in which infection was produced with a strain of *C. perfringens* that was susceptible to all tested antibiotics and survival was the end point. Penicillin-treated animals fared no better than untreated controls, but improved outcomes were achieved with clindamycin, metronidazole, rifampin, and tetracycline.[62] This group also found that protein synthesis inhibitors were better inhibitors of toxin synthesis than were cell wall–active agents and that the combination of penicillin plus clindamycin had considerably better efficacy than did penicillin alone.[63,64] The impact that such studies should have on antibiotic recommendations is not obvious. However, in view of these observations and the severity of clostridial myonecrosis, it would seem prudent to combine penicillin with clindamycin, tetracycline, or metronidazole. If Gram

FIGURE 244-2. Algorithm for management of gas gangrene.

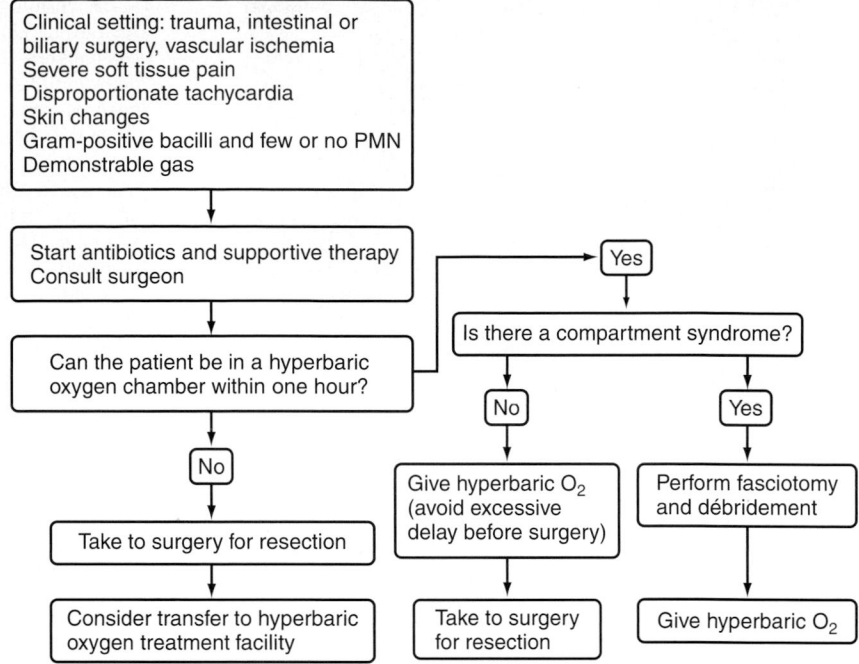

stain of exudate demonstrates polymicrobial infection, other antibiotics should be added accordingly.

Antitoxin for gas gangrene was introduced in 1918 and was later commercially developed and used widely in World War II. Later studies of this horse serum prepared against the toxins of five clostridial species known to cause gas gangrene showed a lack of efficacy and a high frequency of allergic reaction.[56] Antitoxin is no longer available commercially.

Hyperbaric oxygen treatment for gas gangrene has been used for over 30 years, but consensus has still not been reached on its value. Adequately controlled trials do not exist,[65] and many reports include patients who did not have confirmed myonecrosis. The debate about efficacy continues, with passionate voices on both sides.[44-47,49,51] The rationale for the use of hyperbaric oxygen includes the observations that raising local tissue oxygen concentrations arrests clostridial replication and α-toxin production and that hyperbaric oxygen treatment of experimental animals reduces mortality.[52,56] Using a murine model of clostridial myonecrosis, Stevens and colleagues showed an additive beneficial effect of hyperbaric oxygen combined with metronidazole or penicillin in animals challenged with a large inoculum of *C. perfringens*. In this model, clindamycin was superior to both penicillin and metronidazole, and its efficacy was not enhanced further by adjunctive treatment with hyperbaric oxygen.[66] The weight of clinical evidence indicates that hyperbaric oxygen therapy reduces morbidity and mortality when combined with surgery and antibiotics; however, efficacy is generally determined by comparison to historical controls, and some argue that institutions with hyperbaric chambers are referral centers more likely to provide aggressive surgery and medical support and, therefore, more likely to obtain good results. In uterine myonecrosis, hyperbaric oxygen has been less efficacious, and most authorities do not advocate its use.

Controversy continues about the timing of hyperbaric oxygen treatment and surgery. If fasciotomy is indicated, it should not be delayed for hyperbaric oxygen therapy. Use of hyperbaric oxygen before surgery has the potential benefit of (1) more clearly demarcating involved muscle, thus enabling the surgeon to define the extent of resection necessary and spare some viable tissue; and (2) potentially halting toxin production. The standard treatment regimen includes five "dives" of 3 atm of pressure within the first 48 hours. Ideally, the first treatment would be given before surgery, but surgery should not be de-

layed if a chamber is not immediately at hand or available at a referral center within a 1-hour time frame. The aerotolerance of *C. septicum* may reduce the efficacy of hyperbaric oxygen treatment for myonecrosis caused by this pathogen.

Prognosis. Before the availability of penicillin, mortality rates reported for gas gangrene encountered in the world wars were approximately 30%. In the antibiotic era, mortality rates are generally around 20% to 25%, but many patients are left severely crippled or disfigured by the necessary surgery. Poor prognostic findings include leukopenia, intravascular hemolysis, renal failure, advanced age, involvement of the abdominal wall, "spontaneous gas gangrene," and underlying colorectal cancer or leukemia and *C. septicum* infection. Without treatment, mortality approaches 100% within 48 hours of the onset of symptoms. Prompt treatment is essential, and treatment delay is associated with increased mortality.

Enteric Infections

Four histotoxic clostridial syndromes that involve the gastrointestinal tract are recognized: *C. perfringens* food poisoning, enteritis necroticans, *Clostridium difficile*–induced diarrhea or colitis, and neutropenic enterocolitis (Table 244-4). In all but neutropenic enterocolitis, the responsible toxin has been defined, and when that toxin is used, the disease has been reproduced in experimental animals. In neutropenic enterocolitis, in which *C. septicum* is the usual but not exclusive pathogen, the responsible toxin is not known, although β-toxin is an attractive candidate because of similarities to enteritis necroticans. These conditions show considerable variation in pathophysiologic mechanisms, risk factors, clinical features, and treatment (see Table 244-4). *C. difficile* colitis is discussed in Chapter 92. Neonatal necrotizing enterocolitis has been associated with clostridial species, particularly *Clostridium butyricum* and *C. perfringens*, but the role of these bacteria in its pathogenesis remains unclear.[67]

Enteritis Necroticans

Enteritis necroticans is a necrotizing infection of the small intestine caused by the β-toxin of *C. perfringens* type C. An important enteric disease of sheep, calves, and piglets in veterinary medicine, its human equivalent appears to occur in the presence of a unique combination of societal and nutritional factors in which protein malnutrition, pig feasts, sweet potatoes, and nematodes all play contributing roles.

TABLE 244-4 Enteric Diseases That Are Due to Histotoxic Clostridia

Feature	Clostridium perfringens Food Poisoning	Enteritis Necroticans	C. difficile Colitis	Neutropenic Enterocolitis
Pathogen	C. perfringens type A	C. perfringens type C	C. difficile	C. septicum (C. tertium. C. perfringens, others)
Toxin	Enterotoxin (cytotoxin)	β-Toxin	Toxin A	Unknown; β-toxin?
MW (daltons)	35,000	48,000	440,000	?
Trypsin sensitivity	No	Yes	Yes	?
Mouse LD$_{50}$ (ng)	1400	8	26	?
Rabbit ileal loop	Fluid flux, epithelial damage	Segmental transmural necrosis	Mucosal hemorrhage, fluid flux	?
Distribution	Worldwide	Papua New Guinea; other Third World countries	Worldwide	Worldwide
Carrier rate (stool)	90%-95% for C. perfringens; up to 30% for enterotoxin-producing strains	20%-70% in endemic areas	3% in healthy adults	2% for C. septicum (10%-63% in appendix)
Diagnosis	Serology, enterotoxin assay of stools, quantitative culture of food source and stools	Serology, fluorescence-labeled antibody to demonstrate organism	Tissue culture assay for toxin B	Blood cultures
Clinical findings	Diarrhea, abdominal cramps, minimal systemic toxicity	Bloody diarrhea, vomiting, abdominal pain	Diarrhea, fever	Bacteremia, abdominal pain, vomiting, diarrhea, shock
Pathology	Small bowel epithelial damage, polymorphonuclear infiltrate	Small bowel segmental transmural necrosis	Colitis ± pseudomembranes	Colitis (usually cecal) with hemorrhagic necrosis
Treatment	None (self-limited)	Penicillin ± surgery	Metronidazole or vancomycin orally	Penicillin ± surgery
Mortality	Extremely rare	15%-45% (serious cases)	10%-30% (serious cases; untreated)	50%-75%

LD$_{50}$, lethal dose for 50%; MW, molecular weight.

History. After the end of World War II, hundreds of cases of enteritis necroticans occurred in malnourished individuals in northwestern Germany, where the disease was named Darmbrand. Workers at that time suspected *C. perfringens* type F (later reclassified as type C) on the basis of its recovery in stool from afflicted patients and the production of a similar disease by injecting broth cultures of the organism into the small intestine of experimental animals. Subsequent work demonstrated that the pathologic lesion could be attributed to an exotoxin. Renewed interest in the disease occurred in the 1960s, when enteritis necroticans, known locally as "pig-bel," was found to be endemic in the highlands of Papua New Guinea.[68-70]

Pathogen. *C. perfringens* type C is widely distributed in soil and has been found in the stools of many asymptomatic humans, as well as animals; carrier rates are reportedly 20% to 70% in endemic areas. Exposure to the etiologic organism is therefore common, and other factors must be invoked in the pathophysiology of the disease. Especially important is the β-toxin, a protein exotoxin of about 48,000 Da that is extremely sensitive to proteolytic enzymes.

Epidemiology. Enteritis necroticans is endemic in the highlands of Papua New Guinea, where surveys in 1964 showed a prevalence of 50 cases per 10,000 population with a mortality rate of 14 per 100,000.[70] At the time it was the most common cause of acute abdomen in surgical practice and the most common cause of death in children older than 12 months in the region; over 86% of adults in the area had circulating antibody to the β-toxin. Sporadic outbreaks have been reported from Southeast Asia, the South Pacific, Africa, China, and Western countries. It is thought that the disease is more frequent than generally appreciated, especially in areas with widespread malnutrition. This contention is supported by a report of 30 cases in a Khmer refugee camp at the Thai-Kampuchean border in 1985.[71] An unusual case occurred in a well-nourished but poorly controlled diabetic boy from the United States after ingestion of pig intestines (chitterlings).[72]

The high prevalence of the disease in Papua New Guinea is attributed to unique cultural habits. Although all people are presumably exposed, it is postulated that the inoculum is especially high during pig feasts, in which cooking is usually inadequate to eliminate clostridial spores or inactivate preformed toxin; the sudden protein intake is thought to encourage the growth of *C. perfringens* and toxin production. The organism appears to adhere to the small bowel, probably through specific pili, and produce β-toxin, which is protected from normal proteolytic enzyme destruction by several contributing factors,

including (1) protein malnutrition, which results in depletion of protease enzymes; (2) the dietary staple of sweet potato (*Ipomoea batatas*), which contains heat-stable inhibitors of trypsin; and (3) a high incidence of colonization (70% to 80%) with *Ascaris lumbricoides,* which secretes trypsin inhibitors. Trigger meals with peanuts and meats other than pork are reported. The high prevalence of the disease in children appears to reflect immunologic naiveté. Experimental support for the proposed mechanism is based on studies showing that inocula of broth cultures or culture filtrates produce typical segmental, transmural necrosis, which can be prevented by combining the filtrate with pancreatin (which destroys β-toxin) or by challenge to animals immunized with β-toxoid vaccine.

Clinical and Pathologic Features. Enteritis necroticans is a segmental disease of the small intestine chiefly involving the jejunum and rarely the ileum; the colon is never involved. The pathologic spectrum of disease ranges from small necrotic patches with normal intervening mucosa to full-thickness necrosis involving large segments.[73] With advanced lesions the bowel wall becomes thin and subject to perforation. Microscopic studies show necrotic villi, mucosal infarction with edema, hemorrhage, and a transmural neutrophilic infiltrate.

The usual initial symptoms are severe upper abdominal pain, distention, vomiting, passage of bloody stool, and later, signs of small bowel obstruction.[69,70] The incubation period after ingestion of the high-protein meal is usually about 1 to 4 days but varies from hours to a week.

Considerable variation is noted in the spectrum of clinical features, which range from mild diarrhea mimicking common forms of gastroenteritis to acute enteritis, intestinal obstruction, and a fulminant course with death in 24 hours.

Diagnosis. In the endemic area, the diagnosis is usually made by clinical observations, sometimes supported by typical pathologic changes in the small bowel noted at surgery or autopsy. Fluorescent-stained antibody to the clostridial capsular antigen has been used to identify the causative agent in stool or bowel contents. Cultures are difficult to interpret because of the relatively high carrier rates in asymptomatic persons and the frequent overgrowth of *C. perfringens* type A in stool cultures.

Treatment. The preferred antibiotics are penicillin G, metronidazole, or chloramphenicol. Indications for surgical intervention include persistent toxicity, persistent intestinal obstruction, suspected perforation, and severe recurrent bleeding. Approximately 50% of patients with serious disease require surgery, which generally consists of resecting 50 to 200 cm of jejunum. Excluding patients with mild disease, the mortality rate is reported at 15% to 45%. Administration of antiserum has no role. A very promising development has been prevention of the disease by using a β-toxoid vaccine prepared from culture filtrates of *C. perfringens* type C. In 1980, after a successful controlled trial of this toxoid demonstrated protection for over 2 years, the Papua New Guinea health services initiated an immunization program with pig-bel vaccine (Wellcome, Beckenham, UK) for children at 2, 4, and 6 months of age.[74] Within 2 years, hospital admissions that were due to enteritis necroticans dropped to less than one fifth of prevaccination levels.

Neutropenic Enterocolitis

Neutropenic enterocolitis (typhlitis) is seen with congenital neutropenia, leukemia, or neutropenia resulting from cytotoxic chemotherapy.[75,76] It characteristically involves the cecum but may extend throughout the bowel. *C. septicum* is the usual cause, and the major risk factor is neutropenia, but antecedent mucosal damage may be important inasmuch as some patients have severe mucositis. Common initial findings are fever, abdominal pain, and diarrhea, which is watery and occasionally bloody. Abdominal distention, tenderness often localizing to the right lower quadrant, and decreased bowel sounds are found. At autopsy or laparotomy, the cecum and adjacent bowel show edema, hemorrhage, and necrosis, with typical organisms invading the bowel wall. Physicians should consider clostridial infection in any patient with known gastrointestinal or pelvic malignancy or neutropenia in whom abdominal pain, tenderness, and fever develop, because early institution of antibiotics will salvage up to one half of patients.[77] The role of surgery is controversial.[75,76,78] Some cases respond to bowel rest and antibiotics; in others, extensive surgery is sometimes necessary to débride gangrenous lesions of the bowel. In addition to *C. septicum,* other clostridia that are less commonly implicated in neutropenic enterocolitis include *C. perfringens, C. sporogenes, C. sphenoides, C. sordellii, C. paraperfringens,* and *C. tertium.*[79] *C. tertium,* a rare cause of bacteremia overall, is the second most frequent blood culture isolate in this setting but is clinically distinctive in that it causes a milder illness than does *C. septicum* and has a favorable prognosis with antibiotic treatment. Fecal carriage of *C. tertium* in the setting of neutropenia may be increased when compared with healthy people and may be related to selection by previously administered antibiotics.[21]

Clostridium perfringens Food Poisoning

Enterotoxin-producing strains of *C. perfringens* type A cause a mild form of food poisoning that is found worldwide,[80] and is one of the most common causes of foodborne illness in the United States.[81] Less commonly, they produce sporadic diarrhea that may or may not be associated with antibiotic use.[82]

Pathogen. *C. perfringens* type A is responsible for nearly all cases of *C. perfringens* food poisoning. In a food product in which the toxin survives cooking, spores germinate, and vegetative cells multiply during slow cooling or inadequate reheating. Illness results after ingestion of food containing large amounts of vegetative cells, which undergo sporulation in the small intestine, producing an enterotoxin in the process. Some authors refer to the responsible toxin as a cytotoxin because it produces cellular damage, in order to distinguish it from true enterotoxin, which produces no such cell toxicity. Some investigators believe that the enterotoxin is a structural, but not essential component of the spore coat; others claim that high levels are produced in the cytoplasm after activation of the enterotoxin gene (*cpe*) by transcriptional factors that also control sporulation genes.[5] Methods of detecting toxigenic potential include techniques for enhancing sporulation. Enterotoxin was produced by 51 of 66 strains from foodborne disease cases as compared with 1 of 117 strains recovered from the stools of healthy controls.[83] One study showed that 11 of 35 healthy persons (31%) harbored toxigenic strains.[84]

The enterotoxin is a polypeptide of 320 amino acids, has a molecular weight of about 35,000 Da, and is susceptible to pronase, but not trypsin, chymotrypsin, or papain.[2,5] Biologic activities of the heat-labile toxin include fluid accumulation in the rabbit ileal loop 90 minutes after challenge, induction of vomiting in cynomolgus monkeys with orogastric challenge, lethality after an intravenous challenge to mice with a median lethal dose of 80 μg, and cytotoxicity to Vero cells.[2,85] In the small bowel, the enterotoxin binds to a brush-border membrane receptor and then induces a calcium ion–dependent breakdown in permeability that results in the loss of low-molecular-weight metabolites and ions.[5,85,86] This loss alters intracellular metabolic function, including macromolecular synthesis, and is associated with morphologic damage and eventual cell lysis.

Bowness and associates demonstrated that *C. perfringens* enterotoxin acts as a superantigen and, in the absence of antigen processing, significantly stimulates human lymphocytes.[87] Thus the pathogenesis of *C. perfringens* food poisoning may involve a massive release of inflammatory mediators through superantigen reacting with a large proportion of T lymphocytes.

Epidemiology. *C. perfringens* food poisoning follows the ingestion of food containing at least 108 enterotoxin-producing organisms and is virtually always associated with food that was inadequately stored. The most frequent vehicles are animal protein foods such as cooked meat, poultry, stews, meat pies, and gravies that have become grossly contaminated during long periods of slow cooling after cooking and storage at ambient temperature. On occasion, vegetable protein sources such as beans have been the vehicle for *C. perfringens* food poisoning. The spores survive cooking, the heat-activated spores germinate as the food cools, and optimal growth in meat is achieved at 43° to 47° C, with a generation time of 10 to 12 minutes. Most outbreaks have been associated with commercially prepared food in restaurants and institutions; home outbreaks are uncommon, in contrast to those caused by *S. aureus* and *Salmonella* spp. To prevent disease, cooked meat should be refrigerated if not served immediately to prevent the growth of vegetative cells; rewarmed meats should be heated to an internal temperature of greater than 75° C before serving.

C. perfringens is a relatively common cause of foodborne outbreaks, accounting for approximately 3% to 10% of such outbreaks in the United States, with an average of 24 victims per outbreak.[80,82] About 25 outbreaks are reported annually. It is likely that many outbreaks go undetected as a result of the relatively mild clinical symptoms and the specialized laboratory techniques required to confirm *C. perfringens* as the cause. Recent studies have expanded the epidemiologic spectrum of *C. perfringens*–induced diarrheal disease, and the organism has been implicated in sporadic cases of diarrhea, antibiotic-associated diarrhea, and diarrhea in chronic care facilities.[82,88] The diarrhea in these alternative forms lasts longer, with an average duration of 11 days.

Clinical Features. Most cases occur in the setting of a common-source outbreak, with meat being the most frequent vehicle. Sporadic cases are presumably common as well but are unlikely to be investigated. In outbreaks, the attack rate in exposed persons averages 50% to 60%. One of the largest outbreaks was seen after a banquet in New York City attended by 1800 people, over 900 of whom later had symptomatic disease.[89] The incubation period after exposure is brief, usually 7 to 15 hours with a range of 6 to 24 hours. The usual symptoms are watery diarrhea in over 90% and abdominal cramps in about 80%. Less frequent symptoms are nausea (25%), vomiting (9%), and fever (24%). Nearly all patients have spontaneous resolution of symptoms within 6 to 24 hours; fatalities are extremely rare.

Diagnosis. *C. perfringens* food poisoning is suspect in any outbreak of diarrhea occurring 7 to 15 hours after ingestion of a common food source. Suggested diagnostic criteria include (1) detection of 10^5 *C. perfringens* colony-forming units per gram in the suspected food source and (2) stools obtained within 48 hours of symptoms that show 10^6 *C. perfringens* spores per gram. However, mean fecal spore counts of this magnitude may be seen in patients without symptoms. A more preferred method is direct analysis of stool for enterotoxin, which can be achieved by using a reverse passive latex agglutination assay, an enzyme-linked immunoassay, or a tissue culture assay using

Vero cells with neutralizing antibody to inhibit cytopathic effects; polymerase chain reaction assays have been used to detect the enterotoxin gene.[1]

Several molecular epidemiologic techniques have been used to show identity of patient isolates with food sources, including phage typing, bacteriocin typing, plasmid profiles, and DNA probes.[5]

PREVENTION AND TREATMENT

Clostridial species are involved in a very heterogeneous group of human infections. Specific treatment recommendations have been discussed earlier in the context of unique clinical syndromes. Some general principles are reviewed here.

Because the histotoxic clostridial syndromes (see Table 244-2) are due to antigenic protein exotoxins, active or passive immunization is a possibility. Tetanus toxoid vaccine is universally recommended, and β-toxoid vaccine has been used with great success to prevent enteritis necroticans in Papua New Guinea. Tetanus immune globulin is recommended for patients with tetanus and botulinum antitoxin for adults with botulism. Horse serum antitoxin was once available for use in gas gangrene, but efficacy was not established, toxicity was significant, and the antiserum is no longer commercially available. A *C. sordellii* antitoxin reacts with *C. difficile* toxins and, in vitro, neutralizes both toxin A and toxin B. It has never been tested for potential clinical efficacy. Thus, although potentially useful in principle, immunotherapy plays a small role in the treatment of histotoxic clostridial syndromes.

Traumatic wounds should be irrigated copiously and meticulously débrided of all dirt, foreign bodies, and devitalized tissue. Appropriate antimicrobial prophylaxis should be given for surgery of the intestine and biliary tract, for limb surgery associated with vascular insufficiency, and for contaminated trauma. Intramuscular epinephrine should not be given in the buttock.

Surgical intervention depends on the specific infection. Most clostridial infections are polymicrobial, and physicians should follow the standard guidelines for surgery that would apply if clostridia were not present. Some clostridial infections may require aggressive surgical intervention in terms of timing or the extent of resection. Included in this group are emphysematous cholecystitis, neutropenic enterocolitis, enteritis necroticans, wounds associated with tetanus, some cases of crepitant cellulitis, and all cases of gas gangrene.

Penicillin G is generally considered the drug of choice for clostridial infections. Exceptions are *C. difficile*–induced diarrheal disease, for which oral metronidazole or vancomycin is effective, and botulism and *C. perfringens* food poisoning, for which antibiotics are not indicated. Alternative agents that are highly active in vitro against most clostridial strains are chloramphenicol, imipenem, meropenem, ertapenem, metronidazole, clindamycin, most expanded-spectrum cephalosporins, and combinations of a β-lactam and β-lactamase inhibitor.[58,59] Extended-spectrum penicillins, including ampicillin, and the antipseudomonal penicillins are also very active. Despite their in vitro activity, the clinical efficacy of cephalosporins and clindamycin is uncertain. Gas gangrene has developed in some patients while receiving cephalothin,[60] and the published clinical experience with cephalosporins is limited. Clindamycin is relatively inactive in vitro against some species other than *C. perfringens,* but this drug has shown excellent in vivo activity in an animal model of gas gangrene.[62] *C. sordellii* displays susceptibilities similar to those of *C. perfringens,* and the same is true for *C. septicum,* although resistance to clindamycin and extended-spectrum penicillins has occasionally been reported.[14,15,59] *C. tertium* is resistant to the newer cephalosporins.[21]

Concern can be raised about the continued recommendation of penicillin G as the drug of choice for clostridial infections. Some studies have shown increasing resistance of clostridia to penicillin, although nearly all strains of *C. perfringens* remain susceptible to levels easily achieved with parenteral doses. β-Lactamase production has been noted with *C. butyricum,* *Clostridium clostridiiforme,* and *C. ramosum,* and decreased affinity for penicillin-binding proteins has been demonstrated for some strains of *C. perfringens.* Plasmid-mediated transferable resistance to tetracycline-chloramphenicol and clindamycin-erythromycin has been observed with *C. perfringens.* Additionally, penicillin is ineffective in animal models of gas gangrene in which metronidazole, clindamycin, rifampin, and tetracycline are effective.[43,61,62] Most authorities continue to recommend penicillin as the preferred agent for clostridial infections, but because of concerns raised by in vitro data and animal studies, alternative drugs should be considered.

REFERENCES

1. Allen SD, Emery CL, Lyerly DM. *Clostridium.* In: Murray PR, Baron EJ, Jorgensen JH, et al, eds. Manual of Clinical Microbiology. 8th ed. Washington, DC: ASM Press; 2003:461-471.
2. Hatheway CL. Toxigenic clostridia. Clin Microbiol Rev. 1990;3:66-98.
3. Smith LDS. The Pathogenic Anaerobic Bacteria. 2nd ed. Springfield, IL: Charles C Thomas; 1975:115-324.
4. Finegold SM, Attebery HR, Sutter VL. Effect of diet on human fecal flora: Comparison of Japanese and American diets. Am J Clin Nutr. 1974;27:1456-1469.
5. Rood JI, Cole ST. Molecular genetics and pathogenesis of *Clostridium perfringens.* Microbiol Rev. 1991;55:621-648.
6. Caya JG, Truant AL. Clostridial bacteremia during the first year of life: An analysis of 53 patients including two new cases. Anaerobe. 2000;6:1-9.
7. Dorsher CW, Rosenblatt JE, Wilson WR, et al. Anaerobic bacteremia: Decreasing rate over a 15 year period. Rev Infect Dis. 1991;13:633-636.
8. Bodey GP, Rodriquez S, Fainstein V, et al. Clostridial bacteremia in cancer patients: A 12-year experience. Cancer. 1991;67:1928-1942.
9. Gorbach SL, Thadepalli H. Isolation of *Clostridium* in human infections: Evaluation of 114 cases. J Infect Dis. 1975;131(Suppl):S81-S85.
10. Myers G, Ngoi SS, Cennerazzo W, et al. Clostridial septicemia in an urban hospital. Surg Gynecol Obstet. 1992;174:291-296.
11. Rechner PM, Agger WA, Cogbill TH. Clinical features of clostridial bacteremia: A review from a rural area. Clin Infect Dis 2001;33:349-353.
12. Miguélez M, Aguado JM. Recurrent episodes of spontaneous clostridial myonecrosis related to colorectal carcinoma. Clin Infect Dis. 1996;22:582-583.
13. Larson CM, Bubrick MP, Jacobs DM, et al. Malignancy, mortality and medicosurgical management of *Clostridium septicum* infection. Surgery. 1995;118:592-598.
14. Kornbluth AA, Danzig JB, Bernstein LH. *Clostridium septicum* infection and associated malignancy. Medicine (Baltimore). 1989;68:30-37.
15. Stevens PL, Musher DM, Watson DA, et al. Spontaneous, nontraumatic gangrene due to *Clostridium septicum.* Rev Infect Dis. 1990;12:286-296.
16. Case Records of the Massachusetts General Hospital (case 5-1993). N Engl J Med. 1993;328:340-346.
17. Rifkin GD. Neutropenic enterocolitis and *Clostridium septicum* infection in patients with agranulocytosis. Arch Intern Med. 1980;140:834-835.
18. Bar-Joseph G, Halberthal M, Sweed Y, et al. *Clostridium septicum* infection in children with cyclic neutropenia. J Pediatr. 1997;131:317-319.
19. Barnham M, Weightman N. *Clostridium septicum* infection and hemolytic uremic syndrome. Emerg Infect Dis. 1998;4:321-324.
20. George WL, Finegold SM. Clostridia in the human gastrointestinal flora. In: Boriello SP, ed. Clostridia in Gastrointestinal Disease. Boca Raton, FL: CRC Press; 1985:1-37.
21. Speirs G, Warren RE, Rampling A. *Clostridium tertium* septicemia in patients with neutropenia. J Infect Dis. 1988;158:1336-1340.
22. Miller DL, Brazer S, Murdoch D, et al. Significance of *Clostridium tertium* bacteremia in neutropenic and nonneutropenic patients: Review of 32 cases. Clin Infect Dis. 2001;32:975-978.
23. Abdulla A, Yee L. The clinical spectrum of *Clostridium sordellii* bacteraemia: Two case reports and a review of the literature. J Clin Pathol. 2000;53:709-712.
24. Lorber B, Swenson RM. The bacteriology of intra-abdominal infections. Surg Clin North Am. 1975;55:1349-1354.
25. Dunn DL, Simmons RL. The role of anaerobic bacteria in intraabdominal infections. Rev Infect Dis. 1984;6(Suppl):S139-S147.
26. Shimada K, Inamatsu T, Yamashiro M. Anaerobic bacteria in biliary disease in elderly patients. J Infect Dis. 1977;135:850-854.
27. Mentzer RM Jr, Golden GT, Chandler JG, et al. A comparative appraisal of emphysematous cholecystitis. Am J Surg. 1975;129:10-15.
28. Thadepalli H, Gorbach SL, Keith L. Anaerobic infections of the female genital tract: Bacteriologic and therapeutic aspects. Am J Obstet Gynecol. 1973;117:1034-1040.
29. Sweet RL. Anaerobic infections of the female genital tract. Am J Obstet Gynecol. 1975;122:891-901.
30. Bartlett JG, Onderdonk AB, Drude E, et al. Quantitative bacteriology of the vaginal flora. J Infect Dis. 1977;136:271-277.
31. Holtz F, Mauch EW. Gas gangrene of the uterus: Survival following hysterectomy. Obstet Gynecol. 1962;19:545-548.
32. Dylewski J, Wiesenfeld H, Latour A. Postpartum uterine infection with *Clostridium perfringens.* J Infect Dis. 1989;11:470-473.
33. Hovav Y, Hornstein E, Pollack RN, et al. Sepsis due to *Clostridium perfringens* after second-trimester amniocentesis. Clin Infect Dis. 1995;21:235-236.
34. Bartlett JG. Anaerobic bacterial infections of the lung. Chest. 1988;91:901-909.
35. Bekemeyer WB Jr. Clostridial infections of the lungs and pleura. South Med J. 1986;79:1393-1397.
36. Bartlett JG, Gorbach SL, Finegold S. The bacteriology of aspiration pneumonia. Am J Med. 1974;56:202-207.

37. Domingo Z. Clostridial brain abscesses. Br J Neurosurg. 1994;8:691-694.

38. Lew JF, Wiedermann BL, Sneed J, et al. Aerotolerant *Clostridium tertium* brain abscess following a lawn dart injury. J Clin Microbiol. 1990;28:2127-2129.

39. Bryant P, Carapetis J, Matussek J, et al. Recurrent crepitant cellulitis caused by Clostridium perfringens. Pediatr Infect Dis J. 2002;21:1173-1174.

40. Centers for Disease Control and Prevention. Update: *Clostridium novyi* and unexplained illness among injecting-drug users—Scotland, Ireland, and England, April-June 2000. MMWR Morb Mortal Wkly Rep. 2000;49:543-545.

41. Willis AT. History. In: Finegold SM, George L, eds. Anaerobic Infections in Humans. New York: Academic; 1989:1-22.

42. MacLennan JD. The histotoxic clostridial infections of man. Bacteriol Rev. 1962;26:177-276.

43. Altemeier WA, Furste WL. Gas gangrene. Surg Gynecol Obstet. 1947;84:507-523.

44. Brown PW, Kinman PB. Gas gangrene in a metropolitan community. J Bone Joint Surg Am. 1974;56:1445.

45. Stevens DL, Bryant AE. Pathogenesis of *Clostridium perfringens* infection: Mechanisms and mediators of shock. Clin Infect Dis. 1997;25(Suppl 2):S160-S162.

46. Johnson S, Driks MR, Tweten RK, et al. Clinical course of seven survivors of *Clostridium septicum* infection and their immunologic responses to α-toxin. Clin Infect Dis. 1994;19:761-764.

47. Altemeier WA, Furste WL. Studies in virulence of *Clostridium welchii*. Surgery. 1949;25:12.

48. Bangsberg DR, Rosen JI, Aragon T, et al. Clostridial myonecrosis cluster among injection drug users. Arch Intern Med. 2002;162:517-522.

49. Hallagan LF, Scott JL, Horowitz BC, et al. Clostridial myonecrosis resulting from subcutaneous epinephrine suspension injection. Ann Emerg Med. 1992;21:434-436.

50. Jamieson NF, Willoughby CP. Gas gangrene after colonoscopy. Postgrad Med J. 2001;77:47-49.

51. Eickhoff TC. An outbreak of surgical wound infections due to *Clostridium perfringens*. Surg Gynecol Obstet. 1962;114:102-108.

52. Cline KA, Turnbull TL. Clostridial myonecrosis. Ann Emerg Med. 1985;14:459-466.

53. Stevens DL, Tweten RK, Awad MM, et al. Clostridial gas gangrene: Evidence that α and θ toxins differentially modulate the immune response and induce tissue necrosis. J Infect Dis. 1997;176:189-195.

54. Bryant AE, Chen RYZ, Nagata Y, et al. Clostridial gas gangrene. I. Cellular and molecular mechanisms of microvascular dysfunction induced by exotoxins of *Clostridium perfringens*. J Infect Dis. 2000;182:799-807.

55. Bryant AE, Bayer CR, Hayes-Schroer SM, et al. Activation of platelet gpIIbIIIa by phospholipase C from *Clostridium perfringens* involves store-operated calcium entry. J Infect Dis. 2003;187:408-417.

56. Demello FJ, Maglin JJ, Hitchcock CR. Comparative study of experimental *Clostridium perfringens* infection in dogs treated with antibiotics, surgery and hyperbaric oxygen. Surgery. 1973;73:936-941.

57. Darke SG, King AM, Slack WK. Gas gangrene and related infection: Classification. Clinical features and etiology, management and mortality. A report of 88 cases. Br J Surg. 1977;64:104-112.

58. Alexander CJ, Citron DM, Brazier JS, et al. Identification and antimicrobial resistance patterns of clinical isolates of *Clostridium clostridiiforme, Clostridium innocuum,* and *Clostridium ramosum* compared with those of clinical isolates of *Clostridium perfringens*. J Clin Microbiol. 1995;33:3209-3215.

59. Brazier JS, Levett PN, Stannard AL, et al. Antibiotic susceptibility of clinical isolates of *clostridia*. J Antimicrob Chemother. 1985;15:181-185.

60. Mohr JA, Griffiths W, Holm R, et al. Clostridial myonecrosis (gas gangrene) during cephalosporin prophylaxis. JAMA. 1978;239:847-849.

61. Altemeier WA, McMurrin JA, Alt AP. Chloromycetin and aureomycin in experimental gas gangrene. Surgery. 1950;28:621-631.

62. Stevens DL, Maier KA, Laine BM, et al. Comparison of clindamycin, rifampin, tetracycline, metronidazole, and penicillin for efficacy in prevention of experimental gas gangrene due to *Clostridium perfringens*. J Infect Dis. 1987;155:220-228.

63. Stevens DL, Maier KA, Mitten JE. Effect of antibiotics on toxin production and viability of *Clostridium perfringens*. Antimicrob Agents Chemother. 1987;31:213-218.

64. Stevens DL, Laine BM, Mitten JE. Comparison of single and combination antimicrobial agents for prevention of experimental gas gangrene caused by *Clostridium perfringens*. Antimicrob Agents Chemother. 1987;31:312-316.

65. Wang C, Schwaitzberg S, Berliner E, et al. Hyperbaric oxygen for treating wounds: A systematic review of the literature. Arch Surg. 2003;138:272-279.

66. Stevens DL, Bryant AE, Adams K, et al. Evaluation of therapy with hyperbaric oxygen for experimental infection with *Clostridium perfringens*. Clin Infect Dis. 1993;17:231-237. (2 editorial responses: Thom S. Editorial response: A role for hyperbaric oxygen in clostridial myonecrosis. Clin Infect Dis. 1993;17:238; and Heimbach D. Editorial response: Use of hyperbaric oxygen. Clin Infect Dis. 1993;17:239-240.)

67. Kliegman RM. The role of clostridia in the pathogenesis of neonatal necrotizing enterocolitis. In: Borriello SP, ed. Clostridia in Gastrointestinal Disease. Boca Raton, FL: CRC Press; 1985:67-92.

68. Murrell TGC. Enteritis necroticans. In: Finegold SM, George WL, eds. Anaerobic Infections in Humans. New York: Academic; 1989;639-659.

69. Murrell TGC. Pig-bel in Papua New Guinea: An ancient disease rediscovered? Int J Epidemiol. 1983;12:211-214.

70. Davis M. A review of pig-bel (necrotizing enteritis) in Papua New Guinea 1961-1984. Papua New Guinea Med J. 1985;2:75-82.

71. Karanth S, Coninx R, Dickson C, et al. Enteritis necroticans (pig-bel) on Thai/Kampuchean border? Lancet. 1986;1:1437.

72. Petrillo TM, Beck-Sague CM, Songer JG, et al. Enteritis necroticans (pigbel) in a diabetic child. N Engl J Med. 2000;342:1250-1253.

73. Walker PD, Murrell TGC, Nagy LK. Scanning electron microscopy of the jejunum in enteritis necroticans. J Med Microbiol. 1980;13:445-450.

74. Murrell TGC, Walker PD. The pigbel story of Papua New Guinea. Trans R Soc Trop Med Hyg. 1991;85:119-122.

75. Alt B, Glass NR, Sollinger H. Neutropenic enterocolitis in adults: Review of the literature and assessment of surgical intervention. Am J Surg. 1985;149:405-408.

76. Mower WJ, Hawkins JA, Nelson EW. Neutropenic enterocolitis in adults with acute leukemia. Arch Surg. 1986;121:571-573.

77. Koransky JR, Stargel MD, Dowell VR. *Clostridium septicum* bacteremia: Its clinical significance. Am J Med. 1979;66:63-66.

78. Shamberger RC, Weinstein HJ, Delorey MJ, et al. The medical and surgical management of typhlitis in children with acute nonlymphocytic (myelogenous) leukemia. Cancer. 1986;57:603-609.

79. Thaler M, Gill V, Pizzo PA. Emergence of *Clostridium tertium* as a pathogen in neutropenic patients. Am J Med. 1986;81:596-600.

80. Aucott JN. Food poisoning. In: Blaser M, Smith PD, Rardin JI, et al, eds. Infections of the Gastrointestinal Tract. New York: Raven; 1995:237-250.

81. Olsen SJ, MacKinnon LC, Goulding NH, et al. Surveillance for foodborne disease outbreaks—United States, 1993-1997. Mor Mortal Wkly Rep CDC Surveill Summ. 2000;49:1-62.

82. Borriello SP. Clostridial diseases of the gut. Clin Infect Dis. 1995;20(Suppl 2):S242-S250.

83. Yasukawa A, Okada Y, Kitase T, et al. Distribution of enterotoxin producing strains of *Clostridium perfringens* type A in human beings, food and soils. J Food Hyg Soc Jpn. 1975;16:313-317.

84. Uemura T. Incidence of enterotoxigenic *Clostridium perfringens* in healthy humans in relation to the enhancement of enterotoxin production by heat treatment. J Appl Bacteriol. 1978;44:411-419.

85. McDonel JL. Binding of *Clostridium perfringens* (^{125}I) enterotoxin in rabbit intestinal cells. Biochemistry. 1980;19:4801-4807.

86. McClane BA, McDonel JL. The effects of *Clostridium perfringens* enterotoxin on morphology viability and macromolecular synthesis in Vero cells. J Cell Physiol. 1979;99:191-199.

87. Bowness P, Moss PA, Tranter H, et al. *Clostridium perfringens* enterotoxin is a superantigen reactive with human T cell receptors: V beta 6.9 and V beta 22. J Exp Med. 1992;176:893-896.

88. Jackson SG, Yip-Chuck DA, Clark JB, et al. Diagnostic importance of *Clostridium perfringens* enterotoxin analysis in recurring enteritis among elderly, chronic care psychiatric patients. J Clin Microbiol. 1986;23:748-751.

89. Finegold SM. *Clostridium perfringens* food poisoning. In: Anaerobic Bacteria in Human Disease. New York: Academic; 1977:511-512.

ADDITIONAL READING

Rood JI, McClane BA, Songer JG, et al, eds. The Clostridia: Molecular Biology and Pathogenesis. San Diego: Academic; 1997.

CHAPTER **245**

Bacteroides, Prevotella, Porphyromonas, and Fusobacterium Species (and Other Medically Important Anaerobic Gram-Negative Bacilli)

BENNETT LORBER

The anaerobic gram-negative bacilli that make up the genus *Bacteroides* are among the most important constituents of the normal human flora and are plentiful in the oral cavity, the gastrointestinal tract, and the vagina. From these endogenous sources, a wide variety of human infections may occur, many of which (1) are polymicrobial and involve multiple anaerobic species, as well as facultative organisms, and (2) have a tendency for abscess formation. Among the common infections caused by these bacteria are periodontal disease, postaspiration pleuropulmonary infection, genital tract infections in

TABLE 245-1 Characteristics of Anaerobic Gram-Negative Rods

Genus and Species	Growth in 20% Bile	Kanamycin, 1000 μg	Vancomycin, 5 μg	Colistin, 10 μg	Catalase	Indole	Lipase	Pigment	Brick Red Fluorescence
Bacteroides fragilis group	Yes	Resistant	Resistant	Resistant	Variable	Variable	Negative	No	No
Prevotella	No	Resistant	Resistant	Variable	Negative usually	Variable	Variable	Yes	Usually
Porphyromonas	No	Resistant	Sensitive	Resistant	Negative usually	Positive	Variable	Yes	Usually
Fusobacterium	Variable	Sensitive	Resistant	Sensitive	Negative	Variable	Variable	No	No
Bilophila	Yes	Sensitive	Resistant	Sensitive	Positive	Negative	Negative	No	No

women, and intra-abdominal abscesses. *Bacteroides fragilis* is the most important species, and its putative presence has implications for antimicrobial selection.

MICROBIOLOGY

More than 30 genera of anaerobic gram-negative bacilli are recognized,[1] but human infection is largely restricted to 4 of these, namely, *Bacteroides, Prevotella, Porphyromonas,* and *Fusobacterium.* Unlike clostridial species, none of these anaerobic bacteria form spores. These bacteria are identified presumptively (Table 245-1) on the basis of colonial morphology, Gram-stain characteristics, pigment production, fluorescence with long-wave ultraviolet light, susceptibility to special-strength antibiotic disks, and biochemical tests.[1] Definitive identification requires multiple biochemical tests that are tedious to perform and, because of expense, not feasible for most clinical laboratories. Because of its clinical importance and relative antimicrobial resistance, identification of *B. fragilis* is essential.

The *B. fragilis* group can be distinguished from other species of anaerobic gram-negative bacilli by growth in 20% bile and resistance to special-strength kanamycin, vancomycin, and colistin antibiotic disks. *B. fragilis* forms 1- to 3-mm nonhemolytic, glistening colonies on blood agar and is aerotolerant. On Gram stain, *B. fragilis* usually appears as a pale gram-negative bacillus but may appear pleomorphic (coccobacillary) and may be gram-variable with irregular or bipolar staining.

The pigmenting anaerobic gram-negative bacilli are made up of saccharolytic and asaccharolytic species of the genera *Prevotella* and *Porphyromonas,* respectively. These organisms form brown to black colonies after about a week when grown on rabbit laked blood agar; under ultraviolet light, young unpigmented colonies exhibit brick red fluorescence. On Gram stain they appear as small, pale-staining, coccobacillary gram-negative rods.

Fusobacterium organisms are long, thin, gram-negative rods with pointed ends, often arranged end to end in pairs. *Bilophila wadsworthia* is a recently described slow-growing, asaccharolytic, nonmotile bacillus that is strongly catalase positive and derives its name from its resistance to 20% ox bile.

The commercial development and widespread clinical use of anaerobic culture environments, such as anaerobic chambers, jars, or pouches, has led in the last 30 years to an appreciation of the major role that these anaerobic gram-negative bacilli play in human infection.

NORMAL FLORA

Anaerobes are the predominant constituents of the normal human bacterial flora, and anaerobic gram-negative bacilli, particularly *Bacteroides* and *Prevotella* spp., are numerically the most prevalent organisms. These bacteria are not prominent skin flora but are abundant on all mucosal surfaces and reach their largest concentrations in the tonsillar crypts, the crypts of the tongue, dental plaque, and the gingival crevices in the oral cavity; the colon in the gastrointestinal tract; and the vagina.

Colonization of the oral cavity begins at or shortly after birth, with specific bacterial adherence being an important determinant of the microecology.[2,3] Anaerobes become prominent in childhood in association with the eruption of teeth and the anaerobic environment created

by the establishment of gingival crevices (redox potential as low as −350 mV).[4] *Prevotella melaninogenica* is found in the gingival crevices of 18% to 40% of 5-year-olds and virtually 100% of teenagers. *Porphyromonas gingivalis* is found in 37% of subjects, with similar frequencies at all ages, and may be acquired in the first days of life.[5] Colonization concordance is found in families, which suggests that *P. gingivalis* is transmitted by contact within the home.[6] Other important oral anaerobes include *Fusobacterium nucleatum, Fusobacterium necrophorum, Prevotella oralis, Prevotella disiens, Prevotella oris, Prevotella buccae,* and *Bacteroides forsythus.* In dental plaque and gingival sulci, concentrations of bacteria may reach 10^{12}/mL, which approximates the physical limits of space. The microecology in the mouth is complex, and many bacteria are dependent on other species for survival; for example, *P. melaninogenica* requires vitamin K produced by other species, and oral spirochetes are dependent on metabolites produced by *Fusobacterium* spp.[7]

The largest concentration of bacteria in the human body is found in the colon, where more than 400 genera may coexist. Anaerobes outnumber aerobes 1000:1, reach numbers of 10^{11}/g of fecal material,[8] and are usually found in intimate association with the mucosa and mucous sheath. The infant alimentary tract, sterile at birth, is rapidly colonized by aerobic bacteria and later by anaerobes, with the fecal flora resembling that of an adult by the end of the second year of life.[9] The small bowel contains fewer anaerobes (10^2 to 10^4/g) and an equal number of aerobes, but if intestinal motility is interrupted by obstruction or if a diverticulum or surgical blind loop is present, the flora changes to resemble that of the colon.[10] Numerically, the major colonic organisms are *Bacteroides* spp., with *Bacteroides vulgatus* and *Bacteroides thetaiotaomicron* being the most common. *B. fragilis,* the most important anaerobe in clinical infection, is present in virtually all humans but accounts for only 0.5% of the flora. The intestinal anaerobic flora carries out a variety of metabolic activities[7] and may be important in protecting the host from colonization with potential pathogens ("colonization resistance").[11]

The adult vaginal flora, which contains bacterial concentrations of 10^5 to 10^8/mL, is dominated by anaerobes, of which the gram-positive lactobacilli are most plentiful, but as many as 20% of women have no detectable anaerobes or very low concentrations.[12] *B. fragilis* is found in only 2% to 4% of subjects, and the most commonly found anaerobic gram-negative bacilli are *P. melaninogenica, Prevotella bivia,* and *P. disiens,* which are present in one quarter to one third of women. Anaerobes predominate in the normal vaginal flora of prepubertal girls in numbers higher than those found in premenopausal adults,[13] and gram-negative anaerobes are less prevalent in postmenopausal women than in women of reproductive age.[14] The flora of the vagina is dynamic and less stable than that of the gastrointestinal tract and may vary with the menstrual cycle, pregnancy, postmenopausal state, gynecologic surgery, and antimicrobial therapy.

PATHOGENESIS

Synergy

Infections involving anaerobic bacteria characteristically contain multiple anaerobes and often facultative organisms as well. Considerable evidence points to true synergy between unrelated bacterial species in the pathogenesis of these infections. In 1930, Smith[15] isolated multiple bacterial types from patients with purulent gingivitis and used these organisms singly and in combinations in an animal model of lung abscess. He demonstrated that multiple agents together might produce an infection that could not be produced with the individual components used singly. Anaerobic bacilli in combination with facultative bacteria induce the formation of intra-abdominal abscesses more readily than either component does alone,[16] and mixtures containing *Bacteroides* spp. enhance the growth of some facultative bacteria.[17]

It is postulated that, by lowering the oxidation-reduction potential in the microenvironment, facultative organisms may promote more favorable conditions for anaerobic growth and that the anaerobic component in mixed infection may facilitate the growth of facultative bacteria through inhibition of phagocytes.[18] *B. fragilis* produces detectable levels of β-lactamase in abscess fluid that may protect normally susceptible components of mixed infections from the actions of antimicrobials.[19]

Virulence

The importance of virulence factors (Table 245-2) in the pathogenesis of infections caused by anaerobic gram-negative bacilli is indicated by the fact that *B. fragilis* and *Fusobacterium* spp. are isolated from clinical infections with a frequency disproportionate to their prevalence in the normal gastrointestinal and oral flora.

Bacteroides fragilis has an immunologically distinct capsule composed of two polysaccharides,[20] and studies have indicated the important role of the capsule as a virulence factor.[21,22] A similar capsule is found in *P. melaninogenica.* The capsule seems to promote abscess formation, possibly by inhibiting opsonophagocytosis,[23] and is capable of inducing experimental abscess formation even in the absence of viable bacteria.[24]

The adherence of *B. fragilis* and *Bacteroides ovatus* to intestinal epithelium and mucus is promoted by pili; the adherence of piliated and encapsulated strains is five times that of nonpiliated and nonencapsulated or encapsulated-only counterparts.[25] Similar surface structures have been identified as important attachment factors in *P. gingivalis.*

Lipopolysaccharide endotoxin is formed by *Fusobacterium* and *Bacteroides* spp., but although this virulence factor contributes to abscess formation, the lipopolysaccharide formed by *Bacteroides* does not contain lipid A and is 100- to 5000-fold less biologically active than conventional endotoxin.[26]

B. fragilis, like many other anaerobes, produces the short-chain fatty acid succinic acid, which inhibits phagocytosis. Through this product, as well as others, anaerobic bacteria may protect coinfecting facultative organisms from the action of phagocytic cells.[27]

TABLE 245-2 Virulence Factors of Anaerobic Gram-Negative Bacilli

Factor	Comment
Capsular polysaccharide	Found in *Bacteroides fragilis* and *Prevotella melaninogenica,* inhibits opsonophagocytosis, promotes abscess formation, promotes adherence to epithelial cells
Pili and fimbriae	Found in the *B. fragilis* group and *Porphyromonas gingivalis,* promotes adherence to epithelial cells and mucus
Endotoxin	*Fusobacterium* spp. have a biologically active form; *Bacteroides* lipopolysaccharide lacks lipid A and is biologically impotent
Succinic acid	Produced by many species, inhibits phagocytosis and intracellular killing of the producer and others in its milieu
Enzymes	
Hyaluronidase, hemolysin, peroxidase, collagenase, phospholipase, protease, fibrinolysin, heparinase, neuraminidase	Produced by many species, contribute to tissue damage and/or promote invasion and spread
Superoxide dismutase	Produced by many clinically important anaerobes, defends against oxygen radicals and enhances aerotolerance

A variety of enzymes produced by *Bacteroides* spp. may contribute to tissue damage or enable these pathogens to escape host defenses.[28,29] Among these enzymes are hyaluronidase, collagenase, neuraminidase, heparinase, and fibrinolysin. *P. melaninogenica* and *Prevotella intermedia* produce a phospholipase A that may disrupt the integrity of epithelial cells.[30] *P. gingivalis,* in addition to having hemagglutination properties, specifically degrades human fibrinogen and possesses a potent collagenase.[31] Many clinically important anaerobes, including *B. fragilis,* have some degree of oxygen tolerance, presumably through production of the important enzyme superoxide dismutase.[32]

Toxins that are so important in disease caused by *Clostridium* spp. do not contribute significantly to the pathogenesis of infection caused by anaerobic gram-negative rods. An exception is an enterotoxin produced by *B. fragilis* that has been associated with diarrheal disease.[33]

Immunity and Resistance

The role of humoral immunity in *Bacteroides* infection is unclear. Pathogenic anaerobic gram-negative bacilli activate complement[34] and induce B-cell activation and the production of antibody.[35] Both the alternative and classic pathways of the complement system contribute to opsonization. The alternative complement pathway is important for effective in vitro opsonization of *B. fragilis* and *B. thetaiotaomicron*[36] and is activated in the absence of antibody. Pooled human immunoglobulin has been shown to facilitate in vitro killing of *B. thetaiotaomicron* and *B. fragilis.* Antibody to capsular polysaccharide enhances killing primarily by the classic complement pathway.[37] Specific hyperimmune globulin to *B. fragilis* capsular polysaccharide does not seem to play a protective role in experimental intra-abdominal abscesses but did facilitate clearance of *B. fragilis* bacteremia.[38]

Cell-mediated immunity surprisingly appears to be more important with regard to *B. fragilis*–induced abscesses than is humoral immunity, as demonstrated in an animal model.[20,38,39] Immunization of rats with *B. fragilis* capsular polysaccharide protected against *B. fragilis*–induced abscesses. However, passive transfer of immunoglobulin from immunized animals did not protect naive animals, whereas transfer of splenic cells and fractionated T cells was protective.

Neutrophils are prominent in exudates associated with clinical infection caused by anaerobic gram-negative bacilli and are abundant in abscesses caused by these bacteria. These organisms induce neutrophil chemotaxis, phagocytosis, and chemiluminescence,[18] and phagocytic leukocytes are active against anaerobic bacteria[40] and kill *Bacteroides* spp. under anaerobic conditions.

In spite of the considerable laboratory evidence for roles of host complement, antibody, cellular immunity, and phagocytes in protecting against anaerobic gram-negative bacillary infection, few clinical observations support the relative importance of these defense mechanisms. In an intriguing clinical observation, Fisher and colleagues[41] described *B. fragilis* as the most common cause of postoperative bacteremia in children who had elective appendectomy at the time of renal transplantation; profound lymphopenia was a risk factor for infection. Generally speaking, however, patients with complement or antibody deficiencies, as well as those with impaired cellular immunity or neutropenia, rarely acquire infections with *Bacteroides* or *Prevotella* spp. unless the underlying illness is associated with a more obvious predisposition to infection, such as colon carcinoma with perforation.

INFECTIONS

Central Nervous System Infections

Meningitis

Anaerobic bacterial meningitis is so rare that most laboratories do not culture cerebrospinal fluid anaerobically. Durand and associates[42] reviewed 493 episodes of bacterial meningitis in adults seen over a 27-year period and found anaerobes involved in only 3 instances; the species were not identified. When anaerobic meningitis has been described, *B. fragilis* has been the most frequently cited etiologic agent.

Feder[43] reviewed nine cases of *B. fragilis* meningitis reported from 1963 to 1985, seven of which occurred in premature infants and neonates. Underlying conditions included necrotizing enterocolitis, bowel perforation, chronic otitis media (the two cases seen after the neonatal period), and a cerebrospinal fluid shunt infection.

Brain Abscess

In contrast to their rare association with meningitis, anaerobes are frequently implicated as causative agents in brain abscess,[44,45] which is not surprising given that the predisposing condition in 20% to 40% of brain abscess cases is chronic sinusitis or chronic otitis media, conditions commonly caused by anaerobes. *Prevotella* spp., *Bacteroides* spp., and *Fusobacterium* spp. are all commonly isolated, often in mixed culture and often in association with other anaerobes and streptococcal species, including *Streptococcus intermedius.*

Anaerobic gram-negative bacilli have also been reported to cause subdural empyema, cranial epidural abscess, and, less commonly, spinal epidural abscess and lateral sinus thrombophlebitis.[45]

Infections of the Oral Cavity and Upper Respiratory Tract

Many infections of the oral cavity and adjacent structures involve anaerobic bacteria. The pattern of bacteria found tends to be similar for most of these infections. The predominant pathogens include peptostreptococci and anaerobic gram-negative bacilli, particularly *P. melaninogenica, P. oralis, P. oris, P. buccae, P. disiens, F. nucleatum, F. necrophorum, Porphyromonas asaccharolytica,* and *Bacteroides ureolyticus.* Most infections involve multiple anaerobes and in many instances facultative organisms as well, including *Eikenella* and *Capnocytophaga. B. fragilis* is not part of the oral flora, and reports indicating the presence of *B. fragilis* in infections of the oral cavity and upper respiratory tract probably represent misidentification in many instances.

Odontogenic Infections

Virtually all clinically important dental infections, including endodontic infection[46] and periapical abscess,[47] involve anaerobes. From these sites, infection may spread to a number of potential spaces bounded by muscles and fascia; some of these infections can be quite severe and even life threatening.[48] One such process is Ludwig's angina, a cellulitis of the sublingual and submandibular spaces that can progress to elevation of the floor of the mouth with the tongue forced posteriorly, thereby resulting in strangulation. Surgical decompression is the mainstay of treatment. Another serious complication of perimandibular infection is Lemierre syndrome, or postanginal septicemia, a suppurative infection of the lateral pharyngeal space associated with *F. necrophorum* bacteremia and septic jugular vein thrombophlebitis that can lead to septic embolization to the lung with metastatic abscess formation.[49]

Odontogenic orofacial infections caused by anaerobic gram-negative bacilli are associated with more severe clinical illness than are such infections caused by other bacterial species; especially severe are those involving *F. nucleatum.*[50]

Periodontal disease, including pyorrhea and gingivitis, is extremely common and a major contributor to tooth loss as infection progresses from spongy, easily bleeding gums to abscess formation around teeth and bone destruction.[51-53] *P. melaninogenica, P. intermedia, P. gingivalis,* and *B. forsythus* are thought to be important pathogens in this setting.[54] An uncommon but severe and distinctive form of gingivitis is Vincent's angina, or "trench mouth," also known as acute necrotizing ulcerative gingivitis.[55] In this infection, an acute destructive and ulcerative gingivitis causes a putrid breath odor and severe pain; fever may be present. Imputed etiologies include oral fusospirochetes along with the usual mouth anaerobes. Antibiotic treatment should be directed at anaerobes.

Pharyngitis

Anaerobic bacteria do not play an important role in acute pharyngitis, but they are important pathogens when peritonsillar abscess, also known as quinsy, occurs.[56] *P. melaninogenica* is commonly isolated along with other mouth anaerobes, facultative flora, and group A streptococci.

Sinusitis

Although rarely found in acute sinusitis, anaerobes are the predominant pathogens found in chronic sinusitis (of more than 3 months' duration). Using surgically obtained specimens from 83 patients with chronic paranasal sinusitis, Frederick and Braude[57] found that 31% had only anaerobes, 23% had only aerobes, 20% had mixed flora, and 25% had sterile specimens. Predominant anaerobic isolates in chronic sinusitis include *Peptostreptococcus* spp., *Prevotella* spp., *Bacteroides* spp. (non-*fragilis* group), and *Fusobacterium* spp.[57,58] The common isolation of these bacteria from intracranial suppurative infection complicating chronic sinusitis supports their important role in chronic sinus infection.

Otitis

Oral cavity anaerobes are found very uncommonly in acute otitis media but are isolated from 15% to 50% of cultures obtained from patients with chronic otitis media.[59] In cases complicated by mastoiditis or cholesteatoma, the frequency of anaerobes isolated from surgical specimens rises to 65% to 95%.[60,61]

Parotitis

Suppurative infection of the parotid salivary gland is usually due to *Staphylococcus aureus,* but recent reports indicate a pathogenic role for anaerobes, including *Prevotella* spp., *Fusobacterium* spp., and *Peptostreptococcus* spp.[62] A Gram stain of pus expressed from the salivary duct may provide an immediate clue to the etiology.

Pleuropulmonary Infections

Pleuropulmonary infections, including community-acquired aspiration pneumonia, necrotizing pneumonia, lung abscess, and empyema, are among the most common and important clinical infections in which anaerobic gram-negative bacilli play a role.[63-65] These infections are thought to follow aspiration of oropharyngeal flora, and many patients have obvious periodontal disease, the likely reservoir for the infecting bacteria. The clinical picture is similar to pyogenic lung infection of any etiology, although the tempo of the illness is typically slower. In advanced disease with cavitation, empyema, or both, as many as one half to two thirds of patients will have putrid sputum or pleural fluid, but in early infection this important clinical clue to the anaerobic etiology is often absent. Gram stain of empyema fluid demonstrating a mixed flora with morphologies consistent with *Prevotella* and *Fusobacterium* spp. will often provide prompt diagnosis.

The bacteriology of these infections is similar to that found in odontogenic infections: most are polymicrobial and usually contain three to four anaerobic species and often, but not always, a facultative organism such as a viridans streptococcus. *P. melaninogenica, P. intermedia, F. nucleatum,* and *B. ureolyticus* are among the most commonly isolated bacterial species. Many of these infections are probably truly synergistic. *B. fragilis* is virtually never found in the oropharyngeal flora, and earlier studies of the bacteriology of anaerobic pleuropulmonary infection citing a *B. fragilis* isolation rate of approximately 15% probably represent misidentification of penicillin-resistant organisms such as *P. buccae* and *P. disiens.*

Concern about increasing antimicrobial resistance among mouth anaerobic species has caused most authorities to substitute new regimens for penicillin, the long-standing drug of choice in this setting (see later).

Intra-abdominal Infections

Bacteroides spp., particularly *B. fragilis,* are the organisms most frequently recovered from intra-abdominal abscesses (intraperitoneal and visceral), as well as from peritonitis occurring after a breach of the integrity of the intestinal mucosa, whether it be from a surgeon's scalpel, a ruptured appendix, or a perforating cancer of the colon. The fact that *B. fragilis* makes up a small part of the fecal inoculum (0.5% of the colonic microflora) but is the dominant anaerobe isolated from clinical infection attests to the virulence of this organism. The pathogenic role played by *B. fragilis* in the formation of abdominal abscesses has been suggested by the study of animal models.[38,66]

Generally, intra-abdominal infections are mixed and polymicrobial and contain an average of five organisms, three anaerobic and two facultative (often coliforms), with anaerobes being present in 80% to 90% of infections and *Bacteroides* spp. in roughly two thirds of these.[67,68] Exceptions to these generalizations include "spontaneous" peritonitis, pancreatic abscesses or infected pancreatic pseudocysts, and acute cholecystitis, which are often due to a single coliform or streptococcal species; another exception is peritonitis complicating peritoneal dialysis, which is often due to a single staphylococcal or coliform organism. *Bacteroides* spp. are important pathogens in liver abscess, the most common of visceral abdominal infections. This finding is not surprising given that the most common ways in which infecting bacteria are introduced into the hepatic parenchyma are from the intestinal flora via the biliary tract or the portal venous system.

Although *B. fragilis* is the predominant isolate from intra-abdominal infections, other members of the *B. fragilis* group, including *B. thetaiotaomicron, Bacteroides distasonis,* and *B. vulgatus,* are commonly recovered, as is *P. melaninogenica.*

Bilophila wadsworthia was described in 1989 as a novel genus of a bile-tolerant gram-negative anaerobe that was isolated from appendicitis specimens and human feces.[69] Occasionally it has been found in the vagina and in saliva.[70] Although it is found in the stool in mean counts of only 10^5 to 10^6/g (total bacterial counts, 10^{12}/g), it is the third most common anaerobe isolated from infections in the setting of gangrenous or perforated appendices, and its presence can be demonstrated in nearly one half of such cases.[71] It has occasionally been reported in other infections, including hepatic abscess, cholecystitis, and soft tissue infections, usually as part of a polymicrobial flora, but it has been reported to cause bacteremia.[72] Another bile-tolerant, asaccharolytic, anaerobic, gram-negative rod, *Sutterella wadsworthensis,* is found most frequently in association with appendicitis, peritonitis, and intra-abdominal abscesses.[73,74]

Diarrhea

In case-control studies, enterotoxin-producing strains of *B. fragilis* have been implicated as the cause of self-limited, watery diarrhea. Disease appears limited to children 1 to 5 years old, and 5% to 20% of cases of diarrhea in this age range are thought to be due to this etiology.[75,76] The toxin is an extracellular, heat-labile metalloproteinase with a mass of about 20 kDa that possesses both secretory and cytotoxic effects.[33] As with other enteric pathogens, carriage of enterotoxigenic *B. fragilis* may be clinically silent and has been reported in 6.5% of healthy persons. It may be transmitted through contaminated water.

Genital Tract Infections in Women

Anaerobic gram-negative bacilli figure prominently in the normal vaginal flora and are important pathogens in most genital tract infections in women, excluding those resulting from sexually transmitted organisms. A wide variety of infections can involve anaerobes, including Bartholin's cyst abscess, pelvic inflammatory disease, tuboovarian abscess, endometritis, amnionitis, and wound infections complicating obstetric procedures or gynecologic surgery.[77,78]

These infections are characteristically polymicrobial and involve anaerobes, particularly anaerobic gram-negative rods and peptostreptococci, along with aerobes, including possibly *Gardnerella vaginalis, Escherichia coli* (coliforms are less common than in intra-abdominal infections), and group B streptococci. In a study of salpingitis,[79] Sweet demonstrated that patients typically had mixed anaerobic infection in the fallopian tubes even when the sexually transmitted pathogens *Neisseria gonorrhoeae* and *Chlamydia trachomatis* were isolated from the endocervix.

P. bivia and *P. disiens* are important pathogens in genital tract infections of women, and earlier reports indicating a high isolation rate for *B. fragilis* probably represent organism misidentification in many instances.[80]

An extremely common infection involving anaerobic gram-negative bacilli is bacterial vaginosis, which is characterized by a foul-smelling discharge, increased concentration of succinic acid and an elevated pH in vaginal fluid, loss of the normally predominant lactobacilli, a marked quantitative increase in *Prevotella* spp., and response to metronidazole or topical clindamycin.[81] Other bacteria commonly found are *G. vaginalis* and the curved, anaerobic gram-positive rod *Mobiluncus.* Bacterial vaginosis is associated with an increased risk of pelvic inflammatory disease,[82] and heavy anaerobic colonization of the vagina is associated with an increased risk of intra-amniotic infection, as well as preterm delivery (see also Chapter 103).[83]

Bacteremia

B. fragilis is not uncommonly isolated from blood cultures, and it is the dominant isolate (70%) in cases of anaerobic bacteremia.[84-86] Additional common isolates are other members of the *B. fragilis* group, particularly *B. thetaiotaomicron,* and *Fusobacterium* spp. Unlike anaerobic gram-positive cocci and rods, which often represent contaminants when found in blood cultures, isolation of anaerobic gram-negative bacilli from blood is virtually always associated with clinical infection.[85] The significance of *Bacteroides* bacteremia is indicated by an associated mortality of 15% to 30%, with a 60% mortality reported in cases when therapy was not directed at these organisms.[87] In one controlled study, *B. fragilis* group bacteremia resulted in 16 days of additional hospitalization and an attributable mortality of 19%.[88]

A decline in the frequency of anaerobic gram-negative rod bacteremia has been reported in the last 2 decades.[86,89,90] This decline may be due to improved surgical prophylaxis, newer imaging techniques permitting earlier diagnosis and drainage of abscesses, and heightened awareness of the role of anaerobes in infection, with specific antimicrobial treatment directed at these organisms. Noting this decline, some authorities have suggested abandoning routine anaerobic blood cultures.[91] In some recent reports, anaerobes have accounted for about 4% of all bacteremias without demonstrable decline. Because of attributable morbidity and mortality, along with increasing antibiotic resistance and the fact that anaerobic blood cultures enhance the isolation of *Streptococcus pneumoniae,* other streptococci, enterococci, many enteric gram-negative rods, and *Listeria monocytogenes,* routine anaerobic blood cultures remain warranted.[92,93] Failure to culture blood anaerobically has led to delay in diagnosis of a life-threatening infection.[94]

The source of bacteremia caused by anaerobic gram-negative bacilli is found to be intra-abdominal infections in one half to two thirds of cases (particularly when associated with abscesses, malignancy, surgery, and intestinal obstruction or perforation); female genital tract infections in about 8% to 25%; soft tissue infections, including decubitus ulcers, in about 5% to 10%; and the oropharynx and lower respiratory tract in about 5% each. *Fusobacterium* bacteremia is usually associated with oropharyngeal and lung infection, and *P. disiens* or *P. bivia* bacteremia generally correlates with obstetric and gynecologic sources of infection. In one study,[95] an increase in anaerobic bacteremia, primarily due to *Fusobacterium nucleatum,* was seen in bone marrow transplant recipients accounting for 17% of blood stream infections in this group, and was associated with severity of mucositis. When *B. fragilis* is isolated from the blood of a febrile patient without obvious localizing signs or symptoms, an intra-abdominal source should be investigated.

The clinical picture of *Bacteroides* bacteremia is similar to that produced by anaerobic gram-negative bacilli, with the exception that the "gram-negative sepsis syndrome," shock, and disseminated intravascular coagulation appear to be less common in anaerobic bacteremia, perhaps related to the absence of lipid A from *B. fragilis* endotoxin.[26]

Endocarditis

Anaerobic bacteria are uncommon causes of infective endocarditis, with incidences reported to range from 1% to 16% of total cases. Anaerobic streptococci and *B. fragilis* are the most frequent causes,[96] with *B. fragilis* being the etiologic agent in approximately one third of cases. A polymicrobial etiology is more commonly found in anaerobic endocarditis than in cases caused by facultative bacteria, with more than one organism isolated from 14% to 24% of the former; in polymicrobial cases, *P. melaninogenica* is often found in combination with anaerobic or facultative streptococcal species.[96,97] *Fusobacterium* spp., particularly *F. necrophorum,* are second only to *B. fragilis* as the etiology of endocarditis caused by anaerobic gram-negative bacilli. The valve distribution and subacute clinical course in most instances of anaerobic endocarditis are similar to that caused by viridans streptococci, but underlying heart disease is less common, being present in 43% to 64% of patients. *B. fragilis* endocarditis is associated with the formation of large vegetations, with systemic embolization reported in 60% to 70% of cases. It has been suggested that the high frequency of thromboembolic complications in *B. fragilis* endocarditis may be related to the heparinase that it produces. Mortality in cases caused by anaerobic gram-negative bacilli is higher than in those caused by anaerobic gram-positive cocci, with a rate of 46% reported for cases caused by *B. fragilis. F. necrophorum* can cause acute endocarditis with rapid valve destruction and a 75% mortality.[97] Pericarditis secondary to anaerobes is rare.[98]

Skin and Soft Tissue Infections

Anaerobic gram-negative bacilli do not contribute significantly to the normal skin flora, but these bacteria are important pathogens when the skin and underlying soft tissue are damaged by trauma or vascular insufficiency and contaminated with fecal or upper airway flora. Examples of infections commonly involving *Bacteroides* and *Prevotella* spp. are wound infections after intestinal or gynecologic surgery, dog and human bite infections,[99] infected pilonidal cysts, necrotizing fasciitis,[100] and infections complicating decubitus and diabetic ulcers.

   B. fragilis is the most common species found in the mixed flora colonizing both diabetic[101] and decubitus ulcers. When these ulcers lead to cellulitis, osteomyelitis, bacteremia, or a combination of these conditions, *B. fragilis* is commonly recovered from clinical specimens.[102,103]

   Cutaneous abscesses below the waist have often been found to be caused by colonic flora anaerobes, including *B. fragilis* and *P. melaninogenica.*[104] Breast abscesses, although usually caused by *S. aureus,* may result from anaerobic gram-negative bacilli, particularly in nonpuerperal women; *P. bivia, B. ureolyticus,* and *P. asaccharolytica* have been common isolates and are often present with anaerobic cocci.[105]

Bone and Joint Infections

Osteomyelitis

Hematogenous anaerobic osteomyelitis is very rare, but anaerobes play a prominent role in osteomyelitis of the long bones after trauma and fracture; osteomyelitis associated with vascular insufficiency; osteomyelitis of the skull bones complicating odontogenic infection, chronic sinusitis, or chronic otitis; osteomyelitis contiguous to deep diabetic or decubitus ulcers; and osteomyelitis complicating human bites or clenched-fist injuries.[106-108] Anaerobic osteomyelitis of the pubis has been described in women after pelvic surgery. *B. fragilis,* the most common isolate, is found in about one third of cases in which anaerobes are found; *P. melaninogenica, F. nucleatum,* and *Porphyromonas* spp. are common pathogens in osteomyelitis of the facial bones and in human bite wounds. Purulent drainage has a foul odor in 48% of cases.[108] A rare form of hematogenous osteomyelitis is that seen complicating Gaucher's disease, and, interestingly, most of these cases have been due to anaerobic gram-negative bacilli.[109]

Septic Arthritis

Infectious arthritis caused by anaerobic bacteria is rare, but infection has occurred secondary to hematogenous spread, including cases complicating rheumatoid arthritis.[110] A number of prosthetic joint infections have been reported,[107] the presumption being that the infecting agents

were introduced at the time of surgery. Brook and Frazier[108] reported 65 cases seen at a military hospital over a 10-year period. The hip and knee were most commonly affected. Unlike other anaerobic infections, including osteomyelitis, polymicrobial infection was uncommon. One anaerobe was typically found per infection, and facultative organisms were coinfecting agents in only 11% of cases. Anaerobic gram-positive cocci were the most commonly isolated pathogens and were often associated with prosthetic device infections. *B. fragilis* group organisms were isolated in nine instances, five in association with distant-site infection; *Fusobacterium* spp. were implicated in five cases, three of which had concomitant oropharyngeal infection. The mean symptom duration before diagnosis was 4.5 days, fever was present in 80%, blood cultures were negative in all cases when obtained, and purulent joint fluid had a foul odor 37% of the time.

TREATMENT

Surgical Treatment

Drainage of abscesses and débridement of necrotic tissue continue to be mainstays of the treatment of anaerobic infections. For localized, accessible abscesses, particularly in the abdomen, it is now possible in many instances to achieve adequate drainage through the use of percutaneous catheters placed under radiographic guidance.[111] An attempt at percutaneous drainage is a reasonable first step, with open drainage reserved if the abscess is inaccessible, if drainage is incomplete, or if the clinical response is inadequate. Although surgical drainage is generally a critical determinant in the treatment of abscesses, there are exceptions involving anaerobic gram-negative bacilli that have been successfully managed with antimicrobial therapy alone. Brain, liver, and tuboovarian abscesses have been managed with antimicrobials after diagnostic aspiration or with empirical antimicrobials without diagnostic aspiration.[112-114] Lung abscesses rarely require drainage.

Hyperbaric Oxygen

In certain infections involving anaerobic gram-negative bacilli, including necrotizing fasciitis and osteomyelitis, hyperbaric oxygen has been used as adjunctive therapy to débridement and antimicrobials.[115] In animal experiments, hyperbaric oxygen has been reported to improve survival in mixed aerobic and anaerobic infection.[116] However, despite occasional testimonials and some experimental data to support its use, no controlled trials have studied the efficacy of hyperbaric oxygen, and its value in the treatment of infections involving anaerobic gram-negative bacilli remains to be proved.[115]

Antibiotic Therapy

The selection of antimicrobials to treat infections imputed or proved to be due to *B. fragilis* and other anaerobic gram-negative bacilli is largely empirical. This approach is necessary because most of the infections involving these bacteria are polymicrobial, and considerable laboratory time is required to separate and identify all species, in addition to the fact that most laboratories cannot reliably perform susceptibility testing for anaerobic bacteria. The choice of antimicrobials is generally based on (1) studies of the activity of new agents, (2) ongoing studies that monitor national susceptibility patterns to determine changes in susceptibility to commonly used agents, and (3) studies of clinical efficacy. In vitro susceptibility testing is advisable for anaerobic isolates recovered from patients with certain infections, including brain abscess, endocarditis, prosthetic device infections, and refractory bacteremia. A prospective observational multicenter study of *Bacteroides* bacteremia confirmed that in vitro activity of antimicrobials reliably predicts treatment outcome and provides compelling evidence that more routine antimicrobial susceptibility testing may be indicated for patients whose blood cultures grow *Bacteroides* species.[117]

   For a long time penicillin was considered the drug of choice for anaerobic infections above the diaphragm because penicillin resistance was largely confined to *B. fragilis,* a pathogen usually restricted to infections found below the diaphragm. Oropharyngeal anaerobes,

TABLE 245-3 Antimicrobial Activity against Anaerobic Gram-Negative Bacilli

	% Susceptible at Breakpoint					
Antibiotic	Bacteroides fragilis	B. fragilis Group*	Porphyromonas *and* Prevotella	Fusobacterium	Bilophila	Sutterella
Amoxicillin-clavulanate	>95	>95	>95	>95	>95	>95
Ampicillin-sulbactam	>95	>95	>95	>95	>95	>95
Cefotaxime	50-70	<50	>95	85-95	70-85	>95
Cefotetan	85-95	50-70	85-95	85-95	70-85	—
Cefoxitin	85-95	70-85	>95	85-95	>95	>95
Ceftizoxime	70-85	70-85	>95	>95	<50	85-95
Ciprofloxacin	<50	<50	50-85	50-85	>95	—
Chloramphenicol	>95	>95	>95	>95	>95	>95
Clindamycin	70-85	65-80	>95	>95	85-95	65-75
Gatifloxacin	>95	>95	>95	>95	>95	>95
Imipenem	>95	>95	>95	>95	>95	>95
Levofloxacin	50-85	<50	75-85	50-85	>95	—
Meropenem	>95	>95	>95	>95	>95	>95
Metronidazole	>95	>95	>95	>95	>95	70-80
Moxifloxacin	>95	>95	>95	>95	>95	>95
Penicillin	<50	<50	50-85	85-95	<50	—
Piperacillin	70-85	70-85	>95	>95	>95	85-95
Piperacillin-tazobactam	>95	>95	>95	>95	>95	85-95
Ticarcillin-clavulanate	>95	>95	>95	>95	>95	>95

*Includes *B. distasonis, B. ovatus, B. thetaiotaomicron,* and *B. vulgatus.*
Data from references 1, 124-130, 138.

particularly *P. melaninogenica,* have shown increasing resistance to penicillin as a result of β-lactamase production, and these organisms have been associated with penicillin treatment failure.[118]

Most *Fusobacterium* spp. remain susceptible to penicillin, but treatment failure because of β-lactamase production has been reported.[119] *Campylobacter gracilis,* a pathogen found in serious head and neck infections, is also often penicillin resistant.[120] Although some odontogenic and pulmonary infections will still respond to penicillin, it should not be used as initial therapy for serious infections involving mouth anaerobes. Such infections include Ludwig's angina, peritonsillar abscess, necrotizing anaerobic pneumonia, anaerobic empyema, and human bite infections, as well as infections after clenched-fist injuries.

Antimicrobial susceptibilities for the *B. fragilis* group are shown in Table 245-3. The antibiotics that are most predictably active against anaerobic gram-negative bacilli, including the *B. fragilis* group, are metronidazole, chloramphenicol, clindamycin, carbapenems (imipenem, meropenem, and ertapenem), cefoxitin, and combinations of a β-lactam plus a β-lactamase inhibitor (amoxicillin-clavulanate, ampicillin-sulbactam, ticarcillin-clavulanate, and piperacillin-tazobactam).[1,121-125] Cefotetan and cefmetazole have activity similar to that of cefoxitin, although these agents tend to be less active against the non-fragilis species.[126] *B. fragilis* has shown increasing resistance in recent years to some of the antimicrobials commonly used to treat infections with this organism, including cefoxitin, clindamycin, and the anti-*Pseudomonas* penicillins. For many years clindamycin has been widely used and relied upon for its broad activity against anaerobic organisms, including those of the *B. fragilis* group, but caution is now advised because in recent surveys almost 30% or more of *B. fragilis* isolates were clindamycin resistant.[127,128] Drugs having poor activity against anaerobic gram-negative bacilli include aminoglycosides, trimethoprim-sulfamethoxazole, and most third-generation cephalosporins, quinolones, and monobactams. Two currently available quinolones, moxifloxacin and gatifloxacin, are highly active against all anaerobic gram-negative rods.[129,130]

In the treatment of cerebral abscess, metronidazole has proved to be a useful drug because of its activity and good penetration into the brain. Because metronidazole has poor activity against anaerobic gram-positive cocci and no activity against commonly found aerobes such as *S. intermedius,* it is generally combined with penicillin, ampicillin, or a third-generation cephalosporin.[112]

Common bacterial isolates from human bite infections and infected clenched-fist injuries include *Prevotella* spp., which may be penicillin resistant, *Eikenella corrodens,* which is clindamycin and metronida-

zole resistant, and often staphylococci.[99] Therefore, appropriate therapies would include two-drug regimens such as clindamycin and penicillin, clindamycin and a quinolone, or a β-lactam and a β-lactamase combination such as amoxicillin-clavulanate.

In pulmonary infections caused by anaerobic mouth flora, commonly used regimens are clindamycin alone, which was superior to penicillin in two randomized studies of the treatment of lung abscess,[131,132] and the combination of penicillin with metronidazole.[64] Metronidazole should not be used alone because of its lack of activity against the frequently present streptococcal species and its poor efficacy as monotherapy in clinical trials.[133]

Intra-abdominal infections characteristically involve *B. fragilis,* other anaerobes, and coliforms. Typical treatment regimens include two drugs, one for the anaerobes (clindamycin, metronidazole, cefoxitin) and a second for the coliforms (aminoglycoside, third-generation cephalosporin, quinolone, monobactam). Agents having activity against both components, including imipenem, meropenem, ertapenem, and piperacillin-tazobactam, have been used as monotherapy. Many comparative trials have shown that, as long as the regimen is active against coliforms and anaerobes, including *B. fragilis,* efficacy is similar.[134-137] Almost all strains of *B. wadsworthia,* an important pathogen in appendicitis, produce β-lactamase; they are susceptible to agents active against *B. fragilis.* Virtually all anaerobic gram-negative rods are susceptible to metronidazole with the exception of *Sutterella wadsworthensis,* which shows almost 20% resistance.[138]

Genital tract infections in women are typically mixed and involve coliforms, streptococcal species, and anaerobes. Although *B. fragilis* is not as frequent a pathogen as it is in intra-abdominal infections, it is present in a significant number of patients. *P. bivia* is a common anaerobe recovered in genital tract infections of women and has susceptibilities similar to those of *B. fragilis.*[139] Therefore, therapeutic options for these infections are like those used in the treatment of abdominal infections.[139-141]

Guidelines for treatment of skin and soft tissue infections involving mixed aerobic-anaerobic flora are like those for intra-abdominal infections.

Antimicrobial resistance in *Bacteroides* and *Prevotella* spp. has a direct impact on the choice of agents used to treat infections thought to involve anaerobic bacteria. A number of resistance mechanisms have been defined[142]; among these mechanisms, the production of β-lactamase is currently considered to be of greatest clinical importance. Resistance to metronidazole and clindamycin occurs through other unique mechanisms, and, disturbingly, resistance to multiple antibiotic classes has been seen in a single organism. Because susceptibility testing of anaerobic bacteria is problematic[143] and not routinely available, physicians must continue to monitor susceptibility data provided through reference centers to be aware of changing patterns of antimicrobial activity and to ensure optimal treatment of their patients.

REFERENCES

1. Jousimies-Somer HR, Summanen PH, Wexler H, et al. *Bacteroides, Porphyromonas, Prevotella, Fusobacterium,* and other anaerobic gram-negative bacteria. In: Murray PR, Baron EJ, Jorgensen JH, et al, eds. Manual of Clinical Microbiology. 8th ed. Washington, DC: ASM Press; 2003:880-901.
2. Gibbons RJ, van Houte J. Bacterial adherence in oral microbial ecology. Annu Rev Microbiol. 1975;29:19-44.
3. Long SS, Swenson RM. Determinants of the developing oral flora in normal newborns. Appl Environ Microbiol. 1976;32:494-497.
4. Socransky SS, Manganiello SD. The oral microbiota of man from birth to senility. J Periodontol. 1971;42:485-496.
5. McClellan DL, Griffen AL, Leys EJ. Age and prevalence of *Porphyromonas gingivalis* in children. J Clin Microbiol. 1996;34:2017-2019.
6. Tuite-McDonnell M, Griffen AL, Moeschberger ML, et al. Concordance of *Porphyromonas gingivalis* colonization in families. J Clin Microbiol. 1997;35:455-461.
7. Hentges DJ. The anaerobic microflora of the human body. Clin Infect Dis. 1993;16(Suppl):S175-S180.
8. Moore WEC, Holdeman LV. Human fecal flora: The normal flora of 20 Japanese-Hawaiians. Appl Microbiol. 1974;27:961-979.
9. Stark PL, Lee A. The microbial ecology of the large bowel of breast-fed and formula-fed infants during the first year of life. J Med Microbiol. 1982;15:189-203.
10. Gorbach SL. Intestinal microflora. Gastroenterology. 1971;60:1110-1129.
11. van der Waaij D, Berghuis de Vries JM, Lekkerkerk van der Wees JEC. Colonization resistance of the digestive tract in conventional and antibiotic treated mice. J Hyg. 1971;69:405-411.
12. Barlett JG, Polk BF. Bacterial flora of the vagina: Quantitative study. Rev Infect Dis. 1984;(Suppl):S67-S72.
13. Hill GB, St Claire KK, Gutman LT. Anaerobes predominate among the vaginal microflora of prepubertal girls. Clin Infect Dis. 1995;20(Suppl 2):S269-S270.
14. Hillier SL, Lau RJ. Vaginal microflora in postmenopausal women who have not received estrogen replacement therapy. Clin Infect Dis. 1997;25(Suppl 2):S123-S126.
15. Smith DT. Fusospirochetal disease of the lungs produced with cultures from Vincent's angina. J Infect Dis. 1930;46:303-310.
16. Onderdonk AB, Bartlett JG, Louie T, et al. Microbial synergy in experimental intraabdominal abscess. Infect Immun. 1976;13:22-26.
17. Brook I. Enhancement of growth of aerobic and facultative bacteria in mixed infections with *Bacteroides* species. Infect Immun. 1985;50:929-931.
18. Styrt B, Gorbach SL. Recent developments in the understanding of the pathogenesis and treatment of anaerobic infections. N Engl J Med. 1989;321:240-246.
19. Brook I. Presence of beta-lactamase-producing bacteria and beta-lactamase activity in abscesses. Am J Clin Pathol. 1986;86:97-101.
20. Tzianabos AO, Kasper DL, Onderdonk AB. Structure and function of *Bacteroides fragilis* capsular polysaccharides: Relationship to induction and prevention of abscesses. Clin Infect Dis. 1995;20(Suppl 2):S132-S140.
21. Onderdonk AB, Kasper DL, Cisneros RL, et al. The capsular polysaccharide of *Bacteroides fragilis* as a virulence factor: Comparison of the pathogenic potential of encapsulated and unencapsulated strains. J Infect Dis. 1977;136:82-89.
22. Gibson FC 3rd, Onderdonk AB, Kasper DL, et al. Cellular mechanism of intraabdominal abscess formation by Bacteroides fragilis. J Immunol. 1998;160:5000-5006.
23. Simon GL, Klempner MJ, Kasper DL, et al. Alterations in opsonophagocytic killing by neutrophils of *Bacteroides fragilis* associated with animal and laboratory passage: Effect of capsular polysaccharide. J Infect Dis. 1982;145:72-77.
24. Kasper DL, Onderdonk AB, Polk BF, et al. Surface antigens as virulence factors in infection with *Bacteroides fragilis*. Rev Infect Dis. 1979;1:278-290.
25. Brook I, Myhal ML. Adherence of *Bacteroides fragilis* group species. Infect Immun. 1991;59:742-744.
26. Delahooke DM, Barclay GR, Poxton IR. A re-appraisal of the biological activity of *Bacteroides* lipopolysaccharide. J Med Microbiol. 1995;42:102-112.
27. Rotstein OD. Interactions between leukocytes and anaerobic bacteria in polymicrobial surgical infections. Clin Infect Dis. 1993;16(Suppl):S190-S194.
28. Duerden BI. Virulence factors in anaerobes. Clin Infect Dis. 1994;18(Suppl):S253-S259.
29. Botta GA, Araese A, Minisini R, et al. Role of structural and extracellular virulence factors in gram-negative anaerobic bacteria. Clin Infect Dis. 1994;18(Suppl):S260-S264.
30. Bulkacz J, Schuster GS, Singh B, et al. Phospholipase A activity of extracellular products from *Bacteroides melaninogenicus* on epithelium tissue cultures. J Periodont Res. 1985;20:146-153.
31. Grenier D, Mayrand D. Selected characteristics of pathogenic and non-pathogenic strains of *Bacteroides gingivalis*. J Clin Microbiol. 1987;25:738-740.
32. Tally FP, Goldin BR, Jabobus NV, et al. Superoxide dismutase in anaerobic bacteria of clinical significance. Infect Immun. 1977;16:20-25.
33. Sears CL. The toxins of Bacteroides fragilis. Toxicon. 2001;39:1737-1746.
34. Bjornson AB. Role of complement in host resistance against members of the Bacteroidaceae. Rev Infect Dis. 1984;6(Suppl):S34-S39.
35. Mangan DF, Lopatin DE. Polyclonal activation of human peripheral blood B lymphocytes by *Fusobacterium nucleatum*. Infect Immun. 1983;40:1104-1110.
36. Bjornson AB, Magnafichi PI, Schrieber RD, et al. Opsonization of *Bacteroides* by the alternative complement pathway reconstructed from isolated plasma proteins. J Exp Med. 1987;164:777-798.
37. Zalezvik DF, Farmer T, Kasper DL. Antibody mediated killing of *Bacteroides fragilis* is strain specific and proceeds via the classical complement pathway (Abstract). Clin Res. 1988;36:583.
38. Onderdonk AB, Markham RB, Zaleznik DF, et al. Evidence for T cell-dependent immunity to *Bacteroides fragilis* in an intraabdominal abscess model. J Clin Invest. 1982;69:9-16.
39. Tzianabos AO, Kasper DL. Role of T cells in abscess formation. Curr Opin Microbiol. 2002;5:92-96.
40. Klempner MS. Interactions of polymorphonuclear leukocytes with anaerobic bacteria. Rev Infect Dis. 1984;6(Suppl):S40-S44.
41. Fisher ML, Baluarte HJ, Long SS. Bacteremia due to *Bacteroides fragilis* after elective appendectomy in renal transplant recipients. J Infect Dis. 1981;143:635-638.
42. Durand ML, Calderwood SB, Weber DJ, et al. Acute bacterial meningitis in adults: A review of 493 episodes. N Engl J Med. 1993;328:21-28.
43. Feder HM Jr. *Bacteroides fragilis* meningitis. Rev Infect Dis. 1987;9:783-786.
44. Brook I. Bacteriology of intracranial abscess in children. J Neurosurg. 1981;54:484-488.
45. Swartz MN. Central nervous system infections. In: Finegold SM, George WL, eds. Anaerobic Infections in Humans. New York: Academic Press; 1989:155-212.
46. Zavistoski J, Dzink JA, Onderdonk AB, et al. Quantitative bacteriology of endodontic infections. Oral Surg Oral Med Oral Pathol. 1980;49:171-174.
47. Dymock D, Weightman AJ, Scully C, et al. Molecular analysis of microflora associated with dentoalveolar abscesses. J Clin Microbiol. 1996;34:537-542.
48. Chow AW. Life-threatening infections of the head and neck. Clin Infect Dis. 1992;14:991-1004.
49. Chirinos JA, Lichstein DM, Garcia J, et al. The evolution of Lemierre syndrome: Report of 2 cases and review of the literature. Medicine. 2002;81:458-465.
50. Heimdahl A, von Konow L, Satoh T, et al. Clinical appearance of orofacial infections of odontogenic origin in relation to microbiological findings. J Clin Microbiol. 1985;22:299-302.
51. Tanner A, Stillman N. Oral and dental infections with anaerobic bacteria: Clinical features, predominant pathogens, and treatment. Clin Infect Dis. 1993;16(Suppl):S304-S309.
52. Ishikawa I, Nakashima K, Koseki T, et al. Induction of the immune response to periodontopathic bacteria and its role in the pathogenesis of periodontitis. Periodontol 2000. 1997;14:79-111.
53. Loesche WJ, Grossman NS. Periodontal disease as a specific, albeit chronic, infection: Diagnosis and treatment. Clin Microbiol Rev. 2001;14:727-752.
54. Gersdorf H, Meissner A, Pelz K, et al. Identification of *Bacteroides forsythus* in subgingival plaque from patients with advanced periodontitis. J Clin Microbiol. 1993;31:941-946.
55. Loesche WJ, Syed SA, Laughon BE, et al. The bacteriology of acute necrotizing ulcerative gingivitis. J Periodontol. 1982;53:223-230.
56. Brook I, Frazier EH, Thompson DH. Aerobic and anaerobic microbiology of peritonsillar abscess. Laryngoscope. 1991;101:289-292.
57. Frederick J, Braude AI. Anaerobic infection of the paranasal sinuses. N Engl J Med. 1974;290:135-137.
58. Nord CE. The role of anaerobic bacteria in recurrent episodes of sinusitis and tonsillitis. Clin Infect Dis. 1995;20:1512-1524.
59. Brook I, Finegold SM. Bacteriology of chronic otitis media. JAMA. 1979;241:487-488.
60. Brook I. Aerobic and anaerobic bacteriology of chronic mastoiditis in children. Am J Dis Child. 1981;135:478-479.
61. Brook I. Aerobic and anaerobic bacteriology of cholesteatoma. Laryngoscope. 1981;91:250-253.
62. Brook I. Acute bacterial suppurative parotitis: Microbiology and management. J Craniofacial Surg. 2003;14:37-40.
63. Lorber B, Swenson RM. Bacteriology of aspiration pneumonia: A prospective study of community- and hospital-acquired cases. Ann Intern Med. 1974;81:329-331.
64. Bartlett JG. Anaerobic bacteria infections of the lung and pleural space. Clin Infect Dis. 1993;16(Suppl):S248-S255.
65. Levison ME. Anaerobic pleuropulmonary infection. Curr Opin Infect Dis. 2001;14:187-191.
66. Weinstein WM, Onderdonk AB, Bartlett JG, et al. Antimicrobial therapy of experimental intraabdominal sepsis. J Infect Dis. 1975;132:282-286.
67. Lorber B, Swenson RM. The bacteriology of intra-abdominal infections. Surg Clin North Am. 1975;55:1349-1354.
68. McClean KL, Shechan GJ, Harding GKM. Intraabdominal infection: A review. Clin Infect Dis. 1994;19:100-116.
69. Baron EJ, Summanen P, Downes J, et al. *Bilophila wadsworthia,* gen. nov. and sp. nov., a unique gram-negative anaerobic rod recovered from appendicitis specimens and human faeces. J Gen Microbiol. 1989;135:3405-3411.
70. Baron EJ, Corren M, Henderson G, et al. *Bilophila wadsworthia* isolates from clinical specimens. J Clin Microbiol. 1992;30:1882-1884.
71. Baron EJ, Bennion R, Thompson J, et al. A microbiologic comparison between acute and advanced appendicitis. Clin Infect Dis. 1992;14:227-231.
72. Summanen PH, Jousimies-Somer H, Manley S, et al. *Bilophila wadsworthia* isolates from clinical specimens. Clin Infect Dis. 1995;20(Suppl 2):S210-S211.
73. Molitoris E, Wexler HM, Finegold SM. Sources and antimicrobial susceptibilities of *Campylobacter gracilis* and *Sutterella wadsworthensis.* Clin Infect Dis. 1997;25(Suppl 2):S264-S265.
74. Finegold SM, Jousimies-Somer H. Recently described clinically important anaerobic bacteria: Medical aspects. Clin Infect Dis. 1997;25(Suppl 2):S88-S93.

75. Sears CL, Myers LL, Lazenby A, et al. Enterotoxigenic *Bacteroides fragilis*. Clin Infect Dis. 1995;20(Suppl 2):S142-S148.

76. Zhang G, Svenungsson B, Karnell A, et al. Prevalence of enterotoxigenic *Bacteroides fragilis* in adult patients with diarrhea and healthy controls. Clin Infect Dis. 1999;29:590-594.

77. Eschenbach DA. Bacterial vaginosis and anaerobes in obstetric-gynecologic infections. Clin Infect Dis. 1993;16(Suppl):S282-S287.

78. Eschenbach DA, Buchanan TM, Pollock HM, et al. Polymicrobial etiology of acute pelvic inflammatory disease. N Engl J Med. 1975;293:166-171.

79. Sweet RL. Pelvic inflammatory disease. Sex Transm Dis. 1986;13:192-198.

80. Snydman PR, Tally FP, Knoppel R, et al. *Bacteroides bivius* and *Bacteroides disiens* in obstetrical patients: Clinical findings and antimicrobial susceptibilities. J Antimicrob Chemother. 1980;6:519-525.

81. Spiegel CA. Bacterial vaginosis. Clin Microbiol Rev. 1991;4:485-502.

82. Sweet RL. Role of bacterial vaginosis in pelvic inflammatory disease. Clin Infect Dis. 1995;20(Suppl 2):S271-S275.

83. Krohn MA, Hillier SL, Nugent RP, et al. The genital flora of women with intraamnionotic infection. J Infect Dis. 1995;171:1475-1480.

84. Wilson WR, Martin WM, Wilkowski CJ, et al. Anaerobic bacteremia. Mayo Clin Proc. 1972;47:639-646.

85. Weinstein MP, Reller LB, Murphy JR, et al. The clinical significance of positive blood cultures: A comprehensive analysis of 500 episodes of bacteremia and fungemia in adults. I. Laboratory and epidemiologic observations. Rev Infect Dis. 1983;5:35-53.

86. Lombardi DP, Engleberg NC. Anaerobic bacteremia: Incidence, patient characteristics, and clinical significance. Am J Med. 1992;92:53-60.

87. Chow AW, Guze LB. Bacteroidaceae bacteremia: Clinical experience with 112 patients. Medicine (Baltimore). 1974;53:93-123.

88. Redondo MC, Arbo MDJ, Grindlinger J, et al. Attributable mortality of bacteremia associated with the *Bacteroides fragilis* group. Clin Infect Dis. 1995;20:1492-1496.

89. Dorsher CW, Rosenblatt JE, Wilson WR, et al. Anaerobic bacteremia: Decreasing rate over a 15 year period. Rev Infect Dis. 1991;13:633-636.

90. Weinstein MP, Towns ML, Quartey SM, et al. The clinical significance of positive blood cultures in the 1990s: A prospective comprehensive evaluation of the microbiology, epidemiology, and outcome of bacteremia and fungemia in adults. Clin Infect Dis. 1997;24:584-602.

91. James PA, al-Shafi KM. Clinical value of anaerobic blood culture: A retrospective analysis of positive patient episodes. J Clin Pathol. 2000;53:231-233.

92. Cockerill FR, Hughes JG, Vetter EA, et al. Analysis of 281,797 consecutive blood cultures performed over an eight-year period: Trends in microorganisms isolated and the value of anaerobic culture of blood. Clin Infect Dis. 1997;24:403-418.

93. Bartlett JG, Dick J. The controversy regarding routine anaerobic blood cultures. Am J Med. 2000;108:505-506.

94. O'Donnell JA, Asbel LE. *Bacteroides fragilis* bacteremia and infected aortic aneurysm presenting as fever of unknown origin: Diagnostic delay without routine anaerobic blood cultures. Clin Infect Dis. 1999;29:1309-1311.

95. Lark RL, McNeil SA, VanderHyde K, et al. Risk factors for anaerobic bloodstream infections in bone marrow transplant recipients. Clin Infect Dis. 2001;33:338-343.

96. Felner JM, Dowell VR Jr. Anaerobic bacterial endocarditis. N Engl J Med. 1970;282:1188-1192.

97. Nastro LJ, Finegold SM. Endocarditis due to anaerobic gram-negative bacilli. Am J Med. 1973;54:482-496.

98. Skeist DJ, Steiner D, Werner M, et al. Anaerobic pericarditis: Case report and review. Clin Infect Dis. 1994;19:435-440.

99. Goldstein EJC, Citron DM, Finegold JM. Role of anaerobic bacteria in bite-wound infections. Rev Infect Dis. 1984;6(Suppl):S177-S183.

100. Brook I, Frazier EH. Clinical and microbiological features of necrotizing fasciitis. J Clin Microbiol. 1995;33:2382-2387.

101. Louie TJ, Bartlett JG, Tally FP, et al. Aerobic and anaerobic bacteria in diabetic foot ulcers. Ann Intern Med. 1976;85:461-463.

102. Bryan CS, Dew CE, Reynolds KL. Bacteremia associated with decubitus ulcers. Arch Intern Med. 1983;143:2093.

103. Gerding D. Foot infections in diabetic patients: The role of anaerobes. Clin Infect Dis. 1995;20(Suppl 2):S283-S288.

104. Meislin HW, Lerner SA, Graves MH, et al. Cutaneous abscesses: Anaerobic and aerobic bacteriology and outpatient management. Ann Intern Med. 1977;87:145-149.

105. Edmiston CE, Walker AP, Krepel CJ, et al. The nonpuerperal breast infection: Aerobic and anaerobic microbial recovery from acute and chronic disease. J Infect Dis. 1990;162:695-699.

106. Raff MJ, Melo JC. Anaerobic osteomyelitis. Medicine (Baltimore). 1978;57:83-103.

107. Nakata MN, Lewis RP. Anaerobic bacteria in bone and joint infections. Rev Infect Dis. 1984;6(Suppl):S165-S170.

108. Brook I, Frazier EH. Anaerobic osteomyelitis and arthritis in a military hospital: A 10-year experience. Am J Med. 1993;94:21-28.

109. Finkelstein R, Nachum Z, Reissman P, et al. Anaerobic osteomyelitis in patients with Gaucher's disease. Clin Infect Dis. 1992;15:771-773.

110. Rosenkranz P, Lederman MM, Gopabkrishna KV, et al. Septic arthritis caused by *Bacteroides fragilis*. Rev Infect Dis. 1990;12:20-30.

111. Mueller PR, van Sonnenberg E. Interventional radiology in the chest and abdomen. N Engl J Med. 1990;322:1364-1374.

112. Boom WH, Tuazon CU. Successful treatment of multiple brain abscesses with antibiotics alone. Rev Infect Dis. 1985;7:189-199.

113. Herbert DA, Fogel DA, Rothman J, et al. Pyogenic liver abscesses: Successful non-surgical therapy. Lancet. 1992;1:134-136.

114. Landers DV, Sweet RL. Current trends in the diagnosis and treatment of tuboovarian abscess. Am J Obstet Gynecol. 1985;151:1098-1110.

115. Wang C, Schwaitzberg S, Berliner E, et al. Hyperbaric oxygen for treating wounds: A systematic review of the literature. Arch Surg. 2003;138:272-279.

116. Thom SR, Lauermann MW, Hart G-B. Intermittent hyperbaric oxygen therapy for reduction of mortality in experimental polymicrobial sepsis. J Infect Dis. 1986;154:504-510.

117. Nguyen MH, Yu VL, Morris AJ, et al. Antimicrobial resistance and clinical outcome of Bacteroides bacteremia: Findings of a multicenter prospective observational trial. Clin Infect Dis. 2000;30:870-876.

118. Heimdahl A, von Konow L, Nord CE. Isolation of β-lactamase-producing *Bacteroides* strains associated with clinical failures with penicillin treatment of human orofacial infections. Arch Oral Biol. 1980;25:689-692.

119. Goldstein EJC, Summanen PH, Citron DM, et al. Fatal sepsis due to a β-lactamase-producing strain of *Fusobacterium nucleatum* subspecies *polymorphum*. Clin Infect Dis. 1995;20:798-800.

120. Johnson CC, Reinhardt JF, Edelstein MAC, et al. *Bacteroides gracilis*, an important anaerobic bacterial pathogen . J Clin Microbiol. 1985;22:799-802.

121. Cuchural GJ Jr, Tally FP, Jacobus NV, et al. Comparative activities of newer β-lactam agents against members of the *Bacteroides fragilis* group. Antimicrob Agents Chemother. 1990;34:479-480.

122. Appelbaum P, Spangler S, Jacobs MR. Susceptibilities of 394 *Bacteroides fragilis*, non-B. fragilis group *Bacteroides* species, and *Fusobacterium* species to newer antimicrobial agents. Antimicrob Agents Chemother. 1991;35:1214-1218.

123. Snydman DR, McDermott L, Cuchural GJ Jr, et al. Analysis of trends in antimicrobial resistance patterns among clinical isolates of *Bacteroides fragilis* group species from 1990 to 1994. Clin Infect Dis. 1996;23(Suppl 1):S54-S65.

124. Hoellman DB, Kelly LM, Jacobs MR, et al. Comparative antianaerobic activity of BMS 284756. Antimicrob Agents Chemother. 2001;45:589-592.

125. Hoellman DB, Kelly LM, Credito K, et al. In vitro antianaerobic activity of ertapenem (MK-0826) compared to seven other compounds. Antimicrob Agents Chemother. 2002;46:220-224.

126. Wexler HM, Finegold SM. In vitro activity of cefotetan compared with that of other antimicrobial agents against anaerobic bacteria. Antimicrob Agents Chemother. 1988;32:601-604.

127. Aldridge KE, Ashcraft D, Cambre K, et al. Multicenter survey of the changing in vitro antimicrobial susceptibilities of clinical isolates of *Bacteroides fragilis* group, *Prevotella, Fusobacterium, Porphyromonas,* and *Peptostreptococcus* species. Antimicrob Agents Chemother. 2001;45:1238-1243.

128. Teng L-J, Hsueh P-R, Tsai J-C, et al. High incidence of cefoxitin and clindamycin resistance among anaerobes in Taiwan. Antimicrob Agents Chemother. 2002;46:2908-2913.

129. Wexler HM, Molitoris E, Molitoris D, et al. In vitro activity of moxifloxacin against 179 strains of anaerobic bacteria found in pulmonary infections. Anaerobe. 2000;6:227-231.

130. Wexler HM, Molitoris D, Finegold SM. In vitro activity of gatifloxacin against 238 strains of anaerobic bacteria. Anaerobe. 2001;7:285-289.

131. Levison ME, Mangura CT, Lorber B, et al. Clindamycin compared with penicillin for the treatment of anaerobic lung abscess. Ann Intern Med. 1983;98:466-471.

132. Gudiol F, Manresa F, Pallares R, et al. Clindamycin vs penicillin for anaerobic lung infections: High rate of penicillin failures associated with penicillin-resistant *Bacteroides melaninogenicus*. Arch Intern Med. 1990;150:2525-2529.

133. Sanders CV, Hanna BJ, Lewis AC. Metronidazole in the treatment of anaerobic infections. Am Rev Respir Dis. 1979;120:337-343.

134. Harding GKM, Buckwold FJ, Ronald AR, et al. Prospective, randomized comparative study of clindamycin, chloramphenicol, and ticarcillin, each in combination with gentamicin, in therapy for intra-abdominal and female genital tract sepsis. J Infect Dis. 1980;142:384-393.

135. Smith JA, Skidmore AG, Forward AD, et al. Prospective, randomized, double-blind comparison of metronidazole and tobramycin with clindamycin and tobramycin in the treatment of intra-abdominal sepsis. Ann Surg. 1980;192:213-220.

136. Solomkin JS, Dellinger EP, Christou NV, et al. Results of a multicenter trial comparing imipenem/cilastatin to tobramycin/clindamycin for intra-abdominal infections. Ann Surg. 1990;212:581-591.

137. Younes Z, Johnson DA. New developments and concepts in antimicrobial therapy for intraabdominal infections. Curr Gastroenterol Rep. 2000;2:277-282.

138. Wexler HM, Molitoris D, St. John S, et al. In vitro activities of faropenem against 579 strains of anaerobic bacteria. Antimicrob Agents Chemother. 2002;46:3669-3675.

139. Hill GB, Ayers OM. Antimicrobial susceptibilities of anaerobic bacteria isolated from female genital tract infections. Antimicrob Agents Chemother. 1985;27:324-331.

140. Landers DV, Sweet RL. Tubo-ovarian abscess: Contemporary approach to management. Rev Infect Dis. 1983;5:876-884.

141. Pastorek JG II, Sanders CV Jr. Antibiotic therapy for post cesarean endomyometritis. Rev Infect Dis. 1991;13(Suppl):S752-S757.

142. Rasmossen BA, Bush K, Tally FP. Antimicrobial resistance in anaerobes. Clin Infect Dis. 1997;24(Suppl 1):S110-S120.

143. Wexler HM. Susceptibility testing of anaerobic bacteria—The state of the art. Clin Infect Dis. 1993;16(Suppl):S328-S333.

Anaerobic Cocci

ELLEN M. MASCINI

JAN VERHOEF

Anaerobic cocci are found as commensal flora of all skin and mucosal surfaces and are, after the gram-negative bacilli, the second most common group of anaerobes encountered in human infection. The most clinically important anaerobic cocci are included in the genera *Peptostreptococcus, Streptococcus,* and *Veillonella.* Often they are recovered mixed with other bacteria, which always makes it difficult to define their exact role in the cause of the infection. Other genera are seldom cultured from relevant clinical specimens.[1] The microaerophilic gram-positive cocci *Streptococcus anginosus, Streptococcus constellatus,* and *Streptococcus intermedius,* as well as *Gemella morbillorum,* which are often isolated in primary anaerobic culture but adapt to microaerophilic growth on successive subculture,[1,2] are discussed in Chapter 201.

TAXONOMY AND MICROBIOLOGY

In 1977 Watt and Jack defined anaerobic cocci as cocci that grow well under satisfactory conditions of anaerobiosis and do not grow on suitable solid media in 10% carbon dioxide in air even after incubation for 7 days at 37° C.[2] Until recently, classification and definition of these organisms were always extremely difficult because the earlier attempts at identification had included cocci that were likely to be microaerophilic. The genus *Peptostreptococcus* consists of obligatory anaerobic gram-positive cocci that neither require fermentable carbohydrate for growth nor produce lactic acid as their sole major metabolic end product.[3-5] Cell size was the method usually recommended to distinguish two of the most important species, *Peptostreptococcus magnus* and *Peptostreptococcus micros.*[6] Most gram-positive anaerobic cocci use proteins and amino acids as their major energy source and are not amenable to identification methods based on carbohydrate fermentation reactions.[4] In the past, inadequate taxonomy yielded misleading descriptions of the mean pathogenicity and biochemistry of gram-positive anaerobic cocci "species," which were in fact mixed groups. The difficulties in identification and a poor predictive value of identification discouraged clinical microbiologists for a long time, but this circle has been broken: The introduction of nucleic acid techniques (guanosine plus cytosine content, 16S ribosomal RNA [rRNA] sequencing, DNA homology) in the 1980s has revolutionized the taxonomy of these bacteria.[7,8] All but one species formerly classified as *Peptococcus* have been transferred to the genus *Peptostreptococcus.*[1,4,5,8,9] The only species in the genus is *Peptococcus niger,* the former type species of the genus. In fact, *P. niger* phylogenetically clusters within the Actinomycetales and might be renamed accordingly.[1,4,7] *Peptococcus saccharolyticus* has been reclassified as *Staphylococcus saccharolyticus* and is aerotolerant on subculture. Besides genetic analysis, preformed enzyme profiles based on tests for the presence of saccharolytic and proteolytic enzymes provide a simple method for identification in clinical surveys.[3,4,6,8] Unlike the true anaerobic cocci, microaerophilic streptococci are resistant to metronidazole; this characteristic is useful for differentiation of species and is an important factor to be taken into account in predicting therapeutic antimicrobial coverage.[1,2] The major features that differentiate these microaerophilic cocci from *Peptostreptococcus* species are their strong saccharolytic nature and their production of lactic acid as the sole major end product.[1] Together, these developments now allow routine laboratory identification of gram-positive anaerobic cocci to groups with defined and distinct clinical properties, thus giving predictive value to the identification of gram-positive anaerobic cocci.

Currently, the genus *Peptostreptococcus* consists of two species of human origin: *Peptostreptococcus anaerobius* and *Peptostreptococcus productus.* New genera have been proposed for *Peptostreptococcus asaccharolyticus, Peptostreptococcus hydrogenalis, Peptostreptococcus lacrimalis, Peptostreptococcus lactolyticus, P. magnus, P. micros, Peptostreptococcus prevotii, Peptostreptococcus tetradius,* and *Peptostreptococcus vaginalis.*[10,11] Several tests, including sequence analysis of the 16S rRNA gene, indicated that *Peptostreptococcus* was not a well-defined genus but contained some very heterogeneous species with differences marked enough to designate new genera.[3,4,7,8,10,12-14] *P. asaccharolyticus* and *P. lacrimalis* have been reclassified into a genus of unsettled status, either *Schleiferella* or *Peptoniphilus,* with the first of the two probably having precedence. *P. prevotii, P. lactolyticus, P. hydrogenalis, P. vaginalis,* and *P. tetradius* have been moved to the genus *Anaerococcus.*[15] *P. magnus* has been reclassified in the new genus *Finegoldia* as *Finegoldia magna. P. micros* has been reclassified in the new genus *Micromonas* as *Micromonas micros* (though the name *Micromonas micros* is illegitimate because of the preexistence of the fungal genus *Micromonas*).[12-14,16] *P. anaerobius* clusters with some members of the genus *Clostridium. P. anaerobius* may soon prove to be the only remaining member of the genus *Peptostreptococcus.*[3,7,8,10,12,14] Unfortunately, the continual changes in nomenclature are confusing, and for most diagnostic microbiology laboratories, the advanced DNA techniques for identification of gram-positive anaerobic cocci are not applicable.

Veillonella is a small, nonmotile, nonfermentative, obligatory anaerobic gram-negative coccus that fluoresces red under ultraviolet light and reduces nitrate.[3,17,18] Several species have been described, of which *Veillonella parvula* appears to be the most common in specimens from humans.[3,9]

NORMAL FLORA

Peptostreptococcus species are part of the normal flora of the mouth, upper respiratory tract, intestinal tract, vagina, and skin.[8,19,20] *V. parvula* is universally present in the upper airways and normally inhabits the mouth, gastrointestinal tract, and vagina in humans.[3,17,18,21] It has been suggested that their production of volatile fatty acids may be important in inhibiting the growth of enteropathogens in vivo.[16]

CLINICAL ISOLATES

Clinically important obligatory anaerobic cocci include *Peptostreptococcus* and *Veillonella.*[3,5,18,22] Additional anaerobic cocci, including *Coprococcus, Peptococcus, Ruminococcus,* and *Staphylococcus saccharolyticus,* are rarely isolated from clinical specimens.[5,9] Most anaerobic cocci express their pathogenicity via synergistic interaction with other (facultative) anaerobic organisms. Very little is known of the pathogenesis of infections caused by anaerobic cocci. Studies of virulence factors might clarify the pathogenic potential of different species of anaerobic cocci.

Peptostreptococcus and Related Species

Current and former members of the genus Peptostreptococcus are the second most common group of anaerobes, consistently account for 20% to 40% of all anaerobes isolated from clinical sources, and are involved in a wide variety of clinically significant infections.[3,6,8,9,19,22] *P. magnus* (*Finegoldia magna*), *P. micros* (*Micromonas micros*), *P. asaccharolyticus* (*Schleiferella asaccharolytica* or *Peptoniphilus asaccharolyticus*), and *P. anaerobius* are the most important clinical isolates. Their contribution to anaerobic clinical isolates was reported to amount to 27%.[6,8] *Peptostreptococcus* and related species are among the most important causative microbes in abscesses (e.g., brain abscesses), especially in association with chronic otitis media, mastoiditis, chronic sinusitis, and pleuropulmonary infections.[8,19,23,24] These species have been recognized as common causative microbes in anaerobic pleuropulmonary disease, usually in mixed culture.[8,19,24-26] *Peptostreptococcus* and related species recovered from blood were associated with many different sources, but especially with oropharyngeal, pulmonary, and female genital tract sources.[3,8,27,28] They appear to cause significant morbidity much less often than do gram-negative anaerobes, particularly *Bacteroides* species. Predisposing factors to peptostreptococcal bacteremia include malignancy[27,28]; recent gastrointestinal, obstetric, or gynecologic surgery; ulceration of the extremities; dental extraction; and immunosuppression.[3,28] Current and former *Peptostreptococcus* species are among the most common organisms in anaerobic osteomyelitis and arthritis at all sites, including bites and cranial infections.[19,29] When mixed with other aerobes and anaerobes, they may be involved in chronic wounds such as venous leg ulcers and severe soft tissue infections such as cellulitis, streptococcal myonecrosis, necrotizing fasciitis, and Fournier's gangrene.[6,8,19,30,31]

Different species are associated with different sites, as shown in Figure 246-1.[3,6,8,12] *P. magnus* (*Finegoldia magna*) stands out as the most pathogenic species of anaerobic cocci; it is the most frequently isolated species and by far the most common species isolated in pure culture. It is associated with abscesses arising from sebaceous cysts

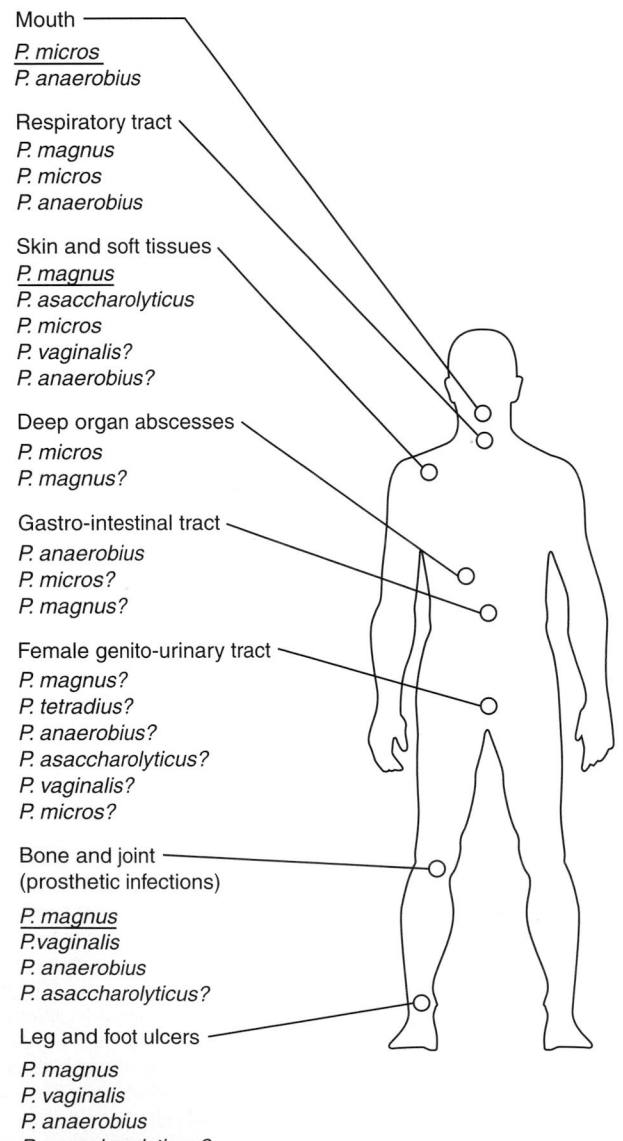

Mouth
P. micros
P. anaerobius

Respiratory tract
P. magnus
P. micros
P. anaerobius

Skin and soft tissues
P. magnus
P. asaccharolyticus
P. micros
P. vaginalis?
P. anaerobius?

Deep organ abscesses
P. micros
P. magnus?

Gastro-intestinal tract
P. anaerobius
P. micros?
P. magnus?

Female genito-urinary tract
P. magnus
P. tetradius?
P. anaerobius?
P. asaccharolyticus?
P. vaginalis?
P. micros?

Bone and joint
(prosthetic infections)
P. magnus
P.vaginalis
P. anaerobius
P. asaccharolyticus?

Leg and foot ulcers
P. magnus
P. vaginalis
P. anaerobius
P. asaccharolyticus?

FIGURE 246-1. Sites of pathology for species of *Peptostreptococcus*. Species of major importance are underlined. Question mark (?) denotes uncertain pathology. (*Adapted from Murdoch DA. Gram-positive anaerobic cocci. Clin Microbiol Rev. 1998;11:81–120.*)

and superficial wound infections, and is isolated in 15% to 20% of diabetic foot infections.[3,6,8] In addition, *F. magna* is recognized as a significant cause of septic arthritis, usually in the presence of joint prostheses, nonpuerperal breast infections, and puerperal sepsis.[3,6,29] Case reports of fatal endocarditis, paravalvular abscess around a bioprosthetic aortic valve, purulent pericarditis, and mediastinitis have very rarely been documented.[6,8,32] The pathogenic potential of other species is very poorly understood, mainly because of problems with identification, but also because most isolates come from mixed cultures, often from superficial sites where they could be part of the normal commensal flora. *M. micros* was usually isolated from soft tissue abscesses, never from the skin, and with a characteristic mixed flora consisting of the *Streptococcus anginosus (milleri)* group and anaerobic gram-negative rods. It might be the predominant anaerobic coccus in oral pathology because it is associated with endodontic abscesses, dental implant infections, progressive periodontitis, and peritonsillar abscesses.[6,8,19] Sporadically, it has also been implicated in vertebral and mastoid ethmoid osteomyelitis, nonpuerperal mastitis, bacteremia, and diabetic foot infections.[6,29] *P. anaerobius* is associated with polymicrobial, soft tissue, and dental abscesses; however, most isolates are from intra-abdominal sepsis or the female genitourinary tract in association with fecal flora.[3,6] The former *P. asaccharolyticus* is cultured from a wide variety of sites, typically mixed with both aerobes and anaerobes, and frequently from abscesses not associated with any particular site or infection.[6,10] Remarkably, this species has been described as a rare causative agent of renal abscess.[33] *A. vaginalis* is usually cultured from superficial sites, often from postoperative wound infections with *Staphylococcus aureus*.

Veillonella

Veillonella species were recovered in less than 0.5% to 4% of clinical specimens cultured for anaerobic bacteria.[3,9,19,22,34] *V. parvula* appears to be the most common species in human specimens.[9,17] When isolated from clinical specimens, it is often regarded as a contaminant or a commensal.[17,18,35] However, it has been isolated in pure culture from various sites and implicated as a pathogen in the sinuses, lungs, liver, central nervous system, heart, and bone.[17,19] The most frequently reported infection caused by *V. parvula* is osteomyelitis,[17,29] and it is also an important pathogen for periodontitis.[18] Occasionally, *V. parvula* has been recovered from blood in association with osteomyelitis, malignancy, low-birth-weight neonates, and gastrointestinal endoscopy.[17,18,27,28,34] *Veillonella* species have been reported as a cause of (prosthetic valve) endocarditis, pleuropulmonary infections, chronic sinusitis, abscesses, burn site infections, meningitis, myositis, and prosthetic joint infection.[17,18,36-38] *V. parvula* is usually isolated as part of a polymicrobial process,[34] which, combined with the fact that *V. parvula* is a normal inhabitant of the mouth, upper airways, gastrointestinal tract, and vagina, has made elucidation of its pathogenetic role difficult. In situations in which it is cultured as a single organism, *V. parvula* should be considered a pathogen, especially in patients with underlying disease or immune suppression. When *V. parvula* is isolated from a specimen such as cerebrospinal fluid, a search should be done for a source, such as imaging of the head to rule out brain abscess, and imaging of the sinuses.[18]

TREATMENT

Successful treatment is often the result of a combination of surgical management involving débridement of necrotic tissue, removal of foreign bodies, drainage, and improvement in circulation with the administration of antimicrobial agents. Because anaerobic cocci are generally recovered mixed with aerobic or other anaerobic organisms, selection of proper therapy becomes more complicated. The appropriate antibiotics should have efficacy against all target organisms. It may be difficult to achieve reliable culture because of problems in obtaining appropriate specimens. Another problem is the lack of consensus about the best method for routine sensitivity testing of anaerobic cocci or, indeed, of any anaerobes.[39,40] Moreover, because both procedures are time consuming, empirical treatment of many patients is necessary until culture results become available. Gram-positive anaerobic cocci and *V. parvula* typically respond well to therapy with a penicillin or clindamycin, but occasional isolates may show resistance to these agents.[3,9,18,24,25,27,34,36,40-42] Metronidazole is effective against most obligate anaerobic cocci and has superior penetration into pus.[8,42] Tetracyclines and macrolides have variable activity against gram-positive anaerobic cocci, but the newer quinolones, as well as quinupristin/dalfopristin and linezolid, show promise.[3,8,40-45] *Veillonella* species are generally resistant to vancomycin, ciprofloxacin, and tetracycline and have only intermediate susceptibility to erythromycin.[17,18,34] Other antimicrobial agents to which the anaerobic cocci are usually susceptible in vitro include cephalosporins, imipenem, and chloramphenicol.[3,9,17,25,34,40-42] Drugs that have virtually no activity are aminoglycosides, aztreonam, and trimethoprim-sulfamethoxazole.[26]

REFERENCES

1. Jousimies-Sommer H. Recently described clinically important anaerobic bacteria: Taxonomic aspects and update. Clin Infect Dis. 1997;25(Suppl 2):S78-S87.
2. Watt B, Jack EP. What are anaerobic cocci? J Med Microbiol. 1977;10:461-468.
3. Wren MWD. Anaerobic cocci of clinical importance. Br J Biomed Sci. 1996;53:294-301.
4. Murdoch DA, Magee JT. A numerical taxonomic study of the gram-positive anaerobic cocci. J Med Microbiol. 1995;45:148-155.
5. Summanen S. Recent taxonomic changes for anaerobic gram-positive and selected gram-negative organisms. Clin Infect Dis. 1993;16(Suppl 4):S168-S174.
6. Murdoch DA, Mitchelmore IJ, Tabaqchali S. The clinical importance of gram-positive anaerobic cocci isolated at St Bartholomew's Hospital, London, in 1987. J Med Microbiol. 1994;41:36-44.
7. Collins MD, Lawson PA, Willems A, et al. The phylogeny of the genus clostridium: Proposal of five new genera and eleven new species combinations. Int J Syst Bacteriol. 1994;44:812-826.
8. Murdoch DA. Gram-positive anaerobic cocci. Clin Microbiol Rev. 1998;11:81-120.
9. Koneman EW, Allen SE, Janda WM, et al. The anaerobic bacteria. In: Color Atlas and Textbook of Diagnostic Microbiology. 5th ed. Philadelphia: Lippincott; 1997:709-784.
10. Pelz K, Mutters R. Taxonomic update and clinical significance of species within the genus *Peptostreptococcus*. Clin Infect Dis. 1997;25(Suppl 2):S94-S97.
11. Moncla BJ, Hillier SL. Peptococcus, Propionibacterium, Lactobacillus, Actinomyces, and other non-spore-forming anaerobic gram-positive bacteria. In: Murray PR, Baron EJ, Jorgensen JH, et al, eds. Manual of Clinical Microbiology. 8th ed. Washington, DC: ASM Press; 2003:857.
12. Song Y, Liu C, McTeague M, et al. Rapid identification of gram-positive anaerobic coccal species originally classified in the genus Peptostreptococcus by multiplex PCR assays using genus- and species-specific primers. Microbiology. 2003;149:1719-1727.
13. Song Y, Liu C, McTeague M, Finegold SM. 16S ribosomal DNA sequence-based analysis of clinically significant gram-positive anaerobic cocci. J Clin Microbiol. 2003;41:1363-1369.
14. Murdoch DA, Shah HN, Gharbia SE, Rajendram D. Proposal to restrict the genus *Peptostreptococcus* (Kluyver & van Niel 1936) to *Peptostreptococcus anaerobius*. Anaerobe. 2000;6:257-260.
15. Ezaki T, Kawamura Y, Li N, et al. Proposal of the genera Anaerococcus gen. nov., Peptoniphilus gen. nov. and Gallicola gen. nov. for members of the genus Peptostreptococcus. Int J Syst Evol Microbiol. 2001;51:1521-1528.
16. Riggio MP, Lennon A. Specific PCR detection of *Peptostreptococcus magnus*. J Med Microbiol. 2003;52:309-313.
17. Fisher RG, Denison MR. *Veillonella parvula* bacteremia without an underlying source. J Clin Microbiol. 1996;34:3235-3236.
18. Bhatti MA, Frank MO. Veillonella parvula meningitis: Case report and review of Veillonella infections. Clin Infect Dis. 2000;31:839-840.
19. Finegold SM. Anaerobic Bacteria in Human Disease. New York: Academic Press, 1977.
20. Evaldson G, Heimdahl A, Kager L, Nord CE. The normal human anaerobic microflora. Scand J Infect Dis Suppl. 1982;35:9-15.
21. Hinton A, Hume ME. Inhibition of *Listeria monocytogenes* growth by *Veillonella* cultured on tartrate medium. Clin Infect Dis. 1997;25(Suppl 2):S120.
22. Bernard K, Cooper C, Johnson W. Prevalence of anaerobes referred to the Canadian National Reference Centre from 1984 to 1996. Clin Infect Dis. 1997;25(Suppl 2):S241-S243.
23. Brook I. Brain abscess in children: Microbiology and management. J Child Neurol. 1995;10:283-288.
24. Brook I. Anaerobic infections in children. Microb Infect. 2002;4:1271-1280.
25. Marina M, Strong CA, Civen R, et al. Bacteriology of anaerobic pleuropulmonary infections: Preliminary report. Clin Infect Dis. 1993;16(Suppl 4):S256-S262.
26. Bartlett, JG. Anaerobic infections of the lung and pleural space. Clin Infect Dis. 1993;16(Suppl 4):S248-S255.
27. Fainstein V, Elting LS, Bodey GP. Bacteremia caused by non-sporulating anaerobes in cancer patients. Medicine. 1989;68:151-162.
28. Brook I. Anaerobic bacterial bacteremia: 12-year experience in two military hospitals. J Infect Dis. 1989;160:1071-1075.
29. Brook I, Frazier E. Anaerobic osteomyelitis and arthritis in a military hospital: A 10-year experience. Am J Med. 1993;94:21-28.
30. Gorbach SL. IDCP guidelines: Necrotizing skin and soft tissue infections. Part II: Myositis, Meleney's gangrene, pyomyositis, necrotizing cellulitis, and Fournier's gangrene. Infect Dis Clin Pract. 1997;5:463-471.
31. Stephens P, Wall IB, Wilson MJ, et al. Anaerobic cocci populating the deep tissues of chronic wounds impair cellular wound healing responses in vitro. Br J Dermatol. 2003;148:456-466.
32. Van der Vorm ER, Dondorp AM, Van Ketel RJ, Dankert J. Apparent culture-negative prosthetic valve endocarditis caused by *Peptostreptococcus magnus*. J Clin Microbiol. 2000;38:4640-4642.
33. Mas Casullo VA, Bottone E, Herold BC. Peptostreptococcus asaccharolyticus renal abscess: A rare cause of fever of unknown origin. Pediatrics. 2001;107:E11.
34. Brook I. *Veillonella* infections in children. J Clin Microbiol. 1996;34:1283-1285.
35. Bartlett JG. Bacteriologic diagnosis in anaerobic pleuropulmonary infections. Clin Infect Dis. 1993;16(Suppl 4):S443-S445.
36. Beumont MG, Duncan J, Mitchell SD, et al. *Veillonella* myositis in an immunocompromised patient. Clin Infect Dis. 1995;21:678-679.
37. Borowski AD, Stein SM, Tulipan NB, Dermody TS. Meningitis caused by mixed anaerobic species complicating tethered cord syndrome. Clin Infect Dis. 1995;21:706-707.
38. Marchandin H, Jean-Pierre H, Carrière C, et al. Prosthetic joint infection due to *Veillonella dispar*. Eur J Clin Microbiol Infect Dis. 2001;20:340-342.
39. Rosenblatt JE, Brook I. Clinical relevance of susceptibility testing of anaerobic bacteria. Clin Infect Dis. 1993;16(Suppl):S446-S448.
40. Duerden BI. Role of the reference laboratory in susceptibility testing of anaerobes and a survey of isolates referred from laboratories in England and Wales during 1993-1994. Clin. Infect. Dis. 1995;20(Suppl 2):S180-S186.
41. Cullman W, Frei R, Krech T. Antibacterial activity of oral antibiotics against anaerobic bacteria. Chemotherapy. 1993;39:169-174.
42. Brazier JS, Hall V, Morris TE, et al. Antibiotic susceptibilities of gram-positive anaerobic cocci: Results of a sentinel study in England and Wales. J Antimicrob Chemother. 2003;52:224-228.
43. Lamb HM, Figgitt DP, Faulds D. Quinupristin/dalfopristin: A review of its use in the management of serious gram-positive infections. Drugs. 1999;58:1061-1097.
44. Perry CM, Jarvis B. Linezolid: A review of its use in the management of serious gram-positive infections. Drugs. 2001;61:525-551.
45. Behra-Miellet J, Calvet L, Dubreuil L. Activity of linezolid against anaerobic bacteria. Int J Antimicrob Agents. 2003;22:28-34.

CHAPTER **247**

Anaerobic Gram-Positive Nonsporulating Bacilli

ELLEN M. MASCINI

JAN VERHOEF

Gram-positive, anaerobic, non–spore-forming rods include species of *Actinomyces, Atopobium, Bifidobacterium, Eubacterium, Lactobacillus, Mobiluncus,* and *Propionibacterium*. These bacilli share a preference for anaerobic growth conditions, although some of them can be cultured in the presence of 5% to 10% CO_2 as well. *Actinomyces* and *Propionibacterium propionicum* cause actinomycosis and are discussed in Chapter 253. Other species of *Propionibacterium* are discussed here. *Propionibacterium, Eubacterium, Bifidobacterium,* and *Lactobacillus* are the most frequently isolated species, apart from those that cause actinomycosis. Their contribution to anaerobic isolates amounts to about 20% to 40%, *Propionibacterium* spp. being the most common isolates.[1-5]

TAXONOMY AND MICROBIOLOGY

In routine microbiologic laboratories, anaerobic gram-positive, nonsporulating bacilli are differentiated to the genus level phenotypically according to their metabolic end products and their morphology. *Propionibacterium* spp., which are occasionally branching, irregularly or regularly shaped rods, produce propionic and acetic acids as major end products (Fig. 247-1A). They are distinguished from

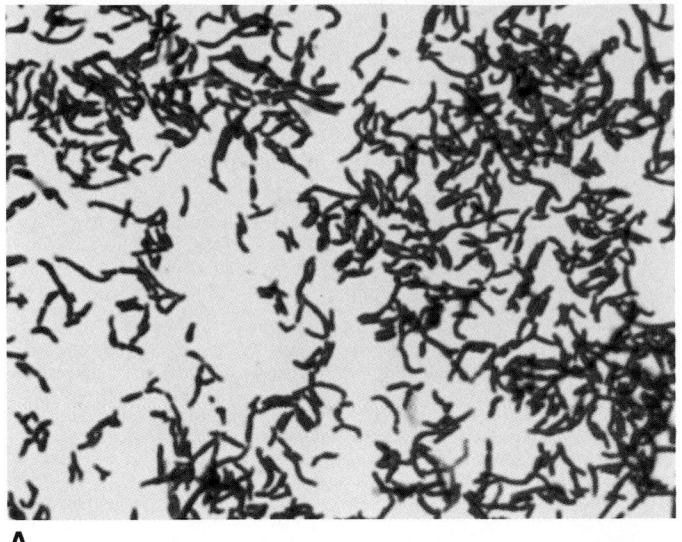

A

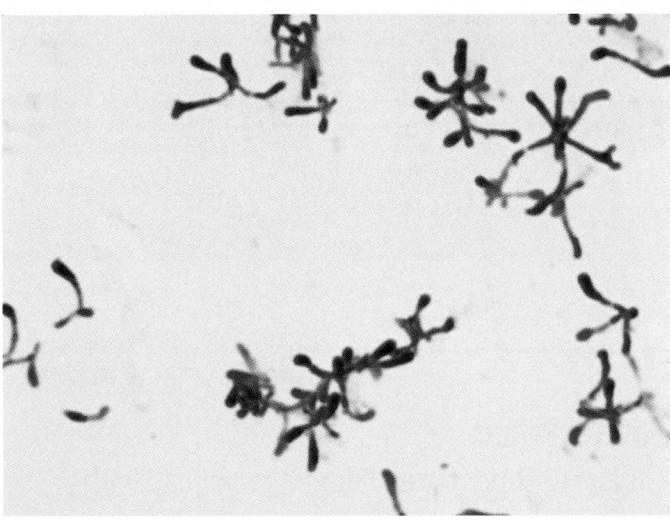

B

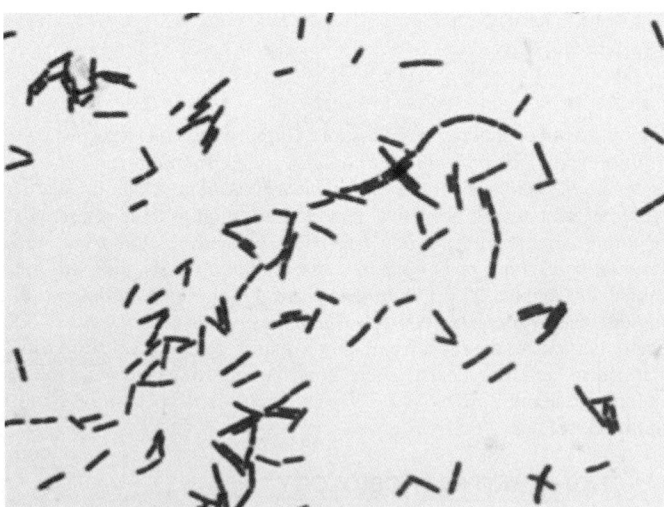

C

FIGURE 247-1. Gram stain of *Propionibacterium* spp. (**A**), *Bifidobacterium* spp. (**B**), and lactobacilli (**C**).

Bifidobacterium, Lactobacillus, and *Eubacterium* spp. by a positive catalase reaction.[1] *Bifidobacterium* appears as very irregular rods with bifid and branching forms that produce acetic and lactic acid (Fig. 247-1B). Short to long and slender rods with chain formation are observed in *Lactobacillus,* which produces lactic acid as its sole major end product (Fig. 247-1C). Eubacteria, nonmotile obligatory anaerobic rods that may form endospores, are distinguished from other genera mainly on the basis of negative metabolic characteristics.[1,6-9] In addition to this marked phenotypic heterogeneity, it is recognized that the eubacteria are not phylogenetically homogeneous either, with species dispersed among many of the different groups of the *Clostridium* genus.[6,7,9] The slow and minimal growth of many strains of gram-positive, nonsporulating rods on the media commonly used in clinical microbiology suggests that these isolates are often missed. Also, the time and effort required to isolate and identify all anaerobic bacteria from mixed infections involving numerous species means that, in many instances, no attempt to isolate these bacteria is made. Even if isolated, anaerobic gram-positive rods have often presented problems with identification, which has led clinical laboratories to report nonclostridial isolates only by Gram stain or to give very presumptive identifications.[10]

Currently, taxonomic assessments are based on nucleic acid analyses (e.g., guanosine plus cytosine content, DNA homology, and RNA sequencing).[6-8] On the basis of 16S ribosomal RNA (rRNA) sequence analysis, a major reorganization is underway, especially among the very heterogeneous organisms classified within the genus *Eubacterium;* new genera such as *Atopobium* and *Mogibacterium* have been introduced.[6,7,9,11] *Atopobium* was created to include one new species (*Atopobium rimae*) and two renamed *Lactobacillus* species, *Atopobium minutum* and *Atopobium parvulum. Atopobium* is phylogenetically located among the Actinomycetales. The clinical significance of these oral organisms is poorly understood.[6,11,12] *Mobiluncus* was tentatively assigned to the family Bacteroidaceae, which includes phenotypically similar organisms. However, electron microscopic studies show a structurally gram-positive cell wall, and lipopolysaccharide was absent. Cells are curved with tapered ends, are motile by multiple subpolar flagella, and appear gram-variable or gram-negative.[1,8] A phylogenetic relationship between *Mobiluncus* and *Actinomyces* was revealed by 16S rRNA sequencing.

NORMAL FLORA

Most bacilli discussed in this chapter are widely distributed and ubiquitous in humans and form part of the indigenous flora of the skin and mucosal layers. Bowel mucosa is inhabited by *Bifidobacterium, Lactobacillus, Eubacterium,* and *Propionibacterium,* which thus contribute to host defense of the enteric ecosystem.[5,13] It has been suggested that the host defense mechanism attributed to bifidobacteria and lactobacilli is related to the fermentative production of acetic and lactic acid, hydrogen peroxide, and antimicrobial substances.[14,15] Several studies have indicated a protective effect of lactobacilli and bifidobacteria against potential pathogens in the gastrointestinal tract,[14,16] linked to prevention of colon cancer in several animals. Therefore, they have been in use as base of so-called probiotics, which are defined as bacteria that provide specific health benefits when consumed as a food component or supplement.[15-17] Lactobacilli are recognized in the oral cavity and the vagina.[5,13] Bifidobacteria are the second most numerous group of microorganisms in the gastrointestinal tract, especially in breast-fed infants.[1,5,13,15] Furthermore, *Propionibacterium acnes* and other *Propionibacterium* spp. are part of the normal flora of the skin, nasopharynx, oral cavity, and genitourinary tract.[1,5,18]

CLINICAL ISOLATES

The rarity of disease caused by *Bifidobacterium, Eubacterium,* and *Lactobacillus* spp. may be secondary to the low pathogenicity of these bacteria, as well as the difficulty in culturing these organisms. The fastidious nature and often prolonged generation time have implicated these bacteria as a possible cause of culture-negative infections (endocarditis, sepsis, abscesses).[19,20]

Propionibacterium

As inhabitants of the skin, propionibacteria are common contaminants of cultures of blood and body fluids. They have traditionally been considered nonpathogenic for humans, but several well-documented cases of infection can be found in association with implanted prostheses or central nervous system shunts.[4,5,21-23] *Propionibacterium* spp. have been identified as causes of brain abscess, subdural empyema, parotid and dental infections, endocarditis, conjunctivitis associated with a contact lens, pulmonary infections, and peritonitis.[5,21,22,24] Significant infections by *Propionibacterium* species have been documented in association with isolates from blood, lymph glands, abscesses, wounds, cysts, and sinuses.[21] *P. acnes,* which produces chemoattractants and activates complement, may result in inflammatory acne.[18] In addition, *P. acnes* has been identified as a frequently recovered cause of anaerobic arthritis in association with prosthetic joints, vascular disease, and peripheral neuropathy.[5,21,25] In addition, isolation of these microorganisms from patients with osteomyelitis has been reported.[25] Because propionibacteria are capable of inducing significant infections, especially in some high-risk patients, efforts should be made to obtain specimens free of contamination by the normal flora of the mucous membranes and skin, where *Propionibacterium* species reside. Determination of the clinical significance of each isolate must be made with caution because such determination influences the need to direct therapy against that isolate.

Bifidobacterium, Eubacterium, and Lactobacillus

These organisms have been found most commonly in infections associated with predisposing or underlying conditions such as previous surgery, malignancy, immunodeficiency, diabetes mellitus, dental extraction, broad-spectrum antibiotics, and the presence of a foreign body.[2,4,5,19,21,26,27] Many (30% to 44%) of these isolates were reported to cause significant infection.[26] Most infections from which these species are recovered are polymicrobial and yield a mixture of aerobic and anaerobic bacteria. Although *Bifidobacterium, Eubacterium,* and *Lactobacillus* spp. are infrequently associated with infections (each < 5% of anaerobic isolates), they do occasionally cause serious illness.[2-4,15,17,26] Mortality associated with infection caused by anaerobic, nonsporulating, gram-positive rods was reported to be very low.[4]

Lactobacillus

Unrelated to particular species, lactobacilli have infrequently been reported as a cause of serious infections in either immunocompetent or immunocompromised hosts. Subacute endocarditis, the most commonly reported severe clinical infection, is characterized by a high mortality rate of 23% to 27%.[20,28,29] Typically, it occurs in patients with preexisting structural heart disease and often with some form of recent dental infection or manipulation.[5,20,28-30] Relapses were observed in 24% to 39%, especially in patients treated with a single antibiotic. Embolization is a common complication, observed in about 40% of patients, and occasionally cardiac surgery is required.[20,28,29] In addition, published cases have reported involvement of *Lactobacillus* in pleuropulmonary infections, (intra-abdominal) abscesses, meningitis, conjunctivitis, dental caries, and endometritis.[2,5,24,26,27,31] *Lactobacillus* septicemia, a rare condition usually seen in patients with severe underlying illnesses, may develop subsequent to a documented infection with the same organisms related to the urogenital or gastrointestinal tract.[2,19,28,30,32] The fact that *Lactobacillus* is not part of the skin flora supports true infection. The actual mortality rate associated with *Lactobacillus* sepsis was reported to be low; some patients have survived without therapy or with therapy that would be unlikely to be active against these pathogens.[19,20,26] Additionally, low virulence of the organism is suggested by the infrequent association of lactobacilli with bacteremic infections in spite of the ubiquitous presence of these organisms in the gastrointestinal tract and their widespread consumption in fermented milk products.[19,20,26,30] However, two cases, one of

endocarditis and the other of liver abscess, have been reported in which the lactobacillus that was isolated was indistinguishable from the probiotic strains recently consumed by the patient.[17]

Bifidobacterium

Because bifidobacteria are usually recovered together with other commensals, little is known of their pathogenic potential. Blood stream infections by bifidobacteria are diagnosed rarely, usually along with other flora, in patients with complications associated with childbirth, gastrointestinal disorders, malignancies, or systemic lupus erythematosus.[26-28,32] Involvement of *Bifidobacterium* species has occasionally been reported in chronic otitis media, pleuropulmonary infections, cholesteatoma, peritonitis, abscesses in the head and neck, meningitis, and paronychia.[2,23,24,26]

Eubacterium

Eubacteria have been recognized as pathogens in infections of the female genital tract associated with intrauterine devices[10] and in chronic periodontal disease.[8,9,33] The endogenous mouth flora, particularly in the presence of oral infection, can serve as a reservoir of opportunistic species that can infect sites in the head, neck, and lung, so numerous sites of infections by eubacteria may not be unexpected.[10] *Eubacterium* spp. have been recovered from pleuropulmonary infections, (brain) abscesses, osteomyelitis of the skull, peritonitis, wound infections, genitourinary sites, decubitus ulcers, and bites.[2,5,10,24,26] Occasionally, *Eubacterium* spp. have been reported as a cause of clinically significant bacteremia in patients with malignancies, gastrointestinal or obstetric disorders, and endocarditis.[2,4,5,27,32] *Eubacterium alactolyticum* has been proposed to be reclassified as *Pseudoramibacter alactolyticus.*[7] These organisms are isolated from dental calculus and the gingival crevices of patients with periodontal disease, from root canals, and from patients with various infections, including purulent pleurisy, cellulitis, postoperative wounds, and abscesses of the brain, lung, intestinal tract, and mouth.[7,34]

Mobiluncus

Mobiluncus has been isolated from vaginal samples of women with nonspecific vaginitis (or bacterial vaginosis), but an etiologic role has not been established.[1,8,35,36] Incidentally, *Mobiluncus* species were recovered from blood after a gynecologic infection and from anaerobic breast abscesses.[36]

TREATMENT

Eradication of organisms from deep-seated sites of infection may be difficult. Surgical intervention, such as drainage of abscesses and removal of foreign bodies, is commonly required in the treatment of infections with anaerobic, gram-positive, nonsporulating bacilli. Prolonged antimicrobial therapy is the other major approach in the elimination of anaerobic bacteria. The frequently polymicrobial nature of these infections should be taken into account when antibiotics are prescribed.[23] In addition, antimicrobial susceptibility patterns of anaerobic bacteria in vitro are available only after a considerable number of days, so therapy often has to be started empirically. Unfortunately, consensus has not been reached about performance of susceptibility patterns because no specific method has proved to be satisfactorily reliable.[37] Thus determination of susceptibility is not routinely performed in most diagnostic microbiologic laboratories, except for isolates obtained from blood or otherwise normally sterile material.

Anaerobic, gram-positive, nonsporulating bacilli are generally susceptible to most antibiotics used for the treatment of anaerobic infections, including penicillins, carbapenems, and clindamycin.[1,2,5,21,24,32,36,38-40] Most eubacteria are susceptible to metronidazole, whereas *Lactobacillus, Propionibacterium,* and other facultatively anaerobic microorganisms regularly show resistance to nitroimidazoles.[1,5,21,23,38] Erythromycin, tetracycline, and cephalosporins showed variable activity.[2,38-40] During treatment of acne, acquisition of antibiotic resistance by *P. acnes* has increasingly been documented, especially in association with topical use of erythromycin and clindamycin.[18] The new antibiotics linezolid and ramoplanin exhibit potent in vitro activity against gram-positive, non-sporulating, anaerobic bacilli and may be promising candidates to treat infections in which these microorganisms are involved.[41,42]

Lactobacilli appear to be uniformly resistant to vancomycin and variably resistant to the cephalosporins and quinolones.[19,29,34,42] Synergistic therapy with a penicillin and an aminoglycoside appeared to provide optimal medical treatment of *Lactobacillus* endocarditis and should possibly be considered for other deep-seated infections.[19,20,29,38] Neither vancomycin nor cephalosporins, both often used as alternatives to penicillins in the treatment of gram-positive bacterial infections, should be prescribed for the treatment of *Lactobacillus* endocarditis.[29] Poor response to antimicrobial therapy in *Lactobacillus* endocarditis may lead to relapse of infection and a need for valve replacement.

REFERENCES

1. Koneman EW, Allen SE, Janda WM, et al. The anaerobic bacteria. In: Color Atlas and Textbook of Diagnostic Microbiology. 5th ed. Philadelphia: Lippincott; 1997:709-784.
2. Brook I. Isolation of non-sporing anaerobic rods from infections in children. J Med Microbiol. 1996;45:21-26.
3. Bernard K, Cooper C, Johnson W. Prevalence of anaerobes referred to the Canadian National Reference Centre from 1984 to 1996. Clin Infect Dis. 1997;25(Suppl 2):S241-S243.
4. Brook I. Anaerobic bacterial bacteremia: 12-year experience in two military hospitals. J Infect Dis. 1989;160:1071-1075.
5. Finegold SM. Anaerobic Bacteria in Human Disease. New York: Academic Press; 1977.
6. Jousimies-Sommer H. Recently described clinically important anaerobic bacteria: Taxonomic aspects and update. Clin Infect Dis. 1997;25(Suppl 2):S78-S87.
7. Willems A, Collins MD. Phylogenetic relationships of the genera *Acetobacter* and *Eubacterium* sensu stricto and reclassification of *Eubacterium alactolyticum* as *Pseudoramibacter alactolyticus* gen. nov., comb. nov. Int J Syst Bacteriol. 1996;46:1083-1087.
8. Summanen P. Recent taxonomic changes for anaerobic gram-positive and selected gram-negative organisms. Clin Infect Dis. 1993;16(Suppl 4):S168-S174.
9. Downes J, Munson MA, Spratt DA, et al. Characterisation of *Eubacterium*-like strains isolated from oral infections. J Med Microbiol. 2001;50:947-951.
10. Hill GB, Ayers OM, Kohan AP. Characteristics and sites of infection of *Eubacterium notatum*, *Eubacterium timidum*, *Eubacterium brachy*, and other asaccharolytic *Eubacteria*. J Clin Microbiol. 1987;25:1540-1545.
11. Geissdörfer W, Böhmer C, Pelz K, et al. Tuboovarian abscess caused by *Atopobium vaginae* following transvaginal oocyte recovery. J Clin Microbiol. 2003;41:2788-2790.
12. Collins MD, Wallbanks S. Comparative sequence analyses of the 16S rRNA genes of *Lactobacillus minutus*, *Lactobacillus rimae* and *Streptococcus parvulus*: Proposal for the creation of a new genus *Atopobium*. FEMS Microbiol Lett. 1992;95:235-240.
13. Evaldson G, Heimdahl A, Kager L, Nord CE. The normal human anaerobic microflora. Scand J Infect Dis Suppl. 1982;35:9-15.
14. Lidbeck A, Nord CE. *Lactobacilli* and the normal human anaerobic microflora. Clin Infect Dis. 1993;16(Suppl):S181-S187.
15. Guarner F, Malagelada J-R. Gut flora in health and disease. Lancet. 2003;360:512-519.
16. Gibson GR, Wang X. Regulatory effects of bifidobacteria on the growth of other colonic bacteria. J Appl Bacteriol. 1994;77:412-420.
17. Borriello SP, Hammes WP, Holzapfel W, et al. Safety of probiotics that contain lactobacilli or bifidobacteria. Clin Infect Dis. 2003;36:775-780.
18. Webster GF. Acne vulgaris. BMJ. 2002;325:475-478.
19. Antony SJ, Stratton CW, Dummer JS. *Lactobacillus* bacteremia: Description of the clinical course in adult patients without endocarditis. Clin Infect Dis. 1996;23:773-778.
20. Sussman JI, Baron EJ, Goldberg SM, et al. Clinical manifestations and therapy of *Lactobacillus* endocarditis: Report of a case and review of the literature. Rev Infect Dis. 1986;8:771-776.
21. Brook I, Frazier EH. Infections caused by *Propionibacterium species*. Rev Infect Dis. 1991;13:819-822.
22. Zedtwitz-Liebenstein K, Gabriel H, Graninger W. Pacemaker endocarditis due to *Propionibacterium acnes*. Infection. 2003;31:184-185.
23. Brook I. Anaerobic infections in children. Microb Infect. 2002;4:1271-1280.
24. Marina M, Strong CA, Civen R, et al. Bacteriology of anaerobic pleuropulmonary infections: Preliminary report. Clin Infect Dis. 1993;16(Suppl 4):S256-S262.
25. Brook I, Frazier E. Anaerobic osteomyelitis and arthritis in a military hospital: A 10-year experience. Am J Med. 1993;94:21-28.
26. Brook I, Frazier EH. Significant recovery of nonsporulating anaerobic rods from clinical specimens. Clin Infect Dis. 1993;16:476-480.
27. Fainstein V, Elting LS, Bodey GP. Bacteremia caused by non-sporulating anaerobes in cancer patients. Medicine. 1989;68:151-162.
28. Gasser F. Safety of lactic acid bacteria and their occurrence in human clinical infections. Bull Inst Pasteur. 1994;92:45-67.
29. Griffiths JK, Daly DS, Dodge RA. Two cases of endocarditis due to *Lactobacillus species*: Antimicrobial susceptibility, review, and discussion of therapy. Clin Infect Dis. 1992;15:250-255.
30. Saxelin M, Chuang NH, Chassy B, et al. *Lactobacilli* and bacteremia in southern Finland, 1989-1992. Clin Infect Dis. 1996;22:564-566.
31. van Houte J. Role of micro-organisms in caries etiology. J Dent Res. 1994;73:672-681.
32. Bourne KA, Beebe JL, Lue YA, Ellner PD. Bacteremia due to *Bifidobacterium*, *Eubacterium* or *Lactobacillus*: Twenty-one cases and review of the literature. Yale J Biol Med. 1978;51:505-512.
33. Kumar PS, Griffen AL, Barton JA, et al. New bacterial species associated with chronic periodontitis. J Dent Res. 2003;82:338-344.
34. Finegold SM, Jousimies-Somer H. Recently described clinically important anaerobic bacteria: Medical aspects. Clin Infect Dis. 1997;25(Suppl 2):S88-S93.
35. Wathne B, Holst E, Hovelius B, Mårdh P-A. Erythromycin versus metronidazole in the treatment of bacterial vaginosis. Acta Obstet Gynecol Scand. 1993;72:470-474.
36. Mayer J, Hegewald S, Sartor VE, Carroll K. Extragenital infection due to *Mobiluncus mulieris*: Case report and review. Diagn Microbiol Infect Dis. 1994;20:163-165.
37. Rosenblatt JE, Brook I. Clinical relevance of susceptibility testing of anaerobic bacteria. Clin Infect Dis. 1993;16(Suppl):S446-S448.
38. Bayer AS, Chow AW, Conception N, Guze LB. Susceptibility of 40 lactobacilli to 6 antimicrobial agents with broad gram-positive anaerobic spectra. Antimicrob Agents Chemother. 1978;14:720-722.
39. Cullman W, Frei R, Krech T. Antibacterial activity of oral antibiotics against anaerobic bacteria. Chemotherapy. 1993;39:169-174.
40. Spiegel CA. Susceptibility of *Mobiluncus* species to 23 antimicrobial agents and 15 other compounds. Antimicrob Agents Chemother. 1987;31:249-252.
41. Behra-Miellet J, Calvet L, Dubreuil L. Activity of linezolid against anaerobic bacteria. Int J Antimicrob Agents. 2003;22:28-34.
42. Citron DM, Merriam CV, Tyrrel KL, et al. In vitro activities of ramoplanin, teicoplanin, vancomycin, linezolid, bacitracin, and four other antimicrobials against intestinal anaerobic bacteria. Antimicrob Agents Chemother. 2003;47:2334-2338.

CHAPTER **248**

Mycobacterium tuberculosis

DANIEL FITZGERALD

DAVID W. HAAS

The term *tuberculosis* describes a broad range of clinical illnesses caused by *Mycobacterium tuberculosis* (or less commonly *Mycobacterium bovis*). It is second only to human immunodeficiency virus (HIV) as a cause of death worldwide resulting from a single infectious agent, and in 1993 the World Health Organization declared tuberculosis a global public health emergency. Tuberculosis can affect virtually every organ, most importantly the lungs, and is typically associated with granuloma formation.

HISTORY

There is evidence of spinal tuberculosis in Neolithic, pre-Columbian, and early Egyptian remains. However, tuberculosis did not become a major problem until the Industrial Revolution, when crowded living conditions favored its spread. In the 17th and 18th centuries, tuberculosis caused one fourth of all adult deaths in Europe. Before antimicrobial agents became available, the cornerstone of treatment was rest in the open air in specialized sanatoria. Sanatorium regimens probably benefitted cases diagnosed before cavitation but had little impact on cavitary disease. When it became clear that cavitation was the pivotal event in progressive pulmonary tuberculosis, most special therapies focused on cavity closure.

The modern era of tuberculosis began in 1946 with demonstration of the efficacy of streptomycin (STM). In 1952, the much more effective drug isoniazid (INH) became available, making tuberculosis curable in the great majority of patients, and in 1970 rifampin (RMP) came to be recognized as at least equal to INH. The availability of drugs led to new treatment principles. With drug coverage it became possible to resect tuberculous tissue successfully, but with drug treatment resection was rarely necessary. Bed rest and collapse therapy added nothing to chemotherapy; treated patients rapidly became non-infectious; and specialized sanatoria ultimately disappeared. The duration of chemotherapy progressively decreased from approximately 2 years before the availability of RMP, to 9 months with INH and RMP given together, and to 6 months using multidrug therapy including INH, RMP, and pyrazinamide (PZA). With INH it also became practical to treat asymptomatic people thought to harbor tubercle bacilli based on positive tuberculin tests.

In the United States, reported cases of tuberculosis had declined nearly every year since accurate statistics became available. However, in 1985 case rates began increasing for the first time in more than 20 years, largely because of infections in individuals coinfected with HIV and transmission of infection from them to others. Unfortunately, tuberculosis control programs in some large cities were not equipped to manage this emerging problem. The often-interrelated factors of illicit drug use, homelessness, and HIV infection predispose to reactivation of remote tuberculosis, to the acquisition and at times epidemic spread of new disease, and, because of irregular adherence to drug therapy, to the development and spread of drug-resistant strains. Epidemics of multidrug-resistant (MDR) tuberculosis emerged in these populations and spread to HIV-negative persons, including health care workers. Treatment programs were often unsuccessful because of drug resistance and patient nonadherence. Since 1992, tuberculosis case rates in the United States have again declined and in 2002 reached the lowest in recorded history.[1] This is a tribute to the success of intensified diagnostic, treatment, and prevention efforts and to the control of HIV-induced immunosuppression by newer antiretroviral agents.[2] Adequate funding for tuberculosis control and research programs must be maintained if recent favorable epidemiologic trends are to continue.

MICROBIOLOGY

The term *tubercle bacillus* designates two species of the family Mycobacteriaceae, order Actinomycetales: *M. tuberculosis* and *M. bovis.* They differ from many other mycobacterial species that share the staining characteristic referred to as *acid fastness.* Three other species—*Mycobacterium microti,* a pathogen for rodents, and *Mycobacterium africanum* and *Mycobacterium canetti,* both rare causes of tuberculosis in Africa—are closely related and are the other members of the *M. tuberculosis* complex. The progenitor of these organisms likely arose from a soil bacterium, and the human bacillus may have arisen from *M. bovis* following the domestication of cattle.[3] Disease caused by *M. bovis* is relatively rare, and the terms *tubercle bacillus* and *M. tuberculosis* are, practically speaking, synonymous.

Humans are the only reservoir for *M. tuberculosis,* although many animals are susceptible to infection.[4] It is an aerobic, non–spore-forming, nonmotile bacillus with a high cell wall content of high-molecular-weight lipids. Growth is slow, the generation time being 15 to 20 hours, compared with much less than 1 hour for most common bacterial pathogens, and visible growth takes from 3 to 8 weeks on solid media. The organism tends to grow in parallel groups, producing the colonial characteristic of serpentine cording. The complete 4.4-Mb circular genome sequence of the H37Rv strain of *M. tuberculosis* was recently reported.[3] Initial analyses indicate that, in radical contrast to other bacteria, a very large portion of *M. tuberculosis* genes encode enzymes involved in lipogenesis and lipolysis. Knowing the genome sequence should accelerate progress in tuberculosis research.

A wide spectrum of laboratory techniques have been developed to diagnose active tuberculosis. Advantages and limitations of various methods are presented in Table 248-1.

Acid-Fast Staining

The term *acid-fast bacilli* is practically synonymous with mycobacteria, although *Nocardia* and some other organisms are variably acid fast. In the Ziehl-Neelsen stain, a fixed smear covered with carbolfuchsin is heated, rinsed, decolorized with acid-alcohol, and counterstained with methylene blue. The Kinyoun stain is modified to make

heating unnecessary. The organisms appear as slightly bent, beaded rods 2 to 4 μm long and 0.2 to 5 μm wide. In sputum they often lie parallel, or two organisms adhere at one end to form a V. An estimated 10,000 organisms/mL of sputum are required for smear positivity, and a single organism on an entire slide is highly suspicious. Most laboratories now use a fluorochrome stain with phenolic auramine or auramine-rhodamine, a slightly modified acid-alcohol decolorization step, and potassium permanganate counterstaining. The fluorescent mycobacteria can be easily seen with a ×20 or ×40 low-magnification objective. Any biologic fluid or material can be examined directly, although thin fluids are best examined after sedimentation by centrifugation. When sputum digestion and concentration are carried out for culture, a smear of the concentrate is productive. Positive smears from concentrated gastric aspiration material are usually due to *M. tuberculosis.* On Gram staining of sputum, *M. tuberculosis* either is weakly gram-positive or appears as colorless rods or "ghosts."

Culture Methods for *M. tuberculosis*

Culture is the "gold standard" for detecting mycobacteria in clinical specimens. Samples of sputum or tissue require initial decontamination to remove fast-growing nonmycobacterial organisms, and liquefaction to allow access of decontaminants to nonmycobacterial organisms and media nutrients to surviving mycobacteria. Decontamination-liquefaction is most commonly done using *N*-acetyl-L-cysteine as a mucolytic in 1% sodium hydroxide solution. Mycobacteria are relatively protected during this procedure by a fatty acid–rich cell wall. However, normally sterile tissues or fluids such as cerebrospinal fluid (CSF) or pleural fluid should not be decontaminated, as some loss of mycobacterial viability does occur. The sample is then neutralized and centrifuged, and the sediment is inoculated onto media.

Three types of media may be used for culture of mycobacteria: solid egg based (e.g., Lowenstein Jensen), solid agar based (e.g., Middlebrook 7H11), and liquid broth (e.g., Middlebrook 7H12). Media are made selective for mycobacteria by adding antibiotics. Nonselective media, on which growth is more rapid, are available. Growth is more rapid in 5% to 10% carbon dioxide. Liquid broth cultures require 1 to 3 weeks of incubation for detection of organisms, as compared to solid media, which require 3 to 8 weeks. However, solid media allow examination of colony morphology, detection of mixed cultures, and quantification of growth. Further, occasional strains of mycobacteria may only grow on solid media. For these reasons, experts suggest using liquid and solid media in conjunction, with inoculation of at least one solid medium culture.[5]

Commercial automated liquid broth systems greatly facilitate mycobacterial culture. The BACTEC 460 TB system (Becton Dickinson Microbiology Systems, Sparks, MD), which detects growth in 1 to 3 weeks by a radiometric method, has been the most widely used. The newer BACTEC 960 mycobacterial growth indicator tube (MGIT) system detects growth by a fluorometric method, removing the need for radioisotopes in culture broth. The BACTEC MGIT is comparable to the BACTEC 460TB for rapid recovery of *M. tuberculosis* from clinical specimens, although some studies report higher contamination rates with the BACTEC MGIT system.[6,7]

The lysis-centrifugation culture method detects intracellular pathogens in peripheral blood. Whole blood is directly introduced into a tube containing a chemical that lyses blood cells, the specimen is centrifuged, and the pellet is used for stain and culture (e.g., Isolator System, Wampole Laboratories, Princeton NJ). Although useful for diagnosing both fungal and mycobacterial blood stream infection in patients with acquired immunodeficiency syndrome (AIDS), it offers no advantage over the BACTEC system for culturing mycobacteria from blood.

Nucleic Acid Amplification

Nucleic acid amplification assays offer another technique for the direct detection of *M. tuberculosis* in clinical specimens. There are at least two commercially available and U.S. Food and Drug Administration (FDA)-approved amplification assays: the Amplified *M. tuberculosis*

TABLE 248-1 Comparison of Assays Used in the Diagnosis of Active Tuberculosis

Clinical Laboratory Question	Diagnostic Assay	Advantages	Limitations
Are mycobacteria present in a clinical specimen?	Culture on solid media (Lowenstein-Jensen egg-based or Middlebrook agar-based media)	Gold standard for isolating *M. tuberculosis;* detects 10-100 organisms/mL; shows colony morphology, detects mixed infection, allows quantification of growth; provides organisms for speciation, strain identification, susceptibility testing	Visible growth takes 3-8 weeks
	Culture in liquid broth	Sensitivity and specificity similar to solid media; automated systems decrease workload; provides organisms for speciation, strain identification, and susceptibility testing; growth detected in 7-21 days	Does not show colony morphology, detect mixed cultures, or quantify growth
	Acid-fast stain	Same-day results; simple technology; inexpensive	Less sensitive than culture, requiring 10,000 organisms/mL; cannot distinguish *M. tuberculosis* from other mycobacteria
	Nucleic acid amplification (e.g., polymerase chain reaction)	Same-day results; sensitivity intermediate between acid-fast stain and culture; identifies organisms as members of *M. tuberculosis* complex	Requires advanced laboratory techniques; cannot distinguish dead from viable organisms; culture still needed for speciation, strain identification, and susceptibility testing
Is a mycobacterium isolated from a clinical specimen a member of *M. tuberculosis* complex? (*M. tuberculosis, M. bovis, M. bovis-BCG, M. africanum, M. microti,* or *M. canetti*)	Nucleic acid amplification	(See above)	(See above)
	Nucleic acid probes	Results available in 2 hr; sensitivity and specificity approach 100%; does not require amplification	Requires at least 10^5 organisms; most useful for pure culture, not directly on clinical specimen; cannot distinguish among members of *M. tuberculosis* complex
	BACTEC *p*-nitroacetyl-aminohydroxypropiophenone (NAP) assay	Provides preliminary identification of *M. tuberculosis*	Need for paired cultures increases cost
	High-performance liquid chromatography (HPLC)	Same-day results; sensitivity and specificity approach 100%; can distinguish *M. bovis-BCG* from other members of *M. tuberculosis* complex	Requires HPLC technology; only useful with pure culture
To which species of *M. tuberculosis* complex does a clinical isolate belong?	Colony morphology and biochemical assays (niacin test, heat sensitive catalase, nitrate reduction, PZA monodrug resistance, etc.)	Classic approach for speciation of *M. tuberculosis*	Time consuming and labor intensive
	Polymerase chain reaction (PCR) genomic analysis	May rapidly distinguish among *M. tuberculosis* complex species	Not yet commercially available for this purpose
Do different *M. tuberculosis* isolates represent the same strain?	Genotyping by restriction fragment length polymorphism (RFLP) analysis	The CDC offers free strain typing through the National Tuberculosis Genotyping and Surveillance Network	Sophisticated assay available only at specialized centers
Is an *M. tuberculosis* isolate drug resistant?	Agar proportion method	Quantifies the proportion of organisms resistant to a drug	Requires as long as 8 wk
	Liquid BACTEC method	Results within 5-14 days	Does not quantify proportion of resistance
	Molecular tests for chromosomal mutations associated with drug resistance	Allow same-day determination of drug resistance; most promising for rifampin resistance mutations	Simple and standardized assays needed before widespread application

Direct Test (Gen-Probe, San Diego CA), which targets ribosomal RNA, and the AMPLICOR *M. tuberculosis* Test (Roche Diagnostic Systems, Basel, Switzerland), which targets DNA. Other nucleic acid amplification tests are commercially available outside of the United States but are not yet FDA approved. The sensitivity of nucleic acid amplification is intermediate between acid-fast staining and culture. For smear-positive specimens, the sensitivity and specificity of nucleic acid amplification exceed 95%. For smear-negative cases, sensitivity has ranged from 40% to 77% and the specificity remains over 95%.[8]

Nucleic acid amplification complements but does not replace clinical judgment, acid-fast smear, and culture in the diagnosis of tuberculosis.[9] In sputum acid-fast smear-positive cases, positive nucleic acid amplification indicates the presence of *M. tuberculosis* complex and confirms active tuberculosis. When there is a high clinical index of suspicion for pulmonary tuberculosis but with a negative acid-fast

smear, a positive nucleic acid amplification test is highly predictive of tuberculosis and allows early initiation of therapy. Nucleic acid amplification tests perform less well when the clinical index of suspicion for tuberculosis is low, in which case the frequency of false-positive tests may approach that of true positives.[10] Case series of suspected extrapulmonary tuberculosis suggest that nucleic acid amplification of nonrespiratory specimens (pleural fluid, urine, CSF, tissue, etc.) may aid in diagnosis.[11-13] However, data are currently inadequate to provide clear usage guidelines for amplification assays in the diagnosis of extrapulmonary tuberculosis. Of note, nucleic acid amplification tests cannot distinguish viable from dead organisms and should not be used to monitor treatment response.

Nucleic acid amplification requires strict adherence to good laboratory practices. In one disquieting study, 20 blinded sputum samples were sent to laboratories in 18 different countries. Only 5 (16%) of 30 laboratories correctly identified the presence or absence of mycobacterial nucleic acid in all 20 samples, and 17 (57%) reported false-positive results.[14]

Speciation of Mycobacteria

Once mycobacteria have been identified in a clinical specimen, speciation may be needed for clinical diagnosis and epidemiologic investigation. For example, speciation may be important in immunocompromised patients at risk for nontuberculous mycobacterial infection, in localities where *M. bovis* transmission from animals to humans is possible, or in bladder cancer patients receiving bacille Calmette-Guérin (BCG) immune stimulatory therapy. Speciation generally involves two steps: first, mycobacteria are identified as members of the *M. tuberculosis* complex (*M. tuberculosis, M. bovis, M. bovis-BCG, M. africanum, M. microti,* or *M. canetti*); subsequently, if necessary, mycobacteria can be further identified as an individual species within the complex. Nucleic acid amplification tests, growth in selective antibiotic media, nucleic acid probes, and high-performance liquid chromatography are all used to place mycobacteria within the *M. tuberculosis* complex.[15] Each has advantages and limitations that are detailed in Table 248-1. Identifying individual species within the *M. tuberculosis* complex is more challenging. *M. tuberculosis* grows slowly, lacks pigment, produces niacin, reduces nitrates, has weak catalase activity that is lost by heating to 68° C at pH 7.0, does not demonstrate monodrug resistance to PZA, is resistant to thiophen-2-carboxylic acid hydrazide, and prefers aerophilic conditions. Other members of the complex show different patterns on these tests. Newer molecular techniques to identify species within the *M. tuberculosis* complex, such as polymerase chain reaction (PCR)-based genomic deletion analysis, are on the horizon.[16]

DNA Fingerprinting for *M. tuberculosis*

Once tuberculosis is diagnosed, characterizing the particular strain of *M. tuberculosis* may be important for clinical and epidemiologic purposes, such as tracing transmission from person to person, distinguishing exogenous reinfection from endogenous reactivation in cases of recurrent tuberculosis, and identifying laboratory cross-contamination of cultures. A standardized protocol of strain identification by DNA fingerprinting based on restriction fragment length polymorphism (RFLP) permits comparison of different genotypes from geographically remote regions.[17] DNA fragments produced by the restriction endonuclease *pvuII* are separated by electrophoresis and visualized using a probe to a repetitive DNA sequence, insertion sequence (IS) *6110.* Because numerous copies of IS*6110* are present in the chromosome of most *M. tuberculosis* isolates, and at highly variable locations, isolates with identical RFLP patterns represent the same strain. The Centers for Disease Control and Prevention (CDC) offers free strain typing through the National Tuberculosis Genotyping and Surveillance Network.

Drug Susceptibility Testing

Testing of *M. tuberculosis* isolates for drug susceptibility is important to guide therapy. In the United States the agar proportion method and the BACTEC liquid radiometric method are most commonly used. The absolute concentration method and resistance ratio method are used less commonly. The agar proportion method compares growth of appropriately diluted inocula on drug-containing media to growth on drug-free media and is reported as proportion resistant. For most drugs, resistance is significant when growth on drug-containing media exceeds 1% of control; 6% to 10% resistance or more indicates that the drug will add nothing to multiple drug therapy. The BACTEC liquid radiometric method compares growth in liquid media containing the test drug to growth in media free of the test drug. The BACTEC method does not provide the proportion of resistant organisms but has the advantage of rapid turnaround time of 5 to 14 days, which is critical for clinical management. The newer BACTEC 960 fluorometric system can also be used for drug susceptibility testing, and studies suggest results comparable to the radiometric method.[18,19]

Molecular tests to detect chromosomal mutations associated with mycobacterial drug resistance are being developed.[20-23] Most promising are tests for RMP resistance, which predicts poor treatment outcomes and is a surrogate marker for MDR tuberculosis.[6] Assays detect mutations in the 81-bp *rpoB* gene, which encodes the β-subunit of RNA polymerase and correlates with greater than 96% of RMP resistance. Resistance to INH is more complex and is encoded by multiple genes, including the catalase peroxidase gene *katG*, the *inhA* gene involved in fatty acid biosynthesis, the *ahpC* gene, the *oxyR* gene, and the *kasA* gene.[24] Mutations associated with resistance to PZA, ethambutol (EMB), STM, and fluoroquinolones have also been identified.[25] Simplification and standardization of molecular assays for the detection of genomic markers of drug resistance will be necessary before widespread application.[15]

EPIDEMIOLOGY

General Considerations

M. tuberculosis infects one third of the world's population and causes 8 million new cases of tuberculosis and approximately 2 million deaths each year.[26] Tuberculosis is second only to HIV as a cause of death worldwide resulting from a single infectious agent.[27] The two factors essential for its rapid spread are crowded living conditions and a population with little native resistance. In the 19th century, tuberculosis caused more than one quarter of all adult deaths in Europe, eliminating those with the least native resistance. A downward trend had been established before the turn of the century. Epidemiologists once believed the disease would eventually disappear, based on the assumptions that 10% of infections result in active disease and that half of diseased persons acquire pulmonary cavities (i.e., become contagious). Thus each cavitary case would have to infect 20 persons to maintain case rates.[28] In Holland before World War II, one infectious case produced only 13 new infections,[28] and since the turn of the century and before drug treatment, the annual decrement in mortality and morbidity was 4% to 6% in developed countries. This rate approximately doubled after chemotherapy became widespread. The prechemotherapy trend was probably due to progressively higher natural residual resistance in those who survived infection and to living conditions less conducive to airborne spread. Epidemics appeared much later in previously unexposed populations such as Native Americans, Eskimos, and remote tribes in the Amazonian rain forest.[29]

Recent Morbidity and Mortality Trends

In the United States the steady decline in tuberculosis morbidity reached a transient nadir in 1984, but from 1985 to 1992 an estimated 64,000 "excess" cases of active tuberculosis were reported, which peaked at 10.5 reported cases per 100,000 population.[30,31] Factors responsible for this increase included urban homelessness, intravenous drug abuse, growing neglect of tuberculosis control programs, and most notably the AIDS epidemic. After 1992, reported cases declined, reaching 5.2 cases per 100,000 population in 2002, the lowest in recorded history, with only Hawaii and the District of Columbia reporting over 10 cases per 100,000 population.[1] Although declines occurred in all age groups, tuberculosis cases have not declined among foreign-born persons, who now account for approximately one half of all reported cases in the United States (Fig. 248-1).[32] This reflects increased immigration from high-prevalence countries. In one half of all immigrants, the duration of U.S. residence was less than 5 years at the time tuberculosis was diagnosed, suggesting that infection was acquired abroad; the risk declines with duration of residency, indicating that most infections were acquired before immigration.[33] The likelihood of developing tuberculosis after immigrating varies by country of origin, with persons from established market economies at lowest risk (Table 248-2).[34]

Tuberculosis has also become concentrated in certain medically underserved populations—the urban poor, alcoholics, intravenous drug users, the homeless, migrant farm workers, and prison inmates—often occurring in contact-based microepidemics. In 1990, the annual

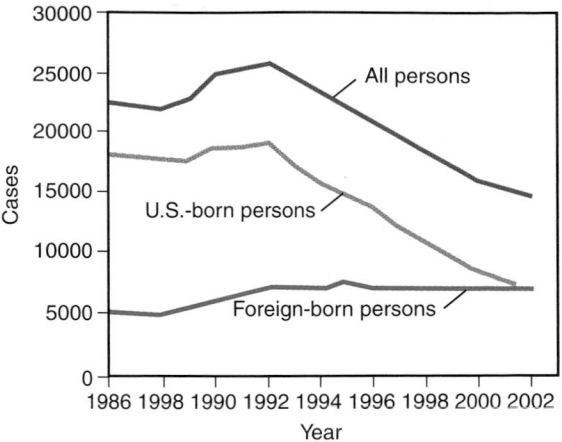

FIGURE 248-1. Number of reported cases of tuberculosis in the United States by country of birth, 1996-2002. *(Adapted from Centers for Disease Control and Prevention. Tuberculosis morbidity—United States, 1997. MMWR Morb Mortal Wkly Rep. 1998;47:253-257; and Centers for Disease Control and Prevention. Tuberculosis morbidity among U.S.-born and foreign-born populations—United States, 2000. MMWR Morb Mortal Wkly Rep. 2002;51:101-104.)*

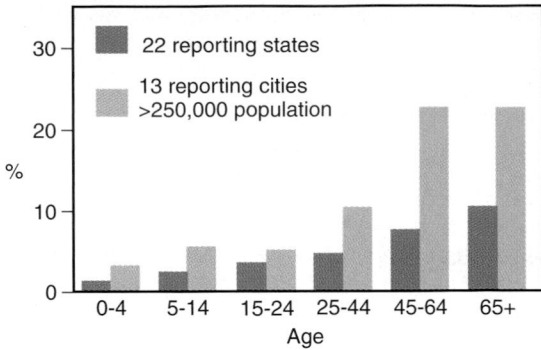

FIGURE 248-2. Percentage of positive tuberculin reactors by age, selected areas, United States, 1979. *(From Centers for Disease Control and Prevention, Tuberculosis Control Division. Tuberculosis in the United States, 1979. Atlanta: Centers for Disease Control and Prevention; 1981:4-31.)*

new-case rate was 5 to 10 times higher in African Americans, Hispanic Americans, Asian Pacific Islanders, and Native Americans than in whites; two thirds of all cases occurred in racial and ethnic minorities.[35] The age distribution of tuberculosis reflects the degree of ongoing transmission in a given population. Disease in the elderly is generally due to reactivation of infection acquired in the remote past, whereas tuberculosis in young children indicates ongoing active transmission in the community. In this regard, 80% of childhood cases were diagnosed in racial and ethnic minorities. Tuberculosis is frequent in geographic regions and demographic groups where AIDS is most prevalent, notably urban blacks and Hispanic Americans between 25 and 45 years of age.[35] Persons with active tuberculosis are more frequently HIV positive than is the general population. In the United States, tuberculosis continues to be an important problem in patients with HIV infection, with 6000 to 9000 new cases annually.[36] Among populations with a high prevalence of tuberculin positivity, waning immunity caused by HIV infection results in enormous tuberculosis

case rates. For example, development of AIDS in Haitians, in whom tuberculin conversion in childhood is almost universal, has resulted in active tuberculosis in 60%.[37] Since 1993, the CDC AIDS surveillance case definition has included any form of active tuberculosis in an HIV-positive person with fewer than 200 CD4+ cells/mm^3.[38]

Despite a predominantly urban epidemiology, large tuberculosis outbreaks have also affected small communities.[39,40] One well-characterized outbreak began in a coastal Maine village (population 10,200) in 1988.[40] Tuberculosis had not been reported in this town in the previous 3 years. However, a shipyard worker with cavitary tuberculosis was the source of 21 subsequent active cases and 697 new tuberculous infections. In retrospect, the source patient had repeatedly sought medical attention for cough, sore throat, and hoarseness during 8 months before tuberculosis was diagnosed and treated. This report highlights the need for vigilance among all segments of the population, not just those known to have high tuberculosis case rates.

Figure 248-2 presents tuberculin positivity by age group in the United States in 1979.[41] These figures are probably representative of other Western developed countries. The estimated annual risk of new tuberculous infection among white men in the United States is currently 0.03%. Immigrants for the most part retain the tuberculin positivity and tuberculosis rates of their country of origin (see Table 248-2).[34] Other groups, such as intravenous drug users, patients with end-stage renal disease, residents of institutions for the homeless, and, to a lesser degree, nursing home residents, demonstrate morbidity rates greatly in excess of the general population (Table 248-3).[42-49]

On a global scale, tuberculosis has a devastating impact in developing nations, with 12 countries accounting for 70% of all cases

TABLE 248-2 Reported Tuberculosis Cases and Rates in Immigrants to the United States According to Place of Birth: 1986-1994

World Region of Origin	Number of Cases	Crude Rate (per 100,000 Person-Years)
United States	160,839	7.8
Asia		
Philippines	7342	89.2
Vietnam	5818	120.0
Korea	2897	57.0
Mainland China	2689	56.4
Other	6038	37.7
Latin America		
Mexico	13,902	36.2
Haiti	2650	133.0
Other	7935	22.8
Sub-Saharan Africa	1426	58.5
Middle East	1459	20.4
Formerly socialist Europe	1328	11.9
Established market economies*	1903	5.4
Total foreign-born cases	55,387	32.6

*Excluding the United States.
Adapted from Zuber PLF, McKenna MT, Binken NJ, et al. Long-term risk of tuberculosis among foreign-born persons in the United States. JAMA. 1997;278:304-307.

TABLE 248-3 Incidence of Active Tuberculosis in Certain Groups

Group	Incidence per 100,000	Reference
Hostel residents in Glasgow	1946	43
Hostel residents in Boston	317	44
Nursing home residents, tuberculin positive on admission	2400	45
Nursing home residents, tuberculin converters	5900	45
Tuberculin-positive Indochinese refugees		46
All ages, both sexes	926	
Older than 65 yr, both sexes	7160	
Males older than 65 yr	14,180	
Dialysis patients, San Francisco	5800	47
East Indian dialysis patients, London	25,000	48
AIDS patients, New York, 1986	7000 (approx.)	49
Haitian AIDS patients, 1984	60,000	42

TABLE 248-4 Estimated Tuberculosis Case Rates among Countries That Account for 70% of Cases Worldwide, 1997

Country	Cases	Rate per 100,000 population
India	1,799,000	187
China	1,402,000	113
Indonesia	583,000	285
Bangladesh	300,000	246
Pakistan	261,000	181
Nigeria	253,000	214
Philippines	222,000	314
South Africa	170,000	392
Russian Federation	156,000	106
Ethiopia	156,000	260
Vietnam	145,000	189
Democratic Republic of Congo	129,000	269

Adapted from Dye C, Scheele S, Dolin P, et al. Consensus statement. Global burden of tuberculosis: Estimated incidence, prevalence, and mortality by country. WHO Global Surveillance and Monitoring Project. JAMA. 1999;282:677-686.

(Table 248-4).[26] In 1993, the World Health Organization declared tuberculosis a global public health emergency and intensified major initiatives to address the problem. Central to this strategy is universal implementation of directly observed therapy (DOT). However, the challenges are daunting. Profound poverty, civil war, and refugee migration all impede success. Some countries have made considerable progress in recent years. In China DOT has been expanded since 1990 to cover more than 500 million persons. Dramatic progress has also been made in India, where from 1993 to 2001 a national tuberculosis control program has prevented an estimated 200,000 deaths.[50] However, in Pakistan it is estimated that fewer than one fourth of tuberculosis cases are ever diagnosed.[27]

Data on the prevalence of drug-resistant tuberculosis are not available from many countries, but much information has been gathered. In a survey conducted between 1996 and 1999, that involved 58 sites globally, the estimated median prevalence of multidrug resistance among cases of tuberculosis was 1.0%, with wide regional variability.[51] Data from the eastern European country of Estonia were concerning, with 14.1% of new cases of tuberculosis being MDR, and 8.5% at least four-drug resistant to INH, RMP, EMB, and STM. In the Henan Province of China, the prevalence of MDR tuberculosis was 11%, and in Latvia, the Russian oblasts of Ivanovo and Tomsk, and Iran it was at least 5%. Most African countries surveyed were not seriously affected by MDR tuberculosis, perhaps reflecting the only recent introduction of RMP and expanded use of DOT, but also limited access to antituberculous therapy.

An estimated 40 million persons worldwide are now living with HIV. The potential for continued interaction between AIDS and tuberculosis is therefore immense. In some developing countries where most persons harbor tubercle bacilli before adulthood, the prevalence of HIV infection becomes the only determinant of coinfection. The situation is currently worst in Africa, where in 1990 half of the estimated 5 million HIV-infected persons between the ages of 15 and 49 years were also infected with *M. tuberculosis,* accounting for 78% of persons in the world dually infected with HIV and tuberculosis. In 1995, annual death rates resulting from tuberculosis in sub-Saharan Africa were greater than 100 per 100,000 population.[27] Many other regions are also being profoundly affected by the coepidemics of tuberculosis and AIDS.

Mode of Spread

Although now rare, *M. bovis* infection from ingestion of contaminated milk was once commonplace. Skin inoculation of *M. tuberculosis* from contamination of an abrasion occurs in pathologists and laboratory personnel (prosector's wart), and venereal transmission has been recorded. However, almost all infections are due to inhalation of droplet nuclei—infectious particles aerosolized by coughing, sneezing, or talking—which dry while airborne, remain suspended for long periods, and reach the terminal air passages. Although the source is pulmonary in the vast majority of cases, aerosolization of organisms during irrigation of cutaneous lesions or at autopsy has caused spread to health care workers.[52,53] A cough can produce 3000 infectious droplet nuclei, talking for 5 minutes an equal number, and sneezing many more than that.[54] Accordingly, the air in a room occupied by a person with pulmonary tuberculosis may remain infectious even after his or her absence. Although in theory one droplet nucleus may be sufficient to establish infection, prolonged exposure and multiple aerosol inocula are usually required, and brief contact carries little risk. Infection does not generally occur out of doors. However, *M. tuberculosis* strains may vary widely in their transmissibility, and a recent outbreak in Kentucky included persons infected despite brief casual contact with the index case.[39] Large drops of respiratory secretions and fomites are unimportant in transmission, and special housekeeping measures for dishes and bed linens are unnecessary.

Risk of Infection

The most important determinants of infection of tuberculin-negative persons are closeness of contact and infectiousness of the source. Cases with positive smears are highly infectious; those positive only on culture are much less so. The degree of sputum positivity and pattern of coughing are important. Compared with measles, one case of which will infect 80% of susceptible casual contacts, tuberculosis is only moderately infectious in most circumstances.

Tuberculosis morbidity in a population is determined both by the risk of infection and the risk of acquiring active disease once infected. In Holland in the 1970s, 50% of 0- to 14-year-old household contacts of smear-positive cases became tuberculin positive, but only 5% did so when the contact case was culture positive but smear negative.[28] In the United States, approximately 27% of household contacts of smear-positive cases become infected, although rates as high as 80% occur in closed environments.[55] A large epidemiologic investigation in San Francisco from 1991 to 1996 estimated that 17% of new active tuberculosis cases arose from smear-negative, culture-positive index cases.[56]

In the pre-AIDS era, cavity formation was almost always necessary for contagiousness. However, patients with AIDS and pulmonary tuberculosis may be highly contagious in the absence of cavitation and even with normal chest roentgenograms, although not inherently more infectious than HIV-negative patients with sputum smear-positive pulmonary tuberculosis.[57-60] In one large study from Democratic Republic of Congo, household contacts of HIV-positive patients with pulmonary tuberculosis were no more likely to become infected with *M. tuberculosis* than were household contacts of HIV-negative tuberculosis patients.[57]

Influence of Chemotherapy on Spread of Infection

Patients receiving appropriate chemotherapy promptly become noninfectious as cough subsides and the concentration of organisms in sputum decreases. There is abundant, albeit indirect, evidence that this occurs within 2 weeks in patients with drug-sensitive tuberculosis.[60] Thus case finding and treatment is the most effective method of tuberculosis control.

In reaction to outbreaks of MDR tuberculosis, the CDC in 1994 established very stringent criteria for removing patients from respiratory isolation, including three consecutive negative sputum smears on different days, which was a marked change from previous practice.[61] Although a report from a New York City hospital noted that one half of their patients with pulmonary tuberculosis did not achieve three consecutive negative smears until after 3 weeks of treatment (especially those with cavitary disease or numerous bacilli on initial smear),[62] the occurrence of new infections is virtually eliminated soon after initiating effective chemotherapy, and many smear-positive sputum specimens in treated patients are culture negative.[63] It has been appropriately argued that the CDC guidelines requiring three negative smears for removal from isolation represent "an exaggerated response to some unusual circumstances" that are quite uncommon today, and strict adherence will increase the cost of care immensely and unnecessarily. Rather, the focus should be rapid screening for drug resistance in smear-positive cases.[64]

Risk of Progression from Infection to Active Disease

In general, approximately 3% to 4% of infected individuals acquire active tuberculosis during the first year after tuberculin conversion, and a total of 5% to 15% do so thereafter. These estimates are based on heavy exposures during disease-prone periods of life. Persons infected with small inocula or during disease-resistant periods probably have a much smaller risk,[54] whereas the risk of progression in immunocompromised persons is greater. In one study of 12,876 unvaccinated adolescents, 10.4% of those who converted their tuberculin tests acquired clinical tuberculosis, 54% of these within 1 year and 78% within 2 years.[28] The three periods of life during which infection is most likely to produce disease are infancy, ages 15 to 25 years, and old age. (The effect of age on disease progression is discussed in "Influence of Age on Tuberculous Infection.")

The likelihood of active disease developing varies with the intensity and duration of exposure. Persons with intense exposures are most at risk not only for infection but also for disease.[55] The degree of tuberculin positivity has some predictive value. Malnutrition, alcoholism, homelessness, incarceration, renal failure, and immunosuppression all favor progression of infection to active disease, but by far the strongest risk factor is AIDS (see Table 248-3). Among tuberculin-positive, HIV-positive intravenous drug users in one methadone clinic population, 8% per year acquired active tuberculosis.[65] It seems likely that active tuberculosis may ultimately develop in all persons with AIDS who are tuberculin positive unless prophylactic therapy is given, another fatal complication of AIDS supervenes, or HIV-induced immunosuppression is reversed with antiretroviral therapy. During outbreaks in hospitals or hospices, as many as 40% of patients with AIDS exposed to an active case have contracted active tuberculosis, often within 2 months.[66]

Host genetic factors also influence disease expression. Reports from India have shown that HLA-DR2 is associated with increased risk of progression to advanced pulmonary disease,[67] that the DRB1*1501 allele correlates with advanced disease and treatment failure, and that DRB1*1502 correlates with decreased risk.[68] A study from Gambia examined polymorphisms of *NRAMP1* (a homologue of the natural resistance–associated macrophage protein 1 gene of mice, also known as *Bcg, Lsh/Ity,* and *Nramp1*) in HIV-negative adults with smear-positive tuberculosis. Three *NRAMP1* alleles were much more frequent among the 410 tuberculosis patients than among 417 ethnically matched controls.[69] Polymorphisms of the interferon-γ pathway clearly predispose to severe mycobacterial infections (see Chapter 11).[70]

Institutional Spread of Tuberculosis

Hospitals

Tuberculosis has long been a recognized risk to health care workers. However, with declining disease rates and rising confidence in chemotherapy, hospital tuberculosis control programs atrophied. Occasional microepidemics of nosocomial tuberculosis in intensive care units were reported, but generally little attention was paid to the problem. However, beginning in the 1980s, numerous explosive outbreaks of tuberculosis occurred among AIDS patients on specialized wards and hospices in the United States and Europe.[66,71-74] In the first reported outbreak on an HIV ward, the index patient had fever, cough, a normal chest roentgenogram, and negative acid-fast smears but a positive sputum culture for *M. tuberculosis.*[71] Thirty-nine percent of other AIDS patients on the same ward acquired active tuberculosis within 60 days. Major factors contributing to these outbreaks have included (1) delays in diagnosis, especially in AIDS patients with noncavitary pulmonary disease; (2) inadequate negative-pressure ventilation in patient rooms; (3) use of aerosol-generating procedures such as bronchoscopy, sputum induction, and aerosolized pentamidine treat-

ments; (4) rapid progression to active, infectious tuberculosis in a large percentage of AIDS patients secondarily exposed; and (5) in the case of MDR tuberculosis, prolonged infectivity despite antituberculous chemotherapy.[75] Health care workers are also at risk. Patients with AIDS and tuberculosis may be highly infectious in the absence of cavitation and even when the chest roentgenogram is normal.[71,72]

Phage typing and antibiotic susceptibility patterns as ways of tracing spread of individual strains of *M. tuberculosis* from patient to patient have largely been replaced by DNA fingerprinting by restriction fragment length polymorphism analysis.[17] This method has confirmed the nosocomial spread of tuberculosis among AIDS patients and to HIV-negative health care workers,[66] demonstrated that AIDS patients treated for one strain of *M. tuberculosis* may be reinfected with a different strain,[76] and has confirmed cross-contamination of cultures in the laboratory.

Shelters for the Homeless

Poor nutrition, intravenous drug use, alcoholism, and crowding increase the risk for both endogenous reactivation of remote infection and acquisition of new (exogenous) infection in homeless shelter clients.[44] A study from New York City demonstrated that HIV infection was also a major factor in homeless shelter tuberculosis. Of 169 men seen at one shelter between 1986 and 1989, 62% were HIV positive and 26% also had active tuberculosis. Conversely, 90% of those with active tuberculosis were HIV positive.[77] The extraordinary frequency of HIV positivity and tuberculosis in homeless men prompted aggressive public health measures, which included identifying active cases and administering effective therapy under supervision. Rates of tuberculosis have since declined considerably.

Correctional Facilities

In the New York State prison system, the incidence of tuberculosis increased sevenfold from 1976 to 1986, reaching 105.5 cases per 100,000. High-risk populations—including young black and Hispanic men, intravenous drug users, and HIV-infected persons—are overrepresented in prison populations.[78] Although most prison cases are due to reactivation of old infections, outbreaks of MDR tuberculosis have shown that transmission of new (exogenous) infection occurs as well. Although difficult for obvious reasons, preventive and curative services in correctional facilities have been identified as high public health priorities. Crowding may be the strongest risk factor for transmission in prisons, but this may be offset by effectively treating latent tuberculous infection.[78] Transmission in prisons and jails may also serve as a reservoir for spread to the community, especially to inner city populations.

Outbreaks of Multidrug-Resistant Tuberculosis

Since the early 1990s, there have been numerous well-documented hospital outbreaks of MDR tuberculosis. Most cases of MDR tuberculosis have been from New York City and Miami. By DNA fingerprinting it has been shown that nearly one fourth of all MDR isolates in the United States between 1990 and 1993, and isolates from patients in 41 different hospitals, had the same DNA fingerprint, designated strain "W."[79] However, outbreaks in suburban areas underscore the potential for MDR tuberculosis to spread much more widely. Fortunately, more recent trends in the United States have also been associated with declines in MDR tuberculosis cases.[80]

Controlling Nosocomial Spread

Spread of tuberculosis in the health care setting has raised justifiable concern. Tuberculin conversion rates as high as 50% among health care workers on HIV wards were reported early in the AIDS epidemic.[72] Delays in diagnosis and initiation of therapy are critical for both outcome and infectiousness for others.[75,81] The HIV status of patients may not be known on admission, tuberculosis is often not an early consideration, an appropriate number of sputum specimens for examination (three) is often not submitted, and sputum acid-fast stains may be negative. Further, the clinical picture of extrapulmonary or disseminated tuberculosis may be confusing. Accordingly, tuberculosis must be considered in any HIV-positive patient with subacute or chronic pulmonary symptoms or symptoms compatible with extrapulmonary tuberculosis. Rapid culture methods including the BACTEC system and the lysis centrifugation technique applied to blood, liver, and bone marrow biopsy specimens, needle aspiration of peripheral nodes, determination of adenine deaminase in body fluids, and PCR methods may expedite diagnosis.[8,75,82]

Hospitalized HIV-positive patients with respiratory symptoms should be admitted to negative-pressure isolation rooms (so that air flows from the corridor into the room and is safely exhausted to the outside) with six air changes per hour. Procedures that stimulate coughing, such as sputum induction, bronchoscopy, and aerosolized pentamidine treatment, should be carried out in negative-pressure rooms or special booths. The use of particulate respirator masks further reduces risk and is recommended by the CDC. Ultraviolet radiation of the air—either pulled by a fan through a radiation chamber or with the ultraviolet beam directed into the uppermost parts of the room so as to avoid direct radiation of personnel—is also advised. The CDC has published guidelines for control of transmission of tuberculosis in health care settings.[61]

IMMUNOLOGY

Tuberculosis is the prototype of infections that require a cellular immune response for their control (see Chapter 9).[83] Although abundant antibodies are also produced during infection, these play no apparent role in host defense mechanisms. In the first few weeks after exposure, the host has almost no immune defense against infection by *M. tuberculosis*. Small inhaled inocula multiply freely in alveolar spaces or within alveolar macrophages. Entry into macrophages involves interactions with complement receptors, mannose receptors, and Fc receptors.[84] The bacteriostatic influence of alveolar macrophages on intracellular bacilli at this stage is probably minimal. Unrestrained replication proceeds for weeks, both in the initial focus and in lymphohematogenous metastatic foci. A heparin-binding hemagglutinin of *M. tuberculosis* may be important for extrapulmonary dissemination.[85] The development of tissue hypersensitivity and cellular immunity ultimately supervenes. Tissue hypersensitivity is florid in comparison to other intracellular infections, perhaps because of the adjuvant activity of mycobacterial lipids.

All persons have a native population of lymphocytes, mostly CD4$^+$ cells bearing $\alpha\beta$ T-cell receptors, capable of recognizing mycobacterial antigens that have been processed and presented by macrophages in a major histocompatibility complex class II context. When the lymphocyte encounters antigen in this manner, it is activated (transformed) and proliferates, producing a clone of similarly reactive lymphocytes. T cells, in turn, produce many distinct secretory proteins (lymphokines), which attract, retain, and activate macrophages at the site of antigen. Activated macrophages accumulate high concentrations of lytic enzymes and reactive metabolites that greatly increase their mycobactericidal competence, but if released into surrounding tissues, they may cause tissue necrosis. Activated macrophages also secrete a number of regulatory factors (tumor necrosis factor-α [TNF-α], platelet-derived growth factor, transforming growth factor-β, and fibroblast growth factor), which in concert with lymphocyte secretory proteins (interferon-γ, migration-inhibitory factor) determine the character of the pathologic and clinical response. Epithelioid cells, characteristic of the tuberculous granuloma, are highly stimulated macrophages. The Langhans giant cell consists of fused macrophages oriented around tuberculosis antigen with the multiple nuclei in a peripheral position, representing the most successful type of host tissue response. Cytotoxic CD8$^+$ T cells specific for *M. tuberculosis* are also generated during infection,[86] and are able to lyse infected mononuclear phagocytes directly. A subset of T cells that expresses the $\gamma\delta$ form of the T-cell receptor also expands in response to mycobacterial antigens.[83]

When the population of activated lymphocytes reaches a certain size, cutaneous delayed reactivity to tuberculin, or tissue hypersensi-

tivity, becomes manifest. The speed with which this occurs varies, but it generally develops within 3 to 9 weeks after infection. At the same time, enhanced macrophage microbicidal activity, or cellular immunity, appears. It is a matter of dispute whether cellular immunity, which connotes resistance to infection, and tissue hypersensitivity, which describes altered cellular reactivity (granuloma formation, tissue necrosis), are end points of the same sequence of immunologic and chemical events or are parallel and closely associated phenomena that depend on different antigens or lymphocyte populations, or both.

The pathologic features of tuberculosis are the result of the degree of hypersensitivity and the local concentration of antigen. When the antigen load is small and tissue hypersensitivity is high, organization of lymphocytes, macrophages, Langhans giant cells, fibroblasts, and capillaries results in granuloma formation. Foci characterized by the resulting hard tubercles are termed *proliferative* or *productive* and constitute a successful tissue reaction with containment of infection, healing with eventual fibrosis, encapsulation, and scar formation. When both antigen load and degree of hypersensitivity are high, epithelioid cells and giant cells are sparse or entirely lacking; lymphocytes, macrophages, and granulocytes are present in a less organized fashion; and tissue necrosis may be present, a type of tissue reaction that has been called *exudative*. In the absence of necrosis, exudative lesions may heal completely, but more frequently some degree of tissue necrosis persists. Necrosis in tuberculosis tends to be incomplete, resulting in solid or semisolid acellular and amorphous material referred to as *caseous* because of its cheesy consistency. The chemical environment and oxygen tension in solid caseous material tend to inhibit microbial multiplication. However, caseous necrosis is inherently unstable, especially in the lungs, where it tends to liquefy and discharge through the bronchial tree, producing a tuberculous cavity and providing conditions in which bacterial populations reach titers 5 to 6 logs greater than in noncavitary lesions. Infectious material sloughed from a cavity results in new exudative foci in other parts of the lung (bronchogenic spread). A cross section of a pulmonary cavity demonstrates all these pathologic reactions, from the least to the most successful in terms of containment of infection. The central cavity, which contains myriad bacilli, is surrounded by a layer of caseous material with fewer organisms, a more peripheral layer of macrophages and lymphocytes with little organization and still fewer organisms, an area that is even more peripheral with epithelioid cells and giant cells in which the bacterial content is quite low, and, most peripherally, a bacillus-free layer of encapsulating fibrosis.

When the degree of hypersensitivity is very low, the tissue reaction may be nonspecific, consisting of a few polymorphonuclear leukocytes and mononuclear cells with huge numbers of tubercle bacilli, a condition termed *nonreactive tuberculosis*.[87] The immunologic spectrum from florid hypersensitivity to little or no specific tissue reaction is similar to that seen in leprosy and is recapitulated in HIV-infected persons as the CD4$^+$ T count decreases.

The sustained immunity to new infection that follows natural infection is most likely due to persistence of viable tubercle bacilli in the tissues with in vivo boosting. In tuberculin-positive persons, endogenous foci may reactivate repeatedly, and active CD4 surveillance is necessary to maintain quiescence.[88] However, reactivation disease may arise from these sites of boosting. In murine models of protective immunity to tuberculosis, CD4 cells are more important than CD8 and $\gamma\delta$ T cells, and the cytokines interferon-γ and TNF-α are essential. However, activation of human monocytes with TNF-α, not interferon-γ, most effectively inhibits intracellular replication of *M. tuberculosis*. Conversely, transforming growth factor-β has an opposite influence, favoring bacterial survival and multiplication.[89] In humans, an effective response to *M. tuberculosis* tends to follow a Th1 CD4 pattern with preferential expression of interferon-γ, interleukin (IL)-2, and IL-12 by mononuclear cells.

When macrophages from patients with established tuberculosis encounter *M. tuberculosis*, they produce cytokines that modulate the activity to CD4 cells. These CD4 cells are essential for optimal macrophage bactericidal activity. Costimulatory cytokines elaborated by macrophages (IL-1, TNF-α, and IL-6) activate CD4 cells and induce interferon-γ production. However, macrophages also produce cytokines (transforming growth factor-β and IL-10) that depress interferon-γ production, inhibit blastogenesis, and block the activity of IL-12. Mycobacterial antigens have a unique ability to promote expression of inhibitory cytokines, and it has been suggested that the suppression of CD4 cell responses contributes to immunosuppression, deactivation of macrophage effector function, and disease progression in tuberculosis.[88]

The antigens of *M. tuberculosis* necessary for protective immunity are not known, and there are currently no validated human surrogate markers for protective immunity. Two antigens of *M. tuberculosis,* ESAT-6 and the 30-kD (or 85B) antigen, are leading candidates.[88]

A gene designated *Bcg* (also known as *Nramp1* and *Lsh/Ity*) is important for immunity to some intracellular pathogens in inbred mice. This gene encodes the natural resistance–associated macrophage protein 1 and is expressed only in reticuloendothclial cells.[90] Specific alleles of *Bcg* in mice confer resistance to the early stages of infection by *M. bovis* (BCG), *Mycobacterium avium* complex, and other intracellular pathogens, although its role for *M. tuberculosis* is less clear. However, an epidemiologic study from West Africa suggests that a homologue of *Bcg* may play an important role in human immunity to tuberculosis[69] (see "Risk of Progression from Infection to Active Disease").

TUBERCULIN TEST

Koch's tuberculin (old tuberculin) was an extract of a boiled culture of tubercle bacilli. In 1934, Siebert made a simple protein precipitate (purified protein derivative [PPD]) of old tuberculin, which became the preferred reagent in most areas. In 1941, a large single lot was adopted as the biologic standard (PPD-S) to which other preparations are now standardized. A 5-tuberculin unit (TU) dose of PPD is equivalent to 0.0001 mg of PPD-S protein in 0.1 mL of solution. It is slightly stronger than first-strength (1:10,000) old tuberculin. The 250-TU dose is roughly bioequivalent to second-strength (1:100) old tuberculin.[91]

Dosage

The sensitivity and specificity of the 5-TU dose were derived in populations in which the incidence of tuberculosis was accurately known. A 5-TU dose of tuberculin clearly separated groups with 100% infection, such as sanatorium patients, from groups with a very low incidence of tuberculosis, such as infants from noninfectious environments. In the former, tuberculin reactions peaked at 16 to 17 mm; in the latter 0- to 5-mm reactions were elicited.

Technical Aspects

Although multiple puncture techniques (Heaf and Tine tests) are preferred in Britain, quantitative tuberculin testing is best performed by intracutaneous injection of 5 TU of PPD in 0.1 mL of solution, usually on the volar aspect of the forearm, using a short, beveled 26- or 27-gauge needle (Mantoux test). Precise injection producing a raised, blanched wheal is necessary. Deeper injections may be washed out by vascular flow, resulting in false-negative results. The loss of potency that occurs when PPD adsorbs to glass surfaces is prevented by the addition of the detergent polysorbate 80 (Tween 80). Tween-stabilized tuberculin in solution is light sensitive and must be refrigerated. The reaction is usually read in 48 to 72 hours, although it can be accurately read up to a week later. A positive test is defined by the diameter of induration, not erythema, in response to 5 TU, and can be measured by viewing the reaction tangentially against a light background. An alternative is to use a medium-point ballpoint pen to draw a line starting 1 to 2 cm away from the skin reaction and moving toward its center. The pen is lifted when resistance is felt, the procedure repeated from the opposite direction, and the distance between opposing line ends measured.

Targeted Tuberculin Testing

Recently a group of expert consultants from the American Thoracic Society and the CDC revised existing recommendations on tuberculin testing.[92] The newer guidelines emphasize targeted tuberculin testing only of persons at high risk for developing tuberculosis without treatment of latent infection, and for whom treatment will be prescribed if the test is positive. These include persons at high risk for recent infection, and persons with clinical conditions that increase the risk for tuberculosis, regardless of age. Testing of persons at lower risk is discouraged. Initial testing is also recommended for persons whose activities will place them at increased risk of exposure, such as employees in settings where transmission may occur.

Interpretation

Ninety percent of persons with 10 mm of induration and virtually all with greater than 15 mm of induration to 5 TU are infected with *M. tuberculosis.* Lesser induration, or reactions requiring 250 TU to be elicited, are frequently cross-reactions caused by infection with other mycobacterial species. However, even 5- to 10-mm reactions are suspicious for tuberculous infection in geographic areas substantially free of other mycobacteria, such as the northeastern United States, and among persons with a high likelihood of tuberculosis, such as contacts of active cases (although this latter point is debated).[93,94] Reactions of 5 to 10 mm may also be due to BCG vaccination. However, unless the vaccination was very recent, tuberculin reactions of greater than 10 mm should not be attributed to BCG.[95] Based on sensitivity and specificity of tuberculin testing, three cutoff levels have been recommended for defining positive reactions (see "Treatment of Latent Tuberculous Infection").[92]

Booster Effect

Although tuberculin cannot sensitize an uninfected person, it can restimulate remote hypersensitivity that has deteriorated. This booster effect (a positive tuberculin test after a negative one) develops within several days after a first injection and may be persistent. This causes interpretative problems, because a negative test result followed by a positive test result approximately 10 weeks later may be a product of either a recent infection or a booster effect. This problem is circumvented by retesting nonreactors 1 week later. If the second test result is positive, this indicates boosting rather than recent tuberculin conversion. Tuberculin positivity only after boosting is more common in older persons, in persons infected with nontuberculous mycobacteria, and in BCG vaccinees. Persons with a booster response are at low risk and can be managed as nonreactors.

False-Positive and False-Negative Reactions

False-positive reactions represent nontuberculous mycobacterial infection. False-negative reactions, although uncommon in otherwise healthy patients with tuberculosis, occur in at least 20% of all persons with known active tuberculosis. In one study, 25% of 200 patients with active tuberculosis were nonreactive to 5 TU, and 10% were also nonreactive to 250 TU.[96] Both false-positive and false-negative reactions to 250 TU limit the usefulness of this dose.[91] (The 1-TU dose is occasionally used in very young children.) Most false-negative test results in patients with tuberculosis are attributed to general illness and become positive 2 to 3 weeks after effective treatment is initiated. Protein malnutrition diminishes all cutaneous delayed hypersensitivity reactions. Sarcoidosis may cause false-negative tuberculin test results, although most sarcoidosis patients with tuberculosis are tuberculin positive. Intercurrent viral infections, reticuloendothelial disease, and corticosteroid therapy may cause false-negative tuberculin reactions. Control antigens (e.g., mumps, *Candida,* tetanus toxoid) are commonly applied to detect cutaneous anergy. However, attempts to correlate negative tuberculin tests with generalized anergy have not been illuminating, and such "anergy testing" is no longer recommended (see "Tuberculin Testing and Human Immunodeficiency Virus Infection").[97] Intraobserver reliability in reading reactivity may vary by as much as 3 mm, causing some classification uncertainty if induration is close to the cutoff value.[98]

Variant ("Delayed") Tuberculin Reactivity

An unusual form of tuberculin response (so-called delayed reactivity) has been described among Indochinese immigrants. This involves induration of less than 10 mm at 48 to 72 hours, which increases to

TABLE 248-5 Annual Tuberculin Conversion Rates (Positive to Negative) According to Age Groups, Victoria County, Canada, 1959-1962

Age Groups	Positive Reactors Retested after 1 Year	Number of Reversions to Negative	Reversion Rate (%)
0-19	99	22	22.2
20-39	200	16	8.0
40-59	525	25	4.8
60 and older	377	34	9.0
Total	1201	97	8.1

From Grzybowski S, Allen EA. The challenge of tuberculosis in decline: A study based on the epidemiology of tuberculosis in Ontario, Canada. Am Rev Respir Dis. 1964;90:707-720. © American Lung Association.

greater than 10 mm when the skin test is read again at 6 days. In a study of Vietnamese immigrants in North Carolina, 32 (26%) of 121 persons demonstrated delayed reactivity, 65% of whom boosted to a positive test 10 to 12 weeks later.[99] The authors concluded that Indochinese persons should have tuberculin tests read at 24 to 72 hours and again at 6 days, that delayed tuberculin responses should be considered true positives, and that those demonstrating less than 10 mm induration at 48- to 72-hour and 6-day readings should be booster-tested at 1 to 2 weeks.

Loss of Tuberculin Reactivity

Earlier in the 20th century, lifelong tuberculin positivity was maintained by frequent reexposure to tubercle bacilli or to continued active disease. However, a positive tuberculin test will revert to negative unless restimulated by new aerosol inocula or persisting infection. In one tuberculin survey, 8.1% of positive reactors reverted to true negative when retested 1 year later (Table 248-5).[100] Persons with a history of a positive skin test result can be safely retested. Two negative tests a week apart (to exclude boosting) indicate true negativity and resumed susceptibility to new infection.

Tuberculin Testing and Human Immunodeficiency Virus Infection

During HIV infection, tuberculin reactivity decreases as the CD4 cell count falls. One study of patients with active tuberculosis demonstrated 10 mm or greater of induration in response to 5 TU in only 60% of persons with HIV infection and in 35% of those with AIDS.[101] Induration of 5 mm in persons with HIV infection is sufficient to warrant treatment of latent tuberculous infection (see "Treating Latent Tuberculous Infection in Persons with Human Immunodeficiency Virus Infection")[102]; it has even been suggested that a 2-mm induration be considered positive in this setting. Testing simultaneously for cutaneous anergy with ubiquitous antigens such as mumps, tetanus toxoid, and *Candida* was once advocated by the CDC.[102] However, the usefulness of anergy testing suffers from lack of standardization and reproducibility, from variable risk of tuberculosis among anergic persons, because cutaneous anergy does not predict *M. tuberculosis* infection, and because responsiveness to control antigens but not PPD does not exclude tuberculous infection. Two studies failed to demonstrate that 6 months of INH preventive therapy administered to anergic HIV-positive persons significantly reduced tuberculosis rates.[103,104] Based on these considerations, routine anergy testing is no longer recommended for HIV-positive persons at risk for tuberculosis (see "Treatment of Latent Tuberculous Infection").[105]

Newer Assays for Latent *M. tuberculosis* Infection

The tuberculin test has limitations, including false-positive results from environmental mycobacterial exposure or BCG vaccination and operator-dependent variability in test placement and reading. Therefore, several new tests to detect latent *M. tuberculosis* infection are being developed that measure host cellular immune response to *M.*

tuberculosis in whole blood samples. The Quantiferon-TB (QFT) test (Cellestis Limited, Carnegie, Victoria, Australia) quantifies release of interferon-γ from lymphocytes in whole blood incubated overnight with PPD. The U.S. FDA has approved the QFT, and the CDC has established guidelines for its use to detect latent tuberculosis in people who are at increased risk and for people at lower risk for latent tuberculosis being screened for other reasons, such as military personnel and hospital staff.[106] In a U.S. multisite comparison of QFT and the tuberculin test, the two assays were moderately concordant with 83% overall agreement.[107] However, in a study of the QFT in Ethiopia, a highly endemic population, the agreement between the two tests was only 35%.[108] A second-generation QFT is being developed.

Another assay, an enzyme-linked immunospot (ELISPOT) assay, detects T cell responses to *M. tuberculosis* antigens.[109] The two *M. tuberculosis* antigens used in the assay, the early secretory antigen target-6 (ESAT-6) and culture filtrate protein-10 (CFP10), are absent from BCG and most environmental mycobacteria. In an investigation of a large school outbreak of tuberculosis in the United Kingdom, the ELISPOT had 89% agreement with the tuberculin skin test and correlated more closely with exposure to the index case than the tuberculin test. This test will need to be simplified and standardized before widespread use. Both the QFT and the ELISPOT to *M. tuberculosis* antigens appear to identify different subpopulations of people exposed to tuberculosis than the tuberculin tests. Because there is no gold standard for the detection of latent tuberculosis, prospective studies of the new assays are needed to evaluate their predictive value for future development of active tuberculosis.

PATHOGENESIS

Airborne droplet nuclei containing tubercle bacilli reach the terminal air spaces where multiplication begins. The initial focus is usually subpleural and in the midlung zone (the lower parts of the upper lobes and the upper parts of the lower and middle lobes), where greater airflow favors deposition of bacilli. (Very rarely, nonpulmonary initial foci will involve abraded skin, the intestine, the oropharynx, or the genitalia, all associated with foci in regional lymph nodes.)

The initial pulmonary focus is typically single, although multiple foci are present in about one fourth of cases. The bacteria are ingested by alveolar macrophages, which may be able to eliminate small numbers of bacilli. However, bacterial multiplication tends to be mostly unimpeded, destroying the macrophage. Blood-borne lymphocytes and monocytes are attracted to this focus, the latter differentiating into macrophages, which ingest bacilli released from degenerating cells, and pneumonitis slowly develops. Infected macrophages are carried by lymphatics to regional (hilar, mediastinal, and sometimes supraclavicular or retroperitoneal) lymph nodes, but in the nonimmune host may spread hematogenously throughout the body. During this occult preallergic lymphohematogenous dissemination, some tissues favor retention and bacillary multiplication. These include the lymph nodes, kidneys, epiphyses of the long bones, vertebral bodies, and juxtaependymal meningeal areas adjacent to the subarachnoid space, but most importantly, the apical posterior areas of the lungs. Before the development of hypersensitivity (tuberculin reactivity), microbial growth is uninhibited, both in the initial focus and in metastatic foci, providing a nidus for subsequent progressive disease in the lung apices and in extrapulmonary sites, either promptly or after a variable period of latency.

Evolution of the Primary Infection

Tuberculin positivity appears 3 to 8 weeks after infection and marks the development of cellular immunity and tissue hypersensitivity. In most instances the infection is controlled, with the only evidence of infection being a positive skin test result. In a minority of cases, antigen concentration in the primary complex, consisting of the initial pulmonary focus (the Ghon focus) and the draining regional nodes, will have reached sufficient size that the development of hypersensitivity results in necrosis and roentgenographically visible calcification, producing the Ranke complex (parenchymal and mediastinal calcific foci). Much less commonly, pulmonary apical and subapical metastatic foci contain sufficient bacilli that necrosis ensues with the onset of hypersensitivity, producing tiny calcific deposits (Simon's foci) in which viable bacilli may persist.

The onset of tuberculin hypersensitivity may be associated with erythema nodosum or phlyctenular keratoconjunctivitis (a severe unilateral inflammation of the eye), although these manifestations are unusual in the United States. The primary complex may progress. In children, large hilar or mediastinal lymph nodes may produce bronchial collapse with distal atelectasis or may erode into a bronchus and spread infection distally. Also, typically in children but also in nonwhite races with less constitutional resistance to tuberculosis, those infected in advanced age,[45] and AIDS patients,[110] the primary focus may become an area of advancing pneumonia, the so-called progressive primary, which may cavitate and spread via the bronchi. Again typically in the very young, preallergic lymphohematogenous dissemination may progress directly to hyperacute miliary tuberculosis as a result of caseous material directly reaching the blood stream, either from the primary complex or from a caseating metastatic focus in the wall of a pulmonary vein (Weigart focus). Hematogenous dissemination in the very young is often followed within weeks by tuberculous meningitis. In adolescents and young adults, the subpleural primary focus may rupture, delivering bacilli and antigen into the pleural space to produce serofibrinous pleurisy with effusion. Overwhelmingly, the most important consequence of preallergic lymphohematogenous dissemination is seeding of the apical posterior areas of the lung, where disease may progress without interruption or after a latent period of months or years, resulting in pulmonary tuberculosis of the adult or reactivation-type tuberculosis (endogenous reinfection).

Primary (Childhood) and Reinfection (Adult) Tuberculosis

The traditional terms *primary* or *childhood pulmonary tuberculosis* and *reinfection* or *adult pulmonary tuberculosis* followed roentgenographic observations early in the 20th century when initial (primary) infection in childhood was thought to be universal.[111] Children's roentgenograms characteristically demonstrated large mediastinal or hilar lymph nodes with inconspicuous pneumonitis in the lower or middle lung field, whereas in adolescents and adults, apical or subapical infiltrates, often with cavitation and no hilar adenopathy, were the rule. These clinical and roentgenographic differences are due to age-related immunologic factors. Although many primary infections in adolescents and adults resemble primary infection in childhood, in others in this age group, an apical posterior metastatic pulmonary focus progresses within weeks to "adult"-type pulmonary disease, whereas the initial focus in the lower lung field and hilar nodes involutes undetected.

Chronic Pulmonary Tuberculosis

Apical Localization

In adults, apical localization of pulmonary tuberculosis has often been attributed to the hyperoxic environment of the apices and the aerobic nature of the tubercle bacillus. A more plausible theory attributes it to deficient lymphatic flow at the lung apices, especially the posterior apices, where the pumping effect of respiratory motion is minimal. Deficient lymph traffic would favor retention of bacillary antigen and, when hypersensitivity ensues, tissue necrosis. Apical posterior localization with a tendency to cavitation and progression is characteristic of pulmonary tuberculosis in adolescents and adults. In contrast, infection contracted in the elderly often causes nondescript lower lobe pneumonia similar to progressive primary infection of childhood.[45]

Endogenous versus Exogenous Reinfection

Resistance to exogenous reinfection in the previously infected host is generally so great that new inocula are destroyed before significant multiplication occurs, with nearly all cases of active tuberculosis in such patients reflecting reactivation of latent foci.[111] Although probably true in developed countries where the level of contagion is low,

when contagion is high exogenous reinfection is the rule.[28,112] Airflow in the apical posterior areas of the lung is low, but when inhaled droplet nuclei reach that location, as is more likely with high levels of contagion, bacillary multiplication will be favored by the same local factors that enhance multiplication of blood-borne organisms. Support for this comes from a study from India that showed that disease in household contacts of active cases was most common in the middle-aged and elderly, who were certain to have been previously infected.[113] A microepidemic in a shelter for homeless men demonstrated that a single strain of *M. tuberculosis* caused infection among men known to have been previously infected.[44] Repeated inhalational exposures to tubercle bacilli maintain high degrees of tissue hypersensitivity and cellular immunity, making superinfection more difficult; however, when the airborne inoculum is large, or in immunocompromised hosts, superinfection may occur.

Influence of Age on Tuberculous Infection

Many of the best clinical descriptions of tuberculosis come from the preantimicrobial era, when infection occurred early in life and cellular immunity was maintained by frequent exposure to tubercle bacilli. However, in industrialized countries, infection more often occurs later in life, and cellular immunity may wane in the absence of restimulation. Accordingly, clinical patterns have changed. At one time, most patients were adolescents and young adults with apical cavitary disease. In developed countries, the incidence of tuberculosis (cases per 100,000) is now greatest in older persons, in whom hypersensitivity is less marked and in whom the clinical manifestations may be different and more subtle. Hypersensitivity and cellular immunity likely become less vigorous with age (see "Epidemiology").

Infection in Infancy and Childhood

Infection in infants often results in disease, with local progression and dissemination (miliary-meningeal disease). The younger the patient, the greater is the risk of progressive disease until the age of 5 years. From age 5 until puberty is a time of relative resistance to progressive disease, although not to infection. When disease occurs, it is usually the childhood type of pulmonary tuberculosis. Involvement of lymph nodes, bones, and, less commonly, other progressive extrapulmonary foci may develop, but tuberculosis confined to the lung in this age group usually heals spontaneously. The short-term prognosis in these cases is good even if untreated, but there is a high frequency of relapse with chronic cavitary tuberculosis when the more disease-prone periods of adolescence and young adulthood arrive.[114]

Infection in Adolescence and Young Adulthood

Clinical disease developing after infection in adolescence or young adulthood may resemble childhood infection (lower lung field pneumonitis, hilar adenitis) but with less parenchymal and hilar calcification (Fig. 248-3). This is particularly the case in dark-skinned races and in immunocompromised patients, including those with AIDS.[110] Rarely the roentgenographic picture may be mixed, with features of childhood disease subsiding while chronic upper lobe (adult) disease progresses. However, disease in this age group frequently first appears as chronic upper lobe tuberculosis with no clinical features of childhood disease. The tendency toward apical cavitation soon after the initial infection appears soon after puberty and is marked in young adults.[92] Because most young people in industrialized countries are tuberculin negative (see Fig. 248-2), most pulmonary tuberculosis in adolescents and young adults is due to recent initial infections rather than to late progression of childhood infections.

Infection in Midadulthood

Infection acquired during the middle years has a much better immediate and probably long-term prognosis than infection acquired in the teens and early 20s, presumably because of a reduced tendency to tissue necrosis.[114,115] One study demonstrated progression from infection (tuberculin conversion) to cavitary tuberculosis in 23% of patients infected from 15 to 19 years of age, 13% of those infected from 20 to 24

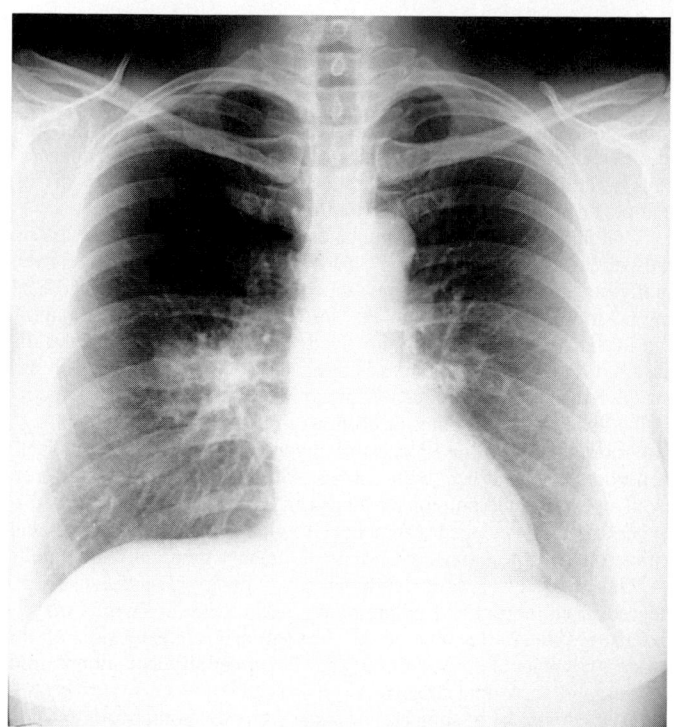

FIGURE 248-3. Chest roentgenogram showing marked right hilar lymphadenopathy and lower lobe opacity in a 58-year-old woman with primary tuberculosis.

years of age, 4% of those infected from 25 to 29 years of age, and only 2% of those infected after 30 years of age. Progression occurred in 3 months in many and within 1 year in most.[116] (Elderly individuals were not included in the study.)

Infection in Old Age

The incidence of tuberculosis is highest in the elderly. Infections acquired years earlier can progress as age compromises immunity, producing typical apical-posterior disease. Studies of tuberculosis in nursing homes, however, have demonstrated that elderly patients are often tuberculin negative, either because they had never been infected or because ancient infections had been completely cleared, with a loss of tissue hypersensitivity. Such tuberculin-negative persons are susceptible to new infection, and if this occurs, they acquire active disease with a frequency similar to that of adolescents. This is typically a nondescript, poorly resolving pneumonitis in the lower or middle lobes or anterior segments of the upper lobes, sometimes with pleural effusion and resembling primary infection in children except for much less hilar-mediastinal lymphadenopathy.[45] Even with prompt diagnosis and treatment, death from tuberculosis appears to be more frequent after age 65.

Late Hematogenous Tuberculosis

Chronic tuberculosis is probably always associated with recurrent abortive episodes of hematogenous spread. However, when aging or other factors compromise cellular immunity, such episodes may become progressively frequent, producing the subtle and often fatal syndrome of late hematogenous or progressive generalized tuberculosis.

Intercurrent Events

General stress, poor health, and malnutrition favor progression of infection. During pregnancy, the time of special risk is probably the early postpartum period. Therapy with corticosteroids or other immunosuppressive agents compromises host defenses, as do hematopoietic-reticuloendothelial diseases, particularly malignancies. Development of tuberculosis in patients with myeloproliferative disorders may cause

confusion because disseminated tuberculosis can cause aplastic anemia, thrombocytopenia, leukopenia, and leukemoid reactions that may mimic leukemia. However, most patients with tuberculosis and hematologic findings suggesting leukemia will have both diseases. Infliximab, a humanized monoclonal anti–TNF-α antibody used to treat rheumatoid arthritis and other conditions, can cause reactivation tuberculosis, including extrapulmonary and disseminated disease.[117]

The postgastrectomy state, jejunal-ileal bypass surgery, and end-stage renal disease are all risk factors (see "Treatment of Latent Tuberculous Infection"). Viral illnesses, particularly in children, may predispose to progression of infection. Destructive local pulmonary processes such as lung abscess, carcinoma, cavitary histoplasmosis, and pulmonary resection occasionally are followed by activation of previously quiescent pulmonary foci. The development of bone and joint tuberculosis after physical injury, tuberculous peritonitis after tubal insufflation, progressive hematogenous tuberculosis after curettage of a tuberculous endometrium, and late generalized hematogenous tuberculosis after major trauma all illustrate that the balance between host and infection can be altered by both systemic factors and local physical disturbance.

Tuberculosis in Acquired Immunodeficiency Syndrome

The earliest descriptions of tuberculosis in AIDS emphasized the very great risk of reactivation of remote infection as a result of progressively compromised cellular immunity. In studies in Haitians, all of whom were likely infected with *M. tuberculosis* in childhood, AIDS was associated with development of active tuberculosis in 60%.[42] Subsequent studies of HIV-positive and tuberculin-positive methadone clinic patients in New York City showed that active tuberculosis developed in 8% yearly.[65] This and other studies suggest that nearly all tuberculin-positive patients with HIV infection eventually develop active tuberculosis unless either HIV or the tuberculous infection, or both, are effectively treated, or another fatal complication of AIDS occurs.

As discussed in "Epidemiology," HIV-infected patients are predisposed not only to reactivation of remote infection but also to rapid progression of recently acquired infection.[66,71] It is also probable that AIDS increases susceptibility to acquisition of new infection, although this has not been rigorously established.

Management of tuberculosis in AIDS may be complicated by concomitant intravenous drug use and homelessness. The difficulty in isolating and completing treatment in such patients is the underlying reason for outbreaks of MDR tuberculosis in this population. It is of interest that long before (and independent of) the AIDS epidemic, illicit intravenous drug use was shown to favor an increased incidence of extrapulmonary disease.[118]

PULMONARY TUBERCULOSIS

Primary Tuberculosis in Childhood

The initial focus of pulmonary tuberculosis in children occurs most frequently in the midlung zones but may develop anywhere. At the time of tuberculin conversion, fever and lassitude and rarely erythema nodosum or phlyctenar keratoconjunctivitis may be present briefly. Clinical manifestations of the initial infection depend on the age of the patient. It is most often symptomatic in childhood because of an age-related tendency to extensive regional lymphadenitis. This may compress central bronchi, causing a brassy cough or atelectasis of a segment or lobe, or may rupture into a bronchus, seeding infection distally and causing pneumonia. In the very young, there is a tendency to progressive lymphohematogenous dissemination with miliary meningeal disease. Uncommonly, again more in infants, local progression of the initial pneumonia results in progressive primary disease, which may cavitate and spread via the bronchial tree or the blood stream. However, most infections during the relatively disease-resistant period of childhood (ages 4 to 15 years) are nonprogressive over the short term; healing by involution, encapsulation, and frequently calcification does not seem to be accelerated by chemotherapy.[114] Progression, if any, usually occurs in extrapulmonary metastatic foci or with the development of apical posterior pulmonary tuberculosis when the patient reaches puberty and young adulthood. Treatment of asymptomatic childhood infection is usually with INH alone for a year except when drug resistance seems likely. The recommended dose is larger (10 to 15 mg/kg) than the adult dose, the risk of INH toxicity being negligible in the young. Symptoms of bronchial compression often respond to brief corticosteroid treatment (prednisone, 20 to 40 mg/day). Progressive disease with caseation should be treated with a multidrug regimen.

Primary infection in adolescents and adults (1) may occur without symptoms and signs, (2) may produce a typical primary complex, or (3) may result in typical chronic pulmonary tuberculosis without a demonstrable primary complex. Any pneumonic infiltrate, especially if rounded, associated with a hilar or mediastinal node, or in an unusual location, particularly anterior to the tracheal plane, may represent primary infection. These lesions may undergo caseation, liquefaction, and bronchogenic spread just as with classic chronic pulmonary tuberculosis.

Postprimary (Adult-type) Pulmonary Tuberculosis

Postprimary pulmonary tuberculosis in adults is usually asymmetrical and characterized by caseation, cavity formation, and fibrosis. It begins as a patch of pneumonitis in the subapical posterior aspect of an upper lobe, usually just below the clavicle or first rib (Fig. 248-4). A less frequent location is the apex of the lower lobe, where it may be obscured by the heart and hilum on chest roentgenogram. The inflammatory response in the sensitized host produces a fibrin-rich alveolar exudate containing a mixture of inflammatory cells. Serial roentgenograms may demonstrate waxing and waning and sometimes complete regression. If the process accelerates, however, an area of caseous necrosis surrounded by epithelioid cells, granulation tissue, and eventually fibrosis develops. This may arrest by inspissation of the caseous area, fibrous encapsulation, and healing. Caseation, however, tends to liquefy and drain into the bronchial tree, spreading bacillary contents by coughing. The cavity is prevented from collapsing by the fibrous capsule and the inelasticity of the surrounding lung. For un-

clear reasons, the pulmonary cavity favors bacillary multiplication to enormous titers, 5 to 6 logs greater than in noncavitary lesions.[119] The progressive nature of pulmonary tuberculosis in the sensitized host is due to (1) the tendency of apical caseous foci to liquefy, (2) the enormous concentrations of organisms in the resulting pulmonary cavities, and (3) spread of this bacilli-rich material through the bronchial tree. Progression from minimal infiltrate to far-advanced cavitary disease can occur within a few months (Fig. 248-5).

Coughing aerosolizes infectious cavity secretions that may distribute widely throughout the lung (bronchogenic spread). New foci eventually develop that, in turn, may undergo caseation, fibrosis, and healing or slough, resulting in new cavities. The segment or lobe containing the initial cavity is typically involved first with scattered patchy disease, but the contralateral apex is often secondarily involved with progressive disease. Bronchogenic spread may establish foci of infection in the lower lobe and anterior portions of the upper lobe, producing a polymorphous mottling on chest roentgenogram, but these are usually nonprogressive and heal with fibrosis. Although hematogenous spread from an established pulmonary focus can occur, it is usually limited by hypersensitivity-induced thrombosis. Regional lymphadenitis and calcification are not features of chronic pulmonary tuberculosis in adults.

The highly infectious secretions from a cavity always cause some degree of endobronchial inflammation and ulceration, which may be extensive. Ulcerative tuberculous laryngitis is an extension of this process, as is local disease throughout the upper airways, mouth, middle ear, and gastrointestinal tract.

Mechanisms of healing are the same whether spontaneous or under the influence of chemotherapy. Without drug therapy, solid caseous foci surrounded by contracting fibrous tissue occasionally arrest. However, viable bacilli almost always persist in such lesions, and can

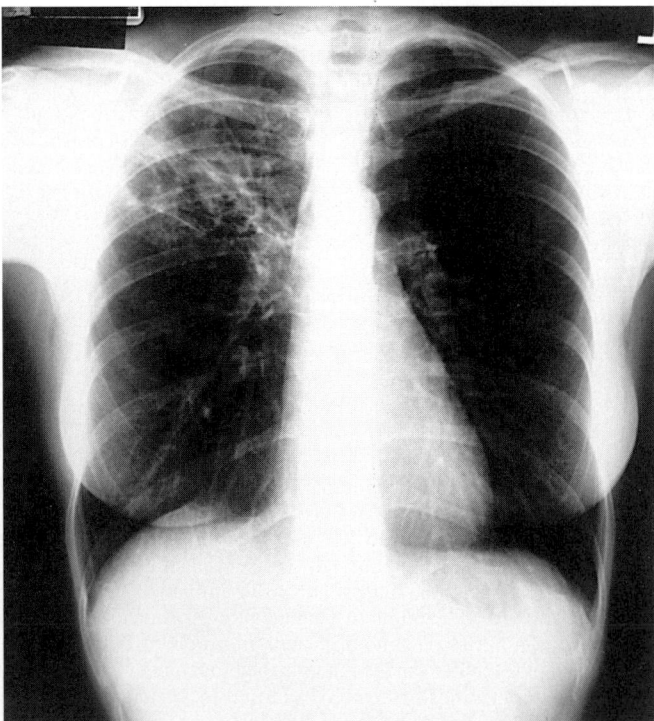

FIGURE 248-4. Chest roentgenogram showing a right apical infiltrate in a patient with moderately advanced postprimary tuberculosis.

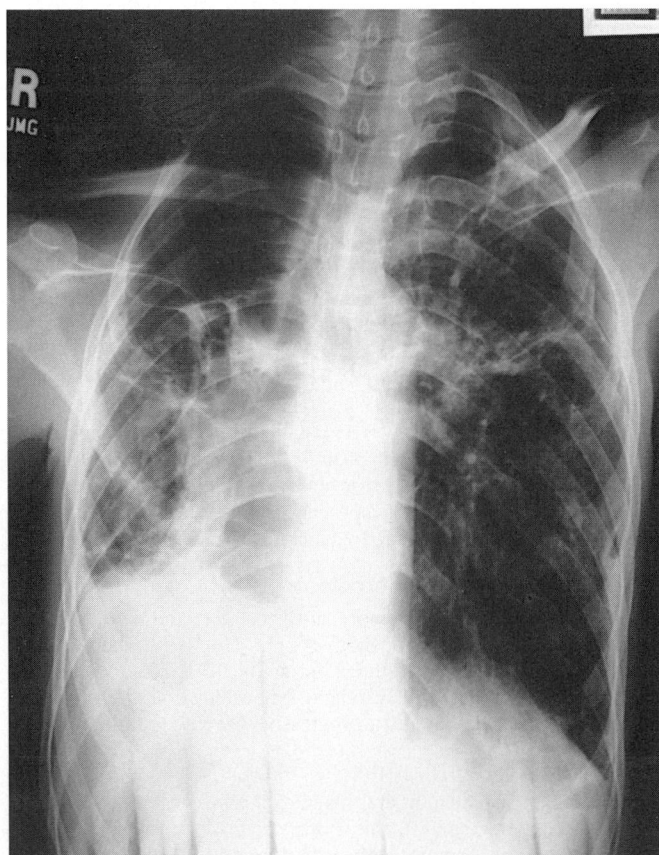

FIGURE 248-5. Chest roentgenogram showing far-advanced bilateral apical cavitary pulmonary tuberculosis in a 32-year-old woman from Ethiopia.

later reactivate. Before drug therapy, open healing of persisting cavities never occurred, although some large, thick-walled cavities in shrunken fibrotic lobes could persist for years with minimal symptoms while remaining highly infectious (chronic fibroid tuberculosis). With drug therapy, open healing of cavities is typical when sputum conversion has been prompt, sometimes with complete reepithelialization. Their major risk is superinfection with organisms such as *Aspergillus* or nontuberculous mycobacteria.

Lower Lobe and Endobronchial Tuberculosis

These terms are not appropriate for chronic pulmonary tuberculosis of the ordinary kind that happens to involve the apex of the lower lobes. In adults, *lower lung field tuberculosis* describes three different but often associated processes: progressive lower lobe pneumonia in recently infected older individuals; endobronchial tuberculosis, often with parenchymal consolidation-collapse; and tuberculosis complicating AIDS. These processes do not suggest tuberculosis roentgenographically, and the former two have a low bacterial content.

Progressive Lower Lobe Disease in Older Persons. Tuberculous infection in an older tuberculin-negative individual frequently causes a nonspecific, nonresolving pneumonitis in the lower or middle lobes or anterior segments of the upper lobes, similar to primary infection in childhood, except with much less hilar and mediastinal adenopathy.[55] Tuberculosis should be considered in any slowly or nonresolving pneumonitis in an older patient.

Endobronchial Tuberculosis. In the past, superficial endobronchial lesions resulting from infectious secretions were common, sometimes spreading to the larynx and beyond or causing obstructive atelectasis with collapse. These superficial lesions responded quickly to chemotherapy. Now endobronchial disease is most frequently caused by rupture of an adjacent node into the bronchial tree, or less frequently by direct spread from parenchymal tuberculosis.[120] The chest roentgenogram typically reveals collapse-consolidation but may be normal in as many as 20% of cases. Sputum smear results are usually negative, but the bronchial wash result is frequently positive.[120]

The usual bronchoscopic findings are mucosal edema, ulceration, and narrowing, but in 30% of cases, bulky granulation tissue may re-

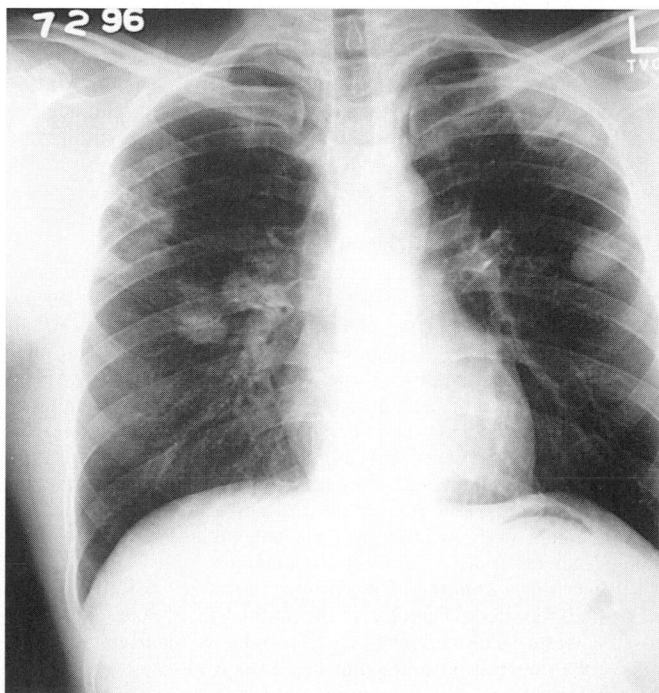

FIGURE 248-6. Chest roentgenogram demonstrating multiple bilateral pulmonary tuberculomas in an asymptomatic 35-year-old man from Poland.

semble bronchogenic carcinoma. Endobronchial involvement is usual in lower lung field tuberculosis,[121] and endobronchial ulcers occasionally produce positive sputum smears with normal chest roentgenograms. Large parenchymal cavities may be present, at times associated with an air-fluid level resulting from intermittent obstruction and poor drainage. Bronchial perforation by tuberculous nodes with endobronchial mass formation and lower lobe consolidation has been observed during AIDS.

Calcified nodes can erode into the bronchial tree and cause hemoptysis, expectoration of calcific material (lithoptysis), or spread of previously quiescent bacilli. The atelectatic pneumonitis, with or without new active disease, that may result is most frequently seen in the anterior segment of the upper lobe and medial segment of the middle lobe.

Tuberculomas. Asymptomatic rounded lesions may develop as the parenchymal residua of the initial infection or as an upper lobe caseous lesion encapsulates (Fig. 248-6). These are ordinarily static, but larger ones may cavitate to produce new spread of disease. In some persons, excessive fibrosis occurs with small caseous or granulomatous residua becoming surrounded by concentric layers of fibrous tissue, at times with central or concentric calcification resembling histoplasmomas. Most such lesions are stable and important only in being confused with cancer.

Pulmonary Tuberculosis in Acquired Immunodeficiency Syndrome. Tuberculosis as first described in Haitians with advanced AIDS was characterized by middle or lower lung field location, absence of cavitation, a greatly increased incidence of extrapulmonary disease, and usually a negative tuberculin test result.[122] Although it was certain on epidemiologic grounds that this represented recrudescence of earlier infection, it resembled childhood tuberculosis clinically except for a negative tuberculin test result and less prominent hilar and mediastinal lymphadenopathy. A later study of tuberculosis in a much less ill population in clients of tuberculosis clinics unaware of their HIV infection found a clinical picture no different from ordinary reactivation tuberculosis in HIV-negative patients, with apical, often cavitary, disease and tuberculin positivity being the rule.[123] The clinical picture of tuberculosis during HIV infection is determined by the degree of immunocompromise (Table 248-6).[110]

HIV-positive persons may also acquire new infection from others in their environment, a risk that was first observed in HIV wards and domiciles. The clinical picture in these patients was diffuse, rapidly progressive, noncavitary disease that was often fatal. In some instances, the infecting person had a normal chest roentgenogram and a negative sputum stain at the time infection of others took place.[66,71]

It is important to consider tuberculosis in HIV-positive individuals with respiratory failure in the intensive care unit. Patients may have adult respiratory distress or sepsis syndrome with multiple organ system failure. The diagnosis can be made readily by stain and culture if appropriate samples are submitted to the laboratory.

Symptoms

Early pulmonary tuberculosis is asymptomatic, usually discovered by chance on a chest roentgenogram. As the bacillary population grows, however, nonspecific constitutional symptoms such as anorexia, fatigue,

TABLE 248-6 Clinical Manifestations of Active Tuberculosis in Early versus Late Human Immunodeficiency Virus Infection*

	Early	Late
Tuberculin test	Usually positive	Usually negative
Adenopathy	Unusual	Common
Pulmonary distribution	Upper lobe	Lower and middle lobe
Cavitation	Often present	Typically absent
Extrapulmonary disease	10%-15% of cases	50% of cases

*For practical purposes, early and late may be defined as CD4+ cell counts greater than 300 cells/mm³ and less than 200 cells/mm³, respectively.

Adapted from Murray JF. Cursed duet: HIV infection and tuberculosis. Respiration. 1990;57:210-220. Reproduced with permission of S. Karger AG, Basel.

weight loss, chilly sensations, afternoon fever, and night sweats may ensue. These late manifestations are gradual in onset, surprisingly well tolerated, and often not even recognized by the patient. Local symptoms also indicate advanced disease. A productive cough is usually present. Coughing to clear cavitary secretions is usually mild and well tolerated but may become bothersome when bronchial involvement is extensive. The mucopurulent sputum is nonspecific, and both cough and sputum may be ignored by patients with chronic bronchitis. Hemoptysis resulting from caseous sloughing or endobronchial erosion is usually minor but connotes advanced disease. Sudden massive hemoptysis resulting from erosion of a pulmonary artery by an advancing cavity (Rasmussen's aneurysm) was an occasional terminal event in the pre-drug era but is now seldom seen. In inactive disease, brisk hemoptysis may be due to *Aspergillus* superinfection of residual cavities (aspergilloma). Chest pain is usually due to extension of inflammation to the parietal pleura. Pleural involvement adjacent to an established cavity tends to cause visceral-parietal pleural symphysis without effusion (dry pleurisy). Serofibrinous pleurisy with effusion is often an early postprimary event but may complicate chronic pulmonary tuberculosis. Rarely, chest pain leads to discovery of tuberculous empyema. Some patients do not seek help until disease occurs in tissues bathed in highly infectious pulmonary secretions, such as painful pharyngeal ulcers; indolent and nonhealing ulcers of the mouth or tongue; hoarseness and dysphagia that are due to laryngeal involvement; tuberculous otitis media; gastrointestinal symptoms that are due to enteric ulceration, perforation, or mass formation; or anal pain that is due to tuberculous perirectal abscess and fistula formation. Lower lobe tuberculosis resulting from bronchial lymph node perforation may be associated with lithoptysis (stone spitting) and characteristically produces symptoms of severe endobronchial disease with serious cough and often hemoptysis.

Physical Examination

Physical findings are not specific, in general underestimating the extent of the illness, and may be absent in spite of extensive disease. Dullness with decreased fremitus may indicate pleural thickening or fluid. Rales may be appreciated only when the patient breathes in after a short cough (post-tussive rales) and may persist long after healing owing to permanent distortion of small airways. With large lesions, signs of consolidation with open bronchi (whispered pectoriloquy, tubular breath sounds) can be heard. Distant hollow breath sounds heard over cavities are called *amphoric,* like the sound made by blowing across the mouth of a jar (amphora).

Roentgenologic Findings

The chest roentgenogram is central to diagnosis, determination of the extent and character of disease, and evaluation of the response to therapy. Certain patterns are highly suggestive, although not diagnostic, of tuberculosis. A patchy or nodular infiltrate in the apical or subapical posterior areas of the upper lobes or the superior segment of a lower lobe is highly suspicious for early chronic tuberculosis, especially if bilateral or associated with cavity formation (see Fig. 248-4). Cavities may be more apparent by computed tomography (CT) or magnetic resonance imaging. Cavitation in the apical segment of the lower lobe may be obscured by the heart shadow and, in the lateral view, by the dorsal spine. Air-fluid levels are uncommon in upper lobe tuberculosis (less than 10%) but occur more frequently in lower lobe cavities.[91] Fresh bronchogenic spread from recent spillage of infectious cavity contents appears as multiple, discrete, soft, fluffy infiltrates, or a confluent infiltrate adjacent to a cavity, or in the middle or lower lung field on the same or opposite side. These latter types of spread are seldom progressive and heal by rounding up into more discrete lesions with regular borders.

Both chronicity and histopathologic features can be estimated based on the chest roentgenogram. Productive lesions (granulomatous) tend to be small, nodular, and sharply defined, indicating few organisms and a good host response. Exudative lesions (pneumonic) tend to have soft, indistinct borders and are more unstable. Fibrotic scars have sharp margins and tend to contract. Caseation causes in-

creased density. Healing exudative lesions first become smaller and less dense and then, as scarring develops, become more sharply defined. Lower lobe tuberculosis is nonspecific roentgenographically. Other patterns include poorly resolving pneumonia, atelectasis, mass lesions, and large cavities with air-fluid levels; initial misdiagnosis is the rule. Pneumonia associated with hilar adenopathy should always suggest primary tuberculosis, regardless of the lung fields involved and patient age.

Other Laboratory Findings

Normocytic, normochromic anemia, hypoalbuminemia, and hypergammaglobulinemia are characteristic of advanced disease. The white blood cell count is usually normal but may be between 10,000 and 15,000 cells/mm³. Many HIV-negative patients with active tuberculosis have CD4+ T cell counts much lower than 500 cells/L, which return toward normal with treatment.[124] Monocytosis is seen in less than 10% of cases. Hematuria or pyuria should suggest coexisting renal tuberculosis. Hyponatremia with features of inappropriate secretion of antidiuretic hormone is characteristic of tuberculous meningitis but also occurs with isolated pulmonary involvement. Hyponatremia should also suggest associated Addison's disease. Hypercalcemia is also seen during pulmonary tuberculosis, usually in the first weeks of therapy.

Diagnosis

A strong presumptive diagnosis can often be made based on the roentgenographic pattern. A positive sputum smear, usual in extensive disease, is almost conclusive in the proper setting. However, an intercurrent cancer or lung abscess, particularly in the apices, may erode a quiescent focus and cause brief shedding of tubercle bacilli without causing active disease. The best diagnostic sputum specimen is an early morning sample. Three daily collections suffice for almost all cases. Aspiration of gastric contents, obtained early in the morning to sample sputum swallowed during sleep, is an alternative when sputum is not produced. Sputum induction by heated saline aerosols is also an effective substitute in ambulatory patients. Although pulmonary tuberculosis in AIDS patients is often noncavitary, both sensitivity and specificity of sputum acid-fast stains are comparable to those in HIV-negative patients.[124] In addition, positive sputum smears are much more likely to indicate *M. tuberculosis* than *M. avium* complex, even in areas where both diseases are common.[125] A negative tuberculin reaction does not exclude tuberculosis even when the dose is 250 TU.[96,126] In AIDS patients, tuberculin negativity is the rule.[110] Granuloma formation on histologic examination, even with acid-fast bacilli, is still only strong presumptive evidence, because similar findings may be produced by mycobacteria other than tuberculosis. Definitive diagnosis requires culture and speciation.

Fiberoptic Bronchoscopy. Diagnostic fiberoptic bronchoscopy with transbronchial biopsy and bronchial washings is an efficient way to obtain diagnostic materials when sputum does not suffice. In most cases of other than miliary disease, however, it is culture of washings rather than acid-fast staining or histologic features that provides the diagnosis, and most cases diagnosed by bronchoscopy are later found to have been positive using specimens obtained less invasively. Bronchoscopy specimens cultured by radiometric methods more frequently grow saprophytic nontuberculous mycobacteria than tuberculosis.[127] In AIDS patients with pulmonary tuberculosis but negative smears, bronchoscopy yields a rapid diagnosis (based on smears and histologic features) in only one third of cases.[128-130] Thus a negative acid-fast stain at bronchoscopy does not exclude tuberculosis, although such cases are certainly less contagious.

Tuberculosis Diagnosed at Autopsy. From 1985 through 1988, 5.1% of all reported tuberculosis cases in the United States were diagnosed at death.[131] Usually, the patient is old, has underlying diseases, and very frequently is tuberculin negative. Both nonresolving pulmonary processes and extrapulmonary tuberculosis, particularly chronic miliary and meningeal disease, are represented in this group. The usual reason for failure to diagnose tuberculosis in this setting is failure to look for it.

Tuberculosis and Cancer

It has been estimated that 1% to 5% of tuberculosis patients also have cancer, most being male smokers. It is possible that cancer can arise in tuberculous scars, and it is certain that cancer can erode old quiescent tuberculous foci, causing active disease. However, in many patients the diseases will be anatomically remote. No one cancer cell type predominates.

When tuberculosis and cancer occur together, diagnosis of the latter is often difficult but should be kept in mind in older smoking men with tuberculosis, and sputum cytologic studies should be performed. There are certain roentgenographic findings that suggest concomitant cancer, such as progression of one area while the remainder of the lesion is regressing, a large (>3 cm) mass lesion admixed with infiltrative disease, the presence of hilar nodes in adult chronic pulmonary tuberculosis, and postobstructive atelectasis.[132]

TREATMENT OF TUBERCULOSIS

Before effective drugs were available, 50% of patients with active pulmonary tuberculosis died within 2 years, and only 25% were cured.[28] With the advent of chemotherapy, successful treatment became a reasonable goal in all adults. In practice, failures occur because of drug resistance or an inappropriate regimen but most importantly because of nonadherence, which is often carefully concealed by the patient as health returns and motivation declines. It is for this reason that the responsibility for adequate treatment has been shifted from the patient to the prescribing physician and to the health department, emphasizing the importance of DOT.[133] Resistance to antituberculous agents can be either *primary*, that is, present before initiating therapy, or *secondary*, indicating emergence of resistance in the setting of inadequately prescribed or taken therapy. Risk factors for infection with drug-resistant tuberculosis are listed in Table 248-7.

Primary Resistance

During the 1970s, primary resistance to at least one drug was observed in less than 3% of cases in the United States. In 1997, approximately 8% of *M. tuberculosis* isolates in the United States were resistant to at least INH, and 1.3% were resistant to at least INH and RMP.[30] Resistance rates are not uniform across the United States. Fortunately, worrisome resistance trends in New York City and other areas have reversed in response to vigorous efforts by physicians and public health personnel.[77]

Secondary Resistance

Historical clues that suggest drug resistance include prior antituberculous chemotherapy or prophylaxis, infection acquired in regions where resistance is prevalent, and contact with a drug-resistant case. One study from southern California recorded resistance in 71% of patients with tuberculosis who had been previously treated and had cavitary disease.[134] Homelessness, illicit drug use, and AIDS all favor acquisition or development of drug-resistant infections.[44,135] Adherence to treatment is unlikely in persons facing the more pressing problems of homelessness. Resistance to at least one drug was present in 33% of *M. tuberculosis* isolates during 1 month in 1991 in New York City and to both INH and RMP in a remarkable 19%.[136] By 1994, these numbers had declined to 24% and 13%, respectively.[77] Fluoroquinolone resistance was also noted.[137]

Effect of Resistance to Different Drugs on Response to Chemotherapy

Surprisingly, studies of four-drug, 6-month chemotherapy demonstrated that initial INH or STM resistance did not compromise outcome, but results were very poor (>50% lack of conversion or relapse) when initial RMP resistance was present. Six- or 9-month therapy is contraindicated in RMP-resistant cases.[138]

Antituberculous Drugs. Information on dosage and pharmacology of antituberculous drugs is provided in Chapter 36.

Isoniazid. INH is the cornerstone of therapy and should be included in all regimens unless a high degree of INH resistance exists and the regimen includes RMP. The increased hepatotoxicity of INH and RMP given together likely outweighs any advantage of continuing INH in the face of INH resistance.

Rifampin. RMP is the second major antituberculous agent. The most important complication of RMP is hepatitis. This occurs four times more frequently in regimens containing both INH and RMP than in those containing INH alone.[139] Although biochemical evidence of hepatic toxicity may occur promptly after administration of INH alone, clinical hepatitis rarely occurs in the first month.[140] In contrast, fulminant hepatitis complicating INH and RMP may occur within the first 2 weeks of therapy. This appears to be due to accelerated production of a hepatotoxic product of INH oxidation by RMP, a hypothesis supported by the observation that phenobarbital and phenytoin, also inducers of the microsomal P-450 system, have been associated with fulminant hepatic failure in persons receiving INH and RMP.[139] INH hepatotoxicity is rare in children, but as many as 25% of children taking INH and RMP together acquire jaundice. This may not be the same phenomenon as in adults.

Of special concern is that RMP, by inducing hepatic P-450 cytochrome oxidases, causes many drug-drug interactions. This can lead to suboptimal HIV-1 protease inhibitor levels, inadequate control of viral replication, and emergence of drug-resistant virus. In this setting, RMP may be replaced by rifabutin, which has comparable antituberculous activity but is a weaker enzyme inducer.[141] This is often preferable to discontinuing the protease inhibitor. Monitoring protease inhibitor blood levels may also be justified. Rifapentine, a newly approved rifamycin antibiotic, has a long half-life that allows once-weekly administration in immunocompetent patients.[142]

Pyrazinamide. PZA is an essential component of 6-month regimens. Early studies of PZA using high doses recorded such serious hepatotoxicity that it was largely abandoned. At currently recommended doses and durations, PZA generally does not add to the hepatotoxicity of INH and RMP,[143] but severe hepatic injury and deaths have been reported among HIV-negative adults receiving short-course RMP plus PZA for latent tuberculous infection.[144] PZA is thought to be ineffective in preventing emergence of resistance to companion drugs, and its beneficial effect is limited to the first 2 months in regimens containing both INH and RMP. Side effects include hyperuricemia, mild nongouty polyarthralgias that respond to nonsteroidal anti-inflammatory agents, and gout. *M. bovis* is uniformly resistant to PZA.[145]

Ethambutol. EMB is a component of most regimens. It is given at a daily dosage of 15 mg/kg. When multidrug resistance is highly likely, 25 mg/kg daily may be warranted but is associated with an increased risk of ocular toxicity.

Streptomycin. STM, the first major antituberculous drug, was promptly replaced by INH as the cornerstone of therapy.

TABLE 248-7 Epidemiologic Circumstances in Which an Exposed Person Is at Increased Risk of Infection with Drug-Resistant *Mycobacterium tuberculosis*[*]

- Exposure to a person who has known drug-resistant tuberculosis
- Exposure to a person with active tuberculosis who has had prior treatment for tuberculosis (treatment failure or relapse) and whose susceptibility test results are not known
- Exposure to persons with active tuberculosis from areas in which there is a high prevalence of drug resistance
- Exposure to persons who continue to have positive sputum smears after 2 months of combination chemotherapy
- Travel in an area of high prevalence of drug resistance

[*]This information is to be used in deciding whether or not to add a fourth drug (usually EMB) for children with active tuberculosis, not to infer the empirical need for a second-line treatment regimen.

From Centers for Disease Control and Prevention. Treatment of tuberculosis. American Thoracic Society, CDC and Infectious Diseases Society of America. MMWR Morb Mortal Wkly Rep. 2003;52(RR-11):1-88.

Fluoroquinolones. Although experience with these agents is not extensive, their in vitro activity and favorable clinical results suggest that some fluoroquinolones, such as levofloxacin, are as effective as traditional first-line agents.[146] However, fluoroquinolones should not be used as first-line therapy but rather reserved for treatment of MDR cases as part of a well-designed multidrug regimen.

Second-Line Agents. Second-line agents are less efficacious or more toxic, or both, than first-line drugs. These include ethionamide, prothionamide, cycloserine, kanamycin, capreomycin, thiacetazone, para-aminosalicylic acid (PAS), and other agents discussed in Chapter 36.

Selecting a Drug Regimen

Before RMP was available, excellent results in drug-sensitive infections were obtained with INH plus either PAS or EMB given for 18 to 24 months, "reinforced" in extensive disease by STM for the first 6 to 12 weeks. Relapse rates were unacceptably high with shorter courses. However, demonstration that RMP was equal to INH in efficacy led to studies of shorter treatment regimens. In definitive studies, drug-sensitive infections responded as effectively to 9 months of INH and RMP as to 18- to 24-month regimens not containing RMP.[147,148] It was subsequently demonstrated that 6-month regimens based on an initial 2-month intensive "bactericidal phase" of INH, RMP, PZA, and either STM or EMB, followed by a "continuation phase" of INH and RMP for 4 more months, performed as well.[149] It was also established that "continuation phase" drugs could be administered twice or thrice weekly, facilitating DOT. Next it was shown that neither STM nor EMB improved results over a three-drug regimen (INH, RMP, and PZA) during the first 2 months of intensive therapy when the isolate was fully susceptible.[149] This 6-month three-drug regimen is perfectly acceptable for drug-sensitive infections. However, given concerns about resistance, EMB is almost always included until susceptibility testing results are known. Regimens lacking RMP are used very infrequently in Western nations.

Standard Nine-Month Regimens Based on Isoniazid and Rifampin

The combination of INH (300 mg) plus RMP (600 mg) daily by mouth on an empty stomach for 9 months is highly effective for almost all forms of drug-sensitive tuberculosis, both pulmonary and extrapulmonary.[150] Most authorities, however, advise addition of PZA (25 mg/kg) plus either EMB (15 mg/kg) or STM (1 g) initially pending sensitivity results, especially when primary drug resistance is suspected.

An intermittent 9-month regimen consisting largely of twice-weekly doses of INH and RMP is an acceptable alternative.[151] INH and RMP are administered daily, as described for 1 to 2 months, and twice weekly thereafter with the same dose of RMP but a larger (900-mg) dose of INH. This is not advised in cases with any likelihood of antimicrobial resistance.

Six-Month Regimens

The CDC has endorsed several regimens for the initial treatment of tuberculosis.[152] The degree to which INH resistance compromises the efficacy of a three-drug (INH, RMP, and PZA) regimen is not known, whereas it appears to make little difference with four-drug regimens (INH, RMP, PZA, and either EMB or STM).[138] Considering the current incidence of drug resistance, and the safety of EMB when given under proper supervision, there is little to be lost and potentially much to be gained by routinely using such a four-drug regimen in the initial 2 months of treatment. Results of all 6-month regimens in patients with initial resistance to RMP are poor, and such cases probably require 18- to 24-month courses, as was the case before RMP was available.[138]

When hepatitis occurs in patients receiving both INH and RMP, both drugs should be discontinued until hepatic transaminase levels normalize. INH may then be cautiously reintroduced in graduated doses while monitoring serum transaminase levels, and a more prolonged (18- to 24-month) regimen based on INH and at least one companion drug other than RMP can be continued. Similarly, when patients in whom drug-related hepatitis develops with INH and RMP

have demonstrated microbial resistance to INH but not RMP, RMP can usually be gradually reintroduced and a more prolonged (18- to 24-month) regimen based on RMP and preferably two new companion drugs other than INH continued. In the uncommon situation in which both INH and RMP must be reintroduced, this can be carried out sequentially with close supervision in many patients.[139]

Directly Observed Therapy in Nonadherent Patients

The failure of conventional treatment programs to cure persons who do not adhere to therapy, together with the fact that most of a 6-month regimen can be given on a less than daily basis, has led to regimens in which the total number of doses is small and DOT is practical. Several acceptable regimens have been endorsed by the CDC.[152] A commonly used regimen consists of INH, RMP, PZA, and either STM or EMB administered daily for 8 weeks, followed by INH and RMP given daily, twice a week, or three times a week for 16 weeks.[153] Another well-studied regimen is presented in Table 248-8.[154] EMB may be substituted for STM without loss of efficacy. Importantly, DOT is cost effective, especially when considering the cost of caring for MDR cases. Because all doses are observed, compliance is assured and the likelihood of emergence of resistance minimized. The ability of mandatory DOT to control drug resistance in a community is well established.[80,155] In some cases, recalcitrant patients must be detained for completion of therapy. It has been recommended that all patients with organisms resistant to either INH or RMP and all patients receiving less than daily therapy receive DOT.[151] Many health departments strive to use DOT for all cases of active tuberculosis.

Regimens of Less than Six Months for Minimal Disease

Extent of disease can be quantified by the mycobacterial content of sputum, with smear- and culture-positive sputum representing most severe disease, smear-negative and culture-positive sputum representing intermediate disease, and smear- and culture-negative sputum representing the least amount of disease. Good results have been obtained with as little as 2 to 4 months of four-drug therapy in patients with less than extensive tuberculosis.[156] Although these abbreviated courses are not recommended, the fact that even short periods of intense therapy cure many patients further supports the use of DOT because it avoids irregular drug taking and has some chance of cure even when terminated prematurely. (The good results with 3 months of therapy in smear- and culture-negative cases also suggest a role for multiple-drug treatment for latent tuberculous infection when exposure to resistant organisms is suspected.)

Combination Tablets

Fixed-dose preparations containing either 300 mg of INH and 600 mg of RMP (Rifamate), or INH, RMP, and PZA (Rifater) are available. These prevent the patient from omitting one of the drugs at the risk of inducing resistance to the others.

TABLE 248-8 A 62-Dose, Four-Drug Regimen for Tuberculosis in Adults

First 2 wk (once-daily dose for 14 consecutive days)
INH	300 mg
RMP	600 mg
PZA	1.5 g if ≤ 50 kg body weight, 2.0 g if 51-74 kg, 2.5 g if ≥ 75 kg
STM	750 mg if ≤ 50 kg body weight, 1.0 g if > 50 kg

Wk 3-8 (twice weekly)
INH	15 mg/kg
RMP	600 mg
PZA	3.0 g if ≤ 50 kg body weight, 3.5 g if 51-74 kg, 4.0 g if ≥ 75 kg
STM	1.0 g if ≤ 50 kg body weight, 1.25 g if 51-74 kg, 1.5 g if ≥ 75 kg

Wk 9-26 (twice weekly)
INH	15 mg/kg body weight
RMP	600 mg

INH, isoniazid; PZA, pyrazinamide; RMP, rifampin; STM, streptomycin.
From Cohn DL, Catlin BJ, Peterson KL, et al. A 62-dose, 6-month therapy for pulmonary and extrapulmonary tuberculosis: A twice-weekly, directly observed, and cost-effective regimen. Ann Intern Med. 1990;112:407-415.

Regimens Based on Isoniazid and Ethambutol

For drug-sensitive infections, the only advantage of shorter regimens is improved compliance. Because RMP increases the risk of hepatotoxicity when given with INH, this needs to be justified when treating drug-sensitive disease of limited extent in highly compliant patients. Treatment with 18 to 24 months of INH plus EMB is a low-cost, effective alternative to shorter regimens for all forms of drug-sensitive tuberculosis, often with daily STM (1 g) added in more advanced or symptomatic cases during the first 2 months. This may be the preferred regimen (1) for patients with less than extensive disease whose compliance is certain and for whom supervision consists of no more than monthly clinic visits, (2) for patients who are likely to be noncompliant but who absolutely cannot receive supervised therapy (this should be exceptionally rare), and (3) for patients with severe liver disease.

Treatment of Multidrug-Resistant Tuberculosis

When initiating treatment for tuberculosis that is resistant to both INH and RMP, extensive susceptibility testing should be performed and expert advice sought. If a suboptimal regimen is prescribed, resistance to additional drugs may emerge and the opportunity for success may be lost. In a discouraging study from Denver, only one half of 171 HIV-negative patients with MDR tuberculosis ever converted sputum cultures to negative despite prolonged administration of carefully selected regimens (not including fluoroquinolones).[157] In contrast, a more recent report from New York City noted remission in virtually all evaluable HIV-negative patients treated for MDR tuberculosis using fluoroquinolone-based regimens.[146] Therapy was administered for a median of 18 months. For tuberculosis that is INH and RMP resistant but fluoroquinolone susceptible, a fluoroquinolone should always be administered along with other drugs to which the organism is susceptible. Levofloxacin may be preferred, although there is experience with ciprofloxacin. Companion drugs may include aminoglycosides (STM, kanamycin, or amikacin) or capreomycin, ethionamide, and cycloserine.[146,150,152,158] To prevent the emergence of resistant strains, fluoroquinolones should be reserved for known drug-resistant cases but not be a routine part of initial therapy for tuberculosis.[137]

Course of Treatment and Duration of Observation

The diagnosis of tuberculosis is usually relatively well established before therapy is initiated. In smear-negative cases, five or six sputum samples and, if available, specimens obtained at bronchoscopy should be submitted before beginning treatment. In severely ill patients with presumed tuberculosis, treatment should be initiated immediately; a few days of antituberculous treatment will not interfere with bacteriologic diagnosis. If treatment is initiated before a microbiologic diagnosis is established, the response to treatment often confirms the diagnosis. Periodic chest roentgenograms are helpful, although monthly films are not necessary. Beginning 1 month after initiation of therapy, an early morning sputum specimen culture should be obtained for culture to monitor conversion or, if sputum positivity persists, to detect the emergence of drug resistance. It may be more practical to obtain several sputum specimens for culture at 2, 4, and 6 months of therapy. Sputum cultures should convert to negative within 2 months with regimens containing both INH and RMP and not much longer with INH plus EMB.[63] In a minority of patients, smears remain positive after cultures revert to negative. Sporadic positive smears for long periods presumably represent inactive bacilli released from caseous foci. When cultures remain positive beyond 4 months, emerging drug resistance is a major concern. This almost never occurs when both INH and RMP are reliably taken as initial therapy for drug-sensitive tuberculosis and suggests initial drug resistance or noncompliance, or both. Sensitivity testing should be performed and consideration given to adding at least two new drugs to which the organism was sensitive at the outset of treatment, at least until sensitivities are known. Addition of only one drug risks rapid resistance to the added drug.

Patients receiving INH should be instructed about symptoms of hepatitis and, when possible, hepatic transaminase levels should be monitored every 1 to 2 months. This is more important in patients receiving both INH and RMP. Patients receiving EMB should be regularly questioned regarding visual symptoms and their visual acuity should be measured (Snellen chart). Testing of red-green color discrimination is desirable when the 25-mg/kg dosage is given. Patients receiving STM should be examined for balance and high-frequency hearing loss if they are older than 50 years of age.

Relapse after adequate treatment of drug-sensitive infections is very infrequent. Prolonged follow-up of appropriately treated patients is not necessary except in the case of unusually extensive disease, slow bacteriologic response to treatment, suspicion of poor compliance, or high-risk patients with intercurrent diseases. Although observation may be discontinued on completion of a 6- or 9-month regimen containing both INH and RMP, continued observation for 2 years is preferred when practical. Interestingly, a randomized study involving HIV-infected adults in Haiti showed that prescribing an additional 12 months of INH after completing a 6-month RMP-containing regimen reduced the tuberculosis recurrence rate,[159] although another study showed no benefit of 1 year of empirical INH in asymptomatic, HIV-infected but tuberculin-negative individuals in the same endemic area.[160]

Treatment Algorithm

A committee from the CDC, the American Thoracic Society, and the Infectious Diseases Society of America has published an algorithm that embodies the principles above but also takes into account the significance of cavitation on the duration of treatment (Fig. 248-7).[133] Presence of pulmonary cavitation and a positive sputum culture after 2 months of therapy would indicate the need for extending therapy to a total of 9 months.

Re-treatment

Clinical judgment based on experience is critical in re-treatment cases, and testing of susceptibility to all potentially useful drugs is required.[150] Some generalizations concerning re-treatment can be made:

1. A relapse after prompt sputum conversion indicates that drugs were stopped too soon. When drugs are taken reliably but stopped prematurely, the infection usually remains susceptible and will respond again to the initial regimen.
2. If relapse occurs with organisms resistant to INH when initial treatment was with INH and EMB or INH, EMB, and STM, retreatment with RMP plus two other drugs to which the organism is susceptible for at least 24 months is highly effective. A 9-month regimen that uses RMP, STM, PZA, and EMB for 2 months, followed by RMP and EMB for 7 months, has performed well in infections resistant to INH but sensitive to RMP and EMB.[161]
3. If compliance has been irregular, resistant organisms will probably be present.
4. When drug resistance is suspected, a two- or three-drug combination including at least one "new" strong drug (INH, RMP, STM, EMB at 25 mg/kg, levofloxacin, or PZA) and a "new" weak drug (ethionamide, PAS, or cycloserine) may be added to drugs previously given pending susceptibility results.
5. Capreomycin or amikacin can replace STM. Kanamycin is less effective and more toxic and is used as a last resort.
6. In infections multiply resistant to INH, RMP, STM, EMB, levofloxacin, and PZA, three or four weak drugs (ethionamide, cycloserine, PAS, and capreomycin) may be used together with high-dose INH (15 mg/kg), because INH may retain some suppressive effect even when in vitro resistance is demonstrated.

Other Forms of Treatment

Bed rest does not influence outcome when effective chemotherapy is given. In treatment failures resistant to all drugs, strict bed rest with continued INH may salvage some otherwise hopeless cases and may also be beneficial during re-treatment of cases resistant to all but the weakest drugs. Resection still has a role in the salvage of patients in whom treatment fails and who have localized, resectable disease, and resistance to all but the weakest drugs.

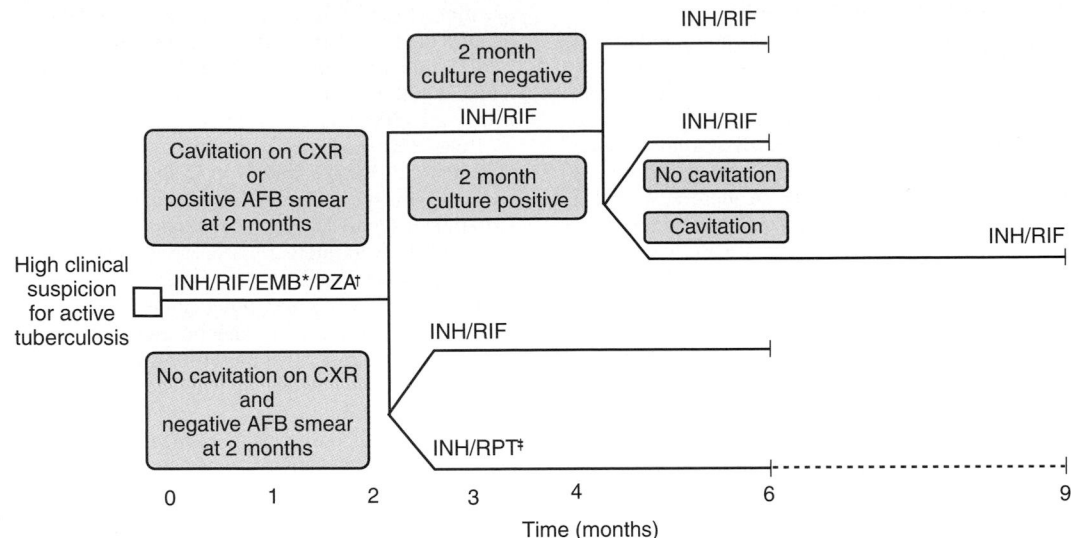

FIGURE 248-7. Treatment algorithm for tuberculosis. Patients in whom tuberculosis is proved or strongly suspected should have treatment initiated with isoniazid, rifampin, pyrazinamide, and ethambutol for the initial 2 months. A repeat smear and culture should be performed when 2 months of treatment has been completed. If cavities were seen on the initial chest radiograph or the acid-fast smear is positive at completion of 2 months of treatment, the continuation phase of treatment should consist of isoniazid and rifampin daily or twice weekly for 4 months to complete a total of 6 months of treatment. If cavitation was present on the initial chest radiograph and the culture at the time of completion of 2 months of therapy is positive, the continuation phase should be lengthened to 7 months (total of 9 months of treatment). If the patient has HIV infection and the CD4+ cell count is less than 100/μL, the continuation phase should consist of daily or three times weekly isoniazid and rifampin. In HIV-uninfected patients having no cavitation on chest radiograph and negative acid-fast smears at completion of 2 months of treatment, the continuation phase may consist of either once-weekly isoniazid and rifapentine, or daily or twice-weekly isoniazid and rifampin, to complete a total of 6 months (*bottom*). Patients receiving isoniazid and rifapentine, and whose 2-month cultures are positive, should have treatment extended by an additional 3 months (total of 9 months). *EMB may be discontinued when results of drug susceptibility testing indicate no drug resistance. †PZA may be discontinued after it has been taken for 2 months (56 doses). ‡RPT should not be used in HIV-infected patients with tuberculosis or in patients with extrapulmonary tuberculosis. Therapy should be extended to 9 months if 2-month culture is positive. CXR, chest radiograph; EMB, ethambutol; INH, isoniazid; PZA, pyrazinamide; RIF, rifampin; RPT, rifapentine. (*From Centers for Disease Control and Prevention. Treatment of tuberculosis. American Thoracic Society, CDC and Infectious Diseases Society of America. MMWR Morb Mortal Wkly Rep. 2003;52[RR-11]:1-88.*)

Corticosteroids. In severely debilitated patients or those with marked constitutional symptoms, adjunctive prednisone (20 to 30 mg daily and slowly tapered) will effect prompt symptomatic improvement, abolish fever, and reverse serious anemia and hypoalbuminemia. When life-threatening hypoxemia complicates extensive pulmonary inflammation, higher doses (60 to 80 mg daily) may improve oxygenation. Disseminated drug-sensitive tuberculosis associated with high fever and clinical deterioration in AIDS patients may respond to corticosteroids.

Treatment of Tuberculosis in Human Immunodeficiency Virus–Infected Patients

A 1998 report from the CDC provides advice in this complicated and rapidly changing arena.[162] The document may be viewed on the CDC website (*http://www.cdc.gov/nchstp/tb/pubs/mmwrhtml/maj_guide.htm*). The 2003 CDC/American Thoracic Society/Infectious Diseases Society of America guidelines update the 1998 report.[133] Another helpful site for information regarding pharmacokinetic interactions with HIV medications is that on the National Institutes of Health website (*http://www.aidsinfo.nih.gov/guidelines*). Updates appear periodically and should be consulted because new antiretroviral agents and new interactions are being discovered. Special attention to drug interactions is required for patients who have tuberculosis and whose HIV infection should be treated with highly active antiretroviral therapy. The rifamycins interact extensively with many protease inhibitors and nonnucleoside reverse transcriptase inhibitors.[163] Among the rifamycins, RMP has the most interactions, rifapentine an intermediate amount, and rifabutin the least. RMP is contraindicated in patients receiving either a protease inhibitor (saquinavir, ritonavir, indinavir, nelfinavir, amprenavir, or lopinavir/ritonavir) or some non-nucleoside reverse transcript inhibitors (nevirapine or delavirdine). RMP modestly lowers

plasma levels of efavirenz and nevirapine. RMP should not affect the antiviral efficacy of efavirenz, and can be administered concomitantly. Rifabutin should not be used with ritonavir, hard-gel saquinavir (Invirase), or delavirdine. Ritonavir increases rifabutin concentrations by 35-fold and causes rifabutin toxicity, such as arthralgia, uveitis, skin discoloration, and leukopenia. Rifabutin decreases serum concentrations of delavirdine and several protease inhibitors, the decrease being most serious for the hard-gel saquinavir because of its low bioavailability. Some authorities recommend that doses of nelfinavir and indinavir should be increased in patients receiving rifabutin. The effect of rifabutin on amprenavir metabolism appears to be insufficient to warrant dose adjustment. The dose of rifabutin should be lowered from 300 mg daily to 150 mg daily in patients receiving indinavir, nelfinavir, or amprenavir in order to avoid rifabutin toxicity. In contrast, in patients taking efavirenz, the rifabutin dose given daily or twice weekly should be increased from 300 mg to 450 mg. Despite this impressive list of interactions, it is not recommended that treatment of tuberculosis be delayed or that highly active antiretroviral therapy be avoided. Because antimycobacterial drugs other than the rifamycins do not have substantial interactions, an alternative regimen with INH, STM, PZA, and EMB can be considered. For adults, one regimen includes STM given as 1 g intramuscularly daily for the first 8 weeks, along with INH 300 mg, PZA 2 g, and EMB 1600 mg daily. For the remainder of the 9- to 12-month treatment (the duration depending on response), the patient is given STM 1.5 g intramuscularly, INH 900 mg, and PZA 3.5 g two times per week. The inconvenience and ototoxicity of STM have made this regimen unpopular. Regimens recommended by the CDC are given in Table 248-9.[162]

The CDC's Tuberculosis Trials Consortium Study 23 prescribed twice-weekly rifabutin-based therapy to HIV-infected adults with active tuberculosis. Study enrollment was suspended after five partici-

TABLE 248-9 Treatment Regimens for Human Immunodeficiency Virus-Related Tuberculosis

Induction Phase		Continuation Phase			
Drugs	*Interval and Duration*	*Drugs*	*Interval and Duration**	*Considerations for Human Immunodeficiency Virus Therapy*	*Comments*
Six-Month RFB-Based Therapy (May Be Prolonged[†] to 9 Mo)					
INH RFB PZA[‡] EMB[‡]	Daily for 2 mo (8 wk)	INH RFB	Daily or 2 times/wk for 4 mo (18 wk)	RFB should not be used concurrently with ritonavir, hard-gel saquinavir (Invirase), or delavirdine.	If the patient also is taking indinavir, nelfinavir, or amprenavir, the daily dose of RFB is decreased from 300 mg to 150 mg. The twice-weekly dose of RFB (300 mg) remains unchanged if the patient is taking these protease inhibitors.
	Or		*Or*	A 20%-25% increase in the dose of protease inhibitors or NNRTIs may be necessary.	
INH RFB PZA[‡] EMB[‡]	Daily for 2 wk, then 2 times/wk for 6 wk	INH RFB	2 times/wk for 4 mo (18 wk)	The patient should be monitored carefully for RFB toxicity (arthralgia, uveitis, leukopenia) if RFB is used concurrently with protease inhibitors or NNRTIs. Evidence of decreased response to antiretroviral therapy should be assessed with HIV RNA levels. No contraindication exists for the use of RFB with NRTIs.	If the patient also is taking efavirenz, the daily or twice weekly dose of RFB is increased from 300 mg to 450 mg. Three-times-a-week RFB in combination with antiretroviral therapy has not been studied.
Nine-Month Non-rifamycin Therapy (May Be Prolonged[†] to 12 Mo)					
INH STM PZA EMB	Daily for 2 mo (8 wk)	INH STM PZA	2-3 times/wk for 7 mo (30 wk)	Can be used concurrently with antiretroviral regimens that include protease inhibitors, NRTIs, and NNRTIs.	STM is contraindicated during pregnancy.
	Or		*Or*		
INH STM PZA EMB	Daily for 2 wk, then 2-3 times/wk for 6 wk	INH STM PZA	2-3 times/wk for 7 mo (30 wk)		Every effort should be made to continue STM for the total duration of treatment. When STM is not used for the recommended 9 mo, EMB should be added and the treatment duration prolonged from 9 mo (38 wk) to 12 mo (52 wk).
Six-Month RMP-Based Therapy (May Be Prolonged[†] to 9 Mo)					
INH RMP PZA[§] EMB[§] (or STM)	Daily for 2 mo (8 wk)	INH RMP	Daily or 2-3 times/week for 4 mo (18 wk)	Protease inhibitors or the NNRTIs nevirapine or delavirdine should not be administered concurrently with RMP. NRTIs can be administered concurrently with RMP.	STM is contraindicated during pregnancy.
	Or		*Or*		
INH RMP PZA[§] EMB[§] (or STM)	Daily for 2 wk, then 2-3 times/wk for 6 wk	INH RMP	2-3 times/wk for 4 mo (18 wk)	If appropriate, patients should be assessed every 3 mo to evaluate the decision to initiate antiretroviral therapy.	
	Or		*Or*	A 2-week "P-450 induction washout" period may be necessary between the last dose of RMP and the first dose of protease inhibitors or nevirapine or delavirdine.	
INH RMP PZA EMB (or STM)	3 times/wk for 2 mo (8 wk)	INH RMP PZA EMB (or STM)	3 times/wk for 4 mo (18 wk)		

*Doses should be given at least 3 times per week if CD4[+] T-cell count is less than 100/mm[3].

[†]Duration should be prolonged if the response to therapy is delayed. Criteria for delayed response should be assessed after 2 months and include (1) lack of culture conversion to negative or (2) lack of resolution of signs or symptoms of tuberculosis.

[‡]Continue PZA and EMB for the total induction phase (8 wk).

[§]Continue PZA for the total induction phase (8 wk). EMB can be stopped after test results indicate *M. tuberculosis* susceptibility to INH and RMP.

EMB, ethambutol; HIV, human immunodeficiency virus; INH, isoniazid, NNRTI, non-nucleoside reverse transcriptase inhibitor; NRTI, nucleoside reverse transcriptase inhibitor; PZA, pyrazinamide; RFB, rifabutin; RMP, rifampin; STM, streptomycin.

From Prevention and treatment of tuberculosis among patients infected with human immunodeficiency virus: Principles of therapy and revised recommendations. MMWR Morb Mortal Wkly Rep. 1998;47:1-58.

pants failed with emergence of rifamycin-resistance strains.[164] In response to this study, the CDC recommends that HIV-infected persons with fewer than 100 CD4[+] T cells/mm[3] should not receive once- or twice-weekly regimens. These patients should receive daily therapy during the intensive phase, and daily doses or three doses a week during the continuation phase.

Other complications of treating tuberculosis in HIV-infected patients include the higher incidence of drug resistance and the paradoxical worsening that may be seen when patients are begun on highly active antiretroviral therapy. HIV-infected patients with tuberculosis who were born in the United States who have not previously been treated for tuberculosis have incidences of INH resistance and RMP resistance higher than in the HIV-negative population.[163] A paradoxical worsening of the signs and symptoms of tuberculosis may occur when patients are treated effectively for their tuberculosis and are begun on effective antiretroviral therapy. High fever, swollen lymph glands, and increased pulmonary infiltrates may appear. The patients usually do not appear toxic despite the new symptoms. In the absence of bacteriologic signs of failure, treatment should not be modified.

If the patient does not require a protease inhibitor or nonnucleoside reverse transcriptase inhibitor, RMP- and INH-containing regimens are very effective in patients with susceptible strains.[165] However, a study from the Democratic Republic of Congo reported an increased relapse rate after "standard" (although admittedly less effective) therapy with INH, thiacetazone, and STM, contrasted with similarly treated HIV-negative patients,[166] and a study of HIV-infected adults in Haiti showed that prescribing an additional 12 months of INH after completing a 6-month RMP-containing regimen reduced the tuberculosis recurrence rate.[159] Patients with AIDS who relapsed after treatment with organisms remaining sensitive to the prescribed drugs have also been reported. It is important to follow response to treatment carefully and prolong therapy if the response is slow or suboptimal.[149] Treatment should be continued for at least 6 months beyond sputum culture conversion. Patients with HIV-related enteropathy may not respond to chemotherapy because of inadequate absorption of oral agents, and in rare cases pharmacokinetic monitoring may be necessary.[167] The optimal regimen for MDR tuberculosis in AIDS patients is uncertain. One group has reported that fever beyond 7 to 14 days of antituberculous therapy in an HIV-positive patient suggests drug resistance and the need to add at least two drugs.[168]

Other Special Treatment Circumstances

Childhood. Pulmonary tuberculosis in childhood should be treated with INH (10 mg/kg, up to 300 mg daily) and RMP (15 mg/kg, up to 600 mg daily) for 1 year. STM (20 mg/kg) or EMB (15 mg/kg) may be added if extensive disease is present, but the inability to monitor visual acuity limits the use of EMB in very young children.[150] PZA is recommended in tuberculous meningitis.

Pregnancy. Treatment should not be deferred during pregnancy. For drug-sensitive tuberculosis, INH plus EMB is the regimen of choice. RMP is also safe and may be used in advanced disease or when a 9-month regimen is desirable. STM should not be used during pregnancy because of eighth nerve toxicity in the fetus. Although PZA is routinely recommended by international organizations, use has not been recommended in the United States because of inadequate teratogenicity data.[150] Because INH treatment for latent tuberculous infection may be associated with a very slightly increased risk of fatal maternal hepatitis, added caution with respect to INH-induced hepatotoxicity is indicated.

Uremia and End-Stage Renal Disease. Dosages of INH and RMP need not be adjusted for renal failure but should be administered after dialysis, and pyridoxine supplementation should be routine. In anephric patients, EMB should be used at 8 to 10 mg/kg. PZA should probably be used at 15 to 20 mg/kg. STM should be used only in very unusual circumstances, and its blood level closely monitored.

Biochemical monitoring of hepatotoxicity during renal failure may be complicated by abnormally low transaminase levels in uremia.

Liver Disease. The selection and dosage of antituberculous agents do not need to be modified in most patients with alcoholism or liver disease, although an 18- to 24-month course of INH and EMB with or without STM may be preferred for patients with severe liver disease and drug-sensitive infections (see "Regimens Based on Isoniazid and Ethambutol"). Preexisting liver disease may complicate the detection of drug-related hepatotoxicity; accordingly, clinical and biochemical supervision should be assiduous.

Patients Receiving Immunosuppressive Drugs. Tuberculosis that develops during immunosuppressive treatment of another disease should be treated with the same regimens used to treat immunocompetent hosts. Immunosuppressive therapy need not be discontinued.

Treatment of Latent Tuberculous Infection

Soon after INH became available, it became widely used in the United States to treat not only persons with active disease or recent infection but also persons who have had positive tuberculin test results. This enthusiasm has never been shared in most of Europe.[93] Arguments for and against treating latent tuberculous infection hinge on estimates of relative risks of tuberculosis and INH-induced hepatotoxicity. Those who support a more conservative approach argue that analyses favoring treatment of latent tuberculous infection have lumped together disparate patient populations with different risks for both disease and toxicity.[169] The value of treating latent tuberculous infection in recent tuberculin converters, especially when young, is well established. There is less agreement, however, concerning positive tuberculin tests of unknown duration. As discussed earlier, long-term tuberculin positivity results either from reexposures to *M. tuberculosis* or, more commonly in the United States, from low-grade or intermittent activity of a chronic focus of tuberculosis. Because INH is effective principally against rapidly metabolizing bacilli, it is unclear whether it is the best prophylactic regimen for old infection, or whether multiple drugs including some with "sterilizing" activity might be preferred.[170] However, pending definitive studies, INH remains the chemoprophylactic agent of choice. Criteria for tuberculin positivity based on recommendations from the CDC are summarized in Table 248-10.[92,93]

It deserves emphasis that, for nonimmunocompromised health care workers, the appropriate cutoff for tuberculin reactivity after exposure has been debated. In contrast to CDC recommendations, Stead argued from personal experience that in this situation new tuberculous infection warranting preventive therapy is almost always associated with induration of at least 15 mm in response to 5 TU of PPD at 8 weeks after exposure, and that the risk of INH hepatotoxicity outweighs the benefit for most lesser reactions (see "Treatment of Contacts of Active Cases" and Fig. 248-8).[94]

Drug Regimens

Nine months of INH, 300 mg daily, is the preferred regimen for treating latent tuberculous infection in adults.[153] Six months of INH may provide a more cost-effective approach, but is not recommended for

---

TABLE 248-10 Criteria for Tuberculin Positivity by Risk Group

Reaction ≥ *5 mm of Induration*	*Reaction* ≥ *10 mm of Induration*	*Reaction* ≥ *15 mm of Induration*
HIV-positive persons	Recent immigrants (within 5 years) from high-prevalence countries	Persons with no risk factors for tuberculosis
Recent contacts of tuberculosis case patients	Injection drug users	
Fibrotic changes on chest radiograph consistent with prior tuberculosis	Residents and employees of high-risk congregate settings (prisons and jails, nursing homes, hospitals and other health care facilities, residential facilities for patients with AIDS, and homeless shelters)	
Patients with organ transplants and other immunosuppressed patients (receiving equivalent of ≥ 15 mg/day of prednisone for at least 1 month)	Children less than 4 years of age, or infants, children, and adolescents exposed to adults at high risk	

Adapted from Centers for Disease Control and Prevention. Targeted tuberculin testing and treatment of latent tuberculosis infection. American Thoracic Society. MMWR Morb Mortal Wkly Rep. 2000;49(RR-6):1-51.

HIV-infected adults, those less than 18 years of age, or those with fibrotic lesions on chest film. When necessary, supervised intermittent treatment of latent tuberculous infection with INH, 900 mg twice weekly, can be used. Pyridoxine supplementation, 10 to 25 mg daily, is recommended for persons older than 65 years of age; pregnant women; persons with diabetes mellitus, chronic renal failure, or alcoholism; persons undergoing treatment with anticonvulsants; and persons who are malnourished. For persons who are intolerant of INH or who are presumed to have INH-resistant infection, 4 months of RMP (10 mg/kg, maximum 600 mg) is an acceptable alternative.[171]

A 2-month regimen of daily RMP/PZA is as effective as a 12-month daily regimen of INH in HIV-infected adults.[172] Unfortunately, initial enthusiasm for this 2-month regimen waned following numerous reports of severe liver injury and death in HIV-negative individuals.[144] Providers choosing to use this nonpreferred regimen should exercise caution, including intensive clinical and laboratory monitoring. It should be avoided in persons with underlying liver disease or those who have had INH-associated hepatotoxicity, and no more than 2 weeks of drug should be dispensed at a time.[144]

Optimal treatment of latent tuberculous infection when drug resistance is likely is not known. Although one study advocated first-line use of RMP-containing regimens for immigrants to the United States from particular countries,[173] routine application of this strategy is premature. When the likelihood of drug resistance is substantial, there is much to recommend treating the patient as if drug-resistant active infection were present, using a 6-month regimen (INH/RMP/STM/PZA or INH/RMP/EMB/PZA for 2 months and INH/RMP for 4 months).

Risk of Isoniazid Hepatotoxicity during Treatment of Latent Tuberculous Infection

A U.S. Public Health Service survey found the incidence of probable hepatitis per 1000 persons to be 0 for those younger than age 20, 3 for ages 20 to 34, 12 for ages 35 to 49, 23 for ages 50 to 64, and 8 for age older than 64.[140] The incidence in daily drinkers of alcohol was also high (26.5 to 1000). The number in the elderly was probably falsely low because of a small sample size. A much larger experience recorded hepatitis in 4.6% of patients older than 65.[174] A large European study reported a hepatitis incidence of 520 per 100,000 population; the figure was 280 per 100,000 for those younger than 35 years and 770 per 100,000 for those older than 54 years.[175] Most hepatitis develops within the first 3 months, and the risk of death, once clinical hepatitis develops, is approximately 9%.[140] Biochemical monitoring will likely prevent some deaths, because there is a subclinical phase of at least several weeks. Byrd and colleagues recorded elevated

serum transaminase levels in 18.3% of patients taking INH but no deaths in a biochemically monitored population. Many patients with severe biochemical hepatitis would not have been detected by monitoring symptoms only.[176] In contrast, one public health clinic reported only 11 cases of clinical hepatotoxicity and no deaths among more than 11,000 persons receiving INH over a 7-year period.[177] Based on this and other considerations, emphasis is now placed on clinic monitoring for signs and symptoms of adverse effects, with prompt evaluation if these develop. Recent recommendations advocate routine baseline and follow-up laboratory monitoring only for persons with HIV infection, pregnant and early postpartum women, and persons with chronic liver disease or who use alcohol regularly.[92]

Snider and Caras analyzed 177 cases of fatal hepatitis from various sources,[178] and estimated a case rate of 14 per 100,000 of those starting and 23 per 100,000 of those completing therapy. Sixty-nine percent were female, and clustering around pregnancy suggested that treatment of latent tuberculous infection should be avoided at this time. However, many experts agree that treating latent tuberculous infection during pregnancy should not be delayed if the infection was recently acquired or in HIV-positive women.[92] Although INH toxicity has been regarded as very rare in young persons, 9% of fatalities were in persons younger than age 20. Israel and co-workers reported three cases of rapidly fatal hepatitis occurring 3 to 6 months into therapy given for indications that in retrospect were questionable.[169]

Assumptions underlying the usual recommendations for treating latent tuberculous infection often group together populations with widely disparate likelihoods of acquiring active tuberculosis. Although the benefits of treatment in many circumstances are well established, these fatalities, together with the fact that INH is given five times more frequently for treating latent tuberculous infection than for primary treatment in the United States, indicate that the decision to prescribe chemoprophylaxis is not trivial.[169] Groups for whom treatment of latent tuberculous infection is indicated are listed in Table 248-10.

Treatment of Contacts of Active Cases

The U.S. Public Health Service contact study showed that treatment of latent tuberculous infection decreased the incidence of subsequent tuberculosis among contacts of active cases from 1550 to 610 cases per 100,000, a 61% reduction over 10 years.[179] In those who were tuberculin negative when first surveyed, the figures (per 100,000) were 510 without and 150 with chemoprophylaxis, a 59% reduction. Estimates of the risk to contacts in some smaller studies are much higher. One year of INH therapy is only 60% to 80% effective in preventing disease, with failures most often caused by nonadherence. INH prophylaxis

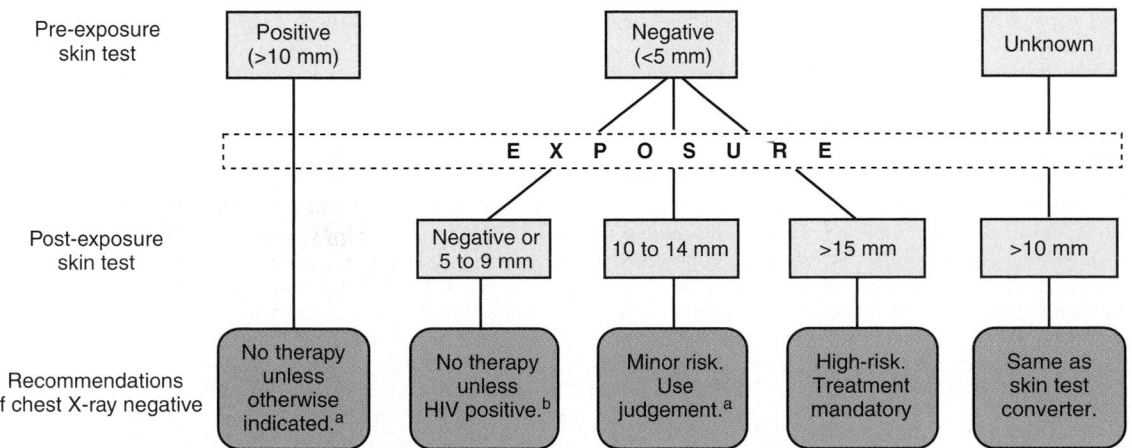

FIGURE 248-8. Proposed strategy for managing health care workers following inadvertent exposure to an active case of tuberculosis. [a]For younger persons preventive therapy should be considered regardless of exposure. [b]If the person has been very heavily exposed, isoniazid should be started. This can be discontinued if the skin test result is still negative. *(From Stead WW. Management of health care workers after inadvertent exposure to tuberculosis: A guide for the use of preventive therapy. Ann Intern Med. 1995;122:906-912.)*

may also fail in drug-resistant infections. It seems unlikely that prophylactic INH monotherapy taken reliably by contacts results in subsequent INH resistance.

Treatment of latent tuberculous infection is indicated for most persons later found to be tuberculin positive after contact with an active case. The advantage is clearest in the young, in whom the risk of INH toxicity is least and the likelihood of recent infection greatest. Tuberculin-positive young adults who are close contacts of active cases should also be treated, but in persons older than 50 years of age, it is reasonable to observe rather than treat in view of the greater risk of INH toxicity and the greater possibility that tuberculin reactions represent remote infections. The case for treating tuberculin-negative contacts of active cases is less secure. Most authorities would advise treatment in those younger than age 5, with repeated tuberculin testing after 3 months. If skin test conversion occurs, a 12-month course can be completed. If the skin test result is negative and the source case is no longer infectious, INH can be discontinued. In older tuberculin-negative contacts, the skin test should be repeated in 2 to 3 months and treatment given only if the test result becomes positive.

To address the risk to health care workers inadvertently exposed to tuberculosis, Stead reviewed 33 previously investigated hospital and nursing home outbreaks.[94] In this setting, on discovering that exposures have occurred, a list of all exposed personnel and their skin test results before exposure should be assembled. Nonreactors should be retested 8 weeks after the exposure to allow time for skin test conversion. However, if exposure is particularly heavy, or in HIV-positive health care workers, preventive therapy should be started even before retesting. Treatment can later be discontinued in HIV-negative persons if they remain tuberculin negative. Based on extensive experience, Stead favored a tuberculin conversion of 15 mm or greater, rather than 5 mm or greater as recommended by the CDC,[92] as a definite indication for preventive therapy after exposure. General guidelines for managing health care workers inadvertently exposed to tuberculosis are presented in Figure 248-8 (see "Treatment of Latent Tuberculous Infection").[94]

Treatment of Quiescent, Previously Untreated Pulmonary Tuberculosis

Tuberculin-positive patients with fibrotic upper lobe lesions and patients who had active tuberculosis before drugs were available relapse frequently that a year of INH prophylaxis is advised. Representative studies demonstrated relapse rates (per 100,000) of 2450 over 5 years in controls compared with 350 with treatment[180]; 1940 over 7 years in controls compared with 560 with treatment[181]; and 1430 over 5 years in controls compared with 360 with treatment.[175] The longer the lesion has been stable, the less is the risk of relapse. In the major European study, the relapse rate in untreated patients (1450 over 5 years) was about 450 in the first year but fell to one third of that by the fifth year, far less than their risk of INH hepatotoxicity.[175] It was concluded that 6 months of INH prophylaxis might be preferred. Conversely, a Canadian study questioned whether INH alone is sufficient if these cases represent low-grade active disease.[180] Of 1017 patients treated for 1 year with INH alone, three relapsed, two with drug-resistant infections, whereas none relapsed when treated with INH and PAS. The declining risk of acquiring active disease over time, and the greater effectiveness of combined drug treatment in the Canadian study, suggest that treatment of presumably quiescent lesions only benefits cases that are low-grade active infections, for which single-drug therapy may not be appropriate. Some have suggested multiple-drug therapy (INH/RMP/STM/PZA or INH/RMP/PZA) for 3 months and then stopping if cultures are negative and the roentgenogram is stable. This has the advantage of being sufficient treatment for sputum- and culture-negative active tuberculosis and includes drugs (RMP and PZA) that kill slowly metabolizing organisms.

Treatment of the Tuberculin Converter

The first 2 years after tuberculin conversion is the period of greatest risk for development of active disease. Most authorities recommend treatment of latent tuberculous infection for any person known to have converted within 2 years, regardless of age. Reactions that require boosting to be elicited are not recent conversions and do not require treatment.

Treatment of Positive Tuberculin Reactions of Uncertain Duration

All infections in children may be presumed to be recent. In developed countries, this is also the case in adolescents and young adults (see Fig. 248-2). Based on a calculation of the relative risk of tuberculosis versus hepatitis, the CDC had previously recommended that tuberculin-positive persons younger than age 35 with no contraindications and no special epidemiologic risks should receive treatment of latent tuberculous infection, but more recent guidelines no longer suggest such an age cutoff. The size of the reaction meriting treatment ranges from 5 to 10 mm, depending on characteristics of the individual and likelihood of recently acquired infection, as indicated in Table 248-10.[92]

Treating Latent Tuberculous Infection in Persons with Human Immunodeficiency Virus Infection

Tuberculin-positive, HIV-positive intravenous drug users acquire active tuberculosis at approximately 8%/year, and treatment of latent tuberculous infection with INH effectively prevents this.[65] Studies in the same population have also shown that the risk of active tuberculosis developing in HIV-positive persons with cutaneous anergy (to tuberculin and a panel of skin-test antigens) was almost as great.[182] As indicated in Table 248-10, the CDC recommends that a tuberculin reaction of 5 mm be considered an indication for treating latent tuberculous infection in persons with known or suspected HIV infection. Some have suggested that 2 mm of induration may be more appropriate. There is general agreement that, when indicated, INH treatment of latent tuberculous infection should be prescribed to HIV-positive persons for 9 months.[92]

Considerable effort has been devoted to determining whether testing for skin test anergy to "control" antigens might be helpful in this situation. The CDC in 1991 recommended that HIV-infected persons who are anergic and members of populations with at least a 10% incidence of tuberculosis should receive treatment of latent tuberculous infection.[102] However, anergy testing in this situation offers no practical advantage, and its utility has since been refuted by two studies.[103,104] Therefore, since 1997 the CDC stopped recommending routine anergy testing for HIV-positive persons at risk for tuberculosis (see "Tuberculin Testing and Human Immunodeficiency Virus Infection").[105]

HIV-infected patients who need treatment of latent tuberculous infection but are not receiving protease inhibitors or the non-nucleoside reverse transcriptase inhibitors nevirapine or delavirdine can be given daily therapy with RMP 600 mg and PZA 2.0 g (adult doses) for 2 months. Efficacy appears comparable to that obtained with 9 months of INH 300 mg daily.[161,183] It is possible that rifabutin may be used with PZA for 2 months provided that the patient is not taking ritonavir, delavirdine, or hard-gel saquinavir, but rifabutin toxicity and decreased antiretroviral effect are possible consequences. The advantages of the 2-month regimens are better likelihood of compliance and an overall cost saving.[183]

Tuberculin-Positive Persons with Additional Risk Factors

Treatment of latent tuberculous infection is advised for tuberculin-positive individuals from groups with a known high incidence of tuberculosis, including immigrants from developing countries, intravenous drug users, the homeless, prisoners, and residents of long-term care facilities.[93] An argument has been made for treating latent tuberculous infection in tuberculin-positive patients after gastrectomy and jejunoileal bypass surgery for obesity. There is a greatly increased incidence of tuberculosis in patients undergoing chronic renal dialysis[47] and in renal transplant patients. The regular occurrence of pyridoxine deficiency in uremia complicates the situation. Preventive therapy has been recommended in tuberculin-positive patients with silicosis, but relapse after preventive therapy has been observed. Treatment of latent tuberculous infection has also been recommended for tuberculin-positive patients with myeloproliferative disorders and hematologic malignancies, especially when corticosteroids are given, but with no real documentation of risks or benefits. Prolonged treatment with high doses of corticosteroids undoubtedly predisposes to activation of latent tuberculosis. Latently infected individuals who are to receive the anti–TNF-α agent infliximab should receive treatment of latent tuberculous infection.[117]

The Nursing Home Problem. A major analysis by Stead and colleagues showed that 3.8% of men and 2.3% of women who were tuberculin positive on admission to nursing homes acquired active disease, and that this could be decreased 10-fold with treatment of latent tuberculous infection.[174] However, because of the high incidence of INH toxicity and drug intolerance, the authors did not recommend treating latent tuberculous infection in this group. Treatment of latent tuberculous infection was clearly beneficial in patients who tuberculin convert after admission, with 11.6% of men and 7.6% of women acquiring active disease without treatment of latent tuberculous infection but only 0.2% with treatment.

Vaccination

BCG, a live-attenuated vaccine derived from a strain of *M. bovis,* is used in young children throughout much of the world. Most evidence indicates that BCG vaccination of children results in a 60% to 80% decrease in the incidence of tuberculosis.[184] Its use is reasonable in high-prevalence situations, greater than those that now exist in the United States and most industrialized nations. It should be administered only to tuberculin-negative persons. Although BCG vaccine does not prevent infection, it usually prevents progression to clinical disease, and it is highly effective in preventing disseminated disease in young children. Infants and children in the United States for whom vaccination is recommended include those at unavoidable risk for exposure to tuberculosis, especially MDR tuberculosis, and for whom other methods of control and prevention are not effective.[150] Vaccination may also be reasonable for certain groups residing in high-prevalence areas, such as some military and foreign service personnel. The risk of disseminated BCG infection after vaccination in infants born to HIV-positive mothers is small. BCG should not be given to persons known to be infected with HIV. Prior BCG vaccination does not alter guidelines for tuberculin skin test interpretation.

The effect of BCG vaccination on tuberculin reactivity depends on the age at vaccination and interval before skin testing. In a study in Montreal, children vaccinated once with BCG before the age of 1 year had a 7.9% prevalence of positive tuberculin skin tests 10 to 25 years later, comparable to those who never received BCG.[185] Prevalence of positive tuberculin skin tests was 18% among those vaccinated between 1 and 5 years of age and 25.4% among those vaccinated after age 5. Although tuberculin reactivity wanes after infant BCG vaccination, later skin testing can cause a booster effect, a potential source of confusion. Interestingly, there is no relationship between tuberculin reactivity after BCG vaccination and protection against development of active tuberculosis.[95]

Intravesicular BCG, used to treat bladder cancer, is a rare cause of miliary granuloma in the liver or lung, psoas abscess, or osteomyelitis.[186-188] This mycobacteriosis responds to treatment with INH and RMP. Developing a more effective vaccine for tuberculosis is a high priority, and candidate vaccines are being developed.[189]

EXTRAPULMONARY TUBERCULOSIS

Extrapulmonary tuberculosis can be divided into three groups based on pathogenesis. The first comprises superficial mucosal foci resulting from the spread of infectious pulmonary secretions via the respiratory and gastrointestinal tracts. Such lesions were once almost inevitable complications of extensive cavitary pulmonary disease but are now rare. The second group comprises foci established by contiguous spread, such as from a subpleural focus into the pleural space. The third group comprises foci established by lymphohematogenous dissemination, either at the time of primary infection or, less commonly, from established chronic pulmonary or extrapulmonary foci. Progression of foci established by lymphohematogenous dissemination implies some degree of compromised immunity.

Acquired Immunodeficiency Syndrome and Extrapulmonary Tuberculosis

Before 1985, cases of pulmonary tuberculosis decreased each year, whereas the number of extrapulmonary cases remained stable at about 4000 per year. The percentage of cases caused by extrapulmonary disease subsequently increased, largely as a result of coinfection with HIV, and in 1991, 21% of extrapulmonary cases in the United States were associated with AIDS.[190,191] Unlike in non-AIDS patients, concomitant pulmonary and extrapulmonary disease was very common in AIDS patients with tuberculosis. Cases of HIV-associated pulmonary and extrapulmonary tuberculosis have declined in the United States since 1992.[30] There are certain distinguishing features of AIDS-associated extrapulmonary tuberculosis. The frequency of disseminated disease (more than one focus or progressive hematogenous disease) is high, 38% in one series,[191] and rapidly progressive forms with diffuse pulmonary infiltrates, acute respiratory failure, and disseminated intravascular coagulation have been observed. Tuberculosis pleuritis, when it occurs, is often bilateral and part of a disseminated process. Visceral lymphadenopathy, both mediastinal and abdominal, is frequent, and a contrast-enhanced CT scan showing nodes with central low attenuation suggests the diagnosis. Abscesses of the liver, pancreas, prostate, spleen, chest, abdominal wall, and other soft tissues have also been described.

General Comments on Treatment of Extrapulmonary Tuberculosis

Extrapulmonary foci usually respond to treatment more rapidly than does cavitary pulmonary tuberculosis. Therapy with three-drug regimens (INH, PZA, and RMP) for 6 months, with PZA stopped after 2 months, is advised in most cases caused by drug-sensitive organisms, the exception being children who have miliary tuberculosis, bone and joint involvement, or tuberculous meningitis. In these cases, at least 12 months of therapy is recommended.[150] Extrapulmonary disease at sites that carry special risk to the patient, such as the central nervous system, the spine, and possibly the pericardium, should be treated with maximal chemotherapy. Other foci of drug-sensitive extrapulmonary tuberculosis respond well to INH and RMP for 9 months or INH and EMB for 18 months.

Miliary Tuberculosis

The term *miliary tuberculosis,* first used to describe the resemblance of the pathologic lesions to millet seeds, now describes any progressive disseminated hematogenous tuberculosis. Miliary tuberculosis can be roughly divided into three groups: (1) acute miliary tuberculosis associated with a brisk and histologically typical tissue reaction; (2) cryptic miliary tuberculosis, a more prolonged illness with subtle clinical findings and an attenuated histologic response; and (3) nonreactive tuberculosis characterized by huge numbers of organisms, little organized tissue response, and often a septic or typhoidal clinical picture.[87]

Usual (Acute) Miliary Tuberculosis

In the prechemotherapy era, miliary tuberculosis occurred either soon after primary infection in children or young adults or as a terminal event in untreated chronic organ tuberculosis. In children, the illness is acute or subacute, with high intermittent fevers, night sweats, and occasional rigors. Pleural effusion, peritonitis, or meningitis occurs in as many as two thirds of persons. The illness in young adults is usually more chronic and initially less severe. However, miliary tuberculosis is now more frequently observed in older individuals, often with underlying illnesses or conditions that may confuse diagnosis.

Four large series in the chemotherapy era[192-195] have emphasized the frequency of miliary tuberculosis in minority racial groups, and the importance of underlying conditions such as alcoholism, cirrhosis, neoplasm, pregnancy, rheumatologic disease, and treatment with

TABLE 248-11 Miliary Tuberculosis

	Study			
	Biehl[192]	*Munt*[193]	*Maartens et al.*[194]	*Kim et al.*[195]
Number of cases	69	68	109	38%*
Mean age	51	50	—	60%*
Minority race	85%	87%	94%	79%*
Predisposing factors	15%	31%	42%	66%*
Weeks of symptoms	2-16	3-24	1-52	—
Meningitis	17%	19%	22%	—
Tuberculin positive	61%	84%	43%	28%
Miliary roentgenogram	93%	97%	—	91%*
Other foci of tuberculosis	32%	23%	—	—
Positive sputum smear	—	39%	33% (21/64)	36% (12/33)
Marrow diagnostic[†]	—	20%	41% (9/22)	9% (2/22)
Transbronchial biopsy diagnostic[‡]	—	—	76% (39/51)	62% (5/8)

*This percentage includes interstitial and diffuse alevolar patterns.
[†]Marrow diagnostic if caseating granuloma or acid-fast bacilli are seen.
[‡]Transbronchial biopsy diagnostic if any granuloma or acid-fast bacilli are seen.

immunosuppressive agents (Table 248-11).[192-195] There is usually no prior history of tuberculosis, and the onset is often subtle. Generalized symptoms of fever, anorexia, weakness, and weight loss are nonspecific. Headache, when present, may indicate meningitis; abdominal pain may be due to peritonitis; and pleural pain may result from pleuritis. Physical findings are likewise usually nonspecific, but a careful search for cutaneous eruptions, sinus tracts, scrotal masses, and lymphadenopathy may yield a prompt biopsy diagnosis. A miliary infiltrate on chest roentgenogram is the most helpful finding and the usual reason miliary tuberculosis is suspected (Fig. 248-9). Unfortunately, many patients, particularly the elderly, succumb to miliary tuberculosis before the chest roentgenogram becomes abnormal.[196] The white

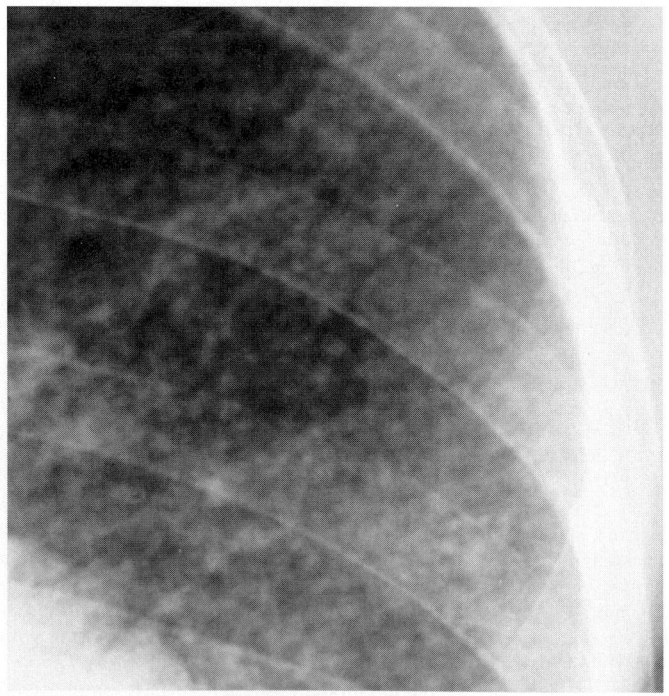

FIGURE 248-9. Detail of a chest roentgenogram (left midlung zone) showing countless 0.5- to 1.0-mm nodules typical of miliary tuberculosis.

blood cell count is usually normal, and anemia is the rule. Hyponatremia with the laboratory features of inappropriate secretion of antidiuretic hormone is frequent, particularly with meningitis.[193] Addison's disease should be considered as a cause of hyponatremia, especially if corticosteroid treatment is anticipated. Elevations of alkaline phosphatase and transaminases are common, and hypoxemia, hypocapnia, and impairment of pulmonary diffusion capacity can be demonstrated. Cultures of sputum, gastric contents, urine, and CSF are positive in some combination in most cases, but smears of sputum and pulmonary secretions alone are positive in less than one third of cases. Immediate diagnosis often results from examination of tissue (lymph nodes, scrotal masses when present, liver biopsy, or bone marrow specimens). Mycobacterial blood cultures may also be positive. Transbronchial biopsy, however, is the best way to obtain tissue and should be performed promptly when the diagnosis is suspected.[197] The finding of caseating granulomas or acid-fast bacilli is virtually diagnostic, but even noncaseating granulomas should prompt therapy.

Rapid diagnosis is mandatory. However, treatment should be initiated immediately based on strong clinical suspicion, as mortality from miliary tuberculosis is most often due to delays in treatment. Therapy with at least INH, RMP, and PZA is advised, especially if meningitis is present. Response may be prompt or may take several weeks. Fulminant miliary tuberculosis may be associated with severe refractory hypoxemia (adult respiratory distress syndrome) and disseminated intravascular coagulation. In such cases, adjunctive corticosteroids (60 to 80 mg of prednisone daily) are indicated. Some also advise corticosteroids in debilitated patients with a poor initial response to therapy.

Cryptic Miliary Tuberculosis and Late Generalized (Chronic Hematogenous) Tuberculosis

Chronic organ tuberculosis is probably always associated with intermittent, nonprogressive seeding of the blood stream. In some individuals, however, especially as age or other factors compromise immunity, this becomes continuous and produces progressive hematogenous tuberculosis long after the primary infection.[198] The term *cryptic miliary tuberculosis* usually describes older patients with miliary tuberculosis in whom the diagnosis is obscure because of normal chest roentgenograms, negative tuberculin test results, and often confounding underlying illnesses to which symptoms are mistakenly attributed[199]; this term has also been applied to miliary tuberculosis diagnosed at autopsy.[196]

The foci responsible for late generalized tuberculosis are often clinically silent, for example, renal, genitourinary, osseous, or visceral lymph nodes.[198] Chronic pulmonary foci are at times involved but are rarely the only source. More than one seeding focus is usually present, suggesting a change in immune status that favors simultaneous reactivation. The clinical picture is frequently fever of unknown origin, often with a normal chest roentgenogram and a negative tuberculin test result. Fever may be absent, and in one series diagnosis was made ante mortem in only 15% of cases.[198] Late generalized tuberculosis may be associated with major hematologic abnormalities (see below).

Nonreactive Tuberculosis

The histologic appearance in this rare form of disseminated hematogenous tuberculosis shows nonspecific necrosis containing disintegrating polymorphonuclear leukocytes and enormous numbers of tubercle bacilli.[87] In the typical case, granulomas and epithelioid cells are lacking, although intermediate cases have areas more typical for tuberculosis. The gross pathologic findings are soft abscesses from minute to 1 cm, which always involve the liver and spleen, usually the marrow, commonly the lungs and kidneys, but never the meninges. The clinical picture may be overwhelming sepsis, with splenomegaly and often an inconspicuous diffuse mottling on the chest roentgenogram. Major hematologic abnormalities are common (see next section).

Miliary Tuberculosis and Hematologic Abnormalities

Some patients with late generalized tuberculosis and most with nonreactive tuberculosis have serious hematologic abnormalities, including leukopenia, thrombocytopenia, anemia, leukemoid reactions, myelofibrosis, and polycythemia.[200] Leukemoid reactions may suggest acute leukemia, although most patients in whom hematogenous tuberculosis coexists with the clinical picture of leukemia have both diseases. Disseminated tuberculosis should be considered when pancytopenia is associated with fever and weight loss or as a cause of other obscure hematologic disorders.

Primary Hepatic Tuberculosis

Rarely, miliary tuberculosis may mimic cholangitis with fever, liver function test abnormalities suggestive of obstructive disease, and little evidence of hepatocellular disease. Diagnosis is made by liver biopsy.

Miliary Tuberculosis in Acquired Immunodeficiency Syndrome

In AIDS patients, 10% with tuberculosis and 38% with extrapulmonary tuberculosis have miliary disease.[128,191] Major constitutional symptoms and hectic fevers are characteristic. The chest roentgenogram is abnormal in 80% and may include typical miliary mottling. Only 10% of patients are tuberculin positive.[128] The sputum smear is positive in only 25%,[191] but cultures of many materials will be positive, including blood in 50% to 60%. Biopsies during life show typical tuberculous histologic appearance but with more stainable organisms than in non-HIV miliary tuberculosis. In fatal cases, in contrast, the histologic picture is often nonreactive tuberculosis.[128]

Miliary tuberculosis in HIV-infected persons may also cause the acute respiratory distress syndrome or tuberculous papular skin lesions. Smears of respiratory secretions are positive in 80%.

Abscesses of various soft tissue and visceral organs have been described in patients with AIDS and tuberculosis, usually with other evidence of disseminated disease. Locations include the liver, spleen, pancreas, psoas muscle without spinal involvement, mediastinum, neck, chest wall, abdominal wall, and prostate.[128,191,201] Diagnosis is usually made by CT or ultrasonography and confirmed by needle or catheter aspiration. Clinical response to chemotherapy and drainage is usually good. An abscess may appear or reappear during therapy and respond to repeated aspiration.

Central Nervous System Tuberculosis

Tuberculous Meningitis

This condition is usually caused by rupture of a subependymal tubercle into the subarachnoid space rather than direct hematogenous seeding. Meningitis complicating miliary disease usually develops several weeks into the illness. In childhood, meningitis is an early postprimary event, and three fourths of these persons have a concurrently active primary complex, pleural effusion, or miliary tuberculosis. Subependymal foci may remain quiescent indefinitely before rupturing. This may follow head trauma or be associated with general depression of host immunity as a result of alcoholism or other factors.

Pathologic Features. Meningeal involvement is most pronounced at the base of the brain. In long-standing cases, a gelatinous mass may extend from the pons to the optic nerves, being most prominent adjacent to the optic chiasm. In more chronic cases, fibrous tissue may encase cranial nerves. Vasculitis of local arteries and veins may lead to aneurysm, thrombosis, and focal hemorrhagic infarction. Perforating vessels to the basal ganglia and pons are most often involved, producing movement disorders or lacunar infarcts; involvement of branches of the middle cerebral artery may cause hemiparesis.

Clinical Findings. The usual illness begins with a prodrome of malaise, intermittent headache, and low-grade fever, followed within 2 to 3 weeks by protracted headache, vomiting, confusion, meningismus, and focal neurologic signs. The clinical spectrum is broad, ranging from chronic headache or subtle mental status changes to sudden, severe meningitis progressing to coma. Fever may be absent, and the peripheral white blood cell count is usually normal. Mild anemia is usual, and hyponatremia resulting from inappropriate antidiuretic hormone secretion is common. Evidence of concomitant extrameningeal tuberculosis is present in roughly three fourths of cases,[202] with mil-

iary shadowing on the chest roentgenogram being most suggestive. In many cases, however, there are no clinical or historical clues to suggest tuberculosis.

The cornerstone of diagnosis is examination of the CSF. The cell count generally ranges from 0 to 1500/mm³; the protein is usually moderately elevated; and the CSF glucose, said to be characteristically low, was greater than 45 mg/100 mL in 83% of cases in one large series.[202] A lymphocytic predominance is usual, although one quarter of cases demonstrate a polymorphonuclear pleocytosis, usually early in the course. Identifying bacilli often requires examination of large volumes of fluid from repeated lumbar punctures. In one study, stains of sediment revealed acid-fast bacilli in 37% of cases on initial examination, but in 90% when fluids from four large-volume lumbar punctures were examined.[202] Initial atypical findings such as a polymorphonuclear pleocytosis, normal glucose, or even entirely normal CSF indices evolve to more typical mononuclear cell predominance with hypoglycorrhachia over time. PCR for *M. tuberculosis* may be very helpful in this setting, although false-negative results have been reported.[203,204] In patients with meningitis, CT or magnetic resonance imaging may reveal rounded lesions presumed to be tuberculomas, basilar arachnoiditis, cerebral infarction, and hydrocephalus (Fig. 248-10).

Prognosis is influenced by age, duration of symptoms, and neurologic deficits. Mortality is greatest in patients younger than age 5 (20%), older than age 50 (60%), or in whom illness has been present for more than 2 months (80%).[202] Clinical staging is based on neurologic status: stage 1 = rational, no focal neurologic signs or hydrocephalus; stage 2 = confusion or focal neurologic deficits; stage 3 = stuporous or dense paraplegia or hemiplegia. Patients who are stage 1 at the start of treatment are likely to recover, but approximately half of stage 3 patients die or recover with severe residual neurologic defects.[202] HIV infection does not appear to alter the clinical and laboratory manifestations or the prognosis of tuberculous meningitis, except that central nervous system mass lesions are more likely.[205]

Treatment. In the presence of meningeal inflammation, both INH and PZA reach concentrations in the CSF equaling those in blood. RMP penetrates the blood-brain barrier less well but still adequately. All three drugs should be used. Increased dosage of INH, 10 mg/kg and

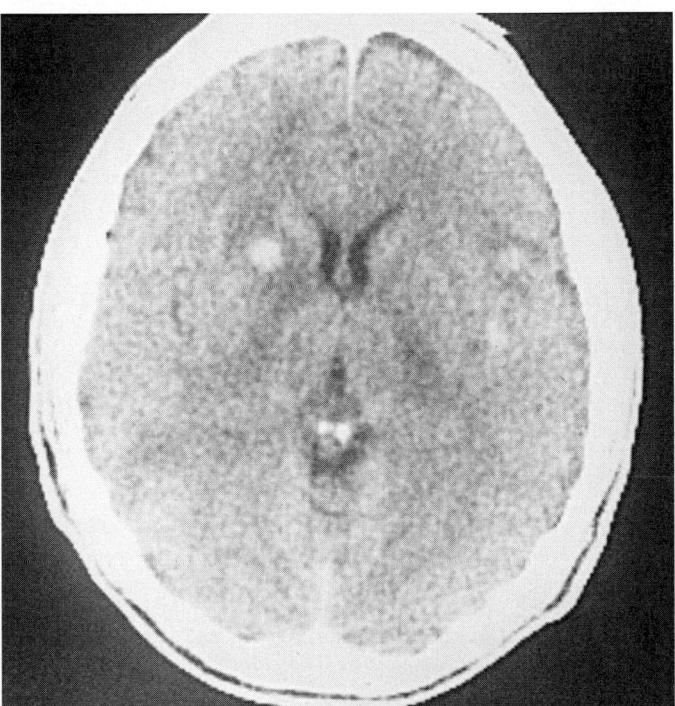

FIGURE 248-10. Multiple cerebral cortical densities on computed tomography of a patient with tuberculous meningitis.

somewhat higher in children, may be preferred until improvement has been established. Otherwise, the dosages are as for pulmonary tuberculosis.

Most authorities recommend adjunctive corticosteroids in stage 2 and stage 3 patients, beginning prednisone at 60 to 80 mg daily. This may be gradually reduced after 1 to 2 weeks and discontinued by 4 to 6 weeks, as guided by symptoms. Symptoms and CSF abnormalities may rebound transiently as steroids are tapered. Ventricular shunting may be beneficial if symptomatic hydrocephalus supervenes.[175]

Tuberculomas

Intracranial tuberculomas are space-occupying lesions that may manifest with seizures. They are most frequently multiple but can be single, appearing on imaging studies as avascular masses with surrounding edema. When diagnosis is secure, chemotherapy should be attempted before resorting to surgery. Corticosteroids reduce edema and decrease symptoms, and chemotherapy prevents spread of infection in cases diagnosed at operation. In India, where tuberculomas are frequent, biopsy confirmation followed by medical therapy without resection is the preferred management.

Tuberculous Spinal Meningitis

Infrequently, tuberculosis causes spinal meningitis with or without intracranial involvement. In advanced cases, the cord may be completely encased in a gelatinous exudate. An intramedullary tuberculoma or an extradural granulomatous mass can cause symptoms without meningeal involvement. Nerve root or cord compression causes pain, bladder or rectal sphincter weakness, hypesthesia, anesthesia, paresthesias in the distribution of a nerve root, or paralysis. Subarachnoid block may cause CSF protein concentrations to be extremely high, with or without cells.

Tuberculous Pleurisy (Serofibrinous Pleurisy with Effusion)

Early Postprimary Pleurisy with Effusion

When infection occurs early in life, tuberculous pleurisy with effusion follows the primary infection within weeks or months. The pathogenesis is rupture of a large subpleural component of the primary infection and delivery of infectious, antigenic material into the pleural space, with inflammation and seeding of foci over the visceral and parietal pleura. In the past, this affected mostly adolescents and young adults, and rarely older adults. Immediate prognosis was excellent, with resolution of the effusion within several months in as many as 90% of cases. However, studies of soldiers during World War II (before chemotherapy) demonstrated that 65% relapsed with chronic organ tuberculosis within 5 years.[206] Early postprimary serofibrinous pleurisy with effusion identifies quantitatively large primary infections with a relatively poor long-term prognosis.

Pleurisy with Effusion Complicating Chronic Pulmonary Tuberculosis

In contrast to early studies,[206] an increasing proportion of pleurisy with effusion since the early 1980s occurs in older individuals with chronic pulmonary tuberculosis, often with complicating illnesses such as cirrhosis or congestive heart failure to which the effusion is mistakenly attributed. In one study, one half of pleurisy cases occurred in the setting of established chronic pulmonary tuberculosis.[207]

Pleurisy with Effusion Complicating Miliary Tuberculosis

Pleural effusions occur in 10% to 30% of cases of miliary tuberculosis.[192,194] These may be associated with other progressive extrapulmonary foci and involvement of other serous membranes. Cases with coexistent pleural (at times bilateral), peritoneal, and pericardial tuberculosis have been referred to as *tuberculous polyserositis*.

Clinical Features and Diagnosis

The clinical presentation may be low grade and subtle or abrupt and severe, easily confused with acute bacterial pneumonia. Cough and pleuritic chest pain are usual, and fever may be high. The effusion is usually less than massive and almost always unilateral except when associated with miliary tuberculosis. The pleural fluid typically contains 500 to 2500 white blood cells/mm^3, with more than 90% lymphocytes in two thirds of cases. However, 38% of cases in one series had predominantly polymorphonuclear leukocytes, and 15% had more than 90% polymorphonuclear leukocytes on the first tap.[208] Repeated taps demonstrate a shift to lymphocytic predominance. Mesothelial cells, characteristic of neoplastic effusions, are sparse or absent, eosinophils are rarely present, and less than 10% of effusions are serosanguineous. The pleural fluid protein usually exceeds 2.5 g/dL, glucose is usually moderately low compared with serum values but rarely less than 20 mg/dL, and the pH is almost always 7.3 or lower and may be as low as 7.0. In the usual case of early postprimary pleurisy with effusion, the acid-fast stain of the fluid sediment is seldom positive, the culture is positive in 25% to 30%, pleural needle biopsy yields granulomas in 75%, and culture of a needle biopsy specimen may be positive even in the 25% of cases with nonspecific pleuritis on histologic examination. Cases complicating chronic pulmonary tuberculosis more often have positive pleural acid-fast smears (50%) and positive cultures (60%) but are less likely (25%) to demonstrate granulomas on pleural biopsy. Repeat pleural biopsy may be necessary to establish the diagnosis, and a small open pleural biopsy or pleuroscopy is diagnostic in virtually all cases. Smears of sputum or gastric fluid are rarely positive in early postprimary cases, and cultures are positive in 25% to 33%. In contrast, sputum smear is positive in 50% and the culture is positive in 60% of "reactivation" cases.[207] Tuberculosis is often not considered as the cause of a pleural effusion in an older person with complicating illnesses such as cirrhosis or congestive heart failure.[208] When pleural effusion complicates miliary tuberculosis, findings associated with the latter condition usually dominate the clinical picture. Elevated levels of adenosine deaminase in pleural fluid may be highly specific for tuberculosis, although this assay is not routinely available in the United States.

Treatment

Early postprimary pleural effusions spontaneously resolve in 2 to 4 months. Chemotherapy does not hasten resolution but prevents active disease elsewhere in the body, which will otherwise occur in two thirds of cases. Therapy is as described for pulmonary tuberculosis. Multiple thoracenteses are not necessary once the diagnosis is established and treatment initiated. A small minority heals with pleural fibrosis. Corticosteroid therapy hastens symptomatic improvement and fluid resorption, but no long-term benefit has been shown.

Tuberculous Empyema and Bronchopleural Fistula

Tuberculous empyema occurs when a major cavity ruptures into the pleural space. This often catastrophic illness is usually associated with bronchopleural fistula formation and frank pus. Before antituberculous drugs were available, tuberculous empyema was almost always rapidly fatal. It virtually never occurs in patients being treated with chemotherapy.

Late Complications of Collapse Therapy

Before the advent of potent antituberculous drugs, cavitary pulmonary tuberculosis was treated by collapse of the affected lung. Repeated instillation of air into the pleural space sometimes led to chronic, often calcified pleural shadows that could increase in size and cause pain, bronchopleural fistulas, and empyemas (both tuberculous and nontuberculous) many years later. CT may reveal collections of fluid under a thickened, calcified pleura. The response to prolonged antibiotic therapy, both antituberculous and routine, should be assessed before undertaking surgery in such cases. A conservative approach may be successful in almost half of cases, an important observation considering the technical difficulty of surgery.

Tuberculous Pericarditis

Tuberculous pericarditis is most often caused by extension from a contiguous focus of infection, usually mediastinal or hilar nodes but also the lung, spine, or sternum. Less commonly, it occurs during miliary tuberculosis. It may develop during the course of otherwise effective drug therapy, probably because the response of caseous lymph nodes to chemotherapy is not always predictable. Tuberculous pericarditis in patients with AIDS is uncommon in the United States, but in a series from Africa, 32 of 37 cases of effusive pericarditis were tuberculous, and 30 were in HIV-positive patients.[209]

Clinical Features and Diagnosis

The onset may be abrupt, resembling acute idiopathic pericarditis, or insidious, resembling congestive heart failure. Symptoms of infection or cardiovascular compromise may be present. Individual cases may present with chronic constrictive pericarditis and may be mistaken for cirrhosis with ascites. As many as 39% also have a pleural effusion, providing a convenient source for diagnostic fluid and tissue.[210,211] Echocardiography demonstrates effusion when present and may reveal multiple loculations suggestive of tuberculosis.

Pericarditis with effusion is usually quickly diagnosed based on physical findings and radiologic examination, but establishing that it is tuberculous in nature is often difficult. The tuberculin test result may be negative and evidence of extrapericardial tuberculosis lacking. In areas of high endemicity, a presumptive diagnosis is often correctly made.[210,211] In the United States, however, many cases are initially misdiagnosed as idiopathic, uremic, or rheumatoid pericarditis.[212]

Pericardiocentesis (ideally performed in a cardiac catheterization laboratory) is indicated for hemodynamic compromise. However, because pericardiocentesis carries risk, and because 90% of acute pericarditis in the United States is idiopathic (presumed viral) and subsides spontaneously in 2 to 3 weeks, some authorities advise against early pericardiocentesis. If improvement has not occurred by that time, a subxiphoid pericardial window can be performed. This provides both fluid and tissue for diagnosis, although in some cases the biopsy demonstrates only nonspecific inflammation.[210,211] Tuberculous pericardial fluid demonstrates many of the characteristics of tuberculous pleural fluid, with acid-fast smears being rarely positive and cultures being positive in approximately 50% of cases. The usefulness of adenosine deaminase determinations on pericardial fluid is not certain, but PCR for *M. tuberculosis* may be useful.

Treatment

Antibiotic treatment is the same as for pulmonary tuberculosis. In a large study from South Africa, treatment with corticosteroids (60 mg/day for 4 weeks, 30 mg/day for 4 weeks, and 15 mg/day for 2 weeks) decreased mortality from 11% in controls to 4% in treated cases. Pericardiectomies were also less frequently necessary in patients given corticosteroids (30% in controls vs. 11% in steroid-treated patients). Surgical drainage via a subxiphoid pericardial window at the outset did not decrease either mortality or the eventual need for pericardiectomy, although it provided diagnostic tissue and obviated the need for recurrent pericardiocenteses. However, 2% surgical mortality was associated with the procedure.[210]

When hemodynamic compromise persists for 6 to 8 weeks, pericardiectomy is usually indicated, and this should probably be performed earlier rather than later. Approximately two thirds of patients, however, do well without surgery.

Skeletal Tuberculosis

Pott's Disease (Tuberculous Spondylitis)

One third of cases of skeletal tuberculosis involve the spine, as a result of past hematogenous foci, contiguous disease, or lymphatic spread from pleural disease. The earliest focus is the anterior superior or inferior angle of the vertebral body. This usually spreads to the intervertebral disk and adjacent vertebra, producing the classic roentgenographic picture of anterior wedging of two adjacent vertebral bodies with destruction of the intervening disk and the physical finding of a tender spine prominence or gibbus. The lower thoracic spine is involved most frequently, the lumbar next, and the cervical and sacral least (Fig. 248-11).

In endemic countries, Pott's disease usually occurs in older children and young adults, but in developed countries it has become a disease of older persons.[213] Evidence of other foci of tuberculosis and

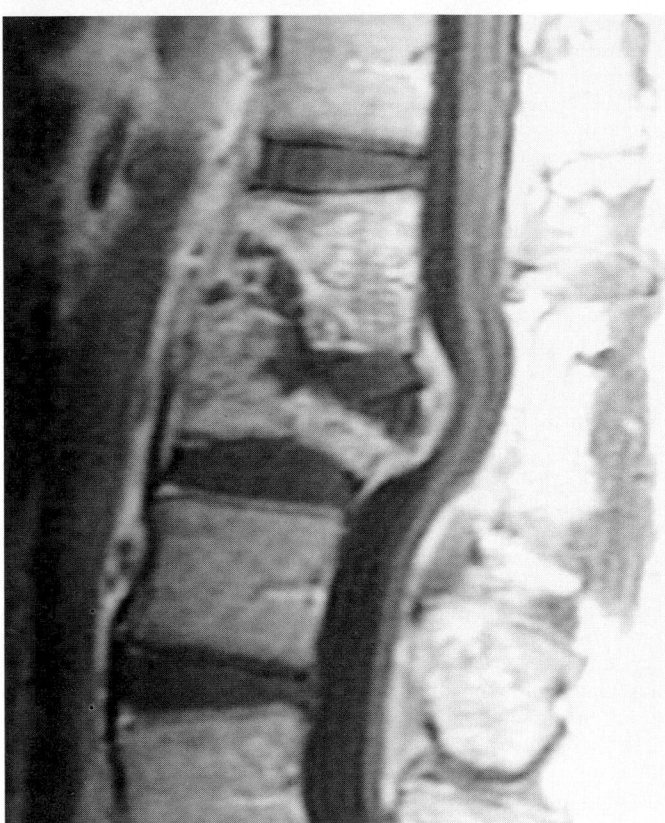

FIGURE 248-11. Magnetic resonance imaging study showing extensive destruction of L1 and L2 vertebral bodies and the intervening disk with posterior extension in a Pakistani man with Pott's disease.

systemic symptoms are often absent, early complaints may be simply back pain or stiffness with an initially normal roentgenogram, and diagnosis may be delayed until signs of advanced disease such as paralysis, deformity, or sinus formation develop. Bacilli are sparse, and smear and culture of pus or tissue are positive in only one half of cases. Histologic studies reveal granulomas with or without caseation in three fourths of cases.

Abscess and Sinus Formation. Paraspinal cold abscesses develop in 50% or more, in some cases appearing after treatment has been initiated, and in some cases visible only by CT or magnetic resonance imaging. The pus, confined by tight ligamentous investments, can dissect along tissue planes for long distances to present as a mass or a draining sinus in the supraclavicular space, above the posterior iliac crest in the Petit triangle, or in the groin, the buttock, or even the popliteal fossa. Perforation into the bowel producing a gas-filled psoas abscess has been reported. The abscess can spread infection to distant vertebral bodies, sometimes without affecting the intervening vertebrae.

Pott's Paraplegia. In approximately half of cases, weakness or paralysis of the lower extremities is present or develops after treatment has begun. Some authorities believe this is due to arachnoiditis and vasculitis.[213] Less frequently, it will be due to compression of the cord by an inflammatory mass or rarely pressure in the abscess producing ischemic changes in the subjacent cord. Inflammatory thrombosis of the anterior spinal artery can occur, and sudden cord compression may result from marked spinal instability.

Treatment. In adults as well as in infants and children, treatment for 12 months may be warranted for skeletal tuberculosis.[150] Major studies from Africa demonstrated a favorable response in 90% of cases without neurologic involvement treated with chemotherapy, modified bed rest until pain abated, and early ambulation, without orthopedic surgery.[214] Even with paraplegia, 40% of this young population did well with conservative management. In another series of older patients, 3 of

26 were treated with laminectomy, 2 without improvement; 12 of 15 cases with abscess required single or multiple needle aspirations; and 3 were drained surgically because of progression on therapy.[213] The authors emphasized that laminectomy should not be undertaken without demonstration of anatomic cord compression and suggested steroid therapy for paraplegia resulting from arachnoiditis. Advanced neurologic defects and severe instability of the spine may require more aggressive surgery.

Peripheral Osteoarticular Tuberculosis

Older reports described peripheral tuberculous arthritis as a chronic, slowly progressive monoarthritis in 90% of cases,[215] often without systemic symptoms or extraskeletal tuberculosis, and most frequently in the hip or knee. A history of trauma was common, followed weeks or months later by indolent progressive inflammation. More recent reports suggest a shift to an older population with a different clinical picture, including more systemic symptoms, multiple joint involvement, and periarticular abscess formation.[216] In one series, most patients older than 60 years had shoulder involvement.[217] Tenosynovitis of the hand, arthritis of the wrist, and carpal tunnel syndrome can be caused by tuberculosis. Clinical confusion occurs when tuberculosis superinfects joints previously involved with gouty or other arthritides.

The earliest manifestation of tuberculous arthritis is pain, which may precede signs of inflammation and roentgenographic changes by weeks or months. Roentgenograms initially may show soft tissue swelling but later demonstrate osteopenia, periarticular bony destruction, periosteal thickening, and eventually destruction of cartilage and bone. Cold abscesses and draining sinuses often develop in chronic cases.

In the absence of coexistent extra-articular tuberculosis, diagnosis almost always requires biopsy. Histologic features compatible with tuberculosis warrant chemotherapy, although other chronic infections (fungi, nontuberculous mycobacteria) can cause identical clinical and histologic pictures. For early cases, prolonged chemotherapy results in complete resolution. Surgery is necessary only when serious joint instability requires fusion, and then only after chemotherapy has failed.

Tuberculous osteomyelitis can affect any bone, including the ribs, skull, phalanx, pelvis, and long bones.[218] Other causes of osteomyelitis of the rib are rare, and tuberculosis is the most common infectious cause of single or multiple osteomyelitic rib lesions. Tuberculous osteomyelitis outside the vertebral body presents as a cold abscess, with swelling and only modest erythema or pain.

Genitourinary Tuberculosis

Renal Tuberculosis

Asymptomatic renal cortical foci may occur during all forms of tuberculosis. An autopsy study of pulmonary tuberculosis revealed unsuspected renal foci in 73% of cases, usually bilateral; 25% of miliary cases have positive urine cultures.[219] Cortical foci tend to be stable unless they penetrate to the medulla, where local factors favor accelerated infection. Most patients have evidence of concomitant extragenitourinary disease, usually pulmonary and most frequently inactive. In normal hosts, the interval between infection and active renal disease is usually years and sometimes decades. Local symptoms predominate, and advanced tissue destruction may occur long before the diagnosis is made. This is mostly a disease of middle-aged adults.

The clinical features in two large series of cases are presented in Table 248-12.[220,221] Although sterile pyuria is typical of renal tuberculosis, positive cultures for routine bacterial pathogens may lead to misdiagnosis, sometimes for years. The intravenous pyelogram is usually abnormal. Early findings are nonspecific, but later changes may be more suggestive, including papillary necrosis, ureteral strictures, "pipe stem" changes, "corkscrewing," "beading," hydronephrosis, gross parenchymal cavitation, and autonephrectomy. Focal calcification is particularly suggestive. The clinical disease is usually unilateral, although microscopic changes are probably always bilateral. Culture of three morning urine specimens for mycobacteria establishes the diagnosis in 80% to 90% of cases. When a renal abnormality is present but urine cultures are negative, cytologic studies and culture of material obtained by fine-needle biopsy may be diagnostic.

TABLE 248-12 Clinical Features of Renal Tuberculosis in Two Series of Patients

Clinical Features	Study Simon et al.[220]	Study Christensen[221]
Number of patients	102	78
Primarily genitourinary symptoms	61%	71%
Back and flank pain	27%	10%
Dysuria, frequency	31%	34%
Constitutional symptoms	33%	14%
Abnormal urine, no symptoms	5%	20%
Abnormal urinalysis	66%	93%
Abnormal intravenous pyelogram	68%	93%
Tuberculin positive	88%	95%
Abnormal chest roentgenogram	75%	66%
Active pulmonary tuberculosis	38%	7%
Other old or active extrapulmonary disease	5%	20%
Urine culture positive For tuberculosis	80%	90%
For routine pathogens	45%	12%
Epididymitis, orchitis	19%	17%
Chronic prostatis	6%	6%

Chemotherapy with drug regimens containing INH and RMP as for pulmonary tuberculosis is recommended. Ureteral cicatrization and obstruction may occur during healing, and the urologic literature recommends frequent pyelograms during therapy, corticosteroid therapy if obstruction develops, and ureteral reimplantation if the obstruction does not resolve.[222] However, obstruction did not develop among 102 treated cases reported by Christensen.[221] Surgery has rarely been required in most recent series.

Hypertension is not a feature of renal tuberculosis, and renal function is usually preserved. However, a rare condition called *tuberculous interstitial nephritis* may cause renal failure.[223] It is characterized by interstitial granulomas and normal-sized kidneys, usually in the presence of active extrarenal tuberculosis. Acid-fast bacilli have been seen but not cultured from renal biopsy specimens, and renal dysfunction responds to corticosteroid therapy but not antituberculous chemotherapy alone. It is unclear that tuberculous interstitial nephritis is actually caused by tuberculous infection.

Male Genital Tuberculosis

Eighty percent of male genital tuberculosis is associated with coexistent renal disease, and most advanced renal tuberculosis is associated with some male genital focus.[224] Spread of infection from renal foci involves the prostate, seminal vesicles, epididymis, and testis in that order. The usual clinical finding is a scrotal mass that may be tender or associated with a draining sinus. Oligospermia is common and may not improve with treatment. Stones may form with treatment of prostatic tuberculosis. Genital foci not associated with renal disease can be established by lymphohematogenous spread and usually present as a painful testicular or scrotal mass. Diagnosis may be suggested by the presence of epididymal or prostatic calcification, although the latter also occurs with nontuberculous chronic prostatitis. The diagnosis is usually established by surgery, and response to chemotherapy is excellent.

Genitourinary Tuberculosis in Acquired Immunodeficiency Syndrome

In a study of 79 HIV-positive patients with tuberculosis, 77% had positive urine cultures, usually as an incidental finding. Only two had male genital involvement, none had symptoms of renal disease, and in only 4% was the genitourinary tract the only apparent site of tuberculosis.[191]

Female Genital Tuberculosis

Female genital tuberculosis begins with a hematogenous focus in the endosalpinx, from which it may spread to the endometrium (50%), ovaries (30%), cervix (10%), and vagina (1%).[225] In the cervix, a granulomatous ulcerating mass may resemble carcinoma. Common complaints are infertility or local symptoms consisting of menstrual disorders and abdominal pain. The clinical picture may suggest pelvic inflammatory disease that is unresponsive to therapy. Systemic symptoms are uncommon, and evidence of old tuberculosis need not be present. Pregnancies that occur in the presence of pelvic tuberculosis are often ectopic. Although cultures of menstrual blood or endometrial scrapings may be positive, the diagnosis is usually made by examination of tissue removed at operation. Response to chemotherapy is excellent, and surgery is needed only for residual large tuboovarian abscesses.

Gastrointestinal Tuberculosis

Before effective chemotherapy was available, 70% of patients with advanced pulmonary disease acquired gastrointestinal tuberculosis from swallowing infectious secretions, and usually developed diarrhea and abdominal pain. Although most cases at present are likely due to swallowed respiratory secretions, roentgenographic evidence of pulmonary tuberculosis is found in fewer than 25% of cases, the diagnosis being discovered unexpectedly by surgery or endoscopy.[226]

Any location from mouth to anus can be involved. Nonhealing ulcers of the tongue or oropharynx and nonhealing sockets after tooth extraction may be due to tuberculosis. Esophageal disease is most frequently caused by an adjacent caseous node, which leads to stricture with obstruction or tracheoesophageal fistula formation, and rarely fatal hematemesis from an aortoesophageal fistula. Stomach involvement may be ulcerative or hyperplastic and may cause gastric outlet obstruction. Isolated duodenal disease can produce symptoms of peptic ulcer or obstruction. Small bowel involvement may lead to perforation, obstruction, enteroenteric and enterocutaneous fistulas, massive hemorrhage, and severe malabsorption. Small bowel lesions are frequently multiple. The ileocecal area is the most typical site of enteric tuberculosis, producing pain, anorexia, diarrhea, obstruction, hemorrhage that may be severe, and often a palpable mass. Clinical, roentgenographic, endoscopic, and even operative findings may suggest carcinoma. A successful diagnosis is usually made by colonoscopy. In a study of 50 cases, ileocecal involvement, with or without involvement of other areas was found in 35 cases, isolated segmental colonic disease was found in 13 cases, and pancolitis was initially misdiagnosed as ulcerative colitis in 2 cases. Evidence of pulmonary tuberculosis was present in only 18 cases.[227] The clinical manifestations of anal tuberculosis are rare and include ulcers, perianal warty growths, and fistulas. The response of gastrointestinal tuberculosis to chemotherapy is excellent. Once the diagnosis is established, surgery should be deferred if possible until the results of chemotherapy have been assessed.

Pancreatic tuberculosis may manifest as an abscess or as a mass involving local nodes and resembling carcinoma. The biliary tract may be obstructed by tuberculous nodes, and tuberculous ascending cholangitis has been described. Tuberculosis is a frequent cause of granulomatous hepatitis. This is usually asymptomatic but may be associated with an elevated alkaline phosphatase level that is out of proportion to bilirubin levels with normal transaminase levels. Very rarely, tuberculous granulomatous hepatitis causes jaundice without evidence of extrahepatic tuberculosis. This is called *primary tuberculosis of the liver. Focal hepatic tuberculosis* describes single or multiple tuberculous abscesses. These appear to occur most frequently in racial groups with little natural immunity to tuberculosis and in children.[228]

Gastrointestinal Tuberculosis in Acquired Immunodeficiency Syndrome

Bowel involvement is not a common feature of extrapulmonary tuberculosis in AIDS patients. One series reported bowel fistulas in less than 4% of such cases,[191] another reported CT evidence of gastrointestinal abnormalities in 4 of 23 cases,[229] and a third study noted positive stool cultures for *M. tuberculosis* in 4 of 10 cases.[230] Tuberculous visceral abscesses, including hepatic, splenic, and pancreatic, may occur in AIDS patients. Pain and fever are usually present. Diagnosis is often made by CT or ultrasonographically guided drainage procedures. Chemotherapy alone has not been effective in all cases.[201]

Tuberculous Peritonitis

Tuberculous peritonitis results either from spread of adjacent tuberculous disease such as an abdominal lymph node, intestinal focus, or fallopian tube, or during miliary tuberculosis. In a summary of 11 series, evidence of associated pleuropulmonary tuberculosis was present in 25% to 83% of cases and the tuberculin test was positive in 30% to 100% of cases.[231] Pleural effusion is the most frequent associated finding, but evidence of tuberculosis in other sites is often present. AIDS patients do not have an increased frequency of peritonitis.[191]

The clinical picture has been divided into *plastic* and *serous* types. The less common plastic type is characterized by tender abdominal masses and a "doughy abdomen." Serous effusions present as ascites with or without signs of peritonitis. Symptoms of fever, abdominal pain, and weight loss are common.[231] The onset may be insidious, and cases diagnosed at routine hernia repair have been described. However, acute presentations resembling bacterial peritonitis also occur. In the past, diagnosis was often made at surgery for a mass or an acute abdomen. Tuberculous peritonitis often goes undiagnosed in patients with concomitant cirrhosis with ascites.[232] Of 20 patients with both conditions, the diagnosis of tuberculous peritonitis was suspected ante mortem in only 11. Tuberculous peritonitis has been reported in peritoneal dialysis patients with the clinical picture of bacterial peritonitis unresponsive to routine antibiotics.[233]

The peritoneal fluid is exudative, usually containing 500 to 2000 cells. Lymphocytes typically predominate, although in some cases polymorphonuclear leukocytes are more abundant early in the process. Acid-fast smear of peritoneal fluid is seldom positive, and culture is positive in only 25% of cases. Measurement of adenosine deaminase activity in ascitic fluid has been reported to have a high degree of sensitivity (86%) and specificity (100%).[234] Analysis of peritoneal fluid by PCR may also yield a specific diagnosis. However, in the absence of other foci of tuberculosis, peritoneal tissue must often be obtained to make the diagnosis. Histologic examination of peritoneal biopsy specimens obtained by a Cope needle were positive in 64% of cases and those obtained by peritoneoscopy in 85% in one series.[235] However, fatal hemorrhages after both Cope needle biopsy and peritoneoscopy have been recorded.[231]

Treatment is the same as for pulmonary tuberculosis. There is some evidence that adjunctive corticosteroids decrease the likelihood of late intestinal obstruction,[235] but pending definitive studies, the routine use of adjunctive corticosteroids cannot be recommended.[236]

Tuberculous Lymphadenitis (Scrofula)

Peripheral Nodes

Lymphadenitis is the most frequent form of extrapulmonary tuberculosis. In HIV-negative persons, it is usually unilateral and cervical in location.[237] The most common site is along the upper border of the sternocleidomastoid muscle, where it presents as a painless, red, firm mass. It is seen most frequently in young adult females of minority races, although it can affect any age or race. Children often have an ongoing primary infection, but in other age groups evidence of extranodal tuberculosis and systemic symptoms are usually absent. Lymphadenopathy outside the cervical and supraclavicular area indicates more serious tuberculosis, usually with systemic symptoms. The tuberculin test result is almost always positive. Fine-needle aspiration demonstrates cytologic evidence of granuloma, but smears or cultures are usually negative.[238] Biopsy with culture is often required for diagnosis, because nodes with a nonspecific histologic appearance have been positive for *M. tuberculosis* on culture, and material with typical histologic features may be due to other mycobacteria or fungi. Complete excision of involved nodes with no drain left in place is recommended to diminish the possibility of postoperative fistula formation. Chemotherapy with a 6-month regimen of INH and RMP, with PZA during the first 2 months, is effective. Untoward events such as node enlargement with pain, suppuration, sinus formation, and appearance of new nodes occur in 25% to 30% of cases, both during and after chemotherapy, and do not indicate failure of drug treatment.

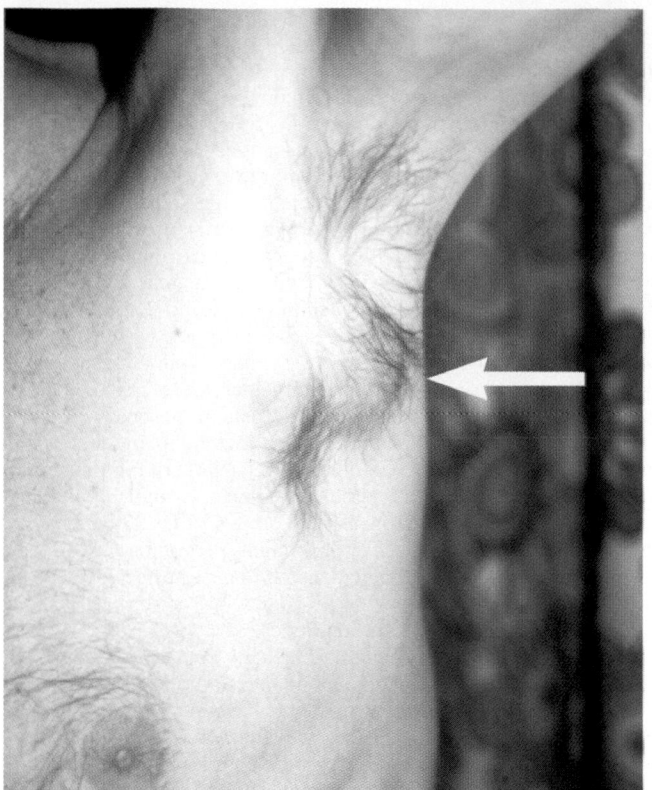

FIGURE 248-12. Axillary lymphadenitis caused by *Mycobacterium tuberculosis* in a patient with acquired immunodeficiency syndrome.

These likely represent reactions to retained tuberculous antigens rather than uncontrolled infection; they usually subside spontaneously, and short courses of corticosteroids may be beneficial when the problem persists.[239]

Conversely, in individuals with AIDS, peripheral tuberculous lymphadenitis is almost always multifocal and associated with major systemic symptoms such as fever, weight loss, and evidence of tuberculosis in the lungs (parenchyma, nodes, or pleura) or elsewhere (Fig. 248-12).[238] In one series from New York City, tuberculosis caused 57% of generalized lymphadenopathy in HIV-positive intravenous drug users.[240] In contrast to non–HIV-infected persons, material removed by fine-needle aspiration is positive on acid-fast stain in the great majority of cases—as frequently as it is by culture. However, both cytologic and histologic findings are less specific than in non–HIV-infected persons.[241]

Mediastinal Tuberculous Lymphadenopathy

Mediastinal adenopathy during primary infection is often visible roentgenologically, especially in children. In minority races, mediastinal adenopathy resulting from tuberculosis may also be seen in young adults, and cases in very old persons have been reported.[242] Associated systemic symptoms may or may not be present, causing confusion with other mediastinal masses such as histoplasmosis, lymphoma, and carcinoma. The finding of low-density areas in the nodes on CT suggests tuberculosis, but diagnosis usually requires mediastinoscopy. In HIV-infected persons with tuberculosis, in contrast, mediastinal lymphadenopathy is frequent. Multiple nodes are usually involved, coalescing into large mediastinal masses with low-density centers, peripheral contrast enhancement, and no calcification.[243,244]

Fibrosing Mediastinitis

Tuberculosis can cause fibrosing mediastinitis, although less commonly than histoplasmosis. Patients present with dyspnea on exertion resulting from compression of pulmonary veins and arteries or, less commonly, superior vena cava syndrome. Hilar adenopathy or active pulmonary disease is rarely found. A perfusion lung scan helps define the extent of pulmonary vascular compression, but thoracotomy is required for diagnosis. Mediastinoscopy is either contraindicated because of superior vena cava syndrome or unsuccessful because of fibrosis.

Mesenteric Tuberculous Lymphadenitis

In HIV-negative persons, isolated symptomatic mesenteric lymphadenitis without bowel disease or peritonitis is rare. It may cause abdominal pain, fever, a palpable mass, or symptoms of partial small bowel obstruction. In AIDS patients with tuberculosis, abdominal lymphadenopathy is common and may be massive.[244,245] Involvement is more often intra-abdominal than retroperitoneal, and occasionally obstruction of the biliary tract, ureters, or bowel is observed. As with thoracic disease, the nodes often are low density or have low-density centers and peripheral enhancement. Other abnormalities on CT may include abscesses in the liver, spleen, pancreas, or kidney; local ileal thickening; extraluminal bowel gas indicating fistula formation; and ascites.

Cutaneous Tuberculosis

In the past, a number of cutaneous conditions were associated with tuberculosis elsewhere in the body, although *M. tuberculosis* could not be identified in the lesions. These have been considered allergic reactions to the infection and termed *tuberculids*. They include erythema induratum of Bazin, papulonecrotic tuberculids, and others. This association has been questioned, and some have attributed tuberculids to other processes, such as sarcoidosis.[246] *M. tuberculosis* DNA has been detected in erythema induratum skin lesions by PCR.[247] Erythema nodosum has been attributed to primary tuberculosis, although organisms cannot be cultured from the lesions.

The pathogenesis of cutaneous involvement in tuberculosis is varied. Skin involvement may result from exogenous inoculation (which in the previously nonsensitized host is associated with regional lymphadenitis), spread from an adjacent focus to the overlying skin (as from lymphadenitis, osteomyelitis, or epididymitis), and hematogenous spread from a distant focus or as a part of the generalized hematogenous dissemination. This last is seen in patients with AIDS and tuberculous bacteremia.[248] The clinical picture of all cutaneous mycobacterial infections, including tuberculosis, is highly variable, and any unexplained skin lesion, especially if it has nodular or ulcerative components, may be due to tuberculosis, particularly in AIDS patients.

Tuberculous Laryngitis

In the prechemotherapy era, laryngeal tuberculosis occurred in more than a third of patients dying of pulmonary tuberculosis, often associated with painful ulcers of the epiglottis, pharynx, tonsils, and mouth, as well as middle ear involvement. Laryngeal disease was highly infectious and often caused terminal widespread bronchogenic dissemination throughout the lungs. At present, however, more than one half of laryngeal tuberculosis cases are due to hematogenous seeding. Such cases are still highly contagious. Lesions vary from erythema to ulceration and exophytic masses resembling carcinoma.[249] Symptoms include cough, wheezing, hemoptysis, dysphagia, odynophagia, and otalgia.

Tuberculous Otitis

Tuberculous otitis media is rare and frequently misdiagnosed. Half of the cases have no other evidence of present or past tuberculosis. The classic clinical picture is painless otorrhea with multiple tympanic perforations, exuberant granulation tissue, early severe hearing loss, and mastoid bone necrosis. The diagnosis has been missed for years by excellent otolaryngologists, even when tissue was available. Tuberculous otitis may be complicated by facial nerve paralysis. Response to drug therapy is excellent, and surgery is usually not required.[250]

Miscellaneous Conditions

Tuberculosis of the aorta with or without aneurysm formation can be caused by spread from contiguous diseased nodes, pericarditis, spondylitis, paravertebral abscesses, or empyema. Extensive hematogenous dissemination or aortic rupture may occur. Tuberculosis produces various ocular syndromes, including choroidal tubercles, uveitis, iritis, and episcleritis. Tuberculosis may also involve the breast, producing abscesses, sclerosing lesions resembling carcinoma, and multiple nodules. Destructive nasal lesions resembling Wegener's granulomatosis both clinically and histologically have been caused by tuberculosis.[251] Tuberculosis of the adrenal glands may cause adrenal enlargement with or without calcification, as may histoplasmosis, but granulomatous adrenal tuberculosis may cause Addison's disease without either calcification or adrenal enlargement.[252]

REFERENCES

1. Trends in tuberculosis morbidity—United States, 1992-2002. MMWR Morb Mortal Wkly Rep. 2003;52:217-220.
2. Palella FJ, Delaney KM, Moorman AC, et al. Declining morbidity and mortality among patients with advanced human immunodeficiency virus infection. N Engl J Med. 1998;338:853-860.
3. Cole ST, Brosch R, Parkhill J, et al. Deciphering the biology of Mycobacterium tuberculosis from the complete genome sequence. Nature. 1998;393:537-544.
4. Oh P, Granich R, Scott J, et al. Human exposure following Mycobacterium tuberculosis infection of multiple animal species in a metropolitan zoo. Emerg Infect Dis. 2002;8:1290-1293.
5. Hale YM, Pfyffer GE, Salfinger M. Laboratory diagnosis of mycobacterial infections: New tools and lessons learned. Clin Infect Dis. 2001;33:834-846.
6. Hanna BA, Ebrahimzadeh A, Elliott LB, et al. Multicenter evaluation of the BACTEC MGIT 960 system for recovery of mycobacteria. J Clin Microbiol. 1999;37:748-752.
7. Leitritz L, Schubert S, Bucherl B, et al. Evaluation of BACTEC MGIT 960 and BACTEC 460TB systems for recovery of mycobacteria from clinical specimens of a university hospital with low incidence of tuberculosis. J Clin Microbiol. 2001;39:3764-3767.
8. Barnes PF. Rapid diagnostic tests for tuberculosis—Progress but no gold standard. Am J Respir Crit Care Med. 1997;155:1497-1498.
9. Centers for Disease Control and Prevention. Nucleic acid amplification tests for tuberculosis. MMWR Morb Mortal Wkly Rep. 1996;45:951.
10. Catanzaro A, Perry S, Clarridge JE, et al. The role of clinical suspicion in evaluating a new diagnostic test for active tuberculosis: Results of a multicenter prospective trial. JAMA. 2000;283:639-645.
11. Pfyffer GE, Kissling P, Jahn EM, et al. Diagnostic performance of amplified Mycobacterium tuberculosis direct test with cerebrospinal fluid, other nonrespiratory, and respiratory specimens. J Clin Microbiol. 1996;34:834-841.
12. O'Sullivan CE, Miller DR, Schneider PS, Roberts GD. Evaluation of Gen-Probe amplified Mycobacterium tuberculosis direct test by using respiratory and nonrespiratory specimens in a tertiary care center laboratory. J Clin Microbiol. 2002;40:1723-1727.
13. Piersimoni C, Scarparo C, Piccoli P, et al. Performance assessment of two commercial amplification assays for direct detection of Mycobacterium tuberculosis complex from respiratory and extrapulmonary specimens. J Clin Microbiol. 2002;40:4138-4142.
14. Noordhoek GT, vanEmbden JDA, Kolk AHJ. Reliability of nucleic acid amplification for detection of Mycobacterium tuberculosis: An international collaborative quality control study among 30 laboratories. J Clin Microbiol. 1996;34:2522-2525.
15. Diagnostic standards and classification of tuberculosis in adults and children. Am J Respir Crit Care Med. 2000;161:1376-1395.
16. Parsons LM, Brosch R, Cole ST, et al. Rapid and simple approach for identification of Mycobacterium tuberculosis complex isolates by PCR-based genomic deletion analysis. J Clin Microbiol. 2002;40:2339-2345.
17. van Embden JD, Cave MD, Crawford JT, et al. Strain identification of Mycobacterium tuberculosis by DNA fingerprinting: Recommendations for a standardized methodology. J Clin Microbiol. 1993;31:406-409.
18. Tortoli E, Benedetti M, Fontanelli A, Simonetti MT. Evaluation of automated BACTEC MGIT 960 system for testing susceptibility of Mycobacterium tuberculosis to four major antituberculous drugs: Comparison with the radiometric BACTEC 460TB method and the agar plate method of proportion. J Clin Microbiol. 2002;40:607-610.
19. Bemer P, Palicova F, Rusch-Gerdes S, et al. Multicenter evaluation of fully automated BACTEC Mycobacteria Growth Indicator Tube 960 system for susceptibility testing of Mycobacterium tuberculosis. J Clin Microbiol. 2002;40:150-154.
20. Telenti A, Honore N, Bernasconi C, et al. Genotypic assessment of isoniazid and rifampin resistance in Mycobacterium tuberculosis—A blinded study at reference laboratory level. J Clin Microbiol. 1997;35:719-723.
21. Williams DL, Spring L, Gillis TP, et al. Evaluation of a polymerase chain reaction-based universal heteroduplex generator assay for direct detection of rifampin susceptibility of Mycobacterium tuberculosis from sputum specimens. Clin Infect Dis. 1998;26:446-450.
22. Kim B-J, Kim S-Y, Park B-H, et al. Mutations in the rpoB gene of Mycobacterium tuberculosis that interfere with PCR-single-strand conformation polymorphism analysis for rifampin susceptibility testing. J Clin Microbiol. 1997;35:492-494.
23. Nachamkin I, Kang C, Weinstein MP. Detection of resistance to isoniazid, rifampin, and streptomycin in clinical isolates of Mycobacterium tuberculosis by molecular methods. Clin Infect Dis. 1997;24:894-900.
24. Khisimuzi M, Slayden RA, Zhu Y, et al. Inhibition of a Mycobacterium tuberculosis β-ketoacyl ACP synthetase by isoniazid. Science. 1998;280:1607-1616.
25. Drobniewski FA, Wilson SM. The rapid diagnosis of isoniazid and rifampicin resistance in Mycobacterium tuberculosis—A molecular story. J Med Microbiol. 1998;47:189-196.
26. Dye C, Scheele S, Dolin P, et al. Consensus statement. Global burden of tuberculosis: Estimated incidence, prevalence, and mortality by country. WHO Global Surveillance and Monitoring Project. JAMA. 1999;282:677-686.
27. World Health Organization Report on the Tuberculosis Epidemic, 1997. Geneva: World Health Organization.
28. Styblo K. Recent advances in epidemiological research in tuberculosis. Adv Tuberc Res. 1980;20:1-63.
29. Sousa AO, Salem JI, Lee FK, et al. An epidemic of tuberculosis with a high rate of tuberculin anergy among a population previously unexposed to tuberculosis, the Yanomami Indians of the Brazilian Amazon. Proc Natl Acad Sci U S A. 1997;94:13227-13232.
30. Centers for Disease Control and Prevention. Tuberculosis morbidity—United States, 1997. MMWR Morb Mortal Wkly Rep. 1998;47:253-257.
31. American Thoracic Society. Control of tuberculosis in the United States. Am Rev Respir Dis. 1992;146:1623-1633.
32. Centers for Disease Control and Prevention. Tuberculosis morbidity among U.S.-born and foreign-born populations—United States, 2000. MMWR Morb Mortal Wkly Rep. 2002;51:101-104.
33. Binkin NJ, Zuber PLF, Wells CD, et al. Overseas screening for tuberculosis in immigrants and refugees to the United States: Current status. Clin Infect Dis. 1996;23:1226-1232.
34. Zuber PLF, McKenna MT, Binkin NJ, et al. Long-term risk of tuberculosis among foreign-born persons in the United States. JAMA. 1997;278:304-307.
35. Jereb JA, Kelly GD, Dooley SW, et al. Tuberculosis morbidity in the United States: Final data, 1990. MMWR Morb Mortal Wkly Rep. 1991;40:23-27.
36. Havlir DV, Barnes PF. Tuberculosis in patients with human immunodeficiency virus infection. N Engl J Med. 1999;340:367-373.
37. Barnes PF, Bloch AB, Davidson PT, et al. Tuberculosis in patients with human immunodeficiency virus infection. N Engl J Med. 1991;100:191-200.
38. Centers for Disease Control. 1993 Revised certification system for HIV infection and expanded surveillance case definition for AIDS among adolescents and adults. MMWR Morb Mortal Wkly Rep. 1992;41:1-19.
39. Valway SE, Sanchez MPC, Shinnick TK, et al. An outbreak involving extensive transmission of a virulent strain of Mycobacterium tuberculosis. N Engl J Med. 1998;338:633-639.
40. Mishu Allos B, Gensheimer KF, Bloch AB, et al. Management of an outbreak of tuberculosis in a small community. Ann Intern Med. 1996;125:114-117.
41. Centers for Disease Control, Tuberculosis Control Division. Tuberculosis in the United States, 1979. Atlanta: Centers for Disease Control; 1981:4-31.
42. Pitchenik AE, Cole C, Russell BW, et al. Tuberculosis, atypical mycobacteriosis, and the acquired immunodeficiency syndrome among Haitian and non-Haitian patients in South Florida. Ann Intern Med. 1984;101:641-645.
43. Patel KR. Pulmonary tuberculosis in residents of lodging houses, night shelters and common hostels in Glasgow: A 5-year prospective study. Br J Dis Chest. 1985;79:60-66.
44. Nardell E, McInnis B, Thomas B, et al. Exogenous reinfection with tuberculosis in a shelter for the homeless. N Engl J Med. 1986;315:1570-1575.
45. Stead WW, Lofgren JP, Warren E, et al. Tuberculosis as an endemic and nosocomial infection among the elderly in nursing homes. N Engl J Med. 1985;312:1483-1487.
46. Centers for Disease Control. Special report: Tuberculosis among Indochinese refugees. In: Tuberculosis in the United States. Atlanta: Centers for Disease Control; 1981:40.
47. Andrew OT, Schoenfeld PY, Hopewell PC, et al. Tuberculosis in patients with end-stage renal disease. Am J Med. 1980;68:59-65.
48. Cuss FM, Carmichael DJ, Linington A, et al. Tuberculosis in renal failure: A high incidence in patients born in the third world. Clin Nephrol. 1986;25:129-133.
49. Louie E, Rice LB, Holzm RS. Tuberculosis in non-Haitian patients with acquired immunodeficiency syndrome. Chest. 1986;90:542-545.
50. Khatri GR, Frieden TR. Controlling tuberculosis in India. N Engl J Med. 2002;347:1420-1425.
51. Espinal MA, Laszlo A, Simonsen L, et al. Global trends in resistance to antituberculosis drugs. World Health Organization–International Union against Tuberculosis and Lung Disease Working Group on Anti-Tuberculosis Drug Resistance Surveillance. N Engl J Med. 2001;344:1294-1303.
52. Frampton MW. An outbreak of tuberculosis among hospital personnel caring for a patient with a skin ulcer. Ann Intern Med. 1992;117:312-313.
53. Templeton GL, Illing LA, Young L, et al. The risk for transmission of Mycobacterium tuberculosis at the bedside and during autopsy. Ann Intern Med. 1995;122:922-925.
54. Bates JH, Stead WW. The history of tuberculosis as a global epidemic. Med Clin North Am. 1993;77:1205-1217.
55. Stead WW. Tuberculosis among elderly persons: An outbreak in a nursing home. Ann Intern Med. 1981;94:606-610.
56. Behr MA, Warren SA, Salamon H, et al. Transmission of Mycobacterium tuberculosis from patients smear-negative for acid-fast bacilli. Lancet. 1999;353:444-449.
57. Klausner JD, Ryder RW, Baende E, et al. Mycobacterium tuberculosis in household contacts of human immunodeficiency virus type 1-seropositive patients with active pulmonary tuberculosis in Kinshasa, Zaire. J Infect Dis. 1993;168:106-111.
58. Elliot AM, Hayes RJ, Halwiindi B, et al. The impact of HIV on infectiousness of pulmonary tuberculosis: A community in Zambia. AIDS. 1993;7:981-987.
59. Nunn P, Mungai M, Nyamwaya J, et al. The effect of human immunodeficiency virus type-1 on the infectiousness of tuberculosis. Tuber Lung Dis. 1994;75:25-32.
60. Cauthen GM, Dooley SW, Onorato IM, et al. Transmission of Mycobacterium tuberculosis from tuberculosis patients with HIV infection or AIDS. Am J Epidemiol. 1996;144:69-77.

61. Centers for Disease Control and Prevention. Guidelines for preventing the transmission of *Mycobacterium tuberculosis* in health-care facilities, 1994. MMWR Morb Mortal Wkly Rep. 1994;43:1-132.

62. Telzak EE, Fazal BE, Pollard CL, et al. Factors influencing time to sputum conversion among patients with smear-positive pulmonary tuberculosis. Clin Infect Dis. 1997;25:666-670.

63. Kim TC, Blackman RS, Heatwole KM, et al. Acid fast bacilli in sputum smears of patients with pulmonary tuberculosis: Prevalence and significance of negative smears pretreatment and positive smears post-treatment. Am Rev Respir Dis. 1984;129:264-268.

64. Iseman MD. An unholy trinity—Three negative sputum smears and release from tuberculosis isolation. Clin Infect Dis. 1997;25:671-672.

65. Selwyn PA, Hartel D, Lewis VA, et al. A prospective study of the risk of tuberculosis among intravenous drug users with human immunodeficiency virus infection. N Engl J Med. 1989;320:545-555.

66. Daley CL, Small PM, Schecter GF. An outbreak of tuberculosis with accelerated progression among persons infected with the human immunodeficiency virus. N Engl J Med. 1992;36:231-235.

67. Brahmajothi V, Pitchappan RM, Kakkanaiah VM, et al. Association of pulmonary tuberculosis and HLA in South India. Tubercle. 1991;72:123-132.

68. Mehra NK, Rajalingam R, Mitra DK, et al. Variants of HLA-DR2/DR51 group haplotypes and susceptibility to tuberculoid leprosy and pulmonary tuberculosis in Asian Indians. Int J Lepr Other Mycobact Dis. 1995;63:241-248.

69. Bellamy R, Ruwende C, Corrah T, et al. Variations in the *NRAMP1* gene and susceptibility to tuberculosis in West Africans. N Engl J Med. 1998;338:640-644.

70. Jouanguy E, Lamhamedi-Cherradi S, Lammas D, et al. A human IFNGR1 small deletion hotspot associated with dominant susceptibility to mycobacterial infection. Nat Genet. 1999;21:370-378.

71. Di Perri G, Danzi MC, DeChecchi G. Nosocomial epidemic of active tuberculosis among HIV-infected patients. Lancet. 1989;2:1502-1504.

72. Pearson ML, Jereb JA, Frieden TR. Nosocomial transmission of multidrug-resistant *Mycobacterium tuberculosis:* A risk to patients and healthcare workers. Ann Intern Med. 1992;117:191-196.

73. Fischl MA, Uttamchandani RB, Daikos GL, et al. An outbreak of tuberculosis caused by multiple-drug resistant tubercle bacilli among patients with HIV infection. Ann Intern Med. 1992;11:177-183.

74. Edlin BR, Tokars JI, Grieco MH, et al. An outbreak of multidrug-resistant tuberculosis among hospitalized patients with the acquired immunodeficiency syndrome. N Engl J Med. 1992;326:1514-1521.

75. Kramer F, Modilevsky T, Waliany AR, et al. Delayed diagnosis of tuberculosis in patients with human immunodeficiency virus infection. Am J Med. 1990;89:451-456.

76. Small PM, Shafer RW, Hopewell PC. Exogenous reinfection with multidrug-resistant *Mycobacterium tuberculosis* in patients with advanced HIV infection. N Engl J Med. 1993;328:1137-1144.

77. Torres R, Mani S, Altholz J, et al. Human immunodeficiency virus infection among homeless men in a New York City shelter. Arch Intern Med. 1990;150:2030-2036.

78. Braun MM, Truman BI, Maguire B. Increasing incidence of tuberculosis in a prison inmate population: Association with HIV infection. JAMA. 1989;261:393-397.

79. Frieden TR, Sherman LF, Maw KL, et al. A multi-institutional outbreak of highly drug-resistant tuberculosis: Epidemiology and clinical outcomes. JAMA. 1996;275:452-457.

80. Fujiwara PI, Cook SV, Rutherford CM, et al. A continuing survey of drug-resistant tuberculosis, New York City, April 1994. Arch Intern Med. 1997;157:531-536.

81. Rao VK, Iademarco EP, Fraser VJ, Kollef MH. Delays in the suspicion and treatment of tuberculosis among hospitalized patients. Ann Intern Med. 1999;130:404-411.

82. ATS Workshop. Rapid diagnostic tests for tuberculosis—What is the appropriate use? Am J Respir Crit Care Med. 1997;155:1804-1814.

83. Orme IM, Andersen P, Boom WH. T cell response to *Mycobacterium tuberculosis*. J Infect Dis. 1993;167:1481-1497.

84. Aderem A, Underhill DM. Mechanisms of phagocytosis in macrophages. Annu Rev Immunol. 1999;17:593-623.

85. Pethe K, Alonso S, Biet F, et al. The heparin-binding haemagglutinin of M. tuberculosis is required for extrapulmonary dissemination. Nature. 2001;412:190-194.

86. van Soolingen D, Hoogenboezem T, de Haas PE, et al. A novel pathogenic taxon of the Mycobacterium tuberculosis complex, Canetti: Characterization of an exceptional isolate from Africa. Int J Syst Bacteriol. 1997;47:1236-1245.

87. O'Brien JR. Nonreactive tuberculosis. J Clin Pathol. 1954;7:216-225.

88. Ellner JJ. The immune response in human tuberculosis: Implications for tuberculosis control. J Infect Dis. 1997;176:1351-1359.

89. Hirsch CS, Hussain R, Toossii Z, et al. Cross-stimulatory role for transforming growth factor _ in tuberculosis: Suppression of antigen driven interferon _ production. Proc Natl Acad Sci U S A. 1996;93:3193-3198.

90. Vidal SM, Malo D, Vogan K, et al. Natural resistance to infection with intracellular parasites: Isolation of a candidate for Bcg. Cell. 1993;73:469.

91. Snider DE Jr. The tuberculin skin test. Am Rev Respir Dis. 1982;125:108-118.

92. Targeted tuberculin testing and treatment of latent tuberculosis infection. American Thoracic Society. MMWR Morb Mortal Wkly Rep. 2000;49(RR-6):1-51.

93. Centers for Disease Control. The use of preventive therapy for tuberculous infection in the United States: Recommendations of the Advisory Committee for the Elimination of Tuberculosis. MMWR Morb Mortal Wkly Rep. 1990;39:9-12.

94. Stead WW. Management of health care workers after inadvertent exposure to tuberculosis: A guide for the use of preventive therapy. Ann Intern Med. 1995;122:906-912.

95. Menzies D. What does tuberculin reactivity after bacille Calmette-Guerin vaccination tell us? Clin Infect Dis. 2000; 31:S71-S74.

96. Nash DR, Douglass JE. Anergy in active pulmonary tuberculosis: A comparison between positive and negative reactors and an evaluation of 5 TU and 250 TU skin test doses. Chest. 1980;77:32-37.

97. Slovis BS, Plitman JD, Haas DW. The case against anergy testing as a routine adjunct to tuberculin skin testing. JAMA. 2000;283:2003-2007.

98. Pouchot J, Grasland A, Collet C, et al. Reliability of tuberculin skin test measurement. Ann Intern Med. 1997;126:210-214.

99. Robertson JM, Burtt DS, Edmonds KL, et al. Delayed tuberculin reactivity in persons of Indochinese origin: Implications for preventive therapy. Ann Intern Med. 1996;124:779-784.

100. Grzybowski S, Allen EA. The challenge of tuberculosis in decline: A study based on the epidemiology of tuberculosis in Ontario, Canada. Am Rev Respir Dis. 1964;90:707-720.

101. Johnson MP, Coberly JS, Clermont HC, et al. Tuberculin skin test reactivity among adults infected with human immunodeficiency virus. J Infect Dis. 1992;166:194-198.

102. Centers for Disease Control. Purified protein derivative (PPD) tuberculin anergy and HIV infection: Guidelines for anergy testing and management of anergic persons at risk of tuberculosis. MMWR Morb Mortal Wkly Rep. 1991;40:27-33.

103. Gordin FM, Matts J, Miller C, et al. A controlled trial of isoniazid in persons with anergy and human immunodeficiency virus infection who are at high risk for tuberculosis. N Engl J Med. 1997;337:315-320.

104. Whalen CC, Johnson JL, Okwera A, et al. A trial of three regimens to prevent tuberculosis in Ugandan adults infected with the human immunodeficiency virus. N Engl J Med. 1997;337:801-808.

105. Centers for Disease Control and Prevention. Anergy skin testing and preventive therapy for HIV-infected persons: Revised guidelines. MMWR Morb Mortal Wkly Rep. 1997;46:1-10.

106. Mazurek GH, Villarino ME. Guidelines for using the QuantiFERON-TB test for diagnosing latent Mycobacterium tuberculosis infection. MMWR Morb Mortal Wkly Rep. 2003;52(RR-2):15-18.

107. Mazurek GH, LoBue PA, Daley CL, et al. Comparison of a whole-blood interferon gamma assay with tuberculin skin testing for detecting latent Mycobacterium tuberculosis infection. JAMA. 2001;286:1740-1747.

108. Bellete B, Coberly J, Barnes GL, et al. Evaluation of a whole-blood interferon-gamma release assay for the detection of Mycobacterium tuberculosis infection in 2 study populations. Clin Infect Dis. 2002;34:1449-1456.

109. Ewer K, Deeks J, Alvarez L, et al. Comparison of T-cell-based assay with tuberculin skin test for diagnosis of Mycobacterium tuberculosis infection in a school tuberculosis outbreak. Lancet. 2003;361:1168-1173.

110. Murray JF. Cursed duet: HIV infection and tuberculosis. Respiration. 1990;57:210-220.

111. Stead WW. Pathogenesis of a first episode of chronic pulmonary tuberculosis in man: Recrudescence of residuals of the primary infection or exogenous reinfection? Am Rev Respir Dis. 1967;95:729-745.

112. Romeyn JA. Exogenous reinfection in tuberculosis. Am Rev Respir Dis. 1970;101:923-927.

113. Kumar RA, Saran M, Verma BL, et al. Pulmonary tuberculosis among contacts of patients with tuberculosis in an urban Indian population. J Epidemiol Community Health. 1984;38:253-258.

114. Dahl RH. First appearance of pulmonary cavity after primary infection with relation to time and age. Acta Tuberc Scand. 1952;27:140-149.

115. Stead WW, Kerby GR, Schlueter DP, et al. The clinical spectrum of primary tuberculosis in adults: Confusion with reinfection in the pathogenesis of chronic tuberculosis. Ann Intern Med. 1968;68:731-745.

116. Gedde-Dahl T. Tuberculous infection in the light of tuberculin matriculation. Am J Hyg. 1952;56:139-214.

117. Keane J, Gershon S, Wise RP, et al. Tuberculosis associated with infliximab, a tumor necrosis factor alpha-neutralizing agent. N Engl J Med. 2001;345:1098-1104.

118. Reichman LB, Felton CP, Edsall JR. Drug dependence, a possible new risk factor for tuberculosis disease. Arch Intern Med. 1979;139:337-339.

119. Canetti G. Present aspects of bacterial resistance in tuberculosis. Am Rev Respir Dis. 1965;92:687-703.

120. Lee JH, Park SS, Lee DH, et al. Endobronchial tuberculosis: Clinical and bronchoscopic features in 121 cases. Chest. 1992;102:990-994.

121. Chang S, Lee P, Perug P. Lower lung field tuberculosis. Chest. 1987;91:230-232.

122. Pitchenik AE, Rubinson HA. The radiographic appearance of tuberculosis in patients with the acquired immune deficiency syndrome (AIDS) and pre-AIDS. Am Rev Respir Dis. 1985;131:393-396.

123. Theuer P, Hopewell PC, Elias D, et al. Human immunodeficiency virus infection in tuberculosis patients. J Infect Dis. 1990;162:8-12.

124. Jones BE, Oo MM, Taikwel EK, et al. CD4 cell counts in human immunodeficiency virus-negative patients with tuberculosis. Clin Infect Dis. 1997;24:988-991.

125. Yajko DM, Nassos PS, Sanders CA, et al. High predictive value of the acid-fast smear for *Mycobacterium tuberculosis* despite the high prevalence of *Mycobacterium avium* complex in respiratory specimens. Clin Infect Dis. 1994;19:334-336.

126. Menzies R, Vissandjee B, Rocher I, et al. The booster effect in two-step tuberculin testing among adults in Montreal. Ann Intern Med. 1994;120:190-198.

127. Russell MD, Torrington KG, Tenholder MF. A ten-year experience with fiberoptic bronchoscopy for mycobacterial isolation: Impact of the BACTEC system. Am Rev Respir Dis. 1986;133:1069-1071.

128. Salzman SH, Schindel ML, Aranda CP, et al. The role of bronchoscopy in the diagnosis of pulmonary tuberculosis in patients at risk for HIV infection. Chest. 1992;102:143-146.

129. Miro AM, Gibilara E, Powell S, et al. The role of fiberoptic bronchoscopy for diagnosis of pulmonary tuberculosis in patients at risk for AIDS. Chest. 1992;101:1211-1214.

130. Kennedy DJ, Lewis WP, Barnes PF. Yield of bronchoscopy for the diagnosis of tuberculosis in patients with human immunodeficiency virus infection. Chest. 1992;102:1040-1044.

131. Reider HL, Kelly GD, Bloch AB, et al. Tuberculosis diagnosed at death in the United States. Chest. 1991;100:678-681.
132. Mok CK, Nandi P, Ong GB. Coexistent bronchogenic carcinoma and active pulmonary tuberculosis. J Thorac Cardiovasc Surg. 1978;76:469-472.
133. Centers for Disease Control and Prevention. Treatment of tuberculosis. American Thoracic Society, CDC and Infectious Diseases Society of America. MMWR Morb Mortal Wkly Rep. 2003;52(RR-11):1-88.
134. Ben-Dov I, Mason G. Drug-resistant tuberculosis in a southern California hospital: Trends from 1969 to 1984. Am Rev Respir Dis. 1987;135:1307-1310.
135. Pablos-Mendez A, Raviglione MC, Battan R, et al. Drug resistant tuberculosis among the homeless in New York City. N Y State J Med. 1990;90:351-355.
136. Frieden TR, Sterling T, Pablos-Mendez A, et al. The emergence of drug resistant tuberculosis in New York City. N Engl J Med. 1993;328:521-526.
137. Sullivan EA, Kreiswirth BN, Palumbo L, et al. Emergence of fluoroquinolone-resistant tuberculosis in New York City. Lancet. 1995;345:1148-1150.
138. Mitchison DA, Nunn AJ. Influence of initial drug resistance on the response to short-course chemotherapy of pulmonary tuberculosis. Am Rev Respir Dis. 1986;133:423-430.
139. Steele MA, Burk RF, Des Prez RM. Toxic hepatitis with isoniazid and rifampin: A metaanalysis. Chest. 1991;99:465-471.
140. Kopanoff DE, Snider DE Jr, Caras GJ. Isoniazid-related hepatitis: A U.S. Public Health Service cooperative surveillance study. Am Rev Respir Dis. 1978;117:991-1001.
141. Centers for Disease Control and Prevention. Clinical update: Impact of HIV protease inhibitors on the treatment of HIV-infected tuberculosis patients with rifampin. MMWR Morb Mortal Wkly Rep. 1996;45:921-925.
142. Jarvis B, Lamb HM. Rifapentine. Drugs. 1998;56:607-616.
143. Steele MA, DesPrez RM. The role of pyrazinamide in tuberculosis chemotherapy. Chest. 1988;94:842-844.
144. Update: Fatal and severe liver injuries associated with rifampin and pyrazinamide treatment for latent tuberculosis infection. MMWR Morb Mortal Wkly Rep. 2002;51:998-999.
145. Dankner WM, Waecker NJ, Essey MA, et al. *Mycobacterium bovis* infections in San Diego: A clinicoepidemiologic study of 73 patients and a historical review of a forgotten pathogen. Medicine. 1993;72:11-37.
146. Telzak EE, Sepkowitz K, Alpert P, et al. Multidrug-resistant tuberculosis in patients without HIV infection. N Engl J Med. 1995;333:907-911.
147. Perez-Stable EJ, Hopewell PC. Current tuberculosis treatment regimens: Choosing the right one for your patient. Clin Chest Med. 1989;10:323-339.
148. Davidson PT, Le HQ. Drug treatment of tuberculosis—1992. Drugs. 1992;43:651-673.
149. Snider DE Jr, Zierski M, Graczyk J, et al. Short-course tuberculosis chemotherapy studies conducted in Poland during the past decade. Eur J Respir Dis. 1986;68:12-18.
150. Treatment of tuberculosis and tuberculous infection in adults and children. Am J Respir Crit Care Med. 1994;149:1359-1374.
151. Dutt AK, Moers D, Stead WW. Short-course chemotherapy for tuberculosis with mainly twice-weekly isoniazid and rifampin: Community physicians' seven-year experience with mainly outpatients. Am J Med. 1984;77:233-242.
152. Centers for Disease Control and Prevention. Initial therapy for tuberculosis in the era of multidrug resistance: Recommendations of the Advisory Council for the Elimination of Tuberculosis. JAMA. 1993;270:694-698.
153. Small PM, Fujiwara PI. Management of tuberculosis in the United States. N Engl J Med 2001;345:189-200.
154. Cohn DL, Catlin BJ, Peterson KL, et al. A 62-dose, 6-month therapy for pulmonary and extrapulmonary tuberculosis: A twice-weekly, directly observed, and cost-effective regimen. Ann Intern Med. 1990;112:407-415.
155. Weis SE, Slocum PC, Blais FX, et al. The effect of directly observed therapy on the rates of drug resistance and relapse in tuberculosis. N Engl J Med. 1994;330:1179-1184.
156. Hong Kong Chest Service Tuberculosis Research Center, Madras, British Medical Research Council. A controlled trial of 3-month, 4-month, and 6-month regimens of chemotherapy for sputum smear-negative pulmonary tuberculosis: Results at 5 years. Am Rev Respir Dis. 1989;139:871-876.
157. Goble M, Iseman MD, Madsen LA. Treatment of 171 patients with pulmonary tuberculosis resistant to isoniazid and rifampin. N Engl J Med. 1993;328:527-532.
158. Iseman MD. Treatment of multidrug-resistant tuberculosis. N Engl J Med. 1993;329:784-791.
159. Fitzgerald DW, Desvarieux M, Severe P, et al. Effect of post-treatment isoniazid on prevention of recurrent tuberculosis in HIV-1-infected individuals: A randomised trial. Lancet. 2000;356:1470-1474.
160. Fitzgerald DW, Severe P, Joseph P, et al. No effect of isoniazid prophylaxis for purified protein derivative-negative HIV-infected adults living in a country with endemic tuberculosis: Results of a randomized trial. J AIDS. 2001;28:305-307.
161. Babu Swai O, Aluoch JA, Githui WA. Controlled clinical trial of a regimen of two durations for the treatment of isoniazid resistant pulmonary tuberculosis. Tubercle. 1988;69:5-14.
162. Prevention and treatment of tuberculosis among patients infected with human immunodeficiency virus: Principles of therapy and revised recommendations. MMWR Morb Mortal Wkly Rep. 1998;47:1-58.
163. Burman WJ, Gallicano K, Peloquin C. Therapeutic implications of drug interactions in the treatment of human immunodeficiency virus-related tuberculosis. Clin Infect Dis. 1999;28:419-429.
164. Acquired rifamycin resistance in persons with advanced HIV disease being treated for active tuberculosis with intermittent rifamycin-based regimens. MMWR Morb Mortal Wkly Rep. 2002;51:214-215.
165. Small PM, Schecter GF, Goodman PC, et al. Treatment of tuberculosis in patients with advanced human immunodeficiency virus infection. N Engl J Med. 1991;324:289-294.
166. Haas DW, Des Prez RM. Tuberculosis and acquired immunodeficiency syndrome: A historical perspective on recent developments. Am J Med. 1994;96:439-450.
167. Berning SE, Huitt DA, Iseman MD, Peloquin CA. Malabsorption of antituberculous medications by a patient with AIDS. N Engl J Med. 1992;327:1817-1818.
168. Busillo CP, Lessnau KD, Sanjana V. Multidrug resistant *Mycobacterium tuberculosis* in patients with human immunodeficiency virus infection. Chest. 1992;102:797-801.
169. Israel HL, Gottlieb JE, Maddrey WC. Perspective: Preventive isoniazid therapy and the liver. Chest. 1992;101:1298-1301.
170. Porter JDH, McAdam KPWJ. Tuberculosis in Africa in the AIDS era: The role of chemoprophylaxis. Trans R Soc Trop Med Hyg. 1992;86:467-469.
171. Jasmer RM, Nahid P, Hopewell PC. Clinical practice. Latent tuberculosis infection. N Engl J Med. 2002;347:1860-1866.
172. Gordin F, Chaisson RE, Matts JP, et al. Rifampin and pyrazinamide vs isoniazid for prevention of tuberculosis in HIV-infected persons: An international randomized trial. Terry Beirn CPCRA, the AACTG, the PAHO, and the CDC Study Group. JAMA. 2000;283:1445-1450.
173. Khan K, Muennig P, Behta M, Zivin JG. Global drug-resistance patterns and the management of latent tuberculosis infection in immigrants to the United States. N Engl J Med. 2002;347:1850-1859.
174. Stead WW, To T, Harrison RW, et al. Benefit-risk considerations in preventive treatment of tuberculosis in elderly persons. Ann Intern Med. 1987;107:843-845.
175. International Union Against Tuberculosis. Efficacy of various durations of isoniazid preventive therapy for tuberculosis: Five years of follow-up in the IUAT trial. Bull World Health Organ. 1982;60:555-564.
176. Byrd RB, Horn BR, Griggs GA, et al. Isoniazid chemoprophylaxis: Association with detection and incidence of liver toxicity. Arch Intern Med. 1970;137:1130-1133.
177. Nolan CM, Goldberg SV, Buskin SE. Hepatotoxicity associated with isoniazid preventive therapy: A 7-year survey from a public health tuberculosis clinic. JAMA. 1999;281:1014-1018.
178. Snider DE Jr, Caras GJ. Isoniazid-associated hepatitis deaths: A review of available information. Am Rev Respir Dis. 1992;145:494-497.
179. Ferebee SH. Controlled chemoprophylaxis trials in tuberculosis: A general review. Bibl Tuberc Med Thorac. 1970;26:28-106.
180. Grzybowski S, Ashley MJ, McKinnon NE, et al. In Canada: A trial of chemoprophylaxis in inactive tuberculosis. Can Med Assoc J. 1969;101:81-86.
181. Falk A, Fuchs GF. Prophylaxis with isoniazid in inactive tuberculosis: A Veterans Administration cooperative study. Chest. 1978;73:44-48.
182. Selwyn PA, Sckell BM, Alcabes P, et al. High risk of active tuberculosis in HIV-infected drug users with cutaneous anergy. JAMA. 1992;268:504-507.
183. Rose DN. Short course prophylaxis against tuberculosis in HIV-infected patients. Ann Intern Med. 1998;129:779-786.
184. Luelmo F. BCG vaccination. Am Rev Respir Dis. 1982;125:70-72.
185. Menzies R, Vissandjee B. Effect of bacille Calmette-Guérin vaccination on tuberculin reactivity. Am Rev Respir Dis. 1992;145:621-624.
186. Hakim S, Heaney JA, Heinz T, et al. Psoas abscess following intravesical bacillus Calmette-Guérin for bladder cancer: A case report. J Urol. 1993;150:188-189.
187. McParland C, Cotton DJ, Gowda KS, et al. Miliary *Mycobacterium bovis* induced by intravesical bacille Calmette-Guerin immunotherapy. Am Rev Respir Dis. 1992;146:1330-1333.
188. Lamm DL, Stogdill VD, Stogdill BJ, et al. Complications of bacillus Calmette-Guérin immunotherapy in 1278 patients with bladder cancer. J Urol. 1986;135:272-274.
189. von Reyn CF, Vuola JM. New vaccines for the prevention of tuberculosis. Clin Infect Dis. 2002;35:465-474.
190. Reider HL, Snider DE, Cauthen GM. Extrapulmonary tuberculosis in the United States. Am Rev Respir Dis. 1990;141:347-351.
191. Shafer RW, Kim DS, Weiss JP, et al. Extrapulmonary tuberculosis in patients with human immunodeficiency virus infection. Medicine. 1991;70:384-397.
192. Biehl JP. Miliary tuberculosis: A review of sixty-eight adult patients admitted to a municipal general hospital. Am Rev Tuberc. 1958;77:605-622.
193. Munt PW. Miliary tuberculosis in the chemotherapy era: With a clinical review in 69 American adults. Medicine. 1972;51:139-155.
194. Maartens G, Willcox PA, Benatar SR. Miliary tuberculosis: Rapid diagnosis, hematologic abnormalities, and outcome in 109 treated adults. Am J Med. 1990;89:291-296.
195. Kim JH, Langston AA, Gallis HA. Miliary tuberculosis: Epidemiology, clinical manifestations, diagnosis, and outcome. Rev Infect Dis. 1990;12:583-590.
196. Yu YL, Chow WH, Humphries MJ, et al. Cryptic miliary tuberculosis. Q J Med. 1986;59:421-428.
197. Willcox PA, Potgieter PD, Bateman ED, et al. Rapid diagnosis of sputum negative miliary tuberculosis using the flexible fiberoptic bronchoscope. Thorax. 1986;41:681-684.
198. Slavin RE, Walsh TJ, Pollock AD. Late generalized tuberculosis: A clinical pathologic analysis and comparison of 100 cases in the pre-antibiotic and antibiotic eras. Medicine. 1980;59:351-366.
199. Proudfoot AT, Akhar AJ, Douglas AC, et al. Miliary tuberculosis in adults. Br Med J. 1969;2:273-276.
200. Cameron SJ. Tuberculosis and the blood: A special relationship. Tubercle. 1974;55:55-72.
201. Lupatkin H, Brau N, Flomenberg P, et al. Tuberculous abscesses in patients with AIDS. Clin Infect Dis. 1992;14:1040-1044.
202. Kennedy DH, Fallon RJ. Tuberculous meningitis. JAMA. 1979;241:264-268.
203. Haas DW. Current and future applications of polymerase chain reaction for *Mycobacterium tuberculosis*. Mayo Clin Proc. 1996;71:311-313.
204. Taylor GR, Dannecker GE, Hoppe JE, et al. Negative polymerase chain reaction in a child with tuberculous meningoencephalitis. Infection. 1997;25:256-257.

205. Dube MP, Holtom PD, Larsen RA. Tuberculous meningitis in patients with and without human immunodeficiency virus infection. Am J Med. 1992;93:520-524.
206. Roper WH, Waring JJ. Primary serofibrinous pleural effusion in military personnel. Am Rev Tuberc. 1955;71:616-634.
207. Antoniskis D, Amin K, Barnes PF. Pleuritis as a manifestation of reactivation tuberculosis. Am J Med. 1990;89:447-450.
208. Epstein DM, Kline LR, Albelda SM, et al. Tuberculous pleural effusions. Chest. 1987;91:106-109.
209. Taelman H, Kagame A, Batungwanayo J, et al. Pericardial effusion and HIV infection. Lancet. 1990;335:924.
210. Strang JIG, Gibson DG, Mitchison DA, et al. Controlled clinical trial of complete open surgical drainage and of prednisolone in treatment of tuberculous pericardial effusion in Transkei. Lancet. 1988;2:759-763.
211. Strang JIG, Gibson DG, Nunn AJ, et al. Controlled trial of prednisolone as adjuvant in treatment of tuberculous constrictive pericarditis in Transkei. Lancet. 1987;23: 1418-1422.
212. Agner RC, Gallis HA. Pericarditis differential diagnostic considerations. Arch Intern Med. 1979;139:407-412.
213. Janssens JP, De Haller R. Spinal tuberculosis in a developed country: A review of 26 cases with special emphasis on abscesses and neurologic complications. Clin Orthop. 1990;257:67-75.
214. Griffiths DL. Tuberculosis of the spine: A review. Adv Tuberc Res. 1980;20:92-110.
215. Davidson PT, Horowitz I. Skeletal tuberculosis: A review with patient presentations and discussion. Am J Med. 1970;48:77-84.
216. LiZares LF, Valcarcel A, Del Castillo JM, et al. Tuberculous arthritis with multiple joint involvement. J Rheumatol. 1991;18:635-636.
217. Garrido G, Gomez-Reino JJ, Fernandez-Dapica P, et al. A review of peripheral tuberculous arthritis. Semin Arthritis Rheum. 1988;18:142-149.
218. Muradali D, Gold WL, Vellend H, et al. Multifocal osteoarticular tuberculosis: Report of four cases and review of management. Clin Infect Dis. 1993;17:204-209.
219. Bentz RR, Dimcheff DG, Nemiroff MJ, et al. The incidence of urine cultures positive for *Mycobacterium tuberculosis* in a general tuberculosis patient population. Am Rev Respir Dis. 1975;111:647-650.
220. Simon HB, Weinstein AJ, Pasternak MS, et al. Genitourinary tuberculosis: Clinical features in a general hospital population. Am J Med. 1977;63:410-420.
221. Christensen WI. Genitourinary tuberculosis: Review of 102 cases. Medicine. 1974;53:377-390.
222. Gow JG. Genitourinary tuberculosis: A study of the disease in one unit over a period of 24 years. Ann R Coll Surg Engl. 1971;49:50-70.
223. Morgan SH, Eastwood JB, Baker LRI. Tuberculous interstitial nephritis: The tip of an iceberg? Tubercle. 1990;71:5-6.
224. Gorse GJ, Belshe RB. Male genital tuberculosis: A review of the literature with instructive case reports. Rev Infect Dis. 1985;7:511-524.
225. Carter JR. Unusual presentations of genital tract tuberculosis. Int J Gynecol Obstet. 1990;33:171-176.
226. Jakubowski A, Elwood RK, Enarson DA. Clinical features of abdominal tuberculosis. J Infect Dis. 1988;158:687-692.
227. Shah S, Thomas V, Mathan M, et al. Colonoscopic study of 50 patients with colonic tuberculosis. Gut. 1992;33:347-351.
228. Kielhofner MA, Hamill RJ. Focal hepatic tuberculosis in a patient with acquired immunodeficiency syndrome. South Med J. 1991;84:401-404.
229. Hulnick DH, Megibow AJ, Naidich DP, et al. Abdominal tuberculosis: CT evaluation. Radiology. 1985;157:199-204.
230. Modilevsky T, Sattler FR, Barnes PF. Mycobacterial disease in patients with human immunodeficiency virus infection. Arch Intern Med. 1989;149:2201-2205.
231. Bastani B, Shariatzadeh MR, Dehdashti F. Tuberculous peritonitis: Report of 30 cases and review of the literature. Q J Med. 1985;56:549-557.
232. Burack WR, Hollister RM. Tuberculous peritonitis. Ann Intern Med. 1960;28:510-523.
233. Cheng IKP, Chan PCK, Chan MK. Tuberculous peritonitis complicating long-term peritoneal dialysis. Am J Nephrol. 1989;9:155-161.
234. Fernandez-Rodriguez CM, Perez-Arguelles BS, Ledo L, et al. Ascites adenosine deaminase activity is decreased in tuberculous ascites with low protein content. Am J Gastroenterol. 1991;86:1500-1503.
235. Singh MM, Bhargava AN, Jain KP. Tuberculous peritonitis: An evaluation of pathogenetic mechanisms, diagnostic procedures and therapeutic measures. N Engl J Med. 1969;281:1091-1094.
236. Haas DW. Are adjunctive corticosteroids indicated during tuberculous peritonitis? Clin Infect Dis. 1998;27:57-58.
237. Summers GD, McNicol MW. Tuberculosis of superficial lymph nodes. Br J Dis Chest. 1980;74:369-373.
238. Dandapat MC, Mishra BM, Dash SP, et al. Peripheral lymph node tuberculosis: A review of 80 cases. Br J Surg. 1990;77:911-912.
239. Campbell IA. The treatment of superficial tuberculous lymphadenitis. Tubercle. 1990;71:1-3.
240. Hewlett D Jr, Duncanson FP, Jagadha V, et al. Lymphadenopathy in an inner city population consisting principally of intravenous drug abusers with suspected acquired immunodeficiency syndrome. Am Rev Respir Dis. 1988;137:1275-1279.
241. Shriner KA, Mathisen GE, Goetz MB. Comparison of mycobacterial lymphadenitis among persons infected with human immunodeficiency virus and seronegative controls. Clin Infect Dis. 1992;15:601-605.
242. Van den Brande P, Vijgen J, Demedts M. Isolated intrathoracic tuberculous lymphadenopathy. Eur Respir J. 1991;4:758-760.
243. Pastores SM, Naidich DP, Arnada CP, et al. Intrathoracic adenopathy associated with pulmonary tuberculosis in patients with human immunodeficiency virus infection. Chest. 1993;103:1433-1437.
244. Perich J, Ayuso MC, Vilana R, et al. Disseminated lymphatic tuberculosis in acquired immunodeficiency syndrome: Computed tomography findings. Can Assoc Radiol J. 1990;41:353-357.
245. Radin DR. Intraabdominal *Mycobacterium tuberculosis* vs *Mycobacterium avium-intracellulare* infections in patients with AIDS: Distinction based on CT findings. AJR Am J Roentgenol. 1991;156:487-491.
246. Beyt BE Jr, Ortbals DW, Santa Cruz DJ, et al. Cutaneous mycobacteriosis: Analysis of 34 cases with a new classification of the disease. Medicine. 1981;60:95-109.
247. Yen A, Rady PL, Cortes-Franco R, et al. Detection of *Mycobacterium tuberculosis* in erythema induratum of Bazin using polymerase chain reaction. Arch Dermatol. 1997;133:532-533.
248. Rohatgi PK, Palazzolo JV, Saini NB. Acute miliary tuberculosis of the skin in acquired immunodeficiency syndrome. J Am Acad Dermatol. 1992;26:356-359.
249. Lindell MM Jr, Jing BS, Wallace S. Laryngeal tuberculosis. AJR Am J Roentgenol. 1977;129:677-680.
250. Lee PY, Drysdale AJ. Tuberculous otitis media: A difficult diagnosis. J Laryngol Otol. 1993;107:339.
251. Harrison NK, Knight RK. Tuberculosis of the nasopharynx misdiagnosed as Wegener's granulomatosis. Thorax. 1986;41:219-220.
252. Kelestimur F, Ozbakir O, Saglam A. Acute adrenocortical failure due to tuberculosis. J Endocrinol Invest. 1993;16:281-284.

CHAPTER 249

Mycobacterium leprae (Leprosy, Hansen's Disease)

WILLIAM R. LEVIS
JOEL D. ERNST

Leprosy has a rich history dating to biblical times.[1] "Leper" is an ancient term used to identify patients with leprosy who were severely stigmatized by the deformity that resulted from *Mycobacterium leprae* infection. Even with the development of modern antibiotic therapy, leprosy continues to place a significant burden on society, and patients continue to be stigmatized by the diagnosis, leading some to avoid proper diagnosis and therapy. In the clinical context, the term Hansen's disease should be used instead of leprosy, out of consideration for the patients. Peripheral nerve damage is the most common complication of leprosy, and early detection and therapy can prevent significant morbidity and disability.

Of the chronic infectious diseases whose clinical and pathologic manifestations arise in a distinct and well-characterized spectrum, leprosy is among the best understood. At one end of the clinical spectrum, tuberculoid leprosy is characterized by a small number of skin lesions, relatively few bacilli in lesions, and development and recruitment of T lymphocytes that contribute to control of the infection.[2,3] At the other extreme of the clinical spectrum, lepromatous leprosy is characterized by a larger number of skin lesions, clinically apparent infiltration of peripheral nerves and skin lesions by a large number of bacilli, and the presence of fewer T lymphocytes in lesions whose effector mechanisms do not contribute to control of the infection.[2,3]

M. leprae was the first bacterium discovered to be associated with a disease. Armauer Hansen, a Norwegian, discovered the microbe in 1874 just before Koch's discovery of *Mycobacterium tuberculosis,* but the inability to cultivate *M. leprae* in vitro (a problem that remains unsolved) allowed Koch to be credited with the discovery and the germ theory of disease. At the time of Hansen's discovery, the disease was endemic in Norway and other northern and southern European countries and is still recognized with a museum at the former Norwegian Leprosarium in Bergen, Norway.

Before the advent of effective antibiotics, treatment consisted of isolating patients diagnosed with leprosy in a leprosarium, which led further to a subculture and even a patients' movement to eradicate the terms leper and leprosy from the English language. Even today, there are still some active leprosaria, but in the past 20 years there has been a major change in both the management and understanding of leprosy. In the 1920s, the United States Public Health Service (USPHS) established a program for patients diagnosed with leprosy, and it has provided a program of global leadership through research and improved therapy that has dramatically changed the manner in which this disease is managed. The United States formally adopted a multidrug treatment policy and an ambulatory care program in 1981, and under USPHS guidance the World Health Organization (WHO) adopted a similar program in 1982. Despite these major advances, it is important to realize that leprosy is still a major bacterial disease that is far from being eradicated.

EPIDEMIOLOGY

Because detection of asymptomatic leprosy can be difficult and because of the persistent stigma associated with the diagnosis, most estimates of leprosy incidence and prevalence are likely to be even less accurate than those of other diseases. Because *M. leprae* cannot be cultured in vitro and there is no sensitive and specific diagnostic test for detection of individuals who are infected without clinical disease, transmission of leprosy is still poorly understood. The predominant mode of transmission is likely to be through respiratory or nasal discharge, as up to 10^7 viable bacilli per day can be shed in respiratory secretions of people with advanced multibacillary leprosy.[4] Modes of nonrespiratory transmission also probably exist. *M. leprae* has been detected in skin, sebaceous gland secretions, and eccrine sweat glands, so that skin-to-skin transmission cannot be excluded. Other modes of transmission such as soil, insect vectors, and armadillos remain speculative and deserve further study.

Global Epidemiology

In 2002, WHO reported detection of 612,110 new cases of leprosy, but active case finding has clearly established that there is an additional hidden case load (http://www.who.int/lep/). The largest number of cases originate in South Asia (India, Bangladesh, Nepal, and Myanmar). Africa and the Americas each reported 40,000 new cases of leprosy in 2002; most of the cases in the Americas were in Brazil.

In 1982, WHO adopted a modification of the U.S. recommended multidrug therapy (MDT) and embarked on a campaign for the elimination of leprosy. The present goal of the WHO program is to reduce the prevalence of leprosy to less than 1 case per 10,000 people. The WHO program has successfully increased the percentage of leprosy patients receiving MDT and has reduced the global prevalence of leprosy from estimates as high as 18 million to less than 2 million in the past 20 years. The long-term effect of the MDT campaign requires continued epidemiologic monitoring with particular scrutiny for late relapses (7 to 10 years after treatment).

United States

The epidemiology of leprosy in the United States reflects immigration patterns, as the vast majority of cases are in Hispanic and Asian immigrants. There are currently 4200 cases registered with the National Hansen's Disease Program, with a documented incidence between 100 and 200 newly diagnosed cases per year (http://bphc.hrsa.gov/nhdp). New York, California, Texas, and Louisiana accounted for the largest number of cases in the 2002 surveillance report, but leprosy has been reported from virtually every state. A marked increase in imported cases occurred with the emigration of Southeast Asian refugees during 1978 to 1988, but it was not accompanied by an increase in cases in people born in the United States, indicating that transmission of leprosy within the United States is rare.[5] However, six endemic cases in the New York City metropolitan area have been identified, including persons who had never traveled outside the continental United States.[6] It is common for cases of leprosy to have a long history of symptoms before diagnosis,[7] which suggests that additional undiagnosed cases exist.

MICROBIOLOGY AND GENOME SEQUENCE

Despite many generations of scientific effort, *M. leprae* remains unculturable in vitro. Consequently, knowledge of the biology of *M. leprae* has been restricted to biochemical and physiologic characterization of bacteria isolated from experimentally infected nine-banded armadillos. *M. leprae* is a straight or slightly curved rod-shaped organism, 1 to 8 μm long and 0.3 μm in diameter. It is gram positive and acid fast, although staining with carbol fuchsin can be irregular. On the basis of assays in footpads of immunodeficient mice, the doubling time of *M. leprae* has been estimated to be 11 to 13 days.[1] Like other mycobacteria, *M. leprae* possesses a highly lipid-rich cell wall, which contains diverse lipids and glycolipids, including an abundant antigenic glycolipid termed phenolic glycolipid 1 (PGL-1). Little information is available on the number or diversity of individual strains of *M. leprae.*

The availability of the genome sequence of one strain of *M. leprae* has provided substantial information on the biology of *M. leprae,* its relationship to other mycobacteria, potential explanations for the inability to culture it in vitro, and potential new targets for drug therapy. The genome of *M. leprae* contains approximately 3.3 million base pairs, with an average G + C content of 57.8%. It compares to the genome of *M. tuberculosis,* which contains approximately 4.4 million base pairs, with an average G + C content greater than 65%.[8] In addition to the reduction in the size of the *M. leprae* genome compared with that of *M. tuberculosis,* only 49.5% of the *M. leprae* genome is predicted to contain protein-coding genes because of a high frequency of randomly distributed pseudogenes (approximately 27% of the genome) and noncoding DNA, which may contain regulatory elements or inactivated genes, or both, that have mutated so extensively that they cannot be identified as genes. Therefore, the functional genome of *M. leprae* appears to be less than 40% of the size of the genome of *M. tuberculosis.* Because it is generally believed that *M. leprae* and *M. tuberculosis* evolved from a common mycobacterial ancestor, *M. leprae* appears to have lost approximately 2000 genes since the divergence, which has left it dependent on highly specialized ecological niches for its survival.

Analysis of the residual functional genes of *M. leprae* in comparison with those of *M. tuberculosis* and the sequenced genomes of other bacteria has provided considerable insight into its biology. On the basis of the presence of intact operons, it appears that *M. leprae* has retained nearly all essential anabolic pathways, including synthesis of amino acids, purines, pyrimidines, nucleosides, nucleotides, and many vitamins and enzyme cofactors. In contrast, it lacks the rich diversity of the apparatus for lipid synthesis and modification characteristic of *M. tuberculosis,* which is consistent with biochemical comparisons of the lipids of the two species. In particular, *M. leprae* lacks methoxymycolates, probably because of the absence of the *mmaA2* and *mmaA3* genes whose products are responsible for methoxy modification of mycolic acids in *M. tuberculosis.*[9] In addition, *M. leprae* has only 6 genes encoding polyketide synthases, compared with 18 in *M. tuberculosis.* Because specific polyketides contribute to pathogenesis of *M. tuberculosis*[10] and *Mycobacterium ulcerans,*[11] the differential polyketide synthase gene content may account for many of the differences in pathogenesis of *M. leprae* compared with other virulent mycobacteria.

One of the polyketide synthases absent from the *M. leprae* genome is encoded by *mbtB,* which is essential for synthesis of salicylate-derived mycobactin siderophores in *M. tuberculosis.* An *M. tuberculosis* mutant that lacks *mbtB* is impaired in its ability to acquire iron and to grow in iron-poor media or macrophages.[10] The absence of the entire *mbt* operon from *M. leprae* implies that this species is impaired in its ability to acquire iron and must depend on other mechanisms for iron acquisition and retention, which may contribute to the narrow ecological niche occupied by *M. leprae.* A glycolipid that is important in *M. leprae* pathogenesis and that is absent from *M. tuberculosis* is PGL-1. PGL-1 is derived from phthiocerol dimycocerosate (PDIM) by addition of O-methylated deoxy sugars, but analysis of the *M. leprae* genome sequence has not revealed the genes encoding the glycosyl-transferases that modify PDIM to produce PGL-1.

The completion of the genome sequence of *M. leprae* provides unique information on potential mechanisms of host and ecological restriction, metabolism, and pathogenesis that has been unavailable in the past because of the inability to culture the bacteria. Further analysis of the *M. leprae* genome and experimental analysis of the functions of specific genes in heterologous systems promise to provide considerable additional understanding of the biology and pathogenesis of *M. leprae*.

IMMUNOLOGY

Clinical and Immunologic Spectrum of Leprosy

On the basis of the number of *M. leprae* present in lesions as determined by acid-fast staining and the histopathologic appearance, clinical leprosy has long been categorized as multibacillary, or lepromatous; or as paucibacillary, or tuberculoid. Some patients' disease and histopathologic appearance fall between these two polar extremes, and a five-category system is now in general use to describe the type of leprosy in an individual patient: lepromatous leprosy (LL), borderline lepromatous (BL), borderline (BB), borderline tuberculoid (BT), and tuberculoid (TT).[2] This classification has been widely used, at least in part because of the clear correlation between the histologic appearance of the local immune response (abundant lymphocytes and well-formed granulomas in tuberculoid; fewer lymphocytes without well-formed granulomas in lepromatous) and the number of bacteria (few in tuberculoid; numerous in lepromatous). From these observations, a correlation between the nature of the immune response, control of bacterial growth, and clinical appearance in leprosy has promoted sophisticated studies of the protective cellular immune response to *M. leprae*.

Mechanisms of Immunity

The early observation that tuberculoid leprosy is associated with large numbers of lymphocytes and low numbers of *M. leprae* in lesions supported the concept that adaptive cellular immunity contributes to control of the infection. Subsequently, with advances in understanding basic cellular immunity, it was found that the patterns of cytokine expression in lesions correlated with protective immunity.[12] A seminal contribution to understanding protective immunity in leprosy was the finding that tuberculoid leprosy was associated with lymphocyte expression of interleukin-2 (IL-2), lymphotoxin, and interferon-γ in lesions, whereas lepromatous leprosy was associated with lymphocyte expression of IL-4, IL-5, and IL-10, and not interferon-γ, in lesions.[3] This pattern of polarity of cytokine production fits the paradigm of helper T cell type 1 (Th1)- or Th2-biased differentiation of the effector functions of T lymphocytes and has been used as the basis of further studies to understand the determinants of an effective immune response to *M. leprae*.

Given the evidence that a Th1-biased CD4⁺ T-cell response to *M. leprae* is associated with control of infection and a Th2-biased response is not, identifying the factors that determine the polarity of the immune response in leprosy has received considerable attention. Although individuals with lepromatous leprosy exhibit little, if any, Th1 immune responses to *M. leprae* antigens, their CD4⁺ T lymphocytes are capable of responding to *M. tuberculosis* antigens with a Th1 (i.e., interferon-γ) response, which demonstrates that lepromatous leprosy is not the result of a global inability to generate a Th1 response.[13] This finding has focused attention on the interactions of *M. leprae* and antigen-presenting cells such as monocytes and dendritic cells because the outcome of these encounters can determine the polarity of naïve CD4⁺ T-cell differentiation (i.e., Th1 versus Th2).

As described in Chapter 9, antigen stimulation of CD4⁺ T lymphocytes is mediated by presentation of pathogen-derived peptide (bound to major histocompatibility complex class II) or glycolipid (bound to CD1a, b, c, or d) antigens on monocytes or dendritic cells for recognition by specific T-cell antigen receptors. The major determinants of the polarity of differentiation of antigen-stimulated naïve T

lymphocytes are imposed by the antigen-presenting cells. One of the major determinants of Th1 differentiation of naïve T lymphocytes is antigen-presenting cell secretion of IL-12. IL-12 expression is approximately 10-fold higher in tuberculoid lesions than in lepromatous lesions,[14] although peripheral blood monocytes and monocyte-derived dendritic cells from patients with lepromatous leprosy and tuberculoid leprosy produce similar amounts of IL-12 in response to a triacylated lipopeptide derived from *M. leprae*.[13] Lipopeptide stimulation of antigen-presenting cell IL-12 production is mediated by Toll-like receptors 1 (TLR1) and 2 (TLR2), and expression of TLR1 and TLR2 is much higher in lesions of tuberculoid compared with lepromatous leprosy.[15] Deficient expression of TLR2 in lepromatous lesions may be secondary to the presence of IL-4, which downregulates expression of TLR2 on monocytes and monocyte-derived dendritic cells in vitro.[15]

These findings imply that circulating monocytes from patients with tuberculoid and lepromatous leprosy do not differ in their ability to respond to *M. leprae*–stimulated, TLR-dependent IL-12 production but that antigen-presenting cells in lepromatous lesions respond to *M. leprae* stimulation less well than those in tuberculoid lesions because of lower expression of TLR1 and TLR2. In addition to TLR-stimulated production of IL-12, stimulation of antigen-presenting cells through CD40 by activated T cells expressing CD40L contributes to production of IL-12. Expression of CD40 and CD40L has also been found to be deficient in lepromatous compared with tuberculoid lesions.[16] The low expression of TLR1, TLR2, and CD40 in lepromatous lesions probably contributes to deficient induction of IL-12, and the resulting deficiency of IL-12 in lepromatous lesions is consistent with failure to generate Th1-biased, interferon-γ–producing CD4⁺ T cells that respond to *M. leprae* antigens.

Although understanding the differences in the immune response in lepromatous compared with tuberculoid leprosy has advanced considerably, the essential initial determinant of the distinct responses remains to be identified. The polarity of the cellular immune response (i.e., Th1 versus Th2) is likely to be determined during the initial encounter of a naïve host with *M. leprae*, but it is not yet clear whether the essential determinant of that outcome is influenced by the route of infection, the precise phenotype of the antigen-presenting cells that present *M. leprae* antigens to naïve T cells, or other host cofactors such as infection with other pathogens. Further investigations of the determinants of T-cell differentiation are needed; at least some of the determinants of the encounter with *M. leprae* are genetically determined.

GENETIC FACTORS IN SUSCEPTIBILITY TO LEPROSY

Cases of leprosy exhibit geographic (e.g., village) and family clustering. Although clustering of leprosy in families can be due at least in part to shared environments and to similarities in exposure, studies in geographically and ethnically diverse populations have provided substantial evidence for genetic determinants of susceptibility to leprosy (reviewed in references 17 and 18). Moreover, there are clearly genetic variations that influence susceptibility to the presence of infection (leprosy per se), whereas other genetic loci influence the clinical form of the disease (multibacillary or paucibacillary). Most early efforts to define the genetic determinants of susceptibility to leprosy were association studies that examined the frequency of human leukocyte antigen (HLA) types with leprosy per se or the clinical form. Although these studies demonstrated associations between HLA-DR2 (now subtyped as DRB1*1501 and DRB1*1502) and tuberculoid leprosy, they also revealed that HLA genes did not fully account for the genetic effects on susceptibility. Susceptibility to leprosy is determined by multiple genes, and some of the genes and chromosomal regions whose variations influence susceptibility to leprosy per se or to either multibacillary or paucibacillary disease have been identified (Table 249-1).

The genes identified in these studies (*NRAMP1*, vitamin D receptor, tumor necrosis factor-α, IL-10, and HLA class II) have established roles or at least plausible roles in innate or adaptive immunity to intracellular pathogens and provide the basis for further studies of the

TABLE 249-1 Genetic Susceptibility in Leprosy

Gene or Chromosomal Region	Leprosy Per Se	Clinical Form of Disease		Reference
		Multibacillary	Paucibacillary	
HLA DRB1*1501		S		55
HLA DRB1*1502			S	56
HLA DRB1*1501+1502				57
NRAMP1 (SLC11A1) 3′ UTR	S	S		58, 59
Vitamin D receptor nucleotide 352; homozygosity for C		S		60
Vitamin D receptor nucleotide 352; homozygosity for T			S	60
TNF-α promoter (−308A)		S		61
TNF-α promoter (−308A)	R	R		62
IL-10 promoter (−819TT)			S	62
TAP2-B allele			S	63
HLA/TNF haplotype segregation		S	S	64
6q25	S			65
10p13			S	65, 66
20p12	S		S	67

HLA, human leukocyte antigen; IL-10, interleukin-10; R, linkage or association with resistance; S, linkage or association with susceptibility; TNF, tumor necrosis factor.

basis of the variable outcomes of exposure to *M. leprae*. In addition to these findings, genetic studies have revealed a lack of association of leprosy susceptibility with the chromosomal region (5p) that contains the Th2 cytokine gene cluster.[19] Because a Th2-biased immune response is characteristic of lepromatous leprosy, this finding suggests that genetic variations in this region are not the primary determinants of the polarization of the immune response to *M. leprae*. Additional studies are necessary to understand more fully the genetic basis of susceptibility to leprosy and to define precisely the polymorphisms in the chromosomal regions linked to susceptibility.

PATHOGENESIS OF NERVE DAMAGE

Peripheral sensory nerve damage is the leading cause of functional morbidity in people infected by *M. leprae* and is characteristic of both multibacillary and paucibacillary disease. Studies have revealed that peripheral nerve damage in leprosy can be mediated by *M. leprae* itself as well as by the immune response to *M. leprae*.[20,21]

Direct Nerve Damage by *Mycobacterium leprae*

M. leprae invades Schwann cells, the glial cells of the peripheral nervous system. Because Schwann cells form a functional unit with peripheral nerve axons and this functional unit is surrounded by a basal lamina, studies have focused on the interaction of *M. leprae* with specific proteins of the basal lamina. These studies revealed that *M. leprae* specifically interacts with the G domain of the α2-subunit of laminin-2, a neural-specific isoform of the 11-member laminin family of extracellular matrix proteins.[22] This domain of laminin-2 can bind simultaneously to *M. leprae* and to the Schwann cell laminin receptor, α-dystroglycan, allowing high-affinity binding of *M. leprae* to Schwann cells by using laminin-2 as a bridging molecule.[23] Laminin-2 recognizes two distinct molecules on the surface of *M. leprae*, a 21-kDa protein and the abundant glycolipid PGL-1. The 21-kDa protein, termed *M. leprae* laminin-binding protein (ML-LBP21), interacts with the G4 module of the α-subunit of laminin-2, and ML-LBP21 is sufficient to mediate invasion of Schwann cells.[24] PGL-1, which is a highly abundant component of *M. leprae*, also binds to the α2-subunit of laminin-2, through the G4 and G5 modules of the G domain.[25] PGL-1, like ML-LBP21, is sufficient to mediate invasion of Schwann cells and interacts with laminin-2 through the unique trisaccharide of PGL-1 (3,6-di-*O*-methylglucose linked α-1→4 to 2,3-di-*O*-methylrhamnose linked β-1→2 to 3-*O*-methylrhamnose).[25,26] These studies provide considerable insight into the molecular mechanism of the direct interaction between *M. leprae* and Schwann cells of peripheral nerves and illustrate that *M. leprae* uses a neural-specific target for its apparently redundant bacterial molecules (ML-LBP21 and PGL-1), to achieve its unique tropism for peripheral nerves.

Once *M. leprae* or its PGL-1 is bound and internalized by Schwann cells, it can cause rapid and direct demyelination of peripheral nerves in vitro and in vivo in the absence of a cellular immune response.[20] Demyelination by *M. leprae* can promote further invasion of Schwann cells by the bacteria, as *M. leprae* preferentially invades nonmyelinated Schwann cell–axon units. *M. leprae*–mediated demyelination occurs without early cell death or toxicity, although Schwann cells and neurons can die by apoptosis later after infection.[20,27] In addition, dead *M. leprae* or PGL-1 shed from live or dying *M. leprae* can mediate peripheral nerve demyelination,[20] which may contribute to the ongoing nerve damage that can follow initiation of active chemotherapy.

In addition to PGL-1, an *M. leprae* 19-kDa lipoprotein can mediate Schwann cell apoptosis as an agonist of TLR2. TLR2 is expressed on Schwann cells in vitro and in vivo, and apoptotic Schwann cells can be found in human leprosy lesions.[27] The results of these studies clearly demonstrate that *M. leprae* is capable of direct peripheral nerve damage, even in the absence of inflammation or a cellular immune response. These mechanisms are likely to be especially responsible for peripheral nerve damage in multibacillary leprosy, in which inflammation and a Th1-biased cellular immune response are less likely to contribute to nerve damage.

Immunologically Mediated Peripheral Nerve Damage in Leprosy

In addition to direct damage to peripheral nerves by *M. leprae*, there is abundant evidence that the immune response in leprosy contributes to nerve damage. This contribution is likely to account for much of the nerve damage that occurs in paucibacillary leprosy, in which the bacteria or PGL-1 or both are present in insufficient quantities to cause widespread nerve damage, and in reversal reactions, in which inflammation is particularly prominent.

Several distinct immunologic mechanisms probably contribute to nerve damage in leprosy.[28] Proinflammatory cytokines such as tumor necrosis factor-α, IL-1β, and interferon-γ are especially prominent in lesions during reversal reactions,[29] when marked and irreversible nerve damage can occur. Because these molecules can directly and indirectly contribute to inflammatory tissue damage and can induce apoptosis of Schwann cells in vitro,[30] it is likely that these mediators play an active role in nerve damage. Reversal reactions are also characterized by an increase in the number of CD4+ T lymphocytes in lesions, and at least some of these CD4+ cells exhibit a cytotoxic phenotype and kill *M. leprae*–infected Schwann cells through antigen- and class II–dependent secretion of cytotoxic granule contents.[21] Whether similar mechanisms of nerve damage occur in chronic tuberculoid leprosy is not established, but qualitatively similar cytokines and T lymphocytes are found in tuberculoid lesions.

CLINICAL MANIFESTATIONS

Diagnosis and Differential Diagnosis

The cardinal manifestations of leprosy are infiltrative skin lesions, hypoesthesia, and peripheral neuropathy; and the clinical manifestations of leprosy are closely related to the polarity of the cellular immune response to *M. leprae* in the individual. Many patients with stable tuberculoid or borderline tuberculoid leprosy may present with skin lesions but without subjective complaints. In contrast, patients with advanced tuberculoid leprosy may present with peripheral neuropathy, which is generally asymmetric. Patients with stable lepromatous or borderline lepromatous leprosy may present with widespread infiltrative skin lesions or prominent peripheral neuropathy with secondary deformities (such as claw hand) or nonhealing painless ulcers. Reversal reactions are most often manifest as increased erythema of skin lesions with progressive peripheral neuropathy, and erythema nodosum leprosum arises with systemic signs, sometimes including fever, and panniculitis, with painful erythematous skin nodules. The history of a patient with suspected leprosy should include whether the person has resided in an area with high prevalence and whether the person has been previously diagnosed or treated for leprosy. Certain patients may deny knowledge of a prior diagnosis or may report that skin lesions or neuropathy or both are acute, as they wish to avoid the stigma of a diagnosis of leprosy, even in emigrants to developed countries.

By following the basic principles of skin examination—distribution, configuration, primary lesions, depth of lesion—it is often possible to classify the type of leprosy accurately. Lepromatous disease is a symmetrical nonscaling infiltrative dermopathy (Figs. 249-1 to 249-3) in which the lesions have intact sensation. Slight asymmetry and a tendency toward annular lesions are seen in subpolar lepromatous disease (Fig. 249-4), and borderline lepromatous (Fig. 249-5) and midborderline disease show striking annularity. The depth of the lesion and degree of lesional hypoesthesia provide additional clues to the type of leprosy. Toward the tuberculoid pole or over reactions the skin begins

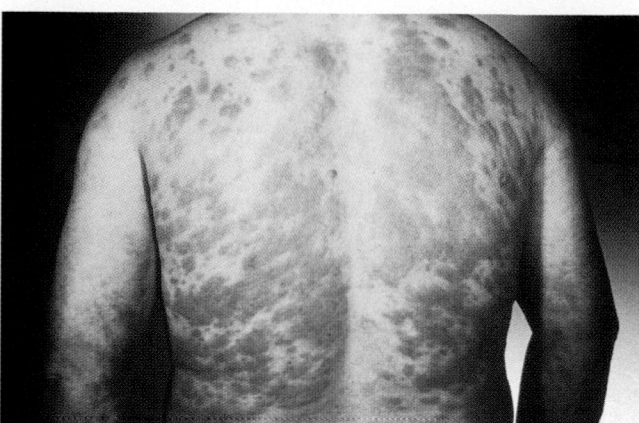

FIGURE 249-2. Lepromatous leprosy can arise as scattered infiltrative papules without scale.

to scale (Figs. 249-6 and 249-7), perhaps because of the production of interferon-γ and its effects on epidermal keratinocytes.[31] Lepromatous disease lacks the fine lesional scale, although occasional large fishlike scales not confined to the lesions can be seen (acquired ichthyosis).

In addition to inspection of the skin, the degree of hypoesthesia aids in clinically classifying leprosy, as tuberculoid lesions are generally hypoesthetic. The degree of hypoesthesia depends on the location of the lesion, the size of the lesion, and the degree of a Th1-biased immune response. Thus, small lesions on the highly innervated face may still have intact sensation even in polar tuberculoid disease. The skin lesions of multibacillary leprosy (borderline lepromatous and lepromatous) generally have intact sensation, although some borderline lepromatous lesions on the body may exhibit hypoesthesia. In addition to lesional hypoesthesia, peripheral neuropathies occur throughout the leprosy spectrum. Marked peripheral nerve (especially in superficial

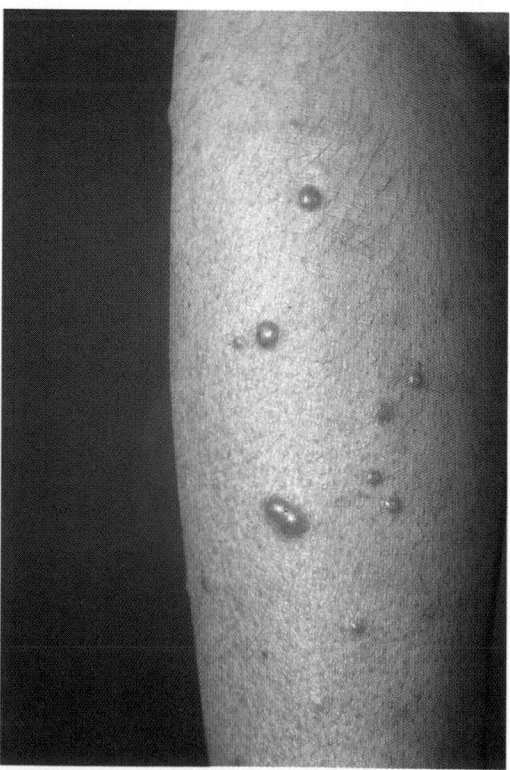

FIGURE 249-1. Lepromatous leprosy arises as a diffuse infiltrative dermopathy without scale. Sensation in the lesions remains intact.

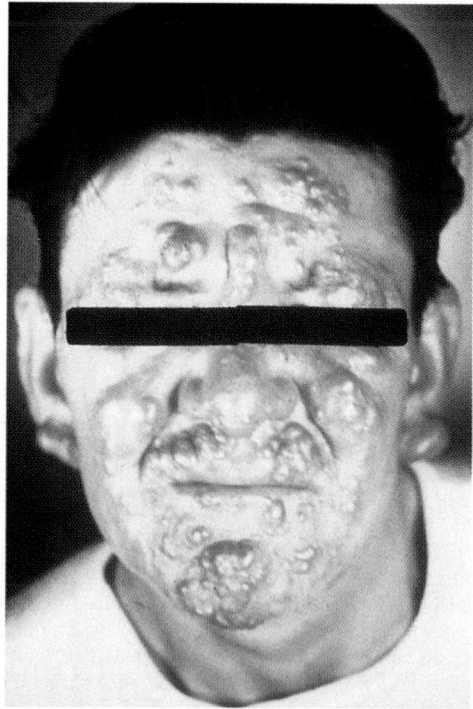

FIGURE 249-3. If lepromatous leprosy is left untreated, it can progress to "leonine" facies.

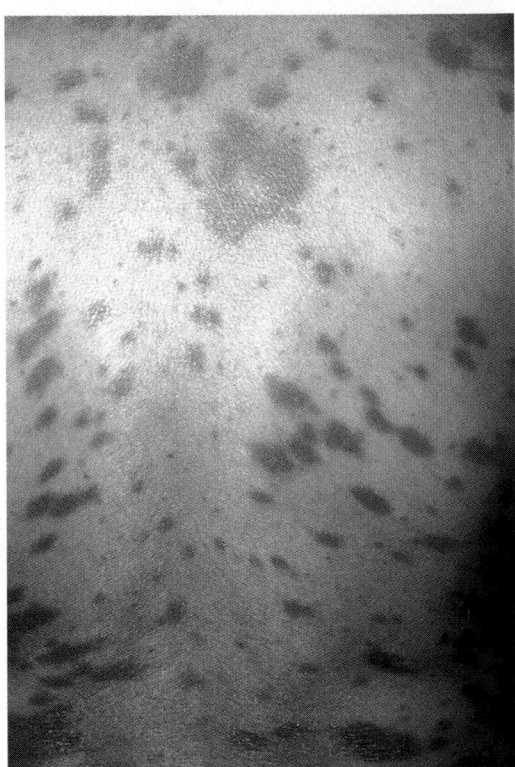

FIGURE 249-4. Subpolar lepromatous leprosy arises as diffuse infiltrative dermopathy with occasional slight annularity and little or no scale.

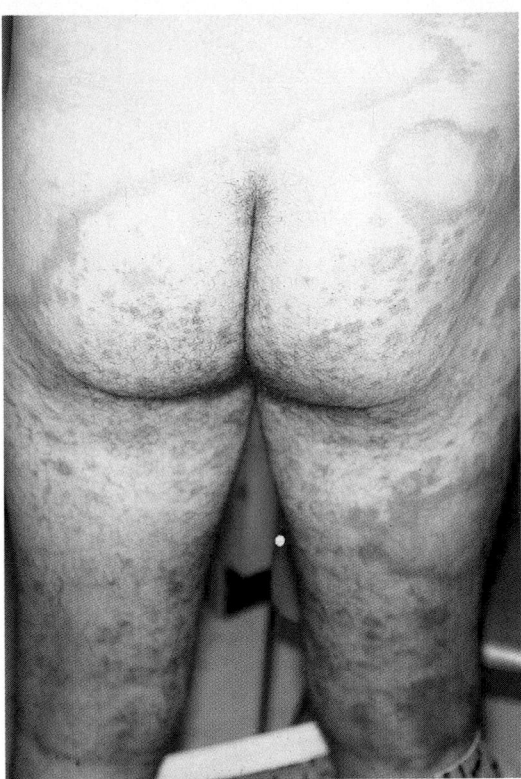

FIGURE 249-5. Borderline lepromatous leprosy—the smaller annular plaques have intact sensation, but large annular plaques are hypoesthetic.

nerves, such as the ulnar, median, and posterior tibial nerves) thickening is characteristic of both borderline and lepromatous disease.

Each of the major clinical manifestations of leprosy has a distinct differential diagnosis. When leprosy arises as an infiltrative dermopathy, there is generally a lack of scale, which distinguishes it from common inflammatory dermatoses such as eczema and psoriasis. There may be a fine scale over tuberculoid lesions or reactions, but the granulomatous response in leprosy is generally more infiltrative than that in typical inflammatory dermatoses. In addition, there is loss of sensation in tuberculoid lesions, which is almost pathognomonic of leprosy. At the lepromatous end of the spectrum, sensation is intact but lesions lack scale. A biopsy and Fite stain distinguish leprosy from other infiltrative disorders, such as cutaneous tuberculosis, sarcoidosis, swimming pool granuloma (*Mycobacterium marinum*), granuloma annulare, Wegener's granulomatosis, tertiary syphilis, leishmaniasis, Lyme disease, deep fungal infections, onchocerciasis, lupus profundus, or cutaneous lymphomas.

Another common presentation of leprosy is as a leprosy reaction simulating lupus erythematosus, rheumatoid arthritis, viral exanthems, urticaria, drug eruptions, and other vascular reaction patterns such as erythema multiforme. As leprosy can itself be associated with autoimmune phenomena, including positive antinuclear antibody, rheumatoid factor, thyroid autoantibodies, and Hashimoto's thyroiditis, a biopsy and Fite stain are required to make the distinction.

The third common way for leprosy to arise is as a peripheral neuropathy. In pure neural leprosy, slit smears are unrevealing, although skin and nasal mucosal biopsies can be abnormal.[32] As the differential diagnosis of peripheral neuropathy is large, a high index of suspicion is required to make the diagnosis of neural leprosy. Palpation of the nerves may reveal thickened nerves, which are suggestive of leprosy, but a nerve biopsy is required to confirm the diagnosis. As biopsy of peripheral nerves sacrifices function, judicious selection is required. The sural nerve is preferred as it results in only a mild loss of sensation on the lateral aspect of the foot that can improve with time. Fite stain of the nerve usually reveals only sparse bacilli and a granulomatous tuberculoid histopathology, but rarely a pure neural leprosy is multibacillary limited to the nerves.

Leprosy and Human Immunodeficiency Virus

Despite the importance of CD4+ T cells and the polarity of the cellular immune response in determining the clinical manifestations of leprosy, current evidence indicates that human immunodeficiency virus (HIV)-associated immunodeficiency has little effect on the course of leprosy. Although HIV is more prevalent in patients with leprosy than in healthy blood donors in some studies, this has not been a widespread finding. In addition, HIV has not been found to affect the clinical form of leprosy (i.e., multibacillary is not more common or paucibacillary less common than in HIV-negative control subjects),[33-35] and HIV infection does not appear to affect the histopathologic appearance of leprosy lesions.[33] *M. leprae* may grow too slowly to affect the clinical form of leprosy in people with HIV in developing countries, as other complications of HIV may dominate. However, as antiretroviral therapy and prophylaxis against other opportunistic infections become more common in the developing world, changes in the course and manifestations of leprosy in people with HIV may become more apparent. Indeed, people with HIV and *M. leprae* coinfection can exhibit reversal reactions as a manifestation of immune reconstitution upon treatment with antiretroviral therapy.[36]

HISTOPATHOLOGY

Histopathology is the only currently established method for diagnosing leprosy. The clinician's index of suspicion needs to be followed up by a pathologist's ability to perform properly Fite staining of tissue biopsy specimens with appropriate positive controls for the staining. It should be emphasized (including to the pathologist) that although *M. leprae* is acid fast, it is particularly sensitive to alcohol decolorization, and the Fite or modified Fite stain is essential; Ziehl-Neelsen staining may produce

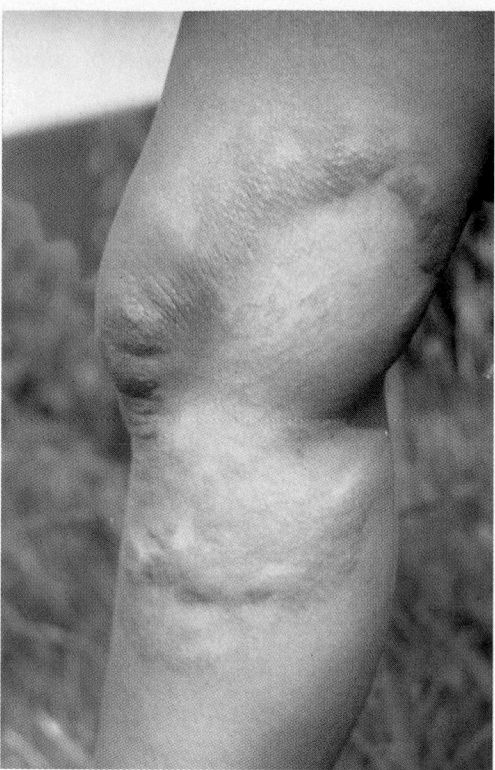

FIGURE 249-6. Borderline tuberculoid leprosy arises as infiltrated plaques and hypesthesia.

false-negative results. With proper Fite staining, lepromatous leprosy reveals numerous (>1000 per high-power [600 to 800×] field) acid-fast bacilli, including clumps, termed globi (Fig. 249-8). With progression toward the tuberculoid pole, the number of bacilli decreases to 100 to 1000/field in borderline lepromatous disease; they are frequent (10 to 100/field) in borderline, scattered to rare (0.1 to 10/field) in borderline tuberculoid, and rare or totally absent in polar tuberculoid disease. At the paucibacillary tuberculoid pole, the diagnosis of leprosy can be made in the absence of acid-fast bacilli with well-formed noncaseating granulomas and nerve involvement (Fig. 249-9).

In addition to the Fite stain, hematoxylin and eosin and immunohistochemistry are helpful in making the diagnosis and identifying the type of leprosy. In lepromatous leprosy the macrophages (or histiocytes) are flaccid, lipid-laden, inactive, foamy (Virchow) cells because of the lack of macrophage activation in the absence of local interferon-γ. There

are also very few lymphocytes, and the lymphocytes that are present produce IL-10 or IL-4, or both, and not interferon-γ.[29] In contrast to leprosy, in tuberculoid and borderline tuberculoid disease, macrophage stimulation by interferon-γ results in a hyaline appearance of an active secretory cell with a surrounding mantle of numerous lymphocytes of both CD4 and CD8 phenotype.[37] Borderline lepromatous, borderline, and borderline tuberculoid give a picture between these two extremes. In an immunohistochemical study of lepromatous skin it was shown that an intradermal injection of interferon-γ upgraded lepromatous leprosy infiltrates toward a borderline tuberculoid picture with attendant epidermal proliferation.[38] Epidermal thickening can be seen over leprosy reactions,[39] probably secondary to the effects of interferon-γ.[31]

REACTIONS

Reversal Reactions (Lepra Type 1 Reactions)

Reversal reactions can occur throughout the leprosy spectrum except for polar tuberculoid disease, as they are the consequence of the development of a more appropriate Th1-biased cellular immune response and represent a vigorous host response against *M. leprae* with local production of interferon-γ and tumor necrosis factor-α[40] as well as the effects of cytolytic CD4+ T cells.[21]

Reversal reactions are recognized clinically by increased erythema of cutaneous plaques and nodules (Fig. 249-10) and by increased swelling of peripheral nerves (especially the ulnar in the ulnar groove at the elbow and the posterior tibial nerve just inferior to the medial malleolus; observing the patient's reaction reveals the degree of inflammation in the nerves). There may be a peripheral lymphocytosis, and skin biopsy may show an accompanying increase in lymphocytes with nerve involvement.

Erythema Nodosum Leprosum (Lepra Type 2 Reactions)

Erythema nodosum leprosum (ENL) is clinically distinguished from reversal reactions by the presence of panniculitis manifest as subcutaneous red nodules (Fig. 249-11), arthralgias or frank arthritis, fever with temperature up to 40° C, and increased urinary protein and active sediment. The peripheral blood may show a polymorphonuclear leukocytosis with a left shift.

Lucio's Phenomenon

Lucio's phenomenon is an uncommon but severe form of reaction in multibacillary leprosy that is distinct from type 1 (reversal reaction) or type 2 (ENL) reactions and can be fatal.[41] It is clinically manifest by bluish or violaceous and hemorrhagic plaques followed by necrotic ulcerations (Fig. 249-12). The epidermis is necrotic, and vasculitis or vasculopathy with endothelial proliferation and thrombus formation is present. Acid-fast bacilli may be present in the endothelial cells.

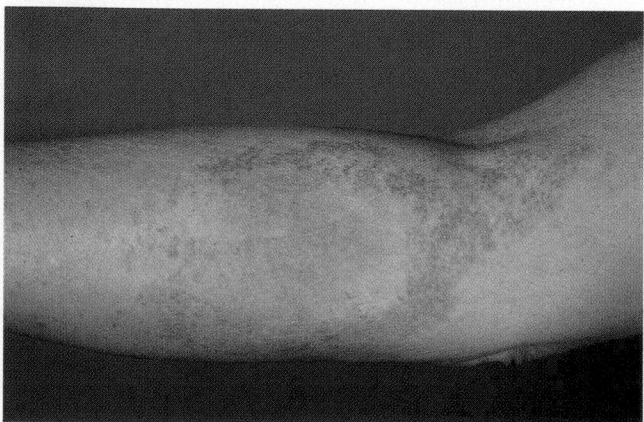

FIGURE 249-7. Polar tuberculoid lesions appear as hypoesthetic infiltrated plaques and sometimes show a fine scale.

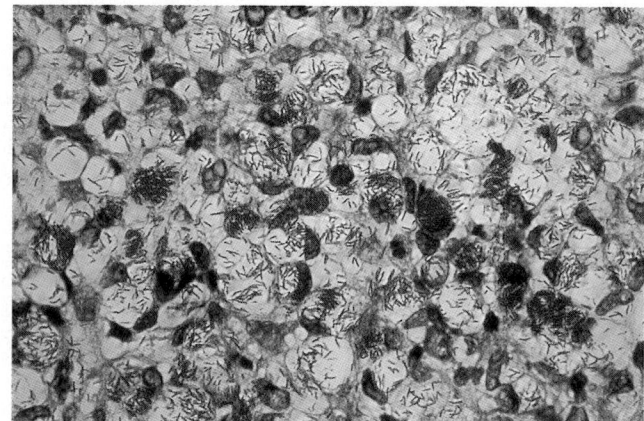

FIGURE 249-8. Multibacillary, or lepromatous, leprosy shows numerous Fite-positive organisms and only rare lymphocytes.

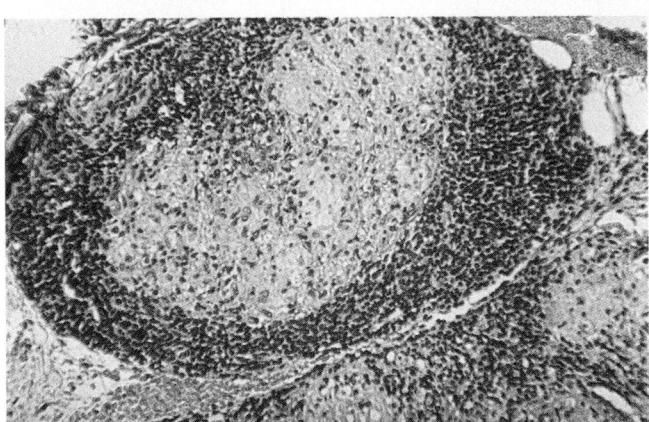

FIGURE 249-9. Paucibacillary, or tuberculoid, leprosy shows a "sarcoidal" granuloma with nerve involvement. Macrophages have an active secretory hyaline appearance with many lymphocytes. Fite staining may be negative or show only a few organisms.

LONG-TERM COMPLICATIONS

The major chronic complications of leprosy are due to peripheral nerve damage. Nerve damage can lead to decreased sweating and skin drying and cracking; to sensory deficits that lead to chronic, nonhealing injuries and ulcers; and to muscle paralysis (especially of the small muscles of the hand and foot) related to motor trunk involvement. Patients should be referred to appropriate rehabilitation medicine specialists, when available, for management of chronic neuropathy and injury prevention. In addition, facial deformity caused by facial nerve palsies and skin infiltration are amenable to reconstructive surgery.

The eye is also a site that requires particular attention in leprosy and all patients should be examined by an ophthalmologist; impaired corneal sensation and corneal opacity are the most common findings.[42] It is important to check patients for an intact corneal reflex and, if it is absent, take appropriate precautions to avoid corneal drying, injury, and opacification. Occasionally, beaded corneal nerves can be seen even without a slit lamp. *M. leprae* can grow in the uveal tract and frank uveitis is common, especially during ENL. It is important to be aware that ocular ENL can still be active even after ENL in the skin and joints is controlled by corticosteroids or thalidomide, or both. Ocular ENL requires topical corticosteroids. Often a low dose of thalidomide (50 to 100 mg/day) can help protect the patient from chronic active uveitis and progressive loss of sight.

The testicles are a site of predilection for multibacillary leprosy, and it is important to screen all multibacillary patients for follicle-stimulating hormone, luteinizing hormone, and testosterone levels.

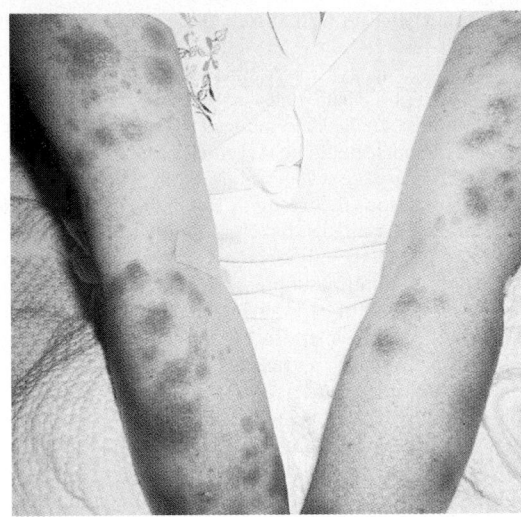

FIGURE 249-11. Erythema nodosum leprosum is recognized clinically by discrete subcutaneous red nodules (panniculitis).

Even patients with multibacillary leprosy who have received adequate antibiotic therapy and are bacillus negative are at risk for progressive testicular dysfunction, including infertility.[43,44] Hypogonadal males are also at greater risk for osteopenia and frank osteoporosis.

THERAPY

Antimicrobial Therapy

Background

Before the advent of antibiotics, there was no effective treatment for leprosy and isolation in leprosaria was the standard approach to disease control and therapy. Dapsone was the first antibiotic found to be effective for leprosy, largely on the basis of trials conducted at the former U.S. Public Health Service Hospital in Carville, Louisiana, in the 1940s and 1950s. Dapsone monotherapy was the standard of care worldwide until the 1970s, when reports of efficacy with rifampin and clofazimine began to appear. In 1981 the USPHS officially adopted the policy of MDT, and WHO followed with a modified protocol shortly thereafter.

Agents to Treat Leprosy

The three established antimicrobial agents are dapsone, rifampin, and clofazimine. Minocycline is also effective[45] and has proved useful when a patient is intolerant of or allergic to the three first-line agents.

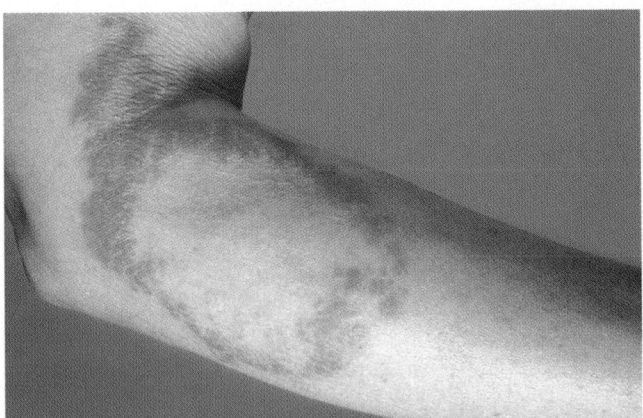

FIGURE 249-10. Reversal reactions are clinically recognized by erythema outlining infiltrative plaques.

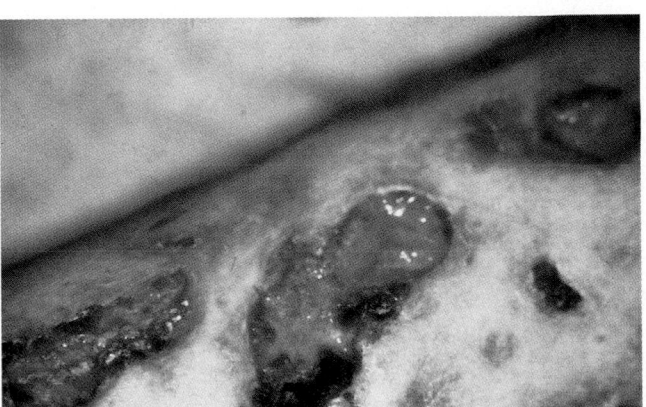

FIGURE 249-12. Lucio's phenomenon is recognized clinically by erosions and ulcerations secondary to underlying vasculitis.

Dapsone is inexpensive, well absorbed after oral administration, has a long serum half-life (28 hours), is well tolerated by most patients, and is safe for use in pregnancy. It is routinely used at a dose of 50 to 100 mg/day. Glucose-6-phosphate dehydrogenase (G6PD)–deficient individuals are susceptible to dapsone-induced methemoglobinemia and hemolysis, and all patients should be screened for G6PD deficiency before starting dapsone. If a patient has mild G6PD deficiency (the African type; caused by mutations that result in instability of the enzyme), dapsone can be started at 25 mg/day but close monitoring for anemia is necessary. In addition to methemoglobinemia and hemolytic anemia, dapsone can cause bone marrow suppression and profound neutropenia. Other rare adverse effects of dapsone include hepatitis, cholestatic jaundice, and a syndrome characterized by exfoliative dermatitis, generalized lymphadenopathy, fever, and hepatosplenomegaly.[1]

Rifampin is the most bactericidal drug against *M. leprae,* as determined by the decrease in viability of bacteria in the mouse foot-pad assay. It is rapidly absorbed after oral administration and has a serum half-life of approximately 3 hours. It is routinely used at a dose of 600 mg/day for treatment of leprosy but should never be used in monotherapy because resistance can develop with single point mutations in its target, RNA polymerase II. Because rifampin is actively bactericidal and rapid release of components from dead bacteria can have proinflammatory effects, rifampin is contraindicated during active reversal reactions or ENL. Adverse effects of rifampin include maculopapular skin rash, hepatotoxicity, an influenza-like syndrome (most frequent with intermittent therapy), and orange discoloration of tears, urine, saliva, and sweat. Thrombocytopenia occurs occasionally, but the platelet count rarely decreases below 10^5/L. If mild thrombocytopenia occurs, rifampin can be continued if the platelet count does not decrease below 10^5/L. Rifampin also induces metabolism and decreases serum concentrations of other drugs, including corticosteroids and oral contraceptives. Rifampin decreases serum concentrations of dapsone, but this is not clinically significant with a dapsone dose of 100 mg/day.

Clofazimine is a lipophilic dye that was originally developed for therapy of tuberculosis and is bacteriostatic against *M. leprae.* Clofazimine has a very long (70-day) half-life and appears to have anti-inflammatory activity as well as direct bacteriostatic activity. The usual dose of clofazimine for leprosy is 100 mg/day, except when used to treat reversal reactions or ENL, when up to 200 to 300 mg/day may be used. Clofazimine is generally very well tolerated; its major side effect is nearly universal discoloration of the skin. The skin discoloration can range from reddish-tan to bluish-black and can be blotchy but is reversible within 6 to 12 months of discontinuing the drug. Clofazimine has very little evidence of either bone marrow toxicity or hepatotoxicity. Chronic reactional patients who are maintained with prolonged high doses of clofazimine (200 to 300 mg/day) need to be monitored for enteropathy as clofazimine is deposited on the serosal surface of the gut and can cause crampy abdominal pain, mild nausea, and diarrhea and may rarely progress to bowel obstruction.

In addition to the four established antimicrobial agents, fluoroquinolones have been used successfully in clinical trials. Ciprofloxacin is ineffective, but ofloxacin, pefloxacin, and sparfloxacin all appear to be bactericidal. These second-generation fluoroquinolones and clarithromycin are currently in field trials in combination with the established agents. Although shortening the course of therapy by use of additional drugs might be possible, it must be remembered that relapses occur after 7 to 10 years and briefer courses need to be given on an informed consent basis.

Regimens to Treat Leprosy

Standard therapy for leprosy uses multiple drugs to increase the cure rate and prevent emergence of drug resistance and treatment failure.

Current Standard U.S. Regimens

Paucibacillary leprosy: Dapsone 100 mg/day plus rifampin 600 mg/day for 6 months, followed by dapsone monotherapy for 3

years for indeterminate and tuberculoid leprosy and 5 years for borderline tuberculoid leprosy.

Multibacillary leprosy: Dapsone 100 mg/day plus rifampin 600 mg/day for 3 years, followed by dapsone monotherapy for 10 years for borderline and indefinitely for borderline lepromatous or lepromatous. (Note: If dapsone resistance is suspected, clofazimine 50 mg/day should be added.)

World Health Organization Regimens

Paucibacillary leprosy: Dapsone 100 mg/day, unsupervised, plus rifampin 600 mg once monthly, supervised for 6 months.

Multibacillary leprosy: Dapsone 100 mg/day, plus clofazimine 50 mg/day, unsupervised, with rifampin 600 mg monthly and clofazimine 300 mg monthly, supervised. This regimen should be continued for at least 2 years and preferably until the skin smears are negative.

It is important to point out that U.S. guidelines for the treatment of leprosy are significantly different from the WHO MDT recommendations, although they are both based on the same principle: use of multiple drugs to avoid drug resistance. Information and a booklet are available through the National Hansen's Disease Program in Baton Rouge, Louisiana (1-800-642-2477). The U.S. recommendations include daily rifampin, the most bactericidal of the antibiotics against *M. leprae,* and recommend daily clofazimine only for chronically reactional patients or patients with suspected resistance. The duration of therapy in the WHO regimens is only 2 years for multibacillary leprosy regardless of the bacillary load. In the U.S. regimens, longer durations of therapy are recommended, but this can be individualized and monotherapy beyond 5 or 10 years is probably not necessary when the patient is clinically bacillus negative. Because of the large initial load of bacilli in multibacillary leprosy, pockets of bacillary persistence may be detected by nerve biopsy even after "adequate" treatment.[46] We routinely monitor such patients at yearly intervals and have not yet seen a full-blown bacillary relapse when they were treated by the recommended U.S. regimens. Some of these patients, however, develop chronic progressive neuropathies, which require further study and improved treatments.

Response to Therapy

Response to therapy is seen clinically as flattening and disappearance of papules, nodules, and plaques and improvement of nerve function. Quantification of bacillary load to assess response to treatment is still cumbersome and at best is semiquantitative. The number of intact Fite-positive organisms in slit smears or skin biopsies is referred to as the morphologic index and in properly treated patients should be zero by the end of therapy. The presence of intact organisms after a patient has received chemotherapy for several months indicates either noncompliance or drug resistance.

Occasionally, patients who have been adequately treated later show evidence of chronic reversal reactions and late neuropathies. Such patients, when bacillus negative, are considered not to have relapses but to have late reversal reactions. To improve nerve function we routinely treat such patients with low-dose clofazimine (50 to 100 mg three times a week) and monitor their nerve function. If the nerves remain stable or improve, we continue clofazimine until all signs of reaction have cleared. If the nerves show evidence of deterioration, additional therapy is warranted, including increasing the dose of clofazimine, adding a second or third antibiotic, or giving a course of corticosteroids, depending on the rate and degree of nerve deterioration.

RELAPSES AND TREATMENT OF RELAPSES

If a patient presents who has a history of adequate treatment but shows evidence of new lesions that are bacillus positive, the patient should be re-treated as a fresh case according to the recommended regimens. We recommend the more thorough U.S. regimens rather than once-monthly rifampin when affordable.

Treatment of Reactions

Treatment of Reversal Reactions

The decision on treatment of reactions should be made clinically, and antimycobacterial chemotherapy with clofazimine or dapsone, or both, should be continued throughout the course of therapy of a reactional state; rifampin should be withheld in the presence of active neuritis. In cases of borderline tuberculoid and borderline leprosy, a sudden loss of sensation requires prompt institution of corticosteroids without waiting for laboratory findings as delay in instituting therapy can lead to permanent nerve damage and residual deformity. In patients with subpolar lepromatous and borderline lepromatous leprosy, and in some patients with borderline and borderline tuberculoid leprosy, reversal reactions may be low grade, and management is based on clinical judgment and the patient's level of discomfort.

If the reaction is confined to the skin, as it often is in lepromatous and occasionally in borderline lepromatous leprosy, it is reasonable to allow it to smolder as the reaction is a manifestation of a more effective cellular immune response. If there is evidence of peripheral nerve deterioration, which is common in borderline lepromatous and nearly universal in borderline and borderline tuberculoid with reversal reactions, it is important to institute prednisone promptly at a dosage of 60 to 80 mg/day. The rate of tapering needs to be individualized and in general should be 10 mg per month or less in order to avoid permanent nerve damage and residual deformity. For chronic neuropathies with intact sensation, adding clofazimine or increasing the dose of clofazimine is an additional option. Rifampin should be withheld until the nerves become quiescent. Thalidomide, because of its ability to upregulate Th1 responses and its potential neurotoxicity, is contraindicated in pure reversal reactions. Occasionally, patients who present with ENL (see the next section) undergo a transition to mixed reactions and reversal reactions, which requires adjustment of therapy.

Treatment of Erythema Nodosum Leprosum

The treatment of choice for ENL is thalidomide. Thalidomide is available from Celgene Corporation (www.celgene.com) and requires that patients and the prescribing physician be enrolled in the System for Thalidomide Education and Prescribing Safety (STEPS) program to avoid the well-known teratogenic effect of phocomelia. The mechanism of action of thalidomide is incompletely understood, and it is likely to have multiple relevant cellular targets in ENL.[47,48] To treat ENL, the clinician should initiate therapy at a dose dictated by the intensity of ENL. If the multibacillary patient has ENL major with large subcutaneous plaques, frank arthritis, and temperature in excess of 38.8° C, a dose of 100 mg four times a day is indicated. With control of the reaction, tapering at a rate of approximately 50 to 100 mg a week can be initiated, to a maintenance dose of 50 to 100 mg at night. For milder cases of ENL with low-grade fever and a few scattered subcutaneous nodules, 50 to 100 mg at night controls these milder reactions. Because the major side effect of thalidomide, other than phocomelia and fatigue, is peripheral neuropathy, it is incumbent on the clinician to attempt periodically to taper patients off thalidomide completely. The peripheral neuropathy side effect is dose dependent with almost no neurotoxicity below 50 mg/day.[49] Because thalidomide may actually enhance Th1 immunity, it should not be used for pure reversal reactions. Occasionally ENL is refractory to thalidomide or the reaction is more of a reversal reaction or mixed reaction. Thalidomide-unresponsive cases may respond to prednisone (60 to 80 mg/day).

There is no current consensus for therapy of Lucio's phenomenon; thalidomide alone may be of little use.[50] Difficult reactional patients with thalidomide-refractory ENL, chronic reversal reactions, mixed reactions, or bullous or necrotic reactions including Lucio's phenomenon have been treated with high-dose clofazimine monotherapy (200 to 300 mg/day) and prednisone (60 to 80 mg/day). If a patient fails to respond to this regimen, low-dose thalidomide (50 to 100 mg at bedtime), additional antimycobacterial chemotherapy, or plasma exchange may be considered.

Management of chronic reactions, often lasting months and years, is among the most challenging problems encountered in clinical leprosy. As with chronic corticosteroid therapy for any indication, patients require monitoring for and management of hypertension, diabetes, peptic ulcers, reactivation of tuberculosis, glaucoma, and osteopenia. Bone density evaluation and prophylactic calcium, vitamin D, and bisphosphonates are necessary, especially for postmenopausal women and hypogonadal men.[51] Alternate-day steroids can be considered during the tapering phrase, but daily and even divided daily doses of prednisone are required for acute reactions. For chronically reactional steroid-dependent patients, there is a great need for steroid-sparing agents. Chronically reactional patients who receive corticosteroids need to be monitored for downgrading reactions, which are best diagnosed by skin biopsy, showing an increase in acid-fast bacilli. Such patients may require additional antimycobacterial chemotherapy.

Supportive Care and Rehabilitation

Rehabilitation is an important component of leprosy management. The most common chronic residual deformity is that of the insensitive foot. Management is similar to that of the diabetic foot, with emphasis on prevention of neurotrophic ulcers. It is important that the clinician examine the plantar surface of both feet of all leprosy patients at each clinic visit. Any callosities on the distal toes, great toe, metatarsal heads, or heels are an indication of lack of proper proprioception and excessive pressure. If a callus shows evidence of a serous or hemorrhagic exudate, it is considered a "preulcer." In any case, careful inspection and sensory examination of the feet and lower extremities followed by proper unloading of the feet are mandatory. Special shoes with molded inserts and education of the patient are major tools to prevent neurotrophic ulcers.

When neurotrophic ulcers have developed, we follow an algorithm similar to that for the diabetic foot.[52] Clinically, we follow the sedimentation rate and radiograph of the foot. If the sedimentation rate is elevated or there is radiographic evidence of bone erosion, a bone scan or magnetic resonance imaging, or both, of the foot is indicated. Antibiotic management of chronic osteomyelitis depends on the extent of the findings and is a matter of clinical judgment and available resources. Judicious use of neurology, physical therapy, occupational therapy, and hand surgery consultation is required for individual patients.

PREVENTION OF LEPROSY

In the United States, the current recommendations for prevention include examination of household contacts and first- and second-degree relatives. The examination should include a complete body skin examination, accompanied by a history of any neurologic symptoms (i.e., numbness, tingling, paresthesias of any kind), and an examination of the peripheral nervous system including palpation of the nerves. Skin biopsy, slit smears, and nerve conduction velocities are obtained for suspected contacts. One report has recommended up to 3 years of full-dose dapsone monotherapy, but because of sporadic compliance and potential side effects, the USPHS National Hansen's Disease Program does not recommend routine dapsone prophylaxis. In some cases, contacts with suspicious skin lesions and peripheral nerve findings who fall short of a definitive diagnosis of leprosy may warrant a therapeutic trial. New strategies for prevention of leprosy depend on further understanding of the transmission of *M. leprae*, which in turn would benefit from high-resolution methods of DNA-based strain typing, such as those that have been used in tuberculosis control.[53,54]

REFERENCES

1. Hastings RC, ed. Leprosy. 2nd ed. Edinburgh: Churchill Livingstone; 1994.
2. Ridley DS, Jopling WH. Classification of leprosy according to immunity. A five-group system. Int J Lepr Other Mycobact Dis. 1966;34:255-273.
3. Yamamura M, Uyemura K, Deans RJ, et al. Defining protective responses to pathogens: Cytokine profiles in leprosy lesions. Science. 1991;254:277-279.
4. Davey TF, Rees RJ. The nasal discharge in leprosy: Clinical and bacteriological aspects. Lepr Rev. 1974;45:121-134.

5. Mastro TD, Redd SC, Breiman RF. Imported leprosy in the United States, 1978 through 1988: An epidemic without secondary transmission. Am J Public Health. 1992;82:1127-1130.

6. Levis WR, Vides EA, Cabrera A. Leprosy in the eastern United States. JAMA. 2000;283:1004-1005.

7. Levis WR, Schuman JS, Friedman SM, et al. An epidemiologic evaluation of leprosy in New York City. JAMA. 1982;247:3221-3226.

8. Cole ST, Eiglmeier K, Parkhill J, et al. Massive gene decay in the leprosy bacillus. Nature. 2001;409:1007-1011.

9. Yuan Y, Barry CE 3rd. A common mechanism for the biosynthesis of methoxy and cyclopropyl mycolic acids in Mycobacterium tuberculosis. Proc Natl Acad Sci USA. 1996;93:12828-12833.

10. De Voss JJ, Rutter K, Schroeder BG, et al. The salicylate-derived mycobactin siderophores of Mycobacterium tuberculosis are essential for growth in macrophages. Proc Natl Acad Sci USA. 2000;97:1252-1257.

11. George KM, Chatterjee D, Gunawardana G, et al. Mycolactone: A polyketide toxin from Mycobacterium ulcerans required for virulence. Science. 1999;283:854-857.

12. Nogueira N, Kaplan G, Levy E, et al. Defective gamma interferon production in leprosy. Reversal with antigen and interleukin 2. J Exp Med. 1983;158:2165-2170.

13. Kim J, Uyemura K, Van Dyke MK, et al. A role for IL-12 receptor expression and signal transduction in host defense in leprosy. J Immunol. 2001;167:779-786.

14. Sieling PA, Wang XH, Gately MK, et al. IL-12 regulates T helper type 1 cytokine responses in human infectious disease. J Immunol. 1994;153:3639-3647.

15. Krutzik SR, Ochoa MT, Sieling PA, et al. Activation and regulation of Toll-like receptors 2 and 1 in human leprosy. Nat Med. 2003;9:525-532.

16. Yamauchi PS, Bleharski JR, Uyemura K, et al. A role for CD40-CD40 ligand interactions in the generation of type 1 cytokine responses in human leprosy. J Immunol. 2000;165:1506-1512.

17. Abel L, Vu DL, Oberti J, et al. Complex segregation analysis of leprosy in southern Vietnam. Genet Epidemiol. 1995;12:63-82.

18. Casanova JL, Abel L. Genetic dissection of immunity to mycobacteria: The human model. Annu Rev Immunol. 2002;20:581-620.

19. Blackwell JM. Genetics of host resistance and susceptibility to intramacrophage pathogens: A study of multicase families of tuberculosis, leprosy and leishmaniasis in north-eastern Brazil. Int J Parasitol. 1998;28:21-28.

20. Rambukkana A, Zanazzi G, Tapinos N, et al. Contact-dependent demyelination by Mycobacterium leprae in the absence of immune cells. Science. 2002;296:927-931.

21. Spierings E, de Boer T, Wieles B, et al. Mycobacterium leprae–specific, HLA class II–restricted killing of human Schwann cells by CD4+ Th1 cells: A novel immunopathogenic mechanism of nerve damage in leprosy. J Immunol. 2001;166:5883-5888.

22. Rambukkana A, Salzer JL, Yurchenco PD, et al. Neural targeting of Mycobacterium leprae mediated by the G domain of the laminin-alpha2 chain. Cell. 1997;88:811-821.

23. Rambukkana A, Yamada H, Zanazzi G, et al. Role of alpha-dystroglycan as a Schwann cell receptor for Mycobacterium leprae. Science. 1998;282:2076-2079.

24. Shimoji Y, Ng V, Matsumura K, et al. A 21-kDa surface protein of Mycobacterium leprae binds peripheral nerve laminin-2 and mediates Schwann cell invasion. Proc Natl Acad Sci USA. 1999;96:9857-9862.

25. Ng V, Zanazzi G, Timpl R, et al. Role of the cell wall phenolic glycolipid-1 in the peripheral nerve predilection of Mycobacterium leprae. Cell. 2000;103:511-524.

26. Hunter SW, Fujiwara T, Brennan PJ. Structure and antigenicity of the major specific glycolipid antigen of Mycobacterium leprae. J Biol Chem. 1982;257:15072-15078.

27. Oliveira RB, Ochoa MT, Sieling PA, et al. Expression of Toll-like receptor 2 on human Schwann cells: A mechanism of nerve damage in leprosy. Infect Immun. 2003;71:1427-1433.

28. Wisniewski HM, Bloom BR. Primary demyelination as a nonspecific consequence of a cell-mediated immune reaction. J Exp Med. 1975;141:346-359.

29. Yamamura M, Wang X, Ohmen J, et al. Cytokine patterns of immunologically mediated tissue damage. J Immunol. 1992;149:1470-1475.

30. Conti G, De Pol A, Scarpini E, et al. Interleukin-1 beta and interferon-gamma induce proliferation and apoptosis in cultured Schwann cells. J Neuroimmunol. 2002;124:29-35.

31. Freedberg IM, Tomic-Canic M, Komine M, et al. Keratins and the keratinocyte activation cycle. J Invest Dermatol. 2001;116:633-640.

32. Suneetha S, Arunthathi S, Kurian N, et al. Histological changes in the nerve, skin and nasal mucosa of patients with primary neuritic leprosy. Acta Leprol. 2000;12:11-18.

33. Sampaio EP, Caneshi JR, Nery JA, et al. Cellular immune response to Mycobacterium leprae infection in human immunodeficiency virus–infected individuals. Infect Immun. 1995;63:1848-1854.

34. Gebre S, Saunderson P, Messele T, et al. The effect of HIV status on the clinical picture of leprosy: A prospective study in Ethiopia. Lepr Rev. 2000;71:338-343.

35. van den Broek J, Chum HJ, Swai R, et al. Association between leprosy and HIV infection in Tanzania. Int J Lepr Other Mycobact Dis. 1997;65:203-210.

36. Lawn SD, Wood C, Lockwood DN. Borderline tuberculoid leprosy: An immune reconstitution phenomenon in a human immunodeficiency virus–infected person. Clin Infect Dis. 2003;36:e5-e6.

37. Van Voorhis WC, Kaplan G, Sarno EN, et al. The cutaneous infiltrates of leprosy: Cellular characteristics and the predominant T-cell phenotypes. N Engl J Med. 1982;307:1593-1597.

38. Nathan CF, Kaplan G, Levis WR, et al. Local and systemic effects of intradermal recombinant interferon-gamma in patients with lepromatous leprosy. N Engl J Med. 1986;315:6-15.

39. Rea TH. Frequency and extent of thickening of the nucleated epidermis in leprosy lesions. Int J Lepr Other Mycobact Dis. 2000;68:410-416.

40. Yamamura M, Wang XH, Ohmen JD, et al. Cytokine patterns of immunologically mediated tissue damage. J Immunol. 1992;149:1470-1475.

41. Ang P, Tay YK, Ng SK, et al. Fatal Lucio's phenomenon in 2 patients with previously undiagnosed leprosy. J Am Acad Dermatol. 2003;48:958-961.

42. Daniel E, Koshy S, Rao GS, et al. Ocular complications in newly diagnosed borderline lepromatous and lepromatous leprosy patients: Baseline profile of the Indian cohort. Br J Ophthalmol. 2002;86:1336-1340.

43. Levis WR, Lanza AP, Swersie S, et al. Testicular dysfunction in leprosy: Relationships of FSH, LH and testosterone to disease classification, activity and duration. Lepr Rev. 1989;60:94-101.

44. Singh N, Arora VK, Jain A, et al. Cytology of testicular changes in leprosy. Acta Cytol. 2002;46:659-663.

45. Gelber RH, Murray LP, Siu P, et al. Efficacy of minocycline in single dose and at 100 mg twice daily for lepromatous leprosy. Int J Lepr Other Mycobact Dis. 1994;62:568-573.

46. Enna CD, Jacobson RR, Mansfield RE. An evaluation of sural nerve biopsy in leprosy. Int J Lepr Other Mycobact Dis. 1970;38:278-281.

47. Haslett PA, Corral LG, Albert M, et al. Thalidomide costimulates primary human T lymphocytes, preferentially inducing proliferation, cytokine production, and cytotoxic responses in the CD8+ subset. J Exp Med. 1998;187:1885-1892.

48. Kaplan G. Potential of thalidomide and thalidomide analogues as immunomodulatory drugs in leprosy and leprosy reactions. Lepr Rev. 2000;71(Suppl):S117-S120.

49. Gaspari A. Thalidomide neurotoxicity in dermatological patients: The next "STEP." J Invest Dermatol. 2002;119:987-988.

50. Rea TH, Levan NE. Lucio's phenomenon and diffuse nonnodular lepromatous leprosy. Arch Dermatol. 1978;114:1023-1028.

51. Ishikawa A, Ishikawa S, Hirakawa M. Osteoporosis, bone turnover and hypogonadism in elderly men with treated leprosy. Lepr Rev. 2001;72:322-329.

52. Patout CA Jr, Birke JA, Wilbright WA, et al. A decision pathway for the staged management of foot problems in diabetes mellitus. Arch Phys Med Rehabil. 2001;82:1724-1728.

53. Kato-Maeda M, Bifani PJ, Kreiswirth BN, et al. The nature and consequence of genetic variability within Mycobacterium tuberculosis. J Clin Invest. 2001;107:533-537.

54. Young D. Prospects for molecular epidemiology of leprosy. Lepr Rev. 2003;74:11-17.

55. Rani R, Fernandez-Vina MA, Zaheer SA, et al. Study of HLA class II alleles by PCR oligotyping in leprosy patients from north India. Tissue Antigens. 1993;42:133-137.

56. Mehra NK, Rajalingam R, Mitra DK, et al. Variants of HLA-DR2/DR51 group haplotypes and susceptibility to tuberculoid leprosy and pulmonary tuberculosis in Asian Indians. Int J Lepr Other Mycobact Dis. 1995;63:241-248.

57. Zerva L, Cizman B, Mehra NK, et al. Arginine at positions 13 or 70-71 in pocket 4 of HLA-DRB1 alleles is associated with susceptibility to tuberculoid leprosy. J Exp Med. 1996;183:829-836.

58. Meisner SJ, Mucklow S, Warner G, et al. Association of NRAMP1 polymorphism with leprosy type but not susceptibility to leprosy per se in west Africans. Am J Trop Med Hyg. 2001;65:733-735.

59. Abel L, Sanchez FO, Oberti J, et al. Susceptibility to leprosy is linked to the human NRAMP1 gene. J Infect Dis. 1998;177:133-145.

60. Roy S, Frodsham A, Saha B, et al. Association of vitamin D receptor genotype with leprosy type. J Infect Dis. 1999;179:187-191.

61. Roy S, McGuire W, Mascie-Taylor CG, et al. Tumor necrosis factor promoter polymorphism and susceptibility to lepromatous leprosy. J Infect Dis. 1997;176:530-532.

62. Santos AR, Suffys PN, Vanderborght PR, et al. Role of tumor necrosis factor-alpha and interleukin-10 promoter gene polymorphisms in leprosy. J Infect Dis. 2002;186:1687-1691.

63. Rajalingam R, Singal DP, Mehra NK. Transporter associated with antigen-processing (TAP) genes and susceptibility to tuberculoid leprosy and pulmonary tuberculosis. Tissue Antigens. 1997;49:168-172.

64. Mira MT, Alcais A, Di Pietrantonio T, et al. Segregation of HLA/TNF region is linked to leprosy clinical spectrum in families displaying mixed leprosy subtypes. Genes Immun. 2003;4:67-73.

65. Mira MT, Alcais A, Van Thuc N, et al. Chromosome 6q25 is linked to susceptibility to leprosy in a Vietnamese population. Nat Genet. 2003;33:412-415.

66. Siddiqui MR, Meisner S, Tosh K, et al. A major susceptibility locus for leprosy in India maps to chromosome 10p13. Nat Genet. 2001;27:439-441.

67. Tosh K, Meisner S, Siddiqui MR, et al. A region of chromosome 20 is linked to leprosy susceptibility in a South Indian population. J Infect Dis. 2002;186:1190-1193.

Mycobacterium avium Complex

FRED M. GORDIN
C. ROBERT HORSBURGH, Jr.

*M*ycobacterium avium complex (MAC) comprises two closely related organisms, *M. avium* and *Mycobacterium intracellulare.* Three major disease syndromes are produced by MAC in humans: pulmonary disease, usually in adults whose systemic immunity is intact; disseminated disease, usually in patients with advanced human immunodeficiency virus (HIV) infection; and cervical lymphadenitis. Also, but rarely, MAC can cause disease in other sites, such as cutaneous disease. The frequency of MAC pulmonary and lymph node disease seems to be increasing, particularly in developed countries, but neither condition is reportable, and increases may be due to improved culture and radiographic techniques. Occurrence of disseminated MAC disease increased precipitously with the HIV pandemic but has declined subsequently with the introduction of effective antiretroviral therapy.

EPIDEMIOLOGY

Reservoir and Route of Acquisition

MAC organisms are common in many environmental sites and are thought to be acquired by inhalation or ingestion. Person-to-person spread has not been observed. Environmental sites harboring MAC are diverse, including water, soil, and animals.[1,2] MAC has been found to colonize natural water sources, indoor water systems, pools, and hot tubs.[3-6] Specific sites from which patients acquire MAC are identified rarely, but exposure to recirculating hot water systems has been identified as one route of acquisition of MAC in patients with acquired immunodeficiency syndrome (AIDS).[6] Less than 15% of cases can be traced to this source, however, suggesting that other environmental reservoirs also may be important. Increased risk for disseminated MAC among patients with AIDS also has been associated with exposure to swimming pools and other water sources,[7] whereas MAC infection of the skin can occur after hot tub use.[8] Aerosols of fresh and salt water may contain MAC, and these have been proposed as vehicles leading to transmission of MAC respiratory disease.[9,10] The frequent occurrence of MAC in milk (even after pasteurization) and the preponderance of cases of cervical lymphadenitis in children younger than 3 years old have led some investigators to speculate that oral exposure to organisms in milk is the route of infection for this clinical presentation.[11]

Pulmonary Disease

MAC pulmonary disease is seen in most developed countries. In the United States[12] and in Japan,[13] there are approximately 1.3 cases per 100,000 persons, whereas in Switzerland, there are 0.9 cases per 100,000 persons.[14] An estimated 3000 cases of MAC pulmonary disease are seen annually in the United States.[12] The average age of patients with MAC pulmonary disease in the United States is 58 years, and most patients are men. Younger persons also seem to be at risk for focal MAC pulmonary disease, however.[15,16] Specific risk factors for MAC pulmonary disease have not been identified, although many reported cases have occurred in persons with a history of prior tuberculosis or heavy smoking. Chronic bronchiectasis is associated with MAC but is likely the result of the disease rather than a predisposition. MAC pulmonary disease can occur in HIV-infected persons without dissemination, although the risk of subsequent dissemination is high.[17-19] Reports have identified MAC in the sputum of patients with cystic fibrosis, and a causal role has been proposed for this organism

in the destruction of pulmonary tissue seen in cystic fibrosis patients.[20-22] MAC also may cause pulmonary disease in patients with pulmonary alveolar proteinosis.[23]

Disseminated Disease

Disseminated MAC disease was extremely rare before 1980,[24] but then the heightened susceptibility of AIDS patients to this disease led to a marked increase in the number of cases. In 1994, an estimated 37,000 cases of disseminated MAC disease were seen in patients with AIDS, making this the most common clinical manifestation of MAC and the most common bacterial disease among patients with AIDS.[25] Since then, with the introduction of preventive antibiotic regimens and effective antiretroviral therapy, the number of patients with MAC has declined substantially.[26,27] Disseminated MAC disease also can be seen in children with primary immunodeficiency diseases and in patients with hairy cell leukemia.[28,29]

The greatest risk for MAC in patients with AIDS is in patients with severe depression of the CD4$^+$ cell count: Disseminated MAC is seen rarely in patients with greater than 100 CD4$^+$ cells/mm^3, and the median CD4$^+$ cell count among patients with disseminated MAC and AIDS is 10 cells/mm^3.[30,31] The risk for MAC increases as the CD4$^+$ count declines,[31] and the prior occurrence of another opportunistic condition increases the risk for MAC at any given CD4$^+$ cell level.[32] Early in the HIV epidemic, similar risks for MAC in HIV-infected patients were seen when patients were compared by age, race, sex, or HIV transmission risk.[33] More recently, patients with AIDS and disseminated MAC are likely to be women and minorities, reflecting lack of preventive care and overall trends in the HIV epidemic.[26] Children with AIDS have a risk for MAC similar to that of adults.[34]

Rates of disseminated MAC disease among patients with AIDS are higher in the southern United States compared with patients in the northern United States or Canada; these differences may be due to decreased environmental exposure to MAC in the north during the winter.[35] Disseminated MAC has been reported with a frequency of 10% to 25% of AIDS patients in Europe, North America, and Australia, but the disease is less common in developing countries, particularly in Africa, where less than 1% of patients with AIDS are affected.[36-38] These differences may be due to several factors, including a smaller proportion of AIDS patients with extremely low CD4$^+$ cell counts, protection from MAC by prior exposure to *Mycobacterium tuberculosis*,[39] or fewer exposures to MAC in piped water systems.

Lymphadenitis

An estimated 300 cases of culture-confirmed MAC lymphadenitis occur in the United States each year.[12] This number is likely to be an underestimate, however, because many cases of lymphadenitis are not cultured or fail to grow an organism. MAC cervical adenitis is largely a disease of children, with most cases occurring in children younger than age 3 years, based on reports from Europe, North America, and Australia. The disease shows a modest female predominance, and nearly all reported cases are in whites.[40] Before 1980, most nontuberculous lymphadenitis in the United States was due to *Mycobacterium scrofulaceum*, but in recent years, MAC has been the cause in most cases.[41] MAC lymphadenitis also is seen in HIV-infected persons, particularly as a manifestation of the immune reconstitution syndrome[42]; cervical, mediastinal, or intra-abdominal nodes may be involved.

PATHOGEN

Classification and Microbiology

Organism

Mycobacteria are aerobic, non-spore-forming, nonmotile bacilli. Their cell walls include mycolic acid-containing, long-chain glycolipids or glycopeptidolipids or both that protect these facultative intracellular parasites from lysosomal attack. The organisms grow slowly (10 to 21 days on solid media) and produce thin-translucent or domed-opaque colonies. Colonies are usually light tan in color, although some MAC strains produce a yellow pigment that increases with light exposure. MAC can be cultured on solid or liquid media; liquid media are more sensitive and yield results in a shorter time but do not allow quantitation of mycobacterial load.[43] Glycolipid typing has divided MAC into 28 serovars; 1 to 6, 8 to 11, and 21 are *M. avium,* and 7, 12 to 20, and 25 are *M. intracellulare.*[44] Pulsed-field gel electrophoresis has been able to resolve greater differences in these isolates, indicating there is considerable diversity in the strains of MAC that infect patients.[45] MAC isolates can be identified as *M. avium* or *M. intracellulare* by DNA probes or polymerase chain reaction restriction analysis.[46] In vitro susceptibility testing of MAC isolates against macrolides and azalides is clinically useful, but susceptibility testing against other antimycobacterial agents (e.g., ethambutol, rifamycins, fluoroquinolones, and aminoglycosides) has not been shown to predict clinical response and is not recommended.[43]

Virulence

MAC is relatively avirulent in the normal host. Serovars 1, 4, and 8 are uncommon in the environment, but they cause most cases of disseminated disease in AIDS patients.[44] These serovars are thought to be associated with virulence and do appear more virulent in an animal model of infection.[47] Possible relative virulence factors include adherence to intestinal epithelial cells, production of catalase, failure to acidify vesicles, and inhibition of phagosome-lysosome fusion.[48-51] Clinical isolates from patients with disseminated disease are always of the smooth-transparent colony type, rather than the domed or opaque type. Colonies that are smooth and transparent are more likely to replicate in vivo, are more likely to induce the cytokines tumor necrosis factor-α and interleukin-1, and usually have decreased susceptibility to antimycobacterial agents in vitro.[52] An isolate from a patient with MAC disease has been shown to produce increased cell lysis and increased ability to stimulate HIV replication in vitro, relative to the abilities of an animal MAC isolate.[53] MAC also seems to be able to exist symbiotically with water-borne amebae, leading to increased virulence of MAC in an animal model.[54]

Pathogenesis

MAC disease results from primary acquisition of the organism by either ingestion or inhalation. No cases of reactivation MAC disease have been reported.

Pulmonary Disease

MAC pulmonary disease develops after inhalation of MAC. The duration from inhalation to disease is unknown but presumably occurs over many months to years. More than one distinct MAC organism can be recovered from some patients,[55] suggesting that disease, superinfection, or colonization may occur concomitantly. Tissue lesions usually are localized and appear grossly as well-circumscribed nodules. Granulomatous pleuritis, bronchitis, vasculitis, and interstitial pneumonia also have been reported.[56] The histologic features vary from poorly formed to well-formed granulomas. Giant cells are seen frequently, and in rare cases, there is central caseating necrosis and cavitation. Thoracic lymph node involvement is uncommon.

Disseminated Disease

Infection is acquired through inhalation or ingestion of MAC, followed by localized disease in the lung or gut. Dissemination ensues from either location over several months.[17] In patients with AIDS, 80% to 90% of infections are acquired by ingestion. Most disseminated disease is due to a single MAC strain, but multiple distinct isolates have been recovered from 15% of patients.[45] The organisms penetrate the gut wall, possibly through Peyer's patches, and subsequently are phagocytized by macrophages and other reticuloendothelial cells.[57,58] Histologically, epithelial cells show only mild inflammatory changes, and ulceration is uncommon. Sheets of foamy macrophages are present in the lamina propria; these massively infected cells may expand the intestinal villi, giving an appearance similar to Whipple's disease. On acid-fast staining, the cells are packed with bacilli.

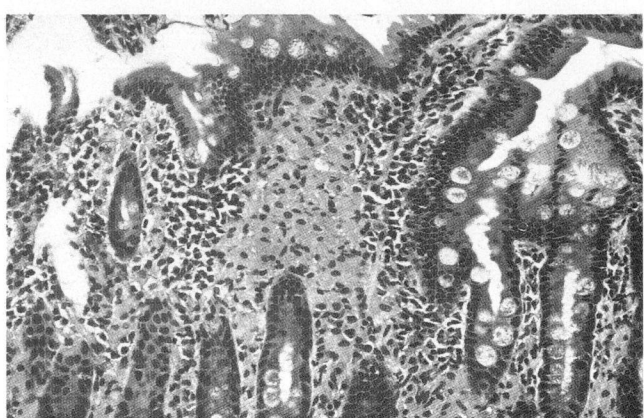

FIGURE 250-1. Photomicrograph of intestinal biopsy specimen from a patient with disseminated *Mycobacterium avium* complex disease and AIDS. Laminae propria of villi are infiltrated with histiocytes. On special stains, the histiocytes were filled with acid-fast bacilli (not evident on this hematoxylin and eosin stain).

The resulting thickening of the bowel wall (Fig. 250-1) can lead to intussusception, gastrointestinal hemorrhage, or obstruction, but these are rare. Mesenteric adenopathy ensues (Fig. 250-2); poorly formed granulomas, abscesses, and necrosis with neutrophilic inflammation are seen in these nodes[59,60]; the cells are filled with acid-fast bacilli. Granulomas with giant cells, epithelioid macrophages, and caseating necrosis can be seen but are less common. Subsequently, hematologic dissemination occurs. Any organ can be seeded secondarily, but the most common sites are liver, spleen, and bone marrow (Fig. 250-3).[59,60] The histologic picture in these organs is similar to that in the lymph nodes. The burden of organisms in the blood is variable, ranging from 1 to greater than 10^5 colony-forming units/mL.[18,61] Higher levels of bacteremia likely represent a longer duration of dissemination and signal a poor prognosis. Untreated disseminated MAC disease leads to death by inanition. Decreased caloric intake and increased metabolic demand seem to play a role in this process.

Entry of MAC into the blood stream leads to elevated serum levels of tumor necrosis factor-α and interleukin-6, which likely are responsible for the predominant symptoms of fever, night sweats, and cachexia.[62,63] The mechanism of the severe anemia seen in disseminated MAC disease is not well understood because bone marrow involvement can be minimal. Erythropoietin levels are variable, and clinical response to exogenous erythropoietin is unpredictable.[64]

A unique pathophysiologic abnormality seen with disseminated MAC disease is marked elevation of serum alkaline phosphatase,

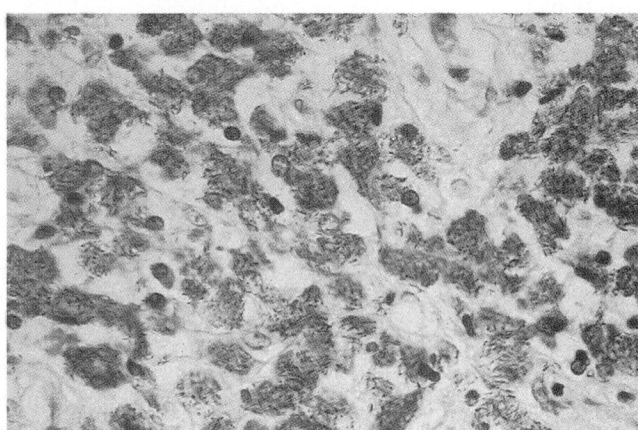

FIGURE 250-2. Photomicrograph of mesenteric lymph node shows histiocytes filled with acid-fast bacilli, stained in red.

FIGURE 250-3. Section of spleen from a patient with disseminated *Mycobacterium avium* complex (MAC) disease and AIDS. Multiple, small, yellow-gray disseminated foci of MAC infection are seen.

which is seen in roughly 5% of patients. Serum enzyme levels may reach 20 to 40 times the normal level, with little elevation of transaminases, bilirubin, or other parameters of hepatic function; nonetheless, fractionation shows it to be of hepatic origin. Patients have little symptomatic discomfort, and the histologic picture in the liver does not show marked abnormality, suggesting interference with enzyme metabolism rather than hepatic tissue destruction.

Lymphadenitis

MAC cervical and abdominal lymphadenitis likely is acquired through ingestion of MAC, whereas thoracic lymphadenitis presumably occurs subsequent to inhalation. Lesions reveal granulomas, usually without caseation. Ulceration and fistula formation are frequent complications, particularly when nodes have been incised or aspirated. In the immunologically normal host, acid-fast bacilli can be seen in macrophages and giant cells, but they often are single, and dissemination of disease does not occur. In HIV-infected patients without antiretroviral therapy, there is little granulomatous response, and unrestrained mycobacterial replication leads to macrophages filled with acid-fast bacilli with eventual dissemination. When antiretroviral therapy is instituted, a vigorous granulomatous response results in elimination of bacilli from the tissues.

Host Immunity

Pulmonary Disease

The fact that many cases of MAC pulmonary disease have occurred in persons with a history of smoking or chronic lung disease, or both, suggests that impaired pulmonary clearance mechanisms may predispose patients to MAC. No specific clearance defects have been identified, however. Patients with MAC lung disease develop antibody and delayed hypersensitivity to MAC antigens, and humoral and cell-mediated immunity remain intact.[65] The host immune response consists of granuloma formation with ingestion and intracellular killing of MAC by macrophages.

Disseminated Disease

Persons with inherited defects in the interferon (IFN)-γ signaling pathway also are exquisitely susceptible to disseminated MAC disease, confirming the importance of this cytokine in host defense against MAC. Sites of defects so far identified include the IFN-γ receptor ligand binding chain, the IFN-γ signal transducing chain, and defective IL-12–mediated modulation of IFN-γ production.[66-69] Exogenously administered IFN-γ overcomes these defects and may lead to clinical improvement.[70]

In patients with AIDS, macrophage phagocytosis of MAC is unimpaired, but intracellular killing does not occur, and organisms multiply unimpeded within macrophages. Macrophages from patients with AIDS can respond normally to cytokines,[71] although cytokine production by T cells is severely impaired in such patients, leading to failure of macrophage activation to eliminate intracellular MAC.[72] Cytotoxic CD4$^+$ cells are important in inhibiting intracellular replication of MAC, but their function also is impaired in HIV infection.[73]

Humoral factors also may play a role in disseminated MAC disease. Antibodies against MAC are produced in response to disease in normal hosts but not in patients with AIDS.[30] Although these antibodies are not known to have a role in protection against MAC disease, they increase MAC killing in vitro.[74] Conversely, MAC growth can be stimulated by high serum levels of triglycerides and by the iron overload seen in patients with AIDS.[75]

Lymphadenitis

Patients with MAC lymphadenitis also develop antibodies and delayed hypersensitivity to MAC antigens, indicating intact humoral and cell-mediated immunity. The histologic response usually consists of noncaseating granuloma formation; few acid-fast bacilli are seen in tissue sections.

CLINICAL PRESENTATION

Pulmonary Disease

The clinical presentation of pulmonary MAC disease is nonspecific and can be confused with other mycobacterial infections and chronic pulmonary diseases. The classic presentation of pulmonary MAC is one of a subacute-to-chronic illness occurring in individuals with a prior history of underlying pulmonary pathology due to smoking, bronchiectasis, cancer, silicosis, prior tuberculosis, or other diseases.[16,76-78] Most of these individuals are middle-aged to older men, predominately white, and frequently with a history of heavy smoking and heavy alcohol consumption. The clinical picture in this population is one of a chronic disease, with the predominant symptoms being productive cough (occurring in >80% of patients), weight loss or weakness (in approximately half), and fever or night sweats (each in 10% to 20% of patients).[77,78] This presentation of pulmonary MAC has been reported to result in death within 2 years of diagnosis in 15% of individuals. Pulmonary MAC alone, without disseminated disease, also may occur in persons with HIV infection.[19]

The chest radiograph in this chronic form of pulmonary MAC typically shows upper lobe fibronodular and cavitary disease, which may be associated with pleural thickening (Fig. 250-4). Rates of cavitation tend to be higher than with tuberculosis: Cavitary disease is reported in 60% to 90% of patients with MAC[77,78] compared with approximately 50% of patients with tuberculosis. The cavities in patients with MAC also are more likely to be thin-walled than in tuberculosis and may be quite large, with most in the 2- to 4-cm range.[79] MAC pulmonary disease is bilateral in almost half of patients. Pleural effusions are uncommon. Other features that may be identified on chest radiographs in patients with pulmonary MAC are pectus excavatum and scoliosis. In one report, 27% of individuals with MAC had pectus excavatum compared with 2.4% in the general population, and 52% of patients with MAC had scoliosis compared with 19% in the general population.[15] Computed tomography (CT) scans of the chest may add some useful clinical information. In a series comparing patients with pulmonary MAC with patients with pulmonary tuberculosis, nodules and consolidation were found equally in both groups; bronchiectasis was found significantly more often, however, in patients with MAC (94% versus 27%).[80] The CT finding of bronchiectasis with multiple nodular infiltrates (Fig. 250-5) is particularly suggestive of MAC pulmonary disease. Tree-in-bud opacities are seen often, but these are not specific for MAC.

Pulmonary MAC also has been recognized with increasing frequency in middle-aged to elderly women with no preexisting lung disease.[16,81,82] This syndrome, sometimes referred to as "the Lady Windermere syndrome," presents with a more indolent clinical picture and with fewer chest radiograph abnormalities. Patients with this

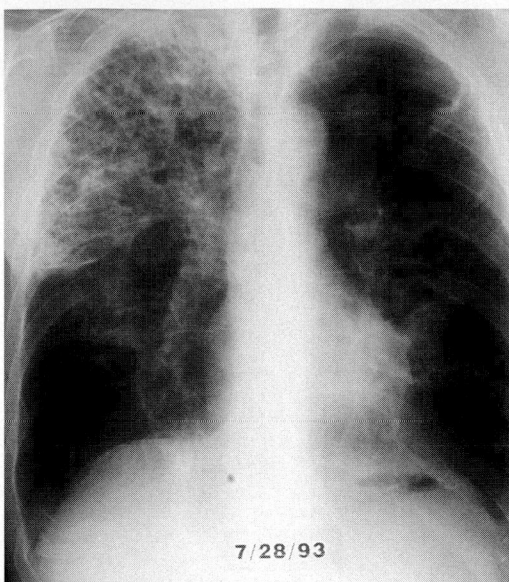

FIGURE 250-4. Chest radiograph of a man with cavitary *Mycobacterium avium* complex disease in the left upper lobe and infiltrative disease in the right upper lobe. *(Courtesy of James L. Cook, MD.)*

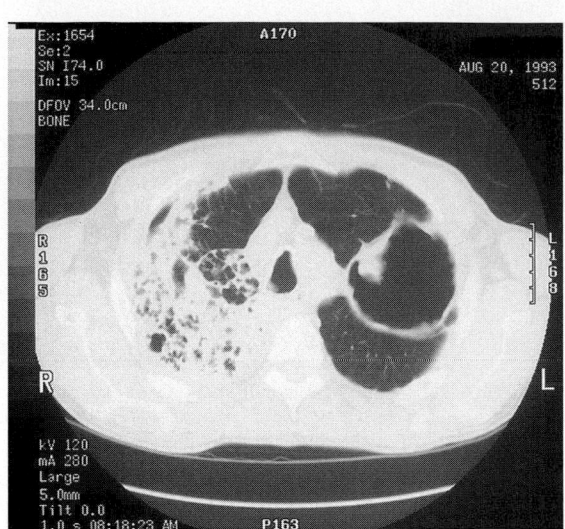

FIGURE 250-5. Computed tomography scan of the lung of the patient in Figure 250-4. Right upper lobe cavity is now apparent, with extensive lung destruction.

syndrome usually present with chronic cough, but other constitutional symptoms, such as weight loss and fever, are uncommon. The chest radiograph in these patients shows less lung involvement than in patients with predisposing lung disease, and changes may occur only over years of follow-up.[79,81,82] Discrete pulmonary nodules may be seen often in the middle lobe or lingular regions, although other areas of the lungs may be involved (Fig. 250-6). Cavities have been reported in only 25% of these patients. High-resolution CT (HRCT) scans can be important as a means of detecting micronodules (<5 mm) and evidence of bronchiectasis in this population (Fig. 250-7).[79,80,83,84]

Patients with cystic fibrosis frequently are colonized with nontuberculosis mycobacteria, but the clinical importance of MAC in this population is not clear. In one multicenter prevalence study of 986 patients with cystic fibrosis, 13% had at least one of three sputum samples positive for nontuberculosis mycobacteria, most (72%) with

MAC.[85] Overall, patients with cystic fibrosis and MAC had similar pulmonary function tests compared with patients without MAC.[86] Serial HRCT scans provided important information because patients with MAC and progression of HRCT abnormalities were more likely to have clinical decline than other cystic fibrosis patients with MAC. In cystic fibrosis patients, HRCT abnormalities suggestive of progressive MAC were progression of areas of cystic or cavitary disease, subsegmental or larger areas of consolidation, pulmonary nodules, and tree-in-bud opacities; these changes are not specific, however, for MAC.[86]

Another pattern of MAC pulmonary disease, known as "hot-tub lung disease,"[5,87-89] occurs in persons exposed to pools of heated water containing MAC. Patients with this condition are presumed to have inhaled aerosolized MAC, resulting in a hypersensitivity pneumonitis. These patients present with mild-to-moderate dyspnea and dry cough, with or without fever. Chest radiographs and CT scans show patterns similar to those seen in other hypersensitivity pneumonitides, with a

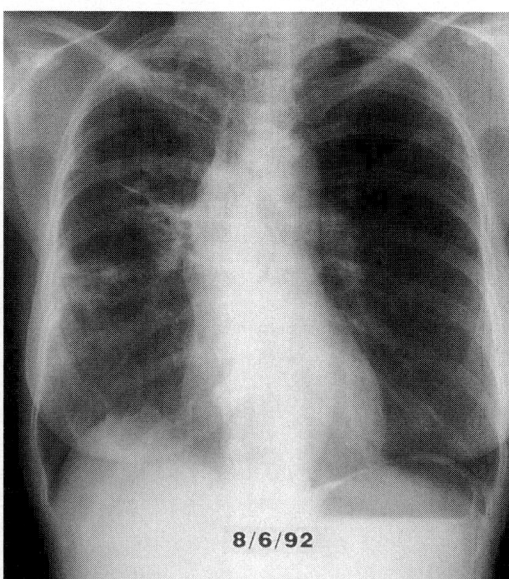

FIGURE 250-6. Chest radiograph of a 67-year-old woman with right-sided bronchiectasis and *Mycobacterium avium* complex pulmonary disease. Nodular densities are seen in the right middle lobe. *(Courtesy of James L. Cook, MD.)*

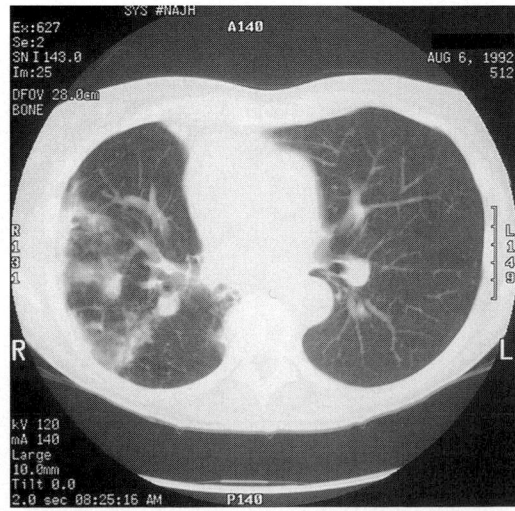

FIGURE 250-7. Computed tomography scan of the lung of the patient in Figure 250-6. Nodules and bronchiectasis are evident.

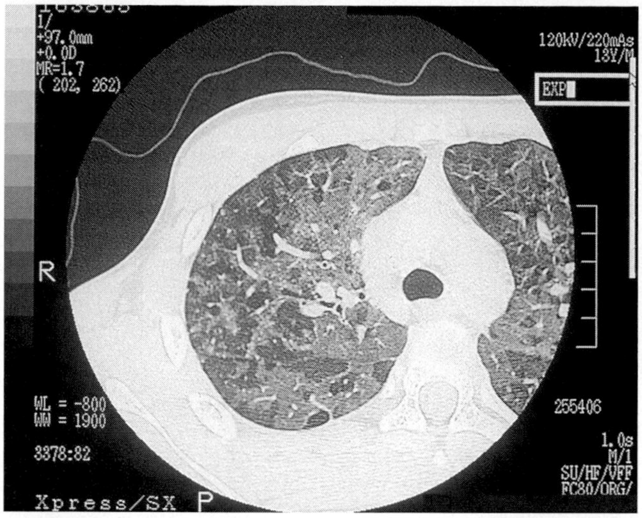

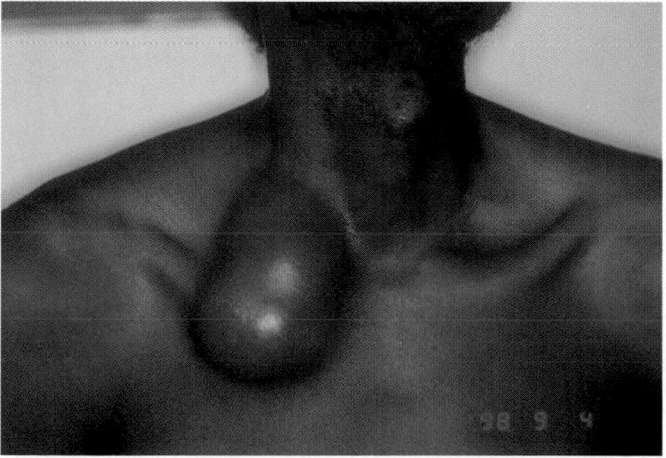

FIGURE 250-8. Computed tomography scan of a patient with hypersensitivity pneumonitis induced by *Mycobacterium avium* complex shows bilateral infiltrates that cleared rapidly with antimycobacterial agents and prednisone. *(Courtesy of James L. Cook, MD.)*

TABLE 250-1 Signs, Symptoms, and Laboratory Abnormalities Associated with Disseminated *Mycobacterium avium* Complex Disease, Showing Evolution of the Clinical Presentation over Time

Presenting Symptom, Sign, or Parameter	% of Patients by Year		
	1991 (n = 114)	1994 (n = 159)	1997 (n = 99)
Fever	86	84	76
Anemia (hematocrit <26%)	76	36	42
Night sweats	44	32	31
Weight loss (≥10%)	40	14	15
Abdominal pain	33	19	29
Diarrhea	33	33	34
Elevated serum alkaline phosphatase level	26	13	19

From Horsburgh CR, Gettings J, Alexander LN, et al. Disseminated *Mycobacterium avium* complex disease among patients infected with human immunodeficiency virus, 1985-2000. Clin Infect Dis. 2001;33:1938-1943.

variety of radiologic patterns, including bilateral alveolar infiltrates, centrilobular nodules, and "ground-glass" opacities (Fig. 250-8).[87-89]

Disseminated Disease

Disseminated MAC occurs almost exclusively in persons with advanced HIV disease. In a large natural history study of patients with HIV infection, MAC bacteremia developed at a median CD4+ cell count of 13 cells/mm³, and the median survival after diagnosis was only 134 days.[31] It is difficult to separate the clinical and laboratory features directly attributable to MAC from abnormalities attributable to advanced HIV disease. In early reports, more than 90% of persons with disseminated MAC had high fever, weight loss, night sweats, or severe anemia (hematocrit <25%).[90-93] Other features associated with MAC include abdominal pain, diarrhea, intra-abdominal lymphadenopathy, hepatosplenomegaly, and an elevated serum alkaline phosphatase level. With the advent of effective antiretroviral therapy and more widespread early detection of MAC, the clinical presentation has evolved.[26] Patients presenting in the late 1990s with MAC were less likely to have severe anemia, significant weight loss, or an elevated alkaline phosphatase than patients presenting in the early and mid 1990s (Table 250-1). The clinical features directly attributable to the onset of disseminated MAC have been described by evaluating patients at risk, with prospective monthly blood cultures for MAC.[94] At the time blood cultures became positive, patients with MAC had more weight loss, fever, anemia, abdominal pain, or elevated alkaline phosphatase than patients who did not develop MAC. The onset of these clinical changes occurred within 2 months of the first positive blood culture for MAC.[94]

In patients with disseminated MAC, other organ-specific localizing signs and symptoms may be present as a manifestation of the involvement of these organ systems. A comprehensive autopsy series of 44 patients with AIDS and disseminated MAC showed the most common organs involved to be the spleen, lymph nodes, liver, intestines, colon, bone marrow, and less commonly, lungs, adrenals, stomach, and central nervous system.[95] Patients may present with clinical manifestations of disease referable to any of these body systems. Patients with AIDS and disseminated MAC may have concurrent pulmonary disease, but this is not common. Although MAC isolated from respiratory specimens may be a harbinger of disseminated MAC,[17] parenchymal lung involvement occurs in less than 10% of patients with disseminated MAC.[19] When parenchymal lung disease does occur in this population, the chest radiograph may reveal alveolar infiltrates, nodules, or cavitary disease.

Local manifestations of disseminated MAC may occur in AIDS patients with severe immune suppression who have been started on antiretroviral therapy; these patients can develop local symptoms as a result of an inflammatory reaction to MAC antigens as the cell-mediated immune response is restored. This phenomenon is called the *immune reconstitution syndrome* or a "paradoxical reaction" (Figs. 250-9 through 250-11).[42,96,97] Most often, patients exhibit painful lymphadenopathy, occurring within 1 to 12 weeks of initiating antiretroviral therapy; abdominal pain and hepatosplenomegaly also have been reported. Patients with immune reconstitution syndrome differ from other patients with disseminated MAC: Fever may be present, but other constitutional symptoms (e.g., weight loss and night sweats) usually are absent, and blood cultures usually do not grow MAC. Biopsy may be required to establish an accurate diagnosis and to exclude other processes.

Disseminated infection with MAC rarely occurs in patients without AIDS. In one review of 37 patients with disseminated MAC but without AIDS, most patients either had received steroids or had an underlying hematopoietic malignancy.[24] The clinical features of disseminated MAC disease in this population were similar to the features in persons with disseminated MAC and AIDS: Fever, weight loss, and local pain occurred in 32% to 54% of patients; night sweats occurred in 14%; anemia occurred in 75%; and lymphadenopathy or hepatosplenomegaly occurred in more than 40%.

FIGURE 250-9. Immune reconstitution reaction in a patient with disseminated *Mycobacterium avium* complex disease and AIDS after initiation of antimycobacterial and antiretroviral therapy. This enlarged supraclavicular lymph node was not painful.

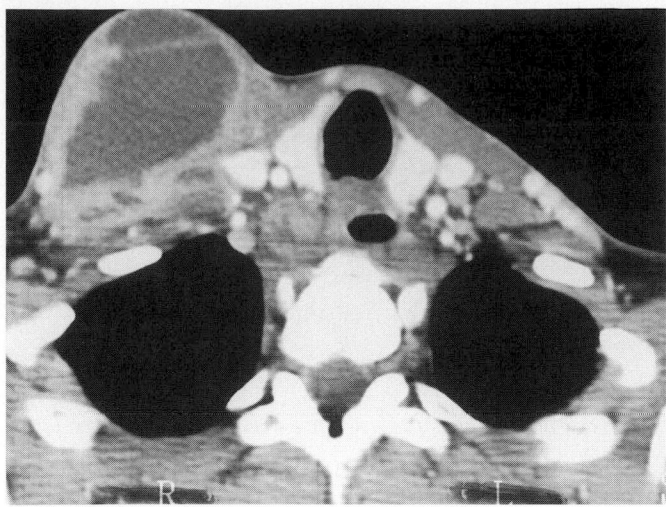

FIGURE 250-10. Computed tomography scan of lymph node shown in Figure 250-9. The node can be seen to be cystic. Multiple enlarged, but noncystic mediastinal lymph nodes also were present.

Lymphadenitis

Cervicofacial lymphadenitis is the most common manifestation of MAC in children, and more than 80% of patients with MAC cervical lymphadenitis are between 1 and 5 years old.[40,41,98-101] The disease also can occur in adults, but tuberculosis as a cause of lymphadenopathy is more common than MAC in patients older than 12 years.[99,100] The clinical presentation is usually painless or minimally painful unilateral enlargement of a node in the submandibular or high jugular region (Fig. 250-12).[40,41,98] Fever is uncommon. Bilateral disease occurs in less than 10% of individuals, and multiple nodes are involved in less than 20% of children. Nodes are most often firm but not fluctulant. Node size may vary from 1 to 7 cm in diameter, with the mean size in one series reported as 2.5 × 3 cm.[98,100]

Other Sites

Cutaneous disease due to MAC is uncommon and not differentiated easily from other chronic skin lesions. Lesions may be ulcers, nodules, or plaques. Cases of cutaneous MAC have been reported in immunocompetent and immunosuppressed hosts.[8,102-104] Most often, cutaneous MAC is due to direct inoculation of the skin by trauma, surgery, or injection. Local swelling, erythema, and tenderness may be present for

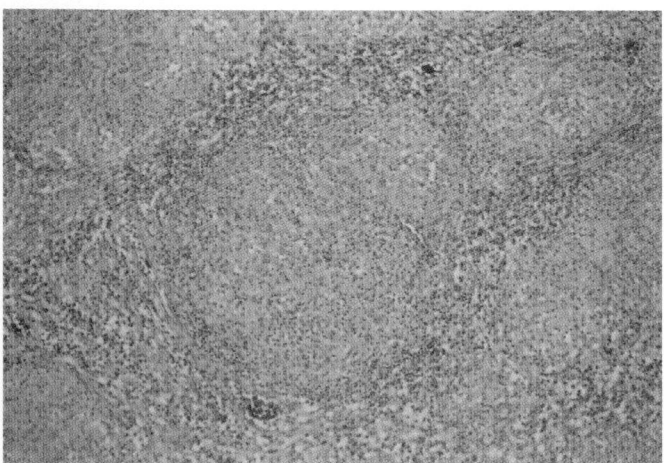

FIGURE 250-11. Histologic section of excised node from the patient with immune reconstitution reaction shown in Figures 250-9 and 250-10. Granulomas are seen, but no acid-fast organisms were identified. Multinucleated giant cells also were present (not shown).

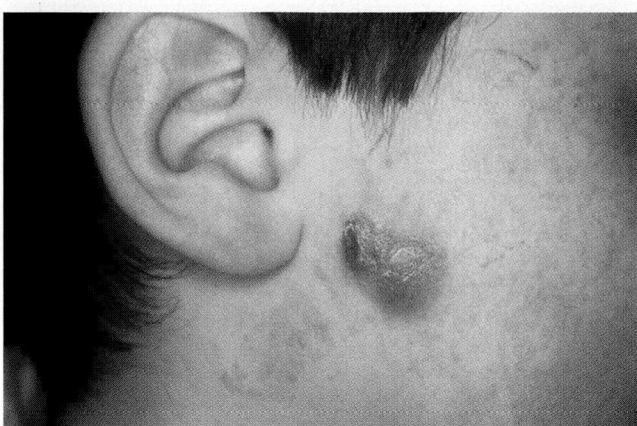

FIGURE 250-12. Preauricular lymph node from a 5-year-old boy with normal immunity and unilateral *Mycobacterium avium* complex lymphadenopathy.

months to years. The lesions are indolent, with little or no lymph node reaction or systemic symptoms. MAC also is a rare cause of renal disease, prostatitis, peritonitis, corneal ulceration, mastoiditis, mastitis, osteomyelitis, endocarditis, septic arthritis, and synovitis.

DIAGNOSIS

Pulmonary Disease

Diagnosis of MAC pulmonary disease is difficult because of the high frequency of positive sputum cultures among persons without disease.[43] A single sputum culture that grows MAC has a low predictive value for disease. The American Thoracic Society has developed a clinical case definition for pulmonary MAC disease: Patients must be symptomatic, have abnormalities on chest radiograph or CT scan of the chest, and have one of the following features: (1) acid-fast bacilli, granulomas, or positive MAC culture from a histopathologic specimen; (2) three positive MAC sputum cultures without positive smears; (3) two positive MAC sputum cultures with one positive smear; or (4) a bronchial wash culture with a 2+ or greater smear or 2+ or greater MAC growth on culture.[43]

Smears are neither sensitive nor specific in the diagnosis of pulmonary MAC disease because they are not commonly positive and, when positive, are less likely to be MAC than to be *M. tuberculosis* or other nontuberculous mycobacteria. Cultures usually turn positive by 21 days when performed on solid media and by 14 days when performed in broth, but the time to growth on culture depends on the inoculum size. Cultures cannot be classified definitively as negative until 6 weeks of observation have failed to yield an organism. Cultures contaminated with bacterial or fungal overgrowth before 6 weeks cannot be interpreted and should be repeated. MAC DNA can be detected directly in sputum, but no licensed tests are available; these tests also would be expected to detect colonization so that the American Thoracic Society diagnostic criteria for MAC pulmonary disease still must be satisfied. Patients who do not meet the American Thoracic Society criteria should be followed closely and re-evaluated because clinical disease may develop over time.

Other conditions that may mimic the infiltrative form of MAC pulmonary disease include tuberculosis and other nontuberculous mycobacterial infections, nocardiosis, histoplasmosis, blastomycosis, coccidioidomycosis, and necrotizing bacterial pneumonia. Bronchiectasis also may be caused by IgG deficiency, pulmonary ciliary disorders, cystic fibrosis, toxin exposure, or allergic bronchopulmonary aspergillosis.

Mycobacterium avium Complex Hypersensitivity Pneumonitis

Patients with hypersensitivity pneumonitis due to MAC usually give a history of exposure to aerosols from pools or hot tubs. Chest radiographs may be normal; show nodules or infiltrates; or, in the acute presentation, show total opacification of the lung fields.[87-89] In the acute stages, lung biopsy may show neutrophilic or lymphocytic infiltrates; later, noncaseating granulomas may be seen. Patients with hypersensitivity pneumonitis usually grow MAC from sputum, bronchoalveolar lavage, or lung biopsy specimens; this entity may be a combination of early infection and hypersensitivity. No test for serum precipitins to MAC antigens is currently available.

Disseminated Disease

Disseminated MAC is diagnosed by recovery of MAC from blood or another usually sterile site, such as bone marrow, liver, or spleen. Although recovery from only one of these sites might indicate localized disease in that organ, such positive cultures are highly predictive of positive cultures from the other sites. MAC growth from lymph nodes may represent localized disease, whereas MAC growth from sputum, bronchial washings, gastrointestinal biopsy specimens, or stool can represent colonization or localized disease; in such cases, positive cultures from more than one organ are needed to establish a diagnosis of disseminated disease. Isolation of MAC from stool by itself does not indicate that the organism is causing disease, and treatment should not be initiated based solely on that finding. The risk of developing MAC-associated disease in severely immunocompromised patients is higher, however, if MAC is present in the stools.

Blood is the preferred specimen for culture, and greater than 90% of cases of disseminated disease are diagnosed by a positive blood culture. Rarely, bone marrow culture may grow MAC when mycobacterial blood cultures are negative. Blood cultures are sensitive and specific for the diagnosis of disseminated MAC disease in patients with AIDS. A single specimen yields the diagnosis in 90% to 95% of cases, and two specimens yield the diagnosis in 99% of cases.[105,106] Additional cultures should be obtained only when clinical suspicion is high. Culture on liquid medium is preferable to culture on solid medium and is more rapid; growth on liquid medium often can be detected in 8 to 14 days, but cultures still must be held for 6 weeks to be negative. When growth is detected in liquid medium, hybridization with DNA or RNA probes can identify MAC definitively in a matter of hours. Blood mycobacterial burden can be quantitated using lysis-centrifugation systems with plating on solid medium, but this information has limited clinical utility.[106] When blood mycobacterial burden is high, mycobacteria may be seen on Kinyoun or auramine stain of buffy coat smears, but this method of diagnosis is neither sensitive nor specific for MAC. Direct detection of MAC in blood by polymerase chain reaction has been reported to be as sensitive and specific as culture, but this assay is not widely available.[107,108]

Disseminated MAC disease has protean manifestations, but none of its features are pathognomonic. The differential diagnosis is broad. Disseminated disease due to histoplasmosis, tuberculosis, or other nontuberculous mycobacteria is especially similar to disseminated MAC. Systemic cryptococcosis, blastomycosis, toxoplasmosis, cytomegalovirus, salmonellosis, lymphoma, and AIDS wasting syndrome also should be considered.

Lymphadenitis

Confirmed diagnosis of MAC lymphadenitis requires growth of MAC from the node. Excision is preferred to needle biopsy or aspirate because fistula formation is common after needle biopsy or aspiration. In the non-HIV-infected host, cultures are likely to yield no growth when obtained more than 1 month after the appearance of adenopathy. Histologic examination that reveals noncaseating granuloma with or without acid-fast bacilli is suggestive but not diagnostic. In these cases, or when excision cannot be performed, dual skin testing that includes specific antigens for MAC is sensitive and specific but these reagents are not licensed for use in the United States at present.[109] Skin testing with *M. tuberculosis* antigen alone (purified protein derivative-standard) has limited sensitivity.[109,110]

Isolated lymphadenopathy has a large differential diagnosis. Tuberculosis and lymphoma are the most commonly encountered entities that present similarly to MAC. Mononucleosis, toxoplasmosis,

syphilis, cat-scratch disease, other malignancies, and lymph nodes reactive to local bacterial infections also should be considered.

Other Sites

Diagnosis of MAC disease in other sites, such as skin, soft tissues, bones, and joints, is suggested by the finding of acid-fast bacilli or granulomas in tissue, but confirmation requires recovery of MAC by culture of the affected site.

TREATMENT

Principles of Treatment

Successful treatment of MAC is a challenge. As with therapy of other mycobacterial infections, the use of at least two active drugs is essential to prevent emergence of resistance and to achieve a long-term cure. Therapy is made difficult by the paucity of drugs that are highly active against MAC and by the frequency of adverse effects associated with the available drugs. In the premacrolide era, success rates of treatment of pulmonary MAC were 50% or less.[76-78,111,112] Treatment regimens included the use of multiple agents, including isoniazid, ethambutol, rifampin, streptomycin, amikacin, para-aminosalicylic acid, clofazimine, cycloserine, and ethionamide. Immediate failure rates were 25%, and eventual failure and relapse rates approached 50%. In addition, these premacrolide regimens required treatment durations of 36 months, and patients had frequent and severe adverse drug reactions-particularly with cycloserine, ethionamide, and the aminoglycosides. AIDS patients with disseminated MAC also responded poorly to nonmacrolide-containing regimens.[113-116] Although the degree of bacteremia was reduced in some trials, overall failure rates and mortality remained high, and drug toxicity was substantial.

Macrolides and azalides exhibit excellent in vitro activity against MAC.[117] Using broth dilution techniques, a minimal inhibitory concentration of less than 8 µg/mL is considered susceptible to clarithromycin, 16 µg/mL is considered moderately susceptible, and greater than 32 µg/mL is considered resistant. Greater than 99% of strains of MAC from patients not previously given a macrolide are susceptible to clarithromycin or azithromycin.[118-120] Macrolide/azalide monotherapy has been evaluated in the treatment of pulmonary MAC in non-AIDS patients. In a trial of clarithromycin monotherapy, 94% of patients showed clinical improvement, but 16% developed clarithromycin resistance.[119] In another trial, azithromycin was given as sole therapy for 4 months to patients with pulmonary MAC, resulting in clinical improvement without the development of macrolide resistance.[120] The clinical effectiveness of clarithromycin and azithromycin has been shown when employed as monotherapy for AIDS patients with disseminated MAC.[118,121,122] Treatment with these drugs resulted in a marked decrease in MAC bacteremia and concomitant reduction in clinical symptoms. When used as monotherapy, however, rates of acquired macrolide resistance are unacceptable. In the largest trial of monotherapy with clarithromycin, 46% of patients developed strains of MAC with a minimal inhibitory concentration equal to or greater than 32 µg/mL, and the development of these resistant strains was associated with recurrence of clinical symptoms.[118]

Other drugs also have been shown to have clinical activity against MAC. Rifabutin is active in vitro against MAC,[123] and in a placebo-controlled trial, rifabutin combined with ethambutol and clofazimine resulted in improvement in bacteremia in 7 of 11 AIDS patients with disseminated MAC compared with 0 of 13 patients receiving placebo with the same two other drugs.[124] Ethambutol has been shown to have activity in vitro against MAC[125] and to be effective in reducing mycobacteremia when used as monotherapy for AIDS patients with disseminated MAC.[126]

Combination therapy is essential in treating MAC to maximize the effectiveness of the macrolides and to minimize the development of macrolide resistance. Many different combination regimens have been evaluated. In pulmonary MAC in patients who have tolerated 6 or more months of macrolide therapy, sputum conversion rates have ranged from 70% to 90%.[127-129] Although there has not been a direct comparative study of azithromycin and clarithromycin in the treatment of MAC pulmonary disease, rates of culture conversion appear lower in studies of azithromycin.[130] Most patients in these macrolide studies received ethambutol, rifabutin (or rifampin), and an aminoglycoside in addition to the macrolide. The importance of the macrolide in the regimens was evident in a study of patients with pulmonary MAC who were being treated with a combination of ethambutol and rifampin without a macrolide: There was a 69% failure rate with 36% mortality.[131]

The addition of macrolides to treatment regimens for AIDS patients with disseminated MAC has shown a marked clinical benefit. Patients receiving a three-drug regimen of clarithromycin, rifabutin, and ethambutol had greater clearance of bacteremia and improved survival compared with patients receiving rifabutin, ethambutol, clofazimine, and ciprofloxacin.[132] Other trials of clarithromycin-containing regimens for the treatment of disseminated MAC have had better clinical outcomes than historical results of patients treated with nonmacrolide-containing regimens.[133-135] Azithromycin also is effective in the treatment of disseminated MAC, although fewer studies have been performed with azithromycin than with clarithromycin. In two comparison trials, patients who received azithromycin were less likely to have MAC bacteremia cleared than patients who received clarithromycin.[136,137]

Tolerability

The maximal dose of clarithromycin is 500 mg twice daily; higher doses have been associated with poorer clinical outcomes and should not be used.[118,138] Many patients, particularly elderly patients, have difficulty tolerating 500 mg twice daily of clarithromycin, largely because of gastrointestinal side effects (Table 250-2). When gastrointestinal side effects occur, doses may be reduced, either to half-dose once a day or full dose thrice weekly, without significant loss of efficacy.[128] Alternatively, azithromycin may be substituted for clarithromycin because azithromycin has similar activity and provokes less gastrointestinal intolerance.[139] Patients initially intolerant of azithromycin may be able to tolerate decreased dose levels or less frequent administration. Ethambutol is well tolerated by most patients, although at higher doses, gastrointestinal intolerance or optic neuritis may occur. Rifabutin is associated with gastrointestinal distress, liver function abnormalities, and neutropenia. When given at higher doses or in combination with drugs that inhibit its metabolism, rifabutin has been associated with uveitis and severe arthralgias.[140,141] For patients unable to tolerate rifabutin, rifampin may be substituted and is often better tolerated.

Aminoglycosides must be administered parenterally; streptomycin usually is given intramuscularly, and amikacin usually is given intravenously. Patients frequently become intolerant of the repeated intramuscular injections associated with long-term streptomycin treatment, so the availability of long-term intravenous access devices makes amikacin the preferable agent. Administration of aminoglycosides twice or thrice weekly is adequate for treatment of MAC, and this relative infrequency lessens inconvenience to the patient. The major toxicities of aminoglycosides are hearing loss and renal function impairment. Audiometry should be performed at baseline and repeated monthly in all elderly patients who are beginning aminoglycoside

therapy for MAC. Similarly, serum creatinine levels should be followed weekly and dosing adjusted accordingly.

Drug Interactions

Neither azithromycin nor ethambutol has clinically important drug interactions, and this is a major advantage of these agents. Clarithromycin inhibits cytochrome P-450 (CYP 3A4) and interferes with the metabolism of drugs that use this enzyme. Increased serum concentrations of theophylline, carbamazepine, omeprazole, digoxin, and terfenadine have been reported when these drugs were coadministered with clarithromycin. Serum levels of theophylline, carbamazepine, and digoxin should be monitored when taken with clarithromycin; coadministration of clarithromycin and terfenadine is contraindicated. Similarly, warfarin (Coumadin) metabolism may be affected, with potentiation of its anticoagulant effect, so prothrombin times should be monitored closely. Serum levels of clarithromycin are increased when the drug is coadministered with fluconazole or ranitidine, but these increased levels do not seem to be associated with alterations in either efficacy or toxicity.

Rifampin and rifabutin decrease clearance of other drugs by induction of the hepatic microsomal enzyme cytochrome P-450 pathway.[142] Many drugs potentially can be affected by rifampin/rifabutin, including clarithromycin, methadone, warfarin, estrogens, theophylline, and several classes of antiretroviral agents. When possible, serum levels of these agents should be monitored when coadministered with rifampin or rifabutin. Rifabutin has a less pronounced effect on hepatic enzyme induction than rifampin and may offer advantages in some cases. Serum levels of clarithromycin and its active metabolite, 14-OH clarithromycin, are decreased by 65% when the drug is coadministered with rifampin; when coadministered with rifabutin, the decrease is 47%.[143] Rifampin and rifabutin have substantial drug interactions with protease inhibitors and non-nucleoside reverse transcriptase inhibitors used in treating HIV infection. Rifampin is not usually recommended for use in these patients, and rifabutin doses need to be adjusted (see Chapter 36).[142] Because fluoroquinolones can affect serum levels of theophylline, dilantin, and warfarin, these agents should be monitored when coadministered with fluoroquinolones. Coadministration of fluoroquinolones with calcium-containing or magnesium-containing antacids or ferrous sulfate tablets can lead to decreased absorption and decreased serum drug levels of the fluoroquinolones.

Drug Dosing in Patients with Impaired Renal Function

Clarithromycin, ethambutol, fluoroquinolones, and aminoglycosides are excreted by the kidney, and doses of these agents should be reduced in patients with renal insufficiency. Rifampin, rifabutin, and azithromycin are excreted largely by the liver and do not require dose reduction when given to patients with renal insufficiency.

Treatment of Macrolide-Resistant *Mycobacterium avium* Complex Disease

Isolates resistant in vitro to clarithromycin are uniformly cross-resistant to azithromycin so that substitution when resistant organisms are present provides no benefit.[144] Neither drug should be continued in patients

TABLE 250-2 Drugs Employed in the Treatment of *Mycobacterium avium* Complex Disease			
Drug	*Usual Daily Dose**	*Usual Intermittent Dose*	*Common Adverse Effects*
Clarithromycin	500 mg bid	1 g 3 times/wk	GI distress, bitter taste, rash, hearing loss, drug interactions
Azithromycin	250 mg qd	500-600 mg 3 times/wk	GI distress, hearing loss
Ethambutol	15 mg/kg qd	25 mg/kg 3 times/wk	At high doses: optic neuritis, GI distress
Rifabutin	300 mg qd	300 mg 3 times/wk	GI distress, hepatitis, neutropenia, drug interactions; at high doses: uveitis, arthralgias
Rifampin	600 mg qd	600 mg 3 times/wk	GI distress, hepatitis, neutropenia, drug interactions
Amikacin	Not recommended	15 mg/kg IV 3 times/wk	Vestibular and auditory abnormalities, renal toxicity
Streptomycin	Not recommended	15 mg/kg IM (maximum 1 g) 3 times/wk	Vestibular and auditory abnormalities, renal toxicity

*Oral dosing unless otherwise indicated.
GI, gastrointestinal.

with MAC disease caused by macrolide-resistant organisms. Choosing the optimal regimen for treatment of MAC disease with macrolide-resistant organisms is challenging because regimens employed before the advent of macrolides were only marginally effective. Most experts recommend a four-drug regimen comprising rifabutin, ethambutol, a fluoroquinolone, and an aminoglycoside. For patient convenience and ease of administration, amikacin is preferable to streptomycin. Choice of the optimal fluoroquinolone is problematic because many MAC isolates are not susceptible in vitro to achievable serum levels of ciprofloxacin or levofloxacin.[145] Moxifloxacin may have a better profile and is effective in animal models of MAC, but clinical experience with it is limited. Ethionamide and cycloserine may be useful but have substantial toxicities; it is advisable to consult a specialist with experience in the use of these agents. Isoniazid, pyrazinamide, and clofazimine are minimally active in vitro and do not provide clinical benefit.[131,146] Newer agents that seem promising in vitro or in animal models include mefloquine and linezolid.[147,148]

Immunomodulatory Treatment of *Mycobacterium avium* Complex Disease

MAC disease in patients with inherited immune defects may have a better response to antimycobacterial therapy when treatment to restore or circumvent immune defects is undertaken. When inherited defects in the IFN-γ signaling pathway are present, subcutaneously administered IFN-γ overcomes these defects and may lead to clinical improvement.[70] IFN-γ also might benefit patients without clearly defined immune defects, but such benefit is less certain.

Specific Treatment Plans

Pulmonary *Mycobacterium avium* Complex

The decision to treat for pulmonary MAC is made difficult by the long duration of therapy required and the likelihood of substantial drug toxicity. Treatment should be initiated only for patients with active clinical symptoms, abnormal imaging studies, and positive cultures, as discussed earlier. Treatment of pulmonary MAC should include a minimum of three drugs-usually clarithromycin, 500 mg twice daily; ethambutol, 15 mg/kg; and rifabutin, 300 mg/day (Table 250-3). An aminoglycoside, usually amikacin or streptomycin, may be valuable for patients with extensive disease. Consensus treatment guidelines suggest daily use of the oral medications, with the aminoglycoside used two to three times weekly.[43] Patients should be evaluated monthly for clinical improvement, ad-

herence to the drug regimen, and occurrence of adverse effects. Sputum should be obtained monthly for mycobacterial smear and culture. The rate of improvement can be expected to be slow, with most patients remaining culture positive for 6 months.[43,127-129,149] Chest radiographs need not be repeated frequently because changes occur slowly. Patients who do not show clinical improvement and whose sputum does not clear of MAC after 6 months should be evaluated for adherence to the regimen. For patients who cannot tolerate the initial regimen, one option is changing from daily clarithromycin to a regimen of thrice-weekly dosing-clarithromycin, 1 g; ethambutol, 25 mg/kg; and rifabutin, 300 mg, all given on a thrice-weekly schedule.[128] Adverse drug effects may require further dose adjustments. Another option for patients who cannot tolerate clarithromycin is to change to azithromycin, 250 mg daily, with ethambutol, 15 mg/kg, and rifabutin, 300 mg, also given daily. Azithromycin may be given at 600 mg thrice weekly, with ethambutol, 25 mg/kg, and rifabutin, 300 mg, each given thrice weekly as well.[130] With patients taking thrice-weekly regimens, it is essential to discuss the extreme importance of adherence to the regimen.

For patients who are not responding despite good adherence to therapy, drug resistance needs to be considered, and drug susceptibility testing for macrolides and azalides should be done. Although almost all MAC isolates from untreated patients are susceptible to macrolides and azalides, resistance can develop on treatment, leading to a poor outcome. Isolates resistant to clarithromycin also are resistant to azithromycin.[144] Drug susceptibility testing is not recommended for drugs other than the macrolides.[43]

The optimal duration of therapy is unknown, but most experts treat at least 12 months after sputum cultures have become negative. Most patients with pulmonary MAC receive a total of 18 to 24 months of therapy.[43] Shorter durations may be reasonable for patients with minimal disease who show a rapid clinical response to treatment. Patients should be followed every few months after therapy is discontinued because relapses can occur. Surgical lung resection has a limited role and is a possibility for select patients who do not respond to medical therapy. Although most surgical procedures for MAC were performed in the premacrolide era,[150,151] surgical resection of MAC-infected lung continues to be required occasionally despite the use of clarithromycin-containing drug regimens.[152] The indication for surgery is usually failure of drug treatment, with the intent of removing major areas of disease, where tissue penetration of antibiotics may be limited. Occasional patients need surgery to control complications of MAC, such as pneumothorax, bronchiectasis, or hemoptysis. Because most patients with MAC have many comorbid conditions, surgery in this population has a high rate of complications, notably prolonged air leaks and bronchopulmonary fistulas.[150-152]

Hypersensitivity Pneumonitis

Most patients with MAC hypersensitivity pneumonitis ("hot-tub lung") have responded well to short-term interventions.[87-89] Some patients have responded simply to avoidance of the source of exposure, with no additional therapy.[89] For patients with progressive pulmonary symptoms, a 1- to 2-month course of prednisone with or without antimycobacterial drugs has been shown to be effective.[87]

Disseminated Disease

Antimycobacterial treatment should be initiated promptly for all patients with culture-confirmed evidence for disseminated MAC. Patients with clinical symptoms suggesting disseminated MAC should have blood cultured, but presumptive treatment is not recommended. If treatment is initiated pending culture results, the clinician should discontinue treatment and evaluate for other illness if the cultures remain negative after 6 to 8 weeks. HIV-infected patients should not be treated if they are colonized with MAC in the sputum or gastrointestinal tract but have no evidence of active infection; these patients should be followed carefully, however, because 60% may develop MAC bacteremia within 1 year.[17]

TABLE 250-3	Regimens for the Treatment and Prevention of *Mycobacterium avium* Complex Disease	
	Preferred	*Alternative*
Treatment		
Pulmonary	Clarithromycin 500 mg/bid+ Ethambutol 15 mg/kg qd+ Rifabutin 300 mg qd± (Aminoglycoside)	Azithromycin 250 mg qd+ Ethambutol 15 mg/kg qd+ Rifabutin 300 mg qd± (Aminoglycoside)
Disseminated	Clarithromycin 500 mg bid+ Ethambutol 15 mg/kg qd± (Rifabutin 300 mg qd)*	Azithromycin 500-600 mg qd+ Ethambutol 15 mg/kg qd± (Rifabutin 300 mg qd)*
Prevention		
Disseminated	Azithromycin 1200 mg every week	Clarithromycin 500 mg bid *or* rifabutin 300 mg qd*

*Rifabutin dose may need to be adjusted if a patient is receiving antiretrovirals (see Chapter 36). Rifampin 600 mg once daily may be substituted for rifabutin if better toleration is needed. Rifampin dose may need adjustment in patients receiving antiretrovirals.

Patients with disseminated MAC should be treated with clarithromycin, 500 mg twice daily, and ethambutol, 15 mg/kg/day (see Table 250-3).[153] Some experts recommend the addition of rifabutin, 300 mg/day, but the addition of this drug is of uncertain benefit. In one trial, the addition of rifabutin did not affect bacteriologic response or survival,[135] but another trial, using a higher dose of rifabutin (450 mg/day), showed modest clinical benefit.[154] Patients with HIV infection and MAC disease have improved clinical outcomes and decreased risk of relapse if antiretroviral therapy for HIV disease is administered concurrently. This treatment is complicated by drug interactions between the rifabutin used to treat MAC disease and the protease inhibitors and non-nucleoside reverse transcriptase inhibitors (or both) used to treat HIV infection. In this situation, treatment of MAC with clarithromycin and ethambutol (alone) is preferred. If rifabutin is to be used, dose adjustment of rifabutin, protease inhibitors, or non-nucleoside reverse transcriptase inhibitors may be required (see Chapters 36 and 124).[142,155]

When effective antimycobacterial therapy of disseminated MAC is instituted, fevers and night sweats usually resolve within 2 to 4 weeks, and mycobacteria are cleared from the blood in 4 to 8 weeks. Severe anemia and fatigue may not resolve, however, for 2 to 6 months. Patients with a hematocrit less than 25% should receive transfusions or exogenous erythropoietin to stimulate erythrocyte production and increase the hematocrit to 28% or greater. Endogenous erythropoietin levels do not seem to be a good predictor of success of exogenous erythropoietin,[64] and symptomatic improvement after transfusion is prompt, so transfusion often is preferable. Hematocrit should be followed monthly to assess the need for subsequent transfusion. The response of anorexia and weight loss to antimycobacterial therapy is variable, but parenteral nutritional supplementation is not indicated. Follow-up blood cultures are not necessary for patients with clinical improvement but should be done for patients who fail to improve after 4 to 8 weeks. MAC isolates from patients failing therapy should be tested for susceptibility to clarithromycin, although most isolates remain sensitive in vitro to this drug.[134,135]

Some patients beginning antiretroviral therapy experience either a local inflammatory reaction or a worsening of systemic symptoms as a manifestation of the immune reconstitution syndrome. This situation is especially likely when antimycobacterial therapy and antiretroviral therapy are initiated concurrently. Common local reactions are painful lymphadenopathy, abdominal pain, or hepatosplenomegaly. Most patients with the immune reconstitution syndrome improve with no change in therapy. For patients with severe symptoms, a short course of steroids (e.g., prednisone, 0.5 to 1 mg/kg daily, tapered as signs and symptoms permit) may relieve symptomatic discomfort.

The duration of treatment depends greatly on the patient's immune status. Therapy should be continued indefinitely for patients with less than 100 CD4+ cells/mm³. In several large series, AIDS patients with disseminated MAC who have had a significant elevation of CD4+ cell counts owing to antiretroviral therapy have had antimycobacterial therapy stopped with no apparent harm.[156-158] Based on these studies, experts suggest that it is reasonable to discontinue treatment for persons who have received MAC therapy for at least 12 months and have had equal to or greater than 100 CD4+ cells/mm³ for at least 6 months.[153] Patients should continue to be followed because there have been occasional reports of patients relapsing with local or systemic MAC after discontinuation of treatment.

Lymphadenitis

Surgical excision is the treatment of choice for lymphadenitis due to MAC.[98-100] Complete excision of the node is recommended as a diagnostic and therapeutic intervention. For individuals for whom surgery poses a high risk, therapy with a clarithromycin-containing regimen may be successful.[43]

PROPHYLAXIS

Patients with AIDS and CD4+ cell counts of less than 50 cells/mm³ are at high risk of developing disseminated MAC disease. Disseminated MAC disease develops in approximately 20% of such patients each year.[30,31] Given the high morbidity and mortality associated with disseminated MAC, chemoprophylaxis of MAC is a crucial component of care for all patients with CD4+ cell counts less than 50 cells/mm³. Drugs that have been proved effective at preventing disseminated MAC in this population are clarithromycin,[159] azithromycin,[160] and rifabutin.[161] In direct comparison studies, the macrolides/azalides were more effective than rifabutin.[162,163] There is no added benefit to using combination therapy to prevent disseminated MAC because resistance rarely emerges with single-agent prophylaxis.

Before beginning antimycobacterial prophylaxis, patients with fever, weight loss, or other symptoms of disseminated MAC should have a mycobacterial blood culture performed to ensure that disseminated disease is not present. Routine screening of sputum or stools for MAC is not indicated. Azithromycin, 1200 mg once weekly, is the preferred regimen, based on ease of administration and low toxicity (see Table 250-3). Clarithromycin also is effective but must be given at a dose of 500 mg twice daily. Rifabutin, 300 mg daily, should be used only when the patient cannot tolerate azithromycin or clarithromycin. Patients receiving rifabutin monotherapy also should be screened for active tuberculosis to avoid the emergence of rifampin-resistant tuberculosis. Patients who have had a nadir CD4+ cell of less than 50 cells/mm³ and who with antiretroviral therapy have achieved an increase in CD4+ cells to greater than 100 cells/mm³ are no longer at increased risk for MAC. Controlled studies have shown the safety of discontinuing antimycobacterial prophylaxis for MAC in this population.[164,165] Current recommendations are to discontinue MAC prophylaxis in persons who have achieved CD4+ counts greater than 100 cells/mm³ for at least 3 months.[153] Patients should be restarted on prophylaxis if their CD4+ cells subsequently decline to less than or equal to 50 cells/mm³.

REFERENCES

1. Horsburgh CR Jr. Epidemiology of *Mycobacterium avium* complex. Lung Biol Health Dis. 1996;87:1-22.
2. Wolinsky E. Nontuberculous mycobacteria and associated diseases. Am Rev Respir Dis. 1979;119:107-159.
3. du Moulin GC, Stottmeier KD, Pelletier PA, et al. Concentration of *Mycobacterium avium* by hospital hot water systems. JAMA. 1988;260:1599-1601.
4. von Reyn CF, Maslow JN, Barber TW, et al. Persistent colonisation of potable water as a source of *Mycobacterium avium* infection in AIDS. Lancet. 1994;343:1137-1141.
5. Kahana LM, Kay M, Yakrus MA, et al. *Mycobacterium avium* complex infection in an immunocompetent young adult related to hot tub exposure. Chest. 1997;111:242-245.
6. Tobin-D'Angelo MJ, Blass MA, del Rio C, et al. Hospital water as a source of *Mycobacterium avium* complex (MAC) isolates in respiratory specimens. J Infect Dis. In press.
7. von Reyn CF, Arbeit RD, Tosteson ANA, et al, and the International MAC Study Group. The international epidemiology of disseminated *Mycobacterium avium* complex infection in AIDS. AIDS. 1996;10:1025-1032.
8. Sugita Y, Ishii N, Katsuno M, et al. Familial cluster of cutaneous *Mycobacterium avium* infection resulting from use of a circulating, constantly heated bath water system. Br J Dermatol. 2000;142:789-793.
9. Gruft H, Katz J, Blanchard DC. Postulated source of *Mycobacterium intracellulare* (Battey) infection. Am J Epidemiol. 1975;102:311-318.
10. Parker BC, Ford MA, Gruft H, et al. Epidemiology of infection by nontuberculous mycobacteria: IV. Preferential aerosolization of *Mycobacterium intracellulare* from natural waters. Am Rev Respir Dis. 1983;128:652-656.
11. Chapman JS. The atypical mycobacteria. Hosp Pract. 1970;5:69-80.
12. O'Brien RJ, Geiter LJ, Snider DE. The epidemiology of nontuberculous mycobacterial diseases in the United States: Results from a national survey. Am Rev Respir Dis. 1987;135:1007-1014.
13. Tsukamura M, Kita N, Shimoide H, et al. Studies on the epidemiology of nontuberculous mycobacteriosis in Japan. Am Rev Respir Dis. 1988;137:1280-1284.
14. Debrunner M, Salfinger M, Brandli O, et al. Epidemiology and clinical significance of nontuberculous mycobacteria in patients negative for human immunodeficiency virus in Switzerland. Clin Infect Dis. 1992;15:330-345.
15. Iseman MD, Buschman DL, Ackerson LM. Pectus excavatum and scoliosis: Thoracic abnormalities associated with pulmonary disease caused by *Mycobacterium avium* complex. Am Rev Respir Dis. 1991;144:914-916.
16. Reich JM, Johnson RE. *Mycobacterium avium* complex pulmonary disease: Incidence, presentation, and response to therapy in a community setting. Am Rev Respir Dis. 1991;143:1381-1385.

17. Chin DP, Hopewell PC, Yajko DM, et al. *Mycobacterium avium* complex in the respiratory or gastrointestinal tract and the risk of developing *Mycobacterium avium* complex bacteremia in patients with the human immunodeficiency virus. J Infect Dis. 1994;169:289-295.

18. Horsburgh CR, Metchock B, Gordon SM, et al. Predictors of survival in patients with AIDS and disseminated *Mycobacterium avium* complex disease. J Infect Dis. 1994;170:573-577.

19. Kalayjian RC, Toossi Z, Tomashefski JF Jr, et al. Pulmonary disease due to infection by *Mycobacterium avium* complex in patients with AIDS. Clin Infect Dis. 1995;20:1186-1194.

20. Kilby JM, Gilligan PH, Yankaskas JR, et al. Nontuberculous mycobacteria in adult patients with cystic fibrosis. Chest. 1992;102:70-75.

21. Tomashefski JF Jr, Stern RC, Demko CA, et al. Nontuberculous mycobacteria in cystic fibrosis. Am J Respir Crit Care Med. 1996;154:523-528.

22. Pinto-Powell R, Olivier KN, Marsh BJ, et al. Skin testing with *Mycobacterium avium* sensitin to identify infection with *M. avium* complex in patients with cystic fibrosis. Clin Infect Dis. 1996;22:560-562.

23. Witty LA, Tapson VF, Piantadosi CA. Isolation of mycobacteria in patients with pulmonary alveolar proteinosis. Medicine. 1994;73:103-109.

24. Horsburgh CR Jr, Mason UG, Farhi DC, et al. Disseminated infection with *Mycobacterium avium-intracellulare:* A report of 13 cases and a review of the literature. Medicine. 1985;64:36-48.

25. Horsburgh CR. Epidemiology of human disease caused by *Mycobacterium avium* complex. Can J Infect Dis. 1994;5(Suppl B):5B-9B.

26. Horsburgh CR, Gettings J, Alexander LN, et al. Disseminated *Mycobacterium avium* complex disease among patients infected with human immunodeficiency virus, 1985-2000. Clin Infect Dis. 2001;33:1938-1943.

27. Kaplan JE, Hanson D, Dworkin MS, et al. Epidemiology of human immunodeficiency virus–associated opportunistic infections in the United States in the era of highly active antiretroviral therapy. Clin Infect Dis. 2000;30(Suppl 1):S5-14.

28. Reichenbach J, Rosenzweig S, Doffinger R, et al. Mycobacterial diseases in primary immunodeficiencies. Curr Opin Allergy Clin Immunol. 2001;1:503-511.

29. Winter SM, Bernard EM, Gold JW, et al. Humoral response to disseminated infection by Mycobacterium avium–Mycobacterium intracellulare in acquired immunodeficiency syndrome and hairy cell leukemia. J Infect Dis. 1985;151:523-527.

30. Horsburgh CR. *Mycobacterium avium* complex infection in the acquired immunodeficiency syndrome. N Engl J Med. 1991;324:1332-1338.

31. Nightingale SD, Byrd LT, Southern PM, et al. Incidence of *Mycobacterium avium-intracellulare* complex bacteremia in human immunodeficiency virus positive patients. J Infect Dis. 1992;165:1082-1085.

32. Finkelstein DM, Williams PL, Molenberghs G, et al. Patterns of opportunistic infections in patients with HIV infection. J Acquir Immune Defic Synd. 1996;12:38-45.

33. Horsburgh CR, Selik RM. The epidemiology of disseminated nontuberculous mycobacterial infection in the acquired immunodeficiency syndrome (AIDS). Am Rev Respir Dis. 1989;139:4-7.

34. Horsburgh CR, Caldwell MB, Simonds RJ. Epidemiology of disseminated nontuberculous mycobacterial infection in children with AIDS. Pediatr Infect Dis J. 1993;12:219-222.

35. Horsburgh CR Jr, Schoenfelder JR, Gordin FM, et al. Geographic and seasonal variation in *Mycobacterium avium* bacteremia among North American patients with AIDS. Am J Med Sci. 1997;313:341-345.

36. Gilks CF, Brindle RJ, Mwachari C, et al. Disseminated mycobacterial infection among HIV-infected patients in Kenya. J Acquir Immune Defic Syndr. 1995;8:195-198.

37. Greenberg AE, Lucas S, Tossou O, et al. Autopsy-proven causes of death in HIV-infected patients treated for tuberculosis in Abidjan, Côte d'Ivoire. AIDS. 1995;9:1251-1254.

38. Okello DO, Sewankambo N, Goodgame R, et al. Absence of bacteremia with *Mycobacterium avium-intracellulare* in Ugandan patients with AIDS. J Infect Dis. 1990;162:208-210.

39. Horsburgh CR, Hanson DL, Jones JL, et al. Protection from *Mycobacterium avium* complex disease in HIV-infected persons with a history of tuberculosis. J Infect Dis. 1996;174:1212-1217.

40. Schaad UB, Votteler TP, McCracken GH, et al. Management of atypical mycobacterial lymphadenitis in childhood: A review based on 380 cases. J Pediatr. 1979;95:356-360.

41. Wolinsky E. Mycobacterial lymphadenitis in children: A prospective study of 105 nontuberculous cases with long-term follow-up. Clin Infect Dis. 1995;20:954-963.

42. Phillips P, Kwiatkowski MB, Copland M, et al. Mycobacterial lymphadenitis associated with the initiation of combination antiretroviral therapy. J Acquir Immune Defic Syndr Hum Retrovirol. 1999;20:122-128.

43. American Thoracic Society Official Statement. Diagnosis and treatment of disease caused by nontuberculous mycobacteria. Am J Respir Crit Care Med. 1997;156:S1-S25.

44. Tsang AY, Denner JC, Brennan PJ, et al. Clinical and epidemiological importance of typing of *Mycobacterium avium* complex isolates. J Clin Microbiol. 1992;30:479-484.

45. Arbeit RD, Slutsky A, Barber TW, et al. Genetic diversity among strains of *Mycobacterium avium* causing monoclonal and polyclonal bacteremia in patients with AIDS. J Infect Dis. 1993;167:1384-1390.

46. Smole SC, McAleese F, Ngampasutadol J, et al. Clinical and epidemiological correlates of genotypes within the *Mycobacterium avium* complex defined by restriction and sequence analysis of hsp65. J Clin Microbiol. 2002;40:3374-3380.

47. Gangadharam PR, Perumal VK, Crawford JT, et al. Association of plasmids and virulence of *Mycobacterium avium* complex. Am Rev Respir Dis. 1988;137:212-214.

48. Mapother ME, Songer JC. In vitro interaction of *Mycobacterium avium* with intestinal epithelial cells. Infect Immun. 1984;45:67-73.

49. Pethel ML, Falkinham JO III. Plasmid-influenced changes in *Mycobacterium avium* catalase activity. Infect Immun. 1989;57:1714-1718.

50. Crowle AJ, Dahl R, Ross E, et al. Evidence that vesicles containing living, virulent *Mycobacterium tuberculosis* or *Mycobacterium avium* in cultured human macrophages are not acidic. Infect Immun. 1991;59:1823-1831.

51. Frehel C, de Chastellier C, Lang T, et al. Evidence for inhibition of fusion of lysosomal and prelysosomal compartments with phagosomes in macrophages infected with pathogenic *Mycobacterium avium*. Infect Immun. 1986;52:252-262.

52. Shiratsuchi H, Toossi Z, Mettler MA, et al. Colonial morphotype as a determinate of cytokine expression by human monocytes infected with *M avium*. J Immunol. 1993;150:2945-2954.

53. Birkness KA, Swords WE, Huang PH, et al. Observed differences in virulence-associated phenotypes between a human clinical isolate and a veterinary isolate of *Mycobacterium avium*. Infect Immun. 1999;67:4895-4901.

54. Cirillo JD, Falkow S, Tompkins LS, et al. Interaction of *Mycobacterium avium* with environmental amoebae enhances virulence. Infect Immun. 1997;65:3759-3767.

55. Guthertz LS, Damsker B, Bottone EJ, et al. *Mycobacterium avium* and *Mycobacterium intracellulare* infections in patients with and without AIDS. J Infect Dis. 1989;160:1037-1041.

56. Marchevsky A, Damsker B, Gribetz A, et al. The spectrum of pathology of nontuberculous mycobacterial infections in open-lung biopsy specimens. Am J Clin Pathol. 1982;78:695-700.

57. Horsburgh CR. The pathophysiology of disseminated *M. avium* disease in AIDS. J Infect Dis. 1999;179(Suppl 3):S461-S465.

58. Torriani FJ, Behling CA, McCutchan JA, et al. Disseminated *Mycobacterium avium* complex: Correlation between blood and tissue burden. J Infect Dis. 1996;173:942-949.

59. Klatt EC, Jensen DF, Meyer PR. Pathology of *Mycobacterium avium-intracellulare* infection in acquired immunodeficiency syndrome. Hum Pathol. 1987;709:714.

60. Wallace JM, Hannah JB. *Mycobacterium avium* complex infection in patients with the acquired immunodeficiency syndrome. Chest. 1988;93:926-932.

61. Hafner R, Inderlied CB, Peterson DM, et al. Correlation of quantitative bone marrow and blood cultures in AIDS patients with disseminated *Mycobacterium avium* complex infection. J Infect Dis. 1999;180:438-447.

62. Haug CJ, Aukrust P, Lien E, et al. Disseminated *Mycobacterium avium* complex infection in AIDS: Immunopathogenic significance of an activated tumor necrosis factor system and depressed serum levels of 1,25 dihydroxyvitamin D. J Infect Dis. 1996;173:259-262.

63. Haas DW, Lederman MM, Clough LA, et al. Proinflammatory cytokine and human immunodeficiency virus RNA levels during early *Mycobacterium avium* complex bacteremia in advanced AIDS. J Infect Dis. 1998;177:1746-1749.

64. Gascon P, Sathe SS, Rameshwar P. Impaired erythropoiesis in the acquired immunodeficiency syndrome with disseminated *Mycobacterium avium* complex. Am J Med. 1993;94:41-48.

65. Vankayalapati R, Wizel B, Samten B, et al. Cytokine profiles in immunocompetent persons infected with *Mycobacterium avium* complex. J Infect Dis. 2001;183:478-484 (Epub December 20, 2000).

66. Newport MJ, Huxley CM, Huston S, et al. A mutation in the interferon-gamma-receptor gene and susceptibility to mycobacterial infection. N Engl J Med. 1996;335:1941-1949.

67. Holland SM, Dorman SE, Kwon A, et al. Abnormal regulation of interferon-gamma, interleukin-12, and tumor necrosis factor-alpha in human interferon-gamma receptor 1 deficiency. J Infect Dis. 1998;178:1095-1104.

68. Dorman SE, Holland SM. Mutation in the signal-transducing chain of the interferon-gamma receptor and susceptibility to mycobacterial infection. J Clin Invest. 1998;101:2364-2369.

69. Frucht DM, Holland SM. Defective monocyte costimulation for IFN-gamma production in familial disseminated *Mycobacterium avium* complex infection: Abnormal IL-12 regulation. J Immunol. 1996;157:411-416.

70. Holland SM, Eisenstein EM, Kuhns DB, et al. Treatment of disseminated nontuberculous mycobacterial infection with interferon gamma: A preliminary report. N Engl J Med. 1994;330:1348-1355.

71. Johnson JL, Shiratsuchi H, Toba H, et al. Preservation of monocyte effector functions against *Mycobacterium avium-M. intracellulare* in patients with AIDS. Infect Immun. 1991;59:3639-3645.

72. Havlir DV, Schrier RD, Torriani FJ, et al. Effect of potent antiretroviral therapy on immune responses to *Mycobacterium avium* in human immunodeficiency virus-infected subjects. J Infect Dis. 2000;182:1658-1663 (Epub October 18, 2000).

73. Ravn P, Pedersen BK. *Mycobacterium avium* and purified protein derivative-specific cytotoxicity mediated by CD4+ lymphocytes from healthy HIV-seropositive and -seronegative individuals. J Acquir Immune Defic Syndr. 1996;2:433-441.

74. Schnittman SH, Lane C, Witebsky FG, et al. Host defense against *Mycobacterium-avium* complex. J Clin Immunol. 1988;8:234-243.

75. Douvas GS, May MH, Pearson JR, et al. Hypertriglyceridemic serum, very low density lipoprotein, and iron enhance *Mycobacterium avium* replication in human macrophages. J Infect Dis. 1994;170:1248-1255.

76. Rosenzweig DY. Pulmonary mycobacterial infections due to *Mycobacterium intracellulare-avium* complex. Chest. 1979;72:115-119.

77. Yeager H Jr. Pulmonary disease due to *Mycobacterium intracellulare*. Am Rev Respir Dis. 1973;108:547-552.

78. Contreras MA, Cheung OT, Sanders DE, et al. Pulmonary infection with nontuberculous mycobacteria. Am Rev Respir Dis. 1988;137:149-152.

79. Levin DL. Radiology of pulmonary *Mycobacterium avium-intracellulare* complex. Clin Chest Med. 2002;23:603-612.

80. Primack SL, Logan PM, Hartman TE, et al. Pulmonary tuberculosis and *Mycobacterium avium-intracellulare:* A comparison of CT findings. Radiology. 1995;194:413-417.

81. Prince DS, Peterson DD, Steiner RM, et al. Infection with *Mycobacterium avium* complex in patients without predisposing conditions. N Engl J Med. 1989;321:863-868.
82. Reich JM, Johnson RE. *Mycobacterium avium* complex pulmonary disease presenting as an isolated lingular or middle lobe pattern. Chest. 1992;101:1605-1609.
83. Hartman TE, Swensen SJ, Williams DE. *Mycobacterium avium-intracellulare* complex: Evaluation with CT. Radiology. 1993;187:23-26.
84. Swenson SJ, Hartman TE, Williams DE. Computer tomographic diagnosis of *Mycobacterium avium-intracellulare* complex in patients with bronchiectasis. Chest. 1994;105:49-52.
85. Olivier KN, Weber DJ, Wallace RJ Jr, et al. Nontuberculous mycobacteria: I. Multicenter prevalence study in cystic fibrosis. Am J Respir Crit Care Med. 2003;167:828-834.
86. Olivier KN, Weber DJ, Lee J-H, et al. Nontuberculous mycobacteria: II. Nested-cohort study of impact on cystic fibrosis lung disease. Am J Respir Crit Care Med. 2003;167:835-840.
87. Khoor A, Leslie KO, Tazelaar HD, et al. Diffuse pulmonary disease caused by nontuberculous mycobacteria in immunocompetent people (hot tub lung). Am J Clin Pathol. 2001;115:755-762.
88. Mangione EJ, Huitt G, Lenaway D, et al. Nontuberculous mycobacterial disease following hot tub exposure. Emerg Infect Dis. 2001;7:1039-1042.
89. Rickman OB, Ryu JH, Fidler ME, et al. Hypersensitivity pneumonitis associated with *Mycobacterium avium* complex and hot tub use. Mayo Clin Proc. 2002;77:1233-1237.
90. Wong B, Edwards FF, Kiehn TE, et al. Continuous high-grade *Mycobacterium avium-intracellulare* bacteremia in patients with the acquired immune deficiency syndrome. Am J Med. 1985;78:35-40.
91. Zakowski P, Fligiel S, Berlin GW, et al. Disseminated *Mycobacterium avium-intracellulare* infection in homosexual men dying of acquired immunodeficiency. JAMA. 1982;248:2980-2982.
92. Greene JB, Sidhu GS, Lewin S, et al. *Mycobacterium avium-intracellulare:* A cause of disseminated life-threatening infection in homosexuals and drug abusers. Ann Intern Med. 1982;97:539-546.
93. Hawkins CC, Gold JWM, Whimbey E, et al. *Mycobacterium avium-intracellulare* complex in patients with acquired immunodeficiency syndrome. Ann Intern Med. 1986;105:184-188.
94. Gordin FM, Cohn DL, Sullam PM, et al. Early manifestations of disseminated *Mycobacterium avium* complex disease: A prospective evaluation. J Infect Dis. 1997;176:126-132.
95. Torriani FJ, McCutchan JA, Bozzette SA, et al. Autopsy findings in AIDS patients with *Mycobacterium avium* complex bacteremia. J Infect Dis. 1994;170:1601-1605.
96. Hassell M, French MA. *Mycobacterium avium* infection and immune restoration disease after highly active antiretroviral therapy in a patient with HIV and normal CD4+ counts. Eur J Clin Microbiol Infect Dis. 2001;20:889-891.
97. Race EM, Adelson-Mitty J, Kriegel GR, et al. Focal mycobacterial lymphadenitis following initiation of protease-inhibitor therapy in patients with advanced HIV-1 disease. Lancet. 1998;351:252-255.
98. Stewart MG, Starke JR, Coker NJ. Nontuberculous mycobacterial infections of the head and neck. Arch Otolaryngol Head Neck Surg. 1994;120:873-876.
99. Rahal A, Abela A, Arcand PH, et al. Nontuberculous mycobacterial adenitis of the head and neck in children: Experience from a tertiary care pediatric center. Laryngoscope. 1002;111:1791-1796.
100. Castro DJ, Hoover L, Castro DJ, et al. Cervical mycobacterial lymphadenitis. Arch Otolaryngol. 1985;111:816-819.
101. Lai KK, Stottmeier KD, Sherman IH, et al. Mycobacterial cervical lymphadenopathy. JAMA. 1984;251:1286-1288.
102. Hellinger WC, Smilack JD, Greider JL Jr, et al. Localized soft-tissue infections with *Mycobacterium avium/Mycobacterium intracellulare* complex in immunocompetent patients: Granulomatous tenosynovitis of the hand and wrist. Clin Infect Dis. 1995;21:65-69.
103. Kayak JD, McCall CO. Sporotrichoid cutaneous *Mycobacterium avium* complex infection. J Am Acad Dermatol. 2002;47:S249-S250.
104. Kullavanijaya P, Sirimachan S, Surarak S. Primary cutaneous infection with *Mycobacterium avium-intracellulare* complex resembling lupus vulgaris. Br J Dermatol. 1997;136:264-266.
105. Stone BL, Cohn DL, Kane MS, et al. Utility of paired blood cultures and smears in diagnosis of disseminated *Mycobacterium avium* complex infections in AIDS patients. J Clin Microbiol. 1994;32:841-842.
106. Havlir D, Kemper CA, Deresinski SC. Reproducibility of lysis-centrifugation cultures for quantification of *Mycobacterium avium* complex bacteremia. J Clin Microbiol. 1993;31:1794-1798.
107. Gamboa F, Manterola JM, Lonca J, et al. Detection and identification of mycobacteria by amplification of RNA and DNA in pretreated blood and bone marrow aspirates by a simple lysis method. J Clin Microbiol. 1997;35:2124-2128.
108. De Francesco MA, Colombrita D, Pinsi G, et al. Detection and identification of *Mycobacterium avium* in the blood of AIDS patients by the polymerase chain reaction. Eur J Clin Microbiol Infect Dis. 1995;15:551-555.
109. von Reyn CF, Williams D, Horsburgh CR, et al. Dual skin testing with *Mycobacterium avium* sensitin and purified protein derivative to discriminate pulmonary disease due to *M. avium* complex from pulmonary disease due to *Mycobacterium tuberculosis.* J Infect Dis. 1998;177:730-736.
110. Daley AJ, Isaacs D. Differential avian and human tuberculin skin testing in nontuberculous mycobacterial infection. Arch Dis Child. 1999;80:377-379.
111. Dutt AK, Stead WW. Long-term results of medical treatment in *Mycobacterium intracellulare* infection. Am J Med. 1979;67:449-453.
112. Ahn CH, Ahn SS, Anderson RA, et al. A four-drug regimen for initial treatment of cavitary disease caused by *Mycobacterium avium* complex. Am Rev Respir Dis. 1986;134:438-441.
113. Kemper CA, Meng T-C, Nussbaum J, et al. Treatment of *Mycobacterium avium* complex bacteremia in AIDS with a four-drug oral regimen. Ann Intern Med. 1992;116:466-472.
114. Hoy J, Mijch A, Sandland M, et al. Quadruple-drug therapy for *Mycobacterium avium-intracellulare* bacteremia in AIDS patients. J Infect Dis. 1990;161:801-805.
115. Chiu J, Nussbaum J, Bozzette S, et al. Treatment of disseminated *Mycobacterium avium* complex infection in AIDS with amikacin, ethambutol, rifampin, and ciprofloxacin. Ann Intern Med. 1990;113:358-361.
116. Agins BD, Berman DS, Spicehandler D, et al. Effect of combined therapy with ansamycin, clofazimine, ethambutol, and isoniazid for *Mycobacterium avium* infection in patients with AIDS. J Infect Dis. 1989;159:784-787.
117. Heifets L. Susceptibility testing of *Mycobacterium avium* complex isolates. Antimicrob Agents Chemother. 1996;40:1759-1967.
118. Chaisson RE, Benson CA, Dubé MP, et al. Clarithromycin therapy for bacteremic *Mycobacterium avium* complex disease. Ann Intern Med. 1994;121:905-911.
119. Wallace RJ Jr, Brown BA, Griffith DE, et al. Initial clarithromycin monotherapy for *Mycobacterium avium-intracellulare* complex lung disease. Am J Respir Crit Care Med. 1994;149:1335-1341.
120. Griffith DE, Brown BA, Girard WM, et al. Azithromycin activity against *Mycobacterium avium* complex lung disease in patients who were not infected with human immunodeficiency virus. Clin Infect Dis. 1996;23:983-989.
121. Dautzenberg B, Marc TS, Meyohas MC, et al. Clarithromycin and other antimicrobial agents in the treatment of disseminated *Mycobacterium avium* infections in patients with acquired immunodefiency syndrome. Arch Intern Med. 1993;153:368-372.
122. Young LS, Wiviott L, Wu M, et al. Azithromycin for treatment of *Mycobacterium avium-intracellulare* complex infection in patients with AIDS. Lancet. 1991;338:1107-1109.
123. Woodley CL, Kilburn JO. In vitro susceptibility of *Mycobacterium avium* complex and *Mycobacterium tuberculosis* strains to a spiro-piperidyl rifamycin. Am Rev Respir Dis. 1982;126:586-587.
124. Sullam PM, Gordin FM, Wynne BA, and the Rifabutin Treatment Group. Efficacy of rifabutin in the treatment of disseminated infection due to *Mycobacterium avium* complex. Clin Infect Dis. 1994;19:84-86.
125. Heifets LB, Iseman M, Lindholm-Levy PJ. Combinations of rifampin or rifabutin plus ethambutol against *Mycobacterium avium* complex. Am Rev Respir Dis. 1988;137:711-715.
126. Kemper CA, Havlir D, Haghighat D, et al. The individual microbiologic effect of three antimycobacterial agents, clofazimine, ethambutol, and rifampin, on *Mycobacterium avium* complex bacteremia in patients with AIDS. J Infect Dis. 1994;170:157-164.
127. Tanaka E, Kimoto T, Tsuyuguchi K, et al. Effect of clarithromycin regimen for *Mycobacterium avium* complex pulmonary disease. Am J Respir Crit Care Med. 1999;160:866-872.
128. Griffith DE, Brown BA, Cegielski P, et al. Early results (at 6 months) with intermittent clarithromycin-including regimens for lung disease due to *Mycobacterium avium* complex. Clin Infect Dis. 2000;30:288-292.
129. Wallace RJ Jr, Brown BA, Griffith DE, et al. Clarithromycin regimens for pulmonary *Mycobacterium avium* complex. Am J Respir Crit Care Med. 1996;153:1766-1772.
130. Griffith DE, Brown BA, Girard WM, et al. Azithromycin-containing regimens for treatment of *Mycobacterium avium* complex lung disease. Clin Infect Dis. 2001;21:1547-1553.
131. The Research Committee of the British Thoracic Society. Pulmonary disease caused by *Mycobacterium avium-intracellulare* in HIV-negative patients: Five-year follow-up of patients receiving standardized treatment. Int J Tuberc Lung Dis. 2002;6:628-634.
132. Shafran SD, Singer J, Zarowny DP, et al. A comparison of two regimens for the treatment of *Mycobacterium avium* complex bacteremia in AIDS: Rifabutin, ethambutol, and clarithromycin versus rifampin, ethambutol, clofazimine, and ciprofloxacin. N Engl J Med. 1996;335:377-383.
133. May T, Brel F, Beuscart C, et al. Comparison of combination therapy regimens for treatment of human immunodeficiency virus-infected patients with disseminated bacteremia due to *Mycobacterium avium.* Clin Infect Dis. 1997;25:621-629.
134. Dubé MP, Sattler FR, Torriani FJ, et al. A randomized evaluation of ethambutol for prevention of relapse and drug resistance during treatment of *Mycobacterium avium* complex bacteremia with clarithromycin-based combination therapy. J Infect Dis. 1997;176:1225-1232.
135. Gordin FM, Sullam PM, Shafran SD, et al. A randomized, placebo-controlled study of rifabutin added to a regimen of clarithromycin and ethambutol for treatment of disseminated infection with *Mycobacterium avium* complex. Clin Infect Dis. 1999;28:1080-1085.
136. Ward TT, Rimland D, Kauffman C, et al. Randomized, open-label trial of azithromycin plus ethambutol vs. clarithromycin plus ethambutol as therapy for *Mycobacterium avium* complex bacteremia in patients with human immunodeficiency virus infection. Clin Infect Dis. 1998;27:1278-1285.
137. Dunne M, Fessel J, Kumar P, et al. A randomized, double-blind trial comparing azithromycin and clarithromycin in the treatment of disseminated *Mycobacterium avium* infection in patients with human immunodeficiency virus. Clin Infect Dis. 2000;31:1245-1252.
138. Cohn DL, Fisher EJ, Peng GT, et al. A prospective randomized trial of four three-drug regimens in the treatment of disseminated *Mycobacterium avium* complex disease in AIDS patients: Excess mortality associated with high-dose clarithromycin. Clin Infect Dis. 1999;29:125-133.
139. Brown BA, Griffith DE, Girard W, et al. Relationship of adverse events to serum drug levels in patients receiving high-dose azithromycin for mycobacterial lung disease. Clin Infect Dis. 1997;24:958-964.
140. Shafran SD, Deschênes J, Miller M, et al. Uveitis and pseudojaundice during a regimen of clarithromycin, rifabutin, and ethambutol. N Engl J Med. 1994;330:438-439.

141. Siegal FP, Eilbott D, Burger H, et al. Dose-limiting toxicity of rifabutin in AIDS-related complex: Syndrome of arthralgias/arthritis. AIDS. 1990;4:433-441.

142. CDC. Updated guidelines for the use of rifabutin or rifampin for the treatment and prevention of tuberculosis among HIV-infected patients taking protease inhibitors or nonnucleoside reverse transcriptase inhibitors. MMWR Morb Mortal Wkly Rep. 2000;49:185-189.

143. Wallace RJ Jr, Brown BA, Griffith DE, et al. Reduced serum levels of clarithromycin in patients treated with multidrug regimens including rifampin or rifabutin for *Mycobacterium avium-M. intracellulare* infection. J Infect Dis. 1995;171:747-750.

144. Heifets L, Mor N, Vanderkolk J. *Mycobacterium avium* strains resistant to clarithromycin and azithromycin. Antimicrob Agents Chemother. 1993;37:2364-2370.

145. Iseman MD. Medical management of pulmonary disease caused by *Mycobacterium avium* complex. Clin Chest Med. 2002;23:633-641.

146. Chaisson RE, Keiser P, Pierce M, et al. Clarithromycin and ethambutol with or without clofazimine for the treatment of bacteremic: *Mycobacterium avium* complex disease in patients with HIV infection. AIDS. 1997;11:311-317.

147. Bermudez LE, Kolonoski P, Petrofsky M, et al. Mefloquine, moxifloxacin and ethambutol are a triple-drug alternative to macrolide-containing regimens for treatment of *Mycobacterium avium* complex. J Infect Dis. 2003;187:1977-1980.

148. Wallace RJ Jr, Brown-Elliot BA, Ward SC, et al. Activities of linazolid against rapidly growing mycobacteria. Antimicrob Agents Chemother. 2001;45:764-767.

149. Aksamit TR. *Mycobacterium avium* complex pulmonary disease in patients with pre-existing lung disease. Clin Chest Med. 2002;23:643-653.

150. Moran JF, Alexander LG, Staub WW, et al. Long-term results of pulmonary resection for atypical mycobacterial disease. Ann Thorac Surg. 1983;35:597-604.

151. Pomerantz M, Madsen L, Goble M, et al. Surgical management of resistant mycobacterial tuberculosis and other mycobacterial pulmonary infections. Ann Thorac Surg. 1991;52:1108-1112.

152. Nelson KG, Griffith DE, Brown BA, et al. Results of operations in *Mycobacterium avium-intracellulare* lung disease. Ann Thorac Surg. 1998;66:325-330.

153. Masur H, Kaplan JE, Holmes KK. Guidelines for preventing opportunistic infections among HIV-infected persons—2002. Ann Intern Med. 2002;137:435-477.

154. Benson CA, Williams PL, Currier JS, et al. A prospective, randomized trial examining the efficacy and safety of clarithromycin in combination with ethambutol, rifabutin, or both for the treatment of disseminated *Mycobacterium avium* complex disease in persons with acquired immunodeficiency syndrome. Clin Infect Dis. 2003;37:1234-1243.

155. Burman WJ, Gallicano K, Peloquin C. Therapeutic implications of drug interactions in the treatment of human immunodeficiency virus–related tuberculosis. Clin Infect Dis. 1999;28:419-429.

156. Kirk O, Reiss P, Uberti-Foppa C, et al. Safe interruption of maintenance therapy against previous infection with four common HIV-associated opportunistic pathogens during potent antiretroviral therapy. Ann Intern Med. 2002;137:239-250.

157. Shafran SD, Mashinter LD, Phillips P, et al. Successful discontinuation of therapy for disseminated *Mycobacterium avium* complex infection after effective antiretroviral therapy. Ann Intern Med. 2002;137:734-737.

158. Aberg JA, Williams PL, Liu T, et al. A study of discontinuing maintenance therapy in human immunodeficiency virus-infected subjects with disseminated *Mycobacterium avium* complex: AIDS clinical trial group 393 study team. J Infect Dis. 2003;187:1046-1052.

159. Pierce M, Crampton S, Henry D, et al. A randomized trial of clarithromycin as prophylaxis against disseminated *Mycobacterium avium* complex infection in patients with advanced acquired immunodeficiency syndrome. N Engl J Med. 1996;335:384-391.

160. Oldfield EC, Fessel WJ, Dunne MW, et al. Once weekly azithromycin therapy for prevention of *Mycobacterium avium* complex infection in patients with AIDS: A randomized, double-blind, placebo-controlled multicenter trial. Clin Infect Dis. 1998;26:611-619.

161. Nightingale SD, Cameron DW, Gordin FM, et al. Two controlled trials of rifabutin prophylaxis against *Mycobacterium avium* complex infection in AIDS. N Engl J Med. 1993;329:828-833.

162. Benson CA, Williams PL, Cohn DL, et al. Clarithromycin or rifabutin alone or in combination for primary prophylaxis of *Mycobacterium avium* complex disease in patients with AIDS: A randomized, double-blind, placebo-controlled trial. J Infect Dis. 2000;181:1289-1297.

163. Havlir DV, Dubé MP, Sattler FR, et al. Prophylaxis against disseminated *Mycobacterium avium* complex with weekly azithromycin, daily rifabutin, or both. N Engl J Med. 1996;335:392-398.

164. El-Sadr WM, Burman WJ, Grant LB, et al. Discontinuation of prophylaxis against *Mycobacterium avium* complex disease in HIV-infected patients who have a response to antiretroviral therapy. N Engl J Med. 2000;342:1085-1092.

165. Currier JS, Williams PL, Koletar SL, et al. Discontinuation of *Mycobacterium avium* complex prophylaxis in patients with antiretroviral therapy–induced increases in CD4+ cell count. Ann Intern Med. 2000;133:493-503.

Infections Caused by Nontuberculous Mycobacteria

BARBARA A. BROWN-ELLIOTT

RICHARD J. WALLACE, Jr.

The improvement in mycobacterial culture techniques and the advent of new molecular techniques for identification of previously unidentified organisms has evoked a resurgence of interest in disease caused by the nontuberculous mycobacteria (NTM). This group of mycobacteria is composed of species other than *M. tuberculosis, Mycobacterium africanum, Mycobacterium bovis, M. caprae, M. microti,* and *Mycobacterium leprae.* Previous names for this group of organisms include "atypical mycobacteria" or "mycobacteria other than *M. tuberculosis.*"[1-3] Currently there are more than 100 species of NTM, of which approximately 60 are considered to be potential sources of disease. Traditionally, NTM have been categorized into different groups based on characteristic colony morphology, growth rate, and pigmentation (the Runyon system of classification). This system has become less useful as we focus on more rapid molecular systems of diagnostics. Growth rates and colony pigmentation continue to provide practical means for grouping species of mycobacteria within the laboratory and are thus indicated here. *Mycobacterium avium* complex (MAC) is discussed in Chapter 250.

Rapidly Growing Mycobacteria

This group of organisms includes nonpigmented and pigmented species that produce mature growth on agar plates within 7 days. Nonpigmented pathogenic species are usually grouped within the *Mycobacterium fortuitum* complex. This complex now includes the *M. fortuitum* group of *M. fortuitum, M. peregrinum, M. mucogenicum*[4] (formerly *M. chelonae*-like organism), and *M. senegalense,*[5] and the third biovariant complex, including *M. septicum,*[6,7] *M. mageritense,*[8,9] *M. porcinum,*[10,11] *M. houstonense, M. bonickei,* and *M. neworleansense.*[12] The *M. fortuitum* complex[13,14] also includes the *M. chelonae/abscessus* group, which includes *M. chelonae, M. abscessus,*[5] and the newly described species *M. immunogenum.*[13,15-18] A second group of pathogenic organisms within the rapidly growing mycobacteria (RGM) is the *M. smegmatis* group.[19,20] Isolates within this group include late-pigmenting or nonpigmented species. This group is currently composed of three species: *M. smegmatis, M. wolinskyi,* and *M. goodii.*[20] Many of these pathogenic species grow best at 30° C, but none has special nutritional requirements.

(Early) pigmenting RGM are difficult to identify using conventional laboratory methods and are usually not clinically significant. The pigmented species that are occasionally found to cause clinical disease include *M. phlei, M. aurum, M. flavescens, M. neoaurum, M. vaccae,* the thermophilic species *M. thermoresistible,*[3] and two newly described species: *M. elephantis*[21] and *M. novocastrense.*[22]

Slowly Growing Mycobacteria

This group includes species of mycobacteria that require more than 7 days to reach mature growth. Some species may also require nutritional supplementation of routine mycobacterial media.[2,23,24] The major clinically important established species within this group include MAC (*M. avium* and *M. intracellulare*), *M. kansasii, M. xenopi, M. simiae* complex (*M. simiae, M. lentiflavum,* and *M. triplex*), *M. szulgai, M. malmoense, M. scrofulaceum,* and the *M. terrae/ M. nonchromogenicum* complex, and less commonly *M. asiaticum.*[2,3,25] Organisms that require special nutritional supplements include *M. haemophilum,* which requires hemin for growth (hence its name),

TABLE 251-1 Major Clinical Syndromes Associated with Nontuberculous Mycobacterial Infections

Syndrome	Most Common Causes	Less Frequent Causes
Chronic bronchopulmonary disease (adults, patients with cystic fibrosis)	*M. avium* complex (*M. intracellulare* and *M. avium*), *M. kansasii, M. abscessus*	*M. xenopi, M. malmoense, M. szulgai, M. smegmatis, M. scrofulaceum, M. celatum, M. simiae, M. goodii, M. asiaticum, M. heckeshornense, M. branderi, M. lentiflavum, M. triplex, M. fortuitum*
Cervical or other lymphadenitis (especially children)	*M. avium* complex	*M. scrofulaceum, M. malmoense* (northern Europe), *M. abscessus, M. fortuitum, M. lentiflavum, M. tusciae, M. palustre, M. interjectum, M. elephantis, M. heidelbergense*
Skin and soft tissue disease	*M. fortuitum* group, *M. chelonae, M. abscessus, M. marinum, M. ulcerans* (Australia, tropical countries only)	*M. kansasii, M. haemophilum, M. porcinum, M. smegmatis, M. genavense, M. lacus, M. novocastrense, M. houstonense, M. goodii, M. immunogenum, M. mageritense*
Skeletal (bone, joint, tendon) infection	*M. marinum, M. avium* complex, *M. kansasii, M. fortuitum* group, *M. abscessus, M. chelonae*	*M. haemophilum, M. scrofulaceum, M. smegmatis, M. terrae/chromogenicum* complex, *M. wolinskyi, M. goodii*
Disseminated infection		
HIV-seropositive host	*M. avium, M. kansasii*	*M. genavense, M. haemophilum, M. xenopi, M. marinum, M. simiae, M. intracellulare, M. scrofulaceum, M. fortuitum, M. conspicuum, M. celatum, M. lentiflavum, M. triplex*
HIV-seronegative host	*M. abscessus, M. chelonae*	*M. marinum, M. kansasii, M. haemophilum*
Catheter related infections	*M. fortuitum, M. abscessus, M. chelonae*	*M. mucogenicum, M. immunogenum, M. mageritense, M. septicum, M. porcinum*

HIV, human immunodeficiency virus.

M. paratuberculosis and *M. genavense*,[2,24] which require mycobactin J and prolonged incubation in broth culture. Most of these slowly growing mycobacteria grow best at 35° to 37° C, with the exception of *M. haemophilum*, which prefers lower temperatures (28° to 30° C), and *M. xenopi*, which grows well at 42° C. Newly described pigmented organisms in this group include *M. celatum*,[26] *M. interjectum*,[27,28] *M. lentiflavum*,[29] *M. tusciae*,[30] *M. palustre*,[31] *M. conspicuum*,[32] *M. heckeshornense*,[33] and *M. bohemicum*.[34,35] Nonpigmented species include *M. triplex*[36] (also a part of the *M. simiae* complex), *M. branderi, M. shottsii*,[35] and the previously mentioned *M. haemophilum* and *M. genavense*.

Intermediately Growing Mycobacteria

This group of organisms includes *M. marinum* and *M. gordonae*. These organisms are pigmented and require 7 to 10 days to reach mature growth. *M. marinum* grows optimally at 28° to 30° C, whereas *M. gordonae* prefers 35° to 37° C.[37,38]

NONTUBERCULOUS MYCOBACTERIA AND THE ENVIRONMENT

Most NTM species are readily recovered from the environment. Isolates have been recovered from samples of soil, water, animals, plant material, and birds. A few species that are known to cause disease, such as *M. ulcerans*, has yet to be recovered from the environment. Although an association with an environmental source may be present, a direct link to the environment has not been proven except for health care–associated disease and pseudo-outbreak, and no evidence of person-to-person spread has been reported.[2,3,39] Tap water is considered the major reservoir for most common human NTM pathogens, and as such is of increasing public health interest. Species recovered from tap water include *M. kansasii, M. xenopi, M. simiae*, RGM and MAC. NTM produce six major clinical disease syndromes (Table 251-1), which are reviewed in the following sections.

PULMONARY DISEASE

Chronic pulmonary disease in a human immunodeficiency virus (HIV)-negative host is the most common localized clinical disease caused by NTM.[2,3,40] In the United States, MAC, followed by *M. kansasii*, is the most frequently recognized pathogen.[2] In Canada, some parts of the United Kingdom, and Europe,[2,41] *M. xenopi* ranks second after MAC, whereas *M. malmoense* is second in Scandinavia and northern Europe.[42,43] In southeast England, *M. xenopi*[44] and *M.*

kansasii (known to be present in local water supplies) are both more common than *M. avium* complex.[45] In the United States, the third most common cause of NTM pulmonary disease is *M. abscessus*, which produces 80% of pulmonary infections caused by RGM.[46] Other NTM that less commonly cause pulmonary disease include *M. fortuitum, M. smegmatis*,[19] *M. goodii*,[20] *M. szulgai*,[47] *M. simiae*,[48,49] *M. celatum*,[50] *M. asiaticum, M. lentiflavum, M. heckeshornense*,[33] and rarely *M. gordonae*.[2,3,51] In contrast to pneumonia caused by *M. abscessus*, pulmonary disease with *M. goodii*[20] usually infects patients with aspiration-induced lipoid pneumonia.

Because the signs and symptoms of NTM lung disease are often variable and nonspecific, disease with NTM is difficult to diagnose without multiple positive respiratory cultures.[2] Patients often present with chronic cough, sputum production, and fatigue. Less frequently, complaints of malaise, dyspnea, fever, hemoptysis, and weight loss may also be present. Clinical studies should include microbiologic cultures for acid-fast bacilli and routine chest radiographs. High-resolution chest computed tomography is helpful in patients suspected of having nodular bronchiectasis. Recovery of NTM from a single sputum sample is not proof of NTM disease, especially when the acid-fast bacillus smear is negative and NTM are present in low numbers. The American Thoracic Society statement on the diagnosis and treatment of NTM[2] has four suggested diagnostic criteria to determine lung disease caused by NTM and specifically by MAC (Table 251-2). For NTM disease caused by organisms other than MAC, these criteria may need to be adjusted because inadequate data are available to evaluate them. At least three respiratory samples should be evaluated and other lung disease excluded.[2]

Treatment of lung disease caused by *M. kansasii* has traditionally been less difficult than that for MAC since the introduction of rifampin.[52] A regimen of daily rifampin (600 mg), isoniazid (300 mg), and ethambutol (15 mg/kg) has been widely accepted in the United States and is currently recommended by the American Thoracic Society (see Table 251-2).[2] In the United Kingdom, isoniazid is omitted from the regimen.[53] In HIV-positive patients who need to receive a protease inhibitor, rifampin can be replaced by rifabutin, 150 mg daily, if the patient is receiving indinavir, nelfinavir, soft-gel saquinavir (Fortovase), or amprenavir. Rifabutin causes less reduction in the blood level of protease inhibitor than rifampin. If the patient is taking ritonavir, hard-gel saquinavir (Invirase), or delavirdine (a nonnucleoside reverse transcriptase inhibitor), the reduction in blood level is so substantial that neither rifampin nor rifabutin can be used and clarithromycin, 500 mg twice daily, is recommended.[2,54] Patients should be treated for at least 18 months, with at least 12 months of cul-

TABLE 251-2 American Thoracic Society Diagnostic Criteria for Nontuberculous Mycobacterial Lung Disease

In symptomatic patients with reticulonodular or cavitary disease or a high-resolution computed tomography scan revealing multifocal bronchiectasis and/or small nodules:

1. Two positive sputum/bronchial wash cultures within 12 months if one or both specimens is AFB smear positive; *or*

2. Three positive sputum/bronchial wash cultures within 12 months if none of the specimens is AFB smear positive; *or*

3. In patients unable to produce sputum, one positive bronchial wash culture with > 2+ AFB smear and/or growth on solid media; *or*

4. In the absence of diagnostic sputum/bronchial wash evaluations, a transbronchial or lung biopsy yielding an NTM or a biopsy showing mycobacterial histopathologic features (granulomatous inflammation and/or AFB) and one or more respiratory cultures positive for an NTM even in low numbers.

*Applies to HIV negative patients, and has not been studied for most NTM other than *M. avium* complex.

AFB, acid-fast bacillus; NTM, nontuberculous mycobacteria.

From Wallace RJ Jr, Cook JL, Glassroth J, et al. Diagnosis and treatment of disease caused by nontuberculous mycobacteria. American Thoracic Society Statement. Am J Respir Crit Care Med. 1997;156(Suppl):S1-S25.

ture negativity.[2] For patients resistant or intolerant to rifampin, clarithromycin is a reasonable but unproven alternative agent. An intermittent regimen (three times weekly) using the same drugs and drug concentration as for MAC looks very promising, but has been studied with only a small number of patients.[55] Untreated strains of *M. kansasii* are susceptible to low concentrations of rifampin, rifabutin, ethambutol, ethionamide, streptomycin, sulfonamides, clarithromycin, and the newer quinolones, although information is limited on the clinical utility of the latter three agents.[2,56-58] Acquired mutational resistance of rifampin to *M. kansasii* can occur, but this organism is readily treated with multidrug regimens.[56,58]

Treatment of *M. abscessus* lung disease with drugs has generally been unsuccessful.[2] Courses of therapy with clarithromycin and several weeks of high-dose cefoxitin (12 g/day in three or four divided doses) and low-dose amikacin (peaks at 20 μg/mL on once-daily dosing) produce good clinical improvement but do not result in microbiologic cure. Currently, studies are underway to assess the potential efficacy of a new glycylcycline antibiotic called tigecycline. In vitro studies have demonstrated that all species of RGM, including *M. abscessus,* have very low minimum inhibitory concentrations (<1 μg/mL) for this agent.[59]

Treatment of lung disease caused by other slowly growing mycobacteria such as *M. simiae, M. szulgai, M. xenopi,* and *M. malmoense* has not been established.[2,42,47,49,60] Drug combinations similar to what is used with MAC, such as clarithromycin, ethambutol, rifabutin, and perhaps an aminoglycoside with 12 months of negative cultures, seem reasonable at the present time.[42,47,49,60]

Pseudo-outbreaks of pulmonary disease have been described, usually related to contamination of bronchoscopes or the automated endoscope washing machine.[61] *M. immunogenum* is the species most commonly recovered in this setting.[18]

LYMPHADENITIS

Localized lymphadenitis is the most common NTM disease in children, with a peak incidence between 1 and 5 years of age.[62-65] NTM-affected lymph nodes are usually in the anterior cervical chain and are unilateral and painless. The nodes may enlarge rapidly with the formation of fistulas to the skin, and prolonged drainage may occur.[65] Occasionally, other nodes outside the head and neck, such as the mediastinal lymph nodes, may be involved.[63] A definitive diagnosis of NTM lymphadenitis is made by recovery of the etiologic organism from lymph node cultures. The tuberculin skin test is often weakly positive (5 to 10 mm), but it may be more than 10 mm.[63] Efforts to de-velop a useful MAC skin test have thus far been unsuccessful.[66] Routine biopsy or incision and drainage should be avoided because these procedures often result in the formation of fistulas and chronic drainage.[65] Fine-needle aspiration with cytology and culture has been used increasingly with apparently few associated problems.[2]

Treatment of NTM cervical lymphadenitis is still evolving. The potential role of chemotherapy without surgery or as a supplement to surgery in complicated or recurrent disease is being considered with increasing frequency. Clarithromycin combined with ethambutol or rifabutin is the usual suggested regimen (see Table 251-2). However, the established treatment of routine NTM cervical lymphadenitis remains surgical excision without chemotherapy.

Since the early 1980s, 80% of cases of culture-positive NTM lymphadenitis in children in the United States have been caused by MAC.[62] The remainder of the cases in Australia and the United States are caused by *M. scrofulaceum,* and only about 10% of the cases have been caused by *M. tuberculosis.*[62,63,65] In parts of northern Europe, including Scandinavia and the United Kingdom, *M. malmoense* has become the second most common pathogen after MAC.[45,67-69] Rarely, other species are recovered, including RGM,[5] *M. kansasii,* and *M. haemophilum,*[45,69,70] and the newly described *M. interjectum,*[27] *M. palustre,*[31] *M. tusciae,*[30,71] *M. heidelbergense,*[72,73] *M. elephantis,*[21] *M. lentiflavum,*[74,75] and *M. bohemicum.*[76] *M. haemophilum* has a special growth requirement for hemin or iron and may present some diagnostic difficulties if iron- or hemin-supplemented media and lower temperatures (incubation at 28° to 30° C) are not used.[2,23,77] A surprising number of specimens are acid-fast bacillus smear positive and culture negative, so a presumptive diagnosis is often based on typical caseating granulomas and a negative culture for *M. tuberculosis* in the common clinical setting.

LOCALIZED CUTANEOUS AND SOFT TISSUE INFECTIONS

Although most pathogenic species of NTM have been incriminated in cutaneous NTM disease,[2,3] *M. marinum, M. ulcerans,* and the RGM most often cause localized skin infections. *M. marinum* causes an infection historically recognized as "swimming pool" or "fish tank granuloma."[1-3,78] This common name is derived from the epidemiologic niche of the organism. Most infections occur 2 to 3 weeks after contact with contaminated water from one of these sources. The lesions are most often small violet papules on the hands and arms that may progress to shallow, crusty ulcerations and scar formation. Lesions are usually singular. However, multiple ascending lesions resembling sporotrichosis ("sporotrichoid disease") can occasionally occur.[2,78] Most patients are clinically healthy with a previous local hand injury that becomes infected while cleaning a fish tank, or patients may sustain scratches or puncture wounds from saltwater fish, shrimp, fins, and so forth contaminated with *M. marinum.* Swimming pools seem to be a risk only when nonchlorinated. Diagnosis is made from culture and histologic examination of biopsy material, along with a compatible history of exposure.[2,78] No treatment of choice is recognized for *M. marinum* (see Table 251-3). Treatments have traditionally been a two-drug combination of rifampin plus ethambutol or monotherapy with doxycycline, minocycline, clarithromycin, or trimethoprim-sulfamethoxazole given for a minimum of 3 months.[37,79,80] Clarithromycin has been used increasingly because of good clinical efficacy and minimal side effects, although published experience is limited.[2]

The rapidly growing species *M. abscessus, M. fortuitum,* and *M. chelonae* are the most common NTM involved in cases of community-acquired infections of skin and soft tissue in the United States.[81] The *M. fortuitum* group is responsible for 60% of localized cutaneous infections in previously healthy individuals. Unlike infections with the *M. chelonae-M. abscessus* group, the patient with *M. fortuitum* localized infection usually has no predisposing immune suppression. In a series of 42 patients for whom clinical history was available, the majority of infections involved some type of traumatic injury such as metal puncture wounds from stepping on a nail (48%) or motor vehicle accidents (26%), and approximately 40% of the injuries involved the foot or leg.[14] Open lacerations or fractures were common. Community outbreaks of furunculosis caused by RGM, most commonly *M. fortuitum,* have been traced to contaminated footbaths in nail salons.[82] Wax removal of leg hair has been a contributing factor in some cases.

In contrast, localized infections with *M. chelonae* are seen primarily in patients who are immunosuppressed, especially on long-term corticosteroids. Autoimmune diseases such as rheumatoid arthritis and systemic lupus are often predisposing factors. In a study by Wallace and colleagues, 35% of the *M. chelonae* were seen in localized wound infections.[15]

Disease caused by *M. abscessus* is somewhat intermediate, as it causes disease in normal hosts and those with immune suppression. Examples of localized wound infection with *M. abscessus* include soft tissue infection of the cheek following an insect bite and vertebral osteomyelitis.[71]

Occasionally, localized community-acquired infections of the skin, soft tissue, or bone may involve slowly growing species, including MAC, *M. kansasii*, and *M. terrae/M. nonchromogenicum* complex[3] and rarely the newly described species *M. novocastrense*[22] and *M. lacus*.[83]

Sporadic cases of health care–associated skin and soft tissue disease have also been described. These cases include infections of long-term intravenous or peritoneal catheters, postinjection abscesses, surgical wound infections such as after cardiac bypass surgery, and augmentation mammoplasty.[3,39,81,84] In ophthalmology, rapidly growing species may cause keratitis and corneal ulceration after surgery, as well as infection after local accidental trauma.[1] Clustered outbreaks or pseudo-outbreaks of mycobacterial skin, soft tissue, or bone infections have been described and usually result from contaminated fluids such as ice made from tap water, irrigation with or exposure to tap water, injectable medicines, and topical skin solutions/markers.[39,85,86] One recent outbreak involved contamination of liposuction equipment with *M. chelonae*, with the same disease strain found in tap water used for rinsing suction tubing.[87] Most of the skin and soft tissue disease outbreaks have involved the rapidly growing species *M. fortuitum* and *M. abscessus*. The reservoir for these outbreaks has generally been municipal or distilled (hospital) water supplies.[39,85,86] These and other species such as MAC and *M. xenopi* are incredibly hardy, can endure temperatures of 45° C and above (MAC and *M. xenopi*),[44] and may resist the activity of commonly used disinfectants.[3,39,88]

Diagnosis of all types of skin and soft tissue infections is made by culture of specific NTM from drainage material or tissue biopsy. Treatment may include amikacin, cefoxitin, ciprofloxacin, the newer quinolones such as gatifloxacin and moxifloxacin,[89] clarithromycin, doxycycline, sulfonamides, and imipenem for the *M. fortuitum* group, whereas only amikacin, cefoxitin, imipenem, and clarithromycin or only amikacin, imipenem, tobramycin, clarithromycin, and sometimes linezolid[90,91] have activity against *M. abscessus* and *M. chelonae*, respectively.[15,90] Clarithromycin is generally the drug of choice for localized disease caused by *M. chelonae* and *M. abscessus*.[2,15] The duration of therapy is usually 6 months. Antituberculous agents have no efficacy against any of the RGM other than ethambutol for *M. smegmatis*. Monotherapy with quinolones is, however, not recommended because of the high risk of mutational resistance of the RGM to these agents.[2] Treatment of slowly growing species is similar to that for chronic lung disease, except that the duration of therapy may only be 6 to 12 months, depending upon severity of the disease.[2]

Two unusual species causing skin and soft tissue infections in select situations are *M. ulcerans* and *M. haemophilum*. *M. ulcerans* is not endemic in the United States, but it is endemic in areas of Australia and tropical locations of the world, where it is commonly known as the "Buruli ulcer."[92] *M. ulcerans* is extremely slow growing, with an average incubation time of around 8 to 12 weeks, and *M. haemophilum* may take up to 3 to 4 weeks to grow on primary culture. Fortunately, newer molecular techniques for identification of these organisms have expedited diagnosis of infection with the organisms.[71] The *M. ulcerans* infection progresses from an itchy nodule most often on the extremities to a necrotic lesion that may result in severe limb deformity. Treatment success is common in early disease with excisional surgery, rifampin, sulfonamides, and clofazimine, but for advanced ulcerative disease, therapeutic response has generally been poor.[93] Surgical débridement and skin graft-

ing then become the usual therapeutic measures of choice.[1,3,93] Recent studies suggest that clarithromycin is highly active in vitro.[93]

The second unusual species, *M. haemophilum*, causes cutaneous infections (primarily of the extremities) in immunosuppressed patients, especially in the setting of organ transplantation, long-term high-dose steroid use, or HIV.[23,94,95] A recent review by Saubolle and co-workers cited more than 50 cases of *M. haemophilum*, with almost 80% of them involving skin and soft tissue infections.[77] Careful attention to culture technique is essential because this species requires heme or iron to grow in culture. Therapy for this species usually includes clarithromycin and rifampin or rifabutin.[23,70,95]

INFECTION OF TENDON SHEATHS, BONES, BURSAE, AND JOINTS

Both rapidly growing and slowly growing species of NTM have been implicated in chronic granulomatous infections involving tendon sheaths, bursae, bones, and joints after direct inoculation of the pathogen through accidental trauma, surgical incisions, puncture wounds, or injections.[3,15,81,84] Most patients have no underlying immune suppression, but high risk for some pathogens such as *M. chelonae* and *M. haemophilum* is seen in patients who are immunosuppressed. MAC and *M. marinum* have been described as causing tenosynovitis of the hand,[3,80] although the RGM,[81] *M. kansasii*, and *M. terrae* complex (especially *M. nonchromogenicum*)[96-98] have also been associated with a chronic type of disease.[3,51] Osteomyelitis of the sternum caused by *M. fortuitum* and *M. abscessus* has also been found in clustered outbreaks and sporadic cases after cardiac surgery.[84,99-101] Additionally, *M. haemophilum* has a tendency to involve bones and joints, usually with concurrent draining skin lesions and bacteremia.[1,23,77,95]

Management of mycobacterial rheumatologic infections often requires surgical débridement for both diagnosis and therapy, especially for the closed spaces of the hand and the wrist and for patients with infected bones such as fractured long bones or the sternum after cardiac surgery. Drug therapy for the specific pathogen is also essential.

DISSEMINATED DISEASE

In the setting of advanced HIV infection, most disseminated NTM disease is due to *M. avium*. However, other NTM, including *M. kansasii*, *M. genavense*, *M. intracellulare*, *M. haemophilum*, *M. simiae*, *M. celatum*, *M. malmoense*, *M. marinum*, and RGM, have also been cited.[5,24,38,77,102-107] Disseminated disease among the newly described species *M. triplex*,[108] *M. lentiflavum*,[75] and *M. conspicuum*[32] has also been reported.[35,71]

Disseminated infection by NTM species other than MAC has occurred in all age groups and almost exclusively in immunosuppressed patients, such as organ transplant recipients or patients receiving chronic steroids.[2,15,109,110] Nonimmunosuppressed children with disseminated NTM should be tested for congenital defects in the cellular receptors for interferon-γ and interleukin-12 as well as defective production of interleukin-12 (see Chapter 11).

Disseminated *M. kansasii* is the second most frequent cause of disseminated NTM disease after *M. avium*.[3,106] Pulmonary and cutaneous manifestations have occurred[106,110] in patients with chronic lymphocytic leukemia, after organ transplantation, and in those infected by HIV. One study reported five patients with disseminated *M. kansasii* infection, including three patients with pulmonary and extrapulmonary involvement and two patients with exclusive extrapulmonary involvement. All patients had CD4+ lymphocyte counts less than 200 cells/μL. The most common clinical manifestation was pulmonary disease with thin-walled cavitary lesions.[106]

The incidence of *M. conspicuum* in disseminated disease may be underestimated as a result of the low growth temperature requirements.[32] Prior to the advent of antiretroviral therapy, *M. genavense* was the second most frequently isolated species after *M. avium* complex.

Treatment of disseminated disease caused by NTM other than *M. avium* utilizes regimens similar to those used for pulmonary disease (Table 251-3).

TABLE 251-3 Frequently Used Treatment Regimens for Common Nontuberculous Mycobacterial Pathogens

Species	Disease*	Drug	Daily Adult Doses†	Three Times Weekly Adult Dose	Duration
M. kansasii	Pulmonary				
	USA	Isoniazid plus	300 mg		18 mo, culture negative
		Rifampin plus	600 mg	600 mg	at least 12 mo
		Ethambutol	15 mg/kg	25 mg/kg	
		Clarithromycin‡	500 mg bid	1000 mg	
	UK	Rifampin plus	600 mg		9-12 mo
		Ethambutol	15 mg/kg		
	Disseminated	Same as pulmonary			
	HIV positive	Same as pulmonary (USA) but replace rifampin with			Same as pulmonary (USA)
		rifabutin or	150 mg		
		clarithromycin§	500 mg bid		
M. abscessus	Pulmonary	Amikacin IV plus	Depends on age/body weight/renal function; in adults 7- to 10 mg/kg single dose		2 wk (designed to improve, not cure)
		Cefoxitin IV	12 g/day		2 wk
		Clarithromycin	500 mg bid		6 mo
	Cutaneous localized	Clarithromycin	500 mg bid		6 mo
	Disseminated or extensive cutaneous	Same 3 drugs as above			
M. marinum	Cutaneous	Clarithromycin or	500 mg bid		3 mo minimum for
		Minocycline or	100 mg bid		all regimens
		Rifampin plus	600 mg		
		Ethambutol	15 mg/kg		

*Human immunodeficiency virus (HIV)-negative host unless otherwise stated.
†Drugs by mouth unless otherwise stated.
‡Based on preliminary study only.
§Patients on HIV medicines inactivated by rifampin.

CATHETER-RELATED INFECTIONS

Currently, catheter-related infections are the most common health care–associated NTM infections encountered.[3,39] They are seen most often with long-term central intravenous catheters, but they may also occur with peritoneal or shunt catheters. The usual pathogens are RGM (see Table 251-1). These infections may be manifested as fever, local catheter site drainage, or bacteremia or occasionally as lung infiltrates or granulomatous hepatitis. The usual treatment is catheter removal combined with appropriate antibiotics for 6 to 12 weeks.[3,39]

LABORATORY ASPECTS

Stain and Culture

The methods used for staining and culture of M. tuberculosis generally work well for the NTM, although some RGM are adversely affected by harsh decontamination methods that are standard for M. tuberculosis. Middlebrook 7H10 or 7H11 agar, BACTEC broth, and the newer rapid broth systems all support growth of the common NTM.[2] Cultures of skin and soft tissue need to be plated at 28° to 30° C as well as 35° C, because some species such as M. marinum, M. chelonae, and M. haemophilum grow only at low temperatures on primary isolation. M. genavense (BACTEC broth for 6 to 8 weeks)[111] and M. haemophilum (iron or heme in the media)[2,23] have special growth requirements. If M. ulcerans, M. genavense, or M. malmoense is suspected, cultures should be held up 10 to 12 weeks before discarding. Because of the difficulty often encountered in growing M. ulcerans and M. genavense on solid media, molecular techniques may be necessary to identify these species.[71]

Identification

As a consequence of the demand for more rapid diagnosis of M. tuberculosis,[2,112] identification of NTM increasingly focuses on the use of rapid diagnostic systems: high-performance liquid chromatography, which assesses the patterns of long-chain fatty acids (mycolic acids) found in different NTM species[113]; molecular methods such as 16S ribosomal RNA gene sequencing or polymerase chain reaction restriction fragment length polymorphism analysis of a 441-bp fragment of the 65-kDa heat shock protein gene[114,115]; and commercial molecular probes. Commercial genetic probes for mycobacterial RNA are currently available for the identification of M. tuberculosis complex, M. avium, M. intracellulare, M. gordonae, and M. kansasii.[2] For some of the newer species such as M. celatum,[115] M. genavense,[24] M. confluentis, M. interjectum, M. tusciae, M. heidelbergense, M. heckeshornense, M. lacus, M. elephantis, M. novocastrense, and M. triplex,[36] high-performance liquid chromatography, 16S ribosomal DNA sequencing, or both are important or essential to make a species identification.[35,116] Traditional biochemical testing to determine carbohydrate utilization and other standard mycobacterial tests such as arylsulfatase, nitrate reduction, and iron uptake provide alternative, although slower, methods for identification of some species of slowly growing and rapidly growing NTM.[2,13]

Strain Comparison

For epidemiologic studies, standard biochemical and susceptibility testing have been useful in initial strain comparison for most outbreaks involving NTM. Molecular methods such as Southern hybridization with repetitive elements, arbitrarily primed polymerase chain reaction, and pulsed-field gel electrophoresis ("DNA fingerprinting") of NTM are now the standard for definitive strain comparison of NTM outbreaks.[39,117,118]

Susceptibility Testing

Rapidly Growing Mycobacteria

Recently the NCCLS (formerly the National Committee for Clinical Laboratory Standards) published a document for standardization of susceptibility testing of all mycobacteria species, including the NTM. The NCCLS-recommended method for susceptibility testing of the RGM is the broth microdilution technique.[119] The antimicrobials used are selected bacterial agents because antituberculous drugs are not effective against these species. Current minimal recommendations for testing the RGM include clarithromycin (used as a class representative agent for the new macrolides), amikacin, cefoxitin, imipenem, tobramycin, doxycycline, ciprofloxacin, and a sulfonamide.[2,120,121] Linezolid may also be included along with the newer quinolones, gatifloxacin and moxifloxacin.[89,90,119]

Susceptibility Testing: Slowly Growing Nontuberculous Mycobacteria

The proportion method in agar, broth microdilution, Etest, and in some cases BACTEC radiometric detection have been used for determining minimal inhibitory concentrations of the slowly growing NTM.[2,122] Recently the NCCLS has recommended agar proportion, broth microdilution, and broth macrodilution (i.e., BACTEC or another commercial system) for susceptibility testing of the slowly growing mycobacteria.[119] Standard first-line antituberculous agents (ethambutol, rifampin, isoniazid) are commonly tested along with other agents, including clarithromycin (used as the class agent for the macrolides, including azithromycin), rifabutin, streptomycin, amikacin, quinolones (ciprofloxacin, gatifloxacin, levofloxacin, and moxifloxacin), and a sulfonamide. Other agents such as linezolid may also be useful to test.[123] Susceptibility testing to pyrazinamide is not recommended because it has no efficacy against NTM. Currently, susceptibility testing is recommended for isolates of *M. kansasii* (rifampin only), MAC (clarithromycin only), and less commonly encountered slowly growing species such as *M. xenopi* (all of the aforementioned drugs).[2,119]

REFERENCES

1. Hirschel B. Infections due to nontuberculous mycobacteria. In: Fauci AS, Braunwald E, Isselbacher KJ, et al, eds. Harrison's Principles of Internal Medicine. 14th ed. New York: McGraw-Hill; 1998:1019-1022.
2. Wallace RJ Jr, Cook JL, Glassroth J, et al. Diagnosis and treatment of disease caused by nontuberculous mycobacteria. American Thoracic Society Statement. Am J Respir Crit Care Med. 1997;156(Suppl):S1-S25.
3. Wolinsky E. State of the art: Nontuberculous mycobacteria and associated diseases. Am Rev Respir Dis. 1979;119:107-159.
4. Springer B, Böttger EC, Kirschner P, et al. Phylogeny of the *Mycobacterium chelonae*-like organism based on partial sequencing of the 16S rRNA gene and proposal of *Mycobacterium mucogenicum* sp. nov. Int J Syst Bacteriol. 1995;45:262-267.
5. Brown-Elliott BA, Wallace RJ Jr. Clinical and taxonomic status of pathogenic nonpigmented or late-pigmenting rapidly growing mycobacteria. Clin Microbiol Rev. 2002;15:716-746.
6. Hogg GG, Schinsky MF, McNeil MM, et al. Central line sepsis in a child due to a previously unidentified mycobacterium. J Clin Microbiol. 1999;37:1193-1196.
7. Schinsky MF, McNeil MM, Whitney AM, et al. *Mycobacterium septicum* sp. nov., a new rapidly growing species associated with catheter-related bacteraemia. Int J Syst Evol Microbiol. 2000;50:575-581.
8. Domenech P, Jimenez MS, Menendez MC, et al. *Mycobacterium mageritense* sp. nov. Int J Syst Bacteriol. 1997;47:535-540.
9. Wallace RJ Jr, Brown-Elliott BA, Wilson RW, et al. Clinical and laboratory features of *Mycobacterium mageritense*. J Clin Microbiol. 2002;40:2930-2935.
10. Tsukamura M, Nemoto H, Yugi H. *Mycobacterium porcinum* sp. nov., a porcine pathogen. Int J Syst Bacteriol. 1983;33:162-165.
11. Wallace RJ Jr, Brown-Elliott BA, Wilson RW, et al. Clinical and laboratory features of *Mycobacterium porcinum*. J Clin Microbiol. In press.
12. Schinsky MF, Douglas MP, Steigerwalt AG, et al. Taxonomic variation in the *Mycobacterium fortuitum* third-biovariant complex: Description of *Mycobacterium boenickei* sp. nov., *Mycobacterium houstonense* sp. nov., four unnamed *Mycobacterium* genomospecies, *Mycobacterium fortuitum* subsp. *pseudoperegrinum* subsp. nov., and an emended description of *Mycobacterium fortuitum*. Int J Syst Evol Microbiol. 2004, in press.
13. Silcox VA, Good RC, Floyd MM. Identification of clinically significant *Mycobacterium fortuitum* complex isolates. J Clin Microbiol. 1981;14:686-691.
14. Wallace RJ Jr, Brown BA, Silcox VA, et al. Clinical disease, drug susceptibility, and biochemical patterns of the unnamed third biovariant complex of *Mycobacterium fortuitum*. J Infect Dis. 1991;163:598-603.
15. Wallace RJ Jr, Brown BA, Onyi GO. Skin, soft tissue, and bone infections due to *Mycobacterium chelonae*: Importance of prior corticosteroid therapy, frequency of disseminated infections, and resistance to oral antimicrobials other than clarithromycin. J Infect Dis. 1992;166:405-412.
16. Band JD, Ward JI, Fraser DW, et al. Peritonitis due to a *Mycobacterium chelonae*-like organism associated with intermittent chronic peritoneal dialysis. J Infect Dis. 1982;145:9-17.
17. Wallace RJ Jr, Silcox VA, Tsukamura M, et al. Clinical significance, biochemical features, and susceptibility patterns of sporadic isolates of the *Mycobacterium chelonae*-like organism. J Clin Microbiol. 1993;31:3231-3239.
18. Wilson RW, Steingrube VA, Böttger EC, et al. A new mycobacterial species related to *Mycobacterium abscessus* associated with clinical disease, pseudo-outbreaks and contaminated metalworking fluids: *Mycobacterium immunogenum* sp. nov.—An international cooperative study on mycobacterial taxonomy. Int J Syst Evol Microbiol. 2001;51:1751-1764.
19. Wallace RJ Jr, Nash DR, Tsukamura M, et al. Human disease due to *Mycobacterium smegmatis*. J Infect Dis. 1988;158:52-59.
20. Brown BA, Springer B, Steingrube VA, et al. Description of *Mycobacterium wolinskyi* and *Mycobacterium goodii*, two new rapidly growing species related to *Mycobacterium smegmatis* and associated with human wound infections: A cooperative study from the International Working Group on Mycobacterial Taxonomy. Int J Syst Bacteriol. 1999;49:1493-1511.
21. Turenne C, Chedore P, Wolfe J, et al. Phenotypic and molecular characterization of clinical isolates of *Mycobacterium elephantis* from human specimens. J Clin Microbiol. 2002;40:1230-1236.
22. Shojaei H, Goodfellow M, Magee JG, et al. *Mycobacterium novocastrense* sp. nov., a rapidly growing photochromogenic mycobacterium. Int J Syst Bacteriol. 1997;47:1205-1207.
23. Kiehn TE, White M. *Mycobacterium haemophilum*: An emerging pathogen. Eur J Clin Microbiol Infect Dis. 1994;13:925-931.
24. Böttger EC. *Mycobacterium genavense*: An emerging pathogen. Eur J Clin Microbiol Infect Dis. 1994;13:932-936.
25. Weiszfeiler G, Karasseva V, Karczag E. A new mycobacterium species: *Mycobacterium asiaticum* sp. Acta Microbiol Acad Sci Hung. 1971;18:247-252.
26. Butler WR, O'Connor SP, Yakrus MA, et al. *Mycobacterium celatum* sp. nov. Int J Syst Bacteriol. 1993;43:539-548.
27. Lumb R, Goodwin A, Ratcliff R, et al. Phenotypic and molecular characterization of three clinical isolates of *Mycobacterium interjectum*. J Clin Microbiol. 1997;35:2782-2785.
28. Springer B, Kirschner P, Rost-Meyer G, et al. *Mycobacterium interjectum*, a new species isolated from a patient with chronic lymphadenitis. J Clin Microbiol. 1993;31:3083-3089.
29. Springer B, Wu WK, Bodmer T, et al. Isolation and characterization of a unique group of slowly growing mycobacteria: Description of *Mycobacterium lentiflavum* sp. nov. J Clin Microbiol. 1996;34:1100-1107.
30. Tortoli E, Kroppenstedt RM, Bartoloni A, et al. *Mycobacterium tusciae* sp. nov. Int J Syst Bacteriol. 1999;49:1839-1844.
31. Torkko P, Suomalainen S, Iivanainen E, et al. *Mycobacterium palustre* sp. nov., a potentially pathogenic slow-growing mycobacterium isolated from veterinary and clinical specimens, and Finnish stream water. Int J Syst Evol Microbiol. 2002;52:1519-1525.
32. Springer B, Tortoli E, Richter I, et al. *Mycobacterium conspicuum* sp. nov., a new species isolated from patients with disseminated infections. J Clin Microbiol. 1995;33:2805-2811.
33. Roth A, Reischl U, Schönfeld N, et al. *Mycobacterium heckeshornense* sp. nov., a new pathogenic slowly growing *Mycobacterium* sp. causing cavitary lung disease in an immunocompetent patient. J Clin Microbiol. 2000;38:4102-4107.
34. Reischl U, Emler S, Horak Z, et al. *Mycobacterium bohemicum* sp. nov., a new slow-growing scotochromogenic mycobacterium. Int J Syst Bacteriol. 1998;48:1349-1355.
35. Tortoli E. Impact of genotypic studies on mycobacterial taxonomy: The new mycobacteria of the 1990s. Clin Microbiol Rev. 2003;16:319-354.
36. Floyd MM, Guthertz LS, Silcox VA, et al. Characterization of an SAV organism and proposal of *Mycobacterium triplex* sp. nov. J Clin Microbiol. 1996;34:2963-2967.
37. Edelstein H. *Mycobacterium marinum* skin infections. Arch Intern Med. 1994;154:1359-1364.
38. Weinberger M, Berg SL, Feuerstein IM, et al. Disseminated infection with *Mycobacterium gordonae*: Report of a case and critical review of the literature. Clin Infect Dis. 1992;14:1229-1239.
39. Fraser V, Wallace RJ Jr. Nontuberculous mycobacteria. In: Mayhall CG, ed. Hospital Epidemiology and Infection Control. Baltimore: Williams & Wilkins; 1996:1224-1237.
40. Hobby GL, Redmond WB, Runyon EH, et al. A study on pulmonary disease associated with mycobacteria other than *Mycobacterium tuberculosis*: Identification and characterization of the mycobacteria. Am Rev Respir Dis. 1967;95:954-971.
41. Thomas P, Liu F, Weiser W. Characteristics of *Mycobacterium xenopi* disease. Bull Int Union Tuberc Lung Dis. 1988;63:12-13.
42. Henriques B, Hoffner SE, Petrini B, et al. Infection with *Mycobacterium malmoense* in Sweden: Report of 221 cases. Clin Infect Dis. 1994;18:596-600.
43. Portaels F, Denef M, Larsson L. Pulmonary disease caused by *Mycobacterium malmoense*: Comments on the possible origin of infection and methods for laboratory diagnosis. Tubercle. 1991;72:218-222.
44. Bennett SN, Peterson DE, Johnson DR, et al. Bronchoscopy-associated *Mycobacterium xenopi* pseudoinfections. Am J Respir Crit Care Med. 1994;150:245-250.
45. Yates MD, Pozniak A, Uttley AHC, et al. Isolation of environmental mycobacteria from clinical specimens in South-East England: 1973-1993. Int J Tuberc Lung Dis. 1997;1:75-80.
46. Griffith DE, Girard WM, Wallace RJ Jr. Clinical features of pulmonary disease caused by rapidly growing mycobacteria: An analysis of 154 patients. Am Rev Respir Dis. 1993;147:1271-1278.
47. Maloney JM, Gregg CR, Stephens DS, et al. Infections caused by *Mycobacterium szulgai* in humans. Rev Infect Dis. 1987;9:1120-1126.
48. Bell RC, Higuchi JH, Donova WN, et al. *Mycobacterium simiae*: Clinical features and follow-up of twenty-four patients. Am Rev Respir Dis. 1983;127:35-38.
49. Valero G, Peters J, Jorgensen JH, et al. Clinical isolates of *Mycobacterium simiae* in San Antonio, Texas. Am J Respir Crit Care Med. 1995;152:1555-1557.
50. Piersimoni C, Zitti PG, Nista D, et al. *Mycobacterium celatum* pulmonary infection in the immunocompetent: Case report and review. Emerg Infect Dis. 2003;9:399-402.
51. Falkinham JO. Epidemiology of infection by nontuberculous mycobacteria. Clin Microbiol Rev. 1996;9:177-215.
52. Pezzia W, Raleigh JW, Bailey MC, et al. Treatment of pulmonary disease due to *Mycobacterium kansasii*: Recent experience with rifampin. Rev Infect Dis. 1981;3:1035-1039.

53. Jenkins PA, Banks J, Campbell IA, et al. *Mycobacterium kansasii* pulmonary infection: A prospective study of the results of nine months of treatment with rifampicin and ethambutol. Thorax. 1994;49:442-445.

54. Centers for Disease Control and Prevention. Impact of HIV protease inhibitors on the treatment of HIV-infected tuberculosis patients with rifampin. MMWR Morb Mortal Wkly Rep. 1996;45:921-925.

55. Griffith DE, Brown-Elliott BA, Wallace RJ Jr. Three times weekly clarithromycin-containing regimen for treatment of *Mycobacterium kansasii* lung disease: Results of a preliminary study. Clin Infect Dis. 2003;37:1178-1182.

56. Ahn CH, Wallace RJ Jr, Steele LC, et al. Sulfonamide-containing regimens for disease caused by rifampin-resistant *Mycobacterium kansasii*. Am Rev Respir Dis. 1987;135:10-16.

57. Gay JD, DeYoung DR, Roberts GD. In vitro activities of norfloxacin and ciprofloxacin against *Mycobacterium tuberculosis, M. avium* complex, *M. chelonae, M. fortuitum,* and *M. kansasii*. Antimicrob Agents Chemother. 1984;26:94-96.

58. Wallace RJ Jr, Dunbar D, Brown BA, et al. Rifampin-resistant *Mycobacterium kansasii*. Clin Infect Dis. 1994;18:736-743.

59. Wallace RJ Jr, Brown-Elliott BA, Crist CJ, et al. Comparison of the in vitro activity of the glycylcycline tigecycline (formerly GAR-936) with those of tetracycline, minocycline, and doxycycline against isolates of nontuberculous mycobacteria. Antimicrob Agents Chemother. 2002;46:3164-3167.

60. Dautzenberg B, Papillon F, Lepitre M, et al. *Mycobacterium xenopi* infections treated with clarithromycin-containing regimens (Abstract 1125). Presented at the Thirty-third Interscience Conference on Antimicrobial Agents and Chemotherapy, New Orleans, 1993.

61. Fraser VJ, Jones M, Murray PR, et al. Contamination of flexible fiberoptic bronchoscopes with *Mycobacterium chelonae* linked to an automated bronchoscope disinfection machine. Am Rev Resp Dis. 1992;145:853-855.

62. Lai KK, Stottmeier KD, Sherman IH, et al. Mycobacterial cervical lymphadenopathy. JAMA. 1984;251:1286-1288.

63. Wolinsky E. Mycobacterial lymphadenitis in children: A prospective study of 105 nontuberculous cases with long-term follow-up. Clin Infect Dis. 1995;20:954-963.

64. Margileth AM, Chandra R, Altman P. Chronic lymphadenopathy due to mycobacterial infection. Am J Dis Child. 1984;138:917-922.

65. Schaad UB, Votteler TP, McCracken GH, et al. Management of atypical mycobacterial lymphadenitis in childhood: A review based on 380 cases. J Pediatr. 1979;95:356-360.

66. Huebner RE, Schein MF, Cauthen GM, et al. Usefulness of skin testing with mycobacterial antigens in children with cervical lymphadenopathy. Pediatr Infect Dis J. 1992;11:450-456.

67. Zaugg M, Salfinger M, Opravil M, et al. Extrapulmonary and disseminated infections due to *Mycobacterium malmoense:* Case report and review. Clin Infect Dis. 1993;16:540-549.

68. Buchholz UT, McNeil MM, Keyes LE, et al. *Mycobacterium malmoense* infections in the United States, January 1993 through June 1995. Clin Infect Dis. 1998;27 (Suppl):S51-S58.

69. Grange JM, Yates MD, Pozniak A. Bacteriologically confirmed non-tuberculous mycobacterial lymphadenitis in southeast England: A recent increase in the number of cases. Arch Dis Child. 1995;72:516-517.

70. Armstrong KL, James RW, Dawson DJ, et al. *Mycobacterium haemophilum* causing perihilar or cervical lymphadenitis in healthy children. J Pediatr. 1992;121:202-205.

71. Brown-Elliott BA, Griffith DE, Wallace RJ Jr. Newly described or emerging human species of nontuberculous mycobacteria. Infect Dis Clin North Am. 2002;16:187-220.

72. Haas WH, Butler WR, Kirschner P, et al. A new agent of mycobacterial lymphadenitis in children: *Mycobacterium heidelbergense* sp. nov. J Clin Microbiol. 1997;35:3203-3209.

73. Pfyffer GE, Weder W, Strässle A, et al. *Mycobacterium heidelbergense* species nov. infection mimicking a lung tumor. Clin Infect Dis. 1998;27:649-650.

74. Haase G, Kentrup H, Skopnik H, et al. *Mycobacterium lentiflavum:* An etiologic agent of cervical lymphadenitis. Clin Infect Dis. 1997;25:1245-1246.

75. Niobe SN, Bebear CM, Clerc M, et al. Disseminated *Mycobacterium lentiflavum* infection in a human immunodeficiency virus-infected patient. J Clin Microbiol. 2001;39:2030-2032.

76. Torkko P, Suomalainen S, Iivanainen E, et al. Characterization of *Mycobacterium bohemicum* isolated from human, veterinary, and environmental sources. J Clin Microbiol. 2001;39:207-211.

77. Saubolle MA, Kiehn TE, White MH, et al. *Mycobacterium haemophilum:* Microbiology and expanding clinical and geographic spectra of disease in humans. Clin Microbiol Rev. 1996;9:435-447.

78. Collins CH, Grange JM, Noble WC, et al. *Mycobacterium marinum* infections in man. J Hyg Camb. 1985;94:135-149.

79. Black MM, Eykyn S. The successful treatment of tropical fish tank granuloma (*Mycobacterium marinum*) infections with co-trimoxazole. Br J Dermatol. 1977;97:689-692.

80. Donta ST, Smith PW, Levitz RE, et al. Therapy of *Mycobacterium marinum* infections. Arch Intern Med. 1986;146:902-904.

81. Wallace RJ Jr, Swenson JM, Silcox VA, et al. Spectrum of disease due to rapidly growing mycobacteria. Rev Infect Dis. 1983;5:657-679.

82. Sniezak PJ, Graham BS, Busch HB, et al. Rapidly growing mycobacterial infections after pedicures. Arch Dermatol. 2003; 139:629-634.

83. Turenne C, Chedore P, Wolfe J, et al. *Mycobacterium lacus* sp. nov., a new slow-growing non-chromogenic clinical isolate. Int J Syst Evol Microbiol. 2002;52:2135-2140.

84. Wallace RJ Jr, Musser JM, Hull SI, et al. Diversity and sources of rapidly growing mycobacteria associated with infections following cardiac surgery. J Infect Dis. 1989;159:708-716.

85. Maloney S, Welbel S, Daves B, et al. *Mycobacterium abscessus* pseudoinfection traced to an automated endoscope washer: Utility of epidemiologic and laboratory investigation. J Infect Dis. 1994;169:1166-1169.

86. Safranek TJ, Jarvis WR, Carson LA, et al. *Mycobacterium chelonae* wound infections after plastic surgery employing contaminated gentian violet skin-marking solution. N Engl J Med. 1987;317:197-201.

87. Meyers H, Brown-Elliott BA, Moore D, et al. An outbreak of *Mycobacterium chelonae* infection following liposuction. Clin Infect Dis. 2002;34:1500-1507.

88. Gross WN, Hawkins JE, Murphy DB. Origin and significance of *Mycobacterium xenopi* in clinical specimens. Bull Int Union Tuberc Lung Dis. 1976;51:267-269.

89. Brown-Elliott BA, Wallace RJ Jr, Crist CJ, et al. Comparison of in vitro activities of gatifloxacin and ciprofloxacin against four taxa of rapidly growing mycobacteria. Antimicrob. Agents Chemother. 2002;46:3283-3285.

90. Wallace RJ Jr, Brown-Elliott BA, Ward SC, et al. Activities of linezolid against rapidly growing mycobacteria. Antimicrob Agents Chemother. 2001;45:764-767.

91. Brown-Elliott BA, Wallace RJ Jr, Blinkhorn R, et al. Successful treatment of disseminated *Mycobacterium chelonae* infection with linezolid. Clin Infect Dis. 2001;33:1433-1434.

92. Marston BJ, Diallo MO, Horsburgh CR Jr, et al. Emergence of Buruli ulcer in the Daloa region of Cote d'Ivoire. Am J Trop Med Hyg. 1995;52:219-224.

93. Portaels F, Traore H, De Ridder K, et al. In vitro susceptibility of *Mycobacterium ulcerans* to clarithromycin. Antimicrob Agents Chemother. 1998;42:2070-2073.

94. McBride ME, Rudolph AH, Tschen JA, et al. Diagnostic and therapeutic considerations for cutaneous *Mycobacterium haemophilum* infections. Arch Dermatol. 1991;127:276-277.

95. Plemmons RM, McAllister CK, Garces MC, et al. Osteomyelitis due to *Mycobacterium haemophilum* in a cardiac transplant patient: Case report and analysis of interactions among clarithromycin, rifampin, and cyclosporine. Clin Infect Dis. 1997;24:995-997.

96. Edwards MS, Huber TW, Baker CJ. *Mycobacterium terrae* synovitis and osteomyelitis. Am Rev Respir Dis. 1978;117:161-163.

97. May DC, Kutz JE, Howell RS, et al. *Mycobacterium terrae* tenosynovitis: Chronic infection in a previously healthy individual. South Med J. 1987;76:1445-1447.

98. Ridderhof JC, Wallace RJ Jr, Kilburn JO, et al. Chronic tenosynovitis of the hand due to *Mycobacterium nonchromogenicum:* Use of high-performance liquid chromatography for identification of isolates. Rev Infect Dis. 1991;13:857-864.

99. Hoffman PC, Fraser DW, Robiesek F, et al. Two outbreaks of sternal wound infections due to organisms of the *Mycobacterium fortuitum* complex. J Infect Dis. 1981;143:533-542.

100. Kuritsky JN, Bullen MG, Broome CV, et al. Sternal wound infections and endocarditis due to organisms of the *Mycobacterium fortuitum* complex. Ann Intern Med. 1983;98:938-939.

101. Szabó I, Sárközi L. *Mycobacterium chelonae* endemy after heart surgery with fatal consequences. Am Rev Respir Dis. 1980;121:607.

102. Bennett C, Vardiman J, Golomb H. Disseminated atypical mycobacterial infection in patients with hairy cell leukemia. Am J Med. 1986;80:891-896.

103. Horsburgh CR. *Mycobacterium avium* complex infection in the acquired immuno-deficiency syndrome. N Engl J Med. 1991;324:1332-1338.

104. Huminer D, Dux S, Samra Z, et al. *Mycobacterium simiae* infection in Israeli patients with AIDS. Clin Infect Dis. 1993;17:508-509.

105. Jemni L, Hmouda H, Letaief A. Disseminated infection due to *Mycobacterium malmoense* in a patient infected with human immunodeficiency virus. Clin Infect Dis. 1994;19:203-204.

106. Lillo M, Orengo S, Cernoch P, et al. Pulmonary and disseminated infection due to *Mycobacterium kansasii:* A decade of experience. Rev Infect Dis. 1990;2:760-767.

107. Bonomo RA, Briggs JM, Gross W, et al. *Mycobacterium celatum* infection in a patient with AIDS. Clin Infect Dis. 1998;26:243-245.

108. Cingolani A, Sanguinetti M, Antinori A, et al. Disseminated mycobacteriosis caused by drug-resistant *Mycobacterium triplex* in a human immunodeficiency virus-infected patient during highly active antiretroviral therapy. Clin Infect Dis. 2000;31:177-179.

109. Akiyama H, Maruyama T, Uetake T, et al. Systemic infection due to atypical mycobacteria in patients with chronic myelogenous leukemia. Rev Infect Dis. 1991;13:815-818.

110. Patel R, Roberts GD, Keating MR, et al. Infections due to nontuberculous mycobacteria in kidney, heart, and liver transplant recipients. Clin Infect Dis. 1994;19:263-273.

111. Coyle MB, Carlson LDC, Wallis CK, et al. Laboratory aspects of "*Mycobacterium genavense,*" a proposed species isolated from AIDS patients. J Clin Microbiol. 1992;30:3206-3212.

112. Tenover FC, Crawford JT, Huebner RE, et al. The resurgence of tuberculosis: Is your laboratory ready? J Clin Microbiol. 1993;31:767-770.

113. Butler WR, Cage G, Desmond E, et al. Standardized Method for the HPLC Identification of Mycobacteria. Atlanta: Centers for Disease Control and Prevention; 1996.

114. Steingrube VA, Gibson JL, Brown BA, et al. PCR amplification and restriction endonuclease analysis of a 65-kilodalton heat shock protein gene sequence for taxonomic separation of rapidly growing mycobacteria. J Clin Microbiol. 1995;33:149-153.

115. Telenti A, Marchesi F, Balz M, et al. Rapid identification of mycobacteria to the species level by polymerase chain reaction and restriction enzyme analysis. J Clin Microbiol. 1993;31:175-178.

116. Butler WR, Guthertz LS. Mycolic acid analysis by high-performance liquid chromatography for identification of *Mycobacterium* species. Clin Microbiol Rev. 2001;14:704-726.

117. Mazurek GH, Hartman S, Zhang Y-S, et al. Large DNA restriction fragment polymorphism in the *Mycobacterium avium-M. intracellulare* complex: A potential epidemiologic tool. J Clin Microbiol. 1993;31:390-394.

118. Wallace RJ Jr, Zhang Y, Brown BA, et al. DNA large restriction fragment patterns of sporadic and epidemic nosocomial strains of *Mycobacterium chelonae* and *Mycobacterium abscessus.* J Clin Microbiol. 1993;31:2697-2701.
119. Woods GL, Brown-Elliott BA, Desmond EP, et al. Susceptibility Testing of Mycobacteria, Nocardia, and Other Aerobic Actinomycetes: Approved Standard. 2nd ed. NCCLS Publications, v. 20. Wayne, PA: NCCLS; 2003:M24.A.
120. Brown BA, Wallace RJ Jr, Onyi GO, et al. Activities of four macrolides, including clarithromycin, against *Mycobacterium fortuitum, Mycobacterium chelonae,* and *M. chelonae*-like organisms. Antimicrob Agents Chemother. 1992;36:180-184.
121. Swenson JM, Wallace RJ Jr, Silcox VA, et al. Antimicrobial susceptibility of five subgroups of *Mycobacterium fortuitum* and *Mycobacterium chelonae.* Antimicrob Agents Chemother. 1985;28:807-811.
122. Hawkins JE, Wallace RJ Jr, Brown BA. Antibacterial susceptibility tests: Mycobacteria. In: Balows A, ed. Manual of Clinical Microbiology. 5th ed. Washington, DC: American Society for Microbiology; 1991:1138-1152.
123. Brown-Elliott BA, Crist CJ, Mann LB, et al. In vitro activity of linezolid against slowly growing nontuberculous mycobacteria. Antimicrob Agents Chemother. 2003;47:1736-1738.

CHAPTER **252**

Nocardia
Species

TANIA C. SORRELL

DAVID H. MITCHELL

JONATHON R. IREDELL

Nocardia is a genus of aerobic actinomycetes responsible for localized or disseminated infections in animals and humans. The genus is named after Edmond Nocard, who in 1888 described the isolation of an aerobic actinomycete from cattle with bovine farcy. The first human case of nocardiosis was reported by Eppinger in 1890. Cases of human disease have increased substantially in the past two decades, in association with an increasing population of immunocompromised hosts and improved methods for detection and identification of *Nocardia* in the clinical laboratory.

CLASSIFICATION

The aerobic actinomycetes are a large and diverse group of gram-positive bacteria[1] that appear on microscopy as branching filamentous cells. Members of the group are often only distantly related phylogenetically. A subgroup, the "aerobic nocardiform actinomycetes," is the most important cause of human infection and includes *Mycobacterium, Corynebacterium, Nocardia, Rhodococcus, Gordona,* and *Tsukamurella.* The putative cause of Whipple's disease *(Tropheryma whippeli)* also belongs to this group.[2] All members have cell walls containing mesodiaminopimelic acid, arabinose, galactose (type IV cell wall),[1] and mycolic acids of various chain lengths. The last are responsible for varying acid fastness on appropriate staining. In addition, *Nocardia* spp. are characterized by an ability to form aerial hyphae, an ability to grow in media containing lysozyme, and an inability to grow at 50° C.[1]

Traditional laboratory methods for identification of *Nocardia,*[3] which are based on simple biochemical reactions and hydrolysis tests, are limited in their ability to differentiate these organisms. However, in the past few years the application of new molecular methods, particularly 16S ribosomal ribonucleic acid (rRNA) gene sequencing,[4,5] has greatly expanded the spectrum of *Nocardia,* with at least 30 species described[4] and at least 13 of these documented to cause human infection.[5] Of these, *Nocardia asteroides* sensu stricto, *Nocardia farcinica, Nocardia nova, Nocardia brasiliensis, Nocardia pseudobrasiliensis, Nocardia otitidiscaviarum,* and *Nocardia transvalensis* are the most important causes of human infection.[6] Other recently described species, documented to cause human infection, include

Nocardia abscessus,[7] *Nocardia cyriacigeorgica*[8] (both formerly part of the *N. asteroides* complex), *Nocardia paucivarans,*[9] *Nocardia africana,*[10] and *Nocardia veterana.*[11]

ECOLOGY AND EPIDEMIOLOGY

Nocardia is a ubiquitous environmental saphrophyte, occurring in soil, organic matter, and water.[12,13] Human infection usually arises from direct inoculation of the skin or soft tissues or by inhalation. Mycetoma due *to N. brasiliensis* is the most common nocardial infection reported from tropical regions, including the southern United States, Central and South America, and Australia. Worldwide, respiratory and disseminated infections are most often due to members of the *N. asteroides* complex.[12,14]

Nocardia is a well-recognized cause of infection in animals, with bovine mastitis being the most common.[12] There are no reports of animal-to-human transmission. Clusters of invasive nocardiosis acquired by patients in oncology and transplant units, presumed to be associated with inhalation of contaminated dust, have been described.[12,15,16] Concurrent transmission via hands of staff or contaminated fomites appeared likely in one of these outbreaks.[15] A cluster of sternotomy site infections due to *N. farcinica* were linked to hand transmission by an anesthesiologist.[17] Hospital construction work may have been a risk factor in separate clusters of postsurgical wound infections due to *Nocardia.*[16,18] Pulsed-field gel electrophoresis[18] and random amplification of polymorphic deoxyribonucleic acid (DNA) (RAPD) fingerprinting[19,20] have been successfully used for confirming clusters and defining common sources.

PATHOLOGY AND PATHOGENESIS

Sections of tissues infected with *Nocardia* usually demonstrate an acute pyogenic inflammatory reaction. Branching, beaded, filamentous bacteria, similar to those seen in smears taken from cultures (Fig. 252-1), may be demonstrated within the abscesses on Gram staining. "Sulfur granules" (bacterial macrocolonies) similar to those seen in actinomycosis, may be found in nocardial mycetomas. *Nocardia* usually stains acid fast in tissue sections if a method such as that of Fite-Faraco is used, whereas *Actinomyces* spp. do not.[21]

The interaction between the host and parasitizing nocardiae has been comprehensively reviewed.[22] Disease manifestations of nocardiosis are determined principally by portal of entry, tissue tropism, growth rates in vivo, ability to survive phagocyte attack, nature of the host immune reaction, and characteristics of the infecting strain. Protective immune responses to *Nocardia* are primarily T-cell medi-

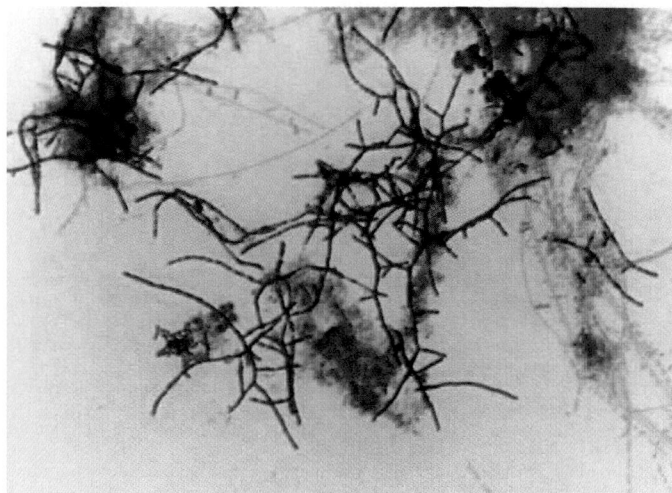

FIGURE 252-1. Photomicrograph of direct Gram-stained smear from a nocardial lung abscess.

ated, and nocardiosis is more problematic in patients with impaired cell-mediated immunity because it elicits little in the way of an effective humoral response.[23,24]

In murine models of infection, virulent nocardiae are cleared from the blood within a few hours of intravenous inoculation and localize in a number of organs (lung, brain, kidneys, liver, spleen). The outcome of infection is largely determined by the ability of a given strain to resist the initial neutrophil leukocyte response and subsequent attack by activated macrophages.[22] Early neutrophil mobilization, although often insufficient to abort infection, appears to retard the process until lymphocyte-mediated cytotoxicity and activated macrophages effect a definitive response.[22,24-26]

Specific Virulence Determinants

The nocardial envelope is structurally similar to that of other actinomycetes: 15% to 25% of the cell wall mass in rapidly growing organisms, and nearly twice that in stationary phase, is composed of peptidoglycan.[27,28] Differences in cell wall ultrastructure and chemical composition are evident during logarithmic and stationary phases of growth. Intrastrain differences in toxicity to host cells as well as virulence in animal models[22,28] may also relate to different virulence factor expression and influence specific cell tropisms. Mycolic acid polymers such as trehalose-6,6'-dimycolate ("cord factor") are members of a group of biologically active cell wall glycolipids found in many actinomycetes including *Nocardia*[27,29,30] and are associated with virulence.[31-34] They are toxic in vitro and in animal models,[33,35] insert themselves into phospholipid bilayers in vitro, and contribute to inhibition of phagosome-lysosome fusion and acidification in macrophages.[31]

Nocardia contains no cell wall lipopolysaccharide, exopolysaccharide capsule, or surface fimbriae. However, strain-dependent specific adhesins and invasion properties influence the outcome of infection in animal models.[36,37] Virulent strains of *N. asteroides* are relatively resistant to neutrophil-mediated killing,[38] and organisms in the logarithmic growth phase are more toxic to macrophages.[27] They inhibit phagosome-lysosome fusion more successfully in vitro,[39] giving rise to L-forms, which can be isolated from within macrophages many days later.[40-42] Cell wall-deficient forms (L-forms) of *Nocardia* have been isolated from serious human and animal infections[43-45] and may explain occasional late relapse of nocardial infections.[22] Nonspecific interactions with neutrophils may contribute to the indolence of nocardiosis in the context of reduced cell-mediated immunity.[14] Patients with specific defects in the phagocyte oxidative burst, for example, those with chronic granulomatous disease,[14] appear to be more vulnerable to this infection. The ability to utilize macrophage lysosomal acid phosphatase as a sole carbon source may be significant in vivo,[41,46] but inhibition of macrophage phagosome acidification and resistance to the oxidative burst of polymorphonuclear neutrophils (PMNs) and macrophages are probably more important. Highly pathogenic *Mycobacterium tuberculosis* and *N. asteroides* secrete superoxide dismutase (SOD) into growth media, whereas nonpathogenic *Mycobacterium* and *Nocardia* do not.[47-49] Antibodies to surface-presented SOD halved the survival of a virulent strain of *N. asteroides* (but not a less virulent strain) in the presence of activated neutrophils in vitro, with added catalase having a protective effect for the less virulent strain.[48] Specific toxins including hemolysins and proteases have been identified but are not thought to be widespread or important virulence factors.[50-52]

Ciliated epithelia appear relatively resistant to invasion by *Nocardia*. However, a range of susceptible lung- and airway-associated cell types has been observed in rat models of infection.[36] Seeding of the central nervous sytem (CNS) may follow hematogenous spread from any focus, and tropism for cerebral tissue is experimentally evident, and neuroinvasiveness and macrophage penetration varies significantly between strains. Acute pyogenic disease is the recognized consequence of neuroinvasion, but experimental evidence of substantia nigra invasion in vivo and apoptosis of dopaminergic cells in vitro[53] as well as a characteristic movement disorder in infected animals[54] has also led to speculation about links with Parkinson's disease. Electron

microscopic studies of infected macrophage and astrocytoma-derived or astrocytoma-related cell lines suggest that the penetration competence of invasive *N. asteroides* is localized to the bacterial apex.[50] Specific lectins have been shown to determine site specificity in the murine brain,[50] intrinsic differences in expression of which may contribute to variations in host susceptibility.[55]

Members of the *N. asteroides* complex are responsible for about 80% of noncutaneous invasive disease and for most systemic and CNS nocardiosis.[22] *N. farcinica* is an important[56] and generally more antibiotic-resistant member of this complex. There is evidence from mouse models that it may be more virulent than other *Nocardia* spp.[57] *N. brasiliensis* is the most frequently reported cause of cutaneous and lymphocutaneous disease, particularly in tropical areas. *N. pseudobrasiliensis,* a new species recently separated from *N. brasiliensis,* appears to be associated with systemic infections, including those in the CNS.[58] Noncutaneous disease is the most frequent presentation of nocardiosis caused by the less common pathogens, *N. transvalensis*[59] and *N. otitidiscavarium,*[22] although both may cause severe cutaneous infection.[60] Superficial nocardiosis following implantation is not necessarily associated with compromised cell-mediated immunity, but may progress to disseminated disease in that setting.[60]

CLINICAL MANIFESTATIONS

Immunocompromise is a well-established risk factor for nocardiosis. *Nocardia* may therefore be considered as an opportunistic pathogen that causes serious and disseminated disease in settings such as organ transplantation and lymphoreticular neoplasia, with the relative risk of progressive disease reflecting the level of immunosuppression. A compilation of more than a thousand randomly selected cases from the literature showed that more than 60% of all reported nocardiosis is associated with preexisting immune compromise, ranging from alcoholism and diabetes to organ transplantation and acquired immunodeficiency syndrome (AIDS).[22] This was also the case in more than one third of *N. farcinica* infections.[56] Persons with chronic pulmonary disorders, notably, pulmonary alveolar proteinosis, and almost any condition requiring long-term corticosteroid usage, are also at risk. Though cases of nocardiosis have been described in patients with AIDS, the overall incidence is low and not fully explained by the use of sulfonamide prophylaxis against *Pneumocystis jirovecii* pneumonia.[12,61,62]

Ubiquitous in soil, all the nocardiae can establish superficial infection following relatively trivial inoculation injuries, which may vary from insect and animal bites to puncture wounds and contaminated abrasions. *N. brasiliensis* is the most common cause of progressive cutaneous and lymphocutaneous (sporotrichoid) disease, whereas *N. asteroides* more commonly causes self-limited infection.[14,22] Because the initial response to *Nocardia* is pyogenic, self-limited skin lesions may initially be disregarded or treated as staphylococcal in origin. Severe and invasive systemic disease is almost certainly overrepresented in the literature, and the extent to which mycetoma is relatively underreported and nocardial infection underdiagnosed overall, is unknown. Mycetoma is a chronically progressive, destructive disease, occurring days to months after inoculation and is typically located distally on the limbs. Eumycetoma (of fungal aetiology) and actinomycetomata (due to actinomycetes) are equally prominent in the literature, the epidemiology varying with geographic location.[63] Overall, *Streptomyces* spp. and *Actinomadura* appear to be of equal or greater importance than *Nocardia* spp. among causative agents of actinomycetoma. Suppurative granulomata, progressive fibrosis and necrosis, sinus formation with destruction of adjacent structures, and macroscopically visible infective granules are regular features of nocardial mycetoma.[63] Inoculation injury occasionally results in infection of the cornea.

Pulmonary disease is the predominant clinical presentation (more than 40% of reported cases), with almost 90% of these caused by members of the *N. asteroides* complex.[22] Pulmonary nocardiosis is usually suppurative in nature, but granulomatous or mixed responses may occur. Clinical manifestations of established infection include endobronchial

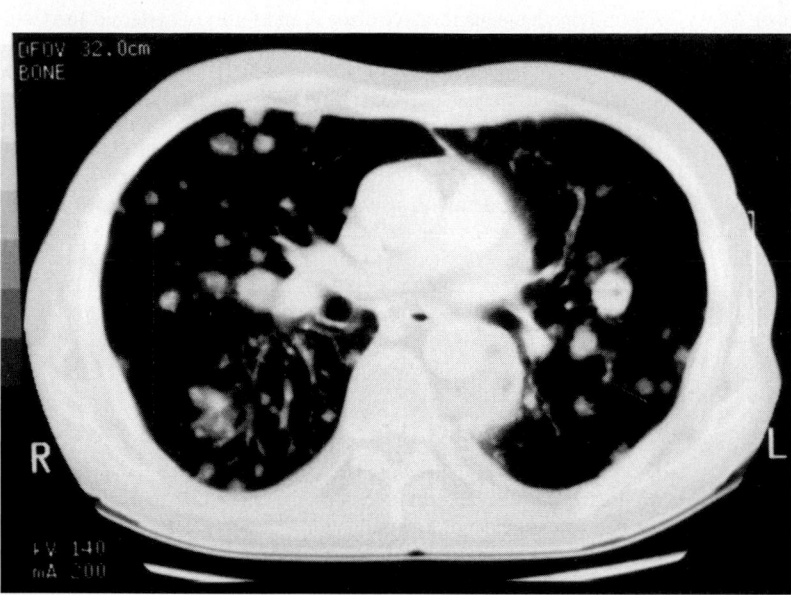

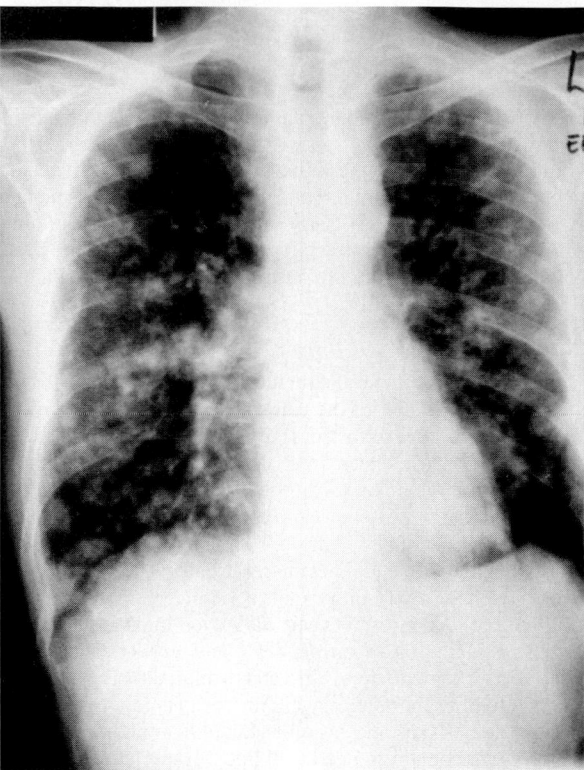

A   **B**

FIGURE 252-2. Computed tomography scan **(A)** and chest radiograph **(B)** from a patient demonstrating multiple abscesses due to *Nocardia farcinica.*

inflammatory masses pneumonia, lung abscess, and cavitary disease with contiguous extension to surface and deep structures, including effusion and empyema. Radiologic manifestations include irregular nodules (usually cavitating when large), reticulonodular or diffuse pneumonic infiltrates, and pleural effusions (Fig. 252-2). The "halo sign," considered characteristic of aspergillosis in neutropenic patients, has been described. Progressive fibrotic disease may develop following inadequate therapy, and diagnosis is often difficult. Pulmonary nocardiosis may be a fatal complication of advanced human immunodeficiency virus (HIV) infection and often manifests as alveolar infiltrates that progress during therapy rather than as cavitary disease.[64-66] It occurs most commonly in severely immunocompromised patients (CD4 200/mm³)[67] in whom nonspecific radiologic appearances oblige a search for a definitive diagnosis. Nocardiosis should always be considered in the differential diagnosis of indolent pulmonary disease, particularly in the setting of cellular immune compromise, along with other actinomycetes (e.g., mycobacteria, *Actinomyces* spp.) and eumycetes (e.g., *Cryptococcus neoformans, Aspergillus* spp.). Clues to a nocardial etiology include spread to contiguous structures, especially with soft tissue swellings or external fistulas, and to the CNS. Secondary cerebral localization and clinically silent destructive infection is sufficiently common that cerebral imaging, preferably magnetic resonance imaging (MRI), should be performed in all cases of pulmonary and disseminated nocardiosis. Invasive diagnostic procedures should be considered early in the immunocompromised host, because disease may follow a rapidly progressive course in patients with severe immunodeficiency, and coincident pathology with similar clinical characteristics (e.g., aspergillosis, tuberculosis, malignancy) is well documented.[68]

CNS involvement was recognized in more than 44% of cases of all systemic nocardiosis in one large survey (Fig. 252-3).[22] Up to 25% of reported nocardial disease other than mycetoma involves the CNS, with nearly 50% of these cases exclusively involving the CNS.[14,69-71] Insidious presentations are often mistaken for neoplasia because of the paucity of clinical and laboratory signs of bacterial inflammation, and silent invasion and persistence make diagnosis and management more

difficult.[14,22] Clinical manifestations of CNS nocardiosis usually result from local effects of granulomata or abscesses in the brain, and less commonly, the spinal cord or meninges. Disease frequently progresses over months to years and causes a broad range of neurologic deficits, including chronic behavioral and psychiatric disturbance, which reflect localization in the cerebral cortices, basal ganglia, and midbrain. Tissue diagnosis of a cerebral mass in the setting of proven pulmonary nocardiosis is not always necessary.[14] However, cerebral biopsy should be considered early in the immunocompromised patient because of the higher incidence of serious coexisting pathology and a more aggressive course than that traditionally ascribed to cerebral nocardiosis.

Disseminated infection is characterized by widespread abscess formation. The most commonly reported sites include the CNS and eyes (particularly the retina), skin and subcutaneous tissues (Fig. 252-4), kidneys, joints, bone, and heart.

Colonization

Occasional instances of transient colonization of sputum and skin by *Nocardia* have been reported and appear to indicate aerosol contamination or soil-derived contamination. Colonization of the sputum is typically found in patients with underlying pulmonary pathology, who are not receiving steroid therapy, and requires no specific therapy. Significant isolates of *Nocardia* should be visible on Gram stain, produce a pure or predominant growth in culture, and be isolated repeatedly from clinical specimens.[71] However, the extent to which spontaneously resolving or subclinical pulmonary infection occurs in the population is not well defined and at least one leading authority warns against dismissing positive sputum cultures as harmless.[22]

LABORATORY DIAGNOSIS

The microbiology laboratory should always be informed when nocardiosis is suspected, because the diagnosis may be missed by routine laboratory methods. Respiratory secretions, skin biopsies, or aspirates from deep collections are the most common specimens from which

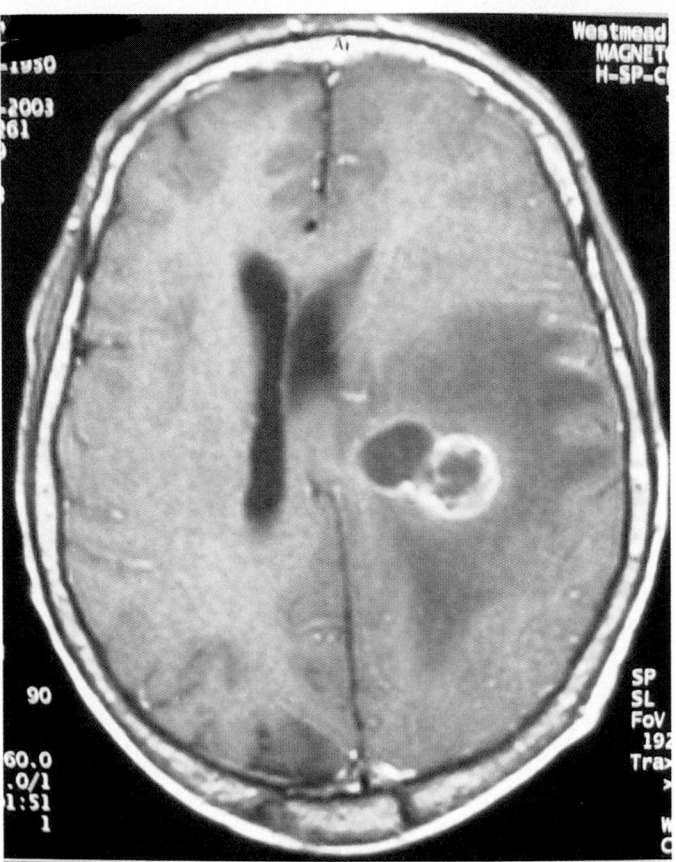

FIGURE 252-3. Cerebral magnetic resonance scan showing a brain abscess due to *Nocardia farcinica.*

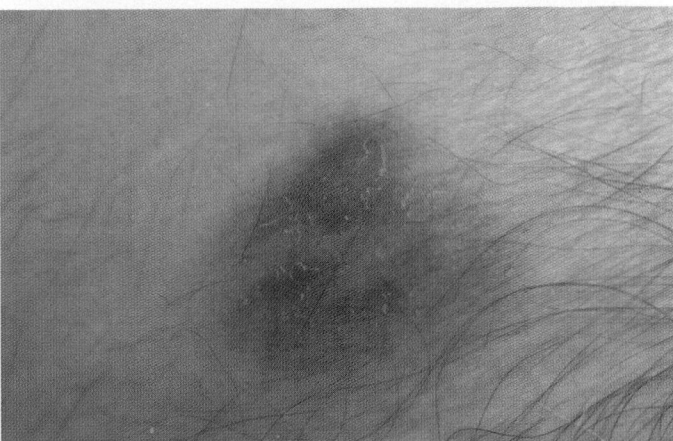

FIGURE 252-4. Nocardial skin nodule in a patient with disseminated infection due to *Nocardia farcinica.*

N. asteroides sensu stricto. Although resistance to third-generation cephalosporins is considered characteristic of *N. farcinica,*[79] this is variable and should not be used as the sole criterion for differentiating this species from *N. asteroides* sensu stricto.[78]

Commercially available identification systems, including Microscan RAI/HNID panels,[81] the 1D32C Yeast Identification System,[82] and the API 20C[6] may provide more rapid methods for differentiating *Nocardia* spp. Molecular techniques including restriction endonuclease analysis following PCR[83,84] and 16S rRNA sequencing[5] have been used to differentiate among the *Nocardia* and to characterize new species and are likely to become the methods of choice for identification of *Nocardia* spp. as they become more available. Immunodominant antigens of *Nocardia* have been described and serologic tests developed; these have proven useful in the diagnosis of *N. brasiliensis* mycetoma[85] but at present remain experimental.

MANAGEMENT

Successful therapy requires the use of an antimicrobial drug or drugs in combination with appropriate surgical drainage or débridement. Optimal antimicrobial regimens have not been established by controlled clinical trial. Initial selection of a therapeutic regimen should take into account the site and severity of infection, the host immune status, potential drug interactions/toxicity and the species of *Nocardia.* Antimicrobial susceptibility testing is a useful guide to therapy in some settings (see later), but results should be interpreted with caution, given the paucity of studies correlating laboratory data with clinical outcome. Indeed, discrepancies between in vitro data and clinical outcome are well documented. The National Committee for Clinical Laboratory Standards (NCCLS) has recently approved a method for antimicrobial testing of the aerobic actinomycetes[86] using broth microdilution. The Etest and the BACTEC radiometric method have been correlated with broth microdilution[87,88] and may be more useful in the routine clinical laboratory. At present it is appropriate that isolates be sent to a specialized reference laboratory for confirmatory testing. Susceptibility testing is indicated when patients present with deep-seated or disseminated infection fail to respond to initial therapy or relapse after therapy, and when alternatives to sulfonamides are being considered. Testing is also indicated when relatively resistant *Nocardia* spp. such as *N. farcinica* or a newly described species has been isolated. Susceptibility profiles of selected *Nocardia* spp. are summarized in Table 252-1.

Sulfonamides have been the mainstay of therapy since their introduction in the 1940s. However, in severely ill patients, those with cerebral involvement or disseminated nocardiosis, and in immunosuppressed patients, two or more drugs, which may include sulfonamides, are frequently prescribed because the mortality with sulfonamide monotherapy may be as high as 50%.[89,90] In immunosuppressed patients

Nocardia is isolated. Direct smears from such specimens typically show gram-positive, beaded, branching filaments, which are usually acid fast. Standard blood culture media support the growth of *Nocardia* organisms, but prolonged incubation (up to 2 weeks) and blind subcultures may be required for their detection.[1] Bacteremia as demonstrated by positive blood cultures is rarely reported in patients with nocardiosis[72] but has been described in cases of central venous catheter infection.[73] *Nocardia* spp. will grow on most nonselective media used routinely for culture of bacteria, fungi, and mycobacteria. However, in specimens containing mixed flora (e.g., respiratory secretions), nocardial colonies are easily obscured by those of more rapidly growing bacteria, and the yield is increased by use of selective media, such as Thayer-Martin agar with antibiotics[74] or paraffin agar.[75] Buffered charcoal-yeast extract (BCYE) medium, which is commonly used for selective growth of *Legionella* spp., may also be used for isolation of *Nocardia* from respiratory specimens.[76] Decontamination methods used for mycobacterial culture are too harsh for *Nocardia* and may substantially reduce the numbers of viable organisms present in the specimen.[77]

Growth of *Nocardia* may take from 48 hours to several weeks, but typical colonies are usually seen from 3 to 5 days. *Nocardia* appear as either buff or pigmented waxy cerebriform colonies or as chalky white if aerial hyphae are produced.[1] Most isolates are acid fast by a method such as the modified Kinyoun technique, but this characteristic may vary with strain and culture media used.

Isolates identified presumptively as *Nocardia* can be assigned to traditional groupings based on the hydrolysis of casein, tyrosine, xanthine, hypoxanthine, and testosterone.[3] These methods are relatively expensive, slow, and limited by their inability to differentiate members of the *N. asteroides* complex or to identify newly described species. Expanded biochemical tests and patterns of resistance to antibiotics can be used to differentiate *N. farcinica*[78,79] and *N. nova*[78,80] from

TABLE 252-1 Antimicrobial Susceptibility of Selected *Nocardia* Species (% Isolates Susceptible)

Antimicrobial	N. asteroides	N. farcinica	N. nova	N. brasiliensis	N. transvalensis	N. otitidiscaviarum
Sulfamethoxazole	(8) 96-199*	(20) 89-100	89-97	99-100	90	V
Trimethoprim-sulfamethoxazole	(8) 100*	(0)*	NR	100	88	V
Ampicillin	40-93	0-5	100	14	10	NR
Amoxicillin clavulanate	53-67	47-71	3-6	65-97	30	R
Ceftriaxone	94-100	0-73	100	88-100	50	NR
Imipenem	77-98	64-87	100	20-30	90	R
Amikacin	100	100	100	100	82	S
Doxycycline	48-88	0-14	19-94	NR	NR	NR
Minocycline	78-94	20-96	89-100	75-90	54	S
Ciprofloxacin	38-98	68-88	0	12-30	60	R
Moxifloxacin	50	NR	NR	NR	NR	NR
Erythromycin	23-93	0-3	100	40	50	NR
Clarithromycin	42	NR	NR	NR	NR	NR
Linezolid	100	100	100	100	100	100

Composite data from multiple references. Interpretation of sensitivity is based on NCCLS breakpoints. Linezolid data based on breakpoint minimal inhibitory concentration (MIC) of 8 mg/L.[129]

NR, not reported; R, resistant; S, sensitive; V, variable susceptibility.
*Discrepant results from a continental European study.

in particular, combination therapy with amikacin and a carbapenem or third-generation cephalosporin should be considered for primary therapy in the setting of severe, progressive infection. Sulfonamides are the treatment of choice for nocardiosis due to *N. brasiliensis*,[91,92] *N. asteroides* complex, and *N. transvalensis*.[14,59] Although sulfonamides are less effective in vitro against *N. otitidiscaviarum*,[19,93,94] they have been curative in cases of cutaneous infection.[95] Trimethoprim-sulfamethoxazole (TMP-SMX) is the formulation currently preferred by most clinicians, despite the absence of conclusive clinical data supporting increased efficacy of the combination compared with the traditional sulfadiazine and sulfisoxazole, and increased myelotoxicity of the TMP-SMX combination, especially in patients receiving myelosuppressive drugs.[91] TMP-SMX (available in the fixed ratio of 1:5) has potential advantages over the older sulfonamide drugs. In vitro, synergistic activity has been demonstrated against a majority of *Nocardia* isolates.[89,91] Optimal drug ratios for demonstration of synergy vary between 1:10 and 1:5 or less in different studies.[89,96,97] The usual ratio of these drugs in serum and cerebrospinal fluid (CSF) is 1:20.[89] Relative levels in tissues and pus, including cerebral nocardial abscesses, approximate 1:7 or less.[91,98] Therapeutic responses to the combination have been reported despite high minimal inhibitory concentrations (MICs) of TMP compared with achievable serum levels and evidence of antagonism between TMP and SMX in vitro.[99]

In adults with normal renal function and localized disease, the recommended dose of TMP-SMX is 5 to 10 mg/kg (TMP) and 25 to 50 mg/kg (SMX) in two to four divided doses, depending on the extent of disease.[91] In patients with primary cutaneous infection, including sporotrichoid nocardiosis, 5 mg/kg/day (TMP component) is sufficient, in combination with appropriate surgical débridement.[91] Higher initial doses (15 mg/kg TMP and 75 mg/kg SMX) intravenously or by mouth are frequently used in patients with cerebral abscesses, severe, extensive or disseminated infection, and patients with AIDS.[67,89] Doses can generally be reduced and therapy changed from intravenous to oral after 3 to 6 weeks, depending on clinical response. Cure of cerebral nocardiosis has been noted with lower doses of TMP-SMX (approximately 10 mg/kg/day of the TMP component)[99,100] or less.[98] Immunocompromised patients do not necessarily need higher doses of TMP-SMX, for example, 5 mg/kg/day (TMP component) in two doses has been successful in the treatment of pulmonary infection in renal transplant patients.[101] It has been recommended that a serum sulfonamide level performed 2 hours after an oral dose at steady state is useful to confirm that gastrointestinal absorption is adequate and that recommended therapeutic levels of sulfonamide (100-150 mg/L) have been achieved.[12] In practice, measurement of serum drug levels should be considered when absorption from the gastrointestinal tract is un-

certain, and in patients who are at risk of dose-related toxicity (for example, renal and bone marrow failure), who require high doses of TMP-SMX, and in cases of poor therapeutic response.

Alternative antimicrobial regimens should be considered in infections caused by *N. otitidiscaviarum*, which demonstrates inconsistent susceptibility to sulfonamides (see Table 252-1), those failing sulfonamide therapy, and those intolerant of sulfonamide-containing regimens because of hypersensitivity, gastrointestinal toxicity, or myelotoxicity. Sulfonamide intolerance occurs in up to 55% of patients with AIDS.[67,102] Desensitization is an option for continuation of TMP-SMX in the presence of hypersensitivity reactions. Although desensitization has been used successfully in patients with AIDS,[103] severe reactions have been reported in other settings.[104] Renal transplantation is associated with an increased risk of myelotoxicity in patients receiving azathioprine[105] and of nephrotoxicity in patients receiving cyclosporine A or tacrolimus. Anecdotal data indicate that immunocompromised patients with severe, progressive nocardial infection may respond to primary therapy with nonsulfonamide-containing regimens.[90]

The choice of alternative therapeutic drugs has been based on in vitro susceptibility data and efficacy in animal models, especially short-term murine models of cerebral and pulmonary nocardiosis.[106,107] Assessment of these regimens in human nocardiosis is complicated by the paucity of case reports, the fact that multiple antimicrobial drugs have often been employed either in combination or sequentially,[108] and the variable, long-term course of nocardiosis. Most clinical experience has been obtained with amikacin and imipenem, which appear to be the most active agents in vitro and in animal models.[14,108] Though amikacin is potentially nephrotoxic and ototoxic, once-daily dose regimens make it a desirable drug for use in home intravenous therapy programs. In one study, cure was effected in seven of eight patients given amikacin in combination with drugs which demonstrated synergy in vitro.[109] In vitro, amikacin exhibits excellent activity against all species of *Nocardia*, with the possible exception of *N. transvalensis* (see Table 252-1). Imipenem is highly active in vitro except against *N. brasiliensis*, though more than 10% of isolates of *N. farcinica*, *N. transvalensis*, and in one study, *N. asteroides* sensu strictu, were resistant (see Table 252-1). Synergy between TMP-SMX and amikacin has been demonstrated in vitro; with imipenem, the effect is predominantly additive.[110] In the short-term murine models of cerebral and pulmonary nocardiosis, imipenem and amikacin were significantly more effective than TMP-SMX.[106,107] The effect of imipenem was not enhanced by TMP-SMX despite demonstration of synergy in vitro.[111] But the apparent inferior efficacy of TMP-SMX may be model dependent.[112] Amikacin has been used successfully, usually in combination with other agents, including sulfonamides, in patients with nocardiosis involving several different body sites, and in immunocompromised patients.[108,113] An initial parenteral regimen of imipenem and amikacin (10-15 mg/kg/day in two divided doses) has been recommended as primary therapy in pulmonary nocardiosis[114] and in the very ill patient,[14] though there are few clinical reports that support this approach. Meropenem is an attractive alternative to imipenem in patients with cerebral nocardiosis because it has a similar pharmacokinetic profile, good CSF penetration, activity against *Nocardia,* and is associated with a lower incidence of seizures.[115,116]

Third-generation cephalosporins have the advantages of excellent CSF penetration and low toxicity. Those with long serum half-lives are suitable for use in ambulatory intravenous therapy programs. In several case reports the efficacy of ceftriaxone-containing regimens in the treatment of nocardiosis has been documented.[108] Ceftriaxone, cefotaxime (see Table 252-1), and cefuroxime[14] exhibit significant in vitro activity against *Nocardia* with the exception of *N. farcinica, N. transvalensis,* and *N. ototidiscaviarum.* Synergy between cefotaxime and imipenem has been noted against susceptible strains of *Nocardia* in vitro, though not in a murine model of cerebral nocardiosis.[111] Cefuroxime and amikacin are synergistic in vitro.[109]

The most frequently used oral alternatives to sulfonamides are minocycline and amoxicillin clavulanate. Minocycline (100-200 mg twice daily) has been effective when used alone, in combination with other drugs, or as sequential therapy. Amoxicillin clavulanate has also been effective in individual patients when used as sequential therapy or in combination with other agents and may be especially useful in treatment of cutaneous infections due to *N. brasiliensis,* a consistent β-lactamase producer.[117] However, mutation in the β-lactamase gene of *N. brasiliensis* has resulted in relapse during therapy with amoxicillin clavulanate.[118] In continental Europe, amoxicillin clavulanate or imipenem combined with amikacin has been recommended, especially for infections due to *N. farcinica.*[90] The use of amoxicillin clavulanate should be guided by in vitro sensitivity data because susceptibility is variable and species dependent (see Table 252-1), demonstration of β-lactamase production is not necessarily predictive of resistance to β-lactam drugs, and species such as *N. nova* may be sensitive to ampicillin but not to amoxicillin clavulanate.[80] Susceptibility data should also be used to guide the choice of alternative agents for which in vitro data are inconsistent and few clinical data are available. These include doxycycline, macrolides, and fluoroquinolones. Linezolid is a new oxazolidinone that appears active in vitro against all clinically important species of *Nocardia.* It offers promise for the future because it is effective orally (bioavailability is close to 100%), CSF penetration is good, and efficacy has been demonstrated in a few patients unable to tolerate TMP-SMX.[104] However, it is expensive, has only been approved for short-term use, and significant toxicity (including bone marrow suppression) has been reported.

The place of surgery in the management of nocardiosis depends on the site and extent of infection. In extraneural disease, indications for aspiration, drainage, or excision of abscesses are similar to those for other chronic bacterial infections. Therapeutic aspiration is generally inadequate in patients with thick-walled multiloculated abscesses, which contain little free-flowing pus, including patients with mycetomas.[119] In patients with brain abscesses, surgery should be performed when abscesses are accessible and relatively large, the patient's condition deteriorates or lesions progress within 2 weeks of therapy, or there is no reduction in abscess size within a month.[120] Decompression of lesions can be accomplished by stereotactic aspiration, though cure is often achieved only after craniotomy and total excision.[100,120] Small abscesses can be cured by prolonged antimicrobial therapy. Because abscesses may progress in the face of appropriate therapy, all patients must be monitored frequently with cranial computed tomography or other imaging modalities.

Duration of Therapy and Prognosis

Clinical improvement is generally evident within 3 to 5 days[112] or at the most, 7 to 10 days[12] after the initiation of appropriate therapy. Parenteral therapy can usually be safely changed to an oral regimen, after 3 to 6 weeks, depending on clinical response. Initial high doses of TMP-SMX

can also be reduced at this time. Patients with extensive nocardiosis or necrotic foci not amenable to surgery or those who respond slowly may benefit from prolongation of parenteral and subsequently, oral, therapy.[14] Lack of response to initial therapy may be due to primary drug resistance, inadequate penetration of drug into sites of infection (dependent on dose, bioavailability of oral drugs, abscess location and pathology, and on patient compliance), or the presence of a sequestered abscess requiring surgical drainage. In immunocompromised hosts, primary treatment failure may also be due to overwhelming nocardial infection or a coexisting or secondary opportunistic infection.

In patients receiving immunosuppressive medication, therapy should generally be continued during treatment of nocardiosis in order to contain the underlying disease or to prevent transplant rejection, or both. Reduction or cessation of immunosuppressive drugs may be required when the *Nocardia* infection is uncontrolled and progressive despite therapeutic serum levels of the antimicrobial drugs.

Recommendations on the duration of therapy are necessarily empirical and based primarily on reports of relapse after sulfonamide therapy of different durations.[66,89,91,92,100,121] There are rare case reports of cure of extrapulmonary abscesses following short course parenteral therapy (7-8 weeks) with amikacin and surgical drainage,[56,122] or amikacin plus ceftriaxone, as in a case of cerebral nocardiosis.[123] One-to 3-month courses of therapy are curative in patients with primary cutaneous infection including sporotrichoid nocardiosis and superficial ulcers.[71,91] Prolonged therapy is required in patients with mycetoma.[119] Nonimmunosuppressed patients with pulmonary or systemic nocardiosis (excluding CNS involvement) should be treated for at least 6 months and those with CNS involvement, for 12 months. These patients should be monitored for at least a year after completion of therapy to detect late relapses.[100,121] In HIV-negative immunosuppressed patients, therapy should be continued for 12 months or longer if there are intercurrent increases in immunosuppression, for example, due to episodes of graft rejection. For patients who must be maintained on steroid or cytotoxic therapy, prolonged low-dose maintenance therapy may be required. The most suitable maintenance regimen has not been defined, but daily low-dose therapy seems appropriate because TMP-SMX administered twice or three times weekly did not prevent the development of nocardiosis after bone marrow transplantation.[113,124] In patients with AIDS, early institution of a prolonged primary course of antinocardial therapy is essential because treatment of patients with late presentations or whose *Nocardia* infection has relapsed has usually been unsuccessful.[66] In this group, low-dose maintenance therapy should be continued for life.

Primary prophylaxis against nocardial infection is not generally necessary for patients who are immunosuppressed after transplantation, because of the low incidence of nocardiosis, especially since the introduction of cyclosporine A.[125] The daily use of TMP-SMX as prophylaxis against alternative infections may prevent some cases of nocardiosis, as has been observed after renal transplantation,[126] though the overall impact of such therapy is reduced by post-transplantation cases of nocardiosis.[125] TMP-SMX prophylaxis has not been of benefit in the prevention of nocardiosis in patients with AIDS, possibly because the overall incidence based on autopsy series is low.[12,62] It is notable that cases of nocardiosis in this group were usually found in patients who had not been receiving sulfonamide prophylaxis against other pathogens.[61,67]

The clinical outcome of therapy for nocardiosis is dependent on the site and extent of disease and underlying host factors. Cure rates of almost 100% are found in patients with skin or soft tissue involvement, compared with rates of 90% in pleuropulmonary disease, 63% in disseminated infection, and 50% in brain abscess.[89] Mortality in patients with brain abscesses diagnosed antemortem approximates 31% but is higher (41%) in patients with multiple abscesses and in immunocompromised patients (55%).[120] In an early large series of patients with nocardiosis, mortality was increased significantly in patients with Cushing's disease and in those receiving corticosteroids or antineoplastic drugs but was not related to the severity of the underlying disease.[127] Although immunosuppressive therapy increases the risk of pulmonary and disseminated nocardiosis in recipients of organ transplants, it is not clear to what extent maintenance of immunosuppressive therapy during treatment of nocardiosis interferes with outcome. In fact, most patients can be cured with appropriate antimicrobial therapy even if immunosuppressive drugs are continued, provided the diagnosis is made early and appropriate full-dose therapy is continued for an adequate period.[124,125,128] However, delay in diagnosis and early cessation of therapy are poor prognostic factors, which in patients with AIDS have been associated with failure of subsequent therapy.[66]

In summary, the choice and dose of antimicrobial drugs, and the duration of therapy, depend on the site or sites and extent of infection, the underlying host factors, the species of *Nocardia,* and the clinical response to initial management. Sulfonamide therapy with TMP-SMX remains the mainstay of treatment for patients with nocardiosis. The use of additional or alternative drugs in severely ill patients, for example, amikacin, a carbapenem, or ceftriaxone, may improve prognosis, especially in the immunocompromised patient. Alternative regimens are required for patients unable to tolerate, or who fail therapy with, sulfonamides and often in those with infections due to *N. otitidiscaviarum.* Linezolid, new quinolones, and macrolides that are effective orally offer promise for the future.

REFERENCES

1. Brown JM, McNeil MM. *Nocardia, Rhodococcus, Gordona, Actinomadura, Streptomyces,* and other aerobic actinomycetes. In: Murray PR, Baron EJ, Jorgensen JH, et al, eds. Manual of Clinical Microbiology. Washington, DC: ASM Press; 2003:502-531.
2. Bentley SD, Maiwald M, Murphy LD, et al. Sequencing and analysis of the genome of the Whipple's disease bacterium *Tropheryma whipplei.* Lancet. 2003;361:637-644.
3. Mishra SK, Gordon RE, Barnett DA. Identification of nocardiae and streptomycetes of medical importance. J Clin Microbiol. 1980;11:728-736.
4. Roth A, Andrees S, Kroppenstedt RM, et al. Phylogeny of the genus *Nocardia* based on reassessed 16S rRNA gene sequences reveals underspeciation and division of strains classified as *Nocardia asteroides* into three established species and two unnamed taxons. J Clin Microbiol. 2003;41:851-856.
5. Wellinghausen N, Pietzcker T, Kern WV, et al. Expanded spectrum of Nocardia species causing clinical nocardiosis detected by molecular methods. Int J Med Microbiol. 2002;292:277-282.
6. Kiska DL, Hicks K, Pettit DJ. Identification of medically relevant *Nocardia* species with an abbreviated battery of tests. J Clin Microbiol. 2002;40:1346-1351.
7. Yassin AF, Rainey FA, Mendrock U, et al. *Nocardia abscessus* sp. nov. Int J Syst Evol Microbiol. 2000;50:1487-1493.
8. Yassin AF, Rainey FA, Steiner U. *Nocardia cyriacigeorgici* sp. nov. Int J Syst Evol Microbiol. 2001;51:1419-1423.
9. Eisenblatter M, Disko U, Stoltenburg-Didinger G, et al. Isolation of *Nocardia paucivorans* from the cerebrospinal fluid of a patient with relapse of cerebral nocardiosis. J Clin Microbiol. 2002;40:3532-3534.
10. Hamid ME, Maldonado L, Sharaf Eldin GS, et al. *Nocardia africana* sp. nov., a new pathogen isolated from patients with pulmonary infections. J Clin Microbiol. 2001;39:625-630.
11. Gurtler V, Smith R, Mayall BC, et al. *Nocardia veterana* sp. nov., isolated from human bronchial lavage. Int J Syst Evol Microbiol. 2001;51:933-936.
12. McNeil MM, Brown JM. The medically important aerobic actinomycetes: Epidemiology and microbiology. Clin Microbiol Rev. 1994;7:357-417.
13. Pier AC, Fichtner RE. Distribution of serotypes of *Nocardia asteroides* from animal, human, and environmental sources. J Clin Microbiol. 1981;13:548-553.
14. Lerner PI. Nocardiosis. Clin Infect Dis. 1996;22:891-903.
15. Houang ET, Lovett IS, Thompson FD, et al. *Nocardia asteroides* infection—A transmissible disease. J Hosp Infect; 1980;1:31-40.
16. Sahathevan M, Harvey FA, Forbes G, et al. Epidemiology, bacteriology and control of an outbreak of *Nocardia asteroides* infection on a liver unit. J Hosp Infect. 1991;18(Suppl A):473-480.
17. Wenger PN, Brown JM, McNeil MM, Jarvis WR. *Nocardia farcinica* sternotomy site infections in patients following open heart surgery. J Infect Dis. 1998;178:1539-1543.
18. Blumel J, Blumel E, Yassin AF, et al. Typing of *Nocardia farcinica* by pulsed-field gel electrophoresis reveals an endemic strain as source of hospital infections. J Clin Microbiol. 1998;36:118-122.
19. Provost F, Laurent F, Uzcategui LR, Boiron P. Molecular study of persistence of *Nocardia asteroides* and *Nocardia otitidiscaviarum* strains in patients with long-term nocardiosis. J Clin Microbiol. 1997;35:1157-1160.
20. Laurent F, Provost F, Couble A, et al. Genetic relatedness analysis of nocardia strains by random amplification polymorphic DNA: Validation and applications. Res Microbiol. 2000;151:263-270.
21. Robboy SJ, Vickery AL. Tinctorial and morphologic properties distinguishing actinomycosis and nocardiosis. N Engl J Med. 1970;282:593-596.
22. Beaman BL, Beaman L. *Nocardia* species: host-parasite relationships. Clin Microbiol Rev. 1994;7:213-264.
23. Beaman BL, Gershwin ME, Ahmed A, et al. Response of CBA/N x DBA2/F1 mice to *Nocardia asteroides.* Infect Immun. 1982;35:111-116.
24. Deem RL, Doughty FA, Beaman BL. Immunologically specific direct T lymphocyte-mediated killing of *Nocardia asteroides.* J Immunol. 1983;130:2401-2406.
25. Beaman BL, Goldstein E, Gershwin ME, et al. Lung response to congenitally athymic (nude), heterozygous, and Swiss Webster mice to aerogenic and intranasal infection by *Nocardia asteroides.* Infect Immun. 1978;22:867-877.
26. Deem RL, Beaman BL, Gershwin ME. Adoptive transfer of immunity to *Nocardia asteroides* in nude mice. Infect Immun. 1982;38:914-920.
27. Beaman BL. Structural and biochemical alterations of *Nocardia asteroides* cell walls during its growth cycle. J Bacteriol. 1975;123:1235-1253.
28. Beaman BL, Moring SE. Relationship among cell wall composition, stage of growth, and virulence of *Nocardia asteroides* GUH-2. Infect Immun. 1988;56:557-563.
29. Beaman B, Serrano J, Serrano A. Comparative ultrastructure within the nocardia. Zentralbl Bakteriol Mikrbiol Hyg Abt. 1977;1(Suppl 6):201-220.
30. Goren MB. Mycobacterial fatty acid esters of sugars and sulfosugars. In: Kates M, ed. Glycolipids, Phospholipids and Sulfoglycolipids of Lipid Research. New York: Plenum Press; 1990:363-461.
31. Spargo BJ, Crowe LM, Ioneda T, et al. Cord factor (alpha,alpha-trehalose 6,6'-dimycolate) inhibits fusion between phospholipid vesicles. Proc Natl Acad Sci U S A. 1991;88:737-740.
32. Beaman BL. An ultrastructural analysis of *Nocardia* during experimental infections in mice. Infect Immun. 1973;8:828-840.
33. Tamplin M, McClung NM. Quantitative studies of the relationship between trehalose lipids and virulence of *Nocardia asteroides* isolates. In: Ortiz-Ortiz L, Bojalil LF, Yakeloff V, eds. Biological, Biochemical and Biomedical Aspects of Actinomycetes. Orlando, Fla: Academic Press Inc; 1984:251-258.
34. Beaman B. Possible mechanisms of nocardial pathogenesis. In: Goodfellow M, Brownell GH, Serrano JA, eds. Biology of the Nocardiae. London: Academie Press Ltd; 1976:386-417.
35. Silva CL, Tincani I, Brandao Filho SL, Faccioli LH. Mouse cachexia induced by trehalose dimycolate from *Nocardia asteroides.* J Gen Microbiol. 1988;134:1629-1633.
36. Beaman BL. Differential binding of *Nocardia asteroides* in the murine lung and brain suggests multiple ligands on the nocardial surface. Infect Immun. 1996;64:4859-4862.
37. Beaman B. The cell wall as a determinant of pathogenicity in Nocardia: The role of L-forms in pathogenesis. In: Ortiz-Ortiz L, Bojalil LF, Yakeloff V, eds. Biological, Biochemical and Biomedical Aspects of Actinomycetes. Orlando, Fla: Academic Press Inc; 1984:89-105.
38. Filice GA, Beaman BL, Krick JA, Remington JS. Effects of human neutrophils and monocytes on *Nocardia asteroides:* Failure of killing despite occurrence of the oxidative metabolic burst. J Infect Dis. 1980;142:432-438.
39. Davis-Scibienski C, Beaman BL. Interaction of *Nocardia asteroides* with rabbit alveolar macrophages: Association of virulence, viability, ultrastructural damage, and phagosome-lysosome fusion. Infect Immun. 1980;28:610-619.
40. Bourgeois L, Beaman BL. Probable L-forms of *Nocardia asteroides* induced in cultured mouse peritoneal macrophages. Infect Immun. 1974;9:576-590.
41. Black CM, Beaman BL, Donovan RM, Goldstein E. Effect of virulent and less virulent strains of *Nocardia asteroides* on acid-phosphatase activity in alveolar and peritoneal macrophages maintained in vitro. J Infect Dis. 1983;148:117-124.
42. Beaman BL, Smathers M. Interaction of *Nocardia asteroides* with cultured rabbit alveolar macrophages. Infect Immun. 1976;13:1126-1131.
43. Beaman BL, Scates SM. Role of L-forms of *Nocardia caviae* in the development of chronic mycetomas in normal and immunodeficient murine models. Infect Immun. 1981;33:893-907.
44. Buchanan AM, Davis DC, Pedersen NC, Beaman BL. Recovery of microorganisms from synovial and pleural fluids of animals using hyperosmolar media. Vet Microbiol. 1982;7:19-33.
45. Beaman B. Nocardiosis: Role of the cell wall deficient state of *Nocardia.* In: Domingue GJ, ed. Cell Wall Defective Bacteria: Basic Principles and Clinical Significance. Reading, Mass: Addison-Wesley Publishing Co Inc; 1990:231-255.
46. Black CM, Beaman BL, Donovan RM, Goldstein E. Intracellular acid phosphatase content and ability of different macrophage populations to kill *Nocardia asteroides.* Infect Immun. 1985;47:375-383.
47. Beaman BL, Scates SM, Moring SE, et al. Purification and properties of a unique superoxide dismutase from *Nocardia asteroides.* J Biol Chem. 1983;258:91-96.
48. Beaman L, Beaman BL. Monoclonal antibodies demonstrate that superoxide dismutase contributes to protection of *Nocardia asteroides* within the intact host. Infect Immun. 1990;58:3122-3128.
49. Kusunose E, Ichihara K, Noda Y, Kusunose M. Superoxide dismutase from *Mycobacterium tuberculosis.* J Biochem (Tokyo). 1976;80:1343-1352.
50. Beaman BL, Ogata SA. Ultrastructural analysis of attachment to and penetration of capillaries in the murine pons, midbrain, thalamus, and hypothalamus by *Nocardia asteroides.* Infect Immun. 1993;61:955-965.
51. Beaman L, Beaman BL. Differences in the interactions of *Nocardia asteroides* with macrophage, endothelial, and astrocytoma cell lines. Infect Immun. 1994;62:1787-1798.
52. Licon-Trillo A, Angeles Castro-Corona M, Salinas-Carmona MC. Immunogenicity and biophysical properties of a *Nocardia brasiliensis* protease involved in pathogenesis of mycetoma. FEMS Immunol Med Microbiol. 2003;37:37-44.
53. Tam S, Barry DP, Beaman L, Beaman BL. Neuroinvasive *Nocardia asteroides* GUH-2 induces apoptosis in the substantia nigra in vivo and dopaminergic cells in vitro. Exp Neurol. 2002;177:453-460.
54. Kohbata S, Beaman BL. L-dopa-responsive movement disorder caused by *Nocardia asteroides* localized in the brains of mice. Infect Immun. 1991;59:181-191.
55. Kuipers S, Aerts PC, van Dijk H. Differential microorganism-induced mannose-binding lectin activation. FEMS Immunol Med Microbiol. 2003;36:33-39.
56. Schiff TA, McNeil MM, Brown JM. Cutaneous *Nocardia farcinica* infection in a non-immunocompromised patient: case report and review. Clin Infect Dis. 1993;16:756-760.

57. Desmond EP, Flores M. Mouse pathogenicity studies of *Nocardia asteroides* complex species and clinical correlation with human isolates. FEMS Microbiol Lett. 1993;110:281-284.

58. Ruimy R, Riegel P, Carlotti A, et al. *Nocardia pseudobrasiliensis* sp. nov., a new species of *Nocardia* which groups bacterial strains previously identified as *Nocardia brasiliensis* and associated with invasive diseases. Int J Syst Bacteriol. 1996;46:259-264.

59. McNeil MM, Brown JM, Georghiou PR, et al. Infections due to *Nocardia transvalensis:* Clinical spectrum and antimicrobial therapy. Clin Infect Dis. 1992;15:453-463.

60. Forbes GM, Harvey FA, Philpott-Howard JN, et al. Nocardiosis in liver transplantation: Variation in presentation, diagnosis and therapy. J Infect. 1990;20:11-19.

61. Kim J, Minamoto GY, Grieco MH. Nocardial infection as a complication of AIDS: Report of six cases and review. Rev Infect Dis. 1991;13:624-629.

62. Niedt GW, Schinella RA. Acquired immunodeficiency syndrome. Clinicopathologic study of 56 autopsies. Arch Pathol Lab Med. 1985;109:727-734.

63. Mahgoub ES. Agents of mycetoma. In: Mandell GL, Bennett JE, Dolin R, eds. Principles and Practices of Infectious Diseases. New York: Churchill Livingstone; 1995:2327-2330.

64. Kramer MR, Uttamchandani RB. The radiographic appearance of pulmonary nocardiosis associated with AIDS. Chest. 1990;98:382-385.

65. Lucas SB, Hounnou A, Peacock C, et al. Nocardiosis in HIV-positive patients: An autopsy study in West Africa. Tuber Lung Dis. 1994;75:301-307.

66. Uttamchandani RB, Daikos GL, Reyes RR, et al. Nocardiosis in 30 patients with advanced human immunodeficiency virus infection: Clinical features and outcome. Clin Infect Dis. 1994;18:348-353.

67. Javaly K, Horowitz HW, Wormser GP. Nocardiosis in patients with human immunodeficiency virus infection. Report of 2 cases and review of the literature. Medicine (Baltimore). 1992;71:128-138.

68. Farina C, Boiron P, Goglio A, Provost F. Human nocardiosis in northern Italy from 1982 to 1992. Northern Italy Collaborative Group on Nocardiosis. Scand J Infect Dis. 1995;27:23-27.

69. Boiron P, Provost F, Chevrier G, Dupont B. Review of nocardial infections in France 1987 to 1990. Eur J Clin Microbiol Infect Dis. 1992;11:709-714.

70. Schaal KP, Lee HJ. Actinomycete infections in humans—A review. Gene. 1992;115:201-211.

71. Georghiou PR, Blacklock ZM. Infection with *Nocardia* species in Queensland. A review of 102 clinical isolates. Med J Aust. 1992;156:692-697.

72. Kontoyiannis DP, Ruoff K, Hooper DC. Nocardia bacteremia. Report of 4 cases and review of the literature. Medicine (Baltimore). 1998;77:255-267.

73. Lui WY, Lee AC, Que TL. Central venous catheter-associated *Nocardia* bacteremia. Clin Infect Dis. 2001;33:1613-1614.

74. Ashdown LR. An improved screening technique for isolation of *Nocardia* species from sputum specimens. Pathology. 1990;22:157-161.

75. Shawar RM, Moore DG, LaRocco MT. Cultivation of *Nocardia* spp. on chemically defined media for selective recovery of isolates from clinical specimens. J Clin Microbiol. 1990;28:508-512.

76. Vickers RM, Rihs JD, Yu VL. Clinical demonstration of isolation of *Nocardia asteroides* on buffered charcoal-yeast extract media. J Clin Microbiol. 1992;30:227-228.

77. Murray PR, Heeren RL, Niles AC. Effect of decontamination procedures on recovery of *Nocardia* spp. J Clin Microbiol. 1987;25:2010-2011.

78. Workman MR, Philpott-Howard J, Yates M, et al. Identification and antibiotic susceptibility of *Nocardia farcinica* and *N. nova* in the UK. J Med Microbiol. 1998;47:85-90.

79. Wallace RJ, Tsukamura M, Brown BA, et al. Cefotaxime-resistant *Nocardia asteroides* strains are isolates of the controversial species *Nocardia farcinica*. J Clin Microbiol. 1990;28:2726-2732.

80. Wallace RJ, Brown BA, Tsukamura M, et al. Clinical and laboratory features of *Nocardia nova*. J Clin Microbiol. 1991;29:2407-2411.

81. Biehle JR, Cavalieri SJ, Felland T, Zimmer BL. Novel method for rapid identification of *Nocardia* species by detection of preformed enzymes. J Clin Microbiol. 1996;34:103-107.

82. Muir DB, Pritchard RC. Use of the BioMerieux ID 32C yeast identification system for identification of aerobic actinomycetes of medical importance. J Clin Microbiol. 1997;35:3240-3243.

83. Steingrube VA, Brown BA, Gibson JL, et al. DNA amplification and restriction endonuclease analysis for differentiation of 12 species and taxa of *Nocardia,* including recognition of four new taxa within the *Nocardia asteroides* complex. J Clin Microbiol. 1995;33: 3096-3101.

84. Wilson RW, Steingrube VA, Brown BA, Wallace RJ. Clinical application of PCR-restriction enzyme pattern analysis for rapid identification of aerobic actinomycete isolates. J Clin Microbiol. 1998;36:148-152.

85. Salinas-Carmona MC, Castro-Corona MA, Sepulveda-Saavedra J, Perez LI. Monoclonal antibodies to P24 and P61 immunodominant antigens from *Nocardia brasiliensis*. Clin Diagn Lab Immunol. 1997;4:133-137.

86. National Center for Clinical Laboratory Standards (NCCLS). Susceptibility testing of Mycobacteria, Nocardia and other aerobic actinomycetes. Tentative Standard M24-T2, NCCLS, 2000.

87. Biehle JR, Cavalieri SJ, Saubolle MA, Getsinger LJ. Comparative evaluation of the E test for susceptibility testing of *Nocardia* species. Diagn Microbiol Infect Dis. 1994;19:101-110.

88. Ambaye A, Kohner PC, Wollan PC, et al. Comparison of agar dilution, broth microdilution, disk diffusion, E-test, and BACTEC radiometric methods for antimicrobial susceptibility testing of clinical isolates of the *Nocardia asteroides* complex. J Clin Microbiol. 1997;35:847-852.

89. Smego RA, Moeller MB, Gallis HA. Trimethoprim-sulfamethoxazole therapy for *Nocardia* infections. Arch Intern Med. 1983;143:711-78.

90. Beaman BL, Boiron P, Beaman L, et al. Nocardia and nocardiosis. J Med Vet Mycol. 1992;30(Suppl 1):317-331.

91. Wallace RJ, Septimus EJ, Williams TW, et al. Use of trimethoprim-sulfamethoxazole for treatment of infections due to *Nocardia*. Rev Infect Dis. 1982;4:315-325.

92. Smego RA, Gallis HA. The clinical spectrum of *Nocardia brasiliensis* infection in the United States. Rev Infect Dis. 1984;6:164-180.

93. Berkey P, Moore D, Rolston K. In vitro susceptibilities of *Nocardia* species to newer antimicrobial agents. Antimicrob Agents Chemother. 1988;32:1078-1079.

94. Boiron P, Provost F. In-vitro susceptibility testing of *Nocardia* spp. and its taxonomic implication. J Antimicrob Chemother. 1988;22:623-629.

95. Clark NM, Braun DK, Pasternak A, Chenoweth CE. Primary cutaneous *Nocardia otitidiscaviarum* infection: Case report and review. Clin Infect Dis. 1995;20:1266-1270.

96. Bennett JE, Jennings AE. Factors influencing susceptibility of *Nocardia* species to trimethoprim-sulfamethoxazole. Antimicrob Agents Chemother. 1978;13:624-627.

97. Beaumont RJ. Trimethoprim as a possible therapy for nocardiosis and melioidosis. Med J Aust. 1970;2:1123-1127.

98. Maderazo EG, Quintiliani R. Treatment of nocardial infection with trimethoprim and sulfamethoxazole. Am J Med. 1974;57:671-675.

99. Smith PW, Steinkraus GE, Henricks BW, Madson EC. CNS nocardiosis: Response to sulfamethoxazole-trimethoprim. Arch Neurol. 1980;37:729-730.

100. Byrne E, Brophy BP, Perrett LV. Nocardia cerebral abscess: New concepts in diagnosis, management, and prognosis. J Neurol Neurosurg Psychiatry. 1979;42:1038-1045.

101. Wilson JP, Turner HR, Kirchner KA, Chapman SW. Nocardial infections in renal transplant recipients. Medicine (Baltimore). 1989;68:38-57.

102. Gordin FM, Simon GL, Wofsy CB, Mills J. Adverse reactions to trimethoprim-sulfamethoxazole in patients with the acquired immunodeficiency syndrome. Ann Intern Med. 1984;100:495-499.

103. Smith RM, Iwamoto GK, Richerson HB, Flaherty JP. Trimethoprim-sulfamethoxazole desensitization in the acquired immunodeficiency syndrome. Ann Intern Med. 1987;106:335.

104. Moylett EH, Pacheco SE, Brown-Elliott BA, et al. Clinical experience with linezolid for the treatment of nocardia infection. Clin Infect Dis. 2003;36:313-318.

105. Bradley PP, Warden GD, Maxwell JG, Rothstein G. Neutropenia and thrombocytopenia in renal allograft recipients treated with trimethoprim-sulfamethoxazole. Ann Intern Med. 1980;93:560-562.

106. Gombert ME, Aulicino TM, duBouchet L, et al. Therapy of experimental cerebral nocardiosis with imipenem, amikacin, trimethoprim-sulfamethoxazole, and minocycline. Antimicrob Agents Chemother. 1986;30:270-273.

107. Gombert ME, Berkowitz LB, Aulicino TM, duBouchet L. Therapy of pulmonary nocardiosis in immunocompromised mice. Antimicrob Agents Chemother. 1990;34: 1766-1768.

108. Threlkeld SC, Hooper DC. Update on management of patients with *Nocardia* infection. Curr Clin Top Infect Dis. 1997;17:1-23.

109. Goldstein FW, Hautefort B, Acar JF. Amikacin-containing regimens for treatment of nocardiosis in immunocompromised patients. Eur J Clin Microbiol. 1987;6:198-200.

110. Gombert ME, Aulicino TM. Synergism of imipenem and amikacin in combination with other antibiotics against *Nocardia asteroides*. Antimicrob Agents Chemother. 1983;24:810-811.

111. Gombert ME, duBouchet L, Aulicino TM, Berkowitz LB. Antimicrobial synergism in the therapy of experimental cerebral nocardiosis. J Antimicrob Chemother. 1989;24:39-43.

112. Filice GA, Simpson GL. Management of *Nocardia* infections. Curr Clin Top Infect Dis. 1984;5:49-64.

113. Choucino C, Goodman SA, Greer JP, et al. Nocardial infections in bone marrow transplant recipients. Clin Infect Dis. 1996;23:1012-1019.

114. Menendez R, Cordero PJ, Santos M, et al. Pulmonary infection with *Nocardia* species: A report of 10 cases and review. Eur Respir J. 1997;10:1542-1546.

115. Yazawa K, Mikami Y, Ohashi S, et al. In-vitro activity of new carbapenem antibiotics: Comparative studies with meropenem, L-627 and imipenem against pathogenic *Nocardia* spp. J Antimicrob Chemother. 1992;29:169-172.

116. Wiseman LR, Wagstaff AJ, Brogden RN, Bryson HM. Meropenem. A review of its antibacterial activity, pharmacokinetic properties and clinical efficacy. Drugs. 1995;50:73-101.

117. Wallace RJ, Nash DR, Johnson WK, et al. Beta-lactam resistance in *Nocardia brasiliensis* is mediated by beta-lactamase and reversed in the presence of clavulanic acid. J Infect Dis. 1987;156:959-966.

118. Steingrube VA, Wallace RJ, Brown BA, et al. Acquired resistance of *Nocardia brasiliensis* to clavulanic acid related to a change in beta-lactamase following treatment with amoxicillin-clavulanic acid. Antimicrob Agents Chemother. 1991;35:524-528.

119. Lopes CF. Trimethoprim-sulfamethoxazole in the treatment of actinomycotic mycetoma by *Nocardia brasiliensis*. Folha Medica. 1996;73:89-92.

120. Mamelak AN, Obana WG, Flaherty JF, Rosenblum ML. Nocardial brain abscess: treatment strategies and factors influencing outcome. Neurosurgery. 1994;35:622-631.

121. Geiseler PJ, Andersen BR. Results of therapy in systemic nocardiosis. Am J Med Sci. 1979;278:188-194.

122. Meier B, Metzger U, Muller F, et al. Successful treatment of a pancreatic *Nocardia asteroides* abscess with amikacin and surgical drainage. Antimicrob Agents Chemother. 1986;29:150-151.

123. Garlando F, Bodmer T, Lee C, et al. Successful treatment of disseminated nocardiosis complicated by cerebral abscess with ceftriaxone and amikacin: Case report. Clin Infect Dis. 1992;15:1039-1040.

124. van Burik JA, Hackman RC, Nadeem SQ, et al. Nocardiosis after bone marrow transplantation: A retrospective study. Clin Infect Dis. 1997;24:1154-1160.

125. Arduino RC, Johnson PC, Miranda AG. Nocardiosis in renal transplant recipients undergoing immunosuppression with cyclosporine. Clin Infect Dis. 1993;16:505-512.

126. Peterson PK, Ferguson R, Fryd DS, et al. Infectious diseases in hospitalized renal transplant recipients: A prospective study of a complex and evolving problem. Medicine (Baltimore). 1982;61:360-372.

127. Presant CA, Wiernik PH, Serpick AA. Factors affecting survival in nocardiosis. Am Rev Respir Dis. 1973;108:1444-1448.
128. Simpson GL, Stinson EB, Egger MJ, Remington JS. Nocardial infections in the immunocompromised host: A detailed study in a defined population. Rev Infect Dis. 1981;3:492-507.
129. Brown-Elliott BA, Ward SC, Crist CJ, et al. In vitro activities of linezolid against multiple *Nocardia* species. Antimicrob Agents Chemother. 2001;45:1295-1297.

CHAPTER **253**

Agents of Actinomycosis

THOMAS A. RUSSO

Actinomycosis is an indolent, slowly progressive infection caused by anaerobic or microaerophilic bacteria, primarily from the genus *Actinomyces,* which normally colonize the mouth, colon, and vagina. Disruption of mucosa may lead to infection of virtually any site. When the organisms invade tissue, they form tiny but visible clumps, called grains or sulfur granules. Lesions of actinomycosis are purulent foci surrounded by dense fibroses. Clinical presentations are myriad. Once common in the preantibiotic era, today the incidence of actinomycosis is diminished and, as a result, so is its timely recognition.[1] It has been called "the most misdiagnosed disease," and it has been stated that "no disease is so often missed by experienced clinicians."[2] Actinomycosis remains a diagnostic challenge. Three clinical presentations that should prompt consideration of this unique infection include (1) the combination of chronicity, progression across tissue boundaries, and masslike features, which mimics malignancy (with which it is often confused); (2) the development of a sinus tract, which may spontaneously resolve and recur; and (3) a refractory or relapsing infection after a short course of therapy, because cure of established actinomycosis requires prolonged treatment. An awareness of the full spectrum of disease manifestations will expedite diagnosis and treatment and minimize unnecessary surgical interventions and morbidity and mortality that all too often occur with actinomycosis.

ETIOLOGIC AGENTS

Actinomycosis is most commonly caused by the gram-positive higher bacterium *Actinomyces israelii.* Additional species that are established but less common causes of actinomycosis include *A. naeslundii/viscosus* complex,[3-7] *A. odontolyticus,*[8-11] *A. meyeri,*[12] and *A. gerencseriae* (formerly *A. israelii* serotype II). Although *Propionibacterium propionicum* (formerly *Arachnia propionica*) has been described to cause actinomycosis,[13,14] recent reports primarily describe this pathogen as causing lacrimal canaliculitis.[15,16]

Until recently, classification of *Actinomyces* spp. was based on differences in phenotypic testing (see "Diagnosis"). However, advances in microbiologic taxonomy, using genotypic methods such as comparative 16S ribosomal RNA (rRNA) gene sequencing or DNA probes, have demonstrated that certain "classic" *Actinomyces* species were misclassified within the genera.[16] These methods have also led to the identification of several new *Actinomyces* species from both human and animal specimens and the reclassification of some actinomycetes as *Arcanobacterium* spp. or *Actinobaculum* spp.[16,17] Although their role in causing human disease has not always been optimally established, an increasing body of data supports that *A. europaeus,*[16-19] *A. neuii,*[19,20] *A. radingae,*[16,17,19,21] *A. graevenitzii, A. turicensis,*[16,17,19,21] *Arcanobacterium (Actinomyces) pyogenes,*[22,23] *Arcanobacterium (Actinomyces) bernardiae,*[24,25] *A. funkei,*[19,26,27] *A. lingnae,*[19] *A. housto-*

nensis,[19] and *A. cardiffensis*[28] are capable of causing a variety of human infections, including the syndrome of actinomycosis.[16] Although *Eubacterium* species have been reported to cause pelvic disease in association with intrauterine contraceptive devices (IUCDs) and "lumpy jaw,"[29,30] additional reports would be desirable to confirm the species of this genus as agents of actinomycosis.

Despite some conflicting reports,[7,31,32] the bulk of evidence supports the concept that most if not all actinomycotic infections are polymicrobial in nature.[1,33,34] Although monomicrobial infections undoubtedly occur, inadequate bacteriologic evaluation or diagnoses made on clinical or pathologic grounds will result in a failure to identify concomitant bacterial species. *Actinobacillus actinomycetemcomitans, Eikenella corrodens, Fusobacterium, Bacteroides, Capnocytophaga, Staphylococcus, Streptococcus,* and Enterobacteriaceae have been commonly isolated in various combinations depending on the site of the infection. The contribution of these additional isolates to the pathogenesis of actinomycosis is difficult to assess; however, it seems reasonable to consider them as being potential copathogens when designing therapeutic regimens.

EPIDEMIOLOGY

In 1890 Bostroem reported culturing an aerobic organism responsible for actinomycosis from grain, grasses, and soil. This resulted in the misconception that actinomycosis is an exogenous infection and that chewing grass or straw or occupations such as farming were risk factors. This myth, though long in dying, has been dispelled. The agents of actinomycosis have been clearly established as members of the endogenous flora of mucous membranes. The frequency of oral cavity colonization with *Actinomyces* is nearly 100% by 2 years of age.[35] It is also often cultured from the gastrointestinal tract, bronchi, and female genital tract.[36] It has never been cultured from nature, and there are no documented cases of person-to-person transmission.[37] Although the normal habitats for the more recently identified *Actinomyces* spp. have not been optimally defined, data to date suggests that these species are also members of the endogenous oral, gastrointestinal, and genital flora.[19]

Infection may occur in individuals of all ages. The peak incidence of actinomycosis is reported to be in the mid-decades, with cases in individuals younger than 10 and older than 60 years being less frequent.[38] Nearly all series have reported males to be infected more frequently than females, at an approximately 3:1 ratio.[1,32,38-41] Plausible, but unproven explanations for this discordance include poorer dental hygiene and increased oral trauma in males.[38,42]

Studies on the occurrence of actinomycosis estimated a yearly incidence of 1:100,000 in the Netherlands and Germany in the 1960s and 1:300,000 in the Cleveland area during the 1970s, making this disease uncommon but not rare.[38] Its frequency is undoubtedly diminished since the preantibiotic era, when this disease was not only common but more malignant in nature. Improved dental hygiene and early antimicrobial treatment of infections prior to the development of a characteristic actinomycotic syndrome are likely contributing factors. However, individuals or populations that do not have access to dental and/or medical care are undoubtedly at higher risk than the population at large in this country. Furthermore, many unrecognized cases probably occur, especially oral-cervicofacial disease, that are successfully treated empirically.

PATHOGENESIS AND PATHOLOGY

A pivotal step in the pathogenesis of actinomycosis is disruption of the mucosal barrier. Oral and cervicofacial disease is frequently associated with dental procedures, trauma, oral surgery, and head and neck radiotherapy or oncologic surgical procedures.[43,44] Likewise, pulmonary infections often arise in the setting of aspiration, and abdominal infection is usually preceded by conditions that result in loss of mucosal integrity, such as gastrointestinal surgery, diverticulitis, appendicitis, or foreign bodies (e.g., fish bones).[1,38,39] Recognition of factors that enable bacterial entry into deep tissues, however, may be absent.[32] The lack of such a history should not prevent consideration of this disease when the clinical circumstance is appropriate.

Other bacterial species concomitantly present have been designated "companion microbes." They may serve as copathogens by aiding in the inhibition of host defenses or by reducing oxygen tension. The difficulty in establishing an animal model of infection with *Actinomyces* alone and enhancement of infection by coinoculation of *E. corrodens* support the concept that additional organisms are important for the initiation of infection.[45] Further, coaggregation of *Actinomyces* and *Streptococcus* spp. occurs and results in increased resistance to phagocytosis and killing.[46]

An acute inflammatory phase manifested by a painful, cellulitic reaction is occasionally observed with oral-cervicofacial disease or with soft tissue infection elsewhere in the body. The chronic phase of this disease is more often seen.[32,47] Classic disease is characterized as a densely fibrotic lesion that undergoes slow, contiguous spread and ignores tissue planes. However, no studies have addressed the factor (? bacterial and/or host) responsible for the unique pathogenesis of this disease. Lesions usually appear as either single or multiple indurated swellings. As the lesion matures, it becomes soft and fluctuant and suppurates centrally. The fibrous walls of the mass have been characteristically described as "wooden" and, in the absence of suppuration, have been frequently confused with neoplasms. This extensive fibrosis, which is one of the hallmarks of this disease, may be minimal, especially in pulmonary and central nervous system lesions. Given time, sinus tracts will often extend from the abscess to either the skin or adjacent organs or bone, depending on the location of the lesion. Sinus tracts can spontaneously close and then re-form. Overlying skin may assume a red to bluish hue. Hematogenous dissemination can occur from these local sites and occasionally be fulminant, although in the antibiotic era this clinical syndrome has become rare.[48]

Microscopically, lesions have an outer zone of granulation, consisting of collagen fibers and fibroblasts. There is a central purulent loculation that contains neutrophils that surround the sulfur granules present. Granules are conglomerations of organisms and are virtually diagnostic of this disease. One to six may be present per loculation, and they range from microscopic to macroscopic in size (see "Diagnosis"). As many as 50 loculations may be present per lesion, and these loculations are separated by granulation tissue or foamy macrophages and may undergo coalescence. Lymphocytes and plasma cells are usually present, and eosinophils were seen in 15% of abscesses. Multinucleated giant cells were occasionally seen, primarily in pulmonary lesions, but they have also been described in disease elsewhere.[32] Suppuration is a constant feature of active disease but may not be present in all areas of the lesion.

The association of pelvic actinomycosis with IUCDs suggests that at least this foreign body contributes to pathogenesis. Associations with actinomycosis and foreign material elsewhere are less strong. Several reports describe periapical actinomycosis associated with root canal fillings,[49] mandibular osteomyelitis associated with wire used in the treatment of a fracture,[39,50] and infection of the tongue in the presence of a foreign body.[51] *Actinomyces* infecting prosthetic joints, through presumed hematogenous spread, is rare but reported.[52,53] Whether aspirated or ingested foreign bodies contribute to pathogenesis via mucosal disruption, or facilitate the growth and survival of *Actinomyces,* or both, is unclear.

Cases of actinomycosis have been described in the setting of steroid use,[54] acute leukemia during chemotherapy,[55,56] lung and renal transplantation,[11,57] and human immunodeficiency virus infection.[58-66] Ulcerative mucosal lesions (herpes simplex virus, cytomegalovirus, chemotherapy) and abnormalities in host defenses likely facilitated the development of actinomycosis in these cases; however, it remains unclear which arm(s) of the host defense are critical in preventing or controlling this infection and the degree to which (if at all) the incidence of infection is increased in these settings.

CLINICAL MANIFESTATIONS

Oral-Cervicofacial Disease

Actinomycosis most commonly occurs and is best recognized in this location. Its frequency varies in different series, ranging from a low of 11% to a high of 97.7% with a mean of 55%.[38,47] Oral-cervicofacial disease probably accounts for even a greater majority because it is underrepresented in autopsy and referral center series.

Oral-cervicofacial disease can present as a soft tissue swelling, an abscess, a mass lesion,[38,39,67] or occasionally an ulcerative lesion.[68,69] The diagnosis of actinomycosis should not only be considered in the classic setting of a painless mass at the angle of the jaw (Fig. 253-1)[114] but should be included in the differential diagnosis of any lesion in the head and neck region. When lesions appear solid, neoplasm is the usual diagnostic consideration.[70] Soft tissue infections of the head and neck may also present as chronic, recurring abscesses. This common scenario of temporary improvement with a short course of empirical antibiotic therapy, followed by relapse, should always arouse suspicion for actinomycosis, regardless of the location.[41] As the disease spreads to adjacent structures, there is little regard for normal tissue planes. Lymphatic spread and associated lymphadenopathy are uncommon. Computed tomography (CT) or magnetic resonance images usually reveal an infiltrative, well- or ill-defined mass with inflammatory changes.[71] Extension to any contiguous structure may occur, including the carotid artery, orbital cavity, cranium, cervical spine, trachea, or thorax.[72-75] Pain, fever, and leukocytosis are variably present.[38,39]

Periapical and endodontic infection caused by *Actinomyces* probably occurs far more frequently than is recognized.[76-78] Appropriate dental intervention and antibiotic therapy usually result in cure before more extensive disease develops.

The most common location for diagnosed actinomycosis is the perimandibular region. Periapical infection or trauma is often, but not always, the inciting event. The classic lesion located at the angle of the jaw is the most frequent location (submandibular) but the cheek, submental space, retromandibular space, and temporomandibular joint may be affected.[79-84] As noted, a hallmark of this disease is the potential for unrestricted contiguous extension. Spread to the skin may result in sinus tract(s) formation, and these can spontaneously close and open elsewhere. The overlying skin often develops a bluish or purplish red hue. Involvement of the muscles of mastication frequently occurs, resulting in trismus.[1,70] Associated mandibular periostitis or osteomyelitis may also be present but is surprisingly infrequent.[85] A lytic lesion, rarefaction with sclerosis, or sclerosis alone may be seen, and this latter pattern may be confused with tumor.[86,87]

Maxillary disease, including osteomyelitis, occurs less frequently.[88] Associated soft tissue lesions[10] and maxillary sinus or cutaneous fistulas, or both, can occur. Maxillary and ethmoid sinusitis may present as

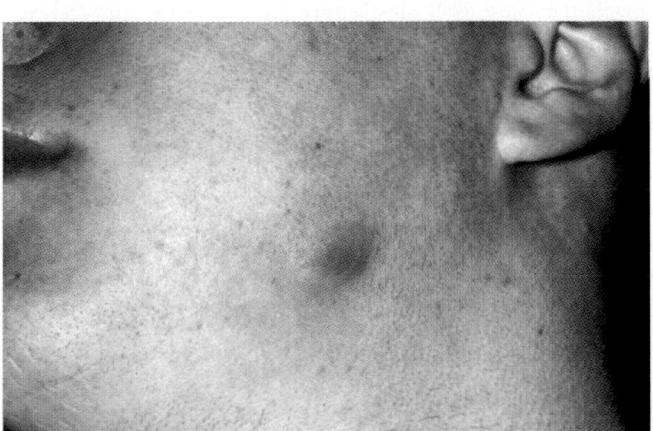

FIGURE 253-1. Submandibular actinomycotic abscess.

isolated disease or can be concomitant with infection of the maxilla.[89] The hard palate may also be involved, with presentation as a mass lesion.[1]

Isolated masses or ulcerative lesions can also occur in the tongue,[69,90] vallecula,[91] nasal septum,[59] nasopharynx,[92] soft tissues of the head and neck,[38,93] salivary glands,[94-96] patent thyroglossal duct,[97] thyroid,[98,99] branchial cleft cyst,[100] and hypopharynx, larynx, or both.[69,101] It is unclear whether *Actinomyces* causes tonsillitis. Although *Actinomyces* is frequently isolated and sulfur granules are occasionally identified in the setting of tonsillitis or tonsillar hypertrophy, the absence of a pathologic tissue reaction characteristic of actinomycosis and the isolation of *Actinomyces* from normal tonsillar tissue make a causal role of *Actinomyces* unclear.[102,103] Mass lesions in tonsils resulting from actinomycosis and expectoration of debris from tonsillar involvement have been described.[104,105]

Infection of the external ear and temporal bone may occur from the spread of facial disease. Actinomycosis is also an uncommon but important cause of primary otitis media; untreated cases may result in fatal extension into the mastoid and then the central nervous system. It is characterized by numerous episodes of otitis media that transiently respond to conventional short course therapy and resistance to myringotomy. Diagnosis can be made by the pathologic and microbiologic examination of infected material from the affected middle ear that may appear to be a cholesteatoma.[106-108]

Actinomyces and more commonly *P. propionicum* can cause lacrimal caniculiticis.[15,16] *Actinomyces* has also caused postoperative endophthalmitis after intraocular lens implant.[109,110] Rarely, secondary extension into the orbit from infected maxillary or ethmoid sinuses can occur.[39]

Thoracic Disease

Thoracic involvement comprises approximately 15% of cases of actinomycosis.[111] Aspiration of organisms from the oropharynx is the usual source of infection. Direct extension may occur from disease in either the head and neck or abdominal cavity; however, such secondary spread has become increasingly uncommon since the advent of efficacious antimicrobial therapy.[40,111]

The most common clinical presentation is an indolent, slowly progressive process that involves some combination of the pulmonary parenchyma and pleural space. Chest pain, fever, weight loss, and less commonly hemoptysis are prominent symptoms, and a cough, when present, is variably productive.[40,112] There are no specific radiographic manifestations and any lobe may be involved. The usual appearance is either a mass lesion or pneumonia with or without pleural involvement (Fig. 253-2).[113,114] The presence of an air bronchogram within a mass lesion (the open bronchus sign) should suggest the possibility of a non-neoplastic process, such as actinomycosis.[115] Pleural thickening, effusion, or empyema is present in greater than 50% of cases of thoracic actinomycosis (Fig. 253-2B). Rarely, actinomycosis may present as an isolated effusion.[116] The spontaneous drainage of an empyema through the chest wall should raise suspicion for this disease.[117] Cavitary disease may develop and is more readily detected by CT scans, because multiple small cavities are more common than large ones.[118] Hilar adenopathy may be present.[119] Pulmonary disease that extends across fissures or pleura (Fig. 253-2C), involves the mediastinum, or has contiguous bony disease should suggest actinomycosis and is also more readily appreciated by CT.[114,115,118] Extension to the chest wall with the development of a soft tissue mass, a draining sinus, or both is a telltale sign when present (Fig. 253-2A). In the absence of this classic scenario, however, thoracic actinomycosis is almost never suspected. It is mistaken for either malignant disease,[120] with the diagnosis made by the pathologist postresection, or for an empyema or pneumonia secondary to more usual causes. Tuberculosis, nocardiosis, histoplasmosis, blastomycosis, cryptococcosis, mixed anaerobic infection, bronchogenic carcinoma, lymphoma, mesothelioma, and pulmonary infarction are among the entities confused with pulmonary actinomycosis.

Mediastinal actinomycosis is an uncommon event. The structures within the anterior or posterior mediastinum and the heart can be involved alone or in combination, resulting in a diverse array of clinical presentations. Infection usually results from contiguous spread from the thorax, but can arise from perforation of the esophagus, chest trauma, or extension of head and neck or abdominal disease.[121] Involvement of cardiac structures represents the majority of mediastinal infections reported. Pericarditis is most common and may be initially asymptomatic or hemodynamically insignificant, but if allowed to progress, cardiac tamponade and constrictive or adhesive pericarditis will develop.[122] Less frequently, myocardial or endocardial infection occurs, either via extension from the pericardium or by initial hematogenous seeding of the endocardium.[123,124] Anterior mediastinal involvement may present as an isolated mass or rarely superior vena cava syndrome.[125,126] Concomitant anterior chest wall infection is common, but associated sternal disease is rare.[111] Posterior mediastinal involvement may result in paraspinous muscle and soft tissue disease, esophageal fistula, or encasement or vertebral body infection, or both. Because of the slow progression of the disease, both vertebral body destruction and new bone formation occur, resulting in a mottled, sawtoothed or honeycombed appearance of bone on x-ray. The transverse processes, and with disease progression the pedicles and spinous processes, are similarly involved as the bodies, in contrast to their usual sparing with tuberculosis. The corresponding posterior ends of ribs are usually involved, and a typical wavy periostitis may be present, but, unlike tuberculosis, vertebral body collapse and disk space narrowing are not usually seen.[115] Extension to the epidural space with spinal cord compression may occur.[127] Primary esophageal disease in the setting of acquired immunodeficiency syndrome has also been described.[60,128]

Other less common manifestations of thoracic actinomycosis include multiple pulmonary nodules,[129] miliary disease,[115,130] and endobronchial lesions, which may be associated with aspirated foreign bodies.[131-133] Primary breast disease either presents as a persistent or recurring abscess(es) or mimics malignancy,[134] and infection of a mammary prosthesis has also been described.[135]

Abdominal Disease

The proportion of reported cases involving the abdomen averages 20%, with a range of 0% to 63%.[38,39,41] Any disease or event that allows the agents of actinomycosis to breach the gastrointestinal mucosa has the potential to be complicated by this infection. The majority of abdominal infections are due to this mechanism, although the inciting conditions are not always apparent. However, it is important to note that ascension from the female genital tract of IUCD-associated actinomycosis has become an increasingly recognized source of abdominal disease.[136] Hematogenous dissemination and extension from the thorax are other portals of entry. As a consequence of the flow of peritoneal fluid, direct extension of primary disease, or both, virtually any abdominal organ, region, or space can be involved either alone or in combination regardless of the initial site of infection. Abdominal actinomycosis is perhaps the greatest diagnostic challenge. This infection is rarely considered prior to the clinical laboratory or pathologist establishing the diagnosis. Months to years usually pass from the time of the inciting event to clinical recognition of this indolent disease.[32] Associated symptoms are generally nonspecific, with fever, weight loss, change in bowel habits, abdominal pain, or a sensation of a mass being most common. Abdominal actinomycosis usually presents either as an abscess or as a firm to hard mass lesion that is often fixed to the underlying tissue and mistaken for tumor.[137] Sinus tracts with drainage from either the abdominal wall or perianal region may develop (Fig. 253-3).[138,139] CT findings usually demonstrate a mass lesion with focal areas of decreased attenuation or a thick-walled cystic mass, both of which frequently enhance with contrast. Lesions often appear invasive, suggesting a tumor, but associated lymphadenopathy is uncommon.[140,141] With colonic involvement, mucosal nodules with associated inflammation may be observed.[142]

Appendicitis, especially with perforation, is the most common predisposing event and is associated with 65% of the cases of abdominal actinomycosis.[143] As a result, the right iliac fossa is the most frequent primary site of abdominal disease and right-sided abdominal infection

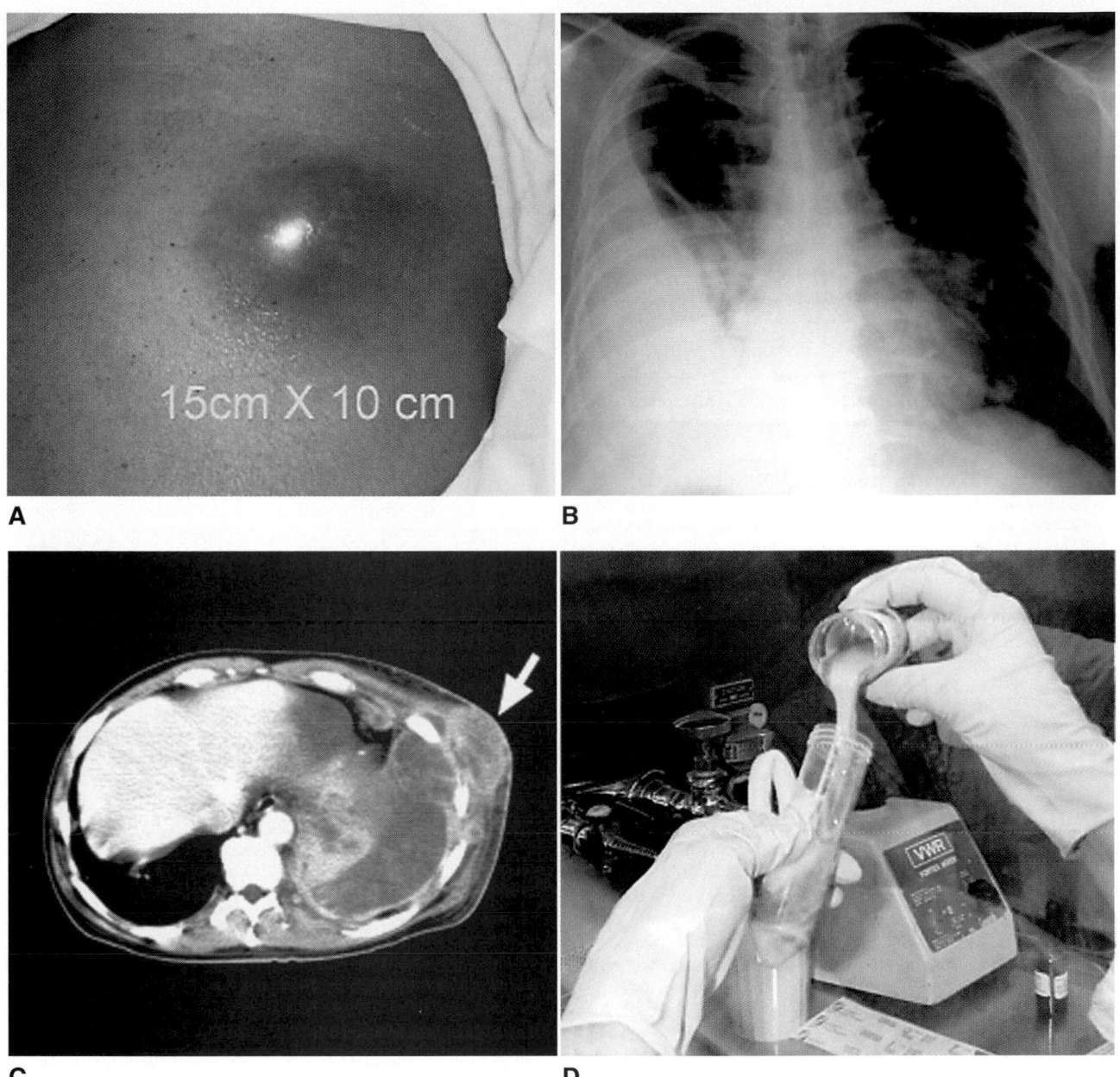

FIGURE 253-2. A, Chest wall mass. **B** and **C,** Chest x-ray and computed tomography demonstrating the pulmonary infiltrate, pleural effusion, and pleural and chest wall extension (*arrow*). **D,** Purulent pleural fluid obtained from aspiration. *(Courtesy of Dr. C.-B. Hsiao.)*

is more common than left. It is also one of the potential inciting events for tuboovarian infection. Diverticulitis or foreign body perforation of the transverse or sigmoid colon tends to be associated with left-sided disease and accounts for 7.3% of cases, a surprisingly low percentage considering the incidence of diverticulitis. The loss of gastric mucosal integrity from peptic ulcer disease or gastrectomy may result in infection and is associated with 4.4% of cases. Isolated esophageal and gastric disease has also been described.[144,145] Additional associations include antecedent bowel surgery, typhoid fever, amebic dysentery, chicken or fish bones, trauma, and hemorrhagic pancreatitis.[39,146] Interestingly, actinomycosis rarely develops as a consequence of Crohn's disease or ulcerative colitis.

Perirectal or perianal disease may result from extension of pelvic infection or, less commonly, more distant disease. Primary disease occurs with either local mucosal damage or infection of anal crypts. The most common presentation is single or multiple perianal abscesses, sinus or fistula tract formation, or both. Infiltrating masses may develop

in the buttock, posterior thigh, scrotum, or inguinal region.[147,148] Recurrent disease over months to years or wounds that fail to heal after drainage or fistulotomy are clues that should suggest actinomycosis, particularly in the absence of documented inflammatory bowel disease. Strictures of the rectum can also occur and cause an alteration of bowel habits, mimicking primary bowel or metastatic prostatic or pelvic tumors.[149] This presentation is most often due to extension of pelvic disease.

Hepatic infection was present in 5% of all cases of actinomycosis[32] and in 16% (19 of 122) of abdominal disease cases.[146] Spread to the liver occurs via extension from a contiguous abdominal focus or hematogenously from more distant but established abdominal or extraabdominal foci. A case associated with a pancreatic stent has also been described.[150] Hepatic involvement is common in disseminated actinomycosis. The entity of primary or isolated disease is presumably hematogenous seeding from cryptic foci. Single or multiple abscesses or lesions suggesting neoplasia are the usual presentation.[151] Generally

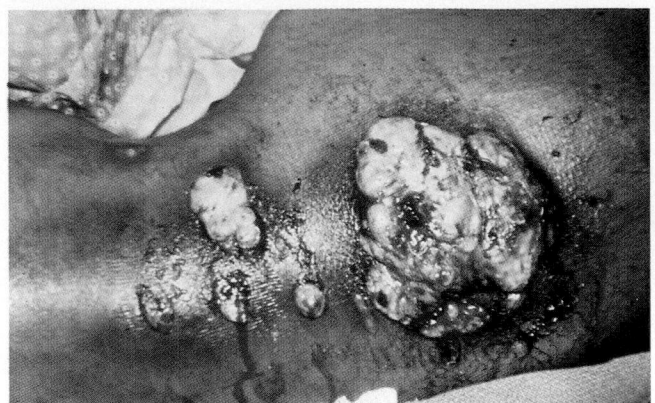

FIGURE 253-3. Multiple draining sinuses of the right flank secondary to intra-abdominal actinomycosis associated with appendicitis.

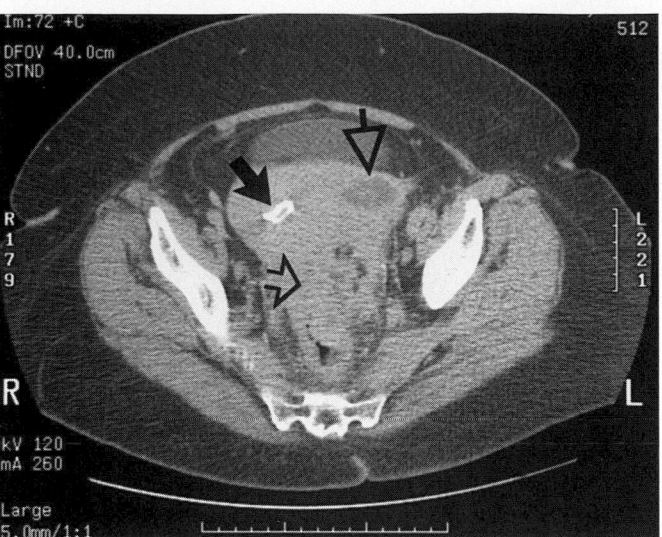

FIGURE 253-4. IUCD-associated pelvic actinomycosis. An IUCD encased by endometrial fibrosis (*solid arrowhead*), paraendometrial fibrosis (*open arrow*), and an area of suppuration (*open arrowhead*) can be appreciated.

a more indolent course is observed compared to the more usual causes of pyogenic hepatic abscesses, but "companion organisms" may contribute to a more acute presentation.[152] Symptoms and laboratory findings often point to the right upper quadrant, but liver functions tests may be normal. The presently available imaging modalities and percutaneous diagnostic techniques have allowed for an increasing number of cases to be diagnosed without surgery. Uncommon presentations or sequelae of hepatic actinomycosis include cholangitis, portal vein occlusion/thrombosis, cholestasis, and extension into the thorax.[153-155]

All levels of the urogenital tract can be infected by the agents of actinomycosis. Renal involvement can occur as either a result of hematogenous dissemination from a cryptic or defined focus, or via direct extension within the pelvis, peritoneum, or thorax. The disease usually manifests as pyelonephritis, renal carbuncle, perinephric abscess, or tumor. Tuberculosis, neoplasm, or more usual bacterial agents are usually considered as the causative agents.[156,157] Hematuria and pyuria are often present, and *Actinomyces* can be successfully detected in the urine if appropriate stains and anaerobic cultures are performed.[158] Renal arteriography usually demonstrates a normal or diminished pattern of vascularization. Ureteric obstruction is most commonly a sequela of contiguous spread from abdominal disease and especially pelvic infection, and may lead to hydronephrosis and renal failure.[159-161] Because the incidence of pelvic disease appears to be increasing, this is presently the most likely site for urinary tract involvement.[162] Infiltration, compression or encasement of the bladder, a pubic mass, or vesicocolic, ileovesical, vesicouterine, or vesicocutaneous fistulas are usually a consequence of secondary involvement from pelvic infection[158,163,164] or occasionally from extension from the rectum.[165] Prostatic, testicular, and urachal involvement may also occur.[166,167]

Actinomycosis of the gallbladder presenting as cholecystitis or suspected neoplasm can occur but is exceedingly rare,[168,169] as is pancreatic involvement.[170] "Primary" actinomycosis of the omentum, abdominal wall, and retroperitoneum has been reported, but the majority of these cases are likely due to secondary spread from a cryptic or obscured abdominal source.[171,172] Isolated peritonitis associated with peritoneal dialysis[173] has also been reported.

Pelvic Disease

Actinomycotic involvement of the pelvis may occur as a consequence of an intra-abdominal inciting event, such as appendicitis or rectal disease. However, the most common portal of entry is ascension from the uterus in association with the presence of any type of IUCD. This clinical syndrome was first described in conjunction with a "modern" IUCD by Henderson in 1973,[174] although cases had been previously described that were associated with pessaries, an endocervical contraceptive device, and a retained hairpin used for an abortion.[175,176] Since that time an increasing number of cases have been reported in the literature. Data from the Public Health Laboratory Service of England and Wales

suggest that the incidence of pelvic actinomycosis is increasing and that it represents an increasing proportion of actinomycosis overall, although increased recognition may be playing a role.[162] In a recent series, although it is unclear if all isolates caused actinomycosis, the greatest proportion of *Actinomyces* were isolated in the presence of an IUCD (30%, or 130 of 432 cases).[16] On average, an IUCD is in place for 8 years in pelvic actinomycosis–associated cases. Disease rarely develops when an IUCD has been in place for less than 1 year, and risk of infection likely increases with time.[177,178] Pelvic actinomycosis has presented months after the removal of the IUCD; therefore, a history of prior use is important when this disease is a diagnostic consideration.[179] Although the precise risk of IUCD-associated actinomycosis has not been quantitated, it would appear to be small.

Presentation is typically indolent, with fever, weight loss, abdominal pain, and abnormal vaginal bleeding or discharge being common symptoms. The earliest form of pelvic actinomycosis associated with IUCD may be an endometritis. A pelvic mass or uni- or bilateral tuboovarian abscesses represents the next stage of disease progression (Fig. 253-4).[17] Unfortunately diagnosis is often delayed. A "frozen pelvis" mimicking malignancy or endometriosis is commonly present by the time of recognition; however, magnetic resonance imaging may suggest actinomycosis.[137] Disease frequently involves the ureters, bladder, or both, resulting in hydroureter and hydronephrosis.[180] Rectal involvement is also common. Extension to the abdominal wall may lead to sinus tract development, and entrapment of small or large bowel may cause fistula or bowel obstruction. Occasionally, the ovaries and fallopian tubes are spared and disease is only evident in contiguous organs. Rarely, the presentation of acute peritonitis, disseminated peritoneal lesions, pelvic bone involvement, extension to the thorax, or hematogenous dissemination may occur.[178,181,182]

One of the management issues that has received considerable attention is whether screening cervical or endometrial specimens for the presence of *Actinomyces* or *Actinomyces*-like organisms (ALOs) can lead to the prevention of IUCD-associated pelvic actinomycosis. Papanicolaou-stained specimens, direct immunofluorescence using fluorescein isothiocyanate–labeled antisera against the agents of actinomycosis, and culture have been assessed to varying degrees for the detection of *Actinomyces* or ALOs.[178] Conflicting results from studies performed to date have made the sensitivity and specificity of these diagnostic modalities for the detection of *Actinomyces* unclear. Nonetheless, these studies have established that (1) in the presence of IUCDs, the prevalence and likely quantitation of *Actinomyces* increases; (2) prevalence is greater in women with IUCDs in place for 2 years or longer and probably increases with time thereafter; and (3) all types of IUCDs have been implicated.[178] However, it is not known whether the detection of *Actinomyces* represents early local disease or colonization, nor has the rate of invasive disease development in women with detectable *Actinomyces* been established. Further, a Papanicolaou smear may fail to detect ALOs even in the presence of active actinomycosis.[178] Although it has not been proven, endometrial disruption and an increased prevalence of endometrial colonization with the agents of actinomycosis as a result of IUCDs are undoubtedly crucial and probably necessary factors in the development of this disease. Considering the overall women-years of IUCD use and the limited number of reported cases of pelvic actinomycosis, the risk appears to be small, but the consequences of infection are significant. Therefore, in the absence of more quantitative data, it would appear prudent to remove IUCDs if symptoms of pain, abnormal bleeding, or discharge cannot be attributed to other pathogens, regardless of whether *Actinomyces* or ALOs are detected. A 14-day course of a penicillin or tetracycline should be given for treatment of possible early pelvic actinomycosis. The detection of *Actinomyces* or ALOs in the absence of symptoms warrants patient education and close follow-up but not removal of the IUCD, unless an equally suitable means of contraception can be agreed upon.[183]

Central Nervous System Disease

Actinomycosis of the central nervous system is rare. The source may be hematogenous, or it may develop through extension of oral-cervico-facial disease. In a recent review, the mean duration of symptoms prior to diagnosis was 2.1 months, longer than with most causes of central nervous system infections.[74,184] Brain abscess is the most common presentation. Headache and focal neurologic findings are the most common clinical features. Fever is variably present. Single or multiple abscesses may be present. The most frequent CT appearance is a ring-enhancing lesion with a thick wall that may be irregular or nodular. Multiloculation, edema, and contiguous areas of low attenuation may be present. These findings are also consistent with brain abscess and tumor.[185] Less commonly, solid nodular or mass lesions termed *actinomycetomas* or *actinomycotic granuloma* occur. A chronic meningitis may develop as a consequence of spread from a parameningeal focus, most commonly the middle ear or paranasal sinuses. Presentation may be acute, particularly with rupture of an abscess into the subarachnoid space, or chronic, with the cerebrospinal fluid having a normal or low glucose level, elevated protein, lymphocytic pleocytosis, and negative culture. Diagnosis can be made by microscopic examination or rarely by culture of cerebrospinal fluid.[186] Extension of disease from foci of cranial osteomyelitis, sinus, or middle ear disease can result in cranial epidural or subdural infection, or both.[187-189] Spinal epidural disease may occur from direct extension of abdominal, thoracic, or cervical disease, is usually associated with a contiguous osteomyelitis, and may result in spinal cord compression.[190,191] Cavernous sinus syndrome and spinal intrathecal infection have also been reported.[192-195]

Musculoskeletal Disease

Actinomycotic infection of the bone is usually a result of an adjacent soft tissue infection, but may also be associated with trauma (e.g., fracture of the mandible), osteoradionecrosis,[196] or hematogenous spread.[87] In the preantibiotic era, the unchecked spread of thoracic and abdominal disease resulted in vertebral infection being the most common site for osseous actinomycosis (see "Thoracic Disease"). Less commonly, hematogenous vertebral osteomyelitis may originate from an occult source and clinically resemble skeletal tuberculosis. Presently, the facial bones, particularly the mandible, are the most frequent site of involvement.[87] Actinomycosis of the skull, ribs, clavicle, sternum, scapula, or pelvis may also occur from extension of oral-facial, thoracic, or abdominal disease. The clinical and radiographic features of infection in these locations have been discussed earlier.

Infection of the extremities, although uncommon, often poses diagnostic difficulties. Blunt or penetrating trauma of the affected area is a frequent inciting event.[197] Some cases are a result of hematogenous dissemination from apparent or cryptic foci.[12,55,198-200] Skin, subcutaneous tissue, muscle, and bone may be involved alone or in various combinations. Cutaneous sinus tracts or abscesses are present in the majority of cases, as is bony involvement in the form of periostitis or acute or chronic osteomyelitis.[198] Presentation is usually indolent. Although actinomycotic infections of the lower extremities have been described as *mycetomas,* this term is best reserved for the group of infections designated as actinomycetoma.

Actinomycotic infections of hip and knee prostheses have been described in several reports.[52,53,201-203] Early presentations suggest that *Actinomyces* may be introduced perioperatively, whereas late presentations suggest hematogenous seeding from a cryptic distant site. Actinomycotic arthritis of the knee has developed in association with trauma or injection of hyaluronate,[204] or as a consequence of hematogenous seeding.[205] Actinomycosis is rarely a result of closed fist injury.[206]

Disseminated Disease

Although uncommon, all of the agents of actinomycosis are capable of hematogenous dissemination resulting in multiorgan involvement. *Actinomyces meyeri* appears to have the greatest capability of causing this syndrome. Disease in any location may serve as the source for spread. The lungs and liver are the most commonly affected organs, and the presentation of multiple nodules mimics disseminated malignancy. The kidneys, brain, spleen, skin, soft tissues of the extremities, and less commonly the heart valves may also be infected in various combinations. The clinical presentation may be surprisingly indolent when the extent of disease is appreciated.[12,55,199,207,208]

DIAGNOSIS

The diagnosis of actinomycosis, particularly when it mimics malignancy, is rarely considered. All too often the first mention of actinomycosis is from the pathologist after extensive surgery has been performed. An increasing body of evidence suggests that medical therapy alone is usually sufficient for cure, including extensive invasive disease. Therefore, the challenge for the clinician is to consider the possibility of actinomycosis so that this unique infection can be diagnosed in the least invasive fashion and unnecessary surgery can be avoided.[160,209] Clinical or radiographic presentations that suggest actinomycosis have been discussed previously. Fine-needle aspiration or biopsy and CT- or ultrasound-guided aspirations or biopsies are being successfully used to obtain clinical material for diagnosis.[184,209-215] Transbronchial biopsies have been less successful in providing diagnostic material for thoracic actinomycosis.[40,216] Surgery may be required for diagnostic purposes. Even when this diagnosis is considered, suitable sampling and handling of clinical specimens is necessary for confirmation. A combination of appropriate microbiologic, molecular, and pathologic studies will maximize the chances of success. The most important step for optimal microbiologic yield is the avoidance of any antimicrobial therapy prior to obtaining the specimen. The agents of actinomycosis are exceedingly sensitive to a wide variety of agents, and even a single dose can interfere with their isolation.

The bacteriologic identification of one of the agents of actinomycosis from a sterile site will confirm the diagnosis. However, the microbiologic identification of the agents of actinomycosis occurs in only a minority of cases.[32] Although 16S rRNA gene amplification and sequencing would be predicted to increase the sensitivity of diagnosis, the utilization of this approach is just beginning to be explored.[217] Because these organisms are normal inhabitants of the oral cavity and female genital tract, the identification of organisms alone, in the absence of sulfur granules or an appropriate clinical syndrome, from sputum, bronchial washings, and cervicovaginal secretions is of little significance.[36,218]

Although most strains of *Actinomyces* are microaerophilic or facultative (except *A. meyeri*), strict anaerobic processing and anaerobic growth should be utilized for primary isolation. The laboratory should

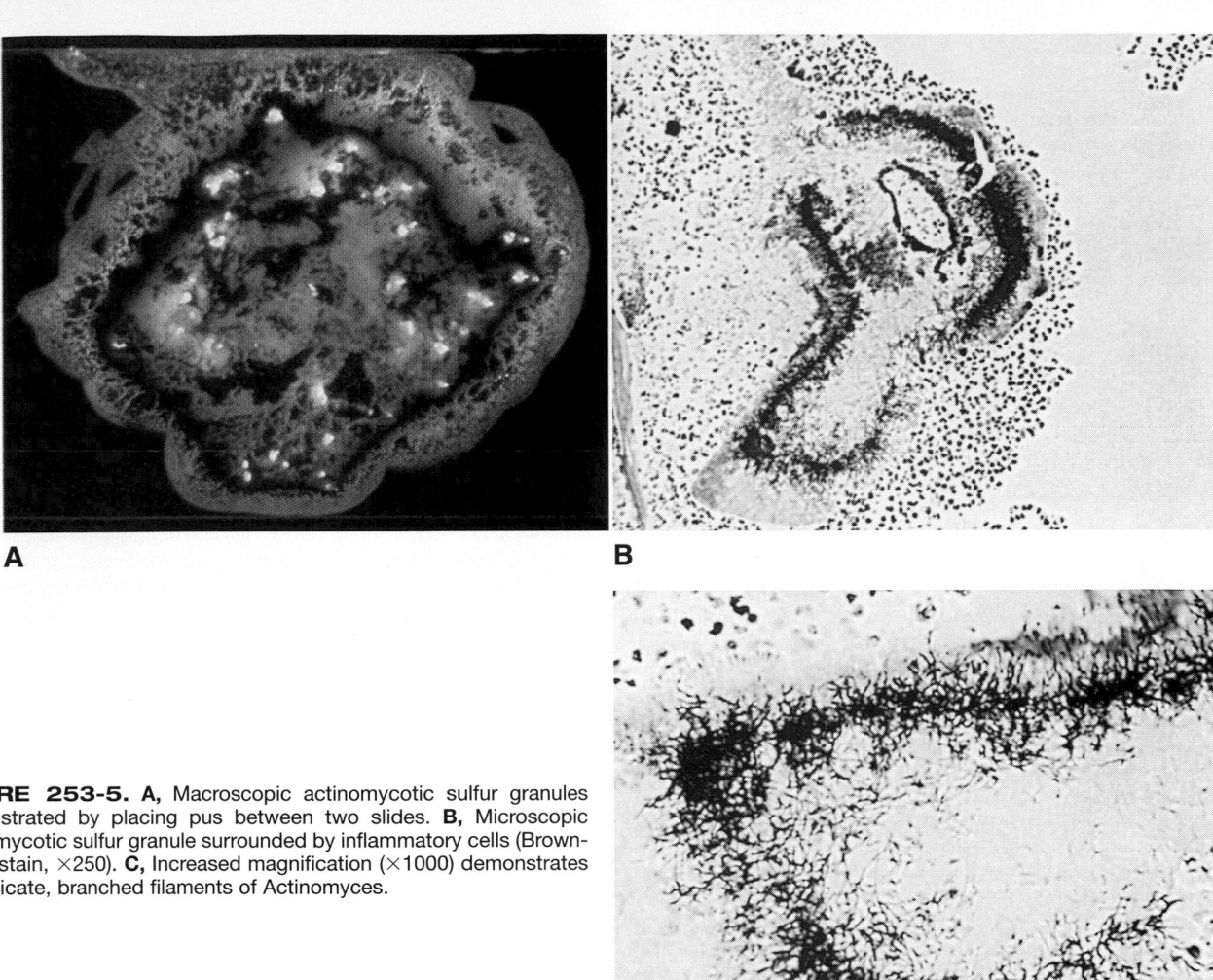

FIGURE 253-5. **A,** Macroscopic actinomycotic sulfur granules demonstrated by placing pus between two slides. **B,** Microscopic actinomycotic sulfur granule surrounded by inflammatory cells (Brown-Brenn stain, ×250). **C,** Increased magnification (×1000) demonstrates the delicate, branched filaments of Actinomyces.

receive specimens expeditiously or in anaerobic transport media. Tissue, pus, or sulfur granules are ideal, and swabs should be avoided. The microbiology laboratory should be alerted prior to receiving any specimen that may harbor the agents of actinomycosis. A Gram stain of the specimen is usually more sensitive than culture, especially if the patient has received prior antibiotics. If granules are identified, they should be washed and crushed between two slides for examination (Fig. 253-5A). The agents of actinomycosis are non–spore-forming rods. Except for *A. meyeri,* which is small and nonbranching, their usual appearance is that of branching, filamentous rods. Growth usually appears within 5 to 7 days, but primary isolation may take up to 2 to 4 weeks. Although specialized media are not required, the use of semi-elective media may increase isolation rates of *Actinomyces,* particularly when more rapidly growing organisms are also present.[219] *A. israelii* characteristically forms a "molar tooth" colony on agar and grows as clumps within broth. *A. odontolyticus* colonies usually appear as rust-brown or red colored. *Actinomyces* are indole negative. Traditional identification is based on these features in combination with tests for urease, catalase, gelatin hydrolysis, and fermentation of cellobiose, trehalose, and arabinose. Occasionally identification of metabolic products by gas-liquid chromatography is contributory.[220] However, classification of *Actinomyces* based on phenotypic tests may result in misidentification.[16] Sequencing or restriction analysis of amplified 16S ribosomal DNA can assist in resolving ambiguities in identification of

the non–spore forming, gram-positive rods.[16,221-224] Suggestive organisms can also be confirmed by immunofluorescence testing, which may be a useful alternative[225] (available through the Centers for Disease Control and Prevention, 404-639-3156 or 404-639-3355). Although a variety of other serologic assays have been developed for diagnostic purposes, improvements in sensitivity, specificity, or both are necessary before they become useful tools in clinical practice.[226]

The single most helpful diagnostic maneuver for actinomycosis is to demonstrate grains (sulfur granules) in pus (Fig. 253-5A) or histologic section of a surgical specimen (Fig. 253-5B, C). Grains represent a conglomeration of microorganisms that forms only in vivo. Hematoxylin-eosin staining of tissue suffices to demonstrate the grain, but a special stain (e.g., Gram, silver) is needed to show that the grain is composed of branching bacteria and not fungi (eumycetoma), cocci, or bacilli (botryomycosis). If branching bacteria are seen on staining of the grain and the infection did not originate in subcutaneous tissue (a characteristic of mycetoma) or tonsillar tissue (see "Oral-Cervicofacial Disease"), then the diagnosis of actinomycosis is established. Grains may be either micro- or macroscopic and are usually yellow (hence their name), but may be white, pinkish gray, gray, or brown. Grains may be identified grossly from draining sinus tracts, other purulent material, or sputum, but may easily escape notice unless sought after. When pus is poured down the side of a glass tube, grains will adhere and are identified more readily. A magnifying glass may aid in their identification. In tissue sections, sulfur granules are most commonly found within microabscesses. Although they may be abundant, they are usually scanty. Only a single granule was identified from 26% of specimens in one series.[32] Because grains are surrounded by neutrophils, several histologic sections containing purulent foci need to be examined to find a grain. Microscopically, grains are round, oval, or horseshoe shaped. Although bacilli within the grain are rarely visible with the hematoxylin-eosin stain, tissue Gram stains, Gomori methenamine silver, and Giemsa stains will demonstrate gram-positive, filamentous, branching bacteria at its periphery (see Fig. 253-4).[226] On hematoxylin-eosin stain the grains may be eosinophilic or variably surrounded by a radiating fringe of eosinophilic clubs. This eosinophilic, proteinaceous coating around organisms in tissue has been called the Splendore-Hoeppli phenomena. It represents an ill-defined host response, but may be accounted for, in part, by eosinophil granule major basic protein.[227] This coating is not specific for actinomycosis and can also be seen in schistosomiasis, sporotrichosis, subcutaneous zygomycosis, botryomycosis, mycetoma, and other indolent infections. A combination of the clinical scenario and stains of the grain can be used to distinguish actinomycotic sulfur granules from others.

Clinically, nocardiosis may closely resemble actinomycosis but does not form grains in visceral lesions.[228] When *Nocardia* is the causative agent of mycetoma, granules are formed. On Gram stain the branching gram-positive bacilli are indistinguishable from *Actinomyces,* but they may be stained by a Fite modified acid-fast stain, whereas *Actinomyces* is not. The granules formed by the fungal agents of mycetoma show branching hyphae on periodic acid–Schiff or Gomori methenamine silver stain. Botryomycosis is a chronic bacterial soft tissue and rarely visceral infection that produces loose clumps of bacteria that resemble grains. Etiologic agents include *Staphylococcus, Streptococcus, Escherichia, Pseudomonas,* and *Proteus,* which are easily distinguished from the agents of actinomycosis by the presence of cocci or nonbranching bacilli.[229-231] Specimens obtained from mucus-producing locations, such as the endocervix, the bronchus, or ventricular colloid cysts, may possess pseudoactinomycotic radiate granules. If hematoxylin-eosin stain alone is used, they may mimic actinomycotic granules, as a central region is bordered by the Splendore-Hoeppli phenomena. However, special stains will reveal the absence of microorganisms.[232,233] When the etiology of a sulfur granule is in question, specific immunofluorescent staining for *A. israelii, A. naeslundii, A. odontolyticus, A. viscosus,* and *P. propionicum* can be utilized.[226]

TREATMENT

The discovery and use of penicillin in the treatment of actinomycosis has dramatically altered the course of this disease.[42] Two principles of therapy, based on the clinical experience of the last 50 years, have evolved. It is necessary to treat this disease both with high doses and for a prolonged period of time. Although therapy needs to be individualized, 18 to 24 million units of penicillin intravenously for 2 to 6 weeks, followed by oral therapy with penicillin or amoxicillin for 6 to 12 months, is a reasonable guideline. Cases with less extensive involvement, particularly in the oral-cervicofacial region, may require less intensive therapy.[234] If the duration of therapy is extended beyond the resolution of measurable disease, then the probability of relapse, one of the clinical hallmarks of this infection, will be minimized.[235] A similar approach is reasonable for immunocompromised patients, although refractory disease has been described in human immunodeficiency virus–infected individuals.[62] For penicillin-allergic patients, tetracycline has been used most extensively with success. Erythromycin, doxycycline, and clindamycin are other suitable alternatives.[236,237] In the pregnant penicillin-sensitive patient, erythromycin is a safe alternative. Little clinical information is available on the newer antimicrobial agents except for anecdotal successes with imipenem,[238-240] ceftriaxone,[241] and ciprofloxacin[242] (Table 253-1). Limited in vitro data demonstrate that the ketolides telithromycin and ABT-773 are active against *Actinomyces* spp.[243,244] In vitro data also suggest that oxacillin, dicloxacillin, cephalexin, metronidazole, and aminoglycosides should be

TABLE 253-1 Antibiotic Therapy for Actinomycosis*

Group 1: Extensive Successful Clinical Experience†
Penicillin (3-4 million units IV q4h or amoxicillin 500 mg PO q6h)
Erythromycin (500-1000 mg IV q6h or 500 mg PO q6h)
Tetracycline (500 g PO q6h)
Doxycycline (100 mg IV q12h or 100 mg PO q12h)
Minocycline (100 mg IV q12h or 100 mg PO q12h)
Clindamycin (900 mg IV q8h or 300-450 mg PO q6h)

Group 2: Anecdotal Successful Clinical Experience
Ceftriaxone
Ceftizoxime
Imipenam
Ciprofloxacin

Group 3: Agents That Should Be Avoided
Metronidazole
Aminoglycosides
Oxacillin
Dicloxacillin
Cephalexin

*Additional coverage for concomitant "companion" bacteria may be required.
†Controlled evaluations have not been performed. Dosing regimens need individulization depending on the site and extent of infection. As a general rule, a maximum antimicrobial dose for 2 to 6 weeks of parenteral therapy followed by oral therapy for a total duration of 6 to 12 months is required for most infections. Monitoring therapeutic effect with computed tomography or magnetic resonance images is advisable when appropriate.

avoided.[245,246] Although the role companion microbes play in actinomycosis is unclear, many of the isolates are pathogens in their own right. Designing a therapeutic regimen that includes coverage for these organisms during the initial treatment course is reasonable.

In the preantibiotic era surgical removal of infected tissue was the only beneficial treatment. Despite the advent of efficacious antimicrobial therapy, combined medical and surgical therapy is still advocated. An increasing body of literature now supports the approach of initially attempting a cure with medical therapy alone, including extensive disease.[156,184,210,247,248] CT and magnetic resonance imaging should be used to monitor the response to therapy.[141,249] In the setting of actinomycosis presenting as a well-defined abscess, percutaneous drainage in combination with medical therapy is a reasonable approach.[250] In a patient with disease in a critical location (e.g., epidural space, selected central nervous system disease), or in whom suitable medical therapy fails, surgical intervention may be appropriate.

REFERENCES

1. Weese WC, Smith IM. A study of 57 cases of actinomycosis over a 36-year period. Arch Intern Med. 1975;135:1562-1568.
2. Cope Z. Visceral actinomycosis. Br Med J. 1949:1311-1316.
3. Coleman RM, George LK, Rozzell AR. Actinomyces naeslundii as an agent in human actinomycosis. Appl Microbiol. 1969;18:420-426.
4. Bonnez WLG, Mohanraj NA. Actinomyces naeslundii as an agent of pelvic actinomycosis in the presence of an intra-uterine device. J Clin Microbiol. 1985;21:273-275.
5. Stenhouse D, MacDonald DG. Low grade osteomyelitis of the jaws with actinomycosis. Int J Oral Surg. 1974;3:60.
6. Eng RHK, Corrado ML, Cleri D, et al. Infections caused by Actinomyces viscosus. Am J Clin Pathol. 1981;75:113-116.
7. Lewis R, Gorbach S. Actinomyces viscosus in man. Lancet. 1972;1:641.
8. Morris JF, Kilbourn P. Systemic actinomycosis caused by Actinomyces odontolyticus. Ann Intern Med. 1974;81:700.
9. Peloux Y, Raoult D, Chardon H, Escarguel JP. Actinomyces odontolyticus infections: Review of six patients. J Infect. 1985;11:125-129.
10. Mitchell P, Hintz C, Haselby R. Malar mass due to Actinomyces odontolyticus. J Clin Microbiol. 1977;5:658-660.
11. Bassiri AG, Girgis RE, Theodore J. Actinomyces odontolyticus thoracopulmonary infections: Two cases in lung and heart-lung transplant recipients and a review of the literature. Chest. 1996;109:1109-1111.
12. Apothéloz C, Regamey C. Disseminated infection due to Actinomyces meyeri: Case report and review. Clin Infect Dis. 1996;22:621-625.
13. Albright J, Toczek S, Brenner V, et al. Osteomyelitis and epidural abscess caused by Arachnia propionica. J Neurosurg. 1974;40:115.
14. Brock D, Georg LK, Brown J, et al. Actinomycosis cause by Arachnia propionica: Report of 11 cases. Am J Clin Pathol. 1973;59:66-77.
15. Brazier JS, Hall V. Propionibacterium propionicum and infections of the lacrimal apparatus. Clin Infect Dis. 1993;17:892-893.

16. Hall V, Talbot P, Stubbs S, Duerden B. Identification of clinical isolates of Actinomyces species by amplified 16S ribosomal DNA restriction analysis. J Clin Microbiol. 2001;39:3555-3562.

17. Sabbe L, Van De Merwe D, Schouls L, et al. Clinical spectrum of infections due to the newly described Actinomyces species A. turicensis, A. radingae, and A. europaeus. J Clin Microbiol. 1999;37:8-13.

18. Funke G, Alvarez N, Pascual C, et al. Actinomyces europaeus sp. nov., isolated from human clinical specimens. Int J Syst Bacteriol. 1997;47:687-692.

19. Clarridge JE 3rd, Zhang Q. Genotypic diversity of clinical Actinomyces species: Phenotype, source, and disease correlation among genospecies. J Clin Microbiol. 2002;40:3442-3448.

20. Funke G, von Graevenitz A. Infections due to Actinomyces neuii (former "CDC Coryneform Group 1" bacteria). Infection. 1995;23:73-75.

21. Wust J, Stubbs S, Weiss N, et al. Assignment of Actinomyces pyogenes-like (CDC coryneform group E) bacteria to the genus Actinomyces as Actinomyces radingae sp. nov. and Actinomyces turicensis sp. nov. Lett Appl Microbiol. 1995;20:76-81.

22. Gahrn-Hansen B, Frederiksen W. Human infections with Actinomyces pyogenes (Corynebacterium pyogenes). Diagn Microbiol Infect Dis. 1992;15:349-354.

23. Reddy I, Ferguson D, Sarubbi F. Endocarditis due to Actinomyces pyogenes. Clin Infect Dis. 1997;25:1476-1477.

24. Funke G, Ramos C, Fernandez-Garayzabal J, et al. Description of human-derived Centers for Disease Control coryneform group 2 bacteria as Actinomyces bernardiae sp. nov. Int J Syst Bacteriol. 1995;45:57-60.

25. Ieven M, Verhoeven J, Gentens P, Goossens H. Severe infection due to Actinomyces bernardiae: Case report. Clin Infect Dis. 1996;22:157-158.

26. Lawson P, Nikolaitchouk N, Falsen E, et al. Actinomyces funkei sp. nov., isolated from human clinical specimens. Int J Syst Evol Microbiol. 2001;51:853-855.

27. Westling K, Lidman C, Thalme A. Tricuspid valve endocarditis caused by a new species of actinomyces: Actinomyces funkei. Scand J Infect Dis. 2002;34:206-207.

28. Hall V, Collins MD, Hutson R, et al. Actinomyces cardiffensis sp. nov. from human clinical sources. J Clin Microbiol. 2002;40:3427-3431.

29. Hill GB, Ayers OM, Kohan AP. Characteristics and sites of infection of Eubacterium nodatum, Eubacterium timidum, Eubacterium brachy, and other asaccharolytic eubacterium. J Clin Microbiol. 1987;25:1540-1545.

30. Hill GB. Eubacterium nodatum mimics Actinomyces in intrauterine device-associated infections and other settings within the female genital tract. Obstet Gynecol. 1992;79:534-538.

31. Garrod LP. Actinomycosis of the lung: Aetiology, diagnosis and chemotherapy. Tubercule. 1952;33:258-266.

32. Brown J. Human actinomycosis: A study of 181 subjects. Hum Pathol. 1973;4:319-330.

33. Holm P. Studies on aetiology of human actinomycosis. I. The "other" microbes of actinomycosis and their importance. Acta Pathol Microbiol Scand. 1950;27:736.

34. Holm P. Studies on aetiology of human actinomycosis. II. Do the "other" microbes of actinomycosis possess virulence? Acta Pathol Microbiol Scand. 1951;28:391.

35. Sarkonen N, Kononen E, Summanen P, et al. Oral colonization with Actinomyces species in infants by two years of age. J Dent Res. 2000;79:864-867.

36. Persson E. Genital actinomycosis and Actinomyces israelii in the female genital tract. Adv Contracept. 1987;3:115-123.

37. Peabody J, Seabury J. Actinomycosis and nocardiosis. J Chronic Dis. 1957;5:374-403.

38. Bennhoff D. Actinomycosis: Diagnostic and therapeutic considerations and a review of 32 cases. Laryngoscope. 1984;94:1198-1217.

39. Harvey J, Cantrell J, Fisher A. Actinomycosis: Its recognition and treatment. Ann Intern Med. 1957;46:868-885.

40. Kinnear W, MacFarlane J. A survey of thoracic actinomycosis. Respir Med. 1990;84:57-59.

41. Spilsbury BW, Johnstone FRC. The clinical course of actinomycotic infections: A report of 14 cases. Can J Surg. 1962;5:33-48.

42. Peabody J, Seabury J. Actinomycosis and nocardiosis: A review of basic differences in therapy. Am J Med. 1960;60:99-115.

43. Zitsch RP 3rd, Bothwell M. Actinomycosis: A potential complication of head and neck surgery. Am J Otolaryngol. 1999;20:260-262.

44. Syed MA, Ayshford CA, Uppal HS, Cullen RJ. Actinomycosis of the post-cricoid space: An unusual cause of dysphagia. J Laryngol Otol. 2001;115:428-429.

45. Jordon H, Kelly D, Heeley J. Enhancement of experimental actinomycosis in mice by Eikenella corrodens. Infect Immun. 1984;46:367-371.

46. Ochiai K, Kurita-Ochiai T, Kamino Y, Ikeda T. Effect of co-aggregation on the pathogenicity of oral bacteria. J Med Microbiol. 1993;39:183-190.

47. Weed L, Baggenstoss A. Actinomycosis: A pathologic and bacteriologic study of twenty-one fatal cases. Am J Clin Pathol. 1949;19:201-216.

48. Hennrikus E, Pederson L. Disseminated actinomycosis. West J Med. 1987;147:201-204.

49. Figures K, Douglas C. Actinomycosis associated with a root-treated tooth: Report of a case. Int Endodon J. 1991;24:326-329.

50. Silbermann M, Chiminello FJ, Doku HC, et al. Mandibular actinomycosis: Report of case. J Am Dent Assoc. 1975;90:162-165.

51. Miller B, Wright J, Colquhoun B. Some etiologic concepts of actinomycosis of the greater omentum. Surg Gynecol Obstet. 1978;146:412-414.

52. Cohen O, Keiser J, Pollner J, Parenti D. Prosthetic joint infection with Actinomyces viscosus. Infect Dis Clin Pract. 1993;2:349-351.

53. Strazzeri JC, Anzel S. Infected total hip arthroplasty due to Actinomyces israelii after dental extraction. Clin Orthop. 1986;210:128-131.

54. Gaffney R, Walsh M. Cervicofacial actinomycosis: An unusual cause of submandibular swelling. J Laryngol Otol. 1993;107:1169-1170.

55. Takeda H, Mitsuhashi Y, Kondo S. Cutaneous disseminated actinomycosis in a patient with acute lymphocytic leukemia. J Dermatol. 1998;25:37-40.

56. Chen CY, Chen YC, Tang JL, et al. Splenic actinomycotic abscess in a patient with acute myeloid leukemia. Ann Hematol. 2002;81:532-534.

57. Rivera M, Marcen R, Aguilera A, et al. Facial actinomycosis in a renal transplant patient. Nephron. 1994;68:149-150.

58. Cendan I, Klapholz A, Talawera W. Pulmonary actinomycosis: A cause of endobronchial disease in a patient with AIDS. Chest. 1993;103:1886-1887.

59. Kingdom T, Tami T. Actinomycosis of the nasal septum in a patient infected with the human immunodeficiency virus. Otolaryngol Head Neck Surg. 1994;111:130-133.

60. Poles MA, McMeeking AA, Scholes JV, Dieterich D. Actinomyces infection of a cytomegalovirus esophageal ulcer in two patients with acquired immunodeficiency syndrome. Am J Gastroenterol. 1994;89:1569-1572.

61. Ossorio MA, Fields CL, Byrd RP, Roy TM. Thoracic actinomycosis and human immunodeficiency virus infection. South Med J. 1997;90:1136-1138.

62. Manfredi R, Mazzoni A, Marinacci G, et al. Progressive intractable actinomycosis in patients with AIDS. Scand J Infect Dis. 1995;27:405-407.

63. Watkins KV, Richmond AS, Langstein IM. Nonhealing extraction site due to Actinomyces naeslundii in a patient with AIDS. Oral Surg Oral Med Oral Pathol. 1991;71:675-677.

64. Yeager B, Hoxie J, Weisman R, et al. Actinomycosis in the acquired immunodeficiency syndrome-related complex. Arch Otolaryngol Head Neck Surg. 1986;112:1293-1295.

65. Arora AK, Nord J, Olofinlade O, Javors B. Esophageal actinomycosis: A case report and review of the literature. Dysphagia. 2003;18:27-31.

66. Chaudhry SI, Greenspan JS. Actinomycosis in HIV infection: A review of a rare complication. Int J STD AIDS. 2000;11:349-355.

67. Sa'do B, Yoshiura K, Yuasa K, et al. Multimodality imaging of cervicofacial actinomycosis. Oral Surg Oral Med Oral Pathol. 1993;76:772-782.

68. Alamillos-Granados FJ, Dean-Ferrer A, Garcia-Lopez A, Lopez-Rubio F. Actinomycotic ulcer of the oral mucosa: An unusual presentation of oral actinomycosis. Br J Oral Maxillofac Surg. 2000;38:121-123.

69. Belmont MJ, Behar PM, Wax MK. Atypical presentations of actinomycosis. Head Neck. 1999;21:264-268.

70. Scott A, Stansbie JM. Actinomycosis presenting as a nasopharyngeal tumour: A case report. J Laryngol Otol. 1997;111:163-165.

71. Park JK, Lee HK, Ha HK, et al. Cervicofacial actinomycosis: CT and MR imaging findings in seven patients. AJNR Am J Neuroradiol. 2003;24:331-335.

72. Balatsouras D, Kaberos A, Eliopoulos P, et al. Cervicofacial actinomycosis presenting as acute upper respiratory tract. J Laryngol Otol. 1994;108:801-803.

73. Freidman HD, Evangelisti PA, Emko P. Postoperative carotid artery rupture caused by actinomyces infection. Otolaryngol Head Neck Surg. 1996;114:145-147.

74. Smego R. Actinomycosis of the central nervous system. Rev Infect Dis. 1987;9:855-865.

75. Nithyanandam S, D'Souza O, Rao SS, et al. Rhinoorbitocerebral actinomycosis. Ophthal Plast Reconstr Surg 2001;17:134-136.

76. Sakellariou P. Periapical actinomycosis: Report of a case and review of the literature. Endod Dent Traumatol. 1996;12:151-154.

77. Kalfas S, Figdor D, Sundqvist G. A new bacterial species associated with failed endodontic treatment: Identification and description of Actinomyces radicidentis. Oral Surg Oral Med Oral Pathol Oral Radiol Endod. 2001;92:208-214.

78. Collins M, Hoyles L, Kalfas S, et al. Characterization of Actinomyces isolates from infected root canals of teeth: Description of Actinomyces radicidentis sp. nov. J Clin Microbiol. 2000;38:3399-3403.

79. Bramley P, Orton H. Cervico-facial actinomycosis: A report on eleven cases. Br Dent J. 1960;109:235-238.

80. Bradley P. Actinomycosis of the temporomandibular joint. Br J Oral Surg. 1971;9:54-56.

81. Friduss M, Maceri D. Cervicofacial actinomycosis in children. Henry Ford Hosp Med J. 1990;38:28-32.

82. Nielsen P, Novak A. Acute cervico-facial actinomycosis. Int J Oral Maxillofac Surg. 1987;16:440-444.

83. Samuels R, Martin M. A clinical and microbiologic study of actinomycetes in oral and cervicofacial lesions. Br J Oral Maxillofac Surg. 1988;26:458-463.

84. Richtsmeier W, Johns ME. Actinomycosis of the head and neck. CRC Crit Rev Clin Lab Sci. 1979;11:175-202.

85. Bartkowski SB, Zapala J, Heczko P, Szuta M. Actinomycotic osteomyelitis of the mandible: Review of 15 cases. J Craniomaxillofac Surg. 1998;26:63-67.

86. Ohlms L, Jones D, Schreibstein J, Ferraro N. Sclerosing osteomyelitis of the mandible. Otolaryngol Head Neck Surg. 1993;109:1070-1073.

87. Lewis R, Sutter S, Finegold V. Bone infections involving anaerobic bacteria. Medicine. 1978;57:279-305.

88. Liu C, Chang K, Ou C. Actinomycosis in a patient treated for maxillary osteoradionecrosis. J Oral Maxillofac Surg. 1998;56:251-253.

89. Roth M, Montone K. Actinomycosis of the paranasal sinuses: A case report and review. Otolaryngol Head Neck Surg. 1996;114:818-821.

90. Vazquez A, Marti C, Renaga I, Salavert A. Actinomycosis of the tongue associated with human immunodeficiency virus infection: Case report. J Oral Maxillofac Surg. 1997;16:879-881.

91. Thomas R, Kameswaran M, Ahmed S, et al. Actinomycosis of the vallecula: Report of a case and review of the literature. J Laryngol Otol. 1995;109:154-156.

92. Chiang CW, Chang YL, Lou PJ. Actinomycosis imitating nasopharyngeal carcinoma. Ann Otol Rhinol Laryngol. 2000;109:605-607.

93. Nagral S, Patel C, Pathare P, et al. Actinomycotic pseudo-tumor of the mid-cervical region. J Postgrad Med. 1990;37:62-64.

94. Appiah S, Tickke M. Actinomycosis—an unusual presentation. Br J Oral Maxillofac Surg. 1995;33:248-249.

95. Chuong R, Goldberg M. CPC, case 60: Preauricular mass. J Oral Maxillofac Surg. 1986;44:214-217.

96. Rice DH. Chronic inflammatory disorders of the salivary glands. Otolaryngol Clin North Am. 1999;32:813-818.
97. Cobb R, Ross H. Actinomycosis in a persistent thyroglossal duct. Br J Surg. 1986;73:751.
98. Yiotakis J, Tzounakos P, Manolopoulos L, et al. Actinomycosis of the thyroid gland masquerading as a neoplasm. J Laryngol Otol. 1997;111:172-174.
99. Trites J, Evans M. Actinomycotic thyroiditis in a child. J Pediatr Surg. 1998;33:781-782.
100. Adeniyi-Jones C, Minielly J, Matthews W, et al. Actinomyces viscosus in a branchial cyst. Am J Clin Pathol. 1973;60:711-713.
101. Hagan M, Klotz S, Bartholomew W, et al. Actinomycosis of the trachea with acute tracheal obstruction. Clin Infect Dis. 1996;22:1126-1127.
102. Bhargava D, Bhusnurmath B, Sundaram KR, et al. Tonsillar actinomycosis: A clinicopathological study. Acta Trop. 2001;80:163-168.
103. Gaffney R, Harrison M, Walsh M, et al. The incidence and role of Actinomyces in recurrent acute tonsillitis. Clin Otolaryngol. 1993;18:268-271.
104. Yadav SP, Chanda K, Gathwala G, Yadav RK. Actinomycosis of tonsil masquerading as tumour in a 12-year old child. Int J Pediatr Otorhinolaryngol. 2002;63:73-75.
105. Blackburn LM, Green ST. Tonsillar actinomycosis presenting as expectorated debris. J Infect. 1997;34:283-284.
106. Tarabichi M, Schloss M. Actinomycosis otomastoiditis. Arch Otolaryngol Head Neck Surg. 1993;119:561-562.
107. Boor A, Jurkovic I, Friedmann I, et al. Actinomycosis of the middle ear. J Laryngol Otol. 1998;112:800-801.
108. Lee ES, Chae SW, Lim HH, et al. Clinical experiences with acute mastoiditis—1988 through 1998. Ear Nose Throat J. 2000;79:884-888, 890-892.
109. Roussel T, Olson R, Rice T, et al. Chronic postoperative endophthalmitis associated with Actinomyces species. Arch Ophthalmol. 1991;109:60-62.
110. Garelick JM, Khodabakhsh AJ, Josephberg RG. Acute postoperative endophthalmitis caused by Actinomyces neuii. Am J Ophthalmol. 2002;133:145-147.
111. Bates M, Cruickshank G. Thoracic actinomycosis. Thorax. 1957;12:99-124.
112. Heffner J. Pleuropulmonary manifestations of actinomycosis and nocardiosis. Semin Respir Infect. 1988;3:352-361.
113. Hsieh M, Liu H, Chang J, Chang C. Thoracic actinomycosis. Chest. 1993;104:366-370.
114. Cheon JE, Im JG, Kim MY, et al. Thoracic actinomycosis: CT findings. Radiology. 1998;209:229-233.
115. Flynn M, Felson B. The roentgen manifestations of thoracic actinomycosis. Am J Roentgenol Radium Ther Nucl Med. 1970;110:707-716.
116. Coodley E, Yoshinaka R. Pleural effusion as the major manifestation of actinomycosis. Chest. 1994;106:1615-1617.
117. Pérez-Castrillon J, Gonzalez-Castaneda C, del Campo-Matias F, et al. Empyema necessitatis due to Actinomyces odontolyticus (Letter). Chest. 1997;111:1144.
118. Kwong J, Muller N, Godwin J, et al. Thoracic actinomycosis: CT findings in eight patients. Radiology. 1992;183:189-192.
119. Hinnie J, Jaques B, Bell E, et al. Actinomycosis presenting as carcinoma. Postgrad Med. 1995;71:749-750.
120. Neijens V, van Heerde P, van der Heijden A, Baas P. Actinomycosis, a sheep in wolves' clothes. Lung Cancer. 1996;15:131-135.
121. Esposti D, Lippolis A, Cipolla M, Bonazzi M. An uncommon cause of pericardial actinomycosis. Ital Heart J. 2000;1:632-635.
122. Fife T, Finegold SM, Grennan T. Pericardial actinomycosis: Case report and review. Rev Infect Dis. 1991;13:120-126.
123. Lam S, Samraj J, Rahman S, Hilton E. Primary actinomycotic endocarditis: Case report and review. Clin Infect Dis. 1993;16:481-485.
124. Mardis JS, Many WJ Jr. Endocarditis due to Actinomyces viscosus. South Med J. 2001;94:240-243.
125. Morgan D, Nath H, Sanders C, et al. Mediastinal actinomycosis. AJR Am J Roentgenol. 1990;155:735-737.
126. Prather J, Eastridge C, Hughes F, et al. Actinomycosis of the thorax. Ann Thorac Surg. 1970;9:307-312.
127. Bentley E, Ostransky D. Unusual manifestations of thoracic actinomycosis. J Am Osteopath Assoc. 1994;94:249-253.
128. Spencer G, Roach D, Skucas J. Actinomycosis of the esophagus in a patient with AIDS: Findings on barium esophagrams. AJR Am J Roentgenol. 1993;161:795-796.
129. Parker J, deBoisblanc B. Case report. Actinomycosis: Multinodular pulmonary involvement. Am J Med Sci. 1994;307:418-419.
130. Fisher M. "Miliary" actinomycosis. J Can Assoc Radiol. 1980;31:149-150.
131. Dalhoff K, Wallner S, Finck C, et al. Endobronchial actinomycosis. Eur Respir J. 1994;7:1189-1191.
132. Kim YS, Suh JH, Kwak SM, et al. Foreign body-induced actinomycosis mimicking bronchogenic carcinoma. Korean J Intern Med. 2002;17:207-210.
133. Ho JC, Ooi GC, Lam WK, et al. Endobronchial actinomycosis associated with a foreign body. Respirology. 2000;5:293-296.
134. Jain B, Sehgal VN, Jagdish S, et al. Primary actinomycosis of the breast: A clinical review and a case report. J Dermatol. 1994;21:497-500.
135. Brunner S, Graf S, Riegel P, Altwegg M. Catalase-negative Actinomyces neuii subsp. neuii isolated from an infected mammary prosthesis. Int J Med Microbiol. 2000;290:285-287.
136. Lee IJ, Ha HK, Park CM, et al. Abdominopelvic actinomycosis involving the gastrointestinal tract: CT features. Radiology. 2001;220:76-80.
137. Meyer P, Nwariaku O, McClelland RN, et al. Rare presentation of actinomycosis as an abdominal mass: Report of a case. Dis Colon Rectum. 2000;43:872-875.
138. Berardi RS. Abdominal actinomycosis. Surg Gynecol Obstet. 1979;149:257-266.
139. Davies M, Keddie NC. Abdominal actinomycosis. Br J Surg. 1973;60:18-22.
140. Ha HK, Lee HJ, Kim H, et al. Abdominal actinomycosis: CT findings in 10 patients. AJR Am J Roentgenol. 1993;161:791-794.
141. Ko S, Ng S, Lee T, Lo C. Retroperitoneal actinomycosis with intraperitoneal spread: Stellate pattern on CT. Clin Imaging. 1996;20:133-136.
142. Kim JC, Ahn BY, Kim HC, et al. Efficiency of combined colonoscopy and computed tomography for diagnosis of colonic actinomycosis: A retrospective evaluation of eight consecutive patients. Int J Colorectal Dis. 2000;15:236-242.
143. Deshmukh N, Heaney S. Actinomycosis at multiple colonic sites. Am J Gastroenterol. 1986;81:1212-1214.
144. Skoutelis A, Panagopoulos C, Kalfarentzos F, Bassaris H. Intramural gastric actinomycosis. South Med J. 1995;88:647-650.
145. Lee SA, Palmer GW, Cooney EL. Esophageal actinomycosis in a patient with AIDS. Yale J Biol Med. 2001;74:383-389.
146. Putman H, Dockerty M, Waugh JM. Abdominal actinomycosis: An analysis of 122 cases. Surgery. 1950;28:781-800.
147. Sarosdy M, Brock W, Parsons C. Scrotal actinomycosis. J Urol. 1979;121:256-257.
148. Alvardo-Cerna R, Bracho-Riquelme R. Perianal actinomycosis—A complication of a fistula-in-ano. Report of a case. Dis Colon Rectum. 1994;37:378-380.
149. Dayan K, Neufeld D, Zissin R, et al. Actinomycosis of the large bowel: Unusual presentations and their surgical treatment. Eur J Surg. 1996;162:657-660.
150. Harsch IA, Benninger J, Niedobitek G, et al. Abdominal actinomycosis: Complication of endoscopic stenting in chronic pancreatitis? Endoscopy. 2001;33:1065-1069.
151. Sharma M, Briski LE, Khatib R. Hepatic actinomycosis: An overview of salient features and outcome of therapy. Scand J Infect Dis. 2002;34:386-391.
152. Miyamoto M, Fang F. Pyogenic liver abscess involving Actinomyces: Case report and review. Clin Infect Dis. 1993;16:303-309.
153. Kasano Y, Tanimura H, Yamaue H, et al. Hepatic actinomycosis infiltrating the diaphragm and right lung. Am J Gastroenterol. 1996;91:2418-2420.
154. Ruutu P, Pentikainen P, Larinkari U, et al. Hepatic actinomycosis presenting as repeated cholestatic reactions. Scand J Infect Dis. 1982;14:235-238.
155. Ubeda B, Vilana R, Bianchi L, Pujol S. Primary hepatic actinomycosis: Association with portal vein thrombosis. AJR Am J Roentgenol. 1995;164:231-232.
156. Khalaff H, Srigley J, Klotz L. Recognition of renal actinomycosis: Nephrectomy can be avoided. Report of a case. Can J Surg. 1995;38:77-79.
157. Ellis L, Kenny G, Nellans R. Urogenital aspects of actinomycosis. J Urol. 1979;122:132-133.
158. Piper J, Stoner B, Mitra S, et al. Ileo-vesical fistula associated with pelvic actinomycosis. Br J Clin Pract. 1969;23:341-343.
159. Ord J, Mishra V, Hudd C, et al. Ureteric obstruction caused by pelvic actinomycosis. Scand J Urol Nephrol. 2002;36:87-88.
160. Haj M, Nasser G, Loberant N, et al. Pelvic actinomycosis presenting as ureteric and rectal stricture. Dig Surg. 2000;17:414-417.
161. de Feiter PW, Soeters PB. Gastrointestinal actinomycosis: An unusual presentation with obstructive uropathy. Report of a case and review of the literature. Dis Colon Rectum. 2001;44:1521-1525.
162. Stringer M, Cameron A. Abdominal actinomycosis: A forgotten disease? Br J Hosp Med. 1987;38:125-127.
163. Richards R, Grayer D. Actinomycosis: A rare cause of vesicocolic fistula. Am J Gastroenterol. 1989;84:677-679.
164. Buckley P, McInerney P, Stephenson T. Actinomycotic vesico-uterine fistula from a wishbone pessary contraceptive device. Br J Urol. 1991;68:206-207.
165. Guermazi A, de Kerviler E, Welker Y, et al. Pseudotumoral vesical actinomycosis. J Urol. 1996;156:2002-2003.
166. Jani AN, Casibang V, Mufarrij WA. Disseminated actinomycosis presenting as a testicular mass: A case report. J Urol. 1990;143:1012-1014.
167. Yeung Y, Cheung MC, Chan GS, et al. Primary actinomycosis mimicking urachal carcinoma. Urology. 2001;58:462.
168. Merle-Melet M, Mory F, Stempfel B, et al. Actinomyces naeslundii, acute cholecystitis and carcinoma of the gallbladder. Am J Gastroenterol. 1995;90:1530-1531.
169. Ormsby AH, Bauer TW, Hall GS. Actinomycosis of the cholecystic duct: Case report and review. Pathology. 1998;30:65-67.
170. Serrano-Rios M, Navarro V, Fontan J, et al. Isolated hepato-pancreatic actinomycosis. Digestion. 1969;2:262-271.
171. Nye F. Primary abdominal actinomycosis. J Infect. 1993;27:105-106.
172. Papachristodoulou AJ, Angouras DC, Papavassiliou VG, et al. Primary actinomycosis of the greater omentum. J Infect. 2001;43:159-160.
173. DeSanto N, Altucci P, Giordano C. Actinomyces peritonitis associated with dialysis. Nephron. 1976;16:236-239.
174. Henderson S. Pelvic actinomycosis associated with an intrauterine device. Obstet Gynecol. 1973;41:726-732.
175. Nieman B, Fahrner A. Actinomycosis of the ovary. Am J Obstet Gynecol. 1943;45:534-538.
176. Brenner R, Gehring S. Pelvic actinomycosis in the presence of an endocervical contraceptive device. Obstet Gynecol. 1964;29:71-73.
177. Schmidt W, Webb J, Bedrossian C, et al. Actinomycosis and intrauterine contraceptive devices: The clinicopathologic entity. Diagn Gynecol Obstet. 1980;2:165-177.
178. Fiorino A. Intrauterine contraceptive device-associated actinomycotic abscess and Actinomyces detection on cervical smear. Obstet Gynecol. 1996;87:142-149.
179. Spagnuolo P, Fransioli M. Intrauterine device-associated actinomycosis simulating pelvic malignancy. Am J Gastroenterol. 1981;75:144-147.
180. Zbar AP, Karayiannakis AJ, Chiappa AC. Obstructive uropathy and pelvic actinomycosis. Dis Colon Rectum. 2002;45:1708; author reply 1708-1709.
181. Dawson JM, O'Riordan B, Chopra S. Ovarian actinomycosis presenting as acute peritonitis. Aust N Z J Surg. 1992;62:161-163.
182. Perlow JH, Wigton T, Yordan EL, et al. Disseminated pelvic actinomycosis presenting as metastatic carcinoma: Association with the Progestasert intrauterine device. Rev Infect Dis. 1991;13:1115-1119.

183. Lippes J. Pelvic actinomycosis: A review and preliminary look at prevalence. Am J Obstet Gynecol. 1999;180:265-269.
184. Pauker S, Kopelman R. A rewarding pursuit of certainty. N Engl J Med. 1993;329:1103-1107.
185. Sharma B, Banerjee A, Sobti M, et al. Actinomycotic brain abscess. Clin Neurol Neurosurg. 1990;92:373-376.
186. Bolton C, Ashenhurst E. Actinomycosis of the brain. Can Med Assoc J. 1964;90:922-928.
187. Kirsch W, Skcess J. Actinomycotic osteomyelitis of the skull and epidural space. J Neurol. 1970;33:347-351.
188. Louie J, Kusske J, Rush JL, et al. Actinomycotic subdural empyema. J Neurosurg. 1979;51:852-855.
189. Soto-Hernandez JL, Morales VA, Lara Giron JC, Balderrama Banares J. Cranial epidural empyema with osteomyelitis caused by Actinomyces: CT, and MRI appearance. Clin Imaging. 1999;23:209-214.
190. Muller P. Actinomycosis as a cause of spinal cord compression: A case report and review. Paraplegia. 1989;27:390-393.
191. Oruckaptan HH, Senmevsim O, Soylemezoglu F, Ozgen T. Cervical actinomycosis causing spinal cord compression and multisegmental root failure: Case report and review of the literature. Neurosurgery. 1998;43:937-940.
192. Holland N, Deibert E. CNS actinomycosis presenting with bilateral cavernous sinus syndrome. J Neurol Neurosurg Psychiatry. 1998;64:4.
193. David C, Brasme L, Peruzzi P, et al. Intramedullary abscess of the spinal cord in a patient with a right-to-left shunt: Case report. Clin Infect Dis. 1997;24:89-90.
194. Ohta S, Nishizawa S, Namba H, Sugimura H. Bilateral cavernous sinus actinomycosis resulting in painful ophthalmoplegia: Case report. J Neurosurg. 2002;96:600-602.
195. Ushikoshi S, Koyanagi I, Hida K, et al. Spinal intrathecal actinomycosis: A case report. Surg Neurol. 1998;50:221-225.
196. Curi MM, Dib LL, Kowalski LP, et al.. Opportunistic actinomycosis in osteoradionecrosis of the jaws in patients affected by head and neck cancer: Incidence and clinical significance. Oral Oncol. 2000;36:294-299.
197. Vandevelde A, Jenkins S, Hardy P. Sclerosing osteomyelitis and Actinomyces naeslundii of surrounding tissues. Clin Infect Dis. 1995;20:1037-1039.
198. Reiner S, Harrelson J, Miller S, et al. Primary actinomycosis of an extremity: A case report and review. Rev Infect Dis. 1987;9:581-589.
199. Liaudet L, Erard P, Kaeser P. Cutaneous and muscular abscesses secondary to Actinomyces meyeri pneumonia. Clin Infect Dis. 1996;22:185-186.
200. Johnston J. Case 29-1993. N Engl J Med. 1993;329:264-269.
201. Petrini B, Welin-Berger T. Late infection with Actinomyces israelii after total hip replacement. Scand J Infect Dis. 1978;10:313-314.
202. Ruhe J, Holding K, Mushatt D. Infected total knee arthroplasty due to Actinomyces naeslundii. Scand J Infect Dis. 2001;33:230-231.
203. Wust J, Steiger U, Vuong H, Zbinden R. Infection of a hip prosthesis by Actinomyces naeslundii. J Clin Microbiol. 2000;38:929-930.
204. Lequerre T, Nouvellon M, Kraznowska K, et al. Septic arthritis due to Actinomyces naeslundii: Report of a case. Joint Bone Spine. 2002;69:499-501.
205. Sherer P, Dobbins J. Actinomycosis arthritis: A case report. Med Ann District Columbia. 1974;43:66-68.
206. Blinkhorn R, Strimbu V, Effron D, et al. 'Punch' actinomycosis causing osteomyelitis of the hand. Arch Intern Med. 1988;148:2668-2670.
207. Mesgarzadeh M, Bonakdarpour A, Redecki P. Case report 365. Skeletal Radiol. 1986;15:584-588.
208. Hilfiker ML. Disseminated actinomycosis presenting as a renal tumor with metastases. J Pediatr Surg. 2001;36:1577-1578.
209. Lee YC, Min D, Holcomb K, et al. Computed tomography guided core needle biopsy diagnosis of pelvic actinomycosis. Gynecol Oncol. 2000;79:318-323.
210. Cintron J, Del Pino A, Duarte B, Wood D. Abdominal actinomycosis: Report of two cases and review of the literature. Dis Colon Rectum. 1996;39:105-108.
211. Hsu W, Chiang C, Chen C, et al. Ultrasound-guided fine needle aspiration biopsy in the diagnosis of chronic pulmonary infection. Respirology. 1997;64:319-325.
212. Das D. Actinomycosis in fine needle aspiration cytology. Cytopathology. 1994;5:243-250.
213. Bakhtawar I, Schaefer RF, Salian N. Utility of Wang needle aspiration in the diagnosis of actinomycosis. Chest. 2001;119:1966-1968.
214. Hyldgaard-Jensen J, Sandstrom HR, Pedersen JF. Ultrasound diagnosis and guided biopsy in renal actinomycosis. Br J Radiol. 1999;72:510-512.
215. Al-Khuwaitir TS, Abdulwahab AA, El-Sharqawy TM, et al. Actinomycotic liver abscess. Saudi Med J. 2000;21:771-774.
216. Lee C-H, Lin M-C, Tsai Y-H, et al. Thoracic actinomycosis—Review of 9 cases. Chang Gung Med. 1991;14:246-252.
217. Siqueira JF, Rocas IN, Moraes SR, Santos KR. Direct amplification of rRNA gene sequences for identification of selected oral pathogens in root canal infections. Int Endod J. 2002;35:345-351.
218. Slack J. The source of infection in actinomycosis. J Bacteriol. 1942;43:193-209.
219. Lewis R, McKenzie D, Bagg J, Dickie A. Experience with a novel selective medium for isolation of Actinomyces spp. from medical and dental specimens. J Clin Microbiol. 1995;33:1613-1616.
220. Sarkonen N, Kononen E, Summanen P, et al. Phenotypic identification of Actinomyces and related species isolated from human sources. J Clin Microbiol. 2001;39:3955-3961.
221. Woo PC, Fung AM, Lau SK, et al. Diagnosis of pelvic actinomycosis by 16S ribosomal RNA gene sequencing and its clinical significance. Diagn Microbiol Infect Dis. 2002;43:113-118.
222. Sato T, Matsuyama J, Takahashi N, et al. Differentiation of oral Actinomyces species by 16S ribosomal DNA polymerase chain reaction-restriction fragment length polymorphism. Arch Oral Biol. 1998;43:247-252.
223. Hall V, O'Neill GL, Magee JT, Duerden BI. Development of amplified 16S ribosomal DNA restriction analysis for identification of Actinomyces species and comparison with pyrolysis-mass spectrometry and conventional biochemical tests. J Clin Microbiol. 1999;37:2255-2261.
224. Ruby JD, Li Y, Luo Y, Caufield PW. Genetic characterization of the oral Actinomyces. Arch Oral Biol. 2002;47:457-463.
225. Hillier S, Moncla B. Anaerobic gram-positive nonsporeforming bacilli and cocci. In Balows EIC, ed. Manual of Clinical Microbiology. Washington, DC: American Society of Microbiology, 1991.
226. Holmberg K. Diagnostic methods for human actinomycosis. Microbiol Sci. 1987;4:72-78.
227. Kephart G, Andrade Z, Gleich G. Localization of eosinophil major basic protein onto eggs of Schistosoma mansoni in human pathologic tissue. Am J Pathol. 1988;133:389-396.
228. Robboy S, Vickery A. Tinctorial and morphologic properties distinguishing actinomycosis and nocardiosis. N Engl J Med. 1970;282:593-595.
229. Multz A, Cohen R, Azeuta V. Bacterial pseudomycosis: A rare cause of haemoptysis. Eur Respir J. 1994;7:1712-1713.
230. Yencha MW, Walker CW, Karakla DW, Simko EJ. Cutaneous botryomycosis of the cervicofacial region. Head Neck. 2001;23:594-598.
231. Bersoff-Matcha SJ, Roper CC, Liapis H, Little JR. Primary pulmonary botryomycosis: Case report and review. Clin Infect Dis. 1998;26:620-624.
232. Sobel R. Pseudopseuodosulfur granules. Am J Clin Pathol. 1982;77:230.
233. Bhagavan B, Ruffier J, Shinn B. Pseudoactinomycotic radiate granules in the lower female genital tract. Hum Pathol. 1982;13:898-904.
234. Martin M. The use of oral amoxicillin for the treatment of actinomycosis. Br Dent J. 1984;156:252-254.
235. Tambay R, Cote J, Bourgault AM, Villeneuve JP. An unusual case of hepatic abscess. Can J Gastroenterol. 2001;15:615-617.
236. Martin MV. Antibiotic treatment of cervicofacial actinomycosis for patients allergic to penicillin: A clinical and in vitro study. Br J Oral Maxillofac Surg. 1985;23:428-435.
237. Fass RJ, Scholand JF, Hodges GR. Clindamycin in the treatment of serious anaerobic infections. Ann Intern Med. 1973;78:853-859.
238. Yew W, Wong P, Wong C, Chau C. Use of imipenem in the treatment of thoracic actinomycosis. Clin Infect Dis. 1994;19:983-984.
239. Garduno E, Rebollo M, Asencio MA, et al. Splenic abscesses caused by Actinomyces meyeri in a patient with autoimmune hepatitis. Diagn Microbiol Infect Dis. 2000;37:213-214.
240. Yew WW, Wong PC, Lee J, et al. Report of eight cases of pulmonary actinomycosis and their treatment with imipenem-cilastatin. Monaldi Arch Chest Dis. 1999;54:126-129.
241. Skoutelis A, Petrochilos J, Bassaris H. Successful treatment of thoracic actinomycosis with ceftriaxone. Clin Infect Dis. 1994;19:161-162.
242. Macfarlane D, Tucker G, Kemp R. Treatment of recalcitrant actinomycosis with ciprofloxacin. J Infect. 1993;27:177-180.
243. Citron DM, Appleman MD. Comparative in vitro activities of ABT-773 against 362 clinical isolates of anaerobic bacteria. Antimicrob Agents Chemother. 2001;45:345-348.
244. Goldstein EJ, Citron DM, Merriam CV, et al. Activities of telithromycin (HMR 3647, RU 66647) compared to those of erythromycin, azithromycin, clarithromycin, roxithromycin, and other antimicrobial agents against unusual anaerobes. Antimicrob Agents Chemother. 1999;43:2801-2805.
245. Lerner P. Susceptibility of pathogenic Actinomycetes to antimicrobial compounds. Antimicrob Agents Chemother. 1974;5:302-309.
246. Shore KP, Pottumarthy S, Morris AJ. Susceptibility of anaerobic bacteria in Auckland: 1991-1996. N Z Med J. 1999;112:424-426.
247. Marty H, Wust J. Disseminated actinomycosis caused by Actinomyces meyeri. Infection. 1989;17:154-155.
248. Schleck W, Gelfand M, Alper B, et al. Medical management of visceral actinomycosis. South Med J. 1983;76:921-922.
249. Hawnaur JM, Reynolds JR, McGettigan C. Magnetic resonance imaging of actinomycosis presenting as pelvic malignancy. Br J Radiol. 1999;72:1006-1011.
250. Goldwag S, Abbitt P, Watts B. Case report: Percutaneous drainage of periappendiceal actinomycosis. Clin Radiol. 1991;44:422-42.

SECTION G

MYCOSES

CHAPTER **254**

Introduction to Mycoses

JOHN E. BENNETT*

The advent of the human immunodeficiency virus epidemic and the ever-increasing use of immunosuppressive drugs has dramatically increased the incidence of deep mycoses and substantially broadened the range of fungi causing potentially lethal disease. Fortunately, the number of effective antifungal drugs has also increased. Together, these changes have made it essential for physicians to increase their awareness and understanding of medically important fungi.

MYCOLOGY

Taxonomy, which is the science of classifying organisms, is drawing increasing reliance on genomic structure. As an example, a second species, called *Coccidioides posadasii,* has been distinguished within *Coccidioides immitis,* using nucleotide sequences. These two species

*The chapter was written by Dr. Bennett in his personal capacity. The views expressed herein do not necessarily represent the views of NIH, DHHS, or the United States.

cannot be distinguished by any of the usual means, such as biochemical tests or appearance. *Candida dubliniensis* was distinguished within *Candida albicans* based originally on molecular tests, though phenotypic differences have now been found. Names and groupings of fungi are now being extensively examined by molecular techniques. However, each name change exacts a price. Infectious diseases are usually named by the organism, so a change in name makes it difficult for the clinician to locate prior published cases. Fungal names present an additional hurdle for the clinician in that many fungi have two names, a phenomenon described later.

Some of specialized terms used in this section of the book are listed in Table 254-1. Although most should be consulted only to help understand one of the chapters in this text, it is important for all infectious disease specialists to understand the distinction between yeasts and moulds (also spelled "molds"). Even at the first recognition in a diagnostic laboratory that a fungus has been found in a smear or culture, the laboratory can distinguish between a yeast and a mould. Yeastlike fungi are typically round or oval, generally form smooth, flat colonies, and reproduce by budding. Biochemical tests are important for identification. Molds are composed of tubular structures called hyphae and grow by branching and longitudinal extension. Mould colonies typically appear fuzzy. Not all pathogenic fungi can be categorized neatly by their appearance in tissue as yeasts or molds. *Coccidioides* species, *Rhinosporidium seeberi,* and *Pneumocystis jirovecii* are round in tissue but do not bud. Instead, the cytoplasm divides up to form numerous internal spores that, on rupture of the "mother" cell, are released to form new spherical structures. Some fungi can grow either yeastlike or as a mold. In candidiasis and tinea versicolor, the fungus is often seen in both tubular and rounded forms. The so-called dimorphic fungi grow in the host as yeastlike forms but grow at room temperature in vitro as molds. These fungi include the agents of histoplasmosis, blastomycosis, sporotrichosis, coccidioidomycosis, paracoccidioidomycosis, and chromoblastomycosis.

Virtually all fungi reproduce by forming spores through mitosis, a process in which the chromosome number remains the same. A fungal

---

TABLE 254-1 A Lexicon of Mycology Terms for the Clinician

Aleurioconidia/aleuriospore: spore growing at the end of a specialized hypha. The spore is released by breakage of the hypha adjacent to the spore.

Anamorph: a fungus forming only asexual spores.

Arthrospore: a spore formed by a hypha breaking at a septum.

Asexual spores: spores formed by mitosis, a form of cell division that creates an exact copy of the original cell.

Basidiomycete: one of the four major classes of fungi; includes mushrooms and *Cryptococcus neoformans.*

Basidiospore: a sexual spore that arises on a specialized structure, usually club shaped, in a basidiomycete (e.g., *Cryptococcus neoformans* forms basidiospores in its sexual state, called *Filobasidiella neoformans*).

Blastospore: an asexual spore formed by budding (e.g., *Cryptococcus neoformans, Candida* species).

Conidiophore: specialized hyphae that bear a conidium (spore) on the end.

Conidium (plural: conidia): an asexual spore usually produced at the tip or side of a hypha.

Dimorphic: capable of producing both hyphae and yeast (e.g., the agents of coccidioidomycosis, blastomycosis, histoplasmosis, sporotrichosis, and chromoblastomycosis).

Diploid: having two sets of chromosomes.

Endemic fungi: fungi having a limited geographic distribution (e.g., blastomycosis, histoplasmosis and coccidioidomycosis).

Endospore: spore formed within a larger cell, such as a *Coccidioides* spherule.

Germ tube: a hypha emerging from a yeastlike structure, characteristic of *Candida albicans* cells placed on specialized culture medium.

Haploid: having a single set of chromosomes.

Heterothallic: a fungus that can only mate between different colonies of an opposite mating type.

Homothallic: a fungus in which mating can take place within the same colony (e.g., *Pseudallescheria boydii*).

Hyaline: colorless, transparent.

Hyalohyphomycosis: infection caused by moulds with light–colored colonies. This term includes most of the pathogenic moulds and is so broad it has not proven useful.

Hypha (plural: hyphae): the tubular element that forms the body of a fungus.

Imperfect state: fungus producing only asexual spores.

Meiosis: process in a dividing cell that allows re-assorting of chromosomes and reduces the number of chromosomes by one half, from diploid to haploid.

Mitosis: process in a dividing cell that produces two genetically identical copies of the original cell.

Morphology: appearance of the fungus.

Mould (or **mold**): filamentous fungus. A colony on agar generally appears fuzzy, rather than smooth.

Mucormycosis: infection by moulds of the order Mucorales.

Perfect state: fungus capable of producing sexual spores.

Phenotype: genetically determined properties that help distinguish an organism from otherwise similar organisms (e.g., requirement for exogenous uracil is useful phenotype in some yeast mutants).

Phaeohyphomycosis: infection caused by moulds with dark-colored colonies because of pigmentation in the hyphae. Individual hyphae may not have enough pigment to be dark colored under the microscope. A colony can be dark colored because of the spores, such as *Sporothrix schenckii,* and not be an agent of phaeohyphomycosis.

Pseudohyphae: a string of budding cells (e.g., those formed by most *Candida* species).

Sexual spores: spores formed by meiosis, a form of division in which the number of chromosomes is reduced by one half.

Spherule: large round cell of *Coccidioides* species that forms spores inside.

Sporangium: a sacklike structure with asexual spores (sporangiospores) inside. Spores are released when the sack breaks.

Spp.: abbreviation for species (plural).

Teleomorph: a fungus forming sexual spores.

Thallus: the vegetative body of a fungus, such as a fungal colony.

Yeast: technically, a fungi of the family Saccharomycetaceae, including *Saccharomyces cerevisiae* (baker's yeast). The terms yeast form or yeast like are generally used to denote fungi that reproduce by budding.

Zygomycete: A class of fungi that includes the order Mucorales, which contains the agents of mucormycosis, and the order Entomophthorales, which has the agents of two tropical mycoses: basidiobolomycosis and entomophthoramycosis.

Zygomycosis: term that includes mucormycosis, basidiobolomycosis, and entomophthoramycosis.

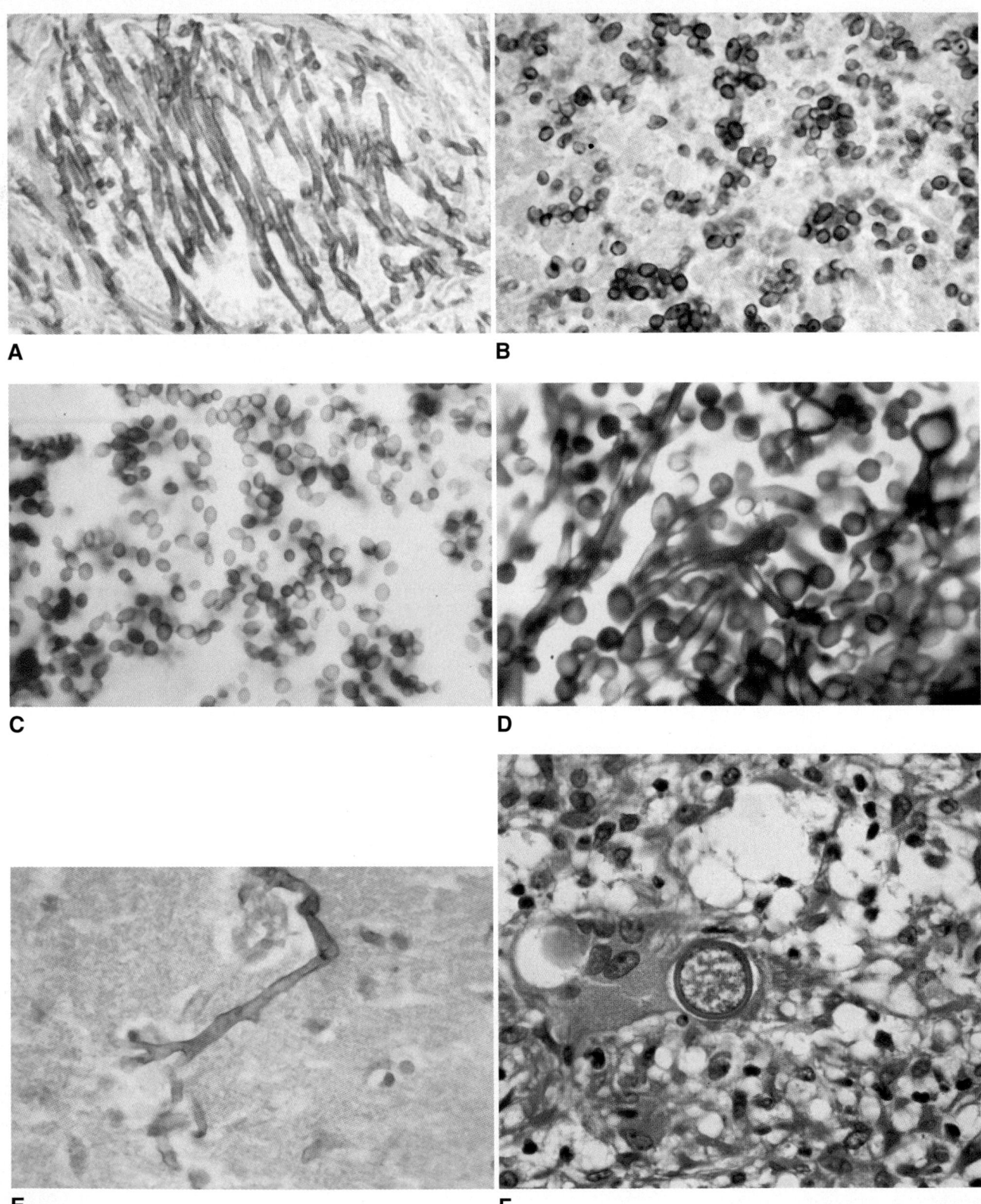

FIGURE 254-1. Appearance of fungi in tissue. **A,** *Aspergillus* sp., periodic acid–Schiff (PAS) stain. **B,** *Histoplasma capsulatum,* Gomori methenamine silver (GMS) stain. **C,** *Candida glabrata* yeast cells, PAS stain. **D,** *Candida albicans,* GMS stain. **E,** *Rhizomucor* sp., GMS stain. **F,** *Coccidioides* sp., hematoxylin and eosin (H&E) stain.

Figure continued on opposite page

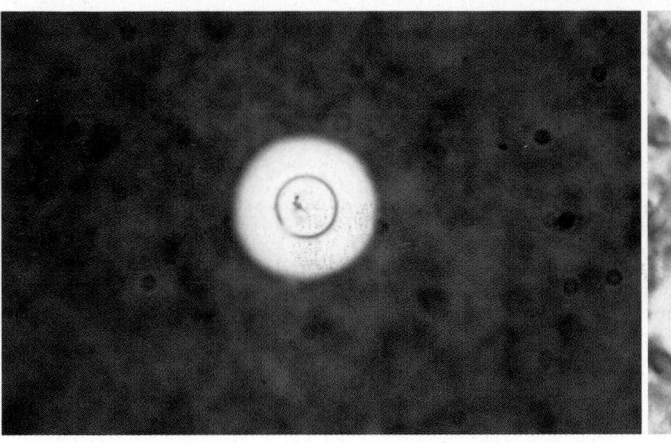

G

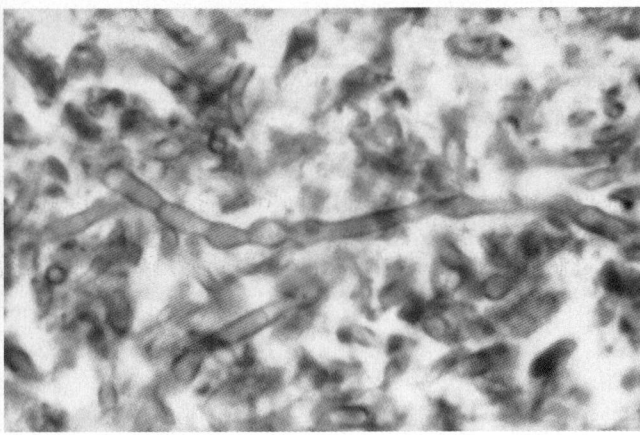

H

FIGURE 254-1—continued. Appearance of fungi in tissue. **G,** *Cryptococcus neoformans,* India ink smear of cerebrospinal fluid. **H,** *Cladophialophora bantiana,* H&E stain. **I,** *Penicillium marneffei,* GMS stain.

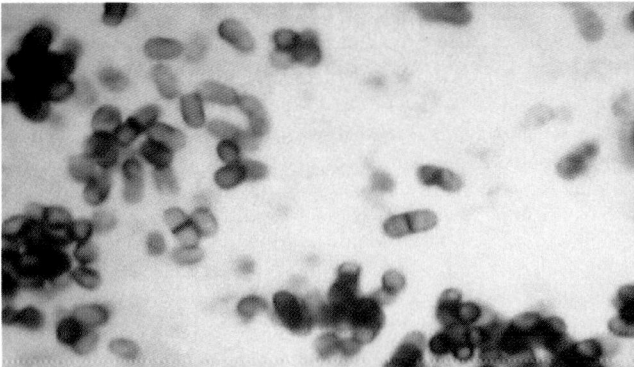

I

colony with only this asexual spore formation or with no spore formation is said to be an "anamorph," or "in the imperfect (asexual) state." Several decades ago, most fungi pathogenic for humans were found only in the imperfect state. Many have subsequently been induced to form sexual spores and have been given names. Fungi growing spores that have the specialized appearance known for "sexual spores" are said to be "teleomorphs," or "in the perfect state." The name given to a fungus in the perfect state shows its similarity to other fungi in their perfect state. Although the fungus may have two names, the diagnostic laboratory uses the single name that is oldest and best established.

Sexual spores arise as a result of nuclear fusion followed by meiosis, a process that reduces the chromosome number by half. If the two nuclei are from the same colony (thallus), the fungus is said to be homothallic. If the nuclei are from different colonies that fuse their cytoplasm when grown adjacent to one another, the fungus is said to be heterothallic. Such fungi only join with colonies having a different, compatible mating type. Heterothallic fungi include the agents of histoplasmosis, blastoplasmosis, and cryptococcosis, as well as some fungi causing ringworm and mucormycosis.

Spores of fungi pathogenic for humans are nonmotile and spread by wind, water, and contact. As a rare exception, motile spores are found in cultures of *Pythium insidiosum,* a fungus-like organism of unsettled classification. Fungal cells have rigid walls of glucans and often chitin. All fungal cell walls are stained by Gomori methenamine-silver, and while the fungus remains viable, the periodic acid–Schiff reagent will stain the polysaccharide in the cell wall. All fungi, including *P. jirovecii,* stain with calcofluor, which appears brilliant white under the fluorescent microscope. This stain has replaced the "wet mount" or KOH stain in many diagnostic laboratories because fungi are easier to see. Gram stain is not usually helpful because most fungi, except *Candida,* remain unstained. India ink smear of cerebrospinal fluid allows visualization of a polysaccharide capsule around the cell wall and is characteristic of only one genus pathogenic for humans, the genus *Cryptococcus.* An India ink smear from a colony on a cul-ture plate is less helpful because the capsule may be too thin to be seen. Inside the fungal cell wall is the sterol-containing cytoplasmic membrane, which is the site affected by azoles, allylamines, and the polyene macrolide antibiotics amphotericin B and nystatin. Some fungi can produce mycotoxins under specialized conditions, including species of *Stachybotrys* and *Aspergillus,* but these toxins are not known to contribute to pathogenesis of mycoses.

Fungi can often be identified in tissue, even in the absence of culture, by taking into account the clinical findings, body site, inflammatory response, and fungal appearance (Fig. 254-1; Table 254-2). Culture diagnosis is potentially more accurate than diagnosis by histologic features, but many smaller laboratories encounter difficulties in isolating and identifying fungi. The histologic features of a biopsy specimen can be more rapidly diagnostic than culture when mycoses are caused by slow-growing fungi. Biopsy slides are more readily mailed to consultants than are cultures, which may arrive nonviable or contaminated. Finally, biopsy may provide proof that the fungus is invading tissue and is not just a contaminant or saprophyte growing on debris in a lung cavity or skin ulcer. Ideally, both histologic examination and culture should be done together. As yet, detection of fungal DNA by polymerase chain reaction has not proved useful in detecting or identifying fungi in tissue. In contrast, luminescent DNA probes for hybridization to fungal RNA are commercially available and valuable for identifying colonies of *Histoplasma capsulatum, Coccidioides* spp., *Blastomyces dermatitidis,* and *Cryptococcus neoformans.* Identification of fungi in tissue by immunohistochemistry remains experimental.

EPIDEMIOLOGY

With rare exception, mycoses are not transmissible from patient to patient. Gown, glove, or mask isolation of hospitalized patients with mycoses is not indicated. Ringworm of the scalp in children is transmissible to other children, so caps and combs should not be shared by infected children and playmates. Airborne transmission of *P. jirovecii* has

TABLE 254-2   Typical Appearance of Fungi in Tissue

Yeastlike Fungi	
Histoplasma capsulatum	2–3 × 3–4-μm oval, budding uninucleate cells; often intracellular; granulomatous inflammation. Caseous necrosis can occur. Cells in African histoplasmosis (var. *duboisii*) are 6–15 μm in diameter.
Penicillium marneffei	2–3 × 2-6-μm oblong yeasts, some with central cross-septum, often intracellular except in areas of necrosis.
Pneumocystis jirovecii	3.5- to 7-μm cysts resemble *H. capsulatum* on methenamine silver stain or calcofluor but do not bud. Clusters of cysts occur in alveoli surrounded by eosinophilic amorphous material.
Candida glabrata	2.5-3 × 4–5-μm oval budding cells; pyogenic necrosis.
Candida albicans	3 × 5-μm oval, budding cells usually by tubular structures (pseudohyphae), with constrictions at septae and branching only at septations.
Cryptococcus neoformans	4 to 6-μm round uninucleate cell with large surrounding capsule; narrow pore between mother and daughter cell; daughter cell detached while small. Stains red with mucicarmine.
Sporothrix schenckii	1–3 × 3–10-μm cigar-shaped cell or 2- to 10-μm round budding cell; pyogenic and granulomatous inflammation.
Blastomyces dermatitidis	8- to 15-μm round multinucleate cell with large pore between mother and daughter cell; daughter cell remains attached until nearly size of mother cell; pyogenic and granulomatous inflammation.
Paracoccidioides brasiliensis	2- to 30-μm multiple, budding, round cells with tiny pore between mother and daughter cell; daughter cell released when small.
Coccidioides spp.	5- to 60-μm thick-walled, nonbudding, round cells that may contain endospores.
Agents of chromoblastomycosis	4- to 12-μm round or oval, brown, thick-walled cells, often in clumps; hyphal forms may be seen in superficial crusts.
Moulds	
Aspergillus spp.	2- to 5-μm-wide hyphae, frequently septate, even diameter, "Y"-shaped branching; vascular invasion; necrosis.
Agents of mucormycosis	4- to 15-μm-wide hyphae, rarely septate, uneven diameter, often branch at broad angles; vascular invasion; necrosis.

been postulated, but isolation of these patients is not routine. Bandages or casts that become contaminated with draining pus from patients with coccidioidomycosis require care to see that the fungus does not remain on the fomite for several days because at room temperature the fungus will grow as the infectious, spore-bearing mold form.

The diagnostic laboratory should be alerted when specimens from patients suspected of having coccidioidomycosis or histoplasmosis are sent for culture. Once these cultures grow in the mold form, they can be hazardous to laboratory personnel.

BIBLIOGRAPHY

Anaissie EJ, Mcginnie MR, Pfaller MA, eds. Clinical Mycology. New York: Churchill Livingstone; 2003.
Connor D. Pathology of Infectious Diseases. Stamford, CT: Appleton & Lange; 1997.
Dismukes WE, Pappas PG, Sobelk JD. Clinical Mycology. New York: Oxford University Press, 2003.
Kwon-Chung KJ, Bennet JE. Medical Mycology. Philadelphia: Lee & Febiger; 1992.
Sugar SM. A Practical Guide to Medically Important Fungi and the Diseases They Cause. Philadelphia: Lippincott-Raven; 1997.

CHAPTER 255

Candida Species

JOHN E. EDWARDS, Jr.

Written descriptions of oral lesions that were probably thrush date to the time of Hippocrates and Galen. Langenbeck, in 1839, found fungi in oral lesions of a patient.[1] By 1841, Berg established the fungal cause of thrush by inoculating healthy babies with aphthous "membrane material." In 1843, Robin attached to the organism the name *Oidium albicans*. There have been more than 100 synonyms for *Candida albicans;* the two that have persisted are *Monilia albicans*, originated by Zopf in 1890, and *C. albicans*, used by Berkhout in 1923.[2]

In 1861, Zenker described the first well-documented case of deep-seated *Candida*. The first case of *Candida*-induced endocarditis was described in 1940.[3] The most interesting period in the history of *Candida* infections began in the 1940s, when the widespread use of antibiotics was introduced. Since then, previously undocumented manifestations of *Candida* infections have occurred, and the incidence of practically all forms of *Candida* infections has risen abruptly.

Candida spp. have been the fourth most common organisms recovered from blood of hospitalized patients in the United States during recent decades.[4] There is evidence that the increase in candidemia may be leveling off and that there is an increase in the proportion of non-*albicans* species occurring now.[5] The burden of this illness in terms of morbidity, mortality, and expense is considerable. The cost of an episode of candidemia in the United States in 1997 was estimated to be $34,123 per Medicare patient and $44,536 for a private insurance patient.[6] More recent estimates describe expenditures adding to hospital costs of approximately $1 billion dollars for the management of candidemia in the United States.[7] Excellent comprehensive reviews detailing the emergence of *Candida* as a common pathogen are now available.[5,8-22] These emerging infections have included arthritis, osteomyelitis, endophthalmitis, myocarditis, pericarditis, pacemaker endocarditis, meningitis, peritonitis, myositis, pancreatitis, and others that are elaborated upon in detail in their respective sections of this chapter. The increasing incidence of human immunodeficiency virus-1 infection, the use of therapeutic modalities for advanced life support, and certain surgical procedures, such as organ transplantation and the implantation of prosthetic devices, have continued to be important in the expanding incidence of *Candida* infections.

PATHOGEN

Candida organisms are yeasts, that is, fungi that exist predominately in a unicellular form. They are small (4- to 6-μm), thin-walled, ovoid cells (blastospores) that reproduce by budding. They grow well in vented routine blood culture bottles and on agar plates and do not require special fungal media for cultivation. Several automated blood culture methods offer more rapid detection of *Candida*.[23,24] Yeast forms, pseudohyphae, and hyphae may be found in microscopic examination of clinical specimens; identification of the hyphae and pseudohyphae is facilitated with 10% potassium hydroxide, which clears the epithelial cells, and with fluorescent microscopic examination of calcofluor white–stained smears. The organism also stains gram positive.

Candida organisms form smooth, creamy white, glistening colonies that may resemble staphylococcal colonies. A rapid, presumptive identification of *C. albicans* can be made by placing the organism in serum and observing germ tube formation—small projections from the cell surface that appear within 90 minutes.[25] However, both false-negative and false-positive germ tube formation may occur. The remainder of the identification and speciation procedures are based primarily on physiologic parameters rather than on morphologic characteristics. Metabolic tests include carbohydrate assimilation and fermentation reactions, nitrate utilization, and urease production. Chlamydospore formation is also used to identify *C. albicans.* Because of variation in species pathogenicity, speciation is desirable. There are more than 150 species of *Candida,* but only nine are regarded as frequent pathogens for humans: *C. albicans, C. guilliermondii, C. krusei, C. parapsilosis, C. tropicalis, C. pseudotropicalis, C. lusitaniae, C. dubliniensis,* and *C. glabrata* (formerly classified as *Torulopsis glabrata*). *C. dubliniensis* is a newly described species that was formerly included within *C. albicans.*[26,27] *C. dubliniensis* forms germ tubes and chlamydospores and is identified as *C. albicans* by the most common methods. However, it will not grow at 45° C, is darker green when initially isolated on CHROMagar candida, and hybridizes poorly to the Ca3 probe.[28] Because it is not yet clear how the clinical features may differ from those of *C. albicans,* if at all, the two are considered synonymous in this chapter. Infections by other species are being reported with increasing frequency, such as the azole-resistant species *Candida inconspicua.*[29-32] The API Yeast 20C strip is a commercial kit that gives accurate identification of most *Candida* spp. in 2 to 5 days.[33]

EPIDEMIOLOGY AND ECOLOGY

C. albicans organisms have been recovered from soil, animals, hospital environments, inanimate objects, and food. Non-*albicans* species may live in animal or nonanimal environments as well. Only rarely are *Candida* spp. laboratory contaminants.[34] That principle has not been generally appreciated, and interpretation of positive cultures as laboratory or skin contaminants has led to important errors in patient management.

The organisms are normal commensals of humans and are commonly found on skin, throughout the entire gastrointestinal (GI) tract, in expectorated sputum, in the female genital tract, and in the urine of patients with indwelling Foley catheters.[35] There is a relatively high incidence of carriage on the skin of health care workers.[32]

Although the vast majority of *Candida* infections are of endogenous origin, human-to-human transmission is possible. Examples are thrush of the newborn, which may be acquired from the maternal vagina, and balanitis in the uncircumcised man, which may be acquired through contact with a partner having *Candida* vaginitis. There is also important, emerging evidence that *Candida* infection can be acquired from the hospital environment.[29,32,36,37] Molecular biology tools are improving considerably the understanding of *Candida* epidemiology.[38-40] Important studies in recent years suggest that *Candida* has many of the genetic components necessary for mating and suggest that mating may actually occur in vivo.[41-45] If *Candida* can be forced to mate in vitro and undergo meiosis, by exploitation of these genetic components, a significant breakthrough will occur in elucidating pathogenetic factors of *Candida* through molecular genetics.

PATHOGENESIS AND PATHOLOGIC FINDINGS

Normal defense mechanisms against *Candida* have been reviewed extensively,[46-50] and a comprehensive compendium of reviews is now available.[8,51] Only highlights of this topic can be discussed herein, and the reader is referred to the cited references for details of this evolving field.

The defense mechanism of intact integument is of importance in maintaining resistance to cutaneous candidiasis. Any process causing skin maceration leaves the involved site susceptible to *Candida* invasion, even in healthy individuals. In recent years the importance of the dendritic cell for maintaining skin and mucosal integrity has been recognized.[51] Once the organism invades the dermis or enters the blood stream, polymorphonuclear leukocytes play a role in defense because they have the capacity to damage pseudohyphae and to phagocytize and kill blastospores.[52-54] In addition to neutrophils, monocytes and eosinophils[55,56] as well as dendritic cells[51,57-59] also ingest and kill *Candida.* Other cells, such as endothelial cells[60] and epithelial cells may also ingest the organisms in vivo, but do not have a direct killing effect. Platelets may also have anti-*Candida* activity.[61,62] A platelet-derived factor stimulates germ tube production, and *Candida* cell wall fractions agglutinate platelets.[63,64] Serum and plasma alone, even

though they contain antibodies and complement components, are incapable of killing *Candida.*

Neutrophils and monocytes lacking myeloperoxidase or the capacity to generate hydrogen peroxide and superoxide anion fail to kill *C. albicans* effectively.[55,56] This observation and additional related studies suggest that the myeloperoxidase, hydrogen peroxide, or superoxide anion system, or all of these, is a major mechanism responsible for intracellular killing of *C. albicans.* In addition, studies have identified a ferrous ion–hydrogen peroxide–iodide system that is operative in intracellular killing.[65] A further intracellular killing mechanism for phagocytes involves chymotrypsin-like cationic proteins.[66-68] These proteins probably act by increasing candidal membrane permeability. The role of macrophages and sessile reticuloendothelial cells has also been investigated.[57] Rabbit and mouse alveolar and peritoneal and human lung macrophages have *Candida*-killing capacities.[69,70] Of interest is a study of Taschdjian and colleagues that showed, by immunofluorescent techniques, organisms within tissue macrophages and sessile reticuloendothelial cells throughout the body in patients with disseminated candidiasis.[71] This observation suggests a defense role for these tissue macrophages. A large number of other components are directly involved with and/or interactive in the mediation of phagocytosis and, in some instances, the regulation of function of lymphocytes by phagocytes; they included mannose receptors, complement receptors, Fc receptors, proinflammatory cytokines, proinflammatory chemokines, interferon-γ (INF-γ); tumor necrosis factor-α; fibronectin; interleukin (IL)-4, IL-8, IL-10, IL-12, and IL-18; and transforming growth factor-β. A source directing a review of these entities is available.[51]

The role of lymphocytes in defense against *Candida* and the regulation of *Candida*-induced cell-mediated immunity, within the context of the Th1/Th2 paradigm, are exceptionally complex subjects and are in a state of evolution.[51,72] They can be only superficially addressed herein. The importance of the defensive role of the lymphocyte can be gleaned from clinical observations: (1) patients with chronic mucocutaneous candidiasis are afflicted with *Candida* infection as a result of dysfunction of their lymphocyte system,[73,74] and (2) patients with acquired immunodeficiency syndrome (AIDS) are highly susceptible to mucocutaneous candidiasis. However, it should be noted that there is experimental evidence for congenitally athymic (nude) mice having more resistance to *Candida* challenge than controls with normal T lymphocytes.[75,76]

A simplified summary of the role of T helper (Th) cells, which are pivotal for regulation of phagocytosis, is as follows. When *Candida* is recognized by both dendritic cells and polymorphonuclear leukocytes, both cell types produce IL-12, which activates Th1 cells. The activated Th1 cells then secrete INF-γ and IL-2, both of which stimulate phagocytic cells. Downregulation of phagocytosis occurs through the stimulation of Th2 cells by IL-4, primarily secreted by the resident dendritic cells. These Th2 cells secrete IL-4 and IL-10, which inhibit phagocytosis.

The role of B lymphocytes and antibody has been investigated for years. Several lines of evidence point to an important role for antibodies in defense against candidiasis. The rate of ingestion of *C. albicans* by neutrophils is increased by both heat-labile and heat-stable serum opsonins.[77] Immunoglobulin (Ig) G and other serum constituents effectively opsonize *C. albicans.*

Evidence exists for the presence of both protective and nonprotective antibodies. Evidence for protective antibody is based in part on experimental data showing that sera from patients who recovered from disseminated candidiasis protect mice when passively transferred. Additionally, clinical trials are currently underway with an antibody to break down products of a heat shock protein from *Candida.*[78] Polyclonal sera and IgM monoclonal antibodies to an adhesin of *Candida* confer protection in mice.[79]

Other humoral factors are likely operative in defense against *Candida* infections. Serum iron-binding proteins have been shown to inhibit the growth of *Candida,* presumably by binding iron, which is a *Candida* growth factor.[80] Finally, there are humoral substances that induce *C. albicans* to form pseudohyphae and to clump the organisms in vitro,[81] and numerous other humoral substances that have inhibitory effects on *Candida* growth.

Complement is necessary for optimal opsonization of *Candida* blastospores[82-84] in vitro, and animals deficient in alternate pathway activation are more susceptible to *Candida* challenge.[85] Furthermore, C3b has been found to bind to *Candida* blastospores.[86] Also, evidence for an important role of complement is the finding of complement components deposited in the basement membrane of cutaneous lesions in patients with chronic mucocutaneous candidiasis.[87] Both the classic and the alternate pathways are activated by *Candida*. The weight of the evidence suggests that the alternate pathway is the most important. *Candida* cells, particularly pseudohyphae, have surface molecules that resemble human complement receptors CR2 and CR3.[88-90]

The capabilities of *Candida* to adhere to vaginal, gastrointestinal, and oral epithelial cells, fibronectin, platelet fibrin clots, acrylic, endothelium, lymphocytes, and plastics have all been demonstrated.[88,89,91-94] The molecular genetics of adherence have been reviewed comprehensively and are beyond the scope of this discussion.[95]

For this human commensal organism to become a pathogen, interruption of normal defense mechanisms is necessary. The factors responsible for this immunocompromise fall into two categories, naturally occurring and iatrogenic. Included in the first category is diabetes mellitus, which predisposes to cutaneous but not disseminated candidiasis.

The most important predisposing factors to *Candida* infection, and especially to disseminated candidiasis, are iatrogenic. The introduction of newer therapeutic modalities for advanced life support into clinical medicine has been primarily responsible for the dramatic change in incidence of this disease. Of these factors, probably the most important have been the introduction of antibiotics and the widespread use of indwelling intravenous catheters. Antibiotics suppress normal bacterial flora and allow *Candida* organisms to proliferate, especially in the GI tract. Sulfonamides decrease neutrophil *Candida* intracellular killing,[96] and tetracycline, doxycycline, and aminoglycosides have been shown to decrease neutrophil phagocytosis.[97,98]

Factors that may provide a route for *Candida* to enter from the environment into the vascular system of susceptible patients include the use of heroin,[99] hyperalimentation fluids, polyethylene catheters,[100] and pressure-monitoring devices. The implantation of prosthetic materials, especially cardiac valves and the artificial heart, is also associated with an increased incidence of *Candida* infection. Clinical situations associated with general immune suppression may be further complicated by the use of antibiotics, hyperalimentation fluid, and the other therapeutic modalities mentioned earlier, usually in the setting of multiple abdominal surgeries, renal transplantation, neoplastic diseases, the use of steroids, and severe burns.

Two observations support the hypothesis that the GI tract is a likely source for entrance of *Candida* into the blood stream. Krause and associates reported drinking a suspension containing a massive amount of *Candida*.[101] Despite no recognizable GI disease, the investigator became candidemic and candiduric. Stone and co-workers have shown that yeasts can cross the GI tract of animals.[102] One would expect patients who have had abdominal surgery and therapy with multiple antibiotics to be at double risk for dissemination from the GI source by having both overgrowth of *Candida* in the GI tract and interruptions of the normal GI-tract mucosal integrity. GI-tract surgery is now a well-recognized predisposing factor to disseminated candidiasis.[103] It is possible that loss of integrity of the GI tract as a result of either the disease or the cytotoxic chemotherapy creates a portal by which *Candida* passes from the GI-tract lumen into the blood stream.[104] Alternatively, the growing body of literature regarding *Candida* as a cause of septic thrombophlebitis suggests that in many cases the skin site of vascular catheter entry, rather than the GI tract, is the most likely portal of entry.[105]

When the organism invades visceral tissue, microabscesses are formed, generally with normal parenchyma between the microabscesses. In tissue, both yeast forms and hyphal forms are present. Whether the formation of filamentous forms of *Candida* is a factor associated with virulence is one of the major unresolved controversies within the field.[106] The initial cellular reaction is granulocytic.

Histiocytes, giant cells, and epithelioid cells appear early, and the reaction may take the form of a granulomatous response. Although organisms may be seen on hematoxylin-eosin stains, optimal staining is accomplished with period acid–Schiff or methenamine silver. In the severely immunocompromised patient, the inflammatory reaction may be minimal or almost nonexistent, leaving the abscess composed only of *Candida* and necrotic tissue.

In superficial candidiasis, the histopathologic change is a chronic dermatitis with the yeast confined to the stratum corneum. However, *Candida* granuloma (see "Clinical Manifestations") is characterized by invasion into both the epidermis and the dermis as well as by marked hyperkeratosis and acanthosis.

The factors associated with the organism rather than the host that are responsible for its virulence are under extensive investigation. An incomplete list includes the germ tube, proteases, phospholipases, adherence capabilities, hydrophobicity, morphologic switching, the presence of human-like integrins, and resistance to platelet-derived microbicidal peptides. A detailed review of the interesting topic of virulence factors is beyond the scope of this discussion, but the reader is referred to the recent compendium of discussions on the topic.[8]

CLINICAL MANIFESTATIONS

As the frequency of diseases caused by *Candida* has increased, a relatively large number of manifestations, which were previously either not recognized or extremely infrequent, have become well documented. The discussion of these clinical manifestations is facilitated by their subdivision into mucocutaneous and deep organ involvement.

Mucous Membrane Infections

Thrush

Oral *Candida* infections are common and have been reviewed.[107-113] The term *thrush* is applied to a specific form of oral candidiasis characterized by creamy white, curdlike patches on the tongue (Fig. 255-1) and on other oral mucosal surfaces; the patches are removable by scraping and leave a raw, bleeding, and painful surface. The patches are actually a pseudomembrane consisting of *Candida,* desquamated epithelial cells, leukocytes, bacteria, keratin, necrotic tissue, and food debris.[114] The diagnosis can be made by the clinical appearance of the

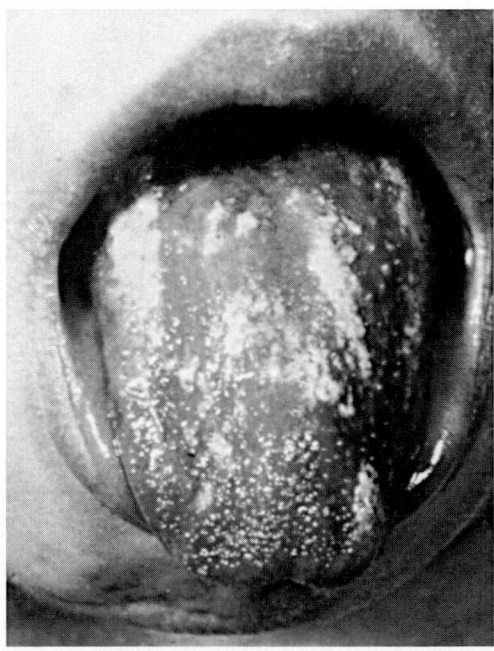

FIGURE 255-1. Typical oral thrush with curdlike white patches over the tongue. *(Courtesy of Dr. Arnold Gurevitch.)*

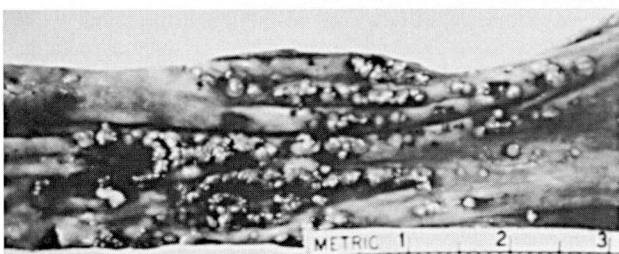

FIGURE 255-2. Severe *Candida* esophagitis at autopsy.

lesion and by scraping, using either a potassium hydroxide smear or Gram stain to show masses of hyphae, pseudohyphae, and yeast forms. Simple culturing does not solidify the diagnosis because *Candida* grows easily from normal mouths. In addition to the classic lesions, which have been described by Lehner,[114] other manifestations include (1) acute atrophic candidiasis, a nonspecific atrophy of the tongue that is thought to be a sequela of acute pseudomembranous candidiasis; (2) chronic atrophic candidiasis or "denture sore mouth," which is a chronic inflammatory reaction and epithelial thinning under the dental plates[109]; (3) angular cheilitis, an inflammatory reaction at the corners of the mouth (not caused exclusively by *Candida*); and (4) *Candida* leukoplakia, firm, white plaques affecting the cheek, lips, and tongue that have a protracted course (and, in rare instances, may be precancerous).[115] Since the introduction of inhaled steroids for the treatment of asthma, especially in children, oral thrush has been reported extensively in patients treated with these agents.[116,117] Incidence has ranged from 0% to 77%. Thrush developing in patients who use inhaled steroids usually resolves spontaneously without a change in the dosage of the agent or is successfully managed with topical nystatin or clotrimazole.

Other patients with a high incidence of thrush are cancer patients and those with AIDS. Patients with thrush for no obvious reason should be evaluated for AIDS. Because of the introduction of potent antiretroviral therapy, the incidence of thrush has declined in patients with AIDS.

Candida Esophagitis

Although there have been a small number of reports of *Candida* esophagitis occurring in patients with no known underlying illness, it is more commonly associated with treatment of malignancy of the hematopoietic or lymphatic systems (Fig. 255-2) and in AIDS patients. Additionally, omeprazole has been implicated as a risk factor.[118] Recently, the expression of a gene family within the organism has been shown when it invades the esophagus, suggesting a role of these genes in the pathogenesis of esophagitis.[119] Esophageal disease was believed to occur by direct spread from oral disease (thrush), but reviews have shown that *Candida* esophagitis may occur frequently without thrush.[120-123] The most common symptoms of *Candida* esophagitis include painful swallowing, a feeling of obstruction on swallowing, and substernal chest pain. Nausea and vomiting may also occur. The diagnosis is made definitively by biopsy during endoscopy[124-126] (Fig. 255-3). However, the appropriate clinical settings, associated with the endoscopic appearance of white patches resembling thrush that show masses of hyphae and pseudohyphae on scraping, are enough evidence to initiate therapy without a histopathologic demonstration of the organisms invading the mucosa.[120-122] It is important to recognize that *Candida* esophagitis can occur simultaneously with herpes simplex virus or cytomegalovirus infection in severely immunocompromised patients. Radiographic examination may be helpful in making a clinical diagnosis; irregularity of the esophageal mucosa as a result of ulcerations may be seen, as well as shoulder defects, diverticula, fistulas, and dilatation of the esophagus from denervation.[127] Endoscopy is the preferred procedure for definitive diagnosis, however. The pseudomembrane that forms may become so extensive that it causes intraluminal protrusions and partial esophageal obstruction. Perforation of the esophagus as a result of esophageal candidiasis is very rare. Generally, if perforation occurs, it is in the lower two thirds of the esophagus. Some patients have had exten-

FIGURE 255-3. Numerous *Candida* plaques seen in the duodenum (*upper panels*) and esophagus (*lower panels*).

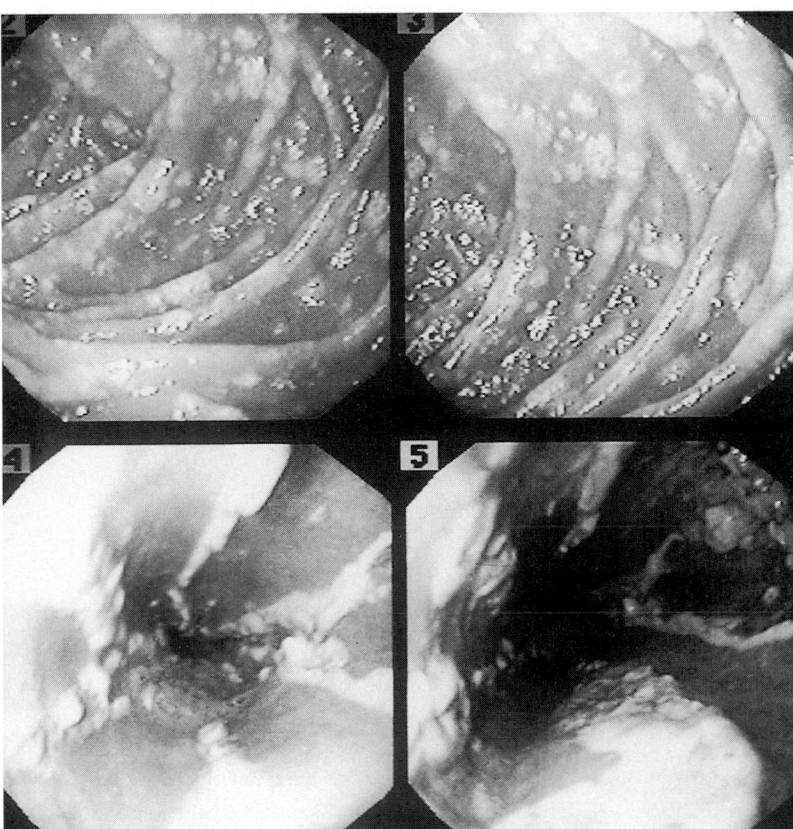

sive esophageal disease and been almost asymptomatic, probably as a result of denervation of the esophagus from the disease.[128] Other complications include bleeding and, presumably, dissemination.

Nonesophageal Gastrointestinal Candidiasis

The most common clinical setting for GI-tract candidiasis is in patients with neoplastic disease. Eras and colleagues reviewed their autopsy experience with candidiasis in a cancer hospital and found that, second only to esophageal candidiasis, involvement of the stomach was by far the next most common site.[129] The most frequent lesions were single or multiple ulcerations containing *Candida* deep in the ulcer beds. In addition, but with lesser frequency, chronic gastric ulcer, gastric perforation, and malignant gastric ulcer with concomitant *Candida* infection were seen. Small bowel and large bowel infection occur also.[130] Ulceration is the most common lesion. Pseudomembrane formation and ulceration in association with tumor occurs also. As in other mucous membrane *Candida* infections, white plaques may be seen on endoscopy of the duodenum, and there may be thickening of mucosal folds in the duodenum and jejunum.[130] Equal in frequency to the involvement of the small bowel is involvement of the large bowel, which again may be characterized by ulceration, superficial erosions, pseudomembrane formation, penetrating ulcers, and perforation. Gastric candidiasis has two forms: diffuse mucosal involvement (rare) and focal invasion of benign gastric ulcers.[131,132]

Candida Vaginitis

This common infection is most frequently seen in a setting of diabetes mellitus, antibiotic therapy, or pregnancy (see Chapter 103).[133-135] In addition, the use of birth control pills may be a predisposing factor, although this association is controversial. However, estimates are that 75% of women have an episode of candidal vaginitis during their lifetime; many have no recognizable underlying predisposing factor.[136] *Candida* has assumed the role of the most common cause of vaginitis, with higher frequency rates than those of *Trichomonas* or bacterial vaginosis.[134] The widespread use of antibiotic therapy may be the most important factor responsible for the emergence of *Candida*-induced vaginitis. Reviews of the current trends in the epidemiology and pathogenesis

of vaginal candidiasis are now available.[113,137-140] In these reviews the rising incidence of non-*albicans Candida* species is emphasized.

Although *Candida*-induced vaginitis may be accompanied by a thick, curdlike discharge, scanty discharge may instead characterize the infection. Edema and intense pruritus of the vulva is almost always present. The discharge consists of epithelial cells and masses of hyphae and pseudohyphae; a polymorphonuclear leukocyte response is not a component of the inflammatory reaction. The vagina and labia are usually erythematous, and extension onto skin of the perineum can occur (Fig. 255-4). In addition, endometritis caused by *Candida* has been reported, and the urethra may become secondarily infected.

Vaginal candidiasis is not clearly more common or more refractory to treatment in patients with AIDS.[141] The causes of recurrent vulvovaginal candidiasis may be related to deficiencies in both systemic cell-mediated immunity and local mucosal immunity.[142]

Cutaneous Candidiasis Syndromes

Generalized Cutaneous Candidiasis

This condition is an unusual form of cutaneous candidiasis and is characterized by widespread eruptions over the trunk, thorax, and extremities with increased severity in the genitocrural folds, anal region, axillae, hands, and feet (Fig. 255-5). The process begins as individual lesions that spread into large confluent areas. It occurs in both adults and children.[143,144]

Erosio Interdigitalis Blastomycetica

This term applies to *Candida* infection occurring between the fingers or toes (Fig. 255-6). It has a red base, may extend onto the sides of the digits, is painful, and is predisposed to maceration.[143,145]

Candida Folliculitis

Infection at the hair follicles with *Candida* can occur (Fig. 255-7).[146,147] Rarely, the condition may become extensive. It must be distinguished from folliculitis caused by the dermatophytes and tinea versicolor. Recently this folliculitis has been described in immunocompromised hosts and intravenous drug abusers.[148,149]

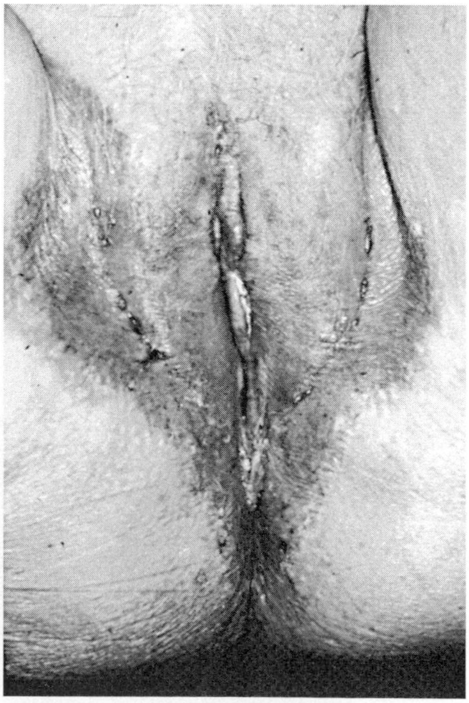

FIGURE 255-4. Extension of *Candida* vaginitis onto the perineum. *(Courtesy of Dr. Victor Newcomer.)*

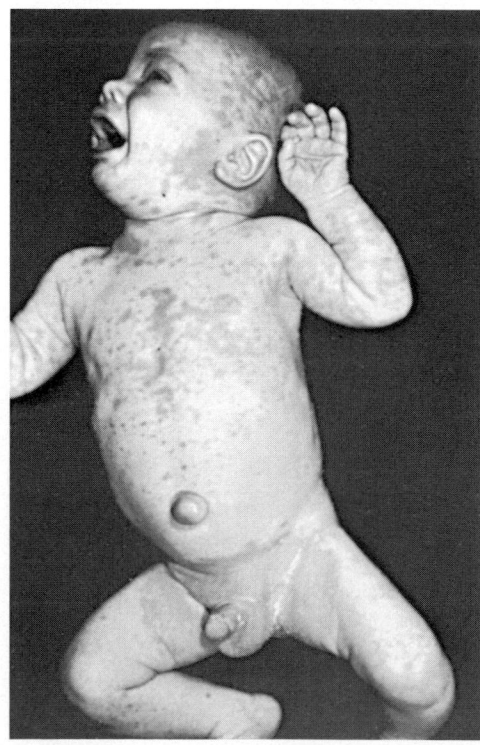

FIGURE 255-5. Generalized candidiasis. *(Courtesy of Dr. Victor Newcomer.)*

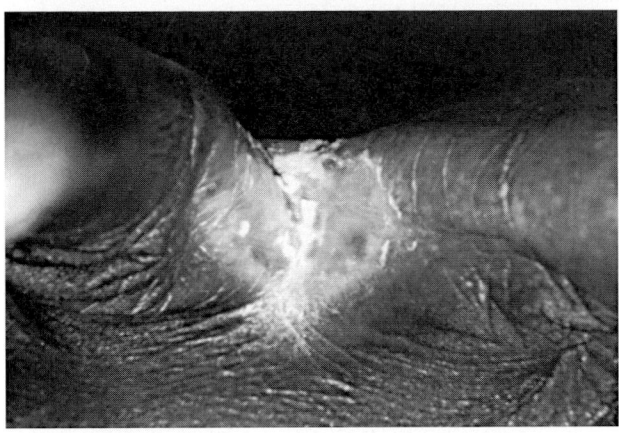

FIGURE 255-6. Erosio interdigitalis blastomycetica. *(Courtesy of Dr. Arnold Gurevitch.)*

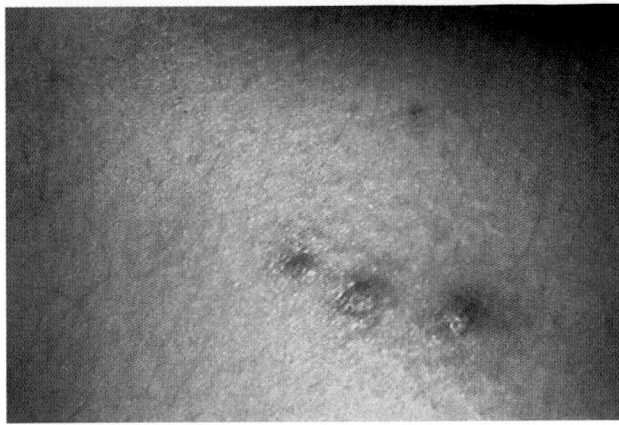

FIGURE 255-8. *Macronodular* lesions of disseminated candidiasis. *(Courtesy of Dr. Richard Meyer.)*

Candida Balanitis

This process begins as vesicles on the penis that develop into patches resembling thrush and are accompanied by severe itching and burning. It may spread to the thighs, gluteal folds, buttocks, and scrotum. It can be acquired through sexual intercourse with a partner having vaginal candidiasis.[150] *Candida* is one of the more common causes of balanitis.[151]

Cutaneous Lesions of Disseminated Candidiasis

Three distinct types of lesions associated with disseminated candidiasis have been described.[152-155] The macronodular lesions (Fig. 255-8) are 0.5 to 1 cm in diameter, are pink to red, and may either be single or occur widely distributed over the entire body.[156,157] The most accurate method of making a specific diagnosis is by punch biopsy and demonstration of organisms on histologic section. Most patients with these lesions are neutropenic, and all have disseminated candidiasis, not local inoculation. Additionally, there may be lesions resembling ecthyma gangrenosum[158] and purpura fulminans.[159] Chronic lesions of pyoderma gangrenosa may become superinfected with *Candida*, delaying their diagnosis.[160]

Intertrigo

This common skin condition affects any site in which skin surfaces are in close proximity and provide a warm, moist environment. It begins as vesicopustules, which enlarge and rupture, causing maceration and fissuring. The area of involvement has a scalloped border with a white rim consisting of necrotic epidermis, which surrounds an erythematous, macerated base. Frequently, satellite lesions are found that may coalesce and extend the affected area. A variant form of cutaneous candidiasis in the intertriginous region has a miliary appearance resembling miliaria rubra with erythematous macules or vesicopustules.[161]

Paronychia and Onychomycosis

Candida is one of the most common causes of paronychia.[162] Many skin bacteria, as well as *Candida,* can usually be recovered by culture of the infected area. The appearance of the reaction is that of a relatively well-localized area of inflammation that becomes warm, glistening, and tense and may extend extensively under the nail (Fig. 255-9). Unless the disease process is stopped, secondary thickening, ridging, and discoloration occur, and nail loss may result.

Candida paronychia occurs in association with frequent immersion of the hands in water. People who may contract paronychia include dishwashers, laundry workers, and young mothers. There is also a higher incidence of paronychia among diabetic patients than in the nondiabetic population. Specific diagnosis is made by Gram stain or potassium hydroxide preparation and culture showing predominantly *Candida* organisms.

In addition to paronychia, *Candida* may cause infection in the nail itself and is a cause of onychomycosis.[163-167]

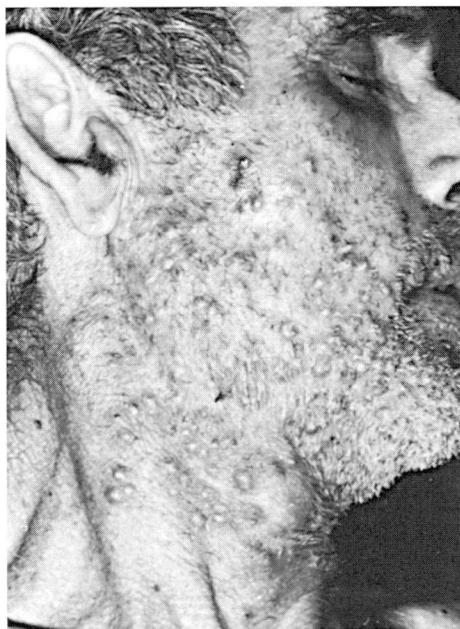

FIGURE 255-7. Severe *Candida* folliculitis in beard distribution. *(Courtesy of Dr. Victor Newcomer.)*

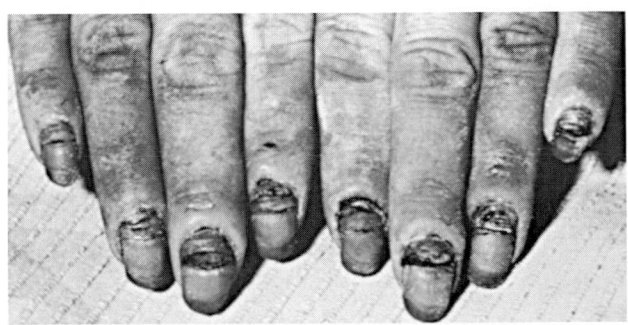

FIGURE 255-9. *Candida* paronychia and onychomycosis. *(Courtesy of Dr. Victor Newcomer.)*

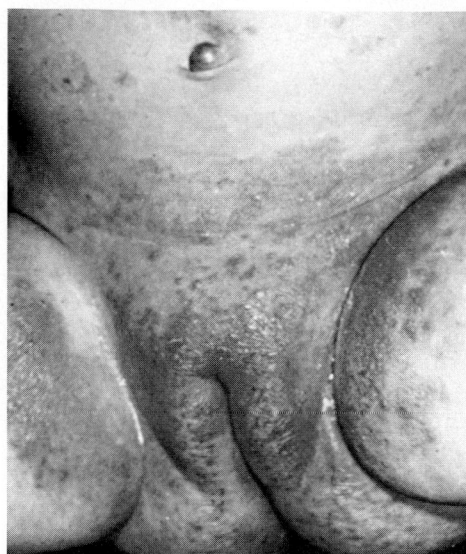

FIGURE 255-10. Severe *Candida* diaper rash. *(Courtesy of Dr. Victor Newcomer.)*

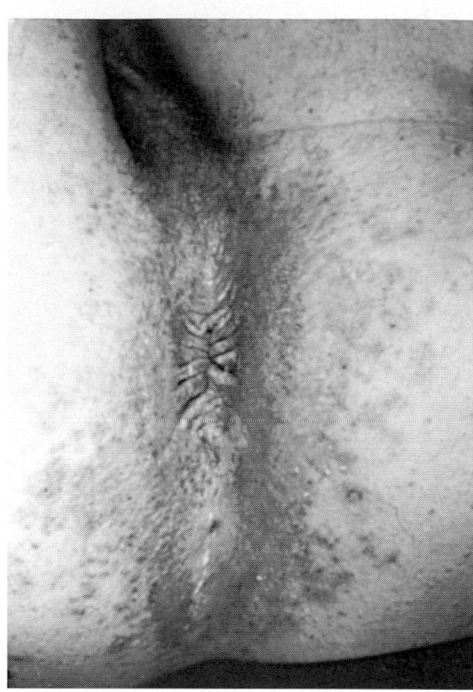

FIGURE 255-11. Perianal candidiasis. *(Courtesy of Dr. Victor Newcomer.)*

Diaper Rash

Candida is a common cause of diaper rash in infants.[168] The condition generally starts in the perianal area and spreads over the perineum in the region of diaper contact (Fig. 255-10). The process is facilitated by maceration caused by wet diapers. The probable origin is the GI tract. Diagnosis is made by scraping the area and demonstrating the organisms on potassium hydroxide preparation.[169]

Perianal Candidiasis

Although numerous organisms and combinations of organisms have been associated with pruritus ani either alone or in combination, *Candida* is a frequent cause.[170] The perianal skin develops marked erythema and progresses to maceration (Fig. 255-11). Intense pruritus results. Complications include involvement of the anal canal and extensive spread over the perineum.

Chronic Mucocutaneous Candidiasis

The term *chronic mucocutaneous candidiasis* (CMC) is used to describe a heterogeneous group of *Candida* infections of the skin, mucous membranes, hair, and nails that have a protracted and persistent course despite what is usually adequate therapy. The subject has been the focus of several reviews.[73,74,171-173] *Candida* esophagitis can occur and, over the years, cause esophageal stenosis. The major problem, however, is disfiguring lesions of the face, scalp, and hands. Alopecia in areas of infection is common and may be permanent. These infections have been associated with definable, relatively specific immunologic abnormalities, which may be responsible for their persistent nature.

The major immune defect associated with CMC is failure of T-cell lymphocytes (thymus derived) to respond to stimulation with *Candida* antigen in vitro by either lymphocyte transformation or the synthesis of cytokines. An in vivo manifestation of this abnormality is reflected in the cutaneous anergy found in approximately one half of the patients. Various combinations of the T-cell function abnormalities exist. Some patients' lymphocytes transform in vitro when stimulated by *Candida* antigen, but their skin tests remain negative to the antigen. Certain patients with positive transformations do not synthesize cytokines; virtually all patients with negative transformations lack cytokine production. Despite these abnormalities of T-cell function (T-cell numbers, lymphocyte proliferative responses to nonspecific mitogens such as phytohemagglutinins and allogenic cells), B-cell lymphocyte numbers and serum immunoglobulins are usually normal. However, a group of patients with selective immunoglobulin has been described.[174] Some patients have other immune abnormalities, such as cutaneous anergy to such antigens as streptokinase-streptodornase, mumps virus, and tetanus toxoid; defective lymphocyte transformations in response to nonspecific mitogens (e.g., phytohemagglutinin); defective monocyte chemotaxis; a lack of anti-*Candida* antibody in salivary IgAs; plasma inhibitors to *Candida*-stimulated lymphocyte transformations; suppressor lymphocytes; and various degrees of thymic aplasia. Not all patients have these identifiable immune abnormalities.

Most forms of CMC begin in infancy or within the first 2 decades; rarely, the onset may be after the age of 30 years. The first manifestation is usually oral thrush followed by nail infections and then skin involvement. There is a considerable spectrum of severity, ranging from chronic involvement of an isolated nail to a severely disfiguring form (*Candida* granuloma) (Fig. 255-12). An additional facet of CMC is the association of several endocrine disorders in approximately one half of the patients. A subset of these patients has a distinct entity, the autoimmune polyendocrinopathy–candidosis–ectodermal dystrophy (APECED) syndrome, an autosomal recessive disorder due to mutations in the *AIRE* gene, mapped to 21q22.3.[175] Prevalence is high in Finns, Iranian Jews, and Sardinians, with a lesser incidence in persons of Northern Italian and Swedish descent. Chronic mucocutaneous candidiasis usually appears by age 5, followed by hypoparathyroidism and later adrenal insufficiency. Autoimmune thyroiditis, Graves' disease, chronic active hepatitis, malabsorption, juvenile-onset pernicious anemia, alopecia, and primary hypogonadism occur with lesser frequency. Dental enamel hypoplasia, pitted nail dystrophy, vitiligo, and calcification of the tympanic membranes may be present. Autoimmune antibodies to adrenal, thyroid, and gastric tissues are common.

Although most patients with CMC survive for a prolonged period with their disease, patients may succumb if the cutaneous condition and immunodeficiencies are severe enough. Disseminated candidiasis has been a rare complication of this disease; the most common cause of death is bacterial sepsis.

The topic of *Candida* skin infection in general has been reviewed extensively.[176]

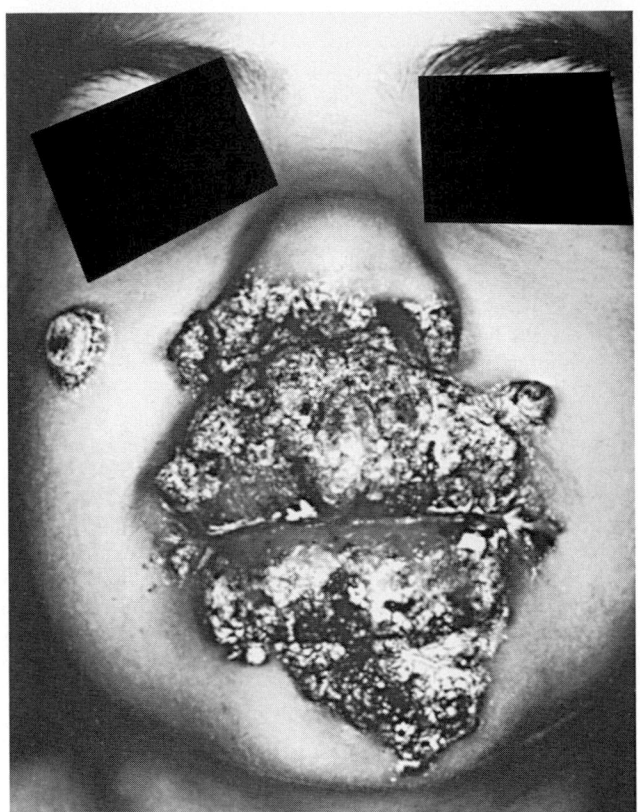

FIGURE 255-12. *Candida granuloma. (Courtesy of Dr. Victor Newcomer.)*

Deep Organ Involvement

Central Nervous System Candidiasis

Candida infects both parenchymal brain tissue and the meninges, usually as a complication of hematogenously disseminated candidiasis.[177-180] Approximately 50% of patients with *Candida* meningitis have had disseminated disease in other organs.[181] *Candida* has emerged as the dominant cerebral mycosis in autopsied patients.[177] When infection occurs in brain parenchyma, it generally forms multiple microabscesses and small macroabscesses scattered throughout the tissue.[182,183] Rarely, larger abscesses have occurred and may be visualized by computed tomography.[184]

Virtually all patients with *Candida* meningitis have had cerebrospinal fluid pleocytosis. Fifty percent have had a lymphocyte pleocytosis with an average count of 600 cells/mm³. Sixty percent have had hypoglycorrhachia and elevated protein levels; organisms have been present on wet mount or Gram stain in approximately 40%.[181] *C. albicans* has been the responsible pathogen in 90% of cases. Occasional cases caused by *C. tropicalis* are being reported.

The clinical manifestations of central nervous system involvement with diffuse microabscesses may be variable. If the patient is comatose or noncommunicative, detection of abnormalities may be exceptionally difficult. When meningitis is present, the signs of meningeal irritation (headache, stiff neck, irritability), typical of any meningeal infection, are frequently present. In the newborn, particularly the very low birth weight neonate, diagnosis is often difficult and delayed, leading to permanent neurologic sequelae. Lumbar puncture should be considered when the blood culture of such infants contains *Candida*.

In addition to occurring as a complication of disseminated candidiasis,[185] *Candida* meningitis may result from infection of a ventricular shunt,[186] or may be introduced by lumbar puncture,[187] trauma, or neurosurgery,[188] or may complicate bacterial meningitis. The signs and symptoms are nonspecific. Untreated, the mortality rate is very high;

it is reduced substantially with antifungal therapy. Hydrocephalus is a reasonably frequently occurring complication of the infection. An increase in the number of cases of *Candida* meningitis reported in neonates is occurring. AIDS is now considered a predisposing factor for *Candida* meningitis.[177,189]

Respiratory Tract Candidiasis

In general, *Candida* pneumonia occurs in two forms: (1) as either local or diffuse bronchopneumonia originating from endobronchial inoculation of the lung,[190,191] a very rare event, or (2) as a hematogenously seeded, finely nodular, diffuse infiltrate, which in its early stages may be difficult to distinguish from congestive heart failure or *Pneumocystis* pneumonia.[192-198] Other forms of *Candida* pneumonia are very rare; those that have been described are necrotizing pneumonia,[193,199] *Candida* pulmonary mycetoma,[200] and transient infiltrates caused by *Candida*.[201] Radiographic and computed tomographic findings are nonspecific, and definitive diagnosis depends on biopsy-proven fungal invasion of pulmonary tissue.[202,203] Because of a relatively high prevalence of yeasts colonizing the respiratory tract, especially in ill patients, a diagnosis of *Candida* pneumonia cannot be made on radiographic findings and recovery of yeasts from sputum or endotracheal tube aspirate.[204] *Candida* has also caused bronchial infection,[205] laryngitis,[206] epiglottitis,[207] and infection of laryngeal prostheses.[208] Recently the entity of "fungal empyema thoracis" has been described as an emerging clinical entity.[209] Infection with *Candida* alone or in association with bacteria has been frequent within the population of patients with this entity. The crude mortality has been very high, and aggressive management has been advocated.

Cardiac Candidiasis

In addition to causing endocarditis, *Candida* infects both the pericardium[210] and the myocardium. *Candida* myocarditis occurs as diffuse microabscesses scattered throughout the myocardium with normal intervening myocardial tissue. The relatively high incidence of myocarditis has been stressed by Franklin and co-workers, who found that 62% of their 50 patients with disseminated candidiasis had myocardial involvement.[211] Other retrospective autopsy studies have shown a range from 8.4% to 93%. *Candida* myocarditis is also occurring in AIDS patients.[212] Autopsy series of disseminated candidiasis reveal a surprisingly high incidence of myocarditis (without associated valvular involvement) and point to the importance of thorough cardiac evaluation in patients who may have disseminated candidiasis. Of interest has been the emergence of *Candida* organisms as a cause of pericarditis.[210,213,214] A review of purulent pericarditis spanning the years 1960 to 1974 revealed that *Candida* organisms were either the single cause or combined with *Aspergillus* in 15% of the 26 cases.[215] The association of *Candida* pericarditis with either cardiac surgery or burns has been emphasized.

Candida Endocarditis

This manifestation of *Candida* was once a distinctly rare phenomenon, but its true incidence has increased simultaneously with the generalized increase in *Candida* infections. Of all the forms of fungal endocarditis, *Candida* is by far the most common. In the last 4 decades, there have been well over 214 reported cases.[216-218] In a detailed review of 319 cases of fungal endocarditis, *Candida* accounted for 67% of the cases.[217] The entity of *Candida* endocarditis has been reviewed extensively.[219-224] In recent years, additional cases have been reported in children.[225-229]

Candida endocarditis occurs in association with six clinical factors: (1) underlying valvular heart disease, (2) heroin addiction, (3) cancer chemotherapy, (4) implantation of prosthetic valves, (5) prolonged use of intravenous catheters (endocarditis, right atrial fungal masses, and infection of atrial myxomas have all been described), and (6) preexisting bacterial endocarditis, on which it is superimposed. Of these associations, by far the most frequent are those related to the postoperative state following cardiac surgery, accounting for approximately 50% of the cases. Of interest is the frequency of species other than *C. albicans* that have caused endocarditis; a minimum of 41% of the cases have been caused by organisms of other species, some of which have been very rarely recovered species.[230] In heroin addicts, *C. parapsilosis* has been the most common causative organism.[231] Of interest is that heroin abuse, in recent years, has diminished in percentage of underlying predisposing conditions relative to iatrogenic causes.[224]

The pathogenic mechanisms for fungal endocarditis are not fully understood, but patients who undergo cardiac surgery are at risk for candidemia by being exposed to multiple antibiotics, prolonged intravenous fluid administration, and intravenous plastic catheters. Both the damaged endocardium and prosthetic material apparently serve as foci for the localization of *Candida* organisms. Also, contamination of suture material has been implicated in cases reported with concentration along the suture line. Contamination of homografts and heterografts before insertion has also been documented.[232] Experimental evidence for a role in the pathogenesis of adherence of *Candida* to platelet fibrin complexes and/or fibronectin is accumulating.[233,234] The mechanisms for adherence and the potential for blocking the adherence are under investigation.

The valves most commonly involved in *Candida* endocarditis have been the aortic and the mitral. In postoperative *Candida* endocarditis, the type of surgery has not been as important as the length of the postoperative course and complications during the postoperative period. *Candida* infection has been seen in simple valvulotomies and in prosthetic material placement, heterografts, and homografts. Pacemaker endocarditis has also been described.[235] The physical findings and usual symptoms of *Candida* endocarditis are not significantly different from those of bacterial endocarditis with the exception of the occurrence of large emboli to major vessels. Osler's nodes, Janeway lesions, splinter hemorrhages, hepatosplenomegaly, hematuria, proteinuria, pyuria, and casts all can occur. In addition, although the lesions of hematogenous *Candida* endophthalmitis have been described much more frequently in the setting of disseminated candidiasis without endocarditis, they may also be seen with endocarditis.

The complications of *Candida* endocarditis are very similar to those of bacterial endocarditis and include valve perforation, myocarditis, congestive heart failure, and major emboli. Although most cases of postoperative *Candida* endocarditis occur in the first 2 postoperative months, some have occurred later,[222,236] and some patients who have been treated have had recurrent active disease after 2 years[237] and perhaps as long as 8 years. Therefore, in following patients treated for postoperative endocarditis, careful follow-up must be extended over a prolonged period.

Most patients with *Candida* endocarditis have positive blood cultures. Seelig and associates, in their 1974 analysis of 91 published cases of *Candida* endocarditis following cardiac surgery, noted that only 24 patients (26%) had negative blood cultures.[238] Modern blood culture methods likely provide better sensitivity. Echocardiography is becoming progressively more helpful, and large vegetations may be detected with this technique. False-negative results are common, especially in cases of mural endocarditis without valvular involvement. Transesophageal echocardiography has improved the sensitivity, particularly in the mitral valve. Serologic tests for *Candida* antibodies are associated with a high incidence of false negatives and false positives and are not clinically useful in the diagnosis of *Candida* endocarditis.

The therapy for *Candida* endocarditis is discussed in detail in the section on treatment. Before the introduction of surgical procedures for the management of *Candida*-induced endocarditis, the mortality rate from this disease was approximately 90%. With combined surgical and medical therapy, this high mortality rate has dropped to approximately 45%. Because of the introduction of newer antifungals, there has been a greater propensity for chronic suppression in selected patients.

Candida endocarditis has been seen in association with bacterial endocarditis. *Candida* is a superinfection introduced by prolonged intravenous catheterization for antibiotic treatment.

Urinary Tract Candidiasis

This topic has been reviewed comprehensively.[239-245] Urethral candidiasis can occur in both men and women. In men, it usually results from sexual contact with women with *Candida* vaginitis. In women, it is generally thought to be acquired from extension of *Candida* vaginitis. *Candida* prostatic infection has also been reported.[246-248] A history of previous antibiotic use has been frequent in most patients.

The presence of *Candida* in the urine is common and usually does not indicate renal tract infection. Antibiotics and Foley catheters have been associated with the acquisition of candiduria.[244] Visualization (cystoscopy) or biopsy proof of either fungus balls or tissue invasion is requisite for linking candiduria to infection. Although the use of colony counting in urine has been attempted to separate colonization from infection, it is not useful.[249] However, finding *Candida* in urine casts may be helpful in diagnosing renal tissue invasion of the upper renal tract.[250] Most patients with iatrogenic candiduria have spontaneous resolution; however, long-term persistence or a bladder fungus ball may be a complication, particularly in patients with diabetes mellitus, urinary stones, or obstruction.[251] Hematogenous dissemination from the urinary tract may occur, usually with instrumention.[252]

Candida cystitis is most commonly a complication of an indwelling Foley catheter. In the absence of bladder instrumentation, *Candida* cystitis has been associated most often with diabetes mellitus. Symptoms may be absent or may be essentially identical to those of bacterial cystitis. The cystoscopic appearance of the condition is that of a chronic nonspecific cystitis. A typical thrush membrane has been observed; it resembles deposits of coagulated milk and bleeds on removal. The condition may be so severe that perforation occurs.[253]

Candida infection of the upper urinary tract has been classified into two distinct forms: primary, that is, presumably from an ascending route; and secondary, from hematogenous spread. Papillary necrosis,[254] calyceal invasion, fungus ball formation, and perinephric abscess[255] can result from ascending infection, particularly in the presence of urinary tract obstruction, renal stones, or diabetes mellitus.[256-259] The hematogenous form of the disease is by far the most common. The pathologic changes are those of multiple microabscesses, especially in the cortical areas. Of interest is one case of emphysematous pyelonephritis in a diabetic drug-addicted patient and a case of cystitis emphysematosa.[260,261] Pneumaturia has occurred.[262] The kidney is one of the organs most frequently involved in disseminated disease.

Candida Arthritis, Osteomyelitis, Costochondritis, and Myositis

These manifestations of *Candida* infections were once extremely rare; however, their true incidence has increased appreciably.[263-270] Sites of localization for hematogenous *Candida*–caused osteomyelitis include the spine (vertebrae and intervertebral disks [Fig. 255-13]),[270] wrist, femur, cervical spine, and costochondral junctions of the ribs, scapula, and proximal humerus. Blood cultures have usually been negative, and diagnosis has been made by percutaneous needle aspiration of the involved area. In children the long bones are generally affected, whereas in adults the axial skeleton predominates. Spinal involvement may be accompanied by disk infection.[271-273] Bone infection may require surgery. Osteomyelitis may be a late complication of candidemia.[265,274] Radiographic examination findings are nonspecific.

Osteomyelitis as a result of contiguous spread from the skin has also been documented, and there is one reported case of extension of thrush of the mouth into the mandibular bone.

Candida arthritis occurs most frequently as a complication of disseminated candidiasis.[275-277] It can also occur from trauma, surgery,[278] and intra-articular injections of steroids, and as a complication of heroin injection, rheumatoid arthritis, and AIDS.[279] The topic of fungal arthritis in general has been reviewed.[275] In *Candida* arthritis occurring unassociated with disseminated candidiasis, non-*albicans* species have been the most common. Although the majority of cases of *Candida* arthritis have been acute, chronic *Candida* arthritis has

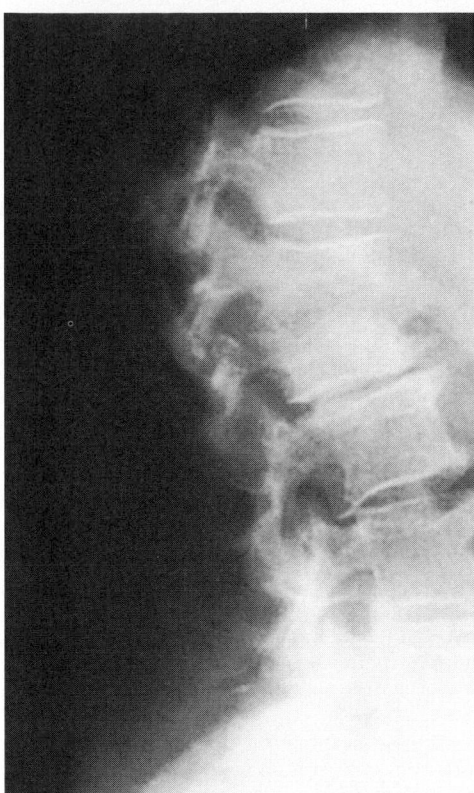

FIGURE 255-13. *Candida* spinal osteomyelitis. Note the involvement of the intervertebral disk and adjacent vertebrae. *(Reprinted from Edwards JE Jr, Turkel SB, Elden HA, et al. Hematogenous candida osteomyelitis. Am J Med. 1975;59:89-94, with permission from Excerpta Medica Inc.)*

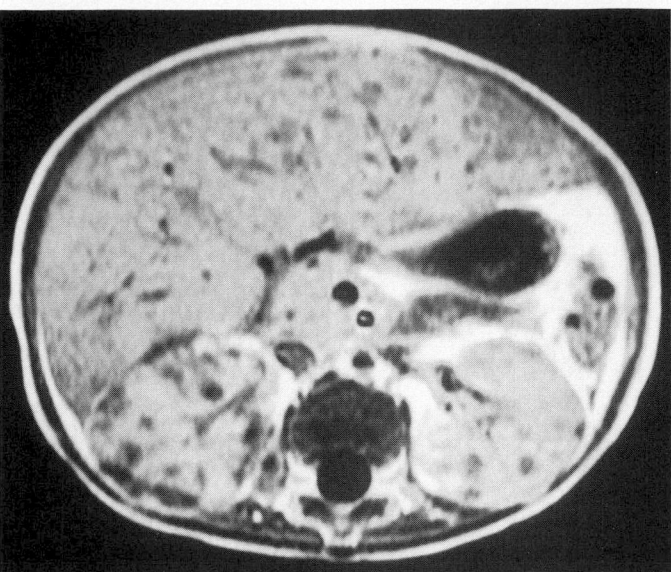

FIGURE 255-14. *Candida* abscesses in the liver, kidney, and spleen on magnetic resonance imaging.

been reported, especially in leukemic patients. Generally, *Candida* arthritis has begun as a suppurative synovitis, and a high percentage of cases have extended to form osteomyelitis. *Candida* costochondritis can occur from hematogenous seeding or as a complication of median sternotomy wound infection.[280]

Candida infection of muscle has been described. The majority of patients have been neutropenic, had hematogenously disseminated candidiasis, and had pain in the involved muscle.[281] The organisms may be seen on biopsy of the involved muscle. Cases have also been reported in drug addicts.[282] Generally, the muscle involvement is diffuse. However, a discrete muscle abscess may occur.[283]

Candida Infection of Peritoneum, Liver, Spleen, and Gallbladder

Candida infection of the peritoneum is a complication of peritoneal dialysis, GI surgery, and perforation of an abdominal viscus.[284-299] Prior antibiotic administration has been an important predisposing factor. For reasons not completely understood, the peritoneal process usually remains localized to the abdomen; the incidence of dissemination is approximately 25% in patients acquiring the disease from GI-tract perforation. In patients with peritonitis caused by chronic ambulatory peritoneal dialysis, dissemination is distinctly uncommon. Infants disseminate more frequently.

Other GI organs infected with *Candida* that have been reported include the gallbladder,[300,301] liver and spleen,[262,302-308] spleen alone,[309,310] and pancreas.[311-314] Hepatosplenic candidiasis has emerged as an important clinical problem in immunocompromised hosts and is particularly difficult to treat successfully. Most of these infections have occurred in severely immunocompromised patients and become manifest during their recovery from neutropenia. When the liver and spleen are involved, there is frequently involvement of other organs also, such as

the kidney. Computed tomography, ultrasonography,[303] or magnetic resonance imaging may visualize liver, kidney, or spleen abscesses (Fig. 255-14).[315] Laparoscopic techniques have been used successfully for diagnosis. The incidence of this entity has diminished in recent years, probably as a function of the increased use of prophylaxis strategies.[308] Fungus balls may form in the gallbladder and bile ducts.[316-320]

Candida Infection of Vasculature

The incidence of *Candida* intravascular infection has increased significantly, probably as a result of the increased number of susceptible patients and the widespread increased use of indwelling intravascular devices for advanced life support.[321-323] Both peripheral and deep vascular structures have been involved as well as both the venous and the arterial sides of the circulation and implanted prosthetic vascular materials.[324,325] Although the exact pathogenesis is not known, presumably the damaged endothelium becomes susceptible to *Candida* invasion. *Candida* adherence to catheters may also play a role. Complications have included superior cava obstruction, mural endocarditis of the right atrium, tricuspid endocarditis, and pulmonary venous thrombosis. Of importance is that, in patients with peripheral septic thrombophlebitis, there may be minimal symptoms and the extent of the disease may be greater than is apparent on initial clinical assessment. Patients with peripheral suppurative thrombophlebitis require aggressive surgical exploration to determine the extent of the disease process. Culture of the blood and involved veins is usually positive.[323]

Ocular Candidiasis

Candida can infect the eye by either hematogenous spread or direct inoculation, especially during eye surgery. *Candida* can infect virtually any eye structure, including conjunctiva, cornea, lens, ciliary body, vitreous humor, and the entire uveal tract. Once endophthalmitis occurs, therapy is difficult, and the incidence of permanent intraocular damage is high.

Through the 1970s there was increased reporting of hematogenous *Candida* endophthalmitis and an actual increase in incidence of this complication of candidemia.[326-339] Estimates of the incidence of the lesions in candidemic patients ranged as high as 28%.[340] Recent studies report a lower incidence.[341-343] An increased use of empirical and prophylactic antifungals may be an explanation for this possible decrease in incidence. A high association of retinopathy of prematurity with candidemia in very low birth weight neonates has been described,

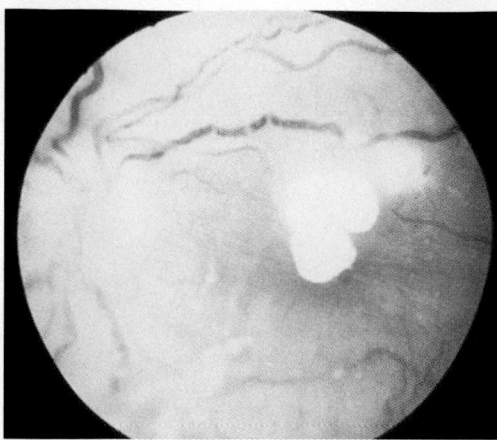

FIGURE 255-15. Advanced hematogenous *Candida* endophthalmitis. *(From Fishman LS, Griffin JR, Sapico FL, et al. Hematogenous Candida endophthalmitis—a complication of candidemia. N Engl J Med. 1972;286:675. Copyright © 1972 Massachusetts Medical Society. All rights reserved.)*

however.[344] More unusual recent cases have included *Candida* endophthalmitis as a complication of tattooing,[345] childbirth,[346] abortion,[347] therapy for human immunodeficiency virus infection,[348] and intravenous administration of contaminated dextrose infusion solution for minor ailments in a rural setting.[349]

The lesions are important because they can cause permanent blindness, and they may indicate underlying disseminated candidiasis. Lesions are white, cotton ball–like, and chorioretinal in origin and rapidly progress to involve the vitreous (Fig. 255-15). Use of the indirect ophthalmoscope facilitates visualization of their three-dimensional characteristics. Neutropenia inhibits the formation of ocular lesions in the experimental rabbit model[350] and may be associated with a lack of formation of easily seen lesions in some neutropenic patients. Diagnosis can be made by the characteristic funduscopic picture plus, in half the cases, an episode of known candidemia. Aspiration of the anterior chamber is rarely diagnostic. However, elective pars plana vitrectomy may be helpful both diagnostically and therapeutically.[351,352] The vitrectomy fluid should be centrifuged and the sediment examined by smear and culture. Diagnosis may also be facilitated with *Candida*-specific polymerase chain reaction.[353] Symptoms include visual blurring, floating scotomas, and bulbar pain. Importantly, many patients in intensive care units are too ill to complain of symptoms. Although *C. albicans* has been the most frequent species causing endophthalmitis, other species have been reported with increasing frequency.

Syndrome of Disseminated Candidiasis and Candidemia

The problems of management of candidemia and detection of underlying disseminated candidiasis present major enigmas for clinicians dealing with patients who are predisposed to the disseminated form of this disease. In recent years, there has been a steady publication stream of issues related to candidemia.[7,14,354-363] The problem is compounded by the absence of positive blood cultures in many patients with disseminated disease. The interpretation of the significance of recovery of increased numbers of *Candida* from sites such as sputum, urine, feces, and skin is difficult, because the organisms can frequently be recovered from these sites without having caused infection.

The clinical setting associated with disseminated candidiasis has been previously described. As expected, the populations of patients most commonly affected are those with neoplastic disease, patients who have had complicated postoperative courses, burn patients, patients who have received organ transplants, and low-birth-weight neonates. In the neoplastic group, the most common association has been with the acute leukemic population. In the postoperative group, the patients who have had organ transplantations, heart surgery, or GI-tract surgery are at greatest risk.

When *Candida* disseminates, multiple organs are usually involved, with the kidney, brain, myocardium, and eye the most common. In cancer patients receiving extensive immunosuppressive therapy, recognition of liver and spleen involvement has increased substantially. Other organs less frequently infected include the lungs, GI tract, skin, and endocrine glands. The hallmarks of the pathologic changes are diffuse microabscesses with a combined acute suppurative and granulomatous reaction and small macroabscesses. Macroabscesses more than 1 cm in diameter may also form, especially in the liver and spleen.

The rate of premortem diagnosis of disseminated candidiasis has been very low; only approximately 15% to 40% of cases have been diagnosed early enough for appropriate therapy. As an aid to earlier diagnosis, considerable attention has been focused on the detection of serum antibodies to *Candida* and the detection of *Candida* antigen. Despite the appearance of a very large number of publications on the serologic diagnosis of disseminated candidiasis, spanning at least 3 decades, controversies remain regarding the value of various serodiagnostic procedures.[364] Problems with the older diagnostic tests have been reviewed in detail.[365-367] Currently, there is no validated serodiagnostic test that is widely used.

The following conclusions can be drawn from available data: (1) the incidence of false-negative test results for antibody has been unacceptably high in most series (probably as a result of severe immunocompromise), and (2) techniques for antigen detection have been associated with a high incidence of false-negative results also (suggesting that antigen may not circulate or circulates in a nondetectable form).

A generalization regarding the application of these experimental serodiagnostic tests, which is an amplification of a similar statement made in 1976,[368] is still appropriate: A "positive" serodiagnostic test in a patient likely to have disseminated candidiasis increases the likelihood of the presence of disseminated disease, but a decision on treatment of a suspect patient cannot be made on serodiagnostic testing alone and must be made on the basis of a comprehensive, multifactorial, repetitive evaluation of the clinical circumstances.

The premortem diagnosis of disseminated candidiasis, therefore, remains a clinical diagnosis. Definitive diagnosis is made by histopathologic demonstration of the organism invading tissues. Of greatest importance in facilitating the diagnosis is awareness of, and persistent evaluation for, the variety of manifestations of disseminated candidiasis that serve as diagnostic clues.

Management of candidemia poses particularly difficult problems. Unquestionably, some patients who have candidemia, especially associated with an indwelling catheter or with the administration of intravenous fluids and competent immune status, have spontaneous resolution simultaneous with the removal of the catheter. Among severely immunosuppressed patients, almost all patients with candidemia have disseminated disease.[369] To assume that a positive blood culture for *Candida* represents "benign" candidemia may be extremely dangerous, and an extensive evaluation of such a patient should be undertaken to disprove the presence of disseminated disease. This evaluation should consist of repeated blood cultures and careful physical examinations for such manifestations as ocular involvement, osteomyelitis, cutaneous manifestations, and the other complications of disseminated disease that may be recognizable on physical examination. In the immunocompetent patient, the catheter, if present, should be removed,[18,370,371] and further blood cultures should be performed. Interpretation of the ensuing resolution of the candidemia should be made with recognition that 50% of the patients with disseminated candidiasis have not had positive blood cultures, and if the patient is bacteremic also, concomitant fungi may not grow in culture.[372] Three factors have resulted in a consensus among clinical mycologists to treat candidemia, regardless of whether it occurs in a compromised host and regardless of whether it is associated with an indwelling intravenous catheter.[18] Those factors are (1) recognition that stratifying patients according to the likelihood of having "benign" candidemia has frequently been unsuccessful, (2) there is at least a 40% mortality rate associated with candidemia,[373] and (3) less toxic antifungals, fluconazole and caspofungin, are now readily available for non-neutropenic patients who would have otherwise not been treated. This increased aggressiveness is a change in approach from previous practices of withholding antifungals in selected patients with candidemia. Of growing concern is the number of patients who have had complications of candidemia, particularly arthritis, endophthalmitis, endocarditis, and osteomyelitis. The incidence of these complications is undefined. The occurrence of these complications is further reason for treating all candidemic patients with antifungals. Removal of an indwelling intravenous catheter is important in management, and a new catheter should not be inserted over a wire in the site of the old one.[370,371]

Neonatal Candidiasis

A striking entity is *Candida* amnionitis, occurring after prolonged rupture of the membranes in mothers given parenteral antibiotics. The neonate's skin may be covered with pustules, vesicles, or diffuse erythema, yet full-term infants respond well to topical therapy. Premature infants with this entity are more likely to have diffuse pulmonary disease, respiratory distress, and a poor outcome despite systemic antifungal therapy. Disseminated candidiasis in the very low birth weight infant typically occurs later as a complication of catheter-acquired candidemia and is often followed still later by an indolent arthritis, osteomyelitis, or chronic meningitis. *Candida* infections of numerous types have been reported with increasing frequency in antenates, neonates, and older children.[374]

Miscellaneous *Candida* Infections

Candida infections that have been described but are beyond the scope of this discussion include ear infections, nasal ulcers, lymphadenitis (in patients with leukemia), laryngeal infection, diarrhea, and the "drunken disease" syndrome described in Japan (thought to be due to *Candida* fermentation of carbohydrate in the GI tract). Additionally, the emergence of *C. glabrata, C. krusei,* and *C. tropicalis* should be noted.[12,15,375,376] The isolation of unusual *Candida* species has been reviewed.[377]

TREATMENT AND PROPHYLAXIS

Treatment strategies have been reviewed in comprehensive detail for both neutropenic and non-neutropenic patients.[378] This review has been formulated into guidelines published under the auspices of the Infectious Diseases Society of America. Although an international consensus review of treatment strategies exists, it does not consider the newer azoles and echinocandins.[379] This discussion relies heavily on both reviews, with an emphasis on the newer guideline document for the newer agents.[378] Significant advances for the treatment of *Candida* infections made in recent years include the introduction of the echinocandins[380-383] and the development of advanced-generation azoles.[384-386] Additionally, an intravenous preparation of itraconazole has been approved[387]; however, data on its use in *Candida* infection are very limited at present. The treatment options included herein are limited to those agents currently approved by regulatory agencies, and do not include ravuconazole, posaconazole, and those echinocandins under development.

Nystatin has been the primary agent used for mucous membrane and cutaneous candidiasis, and most mild to moderate infections in these sites are treatable with it. Clotrimazole and miconazole have been efficacious for these mucocutaneous syndromes and are topical alternatives to nystatin, especially for vaginal infections. Oral clotrimazole has approximately equal efficacy as oral nystatin for thrush, but it is generally more palatable. For cases that cannot be managed with topical agents, itraconazole (solution) has been equal to fluconazole,[388] and the majority of patients with fluconazole-refractory thrush at least initially respond to itraconazole solution.[389] Voriconazole (not yet approved in the United States for disseminated *Candida* infections, but approved in the European Union for "treatment of fluconazole-resistant serious invasive *Candida* infections," and in Australia for all forms of

Candida infections) may be another alternative.[384] Amphotericin B suspension or intravenous amphotericin B, intravenous azoles, or intravenous echinocandins may be alternatives in refractory cases. Orally administered and absorbed, ketoconazole and fluconazole have been effective for mucocutaneous *Candida* infections, especially the chronic mucocutaneous candidiasis syndrome, thrush, and esophagitis. Superior efficacy of fluconazole over ketoconazole in AIDS patients with *Candida* esophagitis has been shown in one large, multicenter study of 169 patients.[390] Voriconazole has been shown to be effective in cases of fluconazole-refractory *Candida* esophagitis.[391]

Amphotericin B generally remains the cornerstone of therapy for disseminated and deep organ *Candida* infection, especially those infections that may be rapidly fatal or refractory to azoles or to echinocandins. There are numerous reports of deep *Candida* infections successfully treated with fluconazole, and these reports were summarized in 1997.[392] Additionally, there are now encouraging data with caspofungin and voriconazole.[384,393] The ease of administration, the availability of fluconazole in both oral and intravenous forms, and the relative lack of toxicity have been factors resulting in its emergence as the most attractive alternative to amphotericin B. However, the emerging non-*albicans* species that are relatively resistant to fluconazole, such as *C. glabrata* and *C. krusei,* are susceptible to caspofungin and to voriconazole, and an expanding role for these agents is anticipated. Although flucytosine has anti-*Candida* activity, its toxicity limits its use. Granulocyte transfusions have been given for *Candida* infection,[364] but they are not used on a wide-scale basis, and their efficacy has not been established from the limited experience to date. Similarly, the roles of human granulocyte colony-stimulating factor and other cytokines or immunomodulators have not been sufficiently evaluated in clinical settings, but are under investigation.[394]

Prophylaxis of *Candida* infection has been highly controversial. However, prospective controlled trials have successful results in allogenic bone marrow transplant recipients.[395,396] Although adequately controlled studies are not available, prophylaxis with fluconazole has also been used in high-risk autologous bone marrow transplantation and liver transplantation.[397] Large controlled trials in neutropenic leukemic patients have failed to show benefit from fluconazole prophylaxis. The use of oral nystatin or ketoconazole has not been associated with an appreciable decrease in systemic candidiasis in leukemic patients.[398-400] Ketoconazole and fluconazole have been efficacious in preventing oral *Candida* infections in cancer patients and AIDS patients. The possibility exists that there are subpopulations who are at high risk for deep candidiasis during neutropenia induced by cytotoxic chemotherapy for leukemia and may benefit.[401] It should be noted that fluconazole prophylaxis does not provide protection against molds.

There is no general consensus regarding prophylaxis in non-neutropenic surgery patients. Most experts do not recommend it. However, there have been successful trials in critically ill surgical patients.[402-404] Prevention must be weighed against the risk of inducing azole resistance in *Candida* strains carried by these patients.

Three lipid formulations of amphotericin B have been marketed in the United States: amphotericin B lipid complex (ABLC; Abelcet), amphotericin B colloidal dispersion (Amphotec), and liposomal amphotericin B (AmBisome).[405-409] Of these preparations, only ABLC and liposomal amphotericin B have been approved for proven candidiasis, and the approval is for patients who are intolerant or refractory to treatment with conventional amphotericin B deoxycholate. The approval stipulations by the Food and Drug Administration for use in patients refractory or intolerant to amphotericin B, high cost, and a lack of randomized trials relegate them to secondary use in candidiasis. The total amount of amphotericin B needed to treat any form of *Candida* infection is not known. Derivation of a specific figure is complicated, because some forms of *Candida* infection resolve spontaneously (often correlated with improvement of the immune status of the host). Because the manifestations of *Candida* infections are so varied, their therapy is discussed individually.

Hematogenously Disseminated Candidiasis

The decision to administer treatment for candidemia has been discussed previously in this chapter, and the consensus that all candidemic patients should be treated with antifungals was described. For neutropenic patients or if the course is consistent with an acute sepsis causing the patient to be in an unstable or rapidly worsening in condition, data with the newer agents remain encouraging but limited in the number of subjects studied compared to amphotericin B. For this subset of patients, although the recommendation is not evidence based, amphotericin B should be selected for initial therapy. As further experience is gained with the newer agents, including the echinocandins, azoles, and lipid formulations of amphotericin B, it may become clear that they are appropriate for such patients, and will have the advantage of being associated with less toxicity.

In patients who are clinically stable and in patients without neutropenia, there are now several options of approved agents, including fluconazole,[21,371,410,411] fluconazole plus amphotericin B, and intravenous caspofungin.[412] Additionally, ABLC and liposomal amphotericin B can be used for patients refractory to or intolerant of amphotericin B. The choice of therapy should be made within the context of the sensitivity of the isolate recovered, because *C. krusei* is resistant to fluconazole and *C. glabrata* is relatively resistant. Removal or changing of intravenous catheters is desirable if feasible.[413]

Candida Endocarditis

The mortality rate is lowest with combined medical and surgical therapy, compared with either medical or surgical treatment alone. McLeod and Remington have reviewed these data,[218] and current experience reflects the same concept.[221,224,236] Once the diagnosis of *Candida*-caused endocarditis is made, the procedure of choice is to initiate amphotericin B therapy and to perform a surgical procedure as soon as possible. After surgery, amphotericin B should be given for 6 to 10 weeks because of the significant incidence of relapse. ABLC or liposomal amphotericin B is an alternative for those patients who develop toxicity from desoxycholate amphotericin B. At the time of removal of the valve and surrounding vegetations, the area can be washed with an amphotericin B–containing solution.[414] Some patients with *Candida* endocarditis have had relapses years after surgery. Patients with *Candida* endocarditis should be monitored carefully for a minimum of 2 years postoperatively. Fluconazole is commonly used as long-term suppressive therapy.[221,415] Occasional cases of successful nonsurgical therapy are reported.[229,416]

Central Nervous System *Candida* Infection

Based on analysis of current literature, combined amphotericin B and 5-fluorocytosine (5-FC) therapy, without intrathecal instillation, is the most rational treatment for both meningitis and diffuse parenchymal infection. This recommendation is based entirely on observational studies. In five of six cases of *Candida* meningitis in newborn infants, liposomal amphotericin B has been successful.[417] If a shunt is in place, it should be removed, if possible.[188] In exceptionally severe cases, intrathecal antifungals should be considered. Indications for surgery of *Candida*-caused brain abscesses remain unclear.

Candida Peritonitis, Gallbladder Infection, and Intra-abdominal Abscesses

Candida peritonitis resulting from peritoneal dialysis of adults, if there is no evidence of spread to other organs, may respond to instillation of local amphotericin B at a concentration of 2 to 4 μg/mL in dialysate fluid.[287] However, many patients experience pain with this treatment. Amphotericin B–induced peritoneal adhesions might reduce access of dialysis fluid to some areas of the peritoneum. Successful treatment with fluconazole has been reported.[295,418] Removal of the catheter is considered helpful whenever feasible.[418,419] However, there are few reports of successful treatment without catheter removal.[420,421] The topic of fungal peritonitis has been reviewed recently without change in the basic therapeutic strategies outlined here.[297]

Candida coming from an abdominal drain placed at the time of GI surgery should not ordinarily prompt antifungal therapy.[18] Discovery of *Candida* in ascites from an undrained abdomen usually means that therapy is required. Hematogenous dissemination from the peritoneum can occur. In general, the threshold for treating *Candida* isolated from the peritoneum is lowering. A prospective study of the significance of the isolation of *Candida* from surgical specimens and freshly placed abdominal drains suggests that this lowering of threshold for treating peritoneal isolates is appropriate.[422] Fluconazole prophylaxis has been successful in preventing the development of *Candida* peritonitis in a population of high-risk surgical patients with interruption of the integrity of the gastrointestinal tract.[423]

The failure rate for the cure of hepatosplenic candidiasis has been high with amphotericin B both alone and in combination with 5-FC. Many experts recommend initial therapy with amphotericin B followed by long-term fluconazole therapy, or the use of fluconazole alone.[18] Reports of cures with liposomal amphotericin have appeared and are promising.[424-426] Successful results have also been obtained with fluconazole, though not during periods of neutropenia.[427] In some instances splenectomy may be necessary for large or refractory abscesses. *Candida*-caused cholecystitis may respond to intravenous amphotericin B or fluconazole.[428] In candidiasis of the gallbladder or biliary tract, drainage may be necessary[301] in addition to antifungal therapy. *Candida* may complicate necrotizing pancreatitis.[429] *Candida* pancreatic abscess has been successfully drained with computed tomography–guided percutaneous aspiration in addition to systemic antifungal therapy.[313]

Urinary Candidiasis

Postcatheterization candiduria usually resolves without specific antifungal therapy. There are several conditions in which it should be treated: in symptomatic patients, in renal transplantation patients, in very low birth weight infants, and in patients undergoing urinary tract instrumentation and possibly in neutropenic patients. Local amphotericin (a solution of 50 mg of amphotericin B in 1 L of sterile water infused at 40 mL/hr through a Foley catheter) is becoming less popular as a result of the use of oral fluconazole (200 mg/day for 7 to 14 days). Selected patients may require irrigation with amphotericin B through nephrostomy tubes placed directly in the collecting systems. If fungus balls form in the urinary tract, they require surgical removal. For kidney involvement, intravenous amphotericin B is indicated. However, oral fluconazole is an alternative to amphotericin B and is much more convenient.[430] The drug is excreted in high concentration in the urine. 5-FC is another alternative.[431] However, it may be less attractive in renal insufficiency, and resistance may develop.[431] Any stents, catheters, or other prosthetic materials in the urinary tract should be removed in order to prevent recurrence.

Eradication of candiduria in patients who require a persistent indwelling Foley catheter is particularly problematic. A placebo-controlled trial found that fluconazole at 200 mg/day for 14 days resulted in eradication of the candiduria, but there was a high rate of recurrence, suggesting the futility of antifungal therapy.[432] A large observational study has also verified the futility of antifungal therapy.[244] Alternatively, it is possible that the urinary tract may be a source for hematogenous dissemination, and the presence of candiduria may indicate hematogenous seeding to the kidney and widespread disseminated candidiasis. The selection of patients requiring persistent indwelling Foley catheters and the approach to their therapy must be individualized according to their clinical setting. As long as the Foley catheter remains in place, the goal of eradicating the candiduria may be impossible to attain. More data are necessary to determine the role of the newer of the azoles under development and of caspofungin.

Mucocutaneous Candidiasis

Oral thrush should be treated with topical agents whenever possible. The least expensive is nystatin. The usual adult dose is 4 to 6 mL of 100,000 units/mL four times daily. Clotrimazole 10-mg troches are also available. These can be sucked four times a day. Clotrimazole is approximately equally effective as nystatin but is not bitter, as is nystatin. Therapy for denture sore mouth is the same as that for thrush, with the addition of meticulous cleaning of the dentures and correction of ill-fitting plates. Angular cheilitis, which is frequently associated with denture sore mouth, should be treated with either topical clotrimazole or miconazole cream. Oral, absorbable fluconazole, ketoconazole, and itraconazole are effective for thrush. Fluconazole is more expensive, is more effective, and has fewer side effects than ketoconazole.[433] Itraconazole capsules are approximately equal to ketaconazole,[434] and the oral solution of itraconazole is equal to fluconazole, because of better absorption of the solution than its capsules.[388,435] Many patients with thrush unresponsive to fluconazole respond at least initially to itraconazole solution.[436]

The diagnosis of *Candida* esophagitis can be made presumptively on the basis of the presence of oral pharyngeal thrush and symptoms of esophagitis in patients with AIDS or cancer. Topical therapy with clotrimazole troches, amphotericin B suspension, or nystatin suspension usually fails. Fluconazole is superior to ketoconazole, itraconazole capsules, and flucytosine.[390,437,438] Itraconazole solution is approximately equal to fluconazole.[439] In one study, itraconazole solution plus 5-FC was approximately equal to fluconazole.[440] A last resort in refractory esophageal infections is low-dose (10 to 20 mg/day) intravenous amphotericin B.[441] Long-term suppressive therapy may be necessary in patients with AIDS.[442] Both caspofungin and voriconazole have been systematically studied for their efficacy in *Candida* esophagitis and their utility has been firmly established.[391,443-445] These agents, as well as itraconazole solution, may be useful in refractory cases.

Candida intertrigo is most successfully managed by decreasing the moisture of the involved area and by the application of amphotericin B lotion or nystatin cream several times a day or topical miconazole or clotrimazole. Management of *Candida* diaper rash has been successful with nystatin powder or cream in combination with a corticosteroid, such as Mycolog-II cream. Amphotericin cream or lotion may also be used. The same agents used for diaper rash are generally successful for pruritus ani.

Uncomplicated *Candida* vaginitis responds to short courses of topical or oral therapy in the vast majority of patients. The following regimens, used from 1 to 7 days, are considered comparable: clotrimazole (over the counter); butoconazole (over the counter); miconazole (over the counter); tioconazole (over the counter); terconazole; oral azoles (ketoconazole [500 mg twice daily for 5 days; not approved in the United States]); itraconazole (200 mg twice daily for 1 day or 200 mg/day for 3 days; not approved in the United States); and fluconazole (150 mg once).[446] Other regimens include nystatin (100,000 units daily for 1 to 2 weeks) and boric acid (600 mg in a gelatin capsule once daily [vaginal] for 14 days[447]). Recurrent *Candida* vaginitis requires eradication of causal factors as much as possible. Then treatment for 2 weeks with topical or oral azoles should be used, followed by 6 months of fluconazole (150 mg orally per week) or itraconazole (100 mg every other day). Ketoconazole (100 mg daily) is another alternative. This topic has been reviewed comprehensively.[448]

Candida-caused paronychia is best managed by preventing immersion of the hands in water as much as possible and applying clotrimazole or miconazole cream twice daily. Drainage is also important.

Chronic Mucocutaneous Candidiasis

Topical therapy to skin and mucous membranes achieves only slight improvement in this disease. Intravenous amphotericin B therapy has been effective, but nearly all patients relapse. Oral 5-FC has not been effective. The most important advance in the therapy of this disease is systemically administered azoles: ketoconazole, fluconazole, or itraconazole.[73] Numerous reports illustrate successful treatment. Therapy for months or years may be necessary. Development of resistance with long-term therapy is a potential problem.

Ocular Candidiasis

Treatment of *Candida* endophthalmitis necessitates the use of parenteral antifungal agents, especially amphotericin B.[449-451] Because of the data demonstrating a synergistic effect of amphotericin B and 5-FC, combination therapy should be used in refractory cases, rapidly developing lesions, or lesions in the vicinity of the macula. There are now many reported successes with fluconazole.[328,334,452] Vitrectomy may be of value in patients with large abscesses in the vitreous, rapidly progressive disease, or lesions threatening the macula. Early consideration for vitrectomy is obligatory in such cases. In addition, vitrectomy may confirm the diagnosis.[328] Hematogenous *Candida* endophthalmitis not extensively involving the vitreous has occasionally healed spontaneously. The use of intraocular antifungals remains controversial. There is a paucity of data on the treatment of *Candida* endophthalmitis with caspofungin, voriconazole, or the echinocandins and azoles under development. Successful therapy with a lipid formulation of amphotericin B has been reported.[453]

Miscellaneous *Candida*-Caused Infections

Candida osteoarthritis has been successfully treated with azoles.[454] One case of successful treatment with antifungals but without removal of the prosthetic joint has been reported.[278] Usually, removal of the prosthetic material is necessary.[455] The topic of *Candida* laryngeal infection has been reviewed.[206] Most patients have been managed with intravenous amphotericin B. Fluconazole may be appropriate as follow-up therapy. The treatment of *Candida*-caused epididymo-orchitis has been reviewed.[456] Although success without surgery has occurred, most patients have required drainage or orchidectomy. Similarly, *Candida*-caused thrombophlebitis of peripheral veins usually requires surgery in addition to antifungals.[105,321,323,457] Most cases of *Candida* pneumonia have been treated with amphotericin B. There is a paucity of information on treatment of this entity.

REFERENCES

1. Langenbeck B. Auffingung von Pilzen aus der Schleimhaut der Speiserohre einer Typhus-Leiche. Neue Not Geb Natur Heilk (Froriep). 1839;12:145-147.
2. Rippon JW. Candidiasis and the pathogenic yeasts. In: Medical Mycology, The Pathogenic Fungi and the Pathogenic Actinomycetes. Philadelphia: WB Saunders; 1988:532-581.
3. Joachim H, Polayes S. Aubacute endocarditis and systemic mycosis (monilia). JAMA. 1940;115:205-208.
4. Pfaller MA, Jones RN, Messer SA, et al. National surveillance of nosocomial blood stream infection due to *Candida albicans:* Frequency of occurrence and antifungal susceptibility in the SCOPE Program. Diagn Microbiol Infect Dis. 1998;31:327-332.
5. Clark TA, Hajjeh RA. Recent trends in the epidemiology of invasive mycoses. Curr Opin Infect Dis. 2002;15:569-574.
6. Rentz AM, Halpern MT, Bowden R. The impact of candidemia on length of hospital stay, outcome, and overall cost of illness. Clin Infect Dis. 1998;27:781-788.
7. Miller LG, Hajjeh RA, Edwards JE Jr. Estimating the cost of nosocomial candidemia in the United States. Clin Infect Dis. 2001;32:1110.
8. In: Calderon RA, ed. *Candida* and Candidiasis. Washington, DC: ASM Press; 2002:450.
9. Sanson GF, Briones MR. Typing of *Candida glabrata* in clinical isolates by comparative sequence analysis of the cytochrome c oxidase subunit 2 gene distinguishes two clusters of strains associated with geographical sequence polymorphisms. J Clin Microbiol. 2000;38:227-235.
10. Costa SF, Marinho I, Araujo EA, et al. Nosocomial fungaemia: A 2-year prospective study. J Hosp Infect. 2000;45:69-72.
11. Ostrosky-Zeichner L, Rex JH, Bennett J, et al. Deeply invasive candidiasis. Infect Dis Clin North Am. 2002;16:821-835.
12. Pappas PG, Rex JH, Lee J, et al. A prospective observational study of candidemia: Epidemiology, therapy, and influences on mortality in hospitalized adult and pediatric patients. Clin Infect Dis. 2003;37:634-643.
13. Snydman DR. Shifting patterns in the epidemiology of nosocomial *Candida* infections. Chest. 2003;123:500S-503S.
14. Gupta N, Mittal N, Sood P, et al. Candidemia in neonatal intensive care unit. Indian J Pathol Microbiol. 2001;44:45-48.
15. Kullberg BJ, Oude Lashof AM. Epidemiology of opportunistic invasive mycoses. Eur J Med Res. 2002;7:183-191.
16. Candidiasis. In: Kwong-Chung KJ, Bennett JE, eds. Medical Mycology. Philadelphia: Lea & Febiger; 1992:280-336.
17. Bodey GP. Candidiasis: Pathogenesis, Diagnosis and Treatment. New York: Raven Press; 1993.
18. Edwards JE Jr, Bodey GP, Bowden RA, et al. International Conference for the Development of a Consensus on the Management and Prevention of Severe Candidal Infections (see Comments). Clin Infect Dis. 1997;25:43-59.
19. Viscoli C, Girmenia C, Marinus A, et al. A surveillance study of fungemia in cancer patients in Europe (Abstract 2). In: Trends in Invasive Fungal Infections 3: meeting of the Invasive Fungal Infections Cooperative Group (IFIG of EORTC), Brussels, 1995.

20. Pfaller MA. Nosocomial candidiasis: Emerging species, reservoirs, and modes of transmission. Clin Infect Dis. 1996;22:S89-S94.

21. Anaissie EJ, Rex JH, Uzun O, et al. Predictors of adverse outcome in cancer patients with candidemia. Am J Med. 1998;104:238-245.

22. Jarvis WR. Epidemiology of nosocomial fungal infections, with emphasis on Candida species. Clin Infect Dis. 1995;20:1526-1530.

23. Body BA, Pfaller MA, Durrer J, et al. Comparison of the lysis centrifugation and radiometric blood culture system for recovery of yeast. Eur J Clin Microbiol Infect Dis. 1988;7:417-420.

24. Yagupsky P, Nolte FS, Menegus MA. Enhanced detection of Candida in blood cultures with the BACTEC 460 system by use of the aerobic-hypertonic (8B) medium. Epidemiol Infect. 1990;105:553-558.

25. Reyolds R, Braude AI. The filament-inducing property of blood for Candida albicans: Its nature and significance. Clin Res Proc. 1956;7:417-420.

26. Hannula J, Saarela M, Dogan B, et al. Comparison of virulence factors of oral Candida dubliniensis and Candida albicans isolates in healthy people and patients with chronic candidosis. Oral Microbiol Immunol. 2000;15:238-244.

27. Schorling SR, Kortinga HC, Froschb M, et al. The role of Candida dubliniensis in oral candidiasis in human immunodeficiency virus-infected individuals. Crit Rev Microbiol. 2000;26:59-68.

28. Pinjon E, Sullivan D, Salkin I, et al. Simple, inexpensive, reliable method for differentiation of Candida dubliniensis from Candida albicans. J Clin Microbiol. 1998;36:2093-2095.

29. D'Antonio D, Violante B, Mazzoni A, et al. A nosocomial cluster of Candida inconspicua infections in patients with hematological malignancies. J Clin Microbiol. 1998;36:792-795.

30. Just-Nubling G, Gentschew G, Dohle M, et al. Fluconazole in the treatment of oropharyngeal candidosis in HIV-positive patients. Mycoses. 1990;33:435-440.

31. Pfaller MA, Diekema DJ, Messer SA, et al. In vitro activities of voriconazole, posaconazole, and four licensed systemic antifungal agents against Candida species infrequently isolated from blood. J Clin Microbiol. 2003;41:78-83.

32. Pfaller MA. Nosocomial candidiasis: Emerging species, reservoirs, and modes of transmission. Clin Infect Dis. 1996;22 Suppl 2:S89-S94.

33. Huppert M, Harper G, Sun SH, et al. Rapid methods for identification of yeasts. J Clin Microbiol. 1975;2:21-34.

34. Hurley R. Pathogenicity of the genus Candida. In: Winner HI, Hurley R, eds. Symposium on Candida Infections. Edinburgh: Churchill Livingstone; 1966:13-25.

35. Odds FC. Candida and Candidosis: A Review and Bibliography. London: Bailliere Tindall; 1988.

36. Fowler SL, Rhoton B, Springer SC, et al. Evidence for person-to-person transmission of Candida lusitaniae in a neonatal intensive-care unit. Infect Control Hosp Epidemiol. 1998;19:343-345.

37. Diekema DJ, Messer SA, Hollis RJ, et al. An outbreak of Candida parapsilosis prosthetic valve endocarditis. Diagn Microbiol Infect Dis. 1997;29:147-153.

38. Pfaller MA. Epidemiology of nosocomial candidiasis: The importance of molecular typing. Braz J Infect Dis. 2000;4:161-167.

39. Shemer R, Weissman Z, Hashman N, et al. A highly polymorphic degenerate microsatellite for molecular strain typing of Candida krusei. Microbiology. 2001;147:2021-2028.

40. Powderly WG, Robinson K, Keath EJ. Molecular typing of Candida albicans isolated from oral lesions of HIV-infected individuals. AIDS. 1992;6:81-84.

41. Lachke SA, Lockhart SR, Daniels KJ, et al. Skin facilitates Candida albicans mating. Infect Immun. 2003;71:4970-4976.

42. Soll DR, Lockhart SR, Zhao R. Relationship between switching and mating in Candida albicans. Eukaryot Cell. 2003;2:390-397.

43. Lockhart SR, Daniels KJ, Zhao R, et al. Cell biology of mating in Candida albicans. Eukaryot Cell. 2003;2:49-61.

44. Magee BB, Magee PT. Induction of mating in Candida albicans by construction of MTLa and MTLalpha strains. Science. 2000;289:310-313.

45. Hull CM, Raisner RM, Johnson AD. Evidence for mating of the "asexual" yeast Candida albicans in a mammalian host. Science. 2000;289:307-310.

46. Murphy JW, Friedman H, Bendinelli M. Fungal Infections and Immune Response. New York: Plenum Press, 1993.

47. Calderone R, Diamond R, Senet JM, et al. Host cell-fungal cell interactions. J Med Vet Mycol. 1994;32(Suppl 1):151-168.

48. Lockhart SR, Joly S, Vargas K, et al. Natural defenses against Candida colonization breakdown in the oral cavities of the elderly. J Dent Res. 1999;78:857-868.

49. Steele C, Fidel PL Jr. Cytokine and chemokine production by human oral and vaginal epithelial cells in response to Candida albicans. Infect Immun. 2002;70:577-583.

50. Fidel PL Jr. Immunity to Candida. Oral Dis. 2002;8(Suppl 2):69-75.

51. Romani L. Immunology of invasive candidiasis. In: Calderone RA, ed. Candida and Candidiasis. Washington, DC: ASM Press; 2002:223-241.

52. Calderone RA. Host-parasite relationships in candidosis. Mycoses. 1989;32(Suppl 2):12-17.

53. Lyman CA, Walsh TJ. Phagocytosis of medically important yeasts by polymorphonuclear leukocytes. Infect Immun. 1994;62:1489-1493.

54. Roos D, Winterbourn CC. Immunology: Lethal weapons. Science. 2002;296:669-671.

55. Lehrer RI. The fungicidal mechanisms of human monocytes: 1. Evidence for myeloperoxidase-linked and myeloperoxidase-independent candidacidal mechanisms. J Clin Invest. 1975;55:338-346.

56. Lehrer RI. Measurement of candidacidal activity of specific leukocyte types in mixed cell populations: II. Normal and chronic granulomatous disease eosinophils. Infect Immun. 1971;3:800-802.

57. Roilides E, Lyman CA, Sein T, et al. Antifungal activity of splenic, liver and pulmonary macrophages against Candida albicans and effects of macrophage colony-stimulating factor. Med Mycol. 2000;38:161-168.

58. Bacci A, Montagnoli C, Perruccio K, et al. Dendritic cells pulsed with fungal RNA induce protective immunity to Candida albicans in hematopoietic transplantation. J Immunol. 2002;168:2904-2913.

59. Willcox MD, Webb BC, Thakur A, et al. Interactions between Candida species and platelets. J Med Microbiol. 1998;47:103-110.

60. Filler SG, Swerdloff JN, Edwards JE Jr. Endothelial cell phagocytosis of Candida albicans is required for endothelial cell injury. Presented at the Infectious Disease Society of America annual meeting, New Orleans, 1994.

61. Tang YQ, Yeaman MR, Selsted ME. Antimicrobial peptides from human platelets. Infect Immun. 2002;70:6524-6533.

62. Yeaman MR, Yount NY. Mechanisms of antimicrobial peptide action and resistance. Pharmacol Rev. 2003;55:27-55.

63. Skerl KG, Calderone RA, Segal E, et al. In vitro binding of Candida albicans yeast cells to human fibronectin. Can J Microbiol. 1984;30:221-227.

64. Robert R, Senet JM, Mahaza C, et al. Molecular basis of the interactions between Candida albicans, fibrinogen, and platelets. J Mycol Med (France). 1992;2:19-25.

65. Levitz SM, Diamond RD. Killing of Aspergillus fumigatus spores and Candida albicans yeast phase by the iron-hydrogen peroxide-iodide cytotoxic system: Comparison with the myeloperoxidase-hydrogen peroxide-halide system. Infect Immun. 1984;43:1100-1102.

66. Selsted ME, Harwig SSL. Purification, primary structure, and antimicrobial activities of a guinea pig neutrophil defensin. Infect Immun. 1987;55:2281-2286.

67. Ganz T, Selsted ME, Szlarek D, et al. Natural peptide antibiotics of human neutrophils. J Clin Invest. 1985;76:1427-1435.

68. Selsted ME, Szlarek D, Ganz T, et al. Activity of rabbit leukocyte peptides against Candida albicans. Infect Immun. 1985;49:202-206.

69. Patterson-Delafield J, Martinez RJ, Lehrer RI. Microbicidal cationic proteins in rabbit alveolar macrophages: A potential host defense mechanism. Infect Immun. 1980;30:180-192.

70. Lehrer RI. Host defense mechanisms against disseminated candidiasis. In: UCLA Conference on Severe Candidal Infections: Clinical Perspective, Immune Defense Mechanisms, and Current Concept of Therapy. Ann Intern Med. 1978;89:91-106.

71. Taschdjian CL, Toni EF, Hsu KC, et al. Immunofluorescence studies of Candida in human reticuloendothelial phagocytes: Implications for immunogenesis and pathogenesis of systemic candidiasis. Am J Clin Pathol. 1971;56:50-58.

72. Spellberg B, Edwards JE. The pathophysiology and treatment of Candida sepsis. Curr Infect Dis Rep. 2002;4:387-399.

73. Kirkpatrick CH. Chronic mucocutaneous candidiasis. Pediatr Infect Dis J. 2001;20:197-206.

74. Lilic D, Gravenor I. Immunology of chronic mucocutaneous candidiasis. J Clin Pathol. 2001;54:81-83.

75. Cutler JE. Acute systemic candidiasis in normal and congenitally thymic-deficient (nude) mice. J Reticuloendothel Soc. 1976;19:121-124.

76. Lee KW, Balish E. Systemic candidiasis in germ free, flora-defined and conventional mice. J Reticuloendothel Soc. 1981;29:71-77.

77. Solomkin JS, Mills EL, Giebink GS, et al. Phagocytosis of Candida albicans by human leukocytes: Opsonic requirements. J Infect Dis. 1978;137:30-37.

78. Matthews RC, Rigg G, Hodgetts S, et al. Preclinical assessment of the efficacy of mycograb, a human recombinant antibody against fungal HSP90. Antimicrob Agents Chemother. 2003;47:2208-2216.

79. Cutler JE, Granger BL, Han Y. Immunoprotection against candidiasis. In: Calderone RA, ed. Candida and Candidiasis. Washington, DC: ASM Press; 2002:243-256.

80. Kirkpatrick CH, Rich RR, Bennett JE. Chronic mucocutaneous candidiasis: Model building in cellular immunity. Ann Intern Med. 1971;74:955-978.

81. Louria DB, Smith JK, Brayton RG, et al. Anti-Candida factors in serum and their inhibitors: I. Clinical and laboratory observations. J Infect Dis. 1972;125:102-114.

82. Triebel T, Grillhosl B, Kacani L, et al. Importance of the terminal complement components for immune defence against Candida. Int J Med Microbiol. 2003;292:527-536.

83. Ashman RB, Papadimitriou JM, Fulurija A, et al. Role of complement C5 and T lymphocytes in pathogenesis of disseminated and mucosal candidiasis in susceptible DBA/2 mice. Microb Pathog. 2003;34:103-113.

84. Kozel TR. Activation of the complement system by pathogenic fungi. Clin Microbiol Rev. 1996;9:34-46.

85. Gelfand JA, Hurley DL, Fauci AS, et al. Role of complement in host defense against experimental disseminated candidiasis. J Infect. Dis. 1978;139:9.

86. Kozel TR, Brown RR, Pformmer GS. Activation and binding of C3 by Candida albicans. Infect Immun. 1987;55:1890-1894.

87. Sohnle PG, Frank MM, Kirkpatrick CH. Deposition of complement components in the cutaneous lesions of chronic mucocutaneous candidiasis. Clin Immunol Immunopathol. 1976;5:340-350.

88. Hostetter MK. Adhesins and ligands involved in the interaction of Candida spp. with epithelial and endothelial surfaces. Clin Microbiol Rev. 1994;7:29-42.

89. Fukazawa Y, Kagaya K. Molecular bases of adhesion of Candida albicans. J Med Vet Mycol. 1997;35:87-99.

90. Edwards JE Jr, Gaither TA, O'Shea JJ, et al. Expression of specific binding sites on Candida with functional and antigenic characteristics of human complement receptors. J Immunol. 1986;137:3577-3583.

91. Calderone RA, Braun PC. Adherence and receptor relationships of Candida albicans. Microbiol Rev. 1991;55:1-20.

92. Klotz SA. Fungal adherence to the vascular compartment: A critical step in the pathogenesis of disseminated candidiasis. Clin Infect Dis. 1992;14:340-347.

93. Edwards JE, Mayer C. Adherence of *Candida albicans* to mammalian cells. In: Ayoub EM, Cassell GH, Branch WC, Henry JJ, eds. Microbial Determinants of Virulence and Host Response. Washington, DC: American Society for Microbiology; 1990:179-194.

94. Ghannoum MA, Edwards JE Jr. *Candida* adherence to epithelial cells. J Mycol Med. 1992;2:10-13.

95. Sundstrom P. Adhesion in *Candida* spp. Cell Microbiol. 2002;4:461-469.

96. Lehrer RI. Inhibition by sulfonamides of the candidacidal activity of human neutrophils. J Clin Invest. 1971;50:2498-2505.

97. Forsgren A, Schmeling D, Quie PG. Effect of tetracycline on the phagocytic function of human leukocytes. J Infect Dis. 1974;130:412-415.

98. Ferrari FA, Pagani A, Marconi M, et al. Inhibition of candidacidal activity of human neutrophil leukocytes by aminoglycoside antibiotics. Antimicrob Agents Chemother. 1980;7:87-88.

99. Bisbe J, Miro JM, Latorre X, et al. Disseminated candidiasis in addicts who use brown heroin: Report of 83 cases and review. Clin Infect Dis. 1992;15:910-923.

100. Nielsen H, Stenderup J, Bruun B. Fungemia in a university hospital 1984-1988: Clinical and mycological characteristics. Scand J Infect Dis. 1991;23:275-282.

101. Krause W, Matheis H, Wulf K. Fungemia and funguria after oral administration of *Candida albicans*. Lancet. 1969;1:598-599.

102. Stone HH, Kolb LD, Currie CA, et al. *Candida* sepsis: Pathogenesis and principles of treatment. Ann Surg. 1974:697-711.

103. Edwards JEJ, Filler SG. Current strategies for treating invasive candidiasis: Emphasis on infections in nonneutropenic patients. Clin Infect Dis. 1992;14(Suppl 1):S106-S113.

104. Cole GT, Halawa AA, Anaissie EJ. The role of the gastrointestinal tract in hematogenous candidiasis: From the laboratory to the bedside. Clin Infect Dis. 1996;22(Suppl 2):S73-S88.

105. Benoit D, Decruyenaere J, Vandewoude K, et al. Management of candidal thrombophlebitis of the central veins: Case report and review. Clin Infect Dis. 1998;26:393-397.

106. Gow NA. Germ tube growth of *Candida albicans*. Curr Top Med Mycol. 1997;8:43-55.

107. Vargas KG, Joly S. Carriage frequency, intensity of carriage, and strains of oral yeast species vary in the progression to oral candidiasis in human immunodeficiency virus-positive individuals. J Clin Microbiol. 2002;40:341-350.

108. Odds FC. Mycology in oral pathology. Acta Stomatol Belg. 1997;94:75-80.

109. Nikawa H, Hamada T, Yamamoto T. Denture plaque-Past and recent concerns. J Dent. 1998;26:299-304.

110. Ellepola AN, Samaranayake LP. Oral candidal infections and antimycotics. Crit Rev Oral Biol Med. 2000;11:172-198.

111. Shepherd J. Thrush and breastfeeding. Pract Midwife. 2002;5:24-27.

112. Sherman RG, Prusinski L, Ravenel MC, et al. Oral candidosis. Quintessence Int. 2002;33:521-532.

113. Vazquez JA, Sobel JD. Mucosal candidiasis. Infect Dis Clin North Am. 2002;16:793-820, v.

114. Lehner T. Classification and clinico-pathological features of *Candida* infections in the mouth. In: Winner HI, Hurley R, eds. Symposium on *Candida* Infections. Edinburgh: Churchill Livingstone; 1966:119-137.

115. Sitheeque MA, Samaranayake LP. Chronic hyperplastic candidosis/candidiasis (candidal leukoplakia). Crit Rev Oral Biol Med. 2003;14:253-267.

116. Fukushima C, Matsuse H, Tomari S, et al. Oral candidiasis associated with inhaled corticosteroid use: Comparison of fluticasone and beclomethasone. Ann Allergy Asthma Immunol. 2003;90:646-651.

117. Simon MR, Houser WL, Smith KA, et al. Esophageal candidiasis as a complication of inhaled corticosteroids. Ann Allergy Asthma Immunol. 1997;79:333-338.

118. Chocarro Martínez A, Galindo Tobal F, Ruiz-Irastorza G, et al. Risk factors for esophageal candidiasis. Eur J Clin Microbiol Infect Dis. 2000;19:96-100.

119. Staib P, Kretschmar M, Nichterlein T, et al. Differential activation of a *Candida albicans* virulence gene family during infection. Proc Natl Acad Sci U S A. 2000;97:6102-6107.

120. Bonacini M, Laine L, Gal AA, et al. Prospective evaluation of blind brushing of the esophagus for *Candida* esophagitis in patients with human immunodeficiency virus infection. Am J Gastroenterol. 1990;85:385-389.

121. Porro GB, Parente F, Cernuschi M. The diagnosis of esophageal candidiasis in patients with acquired immune deficiency syndrome: Is endoscopy always necessary? (see Comments). Am J Gastroenterol. 1989;84:143-146.

122. Gould E, Kory WP, Raskin JB, et al. Esophageal biopsy findings in the acquired immunodeficiency syndrome (AIDS): Clinicopathologic correlation in 20 patients. South Med J. 1988;81:1392-1395.

123. Braegger CP, Albisetti M, Nadal D. Extensive esophageal candidiasis in the absence of oral lesions in pediatric AIDS. J Pediatr Gastroenterol Nutr. 1995;21:104-106.

124. Isaac DW, Parham DM, Patrick CC. The role of esophagoscopy in diagnosis and management of esophagitis in children with cancer. Med Pediatr Oncol. 1997;28:299-303.

125. Geisinger KR. Endoscopic biopsies and cytologic brushings of the esophagus are diagnostically complementary. Am J Clin Pathol. 1995;103:295-299.

126. Redah D, Konutse AY, Agbo K, et al. Is endoscopic diagnosis of *Candida albicans* esophagitis reliable? Correlations with pathology and mycology (in French). Gastroenterol Clin Biol. 2001;25:161-163.

127. Yee J, Wall SD. Infectious esophagitis. Radiol Clin North Am. 1994;32:1135-1145.

128. Jones JM. Necrotizing *Candida* esophagitis: Failure of symptoms and roentgenographic findings to reflect severity. JAMA. 1980;244:2190-2191.

129. Eras P, Goldstein MJ, Sherlock P. *Candida* infections of the gastrointestinal tract. Medicine. 1972;51:367-379.

130. Prescott RJ, Harris M, Banerjee SS. Fungal infections of the small and large intestine. J Clin Pathol. 1992;45:806-811.

131. Trier JS, Bjorkman DJ. Esophageal, gastric, and intestinal candidiasis. Am J Med. 1984;30:39-43.

132. Minolig G, Terruzzi V, Ferrara A, et al. A prospective study of relationships between benign gastric ulcer, *Candida*, and medical treatment. Am J Gastroenterol. 1984;79:95-97.

133. Sobel JD. *Candida* vulvovaginitis. Semin Dermatol. 1996;15:17-28.

134. Sobel JD. Vaginitis. N Engl J Med. 1997;337:1896-1903.

135. Sobel JD, Faro S, Force RW, et al. Vulvovaginal candidiasis: Epidemiologic, diagnostic, and therapeutic considerations. Am J Obstet Gynecol. 1998;178:203-211.

136. Sobel JD. Genital candidiasis. In: Bodey GP, ed. Candidiasis: Pathogenesis, Diagnosis and Treatment. New York: Raven Press; 1993:225-247.

137. Ferrer J. Vaginal candidosis: Epidemiological and etiological factors. Int J Gynaecol Obstet. 2000;71(Suppl 1):S21-S27.

138. Sobel JD. Management of patients with recurrent vulvovaginal candidiasis. Drugs. 2003;63:1059-1066.

139. Sobel JD, Zervos M, Reed BD, et al. Fluconazole susceptibility of vaginal isolates obtained from women with complicated *Candida* vaginitis: Clinical implications. Antimicrob Agents Chemother. 2003;47:34-38.

140. Fidel PL, Sobel JD. Host defense against vaginal candidiasis. In: Calderone RA, ed. *Candida* and Candidiasis. Washington, DC: ASM Press; 2002:193-209.

141. Duerr A, Sierra MF, Feldman J, et al. Immune compromise and prevalence of *Candida* vulvovaginitis in human immunodeficiency virus-infected women. Obstet Gynecol. 1997;90:252-256.

142. Fidel PL Jr. The protective immune response against vaginal candidiasis: Lessons learned from clinical studies and animal models. Int Rev Immunol. 2002;21:515-548.

143. Domonkos AN, Arnold HL Jr, Odom RB. Disease due to fungi. In: Domonkos AN, Arnold HL Jr, Odom RB, eds. Andrews' Diseases of the Skin: Clinical Dermatology. Philadelphia: WB Saunders; 1982:341-403.

144. Alteras I, Feverman EJ, David M, et al. Widely disseminated cutaneous candidosis in adults. Sabouraudia. 1979;17:383-388.

145. Adams SP. Dermacase: Erosio interdigitalis blastomycetica. Can Fam Physician. 2002;48:271-277.

146. Kapdagli H, Ozturk G, Dereli T, et al. *Candida* folliculitis mimicking tinea barbae. Int J Dermatol. 1997;36:295-297.

147. Pierard GE, Pierard-Franchimont C. Folliculites a *Candida*: Dermatose superficielle ou septicemie? (*Candida* folliculitis: Superficial dermatitis or septicemia?) Rev Med Liege. 1996;51:565.

148. Virgili A, Zampino MR, Mantovani L. Fungal skin infections in organ transplant recipients. Am J Clin Dermatol. 2002;3:19-35.

149. Recio C, Pique E, Lluch J, et al. *Candida* folliculitis in intravenous drug users (in Spanish). Enferm Infecc Microbiol Clin. 2003;21:386-387.

150. Edwards S. Balanitis and balanoposthitis: A review (see Comments). Genitourin Med. 1996;72:155-159.

151. Mayser P. Mycotic infections of the penis. Andrologia. 1999;31(Suppl 1):13-16.

152. McQuillen DP, Zingman BS, Meunier F, et al. Invasive infections due to *Candida krusei*: Report of ten cases of fungemia that include three cases of endophthalmitis. Clin Infect Dis. 1992;14:472-478.

153. Leibovitz E, Iuster-Reicher A, Amitai M, et al. Systemic candidal infections associated with use of peripheral venous catheters in neonates: A 9-year experience. Clin Infect Dis. 1992;14:485-491.

154. Marcus J, Grossman ME, Yunakov MJ, et al. Disseminated candidiasis, *Candida* arthritis, and unilateral skin lesions. J Am Acad Dermatol. 1992;26:295-297.

155. Lindblad R, al-Obaidy A, Mobacken H, et al. Diagnostically usable skin lesions in *Candida* septicaemia. Mycoses. 1989;32:416-420.

156. Darcis JM, Etienne M, Demonty J. *Candida albicans* septicemia in heroin addicts. Am J Dermatopathol. 1986;8:501-504.

157. Bodey GP, Luna M. Skin lesions associated with disseminated candidiasis. JAMA. 1974;229:1466-1468.

158. Suster S, Rosen LB. Intradermal bullous dermatitis due to candidiasis in an immunocompromised patient. JAMA. 1987;258:2106-2107.

159. Silverman RA, Rhodes AR, Dennehy PH. Disseminated intravascular coagulation and purpura fulminans in a patient with Candida sepsis: Biopsy of purpura fulminans as an aid to diagnosis of systemic *Candida* infections. Am J Med. 1986;80:679-684.

160. Lysy J, Zimmerman J, Ackerman Z, et al. Atypical auricular pyoderma gangrenosum simulating fungal infection. J Clin Gastroenterol. 1989;11:561-564.

161. Brophy MC, Dunagin WB. Intertriginous dermatoses: Common puzzling problems. Postgrad Med. 1985;78:105-115.

162. Yates YJ, Concannon MJ. Fungal infections of the perionychium. Hand Clin. 2002;18:631-642, vi; discussion 643-646.

163. Hay RJ. Antifungal therapy of yeast infections. J Am Acad Dermatol. 1994;31:S6-S9.

164. Gupta AK, Ryder JE, Baran R, et al. Non-dermatophyte onychomycosis. Dermatol Clin. 2003;21:257-268.

165. Dorko E, Jautova J, Tkacikova L, et al. The frequency of *Candida* species in onychomycosis. Folia Microbiol (Praha). 2002;47:727-731.

166. Ellabib MS, Agaj M, Khalifa Z, et al. Yeasts of the genus *Candida* are the dominant cause of onychomycosis in Libyan women but not men: Results of a 2-year surveillance study. Br J Dermatol. 2002;146:1038-1041.

167. Gautret P, Rodier MH, Kauffmann-Lacroix C, et al. Case report and review: Onychomycosis due to *Candida parapsilosis*. Mycoses. 2000;43:433-435.

168. Concannon P, Gisoldi E, Phillips S, et al. Diaper dermatitis: A therapeutic dilemma. Results of a double-blind placebo controlled trial of miconazole nitrate 0.25%. Pediatr Dermatol. 2001;18:149-155.

169. Rasmusson JE. Classification of diaper dermatitis: An overview. Pediatrician. 1987;14(Suppl 1):6-10.

170. Corno F, Caldart M, Toppino M, et al. La candidosi ano-rettale (Ano-rectal candidiasis). Minerva Chir. 1989;44:2251-2253.

171. Palma-Carlos AG, Palma-Carlos ML. Chronic mucocutaneous candidiasis revisited. Allerg Immunol (Paris). 2001;33:229-232.

172. Tay YK, Seow CS. What syndrome is this? Chronic mucocutaneous candidiasis. Pediatr Dermatol. 2001;18:353-355.

173. de Moraes-Vasconcelos D, Orii NM, Romano CC, et al. Characterization of the cellular immune function of patients with chronic mucocutaneous candidiasis. Clin Exp Immunol. 2001;123:247-253.

174. Kalfa VC, Roberts RL, Stiehm ER. The syndrome of chronic mucocutaneous candidiasis with selective antibody deficiency. Ann Allergy Asthma Immunol. 2003;90:259-264.

175. Buzi F, Badolato R, Mazza C, et al. Autoimmune polyendocrinopathy-candidiasis-ectodermal dystrophy syndrome: Time to review diagnostic criteria? J Clin Endocrin Metab. 2003;88:3146-3148.

176. Chapman SW, Daniel CR. Cutaneous manifestations of fungal infection. Infect Dis Clin North Am. 1994;8:879-910.

177. Chimelli L, Mahler-Araujo MB. Fungal infections. Brain Pathol. 1997;7:613-627.

178. Sánchez-Portocarrero J, Pérez-Cecilia E, Corral O, et al. The central nervous system and infection by Candida species. Diagn Microbiol Infect Dis. 2000;37:169-179.

179. Dorko E, Pilipcinec E, Tkacikova L. Candida species isolated from cerebrospinal fluid. Folia Microbiol (Praha). 2002;47:179-181.

180. Gottfredsson M, Perfect JR. Fungal meningitis. Semin Neurol. 2000;20:307-322.

181. Lipton SA, Hickey VF, Morris JH, et al. Candidal infection in the central nervous system. Am J Med. 1984;76:101-108.

182. Pendlebury WW, Perl DP, Munoz DG. Multiple microabscesses in the central nervous system: A clinicopathologic study. J Neuropathol Exp Neurol. 1989;48:290-300.

183. Lai PH, Lin SM, Pan HB, et al. Disseminated miliary cerebral candidiasis. AJNR Am J Neuroradiol. 1997;18:1303-1306.

184. Hagensee ME, Bauwens JE, Kjos B, et al. Brain abscess following marrow transplantation: Experience at the Fred Hutchinson Cancer Research Center, 1984-1992. Clin Infect Dis. 1994;19:402-408.

185. Treseler CB, Sugar AM. Fungal meningitis. Infect Dis Clin North Am. 1990;4:789-808.

186. Montero A, Romero J, Vargas JA, et al. Candida infection of cerebrospinal fluid shunt devices: Report of two cases and review of the literature. Acta Neurochir (Wien). 2000;142:67-74.

187. Chmel H. Candida albicans meningitis following lumbar puncture. Am J Med Sci. 1973;266:465-467.

188. Nguyen MH, Yu VL. Meningitis caused by Candida species: An emerging problem in neurosurgical patients. Clin Infect Dis. 1995;21:323-327.

189. Casado JL, Quereda C, Oliva J, et al. Candidal meningitis in HIV-infected patients: Analysis of 14 cases. Clin Infect Dis. 1997;25:673-676.

190. Haron E, Vartivarian S, Anaissie E, et al. Primary Candida pneumonia: Experience at a large cancer center and review of the literature. Medicine (Baltimore). 1993;72:137-142.

191. Heurlin N, Bergstrom SE, Winiarski J, et al. Fungal pneumonia: The predominant lung infection causing death in children undergoing bone marrow transplantation. Acta Paediatr. 1996;85:168-172.

192. Armstrong D. Candida species. In: Sarosi GA, Davies SF, eds. Fungal Diseases of the Lung. Orlando, FL: Grune & Stratton, 1986:167-173.

193. Cairns MR, Durack DT. Fungal pneumonia in the immunocompromised host. In: Hoidal JR, ed. Seminars in Respiratory Infection. Orlando, FL: Grune & Stratton, 1986:166-185.

194. Zeluff BJ. Fungal pneumonia in transplant recipients. Semin Respir Infect. 1990;5:80-89.

195. Xu XQ, Shi SY, Han TZ. A retrospective study of 115 cases of fungal pneumonia (in Chinese). Chung Hua Nei Ko Tsa Chih (Chin J Intern Med). 1989;28:7-10, 60.

196. Petrocheilou-Paschou V, Georgilis K, Kontoyannis D, et al. Pneumonia due to Candida krusei. Clin Microbiol Infect. 2002;8:806-809.

197. Saubolle MA. Fungal pneumonias. Semin Respir Infect. 2000;15:162-177.

198. Connolly JE Jr, McAdams HP, Erasmus JJ, et al. Opportunistic fungal pneumonia. J Thorac Imaging. 1999;14:51-62.

199. Patriquin H, Lebowitz R, Perreault G, et al. Neonatal candidiasis: Renal and pulmonary manifestations. AJR Am J Roentgenol. 1980;135:1205-1210.

200. Watanakunakorn C. Acute pulmonary mycetoma due to Candida albicans with complete resolution. J Infect Dis. 1983;148:1131.

201. Wengrower D, Or R, Segal E, et al. Bronchopulmonary candidiasis exacerbating asthma: Case report and review of the literature. Respiration. 1985;47:209-213.

202. McAdams HP, Rosado-de-Christenson ML, Templeton PA, et al. Thoracic mycoses from opportunistic fungi: Radiologic-pathologic correlation. Radiographics. 1995;15:271-286.

203. von Eiff M, Zuhlsdorf M, Roos N, et al. Pulmonary fungal infections in patients with hematological malignancies-Diagnostic approaches. Ann Hematol. 1995;70:135-141.

204. el-Ebiary M, Torres A, Fabregas N, et al. Significance of the isolation of Candida species from respiratory samples in critically ill, non-neutropenic patients: An immediate postmortem histologic study. Am J Respir Crit Care Med. 1997;156:583-590.

205. Wengrower D, Or R, Segal E, et al. Bronchopulmonary candidiasis exacerbating asthma. Respiration. 1985;47:209-213.

206. Wang JN, Liu CC, Huang TZ, et al. Laryngeal candidiasis in children. Scand J Infect Dis. 1997;29:427-429.

207. Walsh TJ, Gray WC. Candida epiglottis in immunocompromised patients. Chest. 1987;91:482-485.

208. Mahieu HF, van Saene HFK, Rosingh HJ, et al. Candida vegetations on silicone voice prostheses. Arch Otolaryngol. 1986;112:321-325.

209. Ko SC, Chen KY, Hsueh PR, et al. Fungal empyema thoracis: An emerging clinical entity. Chest. 2000;117:1672-1678.

210. Rabinovici R, Szewczyk D, Ovadia P, et al. Candida pericarditis: Clinical profile and treatment. Ann Thorac Surg. 1997;63:1200-1204.

211. Franklin WG, Simon AB, Sodeman TM. Candida myocarditis without valvulitis. Am J Cardiol. 1976;38:924-928.

212. Hofman P, Gari-Toussaint M, Bernard E, et al. Myocardites fungiques au cours du syndrome d'immunodeficience acquise (Fungal myocarditis in acquired immunodeficiency syndrome). Arch Mal Coeur Vaiss. 1992;85:203-208.

213. Canver CC, Patel AK, Kosolcharoen P, et al. Fungal purulent constrictive pericarditis in a heart transplant patient. Ann Thorac Surg. 1998;65:1792-1794.

214. McNamee CJ, Wang S, Modry D. Purulent pericarditis secondary to Candida parapsilosis and Peptostreptococcus species. Can J Cardiol. 1998;14:85-86.

215. Rubin RH, Moellering RC. Clinical microbiologic and therapeutic aspects of purulent pericarditis. Am J Med. 1975;59:68-78.

216. McLeod R, Remington JS. Postoperative fungal endocarditis. In: Duma RJ, ed. Infections of Prosthetic Heart Valves and Vascular Grafts: Prevention, Diagnosis and Treatment. Baltimore: University Park Press; 1977:163-236.

217. Reyes MP, Lerner AM. Endocarditis caused by Candida species. In: Bodeg GP, Fainstein V, eds. Candidiasis. New York: Raven Press; 1985:203-209.

218. McLeod R, Remington JS. Infective Endocarditis. New York: Grune & Stratton; 1979:211-290.

219. Ellis M. Fungal endocarditis. J Infect. 1997;35:99-103.

220. Hallum JL, Williams TW Jr. Candida endocarditis. In: Bodey GP, ed. Candidiasis: Pathogenesis, Diagnosis and Treatment. New York: Raven Press; 1993:357-369.

221. Melgar GR, Nasser RM, Gordon SM, et al. Fungal prosthetic valve endocarditis in 16 patients: An 11-year experience in a tertiary care hospital. Medicine (Baltimore). 1997;76:94-103.

222. Nasser RM, Melgar GR, Longworth DL, et al. Incidence and risk of developing fungal prosthetic valve endocarditis after nosocomial candidemia. Am J Med. 1997;103:25-32.

223. Nguyen MH, Nguyen ML, Yu VL, et al. Candida prosthetic valve endocarditis: Prospective study of six cases and review of the literature. Clin Infect Dis. 1996;22:262-267.

224. Pierrotti LC, Baddour LM. Fungal endocarditis, 1995-2000. Chest. 2002;122:302-310.

225. Hauser M, Hess J, Belohradsky BH. Treatment of Candida albicans endocarditis: Case report and a review. Infection. 2003;31:125-127.

226. Posteraro B, Valentini P, Delogu A, et al. Candida albicans endocarditis diagnosed by PCR-based molecular assay in a critically ill pediatric patient. Scand J Infect Dis. 2002;34:145-147.

227. Mogyorosy G, Soos G, Nagy A. Candida endocarditis in a premature infant. J Perinat Med. 2000;28:407-411.

228. Picarelli D, Surraco J, Zuniga C, et al. Surgical management of active infective endocarditis in a premature neonate weighing 950 grams. J Thorac Cardiovasc Surg. 2000;119:380-381.

229. Melamed R, Leibovitz E, Abramson O, et al. Successful non-surgical treatment of Candida tropicalis endocarditis with liposomal amphotericin-B (AmBisome). Scand J Infect Dis. 2000;32:86-89.

230. Kaygusuz I, Mulazimoglu L, Cerikcioglu N, et al. An unusual native tricuspid valve endocarditis caused by Candida colliculosa. Clin Microbiol Infect. 2003;9:319-322.

231. Odds FC. Candida endocarditis, myocarditis, and other cardiovascular Candida infections. In: Candida and Candidosis: A Review and Bibliography. 2nd ed. London: Bailliere Tindall; 1988:175-180.

232. Kuehnert MJ, Clark E, Lockhart SR, et al. Candida albicans endocarditis associated with a contaminated aortic valve allograft: Implications for regulation of allograft processing. Clin Infect Dis. 1998;27:688-691.

233. Yeaman MR, Soldan SS, Ghannoum MA, et al. Resistance to platelet microbicidal protein results in increased severity of experimental Candida albicans endocarditis. Infect Immun. 1996;64:1379-1384.

234. Calderone RA, Scheld WM. Role of fibronectin in the pathogenesis of candidal infections. Rev Infect Dis. 1987;9(Suppl 4):S400-S403.

235. Joly V, Belmatoug N, Leperre A, et al. Pacemaker endocarditis due to Candida albicans: Case report and review. Clin Infect Dis. 1997;25:1359-1362.

236. Gilbert HM, Peters ED, Lang SJ, et al. Successful treatment of fungal prosthetic valve endocarditis: Case report and review (see Comments). Clin Infect Dis. 1996;22:348-354.

237. Galgiani JN, Stevens DA. Fungal endocarditis: Need for guidelines in evaluating therapy. J Thorac Cardiovasc Surg. 1977;73:293-296.

238. Seelig MS, Speth CP, Kozinn PJ, et al. Patterns of Candida endocarditis following cardiac surgery: Importance of early diagnosis and therapy (an analysis of 91 cases). Prog Cardiovasc Dis. 1974;27:125-160.

239. Fisher JF, Newman CL, Sobel JD. Yeast in the urine: Solutions for a budding problem. Clin Infect Dis. 1995;20:183-189.

240. Warren JW. Catheter-associated urinary tract infections. Infect Dis Clin North Am. 1997;11:609-622.

241. Phillips JR, Karlowicz MG. Prevalence of Candida species in hospital-acquired urinary tract infections in a neonatal intensive care unit. Pediatr Infect Dis J. 1997;16:190-194.

242. Oravcova E, Lacka J, Drgona L, et al. Funguria in cancer patients: Analysis of risk factors, clinical presentation and outcome in 50 patients. Infection. 1996;24:319-323.

243. Hitchcock RJ, Pallett A, Hall MA, et al. Urinary tract candidiasis in neonates and infants. Br J Urol. 1995;76:252-256.

244. Kauffman CA, Vazquez JA, Sobel JD, et al. Prospective multicenter surveillance study of funguria in hospitalized patients. The National Institute for Allergy and Infectious Diseases (NIAID) Mycoses Study Group. Clin Infect Dis. 2000;30:14-18.

245. Lundstrom T, Sobel J. Nosocomial candiduria: A review. Clin Infect Dis. 2001;32:1602-1607.

246. Williamson MR, Smith AY, Black WC, et al. Diagnosis of candidal infection of the prostate by transrectal ultrasonography and biopsy. J Clin Ultrasound. 1992;20:618-620.

247. Indudhara R, Singh SK, Vaidyanathan S, et al. Isolated invasive candidal prostatitis. Urol Int. 1992;48:362-364.

248. Golz R, Mendling W. Candidosis of the prostate: A rare form of endomycosis. Mycoses. 1991;34:381-384.

249. Navarro EE, Almario JS, Schaufele RL, et al. Quantitative urine cultures do not reliably detect renal candidiasis in rabbits. J Clin Microbiol. 1997;35:3292-3297.

250. Gregory MC, Schumann GB, Schumann JL, et al. The clinical significance of *Candida* casts. Am J Kidney Dis. 1984;4:179-184.

251. Irby PB, Stoller ML, McAninch JW. Fungal bezoars of the upper urinary tract. J Urol. 1990;143:447-451.

252. Ang BSP, Telenti A, King B, et al. Candidemia from a urinary source: Microbiological aspects and clinical significance. Clin Infect Dis. 1993;17:662-666.

253. Aanestad O, Eilard T. Severe *Candida* cystitis with perforation of the urinary bladder. Scand J Urol Nephrol. 1997;31:311-312.

254. Tomashefski JF Jr, Abramosky CR. *Candida*-associated renal papillary necrosis. Am J Clin Pathol. 1981;75:190-194.

255. High KP, Quagliarello VJ. Yeast perinephric abscess: Report of a case and review. Clin Infect Dis. 1992;15:128-133.

256. Eckstein CW, Kass EJ. Anuria in a newborn secondary to bilateral ureteropelvic fungus balls. J Urol. 1982;127:109-110.

257. Leiter E, Whitehead ED, Desai SB. Fungus balls in renal pelvis. N Y State J Med. 1982;82:64-66.

258. Biggers R, Edwards J. Anuria secondary to bilateral ureteropelvic fungus balls. Urology. 1980;15:161-163.

259. Tennant FS, Remmers AR, Perry JE. Primary renal candidiasis associated perinephric abscess and passage of fungus ball in the urine. Arch Intern Med. 1968;122:435-440.

260. Seidenfeld SM, Lemaistre CF, Setiawan H, et al. Emphysematous pyelonephritis caused by *Candida tropicalis*. J Infect Dis. 1982;146:569.

261. Singh CR, Lytle WF. Cystitis emphysematosa caused by *Candida tropicalis*. J Urol. 1983;130:1171-1173.

262. Sultana SR, McNeill SA, Phillips G, et al. Candidal urinary tract infection as a cause of pneumaturia. J R Coll Surg Edinb. 1998;43:198-199.

263. McCullers JA, Flynn PM. *Candida tropicalis* osteomyelitis: Case report and review. Clin Infect Dis. 1998;26:1000-1001.

264. Jonnalagadda S, Veerabagu MP, Rakela J, et al. *Candida albicans* osteomyelitis in a liver transplant recipient: A case report and review of the literature. Transplantation. 1996;62:1182-1184.

265. Ferra C, Doebbeling BN, Hollis RJ, et al. *Candida tropicalis* vertebral osteomyelitis: A late sequela of fungemia. Clin Infect Dis. 1994;19:697-703.

266. Kerr J. Fungal osteomyelitis of the temporal bone: A review of reported cases (Letter; comment). Ear Nose Throat J. 1994;73:339.

267. Lasday SD, Jay RM. *Candida* osteomyelitis. J Foot Ankle Surg. 1994;33:173-176.

268. Dan M, Priel I. Failure of fluconazole therapy for sternal osteomyelitis due to *Candida albicans* (Letter). Clin Infect Dis. 1994;18:126-127.

269. Heckenkamp J, Helling HJ, Rehm KE. Post-traumatic costochondritis caused by *Candida albicans*: Aetiology, diagnosis and treatment. Scand Cardiovasc J. 1997;31:165-167.

270. Wang YC, Lee ST. Candida vertebral osteomyelitis: A case report and review of the literature. Chang Gung Med J. 2001;24:810-815.

271. Collet P, Biron P, Larbre JP, et al. Spondylodiscites a *Candida*: A propos de 2 observations personnelles et de 28 observations de la litterature.(*Candida* spondylodiscitis: Report of 2 personal cases and 28 cases from the literature.) Rev Med Interne. 1989;10:413-419.

272. Herzog W, Perfect J, Roberts L. Intervertebral diskitis due to *Candida tropicalis*. South Med J. 1989;82:270-273.

273. Parry MF, Grant B, Yukna M, et al. *Candida* osteomyelitis and diskitis after spinal surgery: An outbreak that implicates artificial nail use. Clin Infect Dis. 2001;32:352-357.

274. Dwyer K, McDonald M, Fitzpatrick T. Presentation of *Candida glabrata* spinal osteomyelitis 25 months after documented candidaemia. Aust N Z J Med. 1999;29:571-572.

275. Hansen BL, Andersen K. Fungal arthritis: A review. Scand J Rheumatol. 1995;24:248-250.

276. Silveira LH, Cuellar ML, Citera G, et al. *Candida* arthritis. Rheum Dis Clin North Am. 1993;19:427-437.

277. Murphy O, Gray J, Wagget J, et al. *Candida* arthritis complicating long term total parenteral nutrition. Pediatr Infect Dis J. 1997;16:329.

278. Fukasawa N, Shirakura K. *Candida* arthritis after total knee arthroplasty-A case of successful treatment without prosthesis removal. Acta Orthop Scand. 1997;68:306-307.

279. Belzunegui J, Gonzalez C, Lopez L, et al. Osteoarticular and muscle infectious lesions in patients with the human immunodeficiency virus. Clin Rheumatol. 1997;16:450-453.

280. Malani PN, McNeil SA, Bradley SF, et al. C*andida albicans* sternal wound infections: A chronic and recurrent complication of median sternotomy. Clin Infect Dis. 2002;35:1316-1320.

281. Arena FP, Perlin M, Brahman H. Fever, rash, and myalgias of disseminated candidiasis during antifungal therapy. Arch Intern Med. 1981;14:1233.

282. Belzunegui J, Rodriguez-Arrondo F, Gonzalez C, et al. Musculoskeletal infections in intravenous drug addicts: Report of 34 cases with analysis of microbiological aspects and pathogenic mechanisms. Clin Exp Rheumatol. 2000;18:383-386.

283. Fornadley JA, Parker GS, Rickman LS, et al. *Candida* myositis manifesting as a discrete neck mass. Otolaryngol Head Neck Surg. 1990;102:74-76.

284. Sawyer RG, Rosenlof LK, Adams RB, et al. Peritonitis into the 1990s: Changing pathogens and changing strategies in the critically ill. Am Surg. 1992;58:82-87.

285. Levine J, Bernard DB, Idelson BA, et al. Fungal peritonitis complicating continuous ambulatory peritoneal dialysis: Successful treatment with fluconazole, a new orally active antifungal agent (see Comments). Am J Med. 1989;86:825-827.

286. Alden SM, Frank E, Flancbaum L. Abdominal candidiasis in surgical patients. Am Surg. 1989;55:45-49.

287. Bayer AS, Blumenkrantz MJ, Montgomerie JZ, et al. *Candida* peritonitis: Report of 22 cases and review of the English literature. Am J Med. 1976;61:832-840.

288. Solomkin JS, Flohr AB, Quie PG, et al. The role of *Candida* in intraperitoneal infections. Surgery. 1980;88:524-530.

289. Eisenberg ES, Leviton I, Soeiro R. Fungal peritonitis in patients receiving peritoneal dialysis: Experience with 11 patients and review of the literature. Rev Infect Dis. 1986:309-321.

290. Peoples JB. *Candida* and perforated peptic ulcers. Surgery. 1986;100:758-764.

291. Caesar-TonThat TC, Cutler JE. A monoclonal antibody to *Candida albicans* enhances mouse neutrophil candidacidal activity. Infect Immun. 1997;65:5354-5357.

292. Lo WK, Chan CY, Cheng SW, et al. A prospective randomized control study of oral nystatin prophylaxis for *Candida* peritonitis complicating continuous ambulatory peritoneal dialysis. Am J Kidney Dis. 1996;28:549-552.

293. Petri MG, Konig J, Moecke HP, et al. Epidemiology of invasive mycosis in ICU patients: A prospective multicenter study in 435 non-neutropenic patients. Paul-Ehrlich Society for Chemotherapy, Divisions of Mycology and Pneumonia Research. Intensive Care Med. 1997;23:317-325.

294. Michel C, Courdavault L, al Khayat R, et al. Fungal peritonitis in patients on peritoneal dialysis. Am J Nephrol. 1994;14:113-120.

295. Amici G, Grandesso S, Mottola A, et al. Fungal peritonitis in peritoneal dialysis: Critical review of six cases. Adv Perit Dial. 1994;10:169-173.

296. Goldie SJ, Kiernan-Tridle L, Torres C, et al. Fungal peritonitis in a large chronic peritoneal dialysis population: A report of 55 episodes. Am J Kidney Dis. 1996;28:86-91.

297. Salvaggio MR, Pappas PG. Current concepts in the management of fungal peritonitis. Curr Infect Dis Rep. 2003;5:120-124.

298. Dupont H, Paugam-Burtz C, Muller-Serieys C, et al. Predictive factors of mortality due to polymicrobial peritonitis with *Candida* isolation in peritoneal fluid in critically ill patients. Arch Surg. 2002;137:1341-1346; discussion 1347.

299. Wong PN, Mak SK, Lo KY, et al. A retrospective study of seven cases of *Candida parapsilosis* peritonitis in CAPD patients: The therapeutic implications. Perit Dial Int. 2000;20:76-79.

300. Takano H, Yoshikawa T, Nishida K, et al. *Candida* cholecystitis as an unusual complication of endoscopic retrograde cholangiography. Endoscopy. 1996;28:790-791.

301. Diebel LN, Raafat AM, Dulchavsky SA, et al. Gallbladder and biliary tract candidiasis. Surgery. 1996;120:760-764.

302. Chubachi A, Miura I, Ohshima A, et al. Risk factors for hepatosplenic abscesses in patients with acute leukemia receiving empiric azole treatment. Am J Med Sci. 1994;308:309-312.

303. Gorg C, Weide R, Schwerk WB, et al. Ultrasound evaluation of hepatic and splenic microabscesses in the immunocompromised patient: Sonographic patterns, differential diagnosis, and follow-up. J Clin Ultrasound. 1994;22:525-529.

304. Bjerke JW, Meyers JD, Bowden RA. Hepatosplenic candidiasis—A contraindication to marrow transplantation? Blood. 1994;84:2811-2814.

305. Anttila VJ, Ruutu P, Bondestam S, et al. Hepatosplenic yeast infection in patients with acute leukemia: A diagnostic problem. Clin Infect Dis. 1994;18:979-981.

306. Anttila VJ, Farkkila M, Jansson SE, et al. Diagnostic laparoscopy in patients with acute leukemia and suspected hepatic candidiasis. Eur J Clin Microbiol Infect Dis. 1997;16:637-643.

307. Chanock SJ, Pizzo PA. Infectious complications of patients undergoing therapy for acute leukemia: Current status and future prospects. Semin Oncol. 1997;24:132-140.

308. Kontoyiannis DP, Luna MA, Samuels BI, et al. Hepatosplenic candidiasis: A manifestation of chronic disseminated candidiasis. Infect Dis Clin North Am. 2000;14:721-739.

309. Vasquez TE, Evans DG, Schiffman H, et al. Fungal splenic abscesses in the immunosuppressed patient: Correlation of imaging modalities. Clin Nucl Med. 1987;12:30-38.

310. Helton WS, Carrico CJ, Zaveruha PA, et al. Diagnosis and treatment of splenic fungal abscesses in the immune-suppressed patient. Arch Surg. 1986;121:580-586.

311. Chia N, Clark R, Valainis GT. *Candida albicans* infected pseudocyst in a postpartum woman. South Med J. 1990;83:687-689.

312. Mannell A, Obers V. Pancreatic candidiasis: A case report. S Afr J Surg. 1990;28:26-27.

313. Foust RT. Infection of a pancreatic pseudocyst due to *Candida albicans*. South Med J. 1996;89:1104-1107.

314. Jalan R, Jones HL, Walker RJ. Multiple pancreatic abscesses due to *Candida albicans* following ERCP. Scott Med J. 1994;39:17-18.

315. Semelka RC, Shoenut JP, Greenberg HM, et al. Detection of acute and treated lesions of hepatosplenic candidiasis: Comparison of dynamic contrast-enhanced CT and MR imaging. J Magn Reson Imaging. 1992;2:341-345.

316. Uflacker R, Wholey MH, Amaral NM, et al. Parasitic and mycotic causes of biliary obstruction. Gastrointest Radiol. 1982;7:173-179.

317. Magnussen CR, Olson JP, Ona FV, et al. *Candida* fungus balls in the common bile duct: Unusual manifestations of disseminated candidiasis. Arch Intern Med. 1979;139:821-822.

318. Irani M, Truong LD. Candidiasis of the extrahepatic biliary tract. Arch Pathol Lab Med. 1986;110:1087-1090.

319. Morris AB, Sands ML, Shiraki M, et al. Gallbladder and biliary tract candidiasis: Nine cases and review (see Comments). Rev Infect Dis. 1990;12:483-489.

320. Domagk D, Bisping G, Poremba C, et al. Common bile duct obstruction due to candidiasis. Scand J Gastroenterol. 2001;36:444-446.

321. Garcia E, Granier I, Geissler A, et al. Surgical management of *Candida* suppurative thrombophlebitis of superior vena cava after central venous catheterization. Intensive Care Med. 1997;23:1002-1004.

322. Friedland IR. Peripheral thrombophlebitis caused by *Candida*. Pediatr Infect Dis J. 1996;15:375-377.

323. Khan EA, Correa AG, Baker CJ. Suppurative thrombophlebitis in children: A ten-year experience. Pediatr Infect Dis J. 1997;16:63-67.

324. Ward RA, Wellhausen SR, Dobbins JJ, et al. Thromboembolic and infectious complications of total artificial heart implantation. Ann N Y Acad Sci. 1987;516:638-650.

325. Doscher W, Krishnasastry KV, Deckoff SL. Fungal graft infections: Case report and review of the literature. J Vasc Surg. 1987;6:398-402.

326. Donahue SP, Greven CM, Zuravleff JJ, et al. Intraocular candidiasis in patients with candidemia: Clinical implications derived from a prospective multicenter study. Ophthalmology. 1994;101:1302-1309.

327. Chen SJ, Chung YM, Liu JH. Endogenous *Candida* endophthalmitis after induced abortion. Am J Ophthalmol. 1998;125:873-875.

328. Christmas NJ, Smiddy WE. Vitrectomy and systemic fluconazole for treatment of endogenous fungal endophthalmitis. Ophthalmic Surg Lasers. 1996;27:1012-1018.

329. Moller M, Althaus C, Sundmacher R. Beidseitige *Candida*-Endophthalmitis zweier i.v.-drogenabhngiger Patienten unter oraler L-Methadon-Substitution. (Bilateral *Candida* endophthalmitis in two IV drug-dependent patients with oral L-methadone substitution.) Klin Monatsbl Augenheilkd. 1997;211:53-56.

330. Menezes AV, Sigesmund DA, Demajo WA, et al. Mortality of hospitalized patients with *Candida* endophthalmitis. Arch Intern Med. 1994;154:2093-2097.

331. Coskuncan NM, Jabs DA, Dunn JP, et al. The eye in bone marrow transplantation. VI. Retinal complications. Arch Ophthalmol. 1994;112:372-379.

332. Widder RA, Bartz-Schmidt KU, Geyer H, et al. *Candida albicans* endophthalmitis after anabolic steroid abuse (Letter.) Lancet. 1995;345:330-331.

333. Papanicolaou GA, Meyers BR, Fuchs WS, et al. Infectious ocular complications in orthotopic liver transplant patients. Clin Infect Dis. 1997;24:1172-1177.

334. Essman TF, Flynn HW Jr, Smiddy WE, et al. Treatment outcomes in a 10-year study of endogenous fungal endophthalmitis. Ophthalmic Surg Lasers. 1997;28:185-194.

335. Nolla-Salas J, Sitges-Serra A, Leon C, et al. *Candida* endophthalmitis in non-neutropenic critically ill patients (see Comments.) Eur J Clin Microbiol Infect Dis. 1996;15:503-506.

336. Shmuely H, Kremer I, Sagie A, et al. *Candida tropicalis* multifocal endophthalmitis as the only initial manifestation of pacemaker endocarditis. Am J Ophthalmol. 1997;123:559-560.

337. Wong VK, Tasman W, Eagle RC Jr, et al. Bilateral *Candida parapsilosis* endophthalmitis. Arch Ophthalmol. 1997;115:670-672.

338. Wolfensberger TJ, Gonvers M. Bilateral endogenous *Candida* endophthalmitis. Retina. 1998;18:280-281.

339. Stanbury RM, Chignell AH, Graham EM. Endogenous *Candida* endophthalmitis with no apparent predisposing factors (Letter). Eye. 1998;12(Pt 2):321-323.

340. Brooks RG. Prospective study of *Candida* endophthalmitis in hospitalized patients with candidemia. Arch Intern Med. 1989;149:2226-2228.

341. Rodriguez-Adrian LJ, King RT, Tamayo-Derat LG, et al. Retinal lesions as clues to disseminated bacterial and candidal infections: Frequency, natural history, and etiology. Medicine (Baltimore). 2003;82:187-202.

342. Donahue SP, Hein E, Sinatra RB. Ocular involvement in children with candidemia. Am J Ophthalmol. 2003;135:886-887.

343. Feman SS, Nichols JC, Chung SM, et al. Endophthalmitis in patients with disseminated fungal disease. Trans Am Ophthalmol Soc. 2002;100:67-70; discussion 71.

344. Noyola DE, Bohra L, Paysse EA, et al. Association of candidemia and retinopathy of prematurity in very low birthweight infants. Ophthalmology. 2002;109:80-84.

345. Alexandridou A, Reginald AY, Stavrou P, et al. *Candida* endophthalmitis after tattooing in an asplenic patient. Arch Ophthalmol. 2002;120:518-519.

346. Tsai CC, Chen SJ, Chung YM, et al. Postpartum endogenous *Candida* endophthalmitis. J Formos Med Assoc. 2002;101:432-436.

347. Sikic J, Vukojevic N, Katusic D, et al. Bilateral endogenous *Candida* endophthalmitis after induced abortion. Croat Med J. 2001;42:676-678.

348. Miailhes P, Labetoulle M, Naas T, et al. Unusual etiology of visual loss in an HIV-infected patient due to endogenous endophthalmitis. Clin Microbiol Infect. 2001;7:641-645.

349. Gupta A, Gupta V, Dogra MR, et al. Fungal endophthalmitis after a single intravenous administration of presumably contaminated dextrose infusion fluid. Retina. 2000;20:262-268.

350. Henderson DK, Hockey LB, Vukalcic LJ, et al. Effect of immunosuppression on the development of experimental hematogenous *Candida* endophthalmitis. Infect Immun. 1980;27:628-631.

351. Barrie T. The place of elective vitrectomy in the management of patients with *Candida* endophthalmitis. Graefes Arch Clin Exp Ophthalmol. 1987;225:107-113.

352. McDonald HR, De Bustros S, Sipperley JO. Vitrectomy for epiretinal membrane in *Candida* chorioretinitis. Ophthalmology. 1990;97:466-469.

353. Hidalgo JA, Alangaden GJ, Eliott D, et al. Fungal endophthalmitis diagnosis by detection of *Candida albicans* DNA in intraocular fluid by use of a species-specific polymerase chain reaction assay. J Infect Dis. 2000;181:1198-1201.

354. Appleton SS. Candidiasis: Pathogenesis, clinical characteristics, and treatment. J Calif Dent Assoc. 2000;28:942-948.

355. Marr KA. The changing spectrum of candidemia in oncology patients: Therapeutic implications. Curr Opin Infect Dis. 2000;13:615-620.

356. Uzun O, Anaissie EJ. Predictors of outcome in cancer patients with candidemia. Ann Oncol. 2000;11:1517-1521.

357. Chen YC, Chang SC, Tai HM, et al. Molecular epidemiology of *Candida* colonizing critically ill patients in intensive care units. J Formos Med Assoc. 2001;100:791-797.

358. Kovacicova G, Krcmery V Jr. Nosocomial candidemia in geriatric patients. J Chemother. 2001;13:340-343.

359. Noyola DE, Fernandez M, Moylett EH, et al. Ophthalmologic, visceral, and cardiac involvement in neonates with candidemia. Clin Infect Dis. 2001;32:1018-1023.

360. Blot SI, Vandewoude KH, Hoste EA, et al. Effects of nosocomial candidemia on outcomes of critically ill patients. Am J Med. 2002;113:480-485.

361. Diekema DJ, Messer SA, Brueggemann AB, et al. Epidemiology of candidemia: 3-year results from the Emerging Infections and the Epidemiology of Iowa Organisms Study. J Clin Microbiol. 2002;40:1298-1302.

362. Krcmery VC Jr, Babela R. Candidemia in the surgical intensive care unit. Clin Infect Dis. 2002;34:1537-1538.

363. Pulimood S, Ganesan L, Alangaden G, et al. Polymicrobial candidemia. Diagn Microbiol Infect Dis. 2002;44:353-357.

364. Ponton J, Moragues MD, Guillermo Q. Non-culture-based diagnosis. In: Calderone RA, ed. *Candida* and Candidiasis. Washington, DC: ASM Press; 2002:395-425.

365. Bennett JE. Rapid diagnosis of candidiasis and aspergilloses. Rev Infect Dis. 1987;9:398-402.

366. Edwards JE Jr. Invasive *Candida* infections. N Engl J Med. 1991;324:1060-1062.

367. Mitsutake K, Miyazaki T, Tashiro T, et al. Enolase antigen, mannan antigen, Cand-Tec antigen, and beta-glucan in patients with candidemia. J Clin Microbiol. 1996;34:1918-1921.

368. Krick JA, Remington JS. Opportunistic invasive fungal infections in patients with leukemia and lymphoma. Clin Hematol. 1976;5:249-310.

369. Young RC, Bennett JE, Geelhoed GW, et al. Fungemia with compromised host resistance: A study of 70 cases. Ann Intern Med. 1974;80:605-612.

370. Rex JH. Editorial response: Catheters and candidemia. Clin Infect Dis. 1996;22:467-470.

371. Rex JH, Bennett JE, Sugar AM, et al. A randomized trial comparing fluconazole with amphotericin B for the treatment of candidemia in patients without neutropenia. N Engl J Med. 1994;331:1325-1330.

372. Hockey LJ, Fujita NK, Gibson TR, et al. Detection of fungemia obscured by concomitant bacteremia: In vitro and in vivo studies. J Clin Microbiol. 1982;16:1080-1085.

373. Wey SB, Mori M, Pfaller MA, et al. Hospital-acquired candidemia: The attributable mortality and excess length of stay. Arch Intern Med. 1988;148:2642-2645.

374. Makhoul IR, Kassis I, Smolkin T, et al. Review of 49 neonates with acquired fungal sepsis: Further characterization. Pediatrics. 2001;107:61-66.

375. Rex JH, Rinaldi MG, Pfaller MA. Resistance of *Candida* species to fluconazole. Antimicrob Agents Chemother. 1995;39:1-8.

376. Nguyen MH, Peacock JE Jr, Morris AJ, et al. The changing face of candidemia: Emergence of non-*Candida albicans* species and antifungal resistance. Am J Med. 1996;100:617-623.

377. Dorko E, Kmetova M, Pilipcinec E, et al. Rare non-*albicans Candida* species detected in different clinical diagnoses. Folia Microbiol (Praha). 2000;45:364-368.

378. Pappas PG, Rex JH, Sobel JD, et al. Guidelines for treatment of candidiasis. Clin Infect Dis. 2004;38:161-189.

379. Edwards JE Jr, Bodey GP, Bowden RA, et al. International Conference for the Development of a Consensus on the Management and Prevention of Severe Candidal Infections. Clin Infect Dis. 1997;25:43-59.

380. Deresinski SC, Stevens DA. Caspofungin. Clin Infect Dis. 2003;36:1445-1457.

381. Wiederhold NP, Lewis RE. The echinocandin antifungals: An overview of the pharmacology, spectrum and clinical efficacy. Exp Opin Invest Drugs. 2003;12:1313-1333.

382. Groll AH, Mickiene D, Petraitiene R, et al. Pharmacokinetic and pharmacodynamic modeling of anidulafungin (LY303366): Reappraisal of its efficacy in neutropenic animal models of opportunistic mycoses using optimal plasma sampling. Antimicrob Agents Chemother. 2001;45:2845-2855.

383. Fromtling RA. Micafungin sodium (FK-463). Drugs Today (Barc). 2002;38:245-257.

384. Johnson LB, Kauffman CA. Voriconazole: A new triazole antifungal agent. Clin Infect Dis. 2003;36:630-637.

385. Arikan S, Rex JH. Ravuconazole Eisai/Bristol-Myers Squibb. Curr Opin Invest Drugs. 2002;3:555-561.

386. Courtney R, Pai S, Laughlin M, et al. Pharmacokinetics, safety, and tolerability of oral posaconazole administered in single and multiple doses in healthy adults. Antimicrob Agents Chemother. 2003;47:2788-2795.

387. Willems L, van der Geest R, de Beule K. Itraconazole oral solution and intravenous formulations: A review of pharmacokinetics and pharmacodynamics. J Clin Pharm Ther. 2001;26:159-169.

388. Graybill JR, Vazquez J, Darouiche RO, et al. Randomized trial of itraconazole oral solution for oropharyngeal candidiasis in HIV/AIDS patients. Am J Med. 1998;104:33-39.

389. Eichel M, Just-Nubling G, Helm EB, et al. Itraconazol-Suspension in der Behandlung HIV-infizierter Patienten mit Fluconazol-resistenter oropharyngealer *Candida*-Infektion und Soorosophagitis. (Itraconazole suspension in the treatment of HIV-infected patients with fluconazole-resistant oropharyngeal candidiasis and esophagitis.) Mycoses. 1996;39(Suppl 1):102-106.

390. Laine L, Dretler RH, Conteas CN, et al. Fluconazole compared with ketoconazole for the treatment of *Candida* esophagitis in AIDS: A randomized trial. Ann Intern Med. 1992;117:655-660.

391. Hegener P, Troke PF, Fatkenheuer G, et al. Treatment of fluconazole-resistant candidiasis with voriconazole in patients with AIDS. AIDS. 1998;12:2227-2228.

392. Troke PF. Large-scale multicentre study of fluconazole in the treatment of hospitalised patients with fungal infections. Multicentre European Study Group. Eur J Clin Microbiol Infect Dis. 1997;16:287-295.

393. Keating G, Figgitt D. Caspofungin: A review of its use in oesophageal candidiasis, invasive candidiasis and invasive aspergillosis. Drugs. 2003;63:2235-2263.

394. Kullberg BJ. Trends in immunotherapy of fungal infections. Eur J Clin Microbiol Infect Dis. 1997;16:51-55.
395. Slavin MA, Osborne B, Adams R, et al. Efficacy and safety of fluconazole prophylaxis for fungal infections after marrow transplantation—A prospective, randomized, double-blind study. J Infect Dis. 1995;171:1545-1552.
396. Goodman JL, Winston DJ, Greenfield RA, et al. A controlled trial of fluconazole to prevent fungal infections in patients undergoing bone marrow transplantation. N Engl J Med. 1992;326:845-851.
397. Collins LA, Samore MH, Roberts MS, et al. Risk factors for invasive fungal infections complicating orthotopic liver transplantation. J Infect Dis. 1994;170:644-652.
398. De Gregorio MW, Lee WMF, Ries CA. *Candida* infections in patients with acute leukemia: Ineffectiveness of nystatin prophylaxis and relationship between oropharyngeal and systemic candidiasis. Cancer. 1982;50:2780-2784.
399. Hansen RM, Reinerio N, Sohnle PG, et al. Ketoconazole in the prevention of candidiasis in patients with cancer: A prospective, randomized, controlled, double-blind study. Arch Intern Med. 1987;147:710-712.
400. Meunier F. Prevention of mycosis in immunocompromised patients. Rev Infect Dis. 1987;9:408-416.
401. Kanda Y, Yamamoto R, Chizuka A, et al. Prophylactic action of oral fluconazole against fungal infection in neutropenic patients: A meta-analysis of 16 randomized, controlled trials. Cancer. 2000;89:1611-1625.
402. Slotman GJ, Burchard KW. Ketoconazole prevents *Candida* sepsis in critically ill surgical patients. Arch Surg. 1987;122:147-151.
403. Pelz RK, Hendrix CW, Swoboda SM, et al. Double-blind placebo-controlled trial of fluconazole to prevent candidal infections in critically ill surgical patients. Ann Surg. 2001;233:542-548.
404. Holzheimer RG, Dralle H. Management of mycoses in surgical patients-Review of the literature. Eur J Med Res. 2002;7:200-226.
405. Ostrosky-Zeichner L, Marr KA, Rex JH, et al. Amphotericin B: Time for a new "gold standard." Clin Infect Dis. 2003;37:415-425.
406. Ng AW, Wasan KM, Lopez-Berestein G. Development of liposomal polyene antibiotics: An historical perspective. J Pharm Pharm Sci. 2003;6:67-83.
407. Bellmann R, Egger P, Gritsch W, et al. Amphotericin B lipid formulations in critically ill patients on continuous veno-venous haemofiltration. J Antimicrob Chemother. 2003;51:671-681.
408. Wingard JR. Lipid formulations of amphotericins: Are you a lumper or a splitter? Clin Infect Dis. 2002;35:891-895.
409. Arikan S. Lipid-based antifungal agents. Cell Mol Biol Lett. 2002;7:220-221.
410. Phillips P, Shafran S, Garber G, et al. Multicenter randomized trial of fluconazole versus amphotericin B for treatment of candidemia in non-neutropenic patients. Canadian Candidemia Study Group. Eur J Clin Microbiol Infect Dis. 1997;16:337-345.
411. Nguyen MH, Peacock JE Jr, Tanner DC, et al. Therapeutic approaches in patients with candidemia: Evaluation in a multicenter, prospective, observational study. Arch Intern Med. 1995;155:2429-2435.
412. Mora-Duarte J, Betts R, Rotstein C, et al. Comparison of caspofungin and amphotericin B for invasive candidiasis. N Engl J Med. 2002;347:2020-2029.
413. Rex JH, Bennett JE, Sugar AM, et al. Intravascular catheter exchange and duration of candidemia. NIAID Mycoses Study Group and the Candidemia Study Group. Clin Infect Dis. 1995;21:994-996.
414. Turnier E, Kay JH, Bernstein S, et al. Surgical treatment of *Candida* endocarditis. Chest. 1975;67:262-268.
415. Baddour LM. Long-term suppressive therapy for fungal endocarditis (Letter; comment). Clin Infect Dis. 1996;23:1338-1340.
416. Aaron L, Therby A, Viard JP, et al. Successful medical treatment of *Candida albicans* in mechanical prosthetic valve endocarditis. Scand J Infect Dis. 2003;35:351-352.
417. Scarcella A, Pasquariello MB, Giugliano B, et al. Liposomal amphotericin B treatment for neonatal fungal infections. Pediatr Infect Dis J. 1998;17:146-148.
418. Montenegro J, Aguirre R, Gonzalez O, et al. Fluconazole treatment of candida peritonitis with delayed removal of the peritoneal dialysis catheter. Clin Nephrol. 1995;44:60-63.
419. Chan TM, Chan CY, Cheng SW, et al. Treatment of fungal peritonitis complicating continuous ambulatory peritoneal dialysis with oral fluconazole: A series of 21 patients (see Comments). Nephrol Dial Transplant. 1994;9:539-542.
420. Rodriguez-Perez JC. Fungal peritonitis in CAPD-Which treatment is best? Contrib Nephrol. 1987;57:114-121.
421. Struijk DG, Krediet RT, Boeschoten EW, et al. Antifungal treatment of *Candida* peritonitis in continuous ambulatory peritoneal dialysis patients. Am J Kidney Dis. 1987;9:66-70.
422. Sandven P, Qvist H, Skovlund E, et al. Significance of *Candida* recovered from intraoperative specimens in patients with intra-abdominal perforations. Crit Care Med. 2002;30:541-547.
423. Eggimann P, Francioli P, Bille J, et al. Fluconazole prophylaxis prevents intraabdominal candidiasis in high-risk surgical patients. Crit Care Med. 1999;6:1066-1072.
424. Lopez-Berestin G, Bodeg GP, Frankel LS, et al. Treatment of hepatosplenic candidiasis with liposomal amphotericin B. J Clin Oncol. 1987;5:310-317.
425. Shirkhoda B, Lopez-Berestein G, Hlbert JM, et al. Hepatosplenic fungal infection: CT and pathologic evaluation after treatment with liposomal amphotericin B. Radiology. 1986;159:349-353.
426. Walsh TJ, Whitcomb PO, Revankar SG, et al. Successful treatment of hepatosplenic candidiasis through repeated cycles of chemotherapy and neutropenia. Cancer. 1995;76:2357-2362.
427. Anaissie E, Bodey GP, Kantarjian H, et al. Fluconazole therapy for chronic disseminated candidiasis in patients with leukemia and prior amphotericin B therapy. Am J Med. 1991;91:142-150.
428. Bozzette SA, Gordon RL, Yen A, et al. Biliary concentrations of fluconazole in a patient with candidal cholecystitis: Case report. Clin Infect Dis. 1992;15:701-703.
429. Isenmann R, Schwarz M, Rau B, et al. Characteristics of infection with *Candida* species in patients with necrotizing pancreatitis. World J Surg. 2002;26:372-376.
430. Jacobs LG, Skidmore EA, Freeman K, et al. Oral fluconazole compared with bladder irrigation with amphotericin B for treatment of fungal urinary tract infections in elderly patients. Clin Infect Dis. 1996;22:30-35.
431. Francis P, Walsh TJ. Evolving role of flucytosine in immunocompromised patients: New insights into safety, pharmacokinetics, and antifungal therapy. Clin Infect Dis. 1992;15:1003-1018.
432. Sobel JD, Kauffman CA, McKinsey D, et al. Candiduria: A randomized, double-blind study of treatment with fluconazole and placebo. The National Institute of Allergy and Infectious Diseases (NIAID) Mycoses Study Group. Clin Infect Dis. 2000;30:19-24.
433. DeWit S, Weerts D, Goossens H, et al. Comparisons of fluconazole and ketoconazole for oropharyngeal candidiasis in AIDS. Lancet. 1989;1:746-748.
434. Blatchford NR. Treatment of oral candidosis with itraconazole: A review. J Am Acad Dermatol. 1990;23:565-567.
435. Cartledge JD, Midgely J, Gazzard BG. Itraconazole solution: Higher serum drug concentrations and better clinical response rates than the capsule formulation in acquired immunodeficiency syndrome patients with candidosis. J Clin Pathol. 1997;50:477-480.
436. Phillips P, Zemcov J, Mahmood W, et al. Itraconazole cyclodextrin solution for fluconazole-refractory oropharyngeal candidiasis in AIDS: Correlation of clinical response with in vitro susceptibility. AIDS. 1996;10:1369-1376.
437. Barbaro G, Barbarini G, Calderon W, et al. Fluconazole versus itraconazole for *Candida* esophagitis in acquired immunodeficiency syndrome: *Candida* esophagitis. Gastroenterology. 1996;111:1169-1177.
438. Barbaro G, Barbarini G, Di LG. Fluconazole vs. flucytosine in the treatment of esophageal candidiasis in AIDS patients: A double-blind, placebo-controlled study. Endoscopy. 1995;27:377-383.
439. Wilcox CM, Darouiche RO, Laine L, et al. A randomized, double-blind comparison of itraconazole oral solution and fluconazole tablets in the treatment of esophageal candidiasis. J Infect Dis. 1997;176:227-232.
440. Barbaro G, Barbarini G, Di LG. Fluconazole vs itraconazole-flucytosine association in the treatment of esophageal candidiasis in AIDS patients: A double-blind, multicenter placebo-controlled study. The Candida Esophagitis Multicenter Italian Study (CEMIS) Group. Chest. 1996;110:1507-1514.
441. Medoff G. Controversial areas in antifungal chemotherapy: Short-course and combination therapy with amphotericin B. Rev Infect Dis. 1987;9:403-407.
442. Agresti MG, De BF, Mondello F, et al. Clinical and mycological evaluation of fluconazole in the secondary prophylaxis of esophageal candidiasis in AIDS patients: An open, multicenter study. Eur J Epidemiol. 1994;10:17-22.
443. Vazquez JA. Therapeutic options for the management of oropharyngeal and esophageal candidiasis in HIV/AIDS patients. HIV Clin Trials. 2000;1:47-59.
444. Chocarro Martinez A, Gonzalez A, Garcia I. Caspofungin versus amphotericin B for the treatment of candidal esophagitis. Clin Infect Dis. 2002;35:107; author reply 108.
445. Ally R, Schurmann D, Kreisel W, et al. A randomized, double-blind, double-dummy, multicenter trial of voriconazole and fluconazole in the treatment of esophageal candidiasis in immunocompromised patients. Clin Infect Dis. 2001;33:1447-1454.
446. Reef SE, Levine WC, McNeil MM, et al. Treatment options for vulvovaginal candidiasis, 1993. Clin Infect Dis. 1995;20(Suppl 1):S80-S90.
447. Sobel JD, Chaim W. Treatment of *Torulopsis glabrata* vaginitis: Retrospective review of boric acid therapy. Clin Infect Dis. 1997;24:649-652.
448. Sobel JD. Treatment of vaginal *Candida* infections. Exp Opin Pharmacother. 2002;3:1059-1065.
449. Edwards JE Jr. *Candida* endophthalmitis. In: Bodey GP, Fainstein V, eds. Candidiasis. New York: Raven Press; 1985:211-225.
450. Jones DB. Chemotherapy of experimental endogenous *Candida albicans* endophthalmitis. Trans Am Ophthalmol Soc. 1980;78:846-895.
451. Moyer DV, Edwards JE Jr. *Candida* endophthalmitis and central nervous system infection. In: Bodey GP, ed. Candidiasis: Pathogenesis, Diagnosis and Treatment. New York: Raven Press; 1993:331-355.
452. Luttrull JK, Wan WL, Kubak BM, et al. Treatment of ocular fungal infections with oral fluconazole. Am J Ophthalmol. 1995;119:477-481.
453. Darling K, Singh J, Wilks D. Successful treatment of *Candida glabrata* endophthalmitis with amphotericin B lipid complex (ABLC). J Infect. 2000;40:92-94.
454. Perez-Gomez A, Prieto A, Torresano M, et al. Role of the new azoles in the treatment of fungal osteoarticular infections. Semin Arthritis Rheum. 1998;27:226-244.
455. Dunkley AB, Leslie IJ. *Candida* infection of a silicone metacarpophalangeal arthroplasty. J Hand Surg Br. 1997;22:423-424.
456. Jenkin GA, Choo M, Hosking P, et al. Candidal epididymo-orchitis: Case report and review. Clin Infect Dis. 1998;26:942-945.
457. Walsh TJ, Bustamante CI, Vlahov D, et al. Candidal suppurative peripheral thrombophlebitis: Recognition, prevention, and management. Infect Control. 1986;7:16-22.

CHAPTER **256**

Aspergillus Species

THOMAS F. PATTERSON

Invasive aspergillosis is a major cause of morbidity and mortality in immunosuppressed patients. This infection is caused by *Aspergillus*, a hyaline mold that is the etiologic agent responsible not only for invasive aspergillosis but also a variety of noninvasive or semi-invasive conditions. These syndromes range from colonization with the organism, such as fungus ball due to aspergillus (also known as aspergilloma); allergic responses to *Aspergillus*, including allergic bronchopulmonary aspergillosis (ABPA); and semi-invasive or invasive infections, which span a spectrum from chronic necrotizing pneumonia to invasive pulmonary aspergillosis and other syndromes of tissue invasion.

In recent years *Aspergillus* and aspergillosis have been a major focus of clinical mycology because the number of patients with this disease has risen dramatically and because of the difficulty in diagnosing and treating invasive infection.[1] The increased number of *Aspergillus* infections has occurred because more patients are at risk for this opportunistic pathogen and because no strategies have proved to be successful in preventing the disease it causes.[2] Patients with established invasive aspergillosis have extremely poor outcomes even with recent advances in therapy.[3,4] Successful therapy depends not only on an early diagnosis—which is often difficult to establish—but, even more important, on reversal of underlying host immune defects, such as neutropenia or high doses of immunosuppressive therapy.[1,5] Non–culture-based tests and radiologic approaches can be used to establish an early diagnosis of infection and may result in improved outcomes of infection.[1,6,7] Even when therapy is begun promptly, efficacy of many treatment regimens, including amphotericin B deoxycholate, is poor, particularly in patients with disseminated or central nervous system disease.[1-4] New diagnostic approaches have been introduced and antifungal agents have been developed for this disease, including the newer azoles, lipid formulations of amphotericin B, and a new drug class—the echinocandins.[8-10] In this chapter, clinical mycology, epidemiology, pathogenesis, clinical presentation, diagnosis, treatment, and prevention of aspergillosis are described.

MYCOLOGY

The genus *Aspergillus* was first recognized in 1729 by Micheli, in Florence, who noted the resemblance between the sporulating head of an *Aspergillus* species and an aspergillum used to sprinkle holy water.[11] In 1856, Virchow published the first complete microscopic descriptions of the organism.[12] *Aspergillus flavus* was formally named by Link in 1809.[13] Thom and Church first classified the genus in 1926 with 69 *Aspergillus* species in 11 groups, a figure that has gradually increased to more than 180 species in 18 groups.[14-18]

Most species of *Aspergillus* reproduce asexually, but a teleomorph (or sexual form) has been identified for some species, including at least two pathogenic species: *Aspergillus nidulans* (also referred to as *Aspergillus nidulellus;* teleomorph, *Emericella nidulans*) and *Aspergillus amstelodami* (*Eurotium amstelodami*).[18,19] Even though the correct taxonomic nomenclature would rename these organisms using the sexual form, generally the generic name *Aspergillus* has been retained for all species to simplify nomenclature regardless of their teleomorphs, rather than separating the organisms into unfamiliar species based on discovery of a sexual state.[12] As with other pathogenic fungi, the taxonomy of *Aspergillus* has undergone extensive reclassification with utilization of molecular studies, such as sequencing of ribosomal genes, which has allowed more natural subgroupings of ascomycetous fungi.[18]

The genus *Aspergillus* is an anamorphic member (asexual form) of the family Trichocomaceae. The teleomorphs of *Aspergillus* species are classified in seven genera in the order Eurotiales in the phylum Ascomycota.[18] *Aspergillus* is distinct but is closely related to the genus *Penicillium*.[19] Identification of the genus and of common pathogenic species is usually not difficult, but species level identification of less common members can be laborious.

The most common species causing invasive infection include *Aspergillus fumigatus,* which historically has made up a vast majority of invasive isolates; *A. flavus; Aspergillus terreus;* and, less commonly for invasive infection, *Aspergillus niger.*[4] Recent studies have shown emergence of less common species, including *A. terreus* and unusual less pathogenic species as the etiologic agents of invasive infection (Table 256-1).[20] With more prolonged and profound immunosuppression, the list of rare species causing invasive infection continues to increase, including *A. amstelodami, Aspergillus avenaceus, Aspergillus caesiellus, Aspergillus candidus, Aspergillus carneus, Aspergillus chevalieri, Aspergillus clavatus, Aspergillus flavipes, Aspergillus glaucus, Aspergillus granulosus, A. nidulans (E. nidulans), Aspergillus ochraceus, Aspergillus oryzae, Aspergillus restrictus, Aspergillus sydowii, Aspergillus tetrazonus (Aspergillus quadrilineatus), Aspergillus ustus, Aspergillus versicolor, Aspergillus wentii, Neosartorya fischeri, Neosartorya pseudofischeri,* and others, although the authenticity of at least some of these has been questioned.[1,2,17-19,21,22]

Pathogenic *Aspergillus* species are easily cultured from pathologic samples and grow rapidly (within 24-72 hours) at a broad range of temperatures on a variety of media. Blood cultures are still uncommonly positive and often reflect contamination rather than invasive disease.[23] A distinguishing characteristic of pathogenic *Aspergillus* species is their ability to grow at 37° C. In addition, most strains of *A. fumigatus* are able to grow at temperatures of 45° C and above, which

TABLE 256-1 Characteristics of *Aspergillus* Species Associated with Invasive Infection

Aspergillus Species	Frequency Isolated in Clinical Infection (%)[4]	Colony Characteristics[22]	Microscopic Features[22]	Clinical Significance
A. fumigatus (Fig. 256-1A and B)	66%	Smoky gray green; may have pale yellow or lavender reverse; grows at 50°C	Columnar; uniseriate; smooth to finely roughened conidia 2-3.5 μm	Most common invasive species; most pathogenic
A. flavus (Fig. 256-2A and B)	14%	Olive to lime green	Radiate to loosely columnar; uniseriate or biseriate; rough conidiophore; conidia 3-6 μm	Sinusitis; skin infection; produces aflatoxin
A. terreus (Fig. 256-3A to C)	5%	Beige to cinnamon buff	Columnar; biseriate; globose; small 2-2.5 μm conidia; globose accessory conidia along hyphae	Increasingly detected; resistant to amphotericin B; more susceptible to newer azoles
A. niger. (Fig. 256-4A and B)	5%	Initially white, rapidly turning black with yellow reverse	Radiate; biseriate; globose, black, very rough conidia 4-5 μm	Uncommon in invasive infections; superficial agent of otic disease; colonization

Data from Patterson TF, Kirkpatrick WR, White M, et al. Invasive aspergillosis. Disease spectrum, treatment practices, and outcomes. I3 Aspergillus Study Group. Medicine (Baltimore). 2000;79:250-260; Sutton DA, Fothergill AW, Rinaldi MD, eds. Guide to Clinically Significant Fungi. 1st ed. Baltimore: Williams & Wilkins; 1998.

can also be used to identify that species.[22] Most species initially appear as small, fluffy white colonies on culture plates within 48 hours. Presumptive identification of an *Aspergillus* species is usually readily accomplished by appearance of the fungus on gross and microscopic inspection of the colony growing on medium, which provides typical sporulation.

Microscopic features and colony morphology for the most common clinical isolates, *A. fumigatus, A. flavus, A. terreus,* and *A. niger,* are described in Table 256-1 and shown in Figures 256-1 to 256-4. Species identification of *Aspergillus* has become important because differences in antifungal drug susceptibility and likely pathogenicity may be identified.

A. fumigatus is the most pathogenic species and is the most common species in invasive infection, constituting more than 90% of the isolates in some series, although recently a lower prevalence has been described.[4,18] Colonies of *A. fumigatus* are typically gray-green with a wooly to cottony texture (see Fig. 256-1A).[22] Like other species of *Aspergillus*, hyphae are hyaline (lightly pigmented), have septa, and are usually branched at acute (typically 45 degrees) angles. The conidial head is columnar with conidiophores that are smooth walled and uncolored, or darkened in the upper portion near the vesicle. This species is uniseriate (a term describing phialides that are attached directly to the vesicle), with closely compacted phialides borne only on the upper portion of the vesicle (see Fig. 256-1A). Conidia are smooth

to finely roughened and are 2 to 3.5 μm in diameter. The fruiting head (the conidiophore and conidia) is not commonly seen in clinical specimens, although it may be detected in sites exposed to air, such as wounds or lung cavities.[22] Like other *Aspergillus* spp., it is widespread in nature—found in soil, on decaying vegetation, in the air, and, more recently, in water supplies.[24,25]

A. flavus is a common isolate in sinusitis as well as in skin and invasive infections. This species, which produces an aflatoxin, is found in soil and decaying vegetation.[26] Colonies are olive to lime green and grow at a rapid rate (see Fig. 256-2A). Some isolates are uniseriate, but it is typically biseriate. In biseriate species, sterile cells known as metulae are attached to the vesicle, and these in turn, support the phialides. This species also has noticeably rough conidiophores and smooth conidia 3 to 6 m (see Fig. 256-2B).[22]

A. terreus is a common soil-related isolate that has been increasingly reported in invasive infection in immunocompromised hosts.[20] *A. terreus* conidia are small (2.0-2.5 μm), and the colony color and fruiting structures are characteristic for this species (see Fig. 256-3A and B). Colonies range in color from buff to beige to cinnamon (see Fig. 256-3A).[22] Conidiophores are smooth-walled and hyaline, and the conidial heads are biseriate and columnar (see Fig. 256-3B). A distinguishing feature of this species is the presence of globose aleurioconidia that are produced on hyphae (see Fig. 256-3C). These aleurioconidia, more recently termed *accessory conidia,* may even be detected in

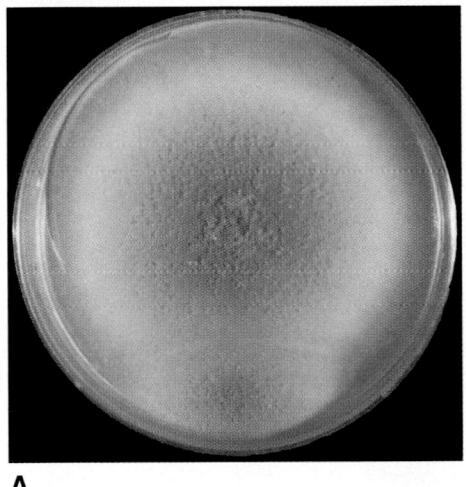

A

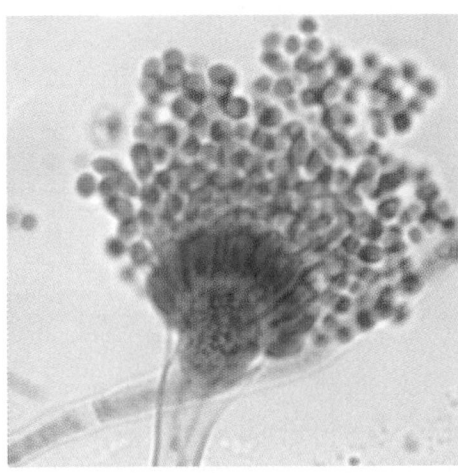

B

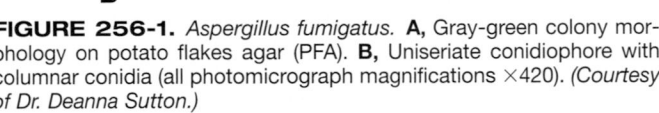

FIGURE 256-1. *Aspergillus fumigatus.* **A,** Gray-green colony morphology on potato flakes agar (PFA). **B,** Uniseriate conidiophore with columnar conidia (all photomicrograph magnifications ×420). *(Courtesy of Dr. Deanna Sutton.)*

A

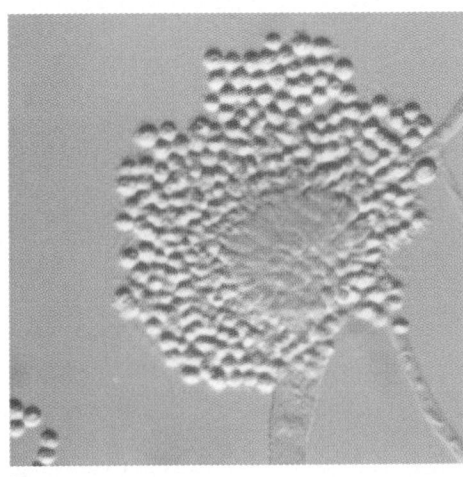

B

FIGURE 256-2. *Aspergillus flavus.* **A,** Olive-lime green colony on PFA. **B,** Radiate, biseriate conidia. *(Courtesy of Dr. Deanna Sutton.)*

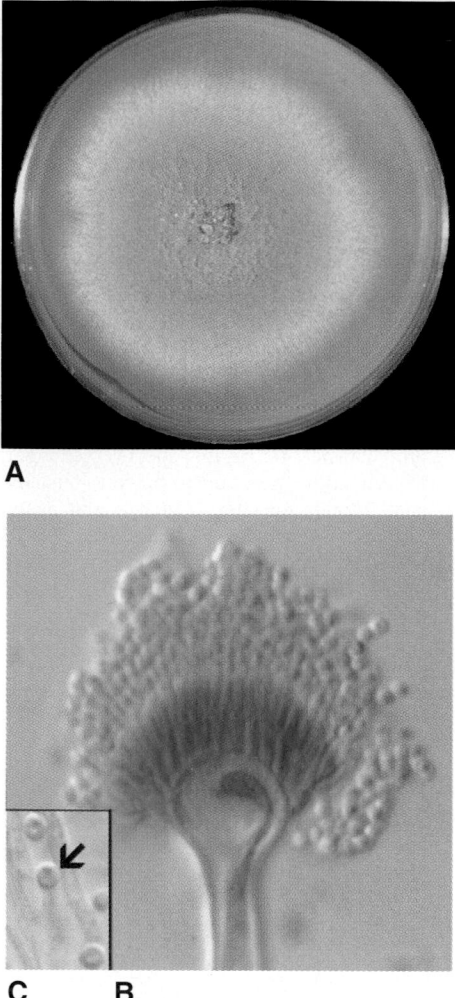

FIGURE 256-3. *Aspergillus terreus.* **A,** Buff-cinnamon colony on PFA. **B,** Columnar, biseriate smooth conidia. **C,** Globose, sessile accessory conidia along hyphae. *(Courtesy of Dr. Deanna Sutton.)*

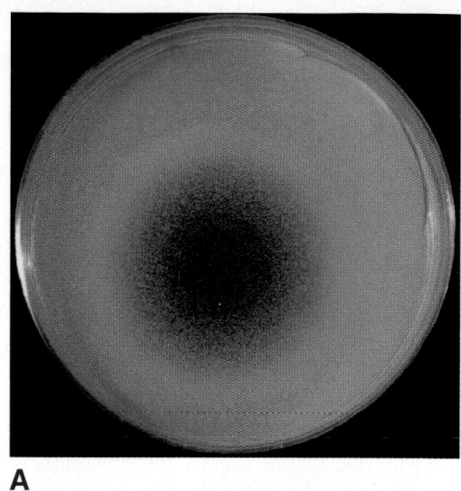

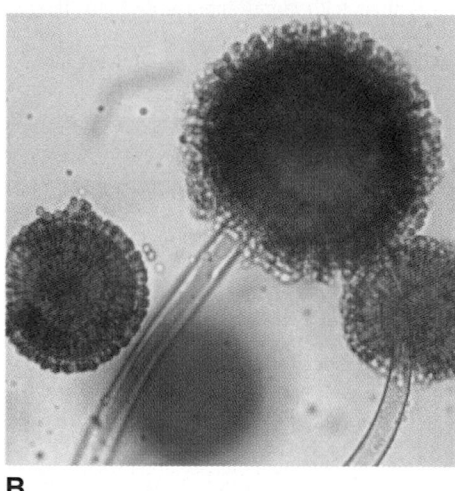

FIGURE 256-4. *Aspergillus niger.* **A,** Black colony on PFA. **B,** Large, radiate, biseriate uniseriate conidia. *(Courtesy of Dr. Deanna Sutton.)*

histopathologic samples, which may be used to establish presumptive identification of the species.[27] Identification of this species has become increasingly important because of its resistance to many antifungals, including amphotericin B, although improved susceptibility and better outcomes with newer azoles have been reported.[20,28,29]

A. niger (see Fig. 256-4A and B) is found in soil, on plants, and even in food and condiments (such as pepper). Colonies are initially white but quickly become black with the production of the pigmented fruiting structures (see Fig. 256-4A). It grows rapidly with a pale yellow reverse. Conidial heads are biseriate and cover the entire vesicle. Conidia are brown to black and are very rough (4-5 μm) (see Fig. 256-4B), although the hyphae are hyaline.[22] The species may produce oxalate crystals in clinical specimens.[30,31] The role of *A. niger* in invasive infection is less well established, with its decreased pathogenicity perhaps due in part to the fact that its larger conidia do not readily reach deep into lung tissues. However, it is a common colonizing isolate and can cause superficial infection, such as otitis externa.[23,32]

Other species of *Aspergillus* are less common in invasive infection, perhaps reflecting an increased awareness of their significance.[4,23] *A. nidulans,* for example, has been reported as a cause of infection in patients with chronic granulomatous disease and is a species that may be resistant to amphotericin B.[33-35] Thus, even these previously "nonpathogenic" *Aspergillus* species must be considered potentially clinically significant in an appropriate clinical setting and host.[36]

EPIDEMIOLOGY

Aspergillus is ubiquitous worldwide. The organism is found in soil, water, food, air, and is particularly common in decaying vegetation.[18] The inoculum for establishing infection is not known, but it is apparent that hosts with normal pulmonary host defenses very rarely develop disease despite routine exposure to the organism with normal daily living—through airborne conidia, through foodstuffs like pepper, and so on. In contrast, patients with altered host immunity, particularly those with reduced pulmonary host defenses (e.g., those who use corticosteroids) that inhibit the activity of pulmonary macrophages or those who are neutropenic, have increased susceptibility to the organism.[37]

Patients with prolonged and profound neutropenia (<100 neutrophils/μl) are at high risk for invasive aspergillosis, but changing treatment patterns in chemotherapy and transplantation, along with the use of growth factors, have limited the numbers of persistently neutropenic patients.[38] Other patients at high risk for invasive aspergillosis include patients undergoing organ and bone marrow transplantation and those receiving corticosteroids or other newer immunosuppressive therapies, including the tumor necrosis factor-α (TNF-α) antagonists such as infliximab and others.[39]

In patients undergoing hematopoietic stem cell or marrow transplantation, a recent increase in the incidence of invasive aspergillosis has been reported, and the epidemiology of infection has changed.[40] In those patients, the major periods of risk are bimodal, with peak incidence occurring at an early time after transplantation (<20 days) but also more than 100 days after transplantation.[41,42] One of the factors in the changing epidemiology in this patient population is the use of non-myeloablative transplantation procedures, which has shifted the major risk factor in these patients from neutropenia to that of the use of high doses of corticosteroids for the treatment of acute or chronic graft-versus-host disease.[41] In fact, only 31% of the hematopoietic stem cell transplant recipients with invasive aspergillosis reported by Wald and colleagues were neutropenic. Acute or chronic graft-versus-host disease may occur an extended time after marrow or stem cell transplantation, which dramatically increases the risk for *Aspergillus* infection and prolongs the period for which these patients are at risk.[41,42]

Although patients undergoing marrow or stem cell transplants and those receiving cytotoxic chemotherapy still constitute a majority of those who develop invasive aspergillosis, other significantly immunosuppressed patients are also at risk. Included in those other groups are patients undergoing organ transplantation, particularly lung transplantation, whose risk is very high with an incidence of infection of 10% to 15%.[43] The increased risk in lung transplantation is because the transplanted organ is constantly exposed to the environment, ciliary clearance is reduced, and many of these patients are colonized with *Aspergillus* in either the native or transplanted lung.[44] In lung transplant recipients, *Aspergillus* infections can range in clinical presentation from an ulcerative tracheobronchitis to disseminated infection.[43,45] Other immunosuppressed patients are also at risk for invasive aspergillosis, although the rates of infection are less, including those with pulmonary diseases, acquired immunodeficiency syndrome (AIDS), chronic granulomatous disease and other hereditary immunodeficiency syndromes, those who use steroids, and others.[4,43,46]

Outbreaks of invasive aspergillosis have occurred in patients exposed to *Aspergillus* conidia in association with construction and other environmental risks.[47,48] In severely immunosuppressed patients, aspergillosis may occur from other exposures as well, including aerosols of contaminated water, which has recently been described.[25,49] Aspergillosis may also occur as endogenous reactivation from prior infection or colonization, so that even when it occurs in a hospital setting it may not be possible to prevent all cases by reducing environmental exposures.[37] It should also be noted that with the prolonged period of risk—more than 100 days after transplantation in some patients—these infections become very difficult to prevent with protective environments as much of their health care will occur in a non-hospital-based setting.[41]

PATHOGENICITY AND HOST DEFENSES

The usual route of infection for invasive aspergillosis is through inhalation of *Aspergillus* conidia into the lungs, although other routes of exposure such as inhalation of water aerosols contaminated with *Aspergillus* conidia have been suggested.[49,50] Although less common, invasive infection may also follow local tissue invasion such as through surgical wounds or contaminated intravenous catheters or armboards, leading to cutaneous infection.[51-53]

In the absence of effective host defenses following pulmonary exposure, the inhaled small resting condida enlarge and germinate, resulting in transformation into hyphae with subsequent vascular invasion and eventual disseminated infection. The incubation period for conidial germination in pulmonary tissue is variable, ranging from 2 days to months and may even vary by species.[27] The growth rate at 37° C may be one determinant of the rate of disease progression and possible pathogenicity of the organism. Hydrocortisone significantly increases the growth rates of *Aspergillus*, further enhancing the role of corticosteroids as a risk factor for invasive disease.[54] The process of hyphal growth and tissue invasion results in a hallmark feature of invasive aspergillosis: vascular invasion (Fig. 256-5) and pulmonary infarction (Fig. 256-6), which are classic features of invasive pulmonary aspergillosis due to the angioinvasive nature of the organism.

Although infection in apparently normal hosts can occur, invasive aspergillosis is extremely uncommon in immunocompetent hosts.[4,55]

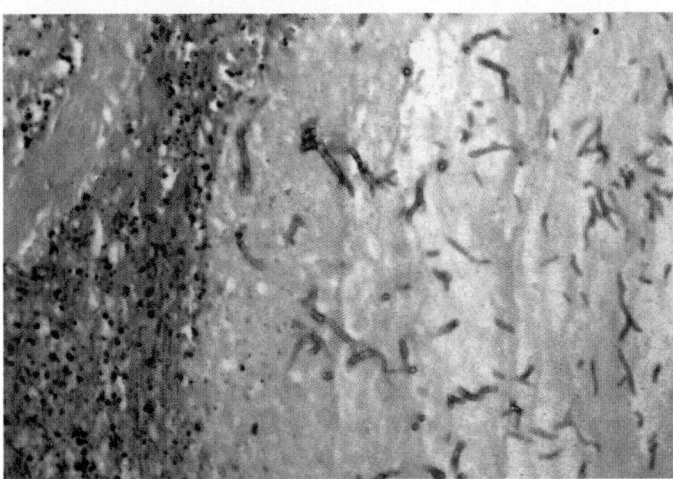

FIGURE 256-5. Lung tissue section showing narrow, acutely branching septated hyphae on hematoxylin-eosin stain showing vascular invasion (original magnification ×420).

Normal pulmonary defense mechanisms are usually able to contain the organism in a host with intact pulmomary defenses. The first line of defense against *Aspergillus* is ciliary clearance of the organism from the airways and limited access to the alveoli due to conidial size. This feature is one reason for the increased pathogenicity of *A. fumigatus* as compared with other species of *Aspergillus*.[54] After conidia reach the alveoli, the major line of defense becomes the pulmonary macrophage, which is capable of ingesting and killing *Aspergillus* conidia.[56,57] After the cells germinate, polymorphonuclear leukocytes act to extracellularly kill both swollen conidia and hyphae.[58] Efficacy

FIGURE 256-6. Infarcted lung tissue due to *Aspergillus* angioinvasion on gross lung specimen.

of host defenses against the organism may be enhanced by opsonization of conidia with complement or other molecules such as mannose-binding protein and surfactant proteins.[59,60] *A. fumigatus* produces a complement inhibitor, which may increase its pathogenicity.[61,62] Antibodies against *Aspergillus* are common because of the ubiquitous nature of the organism, although they are not protective nor are they useful in the diagnosis of infection in high-risk patients owing to the lack of consistent seroconversion following exposure or infection.[63]

Corticosteroids play a major role in increasing susceptibility to *Aspergillus* by decreasing oxidative killing of the organism by pulmonary macrophages and by increasing the linear growth rate by as much as 30% to 40% and cell synthesis by more than 150%.[54,57,64] Studies in a murine model have suggested a role for cellular immunity, in which a Th1 response induced by administration of soluble interleukin-4 (IL-4) was associated with a favorable response.[65] Toll-like receptors (TLRs) have also been described as mediating antifungal defense against *A. fumigatus*.[66] Initially described in *Drosophila* for mediating antifungal defense to *A. fumigatus*, TLRs appear crucial for recognition of *A. fumigatus* by human cells.[67] Recognition of *Aspergillus* (and *Candida*) by TLR2 and TLR4 results in activation of intracellular pathways leading to cytokine production. These events are needed for an effective initial antifungal defense and bridge the gap between the innate and acquired immunity.[67-69]

Many *Aspergillus* species produce toxins including aflatoxins, ochratoxin A, fumagillin, and gliotoxin—the last of which may reduce macrophage and neutrophil function, although the role of these toxins as major virulence factors is not established.[17,70] For example, aflatoxin, produced by *A. flavus*, is important as a carcinogenic and immunosuppressive agent but does not appear to be important in virulence.[26] *Aspergillus* species possess other potential virulence factors including production of proteases and phospholipases, although strains deficient in those genes are still capable of producing experimental infection.[71-73]

In contrast to the deficient host responses that lead to invasive *Aspergillus* infections, the pathogenesis of ABPA and allergic fungal sinusitis relates to aberrant inflammatory host responses to the organism.[1,74,75] The immune response to *Aspergillus* antigens in ABPA as in both asthmatic patients and those with cystic fibrosis is a Th2 CD4[+] cell response.[54] The pathogenesis of ABPA has been an area of active investigation. Currently, the immunopathogenesis of this condition is proposed as beginning with an allergic inflammatory response that follows after *Aspergillus* conidia are inhaled into the bronchi, where they germinate and form hyphae.[54] These mycelial cells release allergens that are processed by antigen-presenting cells bearing HLA-DR2 or HLA-DR5 and presented to T cells within the bronchoalveolar lymphoid tissue. The T-cell response to these allergens favors a Th2 response, with release of cytokines IL-4, IL-5, and IL-13.[54] The inflammatory response in the bronchial submucosa leads to excessive mucin production, extravasation of eosinophils into the bronchial mucin, intermittent bronchial obstruction with atelectasis, and, over time, to bronchiectasis in some patients. Allergic fungal sinusitis is also characterized by submucosal inflammation and eosinophil-rich mucin in the sinus cavity. Aspergilloma, also called *fungus ball of the lung,* is a mass of hyphae in a preexisting cavity. *Aspergillus* causes a brisk IgG antibody response to the organism even though invasion of the cavity wall is rarely observed. Clumps of *Aspergillus* hyphae also may grow in ectatic bronchi of patients with bronchiectasis, but the pathogenesis is poorly understood.[76] Increased risk for chronic forms of pulmonary aspergillosis have been linked to subtle immune defects including polymorphisms in mannose-binding protein or alternations in surfactant D.[77]

CLINICAL PRESENTATION

The spectrum of clinical syndromes associated with aspergillosis is diverse, ranging from allergic responses to the organism, asymptomatic colonization, superficial infection, and acute or subacute invasive disease. Generally, the clinical presentation reflects the underlying immune defects and risk factors associated with each patient group, with greater immune suppression correlating with increased risk for invasive disease.

Allergic Manifestations of Disease

Allergic Bronchopulmonary Aspergillosis

ABPA is a long-term allergic response to *Aspergillus* that is characterized by transient pulmonary infiltrates due to atelectasis. Central bronchiectasis occurs in some patients after several years of disease.[78] The incidence of ABPA is estimated to range from 1% to 2% in patients with persistent asthma and in approximately 7% (with a range from 2%-15%) of patients with cystic fibrosis.[54,79] Specific criteria are used to establish the diagnosis of ABPA because no single finding except for central bronchiectasis in a patient with asthma is diagnostic for the condition. These classic criteria include (1) asthma, (2) central bronchiectasis on chest computed tomography, (3) immediate cutaneous reactivity to *Aspergillus* species (or *A. fumigatus*), (4) total serum IgE concentration greater than 417 IU/mL (1000 ng/mL), (5) elevated serum IgE and/or IgG antibody to *A. fumigatus,* (6) fleeting infiltrates on chest radiograph, (7) serum precipitating antibodies to *A. fumigatus,* and (8) peripheral blood eosinophilia.[54,75,79] It has been suggested that the first five are the minimal essential criteria for ABPA in patients with asthma, with the presence of precipitating antibodies further supporting the diagnosis and total IgE levels correlating with exacerbation of disease.[54] Other clinical features may be present that can be used to support the diagnosis including positive sputum cultures for *Aspergillus* or smears with hyphae consistent with *Aspergillus,* brown mucus plugs with degenerated eosinophils (Charcot-Leyden crystals) in sputa, and chest radiographic findings suggesting bronchial inflammation.[80] These latter chest radiographic findings include the "ring sign," indicating bronchial thickening without mucus plugs, and "parallel lines" or "tram tracks" suggesting bronchiectasis, which contrasts to tapering seen in the normal bronchus.[81]

The diagnosis of ABPA in cystic fibrosis may be particularly difficult because many of the diagnostic criteria overlap with common manifestations of cystic fibrosis. Recently, consensus conference criteria for the diagnosis and management of ABPA in cystic fibrosis have been published (Table 256-2).[54] In these patients eosinophilia is not a useful diagnostic tool because the patients may have elevated peripheral blood eosinophils from other causes such as *Pseudomonas aeruginosa.*

ABPA typically progresses through a series of remissions and exacerbations but can eventually lead to pulmonary fibrosis, which is associated with a poor long-term prognosis.[80] Management of ABPA is directed at reducing acute asthmatic symptoms and avoiding end-stage fibrosis. Corticosteroid therapy is commonly used for treating exacerbations, although few randomized trials have been conducted for their use.[82] Guidelines suggest that worsening diagnostic or clinical parameters may warrant a trial of corticosteroid therapy.[54] The role for antifungal therapy was evaluated with a randomized double-blind, placebo-controlled trial that showed itraconazole at 200 mg per day for 16 weeks significantly reduced daily corticosteroid use, reduced levels of IgE, and improved exercise tolerance and pulmonary function.[83]

Other Allergic Manifestations

Aspergillus is an occasional cause of allergic fungal sinusitis, although most cases are due to dark-walled molds. This entity occurs in patients with a history of chronic allergic rhinitis, often with hyperplastic nasal mucosa forming nasal polyps. A mass of inspisated mucus forms in sinus cavity with *Aspergillus* hyphae and Charcot-Leyden crystals. The sinus mucosa is hyperplastic but not invaded.[84-87,84-86] Management is directed at aerating the sinus and ensuring that tissue invasion is not present.[87] The benefit of treating with either intranasal steroids or systemic antifungal agents has not been shown.[1,87,88]

Saprophytic Colonization and Superficial Aspergillosis

Fungus Balls Due to *Aspergillus*

A pulmonary fungus ball due to *Aspergillus*—or *aspergilloma*—is a solid mass of hyphae growing in a previously existing pulmonary cavity. Typically *Aspergillus* fungus balls of the lung develop in preexisting cavities in the pulmonary apex of patients with chronic lung

TABLE 256-2 Criteria for Diagnosis and Management of Allergic Bronchopulmonary Aspergillosis (ABPA) in Patients with Cystic Fibrosis

Diagnostic Criteria	*Comment*
Clinical deterioration (increased cough, wheezing, exercise intolerance, exercise-induced asthma, increased sputum, decrease in pulmonary function)	Clinical signs not attributed to another etiology
Immediate cutaneous reactivity to *Aspergillus* or presence of IgE to *A. fumigatus*	Pinprick skin test wheal of >3 mm with surrounding erythema while not receiving antihistamines
Total serum IgE concentration >500 IU/mL (>1200 ng/mL)	If ABPA is suspected and level is 200-500 repeat in 1-3 months; if taking steroids, repeat after discontinuation
One of the following: (1) precipitins (or IgG) to *A. fumigatus* or (2) new or recent abnormalities on computed tomography (bronchiectasis) or chest radiograph (mucus plugging/infiltrates)	Failure of infiltrates or abnormalities to clear after antibiotic therapy and standard physiotherapy
Recommendations for screening for ABPA	
Maintain clinical suspicion for diagnosis	Especially in patients older than 6 years
Determine total serum IgE annually	If total IgE >500 IU/mL consider skin test or measure IgE to *Aspergillus*
If IgE 200-500 IU/mL, repeat if clinical suspicion is high	Consider retesting with disease exacerbation and perform other diagnostic tests
Therapy for Exacerbations of ABPA	
Corticosteroids: 0.5-2 mg/kg/day oral prednisone equivalent (maximum 60 mg/day) for 1-2 weeks, tapered over 2-3 months	Recommended for disease exacerbation in all patients except those with steroid toxicity
Antifungal therapy (itraconazole—or other azole with *Aspergillus* activity—voriconazole, posaconazole)	Slow steroid response or toxicity; itraconazole 5 mg/kg/day up to 400 mg/kg/day—levels necessary (other azoles may be effective but not studied); monitor liver function tests; duration 3-6 months
Adjunctive therapy: inhaled corticosteroids; bronchodilators; environmental manipulation	No evidence for efficacy in ABPA but may be useful in asthma; reasonable to search for source of extensive mold exposure

Data from Stevens DA, Moss RB, Kurup VP, et al. Allergic bronchopulmonary aspergillosis in cystic fibrosis—State of the art: Cystic Fibrosis Foundation Consensus Conference. Clin Infect Dis. 2003;37(Suppl 3):S225-S264.

disease such as bullous emphysema, sarcoidosis, tuberculosis, histoplasmosis, congenital cyst, bacterial lung abscess, or, very rarely, in a pulmonary bleb from *Pneumocystis* pneumonia in patients with AIDS.[89-92] *Scedosporium apiospermum* or agents of zygomycosis are rare causes of fungus ball of the lung. On chest radiograph, a pulmonary aspergilloma appears as a solid round mass in a cavity. The detection of *Aspergillus* in sputum cultures or detection of high titers of *Aspergillus* antibodies are further evidence that the radiographic findings are consistent with a diagnosis of fungus ball due to *Aspergillus* so that a biopsy is not usually necessary except to diagnose the underlying lung disease.[93]

In many patients the fungus ball due to *Aspergillus* remains asymptomatic, but in a significant number of patients, hemoptysis occurs and can be fatal.[76,94,95] Surgical resection is considered the definitive therapy but the dense pleural adhesions adjacent the fungus ball and the poor pulmonary reserve of most patients make surgery hazardous. Contamination of the pleural space with *Aspergillus* and the common complication of bronchopleural fistula in the postoperative period can lead to chronic *Aspergillus* empyema. Dense adhesions make pleural drainage difficult, often requiring pleural stripping or an Eloesser procedure, further compromising lung function.[94]

Aspergillus can also be associated with fungus balls of the sinuses without tissue invasion.[91,96] The maxillary sinus is the most common site for a sinus aspergilloma to occur.[91] Clinical presentation is similar to that for any chronic sinusitis. Computed tomography of the sinus can be used to confirm the fungus ball, along with cultures of *Aspergillus,* usually *A. flavus* or *A. fumigatus.* Management is usually directed at surgical removal and a generous maxillary antrostomy for sinus drainage, along with confirmation that invasive disease has not occurred.

Denning and colleagues have described three distinct syndromes of chronic pulmonary aspergillosis to better characterize those patients who develop chronic pulmonary disease related to *Aspergillus.*[77] These conditions include (1) chronic cavitary pulmonary aspergillosis, characterized by the formation and expansion of multiple cavities, which may contain fungus balls; (2) chronic fibrosing aspergillosis, which, as its name suggests, involves extensive fibrosis; and (3) chronic necrotizing, or subacute, aspergillosis, in which slowly progressive infection occurs, usually in a single thin-walled cavity. In all of these conditions, the diagnosis is suggested by radiologic and clinical features and the role of therapy remains speculative, although it

appears that long-term antifungal therapy may be beneficial in a subset of patients.[77]

Other Superficial or Colonizing Syndromes of Aspergillosis

Otomycosis is a condition of superficial colonization typically due to *A. niger.*[97] The clinical features include findings similar to other causes of external otitis, with the external auditory canal potentially revealing mold growing on cerumen and desquamated epithelial debris. *A. fumigatus* looks greenish, and *A. niger* forms a black tuft. Treatment is to focus on the underlying chronic otitis externa rather than the fungus. In immunocompromised patients, invasive otitis externa can occur and resembles that due to *P. aeruginosa* clinically.[32]

Onychomycosis due to *Aspergillus* is another superficial condition that, although rare, can become chronic and respond poorly to antifungal agents.[98] Antifungal agents in the setting of nail infection may empirically target yeasts; thus, a nail culture can be useful in patients with nonresponsive disease to establish a specific fungal etiology so that appropriate therapy can be initiated.

Aspergillus is an occasional etiology of keratitis, particularly following trauma or corneal surgery (see Chapter 107).[99,100] The diagnosis can be established with smears demonstrating hyphae, which may be indistiguishable from other molds like *Fusarium* that also cause keratitis, but culture results are usually positive to confirm the diagnosis. Therapy consists of topical antifungal agents, usually amphotericin B or natamycin (pimaricin) drops administered hourly, although studies demonstrating efficacy of either agent—but particularly the latter—are limited. Surgical intervention may be required for deep lesions or those nonresponsive to medical therapy.[101] Azoles with *Aspergillus* activity, including itraconazole, voriconazole, and posaconazole, have been used (in addition to topical therapy) systemically for this infection, but their role is not well studied. Some of these agents have been also been administered topically. Amphotericin B has been injected intracamerally when corneal penetration has occurred.[102]

Invasive Syndromes Caused by *Aspergillus*

Invasive aspergillosis most frequently begins in the lung following inhalation of *Aspergillus* conidia. Invasion of hyphae into the pulmonary vasculature is common, occurring in as many as a third of patients with invasive pulmonary aspergillosis. Disseminated disease occurs either by hematogenous spread to distant sites or by contiguous extension from the lung.[2] Hematogenous dissemination to the central nervous system or other organs including the thyroid, liver, spleen, kidney, bone, heart, and skin is common in patients with severe immunosuppression such as those undergoing allogeneic hematopoietic stem cell or marrow transplants and heralds an ominously poor prognosis.[4,103]

Invasive Pulmonary Aspergillosis

The most common manifestation of invasive aspergillosis is invasive pulmonary aspergillosis (IPA). Invasive pulmonary aspergillosis rarely manifests before 10 to 12 days of profound neutropenia, which until recently has been the major risk factor for developing infection.[104] In recent series, even with an approximate doubling of disease incidence compared with historical rates of infection, less than a third of patients undergoing marrow or hematopoietic stem cell transplantation were neutropenic at the time of diagnosis of IPA, emphasizing the shifting epidemiology to other forms of immunosuppression, such as the use of high doses of corticosteroids for treating graft-versus-host disease.[41,42] The incubation period for developing IPA after inhalation of conidia is not known, but a significant number of patients have manifestations of IPA on admission or within the first 2 weeks of hospital admission, suggesting that community-acquired exposure is common.[43,105]

Symptoms of IPA include progressive dry cough, dyspnea, pleuritic chest pain, fever despite coverage with broad-spectrum antibiotics, and pulmonary infiltrates. These symptoms may be reduced in patients who are unable to mount an inflammatory response owing to profound neutropenia. In addition, although fever is common, it may be absent in those receiving high doses of corticosteroids. Other clinical features of IPA include hemoptysis, pleural effusion, and pneumothorax. However, all the physical findings are nonspecific and may lag significantly behind the disease process. Clinical characteristics may resemble a pulmonary embolism with pleuritic chest pain, hemoptysis, and dyspnea, which reflect the angioinvasive nature of the organism. Laboratory studies are also nonspecific but may include elevation in bilirubin and lactate dehydrogenase, coagulation abnormalities and elevation in C-reactive protein. Life-threatening hypoxia may occur in patients with extensive or progressive infection.

In extensive infection, multiple diffuse nodular pulmonary infiltrates are readily seen on chest radiographs (Fig. 256-7), but these are not only nondiagnostic but also associated with an extremely poor prognosis.[106] Other pulmonary radiographic findings of IPA include the classic pleural-based, wedge-shaped densities or cavitary lesions, although the former are not commonly detected and the latter are present late in the course of infection.[5] Recent studies suggest that pleural effusions are more common than previously considered,[2] but whether they are actually a manifestation of IPA is not established.[107] The presence of a "halo" of low attenuation surrounding a nodular lesion is an early finding in invasive aspergillosis (Fig. 256-8A).[7,107] Later in the course of infection these nodular lesions may cavitate (usually in temporal association with recovery of neutrophils), forming an "air-crescent" sign (see Fig. 256-8B). These radiographic features are characteristic of IPA, but similar findings can also occur with other angioinvasive organisms, including *Zygomycetes, Fusarium, Scedosporium,* as well as *P. aeruginosa.*

Tracheobronchitis

Aspergillus in the airways can range in significance from colonization, which is common in lung transplantation, to ulcerative tracheobronchitis.[108] Although it may occur in other immunosuppressed patients, the syndrome of *Aspergillus* tracheobronchitis typically occurs in patients undergoing lung transplantation and in patients with AIDS and is characterized by extensive pseudomembranous or ulcerative lesions due to *Aspergillus.*[45,109-111] In patients undergoing lung transplantation, the infection often occurs at the suture line of the lung transplant and can lead to dehiscence of the anastomotic site.[44,108,110] Symptoms of tracheobronchitis are nonspecific and include dyspnea with associated pulmonary function abnormalities, cough, chest pain, fever, or hemoptysis. Symptoms may be mild and can be confused with other causes including rejection. In more severe disease, unilateral wheeze or stridor may develop because of local obstruction.[2,112] Results of plain radiographs may be normal so that clinical suspicion is needed to establish the diagnosis, which is accomplished by bronchoscopy with biopsy to document tissue invasion. A prolonged course of a systemic antifungal agent therapy is usually required for treatment, although aerosols of liposomal formulations of amphotericin B have been used for localized disease.[1,113]

Sinusitis

Aspergillus infection of the sinuses and nasal cavities in immunocompromised patients manifests as acute invasive rhinosinusitis often in association with invasive pulmonary aspergillosis.[114] The clin-

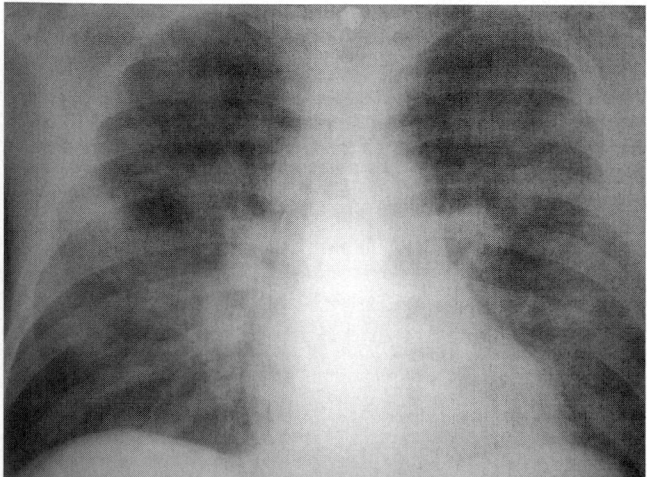

FIGURE 256-7. Chest radiograph showing diffuse pulmonary infiltrates of invasive pulmonary aspergillosis.

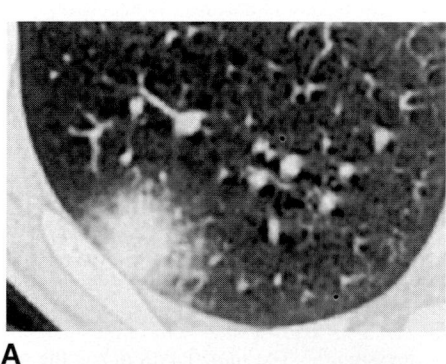

A

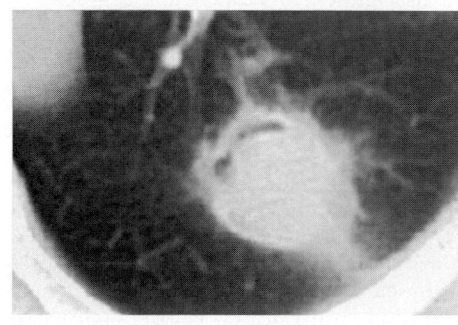

B

FIGURE 256-8. Computed tomography of chest. **A,** "Halo" sign of low attenuation surrounding a nodular lung lesion detected in early pulmonary aspergillosis. **B,** "Air-crescent" sign in a nodular lung lesion found in late disease. *(Radiographs courtesy of Dr. Reginald Greene.)*

ical manifestations are not specific to *Aspergillus* and include fever, cough, epistaxis, sinus discharge, and headaches. Clinical signs are also nondiagnostic but findings of an ulcerative nasal lesion with an eschar or nonsensitive area may be a clue to a fungal diagnosis.[89] Presence of epistaxis or unexplained fever in a high-risk patient may be enough to warrant endoscopy and biopsy of any nasal mucosal lesion. In patients with progressive infection, the disease spreads to contiguous paranasal sinuses, palate, orbit, or brain. The mortality in invasive cases is high, ranging from 20% in patients with leukemia in remission to up to 100% in patients with relapsed leukemia or those undergoing bone marrow transplantation.[115] Plain radiographs are not diagnostic and do not distinguish fungal etiologies from other causes of sinusitis. Sinus computed tomography (CT) scans are useful for establishing extent of infection and determining local tissue invasion (Fig. 256-9). Routine surveillance cultures of the nose have been advocated, but these lack specificity and sensitivity. Cultures from sinus aspirates are useful to demonstrate the presence of *Aspergillus*, but a biopsy with tissue invasion is needed for the diagnosis.[116,117] Therapy for these infections is often difficult and requires long-term administration of antifungal medications.[1] The role of surgery is controversial. Efficacy of antifungal prophylaxis has not been demonstrated, but attempts at reduction of environmental exposures in high-risk patients may be beneficial.[118]

Disseminated Infection

Progressive invasive pulmonary aspergillosis often results in disseminated invasive aspergillosis, a complication associated with an extremely high mortality.[3] In patients with severe and ongoing immunosuppression, such as patients with persistent granulocytopenia, extensive graft-versus-host disease, and progressive underlying malignancy, the efficacy of antifungal therapy for invasive aspergillosis is extremely limited so that infection eventually disseminates to virtually every organ system. In this widespread infection, mortality rates approach 90%, with favorable responses to antifungal therapy seen in less than 20%.[3,4]

Other Invasive Syndromes

Cerebral Aspergillosis

Cerebral aspergillosis is associated with the highest mortality of invasive aspergillosis syndromes, with mortality rates of more than 90% reported in most series.[3] The incidence of cerebral aspergillosis is difficult to determine because the diagnosis is often unsuspected and difficult to confirm, but it has been estimated to occur in 10% to 20% of all cases of invasive aspergillosis, usually in patients with persistent immunosuppression and disseminated disease.[2] In a recent series of patients undergoing allogeneic stem cell transplant, the incidence of proven or suspected cerebral aspergillosis was only 3%, but all suspected cases were fatal.[119] In one series of patients undergoing allogeneic transplantation, *Aspergillus* was found in 58% of biopsied cerebral mass lesions.[120] In transplantation the diagnosis may occur an extended time after transplant (>100 days) and is nearly always associated with extensive immunosuppression, such as therapy for graft-versus-host disease.[119] Concomitant pulmonary infection is usually but not always present.[120] Isolated cerebral aspergillosis can occur in immunocompetent patients or in the setting of injection drug use, in which case it may be associated with a slightly better prognosis provided the diagnosis is made and surgical drainage or removal is performed.[121] *Aspergillus* meningitis is rare. The clinical presentation of cerebral aspergillosis is nonspecific and is characterized by focal neurologic signs, alteration in mental status, and headaches.[122] On CT of the brain the appearance is nonspecific and is similar to that of other infectious causes of brain abscess with ring enhancement of the abscess along with surrounding edema (Fig. 256-10) and may be hemorrhagic.[123] Magnetic resonance imaging (MRI) scans may reveal additional lesions, but the findings are still nonspecific. Confirmation of the diagnosis requires biopsy, but in the setting of documented disseminated disease, the diagnosis is often presumed. However, in patients without a clear diagnosis, biopsy is recommended because the differential diagnosis is extensive, including other fungi and an extensive array of opportunistic diseases. Until recently, the outcome of this infection has been almost universally fatal, although in recent trials voriconazole has been associated with favorable responses in approximately 30% of patients.[121]

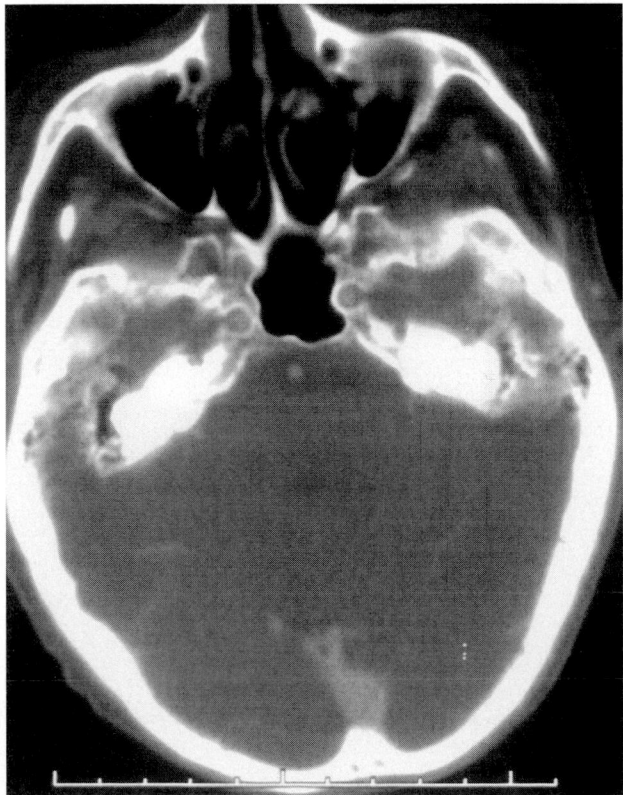

FIGURE 256-9. Computed tomography of sinuses showing sinus wall thickening.

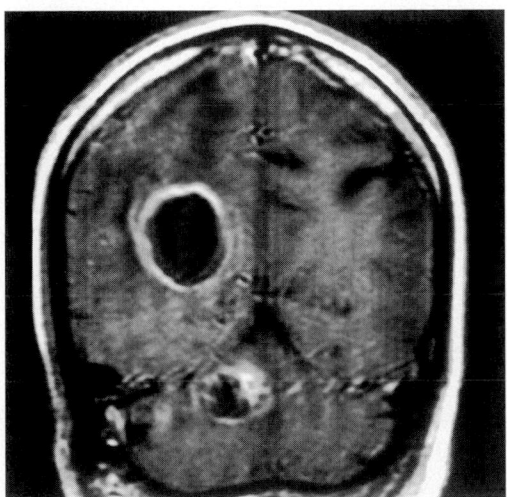

FIGURE 256-10. Brain abscess of invasive aspergillosis with ring enhancement and extensive edema.

Bone Aspergillosis

Aspergillus osteomyelitis is an uncommon finding of invasive aspergillosis. Vertebral osteomyelitis can result from local extension of an *Aspergillus* empyema. *Aspergillus* osteomyelitis can also be seen as a complication of disseminated infection or as a primary infection in certain risk groups such as chronic granulomatous disease or in intravenous drug use.[124] Vertebral osteomyelitis is the most common site for hematogenous spread to bone, usually involving the lumbar region.[125] The lesions can be seen on plain radiographs (Fig. 256-11) as well as on a CT or an MRI scan, which can be useful to stage the infection and to guide needle biopsy of the lesion. Favorable responses in *Aspergillus* osteomyelitis of the spine exceeded 60% in one review, although the need for long-term therapy and surgical intervention in medically nonresponsive patients is noted.[125] Infection of an intervertebral disk is a rare complication of hematogenous spread or surgery on the disk.

Cutaneous Infection

Skin involvement by *Aspergillus* can either represent disseminated hematogenous infection or local inoculation of infection that may arise around an intravenous catheter insertion site or the surrounding areas covered by adhesive dressings.[52] Whereas most lesions occur in patients with neutropenia or in other immunocompromised patients, *Aspergillus* can also invade patients with burns or surgical wounds.[126] Clinically, the lesion is an area of rapidly increasing erythema with a necrotic, often ulcerated, center (Fig. 256-12). The lesions resemble pyoderma gangrenosum. Pathologically, invasion of blood vessels and cutaneous ulceration occurs. Cutaneous disease can also be a manifestation of widespread disseminated disease, and in that setting a skin biopsy can be a relatively easy method to obtain tissue to establish the diagnosis of invasive aspergillosis.

Other Sites

Invasive aspergillosis has also been reported in anecdotal cases to cause infection in virtually all body sites, including the heart, kidney, esophagus, intestine, and others.[2] *Aspergillus* endocarditis can occur in either native or prosthetic heart valves. Diagnosis is difficult because blood cultures usually remain negative even with extensive disease.[126,127] Even with surgical intervention, long-term survival is limited. *Aspergillus* pericarditis is also associated with disseminated infection but can occur because of local extension of invasive pulmonary aspergillosis and can be complicated with cardiac tamponade.[2] Some of these uncommon syndromes appear more common in certain epidemiologic settings. Renal infection occurs in patients with AIDS or with a history of injection drug use.[128] *Aspergillus* keratitis typically occurs following traumatic injury with vegetative material.[129]

DIAGNOSIS AND SUSCEPTIBILITY TESTING

A proven diagnosis of invasive aspergillosis requires a tissue biopsy showing invasion with hyphae and a positive culture for *Aspergillus*.[117] The diagnosis can also be established with positive cultures from a normally sterile site such as a needle biopsy or cerebrospinal fluid (CSF), although blood cultures are rarely positive.[130] Tissue biopsies may not be possible in some immunosuppressed patients because of potential risks, although *Aspergillus* hyphae are easily seen with common fungal stains such as Gomori methenamine silver (GMS) or periodic acid–Schiff (PAS). *Aspergillus* hyphae are hyaline, septate, acute-angle branched, and 3 to 6 μm in width.[22] Although these features usually distinguish *Aspergillus* from agents of zygomycosis, they are not distinguishable from a number of other opportunistic molds, including *Fusarium, Scedosporium (Pseudallescheria),* and others so that a positive culture is needed to confirm the diagnosis.[22]

Cultures for *Aspergillus* in respiratory samples in high-risk patients, particularly if obtained via bronchial alveolar lavage, can support the diagnosis of probable invasive aspergillosis.[131,132] In current definitions of invasive mycoses, a positive respiratory culture with a clinical illness compatible with the diagnosis and new pulmonary infiltrates in an immunosuppressed patient is defined as a probable case of invasive pulmonary aspergillosis for the purposes of clinical trials.[9,117] *Aspergillus* is also cultured from patients in whom no clinical illness is apparent so that positive cultures in patients with a low risk for invasive aspergillosis should be interpreted with caution.[23]

Radiographic findings can also be used in the diagnosis and management of invasive pulmonary aspergillosis. Plain chest radiographs

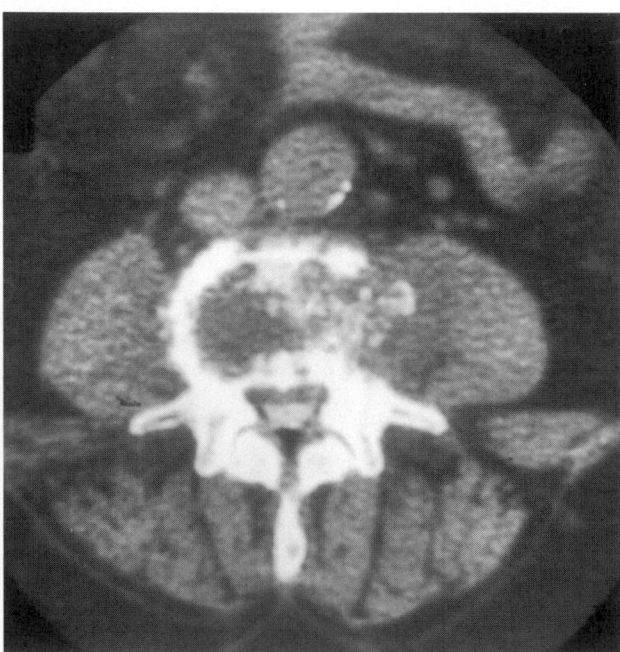

FIGURE 256-11. Radiograph of spine showing bone destruction associated with spinal aspergillosis.

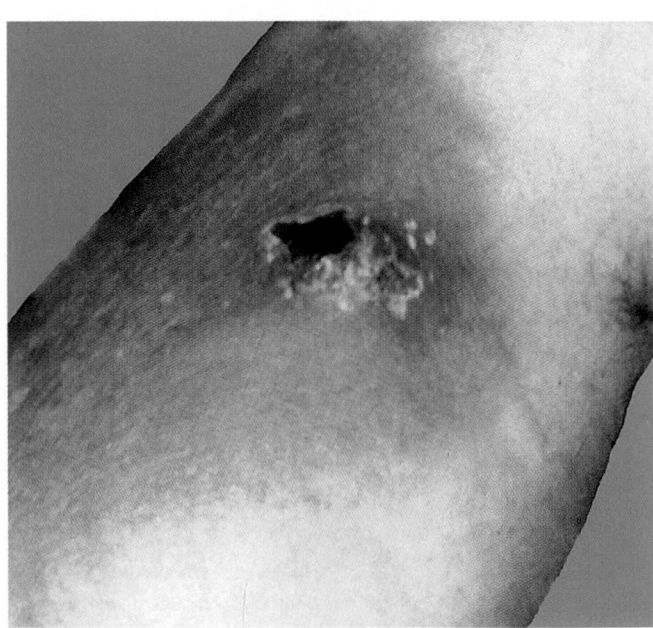

FIGURE 256-12. Necrotic skin lesion of cutaneous aspergillosis.

are of limited diagnostic utility because they are insensitive and findings are nonspecific.[7,133] However, chest CT can be very useful for establishing a diagnosis because the presence of a "halo" of low attenuation surrounding a nodular lesion is an early finding in invasive pulmonary aspergillosis and has been used as a marker for initiating early antifungal therapy.[7,9,107] Notably, the volume of lesions may increase over the first 7 days of infection, even when therapy is successful, so that early radiologic progression should be interpreted cautiously.[134] An "air-crescent" is also suggestive of invasive aspergillosis, but it is a finding that occurs late in the course of infection. The CT findings of IPA have been validated in high-risk, neutropenic, and bone marrow transplant recipients, but in other patients, including solid organ transplant recipients, the CT findings are not as useful. Etiologic agents such as *Nocardia* and other opportunistic pathogens can be associated with nodular or cavitary lesions.

Nonculture methods have been used to establish a rapid diagnosis of invasive aspergillosis.[135] Antibody detection is of limited utility because immunosuppressed hosts fail to mount an antibody response even with invasive infection.[63] Recently, a sandwich enzyme immunoassay (EIA) that utilizes a monoclonal antibody to *Aspergillus* galactomannan has been licensed in the United States for the diagnosis of invasive aspergillosis. This assay (Platelia *Aspergillus,* Sonofi Diagnostics Pasteur, Marnes-la-Coquette, France; BioRad, Redmond, Washington) has been used most extensively in Europe.[6,136-138] A latex agglutination test (Sonofi Diagnostics Pasteur) that also utilizes the monoclonal antibody has limited sensitivity and reproducibility.[139] However, in contrast to the latex agglutination test, the sandwich enzyme-linked immunosorbent assay (ELISA) lowers the detection limit for antigen 10-fold, to 0.5 to 1 ng/mL of galactomannan in serum by using the antibody both as a captor and as a detector.[140] With this ELISA assay, sensitivity for detecting invasive aspergillosis has been reported to be more than 90%, with a specificity that is more than 95%.[6,141] Other studies have found the assay to be less sensitive (30%-50%), perhaps reflecting less extensive infection or the role of antifungal prophylaxis or empirical therapy in reducing the level of circulating galactomannan.[142,143] This has resulted in recommendations for a lower cutoff for a positive test result, but the impact of this lower threshold on potential false-positive results is unresolved. False-positive results have been reported, including some pediatric patients, which may be due to dietary intake,[137] and recently in patients who were receiving antibiotic therapy with piperacillin/tazobactam.[144,145] Although the method has been used for other body fluids such as CSF and in bronchial alveolar lavage fluid, these samples have been less extensively evaluated compared with serum.[135,146] Despite its potential value, several questions of the EIA remain, including the value of routine surveillance testing, frequency of testing, role of false-positive results, importance of prior antifungal therapy, and correlation with clinical outcome.

Other potential markers also include nonspecific fungal marker β-glucan using a variation of the limulus assay to detect endotoxin. This assay also appears promising but remains investigational.[147,148]

Molecular diagnostics including polymerase chain reaction (PCR) have also been developed for *Aspergillus.* Several reports demonstrate the potential for using PCR as an early diagnostic marker, which appears more sensitive than other methods including galactomannan.[149-152] These assays may be associated with false-positive results because of the ubiquitous nature of *Aspergillus* conidia; they are not standardized and remain investigational, although this approach is very promising for improving the diagnosis of invasive aspergillosis.

Susceptibility testing for molds including *Aspergillus* has been standardized, but correlation with clinical responses has not yet been established, and breakpoints have not been determined.[153,154] Antifungal resistance to itraconazole has been reported, which correlated with lack of efficacy in an animal model, suggesting the potential utility of susceptibility testing.[155,156] *Aspergillus terreus* may be resistant to amphotericin B and susceptible to the newer azoles so that testing of that species may be warranted,[22] although the indications for susceptibility testing of *Aspergillus* at the present time are unclear.

THERAPY

Efficacy of antifungal therapy in invasive aspergillosis has been extremely poor. As shown in Table 256-3, favorable responses have been seen in less than 40% of patients, and overall mortality rates are almost 60%.[3,4] Response to antifungal therapy depends on several factors, including the immune status of the host and the extent of infection at time of diagnosis. In severely immunosuppressed patients, such as those undergoing allogeneic bone marrow transplantation, and in patients with widely disseminated infection, extremely poor outcomes have been reported, with mortality rates in the highest risk groups greater than 90%.[4,10,157]

Primary Antifungal Therapy

Amphotericin B Deoxycholate

For more than four decades, amphotericin B deoxycholate has been the gold standard therapy for critically ill patients with invasive aspergillosis.[1] Several recent studies have consistently documented the limited efficacy and substantial toxicity of amphotericin B deoxycholate in high-risk patients.[9,158,159] The overall response rates of amphotericin B deoxycholate are less than 25%, with responses of only 10% to 15% in more severely immunosuppressed patients.[4,9] Wingard and colleagues have recently documented the increased morbidity and mortality associated with standard amphotericin B therapy in patients receiving bone marrow transplantation and those receiving concomitant nephrotoxic agents.[159] Similar findings were documented by Bates and colleagues, who found that renal toxicity occurred in approximately 30% of patients receiving amphotericin B deoxycholate and that this toxicity was associated with a sixfold increase in mortality as well as a dramatic increase in hospital costs.[158] These unacceptably high mortality rates and significant toxicity have highlighted the need for new therapeutic approaches to this disease; thus, for most patients with invasive aspergillosis, primary therapy with amphotericin B can no longer be recommended.[160] New antifungal therapies with activity against *Aspergillus* have been developed, including lipid forms of amphotericin B, the newer azoles (voriconazole, posaconazole, and ravuconazole), and a new class of antifungal therapy, the echinocandins

TABLE 256-3 Clinical Outcomes and Mortality Rates of Invasive Aspergillosis by Underlying Condition and Site of Infection

Underlying Disease/Site of Infection	*Favorable Responses* (%)
Overall	37
Severe immunosuppression	28
Allogeneic bone marrow transplant	13
Autologous bone marrow transplant	21
Hematologic malignancy	44
Less severe immunosuppression	51
Solid organ transplant	60
Human immunodeficiency virus (HIV)/acquired immunodeficiency syndrome (AIDS)	34
Pulmonary diseases/others	54
Invasive pulmonary aspergillosis	40
Disseminated (without central nervous system)	18
Central nervous system (CNS)	9

Underlying Disease/Site of Infection	*Case Fatality Rate* (%)
Overall	58
Bone marrow transplantation	87
Leukemia/lymphoma	49
Lung transplant	42
Liver transplant	63
HIV/AIDS	86
Pulmonary infection	59
CNS or disseminated infection	88

*Favorable responses are complete or partial responses to therapy.

Data from Patterson TF, Kirkpatrick WR, White M, et al. Invasive aspergillosis. Disease spectrum, treatment practices, and outcomes. I3 Aspergillus Study Group. Medicine (Baltimore). 2000;79:250-260; Lin SJ, Schramz J, Teutsch SM. Aspergillosis case—Fatality rate: Systematic review of the literature. Clin Infect Dis. 2001;32:358-366.

TABLE 256-4 Antifungal Agents for Invasive Aspergillosis

Agent	Class	Route of Administration	Dose	Comments
Primary Therapy				
Voriconazole	Azole	IV/oral	4 mg/kg q12h (IV) 6 mg/kg q12h (IV) ×2 loading doses 200 mg bid (PO)	Recommended for primary therapy in most patients due to randomized trial demonstrating improved survival as compared with amphotericin B deoxycholate[9,164]; caution for use in patients with potential liver toxicity and for drug interactions
Other Agents				
Amphotericin B	Polyene	IV	1-1.5 mg/kg/day	Previous gold standard; significant toxicity in higher doses; limited efficacy in high-risk patients[158,159]
Liposomal amphotericin	Polyene	IV	3-5 mg/kg/day	Well tolerated; minimal infusion reactions or nephrotoxicity; higher doses (>5 mg/kg/day) anecdotally more effective[8,168]
Amphotericin B lipid complex	Polyene	IV	5 mg/kg/day	Indicated for patients intolerant or refractory to standard therapy; case-controlled data suggest better efficacy than amphotericin B deoxycholate[169,175]
Amphotericin B colloidal dispersion	Polyene	IV	3-6 mg/kg/day	More infusion-related toxicity than other lipid formulations; efficacy similar to amphotericin B in primary treatment[157]
Itraconazole	Azole	IV/oral	200 mg/day (IV) 200 mg bid (PO)	Oral solution improved bioavailability; limited efficacy data for intravenous formulation[4,178]
Posaconazole	Azole	Oral	Investigational	Oral formulation; efficacy in early trials[182]
Ravuconazole	Polyene	Oral	Investigational	In vitro and animal model studies; early clinical development; long half-life; intravenous formulation under study[184]
Caspofungin	Echinocandin	IV	50-70 mg/day	Approved for refractory infection and intolerance to standard therapy; well tolerated; possible interaction with cyclosporine.[10] Preclinical data showing improved efficacy in combination with azoles[186]
Micafungin	Echinocandin	IV	Investigational [U.S.] (50-100 mg/day)	Phase III studies for prevention and treatment of aspergillosis[191,221]; rabbit model shows improved tissue clearance with a triazole[185]
Anidulafungin	Echinocandin	IV	Investigational (100 mg/day)	Phase III clinical development[222-224]

(caspofungin, micafungin, and anidulafungin) (Table 256-4), all of which offer new options for therapy for this disease.[161]

Voriconazole

Voriconazole is a potent, broad-spectrum triazole that is approved for therapy for invasive aspergillosis and has become the recommended primary therapy for most patients with invasive aspergillosis.[161] Voriconazole has potent fungicidal activity against various *Aspergillus* species, including *A. terreus*.[162,163] The recommendation for voriconazole as the new standard for primary therapy is based on a randomized trial that compared voriconazole with amphotericin B deoxycholate, with each agent followed by other licensed antifungal therapy if needed for intolerance or progression of disease.[9] In this trial, voriconazole was successful in 52% of patients as compared with only 31% in those receiving amphotericin B deoxycholate. Superiority of voriconazole was demonstrated in patients at high risk for mortality, including those undergoing bone marrow transplantation and in those with extrapulmonary disease, including central nervous system involvement, as had previously been seen in open-labeled studies.[9,164] A survival benefit of voriconazole was also shown as compared with amphotericin B.[9] The efficacy of voriconazole is further demonstrated in adult and pediatric patients receiving voriconazole for treatment of invasive aspergillosis in patients who were refractory to or intolerant of conventional antifungal therapy.[29,165] For example, the overall response rate for invasive aspergillosis in pediatric patients who were refractory to or intolerant of standard antifungal therapy was 43%.[165] Finally, voriconazole has also demonstrated efficacy in very difficult to treat clinical conditions, with responses of approximately 34% in central nervous system infection and in 52% of patients with osteomyelitis.[121,166]

In clinical trials, voriconazole has been adequately tolerated, and the drug exhibits a favorable pharmacokinetic profile. There are a number of issues to consider, including important drug interactions, especially those with immunosuppressive agents such as cyclosporine, tacrolimus, and sirolimus, the latter of which is contraindicated for use with voriconazole, and intolerance to the drug. The most common adverse event has been a transient and reversible visual disturbance that

has been reported in approximately 30% of patients receiving the drug.[9,38,167] This effect is dose related and described as an altered or increased light perception that is temporary and not associated with pathologic sequelae. Other adverse events have been less common, including liver abnormalities in 10% to 15%, skin rash in 6%, nausea and vomiting in 2%, and anorexia in 1%.

Other Antifungal Agents

Lipid Amphotericin Formulations

Among these newer compounds with activity against *Aspergillus,* the lipid formulations of amphotericin B were developed to offer the advantage of less toxicity and allow higher doses of therapy.[168-171] The efficacy and role of lipid formulations of amphotericin B in the treatment of invasive aspergillosis remain debatable, in part because few randomized trials have been conducted for patients with this disease.[172] However, clinical experience has been favorable, which is consistent with preclinical studies in animal models, and no studies have suggested less activity when compared with that of amphotericin B deoxycholate.[8,173,174] A small study by Leenders and colleagues documented the utility of liposomal amphotericin B at 5 mg/kg/day as compared with standard amphotericin B at 1 mg/kg/day for proven or suspected invasive mycoses.[168] Overall outcomes of both groups in this small study were equivalent; however, analysis of those patients with proven invasive aspergillosis favored outcomes with the lipid preparation of amphotericin B. Optimal doses of lipid formulations in invasive aspergillosis are not established, but higher doses of 3 to 5 mg/kg/day or more are anecdotally associated with better responses.[175] Notably, the lipid formulations have been evaluated in and are approved for use as salvage therapy of invasive aspergillosis. A recent study evaluated amphotericin B colloidal dispersion for primary therapy for invasive aspergillosis.[157,171] Results of this study were disappointing, because successful responses were not improved as compared with those to amphotericin B deoxycholate, although toxicity was minimally decreased. These results suggest that although lipid formulations of amphotericin B are dramatically more expensive than standard amphotericin B deoxycholate, hidden costs of standard amphotericin B in terms of morbidity and mortality as well as resource utilization may justify the use of lipid formulation of amphotericin B in certain high-risk patients.[176,177]

Other Triazoles

Another approach to the therapy of aspergillosis has been in the development of azole antifungals. Among these compounds, itraconazole is approved for use as salvage therapy of aspergillosis, but its utility has been limited because until recently it has been available only in an oral formulation that is poorly absorbed, and drug interactions further complicate management. An intravenous formulation of itraconazole has only recently been approved for up to 2 weeks of clinical use.[178] For these reasons, itraconazole is more frequently used in less immunosuppressed patients who are able to take oral therapy and for use as sequential oral therapy.[4]

In addition to voriconazole, other second-generation triazoles, including posaconazole and ravuconazole, were developed with an expanded spectrum of activity to include *Aspergillus*.[162,163,179] Posaconazole is available in only an oral formulation but has been shown to have activity against *Aspergillus* in vitro as well as in preclinical in vivo studies.[162,180,181] In an open-labeled trial for salvage therapy of invasive mycoses, posaconazole was also reported to have activity in patients with invasive aspergillosis.[182] Ravuconazole has been evaluated in early phase clinical trials and has also shown activity in animal models of invasive aspergillosis.[183-185]

Echinocandins

The echinocandins are a new class of antifungals with *Aspergillus* activity.[186-189] These agents, which are administered intravenously, target glucan synthase, which is needed for production of β-1,3-glucan in fungal cells walls.[190] These effects are not fungicidal but significantly alter the growing fungal cell wall. Included in these agents are caspofungin, micafungin, and anidulafungin. Caspofungin is approved for treating patients refractory to or intolerant of standard therapies for invasive aspergillosis. In an open-labeled trial for such patients, caspofungin was demonstrated to produce satisfactory clinical responses in 22/54 (41%) of patients studied.[10] Caspofungin has been very well tolerated in clinical trials. Drug discontinuations attributed to caspofungin in the aspergillosis trial occurred in approximately 5% of patients, although drug interactions with cyclosporine have been documented.[10] Micafungin continues to undergo late-stage clinical development in the United States and is approved for use in Japan. In one prophylaxis study, micafungin may have reduced the number of *Aspergillus* infections as compared with standard prophylaxis with fluconazole.[191] Anidulafungin is another echinocandin with *Aspergillus* activity and appears to have favorable toxicity profile similar to those of the other echinocandins.

Combination Antifungal Therapy

The availability of several antifungal drugs and drug classes against *Aspergillus* has increased interest in combination antifungal therapy for this infection.[192,193] None of these combinations has been evaluated in clinical trials, so caution for these approaches is advised. These recommendations are based both on lack of efficacy data for a combination approach and from previous studies showing in vivo (in murine aspergillosis) and in vitro antagonism between amphotericin B and ketoconazole, an early imidazole with limited *Aspergillus* activity.[194] This antagonism occurred with pretreatment of *Aspergillus* with the azole, reducing the cell wall ergosterol and eliminating the site of action of amphotericin B. Other studies with newer azoles have not shown this effect, and clinical demonstrations of this antagonism are limited.[195]

Other combinations have been attempted in the past, including amphotericin B and rifampin, flucytosine, and others (such as terbinafine).[126,196] Unfortunately, preclinical and in vitro studies have had limited utility in guiding clinical combination therapy.[197] Problems with rifampin combinations include increased metabolism of the azoles, which makes that combination not generally recommended.

Similarly, flucytosine has limited activity against *Aspergillus* and can cause pancytopenia that worsens immunosuppression. Recent animal model studies have demonstrated the potential for echinocandins with amphotericin B or with the new azoles in reducing tissue burden and in sterilizing tissues, although clinical studies using combination antifungal therapies are ongoing.[185,186,198,199]

Adjuvant Therapy

Adjuvant therapies including surgical resection or use of granulocyte transfusions and growth factors in invasive aspergillosis can augment antifungal therapy, although their utility has not been established in randomized trials. Surgical resection of isolated pulmonary nodules before additional immunosuppressive therapies has been shown to improve outcome of infection,[7,106] although recent studies suggest that the majority of patients will have bilateral infection at least at baseline diagnosis, which would limit the utility of that approach.[107] Surgical resection may also be indicated in patients with severe hemoptysis or lesions near the hilar vessels or pericardium.

Other adjuvant therapies include granulocyte and granulocyte-macrophage colony-stimulating factors,[200-202] interferon-γ,[203] and granulocyte transfusions, especially granulocyte colony-stimulating factor mobilized cells.[204,205] All these approaches have all been shown in anecdotal reports to improve outcomes but are not generally recommended for routine use.[1]

Approach to Therapy

Guidelines for treating invasive aspergillosis have been published by the Infectious Diseases Society of America.[1] Unfortunately, few randomized controlled trials exist in this area for specific guidelines for therapy. A prompt diagnosis and aggressive initial therapy are both critical in improving the outcome of this infection.[206] Radiography and use of galactomannan EIA may facilitate an early detection of aspergillosis in high-risk patients, for whom outcomes are especially poor.[207] Most patients should receive primary therapy with voriconazole, which has been shown to be superior to amphotericin B, the other agent approved for primary therapy for this infection.[9] However, in patients who are intolerant of voriconazole, have a contraindication to the drug, or have progressive infection, alternative agents include lipid forms of amphotericin B, the echinocandins, or another triazole.[8,169,208] Primary use of combination therapy is not recommended at the present time because of the lack of prospective clinical trial data, but the addition of another agent in a salvage setting may be considered owing to the poor outcomes of a single agent in progressive infection. Sequential therapy with oral azoles after initial intravenous therapy may be a useful option.[4] Although the optimal duration of antifungal therapy is not known, improvement in underlying host defenses is crucial to successful therapy. Substantial advances have recently been made in the management of invasive aspergillosis, but newer approaches to therapy, including the potential of combination therapy and newer diagnostic tools, are needed to improve the outcome of this disease.

PREVENTION AND PROPHYLAXIS

Prevention of invasive aspergillosis in high-risk patients is difficult.[209] Nosocomial outbreaks of aspergillosis have been linked to construction, contaminated ventilation systems, and possibly to contaminated water.[37,49,210,211] For high-risk patients, such as those undergoing hematopoietic stem cell transplantation, the use of high-efficiency particulate air (HEPA) filters, frequent air exchanges, and positive pressure ventilation has been recommended to limit exposures in the hospital setting.[209,212-214] Infection control measures such as construction barriers will limit exposure to aerosols.[43] In addition, attention to routine maintenance and cleaning of showers and water systems may further reduce risk.[215] However, some patients will still develop infection with these precautions, and an increasing number of these patients receive an extensive amount of care outside of the hospital setting so that community-acquired infection is common.[105,212]

Efficacy of antifungal prophylaxis has been limited until recently because of the toxicity of amphotericin B and the limited activity of other oral agents against *Aspergillus*. Agents evaluated in this setting include low-dose amphotericin B, low doses of lipid formulations of amphotericin B, and nasal and aerosolized forms of amphotericin B—none of which has demonstrated conclusively to be beneficial in a large randomized clinical trial.[209] Recent studies of aerosolized lipid forms of amphotericin B demonstrate its safety and potential efficacy in lung transplant recipients at high risk for invasive aspergillosis.[216] Itraconazole has been suggested to have benefit against prevention of molds, but its poor tolerance in high-risk patients has also limited its use.[217-219] In a single, long-term randomized, double-blind, placebo-controlled study of fungal prophylaxis in patients with chronic granulomatous disease, itraconazole appeared to reduce the incidence of serious fungal infections, including those due to *Aspergillus*.[220] No agents are currently recommended for prevention of mold infections in hematopoietic stem cell transplantation,[209] although clinical trials are evaluating the role of the newer azoles as well as the echinocandins in preventing this potentially lethal infection.

REFERENCES

1. Stevens DA, Kan VL, Judson MA, et al. Practice guidelines for diseases caused by *Aspergillus*. Clin Infect Dis. 2000;30:696-709.
2. Denning DW. Invasive aspergillosis. Clin Infect Dis. 1998;26:781-803.
3. Lin SJ, Schranz J, Teutsch SM. Aspergillosis case—Fatality rate: Systematic review of the literature. Clin Infect Dis. 2001;32:358-366.
4. Patterson TF, Kirkpatrick WR, White M, et al. Invasive aspergillosis. Disease spectrum, treatment practices, and outcomes. I3 Aspergillus Study Group. Medicine (Baltimore). 2000;79:250-260.
5. von Eiff M, Roos N, Schulten R, et al. Pulmonary aspergillosis: Early diagnosis improves survival. Respiration. 1995;62:341-347.
6. Maertens J, Verhaegen J, Lagrou K, et al. Screening for circulating galactomannan as a noninvasive diagnostic tool for invasive aspergillosis in prolonged neutropenic patients and stem cell transplantation recipients: A prospective validation. Blood. 2001;97:1604-1610.
7. Caillot D, Casasnovas O, Bernard A, et al. Improved management of invasive pulmonary aspergillosis in neutropenic patients using early thoracic computed tomographic scan and surgery. J Clin Oncol. 1997;15:139-147.
8. Barrett JP, Vardulaki KA, Conlon C, et al. A systematic review of the antifungal effectiveness and tolerability of amphotericin B formulations. Clin Ther. 2003;25:1295-1320.
9. Herbrecht R, Denning DW, Patterson TF, et al. Voriconazole versus amphotericin B for primary therapy of invasive aspergillosis. N Engl J Med. 2002;347:408-415.
10. Maertens J, Raad I, Sable CA, et al. Multicenter, noncomparative study to evaluate safety and efficacy of caspofungin in adults with aspergillosis refractory or intolerant to amphotericin B, amphotericin B lipid formulations, or azoles. 40th Interscience Conference on Antimicrobial Agents and Chemotherapy. Toronto, Canada; 2000.
11. Mackenzie DW. Aspergillus in man. In: Vanden Bossche H, Mackenzie DWR, Cauwenbergh G, eds. Proceedings of the Second International Symposium on Topics in Mycology. Antwerp, Belgium: University of Antwerp; 1987:1-8.
12. Kwon-Chung KJ. *Aspergillus*: Diagnosis and description of the genus. In: Vanden Bossche H, Mackenzie DWR, Cauwenbergh G, eds. Proceedings of the Second International Symposium on Topics in Mycology. Antwerp, Belguim: University of Antwerp; 1987:11-21.
13. Link H. Observations in ordines plantarum naturales. Gesellschaft Naturforschender Freunde zu Berlin, Magazin. 1809;3:1.
14. Thom C, Church M. The Aspergilli. Baltimore: Williams & Wilkins; 1926.
15. Raper B, Fennel J. The Genus *Aspergillus*. Baltimore: Williams & Wilkins; 1965.
16. Pitt J. The current role of *Aspergillus* and *Penicillium* in human and animal health. J Med Vet Mycol. 1994;1:17-21.
17. Denning DW. *Aspergillus* species. In: Mandell GL, Bennett JE, Dolin R, eds. Mandell, Douglas, and Bennett's Principles and Practice of Infectious Diseases. 5th ed. Philadelphia: Churchill Livingstone; 2000:2674-2685.
18. Summerbell R. Ascomycetes. *Aspergillus, Fusarium, Sporothrix, Piedraia,* and Their Relatives. In: Howard DH, ed. Pathogenic fungi in humans and animals. 2nd ed. New York: Marcel Dekker; 2003:237-498.
19. Klich M, Pitt J. A laboratory guide to common *Aspergillus* species and their teleomorphs. North Ryde, New South Wales, Australia: Commonwealth Scientific and Industrial Research Organization; 1988.
20. Iwen PC, Rupp ME, Langnas AN, et al. Invasive pulmonary aspergillosis due to *Aspergillus terreus*: 12-year experience and review of the literature. Clin Infect Dis. 1998;26:1092-1097.
21. Kwon-Chung KJ, Bennett JE. Medical Mycology. Philadelphia: Lea & Febiger; 1992.
22. Sutton DA, Fothergill AW, Rinaldi MG, eds. Guide to Clinically Significant Fungi. 1st ed. Baltimore: Williams & Wilkins; 1998.
23. Perfect JR, Cox GM, Lee JY, et al. The impact of culture isolation of *Aspergillus* species: A hospital-based survey of aspergillosis. Clin Infect Dis. 2001;33:1824-1833.
24. Anaissie EJ, Stratton SL, Dignani MC, et al. Pathogenic *Aspergillus* species recovered from a hospital water system: A 3-year prospective study. Clin Infect Dis. 2002;34:780-789.
25. Warris A, Voss A, Abrahamsen TG, Verweij PE. Contamination of hospital water with *Aspergillus fumigatus* and other molds. Clin Infect Dis. 2002;34:1159-1160.
26. Denning DW. Aflatoxin and human disease. A review. Adverse Drug React Acute Poison Rev. 1987;4:175-209.
27. Walsh TJ, Petraitis V, Petraitiene R, et al. Experimental pulmonary aspergillosis due to *Aspergillus terreus*: Pathogenesis and treatment of an emerging fungal pathogen resistant to amphotericin B. J Infect Dis. 2003;188:305-319.
28. Sutton DA, Sanche SE, Revankar SG, et al. In vitro amphotericin B resistance in clinical isolates of *Aspergillus terreus,* with a head-to-head comparison to voriconazole. J Clin Microbiol. 1999;37:2343-2345.
29. Perfect JR, Marr KA, Walsh TJ, et al. Voriconazole treatment for less-common, emerging, or refractory fungal infections. Clin Infect Dis. 2003;36:1122-1131.
30. Geyer SJ, Surampudi RK. Photo quiz—Birefringent crystals in a pulmonary specimen. Clin Infect Dis. 2002;34:481,551-552.
31. Nakagawa Y, Shimazu K, Ebihara M, Nakagawa K. *Aspergillus niger* pneumonia with fatal pulmonary oxalosis. J Infect Chemother. 1999;5:97-100.
32. Bellini C, Antonini P, Ermanni S, et al. Malignant otitis externa due to *Aspergillus niger*. Scand J Infect Dis. 2003;35:284-288.
33. White CJ, Kwon-Chung KJ, Gallin JI. Chronic granulomatous disease of childhood: An unusual case of infection with *Aspergillus nidulans var. echinulatus*. Am J Clin Pathol. 1987;90:312-316.
34. Ozsahin H, von Planta M, Muller I, et al. Successful treatment of invasive aspergillosis in chronic granulomatous disease by bone marrow transplantation, granulocyte colony-stimulating factor-mobilized granulocytes, and liposomal amphotericin-B. Blood. 1998;92:2719-2724.
35. Kontoyiannis DP, Lewis RE, May GS, et al. *Aspergillus nidulans* is frequently resistant to amphotericin B. Mycoses. 2002;45:406-407.
36. Torres HA, Rivero GA, Lewis RE, et al. Aspergillosis caused by non-*fumigatus Aspergillus* species: Risk factors and in vitro susceptibility compared with *Aspergillus fumigatus*. Diagn Microbiol Infect Dis. 2003;46:25-28.
37. Walsh TJ, Dixon DM. Nosocomial aspergillosis: Environmental microbiology, hospital epidemiology, diagnosis and treatment. Eur J Epidemiol. 1989;5:131-142.
38. Walsh TJ, Pappas P, Winston DJ, et al. Voriconazole compared with liposomal amphotericin B for empirical antifungal therapy in patients with neutropenia and persistent fever. N Engl J Med. 2002;346:225-234.
39. Warris A, Bjorneklett A, Gaustad P. Invasive pulmonary aspergillosis associated with infliximab therapy. N Engl J Med. 2001;344:1099-1100.
40. Marr KA, Carter RA, Crippa F, et al. Epidemiology and outcome of mould infections in hematopoietic stem cell transplant recipients. Clin Infect Dis. 2002;34:909-917.
41. Wald A, Leisenring W, van Burik J-A, Bowden RA. Epidemiology of *Aspergillus* infections in a large cohort of patients undergoing bone marrow transplantation. J Infect Dis. 1997;175:1459-1466.
42. Marr KA, Carter RA, Boeckh M, et al. Invasive aspergillosis in allogeneic stem cell transplant recipients: Changes in epidemiology and risk factors. Blood. 2002;100:4358-4366.
43. Patterson JE, Peters J, Calhoon JH, et al. Investigation and control of aspergillosis and other filamentous fungal infections in solid organ transplant recipients. Transpl Infect Dis. 2000;2:22-28.
44. Kanj SS, Welty-Wolf K, Madden J, et al. Fungal infections in lung and heart-lung transplant recipients. Report of 9 cases and review of the literature. Medicine (Baltimore). 1996;75:142-156.
45. Paterson DL, Singh N. Invasive aspergillosis in transplant recipients. Medicine (Baltimore). 1999;78:123-138.
46. Cohen MS, Isturiz RE, Malech HL, et al. Fungal infection in chronic granulomatous disease. The importance of the phagocyte in defense against fungi. Am J Med. 1981;71:59-66.
47. Opal SM, Asp AA, Cannady PB Jr, et al. Efficacy of infection control measures during a nosocomial outbreak of disseminated aspergillosis associated with hospital construction. J Infect Dis. 1986;153:634-637.
48. Leenders A, van Belkum A, Behrendt M, et al. Density and molecular epidemiology of *Aspergillus* in air and relationship to outbreaks of *Aspergillus* infection. J Clin Microbiol. 1999;37:1752-1757.
49. Anaissie EJ, Costa SF. Nosocomial aspergillosis is waterborne. Clin Infect Dis. 2001;33:1546-1548.
50. Anaissie EJ, Stratton SL, Dignani MC, et al. Pathogenic molds (including *Aspergillus* species) in hospital water distribution systems: A 3-year prospective study and clinical implications for patients with hematologic malignancies. Blood. 2003;101:2542-2546.
51. Walsh TJ. Primary cutaneous aspergillosis—An emerging infection among immunocompromised patients. Clin Infect Dis. 1998;27:453-457.
52. Allo MD, Miller J, Townsend T, Tan C. Primary cutaneous aspergillosis associated with Hickman intravenous catheters. N Engl J Med. 1987;317:1105-1108.
53. Gettleman LK, Shetty AK, Prober CG. Posttraumatic invasive *Aspergillus fumigatus* wound infection. Pediat Inf Dis J. 1999;18:745-747.
54. Stevens DA, Moss RB, Kurup VP, et al. Allergic bronchopulmonary aspergillosis in cystic fibrosis—State of the art: Cystic Fibrosis Foundation Consensus Conference. Clin Infect Dis. 2003;37(Suppl 3):S225-S264.
55. Clancy CJ, Nguyen MH. Acute community-acquired pneumonia due to *Aspergillus* in presumably immunocompetent hosts—Clues for recognition of a rare but fatal disease. Chest. 1998;114:629-634.
56. Schaffner A, Douglas H, Braude A. Selective protection against conidia by mononuclear and against mycelia by polymorphonuclear phagocytes in resistance to *Aspergillus*. Observations on these two lines of defense in vivo and in vitro with human and mouse phagocytes. J Clin Invest. 1982;69:617-631.
57. Kan VL, Bennett JE. Lectin-like attachment sites on murine pulmonary alveolar macrophages bind *Aspergillus fumigatus* conidia. J Infect Dis. 1988;158:407-414.

58. Levitz SM, Selsted ME, Ganz T, et al. In vitro killing of spores and hyphae of *Aspergillus fumigatus* and *Rhizopus oryzae* by rabbit neutrophil cationic peptides and bronchoalveolar macrophages. J Infect Dis. 1986;154:483-489.
59. Allen MJ, Harbeck R, Smith B, et al. Binding of rat and human surfactant proteins A and D to *Aspergillus fumigatus* conidia. Infect Immun. 1999;67:4563-4569.
60. Crosdale DJ, Poulton KV, Ollier WE, et al. Mannose-binding lectin gene polymorphisms as a susceptibility factor for chronic necrotizing pulmonary aspergillosis. J Infec Dis. 2001;184:653-656.
61. Washburn RG, Hammer CH, Bennett JE. Inhibition of complement by culture supernatants of *Aspergillus fumigatus*. J Infect Dis. 1986;154:944-951.
62. Washburn RG, Gallin JI, Bennett JE. Oxidative killing of *Aspergillus fumigatus* proceeds by parallel myeloperoxidase-dependent and -independent pathways. Infect Immun. 1987;55:2088-2092.
63. Young RC, Bennett JE. Invasive aspergillosis. Absence of detectable antibody response. Am Rev Resp Dis. 1971;104:710-716.
64. Schaffner A. Therapeutic concentrations of glucocorticoids suppress the antimicrobial activity of human macrophages without impairing their responsiveness to gamma interferon. J Clin Invest. 1985;76:1755-1764.
65. Cenci E, Perito S, Enssle KH, et al. Th1 and Th2 cytokines in mice with invasive aspergillosis. Infect Immun. 1997;65:564-570.
66. Netea MG, Van Der Graaf CA, Vonk AG, et al. The role of toll-like receptor (TLR) 2 and TLR4 in the host defense against disseminated candidiasis. J Infect Dis. 2002;185:1483-1489.
67. Meier A, Kirschning CJ, Nikolaus T, et al. Toll-like receptor (TLR) 2 and TLR4 are essential for *Aspergillus*-induced activation of murine macrophages. Cell Microbiol. 2003;5:561-570.
68. Marr KA, Balajee SA, Hawn TR, et al. Differential role of MyD88 in macrophage-mediated responses to opportunistic fungal pathogens. Infect Immun. 2003;71:5280-5286.
69. Mambula SS, Sau K, Henneke P, et al. Toll-like receptor (TLR) signaling in response to *Aspergillus fumigatus*. J Biol Chem. 2002;277:39320-39326.
70. Latge JP. *Aspergillus fumigatus* and aspergillosis. Clin Microbiol Rev. 1999;12:310-350.
71. Smith JM, Tang CM, Van Noorden S, Holden DW. Virulence of Aspergillus fumigatus double mutants lacking restriction and an alkaline protease in a low-dose model of invasive pulmonary aspergillosis. Infect Immun. 1994; 62:5247-5254.
72. Tang C, Cohen J, Hrausz T, et al. The alkaline protease of *Aspergillus fumigatus* is not a virulence determinant in two murine models of the invasive pulmonary aspergillosis. Infect Immun. 1993;61:1650-1656.
73. Monod M, Paris S, Sarfati J, et al. Virulence of alkaline protease deficient mutants of *Aspergillus fumigatus*. FEMS Microbiol Lett. 1993;106:39-46.
74. Denning DW. Chronic forms of pulmonary aspergillosis. Clin Microbiol Infect. 2001;7:25-31.
75. Rosenberg M, Patterson R, Mintzer R, et al. Clinical and immunologic criteria for the diagnosis of allergic bronchopulmonary aspergillosis. Ann Intern Med. 1977;86:405-414.
76. Tomlinson J, Sahn S. Aspergilloma in sarcoid and tuberculosis. Chest. 1987;92:505-508.
77. Denning DW, Riniotis K, Dobrashian R, Sambatakou H. Chronic cavitary and fibrosing pulmonary and pleural aspergillosis: Case series, proposed nomenclature change, and review. Clin Infect Dis. 2003;37(Suppl 3):S265-S280.
78. Greenberger PA. Clinical aspects of allergic bronchopulmonary aspergillosis. Front Biosci. 2003;8:s119-s127.
79. Greenberger PA. Allergic bronchopulmonary aspergillosis. J Allergy Clin Immunol. 2002;110:685-692.
80. Patterson R, Greenberger PA, Radin RC, Roberts M. Allergic bronchopulmonary aspergillosis: Staging as an aid to management. Ann Intern Med. 1982;96:286-291.
81. Malo JL, Pepys J, Simon G. Studies in chronic allergic bronchopulmonary aspergillosis. 2. Radiological findings. Thorax. 1977;32:262-268.
82. Wark PA, Gibson PG, Wilson AJ. Azoles for allergic bronchopulmonary aspergillosis associated with asthma. Cochrane Database Syst Rev. 2003:CD001108.
83. Stevens DA, Schwartz HJ, Lee JY, et al. A randomized trial of itraconazole in allergic bronchopulmonary aspergillosis. N Engl J Med. 2000;342:756-762.
84. Corey J, Delsupehe K, Ferguson B. Allergic fungal sinusitis: Allergic, infectious, or both? Otolaryngol Head Neck Surg. 1995;1995:110-119.
85. DeShazo RD, Chapin K, Swain RE. Fungal sinusitis. N Engl J Med. 1997;337:254-259.
86. Washburn RG. Fungal sinusitis. Curr Clin Topics Infect Dis. 1998;18:60-74.
87. Kuhn FA, Javer AR. Allergic fungal sinusitis: A four-year follow-up. Am J Rhinol. 2000;2000:149-156.
88. Kuhn FA, Javer AR. Allergic fungal rhinosinusitis—Perioperative management, prevention of recurrence, and role of steroids and antifungal agents. Otolaryngol Clin N Amer. 2000;33:419-432.
89. de Carpentier J, Ramamurthy M, Taylor P, Denning D. An algorithmic approach to *Aspergillus* sinusitis. J Laryngol Otol. 1994;108:314-318.
90. Gillespie MB, O'Malley BW. An algorithmic approach to the diagnosis and management of invasive fungal rhinosinusitis in the immunocompromised patient. Otolaryngol Clin North Am. 2000;33:323-334.
91. Ferguson BJ. Fungus balls of the paranasal sinuses. Otolaryngol Clin North Am. 2000;33:389-398.
92. Shams MG, Motamedi MH. Aspergilloma of the maxillary sinus complicating an oroantral fistula. Oral Surg Oral Med Oral Pathol Oral Radiol Endod. 2003;96:3-5.
93. Rafferty P, Biggs B, Crompton G, Grant I. What happens to patients with pulmonary aspergilloma? Thorax. 1983;38:579-583.
94. Kauffman CA. Quandary about treatment of aspergillomas persists. Lancet. 1996;347:1640.
95. Aslam P, Eastridge C, Hughes F. Aspergillosis of the lung—An 18 year experience. Chest. 1971;59:28-32.
96. Vennewald I, Henker M, Klemm E, Seebacher C. Fungal colonization of the paranasal sinuses. Mycoses. 1999;42:33-36.
97. Kaur R, Mittal N, Kakkar M, et al. Otomycosis: A clinicomycologic study. Ear Nose Throat J. 2000;79:606-609.
98. Torres-Rodriguez JM, Madrenys-Brunet N, Siddat M, et al. *Aspergillus versicolor* as cause of onychomycosis: Report of 12 cases and susceptibility testing to antifungal drugs. J Eur Acad Dermatol Venereol. 1998;11:25-31.
99. Heidemann DG, Dunn SP, Watts JC. Aspergillus keratitis after radial keratotomy. Am J Ophthalmol. 1995;120:254-256.
100. Kuo IC, Margolis TP, Cevallos V, Hwang DG. *Aspergillus fumigatus* keratitis after laser in situ keratomileusis. Cornea. 2001;20:342-344.
101. Sanitato JJ, Kelley CG, Kaufman HE. Surgical management of peripheral fungal keratitis (keratomycosis). Arch Ophthalmol. 1984;102:1506-1509.
102. Reis A, Sundmacher R, Tintelnot K, et al. Successful treatment of ocular invasive mould infection (fusariosis) with the new antifungal agent voriconazole. Brit J Ophthalmol. 2000;84:932-933.
103. Ribaud P, Chastang C, Latge JP, et al. Survival and prognostic factors of invasive aspergillosis after allogeneic bone marrow transplantation. Clin Infect Dis. 1999;28:322-330.
104. Gerson SL, Talbot GH, Hurwitz S, et al. Prolonged granulocytopenia: The major risk factor for invasive pulmonary aspergillosis in patients with acute leukemia. Ann Intern Med. 1984;100:345-351.
105. Patterson JE, Zidouh A, Miniter P, et al. Hospital epidemiologic surveillance for invasive aspergillosis: Patient demographics and the utility of antigen detection. Infect Control Hosp Epidemiol. 1997;18:104-108.
106. Yeghen T, Kibbler CC, Prentice HG, et al. Management of invasive pulmonary aspergillosis in hematology patients: A review of 87 consecutive cases at a single institution. Clin Infect Dis. 2000;31:859-868.
107. Greene RE, Schlamm HT, Stark P, et al. Radiological findings in acute invasive pulmonary aspergillosis: Utility and reliability of halo sign and air-crescent sign for diagnosis and treatment of IPA in high-risk patients (Abstract O397). Program of the 13th European Congress of Clinical Microbiology and Infectious Diseases. Glasgow, Scotland, May 2003.
108. Mehrad B, Paciocco G, Martinez FJ, et al. Spectrum of aspergillus infection in lung transplant recipients—Case series and review of the literature. Chest. 2001;119:169-175.
109. Denning DW, Follansbee SE, Scolaro M, et al. Pulmonary aspergillosis in the acquired immunodeficiency syndrome. N Engl J Med. 1991;324:654-662.
110. Kramer M, Denning D, Marshall S, et al. Ulcerative tracheobronchitis following lung transplantation: A new form of invasive aspergillosis. Am Rev Resp Dis. 1991;144:552-556.
111. Kemper CA, Hostetler JS, Follansbee SE, et al. Ulcerative and plaque-like tracheobronchitis due to infection with *Aspergillus* in patients with AIDS. Clin Infect Dis. 1993;17:344-352.
112. Tait R, O'Driscoll B, Denning D. Unilateral wheeze due to pseudomembranous *Aspergillus* tracheobronchitis in the immunocompromised patient. Thorax. 1993;48:1285-1287.
113. Palmer SM, Perfect JR, Howell DN, et al. Candidal anastomotic infection in lung transplant recipients: Successful treatment with a combination of systemic and inhaled antifungal agents. J Heart Lung Transplant. 1998;17:1029-1033.
114. Ferguson BJ. Definitions of fungal rhinosinusitis. Otolaryngol Clin North Am. 2000;33:227-235.
115. Iwen PC, Rupp ME, Hinrichs SH. Invasive mold sinusitis: 17 cases in immunocompromised patients and review of the literature. Clin Infect Dis. 1997;24:1178-1184.
116. Schell WA. Histopathology of fungal rhinosinusitis. Otolaryngol Clin North Am. 2000;33:251-276.
117. Ascioglu S, Rex JH, de Pauw B, et al. Defining opportunistic invasive fungal infections in immunocompromised patients with cancer and hematopoietic stem cell transplants: An international consensus. Clin Infect Dis. 2002;34:7-14.
118. Malani PN, Kauffman CA. Prevention and prophylaxis of invasive fungal sinusitis in the immunocompromised patient. Otolaryngol Clin North Am. 2000;33:301-312,VIII.
119. Jantunen E, Volin L, Salonen O, et al. Central nervous system aspergillosis in allogeneic stem cell transplant recipients. Bone Marrow Transplant. 2003;31:191-196.
120. Hagensee ME, Bauwens JE, Kjos B, Bowden RA. Brain abscess following marrow transplantation: Experience at the Fred Hutchinson Cancer Research Center, 1984-1992. Clin Infect Dis. 1994;19:402-408.
121. Troke PF, Schwartz S, Ruhnke M, et al. Voriconazole (VRC) therapy (Rx) in 86 patients (pts) with CNS aspergillosis (CNSA): A retrospective analysis. Abstracts of the 43rd Interscience Conference on Antimicrobial Agents and Chemotherapy, Chicago, September 14-17. Washington, D.C.: American Society for Microbiology; 2003.
122. Walsh TJ, Hier DB, Caplan LR. Aspergillosis of the central nervous system: Clinicopathological analysis of 17 patients. Ann Neurol. 1985;18:574-582.
123. Gotway MB, Dawn SK, Caoili EM. The radiologic spectrum of pulmonary *Aspergillus* infections. J Comput Assist Tomogr. 2002;26:159-173.
124. Van't Wout JW, Raven EJ, van der Meer JW. Treatment of invasive aspergillosis with itraconazole in a patient with chronic granulomatous disease. J Infect. 1990;20:147-150.
125. Vinas FC, King PK, Diaz FG. Spinal aspergillus osteomyelitis. Clin Infect Dis. 1999;28:1223-1229.
126. Denning DW, Stevens DA. Antifungal and surgical treatment of invasive aspergillosis: Review of 2,121 published cases. Rev Infect Dis. 1990;12:1147-1201.
127. Duthie R, Denning DW. *Aspergillus fungemia*: Report of two cases and review. Clin Infect Dis. 1995;20:598-605.
128. Halpern M, Szabo S, Hochberg E, et al. Renal aspergilloma: An unusual cause of infection in a patient with the acquired immunodeficiency syndrome. Am J Med. 1992;92:437-440.
129. Klotz SA, Penn CC, Negvesky GJ, Butrus SI. Fungal and parasitic infections of the eye. Clin Microbiol Rev. 2000;13:662-685,CP664,CP665.

130. Kontoyiannis DP, Sumoza D, Tarrand J, et al. Significance of aspergillemia in patients with cancer: A 10-year study. Clin Infect Dis. 2000;31:188-189.

131. Horvath JA, Dummer S. The use of respiratory-tract cultures in the diagnosis of invasive pulmonary aspergillosis. Am J Med. 1996;100:171-178.

132. Yu VL, Muder RR, Poorsattar A. Significance of isolation of aspergillus from the respiratory tract in diagnosis of invasive pulmonary aspergillosis: Results from a three-year prospective study. Am J Med. 1986;81:249-254.

133. Burch PA, Karp JE, Merz WG, et al. Favorable outcome of invasive aspergillosis in patients with acute leukemia. J Clin Oncol. 1987;5:1985-1993.

134. Caillot D, Couaillier JF, Bernard A, et al. Increasing volume and changing characteristics of invasive pulmonary aspergillosis on sequential thoracic computed tomography scans in patients with neutropenia. J Clin Oncol. 2001;19:253-259.

135. Verweij PE, Poulain D, Obayashi T, et al. Current trends in the detection of antigenaemia, metabolites and cell wall markers for the diagnosis and therapeutic monitoring of fungal infections. Med Mycol. 1998;36:146-155.

136. Verweij PE, Erjavec Z, Sluiters W, et al. Detection of antigen in sera of patients with invasive aspergillosis: Intra- and interlaboratory reproducibility. J Clin Microbiol. 1998;36:1612-1616.

137. Verweij PE, Stynen D, Rijs AJMM, et al. Sandwich enzyme-linked immunosorbent assay compared with Pastorex latex agglutination test for diagnosing invasive aspergillosis in immunocompromised patients. J Clin Microbiol. 1995;33:1912-1914.

138. Maertens J, Verhaegen J, Demuynck H, et al. Autopsy-controlled prospective evaluation of serial screening for circulating galactomannan by a sandwich enzyme-linked immunosorbent assay for hematological patients at risk for invasive aspergillosis. J Clin Microbiol. 1999;37:3223-3228.

139. Verweij PE, Rijs AJ, De Pauw BE, et al. Clinical evaluation and reproducibility of the Pastorex Aspergillus antigen latex agglutination test for diagnosing invasive aspergillosis. J Clin Pathol. 1995;48:474-476.

140. Sulahian A, Tabouret M, Ribaud P, et al. Comparison of an enzyme immunoassay and latex agglutination test for detection of galactomannan in the diagnosis of aspergillosis. Eur J Clin Microbiol Infect Dis. 1996;15:139-145.

141. Swanink CMA, Meis JFGM, Rijs AJMM, et al. Specificity of a sandwich enzyme-linked immunosorbent assay for detecting Aspergillus galactomannan. J Clin Microbiol. 1997; 35:257-260.

142. Herbrecht R, Letscher-Bru V, Oprea C, et al. Aspergillus galactomannan detection in the diagnosis of invasive aspergillosis in cancer patients. J Clin Oncol. 2002;20:1898-1906.

143. Pinel C, Fricker-Hidalgo H, Lebeau B, et al. Detection of circulating Aspergillus fumigatus galactomannan: Value and limits of the Platelia test for diagnosing invasive aspergillosis. J Clin Microbiol. 2003;41:2184-2186.

144. Sulahian A, Touratier S, Leblanc T, et al. False positive Aspergillus antigenemia related to concomitant administration of tazocillin (Abstract M-2062a). Abstracts of the 43rd Interscience Conference on Antimicrobial Agents and Chemotherapy, Chicago, September 14-17. Washington, D.C.: American Society for Microbiology; 2003.

145. Viscoli C, Machetti M, Cappellano P, et al. False-positive platelia Aspergillus (PA) test in patients (pts) receiving piperacillin-tazobactam (P/T) (Abstract M-2062b). Abstracts of the 43rd Interscience Conference on Antimicrobial Agents and Chemotherapy, Chicago, September 14-17. Washington, D.C.: American Society for Microbiology; 2003.

146. Viscoli C, Machetti M, Gazzola P, et al. Aspergillus galactomannan antigen in the cerebrospinal fluid of bone marrow transplant recipients with probable cerebral aspergillosis. J Clin Microbiol. 2002;40:1496-1499.

147. Miyazaki T, Kohno S, Mitsutake K, et al. Plasma (1-3)-beta-D glucan and fungal antigenenia in patients with candidemia, aspergillosis and cryptococcosis. J Clin Microbiol. 1995;33:3115-3118.

148. Obayashi T, Yoshida M, Mori T, et al. Plasma (1→3)-beta-D-glucan measurement in diagnosis of invasive deep mycosis and fungal febrile episodes. Lancet. 1995;345:17-20.

149. Bretagne S, Costa JM, Bart-Delabesse E, et al. Comparison of serum galactomannan antigen detection and competitive polymerase chain reaction for diagnosing invasive aspergillosis. Clin Infect Dis. 1998;26:1407-1412.

150. Jones ME, Fox AJ, Barnes AJ, et al. PCR-ELISA for the early diagnosis of invasive pulmonary aspergillus infection in neutropenic patients. J Clin Pathol. 1998;51:652-656.

151. Hebart H, Loffler J, Meisner C, et al. Early detection of Aspergillus infection after allogeneic stem cell transplantation by polymerase chain reaction screening. J Infec Dis. 2000;181:1713-1719.

152. Loeffler J, Hebart H, Cox P, et al. Nucleic acid sequence-based amplification of Aspergillus RNA in blood samples. J Clin Microbiol. 2001;39:1626-1629.

153. Espinel-Ingroff A, Bartlett M, Bowden R, et al. Multicenter evaluation of proposed standardized procedure for antifungal susceptibility testing of filamentous fungi. J Clin Microbiol. 1997;35:139-143.

154. Espinel-Ingroff A, Warnock DW, Vazquez JA, Arthington-Skaggs BA. In vitro susceptibility methods and clinical implications of antifungal resistance. Med Mycol. 2000;38 (Suppl 1):293-304.

155. Denning DW, Radford SA, Oakley KL, et al. Correlation between in-vitro susceptibility testing to itraconazole and in-vivo outcome of Aspergillus fumigatus infection. J Antimicrob Chemother. 1997;40:401-414.

156. Mosquera J, Denning DW. Azole cross-resistance in Aspergillus fumigatus. Antimicrob Agents Chemother. 2002;46:556-557.

157. Bowden R, Chandrasekar P, White MH, et al. A double-blind, randomized, controlled trial of amphotericin B colloidal dispersion versus amphotericin B for treatment of invasive aspergillosis in immunocompromised patients. Clin Infect Dis. 2002;35:359-366.

158. Bates DW, Su L, Yu DT, et al. Mortality and costs of acute renal failure associated with amphotericin B therapy. Clin Infect Dis. 2001;32:686-693.

159. Wingard JR, Kubilis P, Lee L, et al. Clinical significance of nephrotoxicity in patients treated with amphotericin B for suspected or proven aspergillosis. Clin Infect Dis. 1999;29:1402-1407.

160. Ostrosky-Zeichner L, Marr KA, Rex JH, Cohen SH. Amphotericin B: Time for a new "gold standard." Clin Infect Dis. 2003;37:415-425.

161. Steinbach WJ, Stevens DA. Review of newer antifungal and immunomodulatory strategies for invasive aspergillosis. Clin Infect Dis. 2003;37(Suppl 3):S157-S187.

162. Pfaller MA, Messer SA, Hollis RJ, Jones RN. Antifungal activities of posaconazole, ravuconazole, and voriconazole compared to those of itraconazole and amphotericin B against 239 clinical isolates of Aspergillus spp. and other filamentous fungi: Report from SENTRY Antimicrobial Surveillance Program, 2000. Antimicrob Agents Chemother. 2002;46:1032-1037.

163. Espinel-Ingroff A, Boyle K, Sheehan DJ. In vitro antifungal activities of voriconazole and reference agents as determined by NCCLS methods: Review of the literature. Mycopathologia. 2001;150:101-115.

164. Denning DW, Ribaud P, Milpied N, et al. Efficacy and safety of voriconazole in the treatment of acute invasive aspergillosis. Clin Infect Dis. 2002;34:563-571.

165. Walsh TJ, Lutsar I, Driscoll T, et al. Voriconazole in the treatment of aspergillosis, scedosporiosis and other invasive fungal infections in children. Pediat Inf Dis J. 2002;21:240-248.

166. Lortholary O, Mouas-duPuy H, DuPont B, et al. Voriconazole (VCZ) for bone aspergillosis (BA): A worldwide experience of 19 cases (Abstract M-979). Abstracts of the 43rd Interscience Conference on Antimicrobial Agents and Chemotherapy, Chicago, September 14-17. Washington, D.C.: American Society for Microbiology; 2003.

167. Ally R, Schurmann D, Kreisel W, et al. A randomized, double-blind, double-dummy, multicenter trial of voriconazole and fluconazole in the treatment of esophageal candidiasis in immunocompromised patients. Clin Infect Dis. 2001;33:1447-1454.

168. Leenders ACAP, Daenen S, Jansen RLH, et al. Liposomal amphotericin B compared with amphotericin B deoxycholate in the treatment of documented and suspected neutropenia-associated invasive fungal infections. Br J Haematol. 1998;103:205-212.

169. Walsh TJ, Hiemenz JW, Seibel NL, et al. Amphotericin B lipid complex for invasive fungal infections: Analysis of safety and efficacy in 556 cases. Clin Infect Dis. 1998;26:1383-1396.

170. Ellis M, Spence D, de Pauw B, et al. An EORTC international multicenter randomized trial (EORTC number 19923) comparing two dosages of liposomal amphotericin B for treatment of invasive aspergillosis. Clin Infect Dis. 1998;27:1406-1412.

171. Walsh TJ, Goodman JL, Pappas P, et al. Safety, tolerance, and pharmacokinetics of high-dose liposomal amphotericin B (AmBisome) in patients infected with Aspergillus species and other filamentous fungi: Maximum tolerated dose study. Antimicrob Agents Chemother. 2001;45:3487-3496.

172. Rex JH, Walsh TJ, Nettleman M, et al. Need for alternative trial designs and evaluation strategies for therapeutic studies of invasive mycoses. Clin Infect Dis. 2001;33:95-106.

173. Francis P, Lee JW, Hoffman A, et al. Efficacy of unilamellar liposomal amphotericin B in treatment of pulmonary aspergillosis in persistently granulocytopenic rabbits: The potential role of bronchoalveolar lavage D-mannitol and galactomannan as markers of infection. J Infect Dis. 1994;169:356-368.

174. Patterson TF, Miniter P, Dijkstra J, et al. Treatment of experimental invasive aspergillosis with novel amphotericin B/cholesterol-sulfate complexes. J Infect Dis. 1989;159:717-721.

175. Linden PK, Coley K, Fontes P, et al. Invasive aspergillosis in liver transplant recipients: Outcome comparison of therapy with amphotericin B lipid complex and a historical cohort treated with conventional amphotericin B. Clin Infect Dis. 2003;37:17-25.

176. Bates DW, Su L, Yu DT, et al. Correlates of acute renal failure in patients receiving parenteral amphotericin B. Kidney Int. 2001;60:1452-1459.

177. Rex JH, Walsh TJ. Editorial response: Estimating the true cost of amphotericin B. Clin Infect Dis. 1999;29:1408-1410.

178. Caillot D, Bassaris H, McGeer A, et al. Intravenous itraconazole followed by oral itraconazole in the treatment of invasive pulmonary aspergillosis in patients with hematologic malignancies, chronic granulomatous disease, or AIDS. Clin Infect Dis. 2001;33:E83-E90.

179. Sheehan DJ, Hitchcock CA, Sibley CM. Current and emerging azole antifungal agents. Clin Microbiol Rev. 1999;12:40-79.

180. Kirkpatrick WR, McAtee RK, Fothergill AW, et al. Efficacy of posaconazole in a rabbit model of invasive aspergillosis. Antimicrob Agents Chemother. 2000;44:780-782.

181. Petraitiene R, Petraitis V, Groll AH, et al. Antifungal activity and pharmacokinetics of posaconazole (SCH 56592) in treatment and prevention of experimental invasive pulmonary aspergillosis: Correlation with galactomannan antigenemia. Antimicrob Agents Chemother. 2001;45:857-869.

182. Hachem RY, Raad II, Afif CM, et al. An open, noncomparative multicenter study to evaluate efficacy and safety of posaconazole (SCH 56592) in the treatment of invasive fungal infections refractory to or intolerant of standard therapy. 40th Interscience Conference on Antimicrobial Agents and Chemotherapy. Toronto, Canada: American Society for Microbiology; 2000.

183. Roberts J, Schock K, Marino S, Andriole VT. Efficacies of two new antifungal agents, the triazole ravuconazole and the echinocandin LY-303366, in an experimental model of invasive aspergillosis. Antimicrob Agents Chemother. 2000;44:3381-3388.

184. Kirkpatrick WR, Perea S, Coco BJ, Patterson TF. Efficacy of ravuconazole (BMS-207147) in a guinea pig model of disseminated aspergillosis. J Antimicrob Chemother. 2002;49:353-357.

185. Petraitis V, Petraitiene R, Sarafandi AA, et al. Combination therapy in treatment of experimental pulmonary aspergillosis: Synergistic interaction between an antifungal triazole and an echinocandin. J Infect Dis. 2003;187:1834-1843.

186. Kirkpatrick WR, Perea S, Coco BJ, Patterson TF. Efficacy of caspofungin alone and in combination with voriconazole in a guinea pig model of invasive aspergillosis. Antimicrob Agents Chemother. 2002;46:2564-2568.

187. Petraitis V, Petraitiene R, Groll AH, et al. Dosage-dependent antifungal efficacy of V-echinocandin (LY303366) against experimental fluconazole-resistant oropharyngeal and esophageal candidiasis. Antimicrob Agents Chemother. 2001;45:471-479.

188. Petraitis V, Petraitiene R, Groll A, et al. Comparative antifungal activity of the echinocandin FK463 against disseminated candidiasis and invasive pulmonary aspergillosis in persistently neutropenic rabbits. 40th Interscience Conference on Antimicrobial Agents and Chemotherapy. Toronto, Canada; 2000.

189. Petraitiene R, Petraitis V, Groll AH, et al. Antifungal efficacy of caspofungin (MK-0991) in experimental pulmonary aspergillosis in persistently neutropenic rabbits: Pharmacokinetics, drug disposition, and relationship to galactomannan antigenemia. Antimicrob Agents Chemother. 2002;46:12-23.

190. Bowman JC, Hicks PS, Kurtz MB, et al. The antifungal echinocandin caspofungin ccetate kills growing cells of *Aspergillus fumigatus* in vitro. Antimicrob Agents Chemother. 2002;46:3001-3012.

191. Van Burik J, Ratanatharathorn V, Lipton J, et al. Randomized, double-blind trial of micafungin (MI) versus fluconazole (FL) for prophylaxis of invasive fungal infections in patients (pts) undergoing hematopoietic stem cell transplant (HSCT), NIAID/BAMSG Protocol 46 (Abstract M-1238). 42nd Interscience Conference on Antimicrobial Agents and Chemotherapy. Chicago: American Society for Microbiology; 2002.

192. Kontoyiannis DP, Hachem R, Lewis RE, et al. Efficacy and toxicity of caspofungin in combination with liposomal amphotericin B as primary or salvage treatment of invasive aspergillosis in patients with hematologic malignancies. Cancer. 2003;98:292-299.

193. Aliff TB, Maslak PG, Jurcic JG, et al. Refractory *Aspergillus* pneumonia in patients with acute leukemia: Successful therapy with combination caspofungin and liposomal amphotericin. Cancer. 2003;97:1025-1032.

194. Schaffner A, Frick PG. The effect of ketoconazole on amphotericin B in a model of disseminated aspergillosis. J Infect Dis. 1985;151:902-910.

195. George D, Kordick D, Miniter P, et al. Combination therapy in experimental invasive aspergillosis. J Infec Dis. 1993;168:692-698.

196. Denning DW, Hanson LH, Perlman AM, Stevens DA. In vitro susceptibility and synergy studies of *Aspergillus* species to conventional and new agents. Diagn Microbiol Infect Dis. 1992;15:21-34.

197. Steinbach WJ, Stevens DA, Denning DW. Combination and sequential antifungal therapy for invasive aspergillosis: Review of published in vitro and in vivo interactions and 6281 clinical cases from 1966 to 2001. Clin Infect Dis. 2003;37(Suppl 3):S188-224.

198. Kohno S, Maesaki S, Iwakawa J, et al. Synergistic effects of combination of FK463 with amphotericin B: Enhanced efficacy in murine model of invasive pulmonary aspergillosis. 40th Interscience Conference on Antimicrobial Agents and Chemotherapy. Toronto, Canada; 2000.

199. Nakajima M, Tamada S, Yoshida K, et al. Pathological findings in a murine pulmonary aspergillosis model: Treatment with FK463, amphotericin B, and a combination of FK463 and amphotericin B. 40th Interscience Conference on Antimicrobial Agents and Chemotherapy. Toronto, Canada; 2000.

200. Vose J, Bierman P, Kiessinger A, et al. The use of recombinant human granulocyte-macrophage colony stimulating factor for the treatment of delayed engraftment following high-dose therapy and autologous hematopoietic stem cell transplantation for lymphoid malignancies. Bone Marrow Transplant. 1991;7:139-143.

201. Rowe JM. Treatment of acute myeloid leukemia with cytokines: Effect on duration of neutropenia and response to infections. Clin Infect Dis. 1998;26:1290-1294.

202. Pui CH, Boyett JM, Hughes WT, et al. Human granulocyte colony-stimulating factor after induction chemotherapy in children with acute lymphoblastic leukemia. N Engl J Med. 1997;336:1781-1787.

203. Bernhisel-Broadbent J, Camargo EE, Jaffe HS, Lederman HM. Recombinant human interferon-gamma as adjunct therapy for *Aspergillus* infection in a patient with chronic granulomatous disease. J Infect Dis. 1991;163:908-911.

204. Bhatia S, McCullough J, Perry EH, et al. Granulocyte transfusion: Efficacy in treating fungal infections in neutropenic patients following bone marrow transplantation. Transfusion. 1994;34:226-232.

205. Dignani MC, Anaissie EJ, Hester JP, et al. Treatment of neutropenia-related fungal infections with granulocyte colony-stimulating factor-elicited white blood cell transfusions: A pilot study. Leukemia. 1997;11:1621-1630.

206. Boucher HW, Herbrecht R, Bennett JE, et al. The strategy of following voriconazole (VRC) vs amphotericin B (AMB) with other licensed antifungal therapy (OLAT) for primary therapy of invasive aspergillosis (IA) (Abstract M-964). Abstracts of the 43rd Interscience Conference on Antimicrobial Agents and Chemotherapy, Chicago, September 14-17, 2003. Washington, D.C.: American Society for Microbiology; 2003:446.

207. Herbrecht R. Improving the outcome of invasive aspergillosis: New diagnostic tools and new therapeutic strategies. Ann Hematol. 2002;81(Suppl 2):S52-53.

208. Maertens J, Raad I, Petrikkos G, et al. Update of the multicenter noncomparative study of caspofungin (CAS) in adults with invasive aspergillosis (IA) refractory (R) or intolerant (I) to other antifungal agents: Analysis of 90 patients (Abstract M-868). Abstracts of the 42nd Interscience Conference on Antimicrobial Agents and Chemotherapy, San Diego, Calif, September 27-30, 2002. Washington, D.C.: American Society for Microbiology; 2002.

209. Dykewicz CA, Jaffe HW, Kaplan JE. Guidelines for preventing opportunistic infections among hematopoietic stem cell transplant recipients—Recommendations of CDC, the Infectious Diseases Society of America, and the American Society of Blood and Marrow Transplantation. Biol Blood Marrow Transplant. 2000;6:659-713,715,717-727.

210. Dykewicz CA. Hospital infection control in hematopoietic stem cell transplant recipients. Emerg Infect Dis. 2001;7:263-267.

211. Sherertz RJ, Belani A, Kramer BS, et al. Impact of air filtration on nosocomial aspergillus infections: Unique risk of bone marrow transplant recipients. Am J Med. 1987;83:709-718.

212. Iwen PC, Reed EC, Armitage JO, et al. Nosocomial invasive aspergillosis in lymphoma patients treated with bone marrow or peripheral stem cell transplants. Infect Control Hosp Epidemiol. 1993;14:131-139.

213. Tablan OC, Anderson LJ, Arden NH, et al. Guideline for prevention of nosocomial pneumonia. Infect Control Hosp Epidemiol. 1994;15:588-627.

214. Warris A, Klaassen CH, Meis JF, et al. Molecular epidemiology of *Aspergillus fumigatus* isolates recovered from water, air, and patients shows two clusters of genetically distinct strains. J Clin Microbiol. 2003;41:4101-4106.

215. Anaissie EJ, Owens S, Dignani MC, et al. Cleaning bathrooms: A novel approach to reducing patient exposure to aerosolized *Aspergillus* spp. Blood. 2001;98:207A.

216. Palmer SM, Drew RH, Whitehouse JD, et al. Safety of aerosolized amphotericin B lipid complex in lung transplant recipients. Transplantation. 2001;72:545-548.

217. Morgenstern GR, Prentice AG, Prentice HG, et al. A randomised controlled trial of itraconazole versus fluconazole for the prevention of fungal infections in patients with haematological malignancies. Br J Haematol. 1999;105:901-911.

218. Boogaerts M, Winston DJ, Bow EJ, et al. Intravenous and oral itraconazole versus intravenous amphotericin B deoxycholate as empirical antifungal therapy for persistent fever in neutropenic patients with cancer who are receiving broad-spectrum antibacterial therapy. A randomized, controlled trial. Ann Intern Med. 2001;135:412-422.

219. Winston DJ, Maziarz RT, Chandrasekar PH, et al. Intravenous and oral itraconazole versus intravenous and oral fluconazole for long-term antifungal prophylaxis in allogeneic hematopoietic stem-cell transplant recipients. A multicenter, randomized trial. Ann Intern Med. 2003;138:705-713.

220. Gallin JI, Alling DW, Malech HL, et al. Itraconazole to prevent fungal infections in chronic granulomatous disease. N Engl J Med. 2003;348:2416-2422.

221. Groll AH, Mickiene D, Petraitis V, et al. Compartmental pharmacokinetics and tissue distribution of the antifungal echinocandin lipopeptide micafungin (FK463) in rabbits. Antimicrob Agents Chemother. 2001;45:3322-3327.

222. Vanden Bossche H. Echinocandins—An update. Expert Opin Ther Patents. 2002;12:151-167.

223. Groll AH, Mickiene D, Petraitiene R, et al. Pharmacokinetic and pharmacodynamic modeling of anidulafungin (LY303366): Reappraisal of its efficacy in neutropenic animal models of opportunistic mycoses using optimal plasma sampling. Antimicrob Agents Chemother. 2001;45:2845-2855.

224. Arathoon EG. Clinical efficacy of echinocandin antifungals. Curr Opin Infect Dis. 2001;14:685-691.

CHAPTER **257**

Agents of Mucormycosis and Related Species

ALAN M. SUGAR

Mucormycosis is the common name given to several different diseases caused by fungi of the order Mucorales. Several different species have been implicated as etiologic agents of similar clinical syndromes. The taxonomy of this group is complicated not only by the number of fungi causing similar infections but also because of changes in the names of individual species that are made as new advances in classification are accepted. Table 257-1 summarizes the taxonomic relationships of those Zygomycetes known to be pathogenic for humans. The details of the mycology of the Zygomycetes and problems in taxonomy are beyond the scope of this chapter but can be found elsewhere.[1]

This group of diseases has been known by other names in the past, and the proper terminology to be used in the literature and in clinical discussions still has not been agreed upon. For example, references can be found in the older literature to *phycomycosis* and, more recently, *zygomycosis*. The former is an allusion to an imprecise classification scheme that is no longer used, and the latter reflects the class name of these fungi. As detailed later, not all of the Zygomycetes cause the same type of disease, so the term *zygomycosis* is too vague and does not accurately convey useful information to the physician. Furthermore, the designation *mucormycosis* is well ingrained in the medical literature and evokes certain useful associations, so it is best to continue to refer to the mycoses produced by the organisms in the order Mucorales by this name, a convention that is followed in this chapter.

TABLE 257-1 Classification of Zygomycetes Pathogenic for Humans

Agents of Mucormycosis (Order Mucorales), in Approximate Order of Decreasing Frequency
  Rhizopus arrhizus (*oryzae*)
  Rhizopus microsporus var. *rhizopodiformis*
  Rhizomucor pusillus
  Cunninghamella bertholletiae
  Apophysomyces elegans
  Saksenaea vasiformis
  Rhizopus microsporus var. *microsporus*
  Asbsidia corymbifera
  Mucor circinelloides
  Syncephalastrum racemosum
  Cokeromyces recurvatus
  Mortierella spp.

Agents of Entomophthoramycosis (Order Entomophthorales)
  Conidiobolus coronatus
  Basidiobolus ranarum (*haptosporus*)

Data from Howard DH. An introduction to the taxonomy and nomenclature of zoopathogenic fungi. In: Howard DH, ed. Fungi Pathogenic for Humans and Animals: Part A. Biology. New York: Marcel Dekker; 1983:3-7.

In addition to the order Mucorales, the fungi responsible for mucormycosis, the class Zygomycetes contains the order Entomophthorales. The fungi in this order also cause distinctive clinical syndromes, but they usually are clearly separable from those produced by the agents causing mucormycosis. *Entomophthoramycosis* is the currently accepted general term used to describe disease caused by these fungi. Diseases caused by the Entomophthorales are extremely rare in North America; they are usually found in Africa, Southeast Asia, Indonesia, and South America. Because the clinical and pathologic manifestations of the diseases caused by this group of fungi are for the most part different from those produced by the agents of mucormycosis, they are discussed separately, after a discussion of the more common mucormycosis.

MUCORMYCOSIS

The Pathogens

The medically important Zygomycetes are molds that grow in the environment and in tissue as hyphal forms. The taxonomy of the Zygomycetes is based on a morphologic analysis of the fungus, which is reviewed below. Other taxonomically relevant features include carbohydrate assimilation and maximal temperature compatible with growth. These organisms typically grow in 2 to 5 days on most media.

However, cycloheximide inhibits the growth of these fungi, and media that contain this compound, such as Mycosel and Mycobiotic Agar, should not be used.

Rhizopus species are the most commonly isolated agents of mucormycosis, followed by *Rhizomucor* and *Cunninghamella*. Differentiation between these genera is accomplished by microscopic examination for the presence and location of rhizoids, the presence of apophyses, and the morphology of the columellae[1,2] (Fig. 257-1). The capability to identify these strains to this level should be within the grasp of most tertiary-care hospital laboratories. Speciation of these organisms is desirable for many reasons, including monitoring of the progress of therapy (especially to document the eradication of the original fungus and to determine that a fungus growing from a subsequent clinical specimen is or is not a different contaminating organism) and elucidation of any species-specific responses to different antifungal drugs, an important consideration with the current emphasis on development of new classes of antifungal drugs. Disease caused by *Cunninghamella*,[2,3] *Saksenaea*,[4,5] and *Apophysomyces*[6,7] is indistinguishable from that caused by the more common Mucorales, and these genera are more frequently being recovered in the laboratory as the etiologic agents of mucormycosis.[8] Laboratory confirmation of the identity of the organism is the only way to differentiate among the fungi.

Epidemiology

The Mucoraceae are ubiquitous fungi that are common inhabitants of decaying matter. For example, *Rhizopus* spp. frequently can be recovered from moldy bread. Because of their rapid growth and prolific spore-forming capacity, inhalation of conidia must be a daily experience. The presence of Mucorales spores on nonsterile adhesive tape has been shown to be the source of primary cutaneous mucormycosis.[9-11] Tongue depressors and wooden sticks used in the microbiology laboratory to prepare samples for culture have been found to harbor *Rhizopus* spp. In the former instance, clinical disease secondary to the use of the tongue depressor as a splint in neonates has occurred,[12] and in the latter, a pseudoepidemic was reported in immunocompromised patients.[13] An additional patient with acute lymphoblastic leukemia developed mucormycosis and died of a pulmonary hemorrhage attributed to the use of a tongue depressor.[14] *Apophysomyces* was responsible for a necrotizing cellulitis at a patch test site that used material derived from a snapdragon plant as the test antigen.[15] Thus unusual infections can develop when people are exposed to contaminated material from the environment. Even though these fungi grow in many ecologic niches, the infrequency of disease caused by these organisms attests to their low virulence potential in the human host.

FIGURE 257-1. Diagram of major differentiating morphologic features of three of the most common Mucorales isolated from patients. Note the presence and location of the rhizoids and the columella, and the shape of the sporangia. The infectious spores reside within the sporangia. (*Illustration by Lori Messenger.*)

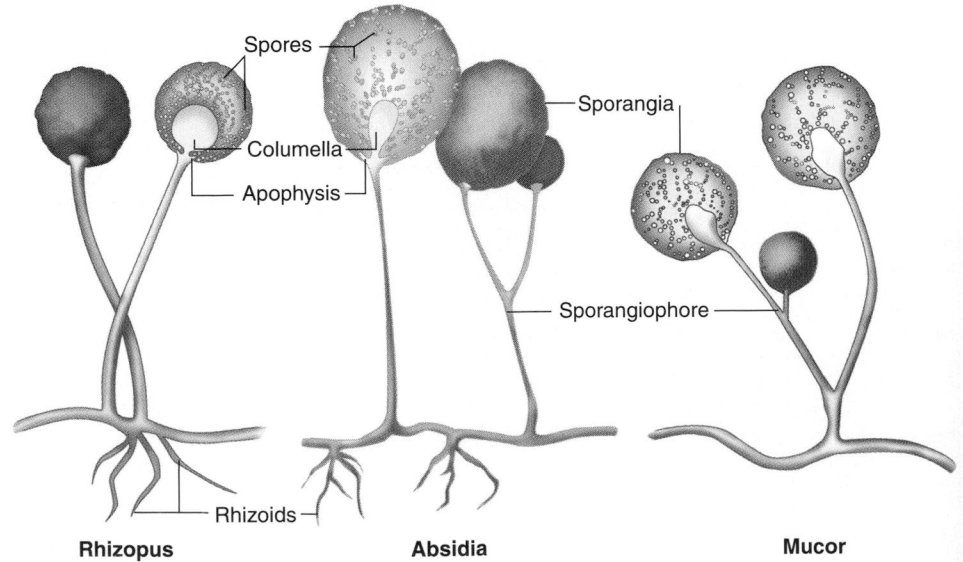

Spores

Columella

Apophysis

Sporangia

Sporangiophore

Rhizoids

Rhizopus   **Absidia**   **Mucor**

In contrast to the widespread distribution of these fungi, disease in humans is limited, in most cases, to people with severe immunocompromise, diabetes mellitus, or trauma. Solid-organ and hematopoietic stem cell transplant recipients represent a growing population at risk.[16-18] In these patients, the disease manifests in all of its diverse forms. More than half of patients have rhinocerebral disease; approximately 10% have pulmonary, cutaneous, or disseminated disease; and 2% have kidney or gastrointestinal involvement. Three quarters of these transplant patients also had diabetes or had received antirejection therapy. Scattered case reports of invasive mucormycosis in apparently normal hosts have appeared,[19-21] but the disease in the immunocompetent person remains a rarity.

Pathogenesis

Most commonly, the fungus gains entry to the body through the respiratory tract. The spores presumably are deposited in the nasal turbinates and may be inhaled into the pulmonary alveoli. In the case of primary cutaneous mucormycosis, spores are introduced directly into abraded skin. They then proliferate and can invade more widely.

To cause disease, spores must overcome the host's natural immunity and specific humoral and cell-mediated immune mechanisms. Most of our understanding of the pathogenesis of mucormycosis is derived from the mouse and rabbit models of infection. Normal animals inoculated with *Rhizopus* do not become ill.[22] However, inhalation of Mucorales spores by animals with diabetes mellitus or those receiving corticosteroids results in death from rapidly progressive pulmonary mucormycosis, often with hematogenous dissemination beyond the lungs.[23-25]

The initial event in fungal cell proliferation is spore germination. In the normal lung, *Rhizopus oryzae* spores are unable to germinate.[23-26] Bronchoalveolar macrophages harvested from normal mice readily ingest *Rhizopus* spores and inhibit their germination.[23-27] However, the spores remain viable and can grow if removed from the phagolysosomes. In the lungs of mice with streptozotocin-induced diabetes and in steroid-treated mice, spore germination readily occurs.[23-27] Bronchoalveolar macrophages recovered from these mice do not possess the normal ability to inhibit spore germination.

Neutrophils are prominent components of the host response to the Mucorales. Recruitment of neutrophils into areas of infection is accomplished by fungus-derived and serum-derived chemotactic factors.[28,29] Activation of the alternative complement pathway is the source of the serum-induced chemotaxis.

The mechanisms responsible for the increased susceptibility to mucormycosis in various patient groups are not clear. Oxidative metabolites generated by the phagocyte respiratory burst (e.g., O_2^-, hydrogen peroxide, hypochlorous acid) have been shown to be fungicidal to *R. oryzae* hyphae.[30] How diabetes and steroids interfere with the ability of this fungus to elicit these toxic phagocyte products or with the activity of the oxidative metabolites is unknown. Defensins, cationic proteins obtained from mammalian phagocytic cells,[31] also have significant ability to kill *R. oryzae* spores and hyphae.[32] The relative importance of oxidative and nonoxidative fungicidal mechanisms in the normal state and in situations of immunosuppression or diabetes remains a mystery.

Hyperglycemia or acidosis per se is not sufficient to permit fungal replication within the alveolar macrophage,[23] although acidosis without hyperglycemia has been associated with invasive mucormycosis of humans on occasion.[33,34] Normal human serum can inhibit the growth of *Rhizopus*.[28] In contrast, serum obtained from patients with diabetic ketoacidosis is not inhibitory and may actually enhance fungal growth.[35,36] Although neither antibody nor complement is responsible for inhibition of growth of the Mucorales, interactions between transferrin and iron molecules and fungal spores have been described and may be important in determining the rate of fungal cell replication.[37,38] Indeed, patients with renal failure who are receiving deferoxamine are at increased risk for developing a rapidly fatal case of mucormycosis, and the importance of iron in fostering growth of the Mucorales is clear.[39,40] In a combination of in vitro and in vivo animal studies,

Boelaert and colleagues showed that, in the presence of feroxamine complex (iron-loaded deferoxamine) and serum, the growth of *Rhizopus* is enhanced more than that of *Aspergillus,* and growth of *Candida* is unaffected.[40] Deferoxamine-treated guinea pigs infected with *Rhizopus, Aspergillus fumigatus,* or *Cryptococcus neoformans* died sooner than untreated animals, but survival of mice infected with *Candida albicans* was unchanged. The importance of the presence of serum, which is inherently fungistatic to *Rhizopus,* in the in vitro studies requires emphasis, because studies performed without the addition of serum fail to demonstrate the growth-enhancing effects of deferoxamine.[41] Feroxamine reverses this serum-associated fungistasis and augments fungal growth.[41]

It is still not possible to develop a unifying concept of the pathogenesis of mucormycosis. It is clear, however, that undefined defects of macrophages and neutrophils, present in diabetic and steroid-treated animals, are important in allowing the replication of the Mucorales. Moreover, immunologically healthy people can suppress the growth of the Mucorales and clear them from the lung with great efficiency. Finally, the relative paucity of cases of mucormycosis in patients with the acquired immunodeficiency syndrome (AIDS) attests to the importance of the neutrophil in inhibiting fungal spore development. However, cases of mucormycosis in AIDS patients do occur and may be secondary to quantitative and qualitative defects in neutrophils.[42-47]

Once the fungus begins to grow, the hyphae invade tissue and have a special affinity for blood vessels. Direct penetration and growth through the blood vessel wall explain the propensity for thrombosis and tissue necrosis, two major hallmarks of the histopathology of mucormycosis. *R. oryzae* spores have been shown to bind laminin and type IV collagen by a lectin-independent mechanism.[48] This binding occurred before spore germination and decreased as the spore germinated. These observations still do not explain the propensity of Mucorales hyphae to invade blood vessels.

Clinical Manifestations

The manifestations of mucormycosis can be arbitrarily divided into at least six separate entities, based on clinical presentation and involvement of a particular body site: (1) rhinocerebral, (2) pulmonary, (3) cutaneous, (4) gastrointestinal, (5) central nervous system, and (6) miscellaneous.[49] In general, the predilection for one of these types of presentation varies with the underlying or predisposing condition. For example, patients with diabetes most often develop rhinocerebral mucormycosis, neutropenic patients who have leukemia or who become neutropenic during bone marrow transplantation for other diseases develop rhinocerebral or pulmonary mucormycosis, and those with protein-calorie malnutrition most often present with gastrointestinal disease. Disseminated disease, resulting from progression from one of the primary anatomic locations, is particularly troublesome in patients with severe immunologic deficits, such as those with bone marrow transplants or acute leukemia.[50-52]

Rhinocerebral Mucormycosis

This form of mucormycosis is most often found in patients with diabetes mellitus, particularly in the presence of acidosis, and in patients with leukemia who have been neutropenic for long periods and who have been receiving broad-spectrum antibacterial drugs.[53-58] Occasional reports of this form of mucormycosis in organ transplant patients have appeared.[59,60]

Patients presenting with uncomplicated diabetic ketoacidosis and altered mental status should have an improvement in consciousness as the metabolic abnormalities are corrected. Persistence of mental status changes beyond the usual 24 to 48 hours after appropriate therapy is begun and metabolic abnormalities are resolving should alert the physician to the possibility that mucormycosis involving the brain may be responsible for the patient's condition.

Patients with this form of mucormycosis virtually always complain of facial pain or headache, or both. Fever and varying degrees of evidence of orbital cellulitis occur. Invasion inferiorly often involves the palate, first with erythema and then, as the disease progresses, the development of an

FIGURE 257-2. **A,** Orbital involvement in a diabetic patient. Note the periorbital ecchymosis, edema, and sanguineous discharge from the eye. **B,** Marked chemosis and proptosis secondary to retro-orbital invasion in rhinocerebral mucormycosis. *(Courtesy of Professor Bertrand Dupont, Paris, France.)*

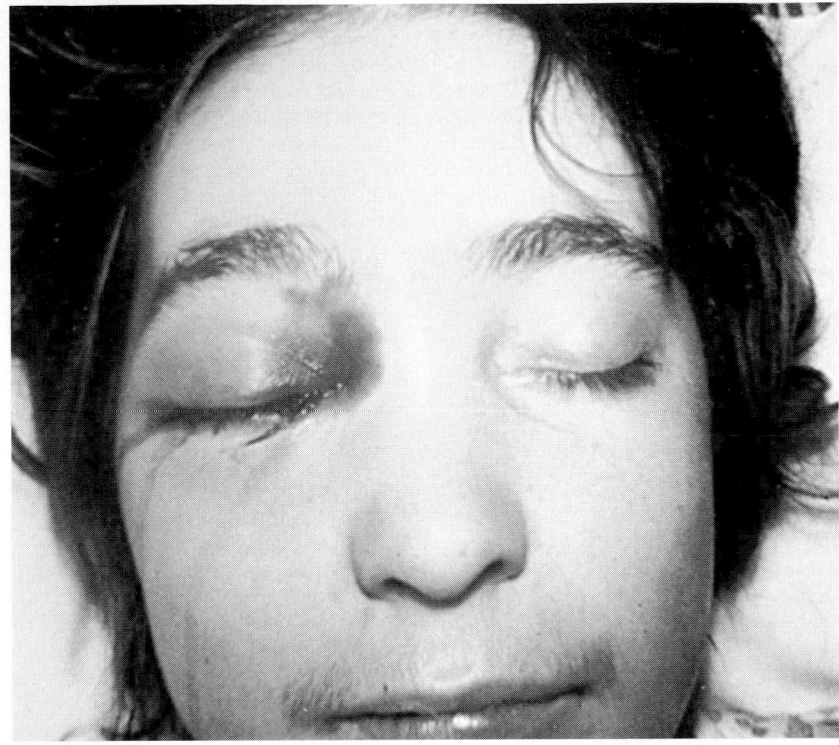

A

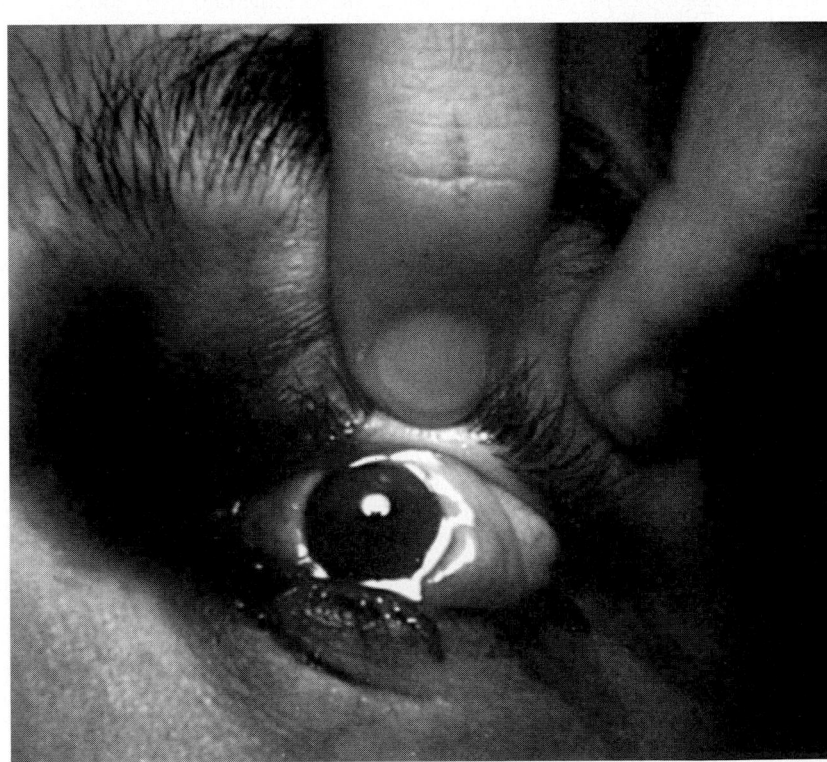

B

ulceration, which may turn black, reflecting the characteristic tissue necrosis associated with the infection. The astute clinician should consider the possibility of mucormycosis before the development of the necrotic ulcer so often associated with this disease. With invasion of the orbit, loss of extraocular muscle function can develop and proptosis becomes evident (Fig. 257-2A). Marked swelling of the conjunctiva also occurs as the disease progresses (Fig. 257-2B). Loss of vision may result from thrombosis of the retinal artery, presumably secondary to direct invasion by fungal elements. The development of cranial nerve dysfunction, especially of nerves V and VII, occurs with progression of the disease, is manifested by ptosis and pupillary dilatation, and represents a serious prognostic event. Cerebral abscess as a complication of mucormycosis involving the nose

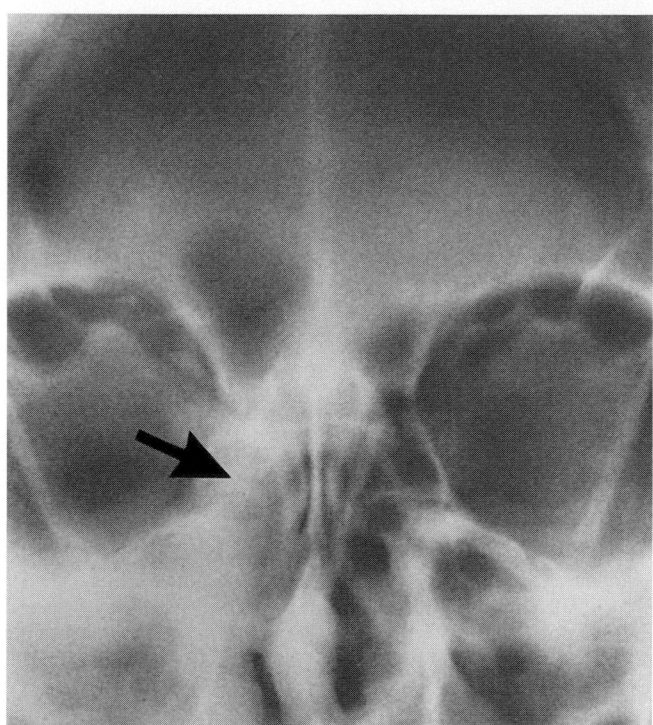

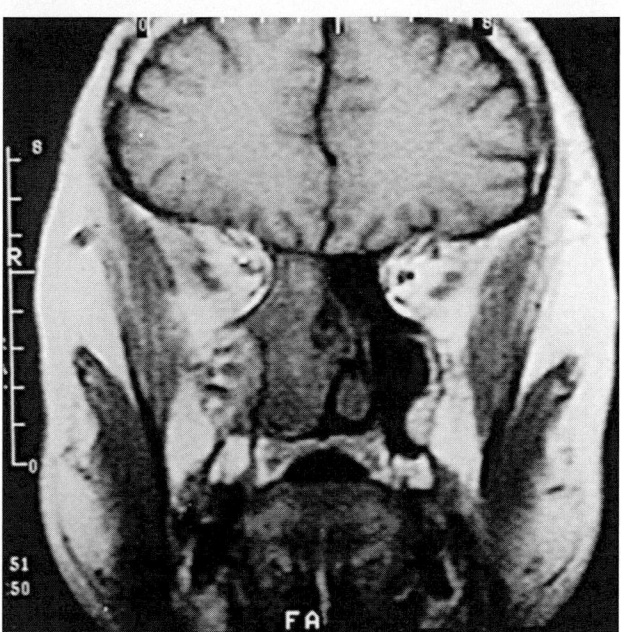

FIGURE 257-4. Magnetic resonance image of mucormycosis of the nasal cavity and ethmoid sinus. Note the contiguity of the frontal lobe to ethmoidal infection.

FIGURE 257-3. Tomogram of the head in a patient with rhinocerebral mucormycosis. Note the presence of clouding in the maxillary and ethmoid (*arrow*) sinuses. *(Courtesy of Dr. David A. Stevens, San José, CA.)*

and eye can also occur.[61,62] Cavernous sinus and internal carotid artery thrombosis[63] are additional complications that reflect the vascular tropism of the fungus. In the terminal stages of the disease, the underlying predisposing condition continues unabated, and patients may lose consciousness. The end result of such progression is death.

Laboratory studies are nonspecific, but suggestive evidence of the presence of disease can be found on roentgenograms of the sinuses. Plain roentgenograms of the sinuses and orbits can reveal sinusoidal mucosal thickening, with or without air-fluid levels (Fig. 257-3).[64] Erosion of bone through the walls of the sinuses or into the orbit can be found as the disease progresses. Destruction of bone in this region is often dramatically revealed by computed tomography (CT). Abnormalities in soft tissues involved in the disease process can also be visualized by CT scans[65] and can be used to guide surgical intervention. Similar changes have been demonstrated by magnetic resonance imaging (Fig. 257-4). Treatment with deferoxamine, usually for chelation therapy in patients receiving hemodialysis, is another risk factor for development of mucormycosis.[40,66-71] Most of these patients die from aggressive infection with *Rhizopus* spp., but *Cunninghamella* spp. have also been recovered from such patients.[39,71] However, iron overload per se may also be an important risk factor for the development of invasive mucormycosis.[67,68]

Finally, chronic presentations or late sequelae after apparently successful therapy can be observed.[71-74] For this reason, all survivors of acute infection should be monitored for signs of indolent residual infection.

Pulmonary Mucormycosis

Most of the patients with this form of mucormycosis are seriously immunocompromised because of an absolute lack of circulating neutrophils. The cause of neutropenia is usually chemotherapy for hematologic malignancies. The patients often have been receiving broad-spectrum antibiotics for unremitting fever. A patient with chronic obstructive pulmonary disease who was being treated with prednisone (10 mg/day) and another with diabetes and renal transplant have been reported, highlighting the increasing spectrum of predisposing factors for mucormycosis and presentations other than the rhinocerebral form.[75,76] Other than fever and perhaps dyspnea and cough, there usually are no other symptoms. With continued tissue necrosis, hemoptysis may develop; should a major blood vessel be eroded, fatal pulmonary hemorrhage can result.[14,77,78] A chest roentgenogram shows evidence of infiltration or cavity formation, usually involving one anatomic segment but typically progressing to involve multiple contiguous areas in the same lung.[79] The most common finding on chest roentgenograms is consolidation (66%).[80] Cavitation occurs in about 40%, usually as neutropenia resolves (Figs. 257-5 and 257-6). In one study, CT scans performed in patients with pulmonary mucormycosis revealed unsuspected abnormalities in 26%, including involvement of spleen, involvement of the kidney, and pulmonary artery pseudoaneurysm.[80] The disease most often begins with unilateral lung involvement but can disseminate more widely as the patient is dying. Patients in intensive care units for prolonged periods are often immunosuppressed as a result of malnutrition and medications (including corticosteroids) and may be hyperglycemic as a result of parenteral hyperalimentation or glucose intolerance. Therefore it is not surprising that nosocomial mucormycosis pneumonia occurs in such patients.

Scattered reports can be found of pulmonary mucormycosis with atypical presentations: as a solitary nodule in a diabetic,[81] in a patient with no underlying predisposing condition,[82] as a cavitary pneumonia in a patient without predisposing conditions,[83] as multiple mycotic pulmonary artery aneurysms,[84] as bronchial obstruction,[85] as pseudoaneurysm of the pulmonary artery,[86] and even in a patient with a normal chest roentgenogram.[87] Patients with diabetes mellitus can also develop pulmonary mucormycosis with a less fulminant, more subacute course than is typically seen in patients with neutropenia.[88]

Cutaneous Mucormycosis

A nationwide epidemic that was caused by contaminated elastic bandages in the 1970s focused attention on primary cutaneous mucormycosis as a distinct entity.[9-11] Since then sporadic cases of cutaneous mucormycosis continue to occur. In cases involving occlusive dressings, failure to recognize the mycotic nature of the underlying infection or to remove the bandages to inspect the area occasionally results in penetration of hyphae into areas below the skin, with subsequent infection of

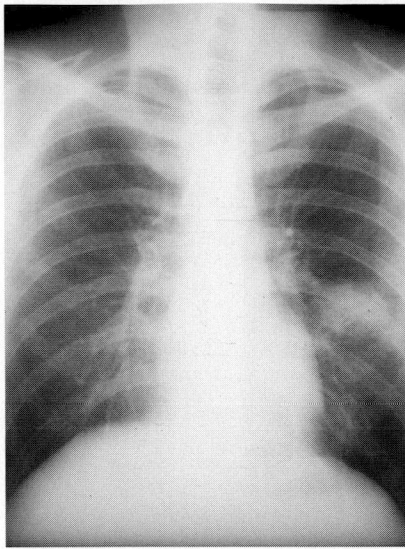

A

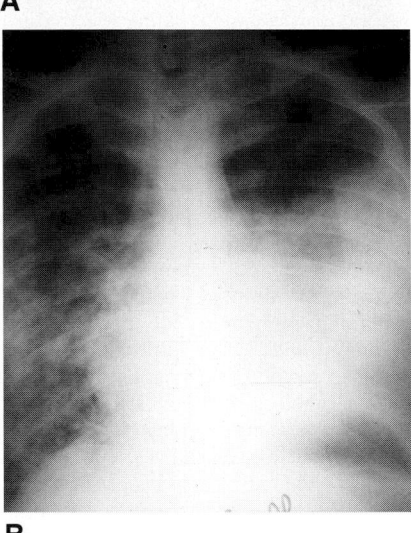

B

FIGURE 257-5. Chest x-rays showing rapidity of progression of pulmonary mucormycosis in a neutropenic leukemic patient. **A,** Day of diagnosis. **B,** At 72 hours later.

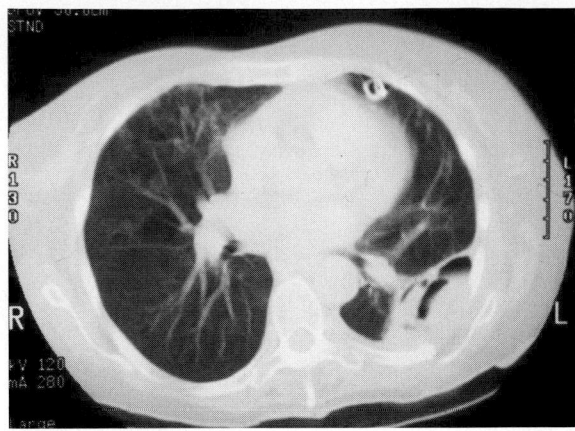

FIGURE 257-6. Computed tomogram showing cavitation in a patient who was recovering from neutropenia and receiving amphotericin B.

muscle, liver, or other viscera. Use of properly sterilized bandages and dressings should eliminate this form of mucormycosis. Dissemination of the organism from the site of primary infection can occur.[89] Rarely, intramuscular injections have been reported to precede the development of this form of mucormycosis.[90] Cases of cutaneous mucormycosis have also been described after minor trauma[91-93]; some of these patients may have had diabetes mellitus. A chronic, nonhealing ulcer at the site of a postoperative drain site has been reported.[94] Contamination of devitalized tissue during major traumatic accidents also can result in cutaneous mucormycosis.[95] Extensive involvement of burn wounds can result in dissemination of the fungus throughout the body and death of the patient.[96]

Cutaneous mucormycosis predominantly involves the epidermis and dermis, and necrosis develops secondary to vascular invasion. Cultures have yielded *R. oryzae* or *Rhizopus rhizopodiformis* in most cases, but recently *Apophysomyces elegans* has been increasingly recovered from patients with mucormycosis of the skin and deeper structures.[97] *Saksenaea vasiformis* was isolated from subcutaneous tissues of a child with thalassemia who sustained trauma and subsequently developed infection in the injured area.[98] *Mucor hiemalis,* a common soil inhabitant, was recovered from an otherwise healthy girl with cutaneous mucormycosis after an insect bite[99] and from a gardener with subcutaneous infection of a finger.[92]

Patients with pulmonary or other forms of mucormycosis can develop skin lesions distant from the site of primary pathology. This secondary cutaneous involvement of the skin is a result of fungemia, which is almost never documented by positive blood cultures and reflects the presence of widely disseminated disease.[51] The involved area is erythematous and painful, with varying degrees of central necrosis.

Gastrointestinal Mucormycosis

Mucormycosis of the gastrointestinal tract is found primarily in patients with extreme malnutrition and is thought to arise from ingestion of the fungi. Reports have highlighted the risk to kidney transplant recipients of gastric mucormycosis.[100,101] All portions of the gastrointestinal tract are susceptible to infection, with the stomach, ileum, and colon being the sites most commonly infected.[102] Because this disease is acute and rapidly fatal, most of the reported cases were diagnosed after the patient died. The initial manifestations of gastrointestinal mucormycosis are abdominal pain and distention associated with nausea and vomiting. Fever and hematochezia may also be found. If the diagnosis is made before death, the patient is often thought to have an intraabdominal abscess. Definitive diagnosis can be made only at surgery with appropriate examination of tissue (see later discussion).

Central Nervous System Mucormycosis

This rare manifestation of mucormycosis occurs in severely debilitated patients. Most often, extension of the fungus from its initial site of invasion in the nose or paranasal sinuses through adjacent bones into the brain is the mode of entry into the central nervous system.[61] This complication is recognizable by decreasing consciousness and development of multiple focal neurologic findings of cranial nerves and motor neurons to the rest of the body.

Occasionally, cerebral mucormycosis may occur after open head trauma, presumably as a result of direct implantation of the fungus at the time of injury,[103] or after intravenous injection of illicit drugs.[104-106] The appearance of a black discharge from the wound heralds necrosis of the underlying dura and brain and should suggest the diagnosis of mucormycosis. Occasional reports of isolated cerebral mucormycosis in patients with leukemia[107] or with no predisposing condition[108] have been published.

Isolated mucormycosis of the brain has also been described in two intravenous drug abusers with AIDS.[109] The appearance of mucormycosis in these patients may reflect the occurrence of cerebral mucormycosis in drug addicts,[104-106] but, as discussed previously, neutropenia complicating AIDS may increase the risk of mucormycosis.

Miscellaneous Forms

Sporadic reports can be found of mucormycosis involving other areas: heart (including endocarditis),[110-113] bones,[7,114-118] kidney,[119] bladder,[120] arterial catheter site with extension to surrounding tissue,[121] mediastinum,[122,123] and trachea.[124] Other reported infections include osteomyelitis of the clivus resulting in chronic meningitis that is caused by parameningeal irritation,[125] superior vena cava syndrome,[126] and possibly bone marrow necrosis in a patient with a *Mucor*-infected renal cyst.[127] A case of allergic sinusitis caused by *Rhizomucor* species presented with a clinical syndrome similar to that of the more common *Aspergillus* sinusitis.[128] Peritonitis in patients undergoing peritoneal dialysis rarely is caused by one of the Mucorales.[129]

Mucormycosis has been reported in patients with human immunodeficiency virus infection, but is usually seen in patients with advanced AIDS, with low CD4+ lymphocyte counts and neutropenia.[47] Various organ systems may be involved and a high degree of suspicion is needed to consider the diagnosis. *Absidia* species, *Rhizopus, Cunninghamella,* and others have been recovered from these patients.

Diagnosis

The hallmarks of disease caused by the Mucorales are vascular invasion and tissue necrosis; black eschars and discharges should be aggressively sought. The presence of a black nasal discharge should not be dismissed as merely dried blood. It may reflect tissue necrosis and may be an important sign of deep infection. Similarly, black necrotic lesions of the nasal mucosa or hard palate may reflect invasive mucormycosis. These manifestations occur only after some time, and attempts at making a diagnosis of mucormycosis should not await the development of necrotic areas. Diagnosis depends on demonstration of the organism in the tissue of a biopsy specimen. Swabs of discharge or abnormal tissue are not appropriate and often result in erroneous information. Fungal hyphae can be seen on potassium hydroxide preparations of touch slides prepared from the biopsy specimen. Fixed tissue can be stained with hematoxylin and eosin, and fungal hyphae can be seen with this routine histologic stain. Grocott methenamine-silver or periodic acid–Schiff (PAS) staining also adequately demarcates fungal elements in tissue in most cases (Fig. 257-7).

Typically, the fungi appear as broad (10 to 20 μm in diameter), nonseptate hyphae with branches occurring at right angles. Rarely, septa can be visualized. The appearance of Mucorales hyphae in tissue is different from that of *Aspergillus, Fusarium,* or *Pseudallescheria* spp., in that the latter organisms appear as thinner, more regularly shaped fungal elements with more frequent, acute-angle branching. These hyphae are also septate. Identification of the genus and species requires culture of tissue and assessment of the morphology of the fungal growth. For unclear reasons, agents of mucormycosis may be difficult to isolate from infected tissue and rarely appear in blood culture.

Affected tissue is typically infiltrated with neutrophils unless the patient is neutropenic. An inflammatory vasculitis involving both arteries and veins is the rule. Tissue necrosis as a result of blood vessel invasion is prominent. Thrombosis and hemorrhage are also commonly found. In more chronic cases, mononuclear cell infiltration is observed, and occasional giant cells may be seen if the infection has been present for a sufficient period.

Antigens that might be useful as reagents in serologic tests have been identified.[130,131] However, serodiagnosis of mucormycosis remains investigational and cannot yet be recommended for routine clinical use.

Differential Diagnosis

There are several other infectious diseases that produce manifestations of tissue necrosis and infarction secondary to direct invasion of the vasculature. Infection with *Aspergillus* is most likely to be confused with the rhinocerebral or pulmonary forms of mucormycosis. The only definitive method of differentiating between these two possibilities is by examination of tissue or culture of a biopsy specimen. Certain aggressive orbital tumors can produce some of the findings of rhinocerebral mucormycosis, but the rapid pace of mucormycosis, the presence of fever, and the evidence of necrosis all favor a fungal cause. Cavernous sinus thrombosis that is caused by extension of staphylococcal lesions of the face can resemble rhinocerebral mucormycosis, but there are no lesions in the nose or paranasal sinuses. Pulmonary mucormycosis can be mistaken for bland pulmonary embolism, but

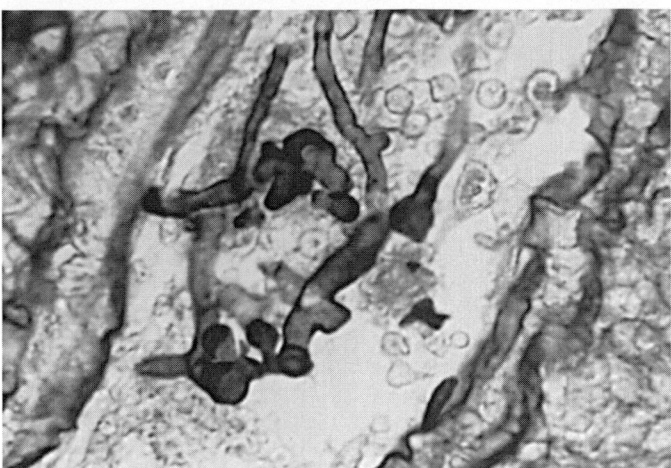

FIGURE 257-7. Photomicrograph of lung demonstrating typical broad, irregularly shaped hyphae with right-angle branching, characteristic of the Mucorales (periodic acid–Schiff stain, ×250). *(Courtesy of Dr. Alayn Waldorf, Oakland, CA.)*

the progressive extension of the fungal lesion distinguishes the two. On rare occasions, patients with acute leukemia develop skin lesions identical to those of ecthyma gangrenosum, which more commonly is caused by *Pseudomonas aeruginosa*. Blood cultures are usually positive in the latter entity.

Therapy and Prevention

As with any opportunistic infection, the first therapeutic maneuver should be to correct the underlying disease. Aggressive correction of hyperglycemia and acidemia should be pursued. If possible, doses of immunosuppressive drugs, including steroids, should be decreased and the drugs stopped. The ultimate outcome of mucormycosis depends, in large part, on the prognosis of the underlying disease and the ability to reverse the predisposing conditions.

The standard therapy for invasive mucormycosis is treatment with amphotericin B. Because the fungus is relatively refractory to medical treatment, the maximum tolerated dose of amphotericin B deoxycholate is usually recommended, typically 1.0 to 1.5 mg/kg/day. High doses are not usually tolerated for more than several days before renal function deteriorates. Several reports have described successful outcomes in patients with rhinocerebral mucormycosis who were treated with lipid preparations of amphotericin B.[132-134]

For mucormycosis the recommended dose of amphotericin B lipid complex (Abelcet) and liposomal amphotericin B (AmBisome) is 5 mg/kg daily. Experts in the treatment of mucormycosis should be sought when faced with a patient with this serious infection.

None of the currently available azoles (ketoconazole, itraconazole, fluconazole, or voriconazole) or echinocandins has a role in the treatment of mucormycosis. A new, broad-spectrum triazole, posaconazole (not yet clinically available), has been shown to be active in a murine model of mucormycosis.[135] In vitro susceptibility testing with posaconazole suggests some difference in susceptibility of different species, with *Absidia* being the most susceptible, but the clinical significance of this difference is unknown.[136,137] Successful use of posaconazole has been reported after initial therapy with amphotericin B and often surgery. Itraconazole was shown to be active in a murine model of *Absidia* and *Apophysomyces*, but inactive against *Rhizopus*, but clinical experience with this drug is limited.[138,139]

The role of colony-stimulating factors as adjuncts to surgical and antifungal therapy still remains unclear, beyond that of increasing the neutrophil count in patients with neutropenia.

Although reports have appeared in the literature of recovery of patients with mucormycosis with antifungal therapy alone,[140-142] these are clearly the exception, and aggressive surgical débridement of necrotic tissue is advisable.[121,144-150] Some patients may recover with minimally disfiguring surgery.[49,56,144,146,151] These patients are probably in the minority, and a well-coordinated medical-surgical approach maximizes the chances of success. Repeated operations may be required for satisfactory removal of continuously appearing necrotic tissue. Frozen section–guided débridement has been advocated as a method for operative intervention and as an alternative to the extensive débridement that has traditionally been performed in patients with invasive mucormycosis.[143] Should the patient survive the acute episode, major reconstructive surgery may also be necessary.[152] Adjunctive oxygen therapy has been considered beneficial in a small number of patients.[153,154] Because of the uncontrolled nature of the observations and the absence of a rationale for treating an obligate aerobic fungus with oxygen, this form of therapy cannot be routinely recommended at present.

In previously normal patients with primary superficial cutaneous involvement, local débridement should be satisfactory. However, with any evidence of progression of the disease beyond the skin into the subcutaneous tissue and muscle, or development of signs and symptoms distant to the focus of infection, systemically administered amphotericin B is advised. Surgical débridement of the primary cutaneous lesion needs to be aggressively performed, and daily (or more frequent) inspection of the wound is mandatory so that necrotic tissue may be removed as soon as possible.[155] The duration of antifungal therapy depends on the response of the infection to treatment and success in resolving the underlying predisposing conditions.

It is almost impossible to determine accurately the effectiveness of any therapeutic approach to mucormycosis. The disease is too rare to warrant appropriately controlled comparative studies, and cases appear in the literature only if therapy is effective. This reporting bias makes generalization of findings in the published literature difficult when attempting to provide the best possible therapy for a given patient. One way of reconciling differences in approach is to assess the extent of infection at the time of diagnosis; early detection can mean less invasion and tissue destruction and therefore less need for extensive removal of devitalized tissue because there are fewer fungi in the tissue. Overall, the earlier the diagnosis of mucormycosis is made, the better the outcome. At present, no one approach is preferred over another, and treatment should be individualized.

It is apparent that two factors determine the outcome in all patients: early diagnosis and resolution of predisposing problems. The overall mortality rate has been about 50%, although higher survival rates (up to 85%) have been reported more recently.[49] Results of treating pulmonary mucormycosis have been poor, probably because diagnosis of this form of mucormycosis is so difficult. By the time the disease is suspected and the diagnosis is made, extensive tissue destruction has occurred, the pace of the disease is rapid, and the general condition of the patient is so poor that medical therapy has minimal effect and surgical options are not possible. Occasionally, surgery alone has appeared to be helpful.[156]

There is no recognized method for preventing systemic infection with the Mucorales. In patients with severe neutropenia, such as those with bone marrow transplant or leukemia, provision of care in rooms equipped with high-efficiency particulate air (HEPA) filters has been shown to reduce the risks of aspergillosis and mucormycosis.[140] However, because of the high cost of this approach and a lack of effect on eventual outcome, most centers do not use such filters in the routine care of these patients. Substitution of hydroxypyridinone chelators for deferoxamine may be one approach to decrease the risk of mucormycosis in patients who require such therapy.[157]

ENTOMOPHTHORAMYCOSIS

The Pathogens

Entomophthoramycosis consist of two different clinical entities caused by different genera of the order Entomophthorales: conidiobolomycosis, caused by *Conidiobolus* spp., and basidiobolomycosis, caused by *Basidiobolus* spp. (see Table 257-1). The former occurs in the head and face and the latter elsewhere in the body, usually the trunk and arms. This nosology is, however, clearly artificial, because

reports of disseminated infection caused by *Conidiobolus* have been published.[158] These rare infections have been reported in the United States,[159-161] Central America,[162] and Australia.[163]

Epidemiology

These fungi are normal inhabitants of soil throughout the world, including the United States.[164] *Basidiobolus ranarum* (also called *B. haptosporus* or *B. meristosporus*) has also been isolated from the gut of amphibians and reptiles, including those found in Florida and other areas of the United States.[165] Isolation of *Basidiobolus ranarum* from a variety of animals in Australia has been documented.[166] However, most reported cases are from Africa,[167] with cases also occurring in India and other parts of Asia.

Pathogenesis

These organisms are ubiquitous in the environment, even in regions where disease caused by the Entomophthorales is almost never found. Entrance into the body via inhalation or direct inoculation has been postulated,[167,168] but proof for this hypothesis is lacking. Likewise, the mechanisms for host resistance to invasive disease are unknown; however, innate immunity must be fairly high, given the low incidence of disease in most areas of the world.

Echetebu and Ononogbu described lipase and proteinase activity in supernatants from *Basidiobolus ranarum (haptosporus).*[169] They postulated that the liberation of lysolecithin from phosphatidylcholine by phospholipase A and a proteinase that can degrade serum proteins may be responsible for the invasive potential of the fungus. Lysolecithin is toxic to mammalian cell membranes, and this may enhance the invasive potential of the organism. However, the ability of the Entomophthorales to produce pathogenetically significant enzymes in vivo is unknown. Moreover, the rarity of disease caused by these agents attests to their low potential for virulence and indicates that some specific abnormality, as yet unknown, must be important in facilitating the initiation and maintenance of infection. The role of nutrition may be important, because most cases are found in less affluent areas of the world.

Clinical Manifestations

Conidiobolomycosis is characterized by swelling of the nose, perinasal tissues, and mouth. This is accompanied by symptoms of nasal stuffiness, drainage, and sinus pain. The infection begins as swelling of the inferior nasal turbinates, with subsequent extension into surrounding structures. Nodular subcutaneous masses can be palpated through intact skin. As the disease progresses, generalized facial swelling occurs and the patient may be unable to open the eyes as a result (Fig. 257-8). Systemic symptoms and signs are conspicuously absent. A particularly lucid and instructive summary of this disease has been published by Martinson.[167]

Basidiobolomycosis also begins as nodular subcutaneous lesions. The lesions are typically firm and are not painful. Most frequently, they are located on the trunk, arms, legs, or buttocks.[170] Deeper invasion of muscle underlying involved subcutaneous disease has been described,[171] as has gastrointestinal involvement.[172] Although the disease may resolve spontaneously, most cases are slowly progressive until appropriate therapy is administered.

Occasionally, disseminated infection occurs.[158] Both a chronic-appearing fibrotic reaction and angioinvasive disease reminiscent of the type of mucormycosis seen in diabetics and immunocompromised patients have been described.

Biopsy of the submucosal or subcutaneous masses of either form of entomophthoramycosis reveals similar histologic features. Acute or chronic inflammatory cells, or both, are found in the vicinity of the typical nonseptate, broad, thin-walled hyphae. Occasional hyphal septations can be observed. The hyphae are readily visible on routine hematoxylin and eosin staining but, in contrast to most other fungal pathogens, are not as well demonstrated by PAS or silver staining. Characteristically, the hyphae are surrounded by eosinophilic material, which can appear in a stellate formation or as a simple sheath sur-

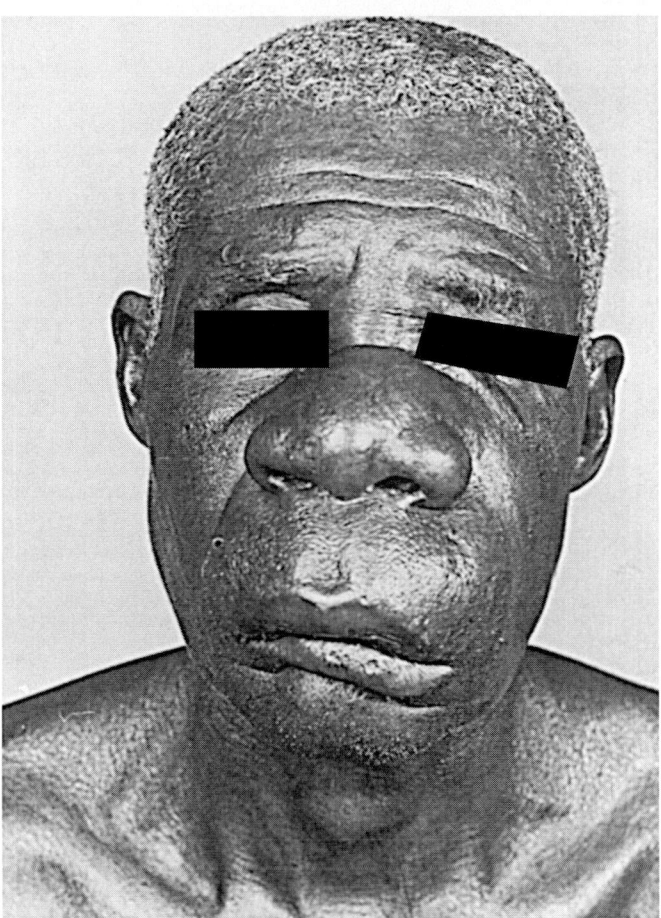

FIGURE 257-8. Photograph of a patient infected with *Conidiobolus* sp. Note the marked swelling of the nose and perinasal tissues extending to the periorbital region. *(Courtesy of Dr. B. C. Okafor, Enugu, Nigeria.)*

method for making the correct diagnosis. The histologic appearance of pythiosis, caused by a fungus-like organism of uncertain taxonomy, *Pythium insidiosum,* is identical to entomophthoramycosis, though the appearance of motile zoospores on water culture of *Pythium* easily distinguishes the two entities.

Therapy and Prevention

Therapeutic recommendations for this disease can be made only on the basis of empirical observations. Potassium iodide, trimethoprim-sulfamethoxazole, imidazoles, triazoles, and amphotericin B have all been used. Anecdotal reports suggest that each of these remedies may work; however, the effect of reporting bias makes the determination of which agent is more efficacious and safer than the others an impossible task. Complicating such analysis of the efficacy of individual treatment regimens is the observation that some cases of entomophthoramycosis, especially those caused by *Basidiobolus* spp., may resolve spontaneously. In patients with chronic infection and without life-threatening complications, any of these antimicrobial agents could be considered for use.[176] Susceptibility testing, as with other fungi, is not reliable and has an uncertain place in guiding therapeutic decisions.[177] One patient infected with *C. coronatus* was apparently cured after receiving ketoconazole (600 mg/day),[178] and others did well while receiving fluconazole[179,180] or itraconazole.[181] However, failures of treatment with azoles have been noted.[173] The role of the newer generation of triazole antifungals is not known.

In addition to medical therapy, a surgical approach to this disease includes removal of accessible nodules and reconstructive surgery to restore a more normal appearance to tissues grossly swollen and deformed by the chronic inflammatory response to the fungus.

Currently, there are no means of preventing this infection or even of identifying those at risk for development of this disease. Therefore, there is no role for the use of prophylactic antifungal agents. Early detection of newly acquired infection seems to be the best hope of reducing the serious morbidity associated with long-standing disease.

rounding the hyphae. This has been termed the *Splendore-Hoeppli phenomenon,* and it is an important histopathologic concomitant of this disease. Similar perihyphal deposition of eosinophilic material can occur with other fungi or parasites. In contrast to the agents of mucormycosis, the Entomophthoraceae do not usually invade blood vessels; tissue infarction and necrosis are not part of the usual pathology seen in this disease. However, reports detail the rare case of invasive disease and tissue destruction that can be observed.[163,173]

Diagnosis

In areas where entomophthoramycosis is relatively common, the diagnosis may be suspected from the clinical appearance of the patient and the lesions. Definitive diagnosis depends on biopsy of the involved site, with microscopic documentation of tissue invasion and the presence of typical hyphae of either genus. Culture of the fungus is the only way to identify correctly the species present in tissue. A preliminary report of an immunodiffusion test for making the diagnosis of *Basidiobolus ranarum* and *Conidiobolus coronatus* infections has appeared,[174] but this has not been confirmed as a useful clinical tool.

Differential Diagnosis

In tropical areas, a variety of diseases can present with submucosal or subcutaneous nodular lesions associated with swelling. Malignancy and abscess must be ruled out. The presentation in one patient was similar to that of Burkitt's lymphoma.[175] Infection with *Sporothrix schenckii, Mycobacterium tuberculosis,* or *Mycobacterium ulcerans* also can mimic entomophthoramycosis. Biopsy of abnormal tissue, with pathologic and microbiologic evaluation, is the most efficient

REFERENCES

1. Kwon-Chung KJ, Bennett JE. Mucormycosis. In: Medical Mycology. Philadelphia: Lea & Febiger; 1992:524-559.
2. Kwon-Chung KJ, Young RC, Orlando M. Pulmonary mucormycosis caused by *Cunninghamella elegans* in a patient with chronic myelogenous leukemia. Am J Clin Pathol. 1975;64:544-548.
3. Kolbeck PC, Makhoul RG, Bollinger RR, et al. Widely disseminated *Cunninghamella* mucormycosis in an adult renal transplant patient: Case report and review of the literature. Am J Clin Pathol. 1985;83:747-753.
4. Torell H, Cooper BH, Helgeson NGP. Disseminated *Saksenaea vasiformis* infection. Am J Clin Pathol. 1981;76:116-121.
5. Gonis G, Starr M. Fatal rhinoorbital mucormycosis caused by *Saksenaea vasiformis* in an immunocompromised child. Pediatr Infect Dis J. 1997;16:714-716.
6. Lakshmi V, Rani TS, Sharma S, et al. Zygomycotic necrotizing fasciitis caused by *Apophysomyces elegans.* J Clin Microbiol. 1993;31:1368-1369.
7. Huffnagle KE, Southern PM Jr, Byrd LT, et al. *Apophysomyces elegans* as an agent of zygomycosis in a patient following trauma. J Med Vet Mycol. 1992;30:83-86.
8. Holland J. Emerging zygomycoses of humans: *Saksenaea vasiformis* and *Apophysomyces elegans.* Curr Top Med Mycol. 1997;8:27-34.
9. Gartenberg G, Bottone EJ, Keusch GT, et al. Hospital-acquired mucormycosis (*Rhizopus rhizopodiformis*) of skin and subcutaneous tissue: Epidemiology, mycology and treatment. N Engl J Med. 1978;299:1115-1117.
10. Dennis JE, Rhodes KH, Cooney DR, et al. Nosocomial *Rhizopus* infection (zygomycosis) in children. J Pediatr. 1980;96:824-828.
11. Mead JH, Lupton GP, Dillavou CL, et al. Cutaneous *Rhizopus* infection: Occurrence as a postoperative complication associated with an elasticized adhesive dressing. JAMA. 1979;242:272-274.
12. Mitchell SJ, Gray J, Morgan MEI, et al. Nosocomial infection with *Rhizopus microsporus* in preterm infants: Association with wooden tongue depressors. Lancet. 1996;34:441-443.
13. Verweij PE, Voss A, Donnelly JP, et al. Wooden sticks as the source of a pseudoepidemic of infection with *Rhizopus microsporus* var. *rhizopodiformis* among immunocompromised patients. J Clin Microbiol. 1997;35:2422-2423.
14. Paydas S, Yavuz S, Disel U, et al. Mucormycosis of the tongue in a patient with acute lymphoblastic leukemia: A possible relation with use of a tongue depressor. Am J Med. 2003;114:618-620.
15. Blair JE, Fredrikson LJ, Pockaj BA, Lucaire CS. Locally invasive cutaneous *Apophysomyces elegans* infection acquired from snapdragon patch test. Mayo Clin Proc. 2002;77:717-720.

16. Singh N, Gayowski T, Singh J, Yu VL. Invasive gastrointestinal zygomycosis in a liver transplant recipient: Case report and review of zygomycosis in solid-organ transplant recipients. Clin Infect Dis. 1995;20:617-620.

17. Marr K, Carter RA, Crippa F, et al. Epidemiology and outcome of mould infections in hematopoietic stem cell transplant recipients. Clin Infect Dis. 2002;34:909-917.

18. Lee DG, Choi JH, Choi SM, et al. Two cases of disseminated mucormycosis in patients following allogeneic bone marrow transplantation. J Korean Med Sci. 2002;17:403-406.

19. Al-Asiri RH, Van Dijken PJ, Mahmood MA, et al. Isolated hepatic mucormycosis in an immunocompetent child. Am J Gastroenterol. 1996;91:606-607.

20. Butala A, Shah B, Cho YT, Schmidt MF. Isolated pulmonary mucormycosis in an apparently normal host: A case report. J Natl Med Assoc. 1995;87:572-574.

21. Larsen K, Buchwald C, Ellefsen B, Francis D. Unexpected expansive paranasal sinus mucormycosis. J Otorhinolaryngol Relat Spec. 2003;65:57-60.

22. Waldorf AR, Halde C, Vedros NA. Murine model of pulmonary mucormycosis in cortisone-treated mice. Sabouraudia. 1982;20:217-224.

23. Waldorf AR, Ruderman N, Diamond RD. Specific susceptibility to mucormycosis in murine diabetes and bronchoalveolar macrophage defense against Rhizopus. J Clin Invest. 1984;74:150-160.

24. Waldorf AR, Peter L, Polak A. Mucormycotic infection in mice following prolonged incubation of spores in vivo and the role of spore agglutinating antibodies on spore germination. Sabouraudia. 1984;22:101-108.

25. Reinhardt DJ, Licata I, Kaplan W, et al. Experimental cerebral zygomycosis in alloxan-diabetic rabbits: Variation in virulence among Zygomycetes. Sabouraudia. 1981;19:245-255.

26. Schaffner A, Davis CE, Schaffner T, et al. In vitro susceptibility of fungi to killing by neutrophil granulocytes discriminates between primary pathogenicity and opportunism. J Clin Invest. 1986;78:511-524.

27. Waldorf AR, Levitz SM, Diamond RD. In vivo bronchoalveolar macrophage defense against Rhizopus oryzae and Aspergillus fumigatus. J Infect Dis. 1984;150:752-760.

28. Chinn RYW, Diamond RD. Generation of chemotactic factors by Rhizopus oryzae in the presence and absence of serum: Relationship to hyphal damage mediated by human neutrophils and effects of hyperglycemia and ketoacidosis. Infect Immun. 1982;38:1123-1129.

29. Marx RS, Forsyth KR, Hentz ZK. Mucorales species activation of a serum leukotactic factor. Infect Immun. 1982;38:1217-1222.

30. Diamond RD, Haudenschild CC, Erickson NF III. Monocyte-mediated damage to Rhizopus oryzae hyphae in vitro. Infect Immun. 1982;38:292-297.

31. Ganz T, Selsted ME, Szklarek D, et al. Defensins: Natural peptide antibiotics of human neutrophils. J Clin Invest. 1985;76:1427-1435.

32. Levitz SM, Selsted ME, Ganz T, et al. In vitro killing of spores and hyphae of Aspergillus fumigatus and Rhizopus oryzae by rabbit neutrophil cationic peptides and bronchoalveolar macrophages. J Infect Dis. 1986;154:483-489.

33. Espinoza CG, Halkias DG. Pulmonary mucormycosis as a complication of chronic salicylate poisoning. Am J Clin Pathol. 1983;80:508-511.

34. Wong KL, Tai YT, Loke SL, et al. Disseminated zygomycosis masquerading as cerebral lupus erythematosus. Am J Clin Pathol. 1986;86:546-549.

35. Gale GR, Welch A. Studies of opportunistic fungi: I. Inhibition of R. oryzae by human sera. Am J Med Sci. 1961;45:604-612.

36. Owens AW, Hacklette MS, Baker RD. An antifungal factor in human serum: I. Studies of Rhizopus rhizopodiformis. Sabouraudia. 1965;4:179.

37. Artis WM, Fountain JA, Delcher HK, et al. A mechanism of susceptibility to mucormycosis in diabetic ketoacidosis: Transferrin and iron availability. Diabetes. 1982;31:1109-1114.

38. Artis WM, Patrusky E, Rastinejad F, et al. Fungistatic mechanism of human transferrin for R. oryzae and Trichophyton mentagrophytes: Alternative to simple iron deprivation. Infect Immun. 1983;41:1269-1278.

39. Maloisel F, Dufour P, Waller J, et al. Cunninghamella bertholletiae: An uncommon agent of opportunistic fungal infection: Case report and review. Nouv Rev Fr Hematol. 1991;33:311-315.

40. Boelaert JR, de Locht M, Van Cutsem J, et al. Mucormycosis during deferoxamine therapy is a siderophore-mediated infection: In vitro and in vivo animal studies. J Clin Invest. 1993;91:1979-1986.

41. Vlasveld LT, van Asbeck BS. Treatment with deferoxamine: A real risk factor for mucormycosis? Nephron. 1991;57:487-488.

42. Smith AG, Bustamante CI, Gilmor GD. Zygomycosis (absidiomycosis) in an AIDS patient. Mycopathologia. 1989;105:7-10.

43. Vesa J, Bielsa O, Arango O, et al. Massive renal infarction due to mucormycosis in an AIDS patient. Infection. 1992;20:234-236.

44. Hopwood V, Hicks DA, Thomas S, et al. Primary cutaneous zygomycosis due to Absidia corymbifera in a patient with AIDS. J Med Vet Mycol. 1992;30:399-402.

45. Diamond HJ, Phelps RG, Gordon ML, et al. Combined Aspergillus and zygomycotic (Rhizopus) infection in a patient with acquired immunodeficiency syndrome: Presentation as inflammatory tinea capitis. J Am Acad Dermatol. 1992;26:1017-1018.

46. Blatt SP, Lucey DR, DeHoff D, et al. Rhinocerebral zygomycosis in a patient with AIDS. J Infect Dis. 1991;164:215-216.

47. Nagy-Agren SE, Chu P, Smith GJ, et al. Zygomycosis (mucormycosis) and HIV infection: Report of three cases and review. J Acquir Immune Defic Syndr Hum Retrovirol. 1995;10:441-449.

48. Bouchara J-P, Oumeziane NA, Lissitzky J-C, et al. Attachment of spores of the human pathogenic fungus Rhizopus oryzae to extracellular matrix components. Eur J Cell Biol. 1996;70:76-83.

49. Parfrey NA. Improved diagnosis and prognosis of mucormycosis: A clinicopathologic study of 33 cases. Medicine (Baltimore). 1986;65:113-123.

50. Myskowski PL, Brown AE, Dinsmore R, et al. Mucormycosis following bone marrow transplantation. J Am Acad Dermatol. 1983;9:111-115.

51. Meyer RD, Kaplan MH, Ong M, et al. Cutaneous lesions in disseminated mucormycosis. JAMA. 1973;225:737-738.

52. St-Germain G, Robert A, Ishak M, et al. Infection due to Rhizomucor pusillus: Report of four cases in patients with leukemia and review. Clin Infect Dis. 1993;16:640-645.

53. Peterson KL, Wang M, Canalis RF, Abemayor E. Rhinocerebral mucormycosis: Evolution of the disease and treatment options. Laryngoscope. 1997;107:855-862.

54. Yanagisawa E, Friedman S, Kundargi RS, et al. Rhinocerebral phycomycosis. Laryngoscope. 1977;87:1319-1335.

55. Pillsbury JC, Fischer ND. Rhinocerebral mucormycosis. Arch Otolaryngol. 1977;103:600-604.

56. Meyers BR, Wormser G, Hirschman SZ, et al. Rhinocerebral mucormycosis: Premortem diagnosis and therapy. Arch Intern Med. 1979;139:557-560.

57. England AC III, Weinstein M, Ellner JJ, et al. Two cases of rhinocerebral zygomycosis (mucormycosis) with common epidemiologic and environmental features. Am Rev Respir Dis. 1981;124:497-498.

58. Abedi E, Sismanis A, Choi K, et al. Twenty-five years' experience treating cerebro-rhino-orbital mucormycosis. Laryngoscope. 1984;94:1060-1062.

59. Morduchowicz G, Shmueli D, Shapira Z, et al. Rhinocerebral mucormycosis in renal transplant recipients: Report of three cases and review of the literature. Rev Infect Dis. 1986;8:441-446.

60. Torre Cisneros J, Kusne S, Martin M, et al. Rhinocerebral mucormycosis after liver transplantation. Transplant Sci. 1992;2:63-64.

61. Berthier M, Palmieri O, Lylyk P, et al. Rhino-orbital phycomycosis complicated by cerebral abscess. Neuroradiology. 1982;22:221-224.

62. Price DL, Wolpow ER, Richardson EP Jr. Intracranial phycomycosis: A clinico-pathological and radiological study. J Neurol Sci. 1971;14:359-375.

63. Lowe JT Jr, Hudson WR. Rhinocerebral phycomycosis and internal carotid artery thrombosis. Arch Otolaryngol. 1975;101:100-103.

64. Lazo A, Wilner HI, Metes JJ. Craniofacial mucormycosis: Computed tomographic and angiographic findings in two cases. Radiology. 1981;139:623-626.

65. Greenberg MR, Lippman SM, Grinnell VS, et al. Computed tomographic findings in orbital Mucor. West J Med. 1985;143:102-103.

66. Boelaert JR, Vergauwe PL, Vandepitte JM. Mucormycosis infection in dialysis patients. Ann Intern Med. 1987;107:782-783.

67. McNab A, McKelvie P. Iron overload is a risk factor for zygomycosis. Arch Ophthalmol. 1997;115:919-921.

68. Gaziev D, Baronciani D, Galimberti M, et al. Mucormycosis after bone marrow transplantation: Report of four cases in thalassemia and review of the literature. Bone Marrow Transplant. 1996;17:409-414.

69. Windus DW, Stokes TJ, Julian BA, et al. Fatal Rhizopus infections in hemodialysis patients receiving deferoxamine. Ann Intern Med. 1987;107:678-680.

70. Kaneko T, Abe F, Ito M, et al. Intestinal mucormycosis in a hemodialysis patient treated with desferrioxamine. Acta Pathol Jpn. 1991;41:561-566.

71. Rex JH, Ginsberg AM, Fries LF, et al. Cunninghamella bertholletiae infection associated with deferoxamine therapy. Rev Infect Dis. 1988;10:1187-1194.

72. Finn DG, Farmer JC Jr. Chronic mucormycosis. Laryngoscope. 1982;92:761-763.

73. Ferstenfeld JE, Cohen SH, Rose HD, et al. Chronic cerebral phycomycosis in association with diabetes. Postgrad Med J. 1977;53:337-342.

74. Harrison AR, Wirtschafter JD. Ocular neuromyotonia in a patient with cavernous sinus thrombosis secondary to mucormycosis. Am J Ophthalmol. 1997;124:122-123.

75. Spira A, Brecher S, Karlinsky J. Pulmonary mucormycosis in the setting of chronic obstructive pulmonary disease: A case report and review of the literature. Respiration. 2003;69:560-563.

76. Bhowmik D, Dinda AK, Khilnani GC, et al. Pulmonary mucormycosis in a diabetic renal transplant patient. Indian J Chest Dis Allied Sci. 2002;44:275-277.

77. Harada M, Manabe T, Yamashita K, et al. Pulmonary mucormycosis with fatal massive hemoptysis. Acta Pathol Jpn. 1992;42:49-55.

78. Watts WJ. Bronchopleural fistula followed by massive fatal hemoptysis in a patient with pulmonary mucormycosis: A case report. Arch Intern Med. 1983;143:1029-1030.

79. Tedder M, Spratt JA, Anstadt MP, et al. Pulmonary mucormycosis: Results of medical and surgical therapy. Ann Thorac Surg. 1994;57:1044-1050.

80. McAdams HP, Rosado de Christenson M, Strollo DC, Patz EF Jr. Pulmonary mucormycosis: Radiologic findings in 32 cases. AJR Am J Roentgenol. 1997;168:1541-1548.

81. Gale AM, Kleitsch WP. Solitary pulmonary nodule due to phycomycosis (mucormycosis). Chest. 1972;62:752-755.

82. Matsushima T, Soejima R, Nakashima T. Solitary pulmonary nodule caused by phycomycosis in a patient without obvious predisposing factors. Thorax. 1980;35:877-878.

83. Butala A, Shah B, Cho YT, Schmidt FJ. Isolated pulmonary mucormycosis in an apparently normal host: A case report. J Natl Med Assoc. 1995;87:572-574.

84. Loevner LA, Andrews JC, Francis IR. Multiple mycotic pulmonary artery aneurysms: A complication of invasive mucormycosis. AJR Am J Roentgenol. 1992;158:761-762.

85. Brown RB, Johnson JH, Kessinger JM, et al. Bronchovascular mucormycosis in the diabetic: An urgent surgical problem. Ann Thorac Surg. 1992;53:854-855.

86. Coffey MJ, Fantone J III, Stirling MC, et al. Pseudoaneurysm of pulmonary artery in mucormycosis: Radiographic characteristics and management. Am Rev Respir Dis. 1992;145:1487-1490.

87. Aderka A, Sidi Y, Garfinkel D, et al. Roentgenologically invisible mucormycosis pneumonia. Respiration. 1983;44:158-160.

88. Rothstein RD, Simon GL. Subacute pulmonary mucormycosis. J Med Vet Mycol. 1986;24:391-394.

89. Wirth F, Perry R, Eskenazi A, et al. Cutaneous mucormycosis with subsequent visceral dissemination in a child with neutropenia: A case report and review of the pediatric literature. J Am Acad Dermatol. 1996;35:336-341.
90. Jain JK, Markowitz A, Khilanani PV, et al. Case report: Localized mucormycosis following intramuscular corticosteroid. Case report and review of the literature. Am J Med Sci. 1978;275:209-216.
91. Rothburn MM, Chambers DK, Roberts C, et al. Cutaneous mucormycosis: A rare cause of leg ulceration. J Infect. 1986;13:175-178.
92. Costa AR, Porto E, Tayah M, et al. Subcutaneous mucormycosis caused by *Mucor hiemalis* Wehmer f. luteus (Linnemann) Schipper 1973. Mycoses. 1990;33:241-246.
93. Hicks WL Jr, Nowels K, Troxel J. Primary cutaneous mucormycosis. Am J Otolaryngol. 1995;16:265-268.
94. Paparello SF, Parry RL, MacGillivray DC, et al. Hospital-acquired wound mucormycosis. Clin Infect Dis. 1992;14:350-352.
95. Vainrub B, Macareno H, Mandel S, et al. Wound zygomycosis (mucormycosis) in otherwise healthy adults. Am J Med. 1988;84:546-548.
96. Rabin ER, Lundberg GD, Mitchell ET. Mucormycosis in severely burned patients: Report of two cases with extensive destruction of the face and nasal cavity. N Engl J Med. 1961;264:1286-1289.
97. Chakrabarti A, Ghosh A, Prasad GS, et al. Apophysimyces elegans: An emerging zygomycete in India. J Clin Microbiol. 2003;41:783-788.
98. Tanphaichitr VS, Chaiprasert A, Suvatte V, et al. Subcutaneous mucormycosis caused by *Saksenaea vasiformis* in a thalassaemic child: First case report in Thailand. Mycoses. 1990;33:303-309.
99. Prevoo RLMA, Starink TM, de Haan P. Primary cutaneous mucormycosis in a healthy young girl. J Am Acad Dermatol. 1991;24:882-885.
100. Winkler S, Susani S, Willinger B, et al. Gastric mucormycosis due to *Rhizopus oryzae* in a renal transplant recipient. J Clin Microbiol. 1996;34:2585-2587.
101. Martinez EJ, Cancio MR, Sinnott JT IV, et al. Nonfatal gastric mucormycosis in a renal transplant recipient. South Med J. 1997;90:341-344.
102. Thomson SR, Bade PG, Taams M, Chrystal V. Gastrointestinal mucormycosis. Br J Surg. 1991;78:952-954.
103. Ignelzi RJ, VanderArk GD. Cerebral mucormycosis following open head trauma: Case report. J Neurosurg. 1975;42:593-596.
104. Hameroff SB, Eckholdt JW, Lindenberg R. Cerebral phycomycosis in a heroin addict. Neurology. 1970;20:261-265.
105. Pierce PF Jr, Soloman SL, Kaufman L, et al. Zygomycetes brain abscesses in narcotic addicts with serological diagnosis. JAMA. 1982;248:2881-2882.
106. Woods KF, Hanna BJ. Brain stem mucormycosis in a narcotic addict with eventual recovery. Am J Med. 1986;80:126-128.
107. Bachor R, Baczako K, Kern W. Isolated cerebral mucormycosis in a patient with leukemia. Mykosen. 1986;29:497-501.
108. Watson DF, Stern BJ, Levin ML, et al. Isolated cerebral phycomycosis presenting as focal encephalitis. Arch Neurol. 1985;42:922-923.
109. Cuadrado LM, Guerrero A, Lopez Garcia Asenjo JA, et al. Cerebral mucormycosis in two cases of acquired immunodeficiency syndrome. Arch Neurol. 1988;45:109-111.
110. Virmani R, Connor D, McAllister HA. A report of five patients and review of 14 previously reported cases. Am J Clin Pathol. 1982;78:42-47.
111. Merchant RK, Louria B, Geisler PH, et al. Fungal endocarditis: Review of the literature and report of three cases. Ann Intern Med. 1958;48:242-266.
112. Khica GJ, Berroya RB, Escano FB, et al. Mucormycosis in a mitral prosthesis. J Thorac Cardiovasc Surg. 1972;63:903-905.
113. Tuder RM. Myocardial infarct in disseminated mucormycosis: Case report with special emphasis on the pathogenic mechanisms. Mycopathologia. 1985;89:81-88.
114. Echols RM, Selinger DS, Hallowell C, et al. *Rhizopus* osteomyelitis: A case report and review. Am J Med. 1979;66:141-145.
115. Gussen R, Canalis RF. Mucormycosis of the temporal bone. Ann Otol Rhinol Laryngol. 1982;91:27-32.
116. Maliwan N, Reyes CV, Rippon JW. Osteomyelitis secondary to cutaneous mucormycosis: Report of a case and a review of the literature. Am J Dermatopathol. 1984;6:479-481.
117. Brown OE, Finn R. Mucormycosis of the mandible. J Oral Maxillofac Surg. 1986;44:132-136.
118. Pierce PF, Wood MB, Roberts GD Jr, et al. *Saksenaea vasiformis* osteomyelitis. J Clin Microbiol. 1987;25:933-935.
119. Davila R, Moser SA, Grosso LE. Renal mucormycosis: A case report and review of the literature. J Urol. 1991;145:1242-1244.
120. Axelrod P, Kwon-Chung KJ, Frawley P, et al. Chronic cystitis due to *Cokeromyces recurvatus*: A case report. J Infect Dis. 1987;155:1062-1064.
121. Oberle AD, Penn RL. Nosocomial invasive *Saksenaea vasiformis* infection. Am J Clin Pathol. 1983;80:885-888.
122. Leong ASY. Granulomatous mediastinitis due to *Rhizopus* species. Am J Clin Pathol. 1978;70:103-107.
123. Connor BA, Anderson RJ, Smith JW. Mucor mediastinitis. Chest. 1979;75:524-526.
124. Andrews DR, Allan A, Larbalestier RI. Tracheal mucormycosis. Ann Thorac Surg. 1997;63:230-232.
125. Jones PG, Gilman RM, Medeiros AA, et al. Focal intracranial mucormycosis presenting as chronic meningitis. JAMA. 1981;246:2063-2064.
126. Helenglass G, Elliott JA, Lucie NP. An unusual presentation of opportunistic mucormycosis. Br Med J (Clin Res Ed). 1981;282:108-109.
127. Caraveo J, Trowbridge AA, Amaral BW, et al. Bone marrow necrosis associated with a mucor infection. Am J Med. 1977;62:404-408.
128. Goldstein MF, Dvorin DJ, Dunsky EH, et al. Allergic *Rhizomucor* sinusitis. J Allergy Clin Immunol. 1992;90:394-404.
129. Nannini EC, Paphitou NI, Ostrosky-Zeichner L. Peritonitis due to *Aspergillus* and Zygomycetes in patients undergoing peritoneal dialysis: Report of 2 cases and review of the literature. Diagn Microbiol Infect Dis. 2003;46:49-54.
130. Levy SA, Schmitt KW, Kaufman L. Systemic zygomycosis diagnosed by fine needle aspiration and confirmed with enzyme immunoassay. Chest. 1986;89:146-148.
131. Wysong DR, Waldorf AR. Electrophoretic and immunoblot analyses of *Rhizopus arrhizus* antigens. J Clin Microbiol. 1987;25:358-363.
132. Strasser MD, Kennedy RJ, Adam RD. Rhinocerebral mucormycosis: Therapy with amphotericin B lipid complex. Arch Intern Med. 1996;156:337-339.
133. Munckhof W, Jones R, Tosolini FA, et al. Cure of *Rhizopus* sinusitis in a liver transplant recipient with liposomal amphotericin B. Clin Infect Dis. 1993;16:183.
134. Ericsson M, Anniko M, Gustafsson H, et al. A case of chronic progressive rhinocerebral mucormycosis treated with liposomal amphotericin B and surgery. Clin Infect Dis. 1993;16:585-586.
135. Sun QN, Najvar LK, Bocanegra R, et al. In vivo activity of posaconazole against Mucor spp. in an immunosuppressed-mouse model. Antimicrob Agents Chemother. 2003;46:2310-2312.
136. Pfaller MA, Messer SA, Hollis RJ, et al. Antifungal activities of posaconazole, ravuconazole, and voriconazole compared to those of itraconazole and amphotericin B against 239 clinical isolates of Aspergillus spp. and other filamentous fungi: Report from SENTRY Antimicrobial Surveillance Program, 2000. Antimicrob Agents Chemother. 2002;46:1032-1037.
137. Sun QN, Fothergill AW, McCarthy DI, et al. In vitro activities of posaconazole, voriconazole, amphotericin B, and fluconazole against 37 clinical isolates of zygomycetes. Antimicrob Agents Chemother. 2002;46:1581-1582.
138. Dannaoui E, Mouton JW, Meis JF, et al. Efficacy of antifungal therapy in a nonneutropenic murine model of zygomycosis. Antimicrob Agents Chemother. 2002;46:1953-1959.
139. Hunter AJ, Bryant RE. Abdominal wall mucormycosis successfully treated with amphotericin and itraconazole. J Infect. 2002;44:203-204.
140. Bogard BN. Pulmonary mucormycosis. N Engl J Med. 1972;286:606.
141. Hauch TW. Pulmonary mucormycosis: Another cure. Chest. 1977;72:92-93.
142. Brown JF Jr, Gottlieb LS, McCormick RA. Pulmonary and rhinocerebral mucormycosis: Successful outcome with amphotericin B and griseofulvin therapy. Arch Intern Med. 1977;137:936-938.
143. Langford JD, McCartney DL, Wang RC. Frozen section-guided surgical debridement for management of rhino-orbital mucormycosis. Am J Ophthalmol. 1997;124:265-267.
144. Henriquez M, Levy R, Raja RM, et al. Mucormycosis in a renal transplant recipient with successful outcome. JAMA. 1979;242:1397-1399.
145. Rosenberger RS, West BC, King JW. Case report: Survival from sino-orbital mucormycosis due to *Rhizopus rhizopodiformis*. Am J Med Sci. 1983;286:25-30.
146. Smith JL, Stevens DA. Survival in cerebro-rhino-orbital zygomycosis and cavernous sinus thrombosis with combined therapy. South Med J. 1986;79:501-504.
147. West BC, Kwon-Chung KJ, King JW, et al. Inguinal abscess caused by *Rhizopus rhizopodiformis*: Successful treatment with surgery and amphotericin B. J Clin Microbiol. 1983;18:1384-1387.
148. Hamill R, Oney LA, Crane LR. Successful therapy for rhinocerebral mucormycosis with associated bilateral brain abscesses. Arch Intern Med. 1983;143:581-583.
149. Breiman A, Sadowsky D, Friedman J. Mucormycosis: Discussion and report of a case involving the maxillary sinus. Oral Surg Oral Med Oral Pathol. 1981;52:375-378.
150. Rakover Y, Vered I, Garzuzi H, et al. Rhinocerebral phycomycosis: Combined approach therapy. Case Report. J Laryngol Otol. 1985;99:1279-1280.
151. Kohn R, Hepler R. Management of limited rhino-orbital mucormycosis without exenteration. Ophthalmology. 1985;92:1440-1444.
152. Kaplan AL, Huerta AR, Chiou SJ. Rhinocerebral mucormycosis. West J Med. 1981;135:326-329.
153. de la Paz MA, Patrinely JR, Marines HM, et al. Adjunctive hyperbaric oxygen in the treatment of bilateral cerebro-rhino-orbital mucormycosis. Am J Ophthalmol. 1992;114:208-211.
154. Ferguson BJ, Mitchell TG, Moon R, et al. Adjunctive hyperbaric oxygen for treatment of rhinocerebral mucormycosis. Rev Infect Dis. 1988;10:551-559.
155. Losee JE, Selber J, Vega S, et al. Primary cutaneous mucormycosis: Guide to surgical management. Ann Plast Surg. 2002;49:385-390.
156. Bribetz AR, Chuang MT, Burrows L, et al. *Rhizopus* lung abscess in renal transplant patient successfully treated by lobectomy. Chest. 1980;77:102-104.
157. Boelaert JR, VanCutsem J, deLocht M, et al. Deferoxamine augments growth and pathogenicity of *Rhizopus*, while hydroxypyridinone chelators have no effect. Kidney Int. 1994;45:667-671.
158. Walsh TJ, Renshaw G, Andrews J, et al. Invasive zygomycosis due to *Conidiobolus incongruus*. Clin Infect Dis. 1994;19:423-430.
159. Nathan MD Jr, Keller AR, Lerner CJ, et al. Entomophthorales infection of the maxillofacial region. Laryngoscope. 1982;92:767-769.
160. Dworzack DL, Pollock AS, Hodges GR, et al. Zygomycosis of the maxillary sinus and palate caused by *Basidiobolus haptosporus*. Arch Intern Med. 1978;138:1274-1276.
161. Akpunonu BE, Ansel G, Karurich JD, et al. Zygomycosis mimicking paranasal malignancy. Am J Trop Med Hyg. 1991;45:390-398.
162. Segura JJ, Gonzalez K, Berrocal J, et al. Rhinoentomophthoramycosis: Report of the first two cases observed in Costa Rica (Central America), and review of the literature. Am J Trop Med Hyg. 1981;30:1078-1084.
163. Davis SR, Ellis DH, Goldwater P, et al. First human culture-proven Australian case of entomophthoromycosis caused by *Basidiobolus ranarum*. J Med Vet Mycol. 1994;32:225-230.

164. Greer DL, Friedman L. Studies on the genus *Basidiobolus* with reclassification on the species pathogenic for man. Sabouraudia. 1966;4:231-241.

165. Nelson RT, Cochrane BJ, Delis PR, et al. Basidioboliasis in anurans in Florida. J Wildl Dis. 2002;38:463-467.

166. Zahari P, Hirst RG, Shipton WA, et al. The origin and pathogenicity of *Basidiobolus* species in northern Australia. J Med Vet Mycol. 1990;28:461-468.

167. Martinson FD. Clinical epidemiological and therapeutic aspects of entomophthoramycosis. Ann Soc Belg Med Trop. 1972;52:329-342.

168. Herstoff JK, Bogaars H, McDonald CJ. Rhinophycomycosis entomophtorae. Arch Dermatol. 1978;114:1674-1678.

169. Echetebu CO, Ononogbu IC. Extracellular lipase and proteinase of *Basidiobolus haptosporus*: Possible role in subcutaneous mycosis. Mycopathologia. 1982;80:171-177.

170. Antonelli M, Vignetti P, Dahir M, et al. Entomophthoramycosis due to *Basidiobolus* in Somalia. Trans R Soc Trop Med Hyg. 1987;81:186-187.

171. Kamalam A, Thambiah AS. Muscle invasion by *Basidiobolus haptosporus*. Sabouraudia. 1984;22:273-277.

172. Schmidt JR, Howard RJ, Chen JL, et al. First culture-proven gastrointestinal entomophthoromycosis in the United States: A case report and review of the literature. Mycopathologia. 1986;95:101-104.

173. Fournier S, Dupont B, Begue P, et al. Infection rhino-faciale a *Conidiobolus coronatus* avec lyse osseuse et adénomégalie: Difficultés thérapeutiques. J Mycol Méd. 1995;5(Suppl 1):35-39.

174. Kaufman L, Mendoza L, Standard PG. Immunodiffusion test for serodiagnosing subcutaneous zygomycosis. J Clin Microbiol. 1990;28:1887-1890.

175. Bittencourt AL, Serra G, Sadigursky M, et al. Subcutaneous zygomycosis caused by *Basidiobolus haptosporus*: Presentation of a case mimicking Burkitt's lymphoma. Am J Trop Med Hyg. 1982;31:370-373.

176. Taylor GD, Sekhon AS, Tyrrell DLJ, et al. Rhinofacial zygomycosis caused by *Conidiobolus coronatus*: A case report including in vitro sensitivity to antimycotic agents. Am J Trop Med Hyg. 1987;36:398-401.

177. Yangco BG, Okafor JI, TeStrake D. In vitro susceptibilities of human and wild-type isolates of *Basidiobolus* and *Conidiobolus* species. Antimicrob Agents Chemother. 1984;25:413-416.

178. Chauvin JL, Drouhet E, Dupont B. Nouveau cas de rhino-entomophthoramycose: Gueiron par le ketoconazole. Ann Otolaryngol (Paris). 1982;99:563-568.

179. Costa AR, Porto E, Pegas JRP, et al. Rhinofacial zygomycosis caused by *Conidiobolum* [sic] *coronatus*: A case report. Mycopathologia. 1991;115:1-8.

180. Gugnani HC. Fluconazole in the therapy of tropical deep mycoses. In: Abstracts of the XII Congress of the International Society for Human and Animal Mycology, PO2.59, Adelaide, Australia, March 1994.

181. Shaoxi W, Ningru G, Guixiz L, et al. Basidiobolomycosis in China successfully treated with itraconazole. J Mycol Méd. 1997;7:40-42.

CHAPTER **258**

Sporothrix schenckii

JOHN H. REX

PABLO C. OKHUYSEN

Sporotrichosis usually begins when the causative agent, *Sporothrix schenckii,* is inoculated into a site of a minor skin injury and produces an ulcerated, verrucous, or erythematous nodule, sometimes associated with local lymphatic spread. On rare occasions the fungus is inhaled and causes a granulomatous pneumonitis that often cavitates, producing a clinical pattern very similar to tuberculosis. The fungus may also disseminate hematogenously and cause isolated osteoarticular, central nervous system, or ocular lesions in the normal host or widespread, multifocal disease in the immunosuppressed host.

MYCOLOGY

S. schenckii is a dimorphic fungus that exists in a hyphal form in vitro at temperatures less than 37° C. Colonies are initially white, but gradually become brown to black as a result of the production of pigmented conidia. In vivo or at 37° C on rich media such as brain-heart infusion, the organism converts to an oval- or cigar-shaped budding yeast. Along with the characteristic morphology of the sporulating mould, identification is based on demonstration of this conversion to a yeast form. The

variety *S. schenckii* var. *luriei* has been rarely isolated from humans and differs by producing a variety of unusual shapes in vivo.[1]

EPIDEMIOLOGY

Sporotrichosis has been reported from locations around the globe, but most case reports come from the tropical and subtropical regions of the Americas.[2] Regions of hyperendemicity are known.[3] *S. schenckii* is most often isolated from soil, plants, or plant products such as straw, wood, sphagnum moss, and thorny plants, though the fungus is not a plant pathogen. Scratches on exposed skin of florists, rose gardeners, horticulturalists, farmers, miners, and armadillo hunters have increased risk of infection.[2,4,5] Because most cases appear to be due to occupational or avocational exposure to these materials, typically in the form of gardening or farming, patients with suggestive syndromes should be asked about these activities. Cases of animal-to-human transmission involving squirrels, horses, dogs, cats, pigs, mules, insects, and birds have been described,[6,7] as well as one case in which sporotrichosis was apparently transmitted from the infected cheek of a mother to her infant.[8]

CLINICAL SYNDROMES

Infections caused by *S. schenckii* can be divided into several syndromes. The lymphocutaneous forms are the most common.

Lymphocutaneous Sporotrichosis

Cutaneous disease arises at sites of minor trauma and inoculation of the fungus into the skin. The initial lesion is most often on a distal extremity, but almost any site may be involved, including such central locations as the nose and the ocular adnexa.[9,10] This preference for cooler parts of the body corresponds to the known intolerance of some strains of *S. schenckii* to growth at 37° C.[11] Initial lesions are papulonodular, often erythematous, and range in size from a few millimeters to 2 to 4 cm. The lesions may be smooth or verrucous, and they often ulcerate and develop raised erythematous borders.[9] Secondary lesions may develop proximally along lymphatic channels—these secondary lesions evolve in the same fashion as the primary lesion (Fig. 258-1). Secondary lesions do not usually involve a lymph node, although lymphadenopathy may develop. The lesions are typically painless, even after they ulcerate. The fixed, or plaque, form of sporotrichosis differs by not demonstrating any tendency to spread locally. Although spontaneous resolution of fixed sporotrichosis has been described,[9] the lesions of sporotrichosis usually wax and wane over months to years. The patient will not have systemic symptoms and laboratory examinations will be normal.

The indolent progression and physical examination features that suggest both lymphocutaneous and fixed sporotrichosis are also pro-

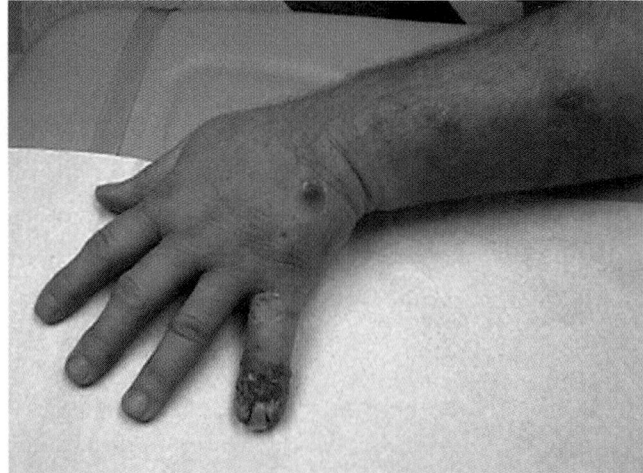

FIGURE 258-1. Sporotrichosis of the fifth finger in a gardener. Three nodular lesions are visible on the hand and arm.

TABLE 258-1 Differential Diagnosis of Sporotrichoid Lesions

Lesions resembling lymphocutaneous sporotrichosis (papulo-nodular lesions with or without central ulceration and with one or more nodules in the proximal skin along paths of presumed lymphatic spread):
  Nocardiosis caused by *Nocardia brasiliensis*
  Cutaneous leishmaniasis
  Mycobacterial infection caused by
    M. tuberculosis (tuberculosis cutis verrucosa)
    M. marinum
    M. chelonae
    M. kansasii
    M. fortuitum
    M. leprae
Lesions resembling plaque sporotrichosis (chronic, indurated hyperkeratotic plaques):
  Infections—as for lymphocutaneous disease and also
    Blastomycosis
    Paracoccidioidomycosis
    Chromoblastomycosis
    Lobomycosis
  Neoplasms
    Squamous carcinoma
    Basal cell carcinoma
    Mycosis fungoides
  Other
    Psoriasis
    Lupus vulgaris
    Pyoderma gangrenosum

Adapted from Kostman JR, DiNubile MJ. Nodular lymphangitis: A distinctive but often unrecognized syndrome. Ann Intern Med. 1993;118:883-888; and Smego RA Jr, Castiglia M, Asperilla MO. Lymphocutaneous syndrome—A review of non-sporothrix causes. Medicine. 1999;78:38-63.

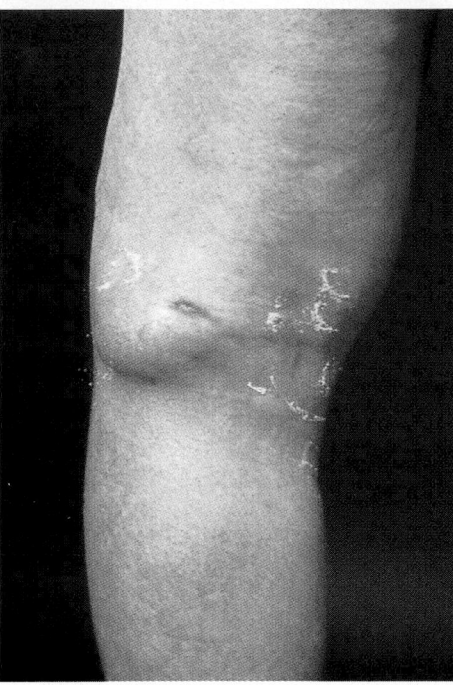

FIGURE 258-3. Sporotrichosis of the knee with formation of a Baker's cyst. *(From Kwon-Chung KJ, Bennett JE. Medical Mycology. Philadelphia: Lea & Febiger; 1992:712, with permission.)*

duced by a number of other organisms (Table 258-1). Cultures of the drainage from skin lesions are occasionally helpful, but culture of biopsy material is preferred and is diagnostic when positive. Microscopic examination will reveal pyogranulomas in the mid and upper dermis, but examination of multiple sections may be required in order to demonstrate the organism.[12]

Extracutaneous Sporotrichosis

Osteoarticular involvement is the most common form of extracutaneous sporotrichosis.[13] Involvement is of the major joints of the extremities (wrist [Fig. 258-2], elbow, ankle, and knee [Fig. 258-3])—the hip, shoulder, and spine are not involved.[14] Most patients present with involvement of a single joint without previously having had sporotrichosis at any another site. The joint is swollen and painful on motion, an effusion is present, and a sinus tract may develop. The overlying skin may or may not be erythematous. Systemic symptoms are minimal and, other than elevation of the erythrocyte sedimentation rate, laboratory examinations are unrevealing. If the infection remains untreated, other joints may become involved. Tenosynovitis associated with carpal tunnel syndrome or nerve entrapment has been reported.[15] The radiologic changes of osteomyelitis develop slowly and include loss of articular cartilage, periosteal reaction, and peri-articular osteopenia and cystic changes. Failure to consider the diagnosis has resulted in an average 25-month delay before diagnosis.[16] Repeated culture of fluid from joint aspiration as well as culture and microscopic examination of tissue from synovial biopsies is often required to make the diagnosis. Differential considerations include pigmented villonodular synovitis, tuberculosis, gout, osteoarthritis, and rheumatoid arthritis.

Pulmonary sporotrichosis is well described.[17] The typical patient is a 30- to 60-year-old male. Approximately one third of the patients are alcoholic, and one third have another concomitant medical illness such as pulmonary tuberculosis, diabetes mellitus, sarcoidosis, or steroid use; one third are apparently normal. Patients are occasionally asymptomatic, but will usually have a productive cough, low-grade fever, or weight loss. Other than elevation of the erythrocyte sedimentation rate, laboratory abnormalities are minimal. The chest x-ray reveals unilateral or bilateral cavitary lesions, usually with an associated parenchymal infiltrate (Fig. 258-4). Pleural effusions and hilar lymphadenopathy are occasionally noted. Gram stain or cytologic examination of sputum or bronchial washings will sometimes reveal elongated budding yeast,[18] and sputum culture will usually yield the organism. With some patients, however, repeated cultures and long-term follow-up are necessary in order to make the diagnosis.[19] Untreated, the cavities of pulmonary sporotrichosis gradually enlarge and produce progressive pulmonary dysfunction. A single case of spontaneous resolution of noncavitary infection has been reported.[20] The differential diagnosis includes mycobacterial infections (caused by both *M. tuberculosis* and the atypical mycobacteria), histoplasmosis, and coccidioidomycosis.

Meningitis caused by *S. schenckii* has been described in a small number of patients. The patients present with an indolent meningitis. Cerebrospinal fluid (CSF) analysis demonstrates a lymphocytic pleocytosis, an elevated protein, and hypoglycorrhachia. Culture of the CSF may be negative, and repeated cultures of large volumes of

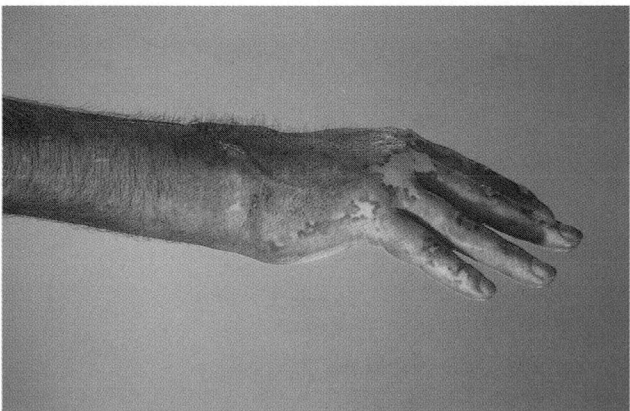

FIGURE 258-2. Sporotrichosis of the bones of the wrist.

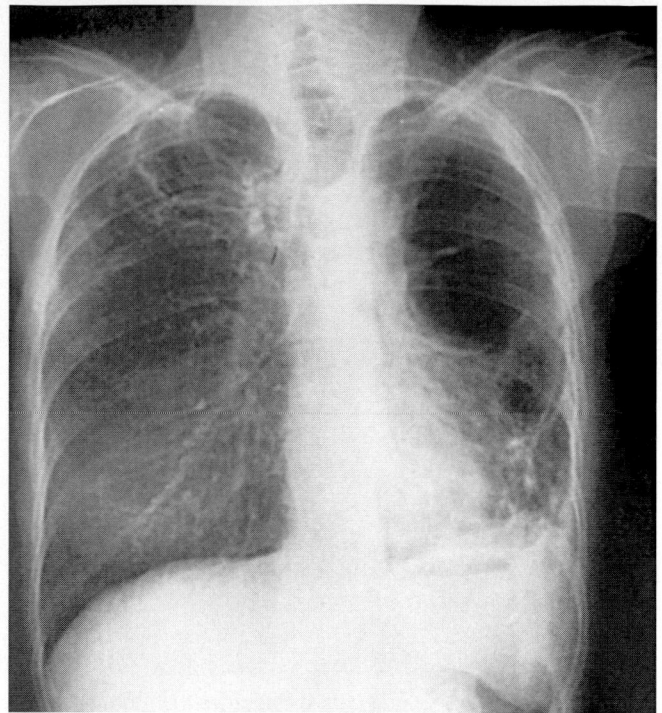

FIGURE 258-4. Chest roentgenogram demonstrating extensive bilateral cavitation resulting from sporotrichosis.

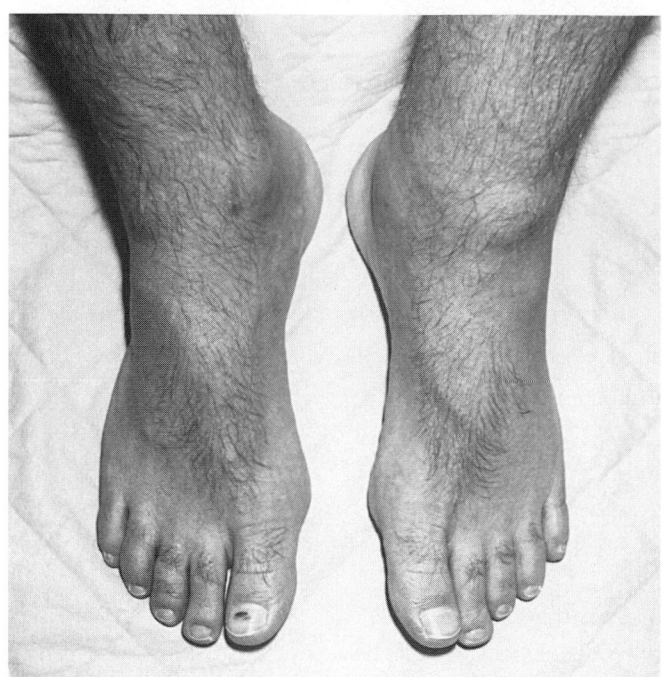

FIGURE 258-5. Extensive multifocal sporotrichosis with tenosynovitis of the toes, arthritis of the ankles, and associated lymphedema in a patient with advanced AIDS. This patient also had tenosynovitis of the wrists and hands along with arthritis of the wrists and knees.

CSF or serologic studies may be required to make the diagnosis.[21] The differential diagnosis is broad and includes tuberculosis, cryptococcosis, coccidioidomycosis, and histoplasmosis.

Infections of a variety of other sites have been reported but are uncommon. Involvement of the ocular adnexa, sometimes with spread to the eye, has been described.[10] Endophthalmitis may even occur without prior trauma or other evidence of sporotrichosis.[22] Cases of isolated involvement of the sinuses, kidney, testes, and epididymis have also been reported.[13,23]

Multifocal Extracutaneous Sporotrichosis

In otherwise normal patients with extracutaneous sporotrichosis, the lesions are generally restricted to a single site and are only locally progressive. Occasionally a patient with osteoarticular sporotrichosis will have involvement of several joints, but the presentation is otherwise identical to that of patients with involvement of only a single joint. A much smaller group of patients, in contrast, present with weight loss and variable low-grade fever, and often have several widely scattered cutaneous lesions. Mild anemia, leukocytosis, and elevation of the erythrocyte sedimentation rate may be present. Osteolytic bone lesions and arthritis are common, and spread to the palate, eyes, and central nervous system may develop.[13,24] Noncavitary lung lesions may also be seen. Untreated infection is ultimately fatal. Patients with this form of sporotrichosis almost always have some form of immunosuppression, commonly hematologic malignancy[13,24] or human immunodeficiency virus (HIV) infection (see below). Cultures of skin lesions and joints are usually positive, and blood and bone marrow cultures are occasionally positive. Immunosuppressed patients who present with what appears to be simple cutaneous sporotrichosis should be carefully examined for other sites of infection and a technetium pyrophosphate bone scan should be obtained.

CLINICAL MANIFESTATIONS OF SPOROTRICHOSIS IN THE HUMAN IMMUNODEFICIENCY VIRUS–INFECTED PATIENT

When CD4 counts are relatively well preserved, localized infection may follow direct cutaneous inoculation in a pattern analogous to that in immunocompetent patients.[25] However, widespread lymphocutaneous sporotrichosis or multifocal extracutaneous disease may be seen in patients with more advanced HIV infection. In a review of acquired immunodeficiency syndrome (AIDS) patients with disseminated sporotrichosis,[26] almost all had fewer than 100 CD4+ T cells/μL. Multiple ulcerative skin lesions are usually present. Sporotrichosis may also present as multifocal tenosynovitis and arthritis with or without overt cutaneous disease or systemic dissemination and thus may resemble disseminated gonococcal infection or the seronegative spondyloarthropathies, such as Reiter's syndrome or psoriatic arthritis (Fig. 258-5), which are seen with a higher frequency in the setting of AIDS.[27] Widespread visceral dissemination also occurs, as evidenced by reports of meningitis with parenchymal brain lesions[28]; lung abscess, liver, and spleen involvement[29]; endophthalmitis[30]; and fungemia with spread to esophagus, colon, testes, bone marrow, and lymph nodes.[30] Sinusitis with invasion of the contiguous bone and soft tissues has also been described,[31] and emphasizes the potential for the respiratory tract as the initial focus of infection in HIV-infected patients.

DIAGNOSIS

Diagnosis is best made by culture of the affected site, though repeated attempts at culture may have to be made. A positive culture from any site is ordinarily diagnostic of infection, although a case of saprophytic involvement of the respiratory tract has been described.[32] A positive blood culture strongly suggests the multifocal form of sporotrichosis seen in immunocompromised hosts, although the lysis-centrifugation system may be more sensitive in detecting fungemia in nonimmunocompromised patients.[33] Serologic techniques have been described and may be useful in such obscure forms of sporotrichosis as meningitis, but are confounded by the presence of antibody in individuals without evidence of sporotrichosis.[34] No standard method of serologic testing is available.

Examination of biopsy specimens reveals a pyogranulomatous response and is diagnostic if characteristic 1- to 3- × 3- to 10-μm cigar-shaped yeast forms are seen. Unfortunately, the yeast may be difficult to detect unless multiple sections are examined,[12] although lesions from immunocompromised hosts may contain numerous yeasts (Fig.

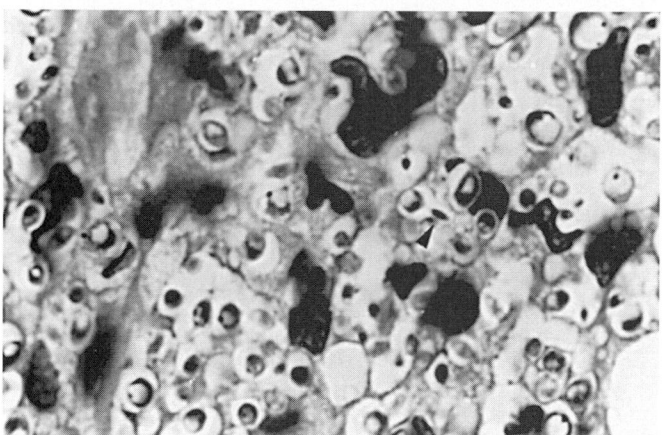

FIGURE 258-6. Numerous yeasts of sporotrichosis in a cutaneous lesion from an immunosuppressed patient. In the normal host, organisms are usually difficult to locate. Although a single cigar-shaped form is present (*arrowhead*), most of the yeasts have a rounded form that is consistent with, but not diagnostic of, sporotrichosis. *(Courtesy of Dr. Ronald Rapini, Houston, TX.)*

258-6). In addition, *S. schenckii* often assumes a more rounded tissue form, making the biopsy suggestive but not diagnostic. The organisms may be surrounded by a stellate, periodic acid–Schiff positive, eosinophilic material known as an asteroid body. In the brain or eye, a capsule has sometimes been demonstrable around the yeastlike cells.

As with other immunosuppressed patients, individuals with advanced AIDS may have a high fungal load that results in positive smears and cultures.[18] Skin biopsy may reveal fungal elements with a limited inflammatory response, and this should prompt the clinician to initiate a search for a systemic immunodeficiency.[35]

THERAPY

Treatment guidelines for sporotrichosis have been proposed.[36] Because of its convenience and consistent efficacy,[37] itraconazole at 100 to 200 mg/day has become the therapy of choice.[36] Therapy with itraconazole usually requires 3 to 6 months to effect a clinical cure. Relapse has been observed on occasion after cessation of therapy. Should relapse develop, anecdotal reports suggest that a repeated, but more prolonged, course of therapy will typically produce a permanent cure. Iodides are an effective and inexpensive but poorly tolerated therapy for cutaneous sporotrichosis. A saturated solution of potassium iodide (SSKI) is prescribed, and therapy is begun with 5 to 10 drops taken orally three times per day. The dose is gradually advanced to 25 to 40 drops three times daily (for children) or 40 to 50 drops three times daily (for adults). SSKI has a bitter taste and is made more palatable by taking it in milk, juice, or a carbonated beverage. Side effects include nausea, anorexia, diarrhea, parotid or lacrimal gland enlargement, and an acneiform rash. These side effects will remit with reduction of the dose of SSKI or temporary cessation of therapy. Therapy at the maximal tolerated dose should be continued until the cutaneous lesions have resolved, a process that usually takes up to 6 months. Some patients are allergic to iodides and in others cutaneous disease may respond slowly to iodide therapy or, rarely, fail to respond at all. Ketoconazole has not proven to be very effective, and amphotericin B is too toxic to be used in this setting. Consistent with its limited in vitro activity,[38] fluconazole has only modest clinical activity.[39] The experience with voriconazole is limited to in vitro data showing limited activity.[38] Although it is not licensed for this indication, limited data suggest that terbinafine is also efficacious for plaque sporotrichosis.[40,41] Because of the temperature sensitivity of this organism, heat is a useful adjunct therapy and on occasion has been curative.[42] Given the toxicity of both the azoles and the iodides in pregnant women (skeletal bone deformities and goiter, respectively),[43] use of heat may be especially valuable during pregnancy.[36,44]

Therapy of extracutaneous sporotrichosis is often difficult. Osteoarticular sporotrichosis has been treated with intravenous amphotericin B,[16] but itraconazole at 400 mg/day is now the preferred agent.[36] Ketoconazole (400 to 800 mg/day) and fluconazole (200 to 400 mg/day) appear less efficacious.[39,45] Intra-articular amphotericin B is sometimes given, although its role has not been clearly defined. Surgical débridement is often employed, but its utility is also uncertain. SSKI has rarely been reported to be effective, but usually is not.

If diagnosed prior to the development of cavities, pulmonary sporotrichosis may be treated with SSKI or amphotericin B.[17] Cure of cavitary disease typically requires pulmonary resection plus a perioperative course of itraconazole or amphotericin B.[36] Treatment failure is often associated with incomplete resection. Data are as yet incomplete on the use of ketoconazole, fluconazole, or itraconazole in this setting—successes and failures have been reported with each[17,37]—and they are not generally recommended.[36]

S. schenckii meningitis does not consistently respond to amphotericin B, and the addition of 5-fluorocytosine may be warranted. Limited data suggest that itraconazole might be useful as suppressive therapy.[36] The number of reported cases of involvement of other specific sites is too limited to permit generalization. Extracutaneous sporotrichosis in the immunocompromised host usually responds at least partially to either amphotericin B or itraconazole, although relapse is common.

Therapy of Patients with Acquired Immunodeficiency Syndrome

Therapy of sporotrichosis in AIDS should be tailored to the presenting syndrome. Itraconazole appears to be the drug of choice, and individuals with limited cutaneous disease can be treated with 200 mg twice daily. Amphotericin B should be used as initial therapy of disseminated disease.[36] Lifetime suppressive itraconazole therapy should follow initial therapy, given the likelihood of relapse and dissemination.[36] Monitoring of itraconazole levels is useful because of the potential for reduced drug absorption as a result of HIV-associated achlorhydria, malabsorption, or diarrhea caused by other opportunistic pathogens. Drug levels may also be altered as a result of drug interactions that interfere with drug metabolism. Although strong data showing the correlation between itraconazole levels and response to sporotrichosis are not available, data from other settings (most notably aspergillosis) suggest that levels of the parent (unmetabolized) itraconazole molecule of 500 ng/mL by high-performance liquid chromatography would likely be adequate to produce a clinical response. The increased bioavailability of the newer itraconazole cyclodextrin suspension is helpful in achieving such blood levels.

Both anecdotal and published experience suggest that multifocal extracutaneous disease in HIV-infected patients may respond poorly, if at all, to current therapies.[46,47] Therapy should be initiated with amphotericin B followed by lifetime suppression with itraconazole. Progression may occur despite amphotericin therapy. Little information exists concerning the use of newer lipid-associated amphotericin B preparations in this setting. Because disseminated disease has been reported to develop despite ongoing fluconazole being given for other indications,[48] fluconazole is not a first-line choice. As has been demonstrated for other opportunistic pathogens, the use of potent new combination antiretroviral therapies with protease inhibitors may also assist in clearing the infection.[49]

PROGNOSIS

Cutaneous sporotrichosis responds well to therapy and has an excellent prognosis. Osteoarticular sporotrichosis may require prolonged therapy but is not life threatening. Other forms of extracutaneous sporotrichosis can be difficult to treat and may have substantial morbidity and mortality.

REFERENCES

1. Ajello L, Kaplan W. A new variant of *Sporothrix schenckii*. Mykosen. 1969;12:633-644.
2. Travassos LR, Lloyd KO. *Sporothrix schenckii* and related species of *Ceratocystis*. Microbiol Rev. 1980;44:683-721.
3. Pappas PG, Tellez I, Deep AE, et al. Sporotrichosis in Peru: Description of an area of hyperendemicity. Clin Infect Dis. 2000;30:65-70.

4. Hajjeh R, McDonnell S, Reef S, et al. Outbreak of sporotrichosis among tree nursery workers. J Infect Dis. 1997;176:499-504.

5. Lyon GM, Zurita S, Casquero J, et al. Population-based surveillance and a case-control study of risk factors for endemic lymphocutaneous sporotrichosis in Peru. Clin Infect Dis. 2003;36:34-39.

6. Saravanakumar PS, Eslami P, Zar FA. Lymphocutaneous sporotrichosis associated with a squirrel bite: Case report and review. Clin Infect Dis. 1996;23:647-648.

7. Reed KD, Moore FM, Geiger GE, Stemper ME. Zoonotic transmission of sporotrichosis—Case report and review. Clin Infect Dis. 1993;16:384-387.

8. Smith LM. Sporotrichosis: Report of four clinically atypical cases. South Med J. 1945;38:505-515.

9. Bargman HB. Sporotrichosis of the nose with spontaneous cure. Can Med Assoc J. 1981;124:1027.

10. Gordon D. Ocular sporotrichosis. Arch Ophthalmol. 1947;37:56-72.

11. Kwon-Chung KJ. Comparison of isolates of Sporothrix schenckii obtained from fixed cutaneous lesions with isolates from other types of lesions. J Infect Dis. 1979;139:424-431.

12. Bullpitt P, Weedon D. Sporotrichosis: A review of 39 cases. Pathology. 1978;10:249-256.

13. Wilson DE, Mann JJ, Bennett JE, Utz JP. Clinical features of extracutaneous sporotrichosis. Medicine. 1967;46:265-279.

14. Janes PC, Mann RJ. Extracutaneous sporotrichosis. J Hand Surg Am. 1987;12:441-445.

15. Stratton CW, Lichtenstein KA, Lowenstein SR, et al. Granulomatous tenosynovitis and carpal tunnel syndrome caused by Sporothrix schenckii. Am J Med. 1981;71:161-164.

16. Crout JE, Brewer NS, Tompkins RB. Sporotrichosis arthritis: Clinical features in seven patients. Ann Intern Med. 1977;86:294-297.

17. Pluss JL, Opal SM. Pulmonary sporotrichosis: Review of treatment and outcome. Medicine. 1986;65:143-153.

18. Gori S, Lupetti A, Moscato G, et al. Pulmonary sporotrichosis with hyphae in a human immunodeficiency virus-infected patient: A case report. Acta Cytol. 1997;41:519-521.

19. Khan FA, Guarneri JJ, Sierra MF. Primary pulmonary sporotrichosis complicated by perirectal abscess. Am Rev Respir Dis. 1975;112:119-123.

20. Pueringer RJ, Iber C, Deike MA, Davies SF. Spontaneous remission of extensive pulmonary sporotrichosis. Ann Intern Med. 1986;104:366-367.

21. Scott EN, Kaufman L, Brown AC, Muchmore HG. Serologic studies in the diagnosis and management of meningitis due to Sporothrix schenckii. N Engl J Med. 1987;317:935-940.

22. Font RL, Jakobiec FA. Granulomatous necrotizing retinochoroiditis caused by Sporotrichum schenckii. Arch Ophthalmol. 1976;94:1513-1519.

23. Friedman SJ, Doyle JA. Extracutaneous sporotrichosis. Int J Dermatol. 1983;22:171-173.

24. Lynch PJ, Voorhees JJ, Harrell ER. Systemic sporotrichosis. Ann Intern Med. 1970;73:23-30.

25. Keiser P, Whittle D. Sporotrichosis in human immunodeficiency virus-infected patients: Report of a case. Rev Infect Dis. 1991;13:1027-1028.

26. Al-Tawfiq JA, Wools KK. Disseminated sporotrichosis and Sporothrix schenckii fungemia as the initial presentation of human immunodeficiency virus infection. Clin Infect Dis. 1998;26:1403-1406.

27. Oscherwitz SL, Rinaldi MG. Disseminated sporotrichosis in a patient infected with human immunodeficiency virus. Clin Infect Dis. 1992;15:568-569.

28. Penn CC, Goldstein E, Bartholomew WR. Sporothrix schenckii meningitis in a patients with AIDS. Clin Infect Dis. 1992;15:741-743.

29. Lipstein-Kresch E, Isenberg HD, Singer C, et al. Disseminated Sporothrix schenckii infection with arthritis in a patient with acquired immunodeficiency syndrome. J Rheumatol. 1985;12:805-808.

30. Heller HM, Fuhrer J. Disseminated sporotrichosis in patients with AIDS: Case report and review of the literature. AIDS. 1991;5:1243-1246.

31. Morgan M, Reves R. Invasive sinusitis due to Sporothrix schenckii in a patient with AIDS. Clin Infect Dis. 1996;23:1319-1320.

32. Lowenstein M, Markowitz SM, Nottebart HC, Shadomy S. Existence of Sporothrix schenckii as a pulmonary saprophyte. Chest. 1978;73:419-421.

33. Kosinski RM, Axelrod P, Rex JH, et al. Sporothrix schenckii fungemia without disseminated sporotrichosis. J Clin Microbiol. 1992;30:501-503.

34. Scott EN, Muchmore HG. Immunoblot analysis of antibody responses to Sporothrix schenckii. J Clin Microbiol. 1989;27:300-304.

35. Fitzpatrick JE, Eubanks S. Acquired immunodeficiency syndrome presenting as disseminated cutaneous sporotrichosis. Int J Dermatol. 1988;27:406-407.

36. Kauffman CA, Hajjeh R, Chapman SW, for the Mycoses Study Group. Practice guidelines for the management of patients with sporotrichosis. Clin Infect Dis. 2000;30:684-687.

37. Sharkey-Mathis PK, Kauffman CA, Graybill JR, et al, for the NIAID Mycoses Study Group. Treatment of sporotrichosis with itraconazole. Am J Med. 1993;95:279-285.

38. Espinel-Ingroff A, Boyle K, Sheehan DJ. In vitro antifungal activities of voriconazole and reference agents as determined by NCCLS methods: Review of the literature. Mycopathologia. 2001;150:101-115.

39. Kauffman CA, Pappas PG, McKinsey DS, et al, for the National Institute of Allergy and Infectious Diseases Mycoses Study Group. Treatment of lymphocutaneous and visceral sporotrichosis with fluconazole. Clin Infect Dis. 1996;22:46-50.

40. Pappas PG, Bustamante B, Nolasco D, et al. Treatment of lymphocutaneous sporotrichosis with terbinafine: Results of a randomized double-blind trial (Abstract No 648). In: Abstracts of the 39th Annual Meeting of the Infectious Diseases Society of America, San Francisco, 2001.

41. Perez A. Terbinafine: Broad new spectrum of indications in several subcutaneous and systemic and parasitic diseases. Mycoses. 1999;42:111-114.

42. Galiana J, Conti-Díaz IA. Healing effects of heat and a rubefacient on nine cases of sporotrichosis. Sabouraudia. 1963;3:64-71.

43. Sobel JD. Use of antifungal drugs in pregnancy: A focus on safety. Drug Safety. 2000;1:77-85.

44. Vanderveen EE, Messenger AL, Voorhees JJ. Sporotrichosis in pregnancy. Cutis. 1982;30:761-763.

45. Calhoun DL, Washkin H, White MP, et al. Treatment of systemic sporotrichosis with ketoconazole. Rev Infect Dis. 1991;13:47-51.

46. Kauffman CA. Old and new therapies for sporotrichosis. Clin Infect Dis. 1995;21:981-985.

47. Donabedian H, O'Donnell E, Olszewski C, et al. Disseminated cutaneous and meningeal sporotrichosis in an AIDS patient. Diagn Microbiol Infect Dis. 1994;18:111-115.

48. Goldani LZ, Aquino VR, Dargel AA. Disseminated cutaneous sporotrichosis in an AIDS patient receiving maintenance therapy with fluconazole for previous cryptococcal meningitis. Clin Infect Dis. 1999;28:1337-1338.

49. Carr A, Marriott D, Field A, et al. Treatment of HIV-1-associated microsporidiosis and cryptosporidiosis with combination antiretroviral therapy. Lancet. 1998;351:256-261.

CHAPTER **259**

Agents of Chromoblastomycosis

DUANE R. HOSPENTHAL

Chromoblastomycosis (chromomycosis) is a chronic localized fungal infection of the skin and subcutaneous tissue that produces raised scaly lesions usually of the lower extremities. The lesions of chromoblastomycosis are frequently warty or cauliflower-like in appearance, with pathognomonic muriform cells (also called "copper penny" or sclerotic bodies) found on histologic examination. This disease of tropical and subtropical distribution is produced by inoculation of the infecting fungi in association with minor trauma. Pedroso, for whom the major etiologic agent is named, first noted the disease in 1911, although the first publication to describe what was likely chromoblastomycosis appeared in 1914 authored by Rudolph.[1] The first reports to include identification of the fungal etiology of this disease were published 1 year later by Medlar and Lane, describing a patient with disease acquired not in the tropics, but in New England.

ETIOLOGIC AGENTS

Infection is caused by one of several dark-walled (dematiaceous) fungi found in the soil, and in association with decaying wood and other vegetation. *Fonsecaea pedrosoi* is the most common cause of chromoblastomycosis, though disease caused by *Fonsecaea compacta*, *Cladophialophora* (*Cladosporium*) *carrionii*, *Phialophora verrucosa*, and *Rhinocladiella aquaspersa* also occurs. In the largest reports from Brazil,[2] Mexico,[3] Sri Lanka,[4] and Japan,[5] *F. pedrosoi* has been responsible for 86% to 96% of all infections. *Botryomyces caespitosus* has been reported in at least two cases of chromoblastomycosis,[1] and case reports of disease secondary to *Exophiala jeanselmei* and *Exophiala spinifera* also exist in the literature.[6]

EPIDEMIOLOGY

Chromoblastomycosis has been described to occur throughout the world, although most cases arise in tropical and subtropical regions, especially those with high annual rainfall. Large numbers of cases have been described from Madagascar, Brazil, and Costa Rica. Disease is more prevalent in males (4:1 ratio) ages 40 to 69,[2] and in association with outdoor activity such as farming and woodcutting, and in the absence of footwear use. In Madagascar, a unique epidemiology has been described in what is probably the largest focus of endemic disease.[7] Madagascar has two distinct foci of infection, with disease secondary to *F. pedrosoi* occurring in the humid, rainy northern evergreen forest region and disease secondary to *C. carrionii* found in the arid southern desert region. In a study of 1343 cases of disease over 40 years in that country, prevalence of 1 case per 1920 inhabitants in the southern desert region has been described, with an incredible 1 in 910 prevalence in a single district of that region.

PATHOLOGY AND PATHOGENESIS

The traumatic inoculation of the agents of chromoblastomycosis results in a mixed chronic suppurative and granulomatous host response.[8] The epidermis typically becomes thickened in a process called pseudoepitheliomatous hyperplasia, a histologic morphology that may be misidentified as malignancy by more inexperienced microscopists. Foci of polymorphonuclear cells and microabscesses are seen in both the epidermis and dermis. In the dermis, granulomas that include multinucleated giant cells and epithelioid cells are present along with varying amounts of fibrosis. Fibrosis is increased in older lesions and can extend into the subcutaneous tissue, though disease rarely extends deep into the subcutaneous tissue. The hallmark of chromoblastomycosis, the muriform cells (also called sclerotic, copper penny, or Medlar bodies) may be found intracellularly in macrophages or extracellularly in abscesses. These are darkly pigmented (brown-golden), thick-walled, rounded cells, 4 to 12 μm wide with cross walls in one or two planes. Hyphae may also occasionally be seen, usually in the epidermis. The host response to these structures results in a process termed *transepithelial elimination,* in which fungi and damaged tissue are expelled through the epidermis, a process similar to that seen in calcinosis cutis.[9] Little has been described regarding the immunologic response of the host in this mycosis. Antibody responses have shown association with disease chronicity and extent but do not appear to provide any degree of protection in this infection.[10]

CLINICAL MANIFESTATIONS

Weeks to months following inoculation of the causative organisms through minor trauma, individuals typically develop a small scaly papule on the lower extremity at the site of the trauma (Figs. 259-1 through 259-3). This lesion slowly develops into a superficial nodule, commonly with an irregular friable surface. Frequently, these nodules later spread out to become purplish irregular raised plaques. In descriptions by Carrion, lesions of chromoblastomycosis were catego-

FIGURE 259-2. Chromoblastomycosis with multiple verrucous nodules. *(From McGinnis MR, Chandler FW. Chromoblastomycosis. In: Connor DH, Chandler FW, Schwartz DA, et al, eds. Pathology of Infectious Diseases. Norwalk, CT: Appleton & Lange; 1997, with permission of the McGraw-Hill Companies.)*

rized into five types[11]: (1) early nodular lesions, which were described as soft and pink-violaceous in color, with smooth, verrucous, or scaly surfaces; (2) tumorous lesions, which are large, papillomatous, often lobulated masses with crusting, sometimes described as cauliflower-like; (3) verrucous lesions with prominent hyperkeratosis; (4) plaque lesions; and (5) cicatricial lesions. Most lesions have "black dots" associated with their outer surface that are composed of fungi and necrotic debris, the products of transepithelial elimination. Though not typically painful, lesions may be associated with pruritus, are easily traumatized, and bleed readily. Ulceration is generally limited to those lesions with bacterial superinfection. Large lesions may become hyperkeratotic, and limb distortion can occur as a result of blockage of normal lymphatic drainage (including elephantiasis).

Although lesions have been described to occur chiefly on the lower extremities (80% to 85%)[2,12] of persons with outdoor exposures in most regions of the world, an exception to this pattern is reported from Japan. Evaluation of 290 lesions from that country found chromoblastomycosis to occur most commonly on the upper extremities of male subjects and on the face or neck of females.[5]

Persistence of the lesions of chromoblastomycosis for 30 years has been reported, and delays in diagnosis of 1 to 3 years are not unusual.

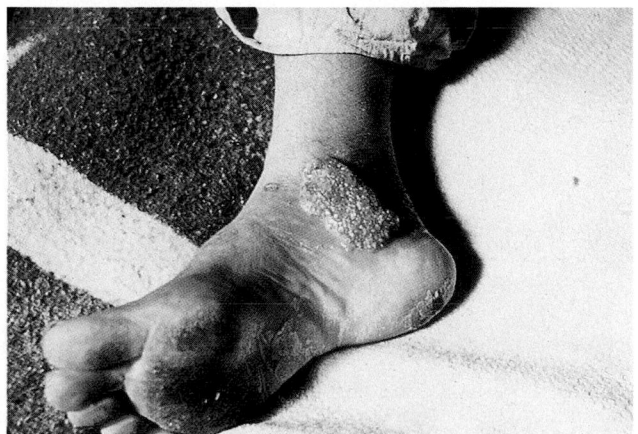

FIGURE 259-1. Chromoblastomycosis of the foot. *(From Beneke ES, Rogers AL. Medical Mycology and Human Mycoses. Belmont, CA: Star Publishing Company; 1996; reprinted with permission.)*

FIGURE 259-3. Chromoblastomycosis of the lower leg with lobulated, confluent nodules with focal ulcerations. *(From McGinnis MR, Chandler FW. Chromoblastomycosis. In: Connor DH, Chandler FW, Schwartz DA, et al, eds. Pathology of Infectious Diseases. Norwalk, CT: Appleton & Lange; 1997, with permission of the McGraw-Hill Companies.)*

Although most lesions remain localized without spread to deeper structures, localized dissemination may occur via autoinoculation or via the lymphatics. Hematogenous spread has only rarely been described, but does include reports of dissemination to the central nervous system.[5] The occurrence of secondary bacterial infection has been reported to affect as many as 63% of persons with chromoblastomycosis.[3] Though apparently rare, at least seven cases of malignant transformation of chromoblastomycosis lesions have been reported in the literature.[13] All of the associated malignancies have been squamous cell carcinomas and have occurred after 10 or more years of disease.

The differential diagnosis of chromoblastomycosis includes psoriasis, other mycoses (blastomycosis, coccidioidomycosis, lobomycosis, mycetoma, paracoccidioidomycosis, cutaneous phaeohyphomycosis, sporotrichosis, tinea), tuberculosis, leprosy, leishmaniasis, protothecosis, keratoacanthoma, squamous cell carcinoma, and sarcoidosis.

DIAGNOSIS

Chromoblastomycosis should be suspected in persons with chronic scaly or friable lesions of the extremities, especially in rural tropical climates. Microscopic examination of skin scrapings can provide a rapid diagnosis of chromoblastomycosis because the characteristic muriform cells may be seen in potassium hydroxide preparations, especially those containing black dots (Fig. 259-4). These unique structures may also be readily observed with standard staining of skin punch biopsy specimens with hematoxylin and eosin (Fig. 259-5). Although not absolutely necessary, culture should be performed to identify the specific cause of infection. Standard mycologic media (Sabouraud glucose agar) with and without cycloheximide should be used and cultures incubated for at least 4 weeks. In culture, the fungal agents of chromoblastomycosis appear as dark molds. Under standard culture conditions, these fungi may be identified by the microscopic appearance of hyphae and reproductive structures. The muriform structures seen in tissue have been produced in vitro using low pH and the addition of propranolol, but this is not necessary for clinical diagnoses.[14] Exoantigen testing has been developed to aid in the diagnosis, though this is not commonly used.[15] Serologic and skin tests have also been developed, but their use in this rare disease is limited to specialized centers in more endemic regions of the world.

TREATMENT

Although spontaneous resolution has been reported,[16] this is only a rare occurrence. Most chromoblastomycosis is a chronic indolent infection, which when caused by its most common etiologic agent, *Fonsecaea pedrosoi*, has proven difficult to eradicate even with pro-

longed therapy. Multiple modalities have been used to treat individuals with chromoblastomycosis, including surgery, local (physical) treatments, and antifungal agents. Surgical removal of small lesions appears to be effective, as does local application of liquid nitrogen, topical heat, and photocoagulation. Local curettage or electrocautery has been reported to sometimes result in disease spread and is to be discouraged. Heat therapy (42° to 46° C) with pocket warmers and other devices providing prolonged daily warmth directly to the lesions has been described as effective with 2 to 12 months of treatment.[17] Cryotherapy with liquid nitrogen sprays or applied with soaked cotton swabs or balls has been successful in the cure of small, early lesions, and may be used effectively in combination with antifungal medications on larger lesions.

Currently the best therapy appears to be either itraconazole or terbinafine, perhaps with adjunctive cryotherapy with liquid nitrogen or other local treatments. Other antifungal agents, including amphotericin B (intravenous or intralesional), 5-fluorocytosine, ketoconazole, and fluconazole, have been used with poor to mixed success, both alone and in combination. Thiabendazole, an antiparasitic drug and the first agent used successfully in this disease, has produced cure rates of 25% to 50% with 3 to 8 months of therapy. This drug is associated with gastrointestinal adverse effects, including liver toxicity, and is no longer used with any frequency. Prior to the more recent availability of itraconazole and terbinafine, thiabendazole, ketoconazole, and fluorocytosine were the most commonly used agents.

Itraconazole has been shown to be effective in many patients in uncontrolled, nonrandomized studies. Early study with lower doses (100 to 200 mg daily) of itraconazole documented high response rates with this azole antifungal agent, but the numbers of cures were small (3 of 10 patients treated for 12 to 24 months).[18] Treatment of chromoblastomycosis caused by *C. carrionii* with itraconazole has met with much greater success than treatment of that caused by other agents. One study reported cure in two of five individuals with disease secondary to *F. pedrosoi* and eight of nine patients with *C. carrionii*, all given 100 to 400 mg of the drug daily for 4 to 8 months.[19] Queiroz-Telles and colleagues reported the cure of 42% of patients (8 of 19) treated with 200 to 400 mg of itraconazole for a median of 7 months.[20] Another group described the therapy of 10 patients with disease secondary to *F. pedrosoi*, 4 of whom had failed prior therapy with ketoconazole.[21] All patients received 200 to 400 mg of itraconazole daily, and eight also received monthly cryotherapy with liquid nitrogen. Nine patients were cured with 3 to 12 months of therapy; two of these responded with sustained cures after only 3 months of itraconazole at the lower dose of 200 mg daily. The remaining patient had marked improvement without cure. Recurrence was noted in a single patient who

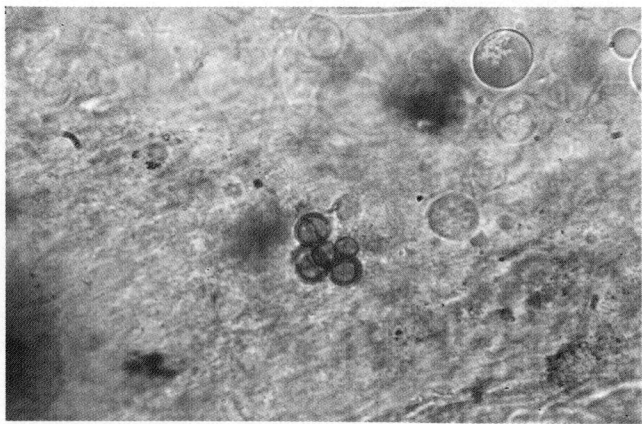

FIGURE 259-4. Sclerotic bodies of chromoblastomycosis. *(From Beneke ES, Rogers AL. Medical Mycology and Human Mycoses. Belmont, CA: Star Publishing Company; 1996; reprinted with permission.)*

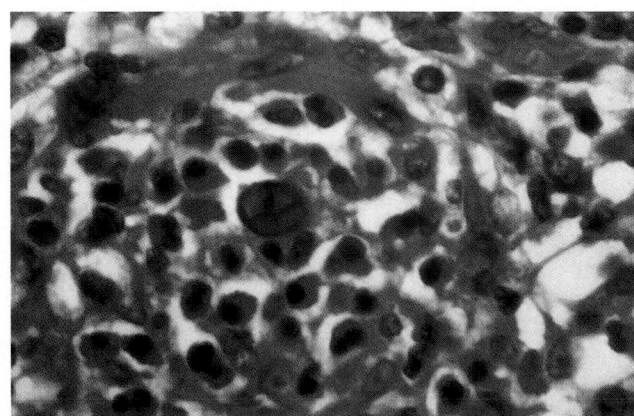

FIGURE 259-5. Dermal abscess with quadrate cluster of organisms in a mixture of neutrophils, macrophages, eosinophils, and a giant cell (hematoxylin and eosin). *(From McGinnis MR, Chandler FW. Chromoblastomycosis. In: Connor DH, Chandler FW, Schwartz DA, et al, eds. Pathology of Infectious Diseases. Norwalk, CT: Appleton & Lange; 1997, with permission of the McGraw-Hill Companies.)*

had been cured with a 6-month course of itraconazole (400 mg daily) and cryotherapy. Bonifaz and associates described good success with smaller lesions treated with itraconazole or cryosurgery, and in larger lesions treated with itraconazole followed by cryosurgery.[22] In that study, which included four patients in each group and dosing of itraconazole at 100 mg three times daily for 5 to 14 months, 8 of 12 patients (67%) were cured and the remaining 4 showed improvement.

The allylamine antifungal agent terbinafine has produced excellent results in treatment of chromoblastomycosis. In the largest study to date, terbinafine at 500 mg daily was given to 35 patients for up to 12 months.[23] In that study, 16 patients had failed thiabendazole in the past and almost half had lesions of greater than 10 years' duration. Improvement defined as lack of bacterial superinfection and resolution of edema was seen after 2 to 4 months of therapy, and after 12 months, 86% of persons obtained mycologic cures[12] (72% with clinical cures). Patients with *C. carrionii* infections were noted to respond more quickly than those with *F. pedrosoi* infection in that study. Unexpectedly, partial reversal of fibrosis of the lesions of chromoblastomycosis has also been reported to occur with terbinafine therapy. This reversal has been suggested to be independent of mycologic cure of infection in persons receiving terbinafine.[24,25] Terbinafine used in alternate-week or combination therapy with itraconazole to successfully treat four patients with resistant infections has also been reported.[26]

The newer broad-spectrum azole antifungals may potentially be useful in this disease. In vitro testing has shown that the minimum inhibitory concentration of voriconazole for *F. pedrosoi* and *F. compacta* is lower than those seen with itraconazole.[27] *F. pedrosoi* has also been shown to be susceptible to the echinocandin caspofungin in one small in vitro study.[28]

No vaccinations exist to prevent chromoblastomycosis. Proper protective clothing, especially footwear, and early treatment of the lesions are the only available preventive measures against this disease.

REFERENCES

1. Kwon-Chung KJ, Bennett JE. Medical Mycology. Philadelphia: Lea & Febiger, 1992.
2. Minotto R, Bernardi CD, Mallmann LF, et al. Chromoblastomycosis: A review of 100 cases in the state of Rio Grande do Sul, Brazil. J Am Acad Dermatol. 2001;44:585-592.
3. Bonifaz A, Carrasco-Gerard E, Saul A. Chromoblastomycosis: Clinical and mycologic experience of 51 cases. Mycoses. 2001;44:1-7.
4. Attapattu MC. Chromoblastomycosis—A clinical and mycological study of 71 cases from Sri Lanka. Mycopathologia. 1997;137:145-151.
5. Fukushiro R. Chromomycosis in Japan. Int J Dermatol. 1983;22:221-229.
6. Barba-Gomez JF, Mayorga J, McGinnis MR, Gonzalez-Mendoza A. Chromoblastomycosis caused by *Exophiala spinifera*. J Am Acad Dermatol. 1992;26:367-370.
7. Esterre P, Andriantsimahavandy A, Ramarcel ER, Pecarrere JL. Forty years of chromoblastomycosis in Madagascar: A review. Am J Trop Med Hyg. 1996;55:45-47.
8. Uribe F, Zuluaga AI, Leon W, Restrepo A. Histopathology of chromoblastomycosis. Mycopathologia. 1989;105:1-6.
9. Batres E, Wolf JE Jr, Rudolph AH, Knox JM. Transepithelial elimination of cutaneous chromomycosis. Arch Dermatol. 1978;114:1231-1232.
10. Esterre P, Jahevitra M, Andriantsimahavandy A. Humoral immune response in chromoblastomycosis during and after therapy. Clin Diagn Lab Immunol. 2000;7:497-500.
11. Carrion AL. Chromoblastomycosis. Ann N Y Acad Sci. 1950;50:1255-1282.
12. Silva JP, de Souza W, Rozental S. Chromoblastomycosis: A retrospective study of 325 cases in Amazonic Region (Brazil). Mycopathologia. 1999;143:171-175.
13. Paul C, Dupont B, Pialoux G, et al. Chromoblastomycosis with malignant transformation and cutaneous-synovial secondary localization: The potential therapeutic role of itraconazole. J Med Vet Mycol. 1991;29:313-316.
14. da Silva JP, Alviano DS, Alviano CS, et al. Comparison of *Fonsecaea pedrosoi* sclerotic cells obtained in vivo and in vitro: Ultrastructure and antigenicity. FEMS Immunol Med Microbiol. 2002;33:63-69.
15. Espinel-Ingroff A, Shadomy S, Dixon D, Goldson P. Exoantigen test for *Cladosporium bantianum, Fonsecaea pedrosoi,* and *Phialophora verrucosa*. J Clin Microbiol. 1986;23:305-310.
16. Nishimoto K, Yoshimura S, Honma K. Chromomycosis spontaneously healed. Int J Dermatol. 1984;23:408-410.
17. Tagami H, Ginoza M, Imaizumi S, Urano-Suehisa S. Successful treatment of chromoblastomycosis with topical heat therapy. J Am Acad Dermatol. 1984;10:615-619.
18. Restrepo A, Gonzalez A, Gomez I, et al. Treatment of chromoblastomycosis with itraconazole. Ann N Y Acad Sci. 1988;544:504-516.
19. Borelli D. A clinical trial of itraconazole in the treatment of deep mycoses and leishmaniasis. Rev Infect Dis. 1987;9(Suppl 1):S57-S63.
20. Queiroz-Telles F, Purim KS, Fillus JN, et al. Itraconazole in the treatment of chromoblastomycosis due to *Fonsecaea pedrosoi*. Int J Dermatol. 1992;31:805-812.
21. Kullavanijaya P, Rojanavanich V. Successful treatment of chromoblastomycosis due to *Fonsecaea pedrosoi* by the combination of itraconazole and cryotherapy. Int J Dermatol. 1995;34:804-807.
22. Bonifaz A, Martinez-Soto E, Carrasco-Gerard E, Peniche J. Treatment of chromoblastomycosis with itraconazole, cryosurgery, and a combination of both. Int J Dermatol. 1997;36:542-547.
23. Esterre P, Inzan CK, Ratsioharana M, et al. A multicentre trial of terbinafine in patients with chromoblastomycosis. Effect on clinical and biologic criteria. J Dermatol Treat. 1998;9(Suppl 1):S29-S34.
24. Esterre P, Risteli L, Ricard-Blum S. Immunohistochemical study of type I collagen turn-over and of matrix metalloproteinases in chromoblastomycosis before and after treatment by terbinafine. Pathol Res Pract. 1998;194:847-853.
25. Ricard-Blum S, Hartmann DJ, Esterre P. Monitoring of extracellular matrix metabolism and cross-linking in tissue, serum and urine of patients with chromoblastomycosis, a chronic skin fibrosis. Eur J Clin Invest. 1998;28:748-754.
26. Gupta AK, Taborda PR, Sanzovo AD. Alternate week and combination itraconazole and terbinafine therapy for chromoblastomycosis caused by *Fonsecaea pedrosoi* in Brazil. Med Mycol. 2002;40:529-534.
27. Radford SA, Johnson EM, Warnock DW. *In vitro* studies of activity of voriconazole (UK-109,496), a new triazole antifungal agent, against emerging and less-common mold pathogens. Antimicrob Agents Chemother. 1997;41:841-843.
28. Del Poeta M, Schell WA, Perfect JR. *In vitro* antifungal activity of pneumocandin L-743,872 against a variety of clinically important molds. Antimicrob Agents Chemother. 1997;41:1835-1836.

CHAPTER **260**

Agents of Mycetoma

DUANE R. HOSPENTHAL

Mycetoma is a chronic progressive granulomatous infection of the skin and subcutaneous tissue most often affecting the lower extremities, typically a single foot. Disease is unique from other cutaneous/subcutaneous diseases in its triad of localized swelling, underlying sinus tracts, and production of grains or granules (comprised of aggregations of the causative organism) within the sinus tracts. These infections may be caused by fungi and termed *eumycotic mycetoma* or *eumycetoma,* or by filamentous higher bacteria and called *actinomycotic mycetoma* or *actinomycetoma.* The term *mycetoma* can also be found in the literature incorrectly referring to a fungus ball found in a preexisting cavity in the lung or within a paranasal sinus, most often caused by *Aspergillus* spp. The formation of grains by the infecting organism is confined to mycetoma, actinomycosis (see Chapter 253), and botryomycosis. Actinomycosis is a disease produced by the anaerobic and microaerophilic higher bacteria that normally colonize the mouth and gastrointestinal and urogenital tracts. The portal of entry in actinomycosis is from those colonized sites, whereas in mycetoma the portal is the skin and subcutaneous tissue into which the organism was inoculated by minor trauma. Botryomycosis is a chronic bacterial infection of soft tissues in which the causative organism, often *Staphylococcus aureus,* is found in loose clusters among the pus. In a rare form of ringworm called *dermatophyte mycetoma* there are also loosely compacted clusters of hyphae in subcutaneous pus. In contrast, mycetoma grains are dense clusters of organisms.

ETIOLOGIC AGENTS

The agents of mycetoma are fungi and aerobic filamentous bacteria that have been found on plants and in the soil.[1] Mycetoma caused by the actinomycetes appears to occur at a higher incidence than that caused by fungi. Eumycotic ("true fungal") disease is caused by a variety of fungal organisms. These can be divided into those that form dark grains

The views expressed are those of the author and do not reflect the official policy or position of the Department of the Army, the Department of Defense, or the U.S. Government.

TABLE 260-1 Typical Morphologic Features of Mycetoma Grains

Grain Color	Etiologic Agent
Eumycetoma (Eumycotic Mycetoma)*	
Black grains	*Madurella* spp., *Leptoshaeria* spp., *Curvularia* spp., *Exophiala jeanselmei*, *Phialophora verrucosa*, *Pyrenochaeta mackinnonii*, *P. romeroi*
Pale grains (white to yellow)	*Pseudallescheria boydii* (*Scedosporium apiospermum*), *Acremonium* spp., *Aspergillus* spp., *Fusarium* spp., *Neotestudina rosatii*
Actinomycetoma (Actinomycotic Mycetoma)†	
Pale grains (white to yellow)	*Actinomadurae madurae, Nocardia* spp.
Yellow to brown grains	*Streptomyces somaliensis*
Red to pink grains	*Actinomadurae pelletieri*

*Two- to 5-μm diameter hyphae are observed within grain.
†One-half to 1 μm diameter filaments are observed within grain.

and those that form pale or white grains (Table 260-1). The color must be observed in unstained specimens. Among the fungi causing dark-grained mycetoma, the most common are *Madurella mycetomatis, Leptosphaeria senegalensis,* and *Madurella grisea.* Other agents include *Corynespora cassicola, Curvularia geniculata, Curvularia lunata, Exophiala jeanselmei, Leptosphaeria tompkinsii, Phialophora verrucosa, Plenodomas avramii, Pseudochaetosphaeronema larense, Rhinocladiella atrovirens, Pyrenochaeta mackinnonii,* and *Pyrenochaeta romeroi. Pseudallescheria boydii* (anamorph *Scedosporium apiospermum*) is the most common cause of pale-colored grains. Other fungi in that category include *Acremonium falciforme, Acremonium kiliensis, Acremonium recifei, Aspergillus flavus, Aspergillus nidulans, Cylindrocarpon cyanescens, Cylindrocarpon destructans, Fusarium solani, Fusarium moniliforme (verticillioides), Neotestudina rosatii, Phaeoacremonium inflatipes,* and *Polycytella hominis.*[2-4] Actinomycetoma is caused by members of the order Actinomycetales, most commonly *Nocardia brasiliensis, Actinomadura madurae, Streptomyces somaliensis,* and *Actinomadura pelletieri.* A few cases have been reported caused by *Actinomadura latina, Nocardia asteroides, Nocardia otitidiscaviarum, Nocardia transvalensis,* and *Nocardiopsis dassonvillei.*[2,5] Actinomycetoma grains are white or pale yellow, except those caused by *Actinomadura pelletieri,* which are red to pink.

EPIDEMIOLOGY

The oldest description of this disease appears to date back to the ancient Indian Sanskrit text Atharva Veda, in which reference is made to "pada valmikam," translated to mean "anthill foot."[2] More modern descriptions from Madras, India, in the 19th century led to this disease initially being called "madura foot" or *maduromycosis,* a term still used by some today to describe eumycotic mycetoma. Mycetoma is most commonly found in tropical and subtropical climates, with highest incidence being reported from endemic areas in the India subcontinent, the Middle East, Africa, and Central and South America. Recently, reports have described the greatest number of new cases to occur in the Sudan. Only scattered reports describe cases originating in the United States, Europe, and Japan. Disease occurs around five times more frequently in males, commonly in the 20- to 40-year-old age range. Disease is more common in agricultural workers and outdoor laborers, but is not exclusively seen in rural areas. Disease occurs sporadically throughout most areas of the world, and some postulate that the increased numbers in tropical regions may also be in part due to decreased use of protective clothing, chiefly shoes in the warmer, poorer endemic regions.

The etiologic agents causing mycetoma vary from region to region and with climate. Worldwide, *M. mycetomatis* is the most common cause of this affliction, but *A. madurae, M. mycetomatis,* and *S. somaliensis* are more commonly reported from drier regions, whereas *P. boydii, Nocardia* species, and *A. pelletieri* are more common in those

areas with higher annual rainfall. In India, *Nocardia* species and *M. grisea* are the most common causes of mycetoma; in the Middle East, *M. mycetomatis* and *S. somaliensis;* in West Africa, *L. senegalensis;* and in East Africa, *M. mycetomatis* and *S. somaliensis.* In Central and South America, *M. grisea* and *Nocardia* species are the common causes of mycetoma, and in the United States, *P. boydii* (*S. apiospermum*) is the most commonly recovered etiologic agent.[6]

PATHOLOGY AND PATHOGENESIS

Infection follows inoculation of organisms, frequently through thorn punctures, wood splinters, or preexisting abrasions or trauma. After inoculation, these normally nonpathogenic organisms grow and survive through the production of grains (also called granules or sclerotia), structures composed of masses of mycelial fungi or bacterial filaments and a matrix component. The matrix material has been shown to be host derived with some pathogens. In eumycetoma, hyphal elements often have thickened cell walls toward the periphery of grains, potentially conferring protection against the host immune system.[7] Grains are seen in histopathology within abscesses containing polymorphonuclear cells. Complement-dependent chemotaxis of polymorphonuclear leukocytes has been shown to be induced by both fungal (*M. mycetomatis* and *P. boydii*) and actinomycotic (*S. somaliensis*) antigens in vitro.[8] Cells of the innate immune system attempt to engulf and inactivate these organisms, but in disease ultimately fail to accomplish this goal. Abscesses containing grains are seen in association with granulomatous inflammation and fibrosis. Three types of immune responses have been described in response to the grains of mycetoma.[9] The type I response is seen as neutrophils degranulate and adhere to the grain surface, leading to gradual disintegration of the grain. Type II response is characterized by the disappearance of neutrophils and arrival of macrophages to clear grains and neutrophil debris. Type III response is marked by the formation of epithelioid granuloma. This host response does not appear to be able to control infection, but likely accounts for the partial spontaneous healing that is seen in the disease.

It is not clear whether persons who develop mycetoma have predisposing immune deficits. Disease does not appear to be more common in immunocompromised hosts, and early study of immune function in persons with mycetoma has not clearly documented a common deficit.[10,11] Establishment of mycetoma in an animal model has only been accomplished in athymic nude (cell-mediated immune deficient) mice, suggesting an important role of the cell-mediated immune system. It has been suggested that the greater prevalence of disease in men is not completely explained by increased frequency of exposure to soil and plant material. Progesterone has been shown in vitro to inhibit the growth of *M. mycetomatis, P. romeroi,* and *N. brasiliensis.*[12,13] In the study of *N. brasiliensis,* estradiol limited disease produced in animals.[12] If immune dysfunction plays any role influencing which persons develop mycetoma, it is likely a minor deficit in cell-mediated immunity.

CLINICAL MANIFESTATIONS

Over three quarters of persons with mycetoma have a lesion of a lower extremity, most commonly in the foot (70%) (Figs. 260-1 and 260-2). Next in prevalence is disease of the hand (15%), followed by the upper extremities and other areas of the body that may be exposed by carrying firewood or thorny brush, including the upper back and adjacent neck, top of the head, and rarely the face (Fig. 260-3). Lesions in more than one anatomic site are extraordinarily rare. Disease begins in most cases as a single, small, painless subcutaneous nodule. This nodule slowly increases in size, becomes fixed to the underlying tissue, and ultimately develops sinus tracts beneath the lesion. These tracts open to the surface and drain purulent material with grains. Grains are several millimeters in diameter and may be seen by close inspection of a gauze bandage covering the sinus tract. Progression to draining sinus tracts can take weeks, months, and even years, occurring more rapidly in actinomycetoma. In a study of patients in India, the average time to presentation with disease from his-

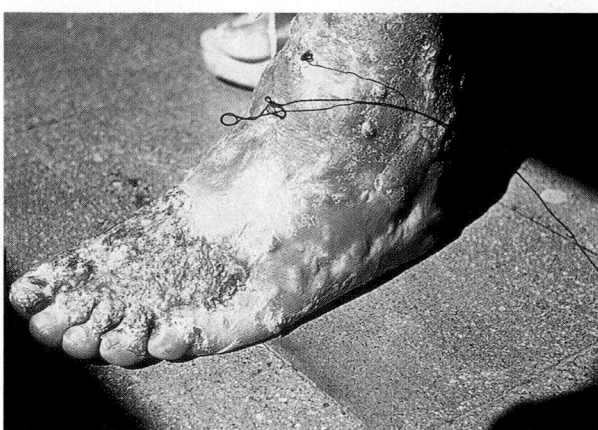

FIGURE 260-1. Mycetoma of the foot. *(From Beneke ES, Rogers AL. Medical Mycology and Human Mycoses. Belmont, CA: Star Publishing Company; 1996, reprinted with permission.)*

tory of probable inciting trauma was 3 years for *N. brasiliensis,* 7 years for *A. madurae,* and 9 years for *M. grisea.*[14]

Disease can affect the skin, subcutaneous tissue, and eventually contiguous bone, spreading along fascial planes. Overlying skin appears smooth and shiny, and is commonly fixed to the underlying tissue. Skin may be hypo- or hyperpigmented with signs of both old healed and active sinuses, displaying the cycle of spontaneous healing of older sinuses tracts and simultaneous spread of infection to new areas typical of this disease. Swelling is often firm and nontender, and the overlying skin is not erythematous. Muscle, tendons, and nerves are generally spared direct infection, but extensive local damage may lead to muscle wasting, bone destruction, and limb deformities. Lymphatic spread is rare, though it may follow surgical manipulation. Hematogenous spread has not been documented. This disease and its effects are generally localized, and thus no signs or symptoms of systemic illness are usually seen in mycetoma unless secondary bacterial infection occurs. When left untreated, disease continues to progress, and bacterial superinfection can lead to increased morbidity from local abscess formation, cellulitis, bacterial osteomyelitis, and, rarely, septic death.

Differential diagnosis includes botryomycosis, chronic bacterial osteomyelitis, and chromoblastomycosis.

DIAGNOSIS

A diagnosis of mycetoma can be made by the classic triad of painless soft tissue swelling, draining sinus tracts, and extrusion of grains. Diagnosis of the causative organism can be made by microscopic observation and culture of a grain. Deep biopsy with histopathology and

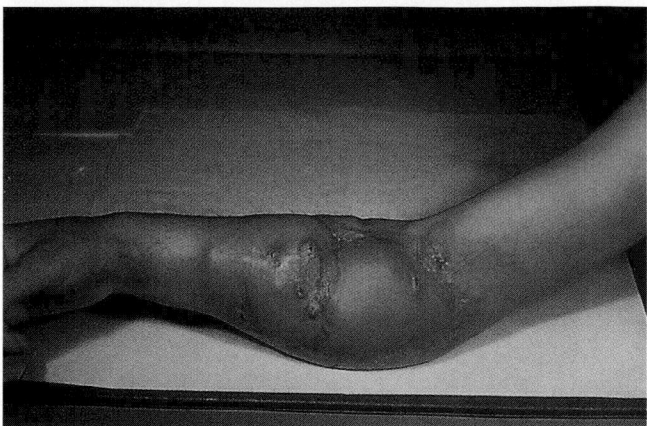

FIGURE 260-3. Mycetoma of the arm caused by *Madurella mycetomatis. (From Chandler FW, Ajello L. Mycetoma. In: Connor DH, Chandler FW, Schwartz DA, et al, eds. Pathology of Infectious Diseases. Norwalk, CT: Appleton & Lange; 1997, with permission of the McGraw-Hill Companies.)*

culture is usually not necessary, though obtaining a deep tissue biopsy avoids the bacterial contamination of surface cultures. Grains may not be seen in any one histopathologic section because they are scattered along the tracts. When a grain is present in the section, its large size and surrounding cluster of neutrophils make it difficult to miss, even without fungal or bacterial stains (Figs. 260-4 through 260-9). Organisms are usually not seen outside the grain. An alternate strategy is the aspiration of grains directly from an unopened sinus tract for microscopic observation and culture. Evaluation of spontaneously extruded grains may not allow diagnosis, because these grains may be composed of dead organisms and are frequently associated with contaminating bacteria that grow more rapidly than the mycetoma agent.

The grains (or granules or sclerotia) of mycetoma are usually 0.2 to 5 mm in diameter and thus may be observed grossly without magnification. Microscopic evaluation of crushed grains prepared with potassium hydroxide or stained with Gram stain is useful in differentiating between fungal and bacterial etiologies. Upon inspection, actinomycetes are recognized by the production of 0.5- to 1-μm-wide filaments and fungi by 2- to 5-μm-wide hyphae. Many reports and reviews detail the use of grain color, size, and consistency to diagnose the specific cause of mycetoma, but recovery of the causative agents in culture is more accurate and of greater clinical utility where resources are available.

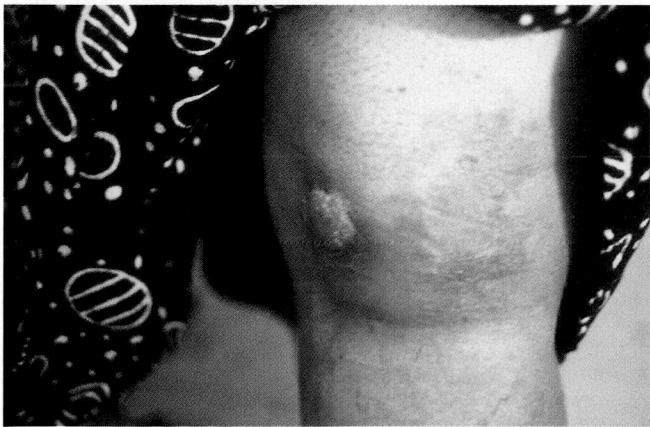

FIGURE 260-2. Mycetoma of the leg (seen from back of knee). *(Courtesy of Glenn W. Wortmann, M.D.)*

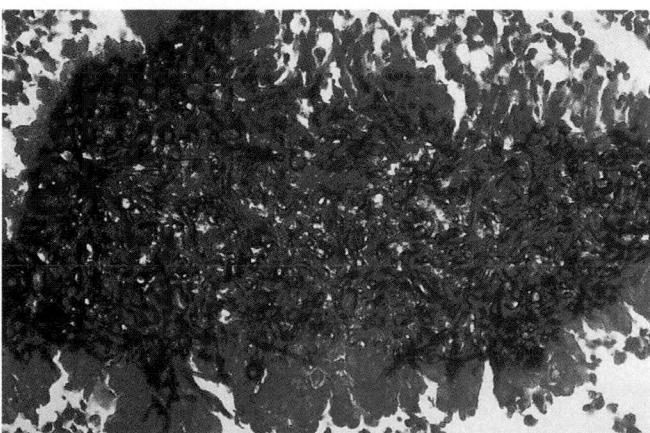

FIGURE 260-4. Eumycetoma grain of *Acremonium falciforme* (Gomori methenamine-silver [GMS] and hematoxylin and eosin [H&E]). *(From Chandler FW, Ajello L. Mycetoma. In: Connor DH, Chandler FW, Schwartz DA, et al, eds. Pathology of Infectious Diseases. Norwalk, CT: Appleton & Lange; 1997, with permission of the McGraw-Hill Companies.)*

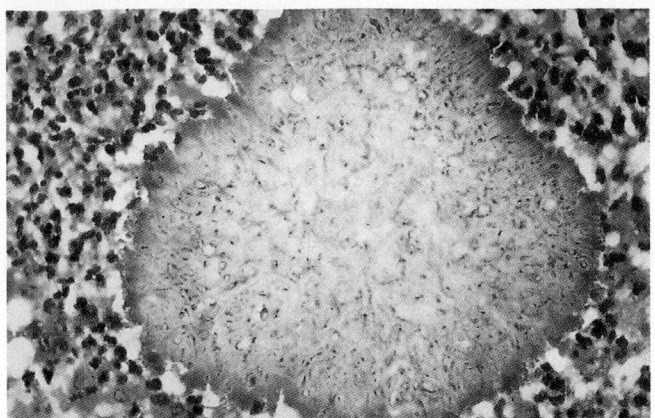

FIGURE 260-5. Eumycetoma grain of *Pseudallescheria boydii* (H&E). *(From Chandler FW, Ajello L. Mycetoma. In: Connor DH, Chandler FW, Schwartz DA, et al, eds. Pathology of Infectious Diseases. Norwalk, CT: Appleton & Lange; 1997, with permission of the McGraw-Hill Companies.)*

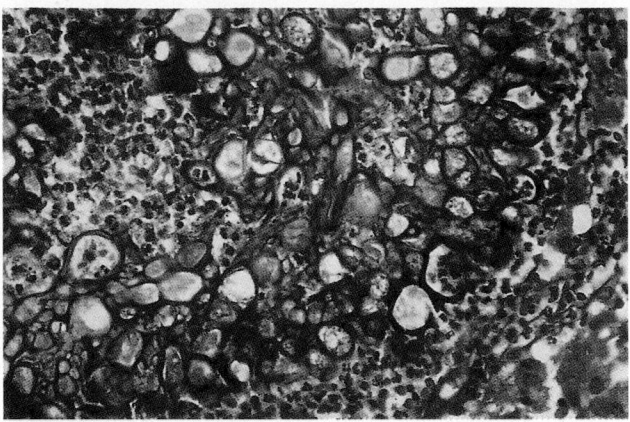

FIGURE 260-6. Eumycetoma grain of *Curvularia geniculata* (H&E). *(From Chandler FW, Ajello L. Mycetoma. In: Connor DH, Chandler FW, Schwartz DA, et al, eds. Pathology of Infectious Diseases. Norwalk, CT: Appleton & Lange; 1997, with permission of the McGraw-Hill Companies.)*

Culture of grains recovered from aspirated material or biopsy specimens can be used to diagnose the specific cause of mycetoma. If extruded grains are used, most experts suggest rinsing these in 70% alcohol, or alternately with antibiotic-containing saline solutions, to decrease bacterial contamination. Specimens should be cultured on both mycologic and mycobacteriologic media and held for at least 4 weeks.

The role of radiology in the management of mycetoma is limited to adjunctive assessment of disease extent, involvement of bone, and perhaps long-term follow-up of disease regression or progression. Radiographic studies can help define the extent of disease and aid in the differentiation of mycetoma from other disease. Standard x-ray studies can reveal bony involvement such as periosteal erosion secondary to invasion, osteoporosis, and changes consistent with osteomyelitis, including lytic lesions. Ultrasonography has been used successfully in the differentiation of mycetoma from other diseases. In a study of 100 patients with foot swelling who underwent ultrasonography prior to surgical excision, these lesions were found to have distinct characteristics that distinguished them from other diseases.[15] Eumycetoma were found to produce single or multiple thick-walled cavities, without acoustic enhancement, with grains represented as distinct hyperreflective echoes. Actinomycetoma produced similar results except grains produced fine echoes that were found at the bottom

of the cavities. Magnetic resonance imaging and computed tomography (CT) have also been evaluated in the management of mycetoma. Both modalities provide accurate assessment of disease extent when compared to surgical finding, especially in the soft tissues.[16] When compared directly, CT appears to be more sensitive in detecting early changes consistent with bone involvement.

Use of serology has been advocated by some authorities in the diagnosis and long-term management of this disease. Of the described tests, counterimmunoelectrophoresis is purported the most commonly used test. Lack of standardization or widespread availability limit the use of these tests except in centers that see a large volume of such patients.

TREATMENT

Treatment of this disease has proven to be quite difficult, and typically includes both antimicrobial agents and surgery. Short of amputation, surgery alone is rarely successful in the treatment of mycetoma, but adjunctive removal of smaller lesions or debulking of larger ones does play an important role in management of this disease. Because chemotherapy varies for actinomycetoma and eumycetoma, at a minimum the clinician must differentiate whether a mycetoma is due to actinomycetes or fungi. Ideally, recovery of the causative organism

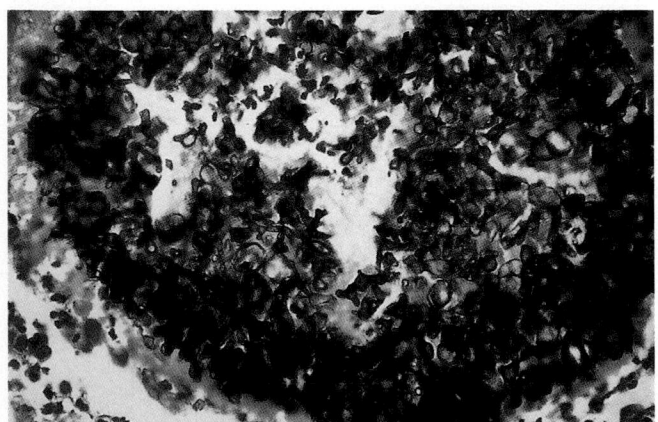

FIGURE 260-7. Eumycetoma grain of *Neotestudina rosatii* (GMS-H&E). *(From Chandler FW, Ajello L. Mycetoma. In: Connor DH, Chandler FW, Schwartz DA, et al, eds. Pathology of Infectious Diseases. Norwalk, CT: Appleton & Lange; 1997, with permission of the McGraw-Hill Companies.)*

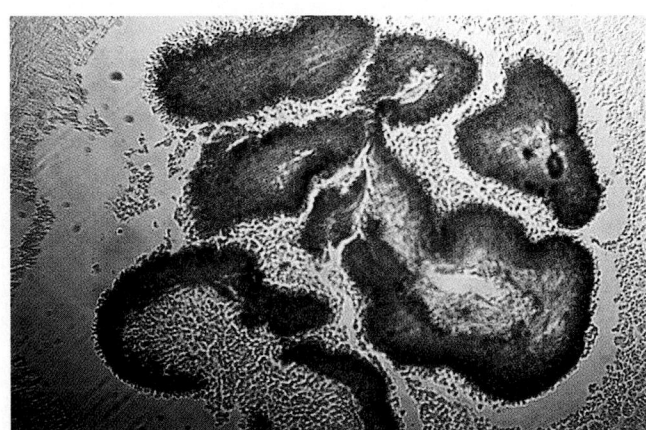

FIGURE 260-8. Actinomycetoma grain (Gridley stain). *(From Beneke ES, Rogers AL. Medical Mycology and Human Mycoses. Belmont, CA: Star Publishing Company; 1996, reprinted with permission.)*

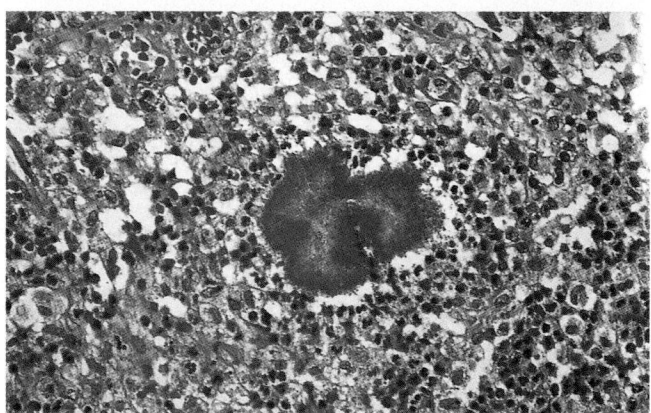

FIGURE 260-9. *Nocardia brasiliensis* grain (H&E). *(From Chandler FW, Ajello L. Mycetoma. In: Connor DH, Chandler FW, Schwartz DA, et al, eds. Pathology of Infectious Diseases. Norwalk, CT: Appleton & Lange; 1997, with permission of the McGraw-Hill Companies.)*

can allow identification of species, and perhaps even susceptibility testing, to guide therapy. Treatment regimens are currently based on expert opinion as no randomized controlled trials have been performed. Duration of therapy is also not defined, with most patients receiving 3 to 24 months of therapy to effect an adequate response.

The most commonly described regimens for actinomycetoma includes streptomycin plus either trimethoprim-sulfamethoxazole or dapsone. In this regimen, streptomycin (14 mg/kg/day) is given intramuscularly for the first month (and sometimes three times weekly thereafter for several months) in addition to a long course of trimethoprim-sulfamethoxazole, usually one double-strength tablet (160 mg trimethoprim and 800 mg sulfamethoxazole) twice daily, or dapsone (1.5 mg/kg/day twice daily). Alternate regimens include trimethoprim-sulfamethoxazole and dapsone,[5] and amikacin with trimethoprim-sulfamethoxazole. Cycled dosing of amikacin (15 mg/kg/day divided into two daily doses for 3 weeks) in addition to trimethoprim-sulfamethoxazole for 5 weeks has also been described.[17] Most patients improved with only one to two cycles of this therapy. Response to trimethoprim-sulfamethoxazole alone has also been reported.[18] Other regimens that have been used include streptomycin with either sulfadoxine-pyrimethamine or rifampin; combination of penicillin, gentamicin, and trimethoprim-sulfamethoxazole followed by amoxicillin and trimethoprim-sulfamethoxazole[19]; and regimens that include amoxicillin-clavulanate,[20] fusidic acid, clindamycin, or imipenem/cilastatin.

Antifungal therapy of eumycetoma most commonly includes use of azole antifungals, because amphotericin B has not proved to be effective in producing long-term cures. Early study using ketoconazole at 200 mg twice daily noted marked improvement or cure in 72% of a group of 50 patients with mycetoma secondary to *M. mycetomatis* receiving 9 to 36 months of therapy.[5] Itraconazole used at a dose of 100 mg twice daily in the same population produced marked improvement in 42% of subjects, but no cures.[17] Multiple case reports and case series have reported mixed success with the use of itraconazole, employing a range of doses.[5,21,22] Fluconazole has proven to be even less effective in the treatment of mycetoma. *P. boydii* (*S. apiospermum*) is not responsive to ketoconazole therapy and is often resistant to itraconazole in vitro and in clinical therapy. In vitro, voriconazole has good activity against many of the agents of eumycetoma, including *M. mycetomatis*, *L. senegalensis*, and *P. boydii* (*S. apiospermum*).[23] Although data on clinical efficacy is lacking, the

minimum inhibitory concentration of voriconazole is commonly lower than that seen with itraconazole against many of the agents of eumycetoma, and thus this azole antifungal could potentially become an important drug in the treatment of fungal mycetoma. Posaconazole is an investigational oral azole that has similar in vitro susceptibility patterns to voriconazole and also may deserve a clinical trial in mycetoma.

PREVENTION

No preventative vaccine is available against any of the agents of mycetoma. Disease prevention is best accomplished by impacting on the incidence of the traumatic inoculation of the causative organisms. The wearing of shoes and clothing to protect against splinters and thorn picks should be stressed. Debilitating disease can be prevented by early identification and treatment of lesions, usually with minor surgery and chemotherapy.

REFERENCES

1. Ahmed A, Adelmann D, Fahal A, et al. Environmental occurrence of *Madurella mycetomatis*, the major agent of human eumycetoma in Sudan. J Clin Microbiol. 2002;40:1031-1036.
2. Kwon-Chung KJ, Bennett JE. Mycetoma. In: Medical Mycology. Philadelphia: Lea & Febiger; 1992:560-593.
3. McGinnis MR. Mycetoma. Dermatol Clin. 1996;14:97-104.
4. McGinnis MR, Padhye AA. Fungi causing eumycotic mycetoma. In: Murray PR, Baron EJ, Jorgensen JH, et al, eds. Manual of Clinical Microbiology. 8th ed. Washington, DC: ASM Press; 2003:1848-1856.
5. Welsh O, Salinas MC, Rodriguez MA. Treatment of eumycetoma and actinomycetoma. Curr Top Med Mycol. 1995;6:47-71.
6. Green WO, Adams TE. Mycetoma in the United States: A review and report of seven additional cases. Am J Clin Pathol. 1964;42:75-91.
7. Wethered DB, Markey MA, Hay RJ, et al. Ultrastructural and immunogenic changes in the formation of mycetoma grains. J Med Vet Mycol. 1986;25:39-46.
8. Yousif MA, Hay RJ. Leucocyte chemotaxis to mycetoma agents—The effect of the antifungal drugs griseofulvin and ketoconazole. Trans R Soc Trop Med Hyg. 1987;81:319-321.
9. Fahal AH, el Toum EA, el Hassan AM, et al. The host tissue reaction to Madurella mycetomatis: New classification. J Med Vet Mycol. 1995;33:15-17.
10. Bendl BJ, Mackey D, Al-Saati F, et al. Mycetoma in Saudi Arabia. J Trop Med Hyg. 1987;90:51-59.
11. Mahgoub ES, Gumaa SA, El Hassan AM. Immunological status of mycetoma patients. Bull Soc Pathol Exot Filiales. 1977;70:48-54.
12. Hernández-Hernández F, López-Martínez R, Méndez-Tovar LJ, Manzano-Gayosso P. *Nocardia brasiliensis*: in vitro and in vivo growth in response to steroid sex hormones. Mycopathologia. 1995;132:79-85.
13. Méndez-Tovar LJ, de Bièvre C, López-Martínez R. Effets des hormones sexuelles humaines sur le dévelopment in vitro des agens d'eumycétomes. J Mycol Méd. 1991;1:141-143.
14. Maiti PK, Ray A, Bandyopadhyay S. Epidemiological aspects of mycetoma from a retrospective study of 264 cases in West Bengal. Trop Med Int Health. 2002;7:788-792.
15. Fahal AH, Sheik HE, Homeida MM, et al. Ultrasonographic imaging of mycetoma. Br J Surg. 1997;84:1120-1122.
16. Sharif HS, Clark DC, Aabed MY, et al. Mycetoma: Comparison of MR imaging with CT. Radiology. 1991;178:865-870.
17. Hay RJ, Mahgoub ES, Leon G, et al. Mycetoma. J Med Vet Mycol. 1992;30(Suppl 1):41-49.
18. Khatri ML, Al-Halali HM, Fouad Khalid M, et al. Mycetoma in Yemen: Clinicoepidemiologic and histopathologic study. Int J Dermatol. 2002;41:586-593.
19. Ramam M, Garg T, D'Souza P, et al. A two-step schedule for the treatment of actinomycotic mycetomas. Acta Derm Venereol. 2000;80:378-380.
20. Wortman PD. Treatment of a *Nocardia brasiliensis* mycetoma with sulfamethoxazole and trimethoprim, amikacin, and amoxicillin and clavulanate. Arch Dermatol. 1993;129:564-567.
21. Resnik BI, Burdick AE. Improvement of eumycetoma with itraconazole. J Am Acad Dermatol. 1995;33:917-919.
22. Smith EL, Kutbi S. Improvement of eumycetoma with itraconazole. J Am Acad Dermatol. 1997;36:279-280.
23. Radford SA, Johnson EM, Warnock DW. In vitro studies of activity of voriconazole (UK-109,496), a new triazole antifungal agent, against emerging and less-common mold pathogens. Antimicrob Agents

Cryptococcus neoformans

JOHN R. PERFECT

Cryptococcus neoformans is an encapsulated, heterobasidiomycetous fungus that has progressed from being a rare human pathogen, with just over 300 cases of cryptococcosis reported in the literature before 1955, to being a common worldwide opportunistic pathogen as immunocompromised human populations have dramatically increased over the past two decades. Cryptococcosis crosses the entire spectrum of patient populations, from the apparently immunocompetent host without an underlying disease to those severely immunocompromised from infection with the human immunodeficiency virus (HIV), an organ transplantation, or a malignancy.[1] Furthermore, it has a wide range of clinical presentations, which can vary from asymptomatic colonization of the respiratory airways to dissemination of infection into any part of the human body. *C. neoformans* enters the host primarily through the lungs but has a special predilection for invading the central nervous system (CNS) of the susceptible host. Pulmonary infections are common and may have multiple clinical presentations and management issues. On the other hand, cryptococcal meningoencephalitis represents the primary life-threatening infection for this fungal pathogen and has required the most clinical attention.

HISTORY

The first identification of *Cryptococcus* from an environmental source was made by Sanfelice in 1894, from peach juice in Italy.[2] Within a year, Busse and Buschke[3] independently reported the first human case of cryptococcosis in a young woman who developed a chronic ulcer over the skin above her tibia, with yeasts identified in the tissue and later at autopsy; this yeast was also found to have spread to multiple organs in her body. By 1914, Versé described a human case of cryptococcal meningitis,[3a,3b] and in 1916 Stoddard and Cutler gave a complete description of the CNS pathology for this infection, including in their report that the yeast forms had surrounding areas of clearing within the tissue. This finding was the first description of the signature structure for this yeast, the polysaccharide capsule. During the early years of clinical cryptococcosis, the names of this yeast were several and included *Saccharomyces neoformans, Cryptococcus hominis,* and *Torula histolytica.* In 1935, Benham attempted to categorize these poorly defined yeasts based on morphology, fermentation, and serologic studies.[4] She named one yeast *C. hominis,* and its disease, cryptococcosis. The name was later changed to *C. neoformans* based on temporal priority, as Sanfelice had first used the species name of *neoformans.* However, despite Benham's proposal, it took another 25 years before cryptococcosis became the primary nomenclature for this infection rather than torulosis. In 1976, Kwon-Chung discovered and characterized the sexual stage of *C. neoformans,* and the teleomorph was named *Filobasidiella neoformans.*[5] In a culmination of studies identifying this encapsulated yeast, in 2003 the genome of *C. neoformans* was sequenced.

MYCOLOGY

Life Cycle and Genetics

The life cycle of *C. neoformans* involves two distinct forms: asexual and sexual. The asexual stage exists as encapsulated yeast cells that reproduce by simple, narrow-based budding. The haploid (occasionally diploid in nature), unicellular yeasts are the primary forms recovered from environmental sources and human infections. The asexual forms represent the primary structures seen in tissue and recovered from cultures during clinical disease. However, this fungus has a more complex life cycle, with a bipolar mating system that can be observed under certain in vitro conditions. For example, yeasts exist in one of two mating types, "alpha" or "a." When two strains of opposite mating types are physically placed together on specific, nutrient-poor media such as V-8 juice agar, the cells undergo conjugation, producing filaments with true clamp connections. At the ends of these filaments, basidia form, and within these basidia, meiosis occurs and chains of basidiospores are produced. The 1- to 2-micron basidiospores, with their size and shape, have been hypothesized to be the infectious propagules. They deposit in the lung, where the spores rapidly convert to the yeast form. However, the sexual stage at present remains a laboratory observation, and the sexual structures such as basidiospores have yet to be identified in nature. Recent studies have made substantial progress in understanding the molecular signaling networks that control the sexual cycle, and in some cases genes in these mating pathways have been linked to both morphogenesis and virulence of the yeast.[6]

In the 1980s, an interesting epidemiologic observation was made and confirmed by others that more than 95% of environmental and clinical *C. neoformans* isolates appear to contain only the alpha mating locus.[7] The reason for this genetic bias remains unclear, but it has been discovered that under certain environmental conditions *C. neoformans* undergoes haploid fruiting.[8] Haploid fruiting occurs when haploid yeast strains under specific conditions produce hyphae and basidiospores without mating and exchange genetic information through meiosis. It is possible that this fruiting with sporulation allows wider dissemination of the fungus in the environment and thus more exposure leading to clinical disease. The alpha-mating–type strains are much more likely to produce haploid fruiting structures. An alternative explanation for the alpha-mating locus bias is that the approximately 100-kilobase locus or its adjacent genomic areas contain virulence genes that make the strains more fit in the environment (or in the host). Initial studies with congenic strains of *C. neoformans* var. *neoformans* differing primarily in mating-type locus did suggest that the alpha-mating strain was more virulent in mice.[9] On the other hand, the alpha and "a" mating-type loci have been identified in *C. neoformans* var. *grubii,* and recent experiments with two congenic strains in this variety differing only in the mating locus appear to be identical in virulence.[10] It is still uncertain how much the mating loci contribute to the virulence of this yeast, and the alpha-mating–type bias is not yet precisely explained.

Taxonomy

The genus *Cryptococcus* comprises 19 species, loosely characterized as a variety of encapsulated yeasts. There have been occasional reports of human infections with several of these non-*neoformans* species, such as *Cryptococcus albidus* and *Cryptococcus laurentii.*[11,12] However, such clinical reports are uncommon, and the infection is occasionally poorly documented. Therefore any human infection with a cryptococcal species other than *C. neoformans* needs rigorous histopathology and cultural proof of infection.

For several decades, *C. neoformans* strains have been grouped into two varieties that included five serotypes based on capsule structure. *C. neoformans* var. *neoformans* included strains with serotypes A, D, and AD, and *C. neoformans* var. *gattii* contained strains with serotypes B and C. The serotype classification (A-D) describes antigenic differences in the structure of the polysaccharide capsule; these differences can be detected by antibodies from rabbit sera[13] or by specific monoclonal antibodies.[14,15]

The stable taxonomic classification of these varieties and serotypes has been updated through new genomic analyses, and several changes have been proposed. With the use of specific DNA typing methods and other physiologic factors, it has been proposed that the serotype A strains be classified into a separate variety, *C. neoformans* var. *grubii.*[16] Serotype D isolates are to remain in the var. *neoformans.* The varietal status of serotype AD strains has not been proposed. It has also become clear that many of the serotype AD strains represent stable diploid strains, possibly occurring as incomplete genetic crosses between varieties *neoformans* and *grubii*. However, genetic mapping of A and D strains suggests that these varieties biologically diverged from each other more than 18 million years ago.[17] Thus, there are proposals to abolish the varietal system and replace it with three separate species that contain a grouping of several genotypes in each species. A strong argument has recently been made to change *C. neoformans* var. *gattii* (serotypes B and C) to a separate species named *Cryptococcus bacillospora*. As rapid advances in the understanding of genetic diversity are made among these fungi in the genome era, taxonomic relationships and nomenclature will remain in some flux. However, at present, for clinicians the standard serotype classification used for half a century and the split into two varieties, var. *neoformans* and var. *gattii*, still remain useful nomenclature for describing the clinical strain differences in epidemiology, pathogenesis, and clinical features. In this chapter, the term var. *grubii* will be appended to the designation of serotype A because most isolates continue to be identified by serotype, not by genotype, and the taxonomic status of var. *grubii* remains controversial.

The anamorph (yeast or asexual stage) dominates clinical discussion of this encapsulated yeast. On the other hand, the teleomorph and its more complex structure places this fungus in the basidiomycete family, and its sexual state genus name is *Filobasidiella*. The sexual state of serotypes A and D strains is called *Filobasidiella neoformans;* serotype B and C strains are designated *Filobasidiella bacillospora*.

Epidemiologic and clinical studies have usually used a colored growth medium, described later, to distinguish serotype A, D, and AD isolates, designated var. *neoformans,* from serotype B and C isolates, designated var. *gattii*. When referring to the results of such studies, the term var. *neoformans* should be understood to include what some authorities call var. *grubii*.

Identification

On most routine laboratory agar media, colonies of *C. neoformans* appear within 48 to 72 hours after plating a specimen. Some selective media containing cycloheximide inhibit the growth of this yeast and thus should not be used. For blood cultures, the lysis–centrifugation method works very well for isolating *Cryptococcus,* but is no longer necessary because automated blood culture methods have been improved, and cryptococcemia is commonly detected in severely immunosuppressed patients.[18] In some populations of the world with high rates of HIV infection, cryptococcemia has become a common finding in patients with fever. However, it rarely produces symptoms of hypotension or shock.

On agar plates, the yeast colony grows as a white-to-cream–colored, opaque colony several millimeters in diameter. The colonies typically become mucoid with prolonged incubation, reflecting polysaccharide capsule formation. Colonies occasionally develop sectors that differ in pigmentation or exhibit morphologic changes (e.g., smooth or wrinkled). *C. neoformans* has been shown to possess the ability to produce a morphologic switching phenotype, which explains this variety of colony shapes in some strains.[19,20] The optimal environmental growth temperature for the majority of *C. neoformans* strains is between 30° and 35° C, with a maximum tolerated temperature for most strains at 40° C. Serotype A strains tend to tolerate higher temperatures than serotype D and serotype B/C strains.[21] *C. neoformans* strains generally grow well at 37° C, with generation times of 3 to 6 hours, and this is a primary virulence phenotype that separates it from other cryptococcal species that do not tolerate mammalian body temperatures.

In the clinical laboratory, *C. neoformans* can be readily differentiated from other yeasts on the basis of its morphology and biochemical tests. The specific identification can be confirmed by a battery of biochemical tests available commercially in kits.[22,23] However, there are three direct tests that predict that a yeast may be *C. neoformans*. First, placing the yeast into an India ink preparation may reveal the encapsulated yeast. The capsule is generally better seen in direct clinical specimens and may not be apparent in wet mounts made from cultures. This finding occurs because capsule

production is induced by environmental cues, such as elevated carbon dioxide concentrations or limited iron conditions. The host environment is ideal for capsule production.

Second, a rapid urease test is positive in most *Cryptococcus* species. *Cryptococcus* species, unlike *Candida* species, possess urease, an enzyme that hydrolyzes urea to ammonia and increases the ambient pH. A positive urease test can be detected within minutes.[24] Several nonpathogenic yeasts produce abundant urease and *Trichosporon* species may be weakly urease positive.

Third, *C. neoformans* is one of the few yeast species that possess prominent laccase activity,[25] an enzyme that allows the conversion of diphenolic compounds into melanin. Detection of this unique biologic characteristic is possible with media containing, for example, niger seed (birdseed), caffeic acid, or dopamine. Yeast colonies that turn brown to black on these special agars are identified as melanin positive. In a clinical specimen, such a yeast colony might well be *C. neoformans*. (However, other cryptococcal species also possess laccase.) These selective agar assays are particularly helpful when attempting to identify pigmented cryptococcal colonies from environmental samples contaminated by other fungi and bacteria.

Histopathologically, *C. neoformans* has several important features. In most cases, *C. neoformans* in tissue exhibits a prominent capsule. Microscopically, most clinical isolates appear as spherical, narrow-based, budding, encapsulated yeast cells in both tissue and culture. Short hyphal or pseudohyphal structures may exist in vivo or under certain stress conditions in vitro, but these structures are rarely observed unless certain in vitro nutrient conditions for mating or haploid fruiting are met. The yeast cells vary in size from 5 to 10 μ in diameter, and they exhibit single or multiple buds. Because the buds are readily detached from their parental cells, the majority of yeast cells in both tissue and culture lack buds. Finally, the size of the capsule under direct observation varies with the individual strain and with the immediate environment.

There are three methods for identifying the four serotypes. First, commercially available antibodies can distinguish differences in the capsular structures. Second, there are known differences between the biochemistry pathways of the serotypes. Most serotype B and C isolates assimilate glycine as a sole carbon source, whereas serotype A and D isolates generally do not. An agar containing L-canavanine, glycine, and bromothymol blue (CGB) uses a color change to separate serotypes A and D from B and C. Third, analysis of DNA base composition is extremely accurate. Early examination of the genomes of these serotypes shows an approximately 6% to 8% difference in nucleotides between serotype A and D strains and a slightly greater difference between these strains and serotype B and C strains. It is clear from a variety of methods, including random amplified polymorphic DNA (RAPD), karyotypes, polymerase chain reaction (PCR) fingerprinting, and direct sequencing of strains, that molecular techniques can be used to readily identify an isolate as belonging to a certain serotype. Furthermore, strains can even be classified into certain genotypes by PCR fingerprint patterns. There are presently eight distinct genotypes for *C. neoformans*: VN1 to VN4 for serotype A, and VG1 to VG4 for serotypes B and C.[26] Serotype D isolates have proven difficult to cluster into distinct genotypes.

ECOLOGY

C. neoformans is a saprobe in nature.[27] It was first described in fruits, but after years of investigation it is clear that it has an environmental niche or habitat associated with certain trees and rotting wood. A second consistent finding is that *C. neoformans* has frequently been isolated from soil contaminated by guano from birds.[28,29]

C. neoformans Serotypes A, D, and AD (var. *neoformans* and var. *grubii*)

In the 1950s, Emmons first isolated *C. neoformans* from soil and from the droppings and nests of pigeons.[28,29] Since the original reports, the fungus has been found in soil samples from around the world.

However, the soils most enriched in *C. neoformans* are those that are frequented by birds, especially pigeons, turkeys, and chickens. Guano from other birds, such as canaries and parrots, has also yielded the yeast. Despite this consistent ecologic observation, it is still not certain the precise link between natural habitat and the birds. Occasionally, birds develop disease that involves *C. neoformans,* but this is relatively unusual. The resistance of birds to disease may result from their very high body temperature, which is not conducive to growth of *C. neoformans.* The yeast may transiently colonize the gastrointestinal tract of the birds, however. The most likely environmental niche for these serotypes is rotting vegetation or wood of certain trees. The birds may simply represent vectors, spreading the fungus from vegetations into the soils and dusts of human traffic.

C. neoformans Serotypes B and C (var. *gattii*)

Unlike the two other varieties, *C. neoformans* var. *gattii* has never been cultured from bird guano. Furthermore, there appears to be a certain geographic limitation to the occurrence of infections with this variety. With this knowledge base, Ellis and Pfeiffer were able to culture *C. neoformans* var. *gattii* from vegetation around and associated with the river red gum trees *(Eucalyptus camaldulensis)* and forest red gum trees *(E. tereticornis)* in Australia.[30] Because these trees were exported to other areas of the world where this variety of infection is also observed, Ellis and Pfeiffer reasoned that these tree species may be a vector for infection. Others have found this cryptococcal variety associated with many species of eucalyptus trees in other parts of the world. It was suggested that the yeasts or basidiospores might be released in relationship to the flowering of these trees, but this has not been proven. The association of these trees with var. *gattii* remains strong, but a recent outbreak of cryptococcosis on Vancouver Island, British Columbia, suggests that other trees such as firs, maples, and oaks may also be an ecologic niche for this variety of *Cryptococcus.*[31]

Another ecologic factor may be important to the human pathogenicity of this fungus: it has been found in soil associated with a variety of soil bacteria, amebas, mites, worms, and sow bugs. The stress of this biotic area with its abundant predatory scavengers may have selected for a yeast species that can survive such harsh conditions. In fact, recent work has shown that *C. neoformans* can survive within amebas, which in some respects may provide an environment similar to that in a human macrophage.[32] Furthermore, nonpathogenic cryptococci can act as food for the nematode *Caenorhabditis elegans,* but *C. neoformans* can actually kill the worm.[33]

EPIDEMIOLOGY

C. neoformans is not generally considered to be a routine constituent of the human microbial biota. Although there are clinical reports of its being isolated from nonsterile sites on patients with no signs or symptoms of cryptococcosis,[34] and although it can be detected as a commensal in dogs, endobronchial colonization is more frequently observed in humans with underlying chronic pulmonary disease. When *C. neoformans* is isolated from nonsterile clinical specimens, the clinician must examine for evidence of disease, or of risk factors for the development of disease, before planning further management strategies. Several methods have been used to study the existence of prior infection with *C. neoformans* without evidence for disease. Research has shown that patients with cryptococcosis have delayed hypersensitivity to cryptococcal antigens,[35] and the prevalence of positive skin test reactions in pigeon fanciers and laboratory workers engaged in research activities with this yeast have been reported to be high.[36] Unfortunately, there is no established skin test for routine clinical use in patients with cryptococcosis, and this reduces our ability to assess the magnitude of infection. However, most adults possess antibody to *C. neoformans* antigens; in New York City, most children acquire antibodies to cryptococcal antigens before the age of 10.[37,38] These observations suggest that there are frequent asymptomatic infections. Although exposure to this yeast is limited in certain areas of the world, infections have been reported in all continents.

TABLE 261-1 Conditions Known or Possibly Associated with Predisposition to *Cryptococcus neoformans* Infections

HIV infection	Systemic lupus erythematosus*
Lymphoproliferative disorders	HIV-negative CD4+ T-cell lymphopenia
Sarcoidosis	Diabetes mellitus†
Corticosteroid therapy	Organ transplantation*
Hyper-IgM syndrome	Peritoneal dialysis
Hyper-IgE syndrome	Cirrhosis
Monoclonal antibodies (e.g., infliximab)	

*Immunosuppressive therapy may account for the predisposition.
†Diabetes mellitus has historically been considered a risk factor for cryptococcal infection. However, diabetes is a common disease, and it is unclear whether this condition is truly a specific risk factor for cryptococcosis.
From Casadevall A, Perfect JR. *Cryptococcus neoformans.* Washington: ASM Press; 1998:410.

The vast majority of patients with symptomatic disseminated cryptococcosis have an identified underlying immunocompromised condition (Table 261-1). The most common underlying conditions worldwide include the acquired immunodeficiency syndrome (AIDS), prolonged treatment with corticosteroids, organ transplantation, advanced malignancy, diabetes, and sarcoidosis. It has been estimated that approximately 20% of patients who have cryptococcosis without HIV infection have no apparent underlying disease or risk factor.[39]

The best estimates for rates of cryptococcosis in the United States in the pre-AIDS era predicted an overall incidence of 0.8 case per million persons per year. In 1992, during the peak of the AIDS epidemic in the United States, the rate reached almost five cases of cryptococcosis per 100,000 persons per year in several large cities. In the mid 1990s, before highly active antiretroviral therapy (HAART) but with widespread use of fluconazole for oral candidiasis, the rate was reduced, and it stabilized in the cities at approximately one case per 100,000 per year.[40,41] With the widespread use of HAART in developed countries by the beginning of the 21st century, the incidence of cryptococcosis has declined and appears to have reached a stable number of new infections.[42] In the AIDS population in developed countries, it now represents an infection that identifies a disadvantaged patient or an untreated and undiagnosed HIV infection. Thus, cryptococcosis in patients with AIDS identifies this group as having less access to medical care.[43]

In less well-developed countries with major epidemics of HIV, such as sub-Saharan Africa, cryptococcosis appears to reach very high prevalences. Although the data are not precise, some reports indicate that 15% to 45% of those with advanced HIV infection succumb to cryptococcosis.[44,45] In many African medical centers, cryptococcosis represents the most common cause of culture-proven meningitis, even surpassing *Neisseria meningitidis* and *Streptococcus pneumoniae* meningitis.[46] In fact, the risk of cryptococcosis appears higher for African-born individuals even when they move to industrialized nations.[47] Increasing cases of cryptococcosis have consistently followed the pattern of HIV infections, and in countries such as Thailand, blood cultures containing this yeast have become common.[48]

The varieties of *C. neoformans* that are identified as causing disease differ by geographic location and by whether the patient has a concomitant HIV infection. Prior to the AIDS epidemic, Kwon-Chung and Bennett found that at least 80% of clinical isolates worldwide were *C. neoformans* serotype A (var. *grubii*).[49] *C. neoformans* serotype B was almost exclusively found in tropical and subtropical areas such as southern California, Hawaii, Brazil, Australia, Southeast Asia, and central Africa. Serotype C was rare in all localities but seemed to follow the same geographic distribution as serotype B. *C. neoformans* serotype D (var. *neoformans*) was predominantly isolated from Europe, especially Denmark, Germany, Italy, France, and Switzerland, and some strains of this variety were found in the United States.[49-51] In AIDS patients, the vast majority of isolates are serotype A (var. *grubii*), although serotype D has constituted a significant percentage of isolates in several areas of France. Only a small portion of cases have been reported to be var. *gattii*. The numbers of var. *gattii* infections were very small even in areas where this variety was commonly observed to cause disease in the pre-AIDS era.

Cryptococcosis has a measurable rate of infection in two other major risk groups: cancer patients and recipients of solid organ transplants. Since the 1950s, it has been known that patients with lymphoproliferative disorders and certain hematologic malignancies, such as chronic lymphocytic leukemia, were at higher risk than the general population for cryptococcosis.[52-55] A retrospective analysis of case reports from a single large cancer center from 1989 to 1999 reported that the incidence of cryptococcosis was 18 cases per 100,000 admissions.[56] Because of their profound and prolonged immunosuppression, organ transplant recipients also became a target for this infection. In one study, cryptococcosis occurred in 2.8% of all solid organ transplant recipients.[57] Kidney and liver transplant recipients appeared to have the highest risk for cryptococcosis.[57,58] However, in bone marrow transplant recipients, who have a very high incidence of fungal infections, cryptococcosis is not common. In rare circumstances, the transplanted organ (e.g., cornea, lung) has been shown to carry the cryptococcal infection into a susceptible recipient.[59,60]

Sarcoidosis, with or without corticosteroid therapy, predisposes to cryptococcosis. The lung, skin, and bone lesions of the two diseases overlap clinically and by histopathology.

Before the AIDS epidemic, there was a small but consistently higher rate of cryptococcosis in males than in females. Cryptococcosis can occur before puberty, but even in children with several known risk factors, the incidence is uncommon. Interestingly, there have been several reports of cryptococcosis in children with a hyper-IgM syndrome.[61,62] In adults, idiopathic CD4+ T-cell lymphopenia may be identified by the development of disseminated cryptococcosis.[63] With much less preciseness, it has been suggested that smoking and outdoor activities may increase the risk of cryptococcosis.[40,64] Finally, it is likely that as there is more clinical use of monoclonal antibodies, such as infliximab,[65] against immune factors for other diseases, this group of patients may become at higher risk for cryptococcal infections.

There is general agreement that most cryptococcal infections are acquired primarily by inhalation of infectious propagules, and there are occasional cases of direct traumatic inoculation through contaminated environmental projectiles or laboratory/clinical accidents such as needlesticks.[66,67] However, neither the environmental source of infection nor the infectious form of *C. neoformans* has been precisely established in most cases of cryptococcosis. It is hypothesized that either dehydrated, poorly encapsulated yeast cells or basidiospores (<5 μm) are needed as infectious propagules for alveolar deposition in the lungs. Studies at sites with contaminated soils have found that the air contains the correct size of propagule.[68-70] Molecular typing methods have confirmed that clinical isolates can be indistinguishable from environmental isolates.[71-73] Although associations between infection and environmental exposure have been reported for many of the classic dimorphic fungi, this association is rare for *C. neoformans*. However, a recent outbreak of var. *gattii* infections on Vancouver Island has been potentially linked to a common environmental exposure.[31] There has not been a consistent seasonal association for the occurrence of cryptococcosis, but one study did find more cases in the fall and winter.[74] However, another study found no seasonal association despite the finding that *Penicillium marneffei* infections increased during the dry season.

Human-to-human transmission of cryptococcosis has not been reported except in cases of contaminated transplant tissue.[59,60] Many species of animals, including dogs and cats, can develop cryptococcosis,[75-77] but there is little evidence of zoonotic transmission between them. However, in one case, *C. neoformans* isolated from the cage of a pet cockatoo was molecularly linked with the strain that caused infection in a transplant recipient who was exposed to the cage.[78] Also, several cryptococcal cases have been linked to intense bird exposures.[79]

PATHOGENICITY

The encapsulated yeast *C. neoformans* has been studied extensively for more than 50 years. In the past decade, genetic and molecular biologic research, in concert with well-established and robust animal models, has rapidly increased our understanding of its pathobiology. Progress in cryptococcal molecular biology has led to the use of karyotypes, repetitive elements, and transposons to identify yeast strains through a variety of analyses including restriction fragment length polymorphism (RFLP), RAPD, and PCR fingerprints. Recently, the entire genomes of several strains of *C. neoformans* have been sequenced. Several transformation systems are available for introducing DNA into this yeast, and site-specific gene disruptions and replacements are now routine. Dozens of specific null mutants have been made to examine their impact on the virulence composite of the yeast. Furthermore, differential display PCR, cDNA subtraction techniques, serial analysis of gene expression (SAGE), and microarray analysis have been used to document and understand *C. neoformans* transcription profiles.[32,80] Proteomic approaches have also been used.

All these molecular tools have been employed to determine the components and mechanisms that make this yeast such an efficient and deadly pathogen. The following paragraphs describe its most prominent virulence phenotypes.

Capsule

The most distinctive feature of *C. neoformans* is a polysaccharide capsule containing an unbranched chain of α-1,3-linked mannose units substituted with xylosyl and β-glucuronyl groups. The serotype specificity appears to be determined by structural differences in the glucuronoxylomannan (GXM) related to the number of xylose residues and the degree of *O*-acetylation of hydroxyl groups. The capsular polysaccharide has a high negative cell surface charge and is attached to the cell wall by α-1,3-glucan residues. However, it is easily released into the immediate growth media or tissue. Capsular thickness, which varies between isolates, is regulated by several environmental cues, including both ambient P_{CO_2}, serum and low iron concentrations, which increase capsular size in many strains. These environmental signals appear to augment the yeast's ability to produce disease and may help explain why the capsule may be small in in vitro cultures but is much larger when observed in the host. Mutant cryptococci that are made to be hypocapsular or acapsular are dramatically less virulent than the parental strains in animal models.[81] Infections caused by capsule-free or poorly encapsulated strains are rarely observed in the host.

The impact of the capsular polysaccharide on host immunity can be profound at many pathophysiologic levels. For example, it has been shown to produce the following effects on the host[82]:

1. It acts as antiphagocytosis barrier.
2. It depletes complement.
3. It produces antibody unresponsiveness.
4. It dysregulates cytokine secretion.
5. It interferes with antigen presentation.
6. It produces brain edema.
7. It creates selectin and tumor necrosis factor receptor loss.
8. It allows a highly negative charge around yeast cells.
9. It extrudes itself into the intracellular environment with the potential for local toxicity on cellular organelles.
10. It enhances HIV replication.

The attached capsule with its ability to shed the structural GXM component has multiple mechanisms to abrogate a successful host immune challenge. When the GXM is shed into the host environment, it affects host immunity, but fortunately its detection in host fluids permits a very successful diagnostic test.

The biochemistry of this imposing structure remains poorly understood. On the other hand, multiple genes related to capsule synthesis have been identified. Through creation of specific null mutants, it has been shown that any disturbance in efficient capsular synthesis (e.g., reduced formation, secretion or elimination of the structure) attenuates the ability of the mutated yeast to produce disease.[81] Furthermore, there has been new insight into the molecular signaling pathways that control expression of the capsule. One critical pathway necessary for efficient capsular production uses a G-protein that signals through a cyclic AMP-mediated pathway.[83] Downregulation of this pathway with a concomitant reduction in capsule size produces an attenuated virulence phenotype, but if a mutation in the pathway upregulates capsule production, the mutant yeast becomes hypervirulent.

Melanin

The production of melanin is observed in many fungi including some pathogenic species.[25] *C. neoformans* possesses laccase, an enzyme that catalyzes the conversion of diphenolic compounds such as L-DOPA, norepinephrine, epinephrine, and other related aromatic compounds to quinones, which rapidly autopolymerize to form melanin. The production of this pigment can help identify the yeast in the laboratory, but it is also a major virulence factor for the yeast. A gene encoding for this laccase is bound to the inner aspect of the yeast's cytoplasmic membrane, and a site-directed mutant has been created. This laccase-negative or albino mutant has been attenuated for virulence in animal models.[84]

One proposed mechanism by which melanin may protect the yeast is through its ability to act as an antioxidant, and it has been shown that yeast cells without the ability to form melanin are more susceptible to oxidative stress. Other mechanisms by which melanin protects the yeast from host damage involve the following:

1. Cell wall support or integrity
2. Alteration in cell wall charge
3. Interference with T-cell response
4. Abrogation of antibody-mediated phagocytosis
5. Protection from temperature changes and antifungal agents

It remains unclear whether the catecholamine-rich CNS with its excellent substrates for melanin formation provides some tissue tropism or rich environment that enhances this yeast's ability to produce disease. However, it has clearly been shown that melanin is formed in yeast cells within the brain.[85,86]

High-Temperature Growth

A basic trait of all pathogenic fungi is their ability to grow well at mammalian body temperature. For example, *C. neoformans* is the only cryptococcal species to grow at 37° C, and when mutants are made that cannot grow well at this temperature, they are avirulent even when they possess the ability to make capsules and produce melanin. There appears to be some evolutionary drift in high-temperature growth, in that isolates of serotypes B and C (var. *gattii*) and serotype D (var. *neoformans*) generally appear to be more sensitive to growth inhibition and killing at high temperatures than serotype A (var. *grubii*), and the less heat-tolerant isolates quickly lose viability at temperatures of 40° C and above.[21]

There has been progress in understanding the genetic controls for high-temperature growth in *C. neoformans*. First, two signaling pathways (calcineurin and RAS) have been associated with the yeast's ability to grow at mammalian body temperatures, and these are linked to its virulence composite.[87,88] It is also clear that a vacuolar ATPase activity[89] and the stress sugar (trehalose) are important for high-temperature growth of this yeast. *C. neoformans* has evolved a series of molecular pathways and mechanisms to withstand host temperatures, and this is a major reason it is a pathogen.

Other Pathogenicity Factors

Detailed research has focused on the three classic virulence factors of *C. neoformans* (capsule, melanin, and growth at 37° C), but this complex pathogen has many other tools to produce disease. First, individual clinical or environmental strains vary in their ability to produce disease in animal models despite possessing all known virulence factors. Strains can also rapidly change their virulence potential by passage through animals.

Second, a series of genetic loci have been associated with the virulence composite.[1] Phospholipase activity has been linked to virulence by a gene knockout of the phospholipase B gene (PLB1). Null mutants of PLB1 are hypovirulent[90] and may have an impact on the immunologic response of the host to infection.[2] *C. neoformans* makes large amounts of urease, and if the gene for this enzyme (URE1) is disrupted, infection with the mutant is attenuated in mice but not in rabbits.[3,91] A vacuolar ATPase appears to impact on several virulence phenotypes, and the absence of the encoding gene attenuates virulence of the strain.[4,89] Besides melanin as an antioxidant, several other genes such as those for superoxide dismutase, alternative oxidase, and flavohemoglobin are associated with oxidative or nitrosative stress and have been linked to the virulence composite of this yeast.

It is clear that mechanisms for stress responses are important for the yeast to establish a robust infection, but there is also some redundancy in these systems because the yeast can still survive in the host without these protective features.[5] The alpha mating locus has been linked to the virulence of *C. neoformans* serotype D (var. *neoformans*) strains by the demonstration that the alpha mating strain was more virulent than its congenic "a" mating pair.[9] These results suggest that the mating locus, which is over 100 kilobases in size, may contain some virulence genes. On the other hand, recent studies have found that congenic *C. neoformans* serotype A (var. *grubii*) strains had no apparent difference in virulence between alpha and "a" strains in several animal models.[92] It has also been shown with several other genetic loci that virulence genes in one variety are not used by another variety, and vice versa. Thus, evolutionary drift may explain the variability and complexity of the entire virulence composite of strains and serotypes.

HOST RESPONSES

Because serologic and skin hypersensitivity studies frequently identify cryptococcal infections and yet the incidence of cryptococcosis is low, it has been concluded that host immunity in humans is generally very effective after initial exposure to this yeast.[93,94] In fact, the vast majority of cryptococcal infections are diagnosed in patients with a compromised cell-mediated immunity.[93] Furthermore, there is general agreement among researchers that a strong cellular immune response producing granulomatous inflammation is essential for containment of infection.[94-97] Because granuloma formation is a result of a helper T cell 1 (Th1)-polarized response, cytokines such as tumor necrosis factor, interferon-γ, and interleukin (IL)-2 are required.[98,99] Proinflammatory cytokines, such as IL-12, IL-18, and chemokines, such as monocyte chemotactic protein (MCP)-1 and macrophage inflammatory protein (MIP)-1α, are critically important for recruitment of inflammatory cells to the site of infection.[100,101]

Several immune cell populations, such as natural killer cells, and certain types of lymphocytes have been shown to possess direct anticryptococcal effects. Human lymphocytes (CD4, CD8) inhibit growth of *C. neoformans* by direct contact.[102] A primary effector cell against *C. neoformans* is the macrophage, which produces anticryptococcal activity when it is "activated."[103] Other professional phagocytes, such as monocyte-derived macrophages, microglial cells, and polymorphonuclear neutrophils, may kill or at least significantly inhibit *C. neoformans*. It has been shown that a major factor in the infectivity of *C. neoformans* is its ability to survive inside cells.[104,105]

It is not only the state of cellular activation or the type of host cell but also the number of cells at the site of infection that appear to provide an effective host immune response. It is clear from natural history studies in patients with AIDS that the risk of infection dramatically increases as total CD4 lymphocyte counts drop below 50 to 100 cells/μL of blood.[106] In these patients, the paucity of inflammatory cells at the site of infection, such as the subarachnoid space, is impressive. Animal studies further confirm the importance of cell-mediated immunity by showing that T-cell–depleted mice are dramatically more susceptible to infection.

A series of innate factors, such as the anticryptococcal activity of saliva and serum, may discourage active infection or disease with

C. neoformans. Phagocytosis of *C. neoformans* is optimally performed in the presence of complement or antibody. The intracellular fate of yeasts depends on cytokines such as interferon-γ or granulocyte-macrophage colony-stimulating factor (GM-CSF) to improve intracellular inhibition or killing of the yeasts by either host oxidative or nonoxidative mechanisms. Human genome and immunogenetic studies in the future should reveal whether patients who have cryptococcosis, despite having an apparently normal immune system and no risk factors, might have subtle defects in innate or acquired immunity to this yeast. For example, it has already been shown that long-term survivors of cryptococcal meningitis have measurable persistent specific cell-mediated defects against *C. neoformans.*[107]

It appears that *C. neoformans* has both extracellular and intracellular components or stages of infection. The results of histologic examination of tissues and fluids range from virtual absence of an inflammatory reaction to intense granulomatous inflammation with caseous necrosis. The immune reaction appears to be primarily a function of the host status, but the yeast can participate in the inflammatory response, as switch variants in a single strain can produce vastly different histologic responses.[19] The immune response may be influenced by not only the shedding of polysaccharide into tissue but also other yeast factors such as mannitol,[108] melanin,[109] and prostaglandins,[110] which may have profound direct effects on immunomodulation of these infections.

There is substantial evidence that the humoral immunity arm can contribute to an effective immune response.[111-115] Several groups have shown that monoclonal antibody strategies directed against the polysaccharide capsule can reduce the burden of yeasts and improve survival in animal models. In fact, a polysaccharide–tetanus toxoid conjugate vaccine was shown to elicit high titers of antibody to the capsule and subsequently to protect against an intravenous inoculation of cryptococci in mice. These antibodies provide for (1) efficient phagocytosis, (2) enhanced natural killer cell function, and (3) improvement in clearing capsular polysaccharide. Antibodies to other structural components such as melanin[116] and glucosyl-ceramide in the cell wall[117] have also been able to improve the host's ability to fight infection. Sophisticated serologic studies of the host have suggested that there are both qualitative and quantitative differences in the individual types of immunoglobulins that may predispose to disseminated cryptococcal disease.[118]

PATHOGENESIS

The pathogenesis of cryptococcosis is determined by three broad factors: (1) the status of the host defenses, (2) the virulence of the strain of *C. neoformans,* and (3) the size of the inoculum. The relative importance of each factor as a determinant of clinical disease remains uncertain, but it is clear that the complexities of these interactions together produce the ultimate presentation.

A reasonable scenario for the pathophysiology of cryptococcosis is that the susceptible host comes into contact with cryptococci from the environment through inhalation of infectious propagules. In the alveoli, the yeasts contact the alveolar macrophages, which recruit other inflammatory cells through cytokines/chemokines, and a proper Th1 response and granulomatous inflammation is elicited. The infection can then take one of three pathways:

1. In an immunosuppressed host, the yeast continues to proliferate and disseminate, causing clinical disease.
2. The effective immune response completely eliminates the yeast from the host.
3. The yeasts produce a small lung/lymph-node complex and remain dormant in tissues but are not dead.

The third scenario may be a common occurrence. Baker, in elegant postmortem studies of asymptomatic individuals, showed the existence of pulmonary foci and hilar nodes containing yeasts in individuals with no antecedent complaints.[119,120] The yeasts remain dormant and the host is clinically asymptomatic until loss of local immunity occurs through, for example, corticosteroid use or progression of an HIV infection. Then the yeasts begin to replicate in the pulmonary lymph node complex and eventually disseminate into organs outside the lung. This pathophysiology is similar to the scenario proposed for reactivation of tuberculosis and histoplasmosis. Studies in France have given epidemiologic support for this concept of reactivation. In African expatriots who lived in Europe for many years prior to their development of cryptococcosis, the infecting strain possessed a genotype consistent with strains from an African origin.[121]

CLINICAL MANIFESTATIONS

The two common sites for infection with this encapsulated yeast, the lung and the CNS,[122] were emphasized in a recent review of cryptococcosis in HIV-negative patents. In this cohort, 109 (36%) were diagnosed with only pulmonary involvement and 157 (51%) presented with initial evidence of CNS disease.[39] Three other sites of infection (skin, prostate, and eye) have clinical features that are worthy of mention. However, it should be noted that *C. neoformans* has been found to infect any organ of the human body (Table 261-2), and in the severely immunosuppressed patient cryptococcosis may present with involvement of multiple body sites.

Cryptococcosis demonstrates a few differences depending on whether the patient has or does not have an underlying HIV infection.[74,123-126] HIV-infected patients present with more CNS and extrapulmonary infections, higher rates of positive India ink examinations, higher polysaccharide antigen titers, more frequent positive blood cultures, and fewer cerebrospinal fluid (CSF) inflammatory cells. These clinical distinctions are primarily a function of the severity of immunosuppression and the resulting high burden of yeast. It most likely does not reflect a specific interaction between HIV and *C. neoformans* growth.

Lung

The respiratory tract is the most common portal of entry for this yeast, and symptoms there range from asymptomatic colonization of the airway[127] to life-threatening pneumonia with evidence of an acute respiratory distress syndrome.[128-130] In at least a third of normal hosts, the infection is asymptomatic on presentation and is detected by an abnormal chest radiograph. On the other hand, patients can present with acute symptoms of fever, chest pain, cough, weight loss, and sputum production.[131] Common and unusual pulmonary presentations are listed in Table 261-2. Cryptococcosis occasionally occurs with another pathogen; coinfections of the lung have been reported with tuberculosis, nocardiosis, and echinococcosis.[132-134] Also, *C. neoformans* may be isolated from the sputum repeatedly over months and years in patients with prior chronic lung disease but no immunosuppression, no evidence of active pulmonary parenchymal disease, negative serum cryptococcal antigen, and negative fungal cultures from urine and CSF. These patients are considered to have chronic endobronchial colonization. A pulmonary nodule in such a patient may be considered to be cryptococcal in origin but may represent a malignancy.

In normal hosts, chest radiographs commonly show well-defined, noncalcified single (Fig. 261-1) or multiple nodules. An initial presentation may be that of a radiographic lesion (or more than one) that is worrisome for a lung malignancy but then is proven by lung biopsy to be a cryptococcal infection. Other radiographic characteristics include indistinct masslike infiltrates, hilar lymphadenopathy, lobar infiltrates (Fig. 261-2), pleural effusions, and lung cavitation.[135] When infection is limited to the lung, the test for serum cryptococcal antigen is generally negative. If there is pulmonary cryptococcosis with a positive test for serum cryptococcal antigen, it is prudent to examine for an extrapulmonary source of infection although workups may still be negative for another infection site (e.g., blood, skin, CSF). When *C. neoformans* has been isolated from the lung in patients at high risk for dissemination, a lumbar puncture should be considered to rule out CNS infection, even in the absence of symptoms. Early, asymptomatic spread to the CNS may be manifested only by a positive CSF fungal culture, with otherwise normal CSF and a negative antigen test. The number of cryptococci may be so low that several milliliters of CSF must be cultured for a pos-

TABLE 261-2 **Clinical Manifestations of Cryptococcosis**

Central nervous system	Eye	Gastrointestinal tract
Acute, subacute, chronic meningitis	Papilledema	Esophageal nodule
Cryptococcomas of brain (abscesses)	Extraocular muscle paresis	Nodular or ulcerated lesions in stomach or intestines
Spinal cord granuloma	Keratitis	(may resemble Crohn's)
Chronic dementia (from hydrocephalus)	Chorioretinitis	Hepatitis
Lung	Endophthalmitis	Peritonitis
Nodules (single or multiple)	Optic nerve atrophy	Pancreatic mass
Lobar infiltrates	Genitourinary tract	Breast
Interstitial infiltrates	Prostatitis	Breast abscess
Cavities	Renal cortical abscess	Lymph nodes
Endobronchial masses	Positive urine culture from occult source	Lymphadenopathy
Endobronchial colonization	Genital lesions	Thyroid
Acute respiratory distress syndrome	Bone and joints	Thyroiditis
Mediastinal adenopathy	Osteolytic lesion (single or multiple sites)	Thyroid mass
Hilar adenopathy	Arthritis (acute/chronic)	Adrenal gland
Pneumothorax	Muscle	Adrenal insufficiency
Pleural effusions/empyema	Myositis	Adrenal mass
Miliary pattern	Heart, blood vessels	Head and neck
Skin	Cryptococcemia	Gingivitis
Papules and maculopapules	Endocarditis (native and prosthetic)	Sinusitis
Subcutaneous abscess	Mycotic aneurysm	Salivary gland enlargement
Vesicles	Myocarditis	
Plaques	Pericarditis	
Cellulitis	Infected vascular graft	
Purpura		
Acne		
Draining sinuses		
Ulcers		
Bullae		
Herpetiformis-like		
Molluscum contagiosum-like		

From Casadevall A, Perfect JR. Cryptococcus neoformans. Washington: ASM Press; 1998:409.

itive culture to be obtained. Because positive CSF cultures are infrequent, some clinicians advocate treating previously normal patients who are asymptomatic and have no apparent underlying disease with long-term fluconazole and omitting the lumbar puncture.[136]

In the severely immunosuppressed host with AIDS or receiving high-dose corticosteroids, cryptococcal pneumonia can progress more rapidly (over days instead of weeks).[128,130] Unlike immunocompetent hosts, most immunosuppressed individuals have constitutional symptoms such as fever, malaise, chest pain, shortness of breath, and weight loss. In these patients, pneumonia can progress to features of acute respiratory compromise even without evidence of CNS involvement. However, because of the ability of the yeast to disseminate outside the primary lung focus to the CNS, these very high risk patients frequently present with a meningeal rather than a pulmonary syndrome. In AIDS patients, cryptococcal pneumonia may not be symptomatic, and over 90% may present with concomitant CNS infection at the initial diag-

nosis. Chest radiographs in these immunocompromised hosts are similar in their range of presentations to those of immunocompetent hosts. However, alveolar and interstitial infiltrates are particularly common and thus might be confused with *Pneumocystis* infection. Because the severely immunosuppressed patient with pulmonary cryptococcosis and AIDS generally has a CD4 count substantially below 100 cells/μL, it is always prudent to consider the possibility of coinfection with other opportunists such as typical and atypical mycobacterium, cytomegalovirus, *Nocardia,* and *Pneumocystis.*

Central Nervous Systems

Most patients with cryptococcosis of the CNS present with signs and symptoms of subacute meningitis or meningoencephalitis, such as headache, fever, cranial nerve palsies, lethargy, coma, or memory loss over several weeks (see Table 261-2).[122] Symptoms may not be typical, and patients may present with acute (several days) symptoms of

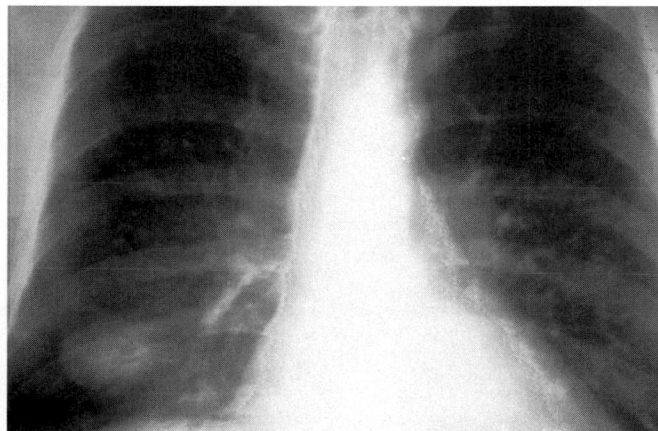

FIGURE 261-1. Cryptococcal nodule. Previously healthy, asymptomatic patient with a right lung nodule.

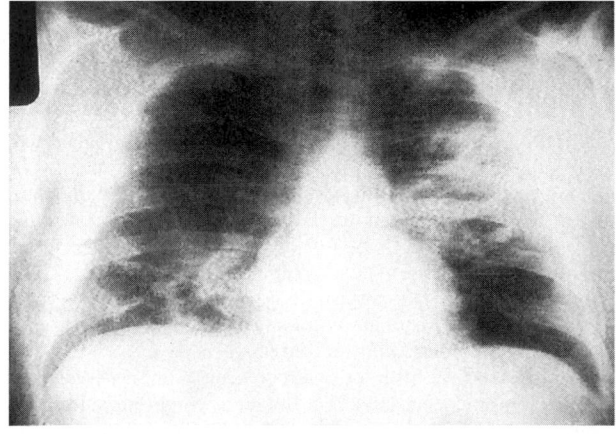

FIGURE 261-2. Cryptococcal pneumonia. Previously healthy patient with fever, cough, shortness of breath, and left lobar infiltrate.

severe headaches, with intermittent headaches, or even with no headache but with altered mental status.

HIV-infected patients with cryptococcal meningitis exhibit few differences at presentation from those without HIV. However, several clinical aspects may be more prominent in patients with AIDS.[39] First, the burden of yeast is generally higher, and this may be reflected in higher polysaccharide antigen titers, slower conversion of CSF to sterilization during treatment, and a tendency toward a higher incidence of increased intracranial pressure. Second, there is a greater likelihood of finding the yeast in extracranial locations during the initial workup. Third, the possibility is greater that a second CNS event may occur, such as infection with *Toxoplasma gondii* or development of a lymphoma.

Fourth, the use of HAART in AIDS patients has created a new immune reconstitution syndrome in cryptococcal infections.[137] After starting HAART, some patients develop acute symptoms of cryptococcal meningitis or pain and swelling in peripheral, hilar, or mediastinal lymph nodes. This syndrome may also occur during treatment of cryptococcal meningitis in the first few months after HAART is introduced. It appears to correlate with a significant drop in HIV load, but there may be only a modest rise in the number of CD4 cells.[138] It is hypothesized that as immunity improves with HAART, silent or latent cryptococcal infections are made clinically apparent as inflammation is mobilized to interact with the yeasts or polysaccharide antigen. During treatment for cryptococcal meningitis, this immune reconstitution syndrome may be marked by increasing headaches, new neurologic signs, appearance of more inflammatory cells in the CSF, and possibly increased intracranial pressure.[139] Distinction between immune reconstitution and progressive infection can be difficult, but cultures from the CSF and lymph node aspirates are negative in immune reconstitution syndromes, even though cryptococci may be present on a smear.

There are limited data that relate the severity of the meningitis to the particular infecting strain, and in most cases the host defense responses determine the clinical manifestations. However, some clinical presentations may depend on the particular infecting strain. For example, in areas of the world that have infections with both *C. neoformans* serotypes A, D, and AD (var. *neoformans/grubii*) and *C. neoformans* serotypes B and C (var. *gattii*), cerebral cryptococcomas (Fig. 261-3) and hydrocephalus with or without large pulmonary mass lesions in immunocompetent hosts were found more commonly with the var. *gattii* infections.[140-142] Although patients infected with this variety have higher survival rates, a subgroup of patients with var. *gattii* infections have brain parenchymal lesions by scan, complications of hydrocephalus and increased intracranial pressure, cranial neuropathies, and a poor response to therapy. These observations suggest that some strains may have a greater propensity for invading the brain parenchyma than for producing a primary presentation of meningitis.

Skin

C. neoformans can produce almost any type of skin lesion (see Table 261-2). A common lesion is a papule or maculopapule with a soft or ulcerated center (Fig. 261-4). A draining sinus usually originates in an underlying bone lesion or occasionally a subcutaneous abscess. Some lesions are easily mistaken for molluscum contagiosum, acne vulgaris, squamous carcinoma, or basal cell carcinoma. After pulmonary and CNS sites of infection, the skin is the third most common organ for appearance of infection. Skin manifestations can be extraordinarily varied.[143-146] In severely immunocompromised patients, skin infections may present as a cellulitis (Fig. 261-5) or an abscess that mimics a bacterial skin infection in both appearance and rapidity of onset.[147,148] Because of the variety of skin manifestations, a correct diagnosis requires a biopsy with proper histopathology and culture. This is extremely important in the immunocompromised host.

In most cases, the skin lesions represent a sentinel finding for disseminated cryptococcal infection. In fact, severely immunosuppressed patients can present with both cutaneous cryptococcosis and another pathogenic fungus in the skin as a manifestation of disseminated fungal disease.[149] However, there is strong evidence that rare cases of skin

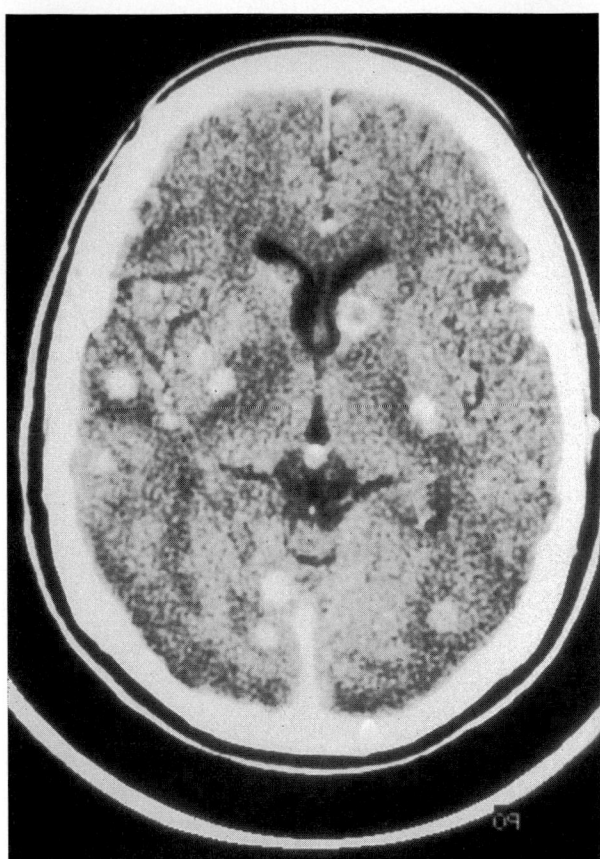

FIGURE 261-3. CT scan of previously healthy patient with multiple cryptococcomas.

cryptococcosis represent primary cutaneous cryptococcosis from direct inoculation or exposure rather than being a marker of disseminated disease. In a large retrospective review of patients with cutaneous findings, a series of immunocompetent patients had (1) solitary skin lesion on unclothed areas of the skin, (2) a history of skin injury, participation in outdoor activities, or exposure to bird droppings, (3) isolation of *C. neoformans,* and (4) no evidence of disseminated disease.[150] There are reports of direct inoculation of yeast into skin by laboratory or clinical accidents and defined episodes of trauma.[66,67] In these cases, there has been no evidence for dissemination of infection from this body site of infection.

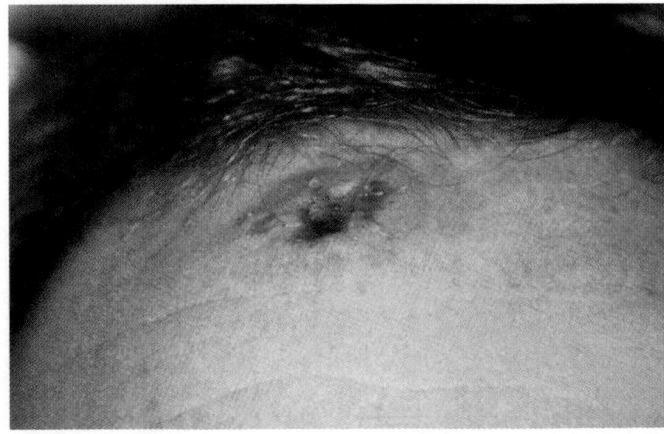

FIGURE 261-4. Forehead ulcer in an HIV-infected host with *Cryptococcus neoformans* seen in histopathology.

Involvement of skin may be influenced by several factors. First, some strains of *C. neoformans* have been described as being dermotropic in animal models. Second, an observation made in a cohort of recipients of solid organ transplant suggests that patients receiving tacrolimus appeared to develop a higher ratio of skin and soft tissue infections to CNS infections when compared to previous immunosuppressive regimens.[58] Because tacrolimus has anticryptococcal activity at temperatures of 37° to 39° C[151] but loses its anticryptococcal activity at environmental temperatures, the skin involvement might result from the lower temperatures at this body site.

Prostate

Like *Blastomyces* and *Mycobacterium tuberculosis, C. neoformans* can invade the prostate gland, although in most cases of cryptococcal infection this involvement is asymptomatic.[152] In fact, asymptomatic or silent prostate infection may first be identified during urologic surgery and may spread into the bloodstream during surgery.[153] For *C. neoformans,* this gland was considered an important site for sanctuary of this yeast from antifungal treatment in HIV-infected patients prior to HAART.[154,155] Frequently, in follow-up of patients with AIDS and cryptococcal meningitis after initial antifungal therapy, cultures of urine (with or without prostatic massage) or seminal fluid were positive for the yeast. In many patients, the location of relapse after therapy remains uncertain, but the prostate is clearly a site that requires prolonged therapy to clear infection in the severely immunosuppressed patients. Besides the prostate, penile[156] and vulvar[157] lesions with *C. neoformans* have been reported, but there has been no evidence for conjugal spread of this yeast.

Eye

In the early reviews of cryptococcal meningitis, ocular signs and symptoms were reported in 45% of the cases.[158] The most common manifestations are ocular palsies and papilledema. Small white retinal exudates, without overlying vitritis, are probably the next most common finding. In this era of severely immunosuppressed patients, several new features of ocular involvement have arisen. First, cryptococcal eye infections can occur simultaneously with infections with other pathogens such as HIV and cytomegalovirus.[159] Second, the presence of extensive retinal lesions, particularly with vitritis, frequently leads to blindness and only occasionally is it successfully managed.[160,161] Third, there are reports of catastrophic loss of vision without evidence for endophthalmitis.[162,163]

In these cases of blindness, which may occur while receiving therapy, two pathogenic processes have been identified. First, there is a visual loss secondary to an optic neuritis produced by infiltration of the optic nerve with yeasts, and, as for endophthalmitis, there are few options for successful management. Second, other patients present with visual loss in one or both eyes during antifungal therapy. In these pa-

tients, symptoms are probably related to the development of cerebral edema and unrelieved high intracranial pressure. The probable pathogenesis is compression of the ophthalmic artery within the optic sheath. Treatment is decrease of CSF pressure by repeated lumbar punctures, CSF shunting, or perhaps slitting the optic sheath within the posterior orbit. Once blindness has occurred, return of visual acuity is rare. A central scotoma or optic atrophy may be the only sequela of cured cryptococcosis.

Other Body Sites

Cryptococcus neoformans can produce infection in most areas of the body (see Table 261-2), and several require further discussion. Cryptococcemia occurs during severe immunosuppression and when there is a high burden of yeast in the body. Cryptococcemia rarely produces vascular instability, and only a few cases of endocarditis have been described.

Bone lesions prior to the AIDS epidemic were reported in up to 5% of disseminated cases.[164] Bone lesions are typically one or more well-circumscribed osteolytic lesions in almost any bone and may have a contiguous soft tissue abscess ("cold abscess"). Bone lesions of sarcoidosis resemble cryptococcal lesions on x-ray films but are more often on the hands or feet and have no contiguous soft tissue abscess.[165] In AIDS patients, the yeast may be found in bone marrow biopsies cultured for other reasons.

Cryptococcal peritonitis can present in two distinct patient groups: (1) those receiving chronic ambulatory peritoneal dialysis, and (2) those with underlying liver disease and cirrhosis.[166,167]

Rare body sites for cryptococcosis (less than a dozen reported cases) include genital and urinary tracts (renal cortical abscess, positive urine culture from an occult site), muscle (myositis), heart (native and prosthetic valve endocarditis), mycotic aortitis or aneurysm, myocarditis, pericarditis, vascular foreign body, thyroid (thyroiditis, mass), adrenal gland (adrenal insufficiency), head and neck (gingivitis, sinusitis, salivary gland enlargement), gastrointestinal nodules or ulcers, hepatitis, breast (inflammatory mass), and lymph node (lymphadenopathy).

LABORATORY DIAGNOSIS

Microscopic Examination

The simple procedure of mixing together India ink and biologic fluids to identify the 5- to 10-μ-diameter encapsulated yeasts remains a rapid and effective method for diagnosing cryptococcal meningitis (Fig. 261-6). Approximately 50% of non-AIDS patients with cryptococcal meningitis and over 80% of patients with AIDS have a positive India ink examination of the CSF. Experience is required to distinguish an encapsulated yeast from a lymphocyte with surrounding proteinaceous debris. India ink smears of urine, sputum, and bronchoalveolar lavage

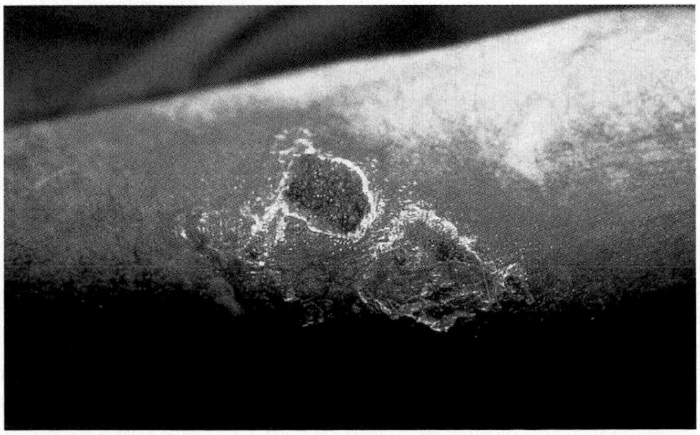

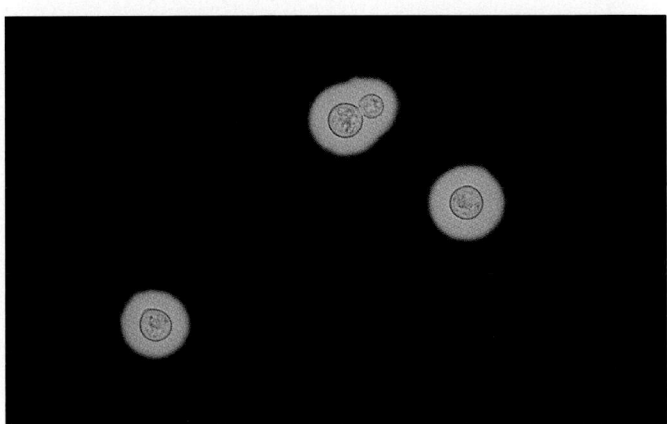

FIGURE 261-5. Severely immunosuppressed patient with cellulitis of the arm caused by *Cryptococcus neoformans.*

FIGURE 261-6. India ink preparations from cerebrospinal fluid of patient with meningitis (note encapsulated yeasts).

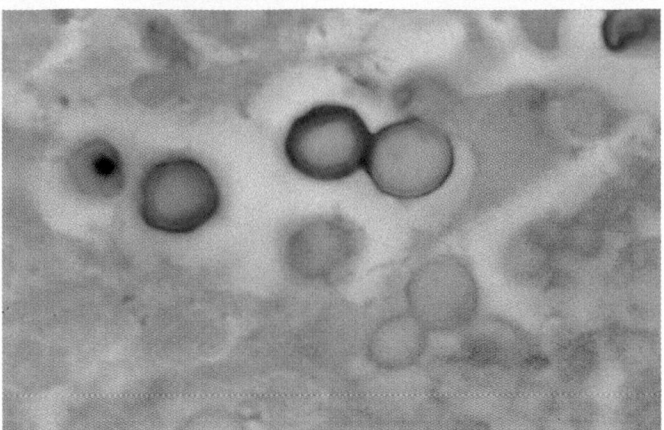

FIGURE 261-7. Alcian blue stain of lung tissue from patient with cryptococcal pneumonia (note blue stain of polysaccharide capsule).

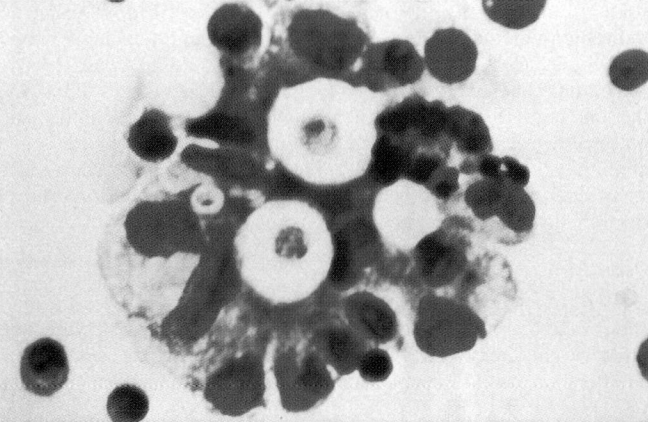

FIGURE 261-9. Cytospin preparation of a host with cryptococcal meningitis showing encapsulated yeast surrounded by a mixed inflammatory reaction.

specimens are almost impossible to interpret. With calcofluor white and a fluorescent microscope, yeasts can be detected in a specimen when numbers are reduced. With routine histopathologic stains such as hematoxylin and eosin, the yeasts are surrounded by empty spaces, which reflect the capsule. The polysaccharide capsule can be identified with stains such as mucicarmine and alcian blue (Fig. 261-7), and its ability to produce melanin allows it to be stained with the Fontana-Masson stain. Gomori's methenamine silver (GMS) fungal stain identifies the narrow-based budding yeast in tissue (Fig. 261-8), and a Gram stain usually reveals a poorly stained gram-positive yeast. Both biopsies and cytologies (Fig. 261-9) can be extremely helpful in the diagnosis of cryptococcosis.

Cultures

Cryptococcus neoformans can grow on most bacterial and fungal media. Both automated and lysis–centrifugation methods are effective in detecting cryptococcemia, and the finding of positive blood cultures has been more common during the AIDS epidemic. Most *C. neoformans* isolates from untreated patients can be detected in culture 3 to 7 days after the specimen is collected and placed into or on culture media.

Isolates can be identified by biochemical reactions[22,23] or DNA-based methods.[168,169] Other methods to presumptively identify the yeast are to perform a rapid urease test or to inoculate the yeast onto Staib's birdseed,[170] DOPA, or caffeic acid media (in which colonies

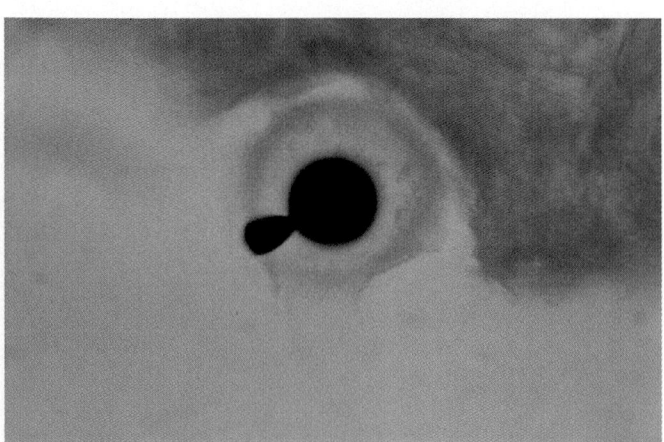

FIGURE 261-8. Gomori's methenamine silver stain shows narrow-based yeast with a faint capsule.

will produce melanin and turn brown to black). However, some other yeasts produce urease, and the highly mucoid colonies of *C. neoformans* may not produce enough melanin to be clearly positive.

The identification of the varieties for *C. neoformans* can be made by several methods: (1) a color reaction on concanavaline-glycine-thymol agar, which distinguishes serotypes A, D, and AD from B and C[171]; (2) an antibody kit for serotyping[172]; (3) fingerprinting with DNA-based methods, which can further separate strains into eight genotypes.[173-175]

Serology

The serologic tests for detection of cryptococcal polysaccharide antigen in serum and CSF are extremely accurate for the diagnosis of invasive disease.[176] Both latex agglutination and enzyme immunoassay tests are greater that 90% sensitive and specific.[177] With the proper treatment of specimens (boiling and pronase/2-mercaptoethanol treatment), false-positive tests are not common when CSF titers are 1:4 or greater.[178] False-positive latex agglutination tests are usually negative by enzyme immunoassay, and vice versa. An occasional false-positive test is observed when there is a cross-reactive antigen in the specimen, and this may occur with microorganisms such as *Trichosporon asahii (beigelii)*[179] or other infections.[180] The false-negative tests may be present in early asymptomatic meningitis and in chronic, indolent meningitis. The clinical experience with, and preciseness of, this test has been studied in sera and in CSF, and it is not recommended to detect polysaccharide antigen in the urine and bronchoalveolar lavage fluid, despite some reports to the contrary.[181]

There are a number of clinical issues related to the use of cryptococcal polysaccharide antigen. Serum cryptococcal polysaccharide antigen tests have been used successfully to screen very high risk, febrile AIDS patients, particularly those with headache, in areas where the incidence of cryptococcal meningitis is high,[182] but these tests may be less useful in areas where the prevalence of infection is low.[183] In patients with cryptococcal infection of the lung who have a positive serum polysaccharide antigen test, there is heightened concern that the infection has become extrapulmonary. It is also unlikely that this large-molecular-weight molecule can cross the blood–CSF barrier, and thus its presence in CSF probably confirms the presence of the yeast in this compartment. In fact, there are occasional cases of meningitis in which CSF antigen is detected early in infection before there is a high enough colony count for the routine laboratory to detect a positive culture, particularly with small volumes of CSF. There are also isolated cases of serum cryptococcal polysaccharidemia in HIV-infected patients with negative fungal cultures from CSF and urine. Management of these cases can be confusing, but in these high-risk patients it is probably wise to start empiric therapy because many of them will eventually develop cryptococcosis.[184,185] It is advisable to confirm a positive latex agglutination with an enzyme immunoassay, and vice versa, before beginning prolonged therapy with fluconazole.

Despite its excellence as a diagnostic test, the polysaccharide antigen is not sufficiently accurate to use in making treatment decisions. In fact, serial polysaccharide antigen titers are imprecise and should not be used to develop treatment guidelines.[186] The cryptococcal polysaccharide antigen titer, however, does give general prognostic information. Initial high titers ($\geq$1:1024) demonstrate a high burden of yeasts in the host, poor host immunity, and a greater chance of therapeutic failure. Antibodies to *C. neoformans* may be detected during infection, but because many of these patients with disease are immunosuppressed, the titers are inconsistent and not generally used for diagnostic or treatment decisions.

Radiology

The chest radiograph of pulmonary cryptococcosis can show a variety of characteristics including local or diffuse infiltrates, nodules, hilar lymphadenopathy, cavitation, and pleural effusion(s).[187-191] In AIDS patients, the diffuse interstitial infiltrates may be confused with coexistent *Pneumocystis* infection.[192,193]

Computed tomography (CT) and magnetic resonance imaging (MRI) of the brain are frequently used in the management of cryptococcal meningoencephalitis.[194-198] Approximately half of CT scans are normal in CNS infection. However, CT can reveal hydrocephalus, gyral enhancement, or single or multiple nodules that may or may not be enhancing. Cryptococcomas may be single or multiple, and in some populations (such as those with var. *gattii* infection) they can occur in up to 25% of non-AIDS and apparently immunocompetent patients. In patients with AIDS, the CT scan differs only in that approximately a third of patients demonstrate cortical atrophy from the underlying HIV infection. The MRI scans are more sensitive than CT scans for detecting abnormalities. MRI findings can include numerous, clustered foci that are hyperintense on T_2-weighted images and nonenhancing on postcontrast T_1-weighted images in the basal ganglia or midbrain. Rarely, there may also be multiple miliary enhancing parenchymal and leptomeningeal nodules.

There are several points to emphasize with regard to CNS radiology. First, there is no pathognomonic scan, and patients with cryptococcal meningitis may simply present with evidence of idiopathic hydrocephalus.[199] Second, in AIDS patients, CNS parenchymal lesions may represent lymphoma or a second infection such as toxoplasmosis or nocardiosis.

Third, follow-up scans may actually show worsening of lesions, with enlargement, new lesions, or persistence of cryptococcomas. Lesions on MRI scans may not decrease in size for months or years.[200] This finding is not necessarily a sign of treatment failure. It simply represents enhancement by inflammation as microscopic yeast foci are being eliminated. Especially with the use of HAART and the potential for immune reconstitution, these radiographs need to be judged carefully in the context of the patient's cultures and clinical signs and symptoms before deciding that the radiograph signifies treatment failure.

MANAGEMENT

The management of cryptococcosis has been the subject of a series of evidence-based studies. Guidelines have been established for therapy,[201] and the general recommendations should be helpful to clinicians, but there remain many unanswered questions. It is clear that cryptococcal meningitis is uniformly fatal without antifungal treatment. However, prior to the availability of antifungals, there were several reports of patients who survived for years before succumbing to infection. Today, in contrast, with the severe immunosuppression of HIV infection and if adequate treatments are not available, a very high percentage of untreated patients die within the first 2 weeks of hospitalization.[202] The rapidity of the progression is likely to depend on host factors. On the other hand, it has been shown that some individuals have asymptomatic endobronchial colonization, no detectable pulmonary lesions on CT scan, negative serum cryptococcal antigen, and negative fungal cultures from CSF and urine. These patients do not need antifungal treatment. In a recent review of non-AIDS patients with positive pulmonary cultures for *C. neoformans,* approximately 20% did not receive treatment.[39] Previously healthy patients with cryptococcosis confined to the lung may heal spontaneously. However, because pulmonary cryptococcosis in some patients progresses or becomes chronic in the lung, and in others it disseminates later to the CNS, all such patients should be treated.

In Vitro Drug Analysis

Methods for in vitro susceptibility testing of *Cryptococcus neoformans* have been modified and standardized.[203] Most initial isolates have low minimal inhibitory concentrations (MICs) to amphotericin B, flucytosine, and azoles but high MICs to caspofungin. By in vitro susceptibility testing, isolates have been detected that are resistant to flucytosine, azoles, and polyenes. In fact, there appears to be some correlation between MICs and clinical resistance,[204-206] but by molecular typing methods, most of the refractory cases represent relapse isolates rather than reinfection,[207] and they possess MICs that are similar to those of the primary isolates.[208] However, in one case it was suggested by molecular techniques that reinfection occurred with a novel strain.[209] When MICs of isolates rise while the patient is being treated, or when the MICs were initially 16 μg/mL or greater for fluconazole, or 128 μg/mL or greater for flucytosine, failure of treatment might possibly be related directly to drug resistance.[210] *C. neoformans* strains have been isolated that possess known drug resistance mechanisms.[210]

Treatment Strategies

Cryptococcal Meningitis

Amphotericin B remains the cornerstone of therapy for cryptococcal meningitis, and from the early studies when it was used alone[211] to its use in combinations, it has performed reasonably well for this infection, with successes in the non-AIDS era of between 60% and 75%.[212,213] With polyene therapy, two issues have been noted. First, recent studies have suggested that higher daily doses of amphotericin B might be more effective in sterilization of the CSF.[214] A standard induction dose for amphotericin B deoxycholate has now been established at 0.7 mg/kg/day. Second, liposomal amphotericin B (AmBisome) at 4 mg/kg/day has had treatment success similar to that of amphotericin B deoxycholate, with reduced toxicity,[215] and it can be recommended as an alternative therapy.

Flucytosine has been used alone in treatment of cryptococcal meningitis,[216] but development of drug resistance on monotherapy has meant that it cannot be recommended as a single agent for treatment of this infection. It is primarily used in combination therapy with amphotericin B,[212,213,217-220] and doses in patients with normal renal function are typically 100 mg/kg/day. Drug levels should be monitored to keep 2-hour postdose levels under 100 μg/mL[221] to reduce the development of bone marrow depression in those with risk for this toxicity, such as patients with renal dysfunction or those receiving high doses of polyenes. One report concluded that adding flucytosine to amphotericin B reduced the rates of relapse compared to amphotericin B monotherapy, although this secondary analysis had serious limitations.[222]

Azoles have been used effectively in the management of cryptococcal meningitis. Fluconazole has been used extensively in cryptococcal meningitis because of its excellent CSF pharmacokinetics and long-term oral safety.[223-227] Clinical trials have shown that it penetrates well into CSF and is excellent for use in the suppressive phase of cryptococcal meningitis management.[228,229] However, it tends to be fungistatic and is probably best used in the stage of infection in which there is a low burden of yeasts in the CSF.

Itraconazole, despite its poor CSF penetration and inconsistent oral bioavailability, has been successfully used in the treatment of cryptococcal meningitis.[230,231] However, it has been shown to be inferior to fluconazole for the suppressive phase of treatment.[222] Its place in therapy for cryptococcal meningitis is probably as an alternative to the first-line therapy with fluconazole, and it can be used in the clearance and suppressive phases of meningitis management if the drug levels are monitored. Other azoles have been studied as treatment of cryptococcosis, but miconazole and ketoconazole are no longer used. The new triazole, voriconazole, has been studied in a small number of refractory cases of cryptococcosis with moderate success.[232]

The new antifungal class of β-glucan synthase inhibitors such as caspofungin, micafungin, and anidulafungin does not possess reliable anticryptococcal activity and are not likely to be used for cryptococcal infections.

Combination therapy for the management of cryptococcal meningitis has been extremely well studied. The combination of amphotericin B and flucytosine has become the standard therapy for meningitis, and in patients without AIDS it reliably sterilizes CSF after 2 weeks of therapy. Flucytosine and fluconazole have been studied in animals and in a single open clinical trial.[233] This report awaits confirmation. Finally, three-drug regimens have occasionally been reported with a polyene, an azole, and flucytosine, but the added benefit of a three-drug regimen has not been defined. Also, a recent study did not show improved killing of yeasts in CSF compared to the amphotericin B plus flucytosine regimen.[233]

A standard algorithm for the management of cryptococcal meningitis in patients with HIV is a three-stage regimen.[218] Treatment is initiated with amphotericin B 0.7 mg/kg/day plus flucytosine 100 mg/kg/day for at least 2 weeks. Patients who have responded clinically may be changed to fluconazole 400 to 800 mg/day for 8 to 10 weeks. Finally, a chronic suppressive phase is begun with fluconazole 200 mg once daily. The use of suppressive or maintenance therapy for cryptococcal meningitis became a concept during the pre-HAART AIDS epidemic, when 50% to 60% of patients relapsed after therapy was stopped. With the use of fluconazole daily, suppression was better than that obtained with intermittent amphotericin B or itraconazole, and there was a reduction in the relapse rate to less than 5%.[228,229] Recent data in several studies have shown that administration of HAART, with its ability to produce immune reconstitution (rising CD4 counts and lower HIV loads), allows antifungal therapy to be stopped after 1 to 2 years in patients with a CD4 count above 200/L for at least 6 months, a nondetectable viral load, and a negative serum cryptococcal antigen.[234,235]

Patients without AIDS can be given either a 6- to 10-week regimen of amphotericin B, with or without initial flucytosine, or, more commonly, the above regimen for AIDS patients. Criteria for stopping therapy are not well defined but include resolution of symptoms, at least two negative CSF cultures from several milliliters of CSF, and a normal CSF glucose. A negative CSF or serum cryptococcal antigen or a normal CSF does not appear to be required to discontinue therapy. Patients with continuing immunosuppression may benefit from prolonged fluconazole therapy after these criteria are met because relapse rates are substantial. Most patients will receive 6-12 months of fluconazole therapy.

The site of infection may modify the treatment recommendation.[201] Any presentation of disseminated cryptococcosis should probably follow recommendations for cryptococcal meningitis. On the other hand, cryptococcosis confined to the lung in previously healthy persons responds very well to fluconazole at 200 to 400 mg/day for 3 to 6 months.[39,224,225] Nonimmunosuppressed patients with endobronchial colonization but without radiologic evidence of pulmonary parenchymal disease do not require antifungal treatment. However, if the patient becomes immunocompromised, treatment should be considered. CNS cryptococcomas tend to be treated for longer periods with fluconazole, but they rarely need surgical removal.[236] MRI scans of the brain may not show a decrease in lesion size for many months. Edema around a lesion, if present, decreases more rapidly.[200]

Identifying a relapse can be difficult in patients with cryptococcal infections. The two clearest signs of relapse that suggest a change in management are development of new clinical signs and symptoms and repeat positive cultures. The persistence of a positive India ink examination or changing versus fixed polysaccharide antigen titers are not precise indications of relapse. In the era of HAART, an immune re-

constitution syndrome in cryptococcosis has been described.[138] It is marked by a rapid return of an inflammatory response that may produce new symptoms such as fever, headaches, and increased number of host cells in the CSF. This syndrome may occur from several months to a year after beginning HAART, and it is still not certain when it is best to initiate HAART in the treatment of cryptococcal meningitis to prevent this syndrome. It is important to recognize that this syndrome is not an indication of direct antifungal failure and might be improved with corticosteroid therapy.

A critical management issue in cryptococcal meningitis is the role of increased intracranial pressure.[237,238] Patients with severe infection often present with CSF opening pressures in excess of 250 mm of water and rapidly progressing signs of cerebral edema. Symptoms include confusion, somnolence, severe headache, emesis, cranial nerve palsies, and fading vision. The pathophysiology for this elevated subarachnoid pressure even as antifungal treatment is started remains uncertain, but cerebral edema is obvious at autopsy, with uncal grooving, midbrain compression, and herniation of the cerebellar tonsils. Control of increased intracranial pressures with external drainage, such as by repeated lumbar punctures with large-bore needles and ventricular or lumbar drains, may be necessary during the early treatment phase.[239] Persistent, symptomatic, high CSF pressures may warrant placement of a permanent CSF shunt. In a retrospective review, corticosteroid treatment was not found to be generally useful.[237,238] but cases need to be examined on an individual basis. Unfortunately, despite intervention, blindness, permanent dementia, or death may result.

It is vital to distinguish cerebral edema from hydrocephalus. The latter is diagnosed by the presence of dilated cerebral ventricles and dementia, with or without gait ataxia or urinary incontinence. CSF pressure may or may not be elevated. A loculated temporal horn of the lateral cerebral ventricle may present as a space-filling mass and cause transfalciform herniation. Symptoms of hydrocephalus need to be identified in the follow-up period and can occur months after the initial diagnosis. A shunt for hydrocephalus can be placed successfully during effective therapy for cryptococcal meningitis.[199,240] There is nothing to suggest that a shunt after institution of antifungal therapy presents a foreign body that impairs cure.

Every attempt to improve the immunity of the patient with cryptococcosis should be made. For example, a goal is to reduce the daily dose of prednisone to less than or equal to 20 mg/day during therapy. Adjunctive cytokine therapies, such as with granulocyte colony-stimulating factor (G-CSF), GM-CSF, and interferon-γ, have in vitro support, and preliminary human studies with interferon-γ as adjunctive therapy have begun. However, clinical trials of immunomodulation for management of cryptococcosis await further definitive studies. Specific monoclonal antibodies have been shown to be helpful in experimental cryptococcal infections and to be safe in humans, but they have yet to reach therapeutic trials. Finally, HAART has a major influence on improving immunity and can have a significant impact on the patient's long-term prognosis. It should be instituted and monitored in all HIV-infected patients during treatment for cryptococcal meningitis. It is essential to gain control of the HIV infection for long-term success.

PROGNOSIS

The most important prognostic factor for success in the treatment of cryptococcosis remains the ability to control the patient's underlying disease. In fact, it has been shown that cancer victims have shorter survival than patients with AIDS because of the inability to control their underlying neoplasm.[241] In another major group of patients with cryptococcosis, those who received solid organ transplants, the results are conflicting. Some studies show an outcome similar to that in patients without an underlying disease,[39] but another study reported a death rate of 42%.[57]

Several studies have examined the prognostic features of cryptococcal meningitis,[212,217,242] and a summary of the different populations, treatment modalities, and end-point evaluations suggests that there are two major prognostic findings: (1) burden of yeasts at presentation, and

(2) level of the patient's sensorium at presentation. A poor prognosis is indicated by a strongly positive India ink examination, a high polysaccharide antigen titer (1:1024), and a poor inflammatory response in the CSF (<20 cells/μL). Patients who present with a lucid sensorium have a better prognosis than those who are stuporous or in a coma. The prognosis is also influenced by the ability to manage the underlying disease and to detect and treat elevated intracranial pressure. Identification of these high-risk patients so that failure and relapse can be predicted may allow the clinician to design a specific antifungal regimen for this refractory subset. In most cases in developed countries, the immediate mortality rate (at 6 months to a year) of cryptococcal meningitis remains at 10% to 25%, and in undeveloped countries with limited resources the mortality rate at 6 months reaches 100%.[202]

PREVENTION

There are four potential methods for preventing infection in high-risk patients. First, in the pre-HAART era, fluconazole prophylaxis in patients with AIDS and CD4 counts under 100 cells/μL has been shown to be effective in reducing the incidence of cryptococcosis.[243,244] However, both the use of HAART and concern about drug resistance with its widespread use have reduced enthusiasm for this approach. Second, active immunization with a vaccine in high-risk patients has been considered. A cryptococcal GXM–tetanus toxoid conjugate vaccine was developed that protected mice,[245] and several new potential protective antigens have been identified. However, human trials have not yet been conducted, and the use of a vaccine in nonimmunosuppressed populations with potential risk factors for disease are hard to define. Third, the use of protective serotherapy with specific monoclonal antibodies[246,247] could be attempted in high-risk patients, but protection would require repeated injections. Finally, high-risk patients can attempt to avoid high-risk environments, such as sites where high numbers of yeasts might be aerosolized from bird droppings.

REFERENCES

1. Perfect JR, Casadevall A. Cryptococcosis. Infect Dis Clin North Am. 2002;16:837-874.
2. Sanfelice F. Contributo alla morfologia e biolgia dei blastomiceti che si sviluppano nei succhi di alcuni frutti. Ann d'Igiene. 1894;4:463-495.
3. Buschke A. Ueber eine durch coccidien hemgerufene krankheit des menschen. Dtsch Med Wochenschr. 1895;21:14.
3a. Versé M. Über einen Fall von generalisicrtcr Blastomykosc beim Menschen. Ver Dtsch Path Ges. 1914;17:275-278.
3b. Stoddard JL, Cutler EC. Torula infections in man. Rockefeller Institute for Medical Research. Monograph No. 6, 1916:1-98.
4. Benham RW. Cryptococcosis and blastomycosis. Ann N Y Acad Sci. 1950;50:1299-1314.
5. Kwon-Chung KJ. Morphogenesis of *Filobasidiella neoformans*, the sexual state of *Cryptococcus neoformans*. Mycologia. 1976;68:821-833.
6. Hull C, Heitman J. Genetics of *Cryptococcus neoformans*. Ann Rev Genet. 2002; 36:557-615.
7. Kwon-Chung KJ, Bennett JE. Distribution of "alpha" and "a" mating types of *Cryptococcus neoformans* among natural and clinical isolates. Am J Med. 1978;108:337-340.
8. Wickes BL, Mayorga ME, Edman U, et al. Dimorphism and haploid fruiting in *Cryptococcus neoformans:* Association with the alpha-mating type. Proc Natl Acad Sci. 1996;93:7327-7331.
9. Kwon-Chung KJ, Edman JC, Wickes BL. Genetic association of mating types and virulence in *Cryptococcus neoformans*. Infect Immun. 1992;60:602-605.
10. Nielsen K, Cox GM, Wang P, et al. Sexual cycle of *Cryptococcus neoformans* variety *grubii* and virulence of congenic a and alpha isolates. Infect Immun. 2003;71:4831-4841.
11. Luna T, Lusins J. *Cryptococcus albidus* meningitis. South Med J. 1973;66:1230.
12. Kromery V, Kunova A, Mardiak J. Nosocomial *Cryptococcus laurentii* fungemia in a bone marrow transplant patient after prophylaxis with ketoconazole successfully treated with oral fluconazole. Infection. 1997;25:130.
13. Ikeda R, Shinoda T, Fukuzawa Y, et al. Antigenic characterization of *Cryptococcus neoformans* serotypes and its application to serotyping of clinical isolates. J Clin Microbiol. 1982;36:22-29.
14. Dromer F, Gueho E, Ronin O, et al. Serotyping of *Cryptococcus neoformans* by using a monoclonal antibody specific for capsular polysaccharide. J Clin Microbiol. 1993;31:359-363.
15. Cleare W, Casadevall A. The different binding patterns of two IgM monoclonal antibodies to *Cryptococcus neoformans* serotype A and D strains correlates with serotype classification and differences in functional assays. Clin Diagn Lab Immunol. 1998;5:125-129.
16. Franzot SP, Salkin IF, Casadevall A. *Cryptococcus neoformans* var. *grubii:* Separate variety status for *Cryptococcus neoformans* serotype A isolates. J Clin Microbiol. 1999;37:838-840.
17. Xu J, Vilgalys R, Mitchell TG. Multiple gene genealogies reveal recent dispersion and hybridization in the human fungus, *Cryptococcus neoformans*. Mol Ecol. 2002;9:1471-1481.
18. Perfect JR, Durack DT, Gallis HA. Cryptococcemia. Medicine. 1983;62:98-109.
19. Goldman DL, Fries BC, Franzot SP, et al. Phenotypic switching in the human pathogenic fungus, *Cryptococcus neoformans*, is associated with changes in virulence and pulmonary inflammatory response in rodents. Proc Natl Acad Sci. 1998;95:14967-14972.
20. Fries BC, Goldman DL, Casadevall A. Phenotypic switching in *Cryptococcus neoformans*. Microbiol Infect Dis. 2002;4:1345-1352.
21. Martinez LR, Garcia-Rivera J, Casadevall A. *Cryptococcus neoformans* var. *neoformans* (serotype D) strains are more susceptible to heat than *C. neoformans* var. *grubii* (serotype A strains). J Clin Microbiol. 2001;39:3365-3367.
22. el-Zaatari M, Pasarell L, McGinnis MR, et al. Evaluation of the updated Vitek yeast identification data base. J Clin Microbiol. 1990;28:1938-1941.
23. St.Germain G, Beauchesne D. Evaluation of the microscan rapid yeast identification panel. J Clin Microbiol. 1991;29:2296-2299.
24. Zimmer BL, Roberts GD. Rapid selective urease test for presumptive identification of *Cryptococcus neoformans*. J Clin Microbiol. 1979;10:380-381.
25. Langfelder K, Streibel M, John B, et al. Biosynthesis of fungal melanins and their importance for human pathogenic fungi. Fungal Genet Biol. 2003;38:143-158.
26. Meyer W, Castaneda A, Jackson S, et al. Molecular typing of Ibero American *Cryptococcus neoformans* isolates. Emerg Infect Dis. 2003;9:189-195.
27. Levitz SM. The ecology of *Cryptococcus neoformans* and the epidemiology of cryptococcosis. Rev Infect Dis. 1991;13:1163-1169.
28. Emmons CW. Isolation of *Cryptococcus neoformans* from soil. J Bacteriol. 1951; 62:685-690.
29. Emmons CW. Saprophytic sources of *Cryptococcus neoformans* associated with the pigeon. Am J Hyg. 1955;62:227-232.
30. Ellis DH, Pfeiffer TJ. Ecology, *life cycle*, and infectious *propagule* of *Cryptococcus neoformans*. Lancet. 1990;336:923-925.
31. Stephen C, Lester S, Black W, et al. Multispecies outbreak cryptococcosis on southern Vancouver Island, British Columbia. Can J Vet Res. 2002;43:792-794.
32. Steenbergen JN, Shuman HA, Casadevall A. *Cryptococcus neoformans* interactions with amoebae suggest an explanation for its virulence and intracellular pathogenic strategy in macrophages. Proc Natl Acad Sci. 2001;98:15245-15250.
33. Mylonakis E, Ausubel FM, Perfect JR, et al. Killing of *Caenorhabditis elegans* by *Cryptococcus neoformans* as a model of yeast pathogenesis. Proc Natl Acad Sci. 2002;99:15675-15680.
34. Howard DH. The commensalism of *Cryptococcus neoformans*. Sabouraudia. 1973; 11:171-174.
35. Schimpff SC, Bennett JE. Abnormalities in cell-mediated immunity in patients with *Cryptococcus neoformans* infection. J Allergy Clin Immunol. 1975;55:430-441.
36. Newberry WM Jr, Walter JE, Chandler JW Jr, et al. Epidemiologic study of *Cryptococcus neoformans*. Ann Intern Med. 1967;67:724-732.
37. Chen L-C, Goldman DL, Doering TL. Antibody response to *Cryptococcus neoformans* proteins in rodents and humans. Infect Immun. 1999;67:2218-2224.
38. Goldman DL, Khine H, Abadi J. Serologic evidence for *Cryptococcus* infection in early childhood. Pediatrics. 2001;107:66.
39. Pappas PG, Perfect JR, Cloud GA, et al. Cryptococcosis in HIV-negative patients in the era of effective azole therapy. Clin Infect Dis. 2001;33:690-699.
40. Hajjman A, Conn LA, Stephens DS. Cryptococcosis: Population-based multistate active surveillance and risk factors in human immunodeficiency virus-infected persons. Cryptococcal Active Surveillance Group. J Infect Dis. 1999;179:449-454.
41. McNeil JI, Kan VL. Decline in the incidence of cryptococcosis among HIV-related patients. J Acquir Immune Defic Syndr Hum Retrovirol. 1995;9:206-208.
42. van Elden LJ, Walenkamp AM, Lipovsky MM. Declining number of patients with cryptococcosis in the Netherlands in the era of highly active antiretroviral therapy. AIDS. 2000;14:2787-2788.
43. Mirza S, Phelan M, Rimland D, et al. The changing epidemiology of cryptococcosis: An update from population-based active surveillance in 2 large metropolitan areas, 1992-2000. Clin Infect Dis. 2002;36:789-794.
44. Clumeck N, Sonnet J, Taelman H, et al. Acquired immunodeficiency syndrome in African patients. N Engl J Med. 1984;310:492-497.
45. Van de Perre P, Lepage P, Kestelyn P. Acquired immunodeficiency syndrome in Rwanda. Lancet. 1984;2:62-65.
46. Hakim JG, Gangaidzo IT, Heyderman RS. Impact of HIV infection on meningitis in Harare, Zimbabwe: A prospective study of 406 predominantly adult patients. AIDS. 2000;14:1401-1407.
47. Dore GJ, Li Y, McDonald A, et al. Spectrum of AIDS-defining illnesses in Australia, 1992 to 1998: Influence of country/region of birth. J Acquir Immune Defic Syndr. 2000;26:283-290.
48. Archibald LK, McDonald LC, Rheanpumikankit S. Fever and human immunodeficiency virus infection as sentinels for emerging mycobacterial and fungal bloodstream infections in hospitalized patients >15 years old, Bangkok. J Infect Dis. 1999;180:87-92.
49. Kwon-Chung KJ, Bennett JE. Epidemiologic differences between the two varieties of *Cryptococcus neoformans*. Am J Epidemiol. 1984;120:123-140.
50. Bennett JE, Kwon-Chung KJ, Howard DH. Epidemiology differences among serotypes of *Cryptococcus neoformans*. Am J Epidemiol. 1977;105:582-586.
51. Steenbergen JN, Casadevall A. Prevalence of *Cryptococcus neoformans* var *neoformans* (serotype D) and *Cryptococcus neoformans* var. *grubii* (serotype A) isolates in New York City. J Clin Microbiol. 2000;38:1974-1976.

52. Collins VP, Gellhorn A, Trimble JR. The coincidence of cryptococcosis and disease of the reticulo-endothelial and lymphatic systems. Cancer. 1995;4:883-889.

53. Zimmerman LE, Rappaport H. Occurrence of cryptococcosis in patients with malignant disease of reticuloendothelial system. Am J Clin Pathol. 1954;24:1050.

54. Kaplan MH, Rosen PP, Armstrong D. Cryptococcus in a cancer hospital: Clinical and pathological correlates in forty-six patients. Cancer. 1977;39:2265-2274.

55. Hutter RVP, Collins HS. The occurrence of opportunistic fungus infections in a cancer hospital. Lab Invest. 1962;11:1035-1045.

56. Kontoyiannis DP, Peitsch WK, Reddy BT. Cryptococcosis in patients with cancer. Clin Infect Dis. 2001;32:145-150.

57. Husain A, Wagener MM, Singh N. *Cryptococcus neoformans* infection in organ transplant recipients: Variables influencing clinical characteristics and outcome. Emerg Infect Dis. 2001;7:375-381.

58. Singh N, Gayowski T, Wagener MM, et al. Clinical spectrum of invasive cryptococcosis in liver transplant recipients receiving tacrolimus. Clin Transpl. 1997;11:66-70.

59. Beyt BE, Waltman SR. Cryptococcal endophthalmitis after corneal transplantation. N Engl J Med. 1978;298:825-826.

60. Kanj SS, Welty-Wolf K, Madden J, et al. Fungal infections in lung and heart-lung transplant recipients, report of 9 cases and review of the literature. Medicine. 1996;75:142-156.

61. Iseki M, Anzo M, Yamashita N, et al. Hyper-IgM immunodeficiency with disseminated cryptococcosis. Acta Paediatr. 1994;83:780-782.

62. Tabone MD, Leverger G, Landman J, et al. Disseminated lymphonodular cryptococcosis in a child with x-linked hyper-IgM immunodeficiency. Pediatr Infect Dis J. 1994;13:77-79.

63. Dev D, Basran GS, Slater D. Consider HIV negative immunodeficiency in cryptococcosis. BMJ. 1994;308:1436.

64. Olson PE, Earhart KC, Rossetti RJ. Smoking and risk of cryptococcosis in patients with AIDS. JAMA. 1997;277:629.

65. True DG, Penmetaha M, Peckham SJ. Disseminated cryptococcal infection in rheumatoid arthritis treated with methotrexate and infliximab. J Rheumatol. 2002; 29:1561-1563.

66. Casadevall AJ, Mukherjee J, Ruong R, et al. Management of *Cryptococcus neoformans* contaminated needle injuries. Clin Infect Dis. 1994;19:951-953.

67. Glaser JB, Garden A. Inoculation of cryptococcosis without transmission of the acquired immunodeficiency syndrome. N Engl J Med. 1985;313:264.

68. Powell KE, Dahl BA, Weeks RJ, et al. Airborne *Cryptococcus neoformans*: Particles from pigeon excreta compatible with alveolar deposition. J Infect Dis. 1972;126:412-415.

69. Wiest PM, Flanigan T, Salata RA, et al. Serious infectious complications of corticosteroid therapy for COPD. Chest. 1989;95:1180-1183.

70. Ruiz A, Bulmer GS. Particle size of airborne *Cryptococcus neoformans* in a tower. Appl Environ Microbiol. 1980;41:1225-1229.

71. Sorrell TC, Chen S, Ruma P, et al. Concordance of clinical and environmental isolates of *Cryptococcus neoformans* var. *gattii* by random amplification of polymorphic DNA analysis and PCR fingerprinting. J Clin Microbiol. 1996;34:1253-1260.

72. Currie BP, Freundlich LF, Casadevall A. Restriction fragment length polymorphism analysis of *Cryptococcus neoformans* isolates from environmental (pigeon excreta) and clinical sources in New York City. J Clin Microbiol. 1994;32:1188-1192.

73. Yamamoto Y, Kohno S, Koga H, et al. Random amplified polymorphic DNA analysis of clinically and environmentally isolated *Cryptococcus neoformans* in Nagasaki. J Clin Microbiol. 1995;33:3328-3332.

74. Sorvillo F, Beall G, Turner PA. Incidence and factors associated with extrapulmonary cryptococcosis among persons with HIV infection in Los Angeles County. AIDS. 1997;11:673-679.

75. Faggi E, Gargani G, Pizzirani C, et al. Cryptococcosis in domestic mammals. Mycoses. 1993;36:165-170.

76. Malik R, Dill-Mackey E, Martin P, et al. Cryptococcosis in dogs: A retrospective study of 20 consecutive cases. J Med Vet Mycol. 1995;33:291-297.

77. Malik R, Wigney DI, Muir DB, et al. Cryptococcosis in cats: Clinical and mycological assessment of 29 cases and evaluation of treatment using orally administered fluconazole. J Med Vet Mycol. 1992;30:133-144.

78. Nosanchuk JD, Shoham S, Fries BC, et al. Evidence for zoonotic transmission of *Cryptococcus neoformans* from a pet cockatoo to an immunocompromised patient. Ann Intern Med. 2000;132:205-208.

79. Fessel WJ. Cryptococcal meningitis after unusual exposures to birds. N Engl J Med. 1993;328:1354-1355.

80. Del Poeta M, Toffaletti DL, Rude TH, et al. *Cryptococcus neoformans* differential gene expression detected *in vitro* and *in vivo* with green fluorescent protein. Infect Immun. 1999;67:1812-1820.

81. Chang YC, Kwon-Chung KJ. Complementation of a capsule-deficiency mutation of *Cryptococcus neoformans* restores its virulence. Mol Cell Biol. 1994;14:4912-4919.

82. Casadevall A, Perfect JR. *Cryptococcus neoformans*. Washington: ASM Press; 1998:409.

83. Alspaugh JA, Perfect JR, Heitman J. *Cryptococcus neoformans* mating and virulence are regulated by the G-protein gamma subunit GPA1 and cAMP. Genes Dev. 1997;11:3206-3217.

84. Salas SD, Bennett JE, Kwon-Chung KJ, et al. Effect of the laccase gene, CNLAC1, on virulence of *Cryptococcus neoformans*. J Exp Med. 1996;184:377-386.

85. Nosanchuk JD, Rosas AL, Lee SC. Melanisation of *Cryptococcus neoformans* in human brain tissue. Lancet. 2000;355:2049-2050.

86. Rosas AL, Nosanchuk JD, Feldmesser M. Synthesis of polymerized melanin by *Cryptococcus neoformans* in infected rodents. Infect Immun. 2000;68:2845-2853.

87. Odom A, Muir S, Lim E, et al. Calcineurin is required for virulence of *Cryptococcus neoformans*. EMBO J. 1997;16:2576-2589.

88. Alspaugh JA, Cavallo LM, Perfect JR, et al. *RAS1* regulates filamentation, mating, and growth at high temperature of *Cryptococcus neoformans*. Mol Microbiol. 2000;36:352-365.

89. Erickson T, Liu L, Gueylkian A, et al. Multiple virulence factors of *Cryptococcus neoformans* are dependent on VPH1. Mol Microbiol. 2001;42:1121-1131.

90. Cox GM, McDade HC, Chen SC, et al. Extracellular phospholipase activity is a virulence factor for *Cryptococcus neoformans*. Mol Microbiol. 2001;39:166-175.

91. Cox GM, Mukherjee J, Cole GT, et al. Urease as a virulence factor in experimental cryptococcosis. Infect Immun. 2000;68:443-448.

92. Del Poeta M, Cruz MC, Cardenas ME, et al. Synergistic antifungal activities of bafilomycin A(1), fluconazole, and the pneumocandin MK-0991/caspofungin acetate (L-743,873) with calcineurin inhibitors FK506 and L-685,818 against *Cryptococcus neoformans*. Antimicrob Agents Chemother. 2000;44:739-746.

93. Murphy JW. Cryptococcal immunity and immunostimulation. Adv Exp Med Biol. 1992;319:225-230.

94. Levitz SM. Overview of host defenses in fungal infections. Clin Infect Dis. 1992; 14:S37-S42.

95. Schwartz DA. Characterization of the biological activity of *Cryptococcus* infections in surgical pathology. Ann Clin Lab Sci. 1988;18:388-397.

96. Lipscomb MF. Lung defenses against opportunistic infections. Chest. 1989;96:1393-1399.

97. Lee SC, Dickson DW, Casadevall A. Pathology of cryptococcal meningoencephalitis: Analysis of 27 patients with pathogenetic implications. Hum Pathol. 1996;27:839-847.

98. Aguirre K, Havell EA, Gibson GW, et al. Role of tumor necrosis factor and gamma interferon in acquired resistance to *Cryptococcus neoformans* in the central nervous system of mice. Infect Immun. 1995;63:1725-1731.

99. Kawakami K, Tohyama M, Teruya K. Contribution of interferon-gamma in protecting mice during pulmonary and disseminated infection with *Cryptococcus neoformans*. FEMS Immunol Med Microbiol. 1996;13:133-140.

100. Huffnagle GB, Strieter RM, McNeil LK. Macrophage inflammatory protein-1 alpha (MIP-alpha) is required for the efferent phase of pulmonary cell-mediated immunity to a *Cryptococcus neoformans* infection. J Immunol. 1997;159:318-327.

101. Huffnagle GB, Traynor TR, McDonald RA. Leukocyte recruitment during pulmonary *Cryptococcus neoformans* infection. Immunopharmacology. 2000;48:231-236.

102. Hill JO. CD4+ T cells cause multinucleated giant cells to form around *Cryptococcus neoformans* and confine the yeast within the primary site of infection in the respiratory tract. J Exp Med. 1992;175:1685-1695.

103. Levitz SM. Macrophage-*Cryptococcus* interactions. In: Zwilling BS, Eisenstein TK, eds. Macrophage-Pathogen Interactions. New York: Marcel Dekker; 1994:533-543.

104. Feldmesser M, Kress Y, Novikoff P, et al. *Cryptococcus neoformans* is a facultative intracellular pathogen in murine pulmonary infection. Infect Immun. 2000;68:4225-4237.

105. Feldmesser M, Tucker SC, Casadevall A. Intracellular parasitism of macrophages by *Cryptococcus neoformans*. Trends Microbiol. 2001;9:273-278.

106. Crowe SM, Carlin JB, Stewart KI, et al. Predictive value of CD4 lymphocyte numbers for the development of opportunistic infections and malignancies in HIV-infected persons. J Acquir Immune Defic Syndr. 1991;4:770-776.

107. Henderson DK, Bennett JE, Huber MA. Long-lasting specific immunologic unresponsiveness associated with cryptococcal meningitis. J Clin Invest. 1982;69:1185-1190.

108. Wong B, Perfect JR, Beggs S, et al. Production of the hexitol D-mannitol by *Cryptococcus neoformans* in vitro and in rabbits with experimental meningitis. Infect Immun. 1990;58:1664-1670.

109. Williamson PR. Biochemical and molecular characterization of the diphenol oxidase of *Cryptococcus neoformans*: Identification as a laccase. J Bacteriol. 1994;176:656-664.

110. Noverr MC, Phare SM, Toews GB, et al. Pathogenic yeasts *Cryptococcus neoformans* and *Candida albicans* produce immunomodulatory prostaglandins. Infect Immun. 2001;69:2957-2963.

111. Vecchiarelli A, Casadevall A. Antibody-mediated effects against *Cryptococcus neoformans*: Evidence for interdependency and collaboration between humoral and cellular immunity. Res Immunol. 1998;149:321-333.

112. Mukherjee J, Sharff MD, Casadevall A. Protective murine monoclonal antibodies to *Cryptococcus neoformans*. Infect Immun. 1992;60:4534-4541.

113. Sanford JE, Lupan DM, Schlageter AM, et al. Passive immunization against *Cryptococcus neoformans* with an isotype-switch family of monoclonal antibodies reactive with cryptococcal polysaccharide. Infect Immun. 1990;58:1919-1923.

114. Dromer F, Charreire J, Contrepois A, et al. Protection of mice against experimental cryptococcosis by anti-*Cryptococcus neoformans* monoclonal antibody. Infect Immun. 1987;55:749-752.

115. Casadevall A. Antibody immunity and invasive fungal infections. Infect Immun. 1995;63:4211-4218.

116. Rosas AL, Nosanchuk JD, Casadevall A. Passive immunization with melanin-binding monoclonal antibodies prolongs survival in mice with lethal *Cryptococcus neoformans* infection. Infect Immun. 2001;69:3410-3412.

117. Rodriques ML, Travassos LR, Miranda KR. Human antibodies against a purified glucosylceramide from *Cryptococcus neoformans* inhibit cell budding and fungal growth. Infect Immun. 2000;68:7049-7060.

118. Fleuridor R, Lyles RH, Pirofski L. Quantitative and qualitative differences in the serum antibody profiles of human immunodeficiency virus-infected persons with and without *Cryptococcus neoformans* meningitis. J Infect Dis. 1999;180:1526-1535.

119. Baker RD. The primary pulmonary lymph node complex of cryptococcosis. Am J Clin Pathol. 1976;65:83-92.

120. Salyer WR, Salyer DC, Baker RD. Primary complex of *Cryptococcus* and pulmonary lymph nodes. J Infect Dis. 1974;130:74-77.
121. Garcia-Hermoso D, Janbon G, Dromer F. Epidemiological evidence for dormant *Cryptococcus neoformans* infection. J Clin Microbiol. 1999;37:3204-3209.
122. Perfect JR. Cryptococcosis. Infect Dis Clin North Am. 1989;3:77-102.
123. Kovacs JA, Kovacs AA, Polis M, et al. Cryptococcosis in the acquired immunodeficiency syndrome. Ann Intern Med. 1985;103:533-538.
124. Zuger A, Louie E, Holzman RS, et al. Cryptococcal disease in patients with acquired immunodeficiency syndrome: Diagnostic features and outcome of treatment. Ann Intern Med. 1986;104:234-240.
125. Chuck SL, Sande MA. Infections with *Cryptococcus neoformans* in the acquired immunodeficiency syndrome. N Engl J Med. 1989;321:794-799.
126. Clark RA, Greer D, Atkinson W, et al. Spectrum of *Cryptococcus neoformans* infection in 68 patients infected with acquired immunodeficiency virus. Rev Infect Dis. 1990;12:768-777.
127. Duperval R, Hermans PE, Brewer NS, et al. Cryptococcosis, with emphasis on the significance of isolation of *Cryptococcus neoformans* from the respiratory tract. Chest. 1977;72:13-19.
128. Henson DJ, Hill AR. Cryptococcal pneumonia: A fulminant presentation. Am J Med. 1984;228:221.
129. Kent TH, Layton JM. Massive pulmonary cryptococcosis. Am J Clin Pathol. 1962;38:596-604.
130. Murray RJ, Becker P, Furth P, et al. Recovery from cryptococcemia and the adult respiratory distress syndrome in the acquired immunodeficiency syndrome. Chest. 1988;93:1304-1307.
131. Warr W, Bates JH, Stone A. The spectrum of pulmonary cryptococcosis. Ann Intern Med. 1968;69:1109-1116.
132. Kahn FW, England DM, Jones JM. Solitary pulmonary nodule due to *Cryptococcus neoformans* and *Mycobacterium tuberculosis*. Am J Med. 1985;78:677-681.
133. Riley E, Cahan WG. Pulmonary cryptococcosis followed by pulmonary tuberculosis: A case report. Am Rev Respir Dis. 1972;106:594-599.
134. Dalgleish AG. Concurrent hydatid disease and cryptococcosis in a 16-year-old girl. Med J Aust. 1981;2:144-145.
135. Feigin DS. Pulmonary cryptococcosis: Radiologic-pathologic correlates of its three forms. AJR Am J Roentgenol. 1983;141:1263-1272.
136. Aberg JA, Mundy LM, Powderly WG. Pulmonary cryptococcosis in patients without HIV infection. Chest. 1999;115:734-740.
137. Woods ML, MacGinley R, Eisen DP, et al. HIV combination therapy: Partial immune restitution unmasking latent cryptococcal infection. AIDS. 1998;12:1491-1494.
138. Jenny-Avital ER, Abadi M. Immune reconstitution cryptococcosis after initiation of successful highly active antiretroviral therapy. Infect Immun. 2002;35:128-133.
139. Cinti SK, Armstrong WS, Kaufman CA. Recurrence of increased intracranial pressure with antiretroviral therapy in an AIDS patient with cryptococcal meningitis. Mycoses. 2003;44:497-501.
140. Mitchell DH, Sorrell TC, Allworth AM, et al. Cryptococcal disease of the CNS in immunocompetent hosts: Influence of cryptococcal variety on clinical manifestations and outcome. Clin Infect Dis. 1995;20:611-616.
141. Speed B, Dunt D. Clinical and host differences between infections with the two varieties of *Cryptococcus neoformans*. Clin Infect Dis. 1995;21:28-34.
142. Chen S, Sorrell T, Nimmo G, et al. Epidemiology and host and variety-dependent characteristics of infection due to *Cryptococcus neoformans* in Australia and New Zealand. Clin Infect Dis. 2000;31:499-508.
143. Borton LK, Wintroub BU. Disseminated cryptococcosis presenting as herpetiform lesions in a homosexual man with acquired immunodeficiency syndrome. J Am Acad Dermatol. 1984;10:387-390.
144. Schupbach CW, Wheeler CE, Briggaman RA. Cutaneous manifestations of disseminated cryptococcosis. Arch Dermatol. 1976;112:1734-1744.
145. Concus AP, Helfand RF, Imber MJ, et al. Cutaneous cryptococcosis mimicking *Molluscum contagiosum* in a patient with AIDS. J Infect Dis. 1988;158:897-898.
146. Pema K, Diaz J, Guerra LG, et al. Disseminated cutaneous cryptococcosis: Comparison of clinical manifestations in the pre-AIDS and AIDS eras. Arch Intern Med. 1994;154:1032-1034.
147. Gauder JP. Cryptococcal cellulitis. JAMA. 1977;237:672-673.
148. Mayers DL, Martone WJ, Mandell GL. Cutaneous cryptococcosis mimicking gram-positive cellulitis in a renal transplant patient. South Med J. 1981;74:1032.
149. Pierard GE, Pierard-Franchimont C, Estrada JA, et al. Cutaneous mixed infections in AIDS. Am J Dermatopathol. 1990;12:63-66.
150. Neuville S, Dromer F, Morin O, et al. Primary cryptococcosis: A distinct clinical entity. Clin Infect Dis. 2003;36:347.
151. Odom A, Del Poeta M, Perfect J, et al. The immunosuppressant FK506 and its non-immunosuppressive analog L-685,818 are toxic to *Cryptococcus neoformans* by inhibition of a common target protein. Antimicrob Agents Chemother. 1997;41:156-161.
152. Braman RT. Cryptococcosis (Torulopsis) of prostate. Urology. 1981;17:284-286.
153. Plunkett JM, Turner BI, Tallent MB. Cryptococcal septicemia associated with urologic instrumentation in a renal allograft recipient. J Urol. 1981;125:241-242.
154. Larsen RA, Bozzette S, McCutchan JA, et al. Persistent *Cryptococcus neoformans* infection of the prostate after successful treatment of meningitis. Ann Intern Med. 1989;111:125-128.
155. Staib F, Seibold M, L'age M, et al. *Cryptococcus neoformans* in the seminal fluid of an AIDS patient: A contribution to the clinical course of cryptococcosis. Mycoses. 1989;32:171-180.
156. Perfect JR, Seaworth B. Penile cryptococcosis with a review of mycotic infections of the penis. Urology. 1985;25:528-531.
157. Blocher KS, Weeks JA, Noble RC. Cutaneous cryptococcal infection presenting as vulvar lesion. Genitourin Med. 1987;63:341-343.
158. Okun E, Butler WT. Ophthalmologic complications of cryptococcal meningitis. Arch Ophthalmol. 1964;71:52-57.
159. Doft BH, Curtin VT. Combined ocular infection with cytomegalovirus and cryptococcosis. Arch Ophthalmol. 1982;100:1800-1803.
160. Crump JR, Elner SG, Elner VM, et al. Cryptococcal endophthalmitis: Case report and review. Clin Infect Dis. 1992;14:1069-1073.
161. Denning DW, Armstrong RW, Fishman M, et al. Endophthalmitis in a patient with disseminated cryptococcosis and AIDS who was treated with itraconazole. Rev Infect Dis. 1991;13:1126-1130.
162. Johnston SR, Corbett EL, Foster O, et al. Raised intracranial pressure and visual complications in AIDs patients with cryptococcal meningitis. J Infect. 1992;24:185-189.
163. Rex JH, Larsen RA, Dismukes WE, et al. Catastrophic visceral loss due to *Cryptococcus neoformans* meningitis. Medicine. 1993;72:207-224.
164. Behrman RE, Masci JR, Nicholas P. Cryptococcal skeletal infections: Case report and review. Rev Infect Dis. 1990;12:181-190.
165. Ross JJ, Katz JD. Cryptococcal meningitis and sarcoidosis. J Infect Dis. 2002;34:937-939.
166. Yinnon AM, Solages A, Treanor JJ. Cryptococcal peritonitis: report of a case developing during continuous ambulatory peritoneal dialysis and review of the literature. Clin Infect Dis. 1993;17:736-741.
167. Sungkanuparph S, Vibhagool A, Pracharktam R. Spontaneous cryptococcal peritonitis in cirrhotic patients. J Postgrad Med. 2002;48:201-202.
168. Huffnagle KE, Gander RM. Evaluation of Gen-probe's *Histoplasma capsulatum* and *Cryptococcus neoformans* ACCU probes. J Clin Microbiol. 1993;31:419-421.
169. Mitchell TG, Freedman EZ, White TJ, et al. Unique oligonucleotide primers in PCR for identification of *Cryptococcus neoformans*. J Clin Microbiol. 1994;32:253-255.
170. Staib F. *Cryptococcus neoformans* und *Guizotia abyssinica* (Syn. *G. oleifera*) Farbreaktion fur *C. neoformans*. Zbl Hyg. 1962;148:466-475.
171. Kwon-Chung KJ, Polacheck I, Bennett JE. Improved diagnostic medium for separation of *Cryptococcus neoformans* var. *neoformans* (serotypes A and D) and *Cryptococcus neoformans* var *gattii* (serotypes B and C). Ann Intern Med. 1985;103:533-538.
172. Ikeda R, Shinoda R, Fukazawa Y, et al. Antigenic characterization of *Cryptococcus neoformans* serotypes and its application of serotyping of clinical isolates. J Clin Microbiol. 1982;16:22-29.
173. Crampin AC, Matthews RC, Hall D, et al. PCR fingerprinting *Cryptococcus neoformans* by random amplification of polymorphic DNA. J Med Vet Mycol. 1993;31:463-465.
174. Spitzer ED, Spitzer SG. Use of a dispersed repetitive DNA element to distinguish clinical isolates of *Cryptococcus neoformans*. J Clin Microbiol. 1992;30:1094-1097.
175. Varma A, Kwon-Chung KJ. DNA probe for strain typing of *Cryptococcus neoformans*. J Clin Microbiol. 1992;30:2960-2967.
176. Goodman JS, Kaufman L, Loening MG. Diagnosis of cryptococcal meningitis: Detection of cryptococcal antigen. N Engl J Med. 1971;285:434-436.
177. Kauffman CA, Bergman AG, Severance PJ, et al. Detection of cryptococcal antigen. Comparison of two latex agglutination tests. Am J Clin Pathol. 1981;75:106-109.
178. Snow RM, Dismukes WE. Cryptococcal meningitis: Diagnostic value of cryptococcal antigen in cerebrospinal fluid. Arch Intern Med. 1975;135:1155-1157.
179. McManus EJ, Jones JM. Detection of a *Trichosporon beigelii* antigen cross-reactive with *Cryptococcus neoformans* capsular polysaccharides in serum from a patient with disseminated trichosporon infection. J Clin Microbiol. 1985;21:681-685.
180. Chanock SJ, Toltzis P, Wilson C. Cross-reactivity between *Stomatococcus mucilaginosus* and latex agglutination for cryptococcal antigen. Lancet. 1993;342:1119-1120.
181. Baughman RP, Rhodes JC, Dohn MN, et al. Detection of cryptococcal antigen in bronchoalveolar lavage fluid: A prospective study of diagnostic utility. Am Rev Respir Dis. 1992;145:1226-1229.
182. Desmet P, Kayembe KD, DeVroey C. The value of cryptococcal serum antigen screening among HIV positive AIDS patients in Kinshasa, Zaire. AIDS. 1989;3:77-78.
183. Hoffman S, Stenderup J, Mathiesen LR. Low yield of screening for cryptococcal antigen by latex agglutination assay on serum and cerebrospinal fluid from Danish patients with AIDS or ARC. Scand J Infect Dis. 1991;23:697-702.
184. Feldmesser M, Harris C, Reichberg S, et al. Serum cryptococcal antigen in patients with AIDS. Clin Infect Dis. 1996;23:827-830.
185. Manfredi R, Moroni A, Mazzoni A, et al. Isolated detection of cryptococcal polysaccharide antigen in cerebrospinal fluid samples from patients with AIDS. Clin Infect Dis. 1996;23:849-850.
186. Powderly WG, Cloud GA, Dismukes WE, et al. Measurement of cryptococcal antigen in serum and cerebrospinal fluid: value in the management of AIDS-associated cryptococcal meningitis. Clin Infect Dis. 1994;18:789-792.
187. Hunt KK Jr, Enquist RW, Bowen TE. Multiple pulmonary nodules with central cavitation. Chest. 1976;69:529-530.
188. Khoury MB, Godwin JD, Ravin CE, et al. Thoracic cryptococcosis: Immunologic competence and radiologic appearance. AJR Am J Roentgenol. 1984;141:893-896.
189. McAllister CK, Davis CE Jr, Ognibene AJ, et al. Cryptococcal pleuro-pulmonary disease: Infection of the pleural fluid in the absence of disseminated cryptococcosis—Case report. Milit Med. 1984;149:684-686.
190. Young EJ, Hirsh DD, Fainstein V, et al. Pleural effusions due to *Cryptococcus neoformans*: A review of the literature and report of two cases with cryptococcal antigen determinations. Am Rev Respir Dis. 1980;121:743-746.
191. Zlupko GM, Fochler FJ, Goldschmidt ZH. Pulmonary cryptococcosis presenting with multiple pulmonary nodules. Chest. 1980;77:575.
192. Clark RA, Greer DL, Valainis GT, et al. *Cryptococcus neoformans* pulmonary infection in HIV-1-infected patients. J Acquir Immune Defic Syndr. 1990;3:480-485.
193. Miller WT, Edelman JM. Cryptococcal pulmonary infection in patients with AIDS: Radiographic appearance. Radiology. 1990;175:725-728.

194. Cornell SH, Jacoby CG. The varied computed tomographic appearance of intracranial cryptococcosis. Radiology. 1982;143:703-707.

195. Tan CT, Kuan BB. *Cryptococcus* meningitis, clinical–CT scan considerations. Neuroradiology. 1987;29:43-46.

196. Long JA, Herdt JR, DiChiro G, et al. Cerebral mass lesions in torulosis demonstrated by computer tomography. J Comput Assist Tomogr. 1980;4:766-769.

197. Poprich MJ, Arthur RH, Helmer E. CT of intracranial cryptococcosis. AJR Am J Roentgenol. 1990;154:603-606.

198. Wehn SM, Heinz R, Burger PC. Dilated Virchow-Robin spaces in cryptococcal meningitis associated with AIDS: CT and MR findings. J Comput Assist Tomogr. 1989;13:756-762.

199. Ingram CW, Haywood HB, Morris VM, et al. Cryptococcal ventricular peritoneal shunt infection: Clinical and epidemiological evaluation of two closely associated cases. Infect Immun. 1993;14:719-722.

200. Hospenthal D, Bennett JE. Persistence of cryptococcomas on neuroimaging. Clin Infect Dis. 2000;31:1303-1306.

201. Saag MS, Graybill JR, Larsen RA, et al. Practice guidelines for the management of cryptococcal disease. Infectious Disease Society of America. Clin Infect Dis. 2000;30:710-718.

202. Mwaba P, Mwansa J, Chintu C, ct al. Clinical presentation, natural history and cumulative death rates of 230 adults with primary cryptococcal meningitis in Zambian AIDS patients treated under local conditions. Postgrad Med. 2001;77:769-773.

203. Ghannoun MA, Ibrahim AS, Fu Y, et al. Susceptibility testing of *Cryptococcus neoformans*: A microdilution technique. J Clin Microbiol. 1992;30:2881-2886.

204. Valez JD, Allendoerfer R, Luther M, et al. Correlation of *in vitro* azole susceptibility with *in vivo* response in a murine model of cryptococcal meningitis. J Infect Dis. 1993;168:508-510.

205. Aller AI, Martin-Manzuelos E, Lozano F, et al. Correlation of fluconazole MICs with clinical outcome in cryptococcal infection. Antimicrob Agents Chemother. 2000;44:1544-1548.

206. Witt MD, Lewis RJ, Larsen RA, et al. Identification of patients with acute AIDS-associated cryptococcal meningitis who can be effectively treated with fluconazole: The role of antifungal susceptibility testing. Clin Infect Dis. 1996;22:322-328.

207. Spitzer ED, Spitzer SG, Freundlich LF, et al. Persistence of initial infection in recurrent *Cryptococcus neoformans* meningitis. Lancet. 1993;341:595-596.

208. Casadevall A, Spitzer ED, Webb D, et al. Susceptibilities of serial *Cryptococcus neoformans* isolates from patients with recurrent cryptococcal meningitis to amphotericin B and fluconazole. Antimicrob Agents Chemother. 1993;37:1383-1386.

209. Haynes KA, Sullivan DJ, Coleman DC, et al. Involvement of multiple *Cryptococcus neoformans* strains in a single episode of cryptococcosis and reinfection with novel strains in recurrent infection demonstrated by random amplification of polymorphic DNA and DNA fingerprinting. J Clin Microbiol. 1995;33:99-102.

210. Perfect JR, Cox GM. Drug resistance in *Cryptococcus neoformans*. Drug Resist Updat. 1999;2:259-269.

211. Sarosi GA, Parker JD, Doto IL, et al. Amphotericin B in cryptococcal meningitis: Long-term results of treatment. Ann Intern Med. 1969;71:1079-1087.

212. Bennett JE, Dismukes W, Duma RJ, et al. A comparison of amphotericin B alone and combined with flucytosine in the treatment of cryptococcal meningitis. N Engl J Med. 1979;301:126-131.

213. Utz JP, Garrigues IL, Sande MA, et al. Therapy of cryptococcosis with a combination of flucytosine and amphotericin B. J Infect Dis. 1975;132:368-373.

214. deLalla F, Pellizzer G, Vaglia A. Amphotericin B as primary therapy for cryptococcosis in patients with AIDS: reliability of relatively high doses administered over a relatively short period. Clin Infect Dis. 1995;20:263-266.

215. Leenders AC, Reiss P, Portegies P, et al. Liposomal amphotericin B (Ambisome) compared with amphotericin B followed by oral fluconazole in the treatment of AIDS-associated cryptococcal meningitis. AIDS. 1997;11:1463-1471.

216. Utz JP, Shadomy S, McGehee RF. Flucytosine. N Engl J Med. 1972;286:777-778.

217. Dismukes WE, Cloud G, Gallis HA, et al. Treatment of cryptococcal meningitis with combination amphotericin B and flucytosine for four as compared with six weeks. N Engl J Med. 1987;317:334-341.

218. van der Horst C, Saag MS, Cloud GA, et al. Treatment of cryptococcal meningitis associated with the acquired immunodeficiency syndrome. N Engl J Med. 1997;337:15-21.

219. DeGans J, Portegies P, Tiessens G. Itraconazole compared with amphotericin B plus flucytosine in AIDS patients with cryptococcal meningitis. AIDS. 1992;6:185-190.

220. Larsen RA, Leal MAE, Chan LS. Fluconazole compared with amphotericin B plus flucytosine for cryptococcal meningitis in AIDS. Ann Intern Med. 1990;113:183-187.

221. Stamm AM, Diasio RB, Dismukes WE, et al. Toxicity of amphotericin B plus flucytosine in 194 patients with cryptococcal meningitis. Am J Med. 1987;83:236-242.

222. Saag MS, Cloud GA, Graybill JR, et al. A comparison of itraconazole versus fluconazole as maintenance therapy for AIDS-associated cryptococcal meningitis. Clin Infect Dis. 1999;28:291-296.

223. Stern JJ, Hartman BJ, Sharkey P, et al. Oral fluconazole therapy for patients with the acquired immunodeficiency syndrome and cryptococcosis: Experience with 22 patients. Am J Med. 1988;85:477-480.

224. Dromer F, Mathoulin S, Dupont B, et al. Comparison of the efficacy of amphotericin B and fluconazole in the treatment of cryptococcosis in human immunodeficiency virus-negative patients: Retrospective analysis of 83 cases. Clin Infect Dis. 1996;22(Suppl 2):s154-160.

225. Yamaguchi H, Ikemoto H, Watanabe K, et al. Fluconazole monotherapy for cryptococcosis in non-AIDS patients. Eur J Clin Microbiol Infect Dis. 1996;15:787-792.

226. Saag MS, Powderly WG, Cloud GA, et al. Comparison of amphotericin B with fluconazole in the treatment of acute AIDS-associated cryptococcal meningitis. N Engl J Med. 1992;326:83-89.

227. Berry AJ, Rinaldi MG, Graybill JR. Use of high dose fluconazole as salvage therapy for cryptococcal meningitis in patients with AIDS. Antimicrob Agents Chemother. 1992;36:690-692.

228. Bozette SA, Larsen RA, Chiu J, et al. A placebo-controlled trial of maintenance therapy with fluconazole after treatment of cryptococcal meningitis in the acquired immunodeficiency syndrome. N Engl J Med. 1991;324:580-584.

229. Powderly WG, Saag MS, Cloud GA, et al. A controlled trial of fluconazole or amphotericin B to prevent relapse of cryptococcal meningitis in patients with the acquired immunodeficiency syndrome. N Engl J Med. 1992;326:793-798.

230. Denning DW, Tucker RM, Hanson LH, et al. Itraconazole therapy for cryptococcal meningitis and cryptococcosis. Arch Intern Med. 1989;149:2301-2308.

231. Viviani MA, Tortorano AM, Langer M, et al. Experience with itraconazole in cryptococcosis and aspergillosis. J Infect. 1989;18:151-165.

232. Perfect JR, Marr KA, Walsh TJ, et al. Voriconazole treatment for less common, emerging or refractory fungal infections. Clin Infect Dis. 2003;36:1122-1131.

233. Larsen RA, Bozzette SA, Jones BE, et al. Fluconazole combined with flucytosine for treatment of cryptococcal meningitis in patients with AIDS. Clin Infect Dis. 1994;19:741-745.

234. Martinez E, Garcia-Viejo MA, Marcos MA. Discontinuation of secondary prophylaxis for cryptococcal meningitis in HIV-infected patients responding to highly active antiretroviral therapy. AIDS. 2000;14:2615.

235. Vibhagool A, Sungkanuparph S, Mootsikapun P, et al. Discontinuation of secondary prophylaxis for cryptococcal meningitis in human immunodeficiency virus–infected patients treated with highly active antiretroviral therapy: A prospective, multicenter randomized study. Clin Infect Dis. 2003;36:1329-1331.

236. Fujita NK, Reynard M, Sapico FL, et al. Cryptococcal intracerebral mass lesions. Ann Intern Med. 1981;94:382-388.

237. Graybill JR, Sobel J, Saag M, et al. Diagnosis and management of increased intracranial pressure in patients with AIDS and cryptococcal meningitis. Clin Infect Dis. 2000;30:47-54.

238. Denning DW, Armstrong RW, Lewis BH, et al. Elevated cerebrospinal fluid pressures in patients with cryptococcal meningitis and acquired immunodeficiency syndrome. Am J Med. 1991;91:267-272.

239. Van Gemert HM, Vermeulen M. Treatment of impaired consciousness with lumbar punctures in a patient with cryptococcal meningitis and AIDS. Clin Neurol Neurosurg. 1991;93:257-258.

240. Yadav YR, Perfect JR, Friedman A. Successful treatment of cryptococcal ventriculoatrial shunt infection with systemic therapy alone. Neurosurgery. 1988;23:317-322.

241. White M, Cirrincione C, Blevins A, et al. Cryptococcal meningitis with AIDS and patients with neoplastic disease. J Infect Dis. 1992;165:960-966.

242. Diamond RD, Bennett JE. Prognostic factors in cryptococcal meningitis: A study of 111 cases. Ann Intern Med. 1974;80:176-181.

243. Nightingale SD, Cal SX, Peterson DM, et al. Primary prophylaxis with fluconazole against systemic fungal infections in HIV-positive patients. AIDS. 1992;6:191-194.

244. Powderly WG, Finkelstein DM, Feinberg J, et al. A randomized trial comparing fluconazole with clotrimazole troches for the prevention of fungal infections in patients with advanced human immunodeficiency virus infection. N Engl J Med. 1995;332:700-705.

245. Devi SJ, Scheerson R, Egan W, et al. *Cryptococcus neoformans* serotype A glucuronoxylomannan protein conjugate vaccines: Synthesis, characterization, and immunogenicity. Infect Immun. 1991;59:3700-3707.

246. Mukherjee J, Pirofski LA, Scharff MD, et al. Antibody-mediated protection in mice with lethal intracerebral *Cryptococcus neoformans* infection. Proc Natl Acad Sci U S A. 1993;90:3636-3640.

247. Mukherjee J, Zuckier LS, Scharff MD, et al. Therapeutic efficacy of monoclonal antibodies to *Cryptococcus neoformans* glucuronoxylomannan alone and in combination with amphotericin B. Antimicrob Agents Chemother. 1994;38:580-587.

CHAPTER **262**

Histoplasma capsulatum

GEORGE S. DEEPE, JR.

Histoplasma capsulatum is one of the more common causes of infection in the midwestern and southeastern United States. Histoplasmosis, acquired by inhalation of mycelial fragments and microconidia, is most often self-limiting but can cause potentially lethal infection in patients with preexisting conditions. It remains a frequent cause of opportunistic infection among patients whose immune system is impaired either by pharmaceutical agents or by human immunodeficiency virus (HIV). This accelerating trend is unlikely to abate because the reservoir of *H. capsulatum* (soil) will never disappear.

HISTORY

The discovery of *H. capsulatum* was made in December 1905, when Samuel Darling, a pathologist stationed in Panama, examined visceral tissues and bone marrow from a young man from Martinique whose death was originally attributed to miliary tuberculosis.[1] Peering through his microscope, Darling was struck by the presence of many small bodies, most of which were intracellular. Having been influenced by reports from Leishman and Donovan, he mistakenly thought that this organism was a protozoan. Because it lacked a kinetoplast, Darling assumed that it was a different *Leishmania* species. He termed this new species *Histoplasma capsulatum* because it seemingly exhibited a capsule. It was not until 1912, after reviewing tissue specimens, that da Rocha-Lima suggested that the organism resembled a yeast rather than a protozoan.[2] A little more than 20 years later, the organism was finally isolated on artificial medium and observed to grow as a mold at room temperature and as a yeast at 37° C.[3]

For many years the presence of pulmonary calcifications had become synonymous with healed tuberculosis by physicians. Amos Christie, a pediatrician at Vanderbilt University, dispelled that dictum.[4,5] The presence of cutaneous reactivity to a skin test reagent, prepared from the mycelial phase of the organism, in an infant with disseminated histoplasmosis prompted large-scale testing during the 1930s. This endeavor unearthed the surprising finding that histoplasmosis was highly prevalent in the Ohio and Mississippi river valleys.[5] Moreover, many cases of presumed tuberculosis that were based on the presence of calcified nodules on chest roentgenograms were determined to be histoplasmosis instead.[6] Eventually, many individuals residing in tuberculosis sanatoriums in the midwestern and southeastern United States were recognized to be mistakenly admitted. They suffered from histoplasmosis, not tuberculosis. Some of these individuals contracted tuberculosis while housed in open wards with patients who had active pulmonary tuberculosis.

ECOLOGY AND EPIDEMIOLOGY

Cases of histoplasmosis have been reported from every continent except Antarctica. Although *H. capsulatum* has been detected in many areas of the world, the most highly endemic region is the Ohio and Mississippi river valleys (Fig. 262-1).[6] *H. capsulatum* is a soil-based fungus that has been isolated from many regions of the world and is most often associated with river valleys. The conditions that favor the growth of this fungus in soil are a mean temperature of 22° C to 29° C, an annual precipitation of 35 to 50 inches, and a relative humidity of 67% to 87%. These conditions are typically found in the temperate zone between latitudes 45 degrees north to 30 degrees south.[7] The organism is typically found within 20 cm of the surface, and it prefers soil that is acidic, has a high nitrogen content, and is moist. In areas where avians roost, the fungus is found most often where the guano is decaying and mixed with soil.[8] In such areas, infectious particles can exceed 10^5 per gram of soil. Fresh guano is less likely to contain any infectious particles. There is a strong association between the presence of bird and bat guano and the presence of *H. capsulatum*. In fact, the first isolation of the organism from an environmental source was from an area adjacent to a chicken house. Birds are not infected by the fungus, and attempts to isolate *H. capsulatum* from their cloaca have been unsuccessful. Bats, on the other hand, carry the fungus in their gastrointestinal tracts and shed it.[9]

Disruption of the soil by excavation or construction is one of the most common means of releasing infectious elements that are inhaled

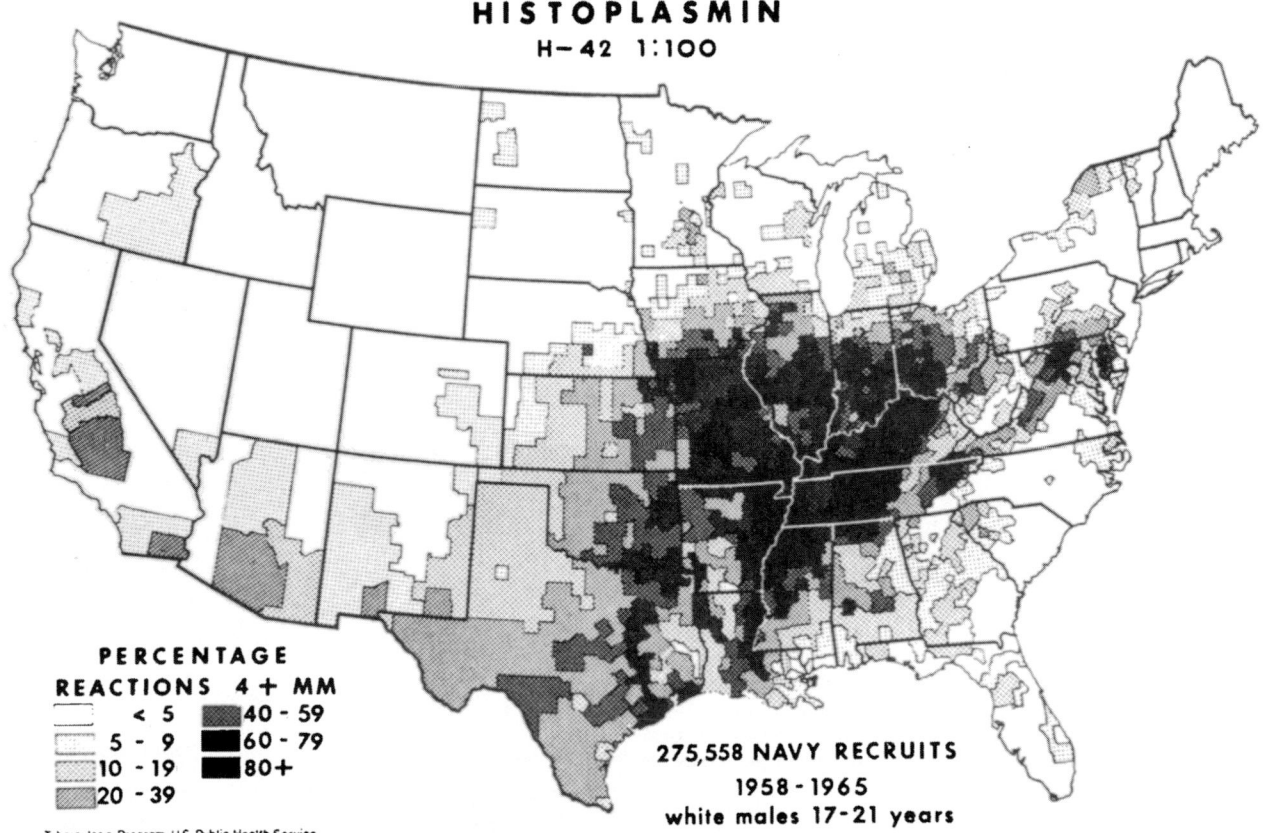

FIGURE 262-1. Histoplasmin reactivity in the continental United States among naval recruits. *(Reprinted from Edwards LB, Acquaviva FA, Livesay VT, et al. An atlas of sensitivity to tuberculin, PPD-B, and histoplasmin in the United States. Am Rev Respir Dis. 1969;99[Part 2]:1-111, with permission.)*

and eventually settle into the lungs. Those involved in recreational or work activities that expose them to disrupted soil are at highest risk for infection. Persons at risk include spelunkers who roam caves where bats reside, those who are engaged in agriculture, outdoor construction, or rehabilitation of buildings that have been inhabited by birds or bats. Human-to-human transmission via the pulmonary route has not been reported.

Although skin test reactivity to histoplasmin is equally distributed among men and women, disease develops in males more frequently than in females by a 4:1 ratio.[10] The disease incidence may be skewed because of the association of chronic pulmonary histoplasmosis with smoking, which for many years was a male-dominated activity. Unlike coccidioidomycosis, there are no known differences in susceptibility or resistance to infection among racial or ethnic groups.

H. capsulatum contains between four to seven chromosomes.[11] Differences in numbers of chromosomes are evident among strains. Originally the organism could be distinguished by two chemotypes, but the advent of molecular biology has improved methods to distinguish strains of *H. capsulatum*. Restriction fragment length polymorphisms (RFLP) of mitochondrial deoxyribonucleic acid (DNA) and of ribosomal and *yps-3* (a yeast-phase specific gene) nuclear genes have segregated *H. capsulatum* into six classes that correlate with geographic distribution and virulence.[12] The vast majority of North American and African *H. capsulatum* var. *duboisii* isolates belong to class 2, and those from Central and South America are in class 3. A thermointolerant strain that is avirulent, the Down's strain, has been assigned to class 1. Interestingly, many of the isolates recovered from acquired immunodeficiency syndrome (AIDS) patients in St. Louis are found to be in class 1.[13] However, genetic differences can be associated with varied clinical manifestation. *H. capsulatum* from specific regions of South America, which are in class 5 or 6, often produce skin lesions, whereas class 2 isolates from North America do not. The findings suggest that *H. capsulatum* is highly diverse at the genetic level, the basis for this may be that the fungus undergoes sexual recombination in nature, thus allowing for exchange of genetic material.

MYCOLOGY

H. capsulatum is classified as a member of the family of Ascomycetes and has a heterothallic form that is designated, *Ajellomyces capsulatum* (see Chapter 254). Mating types (+) and (−) have been described and when combined onto sporulating medium, they produce fruiting bodies containing asci. Isolates from patients carry the (−) mating type from two to seven times more frequently than the (+) type, although the ratio of mating types in soil is 1:1.[14]

The organism has two forms: the mycelial phase and the yeast phase. The former is present at ambient temperature, and the latter at 37° C or higher. The saprobic or mycelial phase can be divided into two colony types, brown (B) and albino (A). The A type grows more rapidly in culture and loses the capability to produce spores after prolonged subculturing. The B type generates a brown pigment. Yeast cells from the B type are more virulent than those from A type.

The basic elements of the nutritional needs of the organism are poorly defined because of the lack of a standardized medium. The organism requires vitamins, thiamine, biotin, and iron. Sulfhydryl groups in the form of cysteine or cystine, are necessary for growth and maintenance of the yeast phase. The mycelial and yeast phase differ in their requirements for calcium. Chelation of this element from medium inhibits the growth of the mycelial but not the yeast phase. The transition from the mycelial to the yeast phase is associated with upregulation in the transcription of a calcium-binding protein messenger RNA (mRNA) and synthesis of the protein. This protein may act as a scavenger of calcium and may be synthesized by yeast cells in order to acquire calcium from intracellular environments that contain little of this element.[15]

Microscopic evaluation of the mycelial phase reveals two types of conidia. Macroconidia are large ovoid bodies that span 8 to 15 μm in diameter. The surface is decorated with slender protrusions that are re-

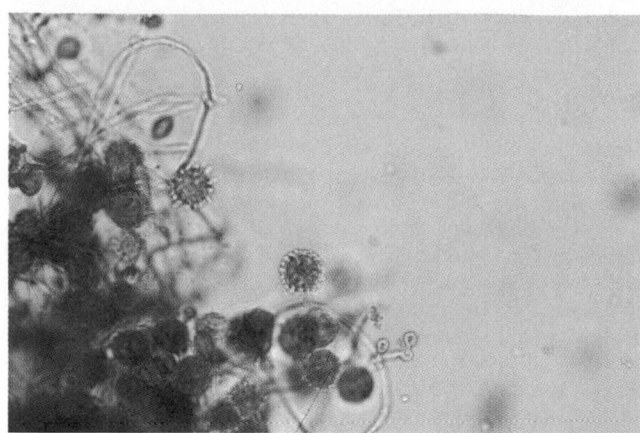

FIGURE 262-2. Mycelial phase of *H. capsulatum*. Both macroconidia and microconidia are evident.

ferred to as tuberculate. Microconidia are small, smooth oval bodies whose diameter ranges from 2 to 5 μm (Fig. 262-2). It is these forms that are believed to be the infective phase because their size is small enough to lodge in the terminal bronchioles and alveoli.

The transition from the saprobic to the yeast phase is a critical step in infectivity of the fungus. Upon exposure to 37° C, the organism undergoes genetic, biochemical, and physical alterations that result in the production of yeast cells that are uninucleate.[16] These forms are small, typically 2 to 5 m in diameter, and reproduce by multipolar budding (Fig. 262-3). The stimulus for the transition is heat, and the shift in temperature may be sensed by a change in the fluidity of the yeast membrane. Genetically, the first genes that are upregulated upon exposure to heat are *cdc2*, a gene involved in cell cycle progression, and *yps-3*, a yeast specific gene whose function remains unknown. There is also increased transcription of genes encoding heat shock proteins, especially heat shock protein 70.

Three biochemical stages have been identified during the conversion following exposure to 37° C. Stage 1 is characterized by an uncoupling of oxidation-phosphorylation and a decrease in ribonucleic acid (RNA) and protein synthesis. In stage 2 no respiration is detectable, and in stage 3 there is a resumption of respiration. Chitin and α- and β-glucan content differ between the two phases.

Within tissues, yeast cells may possess a morphology that differs from the usual ovoid shape. Misshapen or large yeasts have been observed in tissues and epithelial cells. These allomorphs may contain less α-(1,3)-glucan and appear to be less virulent than oval-shaped yeasts. It has been suggested that because of their reduced virulence

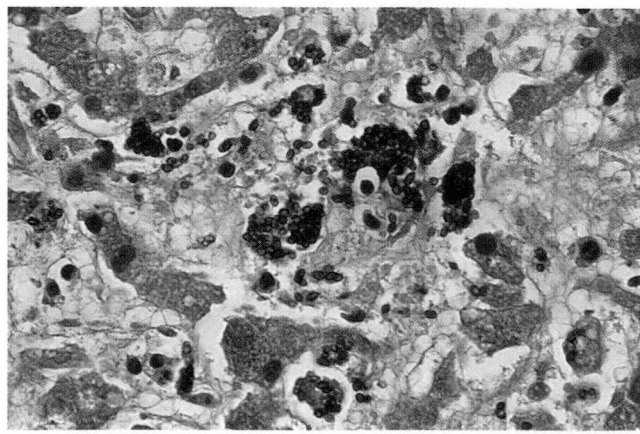

FIGURE 262-3. Yeast cells of *H. capsulatum* in a section of liver. Tissue was stained with Gomori methenamine silver.

potential, the allomorphs may represent a persistent or dormant phase of the fungus.[17]

PATHOGENESIS

The study of the pathogenesis of this fungus has been hampered by the lack of a suitable transformation system to delete genes. This system uses a two-step process to achieve homologous recombination. Recently, this hurdle has been overcome with the development of molecular genetic tools to manipulate genes within the fungus. This advance creates the foundation for the influence of genes or gene regulators on the pathobiology of *H. capsulatum.*[18,19]

The transition from the mycelial to the yeast phase is the most critical determinant in the establishment of infection.[20] This contention is supported by several findings. First, it is quite rare to find mycelial particles in tissues of humans or mammals with established infection. Rather, yeast cells are commonly detected. Second, exposure of *H. capsulatum* mycelia to p-chloromercuriphenylsulfonic acid (PCMS), a sulfhydryl inhibitor, irreversibly blocks the conversion to yeasts but does not alter growth of yeasts or mycelia. PCMS-treated mycelia fail to infect animals.

In addition to calcium, iron is another vital element required for survival of *H. capsulatum.* The organism can acquire iron from the intracellular environment by three means: release of iron scavenging siderophores, production of a ferric reductase, and modulating pH to remove iron from transferrin. Calcium acquisition is mediated in part by a calcium-binding protein. The gene encoding this protein is expressed only in the yeast phase, and its presence is essential for virulence of the fungus both in vitro and in vivo.[18,19]

After conidia settle into the alveoli, they bind to the CD11/CD18 family of integrins and are engulfed by both neutrophils and macrophages.[21] It is likely that the conversion of mycelia to the yeast phase transpires, at least partially if not entirely, intracellularly. The duration of the phase transition ranges from hours to days. Following transformation of the conidia into yeasts within lungs, yeasts migrate, presumably intracellularly, to local draining lymph nodes and subsequently, distant organs that are rich in mononuclear phagocytes such as liver and spleen. The yeasts grow quite readily within resting macrophages. Activation of cellular immunity is necessary for restricting growth, and in primary infection this arm of immunity matures by 2 weeks.

In experimental pulmonary infection, neutrophils constitute one of the prominent cell populations that emigrate early into infected foci of lungs.[22] These cells are capable of inhibiting the growth of yeast cells. Constituents from the azurophilic granules express fungistatic activity, and defensins also inhibit the growth of yeast cells.[23] Elimination of murine neutrophils enhances considerably the susceptibility of mice to sublethal inocula with yeast cells.[24] Neutrophils mount a respiratory burst in response to the fungus, but the oxygen intermediates are trapped intracellularly. Despite the burst, there is little evidence that toxic oxygen intermediates contribute to the anti-*Histoplasma* activity of these phagocytes.

Macrophages and dendritic cells are the principal effector cells in host resistance to this fungus.[21,25] The fate of yeast cells in each of these cell populations differs. Yeast proliferate within resting mononuclear phagocytes, but this form is killed by dendritic cells. As mentioned, macrophages engulf yeast via CD11/CD18 receptors, whereas dendritic cells use the fibronectin receptor. Engagement of two disparate receptors may explain in part the different fates within these cell populations.

In murine macrophages, a high percentage of yeast cells are located within phagolysosomes. Binding to the CD11/CD18 receptors and subsequent entry into macrophages are mediated by heat shock protein 60 that is expressed on the surface of yeast.[26] The fungus must contend with the inimical contents (e.g., acid proteinases) in this intensely hostile environment. One mechanism by which yeasts survive is by alkalization of the phagolysosome.[27] Yeast cells raise the pH of the phagocytic compartment to 6.0 to 6.5. One reason for maintaining the pH within a narrow range is that yeast cells require iron to grow, and if the pH exceeds 6.5, they cannot acquire iron from the host.[21]

Nitric oxide produced by activated murine macrophages is a major mediator of anti-*Histoplasma* activity. The ability of this nitrogen intermediate to oxidize iron may explain its potent fungicidal activity. However, its influence in human infection remains unknown because human macrophages infected with *H. capsulatum* have not been reported to produce nitric oxide.

The interaction between human macrophages and yeast differs substantially from that found with murine macrophages. The former cell population mounts a vigorous respiratory burst in response to unopsonized yeasts,[22] whereas murine cells do not unless yeasts are opsonized with antibody and therefore, engulfed through Fc receptors. Another contrast is that yeast cells do not predominantly reside in phagolysosomes of plastic-bound human macrophages, but rather reside in endosomes. However, if human macrophages that are adherent to collagen gels are exposed to yeast cells, massive phagolysosomal fusion develops.[22] This process is correlated with a pronounced inhibition of growth of *H. capsulatum* yeasts.

Macrophages from HIV-infected individuals manifest defective activity in their interaction with *H. capsulatum.* These cells bind fewer yeasts than cells from uninfected individuals, and a direct correlation exists between the CD4+ T-cell count and the capacity of macrophages to bind yeast cells. Upon entry into cells, yeasts grow more rapidly within macrophages from HIV-infected individuals or in macrophages that have been infected in vitro with a macrophage tropic strain of HIV. The envelope glycoprotein 120 from the virus is responsible for the inhibition of binding yeasts to macrophages,[22] but not the altered growth characteristics of the yeasts within phagocytes.

Within the elements of the acquired immune response, T cells are pivotal in clearance of the fungus. Experimental studies indicate that neither B cells nor antibodies influence host resistance, although the data are limited. CD4+ cells are extremely important in controlling primary infection in mice.[24] The central role of CD4+ cells in this species is supported by the finding that in HIV-infected individuals, most cases of histoplasmosis develop when the CD4+ cell count is less than 200/μl.[29] Mice deficient in CD8+ cells are impaired in their ability to reduce the fungal burden, but they can eventually eliminate the fungus. Likewise, β_2-microglobulin knockout mice that lack CD8+ T cells and major histocompatibility complex I antigens are more susceptible to infection than controls, but they are able to sterilize tissues.[24] In contrast, in secondary infection, the absence of CD4+ or CD8+ cells diminishes the efficiency of yeast elimination, but mice survive. The loss of protective immunity only develops when both subsets are eliminated.

The primary contribution of T cells to host defense is the release of cytokines that eventually activate mononuclear phagocytes. Blockade of endogenous interferon-γ or mice congenitally deficient in this lymphokine are exceptionally susceptible to infection.[24] Other cytokines in mice that are necessary for host clearance are interleukin-12 and tumor necrosis factor-α. Blockade of endogenous production of either of these leads to the death of mice. The effect of interleukin-12 is mediated through the induction of interferon-γ.[24] Interestingly, interleukin-12 is important in primary infection but not in reexposure histoplasmosis.[72] Tumor necrosis factor-α and interferon-γ are both necessary for controlling primary as well as secondary infection.[24]

In vitro, recombinant interferon-γ activates murine peritoneal macrophages to inhibit the growth of yeast cells. Macrophages from other tissue sources are either nonresponsive to this stimulus or require costimulation with lipopolysaccharide.[22] The anti-*Histoplasma* action of interferon-γ is mediated by limiting iron acquisition, and this effect can be reversed by exposure to additional iron.[57] Human macrophages, on the other hand, do not respond to human recombinant interferon-γ to inhibit yeast cell growth.[22] The cytokines that activate these cells are macrophage colony-stimulating factor, granulocyte-macrophage colony-stimulating factor, and interleukin-3,[22] but the mechanism by which these cytokines induce fungistatic activity has not been established.

Although the infection is limited by cell-mediated immunity, tissues are not sterilized. Infected individuals contain yeasts, some of

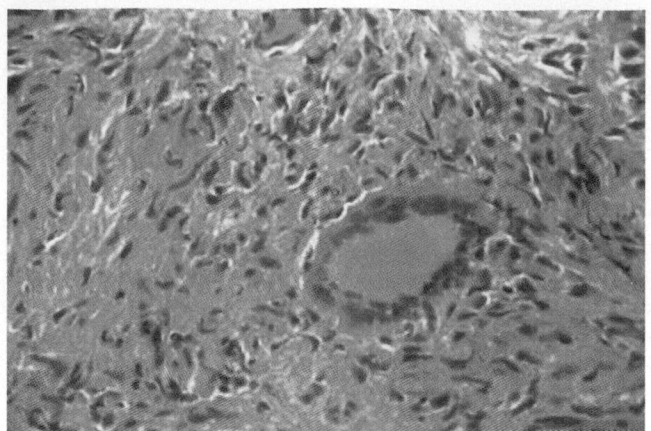

FIGURE 262-4. Granuloma in the lung of a patient with histoplasmosis.

which remain viable for many years. The dormant organisms pose little risk unless the individual becomes immunosuppressed as a result of either potent immunosuppressive agents used to combat various clinical conditions or from immunosuppressive viruses such as HIV. The metabolic state of *H. capsulatum* in tissues is unknown. It is likely that some of the yeasts remain viable, because individuals who have moved from endemic to nonendemic areas many years ago may reactivate infection. Although the cascade of immunologic events that lead to activation of this form of the infection remains largely unknown, reports of patients developing disseminated histoplasmosis after treatment with monoclonal antibody to tumor necrosis factor-α may implicate this cytokine in reactivation.[30] However, most, if not all of these patients, also were prescribed additional immunosuppressive agents such as prednisone and methotrexate. Thus the precise defects of immunity require further examination.

The hallmark of the tissue response to this fungus is the development of caseating or noncaseating granulomas in which calcium may be deposited (Fig. 262-4). The granuloma consists of an admixture of mononuclear phagocytes and lymphocytes, principally T cells. The putative function of the granuloma is to contain fungal growth. Although interferon-γ and tumor necrosis factor-α are important in the generation of granulomas formed in response to other microbes, neutralization of these two cytokines does not prevent their formation in response to *H. capsulatum*. Organized granulomatous inflammation is typically observed in self-limited disease. Conversely, in progressive disseminated histoplasmosis, the more common histopathologic appearance of tissue is a massive influx of macrophages with scattered lymphocytes. Well-circumscribed granulomas are infrequently present, and the lack

of an organized inflammatory response is indicative of a perturbed cellular immune response. Occasionally the inflammatory response in mediastinal lymph nodes is exaggerated, resulting in excessive granuloma formation followed by fibrosis. The progressive scarring may impact on the patency of the airways and major blood vessels.[31,32]

In experimental infection, either cutaneous or in vitro delayed-type hypersensitivity responses to *H. capsulatum* antigens are detected approximately 2 weeks after exposure.[24] In humans, delayed-type hypersensitivity responses are manifest within 3 to 6 weeks after exposure.[33] These values are simply approximations because the precise time in which individuals are exposed in endemic areas is exceptionally difficult to determine. Reexposure to *H. capsulatum* in previously sensitized individuals is characterized by a more rapid tissue response. This finding is not surprising because *H. capsulatum* induces a memory response in which the immune system reacts in a much shorter time frame.

Infection with *H. capsulatum* produces a broad array of clinical and pathologic manifestations that must be recognized in order to correctly diagnose and treat individuals afflicted with this fungus. A summary of the clinicopathologic manifestations is depicted in Table 262-1.

PULMONARY HISTOPLASMOSIS

Acute Primary Infection

The vast majority of primary infections (>90%) go unrecognized medically. Most often they are either asymptomatic or result in mild influenza-like illness for which individuals do not seek medical attention. However, there is a small proportion of patients who become overtly ill. The major determinant for the development of symptoms is likely to be the inoculum size, although differences in strain virulence cannot be excluded.[34,35] Other contributing factors include age and underlying diseases. Thus, the elderly, those younger than 2 years of age, and individuals whose immune systems are compromised are more likely to develop progressive, disseminated disease symptoms.

In those that become ill, the typical incubation time is 7 to 21 days, and most individuals manifest symptoms by day 14.[34-36] Fever that may reach 42° C, headache, nonproductive cough, chills, and chest pain are the most common symptoms noted. The latter is described usually as a substernal discomfort, although in an outbreak in children, it was more often located in the anterior chest.[36] Pleuritic chest pain is uncommon. The chest pain is believed to be caused by enlargement of either mediastinal or hilar lymph nodes, or both. Malaise, weakness, fatigue, and myalgia are observed in a distinctly smaller percentage of patients. Most symptoms resolve within 10 days, but they can persist for several weeks if there is an exposure to a heavy inoculum. Acute pulmonary infection can be accompanied by a number of rheumatologic manifestations. Arthralgias, erythema nodosum, and erythema multiforme are present in approximately 6% of patients, the majority of whom are women.[37] In some, these manifes-

TABLE 262-1 The Spectrum of *H. capsulatum*-Induced Disease*

Manifestations	Acute Pulmonary Disease	Acute Cavitary Pulmonary Disease	Disseminated Disease
Clinical	Often asymptomatic	Fever, productive cough, chest pain	Fever, weight loss, hepatosplenomegaly, hematologic disturbances[†]
Immunologic			
Positive skin test	>90%	70%-90%	30%-55%
Lymphocyte transformation	+++[‡]	+ to +++	±
Antibody to *H. capsulatum*[§]	25%-85%[‖]	75%-95%	70%-90%
Antigenuria	20%[‖]	40%	60%-90%
Pathologic			
Positive culture from lungs	<25%	5%-70%	50%-70%
Histology	Caseating and noncaseating granulomas, few yeasts, giant cells	Noncaseating granulomas, interstitial fibrosis, necrosis, yeasts, cavities, few to moderate yeasts	Diffuse macrophage proliferation, abundant few giant cells

*Reprinted with permission from Deepe GS Jr, Bullock WE. Histoplasmosis: A granulomatous inflammatory response. In: Gallin JI, Goldstein IM, Synderman R, eds. Inflammation: Basic Principles and Clinical Correlates. 2nd ed. New York: Raven Press; 1992:943.
[†]Hematologic disturbances include anemia, leukopenia, and thrombocytopenia.
[‡]"+" indicates a proliferative response to antigen or mitogen that is 3- to 5-fold higher than backgrond; "++" 5-to 10-fold higher than background, and more than 10-fold higher.
[§]Complement-fixation titer of greater than or equal to 1:8.
[‖]Higher incidence in those with symptomatic infection.

tations of histoplasmosis may be the presenting complaint. Frank arthritis is distinctly uncommon.

Physical findings in acute pulmonary histoplasmosis are minimal. Rales may be detected and, rarely, hepatosplenomegaly. The common roentgenographic features are characterized by a patchy pneumonitis that eventually calcifies, and hilar lymphadenopathy (Fig. 262-5). If a heavy exposure has transpired, numerous patches of pneumonitis that calcify may develop, and these produce the so-called buckshot appearance on the chest roentgenogram.[34] Pleural effusions are distinctly uncommon. The white blood cell count is usually within the normal range, but approximately 30% of patients will have either leukocytosis or leukopenia during the course of this infection. Another laboratory abnormality is a transient increase in serum alkaline phosphatase. Pulmonary function studies, performed in only a few patients, have demonstrated reversible restrictive defects, impaired DL_{co}, and obstructive defects.[38]

At least 6% of patients that acquire histoplasmosis suffer from acute pericarditis.[39] This percentage may underestimate the true incidence because only the most seriously affected individuals will seek medical attention. Precordial chest pain and fever are frequent. A high proportion of patients report a respiratory illness approximately 6 weeks before the onset of the pericarditis. A pericardial friction rub is auscultated in greater than 75% of patients with pericarditis, and in a similar percentage, pulsus paradoxus is present. An enlarged cardiac silhouette is usually seen on chest roentgenogram. Electrocardiographic abnormalities indicative of pericarditis, for example, ST segment elevation, are often observed. Only a small percentage of individuals develop cardiac tamponade. The likely cause of the pericarditis is not direct invasion of the organism, because it is rarely found in tissue specimens or in pericardial fluid, but rather the granulomatous inflammatory response that is mounted in mediastinal lymph nodes adjacent to the pericardium.

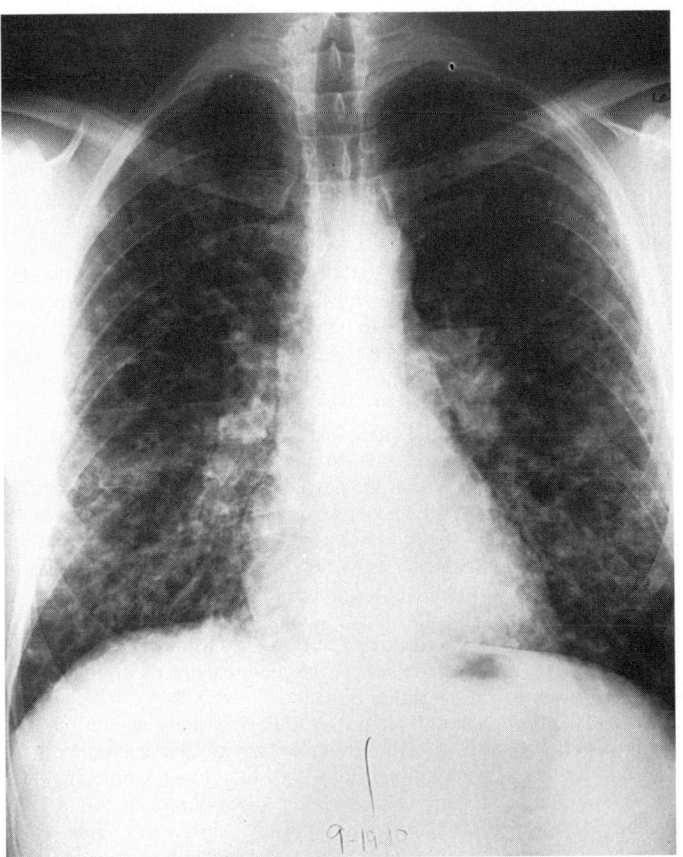

FIGURE 262-5. Chest roentgenogram of patient with acute pulmonary histoplasmosis.

Acute pulmonary histoplasmosis must be distinguished from influenza and from other forms of community-acquired pneumonia.[40] This task is difficult unless a thorough exposure history is obtained. Of greater concern, however, are patients who present with mediastinal lymphadenopathy. This finding is often considered to be caused by a hematologic malignancy rather than histoplasmosis. In such cases, patients may undergo unnecessary surgical procedures in an attempt to establish a diagnosis. Sarcoidosis also should be considered and distinguishing between histoplasmosis and sarcoidosis can be difficult at best. Both may have similar histopathologic features, and serum angiotensin-converting enzyme levels are elevated in each disease.[41] Thus, in all patients who present with mediastinal or hilar lymphadenopathy, it is critically important that histoplasmosis be considered in the differential diagnosis in patients who reside or have recently inhabited an endemic region.

A Ghon complex and pulmonary calcifications are common in healed pulmonary histoplasmosis. Another characteristic feature of resolved primary infection is the presence of splenic or liver calcifications. In fact, the presence of these on a routine roentgenogram should be considered evidence of resolved histoplasmosis if the patient has resided in an endemic area. Although splenic and liver calcifications also are noted in healed tuberculosis, the most likely cause of these findings remains histoplasmosis because the incidence of tuberculosis in the United States is much lower than that of histoplasmosis.

ACUTE REINFECTION PULMONARY HISTOPLASMOSIS

It is not uncommon for those who reside in endemic areas to be exposed more than once to *H. capsulatum*. Those who are reexposed to a large inoculum in heavily endemic areas present with a milder influenza-like illness. The onset can begin within 3 days, which is shorter than in primary infection. The characteristic chest roentgenogram is one of numerous small nodules that are diffusely scattered throughout both lung fields. This feature has been referred to as miliary granulomatosis. Hilar or mediastinal lymphadenopathy is absent. The duration of illness often is briefer than in primary infection.[34,35,42]

HISTOPLASMOMA

A very infrequent complication of primary histoplasmosis is the development of a mass lesion that resembles a fibroma.[43] When it arises, it is found most often in the lung. Instead of resolving, a nidus of infection gradually enlarges over years to form a concentric mass. Presumably, the growth is caused by persistent antigenic stimulus from the yeasts. It is composed of active inflammation at the periphery and fibrous tissue within the inner sphere, and eventually, the central portion calcifies. Roentgenographically, the histoplasmoma may have either a central core of calcium or rings of calcium, and these findings are useful in distinguishing it from a neoplastic growth.

MEDIASTINAL GRANULOMA AND FIBROSIS

Another complication of primary infection is a massive enlargement of the mediastinal lymph nodes that is caused by the granulomatous inflammation mounted in response to the fungus.[34] The diameter of these nodes can reach 8 to 10 cm. The nodes are caseous and contain a fibrotic shell that may be up to 5 mm thick. Often this process is asymptomatic. Occasionally, however, the nodes may impinge upon major airways and impair gas exchange. During the healing process, the fibrotic tissue can cause retraction of the airways leading to postobstructive pneumonias, hypoxemia, and bronchiectasis. The fibrosis also may constrict the esophagus or the superior vena cava, resulting in dysphagia or superior vena cava syndrome, or both.[43,44]

Calcific deposits that originate within the lungs occasionally produce lithoptysis. More common, however, is the penetration of enlarged, calcified nodes into the airways, and the generation of particles of calcium that can be expectorated. If the calcific mass is large, airway obstruction may ensue. Another consequence of enlarged nodes is

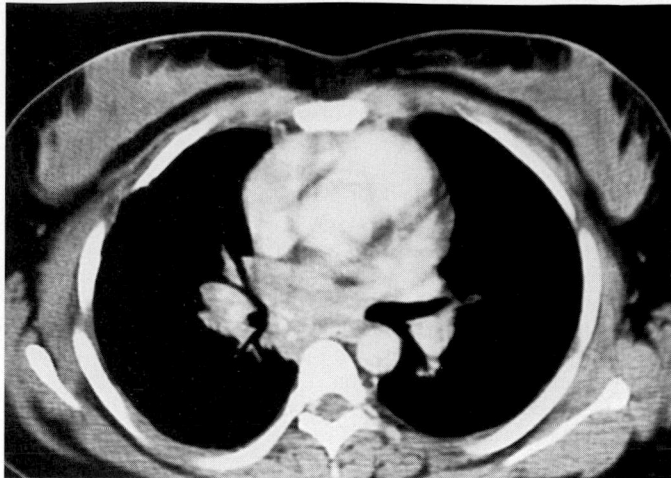

FIGURE 262-6. Computed tomographic image of the mediastinum in a patient with mediastinal fibrosis.

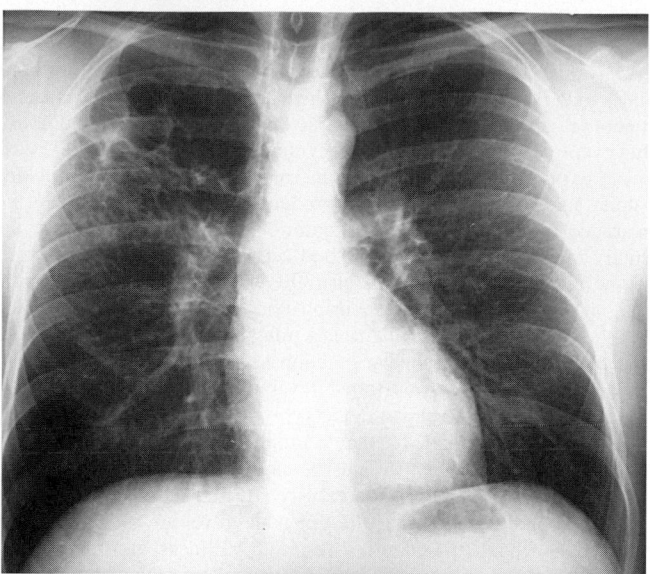

FIGURE 262-7. Chest roentgenogram of patient with cavitary histoplasmosis.

the creation of sinuses or fistulas between the airways and the pericardium or the esophagus.[43]

A rare but dire consequence of mediastinal involvement is mediastinal fibrosis.[45] This syndrome is quite similar to that observed with tuberculosis, in which the infection leads to a massive deposition of fibrotic tissue within the mediastinum (Fig. 262-6). The mechanism underlying this exuberant immune response is unknown. However, it appears not to be triggered by massive numbers of yeast, because they are observed infrequently in lesions. The reaction to the antigen or antigens from *H. capsulatum* must be host-specific, based on its infrequent development. If there exist any genetic susceptibility loci for this entity, they have not been identified. The fibrosis encroaches on all the structures of the mediastinum including the major airways, superior vena cava, and the esophagus. The symptoms that arise from the fibrotic process are attributable to the narrowing of the patency of these structures. Hypoxemia, shortness of breath, superior vena cava syndrome, and dysphagia may ensue as the fibrotic process progresses.

CAVITARY PULMONARY HISTOPLASMOSIS

Cavitary pulmonary histoplasmosis (also known as chronic pulmonary histoplasmosis) is a distinct clinical entity (Fig. 262-7). Although the precise incidence is not known because of the sporadic nature of the disease, approximately 8% of individuals developed this manifestation of disease following two large epidemics in Indianapolis.[46] Cavitary lesions are found in the upper lobes in greater than 90% of cases. Males older than 50 years of age with preexisting chronic lung disease, usually emphysema, constitute the highest proportion of patients, and it is quite unusual in those younger than age 40 (i.e., <5% of all cases).[46,47]

The most frequent symptoms are low-grade fever, productive cough, dyspnea, and weight loss of insidious onset. Night sweats, chest pain, hemoptysis, and malaise are less common. Hemoptysis is rare. Completely asymptomatic intervals with radiologic stability are interspersed with periods of recurrent symptoms and radiologic progression. Both an early and a late stage have been described. The major difference between the two forms is the symptomatology. In the early stage, the illness, characterized by chest pain, productive cough, fever, and weakness, begins abruptly and persists for several weeks before medical attention is sought. In the late stage, the proportion of patients experiencing productive cough and hemoptysis is much higher, whereas chest pain and fever are much less frequent. Bronchogenic transmission from one segment of the lung to another may occur during cough or aspiration.[47]

Roentgenographically, patchy infiltrates appear and develop areas of dense consolidation that progress to cavitation. Over months or years, extensive fibrosis, retraction, and areas of compensatory emphysema appear unless effective treatment is given. The most common location is the upper lobes. Disease is often unilateral originally but the other lung is eventually involved, as are the lower lobes. Bronchogenic transmission from one segment of the lung to another may occur during cough or aspiration.[47] Nearly all patients either have a history of heavy cigarette use or exhibit evidence of emphysema coexisting with chronic obstructive pulmonary disease, and therefore, the cavities must be distinguished from preexisting bullae. Thin-walled or thick-walled cavities may form in response to *H. capsulatum*. Enlarged hilar or mediastinal lymph nodes are notably absent, and distinctive laboratory features are not present. Leukocytosis and elevated alkaline phosphatase levels are detected in about one third of symptomatic patients, and anemia is present in one half.[46,47]

The earliest lesion on histopathology is an interstitial pneumonitis. The inflammatory infiltrate is composed primarily of lymphocytes and macrophages, and it is often found adjacent to bullae. The alveolar walls are thickened, and the peribronchial lymphatics contain a similar type of inflammatory infiltrate. Subsequently, necrosis develops, and it resembles that caused by infarction. Vascular compromise as denoted by subintimal thickening and vessel obliteration is present in inflamed regions. Proteinaceous exudate can be found within bullae, and yeasts are present within the necrotic lining of a cavity or within small encapsulated necrotic lesions. Areas of infarction are slowly replaced by scarring of the involved parenchyma. The healing phase is characterized by fibrosis and retraction, some leaving central areas of caseous necrosis surrounded by epithelioid cells, lymphocytes, and giant cells. Neighboring bullae may enlarge from compensatory emphysema. Following healing, recurrence of cavitary lesions will develop in approximately 20% of patients, but the prognosis of recurrence is not different from that of the initial infection.[47]

Spontaneous resolution of thin-walled and thick-walled cavities ranges from 10% to 60%, and thin-walled cavities have a higher healing rate. Despite shrinking and fibrosis of individual lesions, new lesions continue to appear and radiologic progression occurs in an estimated 79%. In individuals with chronic obstructive pulmonary disease, cavitary histoplasmosis can exacerbate the existing pulmonary dysfunction, and the destructive nature of the inflammation irreversibly compromises pulmonary function. Death caused by cavitary histoplasmosis is distinctly unusual but is attributable to respiratory failure, cor pulmonale, or secondary bacterial pneumonia.

The association between the presence of chronic obstructive pulmonary disease and chronic cavitary histoplasmosis suggests that the anatomic defect present in these lungs predisposes patients to this clinical form of infection and promotes the formation of cavities. This intriguing postulate has been proposed and is most likely correct, although no experimental data exist to support it.[47] The difficulty in testing this hypothesis is that a suitable animal model has not been developed. In addition, the postulate does not explain the development of cavities in other patients. At present, *H. capsulatum* is not known to elaborate any elastinolytic or proteolytic enzymes that digest collagen.

Some have argued that most cases represent reinfection because there is no concomitant enlargement of intrathoracic lymph nodes. However, this finding may argue equally well for reactivation because nodal enlargement may not be expected in local reactivation disease. The distinction will not be made until the molecular genetic tools are used to distinguish individual isolates of *H. capsulatum*.

PROGRESSIVE DISSEMINATED HISTOPLASMOSIS

Although all primary infections can be considered disseminated because yeast cells migrate from the lungs to organs rich in mononuclear phagocytes, the term progressive disseminated histoplasmosis (PDH) refers to the relentless growth of the organism in multiple organ systems. Because *H. capsulatum* is not a reportable disease, only estimates of incidence or prevalence are available. The estimated incidence is 1 per 2000 cases of histoplasmosis.[48] Following the two Indianapolis epidemics, 8% of clinically recognized cases of histoplasmosis were PDH.[48] The major risk factors in those two epidemics for this manifestation of histoplasmosis were age older than 54 years and immunosuppression. Among patients with AIDS, the incidence may approach 25%. The outcome of infection with *H. capsulatum* was poor among HIV-infected individuals including the presence of a chronic medical condition and a history of herpes simplex virus infection. Conversely, the use of antiretrovirals and triazoles was associated with a decreased risk. In an analysis of 1074 renal allograft recipients, 0.4% developed clinically recognized PDH over a 25-year span.[49] This value is moderately different than the one reported during the Indianapolis epidemic, in which 2.1% of renal allograft recipients exhibited PDH.[50] Another risk factor for acquiring PDH is the use of tumor necrosis factor-α antagonists.[30]

The exposure leading to PDH is inapparent, without an antecedent episode of acute pulmonary histoplasmosis. PDH can develop by reexposure to a large inoculum of the fungus or by reactivation of dormant, endogenous foci. The vast majority of cases are believed to arise from endogenous reactivation because cases develop in those who remotely resided in an endemic area. Reactivation of latent infection can develop from transplanted organs.[51] One such case in which kidneys from one donor was associated with infection in recipients who were not residents of an endemic area. These types of cases are difficult to discern in endemic areas. Most cases of PDH are now observed in immunosuppressed individuals.[48,52] However, there still exist cases in previously normal individuals, often at the extremes of age who are not known to exhibit preexisting immunologic dysfunction. The perturbations that cause a breach in the integrity of the immune system and therefore, lead to reactivation of quiescent infected foci, have not been delineated.

Although infection with *H. capsulatum* produces a broad range of disease, PDH also can be categorized by clinical and pathologic manifestations. There is the acute form that is associated with a fulminant course. Histopathologically, massive macrophage infiltration and scattered lymphocytes are apparent. Tissue macrophages are engorged with yeast cells, and tests of cellular immunity often reveal poor to absent responses. At the other extreme is the chronic form characterized by an indolent course and the presence of well-circumscribed granulomas in involved tissues. In tissues, few yeasts are seen, and delayed-type hypersensitivity responses are intact in a high proportion of individuals.

Acute Progressive Disseminated Histoplasmosis

In the era before aggressive immunosuppressive or cytotoxic therapy, this entity was principally seen in infants, hence its moniker, the infantile form. To date, however, it is most often observed in those who are severely immunosuppressed, especially those with AIDS and hematologic malignancies such as Hodgkin's and non-Hodgkin's lymphoma. In infants and young children it is believed that this form of histoplasmosis is a progression of either a primary exposure or reinfection because pulmonary symptoms dominate the early phases of illness. The onset is usually abrupt, extending over just a few days. Fever and malaise are the two most common manifestations followed by weight loss, cough, and diarrhea. Physical findings include hepatosplenomegaly in nearly all patients, lymphadenopathy especially of the cervical chain, in about 30%, and rales. Jaundice is observed in a minority, and oropharyngeal ulcers develop in less than 20%.[32]

Hematologic disturbances are frequent. Anemia is present in more than 90% of cases, of whom the majority have a hematocrit of less than 20%. Leukopenia and thrombocytopenia are observed in more than 80% of children. Serum levels of the liver enzymes alanine aminotransferase and alkaline phosphatase are elevated in a high proportion. Chest roentgenograms most often reveal a patchy pneumonitis with mediastinal and hilar node enlargement. This finding supports the contention that acute PDH in children represents an extension of an exogenous exposure. Untreated, the mortality is 100%, and prior to the introduction of effective antifungal agents, most children died within 5 to 6 weeks after onset of symptoms. Terminal events include disseminated intravascular coagulation, gastrointestinal hemorrhage probably resulting from severe thrombocytopenia, and secondary bacterial sepsis associated with profound granulocytopenia.

In HIV-infected individuals, the risk factors for the development of histoplasmosis are CD4+ cell count of less than 200 cells/μl, history of exposure to chicken coops, and a known positive serology for complement-fixing antibodies prior to illness.[52] Most AIDS patients who develop PDH have had at least one opportunistic infection. Although PDH may develop in approximately 25% of AIDS patients residing in an endemic area, there is no comparable information in the era of highly active antiretroviral therapy, although anecdotal reports suggest a decline in the incidence of cases. Upon seeking medical attention, nearly all patients manifest evidence of disseminated disease. Fever and weight loss are found in more than 90% of those with AIDS and PDH. The most common physical findings include rales, hepatosplenomegaly, and lymphadenopathy. Mucosal ulcers are distinctly uncommon, but as many as 10% of patients will exhibit cutaneous lesions.[53] The common cutaneous findings are a maculopapular eruption, petechiae, or ecchymosis. The maculopapular rash does not display any unique pattern of distribution. The finding of skin lesions is much more common in those infected with the South American strains of *H. capsulatum*.

In a small study, up to 66% of AIDS patients with disseminated histoplasmosis manifested skin lesions. The most common appearance is a papular eruption with crusting. Less frequent are nodular or purely pustular lesions. Histopathology of skin lesions reveals necrosis circumscribing the superficial dermal vessels. There is perivascular cuffing with lymphocytes and neutrophils, but the number of cells is very few. Yeasts are present both intra- and extracellularly. In addition to the skin findings, a number of other unusual manifestations have been reported, including colonic masses, perianal ulcers, and chorioretinitis, meningitis, and encephalitis. It is estimated from results of one series that up to 20% of patients with PDH will have central nervous system involvement.[54] The more aggressive forms include encephalitis, acute meningitis, and encephalopathy in acute PDH. Histoplasmoma of the central nervous system and chronic meningitis are manifestations of a more indolent form of PDH.

Anemia, thrombocytopenia, and leukopenia are common laboratory features of PDH in the immunosuppressed population. In AIDS patients, the alteration in the peripheral blood counts may be attributable in part to the disease or to the drugs they are receiving. Elevated

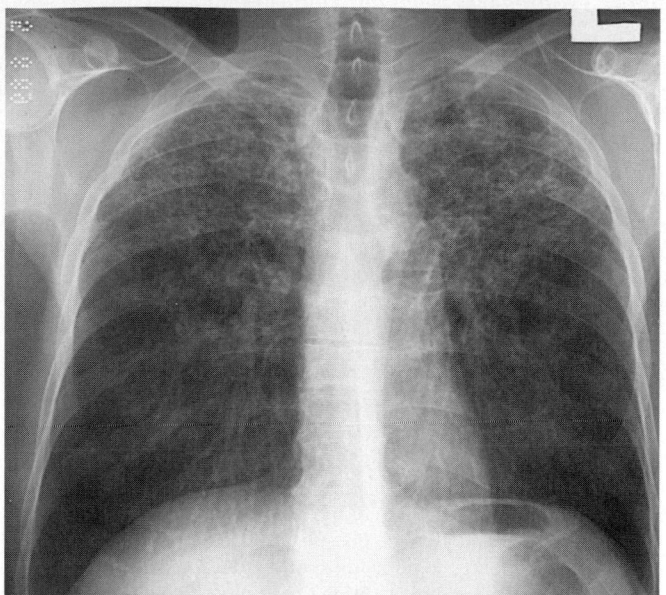

FIGURE 262-8. Diffuse infiltrates in patients with progressive disseminated histoplasmosis and acquired immunodeficiency syndrome.

serum levels of hepatic enzymes are frequently detected. Again, concomitant drugs may obscure the laboratory abnormalities caused strictly by *H. capsulatum*. Chest roentgenograms typically demonstrate widely scattered nodular opacities or diffuse reticular pattern (Fig. 262-8). However, a substantial percentage (30%) may present with a normal roentgenogram.[55]

The fatality rate of acute PDH in the immunocompromised patient is 100% if untreated. With therapy, survival rates of the acute episode exceed 80%. Infrequently, patients exhibit a sepsis-like syndrome characterized by disseminated intravascular coagulation, encephalopathy, acute respiratory distress syndrome, vascular collapse, and subsequently, multiorgan failure. In a portion of the patients, bone marrow biopsy has demonstrated the presence of histiocytes phagocytosing erythrocytes. This form of PDH has been termed the reactive hemophagocytic syndrome, and despite aggressive management and therapy, the outcome is usually catastrophic.

Subacute Progressive Disseminated Histoplasmosis

Subacute PDH is distinguished from the acute form primarily by the more prolonged nature of the symptoms prior to seeking medical attention. Fever and weight loss are common sometime during the course of infection, but fever is a presenting complaint in only about 50%. Physical findings include hepatosplenomegaly and oropharyngeal ulcers. In contrast to the ulcers observed in acute PDH, these are deeper and more likely to be confused with malignancy. Laboratory abnormalities are much less striking than in acute PDH. Although anemia and leukopenia are noted in up to 40%, the percentage of patients with severe depression of either the hematocrit or leukocyte count is small. Thrombocytopenia is evident in about 20%, and it is usually mild. Rarely is the platelet count less than 20,000/μl.[32]

One of the notable features of subacute PDH is the presence of focal lesions in various organ systems, including the gastrointestinal tract, endovascular structures, the central nervous system, and the adrenal glands.[32,56] Aside from liver and spleen, the gastrointestinal tract is one of the most common organs affected in subacute PDH. Yeast cells can be found in the bowel mucosa in up to 70% of autopsy cases. Macroscopic ulcerations of the small and large bowel are present in about 40%, and perforation from a penetrating ulcer has been reported. The terminal ileum and cecum are the sites most frequently involved. Symptoms referable to the bowel are not frequent, but if present, diarrhea and crampy abdominal pain are typical complaints. Intestinal obstruction of the ileum also has been reported.

Endocarditis and infection of other vascular structures may be a manifestation of subacute PDH.[57] The aortic and mitral valves are affected more commonly than right-sided valves, and the aortic valve is the single most common valve involved. In about 50% of the cases, there is prior evidence of valvular disease, such as a bicuspid aortic valve. By echocardiography, the lesions tend to be extensive, and large vessel embolization can be the presenting symptom. Clumps of yeasts embedded in a fibrin mesh is the characteristic histopathologic feature. Occasionally allomorphs that are as large as 20 m in diameter have been observed. In addition, hyphal forms of *H. capsulatum* have been detected in endocarditis. If untreated, death usually ensues. Other endovascular manifestations include prosthetic valve endocarditis, infection of abdominal aortic aneurysms, and prosthetic grafts. Previous reports have indicated that blood cultures are rarely positive. However, those reports precede improved methods for isolating *H. capsulatum* from blood.

Central nervous system infection involves all age groups and causes a number of manifestations including chronic meningitis, mass lesion, and cerebritis. Among these, chronic meningitis is the most frequent.[54] Symptoms of central nervous system histoplasmosis may antedate medical attention for several weeks, and they include headache, altered sensorium, and cranial nerve deficits. Seizures, ataxia, meningismus and other focal deficits constitute much of the remaining symptomatology. It must be emphasized that only half of the patients may complain of symptoms localized to the central nervous system. Associated physical findings consist of hepatosplenomegaly in about a third, lymphadenopathy, and mucocutaneous lesions.

In cases of meningitis, pleocytosis of the cerebrospinal fluid is present in all patients. Cell counts usually range from 10 to 100/μl with a preponderance of lymphocytes. Hypoglycorrhachia and elevated protein are detected in 80%. Histopathology of the brain parenchyma and meninges characteristically reveals granulomatous inflammation. A perivenous granulomatosis in which parasitized macrophages are observed beneath the intima of parenchymal and meningeal veins is commonly seen. The basilar meninges are the most severely affected area of the central nervous system. Hydrocephalus may contribute to the symptomatology.

Histoplasmoma causes a mass effect and may initially be mistaken for a malignancy or abscess by computed tomography because it exhibits ring enhancement with the administration of contrast. Dense fibrotic tissue surrounds a caseous center in which yeasts are detected. Histoplasmomas may be associated with meningitis, but often are independently present. Cerebrospinal fluid pleocytosis is common but hypoglycorrhachia is not.

Although symptoms arising from involvement of adrenal glands is not frequent, autopsy series indicate that yeasts invade this organ system in approximately 80% of cases.[58] Macrophages containing yeasts are found scattered throughout the parenchyma of the adrenal gland. There is no particular predilection for either the cortex or the medulla. The severity of infection ranges from focal areas containing parasitized macrophages to diffuse involvement of the adrenal parenchyma. The former is most commonly detected. Tissue necrosis is seen, but usually involves only a small portion of the gland. Grossly, the adrenal glands are enlarged. This postmortem discovery has been supported by findings on computed tomography in which a high percentage of patients with subacute PDH display enlarged adrenals. Overt Addison's disease is uncommon, occurring in less than 10%. There is little information concerning the incidence of an impaired pituitary-adrenal axis.

Chronic Progressive Disseminated Histoplasmosis

Chronic PDH can be distinguished from subacute PDH by the prolonged chronicity of symptoms that are often very mild. This form is seen almost exclusively in previously normal adults. Malaise and lethargy stand out as the most frequent complaints. Fever is much less

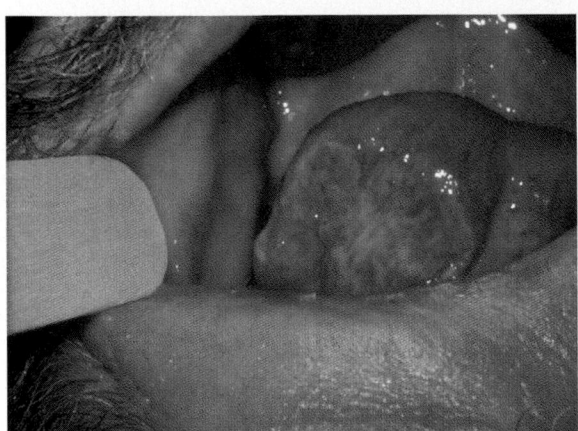

FIGURE 262-9. Tongue ulcer in patient with chronic disseminated histoplasmosis.

frequent (<30%) and is often low grade. The most common physical finding (50%) is an oropharyngeal ulcer that is well circumscribed, indurated, usually deep and painless (Fig. 262-9).[32] The tongue, buccal mucosa, larynx, gums, and lip comprise the majority of affected structures. Occasionally the lesion is on the labia or glans penis. These lesions are often confused with squamous carcinoma oral malignancy. Hence it is incumbent upon the clinician to consider the diagnosis of histoplasmosis; otherwise tissue will be sent only for histology. Histopathologically, the center of the lesion contains macrophages with many yeasts, but the number of such macrophages decreases in the periphery of the lesion. Unlike the histologic reaction in other viscera, the response in the mucosa is an admixture of acute and chronic inflammation. Thus, plasma cells, lymphocytes, eosinophils, and granulocytes are found infiltrating the ulcer, and fibrosis is a characteristic feature. Areas of intact mucosa may show hyperplasia that can be confused with squamous carcinoma on superficial biopsy. Well-circumscribed granulomas are typically found, usually at the periphery.

Other symptoms include hepatosplenomegaly in about a third of patients. Chronic meningitis or chronic granulomatous hepatitis may be the only manifestation of infection. Unlike subacute PDH, there is a notable absence of disease involvement of other organ systems including central nervous system, heart, and adrenals. Bone infection, Addison's disease, and endocarditis all have been described, but these entities are uncommon. Hematologic abnormalities are distinctly uncommon and often not significant. This illness may persist for years, with periods of spontaneous improvement in symptoms, without being recognized. On occasion, there may be an abrupt worsening caused by involvement of a particular organ such as the central nervous system, adrenals, or heart.[32] Usually, however, the illness remains undiagnosed until symptoms arising from a single organ are observed. Without appropriate therapy, infection progresses to death.

OCULAR HISTOPLASMOSIS

Two different syndromes of ocular involvement are described. The less common is a uveitis or panophthalmitis in association with active histoplasmosis. Granulomas are present in the uvea, and yeasts are recovered from lesions. Much more frequent is the presumed ocular histoplasmosis syndrome (POHS), which consists of a posterior uveitis or choroiditis in individuals who manifest skin test positivity to histoplasmin and intrathoracic calcifications.[59] However, it must be stressed that a skin test and the presence of intrathoracic calcifications do not prove cause and effect.

Typically, there are peripheral atrophic scars and a lack of vitreous or anterior segment inflammation. The scars or "histo-spots" are located posterior to the equator of the eye. They range in size from 0.2 to 0.7 disk diameters, and they can vary from 1 to 70 in a single eye. Involvement of both eyes is uncommon (<10%). Most individuals are between 20 and 50 years of age when this syndrome is diagnosed, and the prevalence may be as high as 10% in endemic regions. The major destructive consequence of this lesion is macular hemorrhage, which develops 10 to 20 years after the appearance of scars. Neovascularization and scarring can lead to loss of vision in up to 60% of patients.[59] Because neovascularization can exert such devastating effects, efforts have been made to understand its etiology. It has been shown that the integrin $\alpha_v\beta_3$ is expressed on blood vessels from patients with POHS.

The histopathology of POHS reveals a lymphocytic infiltration in the scarred areas. Yeasts are rarely observed in the eye or elsewhere. Recently, a model for this syndrome has been developed in primates in order to define the cellular immunopathology. Chronic lesions contain a preponderance of B and CD4+ cells. As in affected human eyes, yeasts are not found in the lesions. Within the choroidal lesions there is an increase in the percentage of CD4+ cells and macrophages. There is no definitive proof that *H. capsulatum* causes the scars that are observed in humans although the primate model establishes that this fungus can produce choroidal scars. The pathogenesis appears to be an exuberant cellular immune reaction to inert fungal antigens, thus resembling to some degree the tissue response in mediastinal fibrosis. Corticosteroid treatment of POHS does not activate latent histoplasmosis.

AFRICAN HISTOPLASMOSIS

In Africa, the classical *H. capsulatum* var. *capsulatum* coexists with *H. capsulatum* var. *duboisii*. The yeast form of the latter is typically much larger with a diameter up to 15 μm and has a thicker wall. The mycelial form of both is indistinguishable. The pathogenesis of this fungus is presumed to be inhalation from the soil, although a primary pulmonary infection has not been demonstrated. Cutaneous inoculation is certainly an alternative mode of acquisition of the infection. Spontaneous disease has been reported in baboons and *Cynocephalus* monkeys. Most cases are reported from Uganda, Nigeria, Zaire, and Senegal.

The clinical picture associated with infection by *H. capsulatum* var. *duboisii*.[60] is distinctly different than that caused by *H. capsulatum* var. *capsulatum*.[60] Skin and skeleton are the most frequent organs affected by this pathogen. In the skin, the usual findings are ulcers, nodules, or psoriatic-like lesions that may spontaneously resolve. Involvement of the subcutaneous tissue may present with tender nodules ("cold" abscesses) in which the typical manifestations of inflammation are absent. Osteolytic bone lesions are fairly common and are noted in up to 50% of cases. The skull and ribs are the most frequent bones affected, followed by vertebrae. The organism produces granulomatous inflammation within the bone. This type of inflammation can lead to sinus formation and cystic bone lesions. In a high proportion of patients, multiple bones may be infected. Even in the presence of overt skin or bone lesions, chest roentgenograms are often free of evidence of previous exposure to *H. capsulatum*. Draining lymph nodes also may become inflamed.

A progressive disseminated disease has been recognized. Patients are febrile with hematologic abnormalities. There is multiorgan involvement including liver, spleen, kidney, and lung, and miliary lesions are observed in the latter. The histopathology resembles that induced by *Blastomyces dermatitidis* or *Coccidioides immitis*, that is a pyogranulomatous reaction in which there is a combination of granulomas and suppuration. One likely reason for this pathologic reaction is the large size of *H. capsulatum* var. *duboisii* preventing avid ingestion by macrophages. Thus, neutrophils may ingress to assist in the clearance of the fungus.

Reports of African histoplasmosis in HIV-infected individuals are emerging. A variety of manifestations in individual patients has been observed. Disseminated infection with fever, cutaneous infection, and bone infection have been recognized.[61] The outcome has been favorable only in a minority of patients.

DIAGNOSIS

Histoplasmosis only can be established with assurance by isolation from body fluids or from tissues. The typical medium that is used to recover the fungus includes brain heart infusion agar with a source of blood plus antibiotics and cycloheximide. These chemicals are included to inhibit the growth of saprophytic fungi and bacteria. Cultures are incubated at 30° C for up to 6 weeks. Often, growth is noted within 3 weeks, and greater than 90% of cultures exhibit fungus within 7 days. Previously, confirmation that the fungus was *H. capsulatum* required exoantigen testing or conversion of the mycelial form to the yeast form, but this step is no longer necessary. All mycelial isolates are confirmed using a DNA probe that recognizes recombinant DNA (rDNA).

The success rate varies considerably and often is correlated with the number of specimens collected, the source of the specimen, and the burden of infection. Recovery of *H. capsulatum* from sputa of patients with acute pulmonary histoplasmosis ranges from 10% to 15%, whereas in cavitary histoplasmosis, cultures are positive in up to 60% of patients.[62] The yield of positive cultures increases with the number of specimens collected. Three or more specimens are more likely to display growth of *H. capsulatum*. In AIDS patients with pulmonary manifestations, up to 90% of cultures from the lungs obtained from bronchoscopic samples will grow *H. capsulatum*. Bone marrow and blood cultures are positive in up to 50%.[62] Yields for blood cultures are considerably higher if the lysis centrifugation technique is used. The organism can be frequently isolated from oropharyngeal ulcers in patients with chronic PDH. In endocarditis, valve cultures are positive in a high percentage but blood cultures often are negative. However, much of the data concerning blood cultures utilized the biphasic medium, which may not be as sensitive as lysis centrifugation. In meningitis, the organism is recovered from the cerebrospinal fluid (CSF) in 25% to 65% of patients,[54] and the yield is improved if a large volume (≥ 20 mL) is removed because *H. capsulatum* invades the basilar meninges. The organism is unlikely to be isolated from pericardial or pleural fluid, but more likely from their respective serosal tissues. Likewise, *H. capsulatum* rarely is isolated from mediastinal tissues in patients with mediastinal fibrosis.

Antigen Detection and Polymerase Chain Reaction Analysis

This assay, which detects polysaccharide antigen in serum or urine by enzyme-linked immunosorbent assay (ELISA), is the mainstay of diagnosis especially in those with PDH. Antigen is detected in up to 90% of patients with acute PDH, 40% with cavitary disease, and 20% with acute pulmonary histoplasmosis.[62] The test also has excellent utility in monitoring relapses of acute PDH, especially in immunosuppressed patients. An increase of the arbitrary value of 2 units is significantly associated with relapse of infection. Antigen detection is much more sensitive than serology for identifying relapsing cases, and it has been applied successfully to cerebrospinal fluid in patients with meningitis. In 14 cases, the test was positive in 12. Thus it has a high degree of sensitivity and specificity. Cross-reactivity in the urine test has been found for patients infected with *B. dermatitidis*, *Paracoccidioides brasiliensis*, or *Penicillium marneffei*.

Several reports of the utility of the polymerase chain reaction have been published and although not in clinical use yet, they show promise.

Serology

Since the late 1940s, serology has been a vital instrument in the diagnosis of infection with *H. capsulatum*. Complement-fixing (CF) antibodies and precipitin bands have been the most common tests used in the clinical laboratory. The greatest utility has been in the retrospective diagnosis of acute histoplasmosis, using a fourfold or greater rise in CF titer between acute and convalescent serum. This has been particularly helpful in outbreaks that are recognized in time to collect acute sera but the antibody titer rise occurs too late to be of value in patient management. For chronic pulmonary or progressive disseminated histoplasmosis, fourfold rises are not observed and antibody tests have insufficient sensitivity and specificity to be of clinical value. For CF antibodies, a titer of 1:8 to either yeast or mycelial antigen is considered positive, and a titer of 1:32 indicates the need to pursue a possible diagnosis of histoplasmosis. Titers that fall between these two values neither exclude nor suggest the diagnosis. On occasion, a result is returned that states that the test is anticomplementary. This result signifies that the serum contained a substance or substances that interfered with the CF test. Repeat of the test with a new serum specimen quite frequently yields a result.

Low levels of CF antibodies are detected in approximately 10% of healthy individuals that reside in an endemic region. A low percentage of individuals with acute pulmonary histoplasmosis will develop CF antibodies within the first 3 weeks of infection, but by 6 weeks, at least 75% of patients manifest a positive CF antibody titer or a fourfold rise. Over the course of months, the antibody titer will decline although it may remain serofast for years, especially in those with cavitary pulmonary disease or with chronic PDH. The false-positive rate is estimated to be 15% and is most commonly observed in those with coccidioidomycosis or with blastomycosis.[63] The reason for the cross-reactivity is the presence of a carbohydrate antigen common to the three fungi.

Another test is the detection of H and M bands during the illness. These bands on agar gel precipitin test are identified by lines of identity with bands formed by control sera known to have precipitating antibody to H or M antigens. These two precipitin bands were originally identified using immunodiffusion as specific to sera from patients with histoplasmosis. The H and M antigens are glycoproteins that are released by both mycelial and yeast phase cultures. The H antigen has been cloned and sequenced, and it demonstrates homology to β-glucosidases. It is infrequently (<10%) detected in the sera of patients, but when present, signifies active infection. The M antigen also has been cloned and sequenced, and it has a high degree of homology to catalase. Unlike the H antigen, it is detected in up to 80% of individuals following exposure to the fungus. However, it is present in patients who have recovered from infection or who have active disease. Therefore, it is not useful in discriminating remote from current infection. A major limitation of the serologic tests is that even in the presence of active infection, they are negative in up to 50% of immunosuppressed patients, especially those with AIDS. One explanation for the poor anti-*Histoplasma* antibody response is that the immunosuppressive agents or HIV induce dysfunctional B cells and/or CD4+ T cells, thus rendering serologic assays almost useless.

Histochemical Identification of *H. capsulatum*

Stains for the presence of *H. capsulatum* can be extremely useful in rapid identification of the fungus in various tissues or body fluids. The yeast is visualized poorly by hematoxylin-eosin stain, but it is more apparent using the periodic acid–Schiff (PAS) stain. The most useful stain is either the Gomori-methenamine (GMS) or Grocott silver stain. The organism can be detected in peripheral blood smears stained with Wright-Giemsa in up to 40% of cases of acute PDH (Fig. 262-10). This percentage is much less if the reader of the blood smear is scrutinizing the slide only to determine a differential. Examination of the peripheral blood smear can be very useful if the clinician suspects PDH as a cause of a patient's illness. The yeast must be discriminated from *Pneumocystis jirovecii* in the lung. This organism is larger, nonbudding, and usually extracellular. Moreover, it is exceedingly rare to find *P. jiroveciicarinii* outside the lung or in an area of caseous necrosis. Although *Leishmania* spp. and *Toxoplasma gondii* may on occasion be confused morphologically with *H. capsulatum*, neither stains with silver.

Skin Test

The histoplasmin skin test has been used for several decades to determine who has been exposed to *H. capsulatum*. The skin test reagent is the supernatant from the mycelial growth and has been standardized by the World Health Organization. This reagent has been exceptionally

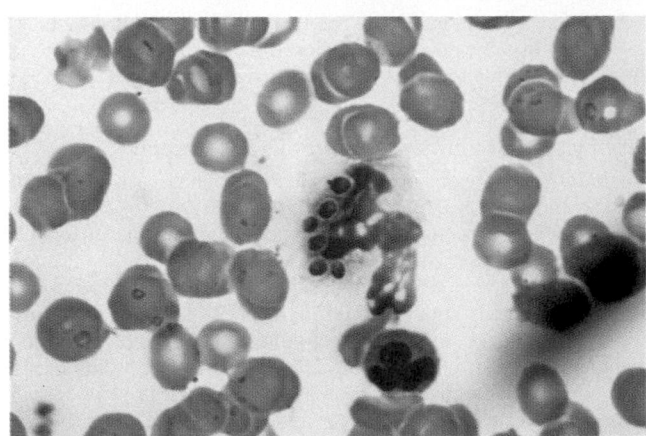

FIGURE 262-10. Wright-Giemsa stain of circulating neutrophil with intracellular yeast cells.

useful as an epidemiologic tool but has practically no value as a diagnostic tool because it only indicates past exposure. This test is no longer available commercially. In past surveys, the prevalence of skin test positivity among inhabitants of an endemic area was as high as 90%, but later surveys have suggested the prevalence to be lower.

Miscellaneous Laboratory Tests

One retrospective study has suggested that patients with AIDS who are admitted to the hospital with pulmonary infiltrates and fever greater than 38° C and serum lactate dehydrogenase (LDH) values greater than 600 IU/mL were highly likely to have disseminated histoplasmosis.[64] Other studies have suggested that elevated serum ferritin levels are strongly suggestive of histoplasmosis.[65]

TREATMENT

The increasing incidence of fungal infections has prompted the development and testing of numerous new antifungal agents, some of which have reached the marketplace. The introduction of azoles has moved the treatment of histoplasmosis from an inpatient to an outpatient setting. In the past, the clinician's principal option was amphotericin B. Now there are several azoles from which to choose, and lipid-based preparations of amphotericin B are also available. Moreover, caspofungin acetate and voriconazole are two additional agents that have been introduced. Caspofungin does not appear to be sufficiently active against *H. capsulatum*, and voriconazole manifests excellent in vitro susceptibility, but there is too little clinical information to recommend it at this time. Practice guidelines for the treatment of various forms of histoplasmosis have been published.[66]

Acute Pulmonary Histoplasmosis

The vast majority of cases of acute pulmonary histoplasmosis do not require therapeutic intervention. Bed rest and antipyretics suffice for these individuals. Treatment should be instituted for those who have not improved after 1 month of illness or who exhibit hypoxemia. In those who have not spontaneously resolved their illness after 1 month, itraconazole 200 mg orally daily for 6 to 12 weeks will be sufficient. Ketoconazole 400 mg/day also is effective but is less well tolerated. Fluconazole is not as active as either itraconazole or ketoconazole and should be avoided. If the patient cannot ingest an oral medication or tolerate an azole, amphotericin B is the preferred agent. A dosage of 0.4 to 0.5 mg/kg intravenously can be given every day until the symptoms subside, often within 2 weeks, and it is uncommon to administer more than 500 mg. Daily administration is useful in those that have large catheters for venous access. If smaller-bore catheters are used, 0.7 to 1 mg/kg every other day is an option. No comparative trials of amphotericin B and azoles have been performed, but clinical experience suggests that resolution of symptoms is faster with the former.

If the patient is hypoxemic and requires mechanical ventilation, amphotericin B 0.7 mg/kg/day is recommended until they improve. When patients improve to the point that they can ingest food and medications, itraconazole 200 mg once or twice a day should be used to complete 12 weeks of therapy. If the patient has renal dysfunction, a lipid-based preparation may be substituted for amphotericin B at a dose of 3 mg/kg/day. The inflammatory response may be responsible in part for the respiratory compromise. Although ample evidence does not exist, corticosteroids may be used to mitigate inflammation. Prednisone or its parenteral equivalents can be used at a dosage of 60 mg/day for 14 days.

Itraconazole is a lipophilic agent that inhibits the cytochrome P-450 system. As such, there are a number of drug interactions with the antihistamines, terfenadine and astemizole. Co-administration of azoles with either of these two drugs can lead to serious ventricular arrthymias because elevated levels of the antihistamines increase the QT interval. The azoles also increase the levels of cyclosporine, warfarin, and digoxin. Rhabdomyolysis has developed in patients taking the cholesterol-lowering agents simvastatin or lovastatin with azoles. Rifampin, isoniazid, phenytoin, and carbamazepine can lower concentrations of itraconazole and ketoconzole by increasing metabolism. Optimal itraconazole absorption is dependent on gastric acidity, and agents that alkalinize the gastric pH may interfere. The cyclodextrin oral liquid formulation of itraconazole increases absorption by 50% and makes administration to young children much easier.

Mediastinal Granuloma, Mediastinal Fibrosis, and Histoplasmoma

Hilar and mediastinal lymphadenopathy from acute pulmonary histoplasmosis usually is asymptomatic but can cause a brassy cough or compress the middle lobe bronchus, leading to temporary atelectasis. Although no therapy is usually necessary, persistent symptoms could be treated with itraconazole 200 mg per day for 3 to 6 months. Rarely, large caseous mediastinal nodes will compress the esophagus or erode into both the esophagus and bronchus, causing a bronchoesophageal fistula. Surgical resection of the nodes may be indicated, though the nodes may be densely adherent to the pulmonary veins and other surrounding structures.

Mediastinal fibrosis is an exceptionally difficult clinical problem for which there is no consensus on optimal management. Surgery, corticosteroids, and antifungal agents have been utilized in the treatment of this condition, with minimal success. Surgery to remove the fibrosis area and placement of intravascular stents can alleviate the life-threatening situation, but the fibrosis often progresses. Moreover, the surgery may jeopardize essential venous collaterals, such as the hemiazygos or azygos veins. Addition of azoles after surgery has been proposed, but the utility of this approach is debatable.[66]

A histoplasmoma of the lung, which is a fibrocaseous nodule resulting from healed acute pulmonary histoplasmosis, does not require any therapy. Surgical resection or biopsy may be needed to exclude malignancy in a solitary pulmonary nodule, should no central calcification be evident. Serology is of no value in proving the nodule is a histoplasmoma.

Cavitary Pulmonary Histoplasmosis

Although a proportion of patients with fibrocavitary disease will eventually stabilize their disease without treatment, the inability to predict which patients will eventually progress has led to the recommendation that all patients should be treated, even those who are currently asymptomatic. Treatment does not improve pulmonary function already lost and, in fact, healing may lead to some further loss of function due to fibrosis. Discontinuing cigarette smoking is an important adjunct in preventing further loss of pulmonary capacity. Many patients with only thin-walled cavities spontaneously resolve infection without therapeutic intervention. Such patients, if untreated, should be followed by serial chest roentgenograms every 2 to 3 months. Those who have thick-walled cavities, progressive pulmonary infiltrates, or persistent cavities associated with declining respiratory function should be treated. Itraconazole or ketoconazole at 400 mg/day (200 mg twice a day) should be given for 12 to 24 months.[66] This regimen will arrest progression in 75% to 85% of patients. Relapse may be difficult to detect radiologically in patients with extensive prior lung damage. Sputum culture is the best means for detecting relapse, though *Aspergillus* and other rapidly growing molds may overgrow the culture plate. Fluconazole is less effective than either itraconazole or ketoconazole for chronic pulmonary histoplasmosis, based on incomplete data. If there is progression of infection while on azoles or the patient has relapsed following azole therapy, amphotericin B is preferable. The total dose is 30 to 35 mg/kg, and can be given as 0.7 mg/kg/day or approximately 50 mg daily.[66] If renal dysfunction is a consideration, a lipid formulation may be used at 3 to 5 mg/kg/day.

The relapse rates for cavitary pulmonary histoplasmosis are as high as 20%, with the highest relapse rates being in patients with thick-walled cavities. If there is a failure of antifungal therapy, surgical resection may be indicated if the patient has sufficient pulmonary reserve.

Acute Progressive Disseminated Histoplasmosis

Prompt institution of amphotericin B therapy is necessary for treatment of patients with acute, life-threatening PDH. Patients should receive 25 mg on the initial dose followed by a rapid escalation to 0.7 to 1 mg/kg daily. Within a week, most patients are symptomatically improved, and laboratory abnormalities begin to return to baseline values. Once the patient has become afebrile and clinically stable, amphotericin B can be administered at a lower dose of 0.4 to 0.5 mg/kg daily. If amphotericin B is utilized throughout the illness, patients should receive a total dose of 30 to 35 mg/kg. Lipid formulations are also effective for PDH at a dosage of 3 to 5 mg/kg/day. Patients who demonstrate resolution of symptoms while on amphotericin B may be switched to itraconazole 400 mg daily for a total duration of 6 months. Ketoconazole should be avoided in immunosuppressed patients because of the high failure rate. In acute PDH that is not associated with hemodynamic instability or severe illness, itraconazole may be used initially. Therapy should begin with 300 mg twice a day for 3 days followed by 200 mg twice a day for at least 6 months. Itraconazole interacts with many antiretrovirals, including elevating serum concentrations of several protease inhibitors.

In patients with AIDS, lifelong suppressive therapy with itraconazole 200 mg daily is recommended for most patients. Although there are no reliable data to make this decision, it may be reasonable to discontinue maintenance therapy in patients receiving highly active antiretroviral therapy, and who have a CD4 count greater than 150 μl for 6 months, a nondetectable viral load, at least 12 months of antifungal therapy and a negative test for *Histoplasma* antigen in urine. If the patient relapses while receiving azole maintenance therapy, amphotericin B should be given.[66] Following treatment of the relapse, the patient should receive amphotericin B as maintenance therapy with 0.7 to 1 mg/kg once or twice a week. A self-limiting immune reconstitution syndrome has been recognized occasionally in HIV patients being treated for PDH and who have had an effective response to highly active antiretroviral therapy. The syndrome presents as fever, with or without an elevated alkaline phosphatase. Management is supportive.

Relapse of PDH is common in other persistently immunosuppressed patients and may be difficult to detect until far advanced. Indefinite suppressive therapy with itraconazole may be a useful option.

Subacute and Chronic Progressive Disseminated Histoplasmosis

Because many of these cases develop in patients whose immune system is intact, itraconazole 400 mg daily is highly efficacious. The success rate in these individuals approaches 90%. Ketoconazole has a similar success rate but causes more side effects. If the patient requires hospitalization, fails to improve on azole therapy, is immunosuppressed, or demonstrates intolerance to azoles, amphotericin B, 0.7 to

1 mg/kg/day, should be given. The total amphotericin B dose is 30 to 35 mg/kg. In selected patients whose infection is controlled by this drug, it is possible to switch them to an azole to complete a total of 6 months' therapy.

Prophylaxis of Immunocompromised Persons

For immunosuppressed patients who have a high risk of acquiring histoplasmosis from the environment either because of their work or their residence, itraconazole, 200 mg per day, is useful. Such patients would include those with AIDS whose CD4 cell count is <150/μl or those who require potent immunosuppressive therapy. In the former group, prophylaxis with itraconazole reduced the incidence of infection by more than twofold. Another indication for prophylaxis among immunosuppressed patients would be for those residing in areas that have a high incidence of infection as defined by at least 10 cases per 100 patient-years.[67]

Meningitis

Patients with meningitis should be given amphotericin B, 0.7 to 1 mg/kg/day to a total dosage of 30 to 35 mg/kg. This treatment should be followed by 800 mg of fluconazole daily for 9 to 12 months. Cerebrospinal fluid should have a normal glucose and no detectable cerebrospinal fluid *Histoplasma* antigen at the end of therapy. Although fluconazole therapy is less effective than amphotericin B, fluconazole does cross the blood-brain barrier. Lipid formulations of amphotericin B also could be used in dosages from 3 to 5 mg/kg/day. Repeat lumbar punctures should be performed approximately every week for the first 6 weeks and every 2 weeks thereafter to assess therapy. Although a high percentage of patients may respond initially to therapy, they frequently relapse. Overall cure rates are no better than 50%, and immunocompetent patients respond much better to treatment than do immunosuppressed individuals. Itraconazole and ketoconazole do not penetrate the blood-brain barrier well and therefore should not be used.

Endocarditis

As with bacterial causes of endocarditis, a microbicidal agent should be used. Therefore, amphotericin B, 0.7 to 1 mg/kg/day should be given. Alternatively, a lipid formulation of amphotericin may be used at a dosage of 3 to 5 mg/kg/day. Administration of an antifungal agent alone is not sufficient and must be used in combination with surgical removal of the affected valve(s). One issue is how long to treat after the valve has been removed. If there are other foci of active histoplasmosis, then the total dosage should be 30 to 35 mg/kg. However, if the valve was the only site involved, treatment with amphotericin B for 2 weeks following surgical extraction may be sufficient. If the patient cannot undergo surgery, conventional amphotericin B in the highest tolerated dose, or a liposomal amphotericin B should be given daily.[66]

Pericarditis

Pericarditis following acute pulmonary histoplasmosis does not require antifungal therapy. Most patients can be treated symptomatically with nonsteroidal anti-inflammatory agents for 2 to 12 weeks.[66] If patients fail to respond to these agents or if the patient manifests hemodynamic instability, corticosteroids are indicated for 1 to 2 weeks followed by nonsteroidals. One must be cautious because if there are active lesions of histoplasmosis, the infection may become more aggressive during corticosteroid therapy. Cardiac tamponade associated with *H. capsulatum* pericarditis is uncommon, but when it occurs it must be treated as a medical emergency with pericardiocentesis. Despite the severity of illness, antifungal therapy is not indicated. Unlike tuberculous pericarditis, constrictive pericarditis rarely develops, but patients should be monitored for several years after the acute attack. In the uncommon situation in which the pericardium is infected as a manifestation of PDH, antifungal therapy either with amphotericin B or azoles is indicated depending on the severity of illness.

Arthropathies

Nonsteroidal anti-inflammatory agents should be continued until resolution of symptoms. Antifungal therapy should not be used.

Presumed Ocular Histoplasmosis

This condition does not require antifungal therapy. Laser therapy is used to prevent additional neovascularization within the choroid, but lesions that abut the fovea cannot be subjected to this treatment.[59] Photodynamic therapy for this region of the eye appears promising as does the implementation of antiangiogenic agents. The role of retrobulbar local injection of corticosteroids is unclear.

Prevention

Educational efforts must be ongoing to alert those who work in areas in which a substantial risk of infection exists. Dust control and use of N95 masks should be considered. For example, construction workers who are restoring buildings that have served as homes for starlings and bats must be warned about the possibility of exposure and steps taken to remove the guano safely. Spraying 3% formalin on guano deposits will kill the fungus within several days, and the material can then be removed. However, formaldehyde decontamination is rarely employed because the vapor is toxic, it can seep into groundwater and thus poses an environmental hazard, and it does not penetrate dried guano uniformly.

There is a continuing resurgent effort to develop a vaccine preventive against *H. capsulatum* pathogenic fungi because of their escalating incidence. Among those in which animal studies have defined a vaccine is *H. capsulatum*. Vaccine candidates containing heat shock protein 60 and H antigen from *H. capsulatum* have been demonstrated to confer protection in mice given a pulmonary challenge. A region of heat shock protein 60 that spans amino acids 174 to 445 appears to contain the protective activity of the entire protein.

REFERENCES

1. Darling ST. A protozoal general infection producing pseudotubercles in the lungs and focal necrosis in the liver, spleen, and lymph nodes. JAMA. 1906;46:1283-1285.
2. da Rocha-Lima H. Histoplasmose und epizootische Lymphangitis. Arch Schiffs Tropenhyg. 1912;16:79.
3. DeMonbreun WA. The cultivation and cultural characteristics of Darling's *Histoplasma capsulatum*. Am J Trop Med Hyg. 1934;14:93-125.
4. Christie A. Histoplasmosis and pulmonary calcification. Ann N Y Acad Sci. 1950;501283-1298.
5. Furcolow ML, Schubert J, Tosh FE, et al. Serologic evidence of histoplasmosis in sanitariums in the U.S. JAMA. 1962;180:109-114.
6. Ajello L. Distribution of *Histoplasma capsulatum* in the United States. In: Ajello L, Chick W, Furculow MF, eds. Histoplasmosis. Springfield, Ill: Charles C Thomas; 1971:103-122.
7. Zeidberg LD, Ajello L, Webster RH. Physical and chemical factors in relation to *Histoplasma capsulatum* in soil. Science. 1955;122:33-34.
8. Emmons CW. Isolation of *Histoplasma capsulatum* from soil. Public Health Rep. 1949;64:892-896.
9. DiSalvo AF, Ajello L, Palmer JW, Winkler WG. Isolation of *Histoplasma capsulatum* from Arizona bats. Am J Epidemiol. 1969;89:606-614.
10. Schwarz J. Immunity. In: Schwarz J, ed. Histoplasmosis. New York: Praeger; 1981:147.
11. Steele PE, Carle GF, Kobayashi GS, Medoff G. Electrophoretic analysis of *Histoplasma capsulatum* chromosomal DNA. Mol Cell Biol. 1989;9:983-987.
12. Keath EJ, Kobayashi GS, Medoff G. Classification of *Histoplasma capsulatum* by restriction fragment length polymorphisms in a nuclear gene. J Clin Microbiol. 1992;30:2104-2107.
13. Spitzer ED, Keath EJ, Travis SJ, et al. Temperature-sensitive variants of *Histoplasma capsulatum* isolated from patients with acquired immunodeficiency syndrome. J Infect Dis. 1990;162:258-261.
14. Kwon-Chung KJ, Weeks RJ, Larsh HW. Studies on *Emonsiella capsulata* (*Histoplasma capsulatum*). II. Distribution of the two mating types in 13 endemic states of the United States. Am J Epidemiol. 1974;99:44-49.
15. Batanghari JW, Deepe GS Jr, Di Cera E, et al. Histoplasma acquisition of calcium and expression of CBP1 during intracellular parasitism. Mol Microbiol. 1998;27:531-539.
16. Maresca B, Kobayashi GS. Dimorphism in *Histoplasma capsulatum* and *Blastomyces dermatitidis*. Contrib Microbiol. 2000;5:201-216.
17. Eissenberg LG, Poirier S, Goldman, WE. Phenotypic variation and persistence of *Histoplasma capsulatum* yeasts in host cells. Infect Immun. 1996;64:5310-5314.
18. Magrini V, Goldman WE. Molecular mycology: A genetic toolbox for *Histoplasma capsulatum*. Trends Microbiol. 2001;9:541-546.
19. Woods JP. *Histoplasma capsulatum* molecular genetics, pathogenesis, and responsiveness to its environment. Fungal Genet Biol. 2002;35:81-97.
20. Medoff G, Sacco M, Maresca B, et al. Irreversible block of the mycelial to yeast phase transition of *Histoplasma capsulatum*. Science. 1986;231:476-479.
21. Newman SL. Macrophages in host defense against *Histoplasma capsulatum*. Trends Microbiol. 1999;7:67-71.
22. Baughman RP, Kim CK, Vinegar A, et al. The pathogenesis of experimental pulmonary histoplasmosis. Correlative studies of histopathology, bronchoalveolar lavage, and respiratory function. Am Rev Respir Dis. 1986;134:771-776.
23. Newman SL, Gootee L, Gabay J. Human neutrophil-mediated fungistasis against *Histoplasma capsulatum*. Localization of fungistatic activity to the azurophil granules. J Clin Invest. 1993;92:624-631.
24. Deepe GS Jr, Seder RA. Molecular and cellular determinants of immunity to *Histoplasma capsulatum*. Res Immunol. 1998;149:397-406.
25. Gildea L, Morris RE, Newman SL. *Histoplasma capsulatum* yeasts are phagocytosed via very late antigen-5, killed, and processed for antigen presentation by human dendritic cells. J Immunol. 2001;166:1049-1056.
26. Long KH, Gomez FJ, Morris RE, et al. Identification of heat shock protein 60 as the ligand on *Histoplasma capsulatum* that mediates binding to the CD18 receptors on human macrophages. J Immunol. 2003;170:487-494.
27. Eissenberg LG, Goldman WE, Schlesinger PH. *Histoplasma capsulatum* modulates the acidification of phagolysosomes. J Exp Med. 1993;177:1605-1611.
28. Lane TE, Wu-Hsieh BA, Howard DH. Iron limitation and the gamma interferon-mediated antihistoplasma state of murine macrophages. Infect Immun. 1991;59:2274-2278.
29. Wheat LJ, Connolly-Stringfield PA, Baker RL, et al. Disseminated histoplasmosis in the acquired immune deficiency syndrome: Clinical findings, diagnosis and treatment, and review of the literature. Medicine (Baltimore). 1990;69:361-374.
30. Lee JH, Slifman NR, Gershon SK, et al. Life-threatening histoplasmosis complicating immunotherapy with tumor necrosis factor α antagonists infliximab and etanercept. Arthritis Rheum. 2002;46:2565-2570.
31. Vanek J, Schwarz J. The gamut of histoplasmosis. Am J Med. 1971;50:89-104.
32. Goodwin RA Jr, Shapiro JL, Thurman GH, et al. Disseminated histoplasmosis: Clinical and pathologic correlations. Medicine (Baltimore). 1980;59:1-31.
33. Loosli CG, Grayston JT, Alexander ER, Tanzi F. Epidemiological studies of pulmonary histoplasmosis in a farm family. Am J Hyg. 1952;55:392-401.
34. Goodwin RA Jr, Loyd JE, Des Prez RM. Histoplasmosis in normal hosts. Medicine (Baltimore). 1981;60:231-266.
35. Goodwin RA Jr, Des Prez RM. Histoplasmosis. Am Rev Respir Dis. 1978;117:929-956.
36. Storch G, Burford JG, George RB, et al. Acute histoplasmosis: Description of an outbreak in northern Louisiana. Chest. 1980;77:38-42.
37. Rosenthal J, Brandt KD, Wheat LJ, et al. Rheumatologic manifestations of histoplasmosis in the recent Indianapolis epidemic. Arthritis Rheum. 1983;26:1065-70.
38. Ploy-song-sang YY, Loudon RG, Beach BC, Corbin RP. Pulmonary function studies in acute pulmonary histoplasmosis. South Med J. 1979;72:568-572.
39. Wheat LJ, Stein L, Corya BC, et al. Pericarditis as a manifestation of histoplasmosis during two large urban outbreaks. Medicine (Baltimore). 1983;62:110-119.
40. Wheat LJ, Slama TG, Eitzen HE, et al. A large urban outbreak of histoplasmosis: Clinical features. Ann Intern Med. 1981;94:331-337.
41. Davies SF, Rohrbach MS, Thelen V, et al. Elevated serum angiotensin-converting enzyme (SACE) activity in acute pulmonary histoplasmosis. Chest. 1984;85:307-310.
42. Powell KE, Hammerman KJ, Dahl BA, Tosh FE. Acute reinfection pulmonary histoplasmosis. A report of six cases. Am Rev Respir Dis. 1973;107:374-378.
43. Goodwin RA, Snell JD. The enlarging histoplasmoma. Concept of a tumor-like phenomenon encompassing the tuberculoma and coccidioidoma. Am Rev Respir Dis. 1969;100:1-12.
44. Schwarz J, Schaen MD, Picardi JL. Complications of the arrested primary histoplasmic focus. JAMA. 1976;236:1157-1161.
45. Loyd JE, Tillman BF, Atkinson JB, Des Prez RM. Mediastinal fibrosis complicating histoplasmosis. Medicine. 1988;67:295-310.
46. Wheat LJ, Wass J, Norton J, et al. Cavitary histoplasmosis occurring during two large urban outbreaks: Analysis of clinical, epidemiologic, roentgenographic, and laboratory features. Medicine (Baltimore). 1984;63:201-209.
47. Goodwin RA, Owens FT, Snell JD, et al. Chronic pulmonary histoplasmosis. Medicine (Baltimore). 1976;55:413-452.
48. Wheat LJ, Slama TG, Norton JA, et al. Risk factors for disseminated or fatal histoplasmosis. Ann Intern Med. 1982;96:159-163.
49. Peddi VR, Hariharan S, First MR. Disseminated histoplasmosis in renal allograft recipients. Clin Transplant. 1996;10:160-165.
50. Wheat LJ, Smith EJ, Sathapatayavongs B, et al. Histoplasmosis in renal allograft recipients: Two large urban outbreaks. Arch Intern Med. 1983;143:703-707.
51. Limaye AP, Connolly PA, Sagar M, et al. Transmission of *Histoplasma capsulatum* by organ transplantation. N Engl J Med. 2000;343:1163-1166.
52. McKinsey DS, Spiegel RA, Hutwagner L, et al. Prospective study of histoplasmosis in patients infected with human immunodeficiency virus: Incidence, risk factors, and pathophysiology. Clin Infect Dis. 1997;24:1195-1203.
53. Eidbo J, Sanchez RL, Tschen JA, Ellner KM. Cutaneous manifestations of histoplasmosis in the acquired immune deficiency syndrome. Am J Surg Path. 1993;17:110-116.
54. Wheat LJ, Batteiger BE, Sathapatayavongs B. Histoplasma capsulatum infections of the central nervous system: A clinical review. Medicine (Baltimore). 1990;69:244-260.
55. Conces DJ, Stockberger, SM, Tarver RD, Wheat LJ. Disseminated histoplasmosis in AIDS: Findings on chest radiographs. AJR. 1993;160:15-19.
56. Sturim HS, Kouchoukos NT, Ahluvin RC. Gastrointestinal manifestations of disseminated histoplasmosis. Am J Surg. 1965;110:435-440.
57. Blair TP, Waugh RA, Pollack M, et al. *Histoplasma capsulatum* endocarditis. Am Heart J. 1980;99:783-788.

58. Wilson DA, Muchmore HG, Tisdal RG, et al. Histoplasmosis of the adrenal glands studied by CT. Radiology. 1984;150:779-783.
59. Ciulla TA, Piper HC, Xiao M, et al. Presumed ocular histoplasmosis syndrome: Update on epidemiology, pathogenesis, and photodynamic, antiangiogenic, and surgical therapies. Curr Opin Ophthalmol. 2001;12:442-449.
60. Cockshott WP, Lucas AO. *Histoplasma duboisii*. Q J Med. 1964;33:223-238.
61. Manfredi R, Mazzoni A, Nanetti A, et al. *Histoplasma capsulati* and *duboisii* in Europe: The impact of the HIV pandemic, travel, and immigration. Eur J Epidemiol. 1994;10:675-681.
62. Wheat LJ. Laboratory diagnosis of histoplasmosis: Update 2000. Semin Respir Infect. 2001;16:131-140.
63. Terry PB, Rosenow EC, Roberts GD. False-positive complement fixation serology in histoplasmosis. A retrospective study. JAMA. 1978;239:2453-2456.
64. Corcoran GR, Al-Abdely H, Glanders CD. Markedly elevated serum lactate dehydrogenase levels are a clue to the diagnosis of disseminated histoplasmosis in patients with AIDS. Clin Infect Dis. 1997;24:942-944.
65. Kirn DH, Fredericks D, McCutchan JA, et al. Serum ferritin levels correlate with disease activity in patients with AIDS and disseminated histoplasmosis. Clin Infect Dis. 1995;21:1048-1049.
66. Wheat J, Sarosi G, McKinsey D, et al. Practice guidelines for the management of patients with histoplasmosis. Clin Infect Dis. 2000;30:688-695.
67. Masur H, Kaplan JE, Holmes KK, et al. Guidelines for preventing opportunistic infections among HIV-infected persons. Recommendations of the U.S. Public Health Service and the Infectious Diseases Society of America. Ann Intern Med. 2002;137:435-478.
68. Deepe GS Jr, Bullock WE. Histoplasmosis: A granulomatous inflammatory response. In: Gallin JI, Goldstein IM, Synderman R, eds. Inflammation: Basic Principles and Clinical Correlates. 2nd ed. New York: Raven Press; 1992:943.
69. Edwards LB, Acquaviva FA, Livesay VT, et al. An atlas of sensitivity to tuberculin, PPD-B, and histoplasmin in the United States. Am Rev Respir Dis. 1969;99(Part 2):1-111.

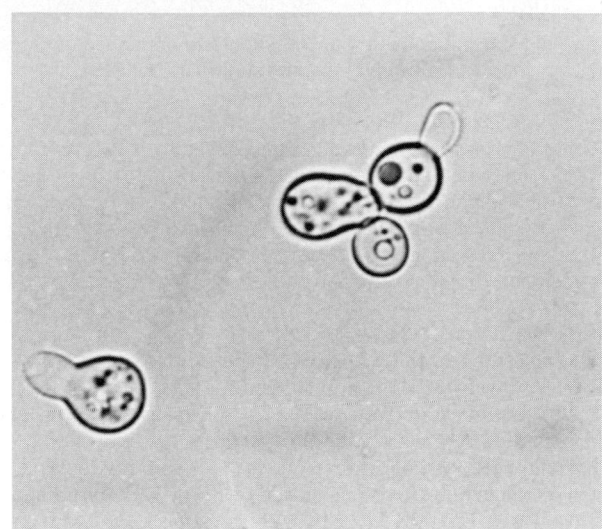

FIGURE 263-1. Yeast cells of *Blastomyces dermatitidis* in wet smear (×1000).

CHAPTER **263**

Blastomyces dermatitidis

STANLEY W. CHAPMAN

*B*lastomyces dermatitidis is the dimorphic fungus that causes the systemic pyogranulomatous disease blastomycosis. Initial infection is through the lungs and is often subclinical. Hematogenous dissemination may occur, culminating in a disease with protean manifestations. Clinical disease most often involves the lungs, skin, bones, and genitourinary system.

HISTORY

Blastomycosis was first reported in 1894 by T. C. Gilchrist,[1] who initially postulated that the disease was caused by a protozoan. In collaboration with Stokes, Gilchrist subsequently isolated the organism, established that the disease was caused by a fungus, and, finally, infected a dog with the newly isolated fungus.[2-4] Although blastomycosis was originally believed to involve only the skin, a number of cases of systemic disease were soon reported. Analysis of these early cases[5,6] led to the concept that two forms of the disease existed—cutaneous and systemic—and that they represented different portals of entry (skin and lung, respectively). This concept was not disproved until the work of Schwartz and Baum.[7] Through careful clinical and pathologic studies, they established definitively that the lung was the primary route of infection and that skin disease or other organ involvement was secondary to dissemination.

THE ORGANISM

B. dermatitidis is the imperfect (asexual) stage of *Ajellomyces dermatitidis.* The imperfect stage exhibits dimorphism, growing as a mycelial form at room temperature and as a yeast form at 37° C.[8,9] The mycelial form grows as a white mold that slowly turns light brown. On primary isolation, colonies appear in 1 to 3 weeks. The branching hyphae are usually 2 to 3 μm in diameter. Arising at right angles to the hyphae are conidiophores that produce single terminal conidia that vary from 2 to 10 μm in diameter and are round or oval in shape. The conidia are thought to be infectious for humans when the mycelia are disturbed. Conversion of the mycelial form to the yeast form at 37° C is necessary for positive identification. The physiologic events associated with this phase shift are similar to those associated with *Histoplasma capsulatum* and include heat-related stress, followed by uncoupling of oxidative phosphorylation.[10,11] Yeastlike colonies are wrinkled and cream or tan in color. The yeast cells (Fig. 263-1) may vary in diameter from 5 to 30 μm but are usually 8 to 15 μm, with a thick cell wall that is highly refractile. The yeast cells are multinucleate, containing 8 to 12 nuclei, and reproduce by single buds with a broad base between parent and bud. The daughter cell is often nearly as large as the mother cell before detachment. The same yeast cell in vitro characteristics are also noted in tissue or secretions and are used to distinguish *B. dermatitidis* from other fungi.

Two serotypes of *B. dermatitidis* have been identified by exoantigen analysis of yeast organisms.[12] Initial studies indicate that the A antigen–deficient serotypes are restricted to Africa.[13] The sexual form, *A. dermatitidis,* is heterothallic and requires opposite mating types (+ and −) for fertile cultures.[14,15] Both mating types are pathogenic, and infection occurs with equal frequency with each mating type.[16] Both types are occasionally isolated from a single patient.

Studies employing genomic restriction fragment length polymorphism analysis among isolates of *B. dermatitidis* obtained from diverse geographic regions in North America and Africa reveal a high degree of genetic similarity among isolates.[17,18] Three major groups, however, could be identified by a polymerase chain reaction (PCR)–based typing system. Strains could be further differentiated by a PCR fingerprinting method employing different primers. The use of this typing system could prove invaluable as a tool for studying the epidemiology of endemic blastomycosis as well as epidemic or case cluster situations. Whether these different groups are also associated with any mycologic differences between isolates of *B. dermatitidis* (e.g., virulence, adaptation to environment) will need further study.

EPIDEMIOLOGY

A complete understanding of the incidence and epidemiology of blastomycosis has been hindered by the lack of a sensitive, specific skin test reagent and the difficulty in establishing the ecologic niche of *B. der-*

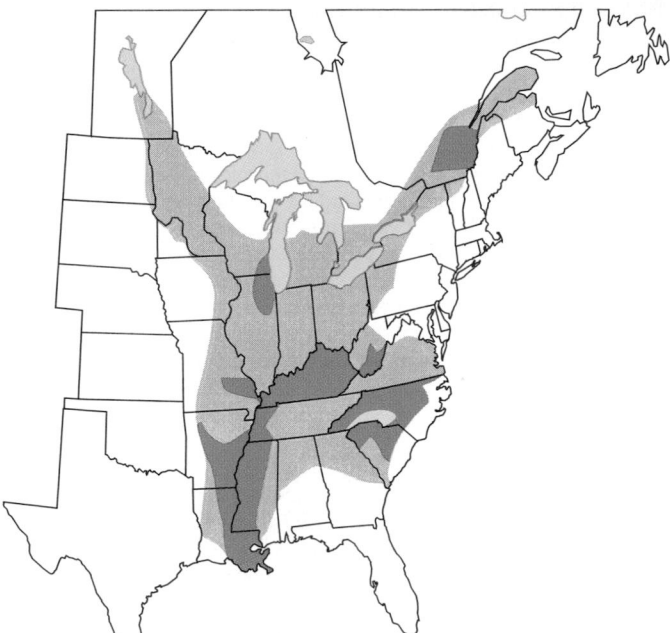

FIGURE 263-2. The incidence and prevalence of blastomycosis in North America. *Brown areas* indicate the known endemic region; *green areas* are those with the highest incidence. *(From Rippon JW. Medical Mycology: The Pathogenic Fungi and Pathogenic Actinomycetes. 3rd ed. Philadelphia: WB Saunders; 1988:474.)*

matitidis in nature. Our knowledge of blastomycosis is based on the collected reports of sporadic cases in humans and dogs,[19-25] as well as the studies of 11 epidemics or clusters of disease.[26-36] On the basis of these data, the endemic area in North America (Fig. 263-2) includes the southeastern and south central states, especially those bordering the Mississippi and Ohio River basins; the midwestern states and Canadian provinces that border the Great Lakes; and a small area in New York and Canada along the St. Lawrence River. Most cases are reported in Mississippi, Arkansas, Kentucky, Tennessee, and Wisconsin. Several studies in these endemic regions have documented hyperendemic areas with unusually high rates of blastomycosis.[24,36] Outside North America, well-documented autochthonous cases have been reported most frequently in Africa.[37] Occasional cases have also been reported in Central America, South America, India, and the Middle East.[38]

Initial analysis of sporadic cases indicated that middle-aged men with outdoor occupations that exposed them to soil were at greatest risk for blastomycosis.[21,22] These findings, however, may reflect only the demographics of the rural states from which most of the cases were reported. In contrast, review of the 12 case clusters reported to date[22,26-36] indicates that there is no sex, age, race, occupational, or seasonal predilection for blastomycosis. In seven of the outbreaks, recreational activities in wooded areas along waterways were the major risk identified. Exposure to dust clouds associated with construction projects or crop harvesting was the only potential risk for infection identified in four of the outbreaks. Thus exposure to soil, whether at work or at play, appears to be the common link in reports of sporadic disease and outbreaks. A recent article, however, indicates that many cases of blastomycosis may result from exposure in the home, especially in the attic or basement. In this same article, repeat cases occurred in different families in four homes and most cases were separated by a year or more. This indicates that *B. dermatitidis* may be relatively persistent at certain properties.[39]

Attempts to isolate the organism in nature have been difficult and the results inconsistent. Denton and co-workers[40-42] reported multiple isolations of *B. dermatitidis* from soil and rotting wood during environmental surveys between 1958 and 1963. Yeast-phase organisms

were purportedly recovered from pigeon manure after a single case of blastomycosis, but this report lacks crucial details.[43] Isolation from soil samples from an earthen floor was also reported after a single case of disease in Canada.[44] The environmental isolations of *B. dermatitidis* by Klein and co-workers[32,33] in association with two outbreaks of disease represented an important breakthrough in defining the ecologic niche of the organism. In both instances, the organism was isolated from soil containing decayed vegetation or from decomposed wood. Humidity probably played an important role in promoting the growth of the organism because of the proximity to water and recent rainfall in both outbreaks. These studies, together with other in vitro work,[45,46] indicate that *B. dermatitidis* exists in nature in warm, moist soil of wooded areas that is also rich in organic debris, such as decaying vegetation. The conditions that support the growth of *B. dermatitidis* in these microfoci probably exist for only short periods of time. Thus, when a sporadic case or outbreak of blastomycosis is recognized, environmental isolation is often impossible because the appropriate local and environmental conditions may no longer exist at the site of exposure. Alternatively, a more complete understanding of the ecology of *B. dermatitidis* may also result from a more sensitive culture technique for the organism. The recently reported isolation of *B. dermatitidis* from environmental sources by Baumgardner and Paretsky using a two-step procedure may be useful in such studies.[46,47]

PATHOGENESIS AND PATHOLOGY

The studies of Schwartz and Baum[7] were the first to establish that the usual portal of entry for blastomycosis in humans is the lungs. Thus disease at other body sites is the result of dissemination from a primary pulmonary infection, even if the infection is clinically undetected. Primary cutaneous blastomycosis has occurred after accidental inoculation in the laboratory or at autopsy[18] and after dog bites.[49] Person-to-person transmission of disease by yeast-phase organisms has not been documented, except for a rare vaginal infection acquired from a man with genitourinary blastomycosis[50] and two instances of perinatal transmission.[51,52]

Pulmonary infection occurs by inhalation of the conidia, which convert to the yeast phase in the lung. The typical inflammatory response consists of clusters of neutrophils and noncaseating granulomas with epithelioid and giant cells. This response is similar to that seen with coccidioidomycosis and sporotrichosis. Although this histopathologic picture is duplicated to a variable degree in extrapulmonary sites, the response in cutaneous disease is unique in that prominent pseudoepitheliomatous hyperplasia is present with microabscess formation that clinically and histologically may mimic a variety of cutaneous diseases, including giant keratoacanthoma and squamous cell carcinoma of the skin.[53] The same pseudoepitheliomatous response may also be seen when mucosal surfaces of the mouth, oropharynx, or larynx are involved.[54,55] The gross and histopathologic appearance of laryngeal disease is similar to that of well-differentiated squamous cell carcinoma and is not infrequently misdiagnosed as such.

IMMUNITY

Our understanding of the immunologic defenses against *B. dermatitidis* is incomplete owing to the lack of appropriate antigens. Advances in characterizing specific yeast antigens have facilitated our study of both humoral and cellular immunity. Specific antibody against *B. dermatitidis* does not appear to confer resistance to or hasten recovery from disease. The major acquired host defense against *B. dermatitidis* is cellular immunity, mediated by antigen-specific T lymphocytes and lymphokine-activated macrophages.

Natural Immunity and Virulence

Investigations of point-source outbreaks indicate that infection rates are high but that symptomatic disease occurs in less than one half of infected individuals.[32,33] Studies using antigen-specific lymphocyte proliferation as a marker of remote infection suggest that subclinical cases of sporadic blastomycosis also occur, probably more commonly than symptomatic cases.[56] This high frequency of asymptomatic infection supports the concept that healthy people are fairly resistant to infection by *B. dermatitidis*. The presence of natural resistance may, in part, explain why blastomycosis is infrequently reported as an opportunistic infection in the immunocompromised host. When conidia are inhaled into the lungs, natural resistance is probably mediated by neutrophils, monocytes, and alveolar macrophages, which can phagocytize and kill the conidia of *Blastomyces*.

Striking differences in the susceptibilities of immature and mature mice to infection with *Blastomyces* have been linked to differences in nonspecific immunity, specifically effector cell function.[57] These studies indicate enhanced susceptibility resulting from depressed capacity of polymorphonuclear leukocytes harvested from immature mice to kill *B. dermatitidis*. Peripheral blood neutrophils from mature animals killed *B. dermatitidis* in greater numbers than those neutrophils from immature animals (41% vs. 10%). Peritoneal inflammatory cells, enriched for neutrophils, showed a similar pattern (70% for peritoneal cells from mature animals vs. 25% for immature).[57] Sugar and Picard[58] have also shown that alveolar macrophages inhibit transformation of conidia to the pathogenic yeast form. Once converted in tissue, the yeast forms are relatively resistant to phagocytosis and killing. This conidia-to-yeast conversion most likely results in a survival advantage for the organism when inhaled into the lungs and contributes to the pathogenicity of *B. dermatitidis*.

Although the thick cell wall of the yeast form has been postulated to be antiphagocytic, specific structural and chemical components of the cell wall have been associated with virulence. Early studies by DiSalvo and Denton[59] reported a higher concentration of lipid in the yeast cells of virulent strains of *B. dermatitidis* than in less virulent strains. Conversely, Cox and Best[60] noted more phospholipid in a single virulent strain than in a less virulent strain. These two studies were limited by the genetic disparity in the strains employed. The elegant work of Klein and associates[61-63] has defined other important virulence factors associated with the yeast form of *B. dermatitidis*. These investigators have identified a novel 120-kDa glycoprotein antigen on the cell wall surface of the yeast form that serves as the major immunodominant epitope for both humoral and cellular immunity. The antigen, designated WI-1, also functions as an adhesin that binds to host cell receptors, including CR3 and CD14 of human macrophages.[68] This adhesin activity is mediated by a 24-amino-acid tandem repeat that shares 90% homology with the *Yersinia* adhesin invasin.[65] Binding to extracellular matrix may also be mediated by a cysteine-rich domain at the carboxyl-terminal end of WI-1 that is similar to epidermal growth factor.[65] Using three genetically related strains, Klein and colleagues[66] have shown that alterations in the quantity of WI-1 expressed on the cell surface, the amount of WI-1 shed, and the modification of shed WI-1 are different in two hypovirulent strains compared with the parental (virulent) strain. Using the same strains, Hogan and Klein[67] have also shown that the quantity and distribution of cell wall α-1,3-glucan are different in the hypovirulent and virulent strains. Collectively, these experiments indicate that the adhesin WI-1 is a major virulence factor of *B. dermatitidis* but that other cell wall components, such as α-1,3-glucan, may modulate the WI-1–mediated interactions between the yeast and host cell and thereby also modulate virulence.[68,69]

In addition to its role as an antigen and adhesin, the WI-1 protein has also been shown to interfere with host immunity by blocking production of tumor necrosis factor-α (TNF-α) by both macrophages and neutrophils.[70,71] Suppression of TNF-α production is mediated through both transforming growth factor-β1–dependent and –independent mechanisms. Finally, the WI-1 antigen (recently named BAD1) inhibits complement activation by *Blastomyces* yeast cells. In contrast, β-glucan supports complement activation.[72] These studies, analogous to the results noted for the adhesin property, indicate that surface glucan and WI-1 (BAD1) have distinct regulatory roles with regard to complement activation.

Polymorphonuclear Leukocytes

The histopathologic response previously noted implicates both a neutrophil response and a cellular immune response. The polymorphonuclear leukocyte reaction is probably initiated by the release of chemotactic factors from the organism.[73] Human neutrophils efficiently phagocytize and kill the conidia of *B. dermatitidis*. Phagocytosis of conidia is optimal when complement and divalent cations are present, and killing is predominantly by oxidative mechanisms.[74,75] Conversely, phagocytosis and killing of yeast forms are inefficient; this is probably an important factor in disease progression. Despite activating the neutrophil NADPH oxidase system, yeast forms do not efficiently stimulate the production of myeloperoxidase-dependent microbicidal products.[76] The fungicidal activity of neutrophils can be enhanced by either lymphokine-rich supernatants from immunologically stimulated T lymphocytes or interferon-γ, providing a link between cellular immunity and neutrophil function.[77,78]

Cellular Immunity

Delayed hypersensitivity can be induced in mice by subcutaneous injections of live or killed *B. dermatitidis*. Decreased susceptibility to infection parallels the development of the cellular immune response,[79,80] and resistance to infection in mice has been transferred by T lymphocytes.[81] Macrophages harvested from mice with experimental blastomycosis have also been reported to inhibit the replication of *B. dermatitidis*, and both in vivo and in vitro interferon-γ treatments have been shown to enhance killing of *B. dermatitidis* by murine alveolar macrophages.[82,83] Interestingly, therapeutic concentrations of hydrocortisone and cyclosporine do not inhibit macrophage activation by interferon-γ.[84]

The study of cellular immunity in humans has been hindered by the lack of a sensitive, specific antigen for both in vitro studies and skin testing. The development of specific cellular immunity, as monitored by antigen-induced lymphocyte proliferation, has been documented in patients with blastomycosis using whole yeast-phase organisms; an alkali-soluble, water-soluble yeast extract; and the surface protein of yeast cells, designated WI-1.[62,85,86] Chang and colleagues investigated peripheral blood mononuclear cell responses from patients with blastomycosis to segments of the WI-1 antigen recognized by T cells.[87] These studies defined a 25-amino-acid segment in the amino terminus of the peptide recognized by T-cell clones and the human leukocyte antigen molecules that display these epitopes to T cells. WI-1 administration produced both antibody and cell-mediated immunity in a murine model of pulmonary blastomycosis.[88] Furthermore, use of interleukin-12 as an adjuvant for WI-1 significantly augmented delayed-type hypersensitivity and enhanced resistance to experimental *B. dermatitidis* infection, although the level of resistance was modest.[89] Macrophages from patients recovering from blastomycosis have also been shown to have enhanced inhibition of intracellular growth of *B. dermatitidis* as compared to control macrophages.[90] Finally, supernatants of antigen-stimulated human lymphocytes have been shown to enhance phagocytosis and intracellular inhibition of the growth of *B. dermatitidis* by both alveolar and monocyte-derived macrophages.[90]

Despite these advances, however, an antigen for skin testing is not yet available. Blastomycin, a culture filtrate of mycelial-phase organisms, lacks both specificity and sensitivity. In the Veterans Administration Cooperative Study, only 40% of patients with blastomycosis had a positive skin test to blastomycin.[19] Further clarification of cellular immunity in human cases of blastomycosis awaits more definitive characterization of the fungal antigens.

Humoral Immunity

Yeast antigens have been used to evaluate humoral immunity in a variety of serologic tests of different sensitivities and specificities. The complement fixation test has not proved useful because it lacks both sensitivity and specificity. At most, 50% of patients with blastomycosis have a positive complement fixation reaction to *B. dermatitidis* antigens.[13] Cross-reactivity with *H. capsulatum* and, to a lesser degree, *Coccidioides immitis* has also been a problem.

The immunodiffusion test, which detects precipitin antibodies to the A and B antigens located in the cell wall of the yeast, is more specific for blastomycosis. Using the modifications suggested by Kaufman and associates, the presence of antibody to the A antigen has been noted in as many as 70% to 80% of patients with blastomycosis.[91,92] However, patients with localized disease or those with symptoms of less than 50 days' duration are less likely to have a positive antibody response.[93,94] Furthermore, detectable antibody is present only a short time after cure of disease. These findings emphasize the limitations of immunodiffusion serology for both clinical and epidemiologic studies. Using the A antigen in an enzyme immunoassay has improved sensitivity, but false-positive reactions, especially in patients with histoplasmosis and other fungal infections, are more common.[94-96] Studies by Klein and Jones[97] indicate that the cross-reactive determinants reside in the carbohydrate component of the A antigen. Commercial kits for both the immunodiffusion assay and enzyme immunoassay are available.

As noted previously, Klein and Jones[61] identified the novel 120-kDa surface protein of *B. dermatitidis* yeasts that they have designated WI-1. These investigators purified and characterized WI-1 and compared it immunologically with the commercially available A antigen.[97] The results of this study indicate that the tandem repeat of WI-1 is the major antibody recognition site of both WI-1 and A antigen. When used in a radioimmunoassay, antibody to WI-1 was detected in 85% of patients with blastomycosis and in only 3% of patients with other fungal infections.[61] In a second study from the same laboratory, similar sensitivity (83%) was noted for the detection of anti–WI-1 antibodies by radioimmunoassay.[98] All patients with proven blastomycosis whose serum was obtained within 60 days of onset of symptoms or diagnosis had at least one serum sample positive for anti–WI-1. Furthermore, anti–WI-1 antibody titers fell as the infection resolved, and antibody titers in most patients were undetectable after 8 months from the onset of symptoms. Enhanced diagnostic sensitivity did not result from modification of the radioimmunoassay to detect immunoglobulin M antibody. Comparison of antibody detection of WI-1 antigen by radioimmunoassay or A antigen by agar gel diffusion in dogs revealed a WI-1 sensitivity of 92% compared to 41% for antigen A; both tests had 100% specificity in this study.[99] Further studies, including the development of a nonradiometric test, will be necessary to clarify the role of the WI-1 antigen in the serodiagnosis of blastomycosis.

CLINICAL MANIFESTATIONS

Our knowledge of the clinical manifestations of blastomycosis is derived from careful studies of symptomatic, sporadic cases and the few case clusters reported.[100] It must be emphasized that blastomycosis is a systemic disease with a wide variety of pulmonary and extrapulmonary manifestations. Pulmonary disease may be acute or chronic and mimics infection with pyogenic bacteria, tuberculosis, infection with other fungi, and malignancy. Cutaneous disease, the most common extrapulmonary manifestation, appears similar to disease seen with bromoderma, pyoderma gangrenosum, Majocchi's granuloma, leishmaniasis, *Mycobacterium marinum* infection, giant keratoacanthoma, and squamous cell carcinoma.

B. dermatitidis infection may involve almost every organ of the body (Table 263-1), resulting in the diversity of clinical manifestations. Skin, bone, and genitourinary sites of infection are the most common and are most likely to be clinically manifest. Extrapulmonary disease is seen most commonly during the chronic form of illness, in which approximately two thirds of patients have been reported with multiple organ involvement. Many of the reports noting this high frequency of extrapulmonary dissemination, however, were autopsy based or appeared before the availability of effective treatments. In contrast to these earlier studies, later clinical experience in Arkansas,[107] Wisconsin,[108] and Mississippi,[109] three states in which blastomycosis is endemic, has indicated a lower frequency of extrapulmonary disease (Table 263-2). Approximately three fourths of the patients reported in these studies had isolated pulmonary disease. Similar results were recently reported by Crampton and associates for cases of blastomycosis diagnosed in Manitoba hospitals.[25] Specifically, isolated pulmonary involvement was reported in 70% of 143 patients with blastomycosis. Extrapulmonary disease is usually seen in conjunction with active pulmonary infection. In some patients, however, especially those with skin involvement, extrapulmonary lesions may be present without clinically overt pulmonary infection.

Although a variety of clinical schemata may be used in discussing blastomycosis, that proposed by Sarosi and Davies[110] appears most comprehensive. A modification of this schema is presented in Figure 263-3. It should be noted that the occurrence of reactivation blastomycosis is a controversial issue, with only a few cases being suggestive.[111] Cases attributed to extrapulmonary reactivation may represent

TABLE 263-1 Organ Involvement in Blastomycosis from Clinical and Autopsy Findings in Seven Studies

Organ System Involved	*Cherniss and Waisbren*[101] *[40]*	*Abernathy*[102] *[35]*	*Veterans Administration Cooperative Study*[19] *[198]*	*Witorsch and Utz*[103] *[40]*	*Lockwood et al*[104] *[63]*	*Duttera and Osterhout*[105] *[63]*	*Busey and Veterans Administration Cooperative Group*[106] *[84]*	*Total*[†]
Lungs	28 (70)[‡]	27 (77)	118 (60)	28 (70)	59 (80)	33 (52)	76 (90)	369/534 (69)
Skin	30 (75)	28 (80)	118 (60)	29 (73)	33 (45)	36 (57)	32 (38)	306/534 (57)
Bone	19 (48)	12 (34)	46 (23)	11 (28)	10 (14)	12 (19)	6 (7)	116/534 (22)
Genitourinary	11 (28)	5 (14)	32 (16)	13 (33)	13 (18)	6 (10)	12 (14)	92/534 (17)
Reticuloendothelial system (liver, spleen, lymph nodes)	5 (13)	13 (37)	25 (13)	7 (18)	NS[†]	3 (5)	3 (4)	56/460 (12)
Central nervous system	4 (10)	1 (3)	9 (5)	1 (3)	5 (7)	4 (6)	4 (5)	29/534 (5)
Mucous membranes	3 (8)	2 (6)	11 (6)	10 (25)	NS	NS	NS	26/273 (10)
Subcutaneous	25 (63)	NS	NS	15 (38)	NS	NS	NS	40/80 (30)
Others[§]	5 (13)	9 (26)	18 (9)	5 (13)	NS	7 (11)	2 (2)	46/460 (10)

*Number of cases given in square brackets; reference numbers after authors.
[†]Total based on studies where stated; NS, not stated.
[‡]Number of cases followed by percentage in parentheses.
[§]Other: thyroid, 10; gastrointestinal, 8; adrenal, 7; pleura, 6; joints, 5; heart, 2, peritoneum, 1, eye, 1; psoas, 1; retropharynx, 1.

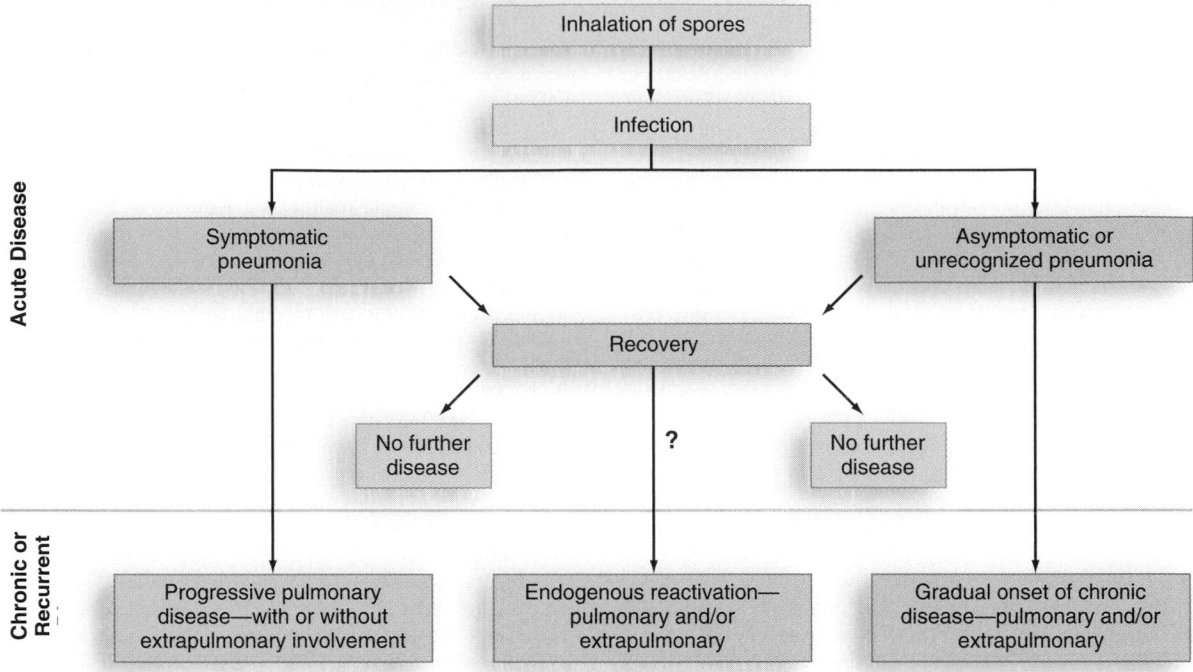

FIGURE 263-3. Clinical classification of blastomycosis. *(Adapted from Sarosi GA, Davies SF. Blastomycosis. Am Rev Respir Dis. 1979;120:911-938.)*

TABLE 263-2   Clinical Experience with Blastomycosis*

Involvement	Arkansas[107] [44]	Wisconsin[108] [73]	Mississippi[109] [326]	Total [443]
Single-organ disease	30 (69)†	62 (85)	270 (83)	362 (82)
Lung	26 (50)	56 (77)	245 (75)	327 (74)
Skin	2 (5)	3 (4)	16 (5)	21 (5)
Other	2 (5)	3 (4)	9 (3)	14 (3)
Multiorgan disease	14 (31)	11 (15)	56 (17)	81 (18)

*Number of cases given in square brackets; reference numbers after state names.
†Number of cases followed by percentage in parentheses.

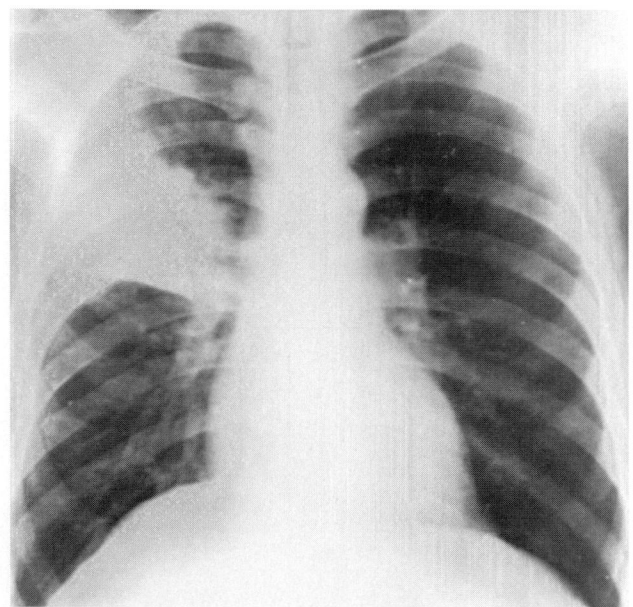

FIGURE 263-4. A confluent infiltrate with a segmental distribution in a patient with blastomycosis.

the late clinical manifestations of chronic, subclinical disease that remains active after pulmonary healing. The factors determining the clinical course after acute infection are not well defined but probably involve a complex interaction of pulmonary anatomy, host defenses, and microbial factors.

Acute Infection

Acute pulmonary infection is often unrecognized unless related to group exposure. Analysis of point-source outbreaks indicates that only about one half of infected individuals develop symptomatic disease and that the median incubation period is 30 to 45 days.[24,30-33] Symptoms are nonspecific and tend to mimic those of influenza or bacterial infection with abrupt onset of myalgias, arthralgias, chills, and fever. Pleuritic pain may be prominent but is usually transient. Cough is initially nonproductive, but in many cases becomes productive of purulent sputum. The radiologic findings in the acute stage of disease, whether symptomatic or asymptomatic, are also nonspecific but are usually those of lobar or segmental consolidation (Fig. 263-4).[112,113] Pleural effusion is uncommon and, if present, is found only in small amounts. Hilar adenopathy is also uncommon.

Spontaneous resolution of symptomatic acute pneumonia has been recognized in a few sporadic cases, in case clusters, and after accidental laboratory infection.[114-116] The frequency of this has not been established. In these cases symptoms have usually resolved in less than 4 weeks, but radiologic abnormalities have taken longer to clear.

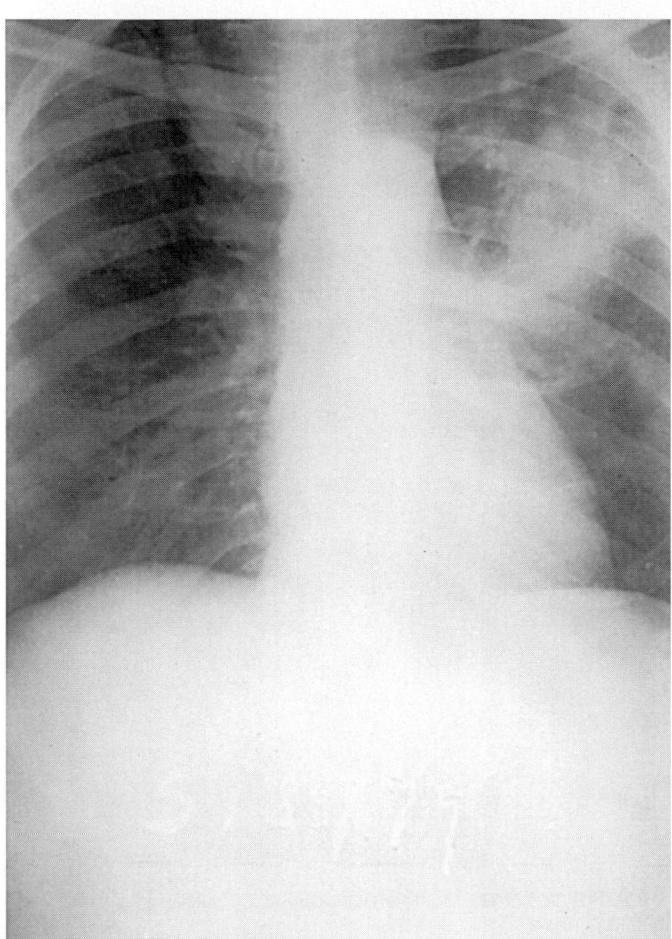

FIGURE 263-5. Multinodular densities with consolidation of the left upper lobe in a patient with blastomycosis.

Chronic or Recurrent Infection

Most patients in whom blastomycosis is diagnosed have an indolent onset and progressive disease. The clinical manifestations are diverse, including pulmonary or extrapulmonary disease or both. For clarity, these are discussed separately.

Pulmonary Manifestations

The clinical manifestations of pulmonary disease are those of chronic pneumonia, including productive cough, hemoptysis, weight loss, and pleuritic chest pain. Fever, if present, tends to be low grade. The radiologic findings in these patients are variable. Lobar or segmental alveolar infiltrates, with or without cavitation, are most frequently reported (Fig. 263-5).[112,113] The specific lobar distribution of infiltrates is not clinically helpful, although upper lobe infiltrates are reported more commonly. Mass lesions that mimic bronchogenic carcinoma occur almost as frequently as do alveolar infiltrates (Fig. 263-6).[117] Other radiographic features include intermediate-size nodules, solitary cavities, and fibronodular infiltrates, often with cavities (Fig. 263-7). Hilar adenopathy is variably reported. Postinfectious calcification of lymph nodes or pulmonary parenchyma is rare. An occasional patient has acute deterioration associated with miliary disease resulting from hematogenous spread[118] (Fig. 263-8) or diffuse pneumonitis from presumed endobronchial spread.[119] When either of these radiographic findings is accompanied by respiratory failure, mortality usually exceeds 50%.[119] Although pleural thickening and small pleural effusions may occur, large pleural effusions are uncommon. One report noted an unfavorable response to therapy in patients with major pleural disease.[120]

Skin

Skin disease is the most common extrapulmonary manifestation of blastomycosis, being reported in 40% to 80% percent of cases (see Tables 263-1 and 263-2). Although extrapulmonary disease is usually seen in conjunction with active pulmonary disease, skin involvement may occur alone.[121] In some patients with skin disease, asymptomatic pulmonary disease is found. In my experience, skin disease occurs in approximately one third of patients with blastomycosis, but is a marker for multiorgan infection, being present in three quarters of patients with disease in two or more organs.[109]

Two types of skin lesions may be seen. The first are the more characteristic verrucous lesions that usually appear on exposed body areas. These often begin as small papulopustular lesions (Fig. 263-9) and

FIGURE 263-6. A perihilar mass lesion in a patient with blastomycosis. This radiographic appearance mimics that of carcinoma of the lung. To rule out a coexisting malignancy, patients with this radiographic picture should have bronchoscopy even if wet preparations of sputum reveal the organism.

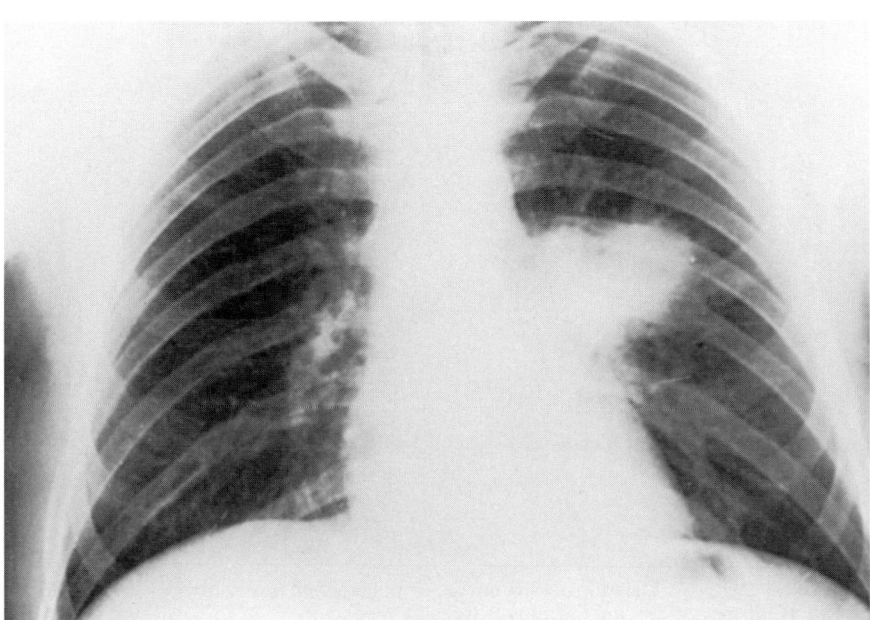

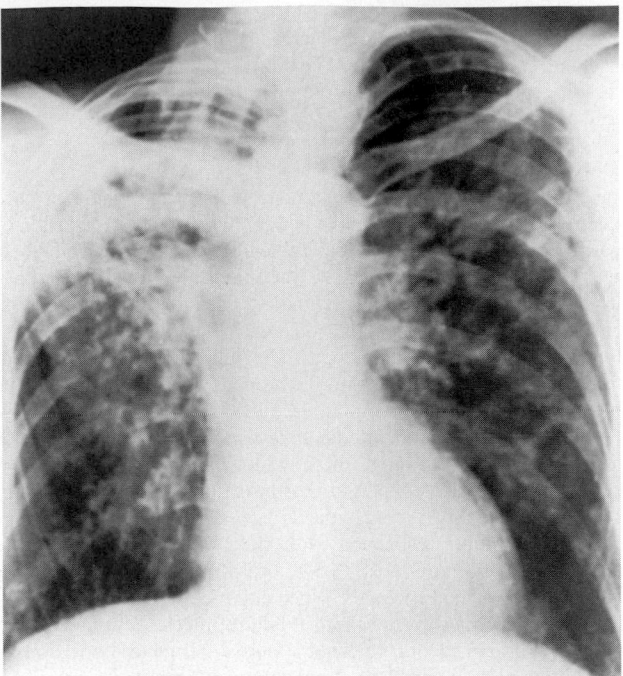

FIGURE 263-7. Bilateral fibronodular infiltrates with cavitation and volume loss in the right upper lobe. This radiographic appearance cannot be distinguished from that of tuberculosis or other granulomatous diseases.

slowly spread to form crusted, heaped-up lesions that can vary in color from gray to a violaceous hue (Fig. 263-10). These lesions are often mistaken for squamous cell carcinoma. Older lesions may show central clearing with scar formation and depigmentation. Microabscess formation tends to occur at the periphery of such lesions, and removal of the eschar peripherally reveals purulent material in which the yeast forms are usually visible on wet preparation.

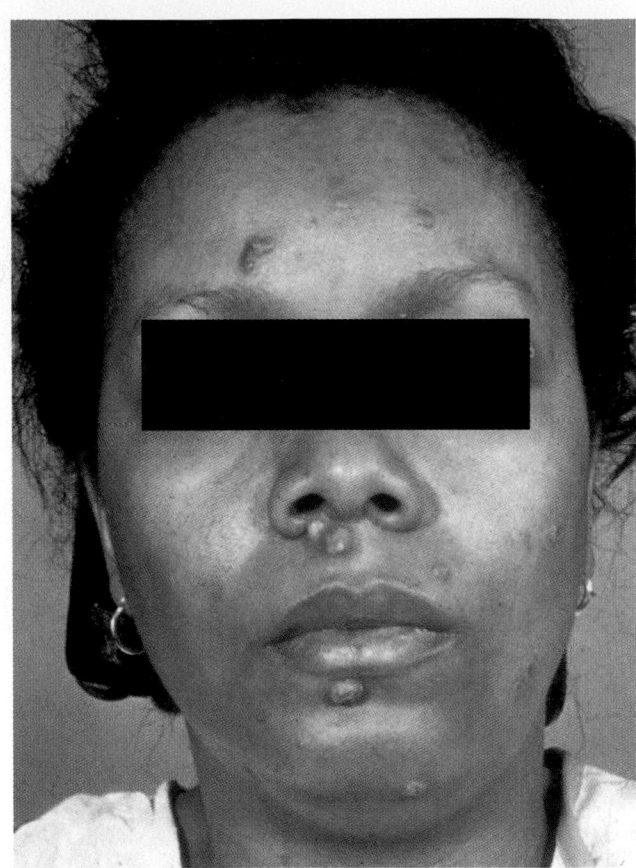

FIGURE 263-9. Multiple papulopustular lesions in a patient with blastomycosis.

The second type of lesion is described as ulcerative (Fig. 263-11); the initial pustule spreads as a superficial ulcer or slightly raised lesion, with a bed of red friable granulation tissue that bleeds easily. Skin lesions of both types may be seen in the same patient. Lesions may also occur on the mucosa of the nose, mouth, and larynx. With skin lesions associated with a pulmonary pathogenesis, there is little or no regional lymph node involvement or lymphadenitis, in contrast to that seen with inoculation blastomycosis.[48,49]

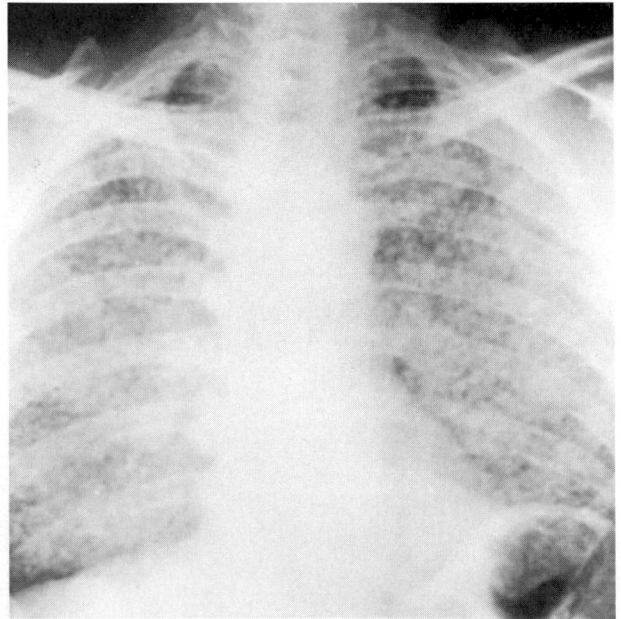

FIGURE 263-8. Miliary blastomycosis in a patient with respiratory failure. *(Courtesy of Dr. Guy Campbell, Jackson, MS.)*

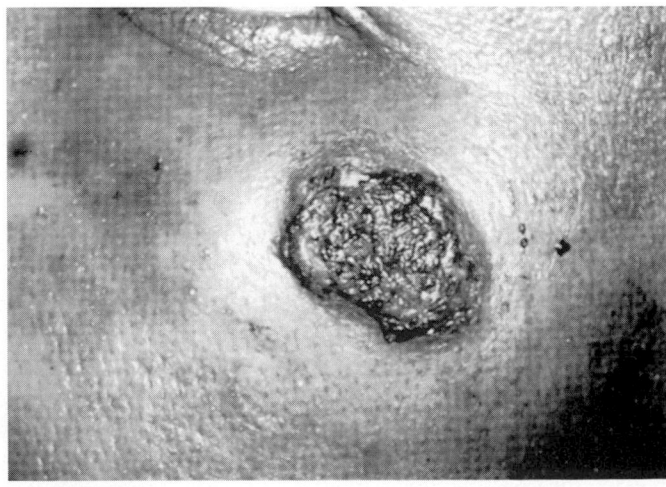

FIGURE 263-10. The typical verrucous skin lesion of blastomycosis on the cheek. Note the circumscribed edges.

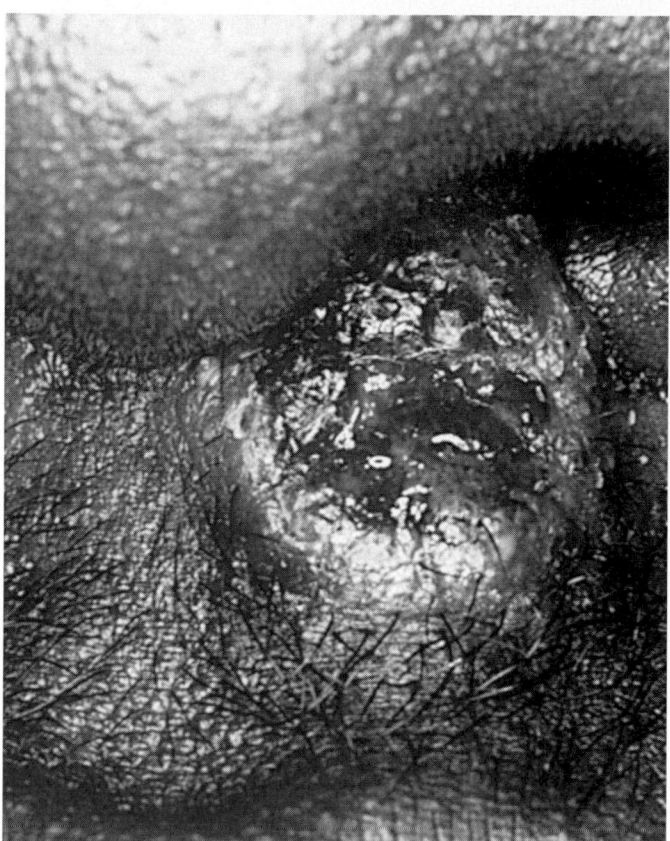

FIGURE 263-11. The ulcerative skin lesion of blastomycosis. These lesions bleed easily.

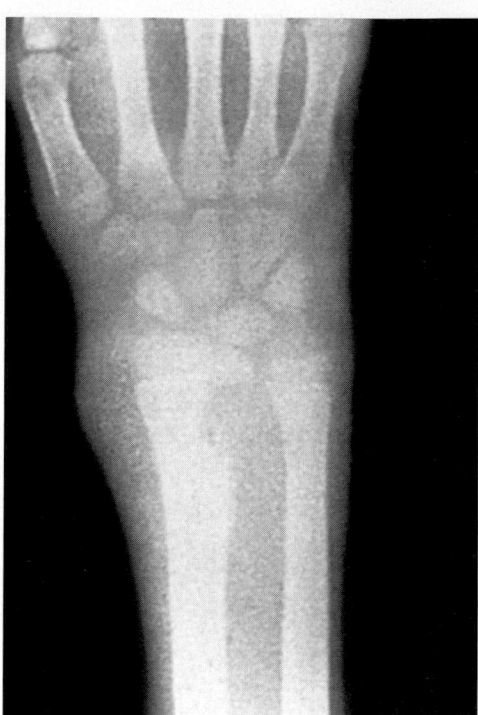

FIGURE 263-12. Osteolytic lesion affecting the ulnar aspect of the distal left radius and extending to the epiphysis. Note the extensive soft tissue swelling. This child had a recent history of chronic pneumonia. *(Courtesy of Dr. Blair Batson, Jackson, MS.)*

Subcutaneous Nodules

Although subcutaneous nodules are often discussed as a skin manifestation, the clinical syndrome seen in patients with subcutaneous nodules is different from that associated with other skin lesions. Subcutaneous nodules are cold abscesses that are usually seen in conjunction with pulmonary and other extrapulmonary disease. The patient often appears acutely ill, systemic manifestations may be prominent, and rapid deterioration may result unless therapy is initiated promptly. Lesions sometimes drain spontaneously. Drainage or aspirated pus has abundant numbers of organisms that are readily visible on microscopic examination.

Bone and Joint

After skin disease, skeletal blastomycosis is next in frequency (see Tables 263-1 and 263-2). Although almost any bone can be infected, the long bones, vertebrae, and ribs are most commonly involved.[122] A well-circumscribed osteolytic lesion is typical (Fig. 263-12). Patients with bone lesions rarely present with bone pain but instead present with contiguous soft tissue abscesses or chronic draining sinuses. Vertebral disease mimics tuberculosis, with anterior involvement of the vertebral body, destruction of the interspace, and development of large paraspinous abscesses.[123]

Arthritis usually occurs by extension from a contiguous osteomyelitis. Signs and symptoms may be acute or chronic. Synovial fluid is usually purulent, with organisms readily visible on wet preparation.[124]

Genitourinary Tract

From 10% to 30% of the cases in men have been reported to involve the genitourinary tract, primarily the prostate and epididymis.[125] Epididymal disease may spread to the testes. The variable incidence reported may reflect the respective authors' tenacity in pursuing the diagnosis. Prostatic involvement is most common and is usually manifested by symptoms of obstruction; an enlarged, tender prostate; and pyuria. Urine cultures, especially after prostatic massage, are often positive.

Central Nervous System

In the normal host, disease involving the central nervous system is uncommon, being reported in less than 5% of cases. In patients with acquired immunodeficiency syndrome (AIDS), however, central nervous system complications of blastomycosis are common. A review noted that 40% of AIDS patients with blastomycosis had central nervous system disease, usually associated with dissemination to multiple organs.[126] When present, it is manifest as either an abscess or meningitis.[127-129] Abscesses present as mass lesions and may be intracranial (Fig. 263-13) or, occasionally, spinal in location. Surgical management of mass lesions may be necessary to establish the diagnosis and to prevent progressive neurologic deterioration.[130] Meningitis is usually a late and fulminant complication of widely disseminated blastomycosis.

Other Sites

Blastomycosis may infrequently affect the liver, spleen, gastrointestinal tract, thyroid, pericardium, adrenal glands, and other sites (see Tables 263-1 and 263-2). Reports of such cases largely represent findings at autopsy in patients with widely disseminated disease. Of note, gastrointestinal disease below the esophagus and overt adrenal insufficiency are rare.

Special Circumstances

Blastomycosis in Children

Although blastomycosis in children is considered rare by some authors, most reviews of blastomycosis note that 2% to 10% of the patients reported are younger than 15 years of age. In a large common-source outbreak of disease involving 46 children, the attack rate for infection was approximately 50%. Of the infected, about one half were symptomatic.[32] Pediatric patients manifest the full clinical spectrum of disease

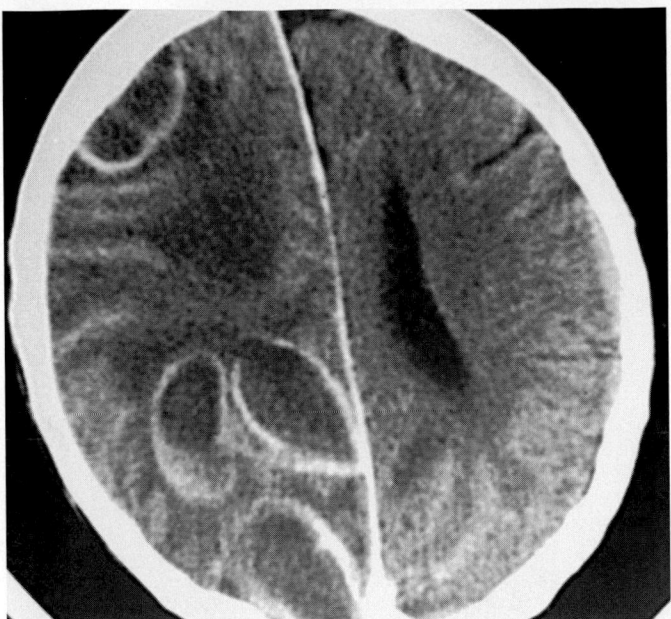

FIGURE 263-13. Multiple ring-enhancing lesions affecting the right frontal and parietal lobes. There is extensive surrounding edema with effacement of the sulci and right ventricle. This patient simultaneously had pulmonary blastomycosis.

as outlined for adults.[131-133] However, a clinical review from Arkansas noted greater difficulty in establishing the diagnosis and a poorer response to oral azole treatment in children with blastomycosis.[134]

Blastomycosis in Pregnancy

Despite the depressed cellular immunity associated with pregnancy, blastomycosis has been reported only infrequently in pregnant women.[135] Disseminated disease is common, and a case of adult respiratory distress syndrome in a woman who developed blastomycosis in the third trimester of pregnancy is noteworthy.[136] Perinatal blastomycosis has been reported in two infants born to mothers with untreated blastomycosis.[51,52] Both infants died as a result of overwhelming pulmonary disease. Infection of the infant may result from aspiration into the lungs of vaginal secretions colonized with *B. dermatitidis*, an ascending vaginal infection associated with partially ruptured membranes, or transplacental intrauterine infection.[52] Although a presumptive case of intrauterine transmission has been reported,[51] the placenta in this case was never examined. It is therefore not possible to state with certainty that the child acquired blastomycosis by intrauterine transmission. In a case reported by MacDonald and Alguire,[136] however, *B. dermatitidis* was demonstrated on both the maternal and fetal sides of the placenta. Regardless of the pathogenesis of infection, perinatal transmission remains a definite possibility, and all pregnant women with blastomycosis should be treated without delay. Amphotericin B has been used successfully for blastomycosis and other fungal infections during pregnancy, with no documented adverse outcome for the pregnancy or fetus.[135]

Blastomycosis in the Compromised Host

Although invasive fungal diseases are common in the immunosuppressed host, only a few reports have indicated that *B. dermatitidis* can act as an opportunistic pathogen.[126,137-139] As suggested previously, this may be related to natural host defenses that are active against the inhaled conidia.

Blastomycosis has been reported as a late infectious complication in AIDS patients.[126] Most patients have had previous AIDS-defining illnesses and their CD4+ counts are usually less than 200 cells/mm³. Disease, whether pulmonary or disseminated, is more aggressive and

more often rapidly fatal than disease in the healthy host. Pulmonary disease is more likely to present with diffuse interstitial infiltrates or a miliary pattern on the chest radiograph. Central nervous system disease is especially common, being noted to occur in 40% of patients.[126]

Blastomycosis has also been reported in other immunocompromised hosts, including transplant recipients, patients receiving glucocorticosteroid therapy, and patients receiving cytotoxic chemotherapy for hematologic malignancies or solid tumors.[137-139] A large series of patients reported by Pappas and colleagues[139] has helped to clarify the clinical spectrum of blastomycosis in the immunocompromised host. Blastomycosis in these patients was more often disseminated, more aggressive, and associated with higher mortality than in the immunocompetent host. Diffuse pulmonary infiltrates, pleural effusions, and respiratory failure were common. Multiple visceral organ dissemination and central nervous system disease occurred frequently but not as often as in AIDS patients.

Mortality rates of 30% to 40% have been reported for immunocompromised patients with blastomycosis. In addition, most deaths attributed to blastomycosis occur within the first few weeks of disease. Thus early aggressive therapy with amphotericin B is indicated. Frequent relapses have been noted in AIDS patients and those with continued immunosuppressive therapy. Chronic suppressive therapy with an oral azole should therefore be strongly considered for individuals who respond to a primary course of amphotericin.[140]

DIAGNOSIS

No clinical syndrome is characteristic of blastomycosis. Definitive diagnosis requires the growth of the organism from clinical specimens. A presumptive diagnosis may be made by visualization of the characteristic yeast in pus, sputum, other secretions, or histopathologic sections. In the appropriate clinical setting, visualization of the fungus can prompt the initiation of antimicrobial therapy.

Direct Examination of Secretions

Sputum or pus is easily examined by wet preparation. A drop of the specimen is placed on a microscope slide, covered with a coverslip, and examined under the high-dry objective. In a retrospective study of patients with a confirmed diagnosis of blastomycosis, Martynowicz and Prakash[141] reported that KOH smears were underutilized and were performed on only 30% of all microbiologic specimens collected. Wet preparations had a relatively low diagnostic yield (e.g., 36% for a single specimen and 46% for multiple specimens). Despite these low diagnostic results, the simplicity and low cost of the procedure, as well as its potential for rapid diagnosis, warrants a wet preparation on all specimens collected. Although 10% potassium hydroxide has been recommended to aid in finding the organism, it is usually not necessary because the large, characteristic yeast cell is easily seen despite cellular debris. Sometimes it is also useful to digest sputum with trypsin and smear the centrifuged sediment. Body fluids such as urine, pleural fluid, and cerebrospinal fluid should be centrifuged and the sediment evaluated in the same way. Calcofluor white stain requires use of a fluorescence microscope but is easy, rapid, and particularly useful when organisms are sparse (see Chapter 15).

Cytology has been shown to be particularly useful in diagnosis, permitting identification of the etiologic agent in 56% of all cases and 72% of pulmonary cases of blastomycosis in a retrospective study at the University of Mississippi Medical Center.[142] When visualized, the yeast cells are easily differentiated from others on the basis of their size, refractile cell wall, and single, broad-based buds (see Fig. 263-1). Occasionally the endospores of *C. immitis* may resemble single yeast cells, but the presence of budding can be used to distinguish *B. dermatitidis*. *Paracoccidioides brasiliensis,* rarely seen in the United States, is distinguished by the presence of multiple, narrow-based buds. *B. dermatitidis* may sometimes be as small as *Cryptococcus neoformans,* although the capsule and narrow-based bud of the latter aid in differentiation.

FIGURE 263-14. A Gomori methenamine-silver stain of a laryngeal biopsy specimen in a patient with suspected carcinoma of the larynx. *(Courtesy of James Gorman, Jackson, MS.)*

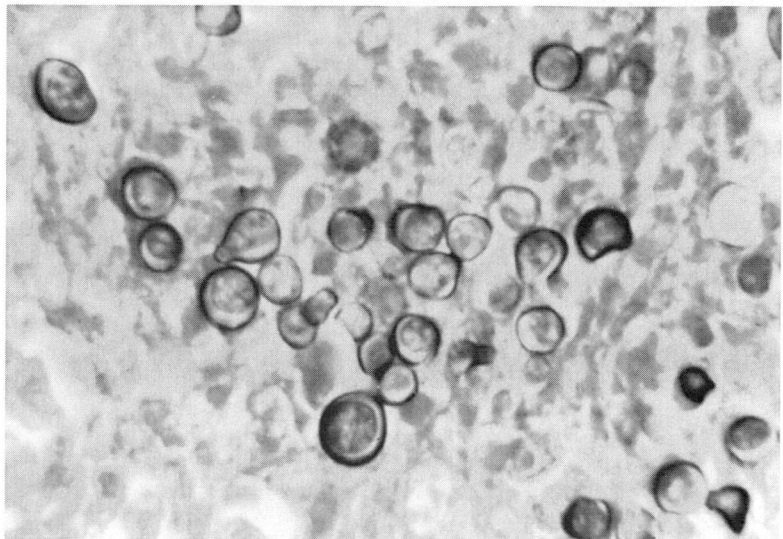

Bronchoscopy is useful for diagnosis, especially in patients who are not producing sputum or in whom the radiograph indicates the possibility of malignancy.[141] Bronchial washings, lavage fluid, and post-bronchoscopy sputum samples should be sent for cytology as well as smear and culture, because the organism is often visualized on Papanicolaou preparations.[143]

Histopathologic Examination

The presence of pyogranulomas should alert one to the possibility of blastomycosis. Yeast forms can be difficult to visualize with routine hematoxylin and eosin stains, and special stains should be used to enhance visualization. The Gomori methenamine-silver stain is best used for screening tissue for the presence of fungal elements (Fig. 263-14). The Gomori methenamine-silver counterstain does not allow evaluation of the inflammatory response in the tissue. The periodic acid–Schiff stain, which colors the cell wall pink or red, has a counterstain that does allow evaluation of cell morphology and tissue response (see Chapter 254). Mayer mucicarmine stains the cell wall of *B. dermatitidis* faintly or not at all, which may be useful in differentiating it from *C. neoformans* when necessary. A variety of fluorescent microscopic techniques and reagents have also been used to facilitate the histopathologic review of specimens.[144-146] Although these are occasionally helpful when fungal elements in a specimen are atypical or sparse, in my experience their routine use is not warranted because a presumptive diagnosis of *B. dermatitidis* can usually be made by review of Gomori methenamine-silver– or periodic acid–Schiff-stained tissue sections.

Culture

Culture of *B. dermatitidis* from environmental sources remains difficult, although Baumgardner and Paretsky have recently reported successful isolation using a two-step procedure.[46,47] In patients with pulmonary blastomycosis, sputum culture has a high positive yield (e.g., 75% per single sample, 86% per patient). Specimens obtained for culture by bronchoscopy yielded a positive diagnosis in 92% of patients. Any material obtained should be placed on Sabouraud's or, preferably, more enriched agar (e.g., Sabhi, brain-heart infusion, Gorman's medium). Because initial growth is more dependable at 30° C, this temperature is recommended. Specimens contaminated with bacteria should also be cultured on medium containing an antibacterial antibiotic such as chloramphenicol. Cycloheximide can be incorporated in the medium to inhibit other fungal contaminants. This selective medium should never be used at 37° C, however, because the yeast phase of *B. dermatitidis* and some opportunistic fungi are sensitive to cycloheximide and growth may be inhibited. The mycelial form of *B. dermatitidis* is not diagnostic, and conversion to the yeast form is required for confirmation. Early identification of mycelial cultures is possible, however, with commercially available chemiluminescent DNA probes that recognize unique RNA sequences of *Blastomyces* (see "Nucleic Acid Detection" below and Chapter 15).[147]

Serologic Methods

As mentioned previously, serum complement fixation tests are neither specific nor sensitive. The immunodiffusion test is more sensitive and specific than the complement fixation test.[13,91-94] Antibody against A antigen has been reported in 52% to 80% of patients with blastomycosis, with almost no cross-reactivity with other fungi. In one report, however, patients with localized disease had a lower rate of positivity (33%) than those with disseminated disease (88%).[93] Furthermore, immunodiffusion serology is of little help in the diagnosis of acute disease. In one large outbreak, only 28% of patients had a positive test and all but one of the positive sera were obtained 50 or more days after the onset of symptoms.[94]

A radioimmunoassay and an enzyme immunoassay employing commercial antigens have been used by George and co-workers[148,149] as rapid screening tests for histoplasmosis and blastomycosis. Both tests are quite sensitive, but their specificity is no better than that of complement fixation. A sensitive enzyme immunoassay using purified A antigen has been reported, but the specificity of this test varies depending on the cutoff titer employed.[150] When this assay was used in evaluating a large common-source outbreak, a positive test was noted in 77% of patients.[94] Although some positive results were noted in the first 2 weeks of illness, both the peak seroprevalence rate and peak geometric mean titer did not occur until 50 to 70 days after the onset of symptoms. A commercial enzyme-linked immunosorbent assay is now available, and the use of this sensitive test for initial screening in conjunction with the more specific immunodiffusion test may be helpful.[95,96]

Klein and co-workers[61] have utilized a 120-kDa cell wall protein antigen (WI-1) to detect antibodies to *B. dermatitidis* in infected patients. When it was employed in a radioimmunoassay, antibodies to WI-1 were detected in 85% of patients with blastomycosis. Specificity was excellent, with positive tests being noted in only 3% to 5% of patients with other fungal infections or patients in whom infection could not be confirmed. Although the use of WI-1 in serologic testing appears promising, this test is not generally available and further studies are necessary to establish its role in the diagnosis of blastomycosis.

In summary, complement fixation, immunodiffusion, and enzyme-linked immunosorbent assay serologic tests are currently available to aid in the diagnosis of blastomycosis. Unfortunately, sensitivity and specificity vary with the test employed. Because false-positive and false-negative results occur commonly, a negative antibody titer, regardless of which test is used, should never be used to rule out disease. Neither should a positive titer alone be an indication for therapy; it should instead stimulate the clinician to look carefully for the disease.

Nucleic Acid Detection

Many molecular techniques for the identification of genetic material for specific fungal pathogens have been described.[151-157] Nucleic acid techniques, both nonamplification and amplification methods, have been developed. The Gen-Probe nonisotopic detection kit (Gen-Probe, San Diego, CA) can detect *B. dermatitidis* in very young cultures, shortening identification time from weeks to days or hours. Amplification techniques such as PCR and its many derivations (nested PCR and multiplex PCR) have also been developed.[155-157] PCR amplification of the ribosomal RNA gene, containing both conserved and unique regions, has been combined with oligonucleotide-specific probe hybridization to identify fungal pathogens with yeast-like morphology in vivo.[157] The gene encoding the WI-1 adhesin has also been employed as a target for nucleic acid amplification in a nested PCR assay.[158] PCR techniques, although promising, are labor intensive, are not generally available, and have not yet been examined in large prospective studies.

Antigen Detection

The detection of fungal antigens in serum and urine has proven useful in the diagnosis and treatment of patients with cryptococcal meningitis and disseminated histoplasmosis. A commercially available Blastomyces antigen assay has recently been developed by MiraVista Diagnostics (*www.miravistalabs.com*). Sensitivity is greatest in urine, but antigen has also been detected in serum and other body fluids, including cerebrospinal fluid. According to MiraVista Diagnostics (Joseph Wheat, M.D., Director), antigenuria is detected in 70% to 80% of cases of disseminated blastomycosis. Sensitivity of antigen detection in the urine of patients with pulmonary disease approaches 100%. Serum antigen is detected in approximately 50% of cases. Cross-reactive antigens are present in specimens obtained from patients with histoplasmosis, paracoccidioidomycosis, and penicilliosis.[159] Specificity is said to be greater than 90% in patients with other fungal infection and healthy volunteers. Antigen levels decline with successful treatment and increase with recurrence of illness. Usefulness in diagnosis is limited by the ease of diagnosis using conventional methods once the possibility is considered.

Cellular Immunity Testing

No reagent is currently available for skin testing patients with suspected blastomycosis. Lymphocyte transformation to yeast-phase organisms, the WI-1 surface protein, and alkali-soluble, water-soluble antigens have been used as indicators of cell-mediated immunity in patients with blastomycosis.[62,85,86] In an outbreak, 81% of definite and probable cases of blastomycosis had positive lymphocyte transformation tests with the alkali-soluble, water-soluble antigen.[32] This test does not appear to be useful early in the acute disease, because positive tests are not obtained in the first 2 weeks of disease. Furthermore, because this immunity appears to be long lived, a positive test does not necessarily indicate recent infection.[86] Finally, there are only limited data on the specificity of this test. Lymphocyte transformation assays are therefore not yet clinically useful and should be considered investigational tests.

TREATMENT

Chemotherapy

Before the availability of chemotherapy for treatment of blastomycosis, the disease as reported had a progressive course with eventual extrapulmonary disease and a mortality exceeding 60%. Even though isolated cutaneous disease had a better prognosis, skin lesions were progressive and spontaneous recovery was uncommon. Thus, after the introduction of effective antifungal therapy, it was accepted that all patients with blastomycosis should be treated. This concept was questioned after the description of self-limited pulmonary blastomycosis.[115] The decision to withhold therapy for patients with acute pulmonary blastomycosis is difficult and remains a controversial issue. Although it is true that in some patients blastomycotic pneumonia may resolve without therapy, there is no way to determine which patients will present later with extrapulmonary disease, often with serious sequelae.[160] Furthermore, some patients while under observation may suffer acute exacerbation with miliary disease or endobronchial spread, both associated with high mortality.[118,119] For these reasons, it is the policy at my medical center that almost all patients with active disease be treated. If a culture-based diagnosis is made after spontaneous recovery from blastomycotic pneumonia, patients are carefully evaluated for the presence of extrapulmonary disease before a decision is made to withhold treatment. If treatment is withheld, patients must be followed carefully for many years for evidence of reactivation or progressive disease.

Amphotericin B was previously considered the treatment of choice for all clinical forms of blastomycosis.[161,162] However, ketoconazole, itraconazole, and fluconazole are now considered effective alternatives for immunocompetent patients with mild to moderate disease (Table 263-3).[162] Azoles should not be used in patients with life-

TABLE 263-3 Treatment Guidelines for Blastomycosis

Type of Disease	Preferred	Alternative
Pulmonary*		
Serious	Amphotericin B, 0.3-0.6 mg/kg/day[†]	Change to itraconazole after the patient's condition has stabilized
Mild to moderate	Itraconazole, 200-400 mg/day[‡]	Ketoconazole, 400-800 mg/day *or* Fluconazole, 400-800 mg/day
Disseminated		
Central nervous system	Amphotericin B, 0.7-1.0 mg/kg/day	For patients unable to tolerate a full course of amphotericin B, consider fluconazole, 800 mg/day
Non–central nervous system		
Serious	Amphotericin B, 0.3-0.6 mg/kg/day	Change to itraconazole after the patient's condition has stabilized
Mild to moderate	Itraconazole, 200-400 mg/day	Ketoconazole, 400-800 mg/day *or* Fluconazole, 400-800 mg/day

*Some patients with acute pulmonary infection may have a spontaneous cure. Thus patients with mild pulmonary disease may be monitored closely for resolution. Patients with extrapulmonary disease or progressive pulmonary disease should be treated.
†Some authors recommend higher initial doses of amphotericin B (0.7 to 1.0 mg/kg/day) for immunocompromised patients and patients with adult respiratory distress syndrome or central nervous system disease. For patients requiring a full course of amphotericin B, a total dose of 1.5 to 2.5 g is associated with the lowest relapse rates.
‡Treatment with an azole should be continued for at least 6 months.

threatening disease or with central nervous system blastomycosis. Hydroxystilbamidine, the first effective drug available for the treatment of blastomycosis, is no longer available. Intravenous miconazole has also been used for the treatment of blastomycosis.

Ketoconazole

In a prospective, randomized multicenter trial of patients treated with ketoconazole for at least 6 months, the cure rates were 100% in patients treated with 800 mg/day and 79% in those treated with 400 mg/day.[163] Toxicity was greater with the higher dose. A second study noted a cure rate of 81% in 43 patients who completed at least 1 month of therapy with 400 mg/day.[107] A retrospective study documented a cure rate of 82% for patients treated with ketoconazole at a daily dose of 400 mg or greater.[109] Therapy should be continued for at least 6 months.[162,164,165] Relapse rates of 10% to 14% have been reported after ketoconazole therapy.[107,109,162]

Itraconazole

Itraconazole has excellent in vitro and in vivo activity against *B. dermatitidis*.[166,167] In a prospective, Phase II clinical trial, itraconazole at doses ranging from 200 to 400 mg/day was effective in 90% of patients.[168] For compliant patients with at least 2 months of therapy, a successful outcome was noted in 95%. Although the study design did not allow comparison of the relative efficacy of the different doses, most patients received 200 mg/day and no further improvement in outcome was noted in patients receiving higher doses. Itraconazole was well tolerated, and only one patient had to discontinue therapy because of drug toxicity. When compared with ketoconazole in a similar study design,[163] itraconazole appeared to be better tolerated. Bradsher[169] noted similar success in 42 patients treated with itraconazole at a daily dose of 200 mg. Thus the recommended initial dose of itraconazole is 200 mg/day, which should effect a cure in most patients with blastomycosis. For patients whose disease persists or progresses, the dose should be increased in increments of 100 mg daily to a maximum daily dose of 400 mg. The optimal duration of therapy has not been determined, but it is recommended that treatment be continued for 6 months. Itraconazole is now the drug of choice for patients with indolent blastomycosis. The greater rapidity of the clinical response to amphotericin B has made both the oral and intravenous formulations of itraconazole less desirable in severely ill patients.

Attention must be paid to the pharmacology of itraconazole, reviewed in Chapter 36. Bioavailability of itraconazole capsules is enhanced when taken with meals, though the suspension should be taken fasting (see Chapter 36).[170,171] Patients receiving antacid therapy or histamine$_2$ or proton pump blockers may have subtherapeutic serum levels. A variety of drugs can decrease itraconazole blood levels to nearly zero and lead to treatment failure.[172] Very little itraconazole is excreted in the urine as active drug.[170,171] It is possible that patients with genitourinary disease may be more resistant to therapy or more likely to have relapses after treatment.[173] Itraconazole can cause metabolism of many other drugs to slow, causing those drugs to be toxic.[174,175] Cardiac failure may be increased by itraconazole, and hepatotoxicity, although rare, may occur.

Fluconazole

Fluconazole, a triazole that is available in both oral and intravenous preparations, has been used to treat only a small cohort of patients with blastomycosis. It is my opinion that, compared with ketoconazole and itraconazole, fluconazole has a limited role in the treatment of blastomycosis. The results of a pilot study employing lower dose fluconazole were disappointing, with a successful outcome noted in only 65% of the 23 patients treated with daily doses of 200 and 400 mg.[176] A study employing higher doses of fluconazole (400 to 800 mg daily) showed enhanced efficacy.[177] A successful outcome was noted in 87% of the 39 patients treated for a mean of 8.9 months. Adverse events were usually mild. Cessation of therapy owing to an adverse event was necessary in only 1 of 39 patients; a second patient required a dosage reduction. In both patients, however, treatment was successful. These results indicate that fluconazole is similar in efficacy to ketoconazole at equivalent doses but has less serious toxicity. However, fluconazole is not as efficacious as itraconazole for the treatment of patients with mild to moderate blastomycosis. Because fluconazole has excellent penetration into the central nervous system, it may have some role in the treatment of blastomycotic meningitis and cerebral abscesses, although clinical experience in treating these conditions is limited to only a few cases.

Newer Azoles

Voriconazole, a newly released triazole, and posaconazole have shown excellent in vitro and in vivo activity against isolates of *B. dermatitidis*. These agents presently do not appear to offer any advantage for blastomycosis but may prove to offer an option in the treatment of patients failing or intolerant to amphotericin B and not tolerating itraconazole.

Amphotericin

Amphotericin B remains the drug of choice for patients who are severely immunocompromised; for patients with life-threatening disease, central nervous system disease, or progression of disease during treatment with an azole; and for those who are unable to tolerate an azole because of toxicity.[138,162] Although the exact dose and optimal duration of therapy are uncertain, relapse appears to be more common if the total dose is less than 1.5 g. Most experts, therefore, recommend a total dose of 1.5 to 2.5 g of amphotericin B. For seriously ill patients, 0.3 to 0.6 mg/kg (usually not exceeding 50 mg) should be administered daily until objective evidence of improvement is noted. Some authors recommend higher doses of amphotericin B (0.7 to 1.0 mg/kg/day) as initial therapy for patients with life-threatening disease (such as adult respiratory distress syndrome) or central nervous system disease.[162] Patients who are immunocompetent and do not have central nervous system disease have been successfully treated at my medical center by the substitution of itraconazole or ketoconazole in their treatment regimen. For patients who must continue to take amphotericin B, 0.6 to 0.8 mg/kg (usually 50 mg) may be administered thrice weekly or every other day on an outpatient basis.[178] Relapse rates of most patients treated with amphotericin B are less than 5%. Relapse is more common in immunocompromised patients, especially those with AIDS.[162] Some authorities recommend long-term suppressive therapy with an azole, and this practice seems prudent.[162] These patients still require close follow-up for relapse of disease, especially in the central nervous system.

Lipid preparations of amphotericin B (Abelcet, Amphocil, AmBisome) have not been adequately evaluated in blastomycosis. Usage should be confined to patients who cannot tolerate conventional amphotericin B.

Echinocandins

The echinocandins (e.g., caspofungin, anidulafungin, and mycafungin) show only variable activity against *B. dermatitidis*. Presently, there are no clinical data to support the use of echinocandins for the therapy of blastomycosis.

Surgery

Apart from diagnosis, surgery has little role in the treatment of blastomycosis.[162,179-181] In conjunction with antifungal therapy, surgery appears indicated for the drainage of large abscesses, for the rare patient with large accumulations of empyema fluid or bronchopleural fistula, and for the débridement of devitalized bone tissue in patients with osteomyelitis who are responding poorly to therapy. Unless patients have repeated relapses in the lung or remain culture positive with appropriate therapy, the surgical resection of large or residual lung cavities is not indicated. Although one report implied that surgical resection alone may be curative,[181] the likelihood of relapse must be considered. Furthermore, we have seen patients who developed acute, life-threatening disease after surgical resection of lung tissue for diagnostic purposes when blastomycosis was left untreated.[149] Therefore, it is our policy to treat any patient whose resected lung tissue contains *B. dermatitidis*.

REFERENCES

1. Gilchrist TC. Protozoan dermatitis. J Cutan Gen Dis. 1894;12:496-499.
2. Gilchrist TC. A case of blastomycetic dermatitis in man. Johns Hopkins Hosp Rep. 1896;1:269-283.
3. Gilchrist TC, Stokes WR. The presence of an oidium in the tissues of a case of pseudo-lupus vulgaris. Johns Hopkins Hosp Rep. 1896;7:129-133.
4. Gilchrist TC, Stokes WR. Case of pseudo-lupus vulgaris caused by *Blastomyces*. J Exp Med. 1898;3:53-78.
5. Martin DS, Smith DT. Blastomycosis I: A review of the literature. Am Rev Tuberc. 1939;39:275-304.
6. Martin DS, Smith DT. Blastomycosis II: A report of thirteen new cases. Am Rev Tuberc. 1939;39:488-515.
7. Schwartz J, Baum GL. Blastomycosis. Am J Clin Pathol. 1951;21:999-1029.
8. Kwon-Chung KJ, Bennett JE. Medical Mycology. Philadelphia: Lea & Febiger; 1992:248.
9. Bradsher, RW. Blastomycosis. In: Dismukes WE, Pappas PG, Sobel JD, eds. Clinical Mycology. New York: Oxford University Press; 2003:299-310.
10. Medoff G, Painter A, Kobayashi GS. Mycelial-to-yeast phase transitions of the dimorphic fungi *Blastomyces dermatitidis* and *Paracoccidioides brasiliensis*. J Bacteriol. 1987;169:4055-4060.
11. Maresca B, Kobayashi, GS, Dimorphism *in Histoplasma capsulatum* and *Blastomyces dermatitidis*. Contrib Microbiol. 2000;5:201-216.
12. Kaufman L, Standard PG, Weeks RJ, et al. Detection of two *Blastomyces dermatitidis* serotypes by exoantigen analysis. J Clin Microbiol. 1983;18:110-114.
13. Turner S, Kaufman L. Immunodiagnosis of blastomycosis. Semin Respir Infect. 1986;1:22-28.
14. McDonough ES, Lewis AL. *Blastomyces dermatitidis:* Production of the sexual state. Science. 1967;156:528-529.
15. McDonough ES, Lewis AL. The ascigerous state of *Blastomyces dermatitidis*. Mycologia. 1968;60:76-83.
16. McDonough ES, McNamara WJ, Chan DM, et al. Geographic distribution of "+" and " − " isolates of *Blastomyces (Ajellomyces) dermatitidis* in North America. Am J Epidemiol. 1973;98:63-67.
17. Yates-Ciilata KE, Sander DM, Keith EJ. Genetic diversity in clinical isolates of the dimorphic fungus *Blastomyces dermatitidis* detected by PCR based random amplified polymorphic DNA assay. J. Clin Microbiol. 1995;33:2171-2175.
18. McCullough MJ, DiSalvo AF, Clemons KV, et al. Molecular epidemiology of *Blastomyces dermatitidis*. Clin Infect Dis. 2003:328-335.
19. Blastomycosis Cooperative Study of the Veterans Administration. Blastomycosis I: A review of 198 collected cases in Veterans Administration hospitals. Am Rev Respir Dis. 1964;89:659-672.
20. Menges RW, Doto IL, Weeks RJ. Epidemiologic studies of blastomycosis in Arkansas. Arch Environ Health. 1969;18:956-971.
21. Furcolow ML, Chick EW, Busey JF, et al. Prevalence and incidence studies of human and canine blastomycosis I: Cases in the United States, 1885-1968. Am Rev Respir Dis. 1970;102:60-67.
22. Furcolow ML, Busey JF, Menges RW, et al. Prevalence and incidence studies of human and canine blastomycosis II: Yearly incidence studies in three selected states, 1960-1967. Am J Epidemiol. 1970;92:121-131.
23. Sekshon AS, Borgorus MS, Sims HV. Blastomycosis: Report of three cases from Alberta with a review of Canadian cases. Mycopathologia. 1979;1:53-63.
24. Klein BS, Vergeront JM, Davis JP. Epidemiologic aspects of blastomycosis, the enigmatic systemic mycosis. Semin Respir Infect. 1986;1:29-39.
25. Crampton TL, Light RB, Berg GM, et al. Epidemiology and clinical spectrum of blastomycoses diagnosed at Manitoba hospitals. Clin Infect Dis. 2002;34:1310-1316.
26. Smith JD Jr, Harris JS, Conant NF, et al. An epidemic of North American blastomycosis. JAMA. 1955;158:641-646.
27. Tosh FE, Hammerman KJ, Weeks RJ, et al. A common source epidemic of North American blastomycosis. Am Rev Respir Dis. 1974;109:525-529.
28. Centers for Disease Control. Blastomycosis: North Carolina. MMWR Morb Mortal Wkly Rep. 1976;25:205-206.
29. Kitchen MS, Reiber CD, Eastin GB. An urban epidemic of North American blastomycosis. Am Rev Respir Dis. 1977;115:1063-1066.
30. Cockerill FR III, Roberts GD, Rosenblatt JE, et al. Epidemic of pulmonary blastomycosis (Nanekagan fever) in Wisconsin canoeists. Chest. 1984; 86:688-692.
31. Armstrong CW, Jenkins SR, Kaufman L, et al. Common source outbreak of blastomycosis in hunters and their dogs. J Infect Dis. 1987;155:568-570.
32. Klein BS, Vergeront JM, Weeks RJ, et al. Isolation of *Blastomyces dermatitidis* in soil associated with a large outbreak of blastomycosis in Wisconsin. N Engl J Med. 1986;314:529-534.
33. Klein BS, Vergeront JM, DiSalvo AF, et al. Two outbreaks of blastomycosis along rivers in Wisconsin: Isolation of *Blastomyces dermatitidis* from riverbank soil and evidence of its transmission along waterways. Am Rev Respir Dis. 1987;136:1333-1338.
34. Baumgardner DJ, Burdick JS. An outbreak of human and canine blastomycosis. Rev Infect Dis. 1991;13:898-905.
35. Frye MD, Seifer FD. An outbreak of blastomycosis in eastern Tennessee. Mycopathologia. 1991;116:15-21.
36. Proctor ME, Klein BS, Jones JM, Davis JP. Cluster of pulmonary blastomycosis in a rural community: Evidence for multiple high-risk environmental foci following a sustained period of diminished precipitation. Mycopathologia. 2002;153:113-120.
37. Baily GG, Robertson VJ, Neill P, et al. Blastomycosis in Africa: Clinical features, diagnosis and treatment. Rev Infect Dis. 1991;13:1005-1008.
38. DiSalvo AF. The ecology of *Blastomyces dermatitidis*. In: Al-Doory Y, DiSalvo AF, eds. Blastomycosis. New York: Plenum; 1992:43.
39. Baumgardner DJ, Paretsky DP. Blastomycosis: More evidence for exposure near one's domicile. WMJ. 2001;100:4-5.
40. Denton JF, McDonough ES, Ajello L, et al. Isolation of *Blastomyces dermatitidis* from soil. Science. 1961;133:1126-1127.
41. Denton JF, DiSalvo AF. Isolation of *Blastomyces dermatitidis* from natural sites in Augusta, Georgia. Am J Trop Med Hyg. 1964;13:716-722.
42. Denton JF, DiSalvo AF. Additional isolations of *Blastomyces dermatitidis* from natural sites. Am J Trop Med Hyg. 1979;28:697-700.
43. Sarosi GA, Serstock DA. Isolation of *Blastomyces dermatitidis* from pigeon manure. Am Rev Respir Dis. 1976;114:1179-1183.
44. Bakerspigel A, Kane J, Schaus D. Isolation of *Blastomyces dermatitidis* from an earthen floor in southwestern Ontario, Canada. J Clin Microbiol. 1986;24:890-891.
45. Dixon DM, Shadomy HJ, Shadomy S. In vitro growth and sporulation of *Blastomyces dermatitidis* on woody plant material. Mycologia. 1977;69:1193-1195.
46. Baumgardner DJ, Laundre B. Studies on the molecular ecology of *Blastomyces dermatitidis*. Mycopathologia. 2001;152:51-58.
47. Baumgardner DJ, Paretsky DP. The in vitro isolation of *Blastomyces dermatitidis* from a woodpile in north central Wisconsin, USA. Med. Mycol. 1999;37:163-168.
48. Larson DM, Eckman MR, Alber RL, et al. Primary cutaneous (inoculation) blastomycosis: An occupational hazard to pathologists. Am J Clin Pathol. 1983;79:253-255.
49. Gnann JW Jr, Bressler GS, Bodet CA, et al. Human blastomycosis after a dog bite. Ann Intern Med. 1983;98:48-49.
50. Craig MW, Davey WN, Green RA. Conjugal blastomycosis. Am Rev Respir Dis. 1970;102:86-90.
51. Watts EA, Gard PD Jr, Tuthill SW. First reported case of intrauterine transmission of blastomycosis. Pediatr Infect Dis. 1983;2:308-310.
52. Maxson S, Miller SF, Tryka AF, et al. Perinatal blastomycosis: A review. Pediatr Infect Dis. 1992;11:760-763.
53. Daniel WP, Danaar SC, Perry HD. Blastomycosis-like pyoderma. Arch Dermatol. 1979;115:170-173.
54. Reder PA, Neel HB III. Blastomycosis in otolaryngology: Review of a large series. Laryngoscope. 1993;103:53-58.
55. Ebeo CT, Olove K, Byrd RP Jr, et al. Blastomycosis of the vocal folds with life threatening upper airway obstruction: A case report. Ear Nose Throat J. 2002;81:852-855.
56. Vaaler AK, Bradsher RW, Davies SF. Evidence of subclinical blastomycosis in forestry workers in northern Minnesota and northern Wisconsin. Am J Med. 1990;89:470-476.
57. Ganer A, Brummer E, Stevens DA. Correlation of susceptibility of immature mice to fungal infection (blastomycosis) and effector cell function. Infect Immun. 2000;68:6833-6839.
58. Sugar AM, Picard M. Macrophage- and oxidant-mediated inhibition of the ability of live *Blastomyces dermatitidis* conidia to transform to the pathogenic yeast phase: Implications for the pathogenesis of dimorphic fungal infections. J Infect Dis. 1991;163:371-375.
59. DiSalvo AF, Denton JF. Lipid content of four strains of *Blastomyces dermatitidis* of different mouse virulence. J Bacteriol. 1963;85:927-931.
60. Cox RA, Best GK. Cell wall composition of two strains of *Blastomyces dermatitidis* exhibiting differences in virulence for mice. Infect Immunol. 1972;5:449-453.
61. Klein BS, Jones JM. Isolation, purification, and radiolabeling of a novel 120-kD surface protein on *Blastomyces dermatitidis* yeasts to detect antibody in infected patients. J Clin Invest. 1990;85:152-161.
62. Klein BS, Sondel PM, Jones JM. WI-1, a novel 120-kilodalton surface protein on *Blastomyces dermatitidis* yeast cells, is a target antigen of cell-mediated immunity in human blastomycosis. Infect Immunol. 1992;60:4291-4300.
63. Klein BS, Hogan LH, Jones JM. Immunologic recognition of a 25-amino acid repeat arrayed in tandem on a major antigen of *Blastomyces dermatitidis*. J Clin Invest. 1993;92:330-337.
64. Newman SL, Chaturvedi S, Klein BS. The WI-1 antigen of *Blastomyces dermatitidis* yeast mediates binding to human macrophage CD11b/CD18 (CR3) and CD14. J Immunol. 1995;154:753-761.
65. Hogan LH, Josvai S, Klein BS. Genomic cloning, characterization and functional analysis of the major surface adhesin WI-1 on *Blastomyces dermatitidis* yeasts. J Biol Chem. 1995;270:30725-30732.
66. Klein BS, Chaturvedi S, Hogan LH, et al. Altered expression of surface protein WI-1 in genetically related strains of *Blastomyces dermatitidis* that differ in virulence regulates recognition of yeasts by human macrophages. Infect Immunol. 1994;62:3536-3542.
67. Hogan LH, Klein BS. Altered expression of surface α-1,3-glucan in genetically related strains of *Blastomyces dermatitidis* that differ in virulence. Infect Immunol. 1994;62:3543-3546.
68. Klein BS, Newman SL. Role of cell-surface molecules of *Blastomyces dermatitidis* in host-pathogen interactions. Trends Microbiol. 1996;4:246-251.
69. Brandhorst T, Klein B. Cell wall biogenesis of *Blastomyces dermatitidis:* Evidence for a novel mechanism of self service localization of a virulence-associated adhesin by an extracellular release and reassociation with cell wall chitin. J Biol Chem. 2000;275:7925-7934.
70. Finkel-Jimenez B, Wuthichm M, Brandhorst T, Klein BS. WI-1 adhesin blocks phagocytic TNF-α production, imparting pathogenicity in *Blastomyces dermatitidis*. J Immunol. 2001;166:2665-2673.
71. Finkel-Jimenez B, Wuthichm M, Klein BS. BAD1, an essential virulence factor of *Blastomyces dermatitidis*, suppresses host TNF-α production through TGF-B-dependent and independent mechanisms. J Immunol. 2002;168:5746-5755.
72. Ahang MX, Brandhorst TT, Kozel TR, Klein BS. Role of glucan and surface protein BAD1 in complement activation of *Blastomyces dermatitidis* yeast. Infect Immun. 2001;69:7559-7564.

73. Thurmond LM, Mitchell TG. *Blastomyces dermatitidis* chemotactic factor: Kinetics of production and biological characterization evaluated by a modified chemotaxis assay. Infect Immun. 1984;46:87-93.

74. Drutz DJ, Frey CL. Intracellular and extracellular defenses against *Blastomyces dermatitidis* conidia and yeasts. J Lab Clin Med. 1985;105:737-750.

75. Schaffner A, Davis CE, Schaffner T, et al. In vitro susceptibility of fungi to killing by neutrophil granulocytes discriminates between primary pathogenicity and opportunism. J Clin Invest. 1986;78:511-524.

76. Brummer E, Kurita N, Yoshida K, et al. A basis for resistance of *Blastomyces dermatitidis* killing by human neutrophils: Inefficient generation of myeloperoxidase system products. J Med Vet Mycol. 1992;30:233-243.

77. Brummer E, Stevens DA. Activation of murine polymorphonuclear neutrophils for fungicidal activity with supernatants from antigen-stimulated immune spleen cell cultures. Infect Immun. 1984;45:447-452.

78. Morrison CJ, Brummer E, Isenberg RA, et al. Activation of murine polymorphonuclear neutrophils for fungicidal activity by recombinant gamma interferon. J Leukoc Biol. 1987;41:434-440.

79. Cozad GC, Chang C. T-cell mediated immunoprotection in blastomycosis. Infect Immun. 1980;78:393-403.

80. Morozumi PA, Brummer E, Stevens DA. Protection against pulmonary blastomycosis. Infect Immun. 1982;37:670-678.

81. Brummer E, Morozumi PA, Vo PT, et al. Protection against pulmonary blastomycosis: Adaptive transfer with T lymphocytes, but not serum, from resistant mice. Cell Immunol. 1982;73:349-359.

82. Brummer E, Morozumi A, Philpott DE, et al. Virulence of fungi: Correlation of virulence of *Blastomyces dermatitidis* in vivo with escape from macrophage inhibition of replication in vitro. Infect Immun. 1981;32:864-871.

83. Brummer E, Hanson LH, Restrepo A, et al. In vivo and in vitro activation of pulmonary macrophages by IFN-γ for enhanced killing of *Paracoccidioides brasiliensis* or *Blastomyces dermatitidis*. J Immunol. 1988;140:2786-2789.

84. Brummer E, Hanson LH, Stevens DA. Kinetics and requirements for activation of macrophages for fungicidal activity: Effect of protein synthesis inhibitors and immunosuppressants on activation and fungicidal mechanisms. Cell Immunol. 1991;132:236-245.

85. Bradsher RW. Live *Blastomyces dermatitidis* yeast-induced responses of immune and non-immune human mononuclear cells. Mycopathologia. 1984;87:159-166.

86. Klein PS, Bradsher RW, Vergeront JM, et al. Development of long-term specific cellular immunity after acute *Blastomyces dermatitidis* infection: Assessments following a large point-source outbreak in Wisconsin. J Infect Dis. 1990;161:97-101.

87. Chang WL, Audet RG, Aizenstein BD, et al. T cell epitopes and human leukocyte antigen restriction elements in an immunodominant antigen of *Blastomyces dermatitidis*. Infect Immun. 2000;68:502-510.

88. Wüthrich M, Chang WL, Klein BS. Immunogenicity and protective efficacy of the WI-1 adhesin of *Blastomyces dermatitidis*. Infect Immun. 1998;66:5443-5449.

89. Wüthrich M, Finkel-Jimenez BE, Klein BS. Interleukin 12 as an adjuvant to WI-1 adhesin immunization augments delayed-type hypersensitivity, shifts the subclass distribution of immunoglobulin G antibodies, and enhances protective immunity to *Blastomyces dermatitidis*. Infect Immun. 2000;68:7172-7174.

90. Bradsher RW, Balk RA, Jacobs RF. Growth inhibition of *Blastomyces dermatitidis* in alveolar and peripheral macrophages from patients with blastomycosis. Am Rev Respir Dis. 1987;135:412-417.

91. Kaufman L, McLaughlin DW, Clark MJ, et al. Specific immunodiffusion test for blastomycosis. Appl Microbiol. 1973;26:244-247.

92. Williams JE, Murphy R, Standard PG, et al. Serologic response in blastomycosis: Diagnostic value of double immunodiffusion assay. Am Rev Respir Dis. 1981;123:209-212.

93. Klein BS, Kuritsky WAC, Kaufman L, et al. Comparison of enzyme immunoassay, immunodiffusion and complement fixation in detecting antibody in human serum to the A antigen in *B. dermatitidis*. Am Rev Respir Dis. 1986;133:144-148.

94. Klein BS, Vergeront JM, Kaufman L, et al. Serological test for blastomycosis: Assessments during a large point-source outbreak in Wisconsin. J Infect Dis. 1987;155:262-268.

95. Bradsher RW, Pappas PG. Detection of specific antibodies in human blastomycosis by enzyme immunoassay. South Med J. 1995;88:1256-1259.

96. Sekhorn AS, Kaufman L, Kobayashi AS, et al. The value of the Premier enzyme immunoassay for diagnosing *Blastomyces dermatitidis* infections. J Med Vet Mycol. 1995;33:123-125.

97. Klein BS, Jones JM. Purification and characterization of the major WI-1 from *Blastomyces dermatitidis* yeast and immunological comparison with A antigen. Infect Immun. 1994;62:3890-3900.

98. Soufleris AJ, Klein BS, Courtney BT, et al. Utility of anti-WI-1 serological testing in the diagnosis of blastomycosis in Wisconsin residents. Clin Infect Dis. 1994;19:87-92.

99. Klein BS, Squires RA, Lloyd JK, et al. Canine antibody response to *Blastomyces dermatitidis* WI-1 antigen. Am J Vet Res. 2000;61:554-558.

100. Bradsher RW, Chapman SW, Pappas PG. Blastomycosis. Infect Dis Clin North Am. 2003;17:21-40.

101. Cherniss EI, Waisbren BA. North American blastomycosis: A clinical study of 40 cases. Ann Intern Med. 1956;44:105-123.

102. Abernathy RS. Clinical manifestations of pulmonary blastomycosis. Ann Intern Med. 1959;51:707-727.

103. Witorsch P, Utz JP. North American blastomycosis: A study of 40 patients. Medicine (Baltimore). 1968;47:169-200.

104. Lockwood WR, Allison F, Batson BE, et al. The treatment of North American blastomycosis: Ten years experience. Am Rev Respir Dis. 1969;100:314-320.

105. Duttera MJ, Osterhout S. North American blastomycosis: A survey of 63 cases. South Med J. 1969;62:295-301.

106. Busey JF, and the Veterans Administrative Cooperative Group. Blastomycosis: III. A comparative study of 2-hydroxystilbamidine and amphotericin B therapy. Am Rev Respir Dis. 1972;105:812-818.

107. Bradsher RW, Rice DC, Abernathy RS. Ketoconazole therapy for endemic blastomycosis. Ann Intern Med. 1985;103:872-879.

108. Baumgardner DJ, Buggy BP, Mattson BJ, et al. Epidemiology of blastomycosis in a region of high endemicity in north central Wisconsin. Clin Infect Dis. 1992;15:629-635.

109. Chapman SW, Lin AC, Hendricks KA, et al. Endemic blastomycosis in Mississippi: Epidemiological and clinical studies. Semin Respir Infect. 1997;12:219-228.

110. Sarosi GA, Davies SF. Blastomycosis. Am Rev Respir Dis. 1979;120:911-938.

111. Ehni W. Endogenous reactivation in blastomycosis. Am J Med. 1989;86:831-832.

112. Sheflin JR, Campbell JA, Thompson GP. Pulmonary blastomycosis: Findings on chest radiographs in 63 patients. AJR Am J Roentgenol. 1990;154:1177-1180.

113. Brown LR, Sweasen SJ, VanScoy RE, et al. Roentgenologic features of pulmonary blastomycosis. Mayo Clin Proc. 1991;66:29-38.

114. Sarosi GA, Davies SF, Phillips JR. Self-limited blastomycosis: A report of 39 cases. Semin Respir Infect. 1986;1:40-44.

115. Sarosi GA, Hammerman KJ, Tosh FE, et al. Clinical features of acute pulmonary blastomycosis. N Engl J Med. 1974;290:540-543.

116. Baum GL, Lerner PI. Primary pulmonary blastomycosis: A laboratory acquired infection. Ann Intern Med. 1970;73:263-265.

117. Poe RH, Vassallo CL, Plessinger VA, et al. Pulmonary blastomycosis versus carcinoma: A challenging differential. Am J Med Sci. 1972;263:145-155.

118. Stelling CB, Woodring JH, Rehm SR, et al. Miliary pulmonary blastomycosis. Radiology. 1984;150:7-13.

119. Meyer KC, McManus EJ, Maki DG. Overwhelming pulmonary blastomycosis associated with the adult respiratory distress syndrome. N Engl J Med. 1993;329:1231-1236.

120. Kinasewitz GT, Penn RL, George RB. The spectrum and significance of pleural disease in blastomycosis. Chest. 1984;86:580-584.

121. Mercurio MG, Elewski BE. Cutaneous blastomycosis. Cutis. 1992;50:422-424.

122. MacDonald PB, Black GB, MacKenzie R. Orthopaedic manifestations of blastomycosis. J Bone Joint Surg Am. 1990;72:860-864.

123. Guler N, Palanduz A, Ones U, et al. Progressive vertebral blastomycosis mimicking tuberculosis. Pediatr Infect Dis J. 1995; 14:816-818.

124. Bayer AS, Scott VJ, Guze LB. Fungal arthritis IV. Blastomycotic arthritis. Semin Arthritis Rheum. 1979;9:145-151.

125. Eikenberg HA, Amin M, Lich RJ. Blastomycosis of the genitourinary tract. J Urol. 1975;113:650-652.

126. Pappas PG, Pottage JC, Powderly WG, et al. Blastomycosis in patients with acquired immunodeficiency syndrome. Ann Intern Med. 1992;116:847-853.

127. Gonyea EF. The spectrum of primary blastomycotic meningitis: A review of central nervous system blastomycosis. Ann Neurol. 1978;3:26-39.

128. Kravitz GR, Davies SF, Eckman MR, et al. Chronic blastomycotic meningitis. Am J Med. 1981;71:501-505.

129. Roos KL, Bryan JP, Maggio WW, et al. Intracranial blastomycoma. Medicine (Baltimore). 1987;66:224-235.

130. Ward BA, Parent AD, Raila F. Indications for the surgical management of central nervous system blastomycosis. Surg Neurol. 1995;43:379-388.

131. Laskey WK, Sarosi GA. Blastomycosis in children. Pediatrics. 1980;65:111-114.

132. Steele RW, Abernathy RS. Systemic blastomycosis in children. Pediatr Infect Dis. 1983;2:304-307.

133. Alkrinawi S, Reed MH, Pasterkamp H. Pulmonary blastomycosis in children: Findings on chest radiographs. AJR Am J Roentgenol. 1995;165:651-654.

134. Schutze GE, Hickerson SL, Fortin EM, et al. Blastomycosis in children. Clin Infect Dis. 1996;22:496-502.

135. Ismail MA, Lerner SA. Disseminated blastomycosis in a pregnant woman: Review of amphotericin B usage in pregnancy. Am Rev Respir Dis. 1982;126:350-353.

136. MacDonald D, Alguire PC. Adult respiratory distress syndrome due to blastomycosis during pregnancy. Chest. 1990;98:1527-1528.

137. Recht AD, Davies SF, Eckman MR. Blastomycosis in immunosuppressed patients. Am Rev Respir Dis. 1982;125:359-362.

138. Serody JS, Mill MR, Detterbeck FC, et al. Blastomycosis in transplant recipients: Report of a case and review. Clin Infect Dis. 1993;16:54-58.

139. Pappas PG, Threlkeld MG, Bedsole GD, et al. Blastomycosis in immunocompromised patients. Medicine (Baltimore). 1993;72:311-325.

140. Wheat J. Endemic mycoses in AIDS: A clinical review. Clin Microbiol Rev. 1995;8:146-159.

141. Martynowicz MA, Prakash UBS. Pulmonary blastomycosis: An appraisal of diagnostic techniques. Chest. 2002;121:768-773.

142. Lemos LB, Guo M, Baliga M. Blastomycosis: Organ involvement and etiologic diagnosis. A review of 123 patients from Mississippi. Ann Diagn Pathol. 2000; 4:391-406.

143. Lemos LB, Baliga M, Taylor BD, et al. Bronchoalveolar lavage for diagnosis of fungal disease: Five years experience in a southern United States rural area with many blastomycosis cases. Acta Cytol. 1995;39:1101-1111.

144. Graham AR. Fungal autofluorescence with ultraviolet illumination. Am J Clin Pathol. 1983;79:231-234.

145. Monheit JG, Cowman DF, Moore DG. Rapid detection of fungi in tissues using calcofluor white and fluorescence microscopy. Arch Pathol Lab Med. 1984;108:616-618.

146. Kaplan W, Kaufman L. Specific fluorescent antiglobulins for the detection and identification of *Blastomyces dermatitidis* yeast phase cells. Mycopathologia. 1963;19:173-180.

147. Stockman L, Clark MA, Hunt JM, et al. Evaluation of commercially available acridine ester-labeled chemiluminescent DNA probes for culture identification of *Blastomyces dermatitidis*, *Coccidioides immitis*, *Cryptococcus neoformans* and *Histoplasma capsulatum*. J Clin Microbiol. 1993;31:845-850.

148. George RB, Lambert RS, Bruce MJ, et al. Radioimmunoassay: A sensitive screening test for histoplasmosis and blastomycosis. Am Rev Respir Dis. 1981;124:407-410.

149. Lambert RS, George RB. Evaluation of enzyme immunoassay as a rapid screening test for histoplasmosis and blastomycosis. Am Rev Respir Dis. 1987;136:316-319.

150. Turner SH, Kaufman L, Jalbert M. Diagnostic assessment of an enzyme-linked immunosorbent assay for human and canine blastomycosis. J Clin Microbiol. 1986;23:294-297.

151. Reiss E, Tanaka K, Bruker G, et al. Molecular diagnosis and epidemiology of fungal infections. Med Mycol. 1998;36:249-257.

152. Walsh TJ, Chanock SJ. Diagnosis of invasive fungal infections: Advances in nonculture systems. Curr Clin Top Infect Dis. 1998;18:101-153.

153. Yeo SF, Wong B. Current status of nonculture methods for diagnosis of invasive fungal infections. Clin Microbiol Rev. 2002;15:465-484.

154. Walsh TJ, Larone DH, Schell WA, Mitchell TG. *Histoplasma, Blastomyces, Coccidioides*, and other dimorphic fungi causing systemic mycoses. In: Murray PR, Barron EJ, Jorgensen JH, et al, eds. Manual of Clinical Microbiology. 8th ed. Washington, DC: ASM Press; 2003:1781-1797.

155. Turenne CY, Sanche SE, Hoban DJ, et al. Rapid identification of fungi by using the ITS2 genetic region and an automated fluorescent capillary electrophoresis system. J Clin Microbiol. 1999;37:1846-1851.

156. Einsele H, Hebart H, Roller G, et al. Detection and identification of fungal pathogens in blood by using molecular probes. J Clin Microbiol. 1997;35:1353-1360.

157. Lindsley MD, Hurst SF, Iqbal NJ, Morrison CJ. Rapid identification of dimorphic and yeast-like fungal pathogens using specific DNA probes. J Clin Microbiol. 2001;39:3505-3511.

158. Bialek R, Cirera AC, Herrmann T, et al. Nested PCR assay for detection of *Blastomyces dermatitidis* DNA in paraffin-embedded canine tissue. J Clin Microbiol. 2003;41:205-208.

159. Wheat J, Wheat H, Connolly P, et al. Cross-reactivity in *Histoplasma capsulatum* variety *capsulatum* antigen assays of urine samples from patients with endemic mycoses. Clin Infect Dis. 1997;24:1169-1171.

160. Lagging LM, Breland CM, Kennedy DJ, et al. Delayed treatment of pulmonary blastomycosis causing vertebral osteomyelitis, paraspinal abscess and spinal cord compression. Scand J Infect Dis. 1994;26:111-115.

161. Sarosi GA. Management of fungal disease. Am Rev Respir Dis. 1983;127:250-253.

162. Chapman SW, Bradsher RW Jr, Campbell GD Jr, et al. Practice guidelines for the management of patient with blastomycosis. Clin Infect Dis. 2000;30:679-683.

163. National Institute of Allergy and Infectious Diseases Study Group. Treatment of blastomycosis and histoplasmosis with ketoconazole: Results of a prospective randomized trial. Ann Intern Med. 1985;103:861-872.

164. Sagg MS, Dismukes WE. Treatment of histoplasmosis and blastomycosis. Chest. 1988;93:848-851.

165. Johnson P, Sarosi G. Current therapy of major fungal diseases of the lung. Infect Dis Clin North Am. 1991;5:635-645.

166. Brummer E, Bhagavathula PR, Hanson LH, et al. Synergy of itraconazole with macrophages in killing *Blastomyces dermatitidis*. Antimicrob Agents Chemother. 1992;36:2487-2492.

167. Chapman SW, Rogers PD, Rinaldi MG, et al. Susceptibilities of clinical and laboratory isolates of *Blastomyces dermatitidis* to ketoconazole, itraconazole and fluconazole. Antimicrob Agents Chemother. 1998;42:978-980.

168. Dismukes WE, Bradsher RW, Cloud GC, et al. Itraconazole therapy for blastomycosis and histoplasmosis. Am J Med. 1992;93:489-497.

169. Bradsher RW. Histoplasmosis and blastomycosis. Clin Infect Dis. 1996;22:5102-5111.

170. Daneshmend TK, Warnock DW. Clinical pharmacokinetics of ketoconazole. Clin Pharmacokinet. 1988;14:13-34.

171. Cleary JD, Taylor JW, Chapman SW. Itraconazole in antifungal therapy. Ann Pharmacother. 1992;26:502-509.

172. Tucker RM, Denning DW, Hanson LH, et al. Interactions of azoles with rifampin, phenytoin, and carbamazepine: In vitro and clinical observations. Clin Infect Dis. 1992;14:165-174.

173. Wise GJ, Goldberg PE, Kozinin PJ. Do the imidazoles have a role in the management of genitourinary fungal infections? J Urol. 1985;133:61-64.

174. Honig PK, Wortham DC, Zamani K, et al. Terfenadine-ketoconazole interaction: Pharmacokinetic and electrocardiographic consequences. JAMA. 1992;269:1513-1518.

175. Itraconazole. Med Lett Drugs Ther. 1993;35:7-9.

176. Pappas PG, Bradsher RW, Chapman SW, et al. Treatment of blastomycosis with fluconazole: A pilot study. Clin Infect Dis. 1995;20:267-271.

177. Pappas PG, Bradsher RW, Kaufman CA, et al. Treatment of blastomycosis with higher dose fluconazole. Clin Infect Dis. 1997;25:200-205.

178. Campbell GD, Chapman SW. Blastomycosis. Semin Respir Med. 1987;9:164-170.

179. Hammon JW, Prager RL. Surgical management of fungal diseases of the chest. Surg Clin North Am. 1980;60:897-912.

180. Newsom BD, Hardy JD. Pulmonary fungal infections: Survey of 159 cases with surgical implications. J Thorac Cardiovasc Surg. 1982;83:218-226.

181. Edson RS, Keys TF. Treatment of primary pulmonary blastomycosis: Results of long-term follow-up. Mayo Clin Proc. 1981;56:683-685.

Coccidioides Species

JOHN GALGIANI

Although the systemic fungal infection now known as *coccidioidomycosis* has been recognized for more than a century,[1] more recently its importance has increased throughout the nonendemic and the endemic regions of the world.[2] A medical intern is credited with identifying in 1892 the first patient who had widespread disease.[3] Organisms seen microscopically mistakenly were thought to be parasites, and only several years later was the true mycotic etiology determined and the agent given the name *Coccidioides immitis*.[4] For 3 decades, coccidioidomycosis was thought to be a rare and nearly always fatal infection. In 1929, an accidental laboratory exposure of a medical student at Stanford University resulted in only a transient respiratory infection. His unexpected survival stimulated a reassessment of the natural history of coccidioidal infections, soon leading to the recognition that a common respiratory condition in the San Joaquin Valley of California (valley fever) was the more usual result of infection.[5] This link was corroborated with the development by Smith and colleagues[6] of a specific skin test and serologic assays for coccidioidomycosis, tests still in clinical use today. With these tools, the clinical spectrum was well described by the mid-1950s (an excellent monograph was published by Fiese[7] and remains a valuable contemporary reference on the disease).

The reemergence of coccidioidomycosis can be attributed to changes in demography and in contemporary medicine. First, the populations at risk of exposure are greatly expanded. Regions in which *Coccidioides* spp. are endemic, which previously were sparsely populated, now encompass major metropolitan centers, such as Phoenix, Arizona. With this growth has come greatly increased tourism and commerce-related movement of people into and out of infected areas. As a result, coccidioidal infections occur in increased numbers. Second, a major segment of the population has emerged with compromised cellular immunity because of either underlying diseases or immunosuppressive therapies to control other diseases.[8-19] These patients are unusually susceptible to serious coccidioidal infections, and as a result the severity of coccidioidal infections as a public health problem has increased. Third, advances in prevention and treatment of fungal infections have been made that offer new opportunities for management. These trends have made coccidioidomycosis more relevant to physicians everywhere. Finally, the emergence of *Coccidioides* spp. as potential agents of bioterrorism was identified by the Centers for Disease Control and Prevention (CDC) in 1997. Since then, awareness of this possibility has become even greater with the increased incidence of terrorism as an international tactic and because of technical advances in genetic transformation, which adds to the potential to weaponize *Coccidioides* spp.[20-23]

MYCOLOGY

Coccidioides spp. are dimorphic fungi that exist as either a mycelium or a unique structure known as a spherule.[24] Both forms of growth are asexual, and it is not possible to classify *Coccidioides* spp. in relation to other fungi by classic taxonomy. By molecular analysis, however, *Coccidioides* spp. appear most related to other ascomycetes, most closely to the medically important organisms *Blastomyces dermatitidis* and *Histoplasma capsulatum*.[25] Although a sexual phase has not been found, population genetic studies suggest that one does exist.[26] More recently, two genetically distinct populations have been identified among the etiologic agents of coccidioidomycosis. The occurrence of two populations correlated with separate endemic regions where patients resided. This finding prompted classification of the previously known single species, *C. immitis,* into two species *C. immitis* and *Coccidioides posadasii.* Most of the *C. immitis* isolates have been obtained from California, whereas *C. posadasii* isolates have been obtained from patients in other states and from countries outside of the United States.[27] Extensive DNA sequence analysis of *C. posadasii* strains offered the means to deduce geographic origin of infection.[28] The two species have shown few phenotypic differences, however, and the clinical manifestations resulting from infection with either species appear similar. Molecular identification methods for routine differentiation of *C. immitis* from *C. posadasii* in clinical laboratories are currently unavailable, and until such methods are developed, references in the literature to *C. immitis* may actually be referring to *C. posadasii.* More appropriately, all isolates that have not been subjected to genetic characterization are designated best as simply *Coccidioides* spp., which is the convention employed in this chapter.

Mycelial (Saprobic) Growth

On routine microbiologic nutrient agar media and presumably in the soil, *Coccidioides* spp. grow as mycelia by apical extension, and true septa form along its course. Maturation within 1 week of growth results in alternating mycelial cells undergoing a process of autolysis and thinning of the cell walls. The remaining cells (arthroconidia), which become barrel shaped and approximately 5 μm in length, develop a hydrophobic outer layer and become capable of remaining viable for long periods. The fragile attachments of arthroconidia to adjacent cell remnants make them prone to separation by physical disruption or mild air turbulence. As a result, arthroconidia become airborne in a form capable of deposition in the lungs if inhaled.

Spherule (Parasitic) Growth

In the lungs, arthroconidia remodel into spherical cells, shedding their hydrophobic outer wall.[29,30] During this phase, nuclear division and cell multiplication occur and septa extend from the internal surface of the wall to transect the growing spherule into scores of subcompartments, each containing viable daughter cells or endospores. In tissue, spherules can become 75 μm in diameter (Fig. 264-1). As a spherule matures, its outer wall thins and eventually ruptures. Early

in the course of experimental infections and in specialized media in vitro, this rupture occurs in approximately 4 days, and with the release of endospores, the number of viable fungal units is amplified approximately 2 logs, each of which may continue to propagate in tissue or to revert to mycelial growth if removed from the site of an infection.

EPIDEMIOLOGY

Geographic Range

Coccidioides spp. are endemic to the soils of only certain regions of the Western Hemisphere, nearly all of which are within the north and south 40-degree latitudes. Well-described transport of arthroconidia, either in soil on fomites[31] or as the result of unusually severe dust storms,[32] has produced infections in persons without endemic exposure, but this generally has not established new areas of endemicity. Regions of the United States in which *Coccidioides* spp. are endemic are shown in Figure 264-2. These regions generally have the characteristics of the "lower Sonoran life zone," which include an arid climate, yearly rainfall of 5 to 20 inches, hot summers, winters with few freezes, and alkaline soil, although small areas of endemnicity have been found unexpectedly elsewhere.[33] Other areas where *Coccidioides* spp. have been identified include Mexico (adjacent to the U.S. border; western portions of Sonora, Nayarit, Jalisco, and Michoacan; central regions, including Coahulia, Durango, and San Luis Potosi), Central America (Guatemala, Honduras, Nicaragua), and South America (Argentina, Paraguay, Venezuela, Colombia, Brazil).[34]

Within the endemic regions, the likelihood of finding *Coccidioides* spp. in soil samples varies considerably among different locations and different seasons. The fungus is recovered most easily toward the end of winter rains.[35] This is opposite to the seasonal relationship for acquisition of new infections, which in California and Arizona occur most frequently during the summer months after the soil has become dry. In Arizona, there is a second peak of new clinical infections in October, which corresponds to a similar dry period after the late summer rains in that region.[36] Colonies of *Coccidioides* spp. seem not to be distributed uniformly within the endemic region and may be quite sparse.[37]

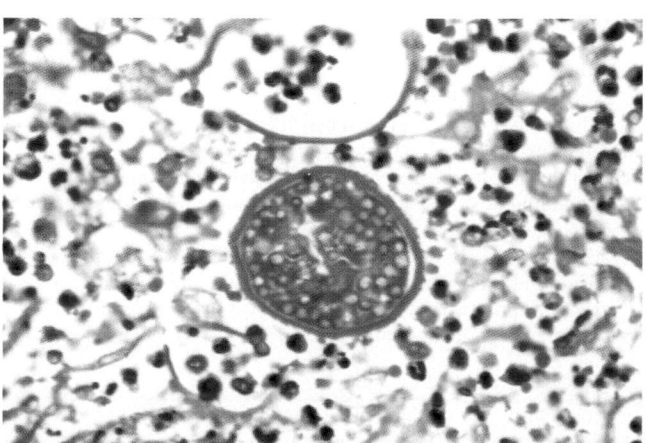

FIGURE 264-1. Photomicrograph of a spherule in a tissue. Hematoxylin and eosin staining. *(Courtesy of Richard Sobonya, M.D., University of Arizona.)*

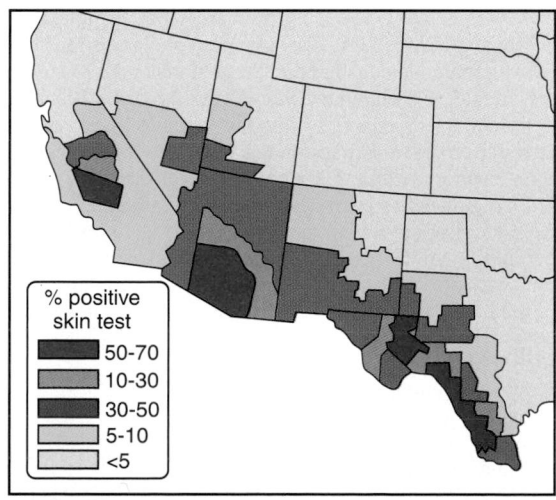

% positive skin test

50-70
10-30
30-50
5-10
<5

FIGURE 264-2. Map of the U.S. regions endemic for coccidioidomycosis as evidence by a survey of skin test reactivity to coccidioidin. *(From Edwards PQ, Palmer CD. Prevalence of sensitivity to coccidioidin, with special reference to specific and nonspecific reactions to coccidioidin and to histoplasmin. Dis Chest. 1957;31:35-60.)*

Rates of Coccidioidal Infection

Prevalence surveys in the 1950s of skin test reactivity to coccidioidal antigens in school-age children of California's central valley suggested that the annual risk of infection was approximately 15%.[38] Smith and co-workers[39] showed that 25% to 50% of military personnel in the San Joaquin Valley experienced conversion of their coccidioidal skin during a single year. More contemporary estimates from the same areas in California and from Tucson, Arizona, indicate that the risk has declined to approximately 3% per year.[40,41] Because of these lower rates and because of the large influx of new residents to the endemic regions from nonendemic locales (in 2005, estimated to total >7 million persons for southern Arizona and southern central California), the proportion of persons within the endemic region with prior infection is approximately 30%. The expected number of infections is on the order of 150,000 annually.

The numbers of infections reported to state departments of public health show significant differences from year to year. Some variation has been associated with total winter rainfall, with more cases occurring in the summers after wetter winters.[42] Occasionally, epidemics also have been associated with disruption of infected soil, by human intent, such as with archaeologic excavation[43]; after natural events, such as severe dust storms or earthquakes[44]; or during military maneuvers.[45] Some fluctuations in rates of infections are not explained, however. Such is the case for an exceptionally large epidemic in California's Central Valley in the period 1992 to 1995, in which the incidence of infection at times was more than 10 times that normally reported.[46] From the second half of the 1990s, Arizona also has been experiencing epidemic rates.[47,48]

PATHOGENESIS AND CONTROL

Nearly all infections are the result of inhaling arthroconidia. Cutaneous inoculations have been reported, producing lymphatic extension to regional lymph nodes and resolving without treatment. These occurrences are exceedingly rare, however.[49] A single arthroconidium may be sufficient to produce a naturally acquired respiratory infection. This is the case for experimental infections in mice,[50] and air sampling within coccidioidal endemic regions suggests that the ambient density of arthroconidia in the air is very low.[51,52] The size of the arthroconidium would allow its deposition within the terminal bronchiole but probably not as far as the alveolar space. As an arthroconidium transforms into a spherule, inflammation ensues, forming a local pulmonary lesion. Extracts of *Coccidioides* spp. have been shown to react with complement, releasing mediators of chemotaxis for neutrophils.[53] In some infections, *Coccidioides* spp. leaves the lungs to establish disseminated lesions in other parts of the body. In this sequence of events, fungal elements must move from the distal bronchiole into the lung parenchyma, gain entry into the vascular space, and leave the vascular space to create extrapulmonary sites of infection. It is possible that endospores within macrophages travel through lymphatics to the blood stream, as has been described for dissemination of tuberculosis and histoplasmosis. This possibility also is compatible with the common finding of infected hilar, peritracheal, and cervical lymph nodes in patients with extrapulmonary coccidioidal infections.[54] Specific details of any of these events are unknown, however.

Histopathology

Microscopic examination of tissue infected with *Coccidioides* spp. shows elements of acute and chronic inflammation. Acute inflammation, including neutrophils and eosinophils, is associated with active infections and rupturing spherules.[54,55] Granulomatous lesions that include lymphocytes, histiocytes, and multinucleated giant cells are associated with chronic or arrested infections and with mature unruptured spherules. In patients with widespread infections, it is common to find both inflammatory responses represented concurrently at different anatomic sites.

Host Defenses

Control of coccidioidomycosis depends on T lymphocytes. This conclusion is supported by studies of experimentally produced infections in mice[56-60] and by the increased severity of naturally acquired infections in T cell–deficient patients.[9-11,14,15-18] Peripheral blood mononuclear cells from patients with disseminated coccidioidomycosis have virtually no interferon-γ response to coccidioidal antigens.[61] This is in contrast to the brisk stimulation of similar leukocyte preparations from patients in whom coccidioidal infections are competently controlled and who have delayed-type dermal hypersensitivity to coccidioidal skin-testing antigens.[62] These findings are consistent with an absent Th1-type response described in some experimental animals[63-65] and human infectious diseases in which cellular immunity plays a role. In humans, however, despite the observed depression of interferon-γ, interleukin-4 and interleukin-10 levels were not reciprocally elevated,[62] which would be indicative of a Th2 response.

In addition to T cell–mediated control of infection, innate cellular responses may contribute to host defense. Inhibition of growth of *Coccidioides* spp. can be shown in vitro by human neutrophils and mononuclear cells from persons with or without prior coccidioidal infection as judged by skin test reactivity to coccidioidal antigens.[66] Although neutrophils do not seem to be fungicidal against *Coccidioides* spp., mononuclear cells or natural killer cells have been shown to reduce fungal viability.[67,68] These innate cellular inhibitory effects are most evident against arthroconidia or endospores and are lost as spherules increase in size and mature.[69] Extrapolating from these in vitro observations, innate defenses may serve primarily to slow fungal proliferation after infection, transforming what otherwise might be a more fulminant infection to a more subacute or chronic process.

Coccidioidal infections engender a variety of humoral responses to several different antigens in patients, and as discussed subsequently, several are diagnostically useful. None have been found so far to play a role in host defenses against *Coccidioides* spp., however.

CLINICAL MANIFESTATIONS

At least one half to two thirds of all infections due to *Coccidioides* spp. are either inapparent or sufficiently mild not to prompt medical evaluation.[39] Many other coccidioidal infections produce a respiratory illness that is indistinguishable from a variety of other diseases without specific testing.[70] Some estimates suggest that within the endemic regions coccidioidomycosis may account for a quarter of all community-acquired pneumonias.[71] Nonetheless, misunderstandings of the manifestations of coccidioidomycosis or the lack of conviction that diagnosis of early infections is important has led to gross disparities between the numbers of expected and reported coccidioidal infections. Public health statistics for Arizona in 2001 represent less than 10% of the expected 30,000 new illnesses due to coccidioidal infections.[48] Underdiagnosis may be even more likely for patients with coccidioidomycosis evaluated outside the endemic region.[72,73] Whether detected or not, most infections follow a self-limited course, with only a few producing residual sequelae or chronic progressive infections. Although complications typically are manifest within weeks or up to 2 years after the original infection, the severity of the initial respiratory infection frequently does not correlate with the likelihood of complications. In this context, the identification of even mild primary infections takes on added significance and clinical relevance.

Early Respiratory Infection

The first symptoms of the primary infection usually appear 7 to 21 days after exposure. Although most infections seem to develop as a result of exposure to small numbers of arthroconidia, when exposure is unusually intense symptoms are more likely to appear early. In an epidemic of coccidioidomycosis that occurred in the San Joaquin Valley of California between 1991 and 1994,[74] the findings for 536 patients with new infections included cough (73%), chest pain (44%), shortness of breath (32%), fever (76%), and fatigue (39%). These findings are typical of earlier reports. Although the infection often is subacute in development, patients occasionally report abrupt onset of symptoms, especially that of pleurisy. Weight loss also is a common sign, and headache has been noted in 21% of patients in the absence of meningeal infection.[36] Skin manifestations develop as part of the primary illness. Most frequent and easily missed is a nonpruritic fine papular rash that occurs early and transiently during the illness. More striking are *erythema nodosum* and *erythema multiforme,* which have strong predilections for women. Migratory arthralgias also are common complaints, and the triad of fever, *erythema nodosum,* and arthralgias (especially of the knees and ankles) has been termed "desert rheumatism." Routine laboratory findings are usually normal except for an increase in the erythrocyte sedimentation rate. Peripheral blood eosinophilia may be present, occasionally accounting for two thirds of the circulating leukocytes. Chest radiograph results are abnormal in more than half of patients. Common findings include unilateral infiltrates, hilar adenopathy, and pleural effusions. Persistent hilar or peritracheal adenopathy is associated with extrathoracic spread of infection. Lung cavities are present initially in approximately 8% of infections recognized in adults but are less frequent in children.

Uncommonly, coccidioidal pneumonia presents as a diffuse process leading to respiratory failure, either because of high-inoculum exposure[75,76] or because of fungi in the blood stream seeding the lung in many sites (Fig. 264-3).[15] The presentation is often fulminant, mimicking that of septic shock or a bacterial infection, and despite treatment, mortality is high. Approximately one third of human immunodeficiency virus (HIV)–infected patients present with this radiographic appearance. Although fungemia associated with diffuse pulmonary infiltrates may occur in immunologically intact patients,[77] it is nearly always due to a recognizable cellular immunodeficiency state. In HIV-infected patients, the CD4+ counts are typically less than 100 cells/mm³, and the viral load is probably high.

Although some of the presenting symptoms are statistically more likely to occur with coccidioidal infections than with respiratory illness of other etiologies, the overlap of clinical syndromes is substantial.[70] For most patients, specific testing is required to secure a definite diagnosis of coccidioidomycosis.

Most coccidioidal respiratory infections resolve without complications, taking several weeks to several months to do so. When resolution of the self-limited illness is protracted, the symptom of fatigue, disproportionate to other evidence of infection, is frequently the last to resolve and may be a source of considerable distress. A few patients with infections develop various pulmonary sequelae, and even fewer patients manifest disseminated infection outside the lungs. Despite their relative infrequency, these complications pose significant difficulties in diagnosis and management (discussed later).

Pulmonary Nodules and Cavities

Approximately 4% of pulmonary infections result in a nodule, ranging up to 5 cm in diameter. Typically a nodule causes no symptoms but may be indistinguishable from a neoplasm without histologic examination.[78] Occasionally, nodules liquefy and drain into a bronchus to form a cavity (Fig. 264-4).

Pulmonary cavities may be present initially or in the later stages of the primary infection. They usually are peripheral and solitary, and with time most develop a distinctive thin wall.[79] Cavities may not cause any symptoms, and half close within 2 years. Others are associated with local symptoms of pleuritic pain, cough, or hemoptysis (Figs. 264-5 and 264-6). Mycetoma may develop within cavities, either from mycelia of *Coccidioides* spp.[80] or with other species of fungi (Fig. 264-7). Another infrequent but well-recognized complication is that a peripheral coccidioidal cavity ruptures into the pleural space. Commonly, ruptures occur in athletic young men and are not associated with underlying immunodeficiency. Because the fungal walls of *Coccidioides* spp. are inflammatory, ruptured coccidioidal cavities produce fluid in the pleural space, and the presence of an air-fluid level within the pleural space is a clue that the process is not a spontaneous pneumothorax or a ruptured pulmonary bleb (Fig. 264-8). Prompt surgical correction of the defect is the preferred treatment, unless there is a delay in diagnosis or other medical conditions preclude an operation.[81]

Chronic Fibrocavitary Pneumonia

In contrast to thin-walled coccidioidal cavities, some patients develop a chronic fibrotic pneumonic process that is characterized by pulmonary infiltrates and pulmonary cavitation.[82] This form of infection is not common among patients with T-cell deficiencies but seems to be associated with diabetes or preexisting pulmonary fibrosis related to smoking or other causes. Involvement of more than one lobe is more common, and these lesions may cause systemic symptoms, such as night sweats and weight loss, and local symptoms.

Extrapulmonary Dissemination

C. immitis spreads beyond the lungs in approximately 0.5% of all infections in the general population. Several factors dramatically increase the risk of dissemination, however. Patients who have immunodeficiency conditions, such as the later stages of HIV infection, therapies to prevent solid organ rejection, high-dose corticosteroid therapy (equivalent to long-term prednisone doses >20 mg/day), therapeutic inhibitors of tumor necrosis factor, and Hodgkin's lymphoma, are at much greater risk of dissemination.[8-10,15-19,21,22] Two thirds of renal transplant recipients who developed coccidioidal infection progressed to dissemination.[10,11] With transplantation, the risk is mostly due to either newly acquired disease or reactivation from prior infection. Instances of transmission by the engrafted organ have been reported, however.[12,13] Men are more likely to develop dissemination than women.[35] Dissemination also is more likely, however, if infection is diagnosed first during pregnancy, especially during the third trimester or in the immediate postpartum period.[83,84] There also seems to be an increased risk of dissemination among

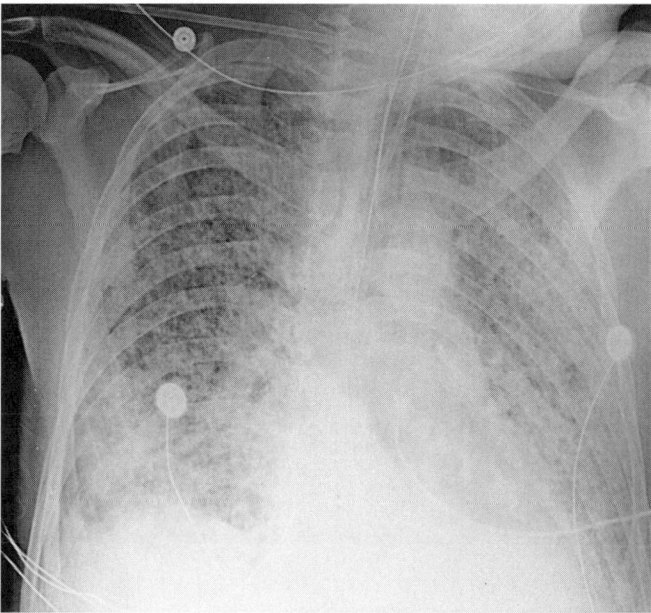

FIGURE 264-3. Diffuse reticulonodular infiltrates due to *Coccidioides immitis* in a patient with human immunodeficiency virus infection.

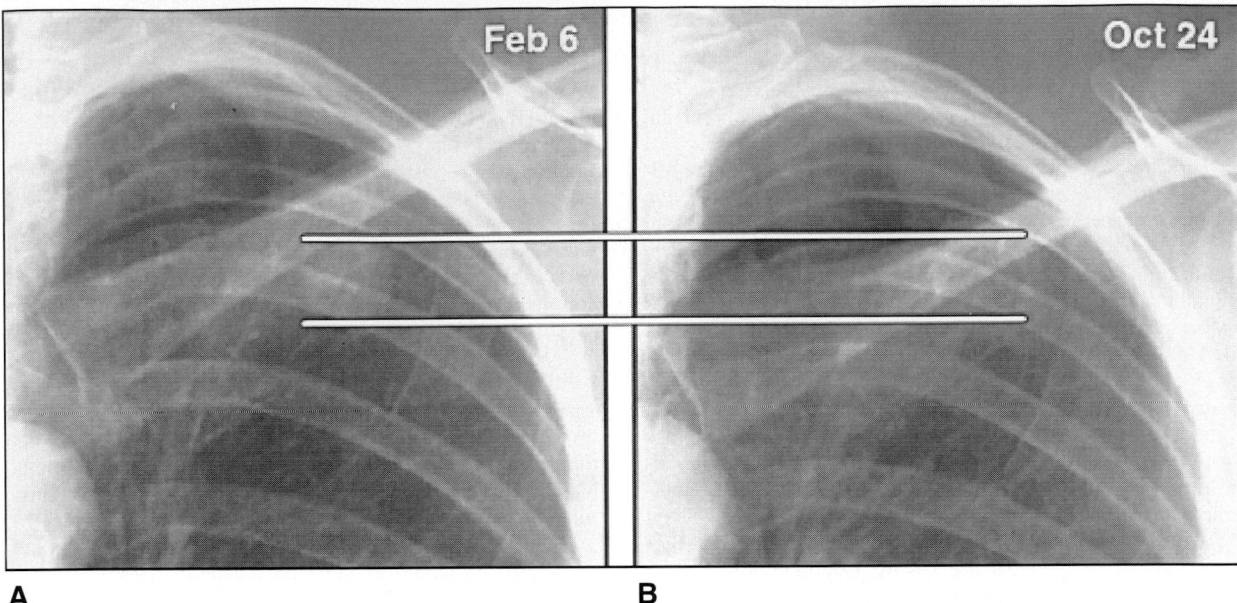

FIGURE 264-4. Cavitation of a coccidiodal nodule. A 1.8-cm nodule can be seen in **A**. Eight months later (**B**), this lesion has become a thin-walled cavity.

persons of African or Filipino ancestry, although the exact magnitude of the risk is controversial.[85]

Extrapulmonary dissemination is not associated often with pulmonary complications. Many patients with disseminated coccidioidal infection have entirely normal chest radiographs. The most common site of dissemination is the skin. Lesions range from superficial maculopapular lesions, to keratotic and verrucose ulcers, to subcutaneous fluctuant abscesses. There is a predilection for lesions at the nasolabial fold (Fig. 264-9). Although most extrapulmonary dissemination is the result of hematogenous spread, supraclavicular and cervical lymphadenopathy also is a frequent presentation and probably represents lymphatic drainage from the primary pulmonary infection.

Joints and bones also are a common site of dissemination. Joint infections differ from the self-limited joint complaints of desert rheumatism in that infections typically are asymmetrically distributed and are associated with a prominent synovitis and effusion. Although any joint can become infected, the knee is involved most frequently; other common locations include the joints of the hands and wrists, the feet and ankles, and the pelvis.[86-88] Infection may be limited to the synovium or may erode to involve the underlying bone. Alternatively, bones may be involved first with secondary extension into the joint.[89] Although long bones may be affected, vertebral infection is much more common. Involvement of multiple vertebrae is typical. These may coalesce to produce anterior or posterior paraspinous abscesses (Fig. 264-10). Magnetic resonance imaging (MRI) is often helpful in defining the exact location of these lesions.[90]

Coccidioidal meningitis is the most serious form of disseminated infection. Untreated, it is nearly always fatal within 2 years of diag-

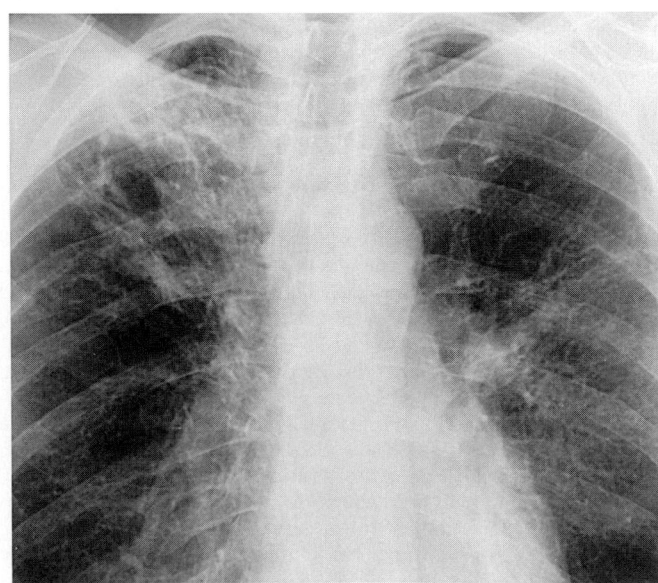

FIGURE 264-5. Pulmonary cavity in the right upper lobe with surrounding fibrosis.

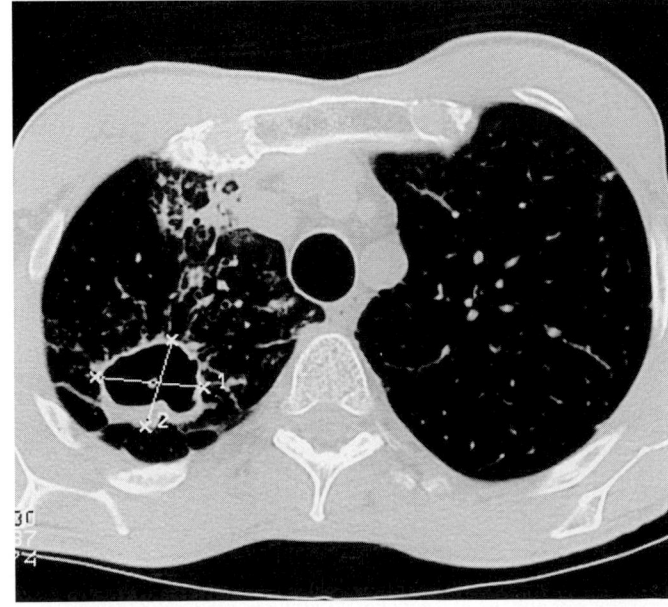

FIGURE 264-6. Computed tomography scan of the cavity shown in Figure 264-4.

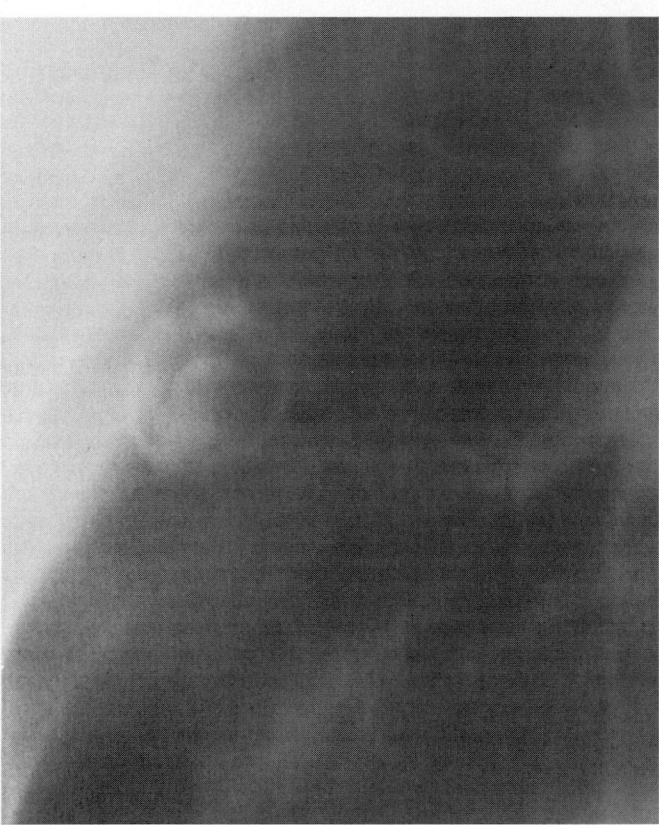

FIGURE 264-7. Mycetoma in the right lung of a coccidoidal cavity. Bronchoscopy specimens yielded *Coccidioides immitis* in culture. *(From Winn RE, Johnson R, Galgiani JN, et al. Cavitary coccidioidomycosis with fungus ball formation. Chest. 1994;105:412-416.)*

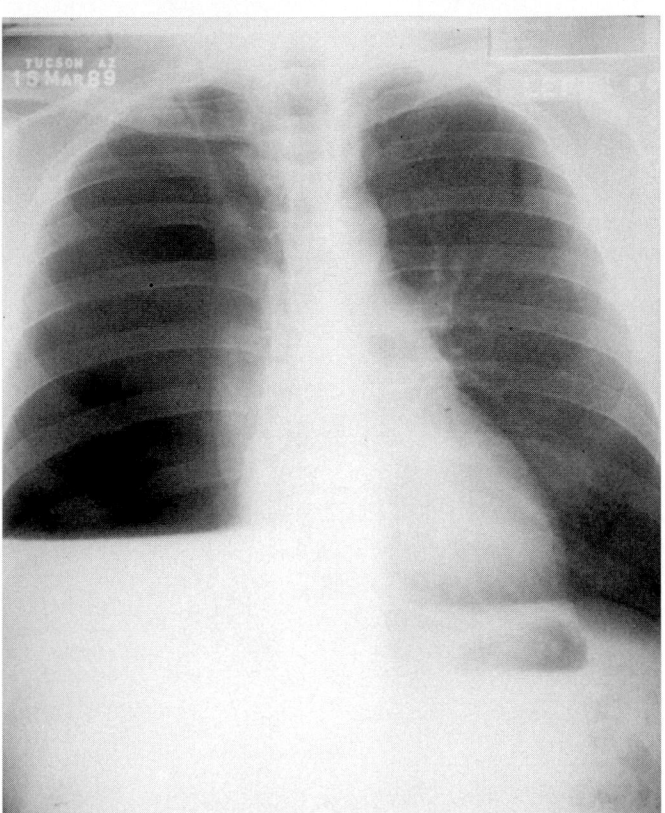

FIGURE 264-8. Pyopneumothorax resulting from a ruptured coccidioidal cavity. *(From Snyder LS, Galgiani JN. Coccidioidomycosis: the initial pulmonary infection and beyond. Semin Respir Crit Care Med. 1997;18:235-247.)*

nosis.[91,92] Similar to most other complications of coccidioidomycosis, meningitis usually develops relatively soon after the initial infection. In one study, all of 22 patients who developed meningitis after a large dust storm did so an average of 5.4 weeks after the onset of symptoms.[93] Similarly, a review of cases from the Department of Veterans Affairs and military records showed that 20 of 25 patients developed meningitis within 6 months of their first symptoms of infection.[91,92] Common presenting symptoms are headache, vomiting, and altered mental status. In addition to an elevated cerebrospinal fluid, white blood cell count, elevated protein, and depressed glucose, eosinophils are occasionally prominent.[94] The main areas of involvement are the basilar meninges. Hydrocephalus is a common complication, especially in children.[95] Attention has been drawn to vasculitis and focal intracerebral coccidioidal abscesses as less frequent complications.[96-99]

DIAGNOSIS

The manifestations of most early coccidioidal infections overlap substantially with those of other respiratory infections.[70] Specific laboratory testing usually is required to establish a diagnosis of coccidioidomycosis. In regions where *Coccidioides* spp. are endemic, this testing is commonplace. In most of the rest of the United States, the possibility of coccidioidomycosis is unlikely to be considered, unless a geographic exposure is identified. It is hard to overestimate the importance of obtaining a detailed travel history as a crucial first step in diagnosis. Because the incubation period usually is 1 to 3 weeks, endemic exposure within this period should raise the possibility of coccidioidomycosis to account for a respiratory condition of new onset. Exposure need not be extensive. Infections have occurred in patients whose only exposure occurred while changing airplanes at the Phoenix airport or during a single drive across California's Central Valley.

Complications of the initial infection, such as chronic pneumonia or extrathoracic dissemination, may take longer to become apparent but nearly always emerge within 2 years after exposure. One exception to this rule is the detection of a pulmonary nodule, which may persist without symptoms for many years after the original infection. Another special case is the setting of waning immunity, such as after the development of acquired immunodeficiency syndrome or with immunosuppressive therapy associated with solid organ transplantation. In such circumstances, exposure to *Coccidioides* spp. in the distant past may be sufficient to account for the current clinical illness.[100]

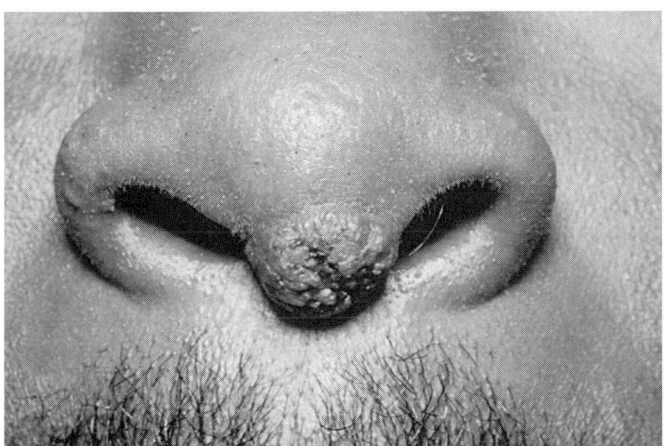

FIGURE 264-9. Ulcerative lesion of disseminated coccidioidal infection. *(From Galgiani JN. Coccidioidomycosis. West J Med. 1993;159:153-171.)*

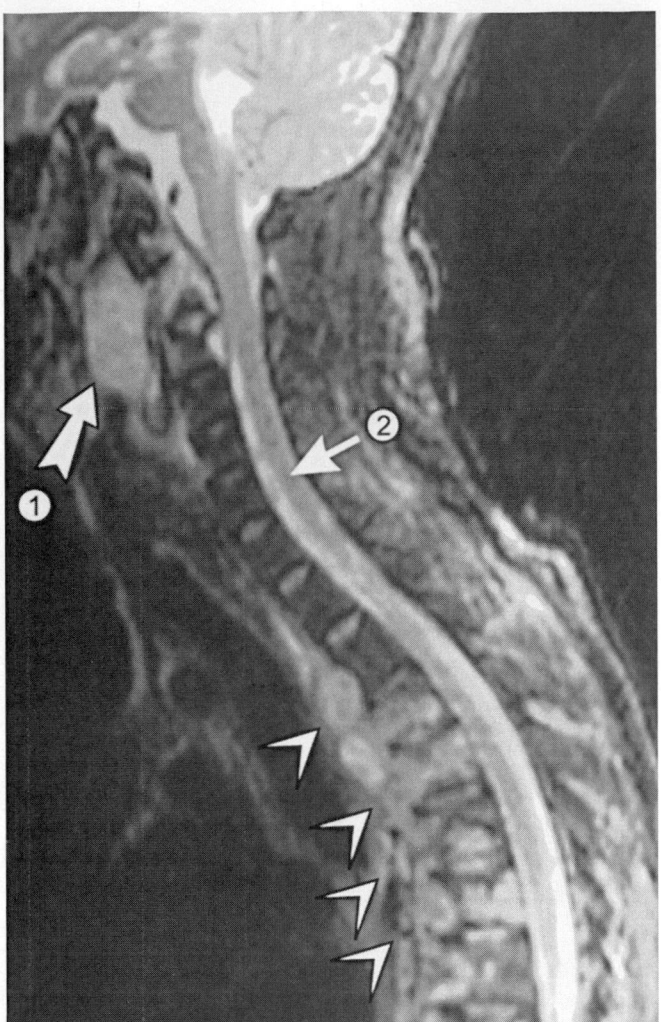

FIGURE 264-10. Sagittal magnetic resonance imaging shows an anterior paraspinous abscess extending from the base of the skull to the midthoracic vertebrae. *Arrow 1* points to an abscess that originated in a cervical vertebra and dissected anteriorly. *Arrow 2* identifies a normal spinal cord. The *other arrows* indicate abscesses anterior to the thoracic vertebrae. Multiple surgical procedures were required to control this infection.

When the possibility of coccidioidomycosis has been raised, diagnosis may be established in three ways: (1) identifying spherules in or recovering *C. immitis* from a clinical specimen; (2) detecting specific anticoccidioidal antibodies in serum, cerebrospinal fluid, or other bodily fluid; or (3) detecting dermal delayed-type hypersensitivity to coccidioidal antigens by skin testing.

Direct Examination and Culture

Isolating *Coccidioides* spp. from a patient is definitive evidence of a coccidioidal infection, and this diagnostic approach is used most frequently for patients with complicated pulmonary or disseminated syndromes. Sputum or other clinical specimens can be collected at no risk to personnel because the infection is not transmitted from the primary specimen. Direct microscopic examination of secretions can be done immediately or after the addition of potassium hydroxide. Calcofluor staining of the cell wall also may help to distinguish spherules from leukocytes. *Coccidioides* spp. cannot be detected by Gram staining. Spherules also can be stained by cytology stains (e.g., in bronchoscopy specimens)[101]; by hematoxylin and eosin stains; and by other specialized procedures, such as silver or periodic acid–Schiff staining.

Hematoxylin and eosin staining of spherules produces a distinctive autofluorescence that may help to identify a few organisms in tissues.[102] Using species-specific probes, in situ hybridization was not as sensitive as silver staining but was more specific.[103] Although culture results are more sensitive, identification of spherules by direct examination is more rapid and may speed diagnosis.

Coccidioides spp. grow well on most mycologic or bacteriologic media after 5 or 7 days of incubation. Aerobic conditions are required. When growth occurs, it is typically as a white (nonpigmented) mold. There are many exceptions to this general appearance, however, and the morphologic appearance is not reliable in determining whether the fungus is *Coccidioides* spp.[104] When growth is evident on culture medium, care should be taken not to open the culture container except in an appropriate biocontainment cabinet. Cultures at this stage are highly infectious, and infections have occurred in laboratory personnel when cultures have not been handled properly.[105]

The mycelial form of growth is not specific for *Coccidioides* spp., and further testing is required for species identification. The two most common ways for microbiologists to do this are to detect a specific coccidioidal antigen (exoantigen) in an extract of the fungus and to detect a specific ribosomal RNA sequence using a DNA probe.[106-108] At present, commercially available molecular procedures are not available to differentiate between *C. immitis* and *C. posadasii*. When the fungal isolate is identified as *Coccidioides* spp., it is subject to strict federal security regulations as are developed for all select agents of bioterrorism as listed by the CDC. Laboratories that are not registered with the CDC are liable for severe criminal penalties if isolates are not transferred to a registered laboratory or destroyed within 7 days after identification. In place of maintaining these capabilities, many clinical laboratories refer the culture to a reference laboratory where identification is completed.

Serologic Testing

Serologic testing is the most frequent means of diagnosing primary coccidioidal infections because the patients may not be able to produce a sputum specimen, and fungal cultures often are not practical in an ambulatory setting. It also may be indispensable in establishing the cause of chronic meningitis because cultures of cerebrospinal fluid are commonly negative in coccidioidal meningitis. Of the variety of tests available, most are highly specific for an active infection.[109] Minimally reactive test results often are diagnostically important and should not be dismissed as insignificant. A negative serologic test never excludes the presence of a coccidioidal infection, however. Performing one or more repeated serologic tests over the course of 2 months increases the sensitivity of serologic diagnosis, especially for recently acquired infections.

Tube Precipitin Antibodies

Tube precipitin antibodies of this type originally were detected by the presence of a precipitin button that formed at the bottom of a test tube after overnight incubation of the patient's serum mixed with coccidioidal antigen.[110] Because IgM is most adept at forming immune precipitins, and these reactions were detected early after the onset of infection, this test sometimes is referred to as the *IgM test*. The antigen responsible for this reaction is a polysaccharide from the fungal cell wall. At some time within the first 3 weeks of symptoms, 90% of patients have tube precipitin antibodies detected, and this value declines to less than 5% more than 7 months after the onset of a self-limited illness.

Complement-Fixing Antibodies

When the patient's serum is mixed with coccidioidal antigen, an immune complex forms that consumes complement.[6] This event is detected by the subsequent addition of antibody-coated red blood cells, which normally lyse in the presence of complement but remain intact if the complement is depleted. Because IgG is the immunoglobulin class usually involved in these immune complexes, this test sometimes is referred to as the *IgG test*. Although this test originally was developed using various complex extracts of *C. immitis,* it now is known that the antigen involved in this reaction is a chitinase, and the gene encoding this enzyme has been cloned.[111-114] In early coccidioidal infections, complement-fixing antibodies are detected later and for longer periods than tube precipitin antibodies. Complex-fixing antibodies can be detected in other body fluids, and their detection in cerebrospinal fluid is an especially important aid to the diagnosis of coccidioidal meningitis. Complex-fixing antibody concentration is expressed as a titer, such as 1:4 or 1:64, indicating the greatest dilution of serum at which complement consumption still is detected. Traditionally, a titer of 1:16 or greater has been associated frequently with extrathoracic dissemination. Because of technical factors, however, end point results for the same serum samples may vary considerably on testing by different laboratories. More useful are serial determinations of complex-fixing antibody concentrations performed by the same laboratory. In general, higher titers reflect more extensive coccidioidal infection, and increasing complex-fixing antibody concentrations are associated with worsening disease.

Immunodiffusion Tests

Antibodies that were detected by the original tube precipitin or complex-fixing tests can be detected by alternative procedures known as the *immunodiffusion tube precipitin* and *immunodiffusion complex-fixing* tests. Although the immunodiffusion tube precipitin and immunodiffusion complex-fixing tests are conducted similarly, they use different antigens to measure different types of antibodies. As with the original tests, the immunodiffusion tube precipitin test result is reported by some laboratories as the IgM test result, and the immunodiffusion complex-fixing result is reported as the IgG test result. Both tests have been found to be at least as sensitive as their original counterparts.[115,116] Immunodiffusion tests are more amenable to being manufactured and distributed as commercially prepared kits, allowing the tests to be performed in laboratories not fully dedicated to a mycology specialty.

Enzyme-Linked Immunoassays

An enzyme immunoassay for coccidioidal antibodies is available commercially (Meridian Diagnostics, Cincinnati, OH). The test kit allows the specific detection of IgM or IgG antibodies. These results are not interchangeable, however, with the IgM test or IgG test results. Positive results with this commercial kit are highly sensitive for coccidioidal infection. Occasionally, false-positive results are noted, especially with the IgM enzyme immunoassay. At present, enzyme immunoassay results normally should be confirmed with immunodiffusion tube precipitin, immunodiffusion complex-fixing, or complex-fixing tests. When the more established tests fail to corroborate the enzyme immunoassay, the diagnosis is less firmly established.[117-119]

Latex Tests

Latex tests for coccidioidal antibodies also are commercially available. They are attractive to clinical laboratories because they are easy to use, and results are obtained rapidly. There are significant numbers of false-positive reactions, however, and the latex test is not as reliable as the other tests described in this section.[109]

Skin Testing

Dermal delayed-type hypersensitivity to coccidioidal antigens is highly specific for coccidioidal infection.[120] Because skin tests remain positive after infection in most people for life, however, a result may not be related to the current illness. In addition, some of the most serious infections may be associated with selective anergy, and the skin test may not show reactivity. As useful as skin test results are for epidemiologic studies, the test has important limitations as a screening procedure for recent infection. For patients in whom coccidioidomycosis has been diagnosed by other means, skin testing may have prognostic significance.[121] At present, coccidioidal skin testing reagents are not available commercially.

Other Approaches to Diagnosis

Antigenemia may occur either with early or with chronic coccidioidal infections and could be the basis of a diagnostic test.[122-125] The specific antigens responsible have not been characterized in any detail, and currently antigen detection remains a research rather than a clinically applicable procedure. It also is possible that polymerase chain reaction methodology could be used to detect *C. immititis*–specific nucleic acid sequences in patient specimens. Primers that seem to be specific for *C. immitis* exist,[126] and a report has suggested that coccidioidal nucleic acid has been detected in a few tissue and fluid samples from patients.[127] This approach has not been implemented yet for clinical use.

MANAGEMENT

General Approaches

The three components of managing coccidioidal infections are (1) assessment of the need for intervention, (2) selection of antifungal agents for patients who would benefit from treatment, and (3) choice of surgical procedures for débridement and reconstruction of destructive lesions. A practice guideline has been published[128] and is available online from the Infectious Diseases Society of America (IDSociety.org).

In patients with newly diagnosed coccidioidal infections, two crucial assessments are the extent of disease at present and factors that increase the risk of future complications. Assessment of the current extent of disease usually can be based on a careful review of systems and physical examination. When new focal complaints of discomfort or swelling are identified, these should be evaluated further with appropriate imaging or, if necessary, biopsy. Pain referable to bones might be assessed with a radionuclide bone scan,[129,130] an effusion that develops in a joint could be aspirated for cell count and culture, a progressively severe headache may require MRI and lumbar puncture to evaluate the possibility of meningitis, or a nonhealing skin lesion may need biopsy.

In the general population, pulmonary or extrapulmonary complications are uncommon. There is a special risk of disseminated infection, however, with conditions that prominently suppress T-cell immunity. The best recognized of these are HIV infection, immunosuppression to prevent rejection of a transplanted solid organ, and treatment with high doses of corticosteroids. Pregnancy, especially during the third trimester or the immediate peripartum period, also seems to predispose patients to a high risk of widespread dissemination. Patients with any of these risk factors nearly always should be treated with antifungal therapy even if there is no evidence of extrapulmonary spread. Patients with diabetes mellitus are not prone to extrapulmonary dissemination. They are more likely to develop pulmonary cavitation or chronic pneumonia, however, and may be more likely to require treatment.

Available antifungal agents include amphotericin B and the azole antifungal agents ketoconazole, fluconazole, and itraconazole. Their pharmacology is described in detail in Chapter 37. In coccidioidomycosis, selecting between amphotericin B and azole antifungals is based primarily on the degree of respiratory compromise in pulmonary infections or rate of progression of disseminated infections. Amphotericin B is perceived to have a more rapid onset of action, so despite its well-known toxicities, it is the preferred initial therapy for patients who have developed serious respiratory compromise or who are deteriorating rapidly. There is no evidence that a lipid formulation of amphotericin B improves on the efficacy of amphotericin B suspended with deoxycholate. Azole antifungals often are selected for patients with chronic processes because possible differences in rate of response to azole antifungals would be outweighed by their ease of administration and lack of toxicity. Ketoconazole is the only orally available azole antifungal approved by the U.S. Food and Drug Administration for the treatment of coccidioidomycosis, although several clinical trials have indicated that fluconazole and itraconazole also are efficacious.[131-138] There are no studies showing superiority of one azole antifungal over another. In a comparison of fluconazole (400 mg/day) and itraconazole (200 mg twice daily), the primary analysis showed that the two drugs were within 20% of each other in producing responses.[139] In a secondary analysis of skeletal lesions, twice as many subjects treated with itraconazole responded compared with subjects treated with fluconazole.

Because the manifestations, locations, and severity of progressive forms of coccidioidomycosis vary among patients, the need for surgery is determined by the nature of specific lesions on a case-by-case basis. In some patients, especially in whom there is extensive skeletal involvement, débridement and drainage of infected sites may be essential to achieving control of the infection. One reason may be that the spherule wall, a strong stimulus of inflammation,[140] is not degraded and cleared easily from large coccidioidal lesions by macrophages and other elements of the reticuloendothelial system. Even if therapy is effective in arresting fungal proliferation, fungal debris already present may continue to produce tissue destruction until it is surgically removed. Patients with persistent fever and malaise may benefit from drainage of large collections of pus. Also, surgery may be needed to stabilize bones that are structurally unsound or may be needed when the spinal cord is at risk of compression. Advances in imaging using computed tomography or MRI have aided greatly in the evaluation of specific lesions.[88,90,141,142] Repeated use of these modalities often helps to identify lesions that are progressing despite the current management strategy and may benefit from additional surgical intervention or other changes in management.

Early Uncomplicated Infections

For patients with neither risk factors nor evidence of extrapulmonary spread, treatment is of unproven benefit. To date, there have been no placebo-controlled trials concerning this self-limited form of infection to determine whether treatment hastens the resolution of symptoms or prevents the risk of complications. Experts familiar with coccidioidomycosis vary widely in their recommendations for management of specific patients in this category. Although some physicians recommend treatment for all patients, others recommend treating only patients with more severe manifestations. Evidence that often is considered to indicate more severe infection includes loss of more than 10% of body weight, intense night sweats for more than 3 weeks, infiltrates involving more than half of one lung or portions of both lungs, prominent or persistent hilar or peritracheal adenopathy, anticoccidioidal complex-fixing antibody titer greater than 1:16, failure to develop dermal hypersensitivity to coccidioidal antigens, inability to work, or symptoms that persist for more than 2 months.[130] Because persons of African or Filipino descent seem to have some increased risk of dissemination, this factor sometimes also weighs in the decision for treatment. If treatment is recommended, commonly prescribed therapies include currently available oral azole antifungal agents, such as ketoconazole, fluconazole, or itraconazole, for courses ranging from 3 to 6 months.

Diffuse Pneumonia

Diffuse bilateral infiltrates represent either hematogenous infection of the lungs or multiple foci of infection resulting from exposure to a high inoculum of arthroconidia. In either case, even early infections are regarded as serious and warranting therapy. Initial therapy in such cases is usually with amphotericin B, at least for the first several weeks and until the illness seems to be improving. Concomitant use of a brief course of corticosteroids in this situation is controversial but advocated by some.[137] After this time, therapy often is switched to an antifungal azole agent for at least 1 year. Fungemia resulting in diffuse pulmonary infiltrates is often the consequence of severe immunodeficiency, and for these patients treatment may need to be continued indefinitely to prevent relapse.

Pulmonary Cavity

Cavitation as a sequela of coccidioidal pneumonia is often asymptomatic and may not need treatment. With the passage of time, some cavities disappear. Cavities that do not close spontaneously over 1 to several years sometimes are resected to prevent future complications, especially if the cavity shows progressive enlargement or is immediately adjacent to the pleura. This potential benefit must be weighed against the risks of the surgical procedure, which vary according to the general health of the patient and the skill of the surgeon.

Pulmonary cavities occasionally produce symptoms, such as local pain, superinfection, or hemoptysis. When this occurs, treatment usually is instituted with oral antifungal azole therapy. This therapy often is accompanied by a diminution of symptoms, but recurrences are frequent if therapy is stopped. For these patients, resection is a reasonable alternative to long-term suppressive medical therapy.

Chronic Fibrocavitary Pneumonia

Persistent coccidioidal pneumonia normally is treated with oral azole antifungal agents. Responses to these agents are approximately 55% to 60% as judged by improved symptoms and radiographic appearance. Treatment options for patients who do not respond include switching to an alternative antifungal azole, for fluconazole raising the dose, or instituting amphotericin B therapy.

Extrapulmonary Dissemination

For most patients with nonmeningeal dissemination, initial therapy is with an oral antifungal azole. Exceptional patients with rapidly progressive infection or infection in critical locations, such as vertebrae, may respond faster to initial therapy with amphotericin B, although this is not proven. As discussed before, surgical débridement or drainage of lesions may be an important component of controlling infection. As with patients with chronic coccidioidal pneumonia, treatment is continued for at least 1 year and for 6 months past the point at which all evidence of further improvement has ceased. Even so, relapses occur in approximately one third of patients when therapy is stopped, and some patients may require suppressive therapy indefinitely.

In the management of coccidioidal meningitis, most patients now are treated initially with fluconazole. This is a major departure from therapy with intrathecal amphotericin B, which until the past several years still was standard treatment.[143] Although there have been no comparative trials of intrathecal amphotericin B and fluconazole, the response rate of approximately 70% with fluconazole at 400 mg/day is probably at least as good as that achieved with intrathecal amphotericin B, and use of fluconazole avoids most of the toxicity associated with amphotericin B. Higher doses of fluconazole have produced responses in some patients who did not respond initially to 400 mg/day. Similar results have been obtained in patients treated with itraconazole, although there is less clinical experience with this drug than with fluconazole. Ketoconazole in doses of at least 1200 mg/day has been effective in some patients,[144] although it has been largely superseded by the newer azoles.

Patients who do not respond to oral azole therapy may benefit from intrathecal amphotericin B.[145] Routes of administration include repeated percutaneous intracisternal injection, injection into Ommaya reservoirs that drain to either the cistern or a ventricle, lumbar puncture with medication in a hyperbaric glucose solution, and lateral cervical injection. The technique, frequency, and dosage of intrathecal amphotericin B vary widely among practitioners. For some patients who could not tolerate intrathecal amphotericin B, miconazole administered intravenously or intrathecally also has been effective treatment.[146]

In addition to antifungal therapy to control the meningeal inflammation, interventions are required for two other manifestations. Hydrocephalus is a common complication of coccidioidal meningitis. Normally, hydrocephalus does not respond to antifungal therapy and requires a shunting procedure. Ventriculoperitoneal shunts become a conduit for *Coccidioides* spp. from the cerebrospinal space to the peritoneum, but this usually does not result in clinically apparent abdominal complications. Although infection predominantly affects the basilar meninges, intracerebral abscesses occasionally develop.[97] These lesions may require drainage or resection in addition to systemic antifungal drug therapy.

New Therapies

Voriconazole (Vfend) has been introduced for treatment of systemic aspergillosis and certain other mycoses that have not responded to conventional therapy. With respect to *Coccidioides* spp., voriconazole's in vitro activity is comparable to that for other dimorphic fungi.[99] Voriconazole treatment of experimental coccidioidal infections in mice or other species has not been reported. One patient with coccidioidal meningitis responded to voriconazole in high doses.[147] So far, no other clinical reports exist.

Because the fungal wall of *Coccidioides* spp. contains β-1,3-glucan and chitin,[29] antifungals that interfere with synthesis of these polysaccharides potentially could be therapeutic for coccidioidomycosis. Caspofungin (Cancidas) has been effective in treatment of experimental coccidioidal infections,[148] but clinical reports have not been published yet. According to preclinical reports, Nikkomycin Z, a chitin synthase inhibitor, has shown considerable promise,[149,150] but it has not begun clinical trials yet.

PREVENTION

Developing a vaccine as a means of preventing coccidioidomycosis has been an attractive goal for many years. This strategy might be useful because immunity develops in most persons who are infected naturally.[151] A formalin-killed, whole-cell spherule vaccine was found to be exceptionally protective for mice against lethal intranasal infections.[50,152-160] The whole-cell vaccine also induced a great deal of local inflammation at the injection site, however, limiting the dose in humans to 1.84 mg.[144] For an average human, this is approximately 1/1000 of the vaccine dose (mg/kg) required for protection in mice. When this dose of formalin-killed spherule vaccine was used in a human field trial, vaccination failed to result in significantly fewer symptomatic cases of coccidioidal pneumonia than were detected in placebo recipients.[161] One plausible explanation for the failure is that the inflammatory reactions to the whole-cell vaccine prevented use of a sufficient dose of the antigens responsible for protection. If this is the case, use of a purified or recombinant antigen might circumvent this limitation.

Several antigens have been expressed as recombinant proteins and when used with Th1-based adjuvants have evoked protection against experimental coccidioidal infections in mice.[162-164] Studies now under way are designed to permit a phase I clinical trial in 2005.

REFERENCES

1. Deresinski SC, Hector RF. The history of coccidioidomycosis. In: Einstein HE, Catanzaro A, eds. Coccidioidomycosis. Proceedings of the Fifth International Conference on Coccidioidomycosis. Washington, DC: National Foundation for Infectious Diseases; 1996:48-76.
2. Galgiani JN. Coccidioidomycosis: A regional disease of national importance: Rethinking approaches for control. Ann Intern Med. 1999;130:293-300.
3. Posada A. Un nuevo caso de micosis fungoidea con psorospermias. Annales del Circulo Medico Argentino. 1892;15:585-597.
4. Ophuls W, Moffitt HC. A new pathogenic mould (formerly described as a protozoon: *Coccidioides immitis*): Preliminary report. Phila Med J. 1900;5:1471-1472.
5. Gifford MA. San Joaquin fever. Kern County Dept Public Health Annu Rep. 1936:22-23.
6. Smith CE, Saito MT, Simons SA. Pattern of 39,500 serologic tests in coccidioidomycosis. JAMA. 1956;160:546-552.
7. Fiese MJ. Coccidioidomycosis. Springfield, IL: Charles C Thomas; 1958.
8. Riley DK, Galgiani JN, O'Donnell MR, et al. Coccidioidomycosis in bone marrow transplant recipients. Transplantation. 1994;56:1531-1533.
9. Hall KA, Copeland JG, Zukoski CF, et al. Markers of coccidioidomycosis before cardiac or renal transplantation and the risk of recurrent infection. Transplantation. 1993;55:1422-1424.
10. Blair JE, Logan JL. Coccidioidomycosis in solid organ transplantation. Clin Infect Dis. 2001;33:1536-1544.
11. Logan JL, Blair JE, Galgiani JN. Coccidioidomycosis complicating solid organ transplantation. Semin Respir Infect. 2001;16:251-256.
12. Wright P, Pappagianis D, Taylor J, et al. Transmission of *Coccidioides immitis* from donor organs: A description of two fatal cases of disseminated coccidioidomycosis. Clin Infect Dis. 2001;33:1194.
13. Tripathy N, Yung GL, Kriett JM, et al. Donor transfer of pulmonary coccidioidomycosis in lung transplantation. Ann Thorac Surg. 2002;73:306-308.
14. Ampel NM, Dols CL, Galgiani JN. Coccidioidomycosis during human immunodeficiency virus infection: Results of a prospective study in coccidioidal endemic area. Am J Med. 1993;94:235-240.
15. Ampel NM, Ryan KJ, Carry PJ, et al. Fungemia due to *Coccidioides immitis*: An analysis of 16 episodes in 15 patients and a review of the literature. Medicine (Baltimore). 1986;65:312-321.
16. Deresinski SC, Stevens DA. Coccidioidomycosis in compromised hosts: Experience at Stanford University Hospital. Medicine (Baltimore). 1974;54:377-395.
17. Rutala PJ, Smith JW. Coccidioidomycosis in potentially compromised hosts: The effect of immunosuppressive therapy in dissemination. Am J Med Sci. 1978;275:283-295.
18. Woods CW, McRill C, Plikaytis BD, et al. Coccidioidomycosis in human immunodeficiency virus-infected persons in Arizona, 1994-1997: Incidence, risk factors, and prevention. J Infect Dis. 2000;181:1428-1434.
19. Ampel NM. Coccidioidomycosis among persons with human immunodeficiency virus infection in the era of highly active antiretroviral therapy (HAART). Semin Respir Infect. 2001;16:257-262.
20. Logan JL, Blair JE, Galgiani JN. Coccidioidomycosis complicating solid organ transplantation. Semin Respir Infect. 2001;16:251-256.
21. Ramzan NN, Shapiro MS, Robinson E, et al. Use of infliximab leading to extensive pulmonary coccidioidomycosis. Am J Gastroenterol. 2002;97:S157.
22. Sun SH, Sekhon SS, Huppert M. Electron microscopic studies of saprobic and parasitic forms of *Coccidioides immitis*. Sabouraudia. 1979;17:265-273.
23. Dixon DM. *Coccidioides immitis* as a select agent of bioterrorism. J Appl Microbiol. 2001;91:602-605.
24. Abuodeh RO, Orbach MJ, Mandel MA, et al. Genetic transformation of *Coccidioides immitis* facilitated by *Agrobacterium tumefaciens*. J Infect Dis. 2000;181:2106-2110.
25. Bowman BH, Taylor JW, Brownlee AG, et al. Molecular evolution of the fungi: Relationship of the basidiomycetes, ascomycetes, and chytridiomycetes. Mol Biol Evol. 1992;9:285-296.
26. Burt A, Carter DA, Koenig GL, et al. Molecular markers reveal cryptic sex in the human pathogen *Coccidioides immitis*. Proc Natl Acad Sci U S A. 1996;93:770-773.
27. Fisher MC, Koenig GL, White TJ, et al. Molecular and phenotypic description of *Coccidioides posadasii* sp nov., previously recognized as the non-California population of *Coccidioides immitis*. Mycologia. 2002;94:73-84.
28. Fisher MC, Rannala B, Chaturvedi V, et al. Disease surveillance in recombining pathogens: Multilocus genotypes identify sources of human *Coccidioides* infections. Proc Natl Acad Sci U S A. 2002;99:9067-9071.
29. Hector RF, Pappagianis D. Enzymatic degradation of the walls of spherules of *Coccidioides immitis*. Exp Mycol. 1982;6:136-152.
30. Huppert M, Sun SH, Harrison JL. Morphogenesis throughout saprobic and parasitic cycles of *Coccidioides immitis*. Mycopathologia. 1982;78:107-122.
31. Ogiso A, Ito M, Koyama M, et al. Pulmonary coccidioidomycosis in Japan: Case report and review. Clin Infect Dis. 1997;25:1260-1261.
32. Pappagianis D, Einstein H. Tempest from Tehachapi takes toll or *Coccidioides* conveyed aloft and afar. West J Med. 1978;129:527-530.
33. Mardo D, Christensen RA, Nielson N, et al. Coccidioidomycosis in workers at an archeologic site—Dinosaur National Monument, Utah, June-July 2001. JAMA. 2001;286:3072-3073 (Reprinted from MMWR Morb Mortal Wkly Rep. 2001;50:1005-1008).
34. Eulalio KD, de Macedo RL, Cavalcanti MA, et al. *Coccidioides immitis* isolated from armadillos (*Dasypus novemcinctus*) in the state of Piaui, northeast Brazil. Mycopathologia. 2001;149:57-61.
35. Pappagianis D. Epidemiology of coccidioidomycosis. Curr Top Med Mycol. 1988;2:199-238.
36. Kerrick SS, Lundergan LL, Galgiani JN. Coccidioidomycosis at a university health service. Am Rev Respir Dis. 1985;131:100-102.
37. Greene DR, Koenig G, Fisher MC, et al. Soil isolation and molecular identification of *Coccidioides immitis*. Mycologia. 2000;92:406-410.
38. Larwood TR. Coccidioidin skin testing in Kern County, California: Decrease in infection rate over 58 years. Clin Infect Dis. 2000;30:612-613.
39. Smith CE, Beard RR, Whiting EG, et al. Varieties of coccidioidal infection in relation to the epidemiology and control of the disease. Am J Public Health. 1946;36:1394-1402.
40. Dodge RR, Lebowitz MD, Barbee RA, et al. Estimates of *C. immitis* infection by skin test reactivity in an endemic community. Am J Public Health. 1985;75:863-865.
41. Larwood TR. Coccidioidin skin testing in Kern County, California: Decrease in infection rate over 58 years. Clin Infect Dis. 2000;30:612-613.
42. Kolivras KN, Comrie AC. 2003: Modeling valley fever incidence based on climate conditions in Pima County, Arizona. Int J Biometeorol. 2003;47:87-101.
43. Werner SB, Pappagianis D, Heindl I, et al. An epidemic of coccidioidomycosis among archeology students in northern California. N Engl J Med. 1972;286:507-512.
44. Jibson RW. A public health issue related to collateral seismic hazards: The valley fever outbreak triggered by the 1994 Northridge, California earthquake. Surveys in Geophysics. 2002;23:511-528.
45. Crum N, Lamb C, Utz G, et al. Coccidioidomycosis outbreak among United States Navy SEALs training in a *Coccidioides immitis*-endemic area—Coalinga, California. J Infect Dis. 2002;186:865-868.
46. Centers for Disease Control and Prevention. Coccidioidomycosis—United States, 1991-1992. MMWR Morb Mortal Wkly Rep. 1993;42:21-24.
47. Leake JA, Mosley DG, England B, et al. Risk factors for acute symptomatic coccidioidomycosis among elderly persons in Arizona, 1996-1997. J Infect Dis. 2000;181:1435-1440.
48. Komatsu K, Vaz V, McRill C, et al. Increase in coccidioidomycosis—Arizona, 1998-2001. JAMA. 2003;289:1500-1502 (Reprinted from MMWR Morb Mortal Wkly Rep. 2003;52:109).
49. Winn WA. Primary cutaneous coccidioidomycosis: Reevaluation of its potentiality based on study of three new cases. Arch Dermatol. 1965;92:221-228.
50. Kong Y-C, Levine HB, Madin SH, et al. Fungal multiplication and histopathologic changes in vaccinated mice infected with *Coccidioides immitis*. J Immunol. 1964;92:779-790.

51. Hoggan MD, Ransom JP, Pappagianis D, et al. Isolation of *Coccidioides immitis* from the air (Abstract). Stanford Med Bull. 1956;14:190.
52. Ajello L, Maddy K, Crecelius G, et al. Recovery of *Coccidioides immitis* from the air. Sabouraudia. 1965;4:92-95.
53. Galgiani JN, Isenberg RA, Stevens DA. Chemotaxigenic activity of extracts from the mycelial and spherule phases of *Coccidioides immitis* for human polymorphonuclear leukocytes. Infect Immun. 1978;21:862-865.
54. Huntington RW Jr, Waldmann WJ, Sargent JA, et al. Pathologic and clinical observations on 142 cases of fatal coccidioidomycosis with necropsy. In: Ajello L, ed. Coccidioidomycosis. Tucson: University of Arizona Press; 1967:221-225.
55. Echols RM, Palmer DL, Long GW. Tissue eosinophilia in human coccidioidomycosis. Rev Infect Dis. 1982;4:656-664.
56. Beaman L, Pappagianis D, Benjamini E. Mechanisms of resistance to infection with *Coccidioides immitis* in mice. Infect Immun. 1979;23:681-685.
57. Beaman L, Benjamini E, Pappagianis D. Role of lymphocytes in macrophage-induced killing of *Coccidioides immitis* in vitro. Infect Immun. 1981;34:347-353.
58. Beaman L, Benjamini E, Pappagianis D. Activation of macrophages by lymphokines: Enhancement of phagosome-lysosome fusion and killing of *Coccidioides immitis*. Infect Immun. 1983;39:1201-1207.
59. Beaman L. Fungicidal activation of murine macrophages by recombinant gamma interferon. Infect Immun. 1987;55:2951-2955.
60. Beaman L. Effects of recombinant gamma interferon and tumor necrosis factor on in vitro interactions of human mononuclear phagocytes with *Coccidioides immitis*. Infect Immun. 1991;59:4227-4229.
61. Ampel NM, Christian L. In vitro modulation of proliferation and cytokine production by human peripheral blood mononuclear cells from subjects with various forms of coccidioidomycosis. Infect Immun. 1997;65:4483-4487.
62. Corry DB, Ampel NM, Christian L, et al. Cytokine production by peripheral blood mononuclear cells in human coccidioidomycosis. J Infect Dis. 1996;174:440-443.
63. Appelberg R, Castro AG, Pedrosa J, et al. Role of gamma interferon and tumor necrosis factor alpha during T-cell-independent and -dependent phases of *Mycobacterium avium* infection. Infect Immun. 1994;62:3962-3971.
64. Kauffman SH. Immunity to intracellular bacteria. Annu Rev Immunol. 1993;11:151-177.
65. Reiner SL, Locksley RM. The regulation of immunity to *Leishmania major*. Annu Rev Immunol. 1995;13:151-177.
66. Galgiani JN, Payne CM, Jones JF. Human polymorphonuclear-leukocyte inhibition of incorporation of chitin precursors into mycelia of *Coccidioides immitis*. J Infect Dis. 1984;149:404-412.
67. Ampel NM, Bejarano GC, Galgiani JN. Killing of *Coccidioides immitis* by human peripheral blood mononuclear cells. Infect Immun. 1992;60:4200-4204.
68. Petkus AF, Baum LL. Natural killer cell inhibition of young spherules and endospores of *Coccidioides immitis*. J Immunol. 1987;139:3107-3111.
69. Frey CL, Drutz DJ. Influence of fungal surface components on the interaction of *Coccidioides immitis* with polymorphonuclear neutrophils. J Infect Dis. 1986;153:933-943.
70. Yozwiak ML, Lundergan LL, Kerrick SS, et al. Symptoms and routine laboratory abnormalities associated with coccidioidomycosis. West J Med. 1988;149:419-421.
71. Campion J, Gardner M, Galgiani JN. Coccidioidomycosis (valley fever) in older adults—an increasing problem needing increasing attention. Arizona Geriatr Soc J. 2003;8:3-12.
72. Standaert SM, Schaffner W, Galgiani JN, et al. Coccidioidomycosis among visitors to a *Coccidioides immitis*–endemic area: An outbreak in a military reserve unit. J Infect Dis. 1995;171:1672-1675.
73. Cairns L, Blythe D, Kao A, et al. Outbreak of coccidioidomycosis in Washington State residents returning from Mexico. Clin Infect Dis. 2000;30:61-64.
74. Johnson RH, Caldwell JW, Welch G, et al. The great coccidioidomycosis epidemic: Clinical features. In: Einstein HE, Catanzaro A, eds. Coccidioidomycosis. Proceedings of the Fifth International Conference. Washington, DC: National Foundation for Infectious Diseases; 1996:77-87.
75. Lopez AM, Williams PL, Ampel NM. Acute pulmonary coccidioidomycosis mimicking bacterial pneumonia and septic shock: A report of two cases. Am J Med. 1993;95:236-239.
76. Arsura EL, Bellinghausen PL, Kilgore WB, et al. Septic shock in coccidioidomycosis. Crit Care Med. 1998;26:62-65.
77. Arsura EL, Kilgore WB. Miliary coccidioidomycosis in the immunocompetent. Chest. 2000;117:404-409.
78. Forseth J, Rohwedder JJ, Levine BE, et al. Experience with needle biopsy for coccidioidal lung nodules. Arch Intern Med. 1986;146:319-320.
79. Smith CE, Beard RR, Saito MT. Pathogenesis of coccidioidomycosis with special reference to pulmonary cavitation. Ann Intern Med. 1948;29:623-655.
80. Winn RE, Johnson R, Galgiani JN, et al. Cavitary coccidioidomycosis with fungus ball formation: Diagnosis by fiberoptic bronchoscopy with coexistence of hyphae and spherules. Chest. 1994;105:412-416.
81. Cunningham RT, Einstein H. Coccidioidal pulmonary cavities with rupture. J Thorac Cardiovasc Surg. 1982;84:172-177.
82. Sarosi GA, Parker JD, Doto IL, et al. Chronic pulmonary coccidioidomycosis. N Engl J Med. 1970;283:325-329.
83. Walker MP, Brody CZ, Resnik R. Reactivation of coccidioidomycosis in pregnancy. Obstet Gynecol. 1992;79:815-817.
84. Peterson CM, Schuppert K, Kelly PC, et al. Coccidioidomycosis and pregnancy. Obstet Gynecol Surv. 1993;48:149-156.
85. Louie L, Ng S, Hajjeh R, et al. Influence of host genetics on the severity of coccidioidomycosis. Emerg Infect Dis. 1999;5:672-680.
86. Bisla RS, Taber TH Jr. Coccidioidomycosis of bone and joints. Clin Orthop. 1976;121:196-204.
87. Bried JH, Galgiani JN. *Coccidioides immitis* infections in bones and joints. Clin Orthop. 1986;211:235-243.
88. Lund PJ, Chan KM, Unger EC, et al. Magnetic resonance imaging in coccidioidal arthritis. Skeletal Radiol. 1996;25:661-665.
89. Dalinka MK, Dinnenberg S, Greendyke WH, et al. Roentgenographic features of osseous coccidioidomycosis and differential diagnosis. J Bone Joint Surg Am. 1971;53:1157-1164.
90. Erly WK, Carmody RF, Seeger JF, et al. Magnetic resonance imaging of coccidioidal spondylitis. Int J Neuroradiol. 1997;3:385-392.
91. Einstein HE, Holeman CW Jr, Sandidge LL, et al. Coccidioidal meningitis: The use of amphotericin B in treatment. Calif Med. 1961;94:339-343.
92. Vincent T, Galgiani JN, Huppert M, et al. The natural history of coccidioidal meningitis: VA-Armed Forces Cooperative Studies, 1955-1958. Clin Infect Dis. 1993;16:247-254.
93. Pappagianis D. Coccidioidomycosis. In: Balows A, Hausler WJ Jr, Lennette EH, eds. Laboratory Diagnosis of Infectious Diseases. Berlin: Springer-Verlag; 1988:600-623.
94. Ismail Y, Arsura EL. Eosinophilic meningitis associated with coccidioidomycosis. West J Med. 1993;158:300-301.
95. Harrison HR, Galgiani JN, Reynolds AF Jr, et al. Amphotericin B and imidazole therapy for coccidioidal meningitis in children. Pediatr Infect Dis. 1983;2:216-221.
96. Mischel PS, Vinters HV. Coccidioidomycosis of the central nervous system: Neuropathological and vasculopathic manifestations and clinical correlates. Clin Infect Dis. 1995;20:400-405.
97. BaZuelos AF, Williams PL, Johnson RH, et al. Central nervous system abscesses due to *Coccidioides* species. Clin Infect Dis. 1996;22:240-250.
98. Williams PL. Vasculitic complications associated with coccidioidal meningitis. Semin Respir Infect. 2001;16:270-279.
99. Li RK, Ciblak MA, Nordoff N, et al. In vitro activities of voriconazole, itraconazole, and amphotericin B against *Blastomyces dermatitidis, Coccidioides immitis* and *Histoplasma capsulatum*. Antimicrob Agents Chemother. 2000;44:1734-1736.
100. Hernandez JL, Echevarria S, Garcia-Valtuille A, et al. Atypical coccidioidomycosis in an AIDS patient successfully treated with fluconazole. Eur J Clin Microbiol Infect Dis. 1997;16:592-594.
101. Sarosi GA, Lawrence JP, Smith DK, et al. Rapid diagnostic evaluation of bronchial washings in patients with suspected coccidioidomycosis. Semin Respir Infect. 2001;16:238-241.
102. Graham AR. Fungal autofluorescence with ultraviolet illumination. Am J Clin Pathol. 1983;79:231-234.
103. Hayden RT, Qian X, Roberts GD, et al. In situ hybridization for the identification of yeastlike organisms in tissue section. Diag Mol Pathol. 2001;10:15-23.
104. Huppert M, Sun SH, Bailey JW. Natural variability in *Coccidioides immitis*. In: Ajello L, ed. Coccidioidomycosis. The Second Symposium on Coccidioidomycosis. Tucson: University of Arizona Press; 1965:323-328.
105. Pappagianis D. Coccidioidomycosis (San Joaquin or valley fever). In: DiSalvo A, ed. Occupational Mycoses. Philadelphia: Lea & Febiger; 1983:13-28.
106. Huppert M, Sun SH, Rice EH. Specificity of exoantigens for identifying cultures of *Coccidioides immitis*. J Clin Microbiol. 1978;8:346-348.
107. Padhye AA, Smith G, Standard PG, et al. Comparative evaluation of chemiluminescent DNA probe assays and exoantigen tests for rapid identification of *Blastomyces dermatitidis* and *Coccidioides immitis*. J Clin Microbiol. 1994;32:867-870.
108. Sandhu GS, Kline BC, Stockman L, et al. Molecular probes for diagnosis of fungal infections. J Clin Microbiol. 1995;33:2913-2919.
109. Pappagianis D, Zimmer BL. Serology of coccidioidomycosis. Clin Microbiol Rev. 1990;3:247-268.
110. Smith CE, Whiting EG, Baker EE, et al. The use of coccidioidin. Am Rev Tuberc Pulm Dis. 1948;57:330-360.
111. Johnson SM, Pappagianis D. The coccidioidal complement fixation and immunodiffusion-complement fixation antigen is a chitinase. Infect Immun. 1992;60:2588-2592.
112. Pishko EJ, Kirkland TN, Cole GT. Isolation and characterization of two chitinase-encoding genes (*cts1, cts2*) from the fungus *Coccidioides immitis*. Gene. 1995;167:173-177.
113. Yang CM, Zhu YF, Magee DM, et al. Molecular cloning and characterization of the *Coccidioides immitis* complement fixation chitinase antigen. Infect Immun. 1996;64:1992-1997.
114. Zimmermann CR, Johnson SM, Martens GW, et al. Cloning and expression of the complement fixation antigen-chitinase of *Coccidioides immitis*. Infect Immun. 1996;64:4967-4975.
115. Huppert M, Bailey JW. The use of immunodiffusion tests in coccidioidomycosis: II. An immunodiffusion test as a substitute for the tube precipitin test. Am J Clin Pathol. 1965;44:369.
116. Wieden MA, Galgiani JN, Pappagianis D. Comparison of immunodiffusion techniques with standard complement fixation assay for quantitation of coccidioidal antibodies. J Clin Microbiol. 1983;18:529-534.
117. Kaufman L, Sekhon AS, Moledina N, et al. Comparative evaluation of commercial Premier EIA and microimmunodiffusion and complement fixation tests for *Coccidioides* immunodiffusion antibodies. J Clin Microbiol. 1995;33:618-619.
118. Wieden MA, Lundergan LL, Blum J, et al. Detection of coccidioidal antibodies by 33-kDa spherule antigen, *Coccidioides* EIA, and standard serologic tests in sera from patients evaluated for coccidioidomycosis. J Infect Dis. 1996;173:1273-1277.
119. Zartarian M, Peterson EM, De la Maza LM. Detection of antibodies to *Coccidioides immitis* by enzyme immunoassay. Am J Clin Pathol. 1997;107:148-153.

120. Drutz DJ, Catanzaro A. Coccidioidomycosis: Part I. Am Rev Respir Dis. 1978;117:559-585.
121. Oldfield EC, Bone WD, Martain CR, et al. Prediction of relapse after treatment of coccidioidomycosis. Clin Infect Dis. 1997;25:1205-1210.
122. Yoshinoya S, Cox RA, Pope RM. Circulating immune complexes in coccidioidomycosis: Detection and characterization. J Clin Invest. 1980;66:655-663.
123. Weiner MH. Antigenemia detected in human coccidioidomycosis. J Clin Microbiol. 1983;18:136-142.
124. Galgiani JN, Dugger KO, Ito JI, et al. Antigenemia in primary coccidioidomycosis. Am J Trop Med Hyg. 1984;33:645-649.
125. Galgiani JN, Grace GM, Lundergan LL. New serologic tests for early detection of coccidioidomycosis. J Infect Dis. 1991;163:671-674.
126. Bowman BH. Designing a PCR/probe detection system for pathogenic fungi. Clin Immunol. 1992;12:66-69.
127. Clark KA, McAllister D. Direct detection of Coccidioides immitis in clinical specimens using target amplification. In: Einstein HE, Catanzaro A, eds. Coccidioidomycosis. Proceedings of the Fifth International Conference. Washington, DC: National Foundation for Infectious Diseases; 1996:129-136.
128. Galgiani JN, Ampel NM, Catanzaro A, et al. Practice guidelines for the treatment of coccidioidomycosis. Clin Infect Dis. 2000;30:658-661.
129. Stadalnik RC, Goldstein E, Hoeprich PD, et al. Diagnostic value of gallium and bone scans in evaluation of extrapulmonary coccidioidal lesions. Am Rev Respir Dis. 1980;121:673-676.
130. Boddicker JH, Fong D, Walsh TE, et al. Bone and gallium scanning in the evaluation of disseminated coccidioidomycosis. Am Rev Respir Dis. 1980;122:279-287.
131. Galgiani JN, Stevens DA, Graybill JR, et al. Ketoconazole therapy of progressive coccidioidomycosis: Comparison of 400- and 800-mg doses and observations at higher doses. Am J Med. 1988;84:603-610.
132. Tucker RM, Denning DW, Dupont B, et al. Itraconazole therapy for chronic coccidioidal meningitis. Ann Intern Med. 1990;112:108-112.
133. Galgiani JN, Catanzaro A, Cloud GA, et al. Fluconazole therapy for coccidioidal meningitis. Ann Intern Med. 1993;119:28-35.
134. Stevens DA. Itraconazole and fluconazole for treatment of coccidioidomycosis. Clin Infect Dis. 1994;18:470-470.
135. Catanzaro A, Galgiani JN, Levine BE, et al. Fluconazole in the treatment of chronic pulmonary and nonmeningeal disseminated coccidioidomycosis. Am J Med. 1995;98:249-256.
136. Holley K, Muldoon M, Tasker S. Coccidioides immitis osteomyelitis: A case series review. Orthopedics. 2002;25:827-831.
137. Shibli M, Ghassibi J, Hajal R, et al. Adjunctive corticosteroids therapy in acute respiratory distress syndrome owing to disseminated coccidioidomycosis. Crit Care Med. 2002;30:1896-1898.
138. Perez JA Jr, Johnson RH, Caldwell JW, et al. Fluconazole therapy in coccidioidal meningitis maintained with intrathecal amphotericin B. Arch Intern Med. 1995;155:1665-1668.
139. Galgiani JN, Catanzaro A, Cloud GA, et al. Comparison of oral fluconazole and itraconazole for progressive, nonmeningeal coccidioidomycosis: A randomized, double-blind trial. Mycoses Study Group. Ann Intern Med. 2000;133:676-686.
140. Williams PL, Sable DL, Sorgen D, et al. Immunologic responsiveness and safety associated with the Coccidioides immitis spherule vaccine in volunteers of white, black and Filipino ancestry. Am J Epidemiol. 1984;119:591-602.
141. Garvin GJ, Peterfy CG. Soft tissue coccidioidomycosis on MRI. J Comput Assist Tomogr. 1995;19:612-614.
142. Erly WK, Bellon RJ, Seeger JF, et al. MR imaging of acute coccidioidal meningitis. AJNR Am J Neuroradiol. 1999;20:509-514.
143. Labadie EL, Hamilton RH. Survival improvement in coccidioidal meningitis by high-dose intrathecal amphotericin B. Arch Intern Med. 1986;146:2013-2018.
144. Craven PC, Graybill JR, Jorgensen JH, et al. High-dose ketoconazole for treatment of fungal infections of the central nervous system. Ann Intern Med. 1983;98:160-167.
145. Stevens DA, Shatsky SA. Intrathecal amphotericin in the management of coccidioidal meningitis. Semin Respir Infect. 2001;16:263-269.
146. Deresinski SC, Lilly RB, Levine HB, et al. Treatment of fungal meningitis with miconazole. Arch Intern Med. 1977;137:1180-1185.
147. Cortez K, Walsh TJ, Bennett JE. Coccidioidal meningitis successfully treated with voriconazole. Clin Infect Dis. 2003;36:1619-1622.
148. Gonzalez GM, Tijerina R, Najvar LK, et al. Correlation between antifungal susceptibilities of Coccidioides immitis in vitro and antifungal treatment with caspofungin in a mouse model. Antimicrob Agents Chemother. 2001;45:1854-1859.
149. Hector RF, Zimmer BL, Pappagianis D. Evaluation of nikkomycins X and Z in murine models of coccidioidomycosis, histoplasmosis, and blastomycosis. Antimicrob Agents Chemother. 1990;34:587-593.
150. Li RK, Rinaldi MG. In vitro antifungal activity of nikkomycin Z in combination with fluconazole or itraconazole. Antimicrob Agents Chemother. 1999;43:1401-1405.
151. Barnato AE, Sanders GD, Owens DK. Cost-effectiveness of a potential vaccine for Coccidioides immitis. Emerg Infect Dis. 2001;7:797-806.
152. Levine HB, Cobb JM, Smith CE. Immunity to coccidioidomycosis induced in mice by purified spherule, arthrospore, and mycelial vaccines. Trans N Y Acad Sci. 1960;22:436-447.
153. Levine HB, Cobb JM, Smith CE. Immunogenicity of spherule-endospore vaccines of Coccidioides immitis for mice. J Immunol. 1961;87:218-227.
154. Levine HB, Miller RL, Smith CE. Influence of vaccination on respiratory coccidioidal disease in cynomolgus monkeys. J Immunol. 1962;89:242-251.
155. Kong Y-C, Levine HB, Smith CE. Immunogenic properties of nondisrupted and disrupted spherules of Coccidioides immitis in mice. Sabouraudia. 1963;2:131-142.
156. Levine HB, Kong Y-C, Smith CE. Immunization of mice to Coccidioides immitis: Dose, regimen and spherulation stage of killed spherule vaccines. J Immunol. 1965;94:132-142.
157. Levine HB. Purification of the spherule-endospore phase of Coccidioides immitis. Sabouraudia. 1961;1:112-115.
158. Kong Y-C, Savage DC, Levine HB. Enhancement of immune responses in mice by a booster injection of Coccidioides spherules. J Immunol. 1966;95:1048-1056.
159. Huppert M, Levine HB, Sun SH, et al. Resistance of vaccinated mice to typical and atypical strains of Coccidioides immitis. J Bacteriol. 1967;94:924-927.
160. Pappagianis D. Histopathologic response of mice to killed vaccines of Coccidioides immitis. J Invest Dermatol. 1967;49:71-77.
161. Pappagianis D. Valley Fever Vaccine Study Group: Evaluation of the protective efficacy of the killed Coccidioides immitis spherule vaccine in humans. Am Rev Respir Dis. 1993;148:656-660.
162. Peng T, Shubitz L, Simons J, et al. Localization within a proline-rich antigen (Ag2/PRA) of protective antigenicity against infection with Coccidioides immitis in mice. Infect Immun. 2002;70:3330-3335.
163. Li K, Yu JJ, Hung CY, et al. Recombinant urease and urease DNA of Coccidioides immitis elicit an immunoprotective response against coccidioidomycosis in mice. Infect Immun. 2001;69:2878-2887.
164. Pappagianis D. Seeking a vaccine against Coccidioides immitis and serologic studies: Expectations and realities. Fungal Genet Biol. 2001;32:1-9.

CHAPTER **265**

Dermatophytosis and Other Superficial Mycoses

RODERICK J. HAY

The superficial fungal infections include some of the most common infectious conditions, such as ringworm or dermatophytosis and pityriasis versicolor, as well as rare disorders including tinea nigra. Their prevalence varies in different parts of the world, but in many tropical countries they are the most common causes of skin disease. Dermatophyte infections and other superficial mycoses are described in this chapter. Superficial candidiasis is discussed in Chapter 255.

DERMATOPHYTOSIS

The dermatophytes are molds that can invade the stratum corneum of the skin or other keratinized tissues derived from epidermis, such as hair and nails. They may cause infections (dermatophytoses) at most skin sites, although the feet, groin, scalp, and nails are most commonly affected.[1] The dermatophytes are among the earliest microorganisms that were found to cause infections in humans. *Trichophyton schoenleinii,* the cause of the scalp infection favus, was isolated from a patient and the culture shown to reproduce the typical lesions after inoculation onto human skin as early as 1841. Dermatophyte infections had been described many years before this even though the identity of the cause had not been recognized. The ancient Greek physicians knew about ringworm, and there are descriptions of the manifestations of dermatophytosis in more unlikely sources, such as the records of the early Dutch explorers of the 16th century who brought back reports of a strange disease of the skin, subsequently known as tinea imbricata caused by *Trichophyton concentricum,* in the islanders of the western Pacific.

The Dermatophytes

There are three genera of pathogenic dermatophyte fungi—*Trichophyton, Microsporum,* and *Epidermophyton.* The last genus is represented by only a single species, *Epidermophyton floccosum.* These keratinophilic organisms probably arose as saprophytic soil fungi, and some dermatophytes, which have been isolated only from soil, have not been shown to cause disease in either animals or humans. Most of the 39 dermatophyte species, however, are parasitic and can cause disease in either humans or animals, often being adapted to a single or narrow range of host species. The dermatophytes are referred to as either zoophilic, anthropophilic, or geophilic, depending on whether their primary source is an animal, human, or soil, respectively.

The taxonomy of these fungi is complicated by the fact that most clinical isolates are imperfect fungi, organisms that do not produce sexual structures in culture. However, sexual forms of many of these species are known and have been assigned to one of two genera, *Arthroderma* and *Nannizzia*, which correspond to the imperfect genera *Trichophyton* and *Microsporum*, respectively. The classification of these fungi is difficult, and their exact taxonomic status remains a subject of debate.[2]

The relationships among different dermatophytes are not simply a subject for intellectual dispute. It is important, for instance, to attempt to differentiate strains of the same species to understand the spread of infections. In the past few years there have been significant advances in both the molecular taxonomy of these organisms and the development of schemes for strain differentiation using molecular tools.[3] These have upheld the conventional classification but enhanced our understanding of key issues in pathogenesis, such as spread of infection in populations and relapse after apparently successful treatment. Attempts have also been made to classify the dermatophytes according to their protein composition[4] and production of antibiotics or enzymes such as urease. Both antibiotics and enzymes may play a role in determining pathogenicity. Proteinases produced by dermatophytes are inducible by, for instance, amino acids. *Trichophyton rubrum* secretes a number of enzymes with different protein affinities, including keratin, the largest of which is a 200-kDa glycosylated metalloprotease.[5] The production of elastase has also been proposed as a factor affecting the development of inflammatory responses in ringworm.[6] The significance of the production of antibiotics by dermatophytes is uncertain. The main groups detected have been the penicillins and fusidates, and these are produced by dermatophytes not only under laboratory culture conditions but also after growth on epidermal sheets in vitro.

Epidemiology

The factors affecting the distribution and transmission of dermatophytosis are largely dependent on the source of the infection[7]—animal, soil, or human.

Zoophilic Dermatophyte Infections

The main zoophilic dermatophyte fungi are shown in Table 265-1. Each organism is primarily an animal pathogen that sometimes causes human infection. In each case there is usually a range of host specificities, from organisms such as *Microsporum nanum*, whose natural host is the pig and which does not infect other animals, to *Trichophyton mentagrophytes*, which affects a range of different rodent species as well as cats, dogs, and horses.

The host preferences of *T. mentagrophytes* coupled with small clinical and cultural differences have led many mycologists to subdivide this group into different species or subspecies (the *mentagrophytes* complex). Under this classification *T. mentagrophytes quinckeanum* (*Trichophyton quinckeanum*) is used to describe the fungus that causes the clinical pattern of favus in mice, an infection associated with the formation of epithelial crusts. In most temperate countries *Trichophyton verrucosum*, the cause of cattle ringworm, and *Microsporum canis*, a dermatophyte that causes infections in cats or dogs, are the most common zoophilic dermatophytes that cause human infections.

Of all the zoophilic dermatophytes, *M. canis* is probably the most prevalent throughout the world. Its appearance in the tropics is a comparatively recent event, and it is mainly found there as a cause of disease in urban communities.[7] Occasionally, the distribution of zoophilic dermatophytes may appear to be difficult to explain, but usually it reflects the distribution of the animal host. For instance, *Trichophyton erinacei* (*T. mentagrophytes*) is mainly confined to Europe and New Zealand. It is carried by hedgehogs, which were introduced into New Zealand in the 19th century from England. *Microsporum persicolor* is a rare cause of human infections in Europe, where it has been isolated from the bank vole, whose distribution is similarly restricted. *Trichophyton simii* is associated with monkeys in India and the Far East, and human infections are seen only in these areas.[8]

Geophilic Dermatophyte Infections

Dermatophytes originating from soil, such as *Microsporum gypseum*, are infrequent causes of human disease, although they may be seen more commonly in certain parts of the tropics such as the western Pacific and Central America. In other areas they usually cause sporadic infections, although occasionally they may be responsible for outbreaks of human disease in appropriately exposed occupational groups such as gardeners or farm workers.[8]

Anthropophilic Dermatophyte Infections

Dermatophytes that are natural pathogens of humans are the most common cause of human dermatophytosis. They include organisms that mainly cause infections of glabrous skin of the feet or hands as well as a range of pathogens whose invasion may involve penetration of the hair shaft. The most common of these organisms in most parts of the world is *T. rubrum*, which causes tinea pedis or tinea cruris in temperate climates and, particularly in the tropics, tinea corporis. Cases of infection that are due to *T. rubrum* were once rare in the Western Hemisphere, but the infection has spread rapidly during the past 40 years. The ability of this dermatophyte to cause noninflammatory chronic infections of the feet, among other sites, that are easily

---

TABLE 265-1 Classification of the Main Dermatophytes (*Trichophyton, Microsporum,* and *Epidermophyton*) Organisms

Anthropophilic	Geophilic	Zoophilic	
		Organism	Sources
Trichophyton concentricum	*Trichophyton ajelloi*	*Trichophyton erinacei**	Hedgehogs
T. gourvilii	*T. terrestre*	*T. equinum*	Horses
T. mentagrophytes interdigitale*	*Microsporum fulvum*	*T. mentagrophytes mentagrophytes**	Rodents
T. megnini	*M. gypseum*	*T. quinckeanum**	Mice
T. rubrum		*T. simii*	Monkeys
T. schoenleinii		*T. verrucosum*	Cattle
T. soudanense		*Microsporum canis*	Cats, dogs
T. tonsurans		*M. gallinae*	Chickens
T. violaceum		*M. nanum*	Pigs
T. yaoundei		*M. persicolor*	Bank voles
Microsporum audouinii			
M. ferrugineum			
Epidermophyton floccosum			

*These organisms are part of the "mentagrophytes" complex and may be classified as a single species.

transmitted is probably an important factor that has determined its spread in recent years.[7] The large population movements during World War II are also thought to have contributed to the spread of the disease. Despite this, a variant with distinct morphologic appearances may be isolated from patients with tinea corporis in remote rural areas of the New World and Old World tropics, which suggests that, although endemic disease caused by this species has been present for a considerable time, the key adaptation leading to spread was the appearance of strains capable of causing indolent and noninflammatory infections of peripheral skin sites.[9]

Spread of the organisms that infect glabrous skin is largely through contact with infected desquamated skin scales. Classically, this occurs in bathing areas or shower rooms where large numbers of individuals share common facilities, for instance, in military camps or factories.[10] In the U.K. coal mining industry as many as 30% to 35% of coal miners had dermatophyte infections affecting their feet. In most cases this was due to *T. rubrum,* although *Trichophyton interdigitale (mentagrophytes)* may also be isolated.[11] Changing rooms in other heavy industrial companies, the police and armed forces, schools, and public swimming pools are also sites for infection. By contrast, transmission within the home as a reflection of conjugal or familial cases is not common,[12] although it has been suggested that some patients show genetic susceptibility. *E. floccosum* may also cause foot infections, although it is particularly associated with tinea cruris either as a sporadic disease or in institutions such as prisons or military barracks. These infections are not geographically restricted, even though there are variations in different countries. In many tropical areas, particularly the Far East, *T. mentagrophytes* is less commonly a cause of interdigital foot disease, and patients are infected by the zoophilic variety of this species on sites other than the feet.[13]

Tinea corporis (tinea imbricata), caused by the anthropophilic dermatophyte *T. concentricum,* has an unusual distribution confined to remote parts of the humid tropics.[14] The main endemic areas are the western Pacific, Malaysia, Assam, and parts of the Amazon basin in Brazil. Infants may be affected shortly after birth, and spontaneous recovery is unusual. Large numbers of viable organisms can be cultured from the houses of infected families. Visitors to endemic areas are rarely infected. Cases have also been described in southern Mexico, where the disease appears to fluctuate in severity with the season.

The distribution of some of the other anthropophilic dermatophytes that cause tinea capitis in children as well as other clinical forms of disease such as tinea corporis or onychomycosis may be more restricted. The reasons for this are not entirely clear unless the prevalence of these infections in children, who form a relatively stable population with little opportunity for travel, limits the spread of the disease to certain localities. Whatever the reason, these scalp infections are often found in defined endemic areas (Table 265-2). The situation is best illustrated by the distribution of *Trichophyton* spp. causing tinea capitis in West Africa, where the endemic areas for *Trichophyton soudanense, Trichophyton yaoundei,* and *Trichophyton gourvilii* are distinct, although there is some overlap.[15] *Trichophyton tonsurans* in the United Kingdom, United States, and Mexico and *Trichophyton violaceum* in India, East Africa, and the Middle East are the predominant causes of scalp infection in some areas. The situation does not always remain stable, and the slow increase in numbers of *T. tonsurans* in the United States was followed by spread to the United Kingdom and some parts of Europe.[7] Endemic anthropophilic scalp infections that are due to *Microsporum* spp. are less common. For instance, *Microsporum ferrugineum* is found occasionally in the Far East or central Europe. *Microsporum rivalieri* is seen in Africa, Democratic Republic of Congo, and Angola. The most widely distributed of this genus is *Microsporum audouinii.* Once common throughout Europe, it is now rare in this area, but it is still an important cause of tinea capitis in West Africa and in parts of the United States and Latin America. *Microsporum canis* has begun to spread in Eastern Europe in the past few years.

The infection caused by *T. schoenleinii,* favus, has characteristic clinical features. It was once common in Europe but has now largely

disappeared from many areas, although there are still pockets of infection in parts of the United States, South America, South Africa (Botswana), and North Africa. One of the features of this disease is the development of crusts or scutula on the scalp. Hairs are invaded, but shedding is delayed because they are not structurally damaged until late in the course of the infection. Although tinea capitis is normally a disease of children, adult women with favus are occasionally seen.

Dermatophytes causing scalp disease may be carried on the skin surface without invading the skin or hair. A small proportion of carriers develop infections within 6 months, others lose the fungus, and the rest remain carriers.[16] It is likely, though, that some carriers are simply patients with limited but undetected infections. The same can also be seen in foot infections, where carriage can also occur.

Age Incidence. Tinea capitis is mainly a disease of childhood, and cases are rare after puberty. Occasionally, this infection may occur in elderly women and is associated with scarring alopecia. The reason for the preponderance of the disease in children is thought to be the presence of medium-chain-length fatty (C_8 to C_{12}) acids in sebum that inhibit the growth of dermatophytes in postpubertal individuals. By contrast, tinea pedis is usually seen in adolescents or young adults.[17] Although foot infections can occasionally occur in young children, in this age group the nails may be invaded without concomitant skin infection.

Pathogenesis

Transfer of infecting organisms from soil, other animals, or humans is accomplished by means of arthrospores, which are vegetative cells with thickened cell walls formed by dermatophyte hyphae in vitro and in vivo. It is likely that these structures are shed by the primary host with shed skin scales or hair. It has been shown that dermatophyte arthrospores can survive for considerable periods outside the host, in some cases for more than 15 months. Direct contact between the infected individual and another is not necessary for the development of dermatophytosis. The process of transfer itself is little understood, but invasion of the skin appears to follow adherence of fungal cells to keratinocytes in vitro, a process that is maximal after about 2 or 3 hours. Keratinocytes from different sites do not appear to differ in their binding capacity for arthrospores. Subsequent germination leads to invasion.[18]

Susceptibility to infection is not universal. Studies of mice experimentally infected with *T. quinckeanum* have shown considerable interstrain variation in susceptibility to dermatophytosis.[19] In humans it has been suggested that susceptibility to tinea imbricata is mediated through an autosomal recessive gene, the evidence being based on population studies among tribes of Papua New Guinea.[20] Similar studies of the more common infections have not been carried out, but familial cases of tinea pedis are not common. The factors determining individual susceptibility to dermatophytosis are not understood,

TABLE 265-2 Distribution of *Trichophyton* and *Microsporum* Species Causing Tinea Capitis

Dermatophyte	Distribution
Trichophyton gourvilii	Central Africa
Trichophyton tonsurans	North America and Central America (Europe—some inner cities)
Trichophyton soudanense	West and central Africa
Trichophyton schoenleinii	North Africa (United States, Middle East, South Africa, South America—sporadic)
Trichophyton verrucosum	Europe
Trichophyton violaceum	Indian subcontinent, Middle East, North Africa
Trichophyton yaoundei	Central Africa
Microsporum audouinii	Central America, West Africa (Europe—uncommon)
Microsporum canis	Worldwide but uncommon in India and Far East
Microsporum ferrugineum	Central Africa, Far East

but variations in the composition of inhibitory fatty acids in sebum (see earlier) offer one explanation. Other skin surface factors thought to be important in determining the outcome of infection include the local carbon dioxide tension and the presence of surface moisture as well as unsaturated transferrin. After invasion, dermatophytes secrete proteinases such as zinc-containing metalloproteinases, which aid penetration.[21] In experimentally infected mice and guinea pigs, the inflammatory response to dermatophytosis is maximal after 9 to 16 days, and after this stage there is resolution of the infection. The main efferent limb of immunologic resistance is the T lymphocyte. Studies of mice with *T. quinckeanum* infections have shown that resistance can be transferred to sublethally irradiated mice with T cells bearing the Thy-1 phenotype (helper-inducer T cells).[19] Suppressor lymphocyte activity can be detected in cells from the draining lymph nodes at the peak of infection. Immunity cannot be transferred to naive animals with antibody. Although it is difficult to extrapolate these data to infected humans, there is evidence that the kinetics of the immune response in humans are similar. For instance, the development of delayed-type hypersensitivity in children with naturally acquired scalp ringworm caused by *T. tonsurans* correlates with recovery. Experimentally infected humans develop both delayed-type skin reactions to trichophytin and T-lymphocyte blastogenic responses at the time of recovery.[22] Patients with chronic *T. rubrum* or *T. concentricum* infections appear to have defective T-lymphocyte–mediated responses suggestive of a Th2 response.[23] These observations suggest that appropriate T-lymphocyte activation is critical for recovery in dermatophytosis.

The afferent limb of the immune response is provided by epidermal Langerhans cells, which have been shown to act as antigen-presenting cells in mixed cultures with human lymphocytes. The mechanisms by which T lymphocytes affect recovery are less well understood. Phagocytes, mainly neutrophils and to a lesser extent macrophages, can kill dermatophytes both intracellularly and extracellularly, mainly via oxidative pathways.[19] Dermatophyte antigens have been shown to be chemotactic to human leukocytes and may activate the alternative pathway of complement activation. However, except in inflammatory ringworm, neutrophils are not commonly seen as part of the inflammatory infiltrate in dermatophytosis, and other mechanisms of fungal clearance must be involved. It has been shown that increased epidermal turnover occurs during infection. Although this also occurs in heterologous skin grafted onto *nu/nu* (T-cell–deficient) mice, suggesting that an intrinsic response is involved, it is maximal at the time of development of the maximal immune responses.[24] It is possible that elimination of dermatophytes is also accomplished by increased shedding of the stratum corneum and that the immune system amplifies an endogenous epidermal response to infection.

Different dermatophyte species vary in their ability to elicit an immune response, with some organisms such as *T. rubrum* causing chronic or relapsing infections and others, including *T. verrucosum*, leading to long-term resistance to reinfection. Some dermatophytes produce glycopeptides, which are capable of reversibly inhibiting T-lymphocyte blastogenesis in vitro.[5] This may account for in vivo modulation of immunity.

Clinical Features

The archetypal lesion of dermatophytosis is an annular scaling patch with a raised margin showing a variable degree of inflammation, the center usually being less inflamed than the edge. The word *tinea* is used to refer to dermatophyte infections, and it is usually followed by the Latin description of the appropriate site. Hence, tinea pedis is an infection of the feet and tinea capitis, the scalp. The phrase *tinea incognito* is used to describe infections that do not show any of the usual characteristic features of dermatophytosis, often because of inappropriate application of corticosteroid creams.

The clinical appearances of the infection vary with the site, the fungal species involved, and the host's immune response. Zoophilic fungi often cause inflammatory lesions, and in some cases large pustular lesions (kerions) may develop. By contrast, lesions caused by anthro-

pophilic dermatophytes often show little inflammation and may become chronic (see "Pathogenesis").

Dermatophytes cause infections irrespective of the patient's underlying immune status. However, in common with other infections, the clinical appearances are altered in immunocompromised individuals. Dermatophyte lesions are usually less inflamed in patients with diseases affecting T-lymphocyte function, but, paradoxically, in some patients lesions are pustular as well as extensive. Often there is a marked follicular component of the rash in these individuals.

Tinea Pedis

Tinea pedis is usually caused by infection with either *T. rubrum* or *T. mentagrophytes (interdigitale)*, less commonly by *E. floccosum*. The infection usually starts in the lateral interdigital spaces of the foot or on the undersurface of the lateral aspects of the toes. The main symptom is itching, although this is variable. The skin usually cracks and may become severely macerated. In some cases, often where *T. mentagrophytes* is the causative organism, bullae are formed, and there is severe itching. The infection may also spread onto the dorsum of the feet, usually on the lateral side of the foot. Involvement of the sole is common in *T. rubrum* infections, and part of or the entire sole becomes erythematous and covered with dry scales. This is most noticeable along the lateral borders of the sole, where the appearance often leads to the term *moccasin* or *dry-type* infection. Blisters may also be formed in small clusters on the sole. The course of infection is variable. In noninflammatory forms the interdigital scaling is often chronic or intermittent, whereas if blisters are formed, the infection usually resolves but may recur several months later. The main complications of tinea pedis are bacterial cellulitis and fungal invasion of the toenails (onychomycosis) or the skin of the dorsum of the foot and leg.

Tinea pedis is usually seen in young adults or teenage children. It is particularly common in institutions or places where common bathing facilities are used. The clinical manifestations of infection are altered in patients with T-lymphocyte abnormalities, including those with acquired immunodeficiency syndrome (AIDS), in whom there is often extensive spread of the lesions onto the dorsal surface of the foot.

Scaling between the toes is often referred to as athlete's foot, but similar clinical signs may be produced by a variety of organisms. Erythrasma that is due to *Corynebacterium minutissimum* may present with scaling and, in particular, maceration between the toe webs. Gram-negative bacteria such as *Pseudomonas* and *Proteus* spp. may contribute to interdigital disease in patients with closely apposed web spaces or whose work involves immersion in water. These organisms may replace the original dermatophytes in this site, an infection known as dermatophytosis complex.[25] *Staphylococcus aureus* may cause secondary infections of foot, but characteristically this starts on the dorsum of the foot over the first two digits. The mold fungi *Scytalidium dimidiatum* and *S. hyalinum* may cause interdigital scaling as well as nail disease and sole involvement that is indistinguishable from dry-type infections caused by dermatophytes.

Tinea Cruris

The most common dermatophytes associated with groin infections are *T. rubrum* and *E. floccosum*. This infection is also called jock itch. The infection starts with scaling and irritation in the groin. The rash usually involves the anterior aspect of the thighs, less commonly the scrotum. The leading edge extending onto the thighs is prominent and may contain follicular papules and pustules. The infection may also spread to the anal cleft. Although tinea cruris is mainly a disease of young adult men, it may affect women, particularly in the tropics, where the infection is often less well delineated and spreads in a band around the waist area.

Tinea cruris, as with tinea pedis, there may be clustering of cases in institutionalized groups such as in military camps. The toe webs are also often infected in patients with tinea cruris.

Erythrasma of the groin may also cause a localized rash with itching. However, here the leading edge is less prominent than in tinea cruris, and the rash is covered with fine wrinkles. Erythrasma fluoresces pink under Wood's light. Candidiasis of the groin may also mimic tinea cruris, but an important clue to the presence of *Candida* is the appearance of small satellite pustules beyond the free margin of the rash. Flexural psoriasis causes a vivid red and uniformly scaling rash in the groin, and there is usually at least one other site with typical psoriatic plaques.

Tinea Corporis

Tinea corporis, or ringworm, is one of the most commonly misdiagnosed skin diseases. Cases of this infection are not common in temperate climates, although it is seen more frequently in the tropics. Generally there are various clinical presentations of this form of dermatophytosis. Most lesions have a prominent edge that may contain pustules or follicular papules, and the center of the lesion is often less inflamed and scaly (Fig. 265-1). Sites commonly involved are the trunk and legs. Itching is variable, and lesions may be single or multiple. Generally, infections caused by anthropophilic dermatophytes such as *T. rubrum* are less inflammatory and less clearly demarcated, and in some patients it is necessary to search for the margin carefully to delineate the rash. Lesions are usually hyperpigmented in pigmented skins. By contrast, zoophilic infections such as those caused by *M. canis* and *T. verrucosum* are more inflammatory, and lesions may become elevated and contain pustules. Infections caused by *M. gypseum* are also usually inflammatory and may have a brick-red appearance.

These clinical patterns vary with the site of infection. *T. rubrum* infections on the lower parts of the legs may lead to the formation of single or multiple deep nodules that may mimic erythema nodosum.[26] The overlying skin is dry, red, and scaly, which is a useful clue to the correct diagnosis. This form of infection, which is known as nodular folliculitis, follows follicular penetration of the hair follicles of the lower portions of the legs by the fungus. It is seen mainly in women. In patients with defective T-lymphocyte function, scaling is often minimal, and the rash of tinea corporis consists of grouped papules or pustules without significant erythema.

Tinea corporis can occur at any age, although in temperate countries it is most often seen in children and is associated with zoophilic infections.

A number of different conditions should be considered in the differential diagnosis of tinea corporis, ranging from eczema to psoriasis or annular erythema. The important points to look for are the annular scaling margin of lesions and follicular prominence, which are features of dermatophytosis. However, it may be necessary to take scrapings for laboratory culture where there is doubt.

Tinea Imbricata

Tinea imbricata is a variant of tinea corporis that is caused by *T. concentricum*. The geographic distribution of the disease is shown in Table 265-2. Patients may be infected at any age, although infants and young children are frequently affected. The main characteristic of the rash is the formation of concentric rings of scales (Fig. 265-2) over large parts of the body that amalgamate to form waves of scaling.[14] There are other clinical varieties of tinea imbricata, including the diffuse scaling variety, in which large flakes of skin are prominent. The disease gets its name *imbricata* (Latin, "tiled") from this clinical pattern. Other patients may have itchy lichenified lesions on the forearms. The face may be affected, as well as the sides of the fingers, but the feet, scalp, axillae, and groin are usually spared. Tinea imbricata is sel-

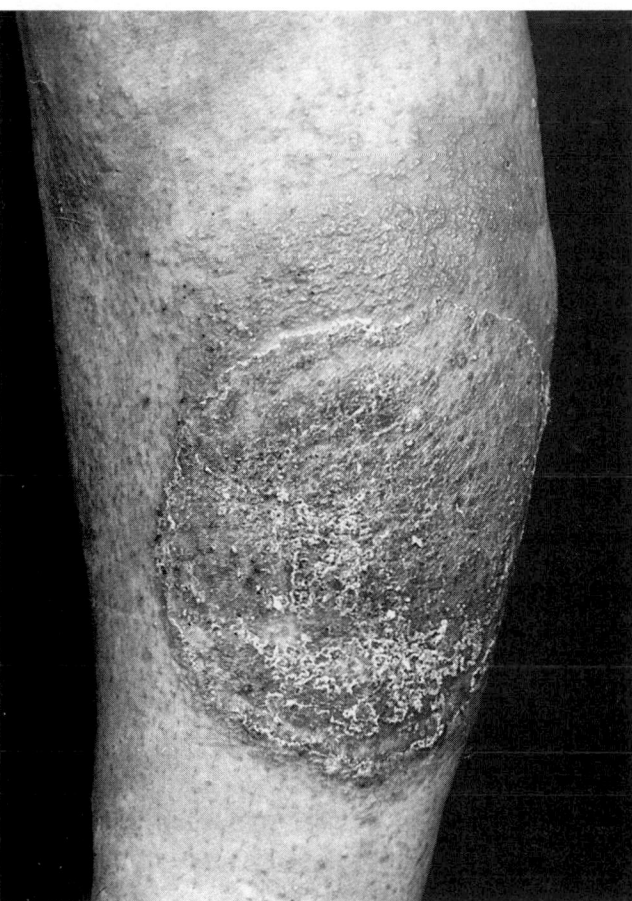

FIGURE 265-1. Inflammatory tinea corporis caused by *Trichophyton erinacei (mentagrophytes).*

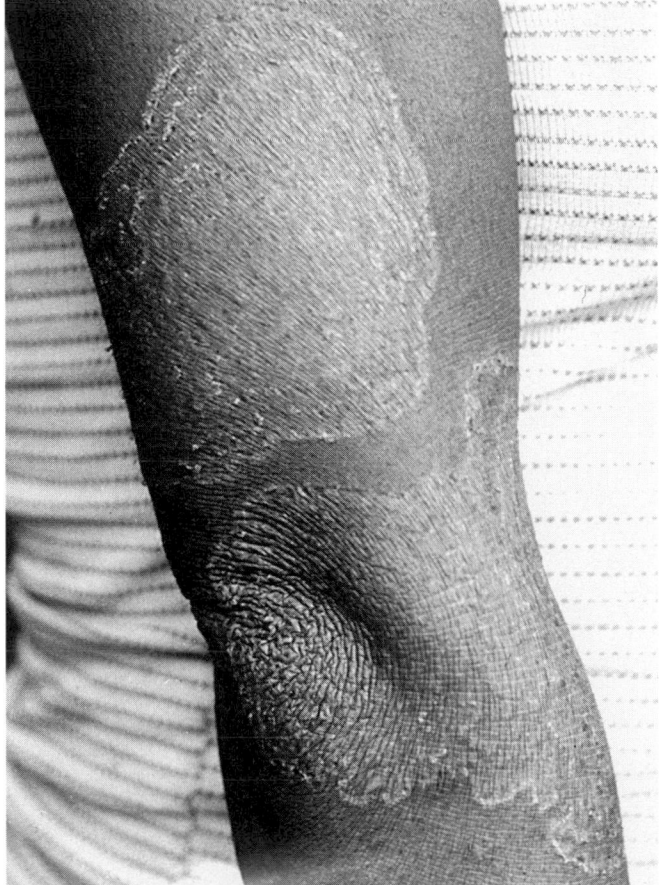

FIGURE 265-2. Early lesions of tinea imbricata showing the first signs of concentric rings.

dom mistaken for other diseases, and the inhabitants of endemic areas easily recognize the appearance of the infection and have specific names for it. In Papua New Guinea, it is called *sipoma* or *grille*.

Dermatophytosis of the Hand (Tinea Manuum)

The term *tinea manuum* is used for dermatophyte infections involving the hand. In some patients the dorsum of the hand may be affected, but most commonly the disease occurs on the palmar surface. It is a characteristic of dry-type infections at this site to find that only one palm is involved, although in some patients both may be infected. The clinical features are identical to those seen with dry-type infections of the sole. The usual cause is *T. rubrum,* and the feet are often involved in addition to the hands.

Dermatophytosis affecting the palm may be confused with eczema, but the unilateral distribution of the infection and the common accompanying findings of onychomycosis and tinea pedis are helpful clues. Patients with palmoplantar keratoderma (tylosis) are particularly susceptible to superinfection of the palms and soles with dermatophytes.[27] This complication may be difficult to identify, but the skin may blister and the hand usually itches. In these patients fungi other than *T. rubrum* may be implicated.

Tinea Faciei

Dermatophyte infections of the face are usually caused by the same organisms associated with tinea corporis. Infections that are due to *T. rubrum* at this site are often particularly difficult to recognize (tinea incognito). The facial skin becomes itchy and red, but the margin of the rash may be difficult to discern (Fig. 265-3). Some patients report that the facial rash is exacerbated by sun exposure. In other instances

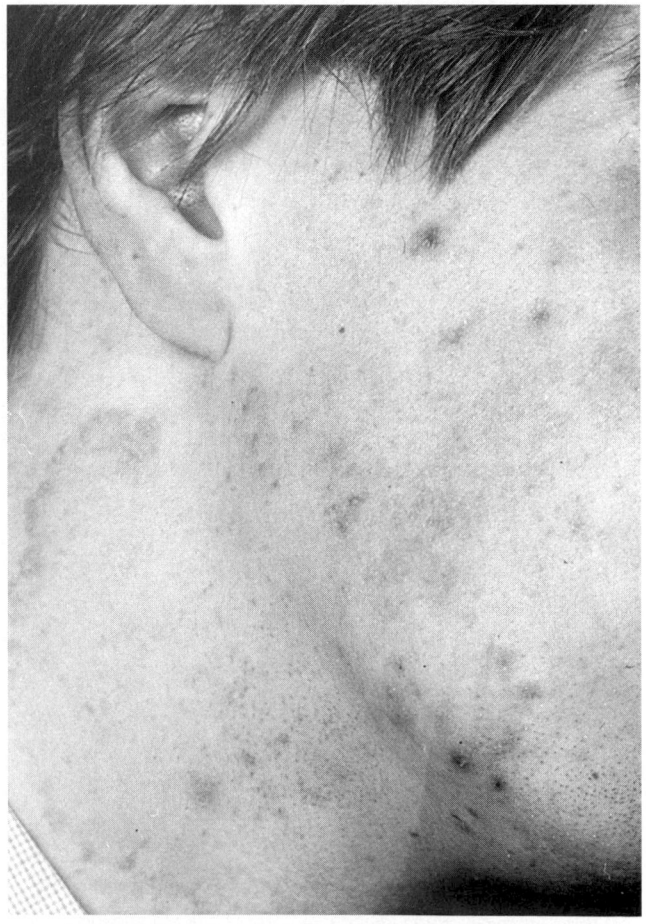

FIGURE 265-3. Tinea faciei caused by *Trichophyton rubrum.*

lesions are more readily noticeable and affect the ears. Tinea faciei has been reported more frequently in AIDS patients.

Tinea barbae, infection of the neck and beard area, may be pustular and inflamed because it is often caused by zoophilic organisms such as *T. verrucosum.* It is more localized than sycosis barbae caused by *S. aureus,* a helpful point in distinguishing the two conditions.

Tinea Capitis

Scalp ringworm, or tinea capitis, is a disease of childhood. Its prevalence varies considerably in different parts of the world. The disease is widespread in some urban areas in the United States, Africa, and Europe. Tinea capitis is also common in parts of India. In northern Europe the disease is sporadic. The main reasons for these differences in the prevalence of infection in different localities are the nature of the infecting organisms and the availability of control measures. Endemic infections affecting large numbers of children are associated with anthropophilic organisms, and sporadic disease with zoophilic fungi. Tinea capitis is usually classified by the pattern of hair shaft invasion. Dermatophyte infections in which arthrospores are formed on the outside of the hair shaft are known as *ectothrix* infections and those in which the spores develop within the hair itself as *endothrix* infections. In *T. schoenleinii* infections the fungi invade the hair medulla but then regress and leave tunnels containing air within the hair shaft (the "favic" pattern). Although it is identified as a childhood disease, adults exposed to *T. tonsurans* infections and patients with AIDS may develop tinea capitis.

The main clinical feature of dermatophyte scalp infections are the appearance of scaling of the scalp skin that is associated with a variable degree of erythema and inflammation and alopecia. In some cases the infection closely resembles seborrheic dermatitis or dandruff of the scalp. The infection is often accompanied by itching. A pathognomonic feature is hair loss. In ectothrix infections hairs often break a few millimeters or more above the skin surface (Fig. 265-4). Broken or infected hairs are also slightly swollen and have a dull appearance. In endothrix infections, parasitized hairs break at the skin level. In some endothrix infections scattered stumps can be seen within areas of hair loss (black-dot ringworm). In such cases inflammation may be minimal. A further element in tinea capitis is the variable amount of inflammation, but in some cases the whole area becomes pustular and covered with a thick scale or exudative crust. Often one of these elements dominates the clinical pattern. For instance, in some children there is little overt hair loss, the whole infection resembling seborrheic dermatitis. Likewise, in some ectothrix infections a pustular form of dermatophytosis, or kerion, develops. This is less common in endothrix infections. In most kerions the pustules are not a sign of secondary bacterial infection,[28] although this may occur under adherent crusts.

Tinea capitis is rare in adults, although it may occasionally be found in elderly patients and is caused by a variety of fungi such as *T. tonsurans.* It has been associated with scarring alopecia of unknown etiology (pseudopelade) in adults.

In favus the same processes occur, but an important clinical characteristic is the formation of an inflammatory crust, or scutulum, composed of neutrophils and serous exudate around individual hair shafts. With time these amalgamate over the surface of the scalp so that the hair appears to be matted together with a thick crust that is said to have a mousy odor. In many patients the signs are indistinguishable from those seen with other forms of scalp ringworm. Two other characteristics of favus are late shedding of hairs and a tendency to develop scarring alopecia. The infection may persist into adult life, particular in women.

Untreated scalp ringworm usually remits spontaneously after puberty. Permanent hair loss is uncommon unless there has been a severe inflammatory response or the patient has favus. A surprising degree of recovery of hair growth occurs, even in children with severe kerions.

Tinea capitis has to be distinguished from seborrheic dermatitis, which usually occurs in older children and does not cause hair loss. Alopecia areata also causes circumscribed areas of hair loss but does not scale, and the "exclamation mark" hairs seen in this condition—

broken hairs tapering from the fractured end toward the skin surface—are pathognomonic.

Onychomycosis Caused by Dermatophytes

Onychomycosis, or fungal infection of the nails, usually occurs in individuals with infections of adjacent toe or palmar skin, except in rare cases of childhood nail infection in which nail plate invasion may develop without skin involvement. There are several different patterns of nail plate invasion.[29]

The most common clinical pattern of onychomycosis is distal and subungual onychomycosis, in which the nail plate is invaded from the distal and lateral borders. There is usually associated thickening of the nail, which becomes white, yellow, or brown. The latter color is more common in the rare instances of *T. mentagrophytes* nail disease. In onychomycosis caused by endothrix scalp fungi such as *T. soudanense,* the thickening may be minimal, and the nail surface is pitted with small fissures.[30] The most common cause of onychomycosis is *T. rubrum,* which often accompanies long-standing disease, and the infection involves the entire nail plate.

Superficial white onychomycosis occurs where the nail plate is invaded from the top surface, which is eventually covered with white crumbly plaques. Other fungi, such as *Fusarium* species, more commonly cause this pattern of nail invasion but this may be followed by deeper penetration. However, in its pure form superficial white onychomycosis can be seen with *T. mentagrophytes,* and it may also accompany distal and subungual onychomycosis in some *T. rubrum* infections.

Rarely, invasion appears to originate from the proximal nail plate. This is usually a feature of relapse of treated nails, but rapidly spreading proximal nail plate invasion has also been described in patients with AIDS.[31]

Onychomycosis can occur at any age, although it is more common with increasing age. Males and females are equally affected.

This infection has to be distinguished from onychomycosis caused by *Candida,* in which there is little nail plate thickening but toenail infection is rare. *Scytalidium* infections may also lead to nail plate invasion. These are difficult to distinguish from infections caused by dermatophytes, but the nail plate is often not grossly thickened and may be severely undermined, and invasion predominantly affects the lateral border of the plate in the early stages of disease. Psoriasis of the nail also causes onycholysis, but the nail plate is typically covered with fine pits.

Deep Dermatophyte Infections

On rare occasions patients known to be immunocompromised or apparently unselected individuals develop dermatophyte infections in which the fungi invade subcutaneous tissues via the lymphatics, usually causing clusters of granulomas, lymphedema (Fig. 265-5), and draining sinuses.[32] Sometimes aggregates of fungal hyphae resembling those found in eumycetomas may be seen in histologic sections. These dermatophyte "pseudomycetoma" grains may be surrounded by neutrophil abscesses, but often the fungal hyphae are engulfed by giant cells in tissue sections. Deep dermatophyte infections may extend further to involve draining lymph nodes or other sites, including the liver and brain, and they may be fatal.

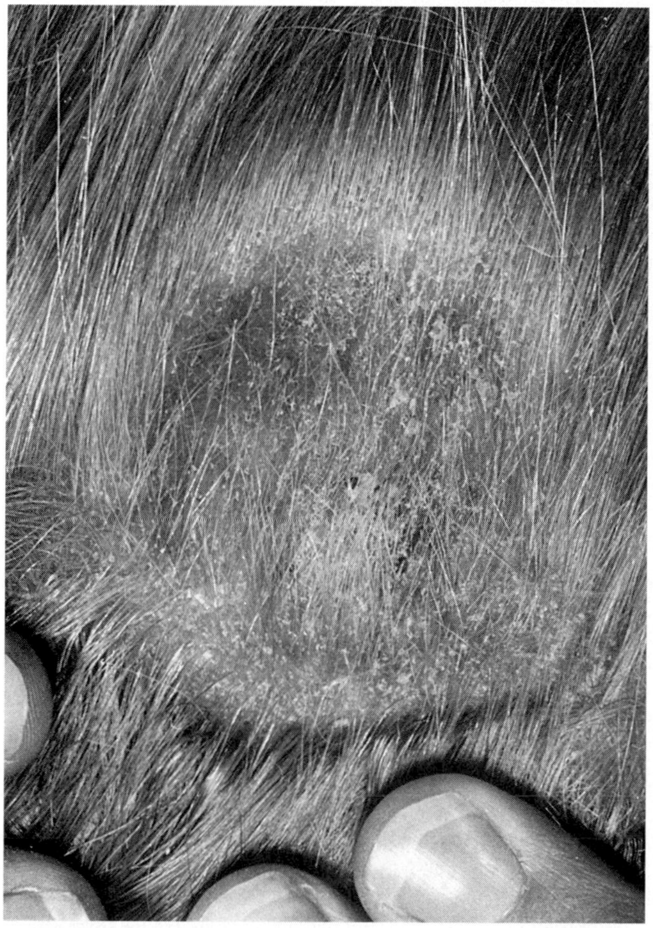

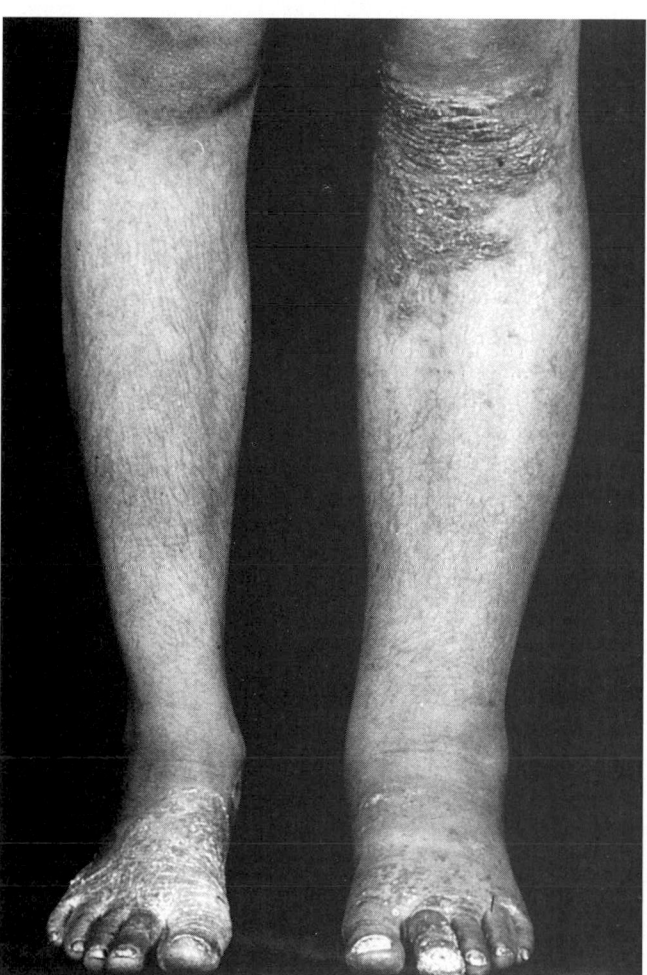

FIGURE 265-4. Scalp ringworm in which an ectothrix infection of the hair is caused by *Microsporum canis.*

FIGURE 265-5. Deep dermatophytosis in which *Trichophyton rubrum* infection is causing unilateral lymphedema after invasion of the lymphatics.

Dermatophyte "Id" Reactions

The immune mechanisms in dermatophytosis may lead to the appearance of secondary rashes called *id reactions*. The most common of these is a type of acute vesicular eczema or pompholyx that occurs on the hands and feet in patients with inflammatory ringworm of the feet, mainly caused by *T. mentagrophytes.* These events are thought to be linked if the original dermatophyte infection becomes inflamed before the appearance of the secondary rash, the latter is maximal on the affected foot, and the patient has a strong delayed-type hypersensitivity reaction to intradermal trichophytin. The histology of this id reaction is that of eczema. A second form of id reaction is seen in patients with inflammatory tinea capitis or corporis and is usually caused by zoophilic organisms. It consists of small follicular papules, some of which appear necrotic. This is a form of cutaneous vasculitis that usually subsides spontaneously. Both reactions may be triggered by antifungal therapy. Other less common types of id reaction include annular erythema and erythema nodosum.

Patients with follicular invasion by dermatophytes may develop a residual granuloma in the late stages of the disease called Majocchi's granuloma. It is usually sterile, although sometimes fragments of mycelium can be seen in histologic sections, and resolves slowly with time.

Laboratory Diagnosis

In some cases it is possible to screen patients with scalp infections by using a filtered ultraviolet light source (Wood's light). Infections caused by *Microsporum* spp. fluoresce green. However, *Trichophyton* infections do not fluoresce, apart from favus, in which the hairs appear yellowish. Fluorescent hairs are infected, and apart from its use as a screening procedure, Wood's light examination may be helpful as a method of selecting hairs for microscopy and culture.

The laboratory diagnosis of dermatophytosis depends on the examination and culture of scrapings or clippings from lesions. It is important to sample the edge of skin lesions and infected nails. In the case of infected hairs, broken stubs are best selected and can be removed with forceps without undue trauma. Material should be allowed to soften in 10% to 20% potassium hydroxide before being examined under the microscope. Nails often take up to 2 hours to soften, although the process can be hastened by gentle warming. Fungal hyphae can be seen as chains of arthrospores in cleared scales or clippings. The fluorescent whitener calcofluor may also be used to stain fungi, but preparations have to be viewed using fluorescence microscopy; however, it may enhance the yield of positive samples.

Dermatophytes infecting hair show characteristic appearances that are helpful in recognition. Some form arthrospores on the outside of the hair shaft (ectothrix infections). The small spores can be seen by focusing the microscope on the edge of the epilated hair shaft. Most of the pathogenic *Microsporum* spp. that cause tinea capitis have small arthrospores clustered around the outside of hair. By contrast, few *Trichophyton* spp. form ectothrix spores, but those that do, such as *T. verrucosum,* produce large arthrospores. The majority of *Trichophyton* spp. causing scalp ringworm form arthrospores within the hair shaft (endothrix infection). With some practice it is possible to make a preliminary identification of the likely genus of invading fungus on the basis of the microscopy of infected hair. *T. schoenleinii* invades hair, but hyphae regress and leave airspaces within the hair shaft.

Scrapings or nail clippings may also be cultured. Primary isolation is carried out at room temperature, usually on Sabouraud's agar containing antibiotics (penicillin-streptomycin or choramphenicol) and cycloheximide (Acti-Dione), an antifungal agent that suppresses the growth of environmental contaminant fungi. In the case of nail disease, it is important to use media without cycloheximide because certain fungi, such as *Scytalidium,* that may infect nails are sensitive to the latter. Most dermatophytes can be identified within 2 weeks, although *T. verrucosum* grows best at 37° C and may only have formed into small and granular colonies at this stage. Identification depends on the gross colonial and microscopic morphology. In some cases,

other tests involving nutritional requirements and hair penetration in vitro are necessary to confirm the identification.

Generally, the identification of dermatophytes in skin material is simple and worth the effort required to obtain samples. It is particularly helpful in scalp infections, in which it is important to identify the likely source of infection.

Treatment

The usual approach to the management of dermatophyte infections is to treat with topical therapy if possible, but most nail and all hair infections and widespread dermatophytosis are best treated with oral drugs (Table 265-3). [33]

The main topical agents used for dermatophytosis are the keratolytics and compounds with specific antifungal activity. The keratolytic agent used most frequently is Whitfield's ointment (salicylic and benzoic acid compound). It is inexpensive but messy to use, although a cream formulation of benzoic acid compound is available in some countries.

In the past, therapy relied on the use of substances including dyes with weak antifungal activity, such as brilliant green and Castellani paint (magenta and resorcinol). There is now a large group of specific antifungals that may be used in dermatophytosis, although the use of some of these is largely confined to the treatment of tinea pedis. They include drugs such as chlorphenesin, undecylenate, and tolnaftate, which are available in cream or, in some cases, powder form. Few comparative studies have examined their relative merits. Nonetheless, they are effective in uncomplicated cases. More attention has been focused on one particular group of antifungal drugs, the azoles, which include miconazole, clotrimazole, econazole, tioconazole, ketoconazole, oxiconazole, bifonazole, isoconazole, and fenticonazole. [34] These are active against all the common skin fungi, and many can be given once daily. Other potent antifungals used in the treatment of dermatophytosis are ciclopiroxolamine, terbinafine, butenafine, and naftifine. It is difficult to choose between the different groups of these agents on the basis of well-constructed comparative studies.

Generally, topical therapy for tinea pedis has to be continued for at least 2 and possibly 4 weeks. Topical terbinafine can be used to clear lesions of tinea pedis in 1 to 7 days. Dry-type infections of the sole respond poorly to topical application, although the topical medication may be useful in relieving the dryness and scaling. Tinea cruris usually responds within 2 or 3 weeks of the outset of treatment. Some of the azole agents can be used only once daily. Topical treatments for scalp and nail infections are generally ineffective, although cures of nail disease have been claimed for topically applied azoles and ciclopiroxolamine. Three other approaches are of potential value in the management of nail disease. The first, a topically applied nail solution containing 28% tioconazole, has been found to produce mycologic and clinical remission on its own or in conjunction with oral griseofulvin. The second such preparation used in nail disease is a combination of 40% urea and bifonazole. Urea is a potent hydrating agent and softens nails after application under occlusion. The 40% urea paste may be used to remove residual areas of infection after oral therapy for onychomycosis. [35] This combination may also prove useful in addition to oral therapy for nail disease. Finally, 5% amorolfine used as a nail lacquer is effective in a proportion of early cases of dermatophyte and *Candida* nail infection and can be applied once or twice weekly or as combination therapy with oral drugs in severe infections. [36]

The main oral antifungals used for dermatophytosis are terbinafine, itraconazole, and fluconazole. Griseofulvin is an alternative treatment but is still the treatment of choice for most cases of tinea capitis. Terbinafine is given in doses of 250 mg daily for 2 weeks for tinea cruris or corporis, 6 weeks for fingernail infections, and 12 weeks for toenail infections. It produces rapid and long-lasting remissions for dry-type dermatophytosis and other skin infections. Itraconazole can be given continuously in doses of 200 mg daily and is curative for tinea cruris or corporis after 1 week. Fluconazole can also be used as a treatment for dermatophytosis, but current regimens employ 150 to 300 mg weekly for infections of the skin. All three drugs are well tolerated and involve

TABLE 265-3 Treatment of Dermatophytosis

Dermatophytosis, Clinical Disease Pattern	Treatment
Tinea pedis	
Interdigital	*Topical cream/ointment:* terbinafine, imidazoles (miconazole, econazole, clotrimazole, etc.), undecenoic acid, tolnaftate
"Dry type"	*Oral:* terbinafine 250 mg/day for 2-4 weeks, itraconazole 400 mg/day for 1 week per month (repeated if necessary), fluconazole 200 mg weekly for 4-8 weeks
Tinea corporis	
Small, well-defined lesions	*Topical cream/ointment:* terbinafine, imidazoles (miconazole, econazole, clotrimazole, etc.)
Larger lesions	*Oral:* terbinafine 250 mg/day for 2 weeks, itraconazole 200 mg/day for 1 week, fluconazole 250 mg weekly for 2-4 weeks
Tinea capitis	Griseofulvin: 10-20 mg/kg daily for minimum 6 weeks
	Terbinafine: < 20 kg: 62.5 mg/day; 20-40 kg: 125 mg/day; > 40 kg: 250 mg/day
	Itraconazole: 4-6 mg/kg pulsed dose weekly
	Fluconazole: 3-8 mg/kg pulsed dose weekly
Onychomycosis	
Fingernails	Terbinafine: 250 mg daily for 6 weeks
	Itraconazole: 400 mg/day for 1 week each month, repeated for 2-3 months
	Fluconazole: 200 mg weekly for 8-16 weeks
Toenails	Terbinafine: 250 mg daily for 12 weeks
	Itraconazole: 400 mg/day for 1 week each month, repeated for 2-4 months
	Fluconazole: 200 mg weekly for 12-24 weeks

a low risk of hepatic injury (less than 1 in 70,000); rarely, terbinafine causes disturbance or loss of taste. All show evidence of efficacy, although there is more information on terbinafine and itraconazole.[37,38]

Griseofulvin is given in doses of 10 to 20 mg/kg daily in either tablet or syrup form and is the main treatment for tinea capitis. Adverse effects include headache, nausea, and abdominal discomfort. Less common reactions are urticaria, diarrhea, and photosensitivity. Griseofulvin may precipitate acute intermittent porphyria and systemic lupus erythematosus in predisposed subjects. Oral ketoconazole may also be used for dermatophytosis, although the risk of hepatitis, albeit rare, makes this a second choice for therapy in most instances.

Oral therapy is used for scalp ringworm and nail infections. Scalp infections take 6 to 12 weeks to respond to griseofulvin. Often it is useful to employ a topical azole cream or shampoo in addition and, if crusts are present, to remove these with saline soaks. For the treatment of large numbers of infected children, intermittent therapy with up to 1 g of griseofulvin has been suggested, with possible retreatment after 6 weeks. A substantial percentage of those infected may respond to single-dose therapy. Itraconazole and terbinafine are also effective in scalp disease but there are few ideal pediatric formulations yet.[39] Terbinafine is very effective for *Trichophyton* scalp infections but less active against *Microsporum,* for which a double dose is advised; treatment is for 4 weeks. It is important to attempt to identify the organism causing scalp infection because, if the infection is of human origin, it can spread to other contacts, and it may be necessary to screen classmates or members of the families of children with anthropophilic infections. Zoophilic infections do not usually spread from child to child, although several family members exposed to the same source of infection may develop scalp disease.

Onychomycosis caused by dermatophytes can be treated with oral therapy. Terbinafine and itraconazole have replaced griseofulvin for this indication. For instance, terbinafine produces 70% to 80% cure rates in 6 weeks for fingernails and 12 weeks for toenails.[40] Itraconazole is also effective at a dose of 200 mg daily for 3 months in toenail infections. However, in nail infections it is usually administered as a "pulsed" treatment given for 1 week of each month at a dose of 400 mg daily, the week's course being repeated once more for fingernail infections (two pulses) and twice or three times for toenail disease (three or four pulses).[41] Reported remission rates are above 60%. Intermittent regimens using fluconazole (300 and 450 mg weekly) are employed in the treatment of onychomycosis.[42] There have been no large comparative studies of fluconazole versus the other two treatments for nail disease. However, one large double-blind comparative study of terbinafine given continuously at 250 mg daily for 12 or 16 weeks versus pulsed itraconazole at 200 mg twice a day for 1 week each month repeated three or four times in toenail onychomycosis showed significantly better responses for both terbinafine groups in both mycologic and clinical remission rates (LION Study results).[43]

SCYTALIDIUM INFECTIONS

Infections caused by the pigmented fungus *S. dimidiatum* (*Hendersonula toruloidea*) closely resemble dry-type dermatophytosis caused by *T. rubrum. S. dimidiatum* was originally described as a plant pathogen, but it appears to be a genuine cause of human infection. A similar type of infection has been ascribed to a nonpigmented mold, *S. hyalinum.* In both cases the affected patients have originated from the tropics.

The precise mechanisms of infection with either organism are unknown. *S. hyalinum* has never been isolated from the environment, and although *S. dimidiatum* is a pathogen of certain plants such as fruit trees, patients do not usually give a specific history of exposure. It has been found that healthy individuals in some tropical areas carry these organisms on the feet but do not have overt disease, suggesting that asymptomatic carriage may be followed under the appropriate conditions by infection. Infections have been described in immigrants from tropical areas to the United Kingdom, Canada, and France. Patients have also been identified in the southern United States, Trinidad, Colombia, Ecuador, and India, and it is likely that the infection is more widespread. Occasionally, it may be seen in patients who have paid short visits to the tropics.

Clinical Features

The clinical signs of skin infection with both *Scytalidium* species are identical to those associated with dry-type *T. rubrum* infections.[44] There is scaling of the lateral interdigital spaces, over the soles, and on one or both palms. Itching is usually minimal. Onychomycosis may also develop. Often there is early invasion of the lateral border of the nail without significant thickening of the nail plate (Fig. 265-6), but eventually the whole nail plate may be undermined and onycholysis may lead to shedding of the complete nail. Hyperpigmented streaks may occur in the nails, although these are not pathognomonic for these infections and can be seen with other forms of inflammatory nail dystrophy.

Diagnosis

Scrapings or nail clippings examined after treatment with potassium hydroxide contain sinuous fungal hyphae. On close inspection the morphology is different from that normally seen with dermatophyte hyphae, but accurate discrimination requires experience. Both organisms grow on Sabouraud's agar but are inhibited if cycloheximide (Acti-Dione) is incorporated in the medium.

Treatment

There is no satisfactory therapy for either infection. Whitfield's ointment may be used to treat *Scytalidium* infections of the sole or the palm. However, none of the specific antifungal drugs currently available produces consistent results.

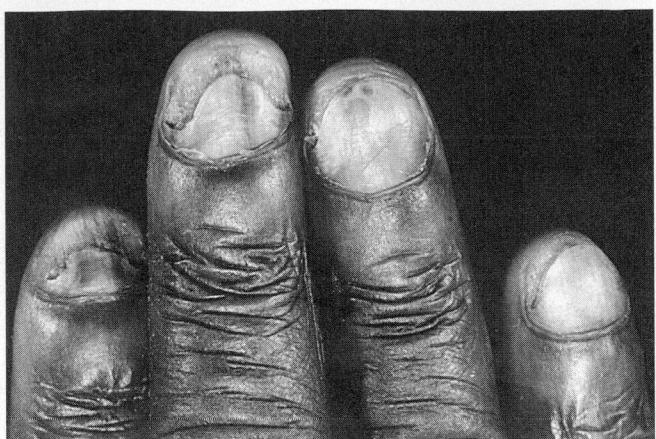

FIGURE 265-6. Onychomycosis caused by *Scytalidium dimidiatum.*

OTHER FORMS OF ONYCHOMYCOSIS

A number of other fungi may cause onychomycosis. The most common of these is *Scopulariopsis brevicaulis,* which usually causes infection of the great toenails. Some patients with this form of infection have previously abnormal toenails (e.g., onychogryphosis). *Scopulariopsis* infections of the nails have a typical cinnamon color that is caused by the presence of fungal spores seen on direct microscopy of the nail. The fungus is easy to isolate in culture. Treatment may be difficult, but chemical nail removal with 40% urea may be useful.

Superficial white onychomycosis may be caused by *Acremonium* or *Fusarium* species. These infections are similar to those caused by *T. mentagrophytes,* and the identity of the causative organisms should be confirmed by culture.

Occasionally, other fungi are isolated from nail material. In many cases they appear to be colonizing the undersurface of dystrophic nail plate. On rare occasions, however, they may contribute to the nail pathology by invasion. This is best established by repeated attempts at culture, and if the organism is isolated on numerous occasions and if hyphae are present in the nail, it is likely that the organism is implicated in the nail disease. Examples of infections caused by a range of different organisms, such as *Aspergillus, Fusarium,* and *Acremonium* spp., have been recorded. *Fusarium* is now known to cause a range of fungal nail infections from superficial white onychomycosis to proximal subungual disease; in severely neutropenic patients nail infection may be followed by systemic dissemination. There is seldom effective oral therapy for these infections,[45] and nail removal with 40% urea is probably the best alternative treatment.

PITYRIASIS VERSICOLOR

Pityriasis or tinea versicolor is a superficial infection caused by *Malassezia* species, lipophilic yeasts that are normal commensals on the skin surface.[46] The infection is confined to the trunk or proximal aspects of the limbs. Hair and nail plate invasions do not occur.

Organisms

The normal skin is colonized in late childhood and adult life by lipophilic yeasts. Morphologically, these are either oval (most common on the scalp) or round (mainly on the trunk), and they were previously called *Pityrosporum ovale* and *Pityrosporum orbiculare,* respectively. These organisms have now been reclassified as members of the genus *Malassezia,* among which there are seven pathogenic species: *Malassezia furfur, M. pachydermatis* (not associated with human skin infections), *M. sympodialis, M. globosa, M. restricta, M. obtusa,* and *M. slooffiae.*[46] Round yeasts, usually *M. globosa,* are seen in lesions of pityriasis versicolor accompanied by short, stubby hyphae; *M. furfur* may produce filaments as well but is less common.

Pathogenesis

The infection is associated with transformation of yeast-phase organisms into hyphal forms, although patients with pityriasis versicolor occasionally have only oval yeasts. The stimulus for this phase change is unknown. Infections are more common in the tropics and may appear after sun exposure, which may therefore be a trigger factor. Patients with Cushing's syndrome may also develop this infection, but diseases related to T-lymphocyte suppression are not necessarily associated with pityriasis versicolor.[47]

A carboxylic acid called *azelaic acid,* thought to be produced by the organism in the stratum corneum, is believed to lead to the depigmentation seen in lesions.[48] *Malassezia* yeasts grow in the presence of medium-chain-length fatty acids.

Different species of *Malassezia* obviously play a role in the development of disease, although it is not known why, for instance, *M. globosa* in particular should be associated with pityriasis versicolor.

Clinical Features

Pityriasis versicolor is usually seen on the trunk or proximal portions of the limbs, although more extensive infections involving the face and waist area are seen in the tropics. Lesions may be hypopigmented or hyperpigmented macules that amalgamate to cover the affected area with scaling plaques. The lesions are usually not itchy. In some patients lesions may remit spontaneously.

The diagnosis can be confirmed by direct microscopy of lesions, on which the characteristic round yeast forms and short hyphae can be seen. The scrapings can be viewed after clearing with potassium hydroxide but are seen more clearly after staining with a mixture of Parker Quink ink and potassium hydroxide. Lesions fluoresce yellow-green under Wood's light, although this may not be seen on all affected areas. *Malassezia* yeasts are difficult to culture unless oil is added to the medium. An overlay of Tween 80 encourages growth.

Treatment

The most appropriate therapy for pityriasis versicolor is a topical azole, terbinafine cream, 2% selenium sulfide lotion, or 20% sodium thiosulfate applied daily for 10 to 14 days. The latter preparations may be irritative. In some cases intermittent applications of 50% propylene glycol in water prevent a relapse.[49] In severe cases, oral ketoconazole or itraconazole produces remissions. The exact doses of ketoconazole needed to induce a remission are not clear, but therapy for 5 to 10 days with 200 mg is usually sufficient, although mycologic recovery is not seen for about 30 days because the organisms can still be seen in skin scrapings. In some patients a single dose of 400 mg is effective. The effective dose of itraconazole is 200 mg daily for 5 days.

Patients usually have to be warned that the pigmentary changes may return to normal only after many months, even when the infection has been successfully treated.

OTHER *MALASSEZIA* INFECTIONS

Two other skin conditions are associated with *Malassezia* yeasts: *Malassezia* folliculitis and seborrheic dermatitis. In addition, this fungus has caused catheter-acquired sepsis (see Chapter 267).

Malassezia Folliculitis

There are three main forms of this condition. The first is a folliculitis on the back or upper part of the chest that consists of scattered follicular papules or pustules. These are itchy and often appear after sun exposure. In the second form, which is seen in patients with seborrheic dermatitis, there are numerous small follicular papules over the upper and lower portions of the back and chest. Erythema and greasy perifollicular scales are often seen in these patients. In the third form multiple pustules are seen on the trunk and face in patients with human immunodeficiency virus infection. This type is similar to the second form, and the patients usually have severe seborrheic dermatitis.

Scrapings or biopsy specimens from lesions show numerous yeasts occluding the mouths of follicles. Treatment with topical azole antifungals may be effective, but oral therapy with ketoconazole or itraconazole is often necessary.

Seborrheic Dermatitis

In the early part of the 20th century, seborrheic dermatitis and dandruff of the scalp were thought to be caused by *Malassezia* yeasts because numerous organisms were present in skin scales. This view was subsequently superseded by the belief that the yeasts were secondary to a hyperproliferative state. However, evidence suggests that *Malassezia* is implicated in the pathogenesis of the condition.[50]

In most cases, seborrheic dermatitis responds to oral ketoconazole or topical azole antifungals. Improvement is associated with disappearance of the organisms, and relapse is associated with recolonization. Furthermore, the clinical appearances can be mimicked in animals with the application of both live and killed organisms to the skin. Some patients with seborrheic dermatitis have high antibody titers to *Malassezia* species.

It is unlikely that invasion of the epidermis is responsible for the appearance of seborrheic dermatitis, but an indirect disease mechanism such as sensitization or toxic damage is possible.

Seborrheic dermatitis can appear in any individual, although it is said to be particularly common in patients with neurologic disease, such as parkinsonism. In patients with AIDS, the onset of seborrheic dermatitis may be sudden and the rash more extensive than in other individuals.[51] The histology of seborrheic dermatitis is similar in all groups. Acanthosis and hyperkeratosis with elongation of dermal papillae are seen. An infiltrate of polymorphs in the epidermis above the dermal papillae is also often seen. Human immunodeficiency virus–positive patients tend to have more plasma cells in the infiltrate. These changes are similar to those seen in some forms of psoriasis.

Clinical Features

The classic features of seborrheic dermatitis comprise a range of different clinical appearances. These include erythema and scaling of the central part of the anterior aspect of the chest and the upper part of the back that are accompanied by a variable degree of itching. On the face there is erythema with greasy scales in the eyebrows, around the alae nasi, behind the ears, and in the external ears. Scaling may also appear in the presternal areas of the chest and on the back. Scaling in the scalp is accompanied by the appearance of pustules in some patients. The clinical appearances are typical, and fungal scrapings are unnecessary.

Other forms of skin disease, including severe erythroderma in infants and an intertriginous rash in adults, have also been called seborrheic dermatitis, but these lesions do not appear to be related to the variety discussed here.

Treatment

The main therapy involves the use of topical azole creams and weak topical corticosteroids such as 1% hydrocortisone. Relapse is common, but retreatment when necessary is the simplest approach to management.

Malassezia is also associated with a form of atopic dermatitis affecting the face in young adults. It is believed that sensitization may play a role in exacerbating the inflammatory responses in eczematous skin.[52]

TINEA NIGRA

Tinea nigra is a superficial form of phaeohyphomycosis caused by *Hortaea (Exophiala) werneckii*. The infection is confined to the stratum corneum of the palms or soles and is mainly seen in the tropics or subtropics in children or young adults.

The typical lesion of tinea nigra is a superficial scaling macule that is brown or black on the palms or soles. The pigmentation is irregularly distributed over larger lesions. Spread of the infection to other sites is rare, and lesions remain asymptomatic.

The main differential diagnosis is a superficial form of melanoma or a pigmented nevus. The pigmented hyphae can be seen by direct microscopy of skin scrapings treated with potassium hydroxide. The organism can also be cultured from scrapings.

The best therapy is treatment with a keratolytic agent such as Whitfield's ointment or 5% to 10% salicylic acid ointment.

WHITE PIEDRA

White piedra is an uncommon infection caused by yeasts of the genus *Trichosporon*, namely, *Trichosporon beigelii*, *T. inkin*, *T. mucoides*, and *T. ovoides*. The infection occurs in both the tropics and temperate zones. It is a superficial infection of the hair shafts of the scalp, body, or pubic hair. *Trichosporon* species may also cause a systemic infection in neutropenic patients (see Chapter 267).

The organisms may be carried on the skin or around the anus. In some patients the infection appears to be sexually transmitted. White piedra is asymptomatic and presents with small yellow concretions on the hair shafts.[53] These are circumscribed and lesions appear as small nodules, unlike the more diffuse coating of axillary or pubic hair seen in trichomycosis axillaris, which is due to the presence of bacteria on the hair.

The diagnosis may be confirmed by examining an epilated hair mounted in potassium hydroxide. Each nodule contains fungal hyphae, and the organisms can be cultured from infected hairs without difficulty.

Treatment is difficult. Nodules may be removed simply by shaving. Otherwise, coating the hairs with an azole such as econazole or treating the patient with oral ketoconazole may cure the infection. Relapse is common after therapy.

BLACK PIEDRA

Black piedra is another infection of the hair shafts that is caused by a black yeast, *Piedraia hortae*. The disease is rare and mainly confined to parts of the humid tropics. The infection manifests with small black nodules on the hairs of the scalp, less commonly elsewhere. These have to be distinguished from pediculosis, but itching is usually absent in black piedra. With direct microscopy these nodules can be shown to be composed of hyphal elements and small ascospores of the causative agent within a dark cement-containing stroma. Treating hairs with a topical salicylic acid, 2% formaldehyde, or an azole cream is usually sufficient, although relapse is common.

REFERENCES

1. Midgley M, Clayton YM, Hay RJ. Medical Mycology. London: Gower; 1997.
2. De Vroey C. Epidemiology of ringworm (dermatophytosis). Semin Dermatol. 1985;4:185-200.
3. Tsuboi R, Okeke CN, Inoue A, et al. Identification and viability assessment of dermatophytes infecting nail based on quantitative PCR of dermatophyte actin (ACT) mRNA. Nippon Ishinkin Gakkai Zasshi. 2002;43:91-93.
4. Jeffries CD, Reiss E, Ajello L. Analytical isoelectric focusing of secreted dermatophyte proteins applied to taxonomic differentiation of *Microsporum* and *Trichophyton* species (preliminary studies). J Med Vet Mycol. 1984;22:364-379.
5. MacGregor JM, Hamilton A, Hay RJ. Possible mechanisms of immune modulation in chronic dermatophytoses—An in vitro study. Br J Dermatol. 1992;127:233-238.
6. Rippon JW. Elastase production by ringworm fungi. Science. 1967;157:947.
7. Ghannoum M, Isham N, Hajjeh R, et al. Tinea capitis in Cleveland: Survey of elementary school students. J Am Acad Dermatol. 2003;48:189-193.
8. Philpot CM. Geographical distribution of the dermatophytes—A review. J Hyg (Lond). 1978;80:301-313.
9. Smith JMB, Rush-Munro FM. An unusual strain of *Trichophyton rubrum* from Fiji. Sabouraudia. 1971;9:153-156.
10. Gentles JC, Evans EGV. Foot infections in swimming baths. Br Med J. 1973;3:260-262.
11. Hope YM, Clayton YM, Hay RJ, et al. Foot infection in coal miners: A reassessment. Br J Dermatol. 1985;112:405-413.
12. Rothman S, Knox G, Windhorst D. Tinea pedis, a source of infection in the family. Arch Dermatol. 1957;75:270-271.
13. Blank H, Taplin D, Zaias N. Cutaneous *Trichophyton mentagrophytes* infections in Vietnam. Arch Dermatol. 1969;99:135-144.
14. Hay RJ. Tinea imbricata. Curr Top Med Mycol. 1987;2:55-72.
15. Verhagen AR. Distribution of dermatophytes causing tinea capitis in Africa. Trop Geogr Med. 1973;26:101-120.
16. Ive FA. The carrier state of tinea capitis in Nigeria. Br J Dermatol. 1966;78:219-221.

17. Blank F, Mann SJ, Peak PA. Distribution of dermatophytosis according to age, ethnic group and sex. Sabouraudia. 1974;12:352-361.

18. Zurita J, Hay RJ. The adherence of dermatophyte microconidia and arthroconidia to human keratinocytes in vitro. J Invest Dermatol. 1987;89:529-534.

19. Hay RJ. Fungal infections. In: Bos JD, ed. Skin Immune System (SIS). Boca Raton, FL: CRC Press; 1997:593-604.

20. Serjeantson S, Lawrence G. Autosomal recessive inheritance of susceptibility to tinea imbricata. Lancet. 1977;1:13-15.

21. Brouta F, Descamps F, Monod M, et al. Secreted metalloprotease gene family of *Microsporum canis*. Infect Immun. 2002;70:5676-5683.

22. Jones HE, Reinhardt JH, Rinaldi MG. Acquired immunity to dermatophytosis. Arch Dermatol. 1974;109:840-848.

23. Hay RJ, Reid S, Talwet E, et al. Immune responses of patients with tinea imbricata. Br J Dermatol. 1983;108:581-589.

24. Green F, Lee KW, Balish E. Chronic *T. mentagrophytes* dermatophytosis of guinea pig skin grafts on nude mice. J Invest Dermatol. 1982;79:125-131.

25. Leyden JJ, Kligman AM. Interdigital athletes foot, the interaction of dermatophytes and residual bacteria. Arch Dermatol. 1978;114:1466-1472.

26. Wilson JW, Plunkett DA. Nodular granulomatous perifolliculitis due to *Trichophyton rubrum*. Arch Dermatol. 1954;64:258-277.

27. Elmros T, Liden S. Hereditary palmo-plantar keratoderma: Incidence of dermatophyte infections and the results of topical treatment with retinoic acid. Acta Derm Venereol. 1983;63:254-257.

28. Birt AR, Wilt JC. Mycology, bacteriology and histopathology of suppurative ringworm. Arch Dermatol. 1957;69:441-448.

29. Baran R, Hay RJ, Tosti A, Haneke E. A new classification of onychomycosis. Br J Dermatol. 1998;139:567-571.

30. Kalter DC, Hay RJ. Onychomycosis due to *Trichophyton soudanense*. Clin Exp Dermatol. 1988;13:221-227.

31. Weismann K, Knudsen EA, Pedersen C. White nails in AIDS/ARC due to *Trichophyton rubrum* infection. Clin Exp Dermatol. 1988;13:24-27.

32. Allen DE, Snyderman R, Meadows L, et al. Generalized *Microsporum audouinii* infection and depressed cellular immunity associated with a missing plasma factor required for lymphocyte blastogenesis. Am J Med. 1977;63:991-1000.

33. Gupta AK, Sauder DN, Shear NH. Antifungal agents: An overview. Parts I and II. J Am Acad Dermatol. 1994;30:911-918.

34. Hay RJ. Recent advances in the management of fungal disease. Q J Med. 1987;244:631-639.

35. Hay RJ, Roberts D, Richardson M, et al. The evaluation of bifonazole 1% and 40% urea paste in the management of onychomycosis. Clin Exp Dermatol. 1988;13:164-167.

36. Baran R, Feuilhade M, Datry A, et al. A randomized trial of amorolfine 5% solution nail lacquer combined with oral terbinafine compared with terbinafine alone in the treatment of dermatophytic toenail onychomycoses affecting the matrix region. Br J Dermatol. 2000;142:1177-1183.

37. Roberts DT, Taylor WD, Boyle J. British Association of Dermatologists: Guidelines for treatment of onychomycosis. Br J Dermatol. 2003;148:402-410.

38. Bell-Syer SE, Hart R, Crawford F, et al. Oral treatments for fungal infections of the skin of the foot. Cochrane Database Syst Rev. 2002:CD003584.

39. Elewski B. Cutaneous mycoses in children. Br J Dermatol. 1996;134(Suppl 46):7-11.

40. Drake LA, Shear NH, Arlette JP, et al. Oral terbinafine in the treatment of toe nail onychomycosis: North American multicenter trial. J Am Acad Dermatol. 1997;37:740-745.

41. Odom RB, Aly R, Scher RK, et al. A multicenter, placebo-controlled, double-blind study of intermittent therapy with itraconazole for the treatment of onychomycosis of the finger nail. J Am Acad Dermatol. 1997;36:231-235.

42. Scher RK, Breneman D, Rich P, et al. Once-weekly fluconazole (150, 300 or 450 mg) in the treatment of distal subungual onychomycosis of the toenail. J Am Acad Dermatol. 1998;38:S77-S86.

43. Evans EG, Sigurgeirsson B. Double blind, randomised study of continuous terbinafine compared with intermittent itraconazole in treatment of toenail onychomycosis. The LION study group. BMJ. 1999;318:1031-1035.

44. Hay RJ, Moore MK. The clinical features of superficial infections caused by *Hendersonula toruloidea* and *Scytalidium hyalinum*. Br J Dermatol. 1984;110:677-684.

45. Gupta AK, Gregurek-Novak T, Konnikov N, et al. Itraconazole and terbinafine treatment of some nondermatophyte molds causing onychomycosis of the toes and a review of the literature. J Cutan Med Surg. 2001;5:206-210.

46. Crespo Erchiga V, Delgado Florencio V. *Malassezia* species in skin diseases. Curr Opin Infect Dis. 2002: 15:133-142.

47. Ashbee HR, Evans EG. Immunology of diseases associated with *Malassezia* species. Clin Microbiol Revs. 2002: 15:21-57.

48. Nazzaro-Porro M, Passi S. Identification of tyrosinase inhibitors in cultures of *Pityrosporum*. J Invest Dermatol. 1978;71:205-208.

49. Faergemann J, Fredriksson T. Propylene glycol in the treatment of pityriasis versicolor. Acta Derm Venereol. 1980;60:92-93.

50. Shuster S. The aetiology of dandruff and the mode of action of therapeutic agents. Br J Dermatol. 1984;111:235-242.

51. Garman ME, Tyring SK. The cutaneous manifestations of HIV infection. Dermatol Clin. 2002;20:193-214.

52. Johansson C, Eshaghi H, Linder MT, et al. Positive atopy patch test reaction to *Malassezia furfur* in atopic dermatitis correlates with a T helper 2-like peripheral blood mononuclear cells response. J Invest Dermatol. 2002;118:1044-1051.

53. Kalter DCA, Tschen JA, Cernoch PL, et al. Genital white piedra: Epidemiology, microbiology and therapy. J Am Acad Dermatol. 1986;14:982-993.

CHAPTER **266**

Paracoccidioides brasiliensis

ANGELA RESTREPO

ANGELA MARÍA TOBÓN

Paracoccidioidomycosis is one of the most important endemic fungal diseases in Latin America. It is a chronic, systemic, and progressive disease that usually afflicts adult men. Although the lungs are the site of primary infection, dissemination is common, mainly to mucous membranes, the skin, the reticuloendothelial system, and the adrenals.

DESCRIPTION OF THE PATHOGEN

The etiologic agent is a thermally dimorphic fungus, *Paracoccidioides brasiliensis,* recently classified in the phylum Ascomycota, order Onygenales, family Onygenaceae, despite the fact that only the anamorph characteristics are known.[1,2] Microscopically, in cultures at 37° C as well as in tissues and exudates, the fungus appears as an oval-to-round yeast cell quite variable in size (4 to 40 μm), and surrounded by a translucent double-contoured cell wall; intracytoplasmic lipid globules are characteristic and prominent. It reproduces by multiple budding; typically, numerous blastoconidia, usually small (4 to 6 μm), surround the mother cell to which they are connected by short cytoplasmic bridges, thus resembling a "pilot wheel"; this cell is a hallmark of *P. brasiliensis* (Figs. 266-1 and 266-2). Colonies produced at 37° C grow in approximately 10 days and are soft, cream colored, and wrinkled.[3,4] The fungus develops as a slow-growing mold (20 to 30 days) at lower temperatures, below 26° C and including 4° C if in liquid substrates. In solid media, colonies demonstrate short tufts of white aerial mycelia, but then they become cottony and adhere strongly to the agar; the area beneath is often brownish. Microscopically, only chlamydospores and thin septate hyphae are observed when the mold is grown in the regular mycologic media.[3,4] Media with reduced carbohydrate content may give rise to arthroconidia and other types of conidia, propagules that are considered to be the infectious particles in nature.[3-5] These propagules are small (4 to 5 μm), and when given to mice intranasally, they convert into yeast cells in approximately 72 hours, giving rise to progressive disease as well as to pulmonary fibrosis. *P. brasiliensis* produces an immunodominant antigen, gp43, which serves in diagnosis, behaves as an adhesin, and has a suppressive role in certain immune functions.[6-8] Several virulence traits (morphologic transition, adherence, proteolytic enzymes, melanin production) have been identified.[1,6,9] Genomic studies are permitting a more precise characterization of genes involved in host adaptation and survival.[6,10,11]

ECOLOGY AND EPIDEMIOLOGY

Perhaps the most notable ecologic characteristic of paracoccidioidomycosis is its restricted geographic distribution. It has been reported only in Latin America from Mexico (23° N) to Argentina (34° S); however, some countries within these latitudes are not affected (e.g., some Caribbean Islands and Chile); furthermore, the disorder does not afflict persons living in every region of the affected areas. Endemicity centers in regions with relatively well defined ecologic characteristics, in the tropical and subtropical forests where temperatures are mild and humidity is relatively high and constant throughout the year.[12,13] Brazil constitutes the heart of the endemic area and is followed at a distance by Colombia, Venezuela, Ecuador, Argentina, and other Latin American countries.[3] The annual incidence rate in Brazil is estimated to vary from 10 to 30 per million inhabitants; the mean mortality rate is 1.4 per million.[14] In Colombia, incidence is much lower

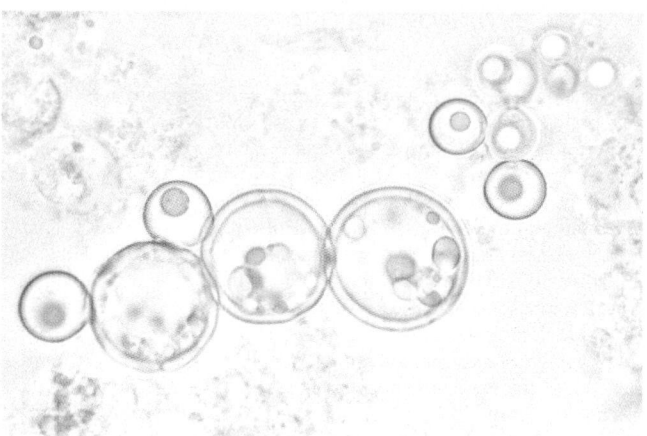

FIGURE 266-1. *Paracoccidioides brasiliensis.* Potassium hydroxide preparation from pus. Multiple budding and variation in cell size are apparent (×1000).

and fluctuates (between 0.5 and 2.2 per million) year to year.[13,15] Although over 55 cases have now been reported in North America, Europe, and Asia, all these patients had previously resided in endemic countries.[3,4,16,17]

Molecular tools have shown that fungal isolates obtained from various endemic countries are restricted geographically, which indicates that they occupy specialized endemic niches in nature.[1,18] Restricted geographic distribution indicates an equally limited habitat for *P. brasiliensis,* one that has proved elusive. The fungus has been isolated from nonhuman sources only sporadically, six times from soils, and once each from a commercial chow and from penguin feces.[19] Naturally acquired animal infection has been convincingly demonstrated only in armadillos *(Dasypus novemcinctus),* a mammal distributed in areas that coincide closely to the distribution of the mycosis.[20,21] Dogs also appear to be infected.[3,22] Despite the clue offered by such isolations, attempts to locate the precise microniche of the fungus have failed.[13] Outbreaks have not been reported, and consequently, valuable information pointing toward the fungus niche is unavailable.[13]

Skin test surveys have revealed a significant prevalence of delayed hypersensitivity reactions to paracoccidioidin (close to 70%) among farm workers, especially in coffee growing areas.[3,13] An ecologic analysis centered on the conditions prevailing in endemic counties has also revealed that coffee and tobacco growing regions, as well as high humidity and heavy annual precipitation, were significantly correlated

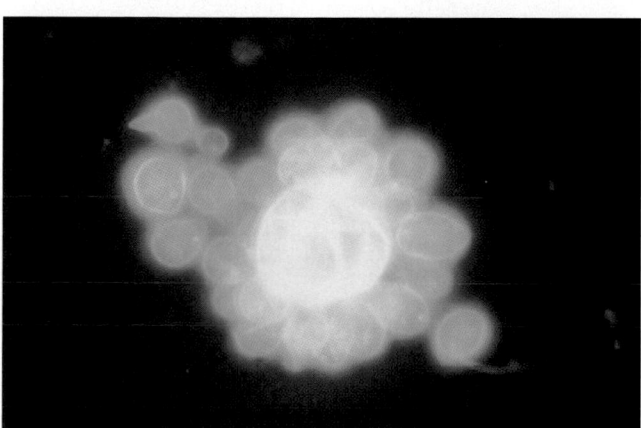

FIGURE 266-2. *Paracoccidioides brasiliensis* from a 37° C culture. Observe multiple buds surrounding the mother cell (calcofluor, ×1000).

with the presence of the mycosis.[12,13] A cross-sectional epidemiologic survey among the indigenous population of the Brazilian Amazon basin,[23] where an unusual number of paracoccidioidomycosis cases had been diagnosed, revealed that changes in the natives' traditional economic system and agricultural practices had resulted in increased contact with the fungus.[23]

Paracoccidioidomycosis is not contagious from person to person. The imprecise knowledge on *P. brasiliensis* habitat has hindered determination of the route of infection; nonetheless, physiopathologic observations and experimental animal studies have ruled out traumatic implantation and point toward inhalation as the infectious route.[4,24]

The age and sex distribution of clinical cases is peculiar. Paracoccidioidomycosis is rare in children and teenagers, and most patients are 30 or more years of age.[3,4,25] Men are more commonly afflicted than women, at a mean ratio of 15:1. This is in contrast to the rate of infection, as determined by a paracoccidioidin skin test, which is similar for both sexes. Of interest, too, is the fact that when the disease occurs in prepubertal patients, this sex difference does not exist.[4] It has been suggested that the marked sex difference seen in adults could be explained by the inhibitory action of estrogens on the conidia or mycelium transition to yeast cells.[4] Male mice infected with *P. brasiliensis* conidia were shown to develop a progressive disseminated disease, whereas female animals were able to arrest the conidia to yeast transition, and promptly controlled the infection.[26] The occupational distribution reveals a predilection for persons who work (or had worked) in agriculture-related occupations.[3,4]

The disease is characterized by long periods of latency, as demonstrated by the non-autochthonous cases reported outside the endemic area; some of these patients developed overt paracoccidioidomycosis 30 or more years after leaving the endemic regions.[3,4,16,17] There are indications suggesting that a certain number of yeasts present in lung tissues adapt to the reduced oxygen tension in walled-off, residual lesions, where they remain dormant.[27]

PATHOGENESIS AND CLINICAL MANIFESTATIONS

Paracoccidioidomycosis encompasses both a subclinical infection resulting from the initial contact with the fungus, and an overt disease manifested later on. The infection is evidenced by a reactive skin test, presence of anti-GP43 antibodies in healthy blood donors,[3,4,25,28] and, exceptionally, also by the demonstration of *P. brasiliensis* in residual lesions.[3,27,29] The overt disease has two main clinical presentations, a chronic adult form that may be either unifocal or multifocal depending on the extent of involvement, and the juvenile form, which is an acute/subacute, more severe disease.[29,30] The latter is characterized by marked involvement of the reticuloendothelial system and occurs in less than 15% of the cases; it is thought to represent progression after a rather recent exposure. The hallmarks of the chronic adult type of disease are significant lung involvement and extrapulmonary lesions; it is the predominant form (occurring in approximately 90% of cases) and represents endogenous reactivation years after the initial contact with the fungus.[3,4,31] Gallium-67 scans have challenged this classification system, however, as even in the unifocal adult form, the mycosis presents with multiorgan involvement, and in patients with the juvenile form, extralymphatic involvement is not infrequent.[32] A residual form represented by fibrotic scarring of previously active lesions is also recognized.[3,4,29]

P. brasiliensis infection may become dormant and then be reactivated under conditions that are not clearly defined but perhaps include immunosuppression, debilitating disease, chronic alcoholism, malnutrition, and smoking.[4,27]

The host's immune defenses directly influence the clinical presentation and the severity of the mycosis.[30] The first line of defense is represented by an array of innate defenses represented by polymorphonuclear leukocytes, alveolar macrophages, natural killer (NK) cells, complement, peptides, proinflammatory cytokines, and chemokines, all of which hinder fungal multiplication but are unable to destroy the invading microorganism.[3,4,30,33] Humoral immunity is intact. In patients with the juvenile form, specific antibodies of the IgA, IgG, and IgE subclasses are markedly increased.[34-36] Patients with the multifocal adult-type disease also have elevated antibody titers, but patients with the unifocal adult form have significantly lower antibody production than other patient groups, suggesting that antibodies bear no direct role in protection.[3,34-36] Additionally, patients with the juvenile form show eosinophilia and increased levels of transforming growth factor (TGF)-β, a switching factor for IgA.[3,34,36]

Cell-mediated immunity is crucial to defense; it is usually depressed at the peak of the infection but is restored with successful treatment. The dichotomy between humoral and cellular immune responses suggests a helper T-cell 2 (Th2) pattern of immune response.[37-39] Thus, the juvenile patients and those with the adult multifocal disease exhibit nonreactive paracoccidioidin skin tests, detectable anti–*P. brasiliensis* antibodies, depressed lymphoproliferative responses to the specific (gp43) antigen, and cytokine patterns corresponding to the Th2 type immunity—for example, low interferon (IFN)-γ secretion; high levels of interleukin (IL)-4, IL-5, and IL-10; and defective synthesis of IL-12.[30,37-39] Addition of IL-12 to patients' macrophages and neutralization of IL-10 increase IFN-γ levels, which suggests the possibility of introducing immune modulation to restore patients' defenses.[40] In patients with the unifocal adult disease, intermediate immune responses are observed; for example, their specific lymphoproliferative response is higher than in the juvenile patients.[37,38] Thus, patient profiles are compatible with the presence of low and high resistance to fungal invasion.[3,34,37-39] In contrast to patients, infected (i.e., skin test–reactive) individuals living in the endemic area who have no clinical manifestation of the disease exhibit an opposite, normal Th1 immune profile.[37] Apoptosis mediated by ligands (Fas-FasL) and engagement of the cytotoxic T lymphocyte antigen 4 are involved in modulation of the immune response in patients infected with *P. brasiliensis*.[41]

Macrophages represent the major cell defense against *P. brasiliensis,* and when activated by IFN-γ they ingest and kill both conidia and yeast cells.[42,43] IFN-γ attaches to its proper macrophage receptor, and once in the cytoplasm it induces nuclear factor (NF)-κ beta production, thus prompting expression of the inducible nitric oxide synthase (iNOS) with activation of the L-arginine–nitric oxide pathway and NO production.[43] Nitric oxide, however, may play a dual role (resistance and susceptibility) depending on the degree of expression.[44]

Compact granulomas are considered to be the most evolved and effective biologic defense weapon against *P. brasiliensis*.[3,29,30] Granuloma formation involves the activity of T lymphocytes (helper and cytotoxic subsets), activated effector cells (mainly macrophages but also neutrophils), and several cytokines, especially IFN-γ and IL-12. Th2 cytokines (IL-4, IL-10, TGF-α or β) are associated with host susceptibility, probably because they interfere with correct macrophage function.[30,37,39,42,43]

Paracoccidioidomycosis is a polymorphic, progressive disease, often severe, although self-limited cases have been occasionally reported.[3,4,14,16,25,45] The lungs are the site of the primary infection, but the patient's symptoms may not reflect this fact.[3,4,27,29] In juvenile patients, the disorder is subacute and severe, and it carries a bad prognosis; it is manifested by marked involvement of the reticuloendothelial system with hypertrophy of various lymph node chains and liver and spleen enlargement; respiratory complaints are minimal.[3,4,14,16,25,45] In the adult-type disease, the course is chronic, but, contingent on specific therapy, recovery usually ensues; however, residual fibrotic sequelae, present in over half of the patients after treatment, hinder complete restoration of health.[3,4,46,47] Lesions occur mainly (>90%) in the lungs but are frequently accompanied by secondary lesions in the mucous membranes, the reticuloendothelial system, the skin, the adrenals, and other organs. Usually, more than one lesion are present at the time of the initial consultation.[3,4,14,16,29,45,47] In both clinical forms, the mycosis is also manifested by constitutional symptoms such as weakness, fever, general malaise, and weight loss.[3,4,16,25,45,46]

CHARACTERISTICS OF THE LESIONS

Lungs

At the time of diagnosis, patients frequently present with a dry cough, although at times expectoration and even hemoptysis is noticed; usually, there is some degree of dyspnea. Auscultation reveals minimal abnormalities in comparison with the radiologic findings, so there is a dissociation between the clinical manifestations and the damage observed radiographically.[3,4,45,47,48] In patients with active disease, plain chest x-ray images reveal mostly interstitial infiltrates (64%), followed by mixed lesions with linear and nodular infiltrates and alveolar patterns, occasionally confluent, located preferentially in the central and lower fields, frequently bilateral and symmetric (Fig. 266-3).[3,4,29,48] At diagnosis, high-resolution computed tomography (CT) may demonstrate pleural involvement, small parahilar cavities, and fibrosis with a characteristic frosted-glass appearance (Fig. 266-4).[47] Gallium-67 scans have revealed pulmonary lesions in all juvenile-form and chronic adult–form patients studied, thus confirming that the lungs are the target organ.[32] At diagnosis, one third of those patients who have had long-lasting disease present with serious pulmonary sequelae such as bilateral fibrosis (38%), bullae (27%), and emphysematous areas; additionally, indirect signs of pulmonary hypertension and enlargement of the right ventricle (core pulmonale in approximately 5.0%) are observed.[4,29,45-48] After therapy, these residual lesions tend to increase with time.[46]

Mucosa

Infiltrated, ulcerated, and painful lesions with ragged borders are observed regularly (60%) in the mouth, lips, gingiva, tongue, and palate, and to a lesser extent also in the nose, larynx, pharynx, and gastrointestinal tract, including the anal mucosa. Dysphagia and dysphonia are common; diarrhea and emaciation are frequent in patients with intestinal involvement. Such lesions have a granulomatous appearance and a mulberry-like aspect, and they may produce edema of the affected area; on healing, they produce scarring and diminished sensation (Fig. 266-5).[3,4,49-51]

Skin

Cutaneous lesions are present in approximately 25% of the cases; they are variable in form and aspect and tend to appear around the natural orifices and in the lower limbs. Most commonly, the lesions are warty,

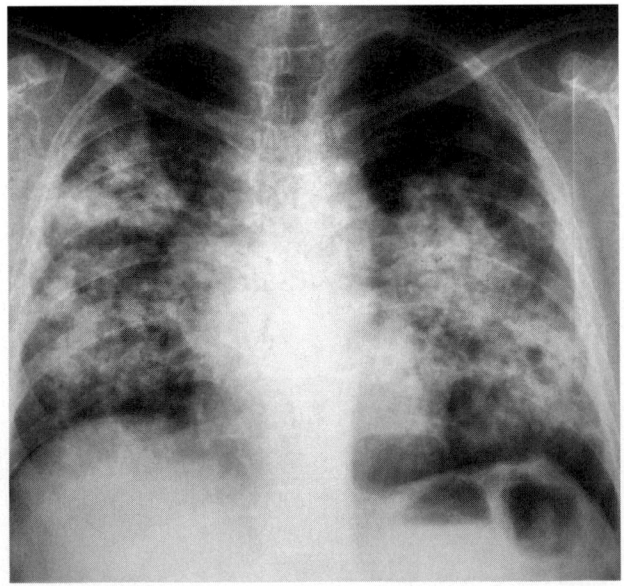

FIGURE 266-3. Paracoccidioidomycosis as seen on a chest radiograph. Infiltrates and nodular lesions are located in the bases of both lungs. Apices are spared.

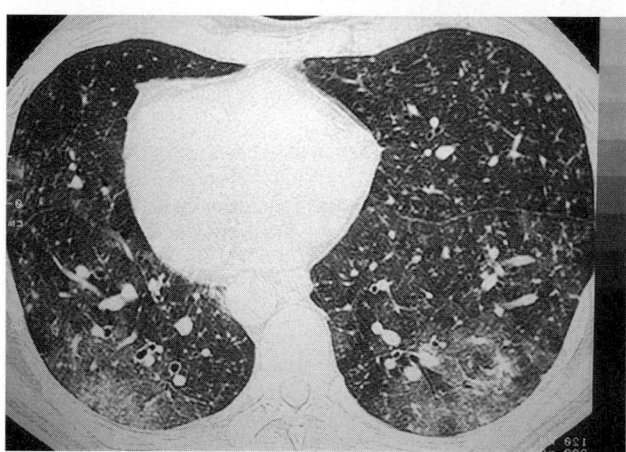

FIGURE 266-4. Paracoccidioidomycosis CT scan showing bronchiectasis, minor bronchial thickening, and interstitial and alveolar infiltrates resembling frosted glass.

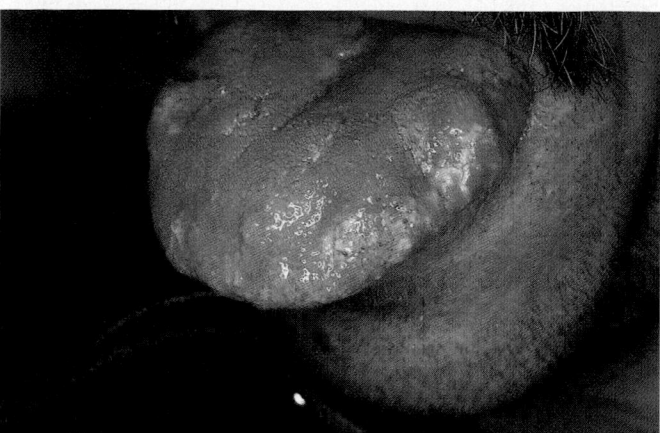

FIGURE 266-6. Paracoccidioidomycosis: granulomatous, infiltrative lesions in the tongue.

ulcerated, and crusted; they infiltrate the subcutaneous tissues and are granulomatous. Often, lung, skin, and mucosal lesions coexist in the same patient (Fig. 266-6).[3,4,25,29]

Lymph Nodes

Although all lymph node chains may be involved, there is a preference for cervical nodes; axillary, mediastinal, mesenteric, and other nodes area also regularly affected. All patients with the juvenile form and at least half of those with the chronic, multifocal forms present with clinically detectable hypertrophied lymph nodes that may impair organ functioning or cause obstructive problems.[3,4,29,32] Reticuloendothelial lesions become more prominent and frequent when gallium-67 scans are performed.[32] Draining fistulas may form. In adult patients with mucosal or skin lesions, enlargement of the neighboring node is frequently noticed.[3,4,29]

Adrenals

Regular evaluation of adrenal function in patients with paracoccidioidomycosis has revealed that 15% experience adrenal insufficiency, whereas only 5% to 9% present with an overt Addisonian crisis. CT shows hypertrophied glands with damage to the cortical and medullary regions; calcifications are rare. Proper patient surveillance allows prompt detection of adrenal damage, facilitating adequate replacement

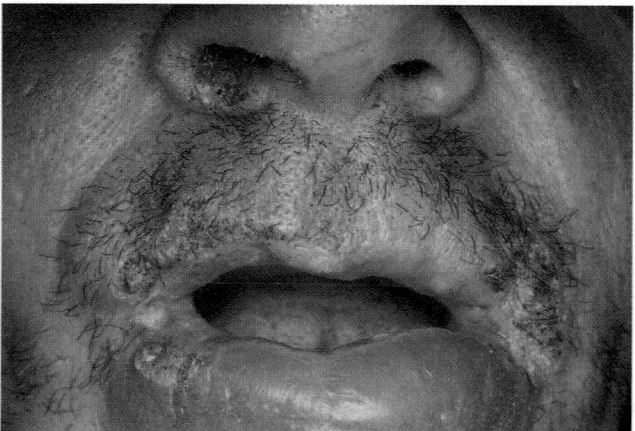

FIGURE 266-5. Paracoccidioidomycosis: mucosal and skin lesions.

therapy.[52,53] A significant inverse correlation between plasma levels of dehydroepiandrosterone sulfate and IL-6 has been found, indicating that this interaction may be of pathogenetic significance in this disease.[53]

Other Lesions

The spleen, liver, gastrointestinal tract, vascular system, bones, central nervous system (CNS), and male genitourinary tract are occasionally involved. Clinical presentations vary according to the organ damaged. Gallium, CT, and magnetic resonance imaging (MRI) have revealed unexpected but common lesions in all organs and systems, reflecting the disseminated nature of this mycosis.[3,29,32,47,54-56]

DIFFERENTIAL DIAGNOSIS

The disease must be differentiated from tuberculosis, which may coexist in 15% of patients with paracoccidioidomycosis.[3,4,57] Other diseases to be considered are neoplastic disorders (including lymphoma), histoplasmosis, leishmaniasis, leprosy, and syphilis. Only the laboratory is capable of establishing the correct diagnosis.[3,4] It should be noticed that paracoccidioidomycosis does not behave as an opportunistic disorder, although it has occasionally been reported in immunosuppressed patients, including those with acquired immunodeficiency syndrome (AIDS).[57,58]

LABORATORY DIAGNOSIS

Direct Examination

When specimens such as sputum, exudates, and pus are available, a simple wet mount suffices to reveal *P. brasiliensis* in 93% of patients. If results are negative, repeated samples should be collected, and sputum should be digested and concentrated. The relatively large size of the fungal cells, their translucent walls, and their multiple budding make diagnosis simple, especially if calcofluor preparations are examined.[3,4] Microscopic diagnosis relies on the presence of the multiple-budding yeast cell; occasionally, however, single buds and small yeast cells may be confused with other fungi, requiring more extensive observations.[3,4] Polymerase chain reaction (PCR) of exudates and tissue samples has been reported to be helpful.[1,59-61]

Histologic Studies

Biopsy is very often diagnostic. Gomori's stain is recommended. If the typical multiple budding cells are not abundant, differentiation from other fungi (*Blastomyces dermatitidis*, *Histoplasma capsulatum*, and *Cryptococcus neoformans*) is necessary. Frequently, infected tissues reveal a mixed inflammatory reaction characterized by the presence of granulomas centered on yeast cells, some of which have been phagocytized. The granuloma is further characterized by the presence of neutrophils, mononuclear cells, epithelioid cells, and multinucleated giant cells, all arranged concentrically around the yeast cells (Fig. 266-7). This type of response is also present in mucocutaneous lesions and in ruptured lymph nodes. Skin lesions reveal pseudoepitheliomatous hyperplasia and intraepithelial microabscesses. In the juvenile form, tissue reactions are diffuse and phagocytosis is sparse. Lymph nodes have hyperplastic germinal centers and increased numbers of plasmocytes.[3,29]

Cultures

Culture should be attempted because a positive culture means the infection is active. When the sample is contaminated, room temperature incubation is preferred. Sabouraud-dextrose or Sabouraud agar with an antibacterial agent and cycloheximide (in Petri dishes) is recommended. Cultures should be kept for 6 weeks.[3,4]

Serologic Tests

Serology for antibody detection is useful not only for diagnosis but also for follow-up studies. Antibodies of the immunoglobulin classes G, M, and E are regularly detected.[3,34,35,62] The easiest method, the agar gel immunodiffusion test, demonstrates circulating antibodies in over 90% of cases. The test is also specific, and the presence of a precipitin band practically makes a diagnosis.[3,4,30,35] However, the diagnosis cannot be based solely on this, because these antibodies can be detected years after apparently successful therapy.[2,4,35] Another useful test, albeit a cumbersome one, is the complement fixation test. Its quantitative nature allows a more precise evaluation of the patient's response to treatment. In this test, and in contrast to the immunodiffusion test, cross-reactions with *H. capsulatum* antigens are important.[3,4] Other tests, such as immunofluorescence, counterimmunoelectrophoresis, the dot-blot test, enzyme-linked immunosorbent assay, and immunoblotting, are also used.[3,63] Improvements in serodiagnosis include the detection of antibodies against chemically characterized and/or recombinant *P. brasiliensis* antigens, notably gp43,[3,30] pb27, and the 87-kilodalton HS protein; a combination of the latter two has resulted in increased sensitivity (92%) and specificity (88%).[64] Monoclonal antibody–based techniques are also important for serologic diagnosis and can be used to demonstrate circulating fungal antigens in patients' sera. Antigen is detected in over 60% of patients, including, most importantly, those immunosuppressed; furthermore, decreasing antigen titers correlate with clinical improvement.[65]

Skin Tests

Paracoccidioidin skin testing is not reliable for diagnosis, because many active cases (35% to 50%) are nonreactive at the time of diagnosis. Cross-reactions with histoplasmin are to be expected, although the use of the purified antigen gp43 appears to be more specific.[3,4,30]

TREATMENT

Paracoccidioidomycosis is the only mycosis amenable to treatment with sulfa drugs. Amphotericin B and various imidazole derivatives are also effective. Because the patients are usually malnourished, treatment directed merely at suppressing the growth of the causative agent may not be successful. Appropriate supportive therapeutic measures (e.g., improved diet, rest, correction of anemia) are essential.[3,4]

Sulfonamides

Either sulfadiazine or the long-acting compounds (sulfamethoxypyridazine, sulfadimethoxine, sulfamethoxazole) can be used. With sulfadiazine, the maximum therapeutic dosage is 4 g/day for adults and 60 to 100 mg/kg/day for children in divided doses. This treatment must be continued without interruption for several months until clinical and mycologic responses become apparent. Then the dosage can be reduced to half. The long-acting compounds require 1 to 2 g/day for adults and half that dose for children during the first 2 to 3 weeks of treatment; after clinical improvement, 500 mg/day suffices. Sulfonamide treatment should be continued for 3 to 5 years to avoid relapses, which occur in 20% to 25% of the cases.[3] The daily use of a combination of sulfamethoxazole (400 mg) and trimethoprim (80 mg) given for a minimum of 3 months is preferred by several investigators.[3]

Amphotericin B

In paracoccidioidomycosis, amphotericin B is administered according to recommendations given for other systemic mycoses. Cumulative total dosages vary from 1000 to 2000 mg. Amphotericin B is not fungicidal in vivo, and all patients thus treated should also receive maintenance sulfonamide or azole therapy. Amphotericin B should be reserved for severe cases and for those unresponsive to other means of therapy.[3,4] Lipid formulations have rarely been prescribed.[3,66]

Treatments with sulfonamides and/or amphotericin B are not always successful, and the mortality rate is rather high (17% to 25%); improvement is obtained in 65% to 70% of cases, and the remainder relapse or fail to improve.[3,66,67]

Imidazole Compounds

Ketoconazole treatment resulted in major improvement (over 84%), with a 10% relapse rate after 5 years.[3,4] Ketoconazole should be given at a dose of 200 to 400 mg/day for a minimum of 6 months and for as long as 12 to 18 months, depending on the patient's response and the results of mycologic tests. Long-lasting ketoconazole therapy mandates regular checkups for hepatic dysfunction and gonadal alterations.[3,4] At present, however, itraconazole is considered to be superior to ketoconazole. This conclusion is based on its shorter treatment period (mean, 6 months), lower daily dose (200 to 100 mg), lack of major interference with endocrine metabolism, little or no liver toxicity, and lower relapse rate (3% to 5%).[4,46] When properly controlled, patients with the severe juvenile form—including AIDS patients—and those with CNS disease respond to itraconazole.[4,46,56,68] Failures, however, are occasionally encountered.[16] A randomized trial conducted with the oral medications (sulfonamides, ketoconazole, and itraconazole) demonstrated their efficacy but failed to reveal differences between sulfonamides and itraconazole, probably because of varying treatment schedules.[69] Fluconazole is not recommended, as there is a need to administer high doses (up to 600 mg/day) for long periods, and also because relapses are too common.[3,4] As yet unpublished clinical studies with a new triazole, posaconazole, have revealed that this compound is effective and well tolerated. Terbinafine has been shown to be active in in vitro tests, comparing favorably with itraconazole; clinical experience is, however, quite limited.[3,70] Immunomodulant therapy has been recommended as an adjuvant to antifungal therapy.[3,40]

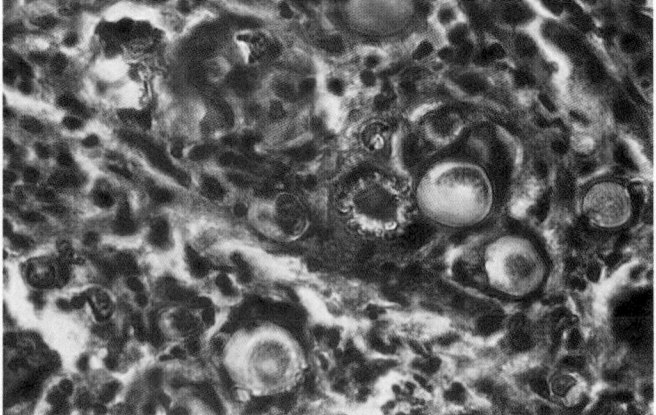

FIGURE 266-7. Paracoccidioidomycosis: yeast cells in tissue demonstrating multiple budding and mononuclear infiltration (hematoxylin and eosin, ×400).

REFERENCES

1. San-Blas G, Nino-Vega G, Iturriaga T. *Paracoccidioides brasiliensis* and paracoccidioidomycosis: Molecular approaches to morphogenesis, diagnosis, epidemiology, taxonomy and genetics. Med Mycol. 2002;40:225-242.
2. Bialek R, Ibricevic A, Fothergill A, et al. Small subunit ribosomal DNA sequence shows *Paracoccidioides brasiliensis* closely related to *Blastomyces dermatitidis*. J Clin Microbiol. . 2000;38:3190-3193.
3. Lacaz CS, Porto E, Martins JEC, et al. Paracoccidioidomicose. In: Lacaz CS, Porto E, Martins JEC, et al, eds. Tratado de Micologia Medica Lacaz. 9th ed. Sao Paulo: Sarvier; 2002:639-729.
4. Restrepo A. Paracoccidioidomycosis. In: Dismukes WE, Pappas PG, Sobel JK, eds. Clinical Mycology. 1st ed. New York: Oxford University Press; 2003:328-345.
5. Cock AM, Cano LE, Vélez D, et al. Fibrotic sequelae in pulmonary paracoccidioidomycosis: Histopathological aspects in BALB/C mice infected with viable and non-viable propagules. Rev Inst Med Trop Sao Paulo. 2000;42:59-66.
6. Borges-Walmsley MI, Chen D, Shu X, Walmsley AR. The pathobiology of *Paracoccidioides brasiliensis*. Trends Microbiol. 2002;10:80-87.
7. Almeida SR, Unterkircher CS, Camargo ZP. Involvement of the major glycoprotein (gp43) of *Paracoccidioides brasiliensis* in attachment to macrophages. Med Mycol. 1998;36:405-411.
8. Flavia-Popi AF, Lopes JD, Mariano M. GP43 from *Paracoccidioides brasiliensis* inhibits macrophage functions: An evasion mechanism of the fungus. Cell Immunol. 2002;218:87-94,
9. Gómez BL, Nosanchuk J. Melanin and fungi. Curr Opin Infect Dis. 2003;16:91-96
10. Felipe MS, Andrade RV, Petrofeza SS, et al. Transcriptome characterization of the dimorphic and pathogenic fungus *Paracoccidioides brasiliensis* by EST analysis. Yeast. 2003;20:263-271.
11. Goldman GH, dos Reis Marques E, Duarte Ribeiro DC, et al. Expressed sequence tag analysis of the human pathogen *Paracoccidioides brasiliensis* yeast phase: Identification of putative homologues of *Candida albicans* virulence and pathogenicity genes. Eukaryotic Cell. 2003;2:34-48, available at http://143.107.203.68/est/default.html.
12. Calle D, Rosero S, Orozco LC, et al. Paracoccidioidomycosis in Colombia: An ecological study. Epidemiol Infect. 2001;126:309-315.
13. Restrepo A, McEwen JG, Castañada E. The habitat of *Paracoccidioides brasiliensis:* How far from solving the riddle? Med Mycol. 2001;39:232-241.
14. Coutinho ZF, Silva D, Lazera M, el at. Paracoccidioidomycosis mortality in Brazil (1980-1995). Cad Saude Publica. 2002;18:1441-1454.
15. Torrado E, Castañeda E, de la Hoz F, Restrepo A. Paracoccidioidomicosis: Definición de las áreas endémicas de Colombia. Biomédica. 2000;20:327-334
16. Manns BJ, Baylis BW, Urbanski SJ, et al. Paracoccidioidomycosis: Case report and review. Clin Infect Dis. 1066;23:1026-1032.
17. Horre R, Schumacher G, Alpers K, et al. A case of imported paracoccidioidomycosis in a German legionnaire. Med Mycol. 2002;40:213-216.
18. Niño-Vega GA, Calgano AM, San Blas G, et al. RFLP analysis reveals marked geographical isolation between strains of *Paracoccidioides brasiliensis*. Med Mycol. 2000;38:437-441.
19. Franco M, Bagagli E, Scapolio S, da Silva Lacaz C. A critical analysis of isolations of *Paracoccidioides brasiliensis* from soil. Med Mycol. 2000;38:185-191.
20. Bagagli E, Sano A, Coelho KI, et al. Isolation of *Paracoccidioides brasiliensis* from armadillos *(Dasypus novemcinctus)* captured in an endemic area of paracoccidioidomycosis. Am J Trop Med Hyg. 1998;58:505-512.
21. Silva-Vergara ML, Martínez R, Camargo ZP, et al. Isolation of *Paracoccidioides brasiliensis* from armadillos *(Dasypus novemcinctus)* in areas where the fungus was recently isolated from soil. Med Mycol. 2000;38:193-199.
22. Ono MA, Bracarense APFRL, Morais HAS, et al. Canine paracoccidioidomycosis: A seroepidemiologic study. Med Mycol. 2000;39:277-282.
23. Coimbra CEA, Wanke B, Santos RV, et al. Paracoccidioidin and histoplasmin sensitivity in the Tupí-Mondé Amerindian populations from Brazilian Amazonia. Ann Trop Med Parasitol. 1994;88:197-207.
24. Roldán JC, Tabares AM, Gómez BL, et al. The oral route in the pathogenesis of paracoccidioidomycosis: An experimental study in BALB/c mice infected with *Paracoccidioides brasiliensis* conidia. Mycopathologia. 2000-2001;151:57-62.
25. Blotta MH, Mamoni RL, Oliveira SJ, et al. Endemic regions of paracoccidioidomycosis in Brazil: A clinical and epidemiological study of 584 cases in the southeast region. Am J Trop Med Hyg. 1999;61:390-394.
26. Aristizábal BH, Clemons KV, Cock AM, et al. Experimental *Paracoccidioides brasiliensis* infection in mice: Influence of the hormonal status of the host on tissue responses. Med Mycol. 2002;40:169-178.
27. Restrepo A. Morphological aspects of *Paracoccidioides brasiliensis* in lymph nodes: Implications for the prolonged latency of paracoccidioidomycosis? Med Mycol. 2000;38:317-322.
28. Botteon FA, Camargo ZP, Benard G, et al. *Paracoccidioides brasiliensis:* Reactive antibodies in Brazilian blood donors. Med Mycol. 2002;40:387-391
29. Montenegro MR, Franco M. Pathology. In: Franco M, Lacaz CS, Restrepo A, et al, eds. Paracoccidioidomycosis. Boca Raton, Fla: CRC Press; 1994:131-150.
30. Camargo ZP, Franco MF. Current knowledge on pathogenesis and immunodiagnosis of paracoccidioidomycosis. Rev Iberoam Micol. 2000;17:41-48.
31. Benard G, Duarte AJ. Paracoccidioidomycosis: A model for evaluation of the effects of human immunodeficiency virus infection on the natural history of endemic tropical diseases. Clin Infect Dis. 2000;31:1032-1039.
32. Yamaga LY, Benard G, Hironaka FH, et al. The role of gallium-67 scan in defining the extent of disease in an endemic deep mycosis, paracoccidioidomycosis: A predominantly multifocal disease. Eur J Nucl Med Mol Imaging. 2003;30:888-894.

33. Gónzalez A, Sahaza J, Ortiz BL, et al. Production of proinflammatory cytokines during the early stages of *Paracoccidioides brasiliensis* infection. Med Mycol. 2003;41:391-399.
34. Mamoni RL, Nouer SA, Oliveira SJ, et al. Enhanced production of specific IgG4, IgE, IgA and TGF-beta in sera from patients with the juvenile form of paracoccidioidomycosis. Med Mycol. 2002;40:153-159.
35. Del Negro GMB, Pereira CN, Andrade HF, et al. Evaluation of tests for antibody response in the follow-up of patients with acute and chronic forms of paracoccidioidomycosis. J Med Microbiol. 2000;49:37-46.
36. Juvenale M, Del Negro GMB, Duarte AJ, et al. Antibody isotypes to a *Paracoccidioides brasiliensis* somatic antigen in subacute and chronic form paracoccidioidomycosis. J Med Microbiol. 2001;50:127-134.
37. Oliveira SJ, Mamoni RL, Musatti CC, et al. Cytokines and lymphocyte proliferation in juvenile and adult forms of paracoccidioidomycosis: Comparison with infected and non-infected controls. Microbes Infect. 2002;4:139-144.
38. Karhawi AS, Colombo AL, Salomão R. Production of IFN-gamma is impaired in patients with paracoccidioidomycosis during active disease and is restored after clinical remission. Med Mycol. 2000;38:225-229.
39. Kashino SS, Fazioli RA, Cafalli-Favati C, et al. Resistance to *Paracoccidioides brasiliensis* infection is linked to a preferential Th1 immune response, whereas susceptibility is associated with absence of IFN-gamma production. J Interferon Cytokine Res. 2000;20:89-97.
40. Romano CC, Mendes-Giannini MJ, Duarte AJ, et al. IL-12 and neutralization of endogenous IL-10 revert the in vitro antigen-specific cellular immunosuppression of paracoccidioidomycosis patients. Cytokine. 2002;18:149-157.
41. Campanelli AP, Martins GA, Souto JT. Fas-Fas ligand (CD95-CD95L) and cytotoxic T lymphocyte antigen-4 engagement mediate T cell unresponsiveness in patients with paracoccidioidomycosis. J Infect Dis. 2003;187:1496-1505.
42. Calvi SA, Peracoli MT, Mendes RP, et al. Effect of cytokines on the in vitro fungicidal activity of monocytes from paracoccidioidomycosis patients. Microbes Infect. 2003;5:107-113.
43. Gónzalez A, Aristizabal BH, Caro, E, et al. Production of nitric oxide and TNF-β, and expression of iNOS and NF κβ in peritoneal macrophages activated with interferon gamma. Ann Rev Biomed Sci. 2003;4:133-139.
44. Nascimento FR, Calich VL, Rodriguez D, Russo M. Dual role for nitric oxide in paracoccidioidomycosis: Essential for resistance, but overproduction associated with susceptibility. J Biol Chem. 2002;168:4593-600,
45. Bethlem EP, Capone D, Maranhao B, et al. Paracoccidioidomycosis. Curr Opin Pulm Med. l999;5:319-325.
46. Tobón AM, Agudelo CA, Osorio ML, et al. Residual pulmonary abnormalities in adult patients with chronic paracoccidioidomycosis. Prolonged follow-up after itraconazole therapy. Clin Infect Dis. 2003;37:898-904.
47. Funari M, Kavakama J, Shikanai-Yasuda MA, et al. Chronic pulmonary paracoccidioidomycosis (South American blastomycosis): High-resolution CT findings in 41 patients. Am J Roentgenol. 1999;173:59-64.
48. Do Valle ACF, Guimaraes RR, Lopes DJ, et al. Thoracic radiologic aspects in paracoccidioidomycosis. Rev Inst Med Trop Sao Paulo. 1992;34:107-116.
49. Bicalho RN, Espírito Santo MF, Aguiar MCF, et al. Oral paracoccidioidomycosis: A retrospective study of 62 Brazilian patients. Oral Dis. 2001;7:56-60.
50. Chojniak R, Viera RA, Lopez A, et al. Intestinal paracoccidioidomycosis simulating colon cancer. Rev Soc Bras Med Trop. 2000;33:309-312.
51. SantAnna GD, Mauri M, Arrarte JL, Camargo H. Laryngeal manifestations of paracoccidioidomycosis (South American blastomycosis). Arch Otolaryngol Head Neck Surg 1999;125:1375-1378.
52. Oñate JM, Tobón AM, Restrepo A. Adrenal gland insufficiency secondary to paracoccidioidomycosis. Biomédica (Bogotá, Colombia). 2002;22:280-286.
53. Leal AM, Magalhaes PK, Martínez R, et al. Adrenocortical hormones and interleukin patterns in paracoccidioidomycosis. J Infect Dis. 2003;187:124-127
54. Doria AS, Taylor GA. Bony involvement in paracoccidioidomycosis. Pediatr Radiol. 1997;27:67-69.
55. Severo LC, Kauer CL, Oliveira FD, et al. Paracoccidioidomycosis of the male genital tract: Report of eleven case a review of the Brazilian literature. Rev Inst Med Tropical Sao Paulo. 2000;42:38-40.
56. Villa LA, Tobón AM, Restrepo A, et al. Central nervous system paracoccidioidomycosis: Report of a case successfully treated with itraconazol. Rev Inst Med Trop Sao Paulo. 2000;42:231-234.
57. Nogueira SA, Caiuby MJ, Vasconcellos V, et al. Paracoccidioidomycosis and tuberculosis in AIDS patients: Report of two cases in Brazil. Int J Infect Dis. 1998;2:168-172.
58. Marques SA, Shikanai-Yasuda MA. Paracoccidioidomycosis associated with immunosuppression, AIDS, and cancer. In: Franco M, Lacaz CS, Restrepo A, et al, eds. Paracoccidioidomycosis. Boca Raton: CRC Press; 1994:393-405.
59. Gomes GM, Cisalpino PS, Taborda CP, Camargo ZP. PCR for diagnosis of paracoccidioidomycosis. J Clin Microbiol. 2000;38:3478-3480.
60. Bialek R, Ibricevic A, Aepinus, C, et al. Detection of *Paracoccidioides brasiliensis* in tissue samples by a nested PCR assay. J Clin Microbiol. 2002;38:2940-2942.
61. Semighini CP, de Camargo ZP, Puccia R, et al. Molecular identification of *Paracoccidioides brasiliensis* by 5′ nuclease assay. Diagn Microbiol Infect Dis. 2002;44:383-386
62. Do Valle ACF, Costa RLB, Fialho-Monteiro PC, et al. Interpretation and clinical correlation of serologic test in paracoccidioidomycosis. Med Mycol. 2001;39:373-377.
63. Cunha DA, Zancopé-Oliveira RS, Sueli M, et al. Heterologous expression, purification, and immunological reactivity of a recombinant HSP60 from *Paracoccidioides brasiliensis*. Clin Diagn Lab Immunol. 2002;9:374-377.

64. Diez S, Gómez BL, McEwen JG, et al. Combined use of *Paracoccidioides brasiliensis* recombinant 27-kilodalton and purified 87-kilodalton antigens in an enzyme-linked immunosorbent assay for serodiagnosis of paracoccidioidomycosis. J Clin Microbiol. 2003;41:1536-1542.

65. Gómez BL, Figueroa JI, Hamilton AJ, et al. Antigenemia in patients with paracoccidioidomycosis: Detection of the 87 kDa determinant during and after antifungal therapy. J Clin Microbiol. 1998;36:3309-3316.

66. Dietze R, Fowler VG, Steiner TS, et al. Failure of amphotericin B colloidal dispersion in the treatment of paracoccidioidomycosis. Am J Trop Med Hyg. 1999;60:837-839.

67. Borgia G, Raynaud L, Cerrini R, et al. A case of paracoccidioidomycosis: Experience with long term therapy. Infection. 2000;28:119-120.

68. Tobón AM, Orozco B, Estrada S, et al. Paracoccidioidomycosis and AIDS: Report of the first two Colombian cases. Rev Inst Med Trop Sao Paulo. 1998;40:377-381.

69. Shikanai-Yasuda MA, Benard G, Higaki Y, et al. Randomized trial with itraconazole, ketoconazole and sulfadiazine in paracoccidioidomycosis. Med Mycol. 2002;40:411-417.

70. Hahn RC, Fontes CJ, Batista RD, et al. In vitro comparison of activities of terbinafine and itraconazole against *Paracoccidioides brasiliensis*. J Clin Microbiol. 2002;40:2828-2831.

CHAPTER **267**

Uncommon Fungi

DUANE R. HOSPENTHAL

PSEUDALLESCHERIA BOYDII

Human infection with *Pseudallescheria boydii* (anamorph [asexual state] *Scedosporium apiospermum*) can produce two distinct rare diseases: mycetoma and pseudallescheriasis (scedosporiosis). Mycetoma is a chronic subcutaneous infection characterized by the production of grains (see Chapter 260), whereas pseudallescheriasis includes all other infections caused by *P. boydii*. The most common sites of pseudallescheriasis are lung, bone, joints, and the central nervous system (CNS).[1] Sinusitis,[2] keratitis, endophthalmitis, skin and soft tissue infections, prostatitis, and endocarditis[3,4] have also been described. The fungus is found in soil and fresh water, especially stagnant or polluted water, throughout the world. Disease is acquired after inhalation of this organism into the lungs or paranasal sinuses or following traumatic inoculation through the skin. There are at least 14 reported cases of pneumonia following near-drowning in contaminated water. Although colonization is more common than infection with this organism, an invasive pulmonary disease similar to invasive pulmonary aspergillosis is seen, usually in immunocompromised patients. Local trauma is the most common cause of eye, soft tissue, and osteoarticular infections in previously healthy persons. CNS infection is seen in both immunocompromised and healthy individuals. Infections in immunocompetent patients usually have subacute to chronic courses, whereas those in immunocompromised patients are frequently acute and severe.

P. boydii can colonize bronchiectatic lungs or intermittently obstructed paranasal sinuses. Masses of *P. boydii* hyphae (fungus balls) have been found in lung cavities.[5] *P. boydii* has also been reported as a cause of allergic bronchopulmonary disease (similar to allergic bronchopulmonary aspergillosis),[6] pleural space infection, lung abscess, pneumonia (including aspiration pneumonia), and invasive sinusitis. As with invasive pulmonary aspergillosis, invasive pulmonary pseudallescheriasis most commonly occurs in patients with prolonged

The views expressed are those of the author and do not reflect the official policy or position of the Department of the Army, the Department of Defense, or the U.S. Government.

neutropenia, those receiving prolonged high-dose corticosteroid therapy, or those who have undergone allogeneic bone marrow transplantation.[7,8] Invasive pulmonary disease with dissemination has also occurred in patients with acquired immunodeficiency syndrome (AIDS) and after solid-organ transplantation.[9] Pulmonary disease in the severely immunocompromised patient usually manifests with fever, cough, pleuritic pain, and often hemoptysis. Chest films show areas of nodularity, alveolar infiltrate or, most commonly, consolidation.[7,8,10] Later, cavitation can be noted.[7,8] Disseminated disease that manifests with only painful cutaneous nodules or endophthalmitis has also been described in this group of patients.[11,12] Invasive pulmonary disease with extension to the vertebrae has been described in a patient without apparent immunocompromise.[13]

Localized disease, including infections of the eye, bone, and cutaneous, subcutaneous (Fig. 267-1), and osteoarticular tissue, may be seen both with and without immunocompromise. Infection is commonly initiated via traumatic implantation of the fungus from soil or water. Surgery, intravenous drug injection, and repeated corticosteroid injections have less frequently been associated with localized infections.[14] Osteoarticular infection in immunocompetent patients often appears as a painful, swollen joint with overlying erythema after penetrating joint injury. Occasionally, weeks to even years may pass between antecedent trauma and the development of septic arthritis.[15,16]

Brain abscesses may result from a known or unsuspected lung lesion in immunocompromised patients, including AIDS patients.[17,18] CNS infection appears to be disproportionately increased in patients with pseudallescheriasis when compared with many other mycoses. For example, 11 of 23 (48%) solid-organ transplant recipients with pseudallescheriasis had CNS involvement.[19] Cerebral abscesses are usually multiple and in the immunocompetent host are often reported in association with near-drownings in polluted water, such as ponds, pig troughs, and roadside ditches.[20,21] CNS infection from contiguous spread of sinusitis[22] and after penetrating trauma[23] has also been described. Indolent, severe neutrophilic meningitis has been reported occasionally, usually in patients with intravenous drug abuse or human immunodeficiency virus (HIV) infection. Cerebrospinal fluid culture and smear have been negative, with the diagnosis made at autopsy.[17] The first described human case of pseudallescheriasis was a meningitis that was likely iatrogenic after a lumbar puncture for the administration of anesthesia.[24]

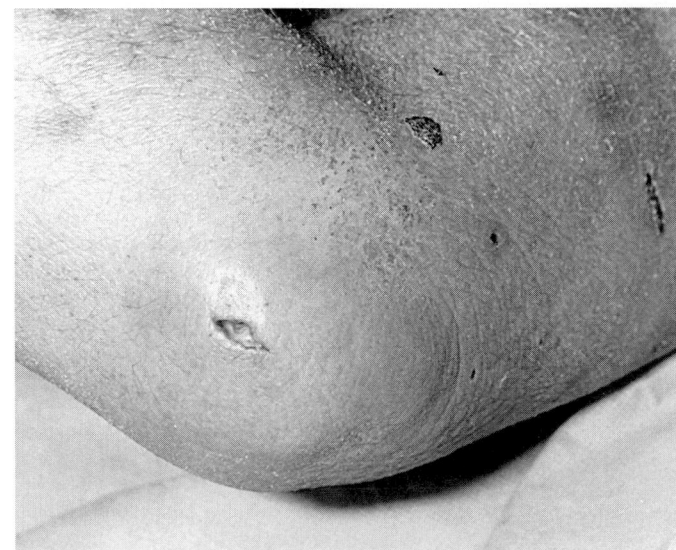

FIGURE 267-1. *Pseudallescheria boydii* olecranon bursitis in a corticosteroid-treated patient who fell on his elbow in the garden. Photograph shows the incision site over the subcutaneous abscess, which began in the bursa.

Isolation of *P. boydii* from normally sterile sites is diagnostic. Rarely, *P. boydii* may be cultured from blood.[3] Growth of the organism from sputum, bronchoalveolar lavage, draining wounds, or paranasal sinus aspirates is less convincing unless accompanied by hyphae on smear or biopsy. Microscopically, *P. boydii* resembles *Aspergillus,* with dichotomously branching septate hyphae seen in tissue. In neutropenic patients, blood vessel invasion and thrombosis are usual. The fungus grows well in standard mycologic media. In a few days, the mold colony takes on a tan color and has sporulating structures that are quite different from *Aspergillus.* Cultures that produce asexual conidia but do not produce the sexual reproductive structure, the cleistothecia, after 2 to 3 weeks are designated by the anamorph name *Scedosporium apiospermum.* No clinically useful serologic or other rapid identification tests are currently available.

Effective antifungal therapy of pseudallescheriasis has not been established. In vitro and clinical resistance to amphotericin B has been reported repeatedly. Surgical débridement has been an important adjunct in treatment of pseudallescheriasis of soft tissue, bone, joint, and pleural and paranasal sinuses, although it is not curative in itself. Intra-articular instillation of amphotericin B may have contributed to success in a few patients. Mortality with brain abscess has traditionally been noted to be greater than 75%.[17,23] In the past intravenous miconazole and surgery had been associated with most successful outcomes in CNS infection.[1,17,23] Successes have been reported with ketoconazole and itraconazole, mostly in patients with localized infection, and in conjunction with débridement.[15,25,26] Combination therapy with liposomal amphotericin B and itraconazole has been used successfully in at least one case of disseminated infection.[27] The new broad-spectrum azole antifungals (including voriconazole, posaconazole, ravuconazole, and albaconazole) and the echinocandin caspofungin have been shown to have activity against *P. boydii* in vitro.[28-33] Clinical response to voriconazole therapy has been reported in numerous case reports,[34-39] as has response to posaconazole in a single reported case of brain abscess.[40] Voriconazole has been approved by the Food and Drug Administration (FDA) for patients with pseudallescheriasis refractory to or intolerant of other approved antifungal agents. This indication was gained based on success reported in 15 of 24 patients treated with this agent (including 6 of 10 with CNS infection). Because of poor response to the only approved agent, amphotericin B, some experts suggest voriconazole as the drug of choice in pseudallescheriasis.[34]

SCEDOSPORIUM PROLIFICANS

Scedosporium prolificans (formerly *S. inflatum*), a fungus found in soil, was first described in 1984 as an agent of human disease.[41] Since that time, several dozen cases have been reported from Spain[42] as well as Australia, Canada, France, Germany, the Netherlands, and the United States, in both immunocompromised and immunocompetent patients.[43] Patients with intact immunity most frequently have focal infections (usually osteoarticular), whereas immunocompromised persons more frequently have disseminated disease. In one recent review 29 of 30 patients with disseminated S. prolificans infections were immunosuppressed.[43]

In immunocompetent patients, infection is usually localized and associated with trauma, including surgery.[44,45] These cases have included infections of bone and joints (Fig. 267-2), onychomycosis, and endophthalmitis. Immunocompromised patients, commonly those undergoing cytoreductive chemotherapy or bone marrow transplantation, present with fungemia and fever during neutropenia.[46-48] Skin lesions, myalgia, endophthalmitis, and pulmonary infiltrates have been described in this setting.[12,49] Skin lesions have been described as a papular rash, later becoming necrotic. Disseminated disease without neutropenia has been described in lung and kidney transplantation.[50] Fatal localized CNS infection has been reported in a child with acute leukemia who had received six intrathecal chemotherapeutic injections.[51] S. prolificans has also been recovered from the external ear and sputum of patients without apparent disease.[42,44,45] Sputum colonization has been seen in patients with AIDS and cystic fibrosis and those who have undergone liver or lung transplantation.[45,52,53]

Diagnosis is most commonly made by recovery of the organism from culture of infected sites, including skin biopsies. Disseminated disease in immunocompromised patients is usually diagnosed by blood culture.[47] Identification of *S. prolificans* is based chiefly on the morphologic characteristics of the asexual structures produced by the mold in culture.[54]

Currently, no effective antifungal therapy is available to treat these infections. *S. prolificans* appears to be intrinsically resistant to most currently available antifungals. Successful therapy of joint infections has been reported with the use of surgical débridement with or without intra-articular amphotericin B.[44] Disseminated infection is usually resistant to antifungal agents and carries a high mortality.[46] Survival has been reported in one patient with disseminated disease and neutropenia who received granulocyte colony-stimulating factor (G-CSF) and amphotericin B followed by itraconazole.[47] In one animal model, liposomal amphotericin B with the addition of G-CSF improved survival.[55] Of the currently available antifungal agents, voriconazole appears most promising in vitro, with better activity than amphotericin B, itraconazole, or posaconazole.[28,31,33] Unfortunately, current dosing regimens of voriconazole are not associated with serum concentrations at which the drug appears to be effective in vitro. Limited reports have described a 29% response (2 of 7) in patients treated with voriconazole.[56] The investigational azole, albaconazole (UR-9825) appears more active than voriconazole in vitro and has shown potential in one animal model.[28,57] Because of the in vitro and in vivo resistance of this organism to currently available agents, the effect of combining agents has been examined. In laboratory studies, synergy has been shown using combinations of amphotericin B plus pentamidine,[58] and terbinafine with voriconazole, itraconazole, or miconazole.[59,60] Clinical support for this in vitro synergy is lacking, although anecdotal experience has been reported with voriconazole and terbinafine.[61]

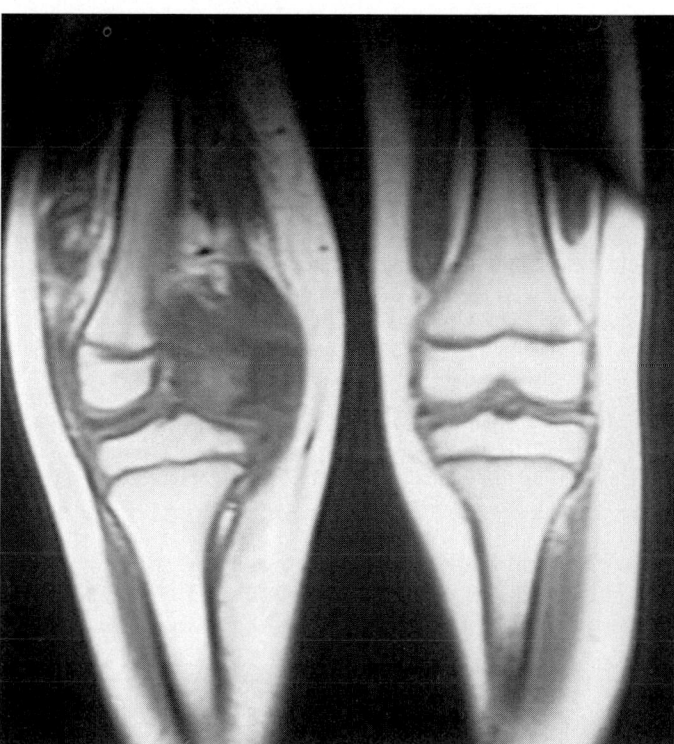

FIGURE 267-2. *Scedosporium prolificans* septic arthritis of the knee in a healthy 12-year-old boy that developed in association with a splinter obtained during a playground fall. T_2-weighted magnetic resonance imaging shows osteomyelitis of the medial condyle.

DARK-WALLED FUNGI/AGENTS OF PHAEOHYPHOMYCOSIS

Phaeohyphomycosis is a loosely defined term used to group infections caused by molds (and a few yeasts) that produce dark cell walls. Also termed *dematiaceous,* these are a diverse group of fungi found in the soil and air, and growing on plants and in organic debris. The number of genera and species of fungi causing phaeohyphomycosis is quite large.[62,63] Frequent changes in species names have compounded the physician's difficulty in looking up similar cases in the literature. Chromoblastomycosis (see Chapter 259) and mycetoma (see Chapter 260) are distinct infections that include dark-walled fungi as etiologic agents that are generally not included in this loose classification (Table 267-1). *Pseudallescheria boydii* and *Scedosporium prolificans* produce dark structures in culture, and currently *S. prolificans* is included in the phaeohyphomycoses by some authorities.[43] The syndromes most commonly produced by the dark-walled fungi include cutaneous and subcutaneous disease (other than chromomycosis or mycetoma), brain abscesses, and sinusitis. Fungemia[64] and disseminated disease[43] are more commonly being described in immunocompromised individuals. Meningitis, pneumonia, prosthetic valve endocarditis, peritoneal dialysis catheter infection, osteomyelitis, and septic arthritis have also been reported. For most clinical purposes, it is preferable to describe disease by the type of infection and species name, such as "*Cladophialophora bantiana* brain abscess" and to reserve the term *phaeohyphomycosis* for patients who have no culture or whose culture has not yet been identified.

Subcutaneous phaeohyphomycosis typically begins as a single red nodule, usually on the extremities. In the immunocompetent person, an indolent, painless expansion in the skin and subcutaneous tissue occurs, sometimes with cyst formation (Fig. 267-3). More rapid local progression, and rarely, extension to the brain, can occur in the immunosuppressed patient. A history of minor trauma is often obtained or a splinter found in the resected lesion. The fungi causing subcutaneous phaeohyphomycosis are extraordinarily diverse, although species of *Bipolaris, Exophiala, Exserohilum, Phialophora,* and *Wangiella* are particularly common.

Brain abscess is one of the best-described syndromes produced by the dark-walled fungi.[62,65,66] Disease presents with headache of indolent onset, low-grade or no fever, and development of focal neurologic signs. There is rarely a history of exposure to dust or mold, no obvious pulmonary portal, and no evidence of dissemination outside the CNS. Males have outnumbered females 3:1, the median age of diagnosis is 38 years, and a majority of patients have been immunocompetent.[66-68] Abscesses may be single or multiple and are well localized within the cerebral cortex on computed tomography or magnetic resonance imaging (Fig. 267-4).[9] Purulent meningitis, with or without brain abscess, may also be seen (Fig. 267-5).[70] On hematoxylin and eosin (H&E) staining, abscesses have purulent centers with surrounding granulomatous reaction and organisms appearing as septate hyphae with golden brown cell walls. As in other forms of infections with the dark-walled fungi, hyphae are commonly irregular in diameter and yeastlike cells are seen with some species. The most common species causing these infections is *Cladophialophora bantiana* (previously named *Xylohypha bantiana, Cladosporium bantianum,* and

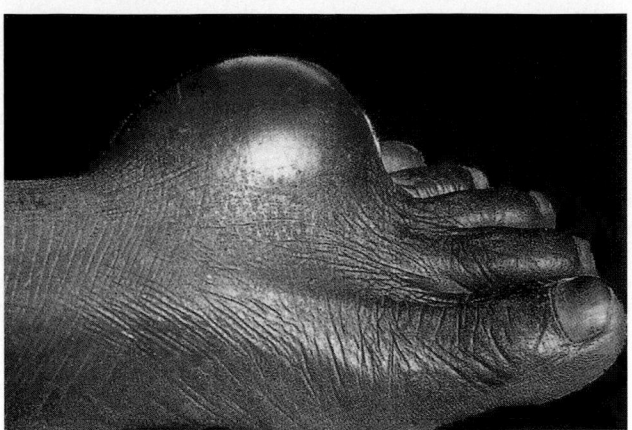

FIGURE 267-3. Phaeohyphomycosis presenting as a cyst. *(From Chandler FW, Watts JC. Phaeohyphomycosis. In: Connor DH, Chandler FW, Schwartz DA, et al, eds. Pathology of Infectious Diseases. Norwalk, CT: Appleton & Lange; 1997, with permission of the McGraw-Hill Companies.)*

C. trichoides), but disease is also caused by *Ramichloridium mackenziei, Ochroconis gallopavum (Dactylaria gallopava), Wangiella dermatitidis, Bipolaris spicifera, Bipolaris hawaiiensis, Chaetomium* species, and, even more rarely, other phaeohyphomycetes.[66,68,71] *R. mackenziei* infections are reported chiefly from the Middle East and India,[72,73] and *W. dermatitidis* cases predominate in the Far East.

Allergic fungal sinusitis may be caused by a wide variety of fungi, though the dark-walled fungi (usually *Bipolaris, Exserohilum, Curvularia,* or *Alternaria* species) and *Aspergillus* species comprise the most common etiology.[74] By definition, disease is allergic and confined

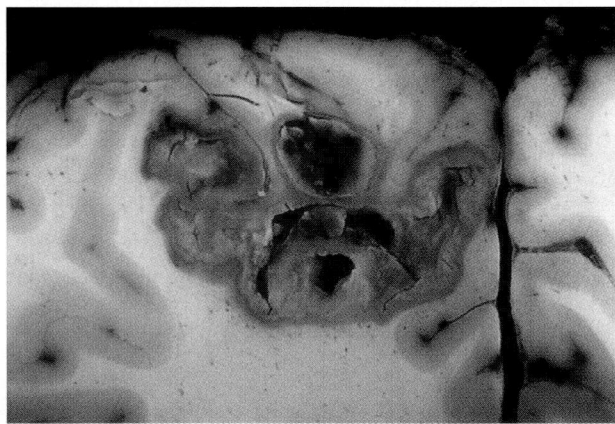

FIGURE 267-4. Phaeohyphomycosis of the brain caused by *Cladophialophora* sp. *(From Chandler FW, Watts JC. Phaeohyphomycosis. In: Connor DH, Chandler FW, Schwartz DA, et al, eds. Pathology of Infectious Diseases. Norwalk, CT: Appleton & Lange; 1997, with permission of the McGraw-Hill Companies.)*

TABLE 267-1 Cutaneous/Subcutaneous Infections Caused by Dark-Walled Fungi

Disease	Lesions	Pathology	Organisms
Chromoblastomycosis	Scaly, friable, often verrucous nodules, commonly pruritic	Muriform cells (golden brown cells with cross walls in more than one plane)	*Fonsecaea pedrosoi, Fonsecaea compacta, Cladophialophora carrionii, Phialophora verrucosa, Rhinocladiella aquaspersa*
Mycetoma (eumycetoma, eumycotic mycetoma)	Nodular with draining sinuses, areas of healing	Grains comprised of septate hyphae	*Madurella* spp., *Leptosphaeria* spp., *Curvularia* spp., *Exophiala jeanselmei, Phialophora verrucosa, Pyrenochaeta mackinnonii, Pyrenochaeta romeroi*
Subcutaneous phaeohyphomycosis	Painless, subcutaneous nodules	Septate hyphae (may also see pseudohyphae or yeasts)	*Bipolaris, Exophiala, Exserohilum, Phialophora, Wangiella,* and many others

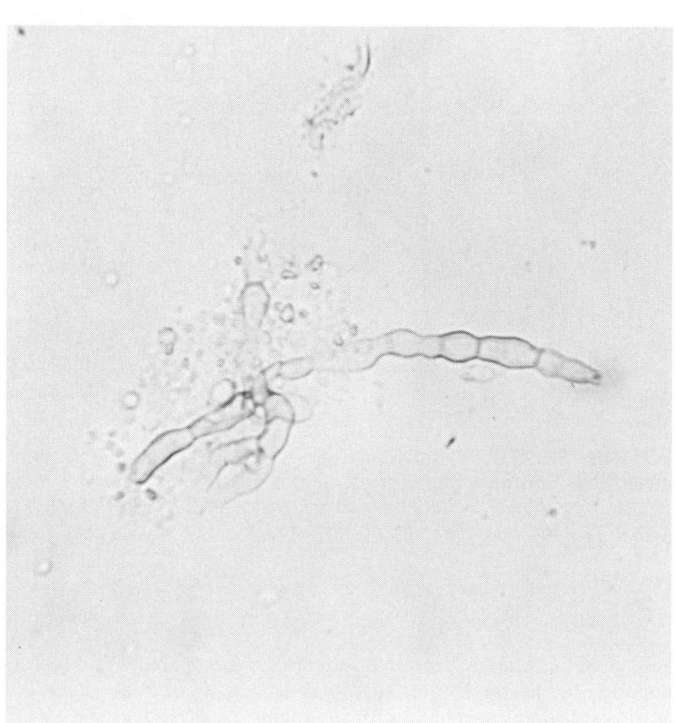

FIGURE 267-5. Weakly pigmented, segmented hyphae of *Cladophialophora bantiana* in the wet mount of pus from the base of the brain.

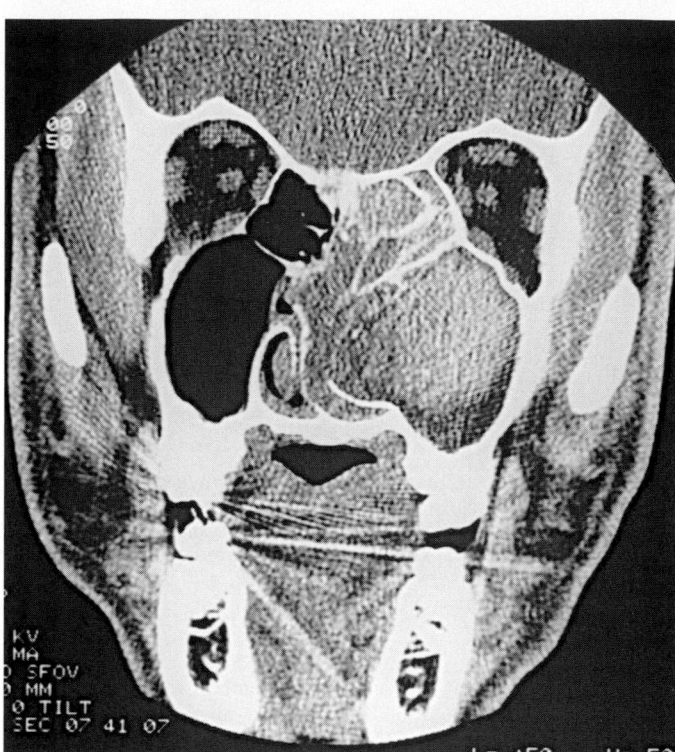

FIGURE 267-6. Computed tomography scan showing outward-bulging mass in the maxillary and ethmoid sinuses of a patient with allergic fungal sinusitis.

to the lumen of the paranasal sinuses. Patients present with an indolent onset of sinus pain or painless proptosis. A history of seasonal or allergic rhinitis is common, and there may be a history of nasal polyps. On computed tomography or magnetic resonance imaging, one or more paranasal sinuses appears full of fluid, with outward pressure on the thinner bony sinus walls, such as the lamina papyracea, medial maxillary wall, or midline sphenoidal septum. Maxillary and ethmoid sinuses are usually involved, but sphenoid and frontal sinuses may be diseased (Fig. 267-6). Surgical débridement of the paranasal sinus removes dark, inspissated mucus that on histopathologic examination has eosinophils with Charcot-Leyden crystals (degenerated eosinophils) and scattered septate hyphae.[75] The walls of the hyphae may not appear as dark as seen in brain abscess. Irregular diameter and bulbous swellings may help distinguish these hyphae from *Aspergillus,* but culture is essential for diagnosis. The most serious sequela of allergic fungal sinusitis is brain invasion, usually in the immunocompromised host (Fig. 267-7). Extension from the ethmoid or frontal sinus into the frontal lobe of the brain can be clinically silent. Erosion into the clivus, pterygoid space, or middle fossa occurs but is rare. Sudden blindness can occur from compression of the optic nerve posterior to the orbital fissure. Compression of the orbit by lateral bulging of the lamina papyracea does not decrease visual acuity but causes proptosis.

Diagnosis of these infections requires observation of the fungi invading tissue or recovery of the fungi in culture from an otherwise sterile site. Lack of tissue invasion is required in the diagnosis of allergic fungal sinusitis by definition. In disease outside the CNS, these organisms may not always appear dark walled on standard histopathologic stains. Cell wall melanin may be visible as a brownish-yellow color on H&E stain (Fig. 267-8). If melanin is not evident on fresh preparations of H&E stain, it can be stained by the Fontana-Masson method, allowing improved diagnosis, especially if culture results are negative or culture is not obtained.[76] One should be aware that Fontana-Masson stain is not 100% specific for the dark-walled fungi because the cell walls of some *Aspergillus* and other fungi with hyaline hyphae have been shown to stain dark using this method.[77]

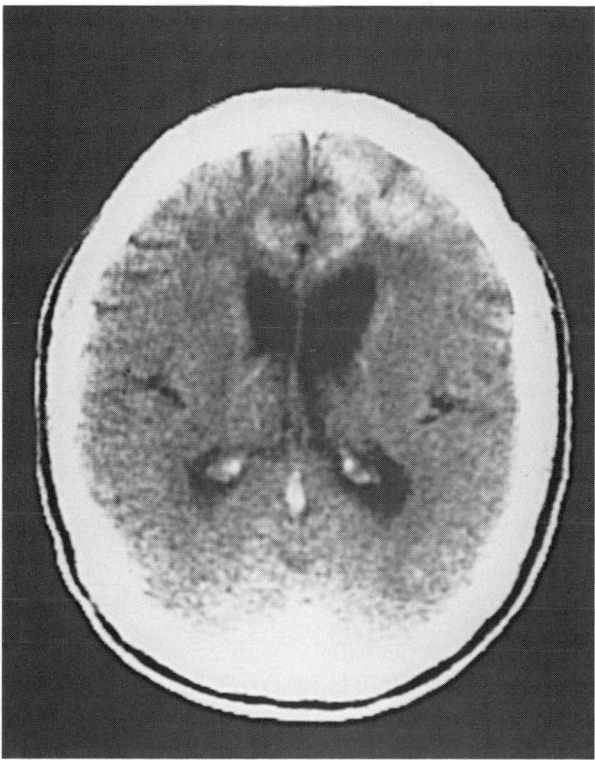

FIGURE 267-7. T$_2$-weighted magnetic resonance imaging showing extension into the frontal lobe of *Bipolaris hawaiiensis* sinusitis.

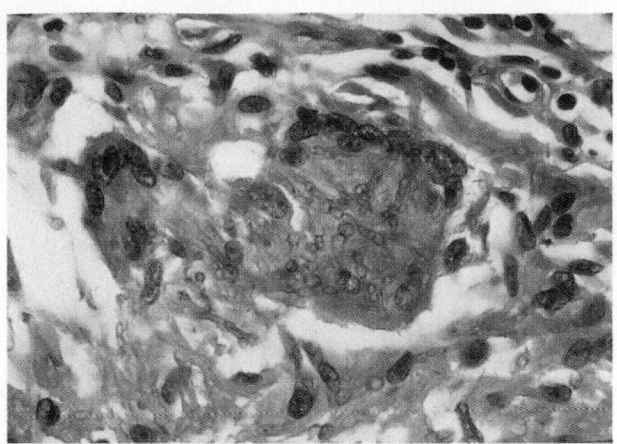

FIGURE 267-8. Cutaneous phaeohyphomycosis caused by *Exophiala jeanselmei*. Note the brown hyphae (hematoxylin and eosin). *(From Chandler FW, Watts JC. Phaeohyphomycosis. In: Connor DH, Chandler FW, Schwartz DA, et al, eds. Pathology of Infectious Diseases. Norwalk, CT: Appleton & Lange; 1997, with permission of the McGraw-Hill Companies.)*

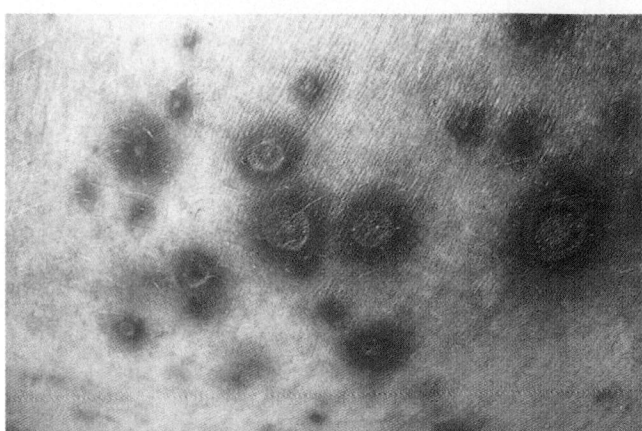

FIGURE 267-9. Cutaneous lesions of disseminated infection caused by *Fusarium moniliforme*. *(From Beneke ES, Rogers AL. Medical Mycology and Human Mycoses. Belmont, CA: Star Publishing Company; 1996, reprinted with permission.)*

Surgical débridement is essential to the cure of most of the infections caused by the dark-walled fungi. Good surgical curettage often suffices in allergic sinusitis if the cranial cavity has not been entered. Amphotericin B is probably the drug of choice for life-threatening infection, including CNS infection. Itraconazole has been used frequently with success in those infections that are not life-threatening.[78,79] In patients who have recurrent allergic fungal sinusitis, long-term itraconazole therapy may be used after repeat surgical drainage to help prevent another recurrence. In vitro, voriconazole commonly produces minimum inhibitory concentrations (MICs) to most of these fungi that are similar to or lower than those seen with itraconazole, making this new drug a potentially useful therapeutic agent.[33] Posaconazole and caspofungin have also been shown to have in vitro activity against many of these fungi.[29,30] Posaconazole has been reported to produce a good clinical response in a woman with disseminated infection caused by *Exophiala spinifera* that did not respond to amphotericin B therapy.[80]

FUSARIUM SPECIES

Species in the genus *Fusarium* are common in soil and organic debris and are frequently the cause of disease in plants. Disease in humans is rare, usually following traumatic inoculation in the healthy host. Inhalation or minor trauma can lead to fusariosis in immunocompromised patients. *Fusarium*, usually *Fusarium solani*, is one of the more common causes of fungal keratitis. *Fusarium* can also cause onychomycosis, endophthalmitis, and skin and musculoskeletal infections (including mycetoma).[81] Since the early 1970s, disseminated infection with *Fusarium* has become an increasingly common problem in persons with hematologic malignancy and other immunocompromising disorders (including AIDS).

Rare cases of dissemination have been described in the clinical setting of severe burns[82] and heat stroke.[83] Most commonly, however, fusariosis occurs in patients with acute leukemia (70% to 80% of cases)[84,85] and prolonged neutropenia (more than 90% of cases).[84,86] In one review of 43 patients, the median duration of neutropenia was greater than 3 weeks.[84] Fusariosis is also increasingly reported in patients undergoing bone marrow transplantation.[87,88] The portal of entry in the majority of these cases of disseminated infection is not known. Inhalation, ingestion, and entry through skin trauma have been suggested.[81] Sinusitis has preceded dissemination in a few reports.[89] Hematogenous spread attributed to indwelling intravascular catheters also has been reported.[90,91] Onychomycosis has been postulated to be a source of this infection in some patients.[84,92] A more recent study has supported the hospital water supply system as a potential source of fusariosis, perhaps accounting for the highly localized endemicity of this infection.[93]

Infection commonly manifests with fever and myalgia that are unresponsive to broad-spectrum antibacterial antibiotics during periods of profound neutropenia. Disseminated fusariosis has been recognized in patients who have been receiving empirical or prophylactic antifungal therapy.[85,87,94] Skin lesions occur in 60% to 80% of infections, usually appearing as multiple papules or deeply set, painful nodules (Fig. 267-9). They may initially be flat (macular) with a central pallor, but later become raised, erythematous, and necrotic (Fig. 267-10).[81,84,86,88] Lesions are most commonly seen on the extremities but have been reported on the trunk and face as well.[87] In profoundly neutropenic patients, this infection can progress rapidly to death, in a manner similar to that seen in invasive aspergillosis. Skin lesions, denoting dissemination, can occur within a day of the onset of fever. In patients whose neutrophils start to return, the infection can progress slowly over weeks until death or can become controlled and eventually cured.

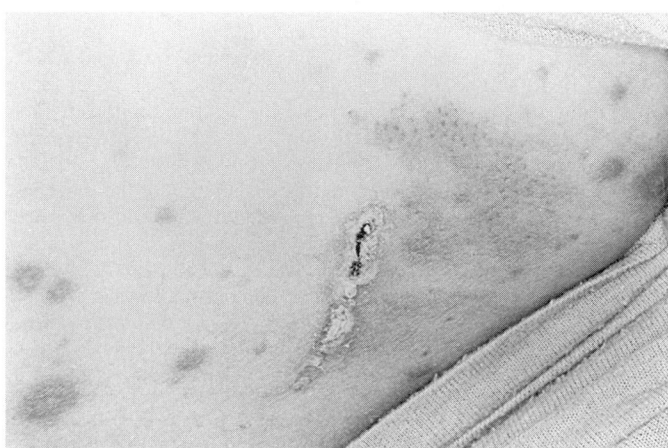

FIGURE 267-10. Multiple necrotic skin lesions in a neutropenic patient with hematogenously disseminated fusariosis.

Recovery of the fungus from the blood and biopsy of suspicious skin lesions are the two most common and effective ways to diagnose this infection. In contrast to aspergillosis, in which blood cultures are nearly always negative, fusariosis is accompanied by positive blood cultures about 50% of the time (48 of 98 patients in one review).[84] Although nonspecific for *Fusarium,* finding septate hyphal elements in a skin biopsy specimen should aid in making rapid therapeutic decisions. *Fusarium* can usually be recovered in culture of skin biopsy tissue and seen in histopathologic studies. The hyphae resemble *Aspergillus. Fusarium* has a predilection for small blood vessels, resulting in angioinvasion and associated thrombosis, although not as prominently as with *Aspergillus.* The septate hyphae of *Fusarium* species are difficult to visualize with routine H&E staining but are easily identified when tissue is prepared with Gomori methenamine-silver or periodic acid–Schiff stains. In culture, the characteristic feature of *Fusarium* is the production of sickle (banana)-shaped multiseptate macroconidia.[95] *F. solani* is the most common species recovered (when speciated), followed by *Fusarium oxysporum,* and *Fusarium moniliforme (verticilloides).*[84,86]

The optimal treatment for disseminated fusariosis has not been established. Overall mortality in this infection has been reported to range from 50% to 80%.[86-88] Survival is almost always associated with the recovery from neutropenia, although corticosteroid use also impairs response to therapy.[84,86,87,96] Analysis of responders versus nonresponders in one study of 43 patients noted an association with malignancy in remission (100% vs. 10%), adequate neutrophil counts (100% vs. 0%), and lack of significant (grade II or greater) graft-versus-host disease (0% vs. 66%).[84] Removal of indwelling venous catheters has been associated with improvement and thus should be considered in all cases of fungemia.[91] Amphotericin B has been included in the regimens of most successfully treated patients, and thus high-dose (0.1 to 1.5 mg/kg/day) amphotericin B is currently the drug of choice. Treatment with lipid-based amphotericin B formulations,[84,97] caspofungin,[98] and combinations of other approved antifungal agents have been reported, all with mixed success. In vitro, voriconazole, posaconazole, and caspofungin have all been shown to be of potential value.[24,230,32,33,99] An interesting laboratory study showed decreased MIC for amphotericin B when combined with azithromycin.[100] Animal models have shown liposomal amphotericin B,[101] posaconazole,[102] and voriconazole[103] to be potentially useful in this difficult-to-treat mycosis. Successful therapy of 9 of 21 (43%) patients who received voriconazole supported FDA approval of this agent for second-line use in fusariosis. The addition of colony-stimulating factors (G-CSF or granulocyte-macrophage colony-stimulating factor) or granulocyte transfusions to specific antifungal therapy has also been reported,[81,84,86,104] but the benefit of these adjunctive therapies is also not proven.

OTHER OPPORTUNISTIC MOLDS

In the immunocompromised host virtually any of the normally nonpathogenic fungi may occasionally cause disease. In addition to more common infections caused by *Aspergillus* and *Fusarium* species, other rare light-colored (hyaline) molds, including species of *Paecilomyces,*[105] *Acremonium,*[106] *Trichoderma,*[107] and *Scopulariopsis,*[108] have been described as more frequently causing clinical disease than other rare fungi. Some authorities have grouped disease caused by molds with light-colored cell walls into a group, termed the *hyalohyphomycoses.* As with the dark-walled fungi, description of these infections based on the causative organisms is preferential to minimize confusion. *Paecilomyces* has been reported to cause keratitis, endophthalmitis, cutaneous and subcutaneous infections, as well as catheter-related fungemia, sinusitis, and disseminated infection. Like *Fusarium,* both *Paecilomyces* and *Acremonium* have been reported to form reproductive structures in vivo in a process called adventitious sporulation.[109] This is believed to account for the much higher frequency of blood culture recovery seen in infections involving these three genera. Also like *Fusarium,* both are typically associated with

poor response to amphotericin B and the older azoles, although resistance varies among species. *P. varioti* is susceptible to amphotericin B, and infections have been treated successfully with this agent. *P. lilacinus* responds poorly to amphotericin B and is resistant to this agent, caspofungin, and the older azoles in vitro. In vitro testing has shown multiple strains of these fungi to be more susceptible to voriconazole, ravuconazole, and posaconazole, but clinical treatment results are not currently available.[33]

TRICHOSPORON SPECIES

The genus *Trichosporon* is characterized by the production of septate hyphae, arthroconidia, yeasts, and pseudohyphae, and yeastlike growth on culture media. Recent revisions in taxonomy have placed most of the agents of deeply invasive human *Trichosporon* infections into the species *Trichosporon asahii* or, less commonly, *Trichosporon mucoides.*[110-113] According to this schema, *Trichosporon asteroides* and *Trichosporon cutaneum* cause superficial infections of humans. White piedra of the scalp is caused by *Trichosporon ovoides* and similar disease of the pubic hair by *Trichosporon inkin* (see Chapter 265). *Trichosporon* can be found in soil and water, on plants, and colonizing human stool, skin, or urine.[114] More than 100 patients with deep trichosporonosis have been described; approximately 60% have been severely neutropenic, usually with acute leukemia.[113,115,116] A few have had organ transplantation, HIV infection, burns, chronic ambulatory peritoneal dialysis, or catheter-acquired fungemia.[117] Seven patients had prosthetic valve infections.[114]

Trichosporonosis is an acute, febrile, often fatal infection with dissemination to multiple deep organs associated with a mortality reaching 64%. Pneumonia is not a consistent or early feature and thus the portal of entry is often not apparent. Renal involvement is common in disseminated disease and is associated with hematuria and funguria. Multiple red papular skin lesions may occur earlier and assist diagnosis.[118,119] On biopsy, a mixture of true hyphae, pseudohyphae, budding yeasts, and arthroconidia is seen, and is easily mistaken for candidiasis. *Trichosporon* grows readily on most culture media, but blood cultures tend to be positive late in the course. Therapy with amphotericin B has been recommended, but poor response and failures with this drug have occurred and there is no obviously effective drug.[114] The MIC of caspofungin and other similar drugs to these fungi is very high and thus echinocandins should not be used to treat trichosporonosis. These fungi are usually susceptible in vitro to fluconazole, itraconazole, and the new broad-spectrum azoles.[120] Therapy should include use of one of the azole antifungals.

MALASSEZIA FURFUR

Malassezia furfur, a lipophilic yeast, may colonize normal human skin and is the cause of the superficial mycosis pityriasis (tinea) versicolor (see Chapter 265). The fungus can also cause catheter-related sepsis, almost always in patients who are receiving parenteral lipids through a central venous catheter.[121] Most reported patients have been neonates with extended stays in intensive care units, although a few have been adults with malignancy or immunosuppression.[122] Fever has been the most common finding, but bradycardia, apnea, thrombocytopenia, and catheter blockage have been observed in some infants. In one autopsied case, the yeast was observed in lipid-containing areas of pulmonary vascular endothelium. *M. furfur* rarely is detected by conventional culture techniques because the yeast requires fatty acids for growth. Optimal recovery has been from culture of blood drawn back through the catheter, using the lysis-centrifugation technique and lipid-enriched agar.[121] The fungus adheres to the lumen of the catheter and has not been eradicated by discontinuing lipid infusions or administering miconazole or amphotericin B through the catheter.[123] Catheter removal and discontinuing parenteral lipids have been curative. In vitro, *M. furfur* appears to be susceptible to both amphotericin B and azole antifungals, including itraconazole and voriconazole.[124,125] Cultures or smears of peripheral blood are occasionally positive.[126]

The yeast is identified on smear by its size and shape and the distinctive collarette between mother and daughter cells. Lipid requirement for growth also aids identification. It seems likely that some cases reported as due to *M. furfur* have been due to other lipid-requiring species that can be termed the *Malassezia furfur* complex, including *Malassezia sympodialis, M. globosa, M. obtusa, M. restricta,* and *M. slooffiae.*[127] *Malassezia pachydermatis* has the same appearance and has caused similar infections, including an outbreak in a neonatal intensive care unit,[128] but does not require lipids for growth.

OTHER UNCOMMON YEASTS

Blastoschizomyces capitatus (formerly *Trichosporon capitatum*) has caused severe infection in about 76 reported cases, most of whom also had acute leukemia.[129,130] Blood cultures are usually positive, and skin lesions similar to those seen in leukemic patients with disseminated candidiasis have been observed. *B. capitatus* may colonize the skin, respiratory tract, and gastrointestinal tract. Intravenous catheters are a possible portal of entry.[131] Intravenous amphotericin B with or without flucytosine,[131] and voriconazole or high-dose fluconazole with amphotericin B[130] have been advocated for treatment of these infections. Catheter removal was associated with improved outcome in the largest and most recent report.[130]

Other noncandidal yeasts may also rarely cause infection in humans.[132] These include *Pichia (Hansenula) anomala,* the black yeast *Exophiala (Wangiella) jeanselmei, Rhodotorula* spp., and *Saccharomyces cerevisiae.* Infection is usually seen in immunocompromised individuals, most commonly as catheter-associated fungemia. Localized outbreaks secondary to *E. jeanselmei* and *P. anomala* have been described.[64,133]

PENICILLIUM MARNEFFEI

Penicillium marneffei is a thermally dimorphic fungus that causes life-threatening disseminated infection (penicilliosis marneffei) in a geographically distinct area of the world. The rapid expansion of the AIDS epidemic in Thailand has led to a marked rise in the incidence of disseminated infection with *P. marneffei.* Before the first reports of this infection in HIV-infected patients in 1988,[134-136] only 29 patients had been described since the first human infection in 1959.[137,138] In 1995, the annual incidence of this disease in Thailand had risen to 1300 cases.[139] In the mid-1990s, this infection was the third most common opportunistic infection seen in HIV-infected individuals in northern Thailand.[140] Infection with *P. marneffei* has a limited geographic distribution, affecting persons residing in or those who have visited Southeast Asia or southern China. Endogenous cases have been reported from Myanmar (Burma), Hong Kong, Indonesia, Laos, Malaysia, Singapore, Taiwan, Thailand, Vietnam, and the Guangxi province of China.[141-143] Although most commonly seen in young adults infected with HIV, disease has been reported in children[144,145] and adults, both with and without detectable immunocompromise.[141,142] *P. marneffei* has been isolated from the organs of apparently healthy bamboo rats *(Rhizomys pruinosis, R. sinensis, R. sumatrensis,* and *Cannomyus badius)*[146,147] and the soil around their burrows.[148] The role of these rats in human infection is unknown. A case-control study of the disease in 80 persons with AIDS found an association with recent history of occupational or other exposure to soil.[149] In that study, no association between infection and exposure to bamboo rats was found. According to one report, infection occurs more commonly during the rainy season in northern Thailand.[150] It is likely that this infection is acquired by inhalation of conidia from an environmental source such as the soil.

Patients typically present with a chronic illness averaging 4 weeks in duration associated with low-grade fever, weight loss, and one or more skin lesions.[140] The most common clinical characteristics are fever, malaise, anemia, leukocytosis, weight loss, and, in 60% to 70%, skin lesions.[140,142] Fungemia, generalized lymphadenopathy, and cough are reported in about 50% of patients. Subcutaneous and mucosal lesions, diarrhea, colonic lesions, hepatomegaly with or without

splenomegaly, hemoptysis, osteoarticular lesions, and pericarditis are also described.[141,151,152] Skin lesions commonly occur on the face, upper trunk, and extremities. They may occur as papules, pustules, nodules, ulcers, or abscesses. In HIV-infected individuals, lesions commonly become umbilicated and resemble those of molluscum contagiosum. Pharyngeal and palatal lesions are also more commonly seen in HIV-infected patients.[152] Lung lesions can appear as reticulonodular, nodular, or diffuse alveolar infiltrates, but on occasion have been cavitary and caused hemoptysis.[153] At autopsy, involvement of lymph nodes, liver, spleen, lung, kidney, skin, bone, bone marrow, adrenal, tonsil, bowel, and meninges has been reported.[141,154]

Consideration of the diagnosis of *P. marneffei* infection should be made in persons who have resided in or visited an endemic area. Laboratory exposure to the organism has been causally linked to disseminated infection in one immunocompromised individual.[155] The duration of incubation is not currently known, and reactivation disease may be possible. In one report, a severely immunocompromised individual acquired disseminated infection more than 10 years after visiting an endemic area.[156] Diagnosis is based on identification of the organism on smear, histopathologic studies, or culture. Diagnosis has most frequently been made from smears of skin lesions and biopsies of lymph node and bone marrow.[140] The organism has also been noted on peripheral blood smear in at least one report.[157] Isolation of *P. marneffei* from culture of bone marrow, blood, lymph node, skin lesions, bronchoalveolar lavage, or sputum can be diagnostic. Microscopic examination of clinical materials reveals yeast forms (2 to 3×2 to $6.5 \mu m$) both within phagocytes and extracellularly.[141] The intracellular forms are smaller, resembling *Histoplasma capsulatum,* whereas the extracellular forms are larger and often have a transverse septum (asexual fission or schizogony) (Fig. 267-11). The extracellular forms may also appear as "sausage forms," consisting of three cells (8 to 13 μm in length) divided by two transverse septa, or rarely as short hyphae. Three types of histopathologic reactions have been noted in association with *P. marneffei* infection. They include granulomatous, suppurative, and necrotizing inflammation.[154] Granulomatous or suppurative changes are most commonly seen in patients with normal immunity. The necrotizing reaction is more commonly seen in immunocompromised patients and is characterized by focal necrosis with surrounding histiocytes and extracellular fungi. Culture at 30° C produces a mold with sporulating structures typical for *Penicillium.* Identification is aided by the formation of a soluble red pigment that diffuses into the agar. This mold form may be converted to a yeast form by incubation at 37° C.[158] This dimorphism is not found in other known members of the genus *Penicillium.* Because disease normally appears

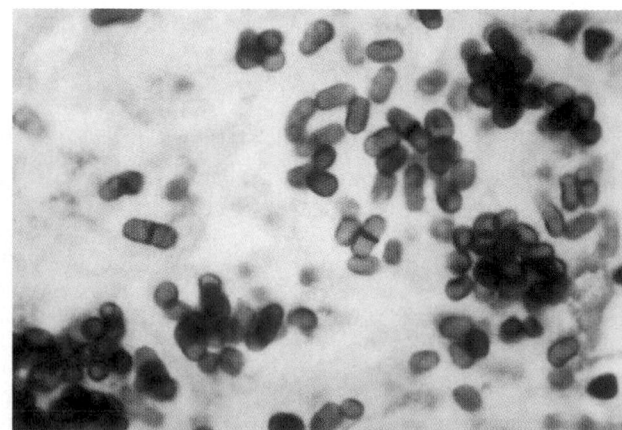

FIGURE 267-11. *Penicillium marneffei* in a splenic abscess. Note the transverse septa (Gomori methenamine-silver [GMS]). *(From McGinnis MR, Chandler FW. Penicilliosis marneffei. In: Connor DH, Chandler FW, Schwartz DA, et al, eds. Pathology of Infectious Diseases. Norwalk, CT: Appleton & Lange; 1997, with permission of the McGraw-Hill Companies.)*

to result from inhalation of conidia, it seems reasonable to use Biosafety Level II precautions when working with the mold form. Diagnosis by immunologic techniques, including serum antibody and antigen tests, as well as identification of organisms in tissue by immunolabeling, are still in the experimental stage.[159-161]

Successful treatment of disseminated infection has been reported with amphotericin B with or without the addition of flucytosine.[141] Therapy with itraconazole has also been successful. Fluconazole therapy has been associated with a high rate of failure. Although no randomized, comparative studies have been performed, the failure rates in a study of 86 HIV-infected patients were as follows: amphotericin B, 8 of 35 patients (22.8%); itraconazole, 3 of 12 (25%); and fluconazole, 7 of 11 (63.6%).[162] Excellent response (97.3%) has been seen with a regimen of intravenous amphotericin B for 2 weeks (0.6 mg/kg/day) followed by oral itraconazole for 10 weeks (200 mg twice daily) in 74 HIV-infected patients.[163] This regimen allowed shortened hospital stays while producing a more rapid clearing of fungemia compared with that seen using itraconazole alone. Itraconazole has been shown to prevent relapse of this disease in patients with HIV infection.[164] Lifelong secondary prophylaxis in HIV-infected patients with itraconazole (200 mg once daily) or ketoconazole has been suggested because relapse in this group of patients is common.[140] Whether and when this can be stopped after immune reconstitution with highly active antiretroviral therapy has not been determined.

LACAZIA LOBOI

Lobomycosis (Lobo's disease, keloidal blastomycosis) is a chronic skin infection most commonly afflicting the indigenous people of the Amazon regions of Columbia and Brazil. The etiologic agent of lobomycosis has never been isolated in culture, but has been shown to be closely related to *Paracoccidioides brasiliensis* by 18S ribosomal DNA (rDNA) sequencing.[165] This fungus has been known by many genus names; most recently, *Lacazia loboi* has been proposed to replace *Loboa loboi* and other previous designations.[166] More than 100 cases have been reported from countries in Central and South America. The disease has not been acquired in the United States except perhaps that reported in dolphins.[62] The fungus remains confined to the skin, progressing slowly over decades. Lesions are typically

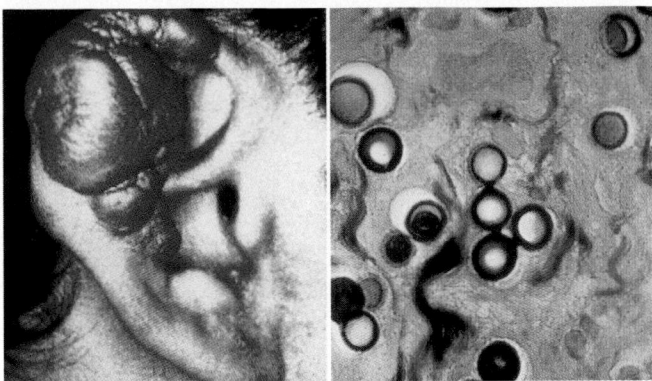

FIGURE 267-13. Lobomycosis of the ear with associated histologic findings (GMS). *(From Herr RA, Herr E, Tarcha PR, et al. Phylogenetic analysis of* Lacazia loboi *places this previously uncharacterized pathogen with the dimorphic Onygenales. J Clin Microbiol. 2001;39:309-314, with permission.)*

nodules or keloidal plaques that are red, hard, and shiny associated with fibrosis and a granulomatous reaction on histology (Figs. 267-12 and 267-13). The diagnosis is made by finding the typical globose to lemon-shaped cells (about 9 μm in diameter), either singly or in short chains (Fig. 267-14). Surgical excision is the only useful therapy.

RHINOSPORIDIUM SEEBERI

Rhinosporidiosis is a chronic, usually painless localized infection of the mucous membranes.[62] Formerly believed to be a fungus, the causative agent *Rhinosporidium seeberi* has also never been cultured. Recent 18S rDNA sequencing has shown this organism to be a protistan parasite.[167,168] Rhinosporidiosis occurs worldwide, with the greatest number of cases found in southern India and Sri Lanka. Lasser and Smith[169] reviewed 28 cases from the United States, 19 affecting the nose and 9 the conjunctiva, with 24 occurring in men and 4 in women. Lesions increase in size over months to years to form friable pedunculated masses, typically in the nose, upper airway, or conjunctiva.[170] Nasal lesions present as nasal obstruction or epistaxis.[171] One or more pedunculated or verrucous skin lesions, with or without nasal or conjunctival lesions, are seen occasionally.[172,173] Rarely, polyps occur in the vagina, urethra, or penis. *R. seeberi* forms round, thick-walled

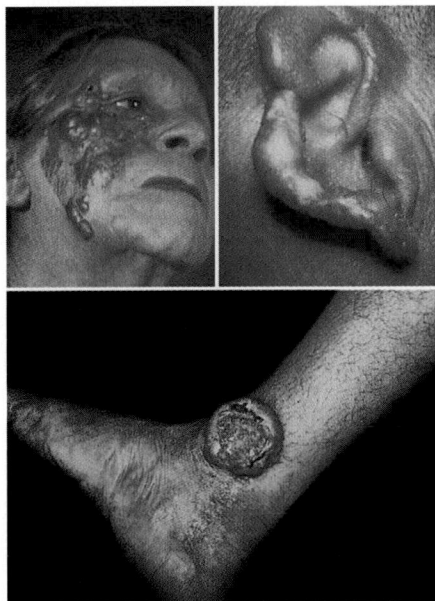

FIGURE 267-12. Lobomycosis. (From the Centers for Disease Control and Prevention, Atlanta.) *(From Nikolaidis G, Rosen T. Lobomycosis. In: Connor DH, Chandler FW, Schwartz DA, et al, eds. Pathology of Infectious Diseases. Norwalk, CT: Appleton & Lange; 1997, with permission of the McGraw-Hill Companies.)*

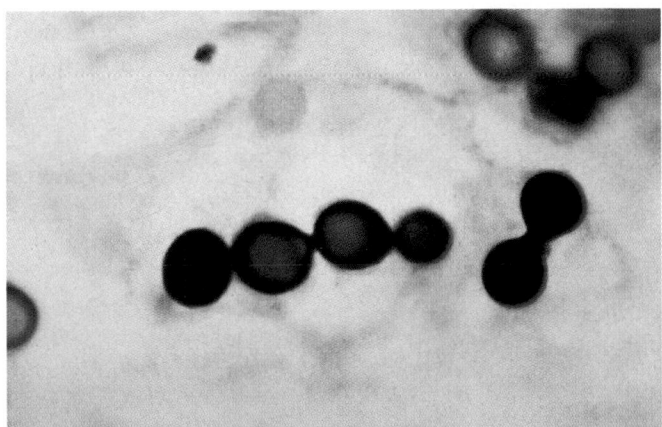

FIGURE 267-14. Histologic appearance of *Lacazia loboi*, the agent of lobomycosis (GMS). *(From Nikolaidis G, Rosen T. Lobomycosis. In: Connor DH, Chandler FW, Schwartz DA, et al, eds. Pathology of Infectious Diseases. Norwalk, CT: Appleton & Lange; 1997, with permission of the McGraw-Hill Companies.)*

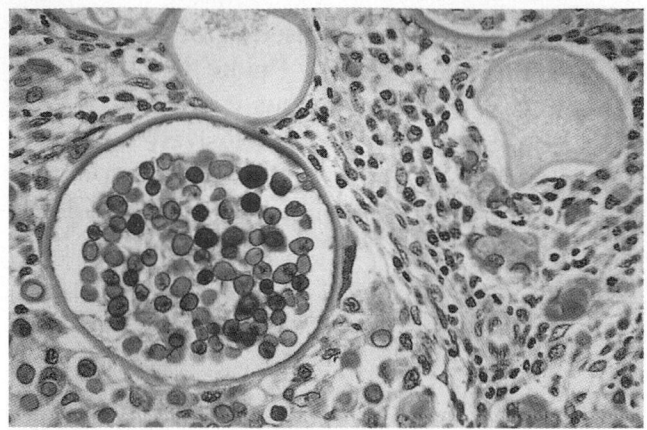

FIGURE 267-15. Mature sporangium of *Rhinosporidium seeberi* (Mayer's mucicarmine). *(From Watts JC, Chandler FW. Rhinosporidiosis. In: Connor DH, Chandler FW, Schwartz DA, et al, eds. Pathology of Infectious Diseases. Norwalk, CT: Appleton & Lange; 1997, with permission of the McGraw-Hill Companies.)*

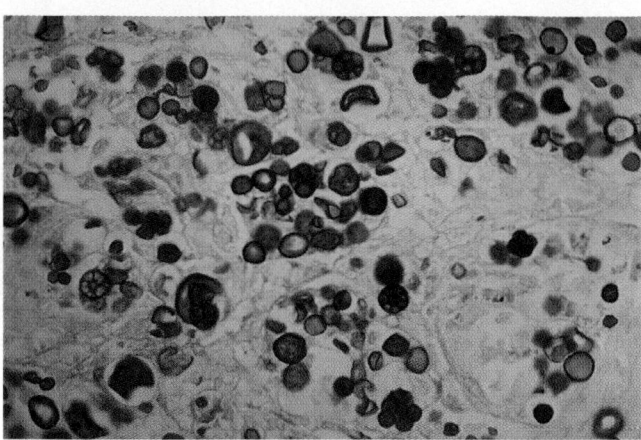

FIGURE 267-16. *Prototheca wickerhamii* in an olecranon bursa biopsy (Gridley stain). *(From Ramsay E, Chandler FW, Connor DH. Prototheosis. In: Connor DH, Chandler FW, Schwartz DA, et al, eds. Pathology of Infectious Diseases. Norwalk, CT: Appleton & Lange; 1997, with permission of the McGraw-Hill Companies.)*

TABLE 267-2 Key Features of the Uncommon Fungi, *Rhinosporidium*, and *Prototheca*

Organism(s)	Risks Factors/ Risk Groups	Geographic Epidemiology	Ecologic Niche	Clinical Manifestation(s)	Tissue forms	Treatment
Pseudallescheria boydii (*Scedosporium apiospermum*)	Trauma, immuno-compromise	Worldwide	Soil, fresh water, respiratory tract colonization	Pneumonia, os-teoarticular, CNS, or dis-seminated in-fection, mycetoma	Septate hyphae	Voriconazole or itraconazole
Scedosporium prolificans	Severe immuno-compromise, trauma	Worldwide	Soil, respiratory tract colonization	Disseminated in-fection, os-teoarticular infection	Septate hyphae	Unknown (consider high-dose L-AMB or voriconazole or itraconazole)
Dark-walled fungi (including *Alternaria, Bipolaris, Cladophialophora, Curvularia, Exophiala, Exserohilum, Wangiella*)	Trauma, allergic rhinitis, immuno-compromise	Worldwide	Soil, decaying organic mat-ter, air, plants	Localized subcu-taneous le-sions, brain abscess, aller-gic sinusitis, rare dissemi-nated infections	Septate hyphae, rarely yeast or pseudohy-phae	High-dose D-AMB or L-AMB or itra-conazole or voriconazole
Fusarium	Severe immuno-compromise	Worldwide	Soil, plants	Disseminated infection, fungemia	Septate hyphae	High-dose D-AMB or L-AMB or voriconazole
Trichosporon	Immunocompro-mise, central venous catheters	Worldwide	Skin and gastro-intestinal flora	Fungemia	Yeast, hyphae, arthroconidia, pseudohy-phae	Fluconazole ± high-dose D-AMB or L-AMB
Penicillium marneffei	AIDS	SE Asia, Southern China	Unknown	Disseminated infection	Yeasts or "sausage forms"	D-AMB ± 5-FC or itraconazole
Lacazia loboi	Rural outdoor labor, minor trauma	Central and South America	Unknown	Localized cuta-neous/subcu-taneous infection	Chains of large yeasts	Surgery
Rhinosporidium seeberi	Rural outdoor labor	India, Sri Lanka, very rare world-wide	Unknown	Localized mu-cous mem-brane poly-poidal lesions	Spores in large (10 to 200 μm) cysts (sporangia)	Surgery
Prototheca	Trauma	Worldwide	Water, soil, foodstuffs	Localized subcutaneous lesions	2-8 endospores in sporangia	Surgery or itraconazole

High-dose D-AMB, deoxycholate amphotericin B at 1.0 to 1.5 mg/kg/day; 5-FC, 5-fluorocytosine (should only be used when monitoring of levels is available lo-cally); L-AMB, lipid preparations of amphotericin B (AmBisome, Abelcet, Amphotec) cysts (sporangium) in the submucosa, varying in diameter from 10 to 200 μm, often visible through the mucosa as white dots. Mature cysts become filled with numerous spores (endospores), which on release become new cysts (Fig. 267-15). Treatment of choice is surgery.[170]

PROTOTHECA SPECIES

Prototheca are unicellular algae that lack chlorophyll and reproduce by endosporulation. Although not fungi, these organisms are included here because they are often preliminarily identified in tissue and culture as a yeast. These organisms are found in a wide range of environmental sites, including tree slime, sewage, fresh and marine water, soil, and foodstuffs. A little more than 100 cases of human infection have been reported,[62,174] almost all in adults and from widely scattered geographic areas. *P. wickerhamii* is the most common cause of human infection, although infection secondary to *P. zofii* has also been reported.

The most common presentation of protothecosis is a single lesion of the skin or subcutaneous tissue. The typical manifestation is a painless, slowly progressive, well-circumscribed plaque or papulonodular lesion that may become eczematoid or ulcerated. Soft tissue lesions favor the olecranon bursa, sites of minor trauma or corticosteroid injection,[175] and surgical wounds exposed to soil or water, such as a hand tendon repair. Gradual enlargement over weeks to months is typically seen. Skin lesions in HIV-infected patients have not differed from those seen in other patients.[176,177] More deeply seated infections such as peritonitis, meningitis, and endocarditis have also been rarely reported.[174]

Protothecosis is best diagnosed by biopsy for histologic study and culture. The inflammatory response shows both microabscesses and granulomas with multinucleate giant cells. *Prototheca* cells usually range from 8 to 20 μm in diameter, stain well with Gomori methenamine silver or periodic acid–Schiff, and often contain two to eight tightly packed endospores in each cell or sporangium (Fig. 267-16). White opaque colonies appear in a few days on standard mycologic media. Identification is made by gross and microscopic appearance plus biochemical testing.

Protothecosis has little, if any, tendency toward self-healing. Surgical excision of lesions and intravenous amphotericin B have both been used successfully.[176] *Prototheca* spp. are resistant to flucytosine, but prolonged therapy with ketoconazole, itraconazole, or fluconazole has been reported to benefit some patients with skin lesions.[175,178,179] Short-course itraconazole (200 mg daily for 2 months) has been used successfully.[180]

SUMMARY

Key features of the uncommon fungi in this chapter are given in Table 267-2.

REFERENCES

1. Travis LB, Roberts GD, Wilson WR. Clinical significance of *Pseudallescheria boydii:* Review of 10 years' experience. Mayo Clin Proc. 1985;60:531-537.
2. Salitan ML, Lawson W, Som PM, et al. *Pseudallescheria* sinusitis with intracranial extension in a nonimmunocompromised host. Otolaryngol Head Neck Surg. 1990;102:745-750.
3. Davis WA, Isner JM, Bracey AW, et al. Disseminated *Petriellidium boydii* and pacemaker endocarditis. Am J Med. 1980;69:929-932.
4. O'Bryan TA, Browne FA, Schonder JF. *Scedosporium apiospermum* (*Pseudallescheria boydii*) endocarditis. J Infect. 2002;44:189-192.
5. Arnett JC, Hatch HB. Pulmonary allescheriasis: Report of a case and review of the literature. Arch Intern Med. 1975;135:1250-1253.
6. Miller MA, Greenberger PA, Amerian R, et al. Allergic bronchopulmonary mycosis caused by *Pseudallescheria boydii*. Am Rev Respir Dis. 1993;148:810-812.
7. Walsh M, Atkinson K, White L, Enno A. Fungal *Pseudallescheria boydii* lung infiltrates unresponsive to amphotericin B in leukaemic patients. Aust N Z J Med. 1992;22:267-268.
8. Winer-Muram HT, Vargas S, Slobod K. Cavitary lung lesions in an immunosuppressed child. Chest. 1994;106:937-938.
9. Patterson TF, Andriole VT, Zervos MJ, et al. The epidemiology of pseudallescheriasis complicating transplantation: Nosocomial and community-acquired infection. Mycoses. 1990;33:297-302.
10. Nomdedeu J, Brunet S, Martino R, et al. Successful treatment of pneumonia due to *Scedosporium apiospermum* with itraconazole: Case report. Clin Infect Dis. 1993;16:731-733.
11. Bernstein EF, Schuster MG, Stieritz DD, et al. Disseminated cutaneous *Pseudallescheria boydii*. Br J Dermatol. 1995;132:456-460.
12. McKelvie PA, Wong EY, Chow LP, Hall AJ. *Scedosporium* endophthalmitis: Two fatal disseminated cases of *Scedosporium* infection presenting with endophthalmitis. Clin Exp Ophthalmol. 2001;29:330-334.
13. Hung CC, Chang SC, Yang PC, Hsieh WC. Invasive pulmonary pseudallescheriasis with direct invasion of the thoracic spine in an immunocompetent patient. Eur J Clin Microbiol Infect Dis. 1994;13:749-751.
14. Halpern AA, Nagel DA, Schurman DJ. *Allescheria boydii* osteomyelitis following multiple steroid injections and surgery. Clin Orthop. 1977;126:232-234.
15. Lavy D, Morin O, Venet G, et al. *Pseudallescheria boydii* knee arthritis in a young immunocompetent adult two years after a compound patellar fracture. Joint Bone Spine. 2001;68:517-520.
16. Tirado-Miranda R, Solera-Santos J, Brasero JC, et al. Septic arthritis due to *Scedosporium apiospermum:* Case report and review. J Infect. 2001;43:210-212.
17. Berenguer J, Diaz-Mediavilla J, Urra D, Munoz P. Central nervous system infection caused by *Pseudallescheria boydii:* Case report and review. Rev Infect Dis. 1989;11:890-896.
18. Montero A, Cohen JE, Fernandez MA, et al. Cerebral pseudallescheriasis due to *Pseudallescheria boydii* as the first manifestation of AIDS. Clin Infect Dis. 1998; 26:1476-1477.
19. Castiglioni B, Dutton DA, Rinaldi MG, et al. *Pseudallescheria boydii* (anamorph *Scedosporium apiospermum*): Infection in solid organ transplant recipients in a tertiary medical center and review of the literature. Medicine. 2002;81:333-348.
20. Hachimi-Idrissi S, Willemsen M, Desprechins B, et al. *Pseudallescheria boydii* and brain abscesses. Pediatr Infect Dis J. 1990;9:737-741.
21. Rüchel R, Wilichowski E. Cerebral *Pseudallescheria* mycosis after near-drowning. Mycoses. 1995;38:473-475.
22. Bryan CS, DiSalvo AF, Kaufman L, et al. *Petriellidium boydii* infection of the sphenoid sinus. Am J Clin Pathol. 1980;74:846-851.
23. Dworzack DL, Clark RB, Borkowski WJ, et al. *Pseudallescheria boydii* brain abscess: Association with near-drowning and efficacy of high-dose, prolonged miconazole therapy in patients with multiple abscesses. Medicine. 1989;68:218-224.
24. Benham RW, Georg LK. *Allescheria boydii*, causative agent in a case of meningitis. J Invest Dermatol. 1948;10:99-110.
25. Galgiani JN, Stevens DA, Graybill JR, et al. *Pseudallescheria boydii* infections treated with ketoconazole: Clinical evaluations of seven patients and *in vitro* susceptibility results. Chest. 1984;82:219-224.
26. Piper JP, Golden J, Brown D, Broestler J. Successful treatment of *Scedosporium apiospermum* suppurative arthritis with itraconazole. Pediatr Infect Dis J. 1990;9:674-675.
27. Barbaric D, Shaw PJ. *Scedosporium* infection in immunocompromised patients: Successful use of liposomal amphotericin B and itraconazole. Med Pediatr Oncol. 2001;37:122-125.
28. Carrillo AJ, Guarro J. *In vitro* activities of four novel triazoles against *Scedosporium* spp. Antimicrob Agents Chemother. 2001;45:2151-2153.
29. Del Poeta M, Schell WA, Perfect JR. *In vitro* antifungal activity of pneumocandin L-743,872 against a variety of clinically important molds. Antimicrob Agents Chemother. 1997;41:1835-1836.
30. Espinel-Ingroff A. Comparison of *in vitro* activities of the new triazole SCH56592 and the echinocandins MK-0991 (L-743,872) and LY303366 against opportunistic filamentous and dimorphic fungi and yeasts. J Clin Microbiol. 1998;36:2950-2956.
31. Meletiadis J, Meis JF, Mouton JW, et al. *In vitro* activities of new and conventional antifungal agents against clinical *Scedosporium* isolates. Antimicrob Agents Chemother. 2002;46:62-68.
32. Pfaller MA, Marco F, Messer SA, Jones RN. *In vitro* activity of two echinocandin derivatives, LY303366 and MK-0991 (L-743,792), against clinical isolates of *Aspergillus, Fusarium, Rhizopus,* and other filamentous fungi. Diagn Microbiol Infect Dis. 1998;30:251-255.
33. Radford SA, Johnson EM, Warnock DW. *In vitro* studies of activity of voriconazole (UK-109,496), a new triazole antifungal agent, against emerging and less-common mold pathogens. Antimicrob Agents Chemother. 1997;41:841-843.
34. Gallagher JC, Dodds Ashley ES, Drew RH, Perfect JR. Antifungal pharmacotherapy for invasive mould infections. Exp Opin Pharmacother. 2003;4:147-164.
35. Girmenia C, Luzi G, Monaco M, Martino P. Use of voriconazole in treatment of *Scedosporium apiospermum*. J Clin Microbiol. 1998;36:1436-1438.
36. Jabado N, Casanova JL, Haddad E, et al. Invasive pulmonary infection due to *Scedosporium apiospermum* in two children with chronic granulomatous disease. Clin Infect Dis. 1998;27:1437-1441.
37. Munoz P, Marin M, Tornero P, et al. Successful outcome of *Scedosporium apiospermum* disseminated infection treated with voriconazole in a patient receiving corticosteroid therapy. Clin Infect Dis. 2000;31:1499-1501.
38. Nesky MA, McDougal EC, Peacock JE Jr. *Pseudallescheria boydii* brain abscess successfully treated with voriconazole and surgical drainage: Case report and literature review of central nervous system pseudallescheriasis. Clin Infect Dis. 2000;31:673-677.
39. Poza G, Montoya J, Redondo C, et al. Meningitis caused by *Pseudallescheria boydii* treated with voriconazole. Clin Infect Dis. 2000;30:981-982.
40. Mellinghoff IK, Winston DJ, Mukwaya G, Schiller GJ. Treatment of *Scedosporium apiospermum* brain abscesses with posaconazole. Clin Infect Dis. 2002;34:1648-1650.

41. Malloch D, Salkin IF. A new species of *Scedosporium* associated with osteomyelitis in humans. Mycotaxon. 1984;21:247-255.

42. Idigoras P, Perez-Trallero E, Pineiro L, et al. Disseminated infection and colonization by *Scedosporium prolificans:* A review of 18 cases, 1990-1999. Clin Infect Dis. 2001;32:e158-e165.

43. Revankar SG, Patterson JE, Sutton DA, et al. Disseminated phaeohyphomycosis: Review of an emerging mycosis. Clin Infect Dis. 2002;34:467-476.

44. Wilson CM, O'Rourke EJ, McGinnis MR, Salkin IF. *Scedosporium inflatum:* Clinical spectrum of a newly recognized pathogen. J Infect Dis. 1990;161:102-107.

45. Wood GM, McCormack JG, Muir DB, et al. Clinical features of human infection with *Scedosporium inflatum.* Clin Infect Dis. 1992;14:1027-1033.

46. Alvarez M, Ponga BL, Rayon C, et al. Nosocomial outbreak caused by *Scedosporium prolificans (inflatum):* Four fatal cases in leukemia patients. J Clin Microbiol. 1995;33:3290-3295.

47. Bouza E, Munoz P, Vega L, et al. Clinical resolution of *Scedosporium prolificans* fungemia associated with reversal of neutropenia following administration of granulocyte colony-stimulating factor. Clin Infect Dis. 1996;23:192-193.

48. Spielberger RT, Tegtmeier BR, O'Donnell MR, Ito JI. Fatal *Scedosporium prolificans* (*S. inflatum*) fungemia following allogeneic bone marrow transplantation: Report of a case in the United States. Clin Infect Dis. 1995;21:1067.

49. Farag SS, Firkin FC, Andrew JH, et al. Fatal disseminated *Scedosporium inflatum* infection in a neutropenic immunocompromised patient. J Infect. 1992;25:201-204.

50. Rabodonirina M, Paulus S, Thevenet F, et al. Disseminated *Scedosporium prolificans* (*S. inflatum*) infection after single-lung transplantation. Clin Infect Dis. 1994;19:138-142.

51. Madrigal V, Alonso J, Bureo E, et al. Fatal meningoencephalitis caused by *Scedosporium inflatum* (*Scedosporium prolificans*) in a child with lymphoblastic leukemia. Eur J Clin Microbiol Infect Dis. 1995;14:601-603.

52. del Palacio A, Garau M, Amor E, et al. Case reports. Transient colonization with *Scedosporium prolificans:* Report of four cases in Madrid. Mycoses. 2001;44: 321-325.

53. Hopwood V, Evans EGV, Matthews J, Denning DW. *Scedosporium prolificans,* a multi-resistant fungus, from a UK AIDS patient. J Infect. 1995;30:153-155.

54. Salkin IF, McGinnis MR, Dykstra MJ, Rinaldi MG. *Scedosporium inflatum,* an emerging pathogen. J Clin Microbiol. 1988;26:498-503.

55. Ortoneda M, Capilla J, Pujol I, et al. Liposomal amphotericin B and granulocyte colony-stimulating factor therapy in a murine model of invasive infection by *Scedosporium prolificans.* J Antimicrob Chemother. 2002;49:525-529.

56. Perfect JR, Marr KA, Walsh TJ, et al. Voriconazole treatment for less-common, emerging, or refractory fungal infections. Clin Infect Dis. 2003;36:1122-1131.

57. Capilla J, Yustes C, Mayayo E, et al. Efficacy of albaconazole (UR-9825) in treatment of disseminated *Scedosporium prolificans* infection in rabbits. Antimicrob Agents Chemother. 2003;47:1948-1951.

58. Afeltra J, Dannaoui E, Meis JF, et al. *In vitro* synergistic interaction between amphotericin B and pentamidine against *Scedosporium prolificans.* Antimicrob Agents Chemother. 2002;46:3323-3326.

59. Meletiadis J, Mouton JW, Meis JF, Verweij PE. *In vitro* drug interaction modeling of combinations of azoles with terbinafine against clinical *Scedosporium prolificans* isolates. Antimicrob Agents Chemother. 2003;47:106-117.

60. Meletiadis J, Mouton JW, Rodriguez-Tudela JL, et al. *In vitro* interaction of terbinafine with itraconazole against clinical isolates of *Scedosporium prolificans.* Antimicrob Agents Chemother. 2000;44:470-472.

61. Howden BP, Slavin MA, Schwarer AP, Mijch AM. Successful control of disseminated *Scedosporium prolificans* infection with a combination of voriconazole and terbinafine. Eur J Clin Microbiol Infect Dis. 2003;22:111-113.

62. Kwon-Chung KJ, Bennett JE. Medical Mycology. Philadelphia: Lea & Febiger; 1992.

63. Rinaldi MG. Phaeohyphomycosis. Dermatol Clin. 1996;14:147-153.

64. Nucci M, Akiti T, Barreiros G, et al. Nosocomial fungemia due to *Exophiala jeanselmei* var. *jeanselmei* and a *Rhinocladiella* species: Newly described causes of bloodstream infection. J Clin Microbiol. 2001;39:514-518.

65. Rossman SNB, Cernoch PL, Davis JR. Dematiaceous fungi are an increasing cause of human disease. Clin Infect Dis. 1996;22:73-80.

66. Revankar SG, Sutton DA, Rinaldi MG. Primary central nervous system phaeohyphomycosis: A review of 101 cases. Clin Infect Dis. 2004;38:206-216.

67. Aldape KD, Fox HS, Roberts JP, et al. *Cladosporium trichoides* cerebral phaeohyphomycosis in a liver transplant recipient. Am J Clin Pathol. 1991;95:499-502.

68. Filizzola MJ, Martinez F, Rauf SJ. Phaeohyphomycosis of the central nervous system in immunocompromised hosts: Report of a case and review of the literature. Int J Infect Dis. 2003;7:282-286.

69. Buxi TBS, Prakash K, Vohra R, et al. Imaging in phaeohyphomycosis of the brain. Case report. Neuroradiology. 1996;38:139-141.

70. Walz R, Bianchin M, Chaves ML, et al. Cerebral phaeohyphomycosis caused by *Cladophialophora bantiana* in a Brazilian drug abuser. J Med Vet Mycol. 1997;35:427-431.

71. Barron MA, Sutton DA, Veve R, et al. Invasive mycotic infections caused by *Chaetomium perlucidum,* a new agent of cerebral phaeohyphomycosis. J Clin Microbiol. 2003;41:5302-5307.

72. Kanj SS, Amr SS, Roberts GD. *Ramichloridium mackenziei* brain abscess: Report of two cases and review of the literature. Med Mycol. 2001;39:97-102.

73. Sutton DA, Slifkin M, Yakulis R, et al. U.S. case report of cerebral phaeohyphomycosis caused by *Ramichloridium obovoideum* (*R. mackenziei*): Criteria for identification, therapy, and review of other known dematiaceous neurotropic taxa. J Clin Microbiol. 1998;36:708-715.

74. deShazo RD, Chapin K, Swain RE. Fungal sinusitis. N Engl J Med. 1997;337:254-259.

75. Washburn RG, Kennedy DW, Begley MG, et al. Chronic fungal sinusitis in apparently normal hosts. Medicine. 1988;67:231-247.

76. Oliveira Ramos AM, Oliveira Sales A, Andrade MC, et al. A simple method for detecting subcutaneous phaeohyphomycosis with light colored fungi. Am J Surg Pathol. 1995;19:109-114.

77. Kimura M, McGinnis MR. Fontana-Masson-stained tissue from culture-proven mycoses. Arch Pathol Lab Med. 1998;122:1107-1111.

78. Sharkey PK, Graybill JR, Rinaldi MG, et al. Itraconazole treatment of phaeohyphomycosis. J Am Acad Dermatol. 1990;23:577-586.

79. Whittle DI, Kominos S. Use of itraconazole for treating subcutaneous phaeohyphomycosis caused by *Exophiala jeanselmei.* Clin Infect Dis. 1995;21:1068.

80. Negroni R, Helou SH, Petri N, et al. Case study: Posaconazole treatment of disseminated phaeohyphomycosis due to *Exophiala spinifera.* Clin Infect Dis. 2004;38:e15-e20.

81. Guarro J, Gené J. Opportunistic fusarial infections in humans. Eur J Clin Microbiol Infect Dis. 1995;14:741-754.

82. Wheeler MS, McGinnis MR, Schell WA, Walker DH. *Fusarium* infection in burned patients. Am J Clin Pathol. 1981;75:304-311.

83. Strum AW, Grave W, Kwee WS. Disseminated *Fusarium oxysporum* infection in a patient with heat stroke. Lancet. 1989;1:968.

84. Boutati EI, Anaissie EJ. *Fusarium,* a significant emerging pathogen in patients with hematologic malignancy: Ten years' experience at a cancer center and implications for management. Blood. 1997;90:999-1008.

85. Krcmery V, Jesenska Z, Spanik S, et al. Fungaemia due to *Fusarium* spp. in cancer patients. J Hosp Infect. 1997;36:223-228.

86. Martino P, Gastaldi R, Raccah R, Girmenia C. Clinical patterns of *Fusarium* infections in immunocompromised patients. J Infect. 1994;28(Suppl 1):7-15.

87. Gamis AS, Gudnason T, Giebink GS, Ramsay NKC. Disseminated infection with *Fusarium* in recipients of bone marrow transplants. Rev Infect Dis. 1991;13:1077-1088.

88. Hennequin C, Lavarde V, Poirot JL, et al. Invasive *Fusarium* infections: A retrospective survey of 31 cases. J Med Vet Mycol. 1997;35:107-114.

89. Anaissie E, Kantarjian H, Ro J, et al. The emerging role of *Fusarium* infections in patients with cancer. Medicine. 1988;67:77-83.

90. Ammari LK, Puck JM, McGowan KL. Catheter-related *Fusarium solani* fungemia and pulmonary infection in a patient with leukemia in remission. Clin Infect Dis. 1993;16:148-150.

91. Raad I, Hachem R. Treatment of central venous catheter-related fungemia due to *Fusarium oxysporum.* Clin Infect Dis. 1995;20:709-711.

92. Girmenia C, Arcese W, Micozzi A, et al. Onychomycosis as a possible origin of disseminated *Fusarium solani* infection in a patient with severe aplastic anemia. Clin Infect Dis. 1992;14:1167.

93. Anaissie EJ, Kuchar RT, Rex JH, et al. Fusariosis associated with pathogenic *Fusarium* species colonization of a hospital water system: A new paradigm for the epidemiology of opportunistic mold infections. Clin Infect Dis. 2001;33:1871-1878.

94. Krcmery V, Spanik S, Kunova A, Trupl J. Breakthrough fungemia appearing during empiric therapy with amphotericin B. Chemotherapy. 1997;43:367-370.

95. Nelson PE, Dignani MC, Anaissie EJ. Taxonomy, biology, and clinical aspects of *Fusarium* species. Clin Microbiol Rev. 1994;7:479-504.

96. Nucci M, Anaissie EJ, Queiroz-Telles F, et al. Outcome predictors of 84 patients with haematologic malignancies and *Fusarium* infection. Cancer. 2003;98:315-319.

97. Wolff MA, Ramphal R. Use of amphotericin B lipid complex for treatment of disseminated cutaneous *Fusarium* infection in a neutropenic patient. Clin Infect Dis. 1995;20:1568-1569.

98. Apostolidis J, Bouzani M, Platsouka E, et al. Resolution of fungemia due to *Fusarium* species in a patient with acute leukemia treated with caspofungin. Clin Infect Dis. 2003;36:1349-1350.

99. Paphitou NI, Ostrosky-Zeichner L, Paetznick VL, et al. *In vitro* activities of investigational triazoles against *Fusarium* species: Effects of inoculum size and incubation time on broth microdilution susceptibility test results. Antimicrob Agents Chemother. 2002;46:3298-3300.

100. Clancy CJ, Nguyen MH. The combination of amphotericin B and azithromycin as a potential new therapeutic approach to fusariosis. J Antimicrob Chemother. 1998;41:127-130.

101. Ortoneda M, Capilla J, Pastor FJ, et al. Efficacy of liposomal amphotericin B in treatment of systemic murine fusariosis. Antimicrob Agents Chemother. 2002;46: 2273-2275.

102. Lozano-Chiu M, Arikan S, Paetznick VL, et al. Treatment of murine fusariosis with SCH 56592. Antimicrob Agents Chemother. 1999;43:589-591.

103. Graybill JR, Najvar LK, Gonzalez GM, et al. Improving the mouse model for studying the efficacy of voriconazole. J Antimicrob Chemother. 2003;51:1373-1376.

104. Spielberger RT, Falleroni MJ, Coene AJ, Larson RA. Concomitant amphotericin B therapy, granulocyte transfusions, and GM-CSF administration for disseminated infection with *Fusarium* in a granulocytopenic patient. Clin Infect Dis. 1993;16:528-530.

105. Gutiérrez-Rodero F, Moragón M, de la Tabla VO, et al. Cutaneous hyalohyphomycosis caused by *Paecilomyces lilacinus* in an immunocompetent host successfully treated with itraconazole: Case report and review. Eur J Clin Microbiol Infect Dis. 1999;18:814-818.

106. Guarro J, Gams W, Pujol I, Gené J. *Acremonium* species: New emerging fungal opportunists—*in vitro* antifungal susceptibilities and review. Clin Infect Dis. 1997;25:1222-1229.

107. Richter S, Cormican MG, Pfaller MA, et al. Fatal disseminated *Trichoderma longibrachiatum* infection in an adult bone marrow transplant patient: Species identification and review of the literature. J Clin Microbiol. 1999;37:1154-1160.

108. Steinbach WJ, Schell WA, Miller JL, et al. Fatal *Scopulariopsis brevicaulis* infection in a paediatric stem-cell transplant patient treated with voriconazole and caspofungin and a review of *Scopulariopsis* infections in immunocompromised patients. J Infect. 2004;48:112-116.

109. Liu K, Howell DN, Perfect JR, Schell WA. Morphologic criteria for the preliminary identification of *Fusarium, Paecilomyces,* and *Acremonium* species by histopathology. Am J Clin Pathol. 1998;109:45-54.
110. Gueho E, Improvisi L, de Hoog GS, et al. *Trichosporon* in humans, a practical account. Mycoses. 1994;37:3-10.
111. Sugita T, Nishikawa A, Shinoda T. Identification of *Trichosporon asahii* by PCR based on sequences of the internal transcribed spacer regions. J Clin Microbiol. 1998;36:2742-2744.
112. Sugita T, Nishikawa A, Shinoda T, et al. Taxonomic position of deep-seated, mucosa associated, and superficial isolates of *Trichosporon cutaneum* from trichosporonosis patients. J Clin Microbiol. 1995;33:1368-1370.
113. Itoh T, Hosokawa H, Kohdera U, et al. Disseminated infection with *Trichosporon asahii.* Mycoses. 1996;39:195-199.
114. Haupt HM, Merz WG, Beschorner WE, et al. Colonization and infection with *Trichosporon* species in the immunosuppressed host. J Infect Dis. 1983;147:199-203.
115. Hung CC, Chang SC, Chen YC, et al. *Trichosporon beigelii* fungemia in patients with acute leukemia: Report of three cases. J Formos Med Assoc. 1995;94:127-131.
116. Hajjeh RA, Blumberg HM. Bloodstream infection due to *Trichosporon beigelii* in a burn patient: Case report and review of therapy. Clin Infect Dis. 1995;20:913-916.
117. Mirza SH. Disseminated *Trichosporon beigelii* infection causing skin lesions in a renal transplant patient. J Infect. 1993;27:67-70.
118. Nahass GT, Rosenberg SP, Leonardi CL, et al. Disseminated infection with *Trichosporon beigelii.* Arch Dermatol. 1993;129:1020-1023.
119. Walsh TJ, Newman KR, Moody M, et al. Trichosporonosis in patients with neoplastic disease. Medicine. 1986;65:268-279.
120. Paphitou NI, Ostrosky-Zeichner L, Paetznick VL, et al. *In vitro* antifungal susceptibilities of *Trichosporon* species. Antimicrob Agents Chemother. 2002;46:1144-1146.
121. Dankner WM, Spector SA, Fierer J, et al. *Malassezia* fungemia in neonates and adults: Complication of hyperalimentation. Rev Infect Dis. 1987;9:743-753.
122. Barber GR, Brown AE, Kiehn TE, et al. Catheter-related *Malassezia furfur* fungemia in immunocompromised patients. Am J Med. 1993;95:365-370.
123. Powell DA, Marcon MJ. Failure to eradicate *Malassezia furfur* Broviac catheter infection with antifungal therapy. Pediatr Infect Dis J. 1987;6:579-588.
124. Gupta AK, Kohli Y, Li A, et al. *In vitro* susceptibility of the seven *Malassezia* species to ketoconazole, voriconazole, itraconazole and terbinafine. Br J Dermatol. 2000;142:758-765.
125. Marcon MJ, Durrell DE, Powell DA, et al. *In vitro* activity of systemic antifungal agents against *Malassezia furfur.* Antimicrob Agents Chemother. 1987;31:951-953.
126. Brooks R, Brown L. Systemic infections with *Malassezia furfur* in an adult receiving long-term hyperalimentation therapy. J Infect Dis. 1987;156:410-411.
127. Boekhout T, Kamp M, Geuho E. Molecular typing of *Malassezia* species with PFGE and RAPD. Mol Mycol. 1998;36:365-372.
128. Chang HJ, Miller HL, Watkins N, et al. An epidemic of *Malassezia pachydermatis* in an intensive care nursery associated with colonization of health care workers' pet dogs. N Engl J Med. 1998; 338:706-711.
129. Perez-Sanchez I, Anguita J, Martin-Rabadan P, et al. *Blastoschizomyces capitatus* infection in acute leukemia patients. Leuk Lymphoma. 2000;39:209-212.
130. Martino R, Salavert M, Parody R, et al. *Blastoschizomyces capitatus* infection in patients with leukemia: Report of 26 cases. Clin Infect Dis. 2004;38:335-341.
131. Sanz MA, Lopez FA, Martinez ML, et al. Disseminated *Blastoschizomyces capitatus* infection in acute myeloblastic leukemia. Support Care Cancer. 1996;4:291-293.
132. Hazen KC. New and emerging yeast pathogens. Clin Microbiol Rev. 1995;8:462-478.
133. Thuler LC, Faivichenco S, Velasco E, et al. Fungaemia caused by *Hansenula anomala*—An outbreak in a cancer hospital. Mycoses. 1997;40:193-196.
134. Ancelle T, Dupouy-Camet J, Pujol F, et al. Un cas de pénicilliose disséminée à *Penicillium marneffei* chez un malade atteint d'un syndrome immunodéficitaire acquis. Presse Med. 1988;17:1095-1096.
135. Peto TEA, Bull R, Millard PR, et al. Systemic mycosis due to *Penicillium marneffei* in a patient with antibody to human immunodeficiency virus. J Infect. 1988;16:285-290.
136. Piehl MR, Kaplan RL, Haber MH. Disseminated penicilliosis in a patient with acquired immunodeficiency syndrome. Arch Pathol Lab Med. 1988;112:1262-1264.
137. DiSalvo AF, Fickling AM, Ajello L. Infection caused by *Penicillium marneffei:* Description of first natural infection in man. Am J Clin Pathol. 1973;59:259-263.
138. Segretain G. *Penicillium marneffei* n. sp., agent d'une mycose du système réticulo-endothélial. Mycopathol Mycol Appl. 1959;11:327-353.
139. Phillips P. *Penicillium marneffei* part of southeast Asian AIDS. JAMA. 1996;276: 86-87.
140. Supparatpinyo K, Khamwan C, Baosoung V, et al. Disseminated *Penicillium marneffei* infections in Southeast Asia. Lancet. 1994;344:110-113.
141. Drouhet E. Penicilliosis due to *Penicillium marneffei:* A new emerging systemic mycosis in AIDS patients traveling or living in Southeast Asia: Review of 44 cases reported in HIV infected patients during the last 5 years compared to 44 cases of non AIDS patients reported over 20 years. J Mycol Med. 1993;4:195-224.
142. Duong TA. Infection due to *Penicillium marneffei,* an emerging pathogen: Review of 155 reported cases. Clin Infect Dis. 1996;23:125-130.
143. Hung C, Hsueh P, Chen M, et al. Invasive infection caused by *Penicillium marneffei:* An emerging pathogen in Taiwan. Clin Infect Dis. 1998;26:202-203.
144. Kwan EYW, Lau YL, Yuen KY, et al. *Penicillium marneffei* infection in a non-HIV infected child. J Paediatr Child Health. 1997;33:267-271.
145. Sirisanthana V, Sirisanthana T. *Penicillium marneffei* infection in children infected with human immunodeficiency virus. Pediatr Infect Dis J. 1993;12:1021-1025.
146. Ajello L, Padhye AA, Sukroongreung S, et al. Occurrence of *Penicillium marneffei* infections among wild bamboo rats in Thailand. Mycopathologia. 1995;131:1-8.
147. Cooper CR. From bamboo rats to humans: The odyssey of *Penicillium marneffei.* ASM News. 1998; 64:390-396.
148. Chariyalertsak S, Vanittanakom P, Nelson KE, et al. *Rhizomys sumatrensis* and *Cannomys badius,* new natural animal hosts of *Penicillium marneffei.* J Med Vet Mycol. 1996;34:105-110.
149. Chariyalertsak S, Sirisanthana T, Supparatpinyo K, et al. Case-control study of the risk factors for *Penicillium marneffei* infection in human immunodeficiency virus-infected patients in northern Thailand. Clin Infect Dis. 1997;24:1080-1086.
150. Chariyalertsak S, Sirisanthana T, Supparatpinyo K, Nelson KE. Seasonal variation of disseminated *Penicillium marneffei* infections in northern Thailand: A clue to the reservoir? J Infect Dis. 1996;173:1490-1493.
151. Ko CI, Hung CC, Chen MY, et al. Endoscopic diagnosis of intestinal penicilliosis marneffei: Report of three cases and review of the literature. Gastrointest Endosc. 1999;50:111-114.
152. Wortmann PD. Infection with *Penicillium marneffei.* Int J Dermatol. 1996;35: 393-399.
153. Cheng NC, Won WW, Fung CP, et al. Unusual pulmonary manifestations of disseminated *Penicillium marneffei* infection in three AIDS patients. Med Mycol. 1998;36:429-432.
154. Deng Z, Ribas JL, Gibson DW, Connor DH. Infections caused by *Penicillium marneffei* in China and southeast Asia: Review of eighteen published cases and report of four more Chinese cases. Rev Infect Dis. 1988;10:640-652.
155. Hilmarsdottir I, Coutellier A, Elbaz J, et al. A French case of laboratory-acquired disseminated *Penicillium marneffei* infection in a patient with AIDS. Clin Infect Dis. 1994;19:357-358.
156. Jones PD, See J. *Penicillium marneffei* infection in patients infected with human immunodeficiency virus: Late presentation in an area of nonendemicity. Clin Infect Dis. 1992;15:744.
157. Supparatpinyo K, Sirisanthana T. Disseminated *Penicillium marneffei* infection diagnosed on examination of a peripheral blood smear of a patient with human immunodeficiency virus infection. Clin Infect Dis. 1994;18:246-247.
158. Cooper CR, McGinnis MR. Pathology of *Penicillium marneffei:* An emerging acquired immunodeficiency syndrome-related pathogen. Arch Pathol Lab Med. 1997;121:798-804.
159. Chaiyaroj SC, Chawengkirttikul R, Sirisinha S, et al. Antigen detection assay for identification of *Penicillium marneffei* infection. J Clin Microbiol. 2003;41:432-434.
160. Desakorn V, Smith MD, Walsh AL, et al. Diagnosis of *Penicillium marneffei* infection by quantitation of urinary antigen by using an enzyme immunoassay. J Clin Microbiol. 1999;37:117-121.
161. Hamilton AJ. Serodiagnosis of histoplasmosis, paracoccidioidomycosis and penicilliosis marneffei: Current status and future trends. Med Mycol. 1998;36:351-364.
162. Supparatpinyo K, Nelson KE, Merz WG, et al. Response to antifungal therapy by human immunodeficiency virus-infected patients with disseminated *Penicillium marneffei* infections and *in vitro* susceptibilities of isolates from clinical specimens. Antimicrob Agents Chemother. 1993;37:2407-2411.
163. Sirisanthana T, Supparatpinyo K, Perriens J, Nelson KE. Amphotericin B and itraconazole for treatment of disseminated *Penicillium marneffei* infection in human immunodeficiency virus-infected patients. Clin Infect Dis. 1998;26:1107-1110.
164. Supparatpinyo K, Perriens J, Nelson KE, Sirisanthana T. A controlled trial of itraconazole to prevent relapse of *Penicillium marneffei* infection in patients infected with the human immunodeficiency virus. N Engl J Med. 1998;339:1739-1743.
165. Herr RA, Tarcha EJ, Taborda PR, et al. Phylogenetic analysis of *Lacazia loboi* places this previously uncharacterized pathogen with the dimorphic Onygenales. J Clin Microbiol. 2001;39:309-314.
166. Taborda PR, Taborda VA, McGinnis MR. *Lacazia loboi* gen. nov., comb. nov., the etiologic agent of lobomycosis. J Clin Microbiol. 1999;37:2031-2033.
167. Fredricks DN, Jolley JA, Lepp PW, et al. *Rhinosporidium seeberi:* A human pathogen from a novel group of aquatic protistan parasites. Emerg Infect Dis. 2000;6:273-282.
168. Herr RA, Ajello L, Taylor JW, et al. Phylogenetic analysis of *Rhinosporidium seeberi's* 18S small-subunit ribosomal DNA groups this pathogen among members of the protoctistan Mesomycetozoa clade. J Clin Microbiol. 1999;37:2750-2754.
169. Lasser A, Smith HW. Rhinosporidiosis. Arch Otolaryngol. 1976;102:308-310.
170. Reidy JJ, Sudesh S, Klafter AB, et al. Infection of the conjunctiva by *Rhinosporidium seeberi.* Surv Ophthalmol. 1997;41:409-413.
171. Snidvongs ML, Supanakorn S, Supiyaphun P. Severe epistaxis from rhinosporidiosis: A case report. J Med Assoc Thai. 1998;81:555-558.
172. Thappa DM, Venkatesan S, Sirka CS, et al. Disseminated cutaneous rhinosporidiosis. J Dermatol. 1998;25:527-532.
173. Ghorpade A, Ramanan C. Verrucoid cutaneous rhinosporidiosis. J Eur Acad Dermatol Venereol. 1998;10:269-270.
174. Krcmery V Jr. Systemic chlorellosis, an emerging infection in humans caused by algae. Int J Antimicrob Agents. 2000;15:235-237.
175. Kim ST, Suh KS, Chae YS, et al. Successful treatment with fluconazole of protothecosis at the site of an intralesional corticosteroid injection. Br J Dermatol. 1996;135:803-806.
176. Carey WP, Kaykova Y, Bandres JC, et al. Cutaneous protothecosis in a patient with AIDS and severe functional defect: Successful therapy with amphotericin B. Clin Infect Dis. 1997;25:1267-1266.
177. Polk P, Sanders DY. Cutaneous protothecosis in association with the acquired immunodeficiency syndrome. South Med J. 1997;90:831-832.
178. Matsumoto Y, Shibata M, Adachi A, et al. Two cases of protothecosis in Nagoya, Japan. Australas J Dermatol. 1996;37(Suppl 1):S42-S43.
179. Tang WY, Lo KK, Lam WY, et al. Cutaneous protothecosis: Report of a case in Hong Kong. Br J Dermatol. 1995;133:479-482.
180. Okuyama Y, Hamaguchi T, Teramoto T, Takiuchi I. A human case of protothecosis successfully treated with itraconazole. Nippon Ishinkin Gakkai Zasshi. 2001;42: 143-147.

CHAPTER 268

Pneumocystis Species

PETER D. WALZER
A. GEORGE SMULIAN

P*neumocystis* was discovered in 1909 by Chagas, who mistakenly interpreted the organism as a trypanosome. Several years later, the Delanöes identified *Pneumocystis* as a separate genus and species and named the organism in honor of Dr. Carini, another early worker. *Pneumocystis* first came to medical attention when it was implicated as the cause of interstitial plasma cell pneumonia, a disorder of institutionalized and debilitated infants in central and Eastern Europe after World War II. In the 1960s, *Pneumocystis* became widely appreciated as an important cause of pneumonia in immunocompromised hosts; however, with the development of safe and effective antimicrobial drugs, interest in the organism waned. The dramatic rise in the incidence of pneumocystosis associated with human immunodeficiency virus (HIV) infection in the 1980s rekindled interest in *Pneumocystis* as a major medical and public health problem. During the 1990s, advances in the treatment of HIV reduced the frequency of *Pneumocystis* pneumonia and other complications. Nevertheless, *Pneumocystis* remains a leading cause of opportunistic infection, morbidity, and mortality in these patients.[1,1a]

THE PATHOGEN

Pneumocystis describes a genus of closely related unicellular fungi of low virulence found in the lungs of humans and a variety of mammals. The taxonomic status of the genus was resolved in the late 1980s when analysis of the rRNA gene in the 1980s suggested that the organism is more closely related to fungi than to protozoa.[2] This conclusion has been strengthened by genomic sequence analysis including genes encoding dihydrofolate reductase, thymidylate synthetase, tubulin, and actins; and by the demonstration of the presence of elongation factor 3, a factor needed for protein synthesis that is found in fungi but not protozoa. Phylogenetic studies have suggested that the organism is most closely related to the ascomycetes as a deep basal branch among the archiascomycetes; however, *Pneumocystis* is unusual among fungi in that the organism lacks ergosterol in its plasma membranes and is insensitive to available antifungal drugs that target ergosterol biosynthesis.

Species within the genus demonstrate genotypic and phenotypic differences manifested by antigenic differences, ultrastructural morphological differences, and host specificity.[2] Genetic studies have demonstrated differences between *Pneumocystis* species at a karyotypic level, in the organization and structure of gene families within specific genomes, and at a sequence level within individual genes. Not only are there genetic differences in *Pneumocystis* between different animal hosts, but there are also species and/or strain differences in organisms from the same host. Ultrastructural morphological differences are evident only at the level of electron microscopy, while other phenotypic differences between species require specialized reagents to determine antigenic characterization or multilocus enzyme electrophoresis.

Experimental models have demonstrated that *Pneumocystis* taken from a given host species appear unable to proliferate in other host species. Associated with a better understanding of the host specificity and genetic differences between members of the genus *Pneumocystis,* a need has arisen to define individual species within the genus. In recognition that the organisms described by the Delanöes were isolated from infected rats, a formal taxonomic description of rat-derived species was made, retaining the name of *P. carinii.*[3] *Pneumocystis* isolated from humans was formally described as *P. jirovecii (jiroveci)* in recognition of Otto Jirovec, whose group first identified *Pneumocystis* as a human pathogen and the causative agent of interstitial plasma cell pneumonia. Subsequently, the Latin was corrected to *jirovecii.* Recently a second species identified in rats has been named *P. wakefieldiae.*

Despite the strenuous efforts by many investigators, the lack of a reliable *Pneumocystis* in vitro cultivation system remains an intractable problem. Limited (up to 10-fold) replication of rat-derived organisms has been achieved in different cell lines and in axenic media.[4] A continuous culture system for rat- and human-derived *Pneumocystis* has been described, but has proven difficult to reproduce and maintain. Short-term culture has been used to study *Pneumocystis* metabolism and susceptibility to antimicrobial drugs, but standardization and reproducibility among laboratories have not yet been achieved.

Studies of the life cycle of *Pneumocystis* have been based mainly on light and electron microscopic analysis of forms seen in infected lungs or in short-term culture (Fig. 268-1).[5] Three developmental stages of the organism are commonly seen in conjunction with additional intermediate forms. The *trophozoite* or *trophic form* is small (1 to 4 μm), pleomorphic, and commonly exists in clusters; this stage can be identified on

FIGURE 268-1. Proposed *Pneumocystis* life cycle involving asexual and sexual stages. *(Adapted from Cushion M. Pneumocystis carinii. In: Collier A, Sussman M, eds. Topley and Wilson's Microbiology and Microbial Infections, v. 4. New York: Oxford University Press; 1998:645–683, with permission.)*

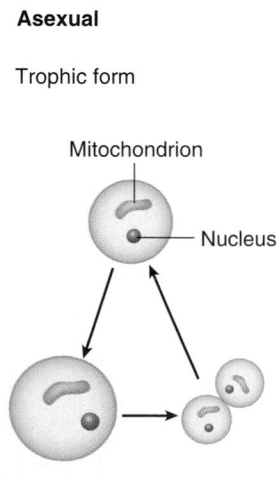

Asexual

Trophic form

Mitochondrion

Nucleus

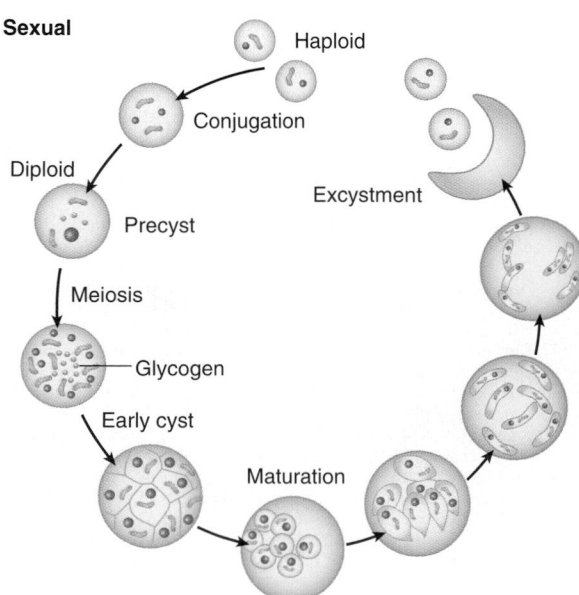

Sexual

Haploid

Conjugation

Diploid

Precyst

Excystment

Meiosis

Glycogen

Early cyst

Maturation

Giemsa stain by its reddish nucleus and blue cytoplasm. In the asexual phase of the life cycle, the trophic forms multiply by binary fission, although trophic binary fission is rarely visualized or documented. In the sexual phase, the haploid trophic forms conjugate to form a diploid zygote that becomes a 4- to 6-μm *precyst* or *sporocyte;* this form is difficult to distinguish from the other developmental stages at the light microscopic level. The precyst undergoes meiosis followed by mitosis, leading to the formation of the *cyst* or *spore case,* which contains eight haploid *intracystic bodies* or *spores.* Genomic studies have confirmed the expression of genes that encode meiosis-specific proteins in the lungs of infected mammalian hosts. The 5- to 8-μm cyst has a thick cell wall that stains well with stains such as methenamine silver and or toluidine blue O. The intracystic bodies are formed by compartmentalization of nuclei and cytoplasmic organelles; exhibit different shapes; and appear to be released through a rent in the cell wall. Studies using echinocandin inhibitors of β-1,3 glucan synthase suggest that the cystic form comprise an integral part of the life cycle.[6]

Biochemical and metabolic studies of *Pneumocystis* have been limited by the problems of culturing the organism.[7] The surface of *Pneumocystis* is rich in glucose/mannose, *N*-acetylglucosamine, and galactose/*N*-acetylgalactosamine residues. The cell walls of cysts and trophic forms contain a number of immunogenic glycoproteins that may be part of a large complex[8] (Fig. 268-2). β-1,3-Glucans are a major component of the cell wall, while little or no chitin has been detected. Lipids have received considerable attention owing to their relationship with antifungal therapy. Cholesterol is the dominant sterol present in *Pneumocystis.*[9] Instead of ergosterol, the organism synthesizes distinct Δ^7, C-24 alkylated sterols. Coenzyme Q10 is the major ubiquinone homologue synthesized by the organism; Co Q homologs, such as 8-aminoquinolones and hydroxynaphthoquinones, have shown good activity against the organism. A variety of enzymes and metabolic pathways have been characterized as potential therapeutic targets.

Several major groups of *Pneumocystis* antigens have been identified. The most widely studied is a 95- to 140-kDa moiety, termed the major surface glycoprotein (MSG) or gpA, is highly immunogenic; exhibits shared and species-specific antigenic determinants; and contains protective B- and T-cell epitopes.[10-15] Immunization with MSG also elicits a protective response in some, but not all, animal models.[16] MSG actually represents a family of proteins encoded by multiple genes that are arranged in clusters at the ends of chromosomes. Transcription of MSG genes occurs at a single expression site, termed the upstream conserved sequence (UCS), which is thought to result in only one MSG isoform being expressed on the surface of *Pneumocystis* at a time.[17,18] Changing the MSG gene at the UCS, by recombination and gene conversion, changes the surface MSG resulting in antigenic variation.

The ability of MSG to undergo antigenic variation may be an important mechanism by which *Pneumocystis* evades the host immune response.[10] The other important function of MSG is to facilitate interaction with host cells by adherence to extracellular matrix proteins fibronectin, vitronectin, possibly laminin, surfactant proteins A and D, and the mannose receptor.[19-23] MSG is composed of up to 10% of *N*-linked carbohydrates, particularly mannose, which participate in the binding to these proteins.

A second family of surface antigens was identified during studies characterizing MSG. A subtilisin-like serine protease encoded by the *PRT1,* also known as *KEX* multigene family, was localized to the surface of rat-derived *Pneumocystis.*[24-26] In other fungi, these proteases are involved in the processing of pre-proteins as they make their way to the cell surface, and may play a role in antigenic variation in *Pneumocystis.*

The third major antigen complex is a glycoprotein that migrates as a broad band of 45 to 55 kDa and 35 to 45 kDa in rat and human *Pneumocystis,* respectively. The gene encoding a rat *Pneumocystis* 45- to 55-kDa antigen (p55) has been cloned and sequenced; the 3' end of the molecule stimulates a host immune response.[27,28] Immunization with recombinant p55 antigen afforded partial protection to subsequent infection.[29] The predicted amino acid sequence of p55 shows a repeated motif rich in glutamic acid residues that, in other microbes, for example, *Plasmodia,* has been suggested as a mechanism to divert the host immune response.[30] The 35- to 45-kDa band of human *Pneumocystis* is frequently found in respiratory tract specimens and is also recognized by serum antibodies.

EPIDEMIOLOGY

When first recognized, *Pneumocystis* pneumonia was known primarily as a disease affecting malnourished and premature infants. Infants are probably the natural host for the disease, becoming colonized in the first few months of life as maternal antibodies wane. This is supported by studies that report finding the organism itself or *Pneumocystis* DNA to be present in clinical or autopsy samples from infants.[31] Similar observations have been made in animal models; in rabbits, for example, the young serve as the primary dispersal host for the agent. Seroepidemiologic surveys have demonstrated that most healthy children have been exposed to *Pneumocystis* by an early age.[30,31] This primary infection is probably asymptomatic, although careful analysis has not been performed to determine if subtle clinical manifestations occur. The serologic studies have shown that *Pneumocystis* has a worldwide distribution, but that the prevalence of antibodies to specific antigens varies among different geographic regions.[10] The frequency of *Pneumocystis* pneumonia among HIV patients in tropical and develop-

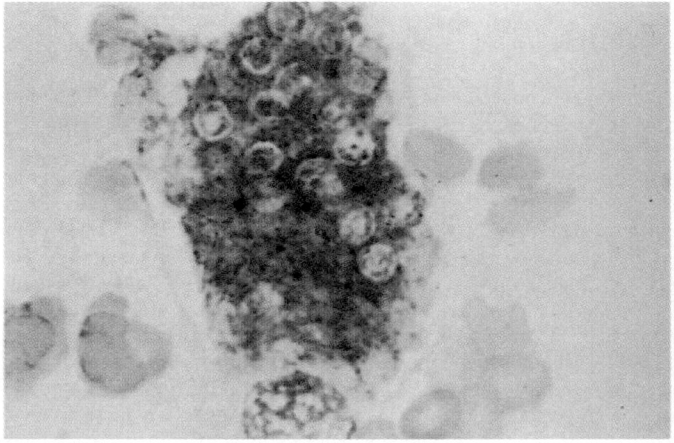
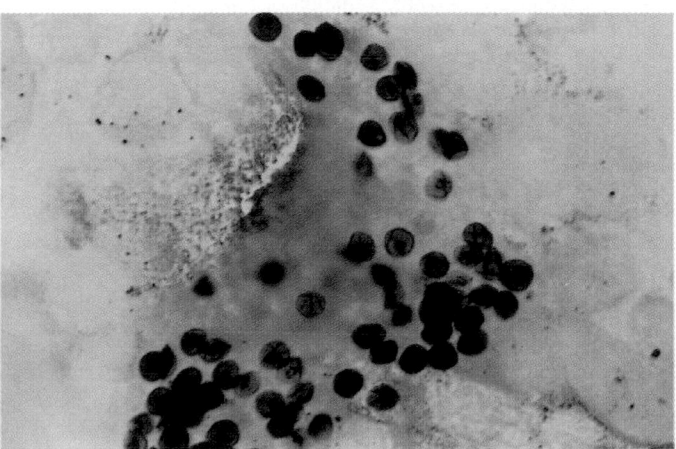

A   **B**

FIGURE 268-2. **A,** Cluster of *Pneumocystis* trophozoites and cysts. (Diff-Quik, ×1000.) **B,** Cluster of *Pneumocystis* cysts. (Methenamine silver stain, ×1250.)

ing countries has generally been thought to be much lower than that in industrialized nations; however recent studies suggest this may reflect rather a failure to diagnose the infection owing to limited access to sophisticated medical care in the third world.[32] Under these conditions, *Pneumocystis* infection is often seen in conjunction with more virulent infections, such as tuberculosis. The demographic features of patients with pneumocystosis generally reflect those of the underlying disease. Pneumocystis pneumonia has also been recognized with increased frequency in Africa in HIV-infected infants.[33] Studies report that *Pneumocystis* organisms can be detected in up to 80% of infants with known or suspected HIV infection presenting with severe pneumonia. Attempts to compare the frequency of *Pneumocystis* pneumonia among different racial and ethnic groups have been complicated by social and cultural factors.[34] There have been conflicting reports about the seasonal occurrence of pneumocystosis.

Animal model studies have shown that *Pneumocystis* is communicable and that the principal mode of transmission is the airborne route, although the infective form of the organism is unknown.[2,3] There is debate about how long the organism resides in the host once *Pneumocystis* infection is acquired. One school of thought holds that the organism becomes part of the host's resident microbial flora and remains quiescent for long periods of time; as immune defenses become compromised, the organism causes disease by reactivation of latent infection. This view is supported by the presence of the same genetic strain of *Pneumocysti* in animal colonies for several years; the high host specificity of *Pneumocystis,* which implies coevolution of the organism and host; and the capability of MSG for antigenic variation. The other view is that *Pneumocystis* infection is transient, but that people are frequently exposed to sources of the organism throughout their lives. One line of support for this hypothesis comes from the limited duration of carriage in recent animal model studies. Healthy adult mice inoculated with *Pneumocystis* clear the infection from the lungs within a short period of time; the process takes slightly longer in neonates. Immunocompromised animals clear *Pneumocystis* form the lungs after normal immune function is restored.

Molecular epidemiological approaches have shed new light on the natural history and epidemiology of *Pneumocystis* infection.[2,3] Although a number of molecular targets have been examined, most information has been obtained from the internal transcribed spacer (ITS) regions of the nuclear rRNA gene, the large subunit mitochondrial rRNA gene, and the dihydropteroate synthase (DHPS) gene sequence. The data indicate that *Pneumocystis* isolates from HIV patients are similar to those from non-HIV patients, and that patients may harbor more than one strain of the organism. Three lines of evidence support the view that active transmission of *Pneumocystis* occurs in humans. AIDS patients with recurrent episodes of pneumocystosis were found to have *Pneumocystis* genotypes that differed from those seen in previous episodes.[35] A second study examined geographic variation of *Pneumocystis* genotypes from pneumocystosis patients in different US cities.[36] This study found that genotypes at the time of an episode of *Pneumocystis* pneumonia reflected the patient's place of diagnosis and not his or her place of birth, suggesting recently acquired infections rather than reactivated latent infection. A third study noted that 53% of AIDS-defining pneumocystosis patients presented with mutant DHPS genotypes.[37] Because these patients had not been receiving prophylactic sulfa, the mutant genotypes could not have resulted from selection but rather as a result of acquisition of a mutant *Pneumocystis* strain. These data strongly suggest that *Pneumocystis* is transmitted directly from person to person, and that active acquisition rather than latency and reactivation results in the majority of pneumocystosis episodes in adults.

The source of exposure for infants as well as adults is probably other individuals with active PCP or transient subclinical colonization. With the advent of AIDS, HIV-infected individuals provide an additional source of exposure. In the pre-HIV era, the prevalence of latent *Pneumocystis* infection in immunocompromised patients autopsy varied from 0% to 8%; the frequency of pneumocystosis at some institutions was related to the type or intensity of immunosuppressive therapy.[38] Subclinical *Pneumocystis* infection has been detected in HIV patients by the polymerase chain reaction (PCR) months before they developed pneumocystosis. Other evidence supporting this concept comes from the occurrence of outbreaks or clusters of *Pneumocystis* pneumonia at orphanages, hospitals, and immunocompromised patients who had prolonged contact with each other. Geographic clustering of pneumocystosis has been reported in two US cities.[39,40] Conflicting results have been reported in surveys to detect subclinical infection in immunocompetent patients or hospital workers that may be attributable to differences in sample size. A number of small studies have demonstrated organisms in patients with obstructive lung disease and other structural lung disease, although it is unknown if these organisms represent colonization or transient infection.

PATHOLOGY AND PATHOGENESIS

Once *Pneumocystis* is inhaled, it escapes the defenses of the upper respiratory tract and is deposited in alveoli. The tropic form preferentially attaches to the alveolar type I cell, and is thought to initiate infection by this act.[38] Ultrastructural analysis has shown that the adherence is characterized by close apposition of the cell surfaces without fusion of the membranes or changes in the intramembranous particles. Although the type I cell does not replicate, in vitro studies using different cell lives have enhanced our understanding about the interaction of the organism and the host. In one report, *Pneumocystis* attachment increased as cultured alveolar type II cells differentiated into type I cell-like phenotype.[41] Other studies have shown that the adherence occurs via extracellular matrix glycoproteins as mentioned earlier, but involves different ligands for the specific glycoproteins.

The attachment for *Pneumocystis* to lung epithelial cells requires an intact cytoskeleton and results in changes in both the organism and the host. One effect is to enhance *Pneumocystis* proliferation. Recent studies have identified *Pneumocystis* genes involved in replication: *Cdc2, Cdc13,* and *Cdc25*; members of the mitogen-activated protein kinase (MAPK) signal transduction pathways; and cell wall genes.[42-46] The functional importance of these genes has been shown by complementation studies in fungi such as *Schizosaccharomyces pombe* and *Saccharomyces cerevisiae. Pneumocystis* maintains an extracellular existence within alveoli, and probably obtains essential nutrients from the alveolar fluid or living cells.[38] Knowledge of how the organism responds to its alveolar microenvironment might lead to an in vitro culture system.

The adherence of *Pneumocystis* suppresses the growth of lung epithelial cells through cyclin-dependent kinase regulatory pathways.[47] Other reports have shown that the organism alters lung GTP-binding regulatory proteins and induces expression of the intracellular adhesion molecule-1 (ICAM-1) and fibrinogen.[48] These properties may influence both the lung damage as well as the host inflammatory and reparative response in *Pneumocystis* pneumonia.

The host immune defects that lead to the unchecked replication of *Pneumocystis,* and hence to the development of pneumocystosis are complex and incompletely understood. Accumulating evidence suggests that one important factor is impaired humoral immunity. *Pneumocystis* pneumonia has been reported in patients and mice with B-cell defects.[30] A positive therapeutic effect has been found with the passive administration of hyperimmune serum or monoclonal antibodies to MSG and other antigens in experimental models of pneumocystosis.[12,13,49] Immunization with live *Pneumocystis* protects T-cell–depleted mice against organism challenge, and is mediated by antibodies that can be produced from Th1 or Th2 type responses.[50-52] Antibodies contribute to host defenses against *Pneumocystis* by acting as opsonins.[30]

In contrast to studies using animal models, analysis of the role of antibodies in humans has been difficult because of the high prevalence of serum antibodies to *Pneumocystis* in the population and the lack of information about which antigen epitopes are protective. Serologic studies of HIV patients have demonstrated a variety of responses, ranging from a fall in serum antibody levels before an episode of pneumocystosis to the development of a vigorous antibody response after recovery.[53-56] Recently developed human *Pneumocystis* MSG recombinant antigen fragments offer powerful new tools to study the antibody responses to the organism in different clinical and immunological settings. The carboxy-terminus fragment is recognized significantly more frequently by HIV patients who had a previous episode of documented pneumocystosis than by patients who never had the disease.[57,58] Although local BALF antibodies have received only limited attention, there is evidence of decreased antibody responses in HIV patients.[59,60]

Impaired cellular immunity has long been considered to be an important predisposing factor in the development of pneumocystosis.[38] Naturally occurring outbreaks of *Pneumocystis* pneumonia have occurred in immunodeficient animals, particularly colonies of severe combined immunodeficiency disease (SCID) mice and athymic nude mice and rats.[61-62] The central role of CD4 cells in host defenses against this organism has been shown by cell depletion and reconstitution experiments, and by knockout mice.[16,63,64] The interaction of T cells with B cells and other cells via the CD40 to CD40L pathway is also important.[65,66] CD8 cells and γδ T cells also contribute to host defenses against *Pneumocystis;* however, their specific roles are complex and incompletely understood.[15,67-69] Pneumocystosis can be induced in normal rodents by the administration of corticosteroids, and these models have been used for more than three decades.[38] Protein malnutrition and an immature immune system also impair host defenses against *Pneumocystis,* although the defect in neonatal mice is related more to factors in the lung milieu than to T cells.[70,71]

The clearest evidence of the role of defective cell-mediated immunity in the development of pneumocystosis in humans comes from persons infected with HIV. The risk of developing *Pneumocystis* pneumonia in adult HIV patients increases greatly when circulating CD4 cells fall below 200/mm^3.[72] Because CD4 counts are much higher in young children than in adults, different criteria must be used. The presence of other clinical complications of HIV, for example, fever and oral candidiasis, increases the risk of pneumocystosis independent of the CD4 count. Cases of pneumocystosis associated with low CD4 counts have been encountered in cancer patients receiving cytotoxic drugs, in adults with idiopathic CD4-lymphopenia, and in otherwise healthy individuals with subtle T-cell defects.[73,74] The issue of evaluating CD4 counts as a risk factor for *Pneumocystis* pneumonia in immunosuppressed patients has also been raised.[75] A few studies have found a correlation between the number of CD4 cells in peripheral blood or bronchoalveolar lavage fluid with poor prognosis.[76]

The interaction of HIV and *Pneumocystis* with CD4 and other T cells in humans is of considerable potential interest, but has received only limited attention. One report has suggested that HIV depletes *Pneumocystis*-specific T cell clones horizontally, that is, by lowering the number of memory cells in the progeny without affecting the number of clones.[77] On the other hand, *Pneumocystis* infection enhances HIV replication in the lung, and may possibly accentuate the depletion of CD4 cells.[78] CD8 cells, which can be infected with HIV, increase in the bronchoalveolar lavage fluid of HIV patients with pneumocystosis, but the pathogenic significance of this accumulation is unknown.[79]

Studies of cellular immune function have shown that HIV patients have a decline in peripheral blood lymphocyte proliferative responses to whole *Pneumocystis* or MSG with progression of the disease and a decline in the number of CD4 cells.[80] A similar decline occurs in Th1-like cytokine response (interferon-α [IFN-α]) but not in the Th2-like cytokine response (interleukin-4 [IL-4]). Patients who have recovered from pneumocystosis exhibit higher proliferative and IL-4 responses to MSG than HIV patients at a similar stage of the infection who have never had pneumocystosis. Thus, *Pneumocystis* patients retain enough CD4 memory cells to recognize the organism, but exhibit a shift from a Th1 to a Th2-like response with progression of HIV.

The occurrence of pneumocystosis in other patient populations with impaired cellular immunity has included premature, debilitated infants; children with primary immunodeficiency diseases, particularly SCID (which involves both T- and B-cell defects) and the hyper IgM syndrome (which involves disruption of the CD40-CD40L pathway)[66]; and patients receiving immunosuppressive drugs for the treatment of a variety of conditions.[38] The principal immunocompromised hosts at risk for pneumocystosis include patients with hematologic malignancies and solid tumors, for example, brain tumors; solid organ and bone marrow transplant recipients; and collagen vascular disorders, for example, Wegener's granulomatosis.[74,81-83] The number of these individuals has grown over the years with better survival and the more widespread use of cytotoxic and immunosuppressive therapy. Corticosteroids, either used alone or in combination with other agents, remain the most common immunosuppressive drugs implicated in the development of pneumocystosis. The relationship of corticosteroids to *Pneumocystis* has been emphasized by the occurrence of pneumocystosis in patients with Cushing's syndrome and children receiving corticosteroids for diseases, for example, asthma, not known to predispose to opportunistic infections.[84,85] Cases of *Pneumocystis* pneumonia in patients on chemotherapy regimens without corticosteroids have also been well documented.[74] Protein malnutrition is an important risk factor for the development of *Pneumocystis* pneumonia, both by itself and as a complication of the patient's underlying disease or its chemotherapy. Lymphopenia and lung factors, for example, radiation and fibrosis, have been suggested as additional predisposing factors in non-HIV patients.[38]

Alveolar macrophages are the first line of defense against *Pneumocystis* and the principal effector cell in clearing the organism from the lung.[86] However, activated macrophages, in the absence of CD4 cells, are unable to control *P. jirovecii* infection.[87] Also needed for *Pneumocystis* clearance is the urokinase-type plasminogen activator, which aids the recruitment of inflammatory cells.[88] An enolase produced by *Pneumocystis* can activate plaminogen, and thus may impair the host plasminogen activator.[89] Recognition and adherence of *Pneumocystis* to macrophages occur by multiple pathways involving MSG and β-glucan in the organism; extracellular matrix and surfactant proteins; and mannose and Fc receptors on the cells.[19-23,90] Macrophages ingest, degrade, and kill *Pneumocystis,* releasing cytokines such as tumor necrosis factor-α (TNF-α), eicosanoids, and reactive oxidants.[91-93] Although nitric acid is released by macrophages, its role in host defenses against *Pneumocystis* is unclear.[94,95]

Alveolar macrophage function is impaired in HIV patients as well as in cancer and transplant patients receiving immunosuppressive drugs. HIV downregulates mannose receptor expression, which results in decreased binding and uptake of *Pneumocystis*.[96,97] HIV also changes the macrophage cytokine response.[98] *Pneumocystis* itself impairs phagocytosis by promoting shedding of the mannose receptor, whereas the administration of a soluble mannose immunoadhesin counteracts this process.[99]

The role of other cells in the host defenses against *Pneumocystis* is poorly understood. One study has shown that neutrophils from *Pneumocystis* patients stimulated with the organism have an impaired respiratory burst when compared with the cells of healthy controls.[100] *Pneumocystis* can also activate natural killer (NK) cells.[101] A role for NK cells has been suggested by reports of the occurrence of pneumocystosis in HIV or other immunodeficient patients who have decreased NK cell numbers or function.[102]

Exposure to *Pneumocystis* or its antigens stimulates production of a multitude of cytokines. Two proinflammatory cytokines, TNF-α and IL-1, have been shown to be important in host defenses against the organism, particularly in the early stages of the infections.[103,104] IL-6, another proinflammatory cytokine, has been produced in response to *Pneumocystis,* but its contributions to host resistance to the organism are unclear.[105] IFN-γ and granulocyte macrophage stimulating factor (GM-CSF) are important contributors to host defense by macrophage activation or in cooperation with TNF-α.[106,107] The role of IFN-γ is particularly complex. One study has shown that the deletion of IFN-γ or TNF-α or IFN-γ receptor genes did not hinder clearance of *Pneumocystis* infection from the lungs; however, deletion of both genes led to severe infection.[108] IFN-γ also influences the host inflammatory response.[109] IL-10 has also been shown to modulate the host inflammatory response, but no role in the host defense against *Pneumocystis* has been found for IL-4 or granulocyte colony stimulating factor (G-CSF).[110,111]

The pathologic changes that occur during the development of pneumocystosis in animal models and in humans are very similar.[38] As the host defenses become compromised, *Pneumocystis* organisms begin to proliferate and gradually fill alveolar lumens. In the corticosteroid-treated rat model, the organism number increases from 10^5 per lung or fewer to 10^9 to 10^{10} per lung after 8 to 10 weeks of corticosteroid administration. The principal histologic finding is the formation of a foamy, eosinophilic alveolar exudate (Fig. 268-3); as the pneumocystosis increases in severity, there may also be hyaline membrane formation along with interstitial fibrosis and edema. The host inflammatory response is usually inconspicuous and is characterized by type II cell proliferation (a typical reparative response) and scanty mononuclear cell infiltrate. SCID mice exhibit cytokine production only late in the course of pneumocystosis, when elevated levels of TNF-α and IL-1 are found in the lungs.[112] Several studies have shown that rats with corticosteroid-induced pneumocystosis, as well as HIV and non-HIV patients with the disease, have elevated levels of proinflammatory cytokines in their respiratory tract but not in the peripheral blood.[113-115] Some patients exhibit atypical findings such as the lack of the alveolar exudate or the development of cavitary lesions, granulomas, or microcalcifications.[116] On electron microscopy, there is increased alveolar-capillary permeability followed by evidence of damage to the type I cell.[38,117]

Physiologic changes include hypoxemia with an increased alveolar-arterial (PAO$_2$-PaO$_2$) oxygen gradient and respiratory alkalosis; impaired diffusing capacity, suggesting alveolar-capillary block; and alterations in lung compliance, total lung capacity, and vital capac-

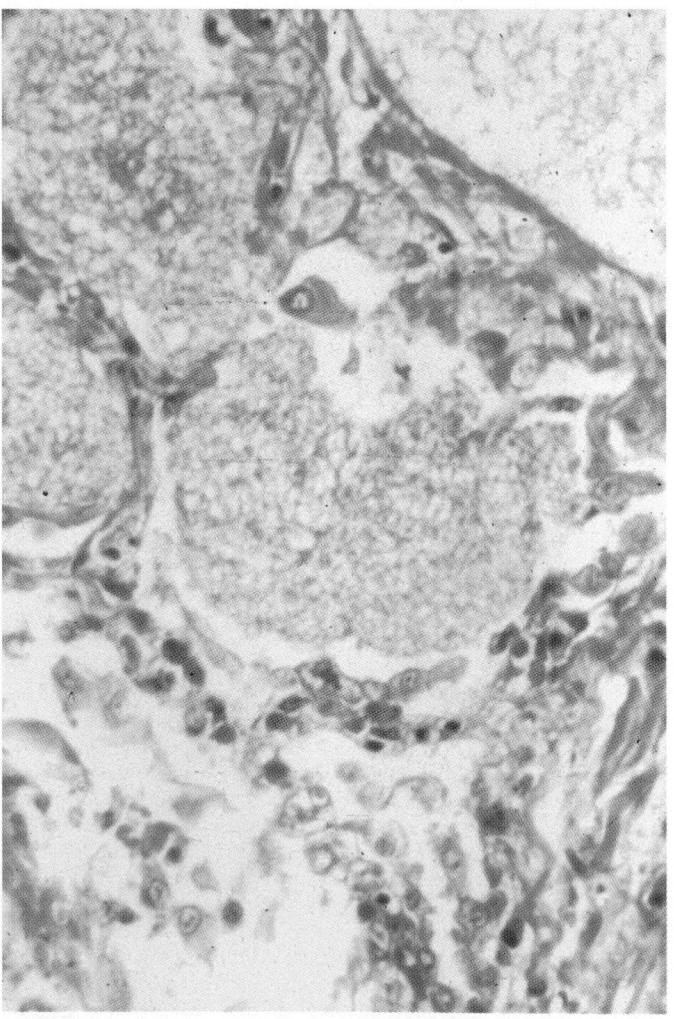

FIGURE 268-3. *Pneumocystis* pneumonia illustrating frothy eosinophillic honeycombed material filling alveolar space. (H&E stain.)

ity.[118,119] The resulting picture suggests diffuse lung damage similar to that seen in the adult respiratory distress syndrome (ARDS).

The pathophysiologic changes described in the preceding are due not only to the effects of *Pneumocystis* on the type I cell, but also to alterations in the surfactant system and host inflammatory response. There is a fall in surfactant phospholipids (mainly phosphatidylcholine) that is due to inhibition of phospholipid secretion mediated by MSG.[120-123] Changes in the surfactant proteins include a decline in SP-B and SP-C and rise in SP-A and SP-D.[124,125] Fractionation of the surfactant has shown that most of the increased SP-A and SP-D levels are localized mainly in the small aggregate compartment.[126] The pathogenic significance of these abnormalities is supported by reports that have shown that the administration of surfactant is of benefit in the treatment of pneumocystosis.

There is now a considerable body of evidence showing that the immune/inflammatory response to *Pneumocystis* can have harmful as well as helpful effects on the host lung. These effects are complex and depend to some degree on the experimental model being used. Immunologic reconstitution of infected SCID mice with immune splenocytes results in clearance of *Pneumocystis* that is associated with a hyperinflammatory response composed of increased proinflammatory cytokines, chemokines, and reduced oxygenation and compliance.[127-129] CD4 cells, particularly those expressing the CD25⁻ phenotype, appear to be the major cell type responsible for these inflammatory changes.[130] The administration of large number of splenocytes or CD4 cells that had been sensitized to MSG to rats with corticosteroid-induced pneumocystosis results in clinical illness and cytokine cascade along with a reduction in Pc burden.[131] The presence of corticosteroids appears to have no influence on the deleterious effects of the inflammatory response. Factors that can ameliorate these effects include hyperimmune serum and CD8 cells. On the other hand, another mouse model has shown that mice depleted of CD4 cells and exposed to *Pneumocystis* develop pneumonia, impaired respiration, and a hyperinflammatory response characterized by the influx of CD8 cells and neutrophils.[127-129] Depletion of CD8 cells abrogates this response.

The contribution of the host inflammatory response to lung damage in HIV patients with pneumocystosis has been suggested by studies that have correlated increased numbers of neutrophils and levels of IL-8 in bronchoalveolar lavage fluid with more severe pneumonia and worse prognosis.[132,133] IL-8 functions as a potent chemoattractant, and its interaction with MSG is mediated by MSG.[134,135] Alterations in eicosanoids, TNF-α, IL-1, other cytokines and inflammatory mediators have also been noted in these studies and other reports; however, the pathogenic significance of these changes is unclear. HIV patients with *Pneumocystis* pneumonia also frequently experience a worsening of respiratory function soon after receiving antimicrobial drugs. Corticosteroids, if given promptly, can ameliorate or prevent this outcome and improve survival.[136] It is thought that the beneficial effects of corticosteroids are attributable to their anti-inflammatory properties or their effects on surfactant components[i]; yet, studies examining these issues have produced inconsistent results.[137-140]

CLINICAL MANIFESTATIONS

Interstitial plasma cell pneumonia, so named because of the distinctive lung infiltrate, has occurred classically in debilitated infants 6 weeks to 4 months of age who are housed in orphanages or foundling homes under crowded conditions.[38] The disease begins insidiously with symptoms such as poor feeding and progresses gradually to overt respiratory distress and cyanosis. Cases sometimes occurred in explosive outbreaks, giving rise to the term "epidemic" form of *Pneumocystis* pneumonia. Interstitial plasma cell pneumonia has largely disappeared from industrialized countries but still exists in parts of the world (and in their refugees) where poor socioeconomic conditions abound, although Pneumocystis pneumonia is being recognized with increasing frequency in HIV-infected children in Africa.

The major presenting symptoms of pneumocystosis in the compromised host are shortness of breath, fever, and a nonproductive cough.[38,141] Occasionally sputum is produced and, rarely, hemoptysis; chest pain may also occur. Patients receiving immunosuppressive drugs frequently develop these clinical manifestations after the corticosteroid dose has been tapered, and are typically sick for about 1 to 2 weeks before seeking medical attention. *Pneumocystis* pneumonia in HIV patients usually is a more subtle disease with symptoms lasting from weeks to months; the organism burden is higher but lung damage is less severe.[142,143] Studies have also compared the clinical features of pneumocystosis in adult HIV patients by age and underlying risk group.[144,145] Yet, in both AIDS and non-AIDS patients the clinical picture is quite variable; for example, lung allograft recipients who develop pneumocystosis frequently are asymptomatic at the time of diagnosis.

On physical examination, tachypnea and tachycardia are found in acutely ill patients. Children may demonstrate cyanosis, flaring of the nasal alae, and intercostal retractions in severe disease. Lung auscultation is usually not helpful, although rales can be heard in about one third of adults with the disease.

The chest radiograph classically exhibits bilateral diffuse infiltrates extending from the perihilar region (Fig. 268-4). Atypical manifestations have ranged from normal films to unilateral infiltrates, nodules, cavities, pneumatoceles, lymphadenopathy, and effusions.[38,146] Patients receiving prophylactic aerosol pentamidine have an increased incidence of apical infiltrates and pneumothoraces.[147] Techniques such as ultrasound and computed tomography (CT) scans have been helpful in studying mass lesions and extrapulmonary infection. High-resolution CT (HRCT) has shown promise in patients with normal or equivocal chest radiographs.[148] Nuclear medicine procedures have demonstrated increased lung uptake on scans using gallium-67 citrate, indium-111, human IgG, and technetium-99 labeled monoclonal antibody to *Pneumocystis* MSG.[149,150]

Impaired oxygenation is the most frequent laboratory abnormality found in pneumocystosis; analysis of the magnitude of hypoxemia or the alveolar-oxygen gradient has been used to evaluate disease severity and monitor progression.[136] Serum lactic dehydrogenase LDH levels, which appear to reflect lung injury, rise frequently in *Pneumocystis* pneumonia and decline with successful therapy; however, the usefulness of serum LDH has been limited because there is much overlap among different patient groups and elevations can be produced by other diseases.[151]

Extrapulmonary Pneumocystosis

In the pre-HIV era, spread of *Pneumocystis* beyond the lungs was considered to be a rare event, with only 16 cases being reported; however, extrapulmonary pneumocystosis has received much more attention in

HIV patients, with 90 cases or more being reported.[152] The precise frequency of this complication in HIV patients has been difficult to determine (estimates have ranged from negligible to 3%) because diagnosis was made by histologic demonstration of *Pneumocystis* at extrapulmonary locations where there were clinical manifestations or at autopsy.[152] A recent survey of autopsies of 233 HIV patients at two medical centers over a 12-year period revealed evidence of *Pneumocystis* pneumonia in 24%, with extrapulmonary involvement in 13%.[153] Studies in animal models have demonstrated *Pneumocystis* outside the lungs histologically, and even more commonly, by PCR analysis; these reports raise the question of whether extrapulmonary dissemination of *Pneumocystis* is more common than generally realized.[154]

Extrapulmonary pneumocystosis occurs mainly in patients with advanced HIV infection who are taking no prophylaxis or only aerosolized pentamidine. The main sites of involvement are lymph nodes, spleen, liver, bone marrow, gastrointestinal tract, eyes, thyroid, adrenal glands, and kidneys. The clinical manifestations, which may occur with or without lung involvement, vary from incidental findings at autopsy to a rapidly progressive multisystem disease. Among the focal manifestations of extrapulmonary pneumocystosis are a rapidly enlarging thyroid mass; pancytopenia from bone marrow necrosis; retinal cotton wool spots; polypoid lesions in the external auditory canal; pleural effusion; numerous hypodense lesions in the spleen on CT scan; and punctate calcifications in the spleen, liver, adrenal, or kidney. Biopsy or fine-needle aspiration shows areas of necrosis filled with foamy material. Gomori methenamine silver or fluorescent monoclonal antibody stain reveals numerous organisms.

DIAGNOSIS

Pneumocystosis should be considered in any immunocompromised patient who develops respiratory symptomatology, fever, and an abnormal chest radiograph. Because these clinical manifestations may be produced by a long list of infectious and noninfectious agents, diagnosis of *Pneumocystis* pneumonia must be made by histopathologic demonstration of the organism. With extrapulmonary pneumocystosis, the diagnosis may be suspected by the presence of the typical eosinophilic, honeycombed material at the affected site.

One approach to the management of patients with suspected *Pneumocystis* pneumonia is presented in Figure 268-5. Patients with a compatible clinical picture and chest radiography demonstrating a reticular or granular infiltrate should undergo a diagnostic procedure to collect respiratory secretions to detect the organism. In patients with a normal chest radiograph, additional testing should be performed to assess the probability of early *Pneumocystis* infection. Either HRCT scan of the chest or pulmonary function testing can be used to identify patients unlikely to have *Pneumocystis* pneumonia and who may be observed without specific anti-*Pneumocystis* treatment. A prospective study found that a normal, unchanged or equivocal chest radiograph and a chest HRCT without ground glass opacities ruled out PcP.[155] Similarly, studies have shown that a normal, or unchanged, chest radiograph and a single breath diffusing capacity for carbon monoxide (DL_{co}) of greater than 75% of predicted virtually ruled out the diagnosis of *Pneumocystis* pneumonia[156] (Fig. 268-6). A DL_{co} of less than 75% of predicted is, however, of low specificity and patients with ground glass opacities on HRCT or a DL_{co} of less than 75% of predicted should undergo a diagnostic workup to detect the organism.

A variety of stains have been used to identify *Pneumocystis* in respiratory tract secretions; in the hands of experienced microscopists, all are highly efficient in detecting the organism.[38,157,158] Stains such as methenamine silver or one of its simpler variants, for example, toluidine blue O, cresyl echt violet, which selectively stain the wall of *Pneumocystis* cysts, have been popular among pathologists because they can be used on imprint smears or tissue sections and are easy to interpret. Reagents such as Wright-Giemsa or one of its more rapid variants, for example, Diff-Quik, stain all *Pneumocystis* developmental stages as well as host cells. Calcofluor white is a chemifluorescent agent that binds to B-linked polymers of *Pneumocystis* and other

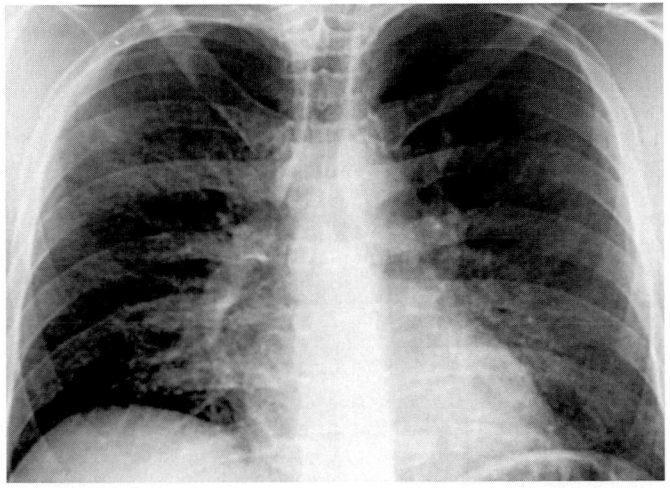

FIGURE 268-4. Chest radiograph showing bilateral infiltrates of *Pneumocystis* pneumonia.

FIGURE 268-5. Algorithm for the diagnostic evaluation and management of patients with suspected *Pneumocystis* pneumonia. DL$_{co}$, Single breath diffusing capacity for carbon monoxide; HRCT, high-resolution computer tomograph; GGO, ground-glass opacities; BAL, bronchoalveolar lavage.

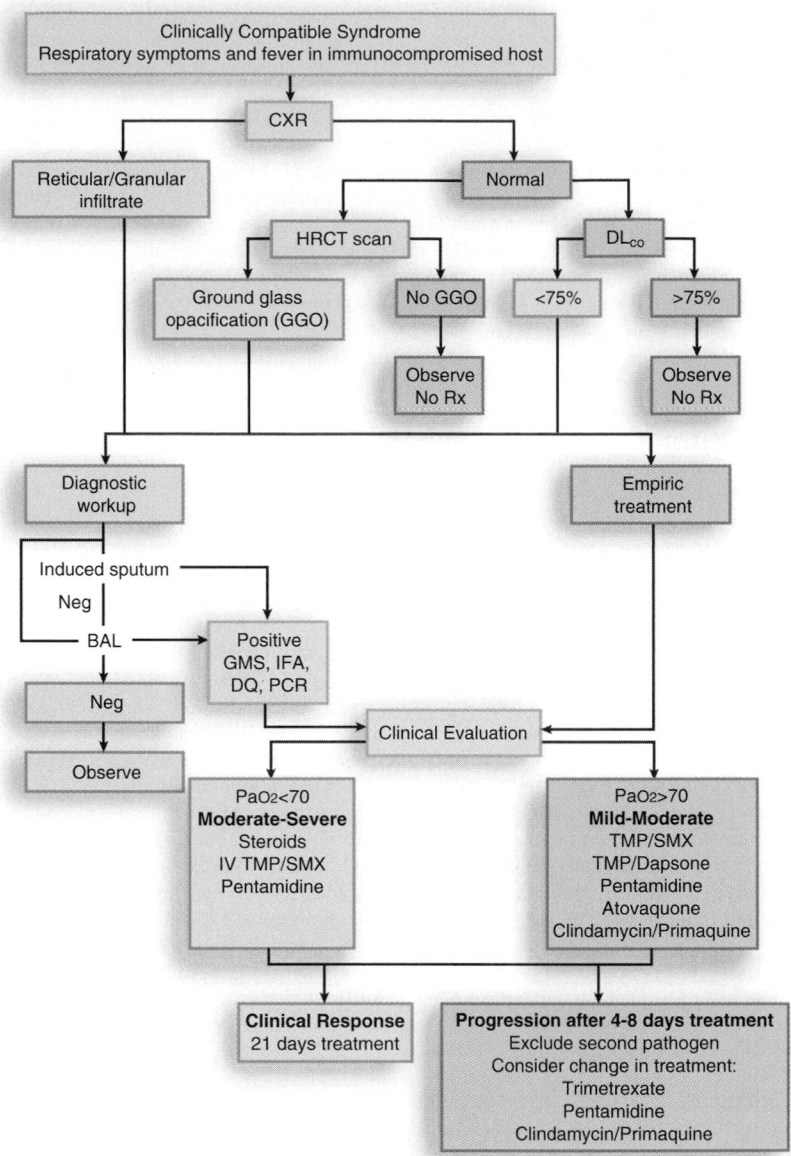

fungi. The Papanicolaou stain, which is used by cytopathologists, is a very sensitive method to detect the foamy, eosinophilic material surrounding *Pneumocystis,* although individual organisms do not stain well. Laboratories may use a rapid staining technique to screen for *Pneumocystis,* which is then followed by a more time-consuming procedure for definitive identification.

Immunofluorescence has been the most widely used immunologic technique for *Pneumocystis* diagnosis.[159,160] Commercial kits employing monoclonal antibodies have been shown to be somewhat more sensitive than histologic stains in detecting *Pneumocystis*; however, this has to be balanced against the need for specialized facilities and increased cost. Immunohistochemistry has been used to detect *Pneumocystis* organisms in tissue sections. Soluble *Pneumocystis* antigens have been found in patients with pneumocystosis by immunoblotting.[161] In some patients, the pattern of immunoreactivity changes after therapy of pneumocystosis or with recurrent episodes of the disease; these results suggest antigenic variation.[10]

The development of DNA amplification by PCR has introduced a new level of sensitivity in *Pneumocystis* detection. In recent years, PCR has proven to be a highly efficient method of detecting *Pneumocystis* in a variety of respiratory specimens; when performed under carefully

controlled conditions, specificity has been reasonable.[162-164] The presence of a positive PCR product in a specimen that cannot be confirmed by other methods of detection presents a diagnostic dilemma. Such a situation might result from the recent administration of anti-*Pneumocystis* drugs or represent subclinical infection or colonization. In the latter case, some patients have gone on to develop *Pneumocystis* pneumonia.[162] Reverse-transcribed PCR has been used to differentiate RNA from viable organisms from DNA and may be of use in following the response to therapy. PCR has been modified so it can be used in the clinical microbiology laboratories; if commercial kits become approved, PCR could gain acceptance as one of the standard techniques available for the diagnosis of pneumocystosis. PCR also offers promise in allowing the use of specimens obtained using noninvasive approaches such as oro-pharyngeal washes to be used to establish the diagnosis. In contrast to respiratory specimens, the results of PCR in detecting *Pneumocystis* in serum have been inconsistent.

The collection of specimens that accurately reflect the disease process in the lungs is an essential component of the diagnostic evaluation of patients with suspected pneumocystosis. The collection procedures used in adults can usually be performed in children, although infants present special problems.[165] In general, the more invasive the

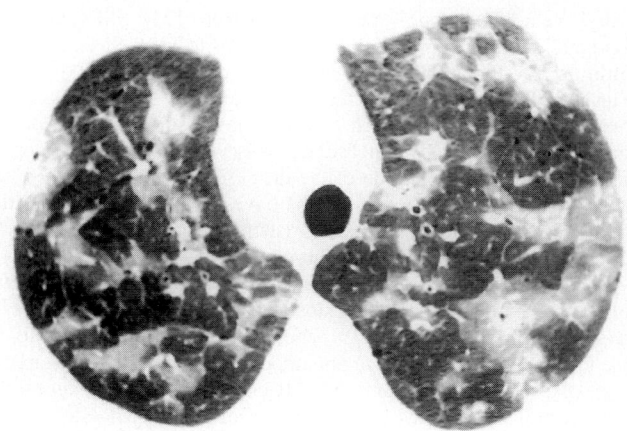

FIGURE 268-6. HRCT scan of an HIV patient with *Pneumocystis* pneumonia who had a normal chest radiograph. HRCT scan demonstrates the characteristic ground-glass opacities. *(Courtesy of L. Huang, with permission.)*

procedure the better the diagnostic yield. These procedures usually have a higher diagnostic yield in AIDS patients than in other immunocompromised hosts because of the higher organism burden. However, chemoprophylaxis (mainly aerosol pentamidine) and the empiric treatment have made the diagnosis of pneumocystosis in AIDS patients more difficult.[147,166,167]

Although *Pneumocystis* organisms are rarely found in expectorated sputum, the organisms can be frequently detected in sputum that has been induced by inhalation of a saline mist. Induced sputum has emerged as a simple, noninvasive technique that can be used to screen for the presence of *Pneumocystis*. The diagnostic yield from induced sputum ranges from less than 50% to 90% at different medical centers, depending on the level of interest and expertise in performing the procedure.[151,158,164] Success in the use of induced sputum requires a serious institutional commitment in terms of specially dedicated and trained personnel, and care in the processing of specimens. Several recent studies comparing PCR assay from oropharyngeal washing specimens with standard microscopy from induced sputum or bronchoalveolar lavage (BAL) specimens have reported promising results, but additional studies are needed prior to recommendation as a standard clinical approach.[168,169]

Fiberoptic bronchoscopy is the most commonly performed invasive procedure, and results in the diagnosis of pneumocystosis in more than 90% of the cases.[38,158,164] BAL is usually performed instead of washings and brushings because it has greater sensitivity and low morbidity. The diagnostic yield of BAL can be increased if multiple lobes are sampled or the procedure is directed toward the sites of greatest involvement[170]; BAL also provides information that cannot be obtained from induced sputum about *Pneumocystis* organism burden, the presence of other infectious agents, and the host inflammatory response.[171] Transbronchial biopsy may provide information not obtainable from a BAL, but is associated with a higher rate of complications, for example, pneumothorax and bleeding.

Open lung biopsy, which requires the use of operating room facilities and general anesthesia, has long served as the standard reference procedure for the diagnosis of *Pneumocystis* because it provides the greatest amount of tissue that can be obtained under direct visualization.[38] Open lung biopsy can be helpful when bronchoscopy is nondiagnostic, in evaluating another infection or condition complicating pneumocystosis, and in diagnosing Kaposi sarcoma of the lung. Open lung biopsy is performed less frequently than in the past and minithoracotomy or thoracoscopically performed biopsies are more commonly performed.

Most serological studies are not specific for *Pneumocystis*. Serum lactic dehydrogenase (LDH) levels are frequently elevated in

Pneumocystis pneumonia and decline with successful therapy; however, the usefulness of serum LDH has been limited because there is much overlap among different patient groups and elevations can be produced by other diseases.[151] Other laboratory tests studied in pneumocystosis include hemoglobin, leukocyte and lymphocyte counts, serum albumin, angiotensin-converting enzyme, thyroxine, triiodothyronine, and carcinoembryonic antigen levels.[141,157] Unfortunately, the specificity of all of these tests for *Pneumocystis* is low. Recently, the measurement of plasma *S*-adenosylmethionine concentrations has been proposed as a sensitive test for *Pneumocystis* pneumonia.[172] In laboratory animal studies, it has shown to be depleted in *Pneumocystis*-infected animals, and in a small clinical study, plasma *S*-adenosylmethionine was undetectable in 14 of 15 HIV-infected patients with confirmed or suspected *Pneumocystis* pneumonia. In addition, serial *S*-adenosylmethionine levels appeared to parallel the clinical course of disease. These promising results will need to be confirmed in larger controlled clinical trials.

Since the onset of the HIV pandemic, pneumocystosis has placed a strain on health care facilities. As managed care with its singular focus on controlling costs has come to dominate health care, *Pneumocystis* pneumonia has served as a model for articles examining the allocation of resources devoted to the care of HIV patients.[173,174] One way to reduce costs has been to replace invasive diagnostic procedures with algorithms and simple diagnostic techniques that are predictive of pneumocystosis.[138,157,158,159] The major problem with this approach is that none of the tests can reliably distinguish *Pneumocystis* infection from multiple other causes of pulmonary infiltrates in HIV patients. Another way to lower costs has been to use empiric therapy.[175] This approach may be appropriate in tropical or developing countries; however, at hospitals in the United States, patients treated empirically for pneumocystosis had higher mortality than patients in whom a specific diagnosis was made by bronchoscopy.[176] Financial considerations were cited as a major contributing factor in the decision not to perform bronchoscopy. Empiric therapy may also impair later attempts to establish a specific etiologic diagnosis.[167]

COURSE AND PROGNOSIS

The natural history of untreated pneumocystosis in HIV patients and other immunocompromised hosts is characterized by progressive respiratory insufficiency, leading to death. Prognosis is related to the degree of hypoxemia at the time of presentation; an arterial oxygen pressure of 70 mmHg while breathing room air has been established to separate the milder from the more serious forms of disease.[136] When this is expressed as the alveolar-arterial oxygen gradient, *Pneumocystis* pneumonia has been classified as mild (less than 35 mmHg), moderate (35 to 45 mmHg), and severe (greater than 45 mmHg). Other prognostic indicators in HIV patients include extensive infiltrates on chest radiograph; interstitial fibrosis and edema on biopsy; increased neutrophils and IL-8 levels in BALF; elevated LDH levels and reduced albumin levels in serum; age over 60 years; CD4 counts in BALF and blood; and general markers of disease severity.[118,132,133,141,151,157] Concurrent pulmonary infection with other microorganisms can complicate management of all patients, and the presence of cytomegalovirus in the respiratory tract of HIV patients may be an independent predictor of poor prognosis.[177] Other prognostic host factors in non-HIV patients include severity of the underlying disease and prior lung damage.

Optimal management of pneumocystosis depends on prompt diagnosis and institution of therapy. Early in the HIV epidemic, survival of *Pneumocystis* patients was better at hospitals with greater familiarity with the disease; however, improvement in management has occurred throughout the medical community. A recent analysis of more than 5000 episodes of pneumocystosis in the United States during the 1990s revealed a mortality rate of 18% at 1 month and 53% at 1 year after diagnosis.[178] Patients who have a milder form of the disease, or are prescribed concurrent anti-retroviral drugs have a better survival.[179] In contrast to HIV patients, the mortality of pneumocystosis in several large series of non-HIV patients is 30% to 50%, a figure that has not changed appreciably in two decades.[81,82,142,143,180] The lack of improvement in the survival in non-HIV patients probably reflects a lack of recognition and delays in diagnosis.

The development of severe pneumocystosis requiring mechanical ventilation and/or admission to the intensive care unit has presented vexing problems for patients, families, and physicians. In the early and mid-1980s the mortality from respiratory failure was so high (80% to 90%) that aggressive measures were often discouraged.[181] Improvements in the diagnosis and treatment of *Pneumocystis* pneumonia have reduced the mortality to 40% to 50%, although there is variability at different medical centers.[180,182,183]

Patients who recover from pneumocystosis are at risk for developing recurrent episodes of the disease as long as the immunosuppressive conditions persist.[38] HIV patients are much more likely to develop recurrence than non-HIV patients. Recent studies have shown that recurrent episodes occurring within 6 months of the first episode are more likely to be relapse, whereas episodes occurring at more than 6 months are more likely to represent a new episode of infection.[184] The prognosis of recurrent episodes of pneumocystosis is similar to that of initial episodes.[185]

Another complication plaguing patients who recover from *Pneumocystis* pneumonia is pneumothorax.[118,141,186] Risk factors include a previous episode of pneumocystosis, the use of aerosol pentamidine, and cigarette smoking. Pneumatoceles, pneumomediastinum, and subcutaneous emphysema also occur. Management is difficult and should be individualized; measures have included chest tube, surgical or chemical pleurodesis, and thoracostomy with stapling. The previous use of corticosteroids may increase risk of morbidity.[186]

TREATMENT

Trimethoprim-sulfamethoxazole (TMP-SMX) is the drug of choice for all forms of pneumocystosis.[1,187] This agent, which acts by inhibiting folic acid synthesis, has been used for two decades against *Pneumocystis* with a high degree of success.[188-191] Among the attractive features of TMP-SMX are its availability in oral and parenteral forms, well-known pharmacokinetics, antibacterial properties, and cost. TMP-SMX is administered orally or intravenously in a dosage of 15 to 20 mg/kg per day (TMP) and 75 to 100 mg/kg per day (SMX) in three or four divided doses. The parenteral preparation should be used in patients who are seriously ill or have gastrointestinal disturbances. As with all anti-*Pneumocystis* drugs, treatment should be continued for 21 days in HIV patients and 14 days in non-HIV patients. The reason for the longer duration in HIV patients is thought to be the fact that these individuals have a higher organism burden and respond more slowly.

TMP-SMX is well tolerated by non-HIV patients, with gastrointestinal symptoms and skin rashes being the most common complaints. By contrast, HIV patients experience a high frequency (up to 80% or more) of adverse reactions which usually begin during the second week of TMP-SMX therapy and may result in discontinuation of the drug in up to 50% of these individuals.[1,192] The side effects include skin rash, fever, cytopenias, nausea and vomiting, hepatitis, pancreatitis, nephritis, hyperkalemia, metabolic acidosis, central nervous system manifestations, and an anaphylactoid reaction. Most of these reactions appear to be caused by the sulfonamide component, but the mechanisms are not well understood. Among the possible contributing factors are elevated serum drug levels, the formation of hydroxylamine metabolites, glutathione deficiency, hypersensitivity, and CD4 counts.[192-194] Hyperkalemia has been attributed to trimethoprim, which acts like a potassium-sparing diuretic.[195]

Some investigators have recommended adjusting the dose of TMP-SMX to achieve serum concentrations of 5 to 8 μg/mL TMP and 100 to 150 μg/mL SMX in order to achieve maximum efficacy and minimum toxicity[190,192]; however, other workers have not found this approach to be beneficial or practical.[196] N-Acetylcysteine and folinic

acid have not helped prevent side effects from TMP-SMX, and folinic acid may actually be harmful. Skin reactions to TMP-SMX range from mild to life-threatening, for example, toxic epidermal necrolysis, Stevens-Johnson syndrome, and anaphylaxis. In some cases, the skin rash and manifestations such as fever may resolve spontaneously or respond to conservative measures, whereas in other instances they may require discontinuation of the drug. Corticosteroids may also be helpful.[197] Desensitization regimens have been successful in patients who have experienced non–life-threatening reactions to TMP-SMX, but should be undertaken with caution.[198]

Several alternative regimens have been developed for the treatment of mild to moderate pneumocystosis.[1,187] Although these studies have been performed mainly in HIV patients, the results should be applicable to non-HIV patients with pneumocystosis. TMP administered at a dose of 15 to 20 mg/kg per day orally combined with dapsone 100 mg per day orally has been shown to be as effective as TMP-SMX and less toxic.[199] The major adverse reactions to dapsone are methemoglobinemia, rash, fever, nausea, and vomiting; hemolysis can occur in patients who have glucose-6-phosphate dehydrogenase (G6PD) deficiency. Dapsone can be administered to patients intolerant of sulfonamides, but must be approached with caution because there are few reliable guidelines to predict who might experience a serious reaction. The serum levels of dapsone and TMP are higher when these drugs are used together than when used alone and suggest bidirectional interference with clearance.[200] The anti-*Pneumocystis* activity of dapsone is reduced when the drug is administered with dideoxyinosine (DDI); this is probably attributable to buffer in the DDI, which raises pH and interferes with dapsone absorption.[201]

Controlled studies have shown that the combination of clindamycin and primaquine exhibits comparable efficacy and toxicity to TMP-SMX and TMP and dapsone in the therapy of pneumocystosis.[199,202] The mechanism of action of clindamycin and primaquine against *Pneumocystis* is not known. The usual doses are clindamycin (600 mg every 6 hours intravenously or 300 to 450 mg every 6 hours orally) and primaquine (15 to 30 mg base per day orally). Treatment may also be initiated with intravenous clindamycin and then switched to oral administration. Adverse effects include skin rash, fever, neutropenia, gastrointestinal complaints, and methemoglobinemia.[1,187] Primaquine also causes hemolysis in patients with G6PD deficiency.

Atovaquone is a hydroxynaphthoquinone that was originally developed as an antimalarial agent. Atovaquone acts on the mitochondrial electron transport chain of Plasmodia, and based on mutations found in *Pneumocystis* isolates from patients failing atovaquone prophylaxis, drug targets are similar in *Pneumocystis*. One study compared atovaquone with TMP-SMX and another with pentamidine isethionate in the treatment of mild to moderate pneumocystosis in HIV patients.[203,204] Atovaquone was less effective than TMP-SMX and about as effective as pentamidine; however, atovaquone was better tolerated in both studies. Adverse reactions to atovaquone include skin rash, fever, gastrointestinal symptoms, and abnormal liver function tests. An oral suspension, administered at a dose of 750 mg/5 mL twice daily with food, results in better absorption than earlier preparations.[205]

Two parenteral drugs, pentamidine isethionate and trimetrexate, are the major alternatives to TMP-SMX for the treatment of moderate to severe pneumocystosis in hospitalized patients.[1,187] Clindamycin at doses of 600 to 900 mg every 6 to 8 hours intravenously has been used with primaquine in these patients, but experience is limited.[206,207] Pentamidine, a diamidine, is an old drug that was first used to treat African trypanosomiasis; pentamidine appears to exert its antimicrobial activity by binding to DNA, but its precise mode of action against *Pneumocystis* is unknown. A number of reports have shown that pentamidine is about as effective as TMP-SMX in the therapy of pneumocystosis in HIV and non-HIV patients.[188-191] Pentamidine is usually administered as a single daily dose of 4 mg/kg, although a dose of 3 mg/kg has been used in some studies. The intravenous route is preferred over the intramuscular route of administration; pentamidine is diluted in 50 to 250 mL of a 5% dextrose solution and infused over a period of at least 1 hour. Pentamidine administered by aerosol has also been used in the treatment of *Pneumocystis* pneumonia; however, since this form of administration is less effective than oral drugs, it is not recommended.

Pharmacokinetic studies have shown that pentamidine follows a three-compartment model with rapid passage to tissues, secondary distribution, and long (about 12 days) elimination half-life; only a small amount of the drug is cleared by the kidney.[192,208] Pentamidine is a toxic drug: adverse reactions occur in 80% or more of HIV and non-HIV patients, and are severe enough to necessitate discontinuation of the drug in about half the cases. Side effects include hypotension, cardiac arrhythmias (e.g., torsades de pointes), azotemia, pancreatitis, dysglycemias, hyperkalemia, hypomagnesemia, hypocalcemia, neutropenia, hepatic disturbances, bronchospasm, and problems at intramuscular injection sites. Hypoglycemia, which is due to damage of pancreatic β cells with insulin release, occurs early in therapy, and may be later followed by diabetes mellitus. The frequency of hypoglycemia and azotemia has been correlated with high serum pentamidine levels, total drug dose, and duration of treatment.[209,210] The mechanism of hyperkalemia caused by pentamidine is similar to that caused by TMP.[211]

Trimetrexate, a lipid-soluble derivative of methotrexate, is a highly potent inhibitor of *Pneumocystis* dihydrofolate reductase (DHFR). A controlled study showed that trimetrexate was less effective but better tolerated than TMP-SMX in the therapy of pneumocystosis in hospitalized patients.[212] Other studies have shown that trimetrexate may be valuable as "salvage" therapy in patients who have failed or cannot tolerate TMP-SMX.[1,187] Trimetrexate is administered intravenously in a single daily dose of 45 mg/m². The principal side effect of trimetrexate is bone marrow suppression, which can be ameliorated or prevented by the administration of folinic acid at a dose of 20 mg/m² intravenously or orally every 6 hours. There is no evidence that folinic acid used at the recommended dose interferes with the therapeutic effect of trimetrexate. Other side effects of trimetrexate include skin rash, peripheral neuropathy, and liver function abnormalities.

The response to anti-*Pneumocystis* drugs generally mirrors other clinical features of the infection. Non-HIV patients, who become ill rather quickly, usually show a clinical response by 4 days of treatment; if there is no response by 4 to 8 days, it is wise to consider switching to another drug. HIV patients typically respond more slowly and take longer to clear *Pneumocystis* from their lungs; it is prudent to wait for at least 8 days before declaring a treatment failure. Adding anti-*Pneumocystis* drugs to the regimen is no more effective than substituting one agent for another, and may increase the risk of adverse reactions.

HIV patients frequently experience worsening of their blood oxygenation during the first few days of therapy; such a clinical deterioration can be particularly dangerous if the initial hypoxemia is marked. Several studies have shown that the administration of corticosteroids during the first 72 hours of treatment can lessen the decline in oxygenation and improve survival. These studies led to a recommendation by an expert panel that steroids be added to the treatment of all patients with moderate to severe pneumocystosis, that is, an arterial oxygen pressure of less than 70 mmHg or an alveolar-arterial oxygen gradient of greater than 35 mmHg in the following dose regimen for adults: prednisone 40 mg orally twice daily, days 1 to 5; 40 mg once daily, days 6 to 10; and 20 mg once daily, days 11 to 20.[136] The use of corticosteroids became widely adopted by the medical community. A subsequent report showed that steroids did not improve the outcome of pneumocystosis other than reducing the frequency of hypersensitivity reactions to TMP-SMX.[213] However, a meta analysis of published controlled studies continued to support the use of these agents.[214]

Corticosteroids used in the manner described in the preceding have generally been well tolerated.[136] The principal side effects are oral candidiasis, mucocutaneous herpes simplex, and metabolic changes such as hyperglycemia. Concerns have been raised about increased frequency of cytomegalovirus, other fungi, and mycobacteria infections

but so far have not materialized. Nevertheless, the lack of efficacy of steroids in some studies,[213,214] along with the risk of other opportunistic infections and other possible complications, for example, increased morbidity of pneumothorax associated with the use of corticosteroids, emphasize the need for careful patient selection and follow-up.

Recommendations about the use of adjunctive corticosteroids in other *Pneumocystis* patient populations are difficult to formulate because of the limited available information. The limited studies that have been performed so far have suggested that corticosteroids may speed clinical improvement, but conflicting results have been obtained about whether survival is enhanced. The problem with non-HIV patients is that most of these individuals have been on corticosteroids shortly before or at the time they developed pneumocystosis. Rapid withdrawal of steroids may have serious adverse consequences, and thus it seems prudent either to maintain the current dose or return to the previous steroid dose when instituting anti-*Pneumocystis* therapy. The steroid dose can then be slowly tapered. The place of corticosteroids in non-HIV patients who have received immunosuppressive drugs other than steroids is unknown.

Future clinical advances in the treatment of pneumocystosis might come from several current lines of investigation. Although the development of a continuous culture system remains elusive, it might be possible to use molecular techniques to identify markers of virulence or antimicrobial resistance. Sequence variation in dihydropteroate synthetase, the target enzyme of sulfonamides, in human *Pneumocystis* have been identified.[215] These mutations at positions associated with sulfonamide resistance in other organisms have been associated with failure in prophylaxis but no clear association with treatment failure or altered outcome has been demonstrated. Mutations have also been described in the gene encoding cytochrome B and have been associated with failure of atovaquone prophylaxis.[216] New drugs with improved efficacy, less toxicity, and different mechanism of action are needed. Animal models, which are the principal test system, have identified several new types of drugs, for example, papulocandins, 8-aminoquinolines, diamidines; however, clinical trials have been held up because of market considerations. Caspofungin, a pneumocandin approved for use in *Aspergillus* and *Candida* infections, had good activity against *Pneumocystis* in animal studies. Manipulation of the host immune or inflammatory response might improve defenses against *Pneumocystis* while lessening their deleterious effects on the host. These studies might develop drugs with greater specificity than corticosteroids. Finally, there is increasing evidence that the physiological changes, which accompany the development of *Pneumocystis* pneumonia and result in lung injury, cannot be reversed by antimicrobial therapy alone; however, they can be improved by the administration of surfactant.[217,218] Clinical trials of surfactant or other agents that improve lung physiology are needed.

PREVENTION

Controlled studies demonstrating the safety and efficacy of daily or intermittent TMP-SMX in preventing pneumocystosis in pediatric cancer patients stimulated considerable interest in developing prophylactic regimens in HIV patients and other immunocompromised hosts.[1] Prophylaxis can be considered either primary (directed at the first bout of *Pneumocystis* pneumonia) or secondary (directed at recurrent episodes). The decision whether to institute chemoprophylaxis depends on such factors as the incidence of pneumocystosis in the target population as well as drug effectiveness, safety, ease of administration, and cost. Because none of the available anti-*Pneumocystis* drugs used in humans have proven to be lethal for *Pneumocystis,* they should be continued for as long as the immunosuppressive conditions exist.

An expert panel convened by the US Public Health Service (USPHS) and Infectious Disease Society of America (IDSA) has reviewed existing data and formulated general guidelines for the prevention of pneumocystosis in adult and pediatric HIV patients.[219] Chemoprophylaxis is indicated for all adults with CD4 counts less than 200/mm³, and adolescents (including those who are pregnant) with oropharyngeal candidiasis or unexplained fever greater than 100° F or 37.7° C for 2 weeks or longer, or who have recovered from a previous episode of pneumocystosis. Chemoprophylaxis is continued for life. Chemoprophylaxis is also indicated for children born to HIV-infected mothers beginning at 4 to 6 weeks of age. Medication should be continued until the child's HIV status is determined. If the child is infected with HIV, prophylaxis should be continued through the first year of life. The subsequent need for chemoprophylaxis is determined by age-specific CD4 counts.

Three drug regimens are currently recommended for *Pneumocystis* prophylaxis. The doses used here are for adults and adolescents; the USPHS/IDSA Guidelines should be consulted for doses in children. TMP-SMX, the drug of choice, is administered at a dose of one-double strength tablet (160 mg TMP to 800 mg SMX) per day. One single-strength tablet (80 mg TMP to 400 mg SMX) per day is very effective and one double-strength tablet three times per week is also acceptable. TMP-SMX protects not only against *Pneumocystis,* but also against *Toxoplasma gondii* and bacterial infections. Adverse reactions to TMP-SMX occur in up to 50% or more of the patients and require discontinuation of the drug in up to 30% to 40% of the cases. The frequency of side effects is somewhat lower with the use of single-strength tablets or three times per week administration. Guidelines for desensitization or rechallenge with TMP-SMX in prophylaxis are similar to those for use of TMP-SMX in treatment.

Recommended drug regimens for HIV patients who cannot tolerate TMP-SMX include dapsone and aerosol pentamidine. Dapsone may be administered at a dose of 100 mg per day alone or at a dose of 50 mg per day combined with 50 mg of pyrimethamine (a DHFR inhibitor) per week and 25 mg of leucovorin per week. Additional dose schedules have also been used. Overall, the dapsone regimens have shown efficacy and toxicity similar to those of the TMP-SMX regimens. Dapsone and pyrimethamine protect against *T. gondii* but not against bacterial infections. Atovaquone suspension at a dose of 1500 mg per day has been shown to have similar efficacy to dapsone in patients intolerant of TMP-SMX. Pentamidine is administered at a dose of 300 mg in a Respirgard nebulizer once per month. Aerosol pentamidine is less effective, better tolerated, and much more expensive than TMP-SMX or dapsone. The major side effects are cough and bronchospasm, which can be controlled by a β-agonist. Aerosol pentamidine requires a negative pressure room with adequate ventilation, and should not be performed in patients with tuberculosis.

A number of other drug regimens have been considered as possible *Pneumocystis* prophylactic agents, but there is insufficient supportive information to recommend their use. Examples include pyrimethamine combined with sulfonamides, for example, Fansidar, or clindamycin; pentamidine administered as an aerosol using other nebulizers or administered intravenously; and clindamycin plus primaquine. Prophylactic regimens for *Mycobacterium avium* complex that contain azithromycin or clarithromycin lower the frequency of pneumocystosis. Mycophenylate mofetil, an immunosuppressive agent, has demonstrated anti-*Pneumocystis* activity in experimental models.

Several studies have documented the safety of discontinuing primary and secondary *Pneumocystis* pneumonia prophylaxis in patients responding to active antiretroviral therapy. It is safe to discontinue primary and secondary prophylaxis in patients who have responded to anti-retroviral therapy with a CD4 cell increase to greater than 200 cells/mm³ that is sustained for longer than 3 months. However, patients who developed a prior episode of *Pneumocystis* pneumonia with CD4 cell levels of greater than 200 cells/mm³ should remain on secondary prophylaxis for life.

The widespread use of *Pneumocystis* chemoprophylaxis has had a major impact on the care of HIV patients.[220] Not only has this practice reduced the incidence of pneumocystosis, but it has also improved survival and quality of life while decreasing resource uti-

lization and cost. Despite this success, studies performed before the introduction of the protease inhibitors showed that breakthrough cases of *Pneumocystis* pneumonia occurred in about 20% of patients.[221] The most important predictor of failure was very low (less than 50 to 100/mm³) CD4 counts.[221,222] These breakthrough infections may also have atypical manifestations, particularly in patients taking aerosol pentamidine.[223] Examples include upper lobe disease, pneumothorax, and extrapulmonary pneumocystosis, and fever of unknown origin.

In contrast to HIV patients, there are no national guidelines for *Pneumocystis* prophylaxis in other immunocompromised hosts. The need for such guidelines is illustrated by the fact that cases of pneumocystosis continue to occur in non-HIV patients despite the availability of safe and effective drugs.[81,224] Based on the available literature, chemoprophylaxis should be considered in patients with the following conditions: (1) primary immune deficiency diseases; (2) severe protein malnutrition; (3) organ transplantation; (4) persistent CD4 counts of less than 200/mm³; and (5) cytotoxic or immunosuppressive therapy for the treatment of cancer of all types, collagen vascular diseases, and other disorders. If a corticosteroid is the sole drug, a reasonable guide for the need for *Pneumocystis* prophylaxis is the equivalent of 20 mg of prednisone for more than 1 month.[81] Some authors have excluded diseases, for example, asthma, which are usually not associated with *Pneumocystis* from this recommendation[81]; however, in light of case reports of pneumocystosis in children with asthma,[85] these recommendations may become blurred.

TMP-SMX is the chemoprophylactic agent of choice and should be used in the same doses as are used in HIV patients. Although there is limited clinical experience with dapsone + pyrimethamine and aerosol pentamidine, there is no reason to doubt the effectiveness of these agents in non-HIV patients.

Another method of preventing pneumocystosis is to boost the host immune response. This could be done either by improving general immune function or focusing on organism-specific immunity. In the latter case, MSG is one potential candidate but other antigens might also be explored. Immunization of immunocompromised patients at an early stage of their disease, for example, HIV patients with a higher than 500 CD4 cell count or newly diagnosed cancer patients might prevent, delay, or lessen the severity of pneumocystosis. Boosting the host immune response might also lessen the need for, or lower the dose of, antimicrobial drugs. Alternate approaches involve administration of specific antibodies or cytokines.

A third method of preventing pneumocystosis is by preventing exposure. The communicability of *Pneumocystis* has been shown in experimental animals.[5] However, infection control guidelines for health care facilities have not recommended isolating *Pneumocystis* patients because person-to-person transmission has seldom been convincingly demonstrated and the disease was thought to occur by reactivation of latent infection. This attitude seems to be changing because of the continued occurrence of outbreaks or cluster of pneumocystosis; the development of sensitive techniques to detect *Pneumocystis* DNA in asymptomatic individuals and the air; and the ability to distinguish among *Pneumocystis* isolates, paticularly in patients with recurrent episodes of pneumocystosis. The practice of isolating *Pneumocystis* patients from direct contact with other immunocompromised hosts, which has long been advocated by the authors and others, is now recommended by the CDC Hospital Infection Control Practice Advisory Committee[225] but not yet by the USPHS/IDSA Opportunistic Infectious Working Group.[226] The conflicting results of studies of the presence of *Pneumocystis* in health care workers and other healthy individuals illustrate the difficulties in investigating the transmission of this infection. Little is also know about the behavior of the organism in the environment, although a recent study suggests *Pneumocystis* is susceptible to common antiseptic agents.[227] Despite these limitations, recent advances in our technology offer promise of providing valuable insight into the epidemiological features of this interesting and enigmatic organism.

REFERENCES

1. Barry SM, Johnson MA. *Pneumocystis carinii* pneumonia: A review of current issues in diagnosis and management. HIV Med. 2001;2:123-132.
1a. Thomas CF, Limper AH. *Pneumocystis* pneumonia. N Engl J Med. 2004;350:2487-2498.
2. Wakefield AE. *Pneumocystis carinii*. Br Med Bull 2002;61:175-188.
3. Stringer JR, Beard CB, Miller RF, Wakefield AE. A new name *Pneumocystis jirovecii* for Pneumocystis from humans. Emerg Infect Dis. 2002;8:891-896.
4. Sloand E, Laughon B, Armstrong M, et al. The challenge of *Pneumocystis carinii* culture. J Euk Microbiol. 1993;40:188-195.
5. Cushion M. *Pneumocystis carinii*. In: Collier L, Balows A, Sussman M, eds. Topley and Wilson's Microbiology and Microbial Infections, v. 4. New York: Oxford University Press; 1998:645-683.
6. Schmatz DM, Powles M, McFadden DC, et al. Treatment and prevention of *Pneumocystis carinii* pneumonia and further elucidation of the *P. carinii* life cycle with 1,3-beta-glucan synthesis inhibitor L-671,329. J Protozool. 1991;38:151S-153S.
7. Kaneshiro ES. *Pneumocystis carinii* pneumonia: The status of Pneumocystis biochemistry. Int J Parasitol. 1998;28:65-84.
8. De Stefano JA, Myers JD, Du Pont D, et al. Cell wall antigens of *Pneumocystis carinii* trophozoites and cysts: Purification and carbohydrate analysis of these glycoproteins. J Euk Microbiol. 1998;45:334-343.
9. Kaneshiro ES. The lipids of *Pneumocystis carinii*. Clin Microbiol Rev. 1998;11:27-41.
10. Smulian AG, Keely SP, Sunkin SM, et al. Genetic and antigenic variation in *Pneumocystis carinii* organisms: Tools for examining the epidemiology and pathogenesis of infection. J Lab Clin Med. 1997;130:461-468.
11. Linke MJ, Sunkin SM, Andrews RP, et al. Expression, structure, and location of epitopes of the major surface glycoprotein of *Pneumocystis carinii* f. sp *carinii*. Clin Diagn Lab Immunol. 1998;5:50-57.
12. Gigliotti F, Hughes WT. Passive immunoprophylaxis with specific monoclonal antibody confers partial protection against *Pneumocystis carinii* pneumonitis in animal models. J Clin Invest. 1988;81:1666-1668.
13. Gigliotti F, Haidaris CG, Wright TW, Harmsen AG. Passive intranasal monoclonal antibody prophylaxis against murine *Pneumocystis carinii* pneumonia. Infect Immun. 2002;70:1069-1074.
14. Theus SA, Smulian AG, Sullivan D, et al. Cytokine responses to the native and recombinant forms of the major surface glycoprotein of *Pneumocystis carinii*. Clin Exp Immunol. 1997;109:255-260.
15. Theus SA, Andrews RP, Steele P, Walzer PD. Adoptive transfer of lymphocytes sensitized to the major surface glycoprotein of *Pneumocystis carinii* confers protection in the rat. J Clin Invest. 1995;95:2587-2593.
16. Theus SA, Smulian AG, Steele P, et al. Immunization with the major surface glycoprotein of *Pneumocystis carinii* elicits a protective response in the rat. Vaccine. 1998;16:1149-1157.
17. Stringer JR, Keely SP. Genetics of surface antigen expression in *Pneumocystis carinii*. Infect Immun. 2001;69:627-639.
18. Kutty G, Ma L, Kovacs JA. Characterization of the expression site of the major surface glycoprotein of human-derived *Pneumcystis carinii*. Mol Microbiol. 2001;42:183-193.
19. Pottratz ST, Paulsrud J, Smith JS, et al. *Pneumocystis carinii* attachment to cultured lung cells by pneumocystis gp 120, a fibronectin binding protein. J Clin Invest. 1991;88:403-407.
20. Ezekowitz RAB, Williams DJ, Koziel H, et al. Uptake of *Pneumocystis carinii* mediated by the macrophage mannose receptor. Nature. 1991;351:155-158.
21. Limper AH. Vitronectin binds to *Pneumocystis carinii* and mediates organism attachment to cultured lung epithelial cells. Infect Immun. 1993;61:4302-4309.
22. McCormack FX, Festa AL, Andrews RP, et al. The carbohydrate binding domain of surfactant protein A mediates binding to the major surface glycoprotein of *Pneumocystis carinii*. Biochemistry. 1997;36:8092-8099.
23. O'Riordan DM, Standing JE, Kwon KY, et al. Surfactant protein D interacts with *Pneumocystis carinii* and mediates organism adherence to alveolar macrophages. J Clin Invest. 1995;95:2699-2710.
24. Lugli EB, Bampton ET, Ferguson DJ, Wakefield AE. Cell surface protease PRT1 identified in the fungal pathogen *Pneumocystis carinii*. Mol Microbiol. 1999;31:1723-1733.
25. Schaffzin JK, Sunkin SM, Stringer JR. A new family of *Pneumocystis carinii* genes related to those encoding the major surface glycoprotein. Curr Genet. 1999;35:134-143.
26. Kutty G, Kovacs JA. A single copy gene encodes Kex 1, a serine endoprogtease of *Pneumocystis jirovecii*. Infect Immun. 2003;71:571-574.
27. Smulian AG, Stringer JR, Linke MJ, et al. Isolation and characterization of a recombinant antigen of *Pneumocystis carinii*. Infect Immun. 1992;60:907-915.
28. Theus SA, Sullivan DW, Walzer PD, et al. Cellular immune response to a 55 kilodalton recombinant *Pneumocystis carinii* antigen. Infect Immun. 1994;62:3479-3484.
29. Smulian AG, Sullivan DW, Theus SA. Immunization with recombinant *Pneumocystis carinii* p55 antigen provides partial protection against infection: Characterization of epitope recognition associated with immunization. Microbes Infect. 2000;2:127-136.
30. Walzer PD. Immunological features of *Pneumocystis carinii* infection in humans. Clin Diag Lab Immunol. 1999;6:149-155.
31. Vargas SL, Hughes WT, Santolaya ME, et al. Search for primary infection by *Pneumocystis carinii* in a cohort of normal, healthy infants. Clin Infect Dis. 2001;32:855-861.
32. Russian DA, Kovacs JA. *Pneumocystis carinii* in Africa: An emerging pathogen? Lancet. 1995;346:1242-1243.
33. Fisk DT, Meshnick S, Kazanjian PH. *Pneumocystis carinii* pneumonia in patients in the developing world who have acquired immunodeficiency syndrome. Clin Infect Dis. 2003;36:70-78.
34. Hu DJ, Fleming PL, Castro KG, et al. How important is race/ethnicity as an indicator of risk for specific AIDS-defining conditions? J Acquir Immun Defic Syndr Hum Retrovirol. 1995;10:374-380.
35. Keely SP, Baughman RP, Smulian AG, et al. Source of *Pneumocystis carinii* in recurrent episodes of pneumonia in AIDS patients. AIDS. 1996;10:881-888.
36. Beard CB, Carter JL, Keely SP, et al. Genetic variation in *Pneumocystis carinii* isolates from different geopgraphic regions: Implications for transmission. Emerg Infect Dis. 2000;6:265-272.
37. Huang L, Beard CB, Creasman J, et al. Sulfa or sulfone prophylaxis and geographic region predict mutations of *Pneumocystis carinii* dihydropteroate synthase gene. J Infect Dis. 2000;182:1192-1198.
38. Walzer PD, Kim CK, Cushion MT. *Pneumocystis carinii*. In: Walzer PD, Genta RM, eds. Parasitic Infections in the Compromised Host. New York: Marcel Dekker; 1989:83-178.
39. Dohn MN, White ML, Vigdorth EM, et al. Geographic clustering of *Pneumocystis carinii* pneumonia in patients with HIV infection. Am J Respir Crit Care Med. 2000; 162:1617-1621.
40. Morris AM, Swanson M, Ha H, Huang L. Geographic distribution of human immunodeficiency virus-associated *Pneumocystis carinii* pneumonia in San Francisco. Am J Respir Crit Care Med. 2000;162:1622-1626.
41. Pottratz ST, Weir AL. Attachment of *Pneumocystis carinii* to primary cultures of rat alveolar epithelial cells. Exp Cell Res. 1995;221:357-362.
42. Smulian AG, Ryan M, Staben C, et al. Signal transduction in *Pneumocystis carinii*: characterization of the genes pcg1 encoding the alpha subunit of the G protein PCG1 of *Pneumocystis carinii carinii* and *Pneumocystis carinii ratti*. Infect Immun. 1996;64:691-701.
43. Gustafson MP, Thomas CF Jr, Rusnak F, et al. Differential regulation of growth and checkpoint control mediated by a Cdc25 mitotic phosphatase from *Pneumocystis carinii*. J Biol Chem. 2001;276:835-843.
44. Fox D, Smulian AG. Mitogen-activated protein kinase Mkp1 of *Pneumocystis carinii* complements the slt2Delta defect in the cell integrity pathway of Saccharomyces cerevisiae. Mol Microbiol. 1999;34:451-462.
45. Smulian AG, Sesterhenn T, Tanaka R, et al. The ste3 pheromone receptor gene of *Pneumocystis carinii* is surrounded by a cluster of signal transduction genes. Genetics 2001;157:991-1002.
46. Kottom TJ, Limper AH. Cell wall assembly by *Pneumocystis carinii*. Evidence for a unique gsc-1 subunit mediating beta -1,3-glucan deposition. J Biol Chem. 2000;275:40628-40634.
47. Limper AH, Edens M, Anders RA, et al. *Pneumocystis carinii* inhibits cyclin-dependent kinase activity in lung epithelial cells. J Clin Invest. 1998;101:1148-1155.
48. Yu ML, Limper AH. *Pneumocystis carinii* induces ICAM-1 expression in lung epithelial cells through a TNF-alpha-mediated mechanism. Am J Physiol. 1997;273:L1103-L1111.
49. Bartlett MS, Angus WC, Shaw MM, et al. Antibody to *Pneumocystis carinii* protects rats and mice from developing pneumonia. Clin Diagn Lab Immun. 1998;5:74-77.
50. Harmsen AG, Chen W, Gigliotti F. Active immunity to *Pneumocystis carinii* reinfection in T-cell-depleted mice. Infect Immun. 1995;63:2391-2395.
51. Zheng M, Shellito JE, Marrero L, et al. CD4+ T cell-independent vaccination against *Pneumocystis carinii* in mice. J Clin Invest. 2001:108:1469-1474.
52. Garvy BA, Wiley JA, Gigliotti F, et al. Protection against *Pneumocystis carinii* pneumonia by antibodies generated from either T helper 1 or T helper 2 responses. Infect Immun. 1997;65:5052-5056.
53. Peglow SL, Smulian AG, Linke MJ, et al. Serologic responses to *Pneumocystis carinii* antigens in health and disease. J Infect Dis. 1990;161:296-306.
54. Elvin K, Bjorkman A, Heurlin N, et al. Seroreactivity to *Pneumocystis carinii* in patients with AIDS verus other immunosuppressed patients. Scand J Infect Dis. 1994;26:33-40.
55. Laursen AL, Andersen PL. Low levels of IgG antibodies against *Pneumocystis carinii* among HIV-infected patients. Scand J Infect Dis. 1998;30:495-499.
56. Lundgren B, Lundgren JD, Nielsen T, et al. Antibody responses to a major *Pneumocystis carinii* antigen in human immunodeficiency virus-infected patients with and without *P. carinii* pneumonia. J Infect Dis. 1992;165:1151-1155.
57. Daly K, Tanka R, Linke MJ, et al. Serologic responses to epitopes of the major surface glycoprotein of *Pneumocystis jirovecii* differ in human immunodeficiency virus-infected and uninfected persons. J Infect Dis. 2002;186:644-651.
58. Daly KR, Koch J, Levin L, Walzer PD. Enzyme-linked immunosorbent assay and serologic responses to *Pneumocystis jirovecii*. Emerg Infect Dis. 2004;10:848-854.
59. Laursen AL, Jensen BN, Andersen PL. Local antibodies against *Pneumocystis carinii* in bronchoalveolar lavage fluid. Eur Respir J. 1994;7:679-685.
60. Jalil A, Moja C, Lambert M, et al. Decreased production of local immunoglobulin A to *Pneumocystis carinii* in bronchoalveolar lavage fluid of human immunodeficiency virus-positive patients. Infect Immun. 2000;68:1054-1060.
61. Walzer PD, Kim CK, Linke MJ, et al. Outbreaks of *Pneumocystis carinii* pneumonia in colonies of immunodeficient mice. Infect Immun. 1989;57:62-70.
62. Furuta T, Fujita M, Machii K, et al. Fatal spontaneous pneumocystosis in nude rats. Lab Anim Sci. 1993;43:551-556.

63. Harmsen AG, Stankiewicz M. Requirement to CD4+ cells in resistance to *Pneumocystis carinii* pneumonia in mice. J Exp Med. 1990;172:937-945.

64. Shellito J, Suzara VV, Blumenfeld W, et al. A new model of *Pneumocystis carinii* infection in mice selectively depleted of helper T lymphocytes. J Clin Invest. 1990;85:1686-1693.

65. Wiley JA, Harmsen AG. CD 40 ligand is required for resolution of *Pneumocystis carinii* pneumonia in mice. J Immunol. 1995;155:3525-3529.

66. Levy J, Espanol-Boren T, Fischer A, et al. Clinical spectrum of X-linked hyper-IgM syndrome. J Pediatr. 1997;131:47-54.

67. Beck JM, Newbury RL, Palmer BE, et al. Role of CD8+ lymphocytes in host defense against *Pneumocystis carinii* in mice. J Lab Clin Med. 1996;128:477-487.

68. Kolls JK, Habetz S, Shean MK, et al. IFN-γ and CD8+ T cells restore host defenses against *Pneumocystis carinii* in mice depleted of CD4+ T cells. J Immunol 1999;162:2890-2894.

69. Steele C, Zheng M, Marrero L, et al. Increased host resistance against *Pneumocystis carinii* in γδ T-cell-deficient mice: Protective role of gamma interferon and CD8+ T cells. Infect Immun. 2002;70:5208-5215.

70. Garvy BA, Qureshi MH. Delayed inflammatory response to *Pneumocystis carinii* infection in neonatal mice due to an inadequate lung environment. J Immunol. 2000;165:6480-6486.

71. Qureshi MH, Garvy BA. Neonatal T cells in an adult lung environment are competent to resolve *Pneumocystis carinii* pneumonia. J Immunol. 2001;166:5704-5711.

72. Phair J, Munoz A, Detels R, et al. The risk of *Pneumocystis carinii* pneumonia among men infected with immunodeficiency virus type 1. N Engl J Med. 1990;322:161-165.

73. Smith,DK, Neal JJ, Holmberg SD, et al. Idiopathic CD4+ T-lymphocytopenia Task Force. Unexplained opportunistic infections and CD4+ T-lymphocytopenia without HIV infection. N Engl J Med. 1993;328:373-379.

74. Kulke MH, Vance EA. *Pneumocystis carinii* pneumonia in patients receiving chemotherapy for breast cancer. Clin Infect Dis. 1997;25:215-218.

75. Mansharamani NG, Balachandran D, Vernofsky I, et al. Peripheral blood CD4 T lymphocyte counts during *Pneumocystis carinii* pneumonia in immunocompromised patients without HIV infection. Chest. 2000;118:712-720.

76. Agostini C, Adami F, Poulter LW, et al. Role of bronchoalveolar lavage in predicting survival of patients with human immunodeficiency virus infection. Am J Respir Crit Care Med. 1997;156:1501-1507.

77. Li Pira G, Fenoglio D, Bottone L, et al. Preservation of clonal heterogeneity of the *Pneumocystis carinii*-specific CD4 T cell repertoire in HIV infected, asymptomatic individuals. Clin Exp Immunol. 2002;128:155-162.

78. Koziel H, Kim S, Reardon C, et al. Enhanced in vivo human immunodeficiency virus-1 replication in the lungs of human immunodeficiency virus-infected persons with *Pneumocystis carinii* pneumonia. Am J Respir Crit Care Med. 1999;160:2048-2055.

79. Semenzato G, Agostini C, Ometto L, et al. CD8+ T lymphocytes in the lung of acquired immunodeficiency syndrome patients harbor human immunodeficiency virus type 1. Blood 1995;85:2308-2314.

80. Theus SA, Sawhney N, Smulian AG, et al. Proliferation and cytokine responses of human T lymphocytes isolated from HIV patients to the major surface glycoprotein of *Pneumocystis carinii*. J Infect Dis. 1998;177:238-241.

81. Sepkowitz KA, Brown AE, Armstrong D. *Pneumocystis carinii* pneumonia without acquired immunodeficiency syndrome. More patients, same risk. Arch Intern Med. 1995;155:1125-1128.

82. Yale SH, Limper AH. *Pneumocystis carinii* pneumonia in patients without acquired immunodeficiency syndrome: associated illness and prior corticosteroid therapy. Mayo Clin Proc. 1996;71:5-13.

83. Godeau B, Coutant-Perronne V, Le Thi Houng D, et al. *Pneumocystis carinii* pneumonia in the course of connective tissue disease: report of 34 cases. J Rheumatol. 1994;21:246-251.

84. Graham BS, Tucker WS. Opportunistic infections in endogenous Cushing's syndrome. Ann Intern Med. 1984;101:334-338.

85. Abernathy-Carver KJ, Fan LL, Boguniewicz M, et al. Legionella and Pneumocystis pneumonias in asthmatic children on high doses of systemic steroids. Pediatr Pulmonol. 1994;18:135-138.

86. Limper AH, Hoyte JS, Standing JE. The role of alveolar macrophages in *Pneumocystis carinii* degradation and clearance from the lung. J Clin Invest. 1997;99:2110-2117.

87. Hanano R, Reifenberg K, Kaufmann SH. Activated pulmonary macrophages are insufficient for resistance against *Pneumocystis carinii*. Infect Immun. 1998;66:305-314.

88. Beck JM, Preston AM, Gyethko MR. Urokinase-type plasminogen activator in inflammatory cell recruitment and host defense against *Pneumocystis carinii* in mice. Infect Immun. 1999;67:879-884.

89. Fox D, Smulian AG. Plasminogen-binding activity of enolase in the opportunistic pathogen *Pneumocystis carinii*. Med Mycol. 2001;39:495-507.

90. Neese LW, Standing JE, Olson EJ, et al. Vitronectin, fibronectin, and gp120 antibody enhance macrophage release of TNF-alpha in response to *Pneumocystis carinii*. J Immunol. 1994;152:4549-4556.

91. Laursen AL, Moller B, Rungby J, et al. *Pneumocystis carinii*-induced activation of the respiratory burst in human monocytes and macrophages. Clin Exp Immunol. 1994;98:196-202.

92. Vassallo R, Kottom TJ, Standing JE, et al. Vitronectin and fibronectin function as glucan binding proteins augmenting macrophage responses to *Pneumocystis carinii*. Am J Respir Cell Mol Biol. 2001;25:203-211.

93. Vassallo R, Standing JE, Limper AH. Isolated *Pneumocystis carinii* cell wall glucan provokes lower respiratory tract inflammatory responses. J Immunol. 2000;164:3755-3763.

94. Shellito JE, Kolls JK, Olariu R, et al. Nitric oxide and host defense against *Pneumocystis carinii* infection in a mouse model. J Infect Dis. 1996;73:432-439.

95. Downing JF, Kachel DL, Pasula R, et al. Gamma interferon stimulates rat alveolar macrophages to kill *Pneumocystis carinii* by L-arginine- and tumor necrosis factor-dependent mechanisms. Infect Immun. 1999;67:1347-1352.

96. Kandil O, Fishman JA, Koziel H, et al. Human immunodeficiency virus type 1 infection of human macrophages modulates the cytokine response to *Pneumocystis carinii*. Infect Immun. 1994;62:644-650.

97. Koziel H, Eichbaum Q, Kruskal BA, et al. Reduced binding and phagocytosis of *Pneumocystis carinii* by alveolar macrophages from persons infected with HIV-1 correlates with mannose receptor downregulation. J Clin Invest. 1998;102:1332-1344.

98. Fraser IP, Takahashi K, Koziel H, et al. *Pneumocystis carinii* enhance soluble mannose receptor production by macrophages. Microbes Infect. 2000;2:1305-1310.

99. Stehle SE, Rogers RA, Harmsen AG, et al. A soluble mannose receptor immunoadhesin enhances phagocytosis of *Pneumocystis carinii* by human polymorphonuclear leukocytes in vitro. Scan J Immunol. 2000;52:131-137.

100. Laursen AL, Rungby J, Andersen PL. Decreased activation of the respiratory burst in neutophils from AIDS patients with previous *Pneumocystis carinii* pneumonia. J Infect Dis. 1995;172:497-505.

101. Warschkau H, Yu H, Kiderlen AF. Activation and suppression of natural cellular immune functions by *Pneumocystis carinii*. Immunobiology. 1998;198:343-360.

102. Bonagura VR, Cunningham-Rundles S, Edwards BL, et al. Common variable hypogammaglobulinemia, recurrent *Pneumocystis carinii* pneumonia on intravenous γ-globulin therapy, and natural killer deficiency. Clin Immunol Immunopathol. 1995;51:216-223.

103. Limper AH. Tumor necrosis factor α-mediated host defense against *Pneumocystis carinii*. Am J Respir Cell Mol Biol. 1997;16:110-111.

104. Chen W, Havell EA, Moldawer LL, et al. Interleukin 1: An important mediator of host resistance against *Pneumocystis carinii* infection. J Exp Med. 1992;176:713-718.

105. Chen W, Havell EA, Gigliotti F, et al. Interleukin-6 production in a murine model of *Pneumocystis carinii* pneumonia: Relation to resistance and inflammatory response. Infect Immun. 1992;61:97-102.

106. Beck JM, Liggitt HD, Brunette EN, et al. Reduction in intensity of *Pneumocystis carinii* pneumonia in mice by aerosol administration of interferon-gamma. Infect Immun. 1991;59:3859-3862.

107. Paine R 3rd, Preston AM, Wilcoxen S, et al. Granulocyte-macrophage colony-stimulating factor in the innate immune response to *Pneumocystis carinii* pneumonia in mice. J Immunol. 2000;164:2602-2609.

108. Rudmann DG, Preston AM, Moore MW, et al. Susceptibility to *Pneumocystis carinii* in mice is dependent on simultaneous deletion of INF-γ and type 1 and 2 TNF receptor genes. J Immunol. 1998;161:360-366.

109. Garvy BA, Ezekowitz RAB, Harmsen AG. Role of gamma interferon in the host immune and inflammatory responses to *Pneumocystis carinii* infection. Infect Immun. 1997;65:373-379.

110. Quereshi MH, Garmsen AG, Garvey BA. IL-10 moculates host responses and lung damage induced by *Pneumocystis carinii* infection. J Immunol. 2003;170:1002-1009.

111. Ikei R, Furuta T, Asano S. Effect of recombinant human granulocyte colony stimulating factor on *Pneumocystis carinii* infection in nude mice. Jpn J Exp Med. 1989;59:51-58.

112. Wright TW, Johnston CJ, Harmsen AG, et al. Analysis of cytokine mRNA profiles in the lungs of *Pneumocystis carinii*-infected mice. Am J Respir Cell Mol Biol. 1997;17:491-500.

113. Perenboom RM, Beckers P, Van Der Meer JW, et al. Pro-inflammatory cytokines in lung and blood during steroid-induced *Pneumocystis carinii* pneumonia in rats. J Leukoc Biol. 1996;60:710-715.

114. Perenboom RM, Sauerwein RW, Beckers P, et al. Cytokine profiles in bronchoalveolar lavage fluid and blood in HIV-seropositive patients with *Pneumocystis carinii* pneumonia. Eur J Clin Invest. 1997;27:333-339.

115. Perenboom RM, van Schijndel AC, Beckers P, et al. Cytokine profiles in bronchoalveolar lavage fluid and blood in HIV-seronegative patients with *Pneumocystis carinii* pneumonia. Eur J Clin Invest. 1996;26:159-166.

116. Travis WD, Pittaluga S, Lipschik GY, et al. Atypical pathologic manifestations of *Pneumocystis carinii* pneumonia in the acquired immune deficiency syndrome. Review of 123 lung biopsies from 76 patients with emphasis on cysts, vascular invasion, vasculitis, and granulomas. Am J Surg Pathol. 1990;14:615-625.

117. Benfield TL, Prento P, Junge J, et al. Alveolar damage in AIDS-related *Pneumocystis carinii* pneumonia. Chest. 1997;111:1193-1199.

118. Stansell JD, Hopewell PC. *Pneumocystis carinii* pneumonia: Risk factor, clinical presentation and natural history. In: Sattler FR, Walzer PD. *Pneumocystis carinii*. London: Bailliére Tindall; 1995:449-459.

119. D'Angelo E, Calderini E, Robatto FM, et al. Lung and chest wall mechanics in patients with acquired immunodeficiency syndrome and severe *Pneumocystis carinii* pneumonia. Eur Respir J. 1997;10:2343-23250.

120. Su TH, Natarajan V, Kachel DL, et al. Functional impairment of bronchoalveolar lavage phospholipids in early *Pneumocystis carinii* pneumonia in rats. J Lab Clin Med. 1996;127:263-271.

121. Hoffman AGD, Lawrence MG, Ognibene FP, et al. Reduction of pulmonary surfactant in patients with human immunodeficiency virus and *Pneumocystis carinii* pneumonia. Chest. 1992;102:1730-1736.

122. Rice WR, Singleton FM, Linke MJ, et al. Regulation of surfactant phosphatidylcholine secretion from alveolar type II cells during *Pneumocystis carinii* pneumonia in the rat. J Clin Invest. 1993;92:2778-2882.

123. Lipschik GY, Treml JF, Moore SD, et al. *Pneumocystis carinii* glycoprotein A inhibits surfactant phospholipid secretion by rat alveolar type II cells. J Infect Dis. 1998;177:182-187.

124. Steinberg RI, Whitsett JA, Hull WM, et al. *Pneumocystis carinii* alters surfactant protein A concentrations in bronchoalveolar lavage fluid. J Lab Clin Med. 1995;125:462-469.

125. Beers MF, Atochina EN, Preston AM, et al. Inhibition of lung surfactant protein B expression during *Pneumocystis carinii* pneumonia in mice. J Lab Clin Med. 1999;133:406-407.

126. Atochina EN, Beck JM, Scanlon ST, et al. *Pneumocystis carinii* pneumonia alters expression and distribution of lung collectins SP-A and SP-D. J Lab Clin Med. 2001;137:429-439.

127. Wright TW, Gigliotti F, Finkelstein JN, et al. Immune mediated inflammation directly impairs pulmonary function contributing to the pathogenesis of *Pneumocystis carinii* pneumonia J Clin Invest. 1999;104:1307-1317.

128. Wright TW, Johnston CJ, Harmsen AG, Finkelstein JN. Chemokine gene expression during *Pneumocystis carinii*-driven pulmonary inflammation. Infect Immun. 1999;67:3452-3460.

129. Wright TW, Notter RH, Wang Z, et al. Pulmonary inflammation disrupts surfactant function during *Pneumocystis carinii* pneumonia. Infect Immun. 2001;69:758-764.

130. Hori S, Thiago L, Demengeot J. CD25+ regulatory T cells suppress CD4+ T cell-mediated pulmonary hyperinflammation driven by *Pneumocystis carinii* in immunodeficient mice. Eur J Iimmunol. 2002;32;1282-1291.

131. Thullen TD, Ashbaugh AD, Daly KR, et al. Sensitized splenocytes result in deleterious response in rats with *Pneumocystis* pneumonia despite the presence of corticosteroids. Infect Immun. 2004;72;757-765.

132. Mason GR, Hashimoto CH, Dickman PS, et al. Prognostic implications of bronochoalveolar lavage neutrophilia in patients with *Pneumocystis carinii* pneumonia and AIDS. Am Rev Respir Dis. 1989;139:1336-1342.

133. Benfield TL, Vestbo J, Junge J, et al. Prognostic value of interleukin-8 in AIDS-associated *Pneumocystis carinii* pneumonia. Am J Respir Crit Care Med. 1995;151:1058-1062.

134. Benfield TL, Kharazmi A, Larsen CG, et al. Neutrophil chemotactic activity in bronchoalveolar lavage fluid of patients with AIDS-associated *Pneumocystis carinii* pneumonia. Scand J Infect Dis. 1997;29:367-371.

135. Benfield TL, Lundgren B, Levine SJ, et al. The major surface glycoprotein of *Pneumocystis carinii* induces release and gene expression of interleukin-8 and tumor necrosis factor alpha in monocytes. Infect Immun. 1997;65:4790-4794.

136. The National Institutes of Health—University of California Expert Panel for Corticosteroids as Adjunctive Therapy for *Pneumocystis carinii* Pneumonia. Consensus statement on the use of corticosteroids as adjunctive therapy for *Pneumocystis* pneumonia in the acquired immunodeficiency syndrome. N Engl J Med. 1990;323:1500-1504.

137. Benfield TL, van Steenwijk R, Nielsen TL, et al. Interleukin-8 and eicosanoid production in the lung during moderate to severe *Pneumocystis carinii* pneumonia in AIDS: A role of interleukin-8 in the pathogenesis of *P. carinii* pneumonia. Respir Med. 1995;89:285-290.

138. Huang ZB, Eden E. Effect of corticosteroids on IL1 beta and TNF alpha release by alveolar macrophages from patients with AIDS and *Pneumocystis carinii* pneumonia. Chest. 1993;104:751-755.

139. Benfield TL, Schattenkerk JK, Hofmann B, et al. Differential effect on serum neopterin and serum beta 2-microglobulin is induced by treatment in *Pneumocystis carinii* pneumonia. J Infect Dis. 1994;169:1170-1173.

140. Dichter JR, Lundgren JD, Nielsen TL, et al. *Pneumocystis carinii* pneumonia in H-infected patients: Effect of steroid therapy on surfactant level. Respir Med. 1999;93:373-378.

141. Dohn MN, Frame PT. Clinical manifestations in adults. In: Walzer PD, ed. *Pneumocystis carinii* Pneumonia. New York: Marcel Dekker; 1994:331-359.

142. Haverkos HW. Assessment of therapy for *Pneumocystis carinii* pneumonia. Am J Med. 1984;76:501-508.

143. Kovacs JA, Hiemenz JW, Macher AM, et al. *Pneumocystis carinii* pneumonia: A comparison between patients with the acquired immunodeficiency syndrome and patients with other immunodeficiencies. Ann Intern Med. 1984;100:663-671.

144. Chen HX, Ryan PA, Ferguson RP, et al. Characteristics of acquired immunodeficiency syndrome in older adults. J Am Geriatr Soc. 1998;46:153-156.

145. Laing R, Brettle R, Leen C, et al. Features and outcome of *Pneumocystis carinii* pneumonia according to risk category for HIV infection. Scand J Infect Dis. 1997;29:57-61.

146. Fishman JA. Radiological approaches to the diagnosis of *Pneumocystis carinii* pneumonitis. In: Walzer PD, ed. *Pneumocystis carinii* Pneumonia. New York: Marcel Dekker; 1994:415-436.

147. Fahy JV, Chin DP, Schnapp LM, et al. Effect of aerosolized pentamidine prophylaxis on the clinical severity and diagnosis of *Pneumocystis carinii* pneumonia. Am Rev Respir Dis. 1992;146:844-848.

148. Richards PJ, Riddell L, Reznek RH, et al. High resolution computer tomography in HIV patients with suspected *Pneumocystis carinii* pneumonia and a normal chest radiograph. Clin Radiol. 1996;51:689-693.

149. Tumeh SS, Belville JS, Pugatch R, et al. Ga-67 scintigraphy and computed tomography in the diagnosis of *Pneumocystis carinii* pneumonia in patients with AIDS. A prospective comparison. Clin Nucl Med. 1992;17:387-394.

150. Goldenberg DM, Sharkey RM, Udem S, et al. *Pneumocystis carinii* pneumonia in AIDS patients: A new method of diagnosis by radioimmunodetection immunoscintigraphy . J Nucl Med. 1994;35:1028-1034.

151. Benson CA, Spear J, Hines D, et al. Combined APACHE II score and serum lactate dehydrogenase as predictors of in-hospital mortality caused by first episode *Pneumocystis carinii* pneumonia in patients with acquired immunodeficiency syndrome. Am Rev Respir Dis. 1991;144:319-323.

152. Ng VL, Yajko DM, Hadley WK. Extrapulmonary pneumocystosis. Clin Microbiol Rev. 1997;10:401-418.

153. Afessa B, Green W, Chiao J, et al. Pulmonary complications of HIV infection: Autopsy findings. Chest. 1998:113:1225-1229.

154. Chary-Reddy S, Graves DC. Identification of extrapulmonary *Pneumocystis carinii* in immunocompromised rats by PCR. J Clin Microbiol. 1996;34:1660-1665.

155. Gruden JF, Huang L, Turner J, et al. High-resolution CT in the evaluation of clinically suspected *Pneumocystis carinii* pneumonia in AIDS patients with normal, equivocal, or nonspecific radiographic findings. AJR. 1997;169:967-975.

156. Huang L, Stansell J, Osmond D, et al. Performance of an algorithm to detect *Pneumocystis carinii* pneumonia in symptomatic HIV-infected persons. Pulmonary Complications of HIV Study Group. Chest. 1999;115:1025-1032.

157. Montaner JS, Zala C. The role of the laboratory in the diagnosis and management of AIDS-related *Pneumocystis carinii* pneumonia. In: Sattler FR, Walzer PD. *Pneumocystis carinii*. London: Bailliére Tindall; 1995:471-485.

158. Kroe DM, Kirsch CM, Jensen WA. Diagnostic strategies for *Pneumocystis carinii* pneumonia. Semin Respir Infect. 1997;12:70-78.

159. Baughman RP. Current methods of diagnosis. In: Walzer PD, ed. *Pneumocystis carinii* Pneumonia. New York: Marcel Dekker; 1994:381-401.

160. Aslanzadeh J, Stelmach PS. Detection of *Pneumocystis carinii* with direct fluorescence antibody and calcofluor white stain. Infection. 1996;24:248-250.

161. Smulian AG, Linke MJ, Baughman RP, et al. Analysis of *Pneumocystis carinii* antigens in bronchoalveolar lavage fluid in patients with pneumocystosis. AIDS. 1994;8:1555-1562.

162. Olsson M, Elvin K, Lidman C, et al. A rapid and simple nested PCR assay for the detection of *Pneumocystis carinii* in sputum samples. Scand J Infect Dis. 1996;28:597-600.

163. Mathis A, Weber R, Kuster H, et al. Simplified sample processing combined with a sensitive one-tube nested PCR assay for detectin of *Pneumocystis carinii* in respiratory specimens. J Clin Microbiol. 1997;35:1691-1695.

164. Caliendo AM, Hewitt PL, Allega JM, et al. Performance of a PCR assay for detection of *Pneumocystis carinii* from respiratory specimens. J Clin Microbiol. 1998;36:979-982.

165. Birriel JA, Adams JA, Saldana MA, et al. Role of flexible bronchoscopy and bronchoalveolar lavages in the diagnosis of pediatric acquired immunodeficiency syndrome-related pulmonary disease. Pediatrics. 1991;87:897-899.

166. Teuscher AU, Opravil M, Theiler R, et al. Predictive value of bronchoalveolar lavage in excluding a diagnosis of *Pneumocystis carinii* pneumonia during prophylaxis with aerosolized pentamidine. Clin Infect Dis. 1993;16:519-522.

167. Gracia JD, Miravitlles M, Mayordomo C, et al. Empiric treatments impair the diagnostic yield of BAL in HIV-positive patients. Chest. 1997;111:1180-1186.

168. Helweg-Larsen J, Jensen JS, Benfield T, et al. Diagnostic use of PCR for detection of *Pneumocystis carinii* in oral wash samples. J Clin Microbiol. 1998;36:2068-2072.

169. Larsen HH, Masur H, Kovacs JA, et al. Development and evaluation of a quantitative, touch-down, real-time PCR assay for diagnosing *Pneumocystis carinii* pneumonia. J. Clin Microbiol. 2002;40:490-494.

170. Cadranel J, Gillet-Juvin K, Antoine M, et al. Site-directed bronchoalveolar lavage and transbronchial biopsy in HIV-infected patients with pneumonia. Am J Respir Crit Care Med. 1995;152:1103-1106.

171. Huang L, Hecht FM, Stansell JD, et al. Suspected *Pneumocystis carinii* pneumonia with a negative induced sputum examination. Is early bronchoscopy useful? Am J Respir Crit Care Med. 1995;151:1866-1871.

172. Skelly M, Hoffman J, Fabbri M, et al. *S*-Adenosylmethionine concentrations in diagnosis of *Pneumocystis carinii* pneumonia. Lancet. 2003;361:1267-1268.

173. Bennett CL, Curtis JR, Achenbach C, et al. U.S. hospital care for HIV-infected persons and the role of public, private, and Veterans Administration hospitals. J Acquir Immune Defic Syndr Hum Retrovirol. 1996;13:416-421.

174. Curtis JR, Ullman M, Collier AC, et al. Variations in medical care for HIV-related *Pneumocystis carinii* pneumonia: A comparison of process and outcome at two hospitals. Chest. 1997;112:398-405.

175. Masur H, Shelhamer J. Empiric outpatient management of HIV-related pneumonia: economical or unwise? Ann Intern Med. 1996;124:451-453.

176. Glassroth J. Empiric diagnosis of *Pneumocystis carinii* pneumonia. Am J Respir Crit Care Med. 1995;152:1433-1434.

177. Benfield TL, Helweg-Larsen J, Bang D, et al. Prognostic markers of short-term mortality in AIDS-associated *Pneumocystis carinii* pneumonia. Chest. 2001;119:844-851.

178. Dworkin MS, Hanson DL, Navin TR. Survival of patients with AIDS, after diagnosis of *Pneumocystis carinii* pneumonia, in the United States. J Infect Dis. 2001;183:1409-1412.

179. Morris A, Wachter RM, Luce J, et al. Improved survival with highly active antiretroviral therapy in HIV-infected patients with severe *Pneumocystis carinii* pneumonia. AIDS. 2003;17:73-80.

180. Mansharamani NG, Garland R, Delaney D, Koziel H. Management and outcome patterns for adult *Pneumocystis carinii* pneumonia, 1985 to 1995: Comparison of HIV-associated cases to other immunocompromised states. Chest. 2000;118:704-711.

181. Gatell JM, Marrades R, El-Ebiary M, et al. Severe pulmonary infectins in AIDS patients. Semin Respir Infect. 1996;11:119-128.

182. Rosen MJ, Clayton K, Schneider RF, et al. Intensive care of patients with HIV infection: utilization, critical illnesses, and outcomes. Pulmonary Complications of HIV Infection Study Group. Am J Respir Crit Care Med. 1997;155:67-71.

183. Randall CJ, Yarnold PR, Schwartz DN, et al. Improvements in outcomes of acute respiratory failure for patients with human immunodeficiency virus-related *Pneumocystis carinii* pneumonia. Am J Respir Crit Care Med. 2000;162:393-398.

184. Keely SP, Stringer JR, Baughman RP, et al. Genetic variation among *Pneumocystis carinii* hominis isolates in recurrent pneumocystosis. J Infect Dis. 1995;172:595-598.

185. Dohn MN, Baughman RP, Vigdorth EM, et al. Equal survival rates for first, second, and third episodes of *Pneumocystis carinii* pneumonia in AIDS patients. Arch Intern Med. 1992;152:2465-2470.

186. Metersky ML, Colt HG, Olson LK, et al. AIDS-related spontaneous pneumothorax. Risk factors and treatmnet. Chest. 1995;108:946-951.

187. Anonymous. Handbook of Antimicrobial Therapy. New Rochelle, NY: The Medical Letter; 2002:137-138.

188. Hughes WT, Feldman S, Chaudhary SC, et al. Comparison of pentamidine isethionate and trimethoprim-sulfamethoxazole in the treatment of *Pneumocystis carinii* pneumonia. J Pediatr. 1978;92:285-291.

189. Wharton JM, Coleman DL, Wofsy CB, et al. Trimethoprim-sulfamethoxazole or pentamidine for *Pneumocystis carinii* pneumonia in the acquired immunodeficiency syndrome: A prospective randomized trial. Ann Intern Med. 1986;105:37-44.

190. Sattler FR, Cowan R, Nielsen DM, et al. Trimethoprim-sulfamethoxazole compared with pentamidine for treatment of *Pneumocystis carinii* pneumonia in the acquired immunodeficiency syndrome: A prospective, noncrossover study. Ann Intern Med. 1988;109:280-287.

191. Klein NC, Duncanson FP, Lenox TH, et al. Trimethoprim-sulfamethoxazole versus pentamidine for *Pneumocystis carinii* pneumonia in AIDS patients: Results of a large prospective randomized treatment trial. AIDS. 1992;6:301-305.

192. Stein DS, Stevens RC. Treatment-associated toxicities: Incidence and mechanisms. In: Sattler FR, Walzer PD. *Pneumocystis carinii*. London: Bailliére Tindall, 1995:505-530.

193. Carr A, Swanson C, Penny R, et al. Clinical and laboratory markers of hypersensitivity to treimethoprim-sulfamethoxazole in patients with *Pneumocystis carinii* pneumonia and AIDS. J Infect Dis. 1993;167:180-185.

194. Veenstra J, Veugelers PJ, Keet IP, et al. Rapid disease progression in human immunodeficiency virus type 1-infected individuals with adverse reactions to trimethoprim-sulfamethoxazole prophylaxis. Clin Infect Dis. 1997;24:936-941.

195. Velazquez H, Perazella MA, Wright FS, et al. Renal mechanism of trimethoprim-induced hyperkalemia. Ann Intern Med. 1993;119:296-301.

196. Joos B, Blaser J, Opravil M, et al. Monitoring of Co-trimoxazole concentrations in serum during treatment of *Pneumocystis carinii* pneumonia. Antimicrob Agents Chemother. 1995;39:2661-2666.

197. Caumes E, Roudier CE, Rogeaux O, et al. Effect of croticosteroids on the incidence of adverse cutaneous reactions to trimethoprim-sulfamethoxazole during treatment of AIDS-associated *Pneumocystis carinii* pneumonia. Clin Infect Dis. 1994;18:319-323.

198. Leung GS, Stanford JF, Giordano MF, et al. Trimethoprim-sulfamethoxazole TMP-SMZ dose escalation versus direct rechallenge for *Pneumocystis carinii* pneumonia prophylaxis in human immunodeficiency virus-infected patients with previous adverse reaction to TMP-SMZ. J Infect Dis. 2001;184:992-997.

199. Safrin S, Finkelstein DM, Feinberg J, et al. Comparison of three regimens for treatment of mild to moderate *Pneumocystis carinii* pneumonia in patients with AIDS. Ann Intern Med. 1996;124:792-802.

200. Lee BL, Medina I, Benowitz NL, et al. Dapsone, trimethoprim, and sulfamethoxazole plasma levels during treatment of *Pneumocystis carinii* pneumonia in patients with the acquired immunodeficiency syndrome AIDS . Evidence of drug interactions. Ann Intern Med. 1989;110:606-611.

201. Metroka CE, McMechan MF, Andrada R, et al. Failure of prophylaxis with dapsone in patients taking dideoxyinosine. N Engl J Med. 1991;325:737.

202. Toma E, Founier S, Dumont M, et al. Clinamycin/primaquine versus trimethoprim-sulfamethoxazole as primary therapy for *Pneumocystis carinii* pneumonia in AIDS: A randomized, double-blind pilot trial. Clin Infect Dis. 1993;17:178-184.

203. Hughes W, Leung G, Kramer F, et al. Comparison of atovaquone 566C80 with trimethoprim-sulfamethoxazole to treat *Pneumocystis carinii* pneumonia in patients with AIDS. N Engl J Med. 1993;328:1521-1527.

204. Dohn MN, Weinberg WG, Torres RA, et al. Oral atovaquone compared with intravenous pentamidine for *Pneumocystis carinii* pneumonia in patients with AIDS. Ann Intern Med. 1994;121:174-180.

205. Rosenberg DM, McCarthy W, Slavinsky J, et al. Atovaquone suspension for treatment of *Pneumocystis carinii* pneumonia in HIV-infected patients. AIDS. 2001;26:211-214.

206. Black JR, Feinberg J, Murphy R, et al. Clindamycin and primaquine therapy for mild-to-moderate episodes of *Pneumocystis carinii* pneumonia in patients with AIDS: AIDS clinical trials group 044. Clin Infect Dis. 1994;18:905-913.

207. Noskin GA, Murphy RL, Black JR, et al. Salvage therapy with clindamycin/primaquine for *Pneumocystis carinii* pneumonia. Clin Infect Dis. 1992;14:183-188.

208. Sattler FR, Jelliffe RW. Pharmacokinetic and pharmacodynamic considerations for drug dosing in the treatment of *Pneumocystis carinii* pneumonia. In: Walzer PD, ed. *Pneumocystis carinii* Pneumonia. New York: Marcel Dekker; 1994.

209. Comtois R, Pouliot J, Vinet B, et al. Higher pentamidine levels in AIDS patients with hypoglycemia and azotemia during treatment of *Pneumocystis carinii* pneumonia. Am Rev Respir Dis. 1992;146:740-744.

210. Bronner LC, Gustafsson LL, Rombo L, et al. Plasma pentamidine concentrations vary between individuals with *Pneumocystis carinii* pneumonia and the drug is actively secreted by the kidney. J Antimicrob Chemother. 1994;33:803-810.

211. Kleyman TR, Roberts C, Ling BN. A mechanism for pentamidine-induced hyperkalemia: inhibition of distal nephron sodium transport. Ann Intern Med. 1995;122:103-106.

212. Sattler FR, Frame P, Davis R, et al. Trimetrexate with leucovorin versus trimethoprim-sulfamethoxazole for moderate to severe episodes of *Pneumocystis carinii* pneumonia in patients with AIDS: A prospective, controlled multicenter investigation of the AIDS clinical trials group protocol 029/031. J Infect Dis. 1994;170:165-172.

213. Walmsley S, Levinton C, Brunton J, et al. A multicenter randomized double-blind placebo-controlled trial of adjunctive corticosteroids in the treatment of *Pneumocystis carinii* pneumonia complicating the acquired immune deficiency syndrome. J Acquir Immune Defic Syndr Hum Retrovirol. 1995;8:348-357.

214. Bozzette SA, Morton SC. Reconsidering the use of adjunctive corticosteroids in *Pneumocystis* pneumonia? J Acquir Immune Defic Syndr Hum Retrovirol. 1995;8:345-347.

215. Kazanjian P, Armstrong W, Hossler PA, et al. *Pneumocystis carinii* mutations are associated with duration of sulfa or sulfone prophylaxis exposure in AIDS patients. J Infect Dis. 2000;182:551-557.

216. Kazanjian P, Armstrong W, Hossler PA, et al. *Pneumocystis carinii* cytochrome b mutations are associated with atovaquone exposure in patients with AIDS. J Infect Dis. 2001;183:819-822.

217. Hughes WT, Sillos E, LaFon S, et al. Effects of aerolized synthetic surfactant, atovaquone, and the combination of these on murine *Pneumocystis carinii* pneumonia. J Infect Dis. 1998;177:1046-1056.

218. Creery WD, Hashmi A, Hutchison JS, et al. Surfactant therapy improves pulmonary function in infants with *Pneumocystis carinii* pneumonia and acquired immunodeficiency syndrome. Pediatr Pulmonol. 1997;24:370-373.

219. Centers for Disease Control and Prevention. Guidelines for Preventing Opportunistic infections among HIV-infected persons—2002 Recommendations of the U.S. Public Health Service and the Infectious Disease Society of America. Morbid Mortal Wkly Rep. 2002;51 RR-8 :1-52.

220. Freedberg KA, Scharfstein JA, Seage GR 3rd, et al. The cost-effectiveness of preventing AIDS-related opportunistic infections. JAMA. 1998;279:130-136.

221. Saah AJ, Hoover DR, Peng Y, et al. Predictors for failure of *Pneumocystis carinii* pneumonia prophylaxis. Multicenter AIDS Cohort Study. JAMA. 1995;273:1197-1202.

222. Bozzette SA, Finkelstein DM, Spector SA, et al. A randomized trial of three antipneumocystis agents in patients with advanced human immunodeficiency virus infection. NIAID AIDS Clinical Trials Group. N Engl J Med. 1995;332:693-699.

223. Sepkowitz KA. Effect of prophylaxis on the clinical manifestations of AIDS-related opportunistic infections. Clin Infect Dis. 1998;26:806-810.

224. Walzer PD. Editorial response: *Pneumocystis carinii* pneumonia in patients without human immunodeficiency virus infection. Clin Infect Dis. 1997;25:219-220.

225. Centers for Disease Control and Prevention. Guideline for isolation precaution in hospitals. Am J Infect Control. 1996;24:24-52.

226. 2001 USPHS/IDSA guidelines for the prevention of opportunistic infections in persons infected with human immunodeficiency virus. HIV Clin Trials 2001;2:493-554.

227. Kuramochi T, Hioki K, Ito M. *Pneumocystis carinii* cysts are susceptible to inactivation by chemical disinfectants. Exp Anim. 1997;46:241-245.

SECTION H

PROTOZOAL DISEASES

CHAPTER **269**

Introduction to Protozoal Diseases

JONATHAN I. RAVDIN
WILLIAM M. STAUFFER

The protozoans known to infect humans are a diverse group, as indicated by phylogeny (Table 269-1), epidemiology (Table 269-2), clinical manifestations (Table 269-3), preferred diagnostic studies (Table 269-4), and chemotherapeutic agents effective in eradicating or arresting infection (see Chapter 41). The phylum protozoa is composed of morphologically simple organisms that are generally unicellular and free living. Protozoa may be divided, for convenience, into four distinct groups based on method of locomotion: mastigophora (flagella), sarcodina (pseudopodia), apicomplexa (microtubule complex, commonly referred to as sporozoa), and ciliophora (ciliates) (see Table 269-1). Protozoans such as *Plasmodium* spp., *Entamoeba histolytica*, *Trypanosoma* spp., and *Leishmania* spp. are major worldwide pathogens and are among the leading causes of morbidity and mortality in areas of Africa, Asia, and Central and South America. *Giardia lamblia* and *Cryptosporidium* are frequent causes of diarrhea in developing areas and established industrialized countries. *Toxoplasma gondii*, *Cryptosporidium* spp., *Microsporidia*, *Cyclospora*, *Trypanosoma cruzi*, and *Leishmania* spp. all have been noted to cause severe diseases in patients with acquired immunodeficiency syndrome. New genetic and molecular biology techniques are leading to better characterization of protozoans.[2]

The new or continued importance of protozoal pathogens has stimulated active research in all areas.[2] Clinicians are encouraged to familiarize themselves with the material in Tables 269-2 through 269-4, which is addressed in depth in the chapters that follow. The key to the recognition of protozoal infection is a knowledge of epidemiologic risk factors such as the parasites' geographic distribution (see Table 269-2) and the most common modes of clinical presentation (see Table 269-3). The clinical diagnosis of protozoal infection presenting outside normal areas of high prevalence is usually dependent on physicians considering this possibility in their differential diagnosis. Given present levels of travel, changing immigration patterns, and the immunosuppressive effects of infection with human immunodeficiency virus, all clinicians need to have a heightened awareness of diseases caused by the protozoans. Diagnosis and therapy often require a specialized expertise with the use of tests (see Table 269-4) or drugs with which most physicians lack experience. Infectious disease consultants will frequently be called on to diagnose and manage protozoal infection; this requires the maintenance of an updated, in-depth database as provided by the chapters within this section.

REFERENCES

1. Committee on Systematics and Evolution of the Society of Protozoologists. A newly revised classification of the protozoa. J Protozool. 1980;27:37-58.
2. Clark CG, Diamond LS. Intraspecific variation and phylogenetic relationships in the genus *Entamoeba* as revealed by riboprinting. M Euk Microbiol. 1997;44:143-154.
3. Ubelaker JE, ed. Stedman's American Society of Parasitology. Parasitic Names. Baltimore: Williams & Wilkins; 1993.
4. Tenter AM, Baverstock PR, Johnson AM. Phylogenetic relationships of *Sarcocystis* species from sheep, goats, cattle and mice based on ribosomal RNA sequences. Int J Parasitol. 1992;22:503-513.

TABLE 269-1   Classification of Protozoans that Infect Humans

Phylum 1. Sarcomastigophora (flagella, pseudopodia)
Subphylum I. Mastiglophora (flagella)
Class 2. Zoomastigophorea
Order 2. Kinetoplastida
Suborder 2. Trypanosomatina
Leishmania, Trypanosoma
Order 5. Diplomonadida
Suborder 2. Diplomonadina
Giardia
Order 7. Trichomonadida
Dientamoeba, Trichomonas
Subphylum III. Sarcodina (pseudopodia)
Super class 1. Rhizopoda
Class 1. Lobosea
Subclass 1. Gymnamoebia
Order 1. Amoebida
Suborder 1. Tubulina
Entamoeba
Suborder 5. Acanthopodina
Acanthamoeba
Order 2. Schizopyrenida
Naegleria

Phylum III. Apicomplexa (apical microtubule complex)
Class 2. Sporozoea
Subclass 2. Coccidia
Order 3. Eucoccidia
Suborder 2. Eimeriina
Cryptosporidium, Isospora, Microsporidia,
Sarcocystis,[3,4] *Toxoplasma*
Suborder 3. Haemosporina
Plasmodium
Suborder 3. Piroplasmia
Order 1. Piroplasmida
Babesia
Phylum VII. Ciliophora (ciliated)
Class I. Kinetofragminophorea
Subclass 2. Vestibuliferia
Order 1. Trichostomatida
Suborder 1. Trichostomatina
Balantidium

Data from Committee on Systematics and Evolution of the Society of Protozoologists. A newly revised classification of the protozoa. J Protozool. 1980;27:37-58.

TABLE 269-2 Geographic Distribution and Mechanism of Transmission of Protozoal Infections

Organism	Geographic Distribution	Means of Transmission
Acanthamoeba spp.	Undefined	Contact lens, ? airborne
Babesia spp.	North America, Europe	Tick-borne, blood transfusions
Balantidium coli.	Worldwide	Zoonosis (pigs), water,* fecal-oral
Blastocystis hominis	Unknown	Fecal-oral, water
Cryptosporidium spp.	Worldwide	Water, fecal-oral, zoonosis
Dientamoeba fragilis	Worldwide	Water, fecal-oral
Entamoeba histolytica	Worldwide	Water, fecal-oral, foodborne
Giardia lamblia	Worldwide	Water, fecal-oral, foodborne
Isospora spp.	Worldwide	Fecal-oral, suspected zoonosis
Leishmania spp.†		Sand fly
L. donovani	India, Pakistan, East Africa, China	
L. tropica	Middle East, Central Asia	
L. major	Middle East, India, Pakistan	
L. aethiopica	Ethiopia, Kenya	
L. mexicana	Central America, Texas	
L. amazonensis	South America	
L. chagasi	Latin America	
L. viannia braziliensis	Latin America	
Naegleria spp.	Worldwide	Fresh water, intranasal exposure
Plasmodium spp.	Africa, Asia, South and Central America, Oceania	Female anopheline mosquitoes, inoculation of infected blood
Sarcocystis spp.	Unknown	Foodborne (meat)
Toxoplasma gondii	Worldwide	Zoonosis (cats), foodborne (meat), blood or organ transplant, congenital
Trichomonas vaginalis	Worldwide	Venereal, during birth, ? nonvenereal
Trypanosoma spp.		
T. cruzi	South and Central America	Reduviid bugs
T. brucei gambiense	West Africa	Tsetse fly
T. brucei rhodesiense	East Africa	Tsetse fly

*Ingestion of water contaminated with fecal material.
†Other *Leishmania* spp. also infect humans but are less common.

TABLE 269-3 Clinical Syndromes Due to Infection by Protozoans

Organism (Disease)	Major Clinical Syndrome	Organism (Disease)	Major Clinical Syndrome
Acanthamoeba spp.	Keratitis, granulomatous encephalitis	*Leptomyxida*	Granulomatous amebic encephalitis
Babesia spp. (babesiosis)	Fever, malaise, hepatosplenomegaly, and hemolytic anemia, especially in the asplenic	*Naegleria* spp.	Meningoencephalitis
		Plasmodium spp. (malaria)	Paroxysmal fever, chills, headache, hepatosplenomegaly
Balantidium coli (balantidiosis)	Colitis	*Sarcocystis* spp.	Myositis, fever, eosinophilia
Blastocystis hominis (blastocystis)	Diarrhea, mild eosinophilia	*Toxoplasma gondii* (toxoplasmosis)	Fever, malaise, lymphadenopathy; chorioretinitis; congenital abnormalities; in immunocompromised host; encephalitis, myocarditis, pneumonitis
Cryptosporidium spp. (crytosporidiosis)	Self-limiting noninflammatory diarrhea; chronic severe diarrhea and cholangitis in AIDS patients		
Dientamoeba fragilis	Diarrhea, eosinophilia	*Trichomas vaginalis* (trichomoniasis)	Vaginitis, urethritis
Entamoeba histolytica (amebiasis)	Rectocolitis, liver abscess		
Giardia lamblia (giardiasis)	Noninflammatory diarrhea with malabsorption	*Trypanosoma* spp. (African sleeping sickness and Chagas' disease)	Fever, lymphadenopathy, meningoencephalitis, myocarditis; megaesophagus and megacolon, congestive cardiopathy
Isospora spp. (isosporiasis)	Diarrhea in AIDS patients		
Leishmania spp. (cutaneous and visceral leishmaniasis)	Cutaneous or mucosal ulceration; visceral disease with fever, hepatosplenomegaly		

AIDS, acquired immunodeficiency syndrome.

TABLE 269-4 Diagnostic Tests for Protozoal Diseases

Disease	Preferred Diagnostic Tests	Disease	Preferred Diagnostic Tests
Amebiasis	Stool for ova and parasites, serologic tests	Malaria	Wright or Giemsa stain of thin and thick blood smear
Intestinal	Fecal antigen		
Liver	Ultrasound examination, serologic tests	Primary amebic meningitis	Cerebrospinal fluid examination, culture for amebae
Amebic keratitis	Corneal scraping for microcscopy and culture		
Babesiosis	Thin and thick blood smears	Toxoplasmosis	Serologic tests, Wright-Giemsa stain of tissue, antigen detection
Cryptosporidiosis	Acid-fast and auramine-rhodamine staining of fecal samples, small bowel biopsy		
		Trichomoniasis	Microscopy, culture, or antigen detection in genital secretions
Giardiasis	Stool for ova and parasites, stool antigen detection, sampling of duodenal contents		
		Trypanosomiasis	
Granulomatous amebic encephalitis	Brain biopsy	Chagas' disease	Fresh blood or stained smear, blood culture, xenodiagnosis; serologic tests for chronic disease
Leishmaniasis		African sleeping sickness	Blood smear, serologic tests
Cutaneous and mucocutaneous	Biopsy, touch preparation, culture, serologic tests		
Visceral	Bone marrow or splenic aspiration, touch preparation, culture, serologic tests, lymph node biopsy		

Entamoeba histolytica (Amebiasis)

JONATHAN I. RAVDIN

WILLIAM M. STAUFFER

If there be among you any man that is not clean by reasons of uncleanness that chanceth him by night, then shall he go abroad out of the camp. . . . And thou shalt have a paddle upon thy weapon; and it shall be, when thou wilt ease thyself abroad, thou shalt dig therewith, and shalt turn back and cover that which cometh from thee.

DEUTERONOMY 23:10 AND 23:13

Acute and chronic diarrhea has been of major concern to humans since earliest recorded history. The invasion of Russia by Napoleon was halted by widespread acute diarrhea. The atrocities affecting prisoners of war, such as at Andersonville during the Civil War and the Bataan Death March in the Philippines during World War II, were caused as much by *Entamoeba histolytica* as by prison officials. Disease caused by *E. histolytica* is expressed most often as ulcerative and inflammatory lesions of the colon resulting in a complete spectrum of colonic signs and symptoms. Occasionally, amebas gain access to extraintestinal sites, most commonly the liver, where marked tissue destruction occurs. This protozoal organism is the third leading parasitic cause of death in developing nations[1] and is one of the important health risks to which travelers are exposed. New information has been acquired on pathogenesis, diagnostic techniques, and host immune response, and dramatic progress has been made in understanding the genetic underpinnings of the organism.[2-6]

In the early 1900s Emile Brumpt, following both animal and human studies, proposed that there were two distinct species in the classification of *E. histolytica:* one that caused disease, which he labeled *Entamoeba dysenteriae,* and one that did not, *E. dispar.* His theory and classification was largely ignored for over 50 years. In the 1970s analyses of zymodemes, the patterns of electrophoretic mobility of certain parasite isoenzymes, revealed an association of distinct zymodemes with symptomatic invasive disease.[7] Subsequently, studies with RNA and DNA probes clearly indicated genetic differences between the potentially pathogenic *E. histolytica* and the nonpathogenic *E. dispar.*[8-10] Restriction enzyme polymorphism analysis of polymerase chain reaction (PCR)–amplified small-subunit ribosomal RNA genes (riboprinting) further defined *Entamoeba* into specific species.[11] Genetic differences between *E. histolytica* and *E. dispar* have been extended to genes encoding important proteins involved in pathogenesis, such as adherence lectins[12] and cysteine proteinases.[4,13] By the mid-1990s there were enough data to officially separate the two species, as Brumpt suggested, into the nonpathogenic *E. dispar* and the potentially pathogenic *E. histolytica.* In fact, Louis Diamond and Graham Clark, using riboprinting, went on to estimate that the genetic distance between the two species was equivalent to the genetic distance between humans and mice.[10]

Losch, in St. Petersburg, Russia, in 1875, is credited with documenting amebas to be pathogenic by inducing lesions in a dog fed dysenteric stool.[14] Kartulis, in Egypt in 1886, settled the role of amebas as a cause of intestinal and hepatic lesions in patients with diarrhea, and Walker and Sellards dispelled all doubt of the pathogenicity of *E. histolytica* with their detailed, though ethically indiscriminant, studies of experimental infection in prisoners in the Philippines in 1913.[15] Councilman and Lafleur, pathologists at Johns Hopkins University, provided the information in 1891 to allow a clear distinction between bacillary and amebic dysentery.[15] The history of amebiasis has been highlighted by a number of well-studied epidemics such as that at the Chicago Century of Progress Exposition in 1933,[16] the Singer Sewing Machine Plant in Indiana in 1950,[17] and a recent outbreak in the Republic of Georgia.[18] However, the main impact has been the ability of *E. dispar* and *E. histolytica* to maintain infection in 20% to 30% of people living in areas of the tropics and in up to 5% of the people in temperate climate nations.[1] The most subtle break in personal sanitation allows the organisms to spread and initiate disease.

ORGANISM

Molecular phylogeny has revealed that *Entamoeba* species (*histolytica* and *dispar*) are close to *Dictyostelium discoideum* on one of the lowest branches of the eukaryotic tree.[3] Although amebae were thought to lack organelles (mitochondria, endoplasmic reticulum, and Golgi apparatus), evidence to the contrary is coming to light. In addition to recently described nuclear-encoded mitochondrial genes and a remnant mitochondrial organelle, a newly described 51-kDa protein of *E. histolytica* has been found to have a significant similarity to the amino acid sequence of the calreticulin-like protein of spinach leaves (77% homology), indicating a system equivalent to the eukaryotic endoplasmic reticulum and Golgi apparatus.[19-21]

Amebas are obligate fermenters that lack pyruvate dehydrogenase and the enzymes for oxidative phosphorylation and the Krebs cycle. *E. histolytica* belongs to the pseudopod-forming protozoal superclass Rhizopoda within the subphylum Sarcodina.[22] Within their family Entamoebidae, order Amoebida, and class Lobosea are many species that infect humans, including *E. histolytica, E. hartmanni, E. polecki, E. coli,* and *E. gingivalis. E. hartmanni,* previously referred to as "small race" *E. histolytica,* is a distinct species by virtue of morphology, unique antigens, and riboprinting.[11] Most experts agree that the noninvasive *Entamoeba*-like Laredo strain, which grows in culture at a lower temperature (25° C), is a separate species.

The distinction between *E. dispar* and *E. histolytica* was first defined by the mobility of four isoenzymes (L-malate: $NADP^+$ oxidoreductase, glucose phosphate isomerase, phosphoglucomutase, and hexokinase) on starch gel electrophoresis. Sargeaunt and co-workers studied more than 6000 clinical isolates and noted more than 22 distinct isoenzyme patterns (zymodemes).[7] However, more recent studies indicate that the true number of distinct zymodemes is much lower.[23] Individual zymodemes have a clear association with the occurrence of asymptomatic infection or symptomatic invasive disease.[7]

Entamoeba histolytica have numerous antigenic differences from *E. dispar.* It was originally found that distinct epitopes of the 170-kDa heavy subunit of the galactose-inhibitable adherence lectin exist in *E. histolytica* but are absent in *E. dispar.*[24] However, it is now clear, and interesting to note, that the gene for the *E. dispar* 170-kDa lectin subunit contains all 97 cysteine residues and conserves the same sequence homology to CD59 found in the *hgl2* lectin gene of *E. histolytica.*[12] Several research groups have been able to further distinguish the two groups by producing monoclonal antibodies that identify antigens utilizing immunofluorescence methodology[25] and immunoblotting.[26-28] Tannich and co-workers were the first to demonstrate genomic DNA differences between *E. histolytica* and *E. dispar.*[29] Subsequently, a complementary DNA (cDNA) clone specific for *E. histolytica* was identified by screening for the expressed protein with pooled human immune sera. Southern blotting of the cDNA probe and restriction mapping of hybridization by an actin cDNA probe both revealed significant genomic DNA differences. These studies were extended by comparison of the restriction fragment pattern of specific PCR-amplified genomic DNA fragments to differentiate isolates. Additional cDNA clones have since been identified that distinguish *E. dispar* from *E. histolytica*[30,31]; studies of ribosomal RNA have also been successful in differentiating strains.[11,32] Early in the 1990s, genetic distance analysis also began to support the existence of at least two distinct groups within the species *E. histolytica.*[33,34] Significant progress has been made in completely sequencing the *E. histolytica* and *E. dispar* genomes, which will further distinguish the organisms as well as highlight the mechanisms that enable *E. histolytica* to invade the host.[4]

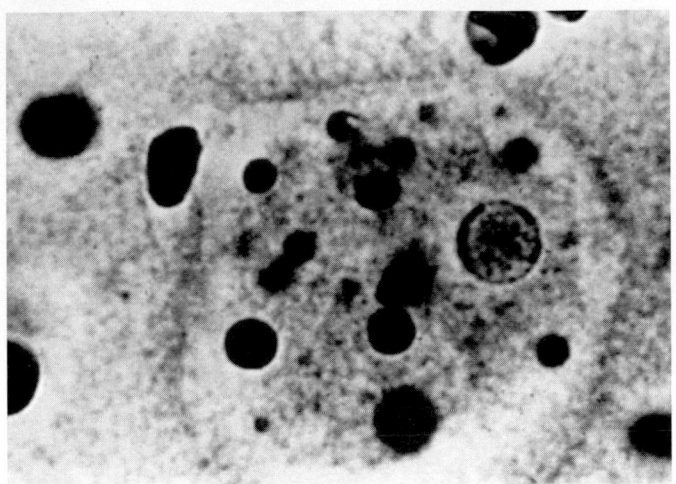

FIGURE 270-1. Trophozoite of *Entamoeba histolytica*. A delicate round nucleus with a small central chromatin dot is seen. The trophozoite contains dense ingested red blood cells.

E. histolytica and *E. dispar* trophozoites are morphologically indistinguishable, ranging in size from 10 to 60 μm, with an average of 25 μm. Trophozoites have a single 3- to 5-μm nucleus containing fine peripheral chromatin and a central nucleolus; *E. histolytica* trophozoites often contain ingested erythrocytes (Fig. 270-1).[35] The cytoplasm consists of a clear ectoplasm and a granular endoplasm that contains numerous vacuoles (Fig. 270-2). Cysts of *E. histolytica* average 12 μm in diameter (range, 5 to 20 μm) and, depending on their maturity, contain one to four nuclei that are morphologically identical to that of trophozoite nuclei (Fig. 270-3). As in other members of the order Amoebida, young *E. histolytica* cysts contain chromatoid bodies with smooth, rounded edges; these are composed of ribosome particles in crystalline arrays. Immature cysts may contain clumps of glycogen that stain with iodine.

Genetics

A joint project between the Institute of Genomic Research (Rockville, MD) and the Pathogen Sequencing Unit based at the Sanger Institute (Cambridge, United Kingdom) is endeavoring to sequence the complete *E. histolytica* genome and, for comparative purposes, to partially

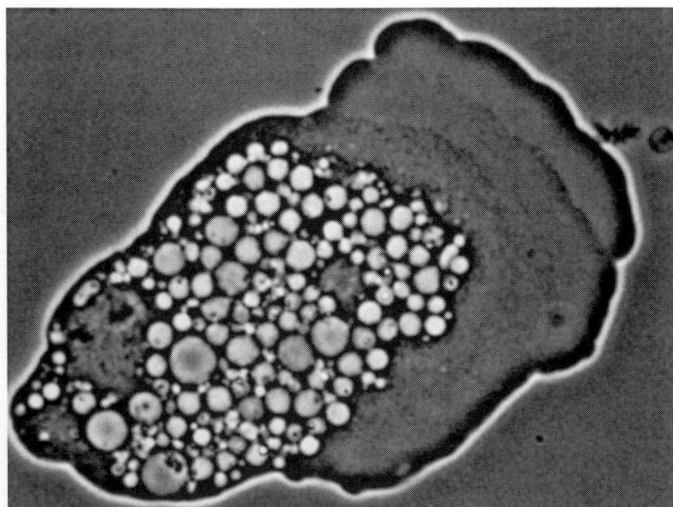

FIGURE 270-2. Phase micrograph of an axenic *Entamoeba histolytica* trophozoite strain HM1:IMSS; note that the cell is oriented with extension of pseudopodia and the highly vesiculated cytoplasm, which is characteristic of virulent axenic strains.

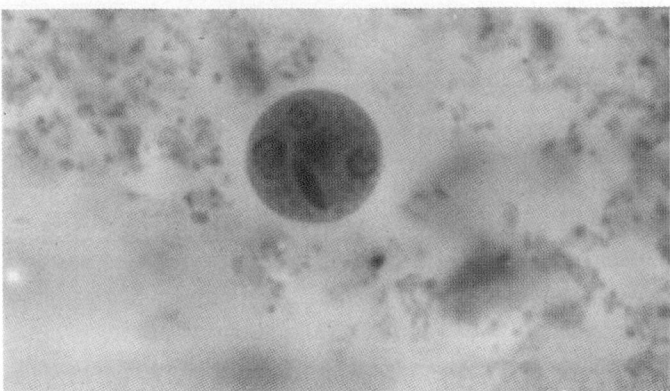

FIGURE 270-3. Mature cyst of *Entamoeba histolytica*. Three of the four nuclei are seen in the plane of focus of this photomicrograph.

sequence four other closely related intestinal protozoa (*E. dispar, E. moshkovskii, E. terrapinae, E. invadins*). It has become clear through this effort that *E. histolytica* has a small genome (~20 MB) that is very repetitive and contains densely packed coding sequences with closely spaced genes that lack introns.[4,36] *E. histolytica* has a complex molecular karyotype composed of six linear DNA molecules ranging from 227 to 1361 kb, multiple circular molecules (5 to 50 kb), and extralinear DNA in the rudimentary mitochondria.[37] It appears that the sequences encoded in the genome arrangement are proteins involved in highly conserved functions and cellular processes; however, there are also areas of the genome that express amazing genetic polymorphisms.[38] For example, in Dhaka, Bangladesh, 25 distinct polymorphisms were observed among 42 stool isolates with an additional 9 distinct patterns among 12 liver abscess isolates.[39] There are several unique features that are proving to be a challenge in decoding the genome, including uncertain ploidy across the genome and a high adenosine-thymidine content making insert cloning difficult.

LIFE CYCLE AND EPIDEMIOLOGY

The life cycle of *E. histolytica* is not complex. A cyst that is excreted into the environment is ingested by a human host though a fecally contaminated product. The cyst then undergoes excystation in the small bowel, becoming a trophozoite. The trophozoite, through the galactose/*N*-acetylgalactosamine (Gal/GalNAc) lectin protein, attaches to the colonic mucin and then reproduces by clonal expansion, most commonly in the cecum. Subsequently, presumably triggered by inhospitable conditions, the Gal/GalNAc lectin, along with mucin glycoproteins, other gut bacteria, or both, initiates the developmental pathway leading to encystment.[40] Encystment of xenic cultures of *E. histolytica* can be induced in vitro by hypo-osmotic conditions resulting in the appearance of two sialylated glycoproteins and a chitinous cell wall (an *N*-acetyl-D-glucosamine polymer).[41] Cysts are then excreted through defecation back into the environment. Cysts may remain viable for weeks or months in an appropriately moist environment outside the body. In fact, cysts may survive for as long as 48 hours at 20° to 25° C on foods and have been found to remain viable in sewage and natural surface water, at 4° C, for 1 month. In contrast, trophozoites are rapidly degraded outside the body and are readily destroyed by the stomach pH and enzymes. The cyst, therefore, is the primary reason for the extensive prevalence of the infection throughout the world.

In a majority of cases, when the host comes into contact with the protozoan, a noninvasive infection and continuation of the natural life cycle will ensue. However, in some individuals the trophozoite will penetrate the mucin layer, directly attaching to a host cell's surface carbohydrates, and causing a cascade of proteolytic and cytolytic events that ultimately lead to invasive disease.

TABLE 270-1 Epidemiologic Risk Factors That Apparently Predispose to *Entamoeba histolytica* Infection and Increased Severity of Disease

Prevalence	Increased Severity
Persons with lower socioeconomic status in endemic area, including those with	Children, especially neonates
	Pregnancy and postpartum states
	Corticosteroid use
Crowding	Malignancy
No indoor plumbing	Malnutrition
Immigrants from endemic area	
Institutionalized populations, especially developmentally and cognitively impaired	
Persons living communally	
Promiscuous male homosexuals	

From Ravdin JI. Intestinal disease caused by *Entamoeba histolytica*. In: Ravdin JI, ed. Amebiasis: Human Infection with *Entamoeba histolytica*. New York: Churchill Livingstone; 1988:495-510.

Entamoeba histolytica has a worldwide distribution but is more commonly encountered in areas of poorer sanitation and nutrition, particularly in the tropics. Knowledge of the epidemiologic risk factors for acquisition of *E. histolytica* infection and for increased severity of the disease (Table 270-1) is essential for the recognition of patients with amebiasis and an understanding of the importance of this parasite. Older epidemiologic surveys for infection are difficult to interpret owing to the low sensitivity of a single stool examination,[42,43] laboratory error,[44] and inability to differentiate between *E. histolytica* and *E. dispar*. Given these limitations, well-collected studies place the worldwide prevalence of *E. dispar* and *E. histolytica* infection at approximately 10%, with some populations in nonindustrialized nations exceeding rates of 50%.[1,45-47] Early studies, using zymodemes analysis, estimated that overall *E. dispar* represented 90% of asymptomatic infections and *E. histolytica* accounted for 10% of asymptomatic infections.[48] Recent studies have utilized diagnostic tools able to differentiate the commensal *E. dispar* from *E. histolytica* in an attempt to determine the latter's true incidence and prevalence.[49] Several cross-sectional studies have attempted to quantify the prevalence of *E. histolytica* and have found great geographic variance ranging from less than 1% in Greece to 21% in Egypt.[8,48,50-53] In one recent study in Bangladeshi children (ages 2 to 5 years), it was found that 55% of children acquired *E. histolytica* infection over a 2-year period, with 80% of these children remaining asymptomatic.[54] Although the high rate of seroconversion is staggering, the rate of disease experienced by infected individuals correlates well with previous estimates of approximately 10% to 20% of infected persons becoming symptomatic.[48,55-59] Another recent cross-sectional study in children in Ecuador found asymptomatic *E. histolytica* infection present in only 7 of 178 children. However, it was interesting to note that greater than 64% of children showed high serologic titers, implying current or recent infection with *E. histolytica*.[60] In endemic areas of Durban, South Africa, approximately 15% of the population is asymptomatically infected with *E. histolytica* each year as determined by prospective seroconversion criteria.[36,61] This high seroprevalence corresponds to an extensive previous serosurvey conducted in Mexico.[49] Asymptomatic *E. dispar* infection elicits an intestinal immunoglobulin A (IgA) antibody response[61] but not a humoral antibody response.[56,62,63] Therefore, in endemic areas worldwide, although the prevalence rate as witnessed by spot stool examinations is relatively low, seroprevalence and seroconversion studies suggest extremely high incidence rates (asymptomatic infection with pathogenic *E. histolytica*). The persistence of this high incidence of amebic infection chiefly depends on cultural habits, sanitation, crowding, and socioeconomic status.[45,49,55]

Approximately 50 million cases of invasive *E. histolytica* disease occur annually, resulting in up to 100,000 deaths, with expression of disease varying with geographic location. For example, in Egypt the predominant presentation is amebic colitis,[64] whereas in South Africa there is an excessive rate of amebic liver abscess (ALA). In a recent study in Hue City, Vietnam, the overall incidence of ALA was estimated to be as high as 21 cases per 100,000 inhabitants—a single hospital reported 1500 cases of ALA over a 5-year period.[65] Although it appears that males and females have an equal frequency of asymptomatic infection and colitis, invasive liver disease (ALA) is much more common in males than females. Other factors, such as hormonal effects, seem to influence the occurrence of ALA. For example, rates are equal in children before puberty and rise in postmenopausal females.[66-68]

Although *E. histolytica* is endemic to the United States, no recent prevalence data exist. However, older data place the overall prevalence of *Entamoeba* infection at approximately 4%, with certain high-risk groups having a much higher incidence of infection and disease. Currently most *E. histolytica* diagnosed in the United States originates abroad, with the majority of the burden of infection and disease occurring among refugees and immigrants or in migrant workers. For example, in 1993, 2790 cases of amebiasis were reported to the Center for Disease Control and Prevention; 33% of these cases were in migrants from Latin America and 17% in recent migrants from Asia and the Pacific Islands.[69] The overwhelming majority of cases of invasive amebiasis reported from academic institutions in the southwestern United States in the 1980s occurred in Mexican Americans.[66,70-74] In areas of the world with low endemicity but having large numbers of immigrants and refugees, like the United States, medical screening policies are frequently employed that include routine stool studies, including ova and parasite exam.[75] Current standard of practice for most screening organizations is to treat all patients with positive microscopy with a luminal anti-protozoan agent. As discussed, unless the stool is positive for a trophozoite that has ingested red blood cells, indicating *E. histolytica*, the routine cyst randomly found in stools is likely that of *E. dispar*. In this scenario, a stool antigen test, serum serologies, or both should be obtained to confirm the diagnosis before initiation of a luminal anti-protozoal agent.[36,76,77]

Increased risk of amebiasis is also associated with foreign travel to any highly endemic area of the world, especially when precautions are not taken to avoid enteric infection.[78] The acquisition of *E. histolytica* infection is usually associated with long-term (greater than 1 month) residence in a highly endemic area and is usually detected only when symptomatic disease results.[79,80] In one study, 10% of 469 individuals with diarrhea after travel to a developing country were diagnosed with amebiasis.[81] In addition, a German study, investigating 2700 returned travelers, found an overall prevalence rate of *E. histolytica* of 0.3%.[82] Institutionalized populations in the United States, especially the developmentally and cognitively impaired, have a very high incidence of *E. histolytica* infection (up to 73% by one serologic survey), with frequent invasive disease and significant mortality.[83-85] Attempts to eradicate amebic infection within individual institutions by the liberal use of anti-amebic drugs or isolation of stool carriers have been unsuccessful.[83,86] Only improved housing and staffing of health care personnel appears to make a substantial impact.[87] In addition, in the late 1970s, there was an increased incidence of infection among sexually promiscuous male homosexuals. The prevalence of *E. dispar* and *E. histolytica* in the male homosexual population of New York City and San Francisco approached 40% to 50% and was one of the many causes considered in the differential diagnosis of bloody diarrhea in these individuals.[88-92] Although the prevalence of amebic infection is undoubtedly declining with the change in sexual practices resulting from human immunodeficiency virus infection,[93] a continued high index of clinical suspicion is indicated.[94,95] Amebiasis is a treatable cause of diarrhea in individuals with acquired immunodeficiency syndrome.[96,97] Although only a few cases of invasive amebiasis have been reported to complicate acquired immunodeficiency syndrome worldwide, it is still an important differential diagnostic consideration.[97-100] Brown and associates have demonstrated that *E. histolytica* trophozoites are capable of taking up human immunodeficiency virus in vitro, although it has never been demonstrated to be transferred through protozoal infection in humans.[101] In addition, amebas isolated from two uninfected individuals were also positive for human immunodeficiency virus.

Many other factors are associated with risk for amebiasis, some unanticipated, such as colonic irrigation without proper sterilization of equipment at a chiropractic clinic in Colorado.[102] Additional high-risk groups include children, who suffer from fulminant invasive disease with a higher mortality than adults,[103,104] and malnourished individuals at any age.[105]

PATHOLOGY AND PATHOGENESIS

Pathology

When the host comes into contact with the protozoan, the result, in a majority of cases, will be establishment of noninvasive infection. The parasite-host interactions that determine the course of disease, although largely still a mystery, are beginning to be understood. *Entamoeba histolytica* exerts a lytic effect on virtually all human tissue, a characteristic for which the organism is named. Reports of initial invasion of amebas via mucosal crypts have not been confirmed; amebas appear to invade the colonic epithelium directly.[106,107] Light and electron microscopic studies have been interpreted as showing lysis of mucosal cells on contact with amebas or, alternatively, diffuse mucosal damage before amebic invasion.[107-109] An amorphous, granular, eosinophilic material surrounds trophozoites in tissue, whether in colon, liver, lung, or brain.[106,110,111] Consistent with the fact that trophozoites have the capacity to destroy leukocytes and inactivated monocytes,[112,113] inflammatory cells are found only at the periphery of established amebic lesions.[106,110] In vivo and in vitro studies demonstrate that lysis of host neutrophils by *E. histolytica* results in the release of toxic nonoxidative neutrophil products that contribute to the destruction of host tissues.[114,115] However, in the severe combined immunodeficient mouse model of experimental ALA, the absence of neutrophils resulted in larger abscesses, suggesting that neutrophils may play a protective role rather than exacerbating tissue destruction.[116]

A spectrum of colonic lesions ranging from nonspecific thickening of the mucosa to the classic "flask-shaped" ulcer may be associated with amebic infection (Fig. 270-4).[108,110] The lateral extension of the ameba through the submucosal tissue that gives the characteristic flask-shaped ulcer is likely triggered when contact is made between amebic trophozoites and the extracellular matrix protein fibronectin, causing signaling cascades to occur within the parasite, and further affecting actin rearrangements that alter the adherence and motility of the organism.[117] However, although classic, one study found that only 20 of 53 patients had the flask-shaped ulcers extending through the mucosa and muscularis mucosa into the submucosa.[110] Amebas can

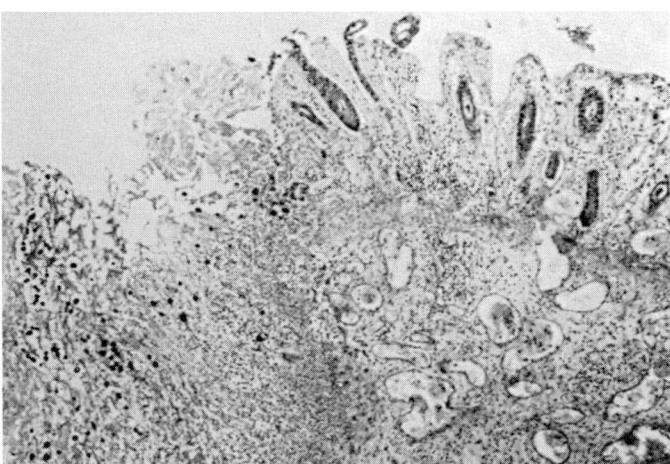

FIGURE 270-4. Light micrograph demonstrating a flask-shaped ulceration in a pathologic specimen from a patient with severe colonic amebiasis (periodic acid–Schiff stain, ×16). (*From Ravdin JI, Guerrant RL. A review of the parasite cellular mechanisms involved in the pathogenesis of amebiasis. Rev Infect Dis. 1982;41:1185-1207.*)

be recognized by a surrounding halo caused by fixation artifact, the presence of characteristic nuclear morphology, ingested erythrocytes, and intense staining with periodic acid–Schiff stain or the Gridley stain to detect ingested erythrocytes.[118] The gross findings commonly resemble, and may be confused with, changes seen in inflammatory bowel disease.

Liver abnormality in amebiasis consists of necrotic abscess or periportal fibrosis. The "abscess" contains acellular, proteinaceous debris rather than white cells and is surrounded by a rim of amebic trophozoites invading tissue.[106,111] Amebas establish hepatic infection by ascending the portal venous system rather than the lymphatics.[119,120] Triangular areas of hepatic necrosis, possibly resulting from ischemia from amebic obstruction of portal vessels, have been observed.[106,119] ALAs probably result from the coalescence of small microabscesses.[119] Liver function abnormalities are frequently present with intestinal amebiasis and are associated with periportal inflammation without demonstrable trophozoites.[111,121] Periportal fibrosis has been reported in such patients; whether this reflects past trophozoite invasion or host reaction to amebic antigens or toxins is unclear.

Pathogenesis

Knowledge of the pathogenic mechanisms of *E. histolytica* has been rapidly expanding; this has been due in part to the development of an axenic culture medium for the parasite and new molecular and genetic techniques.[122,123] The pathogenesis of invasive amebiasis requires adherence of *E. histolytica* trophozoites to the luminal surface of the bowel, amebic cytolytic and proteolytic effects on tissue, resistance of the parasite to host effector mechanisms, and host factors that influence susceptibility to invasive disease.[124]

The trophozoite possesses a surface protein (lectin) that recognizes the sugars galactose and *N*-acetylgalactosamine on the host cell surface. This Gal/GalNAc lectin, which is now well characterized, is essential to the survival of the parasite and its ability to invade the host. It first became apparent that the lectin mediated the parasite's adherence to host cells when it was shown in vitro that *E. histolytica* trophozoites' adherence to Chinese hamster ovary cells and human colonic mucins was dependent on this lectin.[125-128] The adherence lectin was subsequently shown to participate in the in vitro adherence of *E. histolytica* trophozoites to human leukocytes,[113,129] rat and human colonic mucosa and submucosa,[128] human erythrocytes,[125,130] Chang liver cells,[115] opsonized bacteria or bacteria with galactose-containing lipopolysaccharide, and rat colonic epithelial cells.[127] By taking advantage of its carbohydrate-binding activity and adherence-inhibitory monoclonal antibodies,[130,131] the *E. histolytica* galactose-inhibitable lectin was isolated.[126] The lectin is a 260-kDa surface protein that consists of 170- and 35-kDa subunits. The heavy subunit is primarily responsible for attachment, as was originally demonstrated through adherence-inhibitory monoclonal antibodies.[132] The heavy and light subunits are encoded by at least five genes[133-136] that have unique promoter elements.[137] The heavy subunit has a short cytoplasmic domain, a transmembrane domain, and a large extracellular portion with a distinct cysteine-rich area. *Entamoeba dispar* also possesses a distinct gene encoding the functional subunit of the lectin.[12] The light subunit, in contrast, is attached to the membrane via a glycosyl-phosphatidylinositol anchor.[138] There are at least seven discrete epitopes in the lectin heavy subunit, all of which are located in the cysteine-rich domain.[139] Monoclonal antibodies to the lectin heavy subunit abrogate amebic resistance to the lytic effect of the human complement C5b-9 membrane attack complex at the steps of C8 and C9 assembly.[140] The lectin has sequence and antigenic similarities to the human CD59 inhibitor of C8 and C9.[140]

The interface of the Gal/GalNAc lectin with the host mucins lining the intestine is the defining moment of the infection. If the parasite lectin attaches to the host mucin glycoproteins,[127] a noninvasive gut infection is likely. In contrast, if the trophozoite penetrates the mucin layer and the lectin attaches directly to the host cell surface carbohydrates, a cascade of events occurs leading to death of the host cell, and progression to invasive disease may occur. It has been shown that axenic *E. histolytica* trophozoites kill target cells only on direct contact and not via secreted cytotoxins.[125,141] Adherence mediated by the galactose lectin is absolutely required for the in vitro lysis of target cells.[113,125] The death of a target cell may occur up to 20 minutes after amebic adherence; a lethal hit can be delivered within seconds by a trophozoite.[141,142] Amebic cytolytic activity is dependent on parasite microfilament function,[125,141] calcium,[142,143] Ca^{2+}-dependent parasite phospholipase A enzyme activity,[143,144] and maintenance of an acid pH in amebic endocytic vesicles.[145] The presence of a calcium signal pathway in *E. histolytica* is supported by the identification of Ca^2-binding proteins,[146,147] calcium-dependent protein kinases,[146] and a phosphoinositide-3-kinase.[148] Establishment of adherence by *E. histolytica* trophozoites is followed by a marked sustained elevation of the target cell-free intracellular calcium concentration, which contributes to, but may not be totally sufficient for, death of the target cell.[124] Phorbol esters, tumor-promoting agents, and protein kinase C activators specifically augment parasite cytolytic activity.[149] *Entamoeba histolytica* contains an ionophore-like protein of 77 amino acids with sequence homology to NK-lysin, a functionally equivalent protein in the cytotoxic T cells of swine.[133,150] There are three isoforms of the protein, which have been well characterized by protein sequencing and molecular cloning of the cDNA.[133] The polypeptide chain folds into four helical elements; monomers oligomerize after insertion in the membrane to form an ion channel. Amebapore proteins possess potent antibacterial activity, comparable to the role of defensins in mammalian phagocytes, and have been found in the nonpathogenic *E. dispar* spp.[151] Whether these pore-forming proteins function solely as defensins or have a direct role in amebic cytolysis of host cells remains to be determined. Amebic trophozoites cause alterations in intestinal permeability that are independent of their cytolytic activity. For example, when trophozoites are added to the apical surface of a polarized Caco-2 cell line, there is a rapid decrease in transepithelial resistance that precedes any morphologic disruption of monolayer integrity, perhaps indicating disruption of tight-junction proteins.[152] Although it was believed that target cells underwent necrosis rather than apoptosis,[153] recent evidence suggests that apoptosis may be an important component of the pathogenesis of *E. histolytica*.[154] Host-cell apoptosis may be detected in ALAs and invasive intestinal disease in mice, suggesting that this may occur in human invasive disease as well.[155,156] In the murine model of ALA, hepatocyte apoptosis requires activation by caspase, but is independent of Fas and tumor necrosis factor (TNF)–α receptor 1.[155,156] It has been proposed that the parasite's ability to cause apoptosis and then phagocytize the dead cell may substantially limit the host inflammatory response.

Entamoeba histolytica contains numerous proteolytic enzymes, including collagenase and a well-characterized major neutral proteinase.[153,157] Proteinases appear to be involved in dissolution of the extracellular matrix anchoring cells and tissue structure.[153] Kelsall and Ravdin demonstrated that parasite cysteine proteinases are responsible for degradation of human secretory IgA molecules, a possible means of immune evasion.[158] These proteinases have been found to also degrade immunoglobulin G (IgG) molecules and prevent their binding to trophozoites.[159] Conversely, the 56-kDa cysteine proteinase has been associated with activation of complement by cleavage of C3,[160] and pathogenic organisms release greater amounts of the enzyme.[161] Reed and co-workers succeeded in cloning the cysteine proteinase.[157,162] A total of 20 genes, a majority of which are not expressed, have been identified that code for amebic cysteine proteases.[36] *Entamoeba histolytica* trophozoites contain more messenger RNA and secrete 10 to 1000 times the quantity of the proteinase as does *E. dispar*.[157] It is interesting that, even when *E. dispar* genetically engineered cysteine proteinases are intentionally overexpressed, they do not confer virulence.[163,164] Correspondingly, it has been recently demonstrated that the differential expression of these 20 genes varies between *E. histolytica* and *E. dispar*, explaining at least one mechanism that allows *E. histolytica* to invade the host.[36] A direct link between *E. histolytica* cysteine proteinases and the host inflammatory response to amebas was made when it was found that the cysteine proteinases may amplify the interleukin-1–mediated inflammation by mimicking the action of

human interleukin-1 converting enzyme, and cleaving precursor interleukin-1 into its active mature form.[165] In addition to the cysteine proteases, amebic glycosidases, such as β-glucosaminidase[166] and a surface membrane–associated neuraminidase,[167] may be involved in the degradation of colonic mucins or alteration of target cell surface membrane glycoproteins.

In vivo models of ALA[114] and in vitro studies[115] demonstrate that host polymorphonuclear leukocytes constitute the initial host response to *E. histolytica*. Neutrophils demonstrate chemotaxis to amebas,[168] and their lysis by *E. histolytica* enhances tissue destruction in vitro.[115]

HOST IMMUNITY

Humoral and cell-mediated immune responses to *E. histolytica* develop with either asymptomatic or symptomatic infection. *Entamoeba histolytica* has developed multiple immunomodulatory effects on the host response that allow it to successfully invade. Further, it is clear, as with most infectious diseases, that the host responses, likely genetically determined, may not only provide defense for the host but are also a key ingredient in the disease process.[2,169,170] Anecdotal experience suggests that patients cured of amebic colitis or liver abscess are immune to a recurrence of invasive amebiasis. DeLeon followed 1021 patients with ALA for 5 years in Mexico City; only five recurrent abscesses occurred.[171] A study of 982 subjects in a highly endemic area of India found that the rate of gut infection was lower in individuals who possessed serum anti-amebic antibodies.[47] In a longitudinal follow-up of over 1100 subjects in Durban, South Africa, for over 36 months, no recurrences of invasive amebiasis were found.[61] Individuals asymptomatically infected with *E. dispar* spontaneously clear the parasite in 8 to 12 months[58]; it is unknown whether this is due to the acquisition of specific immunity or competition by other intestinal microflora. Further, it has been shown that patients cured of ALA are immune to intestinal infection by *E. dispar* for up to 36 months[61] and children cured of amebic colitis exhibit partial immunity to *E. histolytica* infection.[3]

Both noninvasive and invasive *E. histolytica* infections elicit humoral (IgA and IgG) response to the lectin protein. It has become clear that mucosal IgA response directed at the carbohydrate-recognition domain of the Gal/GalNAc lectin protein is protective against infection.[3] Mucosal immune responses to *E. histolytica* have been well characterized. Studies of colostral antibodies first demonstrated that antiamebic secretory IgA is produced at mucosal surfaces during natural infection.[172,173] Antilectin IgA has been found in the saliva, serum, and feces of subjects with amebic colitis and liver abscess.[61,174–176] Serum IgA antibody responses are found in subjects with asymptomatic *E. histolytica* infection, but not during infection with *E. dispar*. Antilectin intestinal IgA responses persist for up to 36 months in subjects with ALA. A cysteine-rich portion of the galactose-inhibitable lectin heavy subunit (a portion of the 170-kDa subunit designated LC3) appears to be the main epitope on the lectin because it recently was shown to induce humoral (IgA, IgG) immunity in asymptomatic infected patients as well as ALA patients.[36] In addition, epitope-specific mouse monoclonal antibodies against the cysteine-rich region of the Gal/GalNAc lectin's heavy subunit have been shown to inhibit adherence to target cells.[24,36,177,178] Further, oral challenge of BALB/c mice with LC3, using cholera holotoxin as adjuvant, resulted in a high level of intestinal antilectin IgA response, sufficient to block amebic adherence to target cells in vitro.[177] Many investigations are using numerous vaccine strategies and antigens to elicit mucosal immune responses to *E. histolytica*, including the use of an attenuated live *Salmonella* strain with amebic gene inserts or genetically engineered recombinant proteins containing amebic proteins linked to adjuvant proteins.[179]

By the seventh day of illness, patients with ALA develop high titers of serum anti-amebic antibodies.[66] However, patients have progressive, unremitting disease despite possessing serum antibodies, which inhibit amebic adherence in vitro.[180] Further, it has recently been found in a prospective study of Bangladeshi children that a serum IgG response was actually associated with a higher likelihood of future invasive disease.[54] After cure of invasive amebiasis, serum anti-amebic antibodies persist for up to 10 years.[181] Convalescent sera from India, Mexico, Democratic Republic of Congo (formerly Zaire), Egypt, South Africa, and the United States all recognize epitopes on the lectin heavy subunit that was purified from a single *E. histolytica* clone of an axenic strain originally isolated in Mexico City (strain HMI:IMSS).[62,63,174,182,183] In considering the cysteine-rich portion of the heavy subunit as a potential vaccine target, it is important to note recent evidence that demonstrated the Gal/GalNAc lectin heavy subunit from three distinct areas of the world (Bangladesh, Mexico, and the Republic of Georgia) retained remarkable sequence conservation.[184] Highly conserved *E. histolytica* antigens also include a 29-kDa protein,[185] a 125-kDa antigen,[186] a serine-rich surface antigen,[187,188] cysteine proteinases,[31] and an asparagine-rich novel repeat protein.[189]

Sera from both healthy controls and infected patients (with high antibody titers to *E. histolytica*) are amebicidal to trophozoites through activation of the alternate and classic complement pathways.[190,191] However, amebas isolated from a liver abscess or colonic lesions are resistant to complement-mediated lysis[191]; complement-resistant amebas can be selected in vitro by culture in normal human serum.[192] Trophozoites are lysed by the terminal complement components; complement activation occurs at least in part via cleavage of C3 by the parasite's 56-kDa neutral cysteine proteinase.[160] As mentioned previously, the Gal/GalNAc lectin heavy subunit inhibits the assembly of C8 and C9 into the membrane attack complex and apparently has a role in the parasite's resistance to complement-mediated lysis.

Cell-mediated immune defense mechanisms probably have a role in limiting invasive disease and resisting a recurrence after pharmacologic cure. The cell-mediated response consists of antigen-specific lymphocyte blastogenesis with the production of lymphokines (especially interleukin-4, TNF-α, and interferon-γ) capable of activating monocyte-derived macrophages to kill *E. histolytica* trophozoites in vitro.[129,193] Macrophage cytotoxicity is primarily mediated by nitrous oxide, with superoxide and hydrogen peroxide as cofactors.[194] Colonic epithelial cells, induced by contact with *E. histolytica* trophozoites, may have a role in eliciting cellular immune responses by the direct production of cytokines such as interleukin-1β and interleukin-8.[195,196] In addition, in vitro incubation of immune T cells with *E. histolytica* antigen for 5 days elicits cytotoxic T-lymphocyte activity against *E. histolytica* trophozoites.[197,198] However, in acute disease, the T-lymphocyte response to *E. histolytica* may be specifically depressed by a parasite-induced serum factor.[199] The lack of an increased incidence of severe invasive amebiasis in acquired immunodeficiency syndrome patients[93] suggests that host resistance to the initial amebic invasion of the colonic mucosa does not heavily rely on cell-mediated mechanisms. Clinical correlations relating the severity of established invasive disease with cell-mediated immune function include the numerous reports of severe exacerbation of intestinal amebiasis with the occurrence of toxic megacolon during corticosteroid therapy[200] and the fulminant amebic disease in young infants and pregnant women.[103,104]

Nonimmune host defenses may be most important in resistance to symptomatic invasive amebiasis. For example, in animal models, depletion of the colonic mucous blanket is always seen before parasite invasion.[201] Human colonic mucins, rich in terminal galactose residues, act as high-affinity receptors for the *E. histolytica* Gal/GalNAc lectin.[127,202] Colonic mucins inhibit amebic adherence to and lysis of colonic epithelial cells in vitro.[127,203] *E. histolytica* possesses a potent mucus secretogogue activity, comparable to that found with cholera toxin.[204] Therefore, colonic mucin glycoproteins act as an important host defense by binding to the parasite's adherence lectin; however, this interaction probably facilitates intestinal colonization; thus promoting a commensal relationship between *E. histolytica* and the host.

CLINICAL MANIFESTATIONS

The clinical syndromes associated with *E. histolytica* infection are summarized in Table 270-2; familiarity with these diverse manifestations and epidemiologic risk factors greatly facilitates a rapid, correct diagnosis.

TABLE 270-2 Clinical Syndromes Associated with *Entamoeba histolytica* Infection

Intestinal Disease	Extraintestinal Disease
Asymptomatic infection	Liver abscess
Symptomatic noninvasive infection	Liver abscess complicated by
Acute rectocolitis (dysentery)	Peritonitis
Fulminant colitis with perforation	Empyema
Toxic megacolon	Pericarditis
Chronic nondysenteric colitis	Lung abscess
Ameboma	Brain abscess
Perianal ulceration	Genitourinary disease

Intestinal Disease

Many individuals infected with *E. histolytica* will have no or nonspecific gastrointestinal symptoms. Noninvasive intestinal infection may be established by confirmation of *E. histolytica* in the stool in association with Hemoccult-negative stools, and normal mucosa on colonoscopy. In contrast to infection with *E. dispar*, asymptomatic infection with *E. histolytica* is associated with a serum anti-amebic antibody response, and frequently a stool antigen test will be positive.[62,63,174] We do not have a truly controlled prospective study available evaluating the outcome and clinical significance of "noninvasive" amebiasis, although approximately 10% of patients will go on to manifest invasive disease and most individuals will clear their infection within 18 months.

The presentation of invasive intestinal disease caused by *E. histolytica* has been reviewed extensively.[205-207] The signs and symptoms of acute amebic rectocolitis as reported in two large series are summarized in Table 270-3. Its onset is usually gradual over 1 to 3 weeks; although abdominal pain, tenderness, and microscopic hematochezia occur in most patients, a minority experience grossly bloody stools and only one third are febrile. The liver may be enlarged and exhibit percussion tenderness. When diarrhea is marked, the secondary signs of fluid loss and electrolyte imbalance are observed.[206]

Amebic colitis can affect all age groups and both sexes equally. A key point in the differential diagnosis is that virtually all patients have heme-positive stools.[206] Especially in children, colitis can present as rectal bleeding alone without evidence of diarrhea.[208,209] Fecal leukocytes may not be present and are in reduced numbers when compared with patients with shigellosis,[210] presumably as a result of the ability of amebic trophozoites to lyse human neutrophils.[112,113] Charcot-Leyden crystals are often seen in the stool.

Fulminant colitis is an infrequent presentation of amebic infection that has a very high mortality[211] and a predisposition for occurring in malnourished[105] pregnant women,[103] recipients of corticosteroids,[200] or very young patients.[104] Such patients are severely ill with fever, leukocytosis, profuse bloody mucoid diarrhea, and widespread abdominal

TABLE 270-3 Clinical Presentation of Acute Amebic Rectocolitis

Signs and Symptoms	Adams and MacLeod[207] (1958-1972)	Juniper[208] (1957-1962)
Number of cases	3013	55
History < 4 wk	85%	71%
Onset	Gradual	Gradual
Abdominal pain	85%	NA
Diarrhea	100%	94%
Dysentery	99%	94%
Weight loss	NA	44%
Fever	38%	36%
Abdominal tenderness	83%	12%
Heme (+)	100%	100%
Case fatality	1.9%	9.1% (females, twice that of males)
Uncomplicated	10.5%	NA

NA, not available.

pain and are often hypotensive with signs of peritoneal irritation.[210] Fulminant colitis is often associated with liver abscess; segmental or total necrotic involvement of the colon is frequently present and may necessitate total colectomy and result in a fatal outcome despite antiamebic and supportive therapy.[211] Paralytic ileus and colonic mucosal sloughing may occur. Intestinal perforation usually manifests as a slow leakage rather than an acute event; it is unclear whether surgical intervention is beneficial because attempts to suture such necrotic bowels are usually fruitless.[212] Mortality rates with fulminant amebic colitis may exceed 40%.[212]

Toxic megacolon is a well-described complication of acute amebic colitis, occurs in 0.5% of cases, and is a definite complication of inappropriate corticosteroid therapy.[213] Recognition is important because these patients do not respond to drug therapy and require colectomy. Ameboma may be manifested as an annular lesion of the colon that is indistinguishable from colonic carcinoma or as an extrahepatic tender palpable mass, suggesting a pyogenic abscess.[205] Lesions may be single or multiple and are most common in the cecum and ascending colon. Serum anti-amebic antibodies are usually present in this form of amebiasis; in an endemic area, serologic examination or colonoscopy with biopsy should be performed before the surgeon explores the abdomen of such a patient because amebomas tend to respond readily to medical therapy.

Intestinal amebiasis can occur as a chronic nondysenteric syndrome. This was well documented in a series of 159 patients from Pakistan in which most had symptoms for more than 1 year (37% persisted more than 5 years) that consisted of intermittent diarrhea, mucus, abdominal pain, flatulence, and weight loss.[214] This disease is associated with less colonic inflammation and smaller ulcers than in inflammatory bowel disease; amebas are found in the stool, antiamebic serologic tests are positive, and patients respond to antiamebic drug therapy.[214] Chronic amebic infection may be misdiagnosed as inflammatory bowel disease with potentially disastrous consequences if corticosteroid therapy is begun. Examination of stools for ova and parasite, as well as antigen testing, and serologic tests for amebic infection may assist in differentiating chronic *E. histolytica* infection from inflammatory bowel disease.[213]

A chronic, irritative bowel syndrome may also follow acute amebic colitis. This illness usually subsides spontaneously. A more serious but similar illness is that referred to as ulcerative postdysenteric colitis.[206] Fortunately, this is not common. It has a pattern similar to that of ulcerative colitis, with recurrent signs and symptoms of mucus and bloody diarrhea that are unresponsive to antiamebic therapy, but is associated with high antibody titers against *E. histolytica*. Occasionally this can be manifested as a granulomatous colitis with fistula formation.

Perianal amebiasis may result from extension of severe bowel disease to the skin and results from previous trauma, underlying abnormality of the squamous epithelium, or fistulous tracts.[215] Lesions can be ulcerative or condylomatous, slowly enlarge over weeks to months, and result in pain and bleeding. Trophozoites are found in the purulent exudate or on biopsy, and these lesions respond well to antiamebic therapy.

Extraintestinal Amebiasis

An ALA can appear concurrently with colitis, but more frequently there is no evidence or history of recent intestinal infection by *E. histolytica*.[216] In a study of 103 residents of Germany with ALAs after exposure in endemic areas around the world, 95% presented with liver abscesses within 2 to 5 months (median of 3 months) after leaving the endemic area.[217] However, ALA may present years after exposure, and a thorough travel history should be taken in patients with appropriate clinical findings in a low endemic area.[218] Although it has been long accepted that ALA is uniformly a symptomatic and serious disease, recent evidence from Vietnam has shown that this classic paradigm is incorrect. Utilizing abdominal ultrasound, large numbers of asymptomatic people were screened, with confirmatory laboratory examinations, revealing that a substantial number of people may have ALA with no or minimal symptoms, and that this condition may be self-limiting.[65] Thus there is a broad clinical spectrum of disease.

Liver abscess can manifest with an acute onset (less than 10 days) with abdominal pain and fever or subacutely, with weight loss being prominent and less than half the patients having fever or abdominal pain.[66,219-222] Concomitant diarrhea occurs in 30% to 40% of patients; amebas are found in stool by microscopic examination even less frequently.[66] However, Irusen and colleagues demonstrated by fecal culture a high incidence of intestinal colonization at presentation in patients with ALA.[223] In addition, recent studies have indicated that PCR is four to fivefold more sensitive for detecting *E. histolytica* infection than a single culture or microscopy. Failure to eradicate intestinal infection with therapy has been associated with a recurrence of ALA. Abdominal pain is usually localized to the right upper quadrant but can be referred to the shoulder and accompanied by a nonproductive cough.[72,216] On physical examination there is exquisite point tenderness over the liver,[216] hepatomegaly is present in less than half of cases, dullness and rales at the right lung base are common, and peritoneal signs or jaundice are unusual.[216,217,219-222] The presence of diffuse peritonitis or a pericardial friction rub indicates extension of the infection beyond the liver and increased mortality.[217]

Laboratory findings include leukocytosis without eosinophilia in 80% of cases, mild anemia in more than half, elevated alkaline phosphatase levels in 80%, elevated transaminase levels in more aggressive disease, and a high erythrocyte sedimentation rate.[66,216,217,219-222] Serum cholesterol and albumin concentrations have been noted to be decreased in most patients; hyperbilirubinemia is uncommon and present in the setting of severe disease or peritonitis.[66,216] Urinalysis frequently has abnormal findings in acute disease, with proteinuria common.[66]

Pleuropulmonary amebiasis is the most common complication of ALA, usually resulting from the rupture of a superior right lobe abscess with erosion through the diaphragm to involve the pleural space or lung parenchyma.[216,224] Serous pleural effusion and atelectasis are common accompaniments of liver abscesses and do not indicate extension of disease. Patients with pleuropulmonary complications present with cough, pleuritic pain, and dyspnea.[225-227] Empyema resulting from a rupture of the abscess into the pleural cavity presents with sudden respiratory distress and pain and presents a substantial associated mortality risk (15% to 35%).[226,228] Involvement of lung parenchyma may be by direct or hematogenous extension from the liver. Formation of a hepatobronchial fistula is not uncommon and has been associated with spontaneous cure. The sputum contains large amounts of necrotic material, with amebas often demonstrable by sputum ova and parasite examination.[225-227]

Intraperitoneal rupture of liver abscesses occurs in 2% to 7% of cases,[216] with sudden perforation associated with a high mortality.[228] Left lobe abscesses are more likely to progress to rupture because of their later clinical presentation.[216] Such a febrile patient with a rigid distended abdomen may suggest an erroneous diagnosis of a perforated viscus. Pericardial amebiasis is an unusual but serious complication of liver abscesses. Although acute perforation with cardiac tamponade and shock can occur, the usual course is that of fever and abdominal pain progressing to substantial chest pain with signs of congestive heart failure.[216,229] A correct diagnosis is usually dependent on the physician's consideration of the liver as the original source of infection.

Cerebral amebiasis is a rare cause of brain abscess; unfortunately, the onset is abrupt, with rapid progression to death over a period of 12 to 72 hours without adequate therapy.[230] Amebic brain abscesses must be considered in patients with known amebiasis and alteration of mental states or focal signs; on head computed tomography (CT), the lesions appear irregular without a capsule or surrounding enhancement.[231,232] The diagnosis is made directly by examining tissue for amebic trophozoites; medical therapy with metronidazole and surgical decompression for increased intracranial pressure have improved the outcome of cerebral amebiasis.[230-233]

Genitourinary amebiasis is rare; rectovaginal fistulas in females can result in the spread of *E. histolytica* trophozoites to the genitourinary tract.[234,235] Genital disease appears with painful granulation tissue or ulcers; malignancy is often suspected, and diagnosis is again made by biopsy. Penile amebiasis can result via acquisition from vaginal or anal intercourse.[236,237] Medical therapy without surgery is adequate.[238]

DIAGNOSIS

Intestinal Amebiasis

The diagnosis of intestinal amebiasis continues to be most commonly made by identification of E. histolytica or E. dispar in the stool. The finding of either trophozoites or cysts confirms the diagnosis of intestinal infection but does not differentiate the species, although some authors have argued that a microscopic finding of cysts or trophozoites is diagnostic of E. histolytica in a patient with the appropriate clinical syndrome.[35] Substances that interfere with the stool examination should be avoided if possible; these include barium, bismuth, antimicrobials such as tetracyclines or erythromycin, antacids, laxatives, and soap or hypertonic enemas.[207] The best approaches for evaluating stool specimens for amebas are as follows:

1. A specimen obtained during endoscopy should be examined for motile, erythrocyte-containing amebas by direct mount in saline on a warm microscope stage. A small amount of liquid from an area of inflamed bowel is aspirated with a pipette passed through the sigmoidoscope. Liquid stool arriving in the laboratory within 30 minutes after passage can be examined by wet mount in a similar manner. The characteristic motility is that of a directed, linear movement across the microscope stage. Scraping of the ulcer edge or biopsy has a very high yield.
2. Fresh stool specimens should either be smeared and stained with iron hematoxylin or Wheatley trichrome stain or remain fixed in polyvinyl alcohol for later staining (see Figs. 270-1 and 270-3). This allows the best identification of hematophagous E. histolytica trophozoites, the characteristic sign of invasive colonic disease. The nuclear morphology of E. histolytica, such as the central position of the nucleolus and the fine peripheral chromatic pattern, is key to differentiating it from commensals such as Entamoeba coli.
3. Stool specimens are suspended, after a 6% formalin wash and centrifugation, in formalin–ethyl acetate (9 ml 10% formalin, 3 ml ethyl acetate) to allow concentration of E. histolytica cysts at the bottom of the tube after centrifugation.[239] A drop of the sediment is then examined with a drop of dilute iodine solution (1% to 2% iodine in distilled water) to enhance the morphologic features of the cysts (see Fig. 270-3).
4. Because a single stool examination picks up only one third of infected patients, at least three specimens should be submitted before excluding the diagnosis of amebiasis.[42] A saline-purged specimen may increase the likelihood of diagnosis with less than three specimens. Stool culture for E. histolytica is more sensitive[223] and would decrease the need for multiple specimens; however, such cultures are generally not available in clinical practice. The culture media used are not selective for different species of intestinal amebas; therefore, skilled microscopy is still required to determine species identity.

Research has produced promising new diagnostic methodologies to replace fecal microscopy, including direct detection of antigen in the stool and detection of antibodies or antigen in the serum. Detection of serum antibodies to purified defined parasite antigens such as the galactose-inhibitable lectin,[63,183] a 29-kDa surface antigen,[240] and recombinant LC3 subunit antigen[174,182] provides a specific and reproducible means to diagnose infection by E. histolytica. Serum anti-amebic antibody tests are helpful in the diagnosis of invasive intestinal amebiasis.[63,183,241] Asymptomatic cyst passers infected by E. dispar have negative results by standard serologic methods. Eighty-five percent of the patients with biopsy-proven invasive intestinal amebiasis have serum anti-amebic antibodies as determined by various techniques.[63,174,183] Patients with symptoms for more than 1 week are much more likely to have serum anti-amebic antibodies.[183] Indirect hemagglutination anti-amebic antibody titers remain elevated (≥1:128) for years after invasive disease. Other available but less sensitive studies

such as counterimmunoelectrophoresis and gel diffusion precipitation become negative sooner after cure of invasive disease and are helpful in the diagnosis of active amebiasis in an endemic area.[241,242]

Because serum antibodies remain elevated for years after initial exposure, positive serologies in patients from highly endemic areas are difficult to interpret. Therefore, direct detection of E. histolytica antigen in serum and feces is highly desirable. Numerous workers have reported the differentiation of cultivated isolates by binding of monoclonal antibodies to trophozoites.[26,243] Abd-Alla and co-workers[244] and Haque and colleagues[245] (TechLab, Blacksburg, VA) directly detected galactose-inhibitable lectin antigen in fecal samples by enzyme-linked immunosorbent assay and used epitope-specific monoclonal antibodies to differentiate E. histolytica from E. dispar infection. In addition, Abd-Alla and co-workers[244] detected and characterized galactose lectin antigen in serum and found it to be highly specific for infection by E. histolytica. Levels of lectin antigen in feces and serum became undetectable after 7 days of treatment for amebic colitis or liver abscess.[174] Antigen detection provides great advantages in endemic areas where there is a high prevalence of serum anti-amebic antibodies (often 25%).[63] The TechLab assay has gone through a number of improvements and is available for commercial use. In addition, antigen detection facilitates early diagnosis before an antibody response has occurred (<7 days) and differentiates pathogenic from nonpathogenic intestinal infection.[244,245] Another fecal antigen detection method has been developed using polyclonal antibodies (Prospect EIA, Alexon) and is now commercially available; this method was found in one study to be of comparable sensitivity and specificity to microscopy[246]; however, because zymodeme determination was not performed, it is unclear if this assay can differentiate E. dispar from E. histolytica infection. PCR may be so sensitive that it can detect a single trophozoite per gram of feces using amplification of DNA or ribosomal RNA with various methods for performing the study.[247,248] PCR has been utilized successfully for detection of Entamoeba cysts[249] and trophozoites in liver aspirates[250] and can differentiate E. histolytica from E. dispar.[247-250] Recently, real-time PCR, a methodology that distinguishes E. histolytica from E. dispar, has been developed, allowing large numbers of samples to be run with high sensitivity (0.1 parasite per gram of stool) and specificity.[6]

Endoscopy with scraping or biopsy is a valuable technique for the diagnostic evaluation of patients with diarrhea and suspected amebiasis (Table 270-4).[251] Amebic colitis is manifested as punctate hemorrhagic areas or small ulcers (a few millimeters to centimeters in diameter) with exudative centers and hyperemic borders. Rarely, large confluent ulcers are seen. The mucosa may be hyperemic and edematous because of the inflammatory process, and pseudomembranous changes can be present. In the early stage of the disease, endoscopy may be normal; therefore, amebiasis should not be excluded on this basis. In addition, disease may be localized to the cecum or ascending colon and be seen only by total colonoscopy.[212]

There is a broad differential diagnosis in patients presenting with a clinical syndrome consistent with intestinal amebiasis. In patients who excrete Entamoeba cysts and have nonspecific and episodic abdominal complaints such as bloating, cramps, and increased frequency of stools, the differential diagnosis includes giardiasis, viral gastroenteritis, enterotoxigenic E. coli infection, Campylobacter infection,

TABLE 270-4 Indications for Endoscopy with Biopsy or Scrapings in a Patient with a Clinical Syndrome and Risk Factors Consistent with Amebiasis

Stool exam (−), (+) serum anti-amebic antibody test
Stool exam (−), immediate diagnosis required
Stool exam (−), (−) serum anti-amebic antibody test, acute presentation with high suspicion
Chronic syndromes or mass lesions

From Ravdin JI. Intestinal disease caused by *Entamoeba histolytica*. In: Ravdin JI, ed. Amebiasis: Human Infection with *Entamoeba histolytica*. New York: Churchill Livingstone; 1988:495-510.

Salmonella infection, cryptosporidiosis, isosporiasis, malabsorption syndromes, and functional bowel disease. Patients with acute amebic rectocolitis need to be differentiated from those with shigellosis, campylobacteriosis, *Salmonella* colitis, *Clostridium difficile,* toxin-mediated disease, or infection with invasive vibrios, *Yersinia entero-colitica,* or invasive *E. coli* strains.[210] The most difficult distinction is the differentiation of amebiasis from an acute exacerbation of inflammatory bowel disease. Toxic megacolon is a not-infrequent complication of inflammatory bowel disease. Ruling out colitis caused by *E. histolytica* is imperative because corticosteroid therapy exacerbates colonic amebiasis. A complete history with attention to epidemiologic risk factors, stool for fecal leukocytes, use of fecal antigen or toxin detection tests, and examination of stool for amebas may be immediately useful. Appropriate culture of stool for bacterial pathogens, serologic markers for inflammatory bowel disease, and obtaining an amebic serologic examination may be more definitive but generally take a few days.[214] Immediate endoscopy is recommended if the stool examination and stool antigen (by enzyme-linked immunosorbent assay) are negative and amebic colitis is still suspected. A relative contraindication to endoscopy would be patients with fulminant colitis and toxic megacolon, in whom there is a substantial risk of intestinal perforation during endoscopy. Amebomas must be differentiated from other localized processes such as carcinoma, lymphoma, tuberculosis, regional enteritis, or *Yersinia* infection.

Extraintestinal Amebiasis

The diagnosis of ALA, pending serologic results, is based on the clinical presentation and recognition of epidemiologic risk factors, a lack of predisposing conditions for pyogenic liver abscess (such as biliary disease or prior appendicitis), and early use of noninvasive imaging studies.

Most important is performing an imaging study to evaluate for the presence of a hepatic lesion versus biliary tract disease. In one study of 75 patients in an endemic area who presented with fever, right upper quadrant pain, nausea, and vomiting, 9 of the 75 had a liver abscess detected by hepatic sonography and hepatobiliary scans, and all were caused by *E. histolytica.*[221] These patients were clinically indistinguishable from those with cholecystitis except for their younger age (younger than 45 years).[221] Imaging techniques available to establish the presence of cystic liver lesions include ultrasonography, CT, magnetic resonance imaging, and ^{67}Ga scanning.[252] None of these methods is absolutely specific in differentiating an ALA from a pyogenic abscess or tumor.[253] Sonography is rapid, low in cost, and only slightly less sensitive than CT; simultaneously evaluates the gallbladder; and lacks radiation exposure.[252,253] The CT scan is sensitive but not specific

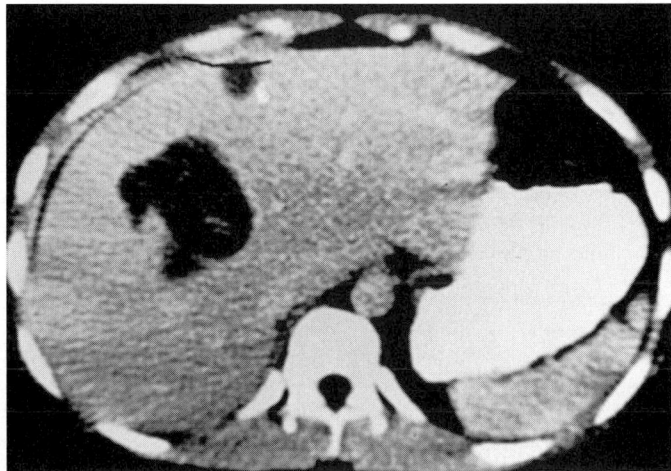

FIGURE 270-5. Abdominal computed tomography scan of a patient with an amebic liver abscess; the irregular multiple defects present in the right lobe of the liver cannot be differentiated from a pyogenic abscess or hepatocellular carcinoma.

for ALA (Fig. 270-5).[252-254] The use of injected contrast material may help differentiate hepatic abscesses from vascular tumors, an important point if liver aspiration is being contemplated. Magnetic resonance imaging is sensitive in the detection of ALA but is no more specific than less costly technology.[255,256] Because of the delay in imaging, gallium scans are not as helpful except if there is uncertainty in regard to a pyogenic versus an amebic abscess. ALAs do not contain leukocytes and therefore appear on gallium scans as cold areas, possibly having a "hot" rim. In contrast, a pyogenic abscess presents as an area of increased isotope concentration.[252]

The presence of serum anti-amebic antibodies is often the definitive study in the diagnosis of ALA; such antibodies are present in up to 99% of patients.[63,66,70,216] One pitfall is in patients with an acute presentation of less than 7 days: serologic studies may be negative.[66] If the diagnosis is still in question, a repeat serologic examination 5 to 7 days later should be positive. The galactose lectin antigen is present in the serum of 75% of subjects with ALA[244,246] and may be an especially useful test in the future for patients who present acutely, before an IgG serum anti-amebic antibody response occurs.

The differential diagnosis for a cystic lesion in the liver that is accompanied by the signs, symptoms, and laboratory abnormalities seen in an ALA might also include pyogenic abscess, echinococcal cyst, and hepatoma. Although older studies emphasize that an ALA presents as a single large lesion in the right lobe of the liver, modern imaging technology demonstrates a high frequency of multiple lesions.[66,252,256] Epidemiologic risk factors, serologic studies, and the presence of calcification aids in the diagnosis of echinococcal disease. If an amebic or pyogenic cause cannot be differentiated on clinical grounds and the patient is not stable enough to await serologic studies, liver aspiration with a "skinny needle" under CT or ultrasound guidance should be performed.[257,258] Aspiration of an ALA yields a sterile, odorless, brown or yellow liquid with amebas not commonly detected on microscopy. A culture of abscess fluid for *E. histolytica* may be helpful, however, most amebas are in the "wall" of the abscess, and the yield of a culture can be low. As indicated, the use of antigen detection enzyme-linked immunosorbent assay on abscess contents is diagnostic.[250] Aspiration of a pyogenic abscess is both diagnostic and therapeutic.[219,220] The main risk of aspiration in all cases is peritoneal spillage; amebic peritonitis complicating a liver abscess markedly increases mortality. In addition, aspiration of an echinococcal cyst is generally to be avoided because of the anaphylactic reaction and seeding with scolices that may accompany leakage into the peritoneum.

Most cases of ALA can be diagnosed and treated without aspiration. In some cases, antimicrobial therapy directed against enteric gram-negative organisms can be added to metronidazole therapy, pending the results of serologic studies. Therapeutic trials of specific antiamebic therapy can be helpful diagnostically; most patients respond within 3 days with decreased pain and fever.[66] The liver abscess cavity usually resolves gradually over months, but persistent cystic lesions are not unusual.[259,260]

TREATMENT

Therapy for amebiasis has been complicated by a number of factors, including (1) variation of drug effects at the three different sites of amebic replication: the lumen of the bowel, the intestinal submucosa, and extraintestinal sites (Table 270-5); (2) the availability of different drugs in different countries; and (3) the development of new drugs and differences of opinion about side effects and efficacy.

It is controversial whether asymptomatic, apparently noninvasive *E. histolytica* infection merits therapy. There is sufficient information to conclude that treatment of *E. dispar* infection in a serum antibody–negative individual is not indicated, especially in a highly endemic area.[48,56-59,63] In contrast, in a low-endemic area all asymptomatic *E. histolytica* infections should be treated[57] because of the potential for invasive disease, antigenic exposure, and risk of transmission of infection to others. Commonly the trophozoites or cysts are detected by routine stool examination performed for

TABLE 270-5 Antimicrobial Agents for Use in Treating Amebiasis

Luminal Agents	Tissue Agents
Diloxanide furoate	Bowel wall only
Paromomycin	Tetracycline
Iodoquinol	Erythromycin
	Liver only
	Chloroquine
	All tissues
	Metronidazole
	Tinidazole
	Emetine hydrochloride
	2-Dehydroemetine

screening purposes on asymptomatic immigrants and refugees migrating from highly endemic areas. If the trophozoites have ingested red blood cells, they may be assumed to be *E. histolytica* and the patient should be treated. If, however, there is no such distinguishing microscopic feature, a serum antibody test, stool antigen test, or both should be utilized to confirm the diagnosis of *E. histolytica* and not *E. dispar* infection, prior to initiation of treatment. In our opinion, given the considerable (>15%) annual risk of infection by *E. histolytica* in highly endemic areas, it is not cost effective or appropriate to screen or to treat asymptomatic patients. An exception to this rule may be members of high-risk groups who, once infected, suffer severe disease, such as malnourished individuals,[105] pregnant women,[103] very young children,[104,261] and patients being administered corticosteroids.[200]

The following recommendations (summarized in Table 270-6) for treating amebiasis are a synthesis of opinions, with emphasis on the easiest, safest, and most effective combination likely to give maximal cure rates with a single course of therapy. When eradication is desired, follow-up stool examination is always necessary because no regimen is completely effective in eradicating intestinal infection. Slightly different treatment regimens in addition to drug toxicities are also summarized in a 1998 *Medical Letter.*[262]

TABLE 270-6 Therapeutic Regimens for the Treatment of Amebiasis*

Type	Efficacy (%)
Cyst Passers	
Diloxanide fuorate,† 500 mg tid for 10 days	87-96
Paromomycin, 30 mg/kg/day in 3 divided doses for 5-10 days	85-90
Tetracycline, 250 mg qid for 10 days then iodoquinol (Yodoxin), 650 mg tid for 20 days	95
Metronidazole, 750 mg tid for 10 days	90
Invasive Rectocolitis	
Metronidazole, 750 mg tid for 5-10 days	>90
Or 2.4 g qd for 2-3 days	>90
Or 50 mg/kg, 1 dose	>86
Plus diloxanide furoate† or paromomycin	
Tetracycline, 250 mg qid for 15 days plus chloroquine (base), 600 mg, 300 mg, then 150 mg tid for 14 days	>94
Dehydroemetine,† 1-1.5 mg/kg/day IM or SC (max. 90 mg) for up to 5 days, plus diloxanide† or paromomycin	>90
Liver Abscess	
Metronidazole, 750 mg tid for 5-10 days or 2.4 g qd for 1-2 days plus diloxanide furoate† or paromomycin	>95
Dehydroemetine,† 1-1.5 mg/kg/day IM or SC (max. 90 mg) for up to 5 days plus diloxanide furoate or paromomycin	>90

*All dosages are for oral administration except dehydroemetine, which is administered intramuscularly; metronidazole can be used intravenously.

†Not commercially available in the United States. Diloxamide furoate is available from the Centers for Disease Control and Prevention.

Intraluminal infection may be treated with diloxanide furoate, 500 mg three times a day for 10 days (this drug is available through the Centers for Disease Control and Prevention).[262-264] Paromomycin (30 mg/kg/day in three divided doses given for 7 days alone) is also an effective treatment of intraluminal infection,[265] has the advantage of being nonabsorbable, and is more available in the United States.[266] Iodoquinol (diiodohydroxyquin, Yodoxin), 650 mg three times daily for 20 days, is effective but difficult to obtain.

Amebic colitis should be treated with a nitroimidazole (metronidazole or tinidazole). Although tinidazole may be slightly more effective and somewhat better tolerated, it is not available in the United States.[208,216,267,268] The recommended dose of tinidazole is 800 mg three times per day for 3 days. Metronidazole is administered in a dose of 750 mg three times a day for 5 to 10 days. This dose of metronidazole may cause nausea and abdominal discomfort in a number of patients, although most can successfully complete a course of therapy. Therapy using 2.4 g/day for 2 days has also been reported to be effective in a small number of patients[269]; there is more extensive experience with single-dose therapy using tinidazole. In view of the side effects, which often begin on the second or third day, this short course may be more palatable to patients.[270] Metronidazole therapy should be followed by specific therapy for intraluminal infection (see Table 270-6).

Extraintestinal amebiasis should be treated with metronidazole or tinidazole and, to prevent continued intraluminal infection, paromomycin or diloxanide furoate.[223] In patients who are seriously ill as a result of complications of amebic infection such as peritonitis or a ruptured amebic abscess, some physicians outside of the United States add parenteral emetine for the first few days (a total of two or three doses once a day, 65 mg/dose). This provides the rapid amebicidal action of emetine with a low incidence of cardiotoxicity; however, there is no published evidence of antiamebic synergy when using these agents in combination. Neither emetine nor its less toxic congener, dehydroemetine, is commercially available in the United States. There is no evidence of metronidazole-resistant *E. histolytica*; although in vitro metronidazole resistance can be induced by axenic culture of trophozoites in increasing concentrations of metronidazole, resulting in increased superoxide dismutase activity,[271] it has not ever been reported to be observed clinically.

The role of invasive procedures in the treatment of amebic abscesses has been an area of debate. Needle aspiration of the liver is a safe procedure in experienced hands,[216] but in most patients it is unnecessary for the relief of symptoms.[66,257] Approximately 10% to 15% of patients, however, are sufficiently ill to consider reducing the size of the abscess before a full therapeutic response is observed. In these patients, needle aspiration is helpful and indicated.[216] Open surgical drainage is not necessary and should be avoided unless the abscess is inaccessible to needle drainage and response to therapy has not occurred in 4 or 5 days. Percutaneous catheter drainage has a higher rate of initial success compared with needle aspiration, but the ultimate outcome in successfully drained patients was no different.[272] Therefore, aspiration is most reasonable when the diagnosis is uncertain (i.e., where pyogenic abscess or bacterial superinfection is suspected), if there is a lack of response to metronidazole/tinidazole therapy after 3 to 4 days, with large left liver abscesses (because of the risk of rupture into the pericardium), and in severely ill patients in whom an accelerated clinical course and large abscesses make rupture seem imminent.[273] Surgical attempts to correct amebic bowel perforation or peritonitis should be avoided, although some patients may benefit from peritoneal lavage.[274] Once a surgeon has performed a laparotomy on a patient with acute abdominal pain of unknown cause and found the damaged bowel of amebiasis, the temptation is to resect it. This is almost always unsuccessful. The surgeon would be better advised simply to obtain confirmatory specimens for examination and bacterial culture and to rely on antiprotozoal and antibacterial agents to control the infection. Maintaining drainage of the peritoneum plus antimicrobial therapy is optimal treatment. Maximal supportive care, including meticulous fluid and electrolyte balance, is essential in the seriously ill patient.

PREVENTION

Amebic infection is prevented by eradicating fecal contamination of food and water. The most commonly contaminated foods are fresh, ground-grown vegetables such as lettuce. Water is always a prime source of spread of infection. Amebic cysts are not killed by low doses of chlorine or iodine; therefore, simply relying on halide tablets in water as a means of preventing amebic infection is not dependable unless adequate concentrations can be guaranteed. Bringing water to a boil ensures the absence of amebas. Vegetables should be treated with a strong detergent soap and then soaked in acetic acid or vinegar for 10 to 15 minutes to ensure eradication of the cysts. In general, when traveling in the tropics, unless the boiling of the water and the preparation of vegetables has been personally observed, these sources of food and refreshment should be omitted. Even in the finest hotels and restaurants, those preparing the food or placing water in bottles for drinking are often not aware of the potential danger of infection to the nonimmune traveler.

Improvement in waste disposal and water purification is the most important factor in reducing the risk of acquiring amebiasis. Avoiding sexual practices that allow fecal-oral contact can prevent infection in the male homosexual population. At present, there is not a clear means to prevent infection in institutionalized individuals, especially the developmentally and cognitively impaired, although case identification, therapy, improved supervision, and hygiene may be beneficial. Studies of the pathogenesis of amebiasis and host immunity may eventually lead to an immunologic or pharmacologic means to prevent invasive amebic disease.

Interruption of transmission of *E. histolytica* depends on extensive changes to complex socioeconomic problems and human behavior. Clearly, applying our knowledge of the pathogenesis of the disease and the immunity of the host to vaccine development would be the most efficient and cost-effective means of preventing disease. The recognition of an extraordinarily high prevalence of *E. histolytica* infection in certain vulnerable populations of the world suggests that an effective and safe vaccine not only would prevent considerable mortality but also would provide a valuable tool in decreasing morbidity in developing nations. This would be particularly true for children in developing nations because the epidemiology indicates that children in poverty are at an extremely high risk for developing infection and are probably instrumental in transmission. Because there is no known natural zoonotic reservoir for the parasite, a safe and effective vaccine could theoretically lead to eradication of *E. histolytica*. Because it appears that acquired immunity to *E. histolytica* is correlated with mucosal immunity, it follows that a vaccine that induces gut-associated lymphoid tissue would be a primary candidate. The amebic native Gal/GalNAc lectin has been demonstrated by Petri and Ravdin to be highly effective as a vaccine in an experimental model of ALA in the gerbil.[204] The recombinant LC3 protein, as mentioned, has also been found efficacious as a vaccine in the gerbil model of ALA via systemic immunization.[182] The use of *Salmonella* expressing different fragments of the lectin 170-kDa subunit provided partial protection.[275] Protective immunity in gerbils immunized with recombinant portions of the lectin 170-kDa subunit was found to correlate with the induction of antibodies to a 25-amino-acid region of the molecule.[276] Immunization with polyclonal antibodies to a recombinant serine-rich protein[277] or with monoclonal antibody to a lipophosphoglycan antigen provided protection against ALA in the severe combined immunodeficient mouse model of ALA.[278] More recently, it was found through an in vivo study conducted in mice that an injectable codon-optimized DNA vaccine targeting a portion of the Gal/GalNAc heavy subunit stimulated a Th1-type Gal/GalNAc lectin–specific cellular immune response as well as inducing development of serum antibodies that recognized a recombinant portion of the heavy subunit.[279] Investigation is underway to assess this vaccine via an oral delivery route. Research on gene expression systems[280-282] and stable episomal transfection[283] provides opportunities to further study unique antigens and their relation to virulence, pathogenesis, and immunity. Numerous research groups are working on the development of different recombinant vaccines to induce amebicidal cell-mediated immunity, adherence-inhibitory secretory IgA responses, or humoral immunity that contributes to protection against invasive amebiasis.[179] The hope is that one day a successful, inexpensive, lectin-based vaccine can be developed and delivered successfully to a large part of the world's population that are at risk for disease from this ancient parasite.

REFERENCES

1. Walsh JA. Prevalence of *Entamoeba histolytica* infection. In: Ravdin JI, ed. Amebiasis: Human Infection by *Entamoeba histolytica*. New York: Churchill Livingstone; 1988:93-105.
2. Petri WA Jr, Haque R, Mann BJ. The bittersweet interface of parasite and host: Lectin-carbohydrate interactions during human invasion by the parasite *Entamoeba histolytica*. Annu Rev Microbiol. 2002;56:39-64.
3. Haque R, Huston CD, Hughs M, et al. Current Concepts: Amebiasis. N Engl J Med. 2003;348:1565-1573.
4. Mann BJ. *Entamoeba histolytica* Genome Project: An update. Trends Parasitol. 2002;18:147-148.
5. Blessman J, Buss H, Phuong A, et al. Real-time PCR for detection and differentiation of *Entamoeba histolytica* and *Entamoeba dispar* in fecal samples. J Clin Microbiol. 2002;40:4413-4417.
6. Haque R, Mollah NU, Ali IKM, et al. Diagnosis of amebic liver abscess and intestinal infection with the TechLab *Entamoeba histolytica* II antigen detection and antibody tests. J Clin Microbiol. 2000;38:3235-3239.
7. Sargeaunt PG, Williams JE, Greene JD. The differentiation of invasive and non-invasive *Entamoeba histolytica* by isoenzyme electrophoresis. Trans R Soc Trop Med Hyg. 1978;72:519-521.
8. Tannich E, Burchard GD. Differentiation of pathogenic from nonpathogenic *Entamoeba histolytica* by restriction fragment analysis of a single gene amplified in vitro. J Clin Microbiol. 1991;29:250-255.
9. Ortner S, Clark CG, Binder M, et al. Molecular biology of the hexokinase isoenzyme pattern that distinguishes pathogenic *Entamoeba histolytica* from nonpathogenic *Entamoeba dispar*. Mol Biochem Parasitol. 1997;86:85-94.
10. Diamond LS, Clark CG. A redescription of *Entamoeba histolytica* Schaudinn 1903 (Emended Walker 1911), separating it from *Entamoeba dispar* Brumpt 1925. J Eukaryot Microbiol. 1993;40:340-344.
11. Clark CG, Diamond LS. Intraspecific variation and phylogenetic relationships in the genus *Entamoeba* as revealed by riboprinting. J Eukaryot Microbiol. 1997;44:143-154.
12. Pillai DR, Britten D, Ackers JP, et al. A gene homologous to *hgl2* of *Entamoeba histolytica* is present and expressed in *Entamoeba dispar*. Mol Biochem Parasitol. 1997;87:101-105.
13. Bruchhaus I, Jacobs T, Leippe M, Tannich E. *Entamoeba histolytica* and *Entamoeba dispar*: Differences in numbers and expression of cysteine proteinase genes. Mol Microbiol. 1996;22:255-263.
14. Losch FA. Massive development of amoebaes in the large intestine. Am J Trop Med Hyg. 1875;24:383-392.
15. Kean BY, Mott KE, Russel AJ. Tropical Medicine and Parasitology: Classic Investigations. Ithaca, NY: Cornell University Press; 1978.
16. Select Committee. Amebiasis outbreak in Chicago: Report of a special committee. JAMA. 1934;102:369.
17. LeMaistre CA, Sappenfield R, Culbertson C, et al. Studies of a water-borne outbreak of amebiasis: South Bend, Indiana. Am J Hyg. 1956;64:30-45.
18. Barwick R, Uzicanin A, Lareau S, et al. Outbreak of amebiasis in Tbilisi, Republic of Georgia, 1998. Am J Trop Med Hyg. 2002;67:623-631.
19. Mai Z, Ghosh S, Frisardi M, et al. Hsp60 is targeted to a cryptic mitochondrion derived organelle ("cryton") in the microaerophilic protozoan parasite *Entamoeba histolytica*. Mol Cell Biol. 1999;19:2198-2205.
20. Tovar J, Fischer A, Clark CG. The mitosome, a novel organelle related to mitochondria in the amitochondriate parasite *Entamoeba histolytica*. Mol Microbiol. 1999;32:1012-1021.
21. Gonzalez E, Rico G, Mendoza G, et al. Calreticulin-like molecule in trophozoites of *Entamoeba histolytica* HM1:IMSS (SWISSPROT: ACCESSION P83003). Am J Trop Med Hyg. 2002;67:636-639.
22. Levine ND, Corliss JO, Cox FEG. A newly revised classification of the protozoa. J Protozool. 1980;27:37-58.
23. Jackson TFHG. *Entamoeba histolytica* and *Entamoeba dispar* are distinct species: Clinical, epidemiological and serological evidence. Int J Parasitol. 1998;28:181-186.
24. Petri WA Jr, Jackson TFHG, Gathiram V, et al. Pathogenic and nonpathogenic strains of *Entamoeba histolytica* can be differentiated by monoclonal antibodies to the galactose-specific adherence lectin. Infect Immun. 1990;58:1802-1806.
25. Tachibana H, Kobayashi S, Nagakura K. Reactivity of monoclonal antibodies to species-specific antigens of *Entamoeba histolytica*. J Protozool. 1991;38:329-334.
26. Tachibana H, Kobayashi S, Cheng X, Hiwatashi E. Differentiation of *Entamoeba histolytica* from *E dispar* facilitated by monoclonal antibodies against a 150-kDa surface antigen. Parasitol Res. 1997;83:435-439.
27. Bhattacharya S, Bhattacharya S, Sharma MP, et al. Metabolic labeling of *Entamoeba histolytica* antigens: Characterization of a 28-kDa major intracellular antigen. Exp Parasitol. 1990;70:255-263.
28. Reed SL, Flores BM, Batzer MA, et al. Molecular and cellular characterization of the 29-kilodalton peripheral membrane protein of *Entamoeba histolytica*: Differentiation between pathogenic and nonpathogenic isolates. Infect Immun. 1992;60:542-549.

29. Tannich E, Horstmann RD, Knobloch J, et al. Genomic DNA differences between pathogenic and nonpathogenic *Entamoeba histolytica.* Proc Natl Acad Sci U S A. 1989;86:5118-5122.

30. Tachibana H, Kobayashi S, Paz KC, et al. Analysis of pathogenicity by restriction-endonuclease digestion of amplified genomic DNA of *Entamoeba histolytica* isolated in Pernambuco, Brazil. Parasitol Res. 1992;78:433-436.

31. Burch DJ, Li E, Reed S, et al. Isolation of a strain specific *Entamoeba histolytica* cDNA clone. J Clin Microbiol. 1991;29:696-701.

32. Que X, Reed SL. Nucleotide sequence of a small subunit ribosomal RNA (16S-like rRNA) gene from *Entamoeba histolytica:* Differentiation of pathogenic from nonpathogenic isolates. Nucleic Acids Res. 1991;19:5438.

33. Blanc DS. Determination of taxonomic status of pathogenic and nonpathogenic *Entamoeba histolytica* zymodemes using isoenzyme analysis. J Protozool. 1992;39:471-479.

34. Baez-Camargo M, Riveron AM, Delgadillo DM, et al. *Entamoeba histolytica:* Gene linkage groups and relevant features of its karyotype. Mol Gen Genet. 1996;253:289-296.

35. Gonzalez-Ruiz A, Hague R, Aquirre A, et al. Value of microscopy in the diagnosis of dysentery associated with invasive *Entamoeba histolytica.* J Clin Pathol. 1994;4:236-239.

36. Stauffer WM, Ravdin JI. *Entamoeba histolytica:* An update. Curr Opin Infect Dis. 2003;16:479-485.

37. Riveron AM, Lopez-Canovas L, Baez-Camargo M, et al. Circular and linear DNA molecules in the *Entamoeba histolytica* complex molecular karyotype. Eur Biophys J. 2000;29:48-56.

38. Ramos MA, Sanchez-Lopez R, Olvera F, et al. *Entamoeba histolytica* genomic organization: Identification, structure, and phylogenetic relationship of 2 serine-threonine protein kinases. Exp Parasitol. 2002;100:135-139.

39. Ayeh-Kumi P, Ali IKM, Lockhart L, et al. *Entamoeba histolytica:* Genetic diversity of clinical isolates from Bangladesh as demonstrated by polymorphisms in the serine-rich gene. Exp Parasitol. 2001;99:80-88.

40. Eichinger D. A role for a galactose lectin and its ligands during encystment of *Entamoeba.* J Eukarot Microbiol. 2001;48:17-21.

41. Chayen A, Avron B, Nuchamowitz Y, et al. Appearance of sialoglycoproteins in encysting cells of *Entamoeba histolytica.* Infect Immun. 1988;56:673-681.

42. Healy GR. Diagnostic techniques for stool samples. In: Ravdin JI, ed. Amebiasis: Human Infection by *Entamoeba histolytica.* New York: Churchill Livingstone; 1988:635-649.

43. Mathur TN, Kaur J. The frequency of excretion of cysts of *Entamoeba histolytica* in known cases of non-dysenteric amebic colitis based on 21 stool examinations. Indian J Med Res. 1973;61:330-334.

44. Krogstad DJ, Spencer HC, Healy GR, et al. Amebiasis: Epidemiologic studies in the United States, 1971-1974. Ann Intern Med. 1978;88:89-97.

45. Caballero-Salcedo A, Viveros-Rogel M, Salvatierra B, et al. Seroepidemiology of amebiasis in Mexico. Am J Trop Med Hyg. 1994;50:412-419.

46. Hossain MM, Ljungstrom I, Glass RI, et al. Amebiasis and giardiasis in Bangladesh: Parasitological and serological studies. Trans R Soc Trop Med Hyg. 1983;77:552-554.

47. Choudhuri G, Prakash V, Kumar A, et al. Protective immunity to *Entamoeba histolytica* infection in subjects with antiamebic antibodies residing in a hyperendemic zone. Scand J Infect Dis. 1991;23:771-776.

48. Gathiram V, Jackson TFHG. A longitudinal study of asymptomatic carriers of pathogenic zymodemes of *Entamoeba histolytica.* S Afr Med J. 1987;72:669-672.

49. Gutierrez G, Ludlow A, Espinos G, et al. National serologic survey. II. Search for antibodies against *Entamoeba histolytica* in Mexico. In: Sepulveda B, Diamond LS, eds. Amebiasis: Proceedings of the International Conference on Amebiasis. Mexico City: Instituto Mexicano del Seguro Social; 1976:609-618.

50. Haque R, Faruque ASG, Hahn P, et al. *Entamoeba histolytica* and *Entamoeba dispar* infection in children in Bangladesh. J Infect Dis. 1997;175:734-736.

51. Braga LL, Mendonca Y, Paiva CA, et al. Seropositivity for and intestinal colonization with *Entamoeba histolytica* and *Entamoeba dispar* in individuals in northeastern Brazil. J Clin Microbiol. 1998;36:3044-3045.

52. Rivera WL, Tachibana H, Kanbara H. Field study on the distribution of *Entamoeba histolytica* and *Entamoeba dispar* in the northern Philippines as detected by polymerase chain reaction. Am J Trop Med Hyg. 1998;59:916-921.

53. Evangelopoulos A, Legakis N, Vakalia N. Microscopy, PCR and ELISA applied to the epidemiology of amebiasis in Greece. Parasitol Int. 2001;50:185-189.

54. Haque R, Duggal P, Ali IM, et al. Innate and acquired resistance to amebiasis in Bangladeshi children. J Infect Dis. 2002;86:547-552.

55. Abdel Hafez MM, el Kady N, Bolbol AS, et al. Prevalence of intestinal parasitic infections in Riyadh district, Saudi Arabia. Ann Trop Med Parasitol. 1986;80:631-634.

56. Jackson TFHG, Gathiram V, Simjee AE. Seroepidemiological study of antibody responses to the zymodemes of *Entamoeba histolytica.* Lancet. 1985;1:716-719.

57. Jackson TFHG. *Entamoeba histolytica* cyst passers—to treat or not to treat (Editorial)? S Afr Med J. 1987;72:657-658.

58. Nanda R, Baveja U, Anand BS. *Entamoeba histolytica* cyst passers: Clinical features and outcome in untreated subjects. Lancet. 1984;2:301-303.

59. Gathiram V, Jackson TFHG. Frequency distribution of *Entamoeba histolytica* zymodemes in a rural South African population. Lancet. 1985;1:719-721.

60. Gatti S, Swierczynski G, Robinson F, et al. Amebic infections due to the *Entamoeba histolytica-Entamoeba dispar* complex: A study of the incidence in a remote rural area of Ecuador. Am J Trop Med Hyg 2002;67:123-127.

61. Ravdin JI, Abd-Alla MD, Welles SL, et al. Intestinal antilectin immunoglobulin A antibody response and immunity to *Entamoeba dispar* infection following cure of amoebic liver abscess. Infect Immun. 2003;71:6899-6905.

62. Abd-Alla M, Jackson TGFH, Ravdin JI. Serum IgM antibody response to the galactose-inhibitable adherence lectin of *Entamoeba histolytica.* Am J Trop Med Hyg. 1998;59:431-434.

63. Ravdin JI, Jackson TF, Petri WA Jr, et al. Association of serum antibodies to adherence lectin with invasive amebiasis and asymptomatic infection with *Entamoeba histolytica.* J Infect Dis. 1990;162:768-772.

64. Abd-Alla M, Wahib A, Ravdin JI. Diagnosis of amebic colitis by antigen capture ELISA in patients presenting with acute diarrhea in Cairo, Egypt. Trop Med Int Health. 2002;7:1-6.

65. Blessman J, Van Linh, Nu PA, et al. Epidemiology of amebiasis in a region of high incidence of amebic liver abscess in Central Vietnam. Am J Trop Med Hyg. 2002;66:578-583.

66. Katzenstein D, Rickerson V, Braude A. New concepts of amebic liver abscess derived from hepatic imaging, serodiagnosis, and hepatic enzymes in 67 consecutive cases in San Diego. Medicine (Baltimore). 1982;61:237-246.

67. Shandera WX, Bollman P, Hashmey RH Jr, et al. Hepatic amebiasis among patients in a public teaching hospital. South Med J. 1998;91:829-837.

68. Blessman J, Van Linh, Nu PA, et al. Epidemiology of amebiasis in a region of high incidence of amebic liver abscess in Central Vietnam. Am J Trop Med Hyg. 2002;66:578-583.

69. Summary of notifiable diseases, United States. MMWR Morb Mortal Wkly Rep. 1994;42:1-73.

70. Shabot JM, Patterson M. Amebic liver abscess: 1966-1976. Dig Dis. 1978;23:110.

71. Abuabara SF, Barrett JA, Hau T, et al. Amebic liver abscess. Arch Surg. 1982;117:239-244.

72. Thompson JE Jr, Forlenza S, Verma R. Amebic liver abscess: A therapeutic approach. Rev Infect Dis. 1985;7:171-179.

73. Barnes PF, DeCock KM, Reynolds TN, et al. A comparison of amebic and pyogenic abscess of the liver. Medicine (Baltimore). 1987;66:472-483.

74. Thompson JE Jr, Glasser AJ. Amebic abscess of the liver: Diagnostic features. J Clin Gastroenterol. 1986;8:550-554.

75. Stauffer WM, Kamat D, Walker PF. Screening of international immigrants, refugees, and adoptees. Prim Care Clin Office Pract. 2002;29:875-905.

76. Stauffer WM, Maroushek S, Kamat D. Medical screening of immigrant children. Clin Pediatr. 2003;42:763-773.

77. Pillai DR, Keystone JS, Sheppard DC, et al. *Entamoeba histolytica* and *Entamoeba dispar:* Epidemiology and comparison of diagnostic methods in a setting of nonendemicity. Clin Infect Dis. 1999;29:1315-1318.

78. Pearson RD, Hewlett EL. Amebiasis in travelers. In: Ravdin JI, ed. Amebiasis: Human Infection by *Entamoeba histolytica.* New York: Churchill Livingstone; 1988:556-562.

79. Pehrson PO. Amebiasis in a non-endemic country. Scand J Infect Dis. 1983;15:207-214.

80. Merson MH, Morris GK, Sack DA, et al. Traveler's diarrhea in Mexico: A prospective study. N Engl J Med. 1976;294:1299.

81. Jelinek T, Peyeri G, Loscher T, Nothdurft HD. Evaluation of an antigen-capture enzyme immunoassay for detection of *Entamoeba histolytica* in stool samples. Eur J Clin Microbiol Infect Dis. 1996;15:752-755.

82. Weinke T, Friedrich-Jaenicke B, Hopp P, Janitshke K. Prevalence and clinical importance of *Entamoeba histolytica* in two high-risk groups: Travelers returning from the tropics and male homosexuals. J Infect Dis. 1990;161:1029-1031.

83. Thacker SB, Simpson S, Gordon TJ, et al. Parasitic disease control in a residential facility for the mentally retarded. Am J Public Health. 1979;69:1279-1281.

84. Sexton DJ, Krogstad DJ, Spencer HC, et al. Amebiasis in a mental institution: Serologic and epidemiologic studies. Am J Epidemiol. 1974;100:414-423.

85. Petri WA, Ravdin JI. Amebiasis in institutionalized populations. In: Ravdin JI, ed. Amebiasis: Human Infection by *Entamoeba histolytica.* New York: Churchill Livingstone; 1988:576-581.

86. Thacker SB, Kimball AM, Wolfe M, et al. Parasitic disease control in a residential facility for the mentally retarded: Failure of selected isolation procedures. Am J Public Health. 1981;71:303.

87. Brooke MM. Epidemiology and control of amebiasis in institutions for the mentally retarded. Am J Ment Defic. 1963;68:187.

88. Kean BH, William DC, Luminais SK. Epidemic of amebiasis and giardiasis in a biased population. Br J Vener Dis. 1979;55:375-378.

89. Quinn TC, Corey L, Chaffee RG, et al. The etiology of anorectal infections in homosexual men. Am J Med. 1981;71:395.

90. Phillips SC, Mildvan D, William DC, et al. Sexual transmission of enteric protozoa and helminths in a venereal-disease-clinic population. N Engl J Med. 1981;305:603-606.

91. Markell EK, Havens RF, Kuritsubo RA, et al. Intestinal protozoa in homosexual men of the San Francisco Bay area: Prevalence and correlates of infection. Am J Trop Med Hyg. 1984;33:239-245.

92. Ortega HB, Borchardt KA, Hamilton R, et al. Enteric pathogenic protozoa in homosexual men from San Francisco. Sex Transm Dis. 1983;11:59.

93. Druckman DA, Quinn TC. *Entamoeba histolytica* infection in homosexual men. In: Ravdin JI, ed. Amebiasis: Human Infection by *Entamoeba histolytica.* Edinburgh: Churchill Livingstone; 1988:563-575.

94. Peters CS, Sable R, Janda WM, et al. Prevalence of enteric parasites in homosexual patients attending an outpatient clinic. J Clin Microbiol. 1986;24:684-685.

95. Sorvillo FJ, Strassburg MA, Seidel J, et al. Amebic infections in asymptomatic homosexual men, lack of evidence of invasive disease. Am J Public Health. 1986;76:1137-1139.

96. Smith PD, Lane HC, Gill VJ, et al. Intestinal infections in patients with the acquired immunodeficiency syndrome (AIDS): Etiology and response to therapy. Ann Intern Med. 1988;108:328-333.

97. Fatkenheuer G, Arnold G, Steffen H, et al. Invasive amebiasis in two patients with AIDS and cytomegalovirus colitis. J Clin Microbiol. 1997;35:2168-2169.

98. Blanshard C, Collins C, Francis N, Gazzard BG. Invasive amebic colitis in AIDS patients. AIDS. 1992;6:1043-1044.

99. Reed SL, Wessel DW, Davis CE. *Entamoeba histolytica* infections and AIDS. Am J Med. 1991;90:269-271.

100. Ohnishi K, Murata M, Okuzawa E. Symptomatic amebic colitis in a Japanese homosexual AIDS patient. Intern Med. 1994;33:120-122.

101. Brown M, Reed S, Levy JA, et al. Detection of HIV-1 in *Entamoeba histolytica* without evidence of transmission to human cells. AIDS. 1991;5:93-96.

102. Istre GR, Kriess K, Hopkins RS, et al. An outbreak of amebiasis spread by colonic irrigation at a chiropractic clinic. N Engl J Med. 1982;309:339-342.

103. Lewis EA, Antia AU. Amebic colitis: Review of 295 cases. Trans R Soc Trop Med Hyg. 1969;63:633-638.

104. Fuchs G, Ruiz Palacios G, Pickering LK. Amebiasis in the pediatric population. In: Ravdin JI, ed. Amebiasis: Human Infection by *Entamoeba histolytica*. New York: Churchill Livingstone; 1988:594-613.

105. Wanke C, Butler T, Islam M. Epidemiologic and clinical features of invasive amebiasis in Bangladesh: A case-control comparison with other diarrheal diseases and post-mortem findings. Am J Trop Med Hyg. 1988;38:335-341.

106. Brandt H, Perez Tamayo R. Pathology of human amebiasis. Hum Pathol. 1970;1:351-385.

107. Griffin JL, Juniper K Jr. Ultrastructure of *Entamoeba histolytica* from human amebic dysentery. Arch Pathol. 1971;91:271-280.

108. Pittman FE, El Hashimi WK, Pittman JC. Studies of human amebiasis. II. Light and electromicroscopic observations of colonic mucosa and exudate in acute amebic colitis. Gastroenterology. 1973;65:588-603.

109. Takeuchi A, Phillips BP. Electron microscopic studies of experimental *Entamoeba histolytica* infection in the guinea pig. I. Penetration of the intestinal epithelium by trophozoites. Am J Trop Med Hyg. 1975;24:34-48.

110. Prathap K, Gilman R. The histopathology of acute intestinal amebiasis. Am J Pathol. 1970;60:229-239.

111. Chatgidakis CB. The pathology of hepatic amebiasis as seen on the Witwatersrand. S Afr J Clin Sci. 1953;4:230.

112. Guerrant RL, Brush J, Ravdin JI, et al. Interaction between *Entamoeba histolytica* and human polymorphonuclear neutrophils. J Infect Dis. 1981;143:83-93.

113. Ravdin JI, Murphy CF, Salata RA, et al. The *N*-acetyl-D-galactosamine-inhibitable adherence lectin of *Entamoeba histolytica*. I. Partial purification and relation to amebic virulence *in vitro*. J Infect Dis. 1985;151:804-815.

114. Tsutsumi V, Mena-Lopez R, Anaya-Velazquez F, et al. Cellular basis of experimental amebic liver abscess formation. Am J Pathol. 1984;117:81-91.

115. Salata RA, Ravdin JI. The interaction of human neutrophils and *Entamoeba histolytica* increases cytopathogenicity for liver cell monolayers. J Infect Dis. 1986;154:19-26.

116. Seydel KB, Zhang T, Stanley JR. Neutrophils play a critical role in early resistance to amebic liver abscesses in severe combined immunodeficient mice. Infect Immun. 1997;65:3951-3953.

117. Meza I. Extracellular matrix-induced signaling in *Entamoeba histolytica*: Its role in invasiveness. Parasitol Today. 2000;16:23-28.

118. Joyce MP, Ravdin JI. Pathology of human amebiasis. In: Ravdin JI, ed. Amebiasis: Human Infection by *Entamoeba histolytica*. New York: Churchill Livingstone; 1988:129-146.

119. Aikat BK, Bhusnurmath SR, Pal AK, et al. The pathology and pathogenesis of fatal hepatic amebiasis: A study based on 79 autopsy cases. Trans R Soc Trop Med Hyg. 1979;73:188-192.

120. Gulati PD, Gupta DN, Chuttani HK. Amebic liver abscess and disturbances of portal circulation. Am J Med. 1967;45:852-854.

121. Tandon BN, Tandon HD, Puri BK. An electron microscopic study of liver in hepatomegaly presumably caused by amebiasis. Exp Mol Pathol. 1975;22:118.

122. Diamond LS, Harlow DR, Cunnick CC. A new medium for the axenic cultivation of *Entamoeba histolytica* and other *Entamoeba*. Trans R Soc Trop Med Hyg. 1978;72:431-432.

123. Clark CG. Axenic cultivation of *Entamoeba dispar* Brumpt 1925, *Entamoeba insolita* Geiman and Wichterman 1937 and *Entamoeba ranarum* Grassi 1879. J Eukaryot Microbiol. 1995;42:590-593.

124. Ravdin JI. Amebiasis, "State of the Art." Clin Infect Dis. 1995;20:1453-1466.

125. Ravdin JI, Guerrant RL. Role of adherence in cytopathogenic mechanisms of *Entamoeba histolytica*. J Clin Invest. 1981;68:1305-1313.

126. Petri WA, Smith RD, Schlesinger PH, et al. Isolation of the galactose-binding lectin which mediates the in vitro adherence of *Entamoeba histolytica*. J Clin Invest. 1987;80:1238-1244.

127. Chadee K, Petri WA, Innes DJ, et al. Rat and human colonic mucins bind to and inhibit the adherence of lectin of *Entamoeba histolytica*. J Clin Invest. 1987;80:1245-1254.

128. Ravdin JI, John JE, Johnston LI, et al. Adherence of *Entamoeba histolytica* trophozoites to rat and human colonic mucosa. Infect Immun. 1985;48:292-297.

129. Salata RA, Pearson RD, Ravdin JI. Interaction of human leukocytes with *Entamoeba histolytica*: Killing of virulent amoebae by the activated macrophage. J Clin Invest. 1985;76:491-499.

130. Kain KC, Ravdin JI. Galactose-specific adhesion mechanisms of *Entamoeba histolytica*: Model for study of enteric pathogens. Methods Enzymol. 1995;253:424-439.

131. Ravdin JI, Petri WA, Murphy CF, et al. Production of mouse monoclonal antibodies which inhibit in vitro adherence of *Entamoeba histolytica* trophozoites. Infect Immun. 1986;53:1-5.

132. Petri WA Jr, Chapman MD, Snodgrass T, et al. Subunit structure of the galactose and *N*-acetyl-D-galactosamine-inhibitable adherence lectin of *Entamoeba histolytica*. J Biol Chem. 1989;264:3007-3012.

133. Leippe M. Amoebapores. Parasitol Today. 1997;13:178-183.

134. Ramakrishnan G, Ragland BD, Purdy JE, Mann BJ. Physical mapping and expression of gene families encoding the *N*-acetyl-D-galactosamine adherence lectin of *Entamoeba histolytica*. Mol Microbiol. 1996;19:91-100.

135. Tannich E, Ebert F, Horstmann RD. Primary structure of the 170-kDa surface lectin of pathogenic *Entamoeba histolytica*. Proc Natl Acad Sci U S A. 1991;88:1849-1853.

136. Mann BJ, Torian BE, Vedvick TS, et al. Sequence of a cysteine-rich galactose-specific lectin of *Entamoeba histolytica*. Proc Natl Acad Sci U S A. 1991;88:3248-3252.

137. Singh U, Rogers JB, Mann BJ, Petri WA. Transcription initiation is controlled by three core promoter elements in the *hgl5* gene of the protozoan parasite *Entamoeba histolytica*. Proc Natl Acad Sci U S A. 1997;94:8812-8817.

138. McCoy JJ, Mann BJ, Vedvick T, et al. Structural analysis of the light subunit of the *Entamoeba histolytica* galactose-specific lectin. J Biol Chem. 1993;24:223-231.

139. Petri WA, Jackson TFHG, Gathiram V, et al. Pathogenic and nonpathogenic strains of *Entamoeba histolytica* can be differentiated by monoclonal antibodies to the galactose-specific lectin. Infect Immun. 1990;58:1802-1806.

140. Braga LL, Ninomiya H, McCoy JJ, et al. Inhibition of the complement membrane attack complex by the galactose-specific adhesion of *Entamoeba histolytica*. J Clin Invest. 1992;90:1131-1137.

141. Ravdin JI, Croft BY, Guerrant RL. Cytopathogenic mechanisms of *Entamoeba histolytica*. J Exp Med. 1980;152:377-390.

142. Ravdin JI, Moreau F, Sullivan JA, et al. The relationship of free intracellular calcium ions to the cytolytic activity of *Entamoeba histolytica*. Infect Immun. 1988;56:1505-1512.

143. Ravdin JI, Murphy CF, Guerrant RL, et al. Effect of calcium and phospholipase A antagonists on the cytopathogenicity of *Entamoeba histolytica*. J Infect Dis. 1985;152:542-549.

144. Long-Krug SA, Hysmith RM, Fischer KJ, et al. The phospholipase A enzymes of *Entamoeba histolytica*: Description and subcellular localization. J Infect Dis. 1985;152:536-541.

145. Ravdin JI, Schlesinger PH, Murphy CF, et al. Acid intracellular vesicles and the cytolysis of mammalian target cells by *Entamoeba histolytica* trophozoites. J Protozool. 1986;33:478-486.

146. Yadava N, Chandok MR, Prasad J, et al. Characterization of EhCaBP, a calcium-building protein of *Entamoeba histolytica* and its binding proteins. Mol Biochem Parasitol. 1997;84:69-82.

147. Gopal B, Swaminathan CP, Bhattacharya S, et al. Thermodynamics of metal ion binding and denaturation of a calcium binding protein from *Entamoeba histolytica*. Biochemistry. 1997;36:10910-10916.

148. Ghosh SK, Samuelson J. Involvement of p21racA, phosphoinositide 3-kinase, and vacuolar ATPase in phagocytosis of bacteria and erythrocytes by *Entamoeba histolytica*: Suggestive evidence for coincidental evolution of amebic invasiveness. Infect Immun. 1997;65:4243-4249.

149. Weikel CS, Murphy CF, Orozco ME, et al. Phorbol esters specifically enhance the cytolytic activity of *Entamoeba histolytica*. Infect Immun. 1988;56:1485-1491.

150. Leippe M, Tannich E, Nickel R, et al. Primary and secondary structure of the pore-forming peptide of pathogenic *Entamoeba histolytica*. EMBO J. 1992;11:3501-3506.

151. Leippe M, Bahr E, Tannich E, et al. Comparison of pore-forming peptides from pathogenic and nonpathogenic *Entamoeba histolytica*. Mol Biol Parasitol. 1997;59:101-110.

152. Leroy A, Lauwaet T, De Bruyne G, et al. *Entamoeba histolytica* disturbs the tight junction complex in human enteric T84 cell layers. FASEB J. 2000;14:1139-1146.

153. Berninghausen O, Leippe M. Necrosis versus apoptosis as the mechanism of target cell death induced by *Entamoeba histolytica*. Infect Immun. 1997;65:3615-3621.

154. Huston CD, Boettner DR, Miller-Sims V, et al. Apoptotic killing and phagocytosis of host cells by the parasite *Entamoeba histolytica*. Infect Immun. 2003;71:964-972.

155. Seydel KB, Stanley SL Jr. *Entamoeba histolytica* induces host cell death in amebic liver abscess by a non-Fas-dependent, non-tumor necrosis factor alpha-dependent pathway of apoptosis. Infect Immun. 1998;66:2980-2983.

156. Yan L, Stanley SL Jr. Blockade of caspases inhibits amebic liver abscess formation in a mouse model of disease. Infect Immun. 2001;69:7911-7914.

157. Que X, Reed SL. The role of extracellular cysteine proteinases in pathogenesis of *Entamoeba histolytica* invasion. Parasitol Today. 1997;13:190-194.

158. Kelsall BL, Ravdin JI. Proteolytic degradation of human IgA by *Entamoeba histolytica*. J Infect Dis. 1993;168:1319-1322.

159. Tran VQ, Herdman DS, Torian BE, Reed SL. The neutral cysteine proteinase of *Entamoeba histolytica* degrades IgG and prevents its binding. J Infect Dis. 1998;177:508-511.

160. Reed SL, Gigli I. Lysis of complement-sensitive *Entamoeba histolytica* by activated terminal complement components. J Clin Invest. 1990;86:1815-1822.

161. Reed SL, Keene WE, McKerrow JH. Thiol proteinase expression and pathogenicity of *Entamoeba histolytica*. J Clin Microbiol. 1989;27:2772-2777.

162. Reed S, Bouvier J, Pollack AS, et al. Cloning of a virulence factor of *Entamoeba histolytica*. J Clin Invest. 1993;91:1532-1540.

163. Que X, Reed SL. Cysteine proteinases and the pathogenesis of amebiasis. Clin Microbiol Rev. 2000;13:196-206.

164. Hellberg A, Nickel R, Lotter H, et al. Overexpression of cysteine proteinase 2 in *Entamoeba histolytica* or *Entamoeba dispar* increases amoeba-induced monolayer destruction in vitro but does not augment amebic liver abscess formation in gerbils. Cell Microbiol. 2001;3:13-20.

165. Zhang Z, Wang L, Seydel KB, et al. *Entamoeba histolytica* cysteine proteinases with interleukin-1 beta converting enzyme (ICE) activity cause intestinal inflammation and tissue damage in amebiasis. Mol Microbiol. 2000;37:542-548.

166. Werries E, Nebinger P, Franz A. Degradation of biogene oligosaccharides by beta-*N*-acetylglucosaminidase secreted by *Entamoeba histolytica*. Mol Biochem Parasitol. 1983;7:127-140.

167. Udezulu IA, Leitch GJ. A membrane-associated neuraminidase in *Entamoeba histolytica* trophozoites. Infect Immun. 1987;55:181-186.

168. Salata RA, Ahmed P, Ravdin JI. *Entamoeba histolytica* contains a chemoattractant for human polymorphonuclear neutrophils. J Parasitol. 1989;75:644-646.

169. Rigothier MC, Khun H, Tavares P, et al. Fate of *Entamoeba histolytica* during the establishment of amebic liver abscess analyzed by quantitative radioimaging and histology. Infect Immun. 2002;70:3208-3215.

170. Arellano J, Perez-Rodriguez M, Lopez-Osuna M, et al. Increased frequency of HLA-DR3 and comploype SCO1 in Mexican mestizo children with amebic abscess of the liver. Parasite Immunol. 1996;18:491-498.

171. DeLeon A. Prognostico tardio en el absceso hepatico amibiano. Arch Invest Med (Mex). 1970;1(Suppl 1):205-206.

172. Grundy MS, Cartwright TL, Lundin L, et al. Antibodies against *Entamoeba histolytica* in human milk and serum in Kenya. J Clin Microbiol. 1983;17:753-758.

173. Islam A, Stoll BJ, Ljungstrom I, et al. The prevalence of *Entamoeba histolytica* in lactating women and in their infants in Bangladesh. Trans R Soc Trop Med Hyg. 1988;82:99-103.

174. Abou-El-Magd I, Soong CG, El-Hawey AM, Ravdin JI. Humoral and mucosal IgA antibody response to a recombinant 52-kDa cysteine-rich portion of the *Entamoeba histolytica* galactose-inhibitable lectin correlates with detection of native 170-kDa lectin antigen in serum of patients with amebic colitis. J Infect Dis. 1996;174:157-162.

175. Carrero JC, Diaz MY, Viveros M, et al. Human secretory immunoglobulin A anti-*Entamoeba histolytica* antibodies inhibit adherence of amoebae to MDCK cells. Infect Immun. 1994;62:764-767.

176. Kelsall BL, Jackson TFHG, Gathiram V, et al. Secretory immunoglobulin A antibodies to the galactose-inhibitable adherence protein in the saliva of patients with amebic liver disease. Am J Trop Med Hyg. 1994;4:454-459.

177. Beving DE, Soong CJ, Ravdin JI. 1996. Oral immunization with a recombinant cysteine-rich section of the *Entamoeba histolytica* galactose-inhibitable lectin elicits an intestinal secretory immunoglobulin A response that has in vitro adherence inhibition activity. Infect Immun. 64;4:1473-1476.

178. Pillai DR, Wan PS, Yau YC, et al. The cysteine-rich region of the *Entamoeba histolytica* adherence lectin (170-kilodalton subunit) is sufficient for high-affinity Gal/GalNAc-specific binding in-vitro. Infect Immun. 1999;67:3836-3841.

179. Stanley SL Jr. Progress toward development of a vaccine for amebiasis. Clin Microbiol Rev. 1997;10:637-649.

180. Petri WA, Joyce MP, Broman J, et al. Recognition of the galactose- or *N*-acetylgalactosamine-binding lectin of *Entamoeba histolytica* by human immune sera. Infect Immun. 1987;55:2327-2331.

181. Joyce MP, Ravdin JI. Antigens of *Entamoeba histolytica* recognized by immune sera from liver abscess patients. Am J Trop Med Hyg. 1988;38:74-80.

182. Soong CJG, Kain KC, Abd-Alla M, et al. A recombinant cysteine-rich section of the *Entamoeba histolytica* galactose-inhibitable adherence lectin is efficacious as a subunit vaccine in the gerbil model of amebic liver abscess. J Infect Dis. 1995;171:645-651.

183. Abd-Alla M, El-Hawey AM, Ravdin JI. Use of an enzyme-linked immunosorbent assay to detect anti-adherence protein antibodies in sera of patients with invasive amebiasis in Cairo, Egypt. Am J Trop Med Hyg. 1992;47:800-804.

184. Beck DL, Tanyuksel M, Mackey AJ, et al. *Entamoeba histolytica*: Sequence conservation of the Gal/GalNAc lectin from clinical isolates. Exp Parasitol. 2002;101:157-163.

185. Torian BE, Flores BM, Stroeher VL, et al. cDNA sequence analysis of a 28 kDa cysteine-rich surface antigen of pathogenic *Entamoeba histolytica*. Proc Natl Acad Sci U S A. 1990;87:6358-6362.

186. Edman U, Meraz MA, Agabian N, et al. Characterization of an immunodominant variable surface antigen from pathogenic and nonpathogenic E histolytica. J Exp Med. 1990;172:879-888.

187. Stanley SL Jr, Becker A, Kunz-Jenkins C, et al. Cloning and expression of a membrane antigen of *Entamoeba histolytica* possessing multiple tandem repeats. Proc Natl Acad Sci U S A. 1990;87:4976-4980.

188. Stanley SL Jr, Tian K, Koester JP, Li E. The serine-rich *Entamoeba histolytica* protein is a phosphorylated membrane protein containing *O*-linked terminal *N*-acetylglucosamine residues. J Biol Chem. 1995;270:4121-4126.

189. Mai Z, Samuelson J. A new gene family (ariel) encodes asparagine-rich *Entamoeba histolytica* antigens, which resemble the amebic vaccine candidate serine-rich *E. histolytica* protein. Infect Immun. 1998;66:353-355.

190. Ortiz-Ortiz L, Capin R, Capin NR, et al. Activation of the alternative pathway of complement by *Entamoeba histolytica*. Clin Exp Immunol. 1978;34:10-18.

191. Reed SL, Sargeaunt PG, Braude AI. Resistance to lysis by human serum of pathogenic *Entamoeba histolytica*. Trans R Soc Trop Med Hyg. 1983;77:248-253.

192. Calderon J, Tovar R. Loss of susceptibility to complement lysis in *Entamoeba histolytica* HM1 by treatment with human serum. Immunology. 1986;58:467-471.

193. Salata RA, Murray HW, Rubin BY, et al. The role of gamma interferon in the generation of human macrophages and T lymphocytes cytotoxic for *Entamoeba histolytica*. Am J Trop Med Hyg. 1987;37:72-78.

194. Campbell D, Chadee K. Survival strategies of *Entamoeba histolytica*: Modulation of cell-mediated immune responses. Parasitol Today. 1997;13:184-190.

195. Yu Y, Chadee K. *Entamoeba histolytica* stimulates interleukin 8 from human colonic epithelial cells without parasite-enterocyte contact. Gastroenterology. 1997;112:1536-1547.

196. Seydel KB, Li E, Swanson PE, Stanley SL Jr. Human intestinal epithelial cells produce proinflammatory cytokines in response to infection in a SCID mouse-human intestinal xenograft model of amebiasis. Infect Immun. 1997;65:1631-1639.

197. Salata RA, Martinez-Palomo A, Murphy CF, et al. Patients treated for amebic liver abscess develop a cell-mediated immune response effective *in vitro* against *Entamoeba histolytica*. J Immunol. 1986;136:2633-2639.

198. Schain DS, Salata RA, Ravdin JI. Human T-lymphocyte proliferation, lymphokine production, and amebicidal activity elicited by the galactose-inhibitable adherence protein of *Entamoeba histolytica*. Infect Immun. 1992;60:2143-2146.

199. Salata RA, Martinez-Palomo A, Conales L, et al. Immune sera suppresses the antigen specific proliferative response in T lymphocytes from patients cured of amebic liver abscess. Infect Immun. 1990;58:3941-3946.

200. Kanani SR, Knight R. Relapsing amebic colitis of 12 years' standing exacerbated by corticosteroids. Be Med J. 1969;2:613-614.

201. Chadee K, Meerovitch E. *Entamoeba histolytica*: Early progressive pathology in the cecum of the gerbil (*Meriones unguiculatus*). Am J Trop Med Hyg. 1985;34:283-291.

202. Belley A, Keller K, Grove J, Chadee K. Interaction of LS174T human colon cancer cell mucins with *Entamoeba histolytica*: An *in vitro* model for colonic disease. Gastroenterology. 1996;111:1484-1492.

203. Chadee K, Innes DJ, Ravdin JI. Mucin and nonmucin secretagogue activity of *Entamoeba histolytica* and cholera toxin in rat colon. Gastroenterology. 1991;100:986-997.

204. Petri WA Jr, Ravdin JI. Protection of gerbils from amebic liver abscess by immunization with the galactose-specific adherence lectin of *Entamoeba histolytica*. Infect Immun. 1991;59:97-101.

205. Ravdin JI. Intestinal disease caused by *Entamoeba histolytica*. In: Ravdin JI, ed. Amebiasis: Human Infection by *Entamoeba histolytica*. New York: Churchill Livingstone; 1988:495-510.

206. Adams EB, MacLeod IN. Invasive amebiasis. I. Amebic dysentery and its complications. Medicine (Baltimore). 1977;56:315-323.

207. Juniper K. Parasitic diseases of the intestinal tract. In: Paulson M, ed. Gastroenterologic Medicine. Philadelphia: Lea & Febiger; 1969:172.

208. Jammal MA, Cox K, Ruebner B. Amebiasis presenting as rectal bleeding without diarrhea in childhood. J Pediatr Gastroenterol Nutr. 1985;4:294-296.

209. Merritt TJ, Coughlin E, Thomas DW, et al. Spectrum of amebiasis in children. Am J Dis Child. 1982;136:785.

210. Speelman P, McGlaughlin R, Kabir I, et al. Differential clinical features and stool findings in shigellosis and amebic dysentery. Trans R Soc Trop Med Hyg. 1987;81:549-551.

211. Takahashi T, Gamboa-Dominguez A, Gomez-Mendez TJM, et al. Fulminant amebic colitis: Analysis of 55 cases. Dis Colon Rectum. 1997;40:1362-1367.

212. Monga NK, Sood S, Kaushik SP, et al. Amebic peritonitis. Am J Gastroenterol. 1976;67:366-373.

213. El-Hennawy M, Abd-Rabbo H. Hazards of cortisone therapy in hepatic amebiasis. J Trop Med Hyg. 1978;81:71-73.

214. Haider Z, Rasul A. Chronic non-dysenteric intestinal amebiasis: A review of 159 cases. J Pakistan Med Assoc. 1975;25:75-78.

215. Ruiz-Moreno F. Perianal skin amebiasis. Dis Colon Rectum. 1967;10:65.

216. Adams EB, MacLeod IN. Invasive amebiasis. II. Amebic liver abscess and its complications. Medicine (Baltimore). 1977;56:325-334.

217. Knobloch J, Mannweiler E. Development and persistence of antibodies to *Entamoeba histolytica* in patients with amebic liver abscess: Analysis of 216 cases. Am J Trop Med Hyg. 1983;32:727-732.

218. Shandera WX, Bollam P, Hashmey RH Jr, et al. Hepatic amebiasis among patients in a public teaching hospital. South Med J. 1998;91:829-837.

219. Conter RL, Pitt HA, Tompkins RK, et al. Differentiation of pyogenic from amebic hepatic abscesses. Surg Gynecol Obstet. 1986;162:114-120.

220. Greenstein AJ, Barth J, Dicker A, et al. Amebic liver abscess: A study of 11 cases compared with a series of 38 patients with pyogenic liver abscess. Am J Gastroenterol. 1985;80:472-478.

221. Boom RA, Fonseca L, Yánez C, et al. Differential diagnosis between amebic liver abscess and acute cholecystitis. J Med Syst. 1983;7:205-212.

222. Overbosch D, Stuiver PC, van der Kaay JH. Hepatic amebiasis: Current concepts and a report of 25 cases in the Netherlands. Acta Leiden. 1983;51:3-17.

223. Irusen EM, Jackson TFGH, Simjee AE. Asymptomatic intestinal colonization by pathogenic *Entamoeba histolytica* in amebic liver abscess: Prevalence, response to therapy and pathogenic potential. Clin Infect Dis. 1992;14:889-893.

224. Rhode FC, Prieto O, Riveros O. Thoracic complications of amebic liver abscess. Br J Dis Chest. 1979;73:302.

225. Adeyemo AO, Aderounmu A. Intrathoracic complications of amebic liver abscess. J R Soc Med. 1984;77:17-20.

226. Kubitschek KR, Peters J, Nickeson D, et al. Amebiasis presenting as pleuropulmonary disease. West J Med. 1985;142:203-207.

227. Nwafo DC, Egbue MO. Intrathoracic manifestations of amebiasis. Ann R Coll Surg Engl. 1981;63:126-128.

228. Eggleston FC, Handa AK, Verghese M. Amebic peritonitis secondary to amebic liver abscess. Surgery. 1982;91:46-48.

229. Wilmot AJ. Clinical Amebiasis. Oxford: Blackwell Scientific; 1962.

230. Orbison JA, Reeves N, Leedham CL, et al. Amebic brain abscess: Review of the literature and report of five additional cases. Medicine (Baltimore). 1951;30:247-282.

231. Becker GL Jr, Knep S, Lance KP, et al. Amebic abscess of the brain. Neurosurgery. 1980;6:192-194.

232. Schmutzhard E, Mayr U, Rumpl E, et al. Secondary cerebral amebiasis due to infection with *Entamoeba histolytica*: A case report with computer tomographic findings. Eur Neurol. 1986;25:161-165.

233. Banerjee AK, Bhatnagar RK, Bhusnurmath SR. Secondary cerebral amebiasis. Trop Geogr Med. 1983;35:333-336.

234. Grisby W. Surgical treatment of amebiasis. Surg Gynecol Obstet. 1969;128:609-627.

235. Heinz KPW. Amebic infection of the female genital tract: A report of three cases. S Afr Med J. 1973;47:1795.

236. Mylius RE, Ten Seldam RE. Venereal infection by *Entamoeba histolytica* in a New Guinea native couple. Trop Geogr Med. 1962;14:20.

237. O'Leary RK, Posen J. Amebiasis of the penis. S Afr Med J. 1984;65:113.

238. Purpon I, Jiminez D, Engelking RL. Amebiasis of the penis. J Urol. 1967;98:372.

239. Young KH, Ballock S, Melvin DM, et al. Ethyl acetate as a substitute for diethylether in the ether-formalin sedimentation technique. J Clin Microbiol. 1979;10:852-853.
240. Reed SL, Flores BM, Batzer MA, et al. Molecular and cellular characterization of the 29-kilodalton peripheral membrane protein of *Entamoeba histolytica:* Differentiation between pathogenic and nonpathogenic isolates. Infect Immun. 1992;60:542-549.
241. Patterson M, Healy GR, Shabot JM. Serologic testing for amebiasis. Gastroenterology. 1980;78:136-141.
242. Healy GR, Sumner CK. The indirect hemagglutination test for amebiasis in patients with inflammatory bowel disease. Am J Dig Dis. 1972;17:97.
243. Gonzalez-Ruiz A, Haque R, Rehman T, et al. A monoclonal antibody for distinction of invasive and noninvasive clinical isolates of *Entamoeba histolytica.* J Clin Microbiol. 1992;30:2807-2813.
244. Abd-Alla MD, Jackson TFGH, Gatherim V, et al. Differentiation of pathogenic from nonpathogenic *Entamoeba histolytica* infection by detection of galactose-inhibitable adherence protein antigen in sera and feces. J Clin Microbiol. 1993;31:2845-2850.
245. Haque R, Kress K, Wood S, et al. Diagnosis of pathogenic *Entamoeba histolytica* infection using a stool ELISA based on monoclonal antibodies to the galactose-specific adhesin. J Infect Dis. 1993;167:247-249.
246. Jelinek T, Peyerl G, Löscher T, Nothdurft HD. Evaluation of an antigen capture enzyme immunoassay for detection of *Entamoeba histolytica* in stool samples. Eur J Clin Microbiol Infect Dis. 1996;15:752-755.
247. Britten D, Wilson SM, McNerney R, et al. An improved colorimetric PCR-based method for detection and differentiation of *Entamoeba histolytica* and *Entamoeba dispar* in feces. J Clin Microbiol. 1997;35:1108-1111.
248. Mirelman D, Nuchamowitz Y, Stolarsky T. Comparison of use of enzyme-linked immunosorbent assay-based kits and PCR amplification of rRNA genes for simultaneous detection of *Entamoeba histolytica* and *E dispar.* J Clin Microbiol. 1997;35:2405-2407.
249. Walderich B, Müller L, Bracha R, et al. A new method for isolation and differentiation of native *Entamoeba histolytica* and *E dispar* cysts from fecal samples. Parasitol Res. 1997;83:719-721.
250. Zengzhu G, Zhengyi W, Yijun A, Hong Z. Application of polymerase chain reaction for diagnosing amebic liver abscess. Chin Med Sci J. 1996;11:100-102.
251. Blumencranz H, Kasen L, Romeu J, et al. The role of endoscopy in suspected amebiasis. Am J Gastroenterol. 1983;78:15-18.
252. Ralls PW, Colletti PM, Halls JM. Imaging in hepatic amebic abscess. In: Ravdin JI, ed. Amebiasis: Human Infection by *Entamoeba histolytica.* New York: Churchill Livingstone; 1988:664-704.
253. Halvorsen RA, Korobkin M, Foster WL, et al. The variable CT appearance of hepatic abscesses. AJR Am J Roentgenol. 1984;142:941-946.
254. Siddiqui JH, Gharib M, Muscat-Baron J, et al. Liver abscess in Dubai: Analysis of 29 cases and an assessment of the value of CAT scan. Trop Med Parasitol. 1985;79:281-286.
255. Elizondo G, Weissleder R, Stark DD, et al. Amebic liver abscess: Diagnosis and treatment evaluation with MR imaging. Radiology. 1987;165:795-800.
256. Ralls PW, Henley DS, Colletti PM, et al. Amebic liver abscess: MR imaging. Radiology. 1987;165:801-804.
257. Ralls PW, Barnes PF, Johnson MB, et al. Medical treatment of hepatic amebic abscess: Rare need for percutaneous drainage. Radiology. 1987;165:805-807.
258. Van Sonnenberg E, Mueller PR, Schiffman RR, et al. Intrahepatic amebic abscesses: Indications for and results of percutaneous catheter drainage. Radiology. 1985;156:631-635.
259. Sharma MP, Dasarathy S, Sushma S, Verma N. Long term follow-up of amebic liver abscess: Clinical and ultrasound patterns of resolution. Trop Gastroenterol. 1995;16:24-28.
260. Simjee A, Patel A, Gathiram V, et al. Serial ultrasound in amebic liver abscess. Clin Radiol. 1985;36:61-68.
261. Scragg J. Amebic liver abscess in African children. Arch Dis Child. 1960;35:171-174.
262. Abramowicz M, ed. Drugs for parasitic infections. Med Lett Drugs Ther. 1998;40:1-12.
263. McAuley JB, Herwaldt BL, Stokes SL, et al. Diloxanide furoate for treating asymptomatic *Entamoeba histolytica* cyst passers: 14 years' experience in the United States. Clin Infect Dis. 1992;15:464-468.
264. Qureshi H, Ali A, Baqai R, Ahmed W. Efficacy of a combined diloxanide furoate-metronidazole preparation in the treatment of amebiasis and giardiasis. J Int Med Res. 1997;25:167-170.
265. Sullam PM, Slutkin G, Gottlieb AB, et al. Paromomycin therapy of endemic amebiasis in homosexual men. Sex Transm Dis. 1986;13:151-155.
266. Norris SM, Ravdin JI. The pharmacology of anti-amebic drugs. In: Ravdin JI, ed. Amebiasis: Human Infection by *Entamoeba histolytica.* New York: Churchill Livingstone; 1988:734-740.
267. Bhatia S, Karnad DR, Oak JL. Randomized double-blind trial of metronidazole versus secnidazole in amebic liver abscess. Indian J Gastroenterol. 1998;17:53-54.
267. Simjee AE, Gathiram V, Jackson TFHG, et al. A comparative trial of metronidazole v tinidazole in the treatment of amebic liver abscess. S Afr Med J. 1985;68:923-924.
269. Powell SJ. Drug trials in amebiasis. Bull World Health Organ. 1969;40:956.
270. Lasserre R, Jaroonvesama N, Kurathong S, et al. Single-day drug treatment of amebic liver abscess. Am J Trop Med Hyg. 1983;32:723-726.
271. Samarawickrema NA, Brown DM, Upcroft JA, et al. Involvement of superoxide dismutase and pyruvate: Ferredoxin oxidoreductase in mechanisms of metronidazole resistance in *Entamoeba histolytica.* J Antimicrob Chemother. 1997;40:833-840.
272. Rajak CL, Gupta S, Jain S, et al. Percutaneous treatment of liver abscesses: Needle aspiration versus catheter drainage. AJR Am J Roentgenol. 1998;170:1035-1039.
273. Stanley SL Jr. Amebiasis. Lancet. 2003;361:1025-1034.
274. Kapoor OP, Joshi VR. Multiple amebic liver abscess: A study of 56 cases. J Trop Med Hyg. 1972;75:4-6.
275. Mann BJ, Burkholder BV, Lockhart LA. Protection in a gerbil model of amebiasis by oral immunization with *Salmonella* by expressing the galactose/*N*-acetyl D-galactosamine inhibitable lectin of *Entamoeba histolytica.* Vaccine. 1997;15:659-663.
276. Lotter H, Zhang T, Seydel KB, et al. Identification of an epitope on the *Entamoeba histolytica* 170-kD lectin conferring antibody-mediated protection against invasive amebiasis. J Exp Med. 1997;185:1793-1801.
277. Stanley SL Jr. Progress toward development of a vaccine for amebiasis. Clin Microbiol Rev. 1997;10:637-649.
278. Marinets A, Zhang T, Guillen N, et al. Protection against invasive amebiasis by a single monoclonal antibody directed against a lipophosphoglycan antigen localized on the surface of *Entamoeba histolytica.* J Exp Med. 1997;186:1557-1565.
279. Gaucher D, Chadee K. Construction and immunogenicity of a codon-optimized *Entamoeba histolytica* Gal-lectin based DNA vaccine. Vaccine. 2002;20:3244-3253.
280. Nickel R, Tannich E. Transfection and transient expression of chloramphenicol acetyltransferase in the protozoan parasite *Entamoeba histolytica.* Proc Natl Acad Sci U S A. 1994;91:7095-7098.
281. Ramakrishnan G, Vines RR, Mann BJ, Petri WA Jr. A tetracycline-inducible gene expression system in *Entamoeba histolytica.* Mol Biochem Parasitol. 1996;84:93-100.
282. Gilchrist CA, Mann BJ, Petri WA Jr. Control of ferredoxin and Gal/GalNAc lectin gene expression in *Entamoeba histolytica* by a *cis*-acting DNA sequence. Infect Immun. 1998;66:2383-2386.
283. Moshitch-Moshkovitch S, Stolarsky T, Mirelman D, Alon RN. Stable episomal transfection and gene expression in *Entamoeba dispar.* Mol Biol Parasitol. 1996;83:257-261.

CHAPTER **271**

Free-Living Amebas

UPINDER SINGH

HISTORY

Infection of humans with free-living amebas is an infrequent but often life-threatening occurrence in both normal and immunocompromised individuals. Central nervous system (CNS) invasion by *Naegleria, Acanthamoeba,* and *Balamuthia mandrillaris* (formerly known as leptomyxid amebas) has been reported in approximately 425 patients worldwide, with numerous cases of *Acanthamoeba* keratitis described in the medical literature.[1-7] A recent report of human infection with *Sappinia diploidea,* a soil ameba, increases the number of potentially pathogenic free-living ameba known to cause human disease and raises the possibility of even more new species being identified as human pathogens in the future.[8,9] Distinct from other pathogenic protozoa by nature of their free-living existence, these organisms have no known insect vectors, there are no human carrier states of epidemiologic importance, and there is little relationship of poor sanitation to the spread of infection. Four distinct clinical syndromes are caused by the species of free-living amebas that infect humans: (1) primary amebic meningoencephalitis (PAM), (2) granulomatous amebic encephalitis, (3) disseminated granulomatous amebic disease (skin, pulmonary, and sinus infection, for example), and (4) amebic keratitis. Primary amebic meningoencephalitis is caused by *Naegleria fowleri* and occurs in healthy children and young adults who usually have been recently swimming in fresh water. The *Naegleria* amoebas gain access to the CNS by direct invasion through the nasal mucosa and the cribriform plate and cause a rapidly fatal meningoencephalitis. Granulomatous amebic encephalitis, caused by *Acanthamoeba* spp. (*A. castellanii, A. culbertsoni, A. astronyxis,* and *A. palestinensis*), *B. mandrillaris,* and *Sappinia diploidea,* is a subacute opportunistic infection that likely spreads hematogenously from pulmonary or skin lesions to the CNS, resulting in focal neurologic deficits that progress over days to weeks to a diffuse meningoencephalitis and death. Disseminated granulomatous amebic disease with skin, pulmonary, and sinus infections but without CNS infection with *Acanthamoeba* and *Balamuthia* has been reported.[3,10-14] *Acanthamoeba* causes a subacute to chronic keratitis that is associated with contact lens use, with rare reports of cases occurring after radial keratotomy.[15]

ORGANISMS

N. fowleri was named after the late Malcolm Fowler of Adelaide Children's Hospital of Australia, who with R.F. Carter described the initial cases of primary amebic meningoencephalitis.[16] *N. fowleri*, also called *Naegleria aerobia* and *Naegleria invadens,* is the predominant pathogenic species of *Naegleria,* although other species with pathogenic potential have been described (*Naegleria australiensis* and *N. italica*).[17] On transfer to distilled water or a nonnutrient medium, *Naegleria* spp. have the ability to transform rapidly from the trophozoite to a flagellate form.[18] The flagellate form can spontaneously revert to the trophozoite, the reproductive stage of the protozoan. The trophozoites are 10 to 30 μm in diameter and have a clear nucleus with a prominent dense central nucleolus, and pseudopodia (Fig. 271-1). The granular cytoplasm can contain ingested red blood cells and leukocytes along with cytoplasmic organelles including rough endoplasmic reticulum and mitochondria. The trophozoites feed predominantly on bacteria and have an aerobic metabolism. Division occurs by a unique nuclear mitosis with retention of the nuclear membrane and nucleolus during karyokinesis. Encystment of the trophozoite results in a 9-μm–diameter spherical cyst with a central nucleus and a single-layered wall containing an average of two pores. The pores, which are plugged with mucus in the cyst, serve as ports for the emergence of the trophozoite during excystation.[17,19] *N. fowleri* is thermophilic, with the trophozoite growing well at temperatures as high as 45° C.[17,20] Interestingly, pathogenic and nonpathogenic *Naegleria* spp. display significant differences in nutritional requirements under tissue culture conditions.[17]

Acanthamoeba (earlier classified as *Hartmanella*)[20] species recognized as pathogenic for humans include *A. castellanii, A. polyphaga, A. culbertsoni, A. palestinensis, A. astronyxis, A. hatchetti,* and *A. rhysodes.*[3] Other species identified to cause disease are *A. divionesis* (CNS disease in an immunocompromised host)[21] and *A. griffini* (corneal disease).[22] Classification of *Acanthamoeba* spp. based on DNA approaches does not correlate well with the classification schemes based on biochemical and morphological criteria, and a revision of the taxonomy of the genus is currently underway.[3] The life cycle of *Acanthamoeba* consists of only the trophozoite and the cyst. Trophozoites are 14 to 40 μm in diameter, contain mitochondria and a single nucleus with a prominent central nucleolus, and have distinctive slender spinelike projections of the plasma membrane (Fig. 271-2). The cysts have a double-layered wall or envelope, are 12 to 16 μm in diameter, and also may contain pores in the cyst wall. *Acanthamoeba* has aerobic metabolism and grows best 25° C to 35° C.[17]

B. mandrillaris, formerly referred to as leptomyxid ameba, is a free-living ameba recently identified as a cause of meningoencephalitis in animals and humans, with approximately 100 cases of human disease reported to date.[1,2,6,7,23-28] Approximately 45 of these cases have been reported from the United States and have included more than 10 cases in patients with acquired immunodeficiency syndrome (AIDS) and 8 in animals.[1,2,27] The trophozoites of *B. mandrillaris* have an average size of 30 μm (range 12 to 60 μm) and are uninucleate. Cysts have a mean diameter of 15 μm (range 6 to 30 μm) and a wavy and irregular outer wall that is composed of three layers[28] (Fig. 271-3). On hematoxylin and eosin–stained specimens, the organism cannot be differentiated reliably from *Acanthamoeba;* thus, definitive diagnosis must be made using immunofluorescent staining with species-specific antibodies. Laboratory growth of *Balamuthia* is significantly different than for *Acanthamoeba* or *Naegleria*[17] and until recently has hampered isolation of environmental samples. However, recent isolation of ameba from potting soil in the home of a fatally infected 3-year-old child that matches the clinical isolate from the patient has been accomplished, confirming its free-living and pathogenic status.[29]

Sappinia diploidea, a free-living ameba, has recently been reported to cause CNS infection in a human.[8,9] First isolated in 1908 and not previously known to be pathogenic to humans,[30] this ameba is found worldwide in soil and animal feces.[31] *S. diploidea* trophozoites are 40 to 70 μm in size, with a single large cytoplasmic vacuole and two nuclei (Fig. 271-4). The double nucleus with a central flattening is a distinctive characteristic of this species and indicative of the sexual reproduction of these parasites, another unusual feature among free-living ameba.[31]

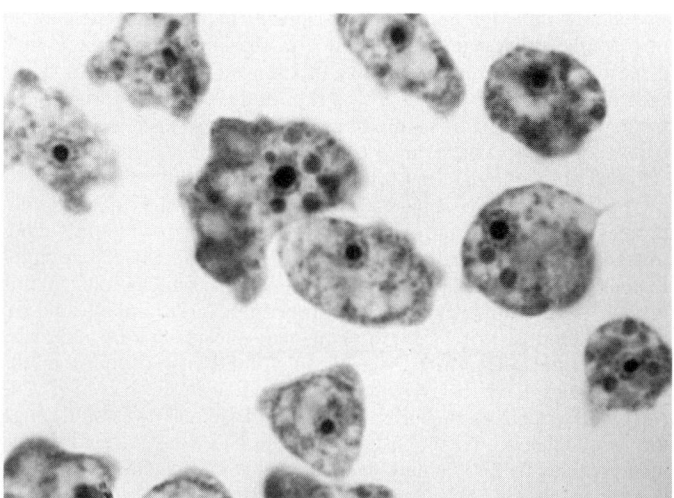

FIGURE 271-1. Trophozoites of *Naegleria fowleri* demonstrating the blunt pseudopodium or lobopodium. The characteristic nucleus contains a centrally placed dense nucleolus. (Iron-hematoxylin, ×800.) *(From Martinez AJ. Free-Living Amebas: Natural History, Prevention, Diagnosis, Pathology, and Treatment of Disease. Boca Raton, FL: CRC Press; 1985, with permission.)*

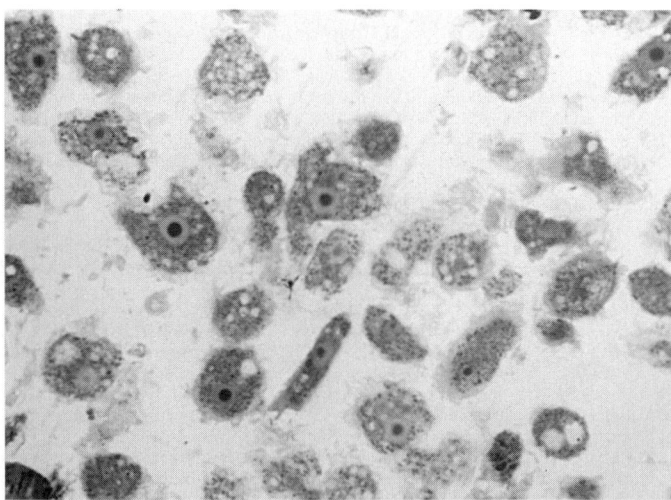

FIGURE 271-2. Trophozoites of *Acanthamoeba glebae* stained with toluidine blue, which demonstrates the round nucleolus surrounded by a nuclear halo and the granular and abundant cytoplasm. (×600.) *(From Martinez AJ. Free-Living Amebas: Natural History, Prevention, Diagnosis, Pathology, and Treatment of Disease. Boca Raton, FL: CRC Press; 1985, with permission.)*

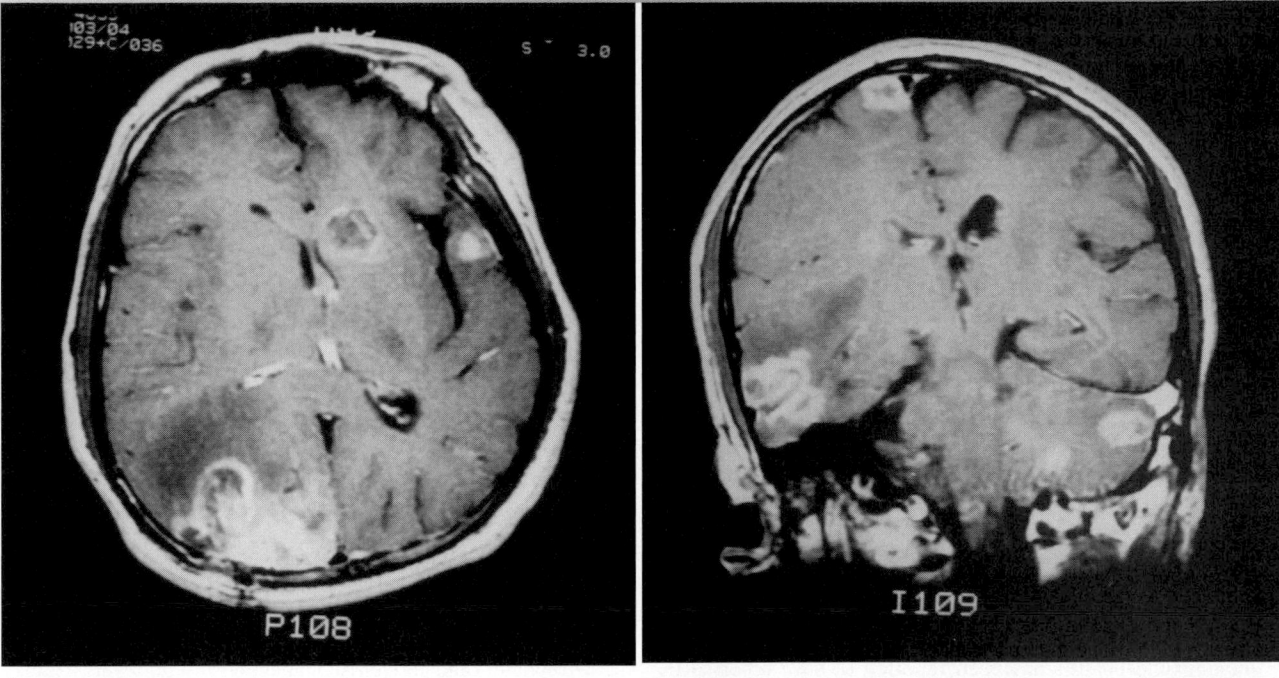

A

B

FIGURE 271-3. **A** and **B,** MR images of the brain of a patient with *Balamuthia mandrillaris* granulomatous amebic encephalitis. Multiple enhancing lesions are seen in the right hemisphere, left cerebellum, midbrain, and brain stem. **C,** Photomicrograph of the brain lesion from the same patient showing perivascular amebic trophozoites. A round amebic cyst with a characteristic double wall is seen in the top center. (H&E ×100.) *(From Deol I, Robledo L, Meza A, et al. Encephalitis due to a free-living amoeba (Balamuthia mandrillaris): Case report with literature review. Surg Neurol. 2000;53:611-616, with permission.)*

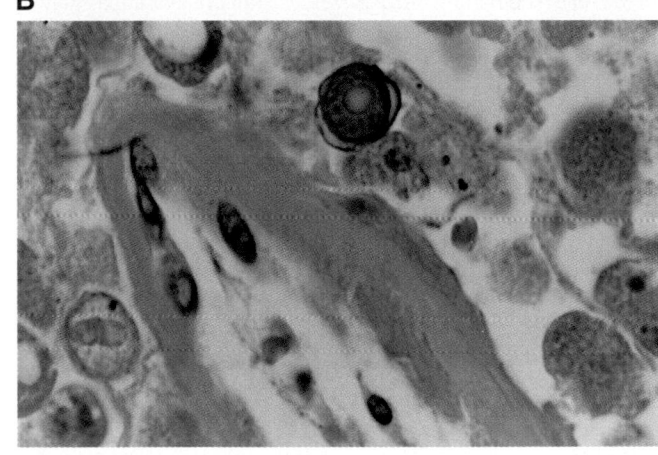

C

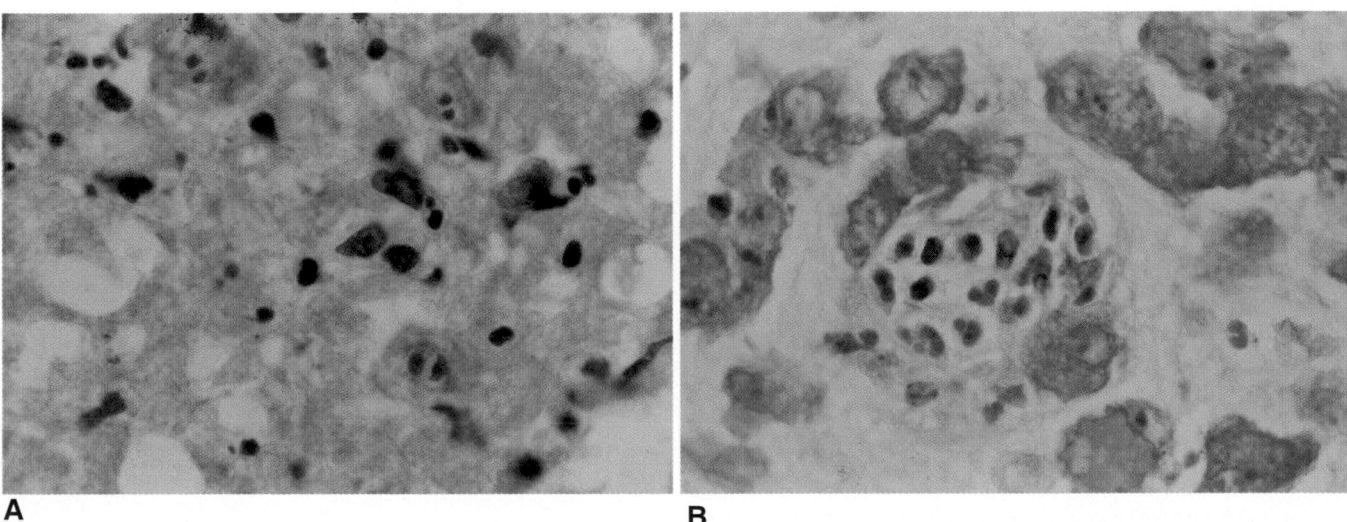

A

B

FIGURE 271-4. **A,** Cryosection of a brain sample from a man infected with *Sappinia diploidea.* The characteristic double nucleus is evident in three trophozoites. (H&E.) **B,** *S. diploidea* trophozoites surrounding a blood vessel from the same patient. Giemsa stains the cytoplasm bright blue and shows the characteristic large vacuole. *(From Gelman BB, Rauf SJ, Nader R, et al. Amoebic encephalitis due to Sappinia diploidea. JAMA. 2001;285:2450-2451, with permission. Copyright © 2001 American Medical Association. All rights reserved.)*

EPIDEMIOLOGY

N. fowleri has been isolated all over the world from soil, river and lake water, and thermally polluted water.[18,20] Pathogenic *N. fowleri* proliferate at higher temperatures, with growth occurring at temperatures up to 45° C, compared with pathogenic *Acanthamoeba*, whose growth is inhibited by temperatures above 35° C to 39° C. The presence of *N. fowleri* in fresh water is directly related to water temperature,[32] and *N. fowleri* has been frequently isolated from thermally polluted waters in temperate climates.[33] In semitropical locations such as Florida, thermal pollution of the already very warm freshwater lakes in summer and fall is less significant, with at least one *N. fowleri* per 25 mL of water frequently isolated.[32] In the winter, as water temperatures drop, *Naegleria* can be isolated only from the lake bottom sediments. *Naegleria* cysts are stable up to 8 months at 4° C.[34] Wellings and colleagues estimated that there had been a billion exposures of people to *Naegleria*-contaminated fresh water, with only seven cases of primary amebic meningoencephalitis in Florida over a 14-year period.[32] The factors that protect most individuals from invasive *Naegleria* infection are not understood. The presence of serum-agglutinating activity for *N. fowleri* in the majority of young adults, but not infants, tested from the southern United States indicates that subclinical infection or exposure to *Naegleria* is common.[35] Primary amebic meningoencephalitis has been reported to have occurred in the central and southern United States,[36] southern Australia, New Zealand, Europe, Africa, and Central America.[20] Clusters of cases of primary amebic meningoencephalitis with common environmental exposures have occurred.[16,19,20] The true incidence of this entity is unknown; however, as of 2000, more than 190 cases of primary amebic meningoencephalitis have been reported worldwide, with 95 cases in the United States.[6,37] New cases continue to be reported in the medical literature and the current incidence is undoubtedly significantly higher.[38-42] The first case of CNS disease caused by *N. fowleri* in an animal was reported in 1997,[43] although previous studies have demonstrated antibodies to *Naegleria* in wild mammals.[44]

Acanthamoeba spp. have also been isolated from soil, water, and air from diverse geographic locations.[3,20] *Acanthamoeba* spp. were cultured from pharyngeal swabs of 38 of 2289 individuals during a study of respiratory viruses in healthy families,[45] and serologic surveys have detected serum antibodies directed against *Acanthamoeba* in 50% to 100% of healthy people.[46,47] Despite such evidence of common exposure of the normal population to *Acanthamoeba,* granulomatous amebic encephalitis caused by *Acanthamoeba* spp. occurs predominantly in debilitated or immunosuppressed individuals.[48,49] Underlying conditions in patients with granulomatous amebic encephalitis have included AIDS,[48,50,51] liver disease, diabetes mellitus, renal and bone marrow transplantation, steroid therapy, and chemotherapy.[52] Disseminated *Acanthamoeba* infection without overt CNS manifestations is increasingly described, with up to 30 cases published in the medical literature.[3,13,53,54] These patients tend to be immunocompromised; the majority have AIDS, but infections in transplant patients and those with long-term steroid use are also reported.[55,56] Most commonly these patients have cutaneous manifestations, although involvement of the liver, lungs, and bone has been reported.[13,54] *Acanthamoeba* keratitis, on the other hand, occurs in healthy people and to date more than 1350 cases have been reported worldwide.[57] Of the first 100 cases of amebic keratitis reported to the Centers for Disease Control and Prevention, 83% occurred in people who were contact lens wearers. Corneal infection was associated with the use of homemade saline to clean the lenses and with the wearing of lenses while swimming.[58] *Acanthamoeba* can survive in many contact lens solutions, which may result in transmission of the disease. Benzalkonium chloride–preserved saline and solutions containing thimerosal with edetate have rendered *A. polyphaga* nonviable and are recommended for cleaning and storing lenses.[59] With the advent of disposable soft contact lenses in the late 1980s, the risk of *Acanthamoeba* keratitis has not declined. The annual incidence during 1985 through

1987 was estimated at 1.65 to 2.01 cases per million contact lens wearers.[5] The disease is now estimated to affect 1 in 250,000 people in the United States.[60]

B. mandrillaris, a soil inhabitant, was first reported to be isolated from water samples from the area around Tulsa, Oklahoma.[61] Water samples taken in the spring and autumn had the highest incidence of contamination with *B. mandrillaris.* The first human cases of infection with this organism were reported in 1990.[24] In contrast to CNS disease caused by *Acanthamoeba* spp., *Balamuthia* infections have been reported to occur in both immunocompetent and immunocompromised human hosts. *Sappinia diploidea* is a newly recognized human pathogen; the first case of a chronic meningoencephalitis involved a healthy 38-year-old man and was reported in 2001.[9]

PATHOGENESIS AND PATHOLOGIC FINDINGS

Primary amebic meningoencephalitis occurs chiefly in healthy children and young adults who have recently swum in warm freshwater lakes or ponds. Animal models[62,63] and autopsy studies[16,18,20,64] indicate that CNS invasion by *N. fowleri* occurs after nasal inoculation with the amebas by disruption of the olfactory mucosa. The amebas penetrate the submucosal nervous plexus and the cribriform plate and gain access to the CNS (Fig. 271-5). *N. fowleri* produces a diffuse meningoencephalitis and purulent leptomeningitis with severest involvement of the cortical gray matter. Cortical hemorrhages and edema with uncal or cerebellar herniation are seen, and the olfactory bulbs are hemorrhagic and necrotic. *Naegleria* trophozoites are found in the olfactory nerves and the adventitia and perivascular spaces of small to midsize arteries and arterioles. No amebic cysts are seen in the brain.[16,18,20,64] A diffuse or focal myocarditis was present in 7 of 16 autopsies of patients with primary amebic meningoencephalitis. The in-

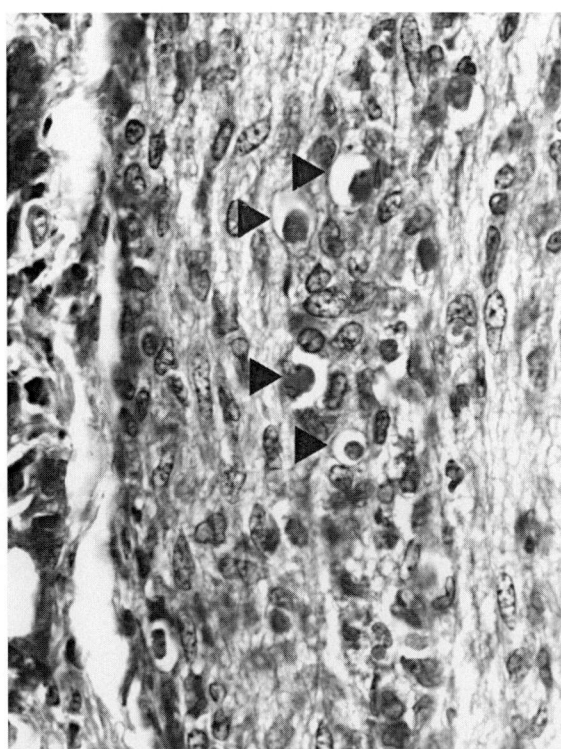

FIGURE 271-5. *Naegleria fowleri* trophozoites *(arrowheads)* within unmyelinated submucosal olfactory nerve bundles of a 27-year-old man who swam in fresh water 4 days before developing primary amebic meningoencephalitis. (H&E, ×500.) *(From Martinez AJ. Free-Living Amebas: Natural History, Prevention, Diagnosis, Pathology, and Treatment of Disease. Boca Raton, FL: CRC Press; 1985, with permission.)*

flammatory infiltrate was predominantly neutrophilic, and no amebae were seen in the myocardium. Retrospective chart review of the patients with primary amebic meningoencephalitis and myocarditis did not reveal evidence of congestive heart failure or arrhythmias in the patients with myocarditis.[65] When searched for, *Naegleria* trophozoites have been identified in the cerebrospinal fluid (CSF) of patients with acute meningoencephalitis.[20,66] The tissue necrosis elicited by *Naegleria* is speculated to be mediated in part by a secreted cysteine protease.[67] Interestingly, *Naegleria gruberi,* a nonpathogenic *Naegleria* that is not thermotolerant above 30° C, expresses a similar protease that is active in vitro at 37° C.[67] Other potential virulence determinants including pore-forming proteins,[68] low-molecular mass thiol compounds,[69] and calcium-mediated complement resistance[70] have also been reported in *Naegleria.*

Granulomatous amebic encephalitis with *Acanthamoeba* spp. occurs in immunocompromised patients, who present with focal neurologic deficits. On macroscopic examinations, the leptomeninges are spared except when directly overlying areas of cortical involvement. Moderate to severe cerebral edema occurs, with bilateral uncal or cerebellar tonsillar herniations occasionally seen. Necrotizing granulomatous lesions containing perivascular trophozoites and cysts are most frequently located in the cerebellum, midbrain, and brain stem. Multinucleated giant cells are occasionally present within the granulomas.[20] A granulomatous tissue reaction may not be present in some immunocompromised individuals with *Acanthamoeba* CNS infection.[26] The preferential location of amebic trophozoites and cysts perivascularly suggests a hematogenous dissemination of *Acanthamoeba* to the CNS. A changing spectrum of *Acanthamoeba* infection with disseminated disease without overt CNS infection is increasingly reported. Hematogenous spread is the likely source of spread and is supported by identification of *Acanthamoeba* in the skin (Fig. 271-6), lung, adrenals, and lymph nodes. Amebic skin lesions,[51,71] sinusitis,[10] and pneumonitis[52] may be sites of primary human infection that lead to hematogenous dissemination.[20]

Acanthamoeba keratitis is a corneal infection associated with minor corneal trauma and the use of soft contact lenses in otherwise healthy people. The histologic appearance of corneal infection is similar to that of *Acanthamoeba* infections of other organs. Both amebic cysts and trophozoites are found within the cornea. There is an acute or mixed inflammatory infiltrate that may contain epithelial and giant cells. However, amebae have also been found in tissue in the absence of an inflammatory infiltrate. Corneal neovascularization occurs to a variable extent.[72,73] Involvement of the posterior chamber of the eye is a rare complication of amebic keratitis but has been observed in enucleation specimens. Sterile inflammation of the posterior segment occurs without isolation or visualization of amebic cysts or trophozoites.[72] The corneal ringlike infiltrate seen with keratitis caused by *Acanthamoeba* and occasionally with gram-negative bacterial, herpes simplex, or fungal causes appears to be caused by the neutrophil chemoattractant effect of antigen-antibody complexes in the cornea.[72,73]

Significant progress has been made toward understanding the molecular basis of pathogenesis in *Acanthamoeba* infections, and molecular techniques are being utilized to differentiate pathogenic from nonpathogenic *Acanthamoeba.*[74] The toxic effect of *Acanthamoeba* in corneal cells is attributed to a variety of pathogenic parasite factors including adhesion, phagocytosis, induction of apoptosis, release of extracellular proteases, temperature and osmotolerance, and phenotypic switching from a trophozoite to a cyst stage.[75] Studies have shown that *Acanthamoeba* keratitis does not stimulate a delayed-type hypersensitivity response or a serum immunoglobulin G (IgG) response, perhaps because of the lack of resident antigen-presenting cells in the cornea.[76] It has long been appreciated that *Legionella* spp. can survive intracellularly within *Acanthamoeba.* A number of other intracellular bacteria are also being described with *Acanthamoeba* including *Chlamydia* spp.,[77,78] *Pseudomonas aeruginosa,*[79] and *Burkholderia pickettii.*[3,80] Models have been developed that can study the intracellular growth of *Legionella* in

Acanthamoeba[81,82] as well as an immortalized hamster corneal epithelial cell line that is susceptible to *Acanthamoeba* infection.[83]

B. mandrillaris causes a subacute or chronic granulomatous meningoencephalitis clinically similar to that caused by *Acanthamoeba* spp. The CNS lesions demonstrate a chronic inflammatory process involving lymphocytes, monocytes, plasma cells, and giant cells.[84] Granulomas can be seen in both immunocompetent and immunocompromised patients with *B. mandrillaris* infection; however, they are often absent.[84] Cysts and trophozoites of *B. mandrillaris* are seen in a perivascular pattern and are associated with angiitis and hemorrhagic necrosis of the underlying meninges and brain tissue. The angiotrophic location as well as the fact that the organism has been isolated from other tissues (skin,[14] adrenals,[85] and kidneys[25]) suggests that it may be spread in a hematogenous manner. An animal model of encephalitis with *B. mandrillaris* has been developed[86] and may be useful in studying the pathogenesis of this infection. As is the case in humans, both immunocompetent and immunocompromised mice are susceptible to intranasal challenge with *B. mandrillaris.*[86] The pathogenic potential of *Sappinia diploidea* for causing disease is humans is not known. Whether the case reported to date is the first of many more such infections or an isolated curiosity remains to be determined.[9]

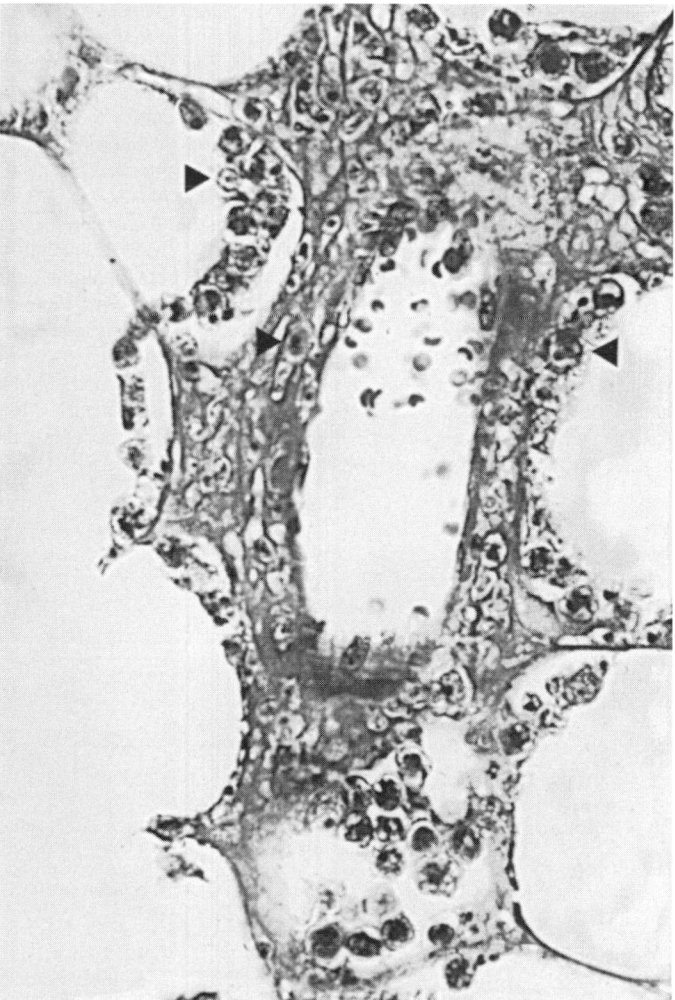

FIGURE 271-6. Skin biopsy from a skin nodule of a patient with granulomatous amebic encephalitis demonstrating perivascular amebic trophozoites *(arrowheads).* (H&E, ×250.) *(From Martinez AJ. Free-Living Amebas: Natural History, Prevention, Diagnosis, Pathology, and Treatment of Disease. Boca Raton, FL: CRC Press; 1985, with permission.)*

CLINICAL MANIFESTATIONS

A comparison of the clinical manifestations of disease by *Naegleria, Acanthamoeba,* and *Balamuthia* are listed in Table 271-1. Primary amebic meningoencephalitis usually occurs in children and young adults who have previously been in excellent health. Most often the patients have been swimming in warm fresh water or have had other exposure to water within 1 week. Rarely will there be no history of water exposure: one episode of primary amebic meningoencephalitis in an arid region of Nigeria was thought to be caused by inhalation of *Naegleria* cysts.[87] The onset of symptoms occurs on average 2 to 5 days after the last exposure to fresh water, but apparent incubation periods of up to 2 weeks have been reported. Very early in the illness, the patient may notice changes in taste or smell followed by an abrupt onset of fever, anorexia, nausea, and vomiting. On initial presentation, headache and meningismus is present in 86% to 100% of patients and mental status changes in two thirds of patients. Patients rapidly progress to coma and death within 1 week after the onset of illness, usually without ever developing focal neurologic signs.[20] Spinal cord involvement has been seen once,[88] and one AIDS patient with *Naegleria* CNS infection has been reported.[89] Myocarditis has been present in almost half of the patients for whom autopsy was performed, but congestive heart failure or arrhythmias are uncommon before death.

Granulomatous amebic encephalitis with *Acanthamoeba* spp. is an illness of immunocompromised and debilitated individuals.[48,49] In contrast to primary amebic meningoencephalitis, granulomatous amebic encephalitis has an insidious onset and presents with focal neurologic deficits. Presenting signs and symptoms of 15 patients with granulomatous amebic encephalitis included mental status abnormalities in 86%; seizures in 66%; fever, headache, and hemiparesis in 53%; meningismus in 40%; visual disturbances in 26%; and ataxia in 20%.[90] Underlying illnesses or conditions in patients with granulomatous amebic encephalitis included AIDS, liver disease, renal transplantation, neoplasm, steroid therapy, chemotherapy, diabetes mellitus, and pregnancy.[48,50-52] The duration of CNS illness until death was 7 to 120 days (average: 39 days). The incubation period of granulomatous amebic encephalitis is difficult to determine as the disease is not associated with freshwater exposure, but *Acanthamoeba* skin ulcers and lesions have often been present for months before the onset of CNS disease.[10,20] The skin lesions can be ulcerative, nodular, or subcutaneous abscesses and on biopsy demonstrate amebic granulomas.[10] Other

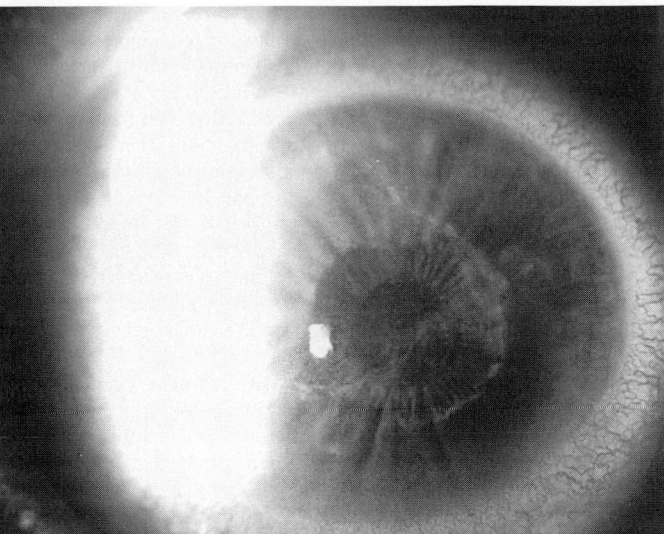

FIGURE 271-7. *Acanthamoeba* keratitis with an early and only partially ring-shaped infiltrate. *(From Lindquist TD, Sher NA, Doughman DJ. Clinical signs and medical therapy of early* Acanthamoeba *keratitis. Arch Ophthalmol. 1988;106:73-77.)*

clinical syndromes that have been described with *Acanthamoeba* infection include pneumonitis,[52] adrenalitis,[52] leukocytoclastic vasculitis,[91] osteomyelitis,[13,54] sinusitis,[72] and infection of a peptic ulcer.[12]

Acanthamoeba keratitis is frequently misdiagnosed initially as herpetic, bacterial, or fungal keratitis, resulting in an average delay to definitive treatment ranging from 11 days to 15 months. The symptoms begin with a foreign-body sensation in the affected eye followed by severe pain, photophobia, tearing, blepharospasm, conjunctivitis, and blurred vision. Periods of temporary remission are common, which lead to further delays in diagnosis because they are interpreted as responses to antibacterial or antiviral therapy. Signs of amebic keratitis in 36 eyes included iritis in 86%; a characteristic corneal ring infiltrate in 78% (Figs. 271-7 and 271-8); recurrent epithelial breakdown or cataracts in 44%; and, in the minority, hypopyon, elevated intraocular pressure, and anterior nodular scleritis. Most patients have an anterior uveitis of fluctuating severity.[72,92] A

TABLE 271-1 Clinical Features and Distinctive Characteristics of Disease Caused by *Naegleria, Acanthamoeba,* and *Balamuthia ameba*

| Characteristic | Acanthamoeba | | | Balamuthia | Naegleria |
	GAE	AK	Cutaneous lesions, sinusitis	GAE	PAME
Portal of entry	Olfactory epithelium, respiratory tract, skin, sinuses	Corneal abrasion	Skin, sinuses, respiratory tract	Olfactory epithelium, skin, respiratory tract	Olfactory epithelium
Incubation period	Weeks to months	Days	Weeks to months	Weeks to months	Days
Clinical signs	Confusion, headache, stiff neck, irritability	Blurred vision, photophobia, inflammation, corneal ring	Skin lesions, nodules, sinus lesions, sinusitis	Slurred speech, muscle weakness, headache, nausea, seizures	Headache, nausea, vomiting, confusion, fever, stiff neck
Pathology	Focal necrosis, granulomas	Ulceration of cornea	Granulomatous reaction in skin, inflammation	Multiple necrotic foci, inflammation, cerebral edema	Hemorrhagic necrosis
Diagnosis	Brain biopsy, CSF smear/wet prep culture, IIF† of tissue, PCR	Corneal scrape, corneal biopsy, calcofluor white, culture of material, confocal microscopy	Skin lesion biopsy, culture, IIF of tissue	Brain biopsy, culture on mammalian cells, IIF of tissue	Brain biopsy, CSF wet prep, CSF culture, IIF of tissue, PCR

From Marciano-Cabral F, Cabral G: *Acanthamoeba* spp. as agents of disease in humans. Clin Microbiol Rev 203;16:273-307, with permission from Clinical Microbiology Reviews.
*Data from references 27, 37, 137.
†IIF, indirect immunofluorescence.
GAE, granulomatous amebic encephalitis; AK, amebic keratitis; PAME, primary amebic meningoencephalitis.

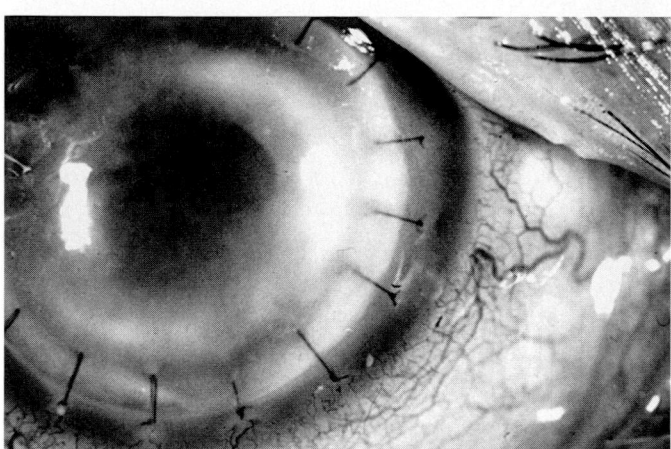

FIGURE 271-8. Progressive ring infiltrate in a corneal graft infected with *Acanthamoeba polyphaga. (Reprinted from Cohen EJ, Parlato CJ, Arentsen JJ, et al. Medical and surgical treatment of* Acanthamoeba *keratitis. Am J Ophthalmol. 1987;103:615-625, with permission from Elsevier Science.)*

dendriform epithelial pattern has been described in three patients as an early sign of *Acanthamoeba* keratitis before stromal involvement (Fig. 271-9). Recognition of this dendriform pattern enabled early and vision-saving therapy in three patients.[5,93]

Infection with *B. mandrillaris* is clinically dissimilar to CNS infection with *Acanthamoeba* spp. in that it can cause disease in both immunocompetent and immunocompromised hosts.[7] Subacute or chronic granulomatous meningoencephalitis, similar to granulomatous amebic encephalitis caused by *Acanthamoeba,* resulting in death within 1 week to several months after the onset of symptoms, is the most common clinical presentation. Important signs and symptoms include fever, headache, nausea, vomiting, seizure, and focal neurologic signs. Hydrocephalus as a complication[94] and initial misdiagnosis as an intracranial neoplasm[85] have been reported. Of the approximately 100 cases reported worldwide, more than 10 have been in patients with AIDS.[6,7] Other underlying illnesses include diabetes, renal failure, alcoholism, and intravenous drug abuse. In nonhuman primates, the disease can manifest in two clinically distinct patterns, one with a short clinical course as an acute necrotizing meningoencephalitis and the other with a more prolonged clinical course and granulomatous ame-

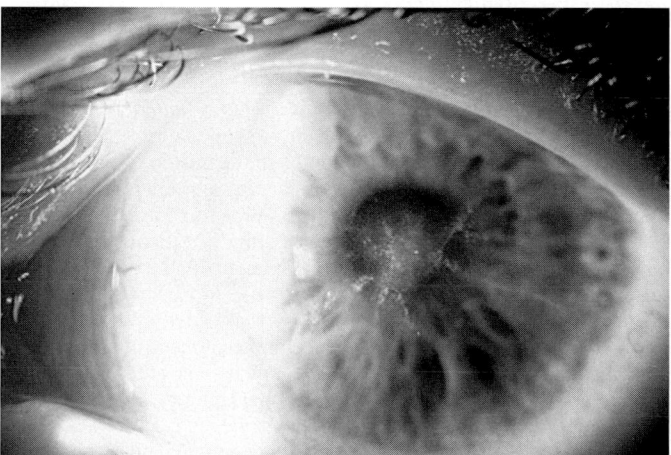

FIGURE 271-9. *Acanthamoeba* keratitis with dendriform epithelial pattern. Radial, linear anterior stromal infiltrates extend nearly to temporal periphery associated with dendriform epithelial irregularity. *(From Lindquist TD, Sher NA, Doughman DJ. Clinical signs and medical therapy of early* Acanthamoeba *keratitis. Arch Ophthalmol. 1988;106:73-77, with permission.)*

bic meningoencephalitis.[1,2,95,96] Only one case of human infection with *Sappinia diploidea* has been reported so it is unclear whether the clinical manifestations seen in this patient will be reproduced in future infections. However, it is important to note that the patient with this infection was previously healthy, had an antecedent sinusitis, and had a single ring-enhancing lesion on brain imaging. The patient was treated with multiple drugs and survived; whether this indicates that infection with *S. diploidea* is less virulent in humans remains to be determined.[9]

LABORATORY DIAGNOSIS

Primary amebic meningoencephalitis should be included in the differential diagnosis of children and young adults with meningoencephalitis. Recent exposure to fresh water should raise suspicions of *N. fowleri* infection. The peripheral white cell count is usually elevated, with a predominance of neutrophils. Head computed tomographic scans in one patient with primary amebic meningoencephalitis showed diffuse contrast enhancement of the gray matter and obliterated ambient, interpeduncular, and quadrigeminal cisterns.[20] The CSF pressure can be elevated, and the CSF is hemorrhagic. White blood cell counts in the CSF may be low early in disease but later range from 400 to 26,000 white blood cells/μL, with neutrophils predominating. The CSF glucose level is low to normal, and the CSF protein level is elevated. In patients with purulent CSF indices and no bacteria demonstrated on Gram stain of CSF sediment, it is very important to examine a wet mount of CSF for amebic trophozoites. These trophozoites are generally destroyed by the fixation procedure for Gram stain and missed if not looked for on a wet mount. Motile trophozoites in the CSF have been seen in 14 of 16 patients with primary amebic meningoencephalitis in which a wet mount of CSF was made.[16,97-99] More recent methods to diagnose *Naegleria* infections rapidly and specifically include molecular methods such as monoclonal antibodies,[4] polymerase chain reaction (PCR),[100,101] isoenzyme profile analysis,[4] and DNA probes.[102] A nested PCR test has recently been developed that appears to be highly sensitive (can detect 5 pg of *N. fowleri* DNA or five intact ameba) and that may make a rapid clinical diagnosis more achievable.[103]

In the past, granulomatous amebic encephalitis with *Acanthamoeba* frequently was diagnosed only at autopsy. Brain biopsy is the only means by which the diagnosis can be made during life because *Acanthamoeba* spp. have never been isolated from the CSF of a patient with granulomatous amebic encephalitis. Head computed tomographic scans have shown multiple lucent nonenhancing lesions in the cortex.[20,51] Lumbar puncture may be contraindicated in patients with granulomatous amebic encephalitis because of the risk of herniation. When it has been performed, the results have been nondiagnostic, with intermediate elevations in the white blood cell count (to 800/μL, lymphocyte predominance) and usually elevated protein and decreased glucose levels.[20,51] *Acanthamoeba* infection of the skin frequently is present with granulomatous amebic encephalitis, and skin nodules or ulcers should be biopsied and examined for *Acanthamoeba* in patients suspected of having granulomatous amebic encephalitis. *Acanthamoeba* and *B. mandrillaris* amebae have been successfully cultured from brain and cutaneous biopsy specimens. Culture of *Acanthamoeba* is best accomplished by the use of tryptic soy agar with rabbit or horse blood, buffered charcoal yeast extract agar, and non-nutrient agar overlaid with live organisms such as *P. aeruginosa, Enterobacter aerogenes,* or *Stenotrophomonas maltophilia.*[104] Specimens should not be frozen and should not be fixed before culture.[17,26]

The successful treatment of *Acanthamoeba* keratitis depends on its early diagnosis and initiation of therapy. Patchy stromal infiltrates[105] and dendriform epithelial involvement without frank corneal ulcerations[93] can be early signs of amebic keratitis (see Figs. 271-7 through 271-9). The ring corneal infiltrate that is characteristic of this disease is a late sign of stromal involvement. Diagnosis rests on demonstrating *Acanthamoeba* in corneal scrapings or biopsy specimens by histopathologic examination or culture. Initial corneal scrapings, Gram stains, and cultures may be misleading because in one third of cases of amebic keratitis these grew *Staphylococcus epidermidis,*

Staphylococcus aureus, β-hemolytic streptococcus, or *Propionibacterium.* A non-nutrient agar overlaid with *Escherichia coli* or *E. aerogenes* has been used to successfully culture *Acanthamoeba* from 10 of 15 amebic keratitis patients whose previous smear or biopsy had been negative.[72] Culture of the contact lenses and contact lens saline solution has also yielded *Acanthamoeba* when initial corneal scrapings were negative.[105] Corneal scrapings should be examined under wet mount for motile trophozoites. Spray fixatives may best preserve the morphology of the trophozoites before air drying occurs.[106] The cysts and trophozoites can be visualized with a number of different stains including hematoxylin-eosin, Wright, Giemsa, and periodic acid–Schiff.[72] Calcofluor white fluorescently stains the cysts and trophozoites in tissue section, facilitating their identification.[107] Molecular techniques that have been used to diagnose infection with *Acanthamoeba* include PCR and DNA probe.[108]

Several of the reported cases of *B. mandrillaris* had initially been described to be caused by *Acanthamoeba* because of the inability to distinguish reliably between the two on the basis of morphologic characteristics. Development of an immunofluorescence assay with the use of rabbit antiserum to the washed trophozoites and cysts from cultures has enabled definitive diagnosis of infection with this organism. Previously, the organism could be grown only on living tissue culture cells such as monkey kidney tissue lines; however, the recent development of a cell-free growth medium and axenization should make the clinical isolation of this organism much easier.[109] In brain biopsy specimens of patients with *B. mandrillaris* infection, both the cysts and trophozoites of the organism have been identified. To date *B. mandrillaris* has not been identified in the CSF; however, wet mount specimens should be examined if this entity is in the clinical differential diagnosis. The CSF findings resemble those of *Acanthamoeba* infections and include a mononuclear pleocytosis (10 to 500 cells), moderate hypoglycorrachia, and an elevated protein level. Imaging studies often reveal multiple hypodense lesions that enhance with a mass effect, thus raising the specter of mass-occupying lesions from malignancy, tuberculosis, and toxoplasmosis. Radiographically, these entities cannot be differentiated reliably, and tissue is required for definitive diagnosis. No diagnostic tests currently exist for *Sappinia diploidia.* The diagnosis therefore rests on the identification of trophozoites with the characteristic diploid nucleus; negative tests for *Naegleria, Acanthamoeba,* and *Balamuthia* species; and a clinical course consistent with subacute encephalitis.[8,9] The development of immunodiagnostic or PCR based tests in the future will be enormously useful for clinical and epidemiological studies.

TREATMENT

Seven patients are known to have survived primary amebic meningoencephalitis.[39,66,110-113] Patients with well-documented primary amebic meningoencephalitis received high-dose systemic and intrathecal amphotericin B. One of the patients was also treated with systemic and intrathecal miconazole, systemic rifampin, and sulfisoxazole.[110] Other agents that have been investigated in animal models include artemisurin, arteether, and sodium artesunic acid; however, these have all been found to be inferior to amphotericin B.[114] A recent report of significant antiamebic activity of azithromycin against *N. fowleri* in a mouse model of primary amebic encephalitis is tantalizing.[115] The authors report that azithromycin had significantly lower activity against *N. fowleri* in vitro, but nonetheless protected 100% of mice challenged in a primary amebic meningoencephalitis model. Because of the overall 95% mortality of primary amebic meningoencephalitis, passive immunotherapy in animal models has been attempted. Intrathecal administration of anti-*Naegleria* immune serum or an anti-*Naegleria* monoclonal antibody prolonged the survival of rabbits inoculated intracisternally with *N. fowleri.*[116] Passive immunotherapy may one day prove to be a useful adjunct to antibiotic treatment of primary amebic meningoencephalitis.

Little is known about the treatment of granulomatous amebic encephalitis caused by *Acanthamoeba.* Most cases have been diagnosed postmortem; premortem diagnosis has generally preceded death by only a few days, making evaluation of therapy difficult. In vitro testing of drug susceptibilities is complicated by interspecies and interstrain differences in antimicrobial sensitivities.[72] Each clinical isolate should be tested for drug sensitivities. In general the diamidine derivatives (propamidine, pentamidine, dibromopropamidine) have the greatest activity against *Acanthamoeba.* Other drugs active in vitro include ketoconazole, miconazole, paromomycin, polymyxin, sulfadiazine, trimethoprim-sulfamethoxazole, azithromycin, neomycin, 5-flucytosine, and, to a lesser extent, amphotericin B.[3,72,117,118] A case of CNS disease reputedly successfully treated with trimethoprim-sulfamethoxazole has been reported.[119] In mice *Acanthamoeba* infections can be treated with sulfadiazine, rifampin, and flucytosine; however, this requires treatment either before or within 24 hours of infection, a scenario unlikely to occur clinically.[120] The mainstay of successful regimens is multidrug therapy such as (1) ketoconazole, rifampin, and trimethoprim-sulfamethoxazole[121]; (2) fluconazole and sulfadiazine[122]; and (3) pentamidine, amphotericin, flucytosine, rifampin, itraconazole, and chlorhexidine[11] (reviewed in ref. 3). Of utmost importance, early diagnosis and drug therapy are essential, as dissemination of the ameba to the CNS has an extremely poor prognosis.

Treatment of *Acanthamoeba* keratitis has been notably more successful than that of granulomatous amebic encephalitis or primary amebic meningoencephalitis.[123] This relates in large part to the accessibility of the infection to surgical débridement and high concentrations of topical antimicrobial drugs. Successful treatment requires early diagnosis and aggressive surgical and medical management. Recognition of the dendriform pattern on the corneal epithelium, the earliest recognized sign of *Acanthamoeba* keratitis, should be followed immediately with débridement of the abnormal epithelium and institution of antiamebic medical therapy.[72,123,124] In vitro susceptibility testing for *Acanthamoeba* spp. is now available and may prove useful to guide medical therapy, although one study reported that in a series of patients with long-standing *Acanthamoeba* keratitis, there was no correlation between in vitro drug susceptibilities and in vivo response.[125] Medical treatment with topical 1% miconazole nitrate, 0.1% propamidine isethionate, and neosporin should continue for a minimum of 3 to 4 weeks. Topical propamidine should be administered at least nine times a day, with some authorities recommending that it be administered as often as every 15 to 60 minutes for the first 3 days.[123,126] Combination therapy with propamidine and polyhexamethyl biguanide[127] and chlorhexidine and propamidine[128] has been shown to be effective.[60] Early recognition and treatment have eliminated the need in some patients for a late penetrating keratoplasty to restore vision and reduce pain.[72,123,124] Propamidine isethionate has caused a reversible epithelial keratopathy after prolonged treatment that can be confused with recurrent amebic keratitis.[129] Other agents with activity against *Acanthamoeba* include pentamidine[130] and ivermectin.[131] Crystalline keratopathy caused by viridans streptococci has occurred after topical corticosteroid therapy of *Acanthamoeba* keratitis in two patients, emphasizing both the risks of using topical steroids in this disease and the need for a complete diagnostic reevaluation of patients with amebic keratitis in whom therapy appears to be failing.[132] The use is somewhat controversial, however, and a more recent study revealed no increased risk of treatment failure in patients treated with adjuvant steroids, with prudent use felt to be justified for the treatment of severe pain or inflammation.[133]

At the present time, there is no known effective treatment for *B. mandrillaris* infections, although successful treatment of two patients has been reported recently.[7] Studies have found some efficacy with pentamidine isethionate, azithromycin, and clarithromycin[109,134] but clarithromycin drug was amebastatic. In the same study, fluconazole and ketoconazole were poor inhibitors of amebic growth, and amphotericin B was marginal, whereas trimethoprim-sulfamethoxazole had minimal effect.[109] One patient has survived *Balamuthia* infection after treatment with clarithromycin, fluconazole, sulfadiazine, and 5-fluorocytosine however suffered significant neurological morbidities.[6] A recent report of two patients successfully treated with flucytosine, pentamidine, fluconazole, sulfadiazine, and a macrolide (azithromycin or clarithromycin) has been published,[7] giving hope that an effective regimen against this ameba can be established. Importantly both these patients had timely diagnosis highlighting the importance of a high index of suspicion and appropriate diagnostic measures in these individuals. The patient with *Sappinia diploidea* was treated with azithromycin, pentamidine, itraconazole, and flucytosine and survived.[8,9]

PREVENTION

Primary amebic meningoencephalitis occurs so rarely that active surveillance for *N. fowleri* in public swimming lakes is probably not justified as a public health measure. However, because of the occurrence of clusters of patients with primary amebic meningoencephalitis with common environmental exposures,[16,64,98] health officials should consider closing the implicated lake to swimming. New water treatment measures are being developed to eliminate free-living ameba.[135]

Acanthamoeba keratitis associated with contact lens use is preventable. Contact lenses should be heat disinfected or cleaned in benzalkonium-preserved saline, as hydrogen peroxide disinfection does not kill *Acanthamoeba*. Homemade saline solutions should not be used to clean or store contact lenses, and individuals should not wear the lenses while swimming in fresh water.[58,60,105,136]

REFERENCES

1. Bakardjiev A, Azimi PH, Ashouri N, et al. Amebic encephalitis caused by *Balamuthia mandrillaris:* Report of four cases. Pediatr Infect Dis J. 2003;22:447-453.
2. Deol I, Robledo L, Meza A, et al. Encephalitis due to a free-living amoeba (*Balamuthia mandrillaris*): Case report with literature review. Surg Neurol. 2000; 53:611-616.
3. Marciano-Cabral F, Cabral G. *Acanthamoeba* sp as agents of disease in humans. Clin Microbiol Rev. 2003;16:273-307.
4. Szenasi Z, Endo T, Yagita K, et al. Isolation, identification and increasing importance of 'free-living' amoebae causing human disease. J Med Microbiol. 1998;47:5-16.
5. Schaumberg DA, Snow KK, Dana MR. The epidemic of *Acanthamoeba* keratitis: Where do we stand? Cornea. 1998;17:3-10.
6. Martinez AJ, Visvesvara GS. *Balamuthia mandrillaris* infection. J Med Microbiol. 2001;50:205-207.
7. Deetz TR, Sawyer MH, Billman G, et al. Successful treatment of *Balamuthia* amoebic encephalitis: Presentation of 2 cases. Clin Infect Dis. 2003;37:1304-1312.
8. Gelman BB, Popov V, Chaljub G, et al. Neuropathological and ultrastructural features of amebic encephalitis caused by *Sappinia diploidea.* J Neuropathol Exp Neurol. 2003;62:990-998.
9. Gelman BB, Rauf SJ, Nader R, et al. Amoebic encephalitis due to *Sappinia diploidea.* JAMA. 2001;285:2450-2451.
10. Dunand VA, Hammer SM, Rossi R, et al. Parasitic sinusitis and otitis in patients infected with human immunodeficiency virus: Report of five cases and review. Clin Infect Dis. 1997;25:267-272.
11. Rivera MA, Padhya TA. *Acanthamoeba:* A rare primary cause of rhinosinusitis. Laryngoscope. 2002;112(7 Pt 1):1201-1203.
12. Thamprasert K, Khunamornpong S, Morakote N. *Acanthamoeba* infection of peptic ulcer. Ann Trop Med Parasitol. 1993;87:403-405.
13. Selby DM, Chandra RS, Rakusan TA, et al. Amebic osteomyelitis in a child with acquired immunodeficiency syndrome: A case report. Pediatr Pathol Lab Med. 1998;18:89-95.
14. Reed RP, Cooke-Yarborough CM, Jaquiery AL, et al. Fatal granulomatous amoebic encephalitis caused by *Balamuthia mandrillaris.* Med J Aust. 1997;167:82-84.
15. Friedman RF, Wolf TC, Chodosh J. *Acanthamoeba* infection after radial keratotomy. Am J Ophthalmol. 1997;123:409-410.
16. Fowler M, Carter RF. Acute pyogenic meningitis probably due to *Acanthamoeba* sp: A preliminary report. Br Med J. 1965;5464:740-742.
17. Schuster FL. Cultivation of pathogenic and opportunistic free-living amebas. Clin Microbiol Rev. 2002;15:342-354.
18. John DT. Primary amebic meningoencephalitis and the biology of *Naegleria fowleri.* Annu Rev Microbiol. 1982;36:101-123.
19. Schuster FL. Ultrastructure of cysts of *Naegleria* spp: A comparative study. J Protozool. 1975:352-359.
20. Martinez AJ, Free-Living Amebas: Natural History, Prevention, Diagnosis, Pathology and treatment of Disease. Boca Raton, FL: CRC Press; 1985.
21. Di Gregorio C, Rivasi F, Mongiardo N, et al. *Acanthamoeba* meningoencephalitis in a patient with acquired immunodeficiency syndrome. Arch Pathol Lab Med. 1992;116:1363-1365.
22. Ledee DR, Hay J, Byers TJ, et al. *Acanthamoeba griffini.* Molecular characterization of a new corneal pathogen. Invest Ophthalmol Vis Sci. 1996;37:544-550.
23. Visvesvara G, Stehy-Green JK. Epidemiology of free-living ameba infections. J Protozool. 1990;37:25S-33S.
24. Visvesvara GS, Martinez AJ, Schuster FL, et al. Leptomyxid ameba, a new agent of amebic meningoencephalitis in humans and animals. J Clin Microbiol. 1990;28:2750-2756.
25. Anzil AP, Rao C, Wrzolek MA, et al. Amebic meningoencephalitis in a patient with AIDS caused by a newly recognized opportunistic pathogen, Leptomyxid ameba. Arch Pathol Lab Med. 1991;115:21-25.
26. Gordon SM, Steinberg JP, DuPuis MH, et al. Culture and isolation of *Acanthamoeba* species and leptomyxid amebas from patients with amebic meningoencephalitis, including two patients with AIDS. Clin Infect Dis. 1992;15:1024-1030.
27. Denney CF, Iragui VJ, Uber-Zak LD, et al. Amebic meningoencephalitis caused by *Balamuthia mandrillaris:* Case report and review. Clin Infect Dis. 1997;25: 1354-1358.
28. Visvesvara GS, Schuster FL, Martinez AJ. Balamuthia mandrillaris, N. G., N. S, agent of amebic meningoencephalitis in humans and other animals. J Eukaryot Microbiol. 1993;40:504-514.
29. Schuster FL, Dunnebacke TH, Booton GC, et al. Environmental isolation of *Balamuthia mandrillaris* associated with a case of amebic encephalitis. J Clin Microbiol. 2003;41:3175-3180.
30. Hartmann M, Nagler K. Copulation bei Ameoba diploidea mit Selbstsamdigbleiben der Gametenkerne wahrend des ganzen lebenscyclus. Sitz-Ber der Ges naturf Freunde Berlin. 1908;5:112-125.
31. Goodfellow L, Belcher J, Page F. A light and electron microscopical study of *Sappinia diploidea,* a sexual amoeba. Protistologica. 1974;Xfas:207-216.
32. Wellings FM, Amuso PT, Chang SL, et al. Isolation and identification of pathogenic *Naegleria* from Florida lakes. Appl Environ Microbiol. 1977;34:661-667.
33. Sykora JL, Keleti G, Martinez AJ. Occurrence and pathogenicity of *Naegleria fowleri* in artificially heated waters. Appl Environ Microbiol. 1983;45:974-979.
34. Warhurst DC, Carman JA, Mann PG. Survival of *Naegleria fowleri* cysts at 4 degrees C for eight months with retention of virulence. Trans R Soc Trop Med Hyg. 1980;74:832.
35. Marciano-Cabral F, Cline ML, Bradley SG. Specificity of antibodies from human sera for *Naegleria* species. J Clin Microbiol. 1987;25:692-697.
36. Primary amebic meningoencephalitis—North Carolina, 1991. Morbid Mortal Wkly Rep. 1992;41:437-440.
37. Martinez AJ, Visvesvara GS. Free-living, amphizoic and opportunistic amebas. Brain Pathol. 1997;7:583-598.
38. Okuda DT, Coons S. *Naegleria fowleri* meningoencephalitis. Neurology. 2003; 61:E1.
39. Jain R, Prabhakar S, Modi M, et al. *Naegleria* meningitis: A rare survival. Neurol India. 2002;50:470-472.
40. Tiewchroom S, Junnu V. Distribution of pathogenic *Naegleria* spp in Thailand. Southeast Asian J Trop Med Publ Hlth. 2001;32(Suppl 2):172-178.
41. Shenoy S, Wilson G, Prashanth HV, et al. Primary meningoencephalitis by *Naegleria fowleri:* First reported case from Mangalore, South India. J Clin Microbiol. 2002;40:309-310.
42. Primary amebic meningoencephalitis—Georgia, 2002. Morbid Mortal Wkly Re 2003;52:962-964.
43. Lozano-Alarcon F, Bradley GA, Houser BS, et al. Primary amebic meningoencephalitis due to *Naegleria fowleri* in a South American tapir. Vet Pathol. 1997;34:239-243.
44. Kollars TM Jr, Wilhelm WE. The occurrence of antibodies to *Naegleria* species in wild mammals. J Parasitol. 1996;82:73-77.
45. Wang SS, Feldman HA. Isolation of hartmannella species from human throats. N Engl J Med. 1967;277:1174-1179.
46. Cerva L. *Acanthamoeba culbertsoni* and *Naegleria fowleri:* Occurrence of antibodies in man. J Hyg Epidemiol Microbiol Immunol. 1989;33:99-103.
47. Cursons RT, Brown TJ, Keys EA. Immunity to pathogenic free-living amoebae. Lancet. 1977;2:875-876.
48. Sison JP, Kemper CA, Loveless M, et al. Disseminated acanthamoeba infection in patients with AIDS: Case reports and review. Clin Infect Dis. 1995;20:1207-1216.
49. Lowichik A, Siegel JD. Parasitic infections of the central nervous system in children. Part I: Congenital infections and meningoencephalitis. J Child Neurol. 1995;10:4-17.
50. Gonzalez MM, Gould E, Dickinson G, et al. Acquired immunodeficiency syndrome associated with *Acanthamoeba* infection and other opportunistic organisms. Arch Pathol Lab Med. 1986;110:749-751.
51. Wiley CA, Safrin RE, Davis CE, et al. *Acanthamoeba* meningoencephalitis in a patient with AIDS. J Infect Dis. 1987;155:130-133.
52. Anderlini P, Przepiorka D, Luna M, et al. *Acanthamoeba* meningoencephalitis after bone marrow transplantation. Bone Marrow Transplant. 1994;14:459-461.
53. Schwarzwald H, Shah P, Hicks J, et al. Disseminated *Acanthamoeba* infection in a human immunodeficiency virus-infected infant. Pediatr Infect Dis J. 2003;22: 197-199.
54. Steinberg JP, Galindo RL, Kraus ES, et al. Disseminated acanthamebiasis in a renal transplant recipient with osteomyelitis and cutaneous lesions: Case report and literature review. Clin Infect Dis. 2002;35:e43-49.
55. Oliva S, Jantz M, Tiernan R, et al. Successful treatment of widely disseminated acanthamoebiasis. South Med J. 1999;92:55-57.
56. Slater CA, Sickel JZ, Visvesvara GS, et al. Brief report: Successful treatment of disseminated acanthamoeba infection in an immunocompromised patient. N Engl J Med. 1994;331:85-87.
57. Martinez AJ. Free-living amebas and the immune deficient host. In: Proceedings of the IXth International Meeting on the Biology and Pathogenicity of Free-Living Amoebae, 2001 Paris, France.
58. Stehr-Green JK, Bailey TM, Brandt FH, et al. *Acanthamoeba* keratitis in soft contact lens wearers. A case-control study. JAMA. 1987;258:57-60.

59. Nauheim RC, Brockman RJ, Stopak SS, et al. Survival of *Acanthamoeba* in contact lens rinse solutions. Cornea. 1990;9:290-293.

60. Kumar R, Lloyd D. Recent advances in the treatment of *Acanthamoeba* keratitis. Clin Infect Dis. 2002;35:434-441.

61. John DT, Howard MJ. Seasonal distribution of pathogenic free-living amebae in Oklahoma waters. Parasitol Res. 1995;81:193-201.

62. Martinez J, Duma RJ, Nelson EC, et al. Experimental *Naegleria* meningoencephalitis in mice. Penetration of the olfactory mucosal epithelium by *Naegleria* and pathologic changes produced: A light and electron microscope study. Lab Invest. 1973;29:121-133.

63. Jaroli KL, McCosh JK, Howard MJ. The role of blood vessels and lungs in the dissemination of *Naegleria fowleri* following intranasal inoculation in mice. Folia Parasitol (Praha). 2002;49:183-188.

64. dos Santos JG. Fatal primary amebic meningoencephalitis. A retrospective study in Richmond, Virginia. Am J Clin Pathol. 1970:737-742.

65. Markowitz SM, Martinez AJ, Duma RJ, et al. Myocarditis associated with primary amebic (*Naegleria*) meningoencephalitis. Am J Clin Pathol. 1974;62: 619-628.

66. Loschiavo F, Ventura-Spagnolo T, Sessa E, et al. Acute primary meningoencephalitis from entamoeba *Naegleria fowleri*. Report of a clinical case with a favourable outcome. Acta Neurol (Napoli). 1993;15:333-340.

67. Aldape K, Huizinga H, Bouvier J, et al. *Naegleria fowleri*: Characterization of a secreted histolytic cysteine protease. Exp Parasitol. 1994;78:230-241.

68. Herbst R, Ott C, Jacobs T, et al. Pore-forming polypeptides of the pathogenic protozoon *Naegleria fowleri*. J Biol Chem. 2002;277:22353-22360.

69. Ondarza RN, Iturbe A, Hernandez E, et al. Low-molecular-mass thiol compounds from a free-living highly pathogenic amoeba, *Naegleria fowleri*. Biotechnol Appl Biochem. 2003;37(Pt 2):195-204.

70. Chu DM, Woodward J, Fritzinger A, et al. Calcium-dependent protection from complement lysis in *Naegleria fowleri* amebae. Cell Calcium. 2002;31:105-114.

71. Wortman PD. *Acanthamoeba* infection. Int J Dermatol. 1996;35:48-51.

72. Auran JD, Starr MB, Jakobiec FA. *Acanthamoeba* keratitis. A review of the literature. Cornea. 1987;6:2-26.

73. Baum J. In: Case records of the Massachusetts General Hospital Case 10-1985. N Engl J Med. 1985;312:634-641.

74. Howe DK, Vodkin MH, Novak RJ, et al. Identification of two genetic markers that distinguish pathogenic and nonpathogenic strains of *Acanthamoeba* sp. Parasitol Res. 1997;83:345-348.

75. Khan NA. Pathogenesis of *Acanthamoeba* infections. Microb Pathog. 2003;34: 277-285.

76. Van Klink F, Leher H, Jager MJ, et al. Systemic immune response to *Acanthamoeba* keratitis in the Chinese hamster. Ocul Immunol Inflamm. 1997;5:235-244.

77. Amann R, Springer N, Schonhuber W, et al. Obligate intracellular bacterial parasites of acanthamoebae related to *Chlamydia* sp. Appl Environ Microbiol. 1997;63: 115-121.

78. Essig A, Heinemann M, Simnacher U, et al. Infection of *Acanthamoeba* castellanii by *Chlamydia pneumoniae*. Appl Environ Microbiol. 1997;63:1396-1399.

79. Michel R, Burghardt H, Bergmann H. [*Acanthamoeba*, naturally intracellularly infected with *Pseudomonas aeruginosa*, after their isolation from a microbiologically contaminated drinking water system in a hospital]. Zentralbl Hyg Umweltmed. 1995;196:532-544.

80. Michel R, Hauroder B. Isolation of an *Acanthamoeba* strain with intracellular *Burkholderia pickettii* infection. Zentralbl Bakteriol. 1997;285: 541-557.

81. Moffat JF, Tompkins LS. A quantitative model of intracellular growth of Legionella pneumophila in *Acanthamoeba castellanii*. Infect Immun. 1992;60: 296-301.

82. Polesky AH, Ross JT, Falkow S, et al. Identification of *Legionella pneumophila* genes important for infection of amoebas by signature-tagged mutagenesis. Infect Immun. 2001;69:977-987.

83. Halenda RM, Grevan VL, Hook RR, et al. An immortalized hamster corneal epithelial cell line for studies of the pathogenesis of *Acanthamoeba* keratitis. Curr Eye Res. 1998;17:225-230.

84. Popek EJ, Neafie RC. Granulomatous meningoencephalitis due to leptomyxid ameba. Pediatr Pathol. 1992;12:871-881.

85. Riestra-Castaneda JM, Riestra-Castaneda R, Gonzalez-Garrido AA, et al. Granulomatous amebic encephalitis due to *Balamuthia mandrillaris* (Leptomyxiidae): Report of four cases from Mexico. Am J Trop Med Hyg. 1997; 56: 603-607.

86. Janitschke K, Martinez AJ, Visvesvara GS, et al. Animal model *Balamuthia mandrillaris* CNS infection: contrast and comparison in immunodeficient and immunocompetent mice: A murine model of "granulomatous" amebic encephalitis. J Neuropathol Exp Neurol. 1996;55:815-821.

87. Lawande RV, John I, Dobbs RH, et al. A case of primary amebic meningoencephalitis in Zaria, Nigeria. Am J Clin Pathol. 1979;71:591-594.

88. Viriyavejakul P, Rochanawutanon M, Sirinavin S. *Naegleria* meningomyeloencephalitis. Southeast Asian J Trop Med Public Hlth. 1997;28: 237-240.

89. De Jonckheere JF, Brown S. Primary amebic meningoencephalitis in a patient with AIDS—Unusual protozoological findings. Clin Infect Dis. 1997;25:943-944.

90. Martinez AJ. Is *Acanthamoeba* encephalitis an opportunistic infection? Neurology. 1980;30:567-574.

91. Helton J, Loveless M, White CR Jr. Cutaneous acanthamoeba infection associated with leukocytoclastic vasculitis in an AIDS patient. Am J Dermatopathol. 1993; 15:146-149.

92. Heffler KF, Eckhardt TJ, Reboli AC, et al. *Acanthamoeba* endophthalmitis in acquired immunodeficiency syndrome. Am J Ophthalmol. 1996;122:584-586.

93. Lindquist TD, Sher NA, Doughman DJ. Clinical signs and medical therapy of early *Acanthamoeba* keratitis. Arch Ophthalmol. 1988;106:73-77.

94. Duke BJ, Tyson RW, DeBiasi R, et al. *Balamuthia mandrillaris* meningoencephalitis presenting with acute hydrocephalus. Pediatr Neurosurg. 1997;26:107-111.

95. Rideout BA, Gardiner CH, Stalis IH, et al. Fatal infections with *Balamuthia mandrillaris* (a free-living amoeba) in gorillas and other Old World primates. Vet Pathol. 1997;34:15-22.

96. Katz JD, Ropper AH, Adelman L, et al. A case of *Balamuthia mandrillaris* meningoencephalitis. Arch Neurol. 2000;57:1210-1212.

97. Lawande RV, Macfarlane JT, Weir WR, et al. A case of primary amebic meningoencephalitis in a Nigerian farmer. Am J Trop Med Hyg. 1980;29:21-25.

98. Callicott JH Jr, Nelson EC, Jones MM, et al. Meningoencephalitis due to pathogenic free-living amoebae. Report of two cases. JAMA. 1968;206:579-582.

99. Duma RJ, Rosenblum WI, McGehee RF, et al. Primary amoebic meningoencephalitis caused by *Naegleria*. Two new cases, response to amphotericin B, and a review. Ann Intern Med. 1971;74:923-931.

100. Sparagano O. Differentiation of *Naegleria fowleri* and other Naegleriae by polymerase chain reaction and hybridization methods. FEMS Microbiol Lett. 1993;110:325-330.

101. Sparagano O, Drouet E, Denoyel G, et al. Differentiation of *Naegleria fowleri* from other species of Naegleria using monoclonal antibodies and the polymerase chain reaction. Trans R Soc Trop Med Hyg. 1994;88:119-120.

102. Sparagano O. Detection of *Naegleria fowleri* cysts in environmental samples by using a DNA probe. FEMS Microbiol Lett. 1993;112:349-351.

103. Reveiller FL, Cabanes PA, Marciano-Cabral F. Development of a nested PCR assay to detect the pathogenic free-living amoeba *Naegleria fowleri*. Parasitol Res. 2002;88:443-450.

104. Penland RL, Wilhelmus KR. Comparison of axenic and monoxenic media for isolation of *Acanthamoeba*. J Clin Microbiol. 1997;35:915-922.

105. Cohen EJ, Parlato CJ, Arentsen JJ, et al. Medical and surgical treatment of *Acanthamoeba* keratitis. Am J Ophthalmol. 1987;103:615-625.

106. Wright P, Warhurst D, Jones BR. *Acanthamoeba* keratitis successfully treated medically. Br J Ophthalmol. 1985;69:778-782.

107. Silvany RE, Luckenbach MW, Moore MB. The rapid detection of *Acanthamoeba* in paraffin-embedded sections of corneal tissue with calcofluor white. Arch Ophthalmol. 1987;105:1366-1367.

108. Lai S, Asgari M, Henney HR Jr. Non-radioactive DNA probe and polymerase chain reaction procedures for the specific detection of *Acanthamoeba*. Mol Cell Probes. 1994;8:81-89.

109. Schuster FL, Visvesvara GS. Axenic growth and drug sensitivity studies of *Balamuthia mandrillaris*, an agent of amebic meningoencephalitis in humans and other animals. J Clin Microbiol. 1996;34:385-388.

110. Seidel JS, Harmatz P, Visvesvara GS, et al. Successful treatment of primary amebic meningoencephalitis. N Engl J Med. 1982;306:346-348.

111. Brown RL. Successful treatment of primary amebic meningoencephalitis. Arch Intern Med. 1991;151:1201-1202.

112. Anderson K, Jamieson A. Primary amoebic meningoencephalitis. Lancet. 1972; 1:902-903.

113. Wang A, Kay R, Poon WS, et al. Successful treatment of amoebic meningoencephalitis in a Chinese living in Hong Kong. Clin Neurol Neurosurg. 1993;95: 249-252.

114. Gupta S, Ghosh PK, Dutta GP, et al. In vivo study of artemisinin and its derivatives against primary amebic meningoencephalitis caused by *Naegleria fowleri*. J Parasitol. 1995; 81: 1012-1013.

115. Goswick SM, Brenner GM. Activities of azithromycin and amphotericin B against *Naegleria fowleri* in vitro and in a mouse model of primary amebic meningoencephalitis. Antimicrob Agents Chemother. 2003;47:524-528.

116. Lallinger GJ, Reiner SL, Cooke DW, et al. Efficacy of immune therapy in early experimental *Naegleria fowleri* meningitis. Infect Immun. 1987;55:1289-1293.

117. Duma RJ, Finley R. In vitro susceptibility of pathogenic *Naegleria* and *Acanthamoeba* species to a variety of therapeutic agents. Antimicrob Agents Chemother. 1976;10:370-376.

118. Nagington J, Richards JE. Chemotherapeutic compounds and Acanthamoebae from eye infections. J Clin Pathol. 1976;29:648-651.

119. Sharma PP, Gupta P, Murali MV, et al. Primary amebic meningoencephalitis caused by *Acanthamoeba* successfully treated with cotrimoxazole. Indian Pediatr. 1993;30:1219-1222.

120. Das SR, Asiri S, el-Soofi A, et al. Protective and curative effects of rifampicin in *Acanthamoeba* meningitis of the mouse. J Infect Dis. 1991;163:916-917.

121. Singhal T, Bajpai A, Kalra V, et al. Successful treatment of *Acanthamoeba* meningitis with combination oral antimicrobials. Pediatr Infect Dis J. 2001;20: 623-627.

122. Seijo Martinez M, Gonzalez-Mediero G, Santiago P, et al. Granulomatous amebic encephalitis in a patient with AIDS: Isolation of acanthamoebas group II from brain tissue and successful treatment with sulfadiazine and fluconazole. J Clin Microbiol. 2000;38:3892-3895.

123. Lindquist TD. Treatment of *Acanthamoeba* keratitis. Cornea. 1998;17:11-16.

124. Holland GN, Donzis PB. Rapid resolution of early *Acanthamoeba* keratitis after epithelial debridement. Am J Ophthalmol. 1987;104:87-89.

125. Perez-Santonja JJ, Kilvington S, Hughes R, et al. Persistently culture positive acanthamoeba keratitis: In vivo resistance and in vitro sensitivity. Ophthalmology. 2003;110:1593-1600.

126. Moore MB, McCulley J. Acanthamoeba keratitis associated with contact lenses: Six consecutive cases of successful management. Br J Opthalmol. 1989;73:271-275.

127. Duguid IG, Dart JK, Morlet N, et al. Outcome of acanthamoeba keratitis treated with polyhexamethyl biguanide and propamidine. Ophthalmology. 1997;104:1587-1592.

128. Seal D, Hay J, Kirkness C, et al. Successful medical therapy of *Acanthamoeba* keratitis with topical chlorhexidine and propamidine. Eye. 1996;10(Pt 4):413-421.

129. Johns KJ, Head WS, O'Day DM. Corneal toxicity of propamidine. Arch Ophthalmol. 1988;106:68-69.
130. Alizadeh H, Silvany RE, Meyer DR, et al. In vitro amoebicidal activity of propamidine and pentamidine isethionate against *Acanthamoeba* species and toxicity to corneal tissues. Cornea. 1997;16:94-100.
131. Rain AN, Radzan T, Sajiri S, et al. In vitro drug susceptibility of *Acanthamoeba* castellani to chloroquine, ivermectin and fungizon. Southeast Asian J Trop Med Public Hlth. 1996;27:319-324.
132. Davis RM, Schroeder RP, Rowsey JJ, et al. *Acanthamoeba* keratitis and infectious crystalline keratopathy. Arch Ophthalmol. 1987;105:1524-1527.
133. Park DH, Palay DA, Daya SM, et al. The role of topical corticosteroids in the management of *Acanthamoeba* keratitis. Cornea. 1997;16:277-283.
134. Schuster FL, Visvesvara GS. Efficacy of novel antimicrobials against clinical isolates of opportunistic amebas. J Eukaryot Microbiol. 1998;45:612-618.
135. Vernhes MC, Benichou A, Pernin P, et al. Elimination of free-living amoebae in fresh water with pulsed electric fields. Water Res. 2002;36:3429-3438.
136. Zanetti S, Fiori PL, Pinna A, et al. Susceptibility of *Acanthamoeba castellanii* to contact lens disinfecting solutions. Antimicrob Agents Chemother. 1995;39:1596-1598.
137. Rowen JL, Doerr CA, Vogel H, et al. *Balamuthia mandrillaris:* A newly recognized agent for amebic meningoencephalitis. Pediatr Infect Dis J. 1995;14:705-710.

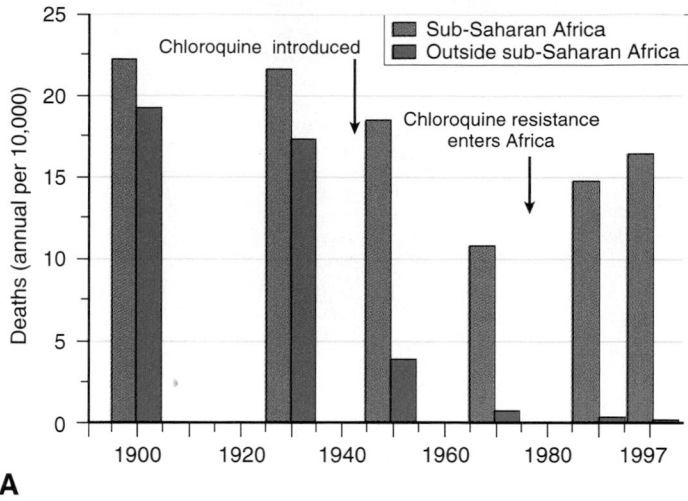

A

CHAPTER **272**

Plasmodium Species (Malaria)

RICK M. FAIRHURST

THOMAS E. WELLEMS

THE MALARIA PROBLEM

Malaria is an overwhelming problem in tropical developing countries, accounting for up to 500 million febrile illnesses and several million deaths annually.[1,2] It is estimated that up to 40% of the world's population is at risk for acquiring malaria. In sub-Saharan Africa, most severe cases and deaths occur in children younger than 5 years old and in pregnant women.

The introduction of chloroquine and dichlorodiphenyltrichloroethane (DDT) at the end of World War II brought dramatic new power to malaria control efforts. With postwar economic recovery and a renewed spirit of international cooperation, optimism ran high that these new tools might be used to eliminate malaria, and in 1955 the World Health Organization launched its campaign to eradicate the disease. This goal soon proved overly optimistic, and the centrally organized DDT-spraying programs at the core of the campaign were discontinued in 1967. The campaign nevertheless brought regional successes that coincided with other factors to reduce malaria rates in many areas of the world (e.g., in Asia)[3] (Fig. 272-1A).

A stark exception to this general progress is sub-Saharan Africa, where malaria remains deeply entrenched. Even the most committed spraying and eradication programs in endemic areas of this region could not defeat malaria's efficient transmission by the African mosquito, *Anopheles gambiae*.[4] The wide availability and use of chloroquine did, however, boost the health of young African children who suffer most from *Plasmodium falciparum,* the species responsible for the deadliest form of malaria. As chloroquine became increasingly available in the 1970s, death rates from malaria in Africa began to drop, approaching half the level of the pre-chloroquine years.[5] Unfortunately, the massive use of chloroquine (hundreds of tons sufficient for hundreds of millions of treatments annually) in the 1980s[6] selected for chloroquine-resistant *P. falciparum* strains that entered and spread across Africa. In the 1980s and 1990s, malaria resurged and death rates increased. The impact of chloroquine resistance was especially evident in young children, who do not have the partially protective antimalarial immunity that usually develops after repeated episodes of the ill-

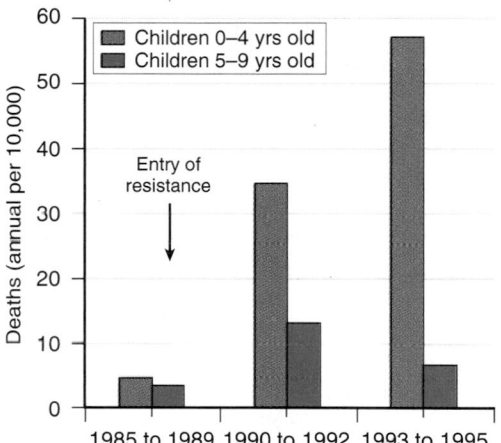

B

FIGURE 272-1. Malaria death rates after the introduction of chloroquine and subsequent evolution of chloroquine-resistant *P. falciparum*. **A,** Malaria death rates in the 20th century. Dramatic reductions in mortality have been achieved outside sub-Saharan Africa. Mortality rates declined after the introduction of chloroquine but rose again after the spread of chloroquine resistance across the continent. **B,** Rise in mortality among children in the village of Mlomp, Senegal. Increased death rates were observed after chloroquine resistance entered the village, chiefly among children younger than 5 years old, the most susceptible age group in highly endemic areas. (**A,** Adapted from Carter R, Mendis KN. Evolutionary and historical aspects of the burden of malaria. Clin Microbiol Rev. 2002;15:564-594. **B,** Adapted from Trape JF, Pison G, Preziosi MP, et al. Impact of chloroquine resistance on malaria mortality. C R Acad Sci III. 1998;321:689-697.)

ness[7,8] (Fig. 272-1B). Unfortunately, the safety and low cost of chloroquine were unmatched by other more expensive drugs that have been largely unaffordable in developing countries.[9] In the absence of an effective vaccine, successful treatment of malaria in Africa will depend on new drugs becoming affordable and readily available.

PLASMODIUM AND ITS LIFE CYCLE

Plasmodium parasites belong to the *Apicomplexa* group of protozoa, which includes other pathogens such as *Babesia, Toxoplasma,* and *Cryptosporidium* species. *Apicomplexa* are distinguished morphologically by the presence of a specialized complex of apical organelles (micronemes,

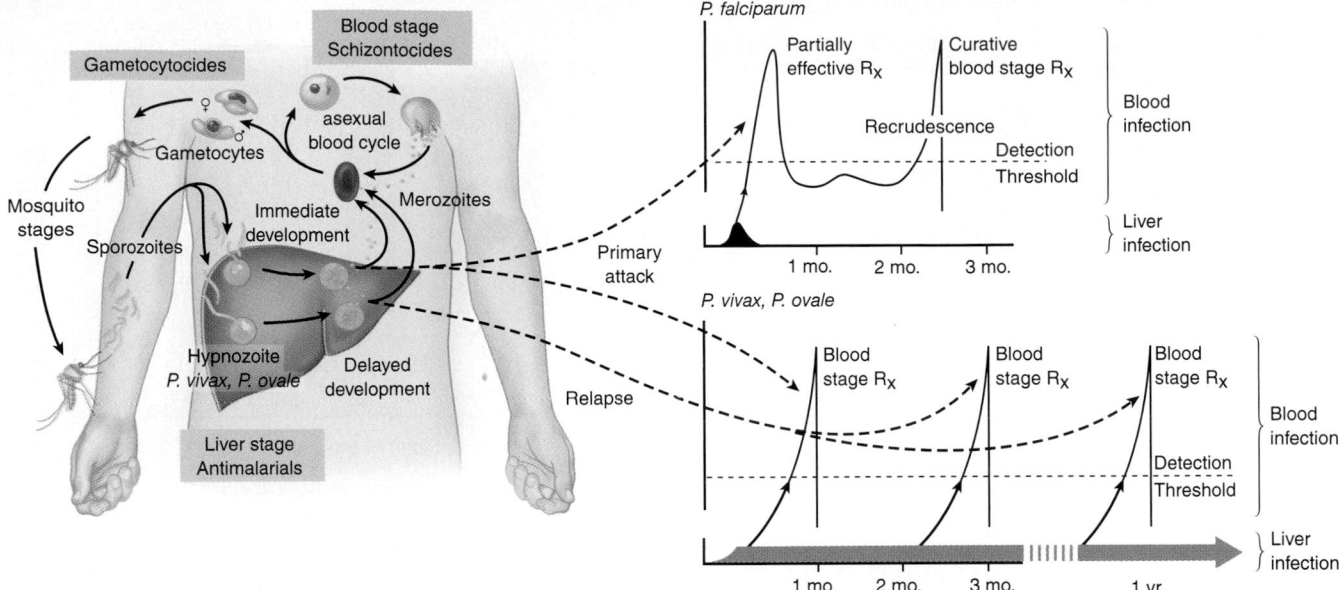

FIGURE 272-2. The *Plasmodium* life cycle and disease patterns of recrudescence and relapse. Anopheline mosquitoes transmit malaria by injecting sporozoites into the human host. The sporozoites then invade hepatocytes, in which they develop into schizonts. Each infected hepatocyte ruptures to liberate 10,000 to 30,000 merozoites that invade circulating erythrocytes. Growth and development of the parasites in red cells result in subsequent waves of merozoite invasion. This asexual blood cycle repeats every 48 or 72 hours, leading to amplification of parasite density; paroxysms of chills, fevers, and sweats; and other manifestations of disease. Malaria symptoms are typically experienced 2 to 4 weeks after the mosquito bite. If the parasites are not cleared (e.g., patient receives partially effective therapy), recrudescence of parasitemia and malaria symptoms can occur. Eradicating parasites with an effective drug regimen cures malaria. Some *P. vivax* and *P. ovale* parasites can postpone their development in the liver, persisting as latent forms called hypnozoites. Hypnozoites are not eradicated by standard therapy (e.g., chloroquine) directed against blood stages. Resumption of hypnozoite development months to years after initial infection can lead to malaria relapse that requires an additional round of drug therapy to treat recurrent symptoms and eradicate blood stages. Treating hypnozoites with primaquine can prevent relapses of malaria.

rhoptries, and dense granules) involved in host cell invasion (Fig. 272-4A).[10] Four *Plasmodium* species cause human malaria: *Plasmodium falciparum, P. vivax, P. ovale,* and *P. malariae.* Some malaria parasites of other primates (e.g., *P. knowlesi, P. cynomolgi,* and *P. simium*) also rarely infect humans under natural conditions.[11]

In 1880, Alphonse Laveran first observed malaria parasites in a human blood sample, including the exflagellation of microgametes that usually emerge in the mosquito.[12] It was eventually established that parasites in the blood stream reproduce asexually in the haploid state (Fig. 272-2). During erythrocytic development, some parasites undergo a poorly understood switch to sexual forms: male and female gametocytes. These are the forms that are taken up by and infect anopheline mosquitoes, as proven by Ronald Ross and Battista Grassi in the 1890s.[13,14] Gametocytes emerge from erythrocytes in the mosquito midgut as male and female gametes that cross-fertilize to form diploid zygotes, which in turn differentiate into ookinetes that burrow across the midgut wall. Each ookinete develops into an oocyst containing up to 1000 sporozoites that emerge and are then carried by the insect hemolymph to invade the salivary glands. These processes in the mosquito require an extrinsic incubation period of about 1 to 2 weeks.

Mosquitoes inject sporozoites into humans when they bite. Shortt and Garnham demonstrated in 1948 that sporozoites must first invade and replicate in hepatocytes before they can differentiate into merozoites capable of entering the intraerythrocytic cycle.[15] This invasion process is mediated by the sporozoite's attachment through its surface protein coat to the hepatocyte's heparan sulfate glycoproteins and low-density lipoprotein (LDL) receptor.[16] Individual infected hepatocytes support the development of 10,000 to 30,000 merozoites, a process that is not associated with symptoms. All *P. falciparum* and *P. malariae* parasites complete their liver stage development in about 1 to 2 weeks.[17] *P. vivax* and *P. ovale* liver stages also can develop promptly or can remain latent as hypnozoites in the liver for months to years before emerging to produce relapses of malaria (Fig. 272-2).

On rupture of infected hepatocytes, merozoites enter the blood stream where they invade erythrocytes. In *P. falciparum* infection, this invasion process can be supported by multiple different interactions between parasite molecules and erythrocyte surface molecules, including glycophorins. Successful invasion of *P. vivax,* by contrast, depends on an interaction with erythrocyte Duffy antigen. Within erythrocytes, merozoites develop from ring forms into trophozoites and then into schizonts over 48 hours *(P. falciparum, P. vivax, P. ovale)* or 72 hours *(P. malariae).* Schizont rupture releases another 24 to 32 merozoites, each of which is capable of infecting a new erythrocyte. Cycles of invasion and growth in erythrocytes produce a parasite biomass that enlarges exponentially, causing fever and leading to pathological processes such as erythrocyte loss (anemia) and sequestration in microvascular beds (cerebral malaria).

PATHOPHYSIOLOGY

The Malaria Paroxysm and General Considerations

Malaria presents as an acute febrile illness that is sometimes but not always characterized by the classic malaria paroxysm: chills and rigors, followed by fever spikes up to 40° C (104° F), then profuse sweating that can ultimately give way to extreme fatigue and sleep. Paroxysms last several hours, occur with a regular periodicity coinciding with the synchronous rupture of blood schizonts, may alternate with relatively asymptomatic periods, and are associated with extremely high levels of tumor necrosis factor-α (TNF-α).[18] Paroxysms can occur in tertian 48-hour or quartan 72-hour cycles, or in other more complicated patterns.[19] TNF-α may originate from macrophages stimulated by glycosyl phosphatidylinositol moieties or other substances released on schizont rupture.[20,21]

Malaria can be acutely malignant and painful, or more indolent and asymptomatic. It increases the morbidity and mortality associated with other diseases by stressing the host and producing effects such as de-

FIGURE 272-3. Pathogenesis of severe *P. falciparum* malaria. Deaths from severe falciparum malaria are commonly attributable to the effects of severe anemia, cerebral malaria, and respiratory distress in young children. This schematic illustrates how multiple pathogenic events such as cytoadherence, destruction of uninfected erythrocytes, and production of inflammatory cytokines combine to produce the microvascular sequestration and metabolic acidosis that are central to the development of severe disease.

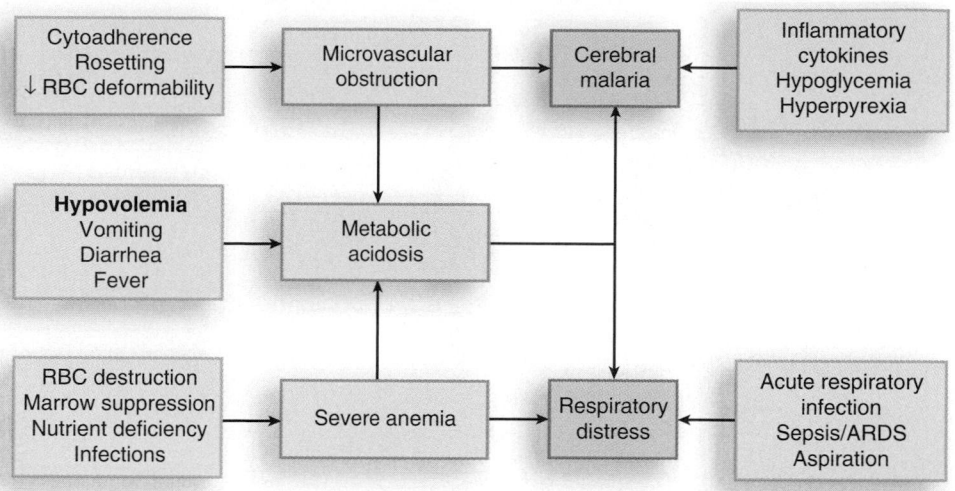

hydration, anemia, and some degree of immune suppression. Malaria is tremendously debilitating and impedes economic development through its adverse effects on fertility, population growth, saving and investment, worker productivity, absenteeism, premature mortality, and medical costs.[22,23] A single episode of malaria has been estimated to result in a loss of 5 to 20 working days, and an agricultural family afflicted by malaria may be up to 60% less productive than a family without malaria.[24]

Plasmodium falciparum

P. falciparum malaria is much more acute and severe than malaria caused by other *Plasmodium* species (Fig. 272-3). Almost all deaths directly attributable to malaria are caused by severe manifestations of *P. falciparum* infection, including cerebral malaria, severe anemia, respiratory failure, renal failure, and severe malaria of pregnancy.[25,26] Important contributory factors include metabolic acidosis, hypoglycemia, and superimposed bacterial infections. Fatal *P. falciparum* infections are often associated with the failure of multiple organ systems.

An important feature of the pathogenesis of *P. falciparum* is its ability to sequester in the deep venous microvasculature. This sequestration is thought to involve a number of processes: cytoadherence—the binding of infected erythrocytes to endothelial cells[27,28] (Fig. 272-4F and G), rosetting—the binding of infected erythrocytes to uninfected erythrocytes[29,30] (see Fig. 272-4H), reduced red cell deformability[31,32] (see Fig. 272-4C and D), and the collection of infected erythrocytes within the proteoglycan matrix of placental spaces. *P. falciparum*-infected erythrocytes sequester throughout the body, including the heart,[33] lung, brain,[34-36] liver, kidney, dermis, bone marrow,[37] and placenta.[38] By this sequestration, *P. falciparum* may avoid filtration and destruction by the spleen and thus multiply to high densities.[39] The survival and propagation of parasites may be aided when they sequester in the low oxygen gas environment of postcapillary venules, where they might have an advantage developing in erythrocytes susceptible to oxidative stress. Attachment points to endothelium have been shown by electron microscopy to be dense protrusions, termed knobs, on the surface of infected erythrocytes (Fig. 272-4D and E), where variant cytoadherence proteins (PfEMP-1; see later) are anchored. Attachment at knobs (Fig. 272-4F) supports cytoadherence in vitro under flow conditions and sequestration in vivo (Fig. 272-4G).[40,41] Under flow conditions, cytoadherence events are reminiscent of leukocyte adhesion, involving distinct phases of tethering, rolling, and stable adhesion.[42]

P. falciparum erythrocyte membrane protein-1 (PfEMP-1) is central to malaria pathogenesis.[43] PfEMP-1 is a family of major antigenically variant proteins encoded by a multicopy gene family termed *var*.[44] Approximately 60 different *var* genes are present in the haploid genome

of each parasite, encoding variants of PfEMP-1 with unique antigenic and cytoadherent properties.[45,46] A single PfEMP-1 variant is thought to be predominantly expressed on the surface of an individual infected erythrocyte[47] while others are silenced.[48] Switches in expression between individual members of the *var* gene family occur at an estimated rate of 2% to 18% per cell per generation[49,50] and produce the antigenic variation in *P. falciparum* populations during the course of an infection. PfEMP-1 proteins exposed on knobs have binding domains that adhere to host molecules, including CD36, intercellular adhesion molecule-1 (ICAM-1), thrombospondin, platelet-endothelial cell adhesion molecule (PECAM/CD31),[42,51-53] and chondroitin sulfate A.[54,55] Broods of parasites infecting a human host may express several variants in their subpopulations.

There is some evidence that *P. falciparum* strains may be associated with pathological developments of different severity because of the particular variants of PfEMP-1 expressed as well as the distribution of host receptors.[27] CD36 is an important cytoadherence ligand expressed on endothelium as well as on monocytes and platelets and is thought to mediate the systemic sequestration of parasites. CD36, however, may have a more limited role in the brain, where ICAM-1 is believed to be a principal cytoadherence ligand. This concept is supported by evidence of ICAM-1 upregulation in autopsy brain specimens and studies that have correlated cerebral malaria with the ability of parasite field isolates to bind ICAM-1.[56-59] Parasites that bind CSA expressed by syncytiotrophoblasts usually do not bind CD36,[60] which accounts for their selective sequestration in placental tissue and role in malaria of pregnancy.

PfEMP-1 is also an important parasite ligand in rosetting,[61] as it can adhere to complement receptor 1 (CR1)[62] and blood group A antigen[63] on the host erythrocyte. A human CR1 polymorphism that reduces *P. falciparum* rosetting was found in one study to protect against severe malaria[64]; data from other studies of rosetting and disease severity have in some cases shown an association[65-69] and in others have not.[70,71]

High parasite densities,[72] increased parasite multiplication rates,[73] and evidence of high parasite biomass (e.g., intraleukocytic pigment, mature trophozoites, and schizonts) on peripheral blood smear, are associated with increased severity of malaria and death.[74,75] *P. falciparum* can infect erythrocytes of all ages, which aids in producing heavy parasite burdens[76]; *P. vivax* is selective for reticulocytes[77,78] and therefore does not achieve high densities.

Cerebral Malaria

The classic histopathological finding of fatal cerebral malaria is the intense sequestration of parasites in the cerebral microvasculature (see Fig. 272-4G), often accompanied by ring hemorrhages, perivascular leukocyte infiltrates, and immunohistochemical evidence for endothelial cell activation.[34,58,79] In one autopsy series of patients who died from

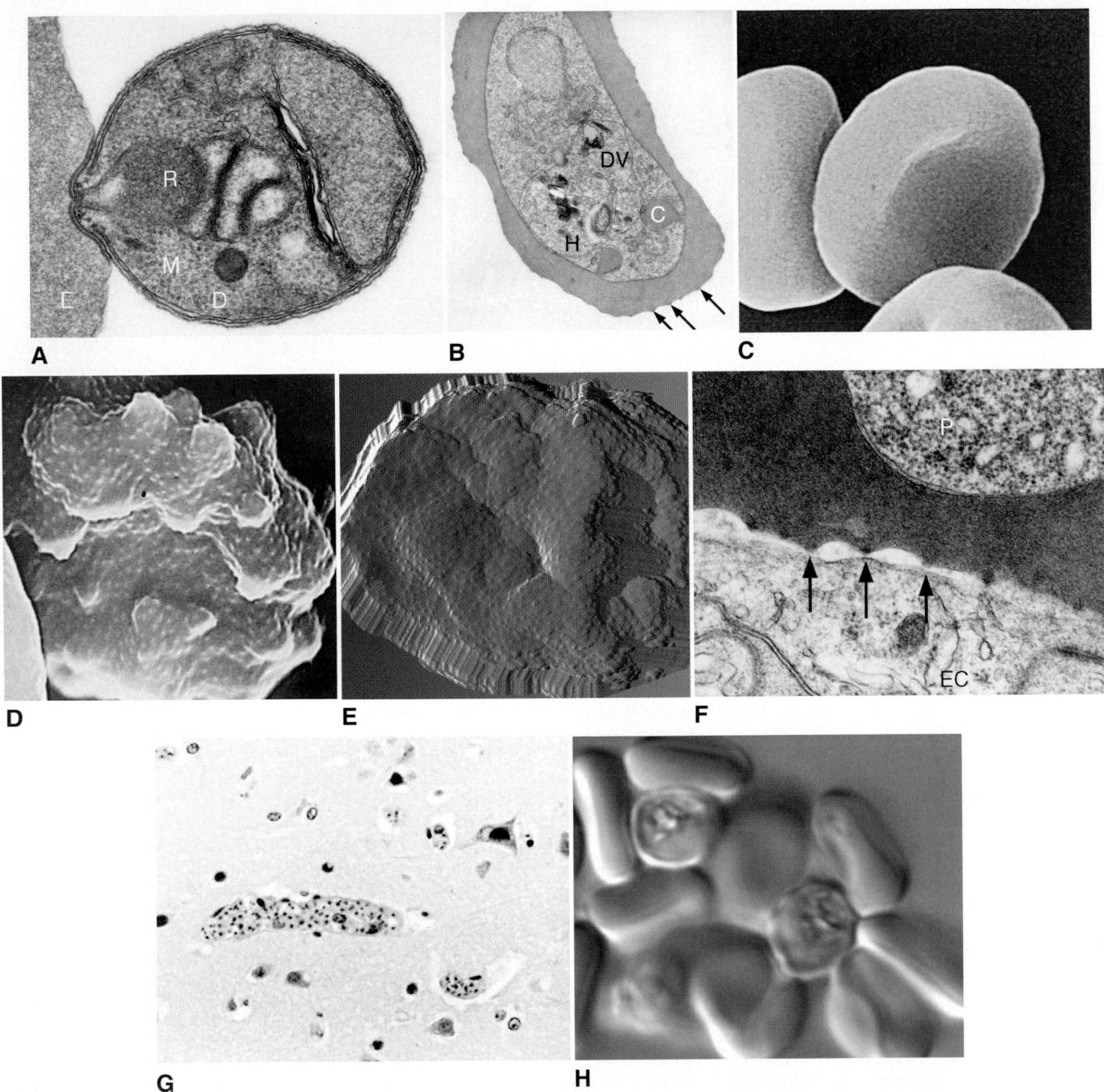

FIGURE 272-4. Morphological features of *P. falciparum*. **A,** Transmission electron micrograph of a *P. knowlesi* merozoite invading an erythrocyte E via its apical end, which contains rhoptries (R), micronemes (M), and dense granules (D). **B,** Transmission electron micrograph of an intraerythrocytic *P. falciparum* trophozoite containing cytosomes (C), digestive vacuole (DV), and crystalline hemazoin (H). *Arrows* identify numerous small electron-dense protrusions termed knobs on the surface of the host erythrocyte. Scanning electron micrographs (**C** and **D**) demonstrate the effects of the malaria parasite on its host erythrocyte. Distension from the growth of the parasite *P. falciparum* converts the erythrocyte from a deformable biconcave disk C to a nondeformable cell D displaying knobs over its surface. **E,** Atomic force microscopic image of the surface of a *P. falciparum*-infected erythrocyte showing numerous knob structures. **F,** Transmission electron micrograph showing adherence via knobs (arrows) between a *P. falciparum*-infected erythrocyte and a host endothelial cell (EC) of a cerebral microvessel. **G,** Histological section of brain tissue showing pigmented mature *P. falciparum* parasites sequestered in microvessels. **H,** Light microscopic image of rosetting, the binding of a *P. falciparum*-infected erythrocyte to multiple uninfected erythrocytes. (*A,* From Fujioka H, Aikawa M. The malaria parasite and its life cycle. In: Wahlgren M, Perlmann P, eds. Malaria: Molecular and Clinical Aspects. Harwood Academic; 1999:19-55. *B,* Courtesy of Hisashi Fujioka, Cleveland, Ohio. *C* and *D,* From Aikawa M, Rabbege JR, Udeinya IJ, et al. Electron microscopy of knobs in Plasmodium falciparum-infected erythrocytes. J Parasitol. 1983;69:435-437. *E,* Courtesy of James Dvorak and Takayuki Arie, Bethesda, Maryland. *F,* Transmission electron micrograph showing adherence via knobs (arrows) between a *P. falciparum*-infected erythrocyte and a host endothelial cell (EC) of a cerebral microvessel. From Atkinson CT, Aikawa M. Ultrastructure of malaria-infected erythrocytes. Blood Cells. 1990;16:351-368. *G,* Courtesy of Hisashi Fujioka, Cleveland, Ohio. *H,* Courtesy of James Dvorak, Bethesda, Maryland (reprinted with permission).

cerebral malaria, 94% of brain microvessels contained adherent parasites versus 13% of controls who died from noncerebral malaria.[80] Parasite sequestration is generally considered to be critical to the pathogenesis of cerebral malaria, although cases of cerebral malaria have been reported in which the microvascular sequestration of parasites was not prominent.

Sequestration of parasites is thought to stimulate the local production of inflammatory cytokines and mediators such as TNF-α and nitric oxide, elevated levels of which may correlate with disease severity.[81-84] These cytokines are believed to upregulate adhesion molecules such as ICAM-1 in the cerebral microvasculature,[85,86] which may lead to further sequestration of infected and uninfected erythrocytes, leukocytes, and activated platelets.[87] This process appears to cause varying degrees of functional obstruction that leads to reduced local delivery of oxygen and glucose. Obstruction by infected erythrocytes does not generally produce neurological sequelae akin to those that follow the physical occlusion in thrombotic stroke, as most patients with cerebral malaria who recover can do so rapidly within 48 hours and without such consequences. Systemic sequestration of metabolically active parasites, blood cells, and platelets likely contributes to the metabolic acidosis and thrombocytopenia commonly seen in severe malaria. Severe metabolic acidosis, hypoglycemia, hyperpyrexia, and nonconvulsive status epilepticus may contribute significantly to the cerebral malaria presentation, as suggested by the rapid clinical improvement of some patients to fluid resuscitation and blood transfusion, dextrose infusion, fever reduction, and anticonvulsants.

Hypoglycemia

Hypoglycemia in malaria can cause coma and convulsions and contributes substantially to the morbidity and mortality associated with cerebral malaria.[25] The pathophysiologic mechanisms of hypoglycemia in children and adults are often different. In children, insulin levels are appropriate and hypoglycemia is associated with impaired hepatic gluconeogenesis and increased consumption of glucose by hypermetabolic peripheral tissues.[88-92] Large amounts of glucose are also consumed by intraerythrocytic parasites.[93] In adults, hypoglycemia is often associated with hyperinsulinemia,[94] which may result from pancreatic islet cell stimulation by parasite-derived factors and/or parenteral quinine or quinidine therapy.[95] Depletion of liver glycogen stores from decreased oral intake during the prodromal period may also contribute to hypoglycemia.

Anemia

The pathophysiology of malarial anemia is multifactorial and complex.[96] The intravascular lysis and phagocytic removal of infected erythrocytes[97] contribute to anemia, but do not always account for the dramatic reductions in erythrocyte mass that can occur with acute *P. falciparum* malaria episodes. Additional processes have therefore been implicated in malarial anemia. Excess removal of uninfected erythrocytes may account for up to 90% of erythrocyte loss[98] and may be mediated by processes (e.g., oxidative stress) that enhance the senescence and impair the deformability of erythrocytes. The contribution of impaired bone marrow responses to malarial anemia is significant and probably involves general processes also found in other diseases. Release of inflammatory cytokines, for example, TNF-α, are associated with impaired production of erythropoietin,[99,100] decreased responsiveness of erythroid progenitor cells to adequate levels of erythropoietin,[101,102] and increased erythrophagocytic activity.[103] These pathogenic processes account for normochromic/normocytic anemia seen in malaria, and explain the notable absence of a robust reticulocyte response. Although microcytosis and hypochromia are seen in malaria, these are often attributable to thalassemias and iron deficiency in endemic areas. Menstruation, nutritional deficiencies, and concomitant infections (e.g., hookworm and *Schistosoma*) may also contribute to the level of anemia experienced during an acute malaria episode by already lowering the baseline from which hemoglobin levels acutely decline. In endemic areas where chloroquine resistance is prevalent, the inability of young children to clear their parasitemias with chloroquine contributes to their higher baseline prevalence of anemia when compared to children treated with more effective drugs.[104]

Pulmonary Edema and Respiratory Distress

The most significant pulmonary manifestation directly attributable to *P. falciparum* is noncardiogenic pulmonary edema.[105,106] Sequestration of infected erythrocytes in the lungs is thought to initiate regional production of inflammatory cytokines that increase capillary permeability, leading sequentially to pulmonary edema, dyspnea, hypoxia, acute lung injury, and acute respiratory distress syndrome (ARDS).[107] Pulmonary edema is common with severe malaria in adults, but rare in children, and is not associated with pleural effusion. Iatrogenic fluid overload and acute renal failure may contribute to the development or worsening of pulmonary edema. Although pulmonary edema usually occurs after other features of severe disease (e.g., coma, acute renal failure) become manifest, it may occur at any time during the clinical course, even when the patient appears to be recovering on antimalarial therapy. Dyspnea and increased respiratory rate are features of impending pulmonary edema and often precede other clinical and radiologic signs (use of accessory muscles of respiration, generalized increase in interstitial markings).

Pulmonary manifestations of deep breathing and respiratory distress associated with severe malaria may also arise from metabolic acidosis,[26] severe acute respiratory infections,[91] sepsis-related ARDS, aspiration (especially with diminished consciousness or convulsions), and nosocomial pneumonia. Cerebral pathological processes may result in abnormal breathing patterns including Cheyne-Stokes and respiratory failure.[108]

Metabolic (Lactic) Acidosis

Metabolic acidosis is a common feature of severe malaria, associated with significant lactic acidemia in up to 85% of cases. Metabolic acidosis is principally caused by reduced delivery of oxygen to tissues, from the combined effects of anemia (decreased oxygen-carrying capacity), sequestration (microvascular obstruction), and hypovolemia (reduced perfusion) as a result of fluid losses caused by fever, decreased intake, vomiting and diarrhea.[109] These effects produce a shift from aerobic to anaerobic metabolism and cause lactate levels to increase.[110] The following factors may also contribute to metabolic acidosis: production of lactate by sequestered parasites by anaerobic glycolysis,[111] reduction of hepatic blood flow leading to diminished lactate clearance,[112,113] induction of lactate production by TNF-α and other pro-inflammatory cytokines,[114] renal impairment,[112] and ingestion of exogenous acids (e.g., salicylate) or the unknown constituents of traditional herbal remedies for fever.[115]

Malaria of Pregnancy

Placental malaria results in maternal morbidity and mortality, intrauterine growth retardation, premature delivery, low birth weight, and increased newborn mortality.[116,117] Selective accumulation of mature parasites in the placenta appears to involve their interaction with syncytiotrophoblastic chondroitin sulfate A (CSA), hyaluronic acid, and immunoglobulins.[118-120] This is in contrast to the sequestration of infected erythrocytes in the systemic microvasculature, where CD36 is the major endothelial receptor. Parasites that accumulate in the placenta express PfEMP-1 variants that bind CSA[121,122] but not CD36.[60] Evidence suggests that women who experience a malaria episode from CSA-binding parasites during their first pregnancy lack immunity to the PfEMP-1 antigenic variants presented by these strains and, despite immunity to CD36-binding variants from previous infections, are highly susceptible to the new infection. Malaria in subsequent pregnancies is typically less severe than in the first pregnancy,[123] presumably because of a woman's previous experience with CSA-binding parasites.

Plasmodium vivax and *P. ovale*

Infections with *P. vivax* and *P. ovale* can be considered similar to each other from a clinical perspective. Although rarely fatal, *P. vivax* infections can be tremendously debilitating and are sometimes associated with serious complications, including acute lung injury[124,125] and splenic rupture and associated pathologies.[126,127] Splenic rupture has been associated with acute and chronic infections and can occur spontaneously or with minor trauma, including manual examination of the spleen. Although more commonly associated with vivax malaria, splenic rupture has been associated with all four *Plasmodium* species infecting humans. Anemia is frequently observed as a consequence of acute or chronic infections, or as a result of repeated acute infections.[97] Suppressed erythrocyte production and hemolysis of both infected and uninfected erythrocytes have been implicated in the pathogenesis of vivax malarial anemia.

The low mortality rates associated with *P. vivax* and *P. ovale* malaria are probably attributable to several factors. The invasion and development of *P. vivax* strongly favors reticulocytes,[78,128] which comprise a small proportion of the total erythrocyte mass. Consequently, parasitemias are usually less than 1%. *P. vivax* and *P. ovale* do not exhibit sequestration as observed for *P. falciparum,* and therefore are not associated with the microvascular obstruction or regional and systemic cytokine effects that characterize falciparum malaria. *P. vivax* parasites may avoid splenic entrapment by actually increasing erythrocyte deformability.[129]

Plasmodium malariae

The quartan malaria of *P. malariae* usually presents with fever and paroxysms similar to those of *P. vivax* but with a 3- rather than 2-day periodicity. *P. malariae* often establishes parasitemias that are below levels of detection by microscopy. Patients can remain infected and asymptomatic for periods of many years before presenting with fevers, malaise, and splenomegaly decades after they have left an endemic area.[130] Chronic *P. malariae* infection can lead to nephrotic syndrome in young children living in endemic areas.[131,132] This complication has features of an immune complex–mediated glomerulonephritis.[133,134]

GENETIC RESISTANCE

Life-threatening *P. falciparum* malaria has been a potent evolutionary force in shaping the human genome. Evidence for selection of genetic polymorphisms can be found in the ethnic and geographic distributions of mutant hemoglobins, thalassemias, glucose-6-phosphate dehydrogenase (G6PD) deficiencies, erythrocyte membrane proteins, human leukocyte antigens (HLA), endothelial cell proteins, and cytokines and other inflammatory mediators. The following paragraphs give brief descriptions of well-established polymorphisms protective against malaria.

Hemoglobins S, E, C

The geographic distributions of mutant hemoglobins overlap considerably with that of *P. falciparum* malaria.[135] Case-control and longitudinal studies have associated malaria protection with hemoglobin S (HbS) heterozygosity (sickle trait), in which the 6th amino acid of the β chain is mutated from glutamate to valine.[136-139] The genetic fitness of SS homozygosity is essentially zero in sub-Saharan Africa, whereas the prevalence of AS heterozygotes can be 25% or more in some areas.[140] The HbS mutation thus exists as a balanced polymorphism: the malaria protective benefit afforded to AS heterozygotes offsets the childhood deaths of SS homozygotes. The mechanisms by which mutant hemoglobins protect against severe malaria have not been definitively established and are likely multifactorial. In vitro culture experiments have shown that parasitized AS erythrocytes are more likely to sickle or support reduced parasite growth rates than their nonparasitized counterparts under conditions of low oxygen tension.[141-144] These effects may have some influence in reducing the hyperparasitemia-related and life-threatening complications of severe malaria in AS individuals. Children with sickle trait, however, are not all protected against cerebral malaria[145,146] and hypotheses of protection based on sickling and reduced growth rates do not account for epidemiological studies showing similar parasite densities in AA and AS children or very high parasite densities in some AS children.[147] Other

mechanisms of protection that include additional genetic or environmental factors are likely to be operative in AS individuals.

Hemoglobins E (HbE) and C (HbC) are also characterized by single point mutations in the β-globin chain: in the case of HbE, this is a glutamate to lysine change at the 26th amino acid, in the case of HbC the mutation is a glutamate to lysine change at the 6th amino acid, the same position as the HbS mutation. HbE and HbC are found predominantly in Asia and West Africa, respectively. Some epidemiological studies have reported a malaria protective effect for HbE.[148,149] In vitro studies have shown that HbE decreases the in vitro multiplication rate of *P. falciparum,*[150] suggesting this mutation may reduce parasite densities in vivo. Two case-control studies in West Africa have associated HbC with malaria protection.[145,151] In in vitro cultures, high proportions of *P. falciparum* parasites in homozygous CC erythrocytes do not develop normally and die.[152-154] It is unlikely, however, that malaria protection by AC erythrocytes can be explained by this mechanism, as in vitro parasite growth and development proceeds as well in AC erythrocytes as in AA erythrocytes.[154]

Thalassemias

Thalassemia arises from deletion of one or more of the four genes encoding the α-globin chain or mutations or deletions in one of the two genes encoding the β-globin chain of hemoglobin. These conditions are generally benign in the heterozygous state and are associated with varying degrees of microcytic, hypochromic anemia. Further loss of expression in the homozygous state causes severe disease and can be incompatible with life. Mutations associated with thalassemias are protective against malaria and exist as balanced polymorphisms in populations.[155-157] Although *P. falciparum* development can be supported by thalassemic erythrocytes, some studies have demonstrated impaired growth, especially under conditions of oxidative stress.[158-160] Other studies have demonstrated that parasitized thalassemic erythrocytes bind increased amounts of antibody from both nonimmune and immune serum, which suggests the possibility of enhanced opsonization in vivo.[161,162] The persistence of small amounts of HbF (see later) in young children may contribute in part to the observed malaria protection in those with thalassemia or sickle-trait.

Hemoglobin F

Hemoglobin F (α2/γ2) is a normal hemoglobin expressed by the fetus in utero and during the first few months of life. The expression of HbF dramatically declines after the 6th month of life as HbA replaces it. The uncommon presentation of malaria in neonates younger than 6 months old led to the hypothesis that HbF contributes to malaria protection, along with maternal antibody. Proteases that are responsible for digesting host cell hemoglobin in the food vacuole of the parasite may work less efficiently on HbF than HbA.[163] Impaired antioxidant capacity of HbF-containing erythrocytes has also been proposed to contribute to malaria protection.[164]

Glucose-6-Phosphate Dehydrogenase Deficiency

Glucose-6-phosphate dehydrogenase (G6PD) is a cytoplasmic enzyme that is essential for an erythrocyte's capacity to withstand oxidant stress, such as that exerted by the developing malaria parasite. The G6PD gene is located on the X-chromosome and is therefore present in only one copy in males. In heterozygous females carrying a mutant allele for deficient G6PD, erythrocytes are present as a mosaic population because of inactivation of one or the other X-chromosome. G6PD deficiency is the most common enzymopathy in humans, with more than 300 allelic polymorphisms identified to date. The most common polymorphism in Africa (the $A-$ allele, 12% enzyme activity) has been associated with malaria protection in children and pregnant women.[139,165] In one large case-control study performed in populations of West and East Africa, male hemizygotes and female heterozygotes carrying the $A-$ allele were 58% and 46% protected against severe malaria.[139] In vitro parasite culture experiments have yielded conflicting results, although most results suggest that parasite development is inhibited in G6PD-deficient erythrocytes.[164,166-168] *P. falciparum* has been reported to adapt to G6PD-deficient erythrocytes after a few cycles of culture by producing its own G6PD.[169,170] In heterozygous women carrying populations of G6PD-normal and G6PD-deficient erythrocytes, malaria protection has been proposed to result from the difficulty parasites have in continually switching between the different host cell types.[170] Early phagocytosis of infected G6PD-deficient erythrocytes has also been proposed to play a role in malaria protection.[171]

Southeast Asian Ovalocytosis

A 27-bp deletion in band 3 (the major anion transporter in erythrocytes) causes Southeast Asian ovalocytosis (SAO) and leads to reduced membrane deformability.[172-174] These properties may be associated with reduced parasite invasion rates of ovalocytes in vitro and reduced parasitemias in heterozygous individuals.[175-177] How these findings relate mechanistically to the dramatic reduction in cerebral malaria episodes among SAO heterozygotes[178] has not yet been established.

Duffy Antigen Negativity

Duffy antigen is the erythrocyte receptor for *P. vivax* merozoite invasion.[77,78] Erythrocytes lacking Duffy antigen are resistant to *P. vivax* invasion, which accounts for the extremely low incidence of vivax malaria in West Africa, where Duffy antigen negativity is highly prevalent.[179,180] Reduced Duffy antigen expression on erythrocytes has also been identified as a protective polymorphism against *P. vivax* malaria in Papua New Guinea.[181] Duffy antigen negativity does not protect against malaria from *P. falciparum, P. ovale,* or *P. malariae.*

ACQUIRED IMMUNITY AND ANTIGENIC VARIATION

Acquired immunity against malaria is not sterilizing immunity against malaria, which does not exist. It is immunity that increases with age, cumulative number of episodes of malaria, and time spent living in an endemic area.[182] As individuals gain the experience of numerous infections in their lifetime, they can be chronically infected yet will have only mild symptoms or none at all, that is, they develop anti-disease immunity. In highly endemic areas, children have multiple bouts of malaria each year and suffer greatly under its morbidity and mortality when they are young, generally less than 5 to 10 years old depending on the transmission level. Pregnant women, especially primagravidae, are an important exception to this general rule because of the ability of antigenically new CSA-binding parasites to sequester in the placenta (see earlier). Nonimmune individuals may develop high parasitemias (up to 80%) within a relatively short period of time.[183] Acquired immunity to malaria is short lived without continual reexposure to infection. Individuals who reside outside an endemic area for more than a year or two can develop symptomatic and/or severe malaria after their return.[184]

Neonates appear to be fairly resistant to malaria during the first 6 months of life. This apparent immunity may be conferred by transplacentally transferred maternal IgG, although the presence of fetal hemoglobin within erythrocytes likely plays a role as well (see above).

Splenomegaly often accompanies malaria and is thought to indicate an important role of the spleen in parasite clearance. Removal of uninfected erythrocytes by the stimulated spleen, however, may contribute to anemia. In asplenic individuals, *P. falciparum* malaria can progress extremely rapidly to high parasitemias that include mature forms not usually found circulating in the blood stream.[39,185,186]

The mechanism by which endemic populations acquire immunity to symptomatic and severe disease has not been defined.[187] Although antibodies and T-cell responses develop against a number of parasite antigens during natural infection, none of them have been found to be superior to age or parasite exposure as correlates of protective immunity.[188] Studies in which humans were infected with a single inoculum of *P. falciparum* in the use of malariotherapy for tertiary syphilis showed that erythrocyte infection peaks decreased in successive waves of parasitemia[189] (Fig. 272-5). Individuals who eventually cleared their infection were not protected against subsequent reinfection with a different *P. falciparum* strain.[190]

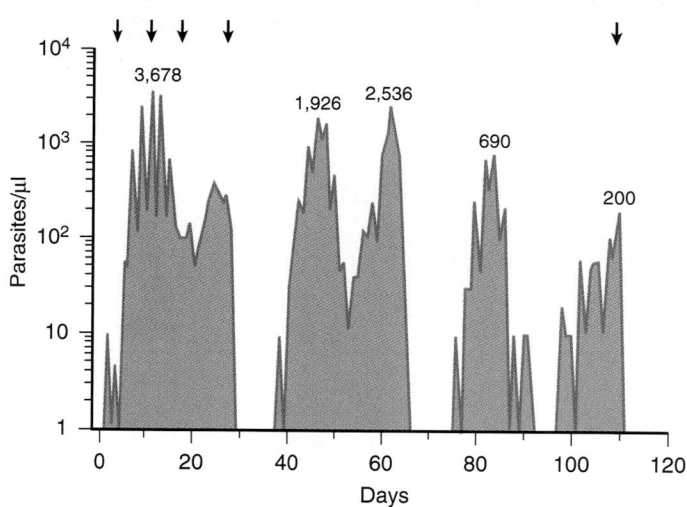

FIGURE 272-5. Premunition and antigenic variation. Parasitemia waves during recrudescence in a patient infected with *P. falciparum* as malariotherapy for tertiary syphilis. Although the individual had previously been infected with *P. falciparum*, drug treatments *(arrows)* were necessary to modify the primary attack and later for radical cure. Following subcurative drug treatments, four recrudescences occurred with parasite density peaks ultimately declining 10-fold. *(Adapted from Collins WE, Jeffery GM. A retrospective examination of sporozoite- and trophozoite-induced infections with* Plasmodium falciparum: *Development of parasitologic and clinical immunity during primary infection. Am J Trop Med Hyg. 1999;611 [Suppl]:4-19.)*

Antigen switching results in new waves of parasitemias that escape the antibody response already produced against previous waves. Waves of *P. falciparum* manifest clinically as recurrent or relapsing fevers reminiscent of those caused by *Borrelia recurrentis* relapsing fever or *Trypanosoma brucei rhodesiense* African sleeping sickness, and may not be cleared for many months. An important component of the eventual acquisition of anti-disease immunity (premunition) after repeated episodes of malaria is the development of an antibody repertoire that can recognize a full spectrum of PfEMP-1 variant antigens. Field studies performed in endemic areas supported this idea by showing that the ability of serum to recognize diverse heterologous parasite strains increased with age and that children tended to be infected with parasites against which they had no preexisting antibody.[191-194] The mechanisms by which variant-specific antibodies act in acquired immunity may include antibody-dependent cellular cytotoxicity and opsonization for uptake and destruction by splenic macrophages.

EPIDEMIOLOGY OF MALARIA

Malaria occurs in most tropical regions of sub-Saharan Africa, Southeast Asia, and Latin America (Fig. 272-6) but its distribution is continually changing. The CDC provides up-to-date information on the geographic distribution of malaria, including drug-resistant malaria, at *www.cdc.gov/travel* and in its publication, Health Information for International Travel 2003-2004, available on-line at *www.cdc.gov/travel/yb/index.htm.*

Generally speaking, *P. falciparum* and *P. malariae* are found worldwide. *P. vivax* is infrequent in most of sub-Saharan Africa, but common elsewhere, *P. ovale* occurs in Africa and in foci within Asia and Oceania, and is often present with other *Plasmodium* species as a mixed infection.[195,196] Malaria is transmitted person to person by anopheline mosquitoes, there is no animal reservoir of human malaria parasites. Its transmission therefore requires competent mosquito vectors, a reservoir of infected humans, and conditions that bring them into proximity. The *Anopheles gambiae* complex of species and *A. funestus* transmit malaria with notoriously high efficiency and are the predominant

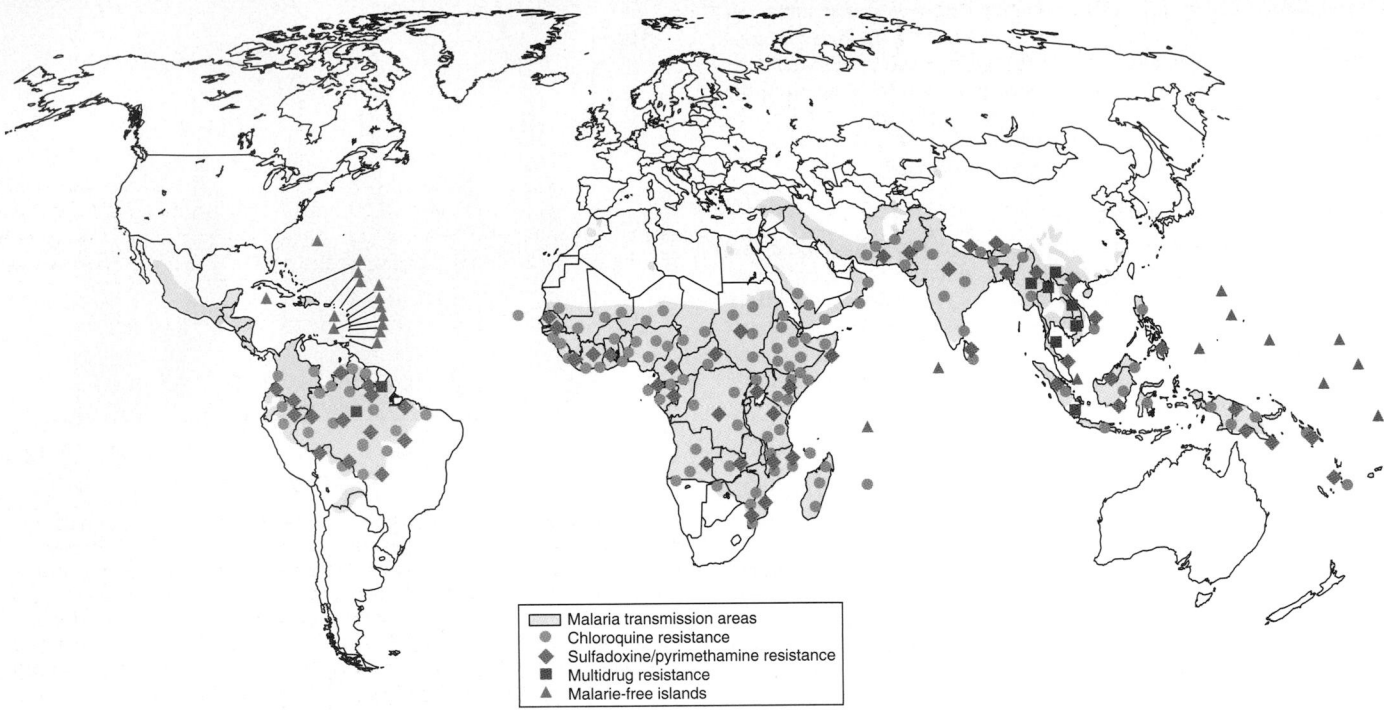

FIGURE 272-6. Distribution of drug-resistant malaria. *(From Wongsrichanalai C, Pickard AL, Wernsdorfer WH, Meshnick SR. Epidemiology of drug-resistant malaria. Lancet Infect Dis. 2002,2:209-218. Reprinted with permission from Elsevier. The CDC provides up-to-date information on the distribution of malaria and drug resistance at www.cdc.gov/travel.)*

vectors in sub-Saharan Africa, where environmental conditions favor their robust reproduction and transmission of parasites to large numbers of people. Malaria is transmitted predominantly during the wet season in endemic areas.

Malaria epidemics may result from the movement of people with no immunity into an endemic area (e.g., nomadic traders, seasonal forest laborers, and military personnel), the breakdown of malaria control measures, or unusually strong rainfalls, which can place indigenous populations at risk for higher than normal transmission.[197-199] Man-made environmental alterations (e.g., damming of rivers, deforestation) can lead to increases in malaria transmission by creating new mosquito habitats. Malaria may also arise in areas previously free of the disease as a result of immigration of populations from malaria endemic areas (e.g., migrating workers, persons displaced by natural disasters or civil strife, resettlement of refugees).[200-203]

In the United States, changes including new agricultural practices, improved housing with screens, water management with swamp drainage, and a radically altered landscape with urban developments led to a steady decline in malaria after the mid-19th century.[204] Final pockets of transmission were removed by the mid-20th century with the help of focused water management and insecticide spraying. Malaria diagnosed in the United States today is therefore almost always acquired in a malaria endemic country by a returning traveler or immigrant. Because of parasite or host factors, immigrants may harbor parasites for months to years and not be recognized as possible sources of transmittable infection. Autochthonous transmission, although infrequent, typically occurs when parasitized individuals infect competent vectors (*A. albimanus, A. quadrimaculatus, A. freeborni*) that remain common in the United States.[205,206] "Airport malaria" occurs when infected mosquitoes arrive from an endemic country on an aircraft from which they escape to bite local residents.[207] Because mosquitoes travel short distances, infections of local residents tend to occur near airports.[208] The spraying of insecticide within aircraft leaving endemic areas reduces the incidence of airport malaria.[209] Malaria

may also be acquired from needles shared among drug users; blood transfusion[210,211]; or solid organ kidney, heart, or liver transplantation.[212] These blood and organ donors are usually asymptomatic persons with low-level parasitemia from endemic areas. The incidence of transfusion-acquired malaria is reduced when returned travelers and immigrants are required to wait for periods of 1 to 3 years prior to donating blood.[210]

DISTRIBUTION OF DRUG RESISTANCE

Chloroquine-resistant *P. falciparum* malaria is widespread in sub-Saharan Africa, Asia, and Latin America (see Fig. 272-6). It has also been reported in areas of the Middle East including Iran, Yemen, Oman, and Saudi Arabia,[213-217] but not from Mexico, other regions of Central America west of the Panama Canal, Haiti, or the Dominican Republic. High-grade resistance of *P. vivax* malaria to chloroquine has been reported in Oceania and parts of Southeast Asia.[218-220] Case reports of patients with chloroquine-resistant vivax malaria have also been reported from Brazil, Guyana, Colombia, Peru, India, and Myanmar.[221-226] Chloroquine-resistant *P. malariae* has been reported in Sumatra, Indonesia.[227]

Mefloquine-resistant *P. falciparum* malaria now occurs in Thailand, Cambodia, Myanmar, and Vietnam[228-230] with scattered cases reported in the Amazon Basin.[231]

Resistance to sulfadoxine-pyrimethamine (SP) is widespread through much of Southeast Asia,[232-234] the Amazon Basin,[235,236] and also occurs in sub-Saharan Africa.[237-239] The prevalence of SP resistance is highly variable in Africa, with some areas of West Africa showing relatively low rates of resistance.[240] In many African countries, SP has replaced chloroquine as first-line therapy or is relied on for treatment of chloroquine-resistant infections.

Reduced susceptibility to quinine has been mostly reported in Southeast Asia,[241] but also in sub-Saharan* Africa and South America.[242,243] Artemisinin resistance has not been detected.

ANTIMALARIAL DRUGS: MECHANISMS OF ACTION AND RESISTANCE

Chloroquine

Intraerythrocytic parasites consume the hemoglobin of their host cells, breaking it down within a large digestive food vacuole (see Fig. 272-4B) and releasing heme molecules that are poisonous if not detoxified. Malaria parasites normally allow these heme molecules to polymerize into inert crystals called hemozoin that can be visualized by light microscopy as intraerythrocytic pigment in thin blood smears (Fig. 272-7E and H). Chloroquine acts by forming toxic complexes with heme molecules and interfering with their crystallization.[244] This mechanism of action explains why chloroquine is effective against intraerythrocytic parasites but ineffective against other parasite stages that do not actively consume hemoglobin.

Chloroquine-resistant *P. falciparum* parasites reduce the amount of drug that accumulates in their digestive vacuoles.[245] The mechanism involves mutations in a highly conserved transport molecule of the digestive vacuole membrane termed PfCRT (*P. falciparum* chloroquine resistance transporter).[246-248] The mutations include a key change from lysine to threonine in the 76th amino acid (K76T) plus additional mutations that depend on their geographic origin.[246,249-251] Drug selection for mutant PfCRT is evident in the association of the K76T marker with increased plasma chloroquine levels[252] and with treatment failures in children receiving the drug.[253] Several lines of evidence now indicate that chloroquine resistance involves a specific interaction between chloroquine and the modified form of PfCRT[247] in an energy-dependent efflux mechanism.[254,255]

While PfCRT is the central determinant of chloroquine resistance, other host and parasite factors also influence treatment outcomes. For example, clearance of phenotypically chloroquine-resistant parasites can occur after chloroquine treatment and becomes increasingly prevalent in children as they grow older, presumably owing to the immunity that develops from repeated episodes of malaria.[253,256] Parasite transport molecules in addition to PfCRT have also been proposed to modulate or contribute to the ability of chloroquine-resistant parasites to cope with the drug.[257,258]

Sulfadoxine-Pyrimethamine

Dihydropteroate synthase (DHPS) and dihydrofolate reductase (DHFR) are sequentially involved in the folate pathway of nucleic acid synthesis. Pyrimethamine inhibits parasite DHFR and the production of tetrahydrofolate, an essential cofactor for one-carbon metabolism required for the synthesis of nucleic acids and certain amino acids. Point mutations in DHFR reduce its affinity for pyrimethamine. The substitution of asparagine for serine at position 108 in DHFR is critical for the initial development of pyrimethamine resistance, with additional mutations (Ile51, Arg59, Leu164) progressively increasing the degree of pyrimethamine resistance.[259-260] Part of sulfadoxine's action is thought to be inhibition of parasite DHPS and point mutations in DHPS reduce its affinity for sulfadoxine.[261,262] Analysis of the mutant *dhfr* and *dhps* alleles in field studies supports conclusions that clinically significant resistance to pyrimethamine arises from multiple mutations in *dhfr* and *dhps* and that *dhps* mutations are thought to be selected after mutations in *dhfr* are already present.[263]

Atovaquone-Proguanil

Atovaquone binds cytochrome *b* and inhibits parasite mitochondrial electron transport, leading to collapse of the mitochondrial membrane potential.[264,265] This effect is potentiated by proguanil.[266] Cycloguanil, the active metabolite of proguanil, inhibits DHFR.[267] The substitution of serine for tyrosine at codon 268 of the cytochrome *b* gene *Y268S* is associated with resistance to atovaquone and the AP combination.[268-271] Single-point mutations in *dhfr* confer resistance to cycloguanil, the pharmacologically active metabolite of proguanil.[272,273]

Doxycycline

Doxycycline inhibits protein synthesis elongation by preventing binding of aminoacyl-tRNA to ribosome 30S subunit. Resistance of human malaria parasites to this drug has not been described.

Mefloquine, Quinidine, and Quinine

Mefloquine, quinidine, and quinine are thought to form drug complexes toxic to the parasite by binding to heme. Mefloquine resistance may be associated in part with increases in expression and mutations in the P-glycoprotein homolog-1 gene *pfmdr1*.[257,274] Decreased quinine sensitivity is associated with resistance to other structurally related drugs such as mefloquine and halofantrine, suggesting that drug resistance mechanisms may share at least some genetic determinants.[275-277] Some studies have implicated *pfmdr1* mutations in mefloquine and halofantrine resistance[257,278] and *pfcrt* mutations in quinine and quinidine responses.[247,248] The different levels of quinine susceptibility among parasites and the relatively slow rate at which quinine resistance has spread throughout the world indicate that quinine resistance is a complex phenotype and is probably affected by other genes in addition to *pfmdr1* and *pfcrt*. The results of a linkage analysis and surveys of parasites from Southeast Asia, Africa, and South America support a model in which multiple genes can combine in different ways to produce similar phenotypes of reduced quinine response.[258,279]

CLINICAL PRESENTATION AND DIAGNOSIS OF MALARIA

The malaria incubation period after an infective mosquito bite includes the time required for the parasites to progress through liver schizogony and produce symptoms by their propagation in the blood stream. For primary attacks, this period is typically approximately 8 to 25 days, but may be much longer depending on the immune status of the infected person, the strain as well as the species of *Plasmodium*, the dose of sporozoites, and if there has been chemoprophylaxis that has been only partially effective. Relapses from latent hypnozoites may develop months or years after mosquito bites. Late-onset or recrudescent *P. falciparum* malaria may also occur in individuals who have suppressed parasitemia of drug-resistant parasites with chemoprophylactic drugs[280] (Fig. 272-2). Febrile patients presenting within 7 days of entering an endemic area are unlikely to have malaria, unless there has been earlier exposure to infective mosquito bites. As a general rule, and because of the dangers of acute *P. falciparum* infection, *all travelers who have visited a malaria endemic area in the 3 months prior to onset of fever or other suggestive symptoms should be considered to have malaria until proven otherwise.* Latent attacks from the reactivation of *P. vivax* or *P. ovale* hypnozoites usually occur within 3 years and are rare more than 5 years after exposure. Recrudescence of *P. malariae* symptoms in individuals with subclinical parasitemia has been reported decades after initial infection.[130,281,282]

History and Physical Examination

Uncomplicated malaria typically presents as an undifferentiated febrile illness.[283] A series of 160 German nationals or residents with imported malaria presented to a travel clinic with the following symptoms: fever, 100%; headache, 100%; weakness, 94%; profuse night sweats, 91%; insomnia, 69%; arthralgias, 59%; myalgias, 56%; diarrhea, 13%, and abdominal cramps, 8%.[284] Fever may be cyclical, recurring every 48 or 72 hours, depending on the species and synchrony of the replicating parasites. Parasite subpopulations on different cycles in the blood stream may produce more complicated fever patterns. *P. falciparum* populations are often asynchronous and may produce continuous fever. Patients with cyclical fevers may be relatively asymptomatic during afebrile periods.

Particular elements from the history and physical examination, when considered together, may be suggestive of the diagnosis of malaria.[285-287] Cyclical paroxysms of chills and rigors, fever, and drenching sweats are characteristic although not necessarily specific for malaria. A travel history that reveals risk of exposure to an endemic region is an alert for malaria and should always be sought in

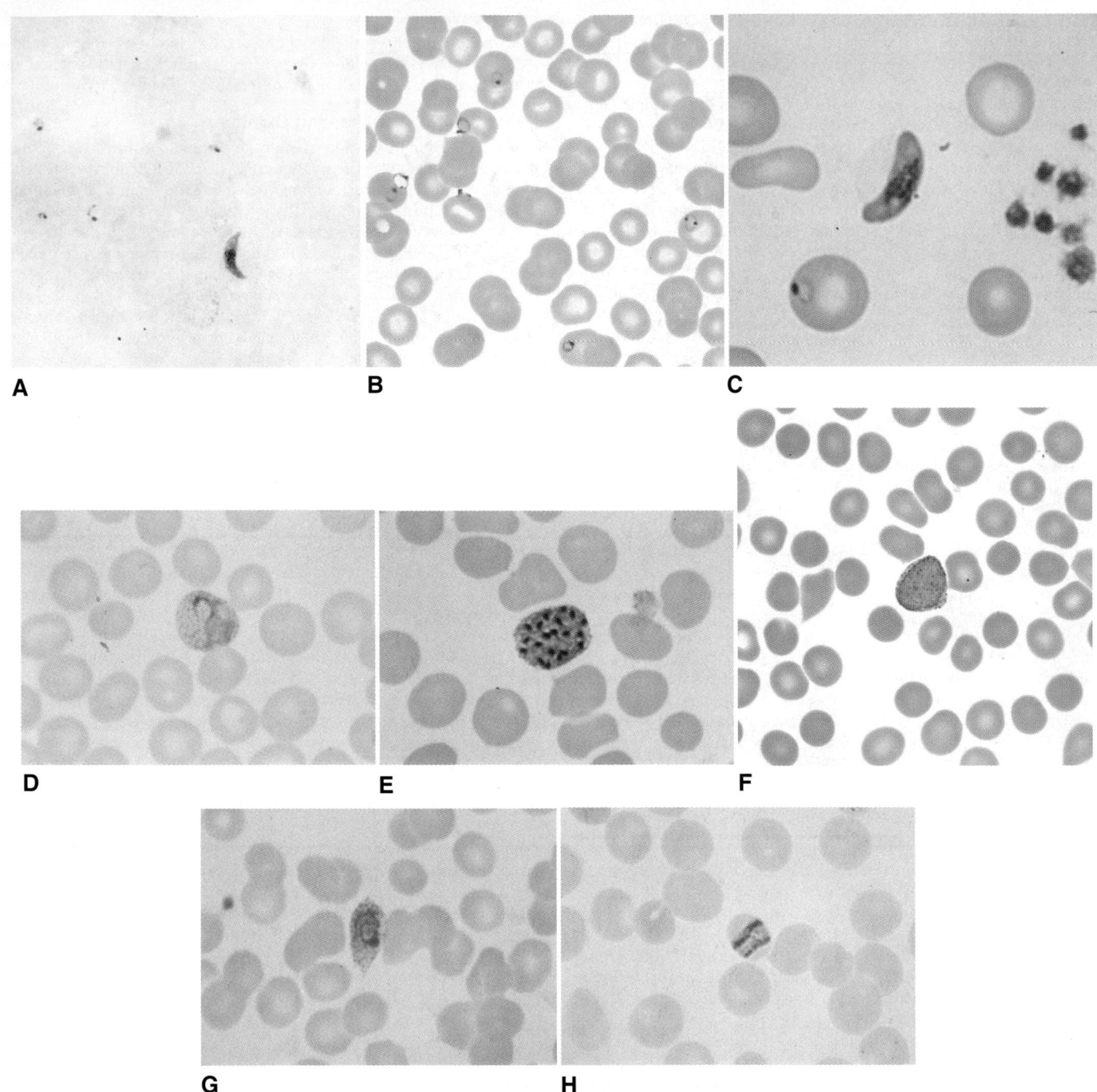

FIGURE 272-7. Giemsa-stained thick **(A)** and thin **(B-H)** smears used for the diagnosis of malaria and the speciation of *Plasmodium* parasites. **A,** Multiple signet-ring *P. falciparum* trophozoites, which are visualized outside erythrocytes. **B,** A multiply infected erythrocyte containing signet-ring *P. falciparum* trophozoites, including an accolade form positioned up against the inner surface of the erythrocyte membrane. **C,** Banana-shaped gametocyte unique to *P. falciparum*. **D,** Amoeboid trophozoite characteristic of *P. vivax*. Both *P. vivax*- and *P. ovale*-infected erythrocytes exhibit Schuffner's dots and tend to be enlarged compared to uninfected erythrocytes. **E,** *P. vivax* schizont. Mature *P. falciparum* parasites, by contrast, are rarely seen on blood smears because they sequester in the systemic microvasculature. **F,** *P. vivax* spherical gametocyte. **G,** *P. ovale* trophozoite. Note Schuffner's dots and ovoid shape of the infected erythrocyte. **H,** Characteristic band form trophozoite of *P. malariae*, containing intracellular pigment hemazoin. *(Images **A, B,** and **F** were kindly provided by DPDx [CDC's website for parasitology identification] at www.dpd.cdc.gov/dpdx/. Images **C, D, E, G** and **H** were contributed by David Wyler, Newton Centre, Massachusetts.)*

presentations of fever. Findings on physical examination may include pallor and hepatosplenomegaly. Rarely, acute *Plasmodium* infections present with splenic rupture requiring surgery or conservative management.[288,289] Findings such as jaundice, diminished consciousness, or convulsions indicate severe malaria (see later). Rash, lymphadenopathy, and signs of pulmonary consolidation are distinctly uncommon.

Thick and Thin Blood Smears

Light microscopy of Giemsa-stained blood smears is the accepted standard for malaria diagnosis. Thick and thin diagnostic blood smears should be *prepared and read immediately by experienced personnel* when the clinical presentation and travel history are compatible with malaria.[290] Preparation instructions and representative images from thick and thin smears are available from DPDx, the CDC's website for parasitological diagnosis: *http://www.dpd.cdc.gov/dpdx/HTML/Malaria.htm.*

Thick smears concentrate red cell layers approximately 40-fold and are used to screen a relatively large amount of blood for the presence of parasites. Because red cells are lysed in the process of staining in the thick smear technique, parasites are visualized *outside* red cells (see Fig. 272-7A). Assuming an average white cell count of 8000 per microliter, parasitemias can be estimated from thick smears by counting the number of parasites until 200 white cells have also been counted. This count, when multiplied by 40, gives an indication of the number of parasites per microliter of blood. The parasitemia % can then be calculated by dividing the parasite density by 4,000,000 (the average number of erythrocytes/μL in blood), and multiplying by 100. Parasite density can be associated with disease severity and must be monitored during and after treatment to ensure adequate resolution of infection. Detectable parasitemia may lag behind aches, fevers, and chills, sometimes for many days; individuals with no antimalarial immunity may have severe manifestations of malaria even though parasites are very difficult to detect on blood smear. A *P. falciparum* infection also may not be apparent on an initial blood smear if the parasites are predominantly mature erythrocytic forms (i.e., trophozoites and schizonts) and are sequestering in the microvasculature. Therefore, if the initial blood smear is negative and malaria remains possible, the smear should be repeated every 12 hours until a diagnosis of malaria is made or ruled out. Before reading a thick blood smear as negative, at least 200 to 500 fields should be examined at × 1000 with an oil immersion objective lens; some experts recommend examining a thick smear for 20 minutes. Blood smear positive cases of malaria diagnosed in the United States should be reported to the CDC using the Malaria Case Surveillance Form provided at: *www.cdc.gov/ncidod/dpd/parasites/malaria/form.htm.*

Giemsa-stained thin smears are prepared from a much smaller amount of blood than thick smears and are used to determine the *Plasmodium* species (see Fig. 272-7B to H). Speciation of malaria parasites has important implications for treatment. *P. falciparum* infections are characterized by thin delicate rings that may be positioned against the inner surface of the red cell membrane (so-called accolade forms) (see Fig. 272-7B), multiply infected cells containing signet-ring forms (see Fig. 272-7B), *absence* of trophozoites and schizonts because they are sequestered in the microvasculature, and banana-shaped gametocytes (see Fig. 272-7C). *P. vivax* is characterized by relatively thicker rings, ameboid trophozoites (see Fig. 272-7D), and schizonts (see Fig. 272-7E) in the peripheral blood, and spherically shaped gametocytes (see Fig. 272-7F). Red cell enlargement and Schuffner's dots (see Fig. 272-7D and G) are common features of *P. vivax* and *P. ovale,* but not *P. falciparum* or *P. malariae*. *P. malariae* can be distinguished by its band forms, if present (see Fig. 272-7H). Thin smear examination can yield additional useful information such as the presence of intraleukocytic pigment (a poor prognostic sign)[291] or other blood pathogens (e.g., filaria, *Borrelia recurrentis*). *Babesia* species produce intraerythrocytic forms that may be confused with *Plasmodium species,*[292] but experienced personnel are able to distinguish between them.

Rapid Diagnostic Tests

While evaluation of Giemsa-stained thick and thin smears is the accepted standard for malaria diagnosis, new rapid diagnostic tests may be useful to complement efforts at microscopic diagnosis.[293-295] In situations in which expert microscopic examination is delayed or difficult to obtain, medical decisions and management of malaria cases can benefit greatly from the appropriate use of rapid tests. Two types of dipstick tests are commercially available and have a sensitivity and specificity of approximately 77% to 100% and 83% to 100%, respectively.[296-299]

The first type, represented by ParaSight F and ICT Malaria Pf tests, is based on the detection of *P. falciparum* histidine-rich protein 2 (HRP-2).[300] Although HRP-2 tests are highly sensitive and specific for malaria diagnosis, they have certain limitations. First, they cannot be used to monitor therapeutic responses, as the tests are persistently positive up to 28 days after treatment. Second, they detect only *P. falci-*

parum, making them less useful for the diagnosis of malaria in returned travelers who typically are infected with *P. vivax* at least as often as with *P. falciparum*.[301] Third, a low percentage of *P. falciparum* infections may not produce HRP-2 detectable by the tests. Fourth, the monoclonal antibody IgG used in the Parasight F test can cross react with rheumatoid factor (RF), causing false-positive results.[302]

The second type of rapid diagnostic test, represented by the OptiMal test, is based on detection of *Plasmodium* lactate dehydrogenase (pLDH).[303] The OptiMal test detects *P. falciparum* infections with sensitivity comparable to that of the HRP-2 tests and has the advantage of also detecting other species of *Plasmodium* that can infect humans: *P. vivax, P. ovale,* and *P. malariae.* Another advantage to this test is that the level of pLDH detection is proportional to parasitemia,[304] allowing for monitoring of therapeutic responses. The OptiMal test has a lower sensitivity for *P. ovale* and *P. malariae* infections,[305] however, and its limit of detection for *P. falciparum* and *P. vivax* is also not as sensitive as state-of-the-art microscopy.

Other Laboratory Tests

The results of routine laboratory tests are not specific for malaria, but may support its diagnosis. Some degree of anemia may be seen with malaria from all *Plasmodium* species. Decreases in hemoglobin, hematocrit, and haptoglobin and increases in lactic dehydrogenase may be marked with large *P. falciparum* parasite burdens. Microcytosis may be seen in patients from malaria endemic areas but is often due to iron deficiency or thalassemia. Leukocyte counts may be high, normal, or low.[306] Platelet counts may be normal or slightly low,[307] but have been observed to be <70,000/μL in *P. falciparum* infection[308] and occasionally in *P. vivax* infection.[309] Sodium may be slightly low, possibly owing to syndrome of inappropriate antidiuretic hormone, excessive vomiting, or urinary losses.[310] Acidemia (pH less than 7.35), acidosis (bicarbonate less than 15 mmol/L), and lactate levels greater than 5 mmol/L can be seen in severe *P. falciparum* malaria (see later). Some degree of renal impairment is common in falciparum malaria and may be associated with increased creatinine, proteinuria, and hemoglobinuria.[311] Serum glucose is often low in children with falciparum malaria, but it is commonly normal in adults. In children with severe falciparum malaria, bacteremia/sepsis may be present at the time of initial clinical evaluation and blood cultures may be positive.[312,313]

Severe *P. falciparum* Malaria

The World Health Organization (WHO) has established clinical and laboratory criteria for severe falciparum malaria that must be treated as an emergency with intensive medical care.[314] By WHO criteria, severe malaria is established by any of the criteria in Table 272-1 in the presence of *P. falciparum* parasitemia and with reasonable exclusion of an alternative diagnosis. Although these WHO criteria are largely based on the clinical presentation of severe malaria among young African children living in endemic areas, they are consistent with the clinical spectrum of severe malaria in travelers who might be encountered in nonendemic developed countries.[315] Nonimmune individuals who do not meet these criteria for severe malaria should be treated with antimalarial drugs as if they have it. In practice, because of the

TABLE 272-1 Diagnostic Features of Severe Malaria

Cerebral malaria (diminished consciousness, seizures)
Respiratory distress
Prostration
Hyperparasitemia
Severe anemia
Hypoglycemia
Jaundice/icterus
Renal insufficiency
Hemoglobinuria
Shock
Cessation of eating and drinking
Repetitive vomiting
Hyperpyrexia

ability of *P. falciparum* infection to progress in just a few hours to severe and life-threatening complications, it is advisable to hospitalize all nonimmune individuals during their initial period of treatment.

Cerebral malaria is a syndrome characterized by diminished consciousness and/or seizures. In endemic areas, it typically occurs in young children and can manifest clinically as varying levels of consciousness, obtundation or coma, or seizures. The Blantyre coma scale is frequently used to measure the level of consciousness.[316] Seizures may be clinically inapparent, subtle motor, partial motor, generalized tonic-clonic, or partial motor with secondary generalization.[317] Multiple factors can contribute to cerebral malaria: hypoglycemia, acidosis, hyperpyrexia, the post-ictal state, and effects of anticonvulsant medication. In endemic areas, there may also be considerable overlap in the clinical presentations of cerebral malaria and other syndromes such as bacterial or viral meningitis, subdural hematoma, or sepsis. Although cerebral malaria commonly resolves without neurological sequelae,[318] some children (especially those with status epilepticus) may develop psychosis, cerebellar ataxia, extrapyramidal rigidity, hemiplegia, or long-term cognitive and language impairment.[319-323]

Respiratory distress is characterized by dyspnea or deep breathing (Kussmaul's respiration), which may be accompanied by nasal flaring or intercostal retraction. In one study, deep breathing was 91% sensitive and 83% specific for the presence of severe metabolic acidosis (base excess less than or equal to -12), the underlying cause of respiratory distress.[26] *Prostration* from fluid and electrolyte depletion is determined by clinical judgement. If a child is 7 months of age or older, prostration may be defined as inability to sit unassisted. *Hyperparasitemia* is defined in endemic areas by WHO as parasite density greater than or equal to 500,000/mm³ ($\sim$ 10% parasitemia) and is associated with severe anemia, hypoglycemia, cerebral malaria, and renal failure. Although severity of disease is generally thought to correlate with parasite density, nonimmune individuals may present with severe malaria at any parasitemia, even at levels that may be difficult to detect by microscopy. *Severe anemia* is defined in endemic areas as hemoglobin less than or equal to 5 g/dL. Nonimmune individuals can present with signs and symptoms of severe anemia at higher hemoglobin levels; in these cases, rapid reductions from baseline hemoglobin can account for the symptoms. *Hypoglycemia* is defined as blood glucose less than or equal to 40 mg/dL and may contribute to diminished consciousness and seizures. *Hyperbilirubinemia* (manifesting as icterus or jaundice) also defines severe malaria, and may reflect underlying liver compromise. *Renal insufficiency* of severe malaria is defined in endemic areas as anuria for at least 24 hours. However, a nonimmune patient with any evidence of renal insufficiency, even that caused by hypovolemia and improved with fluid replacement, should be considered to have severe malaria. *Hemoglobinuria* manifests as dark (cola) colored urine ("blackwater fever"), distinct from the red appearance of hematuria. *Shock* of malaria is essentially indistinguishable from that of sepsis caused by Gram-negative bacteria. Special caution needs to be taken in the evaluation of shock, as concurrent sepsis is frequently present with parasitemia in severe malaria. *Cessation of eating and drinking* contributes to hypovolemia and consequently to severe acidosis and respiratory distress. *Repetitive vomiting* also contributes to hypovolemia and may complicate oral treatment of severe malaria in resource poor countries where parenteral therapy is not readily available. Medications used to treat malaria (e.g., chloroquine) may also cause vomiting, often warranting directly observed therapy. *Hyperpyrexia* is defined as axillary temperature greater than or equal to 40° C and likely contributes to the severity of malaria through its association with febrile seizures.

DISTINGUISHING MALARIA FROM OTHER ILLNESSES WITH SIMILAR CLINICAL PRESENTATION

The differential diagnosis of the malaria presentation is broad and includes many febrile and influenza-like illnesses (Table 272-2). However, malaria should always lead the list in the differential diagnosis of fever in travelers or immigrants who have been in an endemic area within the previous 3 months. Travelers and immigrants often

TABLE 272-2 Differential Diagnosis of the Malaria Presentation: Selected Examples

Influenza
Enteric fever
Bacteremia/sepsis
Classic dengue fever
Acute schistosomiasis (Katayama fever)
Leptospirosis
African tick fever
East African trypanosomiasis (sleeping sickness)
Yellow fever

Reprinted by special permission of the publisher.

present with common ailments and physicians must be alert to recognize and treat malaria to avoid a morbid or fatal outcome,[324-327] especially when they are working in temperate zones and do not often see malaria and other diseases of the tropics. It is estimated that 30 million travelers visit malaria-endemic regions each year. Cases of malaria acquired by international travelers probably number 25,000 annually, of which 10,000 are reported and 150 are fatal.[328]

Clinical criteria to distinguish malaria from other illnesses are critical because rapid diagnostic tests for those illnesses are often limited or not available, and definitive diagnoses often rely on non-routine methods of pathogen isolation or serological testing that rely on comparisons of acute and convalescent antibody titers 2 to 4 weeks later. The probabilities of specific diseases are affected by geographic area visited (e.g., yellow fever is not prevalent in Asia or India); type of travel (e.g., adventure travelers to Lake Malawi are more likely to acquire schistosomiasis or leptospirosis from fresh water contact than are visitors to Nairobi, Kenya); time of travel (e.g., dengue fever is much less likely to be acquired during the dry season, when mosquito transmission is markedly reduced); type of food and water ingested (e.g., enteric fever is relatively unlikely in persons eating only cooked food and bottled water); and vaccination history (e.g., the efficacy of yellow fever, hepatitis A and B vaccines makes these diseases unlikely if patient is vaccinated). Self-reported compliance with mosquito repellents and malaria chemoprophylactic drugs, especially during the post-travel period should *not* be used to rule out malaria, as these reports are often inaccurate and no preventive regimen is 100% effective. Features of selected infectious diseases that may present like malaria are briefly summarized in the following.

Influenza

Like malaria, influenza may present with fever, headache, myalgias, and malaise. Prominent upper respiratory symptoms (rhinorrhea, sore throat, or dry cough) may help to distinguish influenza from malaria. The symptoms of many cases of malaria ultimately fatal to returned travelers in North America have been initially and mistakenly attributed to "the flu."

Enteric Fever

Salmonella serotypes *typhi* and *paratyphi* can be acquired in developing countries worldwide. Like malaria, enteric fever may present with fever, headache, nausea, malaise, anorexia, and myalgias. Prominent gastrointestinal symptoms (abdominal pain, constipation or diarrhea), the findings of rose spots or relative bradycardia, and a history of unsanitary food or water consumption may help to support a diagnosis of enteric fever. A history of prior vaccination against *S. typhi* may not be useful in ruling out enteric fever because it is only 50% to 80% effective and does not protect against paratyphoidal illness.

Bacteremia/Sepsis

The fever, hypotension, evidence of poor peripheral perfusion, altered mental status, and multiorgan dysfunction that characterizes bacteremia and sepsis can mimic severe malaria. One study found that bacteremia accompanied *P. falciparum* infection in 12% of young children who were admitted to hospital with the primary diagnosis of severe malaria.[312]

Dengue Fever

Patients with classic nonhemorrhagic dengue fever may present with fever, headache, nausea, malaise, or anorexia. Myalgias tend to be much more severe than those experienced during malaria episodes. Dengue fever may be distinguished from malaria by its centrifugal rash, petechiae, lymphadenopathy, conjunctival injection, pharyngeal erythema, and relative bradycardia. Although dengue virus is also transmitted by mosquitoes during the rainy season in tropical regions worldwide, its incubation period of 4 to 7 days is not typical of malaria.

Acute Schistosomiasis (Katayama Fever)

Schistosoma trematodes are acquired from fresh water exposure (wading, swimming) in tropical regions worldwide. Patients with acute schistosomiasis may present 4 to 8 weeks after exposure with fever, headache, myalgias, malaise, and anorexia. Acute schistosomiasis can be distinguished from malaria by generalized urticaria, and the findings of a pruritic rash at the site of cercarial penetration (usually on the legs), lymphadenopathy, and blood eosinophilia. Patients may present initially with focal neurological signs as a result of egg dissemination to the central nervous system.

Leptospirosis

Leptospira interrogans spirochetes are acquired from fresh water or soil exposure in tropical and temperate regions worldwide. Patients with leptospirosis usually present within 7 to 12 days of exposure with fever, headache, nausea, and myalgias. Leptospirosis can be distinguished from malaria by the findings of conjunctival suffusion or rash, but may progress to hepatic and renal insufficiency marked by hemorrhagic manifestations and pronounced hyperbilirubinemia (Weil's disease). This complication is similar to the severe malaria presentation, but extremely high bilirubin levels are more characteristic of Weil's disease.

African Tick Fever

Rickettsia africae is transmitted by tick bites, usually acquired during game hunting or safari travel to southern Africa between April and November. African tick fever may present with fever, headache, and myalgias, and can be differentiated from malaria by the findings of lymphadenitis or multiple inoculation eschars.

East African Trypanosomiasis (Sleeping Sickness)

Trypanosoma brucei rhodesiense causes the acute form of African sleeping sickness and is acquired from tsetse fly bites, typically in association with game and brush in eastern and southern Africa. Trypanosomiasis may present with fever, headache, myalgias, malaise, and anorexia, yet it may be differentiated from malaria by a red chancre at the bite site, posterior cervical lymphadenopathy, or rash. Like malaria, it may progress to involve multiple organs, including the central nervous system.

Yellow Fever

Yellow fever virus is acquired from mosquito bites in tropical regions worldwide. It is characterized by fever, headache, myalgias, nausea, anorexia, and jaundice. Yellow fever may be differentiated from malaria by the presence of conjunctival suffusion or relative bradycardia, and by its short incubation period (average 3 to 6 days). Yellow fever is extremely unlikely in patients who have been vaccinated against it within the previous 10 years. As with severe malaria, patients may appear acutely ill and progress to liver failure and hemorrhagic manifestations, multiorgan system failure, and death.

TREATMENT

General Principles

P. falciparum malaria can be fatal if not diagnosed and treated promptly. This is especially true of nonimmune travelers returning from visits to malaria-endemic areas. Malaria is a disease of protean manifestations.[329] Its diagnosis can be delayed by the nonspecificity of the clinical presentation and routine laboratory tests, especially if blood smears are not examined. Life-threatening manifestations of malaria such as seizures, hypoglycemia, and pulmonary edema may develop rapidly in patients who appear relatively well at presentation or appear to respond initially to antimalarial drugs. On the other hand, parasite infection with species other than *P. falciparum* may become symptomatic months to years after exposure to infective mosquitoes.

Although some patients with uncomplicated *P. falciparum* malaria can be treated successfully in an outpatient setting, patients with no immunity against the disease are at increased risk for sudden development of severe complications and should be hospitalized at least 48 hours to ensure adequate response to therapy, regardless of how well they appear at presentation. Acute *P. falciparum* malaria in a nonimmune individual is always highly dangerous and unpredictable; even without adverse signs at presentation, a patient's condition may deteriorate dramatically after prompt hospitalization and apparently adequate treatment.[330] Contributing factors in such cases may include (1) replication of the parasites and their synchronous development into mature forms that sequester in the brain, leading to cerebral malaria, and (2) complications from the infection that lead to acute renal failure, acute lung injury, or hepatic failure, even when the parasitemia is decreasing or the patient appears to be improving in other ways. Pregnant women, young children, and the elderly are at increased risk of morbidity and mortality and should be hospitalized regardless of their clinical state.[331-333]

Patients with non-falciparum malaria *(P. vivax, P. ovale, P. malariae)* rarely require hospitalization.

Uncomplicated Malaria

Treatment of falciparum malaria should always be initiated emergently, as the risk of its morbidity and mortality is increased with even short delays in medical care.[334] Uncomplicated malaria can be treated with oral medication as long as the patient is able to retain the drug; directly observed therapy may be appropriate in some cases to ensure adequate treatment. Drugs currently recommended for the treatment of uncomplicated malaria are listed in Table 272-3. Important adjunct treatment of malaria includes antipyretics, antiemetics, and anticonvulsant medications.

Because of the widespread patterns of drug resistance in the world today, no blanket recommendation suffices and alternatives must be considered when selecting an antimalarial drug. Chloroquine can be used against malaria from those areas where chloroquine resistance has not been reported (certain Central American countries, Haiti, regions of the Middle East). The use of sulfadoxine-pyrimethamine (SP) in the treatment of malaria is now of limited effectiveness where it has encountered drug resistance in South America, Asia, and in parts of southern and eastern Africa. Elsewhere (e.g., some areas of West Africa), SP may be safely used as single-dose therapy for uncomplicated malaria.[335] Oral quinine plus doxycycline can be used for disease acquired in all areas and is particularly useful where chloroquine-resistant strains are present or where mefloquine-resistant strains are present (western and eastern borders of Thailand). Atovaquone-proguanil is being used increasingly in the treatment of uncomplicated malaria, with only limited experience supporting its use in nonimmune individuals. Recrudescence of parasitemia and failure of initial therapy with this combination have now been reported.[268-271] If the patient cannot tolerate oral therapy, parenteral or rectal forms of antimalarial drugs must be administered (see later). Up-to-date information on malaria treatment is available from the CDC's Malaria Hotline (770-488-7788).

Chloroquine Phosphate

Chloroquine is considered safe in pregnant women (all trimesters) and in children of all ages, including newborns.[336] It has a bitter taste and may cause nausea or vomiting (it can be taken with food to ameliorate gastrointestinal symptoms), headache, dizziness, blurred vision, or dysphoria. Chloroquine commonly produces a nonallergic pruritus in dark-skinned persons and may exacerbate psoriasis. It is associated with retinal toxicity at high doses, but not at doses used for malaria treatment.

TABLE 272-3 Malaria Treatment

Drug	Adult Dose	Pediatric Dose	Precautions
Uncomplicated Malaria: P. vivax, P. ovale, P. malariae, or Chloroquine-Susceptible P. falciparum			
Chloroquine phosphate *Supplied in 500-mg salt (300 mg base) tablets.*	One gram (600 mg base), then 500 mg (300 mg base) 6 hours later, then 500 mg (300 mg base) at 24 and 48 hours.	10 mg base/kg (max. 600 mg base), then 5 mg base/kg 6 hours later, then 5 mg base/kg at 24 and 48 hours.	None.
Uncomplicated Malaria: Chloroquine-Resistant P. falciparum			
Mefloquine *Supplied in 250-mg salt (228 mg base) tablets.*	750 mg followed by 500 mg 12 hours later.	<45 kg: 15 mg/kg followed by 10 mg/kg 12 hours later.	*Do not* administer to individuals with cardiac conduction abnormalities, history of seizures, or serious psychiatric illnesses (for example, psychosis, major depression). *Do not* use concomitantly with quinidine, quinine, or halofantrine.
Quinine sulfate *plus* doxycycline *Quinine sulfate supplied in 325 mg or 650-mg tablets. Doxycycline supplied in 100-mg tablets.*	Quinine 650 mg every 8 hours for 3 days* plus doxycycline 100 mg twice daily for 7 days.	Children 8-12 years old: Quinine 8 mg/kg every 8 hours for 3 days* plus doxycycline 2 mg/kg daily for 7 days.	*Do not* use doxycycline in children below the age of 8 years or in pregnant women.†
Atovaquone *plus* proguanil *Supplied in fixed combination tablets containing 250 mg atovaquone and 100 mg proguanil (adult tablets).*	Four adult tablets daily for 3 days (may be administered as 2 tablets twice daily).‡	The number of *adult* tablets taken daily for 3 days depends on patient's weight: 11-20 kg (1 tab), 21-30 kg (2 tabs), 31-40 kg (3 tabs), >40 kg (4 tabs).‡	None.
Artemether *plus* lumefantrine *Supplied in fixed combination tablets containing 20 mg artemether and 120 mg of lumefantrine.*	6 dose regimen: 1st day: 4 tabs initially, then 4 tabs 8 hours later, 2nd day: 4 tabs twice daily, 3rd day: 4 tabs twice daily.	The number of tablets per dose taken according to adult time schedule depends on patient's weight: 10-14 kg (1 tab), 15-24 kg (2 tabs), 25-34 (3 tabs), ≥35 kg or ≥12 years of age (4 tabs).	Safety in pregnant or breastfeeding women is not established.
Severe P. falciparum Malaria			
Quinidine gluconate	Intravenous: 10 mg salt/kg loading dose (max. 600 mg) in normal saline infused slowly at a constant rate over 1-2 hours, followed by continuous infusion of 0.02 mg/kg/min until oral therapy can be started.§	Intravenous: 10 mg salt/kg loading dose (max. 600 mg) in normal saline infused slowly at a constant rate over 1-2 hours, followed by continuous infusion of 0.02 mg/kg/min until oral therapy can be started.§	*Do not* administer as a bolus. Check blood glucose every 4-6 hours during first 24 hours of therapy. Administer 5%-10% dextrose along with quinidine to reduce risk of hypoglycemia. Monitor levels <8 μg/mL.
Quinine dihydrochloride *Not available in the United States.*	Intravenous: 20 mg/kg loading dose in 5% dextrose infused slowly at a constant rate over 4 hours, followed by maintenance dose 10 mg/kg over 3-4 hours at 8-hour intervals (max. 1800 mg/d) until oral therapy can be started.‖	Intravenous: 20 mg/kg loading dose in 5% dextrose infused slowly at a constant rate over 4 hours, followed by maintenance dose 10 mg/kg over 3-4 hours at 8-hour intervals (max. 1800 mg/d) until oral therapy can be started.‖	*Do not* administer as a bolus. Check blood glucose every 4-6 hours during first 24 hours of therapy. Administer 5%-10% dextrose along with quinine to reduce risk of hypoglycemia.
Artemether *Not available in the United States.*	Intramuscular: Artemether 3.2 mg/kg on first day, then 1.6 mg/kg daily for 4 days.¶	Intramuscular: Artemether 3.2 mg/kg on first day, then 1.6 mg/kg daily for 4 days.¶	None.
Prevention (Terminal Prophylaxis) of Relapsing Malaria: P. vivax or P. ovale			
Primaquine phosphate *Supplied in 15-mg base (26.3 salt) tablets.*	15 mg base once daily for 14 days**	0.3 mg base/kg daily for 14 days	Test patient for G6PD deficiency and administer only if enzyme activity is normal.

* For infections acquired in Southeast Asia, where reduced susceptibility to quinine has been reported, treat with quinine for 7 days.
† Doxycycline may be substituted by clindamycin 5 mg/kg (oral) every 8 hours for 7 days.
‡ This regimen can also serve as presumptive treatment in travelers with febrile illness who do not have immediate access to medical care.
§ Complete therapy with quinine *plus* doxycycline regimen to complete a 7-day total course of therapy.
‖ In resource poor countries, treatment usually completed with a standard oral dose of either chloroquine or sulfadoxine-pyrimethamine.
¶ To prevent parasite recrudescence after artemether treatment, complete therapy on day 5 with single dose mefloquine 15 mg/kg, given orally.
** P. vivax acquired in Southeast Asia may show resistance to standard primaquine doses and a regimen of 30 mg daily for 14 days is recommended.
Drug regimens adapted from: Advice for Travelers. The Medical Letter. April 15, 2002;1128;38-39.

Amodiaquine

Although related in structure to chloroquine, and partially susceptible to the chloroquine resistance mechanism, amodiaquine is used in some countries as an available although not entirely satisfactory treatment for chloroquine-resistant *P. falciparum* malaria.[337-340] Rare reports of serious adverse reactions such as agranulocytosis, hepatotoxicity, and aplastic anemia have been associated with long-term prophylactic use,[341,342] and brought its removal from the United States market.

Sulfadoxine *plus* Pyrimethamine (SP)

The use of SP in treating malaria is limited owing to widespread drug resistance. The sulfa component of SP may cause rash or other allergic manifestations. Long-term malaria prophylaxis with SP is no longer approved for use in the United States owing to unacceptably high rates of serious adverse reactions: exfoliative dermatitis, hepatitis, and blood dyscrasias. These same reactions are rare with treatment doses.[341,343] Rarely, hypoglycemic reactions may be seen due to chemical similarity between sulfonamide antibiotics and oral hypoglycemic agents.[344]

Mefloquine

Mefloquine can be used to treat most chloroquine-resistant parasites except for strains in areas such as Thailand, Myanmar, Cambodia, and Vietnam where resistance against this drug is present.[345,346] It may cause gastrointestinal upset, dysphoria, dreams, and mood changes in 5% of people and uncommonly causes transient reversible neuropsychiatric reactions. Mefloquine is cleared slowly, as its elimination half-life is 2 to 3 weeks. Mefloquine may prolong the corrected QT interval and so it cannot be administered concurrently with quinine-like drugs (i.e., quinidine, quinine, halofantrine). Mefloquine should be used only with extreme caution or not at all in individuals with cardiac conduction diseases, as it can aggravate conduction abnormalities.

Quinine *plus* Doxycycline

The combination of quinine plus doxycycline is effective against multidrug-resistant parasites. Quinine has a bitter taste and may cause gastrointestinal upset and cinchonism (nausea, vomiting, dysphoria, tinnitus, and high-tone deafness). Quinine is safely used in pregnancy.[347] Doxycycline also causes gastrointestinal upset and commonly results in vaginal candidiasis, requiring concomitant use of antifungal suppositories. The requirement for multiple doses over 7 days and the gastrointestinal upset caused by both drugs may reduce the compliance and hence effectiveness of this regimen.[348] The use of all tetracyclines is contraindicated in children younger than 8 years old or in pregnant women because of adverse effects on tooth and bone development. In these cases, clindamycin may be a safe and effective substitute for doxycycline.[347,349,350]

Atovaquone *plus* Proguanil (AP)

AP is used to treat multidrug-resistant parasites,[229,351] is well tolerated,[345,352] and has only rarely been associated with severe adverse reactions.[353] AP resistance is rare, being confined to a few case reports in nonimmune individuals in whom both recrudescence and initial treatment failure have been documented.[268,354]

Artemisinins

Artemisinin derivatives are now commonly used in Southeast Asia for the treatment of malaria that is resistant to multiple drugs, including mefloquine and quinine. Resistance to artemisinin derivatives has not been reported. Parasite recrudescence weeks after therapy with artemisinins does occur, but is thought to be due to the elimination of these drugs and recovery of parasitemia without selection of mutant parasites that are truly drug-resistant.[355] The addition of another drug (e.g., chloroquine, SP, or mefloquine) to a 3-day course of an artemisinin derivative was shown in a recent meta-analysis to substantially reduce treatment failure and recrudescence.[356] Artemisinin combination therapy ACT (e.g., artemether *plus* lumefantrine) has recently been registered for use in Europe and in several African countries.

Stand-by Treatment of Uncomplicated Malaria in Travelers

Because treatment delay increases morbidity and mortality associated with malaria, travelers to isolated areas may benefit from stand-by therapy while they actively seek medical care.[357] Stand-by antimalarials in some cases might be advised to travelers for emergency self-treatment of fever or flu-like symptoms that occur at least 1 week after entering a malaria endemic area. Drugs used for this purpose such as chloroquine, sulfadoxine-pyrimethamine, mefloquine, quinine plus doxycycline, or atovaquone-proguanil should be selected based on the resistance pattern of the area visited. Although self-treatment by travelers can be safe, effective, and potentially life-saving, no regimen is currently registered for this use in any country. No randomized con-

trolled clinical trials have been or are likely to be performed owing to the high morbidity and mortality of untreated or inappropriately treated malaria in nonimmune individuals. For example, self-treatment with SP has failed in Kenya, an area with widespread SP-resistant parasites.[358] Finally, travelers should be discouraged from self-treatment using products acquired locally as they may be of poor quality or outright fake.[359]

Presumptive Intermittent Treatment in Infants and Pregnant Women

In areas with intense transmission, infants 6 to 12 months of age suffer multiple episodes of malaria and are therefore at risk for life-threatening severe anemia.[360-362] Weekly chemoprophylaxis of infants protects against malarial fevers as well as anemia, but may compromise development of natural immunity.[363,364] Presumptive intermittent treatment (e.g., amodiaquine every 2 months for a total of 6 months; also known as intermittent preventative treatment) of infants can reduce malaria morbidity by 50% to 65% during the first year of life while still allowing sufficient exposure to parasites and development of immunity.[365,366] In areas of endemic transmission, malaria in pregnancy is associated with severe maternal anemia and low birth weight in newborns. Presumptive intermittent treatment has been shown to reduce the risk of severe anemia in women who received one to three doses of SP over the duration of their first pregnancy.[367]

Severe Malaria

Successful treatment of patients with severe malaria requires frequent clinical monitoring and intensive nursing care and may demand sophisticated interventions such as continuous EKG or hemodynamic monitoring, mechanical ventilation, or hemodialysis. Replacement of blood and fluids may lead to rapid reductions in lactate, resolution of metabolic acidosis, improvement in renal function, and clinical improvement of critically ill patients.[368]

Quinidine gluconate is the only approved parenteral treatment for severe malaria in the United States, on the recommendation of the CDC in recognition of the impracticality of stocking quinine throughout the country.[369,370] However, hospital pharmacies may not carry quinidine on formulary and may not know how to obtain it readily from regional distributors. When the need for quinidine is more acute than can be met by the local or regional distributor, Eli Lilly Company (800-821-0538) can arrange a rapid shipment of the drug. Assistance with the management of patients with severe malaria including the availability and use of quinidine is available from the CDC's Malaria Hotline (770-488-7788). Outside the United States, quinine and artemisinin derivatives (e.g., artemether, artesunate) are widely used to treat severe malaria. In Canada, intravenous formulations of quinine are available through the Canadian Malaria Network *www.hc-sc.gc.ca/pphb-dgspsp/tmp-pmv/quinine/pdf/quinine-cmn_e.pdf.* Antimalarial drug regimens used to treat severe malaria are presented in Table 272-3.

Quinidine Gluconate

Many physicians will be unfamiliar with quinidine as this drug has been largely supplanted with newer antiarrythmic agents. Quinidine has a narrow therapeutic window and must be used with extreme care in an intensive care unit.[369] It is administered intravenously as an infusion until the patient improves clinically and can complete antimalarial treatment with oral medication. Quinidine is *never* administered as a bolus injection, which can lead to fatal hypotension. Potentially fatal adverse reactions can occur even at treatment doses. It can cause postural hypotension, so frequent blood pressure measurements should be made. Quinidine may cause prolongation of the corrected QT interval, putting the patient at risk for ventricular tachycardias (e.g., *torsade de pointes*), and should be administered with continuous EKG monitoring.[371] If QTc prolongation greater than 25% of baseline develops, the infusion rate can be reduced. Since quinidine may cause hyperinsulinemic hypoglycemia, serum glucose must be monitored every 4 to 6 hours and with any acute neurological change (e.g., diminished consciousness, convulsions) that may arise from severe hypoglycemia. Administering 5% or 10% dextrose while infusing quinidine can reduce the incidence of hypoglycemia.

In patients taking medications that also prolong the QT interval, particularly when coadministered with drugs that suppress hepatic metabolism, the use of quinidine can be problematic. Although the initial loading dose of quinidine is not reduced in renal insufficiency, patients with malaria and acute renal failure may not clear quinidine effectively. Case reports illustrating the use of quinidine in the treatment of severe malaria have highlighted common clinical scenarios such as adjustment of infusion rates associated with elevated quinidine blood levels, prolonged QTc intervals, and arrhythmias as well as hypoglycemia, hypotension, and vomiting.[371] Quinidine levels should be maintained below 8 μg/mL, which may require reducing the dose by 30% to 50% to prevent drug accumulation in patients who remain seriously ill after 3 days of treatment. The response to quinidine is assessed by frequent blood smears every 6 to 8 hours to ensure rapid decrease in parasitemia. Once the patient improves and can take oral medications without vomiting, quinidine can be discontinued and a 7-day total course of treatment completed with a combination of quinine tablets and doxycycline.

Sepsis in Severe Malaria

Broad-spectrum antibiotics can be administered while awaiting blood culture results to patients who present with a clinical picture consistent with sepsis syndrome. Bacteremia complicating severe malaria is not uncommon in infants and children and may cause any patient's clinical status to deteriorate abruptly.[312]

Exchange Transfusion in Severe Malaria

High parasitemias have been correlated with mortality in falciparum malaria, leading to the use of exchange transfusion (ET) as an adjunct therapeutic measure. ET may reduce parasite load, remove toxic substances, reduce microcirculatory sludging, and rapidly correct anemia. Although small case series claim beneficial effects of ET (including partial ET in young children),[372-376] a recent meta-analysis concluded that a randomized controlled trial is necessary to determine whether ET is beneficial.[377] ET may be harmful and is associated with fluid overload, risk of transfusion reactions and related infections, and line sepsis. In addition, ET does not remove infected erythrocytes that are sequestered in deep tissue capillary beds, including those in the brain, and achieves only modest reductions in parasitemia.

Quinine Dihydrochloride

Quinine is the only readily available drug in some endemic areas for the parenteral treatment of patients with severe chloroquine-resistant malaria or patients with chloroquine-resistant uncomplicated malaria who cannot take oral medication because of vomiting. Quinine commonly causes hypoglycemia and the unpleasant side effects of cinchonism. Administration of quinine in a glucose infusion and frequent (every 4 to 6 hours) glucose checks help to avoid hypoglycemia, which in some cases can be life threatening. Quinine is much less cardiotoxic than quinidine, requiring no continuous EKG monitoring during its administration. Intravenous formulations of quinine are not commercially available in the United States, nor can they be obtained from the CDC on an emergency basis.

Artemether/Artesunate

Artemisinin derivatives are derived from *Artemesia annua* (qing hao), an herbal plant used in China for millennia as therapy for fevers.[378] Artemisinin derivatives are consistently effective against multidrug-resistant parasites and result in rapid clearance of parasites and clinical improvement usually within 24 to 36 hours. They are well tolerated and safe in adults, children, and pregnant women.[379-381] Several million people have taken artemisinins to date with no significant adverse or treatment-limiting effects being reported.[382] Although neurotoxicity can occur with supraphysiological doses in animals, it has not been documented in humans.[383] A review of 23 trials available in the Cochrane library found artemisinins were at least as effective as quinine for the treatment of severe malaria.[384] Recent studies indicate that intrarectal suppositories of artemether are as effective and safe as qui-

nine infusions in the treatment of both uncomplicated and cerebral malaria.[385] The FDA is currently investigating the use of intrarectal artesunate in the initial treatment of acute malaria in patients who cannot take medication by mouth and for whom parenteral therapy is not available. This medication is not yet approved and remains unavailable in the United States.

Non-falciparum Malaria

All cases of malaria should be treated as falciparum malaria until proven otherwise because *P. falciparum* infections can rapidly become life-threatening. Infections with *P. vivax, P. ovale,* and *P. malariae* are treated with chloroquine, unless (1) they are acquired in geographic regions where these species are known to be chloroquine resistant (Oceania and parts of Southeast Asia), or (2) any doubt exists as to the parasite species or if there is a mixed infection. Mixed infections consisting of two or more *Plasmodium* species may sometimes mask a *P. falciparum* subpopulation that can emerge during or after treatment. Non-falciparum infections likely to be chloroquine resistant are treated with mefloquine, quinine *plus* doxycycline, or atovaquone *plus* proguanil, at doses listed in Table 272-3. Sulfadoxine/pyrimethamine is generally not considered effective for the treatment of vivax malaria.

If there is no contraindication, persistent liver stages (hypnozoites) of *P. vivax* and *P. ovale* may be eradicated with primaquine (see Table 272-3).[386-388] *P. vivax* acquired in Southeast Asia, Papua New Guinea, Solomon Islands, Vanuatu, and parts of Indonesia commonly show resistance to standard primaquine doses and so a higher dose is recommended for infections acquired in these areas.[389-391] After blood stage *P. vivax* and *P. ovale* infections are treated with chloroquine (a drug not effective against hypnozoites), primaquine is administered to prevent relapse. Taking primaquine with food ameliorates gastrointestinal side effects and improves compliance. Patients should be advised to discontinue the drug and seek medical evaluation if their urine becomes dark, as primaquine occasionally can cause some degree of hemolysis in persons with mildly deficient or even normal G6PD activity. Primaquine causes some level of methemoglobinemia in nearly all persons treated, but this is rarely clinically significant (bluish discoloration of mucous membranes may be observed). Primaquine is contraindicated in persons with severe forms of G6PD deficiency (e.g., Mediterranean type or methemoglobin reductase deficiency) because of the danger of massive and potentially fatal hemolysis. Persons with less severe forms of G6PD deficiency have been treated with standard primaquine doses, but significant decreases in hematocrit levels were in some cases observed.[392] Primaquine should not be administered to pregnant women, owing to the risk of hemolytic disease in the fetus. Individuals who do not receive primaquine (including pregnant women) should be monitored for relapses, and if these occur, should be treated with blood-stage antimalarials. Primaquine is not administered to individuals who reside permanently in areas endemic for *P. vivax* or *P. ovale,* as reinfection is likely. Primaquine is also not administered to individuals who acquire infection by transfusion or transplantation, as hypnozoites develop only from mosquito-inoculated sporozoites. Tafenoquine, a primaquine analogue more potent and with a longer half-life than primaquine itself, is currently undergoing advanced clinical testing.[393,394] Primaquine is under evaluation for primary prophylaxis of *P. falciparum* and *P. vivax* malaria in travelers who are not pregnant and have normal G6PD levels.[395]

PREVENTION

Risk Assessment

The risk of acquiring malaria varies according to the geographic region visited, the travel destination within geographic areas (e.g., urban versus rural setting), type of accommodations (e.g., camping versus air-conditioned hotel), duration of stay (e.g., a less than 1-week business trip versus 3-month adventure travel), time of travel (high versus low transmission season), altitude of destination (less than 2000 meters versus higher), and efficacy of and adherence to malaria prophylaxis measures.[396] Immigrants returning home to visit relatives are at high risk for acquiring malaria because they often do not take prophylaxis as they are going home and might not consider malaria a serious threat because of their previous experience with it, are unaware they have lost immunity to malaria and are now at risk for serious disease, do not realize the risks of traveling when pregnant or when taking young nonimmune children to malarious regions, or are medically underserved and are therefore less likely to seek pre-travel advice.

Chemoprophylaxis

Lack of proper chemoprophylaxis is associated with severe complications from malaria and death.[334,397,398] Malaria is effectively prevented in travelers and in pregnant women in endemic areas by the use of antimalarial drugs when prescribed and taken appropriately[399] (Table 272-4). Selection of an effective prophylactic regimen depends on geographic patterns of drug resistance, concomitant illnesses, and other factors that may affect compliance: number of pills, dosing interval (i.e., daily versus weekly), duration of travel, duration of pre- and post-travel medication, cost, and the reputation as well as the actual tolerability of side effects. Chemoprophylaxis recommendations change frequently because of regional and temporal variability in malaria risk even within countries, resurgence of malaria in areas previously free of the disease, and the ongoing spread of drug-resistant parasites.

P. vivax, P. ovale, P. malariae, and *Chloroquine-Susceptible P. falciparum*

Currently, chloroquine can be used in travelers to those limited areas where chloroquine-resistant *P. falciparum* has *not* been reported, such as some areas of Central America and the Caribbean. Although chloroquine has been associated with QT prolongation and hepatic insuffi-

ciency, these effects are unlikely to occur at the doses used for prophylaxis. Chloroquine may cause retinopathy and arrhythmias when it accumulates as a result of excessive or prolonged dosing. Periodic funduscopic examination is therefore recommended with long-term use. Chloroquine prophylaxis has been used extensively and safely in pregnant and breastfeeding women and in children of all ages, including newborns.[400] Chloroquine-containing combinations (e.g., chloroquine *plus* proguanil) are no longer recommended for malaria prophylaxis in areas with chloroquine resistance (this regimen was recently implicated in failure to protect in the death of an American traveler).[397] Travelers who are exposed to *P. vivax* or *P. ovale* and have normal G6PD activity can receive terminal prophylaxis with primaquine on their return, as discussed earlier.

Chloroquine-Resistant *P. falciparum*

Mefloquine can be used in travelers to areas where chloroquine-resistant *P. falciparum* has been reported, *except* in areas where mefloquine resistance has also been reported, such as Thailand, Myanmar, Cambodia, and Vietnam.[401] Mefloquine may prolong the corrected QT interval and so cannot be given to individuals with cardiac conduction abnormalities and should also not be administered concurrently with other quinine-like drugs (quinidine, halofantrine), which can lead to sudden cardiac death. Mefloquine is also contraindicated in individuals with serious psychiatric disorders (e.g., psychosis, major depression, or history of seizures). An estimated 5% of individuals report neuropsychological events such as sleep disturbance, insomnia, nightmares, cognitive changes, anxiety or depression that lead to drug discontinuation.[402,403] However, a systematic review of mefloquine prophylaxis trials available in the Cochrane Library yielded five randomized comparative studies that failed to demonstrate significant differences between the overall adverse event or discontinua-

---

TABLE 272-4 Malaria Chemoprophylaxis

Drug	Adult Dose	Pediatric Dose	Precautions
P. vivax, P. ovale, P. malariae, **and Chloroquine-Susceptible** *P. falciparum*			
Chloroquine phosphate *Supplied in 500 mg salt (300 mg base) tablets.*	500 mg (300 mg base) once weekly*	8.3 mg/kg (5 mg/kg base) once weekly, up to the adult dose of 300 mg base*	Drug accumulation from prolonged use or inadvertent daily dosing may cause retinopathy.
Chloroquine-Resistant *P. falciparum*			
Mefloquine *Supplied in 250 mg salt (228 mg base) tablets.*	250 mg once weekly†	Dosed according to body weight:* <15 kg: 5 mg/kg once weekly 15-19 kg: 1/4 tablet once weekly 20-30 kg: 1/2 tablet once weekly 31-45 kg: 3/4 tablet once weekly	*Do not* use in individuals with cardiac conduction abnormalities, history of seizures, or serious psychiatric illnesses (for example, psychosis, major depression). *Do not* use concomitantly with quinidine, quinine, or halofantrine. *Do not* use in first trimester of pregnancy.
Chloroquine- or Mefloquine-Resistant *P. falciparum*			
Doxycycline *Supplied in 100 mg tablets.*	100 mg once daily‡	For children 8-12 years old: 2 mg/kg once daily, up to adult dose of 100 mg. For children >13 years old: 100 mg once daily‡	*Do not* use doxycycline in children < 8 years old or in pregnant women.
Atovaquone *plus* **proguanil** *Supplied in fixed combination tablets containing 250 mg atovaquone and 100 mg proguanil (adult tablets) or 62.5 mg/25 mg (pediatric tablets).*	250 mg/100 mg (one tablet) once daily§	Dose per body weight§ 11-20 kg: 62.5 mg/25 mg once daily 21-30 kg: 125 mg/50 mg once daily 31-40 kg: 187.5 mg/75 mg once daily >40 kg: 250 mg/100 mg once daily§	Pregnancy category C.

*Beginning 1-2 weeks before travel and continuing weekly for 4 weeks after leaving a malarious area.
†For travelers who will be at immediate high risk of malaria, a loading dose of mefloquine is usually well tolerated: 250 mg daily for 3 consecutive days, followed by weekly dosing as shown.
‡Beginning 1-2 days before travel and continuing daily for 4 weeks after leaving a malarious area.
§Beginning 1-2 days before travel and continuing daily for 7 days after leaving a malarious area.
Drug regimens adapted from: Advice for Travelers. The Medical Letter. April 15, 2002;1128:38-39.
Reprinted by special permission of the publisher.

tion rates associated with mefloquine and other chemoprophylaxis regimens.[404] Although not approved for use during pregnancy, mefloquine prophylaxis has been reported safe and effective during the second and third trimesters[405-407] and possibly during the first trimester.[408] Because most adverse effects are noted within the first three doses, starting prophylaxis 3 weeks prior to travel allows travelers to test their tolerance of the drug before they depart.

Chloroquine- or Mefloquine-Resistant *P. falciparum*

Doxycycline or atovaquone-proguanil (AP) can be used in travelers to areas where mefloquine-resistant *P. falciparum* has been reported, or in those travelers who are at risk of acquiring chloroquine-resistant malaria but who cannot take mefloquine.[401,409-411] Failure of properly taken doxycycline prophylaxis is unlikely, as *Plasmodium* resistance has not been reported against this drug. Failure of AP *treatment* has been documented against resistant *P. falciparum,* so far only for a few cases.[268,354] Doxycycline frequently causes gastrointestinal upset (take with food) and may cause esophageal ulceration (take with water, sit up for 30 minutes), photosensitivity (use sunscreen), vaginal candidiasis (carry over-the-counter antifungal suppositories), and decreased effectiveness of hormonal contraceptive agents (use back-up method). Doxycycline should not be used by pregnant and breastfeeding women or children younger than 8 years old owing to deleterious effects on bone and tooth development. In addition, doxycycline should not be taken with metal-containing antacids, which can decrease its absorption. Actual effectiveness of doxycycline may be slightly lower than that reported from some studies because of frequent noncompliance with its daily dosing requirement. AP is safe, effective, and well tolerated in both short- and long-term nonimmune travelers and there are no contraindications to its use.[412-415] Its safety profile in pregnancy is currently unknown (Category C). Most antimalarial drugs (chloroquine, mefloquine, and doxycycline) are taken for 4 weeks after the individual leaves a malarious area. This is to ensure that all liver stage *P. falciparum* parasites, against which these drugs have no or questionable activity, have entirely completed their development into merozoites and passed into the blood stream, where they can be killed by the drugs. AP eradicates the liver stages of *P. falciparum* although not of *P. vivax*, so the current recommendation is to take this drug for only 7 days after leaving a malarious area.

Mosquito Repellent and Avoidance Measures

No chemoprophylactic regimen is 100% effective. Despite adequate serum mefloquine levels and other laboratory evidence of compliance, mefloquine prophylaxis has failed where mefloquine resistance is not prevalent.[416] This example (as well as others) highlights the recommendation that measures to reduce mosquito bites should always accompany chemoprophylaxis.[417,418] Travelers can reduce mosquito bites by using *N,N*-diethyl-3-methylbenzamide (DEET)-containing insect repellents on exposed skin,[419-421] wearing permethrin-treated clothing, wearing clothes that cover as much skin as possible,[416] sleeping under insecticide-treated bed nets,[416,422,423] staying in housing with air-conditioning and well screened areas cleared of mosquitoes, and refraining from outdoor activity during peak *Anopheles* biting hours from dusk to dawn.[424]

Vaccination

Currently, there is no malaria vaccine. Some recent publications review important concepts in malaria vaccinology and discuss the state of research in the field.[425-428]

REFERENCES

1. Greenwood B. Malaria mortality and morbidity in Africa. Bull WHO. 1999;77: 617-618.
2. Snow RW, Trape JF, Marsh K. The past, present and future of childhood malaria mortality in Africa. Trends Parasitol. 2001;17:593-597.
3. Carter R, Mendis KN. Evolutionary and historical aspects of the burden of malaria. Clin Microbiol Rev. 2002;15:564-594.
4. Molineaux L, Gramiccia G. The Garki Project. Research on the epidemiology and control of malaria in the Sudan savanna of West Africa. World Health Organization Press, 1980.
5. Trape JF, Pison G, Preziosi MP, et al. Impact of chloroquine resistance on malaria mortality. C R Acad Sci III. 1998;321:689-697.
6. Practical chemotherapy of malaria: Report of a WHO Scientific Group. World Health Organization Tech Rep Ser. 1990;805:1-141.
7. Zucker JR, Ruebush TK, Obonyo C, et al. The mortality consequences of the continued use of chloroquine in Africa: Experience in Siaya, western Kenya. Am J Trop Med Hyg. 2003;68:386-390.
8. Zucker JR, Lackritz EM, Ruebush TK, et al. Childhood mortality during and after hospitalization in western Kenya: Effect of malaria treatment regimens. Am J Trop Med Hyg. 1996;55:655-660.
9. Wellems TE. Plasmodium chloroquine resistance and the search for a replacement antimalarial drug. Science. 2002;298:124-126.
10. Blackman MJ, Bannister LH. Apical organelles of *Apicomplexa:* Biology and isolation by subcellular fractionation. Mol Biochem Parasitol. 2001;117:11-25.
11. Bruce-Chwatt LJ. Malaria as a zoonosis. WHO/Zoon/66.90; WHO/Mal/66.578. 1966.
12. Laveran A. Deuxieme note relative a un nouveau parasite trouve dan le sang des maladies atteints de la fievre palustre. Bull Acad Med. 1880;44:1346-1347.
13. Ross R. On some peculiar pigmented cells found in two mosquitoes fed on malarial blood. Br Med J. 1897;1786-1788.
14. Grassi B. Rapporti tra la malaria e peculiari insetti. Atti R Accad Lincei. 1898;7:163-172.
15. Shortt HE, Garnham PCC. The pre-erythrocytic development of *Plasmodium cynomolgi* and *Plasmodium vivax*. Trans R Soc Trop Med Hyg. 1948;41:785-795.
16. Shakibaei M, Frevert U. Dual interaction of the malaria circumsporozoite protein with the low density lipoprotein receptor-related protein LRP and heparan sulfate proteoglycans. J Exp Med. 1996;184:1699-1711.
17. Gilles HM, Warrell DA. Bruce-Chwatt's Essential Malariology. 3rd ed. New York: Oxford University Press, 1993.
18. Karunaweera ND, Grau GE, Gamage P, et al. Dynamics of fever and serum levels of tumor necrosis factor are closely associated during clinical paroxysms in Plasmodium vivax malaria. Proc Natl Acad Sci USA. 1992;89:3200-3203.
19. Boyd MF. Historical Review. In: Boyd MF, ed. Malariology. Phliadelphia: WB Saunders; 1949:3-25.
20. Vijaykumar M, Naik RS, Gowda DC. *Plasmodium falciparum* glycosylphosphatidylinositol-induced TNF-alpha secretion by macrophages is mediated without membrane insertion or endocytosis. J Biol Chem. 2001;276:6909-6912.
21. Wijesekera SK, Carter R, Rathnayaka L, Mendis KN. A malaria parasite toxin associated with *Plasmodium vivax* paroxysms. Clin Exp Immunol. 1996;104:221-227.
22. Sachs J, Malaney P. The economic and social burden of malaria. Nature. 2002;415:680-685.
23. Breman JG. The ears of the hippopotamus: Manifestations, determinants, and estimates of the malaria burden. Am J Trop Med Hyg. 2001;64(Suppl):1-11.
24. Institute of Medicine. Malaria: Obstacles and Opportunities. Oaks SC, Mitchell VS, Pearson GW, Carpenter CCJ, eds. Washington DC: National Academy Press, 1991.
25. Marsh K, Forster D, Waruiru C, et al. Indicators of life-threatening malaria in African children. N Engl J Med. 1995;332:1399-1404.
26. English M, Waruiru C, Amukoye E, et al. Deep breathing in children with severe malaria: Indicator of metabolic acidosis and poor outcome. Am J Trop Med Hyg. 1996;55:521-524.
27. Newbold C, Craig A, Kyes S, et al. Cytoadherence, pathogenesis and the infected red cell surface in *Plasmodium falciparum*. Int J Parasitol. 1999;29:927-937.
28. Sherman IW, Eda S, Winograd E. Cytoadherence and sequestration in *Plasmodium falciparum:* Defining the ties that bind. Microbes Infect. 2003;5:897-909.
29. Chotivanich KT, Dondorp AM, White NJ, et al. The resistance to physiological shear stresses of the erythrocytic rosettes formed by cells infected with *Plasmodium falciparum*. Ann Trop Med Parasitol. 2000;94:219-226.
30. Kaul DK, Roth EF Jr, Nagel RL, et al. Rosetting of *Plasmodium falciparum*-infected red blood cells with uninfected red blood cells enhances microvascular obstruction under flow conditions. Blood. 1991;78:812-819.
31. Dondorp AM, Kager PA, Vreeken J, White NJ. Abnormal blood flow and red blood cell deformability in severe malaria. Parasitol Today. 2000;16:228-232.
32. Miller LH, Usami S, Chien S. Alteration in the rheologic properties of *Plasmodium knowlesi*–infected red cells. A possible mechanism for capillary obstruction. J Clin Invest 1971;50:1451-1455.
33. Luse SA, Miller LH. *Plasmodium falciparum* malaria. Ultrastructure of parasitized erythrocytes in cardiac vessels. Am J Trop Med Hyg. 1971;20:655-660.
34. MacPherson GG, Warrell MJ, White NJ, et al. Human cerebral malaria. A quantitative ultrastructural analysis of parasitized erythrocyte sequestration. Am J Pathol. 1985;119:385-401.
35. Oo MM, Aikawa M, Than T, et al. Human cerebral malaria: A pathological study. J Neuropathol Exp Neurol. 1987;46:223-231.
36. Pongponratn E, Riganti M, Punpoowong B, Aikawa M. Microvascular sequestration of parasitized erythrocytes in human falciparum malaria: A pathological study. Am J Trop Med Hyg. 1991;44:168-175.
37. Wickramasinghe SN, Phillips RE, Looareesuwan S, et al. The bone marrow in human cerebral malaria: Parasite sequestration within sinusoids. Br J Haematol. 1987;66:295-306.
38. Walter PR, Garin Y, Blot P. Placental pathologic changes in malaria. A histologic and ultrastructural study. Am J Pathol. 1982;109:330-342.
39. Pongponratn E, Viriyavejakul P, Wilairatana P, et al. Absence of knobs on parasitized red blood cells in a splenectomized patient in fatal falciparum malaria. Southeast Asian J Trop Med Publ Hlth. 2000;31:829-835.

40. Langreth SG, Peterson E. Pathogenicity, stability, and immunogenicity of a knobless clone of *Plasmodium falciparum* in Colombian owl monkeys. Infect Immun. 1985;47:760-766.

41. Crabb BS, Cooke BM, Reeder JC, et al. Targeted gene disruption shows that knobs enable malaria-infected red cells to cytoadhere under physiological shear stress. Cell. 1997;89:287-296.

42. Yipp BG, Anand S, Schollaardt T, et al. Synergism of multiple adhesion molecules in mediating cytoadherence of *Plasmodium falciparum*-infected erythrocytes to microvascular endothelial cells under flow. Blood. 2000;96:2292-2298.

43. Craig A, Scherf A. Molecules on the surface of the *Plasmodium falciparum* infected erythrocyte and their role in malaria pathogenesis and immune evasion. Mol Biochem Parasitol. 2001;115:129-143.

44. Su XZ, Heatwole VM, Wertheimer SP, et al. The large diverse gene family var encodes proteins involved in cytoadherence and antigenic variation of *Plasmodium falciparum*-infected erythrocytes. Cell. 1995;82:89-100.

45. Smith JD, Chitnis CE, Craig AG, et al. Switches in expression of *Plasmodium falciparum* var genes correlate with changes in antigenic and cytoadherent phenotypes of infected erythrocytes. Cell. 1995;82:101-110.

46. Baruch DI, Pasloske BL, Singh HB, et al. Cloning the P. falciparum gene encoding PfEMP1, a malarial variant antigen and adherence receptor on the surface of parasitized human erythrocytes. Cell. 1995;82:77-87.

47. Chen Q, Fernandez V, Sundstrom A, et al. Developmental selection of var gene expression in *Plasmodium falciparum*. Nature. 1998;394:392-395.

48. Deitsch KW, Calderwood MS, Wellems TE. Malaria. Cooperative silencing elements in var genes. Nature. 2001;412:875-876.

49. Gatton ML, Peters JM, Fowler EV, Cheng Q. Switching rates of *Plasmodium falciparum* var genes: Faster than we thought? Trends Parasitol. 2003;19:202-208.

50. Roberts DJ, Craig AG, Berendt AR, et al. Rapid switching to multiple antigenic and adhesive phenotypes in malaria. Nature. 1992;357:689-692.

51. Roberts DD, Sherwood JA, Spitalnik SL, et al. Thrombospondin binds falciparum malaria parasitized erythrocytes and may mediate cytoadherence. Nature. 1985;318:64-66.

52. Cooke BM, Berendt AR, Craig AG, et al. Rolling and stationary cytoadhesion of red blood cells parasitized by *Plasmodium falciparum:* Separate roles for ICAM-1, CD36 and thrombospondin. Br J Haematol. 1994; 87:162-170.

53. Treutiger CJ, Heddini A, Fernandez V, et al. PECAM-1/CD31, an endothelial receptor for binding *Plasmodium falciparum*-infected erythrocytes. Nat Med. 1997; 3:1405-1408.

54. Reeder JC, Cowman AF, Davern KM, et al. The adhesion of *Plasmodium falciparum*-infected erythrocytes to chondroitin sulfate A is mediated by P. falciparum erythrocyte membrane protein 1. Proc Natl Acad Sci USA. 1999;96:5198-5202.

55. Fried M, Duffy PE. Adherence of *Plasmodium falciparum* to chondroitin sulfate A in the human placenta. Science. 1996;272:1502-1504.

56. Lindenthal C, Kremsner PG, Klinkert MQ. Commonly recognised *Plasmodium falciparum* parasites cause cerebral malaria. Parasitol Res. 2003;91:363-368.

57. Ockenhouse CF, Ho M, Tandon NN, et al. Molecular basis of sequestration in severe and uncomplicated *Plasmodium falciparum* malaria: Differential adhesion of infected erythrocytes to CD36 and ICAM-1. J Infect Dis. 1991;164:163-169.

58. Turner GD, Morrison H, Jones M, et al. An immunohistochemical study of the pathology of fatal malaria. Evidence for widespread endothelial activation and a potential role for intercellular adhesion molecule-1 in cerebral sequestration. Am J Pathol. 1994;145:1057-1069.

59. Newbold C, Warn P, Black G, et al. Receptor-specific adhesion and clinical disease in *Plasmodium falciparum*. Am J Trop Med Hyg. 1997;57:389-398.

60. Gamain B, Smith JD, Miller LH, Baruch DI. Modifications in the CD36 binding domain of the *Plasmodium falciparum* variant antigen are responsible for the inability of chondroitin sulfate A adherent parasites to bind CD36. Blood. 2001;97:3268-3274.

61. Chen Q, Barragan A, Fernandez V, et al. Identification of *Plasmodium falciparum* erythrocyte membrane protein 1 PfEMP1 as the rosetting ligand of the malaria parasite P. falciparum. J Exp Med. 1998;187:15-23.

62. Rowe JA, Moulds JM, Newbold CI, Miller LH. P. falciparum rosetting mediated by a parasite-variant erythrocyte membrane protein and complement-receptor 1. Nature. 1997;388:292-295.

63. Barragan A, Kremsner PG, Wahlgren M, Carlson J. Blood group A antigen is a coreceptor in *Plasmodium falciparum* rosetting. Infect Immun. 2000;68:2971-2975.

64. Cockburn IA, Mackinnon MJ, O'Donnell A, et al. From The Cover: A human complement receptor 1 polymorphism that reduces *Plasmodium falciparum* rosetting confers protection against severe malaria. Proc Natl Acad Sci USA. 2004;101:272-277.

65. Heddini A, Pettersson F, Kai O, et al. Fresh isolates from children with severe *Plasmodium falciparum* malaria bind to multiple receptors. Infect Immun. 2001;69:5849-5856.

66. Treutiger CJ, Hedlund I, Helmby H, et al. Rosette formation in *Plasmodium falciparum* isolates and anti-rosette activity of sera from Gambians with cerebral or uncomplicated malaria. Am J Trop Med Hyg. 1992;46:503-510.

67. Carlson J, Helmby H, Hill AV, et al. Human cerebral malaria: Association with erythrocyte rosetting and lack of anti-rosetting antibodies. Lancet. 1990;336:1457-1460.

68. Rowe A, Obeiro J, Newbold CI, Marsh K. *Plasmodium falciparum* rosetting is associated with malaria severity in Kenya. Infect Immun. 1995;63:2323-2326.

69. Kun JF, Schmidt-Ott RJ, Lehman LG, et al. Merozoite surface antigen 1 and 2 genotypes and rosetting of *Plasmodium falciparum* in severe and mild malaria in Lambarene, Gabon. Trans R Soc Trop Med Hyg. 1998;92:110-114.

70. Ho M, Davis TM, Silamut K, et al. Rosette formation of *Plasmodium falciparum*-infected erythrocytes from patients with acute malaria. Infect Immun. 1991;59: 2135-2139.

71. al Yaman F, Genton B, Mokela D, et al. Human cerebral malaria: lack of significant association between erythrocyte rosetting and disease severity. Trans R Soc Trop Med Hyg. 1995;89:55-58.

72. Field J. Blood examination and prognosis in acute falciparum malaria. Trans R Soc Trop Med Hyg. 1949;43:33-48.

73. Chotivanich K, Udomsangpetch R, Simpson JA, et al. Parasite multiplication potential and the severity of Falciparum malaria. J Infect Dis. 2000;181:1206-1209.

74. Silamut K, White NJ. Relation of the stage of parasite development in the peripheral blood to prognosis in severe falciparum malaria. Trans R Soc Trop Med Hyg. 1993;87:436-443.

75. Amodu OK, Adeyemo AA, Olumese PE, Gbadegesin RA. Intraleucocytic malaria pigment and clinical severity of malaria in children. Trans R Soc Trop Med Hyg. 1998;92:54-56.

76. Simpson JA, Silamut K, Chotivanich K, et al. Red cell selectivity in malaria: A study of multiple-infected erythrocytes. Trans R Soc Trop Med Hyg. 1999;93:165-168.

77. Miller LH, Mason SJ, Dvorak JA, McGinniss MH, Rothman IK. Erythrocyte receptors for (Plasmodium knowlesi) malaria: Duffy blood group determinants. Science. 1975;189:561-563.

78. Horuk R, Chitnis CE, Darbonne WC, Colby TJ, Rybicki A, Hadley TJ, Miller LH. A receptor for the malarial parasite Plasmodium vivax: the erythrocyte chemokine receptor. Science. 1993;261:1182-1184.

79. Nagatake T, Hoang VT, Tegoshi T, et al. Pathology of falciparum malaria in Vietnam. Am J Trop Med Hyg. 1992;47:259-264.

80. Riganti M, Pongponratn E, Tegoshi T, et al. Human cerebral malaria in Thailand: A clinico-pathological correlation. Immunol Lett. 1990;25:199-205.

81. Hobbs MR, Udhayakumar V, Levesque MC, et al. A new NOS2 promoter polymorphism associated with increased nitric oxide production and protection from severe malaria in Tanzanian and Kenyan children. Lancet. 2002;360:1468-1475.

82. Agina AA, Abd-Allah SH. Plasma levels of nitric oxide in association with severe *Plasmodium falciparum* in Yemen. J Egypt Soc Parasitol. 1999;29:215-222.

83. Grau GE, Taylor TE, Molyneux ME, et al. Tumor necrosis factor and disease severity in children with falciparum malaria. N Engl J Med. 1989;320:1586-1591.

84. Al Yaman FM, Mokela D, Genton B, et al. Association between serum levels of reactive nitrogen intermediates and coma in children with cerebral malaria in Papua New Guinea. Trans R Soc Trop Med Hyg. 1996;90:270-273.

85. Dobbie MS, Hurst RD, Klein NJ, Surtees RA. Upregulation of intercellular adhesion molecule-1 expression on human endothelial cells by tumour necrosis factor-alpha in an in vitro model of the blood-brain barrier. Brain Res. 1999;830:330-336.

86. Wong D, Dorovini-Zis K. Upregulation of intercellular adhesion molecule-1 (ICAM-1) expression in primary cultures of human brain microvessel endothelial cells by cytokines and lipopolysaccharide. J Neuroimmunol. 1992;39:11-21.

87. Grau GE, Mackenzie CD, Carr RA, et al. Platelet accumulation in brain microvessels in fatal pediatric cerebral malaria. J Infect Dis. 2003;187:461-466.

88. Molyneux ME, Taylor TE, Wirima JJ, Harper G. Effect of rate of infusion of quinine on insulin and glucose responses in Malawian children with falciparum malaria. Br Med J. 1989;299:602-603.

89. White NJ, Miller KD, Marsh K, et al. Hypoglycaemia in African children with severe malaria. Lancet. 1987;1:708-711.

90. Krishna S, Waller DW, ter Kuile F, et al. Lactic acidosis and hypoglycaemia in children with severe malaria: Pathophysiological and prognostic significance. Trans R Soc Trop Med Hyg. 1994;88:67-73.

91. English M, Punt J, Mwangi I, et al. Clinical overlap between malaria and severe pneumonia in Africa children in hospital. Trans R Soc Trop Med Hyg. 1996;90:658-662.

92. Dekker E, Hellerstein MK, Romijn JA, et al. Glucose homeostasis in children with falciparum malaria: Precursor supply limits gluconeogenesis and glucose production. J Clin Endocrinol Metab. 1997;82:2514-2521.

93. Homewood CA. Carbohydrate metabolism of malarial parasites. Bull WHO. 1977;55:229-235.

94. White NJ, Warrell DA, Chanthavanich P, et al. Severe hypoglycemia and hyperinsulinemia in falciparum malaria. N Engl J Med. 1983;309:61-66.

95. Phillips RE, Looareesuwan S, White NJ, et al. Hypoglycaemia and antimalarial drugs: Quinidine and release of insulin. Br Med J Clin Res Ed. 1986;292:1319-1321.

96. Ekvall H. Malaria and anemia. Curr Opin Hematol. 2003;10:108-114.

97. Selvam R, Baskaran G. Hematological impairments in recurrent *Plasmodium vivax* infected patients. Jpn J Med Sci Biol. 1996;49:151-165.

98. Jakeman GN, Saul A, Hogarth WL, Collins WE. Anaemia of acute malaria infections in nonimmune patients primarily results from destruction of uninfected erythrocytes. Parasitology. 1999;119(Pt 2):127-133.

99. Vedovato M, De P, V, Dapporto M, Salvatorelli G. Defective erythropoietin production in the anaemia of malaria. Nephrol Dial Transplant. 1999;14: 1043-1044.

100. Burgmann H, Looareesuwan S, Kapiotis S, et al. Serum levels of erythropoietin in acute *Plasmodium falciparum* malaria. Am J Trop Med Hyg. 1996;54:280-283.

101. Verhoef H, West CE, Kraaijenhagen R, et al. Malarial anemia leads to adequately increased erythropoiesis in asymptomatic Kenyan children. Blood. 2002;100: 3489-3494.

102. Burchard GD, Radloff P, Philipps J, et al. Increased erythropoietin production in children with severe malarial anemia. Am J Trop Med Hyg. 1995;53:547-551.

103. Abdalla SH. Hematopoiesis in human malaria. Blood Cells. 1990;16:401-416.

104. Bloland PB, Lackritz EM, Kazembe PN, et al. Beyond chloroquine: implications of drug resistance for evaluating malaria therapy efficacy and treatment policy in Africa. J Infect Dis. 1993;167:932-937.

105. Charoenpan P, Indraprasit S, Kiatboonsri S, et al. Pulmonary edema in severe falciparum malaria. Hemodynamic study and clinicophysiologic correlation. Chest. 1990;97:1190-1197.

106. Feldman RM, Singer C. Noncardiogenic pulmonary edema and pulmonary fibrosis in falciparum malaria. Rev Infect Dis. 1987;9:134-139.

107. Taylor WR, White NJ. Malaria and the lung. Clin Chest Med. 2002;23:457-468.

108. Crawley J, English M, Waruiru C, et al. Abnormal respiratory patterns in childhood cerebral malaria. Trans R Soc Trop Med Hyg. 1998;92:305-308.

109. Maitland K, Levin M, English M, et al. Severe *P. falciparum* malaria in Kenyan children: Evidence for hypovolaemia. Q J Med. 2003;96:427-434.

110. Agbenyega T, Angus BJ, Bedu-Addo G, et al. Glucose and lactate kinetics in children with severe malaria. J Clin Endocrinol Metab. 2000;85:1569-1576.

111. Vander Jagt DL, Hunsaker LA, Campos NM, Baack BR. D-Lactate production in erythrocytes infected with *Plasmodium falciparum*. Mol Biochem Parasitol. 1990;42:277-284.

112. Day NP, Phu NH, Mai NT, et al. The pathophysiologic and prognostic significance of acidosis in severe adult malaria. Crit Care Med. 2000;28:1833-1840.

113. Pukrittayakamee S, White NJ, Davis TM, et al. Hepatic blood flow and metabolism in severe falciparum malaria: Clearance of intravenously administered galactose. Clin Sci Lond. 1992;82:63-70.

114. Tureen J. Effect of recombinant human tumor necrosis factor-alpha on cerebral oxygen uptake, cerebrospinal fluid lactate, and cerebral blood flow in the rabbit: Role of nitric oxide. J Clin Invest. 1995;95:1086-1091.

115. English M, Marsh V, Amukoye E, et al. Chronic salicylate poisoning and severe malaria. Lancet. 1996;347:1736-1737.

116. Guyatt HL, Snow RW. Malaria in pregnancy as an indirect cause of infant mortality in sub-Saharan Africa. Trans R Soc Trop Med Hyg. 2001;95:569-576.

117. Steketee RW, Wirima JJ, Hightower AW, et al. The effect of malaria and malaria prevention in pregnancy on offspring birthweight, prematurity, and intrauterine growth retardation in rural Malawi. Am J Trop Med Hyg. 1996;55(Suppl):33-41.

118. Beeson JG, Rogerson SJ, Cooke BM, et al. Adhesion of *Plasmodium falciparum*-infected erythrocytes to hyaluronic acid in placental malaria. Nat Med. 2000;6:86-90.

119. Flick K, Scholander C, Chen Q, et al. Role of nonimmune IgG bound to PfEMP1 in placental malaria. Science. 2001;293:2098-2100.

120. Beeson JG, Amin N, Kanjala M, Rogerson SJ. Selective accumulation of mature asexual stages of *Plasmodium falciparum*-infected erythrocytes in the placenta. Infect Immun. 2002;7:5412-5415.

121. Khattab A, Kun J, Deloron P, et al. Variants of *Plasmodium falciparum* erythrocyte membrane protein 1 expressed by different placental parasites are closely related and adhere to chondroitin sulfate A. J Infect Dis. 2001;183:1165-1169.

122. Khattab A, Kremsner PG, Klinkert MQ. Common surface-antigen var genes of limited diversity expressed by *Plasmodium falciparum* placental isolates separated by time and space. J Infect Dis. 2003;187:477-483.

123. van Eijk AM, Ayisi JG, ter Kuile FO, et al. Risk factors for malaria in pregnancy in an urban and peri-urban population in western Kenya. Trans R Soc Trop Med Hyg. 2002;96:586-592.

124. Carlini ME, White AC Jr, Atmar RL. Vivax malaria complicated by adult respiratory distress syndrome. Clin Infect Dis. 1999;28:1182-1183.

125. Torres JR, Perez H, Postigo MM, Silva JR. Acute non-cardiogenic lung injury in benign tertian malaria. Lancet. 1997;350:31-32.

126. Oscherwitz SL. Chronic malaria with splenic rupture. J Travel Med. 2003;10:64-65.

127. Zingman BS, Viner BL. Splenic complications in malaria: Case report and review. Clin Infect Dis. 1993;16:223-232.

128. Horuk R, Chitnis CE, Darbonne WC, et al. A receptor for the malarial parasite *Plasmodium vivax*: the erythrocyte chemokine receptor. Science. 1993;261: 1182-1184.

129. Suwanarusk R, Cooke BM, Dondorp AM, et al. The Deformability of Red Blood Cells Parasitized by *Plasmodium falciparum* and *P. vivax*. J Infect Dis. 2004;189: 190-194.

130. Vinetz JM, Li J, McCutchan TF, Kaslow DC. *Plasmodium malariae* infection in an asymptomatic 74-year-old Greek woman with splenomegaly. N Engl J Med. 1998; 338:367-371.

131. Okoro BA, Okafor HU, Nnoli LU. Childhood nephrotic syndrome in Enugu, Nigeria. West Afr J Med. 2000;19:137-141.

132. Abdurrahman MB. The role of infectious agents in the aetiology and pathogenesis of childhood nephrotic syndrome in Africa. J Infect. 1984;8:100-109.

133. Abdurrahman MB, Aikhionbare HA, Babaoye FA, et al. Clinicopathological features of childhood nephrotic syndrome in northern Nigeria. Q J Med. 1990;75:563-576.

134. Ward PA, Kibukamusoke JW. Evidence for soluble immune complexes in the pathogenesis of the glomerulonephritis of quartan malaria. Lancet. 1969;1:283-285.

135. Flint J, Harding RM, Boyce AJ, Clegg JB. The population genetics of the haemoglobinopathies. Baillieres Clin Haematol. 1998;11:1-51.

136. Aidoo M, Terlouw DJ, Kolczak MS, et al. Protective effects of the sickle cell gene against malaria morbidity and mortality. Lancet. 2002;359:1311-1312.

137. Allison AC. Protection afforded by sickle-cell trait against subtertian malareal infection. Br Med J. 1954;4857:290-294.

138. Willcox M, Bjorkman A, Brohult J, et al. A case-control study in northern Liberia of *Plasmodium falciparum* malaria in haemoglobin S and beta-thalassaemia traits. Ann Trop Med Parasitol. 1983;77:239-246.

139. Ruwende C, Khoo SC, Snow RW, et al. Natural selection of hemi- and heterozygotes for G6PD deficiency in Africa by resistance to severe malaria. Nature. 1995; 376: 246-249.

140. Fleming AF, Storey J, Molineaux L, et al. Abnormal haemoglobins in the Sudan savanna of Nigeria. I. Prevalence of haemoglobins and relationships between sickle cell trait, malaria and survival. Ann Trop Med Parasitol. 1979;73:161-172.

141. Friedman MJ. Erythrocytic mechanism of sickle cell resistance to malaria. Proc Natl Acad Sci USA. 1978;75:1994-1997.

142. Roth EF Jr, Friedman M, Ueda Y, et al. Sickling rates of human AS red cells infected in vitro with *Plasmodium falciparum* malaria. Science. 1978;202:650-652.

143. Luzzatto L, Nwachuku-Jarrett ES, Reddy S. Increased sickling of parasitised erythrocytes as mechanism of resistance against malaria in the sickle-cell trait. Lancet. 1970;1:319-321.

144. Pasvol G. The interaction between sickle haemoglobin and the malarial parasite *Plasmodium falciparum*. Trans R Soc Trop Med Hyg. 1980;74:701-705.

145. Agarwal A, Guindo A, Cissoko Y, et al. Hemoglobin C associated with protection from severe malaria in the Dogon of Mali, a West African population with a low prevalence of hemoglobin S. Blood. 2000;96:2358-2363.

146. Olumese PE, Adeyemo AA, Ademowo OG, et al. The clinical manifestations of cerebral malaria among Nigerian children with the sickle cell trait. Ann Trop Paediatr. 1997;17:141-145.

147. Achidi EA, Salimonu LS, Asuzu MC, et al. Studies on *Plasmodium falciparum* parasitemia and development of anemia in Nigerian infants during their first year of life. Am J Trop Med Hyg 1996;55:138-143.

148. Kitayaporn D, Nelson KE, Charoenlarp P, Pholpothi T. Haemoglobin-E in the presence of oxidative substances from fava bean may be protective against *Plasmodium falciparum* malaria. Trans R Soc Trop Med Hyg 1992;86:240-244.

149. Hutagalung R, Wilairatana P, Looareesuwan S, et al. Influence of hemoglobin E trait on the severity of Falciparum malaria. J Infect Dis. 1999;179:283-286.

150. Chotivanich K, Udomsangpetch R, Pattanapanyasat K, et al. Hemoglobin E: A balanced polymorphism protective against high parasitemias and thus severe *P. falciparum* malaria. Blood. 2002;100:1172-1176.

151. Modiano D, Luoni G, Sirima BS, et al. Haemoglobin C protects against clinical *Plasmodium falciparum* malaria. Nature. 2001;414:305-308.

152. Fairhurst RM, Fujioka H, Hayton K, et al. Aberrant development of Plasmodium *falciparum* in hemoglobin CC red cells: Implications for the malaria protective effect of the homozygous state. Blood. 2003;101:3309-3315.

153. Olson JA, Nagel RL. Synchronized cultures of *P. falciparum* in abnormal red cells: The mechanism of the inhibition of growth in HbCC cells. Blood. 1986;67:997-1001.

154. Friedman MJ, Roth EF, Nagel RL, Trager W. The role of hemoglobins C, S, and Nbalt in the inhibition of malaria parasite development in vitro. Am J Trop Med Hyg. 1979;28:777-780.

155. Oppenheimer SJ, Hill AV, Gibson FD, et al. The interaction of alpha thalassaemia with malaria. Trans R Soc Trop Med Hyg. 1987;81:322-326.

156. Flint J, Hill AV, Bowden DK, et al. High frequencies of alpha-thalassaemia are the result of natural selection by malaria. Nature. 1986;321:744-750.

157. Weatherall DJ. Thalassaemia and malaria, revisited. Ann Trop Med Parasitol. 1997;91:885-890.

158. Pattanapanyasat K, Yongvanitchit K, Tongtawe P, et al. Impairment of *Plasmodium falciparum* growth in thalassemic red blood cells: Further evidence by using biotin labeling and flow cytometry. Blood. 1999;93:3116-3119.

159. Senok AC, Li K, Nelson EA, et al. Invasion and growth of Plasmodium *falciparum* is inhibited in fractionated thalassaemic erythrocytes. Trans R Soc Trop Med Hyg. 1997;91:138-143.

160. Senok AC, Nelson EA, Li K, Oppenheimer SJ. Thalassaemia trait, red blood cell age and oxidant stress: Effects on *Plasmodium falciparum* growth and sensitivity to artemisinin. Trans R Soc Trop Med Hyg. 1997;91:585-589.

161. Luzzi GA, Merry AH, Newbold CI, et al. Protection by alpha-thalassaemia against *Plasmodium falciparum* malaria: Modified surface antigen expression rather than impaired growth or cytoadherence. Immunol Lett. 1991;30:233-240.

162. Luzzi GA, Merry AH, Newbold CI, et al. Surface antigen expression on *Plasmodium falciparum*-infected erythrocytes is modified in alpha- and beta-thalassemia. J Exp Med. 1991;173:785-791.

163. Shear HL, Grinberg L, Gilman J, et al. Transgenic mice expressing human fetal globin are protected from malaria by a novel mechanism. Blood. 1998;92:2520-2526.

164. Friedman MJ. Oxidant damage mediates variant red cell resistance to malaria. Nature. 1979;280:245-247.

165. Mockenhaupt FP, Mandelkow J, Till H, et al. Reduced prevalence of *Plasmodium falciparum* infection and of concomitant anaemia in pregnant women with heterozygous G6PD deficiency. Trop Med Int Hlth. 2003;8:118-124.

166. Golenser J, Miller J, Spira DT, et al. Inhibition of the intraerythrocytic development of *Plasmodium falciparum* in glucose-6-phosphate dehydrogenase deficient erythrocytes is enhanced by oxidants and by crisis form factor. Trop Med Parasitol. 1988;39:273-276.

167. Luzzatto L, Usanga FA, Reddy S. Glucose-6-phosphate dehydrogenase deficient red cells: Resistance to infection by malarial parasites. Science. 1969;164:839-842.

168. Roth EF Jr, Raventos-Suarez C, Rinaldi A, Nagel RL. Glucose-6-phosphate dehydrogenase deficiency inhibits in vitro growth of *Plasmodium falciparum*. Proc Natl Acad Sci USA. 1983;80:298-299.

169. Yoshida A, Roth EF Jr. Glucose-6-phosphate dehydrogenase of malaria parasite *Plasmodium falciparum*. Blood. 1987;69:1528-1530.

170. Usanga EA, Luzzatto L. Adaptation of *Plasmodium falciparum* to glucose 6-phosphate dehydrogenase-Deficient host red cells by production of parasite-encoded enzyme. Nature. 1985;313:793-795.

171. Cappadoro M, Giribaldi G, O'Brien E, et al. Early phagocytosis of glucose-6-phosphate dehydrogenase G6PD-deficient erythrocytes parasitized by *Plasmodium falciparum* may explain malaria protection in G6PD deficiency. Blood. 1998;92:2527-2534.

172. Jarolim P, Palek J, Amato D, et al. Deletion in erythrocyte band 3 gene in malaria-resistant Southeast Asian ovalocytosis. Proc Natl Acad Sci USA. 1991;88:11022-11026.

173. Mohandas N, Lie-Injo LE, Friedman M, Mak JW. Rigid membranes of Malayan ovalocytes: A likely genetic barrier against malaria. Blood. 1984;63:1385-1392.

174. Liu SC, Palek J, Yi SJ, et al. Molecular basis of altered red blood cell membrane properties in Southeast Asian ovalocytosis: Role of the mutant band 3 protein in band 3 oligomerization and retention by the membrane skeleton. Blood. 1995;86:349-358.

175. Dluzewski AR, Nash GB, Wilson RJ, et al. Invasion of hereditary ovalocytes by *Plasmodium falciparum* in vitro and its relation to intracellular ATP concentration. Mol Biochem Parasitol. 1992;55:1-7.

176. Foo LC, Rekhraj V, Chiang GL, Mak JW. Ovalocytosis protects against severe malaria parasitemia in the Malayan aborigines. Am J Trop Med Hyg. 1992;47:271-275.

177. Cattani JA, Gibson FD, Alpers MP, Crane GG. Hereditary ovalocytosis and reduced susceptibility to malaria in Papua New Guinea. Trans R Soc Trop Med Hyg. 1987;81:705-709.

178. Allen SJ, O'Donnell A, Alexander ND, et al. Prevention of cerebral malaria in children in Papua New Guinea by southeast Asian ovalocytosis band 3. Am J Trop Med Hyg. 1999;60:1056-1060.

179. Welch SG, McGregor IA, Williams K. The Duffy blood group and malaria prevalence in Gambian West Africans. Trans R Soc Trop Med Hyg. 1977;71:295-296.

180. Miller LH, Mason SJ, Clyde DF, McGinniss MH. The resistance factor to *Plasmodium vivax* in blacks. The Duffy-blood-group genotype, FyFy. N Engl J Med. 1976;295:302-304.

181. Zimmerman PA, Woolley I, Masinde GL, et al. Emergence of FY*Anull in a Plasmodium vivax-endemic region of Papua New Guinea. Proc Natl Acad Sci USA. 1999;96:13973-13977.

182. Baird JK, Krisin, Barcus MJ, et al. Onset of clinical immunity to *Plasmodium falciparum* among Javanese migrants to Indonesian Papua. Ann Trop Med Parasitol. 2003;97:557-564.

183. Wichmann O, Loscher T, Jelinek T. Fatal malaria in a German couple returning from Burkina Faso. Infection. 2003;31:260-262.

184. Deloron P, Chougnet C. Is immunity to malaria really short-lived? Parasitol Today. 1992;8:375-378.

185. Chotivanich K, Udomsangpetch R, McGready R, et al. Central role of the spleen in malaria parasite clearance. J Infect Dis. 2002;185:1538-1541.

186. Grobusch MP, Borrmann S, Omva J, et al. Severe malaria in a splenectomised Gabonese woman. Wien Klin Wochenschr. 2003;115:63-65.

187. Artavanis-Tsakonas K, Tongren JE, Riley EM. The war between the malaria parasite and the immune system: immunity, immunoregulation and immunopathology. Clin Exp Immunol. 2003;133:145-152.

188. Marsh K, Otoo L, Hayes RJ, Carson DC, Greenwood BM. Antibodies to blood stage antigens of *Plasmodium falciparum* in rural Gambians and their relation to protection against infection. Trans R Soc Trop Med Hyg. 1989;83:293-303.

189. Collins WE, Jeffery GM. A retrospective examination of sporozoite- and trophozoite-induced infections with *Plasmodium falciparum:* Development of parasitologic and clinical immunity during primary infection. Am J Trop Med Hyg. 1999;61(Suppl):4-19.

190. Collins WE, Jeffery GM. A retrospective examination of secondary sporozoite- and trophozoite-induced infections with *Plasmodium falciparum:* Development of parasitologic and clinical immunity following secondary infection. Am J Trop Med Hyg. 1999;61(Suppl):20-35.

191. Bull PC, Kortok M, Kai O, et al. *Plasmodium falciparum*-infected erythrocytes. Agglutination by diverse Kenyan plasma is associated with severe disease and young host age. J Infect Dis. 2000;182:252-259.

192. Ofori MF, Dodoo D, Staalsoe T, et al. Malaria-induced acquisition of antibodies to *Plasmodium falciparum* variant surface antigens. Infect Immun. 2002;70:2982-2988.

193. Tebo AE, Kremsner PG, Piper KP, Luty AJ. Low antibody responses to variant surface antigens of *Plasmodium falciparum* are associated with severe malaria and increased susceptibility to malaria attacks in Gabonese children. Am J Trop Med Hyg. 2002;67:597-603.

194. Bull PC, Lowe BS, Kortok M, et al. Parasite antigens on the infected red cell surface are targets for naturally acquired immunity to malaria. Nat Med 1998;4:358-360.

195. Win TT, Lin K, Mizuno S, et al. Wide distribution of Plasmodium ovale in Myanmar. Trop Med Int Health 2002;7:231-239.

196. Lysenko AJ, Beljaev AE. An analysis of the geographical distribution of Plasmodium ovale. Bull World Health Organ 1969;40:383-394.

197. Jordan S, Jelinek T, Aida AO, et al. Population structure of *Plasmodium falciparum* isolates during an epidemic in southern Mauritania. Trop Med Int Hlth. 2001;6:761-766.

198. Tuck JJ, Green AD, Roberts KI. A malaria outbreak following a British military deployment to Sierra Leone. J Infect. 2003;47:225-230.

199. Das P. Ethiopia faces severe malaria epidemic. WHO predicts 15 million people could be infected. Lancet. 2003;362:2071.

200. Baomar A, Mohamed A. Malaria outbreak in a malaria-free region in Oman 1998: Unknown impact of civil war in Africa. Publ Hlth. 2000;114:480-483.

201. Schlagenhauf P, Steffen R, Loutan L. Migrants as a major risk group for imported malaria in European countries. J Travel Med. 2003;10:106-107.

202. Dar FK, Bayoumi R, al Karmi T, et al. Status of imported malaria in a control zone of the United Arab Emirates bordering an area of unstable malaria. Trans R Soc Trop Med Hyg. 1993;87:617-619.

203. Paxton LA, Slutsker L, Schultz LJ, et al. Imported malaria in Montagnard refugees settling in North Carolina: Implications for prevention and control. Am J Trop Med Hyg. 1996;54:54-57.

204. Barber MA. The history of malaria in the United States. 44;2575-2587. 1929. Public Health Reports.

205. Local transmission of *Plasmodium vivax* malaria—Palm Beach County, Florida, 2003. MMWR Morb Mortal Wkly Rep. 2003;52:908-911.

206. Zucker JR. Changing patterns of autochthonous malaria transmission in the United States: A review of recent outbreaks. Emerg Infect Dis. 1996;2:37-43.

207. Thang HD, Elsas RM, Veenstra J. Airport malaria: Report of a case and a brief review of the literature. Neth J Med. 2002;60:441-443.

208. Lusina D, Legros F, Esteve V, et al. Airport malaria: Four new cases in suburban Paris during summer 1999. Euro Surveill. 2000;5:76-80.

209. Gratz NG, Steffen R, Cocksedge W. Why aircraft disinsection? Bull WHO. 2000;78:995-1004.

210. Mungai M, Tegtmeier G, Chamberland M, Parise M. Transfusion-transmitted malaria in the United States from 1963 through 1999. N Engl J Med. 2001;344:1973-1978.

211. Bruce-Chwatt LJ. Transfusion malaria revisited. Trop Dis Bull. 1982;79:827-840.

212. Chiche L, Lesage A, Duhamel C, et al. Posttransplant malaria: First case of transmission of *Plasmodium falciparum* from a white multiorgan donor to four recipients. Transplantation. 2003;75:166-168.

213. al Arishi HM, el Awad AF, al Bishi LA. Chloroquine-resistant *Plasmodium falciparum* malaria among children seen in a regional hospital, Tabuk, Saudi Arabia. Trans R Soc Trop Med Hyg. 2001;95:439-440.

214. Ghalib HW, Al Ghamdi S, Akood M, et al. Therapeutic efficacy of chloroquine against uncomplicated, *Plasmodium falciparum* malaria in south-western Saudi Arabia. Ann Trop Med Parasitol. 2001;95:773-779.

215. Jafari S, Le Bras J, Asmar M, Durand R. Molecular survey of *Plasmodium falciparum* resistance in south-eastern Iran. Ann Trop Med Parasitol. 2003;97:119-124.

216. Al Maktari MT, Bassiouny HK. Malaria status in Al-Hodeidah Governorate, Republic of Yemen. Part II: Human factors causing the persistence of chloroquine resistant P. falciparum local strain. J Egypt Soc Parasitol. 2003;33:829-839.

217. Bayoumi RA, Dar FK, Tanira MO, et al. Effect of previous chloroquine intake on in vivo P. falciparum drug sensitivity. East Afr Med J. 1997;74:278-282.

218. Sumawinata IW, Bernadeta, Leksana B, et al. Very high risk of therapeutic failure with chloroquine for uncomplicated *Plasmodium falciparum* and P. vivax malaria in Indonesian Papua. Am J Trop Med Hyg. 2003;68:416-420.

219. Murphy GS, Basri H, Purnomo, et al. Vivax malaria resistant to treatment and prophylaxis with chloroquine. Lancet. 1993;341:96-100.

220. Baird JK, Wiady I, Fryauff DJ, et al. In vivo resistance to chloroquine by *Plasmodium vivax* and *Plasmodium falciparum* at Nabire, Irian Jaya, Indonesia. Am J Trop Med Hyg. 1997;56:627-631.

221. Soto J, Toledo J, Gutierrez P, et al. *Plasmodium vivax* clinically resistant to chloroquine in Colombia. Am J Trop Med Hyg. 2001;65:90-93.

222. Garavelli PL, Corti E. Chloroquine resistance in *Plasmodium vivax:* The first case in Brazil. Trans R Soc Trop Med Hyg. 1992;86:128.

223. Ruebush TK, Zegarra J, Cairo J, et al. Chloroquine-resistant *Plasmodium vivax* malaria in Peru. Am J Trop Med Hyg. 2003;69:548-552.

224. Marlar T, Myat PK, Aye YS, et al. Development of resistance to chloroquine by *Plasmodium vivax* in Myanmar. Trans R Soc Trop Med Hyg. 1995;89:307-308.

225. Garg M, Gopinathan N, Bodhe P, Kshirsagar NA. Vivax malaria resistant to chloroquine: Case reports from Bombay. Trans R Soc Trop Med Hyg. 1995;89:656-657.

226. Barrett JP, Behrens RH. Prophylaxis failure against vivax malaria in Guyana, South America. J Travel Med. 1996;3:60-61.

227. Maguire JD, Sumawinata IW, Masbar S, et al. Chloroquine-resistant *Plasmodium malariae* in south Sumatra, Indonesia. Lancet. 2002;360:58-60.

228. Wongsrichanalai C, Sirichaisinthop J, Karwacki JJ, et al. Drug resistant malaria on the Thai-Myanmar and Thai-Cambodian borders. Southeast Asian J Trop Med Publ Hlth. 2001;32:41-49.

229. Giao PT, De Vries PJ, Hung LQ, et al. Atovaquone-proguanil for recrudescent *Plasmodium falciparum* in Vietnam. Ann Trop Med Parasitol. 2003;97:575-580.

230. Nosten F, ter Kuile F, Chongsuphajaisiddhi T, et al. Mefloquine-resistant falciparum malaria on the Thai-Burmese border. Lancet. 1991;337:1140-1143.

231. Chia JK, Nakata MM, Co S. Smear-negative cerebral malaria due to mefloquine-resistant *Plasmodium falciparum* acquired in the Amazon. J Infect Dis. 1992;165:599-600.

232. Maguire JD, Lacy MD, Sururi, et al. Chloroquine or sulfadoxine-pyrimethamine for the treatment of uncomplicated, *Plasmodium falciparum* malaria during an epidemic in Central Java, Indonesia. Ann Trop Med Parasitol. 2002;96:655-668.

233. Mayxay M, Newton PN, Khanthavong M, et al. Chloroquine versus sulfadoxine-pyrimethamine for treatment of *Plasmodium falciparum* malaria in Savannakhet Province, Lao People's Democratic Republic: an assessment of national antimalarial drug recommendations. Clin Infect Dis. 2003;37:1021-1028.

234. Hurwitz ES, Johnson D, Campbell CC. Resistance of *Plasmodium falciparum* malaria to sulfadoxine-pyrimethamine 'Fansidar' in a refugee camp in Thailand. Lancet. 1981;1:1068-1070.

235. Aramburu GJ, Ramal AC, Witzig R. Malaria reemergence in the Peruvian Amazon region. Emerg Infect Dis. 1999;5:209-215.

236. Vasconcelos KF, Plowe CV, Fontes CJ, et al. Mutations in *Plasmodium falciparum* dihydrofolate reductase and dihydropteroate synthase of isolates from the Amazon region of Brazil. Mem Inst Oswaldo Cruz. 2000;95:721-728.

237. Deloron P, Mayombo J, Le Cardinal A, et al. Sulfadoxine-pyrimethamine for the treatment of *Plasmodium falciparum* malaria in Gabonese children. Trans R Soc Trop Med Hyg. 2000;94:188-190.

238. Bijl HM, Kager J, Koetsier DW, van der Werf TS. Chloroquine- and sulfadoxine-pyrimethamine-resistant Falciparum malaria in vivo—a pilot study in rural Zambia. Trop Med Int Hlth. 2000;5:692-695.

239. Gasasira AF, Dorsey G, Nzarubara B, et al. Comparative efficacy of aminoquinoline-antifolate combinations for the treatment of uncomplicated falciparum malaria in Kampala, Uganda. Am J Trop Med Hyg. 2003;68:127-132.

240. Landgraf B, Kollaritsch H, Wiedermann G, Wernsdorfer WH. *Plasmodium falciparum:* Susceptibility in vitro and in vivo to chloroquine and sulfadoxine-pyrimethamine in Ghanaian schoolchildren. Trans R Soc Trop Med Hyg. 1994;88:440-442.

241. Pukrittayakamee S, Supanaranond W, Looareesuwan S, et al. Quinine in severe falciparum malaria: Evidence of declining efficacy in Thailand. Trans R Soc Trop Med Hyg. 1994;88:324-327.

242. Jelinek T, Schelbert P, Loscher T, Eichenlaub D. Quinine resistant falciparum malaria acquired in east Africa. Trop Med Parasitol. 1995;46:38-40.

243. Segurado AA, di Santi SM, Shiroma M. In vivo and in vitro *Plasmodium falciparum* resistance to chloroquine, amodiaquine and quinine in the Brazilian Amazon. Rev Inst Med Trop Sao Paulo. 1997;39:85-90.

244. Chou AC, Chevli R, Fitch CD. Ferriprotoporphyrin IX fulfills the criteria for identification as the chloroquine receptor of malaria parasites. Biochemistry. 1980;19:1543-1549.

245. Verdier F, Le Bras J, Clavier F, et al. Chloroquine uptake by *Plasmodium falciparum*-infected human erythrocytes during in vitro culture and its relationship to chloroquine resistance. Antimicrob Agents Chemother. 1985;27:561-564.

246. Fidock DA, Nomura T, Talley AK, et al. Mutations in the *P. falciparum* digestive vacuole transmembrane protein PfCRT and evidence for their role in chloroquine resistance. Mol Cell. 2000;6:861-871.

247. Cooper RA, Ferdig MT, Su XZ, et al. Alternative mutations at position 76 of the vacuolar transmembrane protein PfCRT are associated with chloroquine resistance and unique stereospecific quinine and quinidine responses in *Plasmodium falciparum*. Mol Pharmacol. 2002;61:35-42.

248. Sidhu AB, Verdier-Pinard D, Fidock DA. Chloroquine resistance in *Plasmodium falciparum* malaria parasites conferred by pfcrt mutations. Science. 2002;298:210-213.

249. Wootton JC, Feng X, Ferdig MT, et al. Genetic diversity and chloroquine selective sweeps in *Plasmodium falciparum*. Nature. 2002;418:320-323.

250. Nagesha HS, Casey GJ, Rieckmann KH, et al. New haplotypes of the *Plasmodium falciparum* chloroquine resistance transporter pfcrt gene among chloroquine-resistant parasite isolates. Am J Trop Med Hyg. 2003;68:398-402.

251. Chen N, Kyle DE, Pasay C, et al. pfcrt Allelic types with two novel amino acid mutations in chloroquine-resistant *Plasmodium falciparum* isolates from the Philippines. Antimicrob Agents Chemother. 2003;47:3500-3505.

252. May J, Meyer CG. Association of *Plasmodium falciparum* chloroquine resistance transporter variant T76 with age-related plasma chloroquine levels. Am J Trop Med Hyg. 2003;68:143-146.

253. Djimde A, Doumbo OK, Cortese JF, et al. A molecular marker for chloroquine-resistant falciparum malaria. N Engl J Med. 2001;344:257-263.

254. Sanchez CP, Stein W, Lanzer M. Trans stimulation provides evidence for a drug efflux carrier as the mechanism of chloroquine resistance in *Plasmodium falciparum*. Biochemistry. 2003;42:9383-9394.

255. Krogstad DJ, Gluzman IY, Herwaldt BL, et al. Energy dependence of chloroquine accumulation and chloroquine efflux in *Plasmodium falciparum*. Biochem Pharmacol. 1992;43:57-62.

256. Djimde AA, Doumbo OK, Traore O, et al. Clearance of drug-resistant parasites as a model for protective immunity in *Plasmodium falciparum* malaria. Am J Trop Med Hyg. 2003;69:558-563.

257. Reed MB, Saliba KJ, Caruana SR, et al. Pgh1 modulates sensitivity and resistance to multiple antimalarials in *Plasmodium falciparum*. Nature. 2000;403:906-909.

258. Mu J, Ferdig MT, Feng X, et al. Multiple transporters associated with malaria parasite responses to chloroquine and quinine. Mol Microbiol. 2003;49:977-989.

259. Peterson DS, Walliker D, Wellems TE. Evidence that a point mutation in dihydrofolate reductase-thymidylate synthase confers resistance to pyrimethamine in falciparum malaria. Proc Natl Acad Sci USA. 1988;85:9114-9118.

260. Cowman AF, Morry MJ, Biggs BA, et al. Amino acid changes linked to pyrimethamine resistance in the dihydrofolate reductase-thymidylate synthase gene of Plasmodium falciparum. Proc Natl Acad Sci USA. 1988;85:9109-9113.

261. Wang P, Read M, Sims PF, Hyde JE. Sulfadoxine resistance in the human malaria parasite Plasmodium falciparum is determined by mutations in dihydropteroate synthetase and an additional factor associated with folate utilization. Mol Microbiol. 1997;23:979-986.

262. Triglia T, Menting JG, Wilson C, Cowman AF. Mutations in dihydropteroate synthase are responsible for sulfone and sulfonamide resistance in Plasmodium falciparum. Proc Natl Acad Sci USA 1997;94:13944-13949.

263. Plowe CV, Cortese JF, Djimde A, et al. Mutations in Plasmodium falciparum dihydrofolate reductase and dihydropteroate synthase and epidemiologic patterns of pyrimethamine-sulfadoxine use and resistance. J Infect Dis. 1997 Dec;176:1590-6.

264. Srivastava IK, Morrisey JM, Darrouzet E, Daldal F, Vaidya AB. Resistance mutations reveal the atovaquone-binding domain of cytochrome b in malaria parasites. Mol Microbiol. 1999;33:704-711.

265. Srivastava IK, Rottenberg H, Vaidya AB. Atovaquone, a broad spectrum antiparasitic drug, collapses mitochondrial membrane potential in a malarial parasite. J Biol Chem. 1997;272:3961-3966.

266. Srivastava IK, Vaidya AB. A mechanism for the synergistic antimalarial action of atovaquone and proguanil. Antimicrob Agents Chemother. 1999;43:1334-1339.

267. Fidock DA, Nomura T, Wellems TE. Cycloguanil and its parent compound proguanil demonstrate distinct activities against *Plasmodium falciparum* malaria parasites transformed with human dihydrofolate reductase. Mol Pharmacol. 1998;54:1140-1147.

268. Fivelman QL, Butcher GA, Adagu IS, et al. Malarone treatment failure and in vitro confirmation of resistance of *Plasmodium falciparum* isolate from Lagos, Nigeria. Malar J. 2002;1:1.

269. Schwobel B, Alifrangis M, Salanti A, Jelinek T. Different mutation patterns of atovaquone resistance to *Plasmodium falciparum* in vitro and in vivo: Rapid detection of codon 268 polymorphisms in the cytochrome b as potential in vivo resistance marker. Malar J. 2003;2:5.

270. Schwartz E, Bujanover S, Kain KC. Genetic confirmation of atovaquone-proguanil-resistant *Plasmodium falciparum* malaria acquired by a nonimmune traveler to East Africa. Clin Infect Dis. 2003;37:450-451.

271. David KP, Alifrangis M, Salanti A, et al. Atovaquone/proguanil resistance in Africa: A case report. Scand J Infect Dis. 2003;35:897-898.

272. Basco LK, Ringwald P. Molecular epidemiology of malaria in Yaounde, Cameroon. VI. Sequence variations in the *Plasmodium falciparum* dihydrofolate reductase-thymidylate synthase gene and in vitro resistance to pyrimethamine and cycloguanil. Am J Trop Med Hyg. 2000;62:271-276.

273. Basco LK. Molecular epidemiology of malaria in Cameroon. XII. In vitro drug assays and molecular surveillance of chloroquine and proguanil resistance. Am J Trop Med Hyg. 2002;67:383-387.

274. Pickard AL, Wongsrichanalai C, Purfield A, et al. Resistance to antimalarials in Southeast Asia and genetic polymorphisms in pfmdr1. Antimicrob Agents Chemother. 2003;47:2418-2423.

275. Basco LK, Le Bras J. In vitro activity of halofantrine and its relationship to other standard antimalarial drugs against African isolates and clones of *Plasmodium falciparum*. Am J Trop Med Hyg. 1992;47:521-527.

276. Brasseur P, Kouamouo J, Moyou-Somo R, Druilhe P. Multi-drug resistant falciparum malaria in Cameroon in 1987-1988. II. Mefloquine resistance confirmed in vivo and in vitro and its correlation with quinine resistance. Am J Trop Med Hyg. 1992;46:8-14.

277. Warsame M, Wernsdorfer WH, Payne D, Bjorkman A. Susceptibility of *Plasmodium falciparum* in vitro to chloroquine, mefloquine, quinine and sulfadoxine/pyrimethamine in Somalia: relationships between the responses to the different drugs. Trans R Soc Trop Med Hyg. 1991;85:565-569.

278. Cowman AF, Galatis D, Thompson JK. Selection for mefloquine resistance in *Plasmodium falciparum* is linked to amplification of the pfmdr1 gene and cross-resistance to halofantrine and quinine. Proc Natl Acad Sci USA. 1994;91:1143-1147.

279. Ferdig MT, Cooper RA, Mu J, et al. Dissecting the loci of low level quinine resistance in malaria parasites. Mol Microbiol 2004;52:985-997.

280. Schwartz E, Parise M, Kozarsky P, Cetron M. Delayed onset of malaria—implications for chemoprophylaxis in travelers. N Engl J Med. 2003;34916:1510-15.

281. Chadee DD, Tilluckdharry CC, Maharaj P, Sinanan C. Reactivation of *Plasmodium malariae* infection in a Trinidadian man after neurosurgery. N Engl J Med. 2000;342:1924.

282. Tsuchida H, Yamaguchi K, Yamamoto S, Ebisawa I. Quartan malaria following splenectomy 36 years after infection. Am J Trop Med Hyg. 1982;31:163-165.

283. Kockaerts Y, Vanhees S, Knockaert DC, et al. Imported malaria in the 1990s: a review of 101 patients. Eur J Emerg Med. 2001;8:287-290.

284. Jelinek T, Nothdurft HD, Loscher T. Malaria in nonimmune travelers: A synopsis of history, symptoms, and treatment in 160 patients. J Travel Med. 1994;1:199-202.

285. Hu KK, Maung C, Katz DL. Clinical diagnosis of malaria on the Thai-Myanmar border. Yale J Biol Med. 2001;74:303-308.

286. Casalino E, Le Bras J, Chaussin F, et al. Predictive factors of malaria in travelers to areas where malaria is endemic. Arch Intern Med. 2002;162:1625-1630.

287. van der HW, Premasiri DA, Wickremasinghe AR. Clinical diagnosis of uncomplicated malaria in Sri Lanka. Southeast Asian J Trop Med Publ Hlth. 1998;29:242-245.

288. Hamel CT, Blum J, Harder F, Kocher T. Nonoperative treatment of splenic rupture in malaria tropica: review of literature and case report. Acta Trop. 2002;82:1-5.

289. Davies GR, Venkatesan P. Successful conservative management of splenic rupture in vivax malaria. Trans R Soc Trop Med Hyg. 2002;96:149-150.

290. Milne LM, Kyi MS, Chiodini PL, Warhurst DC. Accuracy of routine laboratory diagnosis of malaria in the United Kingdom. J Clin Pathol. 1994;47:740-742.

291. Nguyen PH, Day N, Pram TD, et al. Intraleucocytic malaria pigment and prognosis in severe malaria. Trans R Soc Trop Med Hyg. 1995;89:200-204.

292. Gutman JD, Kotton CN, Kratz A. Case records of the Massachusetts General Hospital. Weekly clinicopathological exercises. Case 29-2003. A 60-year-old man with fever, rigors, and sweats. N Engl J Med. 2003;349:1168-1175.

293. Jelinek T, Grobusch MP, Nothdurft HD. Use of dipstick tests for the rapid diagnosis of malaria in nonimmune travelers. J Travel Med. 2000;7:175-179.

294. Moody A. Rapid diagnostic tests for malaria parasites. Clin Microbiol Rev. 2002;15:66-78.

295. Craig MH, Sharp BL. Comparative evaluation of four techniques for the diagnosis of *Plasmodium falciparum* infections. Trans R Soc Trop Med Hyg. 1997;91:279-282.

296. Wongsrichanalai C, Chuanak N, Tulyayon S, et al. Comparison of a rapid field immunochromatographic test to expert microscopy for the detection of *Plasmodium falciparum* asexual parasitemia in Thailand. Acta Trop. 1999;73:263-273.

297. Humar A, Ohrt C, Harrington MA, et al. Parasight F test compared with the polymerase chain reaction and microscopy for the diagnosis of *Plasmodium falciparum* malaria in travelers. Am J Trop Med Hyg. 1997;56:44-48.

298. Palmer CJ, Lindo JF, Klaskala WI, et al. Evaluation of the OptiMAL test for rapid diagnosis of Plasmodium vivax and *Plasmodium falciparum* malaria. J Clin Microbiol. 1998;36:203-206.

299. Pieroni P, Mills CD, Ohrt C, et al. Comparison of the ParaSight-F test and the ICT Malaria Pf test with the polymerase chain reaction for the diagnosis of *Plasmodium falciparum* malaria in travelers. Trans R Soc Trop Med Hyg. 1998;92:166-169.

300. Beadle C, Long GW, Weiss WR, et al. Diagnosis of malaria by detection of *Plasmodium falciparum* HRP-2 antigen with a rapid dipstick antigen-capture assay. Lancet. 1994;343:564-568.
301. Filler S, Causer LM, Newman RD, et al. Malaria surveillance—United States, 2001. MMWR Surveill Summ. 2003;52:1-14.
302. Laferi H, Kandel K, Pichler H. False positive dipstick test for malaria. N Engl J Med. 1997;337:1635-1636.
303. Singh N, Valecha N, Sharma VP. Malaria diagnosis by field workers using an immunochromatographic test. Trans R Soc Trop Med Hyg. 1997;91:396-397.
304. Makler MT, Hinrichs DJ. Measurement of the lactate dehydrogenase activity of *Plasmodium falciparum* as an assessment of parasitemia. Am J Trop Med Hyg. 1993;48:205-210.
305. Grobusch MP, Hanscheid T, Zoller T, et al. Rapid immunochromatographic malarial antigen detection unreliable for detecting *Plasmodium malariae* and *Plasmodium ovale*. Eur J Clin Microbiol Infect Dis. 2002;21:818-820.
306. Ladhani S, Lowe B, Cole AO, et al. Changes in white blood cells and platelets in children with falciparum malaria: Relationship to disease outcome. Br J Haematol. 2002;119:839-847.
307. Alfandari S, Santre C, Chidiac C, et al. Imported malaria: Presentation and outcome of 111 cases. Clin Microbiol Infect. 1996;2:86-90.
308. Looareesuwan S, Davis JG, Allen DL, et al. Thrombocytopenia in malaria. Southeast Asian J Trop Med Publ Hlth. 1992;23:44-50.
309. Oh MD, Shin H, Shin D, et al. Clinical features of vivax malaria. Am J Trop Med Hyg. 2001;65:143-146.
310. Ustianowski A, Schwab U, Pasvol G. Case report: Severe acute symptomatic hyponatraemia in falciparum malaria. Trans R Soc Trop Med Hyg. 2002;96:647-648.
311. Eiam-Ong S. Malarial nephropathy. Semin Nephrol. 2003;23:21-33.
312. Berkley J, Mwarumba S, Bramham K, et al. Bacteraemia complicating severe malaria in children. Trans R Soc Trop Med Hyg. 1999;93:283-286.
313. Graham SM, Walsh AL, Molyneux EM, et al. Clinical presentation of non-typhoidal Salmonella bacteraemia in Malawian children. Trans R Soc Trop Med Hyg. 2000;94:310-314.
314. Severe falciparum malaria. World Health Organization, Communicable Diseases Cluster. Trans R Soc Trop Med Hyg. 2000;94(Suppl 1):S1-S90.
315. Bruneel F, Hocqueloux L, Alberti C, et al. The clinical spectrum of severe imported falciparum malaria in the intensive care unit: report of 188 cases in adults. Am J Respir Crit Care Med. 2003;167:684-689.
316. Newton CR, Chokwe T, Schellenberg JA, et al. Coma scales for children with severe falciparum malaria. Trans R Soc Trop Med Hyg. 1997;91:161-165.
317. Crawley J, Smith S, Kirkham F, et al. Seizures and status epilepticus in childhood cerebral malaria. Q J Med. 1996;89:591 597.
318. Muntendam AH, Jaffar S, Bleichrodt N, van Hensbroek MB. Absence of neuropsychological sequelae following cerebral malaria in Gambian children. Trans R Soc Trop Med Hyg. 1996;90:391-394.
319. Boivin MJ. Effects of early cerebral malaria on cognitive ability in Senegalese children. J Dev Behav Pediatr. 2002;23:353-364.
320. Carter JA, Neville BG, Newton CR. Neuro-cognitive impairment following acquired central nervous system infections in childhood: A systematic review. Brain Res Brain Res Rev. 2003;43:57-69.
321. Steele RW, Baffoe-Bonnie B. Cerebral malaria in children. Pediatr Infect Dis J. 1995;14:281-285.
322. van Hensbroek MB, Onyiorah E, Jaffar S, et al. A trial of artemether or quinine in children with cerebral malaria. N Engl J Med. 1996;335:69-75.
323. Bajiya HN, Kochar DK. Incidence and pattern of neurological sequelae in survivors of cerebral malaria. J Assoc Phys India. 1996;44:679-681.
324. D'Acremont V, Landry P, Darioli R, et al. Treatment of imported malaria in an ambulatory setting: prospective study. Br Med J. 2002;324:875-877.
325. Moore TA, Tomayko JF Jr, Wierman AM, et al. Imported malaria in the 1990s. A report of 59 cases from Houston, Tex. Arch Fam Med. 1994;3:130-136.
326. Humar A, Sharma S, Zoutman D, Kain KC. Fatal falciparum malaria in Canadian travellers. CMAJ 1997;156:1165-1167.
327. Kain KC, Harrington MA, Tennyson S, Keystone JS. Imported malaria: Prospective analysis of problems in diagnosis and management. Clin Infect Dis. 1998;27:142-149.
328. Loutan L. Malaria: still a threat to travellers. Int J Antimicrob Agents. 2003;21:158-163.
329. Osler W. The study of fevers in the South. JAMA. 1896;26:999-1004.
330. Moore DA, Jennings RM, Doherty TF, et al. Assessing the severity of malaria. Br Med J. 2003;326:808-809.
331. Hammerich A, Campbell OM, Chandramohan D. Unstable malaria transmission and maternal mortality—experiences from Rwanda. Trop Med Int Hlth. 2002;7:573-576.
332. Muhlberger N, Jelinek T, Behrens RH, et al. Age as a risk factor for severe manifestations and fatal outcome of falciparum malaria in European patients: Observations from TropNetEurop and SIMPID Surveillance Data. Clin Infect Dis. 2003;36:990-995.
333. Luxemburger C, Ricci F, Nosten F, et al. The epidemiology of severe malaria in an area of low transmission in Thailand. Trans R Soc Trop Med Hyg. 1997;91:256-262.
334. Greenberg AE, Lobel HO. Mortality from *Plasmodium falciparum* malaria in travelers from the United States, 1959 to 1987. Ann Intern Med. 1990;113:326-327.
335. Driessen GJ, van Kerkhoven S, Schouwenberg BJ, et al. Sulphadoxine/pyrimethamine: An appropriate first-line alternative for the treatment of uncomplicated falciparum malaria in Ghanaian children under 5 years of age. Trop Med Int Hlth. 2002;7:577-583.
336. McGready R, Thwai KL, Cho T, et al. The effects of quinine and chloroquine antimalarial treatments in the first trimester of pregnancy. Trans R Soc Trop Med Hyg. 2002;96:180-184.
337. Brasseur P, Guiguemde R, Diallo S, et al. Amodiaquine remains effective for treating uncomplicated malaria in west and central Africa. Trans R Soc Trop Med Hyg. 1999;93:645-650.
338. Olliaro P, Mussano P. Amodiaquine for treating malaria. Cochrane Database Syst Rev. 2003,2:CD000016.
339. Ndounga M, Basco LK. Rapid clearance of *Plasmodium falciparum* hyperparasitaemia after oral amodiaquine treatment in patients with uncomplicated malaria. Acta Trop. 2003;88:27-32.
340. Olliaro P, Nevill C, LeBras J, et al. Systematic review of amodiaquine treatment in uncomplicated malaria. Lancet. 1996;348:1196-1201.
341. Phillips-Howard PA, West LJ. Serious adverse drug reactions to pyrimethamine-sulphadoxine, pyrimethamine-dapsone and to amodiaquine in Britain. J R Soc Med. 1990;83:82-85.
342. Hatton CS, Peto TE, Bunch C, et al. Frequency of severe neutropenia associated with amodiaquine prophylaxis against malaria. Lancet. 1986;1:411-414.
343. Bjorkman A, Phillips-Howard PA. Adverse reactions to sulfa drugs: Implications for malaria chemotherapy. Bull WHO. 1991;69:297-304.
344. Fairhurst RM, Sadou B, Guindo A, et al. Life-threatening hypoglycaemia associated with sulfadoxine-pyrimethamine, a commonly used antimalarial drug. Trans R Soc Trop Med Hyg. 2004;in press.
345. Looareesuwan S, Wilairatana P, Chalermarut K, et al. Efficacy and safety of atovaquone/proguanil compared with mefloquine for treatment of acute *Plasmodium falciparum* malaria in Thailand. Am J Trop Med Hyg. 1999;60:526-532.
346. Marquino W, Huilca M, Calampa C, et al. Efficacy of mefloquine and a mefloquine-artesunate combination therapy for the treatment of uncomplicated *Plasmodium falciparum* malaria in the Amazon Basin of Peru. Am J Trop Med Hyg. 2003;68:608-612.
347. McGready R, Cho T, Samuel, et al. Randomized comparison of quinine-clindamycin versus artesunate in the treatment of falciparum malaria in pregnancy. Trans R Soc Trop Med Hyg. 2001;95:651-656.
348. Fungladda W, Honrado ER, Thimasarn K, et al. Compliance with artesunate and quinine + tetracycline treatment of uncomplicated falciparum malaria in Thailand. Bull WHO 1998;76(Suppl 1):59-66.
349. Pukrittayakamee S, Chantra A, Vanijanonta S, et al. Therapeutic responses to quinine and clindamycin in multidrug-resistant falciparum malaria. Antimicrob Agents Chemother. 2000;44:2395-2398.
350. Lell B, Kremsner PG. Clindamycin as an antimalarial drug: review of clinical trials. Antimicrob Agents Chemother. 2002;46:2315-2320.
351. van Vugt M, Leonardi E, Phaipun L, et al. Treatment of uncomplicated multidrug-resistant falciparum malaria with artesunate-atovaquone-proguanil. Clin Infect Dis. 2002;35:1498-1504.
352. de Alencar FE, Cerutti C Jr, Durlacher RR, et al. Atovaquone and proguanil for the treatment of malaria in Brazil. J Infect Dis. 1997;175:1544-1547.
353. Emberger M, Lechner AM, Zelger B. Stevens-Johnson syndrome associated with Malarone antimalarial prophylaxis. Clin Infect Dis. 2003;37:e5-e7.
354. Farnert A, Lindberg J, Gil P, et al. Evidence of *Plasmodium falciparum* malaria resistant to atovaquone and proguanil hydrochloride: Case reports. Br Med J. 2003;326:628-629.
355. White NJ. The assessment of antimalarial drug efficacy. Trends Parasitol. 2002;18:458-464.
356. Adjuik M, Babiker A, Garner P, et al. Artesunate combinations for treatment of malaria: Meta-analysis. Lancet. 2004;363:9-17.
357. Nothdurft HD, Jelinek T, Pechel SM, et al. Stand-by treatment of suspected malaria in travellers. Trop Med Parasitol. 1995;46:161-163.
358. Malaria in travelers returning from Kenya: Failure of self-treatment with pyrimethamine/sulfadoxine. MMWR Morb Mortal Wkly Rep. 1989;38:363-364.
359. Rozendaal J. Fake antimalaria drugs in Cambodia. Lancet. 2001;357:890.
360. Binka FN, Morris SS, Ross DA, et al. Patterns of malaria morbidity and mortality in children in northern Ghana. Trans R Soc Trop Med Hyg. 1994;88:381-385.
361. Kitua AY, Smith T, Alonso PL, et al. *Plasmodium falciparum* malaria in the first year of life in an area of intense and perennial transmission. Trop Med Int Hlth. 1996;1:475-484.
362. Cornet M, Le Hesran JY, Fievet N, et al. Prevalence of and risk factors for anemia in young children in southern Cameroon. Am J Trop Med Hyg. 1998;58:606-611.
363. Lemnge MM, Msangeni HA, Ronn AM, et al. Maloprim malaria prophylaxis in children living in a holoendemic village in north-eastern Tanzania. Trans R Soc Trop Med Hyg. 1997;91:68-73.
364. Menendez C, Kahigwa E, Hirt R, et al. Randomised placebo-controlled trial of iron supplementation and malaria chemoprophylaxis for prevention of severe anaemia and malaria in Tanzanian infants. Lancet. 1997;350:844-850.
365. Schellenberg D, Menendez C, Kahigwa E, et al. Intermittent treatment for malaria and anaemia control at time of routine vaccinations in Tanzanian infants: A randomised, placebo-controlled trial. Lancet. 2001;357:1471-1477.
366. Massaga JJ, Kitua AY, Lemnge MM, et al. Effect of intermittent treatment with amodiaquine on anaemia and malarial fevers in infants in Tanzania: A randomised placebo-controlled trial. Lancet. 2003;361:1853-1860.
367. Shulman CE, Dorman EK, Cutts F, et al. Intermittent sulphadoxine-pyrimethamine to prevent severe anaemia secondary to malaria in pregnancy: A randomised placebo-controlled trial. Lancet. 1999;353:632-636.
368. English M, Waruiru C, Marsh K. Transfusion for respiratory distress in life-threatening childhood malaria. Am J Trop Med Hyg. 1996;55:525-530.
369. Availability and use of parenteral quinidine gluconate for severe or complicated malaria. MMWR Morb Mortal Wkly Rep. 2000;49:1138-1140.
370. Treatment of severe *Plasmodium falciparum* malaria with quinidine gluconate: Discontinuation of parenteral quinine from CDC drug service. MMWR Morb Mortal Wkly Rep. 1991;40:240.

371. Bhavnani SM, Preston SL. Monitoring of intravenous quinidine infusion in the treatment of *Plasmodium falciparum* malaria. Ann Pharmacother. 1995;29:33-35.

372. Rego SJ, Subba Rao SD, Hejmadi A, Rekha S. Partial exchange transfusion as an adjunct to the treatment of severe falciparum malaria in children. J Trop Pediatr. 2001;47:118-119.

373. Looareesuwan S, Phillips RE, Karbwang J, et al. *Plasmodium falciparum* hyperparasitaemia: Use of exchange transfusion in seven patients and a review of the literature. Q J Med. 1990;75:471-481.

374. Miller KD, Greenberg AE, Campbell CC. Treatment of severe malaria in the United States with a continuous infusion of quinidine gluconate and exchange transfusion. N Engl J Med. 1989;321:65-70.

375. Burchard GD, Kroger J, Knobloch J, et al. Exchange blood transfusion in severe falciparum malaria: Retrospective evaluation of 61 patients treated with, compared to 63 patients treated without, exchange transfusion. Trop Med Int Hlth. 1997;2:733-740.

376. Hoontrakoon S, Suputtamongkol Y. Exchange transfusion as an adjunct to the treatment of severe falciparum malaria. Trop Med Int Hlth. 1998;3:156-161.

377. Riddle MS, Jackson JL, Sanders JW, Blazes DL. Exchange transfusion as an adjunct therapy in severe *Plasmodium falciparum* malaria: A meta-analysis. Clin Infect Dis. 2002;34:1192-1198.

378. van Agtmael MA, Eggelte TA, van Boxtel CJ. Artemisinin drugs in the treatment of malaria: From medicinal herb to registered medication. Trends Pharmacol Sci. 1999;20:199-205.

379. McGready R, Brockman A, Cho T, et al. Randomized comparison of mefloquine-artesunate versus quinine in the treatment of multidrug-resistant falciparum malaria in pregnancy. Trans R Soc Trop Med Hyg. 2000;94:689-693.

380. McGready R, Cho T, Keo NK, et al. Artemisinin antimalarials in pregnancy: A prospective treatment study of 539 episodes of multidrug-resistant *Plasmodium falciparum*. Clin Infect Dis. 2001;33:2009-2016.

381. Arnold K, Tran TH, Nguyen TC, et al. A randomized comparative study of artemisinine qinghaosu suppositories and oral quinine in acute falciparum malaria. Trans R Soc Trop Med Hyg. 1990;84:499-502.

382. Price R, van Vugt M, Phaipun L, et al. Adverse effects in patients with acute falciparum malaria treated with artemisinin derivatives. Am J Trop Med Hyg. 1999;60:547-555.

383. Hien TT, Turner GD, Mai NT, et al. Neuropathological assessment of artemether-treated severe malaria. Lancet. 2003;362:295-296.

384. McIntosh HM, Olliaro P. Artemisinin derivatives for treating severe malaria. Cochrane Database Syst Rev. 2000;2:CD000527.

385. Hien TT, Arnold K, Vinh H, et al. Comparison of artemisinin suppositories with intravenous artesunate and intravenous quinine in the treatment of cerebral malaria. Trans R Soc Trop Med Hyg. 1992;86:582-583.

386. Gogtay NJ, Desai S, Kamtekar KD, et al. Efficacies of 5- and 14-day primaquine regimens in the prevention of relapses in *Plasmodium vivax* infections. Ann Trop Med Parasitol. 1999;93:809-812.

387. Rowland M, Durrani N. Randomized controlled trials of 5- and 14-days primaquine therapy against relapses of vivax malaria in an Afghan refugee settlement in Pakistan. Trans R Soc Trop Med Hyg. 1999;93:641-643.

388. Buchachart K, Krudsood S, Singhasivanon P, et al. Effect of primaquine standard dose 15 mg/day for 14 days in the treatment of vivax malaria patients in Thailand. Southeast Asian J Trop Med Publ Hlth. 2001;32:720-726.

389. Wilairatana P, Silachamroon U, Krudsood S, et al. Efficacy of primaquine regimens for primaquine-resistant *Plasmodium vivax* malaria in Thailand. Am J Trop Med Hyg. 1999;61:973-977.

390. Bunnag D, Karbwang J, Thanavibul A, et al. High dose of primaquine in primaquine resistant vivax malaria. Trans R Soc Trop Med Hyg. 1994;88:218-219.

391. Collins WE, Jeffery GM. Primaquine resistance in *Plasmodium vivax*. Am J Trop Med Hyg. 1996;55:243-249.

392. Buchachart K, Krudsood S, Singhasivanon P, et al. Effect of primaquine standard dose 15 mg/day for 14 days in the treatment of vivax malaria patients in Thailand. Southeast Asian J Trop Med Publ Hlth. 2001;32:720-726.

393. Shanks GD, Kain KC, Keystone JS. Malaria chemoprophylaxis in the age of drug resistance. II. Drugs that may be available in the future. Clin Infect Dis. 2001;33:381-385.

394. Nasveld P, Kitchener S, Edstein M, Rieckmann K. Comparison of tafenoquine WR238605 and primaquine in the post-exposure (terminal) prophylaxis of vivax malaria in Australian Defence Force personnel. Trans R Soc Trop Med Hyg. 2002;96:683-684.

395. Baird JK, Fryauff DJ, Hoffman SL. Primaquine for prevention of malaria in travelers. Clin Infect Dis. 2003;37:1659-1667.

396. Moore DA, Grant AD, Armstrong M, et al. Risk factors for malaria in UK travellers. Trans R Soc Trop Med Hyg. 2004;98:55-63.

397. Malaria deaths following inappropriate malaria chemoprophylaxis—United States, 2001. MMWR Morb Mortal Wkly Rep 2001;50:597-599.

398. Muehlberger N, Jelinek T, Schlipkoeter U, et al. Effectiveness of chemoprophylaxis and other determinants of malaria in travellers to Kenya. Trop Med Int Hlth. 1998;3:357-363.

399. Lobel HO, Baker MA, Gras FA, et al. Use of malaria prevention measures by North American and European travelers to East Africa. J Travel Med. 2001;8:167-172.

400. Cot M, Roisin A, Barro D, et al. Effect of chloroquine chemoprophylaxis during pregnancy on birth weight: results of a randomized trial. Am J Trop Med Hyg. 1992;46:21-27.

401. Ohrt C, Richie TL, Widjaja H, et al. Mefloquine compared with doxycycline for the prophylaxis of malaria in Indonesian soldiers. A randomized, double-blind, placebo-controlled trial. Ann Intern Med. 1997;126:963-972.

402. Weinke T, Trautmann M, Held T, et al. Neuropsychiatric side effects after the use of mefloquine. Am J Trop Med Hyg. 1991;45:86-91.

403. Boudreau E, Schuster B, Sanchez J, et al. Tolerability of prophylactic Lariam regimens. Trop Med Parasitol. 1993;44:257-265.

404. Croft AM, Garner P. Mefloquine for preventing malaria in nonimmune adult travellers. Cochrane Database Syst Rev. 2000;4:CD000138.

405. Nosten F, ter Kuile F, Maelankiri L, et al. Mefloquine prophylaxis prevents malaria during pregnancy: A double-blind, placebo-controlled study. J Infect Dis. 1994;169:595-603.

406. Smoak BL, Writer JV, Keep LW, et al. The effects of inadvertent exposure of mefloquine chemoprophylaxis on pregnancy outcomes and infants of US Army servicewomen. J Infect Dis. 1997;176:831-833.

407. Vanhauwere B, Maradit H, Kerr L. Post-marketing surveillance of prophylactic mefloquine Lariam use in pregnancy. Am J Trop Med Hyg. 1998;58:17-21.

408. Phillips-Howard PA, Steffen R, Kerr L, et al. Safety of mefloquine and other antimalarial agents in the first trimester of pregnancy. J Travel Med. 1998;5:121-126.

409. Taylor WR, Richie TL, Fryauff DJ, et al. Malaria prophylaxis using azithromycin: A double-blind, placebo-controlled trial in Irian Jaya, Indonesia. Clin Infect Dis. 1999;28:74-81.

410. Sukwa TY, Mulenga M, Chisdaka N, et al. A randomized, double-blind, placebo-controlled field trial to determine the efficacy and safety of Malarone (atovaquone/proguanil) for the prophylaxis of malaria in Zambia. Am J Trop Med Hyg. 1999;60:521-525.

411. Shanks GD, Gordon DM, Klotz FW, et al. Efficacy and safety of atovaquone/proguanil as suppressive prophylaxis for *Plasmodium falciparum* malaria. Clin Infect Dis. 1998;27:494-499.

412. Petersen E. The safety of atovaquone/proguanil in long-term malaria prophylaxis of nonimmune adults. J Travel Med. 2003;10(Suppl 1):S13-S15.

413. Hogh B, Clarke PD, Camus D, et al. Atovaquone-proguanil versus chloroquine-proguanil for malaria prophylaxis in nonimmune travellers: A randomised, double-blind study. Malarone International Study Team. Lancet. 2000;356:1888-1894.

414. Overbosch D, Schilthuis H, Bienzle U, et al. Atovaquone-proguanil versus mefloquine for malaria prophylaxis in nonimmune travelers: Results from a randomized, double-blind study. Clin Infect Dis. 2001;33:1015-1021.

415. Kofoed K, Petersen E. The efficacy of chemoprophylaxis against malaria with chloroquine plus proguanil, mefloquine, and atovaquone plus proguanil in travelers from Denmark. J Travel Med. 2003;10:150-154.

416. Wallace MR, Sharp TW, Smoak B, et al. Malaria among United States troops in Somalia. Am J Med. 1996;100:49-55.

417. Lillie TH, Schreck CE, Rahe AJ. Effectiveness of personal protection against mosquitoes in Alaska. J Med Entomol. 1988;25:475-478.

418. Schoepke A, Steffen R, Gratz N. Effectiveness of personal protection measures against mosquito bites for malaria prophylaxis in travelers. J Travel Med. 1998;5:188-192.

419. Durrheim DN, Govere JM. Malaria outbreak control in an African village by community application of 'deet' mosquito repellent to ankles and feet. Med Vet Entomol. 2002;16:112-115.

420. Alexander B, Cadena H, Usma MC, Rojas CA. Laboratory and field evaluations of a repellent soap containing diethyl toluamide DEET and permethrin against phlebotomine sand flies Diptera: Psychodidae in Valle del Cauca, Colombia. Am J Trop Med Hyg. 1995;52:169-173.

421. Fradin MS. Mosquitoes and mosquito repellents: A clinician's guide. Ann Intern Med. 1998;128:931-940.

422. Lengeler C. Insecticide-treated bednets and curtains for preventing malaria. Cochrane Database Syst Rev. 2000;2:CD000363.

423. Nevill CG, Some ES, Mung'ala VO, et al. Insecticide-treated bednets reduce mortality and severe morbidity from malaria among children on the Kenyan coast. Trop Med Int Hlth. 1996;1:139-146.

424. Kitchener S, Nasveld P, Russell B, Elmes N. An outbreak of malaria in a forward battalion on active service in East Timor. Mil Med. 2003;168:457-459.

425. Moorthy V, Hill AV. Malaria vaccines. Br Med Bull. 2002;62:59-72.

426. Miller LH, Hoffman SL. Research toward vaccines against malaria. Nat Med. 1998;4(5 Suppl):520-524.

427. Graves P, Gelband H. Vaccines for preventing malaria. Cochrane Database Syst Rev. 2003,1:CD000129.

428. Duffy PE. Maternal immunization and malaria in pregnancy. Vaccine. 2003;2:3358-3361.

CHAPTER **273**

Leishmania Species: Visceral (Kala-Azar), Cutaneous, and Mucocutaneous Leishmaniasis

SELMA M. B. JERONIMO
ANASTÁCIO DE QUEIROZ SOUSA
RICHARD D. PEARSON

Leishmaniasis refers to the spectrum of disease caused by *Leishmania* spp., protozoa of the order Kinetoplastida, family Trypanosomatidae. The leishmania are found as intracellular amastigotes in macrophages in humans and other mammalian hosts and as extracellular promastigotes in the gut of their invertebrate sand fly vectors. The clinical manifestations of leishmaniasis vary. They depend on complex interactions resulting from the parasite's inva-siveness, tropism, and pathogenicity, and the host's genetically determined cell-mediated immune responses. The spectrum of disease can be divided into visceral, cutaneous, and mucocutaneous leishmaniasis. A single *Leishmania* sp. can produce more than one of these clinical syndromes, and each of the syndromes is caused by more than one species. The *Leishmania* spp. that infect humans, their geographic distributions, and the clinical syndromes that they most commonly produce are summarized in Table 273-1.[1,2]

The leishmaniases threaten 350 million women, men, and children in widely scattered areas in 88 countries, 72 of which are in developing areas of the world.[3] An estimated 12 million people suffer from the disease. Approximately 90% of all cases of visceral leishmaniasis are found in three areas: eastern India and Bangladesh[4,5]; the Sudan, where a large epidemic has occurred among displaced people[6-8]; and Brazil, where visceral leishmaniasis is endemic in rural areas and large peri-urban outbreaks have been reported from cities in the northeast.[9,10] In addition, a viscerotropic syndrome caused by *Leishmania tropica,* a species historically associated with cutaneous leishmaniasis, was identified among American troops who served in the Persian Gulf War, leading to a temporary ban on blood donations by personnel who served in that theater.[11,12] Visceral leishmaniasis has also emerged as an important opportunistic disease in persons with acquired immunodeficiency syndrome (AIDS) in Southern Europe and other areas of the world where the two diseases coexist,[3,13-16] in persons who have had organ transplants,[17,18] and in association with other conditions in which cell-mediated immunity is compromised. Cutaneous leishmani-

TABLE 273-1 Leishmaniasis*

Clinical Syndromes	*Leishmania* Spp.	Location
Visceral leishmaniasis (kala-azar): generalized involvement of the reticuloendothelial system (spleen, bone marrow, liver and so on)	*L. (Leishmania) donovani*	Indian subcontinent, northern and eastern China, Pakistan, Nepal, eastern Africa, Sudan and Kenya
	L. (L.) infantum/chagasi	Middle East, Mediterranean littoral, Balkans, central and southwestern Asia, northern and western China, North and sub-Saharan Africa, Latin America
	L. (L.) spp.	Kenya, Ethiopia, Sudan, Somalia
	L. (L.) amazonensis	Brazil (Bahia state)
	L. (L.) tropica (rare)	Middle East, Saudi Arabia (U.S. troops), India, North Africa, Pakistan, Mediterranean littoral, central and western Asia
Post–kala-azar dermal leishmaniasis	*L. (L.) donovani*	Indian subcontinent and Sudan
	L. (L.) spp.	Kenya, Ethiopia, and Somalia
Old World cutaneous leishmaniasis: Single or limited number of skin lesions	*L. (L.) major*	Middle East, India, Pakistan, Africa, central and western Asia, northern and western China
	L. (L.) tropica	Mediterranean littoral, Middle East, North Africa, India, Pakistan, central and western Asia
	L. (L.) aethiopica	Ethiopian highlands, Kenya, Yemen
	L. (L.) infantum/chagasi (rare)	Middle East, Mediterranean littoral, central Asia, northern and western China, North and sub-Saharan Africa
	L. (L.) donovani	East Africa
	L. (L.) spp.	Kenya, Ethiopia, Somalia
Diffuse cutaneous leishmaniasis	*L. (L.) aethiopica*	Ethiopian highlands, Kenya, Yemen
New World cutaneous leishmaniasis: single or limited number of skin lesions	*L. (L.) mexicana* (chicle ulcer)	Central and South America, Texas
	L. (L.) amazonensis	Amazon Basin, neighboring areas, Bahia and other states of Brazil
	L. (L.) pifanoi	Venezuela
	L. (L.) garnhami	Venezuela
	L. (L.) venezuelensis	Venezuela
	L. (Viannia) braziliensis	Central and South America
	L. (V.) guyanensis (forest yaws)	Guyana, Surinam, northern Amazon Basin
	L. (V.) peruviana (uta)	Peru (western Andes)
		Argentinian highlands
	L. (V.) panamensis	Panama, Costa Rica, Colombia
	L. (V.) colombiensis	Colombia and Panama
	L. (L.) infantum/chagasi	Central and South America
Diffuse cutaneous leishmaniasis	*L. (L.) amazonensis*	Amazon Basin, neighboring areas, Bahia and other states of Brazil
	L. (L.) pifanoi	Venezuela
	L. (L.) mexicana	Central and South America, Texas
	L. (L.) spp.	Dominican Republic
American mucocutaneous leishmaniasis	*L. (V.) braziliensis* (espundia)	Central and South America
	Other *Leishmania (V.)* spp.	Central and South America

*The taxonomy of *Leishmania* spp. is still in a state of flux.
Data from refs. 1, 2, 100, 101.

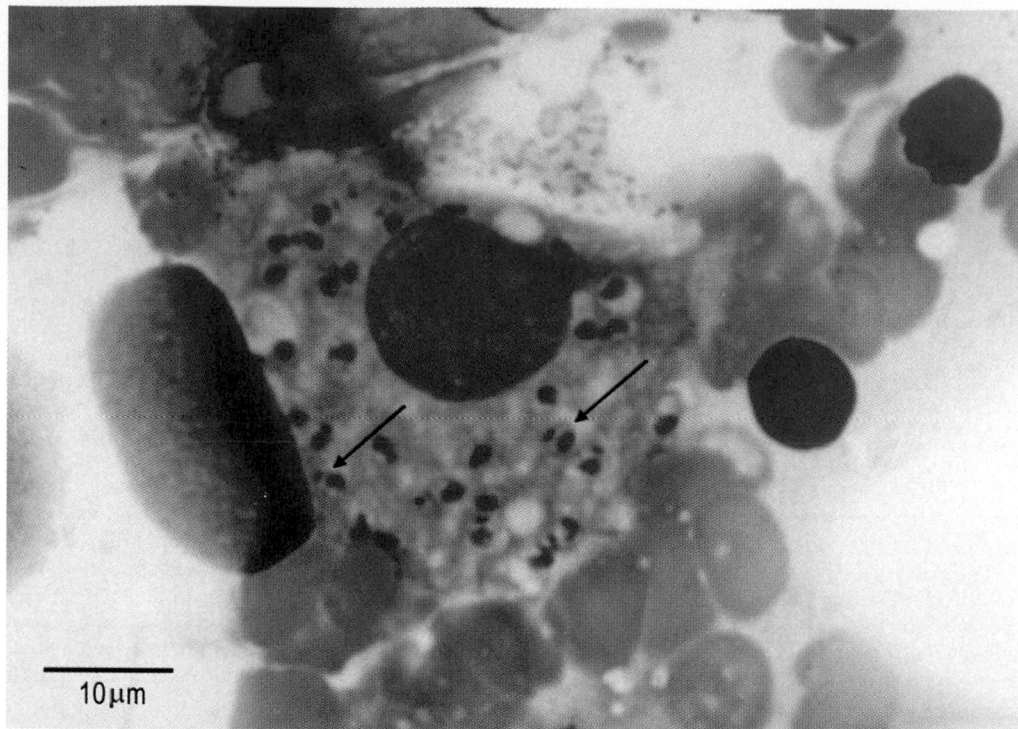

FIGURE 273-1. *Leishmania donovani* amastigotes *(arrows)* in a touch preparation made from a patient with visceral leishmaniasis. The bar equals 10 μm.

asis is an important problem for residents, settlers, troops, and visitors in endemic areas. Approximately 90% of the world's cases occur in Iran, Saudi Arabia, and Syria in the Middle East[3,19]; in Afghanistan in Central Asia; and in Brazil and Peru in Latin America.[3] More than 500 cases have been reported among American troops serving in Iraq and Afghanistan since 2002.[20] Other cases occur among North American civilians following exposure in endemic regions. Finally, 90% of the cases of mucocutaneous leishmaniasis occur in three Latin American countries: Brazil, Bolivia, and Peru.

LEISHMANIA SPECIES

Leishmania spp. are diploid protozoa and have a dimorphic life cycle.[2,21] A sexual stage has not yet been identified. In humans and other susceptible mammals, leishmania are found in cells of reticuloendothelial origin as intracellular amastigotes, which are 2 to 3 μm in length, oval or round, and lack an exteriorized flagellum (Fig. 273-1). In Wright- and Giemsa-stained preparations, the cytoplasm appears blue, and the nucleus is relatively large, eccentrically located, and red. The distinct, rod-shaped, red-staining kinetoplast is a specialized mitochondrial structure that contains a substantial amount of extranuclear DNA arranged as catenated minicircles and maxicircles. Parasite multiplication occurs by simple division within parasitophorous vacuoles in mononuclear phagocytes. Amastigotes are eventually released and go on to infect other mononuclear phagocytes.

In the digestive tract of the invertebrate vectors, female phlebotomine sand flies, leishmania develop through a series of flagellated, intermediate stages to become metacyclic promastigotes (Fig. 273-2).[22] Promastigotes can be grown in vitro in a number of culture media provided that the temperature is kept in the range of 22° C to 26° C. They have pear- or spindle-shaped bodies of variable dimensions, ranging from 10 to 15 μm in length to 1.5 to 3.5 μm in width. A single flagellum, which emerges from a basal body within the parasite, extends 15 to 28 μm and pulls the promastigote forward.

Female sand flies of the genus *Lutzomyia* in the Americas and *Phlebotomus* elsewhere transmit *Leishmania* spp.[2,23] They are modified pool feeders. Sand flies breed in cracks in the walls of dwellings, in

rubbish or rubble, or in rodent burrows. They are weak fliers and tend to remain close to the ground near their breeding sites.[24] Sand flies ingest amastigotes when they feed on an infected mammalian reservoir. Amastigotes convert to promastigotes in the sand fly gut, replicate, and differentiate to metacyclic promastigotes over a period of approximately 1 week. The life cycle is completed when the sand fly attempts to take its next blood meal. Saliva from the sand fly enhances the infectivity of promastigotes through the effects of maxadilan, a potent vasodilator and immunomodulator, and possibly other factors.[25] Depending on the *Leishmania* sp., the sand fly genus, and the geographic location, the major reservoirs are canines, rodents, or humans.

The *Leishmania* spp. that infect humans are summarized in Table 273-1.[2,3] Future revisions in taxonomy are likely as more is learned about their genetic diversity. The genus *Leishmania* has been divided into two subgenera, *Viannia* and *Leishmania*. Species in the *Viannia*

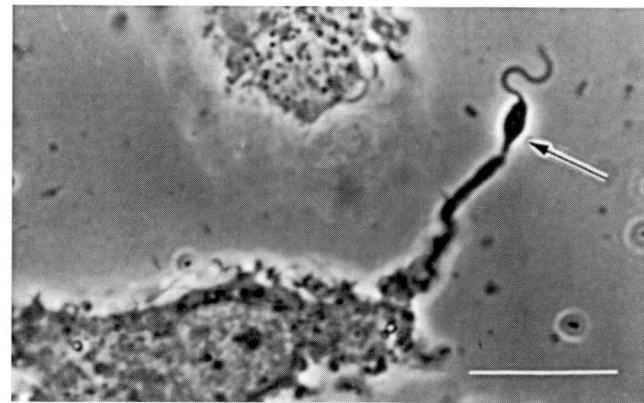

FIGURE 273-2. *Leishmania donovani* promastigote *(arrow)* attached by its alfagellar pole to a human mononuclear phagocyte in vitro. The bar equals 10 μm. *(From Pearson RD, Sullivan JA, Roberts D, et al. Interaction of* Leishmania donovani *promastigotes with human phagocytes. Infect Immun. 1983;40:411-416, with permission.)*

subgenus develop in the hindgut of the sand fly before migrating to the midgut and foregut (peripylaria) while those of the *Leishmania* subgenus develop in the midgut and foregut (suprapylaria). Species of the *Viannia* subgenus are endemic in Central and South America. Members of the *Leishmania* subgenus are found throughout the world. Several assays are used to speciate isolates. They include isoenzyme analysis, which is available at World Health Organization reference laboratories; species-specific monoclonal antibodies,[26] and polymerase chain reaction assays using *Leishmania* spp.-specific oligonucleotide primers, which are currently available in research laboratories.[27-29]

VISCERAL LEISHMANIASIS (KALA-AZAR)

Leishmania donovani and *Leishmania infantum/Leishmania chagasi* are responsible for most of the cases of visceral leishmaniasis (see Table 273-1). Once considered separate species, *L. chagasi,* which is present in Latin America, now appears to be the same as *L. infantum,* which is endemic in the Mediterranean and was probably introduced into the New World by early explorers.[30] On occasion, *Leishmania* spp. that are most commonly associated with cutaneous leishmaniasis such as *Leishmania amazonensis* in Latin America[31] and *Leishmania tropica* in the Middle East[11] or Africa[32] are isolated from patients with visceral syndromes.

L. donovani and *L. infantum/L. chagasi* infections are associated with a spectrum of symptoms and findings. At one extreme are persons with inapparent, self-resolving infections. At the other are those with classic visceral leishmaniasis (*kala-azar*), who present with fever, weight loss, hepatosplenomegaly, anemia, leukopenia, thrombocytopenia, and hypergammaglobulinemia, and in the Indian subcontinent, hyperpigmentation. *Kala-azar* means black fever in Hindi. Visceral leishmaniasis has been called *Dumdum fever, Assam fever,* and *infantile splenomegaly* in different geographic regions.

The ratio of self-resolving infection to frank visceral leishmaniasis varies geographically and with a person's age; it has been reported to range from 6.5:1 in children to 18:1 in adults with *L. infantum/L. chagasi* in northeastern Brazil.[33-35] Although many of those infected have no clinical manifestations of infection, some experience mild symptoms or develop splenomegaly before either progressing to frank visceral leishmaniasis or undergoing spontaneous cure.[33] Persons who are immunocompromised by AIDS, neoplasm, or immunosuppressive therapy are at increased risk of developing progressive disease.[36]

Epidemiology

Visceral leishmaniasis occurs in widely dispersed areas of the world (see Table 273-1).[3-10] Approximately 90% of the cases occur in India, Bangladesh, the Sudan, and Brazil.[3] Transmission depends on the sand fly vector, the presence of a suitable reservoir, and susceptible humans. On rare occasions, visceralizing *Leishmania* spp. cause congenital leishmaniasis.[37,38] Visceralizing leishmania can also be acquired through transfusion of contaminated blood,[39,40] accidental needle stick injuries in the laboratory,[41,42] and sharing of contaminated needles and syringes by intravenous drug users.[43]

L. donovani is responsible for visceral leishmaniasis in eastern India and Bangladesh.[3-5] In India infection is concentrated in the states of Assam and Bihar.[44] Children and young adults are the most frequently affected. Humans serve as the reservoir, and transmission is by *Phlebotomus argentipes* and other anthropophilic *Phlebotomus* spp. Persons with post-kala-azar dermal leishmaniasis may serve as the reservoir during interepidemic periods. Visceral leishmaniasis also occurs in Central Asia and historically in southern China where dogs and other canines are reservoirs. Disease is observed primarily in children. The number of cases in China is now small.[3]

In East Africa, *L. donovani* has been responsible for a very large epidemic among displaced persons in southern Sudan.[6-8] Visceral leishmaniasis occurs in a sporadic manner in Kenya and other areas of eastern Africa. Children and young adults are most frequently affected. Putative reservoirs include rats, gerbils, other rodents, and small carnivores. Humans may also be a reservoir during epidemics.

Visceral leishmaniasis occurs sporadically in the Mediterranean littoral and the Middle East, where rodents such as the black rat and dogs are reservoirs for *L. donovani* and *L. infantum,* respectively. Cases are typically encountered among children and immunocompromised persons. Visceral leishmaniasis has emerged as an important opportunistic disease among persons with AIDS in southern Europe in Spain, France, and Italy.[13-16] Although the incidence decreased following the introduction of highly active antiretroviral therapy (HAART),[36] HAART has not prevented later relapses of visceral leishmaniasis.[45] The sharing of leishmania-contaminated needles and syringes by intravenous drug users has resulted in artificial anthroponotic transmission there.[43]

In Latin America *L. infantum/L. chagasi* has historically caused sporadic cases in rural areas.[33-35] Major outbreaks have been reported during the past decade from cities in northeastern Brazil where suburbs have extended into endemic areas.[9,10] Children are most frequently affected. *Lutzomyia longipalpis* is the major vector. Domestic dogs and wild foxes are reservoirs of infection. The clustering of cases in households suggests that humans may also be reservoirs.[35]

On occasion *L. amazonensis, L. tropica,* or other *Leishmania* spp. that are more commonly associated with cutaneous leishmaniasis are isolated from persons with visceral disease. For example a small group of American military personnel who served in the Persian Gulf War acquired a "viscerotropic" form of *L. tropica* infection.[11,39] The epidemiology of those species is discussed later.

Pathogenesis and Immunology

After inoculation by a sand fly, promastigotes are phagocytosed by macrophages in the skin, convert to amastigotes, and multiply within acidic parasitophorous vacuoles.[21] Leishmania use the macrophage much like a Trojan horse. Additional mononuclear phagocytes are attracted to the site of the initial lesion and become infected. Amastigotes in time disseminate through regional lymphatics and the vascular system to infect mononuclear phagocytes throughout the reticuloendothelial system.

The site where promastigotes are inoculated is usually not apparent in persons with visceral leishmaniasis, but a small papule may be noticed. Larger skin lesions are rare. Increasing numbers of amastigote-infected mononuclear phagocytes in the liver and spleen result in progressive hypertrophy. The spleen often becomes massively enlarged as splenic lymphoid follicles are replaced by parasitized mononuclear cells. In the liver there is a marked increase in the number and size of Kupffer cells, many of which contain amastigotes. Infected mononuclear phagocytes are also found in the bone marrow, lymph nodes, skin, and other organs.

The outcome of leishmanial infection and the manifestations of disease depend on genetically determined human immune responses and environmental factors.[46] There is evidence of both protective and disease-enhancing elements. Cytokines and chemokines play key roles in mediating the outcome of infection, but despite extensive studies in murine models and in naturally infected humans, the precise sequence of events that determines the outcome of infection has not been fully elucidated.[47]

Persons with self-resolving infection with *L. donovani* or *L. infantum/ L. chagasi* and those who have undergone successful chemotherapy develop protective immunity against visceral leishmaniasis, but the disease can develop years later if they become immunocompromised.[48] The majority display delayed type hypersensitivity responses to intradermally administered leishmanial antigens.[33,34] The resolution of infection and the development of immunity are associated with expansion of leishmania-specific CD4[+] T cells of the Th1 type that secrete interferon-γ (INF-γ) and interleukin-2 (IL-2) in response to parasite antigens.[46,47,49] Evidence of leishmania-specific Th1 responses is missing in progressive disease. IL-12 play an important early role in the development of protective immune responses.[50] At the cellular level, INF-γ activates macrophages to kill amastigotes through L-arginine-dependent nitric oxide production, which follows induction of nitric oxide synthase, and oxidative killing mechanisms.[51-54] IL-1 and tumor necrosis factor-α (TNF-α) prime macrophages for activation by INF-γ.

In persons with progressive visceral leishmaniasis, development of leishmania-specific Th1 responses is inhibited. Peripheral blood mononuclear cells neither proliferate nor produce INF-γ or IL-2 in response to leishmanial antigens in vitro. There is no evidence of delayed type cutaneous hypersensitivity responses to leishmanial antigens. Paradoxically, antileishmanial antibodies are produced in high titer during progressive visceral leishmaniasis, but they are not protective. There is evidence of polyclonal B-cell activation. Progressive disease in humans is associated with production of IL-10 and transforming growth factor (TGF)-β. IL-10 is known to suppress the development of Th1 responses and the activation of macrophages by INF-γ.[55,56] TGF-β appears to play an important role early in infection.[57] It also suppresses inducible nitric oxide synthase and IFN-γ production, and it inhibits Th1 expansion.[58] IL-4 is found early, but not later in infection, and leishmania-specific IgE is present.[59] Soluble IL-2 and soluble IL-4 receptors may play a role in evolving immune responses.[60,61] In addition, intracellular amastigotes induce alterations in macrophage signaling and cytokine responses.[62] They decrease expression of class I and class II histocompatibility antigens on macrophages[63] and stimulate macrophage secretion of prostaglandins.[64]

The critical question is why protective Th1 responses arise and dominate in some persons and not in others. The sequence of early cytokine responses; the manner in which leishmanial antigens are presented by macrophages and dendritic cells;[65] parasite virulence factors; and the size of the infecting inoculum[66] may all be important variables. Studies are ongoing to identify the precise sequence of events that leads to the development of immunity and to identify the immunogenetic determinants of human disease.

Clinical Manifestations of Kala-Azar

The clinical features of fully manifest visceral leishmaniasis (*kala-azar*) are similar throughout the world. The incubation period typically varies from 3 to 8 months, but it can be as short as 10 days or longer than a year.[67] Clinical disease may first become symptomatic years after exposure in persons who become immunocompromised.[48]

In cases with a subacute or chronic course, there is an insidious onset of fever, weakness, loss of appetite, weight loss, and abdominal enlargement caused by hepatosplenomegaly. Hyperpigmentation is seen in patients in India and Bangladesh. The symptoms may persist for weeks to months before the infected person comes to medical attention. Fever may be intermittent, remittent with twice-daily temperature spikes, or less commonly, continuous. It is relatively well tolerated. In acute cases, there may be an abrupt onset of high fever and chills, sometimes with a periodicity that suggests malaria. Chills, but seldom rigors, accompany the temperature spikes. As time passes, the spleen can become massively enlarged. It is usually soft and nontender. The presence of a hard spleen suggests a hematologic disorder or another diagnosis such as schistosomiasis. The liver also enlarges; it usually has a sharp edge, soft consistency, and a smooth surface. Lymphadenopathy is common in patients in Sudan[6-8] but uncommon in other geographic areas. Elevated liver enzymes and bilirubin may be observed.[10,68,69]

The skin in persons with visceral leishmaniasis often becomes dry, thin, and scaly, and hair may be lost. As the disease progresses, particularly in light-colored persons in India, the skin on the hands, feet, abdomen, and face may become dark. Darkening of the skin seems to be related to an increase in melanocytes.[70] Peripheral edema may be seen late in disease, particularly in malnourished children. Hemorrhage can occur from one or more sites; epistaxis and gingival bleeding may be noted as well as petechiae and ecchymoses on the extremities.

Many patients with visceral leishmaniasis become cachectic. This appears to be mediated in part by TNF-α and other cytokines that are known to have catabolic and anorectic effects.[71,72] Secondary bacterial infections are common in persons with advanced visceral leishmaniasis.[73,74] Death may result from pneumonia, septicemia, tuberculosis, dysentery, or measles or it may be the consequence of malnutrition, severe anemia, or hemorrhage.

The laboratory findings include anemia, leukopenia, thrombocytopenia, and hypergammaglobulinemia.[67] Anemia is almost always present and may be severe. It is usually normocytic and normochromic. It appears to be due to a combination of factors including hemolysis, marrow replacement with leishmania-infected macrophages, hemorrhage, splenic sequestration of erythrocytes, hemodilution, and marrow suppressive effects of cytokines such as TNF-α.[72-75]

Leukopenia is also prominent, with white blood cell counts occasionally as low as 1000/mm³. It is not known whether the observed neutropenia is due to increased margination, splenic sequestration, or an autoimmune process, or a combination of those factors. Eosinopenia or absence of eosinophils is frequently observed. Of note, anemia and neutropenia have not been prominent in patients with visceral leishmaniasis who have undergone splenectomy.

Hypergammaglobulinemia, circulating immune complexes, and rheumatoid factors are present in the sera of most patients with visceral leishmaniasis.[76,77] There is evidence of polyclonal B-cell activation. The globulin level may be as high as 9 g/dL; the ratio of globulin to albumin is typically high. The erythrocyte sedimentation rate is usually elevated.[10,78] The kidneys may show evidence of immune complex deposition. Mild glomerulonephritis has been reported,[79,80] but renal failure is rarely seen.[81]

Visceral Leishmaniasis in Patients with AIDS

Visceral leishmaniasis may be the first opportunistic infection in persons with AIDS, or it may complicate the terminal stages of disease. Studies in Spain indicate that the majority of human immunodeficiency virus (HIV)-infected persons with visceral leishmaniasis present late in the course of HIV infection with fever, hepatomegaly, splenomegaly, and pancytopenia, but atypical presentations are common.[13-16,82-89] Splenomegaly may be absent. Patients may have involvement of the lungs, pleura, oral mucosa, esophagus, stomach, small intestine, skin, or bone marrow, the latter presenting as aplastic anemia. The number of persons with HIV who develop visceral leishmaniasis has decreased in Europe following the introduction of highly active antiretroviral therapy,[36,90] but the number of cases of visceral leishmaniasis worldwide may increase dramatically as HIV infection continues to spread into leishmania-endemic regions.

Viscerotropic Leishmaniasis

A viscerotropic syndrome due to *L. tropica* was observed among American troops who served in the Persian Gulf War[11] and has been reported in other settings. The symptoms included chronic low-grade fever, malaise, fatigue, and in some cases, diarrhea. Mild splenomegaly was observed in some. None of the troops developed classical kala-azar or progressive visceral leishmaniasis. Subsequent studies failed to show an association between *L. tropica* infection and chronic fatigue and other symptoms associated with the Gulf War syndrome.

Post–Kala-Azar Dermal Leishmaniasis

Post–kala-azar dermal leishmaniasis follows the treatment of visceral leishmaniasis due to *L. donovani* in 5% to 10% of persons in India and approximately 50% of those in Sudan.[91,92] The syndrome is rarely seen following treatment of visceral leishmaniasis in Latin America, but it has been reported in a small number of persons with concurrent AIDS. Skin lesions typically appear in India 1 to 2 years after treatment and may persist for as long as 20 years. In the Sudan they usually appear at the end of or within 6 months of therapy and persist for only a few months to a year. Persistence of lesions beyond 1 year is associated with high antileishmanial antibody titers and negative leishmanial skin test responses.[93] The skin lesions vary from hyperpigmented macules to frank nodules. They are found on the face, trunk, extremities, oral mucous membranes, and occasionally, on the genitals. They may be confused clinically and pathologically with leprosy. Those affected generally feel well. The diagnosis is mainly clinical, but amastigotes can be detected in the skin in more than 80% of cases in the Sudan.[91,92]

Antileishmanial treatment is indicated in Indian post–kala-azar dermal leishmaniasis. In the Sudan, most cases cure spontaneously, but chronic or severe cases are treated.[91,92] In a few instances in India, visceral leishmaniasis has recurred in patients with post–kala-azar dermal leishmaniasis.

Diagnosis

In an endemic area, the constellation of prolonged fever, progressive weight loss, weakness, pronounced splenomegaly, hepatomegaly, anemia, leukopenia, and hypergammaglobulinemia is highly suggestive of visceral leishmaniasis. The diagnosis is more difficult in persons in whom fever or splenomegaly are absent; in travelers who develop symptoms after leaving endemic areas; and in those with concurrent AIDS who present with atypical manifestations.

The diagnosis can be confirmed by demonstrating amastigotes in tissue or isolating promastigotes in culture. Splenic aspiration[94] for Wright-Giemsa stained smears and for culture is the most sensitive method for parasite identification. It is routinely performed in some areas, but it can be associated with substantial hemorrhage, particularly in patients with advanced stages of disease who have undergone aspirations by inexperienced operators. The risk is less when aspiration is performed quickly with a small-bore needle by an experienced healthcare worker in patients with no laboratory evidence of coagulopathy. Bone marrow aspiration is safer, but less sensitive. Amastigotes are seen in approximately two thirds of patients. Liver biopsy is less likely to yield the diagnosis than is splenic puncture or bone marrow biopsy and carries the risk of hemorrhage. Lymph node aspiration or biopsy may be diagnostic when enlarged nodes are present, as is often the case in Sudan. Amastigotes may also be seen within mononuclear cells in Wright- and Giemsa-stained smears of the buffy coat or in biopsy specimens of various organs. The latter is particularly true in patients with AIDS in whom amastigotes in macrophages have been identified in bronchoalveolar lavage fluid, pleural effusions, or biopsy specimens of the oropharynx, stomach, or intestine.[82-89] On occasion, parasites have been cultured from the buffy coat or blood.

Aspirates from the spleen, bone marrow, liver, or lymph node should be cultured. Specimens can be inoculated into one of several media and maintained at ambient temperatures, 22° C to 26° C. In the United States culture media and instructions are available from the Centers for Disease Control and Prevention (CDC). Motile promastigotes develop from amastigotes and multiply in vitro. When the inoculum is high, they may be seen in culture within a few days, but it may take several weeks for the concentration to reach the level of detection. Isolates can be forwarded to the CDC or other WHO reference laboratories for speciation.

Antileishmanial antibodies are typically present in high titer in immunocompetent patients with visceral leishmaniasis. Enzyme-linked immunosorbent assay (ELISA) and dipstick tests using *L. infantum*/ *L. chagasi* recombinant k39, a kinesin-like antigen, have good sensitivity and specificity for the diagnosis of visceral leishmaniasis in immunocompetent persons.[95,96] A number of other serological tests using different antigens and assays are available. In general, they are sensitive,[97] but false-positive results may occur due to cross-reacting antibodies in patients with leprosy, Chagas' disease, cutaneous leishmaniasis, and other infections. Antileishmanial antibodies may be absent or present at low titer in patients with AIDS, resulting in false-negative serological results.

The leishmanin (Montenegro) skin test is negative in patients with active visceral leishmaniasis. It becomes positive in the majority of those in whom infection spontaneously resolves and in patients who have undergone successful chemotherapy. Although the skin test is useful in studies of the epidemiology, it has no value in the diagnosis of visceral leishmaniasis. The leishmanin skin test may be negative or positive in persons with post–kala-azar dermal leishmaniasis.[91-93]

Differential Diagnosis

The clinical picture of visceral leishmaniasis is often indistinguishable from that of other infectious diseases. The differential diagnosis of acute visceral leishmaniasis includes malaria, typhoid fever, typhus, acute Chagas' disease (in Latin America), acute schistosomiasis, miliary tuberculosis, and amebic liver abscess. Subacute or chronic visceral leishmaniasis may be confused with brucellosis, prolonged *Salmonella* bacteremia, histoplasmosis, infectious mononucleosis, lymphoma, leukemia, myeloproliferative disease, hepatosplenic schistosomiasis, and chronic malaria. Post–kala-azar dermal leishmaniasis must be differentiated from leprosy, yaws, and syphilis.

CUTANEOUS LEISHMANIASIS

Cutaneous leishmaniasis is endemic in widely scattered areas throughout the world. The classic form of Old World cutaneous leishmaniasis is the "oriental sore."[1-3,98] It has also been termed *bouton d'orient, bouton de Crete, bouton d'Alep, bouton de Biskra, Aleppo evil, Baghdad boil,* and *Dehli boil* in various regions of the Middle East, the Mediterranean littoral, Africa, India, and Asia (see Table 273-1). It is most frequently caused by *L. major, L. tropica,* or *Leishmania aethiopica,* but *L. donovani* and *L. infantum*/*L. chagasi* can also cause simple cutaneous leishmaniasis.[99] The resulting skin lesions can be troublesome and unsightly, but they generally are not life-threatening. Diffuse cutaneous leishmaniasis due to *L. aethiopica* infection is reported from Ethiopia and adjacent areas of Africa.

American cutaneous leishmaniasis is endemic in widespread areas of Latin America.[1-3,100-102] The causative species include *L. braziliensis, L. mexicana, L. panamensis*/*L. guyanensis,* which are closely related if not identical, and several others (see Table 273-1). *L. infantum*/ *L. chagasi* is associated with simple cutaneous leishmaniasis in Central America. Depending on the clinical presentation and geographic location, American cutaneous leishmaniasis is variously known as *pian bois* (bush yaws), *uta,* or *Chiclero's ulcer.* The spectrum of disease includes single or multiple, localized, cutaneous ulcers (Fig. 273-3); diffuse cutaneous leishmaniasis (Fig. 273-4); and mucocutaneous disease (espundia) caused by *L. braziliensis* or less commonly, other related *Leishmania* spp. (Fig. 273-5).

Epidemiology

In the Old World, cutaneous leishmaniasis is usually a sporadic disease in endemic areas, but occasionally it occurs in an epidemic pattern, particularly when large groups of susceptible persons are exposed during road construction, refugee movements, or military activities.[98] A large number of American troops have been infected in Iraq and Afghanistan while stationed there. *Phlebotomus* species are the vectors. A number of mammals serve as reservoirs in different regions.

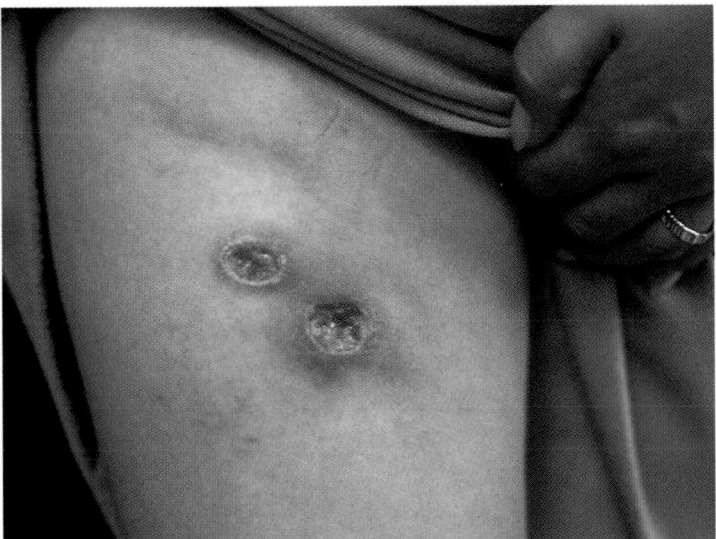

FIGURE 273-3. American cutaneous leishmaniasis. Two leg lesions.

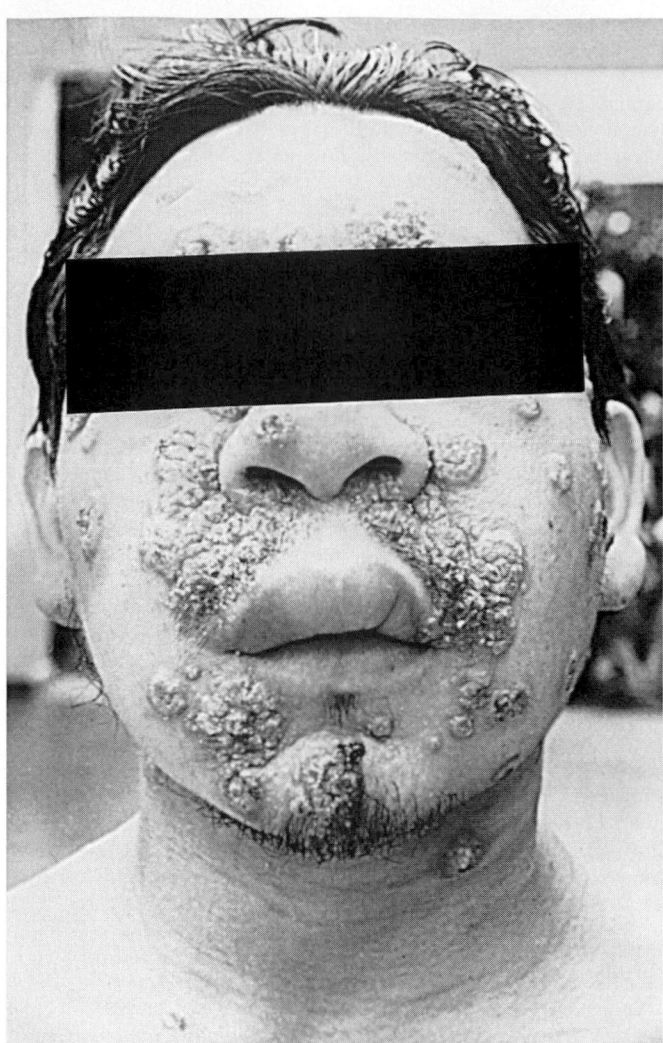

FIGURE 273-4. Brazilian patient with diffuse cutaneous leishmaniasis.

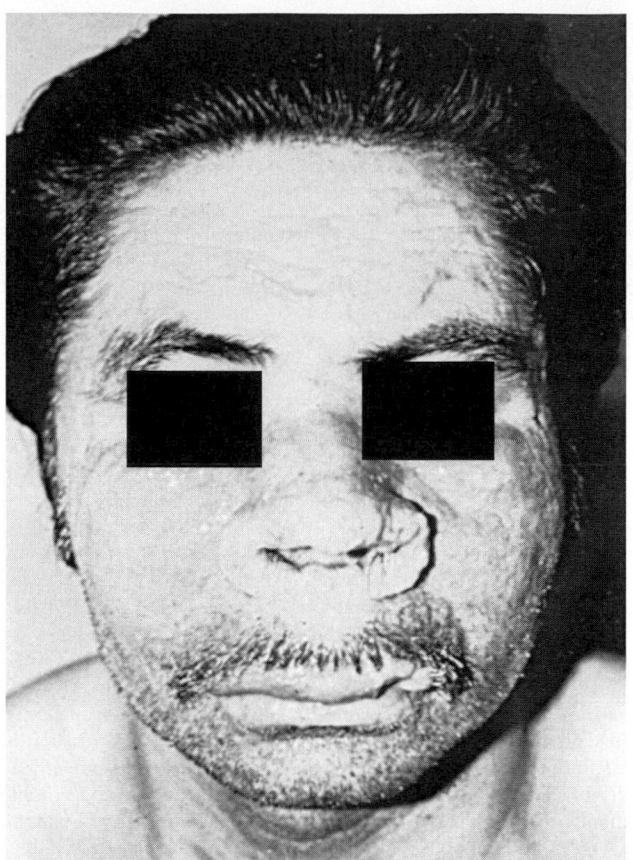

FIGURE 273-5. American mucosal leishmaniasis. There is extensive involvement of the nose and upper lip with destruction of the nasal septum. *(From Pearson RD, Wheeler DA, Harrison LH, et al. The immunology of leishmaniasis. Rev Infect Dis. 1983;5:907-927, with permission.)*

L. major is an infection of desert rodents, primarily gerbils, and affects humans in uninhabited areas or in villages in arid regions of the Middle East, North Africa, and central Asia. It has been a major problem for troops operating in endemic regions in the Middle East. The lesions tend to be larger and "wet" with an overlying exudate. *Phlebotomus papatasi* and other *Phlebotomus* spp. are the vectors.

L. tropica infects dogs and humans in urban areas of the Middle East such as Baghdad, Teheran, and Damascus as well as cities in the Mediterranean littoral, India, and Pakistan. The lesions tend to be crusted and "dry." The vectors include *Phlebotomus sergenti* and *P. papatasi.*

L. aethiopica is endemic in Ethiopia, Kenya, and southwest Africa. The primary reservoirs are hyrax (small mammals); rodents are secondary reservoirs. *Phlebotomus longipes* is one of the vectors. Occasionally *L. donovani* and *L. infantum/L. chagasi* cause simple cutaneous leishmaniasis.[99]

New World cutaneous leishmaniasis is usually a rural zoonosis.[100-102] The main reservoirs are forest rodents, except in the case of *Leishmania peruviana,* in which dogs are the primary reservoir. The vectors are ground-dwelling or arboreal *Lutzomyia* spp. Disease is common in persons working at the edge of the forest and among rural settlers. Outbreaks occur when areas of forest are cleared for roads, villages, or farms, or when military personnel or tourists enter endemic regions.

L. mexicana is responsible for American cutaneous leishmaniasis from northern Argentina to Texas, where a small number of autochthonous cases have been reported.[103] It is an occupational disease of gum, or chicle, collectors in Central America as well as persons living, working, or touring in endemic areas. Lesions typically appear on exposed areas of the extremities, face or ears. A number of sylvatic rodents are reservoirs. *Lutzomyia* species are the vectors.

L. amazonensis produces a spectrum of disease in South America that includes simple cutaneous, diffuse cutaneous, and visceral leishmaniasis.[31] The vectors are *Lutzomyia* spp., and the reservoirs are forest animals.

L. braziliensis is found in widely scattered areas of Central and South America.[100-102] It is responsible for cutaneous as well as mucocutaneous leishmaniasis. Cutaneous leishmaniasis caused by *L. braziliensis* has been diagnosed among American tourists returning from Belize and other Latin American areas. *L. panamensis* is found in Panama and adjacent countries. It was an important problem for US military personnel training in jungle areas of Panama. *Leishmania guyanensis,* which is closely related if not identical, is responsible for *pian bois* or *bush yaws* in the Amazon basin. *Leishmania peruviana* is the cause of *uta* in Peru. It typically causes dry lesions.

Pathogenesis and Immunology

The clinical manifestations of cutaneous leishmaniasis depend on the virulence factors of the infecting *Leishmania* spp. and the genetically determined immune responses of their human hosts. After promastigotes are inoculated into the skin, they convert to amastigotes and multiply within macrophages. A papule forms, enlarges, and, in most instances, ulcerates.

Cutaneous leishmaniasis is characterized by a mixed acute and chronic inflammatory infiltrate with infected and noninfected mononuclear phagocytes, lymphocytes, and plasma cells. There are areas of focal necrosis.[104,105] Early in infection, amastigote-containing macrophages dominate. Eventually, parasitized mononuclear phagocytes are eliminated, lymphocytes become more prevalent, and a granulomatous response containing epithelioid cells and giant cells evolves. Lesions heal slowly leaving a flat, atrophic, burn-like scar as evidence of disease. Recovery is associated with a high level of resistance to reinfection by the homologous *Leishmania* spp.

In some respects, the range of clinical features in cutaneous leishmaniasis parallels that of leprosy. At one end of the spectrum lies diffuse cutaneous leishmaniasis, a relatively uncommon syndrome, in which there is little evidence of effective cell-mediated immune response. Heavily parasitized macrophages are abundant throughout the dermis, and few lymphocytes are present.[106] Peripheral blood mononuclear cells neither proliferate nor produce INF-γ nor IL-2 in response to leishmanial antigens in vitro and cutaneous delayed type hypersensitivity reactions are absent.[107] Diffuse cutaneous leishmaniasis has been compared to lepromatous leprosy in which there is a large number of mycobacteria in macrophages and no evidence of protective, Th1 cell–mediated immune responses.

At the other extreme lies leishmaniasis recidivans, a hyperergic variant of cutaneous leishmaniasis, in which chronic lesions slowly expand while healing at the center. Amastigotes are sparse and a mononuclear cell infiltrate predominates. This is somewhat analogous to tuberculoid leprosy in which there is an intense mononuclear infiltrate with few mycobacteria. But cutaneous leishmaniasis and leprosy differ in important ways. Although the character and organization of the granuloma in leprosy are invariably characteristic of the position in the clinical spectrum, this is not true in simple cutaneous leishmaniasis in which lesions progress over time from a predominance of amastigote-containing macrophages and few lymphocytes to a granulomatous response with a predominance of lymphocytes and few parasites before healing.[104,105]

Persons with cutaneous or mucosal leishmaniasis have evidence of both Th1 and Th2 lymphocytes in their lesions, but the systemic response is predominantly Th1.[108] Their peripheral blood mononuclear cells proliferate and produce INF-γ and IL-2 in response to leishmanial antigens in vitro, and those infected exhibit delayed-type cutaneous hypersensitivity responses as evidenced by positive leishmanin skin tests in vivo. Complex chemokine and cytokine responses govern the tissue localization of effector cells and the resulting immune responses,[106,109] but the precise sequence of events that results in skin necrosis and eventual healing has not yet been characterized.

Clinical Manifestations

The incubation period of cutaneous leishmaniasis typically varies from 2 weeks to several months, but can be as long as several years.[110] A wide variety of skin manifestations ranging from small, dry, crusted lesions to large, deep, mutilating ulcers may be seen. The characteristics vary among *Leishmania* spp. and from one geographic area to another, but overlap occurs. Lesions with different characteristics may even be seen in the same patient. There may be a single lesion or multiple ones. They are usually found on exposed areas of the body. No characteristic of the skin lesion is pathognomonic for cutaneous leishmaniasis or can be used to identify the causative *Leishmania* spp.

In general *L. tropica* tends to cause "dry," crusted, slowly enlarging lesions that can persist for a year or more, whereas *L. major* and *L. braziliensis* are associated with "moist," exudative lesions that are larger, have a granulating base with overlying exudate, mature more rapidly, and typically heal after many months.

Ulcerative lesions are usually shallow and circular with well-defined, raised borders and a central bed of granulation tissue. They gradually increase in size and may develop a "pizza-like" appearance with a raised, circular outer margin, beefy red granulating base, and yellowish exudate on the surface. Satellite lesions may be present, and

they may fuse with the original ulcer. Despite substantial tissue destruction, they are usually not painful. The center of the granulating base of the ulcer may develop a hard excrescence, and a cutaneous horn may arise. Secondary staphylococcal or streptococcal cellulites can occur. After a variable period ranging from several months to longer than a year, ulcers heal leaving flat, atrophic, depigmented, burn-like scars.

In *L. braziliensis* infection, regional lymphadenopathy may precede the development of cutaneous lesions by 1 to 12 weeks.[111,112] Patients may experience constitutional symptoms including malaise, anorexia, weight loss, and low-grade fever. As the skin ulcer develops, the lymphadenopathy and systemic symptoms subside. In *L. guyanensis* and occasionally in *L. braziliensis* infection, a chain of nodules may develop along lymphatics proximal to the lesion, particularly if it is on an extremity, and mimic sporotrichosis.

Diffuse Cutaneous Leishmaniasis

The condition starts as a localized papule that does not ulcerate. Satellite lesions develop around the initial papule, and organisms gradually spread in the skin, resulting in disseminated nodules primarily on the face and extremities. Diffuse cutaneous leishmaniasis has a protracted course and may last for the patient's lifetime.[113]

Leishmaniasis Recidivans

This is a relapsing, tuberculoid form of cutaneous leishmaniasis caused by *L. tropica*. It is observed in Iran and elsewhere in Central Asia. The lesions are usually on the face. They spread outward while healing at the center. Leishmaniasis recidivans is chronic and can last for decades.

Disseminated Cutaneous Leishmaniasis

Disseminated cutaneous lesions have been reported in a small subset of immunocompetent patients with *L. braziliensis* infection in Brazil.[114] Affected persons typically have a large number of acneiform, papular, nodular, or ulcerated lesions. Parasites are scant. Mucosal involvement is common. The syndrome is most commonly observed in adult male agricultural workers in Brazil. Usually more than one course of pentavalent antimony therapy is needed for adequate treatment. Disseminated cutaneous lesions have also been observed in a limited number of patients with cutaneous leishmaniasis and AIDS[115,116] and in patients with organ transplants.[117] Individuals with AIDS and skin lesions may also present with evidence of visceralization.[115,116]

Diagnosis

The development of one or more chronic skin lesions with the appropriate characteristics and a history of exposure in an endemic area suggest cutaneous leishmaniasis. A definite diagnosis is usually made by identifying amastigotes in tissue or promastigotes in culture. Species-specific monoclonal antibodies and DNA probes have been used successfully to identify leishmania in tissue samples in experimental studies, but they are not routinely available. They have the advantage of allowing immediate speciation, which has relevance for chemotherapy.

Punch or incisional biopsies should be taken from the border of the lesion in persons suspected of having cutaneous leishmaniasis. Meticulous cleaning is necessary before the biopsy to prevent bacterial and fungal contamination of cultures.[118] Touch preparations are made from biopsy samples, stained with a Wright-Giemsa preparation, and examined for amastigotes.[119,120] A portion is fixed for histological examination. The diagnosis can also be made by culturing tissue in nonbacteriostatic saline that has been injected and aspirated from the margin of the lesion. Specimens can be cultured using the media and conditions described for visceral leishmaniasis. Scrapings made from ulcerative lesions may also be positive.[121] The sensitivity of direct parasite identification and culture varies with the type and duration of the lesion and the infecting *Leishmania* sp. The combined sensitivity of these methods is estimated to be in the range of 50% to 70%. When lymphadenopathy precedes or accompanies skin ulcers in *L. braziliensis* infection, the diagnosis can sometimes be made by aspirating an enlarged lymph node.[111,112] Organisms isolated in culture can be sent to WHO reference laboratories for speciation. Biopsy specimen should also be examined and cultured for fungi and mycobacteria that can cause similar lesions.

Serological assays are not generally helpful in the diagnosis of cutaneous leishmaniasis. Antileishmanial antibodies are detectable in the serum of only a minority of patients with cutaneous leishmaniasis and the titers are usually low. Cross-reacting "natural" antibodies are also present at low titer in the serum of persons who have never been exposed to *Leishmania* spp. The leishmanin skin test is usually positive in patients with simple cutaneous leishmaniasis.

The differential diagnosis includes sporotrichosis, blastomycosis, chromomycosis, lobomycosis, cutaneous tuberculosis, atypical mycobacterial infection, syphilis, yaws, leprosy, sarcoidosis, lupus vulgaris, and neoplasms of the skin. Rarely, lesions may assume a keloidal form and give the appearance of lobomycosis.

AMERICAN MUCOCUTANEOUS LEISHMANIASIS (ESPUNDIA)

A subset of persons infected with *L. braziliensis* or related *Leishmania* spp. develop mucous membrane involvement of the nose, oral cavity, pharynx, or larynx months to years after their skin lesions have healed.[122] The percentage of patients infected with *L. braziliensis* who develop mucosal disease is relatively small. In one study, mucosal involvement occurred in 2.7% of persons with primary skin lesions after a median duration of 6 years.[123] The time between the primary lesion(s) and mucosal involvement may be as short as 1 month or as long as 2 decades.[123,124]

The initial symptoms are often nasal stuffiness, discharge, discomfort, or epistaxis. Over time, the nasal septum may be destroyed, resulting in nasal collapse ("tapir" nose). Perforation can occur through the skin of the nose or through the soft palate. The upper lip may be involved in addition to the buccal, pharyngeal, or laryngeal mucosa, in that approximate order.[125] Involvement of the trachea as well as the genital mucosa has been reported. On rare occasions, mucosal lesions are so extensive that the individual is unable to eat or experiences fatal aspiration pneumonia.

Histopathologically, chronic mucosal lesions are characterized by an intense mononuclear cell infiltrate with few parasites. Persons with mucosal leishmaniasis demonstrate strong systemic Th1 responses. Their peripheral blood mononuclear cells proliferate and produce INF-γ in response to leishmanial antigens in vitro, and their leishmanin skin tests are usually positive.[108]

Various theories have been advanced to explain mucosal involvement. They include lower temperature, which favors parasite growth; failure of cell-mediated immune responses to be effective in mucosal tissue; local trauma; and capillary plexus trapping of amastigotes in the nose. Spontaneous cure of mucosal leishmaniasis has been reported, but it is rare. The lack of an appropriate animal model has hindered research on the immunopathology of the syndrome.

Mucosal involvement is seen on occasion owing to the contiguous spread of cutaneous lesions caused by *L. tropica* or other *Leishmania* spp. It is also observed in some persons with visceral leishmaniasis, particularly those with concurrent AIDS. The pathophysiology and natural history in those cases is thought to resemble cutaneous and visceral leishmaniasis, respectively, as discussed earlier.

Diagnosis

The diagnosis of mucocutaneous leishmaniasis is confirmed when amastigotes are identified in touch preparations or tissue sections or when promastigotes are isolated in culture. However, these measures are not particularly sensitive since the parasite burden is usually low and *L. braziliensis* is relatively difficult to grow in culture.

A putative diagnosis of mucocutaneous leishmaniasis can be made in an endemic area on the basis of the clinical findings, a char-

acteristic scar representing previous cutaneous infection, a positive leishmanin skin test result, and/or the presence of antileishmanial antibodies in serum.[123,126] In general, mucosal disease caused by *L. braziliensis* is associated with higher antileishmanial antibody titers and stronger delayed-type hypersensitivity responses than simple cutaneous leishmaniasis. The leishmanin skin test is positive in 86% to 100% of cases. The sensitivity of tests for antileishmanial antibodies varies with the assay and antigen, with reported sensitivities ranging from 62% to 100%.[126,127] When positive, subsequent antibody studies can be useful in evaluating the response to chemotherapy. The titer should fall after successful chemotherapy; a subsequent rise in titer suggests a relapse.[128]

The differential diagnosis of mucosal leishmaniasis includes paracoccidioidomycosis, syphilis, tertiary yaws, histoplasmosis, sarcoidosis, basal cell carcinoma, and lethal midline granuloma and T/NK cell lymphoma. The polyp-like nasal lesions that occur in some persons with mucosal leishmaniasis may occasionally mimic rhinosporidiosis.

TREATMENT OF LEISHMANIASIS

The treatment of choice for leishmaniasis depends on the infecting *Leishmania* spp., the clinical syndrome, the immunologic status of the host, and the availability and cost of drugs.[129] There are a number of options. Liposomal amphotericin B is the only drug licensed for the treatment of visceral leishmaniasis in the United States, but cost and availability have limited its use in developing areas.[130-134] Two pentavalent antimony–containing compounds, stibogluconate sodium and meglumine antimoniate, are still used in many sites where *Leishmania* spp. are sensitive, but resistance and treatment failures are common in India and some other areas, immunocompromised patients often relapse after treatment, and side effects are frequent.[135,136] Amphotericin B deoxycholate and pentamidine isethionate are effective, but potentially toxic alternatives.[137-139] The most exiting recent advance has been the introduction of miltefosine, an orally administered compound that has been used successfully for the treatment of pentavalent antimony–resistant visceral leishmaniasis in India.[140-143] It is not licensed in the United States. Studies are ongoing to determine the efficacy of miltefosine in other geographic areas and in other forms of leishmaniasis.[144] Several additional drugs and treatment modalities are also discussed in the following subsections.

Visceral Leishmaniasis

Liposomal amphotericin B (AmBisome) is the drug of choice for the treatment of visceral leishmaniasis in North America and other industrialized countries.[130-134] Several dosage regimens have been studied. For immunocompetent patients, the manufacturer recommends 3.0 mg/kg body weight/day on days 1 to 5, 14, and 21. Shorter courses with higher daily doses have been used in studies in endemic areas with good results. For immunocompromised patients, the manufacturer recommends a dose of 4.0 mg/kg body weight/day on days 1 to 5, 10, 17, 24, 31, and 38. Relapses can occur after liposomal amphotericin B and other forms of therapy in persons with AIDS, and an additional course(s) of liposomal amphotericin B may be necessary. Other lipid-associated amphotericin B preparations appear to be effective in the treatment of visceral leishmaniasis, but the data to support their use are less extensive.[145]

Pentavalent antimony is still used for the treatment of visceral leishmaniasis in many developing areas where isolates are susceptible. It is no longer used in India, where 40% of cases are now resistant.[146] The dosage recommended is 20 mg of pentavalent antimony (Sb^v)/kg body weight/day for 28 days. Persons who respond slowly to the initial course of therapy or relapse may respond to a second course. Persons who fail to respond to pentavalent antimony or acquire infection in areas where resistance is prevalent can be treated with liposomal amphotericin B, amphotericin B deoxycholate, or miltefosine in India. Primary failures and relapses are often observed in patients with concurrent AIDS. Longer durations of therapy have been used to treat post–kala-azar dermal leishmaniasis in India.[147]

Common side effects with stibogluconate sodium and meglumine antimoniate include abdominal pain, anorexia, vomiting, nausea, myalgia, arthralgia, headache, and malaise, but these complications seldom prevent completion of therapy. Elevated amylase and lipase occur in most recipients, but only a minority manifest clinically apparent pancreatitis. Persons with renal insufficiency seem to be at increased risk of this complication. Electrocardiographic changes are dose dependent and include T-wave inversion and a prolonged QT interval. Arrhythmias and sudden death have been reported with doses greater than 20 mg of Sb^v/kg body weight/day. Pentavalent antimonials should be used cautiously in the elderly and in patients with heart disease. Renal failure is a rare side effect.

A major advance in the treatment of visceral leishmaniasis has been the development of miltefosine, an orally administered phosphocholine analogue that is now being used to treat patients with visceral leishmaniasis in India, where pentavalent antimony resistance is common. Miltefosine was initially developed as an antineoplastic agent.[140] It has been associated in some patients with nausea, vomiting, and at higher doses, motion sickness, but the side effects seldom interfere with completion of therapy. While additional post marketing studies are needed, miltefosine may assume an increasingly important role in the treatment of visceral and other forms of leishmaniasis worldwide in the future.

Several other compounds have been used successfully to treat patients with visceral leishmaniasis. Amphotericin B deoxycholate is effective in the treatment of visceral leishmaniasis, but it requires parenteral administration over prolonged periods of time and is associated with nephrotoxicity and other side effects.[137] Various doses and durations of therapy have been used; 1.0 mg per kg body weight per day for 15 days or 1.0 mg per kg body weight every other day for 30 days are two alternatives. Pentamidine isethionate, 2 to 4 mg/kg body weight/day for up to 15 days, is an effective but potentially toxic alternative.[138] Pentamidine has a number of side effects including hypotension, life-threatening hypoglycemia caused by pancreatic β-cell injury, and later insulin-dependent diabetes mellitus. Aminosidine (paromomycin), a parenterally administered aminoglycoside, has appeared promising in limited studies. The imidazoles, ketoconazole and itraconazole, have been used successfully in some cases, but primary failures occur and they are not recommended for general use.

Patients with visceral leishmaniasis are frequently malnourished. It is important to address their nutritional deficiencies. Associated bacterial infections are prevalent and can be life-threatening. They must be diagnosed and treated promptly. Unfortunately, there are no tests or rigid criteria to document cure after treatment of visceral leishmaniasis. The cessation of fever; weight gain; correction of anemia, leukopenia, and thrombocytopenia; and the resolution of splenomegaly and hepatomegaly are all indicative of a response, but viable amastigotes may persist even after clinically successful chemotherapy. When relapses occur, they are usually within 6 months of treatment. Relapses are common in patients with AIDS. In addition to antileishmanial chemotherapy, patients with AIDS should receive highly active antiretroviral therapy. Chronic suppressive antileishmanial therapy is also a consideration, but the optimal drug and regimen have not been defined.

Patients with post–kala-azar dermal leishmaniasis in the Sudan are typically treated with stibogluconate sodium 20 mg/kg body weight per day for 2 months, when treatment is necessary.[91,92] Treatment courses up to 4 months have been used in India, but pentavalent antimony resistance is now common there. Additional studies are needed to define the role of miltefosine and liposomal amphotericin B in the treatment of post–kala-azar dermal leishmaniasis.

Cutaneous Leishmaniasis

The decision whether and how to treat cutaneous leishmaniasis depends on the location and extent of the lesion or lesions and on the infecting *Leishmania* spp. In geographic areas where there is no mucosal leishmaniasis and a cutaneous lesion is healing or cosmetically insignificant, it can be followed expectantly without therapy, or it can be treated topically. Large or disfiguring lesions and those caused by *L. braziliensis* or

other New World *Leishmania* species associated with mucocutaneous leishmaniasis warrant systemic antileishmanial therapy.

The pentavalent antimonial drugs have been the most widely used for cutaneous leishmaniasis. Although the optimal dosage and duration of therapy may vary from one geographic area to another, 20 mg of Sb^v per kg body weight daily for 20 days is recommended.[135,136] Healing of cutaneous lesions occurs slowly over a period of weeks and is often incomplete at the end of the treatment course. In persons who fail to respond, a second or even third course of therapy may be successful, or an alternative drug may be necessary. Attention should be directed to local wound care. Antibiotics should be administered if there is evidence of cellulitis. Leishmaniasis recidivans is relatively resistant to most forms of therapy, although some success has been achieved with intralesional injections of pentavalent antimony, with or without concomitant parenteral pentavalent antimony therapy.

The toxicity associated with pentavalent antimony, the need for parenteral administration over a prolonged period, and concern over resistance has fueled the search for alternatives. Fluconazole, 200 mg daily for 6 weeks, cured 79% of persons with cutaneous leishmaniasis due to *L. major* in one study.[148] Ketoconazole, 400 to 600 mg orally each day for 4 to 6 weeks, has been reported to be effective in approximately 70% of persons with *L. major* or *L. panamensis* infections, but it is not as effective against *L. tropica, L. aethiopica,* or *L. braziliensis.* Amphotericin B deoxycholate is an effective alternative, but it is associated with substantial toxicity.

Miltefosine, which is administered orally, appears promising for cutaneous leishmaniasis,[144] but more experience is needed before it can be recommended. The efficacy of liposomal amphotericin B for cutaneous leishmaniasis likewise has not yet been systematically accessed, but the drug is costly and difficult to obtain in many endemic areas and failures have been observed. In cutaneous and diffuse cutaneous leishmaniasis caused by *L. aethiopica,* pentamidine has been used successfully, but it has substantial toxicity.

A number of other approaches have been used. The topical administration of 15% paromomycin and 12% methylbenzethonium chloride in soft white paraffin has been successful in *L. major* infections.[149] Immunotherapy with Bacillus Calmette-Guérin (BCG) administered with dead leishmania promastigotes has been used in Latin America. The response rate has been similar to that with pentavalent antimony.[150] Intralesional injection of recombinant human granulocyte macrophage colony stimulating factor (GM-CSF) plus standard parenteral pentavalent antimony therapy has shortened the time to healing.[151] Local hyperthermic therapy has also been successful, but it is difficult to administer.[152] Success has been reported using azithromycin for the treatment of cutaneous lesions due to *L. braziliensis.*[153] There have been reports of cures with other antibiotics, but many have been uncontrolled observations. Unless a study is properly designed, generalizations are difficult because cutaneous leishmaniasis resolves spontaneously over time.

American Mucocutaneous Leishmaniasis

Pentavalent antimony has been used for the treatment of American mucocutaneous leishmaniasis, but the response is variable and relapses are common.[154,155] The treatment regimens have varied, but a dose of 20 mg Sb^v per kg body weight per day is typically administered for 28 days. Some patients require longer courses. There are no tests or rigid criteria to document cure. In some regions of South America, relapse after apparent cure occurs in half of the patients with American mucocutaneous leishmaniasis. Those who do not respond or those who relapse can be treated with amphotericin B deoxycholate.[156,157] Depending on the patient's tolerance, 1.0 mg/kg body weight is given intravenously daily or every other day, respectively, for up to 30 days. Liposomal amphotericin B has been used successfully in a small number of cases. Pentamidine isethionate is an alternative, but associated with substantial toxicity. Miltefosine is of interest, but it has not yet been assessed in patients with mucocutaneous leishmaniasis. Plastic surgery may be necessary to ameliorate the sequelae of mucosal leishmaniasis. It should be delayed for a year after successful therapy because grafts may be lost if relapse occurs.

PREVENTION

There are three theoretical approaches to the prevention of leishmaniasis: vector control, reservoir control, or immunoprophylaxis. Personal protective measures are currently the most effective. Permethrin or other insecticides applied to clothing, diethyltoluamide (DEET) applied to exposed skin, and insecticide-impregnated fine mesh bed nets all provide partial protection against sand flies and can prevent transmission of leishmania.[158,159] Residual insecticides applied in houses and other buildings have yielded good results in sites where peridomestic transmission occurs. Unfortunately, spraying is necessary at intervals, sand flies may become resistant, and there is concern about the environmental impact. Of note, the cessation of dichlorodiphenyltrichloroethane (DDT) spraying for malaria in India, Bangladesh, and southern Iran was followed by major epidemics of visceral leishmaniasis. In areas where transmission occurs away from dwellings, residual insecticides are obviously of no benefit. In countries such as Spain where visceral leishmaniasis has been spread among intravenous drug users, needle exchange programs might limit transmission.

Reservoir control is another option in areas with domestic animal or human reservoirs. In northeastern Brazil, infected domestic dogs have been identified by mass serologic testing and exterminated, but the efficacy of the program has been debated. Recent studies suggest that insecticide impregnated collars may protect dogs from sand fly bites and reduce the risk of human disease.[160] In areas of person-sand fly-person transmission, case identification and treatment is important in control. In sites where leishmaniasis is a zoonosis involving sylvatic mammals, reservoir control is rarely possible.

Although no vaccine is currently available, there is reason to expect one in the future. The spontaneous resolution of human infection is associated with high-level immunity against the infecting *Leishmania* spp. Mothers living in endemic areas of the Middle East have exposed the buttocks of their children to sand flies to ensure that leishmanial infection occurs at an inconspicuous site, thus protecting them from later disfiguring skin lesions. "Immunization" was performed in Israel and the former Soviet Union using live promastigotes taken from culture. Good results were obtained with the "Jericho" strain of *L. major*.[161] Although this practice was effective in preventing naturally acquired disease, it was discontinued in Israel because some of the resulting lesions were slow to heal, others became secondarily infected, and parasites persisted at the site of inoculation even after the lesions healed. An inactive vaccine composed of killed promastigotes from five *Leishmania* strains was administered to troops in Brazil.[162] Although its efficacy in protecting against cutaneous leishmaniasis was not clearly documented, it induced leishmania-specific T-cell responses. Recent efforts have focused on identifying protective leishmanial immunogens[163] and effective adjuvants[164] and also on the development of genetically engineered, live, avirulent strains. It is likely that an effective form of immunoprophylaxis will eventually come from one of these approaches.

REFERENCES

1. Peters W, Killick-Kendrick R, eds. The Leishmaniases in Biology and Medicine. London: Academic Press; 1987.
2. Lainson R, Shaw JJ. Evolution, classification and geographic distribution. In: Peters W, Killick-Kendrick R, eds. The Leishmaniases in Biology and Medicine, v. 1. London: Academic Press; 1987:1-120.
3. Desjeux P. Programme for the surveillance and control of leishmaniasis, World Health Organization, 2001[*www.who.int/emc/diseases/leish/index.html.*]
4. Bryceson A. Visceral leishmaniasis in India. Lancet. 2000;356:1933.
5. Elias M, Rahman AJ, Khan NI. Visceral leishmaniasis and its control in Bangladesh. Bull WHO. 1989;67:43-49.
6. Zijlstra EE, Ali MS, el-Hassan AM, et al. Kala-azar in displaced people from southern Sudan: Epidemiological, clinical and therapeutic findings. Trans R Soc Trop Med Hyg. 1991;85:365-369.
7. Zijlstra EE, Ali MS, el-Hassan AM, et al. Clinical aspects of kala-azar in children from the Sudan: A comparison with the disease in adults. J Trop Pediatr. 1992;38:17-21.
8. Zijlstra EE, el-Hassan AM. Leishmaniasis in Sudan. Visceral leishmaniasis. Trans R Soc Trop Med Hyg. 2001;95(Suppl 1):S27-S58.
9. Costa CH, Pereira HF, Araujo MV. Visceral leishmaniasis epidemic in the State of Piaui, Brazil, 1980-1986. Rev Saude Publica. 1990;24:361-372.
10. Jeronimo SMB, Oliveira RM, Mackay S, et al. An urban outbreak of visceral leishmaniasis in Natal, Brazil. Trans R Soc Trop Med Hyg. 1994;88:386-388.
11. Magill AJ, Grogl M, Gasser RA, et al. Visceral infection caused by *Leishmania tropica* in veterans of Operation Desert Storm. N Engl J Med. 1993;328:1383-1387.
12. Gunby P. Desert Storm veterans now may donate blood; others call for discussion of donor tests. JAMA. 1993;269:451-452.
13. Alvar J, Canavate C, Gutierrez-Solar B, et al. Leishmania and human immunodeficiency virus coinfection: The first 10 years. Clin Microbiol Rev. 1997;10:298-319.
14. Montalban C, Calleja JL, Erice A, et al. Visceral leishmaniasis in patients infected with human immunodeficiency virus. Co-operative Group for the Study of Leishmaniasis in AIDS. J Infect. 1990;21:261-270.
15. Peters BS, Fish D, Golden R, et al. Visceral leishmaniasis in HIV infection and AIDS: Clinical features and response to therapy. Q J Med. 1990;77:1101-1111.
16. Medrano FJ, Hernandez-Quero J, Jimenez E, et al. Visceral leishmaniasis in HIV-1-infected individuals: A common opportunistic infection in Spain? AIDS. 1992;6:1499-1503.
17. Kher V, Ghosh AK, Gupta A, et al. Visceral leishmaniasis: An unusual case of fever in a renal transplant recipient. Nephrol Dial Transplant. 1991;6:736-738.
18. Moulin B, Ollier J, Bouchouareb D, et al. Leishmaniasis: A rare cause of unexplained fever in a renal graft recipient. Nephron. 1992;60:360-362.
19. Norton SA, Frankenburg S, Klaus SN. Cutaneous leishmaniasis acquired during military service in the Middle East. Arch Dermatol. 1992;128:83-87.
20. Aronson N, Ananthakrishnan M, Bernstein W, et al. Two cases of visceral leishmaniasis in U.S. military personnel—Afghanistan, 2002-2004. MMWR Morb Mortal Wkly Rep. 2004;53:265-268.
21. Jeronimo SMB, Pearson RD. The Leishmania: Protozoans adapted for intracellular survival. Subcell Biochem. 1992;18:1-37.
22. Sacks DL, Perkins PV. Identification of an infective stage of Leishmania promastigotes. Science. 1984;223:1417-1419.
23. Lewis DJ, Ward RD. Transmission and vectors. In: Peters W, Killick-Kendrick R, eds. The Leishmaniases in Biology and Medicine, v. 1. London: Academic Press; 1987:235-262.
24. Morrison AC, Ferro C, Morales A, et al. Dispersal of the sand fly *Lutzomyia longipalpis* (Diptera: Psychodidae) at an endemic focus of visceral leishmaniasis in Colombia. J Med Entomol. 1993;30:427-435.
25. Guilpin VO, Swardson-Olver C, Nosbisch L, Titus RG. Maxadilan, the vasodilator/immunomodulator from *Lutzomyia longipalpis* sand fly saliva, stimulates haematopoiesis in mice. Parasite Immunol. 2002;24:437-446.
26. Pratt DM, David JR. Monoclonal antibodies that distinguish between new world species of *Leishmania*. Nature. 1981;291:581-583.
27. Rodriquez N, Guzman B, Rodas A, et al. Diagnosis of cutaneous leishmaniasis and species discrimination of parasites by PCR and hybridization. J Clin Microbiol. 1994;32:2246-2252.
28. Nuzum E, White F III, Thakur C, et al. Diagnosis of symptomatic visceral leishmaniasis by the use of the polymerase chain reaction on patient blood. J Infect Dis. 1995;171:751-754.
29. Schonian G, Nasereddin A, Dinse N, et al. PCR diagnosis and characterization of Leishmania in local and imported clinical samples. Diag Microbiol Infect Dis. 2003;47:349-358.
30. Mauricio IL. Howard MK. Stothard JR. Miles MA. Genomic diversity in the Leishmania donovani complex. Parasitology. 1999;119:237-246.
31. Barral A, Pedral-Sampaio D, Grimaldi JG, et al. Leishmaniasis in Bahia, Brazil: Evidence that *Leishmania amazonensis* produces a wide spectrum of clinical diseases. Am J Trop Med Hyg. 1991;44:536-546.
32. Mebrahtu Y, Lawyer P, Githure J, et al. Visceral leishmaniasis unresponsive to pentostam caused by *Leishmania tropica* in Kenya. Am J Trop Med Hyg. 1989;41:289-294.
33. Badaro R, Jones TC, Lorenco R, et al. A prospective study of visceral leishmaniasis in an endemic area of Brazil. J Infect Dis. 1986;154:639-649.
34. Badaro R, Jones TC, Carvalho EM, et al. New perspectives on a subclinical form of visceral leishmaniasis. J Infect Dis. 1986;154:1003-1011.
35. Evans TG, Teixeira MJ, McAuliffe IT, et al. Epidemiology of visceral leishmaniasis in northeast Brazil. J Infect Dis. 1992;166:1124-1132.
36. de La Rosa R, Pineda JA, Delgado J, et al. Incidence of and risk factors for symptomatic visceral leishmaniasis among human immunodeficiency virus type 1-infected patients from Spain in the era of highly active antiretroviral therapy. J Clin Microbiol. 2002;40:762-767.
37. Eltoum IA, Zijlstra EE, Ali MS, Ghalib HW, et al. Congenital kala-azar and leishmaniasis in the placenta. Am J Trop Med Hyg. 1992;46:57-62.
38. Meinecke CK, Schottelius J, Oskam L, Fleischer B. Congenital transmission of visceral leishmaniasis (kala azar) from an asymptomatic mother to her child. Pediatrics. 1999;104:e65.
39. Grogl M, Daugirda JL, Hoover DL, et al. Survivability and infectivity of viscerotropic *Leishmania tropica* from Operation Desert Storm participants in human blood products maintained under blood bank conditions. Am J Trop Med Hyg. 1993;49:308-315.
40. Shulman IA. Parasitic infections and their impact on blood donor selection and testing. Arch Pathol Lab Med. 1994;118:366-370.
41. Evans TG, Pearson RD. Clinical and immunological responses following accidental inoculation of *Leishmania donovani*. Trans R Soc Trop Med Hyg. 1988;82: 854-856.
42. Herwaldt BL, Juranek DD. Laboratory-acquired malaria, leishmaniasis, trypanosomiasis and toxoplasmosis. Am J Trop Med Hyg. 1993;8:313-323.
43. Cruz I, Morales MA, Noguer I, et al. Leishmania in discarded syringes from intravenous drug users. Lancet. 2002;359:1124-1125.

44. Bora D. Epidemiology of visceral leishmaniasis in India. Natl Med J India. 1999;12:62-68.
45. Lopez-Velez R. The impact of highly active antiretroviral therapy (HAART) on visceral leishmaniasis in Spanish patients who are co-infected with HIV. Ann Trop Med Parasitol. 2003;97:S1143-S1147.
46. Blackwell JM. Genetic susceptibility to leishmanial infections: Studies in mice and man. Parasitology. 1996;112 (Suppl):S67-S74.
47. Sacks D, Noben-Trauth N. The immunology of susceptibility and resistance to *Leishmania* major in mice. Nat Rev Immunol. 2002;2:845-858.
48. Badaro R, Carvalho EM, Rocha H, et al. *Leishmania donovani:* An opportunistic microbe associated with progressive disease in three immunocompromised patients. Lancet. 1986;1:647-649.
49. Scott P, Farrell JP. Experimental cutaneous leishmaniasis: Induction and regulation of T cells following infection of mice with *Leishmania major.* Chem Immunol. 1998;70:60-80.
50. Zaph C, Scott P. Interleukin-12 regulates chemokine gene expression during the early immune response to Leishmania major. Infect Immun. 2003;71:1587-1589.
51. Murray HW, Rubin BY, Rothermel CD. Killing of intracellular *Leishmania donovani* by lymphokine-stimulated human mononuclear phagocytes. Evidence that interferon-gamma is the activating lymphokine. J Clin Invest. 1983;72:1506-1510.
52. Squires KE, Schreiber RD, McElrath MJ, et al. Experimental visceral leishmaniasis: Role of endogenous IFN-gamma in host defense and tissue granulomatous response. J Immunol. 1989;143:4244-4249.
53. Liew FY, Li Y, Moss D, et al. Resistance to *Leishmania major* infection correlates with the induction of nitric oxide synthase in murine macrophages. Eur J Immunol. 1991;21:3009-3014.
54. Green SJ, Meltzer MS, Hibbs JB, et al. Activated macrophages destroy intracellular *Leishmania major* amastigotes by an L-arginine-dependent killing mechanism. J Immunol. 1990;144:278-283.
55. Karp CL, El-Safi SH, Wynn TA, et al. In vivo cytokine profiles in patients with kala-azar; marked elevation of both interleukin-10 and interferon-gamma. J Clin Invest. 1993;91:1644-1648.
56. Holaday BJ, Pompeu MML, Jeronimo S, et al. Potential role for interleukin-10 in the immunosuppression associated with kala-azar. J Clin Invest. 1993;92:2626-2632.
57. Barral-Netto M, Barral A, Brownell CE, et al. Transforming growth factor-beta in leishmanial infection: A parasite escape mechanism. Science. 1992;247:545-548.
58. Gantt KR, Schultz-Cherry S, Rodriguez N, et al. Activation of TGF-beta by *Leishmania chagasi:* Importance for parasite survival in macrophages. J Immunol. 2003;170:2613-2620.
59. Atta AM, D'Oliveira A Jr, Correa J, et al. Anti-leishmanial IgE antibodies: A marker of active disease in visceral leishmaniasis. Am J Trop Med Hyg. 1998;59:426-430.
60. Barral-Netto M, Barral A, Santos SB, et al. Soluble IL-2 receptor as an agent of serum-mediated suppression in human visceral leishmaniasis. J Immunol. 1991;147:281-284.
61. Sang DK, Ouma JH, John CC, et al. Increased levels of soluble interleukin-4 receptor in the sera of patients with visceral leishmaniasis. J Infect Dis. 1999;179:743-746.
62. Nandan D, Knutson KL, Lo R, Reiner NE. Exploitation of host cell signaling machinery: Activation of macrophage phosphotyrosine phosphatases as a novel mechanism of molecular microbial pathogenesis. J Leukoc Biol. 2000;67:464-470.
63. Reiner NE, Ng W, McMaster WR. Parasite-accessory cell interactions in murine leishmaniasis II *Leishmania donovani* suppresses macrophage expression of class I and class II major histocompatibility complex gene products. J Immunol. 1987;138:1926-1932.
64. Reiner NE, Malemud CJ. Arachidonic acid metabolism by murine peritoneal macrophages infected with *Leishmania donovani:* In vitro evidence for parasite-induced alterations in cyclooxygenase and lipoxygenase pathways. J Immunol. 1985;134:556-563.
65. Berberich C, Ramirez-Pineda JR, Hambrecht C, et al. Dendritic cell (DC)-based protection against an intracellular pathogen is dependent upon DC-derived IL-12 and can be induced by molecularly defined antigens. J Immunol. 2003;170:3171-3179.
66. Bretscher PA, Wei G, Menon JN, Bielefeldt-Ohmann H. Establishment of stable, cell-mediated immunity that makes "susceptible" mice resistant to *Leishmania major.* Science. 1992;257:539-542.
67. Evans T, Reis MF, Alencar JE, et al. American visceral leishmaniasis (Kala-azar). West J Med. 1985;142:777-781.
68. di Martino L, Vajro P, Nocerino A, et al. Fulminant hepatitis in an Italian infant with visceral leishmaniasis. Trans R Soc Trop Med Hyg. 1992;86:34.
69. Hervas JA, Alberti P, Ferragut J, et al. Acute hepatitis as a presenting manifestation of kala azar. Pediatr Infect Dis J. 1991;10:409-410.
70. Vasconcelos Ide A, Sousa Ade Q, Vasconcelos AW, et al. Cutaneous parasitism by *Leishmania (Leishmania) chagasi* during South American visceral leishmaniasis. Bull Soc Pathol Exot. 1993;86:101-105.
71. Harrison LH, Naidu TG, Drew JS, et al. Reciprocal relationships between undernutrition and the parasitic disease visceral leishmaniasis. Rev Infect Dis. 1986;8:447-453.
72. Pearson RD, Cox G, Jeronimo SMB, et al. Visceral leishmaniasis: A model for infection-induced cachexia. Am J Trop Med Hyg. 1992;47(Suppl):8-15.
73. Andrade TM, Carvalho EM, Rocha H. Bacterial infections in patients with visceral leishmaniasis. J Infect Dis. 1990;162:1354-1359.
74. Garces JM, Tomas S, Rubies-Prat J, et al. Bacterial infection as a presenting manifestation of visceral leishmaniasis. Rev Infect Dis. 1990;12:518-519.
75. Wickramasinghe SN, Abdalla SH, Kasili EG. Ultrastructure of bone marrow in patients with visceral leishmaniasis. J Clin Pathol. 1987;40:267-275.
76. Carvalho EM, Andrews BS, Martinelli R, et al. Circulating immune complexes and rheumatoid factor in schistosomiasis and visceral leishmaniasis. Am J Trop Med Hyg. 1983;32:61-69.
77. Pearson RD, Alencar JE, Romito R, et al. Circulating immune complexes and rheumatoid factors in visceral leishmaniasis. J Infect Dis. 1983;147:1102.
78. Pagliano P, Rossi M, Rescigno C, et al. Mediterranean visceral leishmaniasis in HIV-negative adults: A retrospective analysis of 64 consecutive cases (1995-2001). J Antimicrob Chemother. 2003;52:264-268.
79. De Brito T, Hoshino-Shimizu S, Neto VA, et al. Glomerular involvement in human kala-azar. Am J Trop Med Hyg. 1975;24:9-18.
80. Dutra M, Martinelli R, de Carvalho EM, et al. Renal involvement in visceral leishmaniasis. Am J Kidney Dis. 1985;6:22-27.
81. Caravaca F, Munoz A, Pizarro JL, et al. Acute renal failure in visceral leishmaniasis. Am J Nephrol. 1991;11:350-352.
82. Chenoweth CE, Singal S, Pearson RD, et al. Acquired immunodeficiency syndrome-related visceral leishmaniasis presenting in a pleural effusion. Chest. 1993;103:648-649.
83. Matheron S, Cable A, Parquin F, et al. Visceral leishmaniasis and HIV infection: Unusual presentation with pleuropulmonary involvement, and effect of secondary prophylaxis. AIDS. 1992;6:238-240.
84. Datry A, Similowski T, Jais P, et al. AIDS-associated leishmaniasis: An unusual gastro-duodenal presentation. Trans R Soc Trop Med Hyg. 1990;84:239-240.
85. Altes J, Salas A, Llompart A, et al. Small intestine involvement in visceral leishmaniasis. Am J Gastroenterol. 1991;86:1283.
86. Delsedime L, Coppola F, Mazzucco G. Gastric localization of systemic leishmaniasis in a patient with AIDS. Histopathology. 1991;19:93-95.
87. Muigai R, Gatei DG, Shaunak S, et al. Jejunal function and pathology in visceral leishmaniasis. Lancet. 1983;2:476-479.
88. Sendino A, Barbado FJ, Mostaza JM, et al. Visceral leishmaniasis with malabsorption syndrome in a patient with acquired immunodeficiency syndrome. Am J Med. 1990;89:673-675.
89. Grau JM, Bosch X, Salgado AC, et al. Human immunodeficiency virus (HIV) and aplastic anemia. Ann Intern Med. 1989;110:576-577.
90. Fernandez Cotarelo MJ, Abellan Martinez J, Guerra Vales JM, et al. Effect of highly active antiretroviral therapy on the incidence and clinical manifestations of visceral leishmaniasis in human immunodeficiency virus-infected patients. Clin Infect Dis. 2003;37:973-977.
91. Zijlstra EE, Musa AM, Khalil EA, et al. Post-kala-azar dermal leishmaniasis. Lancet Infect Dis. 2003;3:87-98.
92. Zijlstra EE, el-Hassan AM. Leishmaniasis in Sudan. Post kala-azar dermal leishmaniasis. Trans Rl Soc Trop Med Hyg. 2001;95(Suppl 1):S59-S76.
93. Musa AM, Khalil EA, Raheem MA, et al. The natural history of Sudanese post-kala-azar dermal leishmaniasis: Clinical, immunological and prognostic features. Ann Trop Med Parasitol. 2002;96:765-772.
94. Chulay JD, Bryceson ADM. Quantitation of amastigotes of *Leishmania donovani* in smears of splenic aspirates from patients with visceral leishmaniasis. Am J Trop Med Hyg. 1983;32:475-479.
95. Burns JM Jr, Shreffler WG, Benson DR, et al. Molecular characterization of a kinesin-related antigen of *Leishmania chagasi* that detects specific antibody in African and American visceral *leishmaniasis.* Proc Natl Acad Sci USA. 1993;90:775-759.
96. Braz RF, Nascimento ET, Martins DR, et al. The sensitivity and specificity of *Leishmania chagasi* recombinant K39 antigen in the diagnosis of American visceral leishmaniasis and in differentiating active from subclinical infection. Am J Trop Med Hyg. 2002;67:344-348.
97. Kar K. Serological diagnosis of leishmaniasis. Crit Rev Microbiol. 1995;21:123-152.
98. Ashford RW, Bettini S. Ecology and epidemiology: Old World. In: Peters W, Killick-Kendrick R, eds. The Leishmaniases in Biology and Medicine, v. 1. London: Academic Press; 1987;365-424.
99. Gramiccia M, Ben-Ismail R, Gradoni L, et al. A *Leishmania infantum* enzymatic variant, causative agent of cutaneous leishmaniasis in north Tunisia. Trans R Soc Trop Med Hyg. 1991;85:370-371.
100. Grimaldi G Jr, Tesh RB, McMahon-Pratt DM. A review of the geographic distribution and epidemiology of leishmaniasis in the new world. Am J Trop Med Hyg. 1989;41:687-725.
101. Desjeux P. Information on the epidemiology and control of the leishmaniasis by country and territory. 1991. WHO/Leish/91.30 World Health Organization.
102. Shaw JJ, Lainson R. Ecology and epidemiology: New world. In: Peters W, Killick-Kendrick R, eds. The Leishmaniases in Biology and Medicine, v. 1. London: Academic Press; 1987;291-363.
103. Nelson DA, Gustafson TL, Spielvogel RL. Clinical aspects of cutaneous leishmaniasis acquired in Texas. J Am Acad Dermatol. 1985;12:985-992.
104. Ridley DS. The pathogenesis of cutaneous leishmaniasis. Trans R Soc Trop Med Hyg. 1979;73:150-160.
105. Ridley MJ, Ridley DS. Cutaneous leishmaniasis: Immune complex formation and necrosis in the acute phase. Br J Exp Pathol. 1984;65:327-336.
106. Ritter U, Korner H. Divergent expression of inflammatory dermal chemokines in cutaneous leishmaniasis. Parasite Immunol. 2002;24:295-301.
107. Barral A, Costa JM, Bittencourt AL, et al.. Polar and subpolar diffuse cutaneous leishmaniasis in Brazil: Clinical and immunopathologic aspects. Int J Dermatol. 1995;34:474-479.
108. Bacellar O, Lessa H, Schriefer A, et al. Up-regulation of Th1-type responses in mucosal leishmaniasis patients. Infect Immun. 2002;70:6734-6740.
109. Ghersetich I, Menchini G, Teofoli P, Lotti T. Immune response to Leishmania infection in human skin. Clin Dermatol. 1999;17:333-338.

110. Smith PAJ. Long incubation period in leishmaniasis. Br Med J. 1955;2:1143.

111. Barral A, Guerreiro J, Bomfim G, et al. Lymphadenopathy as the first sign of human cutaneous infection by *Leishmania braziliensis*. Am J Trop Med Hyg. 1995;53: 256-259.

112. Sousa AQ, Parise ME, Pompeu MM, et al. Bubonic leishmaniasis: A common manifestation of *Leishmania (Viannia) braziliensis* infection in Ceara, Brazil. Am J Trop Med Hyg. 1995;53:380-385.

113. Bryceson ADM. Diffuse cutaneous leishmaniasis in Ethiopia. I: The clinical and histological features of disease. Trans R Soc Trop Med Hyg. 1969;63:708-737.

114. Turetz ML, Machado PR, Ko AI, et al. Disseminated leishmaniasis: A new and emerging form of leishmaniasis observed in northeastern Brazil. J Infect Dis. 2002;186:1829-1834.

115. Agostoni C, Dorigoni N, Malfitano A, et al. Mediterranean leishmaniasis in HIV-infected patients: Epidemiology, clinical and diagnostic features of 22 cases. Infection. 1998;26:93-99.

116. Moses AE, Maayan S, Rahav G, et al. HIV infection and AIDS in Jerusalem: A microcosm of illness in Israel. Isr J Med Sci 1996;32:716-721.

117. Golino A, Duncan JM, Zeluff B, et al. Leishmaniasis in a heart transplant patient. J Heart Lung Transplant. 1992;11:820-823.

118. Pearson RD, Navin TR, Sousa AQ, et al. Leishmaniasis. In: Kass EH, Platt R, eds. Current Therapy in Infectious Diseases-3. Toronto: BC Decker; 1990:3384-3389.

119. Berger RS, Perez-Figaredo RA, Spielvogel RL. Leishmaniasis: The touch preparation as a rapid means of diagnosis. J Am Acad Dermatol. 1987;16:1096-1105.

120. Kalter DC. Laboratory tests for the diagnosis and evaluation of leishmaniasis. Dermatol Clin. 1994;12:37-50.

121. Weigle KA, de Davalos M, Heredia P, et al. Diagnosis of cutaneous and mucocutaneous leishmaniasis in Colombia: A comparison of seven methods. Am J Trop Med Hyg. 1987;36:489-496.

122. Marsden PD. Mucosal leishmaniasis ("espundia," Escomel, 1911). Trans R Soc Trop Med Hyg. 1986;80:859-876.

123. Jones TC, Johnson WD Jr, Barretto AC, et al. Epidemiology of American cutaneous leishmaniasis due to *Leishmania braziliensis braziliensis*. J Infect Dis. 1987;156: 73-83.

124. Walton BC, Chinel LV, Egula OE. Onset of espundia after many years of occult infection with *Leishmania braziliensis*. Am J Trop Med Hyg. 1973;22:696-698.

125. Marsden PD, Nonata RR. Mucocutaneous leishmaniasis-a review of clinical aspects. Rev Soc Bras Med Trop. 1975;9:309-326.

126. Cuba CAC, Marsden PD, Barreto AC, et al. Parasitologic and immunologic diagnosis of American (mucocutaneous) leishmaniasis. Bull Pan Am Health Org. 1981;15:249-259.

127. Walton BC, Brooks WH, Arjona J. Serodiagnosis of American leishmaniasis by indirect fluorescent antibody test. Am J Trop Med Hyg. 1972;21:296-299.

128. Walton BC. Evaluation of chemotherapy of American visceral leishmaniasis by indirect fluorescent antibody test. Am J Trop Med Hyg. 1980;29:747-752.

129. Berman JD. Human leishmaniasis: clinical, diagnostic, and chemotherapeutic developments in the last 10 years. Clin Infect Dis. 1997;24:684-703.

130. Torre-Cisneros J, Villanueva JL, Kindelan JM, et al. Successful treatment of antimony-resistant visceral leishmaniasis with liposomal amphotericin B in patients infected with human immunodeficiency virus. Clin Infect Dis. 1993;17:625-627.

131. Gokhale PC, Kshiragar NA, Khan MU, et al. Successful treatment of resistant visceral leishmaniasis with liposomal amphotericin B. Trans R Soc Trop Med Hyg. 1994;88:228.

132. Davidson RN, di Martino L, Gradoni L, et al. Liposomal amphotericin B (AmBisome) in Mediterranean visceral leishmaniasis: A multi-centre trial. Q J Med. 1994;87:75-81.

133. di Martiono L, Ramondi F, Scotti S, et al. Efficacy and tolerability of liposomal amphotericin B in Italian infants with visceral leishmaniasis. Trans R Soc Trop Med Hyg. 1993;87:477.

134. Seaman J, Boer C, Wilkerson R, et al. Liposomal amphotericin B (AmBisome) in the treatment of complicated kala-azar under field conditions. Clin Infect Dis. 1995;21:188-193.

135. Grogl M, Thomason TN, Franke ED. Drug resistance in leishmaniasis: Its implications in systemic chemotherapy of cutaneous and mucocutaneous disease. Am J Trop Med Hyg. 1992;47:117-126.

136. Herwaldt BL, Berman JD. Recommendations for treating leishmaniasis with sodium stibogluconate (Pentostam) and review of pertinent clinical studies. Am J Trop Med Hyg. 1992;46:296-306.

137. Thakur CP, Sinha GP, Pandey AK, et al. Daily versus alternate-day regimen of amphotericin B in the treatment of kala-azar: A randomized comparison. Bull WHO. 1994;72:931-936.

138. Mishra M, Biswas UK, Jha DN, et al. Amphotericin versus pentamidine in antimony-unresponsive kala-azar. Lancet. 1992;340:1256-1257.

139. Soto-Mancipe J, Grogl M, Berman JD. Evaluation of pentamidine for the treatment of cutaneous leishmaniasis in Colombia. Clin Infect Dis. 1993;16:417-425.

140. Fischer C, Voss A, Engel J. Development status of miltefosine as first oral drug in visceral and cutaneous leishmaniasis. Med Microbiol Immunol. 2001;190:85-87.

141. Jha TK, Sundar S, Thakur CP, et al. Miltefosine, an oral agent, for the treatment of Indian visceral leishmaniasis. N Engl J Med 1999;341:1795-1800.

142. Sundar S, Rosenkaimer F, Makharia MK, et al. Trial of oral miltefosine for visceral leishmaniasis. Lancet 1998;352:1821-1823.

143. Sundar S, Makharia A, More DK, et al. Short-course oral miltefosine for treatment of visceral leishmaniasis. Clin Infect Dis. 2000;31:1110-1113.

144. Soto J, Toledo J, Gutierrez P, et al. Treatment of American cutaneous leishmaniasis with miltefosine, an oral agent. Clin Infect Dis. 2001;33:E57-E61.

145. Sundar S, Agrawal NK, Sinha PR, et al. Short-course, low-dose amphotericin B lipid complex therapy for visceral leishmaniasis unresponsive to antimony. Ann Intern Med. 1997;127:133-137.

146. Sundar S. Drug resistance in Indian visceral leishmaniasis. Trop Med Int Hlth. 2001;6:849-54.

147. Thakur CP, Kumar K. Efficacy of prolonged therapy with stibogluconate in post kala-azar dermal leishmaniasis. Indian J Med Res. 1990;91:144-148.

148. Alrajhi AA, Ibrahim EA, De Vol EB, et al. Fluconazole for the treatment of cutaneous leishmaniasis caused by *Leishmania major*. N Engl J Med. 2002;346:891-895.

149. El-On J, Harvey S, Grumwald MH, et al. Topical treatment of Old World cutaneous leishmaniasis caused by *Leishmania major*. A double blind study. J Am Acad Dernatol. 1992;27:227-231.

150. Convit J, Rondon A, Ulrich M, et al. Immunotherapy versus chemotherapy in localized cutaneous leishmaniasis. Lancet. 1987;1:401-405.

151. Almeida R, D'Oliveira A Jr, Machado P, et al. Randomized, double-blind study of stibogluconate plus human granulocyte macrophage colony-stimulating factor versus stibogluconate alone in the treatment of cutaneous Leishmaniasis. J Infect Dis. 1999;180:1735-1737.

152. Navin TR, Arana BA, Arana FE, et al. Placebo-controlled clinical trial of meglumine antimonate (glucantime) vs. localized controlled heat in the treatment of cutaneous leishmaniasis in Guatemala. Am J Trop Med Hyg. 1990;42:43-50.

153. Prata A, Silva-Vergara ML, Costa L, et al. Efficacy of azithromycin in the treatment of cutaneous leishmaniasis. Rev Soc Bras Med Trop. 2003;36:65-69.

154. Franke ED, Wignall S, Cruz ME, et al. Efficacy and toxicity of sodium stibogluconate for mucosal leishmaniasis. Ann Intern Med. 1990;113:934-940.

155. Report of the workshop on the chemotherapy of mucocutaneous leishmaniasis. UNDP/World Bank/Who Special Programme for Research and Training in Tropical Diseases, Brasilia, July 1979.

156. Sampaio SAP, Godoy JT, Paiva L, et al. The treatment of American (mucocutaneous) leishmanias with amphotericin B. Arch Dermatol. 1960;82:627-635.

157. Crofts MAJ. Use of amphotericin B in mucocutaneous leishmaniasis. J Trop Med Hyg. 1976;79:111-113.

158. Schreck CE, Kline DL, Chaniotis BN, et al. Evaluation of personal protection methods against phlebotomine sand flies including vectors of leishmaniasis in Panama. Am J Trop Med Hyg. 1982;31:1046-1053.

159. Soto J, Medina F, Dember N, Berman J. Efficacy of permethrin-impregnated uniforms in the prevention of malaria and leishmaniasis in Colombian soldiers. Clin Infect Dis. 1995;21:599-602.

160. Gavgani AS, Hodjati MH, Mohite H, Davies CR. Effect of insecticide-impregnated dog collars on incidence of zoonotic visceral leishmaniasis in Iranian children: A matched-cluster randomised trial. Lancet. 2002;360:374-379.

161. Greenblatt CL. The present and future of vaccination for cutaneous leishmaniasis. In: Mizrahi A, Hertman I, Klingberg MA, et al, eds. Progress in Clinical and Biological Research, v 47. New Developments with Human and Veterinary Vaccines. New York: Alan R Liss; 1980:259-285.

162. Antunes CM, Mayrink W, Magalhaes PA, et al. Controlled field trials of a vaccine against New World cutaneous leishmaniasis. Int J Epidemiol. 1986;15:572-580.

163. Reed SG, Campos-Neto A. Vaccines for parasitic and bacterial diseases. Curr Opin Immunol. 2003;15:456-460.

164. Skeiky YA, Coler RN, Brannon M, et al. Protective efficacy of a tandemly linked, multi-subunit recombinant leishmanial vaccine (Leish-111f) formulated in MPL adjuvant. Vaccine. 2002;20:3292-3303.

CHAPTER **274**

Trypanosoma Species (American Trypanosomiasis, Chagas' Disease): Biology of Trypanosomes

LOUIS V. KIRCHHOFF

The genus *Trypanosoma* consists of approximately 20 species of protozoa.[1] Two of the three species that infect humans are pathogenic, and several other species cause severe and economically important diseases in domestic mammals. Broadly defined, the organisms belonging to this genus are protozoan flagellates of the family Trypanosomatidae, order Kinetoplastida, that pass through different morphologic stages (epimastigote, amastigote, and trypomastigote) in their vertebrate and invertebrate hosts. The criterion of three morphologic stages, however, is not fulfilled by each species in the genus. For example, only *Trypanosoma cruzi*, the etiologic agent of American trypanosomiasis, or Chagas' disease, and one other species, multiply in mammalian hosts as intracellular amastigotes similar to those seen in infections caused by *Leishmania*. In contrast, African trypanosomes, which cause sleeping sickness in humans and varying degrees of morbidity in wild and domestic mammals, do not have an intracellular form and multiply as trypomastigotes that circulate in the mammalian blood stream and other extracellular spaces.

The trypomastigote form has a single flagellum originating near the kinetoplast, which is a DNA-containing structure located in the parasite's single, complex mitochondrion. The flagellum runs alongside the body of the parasite and is enveloped in an undulating membrane. It extends beyond the body as a free, threadlike structure. The undulating membrane and the free portion of the flagellum give the organism considerable motility.

According to their course of development in the vector, trypanosomes have been classified into two major groups:

1. *Stercoraria:* Multiplication in the mammalian host is discontinuous, taking place in the amastigote stage. Development in the vector (*Triatominae*, or kissing bugs) is completed in the hindgut (posterior station), and mammalian hosts become infected by contaminative transmission. The subgenus *Schizotrypanum* belongs to this group and includes *T. cruzi*.
2. *Salivaria:* Multiplication in the mammalian host is continuous, taking place in the trypomastigote stage. Development in the vector (*Glossina*, or tsetse fly) is completed in the salivary glands (anterior station), and inoculative transmission to the mammalian host occurs. The subgenus *Trypanozoon* belongs to this group and includes, among others, *Trypanosoma brucei brucei,* which causes disease in animals but does not infect humans. *Trypanosoma brucei gambiense* and *Trypanosoma brucei rhodesiense,* the two causative agents of African sleeping sickness, or human African trypanosomiasis, are also found in this subgenus. As a group, these three organisms are often referred to as the *T. brucei* complex. Endemic areas of Chagas' disease and African sleeping sickness do not overlap (Fig. 274-1). Moreover, there are such important differences in the transmission, pathogenesis, and clinical course of the two diseases that they have little in common except the genetic and morphologic similarities of the causative agents.

CHAGAS' DISEASE

Life Cycle and Transmission

T. cruzi, the causative agent of American trypanosomiasis, is transmitted by various species of bloodsucking triatomine insects, or kissing bugs (Fig. 274-2).[2,3] These vectors are found in large numbers in the wild, where they transmit the parasite among many mammalian species that constitute the natural reservoir, and in endemic areas they live in the nooks and crannies of substandard dwellings. The insects become infected by sucking blood from animals or humans that have circulating trypomastigotes (Fig. 274-3). The ingested parasites multiply in the midgut of the insects as epimastigotes, which are flagellates of a distinct morphologic type, and in the hindgut transform into infective metacyclic trypomastigotes that are discharged with the feces at the time of subsequent blood meals. Transmission to a second vertebrate host occurs when mucous membranes, conjunctivae, or breaks in the skin are contaminated with bug feces containing the infective forms. The parasites then enter a variety of host cell types and multiply in the

Human Trypanosomiasis

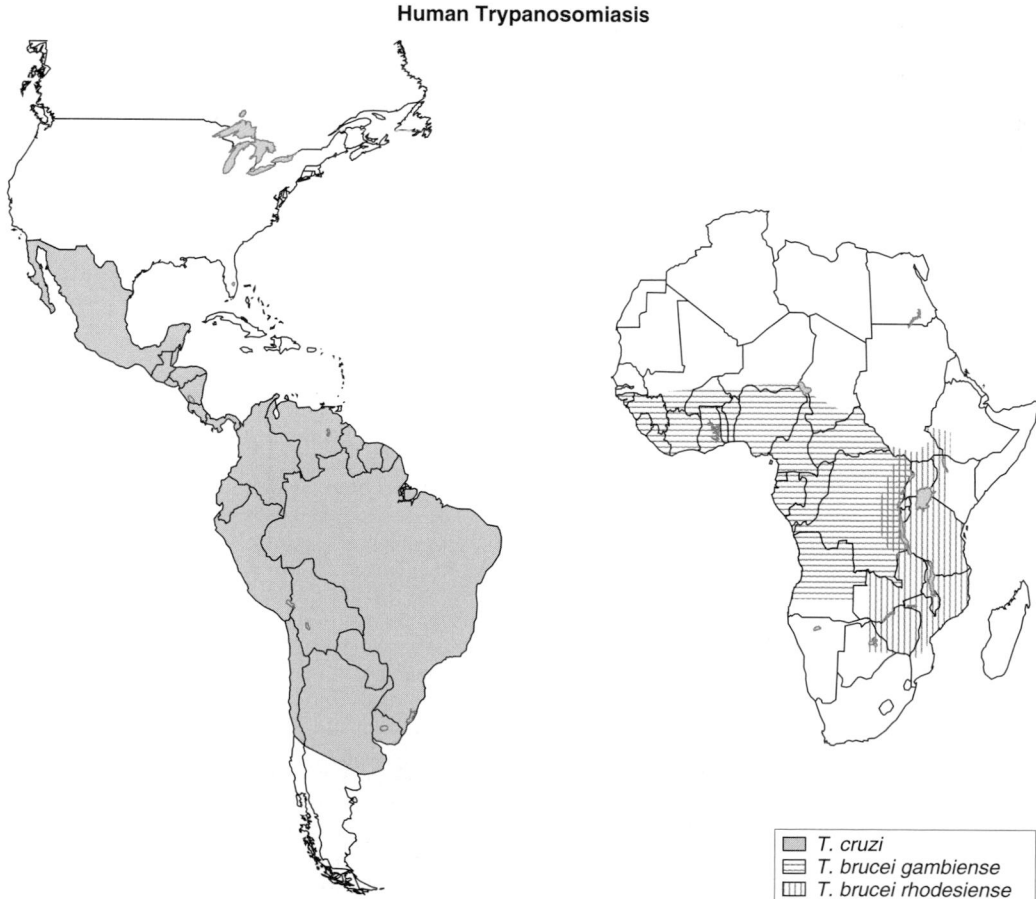

	T. cruzi
	T. brucei gambiense
	T. brucei rhodesiense

FIGURE 274-1. Distribution of human trypanosomiasis.

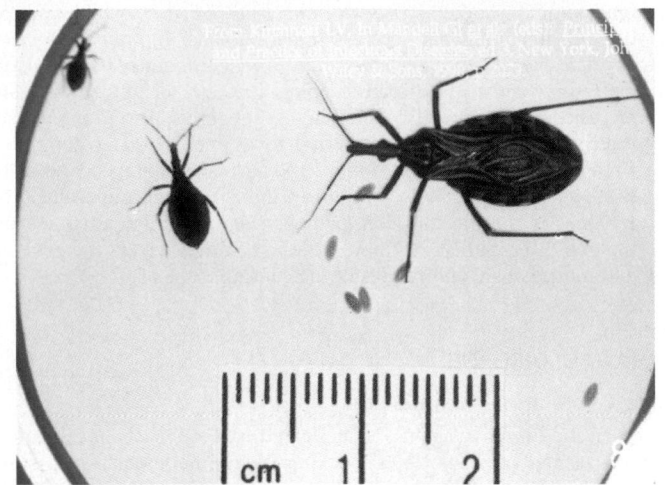

FIGURE 274-2. *Rhodnius prolixus,* a common vector of *Trypanosoma cruzi. Counterclockwise,* Eggs, second stage nymph, and adult.

cytoplasm after transformation into amastigotes. When multiplying amastigotes fill the host cell, they differentiate into trypomastigotes, and the cell ruptures. The parasites released invade local tissues or spread hematogenously to distant sites, thus initiating further cycles of multiplication, primarily in muscle cells, and maintaining a parasitemia infective for vectors.

Transmission of *T. cruzi* also occurs through blood transfusions[4] and typically takes place in cities when infected but asymptomatic migrants from endemic rural areas donate blood. Serologic screening of donated blood has markedly reduced transmission by this route in most endemic areas. *T. cruzi* can also be transmitted by transplantation of organs obtained from chronically infected persons.[5,6] Roughly 5% of infants born to *T. cruzi*-infected women have congenital Chagas' disease. Although some of these infants have severe problems as a result of the infection, about 70% are completely asymptomatic.[7-9] Finally, numerous laboratory accidents resulting in acute Chagas' disease have occurred as a consequence of the facility with which infective forms of the parasite can be produced in the laboratory.[10]

Pathology

In acute Chagas' disease, the inflammatory lesion caused by *T. cruzi* at the site of entry is called a *chagoma.*[11] Local histologic changes in-

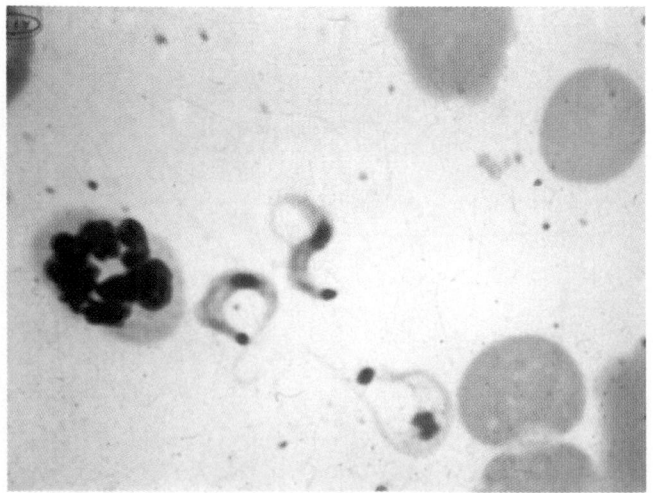

FIGURE 274-3. *Trypanosoma cruzi* trypomastigotes in a smear of mouse blood (Giemsa, ×625). *(Courtesy of Dr. Herbert B. Tanowitz, New York, NY.)*

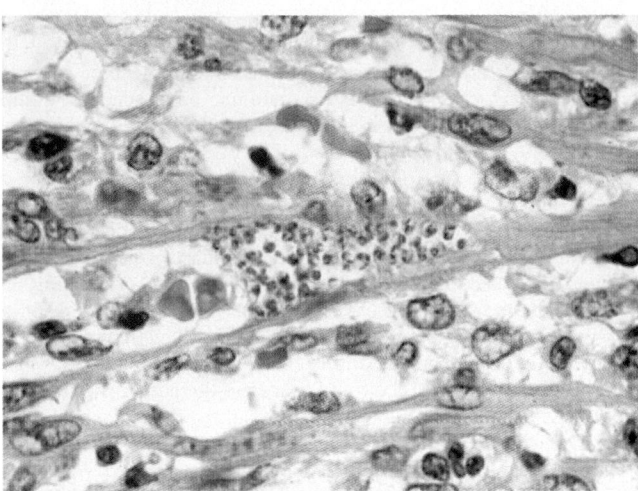

FIGURE 274-4. *Trypanosoma cruzi* in the cardiac muscle of a child who died of acute Chagas' disease in Texas. *(H&E,* ×900.)

clude intracellular parasitism of muscle and other subcutaneous tissues, interstitial edema, lymphocytic infiltration, and reactive hyperplasia of adjacent lymph nodes. Trypomastigotes released when host cells rupture often can be detected by microscopic examination of fresh blood. Muscles, including the myocardium, are the most heavily parasitized tissues. Myocarditis may develop in association with patchy areas of infected cells and necrosis.[12,13] The characteristic pseudocysts seen in sections of infected tissues are intracellular aggregates of amastigotes (Fig. 274-4). A lymphocytosis accompanies the high parasitemias of the acute illness, and mild elevation of transaminase levels is occasionally seen. In some patients, parasites may be found in the cerebrospinal fluid.

The heart is the organ most commonly affected in chronic Chagas' disease. Gross examination of the hearts of chronic chagasic patients who died of heart failure reveals marked bilateral ventricular enlargement, often involving the right side of the heart more than the left. Thinning of the ventricular walls is common, as are apical aneurysms and mural thrombi. Widespread lymphocytic infiltration is present, accompanied by diffuse interstitial fibrosis and atrophy of myocardial cells. Parasites are rarely seen in stained sections of myocardial tissue, but recent studies using polymerase chain reaction (PCR) assays have demonstrated the presence of parasites in areas of focal inflammation.[14-17]

Pathologic changes are also common in the conduction system of chronic chagasic hearts and often correlate with premortem rhythm disturbances.[18] Dense fibrosis and chronic inflammatory lesions most frequently involve the right branch and the left anterior branch of the bundle of His, but lesions of this type are found in other parts of the conduction system as well.

The striking features apparent on gross examination of the esophagus or colon of a patient with chronic Chagas' disease of the digestive tract (megadisease) are the enormous dilation and muscular hypertrophy of the affected organs.[19,20] On microscopic examination, focal inflammatory lesions with lymphocytic infiltration are seen. A marked reduction in the number of neurons in the myenteric plexus is also apparent, and peri- and intraganglion fibrosis in the presence of Schwann cell proliferation and lymphocytosis is found. In most patients, the clinical effects of this parasympathetic denervation are confined to the esophagus or the colon, or both, but similar lesions have been observed in the biliary tree, the ureters, and other hollow viscera.

The pathogenesis of the cardiac and gastrointestinal lesions of chronic Chagas' disease has been debated for many years. In recent years convincing evidence has accumulated indicating that the persistence of parasites in heart muscle stimulates a chronic inflammatory process that often results in rhythm disturbances and cardiomyopathy.[16,21]

Epidemiology

T. cruzi infection is a zoonosis, and humans are merely unfortunate hosts whose involvement in the cycle of transmission is not necessary for the perpetuation of the parasite in nature. The triatomine vectors necessary for natural transmission of *T. cruzi* are found in the Americas from the southern half of the United States to southern Argentina.[3] Although infected insects have been found throughout this range, their distribution is uneven. Burrows, hollow trees, palm trees, and other animal shelters are sites where transmission of *T. cruzi* occurs among infected insects and nonhuman mammalian hosts. Vector transmission to humans occurs only in areas in which triatomine species that defecate during or immediately after blood meals are present. This limitation does not apply to the range of the infection in lower mammals, however, because they can acquire the infection by eating infected insects.[22]

T. cruzi has been isolated from more than 150 species of wild and domestic mammals. The ability of the parasite to adapt to such a wide variety of hosts, coupled with the long-term parasitemias in infected mammals, results in the presence of an enormous sylvatic and domestic reservoir in enzootic areas. Infected mammals have been found in the southern United States[23,24] and from there southward to central Argentina and Chile.

Historically, humans become involved in the cycle of transmission when land is opened up for farming in enzootic areas where vector species adaptable to living in human dwellings, such as *Rhodnius prolixus* and *Triatoma infestans,* are prevalent. As the natural habitat of the vectors and mammalian hosts is disrupted, the insects take up residence in niches in the settlers' primitive wood, mud, and stone houses. In this way, the infected triatomine insects become domiciliary, and the domestic cycle of transmission is established to include domestic animals and humans.[25,26] Thus, human trypanosomiasis in Latin America is primarily a public health problem among poor persons who live in rural areas. Most new vector-borne infections occur in children younger than 10 years old. In a study of selected patients, the case fatality rate for acute Chagas' disease was 12%, but the rate for all new infections is probably less than 1%.[27]

It is currently estimated by the Pan American Health Organization that 10 to 12 million people are infected with *T. cruzi* and that up to 45,000 persons die each year of Chagas' disease.[28] The total annual cost of the morbidity and death associated with Chagas' disease in all endemic countries is thought to be more than US$8 billion.[29] Despite this bleak picture, the current situation relating to the transmission of *T. cruzi* is much brighter. A major international control program in the Southern Cone nations of South America (Argentina, Bolivia, Brazil, Chile, Paraguay, and Uruguay), initiated in 1991, has achieved a marked reduction in transmission rates through education of at risk populations and vector and blood bank control programs. Gradual reduction in prevalence rates in younger age groups and progressive reduction in the percentage of blood donors infected with *T. cruzi* stand as clear evidence of the success of the program.[30-32] Uruguay was certified as transmission-free in 1997 and Chile followed in 1999. It is likely that Argentina and Brazil will be judged free of transmission in 2005 or 2006.[33] Similar control programs have been initiated recently in the Andean countries and also in Central America. In Mexico screening of donated blood for *T. cruzi* infection is likely to be mandated nationwide in the near future, although at the present time only 13% of the blood supply is screened serologically.[28,34] The barriers hindering the elimination of *T. cruzi* transmission to humans throughout the endemic range are economic and political, and no technical breakthroughs are necessary for its completion.

Only about 10% to 30% of persons with chronic *T. cruzi* infections will develop symptomatic Chagas' disease.[35] The age distribution of the onset of the two types of chronic disease is broad. The relatively high frequency of sudden death in young adults observed in some regions in the past was attributed to the disturbances of cardiac rhythm associated with Chagas' disease, and in one highly endemic area in Brazil, chagasic cardiac disease was found to be the leading cause of death in young adults.[36] There is considerable geographic

variation in the prevalence of symptomatic chronic Chagas' disease among infected persons. The prevalence of cardiac disease among persons who harbor the parasite chronically is lower in Venezuela, Colombia, Central America, and Mexico than in the rest of the endemic range. Similarly, megaesophagus and megacolon in association with *T. cruzi* infection are virtually unknown in the northern endemic range, whereas they reach 15% to 20% in the southern endemic regions. It is not known whether host factors or parasite strain differences are the primary determinants of this geographic variation in the patterns of clinical disease.[37]

Despite the presence of *T. cruzi*–infected triatomine vectors in many parts of the southern and western United States, only five autochthonous cases of Chagas' disease have been reported: three in Texas, one in California, and a recent case in Tennessee.[12,38] The rarity of transmission of *T. cruzi* to humans in the United States probably results from our relatively high housing standards and the low overall vector density. In the last 30 years, about 15 laboratory-acquired and imported cases of acute Chagas' disease have been reported to the Centers for Disease Control and Prevention (CDC), but none in the latter group occurred in returning tourists. However, two instances of tourists returning to Europe from Latin America with acute *T. cruzi* infections have been reported.[39] Although the number of autochthonous and imported cases of acute *T. cruzi* infection that go unrecognized may be many times the number reported, the fact remains that acute Chagas' disease is rare in the United States.

In contrast, in recent decades the number of persons in the United States with chronic *T. cruzi* infections has grown considerably. It is estimated that more than 12 million persons born in countries in which Chagas' disease is endemic currently reside here. Eight million of these immigrants are from Mexico.[40] Moreover, a sizable proportion of these immigrants have come from Central America, a region in which the prevalence of *T. cruzi* infection is high. A study of Salvadoran and Nicaraguan immigrants in Washington, D.C., found a 5% prevalence of *T. cruzi* infection.[41] Seroprevalence studies done in a Los Angeles hospital where 50% of blood donors are Hispanic showed that between 1 in 1000 and 1 in 500 harbor *T. cruzi*.[42] In another investigation performed in seven blood banks in three southwestern states, 1 in 603 donors with Hispanic surnames was determined to be infected.[43] Finally, in a study of 300,000 donors in Los Angeles and Miami, the prevalence of *T. cruzi* infection was found to be 1 in 8800 in the general donor population and 1 in 710 among donors who had spent a month or more in an area in which Chagas' disease is endemic.[44,45]

These findings and census data suggest that there are 80,000 to 100,000 *T. cruzi*–infected persons now living in the United States. The presence of infected immigrants poses a risk of transfusion-associated transmission of *T. cruzi,* and to date seven such cases have been reported in the U.S. and Canada[46] (see farther on). Moreover, the recent transplantation of organs obtained from a chronically infected Central American immigrant resulted in three cases of acute Chagas' disease, one of which was fatal.[6]

Clinical Course

The clinical syndromes of acute *T. cruzi* infection and chronic Chagas' disease are quite different. The acute illness results from the first encounter of the host with the parasite, and chronic disease involves late sequelae.

Acute Chagas' disease[47] is usually an illness of children, but it can occur at any age. Only a small portion of acute infections caused by *T. cruzi* are recognized as such because of the mild and nonspecific nature of the symptoms in most patients and the lack of access to medical care. The first signs of illness occur at least a week after invasion by the parasites. When the parasite has entered through a break in the skin, a chagoma may be formed, consisting of an indurated area of erythema and swelling accompanied by local lymph node involvement. The Romaña's sign (Fig. 274-5), the classic sign of acute Chagas' disease, consists of painless edema of the palpebrae and periocular tissues and may appear when the conjunctiva is the portal of entry. These initial local signs can be followed by fever, malaise,

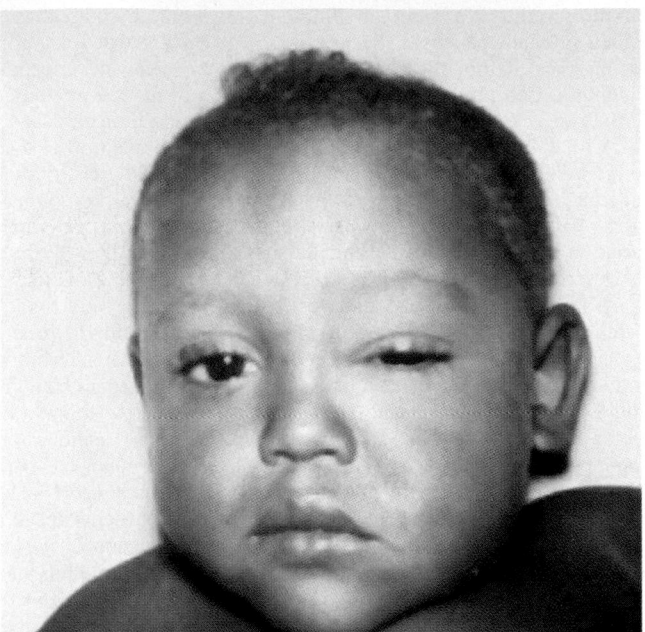

FIGURE 274-5. Romaña's sign in an Argentinean child with acute Chagas' disease. *(Courtesy of Dr. Humberto Lugones, Santiago del Estero, Argentina.)*

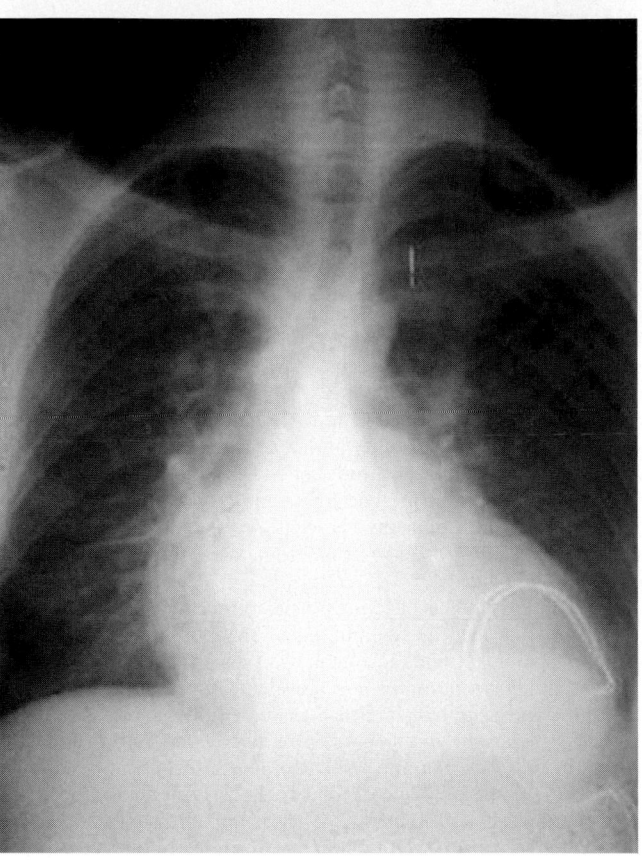

FIGURE 274-6. Chest radiograph of a Bolivian patient with chronic *T. cruzi* infection, congestive heart failure, and rhythm disturbances (described in ref. 49). Pacemaker wires are present in the area of the left ventricle.

anorexia, and edema of the face and lower extremities. Generalized lymphadenopathy and mild hepatosplenomegaly also may appear.

Overt central nervous system signs are not common, but meningoencephalitis develops in some patients and is associated with a very poor prognosis.[48] Severe myocarditis also develops in a small proportion of patients with acute disease, and most deaths are due to the resulting congestive heart failure.[12] Nonspecific electrocardiographic changes are seen, but the life-threatening arrhythmias that are frequent in chronic Chagas' disease generally do not occur. In untreated patients, symptoms resolve gradually over a period of weeks to months. Areas of local reaction around the eye or other sites of parasite entry can persist for several weeks, as can the lymphadenopathy and splenomegaly. After the spontaneous resolution of the acute illness, the patient enters what is called the indeterminate phase of Chagas' disease, which is characterized by asymptomatic and subpatent parasitemia and antibodies to a variety of *T. cruzi* antigens.

Chronic symptomatic Chagas' disease becomes apparent years or even decades after the initial infection. The heart is the organ most commonly involved, and symptoms reflect the rhythm disturbances, congestive heart failure, and thromboembolism that are characteristic of the chronic illness[49,50] (Fig. 274-6). Dizziness, syncope, and, less commonly, seizures result from a wide variety of arrhythmias. The cardiomyopathy that develops insidiously often primarily affects the right ventricle, and the classic signs of right-sided heart failure are frequently present. As in patients with arrhythmias, the progression of symptoms related to the cardiomyopathy may be gradual, but once congestive heart failure develops, death often occurs in a matter of months.[17,36] The clinical course is frequently complicated by emboli to the brain or other areas.

In patients with megaesophagus, symptoms are similar to those of idiopathic achalasia and may include dysphagia, odynophagia, chest pain, cough, and regurgitation[19,20,51] (Figs. 274-7 and 274-8). Hypersalivation and salivary gland hypertrophy have been observed. Aspiration can occur, especially during sleep, and repeated episodes of aspiration pneumonitis are common. Weight loss and even cachexia in patients with megaesophagus can combine with pulmonary infection to result in death. As in idiopathic achalasia, an increased incidence of cancer of the esophagus has been reported in patients with chagasic esophageal disease.[52]

Patients with chagasic megacolon are plagued by chronic constipation and abdominal pain. Individuals with advanced disease can go for several weeks between bowel movements, and acute obstruction, occasionally with volvulus, can lead to perforation, septicemia, and death.

Immunosuppression and Transplantation in *T. cruzi*–Infected Patients

When persons who harbor *T. cruzi* chronically become immunosuppressed, reactivation of the infection can occur, sometimes with a severity that is greater than is typical of acute Chagas' disease in immunocompetent patients. The incidence of reactivation in *T. cruzi*–infected patients who become immunosuppressed is not known, and descriptions of its absence[53] and occurrence[5,54] have been published. There have been several reports of reactivations of chronic *T. cruzi* infections after renal transplantation, and in two of these instances the central nervous system was involved. In my view, *T. cruzi* infection should not be a contraindication for kidney transplantation. In infected patients who do undergo the procedure, however, periodic monitoring for signs and symptoms of chronic Chagas' disease should be carried out, and a specific search for *T. cruzi,* including careful neurologic evaluation, should be performed when acute illnesses occur postoperatively.

Immunosuppression caused by the human immunodeficiency virus (HIV) can also lead to recrudescence of chronic *T. cruzi* infection. To date, several dozen such patients have been described, one of whom was a Latin American immigrant living in the United States.[55-58] It is noteworthy that most of these patients developed *T. cruzi* brain abscesses, which do not occur in immunocompetent *T. cruzi*–infected patients. Calculations based on the epidemiologies of HIV and *T. cruzi*

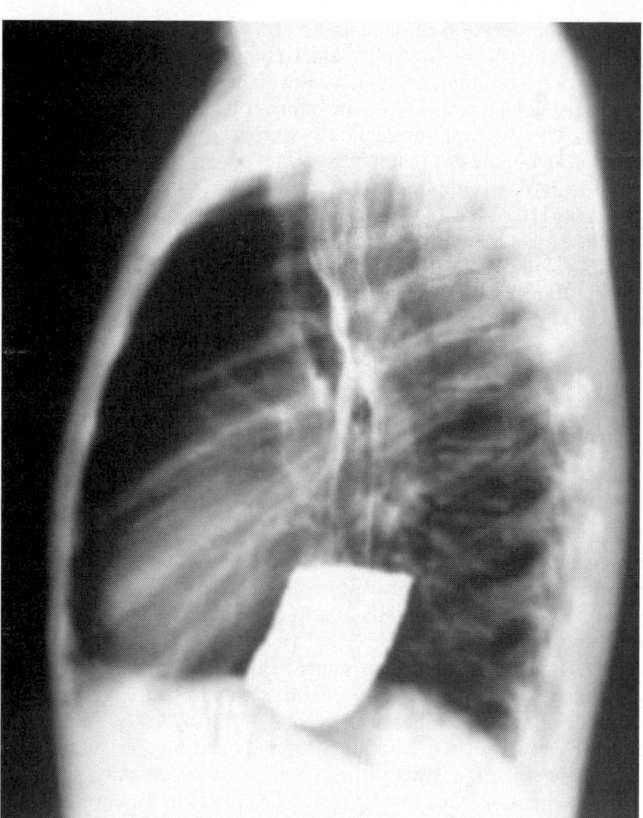

FIGURE 274-7. Barium swallow radiographic study of a Brazilian patient with chronic *T. cruzi* infection and megaesophagus. The markedly increased diameter of the esophagus as well of its failure to empty are typical findings in chagasic patients with megaesophagus. *(Courtesy of Dr. Franklin A. Neva, Bethesda, MD.)*

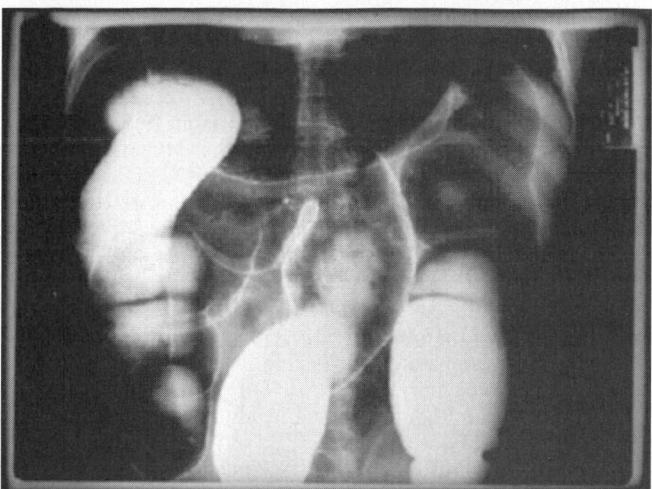

FIGURE 274-8. Air-contrast barium enema of a constipated Bolivian patient with megacolon and chronic Chagas' disease. The markedly increased diameters of the ascending, transverse, and sigmoid segments of the colon are readily apparent.

infections in Latin America suggest that the incidence of brain abscesses caused by the latter in coinfected persons is extremely low.

Heart transplantation is an option in patients with end-stage Chagas' cardiac disease, and more than 100 *T. cruzi*-infected patients have undergone the procedure in Brazil and the United States.[59] Reactivated acute Chagas' disease occurred frequently in the Brazilian patients as a consequence of the postoperative immunosuppression, but this has been less of a problem in the last decade or so because reduced doses of cyclosporine have been used. An additional problem is the fact that the parasitologic approaches usually used to detect acute *T. cruzi* infections were not sensitive detectors of the reactivations. Moreover, a higher than expected incidence of malignant neoplasm was observed in the Brazilian patients.[60] It is also noteworthy that patients who have had transplants for Chagas' heart disease often develop cutaneous lesions containing large numbers of parasites.[61] A similar occurrence has been reported in a Chagas' patient who received a renal transplant,[62] but such lesions have not been observed in coinfected persons with HIV/AIDS. Despite these problems, the long-term survival of Chagas' patients with heart transplants is greater than that of persons transplanted for other reasons, probably because the pathology of chronic *T. cruzi* infection is often limited to the heart.[63]

Diagnosis

The first consideration in the diagnosis of acute Chagas' disease is a history consistent with exposure to *T. cruzi*. This includes residence in an environment in which vector-borne transmission occurs, a recent

transfusion in an endemic area where effective blood screening programs are not in place, birth of an infant to a *T. cruzi*-infected mother, or a laboratory accident involving the parasite. It is important to keep in mind, moreover, that as noted autochthonous *T. cruzi* infections in the United States are extremely rare and that imported cases among tourists returning to the United States have not been reported.

The diagnosis of acute Chagas' disease is made by detecting parasites, and testing for anti–*T. cruzi* immunoglobulin M (IgM) is not useful. Circulating parasites are motile and can often be seen in wet preparations of anticoagulated blood or buffy coat viewed under a cover slip or in microhematocrit tubes. In many cases, the parasites can also be seen in Giemsa-stained smears. In acutely infected immunocompetent patients, examination of blood preparations is the cornerstone of detecting *T. cruzi*. In immunocompromised patients suspected of having acute Chagas' disease, however, other specimens such as lymph node and bone marrow aspirates, pericardial fluid, and cerebrospinal fluid should be examined microscopically. When these methods fail to detect *T. cruzi* in a patient whose clinical and epidemiologic histories suggest that the parasite is present, as is often the case, efforts to grow the organism can be undertaken. This can be attempted by culturing blood or other specimens in liquid media,[64] or by xenodiagnosis, which is a method involving laboratory-reared insect vectors. A major problem with the use of these two methods for diagnosing acute disease is the fact that they take at least several weeks to complete, and this is beyond the time at which decisions regarding drug treatment must be made. Furthermore, although it is thought that culture and xenodiagnosis are more sensitive than microscopic examination of blood and other specimens, their sensitivities may be no greater than 50%. In view of these considerations, it is obvious that improved methods for diagnosing acute *T. cruzi* infections are needed, and PCR assays may fulfill this role (see farther on).

Chronic *T. cruzi* infection is usually diagnosed by detecting IgG antibodies that bind specifically to parasite antigens, and isolating the organism is not of primary importance. Currently more than 30 assays for serologic diagnosis of *T. cruzi* infection are available commercially. The majority are based on enzyme-linked immunosorbent assay, indirect hemagglutination, and indirect immunofluorescence formats, and they are used widely in Latin America for clinical testing and for screening donated blood.[65] Several assays are based on mixtures of recombinant antigens.[66-68] Many of these tests have sensitivities and specificities that are less than ideal, and false-positive reactions occur typically with specimens from patients having illnesses such as leishmaniasis, malaria, syphilis, and other parasitic and nonparasitic diseases. Because of these shortcomings, most authorities recommend that samples be tested in two or three assays based on different formats before diagnostic decisions are made. This latter approach carries with it an enormous economic and logistical burden, particularly for blood banks. For example, in the largest blood donor center in São Paulo, Brazil (22,000 donations per month), three serologic tests for antibodies to *T. cruzi* are used and 1.1% of donated units are thrown out because of reactivity in one or more of the assays. As many as two thirds of these may in fact come from donors who are not infected *T. cruzi,* but the units must be discarded because of inconsistent test results. Thus, as is the case with acute *T. cruzi* infection, improved tests for chronic Chagas' disease are needed. Only one assay is available for use in the United States (Chagas' Kit, Hemagen Diagnostics, Inc., Columbia, MD); it has been cleared by the FDA for clinical testing but cannot be used for screening donated blood.

The possibility of using PCR assays for detecting *T. cruzi* infection has been studied extensively. The numbers of parasites in the blood of patients with chronic *T. cruzi* infections is extremely low, but PCR assays have the potential for detecting such low numbers because the organisms have highly repetitive nuclear and kinetoplast DNA (kDNA) sequences that can be amplified by PCR. Moser and colleagues[69] described a PCR test in which a 188–base pair nuclear repetitive DNA sequence is amplified (TCZ1-TCZ2 primers). Each parasite contains approximately 100,000 copies of this sequence, and in contrived experiments as little as 0.5% of the genome of a single parasite gave a positive result. Studies in mice with acute and chronic *T. cruzi* infections indicated clearly that this PCR assay is much more sensitive than microscopic examination of blood.[70] In a second PCR test, described by Sturm and coworkers,[71] a 330–base pair segment of the *T. cruzi* kinetoplast minicircle is amplified (S35-S36 primers). Each parasite is thought to have approximately 120,000 copies of this sequence, and in mixing experiments the authors were able to detect 0.1% of one parasite genome. In the only head-to-head comparisons of these two assays described to date, it appeared that the TCZ1-TCZ2 assay may have a slight edge in terms of sensitivity.[70,72]

Since the publication of these two original reports in 1989, roughly 100 articles have been published that deal with the detection of *T. cruzi* by PCR tests. Importantly, in a group of nine key human studies published in the 1990s, the sensitivities of the PCR assays ranged from 44.7% to 100%, with most results falling slightly over 90%.[64,73,74] Clearly this level of sensitivity is not high enough to allow use of these assays for testing donated blood. Nonetheless, PCR assays are useful for detecting *T. cruzi* in persons with borderline serology, in infected individuals who have received specific treatment, and in patients suspected of having acute or congenital Chagas' disease in whom parasites are not detected microscopically. In all such persons, only positive results can be taken as truly indicative of their infection status. At the present time no PCR test for the detection of *T. cruzi* is available commercially.

Treatment

Current therapy for persons infected with *T. cruzi* is unsatisfactory. Two drugs are currently being used to treat patients infected with *T. cruzi.*[75,76] The first of these, the nitrofuran derivative nifurtimox (Lampit, Bayer 2502, Leverkusen, Germany),[77] has been in use for more than two decades, and extensive clinical experience has accumulated. In acute and congenital Chagas' disease, nifurtimox markedly reduces the duration and severity of the illness and decreases mortality. However, it results in parasitologic cure in only about 70% of treated patients, can cause severe side effects, and must be taken for prolonged periods. Therapy with nifurtimox should be initiated as early as possible in cases of acute or congenital Chagas' disease. Moreover, when laboratory accidents occur in which there is a reasonable likelihood that *T. cruzi* infection will become established, therapy should be initiated without waiting for clinical or parasitologic indications of infection.

A large proportion of patients treated with nifurtimox experience adverse side effects. Gastrointestinal complaints include abdominal pain, nausea, vomiting, anorexia, and weight loss. Possible neurologic symptoms include restlessness, insomnia, twitching, paresthesias, and seizures. These symptoms generally disappear when the dosage is reduced or therapy is discontinued.

Nifurtimox is supplied as 30- and 120-mg tablets. The recommended oral dosage for adults is 8 to 10 mg/kg body weight/day. The dose for adolescents is 12.5 to 15 mg/kg/day, and for children 1 to 10 years of age it is 15 to 20 mg/kg/day. The drug should be given in four divided doses each day, and therapy should be continued for 90 to 120 days. Nifurtimox can be obtained from the CDC Drug Service (404-639-3670).

Benznidazole (Rochagan, Roche 7-1051, São Paulo, Brazil),[78] a nitroimidazole derivative, is the second agent used to treat patients with Chagas' disease. The efficacy of this drug is similar to that of nifurtimox, with the exception that geographic differences in its efficacy have not been observed. Side effects include peripheral neuropathy, rash, and granulocytopenia. The recommended oral dosage of benznidazole is 5 mg/kg/day for 60 days. Benznidazole is used widely in Latin America, where it is viewed as the drug of choice by many specialists. It also can be obtained from the CDC Drug Service. There are no published data regarding the use of benznidazole and nifurtimox in pregnant women.

The question of whether persons in the indeterminate or chronic symptomatic phases of *T. cruzi* infection should be treated with benznidazole or nifurtimox has been debated for many years. Recent studies of *T. cruzi*–infected laboratory animals and humans suggest that the presence of organisms in heart muscle is specifically associated with inflammation, thus implicating the parasites in the chronic pathogenesis.[14-17] In addition, limited studies in humans have indicated that the appearance and/or progression of cardiac lesions in drug-treated patients may be less than in untreated controls.[79] After reviewing these and other studies, a panel of experts convened by the World Health Organization recommended that all asymptomatic persons in the indeterminate phase of *T. cruzi* infection should be given drug treatment.[80] This recommendation stimulated considerable debate and currently there is no consensus regarding the treatment of persons with long-standing asymptomatic *T. cruzi* infection. It has been argued that there is no convincing evidence that specific treatment affects clinical outcome.[81] Recent reports of long-term studies indicating that parasitological cure rates with nifurtimox and benznidazole are less than 10% have added fuel to the debate.[82-84]

The usefulness of fluconazole, ketoconazole, itraconazole, and allopurinol has been studied extensively in laboratory animals and to a lesser extent in persons with Chagas' disease. None of these drugs has shown a level of anti–*T. cruzi* activity that warrants its use in humans. Posaconazole, which is being studied for treatment of fungal infections, has been shown to cure *T. cruzi* infections in mice[85] and trials in patients with Chagas' disease are being planned. Other promising drugs are being evaluated.[86] Limited studies in mice have shown that recombinant interferon-γ (IFN-γ) reduces the severity of acute *T. cruzi* infection. Two patients with acute Chagas' disease were given IFN-γ in addition to nifurtimox and one is known to have been cured parasitologically. Additional studies must be done before its use in patients with acute Chagas' disease can be recommended.

Most patients with acute Chagas' disease require no therapy other than benznidazole or nifurtimox because symptoms are generally self-limited even in the absence of drug treatment. The management of the occasional severely ill acute-phase patient with myocarditis or meningoencephalitis is largely supportive. The treatment of patients with chronic chagasic heart disease is also supportive. Chronically infected persons should have electrocardiograms performed every 6 months or so because pacemakers have been shown to be useful in the management of bradyarrhythmias seen in chronic Chagas' disease. The congestive heart failure of cardiomyopathic Chagas' disease is generally treated with measures used in patients with cardiomyopathies due to other causes.

Megaesophagus associated with Chagas' disease should be managed as is idiopathic achalasia.[20] The first approach to relieving symptoms is balloon dilation of the lower esophageal sphincter. Patients who fail to respond to repeated attempts at this approach are treated surgically.[87] The procedure used most frequently is wide esophagocardiomyectomy of the anterior gastroesophageal junction, combined with valvuloplasty to reduce reflux. Patients with extreme megaesophagus are often treated with esophageal resection with reconstruction using an esophagogastroplasty. In industrialized countries, laparoscopic myotomy is being used with increasing frequency to treat idiopathic achalasia. This relatively simple procedure may become the approach of choice for both idiopathic achalasia and Chagas' megaesophagus if the encouraging results achieved to date are borne out in larger numbers of patients. A possible role for the injection of botulinum toxin is being studied.[88]

Patients in the early stages of colonic dysfunction associated with chronic Chagas' disease can be managed with a high-fiber diet and occasional laxatives and enemas. Fecal impaction necessitating manual disimpaction may occur, as can toxic megacolon, which requires surgical treatment. Another complication of chagasic megacolon that requires immediate attention is volvulus. This usually occurs when the lengthened and enlarged sigmoid colon twists and folds on itself, causing a constellation of symptoms resulting from the obstruction. Endoscopic emptying can be performed initially in patients without radiographic, clinical, or endoscopic signs of ischemia in the affected area. Complicated cases should be treated with surgical decompression. In either event, however, surgical treatment of the megacolon is eventually necessary because of the high probability of recurrence of the volvulus. A number of surgical procedures have been used to treat advanced chagasic megacolon, and all include resection of the sigmoid colon as well as removal of part of the rectum. The latter is performed to avoid recurrence of megacolon in the segment of the colon that is anastomosed to the rectum.

Prevention

In view of the possible serious consequences of chronic *T. cruzi* infection, I feel that all immigrants from endemic regions should be screened serologically. Identification of infected persons is important because the implantation of pacemakers has been shown to benefit some patients who develop rhythm disturbances. The possibility of congenital transmission is another justification for screening.

As noted earlier, to date seven cases of transfusion-associated transmission of *T. cruzi* have been reported in the United States and Canada. The courses of acute Chagas' disease in these patients were particularly fulminant because of immunosuppressive therapy they were receiving, and this certainly contributed to the definitive diagnoses. Because most transfusions are given to immunocompetent persons in whom acute Chagas' disease would be a mild illness, it is reasonable to infer that many other instances of transfusion-associated transmission of *T. cruzi* have occurred in the United States but have not been noticed. The question as to how best to avoid transmission of the parasite via transfusion in the United States has been debated for more than a decade. Common sense would suggest that if serologic screening is warranted in the endemic countries from which the 12 million immigrants living here have come, then they should be screened when they present for donation here. During the past few years, at the suggestion of the FDA, all prospective donors have been asked questions relating to risk for *T. cruzi* infection, with the goal of deferring persons at high risk for harboring the parasite. The efficacy of the protocol being used is not known, but related data obtained in the United States[89] and Brazil[90] suggest that it may not be serving its purpose. Moreover, it merits mention that one of the transfusion-associated cases occurred after the screening protocol was instituted. Many blood bank authorities here favor serologic screening of all blood donated in the United States, but as noted no assay has been cleared by the FDA for this purpose. The cost of screening of the United States blood supply for *T. cruzi* would be $50 to $100 million per year. Schemes involving regional screening, selective testing of donors having geographic risk, or only testing blood products destined for immunocompromised patients are not likely to be implemented.

Laboratory personnel should wear gloves and eye protection when working with *T. cruzi*, and suitable containment should be used when dealing with infected insects.[91] Persons traveling in endemic areas should avoid sleeping in dilapidated dwellings and should use insect repellent and bed nets to reduce exposure to vectors.[92,93] No vaccine is available for the prevention of transmission of *T. cruzi*. Special precautions for campers, hunters, and others engaging in outdoor activities in the United States are not warranted.

REFERENCES

1. Levine ND, Corliss JO, Cox FEG, et al. A newly revised classification of the protozoa. J Protozool. 1980;27:37-58.
2. Brener Z. Biology of *Trypanosoma cruzi*. Annu Rev Microbiol. 1973;27:347-382.
3. Lent H, Wygodzinsky P. Revision of the Triatominae (Hemiptera, Reduviidae), and their significance as vectors of Chagas' disease. Bull Am Mus Nat Hist. 1979; 163:123-520.
4. Schmunis GA. Prevention of transfusional *Trypanosoma cruzi* infection in Latin America. Mem Inst Oswaldo Cruz 1999;94(Suppl 1):93-101.
5. Riarte A, Luna C, Sabatiello R, et al. Chagas' disease in patients with kidney transplants: 7 years of experience 1989-1996. Clin Infect Dis. 1999;29:561-567.
6. Zayas CF, Perlino C, Caliendo A, et al. Chagas' disease after organ transplantation—United States, 2001. MMWR Morb Mortal Wkly Rep. 2002;51:210-212.
7. Freilij H, Altcheh J. Congenital Chagas' disease: Diagnostic and clinical aspects. Clin Infect Dis. 1995;21:551-555.
8. Schijman AG, Altcheh J, Burgos JM, et al. Aetiological treatment of congenital Chagas' disease diagnosed and monitored by the polymerase chain reaction. J Antimicrob Chemother. 2003;52:441-449.
9. Gurtler RE, Segura EL, Cohen JE. Congenital transmission of *Trypanosoma cruzi* infection in Argentina. Emerg Infect Dis. 2003;9:29-32.
10. Herwaldt BL. Laboratory-acquired parasitic infections from accidental exposures. Clin Microbiol Rev. 2001;14:659-688.
11. Andrade ZA. Patologia da doença de Chagas [Portuguese]. In: Brener Z, Andrade ZA, Barral-Netto M, eds. *Trypanosoma cruzi e Doença de Chagas*. Rio de Janeiro: Guanabara Koogan; 2000:201-230.
12. Ochs DE, Hnilica V, Moser DR, et al. Postmortem diagnosis of autochthonous acute chagasic myocarditis by polymerase chain reaction amplification of a species-specific DNA sequence of *Trypanosoma cruzi*. Am J Trop Med Hyg. 1996;34:526-529.
13. Parada H, Carrasco HA, Anez N, et al. Cardiac involvement is a constant finding in acute Chagas' disease: A clinical, parasitological and histopathological study. Int J Cardiol. 1997;60:49-54.
14. Jones EM, Colley DG, Tostes S, et al. Amplification of a *Trypanosoma cruzi* DNA sequence from inflammatory lesions in human Chagasic cardiomyopathy. Am J Trop Med Hyg. 1993;48:348-357.
15. Bellotti G, Bocchi EA, de Moraes AV, et al. In vivo detection of *Trypanosoma cruzi* antigens in hearts of patients with chronic Chagas' heart disease. Am Heart J. 1996;131:301-307.
16. Zhang L, Tarleton RL. Parasite persistence correlates with disease severity and localization in chronic Chagas' disease. J Infect Dis. 1999;180:480-486.
17. Basquiera AL, Sembaj A, Aguerri AM, et al. Risk progression to chronic Chagas cardiomyopathy: Influence of male sex and of parasitaemia detected by polymerase chain reaction. Heart (Br Cardiac Soc). 2003;89:1186-1190.
18. Andrade ZA, Andrade SG, Oliveira GB, Alonso DR. Histopathology of the conducting tissue of the heart in Chagas' myocarditis. Am Heart J. 1978;95:316-324.
19. Kirchhoff LV. American trypanosomiasis (Chagas' disease). Gastroenterol Clin North Am. 1996;25:517-533.
20. Rezende JM, Moreira H. Forma digestiva da doença de Chagas [Portuguese]. In: Brener Z, Andrade ZA, Barral-Netto M, eds. *Trypanosoma cruzi e Doença de Chagas*. Rio de Janeiro: Guanabara Koogan; 2000:297-343.
21. Anez N, Carrasco H, Parada H, et al. Myocardial parasite persistence in chronic chagasic patients. Am J Trop Med Hyg. 1999;60:726-732.
22. Ryckman RE, Olsen LE. Epizootiology of *Trypanosoma cruzi* in Southwestern North America. Part VI. Insectivorous hosts of Triatominae—the perizootiological relationship to *Trypanosoma cruzi*. J Med Entomol. 1965;2:99-106.
23. Pietrzak SM, Pung OJ. Trypanosomiasis in raccoons from Georgia. J Wildlife Dis. 1998;34:132-136.
24. Bradley KK, Bergman DK, Woods JP, et al. Prevalence of American trypanosomiasis (Chagas' disease) among dogs in Oklahoma. J Am Vet Med Assoc. 2000;217:1853-1857.
25. Cohen JE, Gurtler RE. Modeling household transmission of American trypanosomiasis. Science. 2001;293:694-698.
26. Cecere MC, Gurtler RE, Canale DM, et al. Effects of partial housing improvement and insecticide spraying on the reinfestation dynamics of *Triatoma infestans* in rural northwestern Argentina. Acta Trop. 2002;84:101-116.
27. Laranja FS, Dias E, Nobrega G, Miranda A. Chagas' disease: A clinical, epidemiologic, and pathologic study. Circulation. 1956;14:1035-1060.
28. Anonymous. Publicación Científica y Técnica No. 587 ed. Washington, DC: Pan American Health Organization, 2002.

29. Schmunis GA. American trypanosomiasis and its impact on public health in the Americas [Portuguese]. In: Brener Z, Andrade ZA, Barral-Netto M, eds. *Trypanosoma cruzi e Doença de Chagas*. Rio de Janeiro: Guanabara Koogan; 2000:1-20.

30. Dias JC, Silveira AC, Schofield CJ. The impact of Chagas' disease control in Latin America: A review. Mem Inst Oswaldo Cruz. 2002;97:603-612.

31. Dias JC, Machado EM, Borges EC, et al. [Chagas' disease in Lassance, Minas Gerais State: Clinical-epidemiological re-evaluation ninety years after the discovery by Carlos Chagas]. [Portuguese]. Rev Soc Bras Med Trop. 2002;35:167-176.

32. Sabino EC, Goncalez TT, Salles NA, et al. Trends in the prevalence of Chagas' disease among first-time blood donors in Sao Paulo, Brazil. Transfusion. 2003;43: 853-856.

33. Segura EL, Cura EN, Estani SA, et al. Long-term effects of a nationwide control program on the seropositivity for *Trypanosoma cruzi* infection in young men from Argentina. Am J Trop Med Hyg. 2000;62:353-362.

34. Guzman-Bracho C. Epidemiology of Chagas' disease in Mexico: An update. Trends Parasitol 2001;17:372-376.

35. Mota EA, Guimaraes AC, Santana OO, et al. A nine year prospective study of Chagas' disease in a defined rural population in Northeast Brazil. Am J Trop Med Hyg. 1990;42:429-440.

36. Amorim DS. Chagas' disease. Prog Cardiol. 1979;8:235-279.

37. de Diego JA, Palau MT, Gamallo C, Penin P. Are genotypes of *Trypanosoma cruzi* involved in the challenge of chagasic cardiomyopathy? Parasitol Res. 1998;84: 147-152.

38. Herwaldt BL, Grijalva MJ, Newsome AL, et al. Use of polymerase chain reaction to diagnose the fifth reported US case of autochthonous transmission of *Trypanosoma cruzi*, in Tennessee, 1998. J Infect Dis. 2000;181:395-399.

39. Crovato F, Rebora A. Chagas' disease: A potential problem for Europe? Dermatology. 1997;195:184-185.

40. US Census Bureau. Foreign-born population by country of origin and citizenship status: 2000. Statistical Abstract of the United States: 2001. Washington, DC: US Department of Commerce; 2001.

41. Kirchhoff LV, Gam AA, Gilliam FC. American trypanosomiasis (Chagas' disease) in Central American immigrants. Am J Med. 1987;82:915-920.

42. Shulman IA, Appleman MD, Saxena S, et al. Specific antibodies to *Trypanosoma cruzi* among blood donors in Los Angeles, California. Transfusion. 1997;37:727-731.

43. Winkler MA, Brashear RJ, Hall HJ, et al. Detection of antibodies to *Trypanosoma cruzi* among blood donors in the southwestern and western United States. II. Evaluation of a supplemental enzyme immunoassay and radioimmunoprecipitation assay for confirmation of seroreactivity. Transfusion. 1995;35:219-225.

44. Leiby DA, Read EJ, Lenes BA, et al. Seroepidemiology of *Trypanosoma cruzi*, etiologic agent of Chagas' disease, in U.S. blood donors. J Infect Dis. 1997;176:1047-1052.

45. Leiby DA, Herron RM Jr, Read EJ, et al. *Trypanosoma cruzi* in Los Angeles and Miami blood donors: Impact of evolving donor demographics on seroprevalence and implications for transfusion transmission. Transfusion. 2002;42:549-555.

46. Leiby DA, Lenes BA, Tibbals MA, Tames-Olmedo MT. Prospective evaluation of a patient with *Trypanosoma cruzi* infection transmitted by transfusion. N Engl J Med. 1999;341:1237-1239.

47. Rassi A, Rassi Junior A, Rassi GG. Acute Chagas' disease. [Portuguese]. In: Brener Z, Andrade ZA, Barral-Netto M, eds. *Trypanosoma cruzi e Doença de Chagas*. Rio de Janeiro: Guanabara Koogan; 2000:231-245.

48. Kirchhoff LV. Trypanosomiasis of the central nervous system. In: Scheld WM, Marra CM, Whitely RJ, eds. Infections of the Central Nervous System. 2004.

49. Kirchhoff LV, Neva FA. Chagas' disease in Latin American immigrants. JAMA. 1985;254:3058-3060.

50. Hagar JM, Rahimtoola SH. Chagas' heart disease. Curr Prob Cardiol. 1995;20:827-924.

51. de Oliveira RB, Troncon LE, Dantas RO, Menghelli UG. Gastrointestinal manifestations of Chagas' disease. Am J Gastroenterol. 1998;93:884-889.

52. Camara-Lopes LH. Carcinoma of the esophagus as a complication of megaesophagus. An analysis of seven cases. Am J Dig Dis. 1961;6:742-756.

53. Lopez-Blanco OA, Cavalli NH, Jasovich A, et al. Chagas' disease and kidney transplantation—follow-up of nine patients for 11 years. Transplant Proc. 1992;24:3089-3090.

54. Salgado PR, Gorski AG, Aleixo AR, de Barros EO. Tumor-like lesion due to Chagas' disease in a patient with lymphocytic leukemia. Rev Inst Med Trop Sao Paulo. 1996;38:285-288.

55. Gluckstein D, Ciferri F, Ruskin J. Chagas' disease: Another cause of cerebral mass in the acquired immunodeficiency syndrome. Am J Med. 1992;92:429-432.

56. Sartori AM, Shikanai-Yasuda MA, Amato Neto V, Lopes MH. Follow-up of 18 patients with human immunodeficiency virus infection and chronic Chagas' disease, with reactivation of Chagas' disease causing cardiac disease in three patients. Clin Infect Dis. 1998;26:177-179.

57. Goldani LZ. A 32-year-old Brazilian woman with severe headache and fever. Clin Infect Dis. 2002;35:1512-1550.

58. Sartori AM, Caiaffa-Filho HH, Bezerra RC, et al. Exacerbation of HIV viral load simultaneous with asymptomatic reactivation of chronic Chagas' disease. Am J Trop Med Hyg. 2002;67:521-523.

59. Bocchi EA, Bellotti G, Mocelin AO, et al. Heart transplantation for chronic Chagas' heart disease. Ann Thorac Surg. 1996;61:1727-1733.

60. Bocchi EA, Higuchi ML, Vieira ML, et al. Higher incidence of malignant neoplasms after heart transplantation for treatment of chronic Chagas' heart disease. J Heart Lung Transplant. 1998;17:399-405.

61. Libow LF, Beltrani VP, Silvers DN, Grossman ME. Post-cardiac transplant reactivation of Chagas' disease diagnosed by skin biopsy. Cutis. 1991;48:37-40.

62. La Forgia MP, Pellerano G, las Mercedes PM, et al. Cutaneous manifestation of reactivation of Chagas' disease in a renal transplant patient: Long-term follow-up. Arch Dermatol. 2003;139:104-105.

63. Bocchi EA, Fiorelli A. The paradox of survival results after heart transplantation for cardiomyopathy caused by *Trypanosoma cruzi*. First Guidelines Group for Heart Transplantation of the Brazilian Society of Cardiology. Ann Thor Surg. 2001;71:1833-1838.

64. Castro AM, Luquetti AO, Rassi A, et al. Blood culture and polymerase chain reaction for the diagnosis of the chronic phase of human infection with *Trypanosoma cruzi*. Parasitol Res. 2002;88:894-900.

65. Leiby DA, Wendel S, Takaoka DT, et al. Serologic testing for *Trypanosoma cruzi*: Comparison of radioimmunoprecipitation assay with commercially available indirect immunofluorescence assay, indirect hemagglutination assay, and enzyme-linked immunosorbent assay kits. J Clin Microbiol. 2000;38:639-642.

66. Oelemann W, Vanderborght BO, Verissimo Da Costa GC, et al. A recombinant peptide antigen line immunoassay optimized for the confirmation of Chagas' disease. Transfusion. 1999;39:711-717.

67. Umezawa ES, Bastos SF, Coura JR, et al. An improved serodiagnostic test for Chagas' disease employing a mixture of *Trypanosoma cruzi* recombinant antigens. Transfusion. 2003;43:91-97.

68. Luquetti AO, Ponce C, Ponce E, et al. Chagas disease diagnosis: A multicentric evaluation of Chagas Stat-Pak, a rapid immunochromatographic assay with recombinant proteins of *Trypanosoma cruzi*. Diagn Microbiol Infect Dis. 2003;46:265-271.

69. Moser DR, Kirchhoff LV, Donelson JE. Detection of *Trypanosoma cruzi* by polymerase chain reaction gene amplification. J Clin Microbiol. 1989;27:1744-1749.

70. Kirchhoff LV, Votava JR, Ochs DE, Moser DR. Comparison of PCR and microscopic methods for detecting *Trypanosoma cruzi*. J Clin Microbiol. 1996;34:1171-1175.

71. Sturm NR, Degrave W, Morel C, Simpson L. Sensitive detection and schizodeme classification of *Trypanosoma cruzi* cells by amplification of kinetoplast minicircle DNA sequences: Use in diagnosis of Chagas' disease. Mol Biochem Parasitol. 1989;33:205-214.

72. Virreira M, Torrico F, Truyens C, et al. Comparison of polymerase chain reaction methods for reliable and easy detection of congenital *Trypanosoma cruzi* infection. Am J Trop Med Hyg. 2003;68:574-582.

73. Russomando G, de Tomassone MM, de Guillen I, et al. Treatment of congenital Chagas' disease diagnosed and followed up by the polymerase chain reaction. Am J Trop Med Hyg. 1998;59:487-491.

74. Gomes ML, Galvao LMC, Macedo AM, et al. Chagas' disease diagnosis: Comparative analysis of parasitologic, molecular, and serologic methods. Am J Trop Med Hyg. 1999;60:205-210.

75. Urbina JA. Chemotherapy of Chagas' disease. Curr Pharm Des. 2002;8:287-295.

76. Coura JR, L.de Castro S. A critical review on Chagas' disease chemotherapy. Mem Inst Oswaldo Cruz 2002;97:3-24.

77. Kirchhoff LV. Nifurtimox. In: Yu V, ed. Antimicrobial Therapy and Vaccines. New York: Lippincott Williams & Wilkins; 2004.

78. Kirchhoff LV. Benznidazole. In: Yu V, ed. Antimicrobial Therapy and Vaccines. New York: Lippincott Williams & Wilkins; 2004.

79. Andrade ALSS, Zicker F, Oliveira RM, et al. Randomised trial of efficacy of benznidazole in treatment of early *Trypanosoma cruzi* infection. Lancet. 1996;348:1407-1413.

80. Anonymous. Tratamiento Etiologico de la Enfermedad de Chagas. Conclusiones de una Consulta Tecnica. Pan American Health Organization; 1999:OPS/HCP/HCT/140/99:1-32.

81. Villar JC, Marin-Neto JA, Ebrahim S, Yusuf S. Trypanocidal drugs for chronic asymptomatic *Trypanosoma cruzi* infection. Cochrane Database of Systematic Reviews; 2002:CD003463.

82. Braga MS, Lauria-Pires L, Arganaraz ER, et al. Persistent infections in chronic Chagas' disease patients treated with anti-*Trypanosoma cruzi* nitroderivatives. Rev Inst Med Trop Sao Paulo. 2000;42:157-161.

83. Cancado JR. Long term evaluation of etiological treatment of Chagas' disease with benznidazole. Rev Inst Med Trop Sao Paulo. 2002;44:29-37.

84. Lauria-Pires L, Braga MS, Vexenat AC, et al. Progressive chronic Chagas heart disease ten years after treatment with anti-*Trypanosoma cruzi* nitroderivatives. Am J Trop Med Hyg. 2000;63:111-118.

85. Molina J, Martins-Filho O, Brener Z, et al. Activities of the triazole derivative SCH 56592 (posaconazole) against drug-resistant strains of the protozoan parasite *Trypanosoma (Schizotrypanum) cruzi* in immunocompetent and immunosuppressed murine hosts. Antimicrob Agents Chemother. 2000;44:150-155.

86. Urbina JA, Payares G, Sanoja C, et al. Parasitological cure of acute and chronic experimental Chagas' disease using the long-acting experimental triazole TAK-187. Activity against drug-resistant *Trypanosoma cruzi* strains. Int J Antimicrob Agents. 2003;21:39-48.

87. Pinotti HW, Habr-Gama A, Cecconello I, et al. The surgical treatment of megaesophagus and megacolon. Dig Dis. 1993;11:206-215.

88. Brant C, Moraes-Filho JP, Siqueira E, et al. Intrasphincteric botulinum toxin injection in the treatment of chagasic achalasia. Dis Esophag. 2003;16:33-38.

89. Galel SA, Wolles S, Stumpf R. Evaluation of a selective donor testing strategy for *T. cruzi*. Transfusion. 1997;37:74S.

90. Barjas-Castro ML, Guariento ME, Vincente CS, Castro V. Screening blood donors for *Trypanosoma cruzi* infection in a nonendemic area of Brazil. Transfusion. 1998;38:611-612.

91. Hudson L, Grover F, Gutteridge WE, et al. Suggested guidelines for work with live *Trypanosoma cruzi*. Trans R Soc Trop Med Hyg. 1983;77:416-419.

92. Kroeger A, Villegas E, Ordoñez-Gonzalez J, et al. Prevention of the transmission of Chagas' disease with pyrethroid-impregnated materials. Am J Trop Med Hyg. 2003;68:307-311.

93. Herber O, Kroeger A. Pyrethroid-impregnated curtains for Chagas' disease control in Venezuela. Acta Trop. 2003;88:33-38.

Agents of African Trypanosomiasis (Sleeping Sickness)

LOUIS V. KIRCHHOFF

PARASITES AND THEIR TRANSMISSION

The agents of African sleeping sickness are flagellated protozoan parasites that belong to the genus *Trypanosoma*, subgenus *Trypanozoon*.[1,2] A general description of the members of this genus and specific characteristics of the subgenus are presented in the introduction to Chapter 274. Three trypanosome subspecies, *T. brucei brucei, T. brucei rhodesiense,* and *T. brucei gambiense,* are considered here. They are indistinguishable morphologically, and as a group they are often referred to as the *T. brucei* complex. *T. b. brucei* is a parasite of wild and domestic animals that is not infectious for humans. In contrast, *T. b. rhodesiense,* which is primarily a parasite of wild game, can infect humans, and this difference in host specificity forms the basis of the distinction between the two subspecies. *T. b. gambiense* primarily infects humans, and infections of wild and domestic animals are of limited importance.

The members of the *T. brucei* complex are transmitted by various species of tsetse flies that belong to the genus *Glossina*.[3] These bloodsucking insects are found only in Africa, where their range covers millions of square kilometers of rain forest and savanna. The parasites undergo a developmental cycle in the insect vectors. Tsetse flies of both sexes become infected with trypanosomes when they ingest blood from infected mammalian hosts that contains trypomastigotes, the form of the parasite that circulates in the blood stream. There are two forms of circulating trypomastigotes: long, slender organisms that are capable of dividing and short, stumpy forms thought to be nondividing parasites that are infective for the insect vectors. Once in the midgut of the tsetse flies, stumpy trypomastigotes transform into relatively long, slender procyclic trypomastigotes. After many cycles of multiplication, the procyclic forms migrate to the salivary glands, where they differentiate into epimastigotes and continue to multiply. A final transformation occurs as the epimastigotes become nondividing metacyclic trypomastigotes. Transmission takes place when these infective forms are inoculated during a subsequent blood meal. The cycle is completed when the injected metacyclic forms become blood stream trypomastigotes and begin to multiply in the blood or other extracellular spaces.

The capacity of African trypanosomes to multiply in the blood stream of their mammalian hosts, where they are continually exposed to humoral defenses, constitutes a fundamental difference between the agents of sleeping sickness and *Trypanosoma cruzi,* the cause of Chagas' disease in the Americas. The African trypanosomes are able to evade immune destruction indefinitely because they undergo antigenic variation, a process in which they periodically change the antigenic structure of the coat of glycoproteins that covers the surface of the parasite. The molecular mechanisms that control this complex process have been studied intensively.[4-6] When epimastigotes transform into metacyclic trypomastigotes in the salivary glands of the tsetse fly, each parasite synthesizes a surface coat made up of one of about a dozen types of antigenic glycoproteins, called variant antigen types (VATs). Presumably, this occurs as a preadaptation to the relatively hostile environment of the mammalian host into which the metacyclics must be inoculated if they are to survive. After injection into a mammalian host, the parasites express metacyclic VATs for approximately 5 days, after which they switch to the expression of blood stream VATs. Over time, the host sequentially mounts specific humoral responses directed against the predominantly expressed VATs. The population of parasites survives because an intrinsic rate of VAT switching provides an apparently endless supply of parasites that have surface glycoprotein coats to which the host has not been exposed previously.

Virtually all transmission of African trypanosomes to both wild and domestic animals, as well as to humans, takes place in the cyclic fashion just described. There is no evidence that these parasites can be transmitted by insects other than tsetse flies, and mechanical transmission by vectors is not important, although it may occur occasionally. Congenital transmission can occur, but in humans it is extremely rare,[7] as is transmission by blood transfusion. A small number of laboratory accidents resulting in infection with African trypanosomes have been reported.[8]

PATHOGENESIS AND PATHOLOGY

The pathogenesis of African sleeping sickness is complex, and many aspects of the process are poorly understood.[9-11] The first sign of infection with African trypanosomes can be the acute inflammatory lesion (trypanosomal chancre) that appears a week or so after the bite of an infected tsetse fly and resolves spontaneously over several weeks. Interstitial multiplication of the trypanosomes takes place within the chancre, and there is an intense mononuclear cell reaction to the parasites, as well as edema and local tissue destruction.

After this initial local response, the infection evolves over weeks and months into a systemic hemolymphatic illness as the parasites disseminate widely through the lymphatics and the blood stream. Systemic African trypanosomiasis without central nervous system (CNS) involvement is generally referred to as stage I disease. The parasites first travel from the site of inoculation to regional lymph nodes, where they proliferate and cause an inflammatory response. They then move through the lymphatics into the blood stream, where multiplication continues. Egress of trypanosomes from vessels into interstitial spaces, where multiplication also takes place, is thought to be facilitated by increased vascular permeability.

In stage I trypanosomiasis, there is widespread lymphadenopathy and histiocytic proliferation, which may be followed by fibrosis. Morular cells (Mott cells) are also often present in tissue. These cells are plasmacytes with vacuolated cytoplasm and pyknotic nuclei that are thought to play a role in the production of immunoglobulin M (IgM).[12] The spleen may be enlarged, with generalized cellular proliferation, congestion, and focal necrosis. As the disease evolves, an endarteritis with perivascular infiltration of both parasites and lymphocytes may develop in lymph nodes and the spleen.

The heart is frequently involved in this stage of the disease, especially with *T. b. rhodesiense* infections. A pancarditis may develop involving all layers of the heart, including the mural and valvular endocardia.[13] The conduction system may also be affected, and involvement of the autonomic innervation of the heart has also been reported.[14] At the cellular level, pathologic changes include intense mononuclear infiltration consisting of lymphocytes, plasmacytes, and morular cells. As the infection progresses, myocytolysis and fibrosis may develop.

A number of hematologic manifestations accompany the development of stage I disease. Normocytic anemia is a regular feature in this phase of the illness and is usually accompanied by a brisk reticulocytosis. Several factors are thought to contribute to the anemia, and immune-mediated hemolysis may be important.[12] Platelet counts are often reduced, especially in infections with *T. b. rhodesiense,*[15] and disseminated intravascular coagulation before and during therapy has also been described.[16] A moderate degree of leukocytosis is usually present, especially in the early months of the infection, and this is accompanied by polyclonal B-cell activation.[17] High titers of immunoglobulins are a striking and constant feature of the illness. They consist primarily of polyclonal IgM that, for the most part, is not directed against specific parasite antigens. A number of other factors, including heterophile antibodies, rheumatoid factor, and anti-DNA antibodies, are often detectable. In addition, high levels of circulating antigen-antibody complexes are uniformly present, and these may play a role in the anemia, tissue damage, and increased vascular permeability that facilitate the dissemination of the parasites. Erythrocyte sedimentation rates are elevated, and hypocomplementemia has also been noted.

Stage II African trypanosomiasis involves invasion of the CNS. Parasites reach the brain and meninges via the blood stream and cause meningoencephalitis or meningomyelitis, or both. In the brain, they are found mainly in the frontal lobes, the pons, and the medulla, but other areas may be parasitized as well. Edema and hemorrhages may be evident on gross examination of affected areas at autopsy. Trypanosomes are present in perivascular areas, and nests of organisms can be found without apparent relation to blood vessels. The presence of parasites in the CNS is associated with infiltration of mononuclear cells that are predominantly lymphocytes, plasmacytes, and morular cells. The presence of parasites in the CNS is heralded by abnormal findings in the cerebrospinal fluid (CSF). The CSF may be under increased pressure, and the total protein concentration is elevated, with mononuclear cells predominating in addition to small numbers of morular cells and eosinophils. Trypanosomes are frequently present in the CSF as well.

EPIDEMIOLOGY

Sleeping sickness was a much greater problem in the past than it is at present.[3] The illness has undergone a resurgence in recent years, however, and major epidemics have occurred in the Sudan, the Democratic Republic of Congo, Angola, and several other endemic countries.[18,19] In some areas, wars and the resulting lack of control programs may be the primary factors underlying the outbreaks. Approximately 50 million individuals are at risk for acquiring the disease, and the total number of new cases per year is estimated to be around 100,000,[20] with 66,000 deaths and more than two million disability-adjusted lives-years lost annually.[21] Exact figures are not available because the acquisition of reliable health statistics is difficult in the developing countries where the human trypanosomiases are endemic. West African (gambiense) trypanosomiasis and East African (rhodesiense) trypanosomiasis are epidemiologically distinct diseases. The general geographic distributions of these two illnesses are presented in Figure 274-1, and foci where transmission is known to occur are distributed throughout the indicated areas. Distinguishing epidemiologic and clinical features of the two diseases are presented in Table 275-1.

West African Trypanosomiasis

West African trypanosomiasis is caused by *T. b. gambiense*, which is transmitted primarily by tsetse flies belonging to the *palpalis* group: *Glossina palpalis, Glossina tachinoides,* and *Glossina fuscipes*. These vectors inhabit forests and wooded areas along rivers, where favorable conditions of temperature, moisture, and darkness are combined with the availability of mammalian blood. This distribution of the vectors restricts the occurrence of human infection to the tropical rain forests of Central and West Africa. Despite the fact that these tsetse flies adapt to feeding on a variety of mammals, infected humans constitute the only major reservoir of *T. b. gambiense*. The primary determinant of the risk of acquiring the infection is the frequency of contact with the vector. This risk increases during the dry season, when the density of both vectors and humans increases around limited numbers of water holes. Because of this pattern of transmission, West African trypanosomiasis is primarily a problem in rural populations, and tourists rarely become infected with *T. b. gambiense*. The course of the illness caused by *T. b. gambiense* is less severe than that caused by *T. b. rhodesiense*, although both forms eventually lead to death if not treated. Thus, many persons infected with *T. b. gambiense* are asymptomatic for long periods and continue to have contact with the vectors. This may be an important element in the persistence of the infection in the reservoir between epidemics.

TABLE 275-1 Comparisons of West African and East African Trypanosomiasis

	West African (gambiense)	East African (rhodesiense)
Organism	*Trypanosoma brucei gambiense*	*Trypanosoma brucei rhodesiense*
Vectors	Tsetse flies (*palpalis* group)	Tsetse flies (*morsitans* group)
Primary reservoir	Humans	Antelope and cattle
Human illness	Chronic (late CNS disease)	Acute (early CNS disease)
Duration of illness	Months to years	<9 mo
Lymphadenopathy	Prominent	Minimal
Parasitemia	Low	High
Diagnosis by rodent inoculation	No	Yes
Epidemiology	Rural populations	Tourists in game parks Workers in wild areas Rural populations

East African Trypanosomiasis

The etiologic agent of East African trypanosomiasis is *T. b. rhodesiense*. This subspecies is transmitted by tsetse flies of the *morsitans* group, principally *Glossina morsitans, Glossina pallidipes,* and *Glossina swynnertoni*. These vectors are widely distributed in savanna and woodland areas of central and East Africa. Wild animals are the reservoir of this organism, principally antelope such as the bushbuck and hartebeest. These animals are trypanotolerant and generally do not suffer significant morbidity unless weakened by other illnesses. Cattle are the only domestic animals that can serve as a reservoir of *T. b. rhodesiense*, and infection with the parasite usually causes death if left untreated. Many other wild and domestic animals can be infected with this parasite, but their importance as reservoirs is minimal either because parasitemias are quite low or because they succumb quickly to the infection. The presence of the reservoir of *T. b. rhodesiense* and other trypanosome species in wild game in vast areas of Africa precludes the opening of these lands for cattle grazing.[22] Humans become infected with *T. b. rhodesiense* only incidentally, because for the most part risk results from contact with tsetse flies that principally feed on wild animals. Thus, the illness is an occupational hazard for individuals such as game wardens who work in areas where infected wild animals and vectors are present. In addition, sporadic cases of *T. b. rhodesiense* infection occur among non-African tourists who visit game parks in East Africa.

The natural cycle of the African trypanosomes does not exist outside Africa, and human African trypanosomiasis in the United States and other non-endemic countries is limited to occasional imported cases, most of which are caused by *T. b. rhodesiense*.[23-25] During the past 25 years, roughly two dozen cases of imported African trypanosomiasis have been reported to the Centers for Disease Control and Prevention.[26,27] Most of these cases were caused by *T. b. rhodesiense*, and several patients had CNS involvement. Despite the serious nature of the infection, all the patients were treated effectively.

CLINICAL COURSE

West African Trypanosomiasis

An indurated, painful trypanosomal chancre may develop at the site where parasites were inoculated by an infected tsetse fly. This lesion usually appears 1 to 2 weeks after the bite of the infected fly and resolves spontaneously over several weeks. The chancre may ulcerate and reach a diameter of several centimeters; regional lymphadenopathy may also develop. However, the trypanosomal chancre is seldom seen in clinical practice. Thus, most patients develop systemic trypanosomiasis without experiencing the symptoms of localized disease.

The development of stage I (hemolymphatic) disease with dissemination of the parasites is marked by the onset of fever, which may appear weeks or months after the acquisition of the infection. The fever is characterized by intermittent bouts of high temperatures lasting for several days, and extended periods may intervene during which the patient is afebrile. As the chronic illness evolves, a wide variety of other signs and symptoms develop. Lymphadenopathy is a fairly constant feature of gambiense trypanosomiasis. The nodes are typically discrete, movable, rubbery, and nontender. With time they frequently become indurated as fibrosis occurs. Supraclavicular and cervical nodes are often visibly discernible, and enlargement of the nodes of the posterior cervical triangle, or Winterbottom's sign, is a classic finding in persons infected with *T. b. gambiense*. Mild hepatosplenomegaly may be present as well.

Transient edema is a frequent sign during this phase of the illness and can occur in the face as well as in the hands, feet, and other periarticular areas. Pruritus is common, and an irregular circinate rash is often present. The rash is typically located on the trunk, shoulders, buttocks, and thighs and consists of erythematous areas 5 to 10 cm in diameter with clear centers.[28] Other inconstant findings include malaise, headache, weakness, weight loss, arthralgias, and tachycardia. Amenorrhea and infertility in women as well as a loss of libido and impotence in men as a consequence of neuroendocrine dysfunction have been documented.[29,30]

Stage II (meningoencephalitic) disease is characterized by the insidious development of protean neurologic manifestations, accompanied by progressive alterations in the composition of the CSF.[31] In gambiense trypanosomiasis, CNS findings may develop months or even years after the initiation of the infection. Irritability, a personality change, and a loss of the ability to concentrate may develop before changes in the CSF become evident, and this underscores the arbitrary nature of the distinction between the hemolymphatic and CNS stages of the illness. A picture of progressive indifference develops, associated with daytime somnolence, sometimes alternating with restlessness and insomnia at night. Severe headache is common. The frequency and progressive nature of the somnolence result in the use of the term *sleeping sickness*. A listless gaze reflects a loss of spontaneity, and speech may become indistinct. Extrapyramidal signs often develop and may include choreiform movements of the trunk, neck, and extremities, tremors of the tongue and fingers, and fasciculations of a variety of muscle groups. Ataxia is a frequent sign, and the patient may appear to have Parkinson's disease as a shuffling gait, hypertonia, tremors, and slurred speech develop. The final phase of the CNS disease is one of progressive neurologic impairment ending in coma and death.

Trypanosomiasis in children, which is relatively uncommon because they have less exposure to the vectors, does not differ greatly from the clinical illness seen in adults. However, the illness tends to run a more acute course, and the distinction between the hemolymphatic and CNS stages may be difficult to make.[32] Moreover, due to the protean nature of the symptoms and the lack of pathognomonic signs, the diagnosis is often missed in the early stages of the infection and is made only after neurologic impairment has developed.[33]

East African Trypanosomiasis

The most striking general difference between West African and East African trypanosomiases is that the latter illness tends to follow a more acute course, reflecting a relatively less effective adaptation of *T. b. rhodesiense* to humans.[34,35] The onset of symptoms usually occurs a few days after the patient has been bitten by an infected tsetse fly, but the incubation period may be as long as several weeks. Typically in tourists, systemic signs of infection such as fever, malaise, and headache may appear before the end of the trip or shortly after their return home. As the illness progresses, the pattern of intermittent fever develops, and rash is a nearly constant feature of the early weeks of the illness. Lymph node swelling is not prominent in rhodesiense trypanosomiasis, and thus Winterbottom's sign is generally absent. Persistent tachycardia unrelated to the fevers is frequently present early in the course of the illness, and in some patients death may result from arrhythmias and congestive heart failure due to pancarditis even before CNS disease develops. In general, untreated

rhodesiense trypanosomiasis usually leads to death in a matter of weeks to months, without a clear distinction between the hemolymphatic and CNS stages.

DIAGNOSIS

Epidemiologic information and clinical findings often combine to suggest the diagnosis of African trypanosomiasis, and a high index of suspicion should be maintained with persons who have been in endemic areas. However, there are numerous other illnesses common in the tropics that cause symptoms similar to those seen in both the early and the late stages of sleeping sickness, and a definitive diagnosis of African trypanosomiasis requires demonstration of the parasite.[36]

If a chancre is present, fluid should be expressed and examined directly under light microscopy for the highly motile trypanosomes. Part of the specimen should be fixed and stained with Giemsa. Aspiration of soft lymph nodes early in the course of the infection can also be used to demonstrate the presence of parasites. This method is more effective in patients with West African trypanosomiasis because of the prominence of lymphadenopathy, but even in such patients, multiple aspirates are sometimes necessary before parasites are found. An enlarged node should be punctured and kneaded gently during aspiration, and the sample obtained should be examined directly and also after staining.

Examination of wet preparations and Giemsa-stained thin and thick smears of peripheral blood is also a sensitive method for detection of infection with African trypanosomes (Fig. 275-1). This approach is more likely to be successful in the hemolymphatic stage of the illness, and it is much more useful in patients infected with *T. b. rhodesiense* because of the relatively high parasitemias. Because parasitemia levels vary considerably from one day to the next, serial specimens should be examined. If parasites are not seen in blood from a patient whose history and clinical findings point to African trypanosomiasis as a possible diagnosis, efforts should be made to concentrate the organisms. This can be done most simply by using quantitative buffy coat analysis tubes (QBC, Becton-Dickenson, Franklin Lakes, NJ).[37,38] In these tubes, which are coated with acridine orange, the parasites are separated from blood components by centrifugation and are easily seen under light microscopy because of the stain. Alternatively, the buffy coat obtained by centrifuging 10 to 15 mL of anticoagulated blood can be examined microscopically as a wet preparation and after Giemsa staining, and miniature anion exchange columns, which retain blood cells but not trypanosomes, also can be useful in detecting parasites.[38,39]

Examination of the CSF is mandatory in all patients suspected of having African trypanosomiasis.[40] An increase in the CSF cell count is the first abnormality to be detected. Increased opening pressure of the fluid develops later, as do an elevated IgM level and total protein concentration. Examination of CSF processed by single or double centrifugation

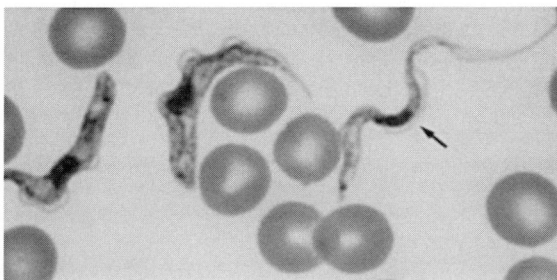

FIGURE 275-1. *Trypanosoma brucei rhodesiense* trypomastigotes in rat blood. The parasite indicated by the *arrow* is typical of the long, slender forms capable of multiplying in the mammalian host. The other two organisms represent the stumpy, nondividing forms infective for the insect vector. (Giemsa, ×1250.) *(Courtesy of Dr. G.A. Cook, Madison, WI.)*

methods often reveals trypanosomes in patients with CNS involvement.[41,42] Any CSF abnormality in a patient in whom trypanosomes have been found in specimens from other sites must be viewed as indicative of CNS involvement, and this has implications for treatment that are discussed later. CSF cell counts and IgM levels may remain elevated for long periods after curative therapy.

An additional approach to patients in whom parasites cannot be demonstrated by the previously described methods is bone marrow aspiration. Trypanosomes may be found by careful examination of Giemsa-stained specimens. Moreover, material aspirated from the bone marrow can be inoculated into special liquid culture medium, as can blood, CSF, or lymph node aspirates obtained from the patient in whom trypanosomiasis is suspected.[43] Finally, a highly sensitive method for the detection of infection with *T. b. rhodesiense* is inoculation of specimens obtained from the patient into mice or rats. Patent parasitemias usually develop within a week or two in animals inoculated with specimens from infected persons. Unfortunately, due to host specificity, it is very difficult to isolate *T. b. gambiense* by this method.

Several serologic assays are available to aid in the diagnosis of African trypanosomiasis, but the variable sensitivity and specificity of these tests mandate that treatment decisions still be based on demonstration of the parasite. Nonetheless, these assays are useful in epidemiologic surveys. Detection of elevated serum IgM levels was used for many years as a screening procedure. Simple agglutination tests for trypanosomes performed on cards (CATT, TrypTect CIATT)[44,45] are available commercially and are easy to use under field conditions. These card assays are useful for screening populations at risk, after which parasitologic studies can be done on persons having positive results. A role for assays based on the polymerase chain reaction for detecting African trypanosomes has not yet been defined.[46,47]

TREATMENT

Suramin, pentamidine, and organic arsenicals have been the mainstay for treating African trypanosomiasis for more than 50 years.[48] Eflornithine, which is effective in both the hemolymphatic and the CNS stages of West African trypanosomiasis, was added to the group in 1990. Therapy of gambiense and rhodesiense trypanosomiases must be individualized based on the presence or absence of CNS disease, side reactions, and occasionally drug resistance of the infecting organisms. Suramin and pentamidine do not penetrate the CNS adequately. Thus eflornithine should be used in patients with gambiense trypanosomiasis who have CNS disease, but because the response of *T. b. rhodesiense* to this drug has been variable,[49] patients with stage II rhodesiense trypanosomiasis must be treated with the arsenical melarsoprol, which is highly toxic (Table 275-2). In the United States these drugs can be obtained from the Drug Service of the Centers for Disease Control and Prevention in Atlanta, Georgia. Currently recommended treatment protocols are summarized in two publications.[50,51]

Patients with the hemolymphatic stage of gambiense trypanosomiasis and normal CSF (stage I disease) should be treated with pentamidine isoethionate (Lomidine).[52] The dosage for both adults and children is 4 mg/kg, up to 300 mg/day, intravenously (IV) or intramuscularly (IM) for 7 days. Intramuscular injections of pentamidine are painful and may cause sterile abscesses. Immediate side effects of pentamidine can include nausea, vomiting, hypotension, and tachycar-

dia. These reactions are generally transient and do not warrant discontinuation of therapy. Other side effects include nephrotoxicity, abnormal liver function tests, neutropenia, rashes, and hypoglycemia.

Eflornithine (difluoromethylornithine [DFMO], Ornidyl) is highly effective in both the hemolymphatic and the CNS stages of gambiense trypanosomiasis. This drug produces a dramatic reduction of symptoms and rapid clearing of parasites from blood and CSF. For adults the recommended dosage is 400 mg/kg/day IV in four divided doses for 14 days, and for children it is 500 to 600 mg/kg/day on the same schedule. Anemia, leukopenia, and thrombocytopenia are frequent in patients treated with eflornithine, but generally they are not clinically significant. Seizures and hearing loss have been reported rarely. Major disadvantages of eflornithine are the requirement that it be given intravenously, the amount of drug that must be given, and the duration of therapy. These factors, combined with the variable drug availability, make widespread use difficult, leaving pentamidine as the better choice for stage I gambiense disease. For patients with gambiense disease and CNS involvement, eflornithine is the drug of choice. It is as effective as melarsoprol, but has far fewer side effects. In persons with HIV/AIDS it is less effective, and thus such dually infected patients should be treated with melarsoprol.[50,53]

Suramin (Bayer 205, Naphuride, Antrypol) is the first-choice drug for stage I rhodesiense trypanosomiasis. A 100- to 200-mg test dose is recommended, although anaphylactic reactions are rare. The dosage for adults is 1 g IV on days 2, 3, 7, 14, and 21. The dosage for children is 20 mg/kg IV on days 1, 3, 7, 14, and 21. The exact spacing of the doses probably is not important because the half-life of suramin is quite long. The drug is administered by slow intravenous infusion of a freshly prepared 10% aqueous solution. Suramin causes a number of side effects and must be administered under the close supervision of a physician. Approximately 1 patient in 20,000 has an immediate, severe, and potentially fatal reaction to the drug consisting of nausea, vomiting, seizures, and shock. A number of less severe reactions can also occur, including fever, pruritus, photophobia, arthralgias, and skin eruptions. The most important side effect of suramin is renal damage. Transient proteinuria is often seen during treatment. Urinalysis should be done before giving each dose, and if proteinuria increases or casts and red cells appear in the urine sediment, the drug should be discontinued. Suramin should not be used in patients with preexisting renal insufficiency.

The drug of choice for rhodesiense trypanosomiasis with CNS involvement is the arsenical melarsoprol (mel B, Arsobal). Melarsoprol cures both stages of the disease. Thus, it is also indicated for treatment of the hemolymphatic stage in patients in whom suramin or pentamidine has failed or could not be tolerated. However, it should never be the first choice for therapy of stage I trypanosomiasis because of its relatively high toxicity. In adults the drug is given in three courses of 3 days each. The recommended dosage is 2 to 3.6 mg/kg/day intravenously in three divided doses for 3 days, followed 1 week later by 3.6 mg/kg/day, also in three divided doses for 3 days. This latter course is then repeated 10 to 21 days later. In debilitated patients, treatment with suramin for 2 to 4 days before starting melarsoprol therapy and an 18-mg initial dose of the latter drug, followed by progressive drug increases, have been recommended. For pediatric patients, 18 to 25 mg/kg total should be given over 1 month. An initial dose of 0.36 mg/kg intravenously should be increased gradually to a maximum of 3.6 mg/kg at 1- to 5-day intervals for a total of 9 to 10 doses.

Melarsoprol is a highly toxic drug and should be administered with great care. The most important side effects involve the CNS. A substantial percentage of patients treated with melarsoprol develop reactive encephalopathy. The risk of this immune-mediated phenomenon and its associated mortality is reduced significantly by concomitant administration of prednisolone. Thus all patients treated with melarsoprol should be given prednisolone at a dose of 1 mg/kg up to 40 mg/day, starting a day or two before initiation of melarsoprol therapy, continued through the period of treatment, and then tapered over several days.[54,55] Clinical indications of reactive encephalopathy include

		Clinical Stage	
TABLE 275-2 Drugs Recommended for Treatment of the African Trypanosomiases			
Causative Agent		*I*	*II*
Trypanosoma brucei gambiense		Pentamidine Alt: Eflornithine	Eflornithine Alt: Melarsoprol
Trypanosoma brucei rhodesiense		Suramin Alt: Pentamidine	Melarsoprol

high fever, headache, tremor, impaired speech, seizures, and finally coma and death. Melarsoprol should be discontinued at the first sign of encephalopathy. It may be restarted cautiously with small doses a few days after the signs have resolved.

A number of other side effects are associated with melarsoprol therapy. Extravasation of the drug results in intense local reactions and, as with administration of other heavy metals, abdominal pain and vomiting are commonly observed. Jarisch-Herxheimer-type reactions have been reported, as have nephrotoxicity, abnormal liver function tests, and myocardial damage.

If a patient with gambiense CNS disease cannot tolerate eflornithine, or if the latter is not available, melarsoprol should be given at a dose of 2.2 mg/kg/day IV for 10 days. This compressed regimen for stage II gambiense disease has been shown in a randomized trial to be equally effective and no more toxic than the traditional regimen outlined above.[56]

PREVENTION

The trypanosomiases constitute complex public health and epizootic problems in many developing countries in Africa. Control programs that focus on eradication of vectors and drug treatment of infected humans and animals have been in operation in some regions for decades. Considerable progress has been made in a number of areas, but the lack of a consensus on the best approach to solving the overall problem of African trypanosomiasis and a paucity of resources stand in the way of effective control.[57,58] Individuals can reduce their risk of acquiring infections with trypanosomes by avoiding areas known to harbor infected insects, by wearing clothing that reduces the biting of the flies, and by using insect repellent. Chemoprophylaxis is not recommended because of the high toxicity of the drugs that are active against African trypanosomes, and no vaccine is available to prevent transmission of the parasites.

REFERENCES

1. Hoare CA. The Trypanosomes of Mammals: A Zoological Monograph. Oxford: Blackwell; 1972.
2. Vickerman K. Developmental cycles and biology of pathogenic trypanosomes. Br Med Bull. 1985;41:105-114.
3. Jordan AM. Trypanosomiasis Control and African Rural Development. London: Longmans; 1986.
4. Borst P, Rudenko G, Blundell PA, et al. Mechanisms of antigenic variation in African trypanosomes. Behring Inst Mitt. 1997;99:1-15.
5. Donelson JE, Hill KL, El-Sayed NMA. Multiple mechanisms of immune evasion by African trypanosomes. Mol Biochem Parasitol. 1998;91:51-66.
6. Donelson JE. Antigenic variation and the African trypanosome genome. Acta Tropica. 2003;85:391-404.
7. Mbala L, Matendo R, Kinkela T, et al. Congenital African trypanosomiasis in a newborn child with current neurologic symptomatology. Trop Doct. 1996;26:186-187.
8. Herwaldt BL. Laboratory-acquired parasitic diseases. Clin Microbiol Rev. 2000;14:659-688.
9. Poltera AA. Pathology of human African trypanosomiasis with reference to experimental African trypanosomiasis and infections of the central nervous system. Br Med Bull. 1985;41:169-174.
10. Hunter CA, Kennedy PGE. Immunopathology in central nervous system human African trypanosomiasis. J Neuroimmunol. 1992;36:91-95.
11. Bentivoglio M, Brassi-Zucconi G, Olsson T, et al. Trypanosoma brucei and the nervous system. Trends Neurosci. 1994;17:325-329.
12. Wery M, Mulumba PM, Lambert PH, Kazyumba L. Hematologic manifestations, diagnosis, and immunopathology of African trypanosomiasis. Semin Hematol. 1982;19:83-92.
13. Poltera AA, Cox JN, Owor R. Pancarditis involving the conducting system and all valves in human African trypanosomiasis. Br Heart J. 1976;38:827-837.
14. Poltera AA, Owor R, Cox JN. Pathological aspects of human African trypanosomiasis (HAT) in Uganda. A post-mortem survey of fourteen cases. Virchows Arch Pathol Histol. 1997;373:249-265.
15. Robins-Browne RM, Schneider J, Metz J. Thrombocytopenia in trypanosomiasis. Am J Trop Med Hyg. 1975;24:226-231.
16. Barrett-Connor E, Ugoreta RJ, Braude I. Disseminated intravascular coagulation in trypanosomiasis. Arch Intern Med. 1973;131:574-577.
17. Lambert PH, Berney M, Kazyumba GL. Immune complexes in serum and in cerebrospinal fluid in sleeping sickness. Correlation with polyclonal B-cell activation and with intracerebral immunoglobulin synthesis. J Clin Invest. 1981;67:77-85.
18. Smith DH, Pepin J, Stich A. Human African trypanosomiasis: An emerging public health crisis. Br Med Bull 1998;54:341-355.
19. Fevre EM, Coleman PG, Odiit M, et al. The origins of a new Trypanosoma brucei rhodesiense sleeping sickness outbreak in eastern Uganda. Lancet. 2001;358:625-628.
20. Pepin J, Meda H. The epidemiology and control of human African trypanosomiasis. Adv Parasitol. 2001;49:71-132.
21. Anonymous. Control and surveillance of African trypanosomiasis. World Health Organization. WHO Technical Report Series No. 881, Geneva, 1998.
22. D'Ieteren GD, Authie E, Wissocq N, Murray M. Trypanotolerance, an option for sustainable livestock production in areas at risk from trypanosomiasis. Rev Sci Tech. 1998;17:154-175.
23. Sahlas DJ, MacLean JD, Janevski J, Detsky AS. Out of Africa. N Engl J Med. 2002;347:749-753.
24. Moore AC, Ryan ET, Waldron MA. Case records of the Massachusetts General Hospital. Weekly clinicopathological exercises. Case 20-2002. N Engl J Med. 2002;346:2069-2076.
25. Lejon V, Boelaert M, Jannin J, et al. The challenge of Trypanosoma brucei gambiense sleeping sickness diagnosis outside Africa. Lancet Infect Dis. 2003;3:804-808.
26. Sinha A, Grace C, Alston WK, et al. African trypanosomiasis in two travelers from the United States. Clin Infect Dis. 1999;29:840-844.
27. Jelinek T, Bisoffi Z, Bonazzi L, et al. Cluster of African trypanosomiasis in travelers to Tanzanian national parks. Emerg Infect Dis. 2002;8:634-635.
28. McGovern TW, Williams W, Fitzpatrick JE, et al. Cutaneous manifestations of African trypanosomiasis. Arch Dermatol. 1995;131:1178-1182.
29. Reincke M, Arlt W, Heppner C, et al. Neuroendocrine dysfunction in African trypanosomiasis. The role of cytokines. Ann NY Acad Sci. 1998;840:809-821.
30. Petzke F, Heppner C, Bulamberi D, et al. Hypogonadism in Rhodesian sleeping sickness: Evidence for acute and chronic dysfunction of the hypothalamic-pituitary-gonadal axis. Fertil Steril. 1996;65:68-75.
31. Haller L, Adams A, Merouze F, Dago A. Clinical and pathological aspects of human African trypanosomiasis (T. b. gambiense) with particular reference to reactive arsenical encephalopathy. Am J Trop Med Hyg. 1986;35:94-99.
32. Buyst H. Sleeping sickness in children. Ann Soc Belge Med Trop. 1977;57:201-212.
33. Koko J, Dufillot D, Gahouma D, et al. Human African trypanosomiasis in children. A pediatrics service experience in Libreville, Gabon (in French). Bull Soc Pathol Exot. 1997;90:14-18.
34. Gear JHS, Miller B. The clinical manifestations of rhodesiense trypanosomiasis: An account of cases contracted in the Okavango swamps of Botswana. Am J Trop Med Hyg. 1986;35:1146-1152.
35. Odiit M, Kansiime F, Enyaru JC. Duration of symptoms and case fatality of sleeping sickness caused by Trypanosoma brucei rhodesiense in Tororo, Uganda. East Afr Med J. 1997;74:792-795.
36. Van Meirvenne N. Diagnosis of human African trypanosomiasis. Ann Soc Belge Med Trop. 1992;72(Suppl 1):53-56.
37. Bailey JW, Smith DH. The use of the acridine orange QBC technique in the diagnosis of African trypanosomiasis. Trans R Soc Trop Med Hyg. 1992;86:630.
38. Truc P, Jamonneau V, N'Guessan P, et al. Parasitological diagnosis of human African trypanosomiasis: A comparison of the QBC® and miniature anion-exchange centrifugation techniques. Trans R Soc Trop Med Hyg. 1998;92:288-289.
39. Lumsden WHR, Kimber CD, Strange M. Trypanosoma brucei: Detection of low parasitemia in mice by a miniature anion-exchanger/centrifugation technique. Trans R Soc Trop Med Hyg. 1977;71:421-424.
40. Miezan TW, Meda HA, Doua F, et al. Assessment of central nervous system involvement in gambiense trypanosomiasis: Value of the cerebro-spinal white cell count. Trop Med Int Health. 1998;3:571-575.
41. Cattand P, Miezan BT, deRaadt P. Human African trypanosomiasis: Use of double centrifugation of cerebrospinal fluid to detect trypanosomes. Bull WHO. 1988;66:83-86.
42. Miezan TW, Meda HA, Doua F, et al. Single centrifugation of cerebrospinal fluid in a sealed Pasteur pipette for simple, rapid and sensitive detection of trypanosomes. Trans R Soc Trop Med Hyg. 2000;94:293.
43. Truc P, Aerts D, McNamara JJ, et al. Direct isolation in vitro of Trypanosoma brucei from man and other animals, and its potential value for the diagnosis of Gambian trypanosomiasis. Trans R Soc Trop Med Hyg. 1992;86:627-629.
44. Nantulya VM. TrypTect CIATT7®-a card indirect agglutination trypanosomiasis test for diagnosis of Trypanosoma brucei gambiense and T. b. rhodesiense infections. Trans R Soc Trop Med Hyg. 1997;91:551-553.
45. Truc P, Lejon V, Magnus E, et al. Evaluation of the micro-CATT, CATT/Trypanosoma brucei gambiense, and LATEX/T. b. gambiense methods for serodiagnosis and surveillance of human African trypanosomiasis in West and Central Africa. Bull WHO. 2002;80:882-886.
46. Penchenier L, Simo G, Grebaut P, et al. Diagnosis of human trypanosomiasis, due to Trypanosoma brucei gambiense in central Africa, by the polymerase chain reaction. Trans R Soc Trop Med Hyg. 2000;94:392-394.
47. Radwanska M, Claes F, Magez S, et al. Novel primer sequences for polymerase chain reaction-based detection of Trypanosoma brucei gambiense. Am J Trop Med Hyg. 2002; 67:289-295.
48. Fairlamb AH. Chemotherapy of human African trypanosomiasis: Current and future prospects. Trends Parasitol. 2003;19:488-494.
49. Iten M, Mett H, Evans A, et al. Alterations in ornithine decarboxylase characteristics account for tolerance of Trypanosoma brucei rhodesiense to D, L-alpha-difluoromethylornithine. Antimicrob Agents Chemother. 1997;41:1922-1925.
50. Pepin J, Milord F. The treatment of human African trypanosomiasis. Adv Parasitol. 1995;33:1-47.
51. Anonymous. Drugs for parasitic infections. Med Lett Drugs Ther. 1998;40:1-12.

52. Doua F, Miezan TW, Sanon Singaro JR, et al. The efficacy of pentamidine in the treatment of early-late stage *Trypanosoma brucei gambiense* trypanosomiasis. Am J Trop Med Hyg. 1997;55:586-588.

53. Meda HA, Doua F, Laveissiere C, et al. Human immunodeficiency virus infection and human African trypanosomiasis: A case-control study in Cote d'Ivoire. Trans R Soc Trop Med Hyg. 1995;89:639-643.

54. Pepin J, Milord F, Guern C, et al. Trial of prednisolone for prevention of melarsoprol-induced encephalopathy in gambiense sleeping sickness. Lancet. 1989;333:1246-1250.

55. Pepin J, Milord F, Khonde N, et al. Risk factors for encephalopathy and mortality during melarsoprol treatment of *T.b. gambiense* sleeping sickness. Trans R Soc Trop Med Hyg. 1995;89:92-97.

56. Burri C, Nkunku S, Merolle A, et al. Efficacy of a new, concise, schedule for melarsoprol in treatment of sleeping sickness caused by *Trypanosoma brucei* gambiense: A randomised trial. Lancet 2000;355:1419-1425.

57. Molyneux DH. Vector-borne parasitic diseases-an overview of recent changes. Int J Parasitol. 1998; 28:927-934.

58. Holmes PH. New approaches to the integrated control of trypanosomiasis. Vet Parasitol. 1997;71:121-135.

CHAPTER **276**

Toxoplasma gondii

JOSE G. MONTOYA

JOSEPH A. KOVACS

JACK S. REMINGTON

Although *Toxoplasma gondii* infects a large proportion of the world's human populations, it is an uncommon cause of disease. Certain individuals are at high risk, however, for severe or life-threatening disease due to this parasite, including congenitally infected fetuses and newborns and immunologically impaired individuals. Congenital toxoplasmosis is the result of maternal infection acquired during gestation, an infection that most often is clinically unapparent. In immunodeficient patients, toxoplasmosis most often occurs in persons with defects in T cell–mediated immunity, such as patients receiving corticosteroids or cytotoxic drugs and patients with hematologic malignancies, organ transplants, or acquired immunodeficiency syndrome (AIDS). In most otherwise immunocompetent individuals, primary or chronic (latent) infection with *T. gondii* is asymptomatic; after the acute infection, a few patients have chorioretinitis, lymphadenitis, or, more rarely, myocarditis and polymyositis.

T. gondii first was observed in the North African rodent *Ctenodactylus gundi* by Nicolle and Manceaux in 1908[1] and was recognized as a cause of human disease in an 11-month-old, congenitally infected infant by Janku in 1923.[2] It was reported as a cause of encephalitis by Wolf and co-workers,[3] who in 1939 observed *T. gondii* in a newborn who presented with seizures, intracranial calcifications, hydrocephalus, and chorioretinitis. Although relatively few cases of severe toxoplasmosis in adults were reported during the ensuing years, a report in 1968 by Vietzke and colleagues[4] from the National Cancer Institute of the National Institutes of Health highlighted *T. gondii* as a cause of life-threatening infection in patients with malignancy, predominantly in patients with hematologic malignancies. Brain involvement with focal areas of encephalitis was the primary finding at autopsy in these patients. Since that time, several hundred cases in non-AIDS immunodeficient patients have been recorded in the literature.[5] In 1983, the first report of toxoplasmosis in AIDS patients appeared.[6] Toxoplasmic encephalitis (TE) subsequently was recognized as the major cause of space-occupying lesions in the brains of these patients, almost all of whom had serologic evidence of prior exposure to the parasite.[6] Despite the significant advances that have been achieved in recent years, major challenges remain in the areas of prevention and management of the acute infection in pregnancy, fetuses,

and newborns[7] and in the understanding and treatment of toxoplasmic chorioretinitis[8] and infection in immunocompromised individuals.[5]

ETIOLOGY

T. gondii is a coccidian parasite of felids with humans and other warm-blooded animals serving as intermediate hosts. It belongs to the subphylum Apicomplexa, class Sporozoa, and exists in nature in three forms: the oocyst (which releases sporozoites), the tissue cyst (which contains and may release bradyzoites), and the tachyzoite (Fig. 276-1).[9]

Population genetic analysis has shown that most organisms isolated from animals and humans can be grouped into one of three clonal genotypes (types I to III), which may identify clinically relevant biologic differences.[10] Clear differences have been observed in the frequency of parasite genotypes when *T. gondii* isolates from animals were compared with isolates from humans. Type III strains are common in animals but observed significantly less often in cases of human toxoplasmosis; most cases in humans are caused by type II strains. Type II strains are associated significantly more often with reactivation of chronic infections and accounted for 65% of strains isolated from AIDS patients.[11] Type I and type II strains have been associated with human congenital toxoplasmosis.[11-13] Type II and type III strains to date have not been detected in immunocompetent individuals with severe ocular disease.[14] Genetic typing of *T. gondii* strains from humans essentially has been limited to strains obtained from patients in Europe and the United States.

Oocyst

Cats shed oocysts after they ingest any of the three forms of the parasite, at which time an enteroepithelial cycle begins. The organisms penetrate the epithelial cells of the small intestine and initiate development of asexual and sexual (gametogony) forms of the parasite. Oocyst wall formation begins around the fertilized gamete, and when mature, oocysts are discharged into the intestinal lumen by rupture of intestinal epithelial cells.[9] Unsporulated oocysts are subspheric to spheric and measure 10×12 μm in diameter (Fig. 276-1A). Oocysts are formed in the small intestine only in felids and are excreted in the feces for periods varying from 7 to 20 days. Ten million oocysts may be shed in the feces in a single day.[9] Sporulation, required for oocysts to become infectious, occurs outside the cat within 1 to 5 days depending on temperature and the availability of oxygen. Sporulated oocysts contain two sporocysts (see Fig. 276-1A), each of which contains four sporozoites. Maturation is more rapid at warm temperatures (2 to 3 days at 24° C compared with 14 to 21 days at 11° C).[9] Oocysts may remain viable for 18 months in moist soil; this results in an environmental reservoir from which incidental hosts may be infected.

Tachyzoite

The tachyzoite form (Fig. 276-1B, C) is oval to crescentic and measures 2 to 3 μm wide and 5 to 7 μm long; it requires an intracellular habitat to multiply and survive, despite having its own Golgi apparatus, ribosomes, and mitochondria. Tachyzoites are seen in primary and reactivated infection; their presence is the hallmark of active infection. They reside and multiply within vacuoles in their host's cells, can infect all phagocytic and nonphagocytic cell types,[9] and multiply approximately every 6 to 8 hours to form rosettes.[15] Continuous multiplication leads to cell disruption and release of organisms that go on to invade contiguous cells or are phagocytosed and transported to other areas of the body by blood and lymph.[16] Tachyzoites seem to migrate actively and rapidly across epithelial cells and may travel to distant sites while extracellular.[17] At the anterior end of the tachyzoite, there is a cone-shaped structure termed the *conoid*. It protrudes during the parasite's entry into host cells. *Rhoptries,* numbering four to eight, are club-shaped organelles that terminate in the conoid. The rhoptries, together with surrounding small, rod-shaped organelles (micronemes), have important secretory functions for parasitic invasion. *Dense granules* are organelles distributed throughout the cytoplasm. Their contents are released

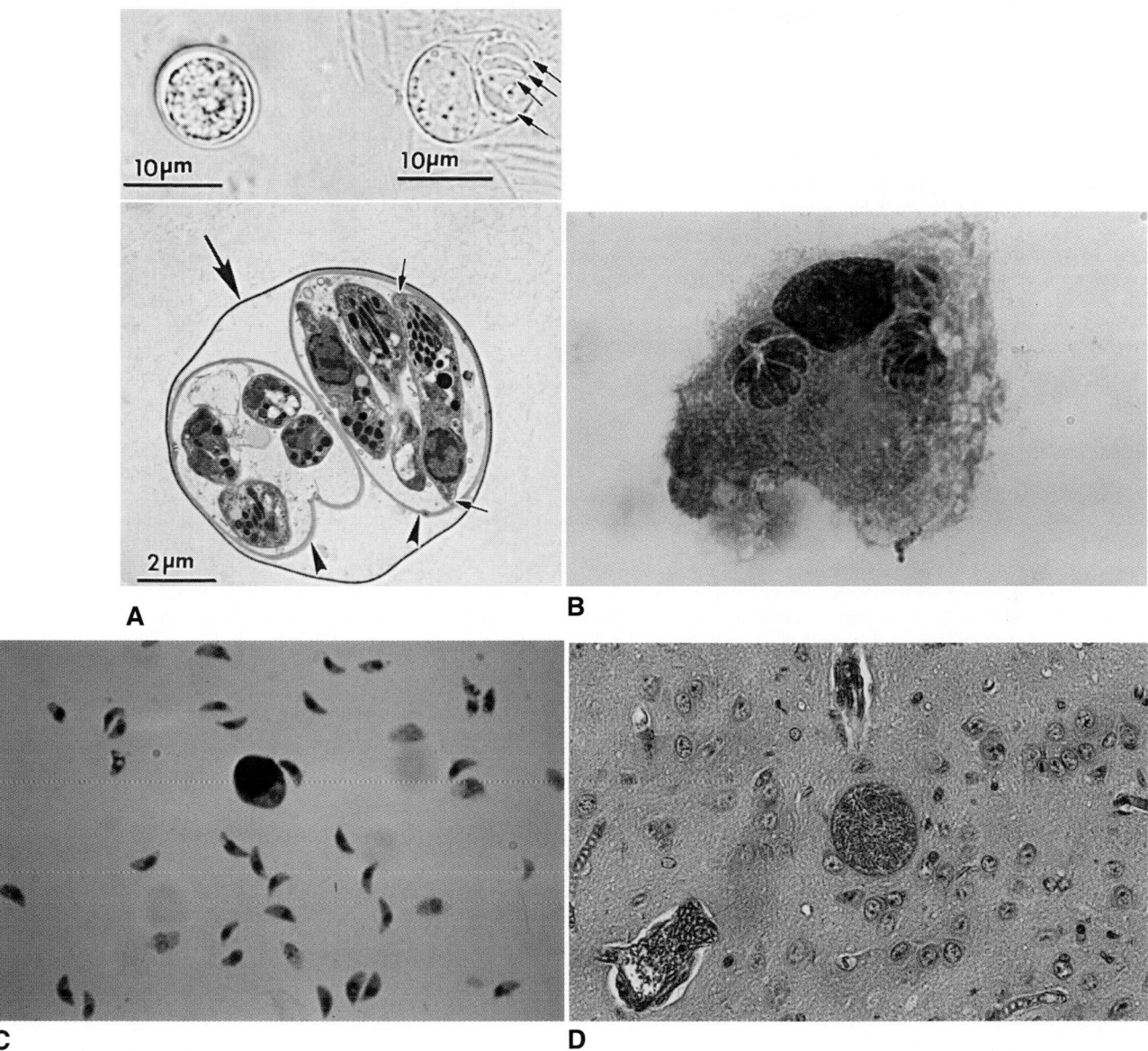

FIGURE 276-1. The three forms of *Toxoplasma gondii* observed in nature. **A,** Oocysts. Unsporulated oocyst *(A)*. Sporulated oocyst with two sporocysts *(B)*. Four sporozoites *(arrows)* are visible in one of the sporocysts. Transmission electron micrograph of a sporulated oocyst *(C)*. Note the thin oocyst wall *(large arrow)*, two sporocysts *(arrowheads)*, and sporozoites, one of which is cut longitudinally. **B,** Giemsa stain showing two rosettes of intracellular tachyzoites in a mouse bone marrow macrophage. **C,** Giemsa-stained smear of mouse peritoneal fluid showing the tachyzoite form. **D,** Hematoxylin and eosin stain of the cyst form in brain. *(**A,** Courtesy of Dr. J. P. Dubey, U.S. Department of Agriculture, Beltsville, MD.)*

into a vacuole, termed the *parasitophorous vacuole,* which is formed around the parasite during entry into the cell and into the external environment as excreted-secreted antigens.[9]

Tachyzoites cannot survive desiccation, freezing and thawing, or extended exposure to gastric digestive juices.[18] They are propagated in the laboratory in the peritoneum of mice and in cultured cells. Tachyzoites can be visualized in sections stained with hematoxylin and eosin but are seen better with Wright-Giemsa and immunoperoxidase stains.[19]

Tissue Cyst

When the tachyzoite has invaded the target cell, it can undergo stage conversion into the bradyzoite form.[9] Tachyzoites and bradyzoites are structurally and phenotypically different. Tachyzoites multiply rapidly and synchronously, forming rosettes and lysing the cell, whereas the more slowly replicating bradyzoites form tissue cysts. Molecules are expressed in a stage-specific manner and are responsible for certain of the phenotypic differences between tachyzoites and bradyzoites. Interferon (IFN)-γ, nitric oxide (NO), heat-shock proteins, and pH and temperature manipulations can trigger conversion of tachyzoites to bradyzoites in vitro and perhaps in vivo.[9]

Tissue cysts grow and remain within the host cell cytoplasm as the intracystic form wherein the bradyzoites continue to divide. Tissue cysts vary in size from younger cysts, which contain only a few bradyzoites, to older tissue cysts, which may contain several thousand bradyzoites and may reach greater than 100 μm in size (see Fig. 276-1D). They appear spheric in the brain and conform to the shape of muscle fibers in heart and skeletal muscles. The central nervous system (CNS); eye; and skeletal, smooth, and heart muscles seem to be the most common sites of latent infection.[20] Because of their persistence in tissues, demonstration of tissue cysts in histologic sections does not mean that the infection was acquired recently or that it is clinically relevant.

Tissue cysts stain well with periodic acid–Schiff, Wright-Giemsa, Gomori–methenamine silver, and immunoperoxidase stains. Tissue cysts in meat are rendered nonviable by gamma-irradiation (0.4 cGy),[21] heating meat throughout to 67° C or freezing to −20° C for 24 hours, then thawing.[22,23]

Although the tachyzoite form appears to be indiscriminate in the type of host cell parasitized, it has been suggested that in brain tissue there is a predilection for tissue cyst formation to occur predominantly within neurons.[24,25] It has been shown, however, that tissue cysts can form within astrocytes cultured in vitro.[26] In an electron microscopic study of the pathologic changes in brains of infected mice, tissue cysts were observed to remain intracellular throughout the period of study (22 months).[24] There is compelling evidence to suggest that bradyzoites can exit from intact tissue cysts and invade contiguous cells (where they convert to the tachyzoite form).[27] This is the likely explanation for the appearance of "daughter" cysts or clumps of cysts in the brain.

TRANSMISSION AND EPIDEMIOLOGY

T. gondii infection is a worldwide zoonosis. The organism infects herbivorous, omnivorous, and carnivorous animals, including birds. Infection in humans most commonly occurs through the ingestion of raw or undercooked meat that contains tissue cysts, through the ingestion of water or food contaminated with oocysts, or congenitally through transplacental transmission from a mother who acquired the infection during gestation (Fig. 276-2). Less common is transmission by transplantation of an infected organ or transfusion of contaminated blood cells. Transmission also has occurred by accidental sticks[28] with contaminated needles or through exposing open lesions or mucosal surfaces to the parasite.[29] Coprophagous invertebrates, including cockroaches, filth flies, earthworms, snails, and slugs, may serve as transport hosts for oocysts to reach the gastrointestinal tract of animals or humans.

Because the sexual cycle of the parasite occurs in the small bowel of members of the cat family, cats play a significant role as powerful amplifiers of the infection in nature (see "Oocyst").[9] Epidemiologic surveys have revealed that in most areas of the world, the presence of cats is of primary importance for the transmission of the parasite. Excretion of oocysts has been reported to occur in approximately 1% of cats in diverse areas of the world.[29]

Although ingestion of raw or undercooked meat that contains viable *T. gondii* tissue cysts results in infection, the relative frequency with which this occurs in relation to the frequency of infection due to ingestion of oocysts is unclear. In countries such as France, where eating undercooked meat is common and the prevalence of the infection is high, meat may be an important cause of the infection. (In Paris, France, the meat-to-human hypothesis of spread of *T. gondii* was proved.[30]) In contrast are countries such as those in Central America, where the prevalence of the infection in humans is high, but the ingestion of undercooked meat is uncommon.

Ingestion of tissue cysts in infected meat (primarily pork and lamb) is a major source of the infection in humans in the United States.[31] *T. gondii* infection is common in many animals used for food, especially sheep and pigs, with a lower prevalence in cattle, horses, and water buffaloes. Organisms may survive in tissue cysts in these animals for years and can be found in nearly all edible portions of an animal.[32] A seminal study on the prevalence of *T. gondii* in samples of meat used for human consumption (obtained from grocery stores) was performed in the United States in the 1960s.[33] The parasite was isolated from 32% of pork chops and 4% of lamb chops; there were no isolations from beef.[33] A polymerase chain reaction (PCR)–based study in England found 33% (19 of 57) of pork samples and 67% (6 of 9) of lamb samples positive for *T. gondii* DNA.[34]

Serologic surveys conducted in the 1980s and 1990s in the United States indicate that the prevalence of *T. gondii* in pigs is declining.[31] In recent studies, seroprevalence in market-weight pigs in North Carolina has been 0.58%.[35] This reduction in *T. gondii* prevalence has been attributed to changing management practices and consolidation of pig production into large-scale operations. Although many pigs in the United States are raised in large-scale operations, however, there still are many isolated small swine farms, and the prevalence of *T. gondii* in some of these pigs is high. Dubey and colleagues[31] reported that *T. gondii* was isolated from tongue and hearts from 51 (92.7%) of 55 pigs destined for human consumption at a small farm in Massachusetts. Meat for human consumption is not inspected routinely for *T. gondii* infection in the United States or elsewhere in the world.[31] Little is known about the prevalence of *T. gondii* infection in lambs. Although *T. gondii* infection of sheep is widely prevalent, the public health importance of this is unclear because in the United States meat from adult sheep usually is not used for human consumption.[29] Reports of suspect transmission by unpasteurized goat's milk have appeared.[36,37]

T. gondii infection also is prevalent in game animals, especially black bears (80% infected), white-tailed deer, and raccoons (60% infected).[32] Infection in raccoons and bears is a good indicator of the prevalence of *T. gondii* in the environment because these animals are scavengers. Wild animal meat can serve as a source of the infection for hunters and their families, especially when care is not taken while eviscerating and handling the game or when meat from these animals is served undercooked or uncooked.[32]

Although *T. gondii* tissue cysts may be found in edible tissues of chickens,[38] poultry products probably are not important in the transmission of *T. gondii* to humans because they usually are frozen for storage and cooked thoroughly to avoid diseases that could be caused by contamination by other organisms.[29] The parasite has been isolated from chicken eggs.[39]

The ingestion of vegetables and other food products contaminated with oocysts probably accounts for infection in seropositive vegetarians. Although isolation of tachyzoites from secretions of people with the acute infection has been claimed, human-to-human transmission of infection by this route has not been established. Outbreaks within fam-

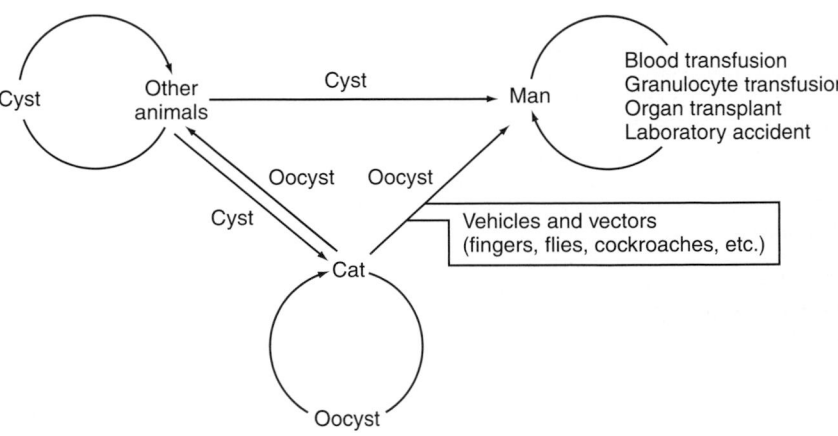

FIGURE 276-2. Transmission and life cycle of *Toxoplasma gondii. (From Knick JA, Remington JS. Toxoplasmosis in the adult—an overview. N Engl J Med. 1978;298:550-553. Copyright © 1978 Massachusetts Medical Society. All rights reserved.)*

ilies and other groups are common,[40-42] but there is no evidence of direct human-to-human transmission other than from mother to fetus.

Epidemiologic studies have identified water as a potential source for *T. gondii* infection in humans and animals.[40,43,44] Population mapping studies of acutely infected individuals and case-control studies linked drinking unfiltered water (presumably contaminated with oocysts) to an outbreak of toxoplasmosis in a municipality in the Western Canadian province of British Columbia[40] and to highly endemic rates of toxoplasmosis in Rio de Janeiro state, Brazil.[44] Coastal freshwater runoff was observed to be a risk factor for *T. gondii* infection among southern sea otters along the California coast.[43]

In humans, the incidence of *T. gondii* antibodies increases with increasing age; the incidence does not vary significantly between sexes. The incidence tends to be less in cold regions, in hot and arid areas, and at high elevations. Slaughterhouse workers may have an increased risk for infection. The prevalence of antibody titers to *T. gondii* varies considerably among different geographic areas and among individuals within a given population. These differences depend on a variety of factors, including culinary habits and cleanliness of surroundings. A decrease in antibody prevalence over the past few decades has been observed in many countries. In the United States, the seroprevalence in U.S. military recruits decreased by one third between 1965 and 1989[45]; the crude seropositivity rate among recruits from 49 states was 9.5% in 1989 compared with 14.4% in 1965.[45] In the 1970s, 24% of women of childbearing age in the Palo Alto, California, area were seropositive, whereas the rate in 2003 was 9%. Seroprevalence rates in the United States among women of childbearing age range from 3% to greater than 35%, whereas rates greater than 50% are present in women of childbearing age in much of Western Europe, Africa, and South and Central America. A woman moving from an area of low prevalence of infection to an area of high prevalence at or before the time of childbearing potential may be at increased risk. The more recent (1988 to 1994) overall age-adjusted seroprevalence of *T. gondii* infection in the United States, based on a study of 17,658 persons, was reported to be 22.5%, with a seroprevalence among women aged 15 to 44 years of 15%.[46] Regional differences were identified, with a higher age-adjusted seroprevalence in the Northeast (29.2%) compared with the South (22.8%), Midwest (20.5%), or West (17.5%) ($P < .05$).[46] For discussion of congenital transmission, see "*Toxoplasma gondii* Infection in Pregnancy."

T. gondii may survive in citrated blood at 4° C for 50 days, and infection has been transmitted through transfusion of whole blood or white blood cells. Leukocyte transfusions may pose a special risk.[47] The transmission of infection by organ transplantation has been documented and may result from the transplantation of an organ (e.g., heart) from a seropositive donor to a seronegative recipient.[48] In bone marrow transplant recipients, toxoplasmosis almost always is a result of recrudescence of a latent infection rather than from the transplant.[49,50]

The incidence of TE among human immunodeficiency virus (HIV)–infected individuals correlates directly with the prevalence of *T. gondii* antibodies among the general HIV-infected population, the degree of immunosuppression (best measured by the CD4⁺ cell count),[51] the immunologic response to antiretroviral drugs, and the use of effective prophylactic treatment regimens against development of TE.[52] AIDS-associated TE and toxoplasmosis involving other organs almost always are due to reactivation of a chronic (latent) infection that results from the progressive immune dysfunction that develops in these patients.[53] It is estimated that 20% to 47% of AIDS patients who are infected with *T. gondii* but are not taking antitoxoplasmic prophylaxis or antiretroviral drugs ultimately develop TE.[51,53] In recent years, a substantial decline in the incidence of TE[54] and toxoplasmosis-associated deaths[55] has been seen in HIV-infected patients who adhere to highly active antiretroviral therapy (HAART) and to effective antitoxoplasmic prophylactic regimens.

In the United States, *T. gondii* seropositivity among HIV-infected patients varies from 10% to 45%[53] and correlates directly with seropositivity in the general non–HIV-infected population. In contrast, the seroprevalence is approximately 50% to 78% in certain areas of Western Europe and Africa.[56,57] In a study in France, 1215 (72.2%) of 1683 HIV-infected patients had serologic evidence of exposure to *T. gondii*.[58] During the study period (1988 to 1995), the overall incidence of toxoplasmosis was estimated to be 1.53 per 100 patient-years, with an increase from 0.68 per 100 patient-years in 1988 to 2.1 per 100 patient-years in 1992 and a subsequent decline to 0.19 per 100 patient-years in 1995. Toxoplasmosis is rare in HIV-infected children: 0.06 cases per 100 patient-years were reported in more than 3000 patients participating in clinical trials in the pre-HAART era, but during a time when *Pneumocystis carinii* pneumonia prophylaxis was recommended.

There is a low reported incidence of TE in Africa despite *T. gondii* seroprevalence rates of 32% to 78%. Lack of autopsy data and a lack of neuroimaging studies likely contribute to the low reported incidence. It also has been suggested that because of poor access to medical care, many HIV-infected patients in Africa die as a result of infection with organisms such as *Mycobacterium tuberculosis* before they develop the opportunistic infections associated with the advanced stage of HIV infection, including toxoplasmosis. In one autopsy series of 175 patients with AIDS-defining abnormalities from the Ivory Coast, however, the prevalence of TE was 21%.[59] *T. gondii* infection may be acquired after the acquisition of HIV infection. Seroconversion rates of 2% to 5.5% have been reported in patients followed for 28 months.[60]

Even before the emergence of AIDS, TE had been recognized as a cause of incapacitating disease and death among immunosuppressed patients,[5,61] especially in patients whose underlying disease or therapy caused a deficiency in cell-mediated immunity. Patients with hematologic malignancies, especially patients with Hodgkin's disease, are at a particularly higher risk to develop recrudescence of the infection. Among organ transplantation patients, heart, lung, kidney, and bone marrow transplant patients develop toxoplasmosis at a higher rate.

PATHOGENESIS AND IMMUNITY

T. gondii multiplies intracellularly at the site of invasion (the gastrointestinal tract is the major route for and the initial site of infection in nature); bradyzoites released from tissue cysts or sporozoites released from oocysts penetrate and multiply within intestinal epithelial cells. Organisms may spread first to the mesenteric lymph nodes then to distant organs by invasion of lymphatics and blood. *T. gondii* infects all cell types, and cell invasion occurs as an active process. Survival of tachyzoites is due to the formation of a parasitophorous vacuole that protects against lysosomal fusion with the vacuole,[62] and consequently acidification does not occur. Active invasion of macrophages by tachyzoites does not trigger oxidative killing mechanisms. With the appearance of humoral and cellular immunity, only parasites protected by an intracellular habitat or within tissue cysts survive. An effective immune response significantly reduces the number of tachyzoites in all tissues. Tachyzoites are killed by reactive oxygen intermediates,[63] acidification,[64] osmotic fluctuations, reactive nitrogen intermediates,[65] intracellular tryptophan depletion,[66] and specific antibody combined with complement.[67] Thereafter, tachyzoites rarely can be shown histologically in tissues of infected immunocompetent humans.

Tissue cyst formation occurs in multiple organs and tissues during the first week of infection. Despite the ability to isolate *T. gondii* from normal brains of chronically infected humans, the tissue cyst form rarely is observed in histologic preparations. It has been isolated from brain and skeletal muscle in 10% of 52 *T. gondii*–seropositive patients who at autopsy had no clinical or pathologic evidence of the infection.[20] The tissue cyst form is responsible for residual (chronic or latent) infection and persists primarily in brain, skeletal and heart muscle, and eye.[20,68]

In immunocompetent individuals, the initial infection and the resultant seeding of different organs leads to a chronic or latent infection without clinical significance. This chronic stage of the infection corresponds to the asymptomatic persistence of the tissue cyst form in multiple tissues. It is believed that periodically bradyzoites are released from tissue cysts or that cysts "rupture"; cyst disruption in this setting is a clinically silent process effectively contained by the immune system and in the CNS likely results in small inflammatory nodules, with a limited degree of neuronal cell death and architectural damage.[27]

Although toxoplasmosis in severely immunodeficient individuals may be caused by primary infection, it most often is the result of recrudescence of a latent infection. It is widely held that reactivation is the result of disruption of the tissue cyst form followed by uncontrolled proliferation of organisms and tissue destruction. In individuals with deficient cell-mediated immunity, rapid, uncontrolled proliferation of T. gondii results in progressively enlarging necrotic lesions. It has been postulated that damage to any organ in these patients, including the brain, eye, heart, lung, skeletal muscle, gastrointestinal tract, and pancreas, can result directly from tissue cyst disruption in the parenchyma of the organ itself or from tissue cyst disruption elsewhere in the body followed by subsequent spread to that organ.[69] Hematogenous spread is supported by the observation of the development of simultaneous lesions in the brain and the presence of parasitemia in 14% to 38% of AIDS patients with TE.[70,71] Lymphocytes obtained from patients with AIDS have impaired production of IFN-γ[72] and interleukin-2 (IL-2)[73] in response to stimulation with T. gondii antigens. Treatment of monocytes and monocyte-derived macrophages from AIDS patients with IFN-γ enhances their activity against T. gondii.[74] Co-infection with other opportunistic pathogens may predispose to reactivation; murine cytomegalovirus (CMV) induces reactivation of latent T. gondii infection in the lungs of experimental animals.[75]

Infection with T. gondii induces humoral and cell-mediated immune responses. A well-orchestrated and effective systemic immune response results in the early disappearance of T. gondii from peripheral blood during the acute infection and limits the parasite burden in other organs. Immunity in the immunocompetent host is lifelong. Exogenous reinfection, which has been shown in laboratory animals, likely also occurs in humans but does not seem to result in clinically apparent disease.

T cells, macrophages, and type 1 cytokines (IFN-γ, IL-12) are crucial for control of T. gondii infection. Adoptive transfer experiments in murine models not only proved that T cells are essential for control of T. gondii infection, but also revealed that CD8+ T cells are primarily responsible for this resistance, although significant protection also is conferred by CD4+ T cells. A rapid and remarkable αβ T-cell response plays an important role in the early events of the immune response against the parasite. In addition, an expansion of γδ T cells occurs in the early stages of infection and may represent an important component of the immune response. These different subsets of T cells are likely to protect the host by secreting cytokines such as IFN-γ, IL-2, and tumor necrosis factor-α and perhaps by lysing T. gondii–infected cells.

The costimulatory molecules CD28 and CD40 ligand are pivotal for the regulation of IL-12 and IFN-γ production in response to the parasite.[76] T. gondii infection of antigen-presenting cells, such as dendritic cells and macrophages, causes upregulation of the counterreceptors for CD28 and CD40L, CD80/CD86 and CD40, respectively.[76] Binding of CD80/CD86 to CD28 enhances production of IFN-γ by CD4+ T cells. In addition, binding of CD40L to CD40 triggers IL-12 secretion, which enhances production of IFN-γ. The relevance of CD40L in the immune response to T. gondii is supported by reports of TE and disseminated toxoplasmosis in children with congenital defects in CD40L signaling (hyper-IgM syndrome).[77] More recent studies have shown that expression of CD40L is defective on CD4+ T cells from HIV-infected patients.[78] This deficiency may play a role in defective IL-12/IFN-γ production associated with HIV infection.

Cytokines play a crucial role in defense against the infection and are important in the pathogenesis of toxoplasmosis and TE.[79] IL-12 enhances survival of T cell–deficient mice during T. gondii infection, possibly through increased production of IFN-γ by natural killer cells.[80] IFN-γ has been shown to play a significant role in the prevention or development of TE in mice.[81] The administration of a monoclonal antibody against IFN-γ to chronically infected mice resulted in a dramatic worsening in the degree of encephalitis.[82] In mice with active TE, treatment with IFN-γ significantly reduced the inflammatory response and numbers of tachyzoites.[83]

Tumor necrosis factor-α is another cytokine pivotal for control of T. gondii infection. Tumor necrosis factor-α is required for triggering of IFN-γ-mediated activation of macrophages for T. gondii-cidal activity[84] and for NO (an inhibitor of T. gondii replication) production by macrophages.[85] The administration of tumor necrosis factor-α–neutralizing antibody to infected mice caused the death of the mice and an increase in the number of T. gondii tissue cysts in the brains of survivors.[86] IL-10 has been shown to deactivate macrophages and result in reduced in vitro killing of T. gondii. IL-4 and IL-6, which usually are considered downregulatory cytokines, have been shown to be important in resistance against TE in the murine model.[87,88] IL-7 also has been shown to have a protective role against T. gondii in mice.[89] During the early stages of the infection, IL-12, IL-1, and tumor necrosis factor-α act in concert with IL-15 to stimulate natural killer cells to produce IFN-γ.[90]

Several hypotheses have been proposed to explain the role of IFN-γ in host resistance to T. gondii. Involvement of reactive nitrogen intermediates (including NO) is suggested by the observation that L-NMMA, a competitive analogue of L-arginine, simultaneously inhibits NO synthesis and intracellular tachyzoite killing by cytokine-activated peritoneal macrophages and microglial cells.[65,91,92] In addition, mice in which NO synthesis is impaired owing to genetic disruptions of the IFN-γ or IFN regulatory factor-1 genes die as a result of the acute infection.[93,94] Similar enhanced susceptibility was observed in mice treated with the reactive nitrogen intermediate inhibitor aminoguanidine[95] and in nitric oxide synthase–deficient mice.[96] The protective role of NO seems to be tissue specific rather than systemic.[96] Because control of the acute infection in vivo was unaffected by NO synthase deficiency, the major role of reactive nitrogen intermediates seems to be to maintain control of established infections in this mouse model.[96]

IgG, IgM, IgA, and IgE antibodies are produced in response to the infection. Extracellular tachyzoites are lysed by specific antibody when it is combined with complement. In mice, humoral immunity results in limited protection against less virulent strains of T. gondii, but not against virulent strains.[97]

Astrocytes and microglia likely play important roles in the immune response against T. gondii within the CNS. In the early stages of TE in humans and mice, there is a remarkable and widespread astrocytosis restricted to areas in which the parasite is detected.[79] Although T. gondii can invade, survive, and multiply within astrocytes, they are killed by activated microglia.[98]

GENETIC SUSCEPTIBILITY

The observations in mice that genetic factors in the host contribute to the development and severity of TE[99-101] and the fact that not all HIV-infected patients with positive T. gondii serologic findings develop TE suggested the possibility that genetic factors also may play a role in the predisposition of AIDS patients for this disease.[102] The major histocompatibility complex (MHC) class II gene DQ3 (HLA-DQ3) has been associated significantly with the development of TE in North American white AIDS patients, whereas HLA-DQ1 was marginally protective.[102] HLA-DQ3 also was associated significantly with the development of hydrocephalus in children with congenital toxoplasmosis.[103] In the latter study, a mouse model transgenic for human MHC class II found higher organism burden with HLA-DQ3 than HLA-DQ1. HLA-DQ3 seems to be associated with susceptibility to disease, whereas HLA-DQ1 may be a resistance marker. Studies are needed to determine if genetic control of susceptibility to disease is similar in other populations.

PATHOLOGY

Knowledge of the pathology of infection in humans has come largely from autopsy studies in severely infected infants and immunodeficient patients. Data in immunocompetent adults are limited almost entirely to results obtained from lymph node biopsy specimens.

Central Nervous System

Damage to the CNS by *T. gondii* is characterized by multiple foci of enlarging necrosis and microglial nodules.[104] Necrosis is the most prominent feature of the disease because of vascular involvement by the lesions. Periaqueductal and periventricular vasculitis with necrosis has been reported to be pathognomonic of toxoplasmosis in the fetus and the newborn.[105] The necrotic areas may calcify and lead to striking radiographic findings suggestive but not pathognomonic of toxoplasmosis. Hydrocephalus may result from obstruction of the aqueduct of Sylvius or foramen of Monro. Tachyzoites and tissue cysts may be seen in and adjacent to necrotic foci, near or in glial nodules, in perivascular regions, and in cerebral tissue uninvolved by inflammatory change. The necrotic brain tissue autolyzes and is shed gradually into the ventricles. The protein content of such ventricular fluid may be in the range of grams per deciliter and has been shown to contain significant amounts of *T. gondii* antigens.

The presence of multiple brain abscesses is the most characteristic feature of TE in severely immunodeficient patients and is particularly characteristic in patients with AIDS.[5,106] Brain abscesses in AIDS patients are characterized by three histologic zones. The central area is avascular. Surrounding this avascular area is an intermediate hyperemic area with a prominent inflammatory infiltrate and perivascular cuffing by lymphocytes, plasma cells, and macrophages. Many tachy-

zoites and, at times, tissue cysts appear at the margins of necrotic areas. An outer peripheral zone contains *T. gondii* tissue cysts.[107] In the areas around the abscesses, edema, vasculitis, hemorrhage, and cerebral infarction secondary to vascular involvement also may be present.[108] Important associated features in TE are the presence of arteritis, perivascular cuffing, and astrocytosis. Because these findings also may be present in patients with viral encephalitis, immunoperoxidase staining is important for differentiating these pathologic processes. Widespread, poorly demarcated, and confluent areas of necrosis with minimal inflammatory response are seen in some patients.[108] Identification of tachyzoites is pathognomonic of active infection, but their visualization may be difficult in hematoxylin and eosin–stained sections. The use of immunoperoxidase staining markedly improves the identification of tissue cyst and tachyzoite forms and highlights the presence of *T. gondii* antigens (Fig. 276-3).[19] *T. gondii* DNA can be amplified from cerebrospinal fluid (CSF) or brain biopsy specimens of patients with TE.[109]

At autopsy in AIDS patients with TE, there is almost universal involvement of the cerebral hemispheres and a remarkable predilection for the basal ganglia.[53] In a consecutive autopsy study of 204 patients who died of AIDS, 46 (23%) had morphologic evidence of cerebral toxoplasmosis. In 38 (83%) of the 46 cases, histologic evidence of toxoplasmosis was restricted to the CNS. The cerebral hemispheres were

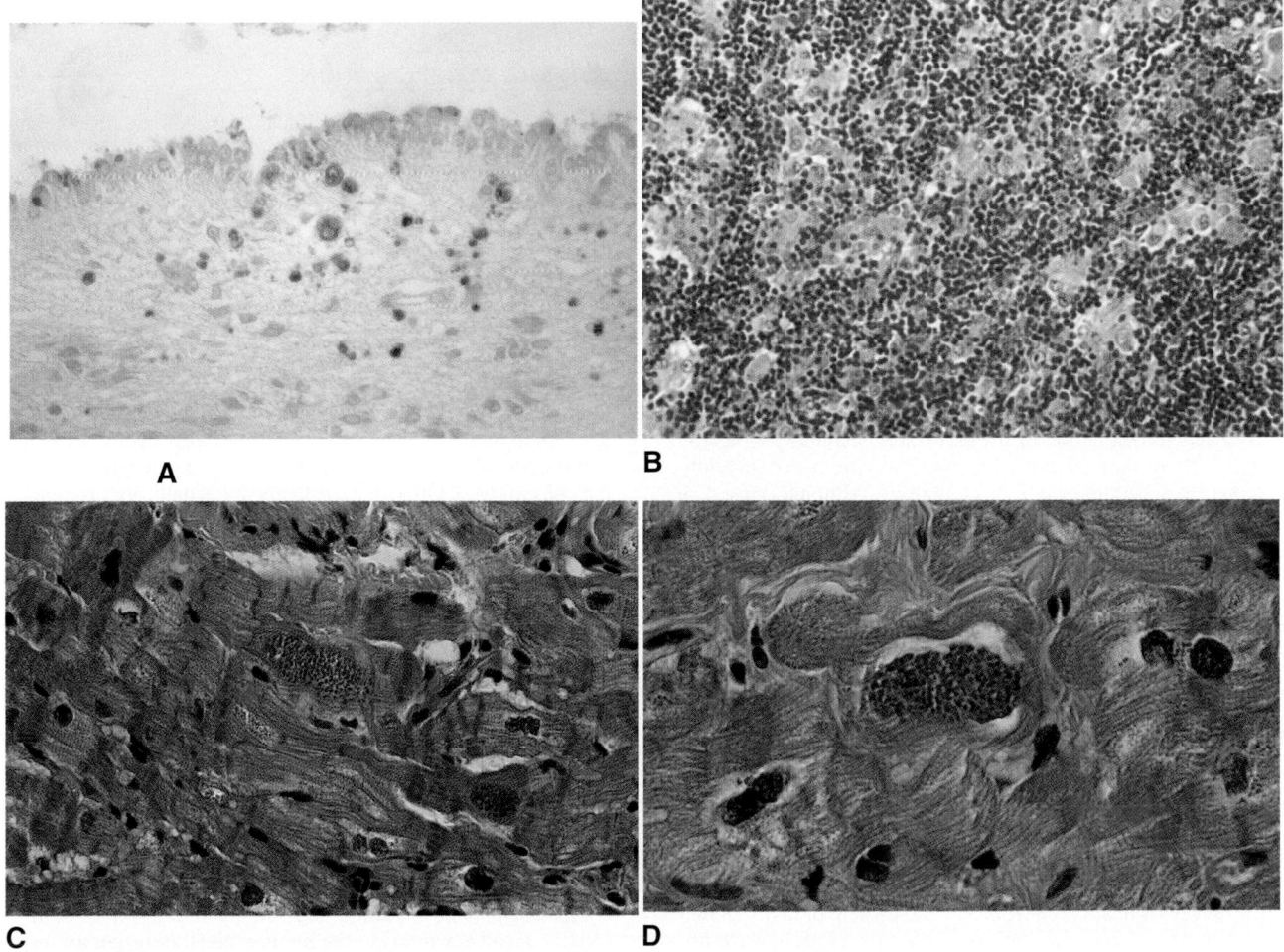

A **B** **C** **D**

FIGURE 276-3. Histologic features of *Toxoplasma gondii* in humans. **A,** Positive immunoperoxidase stain of a brain biopsy specimen in a patient with acquired immunodeficiency syndrome and toxoplasmic encephalitis. **B,** Hematoxylin and eosin (H&E) stain of a lymph node biopsy specimen from an immunocompetent patient with toxoplasmic lymphadenitis. **C,** H&E stain of a right ventricle endomyocardial biopsy specimen from a patient with toxoplasmic myocarditis. Organisms are seen within myocytes (see "Clinical Manifestations"). **D,** H&E stain of a right quadriceps muscle biopsy specimen depicting tissue cyst from the same patient as shown in **B.** She also developed toxoplasmic polymyositis. (**B,** *Courtesy of Dr. Henry Masur, Critical Care Medicine Department, National Institutes of Health, Bethesda, MD.*)

affected in 91% of cases and the rostral basal ganglia in 78%.[108] In cases of congenital toxoplasmosis, necrosis of the brain is most intense in the cortex and basal ganglia and at times in the periventricular areas.[7]

A "diffuse form" of TE has been described with histopathologic findings of widespread microglial nodules without abscess formation in the gray matter of the cerebrum, cerebellum, and brain stem.[110] In these patients, involvement by *T. gondii* was confirmed by immunoperoxidase stains that showed tissue cysts and tachyzoites. In diffuse TE, the clinical course progresses rapidly to death. It has been postulated that in such cases, the lack of characteristic findings on computed tomography (CT) or magnetic resonance imaging (MRI) is due to insufficient time for abscesses to form before death occurs. Leptomeningitis is infrequent and, when present, occurs over adjacent areas of encephalitis. Spinal cord necrotizing lesions are seen at autopsy in approximately 6% of patients with TE.[110] The differential diagnosis of TE lesions includes CNS lymphoma; progressive multifocal leukoencephalopathy; and infection with CMV, *Cryptococcus neoformans, Aspergillus* spp., and *M. tuberculosis*. More than one agent may be present.

Lung

Pulmonary toxoplasmosis in an immunodeficient patient may appear in the form of interstitial pneumonitis, necrotizing pneumonitis, consolidation, pleural effusion, empyema, or all of these.[111] The pneumonitis is associated with the development of fibrinous or fibrinopurulent exudate. Tachyzoites may be found in alveolocytes, in alveolar macrophages, in pleural fluid, or extracellularly within alveolar exudate. *T. gondii* DNA may be shown in bronchoalveolar lavage (BAL) fluid by PCR.[112]

Eye

Chorioretinitis in AIDS patients is characterized by segmental panophthalmitis and areas of coagulative necrosis associated with tissue cysts and tachyzoites.[113] Numerous organisms in the absence of remarkable inflammation may be seen around thrombosed retinal vessels adjacent to necrotic areas. Multiple and bilateral lesions may occur.[113] Amplification of parasite DNA in aqueous humor and vitreous fluid has confirmed or supported the diagnosis of toxoplasmic chorioretinitis in AIDS patients.[114,115]

Eye infection in immunocompetent patients produces acute chorioretinitis characterized by severe inflammation and necrosis.[113] Granulomatous inflammation of the choroid is secondary to necrotizing retinitis. There may be exudation into the vitreous or invasion of the vitreous by a budding mass of capillaries. Although rare, tachyzoites and tissue cysts may be shown in the retina. The pathogenesis of recurrent chorioretinitis is controversial. One school of thought proposes that rupture of tissue cysts releases viable organisms that induce necrosis and inflammation, whereas another school contends that chorioretinitis results from a hypersensitivity reaction triggered by unknown causes.[113] A study showing efficacy of trimethoprim-sulfamethoxazole (TMP-SMX) in preventing recurrences of chorioretinitis is consistent with the hypothesis that active organism replication is necessary for recurrence.[116]

Skeletal and Heart Muscle

Myositis due to *T. gondii* has been reported in 4% of HIV-infected patients who present with neuromuscular symptoms, and the same percentage has been observed in autopsy series of AIDS patients in whom a systematic histologic evaluation of the skeletal muscle was performed.[117] Successful isolation from skeletal muscle biopsy specimens has been reported.[118] Microscopy has revealed necrotic muscle fibers with a variable inflammatory reaction. Skeletal muscle involvement also has been reported in the non-AIDS, immunodeficient patient.[5,119]

Toxoplasmic myocarditis is noted frequently at autopsy in AIDS patients but usually is clinically inapparent,[120] with CNS manifestations predominating.[121] Local necrosis with edema and an inflammatory infiltrate is typical,[120] although abscesses also may be noted.[120,121]

Similar histologic findings are seen in the non-AIDS, immunodeficient population,[5] and in both groups cardiac myocytes may be packed with tachyzoites (to produce pseudocysts) in the absence of an inflammatory response. Biopsy-proven toxoplasmic myocarditis and polymyositis in the setting of acute toxoplasmosis have been reported in otherwise immunocompetent individuals and in patients taking corticosteroids (see Fig. 276-3C and D).[119]

Lymph Node

The histopathologic changes in toxoplasmic lymphadenitis in immunocompetent individuals are frequently distinctive and often diagnostic (see Fig. 276-3B).[122] There is a typical triad of findings: (1) reactive follicular hyperplasia (see Fig. 276-3B), (2) irregular clusters of epithelioid histiocytes encroaching on and blurring the margins of the germinal centers (see Fig. 276-3B), and (3) focal distention of sinuses with monocytoid cells (see Fig. 276-3B).[123] Langerhans giant cells, granulomas, microabscesses, and foci of necrosis typically are not seen. Rarely, tachyzoites or tissue cysts are shown. *T. gondii* DNA infrequently has been amplified from lymph node tissue.[124]

Other Organ Systems

Extensive involvement of the gastrointestinal tract in AIDS patients may occur with tremendous variation in the inflammatory response.[125,126] Hemorrhagic gastritis and colitis have been described.[127] Other organs reported to be involved during toxoplasmosis include liver,[128] pancreas,[129] seminiferous tubules,[130] prostate,[130] adrenals,[131] kidneys,[132] and bone marrow.[133]

CLINICAL MANIFESTATIONS

Toxoplasmosis describes the clinical or pathologic disease caused by *T. gondii* and is distinct from *T. gondii* infection, which is asymptomatic in most immunocompetent patients. Toxoplasmosis is considered in five categories: (1) acquired in the immunocompetent patient, (2) acquired or reactivated in the immunodeficient patient, (3) ocular, (4) in pregnancy, and (5) congenital. In any category, the clinical presentations are not specific for toxoplasmosis, and a wide differential diagnosis must be entertained. Methods of diagnosis and their interpretations may differ for each clinical category.

Toxoplasmosis in Immunocompetent Patients

Only 10% to 20% of cases of *T. gondii* infection in adults and children are symptomatic.[134] Most often, toxoplasmosis manifests as asymptomatic cervical lymphadenopathy, but any or all lymph node groups may be enlarged. On palpation, the nodes usually are discrete and nontender, are rarely greater than 3 cm in diameter, may vary in firmness, and do not suppurate.[135] The nodes may be tender or matted, however. Fever, malaise, night sweats, myalgias, sore throat, maculopapular rash, hepatosplenomegaly, and small numbers of atypical lymphocytes (<10%) may be present. The clinical picture may resemble infectious mononucleosis or CMV infection, but toxoplasmosis probably causes no more than 1% of "mononucleosis" syndromes.[136] Retroperitoneal or mesenteric lymphadenopathy may produce abdominal pain.

Toxoplasmic chorioretinitis as a manifestation of the acute acquired infection is more common than previously recognized.[137,138] Chorioretinitis in the setting of acute acquired toxoplasmosis can occur either sporadically or in the context of an epidemic of acute toxoplasmosis.[138,139] For further discussion of this clinical entity, see "Ocular Toxoplasmosis in Immunocompetent Patients."

In most cases, the clinical course of toxoplasmosis in an immunocompetent patient is benign and self-limited. Symptoms, if present, usually resolve within a few months and rarely persist beyond 12 months. Lymphadenopathy may wax and wane for months and, in unusual cases, for 1 year or longer. Rarely an apparently healthy person develops clinically overt, potentially fatal disseminated disease, with myocarditis, pneumonitis, hepatitis, or encephalitis. None of the clinical presentations of acquired toxoplasmosis is distinctive; the differential diagnosis of toxoplasmic lymphadenitis includes lymphoma, infectious mononucleosis, CMV "mononucleosis," cat-scratch disease, sarcoidosis, tuberculosis, tularemia, metastatic carcinoma, and leukemia. Acute acquired toxoplasmosis associated with multiple-organ involvement has been reported to mimic other causes of pneumonitis, hepatitis, myocarditis, polymyositis, or fever of unknown origin in apparently immunocompetent patients.[134]

T. gondii has been estimated to cause 3% to 7% of clinically significant lymphadenopathy.[135] The major diagnostic confusion with toxoplasmic lymphadenopathy occurs with Hodgkin's disease and the lymphomas. The diagnosis of recently acquired toxoplasmic lymphadenopathy is made easily serologically, but physicians often do not consider this diagnosis in patients with lymphadenopathy. Serologic test titers diagnostic of acute *T. gondii* infection often are obtained after histologic examination of a biopsied node has suggested the possibility of toxoplasmosis.[140]

Myocarditis as a manifestation of acute toxoplasmosis has been reported in relatively few patients.[119,141,142] It may occur clinically as an isolated disease process or as part of a variety of manifestations of the disseminated infection. Manifestations include arrhythmias, pericarditis, and heart failure.[119]

Myositis resembling polymyositis as a manifestation of acute toxoplasmosis also has been reported infrequently.[119,143] Dermatomyositis has been associated with toxoplasmosis, although a cause-and-effect relationship has not been proved.[144,145]

The clinical features of toxoplasmic myocarditis and polymyositis are illustrated by a case in which both were present in the same individual.[119] A 43-year-old woman presented with cardiogenic pulmonary edema followed by progressive sinus bradycardia and subsequent complete heart block; viral myocarditis was considered the most likely diagnosis. During the ensuing months, she developed proximal muscle weakness while being treated with corticosteroids; an endomyocardial biopsy (see Fig. 276-3C) and a quadriceps muscle biopsy (see Fig. 276-3D) revealed *T. gondii*.[119] The patient's symptoms improved on pyrimethamine-sulfadiazine. One year after her initial presentation with myocarditis, retinal lesions characteristic of toxoplasmic chorioretinitis were observed in her right eye. Serologic test results and follow-up were consistent with recently acquired toxoplasmosis.[119]

Toxoplasmosis in Immunodeficient Patients

Although toxoplasmosis in otherwise healthy individuals almost always is benign, its protean clinical manifestations, unusual occurrence, and devastating consequences in immunocompromised individuals emphasize the need for clinical acumen in diagnosis and management of toxoplasmosis in these patients. Immunocompromised individuals include patients with hematologic malignancies (especially Hodgkin's disease and other lymphomas), organ transplant recipients, AIDS patients, and patients receiving immunosuppressive therapy with corticosteroids and cytotoxic drugs. Toxoplasmosis in a non-AIDS, immunodeficient patient has been reviewed elsewhere.[5] In immunodeficient patients, encephalitis, pneumonitis, and myocarditis reflect active infection in the most commonly involved organs. Disseminated infection with multiple-organ involvement is not unusual; clinical manifestations may not reflect the extent and severity of the disseminated infection. Mortality approaches 100% if the infection is not treated or is treated only late in its course. Although serious toxoplasmosis in these patients often reflects recrudescence of a latent infection (from the cyst form of the organism) acquired in the distant past, it also results from recently acquired acute infection with the parasite, usually through the transplanted organ. Although clinical manifestations are similar in patients with different causes for immunosuppression, additional considerations are provided here for organ transplant recipients and patients with AIDS.

At present, TMP-SMZ is used by most transplant teams as prophylaxis against *P. carinii* pneumonia. Its use also has been shown to protect against toxoplasmosis. TMP-SMX is not protective in every case, however, and some patients are not able to tolerate the drug combination. In addition, in some patients, sulfonamides may be con-

traindicated. Alternative drugs for prophylaxis are provided in the section on treatment.

Toxoplasmosis in Solid Organ Transplant Patients

Patients with solid organ transplants develop toxoplasmosis most commonly as a result of acquiring *T. gondii* infection through the transplanted organ when the allograft of a seropositive donor (D+) is given to a seropositive recipient (R−), resulting in a D+/R− mismatch (Table 276-1). Toxoplasmosis also can result from reactivation of a previously acquired infection in the recipient regardless of the serologic status of the donor (D−/R+ or D+/R+) (see Table 276-1).

Knowledge of the overall prevalence of *Toxoplasma* antibodies in a population does not predict accurately the percentage of D+R− *T. gondii* mismatches. This percentage depends on the prevalence of *T. gondii* antibodies in the age groups of the donor and recipient populations. In a given geographic area, the prevalence of antibodies in young heart donors may be 3% to 10%, whereas in an older population of individuals who more likely would be recipients it may be 15% to 30%. Testing for *Toxoplasma* IgG antibodies should be performed in every organ transplant candidate before transplantation and on serum samples from every organ donor. This testing allows for identification of recipients at greatest risk of developing toxoplasmosis because they were seronegative before transplantation and received an organ from a seropositive individual or because they were seropositive before transplantation and are at risk for reactivation of latent (chronic) *Toxoplasma* infection. *Toxoplasma* serologies obtained in the early months posttransplantation frequently are not helpful even in the presence of serious toxoplasmosis in these patients. This is especially true in patients who undergo hematopoietic stem cell transplantation (HSCT), in whom *T. gondii* antibodies demonstrable before transplantation might become negative, increase, or show no change post-transplantation despite life-threatening toxoplasmosis. Transfusion may compound further the difficulties encountered in serodiagnosis.

The actual incidence of toxoplasmosis among various organ transplant recipients is unknown. At present, there is no registry for these cases, and many do not come to autopsy or are not published. There is especially a paucity of objective estimates of mortality due to toxoplasmosis in organ transplant recipients in whom the diagnosis was considered early and treatment begun promptly.

At autopsy, histopathologic evidence of multiorgan involvement by the parasite has been observed in organ transplant patients. The organs most commonly involved are brain, heart, and lungs, but many other organs, including eyes, liver, pancreas, adrenal, and kidney, may reveal the organism. Fever is often the first manifestation in transplant recipients, followed by signs referable to the brain and lungs.

Heart Transplantation

In a review of infections in cardiac transplant recipients at Stanford Medical Center from 1980 to 1996, results of serologic testing for *Toxoplasma* were available for 582 donors (35 [6%] had *T. gondii*–specific IgG antibodies) and 607 recipients (98 [16%] were positive).[146] Results of serologic testing for *Toxoplasma* were available for 575 D/R pairs; of these, 454 (79%) were D−R−, 84 (14.6%) were D−R+, 32 (5.6%) were D+R−, and 5 (0.8%) were D+R+. Of the 32

TABLE 276-1 Source of Toxoplasmosis in the Organ Transplant Patient
Transplant of an Infected Organ (D+R−)
Heart
Heart-lung
Kidney
Liver and liver/pancreas
Bone marrow (rare)
Reactivation of Latent Infection (D−R+ and D+R+)
Bone marrow
Hematopoietic stem cell
Liver
Kidney (rare)

D+R− patients, 16 were receiving TMP-SMX or pyrimethamine prophylaxis or both, and none developed toxoplasmosis; however, 4 (25%) of the 16 D+R− patients who were not taking either TMP-SMZ or pyrimethamine developed toxoplasmosis, and all died of the infection. None of the 98 patients who were seropositive for *T. gondii* preoperatively developed clinical evidence of reactivation of the infection. The importance of prophylaxis is evidenced further from an earlier study at Papworth Hospital in England. Fatal or severe toxoplasmosis developed in 57% (four of seven) of D+R− mismatched heart transplant patients not receiving prophylaxis. Use of pyrimethamine, 25 mg/day for 6 weeks, reduced the transmission rate to 14% (5 of 37). In patients who received pyrimethamine and were infected by the donor heart, only one (20%) developed symptoms of the infection, in contrast to four of four (100%) who did not receive pyrimethamine prophylaxis. Subsequently, prophylaxis with TMP-SMZ (480 mg twice a day orally for 1 year post-transplant and when on oral prednisolone) was used in heart and lung transplant patients. Of patients who were alive at 3 months post-transplantation, 28 (8.75%) were *T. gondii* mismatches; none had evidence of having acquired *Toxoplasma* infection. These investigators observed that use of prophylaxis might prolong the period before observation of seroconversion of donor-acquired infection in heart transplant patients for up to 14 months post-transplantation.[147,148]

Use of TMP-SMZ alone may be sufficient for prevention of toxoplasmosis in patients who are seronegative for *T. gondii* antibodies and who receive heart transplants from seropositive donors (i.e., D+/R− patients). The optimal schedule for administration of TMP-SMZ in heart transplant patients has not been defined. Physicians must decide whether a schedule of daily administration or administration three times a week is to be used. For HIV-infected patients, we routinely recommend daily use of TMP-SMZ whenever feasible.

Toxoplasmosis in heart transplant recipients may simulate organ rejection. In such cases, toxoplasmosis frequently has been diagnosed by endomyocardial biopsy. Many heart transplant recipients with *T. gondii* antibodies before transplantation may show increases in *T. gondii*–specific antibodies (IgG and IgM). These patients have not developed a clinical illness that can be attributed to toxoplasmosis.

Kidney Transplantation

In a review of 31 cases of toxoplasmosis in renal transplant patients, most occurred within the first 3 months after transplantation; 3 cases occurred more than 1 year post-transplantation, and 9 occurred during or immediately after a rejection episode.[149] The greatest risk was in D+R− mismatches. Fever, CNS signs, and pneumonia were the main clinical features. Chest radiographs showed bilateral pneumonia in most cases. The most common organs involved in the 15 cases diagnosed at autopsy were brain, heart, and lungs. *T. gondii* could not be shown in the kidneys. Although the overall mortality rate was 64%, 10 of 11 treated patients survived, emphasizing the importance of early diagnosis and treatment. Acute toxoplasmosis in two recipients of renal allografts from the same donor has occurred.

Liver Transplantation

After orthotopic liver transplantation, toxoplasmosis most often results from activation of a latent infection in the allograft, but also occurs from activation of a quiescent pretransplant infection in the recipient. In most published cases, clinical manifestations of toxoplasmosis appeared within the first 3 months post-transplantation. Fever usually was the first manifestation, and pneumonia, meningitis/encephalitis, and multiorgan failure were observed frequently. Retinochoroiditis requiring enucleation was observed in one patient.[150] Although it is a rare event, it is most often fatal.[151]

Toxoplasmosis in a Hematopoietic Stem Cell Transplant Patient

A report reviewed 41 cases of toxoplasmosis in patients who had undergone HSCT [a term that includes bone marrow transplantation (BMT)] in 15 European transplantation centers from 1994 through 1998.[152] There were no cases among 6787 autologous HSCTs, whereas toxoplasmosis occurred in 0.97% of 4231 allogeneic transplants. The relatively low number of cases in this large survey is likely due to the use of TMP-SMZ prophylaxis after engraftment in all allogeneic HSCTs in 91% of the institutions.[152] Of the patients with available serologies, 94% were seropositive for *T. gondii* before transplantation, and 73% had developed graft-versus-host disease before they developed toxoplasmosis. Thirty (73%) patients had not received prophylaxis for toxoplasmosis, and only 3 were receiving it at the time of disease onset. Median day of onset was day 64 (range 4 to 516 days). Fever with neurologic or pulmonary symptoms was seen most commonly; myocarditis was seen frequently at autopsy. Six patients had fever without evidence of organ involvement. Twenty-two (63%) patients died of toxoplasmosis. Of the 23 patients who received specific therapy for toxoplasmosis for 6 or more days, 11 (48%) had a complete response, and 3 (13%) improved. Survival in this setting is highest in patients with ocular or isolated cerebral toxoplasmosis, primarily when treatment is begun as soon as the diagnosis is suspected.[49,152] Survival in the presence of disseminated toxoplasmosis is rare in HSCT patients.[49,152] Although reactivation of latent *Toxoplasma* infection in allogeneic HSCT recipients most often occurs in the first 6 months post-transplantation (most occur in the first 30 to 90 days), late reactivation has been observed and must be considered in patients in whom late onset (>6 months post-transplantation) graft-versus-host disease occurs.

The incidence of toxoplasmosis in BMT has ranged from 0.3% to 5% and is influenced by the prevalence of pretransplant antibodies in the populations studied and whether toxoplasmosis prophylaxis was used. Major risk factors for toxoplasmosis include the presence of pretransplant *T. gondii* antibodies in recipients and the occurrence of graft-versus-host disease. In a review of 110 published cases of toxoplasmosis after bone marrow transplantation,[49] 96% occurred after allogeneic BMT. Onset post-transplantation occurred on days 1 to 30 in 13%, on days 31 to 100 in 64%, and on days 101 and later in 23%. The infection occurred primarily in recipients who were seropositive before transplant (88%). The diagnosis was made antemortem in only 47% of the cases. Overall mortality was 80% (at a median 87 days post-transplant), and in 66% it was attributed to toxoplasmosis (at a median 74 days post-transplant). Patients with isolated cerebral involvement had a better outcome (58% survival) than patients with disseminated toxoplasmosis (20% survival); underlying disease was the only factor associated with clinical presentation, with acute leukemia being more common in patients with disseminated disease.

Toxoplasmosis in BMT patients frequently involves the lung (usually in the setting of multiorgan disease), with a high associated mortality (>90%). Most patients die within 7 days of onset of pulmonary symptoms and often have adult respiratory distress syndrome. In a review of 25 cases of pulmonary toxoplasmosis in BMT, onset of symptoms referable to the lungs occurred from 7 days to 1 year post-BMT; most occurred in the first 6 weeks.[153] Fever may be the first sign; if pulmonary infiltrates are observed, especially in the setting of rapid deterioration, immediate attempts at diagnosis must be made and empirical treatment begun. The high mortality in many instances has been due to lack of early diagnosis and treatment. The organism can be observed on microscopic examination of BAL material. PCR on material obtained at BAL may be the diagnostic procedure of choice.[153] PCR also can be performed on blood, serum, CSF, and bone marrow aspirates.

Ocular toxoplasmosis has been reported after allogeneic and autologous HSCT. In some cases, the ocular disease was due to reactivation of a previously observed toxoplasmic chorioretinitis, whereas in most it has been associated with disseminated infection. Definitive diagnosis has been by direct observation of the parasite in histopathology sections, culture of tissue samples, or PCR on vitreous fluid.

TMP-SMX prophylaxis, primarily used by transplant teams to prevent *P. carinii* pneumonia, has been successful in prevention of toxoplasmosis. In HSCT patients, this usually is begun after engraftment because of the potential of the drug combination for bone marrow suppression. The delay in instituting prophylaxis, necessitated by potential bone marrow toxicity of the drug, likely results in many more cases of toxoplasmosis than would be expected to occur if adequate prophylaxis was begun early after transplantation. This problem highlights the importance of identifying additional drugs for prophylaxis in these patients.

Toxoplasmosis in Acquired Immunodeficiency Syndrome Patients

Clinical manifestations of toxoplasmosis in AIDS patients commonly reflect involvement of the brain (i.e., TE), the lung (pneumonitis), and the eye (chorioretinitis).[106] Toxoplasmosis with multiorgan involvement manifesting with acute respiratory failure and hemodynamic abnormalities similar to septic shock has been reported, although septic shock has not been proved definitely to be due to *T. gondii*.[154] TE is the most common presentation of toxoplasmosis in AIDS patients[53] and is a frequent cause of focal CNS lesions in AIDS.[53] A wide range of clinical findings, including altered mental state, seizures, weakness, cranial nerve disturbances, sensory abnormalities, cerebellar signs, meningismus, movement disorders, and neuropsychiatric manifestations, is seen in TE. The characteristic presentation usually has a subacute onset with focal neurologic abnormalities in 58% to 89% of patients. In 15% to 25% of cases, the clinical presentation may be more abrupt, however, with seizures or cerebral hemorrhage. Most commonly, hemiparesis, abnormalities of speech, or both are the major initial manifestations. Brain stem involvement often produces cranial nerve lesions, and many patients exhibit cerebral dysfunction with disorientation, altered mental state, lethargy, and coma. Less commonly, parkinsonism, focal dystonia, rubral tremor, hemichorea-hemiballismus, panhypopituitarism, diabetes insipidus, or the syndrome of inappropriate antidiuretic hormone secretion may dominate the clinical picture. In some patients, neuropsychiatric symptoms, such as paranoid psychosis, dementia, anxiety, and agitation, may be the major manifestations.

Diffuse TE[110] has been reported in relatively few AIDS patients; the actual incidence is unknown. This form of TE may manifest acutely and can be rapidly fatal; generalized cerebral dysfunction without focal signs is the most common manifestation, and CT scans are within normal limits or reveal cerebral atrophy.

Spinal cord involvement by *T. gondii* in AIDS patients manifests as motor or sensory disturbances of single or multiple limbs, bladder or bowel dysfunctions or both, and local pain. Patients may present with a clinical syndrome resembling a spinal cord tumor. Reports of cervical myelopathy,[155] thoracic myelopathy,[156] and conus medullaris syndrome[157] have been published.

Pulmonary disease due to toxoplasmosis has been reported in patients with AIDS, and the diagnosis may be made by demonstration of the parasite in BAL fluid.[158] In France, before HAART and routine use of prophylaxis, the prevalence of pulmonary toxoplasmosis in patients dually infected with HIV and *T. gondii* was estimated to be approximately 5%.[159] Pulmonary toxoplasmosis occurs mainly in patients with advanced AIDS (mean CD4+ cell count 40 cells/mm³ ± 75 standard deviation) and primarily presents as a prolonged febrile illness with cough and dyspnea,[158] which may be clinically indistinguishable from *P. carinii* pneumonia. Mortality, even when pulmonary disease is treated appropriately, may be 35%. Extrapulmonary disease may be present in about 50% of cases with toxoplasmic pneumonitis.[154] Often, pulmonary toxoplasmosis is not associated with TE; however, TE may develop after successful treatment of pulmonary toxoplasmosis when therapy is discontinued. The differential diagnosis of toxoplasmic pneumonitis includes *P. carinii* pneumonia and infection with *M. tuberculosis*, *C. neoformans*, *Coccidioides immitis*, and *Histoplasma capsulatum*.

Toxoplasmic chorioretinitis is seen relatively infrequently in AIDS patients[160]; it commonly manifests with ocular pain and loss of visual acuity (Fig. 276-4). Funduscopic examination usually shows necrotizing lesions that may be multifocal or bilateral.[160] Overlying vitreal inflammation often is present and may be extensive. The optic nerve may be involved in 10% of cases. Toxoplasmic chorioretinitis in AIDS

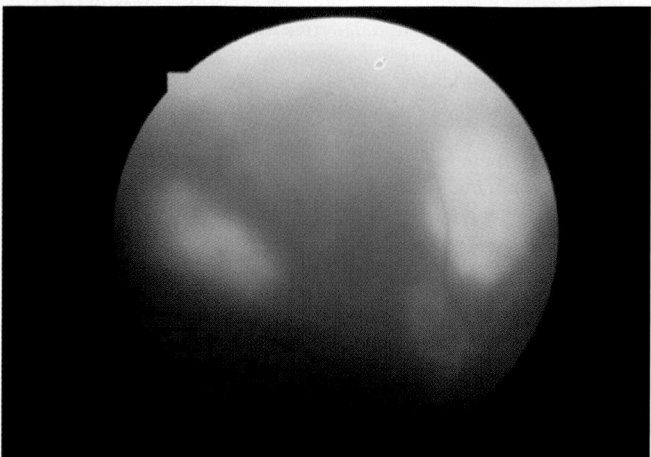

A

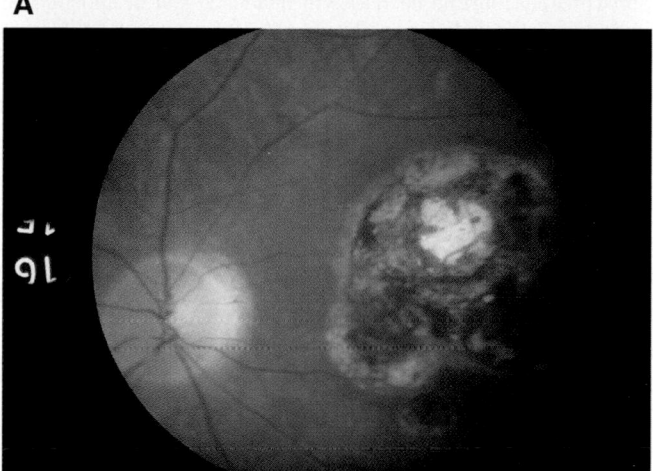

B

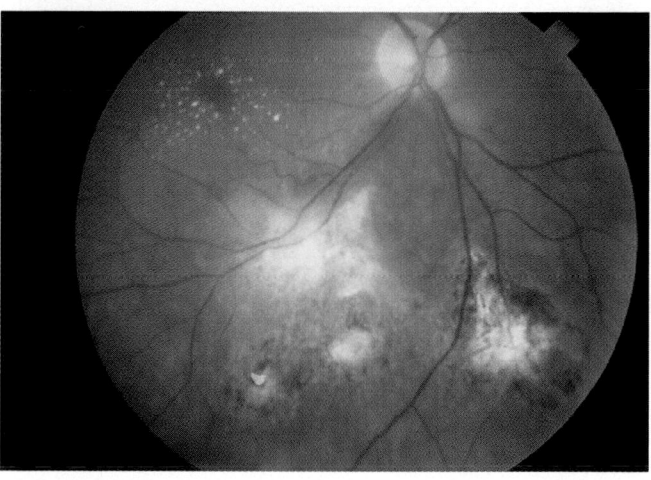

C

FIGURE 276-4. Toxoplasmic chorioretinitis. **A,** Active chorioretinitis with two lesions and vitreous haze, in a human immunodeficiency virus–infected patient. **B,** A large inactive macular lesion typical of congenital disease. **C,** Active chorioretinitis in an immunocompetent patient from an endemic region in Brazil. There is an inactive lesion on the right. Note the macular star, which is due to an exudate around the macula. (*Courtesy of Dr. Robert Nussenblatt, National Eye Institute, Bethesda, MD; Dr. Claudio Silveira, Erechim, Brazil; and Dr. Rubens Belfort, São Paulo, Brazil.*)

patients has been associated with concurrent TE in 63% of patients. The differential diagnosis of toxoplasmic chorioretinitis in AIDS patients includes CMV retinitis, syphilis, herpes simplex, varicella zoster, and fungal infections. The diagnosis relies primarily on clinical findings and the response to anti–*T. gondii* therapy, although definitive diagnosis may be made by demonstration of the organism in retinal biopsy specimens,[160] isolation of the parasite from vitreous aspirates,[161] or amplification of the parasite DNA by PCR.[114]

Other uncommon manifestations of toxoplasmosis in AIDS patients include panhypopituitarism, diabetes insipidus, syndrome of inappropriate antidiuretic hormone secretion, and orchitis. Gastrointestinal involvement may result in abdominal pain, ascites (due to involvement of the stomach, peritoneum, or pancreas), or diarrhea. Acute hepatic failure due to *T. gondii* has been reported,[128] as has musculoskeletal involvement.[117]

Although the incidence of toxoplasmosis in HIV-infected patients began to decrease after the broad use of TMP-SMX for *P. carinii* pneumonia prophylaxis, the incidence decreased dramatically as a result of the immune reconstitution associated with HAART regimens. Approximately fourfold decreases in incidence and death have been reported after the wide availability of HAART regimens.[54,55,162] In patients with CD4+ counts at sustained levels greater than 200 cells/μL for 3 to 6 months, prophylaxis regimens can be discontinued safely, although rare cases of disease can occur even in patients with well-controlled HIV infection.[163-166]

Ocular Toxoplasmosis in Immunocompetent Patients

T. gondii is one of the most frequently identified causes of uveitis and the most commonly identified pathogen to infect the retina of otherwise immunocompetent individuals.[8] Toxoplasmosis is responsible for more than 85% of posterior uveitis cases in southern Brazil, where in one study 9.5% of 21 seroconverters and 8.3% of 131 seropositive patients without ocular involvement developed typical lesions during 7 years of follow-up.[167-169] Chorioretinal lesions may result from congenital or postnatally acquired infection. In both of these situations, lesions may occur during the acute or latent (chronic) stage of the infection.[138,170] Recurrences are frequent, occurring in 79% of patients followed for more than 5 years in one study, with a median time to recurrence of 2 years; lesions were more common in the eye originally involved and may be more common after cataract extraction.[171,172] It frequently is difficult to determine whether the original infection was congenital or acquired in patients who have recurrences of chorioretinitis. Patients who present with chorioretinitis as a late sequela of the infection acquired in utero are more frequently in their second and third decades of life (it is rare after age 40); bilateral disease, old retinal scars, and involvement of the macula are hallmarks of the retinal disease in these cases, as are recurrences (see Fig. 276-4).[7] In contrast, patients who present with toxoplasmic chorioretinitis in the setting of acute toxoplasmosis are more often older than 30, they most often have unilateral involvement, and the eye lesions usually spare the macula and do not present with associated old scars.[138]

Although acquired *T. gondii* infection in otherwise healthy adults is most often subclinical, toxoplasmic chorioretinitis in these individuals may result in complete or partial loss of vision or in glaucoma and may necessitate enucleation.[7,113] Acute chorioretinitis may produce symptoms of blurred vision, scotoma, pain, photophobia, and epiphora. Impairment or a loss of central vision occurs when the macula is involved. As inflammation resolves, vision improves, frequently without complete recovery of visual acuity. In most cases, toxoplasmic chorioretinitis is diagnosed by ophthalmologic examination, and empirical therapy directed against the organism often is instituted based on clinical findings and serologic test results. Typical features of toxoplasmic chorioretinitis include intensely white focal lesions with an overlying, intense, vitreous inflammatory reaction (see Fig. 276-4). Focal necrotizing retinitis initially appears in the fundus as a yellowish white, elevated cotton patch with indistinct margins, usually on the posterior pole. The lesions are often in small clusters, and individual lesions in the cluster may be of varied ages. With healing, the lesions

pale, atrophy, and develop black pigment (see Fig. 276-4). There also can be an associated, secondary iridocyclitis and increased intraocular pressure.[113] The classic "headlight in the fog" appearance is due to the presence of active retinal lesions with severe vitreous inflammatory reaction. The choroid is secondarily inflamed. Recurrent lesions tend to occur at the borders of chorioretinal scars, and scars often are found in clusters. Panuveitis may accompany chorioretinitis, but isolated anterior uveitis has never been proved to occur.

Although the morphology of the lesions of acute toxoplasmic chorioretinitis in the setting of postnatally acquired disease may be indistinguishable from the lesions observed in patients who have acute eye disease in later life due to a congenitally acquired infection, it is important to attempt to establish which type of infection (postnatally acquired or congenital) is occurring in a given patient.[138] Congenitally acquired disease seems to have a more guarded prognosis. From a public health perspective, it is important epidemiologically to establish whether the patient has acute acquired infection to initiate efforts to identify the possible source of *T. gondii* infection and to determine whether other individuals who may be at high risk for developing severe, life-threatening disease (i.e., fetuses of serologically negative pregnant women or immunodeficient individuals) shared the same exposure as the individual with acute acquired toxoplasmic chorioretinitis. Serologic tests have been useful in establishing whether these patients have been infected recently.[137,138] In patients with chorioretinitis and IgG antibodies, additional serologic tests should be performed to determine whether the patient's infection is recently acquired.[138]

T. gondii chorioretinitis may resemble the posterior uveitis of tuberculosis, syphilis, leprosy, or presumed ocular histoplasmosis syndrome. Atypical clinical and serologic manifestations of toxoplasmic chorioretinitis have been reported most commonly in elderly and in immunodeficient individuals.[114,173] Patients are considered to have atypical-appearing lesions when one or more of the following features are present: multiple foci of active retinitis, acute retinal necrosis syndrome (vitritis, peripheral retinitis, retinal vasculitis), significant intraretinal hemorrhage, or an absence of ophthalmoscopically visible chorioretinal scarring. In patients with atypical lesions or an inadequate clinical response to antitoxoplasmal therapy or in whom other diagnostic procedures have not proved helpful, obtaining vitreous or aqueous fluid (in some cases indicated for therapeutic reasons as well) for PCR should be considered early in the workup (see "Diagnosis").[115]

Toxoplasmosis During Pregnancy

As in other immunocompetent individuals, acute *Toxoplasma* infection is asymptomatic in most pregnant women. The most commonly recognized clinical manifestation of recent infection is regional lymphadenopathy. The primary concern is transmission of infection to the fetus. The risk to the fetus does not correlate with whether the infection in the mother was symptomatic or asymptomatic during gestation. Transmission to the fetus has been limited almost solely to women who acquire the infection during gestation. Otherwise healthy women with prior *Toxoplasma* infection are protected from transmitting the infection to their fetuses. Two rare exceptions have been observed. In immunocompetent women infected with *T. gondii* shortly before conception, transmission to the fetus has occurred; in these rare instances, the acute infection was acquired within 3 months of conception.[174-176] Transmission to the fetus has been recognized rarely as a consequence of reactivation of latent *T. gondii* infection in immunocompromised women infected with *T. gondii* before conception (chronic infection) (e.g., pregnant women co-infected with HIV and *T. gondii*,[177] patients with systemic lupus erythematosus who are being treated with corticosteroids).

Congenital Toxoplasmosis

Congenital infection may occur in one of four forms: (1) neonatal disease; (2) disease (mild or severe) occurring in the first months of life; (3) sequelae or relapse of a previously undiagnosed infection during infancy, childhood, or adolescence; or (4) subclinical infection. Data accumulated from prospective studies indicate that the incidence and severity of congenital toxoplasmosis vary with the trimester during which the infection was acquired by the mother.[7] There is an inverse relationship between the frequency of transmission and the severity of disease. The period of highest risk for the development of clinically apparent congenital infection is weeks 10 to 24; the low-risk period is 26 to 40 weeks.[178-180] Infants born to mothers who acquire infection in the first and second trimesters more frequently show severe congenital toxoplasmosis.[181] In contrast, most infants born to women who acquire infection during the third trimester are born with the subclinical form of the infection. If left untreated, 85% of these latter children develop signs and symptoms of the disease, however, in most cases chorioretinitis or developmental delays.[182,183]

Infection acquired in the first trimester by women who were not treated with anti–*T. gondii* drugs resulted in congenital infection in 10% to 25% of cases.[181] For second-trimester and third-trimester infections, the incidences of fetal infection ranged from 30% to 54% and 60% to 65%.[181] Treatment of the mother with spiramycin seems to reduce the incidence of congenital infection by about 60%.[181,184-186] Maternal infection acquired around the time of conception and within the first 2 weeks of gestation and treated with spiramycin usually does not result in transmission.[186] Because of the high transmission rates observed in the late second trimester and during the third trimester, it is recommended that in patients in whom acute infection is highly suspected or confirmed, pyrimethamine-sulfadiazine be used. A group of European investigators have suggested that the beneficial effects of spiramycin or pyrimethamine-sulfadiazine use during pregnancy in preventing vertical transmission or disease in the offspring by *T. gondii* need to be reevaluated (see "Treatment").

Clinical manifestations of congenital toxoplasmosis vary. Most signs and clinical presentations are nonspecific and may mimic disease due to organisms such as herpes simplex virus, CMV, and rubella virus. Signs include chorioretinitis, strabismus, blindness, epilepsy, psychomotor or mental retardation, anemia, jaundice, rash, petechiae due to thrombocytopenia, encephalitis, pneumonitis, microcephaly, intracranial calcification, hydrocephalus, diarrhea, hypothermia, and nonspecific illness.[7] There may be no sequelae, or sequelae may develop or be evident at various times after birth. *T. gondii* infection is not known to cause fetal malformations by affecting the host's DNA.

A detailed examination may be necessary to detect signs of the infection.[7] In one prospective study,[187] 210 congenitally infected infants were identified: 2 patients (0.9%) died, 21 (10.9%) had severe disease, 71 (33.8%) were mildly affected, and 116 (54.4%) had no signs of infection. More intensive examination of the last-mentioned 116 infants revealed abnormalities in 39: Abnormal CSF was detected in 22 infants, chorioretinitis was seen in 17, and intracranial calcifications were found in 10. Premature infants often have CNS disease and ocular disease in the first 3 months of life. Full-term infants frequently develop a milder disease manifested by hepatosplenomegaly and lymphadenopathy that usually appear in the first 2 months of life. In these infants, disease reflecting damage to the CNS may occur later, and eye disease may occur months to years after birth.

Most infants with subclinical infection at birth subsequently develop signs or symptoms of congenital toxoplasmosis.[183] In one study, clinical evaluation at a mean age of 8.3 years showed that 11 of the 13 infected children who had no signs of the disease after detailed examination in the newborn period had sequelae. Some of these children were treated with specific therapy in the newborn period. In each child, the initial manifestation was chorioretinitis, which appeared at a mean age of 3.7 years. Three children had unilateral blindness, whereas the other eight children had no loss of visual function. Five children developed neurologic sequelae, including one child with delayed psychomotor development, microcephaly, and seizure disorder and two children with minor cerebellar signs. Sensorineural hearing loss occurred in 3 of 10 children evaluated. A study from The Netherlands[188] reported that five of nine congenitally infected, untreated children followed for up to 14 years developed chorioretinitis. Information from prospective studies suggests that early instigation of

specific therapy in infants with congenital infection but without clinical signs markedly reduces untoward sequelae.[189,190]

Uncommonly, latent *T. gondii* infection may reactivate in HIV-infected women and result in congenital transmission of the parasite. Congenital toxoplasmosis seems to occur more frequently in the offspring of women infected with HIV and *T. gondii* than in offspring of women who are infected with *T. gondii* but not with HIV.[191] Infants with congenital toxoplasmosis born to HIV-infected mothers also are infected with HIV (suggesting that factors that predispose to the vertical transmission of HIV also favor the transmission of *T. gondii* or vice versa). Congenital toxoplasmosis in an HIV-infected infant seems to run a more rapid course than toxoplasmosis in a non–HIV-infected infant, with the development of failure to thrive, fever, hepatosplenomegaly, chorioretinitis, and seizures. Most children have multiorgan involvement, including CNS, cardiac, and pulmonary disease.

Congenital toxoplasmosis must be differentiated from rubella virus, CMV, and herpes simplex virus infections; syphilis, listeriosis, and other bacterial infections; other infectious encephalopathies; erythroblastosis fetalis; and sepsis. Herpes simplex virus, CMV, rubella virus, and syphilis may cause chorioretinitis; CMV and rubella have been associated with hydrocephalus, microcephaly, and cerebral calcification. A markedly elevated CSF protein concentration is a hallmark of congenital toxoplasmosis.

T. gondii infection acquired during pregnancy has been implicated in spontaneous abortion, stillbirth, and premature births. Rarely, *T. gondii* has been isolated from the abortuses of women with chronic infection, but the frequency of *T. gondii* infection as a cause of abortion is unknown and controversial.

DIAGNOSIS

When considering toxoplasmosis in the differential diagnosis of a patient's illness, emphasis should not be placed on whether the patient has been exposed to cats. Transmission of oocysts virtually always occurs without knowledge of the patient and may be unrelated to direct exposure to a cat (e.g., transmission by contaminated vegetables or water). Patients with an indoor cat or cats that are fed only cooked food are not at risk of acquiring the infection from that cat. Serologic investigation of a cat to establish whether it is a potential source of the infection should be discouraged; the prevalence of *T. gondii* antibodies among cats in a given locale is usually similar to their prevalence in humans. Seropositivity does not predict shedding of oocysts.

Because the clinical manifestations of *T. gondii* infection may be protean and nonspecific, toxoplasmosis must be considered carefully in the differential diagnosis of a large variety of clinical presentations. The correct diagnostic tests must be performed and interpreted appropriately in light of the patient's clinical presentation. The usefulness of a given diagnostic method may differ considerably with the clinical entity, which can be toxoplasmosis in the immunocompetent or immunodeficient patient, ocular toxoplasmosis, toxoplasmosis in pregnancy, or congenital toxoplasmosis.[192]

Acute infection is diagnosed by the isolation of *T. gondii* or amplification of its *T. gondii* DNA in blood or body fluids; demonstration of tachyzoites in histologic sections of tissue or in cytologic preparations of body fluids; demonstration of a characteristic lymph node histologic appearance or of characteristic serologic test results; or demonstration of *T. gondii* tissue cysts in the placenta, fetus, or neonate.[7] Rarely, asymptomatic patients with latent infection have recurrent parasitemia.[193] Isolation of *T. gondii* from the tissues of older children or adults may reflect only the presence of tissue cysts. Finding numerous tissue cysts in tissue sections, especially associated with inflammation, suggests but does not prove the presence of active infection.

Isolation of *Toxoplasma gondii*

Isolation of *T. gondii* from blood or body fluids establishes that the infection is acute. In neonates, isolation of the organism from the placenta is usually diagnostic; isolation from fetal tissues is diagnostic of congenital infection.[7] Attempts at isolation of the parasite can be performed by mouse inoculation or inoculation of tissue cell cultures.[7] In tissue cell cultures, parasite-laden cells can be shown with appropriate staining, and plaques are formed in which tachyzoites are recognized easily. Tissue cell culture has the advantage of widespread availability (e.g., virology laboratories) and yields results more rapidly (within 3 to 6 days) than mouse inoculation. Mouse inoculation is more sensitive, however.

Histologic Diagnosis

Tachyzoites in tissue sections or smears of body fluid (e.g., CSF, amniotic fluid, or BAL) establishes the diagnosis of acute infection.[7] Multiple tissue cysts near an inflammatory necrotic lesion probably establish the diagnosis.[194] It often is difficult to show tachyzoites in stained tissue sections. Fluorescent antibody staining may be useful, but this method often yields nonspecific results.[195] The immunoperoxidase technique, which uses antisera to *T. gondii*, has proved sensitive and specific; it has been used successfully in clinical settings to show the organisms in the CNS of patients with TE.[19] The fluorescent antibody and immunoperoxidase methods are applicable to unfixed or formalin-fixed, paraffin-embedded tissue sections.[19] Fluorescein-labeled monoclonal antibodies to *T. gondii* for staining touch preparations of specimens[196] and rapid electron microscopy[197] have been used successfully to diagnose TE. A rapid, technically simple, but underused method is the detection of *T. gondii* in air-dried, Wright-Giemsa–stained slides of centrifuged (e.g., cytocentrifuge) sediment of CSF or of brain aspirate or in impression smears of biopsy tissue.

Endomyocardial biopsy has been used successfully to diagnose toxoplasmosis in heart transplant recipients.[198] Characteristic histologic criteria alone probably are sufficient to establish the diagnosis of toxoplasmic lymphadenitis in older children and adults.[122]

Polymerase Chain Reaction

PCR amplification for the detection of *T. gondii* DNA in body fluids and tissues has diagnosed congenital,[186,199] ocular,[114,115] cerebral, and disseminated toxoplasmosis successfully.[200,201] PCR of amniotic fluid has revolutionized the diagnosis of intrauterine *T. gondii* infection by enabling an early diagnosis to be made, avoiding the use of invasive procedures on the fetus.[7] PCR also has been used successfully on samples of CSF, blood, urine, placenta, and fetal tissues for diagnosis of congenital infection.[7] PCR has enabled the detection of *T. gondii* DNA in brain tissue,[202] CSF,[109] vitreous and aqueous fluids,[109] BAL,[203] and blood[201] in patients with AIDS. The sensitivity of PCR in CSF varies between 11% and 77%, whereas the specificity is close to 100%.[201,204] PCR also may detect the parasite in buffy coat specimens of AIDS patients with TE.[201,204] The sensitivity of PCR on whole blood or buffy coat is 15% to 85%. PCR on blood seems to be a valuable tool primarily in patients with disseminated disease; it is less sensitive in the detection of TE because a relatively low percentage of AIDS patients with TE have parasitemia.[205,206] Therapy for toxoplasmosis seems to influence the sensitivity of the method; sensitivity is higher in CSF or blood samples collected before or within the first week of therapy.[201]

Because there is no standardized PCR assay, performance characteristics vary widely depending on the laboratory, gene target, primers, and sample preparation.[207] Primers targeting the multicopy *B1* gene seem to be the most sensitive and are the most broadly used.[207,208] For maximal reliability, clinical samples should be sent to reference laboratories experienced in performing this assay.

Serologic Tests for Demonstration of Antibody

The use of serologic tests to show specific antibody to *T. gondii* is the primary method of diagnosis. The problem with serologic diagnosis is that antibody to *T. gondii* is present in relatively high numbers of individuals in most human populations. These antibody titers may persist at high levels for years in healthy people. Many tests have been described, some of which are available only in highly specialized laboratories. Different serologic tests often measure different antibodies that possess unique patterns of rise and fall with the time after infection. False-positive and false-negative results (or both) have been a

problem with certain commercial kits and laboratories in the United States and Europe.[209,210]

There is no single serologic test that can be used to support the diagnosis of acute or chronic infection by *T. gondii*. In most cases, a battery of tests is required to enable the distinction between acute and chronic infection. Which particular combination of tests is used depends on the specific clinical category of the patient (i.e., pregnant versus immunodeficient patient; see "Clinical Manifestations"), the interval between acquisition of infection and sampling of sera,[140] and the question posed by the practitioner. The clinician must be familiar with these problems and consult reference laboratories if the need arises. A panel of tests consisting of the Sabin-Feldman dye test (IgG); IgM, IgA, and IgE enzyme-linked immunosorbent assays (ELISAs); differential agglutination test (measures IgG antibody; also known as the *AC/HS test*); and IgG avidity is used successfully by the Palo Alto Medical Foundation Toxoplasma Serology Laboratory (650-853-4828; http://www.pamf.org/serology/) to determine whether serologic test results are more likely consistent with infection acquired in the recent or more distant past.[119,138,140,211-213]

IgG Antibodies

The most widely used tests for the measurement of IgG antibody are the Sabin-Feldman dye test,[214] ELISA,[215,216] indirect fluorescent antibody (IFA) test,[217] and modified direct agglutination test.[218] In these tests, IgG antibodies usually appear within 1 to 2 weeks of acquisition of the infection, peak within 1 to 2 months, decrease at variable rates, and usually persist for life.

Sabin-Feldman Dye Test. The Sabin-Feldman dye test is the reference serologic test against which other methods have been evaluated.[214] It is a sensitive and specific neutralization test. It measures primarily IgG antibodies that usually appear 1 to 2 weeks after the initiation of infection, reach peak titers in 6 to 8 weeks, then gradually decline over 1 to 2 years.[7] Titers, usually at low levels, probably persist for life. Some patients have high titers for years. The titer does not correlate with the severity of illness.[219] This test is available in only a few reference laboratories, primarily because live organisms are required. A negative Sabin-Feldman dye test practically rules out prior exposure to *T. gondii*. Although rare, cases of documented TE and chorioretinitis have been reported in dye test–negative patients.

Indirect Fluorescent Antibody Test. The IFA test seems to measure the same antibodies as the dye test, and its titers tend to parallel dye test titers.[7] False-positive results may occur with sera that contain antinuclear antibodies,[220] and false-negative results may occur in sera with low IgG antibody titers.

Agglutination Test. The agglutination test using formalin-preserved whole tachyzoites is available commercially (BioMérieux, Marcy-l'Etoile, France) and detects IgG antibody. The test is very sensitive to IgM antibody, and "natural" IgM antibody causes nonspecific agglutination in sera that yield negative results when tested in the dye test and the IFA test. This problem is avoided by including 2-mercaptoethanol in the test. The method is accurate, simple to perform, inexpensive, and excellent for screening purposes.[221] This method should not be used for the measurement of IgM antibodies.

When two different compounds (i.e., acetone and formalin) are used to fix parasites for use in the agglutination test, a "differential" agglutination test (AC/HS test) results because the different antigenic preparations vary in their ability to recognize sera obtained during the acute and chronic stages of the infection.[222] This test has proved useful in helping differentiate acute from chronic infections and is used best in combination with a battery of other tests.

IgG Enzyme-Linked Immunosorbent Assay. The IgG ELISA method is now the most widely used to show IgG antibodies to *T. gondii*. Most commercial IgG antibody test kits are accurate for demonstration of IgG antibodies. One cannot use a single IgG titer, however, no matter what its level, to predict whether the infection was recently acquired or acquired in the distant past.

Immunoglobulin G Avidity Test. Many tests for avidity of *Toxoplasma* IgG antibodies have been introduced to help differentiate between recently acquired and distant infection.[223] This method is based on the observation that during acute *T. gondii* infection, IgG antibodies bind antigen weakly (i.e., have low avidity), whereas chronically infected patients have more strongly binding (high avidity) antibodies.[223] Protein-denaturing reagents, including urea, are used to dissociate the antibody-antigen complex. Low or equivocal avidity test results can persist for months to years after the primary infection,[223] and for this reason a low or equivocal avidity test result must not be used to determine whether the infection was acquired recently. The time of conversion from low or equivocal to high avidity is highly variable among different individuals, including pregnant women.[211,224,225] It has been shown, however, that when the avidity test result is high, the patient was infected at least 3 to 5 months earlier.[225] This timing depends on the method used. High avidity test results by the IgG VI-DAS avidity test (VIDAS Toxoplasma IgG avidity; BioMérieux, Marcy-l'Etoile, France) have been found essentially only in pregnant women who have been infected for at least 4 months.[213,226]

At present, commercial avidity tests have not been released for marketing in the United States. The avidity test should only be employed as an additional confirmatory diagnostic method in patients with positive and/or equivocal IgM test or when the results of a battery of tests are equivocal or interpreted as consistent with the possibility of a recently acquired infection. Health care providers involved in the care of pregnant women should be aware that avidity testing is only a confirmatory test. It should not be used alone as a definitive test for decision making.

IgM Antibodies

IgM antibodies may appear earlier and decline more rapidly than IgG antibodies. IgM antibody tests have been used widely for the diagnosis of acute infection and to determine whether a pregnant woman has been infected during gestation or before conception. There has been a heightened awareness of the fact that titers in tests for IgM antibodies may persist for years after the acute infection and that the reliability of commercially available assays varies considerably.[209,227,228] The laboratory performing the test and the physician requesting the test should be aware of this problem. The U.S. Food and Drug Administration (FDA) has issued a health advisory to obstetricians, gynecologists, pediatricians, clinical pathologists, and infectious diseases specialists warning about the use of *T. gondii* IgM commercial test kits as the sole determinant of recent infection in pregnant women.[229] At present, the decision to treat or undertake other medical interventions, including the termination of pregnancy, should be based on clinical evaluation and additional testing performed in reference or research laboratories with experience in the diagnosis of toxoplasmosis. (For further discussion, see "*Toxoplasma gondii* Infection in Pregnancy.") The persistence of IgM antibodies for several years has not been found to be clinically significant.[7]

Indirect Fluorescent Antibody Test. IgM IFA antibody appears within the first week of infection; titers rise rapidly, then fall to low titers and usually disappear within a few months. Low titers may persist 1 year or longer.[230] Antinuclear antibodies and rheumatoid factor may cause false-positive results.[231] IgG-blocking antibodies can cause false-negative results in this test when IgG is not removed.[232]

IgM Enzyme-Linked Immunosorbent Assay. The double-sandwich IgM ELISA for detection of IgM-specific antibodies to *T. gondii*[233-235] is currently the most widely used method to show IgM antibodies to *T. gondii* in adults, the fetus, and newborns.[7] In contrast to the conventional method in which the wells of microtiter plates are coated with antigen, the wells are coated with specific antibody to IgM. The double-sandwich IgM ELISA is more sensitive than the IgM IFA test for diagnosis of recently acquired infection, and serum samples that are negative in the dye test but that contain either antinuclear antibodies or rheumatoid factor and cause false-positive results in the IgM IFA test are negative in the double-sandwich IgM ELISA. This latter observation is attributed to the fact that serum IgM fractions are separated from IgG fractions during the initial step in the double-sandwich IgM ELISA procedure.[7]

Despite the wide distribution of commercial test kits to measure IgM antibodies, these kits often have low specificity, and the reported results frequently are misinterpreted. False-positive results and the problems associated with the persistence of positive titers years after the initial infection remain major obstacles to correct interpretation of the results obtained in these tests.[209]

IgM Immunosorbent Agglutination Assay. The IgM immunosorbent agglutination assay (ISAGA) (BioMérieux, Marcy-l'Etoile, France), which binds the patient's IgM to a solid surface and uses intact, killed tachyzoites to detect IgM antibodies, is sensitive and specific.[236] The test is simple to perform, does not require the use of enzyme conjugate, and is read in the same manner as the agglutination test. It is more sensitive and specific than the IgM IFA test. The presence of rheumatoid factor or antinuclear antibodies does not cause false-positive results in the IgM ISAGA. The ISAGA method also has been used to detect IgA and IgE antibodies. The IgM ISAGA has been used effectively for diagnosis of congenital infection.[237]

IgA Antibodies

IgA antibodies may be detected in sera of acutely infected adults and congenitally infected infants using ELISA or ISAGA.[238-240] As is true for IgM antibodies to the parasite, IgA antibodies may persist for many months or more than 1 year. For this reason, they are of little additional assistance for the diagnosis of acute infection in an adult. In contrast, the increased sensitivity of IgA assays over IgM assays for the diagnosis of congenital toxoplasmosis represents a major advance in the serologic diagnosis of the infection in the fetus and newborn.[240] IgA antibodies rarely are detectable by ELISA in sera of AIDS patients with TE.[240] If IgA antibodies are detected in the newborn, the test should be repeated at approximately 10 days after birth to ensure that what is being measured is not contaminating maternal IgA antibodies. The possibility that such contamination might occur is the reason that under most circumstances peripheral blood rather than cord serum should be used to measure IgM, IgA, or IgE antibodies in a newborn.

IgE Antibodies

IgE antibodies are detectable by ELISA in sera of acutely infected adults,[241,242] congenitally infected infants,[241,242] and children with congenital toxoplasmic chorioretinitis.[243] The duration of IgE seropositivity is briefer than that of IgM or IgA antibodies, and IgE seems useful for identifying recently acquired infections.[140,242] *T. gondii*–specific IgE antibody has been detected in patients with TE and may be useful as a marker for TE in this population of patients.[242] An IgE ELISA was assessed by studying 2036 sera samples from 792 subjects with and without toxoplasmosis.[244] IgE antibodies were present in 85.7% of asymptomatic seroconverters and in 100% of seroconverters with overt toxoplasmosis. For neonatal diagnosis of congenital toxoplasmosis, IgE was less sensitive than IgM and IgA, but simultaneous measurement of the three immunoglobulins at birth improved the diagnostic yield to 81%.[244] Emergence of specific IgE during postnatal treatment for congenital toxoplasmosis may indicate poor adherence or inadequate dosing.

Radiologic Methods

Radiologic studies are particularly helpful in patients with toxoplasmosis of the CNS. The presence of calcifications in the brain of a newborn, detected by radiography, ultrasonography, or CT, should heighten the suspicion of *T. gondii* as the cause of the disease. In severely affected infants with congenital toxoplasmosis, unilateral or, more often, bilateral and symmetric dilation of the ventricles is a common finding.

In most immunodeficient patients with TE, CT scans show multiple bilateral cerebral lesions.[245] Although multiple lesions are more common in toxoplasmosis, they also may be solitary; a single lesion should not exclude TE as a diagnostic possibility. Clinicians should be aware that toxoplasmosis may manifest as an encephalitis that at autopsy is "diffuse," in which case the neuroimaging study results may appear normal or reveal findings suggestive of HIV encephalopathy.[110]

CT scans in AIDS patients with TE reveal multiple ring-enhancing lesions in 70% to 80% of the cases.[106] In AIDS patients with detectable *Toxoplasma* IgG and multiple ring-enhancing lesions on CT or MRI who are not receiving appropriate antiretroviral treatment or antitoxoplasma prophylaxis, the predictive value for TE is approximately 80%.[246] Lesions tend to occur at the corticomedullary junction (frequently involving the basal ganglia) and are characteristically hypodense.[247,248] The number of lesions frequently is underestimated by CT, although delayed imaging after a double dose of intravenous contrast material may improve the sensitivity of this modality.[247-249] An enlarging hypodense lesion that does not enhance is a poor prognostic sign.[250] TE lesions on MRI appear as high signal abnormalities on T2-weighted studies and reveal a rim of enhancement surrounding the edema on T1-weighted, contrast-enhanced images (Fig. 276-5). MRI

has superior sensitivity (particularly if gadolinium is used for contrast enhancement) compared with CT and often shows a lesion or lesions or more extensive disease not seen by CT.[249,251] MRI should be used as the initial procedure when feasible (or if a single lesion is shown by CT). Nevertheless, even characteristic lesions on CT or MRI are not pathognomonic of TE. The major differential diagnosis of focal CNS lesions in AIDS patients is CNS lymphoma, which may manifest with multiple enhancing lesions in 40% of cases. The probability of TE decreases and the probability of lymphoma increases in the presence of single lesions on MRI.[245] A brain biopsy may be required in a patient with a solitary lesion (especially if confirmed by MRI) to obtain a definitive diagnosis.[252]

In AIDS patients with TE, CT improvement is seen in 90% of patients after 2 to 3 weeks of treatment.[245,247] Complete resolution takes

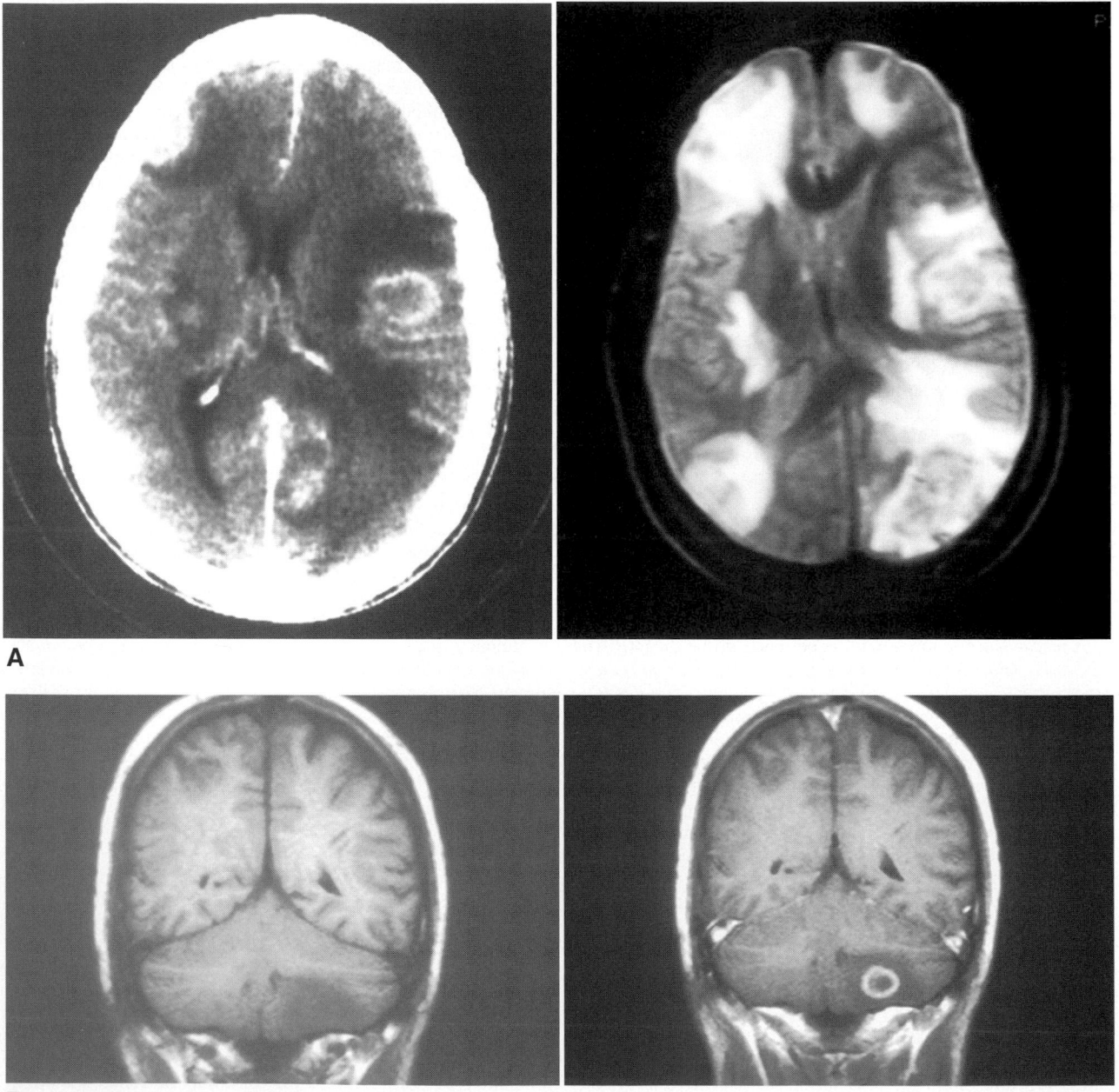

FIGURE 276-5. Imaging studies of toxoplasmic encephalitis. **A,** Computed tomography scan with contrast enhancement *(left)* and T2-weighted magnetic resonance imaging (MRI) scan *(right)* of a patient with multiple lesions, which are identified more easily with MRI. **B,** T1-weighted MRI scan without *(left)* and with *(right)* contrast enhancement. Note the ring-enhancing lesion on the right.

6 weeks to 6 months; peripheral lesions resolve more rapidly than deeper ones. Smaller lesions usually resolve completely on MRI within 3 to 5 weeks, but lesions with a mass effect tend to resolve more slowly and leave a small residual lesion.[253] A radiologic response to therapy lags behind the clinical response with better correlation between them observed by the end of acute therapy.[254]

CT and MRI in toxoplasmic myelopathy usually shows localized enlargement of the spinal cord,[156,255] which may result in obstruction to dye flow on myelography.[156] Gadolinium enhancement of MRI studies usually highlights as an intramedullary lesion at the site of spinal cord enlargement.[255]

Positron emission tomography,[256] radionuclide scanning,[257] and magnetic resonance techniques[258] have been used to evaluate AIDS patients with focal CNS lesions, specifically to differentiate between toxoplasmosis and primary CNS lymphoma.[258] Fluorodeoxyglucose positron emission tomography now is used widely in the evaluation of patients with tumors. There is a significantly higher uptake of fluorodeoxyglucose in patients with cerebral lymphoma than in patients with TE.[259] Radionuclide scanning also has been used to differentiate between CNS toxoplasmosis and lymphoma. Neoplasms usually show increased uptake of thallium 201 on early and late scanning.[258] Although published studies suggest a high sensitivity and specificity of these studies, in practice they often are not helpful, in part because of variability in uptake and in part because they often are used after an empirical trial of antitoxoplasmal therapy.

Proton magnetic resonance spectroscopy to evaluate brain lesions has been used in a few patients. Magnetic resonance spectroscopy in patients with TE reveals an elevation in the lactate and lipid contents[258] and a decrease in the levels of choline. In contrast, magnetic resonance spectroscopy in patients with CNS lymphoma reveals mildly elevated levels of choline.[258]

Cerebrospinal Fluid Abnormalities

CSF abnormalities in patients with TE are nonspecific; mild mononuclear pleocytosis and mild-to-moderate elevations in CSF protein often are observed; hypoglycorrhachia is uncommon.[133,260] Almost unique to infants with neonatal toxoplasmosis is the very high protein content, however, of the ventricular fluid. Although in some infants the protein level is just slightly above normal, in others, it can be measured in grams per deciliter rather than in milligrams per deciliter.[7] Demonstration of intrathecal production of *T. gondii*–specific IgG or IgM in the absence of CSF contamination with blood is diagnostic of TE.[261,262] Demonstration of IgM antibody has been especially useful in congenitally infected newborns.[7]

Diagnosis of Specific Clinical Entities

The initial step in pursuing the diagnosis of *T. gondii* infection or toxoplasmosis is to determine whether the patient has been exposed to the parasite. In virtually all cases, tests for IgG antibodies reliably establish the presence or absence of the infection; a negative IgG test essentially rules out prior or recent exposure to the parasite. Cases of documented toxoplasmic chorioretinitis and TE in adult patients have been observed, however, in which IgG antibodies were not demonstrable; such cases are rare. In addition, IgG antibodies may be absent in bone marrow transplantation patients post-transplant despite being detectable before transplantation.

In the presence of clinical illness, it is important to establish whether the patient's condition is due to a recently acquired infection or to recrudescence of latent infection (chronic infection) or is unrelated to the infection. A true negative IgM test in an otherwise immunologically normal individual essentially rules out that the infection has been acquired in recent months. A positive IgM test is more difficult to interpret correctly. One must not assume that a positive IgM test result is diagnostic of recently acquired infection. The presence of *T. gondii*–specific IgM antibodies can be interpreted as a true positive result consistent with recently acquired infection, a true positive result consistent with a chronic infection (IgM antibodies have been shown to persist for 5 years after the acute infection), or a false-

positive result. To establish which of these is most likely in a given case, confirmatory testing in a reference laboratory should be performed whenever feasible.[209,229]

A combination or battery of tests has been useful for determining whether the patient has been infected recently or in the more distant past.[140,263] Clinicians and laboratories should consider confirmatory testing in all patients in whom IgM test results are positive.[209,229] If the patient has received a blood transfusion, serologic tests may measure exogenously administered rather than endogenous antibody. The use of serologic tests to evaluate the response to therapy should be discouraged.

Toxoplasmosis in an Immunocompetent Patient

Tests for IgG and IgM antibodies should be used for initial evaluation of immunocompetent patients. Testing of serial specimens obtained 3 weeks apart (in parallel) provides the best discriminatory power if the results in the initial specimen are equivocal. Negative results in either of these tests virtually rules out the diagnosis of toxoplasmosis. Early in infection, IgG antibodies may not be detectable, whereas IgM antibodies are present (hence the need for both tests to be performed). Acute infection is supported by documented seroconversion of IgG or IgM antibodies or a greater than two-tube rise in antibody titer in sera run in parallel. A single high titer of any immunoglobulin antibodies is insufficient to make the diagnosis; IgG antibodies may persist at high titers for many years,[7] and IgM antibodies may be detectable for more than 12 months. When only a single serum sample is available, a battery or combination of tests usually is required in determining the likelihood that the infection is acute.

Toxoplasmosis should be considered in the differential diagnosis of lymphadenopathy, whether or not symptoms are present and especially in patients without symptoms. Confirmatory serologic tests should be obtained in these patients. The interval between the clinical onset of lymphadenopathy and the date that the specimen is drawn is crucial for interpretation of the test results.[140] In patients whose serum is available during the first 3 months after the clinical onset, at least the IgG test and the IgM ELISA are positive. In patients in whom sera are obtained more than 3 months after the clinical onset, the IgM ELISA is most likely to be negative, but the IgG test and at least one of the following tests are positive: IgA ELISA, IgE ELISA, IgE ISAGA, or AC/HS test.[140]

Histologic diagnosis can be useful in some cases of suspected toxoplasmosis in an immunocompetent patient. The histologic criteria for the diagnosis of toxoplasmic lymphadenitis have been well established (see Fig. 276-3*B*) (see "Histologic Diagnosis").[122] In this setting, there is no need to visualize the parasite. Endomyocardial biopsy and biopsy of skeletal muscle have been used successfully to establish *T. gondii* as the etiologic agent of myocarditis and polymyositis in the rare cases in immunocompetent patients.[119] Isolation studies and PCR rarely have proved useful in immunocompetent patients.

Toxoplasmosis in an Immunodeficient Patient

Because reactivation of chronic infection is the most common cause of toxoplasmosis in patients with AIDS, malignancies, or organ transplants, initial assessment of these patients routinely should include an assay for *T. gondii* IgG antibodies. Patients with a positive result are at risk of reactivation of the infection; patients with a negative result should be instructed on how they can prevent becoming infected (see "Prevention"). Patients at highest risk (e.g., HIV-infected patients not receiving appropriate antiretroviral therapy or antitoxoplasmal prophylaxis) who are initially seronegative should be retested on an annual basis to determine whether they have seroconverted. Seronegative organ transplant recipients should be identified before transplantation to avoid, when feasible, their receiving an organ from a seropositive donor, particularly if it is a heart.[48] In patients with AIDS and toxoplasmosis, the IgG titer may be relatively low, and tests for IgM, IgA, and IgE antibodies may be negative.[106]

In the early postoperative period in heart transplant recipients with pretransplant *Toxoplasma* antibodies who present with a clinical illness, serologic test results may be misleading.[198,264] In these patients, results indicating apparent reactivation (a rising IgG and IgM titer) may be present in the absence of clinically apparent infection. In addition, serologic test results consistent with chronic infection may be seen in the presence of toxoplasmosis.[198,264] In heart transplant recipients in whom toxoplasmosis is suspected as a cause of altered myocardial function, endomyocardial biopsy has proved useful.[198] The parasite has been shown in the myocardium of patients in whom the biopsy was performed because of a suspicion of rejection.[198]

Diagnosis in the HSCT recipient often requires special consideration. It is crucial in all HSCT patients that a serum IgG titer be performed before the transplant. Toxoplasmosis in these patients almost always is due to recrudescence of a latent infection. After HSCT, the preexisting IgG antibody titer may rise, remain stable, decrease, or become negative. Post-transplant serology frequently is not helpful in these patients and emphasizes the need for knowing the patient's pretransplant serologic status. Clinical evidence of encephalopathy, pneumonia, fever, or any other unexplained syndrome in HSCT patients with pre-existing *T. gondii* IgG antibodies must include toxoplasmosis in the differential diagnosis. The ultimate diagnosis of toxoplasmosis in these patients requires the use of histologic, DNA amplification, or isolation methods to detect the presence of the parasite. Serologic tests in patients with hypogammaglobulinemia or agammaglobulinemia may not be useful to diagnose toxoplasmosis; active infection can occur in these patients in the setting of negative IgG titers.

A definitive diagnosis of toxoplasmosis in an immunodeficient patient relies on histologic demonstration of the parasite (usually in association with an inflammatory process), on detection of *T. gondii* DNA by PCR, or on isolation of the parasite. The presence of tachyzoites is diagnostic of active infection. The presence of a solitary *T. gondii* tissue cyst may reflect only chronic infection, unless it is associated with an area of inflammation (e.g., as seen in myocardial biopsy); however, visualization of several tissue cysts virtually always means that active infection is present.

When clinical signs suggest involvement of the CNS or spinal cord, the workup should include CT or MRI (see "Radiologic Methods") of the brain. These studies should be performed even if the neurologic examination does not reveal focal deficits.

Empirical anti–*T. gondii* therapy for patients with multiple ring-enhancing brain lesions (usually established by MRI), positive IgG antibody titers against *T. gondii,* and advanced immunodeficiency (e.g., AIDS patients with a CD4+ count <200 cells/μL or patients receiving intensive immunosuppressive therapy) is accepted practice. A clinical and radiologic response to specific anti–*T. gondii* therapy essentially confirms the diagnosis of TE.

Brain biopsy should be considered in immunodeficient patients with presumed TE if there is a single lesion on MRI, a negative IgG antibody test, an inadequate clinical response (within a 2- to 3-week period) or progression during optimal therapy, or in patients whom the physician considers have adhered to an effective prophylactic regimen against *T. gondii* (e.g., TMP-SMX). An impression smear of the brain biopsy specimen can be made and examined immediately for the presence of tachyzoites using the conventional Wright-Giemsa stain employed for blood smears in most laboratories. The brain specimen should be submitted to the pathology and microbiology departments for appropriate workup. In addition to hematoxylin and eosin staining, *T. gondii*–specific immunoperoxidase staining should be performed. Because the amount of brain tissue obtained at aspiration or biopsy usually is small, sufficient tissue for mouse inoculation may not be available; however, this should be performed whenever feasible. A positive result often may be obtained with much less than 1 g of brain tissue. PCR has been used successfully in brain tissue to diagnose TE,[202] but a positive result should be interpreted with caution because it may not distinguish between a patient with TE from a patient with latent infection (asymptomatic carrier of brain tissue cysts) who has CNS pathology due to a process other than toxoplasmosis.

If *T. gondii* serologic and radiologic studies are inconclusive or do not support a recommendation for empirical treatment, and if brain

biopsy is not feasible, a lumbar puncture should be considered if it is safe to perform; PCR can be performed on the CSF specimen. CSF also can be sent for isolation studies. PCR examination of the CSF also can be used for the detection of Epstein-Barr virus, JC virus, or CMV DNA in patients in whom primary CNS lymphoma, progressive multifocal leukoencephalopathy, or CMV ventriculitis has been entertained in the differential diagnosis. Especially in HIV-infected patients, a positive Epstein-Barr virus PCR strongly suggests CNS lymphoma.[265] Demonstration of the intrathecal production of *T. gondii*–specific antibody within the CSF may help confirm the diagnosis.[262] Unless sufficient CSF is available, the highest priority should be for PCR and an attempt at isolation of the parasite.

In the appropriate clinical setting, it is important to include toxoplasmosis in the differential diagnosis of pulmonary symptoms, particularly in individuals with interstitial infiltrates. Wright-Giemsa stain and PCR of BAL specimens are useful for the diagnosis of pulmonary toxoplasmosis.[112,266] In patients with visual symptoms in whom toxoplasmic chorioretinitis is a possibility, PCR examination of vitreous or aqueous fluid can be considered and is particularly helpful in patients with atypical clinical features of toxoplasmic chorioretinitis.[115,173,267] PCR examination of the vitreous fluid also can be helpful when other etiologic agents, such as herpes simplex virus, varicella-zoster virus, or CMV, are considered in the differential diagnosis. PCR and isolation studies in peripheral blood can help establish *T. gondii* as the etiologic agent of a febrile syndrome or systemic symptoms of unclear cause.[201,268] These studies tend to have a higher yield early in the disease and before or shortly after specific anti–*T. gondii* therapy is initiated.[201]

In pursuing the diagnosis, histologic examination with the appropriate stains and mouse inoculation can be attempted in virtually any tissue suspected of being involved by *T. gondii*. Body fluids that should be considered for examination by PCR include CSF, blood, vitreous, aqueous, and BAL specimens. Reference laboratories should be contacted before diagnostic procedures to optimize the handling of the specimens and their yield.

Ocular Toxoplasmosis

Low titers of IgG antibody are usual in patients with active chorioretinitis due to reactivation of congenital *T. gondii* infection; IgM antibodies usually are not detected. When sera from these patients are examined in the dye test, they should be titered beginning with undiluted serum because in some cases the conventional initial dilution of 1:16 may be negative.

In most cases, toxoplasmic chorioretinitis is diagnosed by ophthalmologic examination, and empirical therapy directed against the organism often is instituted based on clinical findings and serologic test results. In many patients, the morphology of the retinal lesion or lesions may be nondiagnostic, or the response to treatment may be suboptimal, or both. In such cases (unclear clinical diagnosis or inadequate clinical response or both), the detection of an abnormal *T. gondii* antibody response in ocular fluids (Goldman-Witmer coefficient)[267,269] or demonstration of the parasite by isolation, histopathologic examination, or PCR has been used successfully to establish the diagnosis.[113] PCR has been employed in vitreous and aqueous fluids in an attempt to support or confirm the diagnosis of *T. gondii* as the cause of the retinal lesions.[114,115,173,267] In patients in whom toxoplasmosis is considered in the differential diagnosis but in whom the presentation is atypical, PCR is a useful diagnostic aid. Vitreous biopsy is a potentially hazardous procedure, and its use should be considered only when other diagnostic measures have not revealed a cause.

Toxoplasma gondii Infection in Pregnancy

Acute acquired *T. gondii* infection is diagnosed serologically by the same methods used for immunocompetent adults discussed earlier. Special care is taken to determine whether the infection was acquired before or after conception. This determination frequently is difficult because routine serologic screening is not conducted in pregnant women in the United States. Repeat serologic tests in a pregnant woman who previously has been shown to have *T. gondii* antibodies are not helpful.

The diagnosis of acute *T. gondii* infection or toxoplasmosis in most cases requires demonstration of a rise in titers in serial serum samples (either conversion from a negative to a positive titer or a significant rise from a low to a high titer).[7] These specimens should be obtained at least 3 weeks apart and be tested in parallel. Because the diagnosis frequently is considered relatively late in the course of the patient's pregnancy, serologic test titers already may have reached their peak at the time the first serum sample is obtained for testing. It often is difficult to discriminate between infections acquired recently (possibly during pregnancy) and infections acquired in the more distant past. The initial serum sample should be obtained as early as possible during gestation.

Initial screening of maternal serum involves testing for IgG and IgM antibodies; a lack of both immunoglobulin antibodies essentially excludes active infection but identifies the patient as being at risk for acquisition of the infection (and in need of instruction about primary prevention). The presence of IgG antibodies in the absence of IgM antibodies in the first two trimesters almost always indicates chronic maternal infection with essentially no risk to the fetus (the exceptions are severely immunodeficient patients). In the third trimester, a negative IgM test titer is most likely consistent with a chronic maternal infection but does not exclude the possibility of an acute infection acquired early in pregnancy; this is especially true in patients who exhibit a rapid decline in IgM titers during the acute infection. In these cases, the use of other serologic tests (e.g., IgA, IgE, AC/HS, avidity) may be of particular help.

A positive IgM test result requires further assessment with confirmatory testing at a reference laboratory (see also "Diagnosis of Specific Clinical Entities").[209,229,263] The use of confirmatory testing with a combination of serologic tests in a reference laboratory has proved helpful in discriminating between recently and more distantly acquired infections, and having an expert interpret the results to the patient's physician has been shown to reduce unnecessary induced abortions among pregnant women reported to have IgM antibodies.[263] Women who are informed that they have a positive IgM test titer and that it signifies that their offspring will or might be infected often choose abortion. A positive IgM test may not indicate infection acquired during gestation (a false-positive result), and the abortion may not be indicated. For this reason, confirmatory testing in a reference laboratory has been recommended by many experts and by the Food and Drug Administration.[229]

Many tests for avidity of *Toxoplasma* IgG antibodies have been introduced to help differentiate between recently acquired and distant infection.[223-225] Studies of the kinetics of the avidity of IgG in pregnant women who have seroconverted during gestation have shown that women with high avidity test results have been infected with *T. gondii* for at least 3 to 5 months. It has been shown that when used as a confirmatory test along with a battery of other tests in women in their first 16 weeks of gestation, detection of high avidity IgG antibodies by the VIDAS IgG avidity test (BioMérieux, Marcy-l'Etoile, France) can be a useful addition to the discriminatory power of a combination of tests in distinguishing recently acquired from chronic infection.[192] It is crucial to recognize that the value of the avidity test is in the first 3 to 5 months of gestation (i.e., the fetus of a woman in the 14th week of gestation with a positive IgM test and a high avidity result is not at risk for congenital toxoplasmosis).[213] Because low or equivocal avidity test results may persist for many months, their presence does not indicate recently acquired infection.

Confirmatory testing, using a battery of tests and the VIDAS avidity method in pregnant women during their first 16 weeks of gestation, has the potential to decrease the need for follow-up sera and reduce costs, to make the need for PCR on amniotic fluid and for treatment of the mother with spiramycin unnecessary, to remove the pregnant woman's anxiety associated with further testing, and to decrease unnecessary abortions.[211-213] Although the avidity test is an additional confirmatory method (most useful if high avidity antibodies are detected), it should not be used as the only confirmatory test for pregnant women with positive IgG or IgM antibodies (or both) because of the potential to misinterpret low or borderline avidity antibody results. When the diagnosis of acute acquired infection during pregnancy has been established presumptively, diagnostic efforts should focus on determining whether the fetus has been infected.

Congenital Infection in the Fetus and Newborn

Prenatal diagnosis of fetal infection is advised when a diagnosis of acute infection is established or highly suspected in a pregnant woman. Methods to obtain fetal blood, such as periumbilical fetal blood sampling, have been largely abandoned because of the rate of false-negative prenatal diagnoses, the risk involved for the fetus, and the delay in obtaining definitive results with conventional parasitologic tests.[186]

Prenatal diagnosis of congenital toxoplasmosis presently is based on ultrasonography and amniocentesis. PCR on amniotic fluid for the detection of *T. gondii*–specific DNA performed at 18 weeks of gestation or later is more sensitive, more rapid, and safer than conventional diagnostic procedures involving fetal blood sampling.[186] Amniotic fluid should be tested by PCR in all cases with serologic test results diagnostic of or highly suggestive of acute acquired infection during pregnancy and if there is evidence of fetal damage by ultrasound examination (i.e., hydrocephalus or calcifications or both). In a prospective study conducted by three reference laboratories in France, congenital infection ultimately was documented in 75 of 270 cases. PCR of amniotic fluid had a sensitivity of 64%, specificity of 100%, positive predictive value of 100%, and negative predictive value of 88%.[270] Sensitivity was greatest when maternal infection occurred between 17 and 21 weeks of gestation. In cases in which the approximate date of onset of infection is known, it has been suggested that amniocentesis be performed no earlier than 4 weeks thereafter, with the preferable time for amniocentesis being 17 to 21 weeks. In the United States, systemic monthly screening is not performed as it is in France; we suggest that when feasible, amniocentesis be performed at 18 weeks of gestation. The reliability of the PCR test before 18 weeks of gestation is unknown.[186] Prenatal diagnosis should not be attempted until at least 4 weeks after acute disease has been diagnosed in the mother because of the possibility of a false-negative result.[186]

Maternal IgG antibodies present in the newborn may reflect either past or recent infection in the mother. For this reason, tests for the detection of IgA and IgM antibodies commonly are employed for the diagnosis of infection in the newborn. It is essential that maternal contamination of blood obtained at birth be excluded; serum samples obtained from peripheral blood and not from the umbilical cords are preferred. The demonstration of IgA antibodies seems to be more sensitive than the detection of IgM antibodies for establishing infection in the newborn.[240] If IgG antibodies are detected but serologic tests for IgM and IgA antibodies are negative and *T. gondii* is not isolated, follow-up serologic testing in suspect cases is indicated to attempt to establish the diagnosis. Maternally transferred antibodies usually decline and disappear within 6 to 12 months. Studies using the Western blot technique have shown that maternal and infant sera may recognize different *T. gondii* antigens when the infant is congenitally infected.[271,272] Combining Western blot with conventional serologic analysis (i.e., IgG, IgM, and IgA tests) has been reported to be more sensitive for the diagnosis of congenital toxoplasmosis at birth and within the first 3 months of life than either test alone.[272]

Additional diagnostic methods that have been used successfully to diagnose infection in infants are direct demonstration of the organism by isolation in mice or cell culture (e.g., placental tissue, body fluid) and PCR in body fluids (e.g., CSF, blood, and urine).[273-275] Evaluation of infants with suspected congenital toxoplasmosis always should include ophthalmologic examination, radiologic studies (particularly to detect the presence of cerebral calcifications), and examination of CSF. Diagnostic procedures in congenitally infected infants is discussed in more detail by Remington and colleagues.[7]

Because it is not feasible to screen all pregnant women, a secondary prevention program that consists of serologic testing of all newborns for IgM antibodies against *T. gondii* has been implemented in Massachusetts.[276,277] Using routine screening of all newborns, congenital infection was confirmed in approximately 1 in 12,000 infants. More than 90% of these were identified only through neonatal screening and not through initial clinical examination. Because testing for IgM antibodies in newborns is only 25% to 75% sensitive, this program does not detect many subclinically infected infants or infants infected late in the third trimester (when the frequency of transmission is highest, but antibody formation has not yet occurred).

In infants with congenital toxoplasmosis or congenital infection, a rebound in IgG and IgM antibody titers frequently is observed after discontinuation of therapy. In our experience, such a serologic rebound has not been shown to be clinically significant.[7]

TREATMENT

Currently recommended drugs against *T. gondii* act primarily against the tachyzoite form and do not eradicate the encysted form (bradyzoite). Pyrimethamine is considered to be the most effective anti-*Toxoplasma* agent and, if feasible, always should be included in drug regimens used against the parasite. Pyrimethamine is a folic acid antagonist. The most common side effect is dose-related suppression of the bone marrow, which may be decreased by concomitant administration of folinic acid (calcium leucovorin). It is not well established how often a blood count should be obtained; a reasonable strategy would be to check a peripheral blood cell and platelet count twice weekly until hematologic parameters have stabilized in a nontoxic range, then every 2 to 4 weeks. Folinic acid should be administered concomitantly to avoid bone marrow suppression. The parenteral form of folinic acid is absorbed well orally, and 5 to 10 mg of folinic acid (up to 50 mg/day is used in AIDS patients) may be given orally (e.g., with orange juice at the same time as the pyrimethamine). Although folinic acid does not inhibit the action of pyrimethamine on tachyzoites, folic acid does and should not be used in patients being treated with pyrimethamine. Less serious side effects of pyrimethamine include gastrointestinal distress, rash, headaches, and a bad taste in the mouth.

Unless there are circumstances that preclude the use of more than one drug, there is no role for monotherapy in the treatment of toxoplasmosis. A second drug, such as sulfadiazine or clindamycin, should be added. Sulfadiazine acts synergistically with pyrimethamine; most other sulfonamides have inferior activity. The patient must maintain a good urine output to prevent crystalluria and oliguria. The most common side effects associated with sulfadiazine are skin rashes (which may be life-threatening)[278] and crystal-induced nephrotoxicity.[279] Worsening encephalopathy, hallucinations, or a new onset of psychiatric symptoms in patients with AIDS may be sulfadiazine induced and must be considered in a patient who is nonresponsive to otherwise appropriate antitoxoplasmal treatment.[280] A drug rash with sulfonamide therapy does not preclude its use because successful desensitization protocols have been reported.[281,282] Clindamycin seems to act by targeting translation in the apicoplast of *T. gondii*.[283] Adverse reactions to clindamycin include rash, nausea, vomiting, and diarrhea, which may be associated with *Clostridium difficile* infection. Myopathy with electromyographic abnormalities and elevated serum creatine phosphokinase levels have been described.[284]

The role of other drugs, including azithromycin, clarithromycin, atovaquone, dapsone, and TMP-SMX, is less clear. Other drugs should be used only as alternatives to the above-described regimens and, other than TMP-SMX, should be used in combination with pyrimethamine whenever possible.

Spiramycin has been used in pregnant women to attempt to reduce transmission to the fetus; it has not been shown to be effective for acute therapy, maintenance therapy, or primary prophylaxis of TE in AIDS patients. There is no evidence that spiramycin is teratogenic. Although drugs used to treat toxoplasmosis in the setting of different clinical entities are basically the same, careful attention should be given to the dosing regimen. Recommended doses in immunocompromised patients usually are higher than doses in immunocompetent patients. The recommended dose of pyrimethamine for patients with TE is 50 to 75 mg/day after a loading dose of 200 mg; the dose to treat fetal infection during pregnancy is 25 to 50 mg/day after a loading dose of 100 mg in the mother.

Immunotherapy

Because of the severely impaired immune function in patients with AIDS, immunotherapy has been proposed as adjunctive treatment for life-threatening toxoplasmosis. Of particular interest is IFN-γ, which previously has been identified as the most important mediator of resistance against *T. gondii*.[81] In murine models of toxoplasmosis, the administration of IFN-γ in concert with antimicrobial agents has resulted in synergistic or additive toxoplasmacidal activity. These include IFN-γ in combination with roxithromycin,[285] pyrimethamine,[286] azithromycin,[287] and clindamycin.[286] The combination of IL-12 plus atovaquone or IL-12 plus clindamycin also has proved useful in a mouse model of acute toxoplasmosis.[288]

Treatment Regimens in Specific Clinical Entities

Toxoplasmosis in Immunocompetent Patients

Treatment of immunocompetent adults with the lymphadenopathic form rarely is indicated; this form is self-limited. If visceral disease is clinically overt or symptoms are severe or persistent, treatment may be indicated for 2 to 4 weeks, followed by reassessment of the patient's condition. Infections acquired by laboratory mishap or transfusion of blood products are potentially more severe, and patients who have been infected in these ways probably should be treated.

Toxoplasmosis in Immunodeficient Patients

Because experience with treatment of toxoplasmosis in immunodeficient patients has been studied most extensively in patients with AIDS, this section focuses primarily on this group of patients. Information on treatment in AIDS patients in large part likely can be extrapolated directly to other immunodeficient patients.

If left untreated, toxoplasmosis in immunodeficient patients is often lethal. Treatment is recommended for 4 to 6 weeks after the resolution of all signs and symptoms (often ≥6 months). At one medical center, 80% of non-AIDS, immunodeficient patients with toxoplasmosis improved with specific therapy.[289] This rate of improvement is similar to that observed in appropriately treated AIDS patients with TE.[254,290] Chronic (latent) asymptomatic infection in immunodeficient patients is not treated. The exact dosing schedule for the treatment of toxoplasmosis in non-AIDS, immunocompromised patients has not been defined.[5] Useful information in this regard has resulted, however, from studies performed in AIDS patients with toxoplasmosis.[99]

Therapy for toxoplasmosis in AIDS patients includes acute (primary or induction) treatment, maintenance treatment (secondary prophylaxis), and primary prophylaxis. There are no convincing data from prospective, carefully designed trials to allow the recommendation of monotherapy for induction, maintenance, or primary prophylaxis. Because relapse occurs in 80% of cases[278] after the discontinuation of primary therapy, lifelong maintenance therapy is recommended unless the CD4+ count increases to greater than 200 cells/mm³ for at least 6 months in response to HAART (plasma HIV viral load often is below detection limits during this period).[291]

Acute therapy should be administered for at least 3 weeks[53]; 6 weeks or more may be required for more severely ill patients who have not achieved a complete response. Pyrimethamine combined with sulfadiazine and folinic acid is the therapy of choice for AIDS patients with toxoplasmosis and is the standard to which experimental regimens should be compared. This regimen is associated with clinical response in 68% to 95% of patients with TE.[290,292] Unfortunately, up to 40% of patients develop side effects from one or more of the drugs, often requiring discontinuation of therapy.[133,245] Pyrimethamine-clindamycin and folinic acid seem comparable in efficacy to pyrimethamine-sulfadiazine,[290,293] but this combination also has substantial toxicity. TMP-SMX[294-296] (at 10 mg/kg/day of the trimethoprim component divided in two doses) showed similar efficacy to the pyrimethamine-sulfadiazine regimen (with a more rapid radiologic response in the TMP-SMX group) in a randomized pilot trial in 77 patients with AIDS[297]; this provides an alternative regimen for situations in which parenteral therapy is required. In an international, noncomparative study, the efficacy, safety, and tolerability of atovaquone[298,299] (administered orally as a suspension) combined with either pyrimethamine or sulfadiazine as treatment for acute disease for patients with TE and Karnofsky Performance Scores of greater than 30 were shown, with 6-week response rates of 75% (21 of 28 patients) for atovaquone-pyrimethamine and 82% (9 of 11) for atovaquone-sulfadiazine.[300] Atovaquone-pyrimethamine can be used as an alternative treatment for patients intolerant to sulfonamides, and atovaquone-sulfadiazine can be used for patients who are intolerant to pyrimethamine. Serum levels of atovaquone in patients treated with TE were not predictive of clinical response or failure in one study[301]; in another more extensive study, a direct correlation was noted between clinical and radiologic responses and median atovaquone plasma concentrations.[299]

Promising results were reported in a 13-patient pilot study of TE using the combination of pyrimethamine, 75 mg/day, and clarithromycin, 1 g every 12 hours. In this study, 62% had a complete and 23% a partial clinical response; 15% died by week 3 of therapy.[302] Adverse events resulted in discontinuation of therapy in 27% of patients. Doses of clarithromycin greater than than 500 mg twice daily have been associated with increased mortality in HIV-infected patients receiving therapy for *Mycobacterium avium* infection and should not be used.[303,304]

Dapsone in combination with pyrimethamine has been reported anecdotally to be effective for the treatment of TE when used in an oral dose of 100 mg/day with 25 mg/day of oral pyrimethamine.[305] Doxycycline has been successful in the treatment of TE in a few patients when used at 300 mg/day intravenously in three divided doses.[306] A dosage of 100 mg twice a day was given to six patients intolerant to pyrimethamine-sulfadiazine, but five had associated neurologic and radiologic recurrences while receiving the drug.[307] Further studies are needed to compare the relative efficacy and toxicity of these alternative regimens. Although azithromycin plus pyrimethamine is effective for the treatment of some cases of TE in AIDS patients, its use should be limited based on results of a study showing an inferior response rate, especially during maintenance therapy.[308,309] Alternative regimens used for acute therapy and their dosage schedules are presented in Table 276-2.

Corticosteroids often are given to patients with TE for the reduction of cerebral edema and increased intracranial pressure. The clinical response and survival in patients with TE who received corticosteroids in addition to antimicrobial therapy has been reported to be no different from the response of patients who received antimicrobial agents alone.[254] The use of these agents may complicate the interpretation of empirical therapy of TE because partial clinical and radiologic improvement may be seen solely due to a reduction in cerebral edema and inflammation or a response of CNS lymphoma; they may compromise further the immune systems of these already very immunodeficient patients. Use of corticosteroids should be limited to situations in which clinically significant edema or a mass effect is present.

Seizures occur in 35% of patients with TE.[245] One retrospective study showed a poorer outcome in patients who received anticonvulsant therapy compared with patients who did not.[278] Whether this result represents a true drug effect or a selection bias (given that patients receiving anticonvulsant therapy are likely to be more severely ill) is unclear. Anticonvulsant agents may be responsible for numerous side effects and drug interactions; potentially serious interactions can occur between agents such as carbamazepine, phenobarbital, or phenytoin and other drugs used to treat HIV infection, such as protease inhibitors. Anticonvulsant therapy probably is best administered when seizures have occurred.[278]

The time to clinical response in AIDS patients with TE who were receiving appropriate antitoxoplasmal therapy has been evaluated in a

TABLE 276-2 Guidelines for Acute and Primary Therapy of Toxoplasmic Encephalitis in Patients with AIDS

Drug	Dosage Schedule
Standard Regimens	
Pyrimethamine	Oral 200-mg loading dose, then 50
plus	(<60kg) to 75 (≥60 kg) mg PO qd
Folinic acid (leucovorin)*	Oral, IV, or IM, 10 to 20 mg qd
plus either	(≤50 mg qd)
Sulfadiazine (preferred)	Oral 1000 (<60 kg) to 1500 mg (≥60 kg)
or	q6h
Clindamycin	Oral or IV 600 mg q6h
	(IV ≤1200 mg q6h)
Possible Alternative Regimens	
Trimethoprim-sulfamethoxazole	Oral or IV 5 mg/kg (trimethoprim component) q12h (5-20 mg/kg/day of the trimethoprim component has been used)
Pyrimethamine and folinic acid	As in standard regimens plus one of the following†
Atovaquone	Oral 1500 mg q12h
Clarithromycin	Oral 500 mg q12h
Azithromycin	Oral 900-1200 mg qd
Dapsone	Oral 100 mg qd

*The dose of folinic acid can be titrated based on the hemogram to reduce pyrimethamine-associated myelotoxicity; up to 50 mg/day has been used.

†These agents have been used in clinical studies with a few patients and have response rates lower than the standard regimens (see text for references). They should be used only in patients who are intolerant of the standard regimens. Alternative agents must be used in combination with another antimicrobial agent (most frequently, pyrimethamine with folinic acid) that has proven clinical activity against *Toxoplasma gondii*.

study that included an objective, graded neurologic examination.[254] Of patients with a response, 91% improved with respect to at least half of their baseline abnormalities by day 14.[254] AIDS patients with presumed TE had some degree of improvement within 7 to 10 days of the initiation of appropriate antitoxoplasmal therapy. In contrast, many patients with an alternate diagnosis, including lymphoma, exhibited signs of clinical deterioration 3 to 5 days after the initiation of the empirical regimen for presumed TE.[254] Headaches and seizures were insensitive indicators for a response to therapy. In some cases, toxoplasmosis progressed to death despite the use of appropriate drug regimens.[290,293]

After successful primary therapy, drug dosages generally are decreased for maintenance therapy. No single maintenance regimen that is efficacious with an acceptable adverse reaction profile has been identified yet. Relapse of TE occurs in approximately 20% to 30% of patients who are receiving maintenance therapy, in part because of nonadherence to and patient intolerance of the prescribed regimen.[133] Pyrimethamine (25 mg/day) plus sulfadiazine (500 mg four times daily) has been associated with the lowest relapse rate[290] and is recommended unless there are contraindications to its use. When daily therapy with pyrimethamine-sulfadiazine was compared with a twice-weekly regimen for the prevention of recurrence of TE, the latter was found to be less effective.[310,311] Although a subsequent trial by the same group found that three-times-weekly therapy was equivalent to daily therapy, the relapse rates for both groups (approximately 14.5 per 100 patient-years) was higher than was seen with daily therapy (4.4 per 100 patient-years) in the earlier study.[311,312]

Patients receiving the pyrimethamine-sulfadiazine combination do not require another regimen for *P. carinii* pneumonia prophylaxis. Although 25% of patients receiving pyrimethamine-clindamycin subsequently developed *P. carinii* pneumonia,[313] no patients receiving pyrimethamine-sulfadiazine developed *P. carinii* pneumonia.[311,313] Because of drug toxicity, many patients are unable to continue taking the pyrimethamine-sulfadiazine combination for maintenance therapy. A higher relapse rate has been reported with the use of pyrimethamine-clindamycin compared with pyrimethamine-sulfadiazine for secondary prophylaxis of TE; it is recommended that the clindamycin dose be at least 1200 mg/day.[290,314] Encouraging results have been reported with other drug combinations. These include pyrimethamine-sulfadoxine (Fansidar), which has been used in a dose of one tablet twice weekly,[315] and pyrimethamine-dapsone, administered on an intermittent schedule (two to three times a week).[316-318] The long half-life of these agents allowed the longer dosing interval. When pyrimethamine was used alone as maintenance therapy at 50 mg/day[319,320] and 100 mg/day,[319] the relapse rates were 10% to 28% and 5%. Atovaquone alone or in combination regimens also seems to have activity based on uncontrolled trials; combination therapy (with sulfadiazine or pyrimethamine) should be used whenever possible.[298-300,321]

Primary prophylaxis against *T. gondii* in patients with AIDS has been shown to be effective in preventing acute TE.[322-324] In addition, the use of HAART in HIV-infected patients has had a profound effect in decreasing the incidence of TE in these patients.[54,55] Primary prophylaxis is recommended for patients who have detectable *Toxoplasma* IgG antibodies and whose lowest CD4+ count has been less than 100/mm³ (many experts use <200/mm³ as the cutoff rather than 100/mm³), regardless of the HIV RNA viral load.[291] TMP-SMX (1 double-strength or single-strength tablet/day), dapsone (50 mg/day) plus pyrimethamine (50 mg/week), and Fansidar (twice weekly) have been reported to be effective in preventing the first episode of TE.[291,322,325,326]

Studies have shown that it is safe to discontinue primary or secondary antitoxoplasmal prophylaxis when the recovery of the CD4+ count greater than 200 cells/mm³ is achieved and sustained in patients on effective antiretroviral therapy.[163,164,327,328] Current recommendations are to discontinue primary prophylaxis when the CD4+ count has increased to greater than 200 cells/mm³ for at least 3 months and secondary prophylaxis for at least 6 months.[291] These recommendations should be viewed with caution, however, because the median CD4+ count was greater than 300 cells/mm³ at enrollment, and viral replication had been brought down to levels below detection limits or reasonably controlled in most patients.

Roxithromycin, 900 mg once a week (may be given in three divided doses),[329] has been reported in a small randomized trial to be effective for primary prophylaxis. Many investigators have studied pyrimethamine for primary prophylaxis and have come to different conclusions regarding dosing and efficacy.[51,330,331] In one study, pyrimethamine was associated with a higher death rate,[330] whereas in another no such correlation was found.[51] Patients who developed a rash while receiving prophylactic therapy with pyrimethamine also were noted to be at higher risk of TE.[332] At this time, pyrimethamine alone for primary prophylaxis cannot be recommended. Clarithromycin[333] and spiramycin[334] have been ineffective for primary prophylaxis when used alone. A randomized, placebo-controlled trial showed that when clindamycin was administered at 600 mg/day for primary prophylaxis, there was an unacceptably high rate of associated gastrointestinal disease, in particular, diarrhea, suggesting that poor patient tolerance would prevent its further study for this purpose.[335]

In many studies of TMP-SMX,[322] pyrimethamine-dapsone,[325] and Fansidar[315] for primary prophylaxis, discontinuation of therapy as a result of adverse effects was reported in 29% to 39% of the patients. These regimens may not be satisfactory for many AIDS patients due to intolerance.

Data on the outcome of treatment of AIDS patients with toxoplasmosis outside the CNS are limited. Available information on the therapy of ocular[160,336,337] and pulmonary involvement[154,338] indicate that these forms of toxoplasmosis also are responsive to treatment. Therapy was successful in 50% to 77% of patients with pulmonary toxoplasmosis.[154,338]

The hematologic toxicity associated with zidovudine and the high doses of pyrimethamine used for the treatment of TE are additive. Other drugs used in treating HIV-infected patients that cause myelosuppression include ganciclovir, flucytosine, trimethoprim, trimetrexate, pentamidine, chemotherapy agents, and interferon-alfa.

Ocular Toxoplasmosis

The decision to treat active toxoplasmic chorioretinitis should be made based on a complete ophthalmologic evaluation. Treatment most likely is indicated in the following settings: any decrease in visual acuity, macular or peripapillary lesions, lesions greater than one optic disk diameter, lesions associated with a moderate-to-severe vitreous inflammatory reaction, the presence of multiple active lesions, the persistence of active disease for greater than 1 month, and any ocular lesions associated with recently acquired infection. Because the disease can be self-limited in immunocompetent patients, many clinicians may not treat small, peripheral retinal lesions that are not immediately vision-threatening.[113,339]

The reported benefits of medical therapy are related primarily to the clinical presentation.[113,339] Because there is so much variation in the clinical manifestations of the retinal disease, and because the disease may be self-limited even without treatment, the response to therapy is difficult to interpret. The combination of pyrimethamine (100 mg loading dose given over 24 hours, followed by 25 to 50 mg daily) and sulfadiazine (1 g given four times daily) for 4 to 6 weeks depending on the clinical response, which is considered "classic" therapy for ocular toxoplasmosis, is the most common drug combination used.[339]

Clindamycin (300 mg orally every 6 hours for a minimum of 3 weeks) also has been used with favorable clinical results.[339] Other drugs that may have activity but have not been studied adequately include atovaquone and pyrimethamine plus azithromycin.[340,341] Systemic corticosteroids are indicated when lesions involve the macula, optic nerve head, or papillomacular bundle. Photocoagulation has been used for the treatment of active lesions and for prophylaxis against the spread of lesions because new lesions appear contiguous to old lesions.[339] In some patients, vitrectomy and lensectomy may be necessary.

Given the high relapse rate seen in some patients with ocular toxoplasmosis, prevention of recurrences would be highly desirable. A randomized, open-label trial of 124 patients found that TMP/SMX (1 double-strength tablet every 3 days) was effective in decreasing the frequency of recurrences from 24% to 7% in a population at high risk for recurrences.[116] If confirmed in subsequent studies, such a regimen could be beneficial in patients with frequent or severe recurrences. For the approach to ocular toxoplasmosis during pregnancy, see "Acute Acquired *Toxoplasma* Infection in Pregnant Women," next.

Acute Acquired *Toxoplasma* Infection in Pregnant Women

Treatment of an acutely infected pregnant woman does not eliminate but does seem to decrease the incidence of fetal infection. Because there is usually a delay between the acquisition of acute maternal infection, infection of the placenta, and subsequent infection of the fetus, identification of acute maternal infection necessitates immediate institution of treatment of the mother. Most experience of maternal treatment to prevent transmission to the fetus has been with spiramycin (3 g/day [obtainable in the United States from the Food and Drug Administration; 301-827-2335]). Spiramycin has been accepted by most investigators as being effective in reducing the frequency of maternal transmission of *T. gondii* to the fetus by approximately 60%.[184] If spiramycin cannot be used or is unavailable, it may be replaced by sulfadiazine alone with appropriate precautions at term. There are no data, however, on the efficacy of sulfonamides, including sulfadiazine, when these drugs are used for this purpose.

Because spiramycin does not reliably cross the placenta,[342] if fetal infection is documented, the recommended therapeutic regimen is the combination of sulfadiazine (1 g four times a day), pyrimethamine (25 mg/day), and folinic acid (5 to 15 mg/day). This treatment regimen might be an alternative to the termination of pregnancy when abortion is not allowed by law or for women who desire to continue their pregnancy. Pyrimethamine should not be used in the first 12 to 14 weeks of pregnancy because of a concern for teratogenicity (in this circumstance, we recommend that sulfadiazine be administered alone, although there are no data on its efficacy in this situation).[7] In addition, pyrimethamine-sulfadiazine is recommended for pregnant women in whom a recently acquired acute infection is highly suspected or confirmed during the late second or third trimesters, This recommendation is due to the high rates of vertical transmission observed in those stages of gestation and should be recommended even though fetal infection may not have been confirmed yet.

A group of European investigators reported that in their studies a significant effect of prenatal treatment (in regard to type [i.e., spiramycin versus pyrimethamine-sulfadiazine] and timing [i.e., delay in initiation of the drugs]) on the risk of mother-to-child transmission of toxoplasmosis was not detected.[343-346] These results are not surprising because the studies included few untreated women in their analysis, and most untreated women were infected during the third trimester.[347] The design of the studies performed to date has not permitted a definitive conclusion. Until appropriately designed studies are performed, most authorities continue to recommend spiramycin or pyrimethamine-sulfadiazine for women with suspected or confirmed acute *T. gondii* infection acquired during gestation.

Pregnant women with toxoplasmic chorioretinitis as a result of reactivation of chronic disease do not have a higher risk to transmit the parasite to their offspring than do pregnant women who have been infected before pregnancy and do not have ocular disease. The eye disease should be treated according to the indications discussed in "Ocular Toxoplasmosis." Pregnant women with toxoplasmic chorioretinitis thought to be a manifestation of recently acquired infection should be treated because of the eye disease and the risk of transmission of the infection to the fetus.

Congenital Infection

Detailed information on and recommendations for the postnatal treatment of congenital toxoplasmosis are reviewed elsewhere.[7] We favor continuous sulfadiazine (50 mg/kg twice daily), pyrimethamine (2 mg/kg/day for 2 days, then 1 mg/kg/day for 2 to 6 months, then 1 mg/kg/day three times a week), and folinic acid (10 mg three times weekly) for a minimum of 12 months.[190] Other groups have used pyrimethamine-sulfadiazine-folinic acid alternated with spiramycin (100 mg/kg/day).[7] Serial follow-up to gauge the response of the infant to therapy should include neuroradiology, ophthalmologic examinations, and CSF analysis if indicated.[7]

For guidance on therapy in congenital cases, we recommend that physicians contact Dr. Rima McLeod at the University of Chicago (773-834-4152), where a major study, the National Collaborative Treatment Trial, on the appropriate management of these cases is being performed.[190] Physicians who are treating patients with congenital toxoplasmosis who are younger than 2.5 months of age may wish to contact this multidisciplinary group regarding potential enrollment of their patients in that study.[190] This study has shown that outcomes are substantially better for most, but not all, infants treated from the neonatal period for 12 months with pyrimethamine-sulfadiazine and leucovorin compared with historical controls receiving no or short-course therapy.[190,348-350] Improvement in intellectual function, regression of retinal lesions, reduction in anticonvulsant drug requirements, and prevention of auditory sequelae seem to be the major benefits of such treatment, which was combined with CSF shunting if required.[190] Signs of active infection resolved within weeks of initiation of treatment. In many treated children, cerebral calcifications diminished in size or resolved.[350]

PREVENTION

General Methods

Prevention is most important in seronegative pregnant women and in immunodeficient patients. Prevention is accomplished most readily through education of these patients by their personal physicians (Table 276-3). The goal is to avoid the ingestion of and contact with tissue cysts or sporulated oocysts. Tissue cysts in meat are made noninfectious by heating the meat to 66° C (meat should be cooked to "well done" with no pink meat visible in the center), by smoking or curing it, or by freezing it to −20° (which is not attainable in most home freezers). Hands should be washed thoroughly after handling raw meat

TABLE 276-3 Measures to Prevent Primary *Toxoplasma gondii* Infection
Avoid contact with materials potentially contaminated with cat feces, especially handling of cat litter and gardening; gloves are advised when these activities are necessary
Disinfect cat litter box with near-boiling water for 5 min before handling
Avoid mucous membrane contact when handling raw meat
Wash hands thoroughly after contact with raw meat
Kitchen surfaces and utensils that have come in contact with raw meat should be washed
Cook meat to 66° C or "well done" (meat that is smoked or cured in brine may be infectious)
Avoid ingestion of dried meat
Wash fruits and vegetables before consumption
Refrain from skinning animals

Adapted from Liesenfeld O, Remington JS. Toxoplasmosis. In: Faro S, Soper D, eds. Infectious Diseases in Women. Philadelphia: WB Saunders Company; 2001:75.

or vegetables, eggs should not be eaten raw, and unpasteurized milk (particularly milk from goats) should be avoided. Vectors such as flies and cockroaches should be controlled. Areas contaminated with cat feces should be avoided altogether. Disposable gloves should be worn while disposing of cat litter material, working in the garden, or cleaning a child's sandbox. Oocysts are killed if the cat litter pan is soaked in nearly boiling water for 5 minutes. If the litter pan is cleaned every day, oocysts do not have a chance to sporulate. Serologic testing of cats is unwarranted because testing does not show whether the infected cat is excreting oocysts.

Serologic Screening and Prophylaxis

Acute *Toxoplasma gondii* Infection or Toxoplasmosis in an Immunodeficient Patient

Transmission of *T. gondii* and death as a result of the infection have resulted from the transfusion of leukocyte-rich blood products and by organ transplantation in immunodeficient patients. Transmission of infection by these routes may occur frequently enough to warrant screening for antibody to *T. gondii* in blood product donors and possibly to exclude seropositive people as organ donors to seronegative potential recipients whenever feasible.

Primary prophylaxis can prevent toxoplasmosis in patients dually infected with HIV and *T. gondii* (see "Toxoplasmosis in an Immunodeficient Patient" in the section on treatment). Prophylactic treatment (pyrimethamine, 25 mg orally every day for 6 weeks after transplantation) has been used with apparent success in seronegative recipients of hearts transplanted from seropositive donors.[351] TMP-SMX used for *P. carinii* pneumonia prophylaxis in solid organ transplant patients also is effective as primary prophylaxis against *T. gondii* and can be used without addition of pyrimethamine. Primary prophylaxis in bone marrow transplantation and HSCT patients is particularly challenging because TMP-SMX cannot be used safely early (i.e., before engraftment), whereas in patients with all other transplant organs, it can be used immediately after transplantation.

Congenital *Toxoplasma gondii* Infection or Toxoplasmosis

Congenital toxoplasmosis is a preventable disease. It is the responsibility of physicians who care for pregnant women to educate them on how they can prevent themselves from becoming infected (and not place their fetus at risk). A lack of adoption of a systematic serologic screening program in the United States leaves education as the principal means of preventing this disease. If physicians choose to screen patients serologically, the appropriate tests must be used, the laboratory performing the tests must be competent, and the test results must be interpreted correctly. In some countries (e.g., France and Austria), initially seronegative pregnant women are tested monthly during gestation; this schedule is optimal for detecting infection early enough to institute proper medical management. For further discussion and recommendations

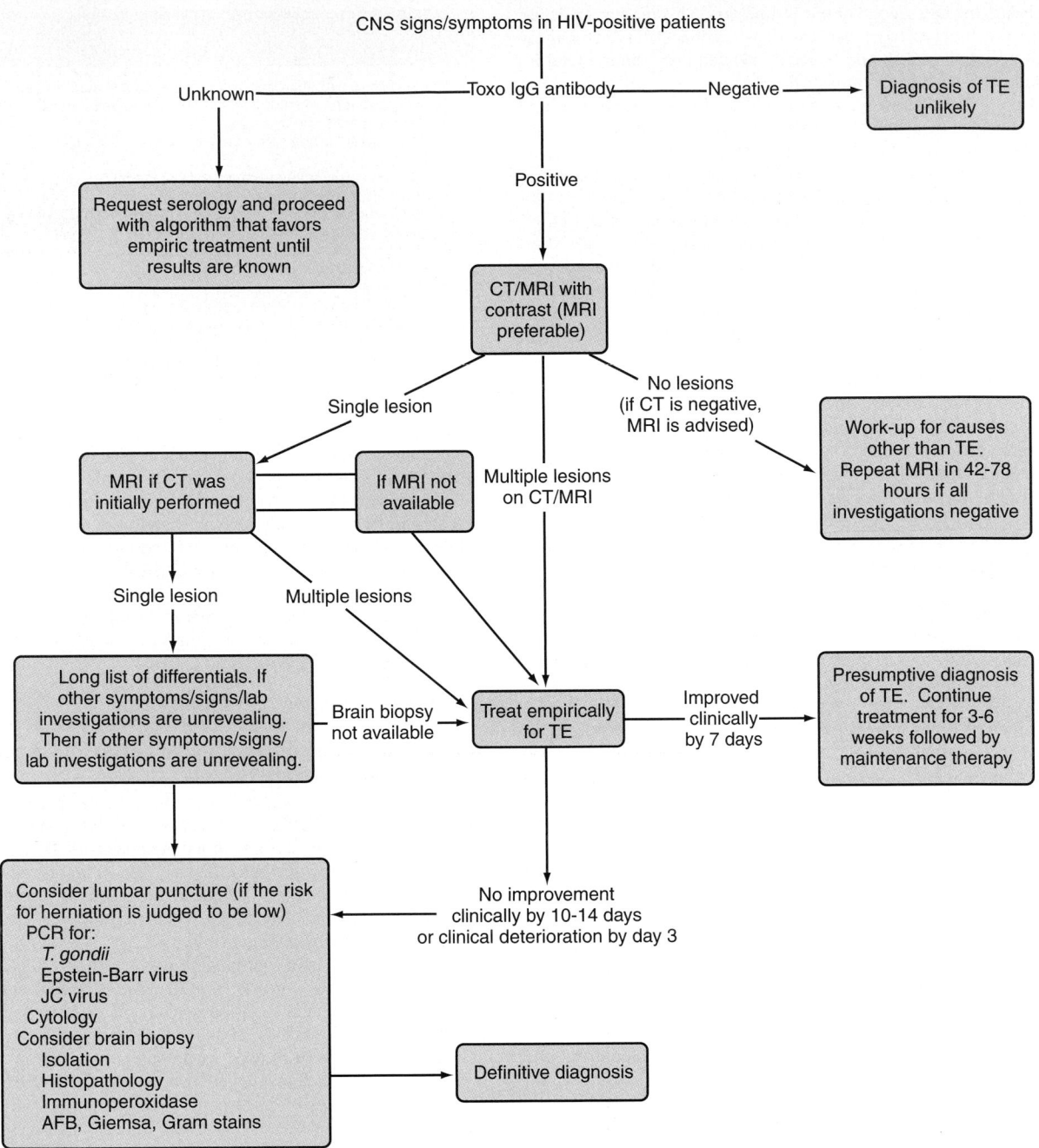

FIGURE 276-6. Treatment algorithm for human immunodeficiency virus (HIV)–infected patients with central nervous system (CNS) symptoms or signs that potentially might be toxoplasmic encephalitis (TE). AFB, acid-fast bacilli; CT, computed tomography; MRI, magnetic resonance imaging; PCR, polymerase chain reaction.

regarding serologic screening, see Remington and colleagues.[7] Women identified as possibly having acquired the infection during gestation can be considered for prenatal diagnosis (see "Congenital Infection in the Fetus and Newborn" in "Diagnosis of Specific Clinical Entities"). The appropriate use of prenatal diagnosis can reduce markedly the incidence of clinically significant congenital toxoplasmosis.[178,180,186]

Women with positive results in the initial IgG antibody test should have a test for IgM antibody performed on the same serum sample. If the IgM assay is positive, the specimen should be sent to a reference laboratory for confirmatory testing (Fig. 276-6) (see "*Toxoplasma gondii* Infection in Pregnancy").[209,229] In patients with IgG antibodies at any titer, a negative IgM antibody test result in the first trimester,

and no clinical signs of acute toxoplasmosis, no further testing would be necessary because the probability of acute acquired infection in these women is extremely low. Given the same circumstances in the second trimester of pregnancy, a negative IgM test result rules out, for practical purposes, recent acquisition of acute infection. A negative IgM test in the third trimester may occur in a patient who acquired the infection earlier in gestation.

The incidence of congenital toxoplasmosis has been shown to be lower in infants born of women who acquire the infection during gestation and are treated with spiramycin.[181,184] Results of a study in France[186] on the incidence of *T. gondii* infection in the fetus of women whose date of acquiring the infection during the gestation was known and who were treated with spiramycin are shown in Table 276-4.

TABLE 276-4 Incidence of Congenital Toxoplasmosis in 2243 Fetuses According to Gestational Age at the Time of Maternal Infection[*]

Weeks of Gestation	Infected Fetuses	All Fetuses	Incidence (%)
0-2	0	100	0
3-6	6	384	1.6
7-10	9	503	1.8
11-14	37	511	7.2
15-18	49	392	13
19-22	44	237	19
23-26[†]	30	116	26
Total	175	2243	7.8

[*]Maternal infection was treated with spiramycin, 1 g tid.
[†] Insufficient data were available after the 32nd week.
Adapted from Hohlfeld P, Daffos F, Thulliez P, et al. Fetal toxoplasmosis: Outcome of pregnancy and infant follow-up after in utero treatment. J Pediatr. 1989;115:765-769.

Studies have suggested that prenatal treatment with spiramycin does not result in significantly lower rates of *T. gondii* vertical transmission.[343-346] These studies have serious limitations in their design, including but not limited to, small sample size, high variability in the method used to diagnose acute infection among different centers, lack of monitoring maternal drug compliance, and short follow-up of the cohort of infected children (see "Treatment"). The current policy for women with highly suspected or confirmed acute toxoplasmosis during the first or second trimesters is to receive spiramycin until delivery, unless a positive prenatal diagnosis is made, in which case pyrimethamine-sulfadiazine should be instituted until delivery. These studies provide no convincing evidence that these recommendations should be changed.[347]

In pregnant women infected with HIV and *T. gondii,* we recommend that primary prophylaxis against *T. gondii* be introduced when the CD4[+] count declines to less than 200/mm.[3] If the patient is receiving TMP-SMX, additional prophylaxis probably is not necessary. Otherwise, spiramycin can be used at a dose of 3 g/day.

REFERENCES

1. Nicolle C, Manceaux L. Sur une infection a corps de Leishman (ou organismes voisins) du gondi. Compte rendu hebdomadaire des seances de l'Academie des sciences 1908;146:207-209.
2. Janku J. Pathogenesa a pathologicka anatomie tak nazvaneho vrozeneho kolobomu zlute skvrny v oku normalne velikem a mikrophthalmickem s nalezem parazitu v sitnici. Cas Lek Ces. 1923;62:1021-1027, 1054-1059, 1081-1085, 1111-1115, 1138-1144.
3. Wolf A, Cowen D, Paige BH. Toxoplasmic encephalomyelitis: III. A new case of granulomatous encephalomyelitis due to a protozoon. Am J Pathol. 1939;15:657-694.
4. Vietzke WM, Gelderman AH, Grimley PM, et al. Toxoplasmosis complicating malignancy: Experience at the National Cancer Institute. Cancer. 1968;21:816-827.
5. Israelski DM, Remington JS. Toxoplasmosis in the non-AIDS immunocompromised host. In: Remington J, Swartz M, eds. Current Clinical Topics in Infectious Diseases, v. 13. London: Blackwell Scientific Publications, 1993:322-356.
6. Luft BJ, Conley F, Remington JS, et al. Outbreak of central-nervous-system toxoplasmosis in western Europe and North America. Lancet. 1983;1:781-784.
7. Remington JS, McLeod R, Thulliez P, et al. Toxoplasmosis. In: Remington JS, Klein J, eds. Infectious Diseases of the Fetus and Newborn Infant. Philadelphia: WB Saunders; 2001:205-346.
8. Holland GN. Reconsidering the pathogenesis of ocular toxoplasmosis. Am J Ophthalmol. 1999;128:502-505.
9. Dubey JP, Lindsay DS, Speer CA. Structures of *Toxoplasma gondii* tachyzoites, bradyzoites, and sporozoites and biology and development of tissue cysts. Clin Microbiol Rev. 1998;11:267-299.
10. Sibley LD, Boothroyd JC. Virulent strains of *Toxoplasma gondii* comprise a single clonal lineage. Nature. 1992;359:82-85.
11. Howe DK, Honore S, Derouin F, et al. Determination of genotypes of *Toxoplasma gondii* strains isolated from patients with toxoplasmosis. J Clin Microbiol. 1997;35:1411-1414.
12. Fuentes I, Rubio JM, Ramirez C, et al. Genotypic characterization of *Toxoplasma gondii* strains associated with human toxoplasmosis in Spain: Direct analysis from clinical samples. J Clin Microbiol. 2001;39:1566-1570.
13. Ajzenberg D, Cogne N, Paris L, et al. Genotype of 86 *Toxoplasma gondii* isolates associated with human congenital toxoplasmosis, and correlation with clinical findings. J Infect Dis. 2002;186:684-689.
14. Boothroyd JC, Grigg ME. Population biology of *Toxoplasma gondii* and its relevance to human infection: Do different strains cause different disease? Curr Opin Microbiol. 2002;5:438-442.
15. Radke JR, Striepen B, Guerini MN, et al. Defining the cell cycle for the tachyzoite stage of *Toxoplasma gondii*. Mol Biochem Parasitol. 2001;115:165-175.
16. Dubey JP. Advances in the life cycle of *Toxoplasma gondii*. Int J Parasitol. 1998;28:1019-1024.
17. Barragan A, Sibley LD. Transepithelial migration of *Toxoplasma gondii* is linked to parasite motility and virulence. J Exp Med. 2002;195:1625-1633.
18. Dubey JP. Advances in the life cycle of *Toxoplasma gondii*. Int J Parasitol. 1998;28:1019-1024.
19. Conley FK, Jenkins KA, Remington JS. *Toxoplasma gondii* infection of the central nervous system: Use of the peroxidase-antiperoxidase method to demonstrate toxoplasma in formalin fixed, paraffin embedded tissue sections. Hum Pathol. 1981;12:690-698.
20. Remington JS, Cavanaugh EN. Isolation of the encysted form of *Toxoplasma gondii* from human skeletal muscle and brain. N Engl J Med. 1965;273:1308-1310.
21. Dubey J, Thayer D. Killing of different strains of *Toxoplasma gondii* tissue cysts by irradiation under defined conditions. J Parasitol. 1994;80:764-767.
22. Dubey J, Kotula A, Sharar A, et al. Effect of high temperature on infectivity of *Toxoplasma gondii* tissue cysts in pork. J Parasitol. 1990;76:201.
23. Jacobs L, Remington JS, Melton ML. The resistance of the encysted form of *Toxoplasma gondii*. J Parasitol. 1960;46:11-21.
24. Ferguson DJP, Graham DI, Hutchinson WM. Pathological changes in the brains of mice infected with *Toxoplasma gondii*: A histological immunocytochemical and ultra structural study. Int J Exp Pathol. 1991;72:463-474.
25. Sims TA, Hay J, Talbot IC. An electron microscope and immunohistochemical study of the intracellular location of *Toxoplasma* tissue cysts within the brains of mice with congenital toxoplasmosis. Br J Exp Pathol. 1989;70:317-325.
26. Jones TC, Bienz KA, Erb P. In vitro cultivation of *Toxoplasma gondii* cysts in astrocytes in the prescence of gamma interferon. Infect Immun. 1986;51:146-156.
27. Ferguson DJ, Hutchison WM, Pettersen E. Tissue cyst rupture in mice chronically infected with *Toxoplasma gondii*. Parasitol Res. 1989;75:599-603.
28. Neu HC. Toxoplasmosis transmitted at autopsy. JAMA. 1967;202:284-285.
29. Dubey J. Toxoplasmosis. J Am Vet Med Assoc. 1994;205:1593-1598.
30. Desmonts G, Couvreur J, Alison F, et al. Etude epidemiologique sur la toxoplasmose: L'influence de la cuisson des viandes de boucherie sur la frequence de l'infectin humaine. Rev Française d'Études Clin Biol. 1965;10:952-958.
31. Dubey JP, Gamble HR, Hill D, et al. High prevalence of viable *Toxoplasma gondii* infection in market weight pigs from a farm in Massachusetts. J Parasitol. 2002;88:1234-1238.
32. Hill D, Dubey JP. *Toxoplasma gondii*: Transmission, diagnosis and prevention. Clin Microbiol Infect. 2002;8:634-640.
33. Remington JS. Toxoplasmosis and congenital infection. Intra-uterine Infection. Birth Defects. Original Article Series. 1968;4:47-56.
34. Aspinall TV, Marlee D, Hyde JE, et al. Prevalence of *Toxoplasma gondii* in commercial meat products as monitored by polymerase chain reaction—food for thought? Int J Parasitol. 2002;32:1193-1199.
35. Davies PR, Morrow WE, Deen J, et al. Seroprevalence of *Toxoplasma gondii* and *Trichinella spiralis* in finishing swine raised in different production systems in North Carolina, USA. Prev Vet Med. 1998;36:67-76.
36. Riemann HP, Meyer ME, Theis JH, et al. Toxoplasmosis in an infant fed unpasteurized goat milk. J Pediatr. 1975;87:573-576.
37. Sacks JJ, Roberto RR, Brooks NF. Toxoplasmosis infection associated with raw goat's milk. JAMA. 1982;248:1728-1732.
38. Dubey JP, Graham DH, Blackston CR, et al. Biological and genetic characterisation of *Toxoplasma gondii* isolates from chickens (*Gallus domesticus*) from Sao Paulo, Brazil: Unexpected findings. Int J Parasitol. 2002;32:99-105.
39. Swartzberg JE, Remington JS. Transmission of *Toxoplasma*. Am J Dis Child. 1975;129:777-779.
40. Bowie WR, King AS, Werker DH, et al. Outbreak of toxoplasmosis associated with municipal drinking water. Lancet. 1997; 350:173-177.
41. Luft BJ, Remington JS. Acute *Toxoplasma* infection among family members of patients with acute lymphadenopathic toxoplasmosis. Arch Intern Med. 1984;144:53-56.
42. Masur H, Jones TC, Lempert JA, et al. Outbreak of toxoplasmosis in a family and documentation of acquired retinochoroiditis. Am J Med. 1978;64:396-402.
43. Miller MA, Gardner IA, Kreuder C, et al. Coastal freshwater runoff is a risk factor for *Toxoplasma gondii* infection of southern sea otters (*Enhydra lutris nereis*). Int J Parasitol. 2002;32:997-1006.
44. Bahia-Oliveira LM, Jones JL, Azevedo-Silva J, et al. Highly endemic, waterborne toxoplasmosis in north Rio de Janeiro state, Brazil. Emerg Infect Dis. 2003;9:55-62.
45. Smith KL, Wilson M, Hightower AW, et al. Prevalence of *Toxoplasma gondii* antibodies in U.S. military recruits in 1989: Comparison with data published in 1965. Clin Infect Dis. 1996;23:1182-1183.
46. Jones JL, Kruszon-Moran D, Wilson M, et al. *Toxoplasma gondii* infection in the United States: Seroprevalence and risk factors. Am J Epidemiol. 2001;154:357-365.
47. Siegel SE, Lunde MN, Gelderman AH, et al. Transmission of toxoplasmosis by leukocyte transfusion. Blood. 1971;37:388-394.
48. Ryning FW, McLeod R, Maddox JC, et al. Probable transmission of *Toxoplasma gondii* by organ transplantation. Ann Intern Med. 1979;90:47-49.
49. Mele A, Paterson PJ, Prentice HG, et al. Toxoplasmosis in bone marrow transplantation: A report of two cases and systematic review of the literature. Bone Marrow Transplant. 2002;29:691-698.
50. Slavin MA, Meyers JD, Remington JS, et al. *Toxoplasma gondii* infection in marrow transplant recipients: A 20 year experience. Bone Marrow Transplant. 1994;13:549-557.
51. Leport C, Chêne G, Morlat P, et al. Pyrimethamine for primary prophylaxis of toxoplasmic encephalitis in patients with human immunodeficiency virus infection: A double-blind, randomized trial. J Infect Dis. 1996;173:91-97.

52. San-Andres FJ, Rubio R, Castilla J, et al. Incidence of acquired immunodeficiency syndrome-associated opportunistic diseases and the effect of treatment on a cohort of 1115 patients infected with human immunodeficiency virus, 1989-1997. Clin Infect Dis. 2003;36:1177-1185.
53. Luft BJ, Remington JS. Toxoplasmic encephalitis in AIDS (AIDS commentary). Clin Infect Dis. 1992;15:211-222.
54. Abgrall S, Rabaud C, Costagliola D. Incidence and risk factors for toxoplasmic encephalitis in human immunodeficiency virus-infected patients before and during the highly active antiretroviral therapy era. Clin Infect Dis. 2001;33:1747-1755.
55. Jones JL, Sehgal M, Maguire JH. Toxoplasmosis-associated deaths among human immunodeficiency virus-infected persons in the United States, 1992-1998. Clin Infect Dis. 2002;34:1161.
56. Clumeck N. Some aspects of the epidemiology of toxoplasmosis and pneumocystosis in AIDS in Europe. Eur J Clin Microbiol Infect Dis. 1991;10:177-178.
57. Zumla A, Savva D, Wheeler RB, et al. *Toxoplasma* serology in Zambian and Ugandan patients infected with the human immunodeficiency virus. Trans R Soc Trop Med Hyg. 1991;85:227-229.
58. Belanger F, Derouin F, Grangeot-Keros L, et al. Incidence and risk factors of toxoplasmosis in a cohort of human immunodeficiency virus-infected patients: 1988-1995. HEMOCO and SEROCO Study Groups. Clin Infect Dis. 1999;28:575-581.
59. Lucas S, Hounnou A, Peacock C, et al. The mortality and pathology of HIV infection in a West African city. AIDS. 1993;7:1569-1579.
60. Wallace MR, Rossetti RJ, Olson PE. Cats and toxoplasmosis risk in HIV-infected adults. JAMA. 1993;269:76-77.
61. Ruskin J, Remington JS. Toxoplasmosis in the compromised host. Ann Intern Med. 1976;84:193-199.
62. Jones TC, Yeh S, Hirsch JG. The interaction between *Toxoplasma gondii* and mammalian cells: I. Mechanism of entry and intracellular fate of the parasite. J Exp Med. 1972;136:1157-1172.
63. Murray HW, Nathans CF, Cohn ZA. Macrophages oxygen-dependent antimicrobial activity: IV. Role of endogenous scavengers of oxygen intermediates. J Exp Med. 1980;152:1610-1624.
64. Sibley LD, Weidner E, Krahenbuhl JL. Phagosome acidification blocked by intracellular *Toxoplasma gondii*. Nature 1985;315:416-419.
65. Adams LB, Hibbs JB Jr, Taintor RR, et al. Microbiostatic effect of murine-activated macrophages for *Toxoplasma gondii*. J Immunol. 1990;144:2725-2729.
66. Pfefferkorn ER. Interferon gamma blocks the growth of *Toxoplasma gondii* in human fibroblasts by inducing the host cells to degrade tryptophan. Proc Natl Acad Sci U S A. 1984;81:908-912.
67. Schreiber RD, Feldman HA. Identification of the activator system for antibody to *Toxoplasma* as the classical complement pathway. J Infect Dis. 1980;141:366-369.
68. Remington JS, Jacobs L, Kaufman HE. Studies on chronic toxoplasmosis: The relation of infective dose to residual infection and to the possibility of congenital transmission. Am J Ophthalmol. 1958;46:261-267.
69. Hofflin JM, Conley FK, Remington JS. Murine model of intracerebral toxoplasmosis. J Infect Dis. 1987;155:550-557.
70. Hofflin JM, Remington JS. Tissue culture isolation of *Toxoplasma* from blood of a patient with AIDS. Arch Intern Med. 1985;145:925-926.
71. Tirard V, Niel G, Rosenheim M, et al. Diagnosis of toxoplasmosis in patients with AIDS by isolation of the parasite from the blood. N Engl J Med. 1991;324:632.
72. Murray H, Rubin BY, Masur H, et al. Impaired production of lymphokines and immune (gamma) interferon in the acquired immunodeficiency syndrome. N Engl J Med. 1984;310:883.
73. Murray H, Welte K, Jacobs J, et al. Production and in vitro response to interleukin-2 in the acquired immunodeficiency syndrome. J Clin Invest. 1985;76:1959-1964.
74. Murray HW, Scavuzzo D, Jacobs JL, et al. In vitro and in vivo activation of human mononuclear phagocytes by interferon-gamma: Studies with normal and AIDS monocytes. J Immunol. 1987;138:2457-2462.
75. Pomeroy C, Filice G, Hitt J, et al. Cytomegalovirus-induced reactivation of *Toxoplasma gondii* in mice: Lung lymphocyte phenotypes and suppressor function. J Infect Dis. 1992;166:677-681.
76. Subauste CS, Wessendarp M, Sorensen RU, et al. CD40-CD40 ligand interaction is central to cell-mediated immunity against *Toxoplasma gondii*: Patients with hyper IgM syndrome have a defective type 1 immune response that can be restored by soluble CD40 ligand trimer. J Immunol. 1999;162:6690-6700.
77. Levy J, Espanol-Boren T, Thomas C, et al. Clinical spectrum of X-linked hyper-IgM syndrome. J Pediatr. 1997;131:47-54.
78. Subauste CS, Wessendarp M, Smulian AG, et al. Role of CD40 ligand signaling in defective type 1 cytokine response in human immunodeficiency virus infection. J Infect Dis. 2001;183:1722-1731.
79. Hunter CA, Remington JS. Immunopathogenesis of toxoplasmic encephalitis. J Infect Dis. 1994;170:1057-1067.
80. Gazzinelli R, Hieny S, Wynn T, et al. Interleukin 12 is required for the T-lymphocyte-independent induction of interferon g by an intracellular parasite and induces resistance in T-cell-deficient hosts. Proc Natl Acad Sci U S A. 1993;90:6115-6119.
81. Suzuki Y, Orellana MA, Schreiber RD, et al. Interferon-γ: The major mediator of resistance against *Toxoplasma gondii*. Science. 1988;240:516-518.
82. Suzuki Y, Conley FK, Remington JS. Importance of endogenous IFN-γ for prevention of toxoplasmic encephalitis in mice. J Immunol 1989;143:2045-2050.
83. Suzuki Y, Conley FK, Remington JS. Treatment of toxoplasmic encephalitis in mice with recombinant gamma interferon. Infect Immun. 1990;58:3050-3055.
84. Sibley LD, Adams LB, Fukutomi Y, et al. Tumor necrosis factor-γ triggers antitoxoplasmal activity of IFN-γ primed macrophages. J Immunol. 1991;147:2340-2345.
85. Langermans J, van der Hulst M, Nibbering P, et al. IFN-γ induced l-arginine-dependent toxoplasmastatic activity in murine peritoneal macrophages is mediated by endogenous tumor necrosis factor. J Immunol. 1992;148:568-574.
86. Chang H, Pechere J, Piguet P. Role of tumour necrosis factor in chronic murine *Toxoplasma gondii* encephalitis. Immunol Infect Dis. 1992;2:61-68.
87. Suzuki Y, Yang Q, Yang S, et al. IL-4 is protective against development of toxoplasmic encephalitis. J Immunol. 1996;157:2564-2569.
88. Suzuki Y, Rani S, Liesenfeld O, et al. Impaired resistance to the development of toxoplasmic encephalitis in interleukin-6-deficient mice. Infect Immun. 1997;65:2339-2345.
89. Kasper LH, Matsuura T, Khan IA. IL-7 stimulates protective immunity in mice against the intracellular pathogen, *Toxoplasma gondii*. J Immunol. 1995;155:4798-4804.
90. Hunter CA, Neyer LA, Gabriel KE, et al. The role of CD28/B7 interaction in the regulation of NK cell responses during infection with *Toxoplasma gondii*. J Immunol. 1997;158:2285-2293.
91. Bohne W, Hessemann J, Gross U. Reduced replication of *Toxoplasma gondii* is necessary for induction of bradyzoite-specific antigens: A possible role for nitric oxide in triggering stage conversion. Infect Immun. 1994;62:1761-1767.
92. Chao C, Gekker G, Hu S, et al. Human microglial cell defense against *Toxoplasma gondii*. J Immunol. 1994;152:1246-1252.
93. Khan IA, Matssuura T, Fonseka S, et al. Production of nitric oxide (NO) is not essential for protection against acute *Toxoplasma gondii* infection in IRF-1$^{-/-}$ mice[1]. J Immunol. 1996;156:636-643.
94. Scharton-Kersten TM, Wynn TA, Denkers EY, et al. In the absence of endogenous IFN-γ mice develop unimpaired IL-12 reponses to *Toxoplasma gondii* while failing to control acute infection. J Immunol. 1996;157:4045-4054.
95. Hayashi S, Chan C, Gazzinelli R, et al. Contribution of nitric oxide to the host parasite equilibrium in toxoplasmosis. J Immunol. 1996;156:1476-1481.
96. Scharton-Kersten TM, Yap G, Magram J, et al. Inducible nitric oxide is essential for host control of persistent but not acute infection with the intracellular pathogen *Toxoplasma gondii*. J Exp Med. 1997;185:1261-1273.
97. Pavia CS. Protection against experimental toxoplasmosis by adoptive immunotherapy. J Immunol. 1986;137:2985-2990.
98. Peterson P, Gekker G, Hu S, et al. Human astrocytes inhibit intracellular multiplication of *Toxoplasma gondii* by a nitric oxide-mediated mechanism. J Infect Dis. 1995;171:516-518.
99. Brown CR, McLeod R. Class I MHC genes and CD8$^+$ T cells determine cyst number in *Toxoplasma gondii* infection. J Immunol. 1990;145:3438-3441.
100. Brown C, Hunter C, Estes R, et al. Definitive identification of a gene that confers resistance against *Toxoplasma* cyst burden and encephalitis. Immunology. 1995;85:419-428.
101. Suzuki Y, Joh K, Orellna MA, et al. A gene(s) within the H-2D region determines the development of toxoplasmic encephalitis in mice. Immunology. 1991;74:732-739.
102. Suzuki Y, Wong S-Y, Grumet FC, et al. Evidence for genetic regulation of susceptibility to toxoplasmic encephalitis in AIDS patients. J Infect Dis. 1996;173:265-268.
103. Mack D, Johnson J, Roberts F, et al. HLA-class II genes modify outcome of *Toxoplasma gondii* infection. Int J Parasitol. 1999;29:1351-1358.
104. Montoya JG, Remington JS. Toxoplasmosis of the central nervous system. In: Peterson PK, Remington JS, eds. In Defense of the Brain: Current Concepts in the Immunopathogenesis and Clinical Aspects of CNS Infections. Boston: Blackwell Scientific Publications; 1997:163-188.
105. Frenkel JK. Pathology and pathogenesis of congenital toxoplasmosis. Bull N Y Acad Med. 1974;50:182-191.
106. Liesenfeld O, Wong SY, Remington JS. Toxoplasmosis in the setting of AIDS. In: Bartlett JG, Merigan TC, Bolognesi D, eds. Textbook of AIDS Medicine. Baltimore: Williams & Wilkins; 1999:225-259.
107. Post MJ, Chan JC, Hensley GT, et al. Toxoplasmosis encephalitis in Haitian adults with acquired immunodeficiency syndrome: A clinical-pathologic-CT correlation. AJNR Am J Neuroradiol. 1983;4:155-162.
108. Strittmatter C, Lang W, Wiestler OD, et al. The changing pattern of human immunodeficiency virus associated cerebral toxoplasmosis: A study of 46 postmortem cases. Acta Neuropathol. 1992;83:475-481.
109. Parmley SF, Goebel FD, Remington JS. Detection of *Toxoplasma gondi* DNA in cerebrospinal fluid from AIDS patients by polymerase chain reaction. J Clin Microbiol. 1992;30:3000-3002.
110. Gray F, Gherardi R, Wingate E, et al. Diffuse "encephalitic" cerebral toxoplasmosis in AIDS. J Neurol. 1989;236:273-277.
111. Mariuz P, Bosler EM, Luft BJ. *Toxoplasma* pneumonia. Semin Respir Infect 1997;12:40-43.
112. Bretagne S, Costa J-M, Fleury-Feith J, et al. Quantitative competitive PCR with bronchoalveolar lavage fluid for diagnosis of toxoplasmosis in AIDS patients. J Clin Microbiol. 1995;33:1662-1664.
113. Holland GN, O'Connor GR, Belfort R Jr, et al. Toxoplasmosis. In: Pepose JS, Holland GN, Wilhelmus KR, eds. Ocular Infection and Immunity. St. Louis: Mosby-Year Book; 1996:1183-1223.
114. Danise A, Cinque P, Vergani S, et al. Use of the polymerase chain reaction assays of aqueous humor in the differential diagnosis of retinitis in patients infected with human immunodeficiency virus. Clin Infect Dis. 1997;24:1100-1106.
115. Montoya JG, Parmley S, Liesenfeld O, et al. Use of the polymerase chain reaction for diagnosis of ocular toxoplasmosis. Ophthalmology. 1999;106:1554-1563.
116. Silveira C, Belfort R Jr, Muccioli C, et al. The effect of long-term intermittent trimethoprim/sulfamethoxazole treatment on recurrences of toxoplasmic retinochoroiditis. Am J Ophthalmol. 2002;134:41-46.

117. Gherardi R, Baudrimont M, Lionnet F, et al. Skeletal muscle toxoplasmosis in patients with acquired immunodeficiency syndrome: A clinical and pathological study. Ann Neurol. 1992;32:535-542.

118. Calico I, Caballero E, Martinez O, et al. Isolation of *Toxoplasma gondii* from immunocompromised patients using tissue culture. Infection. 1991;19:340-342.

119. Montoya JG, Jordan R, Lingamneni S, et al. Toxoplasmic myocarditis and polymyositis in patients with acute acquired toxoplasmosis diagnosed during life. Clin Infect Dis. 1997;24:676-683.

120. Roldan EO, Moskowitz L, Hensley GT. Pathology of the heart in acquired immunodeficiency syndrome. Arch Pathol Lab Med. 1987;111:943-946.

121. Adair OV, Randive N, Krasnow N. Isolated *Toxoplasma* myocarditis in acquired immune deficiency syndrome. Am Heart J. 1989;118:856-857.

122. Dorfman RF, Remington JS. Value of lymph-node biopsy in the diagnosis of acute acquired toxoplasmosis. N Engl J Med. 1973;289:878-881.

123. Negri I, Gualdi C, Negriaagualdi C. Pseudomononucleosi infettiva in corso di malattia linfomatosa [Infectious pseudomononucleosis in lymphomatous diseases]. Minerva Med. 1974;65:78-83.

124. Weiss L, Chen Y, Berry G, et al. Infrequent detection of *Toxoplasma gondii* genome in toxoplasmic lymphadenitis: A polymerase chain reaction study. Hum Pathol. 1992;23:154-158.

125. Pauwels A, Meyohas MC, Eliaszewicz M, et al. *Toxoplasma* colitis in the acquired immunodeficiency syndrome. Am J Gastroenterol. 1992;87:518-519.

126. Smart PE, Weinfeld A, Thompson NE, et al. Toxoplasmosis of the stomach: A cause of antral narrowing. Radiology. 1990;174:369-370.

127. Garcia LW, Hemphill RB, Marasco WA, et al. Acquired immunodeficiency syndrome with disseminated toxoplasmosis presenting as an acute pulmonary and gastrointestinal illness. Arch Pathol Lab Med. 1991;115:459-463.

128. Brion J-P, Pelloux H, Le Marc'hadour F, et al. Acute *Toxoplasmic* hepatitis in a patient with AIDS. Clin Infect Dis. 1992;15:183-184.

129. Bergin C, Murphy M, Lyons D, et al. Toxoplasma pneumonitis: Fatal presentation of disseminated toxoplasmosis in a patient with AIDS. Eur Respir J. 1992;5:1018-1020.

130. Crider SR, Horstman WG, Massey GS. Toxoplasma orchitis: Report of a case and a review of the literature. Am J Med. 1988;85:421-424.

131. Groll A, Schneider M, Althoff PH, et al. Morphology and clinical significance of AIDS-related lesions in the adrenals and pituitary. Dtsch Med Wschr. 1990;115:483-488.

132. Patrick AL, Roberts LA, Burton EN, et al. Focal and segmental glomerulosclerosis in the acquired immunodeficiency syndrome. West Ind Med J. 1986;1986:200-202.

133. Renold C, Sugar A, Chave J-P, et al. *Toxoplasma* encephalitis in patients with the acquired immunodeficiency syndrome. Medicine. 1992;71:224-239.

134. Remington JS. Toxoplasmosis in the adult. Bull N Y Acad Med.1974;50:211-227.

135. McCabe RE, Brooks RG, Dorfman RF, et al. Clinical spectrum in 107 cases of toxoplasmic lymphadenopathy. Rev Infect Dis. 1987;9:754-774.

136. Remington JS, Barnett CG, Meikel M, et al. Toxoplasmosis and infectious mononucleosis. Arch Intern Med. 1962;110:744-753.

137. Couvreur J, Thulliez P. Toxoplasmose acquise à localisation oculaire ou neurologique [Acquired toxoplasmosis with ocular or neurologic involvement]. Presse Med. 1996;25:438-442.

138. Montoya JG, Remington JS. Toxoplasmic chorioretinitis in the setting of acute acquired toxoplasmosis. Clin Infect Dis. 1996;23:277-282.

139. Burnett AJ, Shortt SG, Isaac-Renton J, et al. Multiple cases of acquired toxoplasmosis retinitis presenting in an outbreak. Ophthalmology. 1998;105:1032-1037.

140. Montoya JG, Remington JS. Studies on the serodiagnosis of toxoplasmic lymphadenitis. Clin Infect Dis. 1995;20:781-790.

141. Cunningham T. Pancarditis in acute toxoplasmosis. Am J Clin Pathol. 1982;78:403-405.

142. Prado SP, Pacheco VC, Noemi IH, et al. Pericarditis y miocarditis por toxoplasma [Toxoplasma pericarditis and myocarditis]. Rev Chil Pediatr. 1978;49:179-185.

143. Greenlee JE, Johnson WD Jr, Campa JF, et al. Adult toxoplasmosis presenting as polymyositis and cerebellar ataxia. Ann Intern Med. 1975;82:367-371.

144. Palma S, Reyes H, Guzman L, et al. Dermatomiositis y toxoplasmosis [Dermatomyositis and toxoplasmosis]. Rev Med Chil. 1984;111:164-167.

145. Pollock JL. Toxoplasmosis appearing to be dermatomyositis. Arch Dermatol. 1979;115:736-737.

146. Montoya JG, Giraldo LF, Efron B, et al. Infectious complications among 620 consecutive heart transplant patients at Stanford University Medical Center. Clin Infect Dis. 2001;33:629-640.

147. Wreghitt TG, Gray JJ, Pavel P, et al. Efficacy of pyrimethamine for the prevention of donor-acquired *Toxoplasma gondii* infection in heart and heart-lung transplant patients. Transplant Int. 1992;5:197-200.

148. Wreghitt TG, McNeil K, Roth C, et al. Antibiotic prophylaxis for the prevention of donor-acquired *Toxoplasma gondii* infection in transplant patients (Letter; comment). J Infect. 1995;31:253-254.

149. Renoult E, Georges E, Biava MF, et al. Toxoplasmosis in kidney transplant recipients: Report of six cases and review. Clin Infect Dis. 1997;24:625-634.

150. Singer MA, Hagler WS, Grossniklaus HE. *Toxoplasma gondii* retinochoroiditis after liver transplantation. Retina. 1993;13:40-45.

151. Botterel F, Ichai P, Feray C, et al. Disseminated toxoplasmosis, resulting from infection of allograft, after orthotopic liver transplantation: Usefulness of quantitative PCR. J Clin Microbiol. 2002;40:1648-1650.

152. Martino R, Bretagne S, Rovira M, et al. Toxoplasmosis after hematopoietic stem transplantation: Report of a 5-year survey from the Infectious Diseases Working Party of the European Group for Blood and Marrow Transplantation. Bone Marrow Transplant. 2000;25:1111-1114.

153. Sing A, Leitritz L, Roggenkamp A, et al. Pulmonary toxoplasmosis in bone marrow transplant recipients: Report of two cases and review. Clin Infect Dis. 1999;29:429-433.

154. Oksenhendler E, Cadranel J, Sarfati C, et al. *Toxoplasma gondii* pneumonia in patients with the acquired immunodeficiency syndrome. Am J Med. 1990;88:5-18N-5-21N.

155. Mehren M, Burns PJ, Mamani F, et al. Toxoplasmic myelitis mimicking intramedullary spinal cord tumor. Neurology. 1988;38:1648-1650.

156. Herskovitz S, Siegel SE, Schneider AT, et al. Spinal cord toxoplasmosis in AIDS. Neurology. 1989;39:1552-1553.

157. Overhage JM, Greist A, Brown DR. Conus medullaris syndrome resulting from *Toxoplasma gondii* infection in a patient with the acquired immunodeficiency syndrome. Am J Med. 1990;89:814-815.

158. Rabaud C, May T, Lucet JC, et al. Pulmonary toxoplasmosis in patients infected with human immunodeficiency virus: A French national study. Clin Infect Dis. 1996;23:1249-1254.

159. Derouin F, Sarfati C, Beauvais B, et al. Prevalence of pulmonary toxoplasmosis in HIV-infected patients. AIDS. 1990;4:1036.

160. Holland G, Engstrom R Jr, Glasgow B, et al. Ocular toxoplasmosis in patients with acquired immunodeficiency syndrome. Am J Ophthalmol. 1988;106:653-667.

161. Heinemann MH, Gold JM, Maisel J. Bilateral toxoplasma retinochoroiditis in a patient with acquired immune deficiency syndrome. Retina. 1986;6:224-227.

162. Louie JK, Hsu LC, Osmond DH, et al. Trends in causes of death among persons with acquired immunodeficiency syndrome in the era of highly active antiretroviral therapy, San Francisco, 1994-1998. J Infect Dis. 2002;186:1023-1027.

163. Furrer H, Opravil M, Bernasconi E, et al. Stopping primary prophylaxis in HIV-1-infected patients at high risk of *Toxoplasma* encephalitis. Swiss HIV Cohort Study. Lancet. 2000;355:2217-2218.

164. Kirk O, Reiss P, Uberti-Foppa C, et al. Safe interruption of maintenance therapy against previous infection with four common HIV-associated opportunistic pathogens during potent antiretroviral therapy. Ann Intern Med. 2002;137:239-250.

165. Soriano V, Dona C, Rodriguez-Rosado R, et al. Discontinuation of secondary prophylaxis for opportunistic infections in HIV-infected patients receiving highly active antiretroviral therapy. AIDS. 2000;14:383-386.

166. Stout JE, Lai JC, Giner J, et al. Reactivation of retinal toxoplasmosis despite evidence of immune response to highly active antiretroviral therapy. Clin Infect Dis. 2002;35:e37-e39.

167. Silveira C, Belfort R Jr, Burnier M Jr, et al. Acquired toxoplasmic infection as the cause of toxoplasmic retinochoroiditis in families. Am J Ophthalmol. 1988;106:362-364.

168. Glasner PD, Silveira C, Kruszon-Moran D, et al. An unusually high prevalence of ocular toxoplasmosis in Southern Brazil. Am J Ophthalmol. 1992;114:136-144.

169. Silveira C, Belfort R Jr, Muccioli C, et al. A follow-up study of *Toxoplasma gondii* infection in southern Brazil. Am J Ophthalmol. 2001;131:351-354.

170. Nussenblatt R, Belfort R Jr. Ocular toxoplasmosis. JAMA. 1994;271:302-307.

171. Bosch-Driessen LE, Berendschot TT, Ongkosuwito JV, et al. Ocular toxoplasmosis: Clinical features and prognosis of 154 patients. Ophthalmology. 2002;109:869-878.

172. Bosch-Driessen LH, Plaisier MB, Stilma JS, et al. Reactivations of ocular toxoplasmosis after cataract extraction. Ophthalmology. 2002;109:41-45.

173. Johnson MW, Greven CM, Jaffe GJ, et al. Atypical, severe toxoplasmic retinochoroiditis in elderly patients. Ophthalmology. 1997;104:48-57.

174. Gavinet MF, Robert F, Firtion G, et al. Congenital toxoplasmosis due to maternal reinfection during pregnancy. J Clin Microbiol. 1997;35:1276-1277.

175. Hennequin C, Dureau P, N'Guyen L, et al. Congenital toxoplasmosis acquired from an immune woman. Pediatr Infect Dis. 1997;16:75-76.

176. Vogel N, Kirisits M, Michael E, et al. Congenital toxoplasmosis transmitted from an immunologically competent mother infected before conception. Clin Infect Dis. 1996;23:1055-1060.

177. Minkoff H, Remington JS, Holman S, et al. Vertical transmission of toxoplasma by human immunodeficiency virus-infected women. Am J Obstet Gynecol. 1997;176:555-559.

178. Daffos F, Forestier F, Capella-Pavlovsky M, et al. Prenatal management of 746 pregnancies at risk for congenital toxoplasmosis. N Engl J Med. 1988;318:271-275.

179. Desmonts G. Acquired toxoplasmosis in pregnant women: Evaluation of the frequency of transmission of toxoplasma and of congenital toxoplasmosis. Lyon Med. 1982;248:115-123.

180. Desmonts G, Daffos F, Forestier F, et al. Prenatal diagnosis of congenital toxoplasmosis. Lancet. 1985;1:500-504.

181. Desmonts G, Couvreur J. Congenital toxoplasmosis: A prospective study of the offspring of 542 women who acquired toxoplasmosis during pregnancy. In: Thalhammer O, Baumgarten K, Pollak A, eds. Perinatal Medicine, (6th European Congress, Vienna). Stuttgart, Georg Thieme Publishers, 1979:51-60.

182. Koppe JG, Loewer-Sieger DH, De Roever-Bonnet H. Results of 20-year follow-up of congenital toxoplasmosis. Am J Ophthalmol. 1986;101:248-249.

183. Wilson CB, Remington JS, Stagno S, et al. Development of adverse sequelae in children born with subclinical congenital *Toxoplasma* infection. Pediatrics. 1980;66:767-774.

184. Forestier F. Les foetopathies infectieuses—prevention, diagnostic prenatal, attitude pratique [Fetal diseases, prenatal diagnoses and practical measures]. Presse Med. 1991;20:1448-1454.

185. Hohlfeld P, Daffos F, Thulliez P, et al. Fetal toxoplasmosis: Outcome of pregnancy and infant follow-up after in utero treatment. J Pediatr. 1989;115:765-769.

186. Hohlfeld P, Daffos F, Costa J-M, et al. Prenatal diagnosis of congenital toxoplasmosis with polymerase-chain-reaction test on amniotic fluid. N Engl J Med. 1994;331:695-699.

187. Couvreur J, Desmonts G, Tournier G, et al. Etude d'une serie homogene de 210 cas de toxoplasmose congenitale chez des nourrissons ages de 0 a 11 mois et depistes de facon prospective [A homogeneous series of 210 cases of congenital toxoplasmosis in 0 to 11-month-old infants detected prospectively]. Ann Pediatr (Paris). 1984;31:815-819.

188. De Roever-Bonnet H, Koppe JG, Loewer-Sieger DH. Follow-up of children with congenital *Toxoplasma* infection and children who become serologically negative after 1 year of age, all born in 1964-1965. In: Thalhammer O, Baumgarten K, Pollak A, eds. Perinatal Medicine (6th European Congress, Vienna). Stuttgart, Georg Thieme Publishers, 1979:61-75.
189. Labadie MD, Hazemann JJ. Apport des bilans de sante de l'enfant pour le depistage et l'etude epidemiologique de la toxoplasmose congenitale [Contribution of health check-ups in children to the detection and epidemiologic study of congenital toxoplasmosis]. Ann Pediatr (Paris). 1984;31:823-828.
190. McAuley J, Boyer KM, Patel D, et al. Early and longitudinal evaluations of treated infants and children and untreated historical patients with congenital toxoplasmosis: The Chicago Collaborative Treatment Trial. Clin Infect Dis. 1994;18:38-72.
191. Mitchell CD, Erlich SS, Mastrucci MT, et al. Congenital toxoplasmosis occurring in infants perinatally infected with human immunodeficiency virus 1. Pediatr Infect Dis J. 1990;9:512-518.
192. Montoya JG. Laboratory diagnosis of *Toxoplasma gondii* infection and toxoplasmosis. J Infect Dis. 2002;185:S73-82.
193. Miller MJ, Aronson WJ, Remington JS. Late parasitemia in asymptomatic acquired toxoplasmosis. Ann Intern Med. 1969;71:139-145.
194. Levy RM, Bredesen DE, Rosenblum ML. Opportunistic central nervous system pathology in patients with AIDS. Ann Neurol. 1988;23:S7-S12.
195. Frenkel JK, Piekarski G. The demonstration of *Toxoplasma* and other organisms by immunofluorescence: A pitfall (Editorial). J Infect Dis. 1978;138:265-266.
196. Sun T, Greenspan J, Tenenbaum M, et al. Diagnosis of cerebral toxoplasmosis using fluorescein-labeled antitoxoplasma monoclonal antibodies. Am J Surg Pathol. 1986;10:312-316.
197. Cerezo L, Alvarez M, Price G. Electron microscopic diagnosis of cerebral toxoplasmosis: Case report. J Neurosurg. 1985;63:470-472.
198. Luft BJ, Billingham M, Remington JS. Endomyocardial biopsy in the diagnosis of toxoplasmic myocarditis. Transplant Proc. 1986;18:1871-1873.
199. Grover CM, Thulliez P, Remington JS, et al. Rapid prenatal diagnosis of congenital *Toxoplasma* infection by using polymerase chain reaction and amniotic fluid. J Clin Microbiol. 1990;28:2297-2301.
200. Cinque P, Scarpellini P, Vago L, et al. Diagnosis of central nervous system complications in HIV-infected patients: cerebrospinal fluid analysis by the polymerase chain reaction. AIDS. 1997;11:1-17.
201. Dupouy-Camet J, Lavareda de Souza L, Maslo C, et al. Detection of *Toxoplasma gondii* in venous blood from AIDS patients by polymerase chain reaction. J Clin Microbiol. 1993;31:1866-1869.
202. Holliman RE, Johnson JD, Savva D. Diagnosis of cerebral toxoplasmosis in association with AIDS using the polymerase chain reaction. Scand J Infect Dis. 1990;22:243-244.
203. Bretagne S, Costa J, Vidaud M, et al. *Toxoplasma gondii* DNA amplification from bronchoalveolar lavage samples of AIDS patients. Presented at Ninth International Conference on AIDS, Berlin, 1993.
204. Liesenfeld O, Remington JS. Toxoplasmosis. In: Goldman L, Bennett JC, eds. Cecil Textbook of Medicine. Philadelphia: WB Saunders; 1999:1963-1967.
205. Dannemann BR, Israelski DM, Leoung GS, et al. Toxoplasma serology, parasitemia and antigenemia in patients at risk for toxoplasmic encephalitis. AIDS. 1991;5: 1363-1365.
206. Pelloux H, Dupouy-Camet J, Derouin F, et al. A multicentre prospective study for the polymerase chain reaction detection of *Toxoplasma gondii* DNA in blood samples from 186 AIDS patients with suspected toxoplasmic encephalitis. AIDS. 1997;11:1888-1890.
207. Bastien P. Molecular diagnosis of toxoplasmosis. Trans R Soc Trop Med Hyg. 2002; 96(Suppl 1):S205-215.
208. Jones CD, Okhravi N, Adamson P, et al. Comparison of PCR detection methods for B1, P30, and 18S rDNA genes of *T. gondii* in aqueous humor. Invest Ophthalmol Vis Sci. 2000;41:634-644.
209. Liesenfeld O, Press C, Montoya JG, et al. False-positive results in immunoglobulin M (IgM) toxoplasma antibody tests and importance of confirmatory testing: The Platelia toxo IgM test. J Clin Microbiol. 1997;35:174-178.
210. Wilson M, Remington JS, Clavet C, et al. Evaluation of six commercial kits for detection of human immunoglobulin M antibiodies to *Toxoplasma gondii*. J Clin Microbiol. 1997;35:3112-3115.
211. Liesenfeld O, Montoya JG, Kinney S, et al. Effect of testing for IgG avidity in the diagnosis of *Toxoplasma gondii* infection in pregnant women: Experience in a US reference laboratory. J Infect Dis. 2001;183:1248-1253.
212. Liesenfeld O, Montoya JG, Tathineni NJ, et al. Confirmatory serologic testing for acute toxoplasmosis and rate of induced abortions among women reported to have positive *Toxoplasma* immunoglobulin M antibody titers. Am J Obstet Gynecol. 2001;184:140-145.
213. Montoya JG, Liesenfeld O, Kinney S, et al. VIDAS test for avidity of *Toxoplasma*-specific immunoglobulin G for confirmatory testing of pregnant women. J Clin Microbiol. 2002;40:2504-2508.
214. Sabin AB, Feldman HA. Dyes as microchemical indicators of a new immunity phenomenon affecting a protozoan parasite (toxoplasma). Science. 1948;108:660-663.
215. Balsari A, Poli G, Molina V, et al. ELISA for toxoplasma antibody detection: A comparison with other serodiagnostic tests. J Clin Pathol. 1980;33:640-643.
216. Walls KW, Bullock SL, English DK. Use of the enzyme-linked immunosorbent assay (ELISA) and its microadaptation for the serodiagnosis of toxoplasmosis. J Clin Microbiol. 1977;5:273-277.
217. Walton BC, Benchoff BM, Brooks WH. Comparison of the indirect fluorescent antibody test and methylene blue dye test for detection of antibodies to *Toxoplasma gondii*. Am J Trop Med Hyg. 1966;15:149-152.
218. Thulliez P, Remington JS, Santoro F, et al. A new agglutination test for the diagnosis of acute and chronic toxoplasma infection. Pathol Biol. 1986;34:173-177.
219. Anderson SE, Remington JS. The diagnosis of toxoplasmosis. South Med J. 1975;68:1433-1443.
220. Araujo FG, Barnett EV, Gentry LO, et al. False-positive anti-*Toxoplasma* fluorescent-antibody tests in patients with antinuclear antibodies. Appl Microbiol. 1971;22:270-275.
221. Desmonts G, Remington JS. Direct agglutination test for diagnosis of *Toxoplasma* infection: Method for increasing sensitivity and specificity. J Clin Microbiol. 1980;11:562-568.
222. Dannemann BR, Vaughan WC, Thulliez P, et al. Differential agglutination test for diagnosis of recently acquired infection with *Toxoplasma gondii*. J Clin Microbiol. 1990;28:1928-1933.
223. Hedman K, Lappalainen M, Seppala I, et al. Recent primary *Toxoplasma* infection indicated by a low avidity of specific IgG. J Infect Dis. 1989;159:736-739.
224. Lappalainen M, Koskela P, Koskiniemi M, et al. Toxoplasmosis acquired during pregnancy: Improved serodiagnosis based on avidity of IgG. J Infect Dis. 1993;167:691-697.
225. Montoya JG, Huffman HB, Remington JS. Use of the VIDAS Toxo IgG avidity test for the diagnosis of toxoplasmic lymphadenopathy. Presented at Fortieth Annual Meeting of the Infectious Diseases Society of America (IDSA), Chicago, October 24-27, 2002.
226. Pelloux H, Brun E, Vernet G, et al. Determination of anti-*Toxoplasma gondii* immunoglobulin G avidity: Adaptation to the Vidas system (bioMerieux). Diagn Microbiol Infect Dis. 1998;32:69-73.
227. Bobic B, Sibalic D, Djurkovic-Djakovic O. High levels of IgM antibodies specific for *Toxoplasma gondii* in pregnancy 12 years after primary toxplasma infection. Gynecol Obstet Invest. 1991;31:182-184.
228. Wilson M, Ware DA, Walls KW. Evaluation of commercial serodiagnostic kits for toxoplasmosis. J Clin Microbiol. 1987;25:2262-2265.
229. FDA. Public health advisory: Limitations of toxoplasma IgM commercial test kits. US Food and Drug Administration, Center for Devices and Radiological Health. Limitations of Toxoplasma lgM Commercial Test Kits. Rockville, MD: The Center: 1997;1-3, July 25. Available from URL: http://www.fda.gov/cdrh/toxopha.html
230. Welch PC, Masur H, Jones TC, et al. Serologic diagnosis of acute lymphadenopathic toxoplasmosis. J Infect Dis. 1980;142:256-264.
231. Naot Y, Barnett EV, Remington JS. Method for avoiding false-positive results occurring in immunoglobulin M enzyme-linked immunosorbent assays due to presence of both rheumatoid factor and antinuclear antibodies. J Clin Microbiol. 1981;14:73-78.
232. Filice GA, Yeager AS, Remington JS. Diagnostic significance of immunoglobulin M antibodies to *Toxoplasma gondii* detected after separation of immunoglobulin M from immunoglobulin G antibodies. J Clin Microbiol. 1980;12:336-342.
233. Naot Y, Remington JS. An enzyme-linked immunosorbent assay for detection of IgM antibodies to *Toxoplasma gondii*: Use for diagnosis of acute acquired toxoplasmosis. J Infect Dis. 1980;142:757-766.
234. Naot Y, Desmonts G, Remington JS. IgM enzyme-linked immunosorbent assay test for the diagnosis of congenital *Toxoplasma* infection. J Pediatr. 1981;98:32-36.
235. Siegel JP, Remington JS. Comparison of methods for quantitating antigen-specific immunoglobulin M antibody with a reverse enzyme-linked immunosorbent assay. J Clin Microbiol. 1983;18:63-70.
236. Remington JS, Eimstad WM, Araujo FG. Detection of immunoglobulin M antibodies with antigen-tagged latex particles in an immunosorbent assay. J Clin Microbiol. 1983;17:939-941.
237. Plantaz D, Goullier A, Jouk PS, et al. Interet de la methode ISAGA dans le diagnostic precoce de la toxoplasmose congenitale [Value of the immunosorbent agglutination assay (ISAGA) in the early diagnosis of congenital toxoplasmosis]. Pediatrie. 1987;42:387-391.
238. Decoster A, Slizewicz B, Simon J, et al. Platelia-toxo IgA, a new kit for early diagnosis of congenital toxoplasmosis by detection of anti-P30 immunoglobulin A antibodies. J Clin Microbiol. 1991;29:2291-2295.
239. Pinon JM, Thoannes H, Pouletty PH, et al. Detection of IgA specific for toxoplasmosis in serum and cerebrospinal fluid using a non-enzymatic IgA-capture assay. Diagn Immunol. 1986;4:223-227.
240. Stepick-Biek P, Thulliez P, Araujo FG, et al. IgA antibodies for diagnosis of acute congenital and acquired toxoplasmosis. J Infect Dis. 1990;162:270-273.
241. Pinon JM, Toubas D, Marx C, et al. Detection of specific immunoglobulin E in patients with toxoplasmosis. J Clin Microbiol. 1990;28:1739-1743.
242. Wong SY, Hadju M-P, Ramirez R, et al. The role of specific immunoglobulin E in diagnosis of acute toxoplasma infection and toxoplasmosis. J Clin Microbiol. 1993;31:2952-2959.
243. Poirriez J, Toubas D, Marx-Chemia C, et al. Isotypic characterization of anti-*Toxoplasma gondii* antibodies in 18 cases of congenital toxoplasmic chorioretinitis. Acta Ophthalmol. 1988;67:164-168.
244. Foudrinier F, Villena I, Jaussaud R, et al. Clinical value of specific immunoglobulin E detection by enzyme-linked immunosorbent assay in cases of acquired and congenital toxoplasmosis. J Clin Microbiol. 2003;41:1681-1686.
245. Porter SB, Sande M. Toxoplasmosis of the central nervous system in the acquired immunodeficiency syndrome. N Engl J Med. 1992;327:1643-1648.
246. Haverkos HW, Remington JS, Chan JC. Assesment of *Toxoplasma* encephalitis (TE) therapy: A cooperative study. Am J Med. 1987;82:907-914.
247. Levy RM, Rosenbloom S, Perrett LV. Neuroradiologic findings in AIDS: A review of 200 cases. AJNR Am J Neuroradiol. 1986;147:977-983.
248. Post MJ, Kursunoglu SJ, Hensley GT, et al. Cranial CT in acquired immunodeficiency syndrome: Spectrum of diseases and optimal contrast enhancement technique. AJR Am J Roentgenol. 1985;145:929-940.
249. Levy RM, Mills CM, Posin JP, et al. The efficacy and clinical impact of brain imaging in neurologically symptomatic AIDS patients: A prospective CT/MRI study. J Acquir Immune Defic Syndr. 1990;3:461-471.
250. Post MJ, Chan JC, Hensley GT, et al. Toxoplasma encephalitis in Haitian adults with acquired immunodeficiency syndrome: A clinical-pathologic-CT correlation. AJR Am J Roentgenol. 1983;140:861-868.

251. Ciricillo SF, Rosenblum ML. Use of CT and MR imaging to distinguish intracranial lesions and to define the need for biopsy in AIDS patients. J Neurosurg. 1990;73:720-724.
252. Holloway RG, Mushlin AI. Intracranial mass lesions in acquired immunodeficiency syndrome: Using decision analysis to determine the effectiveness of stereotactic brain biopsy. Neurology. 1996;46:1010-1015.
253. De La Paz R, Enzmann D. Neuroradiology of acquired immunodeficiency syndrome. In: Rosenblum ML, ed. AIDS and the Nervous System. New York: Raven Press; 1988:121-154.
254. Luft BJ, Hafner R, Korzun AH, et al. Toxoplasmic encephalitis in patients with the acquired immunodeficiency syndrome. N Engl J Med. 1993;329:995-1000.
255. Harris TM, Smith RR, Bognanno JR, et al. Toxoplasmic myelitis in AIDS: Gadolinium-enhanced MR. J Comput Assist Tomogr. 1990;14:809-811.
256. O'Doherty MJ, Barrington SF, Campbell M, et al. PET scanning and the human immunodeficiency virus-positive patient. J Nucl Med. 1997;38:1575-1583.
257. Naddaf SY, Akisik MF, Aziz M, et al. Comparison between 201Tl-chloride and 99Tc(m)-sestamibi SPECT brain imaging for differentiating intracranial lymphoma from non-malignant lesions in AIDS patients. Nucl Med Commun. 1998;19:47-53.
258. Ramsey RG, Gean AD. Central nervous system toxoplasmosis. Neuroimag Clin North Am. 1997;7:171-186.
259. Rosenfeld SS, Hoffman JM, Coleman RE, et al. Studies of primary central nervous system lymphoma with [18F]-fluorodeoxyglucose (FDG) PET. J Nucl Med. 1992;33:532-536.
260. Navia BA, Petito CK, Gold JW, et al. Cerebral toxoplasmosis complicating the acquired immune deficiency syndrome: Clinical and neuropathological findings in 27 patients. Ann Neurol. 1986;19:224-238.
261. Orefice G, Carrieri PB, de Marinis T, et al. Use of the intrathecal synthesis of antitoxoplasma antibodies in the diagnositc assessment and in the follow-up of AIDS patients with cerebral toxoplasmosis. Acta Neurol (Napoli). 1990;12:79-81.
262. Potasman I, Resnick L, Luft BJ, et al. Intrathecal production of antibodies against *Toxoplasma gondii* in patients with toxoplasmic encephalitis and the acquired immunodeficiency syndrome (AIDS). Ann Intern Med. 1988;108:49-51.
263. Liesenfeld O, Montoya JG, Tathineni NJ, et al. Confirmatory serological testing results in remarkable decrease in unnecessary abortion among pregnant women in the United States with positive toxoplasma serology. Presented at 35th Annual Meeting of the Infectious Diseases Society of America, San Francisco, September 13-16, 1997.
264. Luft BJ, Naot Y, Araujo FG, et al. Primary and reactivated toxoplasma infection in patients with cardiac transplants: Clinical spectrum and problems in diagnosis in a defined population. Ann Intern Med. 1983;99:27-31.
265. Bossolasco S, Cinque P, Ponzoni M, et al. Epstein-Barr virus DNA load in cerebrospinal fluid and plasma of patients with AIDS-related lymphoma. J Neurovirol. 2002;8:432-438.
266. Roth A, Roth B, Höffken G, et al. Application of the polymerase chain reaction to diagnosis of pulmonary toxoplasmosis in immunocompromised patients. Eur J Clin Microbiol Infect Dis. 1992;11:1177-1181.
267. Fardeau C, Romand S, Rao NA, et al. Diagnosis of toxoplasmic retinochoroiditis with atypical clinical features. Am J Ophthalmol. 2002;134:196-203.
268. Bretagne S, Costa JM, Keuntz M, et al. Late toxoplasmosis evidenced by PCR in marrow transplant reipient. Bone Marrow Transplant. 1995;15:809-811.
269. Turunen HJ, Leinikki PO, Saari KM. Demonstration of intraocular synthesis of immunoglobulin G toxoplasma antibodies for specific diagnosis of toxoplasmic chorioretinitis by enzyme immunoassay. J Clin Microbiol. 1983;17:988-992.
270. Romand S, Wallon M, Franck J, et al. Prenatal diagnosis using polymerase chain reaction on amniotic fluid for congenital toxoplasmosis. Obstet Gynecol. 2001;97:296-300.
271. Remington JS, Araujo FG, Desmonts G. Recognition of different *Toxoplasma* antigens by IgM and IgG antibodies in mothers and their congenitally infected newborns. J Infect Dis. 1985;152:1020-1024.
272. Rilling V, Dietz K, Krczal D, et al. Evaluation of a commercial IgG/IgM Western blot assay for early postnatal diagnosis of congenital toxoplasmosis. Eur J Clin Microbiol Infect Dis. 2003;22:174-180.
273. Cazenave J, Forestier F, Bessieres M, et al. Contribution of a new PCR assay to the prenatal diagnosis of congenital toxoplasmosis. Prenat Diagn. 1992;12:119-127.
274. Fuentes I, Rodriguez M, Domingo CJ, et al. Urine sample used for congenital toxoplasmosis diagnosis by PCR. J Clin Microbiol. 1996;34:2368-2371.
275. van de Ven E, Melchers W, Galama J, et al. Identification of *Toxoplasma gondii* infections by BI gene amplification. J Clin Microbiol. 1991;19:2120-2124.
276. Guerina N, Hsu H-W, Meissner H, et al. Neonatal serologic screening and early treatment for congenital *Toxoplasma gondii* infection. N Engl J Med. 1994;330:1858-1863.
277. Jara M, Hsu HW, Eaton RB, et al. Epidemiology of congenital toxoplasmosis identified by population-based newborn screening in Massachusetts. Pediatr Infect Dis J. 2001;20:1132-1135.
278. Cohn J, McMeeking A, Cohen W, et al. Evaluation of the policy of empiric treatment of suspected *Toxoplasma* encephalitis in patients with the acquired immunodeficiency syndrome. Am J Med. 1989;86:521-527.
279. Carbone LG, Bendixen B, Appel GB. Sulfadiazine-associated obstructive nephropathy occurring in a patient with the acquired immunodeficiency syndrome. Am J Kidney Dis. 1988;12:72-75.
280. Reboli AC, Mandler HD. Encephalopathy and psychoses associated with sulfadiazine in two patients with AIDS and CNS toxoplasmosis. Clin Infect Dis. 1992;15:556-557.
281. Leoung GS, Stanford JF, Giordano MF, et al. Trimethoprim-sulfamethoxazole (TMP-SMZ) dose escalation versus direct rechallenge for *Pneumocystis carinii* pneumonia prophylaxis in human immunodeficiency virus-infected patients with previous adverse reaction to TMP-SMZ. J Infect Dis. 2001;184:992-997.
282. Soffritti S, Ricci G, Prete A, et al. Successful desensitization to trimethoprim-sulfamethoxazole after allogeneic haematopoietic stem cell transplantation: Preliminary observations. Med Pediatr Oncol. 2003;40:271-272.
283. Camps M, Arrizabalaga G, Boothroyd J. An rRNA mutation identifies the apicoplast as the target for clindamycin in *Toxoplasma gondii*. Mol Microbiol. 2002;43:1309-1318.
284. Coppola S, Angarano G, Monno L, et al. Adverse effects of clindamycin in the treatment of cerebral toxoplasmosis in AIDS patients (Abstract). Program and Abstracts of Seventh International Conference on AIDS, v. 2, Florence, Italy, 1991.
285. Hofflin JM, Remington JS. In vivo synergism of roxithromycin (RU 965) and interferon against *Toxoplasma gondii*. Antimicrob Agents Chemother. 1987;31:346-348.
286. Israelski DM, Remington JS. Activity of gamma interferon in combination with pyrimethamine or clindamycin in treatment of murine toxoplasmosis. Eur J Clin Microbiol Infect Dis. 1990;9:358-360.
287. Araujo FG, Remington JS. Synergistic activity of azithromycin and gamma interferon in murine toxoplasmosis. Antimicrob Agents Chemother. 1991;35:1672-1673.
288. Araujo FG, Hunter CA, Remington JS. Treatment with interleukin 12 in combination with atovaquone or clindamycin significantly increases survival of mice with acute toxoplasmosis. Antimicrob Agents Chemother. 1997;41:188-190.
289. Carey RM, Kimball AC, Armstrong D, et al. Toxoplasmosis: Clinical experiences in a cancer hospital. Am J Med. 1973;54:30-38.
290. Katlama C, De Wit S, O'Doherty E, et al. Pyrimethamine-clindamycin vs. pyrimethamine-sulfadiazine as acute and long-term therapy for toxoplasmic encephalitis in patients with AIDS. Clin Infect Dis. 1996;22:268-275.
291. Kaplan JE, Masur H, Holmes KK. Guidelines for preventing opportunistic infections among HIV-infected persons—2002: Recommendations of the U.S. Public Health Service and the Infectious Diseases Society of America. MMWR Recomm Rep. 2002;51:1-52.
292. Luft BJ, Remington JS. AIDS commentary: Toxoplasmic encephalitis. J Infect Dis. 1988;157:1-6.
293. Dannemann BR, McCutchan JA, Israelski DA, et al. Treatment of toxoplasmic encephalitis in patients with AIDS: A randomized trial comparing pyrimethamine plus clindamycin to pyrimethamine plus sulfadiazine. Ann Intern Med. 1992;116:33-43.
294. Canessa A, Del Bono V, De Leo P, et al. Cotrimoxazole therapy of *Toxoplasma gondii* encephalitis in AIDS patients. Eur J Clin Microbiol Infect Dis. 1992;11:125-130.
295. Solbreux P, Sonnet J, Zech F. A retrospective study about the use of cotrimoxazole as diagnostic support and treatment of suspected cerebral toxoplasmosis in AIDS. Acta Clin Belg. 1990;45:85-96.
296. Torre D, Speranza F, Martegani R, et al. A retrospective study of treatment of cerebral toxoplasmosis in AIDS patients with trimethoprim-sulphamethoxazole. J Infect. 1998;37:15-18.
297. Torre D, Casari S, Speranza F, et al. Randomized trial of trimethoprim-sulfamethoxazole versus pyrimethamine-sulfadiazine for therapy of toxoplasmic encephalitis in patients with AIDS. Italian Collaborative Study Group. Antimicrob Agents Chemother. 1998;42:1346-1349.
298. Kovacs JA. Efficacy of atovaquone in treatment of toxoplasmosis in patients with AIDS. Lancet. 1992;340:637-638.
299. Torres R, Weinberg W, Stansell J, et al. Atovaquone for salvage treatment and suppression of toxoplasmic encephalitis in patients with AIDS. Clin Infect Dis. 1997;24:422-429.
300. Chirgwin K, Hafner R, Leport C, et al. Randomized phase II trial of atovaquone with pyrimethamine or sulfadiazine for treatment of toxoplasmic encephalitis in patients with acquired immunodeficiency syndrome. ACTG 237/ANRS 039 Study. AIDS Clinical Trials Group 237/Agence Nationale de Recherche sur le SIDA, Essai 039. Clin Infect Dis. 2002;34:1243-1250.
301. Clumeck N, Katlama C, Ferrero T, et al. Atovaquone (1.4 hydroxynaphtoquione, 566C80) in the treatment of acute cerebral toxoplasmosis (CT) in AIDS patients (P) (Abstract). Presented at Thirty-second Interscience Conference on Antimicrobial Agents and Chemotherapy, Anaheim, CA, 1992.
302. Fernandez-Martin J, Leport C, Morlat P, et al. Pyrimethamine-clarithromycin for therapy of acute toxoplasma encephalitis in patients with AIDS. Antimicrob Agents Chemother. 1991;35:2049-2052.
303. Chaisson RE, Benson CA, Dube MP, et al. Clarithromycin therapy for bacteremic *Mycobacterium avium* complex disease: A randomized, double-blind, dose-ranging study in patients with AIDS. AIDS Clinical Trials Group Protocol 157 Study Team. Ann Intern Med. 1994;121:905-911.
304. Cohn DL, Fisher EJ, Peng GT, et al. A prospective randomized trial of four three-drug regimens in the treatment of disseminated *Mycobacterium avium* complex disease in AIDS patients: Excess mortality associated with high-dose clarithromycin. Terry Beirn Community Programs for Clinical Research on AIDS. Clin Infect Dis. 1999;29:125-133.
305. Ward DJ. Dapsone/pyrimethamine for the treatment of *Toxoplasmic* encephalitis (Abstract). Presented at Eighth International Conference on AIDS, Amsterdam, The Netherlands, 1992.
306. Pope-Pegram L, Gathe J Jr, Bohn B, et al. Treatment of presumed central nervous system toxoplasmosis with doxycycline (Abstract). In Program and Abstracts of Seventh International Conference on AIDS, v. 1, Florence, Italy, 1991.
307. Turett G, Pierone G, Masci J, et al. Failure of doxycycline in the treatment of cerebral toxoplasmosis (Abstract). Presented at Sixth International Conference on AIDS, San Francisco, 1990.
308. Saba J, Morlat P, Raffi F, et al. Pyrimethamine plus azithromycin for treatment of acute toxoplasmic encephalitis in patients with AIDS. Eur J Clin Microbiol Infect Dis. 1993;12:853-856.
309. Jacobson JM, Hafner R, Remington J, et al. Dose-escalation, phase I/II study of azithromycin and pyrimethamine for the treatment of toxoplasmic encephalitis in AIDS. AIDS. 2001;15:583-589.
310. Pedrol E, Gonzales-Clemente JM, Gatell JM, et al. Central nervous system toxoplasmosis in AIDS patients: Efficacy of an intermittent maintenance therapy. AIDS. 1990;4:511-517.

311. Podzamczer D, Miró J, Bolao F, et al. Twice-weekly maintenance therapy with sulfa-diazine-pyrimethamine to prevent recurrent toxoplasmic encephalitis in patients with AIDS. Ann Intern Med. 1995;123:175-180.

312. Podzamczer D, Miro JM, Ferrer E, et al. Thrice-weekly sulfadiazine-pyrimethamine for maintenance therapy of toxoplasmic encephalitis in HIV-infected patients. Spanish Toxoplasmosis Study Group. Eur J Clin Microbiol Infect Dis. 2000;19:89-95.

313. Heald A, Flepp M, Chave J-P, et al. Treatment for cerebral toxoplasmosis protects against *Pneumocystis carinii* pneumonia in patients with AIDS. Ann Intern Med. 1991;115:760-763.

314. Remington JS, Vilde JL, Antunes F, et al. Clindamycin for toxoplasmosis encephali-tis in AIDS (Letter). Lancet. 1991;338:1142-1143.

315. Köppen S, Grunewald T, Jautzke G, et al. Prevention of *Pneumocystis carinii* pneu-monia and toxoplasmic encephalitis in human immunodeficiency virus infected pa-tients: A clinical approach comparing aerosolized pentamidine and pyrimethamine/sulfadoxine. Clin Invest. 1992;70:508-512.

316. Clotet B, Sirera G, Romeu J, et al. Twice-weekly dapsone-pyrimethamine for pre-venting PCP and cerebral toxoplasmosis. AIDS. 1991;5:601-602.

317. Opravil M, Hirschel B, Lazzarin A, et al. Once-weekly administration of dapsone/pyrimethamine vs. aerosolized pentamidine as acombined prophylaxis for *Pneumocystis carinii* pneumonia and toxoplasmic encephalitis in human immunode-ficiency virus-infected patients. Clin Infect Dis. 1995;20:531-541.

318. Torres R, Barr M, Thorn M, et al. Randomized trial of dapsone and aerosolized pen-tamidine for the prophylaxis of *Pneumocystis carinii* pneumonia and toxoplasmic en-cephalitis. Am J Med. 1993;95:573-583.

319. Maslo C, Matheron S, Saimot AG. Cerebral toxoplasmosis: Assessment of mainte-nance therapy. Presented at VIII International Conference on AIDS, v. 2, Amsterdam, The Netherlands, 1992.

320. de Gans J, Portegies P, Reiss P, et al. Pyrimethamine alone as maintenance therapy for central nervous system toxoplasmosis in 38 patients with AIDS. AIDS. 1992;5:137-142.

321. Katlama C, Mouthon B, Gourdon D, et al. Atovaquone as long-term suppressive ther-apy for toxoplasmic encephalitis in patients with AIDS and multiple drug intolerance. AIDS. 1996;10:1107-1112.

322. Carr A, Tindall B, Brew BJ, et al. Low-dose trimethoprim-sulfamethoxazole prophy-laxis for toxoplasmic encephalitis in patients with AIDS. Ann Intern Med. 1992;117:106-111.

323. Bozzette S, Finkelstein D, Spector S, et al. A randomized trial of three antipneumo-cystis agents in patients with advanced human immunodeficiency virus infection. N Engl J Med. 1995;332:693-699.

324. Podzamczer D, Salazar A, Jiménez J, et al. Intermittent trimethoprim-sulfamethoxa-zole compared with dapsone-pyrimethamine for the simultaneous primary prophy-laxis of pneumocystis pneumonia and toxoplasmosis in patients infected with HIV. Ann Intern Med. 1995;122:755-761.

325. Girard P-M, Landman R, Gaudebout C, et al. Dapsone-pyrimethamine compared with aerosolized pentamidine as a primary prophylaxis against *Pneumocystis carinii* pneumonia and toxoplasmosis in HIV infection. N Engl J Med. 1993;328:1514-1520.

326. Schurmann D, Bergmann F, Albrecht H, et al. Effectiveness of twice-weekly pyrimethamine-sulfadoxine as primary prophylaxis of *Pneumocystis carinii* pneumo-nia and toxoplasmic encephalitis in patients with advanced HIV infection. Eur J Clin Microbiol Infect Dis. 2002;21:353-361.

327. Zeller V, Truffot C, Agher R, et al. Discontinuation of secondary prophylaxis against disseminated *Mycobacterium avium* complex infection and toxoplasmic encephalitis. Clin Infect Dis. 2002;34:662-667.

328. Mussini C, Pezzotti P, Govoni A, et al. Discontinuation of primary prophylaxis for *Pneumocystis carinii* pneumonia and toxoplasmic encephalitis in human immunode-ficiency virus type I-infected patients: The changes in opportunistic prophylaxis study. J Infect Dis. 2000;181:1635-1642.

329. Durant J, Hazime F, Carles M, et al. Prevention of *Pneumocystis carinii* pneumonia and of cerebral toxoplasmosis by roxithromycin in HIV-infected patients. Infection. 1995;23:S33-S38.

330. Jacobson M, Besch C, Child C, et al. Primary prophylaxis with pyrimethamine for toxoplasmic encephalitis in patients with advanced human immunodeficiency virus disease: Results of a randomized trial. J Infect Dis. 1994;169:384-394.

331. Klinker H, Langmann P, Richter E. Pyrimethamine alone as prophylaxis for cerebral toxoplasmosis in patients with advanced HIV infection. Infection. 1996;4:324-328.

332. Rousseau F, Pueyo S, Morlat P, et al. Increased risk of toxoplasmic encephalitis in hu-man immunodeficiency virus-infected patients with pyrimethamine-related rash. Clin Infect Dis. 1997;24:396-402.

333. Raffi F, Struillou L, Ninin E, et al. Breakthrough cerebral toxoplasmosis in patients with AIDS who are being treated with clarithromycin. Clin Infect Dis. 1995;20:1076-1077.

334. Leport C, Vilde JL, Katlama C, et al. Failure of spiramycin to prevent neurotoxoplas-mosis in immunosuppressed patients (Letter). Med Clin North Am. 1986;70:677-692.

335. Jacobson M, Besch C, Child C, et al. Toxicity of clindamycin as prophylaxis for AIDS-associated toxoplasmic encephalitis. Lancet. 1992;339:333-334.

336. Cochereau-Massin I, LeHoang P, Lautier-Frau M, et al. Ocular toxoplasmosis in human immunodeficiency virus-infected patients. Am. J. Ophthalmol. 1992;114:130-135.

337. Friedman AH, Orellana J, Gagliuso DJ, et al. Ocular toxoplasmosis in AIDS patients. Trans Am Ophthalmol Soc. 1990;88:63-88.

338. Schnapp L, Geaghan S, Campagna A, et al. *Toxoplasma gondii* pneumonitis in pa-tients infected with the human immunodeficiency virus. Arch Intern Med. 1992;152:1073-1076.

339. Holland GN, Lewis KG. An update on current practices in the management of ocular toxoplasmosis. Am J Ophthalmol. 2002;134:102-114.

340. Pearson PA, Piracha AR, Sen HA, et al. Atovaquone for the treatment of toxoplasma retinochoroiditis in immunocompetent patients. Ophthalmology. 1999;106:148-153.

341. Bosch-Driessen LH, Verbraak FD, Suttorp-Schulten MS, et al. A prospective, ran-domized trial of pyrimethamine and azithromycin vs pyrimethamine and sulfadiazine for the treatment of ocular toxoplasmosis. Am J Ophthalmol. 2002;134:34-40.

342. Forestier F, Daffos F, Rainaut M, et al. Suivi therapeutique foetomaternel de la spi-ramycine en cours de grossesse. Arch Fr Pediatr. 1987;44:539-544.

343. Gilbert R, Gras L. Effect of timing and type of treatment on the risk of mother to child transmission of *Toxoplasma gondii*. Br J Obstet Gynaecol. 2003;110:112-120.

344. Gilbert RE, Gras L, Wallon M, et al. Effect of prenatal treatment on mother to child transmission of *Toxoplasma gondii*: Retrospective cohort study of 554 mother-child pairs in Lyon, France. Int J Epidemiol. 2001;30:1303-1308.

345. Gilbert R, Dunn D, Wallon M, et al. Ecological comparison of the risks of mother-to-child transmission and clinical manifestations of congenital toxoplasmosis according to prenatal treatment protocol. Epidemiol Infect. 2001;127:113-120.

346. Foulon W, Villena I, Stray-Pedersen B, et al. Treatment of toxoplasmosis during preg-nancy: A multicenter study of impact on fetal transmission and children's sequelae at age 1 year. Am J Obstet Gynecol. 1999;180:410-415.

347. Thulliez P. Efficacy of prenatal treatment for toxoplasmosis: A possibility that cannot be ruled out. Int J Epidemiol. 2001;30:1315-1316.

348. McGee T, Wolters C, Stein L, et al. Absence of sensorineural hearing loss in treated infants and children with congenital toxoplasmosis. Otolarygol Head Neck Surg. 1992;106:75-80.

349. Mets MB, Holfels E, Boyer KM, et al. Eye manifestations of congenital toxoplasmo-sis. Am J Ophthalmol. 1996;122:309-324.

350. Roizen N, Swisher CN, Stein MA, et al. Neurologic and developmental outcome in treated congenital toxoplasmosis. Pediatrics. 1995;95:11-20.

351. Wreghitt TG, Hakim M, Gray JJ, et al. Toxoplasmosis in heart and heart lung trans-plant recipients. J Clin Pathol. 1989;42:194-199.

CHAPTER **277**

Giardia lamblia

DAVID R. HILL

Giardia lamblia, a flagellated enteric protozoan, is a common cause of endemic and epidemic diarrhea throughout the world. It is particu-larly seen in waterborne outbreaks of diarrhea, in children who live in resource-poor countries, and occasionally in foodborne outbreaks. In the United States and Canada, it is the most commonly diagnosed en-teric parasite.

DESCRIPTION OF THE PATHOGEN

Giardia has been recognized as an intestinal inhabitant since the late 1600s, when van Leeuwenhoek discovered it in his own stool. It was in the early 1900s that the parasite received the genus name *Giardia*. The designated species name for the human parasite has been *lamblia,* but *intestinalis* and *duodenalis* are also used. The genus *Giardia* falls under the category of intestinal flagellates in the division Protozoa.[1] On the basis of its small subunit ribosomal RNA sequence and the ab-sence of many organelles such as mitochondria and a typical Golgi ap-paratus, it is one of the earliest branching eukaryotes, and it has been used as a model to understand the development of eukaryotic cells.[2-4] However, recent findings of mitochondrial genes in the parasite raise the possibility that *Giardia* was at one time endowed with mitochon-dria but lost its ancestral characteristics.[5]

The differentiation of *Giardia* into species has traditionally de-pended on morphology and the host of origin, with only a few species described: *G. lamblia* in humans, *G. muris* in mice, *G. agilis* in am-phibians, and, more recently, *G. psittaci* in parakeets and *G. microti* in voles and muskrats.[3] However, the understanding of *Giardia* has now moved to molecular typing of isolates within various species.[6] On the basis of this information, *G. lamblia* may be divided into genotypes[3] that have also been designated as groups[7] or assemblages.[8] *G. lamblia* isolates that are genetically distinct (i.e., from separate genotypes [or groups or assemblages]) but morphologically indistinguishable can exhibit differential pathogenicities in human infection[9] or host species infectivity.[10] It is clear from these analyses that *G. lamblia* is a pathogen of both human and other mammalian hosts such as dog, cat, cow, beaver, and sheep. However, many genotypes from dog, cat, and cow have not been isolated from humans, giving these a lower zoonotic potential. Genotypes (or assemblages) associated with human infection are typically A and B.

The *Giardia* genome project that began in 1998 has the goal of sequencing the genome of the WB human isolate (see the website www.mbl.edu/Giardia). This project has estimated the genome size to be 1.2×10^7 base pairs of DNA on five chromosomes, with a GC content of 46%.[11]

Giardia is covered by immunodominant cysteine-rich surface proteins that undergo frequent antigenic variation; these are termed variant-specific surface proteins (VSPs).[12] Antigenic variation occurs during human and animal infection and during the encystation/excystation cycle. It appears that only one VSP is transcribed at a time. The role of VSPs has not been determined, but changes in VSPs may help to protect the parasite against the activity of intestinal proteases, provide oxygen stability, allow adaptation to different hosts, and play a role in immune evasion.

The life cycle of *G. lamblia* is composed of two stages: the trophozoite, or freely living stage, and the cyst. The trophozoite is 9 to 21 μm long and 5 to 15 μm wide (Fig. 277-1A). It has a convex dorsal surface and a flat ventral surface containing the disk, which is often referred to as the *sucking* or *adhesive* disk. There are four pairs of posteriorly directed flagella that are involved in locomotion and perhaps attachment. Their intracytoplasmic projections are termed axonemes. The disk cytoskeleton is composed of a clockwise spiral array of microtubules joined by vertical microribbons.[13] Within these structural components are important antigens: tubulin within microtubules and giardins within microribbons. The disk also contains contractile proteins. The protozoan has two anteriorly placed nuclei, each with a prominent central karyosome and complete copies of the genome.[14] How cloned *Giardia* maintain a high degree of homozygosity with two nuclei is an unanswered question. On stained preparations, the nuclei create the characteristic facelike image. Median bodies, tight collections of microtubules, are placed transversely in a clawlike manner in *G. lamblia* and may be helpful in species differentiation.

Of the *Giardia* species, only *G. lamblia* has been successfully cultured in vitro.[15] Growth is enhanced by the presence of biliary lipids, a high concentration of cysteine, and low oxygen tension, thus helping to explain the predilection of *Giardia* for colonizing the upper small bowel. The trophozoite divides by longitudinal binary fission and has a doubling time in culture of 9 to 12 hours. It is an aerotolerant anaerobe and uses glucose as the major source of carbohydrate energy, metabolizing it to the end products of acetate, ethanol, alanine, and carbon dioxide; ATP is generated during this process.[3] The relative amounts of these end products depends on the oxygen tension in the environment.

Except for alanine, amino acids are taken up from the environment. Metabolism of arginine via the arginine dihydrolase pathway may be another mechanism for ATP generation. Phospholipids, fatty acids, cholesterol, and purine and pyrimidine nucleosides are also scavenged from the environment.

G. lamblia trophozoites encyst to form smooth, oval, thin-walled cysts 8 to 12 μm long and 7 to 10 μm wide (see Fig. 277-1B). Encystation is enhanced by multiple factors, including cholesterol starvation that is followed by an alkaline pH and excess bile salts.[2,16] During encystation, there is downregulation of trophozoite-specific genes and induction of encystation-specific genes.[17] The early phase of this process is characterized by the formation of specific encystment vesicles (ESV), and this is followed by transcription and secretion into the vesicles of cyst wall proteins CWP-1 and CWP-2.[2,18] In the ESVs, the CWPs combine, undergo proteolytic cleavage, are transported to the trophozoite surface, and later appear in the cyst wall. The late phase of encystation consists of assembly of the cyst wall elements and then nuclear division and DNA replication without cell division, so that cysts are generated with a ploidy of 16N.[17] In vitro, the entire process takes about 16 hours.[19] On ultrastructural analysis, the cyst wall has a filamentous character with high concentrations of galactosamine, the synthesis of which is induced during encystation.

Excystation is a highly coordinated process that is initiated when environmental stimuli such as gastric acid and pancreatic enzymes are detected across the cyst wall.[20] During this process, a parasite-derived cysteine protease is activated.[21] Because of the rapidity of excystation, cell-signaling events are likely to be important[22] in addition to new gene expression. A single trophozoite containing four nuclei (4N each) is released; this divides twice without further DNA replication, resulting in four daughter trophozoites.[17]

EPIDEMIOLOGY

Giardia is distributed throughout the world. In the United States, *G. lamblia* has been demonstrated in 4% to 7% of stool specimens, making it the most commonly identified intestinal parasite. A U.S. epidemiologic survey of giardiasis in the mid-1990s found that 25,000 to 28,000 cases were reported annually, with the case rates in different states varying from 0.9 to 42.3 cases per 100,000 persons.[23] Because of underreporting, it is likely that there are 100,000 to 2.5 million cases annually. *Giardia* was most frequently reported in children 0 to 5 years old and adults 31 to 40 years old, and during the late summer and fall months. *Giardia* was the cause of diarrhea in 15% of children presenting to U.S. outpatient offices.[24]

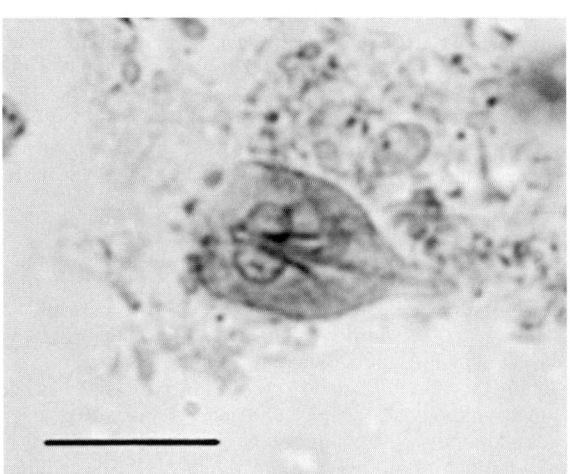

A

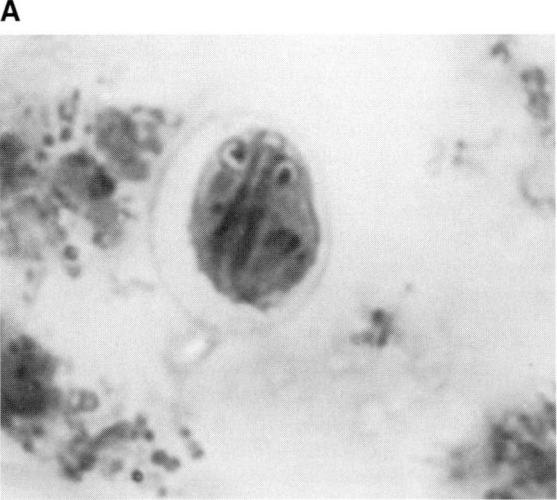

B

FIGURE 277-1. *Giardia lamblia* trophozoite (**A**) and cyst (**B**) are demonstrated in a trichrome stain of fecal material. Note the prominent nuclei in the trophozoite. In the cyst, the cytoplasm has separated from the cyst wall; centrally located axonemes, a clawlike median body, and two eccentrically located nuclei can be detected. (Bar =10 μm.)

In resource-poor regions of the world, *Giardia* is one of the first enteric pathogens to infect infants,[25-27] with peak prevalence rates of 15% to 30% occurring in children younger than 10 years.[25,28-30] Nearly all children in these settings become infected.[26,27,31]

Acquisition of the parasite requires oral ingestion of *Giardia* cysts. Although this frequently occurs after the ingestion of contaminated water, person-to-person and foodborne transmissions are also important. From 1985 through 2000 in the United States, *G. lamblia* was the most common pathogen identified in outbreaks of diarrheal illness from drinking water, causing 41 outbreaks and accounting for 39% of all outbreaks for which an etiology was determined.[32] Recreational water has also been a risk for *Giardia*, but *Cryptosporidium* is far more common as a cause of diarrhea in this setting.[32] Surface water supplies can easily become contaminated by human or animal sources, and *Giardia* cysts survive well in the environment, particularly in cold water. Sampling of surface water demonstrates frequent contamination with *Giardia* cysts as well as those of *Cryptosporidium*. Backpackers who do not adequately treat water may become infected. In an epidemiologic survey from southwest England, swallowing water while swimming and drinking tap water (odds ratio of 1.3 for each additional glass per day) were associated with giardiasis.[33] Common to most waterborne outbreaks has been the use of untreated surface water or well water, or water treated by a faulty purification system or by inadequate chlorination and not subjected to flocculation, sedimentation, and filtration.[34]

In resource-rich regions of the world, person-to-person transmission is the second most commonly identified mode of acquisition and occurs in groups with poor fecal-oral hygiene, such as young children in daycare centers and men who have sex with men. In children in daycare centers, the prevalence of *Giardia* cyst passage has been as high as 20% to 50%.[35] Many of these children are asymptomatic, but they can spread the infection within their homes and may contribute to high endemic rates in their communities.[36] The high North American prevalence of giardiasis in children aged 0 to 5 years would be consistent with this epidemiologic pattern.[23,37] Sexually active gay men have cyst passage rates as high as 20% and frequently report symptoms.[38] Reports that have documented the transmission of *Giardia* in commercial food establishments, corporate office settings, and small gatherings indicate that foodborne transmission may be more common than previously recognized.[39,40] Travelers who acquire *Giardia* have often visited countries in the Indian subcontinent and have traveled for a month or more.[41,42]

Genetic analysis and natural or experimental infection with parasites that are morphologically of the *G. lamblia* species have shown that many mammalian hosts may be infected; these include gerbils, mice, beavers, sheep, cattle, dogs, and cats.[3,10] In some regions, nearly all domestic cattle may become infected,[43] and *Giardia* is the most frequent intestinal parasite of domestic dogs in Australia.[10] However, many of the animal isolates fall under genetic groupings that have not been associated with human infection, lowering their zoonotic potential.[3,43,44] Nevertheless, a study that rigorously analyzed a Canadian waterborne outbreak of giardiasis linked the outbreak to beavers.[45] This emphasizes the importance of protecting water supplies that are used for drinking from surface contamination, and of adequately purifying all public water supplies.

PATHOGENESIS AND IMMUNE RESPONSE

Giardia was once thought to be a harmless commensal, but its association with symptomatic diarrhea, malabsorption in children, and disease after waterborne outbreaks, travel, and experimental human infection[9] has clearly established its pathogenicity. The production of diarrhea, and occasionally malabsorption, is the result of a complex interaction of *Giardia* with the host, with an outcome related to the number and genotype of *Giardia* ingested and the host's previous experience with and immune response to the parasite.

Infection occurs after oral ingestion of as few as 10 to 25 cysts.[46] Although virulence characteristics of individual isolates have not been clearly determined, the ability to establish infection and to cause diarrhea varies between isolates and genotypes.[3,9,47] After excystation, trophozoites colonize and multiply in the upper small bowel. Adherence of *G. lamblia* in the human gut is most likely via the ventral disk, with attachment at the brush border of enterocytes by either a suction or a clasping mechanism. Other specific adherence events have not been completely excluded. The parasite may avoid peristalsis by becoming trapped in intestinal mucus or between villi.

Several pathogenic mechanisms have been postulated: disruption of the enterocyte brush border, mucosal invasion, elaboration of an enterotoxin, and stimulation of an inflammatory infiltration leading to fluid and electrolyte secretion and occasionally to villous changes. This last mechanism is discussed later. Electron microscopy has documented disruption of the brush border in some patients, which could lead to the disaccharidase deficiencies commonly seen in giardiasis. In vitro *G. lamblia* can disrupt tight junctions, increase permeability, and induce apoptosis in small intestinal epithelial cell monolayers.[48] Mucosal invasion is rare, and there is no evidence for the production of an enterotoxin. Simultaneous colonization of the small bowel with *Giardia* and *Enterobacteriaceae* or yeast may contribute to malabsorption in some patients by the deconjugation of bile salts.

The host immune response is the other important component of the host–parasite relationship.[49,50] Host immunity plays a role in clearance of the parasite, in providing some protection against rechallenge, and, in certain instances, in production of disease. Several observations indicate that partially protective immunity may develop to *Giardia*. In rodent models of giardiasis, animals clear infection and become resistant to reinfection. This experimental finding is supported by epidemiologic studies of human giardiasis. The prevalence of *Giardia* in developing countries is higher in younger age groups,[25,30,51] and in endemic areas of North America, lower rates of symptomatic disease have occurred in long-term residents of the area than in visitors or short-term residents.[52,53]

The components of host immunity are humoral and cellular. A systemic antibody response occurs in patients with *Giardia* and has been useful in seroprevalence studies.[25,51,54-56] Although serum immunoglobulin M (IgM) and IgG antibodies develop and with complement can be lethal to *Giardia* trophozoites, it is likely that gastrointestinal, secretory IgA antibodies play a more important role because of the luminal location of trophozoites.[57-60] In mice, IgA has been the predominant antibody class detected in gut secretions, its development correlates temporally with control of the parasite, and its absence is associated with inability to resolve infection.[49,58,60,61] The failure to develop IgA against specific *Giardia* antigens has been suggested to correlate with chronic giardiasis in humans.[57] The mechanism by which IgA prevents or helps to clear infection is probably by binding to trophozoites and preventing a critical adherence step; there is no evidence that IgA can kill trophozoites. *Giardia* species can produce an IgA protease. The cytokine interleukin (IL)-6 is important in the early control of giardiasis in a murine model.[62]

The cellular immune response helps to clear parasites by coordinating the production of anti-*Giardia* secretory IgA and perhaps by engaging in specific anti-*Giardia* cytotoxicity. B-cell–deficient mice are unable to clear infection with either *G. muris* or *G. lamblia*, and this effect goes beyond just the failure of these mice to produce IgA.[60] Athymic, T-cell–deficient mice are unable to clear infection with *G. muris* until the mice are reconstituted with lymphoid cells, particularly the CD4+ helper T lymphocyte.[63] After reconstitution, animals develop an abnormal intestinal histologic appearance that parallels the changes seen in some humans with giardiasis: spruelike lesions with marked flattening of the villi, crypt hypertrophy, and a dense mononuclear cell infiltration of the submucosa.[64-66]

The inflammatory response with damage to enterocytes and the mucosa could initiate a cytokine reaction leading to diarrhea, similar to the proposed mechanism for diarrhea production in adherent or minimally invasive coccidians such as *Cyclospora* and *Cryptosporidium*.[67] It could also stimulate increased epithelial cell turnover in the crypt region, changing the bowel's absorptive capacity. Parasite antigen alone may be sufficient to initiate inflammation.[68]

Human milk may play a role in protection of the host against *Giardia*. Milk is cytotoxic to trophozoites when free fatty acids are released from milk triglycerides by the action of bile salt–stimulated lipase.[69] Both human and animal breast milk have been found to contain anti-*Giardia* antibodies, and several studies have demonstrated protection of breast-feeding infants from symptomatic infection.[70] Local intestinal conditions, nonimmune defenses (e.g., nitric oxide), and microflora may also determine whether *Giardia* can establish infection.[71,72]

Predisposition to giardiasis has been documented in patients with common variable immunodeficiency and in children with X-linked agammaglobulinemia.[73] These patients have symptomatic disease with prolonged diarrhea, malabsorption, and marked changes on small bowel biopsy, as described previously, which can include nodular lymphoid hyperplasia. On administration of anti-*Giardia* therapy, their symptoms improve and the histologic changes resolve. It remains unclear whether selective IgA deficiency is a predisposing factor; many patients with IgA deficiency produce low levels of IgA that may be sufficient to help control *Giardia* infection.[74]

Susceptibility to giardiasis has also been seen in patients with previous gastric surgery and reduced gastric acidity. There appears to be no association of giardiasis with blood group specificity. Patients with acquired immunodeficiency syndrome generally do not have more severe illness with *Giardia*; however, in some cases, the disease may be refractory to treatment.[75]

Although it is clear that different *G. lamblia* isolates have different capacities for establishing infection and causing disease, the exact association of genotypes or assemblages with disease requires ongoing analysis of many isolates from multiple parts of the world. Although *Giardia* organisms change their variant specific surface proteins in vivo, the role that this plays in avoiding immune recognition and allowing persistent infection is speculative.[12,76]

Small bowel biopsy may demonstrate spruelike lesions or may be normal[77]; two studies have correlated the severity of diarrhea with the degree of histologic abnormality on biopsy.[65,78] The variation in the histologic appearance supports the multiple potential mechanisms for the production of diarrhea.

CLINICAL MANIFESTATIONS

Infection with *G. lamblia* includes asymptomatic cyst passage, acute self-limited diarrhea, and a chronic syndrome of diarrhea, malabsorption, and weight loss. Of 100 people ingesting *Giardia* cysts, an estimated 5% to 15% become asymptomatic cyst passers, 25% to 50% become symptomatic with an acute diarrheal syndrome, and the remaining 35% to 70% have no trace of infection. Although many symptomatic patients spontaneously clear their infection, most develop a diarrheal syndrome lasting 1 week to several weeks and will end up being treated with antimicrobial therapy. For children in daycare centers, asymptomatic cyst passage has been documented to last as long as 6 months.

After the ingestion of *G. lamblia* cysts, there is an incubation period of 1 to 2 weeks before the onset of symptoms. The time from ingestion of cysts to detection of cysts in the stool may be longer than the incubation period.[9] Thus, a stool examination at the time of the onset of symptoms could be negative.

Symptomatic giardiasis is characterized by the acute onset of diarrhea, abdominal cramps, bloating, and flatulence (Table 277-1). The patient usually expresses feelings of malaise, nausea, and anorexia and may complain of sulfuric belching. Vomiting, fever, and tenesmus occur less commonly. Initially, stools may be profuse and watery, but later they are commonly greasy and foul smelling and may float. Gross blood, pus, and mucus are usually absent, and if examined microscopically, the stool is found to be free of polymorphonuclear cells.

One of the most important distinguishing features is the prolonged duration of diarrhea with giardiasis. At the time of presentation, most patients have been symptomatic for more than 1 week to 10 days. Weight loss of about 10 pounds occurs more than 50% of the time and is another useful clinical feature.[38] Unusual features include urticaria,

TABLE 277-1	Symptoms of Giardiasis	
	Percentage	*Range*
Diarrhea	89	64-100
Malaise	84	72-97
Flatulence	74	35-97
Foul-smelling, greasy stools	72	57-79
Abdominal cramps	70	44-85
Bloating	69	42-97
Nausea	68	59-79
Anorexia	64	41-82
Weight loss	64	56-73
Vomiting	27	17-36
Fever	13	0-21
Urticaria	9	4-14
Constipation	9	0-17

Data reviewed in Hill DR. Giardiasis: Issues in management and treatment. Infect Dis Clin North Am. 1993;7:503-525.

reactive arthritis, biliary tract disease, and gastric infection. Gastric infection occurs exclusively in the presence of achlorhydria and may be seen in conjunction with *Helicobacter pylori*.[79]

Although most persons with giardiasis have a relatively benign course, some persons, particularly children younger than 5 years and pregnant women, may have severe illness characterized by volume depletion and require hospitalization.[80,81]

Patients who develop chronic diarrhea have profound malaise, lassitude, occasional headache, and diffuse abdominal and epigastric discomfort often exacerbated by eating. Stools may be greasy and foul smelling or frothy, yellowish, occurring in small volume, and frequently passed. Weight loss is usually present. Periods of diarrhea may be interrupted by periods of constipation or normal bowel habits, with the syndrome waxing and waning over months until therapy is given or spontaneous resolution occurs.

Various degrees of malabsorption may be present. Children who present for evaluation for failure to thrive or with a spruelike illness have been found to have giardiasis.[78] Steatorrhea and malabsorption of vitamins A and B_{12}, protein, D-xylose, and iron have been documented.[82,83] The most common disaccharidase deficiency has been that of lactase, occurring in 20% to 40% of cases,[84] with post-*Giardia* lactose intolerance sometimes persisting for several weeks after treatment. This is often confused with relapse or reinfection.

The role that chronic infection with *Giardia* plays in the growth and development of children in the resource-poor regions of the world has been controversial. It is clear that high prevalence rates of *Giardia* exist in both symptomatic and asymptomatic children. Some studies point to a deleterious effect on growth and argue for the need to treat recurrent disease to allow catch-up growth.[28,82,85,86] Others emphasize the high prevalence of *Giardia* infection in asymptomatic children living in areas of poor sanitation and suggest that reinfection occurs so rapidly that repeated therapy is impractical and not indicated.[29,87] In addition, many children may be simultaneously infected with other bacterial, viral, and parasitic infections, making the contribution that *Giardia* makes to their illness less clear.

More recent studies have helped to clarify this issue. Evidence for stunted growth in Ecuadorian children infected with *Giardia*,[88] poor intestinal permeability in Nepali children,[89] low weight-for-age and height-for-age in Brazilian children with persistent symptomatic giardiasis,[90] and decreased cognitive function in Peruvian children with multiple episodes of giardiasis[27] point to a deleterious effect in children who already have a poor underlying nutritional state. In contrast, well-nourished children often have fewer clinical signs of malnutrition.[91,92] Therefore it is likely that prolonged episodes of giardiasis in children with underlying poor nutrition may have more deleterious effects than episodes in normal children.[93] The key in all circumstances is to develop methods to maintain childhood nutrition and to decrease the risk factors for repeated episodes of diarrheal illness.

DIAGNOSIS

The diagnosis of giardiasis should be considered in all patients with prolonged diarrhea, particularly that which is associated with malabsorption or weight loss. If there is a history of recent travel to an endemic area, the presence of small children in the home who attend daycare centers, or sexual risk factors, giardiasis is also more likely. Other diarrheal syndromes caused by viruses, noninvasive bacteria, and protozoans such as *Cryptosporidium* and *Cyclospora*,[67,94,95] as well as tropical sprue, should be considered in the differential diagnosis.

The traditional method of diagnosis has been to perform a stool examination for ova and parasites (O&P), looking for trophozoites or cysts. The O&P examination has been the assay with which other tests are compared. Antigen detection via immunofluorescence, enzyme-linked immunosorbent assays (ELISAs), and nonenzymatic immunoassays are now commonly available and for many laboratories are the tests of choice because they are reproducible and rapid.[96,97]

In an O&P examination, the stool should be examined fresh and after preservation. A saline wet mount of fresh liquid stool obtained in the acute stages of illness may yield motile trophozoites. In semi-formed stool, trophozoites are usually not found. These stools should be examined fresh for cysts after iodine staining or after preservation in 10% buffered formalin or polyvinyl alcohol and subsequent trichrome or iron hematoxylin staining. Formalin-ether or zinc sulfate flotation concentration techniques may increase the yield. *Giardia* should be identified 60% to 80% of the time after one stool, and some report over 90% identification after three stools.[38,98,99] Examination of a purged sample does not increase the yield.

Although antigen assays are used frequently for routine stool diagnostics, they are most helpful when giardiasis is the leading consideration, such as during an outbreak, when screening children in daycare, or when testing patients for cure after the completion of treatment. They are often less expensive than an O&P examination and are 85% to 98% sensitive and 90% to 100% specific.[96,97,100-102] One frequently used assay detects CWP-1 by ELISA (ProSpecT, *Giardia* Microplate Assay, Remel, Lenexa, KS)[103]; a second uses fluorescein-tagged monoclonal antibodies against *Giardia* or *Cryptosporidium* (Merifluor DFA, Meridian Bioscience, Cincinnati, OH).[104]

Because good results can be obtained with a carefully performed stool O&P examination or an antigen assay, sampling of the duodenal contents by string test or biopsy is generally not needed. However, in cases that are particularly difficult to diagnose, these procedures may be helpful. Three methods have been used: the string test or Entero-Test (HDC Corporation, Milpitas, CA), duodenal aspiration, and duodenal biopsy. The string test should yield bile-stained mucus from the duodenum that can be examined for trophozoites in a wet mount or after staining. Duodenal aspiration and biopsy are more invasive. Biopsies require touch preparations, Giemsa staining, and a careful search for trophozoites. An advantage of biopsy, particularly in patients infected with human immunodeficiency virus or persons with malabsorption, is the ability to identify a histologic abnormality that is not caused by giardiasis and to detect other pathogens. An aspirate can be sampled for small bowel overgrowth.

Testing for systemic anti-*Giardia* antibody is not generally available, but it has been useful in seroepidemiologic studies throughout the world.[25,55,56] The IgG antibodies remain elevated for long periods, making them less helpful diagnostically in areas endemic for giardiasis. It is not clear if serum anti-*Giardia* IgM is useful in distinguishing current from past giardiasis.[105]

Although in vitro culture is available in research settings, it is not routinely used because of the difficulty of reproducibly isolating *Giardia* from patient samples.[15] Detection of *Giardia* nucleic acid by polymerase chain reaction or by gene probes is a highly sensitive but experimental methodology. It has been typically applied to the detection of parasites in water samples or to genotype isolates from various mammalian hosts.[43,106] The white blood cell count is usually normal, and eosinophilia is absent. Barium studies are generally nonspecific and show an increased transit time and irregular thickening of small

bowel folds. These studies may interfere with the examination of stools.

TREATMENT

Routine isolation, culture, and susceptibility testing of *Giardia* have been difficult because of the variable success in establishing cultures from clinical specimens and the lack of standardization on sensitivity testing.[107] Drug resistance occurs for *Giardia* and can be induced in vitro,[108] but the clinical significance of this is not known because some isolates that appear clinically resistant are susceptible in vitro, and vice versa. Most information on drug efficacy, therefore, is provided by clinical experience.[107,109]

The drug of choice for the therapy of giardiasis in the United States is metronidazole, a nitroimidazole drug. Although the U.S. Food and Drug Administration has never approved this for giardiasis, most physicians treat giardiasis with metronidazole because of their familiarity with using it for other infections, its favorable side-effect profile, and its ready availability. When metronidazole enters trophozoites, its nitro group becomes reduced, or "activated," by accepting electrons from parasite ferredoxins.[110,111] Once activated, it binds to parasite DNA, causing damage and trophozoite death. Metronidazole also inhibits parasite respiration. When resistance to metronidazole occurs, it correlates with decreased parasite pyruvate:ferredoxin oxidoreductase.[108]

Metronidazole is given in divided doses for 5 to 7 days (Table 277-2), with an efficacy of 80% to 95%. It is tolerated reasonably well in the pediatric age group. Although concerns about potential mutagenicity make its routine use in children debatable, this has not been documented in humans.[112] Side effects that may be noted are a metallic taste in the mouth, some nausea, dizziness, headache, and, rarely, reversible neutropenia. When taken with alcohol, it can produce a disulfiram-like effect. High-dose, short-course regimens have lower efficacy rates and may be poorly tolerated. Although not available in the United States, another nitroimidazole, tinidazole, has excellent efficacy (approximately 90%) when given in a single 2-g dose.[109]

Quinacrine is a very effective agent, but its production in the United States was discontinued in 1992. If quinacrine can be obtained through alternative sources, it can be given in divided doses for 5 to 7 days (see Table 277-2) and should have an efficacy of more than 90%. The most common side effects are a bitter taste, nausea, vomiting, and abdominal cramping. Yellow discoloration of the skin, urine, and sclerae can occasionally occur, and exfoliative dermatitis is a rare side effect.

Nitazoxanide (Alinia, Romark Pharmaceuticals, Tampa, FL) was approved in 2003 for use in pediatric giardiasis and cryptosporidiosis. There is limited clinical experience with this drug, but it is active in vitro, and efficacy appears to be in the range of 70% to 85% when a 3-day course of treatment is given.[113,114] Nitazoxanide has wide activ-

TABLE 277-2 Treatment of Giardiasis

Drug	Dosage	
	Adult	**Pediatric**
Metronidazole*	250 mg tid × 5-7 days	5 mg/kg tid × 7 days
Quinacrine†	100 mg tid × 5-7 days	2 mg/kg tid ×7 days
Nitazoxanide	Not approved	Age 12-47 mo: 100 mg bid × 3 days Age 4-11 yr: 200 mg bid × 3 days
Furazolidone	100 mg qid × 7-10 days	2 mg/kg qid × 10 days
Albendazole*	400 mg qd × 5 days	15 mg/kg/day × 5-7 days (max., 400 mg)
Paromomycin*	500 mg tid × 5-10 days	30 mg/kg/day in 3 doses × 5-10 days
Tinidazole‡	2 g, single dose	50 mg/kg, single dose (max., 2 g)

*Not a U.S. Food and Drug Administration–approved indication.
†No longer produced in the United States; may be obtained from some compounding pharmacies (Panorama Pharmacy, Lake Balboa, CA).
‡Not available in the United States.

ity against a variety of intestinal parasites and some bacteria. Its main side effect is gastrointestinal upset.

Furazolidone, a nitrofuran, has been advocated as another drug in the pediatric age group because of its availability in liquid suspension. It has a success rate of about 80% to 85% and may cause gastrointestinal side effects, turn urine brown, and cause mild hemolysis in glucose-6-phosphate dehydrogenase–deficient individuals.

There is increasing experience with the benzimidazoles. Although efficacy with mebendazole is disappointing, several studies have demonstrated success with albendazole in a single daily dose of 400 mg for 5 days (reviewed in reference 107). The actual role that albendazole will have in therapy remains to be determined, but it is attractive because it has efficacy against many intestinal helminths and may be used in resource-poor regions to decrease intestinal parasitism. Bacitracin has shown efficacy in one study.[115]

For patients in whom one drug course fails or who infrequently relapse, a switch to a drug from a different class is generally effective. For the unusual patient who is not cured with single-drug therapies, combination treatment with metronidazole and quinacrine is often effective.[75] Nitazoxanide may also be effective in patients with resistant giardiasis.[116] When refractory infection is suspected, it is important to establish true persistent infection by obtaining a repeat stool exam; for those patients who simply have post-*Giardia* lactose intolerance, further antiparasitic treatment is not needed.

For pregnant women with giardiasis, there is no consistently recommended therapy because of the theoretical adverse effects of anti-*Giardia* drugs on the fetus.[107] When the disease is mild and hydration and nutrition can be maintained, therapy may be delayed until after delivery, or at least until after the first trimester. If treatment is necessary, paromomycin, an oral aminoglycoside, may be tried. In limited clinical experience, it has an efficacy rate of 60% to 70%, but it has the advantage of not being measurably absorbed from the intestine in persons with normal renal function.[117] It is given in divided doses for 5 to 10 days. Metronidazole has been used extensively in pregnancy for the treatment of trichomoniasis. The teratogenic effect appears to be minimal and, if present, greatest during the first trimester, when the drug should not be used.[107,117,118] If therapy cannot be avoided, then metronidazole can probably be used safely in the last two trimesters of pregnancy. High-dose, short-course regimens should not be used.

PREVENTION

The prevention of giardiasis requires proper handling and treatment of water used for communities, and good personal hygiene on an individual basis. Although chlorination alone is sufficient to kill *G. lamblia* cysts, important variables, such as water temperature, clarity, pH, and contact time, alter the efficacy of chlorine, and higher chlorine levels (4 to 6 mg/L) may be required.[34,119] Thus, in addition to chlorination, public water supplies should also be subjected to flocculation, sedimentation, and filtration.[34]

Travelers to resource-poor regions of the world or to wilderness areas should consider all water potentially contaminated because of the wide array of animal and human reservoirs of giardiasis. Bringing water to a boil is sufficient to kill all protozoal cysts; at high altitudes, boiling for a minute is reasonable. If boiling is impossible, halogenation is generally effective for *Giardia,* but *Cryptosporidium* is resistant,[120] and the sensitivity of *Cyclospora* is likely to be similar to that of *Cryptosporidium*. Chlorine-based (AquaClear; chlorine bleach: 5% to 6%, 2 to 4 drops/L) or iodine-based (tetraglycine hydroperiodide [e.g., Globaline, Potable-Aqua, Coghlan's]; tincture of iodine: 2%, 5 drops/L) preparations may be used.[119] Contact time should be increased for water that is cold, and the concentration of halogen should be increased for turbid water. Small-volume personal water filters with pores of an "absolute" micron size of 0.2 to 1 μm can be used. Filtered water should also be halogenated to kill enteric viruses if they are considered a risk. Uncooked foods that may have been washed or prepared in contaminated water should be avoided.

The endemic foci present in daycare centers are a major problem. It is not clear whether chronic, asymptomatic carriage of *Giardia* in otherwise well-nourished children is deleterious to their health.[91,92,121] For these reasons and because of potential side effects of treatment, some recommend that only symptomatic children be treated.[91,122] On the other hand, infected children transmit *Giardia* to parents and family members and may contribute to high endemic infection rates in communities.[36,123] Because of these conflicting issues, each situation requires an individual decision. However, if strict hand washing and treatment of symptomatic children fail to control an outbreak of diarrhea, consideration can be given to treating all infected children.[124] Venereal transmission of *Giardia* can be decreased by avoidance of oral-anal and oral-genital sex. At present, there is no immuno- or chemoprophylactic strategy for giardiasis in humans, although a veterinary vaccine has been developed.[125]

REFERENCES

1. Garcia LS. Classification of human parasites, vectors, and similar organisms. Clin Infect Dis. 1999;29:734-736.
2. Gillin FD, Reiner DS, McCaffery JM. Cell biology of the primitive eukaryote *Giardia lamblia*. Annu Rev Microbiol. 1996;50:679-705.
3. Adam RD. Biology of *Giardia lamblia*. Clin Microbiol Rev. 2001;14:447-475.
4. Davis-Hayman SR, Nash TE. Genetic manipulation of *Giardia lamblia*. Mol Biochem Parasitol. 2002;122:1-7.
5. Lane S, Lloyd D. Current trends in research into the waterborne parasite *Giardia*. Crit Rev Microbiol. 2002;28:123-147.
6. Monis PT, Andrews RH, Mayrhofer G, Ey PL. Molecular systematics of the parasitic protozoan *Giardia intestinalis*. Mol Biol Evol. 1999;16:1135-1144.
7. Nash TE, McCutchan T, Keister D, et al. Restriction-endonuclease analysis of DNA from 15 *Giardia* isolates obtained from humans and animals. J Infect Dis. 1985;152:64-73.
8. Mayrhofer G, Andrews RH, Ey PL, Chilton NB. Division of *Giardia* isolates from humans into two genetically distinct assemblages by electrophoretic analysis of enzymes encoded at 27 loci and comparison with *Giardia muris*. Parasitology. 1995;111:11-17.
9. Nash TE, Herrington DA, Losonsky GA, Levine MM. Experimental human infections with *Giardia lamblia*. J Infect Dis. 1987;156:974-984.
10. Thompson RC. Giardiasis as a re-emerging infectious disease and its zoonotic potential. Int J Parasitol. 2000;30:1259-1267.
11. Adam RD. The *Giardia lamblia* genome. Int J Parasitol. 2000;30:475-484.
12. Nash TE. Surface antigenic variation in *Giardia lamblia*. Mol Microbiol. 2002;45:585-590.
13. Elmendorf HG, Dawson SC, McCaffery JM. The cytoskeleton of *Giardia lamblia*. Int J Parasitol. 2003;33:3-28.
14. Yu LZ, Birky CW Jr, Adam RD. The two nuclei of *Giardia* each have complete copies of the genome and are partitioned equationally at cytokinesis. Eukaryot Cell. 2002;1:191-9.
15. Clark CG, Diamond LS. Methods for cultivation of luminal parasitic protists of clinical importance. Clin Microbiol Rev. 2002;15:329-341.
16. Lujan HD, Mowatt MR, Byrd LG, Nash TE. Cholesterol starvation induces differentiation of the intestinal parasite *Giardia lamblia*. Proc Natl Acad Sci U S A. 1996;93:7628-7633.
17. Svärd SG, Hagblom P, Palm JE. *Giardia lamblia:* A model organism for eukaryotic cell differentiation. FEMS Microbiol Lett. 2003;218:3-7.
18. Touz MC, Nores MJ, Slavin I, et al. The activity of a developmentally regulated cysteine proteinase is required for cyst wall formation in the primitive eukaryote *Giardia lamblia*. J Biol Chem. 2002;277:8474-8481.
19. Erlandsen SL, Macechko PT, van Keulen H, Jarroll EL. Formation of the *Giardia* cyst wall: Studies on extracellular assembly using immunogold labeling and high resolution field emission SEM. J Eukaryot Microbiol. 1996;43:416-429.
20. Hetsko ML, McCaffery JM, Svard SG, et al. Cellular and transcriptional changes during excystation of *Giardia lamblia* in vitro. Exp Parasitol. 1998;88:172-183.
21. Ward W, Alvarado L, Rawlings ND, et al. A primitive enzyme for a primitive cell: The protease required for excystation of *Giardia*. Cell. 1997;89:437-444.
22. Reiner DS, Hetsko ML, Meszaros JG, et al. Calcium signaling in excystation of the early diverging eukaryote, *Giardia lamblia*. J Biol Chem. 2003;278:2533-2540.
23. Furness BW, Beach MJ, Roberts JM. Giardiasis surveillance: United States, 1992-1997. MMWR CDC Surveill Summ. 2000;49:1-13.
24. Caeiro JP, Mathewson JJ, Smith MA, et al. Etiology of outpatient pediatric nondysenteric diarrhea: A multicenter study in the United States. Pediatr Infect Dis J. 1999;18:94-97.
25. Gilman RH, Brown KH, Visvesvara GS, et al. Epidemiology and serology of *Giardia lamblia* in a developing country: Bangladesh. Trans R Soc Trop Med Hyg. 1985;79:469-473.
26. Fraser D, Dagan R, Naggan L, et al. Natural history of *Giardia lamblia* and *Cryptosporidium* infections in a cohort of Israeli Bedouin infants: A study of a population in transition. Am J Trop Med Hyg. 1997;57:544-549.

27. Berkman DS, Lescano AG, Gilman RH, et al. Effects of stunting, diarrhoeal disease, and parasitic infection during infancy on cognition in late childhood: A follow-up study. Lancet. 2002;359:564-571.

28. Farthing MJG, Mata L, Urrutia JJ, Kronmal RA. Natural history of *Giardia* infection of infants and children in rural Guatemala and its impact on physical growth. Am J Clin Nutr. 1986;43:395-405.

29. Gilman RH, Miranda E, Marquis GS, et al. Rapid reinfection by *Giardia lamblia* after treatment in a hyperendemic Third World community. Lancet. 1988;1:343-345.

30. Cifuentes E, Gomez M, Blumenthal U, et al. Risk factors for *Giardia intestinalis* infection in agricultural villages practicing wastewater irrigation in Mexico. Am J Trop Med Hyg. 2000;62:388-392.

31. Mahmud MA, Chappell C, Hossain MM, et al. Risk factors for development of first symptomatic *Giardia* infection among infants of a birth cohort in rural Egypt. Am J Trop Med Hyg. 1995;53:84-88.

32. Lee SH, Levy DA, Craun GF, et al. Surveillance for waterborne-disease outbreaks: United States, 1999-2000. MMWR Surveill Summ. 2002;51:1-47.

33. Stuart JM, Orr HJ, Warburton FG, et al. Risk factors for sporadic giardiasis: A case-control study in southwestern England. Emerg Infect Dis. 2003;9:229-233.

34. Jakubowski WS. Purple burps and the filtration of drinking water supplies (Editorial). Am J Public Health. 1988;78:123-125.

35. Thompson SC. *Giardia lamblia* in children and the child care setting: A review of the literature. J Paediatr Child Health. 1994;30:202-209.

36. Overturf GD. Endemic giardiasis in the United States: Role of the daycare center (Editorial). Clin Infect Dis. 1994;18:764-765.

37. Greig JD, Michel P, Wilson JB, et al. A descriptive analysis of giardiasis cases reported in Ontario, 1990-1998. Can J Public Health. 2001;92:361-365.

38. Hill DR. Giardiasis: Issues in management and treatment. Infect Dis Clin North Am. 1993;7:503-525.

39. Mintz ED, Hudson-Wragg M, Mshar P, et al. Foodborne giardiasis in a corporate office setting. J Infect Dis. 1993;167:250-253.

40. Olsen SJ, MacKinnon LC, Goulding JS, et al. Surveillance for foodborne-disease outbreaks: United States, 1993-1997. MMWR CDC Surveill Summ. 2000;49:1-62.

41. Jelinek T, Loscher T. Epidemiology of giardiasis in German travelers. J Travel Med. 2000;7:70-73.

42. Okhuysen PC. Traveler's diarrhea due to intestinal protozoa. Clin Infect Dis. 2001;33:110-114.

43. Olson ME, O'Handley RM, Ralston BJ, et al. Update on *Cryptosporidium* and *Giardia* infections in cattle. Trends Parasitol. 2004;20:185-191.

44. Monis PT, Andrews RH, Mayrhofer G, et al. Novel lineages of *Giardia intestinalis* identified by genetic analysis of organisms isolated from dogs in Australia. Parasitology. 1998;116:7-19.

45. Baruch AC, Isaac-Renton J, Adam RD. The molecular epidemiology of *Giardia lamblia*: A sequence-based approach. J Infect Dis. 1996;174:233-236.

46. Rendtorff RC. The experimental transmission of human intestinal protozoan parasites: II. *Giardia lamblia* cysts given in capsules. Am J Hyg. 1954;59:209-220.

47. Homan WL, Mank TG. Human giardiasis: genotype linked differences in clinical symptomatology. Int J Parasitol. 2001;31:822-826.

48. Chin AC, Teoh DA, Scott KG, et al. Strain-dependent induction of enterocyte apoptosis by *Giardia lamblia* disrupts epithelial barrier function in a caspase-3-dependent manner. Infect Immun. 2002;70:3673-3680.

49. Heyworth MF. Immunology of *Giardia* and *Cryptosporidium* infections. J Infect Dis. 1992;166:465-472.

50. Faubert G. Immune response to *Giardia duodenalis*. Clin Micro Rev. 2000;13:35-54.

51. Miotti PG, Gilman RH, Santosham M, et al. Age-related rate of seropositivity of antibody to *Giardia lamblia* in four diverse populations. J Clin Microbiol. 1986;24:972-975.

52. Istre GR, Dunlop TS, Gaspard B, Hopkins RS. Waterborne giardiasis at a mountain resort: Evidence for acquired immunity. Am J Public Health. 1984;74:602-604.

53. Isaac-Renton JL, Lewis LF, Ong CS, Nulsen MF. A second community outbreak of waterborne giardiasis in Canada and serological investigation of patients. Trans R Soc Trop Med Hyg. 1994;88:395-399.

54. Ljungström I, Castor B. Immune response to *Giardia lamblia* in a water-borne outbreak of giardiasis in Sweden. J Med Microbiol. 1992;36:347-352.

55. Soliman MM, Taghi-Kilani R, Abou-Shady AF, et al. Comparison of serum antibody response to *Giardia lamblia* of symptomatic and asymptomatic patients. Am J Trop Med Hyg. 1998;58:232-239.

56. Isaac-Renton J, Blatherwick J, Bowie WR, et al. Epidemic and endemic seroprevalence of antibodies to *Cryptosporidium* and *Giardia* in residents of three communities with different drinking water supplies. Am J Trop Med Hyg. 1999;60:578-583.

57. Char S, Cervallos AM, Yamson P, et al. Impaired IgA response to *Giardia* heat shock antigen in children with persistent diarrhoea and giardiasis. Gut. 1993;34:38-40.

58. Stäger S, Müller N. *Giardia lamblia* infections in B-cell-deficient transgenic mice. Infect Immun. 1997;65:3944-3946.

59. Rosales-Borjas DM, Diaz-Rivadeneyra J, Dona-Leyva A, et al. Secretory immune response to membrane antigens during *Giardia lamblia* infection in humans. Infect Immun. 1998;66:756-759.

60. Langford TD, Housley MP, Boes M, et al. Central importance of immunoglobulin A in host defense against *Giardia* spp. Infect Immun. 2002;70:11-18.

61. Snider DP, Underdown BJ. Quantitative and temporal analyses of murine antibody response in serum and gut secretions to infection with *Giardia muris*. Infect Immun. 1986;52:271-278.

62. Zhou P, Li E, Zhu N, et al. Role of interleukin-6 in the control of acute and chronic *Giardia lamblia* infections in mice. Infect Immun. 2003;71:1566-1568.

63. Heyworth MF, Carlson JR, Ermak TH. Clearance of *Giardia muris* infection requires helper/inducer T lymphocytes. J Exp Med. 1987;165:1743-1748.

64. Ridley MJ, Ridley DS. Serum antibodies and jejunal histology in giardiasis. J Clin Pathol. 1976;29:30-34.

65. Duncombe VM, Bolin TD, Davis AE, Crouch RL. Histopathology in giardiasis: A correlation with diarrhea. Aust N Z J Med. 1978;8:392-396.

66. Scott KG, Logan MR, Klammer GM, et al. Jejunal brush border microvillous alterations in *Giardia muris*–infected mice: Role of T lymphocytes and interleukin-6. Infect Immun. 2000;68:3412-3418.

67. Chen XM, Keithly JS, Paya CV, LaRusso NF. Cryptosporidiosis. N Engl J Med. 2002;346:1723-1731.

68. Jimenez JC, Fontaine J, Grzych JM, et al. Systemic and mucosal responses to oral administration of excretory and secretory antigens from *Giardia intestinalis*. Clin Diagn Lab Immunol. 2004;11:152-160.

69. Reiner DS, Wang CS, Gillin FD. Human milk kills *Giardia lamblia* by generating toxic lipolytic products. J Infect Dis. 1986;154:825-832.

70. Mahmud MA, Chappell CL, Hossain MM, et al. Impact of breast-feeding on *Giardia lamblia* infections in Bilbeis, Egypt. Am J Trop Med Hyg. 2001;65:257-260.

71. Singer SM, Nash TE. The role of normal flora in *Giardia lamblia* infections in mice. J Infect Dis. 2000;181:1510-1512.

72. Eckmann L, Laurent F, Langford TD, et al. Nitric oxide production by human intestinal epithelial cells and competition for arginine as potential determinants of host defense against the lumen-dwelling pathogen *Giardia lamblia*. J Immunol. 2000;164:1478-1487.

73. Rosen FS, Cooper MD, Wedgwood RJP. The primary immunodeficiencies. N Engl J Med. 1995;333:431-440.

74. Burrows PD, Cooper MD. IgA deficiency. Adv Immunol. 1997;65:245-276.

75. Nash TE, Ohl CA, Thomas E, et al. Treatment of patients with refractory giardiasis. Clin Infect Dis. 2001;33:22-28.

76. Singer SM, Elmendorf HG, Conrad JT, Nash TE. Biological selection of variant-specific surface proteins in *Giardia lamblia*. J Infect Dis. 2001;183:119-124.

77. Oberhuber G, Kastner N, Stolte M. Giardiasis: A histologic analysis of 567 cases. Scand J Infect Dis. 1997;32:48-51.

78. Hjelt K, Paerregaard A, Krasilnikoff PA. Giardiasis causing chronic diarrhoea in suburban Copenhagen: Incidence, physical growth, clinical symptoms and small intestinal abnormality. Acta Paediatr. 1992;81:881-886.

79. Berney DM, Rampton D, van der Walt JD. Giardiasis of the stomach. Postgrad Med J. 1994;70:237-238.

80. Lengerich EJ, Addiss DG, Juranek DD. Severe giardiasis in the United States. Clin Infect Dis. 1994;18:760-763.

81. Robertson LJ. Severe giardiasis and cryptosporidiosis in Scotland, UK. Epidemiol Infect. 1996;117:551-561.

82. Solomons NW. Giardiasis: nutritional implications. Rev Infect Dis. 1982;4:859-869.

83. Gillon J. Clinical studies in adults presenting with giardiasis to a gastrointestinal unit. Scot Med J. 1985;30:89-95.

84. Welsh JD, Poley JR, Hensley J, Bhatia M. Intestinal disaccharidase and alkaline phosphatase activity in giardiasis. J Pediatr Gastroenterol Nutr. 1984;3:37-40.

85. Gupta MC, Urrutia JJ. Effect of periodic antiascaris and antigiardia treatment on nutritional status of preschool children. Am J Clin Nutr. 1982;36:79-86.

86. Fraser D, Bilenko N, Deckelbaum RJ, et al. *Giardia lamblia* carriage in Israeli Bedouin infants: Risk factors and consequences. Clin Infect Dis. 2000;30:419-424.

87. Sullivan PS, DuPont HL, Arafat RR, et al. Illness and reservoirs associated with *Giardia lamblia* infection in rural Egypt: The case against treatment in developing world environments of high endemicity. Am J Epidemiol. 1988;127:1272-1281.

88. Sackey ME, Weigel MM, Armijos RX. Predictors and nutritional consequences of intestinal parasitic infections in rural Ecuadorian children. J Trop Pediatr. 2003;49:17-23.

89. Goto R, Panter-Brick C, Northrop-Clewes CA, et al. Poor intestinal permeability in mildly stunted Nepali children: Associations with weaning practices and *Giardia lamblia* infection. Br J Nutr. 2002;88:141-149.

90. Newman RD, Moore SR, Lima AA, et al. A longitudinal study of *Giardia lamblia* infection in north-east Brazilian children. Trop Med Int Health. 2001;6:624-634.

91. Ish-Horowicz M, Korman SH, Shapiro M, et al. Asymptomatic giardiasis in children. Pediatr Infect Dis J. 1989;8:773-779.

92. Moya-Camarena SY, Sotelo N, Valencia ME. Effects of asymptomatic *Giardia intestinalis* infection on carbohydrate absorption in well-nourished Mexican children. Am J Trop Med Hyg. 2002;66:255-259.

93. Lima AA, Moore SR, Barboza MS Jr, et al. Persistent diarrhea signals a critical period of increased diarrhea burdens and nutritional shortfalls: A prospective cohort study among children in northeastern Brazil. J Infect Dis. 2000;181:1643-1651.

94. Marshall MM, Naumovitz D, Ortega Y, Sterling CR. Waterborne protozoan pathogens. Clin Micro Rev. 1997;10:67-85.

95. Herwaldt BL. *Cyclospora cayetanensis*: A review, focusing on the outbreaks of cyclosporiasis in the 1990s. Clin Infect Dis. 2000;31:1040-1057.

96. Garcia LS, Shimizu RY. Evaluation of nine immunoassay kits (enzyme immunoassay and direct fluorescence) for detection of *Giardia lamblia* and *Cryptosporidium parvum* in human fecal specimens. J Clin Microbiol. 1997;35:1526-1529.

97. Aldeen WE, Carroll K, Robison A, et al. Comparison of nine commercially available enzyme-linked immunosorbent assays for the detection of *Giardia lamblia* in fecal specimens. J Clin Microbiol. 1998;36:1338-1340.

98. Hiatt RA, Markell EK, Ng E. How many stool examinations are necessary to detect pathogenic intestinal protozoa? Am J Trop Med Hyg. 1995;53:36-39.

99. Mank TG, Zaat JO, Deelder AM, et al. Sensitivity of microscopy versus enzyme immunoassay in the laboratory diagnosis of giardiasis. Eur J Clin Microbiol Infect Dis. 1997;16:615-619.

100. Zimmerman SK, Needham CA. Comparison of conventional stool concentration and preserved-smear methods with Merifluor Cryptosporidium/Giardia Direct Immunofluorescence Assay and ProSpecT Giardia EZ Microplate Assay for the detection of *Giardia lamblia.* J Clin Microbiol. 1995;33:1942-1943.
101. Chan R, Chen J, York MK, et al. Evaluation of a combination rapid immunoassay for detection of *Giardia* and *Cryptosporidium* antigens. J Clin Microbiol. 2000;38: 393-394.
102. Aziz H, Beck CE, Lux MF, Hudson MJ. A comparison study of different methods used in the detection of *Giardia lamblia.* Clin Lab Sci. 2001;14:150-154.
103. Boone JH, Wilkins TD, Nash TE, et al. TechLab and Alexon *Giardia* enzyme-linked immunosorbent assay kits detect cyst wall protein 1. J Clin Microbiol. 1999;37: 611-614.
104. Johnston SP, Ballard MM, Beach MJ, et al. Evaluation of three commercial assays for detection of *Giardia* and *Cryptosporidium* organisms in fecal specimens. J Clin Microbiol. 2003;41:623-626.
105. Granot E, Spira DT, Fraser D, Deckelbaum RJ. Immunologic response to infection with *Giardia lamblia* in children: Effect of different clinical settings. J Trop Pediatr. 1998;44:241-246.
106. Mahbubani MH, Schaefer FWI, Jones DD, Bej AK. Detection of *Giardia* in environmental waters by immuno-PCR amplification methods. Curr Microbiol. 1998;36: 107-113.
107. Gardner TB, Hill DR. Treatment of giardiasis. Clin Micro Rev. 2001;14:114-128.
108. Upcroft P, Upcroft JA. Drug targets and mechanisms of resistance in the anaerobic protozoa. Clin Microbiol Rev. 2001;14:150-164.
109. Zaat JO, Mank T, Assendelft WJ. Drugs for treating giardiasis. Cochrane Database Syst Rev. 2000:CD000217.
110. Upcroft J, Upcroft P. My favorite cell: *Giardia.* Bioessays. 1998;20:256-263.
111. Samuelson J. Why metronidazole is active against both bacteria and parasites. Antimicrob Agents Chemother. 1999;43:1533-1541.
112. Falagas ME, Walker AM, Jick H, et al. Late incidence of cancer after metronidazole use: A matched metronidazole user/nonuser study. Clin Infect Dis. 1998;26:384-388.
113. Gilles HM, Hoffman PS. Treatment of intestinal parasitic infections: A review of nitazoxanide. Trends Parasitol. 2002;18:95-97.
114. Medical Letter. Nitazoxanide (Alinia): A new anti-protozoal agent. Med Lett Drugs Ther. 2003;45:29-31.
115. Andrews BJ, Panitescu D, Jipa GH, et al. Chemotherapy for giardiasis: Randomized clinical trial of bacitracin, bacitracin zinc, and a combination of bacitracin zinc with neomycin. Am J Trop Med Hyg. 1995;52:318-321.
116. Abboud P, Lemee V, Gargala G, et al. Successful treatment of metronidazole- and albendazole-resistant giardiasis with nitazoxanide in a patient with acquired immunodeficiency syndrome. Clin Infect Dis. 2001;32:1792-1794.
117. Rotblatt MD. Giardiasis and amebiasis in pregnancy. Drug Intell Clin Pharm. 1983;17:187-188.
118. Burtin P, Taddio A, Ariburnu O, et al. Safety of metronidazole in pregnancy: A meta-analysis. Am J Obstet Gynecol. 1995;172:525-529.
119. Backer H. Water disinfection for international and wilderness travelers. Clin Infect Dis. 2002;34:355-364.
120. Juranek DD. Cryptosporidiosis: Sources of infection and guidelines for prevention. Clin Infect Dis. 1995;21(Suppl 1):S57-61.
121. Nunez FA, Hernandez M, Finlay CM. Longitudinal study of giardiasis in three day care centres of Havana City. Acta Trop. 1999;73:237-242.
122. Pickering LK, Woodward WE, DuPont HL, Sullivan P. Occurrence of *Giardia lamblia* in children in day care centers. J Pediatr. 1984;104:522-526.
123. Dennis DT, Smith RP, Welch JJ, et al. Endemic giardiasis in New Hampshire: A case-control study of environmental risks. J Infect Dis. 1993;167:1391-1395.
124. Bartlett AV, Englender SJ, Jarvis BA, et al. Controlled trial of *Giardia lamblia:* Control strategies in day care centers. Am J Public Health. 1991;81:1001-1006.
125. Olson ME, Ceri H, Morck DW. *Giardia* vaccination. Parasitol Today. 2000;16:213-217.

CHAPTER **278**

Trichomonas vaginalis

DAVID H. MARTIN

MICHAEL F. REIN

*T*richomonas vaginalis was first described by Donné in 1836.[1] Its acceptance as a primary pathogen was gradual, and the older literature frequently refers to it as a harmless commensal.[2] Closely related organisms are widespread in nature and are important pathogens of cattle, among which they are venereally transmitted, and fowl. Other organisms in the same family also infect humans. *Trichomonas tenax* resides in the anaerobic, periodontal crevices of some patients with py-

orrhea and occasionally appears to cause respiratory tract infection in patients with underlying pulmonary disease.[2] *Pentatrichomonas hominis* can be recovered from the lower gastrointestinal tract, more frequently from patients with symptomatic bowel disease. Trichomonads are highly site specific, and infection has never followed attempts to inoculate one species into an anatomic site usually inhabited by another.[2] Infected vaginal discharge contains 10^1 to 10^5 protozoa/mL, with most women carrying the larger numbers.[3] In fresh preparations, *T. vaginalis* is actively motile and usually pear-shaped, with average dimensions of approximately 10×7 μm. The organisms vary somewhat in size and shape and are most easily identified by their characteristic twitching motility. There are four free anterior flagella that appear to arise from a single stalk and a fifth flagellum, which is embedded in the undulating membrane that extends about midway across the organism. All areas of the cell surface are capable of phagocytosis and can ingest bacteria, leukocytes, erythrocytes, and epithelial cells. The organism generates metabolic energy with unique organelles called *hydrogenosomes,* reproduces by binary fission, and exists only as a vegetative cell, no cyst forms having been described. More than half of clinical *T. vaginalis* strains carry double-stranded RNA viruses. Parasites infected by viruses differ phenotypically from those that are uninfected but the clinical significance of this observation is unclear.[4,5]

Strains differ with respect to a variety of phenotypic and genotypic variables. However, clear associations with clinical virulence have not been established.[6,7] Trichomonads appear to damage genital epithelium by direct contact[8] that is mediated by surface proteins[8,9] and results in microulcerations. Understanding of attachment mechanisms could lead to the development of new therapeutic and/or preventive agents.[10,11] The human immune response to *T. vaginalis* infection is poorly understood. The organism activates the alternative complement pathway and attracts polymorphonuclear (PMN) neutrophils, which can kill the protozoa.[12] On the other hand, *T. vaginalis* will move away from the products of PMN oxidative metabolism. Monocytes and macrophages can also kill trichomonads in vitro, but their role in natural infection is uncertain. Local and systemic humoral responses and delayed hypersensitivity are manifest in human infection,[2] but they do not appear to be protective and have not proven useful diagnostically.

EPIDEMIOLOGY

Although not a reportable disease, the literature indicates that trichomoniasis is among the most common sexually transmitted diseases (STDs) in women. Rates in female STD clinic clients of 11% to 26% have been reported and rates among newly incarcerated women have approached 50%.[13] Using recently available polymerase chain reaction assays, *T. vaginalis* has been found in 13% to 21% of men with nongonococcal urethritis (NGU)[14-16] and in as high as 12% in asymptomatic men attending an African STD clinic.[14] The age distribution of *T. vaginalis* infections differs dramatically compared to chlamydial and gonococcal infections. For the latter two prevalence rates decline steadily with increasing age. In contrast *T. vaginalis* infection rates are as high or higher in middle aged women compared to adolescents.[17,18] Having a sexual partner who is more than 4 years older is an important risk factor for trichomoniasis among adolescents.[19] The reason that high prevalence rates of trichomoniasis persist in older men and women is unclear, but a likely explanation, at least in part, is that a protective immune response to trichomonal infection either does not develop or is relatively weak.

The venereal nature of trichomoniasis is well established.[2] Its incidence is highest among women with multiple sexual partners[2,20] and in groups with high rates of other sexually transmitted diseases.[2] Thus, patients found to harbor *T. vaginalis* should always be screened for infections with other sexually transmitted pathogens, such as *Neisseria gonorrhoeae, Chlamydia trachomatis,* or HIV,[21] which may be clinically silent but may be of far greater medical consequence than is the protozoon.

The organism is recovered from 66% to 100% of the female partners of infected men and from 22% to 80% of the male sexual partners of infected women.[22] The infection appears to be self limited in only about 20% of women[23] but in at least 40% of men,[22] possibly because of the trichomonacidal action of prostatic secretions or to the mechanical elimination of urethral protozoa during micturition.

Trichomoniasis is occasionally acquired nonvenereally. The organism will survive for several hours in moist environments, including moist cloths. Thus, the potential for nonvenereal transmission clearly exists,[2] and trichomoniasis is found with high prevalence in some institutionalized populations. Transmission via the fingers during mutual masturbation has been suggested,[24] and transmission by sexual toys or shared douche equipment seems a possibility. However, a recent study of incarcerated women revealed no evidence of transmission after entry into the facility.[25]

Like the other genital infections, trichomoniasis may be transmitted to neonates during passage through an infected birth canal and is acquired by 2% to 17% of the female offspring of infected women.[26] Pulmonary infection is rarely acquired by this route.[26] Thereafter, trichomoniasis is rare until menarche. Genital trichomoniasis in an older child should raise the question of sexual abuse[27] but, because of the possibility of nonvenereal transmission, the diagnosis does not prove that abuse has occurred.[28]

HIV infected women are not at greater risk of trichomoniasis than uninfected women.[29] However, there is evidence that *T. vaginalis* infection increases the risk of HIV transmission.[30] HIV viral loads are higher in both men and women with trichomoniasis compared to HIV-infected persons without this organism.[14,31]

CLINICAL FEATURES

The incubation period in women ranges from about 5 to 28 days.[2,21] Symptoms often begin or exacerbate during the menstrual period. Clinical features are summarized in Table 278-1. Approximately 10% to 50% of infected women attending sexually transmitted disease clinics carry the organism asymptomatically.[2] Infected women usually note vaginal discharge and vulvovaginal soreness or irritation.[2,21] Dysuria may be perceived as internal or external, and dyspareunia is common. Abdominal discomfort is described by 5% to 12% of infected women but should still prompt careful evaluation of a second process, such as pelvic inflammatory disease. Unfortunately, none of these symptoms alone or in combination is sufficient to diagnose trichomoniasis reliably because each can accompany other genital infections.[34]

Examination usually reveals a copious discharge that pools in the posterior vaginal fornix. Only about 5% to 40% of the women have a discharge that is distinctly yellow or green.[21] Bubbles are observed in the discharge of 10% to 33% of the cases (Fig. 278-1).[2,21] Although protozoa can be recovered by culture from the endocervix in 90% of infected women, endocervical disease is not caused by *T. vaginalis*.[35] Symptomatic women usually manifest inflammation of the vaginal walls and the exocervix. Punctate hemorrhages (colpitis macularis), including the so-called strawberry cervix, are observed colposcopically in 45% of infected women but in only 2% by visual inspection alone.[2,21] Trichomonal vaginitis is a superficial infection, and invasion of the vaginal walls by the parasite has not been observed. Trichomoniasis is associated with a shift in the vaginal flora away from the normal lactobacillus predominant flora in a majority of cases and approximately a third meet diagnostic criteria for frank bacterial vaginosis.[36,37] Therefore, women with trichomoniasis may complain of a fish-like odor, will have a vaginal secretion pH above 4.5, and will demonstrate clue cells on microscopic examination of the wet mount specimen.[34]

Trichomonads can be recovered from the urethra and paraurethral glands in more than 95% of the women with trichomoniasis, which may explain the association of the infection with urinary frequency and internal dysuria.[21]

Complications of trichomonal vaginitis include vaginitis emphysematosa, an uncommon condition in which gas-filled blebs occur in the vaginal wall. If associated with trichomoniasis, the condition will resolve when the infection is eradicated.[38] Women with trichomoniasis are more likely to suffer vaginal cuff cellulitis after abdominal hysterectomy. Gestational trichomoniasis has been associated with premature labor and low birth weight,[39] and less strikingly with postabortal infection and with premature rupture of the membranes. However, a recent randomized, placebo-controlled treatment trial of trichomoniasis in pregnant women did not demonstrate any benefit of treatment.[40] There has been speculation that bacterial or viral pathogens might be carried into the fallopian tubes by trichomonads, but spread of trichomonads beyond the lower urogenital tract is extremely rare.

TABLE 278-1 Sensitivity of Clinical and Laboratory Features in Vaginal Trichomoniasis

	Clinical Feature	Percent Positive
Symptoms	None	9-56
	Discharge	50-75
	Malodorous	~10
	Irritating, pruritic	23-82
	Dyspareunia	10-50
	Dysuria	30-50
	Lower abdominal discomfort	5-12
Signs	None	~15
	Vulvar erythema	10-20
	Excessive discharge	50-75
	Yellow, green	5-20
	Frothy	10-50
	Vaginal wall inflammation	40-75
	Strawberry cervix (direct visualization)	1-2
	Colpitis macularis (colposcope)	45
Laboratory Findings	pH > 4.5	66-91
	Positive whiff test	~75
	Excess polymorphonuclear neutrophils on wet mount	~75

Data from references 2, 32, 33.

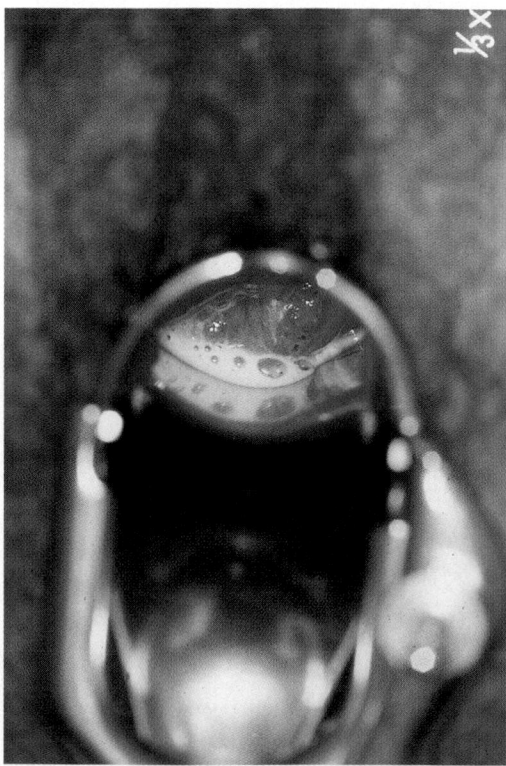

FIGURE 278-1. Vaginal discharge in a patient with trichomoniasis. Note the bubbles, which give the discharge a "frothy" appearance.

The clinical picture of trichomoniasis in men is clouded by the failure of many studies to control observations for the simultaneous presence of *Chlamydia trachomatis, Ureaplasma urealyticum,* or *Mycoplasma genitalium* (see Chapter 102). In any case, most men carrying trichomonads are asymptomatic.[28] Organisms can, however, be isolated from 5% to 15% of patients with NGU,[22] particularly from men with nonchlamydial NGU.[7,22] These men have a syndrome that is not clinically distinguishable from NGU of other etiologies, although the discharge from trichomonal urethritis is usually somewhat milder than with other infections,[22] often so scant that it is noticed only as a small bead at the meatus on arising in the morning. *Trichomonas vaginalis,* as well as some isolates of *Ureaplasma urealyticum,* should be considered in cases of tetracycline-unresponsive NGU.[41] Trichomoniasis occasionally causes epididymitis and superficial penile ulcerations, often beneath the prepuce, and may involve the prostate gland.[22]

DIAGNOSIS

Clinical differentiation of various forms of infectious vaginitis is unreliable, and an accurate diagnosis of trichomoniasis in patients of either gender depends on demonstrating the organism in genital specimens. In clinical practice the most commonly used approach is the direct microscopic examination of vaginal secretions using the wet mount technique (described in Chapter 103) which will detect the organisms in about 60% of infected women.[2,21,42] *T. vaginalis* is most easily recognized by its characteristic movements. The wet mount generally also reveals large numbers of white blood cells,[21] although this is a nonspecific finding, and asymptomatic women may have very few. The clinician should be aware of the fact that about half of women with trichomoniasis have a shift in vaginal bacterial flora away from lactobacillis predominance toward greater numbers of anaerobes and *Gardnerella vaginalis,* although Gram stain criteria for bacterial vaginosis is met in only about 25% of cases.[37] One study showed that 55% of *T. vaginalis* infected women had a vaginal secretion pH greater than or equal to 4.5 and 32% had a positive whiff test.[34] Therefore, identification of *T. vaginalis* in vaginal secretions is very helpful in differentiating this condition from simple bacteria vaginosis. Trichomoniasis can be diagnosed in men with urethritis by direct microscopic examination as well as using material obtained with a platinum loop from the anterior urethra or urine sediments, but the sensitivity is not high and the procedure is seldom performed.[22] As with all microscopic diagnoses the sensitivity and specificity of the wet mount examination are highly dependent on the skill and diligence of the observer. Adequate training of all persons reading wet mounts is essential, and quality assurance protocols should be in place in all settings where this test is performed.

There are several other methods of identifying *T. vaginalis* in clinical specimens. The organism grows readily in a variety of liquid and semisolid artificial media, some of which are available commercially. Culture is regarded as the "gold standard" for determining the performance of other diagnostic tests but it is not entirely clear which of the different media formulations and culture systems is the best. All broth *T. vaginalis* culture systems require that the media be sampled and examined for the appearance of motile organisms every few days for up to 7 days. This is labor intensive and makes culture impractical for use in population-based screening programs. Some of these problems have been alleviated by the recent development of a self-contained liquid culture medium inside a thin, optically clear plastic bag that allows direct microscopic examination of the culture without the need to remove a sample to prepare a microscopic slide.[43]

Several different nonculture tests have been developed for the diagnosis of trichomoniasis. Direct fluorescent antibody staining,[42] latex agglutination, enzyme-linked immunosorbent assay (ELISA) techniques, and a DNA probe assay are more sensitive than wet mount but less sensitive than culture. *T. vaginalis* can be identified in Pap smears with 50% to 60% sensitivity. Specificity has varied, with some authors finding relatively high false-positive test result rates and others not.

This probably reflects interobserver variation. It is reasonable to treat a woman based on a positive Pap smear result (from a laboratory with expertise) but, recalling the potentially damaging psychological effect of diagnosing an STD in a low-risk patient, strong consideration should be given to confirming the diagnosis using culture or one of the new tests described in the following paragraphs.

An RNA probe semi-automated system is now available for the diagnosis of trichomoniasis, bacterial vaginosis, and candida vaginitis. The assay requires about 45 minutes to perform and can be performed by trained clinical personnel as a point-of-care test.[44,45] In the last few years there has been a proliferation of reports in the literature of new nucleic acid amplification tests that are specific for *T. vaginalis.* Originally these assays did not appear to be more sensitive than cultures but more recently developed methods appear to provide sensitivity at least as good as culture if not better.[46,47]

Despite all of the effort that has gone into the development of better diagnostic tests for trichomoniasis, none of these systems is commonly used. The reason is that as yet a compelling case has not been made that this infection is a significant public health problem. However, as noted in the preceding, this perception may be changing based on recent studies suggesting a role for *T. vaginalis* in poor pregnancy outcome and HIV transmission. If further research demonstrates benefit to detecting and treating trichomonal infections not identified by the wet mount examination, *T. vaginalis* screening programs will be needed. One or more of the new diagnostic techniques mentioned earlier will have important roles in supporting such programs.

THERAPY

The development of metronidazole in the early 1960s revolutionized the treatment of trichomoniasis. The drug is activated with reduction of the nitro group by ferredoxin-like proteins possessed only by anaerobic organisms.[48] Short-lived metabolites are felt to act primarily by combining with DNA. Other 5-nitroimidazoles used to treat trichomoniasis outside the United States (nimorazole, tinidazole, and ornidazole) have somewhat different pharmacologic properties but do not vary much in effectiveness or toxicity.[48] Systemic therapy eradicates trichomonads from the urinary tract as well as from the vagina, thereby reducing the risk of relapse.

Numerous studies have confirmed the efficacy of a single oral 2-g dose of metronidazole in women,[2,49] but doses of less than 1.5 g are associated with higher failure rates.[23,50] Data on men are limited and poorly controlled for reinfection, but it is reasonable to assume that the single-dose regimen is effective in men as well as in women. An alternative regimen for either gender consists of 500 mg twice daily for 7 days.[41] The single-dose regimen provides freedom from problems with patient compliance. An apparent disadvantage of the single-dose regimen is a higher rate of reinfection if sexual partners are not treated simultaneously.[51] Metronidazole vaginal gel (0.5%) by itself is inadequate therapy for trichomoniasis.[52]

Adverse events associated with systemic metronidazole are several: Many people taking the drug complain of mild nausea or bad taste, which is more frequent after administration of a large single dose. Metronidazole blocks the metabolism of alcohol, and patients consuming the two concurrently may suffer nausea, vomiting, and flushing. All patients treated with metronidazole should be warned of this. Not merely a narrow-spectrum trichomonacide, metronidazole is active against most anaerobic bacteria and may alter the normal vaginal flora, occasionally causing candidal vaginitis to supervene. Metronidazole may increase the anticoagulatory effect of warfarin. Hypersensitivity reactions to metronidazole are uncommon and desensitization has been employed successfully in a small number of cases.[53]

Attention has been called to the capacity of high-dose, long-term metronidazole to induce lung tumors in animals. However, data linking clinical use of metronidazole to cancer in humans are weak,[2,54] and its advantages in treating trichomoniasis outweigh its risks. The drug should not be administered indiscriminately, and the doses given should be kept as small as possible.

Asymptomatically infected women should be treated because they represent an important reservoir of the disease. In addition, about one third of them will become symptomatic during the following few months. The long-term effects of chronic, asymptomatic trichomoniasis are unknown. A single 2-g dose of metronidazole can be used to treat trichomoniasis in any stage of pregnancy.[41,55]

When confronted with a woman who presents with recurrent infection, the clinician should consider the following possibilities.[1] Reinfection from an untreated sexual partner remains the most common cause of recurrent disease, especially if the patient received a single-dose regimen.[2,51] Nonjudgmental questioning regarding sexual activity may provide necessary information. It is useful to remind women that infected male sexual partners are usually completely asymptomatic.[2] Noncompliance with multidose regimens may be revealed by careful questioning.[3] Very rarely, metronidazole treatment failures have been attributed to increased hepatic inactivation of the drug[56] or even, theoretically, to competitive inactivation by bacteria. Finally, one must consider the possibility of true metronidazole resistance.

Metronidazole Resistance

Metronidazole-resistant *T. vaginalis* has been reported for some years and is estimated to occur in 2% to 5% percent of clinical cases.[2,57-60] Given the lack of a surveillance system it is not clear that this problem is increasing, although a recent report suggests the possibility that it is.[61] Methods for determining the antimicrobial susceptibility of *T. vaginalis* are not standardized, and the apparent level of resistance is highly dependent on assay conditions (e.g., oxygen concentration).[57,58] There have been no treatment trials to establish the optimal approach to patients with metronidazole-resistant trichomoniasis. Current recommendations including those offered in the following paragraphs are based on anecdotal experience only.

The first step in managing a patient who has failed an initial course of metronidazole is to be certain that reinfection is not the problem. One must emphasize the importance of adequate partner treatment, patient and partner compliance with treatment, and abstinence from sexual intercourse until it is clear that a cure has been achieved. Patients and partners then should be retreated with 500 mg of metronidazole orally twice daily for 7 days.[41] One of the problems with single-dose therapy is that patients are protected from reinfection for a relatively short period of time and may be reinfected if the partner is not treated concurrently. With the 7-day regimen this is less likely to happen. If infection persists in a patient treated with a 7-day regimen and reinfection can be ruled out, the next step should be 2 g of metronidazole orally daily for 3 to 5 days.[41] If this regimen fails, cultures should be prepared to document metronidazole resistance and further treatment regimens for such patients should be designed in consultation with an expert. The Centers for Disease Control and Prevention in Atlanta, Georgia provide these services. The patient's physician can call (770) 499-4115 or (404) 639-8363. A culture kit will be mailed to the health care provider with instructions on its use and how to return it to the CDC's laboratory. In addition, advice will be given as to the next therapeutic step. The following are among the approaches that have been tried with varying success in these cases: 1 to 2 g of metronidazole daily for 14 days along with 500 mg intravaginally daily,[2,57,58,62,63] high-dose intravenous metronidazole,[63,64] and intravaginal paromomycin (may cause vaginal mucosa ulceration).[65-67] Intravaginal paromomycin, intravaginal furazolidone, spermacides containing nonoxynl-9,[68] or douching with a 1% solution of zinc sulfate[69] may be tried in conjunction with one of the high-dose systemic metronidazole regimens described earlier. Although not rigorously studied, tinidazole appears to be effective in some cases of metronidazole-resistant *T. vaginalis* infection.[67,68] A recent study found that although in vitro activities of metronidazole and tinidazole against the parasite are highly correlated, the latter does have lower minimum inhibitory concentrations (MICs) than the former.[70] Tinidazole has been used outside of the United States for many years and has an excellent safety profile.

Clinical trials have been completed in the United States and the drug is now approved by the FDA. Finally, postmenopausal women, in at least some cases, may be cured by temporarily discontinuing estrogen replacement therapy.[71]

REFERENCES

1. Kampmeier RH. Description of *Trichomonas vaginalis* by M. A. Donné. Sex Transm Dis. 1978;5:119-122.
2. Honigberg BM, ed. Trichomonads Parasitic in Humans. New York: Springer-Verlag; 1990.
3. Philip A, Carter-Scott P, Rogers C. An agar culture technique to quantitate *Trichomonas vaginalis* from women. J Infect Dis. 1987;155:304-308.
4. Snipes LJ, Gamard PM, Marcisi, EM, et al. Molecular epidemiology of metronidazole resistance in a population of *Trichomonas vaginalis* clinical isolates. J Clin Microbiol 2000;38:3004-3009.
5. Wendel KA, Rompalo AM, Erbelding, EJ, et al. Double-stranded RNA viral infection of *Trichomonas vaginalis* infecting patients attending a sexually transmitted diseases clinic. J Infect Dis 2002;186:558-561.
6. Graves A, Gardner WA Jr. Pathogenicity of *Trichomonas vaginalis*. Clin Obstet Gynecol. 1993;36:145-152.
7. Krieger JN, Wolner-Hanssen P, Stevens C, et al. Characteristics of *Trichomonas vaginalis* isolates from women with and without colpitis macularis. J Infect Dis. 1990;161:307-311.
8. Arroyo R, Engbring J, Alderete JF. Molecular basis of host epithelial cell recognition by *Trichomonas vaginalis*. Mol Microbiol. 1992;6:853-862.
9. Mirhaghani A, Warton A. An electron microscope study of the interaction between *Trichomonas vaginalis* and epithelial cells of the human amnion membrane. Parasitol Res. 1996;82:43-47.
10. Alderete JF, Milsap KW, Lehker MW, Benchimol M. Enzymes on microbial pathogens and *Trichomonas vaginalis*: Molecular mimicry and functional diversity. Cell Microbiol. 2001;3:359-370.
11. Alderete JM, Benchimol M, Kehker MW, Crouch ML. The complex fibronectin— *Trichomonas vaginalis* interactions and trichomonosis. Paristol Int. 2002;51:285-292.
12. Rein MF, Sullivan JA, Mandell GL. Trichomonacidal activity of polymorphonuclear neutrophils: Killing by disruption and fragmentation. J Infect Dis. 1980;142:575-585.
13. Sorvillo F, Smith L, Kerndt P, Ash L. *Trichomonas vaginalis*, HIV, and African-Americans. Emerg Infect Dis. 2001;7:927-932.
14. Hobbs MM, Kazembe P, Reed AW, et al. *Trichomonas vaginalis* as a cause of urethritis in Malawian men. Sex Transm Dis. 1999;26:381-387.
15. Peppin J, Sobela F, Deslandes S, et al. Eteiology of urethral discharge in West Africa: The role of *Mycoplasma genitalium* and *Trichomonas vaginalis*. Bulletin WHO. 2001;79:118-126.
16. Schwebke JR, Lawing LF. Improved detection of DNA amplification of *Trichomonas vaginalis* in males. J Clin Microbiol. 2002;40:3681-3683.
17. Miller JM, Chambers DC, Miller JM. Infection with *Trichomonas vaginalis* in a black population. J Natl Med Assoc. 1989;81:701-702.
18. Shuter J, Bell D, Graham D, et al. Rates of and risk factors for trichomoniasis among pregnant inmates in New York City. Sex Transm Dis. 1998;25:303-307.
19. Crosby R, DiClemente RJ, Wingood GM, et al. Predictors of infection with *Trichomonas vaginalis*: A prospective study of low income African-American adolescent females. Sex Transm Infect. 2002;78:360-364.
20. Cotch MF, Pastorek JG 2nd, Nugent RP, et al. Demographic and behavioral predictors of *Trichomonas vaginalis* infection among pregnant women. Obstet Gynecol. 1991;78:1087-1092.
21. Wolner-Hanssen P, Krieger JN, Stevens CE, et al. Clinical manifestations of vaginal trichomoniasis. JAMA. 1989;264:571-576.
22. Krieger JN. Trichomoniasis in men: Old issues and new data. Sex Transm Dis. 1995;22:83-96.
23. Gulmezoglu AM. Treating trichomoniasis in women. The Cochrane Database of Systematic reviews 1998;3.
24. Kellock D, O'Mahony CP. Sexually acquired metronidazole-resistant trichomoniasis in a lesbian couple. Genitourin Med. 1996;72:60-61.
25. Klausner JD, Baer JT, Contento KM, Bolan G. Investigation of a suspected outbreak of vaginal trichomoniasis among female inmates. Sex Transm Dis. 1999;26:335-338.
26. Danesh IS, Stephen JM, Gorbach J. Neonatal *Trichomonas vaginlis* infection. J Emerg Med. 1995;13:51-54.
27. Jones JG, Yamaguchi T, Lambert B. *Trichomonas vaginalis* infestation in sexually abused girls. Am J Dis Child. 1985;139:846-847.
28. Ross JD, Scott GR, Busuttil A. *Trichomonas vaginalis* infection in pre-pubertal girls. Med Sci Law. 1993;33:82-85.
29. Cu-Uvin S, Ko H, Jamieson DJ, et al. Prevalence, incidence, and persistence or recurrence of trichomoniasis among human immunodeficiency virus (HIV)-positive women and among HIV-negative women at high risk for HIV infection. Clin Infect Dis. 2002;34:1406-1411.
30. Laga M, Manoka A, Kivuvu M, et al. Non-ulcerative sexually transmitted diseases as risk factors for HIV-1 transmission in women. AIDS. 1993;7:95-102.
31. Wang CC, McClelland RS, Reilly M, et al. The effect of treatment of vaginal infections on shedding of human immunodeficiency virus type 1. J Infect Dis. 2001;183:1017-1022.

32. Bickley LS, Krisher KK, Punsalang Jr, et al. Comparison of direct fluorescent antibody, acridine orange, wet mount, and culture for detection of Trichomonas vaginalis in women attending a public sexually transmitted disease clinic. Sex Transm Dis. 1989;16:127-31.

33. Rein MF. Uncertainties and controversies in trichomoniasis. In: Sobel JD, ed. Vulvovaginal Infections: Current Concepts in Diagnosis and Therapy. New York: Academy Professional Information Services; 1990:73-85.

34. Pastorek JG, Cotch MF, Martin DH. Clinical and microbiological correlates of vaginal trichomoniasis during pregnancy. Clin Infect Dis. 1996;23:1075-1080.

35. Kiviat NB, Paavonen JA, Wolner-Hanssen P, et al. Histopathology of endocervical infection caused by Chlamydia trachomatis, herpes simplex virus, Trichomonas vaginalis, and Neisseria gonorrhoeae. Hum Pathol. 1990;21:831-837.

36. James JA, Thomason JL, Gelbart SM, et al. Is trichomoniasis often associated with bacterial vaginosis in pregnant adolescents? Am J Obstet Gynecol. 1992;166:859-863.

37. Hillier SL, Krohn MA, Nugent RP, et al. Characteristics of three vaginal flora pattners assessed by Gram stain among pregnant women. Am J Obstet Gynecol. 1992;166:938-944.

38. Josey WE, Campbell WG Jr. Vaginitis emphysematosa. A report of four cases. J Reprod Med. 1990;35:974-977.

39. Cotch MF, Pastorek JG II, Nugent RP, et al. Trichomonas vaginalis associated with low birth weight and preterm delivery. Sex Transm Dis. 1998, 24:353-360.

40. Klebanoff MA, Carey JC, Hauth JC, et al. Failure of metronidazole to prevent perterm delivery among pregnant women with asymptomatic Trichomonas vaginalis infection. N Engl J Med. 2001;345:487-493.

41. Centers for Disease Control and Prevention. Sexually transmitted diseases treatment guidelines 2002. MMWR Morb Mortal Wkly Rep. 2002;51(No.RR-5):31.

42. Krieger JN, Tam MR, Stevens CE, et al. Diagnosis of trichomoniasis: Comparison of conventional wet-mount examination with cytologic studies, cultures, and monoclonal antibody straining of direct specimens. JAMA. 1988;259:1223-1227.

43. Levi MH, Torres J, Pina C, Klein RS. Comparison of the InPouch TV culture system and Diamond's modified medium for detection of Trichomonas vaginalis. J Clin Microbiol. 1997;35:3308-3310.

44. Ferris DG, Hendrich J, Payne PM, et al. Office laboratory diagnosis of vaginitis. Clinician-performed tests compared with a rapid nucleic acid hybridization test. J Fam Pract 1995;41:575-581.

45. Briselden AM. Hillier S. Evaluation of Affirm VP microbial identification test for Gardenerella vaginalis and Trichomonas vaginalis. J Clin Microbiol. 1994;32:148-152.

46. Madico G, Quin TC, Rampalo A, et al. Diagnosis of Trichomonas vaginalis infection by PCR using vaginal swab samples. J Clin Microbiol. 1998;36:3205-3210.

47. Mayta H, Gilman RH, Calderon MM, et al. 18S ribosomal DNA-based PCR for diagnosis of Trichomonas vaginalis. J Clin Microbiol. 2000;38:2683 2687.

48. Müller M. Mode of action of metronidazole on anaerobic bacteria and protozoa. Surgery. 1983;93:165.

49. Tidwell BH, Lushbaugh WB, Laughlin M, et al. A double-blind placebo-controlled trial of single-dose intravaginal versus single-dose oral metronidazole in the treatment of trichomonas vaginitis. J Infect Dis. 1994;170:242-246.

50. Spence MR, Harwell TS, Davies MC, Smith JL. The minimum oral metronidazole dose for treating trichomoniasis: A randomized blinded study. Obstet Gynecol. 1997;89:699-703.

51. Lyng J, Christensen J. A double-blind study of the value of treatment with a single dose tinidazole of partners to females with trichomoniasis. Acta Obstet Gynecol Scand. 1981;60:199.

52. duBouchet L, McGregor JA, Ismail M, McCormack WM. A pilot study of metronidazole vaginal gel versus oral metronidazole for the treatment of Trichomonas vaginalis vaginitis. Sex Transm Dis. 1998;25:176-179.

53. Pearlman MD, Yashar C, Ernst S, Solomon W. An incremental dosing protocol for women with severe vaginal trichomoniasis and adverse reactions to metronidazole. Am J Obstet Gynecol. 1996;174:934-936.

54. Beard CM, Noller KL, O'Fallon WM, et al. Cancer after exposure to metronidazole. Mayo Clin Proc. 1988;63:147-153.

55. Caro-Paton T, Carvajal A, Martin de Diego I, et al: Is metronidazole teratogenic? A meta-analysis. Br J Clin Pharmacol. 1997;44:179-182.

56. Robertson DHH, Heyworth R, Harrison C, et al. Treatment failure in Trichomonas vaginalis infections in females. 1. Concentrations of metronidazole in plasma and vaginal content during normal and high dosage. J Antimicrob Chemother. 1988;21:373-378.

57. Lossick JG, Müller M, Gorrell TE. In vitro drug susceptibility and doses of metronidazole required for cure in cases of refractory vaginal trichomoniasis. J Infect Dis. 1986;153:948-955.

58. Müller M, Lossick JG, Gorrell TE. In-vitro susceptibility of Trichomonas vaginalis to metronidazole: Treatment outcome in vaginal trichomoniasis. Sex Transm Dis. 1988;15:17-24.

59. Grossman JH 3rd, Galask RP. Persistent vaginitis caused by metronidazole-resistant trichomonas. Obstet Gynecol. 1990;76:521-522.

60. Schmid G, Narcisi E, Mosure D, et al. Prevalence of metronidazole-resistant Trichomonas vaginalis in a gynecology clinic. J Reprod Med. 2001;46:545-549.

61. Sobel JD, Nagappan V, Nyirjesy P. Metronidazole-resistant trichomoniasis: An emerging problem. N Engl J Med. 1999;341:292-293.

62. Lossick JG. Treatment of sexually transmitted vaginosis/vaginitis. Rev Infect Dis. 1990;12(Suppl 6):S665-S681.

63. Lossick JG, Kent HL. Trichomoniasis: Trends in diagnosis and management. Am J Obstet Gynecol. 1991;165:1217-1222.

64. Dombrowski MP, Sokol RJ, Brown WJ, et al. Intravenous therapy of metronidazole-resistant Trichomonas vaginalis. Obstet Gynecol. 1987;69:524-525.

65. Nyirjesy P, Sobel JD, Weitz MV, et al. Difficult to treat trichomoniasis: results with paromomycin cream. Clin Infect Dis. 1998;26:986-988.

66. Coelho DD. Metronidazole resistant trichomoniasis successfully treated with paromomycin. Genitourin Med. 1997;73:397-398.

67. Sobel JD, Nyirjesy P, Brown W. Tinidazole therapy for metronidazole-resistant vaginal trichomoniasis. Clin Infect Dis. 2001;33:1341-1346.

68. Lewis DA, Habgood I, White R, et al. Managing vaginal trichomoniasis resistant to high-dose metronidazole therapy. Int J STD AIDS. 1997;8:780-784.

69. Houang ET, Ahmet Z, Lawrence AG. Successful treatment of four patients with recalcitrant vaginal trichomoniasis with a combination of zinc sulfate douche and metronidazole therapy. Sex Transm Dis. 1997;24:116-119.

70. Crowell AL, Sanders-Lewis KA, Secor WE. In vitro metronidazole and tinidazole activities against metronidazole-resistant strains of Trichomonas vaginalis. Antimicrob Agents Chemother. 2003;47:1407-1409.

71. R, Pickering J, McCormack WM. Trichomoniasis in a postmenopausal woman cured after discontinuation of estrogen replacement therapy. Sex Transm Dis. 1997; 24:543-545.

CHAPTER **279**

Babesia Species

JEFFREY A. GELFAND

EDOUARD VANNIER

Babesiosis is an emerging tick-borne infectious disease caused by the protozoa *Babesia* that, like *Plasmodium,* infects erythrocytes of wild and domestic animals and may cause a malaria-like syndrome including fever, hemolysis, and hemoglobinuria. Babesiosis has long been recognized as an economically important disease of cattle. Only in the last 45 years has *Babesia* been appreciated to be a pathogen in humans. Usually a mild illness in young and healthy people, babesiosis may become fatal in the asplenic or immunocompromised patient, and in the elderly.

The first recorded reference to babesiosis is probably in Exodus 9:3, which describes the plague ("grievous murrain") visited upon the cattle of Pharaoh Rameses II.[1] In 1888, while investigating the febrile hemoglobinuria and death of cattle in Romania, Viktor Babes, a Hungarian pathologist, observed an intraerythrocytic microorganism. In 1893, Smith and Kilbourne described a similar piroplasm in erythrocytes from Texas cattle with fever. Initially named *Pyrosoma,* this organism was later identified as *Babesia bigemina*. This was the seminal observation on the ability of hematophagous arthropods to transmit an infectious pathogen to a vertebrate host. The first well-documented case of human babesiosis was a splenectomized Yugoslavian farmer whose death was reported in 1957 by Skrabalo and Deanovic. Originally identified as *B. bovis,* the causative agent was later reported to be *B. divergens*. *B. divergens* is a parasite of cattle that is transmitted to humans by the tick *Ixodes ricinus,* a species endemic in Europe. Subsequent cases in Europe would confirm the importance of splenectomy to the severity of babesiosis caused by *B. divergens*. In 1969, a 59-year-old resident of Nantucket Island off the Massachusetts coast presented with fever and headache. Unlike the European patients infected with *B. divergens,* this patient had an intact spleen. The causative agent was identified by Spielman and co-workers[2] as *B. microti,* a parasite of white-footed mice transmitted to humans by the tick *Ixodes scapularis* (also known as *I. dammini*). In the decades since, several hundred cases have been reported in the United States alone. In fact, cases of *B. microti* infection have spread from the islands off the coast of New England to the northeast mainland. In addition, human cases of infection with new species of *Babesia* have now been reported in the lakes region of the upper Midwest (Wisconsin,

Minnesota, Missouri), and in the coastal regions of northern California and Washington state.[3,4]

THE PATHOGEN

Babesiosis is a zoonotic disease that requires transmission of a *Babesia* species from a vertebrate reservoir to humans via an invertebrate vector.[5] More than 100 species of *Babesia* have been reported to infect vertebrates, including mammals and birds. Babesias are protozoal parasites classified in the phylum *Apicomplexa,* class *Aconoidasida,* order *Piroplasmidora,* and family *Babesiidae.* In addition to *Babesiidae,* the order *Piroplasmidora* includes the family of *Theileriidae.* As for *Theileria* species, the intraerythrocytic form of *Babesia* species can present a pear-shape appearance, hence the name of piroplasm. *Babesiidae* can also be oval or round. Because of their ring conformation and peripheral location in the erythrocyte, *Babesia* are frequently mistaken for *Plasmodium falciparum.* Babesial trophozoites undergo an asexual division (called merogony) in the vertebrate host erythrocyte. Once ingested by the tick (the invertebrate host), babesial gametocytes will undergo sexual development that ultimately leads to the formation of sporozoites in the salivary glands of the tick.

Events in the Tick

Although some patients acquire babesiosis from blood transfusion,[6] transmission of *Babesia* occurs mostly during the blood meal of infected hard-bodied ticks of the genus *Ixodes.* In Europe, *Ixodes ricinus* feeds primarily on cattle and may transmit *B. divergens* to humans.[7] In the northeastern United States, the deer tick, *I. scapularis,* feeds primarily on deer and white-footed mice (*Peromyscus leucopus*) and occasionally transmits *B. microti* to humans. *I. scapularis* is also the vector for *Borrelia burgdorferi* and *Ehrlichia chaffeensis,* the causative agents of Lyme disease and human granulocytic ehrlichiosis.[8] In the Pacific coastal states of the United States, the vector for transmission of the new *Babesia* species WA1 remains to be identified. To date, the life cycles of *B. microti* and *I. scapularis* are understood best.[5,9]

The life cycle of *I. scapularis* has three active stages (larva, nymph, adult) and requires two years for completion (Fig. 279-1).[5] In the fall, adult stages feed primarily on the white-tailed deer (*Odocoileus virginiamus*). Deer are incompetent reservoirs for *B. microti,* but are essential for maintenance of *I. scapularis.* Adult ticks overwinter in an engorged state, and lay eggs in the spring. Eggs hatch synchronously into larvae in late July. In August and September, larvae feed primarily on the mouse, *P. leucopeus.* Larvae overwinter and molt into nymphs in the spring. Nymphs feed on *P. leucopeus* from May through July, and molt into adults in the fall. *I. scapularis* becomes infected as the larvae feeds on *B. microti*-infected *P. leucopeus.* In endemic areas (Nantucket Island), infection of *P. leucopeus* may be as high as 60%. Other reservoirs include chipmunks, meadow voles, shrews, bats,

passerine and raptorial birds. Once larvae have molted, nymphs remain infected with *B. microti* (trans-stadial transmission). There is no evidence of transovarial transmission of *B. microti* (as it occurs with *B. divergens*). Feeding of infected nymphs early in the summer results in the infection of naïve *P. leucopeus* that become a reservoir of *B. microti* for larvae that feed during the late summer. This favors a high rate of transmission, and therefore maintenance of *B. microti* in the enzootic cycle.

Larvae, nymphs, and adult ticks can all feed on humans, but the nymphal tick is the primary vector for transmission of *B. microti* to humans. Over the last two decades there has been a dramatic increase in the white-tailed deer population in many areas of the northeastern United States. The increased number of deer reflects an increase in suitable deer habitat, usually secondary to revegetation of old farms and fields, and from reduced hunting pressures in suburban areas. The expanding range of *I. scapularis* may be linked to long distance dispersal of this vector by coastal birds that undergo extensive seasonal migration. It is the presence of large numbers of deer, white-footed mice, and ticks that create the conditions for infection of humans with *B. microti.* Cases of babesiosis increase during warmer months when both ticks and people are active and in the same environments. The small size of the nymph (less than 2.5 mm), its pale gray ground color, inconspicuous feeding site, and benign local reaction to blood feeding together make recollection of nymphal tick bite a rare finding. The duration of tick attachment and feeding may range from hours to days. Because sporozoite transmission is optimal as the tick reaches complete repletion with host blood, prompt careful removal of the tick can decrease the likelihood of infection.

Early after attachment (some 10 hours), *B. microti*-infected erythrocytes start to accumulate in the gut of the feeding tick.[5] A novel endocytic organelle, the cytostome, forms in *B. microti.* Some 40 to 60 hours after attachment, microtubules accumulate at the anterior end of the organism to form a ray-like structure known as "Strahlenkorper." On repletion of the feeding tick, these structures contribute to the fusion of gametes into a zygote. Using an arrowhead structure, zygotes penetrate the tick gut epithelium. The arrowhead structure dissociates, and the zygote translocates toward the epithelium basal lamina, enters the hemolymph, and becomes an ookinete. Ookinetes in turn invade the salivary acini of the tick. Once in the secretory or interstitial cells of the acinus, ookinetes undergo hypertrophy to become sporoblasts. Sporoblasts remain dormant while the larva overwinters to molt into a nymph in the spring of the following year. On attachment of the nymphal tick to the host, the temperature of the tick body rises, sporogony is initiated. While the tick is feeding, the sporoblast membrane folds. After 48 hours of feeding, micronemes and rhoptries appear. Cytoplasm starts to separate from the parent sporoblast, nuclear division ensues. Thus, sporogony is a process of budding (not schizogony as in *Plasmodium*). A single sporoblast may generate up to 10,000 sporozoites.

FIGURE 279-1. Giemsa-stained thin blood film. Cytoplasm coalesced into four masses with nuclear material to form the "tetrad" or "maltese cross" of four mature merozoites *(single arrow).* This stage is found infrequently in human blood smears, but is diagnostic of *B. microti.* Note the nearby presence of ring forms. The ring forms have a peripheral location, as with *Plasmodium falciparum,* but the large clear central white vacuole and the absence of brown (hemozoin) pigment are characteristic of *B. microti.* The absence of schizonts and gametocytes on the blood film further distinguishes *B. microti* from *P. falciparum.* (Courtesy of Philip R. Daoust, M.D.)

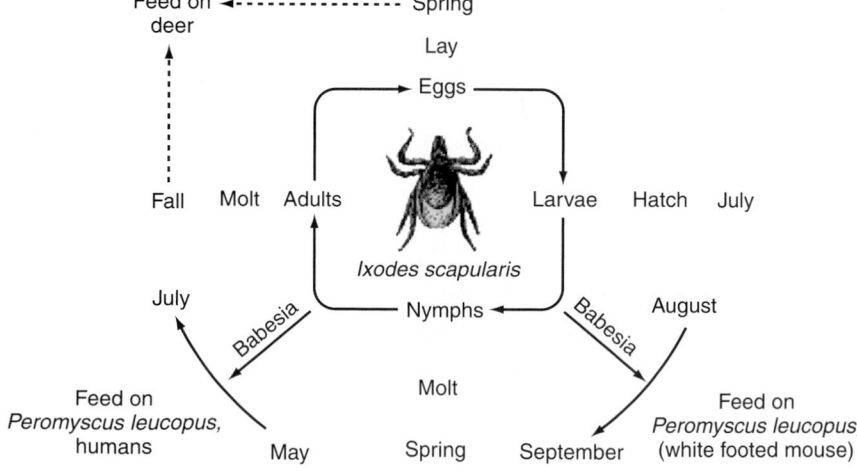

Events in the Vertebrate Hosts

During the last hours of tick feeding, a large number (up to 100,000) of sporozoites is deposited in the dermis of the host.[5] Events that lead sporozoites from the feeding chamber in the dermis to the circulating erythrocytes remain poorly understood. In the case of *Theileria*, sporozoites first invade lymphocytes, divide into merozoites that will, in turn, invade erythrocytes. Sporozoites from *Babesia* species are believed not to undergo merogony in an exoerythrocytic compartment. Instead, *Babesia* sporozoites directly invade erythrocytes. Whether the mode of invasion differs between sporozoites and merozoites is unknown.

Merozoites attach to the erythrocyte by the anterior end. Invagination of the host membrane leads to formation of a parasitophagous vacuole that quickly disappears. The merozoite loses the rhoptry and becomes a trophozoite moving freely in the host cytoplasm. New organelles develop, including large rhoptries and micronemes. The piroplasm undergoes asynchronous, asexual budding resulting into two or four merozoites (daughter cells; Fig. 279-2). The mode of exit from the erythrocyte is unknown. Because budding is asynchronous, massive hemolysis rarely occurs as it does with *Plasmodium* (synchronous schizogony).

Morphologic and Phylogenetic Classifications

Based on the size of the intraerythrocytic form (trophozoite), *Babesia* species have been classified into two groups.[5] Small forms have a diameter between 1.0 to 2.5 μm, and include *B. gibsoni, B. microti,* and *B. rodhaini.* Large forms are 2.5 to 5 μm in diameter, and include *B. bovis, B. canis,* and *B. odocoilei.* Trophozoites of small *Babesia* species multiply by binary fission to create four daughter cells arranged in a tetrad ("Maltese cross"). In contrast, trophozoites of large *Babesia* species bud into two daughter cells only. The size distinction is generally consistent with the phylogenetic classification based on nuclear small subunit-ribosomal DNA (nss-rDNA). Sequence analyses of rDNA revealed that large *Babesia* species form a phylogenetic cluster distinct from small *Babesia* species.[9,10] An exception is the human pathogen *B. divergens,* small in diameter, but genetically related to the large *Babesia* cluster. Phylogenetic analyses also revealed that small *Babesia* are more related to *Theileria* than to large *Babesia* species. This evolutionary link is in agreement with the lack of transovarial transmission of *Theileria* and small *Babesia* species in ticks, a characteristic of large *Babesia* transmission in invertebrate hosts. However, unlike small and large *Babesia* species, Theileria piroplasms first undergo asexual division in lymphocytes before invading erythrocytes as merozoites. *Babesiidae* invade erythrocytes as sporozoites and do not exist in an exoerythrocytic form. The discovery of a lymphocytic exoerythrocytic stage of *B. equi* has led to the reclassification of this equine piroplasm as *Theileria equi.* An exoerythrocytic stage has been suggested for *B. microti,* but remains to be confirmed.

Originally thought to be host specific, some *Babesia* species can infect a wide range of hosts, including humans. *B. microti,* a species that primarily infects rodents, is the main agent of human babesiosis along the Northeastern coastline of the United States.[2] *B. divergens,* a parasite of cattle, is responsible for the majority of cases in Europe.[7] Rare have been the cases of human babesiosis caused by *B. bovis* and *B. canis.* Some new *Babesia* species have been identified as pathogenic in humans in the Northern Pacific states and the Midwest. A hitherto unknown species of *Babesia,* designated WA1, was isolated in 1991 from a 41-year-old immunocompetent resident of Washington state presenting with a moderately severe babesiosis.[3] The patient did not carry the typical risk factors, that is, aging, splenectomy, immunosuppression. WA1 was morphologically indistinguishable from *B. microti.* Trophozoites were typically round or oval and merozoites were found in tetrads, a feature of small *Babesia* species.[11] Unlike *B. microti,* WA1 was lethal to hamsters and birds. The patient's serum failed to immunoreact with *B. microti,* but reacted strongly to antigens from a canine small piroplasm from California (previously identified as *B. gibsoni*), and weakly to antigens from the BH1 strain of *Babesia* that infects the Californian desert bighorn sheep. Phylogenetic analysis re-

vealed that WA1 and the piroplasms obtained from wildlife animals in the western United States form a clade (monophyletic group) closer to the clade of *Theileriae* than to the clades of large (*B. gibsoni, B. bigemina*) and small *Babesia* species (*B. microti, B. rodhaini*).[11,12]

From 1991 to 1993, four cases were reported from California.[13] All patients were asplenic; three (CA1, CA2, CA4) survived the infection. Sera from these three patients immunoreacted strongly to WA1, weakly to the Californian canine small piroplasm, but failed to react to *B. microti.* There was no immunoreactivity in the serum from patient CA3, who died during the acute phase of illness. Interestingly, sera from the four California patients and the index case of WA1 infection all reacted with antigens from piroplasms of wildlife animals living in the western United States.[10] Using the region of ss rDNA that is highly polymorphic among *Babesia* species, it was established that the isolates from CA1 and CA3 were identical, and differed from CA2 and CA4 by one nucleotide (bp) only.[4] Phylogenetic analysis using the entire ss rDNA gene revealed that the California isolates fall into the WA1 clade, and are indistinguishable from the piroplasms MD1 and BH3 isolated from mule deer and bighorn sheep, respectively.[10] Along with serum immunoreactivity, this observation indicates that WA1 and other related piroplasms may use nonrodents as reservoirs. Nonetheless, reservoirs of WA1-type piroplasms have yet to be identified. Given the geography of WA1-related babesiosis, candidate ticks are *Dermacentor variabilis, Dermacentor occidentalis, Ixodes pacificus,* and *Ixodes angustus.*

B. divergens has traditionally been considered a lethal human pathogen in Europe, not in the United States.[7] In 1996, a fatal case of babesiosis was reported from Missouri.[14] The patient was a 73-year-old splenectomized man with a history of systemic lupus erythematosus, taking prednisone. The intraerythrocytic organism MO1 was polymorphic (punctiform, annular, piriform), and budded in tetrads. The patient's serum immunoreacted strongly to *B. divergens* (human isolate Rouen 1987) and weakly to *B. canis.* The ss rDNA region used for phylogenetic analysis was identical in MO1 and *B. divergens.* MO1 was most closely related to *B. divergens,* and is classified in the phylogenetic cluster of large *Babesias* (*B. bigemina, B. bovis, B. odocoilei, B. canis, B. gibsoni*) to which the small *B. divergens* belongs. Surprisingly, MO1 failed to infect calves and birds, although both vertebrates are susceptible to European isolates of *B. divergens.* MO1 is therefore closely related to, but distinct from *B. divergens.* A recent case in Kentucky has confirmed the presence of *B. divergens*-related organism in the central United States.[15] The 56-year-old splenectomized man survived the infection. Examination of Giemsa-stained thin blood smears revealed the presence of single organisms, pairs, and tetrads. Analysis of the fragment of ss rDNA revealed a 98% to 99% homology with several strains of *B. divergens.*

EPIDEMIOLOGY

Babesiosis is still a rarity in Europe, with more than half the cases reported from France and the British Isles.[7] In 2000, 31 cases of babesiosis had been reported.[10] At least 26 of these cases (84%) occurred in splenectomized individuals. *B. divergens* was the pathogen in 23 cases. In the United States, at least two cases with *B. divergens*-like organisms have been reported in the upper and central Midwest.[14,15] Human babesiosis due to *B. divergens* may soon emerge in the northeastern United States, as molecular evidence of *B. divergens* has been found in rabbits and *Ixodes* ticks on Nantucket Island, Massachusetts.[16] In addition, *B. divergens* may not be limited to temperate zones, as this pathogen has been identified in a 34-year-old asplenic resident from the Canary Islands, a subtropical archipelago some 300 km from the west African coast.[17]

In the United States, most cases of human babesiosis are caused by *B. microti.* There have been more than 300 documented human infections with *B. microti,* with additional cases constantly reported.[9,10] Most cases occurred in the coastal region of the northeastern United States, particularly Nantucket Island, Martha's Vineyard, Cape Cod (Massachusetts), Block Island (Rhode Island), eastern Long Island,

Shelter Island, and Fire Island (New York). The geographic range of *B. microti* infection seems to have recently extended to New Jersey.[18] There have been isolated cases of babesiosis in Georgia, Virginia, and Maryland. As with Lyme disease, babesiosis is encountered in the lakes region of the upper Midwest (Wisconsin, Minnesota). Cases of babesiosis caused by a *B. microti*-like piroplasm or *B. microti* itself have been reported from Taiwan.[19,20] Serologic evidence of *B. microti* infection has been obtained from individuals in Germany[21] and Switzerland.[22] Because seroprevalence is higher than incidence of disease in endemic areas such as Cape Cod, Shelter Island, and Block Island,[23,24] most infections with *B. microti* appear to remain subclinical. The incidence of *B. microti* infection may be higher than recognized.

Cases with WA1-type organisms have been documented in Washington state and northern California.[3,4] Outside of Europe and the United States, there have been cases of human babesiosis with species that otherwise infect domestic animals. In Mexico, *B. canis* and *B. bigemina* were identified as human pathogens.[10] On the African continent, human babesiosis has been described in South Africa, Mozambique, Ivory Coast, and Egypt.[10] Because the infection is silent in healthy individuals, and because the pathogen may be mistaken for *Plasmodium* in subtropical zones, human babesiosis may be an underdiagnosed infection worldwide.

With asymptomatic infection the rule and a high seroprevalence rate in certain areas, blood transfusion has become a mode of transmission of babesiosis.[6] Blood components causing transfusion-associated cases include erythrocytes and platelets that are usually contaminated by a small number of erythrocytes. The incubation period in transfusion-associated babesiosis may span up to 9 weeks, as opposed to 1 to 4 weeks in the case of tick-based transmission of *B. microti*. Finally, transplacental transmission of the disease has been described.[25]

CLINICAL MANIFESTATIONS

Babesiosis caused by *B. divergens* occurs mostly (84%) in asplenic patients and is always fulminant and hemolytic.[7] With improved therapy, death occurs in fewer than half (42%) of the cases.[9] In contrast, *B. microti* produces a high incidence of subclinical or mild infections, but clinical infections are likely in asplenic patients, patients with Lyme disease in endemic areas, older individuals and individuals with comorbidities, including human immunodeficiency virus (HIV) infection and other diseases associated with immunosuppression.[26] Symptoms may be severe and even life-threatening, but disease is only occasionally fatal.

Symptoms of *B. microti* infection appear 1 to 4 weeks after the tick bite.[27] Because unengorged nymphs are only 2 mm in diameter, most patients do not recall a tick bite. The onset is gradual with malaise, fatigue, anorexia, shaking, and chills.[28-31] These symptoms are followed within a week by sustained or intermittent fever that may reach 40°C. In acquired immunodeficiency syndrome (AIDS), babesiosis has been associated with a syndrome of fever of unknown origin lasting months.[32] Other less frequent symptoms include myalgia, arthralgia, nausea, vomiting, cough, abdominal pain, depression, emotional lability, photophobia, conjunctival injection, and sore throat.[28-31] Rashes similar to the erythema chronicum migrans are rare, and may result from intercurrent Lyme disease. Because *Ixodes scapularis* is the vector for *B. microti, Borrelia burgdorferi,* and *Ehrlichia chaffeensis,* patients with babesiosis should be evaluated for intercurrent Lyme disease and/or human granulocytic ehrlichiosis.[29] Petechiae, splinter hemorrhages, and ecchymoses have occasionally been noted. Mild splenomegaly and hepatomegaly have been described in some patients, but lymphadenopathy is absent. Dark urine is noted in severe cases.

Hemolytic anemia (occasionally severe), decreased serum haptoglobin levels, and elevated reticulocyte counts are noted.[9,26] The percentage of *B. microti*-infected erythrocytes is usually 1% to 10% in patients with an intact spleen, but may be as high as 85% in asplenic patients.[5] White blood cell counts are normal or mildly decreased, thrombocytopenia is common. The erythrocyte sedimentation rate

may be elevated, and the direct Coombs' test may react positively. Urinalysis reveals proteinuria and hemoglobinuria; blood urea nitrogen and serum creatinine levels may be elevated. About half the patients have a mild elevation of liver function enzymes, including total bilirubin, alkaline phosphatase, aspartate aminotransferase, alanine aminotransferase, and lactic dehydrogenase.[30] On one occasion, bone marrow examination revealed macrophages with hemophagocytosis.

Most patients reported in the United States have intact spleens—fewer than 15% have been asplenic—and almost all of the several hundred patients reported with clinical disease have survived.[9,26] However, babesiosis may be associated with severe complications and ultimately fatal. In one series of hospitalized patients with babesiosis, 25% were admitted to the intensive care unit, 25% required hospitalization for more than 14 days, and 6.5% died.[30] The mean age on admission was 62.5 years. In a more recent series of hospitalized patients, 21% developed acute respiratory failure, 18% had disseminated intravascular coagulation, 12% underwent congestive heart failure, and 9% died.[31] The mean age was 53.1 years, and most patients had significant comorbidities.

Patients with significant clinical illness and intact spleens are usually 50 years of age or older, suggesting that age is a risk factor for severe *B. microti* infection.[33] Previously healthy individuals presenting with babesiosis are generally older (mean, older than 60 years) than babesiosis patients with antecedent medical problems (mean, 48 years). Although the number and duration of symptoms in people older than 50 years of age do not differ from those in younger adults, the rate of hospitalization is higher in older individuals.[34] In one series of 17 patients with symptomatic *B. microti* infection, the mean duration of hospitalization was 19 days, with convalescence lasting from 0 to 18 months.[33] Infection may recrudesce after splenectomy or immunosuppressive therapy.[35] Underscoring the potential severity of this infection were reports of two deaths from babesiosis in Massachusetts within a 2-week period in August 1998, one in a splenectomized patient, the other in a 67-year-old individual.

PATHOGENESIS

Acquired immunity is essential to the control and elimination of *Babesia*. Infection with *B. microti* leads to higher parasitemia if mice are depleted of T cells[36] or genetically lacking T cells.[37] Resistance is restored by reconstitution of T-cell–depleted mice with B-cell–depleted spleen cells. Likewise, transfer of thymocytes from naïve mice overcomes the persistent infection in T-cell–deficient mice. Other studies have confirmed that antibody-independent, T-lymphocyte–mediated mechanisms are important for the resolution of *B. microti* infection in mice. Antibody-based depletion of CD4+ T cells results in increased susceptibility to *B. microti*.[38,39] Mice deficient for CD4+ T cells experience a longer duration of parasitemia when infected with *B. microti* or WA1.[40] These observations indicate that CD4+ T cells are critical for control and elimination of *Babesia* organisms. On the other hand, depletion of CD8+ T cells increases resistance to *B. microti*,[38] but does not render immune mice susceptible to a second challenge with *B. microti*.[39]

A successful immune response to *B. microti* is characterized by the production of inflammatory cytokines typically associated to CD4+ T cell activation, such as tumor necrosis factor-α (TNF)-α and interferon-γ (IFN)-γ. TNF receptor type I-deficient mice exhibit a lower peak parasitemia and a reduced overall parasite burden upon infection with *B. microti*,[40] revealing the detrimental role of TNF-α during *B. microti* infection. In contrast, deletion of the IFN-γ gene renders immune BALB/c mice highly susceptible to rechallenge with *B. microti*,[39] indicating that IFN-γ is critical for the acquisition of protective immunity to *B. microti*. Likewise, mice deficient for the β subunit of the IFN-γ receptor have a higher parasitemia and a greater mortality upon infection with WA1.[41] In humans, infection with *B. microti* is followed by the appearance in the circulation of T cell-derived cytokines such as IFN-γ.[20]

Innate immunity is important for survival from babesiosis. Macrophages are essential to the control of parasitemia and survival from WA1 infection.[41] The role of macrophages in *B. microti* infection is not well understood. Phagocytosis of opsonized erythrocytes and parasites may be an important means of immune protection during *Babesia* infection. Antibodies are unlikely to be the central component of protective immunity against *B. microti* or WA1 in mice.[41,42] The role of humoral immunity in human babesiosis remains unclear.

DIAGNOSIS

Babesiosis is usually diagnosed by microscopic examination of Giemsa-stained thin blood smears. *Babesia* species are annular, oval, or piriform.[1,43] The ring form is most common, and strongly resembles the ring forms of *P. falciparum*. Rings may have a single chromatic dot or two or more chromatic masses. They do not display the brownish pigment deposits (hemozoin) typical of older ring stages of *P. falciparum*. *Babesia* spp. also lack the synchronous stages and schizonts seen with *Plasmodium* spp. Gametocytes cannot be identified. A rare diagnostic feature of the small *Babesia* spp. is the presence of tetrads of merozoites (Fig. 279-2). Larger rings have a central white vacuole that is absent in malaria. Extracellular merozoites are seen in the more severe infections.

An indirect immunofluorescent antibody (IFA; IgG only) test for *B. microti* is available through the Centers for Disease Control and Prevention (Atlanta). In patients with active infection, serum titers may reach 1:1024 or greater within a few weeks, and wane slowly over months.[44] A titer of 1:64 or greater is diagnostic for *B. microti* infection. Titers below 1:64 are generally considered indicative of prior infection, titers as low as 1:16 have been accepted as positive by some. Antibodies to *B. microti* do not react to WA-1 and vice versa.[3] The caveat of serologic testing is that antibody titers are very low during the acute phase of illness, at the time of diagnosis. It is therefore not surprising that serum titers correlate poorly with the severity of symptoms. The IFA may soon be replaced by a synthetic peptide-based assay (EAI). Persing and co-workers[45] have identified immunodominant epitopes in two proteins secreted by *B. microti*. A synthetic peptide combining the two epitopes detects *B. microti*-specific antibodies in sera from infected individuals. This assay is specific for *B. microti* (does not cross-react with *P. falciparum*), and is more sensitive than blood smears. EIA correlates well with polymerase chain reaction (PCR; see later) and IFA, and should become a valuable assay for high-throughput screening of blood samples in blood banks.

Very low levels of parasitemia are detected by PCR.[46,47] In this assay, primers amplify a region of the nuclear small subunit ribosomal DNA that greatly differs between *Babesia* spp., permitting species diagnosis. In chronic babesiosis, the persistence of babesial DNA correlates well with the persistence of symptoms and *B. microti* antibody titers.[35] In an untreated, asymptomatic patient, babesial DNA could be detected for as long as 27 months. Suspected cases of *B. microti* infection can be confirmed by inoculation of 1 mL of edetate-whole blood into the peritoneum of golden hamsters. *B. divergens* replicates readily in gerbils. Giemsa-stained blood smears from these animals will turn positive for the piroplasm 2 to 4 weeks after inoculation with human blood, if infected.

TREATMENT

Most patients infected by *B. microti* appear to have a mild illness and recover without specific chemotherapy. Splenectomized patients are more likely to have high-level parasitemia and be severely ill, but patients with intact spleens may also develop severe infection. In patients with serious disease, a combination of clindamycin (in children, 20 mg/kg/day; in adults, 300 to 600 mg every 6 hours intravenously or intramuscularly) and oral quinine (in children, 25 mg/kg/day; in adults, 650 mg every 6 to 8 hours) taken for 7 to 10 days appears to be an effective regimen.[48] In less severely ill patients, clindamycin can be given orally, 600 mg in adults, every 8 hours with the oral quinine, for 1 week, while reserving intravenous clindamycin and quinine for those with more severe infection. Chloroquine, frequently given because of confusion of *B. microti* with *P. falciparum,* is not effective therapy. A number of other antimalarial and antiprotozoal therapies have likewise been largely unsuccessful, including primaquine, quinacrine, pyrimethamine, pyrimethamine-sulfadoxine, sulfadiazine, tetracycline, minocycline, pentamidine isethionate, and trimethoprim-sulfamethoxazole.[26] Despite the usual success of the clindamycin-quinine combination, failure of this therapy has been reported.

Atovaquone is a potent antiprotozoal agent. Atovaquone has been used along with and in combination with azithromycin for treatment of experimental *B. microti* infection in hamsters. These studies showed atovaquone and azithromycin to be an effective combination for the treatment of experimental babesiosis. Atovaquone monotherapy resulted in recrudescence and resistance. A clinical study by Krause and colleagues[48] compared atovaquone and azithromycin to clindamycin and quinine, both for 7 days. Both regimens were equally effective in clearing parasitemia. Clindamycin-quinine caused untoward drug reactions in 72% of patients, with atovaquone-azithromycin–caused drug reactions in 15% of patients. The atovaquone-azithromycin regimen may not be as rapidly effective but appears preferable because of fewer side effects. The usual dose of atovaquone is 750 mg orally (as suspension), taken with a meal two times daily. Although the pediatric dose has not been established, doses of 40 mg/kg/day of atovaquone and 12 mg/kg/day of azithromycin have been used in children.[49] The dose of azithromycin in adults is 500 mg on day 1 and 250 mg daily thereafter. Higher doses (500 mg to 1000 mg daily) have been employed in *B. microti* infection.[49] A patient with acquired immunodeficiency syndrome and infected with *B. microti* was treated successfully with a combination of clindamycin, doxycycline, and azithromycin after becoming allergic to quinine.[32] The combination of pentamidine

FIGURE 279-2. The life cycle and transmission of *Babesia microti*.

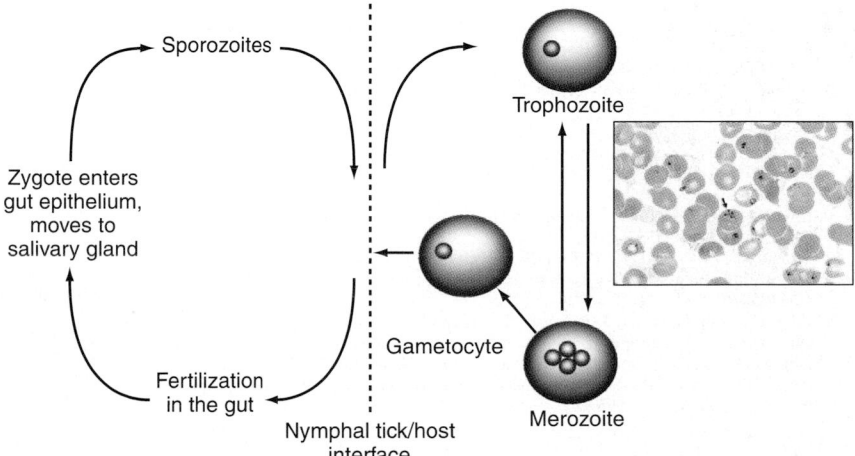

with trimethoprim-sulfamethoxazole was reported to be successful in the treatment of *B. divergens* infection in a splenectomized patient in France.[50] More recently, oral and intravenous quinine with intravenous clindamycin, and exchange transfusion, have been successful in the treatment of *B. divergens*.[51] Exchange transfusions are used in profoundly ill patients with high levels of parasitemia and hemolysis.[52] Used concurrently with chemotherapy, exchange transfusion reduces the level of parasitemia and may remove toxic erythrocytic, babesial, or macrophage-derived factors.

PREVENTION

The prevention of babesiosis requires avoidance of areas endemic for *I. scapularis* between May and September. This is especially important for splenectomized individuals and others who are immunocompromised. It is likely that babesiosis will become a greater problem in the future, as patients with HIV and those older than the age of 50 vacation and live in the ever-increasing geographic areas reporting babesial infection. In endemic areas, clothing should be worn to cover the lower portion of the body (long pants and socks). Because ticks may crawl up pants legs, tucking pants into boots or socks or cinching the legs at the ankles is helpful. Wearing light-colored clothes enables the ticks to be spotted more easily. *N,N*-Diethyl-*m*-toluamide ("DEET") insect repellent applied to the skin in concentrations of 30% to 40%[53] is effective but must be applied every 1 to 2 hours. A spray containing permethrin (Duranon; Permanone) is far more effective but should be applied only to clothes (pants bottoms, socks, shirt sleeves). Strategies for tick avoidance, tick removal, and a review of various acaricides can be found in a recent review from the Division of Vector-Borne Infectious Diseases of the CDC.[54]

Transfusion-associated babesiosis can be reduced by discouraging blood donors from endemic areas between May and September, by avoiding blood donors with fevers during the 2 months before the intended donation, and by not accepting those with a recent history of tick bites.[6] Screening of blood for *Babesia* may be adopted in the near future, and may reduce transfusion-associated babesiosis. Given the increasing confluence of the tick, the parasite, and susceptible people in ever-enlarging areas, clinicians should be increasingly alert to the possibility of this once arcane disease, babesiosis.

REFERENCES

1. Dammin GJ. Babesiosis. In: Weinstein L, Fields B, eds. Seminars in Infectious Disease. New York: Grune & Stratton; 1978:169-199.
2. Spielman A, Wilson ML, Levin JF, et al. Ecology of *Ixodes dammini*-borne human babesiosis and Lyme disease. Annu Rev Entomol. 1985;30:439-460.
3. Quick RE, Herwaldt BL, Thomford JW, et al. Babesiosis in Washington state: A new species of *Babesia*. Ann Intern Med. 1993;119:284-290.
4. Persing DH, Herwaldt BL, Glaser C, et al. Infection with a babesia-like organism in northern California. N Engl J Med. 1995;332:298-303.
5. Telford SR III, Gorenflot A, Brasseur P, Spielman A. Babesial infections in humans and wildlife. In: Kreier JP, ed. Parasitic Protozoa, v. 5. San Diego: Academic Press, 1993:1-47.
6. McQuiston JH, Childs JE, Chamberland ME, Tabor E. Transmission of tick-borne agents of disease by blood transfusion: A review of known and potential risks in the United States. Transfusion. 2000;40:274-284.
7. Gorenflot A, Moubri K, Precigout E, et al. Human babesiosis. Ann Trop Med Parasitol. 1998;92:489-501.
8. Thompson C, Spielman A, Krause PJ. Coinfecting deer-associated zoonoses: Lyme disease, babesiosis, and ehrlichiosis. Clin Infect Dis. 2001;33:676-685.
9. Homer MJ, Aguilar-Delfin I, Telford SR 3rd, et al. Babesiosis. Clin Microbiol Rev. 2000;13:451-469.
10. Kjemtrup AM, Conrad PA. Human babesiosis: An emerging tick-borne disease. Int J Parasitol. 2000; 30:1323-1337.
11. Thomford JW, Conrad PA, Telford SR 3rd, et al. Cultivation and phylogenetic characterization of a newly recognized human pathogenic protozoan. J Infect Dis. 1994; 169:1050-1056.
12. Kjemtrup AM, Thomford J, Robinson T, Conrad PA. Phylogenetic relationships of human and wildlife piroplasm isolates in the western United States inferred from the 18S nuclear small subunit RNA gene. Parasitology. 2000;120:487-493.
13. Persing DH, Conrad PA. Babesiosis: New insights from phylogenetic analysis. Infect Agents Dis. 1995;4:182-195.
14. Herwaldt B, Persing DH, Precigout EA, et al. A fatal case of babesiosis in Missouri: Identification of another piroplasm that infects humans. Ann Intern Med. 1996;124:643-650.
15. Beattie JF, Michelson ML, Holman PJ. Acute babesiosis caused by *Babesia divergens* in a resident of Kentucky. N Engl J Med. 2002;347:697-698.
16. Goethert HK, Telford SR 3rd. Enzootic transmission of *Babesia divergens* in cottontail rabbits on Nantucket Island (Abstract). Am J Trop Med Hyg. 2003;69:455-460.
17. Olmeda AS, Armstrong PM, Rosenthal BM, et al. A subtropical case of human babesiosis. Acta Trop. 1997;67:229-234.
18. Herwaldt BL, McGovern PC, Gerwel MP, et al. Endemic babesiosis in another eastern state: New Jersey. Emerg Infect Dis. 2003;9:184-188.
19. Shih CM, Liu LP, Chung WC, et al. Human babesiosis in Taiwan: Asymptomatic infection with a Babesia microti-like organism in a Taiwanese woman. J Clin Microbiol. 1997;35:450-454.
20. Shaio MF, Lin PR. A case study of cytokine profiles in acute human babesiosis. Am J Trop Med Hyg. 1998;58:335-337.
21. Hunfeld KP, Lambert A, Kampen H, et al. Seroprevalence of *Babesia* infections in humans exposed to ticks in midwestern Germany. J Clin Microbiol. 2002;40: 2431-2436.
22. Foppa IM, Krause PJ, Spielman A, et al. Entomologic and serologic evidence of zoonotic transmission of *Babesia microti*, eastern Switzerland. Emerg Infect Dis. 2002; 8:722-726.
23. Popovsky MA, Lindberg LE, Syrek AL, et al. Prevalance of *Babesia* antibodies in a selected blood donor population. Transfusion. 1988;28:59-61.
24. Krause PJ, Telford SR 3rd, Pollack RJ, et al. Babesiosis: An underdiagnosed disease of children. Pediatrics. 1992; 89:1045-1048.
25. New DL, Quinn JB, Qureshi MZ, Sigler SJ. Vertically transmitted babesiosis. J Pediatr. 1997;131:163-164.
26. Krause PJ. Babesiosis. Med Clin North Am. 2002;86:361-373.
27. Ruebush TK 2nd, Juranek DD, Spielman A, et al. Epidemiology of human babesiosis on Nantucket Island. Am J Trop Med Hyg. 1981;30:937-941.
28. Ruebush TK, Juranek DD, Chisholm ES, et al. Human babesiosis on Nantucket Island: Evidence for self-limited and subclinical infections. N Engl J Med. 1977;297:825-827.
29. Krause PJ, Telford SR 3rd, Spielman A, et al. Concurrent Lyme disease and babesiosis. Evidence for increased severity and duration of illness. JAMA. 1996;275:1657-1660.
30. White DJ, Talarico J, Chang HG, et al. Human babesiosis in New York State: Review of 139 hospitalized cases and analysis of prognostic factors. Arch Intern Med. 1998;158:2149-2154.
31. Hatcher JC, Greenberg PD, Antique J, Jimenez-Lucho VE. Severe babesiosis in Long Island: Review of 34 cases and their complications. Clin Infect Dis. 2001;32: 1117-1125.
32. Falagas ME, Klempner MS. Babesiosis in patients with AIDS: A chronic infection presenting as fever of unknown origin. Clin Infect Dis. 1996; 22:809-812.
33. Benach JL, Habicht GS. Clinical characteristics of human babesiosis. J Infect Dis. 1981; 144:481.
34. Krause PJ, McKay K, Gadbaw J, et al. Increasing health burden of human babesiosis in endemic sites. Am J Trop Med Hyg. 2003; 68:431-436.
35. Krause PJ, Spielman A, Telford SR 3rd, et al. Persistent parasitemia after acute babesiosis. N Engl J Med. 1998; 339:160-165.
36. Ruebush MJ, Hanson WL. Thymus dependence of resistance to infection with *Babesia microti* of human origin in mice. Am J Trop Med Hyg. 1980;29:507-515.
37. Matsubara J, Koura M, Kamiyama T. Infection of immunodeficient mice with a mouse-adapted substrain of the gray strain of *Babesia microti*. J Parasitol. 1993;79:783-786.
38. Shimada T, Shikano S, Hashiguchi R, et al. Effects of depletion of T cell subpopulations on the course of infection and anti-parasite delayed type hypersensitivity response in mice infected with *Babesia microti* and *Babesia rodhaini*. J Vet Med Sci. 1996; 58:343-347.
39. Igarashi I, Suzuki R, Waki S, et al. Roles of CD4(+) T cells and gamma interferon in protective immunity against *Babesia microti* infection in mice. Infect Immun. 1999;67:4143-4148.
40. Hemmer RM, Ferrick DA, Conrad PA. Up-regulation of tumor necrosis factor-alpha and interferon-gamma expression in the spleen and lungs of mice infected with the human *Babesia* isolate WA1. Parasitol Res. 2000;86:121-128.
41. Aguilar-Delfin I, Wettstein PJ, Persing DH. Resistance to acute babesiosis is associated with interleukin-12- and gamma interferon-mediated responses and requires macrophages and natural killer cells. Infect Immun. 2003;71:2002-2008.
42. Clawson ML, Paciorkowski N, Rajan TV, et al. Cellular immunity, but not gamma interferon, is essential for resolution of *Babesia microti* infection in BALB/c mice. Infect Immun. 2002;70:5304-5306.
43. Pantanowitz L, Aufranc S 3rd, Monahan-Earley R, et al. Transfusion medicine illustrated. Morphologic hallmarks of Babesia. Transfusion. 2002; 42:1389.
44. Krause PJ, Telford SR III, Ryan R, et al. Diagnosis of babesiosis: Evaluation of a serologic test for the detection of *Babesia microti* antibody. J Infect Dis. 1994;169:923-926.
45. Houghton RL, Homer MJ, Reynolds LD, et al. Identification of *Babesia microti*-specific immunodominant epitopes and development of a peptide EIA for detection of antibodies in serum. Transfusion. 2002;42:1488-1496.
46. Persing DH, Mathiesen D, Marshall WF, et al. Detection of *Babesia microti* by polymerase chain reaction. J Clin Microbiol. 1992;30:2097-2103.
47. Krause PJ, Telford S 3rd, Spielman A, et al. Comparison of PCR with blood smear and inoculation of small animals for diagnosis of *Babesia microti* parasitemia. J Clin Microbiol. 1996;34:2791-2794.

48. Krause PJ, Lepore T, Sikand VK, et al. Atovaquone and azithromycin for the treatment of babesiosis. N Engl J Med. 2000;343:1454-1458.
49. Weiss LM, Wittner M, Tanowitz HB. The treatment of babesiosis. N Engl J Med. 2001; 344:773.
50. Raoult D, Soulayrol L, Toga E, et al. Babesiosis, pentamidine, and cotrimoxazole. Ann Intern Med 1987;104:944.
51. Berry A, Morassin B, Kamar N, Magnaval JF. Clinical picture: Human babesiosis. Lancet 2001;357:341.
52. Dorman SE, Cannon ME, Telford SR 3rd, et al. Fulminant babesiosis treated with clindamycin, quinine, and whole-blood exchange transfusion. Transfusion. 2000;40:375-380.
53. Fradin MS, Day JF. Comparative efficacy of insect repellents against mosquito bites. N Engl J Med. 2002;347:13-18.
54. Hayes EB, Piesman J. How can we prevent Lyme disease? N Engl J Med. 2003;348:2424-2430.

ACKNOWLEDGMENTS

The authors are supported, in part, by NIA R01 AG19781. Philip R. Daoust, M.D. kindly provided photomicrographs.

CHAPTER **280**

Cryptosporidiosis (*Cryptosporidium hominis, Cryptosporidium parvum,* and Other Species)

A. CLINTON WHITE, Jʀ.

Protozoan parasites of the genus *Cryptosporidium* were first identified in the stomach of mice in 1907.[1] The species name *Cryptosporidium parvum* was proposed in 1912 to describe parasites identified in murine intestines.[2] Although *Cryptosporidium* was linked to gastrointestinal disease in turkeys in 1955 and to bovine diarrhea in 1971, the first human cases were described only in 1976.[3-6] Only a handful of cases had been reported prior to 1982. In the early 1980s, large numbers of cases were noted associated with the emerging epidemic of acquired immunodeficiency syndrome (AIDS).[7,8] Soon studies identified cases among animal handlers and children.[8,9] Shortly thereafter, *Cryptosporidium* was associated with waterborne outbreaks of diarrhea, including an outbreak in Milwaukee, Wisconsin in 1993 that affected an estimated 403,000 persons.[10,11] Studies have now demonstrated that *Cryptosporidium* is an important cause of self-limited diarrhea in normal hosts worldwide, of persistent diarrhea in children in developing countries, and of chronic diarrhea in immunocompromised hosts including patients with AIDS.[12-15]

THE PARASITES

The genus *Cryptosporidium* consists of a group of protozoan parasites within the protist subphylum Apicomplexa (which also includes *Plasmodium* species). *Cryptosporidium* had been classified within the subclass Coccidiasina (coccidia), together with *Eimeria, Sarcocystis, Toxoplasma, Cyclospora,* and *Isospora.* Recent molecular biology studies, however, suggest that *Cryptosporidium* may have diverged earlier from the other apicomplexans and should be reclassified into a separate subclass.[16] Initially, species names were given on the basis of the host species.[17] As of 2000, there were 10 recognized *Cryptosporidium* species, felt to be valid based on host specificity, morphology, and molecular biology studies.[13,18] Most human isolates were thought to belong to a single species, *C. parvum.* Recent molecular biology studies have demonstrated that *C. parvum* includes a number of genotypes and occult species.[19] The bovine genotype is

commonly found in humans and bovines. It infects a wide range of mammalian hosts, including mice. By contrast, the human genotype is found mainly in humans and is not infectious for cattle or mice, but can infect gnotobiotic pigs.[20] In the gnotobiotic pig, the genotypes differ in lesion distribution and intensity of infection.[21] Based on these differences and comparative genomics, a new species name, *C. hominis,* has been proposed for the human genotype.[20] Similarly, the *Cryptosporidium* parasites infecting dogs and humans has been reclassified as *C. canis.*[22] Recent molecular biology studies have demonstrated that humans can also be infected with *C. meleagridis, C. felis,* and *C. muris.*[23-29] The latter has been demonstrated to infect volunteers in experimental challenge studies (PC Okhuysen, personal communication). *C. meleagridis,* formerly thought to mainly infect birds, has been identified in most large series and appears to cause about 1% of cases of human cryptosporidiosis.[24,25,27] Other species have so far been noted to infect only reptiles, fish, birds, or nonhuman mammals.

Cryptosporidium species can complete their entire lifecycle within a single host, including both asexual (merogony) and sexual (sporogony) reproductive cycles (Fig. 280-1). The lifecycle begins with ingestion of the infectious oocyst. The infectious dose varies by several orders of magnitude from isolate to isolate.[32] For one bovine isolate, more than half of volunteers are infected with 10 oocysts.[32] In the stomach and upper intestines, the oocysts are activated, producing serine proteases and aminopeptidases, which allow the organisms to excyst, releasing four infective sporozoites.[33,34] Each sporozoite contains an apical complex with specialized organelles involved in invasion including rhoptries, micronemes, and dense granules. The motile sporozoites bind to receptors on the surface of the intestinal epithelial cells. Several parasite ligands (including the 1300-kDa circumsporozoite-like antigen, gp900, the thrombospondin-related adhesive protein of Cryptosporidium-1 [TRAP C1], the Cpgp40/15, and cp47) have been implicated in parasite attachment to the intestinal epithelium.[35-39] The parasites then induce actin polymerization and protrusion of the intestinal epithelial cell membrane.[40,41] The membrane surrounds the sporozoite and fuses to form the parasitophorous vacuole, which remains in the microvillus layer on the surface of the epithelium. A band of dense cytoskeletal elements separates the parasite from the host cytoplasm. This band prevents free flow of materials between parasite and the host cell cytoplasm.[42] It also contains an ATP binding cassette, which likely functions as an efflux pump, contributing to the resistance of the organisms to chemotherapy.[43] Inside the parasitophorous vacuole, the parasites undergo asexual reproduction (merogony). They enlarge into trophozoite forms and divide to form type I meronts, which mature and rupture to release the motile merozoites. The merozoites bind to receptors on the epithelial cells and are engulfed by the cells. They then either repeat the process of merogony or undergo sexual differentiation. In that case, the merozoites differentiate into the micro- and macrogametocytes. The microgametocyte releases the microgametes, which penetrate the cells infected with macrogametocytes. The macrogametocyte and microgametes fuse to form the zygote form, which then undergoes meiosis to form the oocyst, containing four sporozoites. Two morphologic forms of the oocyst have been described. Thin-walled oocysts are thought to excyst within the same host in a process of self-infection.[31] The thick-walled oocysts are shed into the environment.

EPIDEMIOLOGY

Several factors define the epidemiology of cryptosporidiosis. First, although *Cryptosporidium* does not multiply outside of the host, the infectious dose is low, facilitating transmission from sources with low-grade contamination, such as recreational water.[14] Second, the oocyst stage can survive for prolonged periods in the environment and resists disinfection, including chlorination. Its small size and resistance to chlorination facilitate waterborne transmission. Third, the oocysts are infectious when shed. Thus, parasites are readily transmitted directly from person to person. Fourth, some of the genotypes have important animal reservoirs. Hence, animal contact is associated with transmission. Finally, the host immune response limits the duration and severity of in-

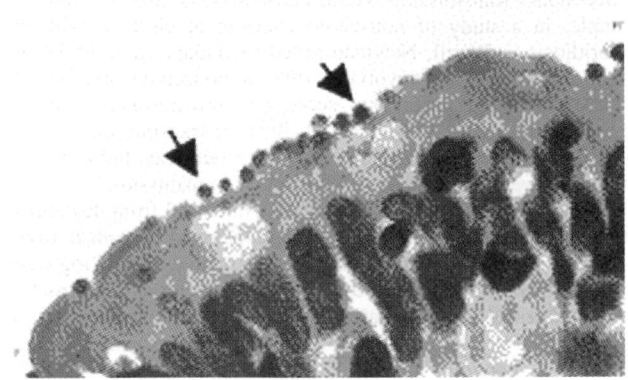

FIGURE 280-2. Intestinal biopsy showing *Cryptosporidium* intracellular forms along the surface of the intestinal epithelium. *(From Petri WA. Therapy of intestinal protozoa. Trends Parasitol. 2003;19:523-526, with permission.)*

hyperplasia, and marked infiltration with lymphocytes, plasma cells, and even neutrophils[121,123,125-127] and is also associated with extraintestinal involvement.

Cryptosporidiosis is characterized clinically by watery diarrhea and malabsorption. The physiologic processes that are thought to account for these symptoms include sodium malabsorption, electrogenic chloride secretion, and increased intestinal permeability. The voluminous, watery diarrhea resembles toxin-mediated illnesses caused by cholera and toxogenic *E. coli*. Some investigators claim to have identified enterotoxic activity in stools, but no secretory activity was detected in formal studies.[128,129]

Infection of intestinal epithelial cells leads to activation of NFκB.[130,131] NFκB then activates anti-apoptotic mechanisms, but also leads to upregulation of a proinflammatory cascade. Murine models, human intestinal xenografts in severe combined immunodeficiency mice (SCID) mice, and both biopsies and stool studies from human infection demonstrate increased expression of proinflammatory cytokines and markers of inflammation including tumor necrosis factor-α (TNF-α), interleukin-1β (IL-1β), IL-8, and lactoferrin.[132-138] Chemokines including IL-8 are produced by the infected epithelial cells.[139-141] The epithelial cells also express proinflammatory cytokines.[134] The chemokines and cytokines recruit inflammatory and immune cells into the intestines. Infection also upregulates expression of COX-2, production of prostaglandins by the epithelial cells, and production of neuropeptides such as substance P by the inflammatory cells.[142,143] The physiologic consequences of infection include increased epithelial permeability, decreased sodium absorption, and chloride secretion.

Prostaglandins mediate decreased sodium in porcine and bovine cryptosporidiosis and are thought to also stimulate cAMP-mediated chloride secretion.[132,142,144,145] In porcine models, diarrhea was induced by prostaglandins and controlled with cyclo-oxygenase inhibitors. Prostaglandin production was stimulated by TNF-α.[132] However, studies in volunteers and AIDS patients with chronic cryptosporidiosis did not demonstrate any correlation between expression or level of proinflammatory cytokines and symptoms.[135,146-148] Furthermore, prostaglandin inhibitors have not proven to be effective symptomatic therapy in human cryptosporidiosis.

More recently neuropeptides have been implicated in the diarrhea. Robinson and colleagues demonstrated a correlation between expression of the neuropeptide substance P and the presence and severity of diarrhea in volunteers challenged with *C. parvum* and AIDS patients with chronic cryptosporidiosis.[143] Similarly, mice were protected against *C. parvum*–induced intestinal inflammation by a substance P receptor antagonist.[149] Octreotide, a somatostatin analogue and substance P antagonist, partially suppresses diarrhea in chronic cryptosporidiosis and reverses altered intestinal function in vitro, suggesting a role for neuropeptides in diarrhea.[144,150]

Cryptosporidiosis is also characterized by defects in intestinal permeability. Increased permeability may result in decreased absorption of fluids and electrolytes as well as solute fluxes into the gut. Studies in AIDS patients with cryptosporidiosis have demonstrated a direct correlation between the severity of disease and altered intestinal permeability (as measured by ratios of excretion in the urine of lactulose and mannitol).[127,151,152] Similar defects have been noted in children with cryptosporidiosis.[153] *Cryptosporidium* infection directly induces defects in intestinal epithelial cell barrier function in vitro.[154-156] The latter can also be mimicked by treatment with proinflammatory cytokines such as interferon-γ (IFN-γ) and reversed by anti-inflammatory cytokines, such as transforming growth factor-β (TGF-β).[156]

Porcine and bovine cryptosporidiosis as well as infection in patients are associated with villous atrophy and crypt hyperplasia, thought to reflect epithelial cell turnover.[124,127,145,157-160] Although infection of epithelial cells stimulates anti-apoptotic mechanisms in infected cells, there is increased apoptosis in adjacent cells likely mediated by the interaction of FAS and FAS ligand.[130,131,161,162] Increased epithelial cell apoptosis has been demonstrated in biopsy specimens from infected intestines.[125] Furthermore, as the organisms complete their cycle, they cause necrotic death of the infected cells.[155,163,164] The resultant loss of villous surface was, in turn, associated with decreased expression of glucose-stimulated sodium pumps.[145,160] Similarly, loss of villous surface area has been demonstrated in human infection as D-xylose malabsorption.[121,127,152,158] Studies of AIDS patients with severe cryptosporidiosis have also demonstrated malabsorption of bile acids, vitamin B₁₂, and fatty acids.[127,165,166] Metabolic studies of AIDS patients with chronic cryptosporidiosis demonstrate fat wasting with a decreased metabolic rate, consistent with decreased absorption.[167]

HOST RESPONSE AND IMMUNITY

CD4⁺ T cells play a key role in the control of cryptosporidiosis. In patients with HIV infection, cryptosporidiosis is self-limited in individuals with CD4 cell counts higher than 180/μL, chronic in patients with CD4 cell depletion to less than 100/μL, and fulminant in some of those with counts below 50/μL.[102,168,170] Similarly, infection is chronic in mice without functional CD4 cells (anti-CD4 treatment, nude mice, SCID mice, major histocompatibility complex [MHC] class II knockout mice).[171-174] These defects can be reversed by infusion of CD4⁺ cells, particularly CD4⁺ intraepithelial lymphocytes.[175-177] Furthermore, resolution of cryptosporidiosis among AIDS patients in response to effective antiretroviral therapy is associated with an influx of CD4 cells into the intestines.[178] The role of other cell populations has been less clear. CD8⁺ cells are found at the site of infection in human and bovine infection,[133,179] but MHC class I deficiency and CD8 depletion have little effect on murine cryptosporidiosis.[174,175]

X-linked immunodeficiency with hyperimmunoglobulin M, caused by a defect in CD40 ligand (also termed CD154), is associated with increased frequency and severity of *Cryptosporidium* infection.[118,119] This syndrome is associated with profound defects in the ability of antigen-presenting cells to produce IL-12 and TNF-α and to stimulate production of IFN-γ.[180] SCID mice can resolve infection if given spleen cells that express CD40L.[181-184] This does not require cognate recognition, as similar effects were seen with cells from RAG knockout mice with a transgenic ovalbumin-specific T-cell receptor.[183] Recovery required expression of CD40 on donor spleen cells, but not recipient epithelial cells.[84]

Production of IFN-γ is a key mediator of the immune response to *Cryptosporidium*. In murine models, IFN-γ knockout mice develop chronic infection.[185,186] Furthermore, inactivation or depletion of IFN-γ causes further exacerbation of infection even beyond that noted with CD4 depletion.[171,173,187] IFN-γ is expressed in the intestines in both mice and cattle, peaking at the time of control of oocyst shedding.[188-190] Lymphocytes from people who have recovered from cryptosporidiosis produced IFN-γ after antigen stimulation in vitro.[191] About half of volunteers challenged with *C. parvum* express IFN-γ in the intestinal mucosa.[192] Treatment with IFN-γ can directly activate intestinal epithelial cell lines to partially clear *C. parvum* infection.[193] Similarly, inactivation of IL-12, the major factor stimulating production of IFN-γ, causes chronic infection.[194,195]

Surprisingly, IFN-γ expression in normal volunteers was limited to the subset with evidence of prior exposure (either seropositive before challenge or demonstrating resistance to infection).[192] Similarly, IFN-γ production by cells from HIV patients during active cryptosporidiosis and from Haitian children with active cryptosporidiosis was very low despite the fact that they had self-limited disease.[137,191] Thus, other factors appear to be involved in limiting human infection after initial exposure. In murine models, inactivation of IFN-γ expression resulted in only a mild chronic infection in BALB/c mice, but fatal infection in C57BL/6 mice.[186] Mild disease in BALB/c mice was associated with expression of IL-12, IL-4, and TNF-α.[136,196] In the absence of IFN-γ, IL-12 treatment only worsened cryptosporidiosis.[197] Similarly, treatment of AIDS patients with chronic cryptosporidiosis was associated with gastrointestinal side effects (Okhuysen PC, Chappell CL, Lewis D, et al., submitted for publication). While IL-4 synergizes with IFN-γ in eliminating infection of epithelial cells and IL-4 knockout mice displayed prolonged oocyst shedding, IL-4 treatment did not modulate infection in IFN-γ knockout mice.[197-199] By contrast, TNF-α limited infection in IFN-γ knockout mice, activated human epithelial cells to limit infection, and has been associated with control of infection in cattle.[133,136,193] In seronegative normal volunteers experimentally infected and AIDS patients recovering from cryptosporidiosis in response to antiretrovirals, control of infection was associated with expression of IL-15.[147,200] This effect is likely mediated by activation of natural killer (NK) cells. However, the role of NK cells in murine models has not been clearly demonstrated.[201-203]

The role of antibody in the immune response to cryptosporidiosis is controversial.[203] Early studies noted cases of chronic cryptosporidiosis in patients with low antibody levels, but in most cases studies were not performed to exclude coexisting T-cell dysfunction. In animal models, inactivation of B cells by antibody to the μ-chain or inactivation of the *muMT* gene did not affect clearance of cryptosporidiosis.[204,205] By contrast, treatment with high concentrations of anti-*Cryptosporidium* antibody did facilitate clearance.[203,206-209] Anecdotes suggested that hyperimmune bovine colostrums might improve cryptosporidiosis in AIDS, but a large randomized controlled trial demonstrated no clinical benefit and decreases in oocyst shedding only at very high doses.[210] High levels of serum and fecal antibodies to *C. parvum* have been found in AIDS patients with chronic cryptosporidiosis.[211,212] Studies of the fecal antibody response in volunteers challenged with *C. parvum* demonstrated specific fecal antibody in most volunteers.[213] However, the presence and timing of antibody correlated with oocyst shedding rather than clearance or resistance to infection. Similarly, cytokines such as TGF-β that stimulate immunoglobulin A (IgA) production often develop only after resolution of illness.[214] Thus, the role of antibody in cryptosporidiosis is at most modest.

CLINICAL MANIFESTATIONS

Symptoms of cryptosporidiosis develop after a prepatent period, during which the parasites invade the intestinal epithelium and proliferate. Studies of immunocompetent individuals with discrete exposures (e.g., travelers, point-source outbreaks, or experimental infection) demonstrate a prepatent period of about 1 week.[32,76,215,216] There is, however, considerable variability, with a range of 1 to 30 days. This variability reflects in part strain differences between the organisms rather than dose.[21,32,216,217] Cryptosporidiosis is noted in both males and females. The age distribution varies considerably with the epidemiology of exposure. In developing countries, most cases occur among children younger than 5 years old. This is thought to reflect both high rates of fecal-oral exposure in children and the development of immunity in older children and adults. By contrast, in Finland, nearly all cases occur in adults, reflecting an association with foreign travel.[215] Waterborne epidemics in developed countries affect all ages.[11,14]

Because *Cryptosporidium* infects primarily intestinal epithelial cells, it is not surprising that diarrhea is the most common clinical presentation. However, there are significant differences in the clinical presentation depending on the host population. The major groups include immunocompetent individuals in developed countries, children in developing countries, and immunocompromised hosts (primarily patients with AIDS).

Immunocompetent Individuals in Developed Countries

Most case series of immunocompetent individuals from developed countries have been associated with waterborne outbreaks, infection in travelers, animal contact, or infections of children in daycare and their contacts.[218] Most patients in outbreaks and among travelers are adults. Immunocompetent adults most commonly present with diarrhea. The diarrhea is usually described as watery, but may also be described as mucoid.[76] The median duration of illness in most case series is approximately 5 to 10 days. Accompanying symptoms are similar to those noted with other diarrheal illnesses including abdominal cramps, nausea, vomiting, and fever.[76,218] In comparative studies, cryptosporidiosis is less likely to cause vomiting than other causes of diarrhea. In one study, cryptosporidiosis was more frequently associated with respiratory symptoms.[219] Up to 39% of cases develop recurrent symptoms after initial resolution.[11,76,220] Relapses may follow a diarrhea-free period of several days to weeks.

Several lines of evidence suggest that milder or even asymptomatic infection may also be very common. For example, seroconversion is more common than is clinically diagnosed disease in developed as well as developing countries.[54,221-223] During the large outbreak in Milwaukee only a minority of the estimated 403,000 of cases presented for clinical care.[76,224] Patients identified by active case-finding or in children with negative stool studies were less severely ill and had a shorter duration of diarrhea than patients with laboratory-confirmed cases. Similarly, in a study of a waterborne outbreak involving a drug-treatment facility, immunocompetent cases had a mild illness, lasting only 4 days.[117] In addition, studies of normal volunteers challenged with *C. parvum* demonstrate that among those infected, most presented with a subclinical or mild illness lasting only for fewer than 5 days.[32,48,57,216] Many of the individuals with milder cases did not shed enough organisms to be detected by immunofluoresence, although, in some cases, infection was documented by flow cytometric analysis.[32]

Childhood Diarrhea in Developing Countries

Childhood diarrhea is the most common clinical manifestation of cryptosporidiosis in developing countries. Investigators in Asia, Africa, and Latin America have carefully studied cryptosporidial diarrheal illness among children.[25,93,96,137,220,225-228] These studies have demonstrated that cryptosporidiosis is common, causing about 5% to 10% of cases of diarrhea. Most present with an acute diarrheal syndrome similar to that seen with other enteric pathogens with watery diarrhea, cramps, and abdominal pain.[112] Less common features may include fever, shortness of breath, and foul stools. While most cases resolve quickly, as many as 45% of cases develop diarrhea persisting beyond 14 days.[96,229] Thus, *Cryptosporidium* is among the more common causes of persistent diarrhea in developing countries, causing about a third of cases.[25,112,220,229] Furthermore, an episode of persistent diarrhea, especially if caused by *Cryptosporidium,* is a marker for the onset of increased risk of recurrent episodes of diarrhea, weight loss, and premature death.[226,230-232] A long-term follow-up study of children with onset of cryptosporidiosis before age 1 year suggested an association with poorer physical fitness and poorer cognitive development that persists for years.[233] In a second study, long-term effects of early childhood malnutrition were noted, but there was no significant association with *Cryptosporidium* compared to other pathogens.[234]

Cryptosporidium and Malnutrition

Studies of childhood diarrhea in developing countries have consistently demonstrated an association between cryptosporidiosis and malnutrition. Case series and case-control studies noted that cryptosporidiosis was more severe in children with malnutrition.[25,93,112,116,220,225,232,235-237] For example, most deaths occur in malnourished children. These studies did not clearly distinguish the effects of cryptosporidiosis on nutritional status from the effects of malnutrition on cryptosporidiosis. Studies prospectively examining both nutritional status and *Cryptosporidium* infection in cohorts of children followed from birth demonstrated significant differences in nutritional status prior to *Cryptosporidium* infection.[226,238,239] Onset of cryptosporidiosis was associated with growth faltering, with a decrease of 300 to 400 g.[226,238,239] Older children eventually recovered and experienced catch-up growth. In contrast, children infected prior to 1 year of age often never recovered.[226,238,239] In one study, children who were stunted at the time of *Cryptosporidium* infection also did not recover weight.[239] Furthermore, even asymptomatic infection (i.e., no diarrhea) was associated with mild growth faltering.[240] Thus, *Cryptosporidium* infection clearly causes acute malnutrition, and the long-term consequences of this interaction are likely to be worse in those infected in infancy or with prior malnutrition.

Cryptosporidiosis in HIV Infection

HIV infection has been the most common host defense defect associated with cryptosporidiosis. Prior to the advent of effective antiretroviral combinations, most patients diagnosed with cryptosporidiosis had underlying HIV infection.[102] However, the incidence of cryptosporidiosis in HIV has dramatically decreased with improvements in antiretroviral therapy.[241-243] The clinical manifestations of cryptosporidiosis in HIV patients are variable. Among patients with CD4 cell counts above 150, most cases of cryptosporidiosis are self limited, similar to those in normal hosts.[102,125,169,170] However, even these cases are more likely to relapse if the cellular immune response deteriorates. Surprisingly, some cases are mild and self limited even in patients with advanced HIV infection. Other patients develop a chronic diarrheal illness. The chronic diarrhea is associated with frequent, foul smelling, bulky stools. Most patients suffer weight loss. Not surprisingly, studies have demonstrated nutrient malabsorption. A minority of cases develop a voluminous watery diarrhea or cholera-like illness. The clinical picture is often confused by other concomitant opportunistic infections, including microsporidiosis, disseminated *Mycobacterium* infection, or cytomegaloviral colitis.[102,125]

Cryptosporidiosis in AIDS is also associated with extraintestinal disease, including involvement of the biliary and respiratory tract.[102,244-247] Respiratory tract involvement is often asymptomatic, but may also manifest as bilateral pulmonary infiltrates with dyspnea. Biliary tract involvement in cryptosporidiosis has been limited to patients with profound immunodeficiency. Biliary involvement correlated with low CD4 cell count and a markedly shortened survival.[102,247] Patients may present with acalculous cholecystitis, sclerosing cholangitis, or pancreatitis.[102,247,248] Most patients present with right upper quadrant abdominal pain, which may be intermittent and colicky. Laboratory studies characteristically reveal elevated levels of alkaline phosphatase. Levels of bilirubin and transaminases are often elevated as well. In patients with associated pancreatitis, amylase and lipase are increased. Ultrasound examination may reveal dilation of the biliary duct and/or signs of gallbladder inflammation. However, most patients require endoscopic retrograde cholecystopancreatogram (ERCP) evaluation to make the anatomic diagnosis. Biopsies of the biliary ducts, staining of the bile, or stool studies may demonstrate the parasites. Most cases of biliary disease will reveal evidence of coinfection with cytomegalovirus or microsporidia as well.

DIAGNOSIS

Parasites were first demonstrated by histologic staining of intestinal tissues. The organisms appear along the surface of the epithelial cells and may appear to be in the lumen (see Fig. 280-2). The intracellular forms stain purple with hematoxylin. Tissues are available only after invasive procedures and the organisms are not consistently identified in biopsies.

Like most intestinal parasites, *Cryptosporidium* infection is usually diagnosed by microscopic examination of stool. Generally, stools are preserved in 10% buffered formalin.[249,250] Fresh stools can also be tested, but are infectious to laboratory personnel.[249] Polyvinyl alcohol interferes with staining techniques and is not recommended. Frozen stools can be used for some immunoassays. Potassium dichromate (2.5%) can also be used to preserve organisms, but it does not decrease oocyst viability.

A number of concentration methods have been attempted. Formalin ether and formalin-ethyl acetate methods are commonly used in clinical laboratories. Either technique can improve the yield in cryptosporidiosis. However, oocysts may fail to sediment if centrifugation speeds or time are not increased.[250,251] Flotation methods (e.g., Sheather's sucrose flotation or sodium chloride) facilitate identification of the organisms.[250] All are laborious and are used mainly in research laboratories. Immunomagnetic beads can be used to isolate and concentrate organisms and can dramatically improve sensitivity of stool examination.[252,253]

Wet mounts may be initially screened by direct or phase-contrast microscopy,[249,250] which may allow rapid identification of heavy infection. However, the oocysts are small, 4 to 6 m in diameter, similar in size and shape to yeast forms normally found in stool. They do not stain well with iodine or trichrome and cannot be differentiated from yeast forms by Giemsa staining. Thus, traditional approaches to stool examinations usually miss the organism. Many laboratories will not test for *Cryptosporidium* unless the tests are specifically requested.[254]

Differential staining was first noted with acid-fast stains. Oocysts stain pink or red while yeast cells and fecal debris are green or blue (Fig. 280-3). The most commonly used stain is a modification of the Ziehl-Neelsen stain.[249,250] A number of other modifications have been described including hot and cold techniques, incorporation of dimethyl sulfoxide, and use of the detergent tergetol. The sensitivity of stool examination with acid-fast staining remains poor, requiring an oocyst concentration of greater than 500,000 per mL in formed stools[255] with fewer cases detected than with fluorescent methods.[256,257] Fluorescent stains (e.g., auramine O, auramine-rhodamine) can be read more quickly than other acid-fast stains and may have improved sensitivity (see Fig. 280-3).[258] However, these assays are plagued by false-positive results. All of the acid-fast stains detect other parasites that may cause similar illnesses (e.g., *Isospora* and *Cyclospora*).

Immunofluorescent assays (IFA) employing oocysts specific monoclonal antibodies are now commonly used to test for cryptosporidiosis. IFA has been reported to be as sensitive[259-261] or up to 10 times more sensitive than acid fast staining.[256,257,262,263] Direct immunofluorescence using monoclonal antibodies is now the gold standard for stool examination. Some of the commercial IFAs (Meriflour Cryptosporidium/Giardia, Meridian Diagnostics) are also sensitive and specific assays in giardiasis.[257,261]

Antigen-detection assays are being increasingly used for stool diagnosis. Commercial kits for *Cryptosporidium* are available in ELISA and immunochromatographic formats. The ELISA kits for *Cryptosporidium* have generally performed well for diagnosis of cryptosporidiosis with sensitivities ranging from 66% to 100% with excellent specificity.[259,261,264,265] However, the sensitivity has been poor in some studies.[257,266,267] Quality control may also be an issue. For example, two kits were associated with pseudo-outbreaks stemming from false-positive results.[268,269] One commercial ELISA kit also tests for *Giardia* and *Entamoeba* antigens.[263,264] The immunochromatographic tests are rapid tests for *Cryptosporidium* and *Giardia* antigen.[257,265] The sensitivity is less than with other assays, but the specificity is excellent and results are available in minutes.[257,265] Antigen assays as a group have the advantage of not requiring skills in microscopic identification of organisms.

Research studies have demonstrated that the combination of fluorescent antibodies and flow cytometry provides a more sensitive measure of oocyst shedding than immunofluoresence.[270] Flow cytometry could detect 10^3 organisms/mL in stool seeded with oocysts.[270]

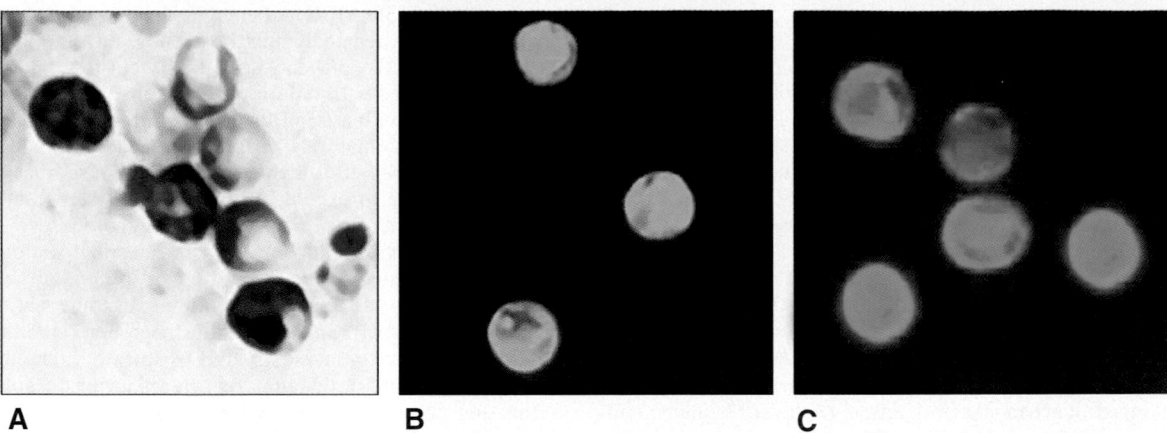

A   **B**   **C**

FIGURE 280-3. Cryptosporidiosis is diagnosed by demonstration of organisms in stool samples. This can be done with immunoassays for antigen or by microscopic demonstration of the organisms. Since the organisms are similar in size and shape to yeast normally found in stool, differential stains are required to identify the organism. These may include modified acid fast stain (**A**) showing the oocysts are red organisms, fluorescent stains such as auramine-rhodamine (**B**), or immunofluorescence (**C**) (green organisms). *(Figures are reproduced from the Centers for Disease Control DpDx: Cryptosporidiosis. http://www.dpd.cdc.gov/dpdx/HTML/Cryptosporidiosis.htm)*

PCR tests for *C. parvum* DNA have also been used to detect organisms. They also have increased sensitivity compared to microscopic studies of stool.[120,249,262] In one study of children with primary immunodeficiencies, PCR was able to detect a number of cases of biliary cryptosporidiosis not detected by stool studies.[120]

MANAGEMENT

Supportive therapy is a key component in the management of cryptosporidiosis. As is the case for all causes of diarrhea, replacement of fluids and electrolytes is a critically important first step in management. Oral rehydration is the preferred, but severely ill patients may require parenteral fluids. Fluids should include sodium, potassium, bicarbonate, and glucose. Cryptosporidiosis is characterized by preferential loss of mature epithelial cells at the tips of the villi, and enzymes expressed on these cells including lactase are lost.[124] Thus, supportive care should include a lactose-free diet. In contrast to glucose-stimulated sodium pumps which are expressed on the villus tips, glutamine-stimulated sodium absorption is not affected.[145,160] Glutamine supplementation may improve fluid absorption.[271] Although nutrition remains important, oral feeding is as effective as parenteral nutrition.[272]

Cryptosporidiosis is associated with increased intestinal transit, which could interfere with absorption of fluids, electrolytes, and drugs.[152,273] Thus, antimotility agents play a key role in therapy. Opiates are usually used as the initial antimotility agents. Loperamide and diphenoxylate/atropine combinations may ameliorate symptoms, but their efficacy is limited in severe disease. More potent opiates including tincture of opium may work in patients who have not responded. Octreotide, a synthetic peptide analogue of somatostatin, is FDA approved for the treatment of tumor-induced secretory diarrhea. Several trials have examined octreotide therapy in AIDS patients with diarrhea. Overall, octreotide was effective but not consistently more effective than other oral antidiarrheal agents.[274,275] Because of its high cost, its use is generally limited to refractory cases. A single study suggested that the enkephalinase inhibitor acetorphan is more effective than somatostatin in AIDS-associated diarrhea.[276]

For immunodeficient patients, restoration of the immune response should be pursued. For AIDS patients with chronic cryptosporidiosis, effective antiretroviral therapy can result in dramatic improvement in diarrhea.[147,277-281] This should generally take the form of combinations of three or more potent antiretroviral drugs including reverse transcriptase inhibitors one or more protease inhibitor. The HIV protease inhibitors have anticryptosporidial activity in vitro and reduced infection by up to 90% in an animal model.[281-283] Cryptosporidiosis can also

cause malabsorption of antiretroviral medications.[273] Several recent studies have combined antiretroviral therapy with antiparasitic agents.[147,280,284] Although unproven, this approach should in theory improve the response to both treatments.

Biliary involvement in cryptosporidiosis usually requires specific interventions. Acalculous cholecystitis should be treated with cholecystectomy.[285] Patients with sclerosing cholangitis can usually be treated by ERCP. Sphincterotomy may result in temporary improvement.[286] However, symptoms often recur unless a stent is placed.[102,287]

The role of antiparasitic therapy in cryptosporidiosis has been difficult to demonstrate. Attempts to screen drugs for anticryptosporidial activity in vitro and in animal models have met with limited success.[288] In vitro screening of more than 200 agents failed to identify any highly effective agent. For some drugs, resistance is attributable to target insensitivity. For example, the *Cryptosporidium* dihydrofolate reductase-thymidylate synthetase contains novel amino acids at sites associated with antifolate resistance in other species.[289] A second reason for drug resistance stems from the unique location of the parasite within the host cell, but segregated in the parasitophorous vacuole, which does not communicate with the epithelial cell cytoplasm.[42]

No agent has proven reliably curative in severely immunocompromised patients. Because cryptosporidiosis is usually self limited in immunocompetent hosts and can be variable in immunocompromised hosts, controlled trials are critically important. In compromised hosts, however, most trials have not been designed to detect partially active agents. Few of the studies of AIDS patients have rigorously excluded patients coinfected with *Mycobacteria,* microsporidia, or cytomegalovirus, all of which are common coinfections that may mask the effects of anticryptosporidial treatments.[290-292] Thus, partially active drugs (which might prove useful in combination or in situations in which the patients immune response can be boosted) may been labeled as ineffective.

Nitazoxanide is a nitrothiazolyl-salicylamide, broad-spectrum antiparasitic drug.[293] Initial studies noted efficacy versus *Taenia saginata* and *Hymenolepis nana.*[294] However, clinical development progressed only after antiprotozoal activity was demonstrated in the early 1990s.[295] Nitazoxanide suspension was approved in the United States for treatment of cryptosporidiosis and giardiasis in children in 2002. Nitazoxanide is active against *Cryptosporidium* in vitro and in animal models. Nitazoxanide inhibits growth in vitro at concentrations of less than 10 μg/mL.[296,297] The metabolite tizoxanide is less active, but tizoxanide glucuronide is nearly as active as the parent compound.[297] Nitazoxanide reduced parasite numbers, but was not curative in neonatal mice, immunosuppressed rats, and gnotobiotic pigs; it was not effective in SCID mice depleted of IFN-γ.[296,298,299]

Doumbo and colleagues reported that 7 of 12 AIDS patients with cryptosporidiosis improved with a 7-day course of nitazoxanide, but diarrhea completely resolved in only 4.[300] A randomized, controlled study of nitazoxanide in HIV patients with cryptosporidiosis was performed in Mexico that compared doses of 500 mg twice a day, 1 g twice a day, or placebo for 2 weeks.[301] Among HIV patients with CD4 cell counts greater than 50, 10 of 14 (71%) responded to 1 g/day and 9/10 (90%) to 2 g per day compared to 3 of 15 (20%) treated with placebo. By contrast, the response was no better than placebo for patients with CD4 cell counts less than or equal to 50.

Two randomized trials were performed in patients with cryptosporidiosis who were not infected with HIV. An outpatient study was performed in Egypt on adults and children with cryptosporidiosis and prolonged diarrhea (mean duration 13 days).[302] Adults, children 4 to 11, or children 1 to 3 years old received nitazoxanide was dosed at 500 mg, 200 mg, or 100 mg twice a day or matching placebo for 3 days. Diarrhea resolved by day 7 in 39 of 49 (80%) in the nitazoxanide group compared to 20 of 49 (41%) treated with placebo. Oocysts were no longer detected in 33 of 49 (67%) treated with nitazoxanide compared to 11 of 50 (22%) treated with placebo. Parallel randomized trials of HIV-infected and HIV-negative children hospitalized with chronic cryptosporidiosis were performed in Zambia.[303] Nearly all of the subjects had moderate to severe malnutrition and persistent diarrhea or chronic diarrhea. All children were treated with nitazoxanide suspension (100 mg twice a day for 3 days) or matching placebo. In the trial of HIV negative children, diarrhea had resolved by day 7 in 14 of 25 (56%) of those treated with nitazoxanide compared to 5 of 22 (23%) for the placebo group. Follow-up stools studies were free of oocysts in 13 of 25 (52%) children in the treatment group compared to 3 of 22 (14%) on placebo. Most of those who did not respond became well after a second course, given open label. Four HIV-negative children died; all were in the placebo group. Among the HIV-infected children, there were no significant differences in clinical and parasitologic responses or in mortality rate with nitazoxanide treatment.[303] Patients with severe defects of the cellular immune response may benefit from higher doses (e.g., 1 g twice a day), longer duration of treatment, or combined therapy with antiretroviral drugs and perhaps other antiparasitic agents.

Paromomycin is an orally administered nonabsorbable aminoglycoside originally approved in the 1960s as a luminal amebicide. Initial in vitro studies noted poor activity against *C. parvum*. However, when AIDS patients with cryptosporidiosis were treated with available antiparasitic drugs, some improved when treated with paromomycin.[304] Subsequently, in vitro studies demonstrated limited activity against *Cryptosporidium* with inhibitory concentrations in the range of 100 to 500 μg/mL.[288] Paromomycin is effective in animal models of cryptosporidiosis, but usually requires doses of 100 to 500 mg/kg/day.[288,296] Human trial have used doses of roughly 25 to 35 mg/kg/day in two to four doses, with estimated drug levels in the intestinal lumen barely above the amount of drug needed to inhibit the organisms in cell culture.[305] The first 12 published case series of AIDS patients treated with paromomycin included more than 300 patients with a response rate of 67%.[102,306] Many of those with initial improvement later relapsed. Three randomized, controlled trials have examined the effects of paromomycin in AIDS patients with cryptosporidiosis in AIDS. Kanyok and colleagues presented preliminary data from a small trial in 1993 demonstrating efficacy of paromomycin.[307] In a small placebo-controlled trial incorporating quantitation of oocyst excretion, the paromomycin arm demonstrated a significant reduction in oocyst shedding (about 70%), decreased stool frequency in those treated with paromomycin, but no cures.[290] Biliary tract involvement and *Mycobacteria* coinfection were common in those not responding. Hewitt and colleagues compared paromomycin with placebo in a

trial including 35 AIDS patients.[308] There was no difference between groups, when analyzing those on treatment, but dropouts occurred only in the placebo arm. By intent-to-treat analysis with dropouts grouped with failures, the response rate was similar to the previous trials with a trend favoring paromomycin over placebo.[292] The trial was prematurely terminated because of poor enrollment and was not powered to detect limited response rates. Limited efforts were made to exclude coinfections. Dose escalation demonstrated no further improvement with higher doses[308] and higher doses have been associated with gastrointestinal and ototoxicity.[305]

Macrolide antibiotics including spiramycin, azithromycin, roxithromycin, and clarithromycin have some activity against *Cryptosporidium*.[288] Spiramycin has been marketed in Europe for treatment of toxoplasmosis and respiratory tract infections. Sáenz-Lloren and colleagues reported shorter duration of symptoms and oocyst shedding when children were treated with 100 mg/kg/day of spiramycin,[309] but a second trial showed no effect.[310] The ACTG conducted a randomized controlled trial in 75 AIDS patients comparing spiramycin with placebo, but noted that spiramycin was not significantly better than placebo.[288] A trial of intravenous spiramycin was associated with significantly decreased oocyst shedding and a partial response in 75% of subjects.[288] However, there were high rates of adverse events including drug-associated intestinal injury.[311] Azithromycin has some activity against *Cryptosporidium* in vitro and in animal studies.[288] Case series note improvement in cryptosporidiosis among HIV and cancer patients treated with azithromycin.[312-315] In a placebo-controlled, multicenter trial, AIDS patients with cryptosporidiosis were randomly assigned to receive azithromycin 900 mg orally daily or placebo. Overall, oocyst shedding, stool frequency and weight loss were not significantly different.[288] A subsequent pilot trial of intravenous azithromycin also did not demonstrate changes in stool frequency or oocyst shedding.[288] Similar results were reported from another prospective study.[306] A pilot study in Egyptian school children suggested more rapid resolution with azithromycin treatment.[316]

Clarithromycin is also active in vitro and in animal studies.[306] There are only limited data on treatment of human cryptosporidiosis with clarithromycin. However, the drug may be useful in chemoprophylaxis (see later). Roxithromycin treatment was associated with improvement in AIDS-associated cryptosporidiosis in two uncontrolled studies.[317,318] Rifaximin, a nonabsorbable rifamycin, was also reported to improve cryptosporidiosis in HIV patients.[319]

Anecdotal reports noted improvement in chronic cryptosporidiosis in patients treated with oral anti-*Cryptosporidium* immunoglobulin preparations.[320] However, two well-controlled trials have examined oral bovine anti-*Cryptosporidium* immunoglobulin (BACI) preparations in cryptosporidiosis. BACI did not significantly decrease symptoms or oocyst shedding in experimental infection of volunteers.[321] In a large trial of BACI for cryptosporidiosis in AIDS patients, there was no effect on symptoms and oocyst shedding only decreased slightly at a dose of 20 g/day.[210] At higher doses, oocyst excretion decreased, but the immunoglobulin preparation caused diarrhea. Letrazuril was initially thought to demonstrate marked reduction in oocyst excretion with minimal change in symptoms.[288,306] Subsequent studies revealed that the treatment mainly interfered with the acid-fast staining of oocysts.

Because individual drugs have limited activity, studies have investigated the effects of combinations. Smith and colleagues conducted a pilot study of the combination of paromomycin combined with azithromycin in AIDS patients with chronic cryptosporidiosis. Overall, there was a 2-log decrease in oocyst shedding, but few patients were cured.[291] Clinical failures were associated with biliary disease, coinfection with other enteric pathogens (especially cytomegalovirus), or side effects of the medications. Thus, combination therapy warrants further study.

PREVENTION

Cryptosporidiosis is transmitted from person to person and via contaminated water and food. Water purification is an important public health measure. Because chlorination has little effect on the oocysts, water purification should generally involve flocculation and filtration.[73] Ultraviolet radiation or ozonation can disinfect contaminated water, but they are rarely used. Recreational waters, such as lakes, may pose a danger for compromised hosts, who should avoid untreated water.[322] Swimming pools are now an important source of infection. Contamination of treated recreational water, such as a fecal accident in a swimming pool, should prompt aggressive measures, including closing the pool temporarily.

Personal measures can be used to decontaminate infected or potentially infected water, such as in travel to developing countries, when the public water supply is contaminated, or as a routine in compromised hosts.[322] Water can be decontaminated by bringing it to a boil or by filtration using a filter with a pore size of 1 μm or less.[322,324]

Although cryptosporidiosis can be transmitted within health care facilities, risk is minimal with standard precautions.[95] Gloves should be worn and hands washed after handling material contaminated with fecal material. Instruments such as endoscopes need to be carefully disinfected between uses. Wearing gloves and handwashing can also prevent infection in daycare centers.

For patients with AIDS (CD4 cell counts less than 200/mm³), water should be boiled or filtered.[322] If HIV-infected persons travel in developing countries, they should be warned to meticulously avoid drinking tap water. They should avoid obvious sources of *Cryptosporidium* oocysts, such as people with diarrhea (particularly avoiding sexual practices that might involve exposure to feces), farm animals (particularly cattle), and domestic pets that are either very young (less than 6 months) or have diarrhea. Chemoprophylaxis should also be considered. Two retrospective studies examined data from trials of prophylaxis of *Mycobacterium avium* for their effects on cryptosporidiosis. Holmberg and colleagues compared the incidence of cryptosporidiosis in those given rifabutin, clarithromycin, or no drug for prevention of *Mycobacterium avium* complex among patients in the HIV Outpatient Study cohort.[324] The incidence of cryptosporidiosis was much lower in those treated with rifabutin and also lower in those treated with clarithromycin. Fichtenbaum and colleagues analyzed patients enrolled in controlled trials of clarithromycin, rifabutin, both, or no drug for *M. avium* complex prophylaxis. They also noted a lower incidence of cryptosporidiosis than in groups treated with rifabutin.[325] However, they could not confirm the efficacy of clarithromycin. However, the incidence of cryptosporidiosis was low in both studies.

Experimental studies suggest that it may be possible to develop a vaccine to prevent cryptosporidiosis.[207,208,326-328] Vaccination would likely have to involve both human and animal hosts and would need to work against a number of species of parasites. Studies have so far not even demonstrated the feasibility of this approach.

REFERENCES

1. Tyzzer EE. A sporozoan found in the peptic glands of the common mouse. Proc Soc Exp Biol Med. 1907;5:12-13.
2. Tyzzer EE. *Cryptosporidium parvum* (sp nov): A coccidium found in the small intestine of the common mouse. Arch Protisten. 1912;26:394-418.
3. Slavin D. *Cryptosporidium meleagridis* (sp nov). J Comp Pathol. 1955;65:262-266.
4. Pancier RJ, Thomassen RW, Garner FM. Cryptosporidial infection in a calf. Vet Pathol. 1971;8:479-484.
5. Nime FA, Burek JD, Page DL, et al. Acute enterocolitis in a human being infected with the protozoan *Cryptosporidium.* Gastroenterology. 1976;70:592-598.
6. Meisel JL, Perera DR, Meligro C, Rubin CE. Overwhelming watery diarrhea associated with a *Cryptosporidium* in an immunosuppressed patient. Gastroenterology. 1976;70:1156-1160.
7. Cryptosporidiosis: Assessment of chemotherapy of males with acquired immune deficiency syndrome (AIDS). MMWR Morb Mortal Wkly Rep. 1982;31:589-592.
8. Current WL, Reese NC, Ernst JV, et al. Human cryptosporidiosis in immunocompetent and immunodeficient persons: Studies of an outbreak and experimental transmission. N Engl J Med. 1983;308:1252-1257.
9. Wolfson JS, Richter JM, Waldron MA, et al. Cryptosporidiosis in immunocompetent hosts. N Engl J Med. 1985;312:1278-1282.
10. D'Antonio RG, Win RE, Taylor JP, et al. A waterborne outbreak of cryptosporidiosis in normal hosts. Ann Intern Med. 1986;103:886-888.
11. MacKenzie WR, Schell WL, Blair KA, et al. Massive outbreak of waterborne *Cryptosporidium* infection in Milwaukee, Wisconsin: Recurrence of illness and risk of secondary transmission. Clin Infect Dis. 1995;21:57-62.
12. Guerrant R. Cryptosporidiosis: An emerging, highly infectious threat. Emerg Infect Dis. 1997;3:51-57.
13. Fayer R, Morgan U, Upton SJ. Epidemiology of *Cryptosporidium:* Transmission, detection and identification. Int J Parasitol. 2000;30:1305-1322.
14. Dillingham RA, Lima AA, Guerrant RL. Cryptosporidiosis: Epidemiology and impact. Microbes Infect. 2002;4:1059-1066.
15. Chen XM, Keithly JS, Paya CV, LaRusso NF. Cryptosporidiosis. N Engl J Med. 2002;346:1723-1731.
16. Zhu G, Keithly JS, Philippe H. What is the phylogenetic position of *Cryptosporidium*? Int J Syst Evol Microbiol. 2000;50 (Pt 4):1673-1681.
17. Xiao L, Sulaiman IM, Ryan UM, et al. Host adaptation and host-parasite co-evolution in *Cryptosporidium:* Implications for taxonomy and public health. Int J Parasitol. 2002;32:1773-1785.
18. Morgan UM, Xiao L, Fayer R, et al. Variation in *Cryptosporidium:* Towards a taxonomic revision of the genus. Int J Parasitol. 1999;29:1733-1751.
19. Xiao L, Morgan UM, Fayer R, et al. *Cryptosporidium* systematics and implications for public health. Parasitol Today. 2000;16:287-292.
20. Morgan-Ryan UM, Fall A, Ward LA, et al. *Cryptosporidium hominis* n. sp. (Apicomplexa: Cryptosporidiidae) from Homo sapiens. J Eukaryot Microbiol. 2002;49:433-440.
21. Pereira SJ, Ramirez NE, Xiao L, Ward LA. Pathogenesis of human and bovine *Cryptosporidium parvum* in gnotobiotic pigs. J Infect Dis. 2002;186:715-718.
22. Fayer R, Trout JM, Xiao L, et al. *Cryptosporidium canis* n. sp. from domestic dogs. J Parasitol. 2001;87:1415-1422.
23. McLauchlin J, Amar C, Pedraza-Diaz S, Nichols GL. Molecular epidemiological analysis of Cryptosporidium spp. in the United Kingdom: Results of genotyping *Cryptosporidium* spp. in 1,705 fecal samples from humans and 105 fecal samples from livestock animals. J Clin Microbiol. 2000;38:3984-3990.
24. Pedraza-Diaz S, Amar CF, McLauchlin J, et al. *Cryptosporidium meleagridis* from humans: Molecular analysis and description of affected patients. J Infect. 2001;42:243-250.
25. Tumwine JK, Kekitiinwa A, Nabukeera N, et al. *Cryptosporidium parvum* in children with diarrhea in Mulago Hospital, Kampala, Uganda. Am J Trop Med Hyg. 2003;68:710-715.
26. Gatei W, Greensill J, Ashford RW, et al. Molecular analysis of the 18S rRNA gene of *Cryptosporidium* parasites from patients with or without human immunodeficiency virus infections living in Kenya, Malawi, Brazil, the United Kingdom, and Vietnam. J Clin Microbiol. 2003;41:1458-1462.
27. Xiao L, Bern C, Limor J, et al. Identification of 5 types of *Cryptosporidium* parasites in children in Lima, Peru. J Infect Dis. 2001;183:492-497.
28. Enemark HL, Ahrens P, Juel CD, et al. Molecular characterization of Danish *Cryptosporidium parvum* isolates. Parasitology. 2002;125:331-341.
29. Gatei W, Suputtamongkol Y, Waywa D, et al. Zoonotic species of *Cryptosporidium* are as prevalent as the anthroponotic in HIV-infected patients in Thailand. Ann Trop Med Parasitol. 2002;96:797-802.
30. Current WL, Reese NC. A comparison of endogenous development of three isolates of *Cryptosporidium* in suckling mice. J Protozool. 1986;33:98-108.
31. Hijjawi NS, Meloni BP, Morgan UM, Thompson RC. Complete development and long-term maintenance of *Cryptosporidium parvum* human and cattle genotypes in cell culture. Int J Parasitol. 2001;31:1048-1055.
32. Okhuysen PC, Chappell CL, Crabb JH, et al. Virulence of three distinct *Cryptosporidium parvum* isolates for healthy adults. J Infect Dis. 1999;180:1275-1281.
33. Forney JR, Yang S, Healey MC. Antagonistic effect of human alpha-1-antitrypsin on excystation of *Cryptosporidium parvum* oocysts. J Parasitol. 1997;83:771-774.
34. Okhuysen PC, Chappell CL, Kettner C, Sterling CR. *Cryptosporidium parvum* metalloaminpeptidase inhibitors prevent in vitro excystation. Antimicrobial Agents Chemother. 1996;40:2781-2784.
35. Langer RC, Riggs MW. *Cryptosporidium parvum* apical complex glycoprotein CSL contains a sporozoite ligand for intestinal epithelial cells. Infect Immun. 1999;67:5282-5291.
36. Barnes DA, Bonnin A, Huang JX, et al. A novel multi-domain mucin-like glycoprotein of *Cryptosporidium parvum* mediates invasion. Mol Biochem Parasitol. 1998;96:93-110.
37. Spano F, Pulignani L, Naitza S, et al. Molecular cloning and expression analysis of a *Cryptosporidium parvum* gene encoding a new member of the thrombospondin family. Mol Biochem Parasitol. 1998;92:147-162.
38. Cevallos AM, Bhat N, Verdon R, et al. Mediation of *Cryptosporidium parvum* infection in vitro by mucin-like glycoproteins defined by a neutralizing monoclonal antibody. Infect Immun. 2000;68:5167-5175.
39. Nesterenko MV, Woods K, Upton SJ. Receptor/ligand interactions between *Cryptosporidium parvum* and the surface of the host cell. Biochim Biophys Acta. 1999;1454:165-173.

40. Elliott DA, Coleman DJ, Lane MA, et al. *Cryptosporidium parvum* infection requires host cell actin polymerization. Infect Immun. 2001;69:5940-5942.

41. Chen XM, Huang BQ, Splinter PL, et al. *Cryptosporidium parvum* invasion of biliary epithelia requires host cell tyrosine phosphorylation of cortactin via c-Src. Gastroenterology. 2003;125:216-228.

42. Griffiths JK, Balakrishnan R, Widmer G, Tzipori S. Paromomycin and geneticin inhibit intracellular *Cryptosporidium parvum* without trafficking through the host cell cytoplasm: Implications for drug delivery. Infect Immun. 1998;66:3874-3883.

43. Perkins ME, Riojas YA, Wu TW, Le Blancq SM. CpABC, a *Cryptosporidium parvum* ATP-binding cassette protein at the host-parasite boundary in intracellular stages. Proc Natl Acad Sci USA. 1999;96:5734-5739.

44. Amin OM. Seasonal prevalence of intestinal parasites in the United States during 2000. Am J Trop Med Hyg. 2002;66:799-803.

45. Dietz V, Vugia D, Nelson R, et al. Active, multisite, laboratory-based surveillance for *Cryptosporidium parvum*. Am J Trop Med Hyg. 2000;62:368-372.

46. Mead PS, Slutsker L, Dietz V, et al. Food-related illness and death in the United States. Emerg Infect Dis. 1999;5:607-625.

47. Kappus KD, Lundgren RG Jr, Juranek DD, et al. Intestinal parasitism in the United States: Update on a continuing problem. Am J Trop Med Hyg. 1994;50:705-713.

48. Okhuysen PC, Chappell CL, Sterling CR, et al. Susceptibility and serologic response of healthy adults to reinfection with *Cryptosporidium parvum*. Infect Immun. 1998;66:441-443.

49. Frost F, de la Cruz AA, Moss DM, et al. Comparison of ELISA and Western blot assays for detection of *Cryptosporidium* antibody. Epidemiol Infect. 1998;121:205-211.

50. Ungar BL, Mulligan M, Nutman TB. Serologic evidence of *Cryptosporidium* infection in US volunteers before and after Peace Corps service in Africa. Arch Intern Med. 1989;149:894-897.

51. Zu SX, Li JF, Barrett LJ, et al. Seroepidemiologic study of *Cryptosporidium* infection in children from rural communities of Anhui, China and Fortaleza, Brazil. Am J Trop Med Hyg. 1994;51:1-10.

52. Frost FJ, Muller T, Craun GF, et al. Serological evidence of endemic waterborne Cryptosporidium infections. Ann Epidemiol. 2002;12:222-227.

53. Lengerich EJ, Addiss DG, Marx JJ, et al. Increased exposure to cryptosporidia among dairy farmers in Wisconsin. J Infect Dis. 1993;167:1252-1255.

54. Kuhls TL, Mosier DA, Crawford DL, Griffis J. Seroprevalence of cryptosporidial antibodies during infancy, childhood, and adolescence. Clin Infect Dis. 1994;18:731-735.

55. Leach CT, Koo FC, Kuhls TL, et al. Prevalence of *Cryptosporidium parvum* infection in children along the Texas-Mexico border and associated risk factors. Am J Trop Med Hyg. 2000;62:656-661.

56. Ungar BLP, Gilman RH, Lanata CF, Perez-Schael I. Seroepidemiology of *Cryptosporidium* infection in two Latin American populations. J Infect Dis. 1988;157:551-556.

57. DuPont H, Chappell C, Sterling C, et al. The infectivity of *Cryptosporidium parvum* in healthy volunteers. N Engl J Med. 1995;332:855-859.

58. Messner MJ, Chappell CL, Okhuysen PC. Risk assessment for *Cryptosporidium*: A hierarchical Bayesian analysis of human dose response data. Water Res. 2001;35:3934-3940.

59. Miller RA, Bronsdon MA, Morton WR. Experimental cryptosporidiosis in a primate model. J Infect Dis. 1990;161:312-315.

60. Chappell CL, Okhuysen PC, Sterling CR, et al. Infectivity of *Cryptosporidium parvum* in healthy adults with pre-existing anti-C. parvum serum IgG. Am J Trop Med Hyg. 1999;60:157-164.

61. Fayer R, Trout JM, Jenkins MC. Infectivity of *Cryptosporidium parvum* oocysts stored in water at environmental temperatures. J Parasitol. 1998;84:1165-1169.

62. Robertson LJ, Campbell AT, Smith HV. Survival of *Cryptosporidium parvum* oocysts under various environmental pressures. Appl Environ Microbiol. 1992;58:3494-3500.

63. Fayer R, Nerad T. Effects of low temperatures on viability of *Cryptosporidium parvum* oocysts. Appl Environ Microbiol. 1996;62:1431-1433.

64. Fayer R. Effect of high temperature on infectivity of *Cryptosporidium parvum* oocysts in water. Appl Environ Microbiol. 1994;60:2732-2735.

65. Harp JA, Fayer R, Pesch BA, Jackson GJ. Effect of pasteurization on infectivity of *Cryptosporidium parvum* oocysts in water and milk. Appl Environ Microbiol. 1996;62:2866-2868.

66. Deng MQ, Cliver DO. Inactivation of *Cryptosporidium parvum* oocysts in cider by flash pasteurization. J Food Prot. 2001;64:523-527.

67. Korich DG, Mead JR, Madore MS, et al. Effects of ozone, chlorine dioxide, chlorine, and monochloramine on *Cryptosporidium parvum* oocyst viability. Appl Environ Microbiol. 1990;56:1423-1428.

68. Quinn CM, Betts WB. Longer term viability of chlorine-treated *Cryptosporidium* oocysts in tap water. Biomed Lett. 1993;48:315-318.

69. Carpenter C, Fayer R, Trout J, Beach MJ. Chlorine disinfection of recreational water for *Cryptosporidium parvum*. Emerg Infect Dis. 1999;5:579-584.

70. Fayer R. Effect of sodium hypochlorite exposure on infectivity of *Cryptosporidium parvum* oocysts for neonatal BALB/c mice. Appl Environ Microbiol. 1995;61:844-846.

71. Fayer R, Speer CA, Dubey JP. General biology of *Cryptosporidium*. In: Dubey JP, Speer CA, Fayer R, eds. Cryptosporidiosis of Man and Animals. Boca Raton, FL: CRC Press; 1990:1-29.

72. LeChevallier MW, Norton WD, Lee RG. Occurrence of *Giardia* and *Cryptosporidium* spp. in surface water supplies. Appl Environ Microbiol. 1991;57:2610-2616.

73. Rose JB, Huffman DE, Gennaccaro A. Risk and control of waterborne cryptosporidiosis. FEMS Microbiol Rev. 2002;26:113-123.

74. Ward PI, Deplazes P, Regli W, et al. Detection of eight *Cryptosporidium* genotypes in surface and waste waters in Europe. Parasitology. 2002;124:359-368.

75. LeChevallier MW, Norton WD, Lee RG. Giardia and *Cryptosporidium* spp. in filtered drinking water supplies. Appl Environ Microbiol. 1991;57:2617-2621.

76. MacKenzie WR, Hoxie NJ, Proctor ME, et al. A massive outbreak in Milwaukee of *Cryptosporidium* infection transmitted through the public water supply. N Engl J Med. 1994;331:161-167.

77. Sulaiman IM, Xiao L, Yang C, et al. Differentiating human from animal isolates of *Cryptosporidium parvum*. Emerg Infect Dis. 1998;4:681-685.

78. Barwick RS, Levy DA, Craun GF, et al. Surveillance for waterborne-disease outbreaks—United States, 1997-1998. MMWR CDC Surveill Summ. 2000;49:1-21.

79. Lee SH, Levy DA, Craun GF, et al. Surveillance for waterborne-disease outbreaks—United States, 1999-2000. MMWR Surveill Summ. 2002;51:1-47.

80. Puech MC, McAnulty JM, Lesjak M, et al. A statewide outbreak of cryptosporidiosis in New South Wales associated with swimming at public pools. Epidemiol Infect. 2001;126:389-396.

81. Robertson B, Sinclair MI, Forbes AB, et al. Case-control studies of sporadic cryptosporidiosis in Melbourne and Adelaide, Australia. Epidemiol Infect. 2002;128:419-431.

82. Xiao L, Sulaiman I, Fayer R, Lal AA. Species and strain-specific typing of *Cryptosporidium* parasites in clinical and environmental samples. Mem Inst Oswaldo Cruz. 1998;93:687-691.

83. Millard PS, Gensheimer KF, Addiss DG, et al. An outbreak of cryptosporidiosis from fresh-pressed apple cider. JAMA. 1994;272:1592-1596.

84. Gelletlie R, Stuart J, Soltanpoor N, et al. Cryptosporidiosis associated with school milk. Lancet. 1997;350:1005-1006.

85. Quiroz ES, Bern C, MacArthur JR, et al. An outbreak of cryptosporidiosis linked to a foodhandler. J Infect Dis. 2000;181:695-700.

86. Ortega YR, Roxas CR, Gilman RH, et al. Isolation of *Cryptosporidium parvum* and *Cyclospora cayetanensis* from vegetables collected in markets of an endemic region in Peru. Am J Trop Med Hyg. 1997;57:683-686.

87. Graczyk TK, Grimes BH, Knight R, et al. Detection of *Cryptosporidium parvum* and *Giardia lamblia* carried by synanthropic flies by combined fluorescent in situ hybridization and a monoclonal antibody. Am J Trop Med Hyg. 2003;68:228-232.

88. Kniel KE, Sumner SS, Lindsay DS, et al. Effect of organic acids and hydrogen peroxide on *Cryptosporidium parvum* viability in fruit juices. J Food Prot. 2003;66:1650-1657.

89. Alpert G, Bell LM, Kirkpatrick CE, et al. Outbreak of cryptosporidiosis in a day-care center. Pediatrics. 1986;77:152-157.

90. Heijbel H, Slaine K, Seigel B, et al. Outbreak of diarrhea in a day care center with spread to household members: The role of *Cryptosporidium*. Pediatr Infect Dis J. 1987;6:532-535.

91. Cordell RL, Addiss DG. Cryptosporidiosis in child care settings: A review of the literature and recommendations for prevention and control. Pediatr Infect Dis J. 1994;13:310-317.

92. Koch KL, Phillips DJ, Aber RC, Current WL. Cryptosporidiosis in hospital personnel. Evidence for person-to-person transmission. Ann Intern Med. 1985;102:593-596.

93. Sarabia-Arce S, Salazar-Lindo E, Gilman RH, et al. Case-control study of *Cryptosporidium parvum* infection in Peruvian children hospitalized for diarrhea: Possible association with malnutrition and nosocomial infection. Pediatr Infect Dis J. 1990;9:627-631.

94. Navarrete S, Stetler HC, Avila C, et al. An outbreak of *Cryptosporidium* diarrhea in a pediatric hospital. Pediatr Infect Dis J. 1991;10:248-250.

95. Bruce BB, Blass MA, Blumberg HM, et al. Risk of *Cryptosporidium parvum* transmission between hospital roommates. Clin Infect Dis. 2000;31:947-950.

96. Newman RD, Zu SX, Wuhib T, et al. Household epidemiology of *Cryptosporidium parvum* infection in an urban community in northeast Brazil. Ann Intern Med. 1994;120:500-505.

97. Jokipii L, Pohjola S, Jokipii AM. Cryptosporidiosis associated with traveling and giardiasis. Gastroenterology. 1985;89:838-842.

98. Jelinek T, Lotze M, Eichenlaub S, et al. Prevalence of infection with *Cryptosporidium parvum* and *Cyclospora cayetanensis* among international travellers. Gut. 1997;41:801-804.

99. Khalakdina A, Vugia DJ, Nadle J, et al. Is drinking water a risk factor for endemic cryptosporidiosis? A case-control study in the immunocompetent general population of the San Francisco Bay Area. BMC Publ Hlth. 2003;3:11.

100. Caputo C, Forbes A, Frost F, et al. Determinants of antibodies to *Cryptosporidium* infection among gay and bisexual men with HIV infection. Epidemiol Infect. 1999;122:291-297.

101. Khalakdina A, Tabnak F, Sun RK, Colford JM Jr. Race/ethnicity and other risk factors associated with cryptosporidiosis as an initial AIDS-defining condition in California, 1980-99. Epidemiol Infect. 2001;127:535-543.

102. Hashmey R, Smith NH, Cron S, et al. Cryptosporidiosis in Houston, Texas. A report of 95 cases. Medicine (Baltimore). 1997;76:118-139.

103. Hellard M, Hocking J, Willis J, et al. Risk factors leading to *Cryptosporidium* infection in men who have sex with men. Sex Transm Infect. 2003;79:412-414.

104. Pohjola S, Jokipii AM, Jokipii L. Sporadic cryptosporidiosis in a rural population is asymptomatic and associated with contact to cattle. Acta Vet Scand. 1986;27:91-102.

105. Miron D, Kenes J, Dagan R. Calves as a source of an outbreak of cryptosporidiosis among young children in an agricultural closed community. Pediatr Infect Dis J. 1991;10:438-441.

106. Hunter PR, Chalmers RM, Syed Q, et al. Foot and mouth disease and cryptosporidiosis: Possible interaction between two emerging infectious diseases. Emerg Infect Dis. 2003;9:109-112.
107. Smerdon WJ, Nichols T, Chalmers RM, et al. Foot and mouth disease in livestock and reduced cryptosporidiosis in humans, England and Wales. Emerg Infect Dis. 2003;9:22-28.
108. Strachan NJ, Ogden ID, Smith-Palmer A, Jones K. Foot and mouth epidemic reduces cases of human cryptosporidiosis in Scotland. J Infect Dis. 2003;188:783-786.
109. Casemore DP. Sheep as a source of human cryptosporidiosis. J Infect. 1989;19:101-104.
110. Molbak K, Aaby P, Hojlyng N, da Silva AP. Risk factors for *Cryptosporidium* diarrhea in early childhood: A case-control study from Guinea-Bissau, West Africa. Am J Epidemiol. 1994;139:734-740.
111. Xiao L, Bern C, Arrowood M, et al. Identification of the *Cryptosporidium* pig genotype in a human patient. J Infect Dis. 2002;185:1846-1848.
112. Sallon S, el-Shawwa R, Khalil M, et al. Diarrhoeal disease in children in Gaza. Ann Trop Med Parasitol. 1994;88:175-182.
113. Bern C, Hernandez B, Lopez MB, et al. The contrasting epidemiology of Cyclospora and *Cryptosporidium* among outpatients in Guatemala. Am J Trop Med Hyg. 2000;63:231-235.
114. Bern C, Ortega Y, Checkley W, et al. Epidemiologic differences between cyclosporiasis and cryptosporidiosis in Peruvian children. Emerg Infect Dis. 2002;8:581-585.
115. Perch M, Sodemann M, Jakobsen MS, et al. Seven years' experience with *Cryptosporidium parvum* in Guinea-Bissau, West Africa. Ann Trop Paediatr. 2001;21:313-318.
116. Hunter PR, Nichols G. Epidemiology and clinical features of *Cryptosporidium* infection in immunocompromised patients. Clin Microbiol Rev. 2002;15:145-154.
117. Pozio E, Rezza G, Boshini A, et al. Clinical cryptosporidiosis and human immunodeficiency virus (HIV)-induced immunosuppression: Findings from a longitudinal study of HIV-positive and HIV-negative fromer injection drug users. J Infect Dis. 1997;176:969-975.
118. Hayward AR, Levy J, Facchetti F, et al. Cholangiopathy and tumors of the pancreas, liver, and biliary tree in boys with X-linked immunodeficiency with hyper-IgM. J Immunol. 1997;158:977-983.
119. Levy J, Espanol-Boren T, Thomas C, et al. Clinical spectrum of X-linked hyper-IgM syndrome. J Pediatr. 1997;131:47-54.
120. McLauchlin J, Amar CF, Pedraza-Diaz S, et al. Polymerase chain reaction-based diagnosis of infection with *Cryptosporidium* in children with primary immunodeficiencies. Pediatr Infect Dis J. 2003;22:329-335.
121. Clayton F, Heller T, Kotler DP. Variation in the enteric distribution of cryptosporidia in acquired immunodeficiency syndrome. Am J Clin Pathol. 1994;102:420-425.
122. Kelly P, Makumbi FA, Carnaby S, et al. Variable distribution of *Cryptosporidium parvum* in the intestine of AIDS patients revealed by polymerase chain reaction. Eur J Gastroenterol Hepatol. 1998;10:855-858.
123. Greenberg PD, Koch J, Cello JP. Diagnosis of *Cryptosporidium parvum* in patients with severe diarrhea and AIDS. Dig Dis Sci. 1996;41:2286-2290.
124. Phillips AD, Thomas AG, Walker-Smith JA. *Cryptosporidium,* chronic diarrhoea and the proximal small intestinal mucosa. Gut. 1992;33:1057-1061.
125. Lumadue JA, Manabe YC, Moore RD, et al. A clinicopathologic analysis of AIDS-related cryptosporidiosis. AIDS. 1998;12:2459-2466.
126. Genta RM, Chappell CL, White AC Jr, et al. Duodenal morphology and intensity of infection in AIDS-related cryptosporidiosis. Gastroenterology. 1993;105.1769-1775.
127. Goodgame RW, Kimball K, Ou C-N, et al. Intestinal function and injury in AIDS-related cryptosporidiosis. Gastroenterology. 1995;108:1075-1082.
128. Guarino A, Canani RB, Casoli A, et al. Human intestinal cryptosporidiosis: Secretory diarrhea and enterotoxic activity in Caco-2 cells. J Infect Dis. 1995;171:976-983.
129. Kelly P, Thillainayagam AV, Smithson J, et al. Jejunal water and electrolyte transport in human cryptosporidiosis. Dig Dis Sci. 1996;41:2095-2099.
130. McCole DF, Eckmann L, Laurent F, Kagnoff MF. Intestinal epithelial cell apoptosis following *Cryptosporidium parvum* infection. Infect Immun. 2000;68:1710-1713.
131. Chen XM, Levine SA, Splinter PL, et al. *Cryptosporidium parvum* activates nuclear factor kappaB in biliary epithelia preventing epithelial cell apoptosis. Gastroenterology. 2001;120:1774-1783.
132. Kandil HM, Berschneider HM, Argenzio RA. Tumour necrosis factor alpha changes porcine intestinal ion transport through a paracrine mechanism involving prostaglandins. Gut. 1994;35:934-940.
133. Wyatt CR, Brackett EJ, Perryman LE, et al. Activation of intestinal intraepithelial T lymphocytes in calves infected with *Cryptosporidium parvum.* Infect Immun. 1997;65:185-190.
134. Seydel KB, Zhang T, Champion GA, et al. *Cryptosporidium parvum* infection of human intestinal xenografts in SCID mice induces production of human tumor necrosis factor alpha and interleukin-8. Infect Immun. 1998;66:2379-2382.
135. Robinson P, Okhuysen PC, Chappell CL, et al. Expression of tumor necrosis factor alpha and interleukin 1 beta in jejuna of volunteers after experimental challenge with *Cryptosporidium parvum* correlates with exposure but not with symptoms. Infect Immun. 2001;69:1172-1174.
136. Lacroix S, Mancassola R, Naciri M, Laurent F. *Cryptosporidium parvum*-specific mucosal immune response in C57BL/6 neonatal and gamma interferon-deficient mice: Role of tumor necrosis factor alpha in protection. Infect Immun. 2001;69:1635-1642.
137. Kirkpatrick BD, Daniels MM, Jean SS, et al. Cryptosporidiosis stimulates an inflammatory intestinal response in malnourished Haitian children. J Infect Dis. 2002;186:94-101.
138. Alcantara CS, Yang CH, Steiner TS, et al. Interleukin-8, tumor necrosis factor-alpha, and lactoferrin in immunocompetent hosts with experimental and Brazilian children with acquired cryptosporidiosis. Am J Trop Med Hyg. 2003;68:325-328.
139. Maillot C, Gargala G, Delaunay A, et al. *Cryptosporidium parvum* infection stimulates the secretion of TGF-beta, IL-8 and RANTES by Caco-2 cell line. Parasitol Res. 2000;86:947-949.
140. Laurent F, Eckmann L, Savidge TC, et al. *Cryptosporidium parvum* infection of human intestinal epithelial cells induces the polarized secretion of C-X-C chemokines. Infect Immun. 1997;65:5067-5073.
141. Lacroix-Lamande S, Mancassola R, Naciri M, Laurent F. Role of gamma interferon in chemokine expression in the ileum of mice and in a murine intestinal epithelial cell line after *Cryptosporidium parvum* infection. Infect Immun. 2002;70:2090-2099.
142. Laurent F, Kagnoff MF, Savidge TC, et al. Human intestinal epithelial cells respond to *Cryptosporidium parvum* infection with increased prostaglandin H synthase 2 expression and prostaglandin E2 and F2alpha production. Infect Immun. 1998;66:1787-1790.
143. Robinson P, Okhuysen PC, Chappell CL, et al. Substance P expression correlates with severity of diarrhea in cryptosporidiosis. J Infect Dis. 2003;188:290-296.
144. Argenzio RA, Armstrong M, Rhoads JM. Role of the enteric nervous system in piglet cryptosporidiosis. J Pharmacol Exp Ther. 1996;279:1109-1115.
145. Cole J, Blikslager A, Hunt E, et al. Cyclooxygenase blockade and exogenous glutamine enhance sodium absorption in infected bovine ileum. Am J Physiol Gastrointest Liver Physiol. 2003;284:G516-24.
146. Snijders F, van Deventer SJ, Bartelsman JF, et al. Diarrhoea in HIV-infected patients: No evidence of cytokine-mediated inflammation in jejunal mucosa. AIDS. 1995;9:367-373.
147. Okhuysen PC, Robinson P, Nguyen MT, et al. Jejunal cytokine response in AIDS patients with chronic cryptosporidiosis and during immune reconstitution. AIDS. 2001;15:802-804.
148. Sharpstone DR, Rowbottom AW, Nelson MR, et al. Faecal tumour necrosis factor-alpha in individuals with HIV-related diarrhoea. AIDS. 1996;10:989-994.
149. Sonea IM, Palmer MV, Akili D, Harp JA. Treatment with neurokinin-1 receptor antagonist reduces severity of inflammatory bowel disease induced by *Cryptosporidium parvum.* Clin Diagn Lab Immunol. 2002;9:333-340.
150. Guarino A, Canani R, Spagnuolo MI, et al. In vivo and in vitro efficacy of octreotide for treatment of enteric cryptosporidiosis. Dig Dis Sci. 1998;43:436-441.
151. Lima AA, Silva TM, Gifoni AM, et al. Mucosal injury and disruption of intestinal barrier function in HIV-infected individuals with and without diarrhea and cryptosporidiosis in northeast Brazil. Am J Gastroenterol. 1997;92:1861-1866.
152. Sharpstone D, Neild P, Crane R, et al. Small intestinal transit, absorption, and permeability in patients with AIDS with and without diarrhoea. Gut. 1999;45:70-76.
153. Zhang Y, Lee B, Thompson M, et al. Lactulose-mannitol intestinal permeability test in children with diarrhea caused by rotavirus and cryptosporidium. Diarrhea Working Group, Peru. J Pediatr Gastroenterol Nutr. 2000;31:16-21.
154. Adams RB, Guerrant RL, Zu S, et al. *Cryptosporidium parvum* infection of intestinal epithelium: Morphologic and functional studies in an in vitro model. J Infect Dis. 1994;169:170-177.
155. Griffiths JK, Moore R, Dooley S, et al. *Cryptosporidium parvum* infection of Caco-2 cell monolayers induces an apical monolayer defect, selectively increases transmonolayer permeability, and causes epithelial cell death. Infect Immun. 1994;62:4506-4514.
156. Roche JK, Martins CA, Cosme R, et al. Transforming growth factor beta1 ameliorates intestinal epithelial barrier disruption by *Cryptosporidium parvum* in vitro in the absence of mucosal T lymphocytes. Infect Immun. 2000;68:5635-5644.
157. Argenzio R, Liacos J, Levy M, et al. Villous atrophy, crypt hyperplasia, cellular infiltration, and impaired glucose-Na absorption in enteric porcine cryptosporidiosis of pigs. Gastroenterology. 1990;98:1129-1140.
158. Kotler DP, Francisco A, Clayton F, et al. Small intestinal injury and parasitic diseases in AIDS. Ann Intern Med. 1990;113:444-449.
159. Moore R, Tzipori S, Griffiths JK, et al. Temporal changes in permeability and structure of piglet ileum after site-specific infection by *Cryptosporidium parvum.* Gastroenterology. 1995;108:1030-1039.
160. Blikslager A, Hunt E, Guerrant R, et al. Glutamine transporter in crypts compensates for loss of villus absorption in bovine cryptosporidiosis. Am J Physiol Gastrointest Liver Physiol. 2001;281:G645-G653.
161. Motta I, Gissot M, Kanellopoulos JM, Ojcius DM. Absence of weight loss during *Cryptosporidium* infection in susceptible mice deficient in Fas-mediated apoptosis. Microbes Infect. 2002;4:821-827.
162. Chen XM, Gores GJ, Paya CV, LaRusso NF. *Cryptosporidium parvum* induced apoptosis in biliary epithelia by a Fas/Fas ligand-dependent mechanism. Am J Physiol Gastrointest Liver Physiol. 1999;277:G599-G608.
163. Chen XM, Levine SA, Tietz P, et al. *Cryptosporidium parvum* is cytopathic for cultured human biliary epithelia via an apoptotic mechanism. Hepatology. 1998;28:906-913.
164. Elliot DA, Clark DP. Host cell fate on *Cryptosporidium parvum* egress from MDCK cells. Infect Immun. 2003;71:5422-5462.
165. Sciarretta G, Bonazzi L, Furno A, et al. Bile acid malabsorption in AIDS-associated chronic diarrhea: A prospective 1-year study. Am J Gastroenterol. 1994;89:379-381.

166. Ribeiro Machado F, Gonzaga Vaz Coelho L, Chausson Y, Greco DB. Fat malabsorption assessed by 14C-triolein breath test in HIV-positive patients in different stages of infection: Is it an early event. J Clin Gastroetnerol. 2000;30:403-408.

167. Sharpstone D, Phelan M, Gazzard B. Differential metabolic response in AIDS-related chronic protozoal diarrhoea. HIV Med. 2000;1:102-106.

168. Flanigan TP, Whalen C, Turner J, et al. *Cryptosporidium* infection and CD4 count. Ann Intern Med. 1992;116:840-842.

169. Blanshard C, Jackson A, Shanson D, et al. Cryptosporidiosis in HIV-seropositive patients. Q J Med. 1992;307/308:813-823.

170. Manabe YC, Clark DP, Moore RD, et al. Cryptosporidiosis in patients with AIDS: Correlates of disease and survival. Clin Infect Dis. 1998;27:536-542.

171. Ungar BLP, Kao T-C, Burris JA, Finkelman FD. *Cryptosporidium* infection in an adult mouse model. Independant roles for IFN-γ and CD4+ T lymphocytes in protective immunity. J Immunol. 1991;147:1014-1022.

172. McDonald V, Deer R, Uni S, et al. Immune responses to *Cryptosporidium muris* and *Cryptosporidium parvum* in adult immunocompetent and immunocompromised (nude and SCID) mice. Infect Immun. 1992;60:3325-3331.

173. Chen W, Harp JA, Harmsen AG. Requirement for CD4+ cells and gamma interferon in resolution of established *Cryptosporidium parvum* infection in mice. Infect Immun. 1993;61:3928-3932.

174. Aguirre SA, Mason PH, Perryman E. Susceptibility of major histocompatibility complex (MHC) class I and MHC class II-deficient mice to *Cryptosporidium parvum* infection. Infect Immun. 1994;62:697-699.

175. McDonald V, Robinson HA, Kelly JP, Bancroft GJ. *Cryptosporidium* muris in adult mice: Adoptive transfer of immunity and protective roles of CD4 versus CD8 cells. Infect Immun. 1994;62:2289-2294.

176. Perryman LA, Mason PH, Chrisp CE. Effect of spleen cell populations in resolution of *Cryptosporidium parvum* infection in SCID mice. Infect Immun. 1994;62:1474-1477.

177. Culshaw RJ, Bancroft GJ, McDonald V. Gut epithelial lymphocytes induce immunity against *Cryptosporidium* infection through a mechanism involving gamma interferon production. Infect Immun. 1997;65:3074-3079.

178. Schmidt W, Wahnschaffe U, Schafer M, et al. Rapid increase of mucosal CD4 T cells followed by clearance of intestinal cryptosporidiosis in an AIDS patient receiving highly active antiretroviral therapy. Gastroenterology. 2001;120:984-987.

179. Abrabamsen MS. Bovine Ta cell responses to *Cryptosporidium parvum* infection. Int J Parasitol. 1998;28:1083-1088.

180. Jain A, Atkinson TP, Lipsky PE, et al. Defects of T-cell effector function and post-thymic maturation in X-linked hyper-IgM syndrome. J Clin Invest. 1999;103:1151-1158.

181. Cosyns M, Tsirkin S, Jones M, et al. Requirement of CD40-CD40 ligand interaction for elimination of *Cryptosporidium parvum* from mice. Infect Immun. 1998;66:603-607.

182. Stephens J, Cosyns M, Jones M, Hayward A. Liver and bile duct pathology following *Cryptosporidium parvum* infection of immunodeficient mice. Hepatology 1999;30:27-35.

183. Lukin K, Cosyns M, Mitchell T, Saffry M, Hayward A. Eradication of *Cryptosporidium parvum* infection by mice with ovalbumin-specific T cells. Infect Immun. 2000;68:2663-2670.

184. Hayward AR, Cosyns M, Jones M, Ponnuraj EM. Marrow-derived CD40-positive cells are required for mice to clear *Cryptosporidium parvum* infection. Infect Immun. 2001;69:1630-1634.

185. Theodos CM, Sullivan KL, Griffiths JK, Tzipori S. Profiles of healing and nonhealing *Cryptosporidium parvum* infection in C57Bl/6 mice with functional B and T lymphocytes: The extent of gamma interferon modulation determines the outcome of infection. Infect Immun. 1997;65:4761-4769.

186. Mead JR, You X. Susceptibility differences to *Cryptosporidium parvum* infection in two strains of gamma interferon knockout mice. J Parasitol. 1998;84:1045-1048.

187. Tzipori S, Rand W, Theodos C. Evaluation of a two-phase scid mouse model preconditioned with anti-interferon-γ monoclonal antibody for drug testing against *Cryptosporidium parvum*. J Infect Dis. 1995;172:1160-1164.

188. Kapel N, Benhamou Y, Burand M, et al. Kinetics of mucosal gamma-Interferon response during cryptosporidiosis in immunocompetent neonatal mice. Parasitol Res. 1996;82:664-667.

189. Urban JF, Fayer R, Chen S-J, et al. Il-12 protects immunocompetent and immunodeficient mice against infection with *Cryptosporidium parvum*. J Immunol. 1996;156:263-268.

190. Fayer R, Gasbarre L, Pasquali P, et al. *Cryptosporidium parvum* infection in bovine neonates: Dynamic clinical, parasitic and immunologic patterns. Int J Parasitol. 1998;28:49-56.

191. Gomez Morales MA, La Rosa G, Ludovisi A, et al. Cytokine profile induced by *Cryptosporidium* antigen in peripheral blood mononuclear cells from immunocompetent and immunosuppressed persons with cryptosporidiosis. J Infect Dis. 1999;179:967-973.

192. White AC, Robinson P, Okhuysen PC, et al. Interferon-gamma expression in jejunal biopsies in experimental human cryptosporidiosis correlates with prior sensitization and control of oocyst excretion. J Infect Dis. 2000;181:701-709.

193. Pollok RC, Farthing MJ, Bajaj-Elliott M, et al. Interferon gamma induces enterocyte resistance against infection by the intracellular pathogen *Cryptosporidium parvum*. Gastroenterology. 2001;120:99-107.

194. Urban JF Jr, Fayer R, Sullivan C, et al. Local TH1 and TH2 responses to parasitic infection in the intestine: Regulation by IFN-gamma and IL-4. Vet Immunol Immunopathol. 1996;54:337-344.

195. Campbell LD, Stewart JN, Mead JR. Susceptibility to *Cryptosporidium parvum* infections in cytokine- and chemokine-receptor knockout mice. J Parasitol. 2002;88:1014-1016.

196. Smith LM, Bonafonte MT, Mead JR. Cytokine expression and specific lymphocyte proliferation in two strains of *Cryptosporidium parvum*-infected gamma interferon knockout mice. J Parasitol. 2000;86:300-307.

197. Smith LM, Bonafonte MT, Campbell LD, Mead JR. Exogenous interleukin-12 (IL-12) exacerbates *Cryptosporidium parvum* infection in gamma interferon knockout mice. Exp Parasitol. 2001;98:123-133.

198. Aguirre SA, Perryman LE, Davis WC, McGuire TC. IL-4 protects adult C57BL/6 mice from prolonged *Cryptosporidium parvum* infection: Analysis of CD4+alpha beta+IFN-gamma+ and CD4+alpha beta+IL-4+ lymphocytes in gut-associated lymphoid tissue during resolution of infection. J Immunol. 1998;161:1891-1900.

199. Lean IS, McDonald SA, Bajaj-Elliott M, et al. Interleukin-4 and transforming growth factor beta have opposing regulatory effects on gamma interferon-mediated inhibition of *Cryptosporidium parvum* reproduction. Infect Immun. 2003;71:4580-4585.

200. Robinson P, Okhuysen PC, Chappell CL, et al. Expression of IL-15 and IL-4 in IFN-gamma-independent control of experimental human *Cryptosporidium parvum* infection. Cytokine. 2001;15:39-46.

201. Rohlman VC, Kuhls TL, Mosier DA, et al. *Cryptosporidium parvum* infection after abrogation of natural killer cell activity in normal and severe combined immunodeficiency mice. J Parasitol. 1993;79:295-297.

202. Enriquez FJ, Sterling CR. *Cryptosporidium* infections in inbred strains of mice. J Protozool. 1991;38:100S-102S.

203. Riggs MW. Recent advances in cryptosporidiosis: The immune response. Microbes Infect. 2002;4:1067-1080.

204. Taghi-Kilani R, Sekla L, Hayglass KT. The role of humoral immunity in *Cryptosporidium* spp. infection: Studies with B cell-depleted mice. J Immunol. 1990;145:1571-1576.

205. Chen W, Harp JA, Harmsen AG. *Cryptosporidium parvum* infection in gene-targeted B cell deficient mice. J Parasitol. 2003;89:391-393.

206. Arrowood MJ, Sterling CR. Comparison of conventional staining methods and monoclonal antibody-based methods for *Cryptosporidium* oocyst detection. J Clin Microbiol. 1989;27:1490-1495.

207. Perryman LE, Kapil SJ, Jones ML, Hunt EL. Protection of calves against cryptosporidiosis with immune bovine colostrum induced by a *Cryptosporidium parvum* recombinant protein. Vaccine. 1999;17:2142-2149.

208. Sagodira S, Iochmann S, Mevelec MN, et al. Nasal immunization of mice with *Cryptosporidium parvum* DNA induces systemic and intestinal immune responses. Parasite Immunol. 1999;21:507-516.

209. Jenkins MC, O'Brien C, Trout J, et al. Hyperimmune bovine colostrum specific for recombinant *Cryptosporidium parvum* antigen confers partial protection against cryptosporidiosis in immunosuppressed adult mice. Vaccine. 1999;17:2453-2460.

210. Fries L, Hillman K, Crabb J, et al. Clinical and microbiologic effects of bovine anti-*Cryptosporidium* immunoglobulin (BACI) on cryptosporidial diarrhea in AIDS (Abstract M31). In: 34th Interscience Conference on Antimicrobial Agents and Chemotherapy. Orlando: American Society for Microbiology; 1994.

211. Cozon G, Biron F, Jeannin M, et al. Secretory IgA antibodies to *Cryptosporidium parvum* in AIDS patients with chronic cryptosporidiosis. J Infect Dis. 1994;169:696-699.

212. Benhamou Y, Kapel N, Hoang C, et al. Inefficacy of intestinal secretory immune response to *Cryptosporidium* in the acquired immunodeficiency syndrome. Gastroenterology. 1995;108:627-635.

213. Dann SM, Okhuysen PC, Salameh BM, et al. Fecal antibodies to *Cryptosporidium parvum* in healthy volunteers. Infect Immun. 2000;68:5068-5074.

214. Robinson P, Okhuysen PC, Chappell CL, et al. Transforming growth factor beta1 is expressed in the jejunum after experimental *Cryptosporidium parvum* infection in humans. Infect Immun. 2000;68:5405-5407.

215. Jokipii L, Jokikii AMM. Timing of symptoms and oocyst excretion in human cryptosporidiosis. N Engl J Med. 1986;315:1643-1647.

216. Okhuysen PC, Rich SM, Chappell CL, et al. Infectivity of a *Cryptosporidium parvum* isolate of cervine origin for healthy adults and interferon-gamma knockout mice. J Infect Dis. 2002;185:1320-1325.

217. Chappell CL, Okhuysen PC, Sterling CR, DuPont HL. *Cryptosporidium parvum:* Intensity of infection and oocyst excretion patterns in healthy volunteers. J Infect Dis. 1996;173:232-236.

218. Public Health Laboratory Service Study Group. Cryptosporidiosis in England and Wales: Prevalence and clinical and epidemiological features. Br Med J. 1990;300:774-777.

219. Egger M, Mäusezahl D, Odermatt P, et al. Symptoms and transmission of intestinal cryptosporidiosis. Arch Dis Childh. 1990;65:445-447.

220. Newman RD, Sears CL, Moore SR, et al. Longitudinal study of *Cryptosporidium* infection in children in northeastern Brazil. J Infect Dis. 1999;180:167-175.

221. Frost FJ, Fea E, Gilli G, et al. Serological evidence of *Cryptosporidium* infections in southern Europe. Eur J Epidemiol. 2000;16:385-390.

222. McDonald AC, Mac Kenzie WR, Addiss DG, et al. *Cryptosporidium parvum*-specific antibody responses among children residing in Milwaukee during the 1993 waterborne outbreak. J Infect Dis. 2001;183:1373-1379.

223. Robin G, Fraser D, Orr N, et al. *Cryptosporidium* infection in Bedouin infants assessed by prospective evaluation of anticryptosporidial antibodies and stool examination. Am J Epidemiol. 2001;153:194-201.

224. Cicirello HG, Kehl KS, Addiss DG, et al. Cryptosporidiosis in children during a massive waterborne outbreak in Milwaukee, Wisconsin: Clinical, laboratory and epidemiologic findings. Epidemiol Infect. 1997;119:53-60.

225. Janoff EN, Mead PS, Mead JR, et al. Endemic *Cryptosporidium* and *Giardia lamblia* infections in a Thai orphanage. Am J Trop Med Hyg. 1990;43:248-256.

226. Agnew DG, Lima AA, Newman RD, et al. Cryptosporidiosis in northeastern Brazilian children: Association with increased diarrhea morbidity. J Infect Dis. 1998;177:754-760.

227. Molbak K, Wested N, Hojlyng N, et al. The etiology of early childhood diarrhea: A community study from Guinea-Bissau. J Infect Dis. 1994;169:581-587.

228. Sallon S, el Showwa R, el Masri M, et al. Cryptosporidiosis in children in Gaza. Ann Trop Paediatr. 1991;11:277-281.

229. Sodemann M, Jakobsen MS, Molbak K, et al. Episode-specific risk factors for progression of acute diarrhoea to persistent diarrhoea in west African children. Trans R Soc Trop Med Hyg. 1999;93:65-68.

230. Molbak K, Hojlyng N, Gottschau A, et al. Cryptosporidiosis in infancy and childhood mortality in Guinea Bissau, west Africa. Br Med J. 1993;307:417-420.

231. Lima AA, Moore SR, Barboza MS Jr, et al. Persistent diarrhea signals a critical period of increased diarrhea burdens and nutritional shortfalls: A prospective cohort study among children in northeastern Brazil. J Infect Dis. 2000;181:1643-1651.

232. Amadi B, Kelly P, Mwiya M, et al. Intestinal and systemic infection, HIV, and mortality in Zambian children with persistent diarrhea and malnutrition. J Pediatr Gastroenterol Nutr. 2001;32:550-554.

233. Guerrant DI, Moore SR, Lima AA, et al. Association of early childhood diarrhea and cryptosporidiosis with impaired physical fitness and cognitive function four-seven years later in a poor urban community in northeast Brazil. Am J Trop Med Hyg. 1999;61:707-713.

234. Berkman DS, Lescano AG, Gilman RH, et al. Effects of stunting, diarrhoeal disease, and parasitic infection during infancy on cognition in late childhood: A follow-up study. Lancet. 2002;359:564-571.

235. Macfarlane DE, Horner-Bryce J. Cryptosporidiosis in well-nourished and malnourished children. Acta Paediatr Scand. 1987;76:474-477.

236. Sallon S, Deckelbaum RJ, Schmid II, et al. Cryptosporidium, malnutrition, and chronic diarrhea. Am J Dis Child. 1988;142:312-315.

237. Javier Enriquez F, Avila CR, Ignacio Santos J, et al. Cryptosporidium infections in Mexican children: Clinical, nutritional, enteropathogenic, and diagnostic evaluations. Am J Trop Med Hyg. 1997;56:254-257.

238. Molbak K, Andersen M, Aaby P, et al. Cryptosporidium infection in infancy as a cause of malnutrition: A community study from Guinea-Bissau, west Africa. Am J Clin Nutr. 1997;65:149-152.

239. Checkley W, Epstein LD, Gilman RH, et al. Effects of Cryptosporidium parvum infection in Peruvian children: Growth faltering and subsequent catch-up growth. Am J Epidemiol. 1998;148:497-506.

240. Checkley W, Gilman RH, Epstein LD, et al. Asymptomatic and symptomatic cryptosporidiosis: Their acute effect on weight gain in Peruvian children. Am J Epidemiol. 1997;145:156-163.

241. Kim LS, Hadley WK, Stansell J, et al. Declining prevalence of cryptosporidiosis in San Francisco. Clin Infect Dis. 1998;27:655-656.

242. Le Moing V, Bissuel F, Costagliola D, et al. Decreased prevalence of intestinal cryptosporidiosis in HIV-infected patients concomitant to the widespread use of protease inhibitors (Letter). AIDS. 1998;12:1395-1397.

243. Miller JR. Decreasing cryptosporidiosis among HIV-infected persons in New York City, 1995-1997. J Urb Hlth. 1998;75:601-602.

244. Lopez-Velez R, Tarazona R, Garcia Camacho A, et al. Intestinal and extraintestinal cryptosporidiosis in AIDS patients. Eur J Clin Microbiol Infect Dis. 1995;14:677-681.

245. Meynard JL, Meyohas MC, Binet D, et al. Pulmonary cryptosporidiosis in the acquired immunodeficiency syndrome. Infection. 1996;24:328-331.

246. Clavel A, Arnal AC, Sanchez EC, et al. Respiratory cryptosporidiosis: Case series and review of the literature. Infection. 1996;24:341-346.

247. Vakil NB, Schwartz SM, Buggy BP, et al. Biliary cryptosporidiosis in HIV-infected people after the waterborne outbreak of cryptosporidiosis in Milwaukee. N Engl J Med. 1996;334:19-23.

248. Teare JP, Daly CA, Rodgers C, et al. Pancreatic abnormalities and AIDS related sclerosing cholangitis. Genitourin Med. 1997;73:271-273.

249. Cryptosporidiosis. *www.dpd.cdc.gov/dpdx/HTML/Cryptosporidiosis/htm.* Accessed October 30, 2003.

250. Arrowood MJ. Diagnosis. In: Fayer R, ed. *Cryptosporidium* and Cryptosporidiosis. Boca Raton, FL: CRC Press, 1997:43-64.

251. Clavel A, Arnal A, Sanchez E, et al. Comparison of 2 centrifugation procedures in the formalin-ethyl acetate stool concentration technique for the detection of *Cryptosporidium* oocysts. Int J Parasitol. 1996;26:671-672.

252. Webster KA, Smith HV, Giles M, et al. Detection of *Cryptosporidium parvum* oocysts in faeces: Comparison of conventional coproscopical methods and the polymerase chain reaction. Vet Parasitol. 1996;61:5-13.

253. Pereira MD, Atwill ER, Barbosa AP, et al. Intra-familial and extra-familial risk factors associated with *Cryptosporidium parvum* infection among children hospitalized for diarrhea in Goiania, Goias, Brazil. Am J Trop Med Hyg. 2002;66:787-793.

254. Jones JL, Lopez A, Wahlquist SP, et al. Survey of clinical laboratory practices for parasitic diseases. Clin Infect Dis. 2004;38:S198-202.

255. Weber R, Bryan R, Bishop H, et al. Threshold for detection of *Cryptosporidium* oocysts in human stool specimens: Evidence for low sensitivity of current diagnostic methods. J Clin Microbiol. 1991;29:963-965.

256. Alles AJ, Waldron MA, Sierra LS, Mattia AR. Prospective comparison of direct immunofluorescence and conventional staining methods for detection of Giardia and Cryptosporidiums pp. in human fecal specimens. J Clin Microbiol. 1995;33:1632-1634.

257. Johnston SP, Ballard MM, Beach MJ, et al. Evaluation of three commercial assays for detection of *Giardia* and *Cryptosporidium* organisms in fecal specimens. J Clin Microbiol. 2003;41:623-626.

258. Tortora GT, Malowitz R, Mendelsohn B, Spitzer ED. Rhodamine-auramine O versus Kinyoun-carbolfuchsin acid-fast stains for detection of *Cryptosporidium* oocysts. Clin Lab Sci. 1992;5:568-569.

259. Dagan R, Fraser D, El-On J, et al. Evaluation of an enzyme immunoassay for the detection of *Cryptosporidium* spp. in stool specimens from infants and young children in field studies. Am J Trop Med Hyg. 1995;52:134-138.

260. Ignatius R, Lehmann M, Miksits K, et al. A new acid-fast trichrome stain for simultaneous detection of *Cryptosporidium parvum* and microsporidial species in stool specimens. J Clin Microbiol. 1997;35:446-449.

261. Garcia LS, Shimizu RY. Evaluation of nine immunoassay kits (enzyme immunoassay and direct fluorescence) for detection of *Giardia lamblia* and *Cryptosporidium parvum* in human fecal specimens. J Clin Microbiol. 1997;35:1526-1529.

262. Balatbat AB, Jordan GW, Tang YJ, Silva J Jr. Detection of *Cryptosporidium parvum* DNA in human feces by nested PCR. J Clin Microbiol. 1996;34:1769-1772.

263. Kehl KS, Cicirello H, Havens PL. Comparison of four different methods for detection of *Cryptosporidium* species. J Clin Microbiol. 1995;33:416-418.

264. Garcia LS, Shimizu RY, Bernard CN. Detection of *Giardia lamblia, Entamoeba histolytica/Entamoeba* dispar, and *Cryptosporidium parvum* antigens in human fecal specimens using the triage parasite panel enzyme immunoassay. J Clin Microbiol. 2000;38:3337-3340.

265. Garcia LS, Shimizu RY, Novak S, et al. Commercial assay for detection of *Giardia lamblia* and *Cryptosporidium parvum* antigens in human fecal specimens by rapid solid-phase qualitative immunochromatography. J Clin Microbiol. 2003;41:209-212.

266. Newman RD, Jaeger KL, Wuhib T, et al. Evaluation of an antigen capture enzyme-linked immunosorbent assay for detection of *Cryptosporidium* oocysts. J Clin Microbiol. 1993;31:2080-2084.

267. Ignatius R, Eisenblatter M, Regnath T, et al. Efficacy of different methods for detection of low *Cryptosporidium parvum* oocyst numbers or antigen concentrations in stool specimens. Eur J Clin Microbiol Infect Dis. 1997;16:732-736.

268. Manufacturer's recall of rapid assay kits based on false positive *Cryptosporidium* antigen tests—Wisconsin, 2001-2002. MMWR Morb Mortal Wkly Rep. 2002;51:189.

269. Doing KM, Hamm JL, Jellison JA, et al. False-positive results obtained with the Alexon ProSpecT *Cryptosporidium* enzyme immunoassay. J Clin Microbiol. 1999;37:1582-1583.

270. Valdez LM, Dang H, Okhuysen PC, Chappell CL. Flow cytometric detection of *Cryptosporidium* oocysts in human stool samples. J Clin Microbiol. 1997;35:2013-2017.

271. Carneiro-Filho BA, Bushen OY, Brito GA, et al. Glutamine analogues as adjunctive therapy for infectious diarrhea. Curr Infect Dis Rep. 2003;5:114-119.

272. Kotler DP, Fogleman L, Tierney AR. Comparison of total parenteral nutrition and an oral, semielemental diet on body composition, physical function, and nutrition-related costs in patients with malabsorption due to acquired immunodeficiency syndrome. J Parenter Enteral Nutr. 1998;22:120-126.

273. Brantley RK, Williams KR, Silva TM, et al. AIDS-associated diarrhea and wasting in Northeast Brazil is associated with subtherapeutic plasma levels of antiretroviral medications and with both bovine and human subtypes of *Cryptosporidium parvum*. Braz J Infect Dis. 2003;7:16-22.

274. Garcia Compean D, Ramos Jimenez J, Guzman de la Garza F, et al. Octreotide therapy of large-volume refractory AIDS-associated diarrhea: A randomized controlled trial. AIDS. 1994;8:1563-1567.

275. Simon DM, Cello JP, Valenzuela J, et al. Multicenter trial of octreotide in patients with refractory acquired immunodeficiency syndrome-associated diarrhea. Gastroenterology. 1995;108:1753-1760.

276. Beaugerie L, Baumer P, Chaussade S, et al. Treatment of refractory diarrhoea in AIDS with acetorphan and octreotide: A randomized crossover study. Eur J Gastroenterol Hepatol. 1996;8:485-489.

277. Carr A, Marriott D, Field A, et al. Treatment of HIV-1-associated microsporidiosis and cryptosporidiosis with combination antiretroviral therapy. Lancet. 1998;351:256-261.

278. Foudraine NA, Weverling GJ, van Gool T, et al. Improvement of chronic diarrhoea in patients with advanced HIV-1 infection during potent antiretroviral therapy. AIDS. 1998;12:35-41.

279. Grube H, Ramratnam B, Ley C, Flanigan TP. Resolution of AIDS associated cryptosporidiosis after treatment with indinavir. Am J Gastroenterol. 1997;92:726.

280. Maggi P, Larocca AM, Quarto M, et al. Effect of antiretroviral therapy on cryptosporidiosis and microsporidiosis in patients infected with human immunodeficiency virus type 1. Eur J Clin Microbiol Infect Dis. 2000;19:213-217.

281. Miao YM, Awad-El-Kariem FM, Franzen C, et al. Eradication of cryptosporidia and microsporidia following successful antiretroviral therapy. J Acquir Immune Defic Syndr. 2000;25:124-129.

282. Hommer V, Eichholz J, Petry F. Effect of antiretroviral protease inhibitors alone, and in combination with paromomycin, on the excystation, invasion and in vitro development of *Cryptosporidium parvum*. J Antimicrob Chemother. 2003;52:359-364.

283. Mele R, Gomez Morales MA, Tosini F, Pozio E. Indinavir reduces *Cryptosporidium parvum* infection in both in vitro and in vivo models. Int J Parasitol. 2003;33:757-764.

284. Maggi P, Larocca AM, Ladisa N, et al. Opportunistic parasitic infections of the intestinal tract in the era of highly active antiretroviral therapy: Is the CD4(+) count so important? Clin Infect Dis. 2001;33:1609-1611.

285. French AL, Beaudet LM, Benator DA, et al. Cholecystectomy in patients with AIDS: Clinicopathologic correlations in 107 cases. Clin Infect Dis. 1995;21:852-858.

286. Bouche H, Housset C, Dumont JL, et al. AIDS-related cholangitis: Diagnostic features and course in 15 patients. J Hepatol. 1993;17:34-39.

287. Cordero E, Lopez-Cortes LF, Belda O, et al. Acquired immunodeficiency syndrome-related cryptosporidial cholangitis: Resolution with endobiliary prosthesis insertion. Gastrointest Endosc. 2001;53:534-535.

288. Blagburn BL, Soave R. Prophylaxis and chemotherapy: Human and animal. In: Fayer R, ed. *Cryptosporidium* and cryptosporidiosis. Boca Raton, Fl: CRC Press, 1997: 111-128.

289. Vasquez JR, Gooze L, Kim K, et al. Potential antifolate resistance determinants and genotypic variation in the bifunctional dihydrofolate reductase-thymidylate synthase gene from human and bovine isolates of *Cryptosporidium parvum*. Mol Biochem Parasitol. 1996;79:153-165.

290. White AC Jr, Chappell CL, Hayat CS, et al. Paromomycin for cryptosporidiosis in AIDS: A prospective, double-blind trial. J Infect Dis. 1994;170:419-424.

291. Smith NH, Cron S, Valdez LM, et al. Combination drug therapy for cryptosporidiosis in AIDS. J Infect Dis. 1998;178:900-903.

292. White AC Jr, Cron SG, Chappell CL. Paromomycin in cryptosporidiosis. Clin Infect Dis. 2001;32:1516-1517.

293. White AC Jr. Nitazoxanide: An important advance in anti-parasitic therapy. Am J Trop Med Hyg. 2003;68:382-383.

294. Rossignol JF, Maisonneuve H. Nitazoxanide in the treatment of *Taenia saginata* and *Hymenolepis nana* infections. Am J Trop Med Hyg. 1984;33:511-512.

295. Gilles HM, Hoffman PS. Treatment of intestinal parasitic infections: A review of nitazoxanide. Trends Parasitol. 2002;18:95-97.

296. Theodos CM, Griffiths JK, D'Onfro J, et al. Efficacy of nitazoxanide against *Cryptosporidium parvum* in cell culture and in animal models. Antimicrob Agents Chemother. 1998;42:1959-1965.

297. Gargala G, Delaunay A, Li X, et al. Efficacy of nitazoxanide, tizoxanide and tizoxanide glucuronide against *Cryptosporidium parvum* development in sporozoite-infected HCT-8 enterocytic cells. J Antimicrob Chemother. 2000;46:57-60.

298. Blagburn BL, Drain KL, Land TM, et al. Comparative efficacy evaluation of dicationic carbazole compounds, nitazoxanide, and paromomycin against *Cryptosporidium parvum* infections in a neonatal mouse model. Antimicrob Agents Chemother. 1998;42:2877-2882.

299. Li X, Brasseur P, Agnamey P, et al. Long-lasting anticryptosporidial activity of nitazoxanide in an immunosuppressed rat model. Folia Parasitol (Praha). 2003;50:19-22.

300. Doumbo O, Rossignol JF, Pichard E, et al. Nitazoxanide in the treatment of cryptosporidial diarrhea and other intestinal parasitic infections associated with acquired immunodeficiency syndrome in tropical Africa. Am J Trop Med Hyg. 1997;56: 637-639.

301. Rossignol JF, Hidalgo H, Feregrino M, et al. A double-'blind' placebo-controlled study of nitazoxanide in the treatment of cryptosporidial diarrhoea in AIDS patients in Mexico. Trans R Soc Trop Med Hyg. 1998;92:663-666.

302. Rossignol JF, Ayoub A, Ayers MS. Treatment of diarrhea caused by *Cryptosporidium parvum:* a prospective randomized, double-blind, placebo-controlled study of Nitazoxanide. J Infect Dis. 2001;184:103-106.

303. Amadi B, Mwiya M, Musuku J, et al. Effect of nitazoxanide on morbidity and mortality in Zambian children with cryptosporidiosis: A randomised controlled trial. Lancet. 2002;360:1375-1380.

304. Gathe J, Piot D, Hawkins K, et al. Treatment of gastrointestinal cryptosporidiosis with paromomycin. In: VIth Annual Conference on AIDS. San Fransisco: London: Welcome Foundation, 1990.

305. White AC Jr, Goodgame RW, Chappell CL. Paromomycin for cryptosporidiosis in AIDS–reply letter]. J Infect Dis. 1995;171:1071.

306. Blanshard C, Shanson DC, Gazzard BG. Pilot studies of azithromycin, letrazuril, and paromomycin in the treatment of cryptosporidiosis. Int J STD AIDS. 1997;8:124-129.

307. Kanyok TP, Novak RM, Danziger LH. Preliminary results of a randomized, blinded, control study of paromomycin vs placebo for treatment of *Cryptosporidium* diarrhea in AIDS patients. In: IX International Conference on AIDS. Berlin: London: Wellcome Foundation, 1993.

308. Hewitt RG, Yiannoutsos CT, Higgs ES, et al. Paromomycin: no more effective than placebo for treatment of cryptosporidiosis in patients with advanced human immunodeficiency virus infection. Clin Infect Dis. 2000;31:1084-1092.

309. Sáez-Llorens X, Odio CM, Umaña MA, Morales MV. Spiramycin vs. placebo for treatment of acute diarrhea caused by *Cryptosporidium*. Pediatr Infect Dis J. 1989;8:136-140.

310. Wittenberg DF, Miller NM, van den Ende J. Spiramycin is not effective in treating *Cryptosporidium* diarrhea in infants: Results of a double-blind randomized trial. J Infect Dis. 1989;159:131-132.

311. Weikel C, Lazenby A, Belitsos P, et al. Intestinal injury associated with spiramycin therapy of *Cryptosporidium* infection in AIDS. J Protozool. 1991;38:147S.

312. Dionisio D, Orsi A, Sterrantino G, et al. Chronic cryptosporidiosis in patients with AIDS: Stable remission and possible eradication after long-term, low dose azithromycin. J Clin Pathol. 1998;51:138-142.

313. Hicks P, Zwiener RJ, Squires J, Savell V. Azithromycin therapy for *Cryptosporidium parvum* infection in four children infected with human immunodeficiency virus. J Pediatr. 1996;129:297-300.

314. Nachbaur D, Kropshofer G, Feichtinger H, et al. Cryptosporidiosis after CD34-selected autologous peripheral blood stem cell transplantation (PBSCT). Treatment with paromomycin, azithromycin and recombinant human interleukin-2. Bone Marrow Transplant. 1997;19:1261-1263.

315. Kadappu KK, Nagaraja MV, Rao PV, Shastry BA. Azithromycin as treatment for cryptosporidiosis in human immunodeficiency virus disease. J Postgrad Med. 2002;48:179-181.

316. Allam AF, Shehab AY. Efficacy of azithromycin, praziquantel and mirazid in treatment of cryptosporidiosis in school children. J Egypt Soc Parasitol. 2002;32:969-978.

317. Sprinz E, Mallman R, Barcellos S, et al. AIDS-related cryptosporidial diarrhoea: an open study with roxithromycin. J Antimicrob Chemother. 1998;419(Suppl B):85-91.

318. Uip DE, Lima AL, Amato VS, et al. Roxithromycin treatment for diarrhoea caused by *Cryptosporidium* spp. in patients with AIDS. J Antimicrob Chemother. 1998;41(Suppl) B:93-97.

319. Amenta M, Dalle Nogare ER, Colomba C, et al. Intestinal protozoa in HIV-infected patients: Effect of rifaximin in *Cryptosporidium parvum* and *Blastocystis hominis* infections. J Chemother. 1999;11:391-395.

320. Greenberg PD, Cello JP. Treatment of severe diarrhea caused by *Cryptosporidium parvum* with oral bovine immunoglobulin concentrate in patients with AIDS. J Acquir Immune Defic Syndr Hum Retrovirol. 1996;13:348-354.

321. Okhuysen PC, Chappell CL, Crabb J, et al. Prophylactic effect of bovine anti-*Cryptosporidium* hyperimmune colostrum immunoglobulin in healthy volunteers challenged with *Cryptosporidium* parvum. Clin Infect Dis. 1998;26:1324-1329.

322. Masur H, Kaplan JE, Holmes KK. Guidelines for preventing opportunistic infections among HIV-infected persons—2002. Recommendations of the U.S. Public Health Service and the Infectious Diseases Society of America. Ann Intern Med. 2002;137:435-478.

323. Addiss DG, Pond RS, Remshak M, et al. Reduction of risk of watery diarrhea with point-of-use water filters during a massive outbreak of waterborne *Cryptosporidium* infection in Milwaukee, Wisconsin, 1993. Am J Trop Med Hyg. 1996;54:549-553.

324. Holmberg SD, Moorman AC, Von Bargen JC, et al. Possible effectiveness of clarithromycin and rifabutin for cryptosporidiosis chemoprophylaxis in HIV disease. HIV Outpatient Study (HOPS) Investigators. JAMA. 1998;279:384-386.

325. Fichtenbaum CJ, Zackin R, Feinberg J, et al. Rifabutin but not clarithromycin prevents cryptosporidiosis in persons with advanced HIV infection. AIDS. 2000;14:2889-2893.

326. Sagodira S, Buzoni-Gatel D, Iochmann S, et al. Protection of kids against *Cryptosporidium parvum* infection after immunization of dams with CP15-DNA . Vaccine. 1999;17:2346-2355.

327. Wheeler C, Berkley S. Initial lessons from public-private partnerships in drug and vaccine development. Bull WHO. 2001;79:728-734.

328. Sagodira S, Buzoni-Gatel D, Iochmann S, et al. Protection of kids against *Cryptosporidium parvum* infection after immunization of dams with CP15-DNA. Vaccine. 1999;17:2346-2355.

CHAPTER **281**

Cyclospora cayetanensis, Isospora belli, Sarcocystis Species, *Balantidium coli,* and *Blastocystis hominis*

TAMARA L. FISK

JAY S. KEYSTONE

PHYLLIS KOZARSKY

Intestinal protozoa have gained increased recognition in the United States in the past decade because of association with foodborne outbreaks and with diarrheal disease, particularly in immunocompromised patients. Veterinary studies of related animal pathogens have provided preliminary information on life cycles and pathology, and molecular studies have been used to clarify relatedness among the coccidian protozoa (*Cyclospora, Isospora,* and *Sarcocystis*) and to classify *Blastocystis*.

CYCLOSPORA

Cyclosporiasis is an emerging infectious disease that was first described in humans in Papua New Guinea in 1977.[1] During the subsequent 15 years, additional cases of diarrheal illness caused by the same organism were reported. It eluded taxonomic classification, however, and was labeled fungal spores, cyanobacterium-like bodies,[2,3] blue-green algae,[4,5] and large cryptosporidia,[6] until 1993, when Ortega and colleagues succeeded in inducing sporulation and thus confirmed its genus, *Cyclospora*.[7,8] It was then named *Cyclospora cayetanensis* after the Universidad Peruana Cayetano Heredia in Lima, Peru, a major site of research on the infection. Phylogenetic analysis confirmed that *Cyclospora* and *Eimeria* belong to the same family and are more distantly related to *Isospora, Sarcocystis,* and *Toxoplasma*.[9]

Cyclospora oocysts are spherical, measure 8 to 10 μm in diameter, and contain two sporocysts that each hold two sporozoites. Ultrastructural studies of the unsporulated oocyst reveal an outer fibrillar coat, cell wall, and membrane. Inside the sporulated oocyst, sporozoites within sporocysts contain a membrane-bound nucleus and micronemes. Sporulation, necessary for infectivity, occurs outside the host[10] and at 27° to 32° C takes from 8 to 11 days.[7] Oocysts in the environment are quite resistant, surviving freezing, 2% formalin, 2% potassium dichromate, and even chlorination.[11-14]

Epidemiology

Cyclospora infections occur worldwide[10,15-18] in clusters and sporadically, with a major increase in reported cases since 1996.[19] Although it is not yet a major cause of diarrhea in travelers,[20] it has been described even in those on usual tourist routes who stay in deluxe facilities.[21] Cyclospora is identified less frequently in residents of and travelers to Africa than in other regions.[18,22-24] This organism has also been identified as an opportunistic infection in those with human immunodeficiency virus infection and other immunosuppressive conditions.[12,13,16,25-27]

Most of the earlier cases were described in Nepal, Peru, and Haiti,[25,26,28,29] but additional study of the organism was prompted by the increase in cases in North America, including the first documented outbreak implicating a contaminated water storage tank in Chicago[5,13] and a large increase in sporadic and clustered cases in 1996-1997 linked to imported raspberries.[30-32] The organism was first identified by microscopy on a suspected food item, basil, in 1998,[33] and identified by polymerase chain reaction (PCR) in raspberry filling in 1999.[34] Later American and European outbreaks were associated with contaminated mixed salad greens.[19] Produce items are presumably contaminated by washing or spraying with contaminated surface water.[19,35] Surveys of stool samples and screening studies from cities in developed countries reveal *Cyclospora* in 0.1% to 0.5% of samples.[6,10,12,29,36,37] In developing countries such as Nepal, the highest risk of diarrhea is in children between the ages of 18 months and 5 years[28]; in Peru, the prevalence decreases with age as well.[38] Infants may be protected by breast-feeding.

In general, infection occurs seasonally, with highest incidence in spring and summer (May through July) in the United States, in the warm season (April through June) in Peru, and before and during the monsoon (May through October) in Nepal.[19,39] Factors that determine seasonality and possible reservoirs during the "off-season" have not yet been defined.

C. cayetensis-like oocysts have been recovered from mice, rats, dogs, and chickens in Nepal,[35] and chickens and ducks in Latin America,[40,41] although not from livestock, poultry, dogs, cats, and guinea pigs in Haiti[42] or dogs in Brazil.[43] Attempts to infect mammals and birds in the laboratory setting have been successful only in albino mice.[44,45] It is unclear whether animals are a source of human infection or if the oocysts recovered from animal feces represent coprophagy or zoonotic organisms that resemble *Cyclospora*.[43,45,46] Oocysts have also been identified in sewage and vegetable washings.[35,47]

Clinical Manifestations

The clinical presentation of *Cyclospora* infection in residents of endemic areas differs from those in travelers to these regions and in exposed persons in nonendemic areas.[8,48] Asymptomatic infections are more common in the indigenous population of endemic areas, particularly in adults from these areas,[8,38,49] although they may occur rarely in others, even in those who are infected with human immunodeficiency virus.[50]

For symptomatic infections, the incubation period is between 1 and 11 days, averaging approximately 1 week.[19] The onset of illness is often abrupt but may be preceded by a flulike illness.[35,36] Watery diarrhea is invariably present with a median of six stools per day. In some patients upper gastrointestinal symptoms predominate.[21,36,48] Fatigue, anorexia, myalgia, abdominal cramps, flatus, and nausea occur frequently.[48] Fever occurs in about 25% of cases.[19] Illness lasts from 2 to 7 weeks or longer,[10] may be cyclic or relapsing, and may result in dehydration and significant weight loss.[6,16-17,52] Clinical signs and symptoms do not distinguish cyclosporiasis from illness caused by cryptosporidia, microsporidia, or *Isospora*. Cases of Reiter's syndrome[53] and Guillian-Barré syndrome[54] following infection with *Cyclospora* have been reported. In patients with AIDS, illness tends to be more severe and prolonged.[26] In these patients, biliary tract disease has been described, as with *Cryptosporidium* infection.[51,55] It is unclear whether antibodies play a role in immunity,[15,56] and whether reinfection occurs.[37] The infectious dose is not known.[31]

In those infected, upper endoscopy appears normal, yet the histologic architecture of the small bowel is altered. Villous atrophy, acute and chronic inflammation in the lamina propria, and vascular dilatation may be seen microscopically.[52,57] It is unknown whether the pathogenesis of infection is caused by enterocyte dysfunction or whether toxins are secreted.

Diagnosis

The diagnosis of cyclosporiasis requires microscopic identification of the oocysts in stool samples (Fig. 281-1). These oocysts are roughly twice the size of cryptosporidia oocysts. Shedding of oocysts in stool can precede the onset of clinical illness, but the disappearance of symptoms and oocysts usually occurs simultaneously.[15,58] With severe diarrhea, xylose absorption may be decreased.[58,59] Although the organism is variably acid-fast on modified Ziehl-Neelsen or Kinyoun stains (Fig. 281-1A), these techniques are superior to the examination of routine wet mounts, which require a trained eye for identification of the organism.[60] If available, the demonstration of blue autofluorescence of the oocysts under ultraviolet epifluorescence microscopy is both rapid and sensitive, although not specific.[61] Safranin stains the oocysts uniformly (Fig. 281-1B)[62] and lacto-phenol cotton blue can also be used.[63] Molecular diagnostic techniques have been developed and are undergoing further evaluation and refinement, as cross-amplification with other coccidian parasites may occur.[9,64] Antibodies to *Cyclospora* can be detected. Cases of cyclosporiasis should be reported to the Centers for Disease Control and Prevention, Division of Parasitic Diseases (Telephone 770-488-7760).[31]

Cyclospora may also be detected in jejunal aspirates or in biopsy specimens, although it is controversial whether routine hematoxylin and eosin staining of the biopsy material permits adequate visualization of the organisms.[3,65] Tissue sections reveal *Cyclospora* in a supranuclear location of the cytoplasm that distinguishes them from *Cryptosporidium,* which are on the surface of the enterocytes.[66] Electron microscopy identifies the organism and its various stages in the cytoplasm of the jejunal epithelial cells.[3,66]

Treatment

The most commonly used treatment is trimethoprim-sulfamethoxazole twice daily for 7 days (160 mg trimethoprim and 800 mg of sulfamethoxazole in adults, 5 mg/kg of trimethoprim, and 25 mg/kg of sulfamethoxazole in children).[38,67] For patients with human immunodeficiency virus infection, because relapse is common, the recommendation is four times daily dosing for 10 days followed by chronic suppression three times per week.[24,68] As an alternative, particularly for patients with sulfa allergy or intolerance, ciprofloxacin is similarly efficacious for both treatment and suppression.[69]

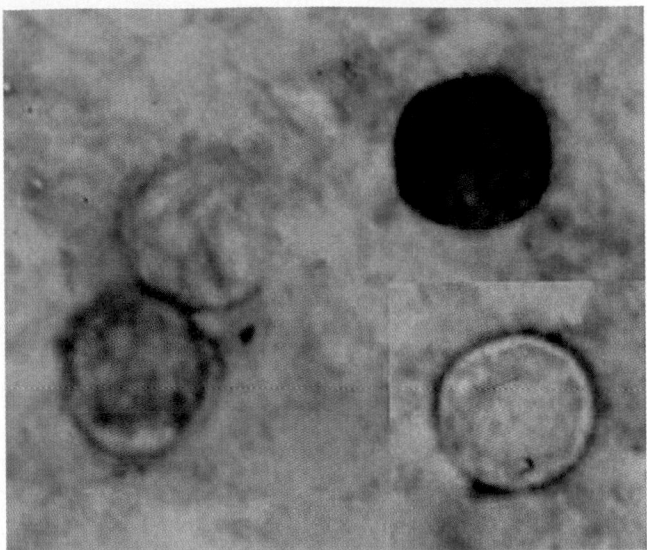

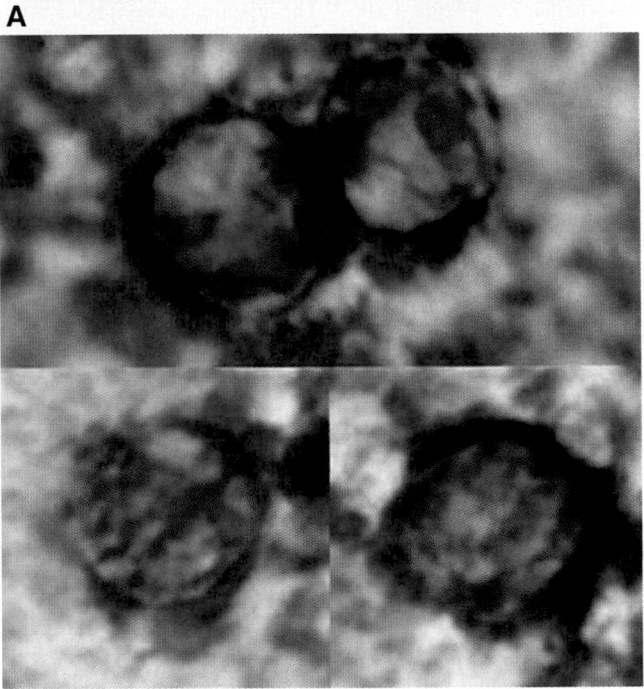

FIGURE 281-1. *Cyclospora* oocysts (from fresh stool fixed in 10% formalin). **A,** Variable staining with modified acid-fast stain. **B,** Uniform staining with modified safranin stain. (Modification consists in heating in a microwave during staining.) *(From DPDx Image Library, Centers for Disease Control and Prevention, Atlanta, GA.)*

ISOSPORA BELLI

Isospora belli, first described in 1915,[70,71] is a coccidian protozoa taxonomically related to *Cyclospora, Toxoplasma, Neospora,* and *Sarcocystis.*[9] Humans are the only recognized host of this species, and no other species that infects humans has been confirmed.[72] Ingestion of infectious sporulated oocysts results in the release of sporozoites that penetrate mucosal epithelial cells of the proximal small intestine where they develop into trophozoites.[73,74] Asexual

multiplication is followed by a sexual cycle in which immature, unsporulated oocysts are passed in the feces (Fig. 281-2A). Within 2 to 3 days, sporulation occurs, resulting in a mature infective elliptical oocyst (22 to 33 × 12 to 15 μm) that contains two sporocysts, each with four sporozoites (Fig. 281-1B). Oocysts can remain viable in the environment for months. The pathogenesis of isosporiasis has not been determined but may be the result of cell damage from direct consequences of parasite invasion, cell-mediated inflammation, or proteins and oxidants released from mast cells.[7]

Epidemiology

Isospora is found predominantly in tropical and subtropical climates, especially in South America, Africa, and Southeast Asia.[76-78] In the United States, isosporiasis has been associated with human immunodeficiency virus infection and other immunosuppressive conditions, immigration from Latin America, daycare centers, and psychiatric institutions.[76,78,79] In patients with acquired immunodeficiency syndrome in the United States, *I. belli* infection accounted for approximately 2% to 3% of AIDS-defining illness in the 1980s but this decreased to less than 0.1% in the late 1990s,[80,81] likely because of the widespread use of trimethoprim-sulfamethoxazole used to prevent *Pneumocystis jirovecii* pneumonia.[79] In contrast, in developing countries, *I. belli* infections are frequently associated with chronic diarrhea in AIDS patients, occurring in 17% to 19% of these patients in Haiti,[82,83] 19% in Democratic Republic of Congo,[84,85] 14% to 16% in Zambia,[86,87] and 10% in Brazil.[88]

Clinical Manifestations

In immunocompetent hosts, *Isospora* infection is indistinguishable from other noninflammatory intestinal infections such as giardiasis, cryptosporidiosis, cyclosporiasis, and enterotoxigenic *Escherichia coli* infection. After an incubation period of approximately 1 week, patients usually develop a self-limited diarrheal illness lasting 2 to 3 weeks characterized by malaise, anorexia, weight loss, abdominal cramps, and profuse watery diarrhea without blood.[89,90] Fever is uncommon and is usually low grade. Oocyst shedding may persist for several weeks after recovery.[91,92] Rarely, in the immunocompetent patient, chronic persistent or intermittent symptoms may continue for many years.[73,93] In contrast, in immunocompromised hosts, including patients with AIDS,[94,95] those with malignancy,[96,97] and those on cytotoxic therapy,[98] infection may result in protracted, severe diarrheal illness, including hemorrhagic colitis,[99] with consequent dehydration and malabsorption that may be life-threatening.[89,99] Disseminated extraintestinal disease has been reported in three patients.[100-102] Other rare, atypical presentations include acalculous cholecystitis[103] and reactive arthritis.[104] Histologic examination of the small bowel of infected patients is relatively nonspecific and reveals villous atrophy, crypt hyperplasia, and lamina propria infiltration with inflammatory cells, particularly eosinophils.[72,73] Asexual and sexual stages of the parasite are identified within parasitophorous vacuoles of enterocytes. Damage to villous absorptive cells has been associated with reports of malabsorption.[73,94,106] In extraintestinal disease, intracellular cysts containing one to three zoites were identified in lymph nodes, liver, and spleen.[100-102] Tissue cysts are proposed as the source of recurrent infections in immunocompromised patients.[110]

Diagnosis

Typically, *I. belli* infection is diagnosed by identification of oocysts in stool in wet mounts[77,93] or acid-fast stained fecal smears[106] (Fig. 281-2C) made from stool concentrates using flotation or sedimentation methods.[107] Direct or concentrated wet mounts are preferable to permanent stain smears because oocysts are difficult to detect in polyvinyl alcohol–preserved stool specimens.[108,109] Auramine-rhodamine, lacto-phenol cotton blue, and heated safranin-methylene blue stains may also be used.[107,110,111] Ultraviolet autofluorescence microscopy is a simple, rapid, and sensitive diagnostic method that is based on the detection of *Isospora* oocyst (blue) auto-

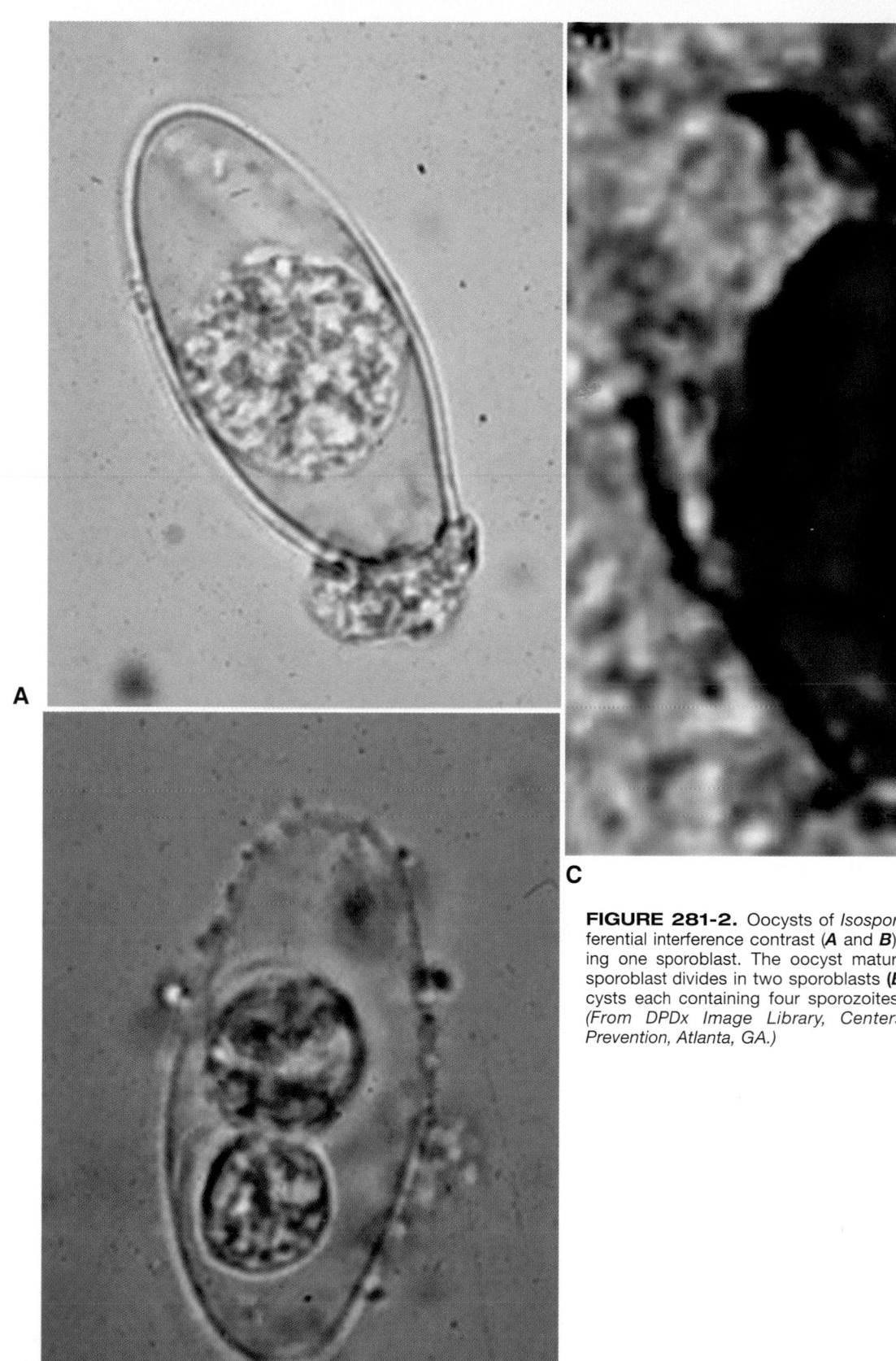

FIGURE 281-2. Oocysts of *Isospora belli* seen in bright-field differential interference contrast (*A* and *B*). *A,* Immature oocyst containing one sporoblast. The oocyst matures after excretion: the single sporoblast divides in two sporoblasts (*B*), which then become sporocysts each containing four sporozoites. **C,** Modified acid-fast stain. *(From DPDx Image Library, Centers for Disease Control and Prevention, Atlanta, GA.)*

fluorescence when a 330- to 380-nanometer ultraviolet filter is used.[112] Because *I. belli* parasites are shed intermittently in low numbers, multiple stool examinations may be required for diagnosis.[77,93] Duodenal aspirates,[113] the string test,[94] and small bowel biopsies[73] may be helpful. Peripheral blood eosinophilia and Charcot-Leyden crystals in stool, both unusual in other protozoal infections, have been reported.[73,114] Molecular diagnostic techniques based on small-subunit rRNA sequences are being developed.[115]

Treatment

Therapeutic modalities have been studied predominantly in HIV-infected patients. Trimethoprim-sulfamethoxazole (160 mg of trimethoprim and 800 mg of sulfamethoxazole), the drug of choice, is administered four times daily for 10 days; AIDS patients with isosporiasis usually respond to antimicrobial therapy within several days[82,83] but lifelong suppressive therapy is recommended because of the 50% chance of recurrence within 6 to 8 weeks of discontinuing initial treatment.[79] Long-term trimethoprim-sulfamethoxazole therapy is efficacious when taken daily or three times each week.[79] When sulfamethoxazole intolerance is present, pyrimethamine (75 mg/day) together with folinic acid (10 to 25 mg/day) has been used successfully,[116] as has ciprofloxacin (500 mg bid for 7 days followed by thrice weekly suppressive therapy).[69] Intravenous therapy may be required if malabsorption is severe.[117] Anecdotal case reports suggest that diclazuril,[118] roxithromycin,[119] nitazoxanide,[120] and a combination of albendazole and ornidazole[121] may be effective. Isolated reports indicating that metronidazole, quinacrine, and furazolidone may be effective have not yet been substantiated.[94,97,122]

SARCOCYSTIS SPECIES

Sarcocystis, previously known as sarcosporidiosis, is a zoonotic coccidian protozoal parasite that has an obligatory two-host cycle.[123] In the definitive host (usually a carnivore) sexual reproduction occurs in the intestinal mucosa and results in the shedding of oocysts and infective sporocysts in the feces. After the ingestion of sporocysts by the intermediate host (usually a herbivore) and gut penetration, asexual multiplication occurs in vascular endothelial cells. Subsequent hematogenous dissemination leads to invasion of cardiac or striated muscle cells where characteristic septate cysts (sarcocysts) containing bradyzoites develop. The cycle is complete when mature muscle cysts are eaten by an appropriate definitive host.

More than 120 species of *Sarcocystis* have been reported from a wide range of domestic and wild animals, but definitive and intermediate hosts are known for only half of these.[123] Through the ingestion of poorly cooked or raw meat, humans may serve as definitive hosts for pork and cattle *Sarcocystis*, excreting fecal oocysts; these often were previously incorrectly identified as *Isospora hominis*. Humans may also serve as incidental intermediate hosts when food or water contaminated with fecal sporocysts is ingested.[124] Sporocysts are hardy, resisting treatment with bleach, chlorhexidine, and the iodophore Betadyne.[125]

Epidemiology

Although worldwide in distribution, most human cases of sarcocystis have been reported from Southeast Asia.[124,126-29] Identification of *Sarcocystis* in stool or muscle or of antibodies in serum are most often incidental findings[124,126,128] with up to 22% prevalence in ethnic groups that consume undercooked pork or beef.[127,129]

Clinical Manifestations

Most individuals with sarcocystis are asymptomatic. Clinical manifestations including myalgia, fever, bronchospasm, transient pruritic rashes and lymphadenopathy, and subcutaneous nodules associated with eosinophilia and elevated creatine kinase have been reported rarely.[130,131] One symptomatic person had transient cardiac conduction abnormalities, possibly indicating myocardial involvement.[132] Muscle cysts vary greatly in size, with diameters from below 50 to 325 μm, and cyst lengths up to 5 cm.[124,133] However, symptoms were noted in only 10 of 52 persons with biopsy-confirmed cases with muscle cysts described in the literature.[132] Naturally occurring gastrointestinal illness, when humans act as definitive hosts, is also rare. In human volunteers who ingested pork or beef containing *Sarcocystis* spp., some developed mild self-limited gastrointestinal illness, while others passed sarcocysts but were asymptomatic.[133,134] Segmental eosinophilic and necrotizing enteritis due to sexual forms of *Sarcocystis* has been reported; however, causation is not clear because of the rarity of the organisms and early confusion with *I. belli*.[135]

Diagnosis

For patients with muscle pain or wasting, muscle biopsy can demonstrate numerous sarcocysts. Differentiation from morphologically indistinguishable *T. gondii* has been achieved by riboprint analysis and PCR of the gene for a surface antigen.[136] Serology using Western blot is highly specific. Sporocysts may be identified in stool of both symptomatic and asymptomatic individuals.[129,133]

Treatment

No specific treatment for *Sarcocystis* infection is known. Albendazole suppressed symptoms in one human case but was not curative.[132] In one small study, sulfadiazine resulted in clearance of cysts from stools.[129] In acute disease of sheep and goats, oxytetracycline, but not cotrimoxazole, prevented death.[130] Corticosteroids may provide symptomatic relief in cases of eosinophilic myositis.

BALANTIDIUM COLI

Balantidium coli, a ciliate, is the largest and possibly least common protozoal pathogen of humans.[137] After ingestion of cysts, trophozoites are released in the small intestine and colonize the large intestine where multiplication in the colonic wall and formation of cysts occurs. The latter is the infective form that survives well in the external environment.[138] The oval trophozoite usually measures 10 to 15 μm, but may reach 200 μm in length. Its surface is covered with tiny cilia that propel it through the intestinal lumen (Fig. 281-3).

Epidemiology

B. coli has a worldwide distribution but is most frequently reported from Latin America, Southeast Asia, and Papua New Guinea.[138,139] Although *B. coli* is found in many mammals, pigs are considered to be the main reservoir for human infection, with prevalence rates of 40% to 90%.[138,139] Human infection is often acquired from the ingestion of produce or water contaminated with pig excrement or during handling of the animal. In humans, the prevalence is usually less than 1%; high rates have been reported in hyperendemic areas and residential institutions. Poor nutrition and achlorhydria appear to be predisposing factors, as humans are usually resistant to infection.[138-140]

Clinical Manifestations

Although most infections are asymptomatic, clinical manifestations usually include a chronic course characterized by intermittent diarrhea, abdominal pain, and weight loss or, rarely, a more fulminant colitis in which stools contain blood and mucus.[138,141,142] The latter may result in intestinal perforation and extraintestinal spread to liver and mesenteric lymph nodes.[138,141,142] A fatal case of *Balantidium coli* pneumonia in a patient with anal carcinoma has been reported,[143] and this organism has been identified in the bladder of a patient with hematuria.[144]

In invasive disease, findings on endoscopy include necrosis and ulceration similar to that found in invasive amebiasis, bacterial

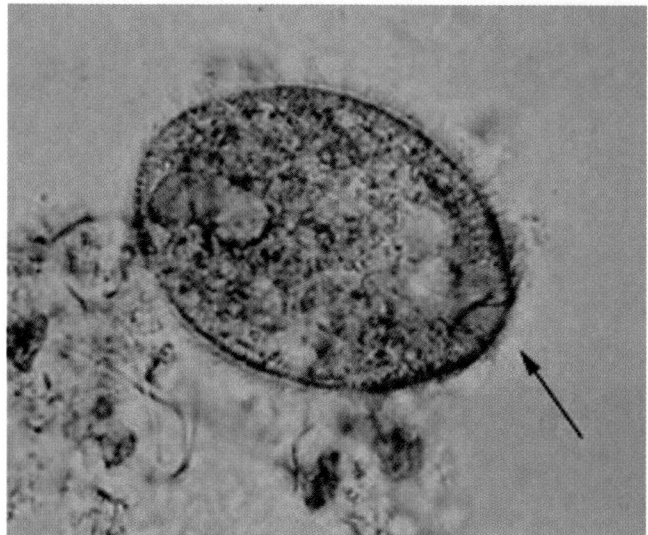

A

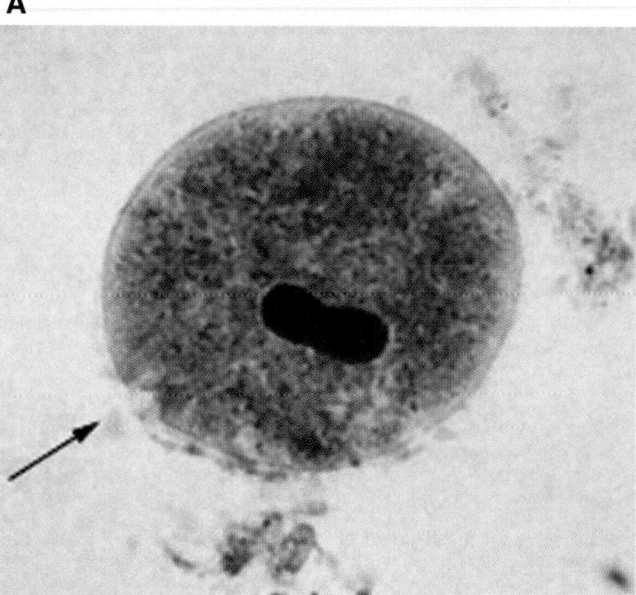

B

FIGURE 281-3. *Balantidium coli* trophozoites. These are large trophozoites (40 μm to more than 70 μm) with cilia on the cell surface, particularly visible in **A**, a bean-shaped macronucleus visible in **B**, and a smaller, less conspicuous micronucleus. *(From DPDx Image Library, Centers for Disease Control and Prevention, Atlanta, GA)*

dysentery, and inflammatory bowel disease. Balantidiasis can be diagnosed by finding the rapidly motile trophozoite in fresh or preserved stool or from scrapings of the periphery of ulcers detected on sigmoidoscopic examination (Fig. 281-2). Cysts are infrequently detected in stool.[138,142]

Treatment

Tetracycline (500 mg qid for 10 days) is the treatment of choice, but other drugs such as iodoquinol, metronidazole, paromomycin, and nitazoxanide have been used successfully.[145-147] Courses of therapy up to 20 days may be required for cure in HIV-infected persons.[148]

BLASTOCYSTIS HOMINIS

Despite its high prevalence throughout the world, major issues about *Blastocystis hominis* remain unresolved, including such fundamental areas as taxonomy and pathogenicity.[149-151] Sequences of the ssrURNA gene place *Blastocystis* in the stramenophiles, a diverse group of organisms that includes brown algae and diatoms[152,153] and under the six-kingdom classification it is not considered a protozoa but is placed in the Kingdom Chromista.[151] Analysis of the elongation factor 1-α gene, however, indicates similarity to *Entamoeba histolytica.*[154] There is considerable morphological variability and karyotype diversity, and it appears that more than one species is present in humans and animals.[152,155,156] In culture, three major forms predominate: vacuolar, granular, and ameboid.[149] Although previously the vacuolated form (usually 10 to 30 μm) was detected most frequently in fecal specimens, more recent studies suggest that smaller forms, including a multivacuolar and cyst form, may be more common.[157,158] The multilayered, thick-walled cyst measures 3 to 10 μm.[155,159] Excystation with differentiation to vacuolar forms has been observed using electron microscopy.[160]

Epidemiology

The prevalence of blastocystosis in humans appears to be higher in developing countries (30% to 50%) than in developed countries (1.5% to 10%), and has been associated with travel.[161-166] *B. hominis* is the most common parasite isolated in stool specimens in symptomatic and asymptomatic persons in a variety of settings.[167-169] Isolates resembling *B. hominis* have been described in a variety of mammals, birds, reptiles, and even insects.[170] The significance of this for human disease is uncertain.

Pathogenicity and Clinical Manifestations

Evidence that *B. hominis* is causally linked to intestinal disease is based on numerous case reports and uncontrolled or retrospective series in which infection was associated with acute or chronic diarrhea, bloating, flatulence, abdominal cramps, and fatigue.[161,166,172,173] In studies including asymptomatic controls, the majority show no correlation between symptoms and identification of *B. hominis* in stool samples or in concentration of organisms in stool.[161,162,171,174-180] A few recent studies have shown a correlation between identification of the organism and symptoms[181] or a decrease of symptoms with treatment with metronidazole or trimethoprim-sulfamethoxasole with consequent decrease or elimination of the organism in stool.[182,183] A recent placebo-controlled trial using metronidazole showed that symptom resolution was significantly correlated with antiparasitic therapy and parasite clearance.[184] Animal models,[185,186] cell cultures,[187] and intestinal permeability studies[188] support its pathogenicity. Also, it has been hypothesized that there may be virulent and avirulent strains of *B. hominis* on the basis of antigen, isoenzyme, and DNA analysis.[156,175,189-191] The pathogenicity of the organism remains unclear because of the difficulty in applying the results of animal models to humans, the uncertainty that other causes of symptoms have been eliminated in case series or treatment trials, and the inability of case-control studies to determine the association of a low-grade pathogen with disease.[166]

Diagnosis

Diagnosis is based on stool examination, preferably using permanent smears for microscopic diagnosis.[192] Concentration methods that involve water washes have been shown to cause lysis of the organism, which also may be difficult to find in wet mounts[94,192,193] (Fig. 281-4).

Treatment

Although treatment of asymptomatic infections is unnecessary, until more is known about the virulence of the organism, therapy for "symptomatic" infections should be withheld until a thorough search has been made to rule out other causes of intestinal symptoms. Treatment of blastocystosis is unsatisfactory; anecdotal studies in which metronidazole and iodoquinol, the most commonly recommended therapies, were used showed variable results.[150,162,193-198] Small studies suggest response to trimethoprim-sulfamethoxazole[183] and nitazoxanide.[199] In vitro studies have shown that emetine dihydrochloride, furazolidone, metronidazole, iodoquinol, and trimethoprim-sulfamethoxazole were inhibitory.[200,201] Adding to the difficulty in the assessment of therapy is the evidence that *B. hominis* is often a self-limited infection.[162,193,194,196]

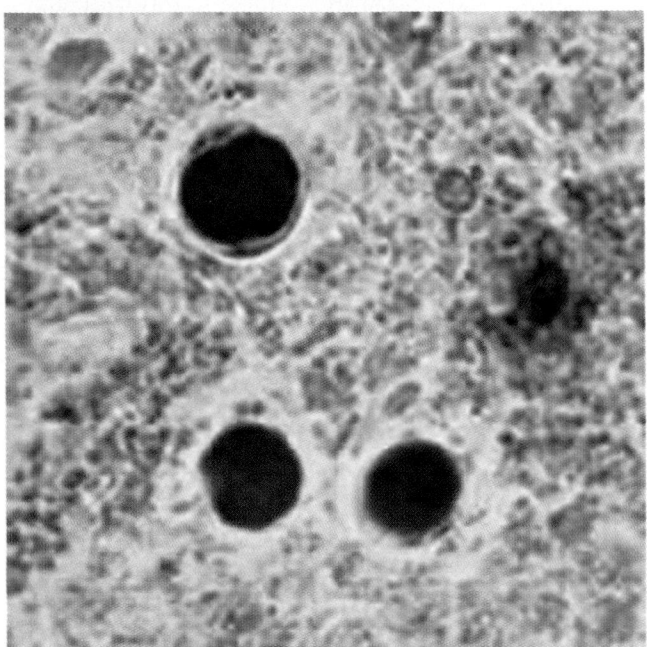

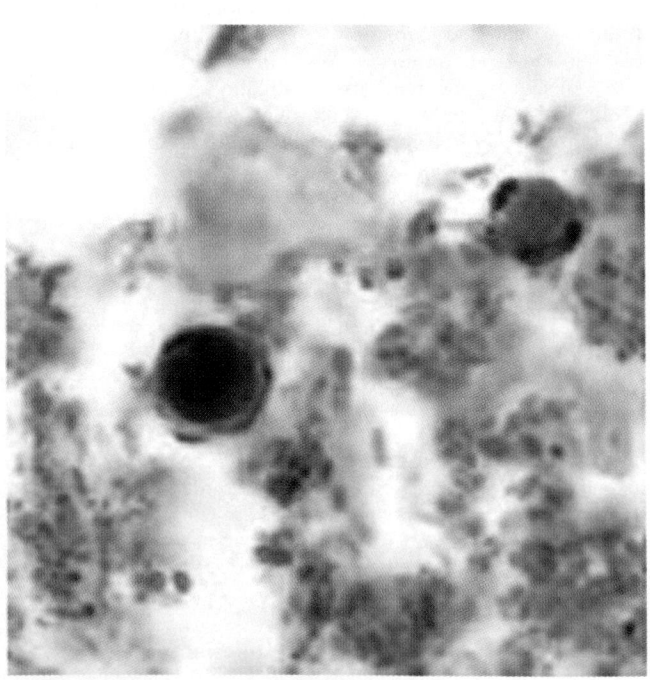

FIGURE 281-4. *Blastocystis hominis* cysts in stool stained with trichrome. Vacuoles vary from red to blue. *(From DPDx Image Library, Centers for Disease Control and Prevention, Atlanta, GA.)*

REFERENCES

1. Ashford RW. Occurrence of an undescribed coccidian in man in Papua New Guinea. Ann Trop Med Parasitol. 1979;73:497-500.
2. Hart AS, Ridinger MR, Soundarajan R, et al. Novel organism associated with chronic diarrhoea in AIDS. Lancet. 1990;335:169-170.
3. Long EG, Ebrahimzadeh A, White EH, et al. Alga associated with diarrhoea in patients with acquired immunodeficiency syndrome and in travelers. J Clin Microbiol. 1990;28:1101-1104.
4. Bendall RP, Luca S, Moody A, et al. Diarrhoea associated with cyanobacterium-like bodies: A new coccidian enteritis of man. Lancet. 1993;341:590-592.
5. Centers for Disease Control. Outbreaks of diarrhoeal illness associated with cyanobacteria (blue-green algae)-like bodies: Chicago and Nepal. MMWR Morb Mortal Wkly Rep. 1991;40:325-327.
6. Soave R. *Cyclospora:* An overview. Clin Infect Dis. 1996;23:429-435.
7. Ortega YR, Sterling CR, Gilman RH, et al. *Cyclospora* species—a new protozoan pathogen of humans. N Engl J Med. 1993;328:1308-1312.
8. Ortega YR, Gilman RH, Sterling CR. A coccidian parasite (Apidocomplexa: Eimeriidae) from humans. J Parasitol. 1994;80:625-629.
9. Franzen C, Muller A, Bialek R, et al. Taxonomic position of the human intestinal protozoan parasite *Isospora belli* as based on ribosomal RNA sequences. Parasitol Res. 2000; 86:669-676.
10. Taylor AD, Davis LJ, Soave R. *Cyclospora*—review. Curr Clin Top Infect Dis. 1997;17:256-268.
11. Rabold JG, Hoge CW, Shlim DR, et al. *Cyclospora* outbreak associated with chlorinated drinking water. Lancet. 1994;344:1360-1361.
12. Ooi WW, Zimmerman SK, Needham CA. *Cyclospora* species as a gastrointestinal pathogen in immunocompetent hosts. J Clin Microbiol. 1995;33:1267-1269.
13. Huang P, Weber JT, Sosin DM, et al. The first reported outbreak of diarrheal illness associated with *Cyclospora* in the United States. Ann Intern Med. 1995;123:409-414.
14. Steiner TS, Thielman NM, Guerrant RL. Protozoal agents: What are the dangers for the public water supply? Annu Rev Med. 1997;48:329-340.
15. Hoge CW, Shlim DR, Rajah R, et al. Epidemiology of diarrhoeal illness associated with coccidian-like organisms among travellers and foreign residents in Nepal. Lancet. 1993;341:1175-1179.
16. Farthing MJG, Kelly MP, Veitch AM. Recently recognised microbial enteropathies and HIV infection. J Antimicrob Chemother. 1996;37(Suppl B):61-70.
17. Chiodini PL. A "new" parasite: Human infection with *Cyclospora cayetanensis*. Trans R Soc Med Hyg. 1994;88:369-371.
18. Markus MB, Frean JA. Occurrence of human *Cyclospora* infection in sub-Saharan Africa. S Afr Med J. 1993;83:862-863.
19. Herwaldt BL. *Cyclospora cayetanensis:* A review, focusing on the outbreaks of cyclosporiasis in the 1990's. Clin Infect Dis. 2000;31:1040-1057.
20. Jelinek T, Lotze M, Eichenlaub S, et al. Prevalence of infection with *Cryptosporidium parvum* and *Cyclospora cayetanensis* among international travellers. Gut. 1997;41:801-804.
21. Berlin OGW, Novak SM, Porschen RK, et al. Recovery of *Cyclospora* organisms from patients with prolonged diarrhea. Clin Infect Dis. 1994;18:606-609.
22. Cegielski JP, Ortega YR, McKee S, et al. Cryptosporidium, enterocytozoon, and cyclospora infections in pediatric and adult patients with diarrhea in Tanzania. Clin Infect Dis. 1999;28:314-321.
23. Gumbo T, Sarbah S, Gangaidzo IT, et al. Intestinal parasites in patients with diarrhea and human immunodeficiency virus infection in Zimbabwe. AIDS. 1999;13:819-821.
24. Gascon J, Alvarez M, Eugenia Valls M, et al. Cyclosporiasis: A clinical and epidemiological study in travellers with imported *Cyclospora cayetanensis* infection. Med Clin. 2001;116:461-464.
25. Pape JW, Levine E, Beaulieu ME, et al. Cryptosporidiosis in Haitian children. Am J Trop Med Hyg. 1987; 36:333-338.
26. Wurtz RM, Kocka FE, Peters CS, et al. Clinical characteristics of seven cases of diarrhea associated with novel acid-fast organism in the stool. Clin Infect Dis. 1993;16:136-138.
27. Rezk H, el-Shazly AM, Soliman M, et al. Coccidiosis among immuno-competent and -compromised adults. J Egypt Soc Parasitol. 2001;31:823-834.
28. Hoge CW, Echeverria P, Rajah R, et al. Prevalence of *Cyclospora* species and other enteric pathogens among children less than 5 years of age in Nepal. J Clin Microbiol. 1995;33:3058-3060.
29. Pape JW, Verdier RI, Boncy M, et al. *Cyclospora* infections in adults with HIV: Clinical manifestations, treatment and prophylaxis. Ann Intern Med. 1994;121:654-657.
30. Herwaldt BL, Ackers M-L, *Cyclospora* Working Group. An outbreak in 1996 of cyclosporiasis associated with imported raspberries. N Engl J Med. 1997;336:1548-1556.
31. Centers for Disease Control and Prevention. Update: Outbreaks of *Cyclospora cayetanensis* infection—United States and Canada. MMWR Morb Mortal Wkly Rep. 1996;45:611-612.
32. Centers for Disease Control and Prevention. Update: outbreaks of cyclosporiasis—United States and Canada 1997. MMWR Morb Mortal Wkly Rep. 1997;46:521-523.
33. Lopez AS, Dodson DR, Arrowood MJ, et al. Outbreak of cyclosporiasis associated with basil in Missouri in 1999. Clin Infect Dis. 2001;32:1010-1017.
34. Ho AY, Lopez AS, Eberhart MG, et al. Outbreak of cyclosporiasis associated with imported raspberries, Philadelphia, Pennsylvania, 2000. Emerg Infect Dis. 2002;8:783-788.
35. Sherchand JB, Cross JH, Jimba M, et al. Study of *Cyclospora cayetanensis* in health care facilities, sewage water and green leafy vegetables in Nepal. Southeast Asian J Trop Med Publ Hlth. 1999;30:58-63.

36. Wurtz R. *Cyclospora:* A newly identified intestinal pathogen of humans. Clin Infect Dis. 1994;18:620-623.

37. Clarke SC, McIntyre M. The incidence of *Cyclospora cayetanensis* in stool samples submitted to a district general hospital. Epidemiol Infect. 1996;117:189-193.

38. Madico G, McDonald J, Gilman RH, et al. Epidemiology and treatment of *Cyclospora cayetanensis* infection in Peruvian children. Clin Infect Dis. 1997;24:977-981.

39. Soave R, Herwaldt BLL, Relman DA. *Cyclospora.* Infect Dis Clin North Am. 1998;12:1-12.

40. Zerpa R, Uchima N, Huicho L. *Cyclospora cayetanensis* associated with water diarrhoea in Peruvian patients. J Trop Med Hyg. 1995;98:325-329.

41. Garcia-Lopez HL, Rodriguez-Tovar LE, Medina de la Garza CE. Identification of *Cyclospora* in poultry. Emerg Infect Dis. 1996;2:356-357.

42. Eberhard ML, Nace EK, Freeman AR. Survey for *Cyclospora cayetanensis* in domestic animals in an endemic area in Haiti. J Parasitol. 1999; 85:562-563.

43. Carollo MC, Amato Neto V, Braz LM, et al. Detection of *Cyclospora* sp oocysts in the feces of stray dogs in Greater Sao Paulo Rev Soc Brasil Med Trop. 2001;34: 597-598.

44. Sadaka HA, Zoheir MA. Experimental studies on cyclosporiosis. J Egypt Soc Parasitol. 2001;31;65-77.

45. Eberhard ML, Ortega YR, Hanes DE, et al. Attempts to establish experimental *Cyclospora cayetanensis* infection in laboratory animals. J Parasitol. 2000;86: 577-582.

46. Connor BA, Shlim DR. Food borne transmission of *Cyclospora.* Lancet. 1995;345:1634.

47. Ortega YR, Roxas CR, Gilman RH, et al. Isolation of *Cryptosporidium parvum* and *Cyclospora cayetanensis* from vegetables collected in markets of an endemic region in Peru. Am J Trop Med Hyg. 1997;57:683-686.

48. Taylor DN, Houston R, Shlim DR, et al. Etiology of diarrhea among travelers and foreign residents in Nepal. JAMA. 1988;260:1245-1248.

49. Chacin-Bonilla L, Mejia de Young M, Estevez J. Prevalence and pathogenic role of *Cyclospora cayetanensis* in a Venezuelan community. Am J Trop Med Hyg. 2003; 68:304-6.

50. Schubach TM, Neves ES, Leite AC, et al. *Cyclospora cayetanensis* in an asymptomatic patient infected with HIV and HTLV-1. Trans R Soc Trop Med Hyg. 1997;91:175.

51. Sifuentes-Osornio J, Porras-Cortes G, Bendall RP, et al. *Cyclospora cayetanensis* infection in patients with and without AIDS: Biliary disease as another clinical manifestation. Clin Infect Dis. 1995;21:1092-1097.

52. Ortega YR, Nagle R, Gilman RH, et al. Pathologic and clinical findings in patients with cyclosporiasis and a description of intracellular parasite life-cycle stages. J Infect Dis. 1997;176:1584-1589.

53. Connor BA, Johnson EJ, Soave R. Reiter syndrome following protracted symptoms of *Cyclospora* infection. Emerg Infect Dis. 2001;7:453-454.

54. Richardson RF Jr, Remler BF, Katirji B, et al. Guillain-Barre syndrome after *Cyclospora* infection. Musc Nerve. 1998;21:669-671.

55. de Gorgolas M, Fortes J, Fernandez Guerrero ML. *Cyclospora cayetanensis* cholecystitis in a patient with AIDS. Ann Intern Med. 2001;134:166.

56. Long EG, White EH, Carmichael WW, et al. Morphologic and staining characteristics of a cyanobacterium-like organism associated with diarrhea. J Infect Dis. 1991;164:199-202.

57. Connor BA, Shlim DR, Scholes JV, et al. Pathogenic changes in the small bowel in nine patients with diarrhoea associated with a coccidia-like body. Ann Intern Med. 1993;119:377-382.

58. Shlim DR, Cohen MT, Eaton M, et al. An alga-like organism associated with an outbreak of prolonged diarrhoea among foreigners in Nepal. Am J Trop Med Hyg. 1991;45:383-389.

59. Pollock RCG, Bendall RP, Moody A, et al. Travellers' diarrhoea associated with cyanobacterium-like bodies. Lancet. 1992;340:556-557.

60. Eberhard ML, Pieniazek NJ, Arrowood MJ. Laboratory diagnosis of *Cyclospora* infections. Arch Pathol Lab Med. 1997;121:792-797.

61. Berlin OGW, Peter JB, Gagne C, et al. Autofluorescence and the detection of *Cyclospora* oocysts. Emerg Infect Dis. 1998;4:127-128.

62. Visvesvara GS, Moura H, Kovacs-Nace E, et al. Uniform staining of *Cyclospora* oocysts in fecal smears by a modified safranin technique with microwave heating. J Clin Microbiol. 1992;35:730-733.

63. Parija SC, Shivaprakash MR, Jayakeerthi SR. Evaluation of lacto-phenol cotton blue (LPCB) for detection of *Cryptosporidium, Cyclospora* and *Isospora* in the wet mount preparation of stool. Acta Trop. 2003;85:349-354.

64. Relman DA, Schmidt TM, Gajadhar A, et al. Molecular phylogenetic analysis of *Cyclospora,* the human intestinal pathogen, suggests that it is closely related to *Eimeria* species. J Infect Dis. 1996;173:440-445.

65. Tran Van Nhieu J, Nin F, Fleury-Feith J, et al. Identification of intracellular stages of *Cyclospora* species by light microscopy of thick sections using hematoxylin. Hum Pathol. 1996;27:1107-1109.

66. Sun T, Ilardi CF, Asnis D, et al. Light and electron microscopic identification of *Cyclospora* species in the small intestine. Evidence of the presence of asexual life cycle in human host. Am J Clin Pathol. 1996;105:216-220.

67. Hoge CW, Shlim DR, Ghirire M, et al. Placebo controlled trail of co-trimoxazole for *Cyclospora* infections among travellers and foreign residents in Nepal. Lancet. 1995;345:691-693.

68. Soave R, Johnson WD Jr. *Cyclospora:* Conquest of an emerging pathogen. Lancet. 1995;345:667-668.

69. Verdier RI, Fitzgerald DW, Johnson WD, et al. Trimethoprim-sulfamethoxazole compared with ciprofloxacin for treatment and prophylaxis of *Isospora belli* and *Cyclospora cayetanensis* infection in HIV-infected patients. A randomized, controlled trial. Ann Intern Med. 2000; 132:885-888.

70. Ledingham JCG, Penfold WJ, Woodcock HM. Recent bacteriological experiences with typhoidal disease and dysentery: With notes on the protozoan parasites in the excreta. Br Med J. 1915;2:704-711.

71. Wenyon CM. Observations on the common intestinal protozoa of man: Their diagnosis and pathogenicity. Lancet. 1915;2:1178-1183.

72. Kirkpatrick CE. Animal reservoirs of *Cryptosporidium* spp and *Isospora belli.* J Infect Dis. 1988;158:909.

73. Trier JS, Moxey PC, Schimmel EM, et al. Chronic intestinal coccidiosis in man: Intestinal morphology and response to treatment. Gastroenterology. 1974;66: 923-935.

74. Lindsay DS, Dubey JP, Blagburn BL. Biology of *Isospora* spp. from humans, nonhuman primates and domestic animals. Clin Microbiol Rev. 1997;10:19-34.

75. Goodgame RW. Understanding intestinal spore-forming protozoa: *Cryptosporidia, Microbporidia, Isospora* and *Cyclospora.* Ann Intern Med. 1996;124:429-441.

76. Faust EC, Giraldo LE, Caicedo G, et al. Human isosporosis in the Western Hemisphere. Am J Trop Med Hyg. 1961;10:343-349.

77. Smitskamp H, Dey-Muller E. Geographic distribution and clinical significance of human coccidiosis. Trop Geogr Med. 1966;18:133-136.

78. Sauve R, Johnson WD. *Cryptosporidium* and *Isospora belli* infections. J Infect Dis. 1988;157:255-259.

79. Sorvillo FJ, Lieb LE, Seidel J, et al. Epidemiology of isosporiasis among persons with acquired immunodeficiency syndrome in Los Angeles County. Am J Trop Med Hyg. 1995;53:656-659.

80. Centers for Disease Control and Prevention. Surveillance for AIDS-defining opportunistic illnesses, 1992-1996. MMWR Morb Mortal Wkly Rep. 1999;48 (SS-2):1-22.

81. Bartlett JG, Belitsos PC, Sears CL. AIDS enteropathy. Clin Infect Dis. 1992;15: 726-735.

82. DeHovitz JA, Pape JW, Boncy M, et al. Clinical manifestations and therapy of *Isospora belli* infection in patients with acquired immunodeficiency syndrome. N Engl J Med. 1986;315:87-90.

83. Pape JW, Verdier RI, Johnson WD Jr. Treatment and prophylaxis of *Isospora belli* infection in patients with acquired immunodeficiency syndrome. N Engl J Med. 1989;320:1044-1047.

84. Colebunders R, Lusakumuni K, Nelson AM, et al. Persistent diarrhoea in Zairian AIDS patients: An endoscopic and histological study. Gut. 1988;29:1687-1691.

85. Henry MC, de Clercq D, Lokombe B, et al. Parasitological observations of chronic diarrhoea in suspected AIDS adult patient Kinshasa (Zaire) Trans R Soc Trop Med Hyg. 1986;80:309-310.

86. Hunter G, Bagshave AF, Baboo KS, et al. Intestinal parasites in Zambian patients with AIDS. Trans R Soc Trop Med Hyg. 1992;86:543-545.

87. Conlon CP, Pinching AJ, Perera CU, et al. HIV-related enteropathy in Zambia: A clinical, microbiological and histological study. Am J Trop Med Hyg. 1990;42:83-88.

88. Sauda FC, Zamarioli LA, Filho WE, et al. Prevalence of *Cryptosporidium* sp and *Isospora belli* among AIDS patients attending Santos Reference for AIDS, Sao Paulo, Brazil. J Parasitol. 1993;79:454-456.

89. Henderson HE, Gillepsie GW, Kaplan P, et al. The human *Isospora.* Am J Hyg. 1963;78:302-309.

90. Leibman WM, Thaler MM, Delorimier A, et al. Intractable diarrhea of infancy due to intestinal coccidiosis. Gastroenterology. 1980;78:579-584.

91. La Via WV. Parasitic gastroenteritis. Pediatr Ann. 1994:556-560.

92. Matsubayashi H, Nozawa T. Experimental infection of *Isospora hominis* in man. Am J Trop Med Hyg. 1948;28:633-637.

93. Shaffer N, Moore L. Chronic travelers' diarrhea in a normal host due to *Isospora belli.* J Infect Dis. 1989;159:596-597.

94. Whiteside ME, Barkin JS, May RG, et al. Enteric coccidiosis among patients with the acquired immunodeficiency syndrome. Am J Trop Med Hyg. 1984;33:1065-1072.

95. Modigliani R, Bories C, Le Charpentier Y, et al. Diarrhea and malabsorption in acquired immune deficiency syndrome: A study of four cases with special emphasis on opportunistic protozoan infestations. Gut. 1985;26:179-187.

96. Greenberg SJ, Davey MP, Zierdt WS, et al. *Isospora belli* infections in patients with human T-cell leukemia virus type 1-associated adult T-cell leukemia. Am J Med. 1988;85:435-438.

97. Hallak A, Yust I, Ratan Y, et al. Malabsorption syndrome, coccidiosis, combined immune deficiency and fulminant lymphoproliferative disease. Arch Intern Med. 1982;142:196-197.

98. Westerman EL, Christensen RP. Chronic *Isospora belli* treated with cotrimoxazole. Ann Intern Med. 1979;91:413-414.

99. Alfandari S, Ajana F, Senneville E, et al. Haemorrhagic ulcerative colitis due to *Isospora belli* in AIDS. Int J STD AIDS. 1995;6:216.

100. Michiels JF, Hofman P, Bernard E, et al. Intestinal and extraintestinal *Isospora belli* infection in an AIDS patient. Pathol Res Pract. 1994;190:1089-1093.

101. Restrepo C, Macher AM, Radany EH. Disseminated extraintestinal isosporiasis in a patient with acquired immune deficiency syndrome. Am J Clin Pathol. 1987;87: 536-542.

102. Bernard E, Delguidice P, Carles M, et al. Disseminated isosporiasis in an AIDS patient. Eur J Clin Micro Infect Dis 1997;16:699-701.

103. Benator DA, French AL, Beaudet LM, et al. *Isospora belli* infection associated with acalculous cholecystitis in a patient with AIDS. Ann Intern Med. 1994;121:663-664.

104. Gonzalez-Dominguez J, Roldan R, Villanueva JL, et al. *Isospora belli* reactive arthritis in a patient with AIDS. Ann Rheum Dis. 1994;53:618-619.

105. Lindsay DS, Dubey JP, Toivio-Kinnuca MA, et al. Examination of extraintestinal tissue cysts of *Isospora belli*. J Parasitol 1997; 83:620-625.
106. Ng E, Markell EK, Fleming RL, et al. Demonstration of *Isospora belli* by acid-fast stain in a patient with acquired immune deficiency syndrome. J Clin Microbiol. 1984;20:384-386.
107. Ma P, Kaufman D, Montana J. *Isospora belli* diarrheal infection in homosexual men. AIDS Res. 1984;1:327-338.
108. Garcia LS, Bruckner DA. Diagnostic Medical Parasitology. Washington, DC: American Society for Microbiology Press; 1993.
109. Wittner M, Tanowitz HB, Weiss LM. Parasitic infections in AIDS patients. Cryptosporidiosis, isosporosis, microsporidiosis, cyclosporiasis. Infect Dis Clin North Am. 1993;7:569-586.
110. Bush JB, Markus MB. Staining of *Isospora belli* oocysts. Trans R Soc Trop Med. 1987;81:244.
111. Parija SC, Bhattacharya S. *Isospora belli* and *Cyclospora cayetanensis* in a case of chronic diarrhoea in an immunocompromised host. J Assoc Phys India. 2000;48:1192.
112. Berlin OGW, Conteas CN, Sowerby TM. Detection of *Isospora* in the stools of AIDS patients using a new rapid autofluorescence technique. AIDS. 1996;10:442-443.
113. Limbos P, Van Ros G, DeMuynck A. Deux noveaux cas de coccidiose a¨ *Isospora belli* observé in Belgique. Bull Soc Pathol Exot. 1972;65:288-292.
114. Brandborg LL, Goldberg SB, Breidenbach WC. Human coccidiosis—a possible cause of malabsorption. N Engl J Med. 1970;24:1306-1313.
115. Muller A, Bialek R, Fatkenheuer G, et al. Detection of *Isospora belli* by polymerase chain reaction using primers based on small-subunit ribosomal RNA sequences. Eur J Clin Microbiol Infect Dis. 2000;19:631-634.
116 Weiss LM, Perlman D, Sherman J, et al. *Isospora belli* infection: Treatment with pyrimethamine. Ann Intern Med. 1988;109:474-475.
117. Bialek R, Binder N, Dietz K, et al. Comparison of autofluorescence and iodine staining for detection of *Isospora belli* in feces. Am J Trop Med Hyg. 2002;67:304-305.
118. Limson-Pobre RNR, Merrick S, Gruen D, et al. Use of diclazuril for the treatment of isosporiasis in patients with AIDS. Clin Infect Dis. 1995;20:201-202.
119. Musey KL, Chidiac C, Beaucaire G, et al. Effectiveness of roxithromycin for treating *Isospora belli* infection. J Infect Dis. 1988;158:646.
120. Doumbo O, Rossignol JF, Pichard E, et al. Nitazoxanide in the treatment of cryptosporidial diarrhea and other intestinal parasitic infections associated with acquired immunodeficiency syndrome in tropical Africa. Am J Trop Med Hyg. 1997;56:637-639.
121. Dionisio D, Sterrantino M, Meli M, et al. Treatment of isosporiasis with combined albendazole and ornidazole in patients with AIDS. AIDS. 1996;10:1301-1302.
122. Forthal DN, Guest SS. *Isospora belli* enteritis in three homosexual men. Am J Trop Med Hyg. 1984;33:1060-1064.
123. Levine ND. The Protozoan Phylum Apicomplexa, v. 2. Bocca Raton, Fl: CRC Press; 1988:1-8.
124. Beaver PC, Gadgil RK, Morera P. *Sarcocystis* in man: A review and report of five cases. Am J Trop Med Hyg. 1979;22:819-844.
125. Dubey JP, Saville WJ, Sreekumar C, et al. Effects of high temperature and disinfectants on the viability of *Sarcocystis neurona* sporocysts. J Parasitol. 2002;88:1252-1254.
126. Wong KT, Pathmananthan R. Review of human skeletal muscle sarcocystosis in Southeast Asia. Trans R Soc Trop Med Hyg. 1992;86:631-632.
127. Kan SP, Pathmananthan R. Review of sarcocystosis in Malaysia. SE Asian J Trop Med Publ Hlth. 1991;22(Suppl):129-134.
128. Wilairatana P, Radomyos P, Radomyos B, et al. Intestinal sarcocystosis in Thai laborers. SE Asian J Trop Med Publ Hlth. 1996;27:43-46.
129. Yu S. Field survey of sarcocystis infection in the Tibet autonomous region. Chung-Kuo i Hsueh Ko Hsueh Yuan Hsueh Pao Acta Academ Med Sinicae. 1991;13:29-32
130. Pamphlett R, O'Donoghue P. *Sarcocystis* infection of human muscle. Aust N Z J Med. 1990;20:705-707.
131. Van den Enden E, Praet M, Joos R, et al. Eosinophilic myositis resulting from sarcocystosis. J Trop Med Hyg. 1995;98:273-276.
132. Arness MK, Brown JD, Dubey JP, et al. An outbreak of acute eosinophilic myositis attributed to human Sarcocystis parasitism. Am J Trop Med Hyg. 1999;61:548-553.
133. Jeffrey HC. Sarcosporidiosis in man. Trans R Soc Trop Med Hyg. 1974;68:17-29.
134. Pena HF, Ogassawara S, Sinhorini IL, Occurrence of cattle *Sarcocystis* species in raw kibbe from Arabian food establishments in the city of Sao Paulo, Brazil, and experimental transmission to humans. J Parasitol. 2001; 87:1459-1465.
135. Bunyaratvej S, Bunyawongwiroj P, Nitiyanant P. Human intestinal sarcosporidiosis: Report of six cases. Am J Trop Med Hyg. 1982;31:36-41.
136. Brindley PJ, Ricardo T, Gazzinelli EY, et al. Differentiation of *Toxoplasma gondii* from closely related coccidia by riboprint analysis and a surface antigen gene polymerase chain reaction. Am J Trop Med Hyg. 1993;48:447-456.
137. Woody NC, Woody HB. Balantidiasis in infancy: Review of the literature and report of a case. J Pediatr. 1960;56:485-489.
138. Arean VM, Koppisch E. Balantidiasis—a review and report of cases. Am J Pathol. 1956;32:1089-1108.
139. Walgzer PD, Judson FN, Murphy KB, et al. Balantidiasis outbreak in Truk. Am J Trop Med Hyg. 1973;22:33-41.
140. Young M. Attempts to transmit human *Balantidium coli*. Am J Trop Med. 1950;30:71-72.
141. Baskerville L. *Balantidium* colitis. Report of a case. Am J Dig Dis. 1970;15:727-731.
142. Ladas SD, Savva S, Frydas A, et al. Invasive balantidiasis presented as chronic colitis and lung involvement. Dig Dis Sci. 1989;34:1621-1623.
143. Vasilakopoulou A, Dimarongona K, Samakovli A, et al. *Balantidium coli* pneumonia in an immunocompromised patient. Scand J Infect Dis. 2003;35:144-146.
144. Maleky F. Case report of *Balantidium coli* in human from south of Tehran, Iran. Indian J Med Sci 1998;52:201-202.
145. Abaza H, El-Zayadi AR, Kabil SM, et al. Nitazoxanide in the treatment of patients with intestinal protozoan and helminthic infections: A report of 546 patients in Egypt. Curr Ther Res. 1998;59:116-121.
146. Drugs for parasitic infections. Med Lett. 2002;44:32-43.
147. Garcia-Laverde A, De Bonilla L. Clinical trials with metronidazole in human balantidiasis. Am J Trop Med Hyg. 1975;24:781-783.
148. Clyti E, Aznar C, Couppie P, et al. A case of coinfection by *Balantidium coli* and HIV in French Guiana. Bull Soc Path Exotique. 1998;91:309-311.
149. Zierdt CH. *Blastocystis hominis*—past and future. Clin Microbiol Rev. 1991;4:61-79.
150. Stenzel DJ, Boreham PFL. *Blastocystis hominis* revisited. Clin Microbiol Rev. 1996;9:563-584.
151. Tan KS, Singh M, Yap EH. Recent advances in *Blastocystis hominis* research: Hot spots in terra incognita. Intl J Parasitol. 2002;32:789-804.
152. Noel C, Peyronnet C, Gerbod D, et al. Phylogenetic analysis of *Blastocystis* isolates from different hosts based on the comparison of small-subunit rRNA gene sequences. Mol Biochem Parasitol. 2003;126:119-123.
153. Silberman JD, Sogin ML, Leipe DD, et al. Human parasite finds taxonomic home. Nature. 1996;380:398.
154. Ho LC, Jeyaseelan K, Singh M. Use of the elongation factor-1 alpha gene in a polymerase chain reaction-based restriction-fragment-length polymorphism analysis of genetic heterogeneity among *Blastocystis* species. Molec Biochem Parasitol. 2001;112:287-291.
155. Zaman V, Howe J, Ng M. Ultrastructure of *Blastocystis hominis* cysts. Parasitol Res. 1995;81:465-469.
156. Stenzel DJ, Lee MG, Boreham PFL. Morphological differences in *Blastocystis* cysts—an indication of different species. Parasitol Res. 1997;83:452-457.
157. Boreham PFL, Stenzel DJ. *Blastocystis* in humans and animals: Morphology, biology and epizootiology. Adv Parasitol. 1993;32:1-70.
158. Stenzel DJ, Boreham PFL, McDougall R. Ultrastructure of *Blastocystis hominis* in human stool samples. Int J Parasitol. 1991;21:807-812.
159. Stenzel DJ, Boreham PFL. A cyst-like stage of *Blastocystis hominis*. Int J Parasitol. 1991;21:613-615.
160. Moe KT, Singh M, Howe J, et al. Observations on the ultrastructure and viability of the cystic stage of *Blastocystis hominis* from human feces. Parasitol Res. 1996; 82:439-444.
161. Doyle PW, Helgason MM, Mathias RG, et al. Epidemiology and pathogenicity of *Blastocystis hominis*. J Clin Microbiol. 1990;28:116-121.
162. Kain KC, Noble MA, Freeman HJ, et al. Epidemiology and clinical features associated with *Blastocystis hominis* infection. Diagn Microbiol Infect Dis. 1987;8:235-244.
163. Puga SL, Figueroa L, Navarrete N. Protozoos y helmintos intestinales en la poblacion prescolar y escolar de la ciudad de Valdivia, Chile. Parasitol Diag. 1991;15:57-58.
164. Torres PJ, Miranda L, Flores J, et al. *Blastocystis* and other intestinal protozoan infections in human riverside communities from Valdiva River Basin, Chile. Rev Inst Med Trop Sao Paulo. 1992;34:557-564.
165. Yamada MH, Matsumoto Y, Tegoshi T, et al. The prevalence of *Blastocystis hominis* infection in humans in Kyoto City, Japan. Jpn J Trop Med Hyg. 1987;15:158-159.
166. Keystone JS. *Blastocystis hominis* and traveler's diarrhea. Clin Infect Dis. 1995;21:102-103.
167. Windsor JJ, Macfarlane L, Hughes-Thapa G, et al. Incidence of *Blastocystis hominis* in faecal samples submitted for routine microbiological analysis. Br J Biomed Sci. 2002; 9:154-157.
168. Giacometti A, Cirioni O, Fiorentini A, et al. Irritable bowel syndrome in patients with Blastocystis hominis infection. Eur J Clin Microbiol Infect Dis. 1999;18:436-439.
169. Amin AM. *Blastocystis hominis* among apparently healthy food handlers in Jeddah, Saudi Arabia. J Egypt Soc Parasitol. 1997;27:817-823.
170. Boreham PF, Stenzel DJ. *Blastocystis* in humans and animals: Morphology, biology and epizootiology. Adv Parasitol. 1993;32:1-70.
171. Cirioni O, Giacometti A, Drenaggi D, et al. Prevalence and clinical relevance of Blastocystis hominis in diverse patient cohorts. Eur J Epidemiol. 1999;15:389-393.
172. O'Gorman MA, Orenstein SR, Proujansky R, et al. Prevalence and characteristics of *Blastocystis hominis* infection in children. Clin Pediatr. 1993;32:91-96.
173. Wilson KW, Winget D. *Blastocystis hominis*: Infection, signs and symptoms in patients at Wilford Hall Medical Center. Mil Med. 1990;155:394-396.
174. Udkow MP, Markell EK. *Blastocystis hominis:* Prevalence in asymptomatic versus symptomatic hosts. J Infect Dis. 1993;168:242-244.
175. Kukoschke KG, Muller HE. Varying incidence of *Blastocystis hominis:* In culture from faeces of patients with diarrhoea and from healthy persons. Int J Med Microbiol Virol Parasitol Infect Dis. 1992;277:112-118.
176. Herwaldt BL, de Arroyave KR, Wahlquist SP, et al. Infections with intestinal parasites in Peace Corps volunteers in Guatemala. J Clin Microbiol. 1994;32:1376-1378.
177. Nimri LF. Evidence of an epidemic of *Blastocystis hominis* infections in preschool children in northern Jordan. J Clin Microbiol. 1993;31:2706-2708.
178. Shlim DR, Hoge CW, Rajah R, et al. Is *Blastocystis hominis* a cause of diarrhea in travelers? A prospective controlled study in Nepal. Clin Infect Dis. 1995;21:97-101.
179. Albrecht H, Stellbrink HJ, Koperski K, et al. Blastocystis hominis in human immunodeficiency virus-related diarrhea. Scand J Gastroenterol. 1995;30:909-914.
180. Brandonisio O, Maggi P, Panaro MA, et al. Intestinal protozoa in HIV-I infected patients in Apulia, South Italy. Epidemiol Infect. 1999;123:457-462.
181. Jelinek T, Peyerl G, Loscher T, et al. The role of *Blastocystis hominis* as a possible intestinal pathogen in travellers. J Infect. 1997;35:63-66.

182. Ghosh K, Ayyaril M, Nirmala V. Acute GVHD involving the gastrointestinal tract and infestation with *Blastocystis hominis* in a patient with chronic myeloid leukaemia following allogeneic bone marrow transplantation. Bone Marrow Transpl. 1998; 22:1115-1117.
183. Ok UZ, Girginkardesler N, Balcioglu C, et al. Effect of trimethoprim-sulfamethaxazole in *Blastocystis hominis* infection. Am J Gastroenterol. 1999;94:3245-3247.
184. Nigro L, Larocca L, Massarelli L, et al. A placebo-controlled treatment trial of *Blastocystis hominis* infection with metronidazole. J Trav Med. 2003;10:128-130.
185 . Phillips PB, Zierdt CH. *Blastocystis hominis:* Pathogenic potential in human patients and gnotobiotes. Exp Parasitol. 1976;39:358-364.
186. Moe KT, Singh M, Howe J, et al. Experimental *Blastocystis hominis* infection in laboratory mice. Parasitol Res. 1997;83:319-325.
187. Walderich B, Bernauer S, Renner M, et al. Cytopathic effects of *Blastocystis hominis* on Chinese hamster ovary (CHO) and adeno carcinoma HT29 cell cultures. Trop Med Int Health. 1998;3:385-390.
188. Dagci H, Ustun S, Taner MS, et al. Protozoon infections and intestinal permeability. Acta Trop. 2002 81:1-5.
189. Bohm-Gloning B, Knobloch J, Walderich B. Five subgroups of *Blastocystis hominis* isolates from symptomatic and asymptomatic patients revealed by restriction site analysis of PCR-amplified I6S-like rDNA. Trop Med Int Hlth. 1997;2:771-778.
190. Boreham PFL, Upcroft JA, Dunn LA. Protein and DNA evidence for two demes of *Blastocystis hominis* from humans. Int J Parasitol. 1992;22:49-53.
191. Gericke AS, Burchard GD, Knobloch J, et al. Isoenzyme patterns of *Blastocystis hominis* patient isolates derived from symptomatic and healthy carriers. Trop Med Int Hlth. 1997;2:245-253.
192. Garcia LS, Bruckner DA. Diagnostic Medical Parasitology. 2nd ed. Washington, DC: American Society for Microbiology Press; 1993.
193. Senay H, MacPherson D. *Blastocystis hominis:* Epidemiology and natural history. J Infect Dis. 1990;162:987-990.
194. Grossman I, Weiss LM, Simon D, et al. *Blastocystis hominis* in hospital employees. Am J Gastroenterol. 1992;87:729-732.
195. Quadris SMH, Al-Okaili GA, Al-Dayel F. Clinical significance of *Blastocystis hominis*. J Clin Microbiol. 1989;27:2407-2409.
196. Markell EK, Udkow MP. *Blastocystis hominis:* Pathogen or fellow traveler? Am J Trop Med Hyg. 1986;35:1023-1026.
197. Babb RR, Wagener S. *Blastocystis hominis:* A potential intestinal pathogen. West J Med. 1989;151:518-519.
198. Sun T, Katz S, Tanenbaum B, et al. Questionable clinical significance of *Blastocystis hominis* infection. Am J Gastroenterol. 1989;84:1543-1547.
199. Zierdt CH, Swan JC, Hosscini J. *In vitro* response of *Blastocystis hominis* to antiprotozoal drugs. J Protozool. 1983;30:332-334.
200. Dunn LA, Boreham PFL. The *in vitro* activity of drugs against *Blastocystis hominis*. J Antimicrob Chemother. 1991;27:507-516.
201. Romero Cabello R, Guerrero LR, Munoz Garcia MR, et al. Nitazoxanide for the treatment of intestinal protozoan and helminthic infections in Mexico. Trans R Soc Trop Med Hyg. 1997;91:701-703.

CHAPTER **282**

Microsporidiosis

LOUIS M. WEISS

The Microsporidia are a group of obligate eukaryotic intracellular parasites first recognized almost 150 years ago with the description of *Nosema bombycis,* a parasite of silkworms that causes the disease pebrine in these economically important insects. The class or order Microsporidia was elevated to the phylum Microspora by Sprague and Vávra in 1977.[1] In 1998 Sprague and Becnel suggested that the term Microsporidia instead be used for the phylum name, as "Microsporidia" is a proper name and should be capitalized.[2]

The term microsporidian should be used, not Microsporidium, which is used at the generic level for Microsporidia of unknown phylogenetic placement (e.g., *Microsporidium ceylonesis*). Microsporidia have historically been considered "primitive" protozoa, although molecular phylogenetic analysis has led to the recognition that these organisms are not "primitive" but degenerate, and that they are related to the fungi and not to other protozoa. Such molecular phylogeny has also led to the recognition that the traditional phylogeny of these organisms based on structural observations may not reflect the "true" relationships among the various microsporidian species and genera.

The Microsporidia infect virtually all animal phyla, including other protists. They are important agricultural parasites in insects, fish, laboratory rodents, rabbits, fur-bearing animals, and primates[3]; and they have been described in dogs and birds kept as household pets.[3,4] Some species of Microsporidia have been used as pesticides for the biologic control of destructive species of grasshoppers and locusts.[5] In their hosts, most Microsporidia infect the digestive tract, but infections of the reproductive, respiratory, muscle, excretory, and nervous systems have been documented.[3,6] Microsporidia were recognized in mammalian tissue samples more than 75 years ago[7] and were first suspected as being a cause of human disease in 1959,[8] when they were found in a child with encephalitis. These organisms are most likely zoonotic or water-borne infections (or both). In the immunnosuppressed host [e.g., those treated with immunosuppressive drugs or infected with human immunodeficiency virus (HIV), particularly at advanced stages of the disease], Microsporidia can produce a wide range of clinical diseases. Reports of diarrheal syndromes associated with microsporidiosis and HIV infection were first reported in 1985,[9] and the number of articles describing human disease increased rapidly after 1990. In addition to gastrointestinal tract involvement, it has been recognized that Microsporidia can infect virtually any organ system; and in patients with encephalitis, ocular infection, sinusitis, myositis, and disseminated infection are well described in the literature. These organisms have also been reported in immunocompetent individuals.

The phylum Microsporidia (Microspora) contains more than 1000 species distributed into 144 genera, of which the following have been demonstrated in human disease (Table 282-1)[3,10]: *Nosema* (*N. corneum* renamed *Vittaforma corneae*[11] and *N. algerae* renamed *Brachiola algerae*[12]), *Pleistophora, Encephalitozoon, Enterocytozoon,*[9] *Septata*[13] (reclassified as *Encephalitozoon*[14]), *Trachipleistophora,*[15,16] *Brachiola,*[12] and *Microsporidium.*[3] *Encephalitozoon hellem (Enc. hellem)* has been associated with superficial keratoconjunctivitis, sinusitis, respiratory disease, prostatic abscesses, and disseminated infection.[3,6,17] *Encephalitozoon cuniculi (Enc. cuniculi)* has been associated with hepatitis, encephalitis, and disseminated disease.[18-20] *Encephalitozoon (Septata) intestinalis* is associated with diarrhea, disseminated infection, and superficial keratoconjunctivitis.[13,21,22] *Nosema, Vittaforma,* and *Microsporidium* have been associated with stromal keratitis associated with trauma in immunocompetent hosts.[17,23] *Pleistophora, Brachiola,* and *Trachipleistophora* have been associated with myositis.[15,24-26] *Trachipleistophora* has been associated with encephalitis and disseminated disease.[15,16,27] *Enterocytozoon bieneusi (Ent. bieneusi),* originally described in humans,[9] is associated with malabsorption, diarrhea, and cholangitis.[28,29]

GENERAL CHARACTERISTICS

The Microsporidia are eukaryotes containing a nucleus with a nuclear envelope, an intracytoplasmic membrane system, chromosome separation on mitotic spindles, and vesicular Golgi.[30] In addition, a mitochondrial "remnant" organelle was reported in the microsporidian *Trachipleistophora hominis.*[31] Microsporidia are ubiquitous in the environment and infect almost all animal phyla (invertebrate and vertebrate hosts).[3,6,10] Microsporidia form characteristic unicellular spores (Fig. 282-1) that are environmentally resistant. The spore size and shape vary depending on the species. Whereas microsporidian spores can be as large as 12 μm, the microsporidia infecting humans have spores that range from 1.0 to 3.0 μm × 1.5 to 4.0 μm in size and are usually ovoid. The structure of the spore is characteristic of the phylum.[3,32] The spore coat consists of an electron-dense, proteinaceous exospore, an electron-lucent endospore composed of chitin and protein, and an inner membrane or plasmalemma.[33] A defining characteristic of all microsporidia is an extrusion apparatus that consists of a polar tube attached to the inside of the anterior end of the spore by an anchoring disk and, depending on the species, forms 4 to approximately 30 coils around the sporoplasm in the spore. During germination the polar tube rapidly everts, forming a hollow tube that brings the sporoplasm into

TABLE 282-1 Microsporidia Identified as Pathogenic to Humans

Genus and Species	Reported Infections	Animal Hosts‡
Encephalitozoon		
Enc. cuniculi*	Hepatitis, peritonitis, encephalitis,† urethritis, prostatitis, nephritis, sinusitis, keratoconjunctivitis, cystitis, diarrhea,† cellulitis, disseminated infection	Mammals (rabbits, rodents, carnivores, primates)
Enc. hellem*	Keratoconjunctivitis, sinusitis, pneumonitis, nephritis, prostatitis, urethritis, cystitis, diarrhea, disseminated infection	Psittacine birds (parrots, lovebirds, budgerigars), birds (ostrich, hummingbirds, finches)
Enc. intestinalis*	Diarrhea,† intestinal perforation, cholangitis, nephritis, keratoconjunctivitis	Mammals (donkeys, dogs, pigs, cows, goats, primates)
Enterocytozoon bieneusi	Diarrhea,† wasting syndrome, cholangitis, rhinitis, bronchitis	Mammals (pigs, primates, cows, dogs, cats), birds (chickens)
Trachipleistophora		
T. hominis*	Myositis, keratoconjunctivitis, sinusitis	None
T. anthropopthera	Encephalitis, disseminated infection	None
Pleistophora sp.		
P. ronneafiei	Myositis	None
Pleistophora sp.	Myositis†	Fish
Brachiola		
B. vesicularum	Myositis	None
B. (Nosema) algerae*	Keratoconjunctivitis, myositis, skin infection	Mosquitoes
B. (Nosema) connori	Disseminated infection	
Nosema		
N. ocularum	Keratoconjunctivitis†	None
Vittaforma corneae*	Keratoconjunctivitis,† urinary tract infection	None
Microsporidium		
M. africanus	Corneal ulcer†	None
M. ceylonesis	Corneal ulcer†	None

*Organism can be grown in tissue culture.
†Cases reported in immunocompetent hosts.
‡Animals in which organism has been found other than humans.

intimate contact with the host cell (Fig. 282-2). The polar tube provides a bridge to deliver the sporoplasm to the host cell. The mechanism by which the polar tube interacts with the host cell membrane is not known, but it may require the participation of host cell proteins such as actin.[34] It is possible that the sporoplasm interacts with the host cell membrane as it emerges from the polar tube. If a spore is phagocytosed by a host cell, germination occurs; and the polar tube can pierce the phagocytic vacuole, delivering the sporoplasm into the host cell cytoplasm. The overall process of germination and formation of the polar tube inoculates the sporoplasm directly into a host cell, functioning essentially like a hypodermic needle.[35,36]

Conditions that promote germination vary widely among species, presumably reflecting the organisms' adaptation to their host and external environment[37,38] (reviewed by Keohane and Weiss[39]). Conditions that promote spore discharge include pH shifts, dehydration followed by rehydration, various cations and anions, mucin or polyanions, hydrogen peroxide, ultraviolet irradiation, and the calcium ionophore A 23187. Inhibitors of spore discharge include magnesium chloride, ammonium chloride, low salt concentrations, sodium fluoride, ultraviolet light, temperatures higher than 40° C, calcium channel antagonists, calmodulin inhibitors, cytochalasin D, demecolcine, and itraconazole. Regardless of the stimuli required for activation, most Microsporidia appear to exhibit the same response to the stimuli: an increase in intrasporal osmotic pressure. This results in an influx of water into the spore accompanied by swelling of the polaroplasts and posterior vacuole prior to spore discharge. In *Brachiola (Nosema) algerae,* it has been proposed that activation brings trehalose in contact with the enzyme trehalase, causing an increase in osmotic pressure.[40,41] The polar tube discharges from the anterior pole of the spore in an explosive reaction, occurring within less than 2 seconds; and it is thought to form a hollow tube by a process of eversion, similar to everting the finger of a glove.[35]

Microsporidia display a number of characteristics that are unusual for eukaryotic organisms. They have prokaryotic-size ribosomes[42] that do not have a 5.8S ribosome subunit but do have sequences homologous to the 5.8S region in the 23S subunit.[43] The small-subunit rRNA of several Microsporidia have been sequenced and found to be signif-

icantly shorter than both eukaryotic and prokaryotic small-subunit rRNA.[44,45] These rRNA genes are in a subtelometeric location on each chromosome of *Enc. cuniculi*[46,47] and lack the paromomycin binding site seen in protozoa and animals.[48] The karyotype of several members of the phylum Microspora has been determined by pulsed-field electrophoresis. The genome size of the microsporidia varies from 2.3 to 19.5 Mb.[49] The genomic size of the Encephalitizoonidae is less than 3.0 Mb, making them the smallest eukaryotic nuclear genomes so far identified.[46] Chromosomal analysis of *Enc. cuniculi* suggests that it is diploid.[50] The karyotypes of a few members of the phylum Microspora have been determined by pulsed-field electrophoresis.[49] Small-subunit rRNA (16S rRNA) diverges greatly from the small-subunit rRNA sequences of other eukaryotes, and microsporidian rRNA genes are significantly shorter than those of both eukaryotes and prokaryotes.[45,51] Sequence data of rRNA from the microsporidia have been used to develop diagnostic polymerase chain reaction (PCR) primers and to study phylogenetic relationships[52,53] (reviewed by Weiss and Vossbrinck[45]).

Use of cloned rRNA genes for the development of a microsporidian molecular phylogeny provides additional evidence for the assignment of a microsporidian to specific genera and gives us the ability to distinguish morphologically similar Microsporidia at the species level. Analysis of the rRNA genes of a variety of Microsporidia highlights the polyphyletic nature of the Microsporidia and brings into doubt the use of any single character for developing higher taxonomic groupings. For example, *Enc. hellem* and *Enc. cuniculi* are indistinguishable at the ultrastructural level, and *Enc. intestinalis* has a distinct extracellular matrix surrounding the sporoblasts and spores; based on rDNA analysis, *Enc. intestinalis* and *Enc. cuniculi* are more similar to each other than to *Enc. hellem.*[54]

Molecular relationships may also be useful for identifying the environmental reservoir for microsporidia that infect humans. *Enc. cuniculi* isolates from various animal species have been identified and separated based on the number of tetranucleotide repeats (5′GTTT3′) in the intergenic spacer region of their rRNA genes.[55] Differences have also been found in the intergenic spacer region of rRNA genes of *Ent. bieneusi.*[56]

FIGURE 282-1. Structure of a microsporidian spore. Depending on the species, the size of the spore can vary from 1 to 10 μm and the number of polar tubule coils can vary from a few to 30 or more. Extrusion apparatus consists of the polar tube (PT), vesiculotubular polaroplast (Vpl), lamellar polaroplast (Pl), anchoring disk (AD) and manubrium (M). This organelle is characteristic of the Microsporidia. A cross section of the coiled polar tube is illustrated. The nucleus (Nu) may be single (such as in *Encephalitozoon* spp.) or a pair of abutted nuclei termed a diplokaryon (such as in *Nosema* spp.). The endospore (En) is an inner thicker electron-lucent region. The exospore (Ex) is an outer electron-dense region. The plasma membrane (Pm) separates the spore coat from the sporoplasm (Sp), which contains ribosomes in a coiled helical array. The posterior vacuole (PV) is a membrane-bound structure. *(Reproduced with permission from Wittner M, Weiss LM, eds. The Microsporidia and Microsporidiosis. Washington, DC: ASM Press; 1999.)*

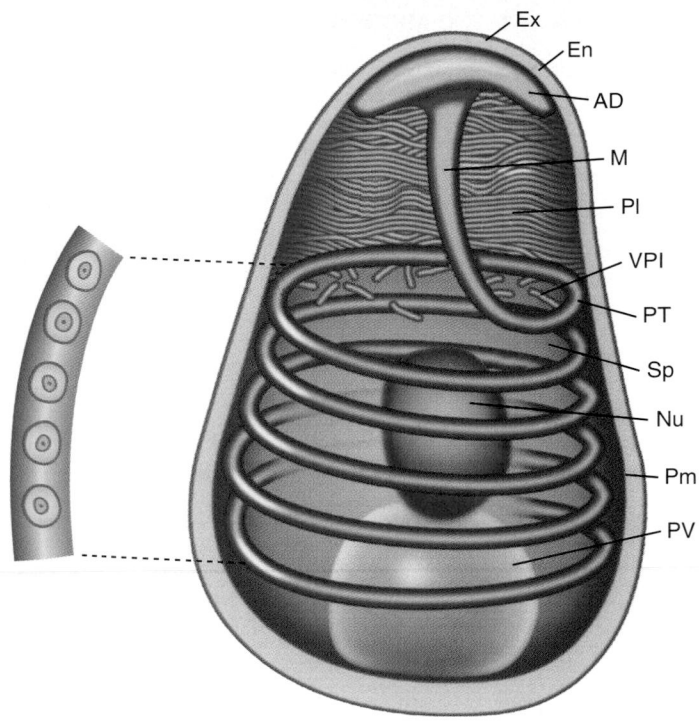

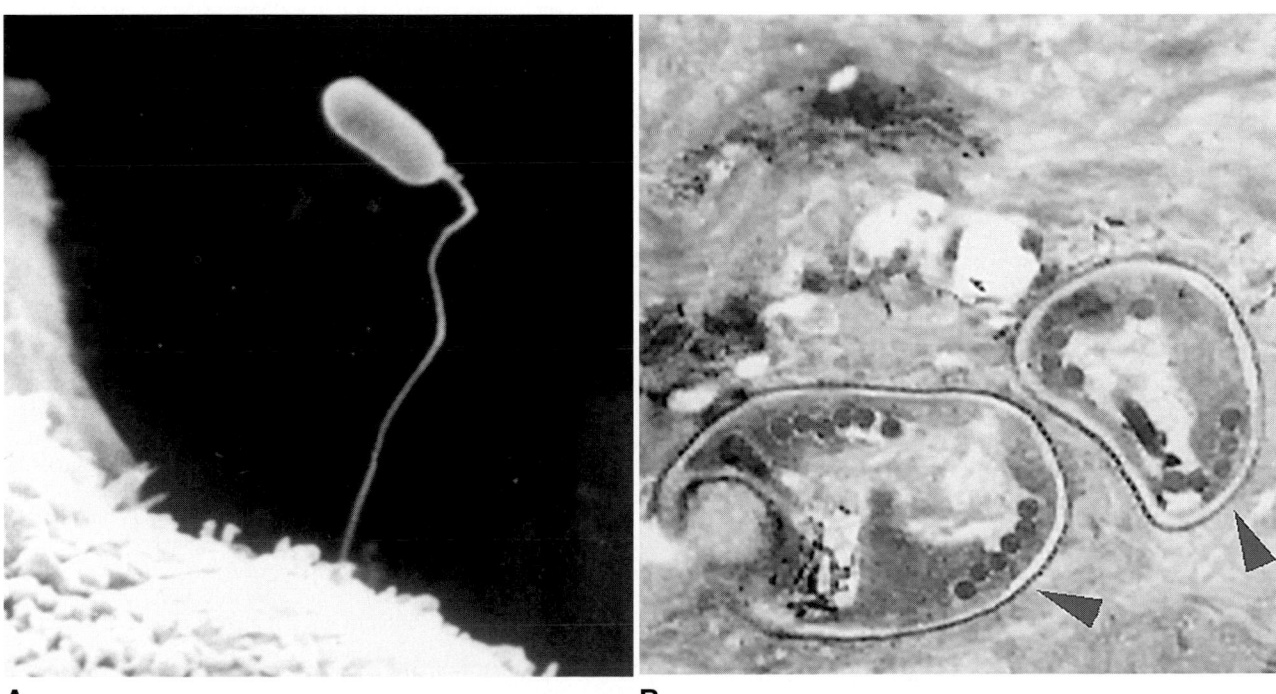

A   B

FIGURE 282-2. Microsporidian polar tube. **A,** Scanning electron micrograph of a tissue culture demonstrating *Encephalitozoon intestinalis* invading a Vero cell in vitro. *(Reproduced with permission from Kock NP. Diagnosis of Human Pathogenic Microsporidia. Dissertation, Berhard Nocht Institiute for Tropical Medicine, Hamburg, Germany. With permission of N.P. Koch, C. Schmertz, and J. Schottelius.)* **B,** Transmission electron micrograph of conjunctival scraping demonstrating Microsporidia *(Encephalitozoon hellem).* **Arrowheads** identify thick-walled spores with single nuclei and five or six coils of polar tubes.

PHYLOGENY OF THE MICROSPORIDIA

Microsporidia are currently classified based on their ultrastructural features, including the size and morphology of the spores, number of coils of the polar tube, developmental life cycle, and host-parasite relationship (see Fig. 282-2). Tuzet et al.,[57] Sprague,[1] Larsson,[58] Issi,[59] Weiser,[60] and Sprague et al.[10] have provided overviews of the history, ultrastructural and structural characteristics, and life cycle differences among taxa of Microsporidia. Microsporidia can be divided into three main groups: (1) The "primitive" (Metchnikovellidae) hyperparasites of gregarines in annelids may be distinguished from the other Microsporidia by the presence of a rudimentary polar filament and the spore being without a polaroplast. (2) The Chytridopsidae, Hesseidsae, and Burkeidae may be seen as "intermediates," having a short polar filament and minimal development of the polaroplast and endospore. (3) The "higher" Microsporidia have a well developed polar filament, polaroplast, and posterior vacuole. Differences among modern classifications of Microsporidia focus on the characteristics used to divide the third group, the "higher" Microsporidia, into subgroups. Molecular analysis of rRNA genes has begun to alter this classification system.[45,61] Antigenic differences between Microsporidia demonstrable by sodium dodecylsulfate polyacyramine gel electrophoresis and Western blot analysis have been used as adjunctive evidence when determining phylogenetic relationships among the Microsporidia infecting humans.[14,62]

The general features of the life cycle are as follows: (1) Spores are ingested or inhaled and then germinate, resulting in extension of the polar tube, which injects the sporoplasm into the host cell. (2) Merogony follows, during which the injected sporoplasm develops into meronts (the proliferative stage), which multiply, depending on the species, by either binary fission or multiple fission, forming multinucleate plasmodial forms. (3) The next step is sporogony, during which meront cell membranes thicken to form sporonts. After subsequent division the sporonts give rise to sporoblasts, which go on to form mature spores without additional multiplication. Once a host cell becomes distended with mature spores, the cell ruptures, releasing mature spores into the environment, thereby completing the life cycle. The combination of multiplication during merogony and sporogony results in a large number of spores being produced from a single infection and illustrates the enormous reproductive potential of these organisms.

Molecular phylogenetic data indicates that the Microsporidia are related to fungi and are not "primitive eukaryotes."[63-65] As early as 1994, based on β-tubulin sequence analysis, it was suggested that the Microsporidia were not ancient eukaryotes but were related to the fungi.[66] Keeling and Doolittle reported similar results for α-tubulin from three species of Microsporidia (*Encephalitozoon hellem, Nosema locustae, Spraguea lophii*) and for β-tubulin from *Encephalitozoon hellem*.[67] Analysis of the heat shock protein gene (*hsp70*) for *Nosema locustae, Vairimorpha necatrix, Encephalitozoon cuniculi, Nosema locustae,* and *Encephalitozoon hellem* provided confirmatory evidence of this relationship.[68-71] Comparative analysis of the largest subunit of the RNA polymerase II (*RPB1*) gene[65] produced a phylogeny similar to the result obtained from an analysis of *hsp70* or the β-tubulin gene. Additional evidence for the relationship of Microsporidia to the fungi includes the following: (1) The *Enc. cuniculi* genes for thymidylate synthase and dihydrofolate reductase are separate genes.[72] (2) The small-subunit rRNA gene of microsporidia lacks a paromomycin binding site, similar to the fungi.[73] (3) The EF-1α sequence of the microsporidian *Glugea plecoglossi* has an insertion that is found only in fungi and animals, not in protozoa.[65,73,74] (4) Microsporidia display similarities to the fungi during mitosis (e.g., closed mitosis and spindle pole bodies[75]) and meiosis.[76] (5) Microsporidia have chitin in their spore wall and store trehalose, as do fungi. (6) Analyses of glutamyl-tRNA synthetase, seryl-tRNA synthetase, vacuolar ATPase, TATA box binding protein, seryl-tRNA synthetase, transcription initiation factor IIB, subunit A of vacuolar ATPase, and a GTP-binding protein and transcription factor IIB sequences[65,77,78] support a relationship between the Microsporidia and fungi. (7) Analysis of the *Enc. cuniculi* genome demonstrates that many of the *Enc. cuniculi* proteins are most similar to fungal homologues.[78] (8) The presence in *Enc. cuniculi* of the principal enzymes for the synthesis and degradation of trehalose confirm that this disaccharide could be the major sugar reserve in Microsporidia, as is seen in many fungi. Analysis of glycosylation pathways suggest that *O*-mannosylation (e.g., *O*-linked glycosylation with mannose), as seen in fungi, also occurs in Microsporidia. Evidence suggests that such *O*-mannosylation does indeed occur on the major polar tube protein PTP1 (L.M. Weiss, unpublished data). Keeling,[79] in an analysis of β-tubulin data that included additional species of Microsporidia and more fungal phyla, suggested that the Microsporidia were a sister group to the Zygomycota.

EPIDEMIOLOGY

Microsporidian spores are commonly found in surface water, and human pathogenic Microsporidia have been found in municipal water supplies, tertiary sewage effluent, and ground water.[80-83] It is possible that many of the microsporidia are water-borne pathogens. Water contact has been found to be an independent risk factor for microsporidiosis in some studies[84,85] but not in others.[86,87] *Enc. cuniculi* spores remain viable for 6 days when in water and 4 weeks when dry at 22° C; and *Nosema bombycis* spores may remain viable for 10 years in distilled water.[88] Spores may be killed, however, by exposure for 30 minutes to 70% ethanol, 1% formaldehyde, or 2% Lysol or by autoclaving at 120° C for 10 minutes.[88] Most microsporidian infections are transmitted by oral ingestion of spores, with the site of initial infection being the gastrointestinal tract. Viable infective spores of Microsporidia are present in multiple body fluids (e.g., stool, urine, respiratory secretions) during infection, suggesting that person-to-person transmission can occur and that ocular infection may be transmitted by external autoinoculation due to contaminated fingers.[89] It has been possible to transmit *Enc. cuniculi* via rectal infection in rabbits, suggesting the possibility of sexual transmission.[90] *Encephalitozoon hellem* has been demonstrated in the respiratory mucosa as well as in the prostate and urogenital tract of patients, raising the possibility of respiratory and sexual transmission in humans.[91,92] Person-to-person transmission is supported by concurrent infections in cohabiting homosexual men.[93] Although congenital transmission of *Enc. cuniculi* has been demonstrated in rabbits, mice, dogs, horses, foxes, and squirrel monkeys, no such congenital transmission has been demonstrated in humans.[94]

It is possible that many of the Microsporidia are zoonotic infections in humans (see Table 282-1). Microsporidia of the genus *Encephalitozoon* are widely distributed parasites of mammals and birds, and the onset of microsporidiosis has been associated with exposure to livestock, fowl, and pets.[95] *Enc. hellem* infections have been described in lovebirds and budgerigars (parakeets),[4] and one case of *Enc. hellem* infection has been reported in a patient who had two pet lovebirds.[96] Up to 30% of dogs in animal shelters may excrete microsporidia in their stools.[95] Microsporidia of the genus *Encephalitozoon* were found in the stools of many animals in an epidemiologic survey in Mexico.[84] *Enterocytozoon bieneusi* has been reported in pigs,[97] dogs,[98] chickens,[99] and simian immunodeficiency virus (SIV)-infected rhesus monkeys.[100] Enterocytozoonidae such as *Nucleospora* (previously *Enterocytozoon*) *salmonis* are pathogens found in fish. *Nosema* and *Vittaforma* infections are believed to be due to traumatic inoculation of environmental spores of insect pathogens into the cornea.[11,23,101]

Although initially regarded as rare, Microsporidia are now believed to be common enteric pathogens that cause self-limited or asymptomatic infections in normal hosts.[95,102] Cases of microsporidiosis have been identified from all continents except Antarctica.[93,95,103-109] Surveys of pathogens seen in stool samples in Africa, Asia, South America, and Central America have demonstrated that Microsporidia are often found during careful stool examinations.

In immunocompetent hosts, most reported cases of microsporidiosis manifested as self-limited diarrhea. They have included cases of *Ent. bieneusi* infections in travelers to and residents of tropical countries[81,102,105,110-116] and *Enc. intestinalis* infections in travelers to and residents of tropical countries.[117] In contrast, in immunodeficient hosts [e.g., those with acquired immunodeficiency syndrome (AIDS) or who have undergone transplantation], most reported cases have manifested as diarrhea with wasting syndrome and disseminated infection. Infections with *Ent. bieneusi* have been reported in patients with liver or heart-lung transplantation; and *Encephalitozoon* sp. infections have been reported in patients with kidney, pancreas, liver, or bone marrow transplantation.[118-125] A case of chronic bilateral keratoconjunctivitis due to *Encephalitozoon* sp. has been reported in a patient taking prednisone (20 mg/day).[126]

Reported prevalence rates in the 25 studies conducted on patients with HIV infection before the widespread use of highly active antiretroviral therapy (HAART) (1989–1998) varied between 2% and 70% depending on the symptoms of the population studied and the diagnostic techniques employed.[6,93,95,103,109,127-132] These studies suggest that asymptomatic carriage can occur in immunocompromised patients. Co-infection with different Microsporidia or other enteric pathogens can occur. There was no overall trend in these prevalence studies with regard to country of origin or other demographic characteristics. When combined, these studies identified 375 *Ent. bieneusi* infections among 2400 patients with chronic diarrhea, for a prevalence of 15% in this population. It is clear that since the institution of HAART and its associated immune reconstitution the prevalence of diarrhea among AIDS patients has decreased, as has the incidence of microsporidiosis. Based on these studies Microsporidia appear to demonstrate strength of association, coherence, and reproducibility with respect to being etiologic for a diarrheal syndrome. Further evidence of the association of Microsporidia with diarrhea is provided by the utility of albendazole in the treatment of microsporidian infection. Therapy with albendazole results in cure of the diarrhea associated with elimination of *Enc. intestinalis* from the stool of infected patients.[133] Treatment with fumagillin has a similar effect in patients with *Ent. bieneusi* infection.[134,135]

Serosurveys in humans have demonstrated a high prevalence of antibodies to *Enc. cuniculi* and *Enc. hellem*, suggesting that asymptomatic infection may be common.[106,136] Serologic cross-reactivity among microsporidia has been demonstrated by both immunofluorescence tests[137] and Western blotting.[138] Singh et al. found positive titers in 6 of 69 healthy adults in England, 38 of 89 Nigerians with tuberculosis, 13 of 70 Malaysians with filariasis, and 33 of 92 Ghanians with malaria.[139] In another study, 14 of 115 travelers returning from the tropics and none of 48 nontravelers were seropositive.[140] In a study of HIV-positive men, 10 of 30 were seropositive, and all had traveled to the tropics.[141] Antibodies to *Enc. intestinalis* were found among 5% of pregnant French women and 8% of Dutch blood donors.[142] In HIV-positive Czech patients 5.3% were seropositive to *Enc. cuniculi* and 1.3% to *Enc. hellem*.[143] In Slovakia, 5.1% of slaughterhouse workers were seropositive to *Encephalitozoon* sp.[144] In a survey of blood donors in the United States, 5% of donors had antibodies to *Enc. hellem* PTP1 antigen (L.M. Weiss, unpublished observations). Overall, these studies suggest that exposure to Microsporidia is common and that asymptomatic infection may be more common than originally suspected.

IMMUNOLOGY

Infection with *Enc. cuniculi* in many mammals results in chronic infection with persistently high antibody titers and ongoing inflammation (e.g., persistent encephalitis in rabbits and chronic renal disease and congenital transmission in foxes). In immunocompetent murine models of *Enc. cuniculi* infection, ascites develops and then clears; however, if corticosteroids are administered, the mice redevelop ascites, consistent with latent persistence of Microsporidia in these animals.[145] In SCID or athymic mice, infection with *Enc. cuniculi* results

in death, with visceral dissemination of the organism and persistent ascites.[146] Adoptive transfer of sensitized syngeneic T-enriched spleen cells protects athymic or SCID mice against lethal *Enc. cuniculi* infection.[147,148] Transfer of naive lymphocytes or hyperimmune serum failed to protect or prolong the survival of these mice. Cytokine-activated murine peritoneal macrophages can inhibit the replication of *E. cuniculi* in vitro.[149] This inhibition is probably mediated by nitric oxide, as studies demonstrate that inhibition of nitric oxide synthesis inhibited such killing.[150] Mice deficient in inducible nitric oxide synthase had no change in susceptibility to *Enc. cuniculi* infection[151]; therefore nitric oxide is not the major mechanism for controlling this organism.

Humoral immunity is not sufficient for protection against *Enc. cuniculi* infection, as adoptive transfer of immune B lymphocytes into athymic BALB/c (nu/nu) or SCID mice or passive transfer of hyperimmune serum into athymic mice does not protect these animals from death after infection. Nonetheless, during *Enc. cuniculi* infection there is a strong antibody response to many components of this organism, and many of these antibodies are cross-reactive with other microsporidia. Maternal antibodies protect newborn rabbits from infection with *Enc. cuniculi* during the first 2 weeks of life.[152] The in vitro infectivity of microsporidia is reduced by treatment with immune serum and complement,[147] monoclonal antibody (mAb 3B6) to the spore coat,[153] or polyclonal antibodies to polar tube protein-1 (PTP1) (L.M. Weiss, unpublished data). It is therefore likely that antibodies play a role in limiting infection in the host, although they are clearly not sufficient to prevent mortality or to cure infection.

Interferon gamma (IFNγ) and interleukin-12 (IL-12) are important for protective immunity against a number of intracellular viral, bacterial, and parasitic infections.[154] Based on in vitro observations, it has been suggested that IFNγ plays an important role in the protective immunity against *Enc. cuniculi* infection. Both natural killer (NK) cells and γδ T cells, which are increased at early stages of infection, are likely important sources of IFNγ production. Studies with *Enc. intestinalis* and *Enc. cuniculi* have demonstrated that INFγ knockout mice cannot clear infection.[155] Treatment of *Enc. cuniculi*-infected mice with neutralizing antibody to INFγ or IL-12 results in increased mortality.[151] The importance of IL-12 is illustrated by the fact that lethal infection with *Enc. cuniculi* also occurs in p40 knockout mice (which are unable to produce IL-12).[156]

The role of individual T cell subtypes during *Enc. cuniculi* infection has been evaluated in murine models.[156] Phenotypic analysis of the spleen cells from infected animals revealed an increase in the CD8+ T cell population starting at day 10 after infection with no significant increase in CD4+ T cells. Mice deficient in CD8+ cells succumb to the parasitic challenge. In contrast, there was no change in mortality for mice deficient in CD4+ cells. The protective effect of CD8+ T cells is mediated by their ability to produce cytokines and to reduce the parasite load by killing the infected targets in the host tissue.[157] The major killing mechanism exhibited by CD8+ T cells is via the perforin pathway, and mice lacking the perforin gene die when infected with *Enc. cuniculi*. These observations suggest that the cytotoxic T cell response is a key factor in the immune response to *Enc. cuniculi*-infected mice.[156] In most cases CD8+ T cells are primed via IL-2-producing CD4+ T cells, although a normal in vivo CD8+ T cell response in the absence of CD4+ T cells has been described with many viral infections and appears also to occur with *Enc. cuniculi* infection. A normal antigen-specific CD8+ T cell response to *Enc. cuniculi* infection has been found to occur in CD4 knockout mice.

There are scant data to confirm the immune response to Microsporidia in humans. It is clear that a strong humoral response occurs during infection and that it includes antibodies that react with the spore wall and polar tube. The immunosuppressive states associated with microsporidiosis (e.g., AIDS and transplantation) are those that inhibit cell-mediated immunity. Microsporidiosis is usually seen in HIV-infected patients when there is a profound defect in cell-mediated immunity (e.g., a CD4+ cell count less than 100/mm³); spontaneous

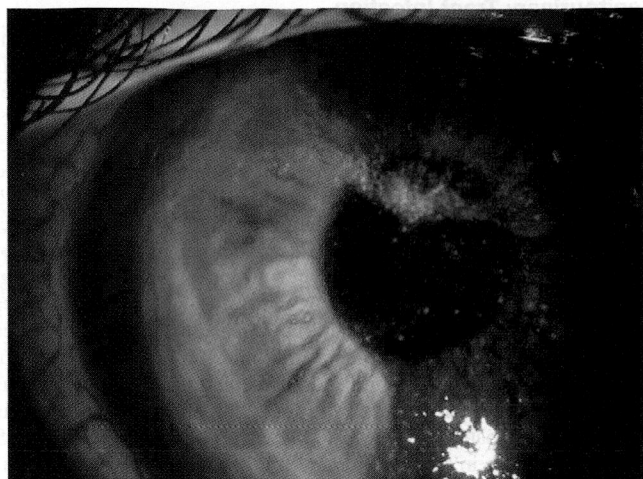

FIGURE 282-4. Ocular examination of a patient with keratoconjunctivitis due to *Encephalitozoon hellem*. Slit lamp examination findings in a patient with punctuate keratoconjunctivitis. A conjunctival scraping from this patient demonstrated spores consistent with *Enc. hellem* (see Fig. 282-2B). Sequencing of the small-subunit rRNA gene obtained by the polymerase chain reaction from this conjunctival biopsy confirmed that the infection was due to *Enc. hellem*.

lens wearers. *Vittaforma corneae, Microsporidium africanum, Microsporidium celonensis,* and *Nosema ocularum* have also been reported to cause infection in immunocompetent patients. Infections with these species of microsporidia have usually involved deeper levels of the corneal stroma and have often been associated with trauma. Biopsies have demonstrated necrosis and acute inflammatory cells with some giant cells in several cases. Clinically, these patients have a corneal stromal keratitis and occasionally uveitis.

Musculoskeletal Infection

Myositis with inflammation due to several Microsporidia has been described in humans. The organisms in these case reports have included *Pleistophora ronneafiei, Pleistophora* sp., *Trachipleistophora hominis, Brachiola vesicularum,* and *Brachiola (Nosema) algerae.*[12,15,25,26,176]

The prevalence or incidence of microsporidian myositis in human is not known. Biopsies from the cases of *Pleistophora* sp. infection demonstrated atrophic and degenerating muscle fibers infiltrated with focal clusters of large microsporidian spores that were up to 3.4 μm in length. There was a mixed inflammatory response consisting of plasma cells, lymphocytes, eosinophils, and histiocytes that was mild in the two cases occurring in AIDS patients but severe in the case involving an HIV-seronegative person.[25,177,178] The *T. hominis* infection that occurred in a patient with AIDS was associated with degeneration, atrophy, scarring, and intense inflammation.[15] The *B. vesicularum* infection occurred in an AIDS patient and was associated with cytolysis around the spores in the muscle fibers, but no cellular immune response was seen.[12] The *B. algerae* infection occurred in a patient with rheumatoid arthritis treated with steroids and monoclonal antibody to tumor necrosis factor-α (TNFα).[176] There was a minimal cellular response to the numerous spores present in the muscle fibers.

Sinus and Respiratory Infection

Respiratory tract involvement is often seen with disseminated infections due to the Encephalitozoonidae.[179] The pathologic features are nonspecific and may include rhinitis, sinusitis, and nasal polyposis in any combination.[180-186] A tongue ulcer containing *Enc. cuniculi* spores was reported in a patient with disseminated infection with this organism.[187] In a study of patients presenting with keratitis due to *Enc. hellem,* spores of this organism were present in many of these patients' sputum samples in the absence of respiratory symptoms.[188] *Encephalitozoon hellem* infection of the entire length of the respiratory tract including the terminal bronchioles, associated with erosive tracheitis, bronchitis, and bronchiolitis, has been described in an autopsy report.[188] Spores were seen in the epithelial cells, neutrophils in the bronchiolar wall, cells lining the aveoli, and extracellularly in the alveolar spaces. Case reports have confirmed that *Enc. cuniculi, Enc. hellem,* and *Enc. intestinalis* can cause bronchiolitis with or without pneumonia. Sinus biopsies in AIDS patients with chronic sinusitis and microsporidiosis have demonstrated spores in epithelium and supporting structures.[180-186,189] The inflammatory response has been variable, with lymphocytes, neutrophils, macrophages, and occasional granuloma formation. Respiratory tract infection due to *Ent. bieneusi* has been reported twice, with spores being found in stool, brochoalveolar lavage fluid, and transbrochial biopsy specimens.[190,191] A case of rinosinusitis due to *Ent. bieneusi* has also been reported.[192] It has been suggested that these cases reflect contamination and colonization of the respiratory tract due to vomiting rather than dissemination of this organism from the gastrointestinal tract.

Skin

Microsporidia infections of the skin have been described. In a child with leukemia, the infection was due to *B. algerae,* with spores infecting the cellular elements of the dermis.[193] In a second case an *Encephalitozoon* sp. was reported to be the cause of nodular skin lesions.[194,195]

CLINICAL MANIFESTATIONS

The clinical manifestations of microsporidiosis are shown in Table 282-1.

Microsporidian Infection in Non-AIDS Patients

Levaditi et al. suggested that Microsporidia were associated with human disease as early as 1923,[196] but the first definitive proof of human infection was not reported for another 50 years. In 1973, a 4-month-old athymic male infant died with severe diarrhea and malabsorption. At autopsy, the microsporidian *Brachiola (Nosema) connori* was discovered in the lungs, stomach, small and large bowel, kidneys, adrenal glands, myocardium, liver, and diaphragm.[197]

In all patients (those with or without HIV infection) the most common symptomatic microsporidian infection is probably diarrhea.[84,93,104,105,110,113,117-119,198] *Ent. bieneusi* has been identified as a cause of self-limited diarrhea in immunocompetent hosts including travelers[93,102,115-117,199,200]; and in epidemiologic studies *Ent. bieneusi* has been identified in 1% to 10% of African children with diarrhea[103,201,202] as well as in patients undergoing liver and bone marrow transplantation.[118-125,172,173,203,204] Clinical manifestations have included watery, nonbloody diarrhea; nausea; diffuse abdominal pain; and fever. Diarrhea tends to be self-limited in immunocompetent patients but is persistent in patients with immunosuppression due to transplantation. *Encephalitozoon intestinalis* was found in 7.8% of the stools of patients in a survey regarding the etiology of diarrhea in Mexico[84] and has been described in travelers with chronic diarrhea.[117]

Ocular infections with ulcer or deep cornea stroma infection associated with eye pain have also been reported in immunocompetent patients. In 1973 and 1981, two cases of corneal microsporidios is due to *Microsporidium africanus* in Botswana[205] and *Microsporidium ceylonesis* in Sri Lanka were described.[206] Additional cases of microsporidian keratitis have been identified in immunocompetent hosts.[3] One of these organisms was classified as *N. ocularum,*[207] and the other, which was successfully propagated in vitro, was named *N. corneum*[23] (now *V. cornea*[11]). *Brachiola algerae* infection of the cornea has also been reported.[193] Among these immunologically normal patients with corneal infections: one patient required enucleation,[205] one underwent unsuccessful penetrating keratoplasty,[206] one was successfully treated with a corneal transplant,[175] and the last was maintained on a variety of topical agents without effect until keratoplasty.[208]

Cerebral infections due to *Enc. cuniculi* are commonly described in many animals but have been reported only rarely in immunocompetent humans. *Encephalitozoon* infection was demonstrated in a 3-year-old boy with seizures and hepatomegaly by positive immunoglobulin G (IgG) and IgM indirect immunofluorescence assays (using *Enc. cuniculi* as the antigen).[136] Recurrent fever infection with *Encephalitozoon* sp. was also reported in a 9-year-old Japanese boy with headache, vomiting, and spastic convulsions.[8]

Pleistophora sp. was identified in the skeletal muscle of an HIV-negative patient as well as HIV-positive patients with myositis associated with normal creatine phosphokinase (CPK) levels.[25,26,177,178] *Brachiola algerae* infection of the skin has been seen in a patient with leukemia[193] and in another patient with myositis who had significant elevations in CPK and muscle pain; the latter patient had rheumatoid arthritis treated with steroids and antibody to TNFα.[176]

Microsporidian Infection in AIDS Patients

Microsporidia were recognized as opportunistic pathogens causing diarrhea and wasting in AIDS patients in 1985.[9] Since then, although most reported cases still involved diarrhea, the spectrum of diseases caused by these organisms has expanded to include keratoconjunctivitis, disseminated disease, hepatitis, myositis, sinusitis, kidney and urogenital infection, ascites, and cholangitis, as well as no symptoms at all.[3,6,29]

Enterocytozoonidae

Gastrointestinal infection is most common with *Ent. bieneusi,* and the presentation classically involves chronic diarrhea (which can last years[209]), anorexia, weight loss, and bloating without associated fever. It is most frequently seen in AIDS patients with CD4+ counts less than 50 cells/mm³. Frequent (3 to 10) bowel movements occur per day, consisting of loose to watery stool that does not contain blood or fecal leukocytes.[6,32,210,211] There is no fever when infection is limited to the intestinal mucosa. Diarrhea is often associated with malabsorption and is worsened by food ingestion.[209] Malabsorption can result in weight loss and a wasting syndrome. The mortality of patients with advanced HIV disease and chronic diarrhea with wasting has been reported to be in excess of 50%.[164,211] Other intestinal pathogens may occur simultaneously or sequentially with the presence of this or other Microsporidia.[212]

Although originally thought to invade only enterocytes, it has been demonstrated that *Ent. bieneusi* can also invade cholangioepithelium.[164] When present in the cholangioepithelium, this organism has been associated with sclerosing cholangitis, AIDS cholangiopathy, and cholecystitis.[213] Presentations include abdominal pain, nausea, vomiting, and fever; jaundice is rarely seen. Fever is most likely the result of concomitant bacterial biliary infection, which produces the typical clinical manifestations of cholangitis. Imaging studies, including abdominal ultrasonography, computed tomography, endoscopic ultrasonography, and endoscopic retrograde cholangiopancreatography (ERCP), usually demonstrate dilated biliary ducts, irregularities of the bile duct wall, and gallbladder abnormalities such as thickening, distention, or the presence of sludge. Papillary stenosis has also been seen. Bilirubin is normal, although most patients have elevated liver function tests (e.g., alkaline phosphatase, γ-glutamyltransferase, aspartate aminotransferase, alanine aminotransferase).[213] Interestingly, an *Ent. bieneusi*-like organism has been identified as an etiologic factor for cholangitis and hepatitis in SIV-infected rhesus monkeys.[100]

Systemic dissemination is rare with *Ent. bieneusi*. One case report described this organism in nasal mucosa, which probably resulted from direct inoculation of spores from gastrointestinal secretions.[214] There are two case reports of respiratory tract involvement with *Ent. bieneusi* associated with chronic diarrhea, persistent cough, dyspnea, wheezing, and chest radiographs showing interstitial infiltrates.[190,209] Spores of *Ent. bieneusi* were detected in these cases in stool, bron-

choalveolar lavage fluid, and transbronchial biopsy specimens. *Ent. bieneusi* has been found to be a cause of proliferative serositis (peritonitis) in macaques (*Macaca mulatta).*

Encephalitozoonidae

Encephalitozoonidae are widely distributed among animals.[215] Three members of the family Encephalitozoonidae have been associated with disease in humans: *Enc. cuniculi, Enc. hellem,* and *Enc. intestinalis* (previously known as *Septata intestinalis*). It appears that these Microsporidia have the capacity to disseminate widely in their hosts, and their involvement in most organs has now been documented.[3,18,29,32] The ability of these organisms to disseminate correlates with their ability to grow in many cell types in vivo and in vitro. These organisms have been associated with gastroenteritis, keratitis, sinusitis, bronchiolitis, nephritis, cystitis/ureteritis, urethritis, prostatitis, hepatitis, fulminant hepatic failure, peritonitis, cerebritis, and disseminated infection.[3,18-20,29,32,166,170,174,216] An *Encephalitozoon* sp. has also been reported in a case of nodular skin lesions.[194,195]

The major syndrome associated with microsporidiosis is diarrhea and wasting. This is usually due to *Ent. bieneusi* (more than 90% of cases in the United States) and occasionally *Enc. intestinalis* (although in Europe this organism may be a more frequent cause of diarrhea[217]). *Enc. intestinalis* also can cause cholangitis,[13,218] keratoconjunctivitis, osteomyelitis of the mandible,[219] upper respiratory infections, renal failure, keratoconjunctivitis, and disseminated infection in AIDS patients.[133,163,220] Elimination of this parasite by treatment with albendazole correlates with the resolution of symptoms.[133,221]

Encephalitozoon cuniculi has been associated with hepatitis,[161] peritonitis,[170] hepatic failure,[19] disseminated disease with fever,[174] renal insufficiency, and intractable cough.[222] Granulomatous encephalitis due to *Enc. cuniculi* was first described in rabbits in 1922, and cases of encephalitis and seizures due to *Enc. cuniculi* have been reported in AIDS patients.[20,174] These infections have been reported to respond to albendazole.[18,20,174,222]

Encephalitozoon hellem has been reported to cause disseminated disease associated with renal failure, nephritis, pneumonia, bronchitis, and keratoconjunctivitis.[188,223,224] Punctate keratoconjunctivitis is the most commonly recognized clinical manifestation of infection with this organism. Most of the reports of ocular infection due to Encephalitozoonidae in the literature have been attributed to *Enc. hellem,* including three cases originally classified as *Enc. cuniculi.*[17,225] The remaining cases have been due to *Encephalitozoon* sp. or *Enc. intestinalis.*[174] Patients present with bilateral coarse punctate epithelial keratopathy and conjunctival inflammation resulting in redness, foreign body sensation, photophobia, excessive tearing, blurred vision, and changes in visual acuity. Ocular microsporidian infection in HIV-1-infected patients has been restricted to the superficial epithelium of the cornea and conjunctiva (i.e., superficial keratoconjunctivitis), and it rarely progresses to corneal ulceration (Fig. 282-4). Physical examination reveals conjunctival hyperemia and superficial punctate keratopathy without deep corneal ulcers or retinal involvement. Slit-lamp examination usually demonstrates punctate epithelial opacities, granular epithelial cells with irregular fluorescein uptake, conjunctival injection, superficial corneal infiltrates, and a noninflamed anterior chamber. Infection may be bilateral or unilateral. It is often associated with disseminated disease.[187,188,223,226,227] Examination of the urine in patients with keratoconjunctivitis often reveals microsporidian spores.[92,187,223,226,227] This organism is also recognized as an important cause infection of the nasal epithelium, which in turn causes sinusitis in AIDS patients.[189]

Other Microsporidia

Trachipleistophora hominis is a pansporoblastic microsporidian that has been described in several patients with disseminated disease in the setting of AIDS.[15] iI has been reported to cause myositis, sinusitis, and keratoconjunctivitis. *Trachipleistophora anthropophthera* infection presents as encephalitis, myositis, and keratoconjunctivitis.[16,27] Several of these patients responded clinically to albendazole.

Brachiola vesicularum caused myositis in an HIV-1-infected patient that responded to a regimen of albendazole and itraconozole.[12] Cases of myositis due to *Pleistophora* sp. and *Pleistophora ronneafiei* have also been reported in patients with AIDS.[25,26,177,228] The myositis presentation of these microsporidia has included myalgias, weakness, elevated serum CPK and aldolase levels, and abnormal electromyography consistent with inflammatory myopathy.[12,15,25,177] A case of urinary tract infection, prostatitis, and *Vit. corneae* infection has been reported in an AIDS patient.[101]

DIAGNOSIS

Examination of stool specimens by light microscopy has become the standard method for diagnosing gastrointestinal microsporidiosis (see Fig. 282-3). As renal involvement with shedding of spores in the urine is common in all of the species of Microsporidia that disseminate, urine specimens should be obtained whenever the diagnosis of microsporidiosis is considered. This has therapeutic implications, as the Microsporidia that disseminate (e.g., *Encephalitozoon*) are usually sensitive to albendazole, whereas those that do not disseminate (e.g., *Ent. bieneusi*) are resistant. Definitive identification of the Microsporidia causing an infection cannot be done with light microscopy and requires either ultrastructural examination (e.g., electron microscopy) or molecular techniques (e.g., species-specific PCR). If stool examination is negative in the setting of chronic diarrhea (more than 2 months' duration), endoscopy should be performed. A summary of the available diagnostic tests and their utility in patients with suspected microsporidiosis are described in Table 282-2.

Demonstration of Microsporidia by light microscopy is accomplished with staining methods that produce differential contrast between the spores of the Microsporidia and the cells and debris in clinical samples in which Microsporidia are found. Adequate magnification using a 60× to 100× objective is required for visualization, as the spores are 1 to 3 μm in size. Chromotrope 2R,[229] calcofluor white (fluorescent brightener 28),[230] and Uvitex 2B[231] are useful selective stains for Microsporidia in stool specimens and other body fluids. The chromotrope 2R-based method of Weber et al.[229] is a modification of a standard trichrome stain using a 10-fold higher chromotrope 2R concentration and a longer staining time. The Weber method, modified by Ryan et al.[232] (which uses aniline blue in place of fast green) and by Kokoskin et al.[233] (which uses a higher temperature), are preferred by some laboratories. With a chromotrope 2R-based stain the spores appear as 1- to 3-μm ovoid, light pink structures with a belt-like stripe girding them diagonally and equatorially against a green (Weber chromotrope stain) or blue (Ryan modification) background (see Fig. 282-3A). A newer rapid (11-minute) stain, the Gram-chromotrope stain, combines chromotrope 2R staining with a Gram staining step and results in violet-staining spores.[234] Microsporidian spores can also be visualized by ultraviolet (UV) microscopy using chemofluorescent optical brightening agents such as Calcofluor white M2R (fluorescent brightener 28; Fungi-Fluor) or Uvitex 2B (Fungiqual A; Dieter Reinehr and Manfred Rembold, Spezialchemikalien fur die Medizinische Diagnostik, Kandern, Germany), which stain chitin in the spore wall (endospore layer) (see Fig. 282-3B). Such stains also stain fungi and other fecal elements; however, microsporidian spores can be distinguished from yeast as they have a uniformly oval shape and are nonbudding.

In a study that examined 50 electron microscopy-proven Microsporidia-positive stool specimens, both the chromotrope 2R and chemofluorescent brightening stains identified 100% of specimens if at least fifty 100× objective fields were examined.[235] With Uvitex 2B, all of the 186 stool samples examined from 19 patients with biopsy-proven *Ent. bieneusi* infection were positive, whereas none of the 55 stool samples from 16 biopsy-negative patients were positive.[231] In another study evaluating Uvitex 2B staining, Microsporidia were identified in all of the samples known to be chromotrope 2R stain-positive as well as in seven additional samples that were chromotrope-negative on initial examination.[236] On reexamination, however, these seven stool samples were found also to be positive with the chromotrope 2R stain. All patients with positive duodenal biopsies had positive stool examinations according to the chromotrope or chemofluorescent methods. The limit of detecting Microsporidia by these techniques appears to be 50,000 organisms/ml.[235] Overall, the sensitivity of the chemofluorescent brightener-based stains is slightly higher than chromotrope-based stains (especially when low numbers of spores are present in a sample); however, the specificity of the chemofluorescent stains is lower (90% vs. 100% in one study).[235] Neither the chromotrope nor the chemofluorescent stain provides information on the species of Microsporidia being identified. Although it has been reported that microsporidian spores in food can give a false-positive result, and despite the fact that Microsporidia are common in the environment, it does not appear to be a common problem when using stool specimens for diagnosing these infections.

Microsporidia in body fluids other than stool (e.g., urine, cerebrospinal fluid), bile, duodenal aspirates, bronchoalveolar lavage fluid, sputum) have been visualized using Chromotrope 2R, chemofluores-

---

TABLE 282-2 Diagnostic Tests for Microsporidiosis

Test	Specimens	Utility
Chromotrope or chemofluorescent stain	Urine	This is often positive in cases of disseminated microsporidiosis (e.g., *Encephalitozoon* spp.). It should be done in all suspected microsporidia cases.
	Stool	At least three stools should be examined. The combination of chromotrope and chemofluorescence stains provides the highest sensitivity and specificity.
	Conjunctival scrapings	This is useful for the diagnosis of keratoconjunctivitis. Urine examination should also be performed in suspected cases to screen for disseminated microsporidiosis.
	Nasal scrapings	This can be useful for the diagnosis of Microsporidian sinusitis. As most of the Microsporidia associated with sinusitis are present in the kidneys, examination or urine should be routine for suspected sinusitis cases. If these tests are negative, biopsy of the nasal mucosa may be useful for diagnosis.
Endoscopy	Touch preparations	Touch preparations are useful for rapid diagnosis (within 24 hours).
	Biliary fluid	Examination is useful for diagnosis of microsporidian cholangitis.
	Biopsy (small intestine)	Biopsy should be considered for all patients with chronic diarrhea of more than 2 months' duration and negative stool and urine examinations. In this group, endoscopy has yielded a diagnosis of microsporidia in up to 30% of patients. Tissue can be examined with chromotrope 2R, tissue Gram stain, orsilver stain. If Microsporidia are demonstrated to invade the lamina propria, urine examination should be repeated as *Encephalitozoon* spp. are the most likely etiologic agents. In this setting, albendazole has high treatment efficacy.
PCR	Urine, stool, or tissue	Available as a research technique, PCR allows species identification.
Electron microscopy	Tissue	It provides species identification and is crucial for identifying new species or for the characterization of Microsporidia in unusual or new locations.
Serology	Serum	Not useful for diagnosis but may be useful for epidemiologic surveys.

cent optical brightening agents, Giemsa, Brown-Hopps Gram stain, acid-fast staining, or Warthin-Starry silver staining.[32,237,238] Generally, it is easier to identify microsporidian spores in body fluids other than in stool owing to the absence of bacteria and debris, which can be confused with microsporidian spores. As microsporidian infections usually involve mucosa or epithelium, cytologic preparations are especially useful for diagnosis.[32] Specimens that have been useful for diagnosing microsporidian infections include intestinal and biliary epithelium, epithelium of the cornea and conjunctivae, epithelium of the sinonasal and tracheobrochial regions, renal tubular epithelium, and urothelium. A diagnosis has also been accomplished by examining touch preparations of biopsy material. Microscopic examination of corneal tissue in patients with microsporidian keratitis, obtained by gently rubbing the conjunctiva and cornea with a tissue swab, usually reveals multiple, gram-positive, oval organisms in epithelial cells.

Histologically, microsporidian spores are easily discernible with a modified tissue chromotrope 2R or tissue Gram stain (Brown-Hopp or Brown-Brenn) in sections prepared from tissue fixed using routine procedures, Most microsporidian spores are gram-positive in tissue sections. With experience, Microsporidia can also be seen on hematoxylin and eosin-stained sections. Other stains that may be useful include periodic acid-Schiff, Giemsa, and Steiner silver stains. Some Microsporidia are also acid-fast stain-positive. Fresh tissue can also be examined by phase contrast microscopy; owing to their thick wall, unstained spores are refractile, appearing green; and such spores can be birefringent. If possible, biopsy or autopsy material should also be placed in electron microscopy fixative when microsporidiosis is suspected, as the definitive diagnosis of species requires ultrastructural information. It is possible, however, to use formalin-fixed tissue for ultrastructural analysis. Molecular methods can also be used on formalin-fixed tissue, although unfixed tissue or tissue fixed in ethanol yields the best results with PCR techniques.

Polyclonal serum prepared to other Microsporidia (*Enc. cuniculi*) has been reported to react with *Ent. bieneusi*.[138,239] Monoclonal antibodies to *Enc. hellem*,[240] *Enc. intestinalis*,[241] and *Ent. bieneusi*[242] have been described. These methods have been used to detect Microsporidia in tissue sections using immunofluorescence techniques. Many of the current antibody reagents have high background staining, limiting their clinical utility for examining stool specimens.

Vittaforma corneae,[23] *Enc. cuniculi, Enc. hellem*,[62] *T. hominis*,[15] and *Enc. intestinalis*[22] have been cultivated in tissue culture systems in vitro (for a review see Visvesvara[243]). *Ent. bieneusi* has not been cultivated continuously in vitro, although limited in vitro cultivation of *Ent. bieneusi* has been reported.[244] Adenovirus can mimic the cytopathologic effect of Microsporidia.[245] Experimental infection of SIV-infected rhesus monkeys with *Ent. bieneusi* from human tissue has been demonstrated.[246] The isolation of Microsporidia from clinical specimens is not a routine procedure and is available in only a few specialized research laboratories.

Serologic tests for diagnosing microsporidiosis have been developed and utilized for epidemiologic studies. Such serologic tests have, for the most part, not been proven useful for diagnosing microsporidiosis. In a study of 12 AIDS patients with *Ent. bieneusi,* 2 AIDS patients with *Enc. intestinalis,* and 2 immunocompetent patients with *Vit. corneae,* enzyme-linked immunosorbent assay (ELISA) titers for *Enc. hellem, Enc. cuniculi,* or *Vit. corneae* were not useful for diagnosis.[247] False-negative titers were present in seven of the patients with microsporidiosis, and half of the control patients (without clinical microsporidiosis) had positive serology to Microsporidia. This is consistent with other AIDS-associated infections in which serology has not proven useful.

A number of molecular diagnostic tests have been developed for pathogenic Microsporidia. For a review of the PCR tests for microsporidiosis, see Weiss and Vossbrinck.[49] Homology cloning of the rRNA genes of many of the Microsporidia pathogenic in humans has been accomplished using PCR techniques, and more than 80 Microsporidia species are now in the GenBank database. It has been

possible to design PCR primers to these small-subunit rRNA genes to identify Microsporidia at the species level in clinical samples without the need for ultrastructural examination. Two main approaches have been employed for constructing PCR primers for Microsporidia: the use of universal pan-Microsporidia primers and of species-specific primer pairs. These PCR techniques have been applied to biopsy specimens, urine, cultures, and more recently stool specimens and should greatly facilitate both diagnosis and epidemiologic studies.[53,248-250] Currently, these molecular tests are available only in reference laboratories such as the Centers for Disease Control (Atlanta, GA, USA).

TREATMENT

Treatment for microsporidiosis is outlined in Table 282-3.

Gastrointestinal and Systemic Disease

Microsporidian infection often occurs in immunocompromised hosts, particularly in those with HIV infection and CD4$^+$ cell counts of less than 50 mm^3. Clinical studies have demonstrated that improved immune function can result in the clinical response of patients with gastrointestinal microsporidiosis, with elimination of the organism and normalization of the intestinal architecture.[159,160,251-253] Relapse has been reported in patients who developed failure of their antiretroviral therapy associated with a decline in immune function and falling CD4$^+$ counts. Overall, these observations suggest that part of the primary treatment of microsporidiosis in the setting of AIDS is the institution of effective HAART. There have been no reports of immune reconstitution syndromes with HAART and microsporidiosis.

Although several species of Microsporidia that infect humans can be grown in vitro (but not without a host cell monolayer), the most common human pathogenic microsporidian, *Ent. bieneusi,* has yet to be grown successfully in vitro. This has limited in vitro testing of antimicrosporidial agents to those active against *Encephalitozoon* spp. and *Vit. corneae*.[11,254,255] Several agents have also been evaluated in animal models of microsporidiosis, but unfortunately no practical animal model has been developed for in vivo studies of *Ent. bieneusi.* For a review of drugs used against microsporidiosis in humans and animals, see Costa and Weiss.[256]

Among the compounds tested in vitro and in vivo for treatment of microsporidiosis, fumagillin and albendazole have demonstrated the most consistent activity and have been demonstrated to have clinical efficacy in human infections with various Microsporidia.[134,135,181,183,220,257-264] Albendazole binds to β-tubulin and is active against all of the Encephalitozoonidae *(Enc. hellem, Enc. cuniculi, Enc. intestinalis)* in vitro at concentrations of less than 0.1 mg/ml; it is also active in animal models of microsporidiosis.[257] Data on Encephalitozoonidae β-tubulin genes demonstrate an amino acid sequence associated with sensitivity to benzimidazoles.[265]

Albendazole is 70% protein-bound. It is distributed to blood, bile, and cerebrospinal fluid; and it is eliminated by the kidneys. Peak serum levels 2 hours after an oral dose are 0.20 to 0.94 μg/ml. Drug absorption is increased if albendazole is taken with food containing relatively high concentrations of fat. After oral administration, the hepatic metabolism converts albendazole to albendazole sulfoxide, which is detectable in the systemic circulation. Albendazole is not carcinogenic or mutagenic, although in rats and rabbits at dosages of 30 mg/kg it is embryotoxic and teratogenic. Albendazole is therefore not recommended for use in pregnant women. Side effects are rare, although the following have been reported: hypersensitivity (rash, pruritus, fever), neutropenia (reversible), CNS effects (dizziness, headache), gastrointestinal disturbances (abdominal pain, diarrhea, nausea, vomiting), hair loss (reversible), and elevated hepatic enzymes (reversible). There is a report of pseudomembranous colitis following albendazole treatment.

There are few placebo-controlled comparative treatment trials of microsporidiosis due to *Encephalitozoon* spp., but there are numerous case reports demonstrating the efficacy of 2 to 4 weeks of albendazole

TABLE 282-3 Current Treatment Options for Microsporidiosis

Organism	Drug	Dosage and Duration
All microsporidian infections	Restoration of immune function can be critical in control of infection. Patients with AIDS should have HAART optimized.	
Enterocytozoon bieneusi	No effective commercial treatment. Oral fumagillin 20 mg TID (e.g., 60 mg/day) has been effective in a clinical trial. Albendazole* resulted in clinical improvement in up to 50% of patients in some studies, but it was not effective in other studies.	
Encephalitozoonidae infection (e.g., systemic, sinusitis, encephalitis, hepatitis)		
Enc. cuniculi	Albendazole	400 mg BID[†]
Enc. hellem	Albendazole	400 mg BID
Enc. intestinalis	Albendazole	400 mg BID
Encephalitozoonidae keratoconjunctivitis	Fumagillin solution[‡] (Fumadil B 3 mg/ml) Patients may also need albendazole if systemic infection is present.	2 drops every 2 hours for 4 days then 2 drops 4 times a day[§]
Trachipleistophora hominis	Albendazole	400 mg BID
Brachiola vesicularum	Albendazole ± Itraconozole	400 mg BID 400 mg QD

*Albendazole 400 mg BID.

†The duration of treatment for microsporidiosis has not been established. Relapse of infection has occurred upon stopping treatment. Patients should be maintained on treatment for at least 4 weeks, and most patients should be on treatment indefinitely.

‡Fumadil B (fumagillin bicylohexylammonium; Mid-Continent Agrimarketing, Overland Park, KS, USA).

§Eye drops should be continued indefinitely; relapse is common on stopping treatment. Adapted from Costa S, Weiss LM. Drug treatment of microsporidiosis. Drug Resistance Updates 2000;3:1-16.

HAART, highly active antiretroviral therapy.

400 mg BID for these infections. In a double-blind, placebo-controlled trial of eight patients with AIDS and diarrhea due to *Enc. intestinalis,* treatment with albendazole (400 mg BID for 3 weeks) resulted in resolution of the diarrhea and elimination of the organism in all eight patients, similar to that seen in several case reports.[133,171,183,220,221,266,267] In case reports of chronic sinusitis, respiratory infection, and disseminated infection due to *Enc. hellem,* treatment with 400 mg of albendazole twice daily resulted in resolution of symptoms and clearance of the organism.[268,269] Clinical improvement was demonstrated with albendazole treatment in a patient with disseminated *Enc. cuniculi* infection involving the CNS, conjunctiva, sinuses, kidneys, and lungs.[20] It has also been reported to be effective in cases of urethritis,[263] renal failure,[262] and disseminated infection.[222] In addition to its efficacy in *Encephalitozoon* spp., disseminated infections with other Microsporidia have also been reported to respond to albendazole treatment. In patients with disseminated infection accompanied by myositis due to *T. hominis* and in a patient with myositis due to a *Brachiola vesicularum,* albendazole (400 mg BID) resulted in clinical improvement.[12,15]

In contrast to its success in treating patients with the species of Microsporidia that disseminate, albendazole has displayed only limited efficacy against *Ent. bieneusi* infection. In two studies examining 66 patients with diarrhea due to *Ent. bieneusi* during the pre-HAART era, symptoms were alleviated in about 50% of the patients treated with albendazole, but the presence of *Ent. bieneusi* persisted during treatment in all patients and there was no improvement in any patient's D-xylose absorption test.[261,264,270] The symptoms rapidly recurred upon discontinuing albendazole therapy in the patients who had reported symptom alleviation with it. Most other studies have found that albendazole had no efficacy against *Ent. bieneusi* infection.[271]

Despite a few case reports indicating that metronidazole was effective for *Ent. bieneusi* intestinal infection, most studies have demonstrated that this drug is not effective against this infection.[171,260,272] In vitro studies have also demonstrated that metronidazole has no activity against Microsporidia (e.g., *Enc. cuniculi*).[254] Other medications used without success to treat gastrointestinal microsporidiosis are azithromycin, paromomycin (Microsporidia lack the rRNA binding site for this drug), and quinacrine. Atovaquone has been anecdotally reported to have limited efficacy in patients with

microsporidiosis,[260,273] although it has no in vitro activity.[254] Transient clinical remission has been reported in a patient treated with furazolidone.[167] Sparfloxacin and chloroquine have demonstrated in vitro activity against Microsporidia but have not been used clinically.[254] Prophylaxis with trimethoprim-sulfamethoxazole is not effective for preventing microsporidiosis, and this drug has no in vitro or in vivo activity against these organisms.[274] Thalidomide and octreotide have both been reported to decrease diarrhea in about 50% of patients with microsporidiosis, which is probably secondary to the effect of these agents on the physiology of enterocytes.[275] Examination of the biopsies of patients treated with thalidomide (100 mg daily for 1 month) demonstrated persistence of the parasite and no change in parasite load.[275]

Fumagillin was isolated from *Aspergillus fumigatus* in 1949, and because of its efficacy against *Entamoeba histolytica* in vitro it was used during the 1950s to treat amebiasis. Fumagillin is used commercially to treat honeybees infected with the microsporidian *Nosema apis* and has been used to treat infections by both microsporidia and myxosporeans in various types of fish.[276,277] Fumagillin and its semisynthetic analogue TNP-470 have been found to have activity in vitro and in vivo against Microsporidia pathogenic for humans, including *Enc. cuniculi, Enc. hellem, Enc. intestinalis, V. corneae,* and *Ent. bieneusi.*[134,135,257,258,260,278] A dose-escalation trial of fumagillin performed on AIDS patients infected with *Ent. bieneusi* employed doses of 10 mg/day for 14 days, 20 mg/day for 14 days, 40 mg/day for 14 days, and 60 mg/day for 14 days.[135] Altogether, 21 of 29 patients exhibited transient clearing of parasites from their stool; all of these patients were in the first three dosage groups. In the 60 mg/day group, 8 of 11 patients did not have spores in their stools at week 6 and remained free of spores in stool specimens for a mean of 11 months. Duodenal biopsies on the same eight patients did not demonstrate Microsporidia by either light or electron microscopy. A subsequent randomized trial based evaluating 12 patients (with either AIDS or transplantation) confirmed that 60 mg/day (given as 20 mg TID) effectively treated *Ent. bieneusi* intestinal infection.[134] Treatment was associated with resolution of diarrhea, clearance of spores, improvement of Karnofsky scores, and improvement in D-xylose absorption tests. The main limiting toxicity of this treatment was thrombocytopenia, which was reversible on stopping fumagillin treatment.

Fumagillin, ovalicin, and their analogues (e.g., TNP-470) bind in a selective, covalent fashion to the metalloprotease methionine aminopeptidase type 2 (MetAP2). Methionine aminopeptidase activity is essential for eukaryotic cell survival, as removal of the terminal methionine of a protein is often essential for its function and post-translational modification. Homology PCR has been used to demonstrate the presence of MetAP2 genes in several microsporidia.[279] Data from the *Enc. cuniculi* genome project[78] indicated that *Enc. cuniculi* does not have a methionine aminopeptidase type 1 gene (MetAP1), unlike mammalian cells, which have both MetAP1 and MetAP2; therefore MetAP2 is an essential enzyme in microsporidia.

Ocular Disease

Solutions of the soluble salt Fumidil B (fumagillin bicylohexylammonium; Mid-Continent Agrimarketing, Overland Park, KS, USA) applied topically have been demonstrated to be nontoxic to the cornea. Treatment of ocular microsporidiosis can be accomplished using a 3 mg/ml solution of Fumidil B in saline (fumagillin 70 mg/ml)[258,259,280-282]; the treatment should be continued indefinitely, as recurrence has been reported upon stopping these drops. Although clearance of Microsporidia from the eye can be demonstrated, the organism is still often present systemically and can be demonstrated in the urine or in nasal smears. In such cases the use of albendazole as a systemic agent is reasonable and effective. Topical treatment with thiabendazole (0.4% suspension), a related benzimidazole, was ineffective in one case of keratitis due to *Enc. hellem*.[258] Two patients with *Encephalitozoon*-like organisms have been reported to respond to imidazole (fluconazole and itraconazole) administration.[283] Yee et al. described complete improvement with oral itraconazole (200 mg BID) in a patient with *Enc. hellem* infection over a 6-week period after debulking the cornea.[96] However, Diesenhouse et al. observed no improvement in a patient with *Enc. hellem* treated with itraconazole 100 mg TID.[258] In vitro data have not confirmed antimicrosporidial activity for imidazole compounds. Sulfa drugs have had variable results in vitro and in vivo and are not recommended for treatment. Polymyxin B, propamidine isethionate 0.1% (Brolene), gramicidin, neomycin sulfate, and tetracycline appear to have limited efficacy for the treatment of microsporidian infection and should not be used except to treat secondary bacterial infections. Keratoplasty appears to provide temporary improvement in some cases, and debulking by corneal scraping may be useful in cases not responding to medical treatment. Steroids may be useful for decreasing the associated inflammatory response but have no direct action on Microsporidia.

PREVENTION

There are limited data on effective preventive strategies for microsporidiosis. Currently, no prophylactic agents have been identified for these organisms. Patients have developed microsporidiosis while on trimethoprim-sulfamethoxazole prophylaxis,[274] and microsporidiosis has occurred in patients receiving dapsone, pyrimethamine, itraconazole, azithromycin, and atovaquone.[158] No studies have evaluated albendazole for prophylaxis; but given its relative lack of efficacy for *Ent. bieneusi* infections, it is unlikely to be effective in preventing most cases of intestinal microsporidiosis. The most effective prophylaxis is the restoration of immune function in immunocompromised hosts. Several studies in AIDS patients have demonstrated that HAART can produce remission of intestinal microsporidiosis.[159,160,251-253] Moreover, the declining incidence of microsporidiosis and other opportunistic infections during the HAART era suggests it also prevents symptomatic infection.

Microsporidian spores can survive and remain infective in the environment for prolonged periods. Experiments with *Enc. cuniculi* have demonstrated that they can survive for years in the environment with the correct humidity and temperature.[88] In the typical hospital environment, *Enc. cuniculi* spores can survive and remain infectious for at least a month. Spores can be rendered noninfectious by a 30-minute exposure to most common disinfectants, so the procedures used to clean most hospital rooms should be sufficient to limit infection. Spores are also killed by the commonly used methods employed for sterilization.

Although the epidemiology of the Microsporidia that infect humans has not been fully elucidated, it is likely they are food- or waterborne pathogens; and the usual sanitary measures that prevent contamination of food and water with animal urine and feces should decrease the chance for infection. Hand washing and general hygienic habits probably reduce the chance of contamination of the conjunctiva and cornea with microsporidian spores. It is not known if person-toperson respiratory transmission occurs. Given the presence of microsporidian spores in respiratory secretions in cases of disseminated microsporidiosis, it may be useful to consider preventing contact of these patients with other immunosuppressed patients until the infection has been treated. Existing guidelines for the prevention of opportunistic infections that address food, water, and animal contact may be useful for preventing microsporidiosis. The presence of these organisms in genitourinary secretions raises the possibility of sexual transmission of these infections. It is reasonable to screen close contacts of patients with index cases of microsporidiosis for the presence of these organisms. Their importance and prevalence in our water supplies is an open question, but severely immunocompromised patients may wish to consider using bottled or filtered water in some settings.

REFERENCES

1. Sprague V. Systematics of the microsporidia. In:Bulla LA, Cheng TC, eds. Comparative Pathobiology, v. 2. New York: Plenum Press; 1977:1-510.
2. Sprague VV, Becnel JJ. Note on the name-author-date combination for the taxon Microsporidies Balbiani, 1882, when ranked as a phylum. J Invertebr Pathol 1998;71:91-94.
3. Wittner M, Weiss LM. The Microsporidia and Microsporidiosis. Washington, DC: ASM Press; 1999:xvii,1:1-553.
4. Black SS, Steinohrt LA, Bertucci DC, et al. Encephalitozoon hellem in budgerigars (Melopsittacus undulatus). Vet Pathol 1997;34:189-198.
5. American Mosquito Control Association. Biological Control of Mosquitoes. AMCA Bulletin No. 6. Fresno, CA: American Mosquito Control Association, 1985:218.
6. Weber R, Bryan RT, Schwartz DA, Owen RL. Human microsporidial infections. Clin Microbiol Rev 1994;7:426-461.
7. Levaditi C, Nicolau S, Schoen R. L'agent etiologique de l'enchalite epizootique du lapin (Encephalitozoon cuniculi). C R Soc Biol 1923;89:984-986.
8. Matsubayashi H, Koide T, Mikata T, Hagiwara S. A case of Encephalitozoon-like body infection in man. Arch Pathol Lab Med 1959;67:181-185.
9. Desportes I, Le Charpentier Y, Galian A, et al. Occurrence of a new microsporidian: Enterocytozoon bieneusi n. g., n. sp., in the enterocytes of a human patient with AIDS. J Protozool 1985;32:250-245.
10. Sprague V, Becnel JJ, Hazard EI. Taxonomy of phylum microspora. Crit Rev Microbiol 1992;18:285-395.
11. Silveira H, Canning EU. Vittaforma corneae n. comb. for the human microsporidium Nosema corneum Shadduck, Meccoli, Davis & Font, 1990, based on its ultrastructure in the liver of experimentally infected athymic mice. J Eukaryot Microbiol 1995;42:158-165.
12. Cali A, Takvorian PM, Lewin S, et al. Brachiola vesicularum, n. g., n. sp., a new microsporidium associated with AIDS and myositis. J Eukaryot Microbiol 1998;45: 240-251.
13. Cali A, Kotler DP, Orenstein JM. Septata intestinalis N. G., N. Sp., an intestinal microsporidian associated with chronic diarrhea and dissemination in AIDS patients. J Eukaryot Microbiol 1993;40:101-112.
14. Hartskeerl RA, Van Gool T, Schuitema AR, et al. Genetic and immunological characterization of the microsporidian Septata intestinalis Cali, Kotler and Orenstein, 1993: reclassification to Encephalitozoon intestinalis. Parasitology 1995;110(Pt 3):277-285.
15. Field AS, Marriott DJ, Milliken ST, et al. Myositis associated with a newly described microsporidian, Trachipleistophora hominis, in a patient with AIDS. J Clin Microbiol 1996;34:2803-2811.
16. Yachnis AT, Berg J, Martinez-Salazar A, et al. Disseminated microsporidiosis especially infecting the brain, heart, and kidneys: report of a newly recognized pansporoblastic species in two symptomatic AIDS patients. Am J Clin Pathol 1996;106:535-543.
17. Rastrelli P, Didier E, Yee R. Microsporidial keratitis. Ophthalmol Clin North Am 1994;7:614-635.
18. Orenstein JM, Gaetz HP, Yachnis AT, et al. Disseminated microsporidiosis in AIDS: are any organs spared? AIDS 1997;11:385-386.
19. Sheth SG, Bates C, Federman M, Chopra S. Fulminant hepatic failure caused by microsporidial infection in a patient with AIDS. AIDS 1997;11:553-554.
20. Weber R, Deplazes P, Flepp M, et al. Cerebral microsporidiosis due to Encephalitozoon cuniculi in a patient with human immunodeficiency virus infection. N Engl J Med 1997;336:474-478.

21. Sheikh RA, Prindiville TP, Yenamandra S, et al. Microsporidial AIDS cholangiopathy due to Encephalitozoon intestinalis: case report and review. Am J Gastroenterol 2000;95:2364-2371.

22. Visvesvara GS, da Silva AJ, Croppo GP, et al. In vitro culture and serologic and molecular identification of Septata intestinalis isolated from urine of a patient with AIDS. J Clin Microbiol 1995;33:930-936.

23. Shadduck JA, Meccoli RA, Davis R, Font RL. Isolation of a microsporidian from a human patient. J Infect Dis 1990;162:773-776.

24. Cali A, Takvorian PM, Lewin S, et al. Identification of a new Nosema-like microsporidian associated with myositis in an AIDS patient. J Eukaryot Microbiol 1996;43:108S.

25. Chupp GL, Alroy J, Adelman LS, et al. Myositis due to Pleistophora (Microsporidia) in a patient with AIDS. Clin Infect Dis 1993;16:15-21.

26. Cali A, Takvorian PM. Ultrastructure and development of Pleistophora ronneafiei n. sp., a microsporidium (Protista) in the skeletal muscle of an immune-compromised individual. J Eukaryot Microbiol 2003;50:77-85.

27. Vavra J, Yachnis AT, Shadduck JA, Orenstein JM. Microsporidia of the genus Trachipleistophora—causative agents of human microsporidiosis: description of Trachipleistophora anthropophthera n. sp. (Protozoa: Microsporidia). J Eukaryot Microbiol 1998;45:273-283.

28. Pol S, Romana CA, Richard S, et al. Microsporidia infection in patients with the human immunodeficiency virus and unexplained cholangitis. N Engl J Med 1993;328:95-99.

29. Franzen C, Muller A. Microsporidiosis: human diseases and diagnosis. Microbes Infect 2001;3:389-400.

30. Desportes-Livage I. Biology of microsporidia. Contrib Microbiol 2000;6:140-65.

31. Williams BA, Hirt RP, Lucocq JM, Embley TM. A mitochondrial remnant in the microsporidian Trachipleistophora hominis. Nature 2002;418:865-9.

32. Weber R, Deplazes P, Schwartz D. Diagnosis and clinical aspects of human microsporidiosis. Contrib Microbiol 2000;6:166-192.

33. Vavra J. Structure of the microsporidia. In: Bulla LA Jr, Cheng TC, eds., Comparative Pathobiology, v. 1. New York: Plenum Press; 1976:1-85.

34. Foucault C, Drancourt M. Actin mediates Encephalitozoon intestinalis entry into the human enterocyte-like cell line, Caco-2. Microb Pathog 2000;28:51-58.

35. Lom J. On the structure of the extruded microsporidian polar filament. Z Parasitenkd 1972;38:200-213.

36. Weidner E. Ultrastructural study of microsporidian invasion into cells. Z Parasitenkd 1972;40:227-242.

37. Undeen AH, Frixione E. The role of osmotic pressure in the germination of Nosema algerae spores. J Protozool 1990;37:561-567.

38. Lom J, Vavra J. The mode of sporoplasm extrusion in microsporidian spores. Acta Protozool 1963;1:81-89.

39. Keohane E, Weiss LM. The structure, function, and composition of the microsporidian polar tube. In: Wittner M, Weiss LM, eds. The Microsporidia and Microsporidiosis. Washington, DC: ASM Press; 1999:196-224.

40. Undeen AH, Solter LF. Sugar acquisition during the development of microsporidian (Microspora: Sosematidae) spores. J Invertebr Pathol 1997;70:106-112.

41. Undeen AH, Vander Meer RK. Microsporidian intrasporal sugars and their role in germination. J Invertebr Pathol 1999;73:294-302.

42. Curgy JJ, Vavra J, Vivares C. Presence of ribosomal RNAs with prokaryotic properties in Microsporidia, eukaryotic organisms. Biol Cell 1980;38:49-52.

43. Vossbrinck CR, Woese CR. Eukaryotic ribosomes that lack a 5.8S RNA. Nature 1986;320:287-288.

44. Vossbrinck CR, Maddox JV, Friedman S, et al. Ribosomal RNA sequence suggests microsporidia are extremely ancient eukaryotes. Nature 1987;326:411-414.

45. Weiss LM, Vossbrinck CR. Microsporidiosis: molecular and diagnostic aspects. Adv Parasitol 1998;40:351-395.

46. Vivares CP, Metenier G. Towards the minimal eukaryotic parasitic genome. Curr Opin Microbiol 2000;3:463-467.

47. Brugere JF, Cornillot E, Metenier G, et al. Encephalitozoon cuniculi (Microspora) genome: physical map and evidence for telomere-associated rDNA units on all chromosomes. Nucleic Acids Res 2000;28:2026-2033.

48. Katiyar SK, Visvesvara GS, Edlind TD. Comparisons of ribosomal RNA sequences from amitochondrial protozoa: implications for processing, mRNA binding and paromomycin susceptibility. Gene 1995;152:27-33.

49. Weiss LM, Vossbrinck CR. Molecular biology, molecular phylogeny, and molecular diagnostic approaches to the microsporidia. In: Wittner M, Weiss LM, eds. The Microsporidia and Microsporidiosis. Washington, DC: ASM Press; 1999:129-171.

50. Brugere JF, Cornillot E, Metenier G, Vivares CP. Occurrence of subtelomeric rearrangements in the genome of the microsporidian parasite Encephalitozoon cuniculi, as revealed by a new fingerprinting procedure based on two-dimensional pulsed field gel electrophoresis. Electrophoresis 2000;21:2576-2581.

51. Vossbrinck CF, Maddox JV, Friedman S, et al. Ribosomal RNA sequence suggests microsporidia are extremely ancient eukaryotes. Nature 1987;326:411-414.

52. Baker MD, Vossbrinck CR, Maddox JV, Undeen AH. Phylogenetic relationships among Vairimorpha and Nosema species (Microspora) based on ribosomal RNA sequence data. J Invertebr Pathol 1994;64:100-106.

53. Franzen C, Muller A. Molecular techniques for detection, species differentiation, and phylogenetic analysis of microsporidia. Clin Microbiol Rev 1999;12:243-285.

54. Baker MD, Vossbrinck CR, Didier ES, et al. Small subunit ribosomal DNA phylogeny of various microsporidia with emphasis on AIDS related forms. J Eukaryot Microbiol 1995;42:564-570.

55. Didier ES, Vossbrinck CR, Baker MD, et al. Identification and characterization of three Encephalitozoon cuniculi strains. Parasitology 1995;111(Pt 4):411-421.

56. Rinder H, Thomschke A, Dengjel B, et al. Close genotypic relationship between Enterocytozoon bieneusi from humans and pigs and first detection in cattle. J Parasitol 2000;86:185-188.

57. Tuzet O, Maurand J, Fize JA, et al. Proposition d'un nouveau cadre systematique pour les genres de Microsporidies. C R Acad Sci (Paris) 1971;272:1268-1271.

58. Larsson JIR. Identification of microsporidian genera: a guide with comments on the taxonomy. Arch Protistenkd 1988;136:1-37.

59. Issi IV. Microsporidia as a phylum of parasitic protozoa. Protozoology 1986;10:6-135 (in Russian).

60. Weiser J. A proposal of the basis for microsporidian taxonomy. Proc Int Congr Protozool 1977;5:267.

61. Baker MD. Phylogenetic Relationships of Five Microsporidian Genera Based on Ribosomal RNA Sequence Data. Urbana-Champaign: University of Illinois; 1987:44.

62. Didier ES, Didier PJ, Friedberg DN, et al. Isolation and characterization of a new human microsporidian, Encephalitozoon hellem (n. sp.) from three AIDS patients with keratoconjunctivitis. J Infect Dis 1991;163:617-621.

63. Keeling PJ, McFadden GI. Origins of microsporidia. Trends Microbiol 1998;6:19-23.

64. Weiss LM, Edlind TD, Vossbrinck CR, Hashimoto T. Microsporidian molecular phylogeny: the fungal connection. J Eukaryot Microbiol 1999;46:17S-18S.

65. Hirt RP, Logsdon JM Jr, Healy B, et al. Microsporidia are related to fungi: evidence from the largest subunit of RNA polymerase II and other proteins. Proc Natl Acad Sci USA 1999;96:580-585.

66. Edlind T, Katiyar S, Visvesvara G, Jing L. Evolutionary origins of microsporidia and basis for benzimidazole sensitivity: an update. J Eukaryot Microbiol 1996;43:109S.

67. Keeling PJ, Doolittle WF. Alpha-tubulin from early-diverging eukaryotic lineages and the evolution of the tubulin family. Mol Biol Evol 1996;13:1297-1305.

68. Arisue N, Sanchez LB, Weiss LM, et al. Mitochondriate-type hsp70 genes of the amitochondriate protists, Giardia intestinalis, Entamoeba histolytica and two microsporidians. Parasitol Int 2002;51:9-16.

69. Germot A, Philippe H, Le GH. Evidence for loss of mitochondria in microsporidia from a mitochondrial-type hsp70 in Nosema locustae. Mol Biochem Parasitol 1997;87:159-168.

70. Hirt RP, Healy B, Vossbrinck CR, et al. A mitochondrial Hsp70 orthologue in Vairimorpha necatrix: molecular evidence that microsporidia once contained mitochondria. Curr Biol 1997;7:995-998.

71. Peyretaillade E, Broussolle V, Peyret P, et al. Microsporidia, amitochondrial protists, possess a 70-kDa heat shock protein gene of mitochondrial evolutionary origin. Mol Biol Evol 1998;15:683-689.

72. Vivares C, Biderre C, Duffieux F, et al. Chromosomal localization of five genes in Encephalitozoon cuniculi (Microsporidia). J Eukaryot Microbiol 1996;43:97S.

73. Edlind T. Phylogenetics of protozoan tubulin with reference to the amitochondriate eukaryotes. In: Coombs GH, Vickerman K, Sleigh MA, Warren A, eds. Evolutionary Relationships Among Protozoa. London: Chapman & Hall; 1998:91-108.

74. Kamaishi T, Hashimoto T, Nakamura Y, et al. Protein phylogeny of translation elongation factor EF-1 alpha suggests microsporidians are extremely ancient eukaryotes. J Mol Evol 1996;42:257-263.

75. Desportes I. Ulatrastructure de Stempellia mutabilis leger et Hess, microsporidie parasite de l'ephemere Ephemera vulgatta. L Protistologica 1976;12:121-150.

76. Flegel TW, Pasharawipas T. A proposal for typical eukaryotic meiosis in microsporidians. Can J Microbiol 1995;41:1-11.

77. Fast NM, Logsdon JM Jr, Doolittle WF. Phylogenetic analysis of the TATA box binding protein (TBP) gene from Nosema locustae: evidence for a microsporidia-fungi relationship and spliceosomal intron loss. Mol Biol Evol 1999;16:1415-1419.

78. Katinka MD, Duprat S, Cornillot E, et al. Genome sequence and gene compaction of the eukaryote parasite Encephalitozoon cuniculi. Nature 2001;414:450-453.

79. Keeling PJ. Congruent evidence from alpha-tubulin and beta-tubulin gene phylogenies for a zygomycete origin of microsporidia. Fungal Genet Biol 2003;38:298-309.

80. Avery SW, Undeen AH. The isolation of microsporidia and other pathogens from concentrated ditch water. J Am Mosq Control Assoc 1987;3:54-58.

81. Cotte L, Rabodonirina M, Chapuis F, et al. Waterborne outbreak of intestinal microsporidiosis in persons with and without human immunodeficiency virus infection. J Infect Dis 1999;180:2003-2008.

82. Sparfel JM, Sarfati C, Liguory O, et al. Detection of microsporidia and identification of Enterocytozoon bieneusi in surface water by filtration followed by specific PCR. J Eukaryot Microbiol 1997;44:78S.

83. Dowd SE, Gerba CP, Pepper IL. Confirmation of the human-pathogenic microsporidia Enterocytozoon bieneusi, Encephalitozoon intestinalis, and Vittaforma corneae in water. Appl Environ Microbiol 1998;64:3332-3335.

84. Enriquez FJ, Taren D, Cruz-Lopez A, et al. Prevalence of intestinal encephalitozoonosis in Mexico. Clin Infect Dis 1998;26:1227-1229.

85. Hutin YJ, Sombardier MN, Liguory O, et al. Risk factors for intestinal microsporidiosis in patients with human immunodeficiency virus infection: a case-control study. J Infect Dis 1998;178:904-907.

86. Conteas CN, Berlin OG, Lariviere MJ, et al. Examination of the prevalence and seasonal variation of intestinal microsporidiosis in the stools of persons with chronic diarrhea and human immunodeficiency virus infection. Am J Trop Med Hyg 1998;58:559-561.

87. Wuhib T, Silva TMJ, Newman RD, et al. Cryptosporidial and microsporidial infections in human immunodeficiency virus-infected patients in northeastern Brazil. J Infect Dis 1994;170:494-497.

88. Waller T. Sensitivity of Encephalitozoon cuniculi to various temperatures, disinfectants and drugs. Lab Anim 1979;13:227-230.

89. Schwartz DA, Visvesvara GS, Diesenhouse MC, et al. Pathologic features and immunofluorescent antibody demonstration of ocular microsporidiosis (Encephalitozoon hellem) in seven patients with acquired immunodeficiency syndrome. Am J Ophthalmol 1993;115:285-292.

90. Fuentealba IC, Mahoney NT, Shadduck JA, et al. Hepatic lesions in rabbits infected with Encephalitozoon cuniculi administered per rectum. Vet Pathol 1992;29:536-540.

91. Schwartz DA, Visvesvara G, Weber R, Bryan RT. Male genital tract microsporidiosis and AIDS: prostatic abscess due to Encephalitozoon hellem. J Eukaryot Microbiol 1994;41:61S.

92. Schwartz DA, Bryan RT, Hewanlowe KO, et al. Disseminated microsporidiosis and AIDS; pathologic evidence for respiratory transmission of Encephalitozoon infection. In: Proceedings of the International Conference on AIDS, July 19-24, 1992, v. 8.

93. Bryan RT, Schwartz DA. Epidemiology of microsporidiosis. In: Wittner M, Weisss LM, eds. The Microsporidia and Microsporidiosis. Washington, DC: ASM Press; 1999:502-516.

94. Hunt RD, King NW, Foster HL. Encephalitozoonosis: evidence for vertical transmission. J Infect Dis 1972;126:212-214.

95. Deplazes P, Mathis A, Weber R. Epidemiology and zoonotic aspects of microsporidia of mammals and birds. Contrib Microbiol 2000;6:236-260.

96. Yee RW, Tio FO, Martinez JA, et al. Resolution of microsporidial epithelial keratopathy in a patient with AIDS. Ophthalmology 1991;98:196-201.

97. Deplazes P, Mathis A, Muller C, Weber R. Molecular epidemiology of Encephalitozoon cuniculi and first detection of Enterocytozoon bieneusi in faecal samples of pigs. J Eukaryot Microbiol 1996;43:93S.

98. Del Aguila C, Izquierdo F, Navajas R, et al. Enterocytozoon bieneusi in animals: rabbits and dogs as new hosts. J Eukaryot Microbiol 1999;46:8S-9S.

99. Reetz J, Rinder H, Thomschke A, et al. First detection of the microsporidium Enterocytozoon bieneusi in non-mammalian hosts (chickens). Int J Parasitol 2002;32:785-787.

100. Mansfield KG, Carville A, Shvetz D, et al. Identification of an Enterocytozoon bieneusi-like microsporidian parasite in simian-immunodeficiency-virus-inoculated macaques with hepatobiliary disease. Am J Pathol 1997;150:1395-1405.

101. Deplazes P, Mathis A, van Saanen M, et al. Dual microsporidial infection due to Vittaforma corneae and Encephalitozoon hellem in a patient with AIDS. Clin Infect Dis 1998;27:1521-1524.

102. Weber R, Bryan RT. Microsporidial infections in immunodeficient and immunocompetent patients. Clin Infect Dis 1994;19:517-521.

103. Drobniewski F, Kelly P, Carew A, et al. Human microsporidiosis in African AIDS patients with chronic diarrhea. J Infect Dis 1995;171:515-516.

104. Aoun K, Bouratbine A, Datry A, et al. Presence of intestinal microsporidia in Tunisia: a case report. Bull Soc Pathol Exot 1997;90:176.

105. Hautvast JL, Tolboom JJ, Derks TJ, et al. Asymptomatic intestinal microsporidiosis in a human immunodeficiency virus-seronegative, immunocompetent Zambian child. Pediatr Infect Dis J 1997;16:415-416.

106. Van Gool T, Luderhoff E, Nathoo KJ, et al. High prevalence of Enterocytozoon bieneusi infections among HIV-positive individuals with persistent diarrhoea in Harare, Zimbabwe. Trans R Soc Trop Med Hyg 1995;89:478-480.

107. Morakote N, Siriprasert P, Piangjai S, et al. Microsporidium and Cyclospora in human stools in Chiang Mai, Thailand. Southeast Asian J Trop Med Public Health 1995;26:799-800.

108. Brazil P, Sodre FC, Cuzzi-Maya T, et al. Intestinal microsporidiosis in HIV-positive patients with chronic unexplained diarrhea in Rio de Janeiro, Brazil: diagnosis, clinical presentation and follow-up. Rev Inst Med Trop Sao Paulo 1996;38:97-102.

109. Weitz JC, Botehlo R, Bryan R. [Microsporidiosis in patients with chronic diarrhea and AIDS, in HIV asymptomatic patients and in patients with acute diarrhea.] Rev Med Chil 1995;123:849-856.

110. Cegielski JP, Ortega YR, McKee S, et al. Cryptosporidium, Enterocytozoon, and Cyclospora infections in pediatric and adult patients with diarrhea in Tanzania. Clin Infect Dis 1999;28:314-321.

111. Maiga I, Doumbo O, Dembele M, et al. [Human intestinal microsporidiosis in Bamako (Mali): the presence of Enterocytozoon bieneusi in HIV seropositive patients.] Sante 1997;7:257-262.

112. Wanke CA, DeGirolami P, Federman M. Enterocytozoon bieneusi infection and diarrheal disease in patients who were not infected with human immunodeficiency virus: case report and review. Clin Infect Dis 1996;23:816-818.

113. Gainzarain JC, Canut A, Lozano M, et al. Detection of Enterocytozoon bieneusi in two human immunodeficiency virus-negative patients with chronic diarrhea by polymerase chain reaction in duodenal biopsy specimens and review. Clin Infect Dis 1998;27:394-398.

114. Albrecht H, Sobottka I. Enterocytozoon bieneusi infection in patients who are not infected with human immunodeficiency virus. Clin Infect Dis 1997;25:344.

115. Sandfort J, Hannemann A, Gelderblom H, et al. Enterocytozoon bieneusi infection in an immunocompetent patient who had acute diarrhea and who was not infected with the human immunodeficiency virus. Clin Infect Dis 1994;19:514-516.

116. Sobottka I, Albrecht H, Schottelius J, et al. Self-limited traveller's diarrhea due to a dual infection with Enterocytozoon bieneusi and Cryptosporidium parvum in an immunocompetent HIV-negative child. Eur J Clin Microbiol Infect Dis 1995;14:919-920.

117. Raynaud L, Delbac F, Broussolle V, et al. Identification of Encephalitozoon intestinalis in travelers with chronic diarrhea by specific PCR amplification. J Clin Microbiol 1998;36:37-40.

118. Rabodonirina M, Bertocchi M, Desportes-Livage I, et al. Enterocytozoon bieneusi as a cause of chronic diarrhea in a heart-lung transplant recipient who was seronegative for human immunodeficiency virus. Clin Infect Dis 1996;23:114-117.

119. Sax PE, Rich JD, Pieciak WS, Trnka YM. Intestinal microsporidiosis occurring in a liver transplant recipient. Transplantation 1995;60:617-618.

120. Gumbo T, Hobbs RE, Carlyn C, et al. Microsporidia infection in transplant patients. Transplantation 1999;67:482-484.

121. Kelkar R, Sastry PS, Kulkarni SS, et al. Pulmonary microsporidial infection in a patient with CML undergoing allogeneic marrow transplant. Bone Marrow Transplant 1997;19:179-182.

122. Mahmood MN, Keohane ME, Burd EM. Pathologic quiz case: a 45-year-old renal transplant recipient with persistent fever. Arch Pathol Lab Med 2003;127:224-226.

123. Metge S, Van Nhieu JT, Dahmane D, et al. A case of Enterocytozoon bieneusi infection in an HIV-negative renal transplant recipient. Eur J Clin Microbiol Infect Dis 2000;19:221-223.

124. Mohindra AR, Lee MW, Visvesvara G, et al. Disseminated microsporidiosis in a renal transplant recipient. Transpl Infect Dis 2002;4:102-107.

125. Sing A, Tybus K, Heesemann J, Mathis A. Molecular diagnosis of an Enterocytozoon bieneusi human genotype C infection in a moderately immunosuppressed human immunodeficiency virus seronegative liver-transplant recipient with severe chronic diarrhea. J Clin Microbiol 2001;39:2371-2372.

126. Silverstein BE, Cunningham ETJ, Margolis TP, et al. Microsporidial keratoconjunctivitis in a patient without human immunodeficiency virus infection. Am J Ophthalmol 1997;124:395-396.

127. Weiss LM. And now microsporidiosis. Ann Intern Med 1995;123:954-956.

128. Van Gool T, Dankert J. Human microsporidiosis: clinical, diagnostic and therapeutic aspects of an increasing infection. Clin Microbiol Infect 1995;1:75-85.

129. Bryan RT, Cali A, Owen RL, Spencer HC. Microsporidia: opportunistic pathogens in patients with AIDS. In: Progress in Clinical Parasitology, v. 2. New York: Field & Wood Medical Publishers; 1991.

130. Coyle CM, Wittner M, Kotler DP, et al. Prevalence of microsporidiosis due to Enterocytozoon bieneusi and Encephalitozoon (Septata) intestinalis among patients with AIDS-related diarrhea: determination by polymerase chain reaction to the microsporidian small-subunit rRNA gene. Clin Infect Dis 1996;23:1002-1006.

131. Voglino MC, Donelli G, Rossi P, et al. Intestinal microsporidiosis in Italian individuals with AIDS. Ital J Gastroenterol 1996;28:381-386.

132. Kyaw T, Curry A, Edwards-Jones V, et al. The prevalence of Enterocytozoon bieneusi in acquired immunodeficiency syndrome (AIDS) patients from the north west of England: 1992-1995. Br J Biomed Sci 1997;54:186-191.

133. Molina JM, Oksenhendler E, Beauvais B, et al. Disseminated microsporidiosis due to Septata intestinalis in patients with AIDS: clinical features and response to albendazole therapy. J Infect Dis 1995;171:245-249.

134. Molina JM, Tourneur M, Sarfati C, et al. Fumagillin treatment of intestinal microsporidiosis. N Engl J Med 2002;346:1963-1969.

135. Molina JM, Goguel J, Sarfati C, et al. Trial of oral fumagillin for the treatment of intestinal microsporidiosis in patients with HIV infection; ANRS 054 Study Group: Agence Nationale de Recherche sur le SIDA. AIDS 2000;14:1341-1348.

136. Bergquist NR, Stintzing G, Smedman L, et al. Diagnosis of encephalitozoonosis in man by serological tests. BMJ 1984;288:902.

137. Aldras AM, Orenstein JM, Kotler DP, et al. Detection of microsporidia by indirect immunofluorescence antibody test using polyclonal and monoclonal antibodies. J Clin Microbiol 1994;32:608-612.

138. Weiss LM, Cali A, Levee E, et al. Diagnosis of Encephalitozoon cuniculi infection by Western blot and the use of cross-reactive antigens for the possible detection of microsporidiosis in humans. Am J Trop Med Hyg 1992;47:456-462.

139. Singh M, Kane GJ, Mackinlay L, et al. Detection of antibodies to Nosema cuniculi (Protozoa: Microscoporidia) in human and animal sera by the indirect fluorescent antibody technique. Southeast Asian J Trop Med Public Health 1982;13:110-113.

140. WHO parasitic diseases surveillance: antibody to Encephalitozoon cuniculi in man. WHO Wkly Epidemiol Rec 1983;58:30.

141. Bergquist R, Morfeldt-Mansson L, Pehrson PO, et al. Antibody against Encephalitozoon cuniculi in Swedish homosexual men. Scand J Infect Dis 1984; 16:389-391.

142. Van Gool T, Vetter JC, Weinmayr B, et al. High seroprevalence of Encephalitozoon species in immunocompetent subjects. J Infect Dis 1997;175:1020-1024.

143. Pospisilova Z, Ditrich O, Stankova M, Kodym P. Parasitic opportunistic infections in Czech HIV-infected patients: a prospective study. Cent Eur J Public Health 1997;5:208-213.

144. Cislakova L, Prokopcakova H, Stef'kovic M, Halanova M. [Encephalitozoon cuniculi—clinical and epidemiologic significance: results of a preliminary serologic study in humans.] Epidemiol Mikrobiol Immunol 1997;46:30-33.

145. Didier ES, Varner PW, Didier PJ, et al. Experimental microsporidiosis in immunocompetent and immunodeficient mice and monkeys. Folia Parasitol 1994;41:1-11.

146. Koudela B, Vitovec J, Kucerova Z, et al. The severe combined immunodeficient mouse as a model for Encephalitozoon cuniculi microsporidiosis. Folia Parasitol (Praha) 1993;40:279-286.

147. Schmidt EC, Shadduck JA. Mechanisms of resistance to the intracellular protozoan Encephalitozoon cuniculi in mice. J Immunol 1984;133:2712-2719.

148. Hermanek J, Koudela B, Kucerova Z, et al. Prophylactic and therapeutic immune reconstitution of SCID mice infected with Encephalitozoon cuniculi. Folia Parasitol (Praha) 1993;40:287-291.

149. Didier ES, Shadduck JA. IFN-gamma and LPS induce murine macrophages to kill Encephalitozoon cuniculi in vitro. J Eukaryot Microbiol 1994;41:34S.

150. Didier ES. Reactive nitrogen intermediates implicated in the inhibition of Encephalitozoon cuniculi (phylum Microspora) replication in murine peritoneal macrophages. Parasite Immunol 1995;17:405-412.

151. Khan IA, Moretto M. Role of gamma interferon in cellular immune response against murine Encephalitozoon cuniculi infection. Infect Immun 1999;67:1887-1893.

152. Bywater JE, Kellett BS. Humoral immune response to natural infection with Encephalitozoon cuniculi in rabbits. Lab Anim 1979;13:293-297.

153. Enriquez FJ, Ditrich O, Palting JD, Smith K. Simple diagnosis of Encephalitozoon sp. microsporidial infections by using a panspecific antiexospore monoclonal antibody. J Clin Microbiol 1997;35:724-729.

154. Shtrichman R, Samuel CE. The role of gamma interferon in antimicrobial immunity. Curr Opin Microbiol 2001;4:251-259.

155. Achbarou A, Ombrouck C, Gneragbe T, et al. Experimental model for human intestinal microsporidiosis in interferon gamma receptor knockout mice infected by Encephalitozoon intestinalis. Parasite Immunol 1996;18:387-392.

156. Khan IA, Schwartzman JD, Kasper LH, Moretto M. CD8+ CTLs are essential for protective immunity against Encephalitozoon cuniculi infection. J Immunol 1999;162:6086-6091.

157. Wong P, Pamer EG. CD8 T cell responses to infectious pathogens. Annu Rev Immunol 2003;21:29-70.

158. Conteas CN, Berlin OG, Speck CE, et al. Modification of the clinical course of intestinal microsporidiosis in acquired immunodeficiency syndrome patients by immune status and anti-human immunodeficiency virus therapy. Am J Trop Med Hyg 1998;58:555-558.

159. Goguel J, Katlama C, Sarfati C, et al. Remission of AIDS-associated intestinal microsporidiosis with highly active antiretroviral therapy. AIDS 1997;11:1658-1659.

160. Foudraine NA, Weverling GJ, van Gool T, et al. Improvement of chronic diarrhoea in patients with advanced HIV-1 infection during potent antiretroviral therapy. AIDS 1998;12:35-41.

161. Terada S, Reddy KR, Jeffers LJ, et al. Microsporidan hepatitis in the acquired immunodeficiency syndrome. Ann Intern Med 1987;107:61-62.

162. Schwartz DA, Anderson DC, Klumpp SA, McClure HM. Ultrastructure of atypical (teratoid) sporogonial stages of Enterocytozoon bieneusi (Microsporidia) in naturally infected rhesus monkeys (Macaca mulatta). Arch Pathol Lab Med 1998;122:423-429.

163. Orenstein JM, Tenner M, Kotler DP. Localization of infection by the microsporidian Enterocytozoon bieneusi in the gastrointestinal tract of AIDS patients with diarrhea. AIDS 1992;6:195-197.

164. Pol S, Romana CA, Richard S, et al. Microsporidia infection in patients with the human immunodeficiency virus and unexplained cholangitis. N Engl J Med 1993;328:95-99.

165. Orenstein JM. Diagnostic pathology of microsporidiosis. Ultrastruct Pathol 2003;27:141-149.

166. Schwartz DA, Sobottka I, Leitch GJ, et al. Pathology of microsporidiosis: emerging parasitic infections in patients with acquired immunodeficiency syndrome. Arch Pathol Lab Med 1996;120:173-188.

167. Schwartz DA, Abou-Ella A, Wilcox CM, et al. The presence of Enterocytozoon bieneusi spores in the lamina propria of small bowel biopsies with no evidence of disseminated microsporidiosis; Enteric Opportunistic Infections Working Group. Arch Pathol Lab Med 1995;119:424-428.

168. Orenstein JM, Dieterich DT, Kotler DP. Systemic dissemination by a newly recognized intestinal microsporidia species in AIDS. AIDS 1992;6:1143-1150.

169. Soule JB, Halverson AL, Becker RB, et al. A patient with acquired immunodeficiency syndrome and untreated Encephalitozoon (Septata) intestinalis microsporidiosis leading to small bowel perforation: response to albendazole. Arch Pathol Lab Med 1997;121:880-887.

170. Zender HO, Arrigoni E, Eckert J, Kapanci Y. A case of Encephalitozoon cuniculi peritonitis in a patient with AIDS. Am J Clin Pathol 1989;92:352-356.

171. Gunnarsson G, Hurlbut D, DeGirolami PC, et al. Multiorgan microsporidiosis: report of five cases and review. Clin Infect Dis 1995;21:37-44.

172. Guerard A, Rabodonirina M, Cotte L, et al. Intestinal microsporidiosis occurring in two renal transplant recipients treated with mycophenolate mofetil. Transplantation 1999;68:699-707.

173. Latib MA, Pascoe MD, Duffield MS, Kahn D. Microsporidiosis in the graft of a renal transplant recipient. Transpl Int 2001;14:274-277.

174. Mertens RB, Didier ES, Fishbein MC, et al. Encephalitozoon cuniculi microsporidiosis: infection of the brain, heart, kidneys, trachea, adrenal glands, and urinary bladder in a patient with AIDS. Mod Pathol 1997;10:68-77.

175. Cali A, Meisler DM, Rutherford I, et al. Corneal microsporidiosis in a patient with AIDS. Am J Trop Med Hyg 1991;44:463-468.

176. Coyle CM, Weiss LM, Rhodes LV III, et al. Fatal myositis due to the microsporidian Brachiola algerae, a mosquito pathogen. N Engl J Med. 2004;351:42-47.

177. Grau A, Valls ME, Williams JE, et al. [Myositis caused by Pleistophora in a patient with AIDS.] Med Clin (Barc) 1996;107:779-781.

178. Ledford DK, Overman MD, Gonzalvo A, et al. Microsporidiosis myositis in a patient with the acquired immunodeficiency syndrome. Ann Intern Med 1985;102:628-630.

179. Schwartz DA, Visvesvara GS, Leitch GJ, et al. Pathology of symptomatic microsporidial (Encephalitozoon hellem) bronchiolitis in the acquired immunodeficiency syndrome: a new respiratory pathogen diagnosed from lung biopsy, bronchoalveolar lavage, sputum, and tissue culture. Hum Pathol 1993;24:937-943.

180. Didier ES, Rogers LB, Orenstein JM, et al. Characterization of Encephalitozoon (Septata) intestinalis isolates cultured from nasal mucosa and bronchoalveolar lavage fluids of two AIDS patients. J Eukaryot Microbiol 1996;43:34-43.

181. Dunand VA, Hammer SM, Rossi R, et al. Parasitic sinusitis and otitis in patients infected with human immunodeficiency virus: report of five cases and review. Clin Infect Dis 1997;25:267-272.

182. Franzen C, Muller A, Salzberger B, et al. Chronic rhinosinusitis in patients with AIDS: potential role of microsporidia. AIDS 1996;10:687-688.

183. Gritz DC, Holsclaw DS, Neger RE, et al. Ocular and sinus microsporidial infection cured with systemic albendazole. Am J Ophthalmol 1997;124:241-243.

184. Josephson GD, Sarlin J, Reidy J, Pincus R. Microsporidial rhinosinusitis: is this the next pathogen to infect the sinuses of the immunocompromised host? Otolaryngol Head Neck Surg 1996;114:137-139.

185. Moss RB, Beaudet LM, Wenig BM, et al. Microsporidium-associated sinusitis. Ear Nose Throat J 1997;76:95-101.

186. Pedro-de-Lelis FJ, Sabater-Marco V, Herrera-Ballester A. Necrotizing maxillary sinus mucormycosis related to candidiasis and microsporidiosis in an AIDS patient. AIDS 1995;9:1386-1388.

187. Degroote MA, Visvesvara G, Wilson ML, et al. Polymerase chain reaction and culture confirmation of disseminated Encephalitozoon cuniculi in a patient with AIDS: successful therapy with albendazole. J Infect Dis 1995;171:1375-1378.

188. Schwartz DA, Bryan RT, Hewanlowe KO, et al. Disseminated microsporidiosis (Encephalitozoon hellem) and acquired immunodeficiency syndrome: autopsy evidence for respiratory acquisition. Arch Pathol Lab Med 1992;116:660-646.

189. Franzen C, Mueller A, Salzberger B, et al. Chronic rhinosinusitis in patients with AIDS: potential role of microsporidia. AIDS 1996;10:687-688.

190. Del Aguila C, Lopez-Velez R, Fenoy S, et al. Identification of Enterocytozoon bieneusi spores in respiratory samples from an AIDS patient with a 2-year history of intestinal microsporidiosis. J Clin Microbiol 1997;35:1862-1866.

191. Weber R, Kuster H, Keller R, et al. Pulmonary and intestinal microsporidiosis in a patient with the acquired immunodeficiency syndrome. Am Rev Respir Dis 1992;146:1603-1605.

192. Hartskeerl RA, Schuitema AR, van Gool T, Terpstra WJ. Genetic evidence for the occurrence of extra-intestinal Enterocytozoon bieneusi infections. Nucleic Acids Res 1993;21:4150.

193. Visvesvara GS, Belloso M, Moura H, et al. Isolation of Nosema algerae from the cornea of an immunocompetent patient. J Eukaryot Microbiol 1999;46:10S.

194. Kester KE, Visvesara GS, McEvoy P. Organism responsible for nodular cutaneous microsporidiosis in a patient with AIDS. Ann Intern Med 2000;133:925.

195. Kester KE, Turiansky GW, McEvoy PL. Nodular cutaneous microsporidiosis in a patient with AIDS and successful treatment with long-term oral clindamycin therapy. Ann Intern Med 1998;128:911-914.

196. Levaditi C, Nicolau S, Schoen R. Nouvelles donnees sur L'Encephalitozoon cuniculi. C R Soc Biol 1923;89:1157-1162.

197. Margileth AM, Strano AJ, Chandra R, et al. Disseminated nosematosis in an immunologically compromised infant. Arch Pathol 1973;95:145-150.

198. Desportes-Livage I, Doumbo O, Pichard E, et al. Microsporidiosis in HIV-seronegative patients in Mali. Trans R Soc Trop Med Hyg 1998;92:423-424.

199. Lopez-Velez R, Turrientes MC, Garron C, et al. Microsporidiosis in travelers with diarrhea from the tropics. J Travel Med 1999;6:223-227.

200. Muller A, Bialek R, Kamper A, et al. Detection of microsporidia in travelers with diarrhea. J Clin Microbiol 2001;39:1630-1632.

201. Orenstein JM, Chiang J, Steinberg W, et al. Intestinal microsporidiosis as a cause of diarrhea in human immunodeficiency virus-infected patients: a report of 20 cases. Hum Pathol 1990;21:475-481.

202. Tumwine JK, Kekitiinwa A, Nabukeera N, et al. Enterocytozoon bieneusi among children with diarrhea attending Mulago Hospital in Uganda. Am J Trop Med Hyg 2002;67:299-303.

203. Goetz M, Eichenlaub S, Pape GR, Hoffmann RM. Chronic diarrhea as a result of intestinal microsporidiosis in a liver transplant recipient. Transplantation 2001;71:334-337.

204. Kelkar R, Sastry PSRK, Kulkarni SS, et al. Pulmonary microsporidial infection in a patient with CML undergoing allogeneic marrow transplant. Bone Marrow Transplant 1997;19:179-182.

205. Pinnolis M, Egbert PR, Font RL, Winter FC. Nosematosis of the cornea: case report, including electron microscopic studies. Arch Ophthalmol 1981;99:1044-1047.

206. Ashton N, Wirasinha PA. Encephalitozoonosis (nosematosis) of the cornea. Br J Ophthalmol 1973;57:669-674.

207. Cali A, Meisler DM, Lowder CY, et al. Corneal microsporidioses: characterization and identification. J Protozool 1991;38:215S-217S.

208. Davis RM, Font RL, Keisler MS, Shadduck JA. Corneal microsporidiosis: a case report including ultrastructural observations. Ophthalmology 1990;97:953-957.

209. Weber R, Muller A, Spycher MA, et al. Intestinal Enterocytozoon bieneusi microsporidiosis in an HIV-infected patient: diagnosis by ileo-colonoscopic biopsies and long-term follow up. Clin Invest 1992;70:1019-1023.

210. Rijpstra AC, Canning EU, Van Ketel RJ, et al. Use of light microscopy to diagnose small-intestinal microsporidiosis in patients with AIDS. J Infect Dis 1988;157:827-831.

211. Molina JM, Sarfati C, Beauvais B, et al. Intestinal microsporidiosis in human immunodeficiency virus-infected patients with chronic unexplained diarrhea: prevalence and clinical and biologic features. J Infect Dis 1993;167:217-221.

212. Hewan-Lowe K, Furlong B, Sims M, Schwartz DA. Coinfection with Giardia lamblia and Enterocytozoon bieneusi in a patient with acquired immunodeficiency syndrome and chronic diarrhea. Arch Pathol Lab Med 1997;121:417-122.

213. Beaugerie L, Teilhac MF, Deluol AM, et al. Cholangiopathy associated with microsporidia infection of the common bile duct mucosa in a patient with HIV infection. Ann Intern Med 1992;117:401-402.

214. Hartskeerl RA, van Gool T, Schuitema ARJ, et al. Genetic and immunological characterization of the microsporidian Septata intestinalis Cali, Kotler and Orenstein, 1993: reclassification to Encephalitozoon intestinalis. Parasitology 1995;110: 277-285.

215. Didier ES, Didier PJ, Snowden KF, Shadduck JA. Microsporidiosis in mammals. Microbes Infect 2000;2:709-720.

216. Schwartz DA, Visvesvara GS, Leitch GJ, et al. Pathology of symptomatic microsporidial (Encephalitozoon hellem) bronchiolitis in the acquired immunodeficiency syndrome: a new respiratory pathogen diagnosed from lung biopsy, bronchoalveolar lavage, sputum, and tissue culture. Hum Pathol 1993;24:937-943.

217. Vangool T, Canning EU, Gilis H, et al. Septata intestinalis frequently isolated from stool of AIDS patients with a new cultivation method. Parasitology 1994;109: 281-289.

218. Willson R, Harrington R, Stewart B, Fritsche T. Human immunodeficiency virus 1-associated necrotizing cholangitis caused by infection with Septata intestinalis. Gastroenterology 1995;108:247-251.

219. Belcher JW Jr, Guttenberg SA, Schmookler BM. Microsporidiosis of the mandible in a patient with acquired immunodeficiency syndrome. J Oral Maxillofac Surg 1997;55:424-426.

220. Dore GJ, Marriott DJ, Hing MC, et al. Disseminated microsporidiosis due to Septata intestinalis in nine patients infected with the human immunodeficiency virus: response to therapy with albendazole. Clin Infect Dis 1995;21:70-76.

221. Weber R, Sauer B, Spycher MA, et al. Detection of Septata intestinalis in stool specimens and coprodiagnostic monitoring of successful treatment with albendazole. Clin Infect Dis 1994;19:342-345.

222. De Groote MA, Visvesvara G, Wilson ML, et al. Polymerase chain reaction and culture confirmation of disseminated Encephalitozoon cuniculi in a patient with AIDS: successful therapy with albendazole. J Infect Dis 1995;171:1375-1378.

223. Weber R, Kuster H, Visvesvara GS, et al. Disseminated microsporidiosis due to Encephalitozoon hellem: pulmonary colonization, microhematuria, and mild conjunctivitis in a patient with AIDS. Clin Infect Dis 1993;17:415-419.

224. Visvesvara GS, Leitch GJ, da Silva AJ, et al. Polyclonal and monoclonal antibody and PCR-amplified small-subunit rRNA identification of a microsporidian, Encephalitozoon hellem, isolated from an AIDS patient with disseminated infection. J Clin Microbiol 1994;32:2760-2768.

225. Lowder CY, Meisler DM, McMahon JT, et al. Microsporidia infection of the cornea in a man seropositive for human immunodeficiency virus. Am J Ophthalmol 1990;109:242-244.

226. Lacey CJN, Clarke AMT, Fraser P, et al. Chronic microsporidian infection of the nasal mucosae, sinuses and conjunctivae in HIV disease. Genitourin Med 1992;68:179-181.

227. Franzen C, Schwartz DA, Visvesvara GS, et al. Immunologically confirmed disseminated, asymptomatic Encephalitozoon cuniculi infection of the gastrointestinal tract in a patient with AIDS. Clin Infect Dis 1995;21:1480-1484.

228. Macher AR, Neafie R, Angritt P, Tuur S. Microsporidia myositis and the acquired immunodeficiency syndrome (AIDS): a four year followup. Ann Intern Med 1988;109:343-344.

229. Weber R, Bryan RT, Owen RL, et al. Improved light-microscopal detection of microsporidia spores in stool and duodenal aspirates. N Engl J Med 1992;326:161-166.

230. Vavra J, Dahbiova R, Hollister WS, Canning EU. Staining of microsporidian spores by optical brighteners with remarks on the use of brighteners for the diagnosis of AIDS associated human microsporidiosis. Folia Parasitol (Praha) 1993;40:267-272.

231. Van Gool T, Snijders F, Reiss P, et al. Diagnosis of intestinal and disseminated microsporidial infections in patients with HIV by a new rapid fluorescence technique. J Clin Pathol 1993;46:694-699.

232. Ryan NJ, Sutherland G, Coughlan K, et al. A new trichrome-blue stain for detection of microsporidial species in urine, stool, and nasopharyngeal specimens. J Clin Microbiol 1993;31:3264-3269.

233. Kokoskin E, Gyorkos TW, Camus A, et al. Modified technique for efficient detection of microsporidia. J Clin Microbiol 1994;32:1074-1075.

234. Moura H, Schwartz DA, Bornay-Llinares F, et al. A new and improved "quick-hot Gram-chromotrope" technique that differentially stains microsporidian spores in clinical samples, including paraffin-embedded tissue sections. Arch Pathol Lab Med 1997;121:888-893.

235. Didier ES, Orenstein JM, Aldras A, et al. Comparison of three staining methods for detecting microsporidia in fluids. J Clin Microbiol 1995;33:3138-3145.

236. DeGirolami PC, Ezratty CR, Desai G, et al. Diagnosis of intestinal microsporidiosis by examination of stool and duodenal aspirate with Weber's modified trichrome and Uvitex 2B strains. J Clin Microbiol 1995;33:805-810.

237. Field AS, Marriott DJ, Hing MC. The Warthin-Starry stain in the diagnosis of small intestinal microsporidiosis in HIV-infected patients. Folia Parasitol (Praha) 1993;40:261-266.

238. Field AS. Light microscopic and electron microscopic diagnosis of gastrointestinal opportunistic infections in HIV-positive patients. Pathology 2002;34:21-35.

239. Zierdt CH, Gill VJ, Zierdt WS. Detection of microsporidian spores in clinical samples by indirect fluorescent-antibody assay using whole-cell antisera to Encephalitozoon cuniculi and Encephalitozoon hellem. J Clin Microbiol 1993;31:3071-3074.

240. Croppo GP, Visvesvara GS, Leitch GJ, et al. Identification of the microsporidian Encephalitozoon hellem using immunoglobulin G monoclonal antibodies. Arch Pathol Lab Med 1998;122:182-186.

241. Beckers PJ, Derks GJ, Gool T, Rietveld FJ, Sauerwein RW. Encephalitozoon intestinalis-specific monoclonal antibodies for laboratory diagnosis of microsporidiosis. J Clin Microbiol 1996;34:282-285.

242. Accoceberry I, Thellier M, Desportes-Livage I, et al. Production of monoclonal antibodies directed against the microsporidium Enterocytozoon bieneusi. J Clin Microbiol 1999;37:4107-4112.

243. Visvesvara GS. In vitro cultivation of microsporidia of clinical importance. Clin Microbiol Rev 2002;15:401-413.

244. Visvesvara GS, Leitch GJ, Pieniazek NJ, et al. Short-term in vitro culture and molecular analysis of the microsporidian, Enterocytozoon bieneusi. J Eukaryot Microbiol 1995;42:506-510.

245. Visvesvara GS, Leitch GJ, Wallace S, et al. Adenovirus masquerading as microsporidia. J Parasitol 1996;82:316-319.

246. Tzipori S, Carville A, Widmer G, et al. Transmission and establishment of a persistent infection of Enterocytozoon bieneusi, derived from a human with AIDS, in simian immunodeficiency virus-infected rhesus monkeys. J Infect Dis 1997;175:1016-1020.

247. Didier ES. Immunology of microsporidiosis. Contrib Microbiol 2000;6:193-208.

248. Katzwinkel-Wladarsch S, Deplazes P, Weber R, et al. Comparison of polymerase chain reaction with light microscopy for detection of microsporida in clinical specimens. Eur J Clin Microbiol Infect Dis 1997;16:7-10.

249. Fedorko DP, Nelson NA, Cartwright CP. Identification of microsporidia in stool specimens by using PCR and restriction endonucleases. J Clin Microbiol 1995;33: 1739-1741.

250. Ombrouck C, Ciceron L, Biligui S, et al. Specific PCR assay for direct detection of intestinal microsporidia Enterocytozoon bieneusi and Encephalitozoon intestinalis in fecal specimens from human immunodeficiency virus-infected patients. J Clin Microbiol 1997;35:652-655.

251. Maggi P, Larocca AM, Quarto M, et al. Effect of antiretroviral therapy on cryptosporidiosis and microsporidiosis in patients infected with human immunodeficiency virus type 1. Eur J Clin Microbiol Infect Dis 2000;19:213-217.

252. Martins SA, Muccioli C, Belfort R Jr, Castelo A. Resolution of microsporidial keratoconjunctivitis in an AIDS patient treated with highly active antiretroviral therapy. Am J Ophthalmol 2001;131:378-379.

253. Miao YM, Awad-El-Kariem FM, Franzen C, et al. Eradication of cryptosporidia and microsporidia following successful antiretroviral therapy. J Acquir Immune Defic Syndr 2000;25:124-129.

254. Beauvais B, Sarfati C, Challier S, Derouin F. In vitro model to assess effect of antimicrobial agents on Encephalitozoon cuniculi. Antimicrob Agents Chemother 1994;38:2440-2448.

255. Franssen FF, Lumeij JT, van Knapen F. Susceptibility of Encephalitozoon cuniculi to several drugs in vitro. Antimicrob Agents Chemother 1995;39:1265-1268.

256. Costa SF, Weiss LM. Drug treatment of microsporidiosis. Drug Resist Update 2000;3.384-399.

257. Didier ES. Effects of albendazole, fumagillin, and TNP-470 on microsporidial replication in vitro. Antimicrob Agents Chemother 1997;41:1541-1546.

258. Diesenhouse MC, Wilson LA, Corrent GF, et al. Treatment of microsporidial keratoconjunctivitis with topical fumagillin. Am J Ophthalmol 1993;115:293-298.

259. Garvey MJ, Ambrose PG, Ulmer JL. Topical fumagillin in the treatment of microsporidial keratoconjunctivitis in AIDS. Ann Pharmacother 1995;29:872-874.

260. Molina JM, Goguel J, Sarfati C, et al. Potential efficacy of fumagillin in intestinal microsporidiosis due to Enterocytozoon bieneusi in patients with HIV infection: results of a drug screening study; the French Microsporidiosis Study Group. AIDS 1997;11:1603-1610.

261. Blanshard C, Peacock C, Ellis D, Gazzard B. Treatment of intestinal microsporidiosis with albendazole. In: Proceedings of the VII International Conference on AIDS: Science Challenging AIDS, Florence, Italy, July 16-21, 1991, v. 1: Clinical Science and Trials.

262. Aarons EJ, Woodrow D, Hollister WS, et al. Reversible renal failure caused by a microsporidian infection. AIDS 1994;8:1119-1121.

263. Corcoran GD, Isaacson JR, Daniels C, Chiodini PL. Urethritis associated with disseminated microsporidiosis: clinical response to albendazole. Clin Infect Dis 1996;22:592-593.

264. Dieterich DT, Lew EA, Kotler DP, et al. Treatment with albendazole for intestinal disease due to Enterocytozoon bieneusi in patients with AIDS. J Infect Dis 1994;169:178-183.

265. Li J, Katiyar SK, Hamelin A, et al. Tubulin genes from AIDS-associated microsporidia and implications for phylogeny and benzimidazole sensitivity. Mol Biochem Parasitol 1996;78:289-295.

266. Molina JM, Chastang C, Goguel J, et al. Albendazole for treatment and prophylaxis of microsporidiosis due to Encephalitozoon intestinalis in patients with AIDS: a randomized double-blind controlled trial. J Infect Dis 1998;177:1373-1377.

267. Sobottka I, Albrecht H, Schafer H, et al. Disseminated Encephalitozoon (Septata) intestinalis infection in a patient with AIDS: novel diagnostic approaches and autopsy-confirmed parasitological cure following treatment with albendazole. J Clin Microbiol 1995;33:2948-2952.

268. Lecuit M, Oksenhendler E, Sarfati C. Use of albendazole for disseminated microsporidian infection in a patient with AIDS. J Infect Dis 1994;19:332-333.

269. Visvesvara GS, Leitch GJ, Dasilva AJ, et al. Polyclonal and monoclonal antibody and PCR-amplified small-subunit rRNA identification of a microsporidian, Encephalitozoon hellem, isolated from an AIDS patient with disseminated infection. J Clin Microbiol 1994;32:2760-2768.

270. Blanshard C, Ellis DS, Tovey DG, et al. Treatment of intestinal microsporidiosis with albendazole in patients with AIDS. AIDS 1992;6:311-313.

271. Leder K, Ryan N, Spelman D, Crowe SM. Microsporidial disease in HIV-infected patients: a report of 42 patients and review of the literature. Scand J Infect Dis 1998;30:331-338.

272. Eeftinck Schattenkerk JK, van Gool T, van Ketel RJ, et al. Clinical significance of small-intestinal microsporidiosis in HIV-1-infected individuals. Lancet 1991;337:895-898.

273. Anwar-Bruni DM, Hogan SE, Schwartz DA, et al. Atovaquone is effective treatment for the symptoms of gastrointestinal microsporidiosis in HIV-1-infected patients. AIDS 1996;10:619-623.

274. Albrecht H, Sobottka I, Stellbrink HJ, Greten H. Does the choice of Pneumocystis carinii prophylaxis influence the prevalence of Enterocytozoon bieneusi microsporidiosis in AIDS patients? AIDS 1995;9:302-303.

275. Sharpstone D, Rowbottom A, Francis N, et al. Thalidomide: a novel therapy for microsporidiosis. Gastroenterology 1997;112:1823-1829.

276. Kano T, Fukui H. Studies on Pleistophora infection in eel, Anguilla japonica. I. Experimental induction of microsporidiosis and fumagillin efficacy. Fish Pathol 1982;16:193-200.

277. Higgins MJ, Kent ML, Moran JD, et al. Efficacy of the fumagillin analog TNP-470 for Nucleospora salmonis and Loma salmonae infections in chinook salmon Oncorhynchus tshawytscha. Dis Aquat Organ 1998;34:45-49.

278. Coyle C, Kent M, Tanowitz HB, et al. TNP-470 is an effective antimicrosporidial agent. J Infect Dis 1998;177:515-518.

279. Weiss LM, Costa SF, Zhang H. Microsporidian methionine aminopeptidase type 2. J Eukaryot Microbiol 2001;48(Suppl):88S-90S.

280. Rosberger DF, Serdarevic ON, Erlandson RA, et al. Successful treatment of microsporidial keratoconjunctivitis with topical fumagillin in a patient with AIDS. Cornea 1993;12:261-265.

281. Wilkins JH, Joshi N, Margolis TP, et al. Microsporidial keratoconjunctivitis treated successfully with a short course of fumagillin. Eye 1994;8(Pt 6):703-704.

282. Lowder CY, McMahon JT, Meisler DM, et al. Microsporidial keratoconjunctivitis caused by Septata intestinalis in a patient with acquired immunodeficiency syndrome. Am J Ophthalmol 1996;121:715-717.

283. Orenstein JM, Seedor J, Friedberg DN, et al. Microsporidian keratoconjunctivitis in patients with AIDS. MMWR Morb Mortal Wkly Rep 1990;39:188-189:

DISEASES DUE TO TOXIC ALGAE

CHAPTER **283**

Human Illness Associated with Harmful Algal Blooms

J. GLENN MORRIS, Jr.

During the past several decades, recognition of human health and environmental problems associated with harmful and toxic algae has been increasing.[1-3] Toxic species constitute a small percentage of the thousands of species of microscopic algae at the base of the marine food chain. However, when these species proliferate, they may cause massive kills of fish and shellfish, the death of marine mammals and seabirds, alterations in marine habitats, and with appropriate exposure human illness and death. Although blooms of certain species such as *Gymnodinium breve* may be manifested as "red tides," adverse events often occur in the absence of visible discoloration of water.

It is generally perceived that harmful algal blooms are increasing in frequency; in the United States, problems that in the past were confined to a few geographic locations are now being seen at multiple sites along the U.S. coastline (Fig. 283-1). The factors leading to this apparent increase in incidence are not well understood, although it has been postulated that human-related phenomena such as nutrient enrichment of waterways, climatic change, and disruption of ecosystems play some role.[1-6]

Six clinical syndromes/illnesses are currently linked with harmful algal blooms (Table 283-1),[7] and as more research is done in this area it is possible that other syndromes will be identified. Ciguatera fish poisoning, paralytic shellfish poisoning, and neurotoxic shellfish poisoning are described in Chapter 95 and so are only briefly discussed in this chapter. Diarrhetic shellfish poisoning, amnesic shellfish poisoning, and *Pfiesteria*-associated syndrome are discussed later in this chapter.

CIGUATERA FISH POISONING

Worldwide, ciguatera fish poisoning (see Chapter 95) is the most common of the clinical syndromes associated with marine biotoxins. It is a major public health problem in the Caribbean and South Pacific, particularly in areas with tropical reefs.[8,9] Illness is caused by toxins that are passed up the marine food chain, with large predatory reef fish (e.g., barracuda, jacks) having the greatest risk of toxicity. Gastrointestinal symptoms are the first manifestation of illness and usually occur within 24 hours of eating a toxic fish. These symptoms are followed by neurologic sequelae, which may persist for weeks to months.[9,10]

PARALYTIC SHELLFISH POISONING

Paralytic shellfish poisoning, or PSP (see Chapter 95), is the most common cause of marine biotoxin-associated illness in the continental United States and Alaska.[11] Illness has traditionally been associated with eating clams and mussels containing saxitoxins produced by *Alexandrium* spp. and related dinoflagellates. Saxitoxins have also been found in pufferfish (presumably related to consumption of mollusks by the fish), with a pufferfish-related PSP outbreak occurring in Florida in 2002.[12] Neurologic manifestations predominate; paresthesias are most common, although severe cases may progress to respiratory paralysis. Prevention is linked with regular monitoring of shellfish populations for saxitoxin by public health authorities.

NEUROTOXIC SHELLFISH POISONING

Illness is caused by brevetoxins produced by *Gymnodynium breve,* a major cause of red tides along the Florida coast. Ingestion of shellfish containing the toxin causes gastrointestinal and neurologic symptoms (see Chapter 95). Aerosolization of toxins by heavy wave action on the

FIGURE 283-1. Sites and types of harmful algal blooms along U.S. coast. *(From The Harmful Algal Page [www.whoi. edu/redtide/].)*

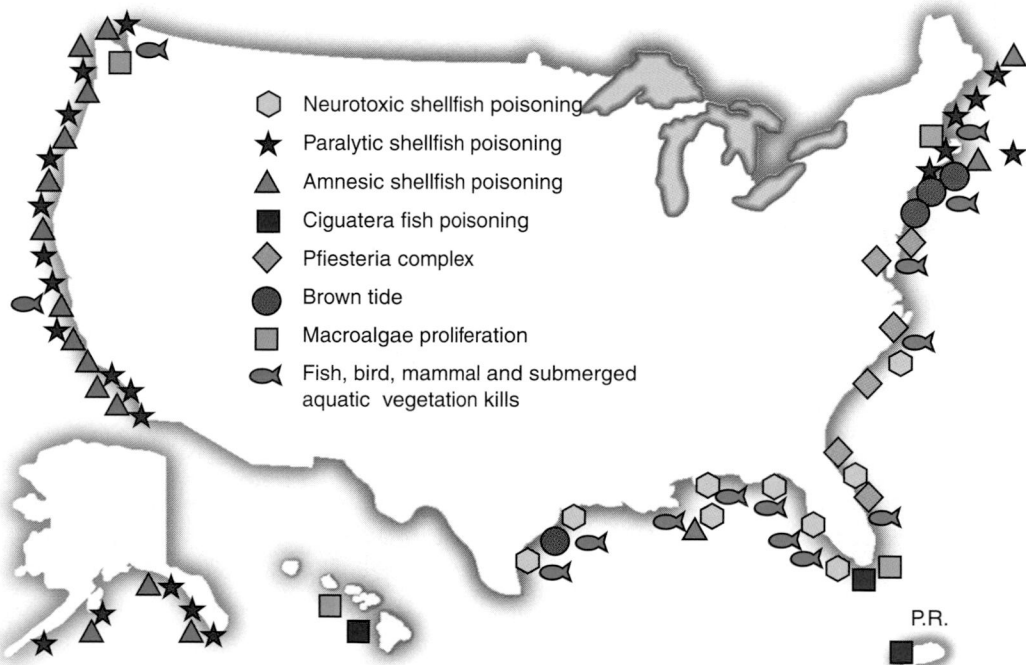

Neurotoxic shellfish poisoning

★ Paralytic shellfish poisoning

▲ Amnesic shellfish poisoning

■ Ciguatera fish poisoning

◆ Pfiesteria complex

● Brown tide

▪ Macroalgae proliferation

Fish, bird, mammal and submerged aquatic vegetation kills

P.R.

TABLE 283-1 Human Illness Associated with Harmful Algal Blooms

Syndrome	Causative Organisms	Toxin Produced	Clinical Manifestations
Ciguatera fish poisoning	*Gambierdiscus toxicus* and others	Ciguatoxin, maitotoxin	Acute gastroenteritis followed by paresthesias and other neurologic symptoms
Paralytic shellfish poisoning	*Alexandrium* spp. and others	Saxitoxins	Acute paresthesias and other neurologic manifestations; may progress rapidly to respiratory paralysis
Neurotoxic shellfish poisoning	*Gymnodinium breve*	Brevetoxins	Gastrointestinal and neurologic symptoms; formation of toxic aerosols by wave action can produce respiratory irritation and asthma-like symptoms
Diarrhetic shellfish poisoning	*Dinophysis* spp.	Okadaic acid and others	Acute gastroenteritis
Amnesic shellfish poisoning	*Pseudo-nitzschia* spp.	Domoic acid	Gastroenteritis, followed by memory loss, neurologic manifestations; may progress to amnesia, coma, and death
Pfiesteria-associated syndrome	*Pfiesteria* spp.	Unidentified to date	Deficiencies in learning and memory; acute respiratory and eye irritation, acute confusional syndrome

Atlantic coast of Florida can result in respiratory irritation and asthma-like symptoms in persons walking along affected beaches.[13]

DIARRHETIC SHELLFISH POISONING

Illness results from eating mussels, scallops, or clams that have been feeding on *Dinophysis fortii* or *Dinophysis acuminata*. In addition to diarrhea, symptoms of diarrhetic shellfish poisoning include nausea, vomiting, and abdominal pain. Although okadaic acid appears to be the primary toxin responsible for the observed clinical syndrome, other toxic compounds have been isolated from these species. Case reports came initially from Japan, but diarrhetic shellfish poisoning has now occurred in France and other parts of Europe, and *Dinophysis* spp. are spreading along the French and Spanish coasts. One episode of diarrhetic shellfish poisoning has occurred in Nova Scotia in association with eating cultured mussels.[3] No U.S. cases have been confirmed, although the causative organisms have been identified in U.S. coastal waters.

AMNESIC SHELLFISH POISONING

Amnesic shellfish poisoning results from the ingestion of shellfish containing domoic acid produced by the diatom *Pseudo-nitzschia pungens*.[1] A series of outbreaks caused by this toxin were reported in the Atlantic provinces of Canada in 1987.[3,14] Symptoms included vomiting, abdominal cramps, diarrhea, headache, and loss of short-term memory. On neuropsychological testing several months after the acute intoxication, patients were found to have severe antegrade memory deficits with relative preservation of other cognitive functions; patients also had clinical and electromyographic evidence of pure motor or sensorimotor neuropathy or axonopathy. Neuropathologic studies in four patients who died demonstrated neuronal necrosis and loss, predominantly in the hippocampus and amygdala.[15] Canadian authorities now analyze mussels and clams for domoic acid, and they close shellfish beds to harvesting when levels exceed 20 mg/g.

Domoic acid has been identified in the marine food web in multiple locations in the United States, including the Monterey Bay and Puget Sound areas. Elevated levels of domoic acid have been linked with neurologic illness and death in seabirds and sea lions in these areas, possibly related to consumption of shellfish or anchovies. Although there have been no confirmed cases of amnesic shellfish poisoning in the United States, a recent study in subsistence shellfish eating by native American tribes in the Puget Sound area found that infants born to shellfish-eating mothers during years when high domoic acid levels were present in shellfish had a significantly lower Mental Developmental Index compared with infants born in other years; children consuming shellfish during these "high" years also had lower memory performance than children who did not eat shellfish.[16] These data suggest that exposure to elevated domoic acid levels presents a health risk to infants and children, and they raise questions about the impact of chronic exposure to levels below the current 20 mg/g limit.

PFIESTERIA-ASSOCIATED SYNDROME

Pfiesteria piscicida was first isolated during the early 1990s as a suspected cause of massive fish kills in the New River and the Albemarle-Pamlico estuarine system of North Carolina.[17] Two *Pfiesteria* species are now recognized: *P. piscicida* and *P. shumwayae*. These microorganisms are widely distributed in estuarine areas in the mid-Atlantic region of the United States and have been identified in northern Europe. The mechanisms by which they affect fish remain controversial: Some investigators believe that it is toxin-mediated, whereas others have proposed a direct micropredation effect.[18] Nutrient loading of waterways may play a role in promoting the growth of *Pfiesteria*, with recent concerns focused on the impact of estuarine runoff of animal feces from large-scale commercial hog and chicken production.[19]

Shortly after identifying the organism, laboratory investigators working with toxic *Pfiesteria* cultures began to note problems with respiratory irritation, skin rashes, and, most disturbingly, cognition.[20] In subsequent studies conducted in the Chesapeake Bay region,[21] a significant association was found between the degree of exposure to waterways where *Pfiesteria* was known to be present and objective deficiencies in learning, memory, and higher-order cognitive function (divided attention). Six months after the cessation of exposure, scores of all affected persons had returned to within the normal range. Exposed persons also complained of headaches, skin lesions, and at times a burning sensation in skin directly exposed to water where *Pfiesteria* organisms appeared to be active. Persons who had been exposed to waterways and who had findings suggestive of extremely high levels of *Pfiesteria* activity (as seen during active fish kills) have reported acute respiratory and eye irritation; an acute, transient confusional syndrome has also been reported in this setting.[22] Studies have suggested that bioactive material produced by the microorganism acts as an inhibitor of the *N*-methyl-D-aspartate (NMDA) neuroreceptor[23] that appears to play a key role in learning and memory.

In contrast to syndromes associated with other marine biotoxins, *Pfiesteria*-associated illness is not connected with eating fish or shellfish. Although exposure routes are not clearly defined, it appears likely that the toxins are transmitted either through aerosols (analogous to what is seen at times with *G. breve* toxins) or by direct contact of skin with water in which the toxin is present.

REFERENCES

1. The Harmful Algal Page (www.whoi.edu/redtide2).
2. Toxic and Harmful Algal Blooms (www.bigelow.org/hab/).
3. Todd ECD. Emerging diseases associated with seafood toxins and other water-borne agents. Ann N Y Acad Sci 1994;740:77-94.
4. Ruff TA. Ciguatera in the Pacific: a link with military activities. Lancet 1989;1:201-205.
5. Thomassin BA, Ali Halidi ME, Quod JP, et al. Evolution of Gambierdiscus toxicus populations in the coral reef complex of Mayotte Island (SW Indian Ocean) during the 1985-1991 period. Bull Soc Pathol Exot 1992;85:449-452.
6. Tester PA. Harmful marine phytoplankton and shellfish toxicity: potential consequences of climatic change. Ann N Y Acad Sci 1994;740:69-76.
7. Morris JG Jr. Pfiesteria, "the cell from hell," and other toxic algal nightmares. Clin Infect Dis 1999;28:1191-1198.

8. Morris JG Jr, Lewin P, Smith CW, et al. Ciguatera fish poisoning: epidemiology of the disease on St. Thomas, U.S. Virgin Islands. Am J Trop Med Hyg 1982;31:574-578.

9. Bagnis R, Kuberski T, Lugier S. Clinical observations on 3009 cases of ciguatera (fish poisoning) in the South Pacific. Am J Trop Med Hyg 1979;28:1067-1073.

10. Morris JG Jr, Lewin P, Hargrett NT, et al. Clinical features of ciguatera fish poisoning: a study of the disease in the U.S. Virgin Islands. Arch Intern Med 1982;142: 1090-1092.

11. Gessner BD, Middaugh JP. Paralytic shellfish poisoning in Alaska: a 20-year retrospective. Am J Epidemiol 1995;141:766-770.

12. Centers for Disease Control. Neurological illness associated with eating Florida pufferfish, 2002. MMWR Morbid Mortal Wkly Rep 2002;51:321-323.

13. Music SI, Howell JT, Brumback CL. Red tide: its public health implications. J Fla Med Assoc 1973;60:27-29.

14. Perl TM, Bedard L, Kosatsky T, et al. An outbreak of toxic encephalopathy caused by eating mussels contaminated with domoic acid. N Engl J Med 1990;322:1775-1780.

15. Teitelbaum JS, Zatorre RJ, Carpenter S, et al. Neurologic sequelae of domoic acid intoxication due to ingestion of contaminated mussels. N Engl J Med 1990;322: 1781-1787.

16. Grattan LM, Lesoing M, Etesamypour-King A, et al. Potential health risks of domoic acid exposure to native American infants/toddlers and children in the Pacific Northwest: a pilot study (Abstract). In: Book of Abstracts, Xth International Conference on Harmful Algae, October 21-25, 2002, St. Pete Beach, Florida

17. Burkholder JM, Noga EJ, Hobbs CH, et al. New "phantom" dinoflagellate is the causative agent of major estuarine fish kills. Nature 1992;358:407-410.

18. Vogelbein WK, Lovko VJ, Shields JD, et al. Pfiesteria shumwayae kills fish by micropredation not exotoxin secretion. Nature 2002;418:967-970.

19. Boesch DF, Brinsfield RB, Magnien RE. Chesapeake Bay eutrophication: scientific understanding, ecosystem restoration, and challenges for agriculture. J Environ Qual 2001;30:303-320.

20. Glasgow HB Jr, Burkholder JM, Schmechel DE, et al. Insidious effects of a toxic estuarine dinoflagellate on fish survival and human health. J Toxicol Environ Health 1995;46:501-522.

21. Grattan LM, Oldach D, Perl TM, et al. Learning and memory difficulties after environmental exposure to waterways containing toxin-producing Pfiesteria or Pfiesteria-like dinoflagellates. Lancet 1998;352:532-539.

22. Haselow DR, Brown E, Tracy JK, et al. Gastrointestinal and respiratory tract symptoms following brief environmental exposure to aerosols during a Pfiesteria-related fish kill. J Toxicol Environ Health A 2001;63:553-564.

23. El-Nabawi A, Quesenberry M, Saito K, et al. The N-methyl-D-aspartate neurotransmitter receptor is a mammalian brain target for the dinoflagellate Pfiesteria piscicida toxin. Toxicol Appl Pharamacol 2000;169:84-93.

CHAPTER **284**

Introduction to Helminth Infections

JAMES H. MAGUIRE

The helminthiases are among the most prevalent infections in the world and a leading cause of morbidity, particularly in developing areas.[1] Literally billions of persons harbor at least one species of parasitic worm.[2] The helminths that parasitize humans include the nematodes (roundworms) and platyhelminths (flatworms), the latter group consisting of cestodes (tapeworms) and trematodes (schistosomes and other flukes). Leeches, ectoparasites belonging to the phylum Annelida (segmented worms) are not discussed here (see Chapter 290). Some helminths are exclusively or primarily human parasites, whereas others parasitize both humans and various other mammals, and others are parasites of lower mammals and infect human beings incidentally.

BIOLOGY OF HELMINTHS

Helminths are multicellular organisms that range from less than 1 cm to more than 10 m in length. They are covered by a cuticle or tegument that protects them from digestion and environmental stresses. Reproductive organs take up a large part of the body regardless of whether the sexes are separate or the species is hermaphroditic, as is the case with cestodes and nonschistosomal trematodes. Neuromuscular, digestive, excretory, and secretory systems typically are smaller and less complex, in keeping with the parasitic state.

The life cycle of all worms includes an egg, one or more larval stages, and the adult. Transmission to humans occurs by ingestion of helminth eggs or larvae, penetration of intact skin by larvae, or inoculation of larvae by biting insects. Depending on the species, humans are the only host, the intermediate host (in which asexual reproduction takes place), or (when there are one or two intermediate hosts) the definitive host in which sexual reproduction occurs. Most helminths are unable to complete their life cycle within the human host, and development of eggs or larvae on soil, in water, or within a plant, arthropod, or other animal intermediate host is necessary. Hence the geographic distribution of these parasites reflects the environmental conditions necessary for development of eggs or larvae or for survival of intermediate hosts and vectors. The only way for the intensity of infection in a person to increase is by further exposure to the infective stage; in the absence of continued exposure, the infection lasts only as long as the life span of the adult worm. In contrast, a few species, most notably *Strongyloides stercoralis,* are able to reproduce and multiply in numbers within the definitive human host. In the case of *Strongyloides,* infectious larvae can be passed directly from one person to another, and transmission is possible in all geographic areas. Infection can persist for the life span of the host, and in the setting of immunosuppression massive infections can result from distant exposure to even small numbers of infectious larvae.

This chapter is based in part on the chapter by Adel A.F. Mahmoud in the 5th edition. All material in this chapter is in the public domain, with the exception of any borrowed figures or tables.

EPIDEMIOLOGY

The prevalence of helminthic disease is highest in warm, developing areas, where climate, environment, and an abundance of vectors favor completion of the life cycle and where poverty leads to increased exposure to parasites because of poor sanitation, lack of clean water, and inadequate housing. Helminthic infections are less common in temperate and industrialized areas, where they have been imported following travel or residence in tropical areas or acquired locally from domestic or wild animals via improperly prepared meat, fish, or vegetables or from close personal contact, as in the case of pinworm infections.

Helminths produce large numbers of eggs or larvae and have a high reproductive capacity, which can lead to an extremely high prevalence of human infection when conditions are conducive to transmission, such as in rural areas in the tropics. Helminths are not uniformly distributed in human populations but are overdispersed, with most infected individuals harboring low worm burdens and only a small number harboring heavy infections.[3] The basis for aggregation of helminths in human populations may be related to the intrinsic biology of the parasites and density-dependent constraints on parasites such as competition for nutrients, parasite-induced pathology, and host factors including genetic susceptibility to infection, immunity, nutrition, and behavioral factors.

PATHOGENESIS AND HOST-PARASITE RELATIONSHIP

Most infected persons harbor few worms and have few or no signs or symptoms of disease, whereas a small proportion of persons with large numbers of worms are at risk for severe disease.[4] Children with even moderate numbers of worms are at risk of malnutrition, impaired growth, and impaired intellectual development.[5] Although mortality rates attributable to helminthic infections are low, rates of chronic morbidity and debilitation are substantial.

Helminths produce disease by a variety of mechanisms, including mechanical effects such as intestinal obstruction (e.g., ascariasis), invasion of host cells or tissues with damage or loss of function (e.g., trichinellosis), or competition for nutrients (e.g., vitamin B_{12} deficiency from fish tapeworm infection). The host responses may lead to immunopathologic lesions such as schistosome egg granulomas, which contribute significantly to disease. In other circumstances, several mechanisms may contribute to disease and chronic sequelae, such as bladder cancer and cholangiocarcinoma associated with *Schistosoma haematobium* and *Opisthorchis viverrini* infection, respectively.

Basic to understanding the pathogenesis of helminthiasis is an appreciation of the size of the organisms, the multiplicity of their antigens, and the chronicity of the infection. Host responses are composed of myriad immunologic and nonimmunologic factors, some of which contribute to disease. Sterilizing immunity to helminthic infections does not develop, and the extent to which previous infections with helminths lead to resistance to subsequent reinfection is not well defined. A degree of acquired immunity has been shown in infected individuals who were cured chemotherapeutically and then continued to live under the same conditions of exposure to infection. These findings suggest that induction of resistance by vaccines may be a viable control strategy.

Eosinophilia is a characteristic of many helminthic infections.[6] Peripheral blood, bone marrow, and tissue eosinophilia is associated with the migration or presence of worms in tissues. Eosinophilia is not observed in infections with helminths that reside in the lumen of the human gut (e.g., tapeworms). Eosinophils have been demonstrated to play a significant role in host resistance to helminthic infections and in the protection against the tissue stages of parasites. The close association of eosinophilia and helminths points to a specific set of interactions and adaptation to this particular class of infectious agents. In addition, chronic infection with worms often leads to a constant state of immune activation characterized by a dominant Th2 type of cytokine profile and high immunoglobulin E (IgE) levels.[7] It is hypothesized that such an immune profile may have an adverse impact on the efficacy of vaccines against other classes of organisms. Helminth infections may affect the expression of allergic disease, and in certain situations it may be associated with increased, decreased, or no risk of asthma and other atopic conditions.[8,9]

Worms have successfully developed multiple strategies to evade host protective responses. Suggested mechanisms include encapsulation within a host fibrous reaction (hydatid cyst), intraluminal location (*Ascaris*), generalized or specific immunosuppression (filariae), and acquisition of host antigens (schistosomes).

DIAGNOSIS AND TREATMENT OF HELMINTHIC INFECTIONS

Recognition of helminthic infections requires knowledge of their clinical presentation, geographic distribution, and epidemiologic risk factors. Persons with light infections may be asymptomatic, and the only clues to diagnosis may be a history of travel and potential exposure to the parasite as well as peripheral blood eosinophilia. It should be kept in mind, however, that eosinophilia may be absent, even in persons with invasive infections. The diagnosis of helminthic infections rests heavily on microscopic examination of stool, urine, blood, other body fluids, and tissue (Table 284–1).[10] When eggs or larvae are produced in abundance, microscopy can be extremely sensitive, but multiple examinations or concentration procedures may be necessary to detect light infections or infections with organisms such as *Strongyloides,* which often sheds low numbers of larvae in the stool. Serologic tests may offer greater sensitivity than microscopic examination and may be the only way to avoid invasive diagnostic procedures for infections with tissue-invading helminths. Many serologic tests for helminths are available only from reference laboratories, and they may lack sensitivity or specificity and not distinguish between past and present infections. Assays to detect helminthic antigens and molecular diagnostic techniques are used mostly for research purposes.

Excellent drugs are available for treating most helminthic infections. Because agents such as albendazole, mebendazole, praziquantel, and ivermectin are highly effective in single orally administered doses, as well as being safe and inexpensive, they are suitable for mass drug administration as well as individual treatment.[11] For infections such as cysticercosis, toxocariasis, and trichinellosis, anti-inflammatory agents are used to minimize tissue damage and symptoms caused by the host's response to the parasite.

TABLE 284-1 Diagnosis of Major Helminthic Infections

Parasite	Microscopic Diagnosis		Other Methods
	Stage	*Specimen*	
Roundworms (Nematodes)			
Intestinal Roundworms			
Ascaris lumbricoides (large intestinal roundworm)	Eggs	Feces	Identification of passed worm
Trichuris trichiura (whipworm)	Eggs	Feces	
Ancylostoma duodenale, Necator americanus (hookworm)	Eggs, larvae	Feces	
Strongyloides stercoralis (threadworm)	Larvae	Feces, duodenal fluid, sputum	Serology*
Enterobius vermicularis (pinworm)	Eggs	Swab of perianal skin; occasionally in feces	Cellophane tape test; identification of adult worms on skin
Tissue Roundworms			
Trichinella spiralis (trichinellosis)	Larvae	Muscle biopsy	Serology*
Dracunculus medinensis (guinea worm)			Identification of emergent adult worm
Wuchereria bancrofti, Brugia malayi (lymphatic filariasis)	Microfilariae	Blood, urine (in setting of chyluria)	Serology, antigen test (blood)
Loa loa (African eye worm)	Microfilariae	Blood	Identification of adult worm in eye, serology
Onchocerca volvulus (river blindness)	Microfilariae	Skin snip	Identification of adult worm in resected nodules
Ancylostoma braziliense, other species (creeping eruption)			Inspection of rash
Toxocara canis, T. cati (visceral larva migrans)	Larvae	Biopsy of liver, other tissues (not recommended)	Serology* (preferred)
Flukes (Trematodes)			
Schistosoma mansoni, S. haematobium, S. japonicum, S. mekongi	Eggs	Feces, rectal snips, urine (S. haematobium)	Serology,* antigen test (serum and urine)
Fasciolopsis buski (intestinal fluke)	Eggs	Feces	
Heterophyes heterophyes (intestinal fluke)	Eggs	Feces	
Metagonimus yokogawai (intestinal fluke)	Eggs	Feces	
Clonorchis sinensis, Opisthorchis spp. (liver fluke)	Eggs	Feces, bile	
Fasciola hepatica (liver fluke)	Eggs	Feces, bile	Serology
Paragonimus spp. (lung fluke)	Eggs	Sputum, feces	Serology*
Tapeworms (Cestodes)			
Intestinal Tapeworms			
Taenia saginata (beef tapeworm)	Eggs	Stool	Identification of passed proglottid (segment)
Hymenolepis nana (dwarf tapeworm)	Eggs	Stool	
Diphyllobothrium latum (fish tapeworm)	Eggs	Stool	Identification of passed proglottid
T. solium (pork tapeworm)	Eggs	Stool	Identification of passed proglottid; stool antigen test; serology
Larval Tapeworms			
Echinococcus granulosus (cystic hydatid disease)	Protoscolices, hooklets	Fluid from cyst	Serology,* CT, MRI, or US can be diagnostic
E. multilocularis (alveolar hydatid disease)	Larvae	Liver biopsy	Serology
Cysticercus (Taenia solium)	Larvae	Brain biopsy	Serology,* CT, or MRI or scan of head can be diagnostic

*Serologic test is available through Division of Parasitic Diseases, Centers for Disease Control and Prevention, Atlanta, GA, USA.
CT, computed tomography; MRI, magnetic resonance imaging; US, ultrasonography.

PREVENTION AND CONTROL

Helminthic infections are prevented by (1) avoiding ingestion of infective eggs, larvae, or intermediate hosts infected with larvae; (2) preventing contact of bare skin with infective larvae; and (3) avoiding bites of infected vectors. At the personal level, these measures entail drinking safe water; properly cleaning, cooking, and otherwise preparing food; adequate hand washing and general hygiene; and employing measures to avoid insect bites, among others. Communities can be protected by interventions such as provision of clean water and sanitation; enforcement of appropriate food-producing practices to prevent infection of fish, meat, and vegetables; vector control; and prevention or treatment of infections in domestic animals.

There are now national and global initiatives to eradicate several helminths and to eliminate or reduce transmission to people and the morbidity caused by other helminths.[11] The guinea worm eradication effort, which relies on community education and participation, provision of filters for drinking water, clean water sources, and case containment, is nearing its goal of zero cases globally. The cornerstone of global programs to eliminate onchocerciasis and lymphatic filariasis and reduce disease due to schistosomiasis and intestinal helminths is periodic administration of anthelmintic drugs to populations at risk. The feasibility of eradicating cysticercosis has been demonstrated at the village level using a variety of measures focused on both human and porcine infections. Research is ongoing to develop vaccines that may provide new approaches to prevent diseases due to hookworms, schistosomes, and other helminths.

REFERENCES

1. Muller R. Worms and Human disease. 2nd ed. Wallingford: CABI Publishing; 2002:1-2.
2. Colley DG, LoVerde PT, Savioli L. Medical helminthology in the 21st century. Science 2001;293:1437-1438.
3. Anderson RM, May RM. Infectious Diseases of Humans: Dynamics and Control. New York: Oxford University Press; 1991:433-606.
4. Awasthi S, Bundy DAP, Savioli L. Helminthic infections. BMJ 2003;327:431-433.
5. Crompton DW, Nesheim MC. Nutritional impact of intestinal helminthiasis during the human life cycle. Annu Rev Nutr 2002;22:35-59.
6. Mahmoud AA. The ecology of eosinophils in schistosomiasis. J Infect Dis 1982;145:613-622.
7. Robinson TM, Nelson RG, Boyer JD. Parasitic infection and the polarized Th2 immune response can alter a vaccine-induced immune response. DNA Cell Biol 2003;22:421-430.
8. Palmer LJ, Celedon JC, Weiss ST, et al. Ascaris lumbricoides infection is associated with increased risk of childhood asthma and atopy in rural China. Am J Respir Crit Care Med 2002;165:1489-1493.
9. Cooper PJ, Chico ME, Bland M, et al. Allergic symptoms, atopy, and geohelminth infections in a rural area of Ecuador. Am J Respir Crit Care Med 2003;168:266-267.
10. Garcia LS. Diagnostic Medical Parasitology. 4th ed. Washington, DC: ASM Press; 2001:1092.
11. Bundy DAP, de Silva NR. Can we deworm this wormy world? Br Med Bull 1998;54:421-432.

CHAPTER 285

Intestinal Nematodes (Roundworms)

JAMES H. MAGUIRE

There are 60 or more species of nematodes or roundworms that infect humans, approximately 80,000 species that infect other invertebrates, and nearly 500,000 free-living species, making the phylum Nematoda one of the largest in the animal kingdom.[1,2] Nematodes are the most common human parasites, with estimates indicating that 1.4 billion, 1.2 billion, and 1.0 billion persons are infected with *Ascaris lumbri-*

coides, hookworm (*Necator americanus, Ancylostoma duodenale*), and *Trichuris trichiura*, respectively.[3] Infections by these four helminths constitute a major health burden in many parts of the world, particularly among the poorest persons in developing countries. Many individuals harbor more than one of these four species as well as other helminths and protozoa throughout much of their lives.[4]

All nematodes are nonsegmented, elongate, cylindrical organisms with a smooth cuticle and a body cavity that contains a tubular digestive tract, reproductive system, and other organs. Sexes are separate; and following mating females produce eggs that give rise to larvae. The larvae then pass through four molts before reaching adulthood and sexual maturity.

Species of nematodes that live in the gut constitute the largest group of human helminths; other species live in or migrate through tissues, including those that are primarily parasites of lower animals. The most common intestinal nematodes—*Ascaris*, hookworm, *Trichuris*—are also referred to as geohelminths because their eggs or larvae must develop on soil before becoming infective to humans (Table 285-1). Because of this requirement, these parasites cannot be transmitted directly from one person to another and cannot multiply in the host. In contrast, another geohelminth, *Strongyloides stercoralis,* is able to complete its life cycle entirely within the human host as well as on soil. Eggs of *Enterobius vermicularis,* the pinworm, become infective within 6 hours of release from the gravid female and exposure to oxygen. Like *Strongyloides,* pinworm can be transmitted directly from person to person.

The inability of the intestinal nematodes other than *Strongyloides* to replicate within the human host explains why they do not behave as opportunistic infections in persons who have acquired immunodeficiency syndrome (AIDS) or are receiving immunosuppressive medications. Rapidly increasing numbers of adult *Strongyloides* and migrating larvae can overwhelm a person receiving corticosteroids, but this complication is surprisingly rare in persons with AIDS. Although intestinal nematodes do not behave as opportunists in persons with human immunodeficiency virus (HIV) infection, they elicit a Th2 type of cytokine response that seems to lead to more rapid HIV infection and progression to AIDS.[5,6] The efficacy of some vaccines against HIV infection is likely to be impaired by chronic helminthiasis.[7]

ASCARIASIS

Ascaris lumbricoides is the most common helminthic infection of humans, infecting more than one-fourth of the world's population.[3] Ascariasis is widely distributed throughout the world, and although most abundant in tropical countries it also occurs in Europe, parts of the southeastern United States, and other temperate areas. Most persons infected with Ascaris are asymptomatic, but mortality is estimated to be 60,000 per year, and more than 15% of infected persons experience some type of morbidity.[2,8-12]

Life Cycle

The white or pinkish adult worms (15 to 35 cm in length) live and mate in the lumen of the small intestine, primarily the jejunum (Fig. 285-1). Each female worm has a daily output of 200,000 ova or more.[10] The fertile ovum is oval, has a thick shell with a mammillated albuminous covering, and is 50 to 70 μm $\times$ 40 to 50 μm (Fig. 285-2). When eggs in the single-cell stage are passed in the feces and reach a favorable environment, they become infective and contain a fully developed larva within 10 to 14 days at 30° C and within 6 weeks at 17° C.[10] Eggs swallowed by humans hatch in the small intestine and release larvae that measure about 250 μm in length. The larvae then penetrate the intestinal wall and migrate via venous blood through the liver to the heart, reaching the lungs approximately 4 days after ingestion of the eggs. By 6 to 10 days later they have attained a length of about 550 μm; they break into the alveoli and ascend the tracheobronchial tree. They are then swallowed and return to the intestines where they develop into mature worms, with egg production beginning about 2 months after ingestion of the eggs. Adult worms live approximately

TABLE 285-1 Features of Major Intestinal Nematodes

Nematode	Transmission	Direct Person-to-Person Transmission	Geographic Distribution	Duration of Infection	Location of Adult Worm(s)	Treatment*
Ascaris lumbricoides	Ingestion of infective eggs	No	Warm, humid areas; temperate zones in warmer months	1–2 Years	Free in lumen of small bowel, primarily jejunum	Albendazole Mebendazole Pyrantel Ivermectin Levamisole Piperazine
Trichuris trichiura (whipworm)	Ingestion of infective eggs	No	Warm, humid areas; temperate zones in warmer months	1–3 Years	Anchored in superfical mucosa of cecum and colon	Albendazole Mebendazole
Necator americanus, Ancylostoma duodenale (hookworm)	Penetration of skin by filariform larvae	No	Warm, humid areas; temperate zones in warmer months	3–5 Years (Necator); 1 year (Ancylostoma)	Attached to mucosa of mid to upper portion of small bowel	Albendazole Mebendazole Levamisole Pyrantel
Strongyloides stercoralis	Penetration of skin or bowel mucosa by filariform larvae	Yes	Primarily warm, humid areas; but can be worldwide	Lifetime of host	Embedded in mucosa of duodenum, jejunum	Ivermectin† Albendazole Thiabendazole
Enterobius vermicularis (pinworm)	Ingestion of infective eggs	Yes	Worldwide	1 Month	Free in lumen of cecum, appendix, adjacent colon	Albendazole Mebendazole Pyrantel Ivermectin Levamisole Piperazine

*Nitazoxanide has been shown to be effective in the treatment of ascariasis, trichuriasis, and enterobiasis in several small trials (Romero R, Guerero LR, Munoz Garcia MR, et al. Nitazoxanide for the treatment of intestinal protozoan and helminthic infections in Mexico. Trans R Soc Trop Med Hyg 1997;91:701-703; Diaz E, Mondragon J, Ramirex E, et al. Epidemiology and control of intestinal parasites with nitazoxanide in children in Mexico. Am J Trop Med Hyg 2003;68:384-385.)
†Drug of choice.

10 to 24 months. Although the host produces specific and nonspecific immunoglobulin E (IgE) antibodies and mounts a cellular immune response, reinfection in endemic areas is common; whatever protection is afforded is partial at best.[8,10]

Epidemiology

The geographic distribution of ascariasis is determined by climate, sanitation, and human behavior. Eggs embryonate and become infective only on soil in warm, humid environments; and transmission may

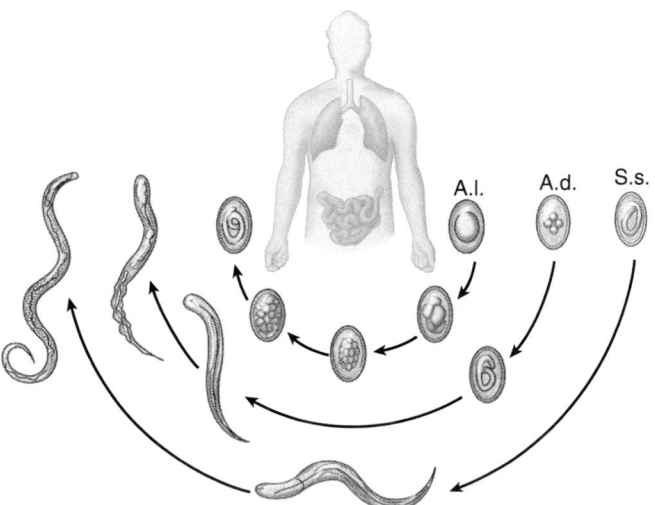

FIGURE 285-1. Life cycle of intestinal nematodes with a migratory phase through the lungs. Eggs are passed with stools in *Ascaris lumbricoides* (A.l.), *Necator americanus,* or *Ancylostoma duodenale* (A.d.), or they hatch on their way out in *Strongyloides stercoralis* (S.s.). *Ascaris* eggs mature in soil, and humans are infected upon ingestion of these eggs. With hookworm and strongyloidiasis, humans are infected via skin penetration by filariform larvae. In all three infections, larvae pass through a migratory phase via the lungs before reaching maturity at their final habitat in the small intestine.

be seasonal in areas where these conditions alternate with periods of extreme temperature and aridity. Children in impoverished rural areas who play on contaminated soil around homes are the most heavily infected and are constantly exposed to reinfection via hand-to-mouth transmission. Infection rates are also high among adults, especially in areas where human excrement ("night soil") is used to fertilize crops. In endemic areas, it is not unusual for more than 80% of the population to be infected.[8-11] The high prevalence of ascariasis worldwide is a consequence of the tremendous egg output from female worms and the remarkable ability of ova to resist unfavorable external environments. *Ascaris* eggs remain viable for up to 6 years in moist, loose soil, and can survive freezing winter temperatures and short periods of desiccation.

In highly endemic communities, most people are infected with a small number of worms, and only a few persons (usually children) have heavy infections; the latter group accounts for the bulk of the worms in the community and most of the eggs shed into the environment, and they are at highest risk of severe disease.[13]

Predisposition to infection is determined by various factors, including the environment and human behavior (which affect the intensity of exposure to infection) and genetic predisposition and host immunity (which underlie individual susceptibility to infection).[14,15] Studies using human genome scans have demonstrated that genes on two chromosomes account for a significant part of the individual variation in susceptibility to infection with *Ascaris*.[16]

Immigrants and travelers account for most cases of ascariasis in nonendemic regions. These persons lose their infections usually within a year of arrival, when the adult worms die. Occasionally *Ascaris* infection is encountered in persons who have never traveled. Imported farm produce contaminated with eggs is the source of infection in some cases. In others, infection was acquired locally by ingesting eggs that were shown by molecular studies to be eggs of the pig roundworm, *Ascaris suum.*[17,18]

Clinical Syndromes

Most persons with *Ascaris* infections are asymptomatic. A small proportion of infected people develop pulmonary symptoms during the second week after ingestion of eggs, when larvae invade lung tissue

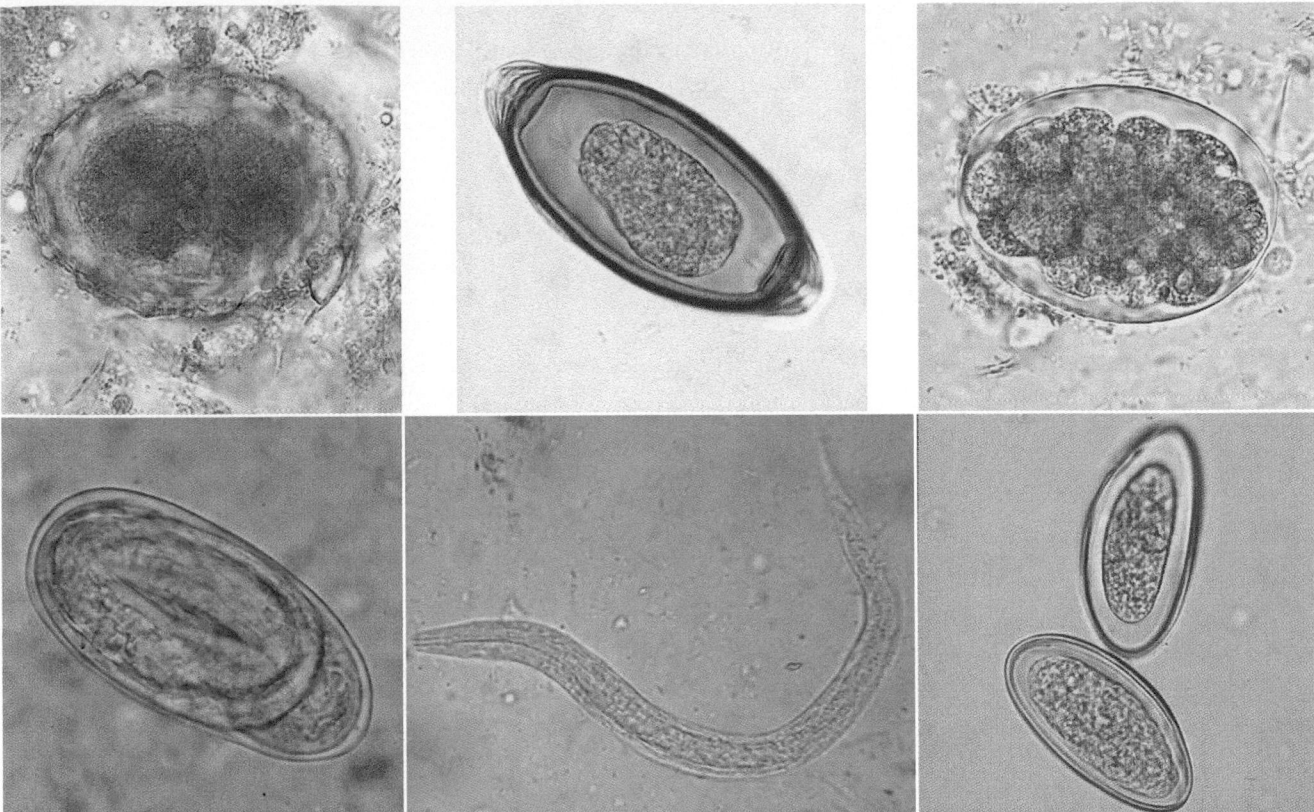

FIGURE 285-2. Eggs and larvae of common intestinal roundworms. Clockwise, beginning at upper left: *Ascaris lumbricoides; Trichuris trichiura;* hookworm; *Enterobius vermicularis; Strongyloides stercoralis;* and embryonated hookworm egg. (From DPDx, website for laboratory diagnosis of parasitic diseases of the Division of Parasitic Diseases, National Centers for Infectious Diseases, Centers for Disease Control and Prevention, Atlanta, GA: [http://www.dpd.cdc.gov/DPDx/].)

and provoke an immune-mediated hypersensitivity response.[19] Symptoms include a nonproductive cough, chest discomfort, fever, and eosinophilia that disappears often by the time the worms reach maturity. In severe cases, patients develop dyspnea and an eosinophilic pneumonia (Löffler syndrome) with transient patchy infiltrates seen on radiographs. Seasonal outbreaks of pneumonitis have occurred in areas such as Saudi Arabia, where transmission of *Ascaris* is seasonal, whereas even isolated cases of pulmonary illness due to ascariasis are uncommon in areas where transmission is continuous.[20]

With most established infections, adult worms in the lumen of the small bowel provoke no symptoms or produce only mild abdominal discomfort, dyspepsia, loss of appetite, or nausea. Moderate and heavy infections, however, can impair the nutritional status of children, especially those living in areas where malnutrition due to other causes is common.[21-23] Infection with *Ascaris* has been shown to depress appetite and food intake by children, and it can interfere with absorption of proteins, fats, lactose, vitamin A, and iodine.[21] The impact on nutrition, cognitive performance, and growth are likely the most important health-related consequences of ascariasis worldwide. Treatment of heavily infected children with anthelmintics has been shown to improve nutritional status.[22-24]

Other complications of chronic ascariasis, such as intestinal obstruction, obstruction of bile and pancreatic ducts, appendicitis, and intestinal perforation, are largely mechanical. Although the rate of serious complications among infected persons is less than 0.1%, the huge number of infected persons makes ascariasis a major cause of surgical admissions in the tropics.[25-27] Entanglement of a large number of adult worms in the lumen of the small bowel, usually near the ileocecal valve, provokes spasmodic contraction and obstruction, especially in children, who may harbor anywhere from 60 to more than 500

worms.[28] Obstruction may be partial or complete, and occasionally it is complicated by perforation, intussusception, volvulus, or death.[29] Intestinal obstruction due to ascariasis occurs in 1 of every 1000 infected children and was responsible for 25% of intestinal obstructions during a 10-year period in Calabar, Nigeria.[25] Individual worms have a tendency to enter and obstruct small orifices, including the common bile duct, pancreatic duct, and appendix.[30-31] Increased migration of worms occurs with general anesthesia, high fevers, fasting, or treatment with certain anthelmintic drugs such as mebendazole or albendazole. Worms may exit the ductal system spontaneously without causing harm or may produce pyogenic cholangitis, liver abscess, hemorrhagic pancreatitis, or appendicitis, or they may die in situ and form the nidus of biliary stones.[32-34] In a series of 500 cases of biliary and pancreatic ascariasis from Kashmir, India, Khuroo et al. described biliary colic in 56% of persons, acute cholangitis in 24%, acute cholecystitis in 13%, acute pancreatitis in 6%, and liver abscess in 1%.[31] Individual worms that wander aberrantly may perforate surgical wounds, Meckel's diverticulum, the appendix, and occasionally portions of the bowel that appear otherwise normal.[34] Occasionally passage of an adult worm per os, per rectum, or less commonly through the nose or a tear duct brings the patient to medical attention. Worms have been found escaping through umbilical and hernial fistulas, in the fallopian tubes and urinary bladder, and in the lungs and heart. Whether chronic ascariasis leads to increased, decreased, or unchanged rates of asthma and other atopic conditions is controversial.[35-36]

Diagnosis

Finding eggs in the feces establishes the diagnosis of ascariasis. Because of the enormous daily output of eggs by gravid female worms, microscopic examination of simple smears is sufficient, and procedures to concentrate stool are not needed. Larvae can be found in sputum or gastric aspirates during their migration through the lungs before eggs are present in the stool.[19] Adult worms passed through the mouth, anus, or nose are readily identified because of their large size and unsegmented cream-colored cuticle. Worms in a gas-filled loop of bowel can be seen on plain radiographs.[37] During barium studies they appear as filling defects, and barium may fill the gut of the worm.[37] Ultrasonography, computed tomography (CT), and endoscopic retrograde cholangiopancreatography (ERCP) readily demonstrate worms in the biliary tree and pancreatic duct.[38-40] Worms visualized in the biliary or pancreatic ducts during ERCP can been extracted with forceps.[41]

Management

All infections, including those that are light or asymptomatic, should be treated, preferably with oral albendazole (400 mg single dose), mebendazole (500 mg single dose or 100 mg twice daily for 3 days), or pyrantel pamoate (11 mg/kg single dose, maximum 1 g).[3,42] Ivermectin is effective for treating ascariasis but is used more commonly for treatment of strongyloidiasis or onchocerciasis. Piperazine citrate, once the drug of choice, can be neurotoxic and hepatotoxic and is no longer available in many countries. Pyrantel pamoate and piperazine citrate have been considered safe for use during pregnancy for years. The World Health Organization (WHO) also recommended use of albendazole and mebendazole during pregnancy based on safety data and concluded that these drugs may be used to treat children as young as 12 months.[3,43]

Intestinal obstruction is best managed conservatively with nasogastric suction, repletion of fluids and electrolytes, and, once bowel motility is restored, anthelmintic therapy.[29] Piperazine produces flaccid paralysis of worms, which can help to relieve the obstruction. If available, the syrup is administered by instillation through a nasogastric tube. Indications for surgery include complete obstruction with inadequate decompression, lack of response within 24 to 48 hours, volvulus, intussusception, or perforation. Worms frequently can be milked into the large bowel at surgery, but enterotomy or resection may be necessary to relieve the obstruction. Conservative management with nasogastric suction, antispasmodics, analgesics, and intravenous fluids is usually effective in cases of biliary ascariasis.[30] Antibiotics are given if there is evidence of bacterial infection, and once acute symptoms subside an anthelmintic is given to prevent recurrence. Indications for endoscopic or surgical removal of worms include those that die or are trapped in ducts or invade the liver.[41] Patients with acute appendicitis or intestinal perforation also require surgical intervention.

TRICHURIASIS

Approximately one billion persons worldwide are infected with the whipworm *Trichuris trichiura,* primarily children living in poverty in the tropics and subtropics.[3,44] Its geographic distribution is similar to that of *A. lumbricoides,* and many persons harbor infections with both *Trichuris* and *Ascaris.*

Life Cycle

Pinkish gray adult worms measuring approximately 4 cm in length reside in the cecum and ascending colon and with heavy infections extend to the lower colon and rectum (Fig. 285-3). The thin whip-like anterior part of the parasite is embedded in a syncytial tunnel in the epithelium of the colon between the mouths of crypts; its thicker posterior extends into the lumen. After mating, the female worm each day produces 7000 to 20,000 barrel-shaped eggs measuring 50×20 μm, with a thick shell and a clear plug at each end (see Fig. 285-2). Eggs shed in the feces onto soil embryonate and become infective under optimal conditions of moisture and shade within 2 to 4 weeks. After the egg has been ingested, the larva emerges from the shell and penetrates mucosal crypts of the cecum. Here it undergoes a series of molts and then moves to the mouth of the crypts. Worms mature into adults and begin to oviposit within about 3 months; they live 1 to 3 years or longer.

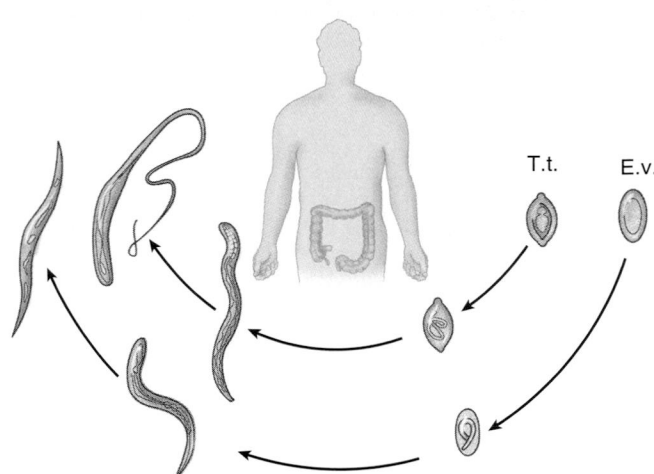

FIGURE 285-3. Life cycle of nematodes without a migratory phase through the lungs. *Trichuris trichiura* (T.t.) eggs are passed with stools; those of *Enterobius vermicularis* (E.v.) are deposited at the perianal region. They embryonate within a short time, and infection is acquired by ingestion. Eggs hatch in the intestine, and larvae migrate to their final habitat in the colon (T.t.) or cecum (E.v.).

Epidemiology

Trichuriasis is found in humid tropical environments and temperate zones, including the southeastern United States during warm and humid months. It is most common in poor rural communities and areas in which sanitary facilities are lacking and hands, food, and drink are easily contaminated. Most infected people harbor fewer than 20 worms, but a small proportion, usually children in the 5- to 15-year age group, harbor more than 200 worms.[44] In endemic communities, persons with these heavy worm burdens typically represent less than 10% of the population and are the only ones to suffer from the disease.[13,45] Genetic studies indicate that about 25% of the variation in susceptibility to infection with *T. trichiura* can be attributed to genetic factors.[46]

Clinical Syndromes

Most persons with trichuriasis have no symptoms or only peripheral blood eosinophilia. In persons with heavy infections, the mucosa is inflamed, edematous, and friable; and there are increased numbers of macrophages in the lamina propria that produce tumor necrosis factor-α (TNFα).[47] These persons are at risk of developing the *Trichuris* dysentery syndrome, an illness resembling inflammatory bowel disease; it is characterized by tenesmus and frequent passage of stools containing large amount of mucus and often blood.[48,49] Recurrent rectal prolapse is common, and adult worms can been seen in the prolapsed mucosa.[50] Children with chronic *Trichuris* colitis usually have severe iron deficiency anemia, growth retardation, and clubbing of the fingers.[51] In persons with moderate or heavy infections, elevated systemic levels of TNFα may contribute to growth retardation and impaired cognitive function.[47,52,53]

Diagnosis

Trichuriasis is diagnosed by identifying the adult worms on the mucosa of the prolapsed rectum or at colonoscopy or by finding the lemon-shaped eggs in the stool.[44] Microscopic examination of a simple fecal smear is sufficient because the level of egg output is high (about 200 eggs/g of feces per worm pair).

Management

Treatment of light to moderate infections with single doses of albendazole or mebendazole achieve cure rates of about 70% to 90% and reductions in egg output of 90% to 99% in persons whose infections are not cured.[3,53,55] For heavy infections, courses of 5 to 7 days of albendazole or a combination of albendazole and ivermectin yield higher rates of cure and a greater reduction in the intensity of the infection.

HOOKWORM

Human infection with the two species of hookworm, *Ancylostoma duodenale* and *Necator americanus,* is estimated to affect approximately one-fourth of the world's population.[3,57,57] Iron-deficiency anemia from hookworm infection is a major health problem throughout the developing world and has especially severe consequences for growing children and women of childbearing age. Hookworm infection occurs in tropical and subtropical zones between 45°N and 30°S latitude.[58] The remarkable success in controlling hookworm infection in the United States during the early part of this century has not occurred in other parts of the world. A low prevalence of the infection still exists in pockets of the southeastern United States.

Life Cycle

Adult hookworms are small, cylindrical, grayish white nematodes measuring approximately 7 to 13 mm in length. They live chiefly in the upper small intestine, attached to the mucosa by their strong buccal capsules and biting plates or teeth. There are major differences between the two species.[58] *N. americanus* is shorter, removes less blood (0.03 ml/day vs. 0.20 ml/day), lives longer (3 to 5 years or more versus 1 to 2 years), and produces fewer eggs (5,000 to 10,000 vs. 10,000 to 25,000 per day) than *A. duodenale.* The ovoid, thin-shelled eggs of the two species measure 58×36 µm and are morphologically identical (see Fig. 285-1).

Under suitable conditions of humidity, temperature, and shade, eggs passed in the stool hatch on loamy soil within 1 to 2 days. The emergent rhabditiform larvae, which are noninfective, molt twice over the next 5 to 10 days and develop into filariform larvae, which are infective. Following contact of human skin with contaminated soil, filariform larvae penetrate through hair follicles and small fissures within minutes. The larvae are carried by the circulation to the lungs, penetrate the alveolar walls, and make their way up the trachea to be swallowed and carried to their final habitat in the small intestine. Gravid females start egg deposition 5 to 6 weeks after skin penetration. *A. duodenale* can be transmitted orally as well as percutaneously, and its larvae can undergo a period of arrested development in the host corresponding to times of the year when environmental conditions are unfavorable.[58]

Epidemiology

The distribution and prevalence of hookworm infections are limited by environmental conditions that include several months of warm weather (ideally 25° C to 32° C) and a minimum annual rainfall of 50 to 60 inches. Larval development is susceptible to extremes of temperature, desiccation, and direct sunlight. Transmission within a community is limited to areas where people defecate and are then visited by people with bare feet or children playing on the ground. The prevalence of infection rises during childhood and levels off during early adulthood. High rates of *A. duodenale* infection in children under the age of 1 year raise the possibility of transplacental or transmammary transmission.[58]

Clinical Syndromes

Most persons harbor light infections and are asymptomatic. Previously sensitized persons may develop a pruritic maculopapular rash known as "ground itch" at the site of larval penetration. Migration of larvae through the lungs may provoke a transient pneumonitis, which occurs less frequently and is less severe than that caused by *Ascaris.* Previously unexposed persons may develop epigastric pain, diarrhea, anorexia, and eosinophilia about 30 to 45 days after penetration as larvae begin attaching to the small bowel mucosa.[59] This syndrome has been recognized most commonly among military troops following contact of skin with fecally contaminated soil during operations in tropical zones.[60]

Persons infected with adult hookworms may experience chronic abdominal pain and persistent eosinophilia. The major manifestations of hookworm disease, however, are iron-deficiency anemia and protein energy malnutrition resulting from blood loss.[56,57] Adult worms draw mucosal plugs into their buccal cavity, secrete enzymes to expose underlying capillaries, and suck blood with powerful esophageal muscles. Bleeding is aggravated by anticoagulants produced by the worm, and continues for some time after the feeding worm attaches to another site.[61] The development of anemia depends on the intensity and duration of the infection, the infecting species of worm, and iron stores, intake, and requirements. Blood loss is gradual, allowing the body to adapt to the chronic anemic state. Features of hookworm-induced anemia include microcytic/hypochromic erythrocytes, pallor, weakness, lassitude, dyspnea, and edema due to hypoproteinemia, especially in malnourished children. Moderate infections and anemia can impair physical, cognitive, and intellectual growth in children, diminish productivity of workers, and threaten the outcome of pregnancy for both mother and child.[62] In the most severe cases, anemia caused by hookworms can lead to congestive heart failure and is responsible for approximately 60,000 deaths per year worldwide.[3]

Diagnosis

Direct fecal smear examination is adequate for diagnosis of clinically significant hookworm infections; concentration techniques are needed only for the lightest infections. For epidemiologic purposes, quantitative egg counts can be performed to determine the intensity of infection, and species can be identified by examining adult worms expelled after treatment or larvae obtained by fecal culture.

Management

A single 400 mg dose of albendazole is the treatment of choice.[3] Mebendazole 100 mg twice daily for 3 days is more effective than a single dose of 500 mg, and several 11 mg/kg doses of pyrantel pamoate may be necessary to eliminate or reduce heavy infections.[63] Iron replacement alone can lead to restoration of a normal hemoglobin level, but anemia recurs unless anthelmintic therapy is given. Although humans do not acquire protective immunity to hookworm infection, the success of experimental immunization of animals with larval vaccines or adult-stage antigens suggest that development of a human vaccine is feasible.[64]

Prevention and Control of Ascariasis, Trichuriasis, and Hookworm Infection

Geohelminth infections are prevented by drinking safe water, properly cleaning and cooking food, hand washing, and wearing shoes. Because provision of safe water sources and adequate sanitation to protect entire communities is too expensive for many poor countries, WHO advocates administering anthelmintic drugs at regular intervals to populations at risk, with the intention of maintaining individual worm burdens at levels below those that cause morbidity and mortality.[11] This strategy is based on studies showing that regular deworming of children and other at-risk populations can prevent and reverse malnutrition, iron-deficiency anemia, impaired growth, poor school performance, and poor-outcome pregnancies.[3,11,65,66] The availability of effective broad-spectrum, safe, inexpensive single-dose drugs such as albendazole and others listed in Table 285-1 make drug administration at the population level feasible. This approach may lower the prevalence and intensity of geohelminth infections but is unlikely to eliminate transmission in the absence of sanitation, clean water supplies, and overall economic development. Major challenges to controlling geohelminthic infections at the population level include implementing and sustaining mass drug administration programs and preventing the emergence of drug resistance, which already has been documented for benzimidazole drugs (e.g., mebendazole) in livestock and has been suspected in humans in a few areas.[67]

STRONGYLOIDIASIS

Although estimates of the global prevalence of strongyloidiasis are imprecise and vary between 3 million and 100 million persons infected, it is clear that infection with *Strongyloides stercoralis* is considerably less common than infections with other major intestinal nematodes.[68] Strongyloidiasis is found throughout the tropics and subtropics and in limited foci in parts of the United States and Europe. Its medical importance lies primarily in its ability to produce overwhelming infection in immunocompromised persons, a consequence of its unique ability to replicate and increase in numbers without leaving its host.[29] A second species, *S. fuelleborni,* a parasite of primates, infects humans in parts of Africa and produces the life-threatening "swollen belly syndrome" with generalized edema and respiratory distress in infants around 2 months of age in Papua New Guinea.[69]

Life Cycle

Semitransparent, colorless female worms measuring 2.2 mm in length live embedded in the mucosal epithelium of the upper small intestine where they deposit their eggs. Eggs are produced by parthenogenesis as parasitic adult males do not exist.[68] The eggs hatch in the mucosa, and the emergent noninfectious rhabditiform larvae measuring 250 to 300 μm in length work their way into the lumen of the bowel (see Fig. 285-1). If excreted with feces onto soil in a warm, humid environment, they can molt and develop into either infective filariform larvae measuring 550 μm or free-living adult males and females. The free-living adults mate and produce rhabditiform larvae, which can develop directly into infective filariform larvae or pass through a free-living cycle first. Filariform larvae penetrate human skin and undergo a migration similar to that of hookworms, which terminates 18 to 28 days later in the small bowel mucosa, where female adult worms begin producing eggs.

A key feature of the biology of *Strongyloides* is that small numbers of rhabditiform larvae develop into filariform larvae within the bowel, reenter the host through the colonic mucosa or perianal skin, and thus complete their life cycle without leaving the host. This process of autoinfection explains how the parasite can increase in numbers in the absence of exogenous reinfection, persist indefinitely in a single host, and be transmitted directly from one person to another during close physical contact.[68]

Epidemiology

Transmission of *S. stercoralis* depends on the suitability of the soil, climatic conditions, sanitation, and human behavior. In addition to the tropics and subtropics, the parasite is endemic in small areas of Appalachia, the southeastern United States, Europe, Australia, and Japan.[68,70] Person-to-person transmission accounts for reports of strongyloidiasis outside of endemic areas in mental institutions and daycare centers and among homosexual men.[71] Infections lasting more than 60 years have been documented in military veterans and immigrants who lived in endemic areas in the distant past.[1,72]

Clinical Syndromes

With acute infections there may be a localized, pruritic, erythematous, papular rash shortly after larval penetration. Pulmonary symptoms with eosinophilia may appear several days later, and diarrhea and abdominal pain develop several weeks after that and just before the appearance of larvae in the stool.[68] In chronic uncomplicated strongyloidiasis, host and parasite live in harmony, autoinfection is well regulated by the host's cell-mediated immunity, and the number of adult worms is low and stable. More than 50% of chronically infected persons are asymptomatic, and up to 75% have a fluctuating eosinophilia, as high as 10% to 15%. Some persons develop recurrent maculopapular or urticarial rashes that involve primarily the buttocks, perineum, and thighs. Migrating larvae may produce the pathognomonic larva currens, a serpiginous urticarial rash that advances as fast as 10 cm/hr. Adult worms and larvae traversing the upper small bowel mucosa may produce epigastric pain that resembles peptic ulcer pain, as well as nausea, diarrhea, and blood loss. Heavy infections can lead to bowel obstruction. Pulmonary symptoms are uncommon, and when present there is often underlying chronic obstructive lung disease.[68]

Hyperinfection, resulting from increased generation of filariform larvae (accelerated autoinfection), occurs when host immunity is impaired, especially by corticosteroid therapy and, less commonly, other immunosuppressive drugs, hematologic malignancies, or malnutrition.[73,74] Infection with human T cell lymphotropic virus-1 (HTLV-1) is associated with hyperinfection, increased susceptibility to infection with *Strongyloides,* and refractoriness to treatment.[75-77] Despite the undoubtedly large numbers of person infected with both *Strongyloides* and human immunodeficiency virus (HIV) worldwide, there have been relatively few case reports of hyperinfection among co-infected persons with acquired immunodeficiency syndrome (AIDS), and some of these persons were also receiving corticosteroids.[78,79]

With hyperinfection, increased numbers of larvae are found in the intestines and lungs, organs involved in the normal autoinfection cycle.[68,73,74] With disseminated strongyloidiasis, larvae are also found in the central nervous system (CNS), kidneys, liver, and almost any other organ. Eosinophilia is often absent. Gastrointestinal manifestations are common and include abdominal pain, nausea, vomiting, diarrhea, ileus, and edema of the bowel, which can lead to intestinal obstruction. Ulceration of the mucosa may produce massive hemorrhage, peritonitis, or bacterial sepsis. Larvae migrating beyond the gastrointestinal tract produce pneumonitis with cough, hemoptysis, and respiratory failure; diffuse interstitial infiltrates or consolidation may be seen on chest radiographs. Occasionally, sputum contains adult worms, rhabditiform larvae, and eggs in addition to the more usual filariform larvae. CNS invasion may cause meningitis and brain abscesses, with larvae in the cerebrospinal fluid and tissue. Biopsy of linear rashes, petechiae, and purpura often shows larvae. Gram-negative bacteria and other bowel flora may gain access to the bloodstream through ulcers in the bowel or by transport on the surface and in the gut of migrating larvae; bacterial sepsis, meningitis, and pneumonia occur frequently. The mortality associated with untreated disseminated strongyloidiasis approaches 100%, and even with treatment it may exceed 25%.[68,74]

Diagnosis

Uncomplicated strongyloidiasis is diagnosed by finding rhabditiform larvae on microscopic examination of the stool, either by direct smear or culture on agar plates, which is the most sensitive of the available concentration methods.[80] A short buccal cavity distinguishes *Strongyloides* larvae from hookworm larvae hatching in stool that is not examined promptly. Repeated stool examinations are often needed because the sensitivity of a single stool examination can be as low as 30%, and it may be necessary to sample duodenal fluid or obtain a small bowel biopsy to demonstrate organisms. Because of their higher sensitivity, the diagnosis is often made by serologic tests, such as the enzyme-linked immunoassay offered by the Centers for Disease Control and Prevention (Atlanta, GA, USA) that has a sensitivity of up to 95%.[81] Hyperinfection and disseminated strongyloidiasis are readily diagnosed by examining stool, sputum, other body fluids, and tissues, which typically contain high numbers of filariform larvae.

Management

All persons infected with S. *stercoralis* should be treated with the aim of eradicating the infection. Uncomplicated strongyloidiasis is treated with oral ivermectin 200 μg once daily for 1 or 2 days, which is at least as effective but better tolerated than thiabendazole 25 mg/kg twice daily for 3 days and is more effective than albendazole 400 mg twice daily for 3 days.[82] The drug of choice for treating hyperinfection and disseminated strongyloidiasis is also ivermectin, which should be administered daily until symptoms have resolved and larvae have not been detected for at least 2 weeks (the length of the autoinfection cycle). Thiabendazole and albendazole are alternatives, and both ivermectin and thiabendazole have been effective when administered by nasogastric tube or per rectum in persons unable to take oral medications or who have ileus.[83,84] If possible, immunosuppressive therapy should be stopped or reduced. Because eradication of infection is the goal for both uncomplicated and complicated strongyloidiasis, follow-up examinations are indicated. Examinations should be repeated frequently, and consideration should be given to administering an anthelmintic drug every few weeks for as long as the immunosuppression or other predisposing condition persists. During long-term follow-up, positive serology and persistent eosinophilia may offer stronger evidence of treatment results than stool examinations.[81]

Prevention of Hyperinfection and Disseminated Strongyloidiasis

Immunosuppressed persons, those about to receive immunosuppressive medications (especially corticosteroids), or persons with HTLV-1 infection should be evaluated for possible strongyloidiasis.[68,80] Those with a history of residence in an endemic area or other potential exposure to *S. stercoralis* at any time during their lives should undergo serologic testing, even in the absence of symptoms or eosinophilia. If serologic tests are positive, stool examinations should be performed. Many authorities recommend treatment even if stool examinations are negative.

ENTEROBIASIS

Enterobius vermicularis, or pinworm, is highly prevalent throughout the world, particularly in countries of the temperate zone. In the United States, it is the most common of all helminthic infections, with an estimated 42 million cases.[85] Pinworm infection is particularly common among children, institutionalized groups, and households; it is not associated with any specific socioeconomic level.[86]

Life Cycle

Enterobius vermicularis is a small white worm measuring 1 cm in length and inhabiting the cecum, appendix, and adjacent gut.[87] Gravid female worms containing an average of 10,000 ova migrate at night to the perianal and perineal regions, where they deposit their eggs and die; ova are infrequently deposited in the bowels. *Enterobius* ova are ovoid but flattened on one side and measure approximately 56×27 μm. The eggs embryonate within 6 hours and are transferred from the perianal region to nightclothes, bedding, and dust and air. The most common mode of transmission, however, is via the hands of the patient, particularly underneath the fingernails, through scratching or handling clothes and bed linen. Enterobiasis may be transmitted between sexual partners, especially those engaging in oral-anal sex. On ingestion, the embryos hatch in the duodenum, molt twice, and within 5 to 6 weeks develop into adult worms that live about 1 month.

Epidemiology

The prevalence of pinworm infection is lowest in infants and reaches its maximum in schoolchildren 5 to 14 years old.[87] The absence of an extended extracorporeal development stage favors both direct transmission to others and autoinfection. Eggs are infective within 6 hours of oviposition and may remain so for 20 days. Pinworm is primarily a familial or institutional infection associated with crowding. Because the life span of the worms is relatively brief, long-standing infections must be due to continuous reinfection.[88]

Clinical Syndromes

Most pinworm infections are asymptomatic. When present, symptoms are related largely to perianal and perineal pruritus and scratching.[89] In a hospital-based study of children 2 to 12 years old, none of the signs and symptoms largely ascribed to enterobiasis was significantly more common in infected than in uninfected children.[90]

The most common complaints are local itching and restless sleep due to nocturnal anal pruritus. Occasionally, the migration of the parasite leads to ectopic disease, such as pelvic, cervical, vulvar, and peritoneal granulomas, which may be mistaken for other pelvic masses or may produce symptoms that mimic pelvic inflammatory disease.[91]

The relationship between pinworm infection and appendicitis is unclear. In one study, more normal than inflamed appendices removed at surgery for suspected appendicitis contained pinworms, suggesting that pinworms may cause symptoms resembling appendicitis without invading the mucosa.[92] Large numbers of larval pinworms, presumably from a single heavy exposure, have caused eosinophilic enterocolitis.[93] Enterobiasis is usually not associated with significant eosinophilia or elevated serum IgE levels.

Diagnosis

Although pinworms can be seen by the naked eye, they may be confused with bits of white thread. Eggs are usually not encountered in stool but are readily identified by microscopic examination of an adhesive cellophane tape pressed against the perianal region early in the morning.[87] A single examination detects 50% of infections, three examinations detect 90%, and five examinations detect 99%.

Management

Single doses of albendazole (400 mg), mebendazole (100 mg), or pyrantel pamoate (11 mg/kg up to 1 g) are highly effective. A second dose is given 2 weeks later because of the frequency of reinfection and autoinfection.[87] Other infected family members, classmates, or residents of long-term care facilities should be treated at the same time as the index case.[86] Treating all close contacts of the index case is effective when rates of infection are high. Reinfections are common, and repeated treatment courses in family members or classmates may be needed.[94] Although personal cleanliness is a useful general principle, its role in the management of enterobiasis is minor, and overemphasis on cleanliness may enhance the psychological trauma and stigma associated with this infection.

REFERENCES

1. Muller R. The nematodes. In: Worms and Human Disease. 2nd ed. Wallingford: CABI Publishing; 2002:109-235.
2. Coombs I, Crompton DWT. A Guide to Human Helminths. London: Taylor & Francis; 1991:1-4.
3. WHO Expert Committee. Prevention and control of schistosomiasis and soil-transmitted helminthiasis. WHO Techn Rep Ser 2002;912:1-53.
4. Awasthi S, Bundy DAP, Savioli L. Helminthic infections. BMJ 2003;327:431-433.
5. Cooper PJ, Chico ME, Sandoval C, et al. Human infection with Ascaris lumbricoides is associated with a polarized cytokine response. J Infect Dis 2000;182:1207-1213.
6. Fincham JE, Markus MB, Adams VJ. Could control of soil-transmitted helminthic infection influence the HIV/AIDS pandemic? Acta Trop 2003;86:315-333.
7. Robinson TM, Nelson RG, Boyer JD. Parasitic infection and the polarized Th2 immune response can alter a vaccine-induced immune response. DNA Cell Biol 2003;22:421-430.
8. Crompton DWT. Ascaris and ascariasis. Adv Parasitol 2001;48:285-375.
9. DeSilva NR, Chan MS, Bundy DA. Morbidity and mortality due to ascariasis: reestimation and sensitivity analysis of global numbers at risk. Trop Med Int Health 1997;2:519-528.
10. Crompton DWT, Nesheim MC, Pawlowski ZS (eds). Ascariasis and Its Prevention and Control. London: Taylor and Francis; 1989.
11. Albonico M, Crompton DW, Savioli L. Control strategies for intestinal nematode infections. Adv Parasitol 1999;42:277-341.
12. O'Lorcain P, Holland CV. The public health importance of Ascaris lumbricoides. Parasitology 2000;121(Suppl):S51-S71.
13. Anderson RM, May RM. Infectious Diseases of Humans: Dynamics and Control. New York: Oxford University Press; 1991:433-606.
14. Wakelin D, Farias SE, Bradley JE. Variation and immunity to intestinal worms. Parasitology 2002;125(Suppl):S39-S50.
15. Williams-Blangero S, VandeBerg JL, Subedi J, et al. Genes on chromosomes 1 and 13 have significant effects on Ascaris infection. Proc Natl Acad Sci USA 2002;99:5533-5538.
16. Quinell RJ. Genetics of susceptibility to human helminth infection. Int J Parasitol 2003;33:1219-1231.
17. Anderson TJ. Ascaris infections in humans from North America: molecular evidence for cross-infection. Parasitology 1995;110:215-219.
18. Anderson TJC. The dangers of using single locus markers in parasite epidemiology: Ascaris as a case study. Trends Parasitol 2001;17:183-188.
19. Gelpi AP, Mustafa A. Ascaris pneumonia. Am J Med 1968;44:377-389.
20. Gelpi AP, Mustafa A. Seasonal pneumonitis with eosinophilia: a study of larval ascariasis in Saudi Arabs. Am J Trop Med Hyg 1967;16:646-657.
21. Strephenson LS. The contribution of Ascaris lumbricoides to malnutrition in children. Parasitology 1980;81:221-233.
22. Stephenson LS, Latham MC, Ottesen EA. Malnutrition and parasitic helminth infections. Parasitology 2000;121:S23-S38.
23. Crompton DW, Nesheim MC. Nutritional impact of intestinal helminthiasis during the human life cycle. Annu Rev Nutr 2002;22:35-59.
24. Willett WC, Kilama WL, Kihamia CM, et al. Ascaris and growth rates: a randomized trial of treatment. Am J Public Health 1979;69:987-991.
25. Archibong AE, Ndoma-Egba R, Asindi AA. Intestinal obstruction in southeastern Nigerian children. East Afr Med J 1994;71:286-289.
26. Blumenthal DS, Schultz MG. Incidence of intestinal obstruction in children infected with Ascaris lumbricoides. Am J Trop Med Hyg 1975;24:801-805.
27. De Silva NR, Chan MS, Bundy DA. Morbidity and mortality due to Ascaris-induced intestinal obstruction. Trans R Soc Trop Med Hyg 1997;91:31-36.

28. De Silva NR, Guyatt HL, Bundy DA. Worm burden in intestinal obstruction caused by Ascaris lumbricoides. Trop Med Int Health 1997;2:189-190.

29. Wasadikar PP, Kulkami AB. Intestinal obstruction due to ascariasis. Br J Surg 1997;84:410-412.

30. Sandouk F, Haffar S, Zada M, et al. Pancreatic-biliary ascariasis: experience of 300 cases. Am J Gastroenterol 1997;92:2264-2267.

31. Khuroo MS, Zargar SA, Mahajan R. Hepatobiliary and pancreatic ascariasis in India. Lancet 1990;335:1503-1508.

32. Javid G, Wani NA, Gulzar GM, et al. Ascaris-induced liver abscess. World J Surg 1999;23:1191-1194.

33. Singh PA, Gupta SC, Agarawal R. Ascaris lumbricoides appendicitis in the tropics. Trop Doct 1997;27:241.

34. Schulman A. Non-western patterns of biliary stones and the role of ascariasis. Radiology 1987;162:425-430.

35. Palmer LJ, Celedon JC, Weiss ST, et al. Ascaris lumbricoides infection is associated with increased risk of childhood asthma and atopy in rural China. Am J Respir Crit Care Med 2002;165:1489-1493.

36. Cooper PJ, Chico ME, Bland M, et al. Allergic symptoms, atopy, and geohelminth infections in a rural area of Ecuador. Am J Respir Crit Care Med 2003;168:266-267.

37. Reeder MM, Palmer PES. The radiology of tropical diseases. 2nd ed. Berlin: Springer-Verlag; 2001:111-139.

38. Ng KK, Wong HF, Kong MS, et al. Biliary ascariasis: CT, MR cholangiopancreatography, and navigator endoscopic appearance—report of a case of acute biliary obstruction. Abdom Imaging 1999;24:470-472.

39. Rocha MdeS, Costa NS, Costa JC, et al. CT identification of ascaris in the biliary tract. Abdom Imaging. 1995;20:317-319.

40. Ferreyra NP, Cerri GG. Ascariasis of the alimentary tract, liver, pancreas and biliary system: its diagnosis by ultrasonography. Hepatogastroenterology 1998;45:932-937.

41. Valgaeren G, Duysburgh I, Fierens H, et al. Endoscopic treatment of biliary ascariasis: report of a case. Acta Clin Belg 1996;51:97-100.

42. Abadi K. Single dose mebendazole therapy for soil-transmitted nematodes. Am J Trop Med Hyg 1985;34:129-133.

43. Montresor A, Awasthi S, Crompton DW. Use of benzimidazoles in children younger than 24 months for the treatment of soil-transmitted helminthiasis. Acta Trop 2003;86:223-232.

44. Cooper ES, Bundy DAP. Trichuriasis. Clin Trop Med Comm Dis 1987;2:629-643.

45. Gilman RH, Chong UH, Davis C, et al. The adverse consequences of heavy Trichuris infection. Trans R Soc Trop Med Hyg 1983;77:432-438.

46. Williams-Blangero S, McGarvey ST, Subedi J, et al. Genetic component to susceptibility to Trichuris trichiura: evidence from two Asian populations. Genet Epidemiol 2002;22:254-264.

47. MacDonald TT, Spencer J, Murch SH, et al. Immunoepidemiology of intestinal helminth infections. 3. Mucosal macrophages and cytokine production in the colon of children with Trichuris trichiura dysentery. Trans R Soc Trop Med Hyg 1994;88:265-268.

48. MacDonald TT, Choy MY, Spencer J, et al. Histopathology and immunochemistry of the caecum in children with the trichoris dysentary syndrome. J Clin Path. 1991;44:194-199.

49. Sandler M. Whipworm infestation in the colon and rectum simulating Crohn's disease. Lancet 1981;2:210.

50. Jung RC, Beaver PC. Clinical observations on Trichocephalus trichuris (whipworm) infestation in children. Pediatrics 1951;8:548-557.

51. Ramdath DD, Simeon DT, Wong MS, et al. Iron status of school children with varying intensities of Trichuris trichiura infection. Parasitology 1995;110:347-351.

52. Cooper ES, Bundy DAP. Trichuris is not trivial. Parasitol Today 1988;4:301-306.

53. Forrester JE, Bailar JC III, Esrey SA, et al. Randomized trial of albendazole and pyrantel in symptomless trichuriasis in children. Lancet 1998;352:1103-1108.

54. Belizario VY, Amarillo ME, de Leon WU, et al. A comparison of the efficacy of single doses of albendazole, ivermectin, and diethylcarbamazine alone or in combinations against Trichuris and Trichuris spp. Bull WHO 2003;81:35-42.

55. Sirivichayakul C, Pojjaroen-Anant C, Wisetsing P, et al. The effectiveness of 3, 5, or 7 days of albendazole for the treatment of Trichuris trichiura infection. An Trop Med Parasitol 2003;97:847-853.

56. Gilles HM, Williams EJW, Ball PAJ. Hookworm infection and anemia: an epidemiological, clinical, and laboratory study. Q J Med 1964;33:1-24.

57. Roche M, Layrisse M. The nature and causes of "hookworm anemia." Am J Trop Med Hyg 1966;15:1032-1102.

58. Migasena S, Gilles HM. Hookworm infection. Clin Trop Med Comm Dis 1987;2: 617-627.

59. Maxwell C, Hussain R, Nutman TB, et al. The clinical and immunological responses of normal human volunteers to low dose hookworm (Necator americanus) infection. Am J Trop Med Hyg 1987;37:126-134.

60. Kelley PW, Takafuji ET, Wiener H, et al. An outbreak of hookworm infection associated with military operations in Grenada. Milit Med 1989;154:55-59.

61. Chadderdon RC, Cappello M. The hookworm platelet inhibitor: functional blockade of integrins GPIIb/IIIa (alphaIIb beta3) and GPIa/IIa (alpha2 beta1) inhibits platelet aggregation and adhesion in vitro. J Infect Dis 1999;179:1235-1241.

62. Sakti H, Nokes C, Hertanto WS, et al. Evidence for an association between hookworm infection and cognitive function in Indonesian school children. Trop Med Int Health 1999;4:322-334.

63. Sacko M, De Clercq D, Behnke JM, et al. Comparison of the efficacy of mebendazole, albendazole and pyrantel in treatment of human hookworm infections in the southern region of Mali, West Africa. Trans R Soc Trop Med Hyg 1999;93:195-203.

64. Hotez PJ, Zhan B, Bethony JM, et al. Progress in the development of a recombinant vaccine for human hookworm and disease: the Human Hookworm Initiative. Int J Parasitol 2003;33:1245-1258.

65. De Silva NR. Impact of mass chemotherapy on the morbidity due to soil-transmitted nematodes. Acta Trop 2003;86:197-214.

66. Stephenson LS. Optimising the benefits of anthelmintic treatment in children. Paediatr Drugs 2001;3:495-508.

67. Geerts S, Gryseels B. Anthelmintic resistance in human helminths: a review. Trop Med Int Health 2001;6:915-921.

68. Grove DI. Human strongyloidiasis. Adv Parasitol. 1996;38:251-309.

69. Ashford RW, Vince JD, Gratten MJ, Miles WE. Strongyloides infection associated with acute infantile disease in Papua New Guinea. Trans R Soc Trop Med Hyg 1978;72:554.

70. Kitchen LW, Tu KK, Kerns FT. Strongyloides-infected patients at Charleston area medical center, West Virginia, 1997-1998. Clin Infect Dis 2000;31:E5-E6.

71. Gatti S, Lopes R, Cevini C. Intestinal parasitic infections in an institution for the mentally retarded. Ann Trop Med Parasitol 2000;94:453-460.

72. Genta RM, Weesner R, Douce RW, et al. Strongyloidiasis in US veterans of the Vietnam and other wars. JAMA 1987;258:49-52.

73. Scowden EB, Schaffner W, Stone WJ. Overwhelming strongyloidiasis: an unappreciated opportunistic infection. Medicine 1978;57:527-544.

74. Adedayo O, Grell G, Bellot P. Hyperinfective strongyloidiasis in the medical ward: review of 27 cases in 5 years. South Med J 2002;95:711-716.

75. Porto AF, Neva FA, Bittencourt H. HTLV-1 decreases Th2 type of immune response in patients with strongyloidiasis. Parasite Immunol 2001;23:503-507.

76. Porto AF, Oliveira Filho J, Neva FA, et al. Influence of human T-cell lymphocytotrophic virus type 1 infection on serologic and skin tests for strongyloidiasis. Am J Trop Med Hyg 2001;65:610-613.

77. Terashima A, Alvarez H, Tello R, et al. Treatment failure in intestinal strongyloidiasis: an indicator of HTLV-I infection. Int J Infect Dis 2002;6:28-30.

78. Gompels MM, Todd J, Peters BS, et al. Disseminated strongyloidiasis in AIDS: uncommon but important. AIDS 1991;5:329-332.

79. Torres JR, Isturiz R, Murillo J, et al. Efficacy of ivermectin in the treatment of strongyloidiasis complicating AIDS. Clin Infect Dis 1993;17:900-902.

80. Siddiqui AA, Berk SL. Diagnosis of Strongyloides stercoralis infection. Clin Infect Dis 2001;33:1040-1047.

81. Loutfy MR, Wilson M, Keystone JS, et al. Serology and eosinophil count in the diagnosis and management of strongyloidiasis in a non-endemic area. Am J Trop Med Hyg 2002;66:749-752.

82. Zaha O, Hirata T, Kinjo F, et al. Strongyloidiasis—progress in diagnosis and treatment. Intern Med 2000;39:695-700.

83. Boken DJ, Leoni PA, Preheim LC. Treatment of Strongyloides stercoralis hyperinfection syndrome with thiabendazole administered per rectum. Clin Infect Dis 1993;16:123-126.

84. Tarr PE, Miele PS, Pergoy KS, et al. Case report: rectal administration of ivermectin to a patient with Strongyloides hyperinfection syndrome. Am J Trop Med Hyg. 2003;68:453-455.

85. Wagner ED, Eby WC. Pinworm prevalence in California elementary school children, and diagnostic methods. Am J Trop Med Hyg 1983;32:998-1001.

86. Lohiya GS, Crinella FM, Lohiya S. Epidemiology and control of enterobiasis in a developmental center. West J Med 2000;172:305-308.

87. Pawlowski ZS. Enterobiasis. Clin Trop Med Comm Dis 1987;3:667-676.

88. Nunez FA, Hernandez M, Finlay CM. A longitudinal study of enterobiasis in three day care centers of Havana City. Rev Inst Med Trop Sao Paulo 1996;38:129-132.

89. Weller TH, Sorenson CW. Enterobiasis: its incidence and symptomatology in a group of 505 children. N Engl J Med 1941;224:143-146.

90. Welsh NM. Recent insights into childhood "social diseases" gonorrhea, scabies, pediculosis, pinworms. Clin Pediatr 1978;17:318-322.

91. Sun T, Schwartz NS, Sewell C, et al. Enterobius egg granuloma of the vulva and peritoneum: review of the literature. Am J Trop Med Hyg 1991;45:249-253.

92. Dahlstrom JE, MacArthur EB. Enterobius vermicularis: a possible cause of symptoms resembling appendicitis. Aust N Z J Surg 1994;64:692-694.

93. Liu LX, Chi JY, Upton MP, et al. Eosinophilic colitis associated with larvae of the pinworm Enterobius vermicularis. Lancet 1995;346:410-412.

94. Matsen JM, Turner JA. Reinfection in enterobiasis (pinworm infection): simultaneous treatment of family members. Am J Dis Child 1969;118:576-581.

Tissue Nematodes Including Trichinosis, Dracunculiasis, and the Filariases

DAVID I. GROVE

The tissue-dwelling roundworms constitute a major global health problem. They are widely scattered around the world, especially in the tropics, and infect millions of people. Some are parasites of humans only, whereas others have an animal reservoir. All these parasites have complex life cycles involving arthropod intermediate hosts, except *Trichinella* species, which are transmitted directly from one host to the next by ingestion of infective larvae. Like most helminths, the adult worms do not multiply in the human host; therefore the worm load and severity of disease depend in large measure on the intensity and frequency of exposure to the infective forms. The relative pathogenicity of the adult worms versus the larval forms varies according to the species of infecting worm. Definitive diagnosis requires isolation and identification of the parasite, but for some infections this is difficult. Effective therapy is available for only some of these infections. Some parasites present almost insurmountable control problems, whereas others can be avoided by simple preventive measures.

Infections acquired by ingestion of contaminated food or water are considered first, and then those transmitted by blood-sucking flies are discussed. Historical information concerning all of these parasites, including the circumstances of their discovery and elucidation of their life cycles together with the clinical illness they cause and modes of treatment that have been developed can be found elsewhere.[1]

TRICHINOSIS

Trichinosis develops when undercooked flesh contaminated with infective larvae of *Trichinella* spp. is eaten. Most infections are asymptomatic, but heavy exposure may lead to diarrhea, periorbital edema, myositis, fever, and prostration.

Trichinella spiralis is the species that has been recognized for years, but the genus has been revised taxonomically. Eight species have now been described based on their genetic, biochemical, physical (tolerance to high and low temperatures), and biologic data (susceptibility of various hosts) (Table 286-1). In addition, three other genotypes are acknowledged in the genus, but their taxonomic level is uncertain at present.[2,3]

Life Cycle

When raw or inadequately cooked meat containing viable larvae of *Trichinella* spp. is eaten, the organisms are freed from the cyst walls by acid pepsin digestion in the stomach and pass into the small intestine. Larvae invade the columnar epithelium at the bases of the villi of the small intestine and develop into adult worms. They are obligate intracellular parasites occupying the cytoplasm of a row of enterocytes. The males are about 1.50×0.05 mm and the females about 3.50×0.06 mm. The number of larvae released by a fertilized female varies with the species of both parasite and host. *T. spiralis* probably produces about 500 larvae over a period of 2 to 3 weeks and then the adult worms are expelled in the feces. The newborn larvae seed the skeletal muscles via the bloodstream. They burrow into individual muscle fibers and over the next 3 weeks increase 10 times in length; they then coil and become capable of infecting a new host. In many species, a cyst wall develops around the larva that may eventually calcify (see Table 286-1). Larvae may remain viable for several years.

Epidemiology

Trichinella spp. are distributed throughout the world and are widely spread in nature among a large number of carnivorous animals, humans being an incidental host (see Table 286-1).[4] The reservoir hosts reflect primarily the fauna present in that region. Humans are an incidental host, most infections being due to *T. spiralis*; a few are caused by *T. britovi*, *T. nativa*, *T. nelsoni*, and *T. pseudospiralis*. *T. spiralis* and *T. papuae* are the species with the highest infectivity for swine. Most swine in the United States are fed with grain, and these animals are generally uninfected. The small proportion fed with garbage may become infected when given uncooked trichinous scraps, usually pig meat, or when the carcasses of infected wild animals such as rats are eaten.[5] In Europe the fox is the primary reservoir of the sylvatic cycle of *Trichinella*, and human infections usually occur in rural areas where traditional swine-rearing practices are used or raw horse meat is eaten.[6]

Fewer than 100 human cases are usually reported each year in the United States. About three-fourths of them are due to inadequately processed pork; most of the rest have been caused by ingestion of poorly cooked bear meat, walrus meat, or cougar jerky.[5] A reemergence of the domestic cycle of trichinosis based in swine in Europe has resulted from the breakdown of veterinary services and state-owned farms in some countries. Game animals as a source of infection has increased greatly in both developing and developed countries.[6]

Pathologic Characteristics

There have been indications that the various species have different pathogenicities for humans and other hosts.[2] For example, trichinosis in the Inuit population in Canada after ingestion of infected walrus seems to be associated with prolonged diarrhea and few muscle symptoms. *T. nativa* produces primarily an enteral illness, whereas *T. britovi* causes few if any intestinal symptoms. *T. nelsoni* is of relatively low pathogenicity during both its enteral and parenteral phases, whereas *T. pseudospiralis* may produce severe enteral and systemic symptoms.[7]

During the first 2 to 3 weeks after infection, the small intestine shows mild, partial villous atrophy and an inflammatory infiltrate of polymorphonuclear cells, eosinophils, lymphocytes, and macrophages in the mucosa and submucosa. Adult worms may be seen in the epithelial layer near the bases of the villi. The most striking changes are in the skeletal muscles. The fibers become edematous, lose their cross-striations, and undergo basophilic degeneration; in addition, their nuclei proliferate. The typical coiled worm, the cyst wall derived from the host cell, and the surrounding lymphocytic and eosinophilic infiltrate may be seen within the muscle fiber (Fig. 286-1). In severe cases, focal interstitial myocarditis, meningitis, and encephalitis may occur.

Clinical Features

Most infections are subclinical. The development of symptoms depends mainly on the size of the inoculum of viable larvae. Consequently, the frequencies of the symptoms and signs of trichi-

TABLE 286-1 Species in the Genus *Trichinella*

Species	Code	Distribution	Most Common Hosts	Cyst Wall
T. spiralis	T1	Worldwide*	Pigs, rodents, horses, bears, foxes	Yes
T. nativa	T2	Arctic, subarctic	Bears, foxes, dogs	Yes
T. britovi	T3	Temperate, subarctic	Dogs, cats, bears	Yes
T. pseudospiralis	T4	Arctic, Tasmania	Birds, omnivorous mammals	No
T. murrelli	T5	North America	Bears	Yes
Uncertain status	T6	Subarctic	Bears	Yes
T. nelsoni	T7	Tropical Africa	Hyenas, cats	Yes
Uncertain status	T8	Southern Africa	Lions, panthers	Yes
Uncertain status	T9	Japan	Sylvatic carnivores	No
T. papuae	T10	Papua New Guinea	Pigs	No
T. zimbawensis	T11	Central Africa	Crocodiles, mammals	Yes

*Except Australia and New Zealand and some Pacific islands.

FIGURE 286-1. Section of muscle showing two cysts, the larger one revealing the coiled larva cut in cross section surrounded by the cyst wall derived from the host muscle fiber (the "nurse" cell) and a predominantly mononuclear infiltrate. H&E.

nosis vary widely from outbreak to outbreak. Their relative frequencies are shown in Table 286-2.

Symptoms attributable to adult worms in the intestines may be found during the first week after infection.[8] Diarrhea is the most common symptom, but patients may also complain of abdominal discomfort and vomiting. Patients with extremely heavy worm burdens may develop fulminating enteritis. Symptoms associated with systemic invasion by larvae are much more common and usually appear during the second week after infection. Fever is frequently present, although it is of variable intensity and duration. Periorbital edema may be associated with subconjunctival hemorrhages and chemosis. Myositis with pain, swelling, and weakness is also common; it usually develops first in the extraocular muscles and then involves the masseters, neck muscles, limb flexors, and lumbar muscles. Some patients complain of headache, cough, shortness of breath, hoarseness, and dysphagia. Occasionally, a macular or petechial rash is observed. Retinal or subungual splinter hemorrhages are sometimes seen. These systemic symptoms usually peak 2 to 3 weeks after infection and then slowly subside, although malaise and weakness may persist for weeks. Occasionally, a patient dies, usually from myocarditis but sometimes from encephalitis or pneumonia. It has been claimed that there may be long-lasting sequelae of infection, including muscle aches, eye disturbances, cardiac complaints, and headaches.[9]

Diagnosis

Trichinosis should be suspected in a patient who has any of the cardinal features of periorbital edema, myositis, fever, and eosinophilia. If questioning reveals the recent consumption of poorly cooked meat, particularly pork products or wildlife, the likelihood of the diagnosis is greatly increased.[10] Further confirmation is provided if others who have eaten the same meat have similar symptoms. Eosinophilia is often found, beginning about the 10th day and sometimes reaching extremely high levels. The erythrocyte sedimentation rate is usually normal. Elevated serum creatine phosphokinase and lactic dehydrogenase levels indicate considerable muscle involvement.

Antibodies are not detectable until at least 3 weeks after infection. They may be measured by a variety of techniques including enzyme-linked, immunofluorescence, indirect hemagglutinin, precipitin, and bentonite flocculation assays. A rising antibody titer may help establish the diagnosis.[8] Tests for detecting *Trichinella* DNA in muscle or blood using the polymerase chain reaction (PCR) are being developed.[11] Muscle biopsy is usually unnecessary; if doubt remains, a specimen obtained from a tender, swollen muscle may confirm the diagnosis, although *Trichinella* species must be differentiated from other nematodes sometimes found in muscles.

The protean manifestations of trichinosis require differentiation of this infection from a large number of other diseases. The gastrointestinal symptoms may mimic those of gastroenteritis. Systemic symptoms may cause confusion with influenza, typhoid fever, sinusitis, dermatomyositis, glomerulonephritis, and angioneurotic edema. The rash may resemble that found with measles, scarlet fever, and typhus.

Treatment

There is no satisfactory treatment for trichinosis. In the rare instance that a patient is known to have ingested trichinous meat within the past week or so, mebendazole (5 mg/kg) or albendazole (5 mg/kg) should be administered orally twice daily for 1 week.[8,12] These drugs are active against intestinal worms but have little effect on muscle-embedded larvae. In a placebo-controlled trial, patients with trichinous myositis treated with mebendazole or thiabendazole improved significantly compared with those given a placebo or the antifungal agent fluconazole.[13] However, the first cases were seen within a day of eating an infected pig, and patients had been ill for a median of only 3 days when treatment was started (G. Watt, personal communication). The apparent improvement in patients given anthelmintics may have been due to accelerated elimination of adult worms from the gut and hence less seeding of muscles by larvae. Furthermore, it has been shown that mebendazole fails to kill parasites encapsulating in muscles.[14] The mainstays of treatment for systemic trichinosis are bed rest and salicylates. Corticosteroids may be used for critically ill patients, but evidence of benefit is equivocal.

Prevention

The most effective method for killing *Trichinella* larvae is proper cooking: The thermal death point is 55° C, so meat should be cooked until there is no trace of pink fluid or flesh. Storage in a home freezer (−15° C) for 3 weeks usually sterilizes meat; smoking, salting, and drying are unreliable.[15]

OTHER MUSCLE NEMATODE INFECTIONS

Haycocknema perplexum Infection

Two Australian patients have been described who presented with severe, progressive muscle weakness, in one case over a period of 2 years. Muscle biopsy disclosed predominantly adult nematodes within muscle fibers and sparse larvae both within and outside of the fibers; capsules did not form around parasites within myofibers.[16] These worms were subsequently described as a new genus and species, *Haycocknema perplexum*.[17] Their life cycle is unknown. It is possible that autoinfection occurs, particularly in patients treated with corticosteroids for polymyositis. Six weeks of treatment with albendazole appeared to be effective.

DRACUNCULIASIS

Dracunculiasis (dracontiasis, guinea worm infection) develops after drinking water containing small crustaceans infected with *Dracunculus medinensis*. It is characterized by a chronic cutaneous ulcer from which the worm protrudes.[18]

TABLE 286-2 Frequency of Symptoms and Signs of Trichinosis Condensed from Nine Reported Outbreaks		
Symptoms or Signs	*Mean (%)*	*Range (%)*
Fever	91	71-100
Myalgia	89	68-100
Weakness and malaise	82	50-94
Periorbital edema	77	29-100
Headache	52	0-100
Cutaneous rash	20	0-67
Trunk and leg edema	18	0-75
Diarrhea	16	0-48
Nausea	15	0-67
Subconjuctival hemorrhage	9	0-65
Subungual splinter hemorrhage	9	0-60
Cough	6	0-40
Vomiting	3	0-13

Life Cycle

When water containing infected copepods is ingested, larvae are released in the host stomach, pass into the small intestine, penetrate the mucosa, and reach the retroperitoneum, where they mature and mate. The female worm (1 to 2 mm in diameter and up to 1 m long) migrates to the subcutaneous tissue, usually of the legs, about 1 year later. The overlying skin ulcerates, and a portion of the worm protrudes. On contact with water, large numbers of larvae are released from a loop of uterus prolapsed through either the mouth or a rupture in the body wall. These larvae are then ingested by crustaceans, in which they undergo further development, continuing the life cycle.

Epidemiology

Dracunculus medinensis is now found mostly in tropical Africa. Shallow ponds, cisterns, and wells are the usual habitat of the crustacean intermediate hosts. The disease is prevalent in areas where people bathe or wade in water used for drinking purposes. Manifestations in a community are highly seasonal. This reflects both the developmental cycle of the parasite, which requires an incubation period of about 1 year, and the influence of climate on the types of water sources used. The disability resulting from infection may be of great socioeconomic importance.

Clinical Features

There are often no clinical signs until the worm reaches the surface and is ready to discharge larvae. A stinging papule develops at this point, usually on the lower portions of the legs. At this time, some patients have a generalized reaction, with urticaria, nausea, vomiting, diarrhea, and dyspnea. Over the next few days the lesion vesiculates, after which the blister ruptures and forms a painful ulcer in which part of the worm is often visible (Fig. 286-2). If the area is douched with fluid, a milky fluid containing larvae wells up. Discharge continues intermittently, and the worm is slowly absorbed or extruded over the next few weeks, after which the ulcer heals. Multiple ulcers are common, and secondary infection is frequent. In endemic areas, patients are often bedridden for a month or so. There is no immunity to reinfection.

Diagnosis

The clinical picture is characteristic. Larvae can be found during microscopic examination of the discharge fluid.

Treatment

Thiabendazole, 25 mg/kg twice daily for 2 days, and metronidazole, 5 mg/kg twice daily for 1 week to 10 days, have no effect on the worms themselves but produce resolution of the inflammation within several days. This permits easy removal of the worm over a week or so by progressively rolling out the emerging worm onto a small stick. (As of this writing, it is not clear whether thiabendazole will continue to be available from its manufacturer, Merck.) Corticosteroid ointments shorten the time to complete healing, and the addition of topical antibiotics reduces the risk of secondary bacterial infection.[19] Ivermectin has no effect on prepatent guinea worms. Mebendazole in high dosage is not recommended because it does not lessen the duration of disease or disability but increases the incidence of nonemerged worms, thereby exacerbating the danger of larvae being released into joints.[20] Alternatively, unerupted worms may be removed completely and painlessly in several minutes by surgical means with local anesthesia.[21] Secondary bacterial infection should be treated as necessary.

Prevention

Guinea worm infection can be prevented by boiling or chlorinating drinking water or by sieving it through a cloth. Control on a public health scale requires health education and improved water supplies. In 1986, the World Health Organization (WHO) initiated a program to eradicate dracunculiasis, and the number of cases has fallen dramatically from an estimated 4 million in 1981. By 2001 dracunculiasis had been restricted to 13 African countries. During the first 6 months of 2002, only 21,000 cases were reported, 71% of those being in the

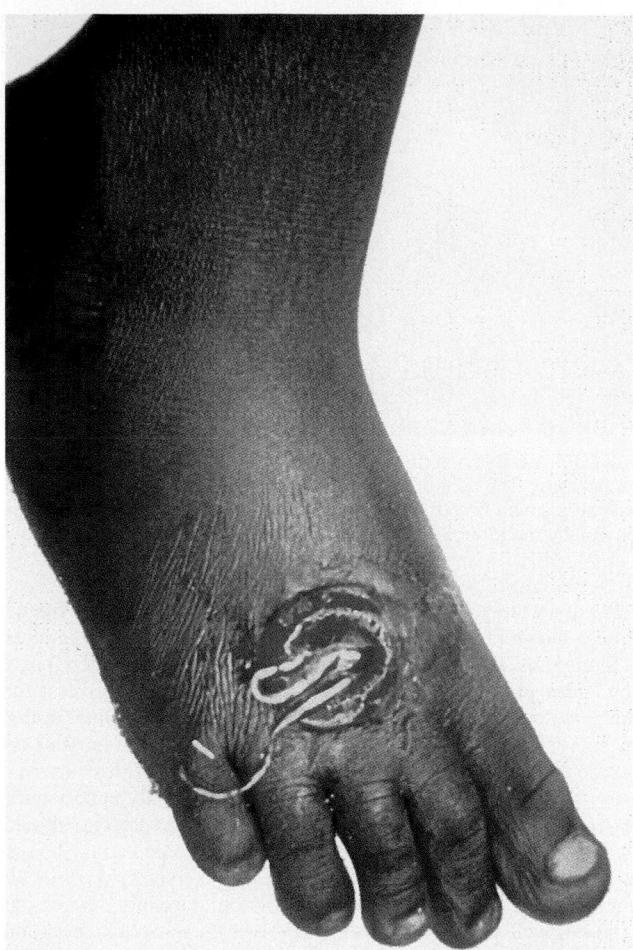

FIGURE 286-2. Guinea worm partially extruded from an ulcer on the dorsum of the foot.

Sudan which is racked by civil war. Guinea worm disease may soon become the second human infection to be eradicated.[22]

BANCROFTIAN AND BRUGIAN FILARIASIS

Bancroftian filariasis and brugian (Malayan) filariasis are similar clinical conditions resulting from the transmission of *Wuchereria bancrofti, Brugia malayi,* and *Brugia timori* to humans by mosquitoes. Symptomatic patients have acute lymphatic inflammation or the effects of chronic lymphatic obstruction such as hydrocele, elephantiasis of the limbs, and chyluria.

Life Cycle

After the bite of an infected mosquito, infective larvae pass into the lymphatics and lymph nodes, where they mature over the next few months into white, thread-like adult worms, the males being about 40.0 × 0.1 mm and the females 100 × 0.25 mm. The adults live for 5 years or more, and the fertilized females discharge microfilariae measuring approximately 150 × 7 μm via the lymphatics into the bloodstream. The number of microfilariae found in the peripheral blood varies. There is usually a surge of microfilariae into the blood during the middle of the night, a phenomenon known as nocturnal periodicity. Patients from the South Pacific with *W. bancrofti* infection have a much less pronounced peak that is maximal during the day. *B. malayi* infections produce nocturnal peaks of varying intensity. If microfilariae are ingested by a mosquito during feeding, the organisms develop into infective larvae over the next 2 weeks and are ready to repeat the cycle.

Epidemiology

Wuchereria bancrofti is distributed widely throughout the tropics and subtropics, *B. malayi* is restricted to South and Southeast Asia, and *B. timori* is restricted to the eastern Indonesian archipelago. It is estimated that 120 million people are infected with these parasites. There is no animal reservoir for *W. bancrofti,* but *B. malayi* has been found in felines and primates.

Even in endemic areas, only a small proportion (less than 1%) of mosquito bites are infective. It is probable that infections with microfilaremia are produced only when a susceptible person receives a large number of infective larvae and that obstructive disease develops only when exposure continues for many years. Although infection often begins during childhood,[23] clinical filariasis is mainly a disease of adults and is more common in men.[24,25] The disability resulting from infection may have profound sexual and socioeconomic effects.

Pathologic Characteristics

Lymphatics harboring adult worms display lymphangiectasia but little inflammation early in the course of infection. Later, there may be endothelial proliferation, fibrin deposition, and a granulomatous inflammatory infiltrate of eosinophils, lymphocytes, and macrophages. Molting and the death of worms exacerbate the inflammation, which is succeeded by fibrosis and obstruction of lymph flow.[26] All of these processes are associated with complex immunologic events.[27] It is possible that a proportion of the population in endemic areas generates protective immunity that may be T cell-mediated. Secondary bacterial infection may be an important cofactor in the development of elephantiasis.[28]

It has been recognized recently that most filariae are infected with endosymbiotic rickettsial bacteria of the genus *Wolbachia*. These bacteria are transmitted transovarially and appear to have evolved a mutualistic association with their filarial hosts.[29] Antibiotic treatment of worms has shown that clearance of bacteria results in embryotoxicity, inhibition of molting, and eventually death of the worms. It is likely that lipolysaccharide released from these bacteria is a major activator of the inflammatory responses. Death of parasites, whether occurring naturally or as a result of antiparasitic treatment,[30] is likely to release large numbers of bacteria, which precipitate an acute inflammatory reaction. Furthermore, chronic release of *Wolbachia* may cause progressive damage to infected lymphatics and desensitization of the immune system.[31]

Clinical Features

Many patients are asymptomatic despite the presence of microfilaremia. Clinical manifestations are due to acute inflammation or chronic lymphatic obstruction. Attacks of lymphangitis or lymphadenitis with fever, headache, backache, and nausea occasionally occur. Acute funiculitis, epididymitis, or orchitis may be seen. These acute episodes usually subside after a few days to several weeks but may recur. Chronic lymphadenopathy is frequently found and may be the only manifestation of filariasis. In long-standing cases, lymphedema may develop. Chronic hydrocele is the most common feature and may cause considerable sexual disability. The lower limbs are involved less frequently; at first there is pitting edema that is most marked pretibially, but eventually nonpitting edema may involve the whole limb (Fig. 286-3). With elephantiasis, the skin of the leg or scrotum becomes thickened, fissured, and warty. Ulceration and secondary infection may occur.[32] Occasionally, lymph varices appear, especially in the genital region. Chyluria develops when swollen lymphatics burst into the urinary tract.

Diagnosis

The definitive diagnosis of bancroftian filariasis and brugian filariasis depends on demonstrating the parasite. Unfortunately, microfilariae are frequently absent from the blood during both the early and late stages of the disease. A blood sample should be taken around midnight unless the patient is from the South Pacific. The smear is stained and examined for microfilariae (Fig. 286-4). If none is found, a concentration method should be used.

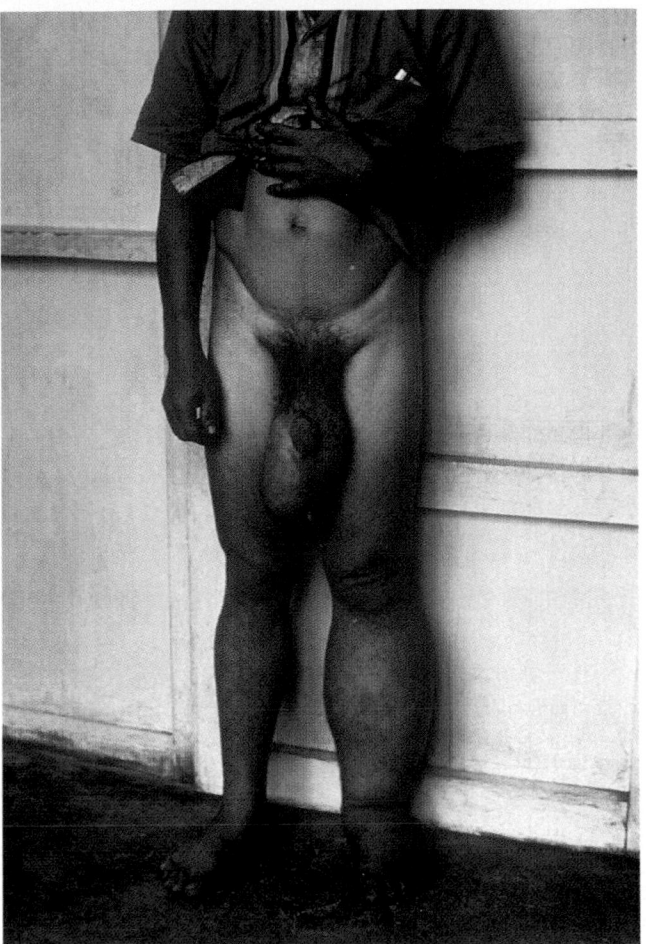

FIGURE 286-3. Man with inguinal lymphadenopathy, large bilateral hydroceles, marked edema of the left lower limb (particularly the leg and foot), and early signs of elephantiasis in the foot.

Microfilariae are occasionally found in hydrocele fluid or chylous urine. Eosinophilia is usually absent except during episodes of acute inflammation. Serologic tests for antibody such as bentonite flocculation, indirect hemagglutination, enzyme-linked immunosorbent assay, and indirect fluorescent antibody tests may be of some help but do not differentiate among the various forms of filariasis or between past and current infection. A commercial card test to detect *W. bancrofti* antigen is available,[33] and assays for brugian filariasis are being developed. Polymerase chain reaction (PCR) tests to detect *W. bancrofti* in blood may be available in research laboratories.[24]

Adult worms are sometimes found in lymph node biopsy specimens, but this procedure is not generally justified. Microfilariae or worm fragments may be seen with fine-needle aspiration cytology.[34] Ultrasonography of the lymphatic vessels in the scrotal area may reveal dilated lymphatics and motile adult worms, the so-called "filarial dance sign," examples of which may be viewed on the Internet.[35] Unfortunately, the adult worms of brugian filariasis are not easily detectable.[36] Abnormal lymphatic drainage in the legs may be demonstrated by lymphoscintigraphy.[37] If microfilariae cannot be found and sophisticated imaging techniques are not available, the diagnosis must be made on clinical grounds by excluding other causes.

Treatment

There is no satisfactory treatment for filariasis. Diethylcarbamazine in an oral dose of 6 mg/kg daily for 2 weeks reduces the number of microfilariae in the peripheral blood but is no panacea. An alternative regimen is as follows: day 1 50 mg, day 2 50 mg tid, day 3 100 mg tid, then 6 mg/kg/day in 3 divided doses for 4-14 days. Diethylcarbamazine kills some adult

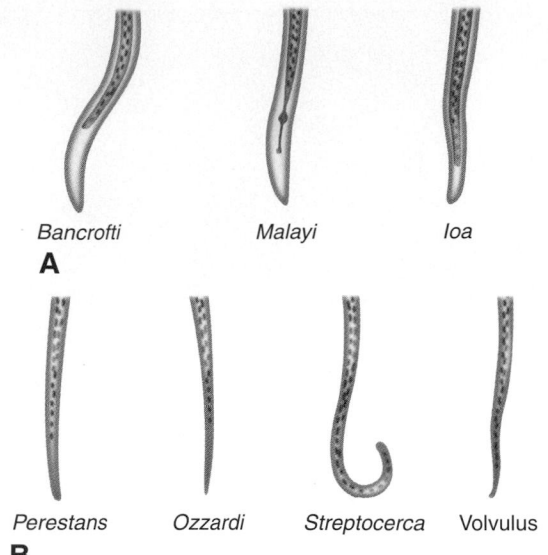

A
Bancrofti   Malayi   Ioa

B
Perestans   Ozzardi   Streptocerca   Volvulus

FIGURE 286-4. Comparative features of sheathed (**A**) and un-sheathed (**B**) microfilariae.

worms but not others. When it does kill worms, it may precipitate acute inflammation that culminates in an exuberant granulomatous process with progressive fibrosis. Ivermectin in a single dose of 200 to 400 µg/kg has been shown to have a microfilaricidal effect similar to that of diethylcarbamazine. Ultrasonography showed that it has no effect on adult worms. Neither diethylcarbamazine nor ivermectin has any significant effect on the clinical course of lymphatic filariasis, and microfilariae often reappear in the peripheral blood after a few months. Furthermore, these drugs may cause severe hypotensive reactions, with dizziness, headache, fever, and vomiting, particularly in patients with high microfilarial loads.

There are conflicting reports on whether a single 400 mg dose of albendazole has any significant effect on microfilaremia. The predominant view is that albendazole alone has minimal effect but, when combined with diethylcarbamazine or ivermectin, there is some further reduction in microfilaremia.[38-40] No studies have yet been reported that examine the effects on filariasis of antibiotic therapy directed against *Wolbachia.*

Acute inflammatory reactions should be treated with anti-inflammatory agents, and secondary bacterial infections should be treated with an appropriate antibiotic. Long-term suppressive therapy with oral penicillin is necessary to suppress streptococcal infections in some patients, together with comprehensive foot care.[41] Mild lymphedema may be controlled with elastic stockings, and a transient response may be seen with sequential intermittent pneumatic compression.[42] Surgery is useful in the management of hydrocele but has little place for patients with elephantiasis of the legs.[43] Operative intervention may be beneficial in patients with intractable chyluria.[44]

Prevention

The most effective preventive measure is avoidance of mosquitoes by the use of screens, nets, and insect repellents. Although diethylcarbamazine and ivermectin have no or limited therapeutic value for the individual patient, repeated administration of either or both drugs every 6 to 12 months may reduce transmission in a community. Rarely, repeated treatment with diethylcarbamazine has succeeded in eradicating the infection. Eradication was achieved in Kinmen Island; the acute inflammatory filarial illnesses disappeared, although chronic obstructive disease persisted for the next two decades.[45] In contrast, eradication could not be achieved on the island of Tahiti despite twice-yearly administration of diethylcarbamazine over 34 years.[46]

Despite the fact that diethylcarbamazine has been available since 1947, some 30 studies evaluating the efficacy of diethylcarbamazine

alone or in combination were reported during the 3 years from 2000 through 2002, suggesting that these drugs alone are not the answer in most endemic areas. Nevertheless, the WHO has embarked on a campaign of mass administration of albendazole (donated by GlaxoSmithKline) together with diethylcarbamazine or ivermectin yearly for 5 years in endemic areas. It is hoped that this "global campaign to eliminate lymphatic filariasis" will lead to elimination of filariasis by 2020.[47] Although the campaign will undoubtedly greatly reduce the burden of filariasis, hopes of sustained control or eradication are likely to be overly optimistic unless ongoing mosquito control campaigns are included.[48]

LOIASIS

Loiasis, caused by *Loa loa,* is transmitted to humans by tabanid flies. It is characterized by transient subcutaneous swellings. Occasionally, the worm is seen migrating through the subconjunctiva or other tissues.

Life Cycle

The white, threadlike adult worms, measuring 30 to 70 × 0.3 mm, migrate through the connective tissues. The sheathed microfilariae, 300 × 8 µm, appear in the blood during the day and may be ingested by tabanid (horse) flies, in which they develop into infective larvae.

Epidemiology

Loa loa is irregularly distributed in West and Central Africa. The vectors are diurnally biting flies (*Chrysops* spp.) that live in the canopy of the rain forest.[49] They are attracted by people moving through open spaces in the jungle. Genetic factors may be important in determining susceptibility to infection.[50] The role of *Wolbachia* in loiasis in unclear.

Clinical Features

Many patients are asymptomatic, although they may have high eosinophil levels in the peripheral blood. Transient swellings of localized subcutaneous edema, called Calabar swellings, may develop.[51] Usually only one swelling occurs at a time. The onset may be preceded by localized pain and itching for several hours. It is nonerythematous, measures 10 to 20 cm in diameter, and lasts several days to weeks. Calabar swellings are commonly seen around joints such as the wrist or the knee and recur irregularly at either the same or different sites. Other patients complain of pruritus or have urticaria. Occasionally, a worm is seen passing through the subconjunctiva (Fig. 286-5), where it produces an intense conjunctivitis lasting several days. Worms have also been seen in the penis or around the nipple.

Visitors to areas of endemicity who are already infected may develop a hyperreactive state characterized by more frequent recurrences of fugitive swellings, more marked eosinophilia, increased debilitation, and more complications. Of particular note is the development of renal disease, either before or after treatment.

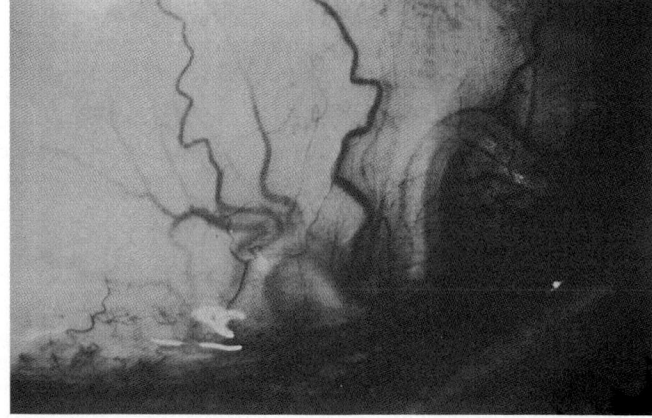

FIGURE 286-5. Serpentine adult *Loa loa* passing through the subconjunctiva.

Other complications that may be seen are endomyocardial fibrosis, retinopathy, encephalopathy, peripheral neuropathy, arthritis, pleural effusion, glomerulonephritis and nephrotic syndrome, venous thrombosis, and breast calcification. Pulmonary infiltrates have also been ascribed to loiasis, but it is difficult to differentiate this condition from tropical pulmonary eosinophilia.

Diagnosis

The disease should be suspected in a patient with a typical history who has lived in West or Central Africa. The diagnosis is established by finding microfilariae in the daytime blood, as described under "Bancroftian and Brugian Filariasis." Failure to find microfilariae does not rule out the diagnosis, and the diagnosis is usually made on clinical grounds. Filarial antibody serology may be available in specialized laboratories.[52] A PCR test has been described that is positive in some nonmicrofilaremic individuals, but it is not generally available.[53] Occasionally, the adult worm can be extracted from the eye or elsewhere, a therapeutic as well as diagnostic measure.

Treatment

Diethylcarbamazine eliminates microfilariae from the blood but often does not kill adult worms. It is administered as described under "Onchocerciasis." Treatment with ivermectin in a single dose of 200 μg/kg decreases microfilarial densities in the peripheral blood. Whether albendazole has any effect is uncertain; conflicting results with albendazole at 600 to 800 mg daily for several days have been found by the same investigators.[54,55] Patients with high microfilarial counts (more than 30,000/ml) often experience fever, pruritus, headache, and arthralgia within 36 hours of diethylcarbamazine or ivermectin therapy. Encephalopathy may be precipitated by treatment with any of these drugs, especially if microfilarial loads are high.[56] Treatment with doxycycline was unsuccessful in two patients.[57]

Prevention

Personal protection depends on avoiding places where biting flies are numerous, wearing protective clothing, and using insect repellents. Mass treatment of villages interrupts transmission; diethylcarbamazine is administered in doses of 5 mg/kg/day for 3 consecutive days each month, or ivermectin may be given at 3-month intervals. Diethylcarbamazine in a dose of 300 mg once weekly is effective in preventing loiasis in persons who are residing temporarily in endemic regions.[58]

OTHER SUBCONJUNCTIVAL NEMATODE INFECTIONS

Dirofilaria repens Infection

There have been a number of reports from around the world of ocular infection with the nematode *Dirofilaria repens,* which is a parasite of canids and felids and is transmitted by mosquitoes. In humans, most worms are found in the subconjunctiva, but they may also be found intraocularly and in the orbit. Treatment is by excision.[59]

Macacanema *formosana* Infection

Macacanema formosana is normally a filarial parasite infection of catarrhine monkeys (*Macaca* cyclopsis), probably transmitted by biting midges (*Culicoides* species). A 7.4 cm long worm was removed from the subconjunctiva of a Taiwanese woman; no microfilariae were seen in the blood.[60]

Onchocerca lupi Infection

Two human cases of subconjunctival infection with a filarial nematode, apparently *Onchocerca lupi,* a parasite of dogs, have been reported from Europe.[61]

Setaria labiatopapillosa Infection

Four cases of subconjunctival infection with *Setaria labiatopillosa,* a filarial nematode, have been described from Romania. The worms were excised, and the patients were treated with diethylcarbamazine. The vector is unknown.[62]

ONCHOCERCIASIS

Onchocerciasis (river blindness) is caused by *Onchocerca volvulus* and is transmitted to humans by blackflies. It is characterized by an itchy dermatitis, subcutaneous nodules, keratitis, and chorioretinitis.

Life Cycle

After the bite of an infected *Simulium* blackfly, larvae penetrate the skin and migrate into the connective tissues. They develop into white filiform adults, the males being 3 × 0.2 mm and the females 400 × 0.3 mm. The worms are often found tangled together in nodules of fibrous tissue, where they may live for years. Each female produces large numbers of unsheathed microfilariae, 200 to 300 × 6 to 8 μm, that migrate through the skin and connective tissues. The life cycle is continued when they are ingested by female blackflies and develop into infective larvae.

Epidemiology

In the recent past, *O. volvulus* has infected 20 million people in West, Central, and East Africa and another 1 million people in scattered foci in Central America and South America. It is possible that the *Onchocerca* causing sowda, which is prevalent in Arabia, may be due to an as yet undescribed species.[63] There is no known animal reservoir. Onchocerciasis tends to have a focal distribution in areas in which it is endemic. In Africa the flies breed in fast-flowing streams in both the savannah and rain forest and tend to bite the lower body. In the Americas the flies breed in small streams on hillsides and bite more frequently around the head. Heavy parasite loads and severe disease are seen only with repeated infection.

Pathologic Characteristics

A granulomatous inflammatory reaction followed by fibrosis develops around the adult worms. The microfilariae in the subcutaneous tissues may produce a low-grade inflammatory reaction, destruction of elastic fibers, and fibrosis. Similarly, immunologically mediated processes cause onchocercal keratitis[64] and retinal disease. As discussed earlier (see "Bancroftian and Brugian Filariasis"), *O. volvulus,* like many other filariae, is infected by *Wolbachia* bacteria.[29] The inflammatory response to microfilariae is thought to be predominantly directed against *Wolbachia.*[65] Furthermore, when patients with onchocerciasis were treated with doxycycline for 6 weeks and the worms excised 4 months later, most bacteria were eliminated and embryogenesis was largely inhibited.[66] When doxycycline was administered with ivermectin, embryogenesis was blocked completely for at least 18 months.[67]

Clinical Features

Early skin lesions produce an itchy, erythematous, papular rash. With severe infections, cutaneous lymphedema with leathery thickening and depigmentation may be seen.[68] Ultimately, loss of elasticity with chronic lymphadenopathy may produce pendulous sacs containing inguinal and femoral lymph nodes. There may be firm, nontender, freely mobile fibrous nodules measuring several millimeters to centimeters and containing the adult worms. They are most commonly located over bony prominences. In addition, there may be systemic changes including weight loss and musculoskeletal pains. Sowda is a form of onchocerciasis that is often localized to one limb with intensely itchy, swollen, darkened skin covered with scaly papules.

Impaired visual acuity is the most serious complication of onchocerciasis. The most common lesion is punctate keratitis followed by pannus formation and corneal fibrosis. Slit lamp examination often reveals microfilariae in the cornea and anterior chamber. Iridocyclitis, glaucoma, choroiditis, and optic atrophy may develop.[69] Not surprisingly, blindness in endemic areas is associated with a three- to fourfold increase in the mortality rate. It has been suggested that onchocerciasis is associated with an increased prevalence of epilepsy.

Diagnosis

The diagnosis is made by demonstrating microfilariae in skin snips or in the cornea or anterior chamber on slit-lamp examination or by finding adult worms in a nodule biopsy specimen. Nonpalpable nodules are sometimes demonstrated by ultrasound techniques. Bloodless skin snips are obtained without anesthesia by raising small cones of skin about 3 mm in diameter with the tip of a needle and then cutting them off with a razor blade. Snips should be taken from over the scapulas and iliac crests and from the buttocks and thighs. They are allowed to stand for half an hour in a drop of 0.9% saline and are then examined under a microscope for microfilariae.

Microfilariae are sometimes found in urine. Ultrasonographic detection of changes in the vitreous humor has been described, and eosinophilia is common. Assays for the detection of onchocercal antibodies and antigens and the PCR test for DNA are available in some research laboratories.[70,71]

If the diagnosis is strongly suspected but parasites are not found, a single oral test dose of 50 mg of diethylcarbamazine can be given. If an exacerbation of the rash occurs within a few hours, the diagnosis is likely (Mazzotti reaction). An alternative method is to apply a diethylcarbamazine patch test to elicit a localized reaction.[72]

Treatment

Traditionally, patients with skin disease have been treated with diethylcarbamazine. This drug kills microfilariae but has little effect on the adult worm. Severe reactions such as rash, fever, generalized body pains, keratitis, and iritis may occur, so the dose must be increased gradually as follows: day 1, 50 mg; day 2, 50 mg three times; day 3, 100 mg three times; and days 4 to 21, 3 mg/kg three times a day.

During the past few years, many studies have shown that ivermectin is safer and more effective than diethylcarbamazine. The rate of decrease in the number of microfilariae in the skin and anterior chamber of the eye and the severity of Mazzotti reactions are less, and the duration of the reduction in microfilarial loads is greater, with ivermectin than with diethylcarbamazine. Ivermectin is currently the drug of choice. Unfortunately, like diethylcarbamazine, ivermectin primarily kills microfilariae but not adult worms. When given in a single dose, it has little effect on the viability or fertility of adult worms, but treatment with 150 μg/kg repeated at 3-month intervals for 2 to 3 years prevents embryogenesis to the microfilarial stage and may cause slow but steady attrition of adult worms.[73] Both single and repeated courses of treatment result in marked reductions in the number of microfilariae in skin and the anterior chamber of the eye, and there is a significant reduction in infection transmission.

Ivermectin therapy leads to alleviation of the severe skin disease and regression of early lesions of the anterior segment of the eye, especially iridocyclitis, but the posterior segment lesions remain stable. Indeed, a Cochrane review has questioned whether ivermectin treatment prevents loss of visual acuity.[74] A practical approach to treatment is to administer ivermectin, 150 μg/kg orally once and repeat it at 3-month intervals if there are continuing symptoms or evidence of eye infection. Side effects appear to be relatively mild in patients in endemic areas but may be more severe in infected expatriates, who often develop fever, pruritus, and an urticarial rash. Patients with concurrent onchocerciasis and loiasis may develop an encephalopathy when treated with ivermectin.[75] Inadvertent administration of ivermectin during pregnancy was not associated with an increased number of birth defects.

Albendazole probably has little place in the treatment of onchocerciasis. It may well be that by the time the next edition of this book appears doxycycline with or without ivermectin will be the standard treatment for onchocerciasis.[76] Nodules should be removed surgically whenever practical. Expert ophthalmologic advice should be sought before treating eye lesions.

Prevention

Personal protection depends on avoiding places where biting flies are numerous and on wearing protective clothing. A major control program is in progress in Sub-Saharan Africa. The vector is being attacked by larvicides applied to breeding places, and there has been repeated mass administration of ivermectin. Although the parasite has not been eradicated, major control has been achieved.[77] In 1991 a program was set in motion in the Americas with the aim of interrupting transmission within the next few years.[78]

OTHER ONCHOCERCAL INFECTIONS

Fewer than 10 cases of zoonotic infections with various species of *Onchocerca* have been reported. The reports have included cases of worms in the subconjunctiva,[61] cornea,[79] wrist,[80] and shoulder.[81]

MANSONELLA INFECTIONS

Mansonella ozzardi Infection

Mansonella ozzardi, transmitted by blackflies and midges, is found in Latin America. Adult worms are found in the visceral fatty tissues. Unsheathed microfilariae that are not periodic may be found in the peripheral blood. Most patients are asymptomatic, although an association with keratitis has been reported.[82] Ivermectin treatment reduces microfilaremia significantly.[83]

Mansonella perstans Infection

Mansonella perstans, also transmitted by midges, is found in Africa and South America. Adult worms live in the body cavities. Unsheathed microfilariae may be found in the peripheral blood, especially at night. Most patients are asymptomatic, although some have conjunctival nodules. If treatment is required, diethylcarbamazine should be tried because ivermectin is minimally effective.[84] Albendazole may be of some value when given at a dose of 400 mg twice daily for at least 1 month.

Mansonella streptocerca Infection

Mansonella streptocerca, transmitted to humans by biting midges, is found in Central Africa. It is characterized by dermatitis. Microfilariae are found in skin snips. The traditional treatment is with diethylcarbamazine, although ivermectin also has some effect.[85]

TROPICAL PULMONARY EOSINOPHILIA

Tropical pulmonary eosinophilia is a disease syndrome caused by microfilariae in the tissues, especially the lungs. It is probably due to immunologic hyperresponsiveness to *W. bancrofti* or *B. malayi*. It is scattered throughout the tropics but is most commonly seen in southern Asia.[86] Patients have recurrent episodes of a paroxysmal dry cough, wheezing, and dyspnea. Malaise, anorexia, and weight loss are frequent.

Physical examination often reveals scattered wheezes and crackles. Some patients may have hepatomegaly and lymphadenopathy. The severity of the symptoms usually fluctuates over many months. The absence of microfilariae from the blood makes a definitive diagnosis

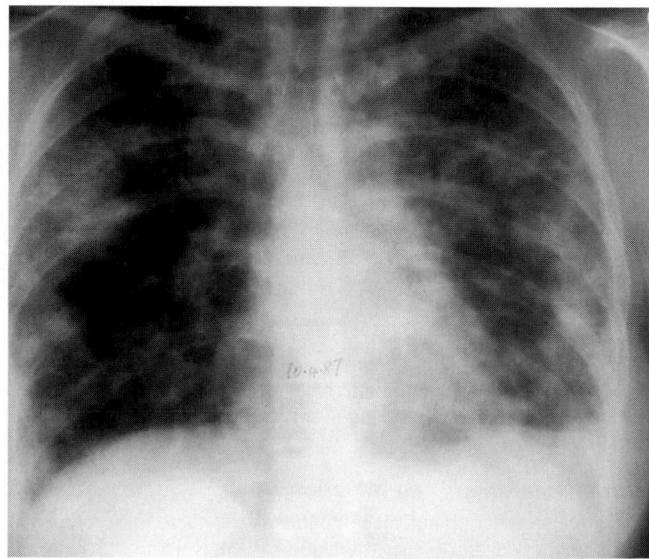

FIGURE 286-6. Chest radiograph of a woman with tropical pulmonary eosinophilia. Reticulonodular opacities are scattered throughout both lung fields.

difficult. Eosinophilia is almost always present at more than 3000 eosinophils/l, often at extremely high levels. Chest radiographs usually reveal scattered reticulonodular opacities (Fig. 286-6). Antibodies to filarial worms are found in the serum. A presumptive clinical diagnosis can usually be made without recourse to lung biopsy, and the diagnosis is established by a successful response to therapy.

Administration of diethylcarbamazine orally in a dose of 3 mg/kg three times daily for 2 weeks is an effective treatment.[87] There may be an initial exacerbation of symptoms, but the eosinophil level falls, and the chest radiograph clears over a few weeks. A small proportion of patients, however, have persistent, subtle clinical, radiologic, or functional abnormalities indicating chronic low-grade alveolitis[77]; in such instances, it may be appropriate to repeat the course of treatment with diethylcarbamazine. The role of ivermectin in the treatment of tropical pulmonary eosinophilia has not yet been determined.

REFERENCES

1. Grove DI. A History of Human Helminthology. Wallingford, UK: CAB International; 1990:1-848; compact disk version obtainable from the author.
2. Murrell KD, Lichtenfels RJ, Zarlenga DS, Pozio E. The systematics of the genus Trichinella with a key to species. Vet Parasitol 2000;93:293-307.
3. Kapel CM. Host diversity and biological characteristics of the Trichinella genotypes and their effect on transmission. Vet Parasitol 2000;93:263-278.
4. Dupouy-Camet J. Trichinellosis: a worldwide zoonosis. Vet Parasitol 2000;93:191-200.
5. Moorhead, A, Grunewald PE, Dietz VJ, Schantz PM. Trichinellosis in the United States 1991-1996: declining but not gone. Am J Trop Med Hyg 1999;60:66-69.
6. Pozio E. New patterns of Trichinella infection. Vet Parasitol 2001;98:13-148.
7. Capo V, Despommier DD. Clinical aspects of infection with Trichinella spp. Clin Microbiol Rev 1996;9:47-54.
8. Kociecka W. Trichinellosis: human disease, diagnosis and treatment. Vet Parasitol 2000;93:365-383.
9. Harms G, Binz P, Feldmeier H, et al. Trichinosis: a prospective controlled trial of patients ten years after acute infection. Clin Infect Dis 1993;17:637-647.
10. Bruschi F, Murrell KD. New aspects of human trichinellosis: the impact of new species. Postgrad Med J 2002;78:15-22.
11. Uparanukraw P, Morakote N. Detection of circulating Trichinella spiralis larvae by polymerase chain reaction. Parasitol Res 1997;83:52-56.
12. Cabie A, Bouchaud O, Houze S, et al. Albendazole versus thiabendazole as therapy for trichinosis: a retrospective study. Clin Infect Dis 1996;22:1033-1035.
13. Watt G, Saisorn S, Jongsakul K, et al. Blinded, placebo-controlled trial of antiparasitic drugs for trichinosis myositis. J Infect Dis 2000;182:371-374.
14. Pozio E, Sacchini D, Sacchi L, et al. Failure of mebendazole in the treatment of humans with Trichinella spiralis infection at the stage of encapsulating larvae. Clin Infect Dis 2001;32:638-642.
15. Gamble HR, Bessanov AS, Cuperlovic K, et al. International Commission on Trichinellosis: recommendations on methods for the control of Trichinella in domestic and wild animals intended for human consumption. Vet Parasitol 2000;93:393-408.
16. Dennett X, Siejka SJ, Andrews JR, et al Polymyositis caused by a new genus of nematode. Med J Aust 1998;168:226-227.
17. Spratt DM, Beveridge I, Andrews JR, Dennett X. Haycocknema perplexum n.g., n. sp. (Nematoda:Robertdollfusidae): an intramyofibre parasite of man. Syst Parasitol 1999;43:123-131.
18. Cairncross S., Muller R, Zagaria N. Dracunculiasis (guinea worm disease) and the eradication initiative. Clin Microbiol Rev 2002;15:223-246.
19. Magnussen P, Yakuba A, Bloch P. The effect of antibiotic- and hydrocortisone-containing ointments in preventing secondary infections in guinea worm disease. Am J Trop Med Hyg 1994;51:797-799.
20. Chippaux JP. Mebendazole treatment of dracunculiasis. Trans R Soc Trop Med Hyg 1991;85:280.
21. Rohde JE, Sharma BL, Patton H, et al. Surgical extraction of guinea worm: disability reduction and contribution to disease control. Am J Trop Med Hyg 1993;48:71-76.
22. Anonymous. Progress toward global dracunculiasis eradication, June 2002. MMWR Morbid Mortal Wkly Rep 2002;51:810-811.
23. Witt C, Ottesen EA. Lymphatic filariasis: an infection of childhood. Trop Med Int Health 2001;6:582-606.
24. Melrose WD. Lymphatic filariasis: new insights into an old disease. Int J Parasitol 2002;32:947-960.
25. Haddix AC, Kestler A. Lymphatic filariasis: economic aspects of the disease and programmes for elimination. Trans R Soc Trop Med Hyg 2000;94:592-593.
26. Figueredo-Silva J, Noroes J, Cedenho A, Dreyer G. The histopathology of bancroftian filariasis revisited: the role of the adult worm in lymphatic vessel disease. Ann Trop Med Parasitol 2002;96:531-541.
27. King C. Transmission intensity and human immune responses in lymphatic filariasis. Parasite Immunol 2001;23:361-371.
28. Olszewski WL, Jamal S, Manokaran G, et al. Bacteriologic studies of skin, tissue fluid, lymph and lymph nodes in patients with filarial lymphedema. Am J Trop Med Hyg 1997;57:7-15.
29. Bandi A, Trees AJ, Brattig NW. Wolbachia in filarial nematodes; evolutionary aspects and implications for the pathogenesis and treatment of filarial diseases. Vet Parasitol 2001;98:215-238.
30. Cross HF, Haarbrink M, Egerton G, et al. Severe reactions to filarial chemotherapy and release of Wolbachia endosymbionts into blood. Lancet 2001;358:1873-1875.
31. Taylor MJ, Cross HF, Ford L, et al. Wolbachia bacteria in filarial immunity and disease. Parasite Immunol 2001;23:401-409.
32. Burri H, Loutan L, Kumaraswami V, Vijayasekaran V. Skin changes in chronic filariasis. Trans R Soc Trop Med Hyg 1996;90:671-674.
33. Chandrasena T, Premaratna R, Abeyewickrema W, de Silva NR. Evaluation of the ICT whole-blood antigen card to detect infection due Wuchereria bancrofti. Trans R Soc Trop Med Hyg 2002;96:60-63.
34. Arora VK, Singh N, Bhatia A. Cytomorphologic profile of lymphatic filariasis. Acta Cytol 1996;40:948-952.
35. Mand S, Marfo-Debrekyi Y, Dittrich M, et al. Animated documentation of the filaria dance sign (FDS) in bancroftian filariasis. Filaria J 2003;2:3.
36. Shenoy RK, John A, Hameed S, et al. Apparent failure of ultrasonography to detect adult worms of Brugia malayi. Ann Trop Med Parasitol 2000;94:77-82.
37. Dissanayake S, Watana L, Piessens WF. Lymphatic pathology in Wuchereria bancrofti microfilaraemic infections. Trans R Soc Trop Med Hyg 1995;89:517-521.
38. Shenoy RK, George LM, John A, et al. Treatment of microfilaraemia of asymptomatic brugian filariasis with single doses of ivermectin, diethylcarbamazine or albendazole, in various combinations. Ann Trop Med Parasitol 1999;93:643-651.
39. Dunyo SK, Nkrumah FK, Simonsen PE. Single-dose treatment of Wuchereria bancrofti infections with ivermectin and albendazole alone or in combination; evaluation for the potential for control at 12 months after treatment. Trans R Soc Trop Med Hyg 2000;94:437-443.
40. Pani S, Subramanyam Reddy G, Das L, et al. Tolerability and efficacy of single dose albendazole, diethylcarbamazine citrate (DEC) or co-administration of albendazole with DEC in the clearance of Wuchereria bancrofti in asymptomatic microfilaraemic volunteers in Pondicherry, South India: a hospital-based study. Filaria J 2002;10:1.
41. Suma TK, Shenoy RK, Kumaraswami V. Efficacy and sustainability of a footcare programme in preventing acute attacks of adenolymphangitis in Brugian filariasis. Trop Med Int Health 2002;7:763-766.
42. Manjula Y, Kate V, Ananthakrishnan N. Evaluation of a sequential intermittent pneumatic compression for filarial lymphoedema. Natl Med J India 2002;15:192-194.
43. Ahorlu CK, Dunyo SK, Asamoah G, Simonsen PE. Consequences of hydrocele and the benefits of hydrocelectomy: a qualitative study in lymphatic filariasis endemic communities on the coast of Ghana. Acta Trop 2001;80:215-221.
44. Hemal AK, Gupta NP. Retroperitoneoscopic lymphatic management of intractable chyluria. J Urol 2002;167:2473-2476.
45. Fan PC, Peng HW, Chen CC. Follow-up investigations on clinical manifestations after filariasis eradication by diethylcarbamazine medicated common salt on Kinmen (Quemoy) Island, Republic of China. J Trop Med Hyg 1995;98:461-464.
46. Esterre P, Plichart C, Sechan Y, Nguyen NL. The impact of 34 years of massive DEC chemotherapy on Wuchereria bancrofti infection and transmission: the Maupiti cohort. Trop Med Int Health 2001;6:190-195.
47. Dean M. Towards the elimination of lymphatic filariasis. Lancet 2002;359:1677.
48. Burkot T, Ichimori K. The PacELF programme: will mass drug administration be enough? Trends Parasitol 2002;18:109-115.
49. Wanji S, Tendongfor N, Esum ME, Enyong P. Chrysops silacea biting densities and transmission potential in an endemic are for human loiasis in south-west Cameroon. Trop Med Int Health 2002;7:371-377.
50. Garcia A, Abel L, Cot M, et al. Genetic epidemiology of host predisposition microfilaraemia in human loiasis. Trop Med Int Health 1999;4:565-574.
51. El Haouri M, Erragragui Y, Sbai M, et al. Filariose cutanée à Loa loa: 26 cas Marocains d'importation. Ann Dermatol Venereol 2001;128:899-202.
52. Klion AD, Vijaykumar A, Oei T, et al. Serum immunoglobulin G4 antibodies to the recombinant antigen, L1-SXP-1, are highly specific for Loa loa infection. J Infect Dis 2003;187:128-133.
53. Toure FS, Kassambara L, Williams T, et al. Human occult loiasis; improvement in diagnostic sensitivity by the use of a nested polymerase chain reaction. Am J Trop Med Hyg 1998;59:144-149.
54. Kamgno J, Boussinesq M. Effect of a single dose (600 mg) of albendazole on Loa loa microfilaraemia. Parasite 2002;9:59-63.
55. Tsague-Dongmo L, Kamgno J, Pion SD, et al. Effects of a 3-day regimen of albendazole (800 mg daily) on Loa loa microfilaraemia. Ann Trop Med Parasitol 2002;96:707-715.
56. Blum J, Wiestner A, Fuhr P, Hatz C. Encephalopathy following Loa loa treatment with albendazole. Acta Trop 2001;78:63-65.
57. Brouqi P, Fournier PE, Raoult D. Doxycycline and eradication of microfilaremia in patients with loiasis. Emerg Infect Dis 2001;7(Suppl 3):604-605.
58. Nutman TB, Miller KD, Mulligan M, et al. Diethylcarbamazine prophylaxis for human loiasis: results of a double-blind study. N Engl J Med 1988;319:752-756.
59. Gautam V, Rustagi IM, Singh S, Arora DR. Subconjunctival infection with Dirofilaria repens. Jpn J Infect Dis 2002;55:47-48.
60. Lau LI, Lee FL, Hsu WM, et al. Human subconjunctival infection of Macacanema formosana: the first case of human infection reported worldwide. Arch Ophthalmol 2002;120:643-646.
61. Streter T, Szell Z, Egyed Z, Varga I. Subconjunctival zoonotic onchocerciasis in man: aberrant infection with Onchocerca lupi? Ann Trop Med Parasitol 2002;96:497-502.
62. Panaitescu D, Freda A, Bain O, Vasile-Bugarin AC. Four cases of human filariosis due to Setaria labiatopapillosa found in Bucharest, Romania. Roum Arch Microbiol Immunol 1999;58:203-207.
63. Richard-Lenoble D, al Qubati Y, Toe L, et al. Onchocercoses humaines et "sowda" en Republique du Yemen. Bull Acad Natl Med 2001;185:1447-1459.

64. Hall LR, Perlman E. Pathogenesis of onchocercal keratitis (river blindness). Clin Microbiol Rev 1999;12:445-453.

65. Saint Andre A, Blackwell NM, Hall LR, et al. The role of endosymbiotic Wolbachia bacteria in the pathogenesis of river blindness. Science 2002;295:1892-1895.

66. Hoerauf A, Volkmann L, Hamelmann C, et al. Endosymbiotic bacteria in worms as targets for a novel chemotherapy of filariasis. Lancet 2000;355:1242-1243.

67. Hoerauf A, Mand S, Adjei O, et al. Depletion of Wolbachia endobacteria in Onchocerca volvulus by doxycycline and microfilaridermia after ivermectin treatment. Lancet 2001;357:415-416.

68. Murdoch ME, Hay RJ, Mackenzie CD, et al. A clinical classification and grading system of the cutaneous changes in onchocerciasis. Br J Dermatol 1993;129:260-269.

69. Kayembe DL, Kasonga DL, Kayembe PK, et al. Profile of eye lesions and vision loss: a cross-sectional study in Lusambo, a forest-savanna area hyperendemic for onchocerciasis in the Democratic Republic of Congo. Trop Med Int Health 2003;8:83-89.

70. Vincent JA, Lustigman S, Zhang S, Weil GJ. A comparison of newer tests for the diagnosis of onchocerciasis. Ann Trop Med Parasitol 2000;94:253-258.

71. Pischke S, Buttner DW, Liebau E, Fischer P. An internal control for the detection of Onchocerca volvulus DNA by PCR-ELISA and rapid detection of specific PCR products by DNA detection test strips. Trop Med Int Health 2002;7:526-531.

72. Toe L, Adjami AG, Boatin BA, et al. Topical application of diethylcarbamazine to detect onchocerciasis recrudescence in West Africa. Trans R Soc Trop Med Hyg 2000;94:519-525.

73. Gardon J, Boussinesq M, Kamgno J, et al. Effects of standard and high doses of ivermectin on adult worms of Onchocerca volvulus: a randomised controlled trial. Lancet 2002;360:203-210.

74. Ejere H, Schwartz E, Wormald R. Ivermectin for onchercercal eye disease (river blindness). Cochrane Database Syst Rev 2002;4:CD002219.

75. Boussinesq M, Gardon J, Gardon-Wendel N, et al. Three probable cases of Loa loa encephalopathy following ivermectin treatment for onchocerciasis. Am J Trop Med Hyg 1998;58:461-469.

76. Hoerauf A, Büttner DW, Adjei O, Pearlman E. Science, medicine and the future: onchocerciasis. BMJ 2003;326:207-210.

77. Hougard JM, Yameogo L, Philippon B. Onchocerciasis in West Africa after 2002: a challenge to take up. Parasite 2002;9:105-111.

78. Dadzie Y, Neira M, Hopkins D. Final report of the conference on the eradicability of onchocerciasis. Filaria J 2003;2:2.

79. Burr WE, Brown MF, Eberhard ML. Zoonotic Onchocerca (Nematoda:Filarioidea) in the cornea of a Colorado resident. Ophthalmology 1998;105:1494-1497.

80. Takaoka H, Bain O, Uni S, et al. Human infection with Onchocerca dewittei japonica, a parasite from wild boar in Oita, Japan. Parasite 2001;8:261-263.

81. Wright, RW, Neafie RC, McLean M, Markman AW. Zoonotic onchocerciasis of the shoulder: a case report. J Bone Joint Surg Am 2002;84;627-629.

82. Garrido C, Campos M. First report of presumed parasitic keratitis in Indians from the Brazilian Amazon. Cornea 2000;19:817-819.

83. Gonzalez AA, Chadee DD, Rawlins SC. Ivermectin treatment of mansonellosis in Trinidad. West Indian Med J 1999;48:231-234.

84. Gardon J, Kamgno J, Gardon-Wendel N, et al. Efficacy of repeated doses of ivermectin against Mansonella perstans. Trans R Soc Trop Med Hyg 2002;96:325-326.

85. Fischer P, Tukesiga E, Büttner DW. Long-term suppression of Mansonella streptocerca microfilariae after treatment with ivermectin. J Infect Dis 1999;180:1403-1405.

86. Ong RK, Doyle RL. Tropical pulmonary eosinophilia. Chest 1998;113:1673-1679.

87. Cooray JH, Ismail MM. Re-examination of the diagnostic criteria of tropical pulmonary eosinophilia. Respir Med 1999;93:655-659.

CHAPTER **287**

Trematodes (Schistosomes and Other Flukes)

JAMES H. MAGUIRE

The trematode flatworms that infect humans include the schistosomes, which live in venules of the gastrointestinal or genitourinary tract, and other flukes, which inhabit the bile ducts, intestines, or bronchi.[1] The geographic distribution of each species of trematode

parallels the distribution of the specific freshwater snail that serves as its intermediate host (Table 287-1). Five major species of schistosomes infect more than 200 million persons, and more than 65 species of other trematodes infect at least 40 million persons.[2-4]

Trematodes vary in length from 1 mm to more than 10 cm, are flattened dorsoventrally, and have an anterior and ventral sucker and a blind bifurcate intestinal tract. Schistosomes differ from other trematodes in several ways: The sexes of adult worms are separate, transmission is via penetration of skin by larvae, and there is only a single intermediate host, whereas other trematodes are hermaphroditic and are transmitted through ingestion of infected fish, crustaceans, or aquatic plants that serve as second intermediate hosts. Most trematode infections are subclinical, and in general it is only the small proportion of persons who have heavy worm burdens who develop severe disease.

SCHISTOSOMES

Of an estimated 200 million persons infected with schistosomes in 74 countries and territories, approximately 120 million have symptoms, 20 million have severe disease, and 100,000 die each year.[2-4] Although control programs and socioeconomic development have nearly eliminated schistosomiasis in some parts of the world, little progress has been made elsewhere, especially in Sub-Saharan Africa, where more than 80% of cases occur. Moreover, water resource development projects and population movements have spread the disease into regions where it was not previously endemic. In addition to the five main species that cause human schistosomiasis or bilharziasis, namely *Schistosoma mansoni, S. japonicum, S. mekongi, S. intercalatum,* and *S. haematobium,* other species of animal schistosomes cause human infection, including schistosomes of birds and small mammals that cannot mature in the human host but die in the skin where they cause a dermatitis.[5,6]

Life Cycle

Adult worms measuring 1 to 2 cm in length and 0.3 to 0.6 mm in width live, mate, and feed on blood in the portal and mesenteric vessels (*S. japonicum, S. mekongi, S. mansoni, S. intercalatum*) or vesical plexus (*S. haematobium*).[7] The male worm folds around and encloses the female in its gynecophoral canal. Egg production varies from approximately 300 eggs per day for female *S. mansoni* and *S. haematobium* and 3000 eggs daily for *S. japonicum* (Fig. 287-1). Eggs, measuring 145 × 55 μm for *S. mansoni* and *S. haematobium* and 85 × 60 μm for *S. japonicum* (Fig. 287-2), are deposited in the venules and make their way into the urine or feces and hatch in fresh water, where the miracidium, a 0.1 mm ciliated larva, emerges. The miracidium penetrates the body of the appropriate snail intermediate host and multiplies asexually. Within 4 to 6 weeks, hundreds of motile, forked-tail cercariae 0.1 to 0.2 mm long emerge. On encountering human skin, the cercariae penetrate with the help of their glandular secretions, and within minutes they lose their tails and change into schistosomula. This transformation occurs in the absence of new protein synthesis and is associated with the unique formation of a heptalaminate membrane.[8] The schistosomula migrate to the lungs and liver, and in about 6 weeks they mature to adult worms and descend via the venous system to their final habitat. Eggs appear in the feces or urine about 4 to 6 weeks after cercariae penetrate the skin.

Epidemiology

Transmission of schistosomiasis requires an appropriate snail intermediate host, fecal or urinary contamination of warm, slowly moving fresh water, and human entry into the snail-infested water. The snail host is specific for each species and strain of schistosome, which have a specific geographic distribution (see Table 287-1).[7] *S. mansoni* occurs in three South American countries, several Caribbean Islands, and along with *S. haematobium,* in Africa and the Middle East, often in areas where the two species overlap. *S. intercalatum* also can overlap with *S. haematobium* in parts of West and Central Africa but is less common. *S. japonicum* and *S. mekongi* occur in various Southeast

TABLE 287-1 Features of Schistosomes and Other Important Trematodes

Parasite	Snail intermediate host (genus)	Second intermediate host	Geographic distribution	Location of adult worms	Treatment
Schistosomes					
Schistosoma mansoni	Biomphalaria	None	South America, Africa, Caribbean, Arabian peninsula	Mesenteric venules	Praziquantel 40 mg/kg/day in 1 or 2 doses × 1 day Oxamniquine*
Schistosoma japonicum	Onchomelania	None	China, Philippines, Indonesia, Thailand	Mesenteric venules	Praziquantel 60 mg/kg/day in 3 doses × 1 day
Schistosoma mekongi	Neotricula	None	Cambodia, Laos	Mesenteric venules	Praziquantel 60 mg/kg/day in 3 doses × 1 day
Schistosoma intercalatum	Bulinus	None	Central and West Africa	Mesenteric venules	Praziquantel 40 mg/kg/day in 1 or 2 doses × 1 day
Schistosoma haematobium	Bulinus	None	Africa, Middle East	Venules of lower urinary tract	Praziquantel 40 mg/kg/day in 1 or 2 doses × 1 day Metriphonate*
Liver Flukes					
Clonorchis sinensis	Bulimos, Parafossarulus	Freshwater fish	China, Taiwan, Korea, Japan, Vietnam	Bile, pancreatic ducts	Praziquantel 75 mg/kg/day in 3 doses × 1–2 days Albendazole† 10 mg/kg/day × 10 days
Opisthorchis viverrini	Bithynia	Freshwater fish	Thailand, Laos, Cambodia	Bile, pancreatic ducts	Praziquantel 75 mg/kg/day in 3 doses × 1–2 days Albendazole† 10 mg/kg/day × 10 days
Opisthorcis felineus	Bithynia	Freshwater fish	Eastern Europe, former Soviet Union	Bile, pancreatic ducts	Praziquantel 75 mg/kg/day in 3 doses × 1–2 days Albendazole† 10 mg/kg/day × 10 days
Fasciola hepatica	Lymneaea	Watercress, other aquatic plants	Americas, Europe, Asia, western Pacific, North Africa	Bile ducts	Triclabendazole‡ 10 mg/kg × 1 day Bithionol* Nitazoxanide§
Intestinal Flukes					
Fasciolopsis buski	Segmentina	Aquatic plants	Far East, India	Small intestine	Praziquantel 25 mg/kg/day × 1 day Niclosamide† 40 mg/kg/day Triclabendazole§
Heterophyes heterophyes	Pirenella, Cerithidea	Freshwater fish	Far East, Egypt, Middle East, southern Europe	Small intestine	Praziquantel 25 mg/kg/day × 1 day Niclosamide† 1 g × 1 day Triclabendazole§
Metagonimus yokogawai	Semisulcospira	Freshwater fish	Far East, Russia, southern Europe	Small intestine	Praziquantel 25 mg/kg/day × 1 day Triclabendazole§
Lung Flukes					
Paragonimus westermani; other species.	Semisulcospira, Onchomelania, Thiara	Freshwater crabs, crayfish	Far East, South Asia, Philippines, West Africa, South and Central America	Lungs	Praziquantel 75 mg/kg/day in 3 doses × 2 days Bithionol*

*Not available or limited availability.
†Alternative drug.
‡In the United States it is available for compassionate use from the manufacturer, Novartis.
§Limited data.

Asian countries, and *S. japonicum* is found in China and the Philippines as well. Cattle, water buffaloes, pigs, dogs, and other mammals are naturally infected with *S. japonicum* and act as reservoir hosts, with a major role in transmission. Infections of rodents, primates, and other animals occur with *S. mansoni* and rarely *S. haematobium,* but they contribute little to maintenance of the life cycle.

Transmission is focal in endemic countries and most intense in poor rural areas with inadequate sanitation and water supplies. The distribution of schistosomiasis is changing in many areas. The risk of infection is now nonexistent or negligible in previously highly endemic countries, including Japan, Morocco, Tunisia, Iran, Surinam, Venezuela, and the Caribbean countries.[2,4] Control programs have significantly reduced the incidence of infection and morbidity in Brazil, China, Saudi Arabia, Egypt, and the Philippines. In most Sub-Saharan African countries, however, high levels of endemicity persist, and dams and irrigation projects have led to major increases in the prevalence and extension of transmission to new areas. Urban transmission now occurs in some large cities of Brazil and Africa.

In endemic communities, the distribution of the infection fits a negative binomial curve, with most infected persons harboring low worm burdens and only a small proportion, usually children ages 8 to 12 years, having heavy infections. Aggregation of the worm burden in a small proportion of infected individuals probably reflects a combination of factors, including the amount of water exposure, partial acquired immunity, age, and genetic susceptibility.[5] Because worms do not multiply in the host, the intensity of the infection depends on the number of cercariae encountered. Persons with heavy infections are at most risk for developing severe disease.

In the United States and other temperate areas, infection cannot be transmitted because of the absence of the appropriate snail intermediate host. Schistosomiasis is seen among immigrants from endemic areas and returning travelers, and sometimes it appears in small epidemics among persons engaging in adventure and nature tourism.[9,10]

Pathogenesis

The disease associated with schistosomiasis is largely due to the host's immune response to the larvae and eggs.[11] Mature adult worms evade the humoral and cellular responses generated against their antigens and contribute little to the immunopathology of the disease. Different mechanisms are responsible for tissue injury during the stage of larval penetration, the acute stage, and the chronic infection.

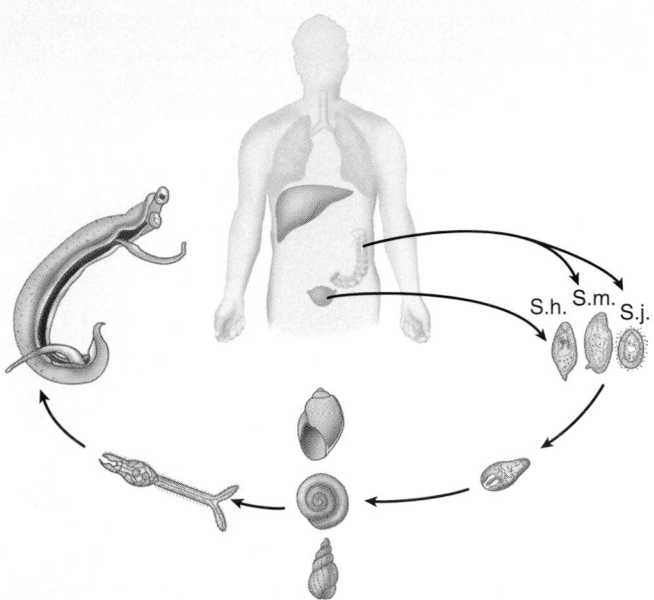

FIGURE 287-1. Life cycle of schistosomes. Eggs are passed in stools for *Schistosoma mansoni* (S.m.) and *Schistosoma japonicum* (S.j.) and in urine for *Schistosoma haematobium* (S.h.). The eggs hatch in fresh water, miracidia invade specific snail intermediate hosts, and in a few weeks forked-tail cercariae are liberated. These infective forms penetrate human skin, pass through a migratory phase in the lung and the liver, and then pass to their final habitat in the portal venous system (S.m. and S.j.) or the urinary bladder venous plexus (S.h.). Two other species infect humans, although less frequently. *Schistosoma intercalatum* produces terminal spined eggs that may be found in feces, whereas *Schistosoma mekongi* produces eggs similar to but smaller than those of *S. japonicum,* which may also be found in stools. These two species of schistosomes have characteristic snail intermediate hosts.

In previously exposed persons, a protective response consisting of specific immunoglobulin G and E (IgG, IgE) antibodies, eosinophils, and macrophages is directed against the schistosomula following cercarial penetration of the skin.[12] As a result, most organisms die in the skin and are surrounded by edema and massive cellular infiltrates in the dermis and epidermis that give rise to a papular dermatitis.

The syndrome of acute schistosomiasis occurs 2 to 8 weeks after a heavy first exposure and just before or at the time egg deposition begins.[13,14] A febrile illness with features of serum sickness is thought to result from the formation of circulating immune complexes and production of high levels of proinflammatory cytokines. As a rule, acute disease develops only in previously unexposed persons; persons who grew up in an endemic area do not develop symptoms perhaps because of sensitization in utero as a result of maternal infection.

Disease during the chronic stage of infection is due to the presence of eggs in host tissues and the immune response directed against the egg antigens. Miracidia in the eggs secrete histolytic enzymes through pores in the egg shell that facilitate passage of the eggs through blood vessel walls and tissues en route to the lumen of the intestinal or urinary tract. One-third to one-half of eggs reach the environment, with the remainder trapped in tissues or embolized to a distant site. The host response to eggs retained in the tissues includes granuloma formation, initially consisting of neutrophils, eosinophils, and mononuclear cells and later mostly lymphocytes, macrophages, multinucleated giant cells, and fibroblasts.[15,16] In *S. mansoni* and *S. haematobium* infections, the granulomatous response has been shown to be orchestrated by CD4+ T lymphocytes and is tightly regulated by several immunologic mechanisms.[13] They involve balanced Th1 and Th2 responses and the production of several cytokines locally in the granulomas and systemically; these responses in turn are regulated by numerous other mechanisms.[17,18] In addition to destroying eggs, granulomas may me-

diate their passage into the lumen of the bowel or urinary tract. This hypothesis is supported by the finding of reduced egg output in persons with advanced human immunodeficiency virus (HIV) disease.[19]

Granulomas initiate tissue injury first through the inflammatory infiltrate and replacement of normal tissue and later through extensive collagen deposition and scarring.[11,20] Large granulomas and fibrosis cause the major pathologic lesions in chronic schistosomiasis. In the case of schistosomes that inhabit the mesenteric vessels, pathology is greatest in the intestines and the liver, the major site of egg embolism. With *S. haematobium* infection, the main system involved is the urinary tract. The result is inflammatory lesions of the mucosa, fibrotic scarring of the bowel, bladder, and lower ureteral walls, and obstruction of portal blood flow in the liver and urine flow through the ureters and bladder. During the early stages of schistosome infection, the granulomatous response is exuberant. Later, modulation of granulomatous hypersensitivity results in smaller granulomas and less fibrosis, which in turn probably plays a significant role in limiting progression of the disease.[12]

The severity of disease in schistosomiasis is determined in part by the duration and intensity of the infection.[21,22] This relation is not exact, however, and other variables such as genetic susceptibility to disease, parasite strain, and co-infections with malaria, hepatitis viruses, HIV, and other infectious agents may be important.[19,23] Chronic schistosomiasis appears to be associated with a partial degree of resistance to reinfection, and several mechanisms for acquired resistance against schistosomiasis have been demonstrated in animals and humans.[24-26] Resistance directed against the invading immature worms has been shown to depend on antibodies and mediation by eosinophils.

Clinical Syndromes

Schistosome Dermatitis

During penetration of cercariae, some previously exposed and unexposed persons experience a prickling sensation and may note a macular rash several hours later.[6,10] In persons exposed for the first time, this rash disappears quickly, but in previously sensitized persons it may persist and progress to a pruritic maculopapular rash that lasts for days. The rash is most severe in persons infected with schistosomes of birds or aquatic mammals, which die in the skin. This "swimmer's itch" is common in the Great Lakes region, New England, and other parts of the United States (see Chapter 289).

Acute Schistosomiasis

Previously uninfected persons from nonendemic areas may develop symptoms of acute schistosomiasis (Katayama fever) 2 to 8 weeks after exposure, particularly to *S. japonicum* or *S. mansoni*.[6,10,13,14] It is unusual with *S. haematobium* and most severe with heavy infections, especially with *S. japonicum*. Onset of fever is often acute and accompanied by chills, headache, myalgia, abdominal pain, diarrhea, and occasionally bloody stools. As many as 70% of patients develop cough, dyspnea, chest pain, and interstitial infiltrates seen on chest radiography. The liver, spleen, and lymph nodes are often enlarged. Eosinophilia occurs in nearly all cases, but eggs may not be seen in the stools until late in the illness. Symptoms and signs usually disappear within a few weeks, but death may occur with heavy infections. Lesions of the central nervous system (CNS), genital tract, and skin due to ectopic deposition of eggs complicate acute schistosomiasis in a small number of cases.

Chronic Schistosomiasis

Symptoms are absent or mild in many patients who have light or moderate egg burdens. Eosinophilia is often present. Studies have demonstrated subtle but important morbidity in children with moderate or heavy infections, such as anemia, malnutrition, stunting, and impaired cognitive function.[27-29] Schistosomiasis in pregnant women appears to affect the health of both mother and fetus adversely.[4]

Patients with heavy infections caused by *S. mansoni, S. japonicum,* or *S. mekongi* may complain of fatigue and colicky abdominal

FIGURE 287-2. Life cycle of important parasitic flukes. Eggs are passed in stools for *Fasciola hepatica* (F.h.), *Clonorchis sinensis* (C.s.), and *Fasciolopsis buski* (F.b.) or in sputum for *Paragonimus westermani* (P.w.) infections. The next stage of multiplication occurs in specific snail intermediate hosts, followed by liberation of cercariae, which encyst on the second intermediate hosts (aquatic plants, fish, or crabs). These metacercariae represent the infective stage, and humans develop the infection after consumption of the second intermediate hosts. The final habitats of these flukes are the liver (F.h. and C.s.), intestines (F.b.), or lungs (P.w.).

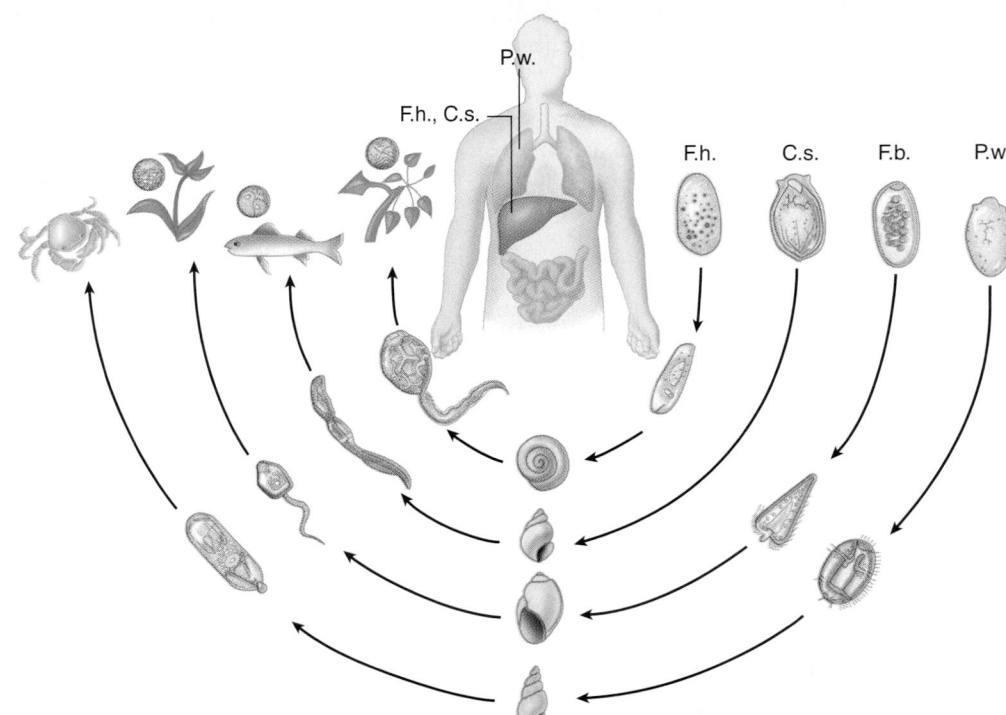

pain with intermittent diarrhea or dysentery. Polyps have been observed, primarily in Egypt.[30] Blood loss from ulcerations may lead to a moderate degree of anemia. Strictures or large inflammatory masses may cause obstruction or mimic carcinoma, but an association between intestinal schistosomiasis and cancer of the bowel has not been demonstrated in a convincing fashion. In some persons, the first sign of chronic schistosomiasis is hepatomegaly from granulomas around embolized eggs that become trapped in small portal venules. After years of infection, about 5% to 10% of persons develop periportal, or Symmers' "pipestem," fibrosis.[11] The granulomas and fibrosis cause a presinusoidal block to portal blood flow and eventually portal hypertension, splenomegaly, hypersplenism, and development of portosystemic collateral blood vessels. In most cases of hepatosplenic schistosomiasis, liver cell perfusion is not reduced, hepatic function is preserved, and liver function tests remain normal.[31] Persons with coexisting alcoholic cirrhosis, chronic hepatitis B, or hepatitis C may develop jaundice and ascites.[6,11] Natural progression of schistosomal disease occasionally leads to decompensated liver disease as well. Repeated episodes of hematemesis from bleeding esophageal varices occur, which usually are associated with low mortality in persons with compensated disease but may lead to hepatic failure and death in persons with decompensated disease. Persons with both schistosomiasis mansoni and chronic hepatitis B may be at higher risk of hepatoma than persons infected with hepatitis B alone.[32]

Infections with *S. intercalatum* tend to be lighter and produce less pathology than infections due to *S. mansoni* or *S. japonicum*.[33] Egg deposition occurs primarily in the colon, and patients may present with blood and mucus in the stool; in these cases, endoscopy shows polyps and inflamed rectal mucosa. Serious pathology can be seen in *S. mekongi* infections with advanced hepatosplenic disease similar to that seen in *S. mansoni* and *S. japonicum* infections.[34]

In schistosomiasis haematobia, hematuria and dysuria from inflammation and small ulcerations in the bladder mucosa may appear within 3 to 4 months of infection.[30,35] Later, polyps, hypertrophic nodules, and "sandy patches" around egg deposits may be visible on cystoscopy. Granulomas, fibrosis, and later calcification of the bladder wall cause reflux and obstruction of urine flow with hydroureter, hydronephrosis, chronic bacteriuria, and ultimately renal failure. Egg deposition in the genital tract is common among women and may cause ulcerative, nodu-

lar, or papillomatous lesions of the vulva, perineum, and cervix.[36,37] These lesions increase the patient's susceptibility to HIV infection and other sexually transmitted diseases, and lesions of internal pelvic organs may cause bleeding and infertility. Hematospermia results from involvement of the prostate and seminal vesicles.[38] Associations have been demonstrated between *S. haematobium* infection, *Salmonella* urinary tract infections, and squamous cell carcinoma of the bladder; the latter has affected primarily young and middle-aged men in Egypt.[30,39,40]

With schistosomiasis mansoni and japonica, eggs may bypass the liver via portosystemic collateral vessels and cause pulmonary disease; in schistosomiasis haematobia, eggs escape the vesical plexus and reach the lungs directly.[41,42] With severe cases, obstruction to pulmonary blood flow due to granulomatous inflammation and arteritis of small pulmonary arteries leads to cor pulmonale. Subclinical glomerulonephritis is not uncommon in persons with chronic schistosomiasis; kidney biopsy has shown deposits of immune complexes containing schistosomal antigens in the glomerular basement membrane.[6,35] Ectopic egg deposition from aberrant migration of adult worms or embolization of eggs from distant sites are common with all species of schistosomes and can involve almost any organ. In most cases, the resulting lesions do not produce symptoms, but involvement of the CNS can cause serious cerebral and spinal cord disease.[43] CNS schistosomiasis is most common with *S. japonicum* infection, occurring in as many as 2% to 5% of infections and accounting for high rates of epilepsy in endemic areas. The brain is the usual site of CNS disease with schistosomiasis japonica, only occasionally with *schistosomiasis mansoni*, and virtually never with schistosomiasis haematobia. Patients present with focal or generalized seizures, focal neurologic deficits, signs of increased intracranial pressure due to the mass effect, and diffuse encephalitis. Computed tomography (CT) and magnetic resonance imaging (MRI) scans of the head show nodular and ring-enhancing lesions with surrounding edema. With *S. haematobium* and *S. mansoni* infections, eggs reach the lower spinal cord through Batson's plexus and produce either granulomatous lesions of the conus medullaris and cauda equina or transverse myelitis with back pain and paraplegia.

Concurrent infection with other organisms may affect the clinical course of schistosomiasis. Prolonged bacteremia with *Salmonella typhi* and other *Salmonella* species has been reported in persons chronically infected with *S. mansoni*, *S. japonicum*, *S. intercalatum*, and

S. haematobium.[44] Unlike typhoid fever, the illness is indolent, with persistent fever, weight loss, and continuous bacteremia; and it can last months. Treatment of the bacterial infection without treating the schistosomiasis often results in relapse of bacteremia and symptoms. *Salmonella* can attach to the tegument and gut of schistosomes, and there is evidence that schistosomes and *Salmonella* share antigens that elicit immunologic tolerance to the bacterial infection.[6,11,44] Chronic *Salmonella* bacteriuria can complicate schistosomiasis haematobia. *Salmonella* bacteremia and bacteriuria have been associated with glomerulonephritis and nephrotic syndrome in persons with *S. haematobium* and *S. mansoni* infections.[35]

Chronic co-infection with hepatitis B or C worsens the prognosis of persons with hepatosplenic schistosomiasis, as already described.[6,11] The high rate of hepatitis C co-infection noted in Egypt probably reflects widespread transmission associated with parenteral antischistosomal treatment that was practiced until the 1980s.[45] HIV co-infection has been associated with decreased egg excretion in persons with *S. mansoni* and *S. haematobium* infections and decreased hematuria with *S. haematobium* infections due to impaired granuloma formation and increased trapping of eggs in tissue.[19,23] HIV infection does not appear to diminish the response to treatment of schistosome infection with praziquantel. Schistosomiasis has been associated with high HIV viral loads, which might accelerate the progression of HIV disease.[46]

Diagnosis

Schistosomiasis should be suspected in persons who have a history of freshwater exposure in endemic areas even in the absence of suggestive clinical findings or eosinophilia.[6,10] Hematuria is common with *S. haematobium* infections, and screening children for blood in their urine using dipsticks has provided reliable estimates of the prevalence of infection in areas of high endemicity. Current diagnostic tests for schistosomiasis include serologic tests and microscopic examination of stool, urine, or tissue for eggs. Microscopy can be performed on a simple smear of feces or a drop of urine. Because eggs may be passed intermittently or in small numbers, repeated examinations or concentration procedures may be needed. Several concentration procedures also allow quantification of egg output, such as the Kato-Katz technique, which uses 20 to 50 mg of fecal material, or filtration of a standard volume of urine through a Nucleopore membrane. Counts higher than 400 eggs per gram of feces or 10 mL of urine are considered heavy and are associated with an increased risk of complications. Microscopic examination of snips of rectal or bladder mucosa obtained at proctoscopy or cystoscopy may reveal eggs when the stool examination is negative. Because persons with inactive infections may continue to shed dead eggs into stool or urine for months, tests for egg viability such as egg hatching or microscopic examination of eggs for movement of flame cells should be performed.

Serologic tests for antibodies to schistosomes are available at the Centers for Disease Control and Prevention (CDC) in Atlanta, Georgia and some commercial laboratories.[47] The CDC uses a combination of tests with purified adult worm antigens. Its Falcon assay screening test–enzyme-linked immunosorbent assay (FAST-ELISA) is 99% specific for all species and has a sensitivity of 99% for *S. mansoni* infection, 95% for *S. haematobium,* but less than 50% for *S. japonicum.* Because the FAST-ELISA may miss some *S. haematobium* and *S. japonicum* infections, immunoblots using species-specific antigens are performed in cases of potential exposure to these parasites. Serologic tests cannot distinguish active from past infections but are useful for screening previously unexposed travelers and expatriates.[19] In such persons, a positive serologic test is presumptive evidence of infection even if microscopic examination of stool or urine fails to reveal schistosome eggs. Serologic tests may turn positive before egg excretion during acute schistosomiasis, but otherwise the diagnosis rests on the epidemiologic history and clinical picture.

Persons with confirmed schistosomiasis should be evaluated for evidence of disease. Urinalysis, urine culture, and serum creatinine determination are indicated for persons with *S. haematobium* infection. Any abnormality should prompt an ultrasound or other imaging study to detect complications such as thickening or calcification of the bladder wall, hydroureter, hydronephrosis, polyps, stones, or carcinoma of the bladder in persons with urinary schistosomiasis.[48] Evaluation of infections due to the intestinal schistosomes includes liver function tests and tests for chronic hepatitis B and C. Persons with evidence of liver disease or heavy infections should undergo imaging to document periportal fibrosis and signs of portal hypertension. Contrast studies, CT, MRI, and ultrasonography are sensitive means of detecting and evaluating urinary tract and hepatic pathology, although ultrasonography has become the preferred modality.[49,50] Standardized protocols have been developed by the World Health Organization (WHO) for ultrasonography in hospitals and the field. Esophageal varices are visualized by barium swallow or endoscopy.[4,10]

Management

Treatment is indicated for all persons with schistosomiasis. Cure of infection is desirable because even a single pair of worms may be responsible for a catastrophic neurologic complication such as transverse myelitis. In endemic areas where reinfection is inevitable, the goal is to reduce worm burdens to levels that are unlikely to produce disease.[4,51] Successful treatment not only prevents the development of complications, but if given early and reinfection is avoided it can cause partial or complete regression of intestinal lesions, urinary bladder wall thickening, bladder polyps, urinary obstruction, and periportal fibrosis.[4,52,53]

The drug of choice for treating all species of schistosomes is praziquantel (see Table 287-1), which affects membrane permeability in the parasite. Paralysis and vacuolation of the tegument immobilize the worm and expose it to attack by the host immune system. After a single treatment, cure rates range from 65% to 90%; and in persons not cured, egg excretion is reduced by more than 90%. Praziquantel does not affect developing schistosomula and may not abort an early infection. Resistance to praziquantel has been documented in the laboratory, and there have been reports of decreased responsiveness in the field.[54-57] Adverse effects, which are usually mild and last less than 24 hours, may be due to reactions to dying worms rather than drug toxicity. Patients may report headache, dizziness, or abdominal discomfort and less commonly nausea, vomiting, diarrhea, bloody stools, fever, and urticaria. WHO now recommends that praziquantel be given to pregnant and lactating women with schistosomiasis.[4,58] Persons with known or suspected cysticercosis should remain under observation during therapy because of the risk of seizures or other neurologic consequences of dying cysticerci.

Oxamniquine, an alternative for treatment of *S. mansoni* infections but with limited availability, is nearly as effective as praziquantel for infections acquired in the Western Hemisphere.[59] Higher doses are needed for strains of the parasite from Africa, and drug resistance has been documented. Metrifonate is effective only against urinary schistosomes; it requires three doses 2 weeks apart and is currently not available. Artemether, which is used as an antimalarial agent, is able to kill schistosomula during the first 3 weeks of infection and is synergistic with praziquantel in killing adult worms.[60,61] It has been shown to be effective as a prophylactic agent when given every 2 weeks. Such use has been proposed to protect persons with unavoidable exposure to infection in areas of high endemicity but not in those areas that are malarious because of the risk of selecting for artemether-resistant *Plasmodia.*

Severely ill persons with acute schistosomiasis should receive antischistosomal drugs and corticosteroids to reduce inflammation and mitigate reactions that develop in response to killing the parasites.[6,10,13,14] Because maturing schistosomes are less susceptible to chemotherapy than adult worms, a second course of therapy should be given several weeks after the first. Persons with neurologic disease should also take corticosteroids to reduce the inflammation and edema around eggs.

Because antischistosomal drugs may temporarily inhibit egg laying by adult worms, stool and urine should be examined up to 6 months after completion of therapy and treatment repeated in persons still excreting eggs. Eosinophilia, hematuria, or persistence of symptoms should prompt repeat parasitologic studies. Serologic tests may remain positive for several years after successful treatment.

Prevention and Control of Schistosomiasis

Travelers to areas where schistosomiasis is endemic should avoid contact with fresh water that may be infested with cercariae.[9] If contact is unavoidable, vigorous toweling of the skin may limit cercarial penetration after leaving the water, and medical follow-up should be sought after return from travel. Topical lotions and soaps have not reliably prevented infection after contact with cercariae, and further data are needed before recommending artemether for prophylaxis, which at any rate should not be used in malarious areas.

Control of schistosomiasis in endemic communities can be approached by providing sanitation and safe water supplies and eliminating snail intermediate hosts or their habitats. Because the cost of these interventions is beyond the reach of most poor countries, WHO recommends regular administration of antischistosomal drugs to populations at risk, primarily to maintain individual worm burdens at levels below those that cause morbidity and mortality and secondarily to decrease transmission and prevalence of infection.[4,62-64] Because of difficulties in sustaining large-scale drug administration programs and the threat of selecting for drug-resistant organisms of resistance, this strategy is a temporary solution. Development of a vaccine to prevent heavy infections seems possible based on experimental studies in animals and evidence of acquired immunity in human populations.[65,66]

LIVER FLUKES

The major liver flukes of humans are *Clonorchis sinensis,* several species of *Opisthorchis* (largely found in the Far East, Southeast Asia, and Russia), and *Fasciola hepatica,* which is widely distributed throughout the world (see Table 287-1).[67,68] Less common liver flukes include *Fasciola gigantica* in South America, Africa, and Southeast Asia; *Metorchis conjunctus* in North America; and *Opisthorchis guayaquilensis* in the Americas. All are infections of various lower animals and are transmitted through food.

Clonorchiasis and Opisthorciasis

Clonorchis sinensis, Opisthorchis viverrini, and *O. felineus,* have similar life cycles, eggs, and capacity to produce disease; they differ primarily in their geographic distribution, the morphology of the adult worms, and the frequency with which the clinical syndromes occur.[69-72] *C. sinensis* is found primarily in eastern Asia, *O. viverrini* in Southeast Asia, and *O. felineus* in the former Soviet Union. Millions of persons are infected, and in some endemic areas it is not uncommon to find prevalence rates of 20% to 80%.

The hermaphroditic adult flukes are flat, elongated worms measuring 5 to 25 mm × 2 to 5 mm that inhabit the intrahepatic bile ducts (see Fig. 287-2). Their yellow-brown operculated eggs (30 × 12 μm) are fully embryonated when they pass out of the body in feces into fresh water (Fig. 287-3). The eggs are ingested by specific snails, inside of which they hatch into miracidia that develop and replicate to produce large numbers of cercariae. Cercariae are released into the water and penetrate susceptible freshwater fish, primarily carp, and then encyst as metacercariae. Humans, cats, dogs, and other fish-eating mammals become infected by ingesting the metacercariae in raw or inadequately cooked fish; the metacercariae excyst in the duodenum and pass through the ampulla of Vater to the bile ducts, where adult worms mature and begin egg laying in about 3 to 4 weeks; they live as long as 30 years.

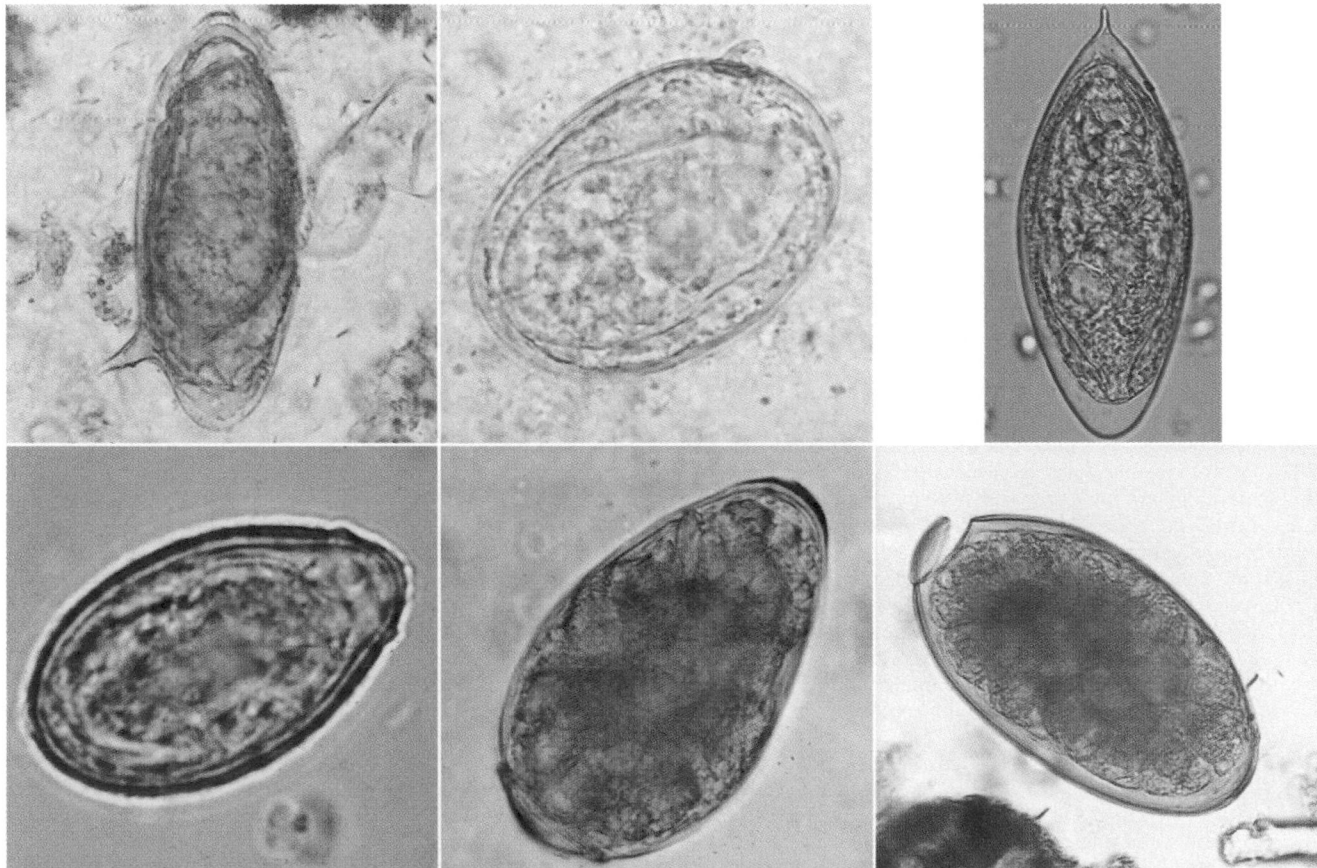

FIGURE 287-3. Eggs of common human trematodes. Clockwise from upper left: *Schistosoma mansoni, Schistosoma japonicum, Schistosoma haematobium, Clonorchis sinensis, Paragonimus westermani,* and *Fasciola hepatica* (note the partially open operculum). *(From DPDx, website for laboratory diagnosis of parasitic diseases of the Division of Parasitic Diseases, National Centers for Infectious Diseases, Centers for Disease Control and Prevention, Atlanta, GA, [http://www.dpd.cdc.gov/DPDx/].)*

Clinical Syndromes

Most patients are asymptomatic but may have eosinophilia. An acute illness resembling acute schistosomiasis with fever, abdominal pain, hepatomegaly, urticaria, and eosinophilia occasionally develops 2 to 3 weeks after the initial exposure.[73,74] No gross changes are detected in the liver with mild or early infection, but irritation of bile duct walls by the suckers of the flukes and secreted metabolic products leads to inflammation and thickening of bile duct walls and localized obstruction in about 10% of persons with heavy chronic infections (more than 10,000 eggs per gram of stool). Patients complain of right upper quadrant discomfort, anorexia, and weight loss. On physical examination, the liver is palpable and firm. Pigment stones, recurring episodes of cholangitis with bacterial sepsis, cholecystitis, liver abscess, and occasionally pancreatitis occur in the most heavily infected persons.[75] An increased incidence of cholangiocarcinoma, an adenocarcinoma originating from hyperplastic biliary epithelium, has been associated with *O. viverrini* infection in Thailand.[76,77]

Diagnosis and Management

Liver fluke infection is diagnosed by finding eggs in the stool or by identifying adult worms during surgery or endoscopic retrograde cholangiopancreatography.[73,74] Eggs may not be found in the stool in infections with fewer than 20 adult flukes, and multiple examinations of concentrated specimens may be necessary. Serologic tests and antigen detection assays are under development but are not widely available outside of endemic areas. Ultrasonography, CT, or MRI can demonstrate dilatation and stricture of bile ducts, thickening of the gallbladder wall, and stones. M-mode ultrasonography may demonstrate moving worms, which appear as thin linear echoes in ducts.

A single course of praziquantel eradicates the infection in more than 85% of cases.[78] Albendazole in a dose of 10 mg/kg for 7 days may also be used. Rarely, surgery is needed to relieve biliary tract obstruction.[75]

Fascioliasis

Infection with the sheep liver fluke *Fasciola hepatica* results from ingesting uncooked watercress or other fresh aquatic vegetation in 61 countries worldwide, especially in sheep- and cattle-raising areas.[79,80] The global prevalence of human infection is in excess of 3 million. Infections have been reported from all continents except Antarctica, with the highest rates of infection in Bolivia, Peru, Egypt, Iran, Portugal, and France. A small number of cases, mostly imported, have been reported in the United States.[81,82] The closely related but larger *F. gigantica* has a more limited distribution.

The hermaphroditic adult fluke is flat, brown, and leaf-shaped; and it measures approximately 3.0 × 1.5 cm. Mature worms in their natural hosts (mainly sheep and cattle) live in the common and hepatic bile ducts, where they deposit their eggs (see Fig. 287-2). The large oval, yellowish brown, operculate ova measuring 140 × 75 μm (see Fig. 287-3) pass to the intestines, are evacuated in the feces, and complete their development in fresh water. Within a few days miracidia hatch and invade their specific snail intermediate host, within which they undergo asexual replication, resulting in the release of cercariae that encyst as metacercariae on aquatic plants, including watercress, water caltrops, water lettuce, mint, and parsley. When swallowed, the infective metacercariae excyst, and the larvae penetrate the intestinal wall into the peritoneum, from whence they pass through the liver capsule and tissues to the biliary tract. Approximately 3 to 4 months are needed from infection to oviposition in humans. Adult flukes can live as long as 10 years.

Clinical Syndromes

Infection with *F. hepatica* has two distinct clinical phases corresponding to the hepatic migratory phase of its life cycle and to the presence of the worms in their final habitat in the bile ducts.[67] Symptoms corresponding to migration of the larval fluke appear within 6 to 12 weeks of ingestion of metacercariae and can last 4 months or longer. Marked eosinophilia is seen in most infected persons, and abdominal pain, intermittent fever, weight loss, and urticaria are common.[83] There may be tender hepatomegaly and elevation of liver function tests. Cough and chest pain occur in 10% to 15% sometimes accompanied by a pleural effusion with eosinophils in the pleural fluid. Aberrant migration may produce migratory nodules in the skin, painful inflammation of the intestinal wall, and lesions in the lung, brain, genitourinary tract, or elsewhere. CT or MRI shows hypodense lesions measuring 1 cm or more in diameter that move to various parts of the liver over the course of several weeks.[84,85] Hypodense tortuous and branching linear tracks under the capsule correspond to necrosis, and eosinophilic inflammatory infiltrates are seen along the path of larval migration.[86,87]

Within several weeks to months, the symptoms and signs of the acute phase subside as the worms enter the bile ducts. Chronic fascioliasis is usually subclinical, but some persons have symptoms due to inflammation and intermittent obstruction of bile ducts that resemble biliary colic and cholecystitis; occasionally there is ascending cholangitis. Ultrasonography may show masses in the common bile duct corresponding to adult worms.

Diagnosis and Management

The diagnosis during the acute stage is based on epidemiology, the clinical picture, and often characteristic lesions seen on CT scans. Biopsy of nodules on the surface of the liver, in the skin, or elsewhere may show inflammatory tracts or immature worms. Serologic tests are useful during acute infection because symptoms develop 1 to 2 months before eggs are detectable in the stool. Whole-worm antigens, coproantigens, and excretory-secretory proteins have been used in enzyme immunoassays and immunoblots; sensitivities of more than 90% are reported, but the specificity may be less owing to cross-reactivity with other helminths.[88] The definitive diagnosis is made by demonstrating eggs in samples of stool, bile, or duodenal aspirates or by recovering worms at surgery. Repeat examinations and concentration procedures may be necessary to detect eggs in the stool.

Unlike infections with other flukes, fascioliasis responds poorly to praziquantel. First-line treatment is with a single oral dose of triclabendazole, a well tolerated benzimidazole used in veterinary practice that is highly effective against mature and immature flukes.[89,90] Rates of cure are around 80%, and persons not cured with a single dose usually respond to a second dose. Treatment should be repeated if radiographic findings or eosinophilia fail to resolve or the titers of serologic tests do not decrease. Alternative therapy is with bithionol, which requires 10 to 15 doses and causes frequent side effects. Limited experience with nitazoxanide suggests cure rates of approximately 60%.[91]

INTESTINAL FLUKES

More than 65 flukes are known to infect the human gastrointestinal tract.[1] Most are found in parts of Asia where the appropriate intermediate hosts and animal reservoirs are found. The best known intestinal flukes include *Fasciolopsis buski* and the heterophytid flukes *Heterophyes heterophyes* and *Metagonimus yokogawai*. *Nanophyetus salmincola*, which is transmitted in the Pacific Northwest of the United States, is discussed in Chapter 289.

Fasciolopsis

Human infection with the large intestinal fluke *Fasciolopsis buski* occurs in the Far East, Southeast Asia, and southern Asia, where pigs are the major reservoir of infection.[92,93] The thick, fleshy adult worms range in length from 2.0 to 7.5 cm and in breadth from 0.8 to 2.0 cm. They inhabit the duodenum and jejunum, where they produce large operculated eggs (135 × 80 μm) (see Fig. 287-2). On reaching fresh water, the eggs hatch, releasing miracidia that penetrate a specific snail intermediate host in which they multiply and develop into free-living cercariae. The cercariae encyst into metacercariae on almost any aquatic plant. The metacercariae survive in most environments for up to 1 year. When raw or poorly cooked infected plants are ingested by humans, the metacercariae excyst in the intestines, and within 3 months the parasites develop into mature worms that survive 6 months or more in the human host.

Adult flukes live in the upper portion of the small intestine, where they attach to the mucosa and produce local inflammation, ulceration, and abscesses. Fasciolopsiasis is mostly subclinical, although eosinophilia is marked in some persons.[67] In some cases, epigastric pain and diarrhea may be seen a month or two after exposure. With heavy infections, flukes may cause transient obstruction and ileus. Edema of the face and extremities may result from hypersensitivity to worm metabolites or from hypoalbuminemia due to malabsorption or protein-losing enteropathy.

Heterophyiasis and Metagonimiasis

There are at least 10 species of flukes in the family Heterophyidae, of which *Heterophyes heterophyes* and *Metagonimus yokogawai* are the most common. *H. heterophyes* is found primarily in the Nile delta region, Tunisia, and Turkey, whereas *M. yokogawai* is most prevalent in the Far East.[94] The adult flukes measure less than 2 mm in length and inhabit the small intestine of human, animal, or avian hosts, where they produce small operculate eggs (30 × 15 μm). The life cycle is similar to that of other trematodes and involves snails and fish living in fresh or brackish water. The metacercariae encyst under the scales of the fish. Infection is acquired by consumption of undercooked or salted fish. Adults begin producing eggs in about 9 days and live only a few months to less than a year.

Flukes attach to the small-intestine wall, where they produce focal inflammation and ulcerations. Infected persons may experience colicky abdominal pain, dyspepsia, diarrhea, and eosinophilia. Flukes may penetrate the mucosa and deposit eggs that pass via lymphatics into the bloodstream. Eggs may embolize to the CNS, where they can cause myocarditis or focal lesions of the brain or spinal cord and occasionally death.

Diagnosis and Management

A definitive diagnosis depends on demonstration of eggs or adult worms in stools. Proper identification of the species by examining eggs is difficult because the morphology and size of eggs of different species are similar.[67] Eggs of *F. buski* can be confused with those of *F. hepatica,* and eggs of *H. heterophyes* and *M. yokogawai* can be confused with each other and with the eggs of *C. sinensis* and *Opisthorchis.* Species identification is best made by examining adult worms expelled after treatment.

The treatment of choice of all intestinal trematodes infections is praziquantel. Triclabendazole is also effective, and niclosamide is effective for treating *Fasciolopsis* and *Heterophyes* infections.[67]

LUNG FLUKES

Paragonimiasis

More than 40 species of *Paragonimus* are recognized as parasites of mammals; however, only eight cause significant infections in humans.[95] *P. westermani,* the most important species infecting humans, is found in the Far East, principally Korea, Japan, Taiwan, China, and the Philippines. The other species are *P. miyazaki* (Japan), *P. skrjabini and P. hueitungensis* (China), *P. heterotrema* (China, Southeast Asia), *P. uterobilateralis* and *P. africanus* (Central and West Africa), *P. mexicanus* (Central and South America), and *P. kellicotti* (North America).[96,97]

Reddish brown adult worms measuring 7 to 16 mm × 4 to 7 mm live in encapsulated cystic cavities in the parenchyma of the lung, usually close to bronchioles. Worms produce golden brown operculate eggs (80 to 120 μm × 50 to 65 μm) that pass into the bronchioles and are coughed up; they are then either passed in sputum or swallowed and passed in feces (see Figs. 287-2 and 287-3). On reaching fresh water, they require 2 to 3 weeks to develop before miracidia hatch at 29° C to 32° C. After 3 to 5 months of development and reproduction in

the snail, stumpy-tailed cercariae emerge. They encyst in the muscles and viscera of crayfish and freshwater crabs. Human infection is initiated by consumption of these freshwater crustaceans if they are uncooked, partially cooked, salted, or pickled. Metacercariae excyst in the duodenum, penetrate the intestinal wall, and enter the peritoneal cavity. After several days, they migrate through the diaphragm to the pleural cavities and then into the lungs. A fibrous cyst wall develops around them, and egg deposition starts 5 to 6 weeks after infection. Worms may develop also in extrapulmonary sites including the liver, lymph nodes, skin, spinal cord, and brain. Adults may live as long as 20 to 25 years but generally are much shorter-lived.

Clinical Syndromes

At 2 to 15 days after ingestion of metacercariae, some persons develop abdominal pain and diarrhea followed by fever, chest pain, cough, urticaria, and eosinophilia. However, these initial symptoms are often absent, and light or moderate infections may remain undetected until first seen on a radiograph obtained for other reasons. The inflammatory reaction to adults encapsulated in the lungs and the shedding of eggs into the bronchial tree are responsible for chronic symptoms. Cough productive of brownish sputum with intermittent hemoptysis are the initial manifestations of chronic infection.[98] Later, the clinical picture resembles chronic bronchitis or bronchiectasis with profuse expectoration and pleuritic chest pain, dyspnea, chronic cough, chest pains, and occasional hemoptysis. Radiographs may be negative or show diffuse infiltration, cysts measuring around 4 cm in diameter, nodules, calcifications, pleural effusion, and pneumothorax. Pleural fluid is exudative and contains large numbers of eosinophils. The illness is often confused with pulmonary tuberculosis, but eosinophilia and the lack of fever suggest the true diagnosis. The most commonly recognized form of extrapulmonary disease is involvement of the CNS, which is seen in as many as 25% of hospitalized cases. Parasite-induced meningitis may be the first manifestation, usually occurring within a year of pulmonary infection. Cerebral infections present as a space-occupying tumor, with seizures, headaches, visual disturbances, and motor or sensory deficits. Radiographs of the skull may show clusters of calcified cysts that resemble soap bubbles, and MRI and CT scans show aggregates of ring-enhancing lesions with surrounding edema.[99]

Other extrapulmonary infections include migratory allergic skin lesions similar to those seen with cutaneous larva migrans; these lesions are common during infections with *P. skrjabini* and other species in addition to infections with *P. westermani.* Flukes may also be found in the liver, spleen, peritoneum, intestinal wall, and intraabdominal lymph nodes.

Diagnosis and Management

The diagnosis of paragonimiasis is established by identifying expectorated eggs in the sputum, swallowed eggs in the feces, or worms and eggs in biopsy specimens. Multiple examinations of stool and sputum may be necessary. Serologic tests are useful for diagnosing light or extrapulmonary infections.[100] Enzyme immunoassay tests are available, and an immunoblot assay performed at the CDC that uses a crude antigen extract of *P. westermani* has a sensitivity of 96% and a specificity of almost 100%.[101,102]

The treatment of choice for paragonimiasis is praziquantel. The alternative, bithionol, has more frequent side effects. Because an inflammatory reaction to dying worms may precipitate seizures or other neurologic complications, corticosteroids should be used simultaneously with praziquantel for cerebral paragonimiasis.

PREVENTION OF FOOD-BORNE FLUKE INFECTIONS

Prevention and control of nonschistosomal trematode infections focuses on food production and preparation because elimination of snail and animal hosts is neither desirable nor feasible. Educational interventions should focus on preventing contamination of water sources with human and animal feces, especially ponds used for the cultivation of fish and aquatic plants. Education about proper preservation, cooking, or other preparation of food must take cultural practices and beliefs into account.

REFERENCES

1. Muller R. The nematodes. In: Worms and Human Disease. 2nd ed. Wallingford: CABI Publishing; 2002:109-235.
2. Engels D, Chitsulo L, Montresor A, et al. The global epidemiological situation of schistosomiasis and new approaches to control and research. Acta Trop 2002;82: 139-146.
3. WHO. Control of foodborne trematode infections: report of a WHO Study Group. WHO Techn Rep Ser 1995;849:1-157.
4. WHO Expert Committee. Prevention and control of schistosomiasis and soil-transmitted helminthiasis. WHO Techn Rep Ser 2002;912:1-5.
5. Jordan P, Webbe G, Sturrock RF. Human schistosomiasis. Wallingford, UK: CAB International; 1993:1-465.
6. Lucey DR, Maguire JH. Schistosomiasis. Infect Dis Clin N Am 1993;7:635-653.
7. Sturrock RF. The schistosomes and their intermediate hosts. In: Mahmoud AAF, ed. Schistosomiasis. London: Imperial College Press; 2001:7-83.
8. Weist PM, Tartakoff AM, Aikawa M, et al. Inhibition of surface membrane maturation in schistosomula of Schistosoma mansoni. Proc Natl Acad Sci USA 1988;85:3825-3829.
9. Corachan M. Schistosomiasis and international travel. Clin Infect Dis 2002;35:446-450.
10. Ross AG, Bartley PB, Sleigh AC, et al. Schistosomiasis. N Engl J Med. 2002; 346:1212-1220.
11. Von Lichtenberg F. Schistosomiasis. In: Connor DH, Chandler FW, Schwartz DA, et al, eds. Pathology of Infectious Diseases. Stamford, CT: Appleton & Lange; 1997: 1537-1551.
12. Pearce EJ, MacDonald AS. The immmunobiology of schistosomiasis. Nat Rev Immunol 2002;2:499-511.
13. Doherty JF, Moody AH, Wright SG. Katayama fever: an acute manifestation of schistosomiasis. BMJ 1996;313:1071-1072.
14. De Jesus AR, Silva A, Santana LB, et al. Clinical and immunological evaluation of 31 patients with acute schistosomiasis mansoni. J Infect Dis 2002;185:98-105.
15. Warren KS, Domingo EO, Cowan RBT. Granuloma formation around schistosome eggs as a manifestation of delayed hypersensitivity. Am J Pathol 1967;51:735-756.
16. Kassis AI, Warren KS, Mahmoud AAF. The Schistosoma haematobium egg granuloma. Cell Immunol 1978;38:310-318.
17. Hoffmann KF, Wynn TA, Dunne DW. Cytokine-mediated host responses during schistosome infections: walking the fine line between immunological control and immunopathology. Adv Parasitol 2002;52:265-307.
18. King D, Mahmoud AAF. Schistosomiasis. In: Blaser M, Smith P, Ravdin J, et al, eds. Infections of the Gastrointestinal Tract. New York: Raven Press; 1995:1209-1222.
19. Karanja DMS, Boyer AE, Strand M, et al. Studies on schistosomiasis in western Kenya. I. Evidence for immune-facilitated excretion of schistosome eggs from patients with Schistosoma mansoni and human immunodeficiency virus coinfections. Am J Trop Med Hyg 1997;56:515-521.
20. Chikunguwo SM, Quinn JJ, Harn DA, et al. The cell-mediated response to schistosome antigens at the clonal level. III. Identification of soluble egg antigens recognized by cloned specific granulomagenic murine CD4+ TH1-type lymphocytes. J Immunol 1993;150:1413-1421.
21. Abdel Salam E, Abdel Fattah M. Prevalence and morbidity of Schistosoma haematobium in Egyptian children: a controlled study. Am J Trop Med Hyg. 1977;26:463-469.
22. Siongok TKA, Mahmoud AAF, Ouma JH, et al. Morbidity in schistosomiasis mansoni in relation to intensity of infection: study of a community in Machakos, Kenya. Am J Trop Med Hyg 1976;25:273-284.
23. Mwanakasale V, Vounatsou P, Sukwa TY, et al. Interactions between Schistosoma haematobium and human immunodeficiency virus type 1: the effects of co-infection on treatment outcomes in rural Zambia. Am J Trop Med Hyg 2003;69:420-428.
24. Karanja DMS, Hightower AW, Colley DG, et al. Resistance to reinfection with Schistosoma mansoni in occupationally exposed adults and effect of HIV-1 co-infection on susceptibility to schistosomiasis: a longitudinal study. Lancet 2002;360:592-596.
25. Zinn-Justin A, Marquet S, Hillaire D, et al. Genome search for additional human loci controlling infection levels by Schistosoma mansoni. Am J Trop Med Hyg 2001;65:754-758.
26. May J, Kremsner PG, Milovanovic D, et al. HLA-DP control of human Schistosoma haematobium infection. Am J Trop Med Hyg 1998;59:302-306.
27. Crompton DW, Nesheim MC. Nutritional impact of intestinal helminthiasis during the human life cycle. Annu Rev Nutr 2002;22:35-59.
28. Nokes C, McGarvey ST, Shiue L, et al. Evidence for an improvement in cognitive function following treatment of Schistosoma japonicum infection in Chinese primary schoolchildren. Am J Trop Med Hyg 1999;60:556-565.
29. Jukes MC, Nokes CA, Alcock KJ, et al. Heavy schistosomiasis associated with poor short-term memory and slower reaction times in Tanzanian schoolchildren. Trop Med Int Health 2002;7:104-117.
30. King CH. Disease in schistosomiasis haematobia. In: Mahmoud AAF, ed. Schistosomiasis. London: Imperial College Press; 2001:265-295.
31. Mies S, Neto OB, Beear A Jr. Systemic and hepatic hemodynamics in hepatosplenic Manson's schistosomiasis with and without propranolol. Dig Dis Sci 1997;42:751-761.
32. Angelico M, Renganathan E, Gandin C, et al. Chronic liver disease in the Alexandria governorate, Egypt: contribution of schistosomiasis and hepatitis virus infection. J Hepatol 1997;26:236-243.
33. King CH. Disease due to Schistoma mekongi, S. intercalatum and other schistosome species. In: Mahmoud AAF, ed. Schistosomiasis. London: Imperial College Press; 2001:391-412.
34. Urbani C, Sinoun M, Socheat D, et al. Epidemiology and control of mekongi schistosomiasis. Acta Trop 2002;82:157-168.
35. Barsoum RS. Schistosomiasis and the kidney. Semin Nephrol 2003;23:34-41.
36. Poggensee G, Feldmeier H. Female genital schistosomiasis: facts and hypotheses. Acta Trop 2001;79:193-210.
37. Mosunjac MB, Tadors T, Beach R, et al. Cervical schistosomiasis, human papilloma virus (HPV), and human immunodeficiency virus (HIV): a dangerous coexistence or coincidence? Gynecol Oncol 2003;90:211-214.
38. Schwartz E, Pick N, Shazberg G, et al. Hematospermia due to schistosome infection in travelers: diagnostic and treatment challenges. Clin Infect Dis 2002;35:1420-1424.
39. Bedwani R, Renegenathan E, El Kwhsky F, et al. Schistosomiasis and the risk of bladder cancer in Alexandria, Egypt. Br J Cancer 1998;77:1186-1189.
40. Badawi AF. Molecular and genetic events in schistosomiasis-associated human bladder cancer: role of oncogenes and tumor suppressor genes. Cancer Lett 1996;105:123-138.
41. Moms W, Knaur CM. Cardiopulmonary manifestations of schistosomiasis. Semin Respir Infect 1997;12:159-170.
42. Schwartz E. Pulmonary schistosomiasis. Clin Chest Med 2002;23:433-443.
43. Pitella JE. Neuroschistosomiasis. Brain Pathol 1997;7:649-662.
44. Young SW, Higashi G, Kamel R, et al. Interaction of salmonellae and schistosomes in host parasite relations. Trans R Soc Trop Med Hyg 1973;67:797-802.
45. Frank C, Mohamed MK, Strickland GT, et al. The role of parenteral antischistosomal therapy in the spread of hepatitis C virus in Egypt. Lancet 2000;355:887-891.
46. Lawn SD, Karanja DMS, Mwinzi P, et al. The effect of treatment of schistosomiasis on blood plasma HIV-1 RNA concentration in coinfected individuals. AIDS 2000;14:2437-2443.
47. Tsang VC, Wilkins PP. Immunodiagnosis of schistosomiasis. Immunol Invest 1997;26:175-186.
48. Medhat A, Zarzoura A, Nafeh M, et al. Evaluation of an ultrasonographic score for urinary bladder morbidity in Schistosoma hematobium infection. Am J Trop Med Hyg 1997;57:16-19.
49. Gerapacher-Lara R, Pinto-Silva RA, Rayes AA, et al. Ultrasonography of periportal fibrosis in schistosomiasis mansoni in Brazil. Trans R Soc Trop Med Hyg 1997;91:307-309.
50. Thomas AK, Dittrich M, Kardorff R, et al. Evaluation of ultrasonographic staging systems for the assessment of Schistosoma mansoni induced hepatic involvement. Acta Trop 1997;68:347-356.
51. Fenwick A, Savioli L, Engels D, et al. Drugs for the control of parasitic diseases: current status and development in schistosomiasis. Trends Parasitol 2003;19:509-515.
52. Frenzel K, Grigull L, Odongo-Aginya E, et al. Evidence for a long-term effect of a single dose of praziquantel on Schistosoma mansoni-induced hepatosplenic lesions in northern Uganda. Am J Trop Med Hyg 1999;60:927-931.
53. Richter J. The impact of chemotherapy on morbidity due to schistosomiasis. Acta Trop 2003;86:161-183.
54. Ismail M, Metwally A, Fargholy A, et al. Characterization of isolates of Schistosoma mansoni from Egyptian villagers that tolerate high doses of praziquantel. Am J Trop Med Hyg 1996;55:214-218.
55. Bennett JL, Dan T, Liang FT, et al. The development of resistance to antihelminthics: a perspective with an emphasis on the antischistosomal drug praziquantel. Exp Parasitol 1997;87:260-267.
56. Ismail M, Botros S, Metwally A, et al. Resistance to praziquantel: direct evidence from Schistosoma mansoni isolated from Egyptian villagers. Am J Trop Med Hyg 1999;60:932-935.
57. Nokes C, McGarvey ST, Shiue L, et al. Evidence for an improvement in cognitive function following treatment of Schistosoma japonicum infection in Chinese primary schoolchildren. Am J Trop Med Hyg 1999;60:556-565.
58. Olds GR. Administration of praziquantel to pregnant and lactating women. Acta Trop 20003;86:185-195.
59. Ferrari ML, Coelho PM, Antunes CM, et al. Efficacy of oxamniquine and praziquantel in the treatment of Schistosoma mansoni infection: a controlled trial. Bull WHO 2003;81:190-196.
60. Utzinger J, Shushua X, N'Goran EK, et al. The potential of artemether for the control of schistosomiasis. Int J Parasitol 2001;31:1549-1562.
61. Utzinger J, Keiser J, Shuhua X, et al. Combination chemotherapy of schistosomiasis in laboratory studies and clinical trials. Antimicrob Agents Chemother 2003;47:1487-1495.
62. Utzinger J, Bergquist R, Shu-Hua X, et al. Sustainable schistosomiasis control—the way forward. Lancet 2003;362:1932-1934.
63. Bergquist NR. Schistosomiasis: from risk assessment to control. Trends Parasitol 2002;18:309-314.
64. Sturrock RF. Schistosomiasis epidemiology and control: how did we get here and where should we go? Mem Inst Oswaldo Cruz 2001;96(Suppl):17-27.
65. Capron A, Capron M, Riveau G. Vaccine development against schistosomiasis from concepts to clinical trials. Br Med Bull 2002;62:139-148.
66. Pearce EJ. Progress towards a vaccine for schistosomiasis. Acta Trop 2003;86: 309-313.

67. Liu LX, Harinasuta KT. Liver and intestinal flukes. Gastroenterol Clin North Am 1996;25:627-636.
68. Kaewkes S. Taxonomy and biology of liver flukes. Acta Trop 2003;88:177-186.
69. Upatham ES, Viyanant V. Opisthorchis viverrini and opisthorchiasis: a historical review and future perspective. Acta Trop 2003;88:171-176.
70. Sripa B, Sithithaworn P, Sirisinha S. Opisthorchis viverrini and opisthorchiasis: the 21st century review. Acta Trop 2003;88:169-170.
71. King S, Scholz T. Trematodes of the family Opisthorchiidae: a minireview. Korean J Parasitol 2001;39:209-221.
72. Sithithaworn P, Haswell-Elkins M. Epidemiology of Opisthorchis viverrini. Acta Trop 2003;88:187-189.
73. Mairiang E, Mairiang P. Clinical manifestation of opisthorchiasis and treatment. Acta Trop 2003;88:221-227.
74. Chan HH, Lai KH, Lo GH, et al. The clinical and cholangiographic picture of hepatic clonorchiasis. J Clin Gastroenterol 2002;34:183-164.
75. Leung JW, Yu AS. Hepatolithiasis and biliary parasites. Baillieres Clin Gastroenterol 1997;11:681-706.
76. Wutanapa P. Cholangiocarcinoma in patients with opisthorchiasis. Br J Surg 1996; 83:1062-1064.
77. Thuluvath PJ, Rai R, Venbrux AC, Yeo CJ. Cholangiocarcinoma: a review. Gastroenterologist 1997;5:306-315.
78. Pungpak S, Viravan C, Radomyos B, et al. Opisthorciasis viverrini infection in Thailand: studies on the morbidity of the infection and resolution following praziquantel treatment. Am J Trop Med Hyg 1997;56:311-314.
79. Esteban JG, Flores A, Angles R, et al. High endemicity of human fascioliasis between Lake Titicaca and La Paz Valley, Bolivia. Trans R Soc Trop Med Hyg 1999;93:151-156.
80. Estaban JG, Gonzalez C, Curtale F, et al. Hyperendemic fascioliasis associated with schistosomiasis in villages in the Nile Delta of Egypt. Am J Trop Med Hyg 2003; 69:429-347.
81. MacLean JD, Graeme-Cook FM. Case records of the Massachusetts General Hospital: weekly clinicopathological exercises; case 12-2002: a 50-year-old man with eosinophilia and fluctuating hepatic lesions. N Engl J Med 2002;346:1232-1239.
82. Graham CS, Brodie SB, Weller PF. Imported Fasciola hepatica infection in the United States and treatment with triclabendazole. Clin Infect Dis 2001;33:1-5.
83. Pulpeiro JR, Armesto V, Varela J, et al. Fascioliasis: findings in 15 patients. Br J Radiol 1991;64:798-801.
84. Van Beers B, Pringot J, Geuber A, et al. Hepatobiliary fascioliasis: noninvasive imaging findings. Radiology 1990;174:809-810.
85. Han JK, Han D, Choi BL, et al. MR findings in human fascioliasis. Trop Med Int Health 1996;1:367-372.
86. Cosme A, Ojeda E, Poch M, et al. Sonographic findings of hepatic lesions in human fascioliasis. J Clin Ultrasound 2003;31:358-363.
87. Cevikol C, Karaali K, Senol U, et al. Human fascioliasis: MR imaging findings of hepatic lesions. Eur Radiol 2003;13:141-148.
88. Hillyer GV, De Galanes MS, Rodriguez Perez J, et al. Use of the Falcon assay screening test enzyme-linked immunosorbent assay (FAST-ELISA) and the enzyme- linked immunoelectrotransfer blot (EITB) to determine the prevalence of human fascioliasis in the Bolivian Altiplano. Am J Trop Med Hyg 1992;46:603-609.
89. Millan JC, Mull R, Freise S, et al. The efficacy and tolerability of triclabendazole in Cuban patients with latent and chronic Fasciola hepatica infection. Am J Trop Med Hyg 2000;63:264-269.
90. Richter J, Freise S, Mull R, et al. Fascioliasis: sonographic abnormailities of the biliary tract and evolution after treatment with triclabendazole. Trop Med Int Health 1999;4:774-781.
91. Favennec L, Jave Ortiz J, Gargala G, et al. Double-blind, randomized, placebo-controlled study of nitazoxanide in the treatment of fascioliasis in adults and children from northern Peru. Aliment Pharmacol Ther 2003;17:265-270.
92. Waikagul J. Intestinal fluke infections in Southeast Asia. Southeast Asian J Trop Med Public Health 1991;22(Suppl):158-162.
93. Graczyk TK, Gilman RH, Fried B. Fasciolopsiasis: is it a controllable food-borne disease? Parasitol Res 2001;87:80-83.
94. Belizario VY Jr, Bersabe MJ, de Leon WU, et al. Intestinal heterophyidiasis: an emerging food-borne parasitic zoonosis in southern Philippines. Southeast Asian J Trop Med Public Health 2001;32(Suppl 2):36-42.
95. Blair D, Xu ZB, Agatsuma T. Paragonimiasis and the genus Paragonimus. Adv Parasitol 1999;42:113-222.
96. DeFrain M, Hooker R. North American paragonimiasis: case report of a severe clinical infection. Chest 2002;121:1368-1372.
97. Procop GW, Marty AM, Scheck DN, et al. North American paragonimiasis: a case report. Acta Cytol 2000;44:75-80.
98. Kagawa FT. Pulmonary paragonimiasis. Semin Respir Infect 1997;12:149-158.
99. Im JG, Chang KH, Reeder MM. Current diagnostic imaging of pulmonary and cerebral paragonimiasis with pathological correlation. Semin Roentgenol 1997;32: 301-324.
100. Mukae O, Taniguchi II, Ashitani J, et al. Case report: paragonimiasis westermani with seroconversion from immunoglobulin (Ig) M to IgG antibody with the clinical course. Am J Trop Med Hyg 2001;65:837-839.
101. Slemenda SB, Maddison SE, Jong EC, et al. Diagnosis of paragonimiasis by immunoblot. Am J Trop Med Hyg 1988;39:469-471.
102. Calvopina M, Guderian RH, Paredes W, et al. Treatment of human pulmonary paragonimiasis with triclabendazole: clinical tolerance and drug efficacy. Trans R Soc Trop Med Hyg 1998;92:566-569.

Cestodes (Tapeworms)

CHARLES H. KING

In humans, parasitic cestode infections occur in either of two forms: as mature tapeworms residing in the gastrointestinal tract or as one or more larval cysts (variously called hydatidosis, cysticercosis, coenurosis, or sparganosis) embedded in liver, lung, muscle, brain, eye, or other tissues.[1,2] The form taken by the infecting parasite depends on which cestode species causes the infection and, to a lesser extent, on the route by which the infection was acquired. Table 288-1 summarizes the common cestode parasites of humans, their typical vectors, and their usual symptoms.

This chapter begins with a discussion of parasite biology and the immunology of cestode infection followed by a description of individual parasite species: intestinal tapeworms (e.g., *Diphyllobothrium latum, Hymenolepis nana, Taenia saginata, Taenia solium*) and invasive cestode parasites [cysticercosis (*T. solium*), hydatid and alveolar cyst disease (*Echinococcus* spp.), sparganosis, and coenurosis (*Taenia multiceps*)]. Diagnosis and therapy, outlined briefly under the individual parasite headings, are discussed in greater detail at the end of each section.

CESTODE BIOLOGY

Parasite Life Cycle

The parasitic cestodes discussed in this chapter are flatworms (platyhelminths) of the orders Pseudophyllidea (*Diphyllobothrium, Spirometra*) and Cyclophyllidea (other species), which divide their life cycle between two animal hosts (Fig. 288-1).[1,2] As mature tapeworms, these parasites reside in the intestinal tract of a definitive host, a carnivorous mammal. Depending on the parasite species, mature tapeworms vary in size from several millimeters (*Echinococcus* spp.) to 25 m (*Diphyllobothrium*).[1]

The tapeworm consists of several parts: a head (*scolex*), a neck, and a tail. The head has two or more suckers and in some cases a *rostellum,* or knob of small hooks, used to attach to the wall of the host's intestine (Fig. 288-2A).[3] The scolex is connected by a short neck to the lower portion of the tapeworm, the *strobila,* which is a ribbon-like chain of independent, but connected, segments called *proglottids* (Fig. 288-2B). Each proglottid has both male and female sexual organs and is responsible for producing the parasite's eggs. Proglottids begin to develop in the neck region of the parasite, then mature and move downward in the strobila as new segments are added from above. The hermaphroditic proglottids become gravid and eventually break free of the tapeworm. Proglottids may degenerate in the stool, releasing eggs (thousands to millions per day) into the feces. Alternatively, intact proglottids may be passed in the stool, with egg release occurring outside the body. In some cases, a section of strobila may be passed in a single day, with no further release of proglottids for several days thereafter. In practical terms, this means that although the number of tapeworm eggs in the stool is usually high, detection of parasite eggs by standard stool examination may be sporadic. It therefore may require multiple stool samples, rectal swabs, and visual examination of stool and perineum for proglottids to detect a tapeworm infection. For some species of tapeworm (e.g., *T. saginata*), the proglottids are motile. They may migrate within the gastrointestinal tract, causing biliary or appendiceal obstruction, or out of the body, to be found in the perineum.

At the point at which eggs are released, two effective biotypes of parasite can be defined. If the eggs released from the parasite are partially

TABLE 288-1 Common Cestode Parasites of Humans, Their Typical Vectors and Their Usual Symptoms

Parasite Species	Developmental Stage Found in Humans	Common Name	Transmission Source	Symptoms Associated with Infection
Diphyllobothrium latum	Tapeworm	Fish tapeworm	Plerocercoid cysts in fresh-water fish	Usually minimal; with prolonged or heavy infection, vitamin B_{12} deficiency
Hymenolepis nana	Tapeworm, cysticercoids	Dwarf tapeworm	Infected humans	Mild abdominal discomfort
Taenia saginata	Tapeworm	Beef tapeworm	Cysts in beef	Abdominal discomfort, proglottid migration
Taenia solium	Tapeworm	Pork tapeworm	Cysticerci in pork	Minimal
Taenia solium (Cysticercus cellulosae)	Cysticerci	Cysticercosis	Eggs from infected humans	Local inflammation, mass effect; if in CNS, seizures, hydrocephalus, arachnoiditis
Echinococcus granulosus	Larval cysts	Hydatid cyst disease	Eggs from infected dogs	Mass effect leading to pain, obstruction of adjacent organs; less commonly, secondary bacterial infection, distal spread of daughter cysts
Echinococcus multilocularis	Larval cysts	Alveolar cyst disease	Eggs from infected canines	Local invasion and mass effect leading to organ dysfunction; distal metastasis possible
Taenia multiceps	Larval cysts	Coenurosis, bladder worm	Eggs from infected dogs	Local inflammation and mass effect
Spirometra mansonoides	Larval cysts	Sparganosis	Cysts from infected copepods, frogs, snakes	Local inflammation and mass effect

CNS, central nervous system.

developed, they are called *embryonated.* If the egg embryo has not yet begun its differentiation, the egg is referred to as *nonembryonated.* In biologic terms, the embryonated egg can immediately infect the next intermediate mammalian or insect host, typically a herbivore or omnivore, through ingestion of food containing the egg.[1] Such eggs, typical of *Echinococcus* spp., *Taenia* spp., and *H. nana,* may lie dormant in grazing areas or become scattered in the home environment and remain infectious for several months to years.[1,4] Once ingested, the egg hatches in the intermediate host's intestine, releasing an *oncosphere,* which penetrates the gut mucosa to reach the circulation. The oncosphere passes to any of several organs to form a parasite cyst, which is variously called a cysticercoid, cysticercus, alveolar cyst, or hydatid cyst, depending on its morphology. The life cycle of these parasites is completed when the carnivorous definitive host consumes the cyst-infected tissues of the intermediate host and the cyst develops into a mature tapeworm in the lumen of the definitive host's intestine.

For nonembryonated eggs, such as those of the fish tapeworm *D. latum,* initial development takes place outside the body in water, after which the eggs hatch to release a free-swimming *coracidium* larva.[5] In time, the coracidium is ingested by a small crustacean called a copepod and develops into a procercoid larva within the copepod's tissues. When the copepod, in turn, is ingested by a fish or other intermediate host, the procercoid infects its musculature, developing into the next larval stage, the *plerocercoid* cyst, or *sparganum.* If an uncooked plerocercoid of *D. latum* is ingested by a human, its definitive host, it develops into a mature, intraluminal "fish tapeworm." However, if the fish containing the plerocercoid is ingested by another, larger fish, it does not become a tapeworm. It reencysts instead as a plerocercoid in the muscles of the second, larger fish.

Plerocercoid encystment or reencystment is significant in terms of human disease (as *sparganosis*) for cestode species for which humans cannot serve as the definitive host (e.g., *Spirometra mansonoides,* a tapeworm of dogs and felines). Plerocercoids can develop in human tissues if *Spirometra*-infested copepods are ingested in drinking water. Alternatively, human plerocercoid cysts may be acquired via the intestine from another intermediate host (e.g., tadpole, frog, snake) if the meat of that aquatic host is eaten uncooked. Migrating plerocercoid cysts can also transfer directly into the skin or the eye if raw flesh of an aquatic intermediate host is used as a poultice in traditional healing.[6]

As a rule, humans are either definitive or intermediate hosts for a given cestode parasite, but not both. For example, humans are solely definitive hosts (i.e., with tapeworms) for *D. latum* (the fish tapeworm) and *T. saginata* ("beef tapeworm") and are solely intermediate hosts for *Echinococcus* spp. (hydatid cysts, alveolar cysts), *Spirometra* (sparganosis), and *T. multiceps* (coenurosis). There are two exceptions to this rule. The first is *T. solium,* which develops in humans as a cysticercus if ingested as an egg or as a tapeworm if ingested as a cysticercus in infected pork. It is thus possible for one patient to harbor both cyst and tapeworm forms of *T. solium.* Such dual infection is seen in about 25% of cysticercosis cases. The second exception is the dwarf tapeworm, *H. nana,* whose eggs after ingestion hatch in the gut and encyst within the wall of the human intestine. After 5 to 7 days the cyst breaks open and the larva develops (within the same host) to become a mature tapeworm. The fertile eggs of this tapeworm may directly infect the mucosa, permitting a continued increase in the number of tapeworms in the affected host, without further exposure to environmental egg contamination. In this fashion, humans serve as both inter-

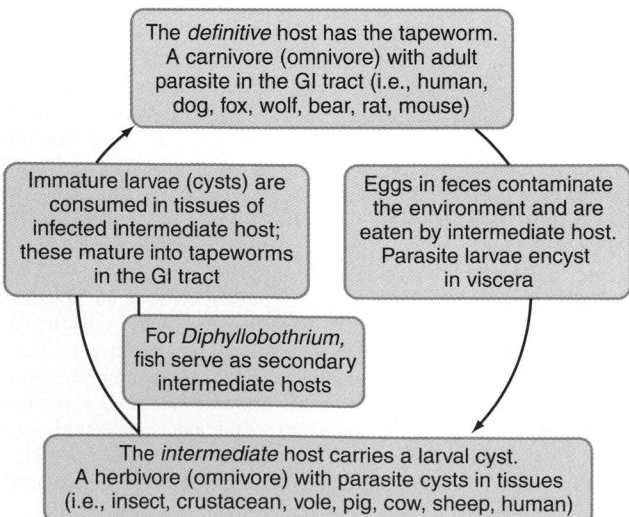

FIGURE 288-1. Cestode parasites alternate larval and adult stages in two different hosts.

FIGURE 288-2. The scolex (**A**) and a proglottid (**B**) of the cestode *Taenia solium. (From Ash LR, Orihel TC. Atlas of Human Parasitology. 3rd ed. Chicago: ASCP; 1990.)*

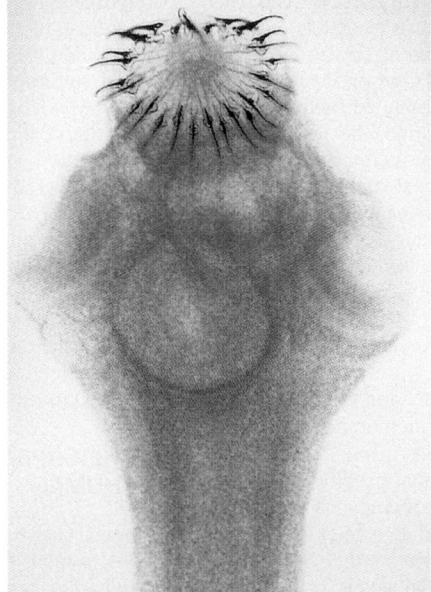

A   **B**

mediate and definitive hosts for *H. nana.* It should be stressed that single-host proliferation such as that of *H. nana* is highly unusual among human cestode infections and helminth infections in general. Normally, heavy cestode infections can be acquired only by repeated environmental exposure to eggs or infectious parasite cysts.

Disease Pathogenesis and Immunology

Adult tapeworms in the intestinal tract generally cause minimal local pathology. Reduced nutrient absorption and alteration of gut motility have been described, but there is no firm association of adult tapeworm infection with specific bowel symptoms. An immune response to adult tapeworms provokes eosinophilia and immunoglobulin E (IgE) elevation in some patients, but the immune response does not appear to alter the course of an intraluminal tapeworm infection. In light of the limited range of potential hosts observed for most adult tapeworms, it has been suggested that host factors, including the presence or absence of specific immunoreactivity, may determine the success of parasite infections in various potential host species.[7]

The immune response to invasive cyst infection is more pronounced but is often unsuccessful in eradicating the cyst in susceptible hosts. Infiltration with neutrophils and eosinophils is followed by local fibrosis, leading to cyst encapsulation and macrophage infiltration. Once the cyst is encapsulated, antigen release may be limited, leading to a reduction in the local inflammatory response. Specific antibody production remains detectable in the serum, however, and delayed-type hypersensitivity may be detected on skin testing. The immune response often increases later as the cyst begins to die and leak antigen or as it erodes into a body cavity, duct, or vessel, increasing local or systemic exposure to antigen. Experimentally, the anticyst immune response appears to limit dissemination of *Echinococcus* spp. after an initial infection.[7,8] Anticyst immunity is also likely to contribute to the spontaneous clearance of *H. nana* infection in older children.

INTESTINAL TAPEWORM INFECTIONS

Diphyllobothrium latum

Diphyllobothrium latum, or fish tapeworm, is one of the pseudophyllidean cestodes transmitted via aquatic species.[5] Human infection with *D. latum* is acquired by eating uncooked freshwater fish containing the parasite's plerocercoid cysts. Some traditional modes of infection include consumption of dried or smoked fish, which may contain viable cysts if not further cooked, or tasting flavored freshwater fish (e.g., gefilte fish) before cooking. The enthusiasm for "raw bar" foods such

as ceviche, sushi, and sashimi prepared from freshwater fish, especially salmon, has increased the transmission potential for *D. latum* in developed areas of North America.[9,10] Areas of the world in which *D. latum* is highly endemic (more than 2% prevalence) include specific lake and delta areas of Siberia, Europe (especially Scandinavia and other Baltic countries), North America, Japan, and Chile. Endemicity in rural areas is favored by stable zoonotic transmission through alternative nonhuman definitive hosts, including seals, cats, bears, minks, foxes, and wolves.

Human *D. latum* tapeworms are large, reaching up to 25 m (3000 to 4000 proglottids) in length. It takes 3 to 6 weeks after exposure for the tapeworm to mature. Once established, a *D. latum* parasite may survive 30 years or more. Multiple tapeworms in the same patient are common. Normally, infection is asymptomatic, but a proportion of infected individuals report nonspecific symptoms of weakness (66%), dizziness (53%), salt craving (62%), diarrhea (22%), and intermittent abdominal discomfort.[5]

Prolonged (more than 3 to 4 years) or heavy *D. latum* infection may lead to megaloblastic anemia caused by vitamin B_{12} deficiency. The vitamin B_{12} deficiency is a consequence of two factors: parasite-mediated dissociation of the vitamin B_{12}–intrinsic factor complex in the gut lumen (making vitamin B_{12} unavailable to the host) and heavy vitamin uptake and use by the parasite. Megaloblastic anemia may be worsened by concurrent folate deficiency, which also occurs as a consequence of *D. latum* infection. Vitamin B_{12} deficiency may be sufficiently severe to cause injury to the nervous system, including peripheral neuropathy and severe combined degeneration of the central nervous system (CNS).

For diagnosis, tapeworm infection may first be suspected based on the patient's history or when contrast studies of the intestine show an intraluminal, ribbon-like filling defect. Definitive diagnosis of *D. latum* infection is made by detection of 45 × 65 mm operculated parasite eggs on stool examination. Recovery of proglottids (with a characteristic central uterus) also establishes the diagnosis.

Treatment is with a single course of niclosamide or praziquantel[11] (see "Treatment of Tapeworm Infection"). Mild vitamin B_{12} deficiency is reversed by eradicating the tapeworm. Severe vitamin B_{12} deficiency should be treated with parenteral vitamin injections.

Hymenolepis nana

Hymenolepis nana, also known as dwarf tapeworm, is a cyclophyllidean tapeworm with embryonated eggs.[6] It is the only tapeworm that can be transmitted directly from human to human. Areas of endemicity (up to

26% prevalence) include Asia, southern and eastern Europe, Central and South America, and Africa. In North America, infection is most frequently found among institutionalized populations (up to 8% prevalence)[12] and among malnourished or immunocompromised patients.

Ingestion of parasite eggs on fecally contaminated food or fomites allows the initial infection. Once in the intestine, the eggs hatch to form oncospheres, which penetrate the mucosa to encyst as cysticercoid larvae. Four to five days later, the larval cyst ruptures into the lumen to form the relatively small, adult *H. nana* tapeworm (15 to 50 mm in length). Internal autoinfection may occur as parasite eggs are released from gravid proglottids in the ileum. In addition, poor sanitary practices promote external (fecal-oral) autoinfection as well as transmission to others sharing the same living quarters. Heavy infection is common among children and may be associated with abdominal cramps, anorexia, dizziness, and diarrhea.

An *H. nana* infection is diagnosed by identifying the 30 × 47 mm parasite eggs (with their characteristic double membrane) in the stool. Treatment is with praziquantel or niclosamide[11] (see "Treatment of Tapeworm Infection"). It is important to note that developing *H. nana* cysticercoids are not as susceptible to drug therapy as adult tapeworms. Because these cysts can emerge several days later to form new tapeworms, effective therapy of *H. nana* requires either higher-than-usual doses of praziquantel to reach cysticidal levels or more prolonged therapy with niclosamide (to eliminate emerging tapeworms) for a period of 5 to 7 days.

Taenia saginata

Taenia saginata, known as the beef tapeworm, is transmitted to humans in the form of infectious larval cysts found in the meat of cattle, which serve as the parasite's usual intermediate host.[1] The *T. saginata* tapeworm is common in cattle-breeding areas of the world. The areas with the highest prevalence (more than 10%) are in central Asia, the Near East, and Central and East Africa. Areas of lower prevalence (less than 1%) are found in Europe, Southeast Asia, Central America, and South America. Consumption of "measly" (i.e., cyst-infected) uncooked or undercooked beef is the usual means of transmission. Rare steak or ke-babs and steak tartare are dishes typically associated with *T. saginata* infection. In the definitive human host, adult *T. saginata* tapeworms are large (10 m in length) and can contain more than 1000 proglottids, each capable of producing thousands of eggs. If, through poor sanitary practices, eggs released in the feces are allowed to reach grazing areas, cattle are subsequently infected with *T. saginata* cysticerci. Alternative intermediate hosts include llamas, buffalo, and giraffes.

Symptoms are absent in most patients with *T. saginata* infection. A small number report mild abdominal cramps or malaise. The proglottids of *T. saginata* are motile and occasionally migrate out of the anus, to be found in the perineum or on clothing. The patient may report seeing moving segments in the feces or passing several feet of strobila at one time. These events are often psychologically distressing and are associated with significant anxiety-associated symptoms.

Specific diagnosis of *T. saginata* infection can be established by recovery of parasite proglottids.[1] If only eggs are found in the stool, it is important to note that *T. saginata* eggs are morphologically indistinguishable from those of *T. solium*. With *T. solium* tapeworms there is potential for autoinfection with cysticercosis; therefore if any *Taenia* spp. eggs are detected, treatment should be given without delay for further speciation. Effective oral treatment for either *Taenia* spp. is obtained with praziquantel or niclosamide[11] (see "Treatment of Tapeworm Infection").

Taenia solium

Humans can serve as either intermediate or definitive hosts for *T. solium*. Individuals who ingest *T. solium* eggs develop tissue infection with parasite cysts, a condition known as cysticercosis (details of this illness are included under "Cysticercosis"). Patients who consume raw or undercooked pork containing infectious larval cysts (cysticerci) acquire the "pork tapeworm," that is, the adult form of *T. solium*, which resides in the intestinal tract.[1] These tapeworms develop to ap-

proximately 2 to 8 m in length and may survive for 10 to 20 years. Some patients harbor both cysticerci and *T. solium* tapeworms, and it is possible for a tapeworm-carrying individual to develop cysticercosis by autoinfection. Areas in which *T. solium* infection is endemic include Mexico, Central America, South America, Africa, Southeast Asia, India, the Philippines, and southern Europe.

Infection with *T. solium* tapeworms is generally asymptomatic unless cysticercosis, caused by autoinfection with parasite eggs, supervenes. The proglottids of *T. solium* are not motile (unlike those of *T. saginata*) and do not migrate. *Taenia* spp. infection is readily diagnosed by detecting eggs during stool examination, but *T. solium* eggs are indistinguishable from those of *T. saginata*. If a proglottid is recovered, the species can be identified based on the characteristic features of the uterine canals in the segment.[1,3] Species identification is not required for therapy, which can be achieved with either praziquantel or niclosamide.[11]

OTHER SPECIES CAUSING TAPEWORM INFECTION IN HUMANS

Human tapeworm infection may also be caused by *Dipylidium caninum*, a more frequent parasite of dogs and cats, or by *Hymenolepis diminuta*, a tapeworm that usually infects rats.[1,6] Such infections are acquired by consumption of insects (fleas or beetles) containing the larval cysticercoids of these species and are most commonly seen among children. Human infection with tapeworm species related to *D. latum*—*Diphyllobothrium klebanovskii*, *Diphyllobothrium dendriticum*, *Diphyllobothrium ursi*, *Diphyllobothrium dalliae*—has been described in the Arctic and parts of Siberia. Rarely, other tapeworm species infect humans, particularly individuals with unusual dietary habits, such as the consumption of uncooked animal viscera. Infection is diagnosed by identifying characteristic parasite eggs in the stool. Effective treatment is obtained with praziquantel or niclosamide.

DIAGNOSIS OF TAPEWORM INFECTION

Because mature tapeworm infection is strictly an intraluminal intestinal infection, the most practical approach to diagnosis is examination of the feces for parasite eggs or proglottids. As was discussed under "Cestode Biology," egg release in the stool may be variable because of an irregular rate of proglottid detachment and degeneration. Thus examination of stool samples on several days may be required to establish a diagnosis. Sensitivity for egg detection may be improved by formyl ethyl acetate or other concentration techniques. Because cestode eggs are relatively heavy, sedimentation procedures (not flotation) provide a more efficient means to isolate tapeworm eggs. When handling specimens, it is important to remember that *T. solium* eggs are infective for humans and cause cysticercosis. For this reason, precautions should be taken to avoid any potential contamination of fingers or clothing with parasite eggs.

In some cases, intact proglottids are passed in the stool. This is most common with *D. latum*, *T. saginata*, *T. solium*, and *D. caninum*. Expelled proglottids tend to degenerate over time, so fixation and staining of specimens are recommended to allow effective microscopic speciation. Although species identification is not essential for treatment, identification of *T. solium* infection is significant and should prompt consideration of possible cysticercosis in the index patient or among his or her household contacts.[13] Proglottids of *D. latum* (fish tapeworm) often pass as short chains of grayish white connected segments, each 11 × 3 mm, with a central uterine structure.[5] Proglottids of the pork tapeworm, *T. solium*, are 11 × 5 mm, with a lateral genital pore and 7 to 13 branches on either side of the central uterine canal. Proglottids of *T. saginata*, the beef tapeworm, have a similar appearance but may be distinguished by the larger number of lateral uterine branches (15 to 20) in the proglottid. *T. saginata* proglottids are motile and may emerge spontaneously from the anus to be found on the perineum, on the legs, or on clothing. Proglottids of *D. caninum* (23 × 8 mm) are also motile and may be described by the patient (or parent) as whitish, moving cucumber seed-like objects in the stool. *D. caninum* proglottids may also become adherent to perianal hairs and then dry to form a whitish yellow object resembling a small grain of rice.

TREATMENT OF TAPEWORM INFECTION

Tapeworm infection should be treated whenever diagnosed. Safe, effective treatment of intestinal tapeworm infection may be achieved with either praziquantel or niclosamide. Both are well tolerated oral agents that have direct parasiticidal effects on intraluminal cestode parasites.

Niclosamide

Niclosamide is a poorly absorbed, narrow-spectrum anthelmintic that is available as 500 mg chewable tablets (Yomesan, Bayer).[11] The drug is normally taken as a 2 g (four-tablet) single dose for adults, as a 1.5 g (three-tablet) dose for children weighing more than 34 kg (75 pounds), or as a 1 g (two-tablet) dose for children weighing 11 to 34 kg (25 to 75 pounds). A single treatment is effective for *D. latum*, *T. saginata*, *D. caninum*, and *T. solium* tapeworms.

Eradication of *H. nana* tapeworm infection requires a more prolonged course of therapy (repeat daily doses for 1 week) because of concomitant infection with maturing *H. nana* cysts, which are not affected by the drug. It is normally recommended that after the first dose subsequent doses for *H. nana* (i.e., days 2 through 7) be reduced to 1 g daily for adults and large children (more than 34 kg) and to 0.5 g daily for small children. These follow-up doses are intended to kill any newly emerging *H. nana* tapeworms and should completely eliminate the infection. Nevertheless, it is appropriate to rescreen the patient's stool for parasite eggs 1 and 3 months after therapy to ensure cure. A repeated cycle of standard dosing (as just outlined) is usually sufficient to eliminate persistent infection.

Niclosamide must be thoroughly chewed before swallowing to obtain the maximal anthelmintic effect. Because the drug is poorly absorbed, the typical side effects of niclosamide are mild, occurring at a rate of approximately 10%.[11] They include malaise, mild abdominal pain, and nausea on the day of administration. High doses of niclosamide have not been shown to have mutagenic effects in animals, and the drug has been placed in Food and Drug Administration (FDA) Pregnancy Category B. Normally, treatment should be delayed until after pregnancy, but with *T. solium* there is concern that patients may develop cysticercosis through autoinfection with parasite eggs. Considering the relative risks and benefits, it may be appropriate to treat pregnant women who have *T. solium* tapeworms at the time of diagnosis and not delay therapy. Concern has also been raised about the possibility of internal autoinfection during *T. solium* therapy because of the release and possible retrograde intestinal movement of eggs during therapy. Although such autoinfection has not been documented, some experts recommend a mild laxative 1 to 2 hours after niclosamide treatment to avoid this possibility in *T. solium*-infected patients.

Praziquantel

Praziquantel is a broad-spectrum anthelmintic used to treat both trematode and cestode infections.[11] It is available as a scored, 600 mg coated tablet (Biltricide, Bayer); it has excellent activity against all tapeworms and is given as a single dose of 5 to 10 mg/kg for both children and adults. The exception to this regimen is *H. nana* infection, for which a higher dose of 25 mg/kg is recommended. If the *H. nana* infection is heavy, it is recommended that the dose be repeated 1 week after the initial therapy. Follow-up stool screening is recommended at 1 and 3 months to ensure eradication of infection.

Mild side effects occur in 10% to 50% of those treated, depending on the population. They include transient dizziness, headache, malaise, abdominal pain, and nausea. Moderate side effects, including sedation, vomiting, diarrhea, urticaria, rash, fever, and mild transaminitis, are not as common (less than 10%) and are also tran-

sient. Like niclosamide, praziquantel is classified in FDA Pregnancy Category B and should be used during pregnancy only if clearly needed. Praziquantel is well absorbed from the gastrointestinal tract and enters breast milk. Because the safety of praziquantel in children younger than 4 years of age is not known, women who are breast-feeding infants should not allow them to nurse for 72 hours after treatment is given.

INVASIVE CESTODE INFECTIONS

Cysticercosis

Cysticercosis is a tissue infection with larval cysts of the cestode *T. solium* in which the patient serves as an intermediate host for the parasite. Infection is acquired by consumption of *T. solium* eggs. Prevalence is high wherever *T. solium* tapeworms are common (i.e., in Mexico, Central America, South America, the Philippines, Southeast Asia). Infected subjects normally harbor multiple cysts in many parts of the body. In areas of endemicity, the cumulative infection risk increases with age, frequent consumption of pork, and poor household hygiene.[14] Symptoms may develop because of local inflammation at the site of involvement; but apart from CNS and cardiac involvement, serious disease is rare.

Neurocysticercosis is the term used for human CNS involvement with *T. solium* cysts.[15] Infection may involve any part of the CNS, but symptomatic disease is most often related to intracerebral lesions (causing mass effects, seizures, or both) (Fig. 288-3), intraventricular cysts (causing hydrocephalus), subarachnoid lesions (causing chronic meningitis), and spinal cord lesions (causing cord compression syndrome or meningitis). Intraparenchymal cerebral cysts typically enlarge slowly, causing minimal symptoms until years or decades after the onset of infection, when the cysts begin to die. At this point, cysts

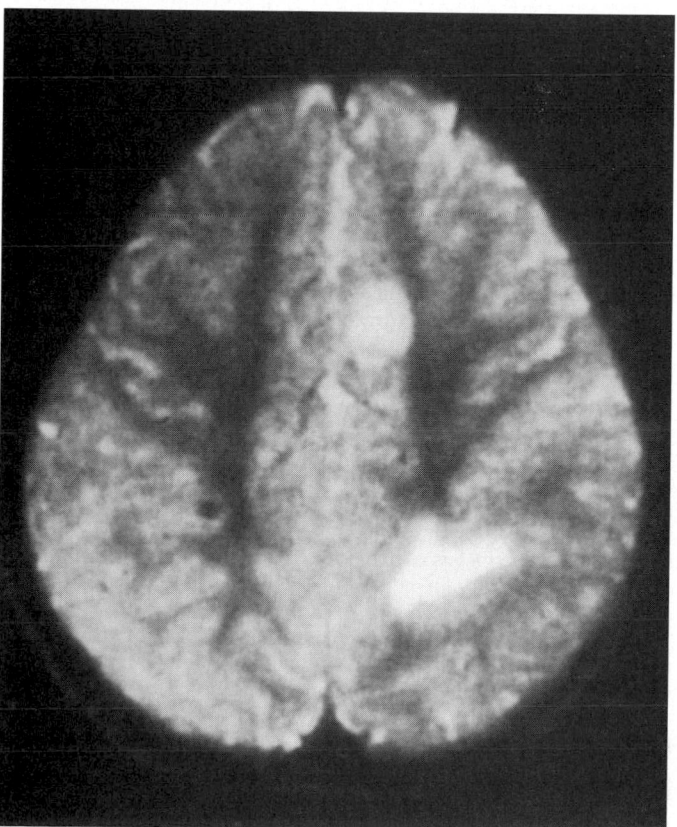

FIGURE 288-3. Magnetic resonance imaging scan of a child with neurocysticercosis. *(From Kruskal BA, Moths L, Teele DW. Neurocysticercosis in a child with no history of travel outside the continental United States. Clin Infect Dis 1993;16:290-292.)*

may lose osmoregulation and begin to swell. They may also leak antigenic material that provokes a severe inflammatory response (cerebritis, meningitis). Both processes contribute to symptoms of focal or generalized seizures, sensorimotor deficits, intellectual impairment, psychiatric disorders, and symptoms of hydrocephalus. In regions where *T. solium* is endemic, as many as 30% to 50% of patients with seizures have antibodies to *T. solium,* compared with the 2% to 11% prevalence in the general population, suggesting the likelihood that neurocysticercosis is an underlying cause of their disease.[15]

Because of their critical location, intraventricular cysts and basilar cysts tend to cause symptoms early during the course of the infection. The symptoms are due to obstruction of cerebrospinal fluid flow (CSF) or local meningeal irritation, which leads to injury to local blood vessels, cranial nerves, or the brain stem.[15] An aggressive form of basilar neurocysticercosis, called *racemose cysticerosis,* has been described in which cysts proliferate at the base of the brain, resulting in mental deterioration, coma, and death. Intraparenchymal spinal cord lesions are often symptomatic early because of direct local pressure effects. When spinal column cysts develop outside the cord itself, the onset of symptoms may be more gradual. The slow onset of external cord compression, arachnoiditis, or radiculopathy may result in a confusing progression of symptoms. In the CNS multiple cysticerci are the rule, and active symptoms may refer to one or several locations.

Diagnosis and treatment of cysticercosis depend on the site of involvement and the symptoms experienced. Travel to or residence in an endemic area significantly increases the likelihood of the diagnosis, although transmission has been documented to occur within the United States in persons living in the same household as a *T. solium*-infected immigrant. Cysts outside the CNS tend not to be symptomatic. These cysts eventually die and calcify, to be detected incidentally on plain radiographs of the limbs.

For symptomatic cysts outside the CNS, the optimal approach is surgical resection. Medical therapy with praziquantel or albendazole may also be employed.[11,15] Deep tissue and CNS lesions are more difficult to diagnose and treat surgically. Lesions may involve critical organs, making surgical removal technically not feasible. Presenting symptoms often suggest a tumor, and a specific diagnosis of cysticercosis is often first suspected on the basis of imaging studies [computed tomography (CT) or magnetic resonance imaging (MRI)], which show multiple enhancing and nonenhancing unilocular cysts.[15] Cerebral cysts are usually multiple (an average of 7 to 10 per patient). CSF examination may show lymphocytic or eosinophilic pleocytosis, hypoglycorrhachia, and elevated protein levels. A suspected diagnosis may be strengthened by serology that is available commercially or through the Centers for Disease Control and Prevention (CDC) in Atlanta, GA. The serology indicates prior exposure to *T. solium* antigens. Patients infected with other helminths, particularly other cestodes, may have circulating antibodies that cross react with antigens of *T. solium* in some assays.[16] However, immunoblotting techniques with the purified glycoprotein fraction of cyst fluid appear to offer a sensitive and specific diagnosis.[16,17] The sensitivity of antibody testing tends to be high for patients with multiple cysts (94%) but substantially lower for patients with single cysts or calcified cysts (28%).[18] CT and MRI remain the most effective means of diagnosis, however; and in the presence of a characteristic scan, negative serology should not exclude the diagnosis of cysticercosis.[15]

The utility of drug therapy for neurocysticercosis is currently controversial. Initially, a number of nonrandomized case series (each involving a small number of treated patients compared with historical control subjects) suggested that both praziquantel and albendazole hastened the clearance of cysticercal lesions seen on CT or MRI.[19] Since these initial reports, concurrently controlled, randomized trials have indicated that anthelmintic therapy given with corticosteroids is not superior to corticosteroid therapy alone for long-term control of seizures or resolution of *intraparenchymal* CNS cysticerci.[15] Other reports have indicated that anthelmintic therapy may exacerbate obstruction of CSF flow, enhance eye inflammation in ocular disease, and increase the risk of pericystic vasculitis, with increased risk of

stroke.[20,21] Thus the risk-benefit ratio for treating disease limited to the CNS parenchyma appears unfavorable. Still, randomized, well controlled trials have not yet evaluated the treatment of other forms of neurocysticercosis (i.e., intraventricular, basilar, and spinal cysticercosis), and the true value of drug treatment for these forms of the disease is not known.[15] However, because drug treatment of *intraventricular* cysts may prove efficacious and because of the higher risk for disease progression, therapy for this form of the disease is currently recommended by experienced groups.

If, on the basis of a review of the latest literature, the decision is made to treat an individual patient with complicated neurocysticercosis medically, treatment should generally be high doses of praziquantel (50 mg/kg/day for 15 to 30 days)[11,19,22] or albendazole (10 to 15 mg/kg/day for 8 days)[11] with the goal of achieving drug levels sufficient to kill any remaining living cysts. As noted earlier, cyst death is often accompanied by increased local inflammation, leading to an increase in symptoms. Before, during, and after drug therapy, seizures should be controlled with appropriate antiepileptic medications, and symptomatic hydrocephalus should be relieved by shunting. Shunt complications caused by blockage and bacterial infection are common in patients with neurocysticercosis.[23] CNS inflammation can be reduced by concurrent administration of pharmacologic doses of corticosteroids (dexamethasone)[24]; however, corticosteroids do not necessarily eliminate the risk of serious complications such as infarction[21,25] or intracranial pressure elevation.[26] Limited pharmacologic evidence suggests that concurrent corticosteroid therapy lowers serum praziquantel levels. In contrast, corticosteroid therapy (variably) increases the circulating levels of albendazole and its active metabolites in some patients. On this basis, some experts favor the use of albendazole for medical treatment of neurocysticercosis.[26]

A poor response to either surgical or drug therapy is more common with intraventricular or cisternal cysts and with racemose neurocysticercosis.[19] For these lesions, the drug levels achieved in the CSF and cyst during medical therapy are likely to be lower than for parenchymal CNS cysts, making drug failure more likely. Surgical approaches to these areas are difficult, and local inflammation may prevent easy removal of the cyst. Retained cyst material may result in postoperative recurrence. Nevertheless, successful therapy of ventricular and basilar cysts has been achieved in a small number of patients by either medical or surgical means.[27,28] Individualized therapy, possibly including a combined surgical-medical approach, is recommended in such cases.[15,22]

Echinococcosis (Hydatid and Alveolar Cyst Disease)

When humans serve as inadvertent intermediate hosts for cestodes of *Echinococcus* spp., which are carried as tapeworms by canines such as dogs, wolves, and foxes, disease may result from the development of expanding parasite cysts in visceral organs.[2,29] This condition, termed *echinococcosis,* has two forms: hydatid or unilocular cyst disease, caused by *Echinococcus granulosus* or *Echinococcus vogeli,* and alveolar cyst disease, caused by *Echinococcus multilocularis.* Sheep, goats, camels, and horses are among the usual intermediate hosts for *E. granulosus;* but because *E. granulosus* is transmitted by domestic dogs in livestock-raising areas, hydatid disease is prevalent worldwide (Africa, Middle East, southern Europe, Latin America, southwestern United States). *E. multilocularis* infections (found in northern forest areas of Europe, Asia, and North America, and in the Arctic regions) and *E. vogeli* infections (found in South American highlands) are transmitted by wild canines and are much less common.

Humans acquire echinococcosis by ingesting viable parasite eggs with their food.[2,29] The parasite eggs are distributed via local environmental contamination by the feces of tapeworm-infected canines. Eggs are partially resistant to desiccation and remain viable for many weeks,[4] allowing delayed transmission to individuals with no direct contact with vector animals. Once in the intestinal tract, the eggs hatch to form oncospheres that penetrate the mucosa and enter the circulation. Oncospheres then encyst in host viscera, developing over time to form mature larval cysts (Fig. 288-4).

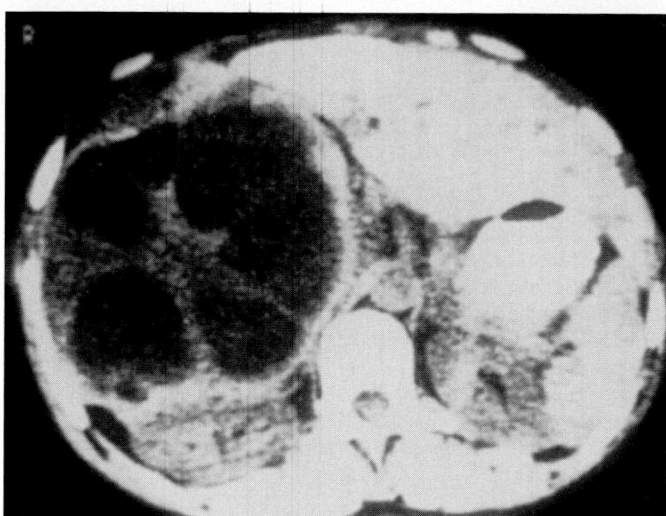

FIGURE 288-4. Hydatid cysts of the liver detected on computed tomographic scan. Note the well demarcated wall and characteristic septate internal structures (daughter cysts).

The hydatid cysts of *E. granulosus* tend to form in the liver (50% to 70% of patients) or lung (20% to 30%) but may be found in any organ of the body, including brain, heart, and bones (less than 10%). They grow to 5 to 10 cm in size within the first year and can survive for years or even decades. Symptoms are often absent, and in many cases infection is detected only incidentally by imaging studies. When symptoms do occur, they are usually due to the mass effect of the enlarging cyst in a confined space. Hydatid cysts contain a germinal layer that allows asexual budding to form "daughter" cysts within the primary cyst (Fig. 288-5). If a cyst erodes into the biliary tree or a bronchus, the cyst contents, including daughter cysts, may enter the lumen and cause obstruction or postobstructive bacterial infection. Bacteria may enter the cyst, causing pyogenic abscess formation in the cyst. Cyst leakage or rupture may be associated with a severe allergic reaction to parasite antigens; in the most extreme cases, patients may have anaphylactoid reactions, including hypotension, syncope, and

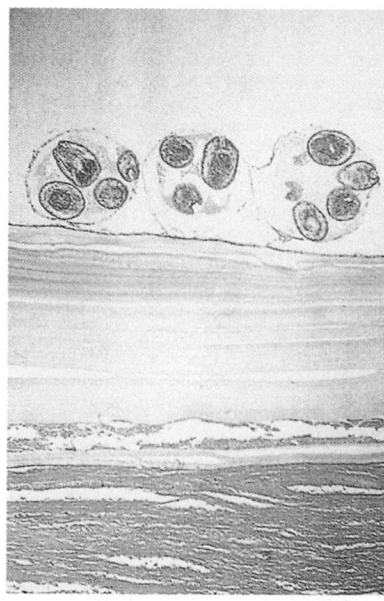

FIGURE 288-5. Daughter cyst formation from the germinal membrane of a hydatid cyst. *(From Ash LR, Orihel TC. Atlas of Human Parasitology. 3rd ed. Chicago: ASCP; 1990.)*

fever, after cyst rupture. A dangerous complication of cyst rupture is secondary seeding of daughter cysts into other areas of the body. Their subsequent enlargement may be associated with critical failure of one or more organs, which is associated with significant morbidity and mortality. Fewer than 10% of patients develop such complications; and because the infection is normally self-limited, it is likely that most infections never come to medical attention.[30] Nevertheless, symptomatic cysts should be treated and asymptomatic cysts carefully observed for a number of years to avert complications of infection.

Infection that is suspected based on imaging studies (ultrasonography, CT, MRI) may be confirmed by a specific enzyme-linked immunosorbent assay (ELISA) and Western blot serology (available in the United States through the CDC), confirming exposure to the parasite.[31,32] Serology is 80% to 100% sensitive and 88% to 96% specific for liver cyst infection but less sensitive for lung (50% to 56%) or other organ (25% to 56%) involvement. Assays are under development using recombinant *Echinococcus* antigens and may provide better diagnostic specificity.[31,32] Imaging remains more sensitive than serodiagnostic techniques, and a characteristic scan in the presence of negative serologic results still suggests the diagnosis of echinococcosis.[30]

Optimal treatment of symptomatic cysts is surgical resection to remove the cyst in toto. Traditionally, because of the risk of spreading infection due to cyst rupture, the recommended approach has been to visualize the cyst, remove a fraction of the fluid, and instill a cysticidal agent [hypertonic (30%) saline, cetrimide, or 70% to 95% ethanol] to kill the germinal layer and daughter cysts before resection.[2] Thirty minutes after instillation, the cyst is totally removed. A number of drains are left in the cyst bed to limit the risk of secondary bacterial infection.

Although time-honored, the efficacy of this approach has not been validated in clinical trials; and given the availability of effective perioperative drug therapy to limit spread, some experts have questioned the need to instill cysticidal agents during surgery.[2] Certainly, cysts communicating with the biliary tree or branches should not have a cysticidal agent instilled because of the risk of postoperative sclerosing cholangitis.[29,33] It may be more prudent to treat the patient perioperatively with an anthelmintic agent active against *Echinococcus* cysts (albendazole, mebendazole)[34-36] to limit the risk of intraoperative dissemination of daughter cysts. Medical therapy for inoperable cysts with albendazole or mebendazole has provided improvement in most patients (55% to 79%) and cure in a smaller number (29%).[34-36]

The preferred agent is albendazole because of its greater absorption from the gastrointestinal tract and higher plasma levels. It is given for three or more cycles at a dose of 400 mg twice a day for 4 weeks followed by a 2-week rest without therapy. The alternative agent, mebendazole, is poorly absorbed and must be taken at higher doses (50 to 70 mg/kg/day) for several months to achieve a therapeutic effect.[36]

The response to drug therapy depends on the cyst size and location.[36,37] Unfortunately, bone cysts, which are frequently not amenable to surgery, respond less well to drug treatment than other cysts. The response to drug therapy is best monitored by serial imaging studies; cyst disappearance or shrinkage along with increasing cyst density is thought to indicate a positive response.

An intermediate intervention for inoperable cysts has been developed, known as the PAIR procedure (puncture, aspiration, injection, reaspiration).[29,37-39] While the patient is receiving anthelmintics to reduce the risk of cyst dissemination, the hydatid cyst may be aspirated with a thin needle under CT guidance. Approximately 30% of the cyst fluid volume is removed. Detection of protoscolices in the cyst fluid allows confirmation of cyst viability. An equal volume of 95% ethanol or other scolicidal agent (e.g., 0.5% cetrimide) is then instilled into the cyst cavity and allowed to react for 30 minutes before removing the needle. Results indicate arrest or involution of cysts after treatment. Although this approach offers possible treatment for inoperable cysts, the risks remain incompletely defined.

Alveolar cyst disease caused by *E. multilocularis* is aggressive. *E. multilocularis* cysts reproduce asexually by lateral budding. Their gradual invasion of adjacent tissue is tumor-like, and sections of the parasite may "metastasize" to distal parts of the body.[2,29] Symptoms are usually of gradual onset, referring to the organ involved, which is most commonly the liver. Complications include biliary tract disease, portal hypertension, and Budd-Chiari syndrome. Initial imaging studies are usually highly suspicious for carcinoma or sarcoma, and biopsy may provide the first indication of infection. Serology, available from the CDC, combined with characteristic imaging studies, is an alternative means of establishing the diagnosis.[31] For operable cases, wide surgical resection (e.g., hepatic lobectomy or liver transplantation) is recommended to ensure total removal of the cyst.[35,40] Adjuvant albendazole therapy to reduce worm size before surgery or limit intraoperative spread has been reported to be beneficial in case series.[2,41] For inoperable cases, drug therapy with mebendazole or albendazole has provided arrest or cure of disease in some patients.[2,35] The efficacy of surgical or drug therapy may be monitored by serial imaging and serology.

Other Invasive Cestodes

Human tissue infection with plerocercoid cysts of several cestode species is referred to, collectively, as *sparganosis*. These parasites, like *Diphyllobothrium latum,* pass through several developmental stages in copepods and vertebrates.[1] The definitive hosts for tapeworms of these species are usually canines or felines. Humans acquire inadvertent parasite infection by ingesting copepods (in water) or by consumption of or prolonged exposure to uncooked meat of plerocercoid-infected animals.[42-44]

Sparganosis has been reported in South America, Japan, China, and other parts of Asia in association with traditional use of frog- or snake-meat poultices. Infection has rarely been reported from Europe and North America. Sparganosis may be the proliferating or nonproliferating type. Infection acquired in the United States is usually due to the species *Spirometra mansonoides,* which is nonproliferating. In other areas of the world, proliferating forms are more common. These forms branch by lateral division and may detach to spread to other, distal areas of the body.[42] Clinical presentation typically involves local inflammation at the site of invasion (skin and eye are the most common sites for poultice application). There is local lymphocytic and eosinophilic inflammation surrounding the parasite(s). Tissue injury may be particularly severe in the eye. Diagnosis is usually by biopsy, although serologic testing is under development.[6] Treatment is by injection with ethanol, surgical resection, or both. Medical therapy with various anthelmintics has not produced a beneficial effect.

Coenurosis is human cyst infection with the cestodes *Taenia multiceps, Taenia crassiceps,* and *Taenia serialis,* which cause tapeworms in dogs.[1] The cysts are unilocular, with multiple protoscolices, but do not contain daughter cysts. Symptomatic disease is usually associated with involvement of the eye or the CNS. Clinically, the cysts may be difficult to distinguish from cysticercosis or hydatid disease. Basal arachnoiditis and hydrocephalus are common. Surgical resection is the recommended mode of therapy.[6]

PREVENTION OF CESTODE INFECTION

Prevention of cestode infection depends on interrupting the parasite life cycle. Transmission of human tapeworm infection can be reduced or eliminated by the following sanitary measures: (1) careful disposal of human sewage to limit environmental spread of parasite eggs; (2) limitation of forage areas and use of safe feed for vector animals such as cattle or swine that serve as common intermediate hosts; (3) meat inspection before marketing to exclude cyst-infested carcasses; and (4) prolonged freezing (at less than $-18°$ C), thorough cooking of meat (at more than $50°$ C), or both to kill any cysts in the tissues. Control of fish tapeworm is more difficult to achieve because the fish vectors can range freely, and there are nonhuman reservoirs for the tapeworm (e.g., bear, seals) that can continue to infect vector fish despite the presence of good human sanitation.

Prevention of invasive cestode infection is more complex. Because this form of human infection results from egg ingestion and the eggs may have been spread throughout an area by free-ranging definitive

hosts such as dogs or humans, infection may be difficult to avoid. It is significant that half of the patients with hydatid cysts do not recall specific exposure to dogs, although they may have resided in or visited an area of endemicity. Successful control of *E. granulosus* transmission has been achieved by regular screening and treatment of dogs in areas of endemicity in New Zealand, Tasmania, and the British Isles[45] to eliminate adult tapeworm carriage and local release of eggs. Treatment of human carriers in areas in which *T. solium* is endemic has proved effective in controlling transmission of cysticercosis.[46] Field trials also indicate that anti-*Echinococcus* and anti-cysticercus vaccines can significantly reduce infection in farm animals (sheep, pigs), which may further lower the level of peridomestic transmission.[47]

In areas of good sanitation (e.g., the United States) autochthonous transmission of cysticercosis is rare but can occur in settings in which a *T. solium* tapeworm-carrying individual shares living or cooking quarters with susceptible individuals.[2,13] Screening of immigrants from *T. solium*-endemic areas and treatment of identified tapeworm infections would eliminate the risk of cysticercosis transmission to nontravelers.

REFERENCES

1. Wittner M, Tanowitz HB. Overview of cestode infections. In: Guerrant RL, Walker DH, Weller PF, eds. Tropical Infectious Diseases: Principles, Pathogens & Practice. Philadelphia: Churchill Livingstone; 1999:985-987.
2. Schantz PM. Echinococcosis. In: Guerrant RL, Walker DH, Weller PF, eds. Tropical Infectious Diseases: Principles, Pathogens & Practice. Philadelphia: Churchill Livingstone; 1999:1005-1025.
3. Ash LR, Orihel TC. Atlas of Human Parasitology. 3rd ed. Chicago: ASCP; 1990.
4. Wachira TM, Macpherson CN, Gathuma JM. Release and survival of Echinococcus eggs in different environments in Turkana, and their possible impact on the incidence of hydatidosis in man and livestock. J Helminthol 1991;65:55-61.
5. Wittner M, Tanowitz HB. Diphyllobothriasis. In: Guerrant RL, Walker DH, Weller PF, eds. Tropical Infectious Diseases: Principles, Pathogens & Practice. Philadelphia: Churchill Livingstone; 1999:1001-1004.
6. Wittner M, Tanowitz HB. Other cestode infections. In: Guerrant RL, Walker DH, Weller PF, eds. Tropical Infectious Diseases: Principles, Pathogens & Practice. Philadelphia: Churchill Livingstone; 1999:1026-1029.
7. Vuitton DA. The ambiguous role of immunity in echinococcosis: protection of the host or of the parasite? Acta Trop 2003;85:119-132.
8. Rau ME, Tanner CE. BCG suppresses growth and metastasis of hydatid infections. Nature 1975;256:318-319.
9. Deardorff TL, Kent ML. Prevalence of larval Anisakis simplex in pen-reared and wild-caught salmon (Salmonidae) from Puget Sound, Washington. J Wildl Dis 1989;25:416-419.
10. Durborow RM. Health and safety concerns in fisheries and aquaculture. Occup Med 1999;14:373-406.
11. Drugs for parasitic infections. Med Lett Drugs Ther 2002 (www.medletter.com).
12. Yoeli M, Most H, Hammond J, et al. Parasitic infections in a closed community: results of a 10-year survey in Willowbrook State School. Trans R Soc Trop Med Hyg 1972;66:764-766.
13. Kruskal BA, Moths L, Teele DW. Neurocysticercosis in a child with no history of travel outside the continental United States. Clin Infect Dis 1993;16:290-292.
14. Sarti E, Schantz PM, Plancarte A, et al. Prevalence and risk factors for Taenia solium taeniasis and cysticercosis in humans and pigs in a village in Morelos, Mexico. Am J Trop Med Hyg 1992;46:677-685.
15. Carpio A. Neurocysticercosis: an update. Lancet Infect Dis 2002;2:751-762.
16. Diaz JF, Verastegui M, Gilman RH, et al. Immunodiagnosis of human cysticercosis (Taenia solium): a field comparison of an antibody-enzyme-linked immunosorbent assay (ELISA), an antigen-ELISA, and an enzyme-linked immunoelectrotransfer blot (EITB) assay in Peru; the Cysticercosis Working Group in Peru (CWG). Am J Trop Med Hyg 1992;46:610-615.
17. Tsang VCW, Brand JA, Boyer AE. An enzyme-linked immunoelectrotransfer blot assay and glycoprotein antigens for diagnosing human cysticercosis (Taenia solium). J Infect Dis 1989;159:50-59.
18. Wilson M, Bryan RT, Fried JA, et al. Clinical evaluation of the cysticercosis enzyme-linked immunoelectrotransfer blot in patients with neurocysticercosis. J Infect Dis 1991;164:1007-1009.
19. Del Brutto OH, Sotelo J. Neurocysticercosis: an update. Rev Infect Dis 1988;10:1075-1087.
20. Evans C, Garcia HH, Gilman RH, Friedland JS. Controversies in the management of cysticercosis. Emerg Infect Dis 1997;3:403-405.
21. Bang OY, Heo JH, Choi SA, Kim DI. Large cerebral infarction during praziquantel therapy in neurocysticercosis. Stroke. 1997;28:211-213. [See comment by Del Brutto OH. Stroke 1997;28:1088.]
22. Garcia HH, Evans CA, Nash TE, et al. Current consensus guidelines for treatment of neurocysticercosis. Clin Microbiol Rev 2002;15:747-756.
23. Sotelo J, Marin C. Hydrocephalus secondary to cysticercotic arachnoiditis: a long-term follow-up review of 92 cases. J Neurosurg 1987;66:686-689.
24. DeGhetaldi LD, Norman RM, Douville AW. Cerebral cysticercosis treated biphasically with dexamethasone and praziquantel. Ann Intern Med 1983;99:179-181.

25. Woo E, Yu YL, Huang CY. Cerebral infarct precipitated by pranziquantel in neuro-cysticercosis: a cautionary note. Trop Geogr Med 1988;40:143-146.

26. Takayangui OM, Jardim E. Therapy for neurocysticercosis: comparison between al-bendazole and pranziquantel. Arch Neurol 1992;49:290-294.

27. Del Brutto OH, Sotelo J. Albendazole therapy for subarachnoid and ventricular cys-ticercosis: a case report. J Neurosurg 1990;72:816-817.

28. Cuetter AC, Garcia-Bobadilla J, Guerra LG, et al. Neurocysticercosis: focus on intra-ventricular disease. Clin Infect Dis 1997;24:157-164.

29. Ammann RW, Eckert J. Cestodes: Echinococcus. Gastroenterol Clin North Am 1996;25:655-689.

30. MacPherson CNL, Milner R. Performance characteristics and quality control of com-munity based ultrasound surveys for cystic and alveolar echinococcosis. Acta Trop 2003;85:203-209.

31. Zhang W, McManus DP. Concepts of immunology and diagnosis of hydatid disease. Clin Microbiol Rev 2003;16:18-36.

32. Ortona E, Rigano R, Butarri B, et al. An update on immunodiagnosis of cystic echinococcosis. Acta Trop 2003;85:165-171.

33. Teres J, Gomez J, Bouguera M, et al. Sclerosing cholangitis after surgical treatment of hepatic echinococcal cysts: report of three cases. Am J Surg 1984;148:694-697.

34. Ammann RW. Improvement of liver resectional therapy by adjuvant chemotherapy in alveolar hydatid disease; Swiss Echinococcosis Study Group (SESG). Parasitol Res 1991;77:290-293.

35. WHO. Guidelines for treatment of cystic and alveolar echinococcosis in humans. Bull WHO 1996;74:231-242.

36. El-On J. Benzimidazole treatment of cystic echinococcosis. Acta Trop 2003;85 :243-252.

37. Todorov T, Mechkov G, Vutova K, et al. Factors influencing the response to chemotherapy in human cystic Echinococcus. Bull WHO 1992;70:347-358.

38. Filice C, Di Perri G, Strosselli M, et al. Parasitologic findings in percutaneous drainage of human hydatid liver cysts. J Infect Dis 1990;161:1290-1295.

39. Mawhorter S, Temeck B, Chang R, et al. Nonsurgical therapy for pulmonary hydatid cyst disease. Chest 1997;112:1432-1436.

40. Mboti B, Van de Stadt J, Carlier Y, et al. Long-term disease-free survival after liver transplantation for alveolar echinococcosis. Acta Chir Belg 1996;96:229-232.

41. Wilson JF, Rausch RL, McMahon BJ, et al. Albendazole therapy in alveolar hydatid disease: a report of favorable results in two patients after short-term therapy. Am J Trop Med Hyg 1987;37:162-168.

42. Kim DG, Paek SH, Chang KH, et al. Cerebral sparganosis: clinical manifestations, treatment and outcome. J Neurosurg 1996;85:1066-1071.

43. Kron MA, Guderian R, Guevara A, et al. Abdominal sparganosis in Ecuador: a case report. Am J Trop Med Hyg 1991;44:146-150.

44. Nakamura T, Hara M, Matsuoka M, et al. Human proliferative sparganosis: a new Japanese case. Am J Clin Pathol 1990;94:224-228.

45. Gemmell MA. Australasian contributions to an understanding of the epidemiology and control of hydatid disease caused by Echinococcus granulosus: past, present and future. Int J Parasitol 1990;20:431-456.

46. Cruz M, Davis A, Dixon H, et al. Operational studies on the control of Taenia solium taeniasis/cysticercosis in Ecuador. Bull WHO 1989;67:401-407.

47. Lightowlers MW, Flisser A, Gauci CG, et al. Vaccination against cysticercosis and hydatid disease. Parisitol Today 2000;16:191-196.

Visceral Larva Migrans and Other Unusual Helminth Infections

THEODORE E. NASH

EOSINOPHILIA: CLINICAL SIGNIFICANCE

Eosinophilia is commonly but not always associated with invasive helminth infections and, when encountered, suggests their presence. The degree of eosinophilia can vary dramatically and is influenced by a number of factors. Helminths whose migrations through tissues are limited (e.g., infections localized to the skin or intestinal lumen) are associated with little or no eosinophilic response. However, helminths that migrate through the internal or visceral organs, either as part of their normal life cycle or ectopically, usually cause eosinophilia. Once the migration is completed and the tissues are no longer exposed to the parasite, eosinophilia wanes.

With some helminth infections, the parasites are effectively sepa-rated from the host by encystment, or a walling off process that limits the eosinophilic response. Acute infections tend to provoke higher re-sponses than do chronic infections, as do heavy compared with light infections. Eosinophilia also depends on the ability of the host to re-spond. Expected responses may not be found in septic patients or in some immunologically impaired patients. Although many helminths may cause eosinophilia, in most instances the possibilities can be nar-rowed by understanding the possible exposures, life cycle, prepatent and incubation periods, usual disease manifestations, and expected laboratory findings.

The diagnostic procedures used to detect infections differ for each parasite, so a clear idea of the potential causes is essential. The physi-cian must understand the sensitivity of the diagnostic procedures and the abilities of the laboratory personnel performing them. For exam-ple, intestinal *Ascaris* infections are readily detected in the stool. On the other hand, the number of *Strongyloides* larvae or *Schistosomia mansoni* ova present in the feces may be difficult to detect, and special stool concentration methods may be needed. Patients may present dur-ing the prepatent period before the parasite can be detected, such as with ascariasis or schistosomiasis. Repeated stool examinations even-tually diagnose both infections. The usefulness of serologic testing varies, but serologic tests can be helpful for suggesting diagnoses and ruling out infections. Few serologic tests for parasitic infections have been standardized, so the sensitivity and specificity may differ from published values and from laboratory to laboratory.

Most helminths that infect humans are relatively host-specific to humans, undergo characteristic migration and development, and are found in typical anatomic locations. However, these helminths some-times undergo atypical or aborted migrations and cause symptoms or signs because of their unusual or ectopic location. A good example of this is the deposition of schistosomal ova and the subsequent granu-lomatous, inflammatory lesions in the spinal cord or brain. In addi-tion, some helminths of animals can also infect humans. Examples are *Echinococcus granulosus* and *Trichinella spiralis,* which com-monly infect humans, migrate and develop normally, and reside in lo-cations similar to those in the animal host. In contrast, other helminths of animals are unable to develop or migrate normally. Commonly, they undergo prolonged, aberrant migrations or locate abnormally in the tissues as underdeveloped larvae and incite an eosinophilic inflammation that is responsible for many of the symp-toms and signs of these infections. Although a large number of ani-mal parasites may infect humans, most do so rarely. In contrast, some helminths of animals infect humans more commonly and cause dis-tinctive clinical syndromes (Table 289-1) sometimes associated with characteristic epidemiology, exposure history, and geographic loca-tions. More often than not, similar clinical syndromes are caused by a group of related parasites. The diagnosis is suggested on clinical and epidemiologic grounds. Although pathologic examination of tis-sue can sometimes establish the diagnosis, the detection of larvae is commonly unrewarding. Serologic tests are sometimes helpful [see "Visceral Larva Migrans (Toxocariasis)"] but usually are not fully evaluated, are experimental, or are unavailable.

VISCERAL LARVA MIGRANS (TOXOCARIASIS)

Visceral larva migrans (VLM) is a syndrome characterized in its most florid state by eosinophilia, fever, and hepatomegaly. It is caused pri-marily by infection with *Toxocara canis* but also by *Toxicara cati* and other helminths less frequently.[1-3]

Life Cycle in the Dog

Toxocara canis infects dogs and related mammals by a number of mechanisms.[1] Most commonly, ingested eggs hatch in the small intes-tine, and the resulting larvae migrate to the liver, lung, and trachea. They are then swallowed and mature in the lumen of the small intes-

TABLE 289-1 Clinical Syndromes Associated with Unusual Helminth Infections in Humans

Clinical Syndrome	Parasite	Usual Host
Visceral larva migrans	*Toxocara canis*	Dogs
	Toxocara cati	Felines
	Balyisascaris procyonis	Raccoons
Eosinophilic gastroenteritis	*Anisakis* spp.	Sea mammals
	Phocanema spp.	Sea mammals
	Ancylostoma caninum	Canines
Cutaneous larva migrans	*Ancylostoma braziliense*	Canines, felines
	Ancylostoma caninum	Dogs and cats
Eosinophilic meningitis	*Angiostrongylus cantonensis*	Rats
	Gnathostoma spinigerum	Felines, other mammals
Pulmonary or cutaneous nodules	*Dirofilaria* spp.	Dogs, other mammals
Abdominal angiostrongyliasis	*Angiostrongylus costaricensis*	Cotton rats
Capillariasis	*Capillaria philippinensis*	?
Diarrhea	*Nanophyetus salmincola*	Mammals, birds
Swimmer's itch	*Trichobilharzia* spp.	Birds

tine, where eggs are shed. Other larvae migrate to and remain dormant in the muscles but are capable of development even years after the primary infection, particularly in pregnant bitches. During pregnancy, larvae again develop and infect the pups transplacentally and transmammarily. Not uncommonly, infective larvae are found in the feces of the pups. Eggs are not infectious when passed in the feces and take 3 to 4 weeks to develop. They are hardy and often remain viable for months. Large numbers of viable eggs contaminate the environment because of the high prevalence of infection in dogs and the ability of eggs to survive relatively harsh environmental conditions.

Infection in Humans

Prevalence

Toxocariasis is prevalent wherever dogs are found and *Toxocara* eggs are able to survive. The prevalence of infection or disease in humans is not known, but seroepidemiologic studies show wide differences in prevalence depending on the population tested. In the United States, seropositivity ranged from 2.8%[4] in an unselected population to 23.1%[5] in a kindergarten population in the southern United States to 54%[6] in a selected rural community. None of the seropositive persons had recognizable disease.

Clinical Manifestations

Visceral larva migrans occurs most commonly in children younger than 6 years.[3,4] Disease manifestations vary and range from asymptomatic infection to fulminant disease and death, but it is increasingly appreciated that most infections are asymptomatic. Those who come to medical attention most commonly complain of cough, fever, wheezing, and other generalized symptoms.[3-7] The liver is the organ most frequently involved, and hepatomegaly is a common finding, although almost any organ can be affected. Splenomegaly occurs in a small number of patients, and lymphadenopathy has been noted. Lung involvement with radiologic findings has been documented in 32% to 44%, but respiratory distress occurs rarely. Skin lesions such as urticaria and nodules have also been described. Seizures have been noted to occur with increased frequency in VLM, but severe neurologic involvement is infrequent. Eye involvement in VLM is unusual but has been documented (see "Ocular Larva Migrans"). Eosinophilia, usually accompanied by leukocytosis, is the hallmark of VLM. Laboratory findings include hypergammaglobulinemia and elevated isohemagglutinin titers to A and B blood group antigens, which are due to the host's immune response to cross-reacting antigens on the surface of *T. canis* larvae.

Diagnosis

The diagnosis of VLM is usually suggested clinically by the presence of eosinophilia, leukocytosis, or both in a young child also presenting with hepatomegaly or signs and symptoms of other organ involvement. A history of pica and exposure to puppies is common. Patients are more commonly black and from rural areas.

The diagnosis is definitively confirmed by finding larvae in the affected tissues by histologic examination or by digestion of tissue; however, larvae are frequently not found. The enzyme-linked immunosorbent assay (ELISA) employing extracts of excretory or secretory products of *T. canis* larvae appears specific and useful for confirming the clinical diagnosis.[8] However, *Toxocara* antibody titers in populations without clinically apparent VLM vary dramatically, and elevated titers cannot definitively establish the diagnosis.

Differential Diagnosis

Eosinophilia, fever, and hepatomegaly are frequently caused by helminths that migrate through the body. *Balyisascaris procyonis* (an ascarid of raccoons) is a recently recognized cause of larval migrans in the United States.[9] Others are acute schistosomiasis, *Fasciola hepatica* infections, *Ascaris lumbricoides* abscess of the liver, acute liver fluke infections (*Clonorchis sinensis, Opisthorchis viverrini*), complications from *Echinococcus* infection of the liver, *Capillaria hepatica*, and other invasive helminths. Diseases not caused by parasitic infections should also be considered. Children with mild disease may manifest only eosinophilia.

Treatment and Management

Most patients recover without specific therapy. Treatment with anti-inflammatory or anthelmintic drugs may be considered for those with severe complications usually due to involvement of the brain, lungs, or heart. There is no proven effective therapy, although albendazole, thiabendazole, mebendazole, diethylcarbamazine, and other anthelmintics have been used. Indeed, injury to the parasite may provoke an intense inflammatory response leading to worsening of the clinical picture. Corticosteroids have been used with and without specific antilarval therapy, with some reports of improvement.

Prevention

Visceral larva migrans can be easily prevented by a number of simple but effective measures that prevent *T. canis* eggs from contaminating the environment and children from ingesting eggs. Dogs, particularly puppies, should be periodically tested and treated for *T. canis* and other worms. Pica should be prevented.

OCULAR LARVA MIGRANS

Ocular larva migrans is caused by an infection of the eye with *T. canis* larvae.[10] Although a present or past history of clinically recognized VLM has occasionally been noted, almost all patients present with unilateral eye involvement without a past history or present systemic symptoms or signs. Presumably, a larva by chance becomes entrapped in the eye, resulting in an eosinophilic inflammatory mass. Children are most commonly affected and, on the average, are older (mean 8.6 years in one study) than those diagnosed with VLM. The findings are most commonly those of a posterior or peripheral subretinal mass. In fact, this entity was first recognized after examining eyes enucleated for the treatment of presumed retinoblastoma.[10] Associated inflammation may be significant.

Eosinophilia, hepatomegaly, and other signs and symptoms of VLM are usually lacking. The diagnosis is established clinically. Although the serum titers to *Toxocara* larvae are higher than those of a control population,[11] many patients with ocular larva migrans have low or negative titers. However, elevated vitreous[12] and aqueous fluid titers[13] to *Toxocara* larvae compared with serum levels have been documented and appear to be useful for establishing the diagnosis. There is no specific therapy.

A characteristic clinically recognizable syndrome, diffuse unilateral subacute neuroretinitis is caused by infection with helminth larvae of *B. procyonis* and *Toxocara* sp.[14] and other unidentified nematodes.[15,16] A motile larva is commonly found in or below the retina. Photocoagulation is curative. Anthelmintic therapy such as albendazole or thiabendazole may be effective.[16]

BAYLISASCARIASIS

Baylisascaris procyonis, an ascarid of raccoons, is a recently recognized cause of visceral larval migrans in humans and many other animals.[17-20] The life cycle is similar to that of dog and cat ascarids, and infection occurs after ingestion of ova excreted in raccoon feces that subsequently contaminates soil and the environment. Although the clinical manifestations are similar to those caused by dog and cat ascarids, severe and commonly fatal eosinophilic meningoencephalitis occurs in more than half the cases.[20] Eye involvement is common and is one of the known causes of diffuse unilateral subacute neuroretinitis.[14,15] The diagnosis is established by detecting typical larvae in tissues; an experimental serologic examination has been reported but is not routinely available. There is no proven therapy. Of the available drugs, albendazole and corticosteroids are most commonly tried.[15,20]

ANISAKIASIS

Anisakiasis is caused by the accidental infection of humans by larvae found in saltwater fish and squid. Definitive hosts are marine mammals. The clinical syndrome is caused by penetration of larvae into the stomach or small intestine; it is characterized by upper or lower abdominal symptoms (or both). The diagnosis is suggested by a history of ingesting raw, salted, pickled, smoked, or poorly cooked fish.

Life Cycle in Marine Mammals

Larvae of the family Anisakidae, including *Anisakis, Pseudoterranova,* and occasionally other genera, can accidentally infect humans.[1,21-23] The adults are found in the stomach of marine mammals. The eggs, passed in the feces, hatch as free-swimming larvae, are ingested by certain crustaceans, and are eaten by fish and squid. When ingested by appropriate marine mammals, such as dolphins, seals, and whales, the larvae burrow head first into the stomach. When consumed by humans, the larvae attempt and many times succeed in burrowing into the stomach or intestine, resulting in typical symptoms.

Clinical Syndrome

Anisakiasis occurs after ingesting raw or improperly cooked marine fish. The disease, initially recognized in The Netherlands after the ingestion of raw herring, is most frequently reported from Japan, where raw fish is commonly eaten. In the United States, infection is still uncommon but is now more frequently recognized because of increased ingestion of raw fish, particularly salmon. Cod, halibut, pollock, greenling, herring, anchovies, hake, tuna, sardines, and mackerel are others that have been implicated.

Clinical manifestations are caused by penetration of worms into the gastrointestinal tract, usually the stomach or lower small intestine, most commonly the ileum.[22-24] Occasionally, throat irritation is followed by coughing up the characteristic worm. Initial invasion is associated with acute symptoms, whereas the presence of worms for longer periods causes chronic symptoms. The location of the worms

and symptoms depend somewhat on the genus, with *Pseudoterranova* commonly associated with infection of the stomach and *Anisakis* with the intestine. Symptoms usually occur within 48 hours after ingestion, but this pattern is variable. With gastric anisakiasis, patients complain of intense abdominal pain, nausea, and vomiting. Small intestinal involvement results in lower abdominal pain and signs of obstruction mimicking appendicitis. Symptoms may be chronic, sometimes lasting for months and, rarely, years. These symptoms are associated with intestinal masses containing the parasite and are sometimes confused with a tumor, regional enteritis, or diverticulitis. Worms are occasionally located ectopically outside the gastrointestinal tract. *Anisakis* larvae in seafood have been implicated as a cause of acute allergic manifestations such as urticaria, angioedema, and anaphylaxis with or without accompanying abdominal gastrointestinal symptoms in patients who ingest raw fish.[25-29] In vitro studies and skin tests indicate that sensitization to *Anisakis* antigen is common in this population, whereas sensitization to fish is uncommon.[23,27-29]

Laboratory Findings

Eosinophilia is usually not present in patients with gastric or intestinal anisakiasis. Leukocytosis is not consistently present with acute anisakiasis but has been noted in almost two-thirds of the patients with intestinal involvement in one series.

Diagnosis

Anisakiasis should be considered in anyone with a history of ingesting raw marine fish and of suggestive abdominal symptoms. A definitive diagnosis can be established by endoscopy, radiographic studies, or pathologic examination of tissue. In the upper gastrointestinal tract, worms are found partially embedded in any area of the stomach and may be associated with localized mucosal edema, erosions, or mass lesions.[30,31] Upper gastrointestinal radiographic studies may reveal the outline of a worm associated with mucosal edema or tumor formation. Removing the worm during endoscopy definitively establishes the diagnosis and is curative.[24] Intestinal anisakiasis is diagnosed clinically. Varied degrees of thickening of the walls and narrowing of the lumen of the ileum or jejunum are found on radiographic studies.[30,31] High-resolution ultrasonography has demonstrated small-intestinal wall thickening and localized ascites around the involved section of bowel. Examination of aspirated ascites has revealed a preponderance of eosinophils.[32] Lesions resolve within 2 to 3 weeks.[30] Occasionally, removal of the intestinal mass is required to establish the diagnosis and effectively treat the patient. Tissues show inflammatory masses, many eosinophils, and the characteristic helminth. Serologic tests are not generally available but may be useful, particularly in patients whose symptoms have lasted longer than 1 week.[33]

Treatment

Symptoms diminish spontaneously in most patients without specific therapy, although the process is hastened by removing worms lodged in the stomach during endoscopy. In one series of intestinal anisakiasis, all 12 patients became asymptomatic by 2 weeks.[30] A report of treatment with albendazole in a case diagnosed only by serology is, at best, suggestive of efficacy.[34] One Japanese investigator commonly prescribes antacids after removing the stomach worms.

Prevention

Larvae resist heating up to 50° C as well as pickling, salting, and some methods of smoking. Infection can be prevented by cooking or freezing fish for 24 hours before ingestion.

CUTANEOUS LARVA MIGRANS (CREEPING ERUPTION)

Cutaneous larva migrans is characterized as serpiginous, reddened, elevated, pruritic skin lesions usually caused by *Ancylostoma braziliense,* the dog and cat hookworm.[1,35] Other animal hookworms including *Ancylostoma caninum, Uncinaria stenocephala, Bunostomum phlebotomum,* and others, as well as the human hookworms *Strongyloides stercoralis* and *Gnathostoma spinigerum* can produce findings. Rarely, insect larvae cause a similar picture.

Like human hookworms, *A. braziliense* larvae infect dogs and cats by burrowing through the skin. The adults reside in the intestine and shed eggs, which undergo development into infectious larvae outside the body in places protected from desiccation and temperature extremes, such as sandy, shady areas around beaches or under houses. Infections are most common in warm climates, such as the southeastern United States, and occur in children more commonly than in adults. Larvae penetrate the skin, causing tingling followed by itching, vesicle formation, and typically raised, reddened, serpiginous tracks that mark the route of the parasite.[1,35,36] With severe infections, persons may have hundreds of tracks. Little further development of the parasite occurs. Usually there are few, if any, systemic symptoms, although some reports have documented lung infiltrates and, rarely, severe lung dysfunction and recovery of parasites in the sputum. Eosinophilia has been noted with some infections.[36] The skin lesions are readily recognized, and the diagnosis is made clinically. Biopsy specimens usually show an eosinophilic inflammatory infiltrate, but the migrating parasite is usually not identified. For this reason, biopsies are usually not indicated to establish the diagnosis.

Without treatment, skin lesions gradually disappear.[37] Thiabendazole administered topically (10% aqueous suspension four times daily)[38] or orally (25 mg/kg twice daily for 2 days)[38] is effective. Albendazole (400 to 800 mg/day PO for 3 to 5 days) and invermectin (200 μg/kg given once) are extremely effective.[39,40]

EOSINOPHILIC MENINGITIS

Infection of humans with larvae of *Angiostrongylus cantonensis,* the rat lung worm, is characterized by invasion of the brain, leading to signs and symptoms of meningitis and encephalitis associated with an eosinophilic pleocytosis in the cerebrospinal fluid (CSF) and peripheral eosinophilia.[34] The adults of *A. cantonensis* reside in the lungs of rats.[1] Eggs hatch in the lungs, and the larvae are swallowed, are expelled in the feces, and seek an appropriate molluscan intermediate host, where the parasite develops into infective third-stage larvae. Infective larvae are found in a number of mollusks including slugs, land snails, and a land planarian; they are also found in a number of unrelated animals, including freshwater prawns, land and coconut crabs, and frogs. After ingestion by rats, the infective larvae migrate to the pulmonary arteries and then the lung, enter the blood vessels, and thereby migrate to the brain. Eventually they return to the lungs via the vasculature. In humans, migration of the larvae to the brain causes eosinophilic meningitis, encephalitis, or both.

Epidemics and sporadic infections occur most commonly in the South Pacific,[41] Southeast Asia,[42] and Taiwan[43] but more recently have been recognized in Jamaica,[44] Cuba,[45] and Egypt.[46] It is likely that cases will be recognized elsewhere because the parasite has been found in other regions. The most commonly recognized sources of human infection are raw or undercooked snails, prawns, or crabs. Contamination of foods such as leafy vegetables by larvae deposited by slugs or snails may also occur. Caesar salad was implicated in one epidemic.[44]

Clinical manifestations vary, and although fatalities occur, particularly with massive infections, most patients have a relatively uncomplicated course.[41-43,47] During one well characterized epidemic, the incubation period ranged from 1 to 6 days after ingestion of infected snails.[41] Symptoms include headache, stiff neck, fever, rash, pruritus, abdominal pain, constitutional complaints, nausea, and vomiting. Neurologic involvement varies from no complaints to paresthesias and pain, weakness, various focal neurologic findings (sixth and fourth cranial nerve palsies are frequently noted), coma, and death. In general, the patients do not appear to be as ill as those who have bacterial meningitis. Signs of meningitis are frequent but nonspecific. CSF leukocytosis with more than 10% eosinophils is frequent. CSF glucose values are usually normal, but depressed values have been noted.

The diagnosis is usually established clinically, although serology, if available, is useful.[44] Occasionally, a characteristic larva is found in the CSF at the time of lumbar puncture. A history of travel or being in an endemic region and ingestion of raw or partially cooked implicated foods should be sought. In severe cases magnetic resonance imaging (MRI) shows meningeal enhancement, tracts in the brain or spinal cord (or both), increased abnormal subcortical and periventricular T2-weighted MRI signals, and enhancing subcortical lesions.[48] A heavy worm burden increases the probability of brain involvement. Analysis of the antibody responses by Western blots showed the development of a characteristic 31 kDa band in infected patients and therefore appears to be a helpful test. However, the lack of availability of the parasite antigen is likely to limit the usefulness of the test.[44,49]

Symptomatic therapy includes corticosteroids, which have been shown to decrease the duration of headaches in a randomized trial.[50] Specific anthelmintic therapy is usually contraindicated, as patients usually recover without specific treatment, and killing larvae in and around the brain may be detrimental. Repeated CSF lumbar punctures appear to be helpful for treating associated headaches, presumably by decreasing CSF pressure. Recovery usually occurs by 2 months, although prolonged symptoms and signs are occasionally noted.

GNATHOSTOMIASIS

A characteristic syndrome of intermittent, nonpitting edematous swellings of subcutaneous tissues associated with eosinophilia is caused by migration throughout the body of larvae from a number of species of helminths of the genus *Gnathostoma* (most commonly *G. spinigerum* in Southeast Asia).[51-53] Although cutaneous symptoms are frequent, any organ may be involved, and the most serious manifestations involve migration of larvae into the brain or spinal cord.[51,52] Most of these infections occur in Southeast Asia, but recently large numbers have been recognized in Mexico.[54] Endogenous human infections have also been documented in Spain, Peru, Ecuador, India, China, Japan, Bangladesh, and other places.

Life Cycle

The adult worms reside in tumorous burrows in the stomachs of a large number of mammals including cats of various types, dogs, opposums, and raccoons.[1,55] Eggs are shed in the feces, hatch after about 1 week, and are subsequently ingested by small crustaceans called *Cyclops*. These crustaceans are subsequently ingested by a variety of other animals including fishes, frogs, and snakes, where they encyst in the muscles as infectious larvae. When eaten by the appropriate definitive host, larvae migrate through the body and eventually invade the stomach, where they mature, mate, and release eggs in the feces. The spectrum of animals that spread infections to humans has broadened considerably because infectious larvae can be passed unaltered from animal to animal after ingestion (paratentic carriage). Most infections occur after eating undercooked freshwater fish, chicken, or pork. However, infectious larvae can also burrow through the skin, or infections may occur after ingesting *Cyclops* in contaminated water. Rarely, prenatal transmission has been documented.

Clinical Manifestations

Acute signs and symptoms such as nausea, vomiting, gastrointestinal pain, and fever may occur shortly after ingestion and likely are caused by the initial invasion of the infecting larva into and out of the intestines.[53,56] The most prominent signs, which occur as early as 3 to 4 weeks after ingestion, are intermittent migratory subcutaneous swellings. They may occur anywhere. They are usually nonpitting, often erythematous, and occasionally pruritic and painful. They may also occur as nodules or abscesses or resemble classic cutaneous larva migrans. Eosinophilia is usually present and may be extreme. Migrating larvae may invade any tissue and give rise to symptoms related to specific organs such as the eye, intestines, spinal cord, and brain. Involvement of the latter results in the most serious complication, eosinophilic encephalomyelitis.[51,52] Although gnathostomiasis is a less frequent cause of encephalomyelitis compared to *A. cantonesis,* it tends to result in permanent neurologic deficits and death because there is more invasion of the brain substance. Consistent with this, the CSF has an increased number of red blood cells.

Diagnosis

In some areas of Southeast Asia gnathostomiasis is a common illness. The diagnosis is suggested when there is a history of intermittent subcutaneous swelling in the presence of eosinophilia and a history of ingesting raw fish or other implicated foods from endemic areas. Serology is helpful and supports or suggests the diagnosis in cryptic cases but is not easily available in nonendemic regions.[57] Occasionally, the worms can be isolated from the migratory swelling, but this endeavor is usually not successful and therefore not recommended.

Differential Diagnosis

The syndrome is relatively distinctive. *Loa loa* may present with calabar swellings and eosinophilia, but the epidemiology is distinctive, and the swellings are not erythematous and do not resemble larval migrans. Cutaneous larval migrans is usually not accompanied by eosinophilia, and there is a distinctive epidemiology. Strongyloidiasis is not commonly associated with larva currens and eosinophilia and can be distinguished by the presence of positive serology for *Strongyloides,* a positive stool examination, or both. *Strongyloides* is one of the causes of eosinophilic meningitis and may be indistinguishable clinically from that caused by *A. cantonesis.* Serologic studies can differentiate between the two infections.

Treatment

Both invermectin (200 μg/kg for one dose) and albendazole (400 mg/day for 21 days) give cure rates of better than 90%.[58,59]

Prevention

Avoiding uncooked, pickled fish and other implicated foods prevents infection in most individuals.

ABDOMINAL ANGIOSTRONGYLIASIS

Clinical manifestations of human infections of *Angiostrongylus costaricensis* are due to penetration and development of the parasite in the lower small bowel and adjacent colon. They are characterized by abdominal pain, vomiting, and a right lower quadrant mass.[60] In the normal host, the rat, adult parasites reside in the arteries and arterioles of the ileocecal area of the intestine. Eggs deposited in the tissue hatch, and the larvae migrate through the intestinal wall into the lumen and are excreted in the feces. Larvae are then ingested by the intermediate host (the slug) and after further development become infectious for rats after ingestion. Following maturation in the lymphatics, the larvae penetrate the arterioles and arteries in the ileocecal area of the rat, where they reside as adults. In humans, the parasite follows a similar pattern of migration, except that eggs are retained in the tissues and larvae do not appear in the feces. Adult parasites are found most commonly in the arteries and arterioles around the ileocecum and deposit eggs there. Both the eggs and worms provoke an inflammatory response, which results in occluded vessels, an accompanying vasculitis, and an eosinophilic, granulomatous, edematous mass.

Infection of humans, most commonly children, has been recognized in Central and South America, occasionally the Caribbean, and, rarely, Africa. The manner of human infection is not usually known, but it may occur after accidental ingestion of infected slugs or of foods contaminated with larvae deposited in the mucous slime trail of slugs. Mint was implicated in one small epidemic.[61]

Patients are mildly to moderately ill and complain of abdominal pain and tenderness, vomiting, and fever; a right lower quadrant mass is noted in about 50% of the cases.[62] Surgery reveals that the cecum, ascending colon, ileum, and appendix are involved to varied degrees. The syndrome resembles appendicitis, except for the usual presence of eosinophilia and leukocytosis in angiostrongyliasis. Perforation occurs uncommonly, and the worms may be found ectopically in extraintestinal sites.[62]

The diagnosis is suspected clinically and confirmed by examination of biopsied or excised specimens. Radiographic findings are nonspecific and show filling defects and spasticity of the ileum, cecum, or colon. Serologic tests have been described that are relatively sensitive and specific, but they are not widely available.[63]

Most patients undergo laparotomy with removal of the inflamed areas; the natural history of infected children is unclear. It is not known if specific anthelmintic therapy is effective, but some clinically diagnosed children have been treated with diethylcarbamazine and thiabendazole (75 mg/kg/day for 3 days; maximum 3 g/day, which may be toxic) without undergoing surgery. An alternative treatment is mebendazole, 200 to 400 mg three times a day for 10 days.

Massive ascaris infections may present with intestinal masses and may be confused with infections due to *Angiostrongylus costaricensis.* Infections can be prevented by treating potentially contaminated vegetables with 1.5% bleach at room temperature for 15 minutes.[64]

EOSINOPHILIC GASTROENTERITIS

One cause of eosinophilic gastroenteritis is infection of humans with *Ancylostoma caninum,* a hookworm of dogs.[65-67] This syndrome is apparently limited to Northern Australia, although the conditions for human infection are likely present in many regions. After invading the skin, the usually single larva migrates to the ileum, and to the colon to a lesser degree, where there is an intense focal response to the worm including ulceration, inflammatory nodules, inflammation, thickening, and stricture formation. Gastrointestinal pain, nausea, vomiting, diarrhea, and bowel obstruction are common and almost always are accompanied by eosinophilia and leukocytosis. Ova are not produced, but the adult worm can sometimes be seen by endoscopy. Patients respond to a standard course of mebendazole 100 mg three times daily for 3 days.

DIROFILARIASIS

Accidental human infections with *Dirofilaria* result most commonly in a lung nodule or subcutaneous mass. Two groups of parasites of the genus *Dirofilaria* accidentally infect humans.[1] The clinical presentations are generally different, which reflects the final location of the adults in the usual animal host. The adult worms of *Dirofilaria immitis,* the dog heartworm and the only important parasite in the first group, reside in the right side of the heart and the right pulmonary vessels; they are usually, but not always, located in the lungs in humans.

Dirofilaria immitis is transmitted by a mosquito to its most common host, the domesticated dog, and other related mammals. After development in subcutaneous tissues, the parasites migrate as young adults to the right side of the heart and the right pulmonary vessels. In humans, the immature filariae migrate similarly but do not fully develop and die instead, which causes a local vasculitis leading to pulmonary infarcts. Histologic examination usually reveals a dead worm in an infarct with vasculitis and with granulomatous and occasionally eosinophilic inflammation.

Most infections occur in the southeastern United States through infections and transmission to dogs and by accidental transmission to humans. Persons are asymptomatic in more than half of the infections and show a coin lesion on a routine chest radiograph.[68,69] Others complain of cough, chest pain, or hemoptysis, most likely due to pulmonary infarction. In some instances, lung infiltrates are noted that resolve into nodules.[70] Eosinophilia occurs in fewer than 15% of cases.

The diagnosis is made with certainty only by biopsy. Although serologic tests are available, their sensitivity and specificity are not adequate to rule out other potential life-threatening conditions such as a tumor.

Adults of the second group of filariae (subgenus *Nochtiella*) reside in the subcutaneous tissues of various mammals and usually cause inflammatory subcutaneous masses in humans.[71] These parasites include *D. tenuis* (raccoon), *D. ursi* (bear), *D. subdermata* (porcupines), and *D. repens* (dogs and cats in Europe and Asia). Patients present with inflammatory subcutaneous masses containing increased numbers of eosinophils. As in infections with *D. immitis,* there are few if any systemic symptoms, and eosinophilia is not usually present. The diagnosis is established by biopsy. However, careful inspection of the entire tissue may be needed to find the parasite.

CAPILLARIASIS

Capillaria philippinensis inhabits the small bowel of humans, causing diarrhea and malabsorption.[72] Infections have been recognized mostly in the Philippines but also in Thailand, Taiwan, Japan, Korea, Egypt, and Iran. The life cycle is incompletely understood, although freshwater fish contain larvae infectious for humans and birds.[73] The latter may be an important reservoir host. After raw freshwater fish are eaten, the larvae invade the jejunum and ileum, and the resulting adults produce both eggs and larvae. Unlike almost all helminths that infect humans, with the exception of *Strongyloides stercoralis,* the parasite multiplies in the gut. This process is known as *autoinfection* and results in an overwhelming infection. In fulminant cases, autopsies reveal a thickened, edematous small bowel with a flattened mucosa containing a mononuclear infiltrate. Numerous adults, larvae, and eggs are present in both the lumen and the mucosa. Larvae infectious for birds, humans, and other mammals develop in certain freshwater fish after ingestion of eggs.[72,73] Almost all the signs and symptoms are related to progressive diarrhea and malabsorption. Patients complain of borborygmi, abdominal pain, vomiting, weight loss, and malaise resulting in wasting, abdominal distention, and edema.

Laboratory examinations document the typical findings of protein-losing enteropathy; fat, mineral, and vitamin malabsorption; and electrolyte loss.[72,73] Fever and eosinophilia are uncommon, although eosinophilia has been noted after therapy. The diagnosis is established by detecting the characteristic *Trichuris trichiura*-like ova or larvae in the stool. No serologic tests are available.

In untreated patients, mortality rates of up to 33% have been documented, but specific anthelmintic therapy is effective and life-saving. Therapy in the past included thiabendazole, 25 mg/kg/day for 30 days, but mebendazole, 200 mg orally twice daily for 20 days, or albendazole[73] has largely supplanted the use of thiabendazole. Relapses are treated with prolonged courses of therapy. Infection is prevented by eating only properly cooked freshwater fish.

NANOPHYETIASIS

Human infections with *Nanophyetus salmincola,* a diminutive small intestine-dwelling trematode, have been increasingly recognized in the Pacific Northwest of the United States.[74] Humans and other mammals and birds become infected after ingesting raw or undercooked freshwater fish (most commonly salminoid fish) or their eggs.

Gastrointestinal symptoms, including diarrhea, abdominal pain, and gas or bloating with accompanying eosinophilia, suggest the diagnosis. However, asymptomatic infections are common. The diagnosis is established by finding the characteristic operculated ova in the feces. They measure 64 to 97 × 34 to 55 µm and are nonembryonated when shed. Because the number of ova shed may be small, methods that concentrate ova in stool should be employed. Praziquantel, 20 mg/kg three times for 1 day, is effective treatment.

Swimmer's Itch or Schistosomal Dermatitis (Cercarial dermatitis, Clam digger's Itch)

Cercariae, the infective form of a large number of blood flukes of birds, such as avian schistosomes (commonly *Trichobilharzia*), those in nonhuman mammals, and less commonly human schistosomes, can cause a characteristic dermatitis in humans associated with penetration of the cercariae into the skin.[1] Although in some animal infection models cercariae from birds may migrate out of the skin and even survive for a limited time in other organs,[75] the clinical manifestations in humans are almost always limited to the skin. Infections are frequent in many areas of the world but are particularly common in persons exposed to the freshwater lakes of the northern United States. However, infections also occur after exposure to saltwater (clam digger's itch).

Although the clinical manifestations vary after the initial exposure, symptoms are typically mild and sometimes go unnoticed.[76,77] The patient complains of itching followed by the appearance of macules at the site of penetration of the cercariae. By 24 hours, the macules have disappeared and begin to be replaced by papules. After repeated exposures, reactions occur earlier than 24 hours after exposure and are more severe. Papules are larger and associated with erythema, itching, and edema. The symptoms subside by 4 to 7 days, but in severe cases they may last weeks.

Cercariae are produced by various species of mollusks, which are the intermediate hosts of these parasites. Control of infection can be obtained by ridding bathing areas of the molluscan intermediate host or the definitive host or by avoiding infected bodies of water. Treatment is symptomatic. There is no specific anthelmintic therapy.

REFERENCES

1. Beaver PC, Jung RC, Cupp EW. Clinical Parasitology. Philadelphia: Lea & Febiger; 1984.
2. Beaver PC, Snyder CH, Carrera GM, et al. Chronic eosinophilia due to visceral larva migrans: report of three cases. Pediatrics 1952;9:7.
3. Huntley CC, Costas MC, Lyerly BS. Visceral larva migrans syndrome: clinical characteristics and immunologic studies in 51 patients. Pediatrics 1965;36:523.
4. Glickman LT, Schantz PM. Epidemiology and pathogenesis of zoonotic toxocariasis. Epidemiol Rev 1981;3:230.
5. Worley G, Green JA, Frothingham TE, et al. Toxocara canis infection: clinical and epidemiological associations with seropositivity in kindergarten children. J Infect Dis 1984;159:591.
6. Jones WE, Schantz PM, Foreman K, et al. Human toxocariasis in a rural community. Am J Dis Child 1980;134:967.
7. Mok CH. Visceral larva migrans: a discussion based on review of the literature. Clin Pediatr 1968;7:565.
8. Glickman L, Schantz P, Dombroske R, et al. Evaluation of serodiagnostic tests for visceral larva migrans. Am J Trop Med Hyg 1978;27:492.
9. Cunningham CK, Kazacos KR, McMillan JA, et al. Diagnosis and management of Baylisascaris procyonis infection in an infant with nonfatal meningoencephalitis. Clin Infect Dis 1994;18:868.
10. Wilder HC. Nematode endophthalmitis. Trans Am Acad Ophthalmol Otolaryngol 1950;55:99.
11. Schantz PM, Meyer D, Glickman LT. Clinical, serologic, and epidemiologic characteristics of ocular toxocariasis. Am J Trop Med Hyg 1979;28:24.
12. Biglan AW, Glickman LT, Lobes LA. Serum and vitreous Toxocara antibody in nematode endophthalmitis. Am J Opthalmol 1979;88:898.
13. Felberg NT, Shields JA, Federman JL. Antibody to Toxocara canis in the aqueous humor. Arch Ophthalmol 1981;99:1563.
14. Gass JD, Braunstein RA. Further observations concerning the diffuse unilateral subacute neuroretinitis syndrome. Arch Ophthalmol 1983;101:1689-1697.
15. De Souza EC, Nakashima Y. Diffuse unilateral subacute neuroretinitis: report of transvitreal surgical removal of a subretinal nematode. Ophthalmology 1995;102:1183.
16. Gass JD, Callanan DG, Bowman CB. Oral therapy in diffuse unilateral subacute neuroretinitis. Arch Ophthalmol 1992;110:675.
17. Fox AS, Kazacos KR, Gould NS. Fatal eosinophilic meningoencephalitis and visceral larva migrans caused by the raccoon ascarid Baylisascaris procyonis. N Engl J Med 1985;312:1619.
18. Park SY, Glaser C, Murray WJ, et al. Raccoon roundworm (Baylisascaris procyonis) encephalitis: case report and field investigation. Pediatrics 2000;106:E56.
19. Rowley HA, Uht RM, Kazacos KR, et al. Radiologic-pathologic findings in raccoon roundworm (Baylisascaris procyonis) encephalitis. AJNR Am J Neuroradiol 2000;21:415.
20. Sorvillo F, Ash LR, Berlin OG, et al. Baylisascaris procyonis: an emerging helminthic zoonosis. Emerg Infect Dis 2002;8:355.
21. Smith JW, Wootten R. Anisakis and anisakiasis. In: Lumsden WHR, Muller R, Baker JR, eds. Advances in Parasitology, v. 16. London: Academic Press; 1978:93.
22. Van Thiel PH, Kuipers FC, Roskam RTH. A nematode parasitic to herring, causing acute abdominal syndromes in man. Trop Geogr Med 1960;2:97.
23. Yokogawa N, Yoshimura H. Clinicopathologic studies of larval anisakiasis in Japan. Am J Trop Med Hyg 1967;16:723.
24. Sugimachi K, Inokuchi K, Ooiwa T, et al. Acute gastric anisakiasis: analysis of 178 cases. JAMA 1985;253:1012.
25. Montoro A, Perteguer MJ, Chivato T, et al. Recidivous acute urticaria caused by Anisakis simplex. Allergy 1997;52:985.
26. Alonso A, Daschner A, Moreno-Ancillo A. Anaphylaxis with Anisakis simplex in the gastric mucosa. N Engl J Med 1997;337:350.
27. Del Pozo MD, Audicana M, Diez JM, et al. Anisakis simplex, a relevant etiologic factor in acute urticaria. Allergy 1997;52:576.
28. Moreno-Ancillo A, Caballero MT, Cabanas R, et al. Allergic reactions to Anisakis simplex parasitizing seafood. Ann Allergy Asthma Immunol 1997;79:246.

29. Daschner A, Alonso-Gomez A, Cabanas R, et al. Gastroallergic anisakiasis: border-line between food allergy and parasitic disease: clinical and allergologic evaluation of 20 patients with confirmed acute parasitism by Anisakis simplex. J Allergy Clin Immunol 2000;105:176.

30. Matsui T, Iida M, Murakami M, et al. Intestinal anisakiasis: clinical and radiologic features. Radiology 1985;157:299.

31. Kusuhara T, Watanabe K, Fukuda M. Radiographic study of acute gastric anisakiasis. Gastrointest Radiol 1984;9:305.

32. Shirahama M, Koga T, Ishibashi H, et al. Intestinal anisakiasis: US in diagnosis. Radiology 1991;185:789.

33. Ishikura H, Kikuchi K, Nagasawa K, et al. Anisakidae and anisakiosis. Prog Clin Parasitol 1993;3:4.

34. Moore DA, Girdwood RW, Chiodini PL. Treatment of anisakiasis with albendazole. Lancet 2002;360:54.

35. KirbySmith JL, Dove WE, White GF. Some observations on creeping eruption. Am J Trop Med Hyg 1929;9:179.

36. Hitch JM. Systemic treatment of creeping eruption. Arch Dermatol Syph 1947;55:664.

37. Katz R, Ziegler J, Blank H. The natural course of creeping eruption and treatment with thiabendazole. Arch Dermatol 1965;91:420.

38. Davis CM, Israel RM. Treatment of creeping eruption with topical thiabendazole. Arch Dermatol 1968;97:325.

39. Caumes E. Treatment of cutaneous larva migrans and Toxocara infection. Fundam Clin Pharmacol 2003;17:213.

40. Bouchaud O, Houze S, Schiemann R, et al. Cutaneous larva migrans in travelers: a prospective study, with assessment of therapy with ivermectin. Clin Infect Dis 2000;31:493.

41. Kliks MM, Kroenke K, Hardman JM. Eosinophilic radiculomyeloencephalitis: an angiostrongyliasis outbreak in American Samoa related to ingestion of Achatina fulica snails. Am J Trop Med Hyg 1982;31:1114.

42. Punyagupta S, Juttijudata P, Bunnag T. Eosinophilic meningitis in Thailand: clinical studies of 484 typical cases probably caused by Angiostrongylus cantonensis. Am J Trop Med Hyg 1975;24:921.

43. Yii CY. Clinical observations on eosinophilic meningitis and meningoencephalitis caused by Angiostrongylus cantonensis in Taiwan. Am J Trop Med Hyg 1976;25:233.

44. Slom TJ, Cortese MM, Gerber SI, et al. An outbreak of eosinophilic meningitis caused by Angiostrongylus cantonensis in travelers returning from the Caribbean. N Engl J Med 2002;346:668.

45. Martinez-Delgado JF, Gonzalez-Cortinas M, Tapanes-Cruz TR, et al. Eosinophilic meningoencephalitis in Villa Clara (Cuba): a study of 17 patients. Rev Neurol 2000;31:417.

46. Brown FM, Mohareb EW, Yousif F, et al. Angiostrongylus eosinophilic meningitis in Egypt. Lancet 1996;348:964.

47. Rosen L, Chappell R, Laqueur GL, et al. Eosinophilic meningoencephalitis caused by a metastrongylid lungworm of rats. JAMA 1962;179:620.

48. Kanpittaya J, Jitpimolmard S, Tiamkao S, et al. MR findings of eosinophilic meningoencephalitis attributed to Angiostrongylus cantonensis. AJNR Am J Neuroradiol 2000;21:1090.

49. Nuamtanong S. The evaluation of the 29 and 31 kDa antigens in female Angiostrongylus cantonensis for serodiagnosis of human angiostrongyliasis. Southeast Asian J Trop Med Public Health 1996;27:291.

50. Chotmongkol V, Sawanyawisuth K, Thavornpitak Y. Corticosteroid treatment of eosinophilic meningitis. Clin Infect Dis 2000;31:660.

51. Chitanondh H, Rosen L. Fatal eosinophilic encephalomyelitis caused by the nematode Gnathostoma spinigerum. Am J Trop Med Hyg 1967;16:638.

52. Punyagupta S, Juttijudata P. Two fatal cases of eosinophilic myeloencephalitis, a newly recognized disease caused by Gnathostoma spinigerum. Trans R Soc Trop Med Hyg 1968;62:801.

53. Rusnak JM, Lucey DR. Clinical gnathostomiasis: case report and review of the English-language literature. Clin Infect Dis 1993;16:33.

54. Diaz Camacho SP, Zazueta Ramos M, Ponce Torrecillas E, et al. Clinical manifestations and immunodiagnosis of gnathostomiasis in Culiacan, Mexico. Am J Trop Med Hyg 1998;59:908.

55. Miyazaki I. On the genus Gnathostoma and human gnathostomiasis, with special reference to Japan. Exp Parasitol 1960;9:338.

56. Migasena S, Pitisuttithum P, Desakorn V. Gnathostoma larva migrans among guests of a New Year party. Southeast Asian J Trop Med Public Health 1991;22(Suppl):225.

57. Dharmkrong-at A, Migasena S, Suntharasamai P, et al. Enzyme-linked immunosorbent assay for detection of antibody to Gnathostoma antigen in patients with intermittent cutaneous migratory swelling. J Clin Microbiol 1986;23:847.

58. Kraivichian P, Kulkumthorn M, Yingyourd P, et al. Albendazole for the treatment of human gnathostomiasis. Trans R Soc Trop Med Hyg 1992;86:418.

59. Nontasut P, Bussaratid V, Chullawichit S, et al. Comparison of ivermectin and albendazole treatment for gnathostomiasis. Southeast Asian J Trop Med Public Health 2000;31:374.

60. Morera P, Cepedes R. Angiostrongylus costaricensis n. sp. (Nematoda: metastrongyloidea), a new lungworm occurring in man in Costa Rica. Rev Biol Trop 1971;18:173.

61. Kramer MH, Greer GJ, Quinonez JF, et al. First reported outbreak of abdominal angiostrongyliasis. Clin Infect Dis 1998;26:365.

62. Loria-Cortes R, Lobo-Sanahuga JF. Clinical abdominal angiostrongylosis: a study of 116 children with intestinal eosinophilic granuloma caused by Angiostrongylus costaricensis. Am J Trop Med Hyg 1980;29:538.

63. Geiger SM, Laitano AC, Sievers-Tostes C, et al. Detection of the acute phase of abdominal angiostrongyliasis with a parasite-specific IgG enzyme linked immunosorbent assay. Mem Inst Oswaldo Cruz 2001;96:515.

64. Zanini GM, Graeff-Teixeira C. Inactivation of infective larvae of Angiostrongylus costaricensis with short time incubations in 1.5% bleach solution, vinegar or saturated cooking salt solution. Acta Trop 2001;78:17.

65. Provic P, Croese J. Human eosinophilic enteritis caused by dog hookworm Ancylostoma caninum. Lancet 1990;335:1299.

66. Croese J, Loukas A, Opdebeeck J, et al. Human enteric infection with canine hookworms. Ann Intern Med 1994;120:369.

67. Croese TJ. Eosinophilic enteritis: a recent North Queensland experience. Aust N Z J Med 1988;18:848.

68. Orihel TC, Eberhard ML. Zoonotic filariasis. Clin Microbiol Rev 1998;11:366.

69. Cifferri F. Human pulmonary dirofilariasis in the United States: a critical review. Am J Trop Med Hyg 1982;31:302.

70. Kochar AS. Human pulmonary dirofilariasis: report of three cases and brief review of the literature. Am J Clin Pathol 1985;84:19.

71. Beaver PC, Wolfson JS, Waldron MA. Dirofilaria ursi-like parasites acquired by humans in the northern United States and Canada: report of two cases and brief review. Am J Trop Med Hyg 1987;37:357.

72. Whalen GE, Strickland GT, Cross HJ, et al. Intestinal capillariasis: a new disease in man. Lancet 1969;1:13.

73. Cross JH. Intestinal capillariasis. Clin Microbiol Rev 1992;5:120.

74. Fritsche TR, Eastburn RL, Wiggens LH, et al. Praziquantel for treatment of human Nanophyetus salmincola (Troglotrema salmincola) infection. J Infect Dis 1989;160:896.

75. Horak P, Kolarova L, Adema CM. Biology of the schistosome genus Trichobilharzia. Adv Parasitol 2002;52:155.

76. Olivier L. Schistosome dermatitis, a sensitization phenomenon. Am J Hyg 1949;49:290.

77. MacFarlane MV. Schistosome dermatitis in New Zealand. Part II. Pathology and immunology of cercarial lesions. Am J Hyg 1949;50:152.

SECTION K

ECTOPARASITIC DISEASES

CHAPTER **290**

Introduction
to Ectoparasitic Diseases

MICHAEL ERIC MATHIEU

BARBARA BRAUNSTEIN WILSON

An ectoparasite is an organism that derives benefit or fulfills a life cycle requirement through interaction with the outer, or cutaneous, surface of the host. Such organisms are generally members of the Arthropoda, a phylum of more than 1 million species. The term ectoparasite includes organisms that live on the host only long enough to obtain a blood meal as well as those that burrow into the superficial layers of the skin and remain there for weeks to months or even years if the host is left untreated.

Arthropods are invertebrates with a chitinous exoskeleton, an internal cavity containing a hemolymph-filled hemocoele and internal organs, a segmented body, and jointed appendages. Five classes of arthropods may affect the skin: Hexapoda, Arachnida, Diplopoda (millipedes), Chilopoda (centipedes), and Crustacea. Selected arthropods from Hexapoda and Arachnida are discussed in the following chapters. The class Hexapoda comprises insects, which are six-legged arthropods, and includes lice, bugs (e.g., bedbugs and kissing bugs), beetles, butterflies and moths, flies (including mosquitoes), fleas, ants, bees, and wasps. The class Arachnida comprises arachnids, which have eight legs, and includes mites, spiders, and ticks.

Stinging or vesicating arthropods, such as spiders, bees, ants, and caterpillars, inflict injury on the skin but do not obtain a blood meal and are therefore not considered true ectoparasites. Adult flies do not parasitize the skin, but their larval forms (maggots) can live off living or necrotic tissue, resulting in a condition known as *myiasis*.

Although ectoparasitic infestations remain a more frequent health problem in nonindustrialized tropical nations of the world, a variety of vector-borne zoonoses are of increasing concern in the United States.[1] In particular, tick-borne bacterial diseases including Lyme disease, human monocytic ehrlichiosis, and human granulocytic ehrlichiosis cause increasing morbidity, occasional mortality, and considerable anxiety among both patients and physicians.

Southern tick-associated rash illness is a recently described entity associated with *Ambylomma americanum,* the Lone Star tick. *Ambylomma americanum* is increasing in importance as a vector of human pathogens in the United States.[2] *Bartonella henselae* and *Bartonella quintana,* the etiologic agents of bacillary angiomatosis-peliosis in patients with acquired immunodeficiency syndrome, have been linked to the age-old ectoparasites fleas and lice, respectively.[3] In tropical climates, few natives escape some type of ectoparasitic disease, and the consequences of such disease can be mutilating, incapacitating, debilitating, or fatal. Not only do ectoparasites cause enormous economic losses to humans by virtue of human parasitism, they also parasitize domestic animals used for food and contribute greatly to the malnutrition found in underdeveloped countries.

Many bacterial, spirochetal, viral, rickettsial, helminthic, and protozoal diseases can be transmitted to humans by arthropod vectors. Table 290-1 lists some arthropod-borne diseases.

ERADICATION, CONTROL, AND PREVENTION

For most ectoparasites, eradication is not a practical approach because of the substantial reservoir of wild animals which allows perpetuation of the species. Elimination of some species from domestic animals is reasonable in certain climates but is a virtual impossibility in other regions of the world. In many instances, improvements in sanitation and improved socioeconomic factors do more to reduce parasitism for humans than do attempts to eliminate the arthropods.

It is sometimes possible, however, to control important diseases in humans and livestock by controlling the arthropod vectors responsible for the transmission of those diseases. Such large-scale programs often require cooperation between governmental agencies at various levels for effective implementation. Methods used to control arthropod vectors include the use of insecticides, biologic interference with the arthropod's life cycle, and environmental manipulations that limit breeding and spread of the undesirable arthropod species. Unfortunately, the widespread use of insecticides may induce the development of resistance in the arthropods, thereby requiring the development of new and different toxic agents. Extensive use of insecticides creates anxiety and controversy because of the possible hazardous effects they may have on people, animals, and the environment.

Diseases spread by arthropods can be limited not only by controlling the arthropod vector but also by preventing access of the arthropod to its host. When possible, fine screening should be used on windows and doors to prevent entrance of flying arthropods into dwellings. Homes built above the ground are less accessible to crawling arthropods. Regular grooming and treatment of infested animals can reduce animal reservoirs of arthropods. Protective clothing and insect repellents applied to the skin or clothes are also effective means of protecting humans from arthropods.

The active ingredient in most of the insect repellents available in the United States is either *N,N*-diethyl-*m*-toluamide (DEET) or ethyl hexanediol. DEET-containing products still offer the longest duration of insect-repelling effect against mosquitoes.[4] This agent is less effective at repelling ticks, however. DEET can damage synthetic plastic material

TABLE 290-1 **Selected Diseases Transmitted by Arthropods**

Infectious Disease	Vector
Anaplasmosis (human granulocytotropic)	Hard ticks
Arbovirus diseases (including yellow fever, dengue fever, encephalitis)	Mosquitoes and ticks
Babesiosis	Hard ticks
Boutonneuse fever (tick bite fever) (*Rickettsia conorii*)	Rabbit flea
Chagas disease	Triatome (kissing) bugs
Colorado tick fever	Hard ticks
Ehrlichiosis, monocytotropic and ewingii	Hard ticks
Endemic relapsing fever (*Borrelia duttonii*)	Soft ticks
Epidemic relapsing fever (*Borrelia recurrentis*)	Human body lice
Epidemic typhus (*Rickettsia prowazekii*)	Human body lice
Filiariasis (*Wuchereria bancrofti, Brugia malayi*)	Mosquitoes
Leishmaniasis (*Leishmania* spp.)	Lutzomyia sandfly in the Americas, Phlebotomid flies elsewhere
Loiasis (*Loa loa*)	Tabanid flies
Lyme disease (*Borrelia burgodorferi*)	Hard ticks
Malaria (*Plasmodium* spp.)	Mosquitoes
Murine typhus (*Rickettsia mooseri*)	Rat fleas, lice
Onchocerciasis (*Onchocerca volvulus*)	Black flies
Plague (*Yersinia pestis*)	Rat fleas
Q fever (*Coxiella burnetii*)	Hard ticks, fleas
Rickettsialpox (*Rickettsia akari*)	Mouse mites and other spotted fevers
Rocky Mountain spotted fever (*Rickettsia rickettsii*)	Hard ticks
Scrub typhus (*Rickettsia tsutsugamushi*)	Mites (chiggers)
Trypanosomiasis, African sleeping sickness	Glossina (tsetse) flies
West Nile fever	Mosquitoes

such as found in clothing or eyeglass frames. The safety of DEET has been considered in a number of analyses. Of 20,764 inappropriate exposure incidents reported to poison control centers in the United States from 1993 to 1997, two deaths, both of adult patients, were reported.[5] Even a cohort of pregnant women deliberately exposed to DEET during the second and third trimesters had no ill effects, nor did their offspring at up to 1 year of follow-up.[6] Other agents with efficacy similar to that of DEET, such as picaridin, may become available in the future.[7]

REFERENCES

1. Walker DH, Barbour AG, Oliver JH, et al. Emerging bacterial zoonotic and vector-borne diseases: ecological and epidemiological factors. JAMA 1996;275:463-469.
2. Childs JE, Paddock CD. The ascendancy of Ambylomma americanum as a vector of pathogens affecting humans in the United States. Annu Rev Entomol 2003;48:307-337.
3. Koehler JE, Sanchez MA, Garrido CS, et al. Molecular epidemiology of Bartonella infections in patients with bacillary angiomatosis-peliosis. N Engl J Med 1997;337:1876-1883.
4. Fradin MS, Day JF. Comparative efficacy of insect repellents against mosquito bites. N Engl J Med 2002;347:13-18.
5. Bell JW, Veltri JC, Page BC. Human exposures to N,N-diethyl-m-toluamide insect repellents reported to the American Association of Poison Control Centers 1993-1997. Int J Toxicol 2002;21:341-352.
6. McGready R, Hamilton KA, Simpson JA, et al. Safety of the insect repellent N,N-diethyl-m-toluamide (DEET) in pregnancy. Am J Trop Med Hyg 2001;65:285-289.
7. Anonymous. Insect repellents. Med Lett Drugs Ther 2003;45:41-42.

BIBLIOGRAPHY

Alexander JO. Arthropods and Human Skin. New York: Springer-Verlag; 1984.
Derbes VJ. Injurious effects in man induced by animals. In: Demis DJ, ed. Clinical Dermatology. Philadelphia: JB Lippincott; 1991.
Honig PJ. Arthropod bites, stings, and infestations: their prevention and treatment. Pediatr Dermatol 1986;3:189-197.
James MT. Herm's Medical Entomology, 7th ed. New York: Macmillan; 1969.

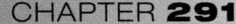

CHAPTER **291**

Lice (Pediculosis)

MICHAEL ERIC MATHIEU

BARBARA BRAUNSTEIN WILSON

THE ORGANISMS

The order Anoplura (sucking lice) contains more than 200 species, of which only two genera, *Pediculus* and *Phthirus,* are parasitic for humans. The species of medical importance are *Pediculus humanus* var. *corporis,* the human body louse; *Pediculus humanus* var. *capitis,* the human head louse; and *Phthirus pubis,* the pubic or crab louse.

The body louse and head louse are morphologically similar, small (2 to 4 mm), grayish white, flattened, wingless, elongated insects with pointed heads. From each segment of the fused triple-segmented thorax, a pair of jointed legs protrudes that end in claw-like projections (Fig. 291-1). The pubic louse is distinctively different in shape, being much wider and shorter than its cousins and resembling a crab, from whence its nickname was derived (Fig. 291-2). Only the body lice transmit disease agents.

Eggs laid by the fertilized adult female are firmly glued to body hairs or fibers of clothing and appear as small globoid or oval protrusions called nits (Fig. 291-3). Approximately 7 to 10 days after deposition, small voracious nymphs emerge that must feed within 24 hours to survive. After 2 to 3 weeks and three successive molts, the mature adults mate. The fertilized females produce 250 to 300 eggs over the next 20 to 30 days and then die.

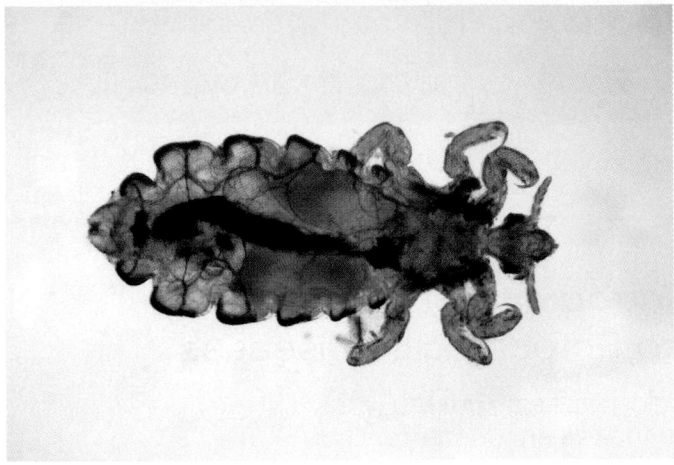

FIGURE 291-1. Pediculus humanus *var.* capitis *(head louse).*

Lice pierce the skin, inject saliva, and defecate while obtaining a blood meal. The pruritic papules that follow are secondary to the hypersensitivity reaction of the host to antigens present in the saliva.

EPIDEMIOLOGY

Lice infestations have been observed in virtually every inhabited area of the world. Major epidemics have occurred at times of war, overcrowding, or widespread inattention to personal hygiene.

Lice are medically important because not only can they cause significant cutaneous disease, they serve as vectors for infectious diseases. The body louse is a known vector for epidemic typhus *(Rickettsia prowazekii),* trench fever *(Bartonella quintana),* and relapsing fever *(Borrelia recurrentis).*

Pediculosis Capitis

Persons from all social and economic backgrounds can become infested with head lice, and infestations can reach epidemic proportions, especially among schoolchildren. The disease is more common in whites than blacks, females than males, and children than adults. Lice are transferred by close personal contact and possibly by the sharing of hats, combs, and brushes.

Pediculosis Corporis

Pediculosis corporis (body louse) is seen primarily where overcrowding and poor sanitation exist. The body louse lays its eggs (nits) and resides in the seams of the clothing rather than on the skin of its host.

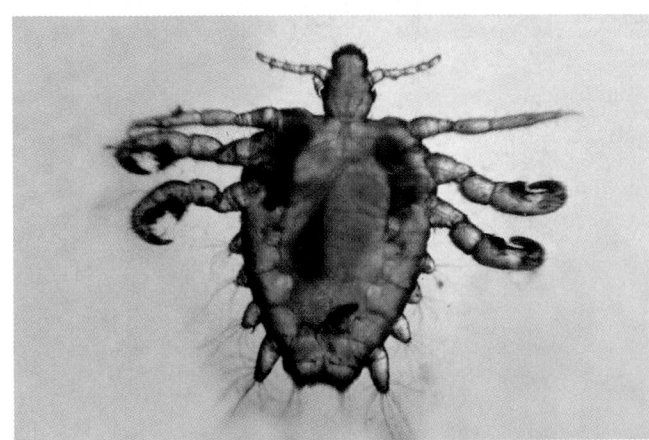

FIGURE 291-2. Phthirus pubis *(pubic louse).*

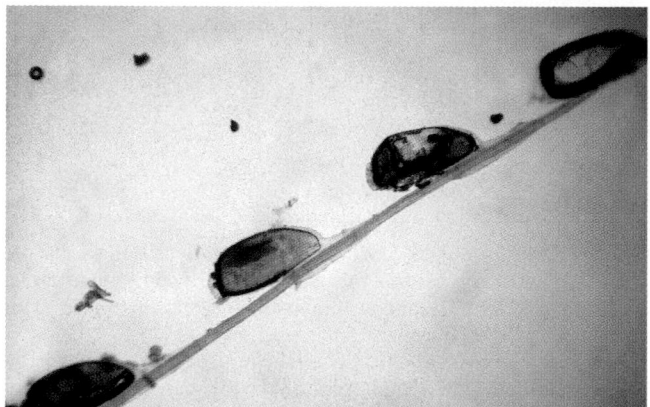

FIGURE 291-3. Nits (ova) of head louse attached to scalp hairs.

It leaves the clothing only to obtain a blood meal from its host. Nits present in the clothing are viable for up to 1 month.

Phthirus pubis

Phthirus pubis (pubic louse) infestation is transmitted by sexual or close body contact. The pubic louse resides primarily in the pubic hair but can also be seen in the eyebrows, eyelashes, axillary hair, and coarse hair on the back and chest of males. The pubic louse also occasionally infests scalp hair.[1] As many as one-third of individuals infested with pubic lice harbor another sexually transmitted disease.[2]

CLINICAL MANIFESTATIONS

Pediculosis Capitis

Adult head lice and nits localize primarily in the temporal and occipital areas of the scalp; however, the entire scalp and the beard area may be involved. The adult lice may be difficult to observe, but the nits that are firmly attached to the base of the hair shaft are easily seen. The major complaint of persons afflicted with head lice is severe pruritus of the scalp. Scratching leads to excoriations and secondary bacterial infection manifested by weeping and crusting of the scalp as well as tender occipital and cervical adenopathy.

The diagnosis of head lice is certain if viable organisms are found on the scalp. Less certain is how one should respond to the presence of nits alone. The presence of nits was associated with eventual clinical disease (conversion) in only 18% of subjects, whereas five or more nits within 0.25 inch of the scalp was associated with conversion in 31.8%.[3] Combing the hair with a fine-toothed, 0.2 to 0.3-mm tooth separation comb may increase the sensitivity and efficiency of louse detection.[4] The diagnosis of head lice infestation in the absence of viable organisms thus requires careful clinical judgment.

Pediculosis Corporis

Except in cases of severe infestation, the adult body louse is not seen on the skin but can be found in the seams of clothing. Patients complain of pruritus and develop small erythematous macules, papules, and excoriations primarily on the trunk. Secondary impetiginization may occur. Persons with long-standing untreated pediculosis corporis may develop generalized hyperpigmentation and thickening of the skin with evidence of numerous healed excoriations, an entity known as vagabonds' disease.

Phthirus pubis

The primary complaint of persons infested with *P. pubis* is marked pruritus of all affected areas, which may include axillary and coarse truncal hairs and eyelashes as well as pubic hair. Erythematous macules and papules with excoriations and secondary infection may be seen, but the cutaneous findings are less severe than those in patients with pediculosis capitis or corporis. The nits and occasionally the adult pubic lice are seen attached to the base of the hairs.

Small gray to bluish macules measuring less than 1 cm in diameter may be seen on the trunk, thighs, and upper parts of the arms. These lesions, known as maculae ceruleae (blue spots), are thought to be caused by an anticoagulant that is injected into the skin by the biting louse. Infestations of the eyelashes by pubic lice can cause crusting of the lid margins. In such cases, the nits are readily seen at the base of the lashes.

THERAPY

Pediculosis Capitis

Therapy has been recently reviewed.[5] Standard pediculicides include 1% lindane, gamma benzene hexachloride shampoo (Kwell), pyrethrins with piperonyl butoxide solution (RID, A-200 pyrinate liquid), 1% permethrin cream rinse (Nix), and 0.5% malathion lotion (Ovide). Although these agents are generally still effective, increasing reports of permethrin-resistant head lice from a number of locations suggest that global dissemination of resistant organisms may eventually occur.[6-8]

Malathion lotion, which has now been reintroduced in the United States, has been shown to be more effective than lindane and the pyrethrins; of the three, it is the only product with excellent ovicidal activity, so a single treatment suffices.[9] Objections to malathion include an unpleasant odor and a treatment time of 8 to 10 hours compared with 10 minutes for the other agents. In the United States, though not in the United Kingdom, a prescription is required to obtain malathion.

The recommended treatment of choice for head lice is 1% permethrin cream rinse.[9] Permethrin is a synthetic pyrethroid with higher activity than the parent compound pyrethrin.[10] Pyrethrins are natural extracts of chrysanthemum species and are combined with piperonyl butoxide, generally in a shampoo vehicle. Such products should be avoided in persons with known allergy to the Compositae family of plants. Both agents are cosmetically acceptable and easy to use, each requiring only a 10-minute application to the scalp. This treatment is repeated in 1 week because nits are more resistant than are living lice, 20% to 30% surviving a single treatment with either pyrethroid. The 1-week interval allows any remaining eggs to hatch into the more susceptible form of the organism.[11]

Lindane offers no advantage over the other agents. Although toxicity resulting from lindane has been reported when it has been improperly used for the treatment of scabies, toxicity is unlikely when treating pediculosis because the short treatment time minimizes the likelihood of systemic absorption of the agent through the skin.

Nits should be removed from the hairs by applying a solution of equal parts of vinegar and water and then combing the hair with a fine-toothed comb that has been dipped in vinegar. Combs and brushes should be soaked in a pediculicide for 1 hour.

Apparent clinical treatment failure may be due to improper use of therapeutic agents, misperception regarding the presence or absence of disease, or the presence of resistant organisms. If, by the process of elimination, resistance is likely, one may consider alternative approaches, such as (1) the application of petrolatum under a shower cap overnight, which is believed to asphyxiate lice; (2) combination therapy with permethrin 1% cream rinse and oral trimethoprim/sulfamethoxazole, which increases the efficacy of permethrin alone from 80% to 95%[12]; or (3) malathion lotion, as discussed above.

Pediculosis Corporis

The patient with body lice does not require treatment, but the patient's clothes must be treated. Body lice can be eradicated by discarding the clothing, when practical, or laundering the clothes in the hot cycle and then carefully ironing the seams of clothing. Body lice can also be eliminated by dusting the clothing with either 1% malathion powder or 10% DDT powder.

Phthirus pubis

Phthirus pubis may be treated with lindane, permethrin, pyrethrin, or malathion, as described for pediculosis capitis. The pediculicides should be applied to all affected areas except the eyelids. Eyelid infestation can be effectively treated by applying a thick layer of petrolatum to the eyelid margins twice a day for 8 days or 1% yellow oxide of mercury four times daily for 2 weeks.[13] Sexual contacts should be treated when possible.

Symptomatic treatment of pruritus due to all three types of infestation consists of adequate doses of antihistamines such as hydroxyzine 25 to 50 mg three or four times daily. Medium- to high-potency topical corticosteroids such as triamcinolone or fluocinolone cream should be applied to affected areas two or three times daily. When secondary bacterial infection is present, *Staphylococcus aureus* is a frequent cause; such patients should be treated with a systemic antibiotic such as dicloxacillin 250 mg four times a day for 10 days.

PREVENTION

The spread of pediculosis capitis can be minimized by improving living conditions, such as eliminating overcrowding, and avoiding the sharing of hats, combs, and hairbrushes. Of particular concern is how the health care professional should respond to an index case of head lice in a school-age child, as such children are often excluded from school as a matter of policy. After assessing the currently available data, the American Academy of Pediatrics has concluded that head lice screening programs have not shown proven efficacy and that "no nit" policies are misguided. Healthy children therefore should not miss school because of actual or suspected head lice infestation.[14] Body lice are rarely seen in those with good personal hygiene who change their clothes frequently. Pubic lice are best prevented by avoiding sexual or close body contact with infested individuals.

REFERENCES

1. Mueller JF. Pubic lice from the scalp hair: a report of two cases. J Parasitol 1973;59:943-944.
2. Chapel TA, Katta T, Kusamar T, et al. Ped. pubis in a clinic for treatment of sexually transmitted diseases. Sex Transm Dis 1979;6:257.
3. Williams LK, Reichert A, MacKenzie WR, et al. Lice, nits, and school policy. Pediatrics 2001;107:1011-1015.
4. Mumcuoglu KY, Friger M, Ioffe-Upensky I, et al. Louse comb versus direct visual examination for the diagnosis of head louse infestations. Pediatr Dermatol 2001;18:9-12.
5. Jones KN, English JC III. Review of common therapeutic options in the United States for the treatment of pediculosis capitis. Clin Infect Dis 2003;36:1355-1361.
6. Downs AM, Stafford KA, Hunt LP, et al. Widespread insecticide resistance in head lice to the over-the-counter pediculocides in England, and the emergence of carbaryl resistance. Br J Dermatol 2002;146:88-93.
7. Mumcuoglu KY, Hemingway J, Miller J, et al. Permethrin resistance in the head louse Pediculus capitis from Israel. Med Vet Entomol 1995;9:427-432.
8. Rupes V, Moravec J, Chmela J, et al. A resistance of head lice (Pediculus capitis) to permethrin in Czech Republic. Central Eur J Public Health 1995;3:30-32.
9. Anonymous. Malathion for treatment of head lice. Med Lett. 1999;41:73-74.
10. Anonymous. Drugs for head lice. Med Lett. 1997;39:6-7.
11. Meinking TL, Taplin D, Kalter DC, Eberle MW. Comparative efficacy of treatments for pediculosis capitis infestations. Arch Dermatol 1986;122:267-271.
12. Hipolito RB, Mallorca FG, Zuniga-Macaraig ZO, et al. Head lice infestation: single drug versus combination therapy with one percent permethrin and trimethoprim/sulfamethoxazole. Pediatrics 2001;107:575.
13. Ashkenazi L, Desatnik HR, Abraham FA. Yellow mercuric oxide: a treatment of choice for phthriasis palpebrum. Br J Ophthalmol 1991;75:356-358.
14. Frankowski BL, Weiner LB, Committee on School Health, Committee on Infectious Disease. American Academy of Pediatrics clinical report: head lice. Pediatrics 2002;110:638-643.

BIBLIOGRAPHY

Alexander JO. Arthropods and Human Skin. New York: Springer-Verlag; 1984.
Hogan DJ, Schachner L, Tanglertsampan C. Diagnosis and treatment of childhood scabies and pediculosis. Pediatr Dermatol 1991;38:941-957.
Honig PJ. Arthropod bites, stings and infestations: their prevention and treatment. Pediatr Dermatol 1986;3:189-197.

CHAPTER 292

Scabies

MICHAEL ERIC MATHIEU
BARBARA BRAUNSTEIN WILSON

THE ORGANISMS

Human scabies is a highly contagious infestation caused by the "itch mite," *Sarcoptes scabiei* var. *hominis,* which belongs to the class Arachnida. The scabies mite is an obligate parasite that burrows into and resides and reproduces in human skin.

Two or three eggs are laid daily by the fertilized female in burrows several millimeters in length created at the base of the stratum corneum of the epidermis. After 72 to 84 hours larvae emerge and after several molts become adult mites; they then mate after about 17 days. The males die shortly, but the gravid females live 4 to 6 weeks.[1] The full-grown adult female measures about 0.35 mm in length, is rounded, and has four pairs of short, stubby legs (Fig. 291-1).

EPIDEMIOLOGY

Scabies is worldwide in distribution and occurs in all races and social classes. Epidemics have been associated with war; however, conditions of poverty, poor hygiene, overcrowding, malnutrition, and sexual promiscuity are probably contributory factors as well. Although the scabies mite can cause significant cutaneous disease, it is not a vector for infectious diseases.

Scabies is transmitted by intimate personal contact, often sexual in nature, although casual contact, including that with nursing attendants, may be adequate for transmission, and institutional epidemics can occur. Live mites can be found in dust samples from homes of infested persons, suggesting that fomites may be an important factor in the transmission of scabies.[2] Studies suggest that an impregnated female mite can survive on human hosts for as long as 2 days.[3]

The clinical picture of scabies is usually fairly characteristic but extremely variable, depending on the degree and duration of the infestation. Fastidious individuals who wash frequently may have fewer, more subtle lesions, whereas those who neglect themselves are more likely to have extensive cutaneous disease.

CLINICAL MANIFESTATIONS

Human Scabies

Most individuals infested with the scabies mite complain of intense itching that is usually more severe at night. Erythematous papules, excoriations, and occasionally vesicles are noted in areas of predilection such as the interdigital web spaces, wrists, anterior axillary folds, peri-

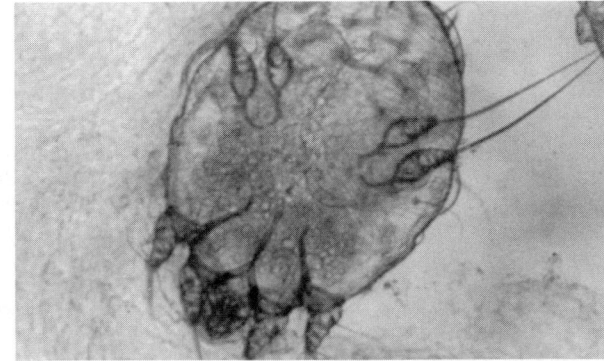

FIGURE 292-1. Scabies organism in a wet mount preparation.

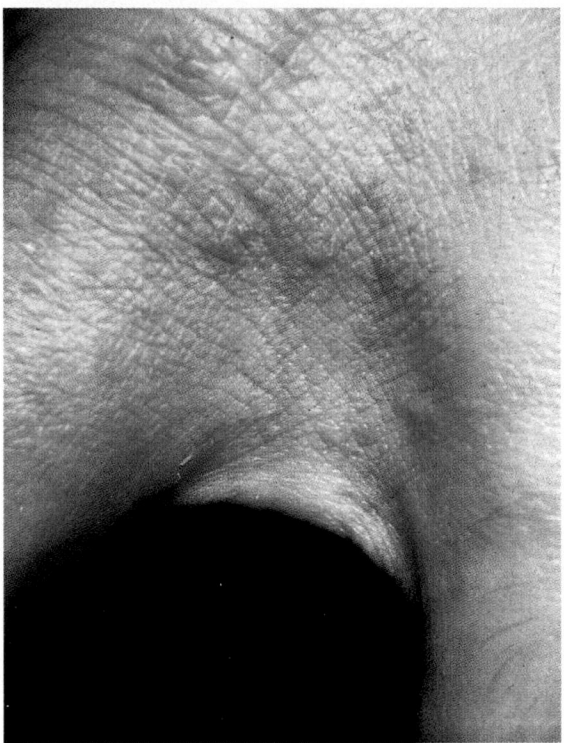

FIGURE 292-2. Erythematous papules and small burrows between fingers in a patient with scabies.

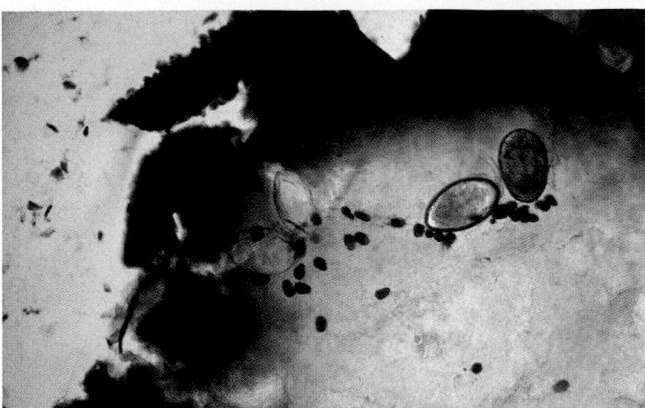

FIGURE 292-3. Eggs and feces can be seen on skin scrapings.

umbilical skin, pelvic girdle, penis, and ankles. In infants and small children the palms, soles, face, neck, and scalp are often involved. One should look carefully for classic linear burrows, particularly in the interdigital spaces and on the wrists and ankles (Fig. 292-2).

Infested male individuals may have pruritic, erythematous papules and nodules on the scrotum and penis (Fig. 292-3). The diagnosis is confirmed microscopically by demonstrating the organism, eggs, or feces in skin scrapings (Fig. 292-4). Skin samples are obtained by scraping or shaving the superficial layers of skin over a burrow with a no. 15 scalpel blade to a depth at which pinpoint bleeding occurs. In the normal host there are usually no more than 5 to 10 adult mites present, most of which reside on the hands and wrists.

Secondary impetiginization, usually caused by *Staphylococcus aureus,* may develop and obscure the underlying condition. A background eczematous eruption may be present and is probably related to the development of hypersensitivity of the host to the scabies mite. Treatment with topical or systemic corticosteroids may alter the clinical picture so the disease remains unrecognized, an entity known as *scabies incognito.* Chronic infestations, especially in children, may lead to the development of pruritic reddish brown nodules, especially on the penis and scrotum and in the axillae (Fig. 292-5). These lesions are thought to be a manifestation of strong delayed hypersensitivity to retained mite products, and it may take weeks or months before they disappear even after adequate therapy.

Norwegian Scabies

A severe variant of scabies known as *Norwegian* or *crusted scabies* can occur, usually in institutionalized persons, particularly those with Down syndrome and in individuals who are debilitated or immunosuppressed, including patients with acquired immunodeficiency syndrome.[4,5] Cutaneous lesions consist of widespread, hyperkeratotic, crusted nodules and plaques (Figs. 292-5 and 292-6). The nails are frequently involved and demonstrate thickening and subungual debris. Secondary bacterial infection, septicemia, and death have been reported.[5] Patients with Norwegian scabies are heavily infested with

mites and harbor tens of thousands of organisms, compared with the 5 or 10 present in immunocompetent hosts with scabies. Patients are therefore highly contagious and require special control measures to prevent transmission of the disease.

Animal Scabies

Occasionally, dogs with sarcoptic mange caused by *S. scabiei* var. *canis* are responsible for minor epidemics of mite bites, usually in members of a family. The lesions are pruritic, papular, or urticarial and are located primarily on the trunk, arms, axillae, and breasts. No burrows are seen because the organisms cannot complete their life cycle on humans. Eradicating the infestation of the animal produces prompt subsidence of the condition.

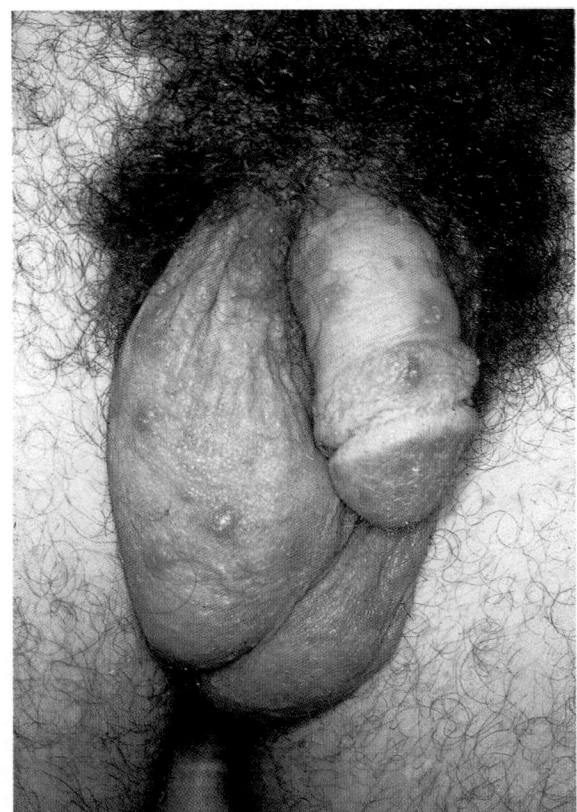

FIGURE 292-4. Typical lesions of scabies on the penis.

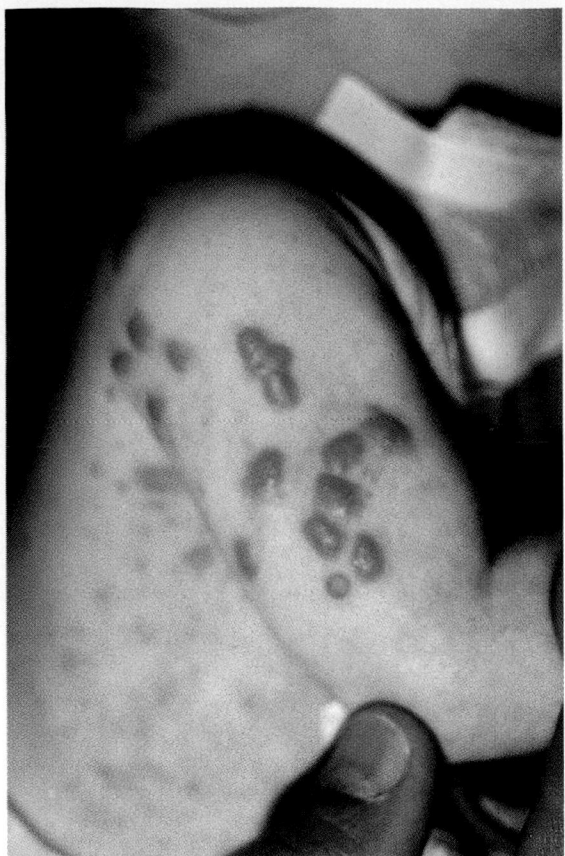

FIGURE 292-5. Nodular scabies on the arm of an infant *(Courtesy of Dr. Kenneth E. Greer, Charlottesville, VA.)*

TREATMENT AND PREVENTION

Lindane 1% lotion is highly effective against scabies and has been the treatment of choice for years. Permethrin 5% cream has become available and has been shown to have an even higher cure rate for scabies than lindane.[6,7] Lindane is not recommended for pregnant women or very young children, especially premature infants, because it is absorbed through the skin and can cause side effects such as irritability, seizures, and even death.[6] In most instances, such side effects have been attributed to overuse or accidental ingestion of the medication. Lindane is applied to the entire skin surface from the chin to the tips of the toes, and it is left on for 8 to 12 hours. Lindane should not be applied immediately after a bath because systemic absorption and possible toxic-

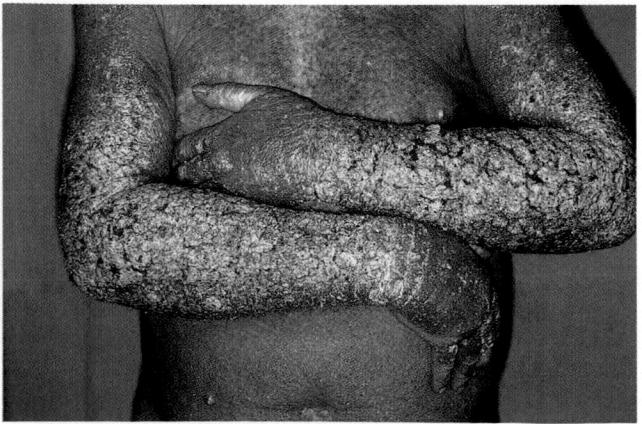

FIGURE 292-6. Marked hyperkeratosis on arms of a patient with Norwegian scabies. *(Courtesy of Dr. Kenneth E. Greer, Charlottesville, VA.)*

ity are enhanced.[2] In children the head is also treated, and the medication is left on for only 6 to 8 hours to minimize transcutaneous absorption. The treatment is repeated in 1 week. Fingernails should be trimmed because they may harbor mites. If the hands are washed for any reason, the medication is reapplied. Patients should be forewarned that even after adequate therapy pruritus may persist up to 2 weeks.

Permethrin 5% cream is cosmetically acceptable. It is poorly absorbed through the skin and is therefore less likely to cause systemic side effects.[7] One application is usually curative. It is applied as was described for lindane and is washed off after 8 to 10 hours. It is safe for use in children 2 months and older; although it may be safe to use during pregnancy, no confirmatory controlled studies have been performed. Pregnant women and infants can be treated with 6% to 10% precipitated sulfur in petrolatum daily for 3 days.[2]

If there is any evidence of secondary bacterial infection, patients should be treated with an antistaphylococcal antibiotic. Pruritus is treated with antihistamines and a topical lotion containing an antipruritic medication such as pramoxine or menthol.

Norwegian scabies is more difficult to treat because of the high mite population as well as a decreased immune response by the host. In such cases, the cure rate may be improved by hydrating the skin via soaking in a tub of lukewarm water for 10 minutes before therapy. Permethrin or lindane is applied immediately after the bath and again in 12 hours; it is then left on for another 12 hours. This regimen should be repeated in 1 week. One week after therapy, skin scrapings should be obtained and the patient retreated if mites are still present. Secondary bacterial infection should be treated.

Orally administered ivermectin is a useful systemic treatment for scabies. Mites become toxic and perish after ingesting host intercellular fluid. The extensive experience with ivermectin for treating other diseases, particularly onchocerciasis and strongyloidiasis, suggests that the drug is safe. Placebo-controlled trials have confirmed the efficacy of single-dose treatment in otherwise normal hosts and in most patients infected with the human immunodeficiency virus, the latter group often being more difficult to treat with standard therapy. In addition to eradication of mites, patients note rapid resolution of pruritus soon after taking the medication.[8] The ease with which ivermectin is administered offers a unique advantage over other forms of therapy.

The overall efficacy of ivermectin in the treatment of scabies relative to standard therapy is not clear. A single dose of ivermectin may be superior to one application of lindane 1% lotion in routine cases, but two applications of lindane yield a similar outcome.[9] One study found that a single application of permethrin 5% cream was modestly superior to a single dose of ivermectin (200 mg/kg body weight) in the treatment of uncomplicated cases, but two doses of ivermectin were as efficacious as a single permethrin cream application.[10] Neither of these comparative studies has been corroborated in separate investigations. Also uncertain is the ideal dose of ivermectin. Although 200 μg/kg is the commonly used dosage, no controlled trials have compared various doses for treating scabies to determine the optimal dose. Patients with more severe disease may require a second or even third treatment, and patients with crusted disease should be treated simultaneously with topical therapy, such as 5% permethrin cream.

The role of ivermectin in the treatment of scabies is thus still under investigation. When compliance with the proper application of topical therapy is difficult, oral ivermectin may be more appropriate. Nursing homes and other instituitions in which treatment of many individuals simultaneously is indicated may be the most appropriate setting for the use of ivermectin at present.

The extensive experience with ivermectin for treating other diseases suggests that the drug is safe in patients weighing more than 15 kg. However, a report of increased mortality among elderly institutionalized patients over a 6-month period after treatment for an outbreak of scabies has given reason to question the safety of ivermectin, although other investigators have refuted such an association.[11,12]

It is important that not only the patient but also household members and close contacts be treated at the same time. Any clothes worn or bed linens used during the 3 days before therapy should be laundered in hot, soapy water and dried in the hot cycle of the dryer. Such high temperatures should be sufficient to kill mites and their eggs.

Institutional Scabies

Scabies outbreaks are a major problem in hospitals and nursing homes, where patients require much hands-on nursing care, leading to transmission of disease between patients and nursing personnel.[7] Juranek and colleagues[13] made several control-measure recommendations to be followed if scabies occurs in a hospitalized patient or hospital employee. The management of scabies outbreaks in institutions depends on whether the index case has typical scabies or Norwegian scabies. If a patient has typical scabies, for at least 8 hours after treatment the nursing personnel should wear gloves while caring for that patient or handling the patient's clothes or bed linens. Close contacts should be treated prophylactically.

Patients with Norwegian scabies are highly contagious and require isolation. When possible, the nurse in charge of the patient with Norwegian scabies should have no responsibility for other patients. Nursing personnel and visitors should wear disposable gowns, gloves, and shoe covers when in contact with the patient. The gown may be sprayed with an insect repellent such as Off or a Cutter brand product if it is necessary to lift or handle the patient. The protective disposable clothing are discarded in a plastic bag. Clothes and bed linens are placed in a plastic laundry bag and handled only by personnel wearing gloves.

REFERENCES

1. Alexander JO. Arthropods and Human Skin. New York: Springer-Verlag; 1984.
2. Hogan DJ, Schachner L, Tanglertsampan C. Diagnosis and treatment of childhood scabies and pediculosis. Pediatr Dermatol 1991;38:941-957.
3. Arlian LG, Estes SA, Vyszenski-Moher DL. Prevalence of Sarcoptes scabiei in the homes and nursing homes of scabietic patients. J Am Acad Dermatol 1988;19:806-811.
4. Glover R, Young L, Goltz RW. Norwegian scabies in acquired immunodeficiency syndrome: report of a case resulting in death from associated sepsis. J Am Acad Dermatol 1987;16:396-399.
5. Orkin M. Scabies in AIDS. Semin Dermatol 1993;12:9-14.
6. Haustein UF, Hlawa B. Treatment of scabies with permethrin vs lindane and benzyl benzoate. Acta Derm Venereol (Stockh) 1989;69:348-351.
7. Taplin D, Meinking TL, Porcelain SL, et al. Permethrin 5% dermal cream: a new treatment for scabies. J Am Acad Dermatol 1986;15:995-1001.
8. Meinking TL, Taplin D, Hermida JL, et al. The treatment of scabies with ivermectin. N Engl J Med 1995;333:26-30.
9. Chouela EN, Abeldano AM, Pellerano G, et al. Equivalent therapeutic efficacy and safety of ivermectin and lindane in the treatment of human scabies. Arch Dermatol 1999;135:651-655.
10. Usha V, Gopalakrishnan N. A comparative study of oral ivermectin and topical permethrin cream in the treatment of scabies. J Am Acad Dermatol 2000;42:236-240.
11. Barkwell R, Shields S. Deaths associated with ivermectin treatment of scabies. Lancet 1997;349:1144-1145.
12. Coyne PE, Addiss DG. Deaths associated with ivermectin for scabies (Correspondence). Lancet 1997;350:215-216.
13. Juranek DD, Currier RW, Milikan LE. Scabies control in institutions. In: Orkin M, Maibach HI, eds. Cutaneous Infestations and Insect Bites. New York: Marcel Dekker; 1985:139-156.

CHAPTER **293**

Myiasis and Tungiasis

MICHAEL ERIC MATHIEU

BARBARA BRAUNSTEIN WILSON

MYIASIS

Myiasis is the infestation of living vertebrates by the larvae (maggots) of dipterous (two-winged) flies, a disease that occurs most frequently, although not exclusively, in tropical climates. The disease in domestic animals is a global agricultural problem. Nosocomial infestation has been reported rarely. The appropriate travel or exposure history in a compatible clinical setting should alert the clinician to the possibility of myiasis.

Classification

Myiasis is enormously important in veterinary medicine, and human disease is due to parasites that usually interact with an animal host. Cutaneous myiasis is the most frequently encountered clinical form. It is further subclassified according to the nature of the manifestation, such as furunculoid subcutaneous infestation with tunnel formation, wound infestation, and subcutaneous infestation with migratory swellings. Nasopharyngeal myiasis has been reported to include infestation of the nose, mouth, sinuses, ear, or eye (ophthalmomyiasis). Intestinal myiasis includes enteric disease caused by ingestion of organisms and anal disease. Urogenital myiasis encompasses urethral, vaginal, and bladder infestations.

Myiasis-Associated Species

Myiasis-inducing flies are members of the superfamily Oestrodiae. Oestrodiae consists of three major families: Oestridae, which includes four subfamilies (Oestrinae, Gasterophiliane, Hypodermatinae, Cuterebrinae); Calliphoridae, or blow flies; and Sarcophagidae, or flesh flies. All Oestridae, at least 151 species, are obligate parasites. The families Calliforidae, with more than 1000 species, and Sarcophagidae, with more than 2000 species, contain both obligate and facultative organisms.

Despite the staggering number of potential agents, a limited number of species actually cause disease (Table 293-1). Travelers returning from the tropics are likely to harbor *Dermatobia hominis* or *Cordylobia anthropophaga*. Other species may infest humans when recreational or occupational activities unite human host and parasite, interactions that can also occur in temperate regions. The reader is referred to an excellent discussion for more detail regarding other potential agents of myiasis in both animals and humans.[1]

Dermatobia hominis, also known as human or tropical botfly, berne, and many other local names, is an Oestridae fly of the Cuterebrinae subfamily, that is endemic to tropical Mexico, South America, Central America, and Trinidad. *Bot* is a term sometimes used for the invading larva. *D. hominis* is an obligate parasite found in humid tropical forests and wooded lowlands. Adults have a blue-black thorax with a metallic violet abdomen and can grow to 2 cm in length. Domesticated animals, especially cattle, and humans may become infested.

The ecology of the fly is fascinating in that egg-bearing female flies intercept blood-sucking arthropods, such as mosquitoes, and attach their eggs to the abdomen of the carrier insect. When the mosquito takes a blood meal from a warm-blooded animal, local heat induces larvae to hatch and drop to the skin of the mammalian host as cylindrical first-instar, or stage I, larvae. Larvae painlessly penetrate the skin of the mammal directly or through the defect produced by the insect proboscis and gain access to the dermis and subcutaneous tissue. Within 5 to 10 weeks, the organisms mature to flask-shaped second-instar, or stage II, larvae and then fusiform third-instar, or stage III, larvae. Second and third instars have sickle-shaped hooks on the bulbous heads and rows of smaller concentric, backward-facing hooks and spines. Eventually, if the cycle is unperturbed, larvae emerge from the host, drop to the ground, and pupate to become flies within 2 to 3 weeks. Adult flies are short-lived, surviving little more than a week.[2] Human and animal disease results from development of larvae in the skin of the infested host.

Cordylobia anthropophaga, the tumbu fly, is a member of the family Calliphoridae, which is endemic to Sub-Saharan Africa. The flies are 8 to 11 mm in length and dull yellow with two broad, dark, longitudinal stripes. Occasional case reports of disease apparently acquired in Europe have suggested the possibility of a more extended range.

Female flies deposit eggs on shaded soil or drying clothes, preferably contaminated with urine or feces. Within 1 to 3 days, larvae hatch and remain near the soil surface until activated by heat, such as the body heat of a potential host, whether human or animal. Larvae from eggs deposited on clothes have direct access to the host when the clothes are worn. As with *D. hominis,* larvae pass through three

TABLE 293-1 Summary of Common Myiasis-Associated Species

Taxonomic Classification, Common Name	Distribution	Mode of Infestation	Disease
Oestrodiae			
Oestridae			
Oestrinae: *Oestrus ovis* (sheep nasal botfly)	Worldwide	Obligate	Ophthalmomyiasis
Gastrophilinae (horse botfly)	Worldwide	Obligate	
Hypodermatinae: *Hypoderma bovis* (cattle botfly)	Worldwide	Obligate	Furunculoid and creeping eruption
Cuterebrinae			
Dermatobia hominis (botfly)	Tropical Latin America, Trinidad	Obligate	Furunculoid
Cuterebra species (North American botfly)	North America	Obligate	Furunculoid rarely ophthalmomyiasis
Calliphoridae (blowflies)			
Calliphorinae			
Cordylobia anthropophaga (tumbu fly)	Tropical Africa	Obligate	Furunculoid
Cordylobia rodhaini	Tropical Africa	Obligate	Furunculoid
Cochliomyia homnivorax (New World screwworm)	Tropical Latin America	Obligate	Wound
Chrysomya bezziana (Old World screwworm)	Tropical Africa and Asia	Obligate	Wound
Lucilia species (green bottle fly)	Worldwide	Facultative	Wound
Calliphora species (blue bottle fly)	Worldwide	Facultative	Wound
Phormia regina (black blowfly)	Worldwide	Facultative	Wound
Nacheromyia senegalensis (Congo floor maggot)	Tropical Africa	Obligate	Bites
Sarcophagidae (flesh flies)			
Wohlfahrtia species			
Wohlfahrtia magnifica	Mediterranean basin, Eastern Europe, Near East	Obligate	Wound
Muscidae			
Musca domestica	Worldwide	Facultative	Wound

stages. *Cordylobia rodhaini,* a related species also known as Lund's fly, is similar to *C. anthropophaga* in terms of distribution and disease manifestations.

Rarely, humans in North America and elsewhere become infested with the horse or cattle botflies *Gasterophilus* spp. and *Hypoderma bovis,* respectively, both of which are Oestridae flies. These organisms produce migratory erythematous lesions. *Cuterebra* spp., large rabbit-parasitizing Oestridae flies, occur in North America and occasionally cause cutaneous myiasis and ophthalmomyiasis in humans, especially children.[3]

Several species occasionally cause wound myiasis by laying eggs directly on compromised tissue. Such parasites are found in both the tropics and in warm temperate zones such as southern North America. Some of the relevant organisms are obligatory species, such as the New World and Old World screwworms *Cochliomyia hominivorax* and *Chrysomya bezziana,* respectively, both being Calliphoridae flies. New World screwworms are endemic in the southern United States, Caribbean, and most of Latin America. Old World screwworms are found in Africa, India, the Arabian peninsula, and the archipelagos of Indonesia, the Philippines, and New Guinea. *Wohlfahrtia magnifica,* an obligate flesh fly Sarcophagidae species of the Mediterranean basin, Near East, and eastern and central Europe, can also cause severe wound myiasis in animals and humans. Facultative wound myiasis, typical maggot-infested wounds, may be due to several frequent Calliphoridae animal pests: *Lucilia* spp., the ubiquitous greenbottle flies; *Calliphora* spp., the ubiquitous bluebottle flies; and *Phormia regina,* the black blow fly of North America. *Musca domestica,* the house fly found throughout the world, may also infest wounds. *Auchmeromyia senegalensis,* the Congo floor maggot, is a unique Calliphoridae obligate parasite of Sub-Saharan Africa that is primarily a human parasite.

Eggs are laid in the soil or sand floors of traditional huts. The larvae hatch in 1 to 3 days, emerging at night to seek a blood meal from sleeping human hosts. All three larval stages are blood-sucking. The bite may be slightly painful, and some patients experience considerable local edema.

Oestrus ovis, the Oestridae sheep nasal botfly found in all major sheep-raising regions, has been particularly implicated in ophthalmomyiasis. The species is found in all areas where shepherding is a major agricultural pursuit. Female flies directly deposit first-instar larvae in the nostrils of sheep for obligate development in the upper respiratory tract.

Clinical Manifestations

Furunculoid Disease

In temperate North America and Europe, the occasional patient presenting with myiasis is likely to be a traveler who has recently returned from tropical Latin America or Equatorial Africa. Both *D. hominis* and *C. anthropophaga,* the most common offending agents, cause furunculoid myiasis. As the term implies, furunculoid disease is characterized by cutaneous nodules, occurring singly or in multiple places, each containing a single larva. The term *warble* is synonymous with a furunculoid lesion.

A central punctum usually develops that may exude serosanguineous or purulent fluid (Fig. 293-1). Frequently, patients are aware of movement within the nodule, and pruritus is common. The tail of the larva may be observed to extrude from the punctum intermittently, the two spiracles simulating tiny black eyes. *D. hominis* infestations are associated with local pain, perhaps because of the larval hooklets, which are believed to assist the organism in boring through tissue to exit.[4] *D. hominis* favors the scalp, face, and extremities, whereas *C. anthropophaga* is more likely to affect the trunk, buttocks, and thighs. *C. rodhaini* is similar to *C. anthropophaga,* but the lesions it produces are larger and more painful.

Associated findings include regional lymphadenopathy, malaise, and fever. Secondary bacterial infection may be present, and a thick purulent discharge suggests typical staphylococcal furunculosis. Tungiasis, a cutaneous disease caused by the chigoe flea *Tunga penetrans,* may also be confused with myiasis, particularly because this infestation is also acquired in New World and Old World tropical regions. The female flea burrows into a distal extremity and feeds on host blood until mature eggs are extruded through the punctum. Tungiasis may be differentiated clinically from myiasis by being virtually confined to the distal extremities, especially the toes, and by the presence of pruritic papules with a central punctum.

Rarer causes of furunculoid disease are rodent and rabbit botflies of the genus *Cuterebra.* This form of myiasis is generally not of tropical origin but has been reported from many regions in the United States. Hypodermatinae species and *Wohlfahrtia magnifica* have also occasionally caused furunculoid disease.

Subcutaneous Infestation with Tunnel Formation

Although they infrequently affect humans, North American *Gasterophilus* species (horse botflies) cause significant morbidity among horses, as the larvae normally develop in the gastrointestinal tract of

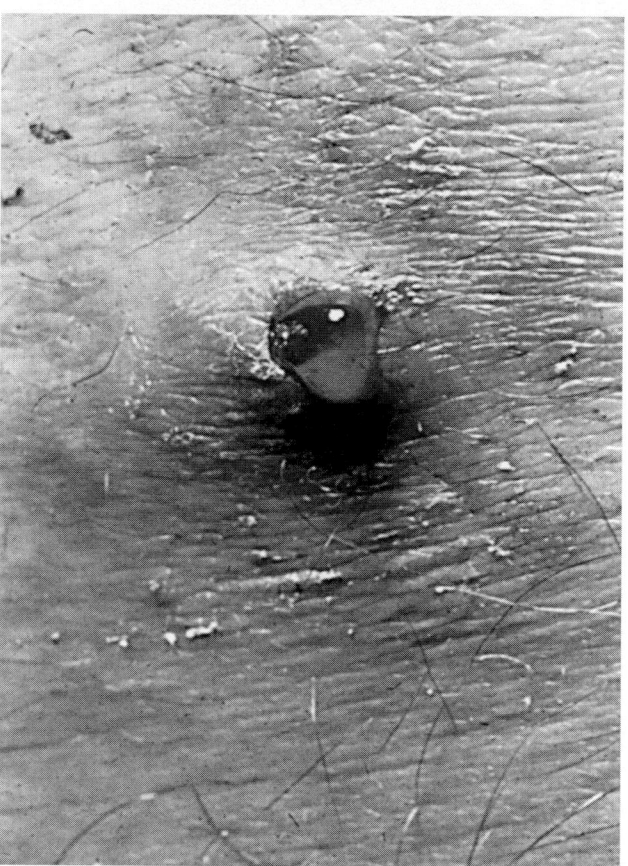

FIGURE 293-1. Typical lesion of furunculoid myiasis consisting of an erythematous nodule draining serosanguineous material from an overlying punctum.

equine hosts. *Gasterophilus intestinalis* and *Gasterophilus hemorrhoidalis* are responsible for migratory integumomyiasis in humans, the so-called creeping eruption as larvae slowly migrate through the skin. The clinical correlate is the development of pruritic, painful, erythematous lesions in a serpiginous configuration. Recurrent disease tends to form large pustules or nodules. Rarely, larvae appear in the lungs and produce nodular parenchymal lesions.

The burden of the clinician is to differentiate this disease from cutaneous larva migrans, a helminthic disease caused by animal intestinal nematode larvae, such as those of *Ancylostoma* species of dogs and cats, which cannot complete their life cycle in humans. The latter condition occurs at sites where skin has been in contact with contaminated warm, sandy soil, such as on the lower extremity; it consists of a thin, erythematous, intensely pruritic, rapidly moving (1 to 2 cm/day) serpiginous eruption that may induce systemic effects such as eosinophilia.

Subcutaneous Infestation with Migratory Swellings

The cattle botfly, or cattle grub, *Hypoderma bovis,* an obligate Oestridae species found in temperate regions including North America and Europe, is a major cause of morbidity in cattle. Humans are occasionally infested, developing a disease that may resemble that caused by *Gasterophilus* infestation but more characteristically involving the formation of furunculoid lesions as the larvae mature. Mature larvae may thus emerge through puncta, as with *Dermatobia hominis* infestation. Rarely, cattle botfly disease leads to severe ophthalmomyiasis, even blindness, or invasion of the central nervous system. As with other invasive parasites too large to be phagocytized, peripheral eosinophilia may occur.

Wound Myiasis

Cochliomyia hominivorax and *Chrysomiyia bezziana,* New World and Old World screwworms, respectively, may cause obligatory wound myiasis. More mature larvae are often more invasive, readily leaving necrotic tissue for viable tissue, which leads to significant local destruction and secondary bacterial infection. Similarly, Wohlfahrtia magnifica may parasitize wounds in an obligatory manner. Lucilia sericata and Musca domestica may facultatively infest wounds when gravid females deposit eggs in and around wounds. One multicenter study suggested that in the United States wound myiasis is likely the most frequent domestically acquired form of the disease and that the green blowfly, Phaenicia sericata, is the most frequent offending species.[5] Of the 42 cases reported, most were in late middle-age men; and homelessness, peripheral vascular disease, and alcoholism were prevalent. Clinical manifestations include secondary bacterial infection and occasional fistula formation.

Other Manifestations

Ophthalmomyiasis is usually caused by *Oestrus ovis.* Ophthalmomyiasis interna involves the globe, whereas ophthalmomyiasis externa is a relatively mild disease, characterized by conjunctivitis, lid edema, and superficial punctate keratopathy in response to movement of larvae across the external surface of the globe.[6] Patients commonly complain of an acute foreign body sensation with lacrimation, often of abrupt onset. Invasion of the globe and severe external inflammation occur occasionally. Non-*O. ovis* eye disease may be more severe.[7] Larvae may appear in the cornea, lens, anterior chamber, or vitreous but rarely undergo continued development when the globe has been entered. A rare devastating consequence is retinitis involving the macula with fibrosis, leading to blindness. Occasionally, enucleation or exenteration is required.

Rarely, other body sites may become infested with dipterous larvae. Virtually any accessible cavity or tissue may provide an environment hospitable for facultative or obligate parasitism. Reported cases have involved the urethra, penis, vagina, bladder, colon, upper respiratory tract, oral cavity, and brain. A report of nosocomial myiasis in the United States involved the nares of two comatose patients in an intensive care unit. The green blowfly, *Phaenicia sericata,* was the causative agent and was linked to parasitized mouse carcasses.[8]

Treatment

Furunculoid and Migratory Myiasis

The goal of treatment is complete removal of larvae from parasitized tissue. *Cordylobia anthropophaga* is reportedly easier to remove than *Dermatobia hominis.*[4] Manual expression of *C. anthropophaga* may be adequate: This procedure is commonly performed by the patient before or in lieu of seeking medical attention. Numerous reports have noted successful eradication of *D. hominis* by occluding the punctum with a substance to prevent gas exchange. To avoid asphyxiation, the organism emerges far enough to be grasped by the forceps of a vigilant physician or patient. Occluding substances have included petrolatum, fingernail polish, makeup cream, adhesive tape, and bacon.[9] Reportedly, occlusion may have to be maintained for 24 hours or more to have the desired effect. The risk of attempted occlusion is that the organism may asphyxiate without emerging through the punctum and the retained larva may elicit an inflammatory response. Surgical excision is therefore often necessary for treatment. In our experience with several cases of furunculoid myiasis in patients returning from tropical Latin America, occlusion alone was unsuccessful and a surgical procedure was required (Fig. 293-2). Surgical excision is almost always required for the migratory forms of the disease, with the formation of furunculoid lesions facilitating localization of the organism. Antibiotic therapy may be necessary for secondary bacterial infection.

Wound Myiasis

Treatment of wound myiasis requires manual removal of all visible larvae followed by débridement. Irrigation may be particularly useful. Chloroform 15% in olive or other oil or ether may help immobilize the

FIGURE 293-2. Larva removed from skin of a patient with furunculoid myiasis.

larvae. Extensive wound exploration may be mandated by the degree of involvement.

Ophthalmomyiasis

External infestation is managed by mechanical removal of larvae from the surface of the anesthetized globe using fine, nontoothed forceps. Slit-lamp examination facilitates the process, but viable larvae have a tendency to avoid bright light. The use of lidocaine or cocaine as an anesthetic has the additional benefit of maggot immobilization, which facilitates removal. As with furuncular myiasis, occlusion with a thick ointment may assist removal by encouraging egress of organisms from the conjunctival sac, if it is involved.[7,10] Careful follow-up examination is necessary to ensure complete removal of the larvae.

The management of internal infestation is more variable and highly dependent on the clinical situation. Dead larvae unassociated with significant inflammation can usually be left in place, as they eventually regress. Inflammation requires management with topical corticosteroids and mydriatics with close follow-up. The presence of persistently viable larvae may require surgical removal, particularly when critical structures are at risk. Living organisms in the appropriate location, such as the subretinal space, may be amenable to destruction by laser photocoagulation. Ivermectin has been used to treat myiasis in animals and in at least one human with subcutaneous *Hypoderma lineatum* infestation.[4]

Prevention

Dermatobia hominis infestation might be thwarted by the application of insect repellents containing diethyltoluamide (DEET) and the use of mosquito netting. Ironing is an effective method for destroying occult eggs laid in clothing by *Cordylobia anthropophaga*. Other general precautions include wearing long-sleeved clothing, covering wounds, and avoiding falling asleep outdoors.

TUNGIASIS

Tungiasis is a syndrome caused by skin penetration by the fertilized female *Tunga* sand flea (*Tunga penetrans*) found in tropical areas of Central South America, the Caribbean, Africa and Asia. Symptoms include local pain and swelling, usually on the toes and feet. There may be a tiny black spot at the site of penetration. Secondary infection may occur, and gas gangrene is reported to be a complication. Treatment consists of surgical removal of the embedded flea.

REFERENCES

1. Hall M, Wall R. Myiasis of humans and domestic animals. Adv Parasitol 1995;35:257-334.
2. Gordon PM, Hepburn NC, Williams AE, Bunney MH. Cutaneous myiasis due to Dermatobia hominis: a report of six cases. Br J Dermatol 1995;132:811-814.
3. Baird JK, Baird CR, Sabrosky CW. North American cuterebrid myiasis. J Am Acad Dermatol 1989;21:673-772.
4. Jelinek T, Nothdurft HD, Rieder N, Löscher T. Cutaneous myiasis: review of 13 cases in travelers returning from tropical countries. Int J Dermatol 1995;34:624-626.
5. Sherman RA. Wound myiasis in urban and suburban United States. Arch Intern Med 2000;160:2004-2014.
6. Harvey JT. Sheep botfly: ophthalmomyiasis externa. Can J Ophthalmol 1986;21:92-95.
7. Chodosh J, Clarridge J. Ophthalmomyiasis: a review with special reference to Cochliomyia hominivorax. Clin Infect Dis 1992;14:444-449.
8. Beckendorf R, Klotz SA, Hinkle N, Bartholomew W. Nasal myiasis in an intensive care unit linked to hospital-wide mouse infestation. Arch Intern Med 2002;162:638-640.
9. Brewer TF, Wilson ME, Gonzalez E, Felsenstein D. Bacon therapy and furuncular myiasis. JAMA 1993;270:2087-2088.
10. Hira PR, Hajj B, al-Ali F, Hall MJ. Ophthalmomyiasis in Kuwait: first report of infections due to the larvae of Oestrus ovis before and after the Gulf conflict. J Trop Med Hyg 1993;96:241-244.

BIBLIOGRAPHY

Canizares O. Myiasis and leeches. In: Canizares O, Harman RRM, eds. Clinical Tropical Dermatology. 2nd ed. Boston: Blackwell Scientific; 1992:404-412.

Garcia LS, Bruckner DA. Medically important arthropods. In: Diagnostic Medical Parasitology. 3rd ed. Washington, DC: American Society for Microbiology; 1997:523-563.

Rossignol PA, Feinsod FM. Arthropods directly causing human injury. In: Warren KS, Mahmoud AAE, eds. Tropical and Geographic Medicine. 2nd ed. New York: McGraw-Hill; 1990:519-522.

CHAPTER **294**

Mites (Including Chiggers)

MICHAEL ERIC MATHIEU

BARBARA BRAUNSTEIN WILSON

THE ORGANISM

Mites belong to the order Acarina, of the class Arachnida. Mites are worldwide in distribution and may be free-living or parasitize plants, insects, animals, or humans.[1] Adult mites have a fused head and thorax and four pairs of legs. The size of the mites varies with the species.

Mites are medically important because not only can they cause significant cutaneous disease in humans but some species are known vectors of infectious diseases such as rickettsialpox, scrub typhus, murine typhus, Q fever, tularemia, plague, and tsutsugamushi fever.

The mites that may affect humans include chiggers (harvest mites), animal mites, bird mites, food mites, grain mites, follicle mites, and scabies. Except for the mite *Sarcoptes scabiei* var. *hominis* (see Chapter 292) and *Demodex* mites (see "Follicle Mites"), which parasitize humans alone, mites are only occasional predators of humans. Unlike the scabies mites, the occasional predators do not burrow into their hosts' skin, and they may remain attached to the skin surface only long enough to obtain a blood meal.

CHIGGERS

The common chigger, also known as the harvest mite or red bug, belongs to the family Trombiculidae. It is prevalent in the southern United States, especially during the summer and fall months. Chiggers live on grasses and shrubs, and it is the larval form that attaches itself to passing animals or humans.

After obtaining a blood meal, the larvae drop off, and within hours extremely pruritic, erythematous papules appear (Fig. 294-1). The larval form is 150 to 300 μm in length and has an unsegmented body and three pairs of legs. Lesions are most frequent on the legs, usually

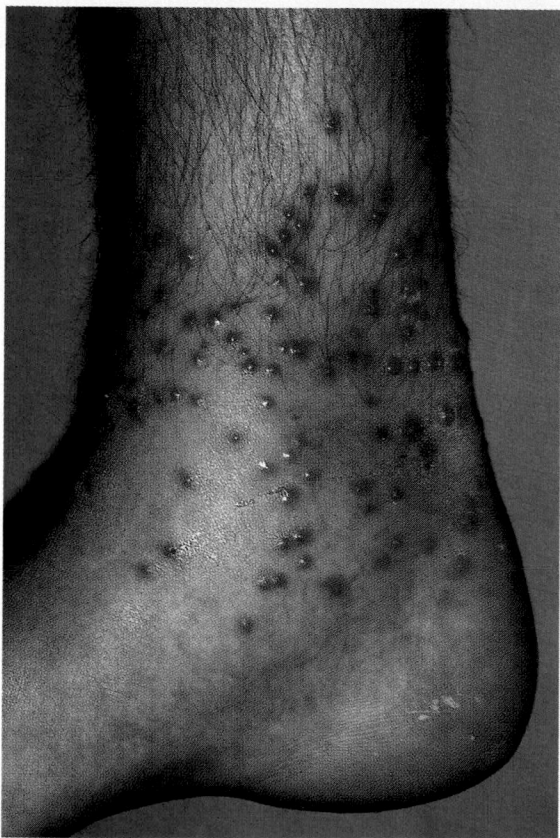

FIGURE 294-1. Intense reaction to chigger bites.

where clothing is snug against the skin, possibly impeding the larvae's migration. The severity of the eruption depends on the allergic sensitivity of the host to the mite's oral secretions. If the reaction is severe, fever or a background eczematous eruption (or both) may develop. Secondary bacterial infection may also be present.

Chiggers are the vector of scrub typhus, caused by *Orientia tsutsugamushi,* which is endemic in southern and eastern Asia. Scrub typhus is a febrile disease associated with a cutaneous eruption. Although most infected individuals recover, a few develop a severe life-threatening illness. Treatment is similar to that of other rickettsial diseases.

ANIMAL MITES

Humans are the occasional hosts of mites that are usually parasites of birds and mammals. Canine mites *(Sarcoptes scabiei* var. *canis)* from infested dogs and *Cheyletiella* spp. (infesting the coats of dogs, cats, and rabbits) can bite humans. *Dermanyssus gallinae* is a common ectoparasite of fowl and other birds. The mouse mite, *Liponyssoides sanguineus,* parasitizes mice and rats and has been documented as a vector for rickettsialpox. *Ornithonyssus bacoti* is an ectoparasite of certain species of rats as well as mice, hamsters, and guinea pigs; it is a probable vector of murine typhus.[2]

FOOD, GRAIN, AND STRAW MITES

Grocery and warehouse workers who handle food such as cheese, flour, or vegetables infested with mites, and farmers exposed to grain or straw mites, may likewise develop pruritic eruptions as a result of mite bites. The clinical appearance of these and animal mite bites consists of pruritic erythematous macules and papules that may show a central red punctum with vesiculation or crusting.

FOLLICLE MITES

Demodex folliculorum and *Demodex brevis* are mites that inhabit the pilosebaceous follicles, especially of the face and eyelids of humans and some animals. Although usually considered harmless saprophytes, *Demodex* spp. can cause "red mange" in dogs, which is manifested by scaling, erythema, nodules, and alopecia.[2] *Demodex* spp. are present in large numbers and are pathogenic in some people, who develop rosacea and blepharitis. Individuals of particular HLA class I phenotypes may be more susceptible to *Demodex*-induced symptoms.[3]

Skin lesions of demodicidosis do not resemble insect bite reactions, as seen with bites of other mites discussed earlier. Instead, they appear as erythematous follicular papulopustules, usually on the face. Treatment with topical sulfur preparations, lindane, or permethrin is often effective for *Demodex* spp. infestations.[4]

MITES AND ALLERGIC DISEASE

There is increasing evidence that hypersensitivity to house dust mites can cause flares in atopic diseases such as asthma, allergic rhinitis, and atopic dermatitis.[5] Allergic disorders related to dust mite exposure is a global problem.[6] The most common species of dust mite in North America are *Dermatophagoides pteronyssinus* and *Dermatophagoides farinae.*[5] The respiratory and cutaneous syndromes caused by dust mite allergy are worldwide in distribution. These disorders may result in morbidity sufficient to compromise the quality of life.[7] Other mite species have been implicated as inducers of allergic sensitization in susceptible individuals. Examples include the spider mite, *Tetranychus urticae,* and the citrus red mite, *Panonychus citri,* which have been linked to sensitization phenomena in individuals working in or living near citrus orchards in Korea.[8,9]

TREATMENT AND PREVENTION

Treatment of mite bites is symptomatic. Oral antihistamines such as hydroxyzine, 25 to 50 mg by mouth three to four times daily, and the application of potent topical steroids such as fluocinonide cream twice a day temporarily relieve the pruritus. Control of severe symptoms may be augmented by a short course of systemic corticosteroids. Secondary bacterial infection should be treated with appropriate antibiotics. Most lesions resolve spontaneously within a week.

Elimination of animal or plant sources of infestation or spraying an infested area with chemicals may reduce or eliminate human mite infestations. Protective clothing and insect repellents are useful for prevention. DEET-containing insect repellents offer some protection against chiggers, although a compound under investigation, *N,N*-diethyl-3-fluorobenzamide, is even more effective.[10]

REFERENCES

1. Moschella SL, Hurley JH, eds. Dermatology. Philadelphia: WB Saunders; 1986.
2. Alexander JO. Arthropods and Human Skin. New York: Springer-Verlag; 1984.
3. Akilov OE, Mumcuoglu KY. Association between human demodicosis and HLA class I. Clin Exp Dermatol 2003;28:70-73
4. Bonnar E, Eustace P, Powell FC. The demodex mite population in rosacea. J Am Acad Dermatol 1993;28:443-448.
5. Platts-Mills TAE, Chapman MD. Dust mites: immunology, allergic disease and environmental control. J Allergy Clin Immunol 1987;80:755-775.
6. Platts-Mills TAE, de Wirk A. Dust mite allergens and asthma: a world-wide problem. J Allergy Clin Immunol 1989;83:416-427
7. Terreehorst I, Duivenvoorden HJ, Tempels-Pavlica Z, et al. The unfavorable effects of concomitant asthma and sleeplessness due to the atopic eczema/dermatitis syndrome (AEDS) on quality of life in subjects allergic to house dust mites. Allergy 2002;57:919-925.
8. Kim YK, Chang YS, Lee MH, et al. Role of environmental exposure to spider mites in the sensitization and the clinical manifestations of asthma and rhinitis in children and adolescents living in rural and urban areas. Clin Exp Allergy 2002;32:1305-1309
9. Kim SH, Kim YK, Lee MH, et al. Relationship between sensitization to citrus red mite (Panonychus citri) and the prevalence of atopic diseases in adolescents living near citrus orchards. Clin Exp Allergy 2002;32:1054-1058.
10. Lerdthusnee K, Khlaimanee N, Monkanna T, et al. Development of an in vitro method for the evaluation of candidate repellents against Leptotombidium (Acari:Trombiculidae) chiggers. J Med Entomol 2003;40:64-67.

BIBLIOGRAPHY

Alexander JO. Arthropods and Human Skin. New York: Springer-Verlag; 1984.

Goddard J. Physicians Guide to Arthropods of Medical Importance. 4th ed. Boca Raton: CRC Press; 2003:229-247.

Hewitt M, Barrow GI, Miller DC, et al. Mites in the personal environment and their role in skin disorders. Br J Dermatol 1973;89:401.

CHAPTER **295**

Ticks (Including Tick Paralysis)

MICHAEL ERIC MATHIEU

BARBARA BRAUNSTEIN WILSON

Ticks are vectors of bacterial, viral, and protozoal diseases throughout the world. Infectious agents are transmitted when the ticks are obtaining blood meals, which are mandatory for their viability and reproductive capacity. Globally, ticks are second only to mosquitoes as vectors of infectious diseases, but in North America ticks are the leading perpetrator of vector-borne infections. Forty-four species are known to parasitize humans in the United States,[1] and a number of tick-borne diseases are recognized, including Lyme disease, Rocky Mountain spotted fever, human monocytic and granulocytic ehrlichiosis, Southern tick-associated rash illness, tularemia, relapsing fever, Colorado tick fever, babesiosis, and tick paralysis, nearly all of which are zoonoses. Humans become infected with microbes usually found in wild animals when an ecologic niche involving mammals and ticks is violated. Ticks may also simply bite without transmitting disease; in such cases, they cause generally benign cutaneous inflammatory reactions.

BIOLOGY AND ECOLOGY

Ticks are blood-sucking arthropods of the class Arachnida. Three families are recognized: Ixodidae (hard ticks); Argasidae (soft ticks); and Nuttalliellidae (a less well known group with characteristics of both hard and soft ticks).

Hard ticks contain a dorsal plate known as the scutum, and adults have mouth parts that extend anteriorly from the head region when viewed from above. In contrast to soft ticks, male and female hard ticks also exhibit distinguishing morphologic characteristics. Some hard ticks have a one-host life cycle, with the larva, nymph, and adult acquiring blood meals from the same host. Many *Ixodes* species, however, require three separate hosts. Adult mating occurs on the first host, and the fully engorged female drops off to lay eggs on the ground and then die. Six-legged larvae hatch in about 1 month and are sometimes referred to as "seed ticks." Larval forms generally feed on small animals such as rodents and, when fully fed, drop to the ground and molt into eight-legged nymphs. Adults similarly develop from nymphs after obtaining a complete blood meal from another host. Ixodidae ticks generally require prolonged attachment to the host, feeding slowly and continuously at first and then rapidly engorging over approximately 24 hours. Hard ticks encounter hosts, including humans, by so-called questing, wherein ticks climb to the top of vegetation and await a potential host. Vibration or carbon dioxide stimulates the tick to wave its legs or move about to facilitate attachment to a passing host. Hard ticks favor brushy, wooded, or weedy areas populated by a variety of mammals. The interface between forest and field is an ideal habitat for most hard ticks. Desiccation is a constant threat that influences activity; ticks thus seek an environment that promotes or preserves hydration (or both).

Soft ticks favor animal dwellings such as burrows, dens, or manmade animal or human shelters in endemic areas. Soft ticks are relatively unaffected by arid conditions. Females often have several opportunities to lay eggs, and many ticks of the family Argasidae undergo several nymphal molts before achieving adult status. Nymphal and adult forms tend to feed rapidly and leave the host quickly.

Ticks penetrate the host epidermis by insertion and lateral motion of chelicerae, sharp structures located on the distal segments of the mouth parts. The hypostome, the tube-like central component of the mouth parts, is inserted into the defect for withdrawal of blood. The depth of penetration of the mouth parts varies with the species. Hard ticks generally elaborate a liquid cement from the salivary glands that hardens and holds the mouth parts in place for the 7 to 14 days required for blood meals. Transmission of tick-borne diseases occurs only after attachment has proceeded for several hours (Table 295-1).

Ticks are important vectors for the transmission of rickettsial, viral, and bacterial diseases (see Table 295-1). Rocky Mountain spotted fever is caused by *Rickettsia rickettsii,* which is transmitted primarily by *Dermacentor andersoni,* the wood tick, in the western United States and *Dermacentor variabilis,* the dog tick (Fig. 295-1), in the eastern United States and Canada.[2] Certain tick species appear to prefer particular body sites for attachment: *D. variabilis* favors the head and neck, whereas *Amblyomma americanum,* the Lone Star tick, often remains below the waist. *Ixodes scapularis,* the deer tick has no particular regional predilection.[3]

Lyme disease (Lyme borreliosis), a zoonosis caused by infection by the spirochete *Borrelia burgdorferi,* is the most common vector-borne disease in the United States. For the year 2000, a total of 17,730 cases from 44 states were reported to the Centers for Disease Control and Prevention (CDC), the largest number of cases to date.[4] Most cases occurred in the Northeast and upper Midwest. The deer tick *Ixodes scapularis,* previously also known as *Ixodes dammini* (Fig. 295-2), is the principal vector for Lyme disease in the northeastern and midwestern United States, and *Ixodes pacificus* is the principal vector in the western United States.[2] The nymph stage of *I. scapularis* is approximately the size of a poppy seed and is therefore frequently overlooked. Nymphs are particularly associated with Lyme disease causation. The adult deer tick, however, can also transmit Lyme disease and can be distinguished from the dog tick by its smaller size (approximately one-half the size) and the presence of an orange crescent along its posterior dorsal plate.

Human ehrlichioses are potentially life-threatening zoonoses transmitted by ticks. Analogous disorders have been recognized in veterinary medicine for nearly a century. Human monocytic ehrlichiosis (HME) is due to *Ehrlichia chaffeensis,* transmitted by the Lone Star tick. Seroprevalence studies suggest that children are more likely to become infected than adults.[5] Human granulocytic anaplasmosis, also known as ehrlichiosis (HGE), is caused by *Anaplasma phagocytophila* and is transmitted by *I. scapularis,* the most important vector for Lyme disease in the United States.[6] Disease caused by *Echaffeensis* is restricted to North America, but *A. phagocytophila* is a cause of disease in both North America and Europe.[7,8] *Ixodes ricinus,* the vector of Lyme borreliosis in Europe (the European disease is caused by *Borrelia afzelii* and *Borrelia garinii*), is also the apparent vector for *A. phagocytophila,* so the epidemiologic pattern of HGE parallels that of Lyme disease. *Ehrlichia ewingii* also causes a granulocytic form of anaplasmosis, particularly in immunocompromised hosts, but this entity is less well understood.[9,10] *E. ewingii* has been associated with disease in both North America and northern and eastern Europe. The white-tailed deer is the emerging reservoir.[11]

Other human diseases that may be transmitted by hard ticks include arboviruses, Colorado tick fever, tularemia, Q fever, babesiosis, boutonneuse fever, and the Southern tick-associated rash illness. Hard ticks emerge during early spring and summer, and sometimes a second peak occurs in autumn.

Tick infestation can cause great economic losses to industries dependent on domestic animals such as cattle and sheep by causing damage to their hides or a decrease in the animals' market weight. Ticks can also transmit infectious diseases such as babesiosis or rickettsial diseases to domestic animals.

TABLE 295-1 Some Ticks of Medical Importance in the United States

Species Name, Common Name	Description	Distribution	Diseases	Comments
Ixodidae, hard ticks				
Ixodes scapularis (black-legged tick)	Dark brown with long mouth parts	Northern form from southern Ontario south through eastern and central United States to Virginia; southern form to northern Mexico	Northern form transmits Lyme disease, babesiosis, and human granulocytic ehrlichiosis; Lyme transmission requires >24 hr for nymphs, 36 hr for adults	Adults active in fall, winter, and spring; immature forms active in spring and summer; favors edges of paths, roads; nymphs important vectors
Ixodes pacificus (western black-legged tick)	Similar to *I. scapularis*	Canadian Pacific coast south through California to Mexico	Lyme disease; Lyme transmission requires 96 hr for nymphs	May cause type I sensitivity reactions
Dermacentor variabilis (American dog tick)	Dark brown with rounded mouth parts	Throughout United States except Rocky Mountains; southern Canada; northern Mexico	RMSF, tularemia; RMSF transmission requires ≥24 hr	Handling ticks picked off dogs may be risky; favor trails or roadsides near clearings
Dermacentor andersoni (Rocky Mountain wood tick)	Dark brown with white markings on scutum	Rocky Mountains and adjacent areas of United States and Canada	RMSF, Colorado tick fever, tularemia, tick paralysis	Favors brushy vegetation
Ambylomma americanum (Lone Star tick)	Red-brown with long mouth parts; females have white spot on back	Central Texas north and east to Iowa and New York; northern Mexico	Tularemia, human monocytic ehrlichiosis, ?Lyme or Lyme-like disease in southeastern United States	Bites aggresively in southern areas; nymphs are common seed ticks
Amblyomma maculatum (Gulf Coast tick)	Brown females have metallic markings on scutum; long mouth parts	Southeastern Atlantic and Gulf coasts, south to South America	None	Bites aggressively
Argasidae, soft ticks				
Ornithodoros hermsi	Characteristic soft tick morphology, gray, mammalated, up to 1 cm	Western United States and Canada	Relapsing fever	Painless bite; often found in cabins
Ornithodoros turicata (relapsing fever tick)	Similar to *O. hermsi*	Southwestern and southcentral United States to northern Florida, eastern Mexico	Relapsing fever	Painless bite but intense local reaction may occur

RMSF, Rocky Mountain spotted fever.

CLINICAL MANIFESTATIONS

Uncomplicated Bites

Most tick bites are asymptomatic. Attached ticks should be removed as soon as possible because of the relation between the feeding interval and disease transmission. Unprotected fingers should not be used to remove ticks, and one should avoid crushing or puncturing the tick. The standard method of removal is to grasp the anterior aspect of the arthropod with blunt, rounded forceps as close to the skin surface as possible and pull upward in a continuous motion. Instruments designed specifically to remove ticks are commercially available and may confer an advantage over standard forceps for removing nymphal forms.[12] Note that the ease of removal varies with the species; *Dermacentor variabilis*, for example, attaches superficially, and *Amblyomma americanum* attaches more deeply.[12] If necessary, the tick may be removed by performing a small shave excision.

With uncomplicated bites, a pruritic erythematous papule or plaque may be present for 1 to 2 weeks after removal. Sometimes, a persistent, firm, pruritic, erythematous papule or nodule known as a tick bite granuloma may develop. Microscopically, this lesion demonstrates a granulomatous reaction, which is thought to represent a response to retained foreign material at the bite site. If a granuloma persists, intralesional corticosteroids and occasionally surgical excision may be required to relieve the pruritus.

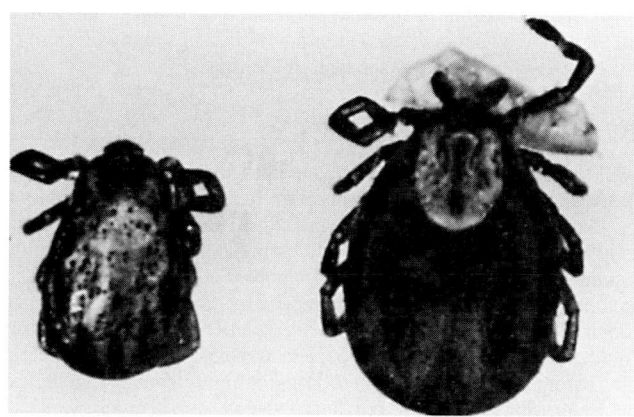

FIGURE 295-1. Nymph and adult dog ticks (*Dermacentor variabilis*). The adult female dog tick is approximately twice as large as the adult female deer tick.

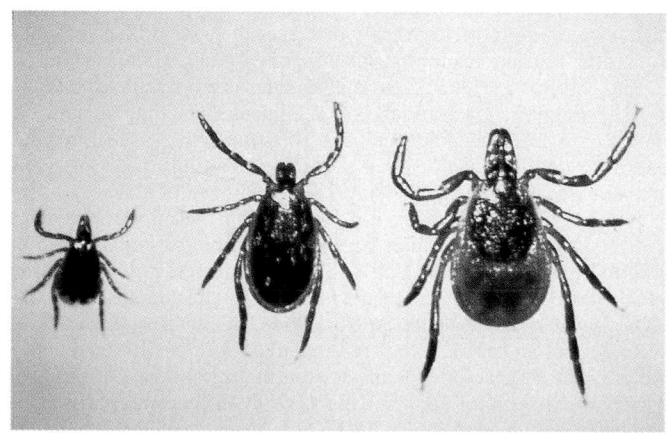

FIGURE 295-2. Nymph, adult male, and adult female ticks (*Ixodes scapularis, Ixodes dammini*). (*Courtesy of Dr. Willy Burgdorfer, Hamilton, MT.*)

Tick Paralysis

A rare but alarming reaction occasionally occurs in which prolonged attachment (5 to 7 days) of certain species of ticks results in paralysis of the host. The paralysis begins in the lower extremities and ascends symmetrically to involve the trunk, upper extremities, and head within a few hours. A neurotoxin isolated from the tick salivary gland is thought to be responsible for the neurologic symptoms. Forty-three species of ticks have been found to cause tick paralysis, but the ticks most often responsible are *Ixodes holocyclus* in Australia, *D. andersoni* in western North America, and *D. variabilis* in eastern North America.[2] A seasonal incidence of tick paralysis corresponds to the breeding season of relevant ticks. In most cases, removal of the tick leads to rapid resolution of symptoms; however, the response may be slow and associated with electromyographic evidence of denervation. Tick paralysis caused by *I. holocyclus* can be especially severe, and the host may die despite removal of the tick. A hyperimmune serum against *I. holocyclus* has been developed and is an effective treatment for tick paralysis caused by this species of tick; however, it is ineffective against other species.

Tick-Borne Relapsing Fever

Between January 1977 and January 2000, a total of 450 cases of tick-borne relapsing fever were acquired in the United States.[13] Forested and mountainous regions of the western United States and Canada are the major endemic areas. *Borrelia* species are the etiologic agents. The incubation period is generally about 1 week. Clinical manifestations include recurring episodes of fever and chills associated with constitutional symptoms such as headache, myalgia, arthralgia, nausea/vomiting, and abdominal pain. Symptomatic periods typically last 3 days, and relapse occurs in approximately 1 week. A similar but more severe syndrome may occur that is caused by *Borrelia* acquired from body lice.

Human Ehrlichioses

Bacteria of the genus *Ehrlichia* are rickettsia-like obligatory intracellular organisms found in the cytoplasmic vacuoles of host phagocytic leukocytes.[14] White-tailed deer and dogs appear to be important reservoir species for *E. chaffeensis,* the principal agent implicated in HME. Lone Star tick larvae or nymphs presumably acquire the organisms from infected reservoir species and then transmit the disease to humans. Most patients with clinical disease are middle-aged men who present during spring or summer. Missouri, Tennessee, Oklahoma, Texas, Arkansas, Virginia, and Georgia have the highest number of serologically confirmed cases in the United States.[15]

Fever, myalgia, headache, nausea, and other nonspecific symptoms are frequent. An exanthem develops in up to 36% of patients. Leukopenia, thrombocytopenia, and elevated hepatic transaminase levels are common laboratory abnormalities. Delay in diagnosis and institution of appropriate therapy increases the risk of fatal complications, such as acute respiratory insufficiency, renal failure, coagulopathy and hemorrhage, shock and multiorgan system failure, among others. The diagnosis is based largely on clinical suspicion, but detection of organism-specific nucleic acids in body fluids by polymerase chain reaction amplification and serologic testing are available. Doxycycline, 100 mg twice a day, is the treatment of choice.

Human granulocytic ehrlichiosis was initially described in the upper Midwest, but cases have since been reported from several states in the eastern United States and California. The epidemiologic features resemble those of Lyme disease, as *I. scapularis* is the principal vector and white-footed mice and deer are reservoirs.[16] Patients with concurrent Lyme disease and HGE have been reported, and ticks from an area in which Lyme disease is endemic have a high prevalence of the HGE agent. Other important mammalian reservoirs include sheep, goats, cattle, horses, and dogs. As with HME, adult men who present during the spring or summer are most frequently affected.[15] Clinical features are generally similar to those of HME, except cutaneous findings are much less frequent. Thrombocytopenia, leukopenia, and transaminase eleva-

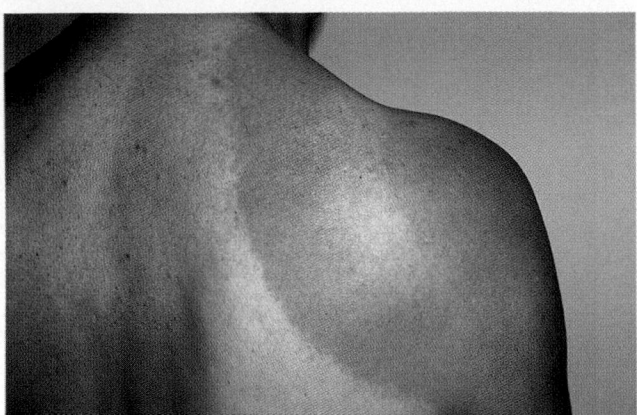

FIGURE 295-3. Expanding erythematous annular lesion of erythema migrans on the shoulder of a patient with Lyme disease.

tions are usual; and intracellular inclusions may be observed in peripheral blood neutrophils. HGE is potentially more severe than HME. Diagnosis and treatment are identical to those for HME.

Lyme Disease

The most common tick-borne disease in the United States is Lyme disease, a multisystem disorder caused by the spirochete *B. burgdorferi* (see Chapter 239). As noted above, *Ixodes* species are the primary vectors for Lyme disease. The seasonal occurrence of Lyme disease parallels the emergence of *Ixodes* ticks between May and November, with most cases occurring during June and July.

An erythematous papule may develop at the site of a tick bite within 4 to 20 days and expand into an erythematous annular lesion with central clearing, an eruption known as erythema migrans (Fig. 295-3). Secondary annular lesions may also develop weeks to months later at locations distant from the original tick bite. Patients with Lyme disease may also have internal involvement, primarily of the heart, joints, and nervous system. Treatment options for early disease include doxycycline and amoxicillin.[17] For a comprehensive review, see Steere.[18]

Southern Tick-Associated Rash Illness

An erythema migrans-like eruption unrelated to *Borrelia burgdorferi* infection has been reported from the southeastern United States.[19] The putative infectious agent is the spirochete *Borrelia lonestari,* which appears to be transmitted by the bite of *Ambylomma americanus.*[20] The white-tailed deer is a likely reservoir.[21]

The eruption develops 2 to 12 days after discovery and removal of the attached tick. Mild systemic symptoms, including fever, may occur. The natural history of this disease is unknown. What, if any, treatment should be given is likewise unknown. Perhaps many of these patients are being treated as cases of Lyme disease.

ERADICATION AND PREVENTION

A well organized, carefully implemented program can successfully control medically or economically important ticks in a limited geographic area. Such programs include the widespread use of acaricides in domestic animals and breeding domestic animals that are resistant to tick infestation. Spraying an area with appropriate chemicals, such as organophosphates, may temporarily reduce the tick population, but such an approach may cause significant adverse effects to both the environment (e.g., toxicity to beneficial species) and exposed humans. Clearing brush, particularly with controlled burns in highly endemic areas, may decrease the tick population; but, again, the effect is temporary.[22,23]

Avoiding exposure to highly endemic areas is the optimal approach to preventing tick-borne illness. People who live and work in such areas are at an unavoidable risk. Persons thus exposed should wear protective clothing (e.g., long-sleeved shirts tucked into long light-colored pants tucked into high socks), use insect repellents, and examine themselves regularly for ticks. *N,N*-Diethyl-*m*-toluamide (DEET)-containing repellents applied to exposed skin combined with permethrin treatment of clothing appears to be an effective approach. Children should be examined periodically by their parents during the tick season (midspring to midsummer). Periodic removal of ticks from household pets is important to prevent spread within the household.

PREVENTION OF LYME DISEASE

Prophylaxis for Lyme disease is an unsettled issue. Most investigators have discouraged the use of prophylactic antibiotics to prevent Lyme disease after *Ixodes scapularis* bites because of the negative results of several studies.[24-27] A general problem with such studies is that the incidence of erythema migrans following tick bites is low, even in endemic areas, so a large number of subjects is required to have enough potential cases to detect a significant difference between treatment and control groups.

A study involving nearly 500 subjects in an endemic area has further stimulated the discussion and makes the best case to date in support of prophylaxis. Results showed that 1 of 235 study subjects who took a single 200 mg dose of doxycycline developed erythema migrans versus 8 of 247 subjects in the placebo (control) group ($P <$ 0.04). The authors concluded that a single 200 mg dose of doxycycline taken within 72 hours after discovery of an *I. scapularis* bite can prevent the development of Lyme disease.[28] This study has been criticized for a number of reasons, such as the limited, 6-week follow-up period, the relatively wide confidence interval, the challenge of determining the tick species, and the degree of engorgement.[29-31]

An effective vaccine for Lyme disease (LYMErix; SmithKline Beecham) was developed from recombinant *Borrelia burgdorferi* outer surface protein A (OspA).[32] The mechanism of action of the OspA vaccine is unique in that antibodies produced from active immunization appear to inactivate the organism in the midgut of the feeding tick (in an animal model).[33-35] The vaccine was withdrawn from the market because sales were poor.

REFERENCES

1. Merten HA, Durden LA. A state-by-state survey of ticks recorded from humans in the United States. J Vector Ecol 2000;25:102-113
2. Spach DH, Liles WC, Campbell GL, et al. Medical progress: tick-borne diseases in the United States. N Engl J Med 1993;329:939-947.
3. Felz MW, Durden LA. Attachment sites of four tick species (Acari: Ixodidae) parasitizing humans in Georgia and South Carolina. J Med Entomol 1999;36:361-364.
4. Marshall GS, Jacobs RF, Schutze GE, et al. Ehrlichia chafeensis seroprevalence among children in the southeast and south-central regions of the United States. Arch Pediatr Adolesc Med 2002;156:166-170.
5. Anonymous. Lyme Disease—United States: 2000. MMWR Morb Mortal Wkly Rep 2002;51:29-31.
6. Matuschka F-R, Spielman A. The vector of the Lyme disease spirochete. N Engl J Med 1992;327:542.
7. Blanco JR, Oteo JA. Human granulocytic ehrlichiosis in Europe. Clin Microbiol Infect 2002;8:763-772.
8. Bjoersdorff A, Wittesjo B, Berglun J, et al. Human granulocytic ehrlichiosis as a common cause of tick-associated fever in southeast Sweden: report from a prospective clinical study. Scand J Infect Dis 2002;34:187-191.
9. Buller RS, Arens M, Hmiel SP, et al. Ehrlichia ewingii, a newly-recognized agent of human ehrlichiosis. N Engl J Med 1999;341:148-155.
10. Paddock CD, Folk SM, Shore GM, et al. Infections with Ehrlichia chaffeensis and Ehrlichia ewingii in persons infected with the human immunodeficiency virus. Clin Infect Dis 2001;33:1586-1594.
11. Yabsley MJ, Varela AS, Tate CM, et al. Ehrlichia ewingii infection in white-tailed deer (Odocoileus virginianus). Emerg Infect Dis 2002;8:668-671.
12. Stewart RL, Burgdorfer W, Needham GR. Evaluation of three commercial tick removal tools. Wilderness Environ Med 1998;9:137-142.
13. Dworkin MS, Shoemaker PC, Fritz CL, et al. The epidemiology of tick-borne relapsing fever in the United States. Am J Trop Med Hyg 2002;66:753-758.
14. Walker DH. Emerging human ehrlichiosis: recently recognized, widely distributed, life-threatening tick-borne diseases. In: Scheld WM, Armstrong D, Hughes JM, eds. Emerging Infections. Washington, DC: ASM Press; 1998:81-91.
15. Bakken JS, Kreuth J, Wilson-Nordskog RL, et al. Human granulocytic ehrlichiosis (HGE): clinical and laboratory characteristics of 41 patients from Minnesota and Wisconsin. JAMA 1996;275:199-205.
16. Fishbein DB, Dawson JE, Robinson LE. Human ehrlichiosis in the United States, 1985 to 1990. Ann Intern Med 1994;120:736-743.
17. Wormser GP, Nadelman RB, Dattwyler RJ, et al. Practice guidelines for the treatment of Lyme disease. Clin Infect Dis 2000;31:1-14.
18. Steere AC. Medical progress: Lyme disease. N Engl J Med 2001;345:115-125.
19. Kirkland KB, Klimko TB, Meriwether RA, et al. Erythema migrans-like rash illness at a camp in North Carolina: a new tick-borne disease? Arch Intern Med 1997;157:2635-2641.
20. James AM, Liveris D, Wormser GP, et al. Borelia lonestari infection after a bite by an Ambylomma americanum tick. J Infect Dis 2001;183:1810-1814.
21. Moore VA 4th, Varela AS, Yabsley MJ, et al. Detection of Borrelia lonestari, putative agent of southern tick-associated rash illness, in white-tailed deer (Odocoileus virginianus) from the southeastern United States. J Clin Microbiol 2003;41:424-427.
22. Schultze TL, Jordan RA, Hung RW. Suppression of subadult Ixodes scapularis (Acari:Ixodidae) following removal of leaf litter. J Med Entomol 1995;32:730-733.
23. Stafford KC III, Cartter ML, Magnarelli LA. Impact of controlled burns on the abundance of Ixodes scapularis (Acari:Ixodidae). J Med Entomol 1998;35:510-513.
24. Costello CM, Steere AC, Pinkerton RE, et al. A prospective study of tick bites in an endemic area for Lyme disease. J Infect Dis 1989;159:136-139.
25. Shapiro ED, Gerber MA, Holabird ND, et al. A controlled trial of antimicrobial prophylaxis for Lyme disease after deer-tick bites. N Engl J Med 1992;327:1769-1773.
26. Agre F, Schwartz R. The value of early treatment of deer tick bites for the prevention of Lyme disease. Am J Dis Child 1993;147:945-947.
27. Poland GA. Prevention of Lyme disease: a review of the evidence. Mayo Clin Proc 2001;76:713-724.
28. Nadelman RB, Nowakowski J, Fish D, et al. Prophylaxis with single-dose doxycycline for the prevention of Lyme disease after an Ixodes scapularis tick bite. N Engl J Med 2001;12:345:79-84.
29. Meyerhoff J. Single-dose doxycycline prevented Lyme disease after an Ixodes scapularis tick bite. ACP J Club 2002;136:56-57.
30. Gonzalez U. Antibiotic prophylaxis for Lyme disease: how the way of reporting a clinical trial can alter the perception of effectiveness. Arch Dermatol 2003;139:373-375.
31. Shapiro ED. Doxycycline for tick bites: not for everyone (Editorial). N Engl J Med 2001;345:133-134.
32. Anonymous. Lyme disease vaccine. Med Lett Drugs Ther 1999;41:29-30.
33. Fikrig E, Telford SR III, Barthold SW, et al. Elimination of Borrelia burgdorferi from vector ticks feeding on OspA-immunized mice. Proc Natl Acad Sci USA 1992;89:5418-5421.
34. Lathrop SL, Ball R, Haber P, et al. Adverse events reported following vaccination for Lyme disease: December 1998–July 2000. Vaccine 2002;20:1603-1608.
35. Steere AC, Sikand VK, Meurice F, et al. Vaccination against Lyme disease with recombinant Borrelia burdorferi outer-surface lipoprotein A with adjuvant. N Engl J Med 1998;339:209-215.

BIBLIOGRAPHY

Edlow JA, ed. Tick-borne diseases. Med Clin North Am 2002;86(2).
Goddard J. Physician's Guide to Arthropods of Medical Importance. 2nd ed. Boca Raton, FL: CRC Press; 1996.
Sonenshine DE. Biology of Ticks, v. 1. New York: Oxford University Press; 1991.
Sonenshine DE. Biology of Ticks, v. 2. New York: Oxford University Press; 1993.
Sonenshine DE, Mather TN, eds. Ecological Dynamics of Tick-Borne Zoonoses. New York: Oxford University Press; 1994.

CHAPTER **296**

Kawasaki Syndrome

FRANK T. SAULSBURY

Kawasaki syndrome is an acute systemic vasculitis that affects primarily infants and young children. It was first reported in the Japanese literature in 1967 by Dr. Tomisaku Kawasaki.[1] The initial reports in the English literature appeared in the 1970s under the designation of "mucocutaneous lymph node syndrome." Kawasaki syndrome is not a new disease; earlier descriptions of infantile periarteritis nodosa almost certainly represented examples of Kawasaki syndrome.

EPIDEMIOLOGY

Although Kawasaki syndrome is recognized throughout the world, it is particularly common in Japan, with an incidence of 90/100,000 children younger than 5 years of age.[2] In the United States, the incidence of Kawasaki syndrome is approximately 9 per 100,000 children younger than 5 years of age.[3] In the United States, the disease is more common in children of Japanese or Korean ancestry.[4] Kawasaki syndrome has been reported in a few adults, but it is overwhelmingly a disease of young children. The peak age of onset is 1 to 2 years, and 80% of patients are younger than 5 years of age. The male-to-female ratio is 1.5:1. Not only are males affected more frequently, but they are at greater risk for developing coronary artery aneurysms, the most serious complication of the disease.[5]

Kawasaki syndrome occurs sporadically and in mini-epidemics. Both endemic and epidemic cases occur more commonly in late winter and spring. Person-to-person spread has not been documented, and secondary cases in contacts of affected patients are unusual. Nevertheless, Kawasaki syndrome occurs in siblings (especially twins) of affected patients more frequently than in the general population.[6] More than half of the secondary cases in siblings develop within 10 days after the first case, suggesting a common exposure to an infectious agent.

CLINICAL FEATURES

The diagnosis of Kawasaki syndrome is established by the presence of the clinical criteria listed in Table 296-1.[7] Fever is usually the initial feature of Kawasaki syndrome. It is characteristically high, spiking, and prolonged, and it persists for 1 to 2 weeks in untreated patients. Bilateral, nonpurulent conjunctivitis ensues shortly after the onset of fever and lasts 1 to 2 weeks in untreated patients. The conjunctival involvement is characterized by hyperemia and injection of the bulbar conjunctivae (Fig. 296-1). Changes of the oropharyngeal mucosa, consisting of (1) erythema progressing to fissuring, cracking, and bleeding of the lips, (2) strawberry tongue, and (3) diffuse erythema of the oropharynx, are prominent during the acute febrile period (see Fig. 296-1).

Changes of the extremities include erythema of the palms and soles accompanied by firm, indurative edema. The swollen extremities may be quite painful. During recovery, a distinctive pattern of skin desqua-

mation develops. Desquamation begins in the periungal region and often extends to involve the entire palms and soles. The erythematous rash of Kawasaki syndrome usually appears shortly after the onset of fever and it persists during the febrile period. Most often, the rash is a raised, deep red, plaquelike eruption (Fig. 296-2). A morbilliform maculopapular rash with multiforme-like target lesions, a scarlatiniform erythroderma, and rarely a fine pustular eruption have also been observed in Kawasaki syndrome. Typically, there is widespread involvement of the trunk and extremities with accentuation in the perineal area.

Cervical lymphadenopathy is the least common of the principal diagnostic criteria. At least one lymph node measuring greater than 1.5 cm in diameter is necessary to fulfill the criterion for this finding. Usually there is enlargement of a single cervical lymph node; the nodes are firm, nonfluctuant, and only moderately tender.

In addition to the clinical features that constitute the diagnostic criteria, there are a wide variety of associated findings in Kawasaki syndrome, owing to the systemic nature of the vasculitis. Some of the more common associated features are listed in Table 296-2.[8]

Up to 10% of patients do not fulfill the requisite clinical criteria, and they are designated having atypical or incomplete Kawasaki syndrome. Atypical disease is especially common in infants less than 12 months of age. Patients with atypical Kawasaki syndrome are at risk for coronary artery aneurysms.[9] Indeed, finding coronary artery aneurysms may be the only way to definitively diagnose atypical Kawasaki syndrome.

TABLE 296-1 Diagnostic Criteria for Kawasaki Syndrome

A. Fever of at least 5 days' duration (100%)
B. Presence of at least four of the following five conditions*:
  1. Bilateral conjunctivitis (85%)
  2. Changes in the lips and oral mucosa (90%)
     Dry, red, fissured lips
     "Strawberry tongue"
     Oropharyngeal erythema
  3. Changes in the extremities (75%)
     Erythema of palms and soles
     Edema of hands and feet
     Periungual desquamation
  4. Polymorphous rash (80%)
  5. Cervical lymphadenopathy (70%)
C. Illness not explained by other known disease processes

*Kawasaki syndrome may be diagnosed in patients with fever and fewer than the required four of five other criteria in the presence of coronary artery abnormalities.

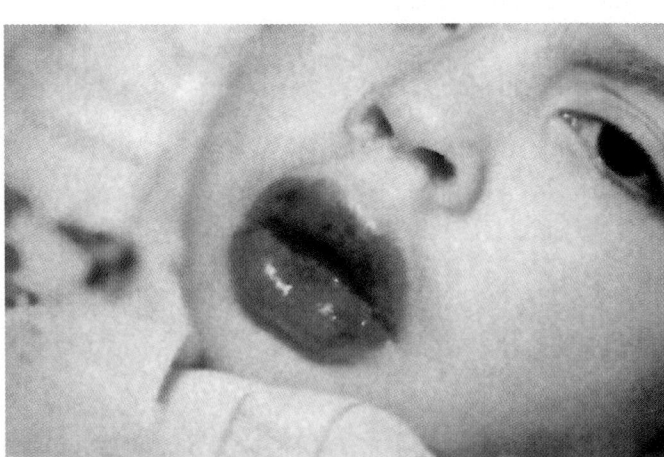

FIGURE 296-1. Conjunctival injection, lip edema, and erythema in a 2-year-old boy on the 6th day of illness. *(From Diagnostic Guidelines for Kawasaki Disease. Circulation 2001;103:335-336. Copyright American Heart Association.)*

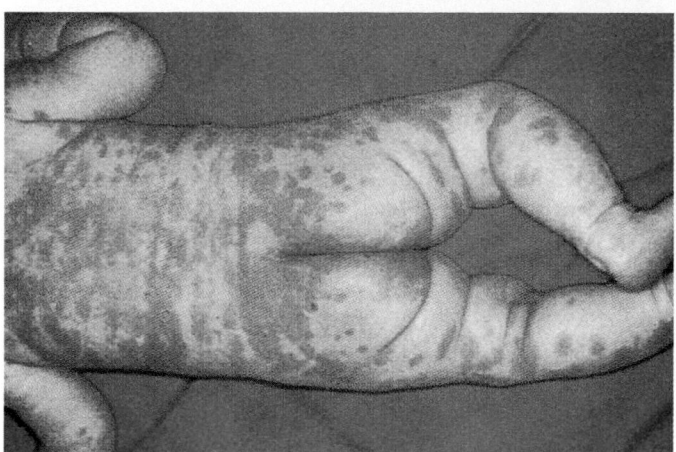

FIGURE 296-2. Rash of Kawasaki disease in a 7-month-old boy on the 4th day of illness. *(From Diagnostic Guidelines for Kawasaki Disease. Circulation 2001;103:335-336. Copyright American Heart Association.)*

The clinical course of untreated Kawasaki syndrome is triphasic. The *acute febrile phase,* lasting 7 to 14 days, is dominated by the features comprising the diagnostic criteria. Irritability, anorexia, aseptic meningitis, and hepatic dysfunction are also prominent features of the acute phase. During the *subacute phase,* which lasts 2 to 4 weeks, fever, rash, and lymphadenopathy resolve, but irritability and conjunctival injection may persist. Arthritis and desquamation of the fingers and toes occur during the subacute phase. Thrombocytosis, often reaching very high levels, is seen during the subacute phase. This is the time when patients are at greatest risk of coronary artery thrombosis. The *convalescent phase* of Kawasaki syndrome begins when all clinical signs have disappeared, and it continues until the sedimentation rate and platelet count return to normal, usually 6 to 10 weeks after the onset of illness.

Recurrent Kawasaki syndrome after apparent resolution is rare, occurring in only 1% to 3% of patients.[8] Most recurrences develop within a few weeks of the original episode.

CARDIAC INVOLVEMENT

Although carditis is not included in the diagnostic criteria, cardiac involvement is the hallmark of Kawasaki syndrome, and it is the major source of morbidity and mortality. During the acute phase, up to 50% of patients have myocarditis manifested by tachycardia and gallop rhythms. Occasionally, myocarditis is severe enough to produce overt congestive heart failure. Pericarditis, conduction disturbances, and regurgitation of the mitral and aortic valves are less frequent manifestations of cardiac involvement during the acute phase.[10]

The most serious cardiac complication of Kawasaki syndrome is aneurysmal dilatation of the coronary arteries, occurring in approximately 20% of untreated patients.[10] Dilatation of the proximal coronary arteries may be detected as early as 7 days after the onset of fever,

with a peak frequency of coronary aneurysm formation occurring within 4 weeks of the onset of illness. If unrecognized and untreated, the coronary aneurysms are prone to clot during the subacute phase of the illness, when the patients are hypercoagulable because of the extreme thrombocytosis. Sudden death from coronary thrombosis and myocardial infraction occurs in 1% to 2% of untreated patients.

The coronary aneurysms regress within 1 to 2 years in the majority of patients.[11] However, even with echocardiographic resolution of the aneurysms, there may be persistent coronary artery stenosis and cardiac ischemia in some patients. The long-term consequences of coronary arteritis are unclear, but ischemic heart disease, myocardial infarction, and sudden death have been reported in young adult survivors of childhood Kawasaki syndrome.[12]

LABORATORY FEATURES

The laboratory features of Kawasaki syndrome are nonspecific and nondiagnostic. The acute phase of the illness is characterized by marked inflammation and immune activation. Most patients have a moderate leukocytosis with a left shift. The sedimentation rate and other acute phase reactants are almost universally elevated during the acute febrile period. Sterile pyuria and elevated alanine aminotransferase levels are present in approximately 50% of patients. The platelet count, which is normal in the first few days of Kawasaki syndrome, begins to rise in the second week of the illness and may ultimately exceed 1,000,000/μL in untreated patients. Tests for antinuclear antibody and rheumatoid factor are routinely negative. A number of immunoregulatory abnormalities have been described in patients with Kawasaki syndrome. These include increased proportions of activated CD4$^+$ lymphocytes, decreased numbers of CD8$^+$ lymphocytes, polyclonal B cell activation, and increased production of a number of proinflammatory cytokines.[8,13]

DIFFERENTIAL DIAGNOSIS

The diagnostic criteria for Kawasaki syndrome are not entirely sensitive or specific. Moreover, there is no diagnostic laboratory test for Kawasaki syndrome. Thus, it is necessary to consider other conditions in the differential diagnosis of Kawasaki syndrome. Some of these conditions are listed in Table 296-3.[8]

PATHOLOGY

Kawasaki syndrome is a generalized vasculitis involving small and medium-sized arteries, with a predilection for the coronary arteries. Histologically, Kawasaki syndrome is characterized by endothelial cell necrosis, leukocyte infiltration of the media and adventitia, medial disruption, aneurysmal dilatation, and intraluminal thrombosis.

ETIOLOGY AND PATHOGENESIS

The clinical and epidemiologic features of Kawasaki syndrome clearly suggest an infectious etiology. However, intensive efforts during the past 30 years have failed to identify a single verifiable infectious cause of Kawasaki syndrome. Recent evidence suggests that Kawasaki syndrome

TABLE 296-2 Associated Features of Kawasaki Syndrome

1. Cardiac disease
   Coronary artery aneurysms
   Myocarditis
   Pericarditis
   Mitral or aortic regurgitation
   Arrhythmias
2. Irritability
3. Arthralgia, arthritis
4. Aseptic meningitis
5. Urethritis with sterile pyuria
6. Hepatitis
7. Hydrops of the gallbladder
8. Pancreatitis
9. Pneumonitis
10. Anterior uveitis
11. Sensorineural hearing loss
12. Peripheral ischemia

TABLE 296-3 Differential Diagnosis of Kawasaki Syndrome

Infections	Other conditions
Measles	Rheumatic fever
Scarlet fever	Stevens-Johnson syndrome
Staphylococcal or streptococcal toxic shock syndrome	Systemic juvenile rheumatoid arthritis
Rocky Mountain spotted fever	Polyarteritis nodosa
Parvovirus B19 infection	Reiter's syndrome
Leptospirosis	Drug reaction
Adenovirus infection	
Enterovirus infection	

may be caused by superantigen bacterial toxins.[14] Superantigens stimulate large populations of T cells expressing particular T-cell-receptor beta-chain variable-region gene products.[15] The immunologic consequences of superantigen stimulation include massive proliferation and expansion of the target T cells with resultant production of pro-inflammatory cytokines.[15] The pathologic consequences of uncontrolled activation of the immune system include the recruitment of endothelial cells into the inflammatory process with resultant vascular damage.[13,14]

A number of toxins elaborated by *Staphylococcus aureus* and *Streptococcus pyogenes* are known to possess superantigen properties.[15] Several lines of evidence support a role for staphylococcal or streptococcal superantigen toxins in the pathogenesis of Kawasaki syndrome. First, selective expansion of Vβ2+ and Vβ8+ T cells in the peripheral blood of patients with Kawasaki syndrome provides indirect evidence of exposure to superantigens.[16-20] Second, selective expansion of Vβ2+ T cells has been found in the myocardium, coronary arteries, and small intestinal mucosa of patients with Kawasaki syndrome.[21,22] Third, staphylococci and streptococci elaborating superantigen toxins (toxic shock syndrome toxin-1 and streptococcal pyrogenic exotoxin, respectively) have been cultured from patients with Kawasaki syndrome.[23,24] Fourth, antibody to toxic shock syndrome toxin-1 is higher in infants less than 6 months of age with Kawasaki syndrome compared to controls, and mothers of infants with Kawasaki syndrome had lower antibody levels to toxic shock syndrome toxin-1 compared to adult controls.[25] However, other studies have not confirmed the expansion of Vβ2+ or Vβ8+ T cells in the peripheral blood of patients with Kawasaki syndrome, and these studies suggest that conventional antigens rather than superantigens are involved in the etiology of Kawasaki syndrome.[26-29] Moreover, culture and serologic data have disputed the role of staphylococcal or streptococcal superantigen toxins in the pathophysiology of Kawasaki syndrome.[30,31] Thus, the etiology of Kawasaki syndrome remains an area of controversy. Nevertheless, the superantigen toxin theory is an attractive explanation for many of the clinical, epidemiologic, and immunologic features of Kawasaki syndrome.

The increased incidence of Kawasaki syndrome in children of Asian ancestry and in siblings of affected children suggests a genetic contribution to the risk of the disease. Early attention focused on major histocompatibility complex (MHC) associations. To date, no clear, consistent MHC class I or class II associations with Kawasaki syndrome have been demonstrated.[32] Recent studies have suggested that genes involved in the inflammatory response or the innate immune system may be associated with Kawasaki syndrome.[33-35] Nevertheless, definitive information concerning the genetic susceptibility to Kawasaki syndrome is lacking.

THERAPY

Despite incomplete knowledge about the etiology and pathogenesis, there has been effective therapy for Kawasaki syndrome for nearly 20 years. Several randomized studies in Japan and the United States have demonstrated that high-dose immune globulin, intravenous (IGIV) is extremely effective therapy for Kawasaki syndrome.[36,37] The use of IGIV has resulted in a substantial decrease in the morbidity and mortality associated with Kawasaki syndrome. IGIV produces rapid resolution of fever and other clinical manifestations of the acute febrile phase and reverses the laboratory indices of systemic inflammation. More importantly, when IGIV is administered within the first 10 days of the illness, the incidence of coronary artery aneurysms is reduced from approximately 20% in untreated patients to 3% to 4%.[36,37] In addition to preventing coronary aneurysms, IGIV is effective in promoting the resolution of established aneurysms.[38] A number of dosage schedules have been studied, but the most effective regimen is a single infusion of IGIV in a dosage of 2 g/kg given over 10 hours.[37]

Approximately 10% of patients have persistent fever or recrudescence of fever more than 48 hours after completion of the IGIV therapy.[39,40] These patients are at increased risk for development of coronary artery aneurysms, and they should be re-treated with IGIV.[39,40]

The optimal management of the rare patient who develops coronary artery aneurysms or who remains persistently febrile despite repeated IGIV infusions remains unclear. There is anecdotal evidence that corticosteroids and low-dose aspirin may be of benefit in such patients, but this has not been studied in a systematic fashion.[41,42]

The mechanisms by which IGIV produces dramatic beneficial effects remain unclear. IGIV is a powerful immunomodulating agent, and it may directly reverse a number of the immunologic abnormalities associated with Kawasaki syndrome. The rapidity with which IGIV works suggests toxin neutralization as a possible mechanism of action. Indeed, commercial IGIV contains specific antibodies to bacterial toxin superantigens.[43]

Aspirin is used as adjunctive therapy in Kawasaki syndrome. Traditionally, aspirin is administered in anti-inflammatory dosages (80-100 mg/kg/day) until the patient is afebrile or until day 14 of the illness. The dosage is then reduced to 3 to 5 mg/kg/day to provide an antiplatelet effect during the period of thrombocytosis when patients are at risk for clotting coronary artery aneurysms.[7] Because IGIV therapy aborts the acute phase of the illness so rapidly, treatment with low-dose aspirin from the outset seems reasonable, but this regimen has not been studied prospectively. Nevertheless, a meta-analysis of published data and a recent retrospective study found no significant difference between the incidence of coronary artery disease in patients treated with IGIV plus high-dose aspirin and those treated with IGIV and low-dose aspirin.[44,45] In patients with no evidence of coronary artery disease, low-dose aspirin is continued until the platelet count returns to normal. In the patients with coronary aneurysms despite IGIV therapy, low-dose aspirin should be continued indefinitely or until 1 year after the aneurysms resolve.

Echocardiography at the time of diagnosis provides valuable baseline information. All patients should have repeat echocardiography 3 to 6 weeks after therapy to guide the duration of aspirin therapy. Patients with coronary artery abnormalities should receive long-term monitoring of cardiac function.

REFERENCES

1. Kawasaki T. Acute febrile mucocutaneous syndrome with lymphoid involvement with specific desquamation of the fingers and toes in children: Clinical observations of 50 cases. Jpn J Allerg. 1967;16:178-222.
2. Yanagawa H, Yashiro M, Nakamura Y, et al. Epidemiologic picture of Kawasaki disease in Japan from the nationwide incidence survey 1991 and 1992. Pediatrics. 1995;95:475-479.
3. Taubert KA, Rowley AH, Shulman ST. Seven-year national survey of Kawasaki disease and rheumatic fever. Pediatr Infect Dis J. 1994;13:704-708.
4. Shulman ST, De Inocencio J, Hirsch R. Kawasaki disease. Pediatr Clin North Am. 1995;42:1205-1222.
5. Beiser AS, Takahashi M, Baker AL, et al. A predictive instrument for coronary artery aneurysms in Kawasaki disease. Am J Cardiol. 1998;81:1116-1120.
6. Fugita Y, Kakamura Y, Sakata K, et al. Kawasaki disease in families. Pediatrics. 1989;84:666-669.
7. Dajani AS, Taubert KA, Gerber MA, et al. Diagnosis and therapy of Kawasaki disease in children. Circulation. 1993;87:1776-1780.
8. Mason WH, Takahashi M. Kawasaki syndrome. Clin Infect Dis. 1999;28:169-187.
9. Fukushige J, Takahashi N, Ueda Y, et al. Incidence and clinical features of incomplete Kawasaki disease. Acta Paediatr. 1994;83:1057-1060.
10. Rose V. Kawasaki syndrome: Cardiovascular manifestations. J Rheumatol. 1990;17(Suppl 24):11-14.
11. Kato H, Ichinose E, Yoshioka F, et al. Fate of coronary aneurysms in Kawasaki disease: A serial coronary angiography and long-term follow-up study. Am J Cardiol. 1982;49:1758-1766.
12. Burns JC, Shike H, Gordon JB, et al. Sequelae of Kawasaki disease in adolescents and young adults. J Am Coll Cardiol. 1996;28:253-257.
13. Leung DYM, Schlievert PM, Meissner HC. The immunopathogenesis and management of Kawasaki syndrome. Arthritis Rheum. 1998;41:1538-1547.
14. Meissner HC, Leung DYM. Superantigens, conventional antigens and the etiology of Kawasaki syndrome. Pediatr Infect Dis J. 2000;19:91-94.
15. Drake CG, Kotzin BL. Superantigens: Biology, immunology, and potential role in disease. J Clin Immunol. 1992;12:149-162.
16. Abe J, Kotzin BL, Jujo K, et al. Selective expansion of T cells expressing T-cell receptor variable regions V beta 2 and V beta 8 in Kawasaki disease. Proc Natl Acad Sci U S A. 1992;89:4066-4070.
17. Brogan PA, Shah V, Klein N, et al. T cell Vβ repertoires in childhood vasculitides. Clin Exp Immunol. 2003;131:517-527.
18. Curtis N, Zheng R, Lamb JR, et al. Evidence for a superantigen mediated process in Kawasaki disease. Arch Dis Child. 1995;72:308-311.

19. Yoshioka T, Matsutani T, Iwagami S, et al. Polyclonal expansion of TCRBV2 and TCRBV6 bearing T cells in patients with Kawasaki disease. Immunology. 1999;96:465-472.
20. Yoshioka T, Matsutani T, Toyosaki-Maeda T, et al. Relation of streptococcal pyrogenic exotoxin C as a causative superantigen for Kawasaki disease. Pediatr Res. 2003;53:403-410.
21. Leung DYM, Giorno RC, Kazemi LV, et al. Evidence for superantigen involvement in cardiovascular injury due to Kawasaki syndrome. J Immunol. 1995;155:5018-5021.
22. Yamashiro Y, Nagata S, Oguchi S, et al. Selective increase of Vβ2+ T cells in the small intestinal mucosa in Kawasaki disease. Pediatr Res. 1996;39:264-266.
23. Leung DYM, Meissner HC, Fulton DR, et al. Toxic shock syndrome toxin-secreting *Staphylococcus aureus* in Kawasaki syndrome. Lancet. 1993;342:1385-1388.
24. Leung DYM, Meissner HC, Shulman ST, et al. Prevalence of superantigen-secreting bacteria in patients with Kawasaki disease. J Pediatr. 2002;140:742-746.
25. Nomura Y, Yoshinaga M, Masuda K, et al. Maternal antibody against toxic shock syndrome toxin-1 may protect infants younger than 6 months of age from developing Kawasaki syndrome. J Infect Dis. 2002;185:1677-1680.
26. Pietra BA, De Inocencio J, Giannini EH, et al. TCR Vβ family repertoire and T cell activation markers in Kawasaki disease. J Immunol. 1994;153:1881-1888.
27. Jason J, Montana E, Donald JF, et al. Kawasaki disease and the T cell antigen receptor. Hum Immunol. 1998;59:29-38.
28. Mancia L, Wahlstrom J, Schiller B, et al. Characterization of the T-cell receptor V-β repertoire in Kawasaki disease. Scand J Immunol. 1998;48:443-449.
29. Rowley AH, Shulman ST, Spike BT, et al. Oligoclonal IgA response in the vascular wall in acute Kawasaki disease. J Immunol. 2001;166:1334-1343.
30. Terai M, Miwa K, Williams T, et al. The absence of evidence of staphylococcal toxin involvement in the pathogenesis of Kawasaki disease. J Infect Dis. 1995;172:558-561.
31. Morita A, Imada Y, Igarashi H, et al. Serologic evidence that streptococcal superantigens are not involved in the pathogenesis of Kawasaki disease. Microbiol Immunol. 1997;41:895-900.
32. Barron KS, Silverman ED, Gonzales JC, et al. Major histocompatibility complex class II alleles in Kawasaki syndrome: Lack of consistent correlation with disease or cardiac involvement. J Rheumatol. 1992;19:1790-1793.
33. Quasney MW, Bronstein DE, Cantor RM, et al. Increased frequency of alleles associated with elevated tumor necrosis factor-alpha levels in children with Kawasaki disease. Pediatr Res. 2001;49:685-690.
34. Ouchi K, Suzuki Y, Shirakawa T, et al. Polymorphism of SLC11A1 (formerly NRAMP1) gene confers susceptibility to Kawasaki disease. J Infect Dis. 2003;187:326-329.
35. Biezeveld MH, Kuipers IM, Geissler J, et al. Association of mannose-binding lectin genotype with cardiovascular abnormalities in Kawasaki disease. Lancet. 2003;361:1268-1270.
36. Newburger JW, Takahashi M, Burns JC, et al. The treatment of Kawasaki syndrome with intravenous gamma globulin. N Engl J Med. 1986;315:341-347.
37. Newburger JW, Takahashi M, Beiser AS, et al. A single intravenous infusion of gamma globulin as compared with four infusions in the treatment of acute Kawasaki syndrome. N Engl J Med. 1991;324:1633-1639.
38. Saalouke MG, Venglarick JS, Baker DR, et al. Rapid regression of coronary dilatation in Kawasaki disease with intravenous gamma globulin. Am Heart J. 1991;121:905-909.
39. Burns JC, Capparelli EV, Brown JA, et al. Intravenous gamma-globulin treatment and retreatment in Kawasaki disease. Pediatr Infect Dis J. 1998;17:1144-1148.
40. Durongpisitkul K, Soongswang J, Laohaprasitiporn D, et al. Immunoglobulin failure and retreatment in Kawasaki disease. Pediatr Cardiol. 2003;24:145-148.
41. Wright DA, Newburger JW, Baker A, et al. Treatment of immune globulin-resistant Kawasaki disease with pulsed doses of corticosteroids. J Pediatr. 1996;128:146-149.
42. Dale RC, Saleem MA, Daw S, et al. Treatment of severe complicated Kawasaki disease with oral prednisolone and aspirin. J Pediatr. 2000;137:723-726.
43. Takei S, Arora YK, Walker SM. Intravenous immunoglobulin contains specific antibodies inhibitory to activation of T cells by staphylococcal toxin superantigens. J Clin Invest. 1993;91:602-607.
44. Terai M, Shulman ST. Prevalence of coronary artery abnormalities is highly dependent on gamma globulin dose but independent of salicylate dose. J Pediatr. 1997;131:888-893.
45. Saulsbury FT. Comparison of high-dose and low-dose aspirin plus intravenous immunoglobulin in the treatment of Kawasaki syndrome. Clin Pediatr. 2002;41:597-601.

CHAPTER 297

Organization for Infection Control

MICHAEL B. EDMOND
RICHARD P. WENZEL

Infection control as a formal discipline in the United States developed during the late 1950s primarily to address the problem of nosocomial staphylococcal infections. Over the ensuing years, the field of infection control was enhanced by incorporating epidemiologic principles and applying statistical analyses. Today, infection control is one facet of the broader discipline of health care epidemiology, the study of clinical performance, which includes the analysis of infectious and noninfectious adverse outcomes.

The primary role of an infection-control program is to reduce the risk of hospital-acquired infection, thereby protecting patients, employees, health care students, and visitors. Nosocomial infections develop in at least 5% of patients admitted to hospitals in the United States[1] and account for 88,000 deaths yearly.[2] In the era of managed care with an intense focus on cost control, the value of effective infection control is obvious.

The functions of a hospital epidemiology program vary from institution to institution but can generally be divided into the following areas: surveillance, outbreak investigation, education, employee health, the monitoring and management of institutional antibiotic utilization, the development of infection-control policies and procedures, environmental hygiene, and new-product evaluation. In some hospitals, quality improvement is also undertaken through the hospital epidemiology program. In the academic setting, additional functions of the program may include research and the provision of consultative services to other acute care and long-term care facilities, public health agencies, and the university campus. The major functions of the effective hospital epidemiology program are listed in Table 297-1, some of which are discussed in further detail here.

SURVEILLANCE

The first aim of surveillance is to determine endemic rates of infection. Once these rates have been established, an outbreak can be identified when its rate of occurrence is significantly higher than the endemic rate. The importance of surveillance was demonstrated by the Study on the Efficacy of Nosocomial Infection Control, which found a 32% reduction in nosocomial infections in hospitals with active surveillance programs compared with hospitals without such programs.[3] Data from hospitals in the National Nosocomial Infection Surveillance System (NNIS) demonstrated that from 1990 to 1999 nosocomial bloodstream infections decreased by 44% in medical intensive care units (ICUs), 32% in pediatric ICUs, and 31% in surgical ICUs.[4]

Surveillance for nosocomial infections is generally targeted to areas of the hospital where the highest rates of infection, highest impact of infection, and antibiotic resistance are likely to be found. These areas include ICUs, cardiothoracic surgery units, and hematology and oncology units. Hospital-wide surveillance (i.e., concurrent surveillance throughout the hospital) is rarely practiced today

because the resources required are prohibitive. Hospitals with sophisticated information systems may be able to streamline surveillance through the development of computer-based algorithms that identify patients at highest risk of a nosocomial infection. Surveillance for some infections (e.g., bloodstream infections, infections with antimicrobial-resistant organisms) is primarily microbiology-based, therefore hospital-wide surveillance for targeted infections can be implemented relatively easily.

The highest quality surveillance methodology for nosocomial infections was developed by the NNIS and is unit-based, infection site-specific, and risk-adjusted (i.e., expressed in terms of device-specific denominators). Because the NNIS methodology is the most widely accepted, hospitals that utilize it are able to compare their institutional rates to those of a large group of hospitals across the country.

Unit-based surveillance trends should be periodically reported back to the health care workers in the unit. It is important that the data be delivered in a nonconfrontational manner. Infectious diseases of public health importance should be reported to public health agencies, whose requirements vary by state.

OUTBREAK INVESTIGATION

Data accumulated by ongoing surveillance allow detection of nosocomial outbreaks. When the monthly rate for a particular infection exceeds the 95% confidence interval based on the previous years' rates for that month, the possibility of an outbreak exists and an investigation is warranted. At other times, an astute observation of a potential cluster of infections by physicians, nurses, or the microbiology laboratory technologists should prompt at least an initial investigation.

When the cluster involves a common organism, hospitals with the capability of performing rapid molecular typing may do so first. If the cluster appears to be polyclonal, it is most likely due to antimicrobial usage patterns, a technical problem, or importation of strains; and a formal case-control study may not be necessary. A clonal outbreak suggests a point source or nosocomial transmission, in which case a case-control study may be warranted.

The primary investigating team should include the hospital epidemiologist, the director of employee health, and the infection-control professionals. External consultants are necessary in some cases. Table 297-2 summarizes the steps of an outbreak investigation.

TABLE 297-1 Functions that May Fall Under the Purview of the Epidemiology Unit
Surveillance for nosocomial infections
Outbreak detection and management
Education of patients and health care workers
Occupational health program for health care workers
Postexposure prophylaxis for health care workers exposed to pathogens in the work setting
Management of the infected health care worker (restriction from work or particular activities)
Respiratory protection program
Antimicrobial usage monitoring and control, and formulary decisions
Development and implementation of policy to decrease the risk of nosocomial infection
Patient safety program
Environmental monitoring for hygiene and infectious hazards
Construction infection control (via design process and monitoring of infectious hazards associated with demolition, renovation, and construction)
Infectious waste management
New product evaluation
Quality assessment
Bioterrorism preparedness
Sterilization and disinfection of medical instruments and devices
Regulatory compliance

TABLE 297-2 Steps for Investigating an Outbreak

1. Contact the microbiology laboratory so all isolates can be saved for further analysis.
2. Develop a case definition.
3. Using the case definition, show statistically that current rates are significantly higher than preoutbreak rates.
4. Review the relevant medical literature.
5. Plot an epidemic curve with the number of cases on the Y-axis and time on the X-axis.
6. Review the charts of case patients and develop line lists containing demographic data (dates of admission and procedures, ward locations, dates) and exposure to potential risk factors.
7. Plot a time line with data for all common events. The number of cases is plotted on the Y-axis, and the time interval between infection and potential risk factor (e.g., procedure, medication, contact with potentially infected patient or health care worker) is plotted on the X-axis.
8. Formulate a hypothesis regarding the source of infection and mechanism of transmission.
9. Perform a case-control study, comparing infected patients of the same age, gender, and service with exposure to potential risk factors.
10. Institute temporary infection-control measures.
11. Obtain cultures of suspected common sources.
12. Perform molecular typing to determine relatedness of isolates.
13. Continue surveillance to document the efficacy of control measures.
14. Summarize the findings of the investigation in a report for the infection-control committee.
15. The infection-control committee should review infection-control policies related to the outbreak and revise if necessary.

EDUCATION

A substantial role for the infection-control professional is to educate hospital personnel in the areas of communicable disease control, sterilization, disinfection, and institutional infection-control policies. In many hospitals, the epidemiology team is responsible for blood-borne pathogen training and in some hospitals for airborne-isolation-mask training and fit testing. Unfortunately, educational efforts aimed at modifying the behavior of health care workers (e.g., increasing hand washing, eliminating needle recapping) have generally had little success. Some hospitals have successfully established an infection-control liaison program, whereby each hospital unit appoints a nurse who attends educational sessions periodically and helps disseminate infection-control information to colleagues.

HOSPITAL EMPLOYEE HEALTH

The hospital epidemiology program must work closely with the employee health service. Issues such as the management of exposure to blood-borne pathogens and other communicable diseases (e.g., varicella, influenza, meningococcal disease, tuberculosis) require a concerted effort by the two groups. In addition, the employee health service is responsible for ensuring that health care workers are fit for duty and free of communicable diseases. At the time of employment, workers should be reviewed to ensure that they have adequate immunity against illnesses such as rubella, measles, tetanus, hepatitis B, and varicella. In addition, baseline and periodic skin testing for tuberculosis should be performed as well as postexposure testing. The employee health service should proactively and creatively devise delivery systems that encourage compliance with annual influenza vaccination by all health care workers.

ANTIMICROBIAL UTILIZATION

Nearly one-half of hospitalized patients receive antimicrobial agents,[5] and antimicrobial usage varies widely across hospitals.[6] The hospital epidemiology program should monitor the antimicrobial susceptibility profiles produced by the microbiology laboratory on a regular basis to observe for trends in the development of antimicrobial resistance. The results should be correlated with the antimicrobial agents currently used in the institution. The best data are obtained if nosocomial isolates are distinguished from community-acquired isolates, if only blood-stream isolates are tested (true pathogens with high mortality), and if only one isolate per patient is counted in the numerator and denominator. To identify the nature of the relation between antibiotic use and resistance, a graph could be plotted with the proportion of unique nosocomial bloodstream isolates that were resistant to the drug on one axis and the total grams of usage for that drug by year on the other axis.

Efforts should be made to optimize antimicrobial prophylaxis for operative procedures, optimize the choice and duration of empiric antimicrobial therapy, and improve antimicrobial prescribing practices. A variety of approaches can be undertaken, including educational, administrative (e.g., formulary restrictions), and direct interventions by a team that manages antimicrobial utilization in real time.

POLICY DEVELOPMENT

The primary administrative function of the infection-control program is to develop, implement, and continually evaluate policies and procedures designed to minimize the risk of nosocomial infection. Some policies are designed to be implemented institution-wide, whereas others apply to specific areas of the hospital. Policies are generally developed by the infection-control committee after a review of data generated in house as well as information available from the medical literature. Recommendations from the infection-control committee may then need to be forwarded to other committees for review and approval before disseminating the new policy.

ENVIRONMENTAL HYGIENE

As the hospitalized population has become more immunosuppressed, the importance of environmental hygiene has significantly increased. Technical issues regarding air handling, construction, demolition, water supply, pest control, and medical waste management may require collaboration with engineers, architects, and other nonmedical professionals, including external consultants. The Centers for Disease Control and Prevention (CDC) has produced a document on environmental infection control[7] that is an excellent resource for hospital epidemiologists on these issues.

NEW-PRODUCT EVALUATION

A large number of new medical products are marketed each year. These products may be introduced into the hospital setting with few data to support their efficacy or their advantage over existing products. Often the new products are significantly more costly. The hospital epidemiology program should play an active role in evaluating data on new products designed to reduce infections or protect health care workers and then make recommendations regarding their introduction to the hospital. It is helpful if hospitals maintain a log of all newly accepted products and their dates of initial use. Such information could suggest the source of a new rise in infections.

QUALITY ASSESSMENT

The components of quality monitoring include data collection, data analysis using epidemiologic methods, interpretation, actions taken to prevent or correct poor quality, and verification that these actions have actually improved quality.[8] Optimally, the assessment of quality should occur at every stage of health care delivery, from access to the hospital through hospitalization and postdischarge follow-up. The determinants of the quality of medical care and the assessment of quality have been categorized into structure, process, and outcome.[9] Process refers to the set of actions required to provide care to the patient, and outcome is the result of those actions. Although assessment of outcome usually is the most meaningful, it is also the most difficult; and Donabedian has argued that case-mix adjustment methodology is not yet sophisticated enough to allow assessment of quality on the basis of outcomes only.[9] Efforts to monitor and improve quality should focus on high-volume diagnoses and procedures as well as high-cost procedures. The use of administrative data sets to assess quality should be avoided, as these data are collected for billing purposes and often utilize imprecise definitions of conditions, a situation that can lead to misclassification of cases.

Organization of the Hospital Epidemiology Program

The organizational structure for infection control should be tailored to meet the demands of the hospital and to use available resources optimally. Large hospitals with a high proportion of tertiary care patients require a more complex system to meet their needs.

Hospital Epidemiologist

The hospital epidemiologist occupies a unique position. He or she must interface with many hospital departments and extramural agencies, directly supervise the infection-control program, and in some hospitals direct the quality assessment program. In areas where subspecialists are available, the position is generally held by a physician who is trained in infectious diseases. Unfortunately, however, many of these physicians have little or no training in the discipline of epidemiology. A recent survey of physicians certifying in infectious diseases since 1992 reported that one-half are performing infection control in their practice. Of those practicing infection control, 55% who completed their infectious disease training prior to 1990 cited their training in infection control as adequate, whereas 69% of those completing training during 1997 to 1999 cited their training as adequate.[10]

Although there has been a trend for hospitals to recognize the importance of the role of the hospital epidemiologist and to compensate physicians for this work, two surveys have shown that only 50% of hospital epidemiologists are compensated.[10,11] Implementation of a prospective payment system for medical services places a new emphasis on the avoidance of complications that prolong hospital stays (e.g., nosocomial infections) and provides an economic impetus for focusing on the quality of medical care. Preventing nosocomial infection is financially advantageous to the hospital because the bulk of the cost of treating the infection is not reimbursed under the prospective payment system.

Before assuming the position of hospital epidemiologist, the physician should meet with key hospital administrators to discuss the responsibilities and expectations of the position and to negotiate the human and material resources, including the salary support that will be made available to implement the infection-control program. An excellent review of resources necessary to operate an infection-control program is found in the Society for Healthcare Epidemiology of America position paper on infrastructure for infection control.[12]

Infection-Control Professionals

Talented infection-control professionals (ICPs) are essential for the operation of an excellent infection-control program. These individuals are usually registered nurses with clinical experience or medical technologists with experience in microbiology. The effective ICP must have a working knowledge of epidemiologic principles and basic microbiology and a sound understanding of the operations of the health care institution. Hoffmann estimated that 30% of the ICP's time should be devoted to surveillance activities, 25% to education, 15% to communication and consultation, and 10% each to quality assurance investigational studies, outbreak investigations, and exposure workups.[13]

During the 1980s, the CDC recommended that hospitals have one ICP for every 250 beds.[3] Since that time, the number of hospital beds has decreased, the severity of illness of hospitalized patients has markedly increased with a corresponding increase in the number of critical care beds, infection control issues in the ambulatory setting have increased, and many new duties have been assumed by infection control programs. In response, the Society for Healthcare Epidemiology of America has recommended that the CDC ratio is no longer valid.[12] In a survey of University Health System Consortium hospitals, a median of one ICP full-time equivalent per 137 occupied beds was documented.[14] A study utilizing the Delphi method determined that for acute care hospitals the optimal ratio is one ICP per 100

to 125 beds.[15] Nonetheless, some health care consulting groups have made recommendations based only on "benchmarks" produced through small, convenience sample surveys of hospitals that (1) may have suboptimal staffing or (2) differ significantly in the scope of services provided (or both).

Infection-Control Committee

A multidisciplinary infection control committee that meets at least quarterly is recommended. This committee should include representatives from the medical and nursing staffs, hospital administration, and the person or persons directly responsible for management of the infection-control program. The committee also typically includes the infection-control professionals and representatives from the microbiology laboratory, pharmacy, operating room, and departments of employee health, housekeeping, central services, and engineering and maintenance. The ideal characteristics of committee members include the following: an interest in infection control, representation of a large group within the hospital, authority in their given specialty, tact, and charisma.

Over the past few decades, controlling nosocomial infections has become highly technical. Therefore the bulk of the committee's work is best accomplished by a core of experts that includes the hospital epidemiologist, infection-control professionals, a microbiologist, and the director of employee health. Policy formulations should be developed by this subgroup and, after thoughtful consideration, be brought to the entire committee for review, ratification, and support from political and administrative standpoints. Thus the full infection-control committee functions to educate key hospital administrators, provide the political support that allows the core members to implement policy, and disseminate new policy.

The chair of the committee should have expertise in hospital epidemiology and infection control. We recommend that the chair be either a physician trained in infectious diseases or a practicing physician trained in clinical epidemiology, because it is generally easier for a clinician to communicate effectively with the hospital staff. Usually it is best if the hospital epidemiologist functions as the committee chair.

The meeting's agenda should be well planned and circulated to committee members before the meeting. In addition, the committee members should receive by mail or e-mail all policies to be reviewed before the meeting to allow adequate time for review by individual committee members and to improve the efficiency of the meeting.

The agenda should begin with an approval of the minutes of the previous meeting. This is followed by brief reports by representatives of the pharmacy, employee health department, and clinical microbiology laboratory. In addition, all communicable disease exposure workups from the previous month are summarized. Ideally, old business is kept to a minimum. The monthly or quarterly infection rates and trends should be reviewed. The focus of the meeting then turns to more in-depth reports of a few current issues, including outbreak investigations. Invited guests may discuss various aspects of these issues. It is also helpful to review, update, and reapprove a few existing policies at each meeting on an ongoing basis.

Joint Commission on Accreditation of Healthcare Organizations

The Joint Commission on Accreditation of Healthcare Organizations (JCAHO) is a nongovernmental, nonprofit organization that develops standards of quality used to accredit hospitals. The commission requires that health care organizations use a coordinated process to reduce the risks of endemic and epidemic nosocomial infections in patients and health care workers. Accreditation is voluntary, although most hospitals view it as mandatory. It is important for the hospital epidemiologist to know and understand the JCAHO standards and to work continually toward achieving compliance with them. JCAHO is currently placing increased emphasis on patient safety and views nosocomial infections as a patient safety issue. Modifications of the survey process are intended to make the survey more data-driven, less predictable, and more customized to the individual health care facility.

FUTURE CHALLENGES

Increasing costs in the provision of medical care with concurrent decreases in reimbursement have created enormous financial pressures on health care institutions. Never has the need for experts in hospital epidemiology been greater. Because nosocomial infections are viewed as a patient safety issue, better educated medical consumers are exhibiting decreasing tolerance for avoidable adverse outcomes in medical care, and the attributable costs of these infections in a prospective payment system has become increasingly more difficult for hospitals to bear. Yet many hospitals have outright reduced funding for infection-control programs or effectively reduced resources by adding significantly to the activities of the hospital epidemiology unit without increasing resources. The hospital epidemiologist as a steward of scarce resources and unfunded mandates must decide how best to appropriate resources within his or her purview but must also justify the cost of the marginal benefits gained by enhanced infection-control activities in light of the impact on other programs with different goals in the health system.

Infection control programs must adopt the approach of interventional epidemiology, which examines issues from a more global perspective. Such an approach focuses on and integrates clinical outcomes, economic impact, and customer (health care provider and patient) satisfaction to balance quality and cost.[16]

Emerging infectious diseases and the threat of bioterrorism require infection control programs to be able to respond more quickly to protect patients and health care workers, even in some cases with few data on the mechanism of disease transmission. Protecting the health care worker with a chronic blood-borne infection and his or her patients remains a challenge, as does the protection of immunosuppressed patients and health care workers from environmental pathogens.

Lastly, and perhaps most importantly, it remains the responsibility of the hospital epidemiologist to evaluate the medical literature and newly collected data critically when making decisions that affect the safety of patients and health care workers. Ensuring that all decisions are evidence-based and free of ideology, politics, or coercion of any form should be a deeply implanted ethic for all involved in this field.

REFERENCES

1. Haley RW, Culver DH, White JW, et al. The nationwide infection rate: a new need for vital statistics. Am J Epidemiol 1985;121:159-167.
2. Jasny BR, Bloom FE. It's not rocket science—but it can save lives. Science 1998;280:1507.
3. Haley RW, Culver DH, White JW, et al. The efficacy of infection surveillance and control programs in preventing nosocomial infections in US hospitals. Am J Epidemiol 1985;121:183-205.
4. CDC. Monitoring Hospital-Acquired Infections to Promote Patient Safety—United States, 1990-1999. MMWR Morb Mortal Wkly Rep 2000;49:149-153.
5. Pallares, Dick R, Wenzel RP, et al. Trends in antimicrobial utilization at a tertiary teaching hospital during a 15-year period (1978-1992). Infect Control Hosp Epidemiol 1993;14:376-382.
6. Polk RE. Antimicrobial formularies: can they minimize antimicrobial resistance? Am J Health Syst Pharm 2003;60 (Suppl 1):S16-19.
7. CDC. Guidelines for environmental infection control in health-care facilities: recommendations of CDC and the Healthcare Infection Control Practices Advisory Committee (HICPAC). MMWR Morb Mortal Wkly Rep 2003;52(No. RR-10).
8. Donabedian A. Contributions of epidemiology to quality assessment and monitoring. Infect Control Hosp Epidemiol 1990;11:117-121.
9. Donabedian A. An Introduction to Quality Assurance in Health Care. Oxford, UK: Oxford University Press; 2003:46-57.
10. Joiner KA, Dismukes WE, Britigan BE, et al. Adequacy of fellowship training: results of a survey of recently graduated fellows. Clin Infect Dis 2001;32:255-262.
11. Membership survey. SHEA Newslett 1996;6:5.
12. Scheckler WE, Brimhall D, Buck AS, et al. Requirements for infrastructure and essential activities of infection control and epidemiology in hospitals: a consensus panel report. Infect Control Hosp Epidemiol 1998;19:114-124.
13. Hoffmann KK. The modern infection control practitioner. In: Wenzel RP, ed. Prevention and Control of Nosocomial Infections. 3rd ed. Baltimore: Williams & Wilkins; 1997:33-45.
14. Friedman C, Chenoweth C. A survey of infection control professional staffing patterns at University Health System Consortium Institutions. Am J Infect Control 1998;26:239-244.
15. O'Boyle C, Jackson M, Henly SJ. Staffing requirements for infection control programs in U.S. health care facilities: Delphi project. Am J Infect Control 2002;30:321-333.
16. Garcia R, Bernard B, Kennedy V. The fifth evolutionary era in infection control: interventional epidemiology. Am J Infect Control 2000;28:30-43.

CHAPTER 298

Isolation

MICHAEL B. EDMOND
RICHARD P. WENZEL

The purpose of isolating patients is to prevent the transmission of microorganisms from infected or colonized patients to other patients, hospital visitors, and health care workers (who may subsequently transmit them to other patients or become infected or colonized themselves). Although isolation guidelines are based on current understanding of the mechanism of the transmission of organisms, few well controlled studies have been performed to demonstrate their efficacy. Because nosocomial infections are relatively uncommon events, any study designed to demonstrate efficacy requires sample sizes that are often prohibitively large. Thus studies evaluating the efficacy of infection-control measures often lack the power to allow one to conclude confidently that there has been a lack of effect (i.e., such studies have a high probability of type II error).

Because the process of isolating patients is expensive and time-consuming and may impede the care of the patient, it should be implemented only when necessary; conversely, failure to isolate a patient with a transmissible disease may lead to morbidity and mortality. Furthermore, such failure may ultimately be quite expensive when one considers both the direct costs of an investigation of an outbreak and an excessive length of stay and the indirect costs of lost productivity. The practice of isolating patients has moved from the requirement for separate infectious disease hospitals to separate wards for these patients, and ultimately to providing precautions in the general hospital environment. However, the emergence of the severe acute respiratory syndrome (SARS) and the potential for the reemergence of smallpox have prompted some hospitals to develop isolation wards because of the high potential for nosocomial transmission with these diseases (see Chapter 14). In 1996, the Centers for Disease Control and Prevention (CDC) and the Hospital Infection Control Practices Advisory Committee issued a revision of the recommended guidelines for isolation.[1] These guidelines outlined a two-tiered approach-standard precautions (which apply to all patients) and transmission-based precautions, which apply to patients with documented or suspected infection or colonization with certain microorganisms. These guidelines are summarized in Table 298-1.

STANDARD PRECAUTIONS

Standard precautions have replaced universal precautions. These guidelines apply to all patients and stipulate that gloves should be worn to touch any of the following: blood; all body fluids, secretions, and excretions except sweat, regardless of whether they are visibly bloody; nonintact skin; and mucous membranes.[1] Hands should be washed immediately after gloves are removed and between patient contacts. For procedures that are likely to generate splashes or sprays of body fluid, a mask with eye protection or a face shield and a gown should be worn. Disposable gowns should be constructed of an impervious material to prevent penetration and subsequent contamination of the skin or clothing. Needles should not be recapped, bent, or broken but should be disposed of in puncture-resistant containers.

Hand Hygiene

Because most nosocomial infections are transmitted by contact, primarily via the hands of health care workers,[2] hand washing remains the single most important means to prevent transmission of nosocomial pathogens. Nonetheless, most observational studies in intensive care units (ICUs) have found that hand-washing compliance by health care workers is less than 50%.[3] It has been estimated that an increase

TABLE 298-1 Essential Elements of Isolation Precautions

Airborne	Droplet	Contact
Room		
Negative pressure, private room with air exhausted to the outdoors or through high-efficiency filtration; door kept closed	Private room; door may remain open	Private room, dedicate use of noncritical patient-care items to a single patient
	[Private room for patients who contaminate the environment or cannot maintain appropriate hygiene.]	
Mask		
N95 mask or portable respirator for those entering room; surgical mask should be placed on patient for transport outside of isolation room	For entering room; surgical mask should be placed on patient for transport outside of isolation room	
	[For procedure/activities likely to generate splashes/sprays of blood, body fluids, secretions, excretions.]	
Face/Eye Protection		
	[For procedure/activities likely to generate splashes/sprays of blood, body fluids, secretions, excretions]	
Gown		
		If clothing will contact patient, surfaces, items in room; if patient has diarrhea, ileostomy, colostomy, uncontained wound drainage; remove gown before leaving room
	[For procedure/activities likely to generate splashes/sprays of blood, body fluids, secretions, excretions.]	
Gloves		
		When entering room
	[When touching blood, body fluids, secretions, excretions, contaminated items, mucous membrane, nonintact skin. Remove promptly after use, before touching noncontaminated items, and before next patient.]	
Hand Hygiene		
	[After touching blood, body fluids, secretions, excretions, contaminated items; immediately after glove removal; between patients]	

Standard precautions are shown in italics in brackets.

in hand-washing compliance by 1.5- to 2.0-fold would result in a 25% to 50% decrease in the incidence of nosocomial infections,[4] but most studies designed to improve hand-washing compliance have not demonstrated a lasting positive effect.[5]

The microorganisms on hands can be divided into transient flora and resident flora.[6] The resident flora include organisms of low virulence (coagulase-negative staphylococci, *Micrococcus,* and *Corynebacterium*) that are rarely transmitted to patients except when introduced by invasive procedures.[7] They are not easily removed through hand washing. The transient flora, however, are important causes of nosocomial infections. These organisms are acquired primarily by contact, are loosely attached to the skin, and are easily washed off. Thus the purpose of hand washing in the hospital is to remove the transient flora recently acquired by contact with patients or environmental surfaces.[7]

Alcohol-based hand rubs have become the recommended agents for hand hygiene in the health care setting.[3] In situations where the hands are visibly soiled, washing with soap (antimicrobial or nonantimicrobial) and water is recommended. Hand decontamination should be performed before and after contact with patients and immediately after removing gloves.[3]

Wall-mounted dispensers with medicated, alcohol-based waterless hand rubs should be installed in all hospital and outpatient rooms. In areas where this is not feasible, individual health care workers should carry small containers of waterless agents.

Nosocomial infections have been attributed to bacterial contamination of artificial fingernails; therefore they should not be worn by health care workers. Because rings have been recently shown to increase the frequency of hand contamination with *Staphylococcus aureus, Candida* spp., and gram-negative bacilli,[8] consideration should be given to ring removal prior to patient care.

Gloves

Gloves should be worn by health care workers to prevent contamination of the hands with microorganisms, to prevent exposure of the health care worker to blood-borne pathogens, and to reduce the risk of transmission of microorganisms from the hands of the health care worker to the patient. However, gloves do not replace the need for hand hygiene. Contamination of the hands can occur with organisms on the surface of the gloves when they are removed, and some gloves have small perforations that may allow organisms to contaminate the hands. Thus, gloves should be viewed as an adjunctive protective barrier but not as a substitute for hand hygiene.

TRANSMISSION-BASED PRECAUTIONS

Transmission-based precautions apply to selected patients based on a suspected or confirmed clinical syndrome, a specific diagnosis, or colonization or infection with epidemiologically important organisms. It is important to note that transmission-based precautions are always implemented in conjunction with standard precautions. Three types of transmission-based precautions have been developed for the major modes of transmission of infectious agents in the health care setting: airborne, droplet, and contact.[1] A few diseases (e.g., varicella) require more than one isolation category. Essential elements of each category are outlined in Table 298-1, and indications for implementation are delineated in Table 298-2.

Airborne Precautions

Airborne precautions are designed to prevent the transmission of diseases by droplet nuclei (particles smaller than 5 μm) or dust particles containing the infectious agent.[1] These particles can remain suspended in the air and travel long distances. If the particles are inhaled, a susceptible host may develop infection. Airborne precautions are indicated for patients with documented or suspected tuberculosis (pulmonary or laryngeal), measles, varicella, or disseminated zoster. Patients who are infected with (or at high risk for infection with) human immunodeficiency virus with fever, cough, and a pulmonary infiltrate should be empirically placed under airborne precautions until tuberculosis can be ruled out.[1] Although open tuberculous skin wounds are uncommon, they have been presumptively associated with nosocomial transmission after manipulation of the wound (surgical débridement, dressing changes, irrigation).[9-11] Therefore placing such patients under airborne precautions should be considered. Patients with nontuberculous (atypical) mycobacterial pulmonary disease need not be isolated because person-to-person transmission does not occur.

Under airborne precautions, patients should be placed in a private room with monitored negative air pressure in relation to surrounding

TABLE 298-2 Indications for Transmission-Based Precautions

Airborne Precautions	Droplet Precautions	Contact Precautions
Scenarios Requiring Empiric Implementation of Precautions		
Vesicular rash*	Meningitis	Acute diarrhea with likely infectious etiology in incontinent or diapered patient
Maculopapular rash with coryza and fever	Petechial or ecchymotic rash with fever	Diarrhea in adult with recent antibiotic use
Cough, fever, upper lobe pulmonary infiltrate	Paroxysmal or severe persistent cough during periods of pertussis activity	Vesicular rash*
Cough, fever, any pulmonary infiltrate in an HIV-infected patient (or patient at risk for HIV infection)		Respiratory infections in infants and young children
Fever, respiratory symptoms in a person with recent contact with SARS patient or recent travel to area with SARS transmission*		History of infection or colonization with MDR organisms
		Skin, wound, or urinary tract infection in a patient with a recent hospital or nursing home stay in a facility where MDR organisms are prevalent
		Abscess or draining wound that cannot be covered
		Fever, respiratory symptoms in a person with recent contact with SARS patient or recent travel to area with SARS transmission*
Known or Suspected Diseases or Pathogens		
Measles	Adenovirus (infants, children)*	Abscess, not covered or drainage not contained
Monkeypox*	Diphtheria, pharyngeal	Adenovirus (infants, children)*
Tuberculosis, pulmonary or laryngeal	*Haemophilus influenzae* meningitis, epiglottitis	Cellulitis (uncontrolled drainage)
SARS*	*H. influenzae* pneumonia (infants, children)	*Clostridium difficile* diarrhea
Smallpox*	Influenza	Conjunctivitis, acute viral
Varicella*	Meningococcal infections	Decubitus ulcer, infected and drainage not contained
Viral hemorrhagic fevers*	Mumps	Diphtheria, cutaneous
Zoster (disseminated or immunocompromised patient)*	*Mycoplasma* pneumonia	*Escherichia coli* O157:H7 colitis (diapered or incontinent patient)
	Parvovirus B19	Enteroviral infections (infants, young children)
	Pertussis	Furunculosis (infants, young children)
	Plague, pneumonic	Hepatitis A (diapered or incontinent patient)
	Rubella	HSV (neonatal; disseminated; severe primary mucocutaneous)
	Streptococcal (group A) pharyngitis, pneumonia, scarlet fever (infants or young children)	Impetigo
		Lice
		MDR bacteria (e.g., MRSA, VRE, VISA, VRSA) infection or colonization
		Monkeypox*
		Parainfluenza infection (infants, children)
		Rotavirus (diapered or incontinent)
		RSV infection (infants, children, immunocompromised)
		Rubella, congenital
		SARS*
		Staphylococcus aureus major skin, wound or burn infection
		Scabies
		Shigella (diapered or incontinent)
		Smallpox*
		Streptococcal (group A) major skin, burn or wound infection
		Varicella*
		Viral hemorrhagic fevers*
		Yersinia enterocolitica enteritis (diapered or incontinent)
		Zoster (disseminated or immunocompromised)*

*Condition requires two types of precaution.

HIV, human immunodeficiency virus; HSV, herpes simplex virus; MDR, multidrug-resistant; MRSA, methicillin-resistant *Staphylococcus aureus;* RSV, respiratory syncytial virus; SARS, severe acute respiratory syndrome; VISA, vancomycin-intermediate *Staphylococcus aureus;* VRE, vancomycin-resistant enterococci; VRSA, vancomycin-resistant *Staphylococcus aureus.*

areas, and the room air must undergo at least six exchanges per hour.[12] The door to the isolation room must remain closed. Air from the isolation room should be exhausted directly to the outside, away from air intakes, and not recirculated. If outdoor exhaust is not possible, air should be exhausted through high-efficiency filters before it is returned to the general ventilation system.[12]

All persons entering the room of patients with suspected or confirmed tuberculosis must wear a personal respirator that filters 1 μm particles with an efficiency of at least 95% (N95 mask). These special masks must fit different facial sizes and characteristics, be fit-tested to obtain leakage of 10% or less, and be able to be checked for fit each time the health care worker puts on the mask. The Occupational Safety and Health Administration requires that health care workers who manage patients with tuberculosis undergo fit testing and training for self-fit checking.[12] Transporting the patient from the isolation room should be limited, and the patient should be fitted with a standard surgical

mask before leaving the room.[1] Before transport, hospital personnel in the area receiving the patient should be notified so proper precautions can be implemented. Gowns and gloves are used as dictated by standard precautions.

Any patient with confirmed or suspected tuberculosis should be instructed to cover his or her mouth and nose with a tissue when coughing or sneezing. Patients should remain in isolation until tuberculosis can be ruled out. Patients with confirmed tuberculosis who are receiving effective antituberculous therapy and clinically improving (three consecutive sputum smears on separate days with no detectable acid-fast bacilli) can be released from isolation.[12] For patients with severe cavitary disease, persistent cough, or laryngeal tuberculosis, and possibly those who will return to an environment with high-risk individuals (e.g., children, immunosuppressed individuals), we recommend maintaining isolation for at least 1 month. Patients with multidrug-resistant disease should remain in isolation for the duration of their hospital stay.[12] Hospitalization is unwarranted solely to provide isolation for clinically stable patients who are compliant with antituberculous therapy and agree to stay in their homes.

Patients with known or suspected measles, varicella, or disseminated zoster require airborne isolation, as do immunocompromised patients with localized zoster. Nonimmune health care workers should avoid entering the rooms of these patients when possible; and if they are required to enter the room, they should wear an N95 mask.[1]

Droplet Precautions

Droplet precautions are used to prevent transmission by large-particle (droplet) aerosols. Unlike droplet nuclei, droplets are larger, do not remain suspended in the air, and do not travel long distances. They are produced when the infected patient talks, coughs, or sneezes and during some procedures (e.g., suctioning, bronchoscopy). A susceptible host may become infected if the infectious droplets land on the mucosal surfaces of the nose, mouth, or eye.

Droplet precautions require patients to be placed in a private room, but no special air handling is necessary.[1] Alternatively, patients with the same disease can be placed in the same room if private rooms are not available. Because droplets do not travel long distances (generally no more than 3 feet), the door to the room may remain open. Health care workers should wear a standard surgical mask when working within 3 feet of the patient, although to improve compliance some hospitals require masks on entry into the room. Gowns and gloves should be worn when dictated by standard precautions. When transported out of the isolation room, the patient should be fitted with a standard surgical mask.[1]

Some illnesses that require droplet precautions include invasive *Haemophilus influenzae* type B and meningococcal infections, multidrug-resistant pneumococcal disease, *Mycoplasma* pneumonia, pertussis, influenza, mumps, rubella, and parvovirus B19 infections.

Contact Precautions

Contact precautions are implemented to prevent the transmission of epidemiologically important organisms from an infected or colonized patient through direct contact (touching the patient) or indirect contact (touching contaminated objects or surfaces in the patient's environment). Patients with contact precautions should be placed in a private room, although patients infected with the same organism may be placed in the same room when private rooms are not available.[1] Multidrug-resistant organisms, such as vancomycin-resistant enterococci and methicillin-resistant *Staphylococcus aureus* contaminate the environment (surfaces and items) in the vicinity of the infected or colonized patient. Therefore barrier precautions to prevent contamination of exposed skin and clothing should be employed. Gloves should be worn when entering the patient's room and removed before leaving it. After removing gloves, the hands must be decontaminated immediately with a medicated hand-washing agent or an alcohol-based hand rub; and care should be taken to prevent recontamination of the hands before leaving the room. Gowns should be worn if the health care worker anticipates substantial contact of his or her clothing with the patient or surfaces in the patient's environment. They should also be worn in situations in which there is an increased risk of contact with potentially infective material (e.g., when the patient is incontinent or has diarrhea, a colostomy, ileostomy, or uncontrolled wound drainage). Gowns should be removed before leaving the isolation room, and care is taken to prevent contamination of clothing while removing the gown before leaving the room.[1]

Numerous studies have documented contamination of noncritical patient care equipment (e.g., stethoscopes, blood pressure cuffs) with vancomycin-resistant enterococci and methicillin-resistant *Staphylococcus aureus* (MRSA). These items should remain in the isolation room and not be used for other patients. If the items must be shared, they should be cleaned and disinfected before reuse. Transport of the patient from the isolation room should be kept to a minimum.

Contact precautions are indicated for patients infected or colonized with multidrug-resistant bacteria (e.g., MRSA or *S. aureus* that have reduced susceptibility to vancomycin and vancomycin-resistant enterococci).[1] Other indications include *Clostridium difficile* enteritis, infections transmitted by the fecal-oral route (e.g., *Shigella*, rotavirus, hepatitis A virus infections) in patients who are diapered or incontinent, and acute diarrheal diseases likely to be infectious in origin. Infants and young children with respiratory syncytial virus, parainfluenza, or enteroviral infections and patients with neonatal, disseminated, or severe primary mucocutaneous herpes simplex virus infections should also be placed under contact precautions. Ectoparasitic infestations (lice and scabies) are additional indications. Patients with varicella or disseminated zoster require both contact and airborne precautions. Infants and children with adenovirus infection require contact and droplet precautions.[1]

Special Guidelines for Vancomycin–Intermediate and Resistant *Staphylococcus aureus*

During the late 1990s, vancomycin-intermediate [minimum inhibitory concentration (MIC) 8 to 16 μg/ml] *S. aureus* emerged. Several cases in the United States have been described, primarily in dialysis patients who were treated with long courses of vancomycin.[13] Two patients in 2002 and a third in 2004 in the United States developed infections due to vancomycin-resistant (MIC more than 32 μg/mL) *S. aureus* strains.[14-15] Patients infected or colonized with vancomycin-intermediate or vancomycin-resistant *S. aureus* should be placed on contact precautions.[16] In addition, we recommend limiting the number of health care workers who are to care for the infected or colonized patient and record their names so follow-up surveillance nasal cultures can be obtained. Health care workers with conditions predisposing to colonization with *S. aureus* (e.g., extensive dermatitides, insulin-requiring diabetes mellitus) should refrain from caring for these patients.[17] To the greatest possible extent, diagnostic and therapeutic procedures should be performed in the patient's room to limit the need for the patient to leave isolation.[17] We recommend placing a monitor at the doorway to remind health care workers of appropriate infection control practices.[18] Isolation precautions should continue for the duration of the hospitalization. After the patient is discharged, the room should undergo terminal disinfection with a quaternary ammonium compound and remain closed to new admissions until environmental cultures are found to be negative. If nosocomial transmission is documented, the hospital unit should be closed to new admissions.[17]

Special Guidelines for Bioterrorism-Associated Infections

The anthrax attack in 2001 heightened awareness to the possibility of bioterrorism. Some bioterrorism-associated infections require transmission-based precautions, although most are not transmitted from person to person. A listing of CDC category A and B bioterrorism agents and their corresponding isolation precautions is contained in Table 298-3. Category A agents include pathogens that are rarely seen naturally in the United States. These high priority agents pose a significant risk to national security, as they can be easily disseminated or transmitted from person to person. Furthermore, the agents result in high mortality rates and have the potential for major public health impact.[19] Category B bioterrorism agents are moderately easy to disseminate and result in moderate morbidity rates and low mortality rates.[19]

Smallpox and viral hemorrhagic fevers require both airborne and contact isolation owing to their ability to cause secondary transmission through inhalation and direct contact.[20-21] Pneumonic plague, caused by *Yersinia pestis*, can also be transmitted from person to person. Because pneumonic plague can be secondarily transmitted in the health care setting by the inhalation of respiratory droplets, droplet precautions are warranted.[22]

TABLE 298-3 Isolation Precautions for Bioterrorism-Associated Diseases

Agent	Precautions			
	Standard	Airborne	Droplet	Contact
Category A				
Anthrax (*Bacillus anthracis*)	X			
Botulism (*Clostridium botulinum* toxin)	X			
Plague (*Yersinia pestis*)	X		X	
Smallpox (variola)	X	X		X
Tularemia (*Francisella tularensis*)	X			
Viral hemorrhagic fevers (filoviruses, arenaviruses)	X	X		X
Category B				
Brucellosis (*Brucella* spp.)	X			
Clostridium perfringens toxin	X			
Glanders (*Burkholderia mallei*)	X			
Melioidosis (*Burkholderia pseudomallei*)	X			
Psittacosis [Chlamydophila (*Chlamydia*) *psittaci*]	X			
Q fever (*Coxiella burnetii*)	X			
Ricin toxin	X			
Staphylococcal enterotoxin B	X			
Typhus (*Rickettsia prowazekii*)	X			
Viral encephalitis (Venezuelan equine, eastern equine, western equine)	X			
Water safety threats (*Vibrio cholera, Cryptosporidium parvum*)	X			

Special Guidelines for SARS

During late 2002, a new respiratory infectious disease, severe acute respiratory syndrome (SARS), emerged in southern China and spread rapidly to other continents. It is characterized by fever, constitutional symptoms, cough, pulmonary infiltrates, and in some cases respiratory failure.[23] The causative pathogen has been shown to be a novel coronavirus. The illness is highly contagious, and many cases have been due to nosocomial transmission.[24]

It appears that the disease is spread by droplets and possibly through airborne aerosols. Environmental contamination has been documented, so transmission via fomites is also suspected. The virus has been detected in stool, blood, sweat, and urine of infected individuals. It is not known when infected persons become contagious, nor is the duration of infectivity known. Based on the current state of knowledge, patients with documented or suspected SARS should be placed in airborne and contact precautions, with strict adherence to standard precautions, including eye protection.

If multiple patients with suspected SARS are hospitalized, it is preferable to house them in a geographically restricted area when possible to minimize exposure of staff and the potential for nosocomial transmission. Limiting visitors to these patients and careful attention to disinfection of the patient's room are also important for limiting the spread of the disease. Health care workers who have unprotected exposure to patients with SARS should be quarantined at home on days 2 through 10 after exposure. During home confinement, it is strongly encouraged that all family members and housemates be transferred out of the house to minimize the risk of transmission. It is important to note that these interim guidelines are based on the current state of knowledge regarding SARS and may have to be revised as the epidemiology of the disease is further elucidated.[25,26] For further discussion of hospital preparedness, see Chapter 14.

REFERENCES

1. Garner JS, Hospital Infection Control Practices Advisory Committee. Guideline for isolation precautions in hospitals. Infect Control Hosp Epidemiol 1996;17:53-80.
2. Bauer TM, Ofner E, Just HM, et al. An epidemiological study assessing the relative importance of airborne and direct contact transmission of microorganisms in a medical intensive care unit. J Hosp Infect 1990;15:301-309.
3. Boyce JM, Pittet D. Healthcare Infection Control Practices Advisory Committee, Society for Healthcare Epidemiology of America, Association for Professionals in Infection Control, Infectious Diseases Society of America Hand Hygiene Task Force. Guideline for hand hygiene in health-care settings: recommendations of the Healthcare Infection Control Practices Advisory Committee and the HICPAC/SHEA/APIC/IDSA Hand Hygiene Task Force. Infect Control Hosp Epidemiol 2002;23(Suppl 12):S3-S40.
4. Doebbeling BN, Stanley GL, Sheetz CT, et al. Comparative efficacy of alternative hand-washing agents in reducing nosocomial infections in intensive care units. N Engl J Med 1992;327:88.
5. Larson E, Kretzer EK. Compliance with handwashing and barrier precautions. J Hosp Infect 1995;30(Suppl):88-106.
6. Price PB. The bacteriology of normal skin: a new quantitative test applied to a study of the bacterial flora and the disinfectant action of mechanical cleaning. J Infect Dis 1938;63:301.
7. Steere AC, Mallison GF. Handwashing practices for the prevention of nosocomial infections. Ann Intern Med 1975;83:683-690.
8. Trick WE, Vernon MO, Hayes RA, et al. Impact of ring wearing on hand contamination and comparison of hand hygiene agents in a hospital. Clin Infect Dis 2003;36:1383-1390.
9. Framptom MW. An outbreak of tuberculosis among hospital personnel caring for a patient with a skin ulcer. Ann Intern Med 1992;117:312-313.
10. Hutton MD, Stead WW, Cauthen GM, et al. Nosocomial transmission of tuberculosis associated with a draining abscess. J Infect Dis 1990;161:286-295.
11. Stead WW. Skin ulcers and tuberculosis outbreaks. Ann Intern Med 1993;118:474.
12. Centers for Disease Control and Prevention. Guidelines for preventing the transmission of Mycobacterium tuberculosis in health-care facilities, 1994. MMWR Morb Mortal Wkly Rep 1994;43:1-132.
13. Fridkin SK. Vancomycin—intermediate and resistant—Staphylococcus aureus: what the infectious disease specialist needs to know. Clin Infect Dis 2001;32:108-115.
14. Chang S, Sievert DM, Hageman JC, et al. Infection with vancomycin-resistant Staphylococcus aureus containing the vanA resistance gene. N Engl J Med 2003;348:1342-1347.
15. Vancomycin-resistant Staphylococcus aureus—Pennsylvania, 2002. MMWR Morb Mortal Wkly Rep 2002;51;902.
16. Centers for Disease Control and Prevention. Interim guidelines for prevention and control of staphylococcal infection associated with reduced susceptibility to vancomycin. MMWR Morb Mortal Wkly Rep 1997;46:626-628, 635.
17. Edmond MB, Wenzel RP, Pasculle AW. Vancomycin-resistant Staphylococcus aureus: perspectives on measures needed for control. Ann Intern Med 1996;124:329-334.
18. Wenzel RP, Edmond MB. Vancomycin-resistant Staphylococcus aureus: infection control considerations. Clin Infect Dis 1998;27:245-249.
19. Centers for Disease Control and Prevention. Public health emergency preparedness and response: biological agents/diseases. Available at: http://www.bt.cdc.gov/agent/agentlist-category.asp#a (accessed July 6, 2003).
20. Henderson DA, Inglesby TV, Bartlett JG, et al. Smallpox as a biological weapon: medical and public health management. JAMA 1999;281:2127-2137.
21. Borio L, Inglesby T, Peters CJ, et al. Hemorrhagic fever viruses as biological weapons: medical and public health management. JAMA 2002;287:2391-2405.
22. Inglesby TV, Dennis DT, Henderson DA, et al. Plague as a biological weapon: medical and public health management. JAMA 2000;283:2281-2290.
23. Poutanen SM, Low DE, Henry B, et al. Identification of severe acute respiratory syndrome in Canada. N Engl J Med 2003;348:1995-2005.
24. Lee N, Hui D, Wu A, et al. A major outbreak of severe acute respiratory syndrome in Hong Kong. N Engl J Med 2003;348:1986-1994.
25. Wenzel RP, Edmond MB. Managing SARS amidst uncertainty. N Engl J Med 2003;348:1947-1948.
26. Wenzel RP, Edmond MB. Listening to SARS: considerations for infection control. Ann Intern Med 2003;139:592-593.

Disinfection, Sterilization, and Control of Hospital Waste

WILLIAM A. RUTALA

DAVID J. WEBER

Each year in the United States there are approximately 27 million surgical procedures and an even larger number of invasive medical procedures.[1] For example, there are at least 10 million gastrointestinal endoscopies per year.[2] Each of these procedures involves contact by a medical device or surgical instrument with a patient's sterile tissue or mucous membranes. A major risk of all such procedures is the introduction of infection. Failure to properly disinfect or sterilize equipment carries not only the risk associated with breach of the host barriers but the additional risk of person-to-person transmission (e.g., hepatitis B virus [HBV]) and transmission of environmental pathogens (e.g., *Pseudomonas aeruginosa*).

Achieving disinfection and sterilization through the use of disinfectants and sterilization practices is essential for ensuring that medical and surgical instruments do not transmit infectious pathogens to patients. Because it is unnecessary to sterilize all patient-care items, health care policies must identify whether cleaning, disinfection, or sterilization is indicated based primarily on the items' intended use.

Multiple studies in many countries have documented lack of compliance with established guidelines for disinfection and sterilization.[3,4] Failure to comply with scientifically based guidelines has led to numerous outbreaks.[4-8] In this chapter, a pragmatic approach to the judicious selection and proper use of disinfection and sterilization processes is presented, based on well-designed studies assessing the efficacy (via laboratory investigations) and effectiveness (via clinical studies) of disinfection and sterilization procedures.

DEFINITION OF TERMS

Sterilization is the complete elimination or destruction of all forms of microbial life and is accomplished in health care facilities by either physical or chemical processes. Steam under pressure, dry heat, ethylene oxide (ETO) gas, hydrogen peroxide gas plasma, and liquid chemicals are the principal sterilizing agents used in health care facilities. Sterilization is intended to convey an absolute meaning, not a relative one. Unfortunately, some health professionals as well as the technical and commercial literature refer to "disinfection" as "sterilization" and to items as "partially sterile." When chemicals are used for the purposes of destroying all forms of microbiologic life, including fungal and bacterial spores, they may be called *chemical sterilants*. These same germicides used for shorter exposure periods may also be part of the disinfection process (i.e., high-level disinfection).

Disinfection describes a process that eliminates many or all pathogenic microorganisms on inanimate objects, with the exception of bacterial spores. Disinfection is usually accomplished by the use of liquid chemicals or wet pasteurization in health care settings. The efficacy of disinfection is affected by a number of factors, each of which may nullify or limit the efficacy of the process. Some of the factors that affect both disinfection and sterilization efficacy are the prior cleaning of the object; the organic and inorganic load present; the type and level of microbial contamination; the concentration of and exposure time to the germicide; the nature of the object (e.g., crevices, hinges, and lumens); the presence of biofilms; the temperature and pH of the disinfection process; and, in some cases, the relative humidity of the sterilization process (e.g., with ETO).

By definition then, disinfection differs from sterilization by its lack of sporicidal property, but this is an oversimplification. A few disinfectants will kill spores with prolonged exposure times (3 to 12 hours) and are called chemical sterilants. At similar concentrations but with shorter exposure periods (e.g., 20 minutes for 2% glutaraldehyde), these same disinfectants will kill all microorganisms with the exception of large numbers of bacterial spores and are called *high-level disinfectants*. *Low-level disinfectants* may kill most vegetative bacteria, some fungi, and some viruses in a practical period of time (<10 minutes), whereas *intermediate-level disinfectants* may be cidal for mycobacteria, vegetative bacteria, most viruses, and most fungi but do not necessarily kill bacterial spores. The germicides differ markedly among themselves primarily in their antimicrobial spectrum and rapidity of action. Table 299-1 is discussed later and consulted in this context.

Cleaning, in contrast, is the removal of visible soil (e.g., organic and inorganic material) from objects and surfaces, and it normally is accomplished by manual or mechanical means using water with detergents or enzymatic products. Thorough cleaning is essential before high-level disinfection and sterilization because inorganic and organic materials that remain on the surfaces of instruments interfere with the effectiveness of these processes. Also, if the soiled materials become dried or baked onto the instruments, the removal process becomes more difficult and the disinfection or sterilization process less effective or ineffective. Surgical instruments should be presoaked or rinsed to prevent drying of blood and to soften or remove blood from the instruments. *Decontamination* is a procedure that removes pathogenic microorganisms from objects so they are safe to handle, use, or discard.

Terms with a suffix "-cide" or "-cidal," for "killing action," also are commonly used. For example, a germicide is an agent that can kill microorganisms, particularly pathogenic organisms ("germs"). The term *germicide* includes both antiseptics and disinfectants. *Antiseptics* are germicides applied to living tissue and skin, whereas *disinfectants* are antimicrobials applied only to inanimate objects. In general, antiseptics are only used on the skin and not for surface disinfection, and disinfectants are not used for skin antisepsis because they may cause injury to skin and other tissues. Other words with the suffix "-cide" (e.g., virucide, fungicide, bactericide, sporicide, and tuberculocide) can kill the type of microorganism identified by the prefix. For example, a bactericide is an agent that kills bacteria.[9-14]

A RATIONAL APPROACH TO DISINFECTION AND STERILIZATION

Over 30 years ago, Earle H. Spaulding[10] devised a rational approach to disinfection and sterilization of patient-care items or equipment. This classification scheme is so clear and logical that it has been retained, refined, and successfully used by infection control professionals and others when planning methods for disinfection or sterilization.[9,11,13,15,16] Spaulding believed that the nature of disinfection could be understood more readily if instruments and items for patient care were divided into three categories based on the degree of risk of infection involved in the use of the items. The three categories he described were critical, semicritical, and noncritical.

Critical Items

Critical items are so called because of the high risk of infection if such an item is contaminated with any microorganism, including bacterial spores. Thus it is critical that objects that enter sterile tissue or the vascular system be sterile because any microbial contamination could result in disease transmission. This category includes surgical instruments, cardiac and urinary catheters, implants, and ultrasound probes used in sterile body cavities. Most of the items in this category should be purchased as sterile or be sterilized by steam sterilization if possible. If heat sensitive, the object may be treated with ETO or hydrogen peroxide gas plasma, or by liquid chemical sterilants if other methods are unsuitable. Table 299-1 lists the sterilization processes that may be used for critical items, and it lists several germicides categorized as

TABLE 299-1 Methods of Sterilization and Disinfection

Object	Sterilization — Critical items (will enter tissue or vascular system or blood will flow through them) Procedure	Exposure time	Disinfection — High-level (semicritical items [except dental]; will come in contact with mucous membrane or nonintact skin) Procedure (exposure time 12-30 min at $\geq 20°$ C)[2,3]	Intermediate-level (some semicritical items[1] and noncritical items) Procedure (exposure time ≤ 10 min)	Low-level (noncritical items; will come in contact with intact skin) Procedure (exposure time ≤ 10 min)
Smooth, hard surface[1,4]	A	MR	D	K	K
	B	MR	E	L[5]	L
	C	MR	F	M	M
	D	10 hr	H	N	N
	E	NA	I[6]		O
	F	6 hr	J		
	G	12 min			
	H	3-8 hr			
Rubber tubing and catheters[3,4]	A	MR	D		
	B	MR	E		
	C	MR	F		
	D	10 hr	H		
	E	NA	I[6]		
	F	6 hr	J		
	G	12 min			
	H	3-8 hr			
Polyethylene tubing and catheters[3,4,7]	A	MR	D		
	B	MR	E		
	C	MR	F		
	D	10 hr	H		
	E	NA	I[6]		
	F	6 hr	J		
	G	12 min			
	H	3-8 hr			
Lensed instruments[4]	A	MR	D		
	B	MR	E		
	C	MR	F		
	D	10 hr	H		
	E	NA			
	F	6 hr			
	G	12 min			
	H	3-8 hr			
Thermometers (oral and rectal)[8]				K[8]	
Hinged instruments[4]	A	MR	D		
	B	MR	E		
	C	MR	F		
	D	10 hr	H		
	E	NA	I[6]		
	F	6 hr	J		
	G	12 min			
	H	3-8 hr			

[1]See text for discussion of hydrotherapy.

[2]The longer the exposure to a disinfectant, the more likely it is that all microorganisms will be eliminated. Ten-minute exposure is not adequate to disinfect many objects, especially those that are difficult to clean because they have narrow channels or other areas that can harbor organic material and bacteria. Twenty-minute exposure at 20° C is the minimum time needed to reliably kill *M. tuberculosis* and nontuberculous mycobacteria with a 2% glutaraldehyde. With the exception of greater than 2% glutaraldehydes, follow the FDA-cleared high-level disinfection claim. Some high-level disinfectants have a reduced exposure time (e.g., *ortho*-phthalaldehyde at 12 minutes at 20° C) because of their rapid activity against mycobacteria or reduced exposure time because of increased mycobactericidal activity at elevated temperature (2.5% glutaraldehyde at 5 minutes at 35° C).

[3]Tubing must be completely filled for disinfection and liquid chemical sterilization; care must be taken to avoid entrapment of air bubbles during immersion.

[4]Material compatibility should be investigated when appropriate.

[5]Used in laboratory where cultures or concentrated preparations of microorganisms have spilled. A concentration of 1000 ppm available chlorine should be considered where cultures of microorganisms or blood have spilled (5.25% to 6.15% household bleach diluted 1:50 provides > 1000 ppm available chlorine). This solution may corrode some surfaces.

[6]Pasteurization (washer-disinfector) of respiratory therapy or anesthesia equipment is a recognized alternative to high-level disinfection. Some data challenge the efficacy of some pasteurization units.

[7]Thermostability should be investigated when appropriate.

[8]Do not mix rectal and oral thermometers at any stage of handling or processing.

A: Heat sterilization, including steam or hot air (see manufacturer's recommendations; steam sterilization processing time from 3 to 30 minutes).

B: Ethylene oxide gas (see manufacturer's recommendations; generally 1 to 6 hours processing time plus aeration time of 8 to 12 hours at 50° to 60° C).

C: Hydrogen peroxide gas plasma (see manufacturer's recommendations; processing time between 45 and 72 minutes; see manufacturer's recommendations for endoscope or medical device restrictions based on lumen internal diameter and length).

D: Glutaraldehyde-based formulations (> 2% glutaraldehyde; caution should be exercised with all glutaraldehyde formulations when further in-use dilution is anticipated); glutaraldehyde (0.95%) and 1.64% phenol/phenate. One glutaraldehyde-based product has a 5 minute exposure time at 35° C.

E: *Ortho*-phthalaldehyde 0.55% (FDA cleared as high-level disinfectant; passes the Sporicidal Activity Test in 32 hours at 20° C but not cleared as a chemical sterilant).

F: Hydrogen peroxide 7.5% (will corrode copper, zinc, and brass).

G: Peracetic acid; concentration variable but 1% or less is sporicidal. Peracetic acid immersion system operates at 50° to 56° C.

H: Hydrogen peroxide (7.35%) and 0.23% peracetic acid; hydrogen peroxide 1% and peracetic acid 0.08% (will corrode metal instruments).

I: Wet pasteurization at 70° C for 30 minutes with detergent cleaning.

J: Hypochlorite greater than 650 to 675 ppm active free chlorine, single-use chlorine generated on site by electrolyzing saline (may corrode metal instruments).

K: Ethyl or isopropyl alcohol (70% to 90%).

L: Sodium hypochlorite (5.25% to 6.15% household bleach diluted 1:500 provides > 100 ppm available chlorine).

M: Phenolic germicidal detergent solution (follow product label for use-dilution).

N: Iodophor germicidal detergent solution (follow product label for use-dilution).

O: Quaternary ammonium germicidal detergent solution (follow product label for use-dilution).

MR: Manufacturer's recommendations.

NA: Not applicable.

Modified from references 11,13,14,48.

chemical sterilants. The chemical sterilants include greater than 2.4% glutaraldehyde-based formulations, 0.95% glutaraldehyde with 1.64% phenol/phenate, 7.5% stabilized hydrogen peroxide, 7.35% hydrogen peroxide with 0.23% peracetic acid, 0.2% peracetic acid, and 0.08% peracetic acid with 1.0% hydrogen peroxide. Liquid chemical sterilants can be relied upon to produce sterility only if cleaning, to eliminate organic and inorganic material, precedes treatment and if proper guidelines as to concentration, contact time, temperature, and pH are met.

Semicritical Items

Semicritical items are those that come in contact with mucous membranes or nonintact skin. Respiratory therapy and anesthesia equipment, some endoscopes, laryngoscope blades, esophageal manometry probes, anorectal manometry catheters, and diaphragm fitting rings are included in this category. These medical devices should be free of all microorganisms, although small numbers of bacterial spores may be present. Intact mucous membranes, such as those of the lungs or the gastrointestinal tract, generally are resistant to infection by common bacterial spores but susceptible to other organisms such as bacteria, mycobacteria, and viruses. Semicritical items minimally require high-level disinfection using chemical disinfectants (see Table 299-1). Glutaraldehyde, hydrogen peroxide, *ortho*-phthalaldehyde, and peracetic acid with hydrogen peroxide are cleared by the Food and Drug Administration (FDA) and are dependable high-level disinfectants provided the factors influencing germicidal procedures are met (Table 299-1). When a disinfectant is selected for use with certain patient-care items, the chemical compatibility after extended use with the items to be disinfected also must be considered.

The complete elimination of all microorganisms in or on an instrument with the exception of small numbers of bacterial spores is the traditional definition of high-level disinfection. The FDA's definition of high-level disinfection is a chemical sterilant used for a shorter contact time to achieve a 6-$\log_{10}$ kill of an appropriate mycobacterium species. Cleaning followed by high-level disinfection should eliminate sufficient pathogens to prevent transmission of infection.[17,18]

Laparoscopes and arthroscopes entering sterile tissue ideally should be sterilized between patients. However, they sometimes undergo only high-level disinfection between patients in the United States.[19-21] As with flexible endoscopes, these devices may be difficult to clean and high-level disinfect/sterilize as a result of intricate device design (e.g., long narrow lumens, hinges). Meticulous cleaning must precede any high-level disinfection/sterilization process. Although sterilization is preferred, there are no published outbreaks resulting following high-level disinfection of these scopes when properly cleaned and high-level disinfected. Newer models of these instruments can withstand steam sterilization that for critical items would be preferable to high-level disinfection.

Semicritical items should be rinsed with sterile water after high-level disinfection to prevent their contamination with organisms that may be present in tap water, such as nontuberculous mycobacteria,[8,22] *Legionella*,[23,24] or gram-negative bacilli such as *Pseudomonas*.[13,15,25-27] In circumstances in which rinsing with sterile water rinse is not feasible, a tap water or filtered water (0.2-μ filter) rinse should be followed by an alcohol rinse and forced-air drying.[19,27,28] Forced-air drying markedly reduces bacterial contamination of stored endoscopes, most likely by removing the wet environment favorable for bacterial growth.[28] After rinsing, items should be dried and stored (e.g., packaged) in a manner that protects them from recontamination.

Noncritical Items

Noncritical items are those that come in contact with intact skin but not mucous membranes. Intact skin acts as an effective barrier to most microorganisms; therefore, the sterility of items coming in contact with intact skin is "not critical." Examples of noncritical items are bedpans, blood pressure cuffs, crutches, bed rails, linens, some food utensils, bedside tables, patient furniture, and floors. In contrast to critical and some semicritical items, most noncritical reusable items may be decontaminated where they are used and do not need to be trans-

ported to a central processing area. There is virtually no documented risk of transmitting infectious agents to patients via noncritical items[26] when they are used as noncritical items and do not contact nonintact skin and/or mucous membranes. However, these items (e.g., bedside tables, bed rails) could potentially contribute to secondary transmission by contaminating hands of health care workers or by contact with medical equipment that will subsequently come in contact with patients.[9,29-32] Table 299-1 lists several low-level disinfectants that may be used for noncritical items. The exposure time listed in Table 299-1 is less than or equal to 10 minutes. Most Environmental Protection Agency (EPA)–registered disinfectants have a 10-minute label claim. However, multiple investigators have demonstrated the effectiveness of these disinfectants against vegetative bacteria (e.g., *Listeria, Escherichia coli, Salmonella,* vancomycin-resistant enterococci [VRE], methicillin-resistant *Staphylococcus aureus* [MRSA]), yeasts (e.g., *Candida*), mycobacteria (e.g., *M. tuberculosis*), and viruses (e.g., poliovirus) at exposure times of 30 to 60 seconds.[30-39] Thus it is acceptable to disinfect noncritical medical equipment (e.g., blood pressure cuff) and noncritical surfaces (e.g., bedside table) with an EPA-registered disinfect or disinfectant/detergent at the proper use-dilution and a contact time of at least 30 to 60 seconds.[40]

Mops and reusable cleaning cloths are regularly used to achieve low-level disinfection. However, they are commonly not kept adequately cleaned and disinfected, and if the water-disinfectant mixture is not changed regularly (e.g., after every three to four rooms, no longer than 60-minute intervals), the mopping procedure may actually spread heavy microbial contamination throughout the health care facility.[41] In one study, standard laundering provided acceptable decontamination of heavily contaminated mop heads but chemical disinfection with a phenolic was less effective.[41] The frequent laundering of mops (e.g., daily) is therefore recommended.

DISINFECTION

A great number of disinfectants are used alone or in combinations (e.g., hydrogen peroxide and peracetic acid) in the health care setting. These include alcohols, chlorine and chlorine compounds, formaldehyde, glutaraldehyde, *ortho*-phthalaldehyde, hydrogen peroxide, iodophors, peracetic acid, phenolics, and quaternary ammonium compounds. With some exceptions (e.g., ethanol or bleach), commercial formulations based on these chemicals are considered unique products and must be registered with the EPA or cleared by the FDA. In most instances, a given product is designed for a specific purpose and is to be used in a certain manner. Therefore, the label should be read carefully to ensure that the right product is selected for the intended use and applied in an efficient manner.

Disinfectants are not interchangeable, and an overview of the performance characteristics of each is provided below so the user has sufficient information to select an appropriate disinfectant for any item and use it in the most efficient way. It should be recognized that excessive costs may be attributed to incorrect concentrations and inappropriate disinfectants. Finally, occupational diseases among cleaning personnel have been associated with the use of several disinfectants, such as formaldehyde, glutaraldehyde, and chlorine, and precautions (e.g., gloves, proper ventilation) should be used to minimize exposure.[42,43] Asthma and reactive airway disease may occur in sensitized individuals exposed to any airborne chemical, including germicides. Clinically important asthma may occur at levels below ceiling levels regulated by the Occupational Safety and Health Administration (OSHA). The preferred method of control is to eliminate the chemical (via engineering controls, or substitution) or relocate the worker.

Chemical Disinfectants

Alcohol

In the health care setting, "alcohol" refers to two water-soluble chemical compounds whose germicidal characteristics are generally underrated: ethyl alcohol and isopropyl alcohol.[44] These alcohols are rapidly bactericidal rather than bacteriostatic against vegetative forms of bacteria; they also are tuberculocidal, fungicidal, and virucidal but do not destroy bacterial spores. Their cidal activity drops sharply when diluted below 50% concentration, and the optimum bactericidal concentration is in the range of 60% to 90% solutions in water (volume/volume).[45,46]

Alcohols are not recommended for sterilizing medical and surgical materials principally because of their lack of sporicidal action and their inability to penetrate protein-rich materials. Fatal postoperative wound infections with *Clostridium* have occurred when alcohols were used to sterilize surgical instruments contaminated with bacterial spores.[47] Alcohols have been used effectively to disinfect oral and rectal thermometers, hospital pagers, scissors, stethoscopes, and fiberoptic endoscopes.[48] Alcohol towelettes have been used for years to disinfect small surfaces such as rubber stoppers of multiple-dose medication vials or vaccine bottles.[48] Beck-Sague and Jarvis described three blood-stream infection outbreaks when alcohol was used to disinfect transducer heads in an intensive care setting.[49]

Alcohols are flammable and consequently must be stored in a cool, well-ventilated area. They also evaporate rapidly, and this makes extended exposure time difficult to achieve unless the items are immersed.

Chlorine and Chlorine Compounds

Hypochlorites are the most widely used of the chlorine disinfectants and are available in a liquid (e.g., sodium hypochlorite) or solid (e.g., calcium hypochlorite) form. The most prevalent chlorine products in the United States are aqueous solutions of 5.25% to 6.15% sodium hypochlorite, which usually are called household bleach. They have a broad spectrum of antimicrobial activity (i.e., bactericidal, virucidal, fungicidal, mycobactericidal, sporicidal), do not leave toxic residues, are unaffected by water hardness, are inexpensive and fast acting,[50] remove dried or fixed organisms and biofilms from surfaces,[51] and a low incidence of serious toxicity.[52] Sodium hypochlorite at the concentration used in domestic bleach (5.25% to 6.15%) may produce ocular irritation or oropharyngeal, esophageal, and gastric burns.[43,53,54] Other disadvantages of hypochlorites include corrosiveness to metals in high concentrations (>500 ppm), inactivation by organic matter, discoloring or "bleaching" of fabrics, release of toxic chlorine gas when mixed with ammonia or acid (e.g., household cleaning agents),[55] and low relative stability.[56]

Reports have examined the microbicidal activity of a new disinfectant, "superoxidized water." The concept of electrolyzing saline to create a disinfectant or antiseptic is appealing because the basic materials of saline and electricity are cheap and the end product (i.e., water) is not damaging to the environment. The main products of this water are hypochlorous acid (e.g., at a concentration of about 144 mg/L) and chlorine. As with any germicide, the antimicrobial activity of superoxidized water is strongly affected by the concentration of the active ingredient (available free chlorine).[57] Data have shown that freshly generated superoxidized water is rapidly effective (<2 minutes) in achieving a 5-$\log_{10}$ reduction of pathogenic microorganisms (i.e., *M. tuberculosis*, *M. chelonae*, poliovirus, human immunodeficiency virus [HIV], MRSA, *E. coli*, *Candida albicans*, *Enterococcus faecalis*, *P. aeruginosa*) in the absence of organic loading. However, the biocidal activity of this disinfectant was substantially reduced in the presence of organic material (5% horse serum).[58,59]

Hypochlorites are widely used in health care facilities in a variety of settings.[50] Inorganic chlorine solution is used for disinfecting tonometer heads[60] and for spot disinfection of countertops and floors. A 1:10 to 1:100 dilution of 5.25% to 6.15% sodium hypochlorite (i.e., household bleach)[61-64] or an EPA-registered tuberculocidal disinfectant[13] has been recommended for decontaminating blood spills. For small spills of blood (i.e., drops of blood) on noncritical surfaces, the area can be disinfected with a 1:100 dilution of 5.25% to 6.15% sodium hypochlorite or an EPA-registered tuberculocidal disinfectant. Because hypochlorites and other germicides are substantially inactivated in the presence of blood,[39,65] large spills of blood require that the surface be cleaned before an EPA-registered disin-

fectant or a 1:10 (final concentration) solution of household bleach is applied. If there is a possibility of a sharps injury, there should be an initial decontamination,[43,66] followed by cleaning and terminal disinfection (1:10 final concentration).[39] Extreme care should always be employed to prevent percutaneous injury. Application of at least 500 ppm of available chlorine for 10 minutes is recommended for decontamination of cardiopulmonary resuscitation training manikins. Other uses in health care include as an irrigating agent in endodontic treatment and for disinfecting manikins, laundry, dental appliances, hydrotherapy tanks,[67] regulated medical waste before disposal,[50] and the water distribution system in hemodialysis centers and hemodialysis machines.[48]

Hyperchlorination of a *Legionella*-contaminated hospital water system[67] resulted in a dramatic decrease (from 30% to 1.5%) in the isolation of *L. pneumophila* from water outlets and a cessation of health care–associated Legionnaires' disease in the affected unit.[68] Chloramine T and hypochlorites have been used in disinfecting hydrotherapy equipment.[48]

Hypochlorite solutions in tap water at a pH greater than 8 stored at room temperature (23° C) in closed, opaque plastic containers may lose up to 40% to 50% of their free available chlorine level over a period of 1 month. Thus, if a user wished to have a solution containing 500 ppm of available chlorine at day 30, a solution containing 1000 ppm of chlorine should be prepared at time 0. There is no decomposition of sodium hypochlorite solution after 30 days when stored in a closed brown bottle.[56]

Glutaraldehyde

Glutaraldehyde is a saturated dialdehyde that has gained wide acceptance as a high-level disinfectant and chemical sterilant.[69] Aqueous solutions of glutaraldehyde are acidic and generally in this state are not sporicidal. Only when the solution is "activated" (made alkaline) by use of alkalinating agents to achieve pH 7.5 to 8.5 does the solution become sporicidal. Once "activated," these solutions have a shelf-life of minimally 14 days because of the polymerization of the glutaraldehyde molecules at alkaline pH levels. This polymerization blocks the active sites (aldehyde groups) of the glutaraldehyde molecules that are responsible for its biocidal activity.

Novel glutaraldehyde formulations (e.g., glutaraldehyde-phenol–sodium phenate, potentiated acid glutaraldehyde, stabilized alkaline glutaraldehyde) produced in the past 30 years have overcome the problem of rapid loss of activity (e.g., use-life of 28 to 30 days) while generally maintaining excellent microbicidal activity.[48,70,71] However, it should be recognized that antimicrobial activity is dependent not only on age but also on use conditions such as dilution and organic stress. The use of glutaraldehyde-based solutions in health care facilities is widespread because of their advantages, which include excellent biocidal properties; activity in the presence of organic matter (20% bovine serum); and noncorrosive action on endoscopic equipment, thermometers, rubber, or plastic equipment. The advantages, disadvantages, and characteristics of glutaraldehyde are listed in Table 299-2.

The in vitro inactivation of microorganisms by glutaraldehydes has been extensively investigated and reviewed.[72] Several investigators showed that greater than 2% aqueous solutions of glutaraldehyde, buffered to pH 7.5 to 8.5 with sodium bicarbonate, were effective in killing vegetative bacteria in less than 2 minutes; *M. tuberculosis*, fungi, and viruses in less than 10 minutes; and spores of *Bacillus* and *Clostridium* species in 3 hours.[72,73] Spores of *Clostridium difficile* are more rapidly killed by 2% glutaraldehyde than are spores of other species of *Clostridium* and *Bacillus*.[74,75] There have been reports of microorganisms with significant resistance to glutaraldehyde, including some mycobacteria (*Mycobacterium chelonae*, *M. avium-intracellulare*, *M. xenopi*),[76,77] *Methylobacterium mesophilicum*,[78] *Trichosporon*, fungal spores (e.g., *Microascus cinereus*, *Cheatomium globosum*), and *Cryptosporidium*.[79] *M. chelonae* persisted in a 0.2% glutaraldehyde solution used to store porcine prosthetic heart valves.[80]

Dilution of glutaraldehyde during use commonly occurs, and studies show a glutaraldehyde concentration decline after a few

TABLE 299-2 Summary of Advantages and Disadvantages of Chemical Agents Used as Chemical Sterilants* or as High-Level Disinfectants

Sterilization Method	Advantages	Disadvantages
Peracetic acid/hydrogen peroxide	• No activation required • Odor or irritation not significant	• Materials compatibility concerns (lead, brass, copper, zinc), both cosmetic and functional • Limited clinical experience • Potential for eye and skin damage
Glutaraldehyde	• Numerous use studies published • Relatively inexpensive • Excellent materials compatibility	• Respiratory irritation from glutaraldehyde vapor • Pungent and irritating odor • Relatively slow mycobactericidal activity • Coagulates blood and fixes tissue to surfaces • Allergic contact dermatitis
Hydrogen peroxide	• No activation required • May enhance removal of organic matter and organisms • No disposal issues • No odor or irritation issues • Does not coagulate blood or fix tissues to surfaces • Inactivates *Cryptosporidium* • Use studies published	• Material compatibility concerns (brass, zinc, copper, and nickel/silver plating), both cosmetic and functional • Serious eye damage with contact
Ortho-phthalaldehyde	• Fast-acting high-level disinfectant • No activation required • Odor not significant • Excellent materials compatibility claimed • Claimed not to coagulate blood or fix tissues to surfaces	• Stains skin, mucous membranes, clothing, and environmental surfaces • Limited clinical experience • More expensive than glutaraldehyde • Eye irritation with contact • Slow sporicidal activity • Anaphylaxis-like reactions in bladder cancer patients
Peracetic acid	• Rapid sterilization cycle time (30-45 minutes) • Low temperature (50° to 55° C) liquid immersion sterilization • Environmentally friendly by-products (acetic acid, O_2, H_2O) • Fully automated • Single-use system eliminates need for concentration testing • Standardized cycle • May enhance removal of organic material and endotoxin • No adverse health effects to operators under normal operating conditions • Compatible with many materials and instruments • Does not coagulate blood or fix tissues to surfaces • Sterilant flows through scope facilitating salt, protein, and microbe removal • Rapidly sporicidal • Provides procedure standardization (constant dilution, perfusion of channel, temperatures, exposure)	• Potential material incompatibility (e.g., aluminum anodized coating becomes dull) • Used for immersible instruments only • Biological indicator may not be suitable for routine monitoring • One scope or a small number of instruments can be processed in a cycle • More expensive (endoscope repairs, operating costs, purchase costs) than high-level disinfection • Serious eye and skin damage (concentrated solution) with contact • Point-of-use system, no sterile storage • Unstable, particularly when diluted

*All products effective in presence of organic soil, relatively easy to use, and have a broad spectrum of antimicrobial activity (bacteria, fungi, viruses, bacterial spores, and mycobacteria). The above characteristics are documented in the literature; contact the manufacturer of the instrument and sterilant for additional information. All products listed above are FDA cleared as chemical sterilants except OPA, which is an FDA-cleared high-level disinfectant.

Modified from Rutala WA, Weber DJ. Disinfection of endoscopes: Review of new chemical sterilants used for high-level disinfection. Infect Control Hosp Epidemiol. 1999; 20:69-76.

days of use in an automatic endoscope washer.[81] This occurs because instruments are not thoroughly dried and water is carried in with the instrument, which increases the solution's volume and dilutes its effective concentration. This emphasizes the need to ensure that semicritical equipment is disinfected with an acceptable concentration of glutaraldehyde. Data suggest that 1.0% to 1.5% glutaraldehyde is the minimum effective concentration for greater than 2% glutaraldehyde solutions when used as a high-level disinfectant.[81-83] Chemical test strips or liquid chemical monitors are available for determining whether an effective concentration of glutaraldehyde is present despite repeated use and dilution. The frequency of testing should be based on how frequently the solutions are used (e.g., used daily, test daily; used weekly, test before use; used 30 times per day, test each 10th use) but the strips should not be used to extend the use life beyond the expiration date. Data suggest the chemicals in the test strip deteriorate with time,[84] and a manufacturer's expiration date should be placed on the bottles. The bottle of test strips should be dated when opened and used for the period of time indicated on the bottle (e.g., 120 days). The results of test strip monitoring should be documented. The glutaraldehyde test kits have been preliminarily evaluated for accuracy and range[84] but the reliability has been questioned. The concentration should be considered unacceptable or unsafe when the test indicates a dilution below the product's minimum effective concentration (generally to 1.0% to 1.5% glutaraldehyde or lower) by the indicator not changing color.

Glutaraldehyde is used most commonly as a high-level disinfectant for medical equipment such as endoscopes,[66] spirometry tubing, dialyzers, transducers, anesthesia and respiratory therapy equipment, and hemodialysis proportioning and dialysate delivery systems, and for reuse of laparoscopic disposable plastic trocars.[48] Glutaraldehyde is noncorrosive to metal and does not damage lensed instruments, rubber, or plastics. The FDA-cleared labels for high-level disinfection with greater than 2% glutaraldehyde at 25° C range from 20 to 90 minutes depending upon the product. However, multiple scientific studies and professional organizations support the efficacy of greater than 2% glutaraldehyde for 20 minutes at 20° C.[13] Minimally, one should follow this latter recommendation. Glutaraldehyde should not be used for cleaning noncritical surfaces because it is too toxic and expensive.

Colitis believed to be due to glutaraldehyde exposure from residual disinfecting solution in endoscope solution channels has been reported and is preventable by careful endoscope rinsing.[43] One study found that residual glutaraldehyde levels were higher and more variable after manual disinfection (<0.2 to 159.5 mg/L) than after automatic disinfection (0.2 to 6.3 mg/L).[85] Similarly, keratopathy and corneal damage were caused by ophthalmic instruments that were inadequately rinsed after soaking in 2% glutaraldehyde.[86]

Glutaraldehyde exposure should be monitored to ensure a safe work environment. In the absence of an OSHA PEL, if the glutaraldehyde level is higher than the ACGIH ceiling limit of 0.05 ppm, it would be prudent to take corrective action and repeat monitoring.[87]

Hydrogen Peroxide

The literature contains several accounts of the properties, germicidal effectiveness, and potential uses for stabilized hydrogen peroxide in the health care setting. Published reports ascribing good germicidal activity to hydrogen peroxide have been published and attest to its bactericidal, virucidal, sporicidal, and fungicidal properties.[88-91] The advantages, disadvantages, and characteristics of hydrogen peroxide are listed in Table 299-2. As with other chemical sterilants, dilution of the hydrogen peroxide must be monitored by regularly testing the minimum effective concentration (i.e., 7.5% to 6.0%). Users should follow the FDA-cleared label claim for high-level disinfection (i.e., 30 minutes at 20° C for 7.5% hydrogen peroxide).

Commercially available 3% hydrogen peroxide is a stable and effective disinfectant when used on inanimate surfaces. It has been used in concentrations from 3% to 6% for the disinfection of soft contact lenses (e.g., 3% for 2 to 3 hours),[88,92] tonometer biprisms, ventilators, fabrics[93] and endoscopes.[48,94] Hydrogen peroxide was effective in spot-disinfecting fabrics in patients' rooms.[93] Corneal damage from a hydrogen peroxide–soaked tonometer tip that was not properly rinsed has been reported.[95] Hydrogen peroxide also has been instilled into urinary drainage bags in an attempt to eliminate the bag as a source of bladder bacteriuria and environmental contamination.[96] Although the instillation of hydrogen peroxide into the bag reduced microbial contamination of the bag, this procedure did not reduce the incidence of catheter-associated bacteriuria.[96]

Iodophors

Iodine solutions, or tinctures, have long been used by health professionals, primarily as antiseptics on skin or tissue. The FDA has not cleared any liquid chemical sterilants/high-level disinfectants with iodophors as the main active ingredient. However, iodophors have been used both as antiseptics and disinfectants. An iodophor is a combination of iodine and a solubilizing agent or carrier; the resulting complex provides a sustained-release reservoir of iodine and releases small amounts of free iodine in aqueous solution. The best known and most widely used iodophor is povidone-iodine, a compound of polyvinylpyrrolidone with iodine. This product and other iodophors retain the germicidal efficacy of iodine but, unlike iodine, are generally nonstaining and are relatively free of toxicity and irritancy.[97]

There are several reports that documented intrinsic microbial contamination of antiseptic formulations of povidone-iodine and poloxamer-iodine.[98,99] It was found that "free" iodine (I_2) contributes to the bactericidal activity of iodophors and that dilutions of iodophors demonstrate more rapid bactericidal action than does a full-strength povidone-iodine solution. Therefore, iodophors must be diluted according to the manufacturers' directions to achieve antimicrobial activity.

Published reports on the in vitro antimicrobial efficacy of iodophors demonstrate that iodophors are bactericidal, mycobactericidal, and virucidal but may require prolonged contact times to kill certain fungi and bacterial spores.[10,48,100-103]

Besides their use as an antiseptic, iodophors have been used for the disinfection of blood culture bottles and medical equipment such as hydrotherapy tanks, thermometers, and, in the past, endoscopes. Antiseptic iodophors are not suitable for use as hard-surface disinfectants because of concentration differences. Iodophors formulated as antiseptics contain less free iodine than those formulated as disinfectants.[104] Iodine or iodine-based antiseptics should not be used on silicone catheters because the silicone tubing may be adversely affected.[105]

Ortho-phthalaldehyde (OPA)

Ortho-phthalaldehyde is a high-level disinfectant that received FDA clearance in October 1999. It contains 0.55% 1,2-benzenedicarboxaldehyde, or OPA. OPA solution is a clear, pale-blue liquid with a pH of 7.5. The advantages, disadvantages, and characteristics of OPA are listed in Table 299-2.

Studies have demonstrated excellent microbicidal activity in vitro,[66,79,106-112] including superior mycobactericidal activity (5-$\log_{10}$ reduction in 5 minutes) compared to glutaraldehyde. Walsh and col-

leagues also found OPA effective (>5-$\log_{10}$ reduction) against a wide range of microorganisms, including glutaraldehyde-resistant mycobacteria and *Bacillus atrophaeus* spores.[109]

OPA has several potential advantages compared to glutaraldehyde. It has excellent stability over a wide pH range (pH 3 to 9), is not a known irritant to the eyes and nasal passages, does not require exposure monitoring, has a barely perceptible odor, and requires no activation. OPA, like glutaraldehyde, has excellent material compatibility. A potential disadvantage of OPA is that it stains proteins gray (including unprotected skin) and thus must be handled with caution.[66] However, skin staining would indicate improper handling that requires additional training, use of personal protective equipment (PPE) (gloves, eye and mouth protection, fluid-resistant gowns), or both. OPA residues remaining on inadequately water-rinsed transesophageal echo probes may leave stains in the patient's mouth. Meticulous cleaning, using the correct OPA exposure time (e.g., 12 minutes), and copious rinsing of the probe with water should eliminate this problem. PPE should be worn when handling contaminated instruments, equipment, and chemicals.[107] In addition, equipment must be thoroughly rinsed to prevent discoloration of a patient's skin or mucous membrane.

Peracetic Acid

Peracetic, or peroxyacetic, acid is characterized by a very rapid action against all microorganisms. Special advantages of peracetic acid include its lack of harmful decomposition products (i.e., acetic acid, water, oxygen, hydrogen peroxide) and the fact that it enhances removal of organic material[113] and leaves no residue. It remains effective in the presence of organic matter and is sporicidal even at low temperatures. Peracetic acid can corrode copper, brass, bronze, plain steel, and galvanized iron, but these effects can be reduced by additives and pH modifications. The advantages, disadvantages, and characteristics of peracetic acid are listed in Tables 299-2 and 299-3.

Peracetic acid will inactivate gram-positive and gram-negative bacteria, fungi, and yeasts in less than 5 minutes at less than 100 ppm. In the presence of organic matter, 200 to 500 ppm is required. For viruses the dosage range is wide (12 to 2250 ppm), with poliovirus inactivated in yeast extract in 15 minutes with 1500 to 2250 ppm. An automated machine using peracetic acid to chemically sterilize medical (e.g., endoscopes, arthroscopes) and surgical instruments is used in the United States.[114,115] The sterilant, 35% peracetic acid, is diluted to 0.2% with filtered water at a temperature of 50° C. Simulated-use trials have demonstrated excellent microbicidal activity,[116-119] and three clinical trials have demonstrated both excellent microbial killing and no clinical failures leading to infection.[120-122] Three clusters of infection using the peracetic acid automated endoscope reprocessor were linked to inadequately processed bronchoscopes when inappropriate channel connectors were used with the system.[123] These clusters highlight the importance of training, proper model-specific endoscope connector systems, and quality control procedures to ensure compliance with endoscope manufacturers' recommendations and professional organization guidelines. An alternative high-level disinfectant available in the United Kingdom contains 0.35% peracetic acid. Although this product is rapidly effective against a broad range of microorganisms,[124,125] it tarnishes the metal of endoscopes and is unstable, resulting in only a 24-hour use life.[125]

Peracetic Acid Plus Hydrogen Peroxide

One chemical sterilants is available that contains peracetic acid plus hydrogen peroxide (0.23% peracetic acid plus 7.35% hydrogen peroxide). The advantages, disadvantages, and characteristics of peracetic acid plus hydrogen peroxide are listed in Table 299-2.

The bactericidal properties of peracetic acid plus hydrogen peroxide have been demonstrated.[126] Manufacturer's data demonstrated that this combination of peracetic acid and hydrogen peroxide inactivated all microorganisms with the exception of bacterial spores within 20 minutes. A 0.08% peracetic acid plus 1.0% hydrogen peroxide product (no longer available) was effective in inactivating a glutaraldehyde-resistant mycobacteria.[127]

TABLE 299-3 Summary of Advantages and Disadvantages of Commonly Used Sterilization Technologies

Sterilization Method	Advantages	Disadvantages
Steam	• Nontoxic to patient, staff, environment • Cycle easy to control and monitor • Rapidly microbicidal • Least affected by organic/inorganic soils among sterilization processes listed • Rapid cycle time • Penetrates medical packing, device lumens	• Deleterious for heat-sensitive instruments • Microsurgical instruments damaged by repeated exposure • May leave instruments wet, causing them to rust • Potential for burns
Hydrogen peroxide gas plasma	• Safe for the environment • Leaves no toxic residuals • Cycle time is 45-73 minutes and no aeration necessary • Used for heat- and moisture-sensitive items because process temperature < 50° C • Simple to operate, install (208-V outlet), and monitor • Compatible with most medical devices • Only requires electrical outlet	• Cellulose (paper), linens, and liquids cannot be processed • Sterilization chamber is small, about 3.5-7.3 ft³ • See manufacturer's recommendations for endoscope or medical device restrictions based on lumen internal diameter or length • Requires synthetic packaging (polypropylene wraps, polyolefin pouches) and special container tray • Hydrogen peroxide may be toxic at levels greater than 1 ppm TWA
100% ethylene oxide (ETO)	• Penetrates packaging materials, device lumens • Single-dose cartridge and negative-pressure chamber minimize the potential for gas leak and ETO exposure • Simple to operate and monitor • Compatible with most medical materials	• Requires aeration time to remove ETO residue • Sterilization chamber is small, 4-8.8 ft³ • ETO is toxic, a carcinogen, and flammable • ETO emission regulated by states but catalytic cell removes 99.9% of ETO and converts it to CO_2 and H_2O • ETO cartridges should be stored in flammable liquid storage cabinet • Lengthy cycle/aeration time
ETO mixtures 8.6% ETO/91.4% HCFC 10% ETO/90% HCFC 8.5% ETO/91.5% CO2	• Penetrate medical packaging and many plastics • Compatible with most medical materials • Cycle easy to control and monitor	• Some states (e.g., CA, NY, MI) require ETO emission reduction of 90%-99.9% • CFC (inert gas that eliminates explosion hazard) banned in 1995 • Potential hazards to staff and patients • Lengthy cycle/aeration time • ETO is toxic, a carcinogen, and flammable • Point-of-use system, no sterile storage
Peracetic acid	• Rapid cycle time (30-45 minutes) • Low temperature (50° to 55° C) liquid immersion sterilization • Environmentally friendly by-products • Sterilant flows through endoscope, which facilitates salt, protein, and microbe removal • Fully automated • Single-use system eliminates need for concentration testing • Standardized cycle	• Biologic indicator may not be suitable for routine monitoring • Used for immersible instruments only • Some material incompatibility (e.g., aluminum anodized coating becomes dull) • One scope or a small number of instruments processed in a cycle • Potential for serious eye and skin damage (concentrated solution) with contact

CFC, chlorofluorocarbon; HCFC, hydrochlorofluorocarbon.
Modified from Rutala WA, Weber DJ. Clinical effectiveness of low-temperature sterilization technologies. Infect Control Hosp Epidemiol. 1998;19:798-804.

The combination of peracetic acid and hydrogen peroxide has been used for disinfecting hemodialyzers.[128] The percentage of dialysis centers using a peracetic acid plus hydrogen peroxide–based disinfectant for reprocessing dialyzers increased from 5% in 1983 to 56% in 1997.[129]

Phenolics

Phenol has occupied a prominent place in the field of hospital disinfection since its initial use as a germicide by Lister in his pioneering work on antiseptic surgery. In the past 30 years, however, work has been concentrated upon the numerous phenol derivatives, or phenolics, and their antimicrobial properties. Phenol derivatives originate when a functional group (e.g., alkyl, phenyl, benzyl, halogen) replaces one of the hydrogen atoms on the aromatic ring. Two phenol derivatives commonly found as constituents of hospital disinfectants are *ortho*-phenylphenol and *ortho*-benzyl-*para*-chlorophenol.

Published reports on the antimicrobial efficacy of commonly used phenolics showed that they were bactericidal, fungicidal, virucidal, and tuberculocidal.[10,48,100,130-135]

Many phenolic germicides are EPA registered as disinfectants for use on environmental surfaces (e.g., bedside tables, bed rails, laboratory surfaces) and noncritical medical devices. Phenolics are not FDA cleared as high-level disinfectants for use with semicritical items but could be used to preclean or decontaminate critical and semicritical devices prior to terminal sterilization or high-level disinfection.

The use of phenolics in nurseries has been questioned because of the occurrence of hyperbilirubinemia in infants placed in bassinets in which phenolic detergents were used.[136] In addition, Doan and co-workers demonstrated bilirubin level increases in phenolic-exposed infants compared to nonphenolic-exposed infants when the phenolic was prepared according to the manufacturers' recommended dilution.[137] If phenolics are used to clean nursery floors, they must be diluted according to the recommendation on the product label. Phenolics (and other disinfectants) should not be used to clean infant bassinets and incubators while occupied. If phenolics are used to terminally clean infant bassinets and incubators, the surfaces should be rinsed thoroughly with water and dried before the bassinets and incubators are reused.[13]

Quaternary Ammonium Compounds

The quaternary ammonium compounds are widely used as surface disinfectants. There have been some reports of health care–associated infections related to contaminated quaternary ammonium compounds used to disinfect patient-care supplies or equipment such as cystoscopes or cardiac catheters.[48] As with several other disinfectants (e.g., phenolics, iodophors), gram-negative bacteria have been found to survive or grow in them.[138]

Results from manufacturers' data sheets and from published scientific literature indicate that the quaternaries sold as hospital disinfectants are generally fungicidal, bactericidal, and virucidal against lipophilic (enveloped) viruses; they are not sporicidal and generally not tuberculocidal or virucidal against hydrophilic (nonenveloped) viruses.[10,36,38,100,130,139-141] Best and colleagues[36] and Rutala and associates[100] demonstrated the poor mycobactericidal activities of quaternary ammonium compounds.

The quaternaries are commonly used in ordinary environmental sanitation of noncritical surfaces such as floors, furniture, and walls.

EPA-registered quaternary ammonium compounds are appropriate to use when disinfecting medical equipment that comes into contact with intact skin (e.g., blood pressure cuffs).

Pasteurization

Pasteurization is not a sterilization process; its purpose is to destroy all pathogenic microorganisms with the exception of bacterial spores. The time-temperature relation for hot-water pasteurization is generally greater than 70° C (158° F) for 30 minutes. The water temperature and time should be monitored as part of a quality assurance program.[142] Pasteurization of respiratory therapy[143,144] and anesthesia equipment[145] is a recognized alternative to chemical disinfection.

STERILIZATION

Most medical and surgical devices used in health care facilities are made of materials that are heat stable and thus are sterilized by heat, primarily steam sterilization. However, since 1950, there has been an increase in medical devices and instruments made of materials (e.g., plastics) that require low-temperature sterilization. Ethylene oxide gas has been used since the 1950s for heat- and moisture-sensitive medical devices. Within the past 15 years, a number of new, low-temperature sterilization systems (e.g., hydrogen peroxide gas plasma, peracetic acid immersion) have been developed and are being used to sterilize medical devices. This section reviews sterilization technologies used in health care and makes recommendations for their optimum performance in the processing of medical devices.[1,14,15,146-152]

Sterilization destroys all microorganisms on the surface of an article or in a fluid to prevent disease transmission associated with the use of that item. Although the use of inadequately sterilized critical items presents a high risk of transmitting pathogens, documented transmission of pathogens associated with an inadequately sterilized critical item is exceedingly rare.[153,154] This is likely due to the wide margin of safety associated with the sterilization processes used in health care facilities. The concept of what constitutes "sterile" is measured as a probability of sterility for each item to be sterilized. This probability is commonly referred to as the sterility assurance level (SAL) of the product and is defined as the probability of a single viable microorganism occurring on a product after sterilization. SAL is normally expressed a 10^{-n}. For example, if the probability of a spore surviving were 1 in 1 million, the SAL would be 10^{-6}.[155,156] In short, a SAL is an estimate of lethality of the entire sterilization process and is a conservative calculation. Dual SALs (e.g., 10^{-3} SAL for blood culture tubes, drainage bags; 10^{-6} SAL for scalpels, implants) have been used in the United States for many years, and the choice of a 10^{-6} SAL was strictly arbitrary and not associated with any adverse outcomes (e.g., patient infections).[155]

Medical devices that have contact with sterile body tissues or fluids are considered critical items. These items should be sterile when used because any microbial contamination could result in disease transmission. Such items include surgical instruments, biopsy forceps, and implanted medical devices. If these items are heat resistant, the recommended sterilization process is steam sterilization, because it has the largest margin of safety as a result of its reliability, consistency, and lethality. However, reprocessing heat- and moisture-sensitive items requires use of a low-temperature sterilization technology (e.g., ETO, hydrogen peroxide gas plasma, peracetic acid).[157] A summary of the advantages and disadvantages for commonly used sterilization technologies is presented in Table 299-3.

Steam Sterilization

Of all the methods available for sterilization, moist heat in the form of saturated steam under pressure is the most widely used and the most dependable. Steam sterilization is nontoxic, inexpensive,[158] rapidly microbicidal, and sporicidal, and rapidly heats and penetrates fabrics (see Table 299-3).[159] Like all sterilization processes, steam sterilization has some deleterious effects on some materials, including corrosion and combustion of lubricants associated with dental handpieces[160]; re-

duction in ability to transmit light associated with laryngoscopes[161]; and increased hardening time (5.6-fold) with plaster cast material.[162]

The basic principle of steam sterilization, as accomplished in an autoclave, is to expose each item to direct steam contact at the required temperature and pressure for the specified time. Thus there are four parameters of steam sterilization: steam, pressure, temperature, and time. The ideal steam for sterilization is dry saturated steam and entrained water (dryness fraction >97%).[148] Pressure serves as a means to obtain the high temperatures necessary to quickly kill microorganisms. Specific temperatures must be obtained to ensure the microbicidal activity. The two common steam-sterilizing temperatures are 121° C (250° F) and 132° C (270° F). These temperatures (and other high temperatures) must be maintained for a minimal time to kill microorganisms. Recognized minimum exposure periods for sterilization of wrapped health care supplies are 30 minutes at 121° C (250° F) in a gravity displacement sterilizer or 4 minutes at 132° C (270° C) in a prevacuum sterilizer. At constant temperatures, sterilization times vary depending on the type of item (e.g., metal versus rubber, plastic, items with lumens), whether the item is wrapped or unwrapped, and the sterilizer type.

The two basic types of steam sterilizers (autoclaves) are the gravity displacement autoclave and the high-speed prevacuum sterilizer. In the former, steam is admitted at the top or the sides of the sterilizing chamber and, because the steam is lighter than air, forces air out the bottom of the chamber through the drain vent. The gravity displacement autoclaves are primarily used to process laboratory media, water, pharmaceutical products, regulated medical waste, and nonporous articles whose surfaces have direct steam contact. With gravity displacement sterilizers the penetration time into porous items is prolonged because of incomplete air elimination. The high-speed prevacuum sterilizers are similar to the gravity displacement sterilizers except that they are fitted with a vacuum pump (or ejector) to ensure air removal from the sterilizing chamber and are loaded before the steam is admitted. The advantage of using a vacuum pump is that there is nearly instantaneous steam penetration even into porous loads.

Like other sterilization systems, the steam cycle is monitored by mechanical, chemical, and biologic monitors. Steam sterilizers usually are monitored using a printout (or graphically) by measuring temperature, the time at the temperature, and pressure. Typically, chemical indicators are affixed to the outside and incorporated into the pack to monitor the temperature or time and temperature. The effectiveness of steam sterilization is monitored with a biologic indicator containing spores of *Geobacillus stearothermophilus* (formerly *Bacillus stearothermophilus*). Positive spore test results are a relatively rare event and may be attributed to operator error, inadequate steam delivery,[163] or equipment malfunction.

Portable steam sterilizers are used in outpatient, dental, and rural clinics. These sterilizers are designed for small instruments, such as hypodermic syringes and needles and dental instruments. The ability of the sterilizer to reach physical parameters necessary to achieve sterilization should be monitored by mechanical, chemical, and biologic indicators.

The oldest and most recognized agent for inactivation of microorganisms is heat. D values (time to reduce the surviving population by 90% or 1 $\log_{10}$) allow a direct comparison of the heat resistance of microorganisms. Because a D value can be determined at various temperatures, a subscript is used to designate the exposure temperature (i.e., D_{121C}). D_{121C} values for *G. stearothermophilus* used to monitor the steam sterilization process range from 1 to 2 minutes. Heat-resistant non–spore-forming bacteria, yeasts, and fungi have such low D_{121C} values that they cannot be experimentally measured.[164]

Steam sterilization should be used whenever possible on all critical and semicritical items that are heat and moisture resistant (e.g., steam-sterilizable respiratory therapy and anesthesia equipment), even when not essential to prevent pathogen transmission. Steam sterilizers also are used in health care facilities to decontaminate microbiologic waste and sharps containers,[165] but additional exposure time is required in the gravity displacement sterilizer for these items.

Flash Sterilization

"Flash" steam sterilization was originally defined by Underwood and Perkins as sterilization of an unwrapped object at 132° C for 3 minutes at 27 to 28 pounds of pressure in a gravity displacement sterilizer.[166] Currently, the time required for flash sterilization depends on the type of sterilizer and the type of item (i.e., porous vs. nonporous items). For example, the minimum flash sterilization cycle time for nonporous items only (i.e., routine metal instruments, no lumens) at 270° F in a prevacuum sterilizer is 3 minutes. Although the wrapped method of sterilization is preferred for the reasons listed below, correctly performed flash sterilization is an effective process for the sterilization of critical medical devices.[167] Flash sterilization is a modification of conventional steam sterilization (either gravity or prevacuum) in which the flashed item is placed in an open tray or in a specially designed, covered, rigid container to allow for rapid penetration of steam. Historically, it is not recommended as a routine sterilization method because of the lack of timely biologic indicators to monitor performance, absence of protective packaging following sterilization, possibility for contamination of processed items during transportation to the operating rooms, and the fact that the sterilization cycle parameters (i.e., time, temperature, pressure) are minimal. To address some of these concerns, many health care facilities have done the following: placed equipment for flash sterilization in close proximity to operating rooms to facilitate aseptic delivery to the point of use (usually the sterile field in an ongoing surgical procedure); extended the exposure time to ensure lethality comparable to sterilized wrapped items (e.g., 4 minutes at 132° C)[168,169]; used biologic indicators that provide results in 1 hour for flash-sterilized items[168,169]; and used protective packaging that permits steam penetration.[1,147,152,167] Furthermore, some rigid, reusable sterilization container systems have been designed and validated by the container manufacturer for use with flash cycles. When sterile items are open to air, they will eventually become contaminated. Thus the longer a sterile item is exposed to air, the greater the number of microorganisms that will settle on it.

A few adverse events have been associated with flash sterilization. When evaluating an increased incidence of neurosurgical infections, the investigators noted that surgical instruments were flash sterilized between cases and that two of three craniotomy infections involved plate implants that were flash sterilized.[170] A report of two patients who received burns during surgery from instruments that had been flash sterilized reinforced the need to develop policies and educate staff to prevent the use of instruments hot enough to cause clinical burns.[171] Staff should use precautions to prevent burns with potentially hot instruments (e.g., transport tray using heat-protective gloves). Patient burns may be prevented by either air-cooling the instruments or immersing them in sterile liquid (e.g., saline).

Flash sterilization is considered acceptable for processing cleaned patient-care items that cannot be packaged, sterilized, and stored before use. It also is used when there is insufficient time to sterilize an item by the preferred package method. Flash sterilization should not be used for reasons of convenience, as an alternative to purchasing additional instrument sets, or to save time.[1] Because of the potential for serious infections, flash sterilization is not recommended for implantable devices (i.e., devices placed into a surgically or naturally formed cavity of the human body); however, flash sterilization may be unavoidable for some devices (e.g., orthopedic screw, plates). If flash sterilization of an implantable device is unavoidable, record keeping (e.g., load identification, patient's name/hospital identifier, biologic indicator result) is essential for epidemiologic tracking (e.g., of surgical site infection, tracing results of biologic indicators to patients who received the item to document sterility), and for an assessment of the reliability of the sterilization process (e.g., evaluation of biologic monitoring records and sterilization maintenance records noting preventive maintenance and repairs with dates).

Ethylene Oxide "Gas" Sterilization

ETO is a colorless gas that is flammable and explosive. Four essential parameters (operational ranges)—gas concentration (450 to 1200 mg/L); temperature (37° to 63° C); relative humidity (40% to 80%) (water molecules carry ETO to reactive sites); and exposure time (1 to 6 hours)—influence the effectiveness of ETO sterilization.[149,172,173] Within certain limitations, an increase in gas concentration and temperature may shorten the time necessary for achieving sterilization.

The main disadvantages associated with ETO are the lengthy cycle time, the cost, and its potential hazards to patients and staff; the main advantage is that it can sterilize heat- or moisture-sensitive medical equipment without deleterious effects on the material used in the medical devices (see Table 299-3). Acute exposure to ETO may result in irritation (e.g., to skin, eyes, gastrointestinal or respiratory tract) and central nervous system depression.[43] Chronic inhalation has been linked to the formation of cataracts, cognitive impairment, neurologic dysfunction, and disabling polyneuropathies.[43] Occupational exposure in health care facilities has been linked to hematologic changes and an increased risk of spontaneous abortions and various cancers.[43] ETO should be considered a known human carcinogen.[174]

The use of ETO evolved when few alternatives existed for sterilizing heat- and moisture-sensitive medical devices; however, favorable properties (see Table 299-3) account for its continued widespread use.[175] Two ETO gas mixtures are available to replace ETO-chlorofluorocarbon (CFC) mixtures for large-capacity, tank-supplied sterilizers. The ETO–carbon dioxide (CO_2) mixture consists of 8.5% ETO and 91.5% CO_2. This mixture is less expensive than ETO-hydrochlorofluorocarbons (HCFCs), but a disadvantage is the need for pressure vessels rated for steam sterilization, because higher pressures (28-psi gauge) are required. The other mixture, which is a drop-in CFC replacement, is ETO mixed with HCFC. HCFCs are approximately 50-fold less damaging to the earth's ozone layer than are CFCs. The EPA will begin regulation of HCFC in the year 2015 and will terminate production in the year 2030. Two companies provide ETO-HCFC mixtures as drop-in replacement for CFC-12; one mixture consists of 8.6% ETO and 91.4% HCFC, and the other mixture is composed of 10% ETO and 90% HCFC.[175] An alternative to the pressurized mixed gas ETO systems is 100% ETO. The 100% ETO sterilizers using unit-dose cartridges eliminate the need for external tanks.

The excellent microbicidal activity of ETO has been demonstrated in several studies[118,119,176-178] and summarized in published reports.[179] ETO inactivates all microorganisms, although bacterial spores (especially *B. atrophaeus*) are more resistant than other microorganisms. For this reason *B. atrophaeus* is the recommended biologic indicator. Like all sterilization processes, the effectiveness of ETO sterilization can be altered by lumen length, lumen diameter, inorganic salts, and organic materials.[118,119,176-178,180] For example, although ETO is not used commonly for reprocessing endoscopes,[19] several studies have shown failure of ETO in inactivating contaminating spores in endoscope channels[180] or lumen test units[118,176,178] and residual ETO levels averaging 66.2 ppm even after the standard degassing time.[94] Failure of ETO also has been observed when dental handpieces were contaminated with *Streptococcus mutans* and exposed to ETO.[181] It is recommended that dental handpieces be steam sterilized.

ETO is used in health care facilities to sterilize critical items (and sometimes semicritical items) that are moisture or heat sensitive and cannot be sterilized by steam sterilization.

Hydrogen Peroxide Gas Plasma

New sterilization technology based on plasma was patented in 1987 and marketed in the United States in 1993. Gas plasmas have been referred to as the fourth state of matter (i.e., liquids, solids, gases, and gas plasmas). Gas plasmas are generated in an enclosed chamber under deep vacuum using radiofrequency or microwave energy to excite the gas (i.e., hydrogen peroxide) molecules and produce charged particles, many of which are in the form of free radicals (e.g., hydroxyls and hydroperoxyls). The biologic indicator used with this system is *G. stearothermophilus* spores.[182]

This process has the ability to inactivate a broad range of microorganisms, including resistant bacterial spores. Studies have been conducted against vegetative bacteria (including mycobacteria), yeasts, fungi, viruses, and bacterial spores.[118,177,178,183-185] Like all sterilization processes, the effectiveness can be altered by lumen length, lumen diameter, inorganic salts, and organic materials.[118,177,178,180]

Materials and devices that cannot tolerate high temperatures and humidity, such as some plastics, electrical devices, and corrosion-susceptible metal alloys, can be sterilized by hydrogen peroxide gas plasma. This method has been compatible with most (>95%) medical devices and materials tested.[186,187]

Peracetic Acid Sterilization

Peracetic acid is a highly biocidal oxidizer that maintains its efficacy in the presence of organic soil. Peracetic acid removes surface contaminants (primarily protein) on endoscopic tubing.[113,114] An automated machine using peracetic acid to sterilize medical, surgical, and dental instruments chemically (e.g., endoscopes, arthroscopes) was introduced in 1988. This microprocessor-controlled, low-temperature sterilization method is commonly used in the United States. Interchangeable trays are available to permit the processing of up to three rigid endoscopes or one flexible endoscope. Connectors are available for most types of flexible endoscopes for the irrigation of all channels by directed flow. Rigid endoscopes are placed within a lidded container, and the sterilant fills the lumens either by immersion in the circulating sterilant or by use of channel connectors to direct flow into the lumen(s) (see later for the importance of channel connectors). As with any sterilization process, the system can only sterilize surfaces that can be contacted by the sterilant. For example, bronchoscopy-related infections occurred when bronchoscopes were processed using the wrong connector.[123,188] Investigation of these incidents revealed that bronchoscopes were inadequately reprocessed when inappropriate channel connectors were used and when there were inconsistencies between the reprocessing instructions provided by the manufacturer of the bronchoscope and the manufacturer of the automatic endoscope reprocessor.[188] The importance of channel connectors to achieve sterilization was also shown for rigid lumen devices.[177,189]

The manufacturers suggest the use of biologic monitors (G. stearothermophilus spore strips) both at the time of installation and routinely to ensure effectiveness of the process. The manufacturer's clip must be used to hold the strip in the designated spot in the machine because a broader clamp will not allow the sterilant to reach the spores trapped under it.[190] The processor is equipped with a conductivity probe that will automatically abort the cycle if the buffer system is not detected in a fresh container of the peracetic acid solution. A chemical monitoring strip that detects that the active ingredient is greater than 1500 ppm is available for routine use as an additional process control.

Peracetic acid will inactivate gram-positive and gram-negative bacteria, fungi, and yeasts in less than 5 minutes at less than 100 ppm. In the presence of organic matter, 200 to 500 ppm is required. For viruses, the dosage range is wide (12 to 2250 ppm), with poliovirus inactivated in yeast extract in 15 minutes with 1500 to 2250 ppm. Bacterial spores in suspension are inactivated in 15 seconds to 30 minutes with 500 to 10,000 ppm (0.05% to 1%).[89]

OSHA BLOOD-BORNE PATHOGEN STANDARD

In December 1991, OSHA promulgated a standard entitled "Occupational Exposure to Bloodborne Pathogens" to eliminate or minimize occupational exposure to blood-borne pathogens.[191] One component of this requirement is that all equipment and environmental and working surfaces be cleaned and decontaminated with an appropriate disinfectant after contact with blood or other potentially infectious materials. Although the OSHA standard does not specify the type of disinfectant or procedure, the OSHA original compliance document[192] suggested that a germicide must be tuberculocidal to kill HBV (e.g., phenolic, chlorine). However, in February 1997, OSHA amended its policy and stated that EPA-registered disinfectants that are labeled as effective against HIV and HBV would be considered as appropriate disinfectants "provided such surfaces have not become contaminated with agent(s) or volumes of or concentrations of

agent(s) for which higher level disinfection is recommended." When blood-borne pathogens other than HBV or HIV are of concern, OSHA continues to require the use of EPA-registered tuberculocidal disinfectants or hypochlorite solution (diluted 1:10 or 1:100 with water).[62,193] Recent studies demonstrate that, in the presence of large blood spills, a 1:10 final dilution of EPA-registered hypochlorite solution initially should be used to inactivate blood-borne viruses[39,194] to minimize risk of disease to the health care worker from percutaneous injury during the cleanup process.

EMERGING PATHOGENS

Emerging pathogens are of growing concern to the general public and infection control professionals. Relevant pathogens include *Cryptosporidium parvum, Helicobacter pylori, E. coli* O157:H7, HIV, hepatitis C virus, rotavirus, human papillomavirus, Norovirus, human severe acute respiratory syndrome (SARS) coronavirus, the Creutzfeldt-Jakob prion, antibiotic-resistant bacteria (VRE, MRSA, multidrug-resistant *M. tuberculosis*), and nontuberculosis mycobacteria (e.g., *M. chelonae*). The susceptibility of each of these pathogens to chemical disinfectants/sterilants has been studied. With the exception of prions (see later), standard sterilization and disinfection procedures for patient-care equipment (as recommended in Table 299-1) are adequate to sterilize or disinfect instruments or devices contaminated with blood or other body fluids from persons infected with blood-borne pathogens and emerging pathogens.[195]

Cryptosporidium is resistant to chlorine at concentrations used in potable water. *C. parvum* is not completely inactivated by most disinfectants used in health care, including ethyl alcohol,[79] glutaraldehyde,[79,196] 5.25% hypochlorite,[79] peracetic acid,[79] ortho-phthalaldehyde,[79] phenol,[79,196] povidone-iodine,[79,196] and quaternary ammonium compounds.[79] The only chemical disinfectants/sterilants able to inactivate greater than 3 $\log_{10}$ of *C. parvum* were 6% and 7.5% hydrogen peroxide.[79] Sterilization methods will fully inactivate *C. parvum*, including steam,[79] ETO,[79,197] and hydrogen peroxide gas plasma.[79] Although most disinfectants are ineffective against *C. parvum*, current cleaning and disinfection practices appear satisfactory to prevent health care–associated transmission. For example, endoscopes are unlikely to represent an important vehicle for the transmission of *C. parvum* because the results of bacterial studies indicate mechanical cleaning will remove approximately 10^4 organisms and drying rapidly results in loss of *C. parvum* viability (e.g., 2.9-$\log_{10}$ decrease in 30 minutes, 3.8-$\log_{10}$ decrease in 60 minutes).[79]

Chlorine at approximately 1 ppm has been found capable of eliminating approximately 4 $\log_{10}$ of *E. coli* O157:H7 within 1 minute in a suspension test.[198] Electrolyzed oxidizing water at 23° C was effective in 10 minutes in producing a 5-$\log_{10}$ decrease in *E. coli* O157:H7 inoculated onto kitchen cutting boards.[199] The following disinfectants eliminated greater than 5 $\log_{10}$ of *E. coli* O157:H7 within 30 seconds: a quaternary ammonium compound, a phenolic, a hypochlorite (1:10 dilution of 5.25% bleach), and ethanol.[35]

Data are available on the susceptibility of *H. pylori* to disinfectants. Using a suspension test, Akamatsu and colleagues assessed the effectiveness of a variety of disinfectants against nine strains of *H. pylori*.[200] Ethanol (80%) and glutaraldehyde (0.5%) killed all strains within 15 seconds; chlorhexidine gluconate (0.05%, 1.0%), benzalkonium chloride (0.025%, 0.1%), alkyldiaminoethylglycine hydrochloride (0.1%), povidone-iodine (0.1%), and sodium hypochlorite (150 ppm) killed all strains within 30 seconds. Both ethanol (80%) and glutaraldehyde (0.5%) retained similar bactericidal activity in the presence of organic matter, whereas the other disinfectants showed reduced bactericidal activity. In particular, the bactericidal activity of povidone-iodine (0.1%) and sodium hypochlorite (150 ppm) was markedly decreased in the presence of dried yeast solution, with killing times increased to 5 to 10 minutes and 5 to 30 minutes, respectively.

Immersion of biopsy forceps in formalin before obtaining a specimen does not affect the ability to culture *H. pylori* from the biopsy specimen.[201] The following methods have been demonstrated to be ineffective for eliminating *H. pylori* from endoscopes: cleaning with soap and water, immersion in 70% ethanol for 3 minutes, instillation of 70% ethanol, instillation of 30 mL of 83% methanol, and instillation of 0.2% Hyamine solution.[202] The differing results with regard to the efficacy of ethyl alcohol are unexplained. Cleaning followed by use of 2% alkaline glutaraldehyde (or automated peracetic acid) has been demonstrated by culture to be effective in eliminating *H. pylori*.[203,204] Epidemiologic investigations of patients who had undergone endoscopy with endoscopes mechanically washed and disinfected with 2.0% to 2.3% glutaraldehyde have revealed no evidence of person-to-person transmission of *H. pylori*.[205] Disinfection of experimentally contaminated endoscopes using 2% glutaraldehyde (10 minutes, 20 minutes, and 45 minutes exposure times) or the peracetic acid system (with and without active peracetic acid) has been demonstrated to be effective in eliminating *H. pylori*.[204] *H. pylori* DNA has been detected by polymerase chain reaction in fluid flushed from endoscope channels following cleaning and disinfection with 2% glutaraldehyde.[206] The clinical significance of this finding is unclear. In vitro experiments have demonstrated a greater than 3.5-log$_{10}$ reduction in *H. pylori* after exposure to 0.5 mg/L of free chlorine for 80 seconds.[207]

An outbreak of health care–associated rotavirus gastroenteritis on a pediatric unit has been reported.[208] Person-to-person via the hands of health care workers was proposed as the mechanism of transmission. Prolonged survival of rotavirus on environmental surfaces (90 minutes to more than 10 days at room temperature) and hands (>4 hours) has been demonstrated. Rotavirus suspended in feces can survive for a longer period of time.[209] Vectors for this infection have included air, hands, fomites, water, and food.[209] Products with demonstrated efficacy (>3-log$_{10}$ reduction in virus) against rotavirus within 1 minute include 95% ethanol, 70% isopropanol, some phenolics, 2% glutaraldehyde, 0.35% peracetic acid, and some quaternary ammonium compounds.[38,210,211] In a human challenge study, a disinfectant spray (0.1% *ortho*-phenylphenol and 79% ethanol), sodium hypochlorite (800 ppm free chlorine), and a phenol-based product (14.7% phenol diluted 1:256 in tap water), when sprayed onto contaminated stainless steel disks, were effective in interrupting the transfer of a human rotavirus from stainless steel disk to fingerpads of volunteers after an exposure time of 3 to 10 minutes. A quaternary ammonium product (7.05% quaternary ammonium compound diluted 1:128 in tap water) and tap water allowed transfer of virus.[34]

There are no data on the inactivation of human papillomavirus by alcohol or other disinfectants because in vitro replication of complete virions has not been achieved. Similarly, little is known about the inactivation of Noroviruses (members of the family Caliciviridae and important causes of gastroenteritis in humans) because they cannot be grown in tissue culture. Inactivation studies with a closely related cultivable virus (i.e., feline calicivirus) have shown the effectiveness of chlorine, glutaraldehyde, and iodine-based products, whereas the quaternary ammonium compounds, detergent, and ethanol failed to inactivate the virus completely.[141]

The Centers for Disease Control and Prevention (CDC) announced that a previously unrecognized human virus from the coronavirus family is the leading hypothesis for the cause of the recently described syndrome known as SARS.[212] Two coronaviruses that are known to infect humans causes one third of common colds. The virucidal efficacy of chemical germicides against coronavirus have been investigated. Sattar and colleagues[213] investigated the activity of several disinfectants against coronavirus 229E and found several disinfectants were effective after a 1-minute contact time, including sodium hypochlorite (at a free chlorine concentration of 1000 ppm and 5000 ppm), 70% ethyl alcohol, and povidone-iodine (1% iodine). Saknimit and co-workers[214] showed that 70% ethanol, 50% isopropanol, 0.05% benzalkonium chloride, 50 ppm iodine in iodophor, 0.23% sodium chlorite, 1% cresol soap, and 0.7% formaldehyde inactivated greater than 3 logs of two animal coronaviruses (mouse hepatitis virus, canine coronavirus) after a 10-minute exposure time. Sizun and associates demonstrated the activity of povidone-iodine against human coronaviruses 229E and OC43.[215] Because the SARS coronavirus is stable in feces and urine at room temperature

for at least 1 to 2 days,[216] surfaces may be a possible source of contamination leading to infection with the SARS coronavirus, and should be disinfected. Until more precise information is available, one should assume the environment in which SARS patients are housed is heavily contaminated and thoroughly disinfect the room and equipment daily and after the patient is discharged. EPA-registered disinfectants or 1:100 dilution of household bleach and water should be used for surface disinfection and disinfection on noncritical patient-care equipment. High-level disinfection and sterilization of semicritical and critical medical devices, respectively, does not need to be altered for patients with known or suspected SARS.

The prions of Creutzfeldt-Jakob disease (CJD) and other transmissible spongiform encephalopathies exhibit an unusual resistance to conventional chemical and physical decontamination methods. Because the CJD agent is not readily inactivated by conventional disinfection and sterilization procedures and because of the invariably fatal outcome of CJD, the procedures for disinfection and sterilization of the CJD prion have been both cautious and controversial for many years. Recommendations for disinfection and sterilization of prion-contaminated medical devices are as follows. Instruments should be kept wet or damp until they are decontaminated and they should be decontaminated as soon as possible after use. Dried films of tissue are more resistant to prion inactivation by steam sterilization compared to tissues that were kept moist. This may relate to the rapid heating that occurs in the film of dried material compared to the bulk of the sample, and the rapid fixation of the prion protein in the dried film.[217] It also appears that prions in the dried portions of the brain macerates are less efficiently inactivated than undisturbed tissue. For high-risk tissues (brain, spinal cord, eyes), high-risk patients, and critical or semicritical medical devices, it is recommended to clean the device and sterilize by one of four methods, preferably using a combination of sodium hydroxide and autoclaving as recommended by the World Health Organization[218] (option 1 or 2), or use autoclaving as recommended in the scientific literature[226] (option 3 or 4).

1. Immerse in 1N NaOH (1N NaOH is a solution of 40 g NaOH in 1 L of water) for 1 hour; remove and rinse in water, then transfer to an open pan and autoclave (121° C gravity displacement or 134° C porous or prevacuum sterilizer) for 1 hour.
2. Immerse instruments in 1N NaOH for 1 hour and heat in a gravity displacement sterilizer at 121° C for 30 minutes; clean; and subject to routine sterilization.
3. Autoclave at 134° C for 18 minutes in a prevacuum sterilizer.
4. Autoclave at 132° C for 1 hour in a gravity displacement sterilizer.

The temperature used for autoclaving should not exceed 134° C because under certain conditions the effectiveness of autoclaving actually declines as the temperature is increased (e.g., 136° C, 138° C).[219] Prion-contaminated medical devices that are impossible or difficult to clean should be discarded. Flash sterilization should not be used for reprocessing. To minimize environmental contamination, noncritical environmental surfaces should be covered with plastic-backed paper, and when contaminated with high-risk tissues, the paper should be properly discarded. Environmental surfaces (noncritical) contaminated with high-risk tissues (e.g., laboratory surfaces) should be cleaned and then spot decontaminated with a 1:10 dilution of hypochlorite solution.

To minimize the possibility of use of neurosurgical instruments that have been potentially contaminated during procedures performed on patients in whom CJD is later diagnosed, health care facilities should consider using the sterilization guidelines outlined above for neurosurgical instruments used during brain biopsy done on patients in whom a specific lesion has not been demonstrated (e.g., by magnetic resonance imaging or computed tomography scans). Alternatively, neurosurgical instruments used in such patients could be disposable[220] or could be quarantined until the pathology of the brain biopsy is reviewed and CJD excluded.

Currently, there are no data to show that antibiotic-resistant bacteria are less sensitive to the liquid chemical germicides than antibiotic-sensitive bacteria at currently used germicide contact conditions and concentrations.[221] Several studies have found antibiotic-resistant hospital strains of common health care–associated pathogens (i.e., *Enterococcus, P. aeruginosa, Klebsiella pneumoniae, E. coli, S. aureus,* and *S. epidermidis*) to be equally susceptible to disinfectants as antibiotic-sensitive strains.[35,222,223] The susceptibility of glycopeptide-intermediate *S. aureus* was similar to that of vancomycin-susceptible MRSA.[224] Based on these data, routine disinfection and housekeeping protocols do not need to be altered because of antibiotic resistance provided the disinfection method is effective.[225] A recent study that evaluated the efficacy of selected cleaning methods (e.g., QUAT-sprayed cloth, and QUAT-immersed cloth) for eliminating VRE found that currently used disinfection processes are likely highly effective in eliminating VRE. However, surface disinfection must involve contact with all contaminated surfaces.[225]

INACTIVATION OF BIOTERRORISM AGENTS

Recent publications have highlighted the concern about the potential for biologic terrorism.[226,227] The CDC has categorized several agents as "high priority" because they can be easily disseminated or transmitted person to person, cause high mortality, and are likely to cause public panic and social disruption.[228] These agents include *Bacillus anthracis* (anthrax), *Yersinia pestis* (plague), variola major (smallpox), *Clostridium botulinum* toxin (botulism), *Francisella tularensis* (tularemia), filoviruses (Ebola hemorrhagic fever, Marburg hemorrhagic fever); and arenaviruses (Lassa [Lassa fever], Junin [Argentine hemorrhagic fever]), and related viruses.[228]

A few comments can be made regarding the role of sterilization and disinfection of potential agents of bioterrorism. First, the susceptibility of these agents to germicides in vitro is similar to that of other related pathogens. For example, variola is similar to vaccinia[101] and *B. anthracis* is similar to *B. atrophaeus* (formerly *B. subtilis*).[229] Thus one can extrapolate from the larger database available on the susceptibility of genetically similar organisms. Second, many of the potential bioterrorism agents are stable enough in the environment that contaminated environmental surfaces or fomites could lead to transmission of agents such as *B. anthracis, F. tularensis,* variola major, *C. botulinum* toxin, and *C. burnetti*.[230] Third, data suggest that current disinfection and sterilization practices are appropriate for the management of patient care equipment and environmental surfaces when potentially contaminated patients are evaluated and/or admitted in a health care facility following exposure to a bioterrorism agent. For example, sodium hypochlorite may be used for surface disinfection.[231] In instances in which the health care facility is the site of a bioterrorist attack, environmental decontamination may require special decontamination procedures (e.g., chlorine dioxide gas for anthrax spores[232]). Use of disinfectants for decontamination following a bioterrorist attack requires a crisis exemption from the EPA.[233] Of only theoretical concern is the possibility that a bioterrorism agent could be engineered to be less susceptible to disinfection and sterilization processes.

CONTROL OF HOSPITAL WASTE

Health care facilities that generate medical, chemical, or radiologic waste have a moral and legal obligation to dispose of these wastes in a manner that poses minimal potential hazard to the environment or public health. The proper disposal of these wastes requires a dynamic waste management plan that conforms to federal, state, and local regulations and provides adequate personnel and financial resources to ensure implementation. This section reviews some of the principles associated with medical waste management; a more detailed description of collection, storage, processing, transporting, treatment, and public health implications of medical waste may be found elsewhere.[234-239]

Despite the attention given to medical waste by the public, the media, and all levels of government, the terms "hospital waste," "medical waste," "regulated medical waste," and "infectious waste" are often used as synonymous. *Hospital waste* refers to all waste, biologic or nonbiologic, that is discarded and not intended for further use. *Medical waste* refers to materials generated as a result of patient diagnosis, immunization, or treatment, such as soiled dressings or intravenous tubing. *Infectious waste* refers to that portion of medical waste that could potentially transmit an infectious disease. Congress and the EPA used the term "regulated medical waste" rather than "infectious waste" in the Medical Waste Tracking Act (MWTA) of 1988 in deference to the remote possibility of disease transmission associated with this waste. Thus "medical waste" is a subset of "hospital waste," and "regulated medical waste" (which is synonymous with "infectious waste" from a regulatory perspective) is a subset of "medical waste."[237,240]

Guidelines produced by the CDC have designated four types of hospital waste as regulated medical waste: microbiology laboratory waste, pathology and anatomy waste, blood, and sharps.[67] The EPA guidelines consider the same types of waste as infectious or regulated medical waste but also designate communicable disease isolation waste.[238] In the MWTA, the EPA modified its position on "communicable disease isolation waste" by including only certain "highly" communicable disease waste, such as Class 4 (e.g., Marburg, Ebola, and Lassa viruses) as regulated medical waste (Table 299-4).[241] In a systematic random survey of all U.S. hospitals conducted in July 1987 and January 1988, the overall compliance rates with the CDC and EPA recommendations were 82% and 75%, respectively. Not only were the majority of hospitals in compliance, but the hospitals frequently treated other hospital waste as infectious, including contaminated laboratory waste (87%), surgery waste (78%), dialysis waste (69%), items contacting secretions (63%), and intensive care (37%) and emergency room waste (41%).[234]

A key component in evaluating the impact of a medical waste management program is the quantity of waste produced per patient. Hospitalized patients generate about 15 pounds of hospital waste per day. The amount of hospital waste generated by U.S. hospital is approximately 6700 tons per day. U.S. hospitals designate approximately 15% of the total hospital waste by weight as infectious (about 1000 tons of infectious waste per day).[234] Not surprisingly, the percentage of medical waste treated as infectious increases with the number and types of medical waste classified as infectious. For example, about 6% of hospital waste would be treated as infectious waste if the CDC guidelines are followed, but 45% of hospital waste could be considered infectious waste under the MWTA.[234,237,240]

The vast majority of U.S. hospitals designate and treat microbiologic, pathologic, isolation, blood, and sharps waste as infectious.[234] Treatment of infectious waste by U.S. hospitals is most commonly accomplished by incineration (range 64% to 93% depending on type of waste). About one third of U.S. hospitals steam sterilize their microbiologic waste and about one fourth pour liquid blood down the drain connected to a sanitary sewer (W. A. Rutala, unpublished data). Several nonincineration alternatives are emerging for treating regulated medical waste (e.g., mechanical/chemical disinfection, microwave decontamination, steam disinfection, and compacting) that require further evaluation.[239] Nonregulated medical waste is generally discarded in a properly sited and operated sanitary landfill because this is a safe and inexpensive disposal method (e.g., landfill disposal, $0.02 to 0.05 per pound, versus contract incinerator, $0.20 to 0.60 per pound).

Federal medical waste regulations have been promulgated by the Department of Transportation (DOT) and OSHA. The DOT regulation involves the transport of infectious substances and medical waste and went into effect January 1996.[242] The OSHA Bloodborne Pathogen Standard requires labeling to designate waste that poses a health threat in the workplace. The OSHA definition of regulated waste is not intended to designate waste that must be treated. In fact, generators who apply the OSHA definition of regulated waste (rather than state regulations) to designate infectious waste for treatment by incineration or other means may unintentionally incur additional expenses.[191] Lastly, nearly all states have developed rules for designation, segregation, handling, storing, transporting, and treating of regulated medical waste.

TABLE 299-4 Types of Medical Waste Designated as Infectious and Recommended Disposal/Treatment Methods—CDC and EPA*

Source/Type of Medical Waste	CDC		EPA		MWTA
	Infectious Waste	Disposal/ Treatment Methods	Infectious Waste	Disposal/ Treatment Methods	Infectious Waste[†]
Microbiologic (e.g., stocks and cultures of infectious agents)	Yes	S,I,In,Al[‡]	Yes	S,I,TI,C	Yes
Blood and blood products	Yes	S,I,In,Al	Yes	S,I,Sew,C	Yes
Pathologic (e.g., tissue, organs)	Yes	S,I,In,Al	Yes	I,SW,CB	Yes[§]
Sharps (e.g., needles)	Yes	S,I,In,Al	Yes	S,I	Yes[§]
Communicable disease isolation	No	—	Yes	S,I	Yes[§]
Contaminated animal carcasses, body parts, and bedding	—	—	Yes	I,SW (not bedding)	Yes
Contaminated laboratory wastes	No	—	Optional.[∥] If considered IW, use S or I		No
Surgery and autopsy wastes	No	—	Optional. If considered IW, use S or I		No
Dialysis unit	No	—	Optional		No
Contaminated equipment	No	—	Optional. If considered IW, use S or I		No

*The Joint Commission for the Accreditation of Healthcare Organizations[243] requires that there be a hazardous waste system designed and operated in accordance with applicable law and regulations.

†The CDC guidelines specify "microbiology laboratory waste" as an infectious waste. This term includes stocks and cultures of microorganisms. The CDC recommends that regulated medical wastes be treated by using a method approved by the authority having jurisdiction (e.g., state) before disposal in a landfill.

‡The Act went into effect on June 22, 1989 and expired June 22, 1991. It affected only four states (New Jersey, New York, Connecticut and Rhode Island). The Act required both treatment (any method, technique or process designed to change the biologic character or composition of medical waste so as to eliminate or reduce its potential for causing disease) and destruction (waste is ruined, torn apart, or mutilated so that it is no longer generally recognizable as medical waste).

§MWTA specified used and unused sharps. The Act regulated wastes from persons with highly communicable diseases such as Class IV etiologic agents (e.g., Marburg, Ebola, Lassa viruses).

∥Optional infectious waste: EPA states that the decision to handle these wastes as infectious should be made by a responsible, authorized person or committee at the individual facility.

CDC, Centers for Disease Control[67]; EPA, Environmental Protection Agency[238]; MWTA, Medical Waste Tracking Act[241]; I, incineration; S, steam sterilization; In, Internment; Al, Alternative treatment technology; TI, thermal inactivation; C, chemical disinfection for liquids only; Sew, sanitary sewer (EPA requires secondary treatment); SW, steam sterilization with incineration or grinding; CB, cremation or burial by mortician; IW, infectious waste.

Modified from Rutala WA, Weber DJ, for the Society of Hospital Epidemiology of America. SHEA position paper: Medical Waste. Infect Control Hosp Epidemiol. 1992; 13:38-48.

CONCLUSION

When properly used, disinfection and sterilization can ensure the safe use of invasive and noninvasive medical devices. However, current disinfection and sterilization guidelines must be strictly followed. Each hospital must develop and maintain a written management plan describing the processes it uses to comply with state and federal medical waste regulations.

REFERENCES

1. Mangram AJ, Horan TC, Pearson ML, et al. Guideline for prevention of surgical site infection, 1999. Hospital Infection Control Practices Advisory Committee. Infect Control Hosp Epidemiol. 1999;20:250-278.
2. American Society for Gastrointestinal Endoscopy. Position statement: Reprocessing of flexible gastrointestinal endoscopes. Gastrointest Endosc. 1996;43:541-546.
3. Uttley AH, Simpson RA. Audit of bronchoscope disinfection: A survey of procedures in England and Wales and incidents of mycobacterial contamination. J Hosp Infect. 1994;26:301-308.
4. Spach DH, Silverstein FE, Stamm WE. Transmission of infection by gastrointestinal endoscopy and bronchoscopy. Ann Intern Med. 1993;118:117-128.
5. Weber DJ, Rutala WA. Lessons from outbreaks associated with bronchoscopy. Infect Control Hosp Epidemiol. 2001;22:403-408.
6. Weber DJ, Rutala WA, DiMarino AJ Jr. The prevention of infection following gastrointestinal endoscopy: The importance of prophylaxis and reprocessing. In: DiMarino AJ Jr, Benjamin SB, eds. Gastrointestinal Diseases: An Endoscopic Approach. Thorofare, NJ: Slack; 2002:87-106.
7. Meyers H, Brown-Elliott BA, Moore D, et al. An outbreak of Mycobacterium chelonae infection following liposuction. Clin Infect Dis. 2002;34:1500-1507.
8. Lowry PW, Jarvis WR, Oberle AD, et al. Mycobacterium chelonae causing otitis media in an ear-nose-and-throat practice. N Engl J Med. 1988;319:978-982.
9. Favero MS, Bond WW. Chemical disinfection of medical and surgical materials. In: Block SS, ed. Disinfection, Sterilization, and Preservation. 5th ed. Philadelphia: Lippincott Williams & Wilkins; 2001:881-917.
10. Spaulding EH. Chemical disinfection of medical and surgical materials. In: Lawrence C, Block SS, eds. Disinfection, Sterilization, and Preservation. Philadelphia: Lea & Febiger; 1968:517-531.
11. Simmons BP. CDC guidelines for the prevention and control of nosocomial infections. Guideline for hospital environmental control. Am J Infect Control. 1983;11:97-120.
12. Block SS. Disinfection, Sterilization, and Preservation. 5th ed. Philadelphia: Lippincott Williams & Wilkins, 2001.
13. Rutala WA, for the 1994, 1995, and 1996 APIC Guidelines Committee. APIC guideline for selection and use of disinfectants. Association for Professionals in Infection Control and Epidemiology, Inc. Am J Infect Control. 1996;24:313-342.
14. Rutala WA. Disinfection, sterilization and waste disposal. In: Wenzel RP, ed. Prevention and Control of Nosocomial Infections. Baltimore: Williams & Wilkins; 1997:539-593.
15. Garner JS, Favero MS. CDC guideline for handwashing and hospital environmental control, 1985. Infect Control. 1986;7:231-243.
16. Rutala WA. APIC guideline for selection and use of disinfectants. Am J Infect Control. 1990;18:99-117.
17. Foliente RL, Kovacs BJ, Aprecio RM, et al. Efficacy of high-level disinfectants for reprocessing gastrointestinal endoscopes in simulated-use testing. Gastrointest Endosc. 2001;53:456-462.
18. Kovacs BJ, Chen YK, Kettering JD, et al. High-level disinfection of gastrointestinal endoscopes: Are current guidelines adequate? Am J Gastroenterol. 1999;94:1546-1550.
19. Rutala WA, Clontz EP, Weber DJ, Hoffmann KK. Disinfection practices for endoscopes and other semicritical items. Infect Control Hosp Epidemiol. 1991;12:282-288.
20. Phillips J, Hulka B, Hulka J, et al. Laparoscopic procedures: The American Association of Gynecologic Laparoscopists' Membership Survey for 1975. J Reprod Med. 1977;18:227-232.
21. Muscarella LF. Current instrument reprocessing practices: Results of a national survey. Gastrointest Nurs. 2001;24:253-260.
22. Wallace RJ Jr, Brown BA, Driffith DE. Nosocomial outbreaks/pseudo-outbreaks caused by nontuberculous mycobacteria. Annu Rev Microbiol. 1998;52:453-490.
23. Meenhorst PL, Reingold AL, Groothuis DG, et al. Water-related nosocomial pneumonia caused by Legionella pneumophila serogroups 1 and 10. J Infect Dis. 1985;152:356-364.
24. Atlas RM. Legionella: From environmental habitats to disease pathology, detection and control. Environ Microbiol. 1999;1:283-293.
25. Rutala WA, Weber DJ. Water as a reservoir of nosocomial pathogens. Infect Control Hosp Epidemiol. 1997;18:609-616.
26. Weber DJ, Rutala WA. Environmental issues and nosocomial infections. In: Wenzel RP, ed. Prevention and Control of Nosocomial Infections. Baltimore: Williams & Wilkins; 1997:491-514.
27. Society of Gastroenterology Nurses and Associates. Standards for infection control and reprocessing of flexible gastrointestinal endoscopes. Gastroenterol Nurs. 2000;23:172-179.
28. Gerding DN, Peterson LR, Vennes JA. Cleaning and disinfection of fiberoptic endoscopes: Evaluation of glutaraldehyde exposure time and forced-air drying. Gastroenterology. 1982;83:613-618.

29. Sattar SA, Lloyd-Evans N, Springthorpe VS, Nair RC. Institutional outbreaks of rotavirus diarrhoea: Potential role of fomites and environmental surfaces as vehicles for virus transmission. J Hyg (Lond). 1986;96:277-289.

30. Weber DJ, Rutala WA. Role of environmental contamination in the transmission of vancomycin-resistant enterococci. Infect Control Hosp Epidemiol. 1997;18:306-309.

31. Ward RL, Bernstein DI, Knowlton DR, et al. Prevention of surface-to-human transmission of rotaviruses by treatment with disinfectant spray. J Clin Microbiol. 1991; 29:1991-1996.

32. Sattar SA, Jacobsen H, Springthorpe VS, et al. Chemical disinfection to interrupt transfer of rhinovirus type 14 from environmental surfaces to hands. Appl Environ Microbiol. 1993;59:1579-1585.

33. Gwaltney JM Jr, Hendley JO. Transmission of experimental rhinovirus infection by contaminated surfaces. Am J Epidemiol. 1982;116:828-833.

34. Sattar SA, Jacobsen H, Rahman H, et al. Interruption of rotavirus spread through chemical disinfection. Infect Control Hosp Epidemiol. 1994;15:751-756.

35. Rutala WA, Barbee SL, Aguiar NC, et al. Antimicrobial activity of home disinfectants and natural products against potential human pathogens. Infect Control Hosp Epidemiol. 2000;21:33-38.

36. Best M, Sattar SA, Springthorpe VS, Kennedy ME. Efficacies of selected disinfectants against *Mycobacterium tuberculosis*. J Clin Microbiol. 1990;28:2234-2239.

37. Best M, Springthorpe VS, Sattar SA. Feasibility of a combined carrier test for disinfectants: Studies with a mixture of five types of microorganisms. Am J Infect Control. 1994;22:152-162.

38. Springthorpe VS, Grenier JL, Lloyd-Evans N, Sattar SA. Chemical disinfection of human rotaviruses: Efficacy of commercially-available products in suspension tests. J Hyg (Lond). 1986;97:139-161.

39. Weber DJ, Barbee SL, Sobsey MD, Rutala WA. The effect of blood on the antiviral activity of sodium hypochlorite, a phenolic, and a quaternary ammonium compound. Infect Control Hosp Epidemiol. 1999;20:821-827.

40. Pentella MA, Fisher T, Chandler S, et al. Are disinfectants accurately prepared for use in hospital patient care areas? Infect Control Hosp Epidemiol. 2000;21:103.

41. Westwood JC, Mitchell MA, Legace S. Hospital sanitation: The massive bacterial contamination of the wet mop. Appl Microbiol. 1971;21:693-697.

42. Hansen KS. Occupational dermatoses in hospital cleaning women. Contact Dermatitis. 1983;9:343-351.

43. Weber DJ, Rutala WA. Occupational risks associated with the use of selected disinfectants and sterilants. In: Rutala WA, ed. Disinfection, Sterilization, and Antisepsis in Healthcare. Champlain, NY: Polyscience Publications; 1998:211-226.

44. Spaulding EH. Alcohol as a surgical disinfectant. AORN J. 1964;2:67-71.

45. Morton HE. The relationship of concentration and germicidal efficiency of ethyl alcohol. Ann N Y Acad Sci. 1950;53:191-196.

46. Ali Y, Dolan MJ, Fendler EJ, Larson EL. Alcohols. In: Block SS, ed. Disinfection, Sterilization, and Preservation. 5th ed. Philadelphia: Lippincott Williams & Wilkins; 2001:229-254.

47. Nye RN, Mallory TB. A note on the fallacy of using alcohol for the sterilization of surgical instruments. Boston Med Surg J. 1923;189:561-563.

48. Rutala WA. Selection and use of disinfectants in healthcare. In: Mayhall CG, ed. Hospital Epidemiology and Infection Control. 2nd ed. Philadelphia: Lippincott Williams & Wilkins; 1999:1161-1187.

49. Beck-Sague CM, Jarvis WR. Epidemic bloodstream infections associated with pressure transducers: A persistent problem. Infect Control Hosp Epidemiol. 1989;10:54-59.

50. Rutala WA, Weber DJ. Uses of inorganic hypochlorite (bleach) in health-care facilities. Clin Microbiol Rev. 1997;10:597-610.

51. Merritt K, Hitchins VM, Brown SA. Safety and cleaning of medical materials and devices. J Biomed Mater Res. 2000;53:131-136.

52. Jakobsson SW, Rajs J, Jonsson JA, Persson H. Poisoning with sodium hypochlorite solution: Report of a fatal case, supplemented with an experimental and clinico-epidemiological study. Am J Forensic Med Pathol. 1991;12:320-327.

53. French RJ, Tabb HG, Rutledge LJ. Esophageal stenosis produced by ingestion of bleach: Report of two cases. South Med J. 1970;63:1140-1144.

54. Ingram TA. Response of the human eye to accidental exposure to sodium hypochlorite. J Endodontics. 1990;16:235-238.

55. Mrvos R, Dean BS, Krenzelok EP. Home exposures to chlorine/chloramine gas: Review of 216 cases. South Med J. 1993;86:654-657.

56. Rutala WA, Cole EC, Thomann CA, Weber DJ. Stability and bactericidal activity of chlorine solutions. Infect Control Hosp Epidemiol. 1998;19:323-327.

57. Sampson MN, Muir AV. Not all super-oxidized waters are the same. J Hosp Infect. 2002;52:227-228.

58. Selkon JB, Babb JR, Morris R. Evaluation of the antimicrobial activity of a new super-oxidized water, Sterilox®, for the disinfection of endoscopes. J Hosp Infect. 1999;41:59-70.

59. Shetty N, Srinivasan S, Holton J, Ridgway GL. Evaluation of microbicidal activity of a new disinfectant: Sterilox® 2500 against *Clostridium difficile* spores, *Helicobacter pylori*, vancomycin resistant *Enterococcus* species, *Candida albicans* and several *Mycobacterium* species. J Hosp Infect. 1999;41:101-105.

60. Nagington J, Sutehall GM, Whipp P. Tonometer disinfection and viruses. Br J Ophthalmol. 1983;67:674-676.

61. Centers for Disease Control. Acquired immune deficiency syndrome (AIDS): Precautions for clinical and laboratory staffs. MMWR Morb Mortal Wkly Rep. 1982;31:577-580.

62. Centers for Disease Control. Recommendations for prevention of HIV transmission in health-care settings. MMWR Morb Mortal Wkly Rep. 1987;36:S3-S18.

63. Centers for Disease Control. Guidelines for prevention of transmission of human immunodeficiency virus and hepatitis B virus to health-care and public-safety workers. MMWR Morb Mortal Wkly Rep. 1989;38:1-37.

64. Garner JS, Simmons BP. Guideline for isolation precautions in hospitals. Infect Control. 1983;4:245-325.

65. Bloomfield SF, Miller EA. A comparison of hypochlorite and phenolic disinfectants for disinfection of clean and soiled surfaces and blood spillages. J Hosp Infect. 1989;13:231-239.

66. Rutala WA, Weber DJ. Disinfection of endoscopes: Review of new chemical sterilants used for high-level disinfection. Infect Control Hosp Epidemiol. 1999;20:69-76.

67. Centers for Disease Control and Prevention. Guidelines for environmental infection control in health-care facilities, 2003. MMWR Morb Mortal Wkly Rep. 2003;52(RR-10):1-44.

68. Helms CM, Massanari RM, Zeitler R, et al. Legionnaires' disease associated with a hospital water system: A cluster of 24 nosocomial cases. Ann Intern Med. 1983;99:172-178.

69. Cheung RJ, Ortiz D, DiMarino AJ Jr. GI endoscopic reprocessing practices in the United States. Gastrointest Endosc. 1999;50:362-368.

70. Miner NA, McDowell JW, Willcockson GW, et al. Antimicrobial and other properties of a new stabilized alkaline glutaraldehyde disinfectant/sterilizer. Am J Hosp Pharm. 1977;34:376-382.

71. Pepper RE. Comparison of the activities and stabilities of alkaline glutaraldehyde sterilizing solutions. Infect Control. 1980;1:90-92.

72. Scott EM, Gorman SP. Glutaraldehyde. In: Block SS, ed. Disinfection, Sterilization, and Preservation. 5th ed. Philadelphia: Lippincott Williams & Wilkins; 2001:361-381.

73. Russell AD. Glutaraldehyde: Current status and uses. Infect Control Hosp Epidemiol. 1994;15:724-733.

74. Rutala WA, Gergen MF, Weber DJ. Inactivation of *Clostridium difficile* spores by disinfectants. Infect Control Hosp Epidemiol. 1993;14:36-39.

75. Dyas A, Das BC. The activity of glutaraldehyde against *Clostridium difficile*. J Hosp Infect. 1985;6:41-45.

76. van Klingeren B, Pullen W. Glutaraldehyde resistant mycobacteria from endoscope washers. J Hosp Infect. 1993;25:147-149.

77. Griffiths PA, Babb JR, Bradley CR, Fraise AP. Glutaraldehyde-resistant *Mycobacterium chelonae* from endoscope washer disinfectors. J Appl Microbiol. 1997;82:519-526.

78. Webster E, Ribner B, Streed LL, Hutton N. Microbial contamination of activated 2% glutaraldehyde used in high-level disinfection of endoscopes (Abstract). Am J Infect Control. 1996;24:153.

79. Barbee SL, Weber DJ, Sobsey MD, Rutala WA. Inactivation of *Cryptosporidium parvum* oocyst infectivity by disinfection and sterilization processes. Gastrointest Endosc. 1999;49:605-611.

80. Laskowski LF, Marr JJ, Spernoga JF, et al. Fastidious mycobacteria grown from porcine prosthetic-heart-valve cultures. N Engl J Med. 1977;297:101-102.

81. Mbithi JN, Springthorpe VS, Sattar SA, Pacquette M. Bactericidal, virucidal, and mycobactericidal activities of reused alkaline glutaraldehyde in an endoscopy unit. J Clin Microbiol. 1993;31:2988-2995.

82. Cole EC, Rutala WA, Nessen L, et al. Effect of methodology, dilution, and exposure time on the tuberculocidal activity of glutaraldehyde-based disinfectants. Appl Environ Microbiol. 1990;56:1813-1817.

83. Collins FM, Montalbine V. Mycobactericidal activity of glutaraldehyde solutions. J Clin Microbiol. 1976;4:408-412.

84. Overton D, Burgess JO, Beck B, Matis B. Glutaraldehyde test kits: Evaluation for accuracy and range. Gen Dent. 1989;37:126, 128.

85. Farina A, Fievet MH, Plassart F, et al. Residual glutaraldehyde levels in fiberoptic endoscopes: Measurement and implications for patient toxicity. J Hosp Infect. 1999;43:293-297.

86. Dailey JR, Parnes RE, Aminlari A. Glutaraldehyde keratopathy. Am J Ophthalmol. 1993;115:256-258.

87. Newman MA, Kachuba JB. Glutaraldehyde: A potential health risk to nurses. Gastroenterol Nurs. 1992;14:296-300, discussion 300-301.

88. Turner FJ. Hydrogen peroxide and other oxidant disinfectants. In: Block SS, ed. Disinfection, Sterilization, and Preservation. 3rd ed. Philadelphia: Lea & Febiger; 1983:240-250.

89. Block SS. Peroxygen compounds. In: Block SS, ed. Disinfection, Sterilization, and Preservation. 5th ed. Philadelphia: Lippincott Williams & Wilkins; 2001:185-204.

90. Sattar SA, Springthorpe VS, Rochon M. A product based on accelerated and stabilized hydrogen peroxide: Evidence for broad-spectrum germicidal activity. Can J Infect Control. 1998;Winter:123-130.

91. Rutala WA, Gergen MF, Weber DJ. Sporicidal activity of chemical sterilants used in hospitals. Infect Control Hosp Epidemiol. 1993;14:713-718.

92. Silvany RE, Dougherty JM, McCulley JP, et al. The effect of currently available contact lens disinfection systems on *Acanthamoeba castellanii* and *Acanthamoeba polyphaga*. Ophthalmology. 1990;97:286-290.

93. Neely AN, Maley MP. The 1999 Lindberg Award: 3% hydrogen peroxide for the gram-positive disinfection of fabrics. J Burn Care Rehabil. 1999;20:471-477.

94. Vesley D, Norlien KG, Nelson B, et al. Significant factors in the disinfection and sterilization of flexible endoscopes. Am J Infect Control. 1992;20:291-300.

95. Levenson JE. Corneal damage from improperly cleaned tonometer tips. Arch Ophthalmol. 1989;107:1117.

96. Thompson RL, Haley CE, Searcy MA, et al. Catheter-associated bacteriuria: Failure to reduce attack rates using periodic instillations of a disinfectant into urinary drainage systems. JAMA. 1984;251:747-751.

97. Gottardi W. Iodine and iodine compounds. In: Block SS, ed. Disinfection, Sterilization, and Preservation. 5th ed. Philadelphia: Lippincott Williams & Wilkins; 2001:159-184.

98. Craven DE, Moody B, Connolly MG, et al. Pseudobacteremia caused by povidone-iodine solution contaminated with *Pseudomonas cepacia*. N Engl J Med. 1981;305:621-623.

99. Berkelman RL, Lewin S, Allen JR, et al. Pseudobacteremia attributed to contamination of povidone-iodine with *Pseudomonas cepacia*. Ann Intern Med. 1981;95:32-36.

100. Rutala WA, Cole EC, Wannamaker NS, Weber DJ. Inactivation of *Mycobacterium tuberculosis* and *Mycobacterium bovis* by 14 hospital disinfectants. Am J Med. 1991;91:267S-271S.

101. Klein M, DeForest A. The inactivation of viruses by germicides. Chem Specialists Manuf Assoc Proc. 1963;49:116-118.

102. Berkelman RL, Holland BW, Anderson RL. Increased bactericidal activity of dilute preparations of povidone-iodine solutions. J Clin Microbiol. 1982;15:635-639.

103. Wallbank AM, Drulak M, Poffenroth L, et al. Wescodyne: Lack of activity against poliovirus in the presence of organic matter. Health Lab Sci. 1978;15:133-137.

104. Favero MS, Bond WW. Chemical disinfection of medical and surgical materials. In: Block SS, ed. Disinfection, Sterilization, and Preservation. 5th ed. Philadelphia: Lea & Febiger; 1991:617-641.

105. Medcomp. Medcomp frequently asked questions. Harleysville, PA: Medcomp; 2000. Available at: *www.medcompnet.com*

106. Gordon MD, Ezzell RJ, Bruckner NI, Ascenzi JM. Enhancement of mycobactericidal activity of glutaraldehyde with α,β-unsaturated and aromatic aldehydes. J Indust Microbiol. 1994;13:77-82.

107. Rutala WA, Weber DJ. New disinfection and sterilization methods. Emerg Infect Dis. 2001;7:348-353.

108. Gregory AW, Schaalje GB, Smart JD, Robison RA. The mycobactericidal efficacy of ortho-phthalaldehyde and the comparative resistances of *Mycobacterium bovis*, *Mycobacterium terrae*, and *Mycobacterium chelonae*. Infect Control Hosp Epidemiol. 1999;20:324-330.

109. Walsh SE, Maillard JY, Russell AD. Ortho-phthalaldehyde: A possible alternative to glutaraldehyde for high level disinfection. J Appl Microbiol. 1999;86:1039-1046.

110. Alfa MJ, Sitter DL. In-hospital evaluation of orthophthalaldehyde as a high level disinfectant for flexible endoscopes. J Hosp Infect. 1994;26:15-26.

111. McDonnell G, Pretzer D. New and developing chemical antimicrobials. In: Block SS, ed. Disinfection, Sterilization, and Preservation. 5th ed. Philadelphia: Lippincott Williams & Wilkins; 2001:431-443.

112. Fraud S, Maillard J-Y, Russell AD. Comparison of the mycobactericidal activity of ortho-phthalaldehyde, glutaraldehyde, and other dialdehydes by a quantitative suspension test. J Hosp Infect. 2001;48:214-221.

113. Tucker RC, Lestini BJ, Marchant RE. Surface analysis of clinically used expanded PTFE endoscopic tubing treated by the Steris process. ASAIO J. 1996;42:306-313.

114. Malchesky PS. Medical applications of peracetic acid. In: Block SS, ed. Disinfection, Sterilization, and Preservation. 5th ed. Philadelphia: Lippincott Williams & Wilkins; 2001:979-996.

115. Mannion PT. The use of peracetic acid for the reprocessing of flexible endoscopes and rigid cystoscopes and laparoscopes. J Hosp Infect. 1995;29:313-315.

116. Bradley CR, Babb JR, Ayliffe GA. Evaluation of the Steris System 1 Peracetic Acid Endoscope Processor. J Hosp Infect. 1995;29:143-151.

117. Duc DL, Ribiollet A, Dode X, et al. Evaluation of the microbicidal efficacy of Steris System I for digestive endoscopes using GERMANDE and ASTM validation protocols. J Hosp Infect. 2001;48:135-141.

118. Alfa MJ, Olson N, DeGagne P, Olson N, Hizon R. New low temperature sterilization technologies: Microbicidal activity and clinical efficacy. In: Rutala WA, ed. Disinfection, Sterilization, and Antisepsis in Healthcare. Champlain, NY: Polyscience Publications; 1998:67-78.

119. Alfa MJ, DeGagne P, Olson N, Hizon R. Comparison of liquid chemical sterilization with peracetic acid and ethylene oxide sterilization for long narrow lumens. Am J Infect Control. 1998;26:469-477.

120. Fuselier HA Jr, Mason C. Liquid sterilization versus high level disinfection in the urologic office. Urology. 1997;50:337-340.

121. Seballos RJ, Walsh AL, Mehta AC. Clinical evaluation of a liquid chemical sterilization system for flexible bronchoscopes. J Bronch. 1995;2:192-199.

122. Wallace CG, Agee PM, Demicco DD. Liquid chemical sterilization using peracetic acid: An alternative approach to endoscope processing. ASAIO J. 1995;41:151-154.

123. Centers for Disease Control and Prevention. Bronchoscopy-related infections and pseudoinfections—New York, 1996 and 1998. MMWR Morb Mortal Wkly Rep. 1999;48:557-560.

124. Middleton AM, Chadwick MV, Gaya H. Disinfection of bronchoscopes, contaminated in vitro with *Mycobacterium tuberculosis*, *Mycobacterium avium-intracellulare* and *Mycobacterium chelonae* in sputum, using stabilized, buffered peracetic acid solution ('Nu-Cidex'). J Hosp Infect. 1997;37:137-143.

125. Holton J, Shetty N. In-use stability of Nu-Cidex. J Hosp Infect. 1997;35:245-248.

126. Alasri A, Roques C, Michel G, et al. Bactericidal properties of peracetic acid and hydrogen peroxide, alone and in combination, and chlorine and formaldehyde against bacterial water strains. Can J Microbiol. 1992;38:635-642.

127. Stanley P. Destruction of a glutaraldehyde-resistant mycobacterium by a per-oxygen disinfectant (Abstract). Am J Infect Control. 1998;26:185.

128. Fleming SJ, Foreman K, Shanley K, et al. Dialyser reprocessing with Renalin. Am J Nephrol. 1991;11:27-31.

129. Tokars JI, Miller ER, Alter MJ, Arduino MJ. National surveillance of dialysis-associated diseases in the United States, 1997. Semin Dialysis. 2000;13:75-85.

130. Sattar SA, Springthorpe VS. Survival and disinfectant inactivation of the human immunodeficiency virus: A critical review. Rev Infect Dis. 1991;13:430-447.

131. Rutala WA, Cole EC. Ineffectiveness of hospital disinfectants against bacteria: A collaborative study. Infect Control. 1987;8:501-506.

132. Prindle RF. Phenolic compounds. In: Block SS, ed. Disinfection, Sterilization, and Preservation. 3rd ed. Philadelphia: Lea & Febiger; 1983:197-224.

133. Cole EC, Rutala WA, Samsa GP. Disinfectant testing using a modified use-dilution method: Collaborative study. J Assoc Off Anal Chem. 1988;71:1187-1194.

134. Goddard PA, McCue KA. Phenolic compounds. In: Block SS, ed. Disinfection, Sterilization, and Preservation. 5th ed. Philadelphia: Lippincott Williams & Wilkins; 2001:255-281.

135. Sagripanti JL, Eklund CA, Trost PA, et al. Comparative sensitivity of 13 species of pathogenic bacteria to seven chemical germicides. Am J Infect Control. 1997;25:335-339.

136. Wysowski DK, Flynt JW Jr, Goldfield M, et al. Epidemic neonatal hyperbilirubinemia and use of a phenolic disinfectant detergent. Pediatrics. 1978;61:165-170.

137. Doan HM, Keith L, Shennan AT. Phenol and neonatal jaundice. Pediatrics. 1979;64:324-325.

138. Rutala WA, Cole EC. Antiseptics and disinfectants—Safe and effective? Infect Control. 1984;5:215-218.

139. Mbithi JN, Springthorpe VS, Sattar SA. Chemical disinfection of hepatitis A virus on environmental surfaces. Appl Environ Microbiol. 1990;56:3601-3604.

140. Petrocci AN. Surface active agents: Quaternary ammonium compounds. In: Block SS, ed. Disinfection, Sterilization, and Preservation. 3rd ed. Philadelphia: Lea & Febiger; 1983:309-329.

141. Doultree JC, Druce JD, Birch CJ, et al. Inactivation of feline calicivirus, a Norwalk virus surrogate. J Hosp Infect. 1999;41:51-57.

142. Cefai C, Richards J, Gould FK, McPeake P. An outbreak of respiratory tract infection resulting from incomplete disinfection of ventilatory equipment. J Hosp Infect. 1990;15:177-182.

143. Gurevich I, Tafuro P, Ristuccia P, et al. Disinfection of respirator tubing: A comparison of chemical versus hot water machine-assisted processing. J Hosp Infect. 1983;4:199-208.

144. Rutala WA, Weber DJ, Gergen MF, Gratta AR. Efficacy of a washer-pasteurizer for disinfection of respiratory-care equipment. Infect Control Hosp Epidemiol. 2000;21:333-336.

145. Jette LP, Lambert NG. Evaluation of two hot water washer disinfectors for medical instruments. Infect Control Hosp Epidemiol. 1988;9:194-199.

146. Association for the Advancement of Medical Instrumentation. Good Hospital Practice: Steam Sterilization and Sterility Assurance. Arlington, VA: AAMI; 1993.

147. Association for the Advancement of Medical Instrumentation. Flash Sterilization: Steam Sterilization of Patient Care Items for Immediate Use. Arlington, VA: AAMI; 1996.

148. Association for the Advancement of Medical Instrumentation. Steam Sterilization and Sterility Assurance in Health Care Facilities. Arlington, VA: AAMI; 2002.

149. Association for the Advancement of Medical Instrumentation. Ethylene Oxide Sterilization in Health Care Facilities: Safety and Effectiveness. Arlington, VA: AAMI; 1999.

150. Association of Operating Room Nurses. Recommended practices for sterilization in perioperative practice settings. In: 2000 Standards, Recommended Practices, and Guidelines. Denver, CO: AORN; 2000:347-358.

151. Association for Peri-Operative Registered Nurses. Recommended practices for cleaning and caring for surgical instruments and powered equipment. AORN J. 2002;75:727-741.

152. Education Design. Best Practices for the Prevention of Surgical Site Infection. Denver Colorado: Education Design; 1998.

153. Singh J, Bhatia R, Gandhi JC, et al. Outbreak of viral hepatitis B in a rural community in India linked to inadequately sterilized needles and syringes. Bull World Health Organ 1998;76:93-98.

154. Eickhoff TC. An outbreak of surgical wound infections due to *Clostridium perfringens*. Surg Gynecol Obstet. 1962;114:102-108.

155. Favero MS. Sterility assurance: Concepts for patient safety. In: Rutala WA, ed. Disinfection, Sterilization and Antisepsis: Principles and Practices in Healthcare Facilities. Washington, DC: Association for Professionals in Infection Control and Epidemiology; 2001:110-119.

156. Oxborrow GS, Berube R. Sterility testing-validation of sterilization processes, and sporicide testing. In: Block SS, ed. Disinfection, Sterilization, and Preservation. 4th ed. Philadelphia: Lea & Febiger; 1991:1047-1057.

157. Rutala WA, Weber DJ. Clinical effectiveness of low-temperature sterilization technologies. Infect Control Hosp Epidemiol. 1998;19:798-804.

158. Adler S, Scherrer M, Daschner FD. Costs of low-temperature plasma sterilization compared with other sterilization methods. J Hosp Infect. 1998;40:125-134.

159. Joslyn L. Sterilization by heat. In: Block SS, ed. Disinfection, Sterilization, and Preservation. 5th ed. Philadelphia: Lippincott Williams & Wilkins; 2001:695-728.

160. Silverstone SE, Hill DE. Evaluation of sterilization of dental handpieces by heating in synthetic compressor lubricant. Gen Dent. 1999;47:158-160.

161. Bucx MJ, Veldman DJ, Beenhakker MM, Koster R. The effect of steam sterilization at 134 degrees C on light intensity provided by Fibrelight Macintoch laryngoscopes. Anaesthesia. 2000;55:185-186.

162. Gilbert JA, Phillips HO 4th. The effect of steam sterilization on plaster casting material. Clin Orthop. 1984;190:241-244.

163. Bryce EA, Roberts FJ, Clements B, MacLean S. When the biological indicator is positive: Investigating autoclave failures. Infect Control Hosp Epidemiol. 1997;18:654-656.

164. Young JH. Sterilization with steam under pressure. In: Morrissey RF, Phillips GB, eds. Sterilization Technology: A Practical Guide for Manufacturers and Users of Health Care Products. New York: Van Nostrand Reinhold; 1993:81-119.

165. Rutala WA, Stiegel MM, Sarubbi FA Jr. Decontamination of laboratory microbiological waste by steam sterilization. Appl Environ Microbiol. 1982;43:1311-1316.

166. Rutala WA. Disinfection and flash sterilization in the operating room. J Ophthal Nurs Technol. 1991;10:106-115.

167. Barrett T. Flash sterilization: What are the risks? In: Rutala WA, ed. Disinfection, Sterilization and Antisepsis: Principles and Practices in Healthcare Facilities. Washington, DC: Association for Professional in Infection Control and Epidemiology; 2001:70-76.

168. Vesley D, Langholz AC, Rohlfing SR, Foltz WE. Fluorometric detection of a *Bacillus stearothermophilus* spore-bound enzyme, α-D-glucosidase, for rapid identification of flash sterilization failure. Appl Environ Microbiol. 1992;58:717-719.

169. Rutala WA, Gergen MF, Weber DJ. Evaluation of a rapid readout biological indicator for flash sterilization with three biological indicators and three chemical indicators. Infect Control Hosp Epidemiol. 1993;14:390-394.

170. Hood E, Stout N, Catto B. Flash sterilization and neurosurgical site infections: Guilt by association. Am J Infect Control. 1997;25:156.

171. Rutala WA, Weber DJ, Chappell KJ. Patient injury from flash-sterilized instruments. Infect Control Hosp Epidemiol. 1999;20:458.

172. Ernst RR, Doyle JE. Sterilization with gaseous ethylene oxide: A review of chemical and physical factors. Biotechnol Bioeng. 1968;10:1-31.

173. Joslyn L. Gaseous chemical sterilization. In: Block SS, ed. Disinfection, Sterilization, and Preservation. 5th ed. Philadelphia: Lippincott Williams & Wilkins; 2001:337-360.

174. National Toxicology Program. 10th Report on Carcinogens. Bethesda, MD: NTP; 2002. Available at: *ehp.niehs.nih.gov/roc/toc.10.html*

175. Anonymous. Ethylene oxide sterilization: How hospitals can adapt to the changes. Health Devices. 1994;23:485-492.

176. Alfa MJ, DeGagne P, Olson N. Bacterial killing ability of 10% ethylene oxide plus 90% hydrochlorofluorocarbon sterilizing gas. Infect Control Hosp Epidemiol. 1997;18:641-645.

177. Rutala WA, Gergen MF, Weber DJ. Comparative evaluation of the sporicidal activity of new low-temperature sterilization technologies: Ethylene oxide, 2 plasma sterilization systems, and liquid peracetic acid. Am J Infect Control. 1998;26:393-398.

178. Alfa MJ, DeGagne P, Olson N, Puchalski T. Comparison of ion plasma, vaporized hydrogen peroxide and 100% ethylene oxide sterilizers to the 12/88 ethylene oxide gas sterilizer. Infect Control Hosp Epidemiol. 1996;17:92-100.

179. Parisi AN, Young WE. Sterilization with ethylene oxide and other gases. In: Block SS, ed. Disinfection, Sterilization, and Preservation. 4th ed. Philadelphia: Lea & Febiger; 1991:580-595.

180. Holler C, Martiny H, Christiansen B, et al. The efficacy of low temperature plasma (LTP) sterilization, a new sterilization technique. Zentralbl Hyg Umweltmed. 1993;194:380-391.

181. Parker HH, Johnson RB. Effectiveness of ethylene oxide for sterilization of dental handpieces. J Dent. 1995;23:113-115.

182. Schneider PM. Low-temperature sterilization alternatives in the 1990s. Tappi J. 1994; 77:115-119.

183. Jacobs PT, Lin SM. Sterilization processes utilizing low-temperature plasma. In: Block SS, ed. Disinfection, Sterilization, and Preservation. 5th ed. Philadelphia: Lippincott Williams & Wilkins; 2001:747-763.

184. Rutala WA, Gergen MF, Weber DJ. Sporicidal activity of a new low-temperature sterilization technology: The Sterrad 50 sterilizer. Infect Control Hosp Epidemiol. 1999;20:514-516.

185. Roberts C, Antonoplos P. Inactivation of human immunodeficiency virus type 1, hepatitis A virus, respiratory syncytial virus, vaccinia virus, herpes simplex virus type 1, and poliovirus type 2 by hydrogen peroxide gas plasma sterilization. Am J Infect Control. 1998;26:94-101.

186. Feldman LA, Hui HK. Compatibility of medical devices and materials with low-temperature hydrogen peroxide gas plasma. Med Dev Diagn Indust. 1997;19:57-62.

187. Jacobs PT, Smith D. The new Sterrad 100S sterilization system: Features and advantages. Zentralbl Steril. 1998;6:86-94.

188. Food and Drug Administration, Centers for Disease Control and Prevention. FDA and CDC Public Health Advisory: Infections from Endoscopes Inadequately Reprocessed by an Automated Endoscope Reprocessing System. Rockville, MD: Food and Drug Administration; 1999.

189. Rutala WA, Weber DJ. Importance of lumen flow in liquid chemical sterilization. Am J Infect Control. 1999;20:458-9.

190. Gurevich I, Qadri SMH, Cunha BA. False-positive results of spore tests from improper clip use with the Steris chemical sterilant system. Infect Control Hosp Epidemiol. 1992;21:42-3.

191. Occupational Safety and Health Administration. Occupational exposure to bloodborne pathogens: Final rule. Fed Regist. 1991;56:64003-182.

192. Occupational Safety and Health Administration, Office of Health Compliance Assistance. OSHA Instruction CPL 2-2.44C. Washington, DC: OSHA; 1992.

193. Occupational Safety and Health Administration. OSHA Memorandum from Stephen Mallinger: EPA-Registered Disinfectants for HIV/HBV. Washington, DC: OSHA; 1997.

194. Payan C, Cottin J, Lemarie C, Ramont C. Inactivation of hepatitis B virus in plasma by hospital in-use chemical disinfectants assessed by a modified HepG2 cell culture. J Hosp Infect. 2001;47:282-287.

195. Rutala WA, Weber DJ. Infection control: The role of disinfection and sterilization. J Hosp Infect. 1999;43:S43-S55.

196. Wilson JA, Margolin AB. The efficacy of three common hospital liquid germicides to inactivate *Cryptosporidium parvum* oocysts. J Hosp Infect. 1999;42:231-237.

197. Fayer R, Graczyk TK, Cranfield MR, Trout JM. Gaseous disinfection of *Cryptosporidium parvum* oocysts. Appl Environ Microbiol. 1996;62:3908-3909.

198. Rice EW, Clark RM, Johnson CH. Chlorine inactivation of *Escherichia coli* O157:H7. Emerg Infect Dis. 1999;5:461-463.

199. Venkitanarayanan KS, Ezeike GO, Hung YC, Doyle MP. Inactivation of *Escherichia coli* O157:H7 and *Listeria monocytogenes* on plastic kitchen cutting boards by electrolyzed oxidizing water. J Food Prot. 1999;62:857-860.

200. Akamatsu T, Tabata K, Hironga M, et al. Transmission of *Helicobacter pylori* infection via flexible fiberoptic endoscopy. Am J Infect Control. 1996;24:396-401.

201. Graham DY, Osato MS. Disinfection of biopsy forceps and culture of *Helicobacter pylori* from gastric mucosal biopsies. Am J Gastroenterol. 1999;94:1422-1423.

202. Rutala WA, Weber DJ. Modern advances in disinfection, sterilization and medical waste management. In: Wenzel RP, ed. Prevention and Control of Nosocomial Infections. Philadelphia: Lippincott Williams & Wilkins; 2003:542-574.

203. Fantry GT, Zheng QX, James SP. Conventional cleaning and disinfection techniques eliminate the risk of endoscopic transmission of *Helicobacter pylori*. Am J Gastroenterol. 1995;90:227-232.

204. Cronmiller JR, Nelson DK, Jackson DK, Kim CH. Efficacy of conventional endoscopic disinfection and sterilization methods against *Helicobacter pylori* contamination. Helicobacter. 1999;4:198-203.

205. Shimada T, Terano A, Ota S, et al. Risk of iatrogenic transmission of *Helicobacter pylori* by gastroscopes. Lancet. 1996;347:1342-1343.

206. Roosendaal R, Kuipers EJ, van den Brule AJ, et al. Detection of *Helicobacter pylori* DNA by PCR in gastrointestinal equipment. Lancet. 1993;341:900.

207. Johnson CH, Rice EW, Reasoner DJ. Inactivation of *Helicobacter pylori* by chlorination. Appl Environ Microbiol. 1997;63:4969-4970.

208. Chapin M, Yatabe J, Cherry JD. An outbreak of rotavirus gastroenteritis on a pediatric unit. Am J Infect Control. 1983;11:88-91.

209. Ansari SA, Spingthorpe S, Sattar SA. Survival and vehicular spread of human rotaviruses: Possible relation to seasonality of outbreaks. Rev Infect Dis. 1991;13:448-461.

210. Sattar SA, Raphael RA, Lochnan H, Springthorpe VS. Rotavirus inactivation by chemical disinfectants and antiseptics used in hospitals. Can J Microbiol. 1983;29:1464-1469.

211. Lloyd-Evans N, Springthorpe VS, Sattar SA. Chemical disinfection of human rotavirus-contaminated inanimate surfaces. J Hyg (Lond). 1986;97:163-173.

212. Centers for Disease Control and Prevention. Update: Severe acute respiratory syndrome—United States, May 14, 2003. MMWR Morb Mortal Wkly Rep. 2003;52:436-438.

213. Sattar SA, Springthorpe VS, Karim Y, Loro P. Chemical disinfection of non-porous inanimate surfaces experimentally contaminated with four human pathogenic viruses. Epidemiol Infect. 1989;102:493-505.

214. Saknimit M, Inatsuki I, Sugiyama Y, Yagami K. Virucidal efficacy of physico-chemical treatments against coronaviruses and parvoviruses of laboratory animals. Jikken Dobutsu. 1988;37:341-345.

215. Sizun J, Yu MW, Talbot PJ. Survival of human coronaviruses 229E and OC43 in suspension and after drying on surfaces: A possible source of hospital-acquired infections. J Hosp Infect. 2000;46:55-60.

216. World Health Organization, Communicable Disease Surveillance and Response. First data on stability and resistance of SARS coronavirus, compiled by members of WHO laboratory network. Geneva: WHO; 2003. Available at: *www.who.int/csr/srs/survival_2003_05_04/en/index.html*

217. Taylor DM. Inactivation of transmissible degenerative encephalopathy agents: A review. Vet J. 2000;159:10-17.

218. World Health Organization. WHO infection control guidelines for transmissible spongiform encephalopathies: Report of a WHO Consultation, Geneva, Switzerland, 23-26 March 1999. Geneva: WHO; 2003. Available at: *www.who.int/csr/resources/publications/bse/en/whocdscsraph2003.pdf*

219. Taylor DM. Inactivation of prions by physical and chemical means. J Hosp Infect. 1999;43(Suppl):S69-S76.

220. Rutala WA, Weber DJ. Creutzfeldt-Jakob disease: Recommendations for disinfection and sterilization. Clin Infect Dis. 2001;32:1348-1356.

221. Weber DJ, Rutala WA. Use of germicides in the home and health care setting: Is there a relationship between germicide use and antimicrobial resistance? Infect Control Hosp Epidemiol. In press.

222. Rutala WA, Stiegel MM, Sarubbi FA, Weber DJ. Susceptibility of antibiotic-susceptible and antibiotic-resistant hospital bacteria to disinfectants. Infect Control Hosp Epidemiol. 1997;18:417-421.

223. Anderson RL, Carr JH, Bond WW, Favero MS. Susceptibility of vancomycin-resistant enterococci to environmental disinfectants. Infect Control Hosp Epidemiol. 1997;18:195-199.

224. Sehulster LM, Anderson RL. Susceptibility of glycopeptide-intermediate resistant *Staphylococcus aureus* (GISA) to surface disinfectants, hand washing chemicals, and a skin antiseptic (Abstract Y-3). In: Abstracts of the 98th General Meeting of the American Society for Microbiology, 1998:547.

225. Rutala WA, Weber DJ, Gergen MF. Studies on the disinfection of VRE-contaminated surfaces. Infect Control Hosp Epidemiol. 2000;21:548.

226. Leggiadro RJ. The threat of biological terrorism: A public health and infection control reality. Infect Control Hosp Epidemiol. 2000;21:53-56.

227. Henderson DA. The looming threat of bioterrorism. Science. 1999;283:1279-1282.

228. Centers for Disease Control and Prevention. Biological and chemical terrorism: Strategic plan for preparedness and response. MMWR Morb Mortal Wkly Rep. 2000;49(RR-4):1-14.

229. Brazis AR, Leslie JE, Kabler PW, Woodward RL. The inactivation of spores of *Bacillus globigii* and *Bacillus anthracis* by free available chlorine. Appl Microbiol. 1958;6:338-342.

230. Weber DJ, Rutala WA. Risks and prevention of nosocomial transmission of rare zoonotic diseases. Clin Infect Dis. 2001;32:446-456.

231. Environmental Protection Agency. Bleach. Washington, DC: EPA; 2003. Available at: *www.epa.gov/pesticides/factsheets/chemicals/bleachfactsheet.htm*

232. Environmental Protection Agency. Chlorine dioxide. Washington, DC: EPA; 2003. Available at: *www.epa.gov/pesticides/factsheets/chemicals/chlorinedioxidefactsheet.htm*

233. Environmental Protection Agency. FIFRA Section 18 emergency exemptions. Washington, DC: EPA; 2003. Available at: *www.epa.gov/opprd001/section18*

234. Rutala WA, Odette RL, Samsa GP. Management of infectious waste by United States hospitals. JAMA. 1989;262:1635-1640.

235. Rutala WA, Sarubbi FA. Management of infectious waste from hospitals. Infect. Control 1983;4:198-204.

236. Agency for Toxic Substances and Disease Registry. The Public Health Implications of Medical Waste: A Report to Congress. Washington, DC: Department of Health and Human Services; 1990.

237. Rutala WA, Weber DJ, for the Society of Hospital Epidemiology of America. SHEA position paper: Medical waste. Infect Control Hosp Epidemiol. 1992;13:38-48.

238. Environmental Protection Agency. EPA Guide for Infectious Waste Management. Washington, DC: EPA; 1986.

239. Office of Technology Assessment. Finding the Rx for Managing Medical Wastes (OTA-0-459). Washington, DC: OTA; 1990.

240. Rutala WA, Weber DJ. Infectious waste: Mismatch between science and policy. N Engl J Med. 1991;325:578-582.

241. Environmental Protection Agency. Standards for the tracking and management of medical waste: Interim final rule and request for comments. Fed Regist. 1989;54:12326-12395.

242. Department of Transportation. Infectious substances: Final rule. Fed Regist. 1995;60:48779-48787.

243. Joint Commission on Accreditation of Healthcare Organizations. Comprehensive Accreditation Manual for Hospitals. Chicago, IL: JCAHO; 2003.

CHAPTER **300**

Infections Caused by Percutaneous Intravascular Devices

SUSAN E. BEEKMANN
DAVID K. HENDERSON

The relentless progress of medical science and technology has been accompanied by the development of a host of new diagnostic and therapeutic medical devices, each of which is associated with its own complications. Included in the list of devices and the complications of their use to be discussed in this chapter are peripheral and central intravenous catheters, including both nontunneled and tunneled (Hickman or Broviac catheters), peripherally inserted central venous catheters (PICCs), totally implanted intravascular access devices, pulmonary artery catheters, and arterial lines.

As early as 1977, Maki suggested that more than 25,000 patients develop device-related bacteremia in the United States each year.[1] More recently, the Centers for Disease Control and Prevention (CDC) has estimated that approximately 80,000 central venous catheter-associated bacteremias currently occur in intensive care units (ICUs) each year.[2] The burgeoning use of an ever-expanding array of vascular access devices in medicine has resulted in even more complications associated with their use. The incidence of bacteremia associated with the use of intravascular devices has increased significantly. In one center the rate of catheter-associated bacteremia rose from 20 episodes per 1000 admissions in 1986 to 50 episodes per 1000 admissions in 1993.[3] Such device-associated infections occur as sporadic cases as well as in case clusters caused by the same organism. Vascular catheters have become an increasingly important source of bacteremias, increasing from 3% in the mid-1970s to 19% in the early 1990s.[4] Primary bacteremias (i.e., no apparent local infection elsewhere caused by the same organism), including intravascular catheter sources, now account for approximately one half of all ICU-related bacteremias.[5,6] The problem of iatrogenic, device-associated bacteremia is not unique to the United States; in one prospective study of bacteremia from Australia, nosocomial bacteremias accounted for 40% of all cases of bacteremia, and half of the nosocomial cases were device associated.[7]

Both local and systemic infection may result from contamination of intravascular devices. Local cellulitis, abscess formation, septic thrombophlebitis, device-associated bacteremia, and endocarditis all occur as complications of intravascular therapy and monitoring.

PATHOGENESIS

In order for intravascular device–related bacteremia to occur, microorganisms must gain access to the extraluminal or intraluminal surface of the device. Microbial adherence and incorporation into biofilms then occurs, resulting first in infection and then, in some instances, hematogenous dissemination.[8] Figure 300-1 illustrates the potential points of access to an intravascular device, each of which has been associated with both sporadic cases and case clusters of nosocomial bacteremia. Whereas the skin entry site has long been thought to be the most important portal of entry for invading microorganisms, the catheter hub–lumen has also been shown to be a major contributor to catheter-related bacteremia.[9,10] The most common point of access appears to vary, depending on the duration of time the catheter has been in place. Each of the three major sources of intravenous device–related bacteremia is discussed below.

Contamination of the Infusate

Contamination of the fluid administered through the device is a major cause of epidemic intravenous device–related bacteremias. Nonetheless, infusate contamination is a rare cause of bacteremia. Infusion-related sepsis has been reviewed in detail,[11] and both manufacture-related[12] and in-use[13] contamination of infusate have been documented as causes of device-associated sepsis.

Another factor influencing the pathogenesis of infusate-associated infection is the composition of the fluid. Different infusion fluids support the growth of differing pathogens. The microbiology of outbreaks of infusate-related sepsis is somewhat monotonous; pathogens such as *Enterobacter, Citrobacter,* and *Serratia* predominate. No infusate is entirely free of risk; even distilled water can support the growth of *Burkholderia cepacia* complex.[14] Parenteral nutrition solutions are su-

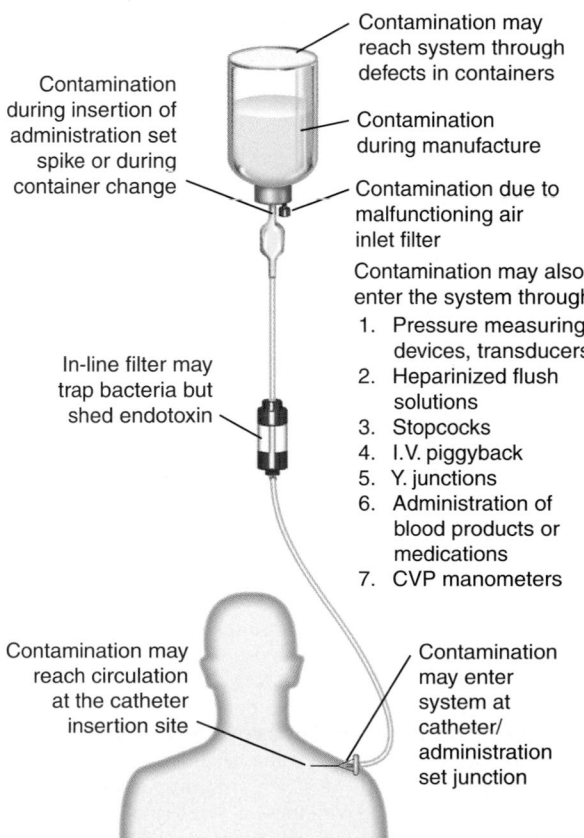

Contamination may reach system through defects in containers

Contamination during insertion of administration set spike or during container change

Contamination during manufacture

Contamination due to malfunctioning air inlet filter

Contamination may also enter the system through
1. Pressure measuring devices, transducers
2. Heparinized flush solutions
3. Stopcocks
4. I.V. piggyback
5. Y. junctions
6. Administration of blood products or medications
7. CVP manometers

In-line filter may trap bacteria but shed endotoxin

Contamination may reach circulation at the catheter insertion site

Contamination may enter system at catheter/ administration set junction

FIGURE 300-1. Points of access for microbial contamination in infusion therapy.

perb substrates for the growth of certain microorganisms.[15] Casein hydrolysate solutions support the growth of many bacteria and fungi.[16] Lipid emulsions support bacterial growth extremely well,[17] and their use has also been associated with a risk for fungemia caused by the lipid-dependent yeast *Malassezia furfur*.[18] This latter risk has been primarily identified in the neonatal intensive care setting and has been less commonly seen in adults.[18] More recently the risk for coagulase-negative staphylococcal bacteremia in neonates has been directly linked to the administration of lipid infusions.[19]

Parenteral nutrition solutions may also become contaminated during compounding in the hospital pharmacy.[20,21] Two similar outbreaks of *Candida parapsilosis* infections were linked to the backflow of yeasts into TPN solution because vacuum pumps were used improperly.[20,21]

The composition of the infusate also influences the degree of irritation of the vascular intima at the site of infusion. Fluids that are not isotonic, those at nonphysiologic pH, and those containing particulates all may irritate the vascular wall, thus provoking thrombus formation. Such thrombi may be seeded with microbes—either hematogenously or by direct extension.

Contamination of the Catheter Hub and Lumen

Contamination of the catheter hub–infusion tubing junction as a significant contributor to device-associated infection has been championed by Sitges-Serra and colleagues (summarized in references 10 and 22-24). These investigators suggested that endemic coagulase-negative staphylococcal bacteremias often arise as a result of contamination of the catheter hub with these organisms. A randomized study examining the effects of a new protective hub found these hubs to be associated with a significantly lower rate of catheter sepsis and culture-positive catheter hubs,[25] indicating that the hub is a common portal of entry for bacteria. Other investigators have incriminated the hub-tubing junction (particularly when it does not allow a good fit) in the pathogenesis of epidemics of coagulase-negative staphylococcal infection.[26] Maki and Ringer found hub contamination to be the second most heavily weighted risk factor for catheter-associated infection in a large, prospective study.[27] Salzman and colleagues noted that more than 50% of episodes of central venous catheter–related sepsis occurring in a neonatal ICU were preceded by colonization of the catheter hub with the incriminated organism.[28] In a subsequent experimental study these investigators found that swabbing the catheter hub with disinfectant substantially reduced the hub's microbial burden and that preparations containing 70% ethanol were both more effective and more likely to be safer for the patient than preparations containing chlorhexidine.[29] Sherertz estimated that the hub, lumen, or both contributed two thirds of the microorganisms that infected long-term catheters and that one fourth of the microorganisms were from the skin.[30] Finally, several outbreaks of bacteremia have been traced to contaminated medications—either those added directly to the system or those piggybacked into a side port.[31,32] Clusters of infection also have been linked to flushing catheters with fluids from a contaminated common source.[33]

Conversely, some new technologies may be associated with increased risks for catheter-associated infection. Whereas the implementation of needleless intravenous admixture systems provided a safer workplace environment for health care providers, some data suggest that use of these devices may be associated with increased risk for device-associated infection. Multiple investigations of bacteremia outbreaks associated with needleless devices have suggested that the mechanism for bacteremia may involve contamination from the end cap.[34-37] Interestingly, different studies have paradoxically found either increased or decreased risk with the same needleless system (e.g., the Interlink device [Baxter, Deerfield, IL][34,35]), leading to the conclusion that the primary risk associated with these devices is related to how the systems are used (e.g., frequency of changing end caps) rather than the intrinsic system. Appropriate staff education regarding use of these devices and ensuring compliance with manufacturer's recommendations is recommended to prevent device-related bacteremia.

Contamination of Skin at the Device Insertion Site

Many authorities believe that the catheter insertion tract provides the major avenue for the ingress of microbial invaders.[1,7,10,11,26,27,38,39] Several studies have focused on microbial colonization around the catheter insertion site as a significant risk factor for catheter-associated infection.[40] Supporting this contention are the studies of Cooper and Hopkins that demonstrated organisms on the exterior surface of catheters, rather than within the catheter lumen.[41] In the prospective study of Maki and Ringer, colonization around the catheter insertion site was the most strongly associated risk factor for local catheter infection.[27] Skin appears to be the primary source of intravenous device–related bacteremia for short-term catheters, placed for an average duration of less than 8 days.[42,43] Nonetheless, skin colonization is a dynamic process. Atela and co-workers conducted a prospective study to assess the turnover of superficial skin colonization by performing serial quantitative cultures of skin and the catheter hub.[38] Strains recovered from the targeted superficial skin sites demonstrated a poor correlation both with strains from previous skin cultures and with catheter tip isolates.[38] Herwaldt and colleagues examined the source of coagulase-negative staphylococcal bacteremias in hematology-oncology patients, and found that the same strain was identified in both skin and blood cultures in only 6 of 20 episodes.[44] The matching strain was isolated only from other sites (primarily nares) in the remaining 70% of episodes, leading these investigators to the conclusion that mucous membranes might be a reservoir for strains of coagulase-negative staphylococci causing bacteremia in immunocompromised patients. Importantly, these investigators were unable to identify colonization with the same strain for the majority of bacteremias; only 4 of the 21 nosocomial blood-stream infections were preceded by colonization with the same strain. Most nosocomial coagulase-negative staphylococcal bacteremias in this study appeared to result from extrinsic introduction of the organism.

EPIDEMIOLOGY

Rates of central venous catheter–associated bacteremia have been reported by the CDC's National Nosocomial Infection Surveillance System since 1970. From 1995 through June 2002, ICU rates of central venous catheter–associated bacteremia ranged from 2.9 (in cardiothoracic ICUs) to 8.8 (in burn ICUs) bacteremias per 1000 central venous catheter days.[45] Intravenous device–related bacteremia rates are influenced by patient-related parameters, catheter-related parameters, and hospital-related parameters (Table 300-1). Because of methodologic difficulties in performing appropriate scientific studies to characterize relative risk, many of these risk factors have been identified either retrospectively or in the epidemic setting. Still, each of the patient-related factors identified in Table 300-1 has been associated with an increased risk of device-associated infection.[46] Alteration of the patient's skin flora, either as a result of antimicrobial therapy or by colonization with an epidemic strain carried on the hands of hospital personnel, is a common event preceding catheter site infection. In addition, certain therapeutic devices (e.g., semipermeable membrane dressings) may actually increase the cutaneous microbial burden surrounding the catheter insertion site.[47,48] Failure of hospital personnel to perform appropriate handwashing, particularly in the ICU setting, has been well documented.[49,50] Numerous epidemics of device-associated bacteremia have been linked to hospital personnel carrying an epidemic strain on their hands. Manipulating the system for repositioning, for obtaining a sample, or for any other reason increases the likelihood that the catheter may become contaminated.[51] This point has been best illustrated in studies of infectious complications associated with catheters used for total parenteral nutrition (TPN) (discussed later).

Several catheter characteristics or properties have been suggested to be associated with an increased risk for catheter-associated infection. Catheters that irritate the vascular intima and provoke thrombogenesis and catheters that are made of materials that are intrinsically thrombogenic are likely to be associated with an increased risk for device-associated infection.[52] Older studies suggest that stiff catheters

TABLE 300-1 Risk Factors for Device-Associated Bacteremia

Granulocytopenia
Immunosuppressive chemotherapy
Loss of skin integrity (e.g., burns, psoriasis)
Severity of underlying illness
Active infection at other site
Alteration in patient's cutaneous microflora
Failure of health care provider to wash hands
Contaminated ointment or cream
Catheter composition/construction
   Flexibility/stiffness
   Thrombogenicity
   Microbial adherence properties and biofilm production
Size of catheter
Number of catheter lumens
Catheter function/use
Catheter management strategies—number of entries into the system
Type of catheter (plastic > steel)
Location of catheter (central > peripheral[228]; jugular > femoral > subclavian[43,71,261]; lower extremity sites > upper extremity sites)
Type of placement (cutdown > percutaneous[126,137,228])
Duration of placement (at least 72 hr . less than 72 hr[27,126,166,228])*
Emergent placement > elective
Skill of venipuncturist (others > IV team[67,166])
Type/use of catheter (balloon-tipped, flow-directed > percutaneously placed central venous > implanted central venous)
Nursing staffing variables (nurse-to-patient ratio[73]; lower regular RN-to-patient ratio and higher float pool RN-to-patient ratio[72,258]

    *Although several studies support this precept, one recent study has questioned it.[128]

were associated with higher infection rates.[53] Such catheters are likely to be more mobile in the insertion tract and are thought to be more thrombogenic. A clear association has been established between the thrombogenicity of a catheter and the risk for device-associated infection.[54] Linder and co-workers confirmed these observations by demonstrating that flexible silicone elastomer and polyurethane catheters are less thrombogenic than polyvinyl chloride catheters.[55] Despite differences in thrombogenicity, some authorities believe that all catheters become coated with a fibrin sheath shortly after placement.[56] Currently, the majority of catheters are manufactured of antithrombogenic polyurethane.

Catheter composition may influence the risk for infection in another way. Sheth and co-workers have shown that certain microorganisms, most notably staphylococci, are able to adhere better to a catheter made from polyvinyl chloride than to a Teflon catheter.[57] Rotrosen and colleagues demonstrated increased adherence of *Candida* spp. to polyvinyl chloride catheters when compared with Teflon catheters.[58] In a rabbit model, silicon catheters are easier to infect with *Staphylococcus aureus* than are those made of polyurethane, Teflon, or polyvinyl chloride.[59] One might hypothesize that materials that facilitate microbial adherence may be associated with an increased risk for device-associated infection. Newer therapeutic interventions have focused on diminishing adherence to the catheter by a variety of different mechanisms.

The physical size of the catheter (and therefore the size of the defect in the skin's intrinsic host defenses) is also likely to be correlated with increased risk. Similarly, increasing the number of lumens in a catheter has been suggested to increase the risk for catheter-associated infections. Several studies have now suggested that the use of triple-lumen catheters is associated with an increased risk for catheter-associated infection when compared with single-lumen catheters.[60] Not all studies have found this difference.[61]

The presence of distant infection resulting in hematogenous seeding of the intravascular device has been incriminated in the pathogenesis of device-associated infection in some series.[40,62] Several factors may influence the risk for catheter seeding, including catheter composition, local thrombus formation at the catheter insertion site, intensity of bacteremia, the infecting pathogen, duration of catheterization, duration of bacteremia, and the patient's ability to mount an immunologic response

to the infection. Some microbes also are able to produce a biofilm, which allows the microbes to embed themselves in this layer and be somewhat protected from the antimicrobial agent activity.[63]

Finally, the manner in which the catheter is used may influence risk. For example, risks for infection with pulmonary artery catheters may be higher because of the manner in which these catheters are used.[64] In critically ill patients these catheters are used intensively: they are frequently repositioned to obtain accurate readings; they are used to obtain samples for the measurement of cardiac output; and they can be used to obtain mixed venous blood to measure oxygen and carbon dioxide tensions.

Catheter management, including both insertion and maintenance, also may influence risk for infection. Several studies[65,66] have shown that catheters placed by less experienced personnel are at increased risk for infection. Another study analyzed the efficacy of using a skilled team for the placement of peripheral intravenous catheters.[67] In this study, an intravenous therapy team significantly reduced both local and bacteremic complications associated with the placement of peripheral intravenous catheters, in part related to the timely replacement of the catheters. Two studies suggest that insertion of central venous catheters with less than maximal sterile barriers increases the risk of catheter-related infection.[43,68] Several studies have suggested that the number of times the system is entered also influences the risk for infection.[51,69,70] Insertion at a subclavian rather than a femoral site is clearly associated with a lesser risk of both infectious and thrombotic complications.[71] In addition to the factors outlined above, the risk of developing catheter-associated bacteremia is related to the patient and her or his intrinsic host defense mechanisms, as well as to factors related to the patient's hospital environment or therapy (see Table 300-1). The physician cannot alter most such patient-related factors; however, these data can be used when evaluating the risks associated with, the necessity for, and the duration of intravenous therapy.

In addition to patient-related risk factors, several hospital-related risk factors for catheter-acquired bacteremia have been either identified or proposed (see Table 300-1). In contraposition to the patient-related factors, such hospital-related factors can often be altered for patient benefit. Nurse staffing variables, including nurse-to-patient ratio, level of training, and permanent assignment to the unit ("float" nurse versus regular unit staff nurse) have been shown to affect bacteremia rates.[72,73]

MICROBIOLOGY

Staphylococci continue to predominate as the most frequently encountered pathogens in device-related infections. Although *S. aureus* is a frequent cause of device-associated infection, the coagulase-negative staphylococci have become the most common causes of these infections in the past two decades—especially in immunocompromised patients and those in whom long-term central venous access is required.[74,75]

Although there are some minor microbiologic differences among the devices or therapies under discussion, as a genus, staphylococci account for two thirds to 90% of the episodes of bacteremia associated with these devices.[4,76] Recent studies have suggested that coagulase-negative staphylococci may be able to adhere to plastic catheters more aggressively than can other organisms.[77] This property would result in a selective advantage for coagulase-negative staphylococci in causing device-associated infections.

Other commonly encountered isolates are listed in Table 300-2. Some institutions have observed a recent increase in catheter-associated infection caused by gram-negative bacilli.[78,79] The occurrence of some of the more unusual isolates (e.g., *Enterobacter* spp., *Burkholderia cepacia* complex, *Citrobacter freundii*) as a clear cause of the device-associated infection should at least suggest the possibility of a contaminated infusion product or of an aqueous environmental reservoir for these pathogens.[33,80-82]

Other organisms may cause such infections (e.g., *Flavobacterium, Acinetobacter* spp.); however, such organisms have been infrequently associated with either infusion-related or cannula-related infections.[13] Concomitant with the increasing empirical use of broad-spectrum

TABLE 300-2 Microbiology of Device-Associated Bacteremia

Coagulase-negative staphylococci including *Staphylococcus epidermidis**
Staphylococcus aureus
Enterococcus spp.
Serratia marcescens†
Candida albicans‡
Candida tropicalis‡
Pseudomonas aeruginosa§
Klebsiella spp.†
Enterobacter spp.†
Citrobacter freundii†
Corynebacterium (especially *C. jeikeium*)‖
Burkholderia cepacia complex§

*Most common pathogen for long-term lines; also associated with lipid infusions in neonates.

†Frequently associated with contaminated infusate.

‡Most often associated with total parenteral nutrition; usually along the catheter path, but occasionally as a result of contaminated infusate.

§May arise from a water source (e.g., infusate) or may reflect cutaneous colonization.

‖*C. jeikeium* bacteremia occurs almost exclusively in severely immunosuppressed patients who are or have been receiving broad-spectrum antibiotics and who have indwelling intravascular devices.

antimicrobials in severely immunosuppressed patients, cases of device-associated blood-stream infection caused by a variety of unusual bacterial and fungal pathogens have been reported with increasing frequency.[7,83-88]

DIAGNOSIS

Clinical detection of catheter-associated septicemia is sometimes difficult. Clinical markers show a poor correlation with intravenous device–related bacteremia.[89] The presence of fever has a high sensitivity for bacteremia but poor specificity, and local inflammation has better specificity but poor sensitivity. In addition to the presence of an indwelling intravascular device, several clinical features should alert the physician to the possibility of device-associated bacteremia. Salient features of device-associated sepsis that help distinguish it from other bacteremic syndromes are listed in Table 300-3. Generally, blood culture results positive for coagulase-negative staphylococci, *S. aureus,* or *Candida* spp., in the absence of any other identifiable source of infection, increase the possibility of intravenous device–related bacteremia.[89] Although none of these criteria specifically identifies the intravascular device as the source of sepsis, the presence of these clinical findings should at least raise the possibility of device-associated bacteremia.

Cultures of the catheter tip itself have been reported to be of variable value. Before the development of the semiquantitative culturing technique reported by Maki and colleagues,[90,91] most clinical microbi-

Local phlebitis, inflammation, or both at catheter insertion site
Lack of other source for bacteremia
Sepsis occurring in a patient not otherwise at high risk for bacteremia
Localized embolic disease distal to cannulated artery[93,217]
Hematogenous *Candida* endophthalmitis in patients receiving total parenteral nutrition[160,161]
Presence of ≥15 colonies of bacteria on semiquantitative culture of the catheter tip[90-92]
Sepsis apparently refractory to "appropriate" antimicrobial therapy
Resolution of febrile syndrome after device removal
Typical (*S. aureus, S. epidermidis,* or other coagulase-negative staphylococci) or unusual (*B. cepacia* complex, *Enterobacter agglomerans, E. cloacae*) microbiology
Clustered infections caused by infusion-related organisms

ology laboratories used broth culture of catheter tips to attempt to detect contaminated catheters. This technique yielded results that were highly variable and unreliable.[90-92]

Using the semiquantitative culture technique, which defines a positive catheter tip culture as yielding 15 or more colonies,[90,91] in combination with a relatively strict definition of catheter-associated sepsis, Maki and colleagues reported a specificity in short peripheral catheters ranging between 76% and 96% and a positive predictive value of a positive catheter tip culture ranging between 16%[91] and 31%[90] in four studies.[90,91,93,94] Data regarding the sensitivity of the semiquantitative culture technique are not available because the authors have incorporated having a positive catheter tip culture as part of their definition of both local catheter infection and catheter-acquired bacteremia.[90,91,93,95] The cutoff point of 15 colonies per catheter as a definition for "infection" appears to have been somewhat arbitrary in these studies. The authors noted that most infected catheters yield confluent growth when using the semiquantitative technique. These original studies from the late 1970s found that *S. aureus,* rather than coagulase-negative staphylococci, *Candida* spp., and *Enterococcus* spp., were the predominate microorganisms causing bacteremia, and short peripheral catheters (5.7 cm) or steel needles comprised most of the catheters studied. Given the current differences in microbiology and in intravascular devices now in use, these studies may be somewhat less relevant in the 21st century than they were 25 years ago.[96]

To culture a catheter using the semiquantitative technique, the point at which the catheter enters the skin should be marked, and the catheter should be removed aseptically. Sterile scissors (plastic catheters) or a sterile hemostat (steel needles) should be used to sever the catheter distal to the skin entry.

Several investigators have tried to modify Maki's technique to improve the predictability of the procedure. Cleri and co-workers reported a technique for quantitatively culturing catheters in broth.[97] This system, which is a bit more cumbersome for the laboratory to use, was considered by these authors to have three advantages over the system described by Maki and colleagues: (1) the ability to detect organisms within the lumen of the insert, (2) the ability to evaluate relative numbers of organisms from different catheter segments, and (3) the ability to compare relative numbers of organisms present in mixed infections.[97] Brun-Buisson and colleagues used a simplified quantitative broth dilution tip culture to evaluate catheters as potential sources for infection and found this technique to be 97.5% sensitive and 88% specific for the diagnosis of device-associated bacteremia, using a strict clinical definition of device-associated bacteremia.[98] Subsequently, Gutierrez and co-workers found a modified broth dilution technique to be only slightly more sensitive, but substantially more labor intensive, than the semiquantitative technique.[99] These latter authors advocated the use of semiquantitative cultures because of the ease with which this test is performed. Hnatiuk and co-workers demonstrated a substantial increase in sensitivity for the semiquantitative technique when the catheter-tip cultures are plated at the patient's bedside, rather than cutting the tip into a sterile tube and sending the tip to the laboratory for culture.[100]

Farr and his co-workers have conducted a meta analysis of catheter culturing techniques and have suggested that the accuracy increases for catheter segment cultures with increasing quantitation (i.e., qualitative < semiquantitative < quantitative).[92] The increase in accuracy is primarily due to the increased specificity of the more quantitative tests. They found that quantitative catheter segment culture was the only method associated with sensitivity and specificity above 90%.[92] Similarly, Sherertz and associates suggested that the common practice of culturing a single segment of a central vascular catheter is inadequate.[101]

Although the relative merits of these various procedures remain to be definitively delineated, the ease of performing the semiquantitative technique described by Maki and co-workers[90,91] has brought it into widespread clinical use.

Other investigators have suggested alternative techniques for diagnosing catheter-associated infections.[41,92,102-105] Cooper and Hopkins evaluated directly Gram staining the catheter segment and found this technique to be more rapid and at least as sensitive and specific as the semiquantitative culture.[41] Collignon and co-workers[102] advocated Gram staining of "impression smears" from the catheter, whereas Zuffrey and associates used direct acridine orange staining of the catheter.[104] Spencer and Kristinsson reported that the Gram stain technique failed to diagnose infection adequately.[106] Although some experience is being gained with the direct Gram stain, none of these newer techniques appears to be effective enough to supplant the semiquantitative method. Kite and co-workers suggested using an endoluminal brush method.[105] These authors suggested that the endoluminal brush method can be employed without sacrificing the intravascular line and argued that the procedure is substantially more sensitive and more specific than the semiquantitative technique.[105] Dobbins and colleagues reported that endoluminal catheter colonization is invariably present in cases of catheter-related bacteremia.[107] Some authors have recommended a combination of direct and microbiologic techniques.[92,102]

Mosca and co-workers emphasized the benefits of obtaining blood cultures by using the Isolator system, which allows for a quantitative estimate of microbial burden in the specimen.[108] Whereas several additional studies have underscored the usefulness of the Isolator system, one study has suggested that results obtained with traditional blood cultures may be complementary to those obtained with the Isolator system and that, whenever feasible, both approaches should be used.[109] Kaditis and colleagues argued that pediatric institutions should develop a standardized method of blood culture collection, suggesting that consistent volumes of blood be drawn for each sample and that a minimum of two cultures be obtained for each febrile episode.[110] Blot and colleagues suggested that the speed with which bacterial isolates can be detected in the microbiology laboratory may distinguish catheter-associated from non–catheter-associated infection.[111] Presumably because of a higher bacterial concentration, the blood cultures from patients with device-associated infections often demonstrate growth much more rapidly than those not associated with an intravascular device.[111] Another group has recently determined that this differential time to positivity (between cultures drawn through the catheter and peripherally) compares favorably with quantitative blood cultures for the diagnosis of device-related bacteremia.[112] This same differential time to positivity was examined in a group of cancer patients and was found not to be useful for many clinical presentations,[113] leaving the validity of this factor undetermined for clinical use.

Occasionally intracellular bacteria may be identified in routine differential blood smears. The finding of intracellular bacteria in such routine studies on a central venous catheter blood specimen often indicates active infection. In one study six such patients were asymptomatic at the time bacteria were detected on their differential blood smears; nonetheless, all six had blood cultures positive for coagulase-negative staphylococci.[114] The identification of intracellular bacteria on differential blood smears from patients who have vascular access devices should prompt consideration for catheter removal, even if the patient is asymptomatic.[114]

On the basis of currently available data, conclusions cannot be drawn regarding the relative merits of various blood culturing techniques in confirming the diagnosis of catheter-acquired sepsis. Several studies have recommended a differential comparison of quantitative cultures obtained peripherally and quantitative cultures obtained by drawing blood back through the putatively contaminated catheter to document the occurrence of catheter-acquired sepsis.[115-117] A study by Quilici and colleagues underscores the utility of obtaining "differential" blood cultures.[118] In their study differential cultures had an overall sensitivity of 92.8% and a specificity of 98.8%. In instances in which the catheters were removed because of suspected infection, the differential cultures exhibited a sensitivity of 92.8% and a specificity of 100%.[118] Because of the complexity of the epidemiology of device-associated bacteremia and the increased technical complexity of the differential blood culturing procedure, the broad applicability of these and the earlier findings nonetheless remains unclear.

The usefulness of "through-the-line" cultures has been questioned repeatedly, because these cultures may become contaminated easily.

Tonnesen and associates reported that blood drawn through venous or arterial catheters gave concordant results with cultures obtained by peripheral venipuncture in 92% of cases.[119] In 5% of cases, results of catheter "pull-back" cultures were considered to represent false positives (most were *S. epidermidis*), and in an additional 2%, catheter-drawn cultures were reported to be falsely negative.[119] Similar results were reported by Felices and co-workers,[120] who compared the results of cultures obtained by peripheral venipuncture with cultures obtained through central venous catheters. A subsequent study reported that rates of contamination for venipuncture versus cultures drawn through the catheter were not significantly different.[121] The incidence of false-positive drawback cultures may greatly depend on the type of intravenous device used to draw the cultures and the care taken in obtaining the specimen. If the details of the method used to obtain the culture are unknown, relying entirely on cultures obtained by drawing blood through an indwelling catheter may be imprudent. In well-defined circumstances in which device-associated bacteria is an important consideration in the patient's differential diagnosis, however, these cultures may provide valuable information.[97-99,108,109,115-117,122] As reported by DesJardin and colleagues, culture of blood drawn through either a central catheter or peripheral vein shows excellent negative predictive value.[123] Blood cultures drawn through a central catheter have a lower positive predictive value than do blood cultures drawn percutaneously, but drawing blood through a catheter may be an acceptable method for ruling out bacteremia. We recommend drawing at least two sets of blood cultures when device-related bacteremia is suspected, with at least one set drawn percutaneously.

Over the past 15 years molecular methods have begun to play an increasingly prominent role in the diagnostic microbiology laboratory. Linares and co-workers recently summarized the importance of molecular techniques in the laboratory.[24] Examples of the usefulness of these new techniques include the use of randomly amplified polymorphic DNA analysis for the rapid fingerprinting of coagulase-negative staphylococci[124]; the use of other molecular typing methods (e.g., pulsed-field electrophoresis, localization and/or probing the vicinity of the *mecA* gene)[24,125]; and the molecular identification of antimicrobial resistance even before speciation can be completed. These molecular techniques are particularly valuable in epidemiologic investigations.

DEVICE-SPECIFIC ISSUES

Peripheral Intravenous Cannulization

In general, peripheral catheters are associated with much lower infection risks than are central catheters. Steel needles have been associated with lower rates of local infections, bacteremic infections, and local phlebitis than have plastic catheters.[126] Tully and associates, however, demonstrated that steel catheters placed by an intravenous team nurse were associated with significantly less phlebitis but significantly more episodes of infiltration than were Teflon catheters.[127] In this study all catheters were removed in less than 72 hours; infection rates for both catheter types were extremely low, and there were no differences in local or systemic infection rates between the two groups.[127] More recently, Bregenzer and colleagues demonstrated that the risks for catheter-related complications—phlebitis, catheter-related infections, and mechanical complications—did not increase during extended (i.e., longer than 72 hours) catheterization.[128] These authors suggested that the CDC's recommendation for routine replacement of peripheral intravenous catheters be reevaluated, particularly considering the additional costs associated with routine catheter replacement, as well as the additional discomfort for the patient.[128] Lai showed similar rates of phlebitis in peripheral catheters left in place for 72 versus 96 hours.[129] Another, more recent, study has similarly demonstrated that prolonged duration of cannulation was not associated with increased risk for phlebitis.[130] The CDC now recommends that peripheral catheters be replaced every 72 to 96 hours in adults to prevent phlebitis.[2] Peripheral catheters should not be routinely replaced in children unless phlebitis or infiltration occurs.

The location of catheter placement also may influence subsequent infection rates. Catheters placed in the lower extremities, particularly those placed in the femoral veins, are associated with increased risk for many complications, including infection.[126,127,131-135] Martin and co-workers evaluated axillary vein cannulation as an alternative to the internal jugular insertion site and found that the rates of catheter-related infection and other complications were similar to those observed after internal jugular vein catheterization.[136]

Catheters placed percutaneously are associated with lower infection rates than are those placed by cutdown.[126,137] Catheters placed emergently are also at higher risk for infection, presumably as a result of breaks in technique at the time of placement. Several authors have suggested that catheters placed by members of an intravenous therapy team are associated with lower complication rates than are those placed by other health care professionals.[67]

Techniques for the placement and care of indwelling venous cannulas have been reviewed in detail.[126] Several aspects of catheter maintenance and care have been controversial, although more definitive studies have answered some questions. These issues are discussed further in the section on "Prevention of Device-Associated Bacteremia."

Finally, two studies have demonstrated that routinely changing intravenous administration sets at 48 rather than 24 hours was not associated with a significant increase in the infusion-related bacteremia rate.[138,139] Snydman and co-workers[140] and Maki and colleagues[141] compared the relative safety of changing administration sets at 72-hour intervals with changing them at 48 hours. Neither study identified an increased risk with the 72-hour interval.

Thus inserting a peripheral catheter, dressing it, hooking up the administration set, and changing all three at 72- to 96-hour intervals now seems both safe and practical and reasonable.

Central Venous Catheters—Short-Term and Total Parenteral Nutrition Issues

Because central venous catheters frequently remain in place longer than peripheral catheters, certain problems either occur with more frequency or are unique to these catheters. In addition, because of the placement of these catheters in the great veins, complications of placement such as infective endocarditis and suppurative thrombophlebitis of the great veins represent life-threatening events.

Michel and colleagues studied 390 catheters placed into the subclavian vein by identical technique, in an attempt to determine risk factors associated with microbial colonization.[142] In this study, the presence of distant infection, bacteremia, or tracheostomy was associated with an increased risk for catheter colonization.[142] Unfortunately, these authors chose to culture the catheters by using the broth culture technique, which yields notoriously unreliable results.[126]

The presence of either intraluminal or extraluminal fibrin has been proposed as predisposing to the development of catheter-associated infection.[54-56,143-146] Stillman and colleagues studied 94 central catheters and found that all 11 catheters categorized as infected in their study and 30 out of 83 not found to be either infected or colonized had gross visible evidence of either intraluminal or surface thrombin at the time of removal.[54] Lloyd and co-workers failed to find a deleterious effect associated with the so-called fibrin sheath when evaluating a rat model of device-associated bacteremia.[147]

Based on three studies, the CDC has recommended against routine replacement of central venous catheters, PICCs, hemodialysis catheters, or pulmonary artery catheters to prevent catheter-related infections. The issue of whether central catheters should be changed over a guide wire remains controversial. Although the guide wire technique is commonly used, little scientific evidence supports its use if catheter-associated infection is suspected. Maher and colleagues used this technique successfully for catheter exchange in situations assessed as "low risk for infection."[148] Two additional studies suggest that guide wire exchange may not be particularly useful if device-associated infection is suspected.[149,150] Use of a guide wire obviates the need for a second percutaneous puncture of the great veins and may be preferable for catheter exchanges judged routine or mandated by some reason other

than suspected infection. In one of the two recently published studies, guide wire catheter exchange was associated with an increased risk of blood-stream infection but a lower risk of mechanical complications.[150] In one experimental study, replacement of a biofilm-colonized central venous catheter over a guide wire was associated with an increased risk for colonization of the new catheter, as well as an increased risk for production of detached, slime-enclosed, antibiotic-resistant aggregates that may disseminate the infection to other sites.[117]

Whereas guide wire exchange of central venous catheters may be associated with a greater risk for catheter-related infection, this technique may result in many fewer mechanical complications than would be the case for repuncture.[151] Specifically, exchange over a guide wire is associated with lower risks for some complications (e.g., bleeding, pneumothorax).[149,150] If a guide wire is to be used for catheter exchange, culture of the removed or "old" catheter tip should be performed. In addition, blood cultures should be drawn through the "old" line before removal. If either of these cultures becomes positive, the most conservative approach would be to remove the "replacement" catheter and perform appropriate cultures. If central access is still desired, a third catheter should be placed at a new puncture site. In situations in which the catheter is being removed for suspected sepsis, in our opinion, exchange over a guide wire should not be attempted. Conversely, one recent study suggested a possible benefit of guide wire exchange for patients who have catheter-associated candidemia.[152]

The umbilical vein catheter that is commonly used for vascular access in neonates presents some unique problems. Because of the extensive microbiologic flora of the umbilical stump, these catheters are at high risk for both colonization and infection.[153,154] Although high rates of umbilical catheter–associated infection have been reported in several studies,[153,154] not all centers report such high rates.[155] One study has reported a much lower incidence of infectious complications when the umbilical artery (rather than the umbilical vein) was cannulated for infusion.[156]

Thrombosis of the great veins, with the attendant risk for suppurative thrombophlebitis, is a major complication of central catheter placement.[134] Thrombosis occurs with increased frequency in patients with malignancies[133] (particularly those who have mediastinal lymphadenopathy) and in patients with sickle cell disease.[157] In instances in which central catheters are placed in patients with these underlying illness, thrombotic and infectious complications should be anticipated, prevented (when possible), diagnosed early, and treated aggressively.

Additional issues relating to catheter composition and effectiveness of subcutaneous tunneling of catheters and risks associated with electronic monitoring devices are discussed in the sections below.

Several aspects of the delivery of TPN separate this mode of intravascular therapy from others. First, the composition of the infusate supports the growth of different microorganisms, most notably certain of the *Candida* spp.[15,16] Second, TPN catheters are often required to remain in place much longer than either peripheral or other central venous cannulas. For this reason, problems with catheter contamination become much more of a concern. Third, the hypertonicity of the solution tends to cause thrombosis, which may result in an increased risk of infection. Fourth, because patients who require TPN are frequently severely ill as a result of neoplasms, trauma, or inflammatory bowel disease, the risk for bacteremia is higher. Therefore, the potential for hematogenous seeding of the catheter is high.

For these and other reasons, the placement, management, and care of catheters used for TPN have received a great deal of attention. Ryan and colleagues, in a prospective study of 200 catheters, documented that the risk of catheter-associated infection increased significantly when the integrity of the delivery system was interrupted.[70] Snydman and colleagues subsequently found that the occurrence of so-called line violations was highly associated with the development of TPN catheter-associated sepsis.[69] For these reasons the CDC has recommended that the administration of TPN be supervised and conducted by members of a team (Table 300-4).[158] In their study, Snydman and colleagues also attempted to correlate the results of twice-weekly 1-mL pour-plate blood cultures with the subsequent de-

TABLE 300-4 Prevention of Infusion-Related Infection in Total Parenteral Nutrition (TPN)

Administration of TPN should be under the supervision of a team of health care professionals (usually a nurse, pharmacist, and physician). Both the decision as to appropriateness of TPN therapy and protocols for insertions, maintenance, and delivery of TPN should be under the responsibility of this team.

TPN solution should be prepared using sterile or aseptic technique when possible in a laminar flow-hood. Once prepared, the solution should be infused immediately or stored at 4°C.

Placement of the catheter should be performed by using sterile technique including, at a minimum, mask, gloves, full drape, and appropriate skin preparation (preferably with chlorhexidine[230,260,262] or 1% iodine).

Once placed, the catheter should be anchored to avoid movement, which may result in local irritation of the insertion site or transport of organisms along the insertion path.

If possible the system should be kept closed, avoiding unnecessary entry for blood drawing and administration of other fluids or blood products via the TPN line

If multiple lumens/ports are present, one lumen/port should be designated as the parenteral nutrition site.

Other aspects of TPN administration are either of empirical or theoretic value, have shown equivocal or borderline results in studies, have shown conflicting results in studies, or have been demonstrated to be of value in small studies. Definitive studies to document the merit of these techniques are needed before they are routinely implemented; they include the following:

- Routine application of antiseptic cream at the site of catheter insertion (either at the time of venipuncture or at routine dressing change)
- Routine dressing changes, skin defatting with acetone, and skin preparation with antiseptics[230,260,262]
- Routine use of semipermeable dressing materials (A meta-analysis of data from several studies suggests that these dressings may actually play a detrimental role in catheter infections[234])
- Routine use of in-line membrane filters (no benefit demonstrated)
- Use of silicone or other less traumatic, nonthrombogenic catheters; use of heparin-bonded catheters; use of low-dose heparin infusions
- Tunneling the catheter subcutaneously to increase the anatomic distance between catheter insertion site and the point at which the catheter enters the vessel (appears to be useful in several small studies)
- Routine use of antibiotic lock prophylaxis with heparin plus vancomycin

Modified from Goldman D, Maki D. Infection control in total parenteral nutrition. JAMA. 1973;223:1360–1364.

velopment of catheter colonization and sepsis. Similar to the previously cited studies,[119,120] although concordance was high among blood cultures, catheter tip cultures, and peripheral blood cultures, cultures obtained through the TPN catheter demonstrated a reasonably high incidence of false positivity, primarily as a result of *S. epidermidis* contamination.[159]

Candida infection has been a particular problem in patients receiving TPN.[160-162] Curry and Quie reported a 16% incidence of candidemia among patients receiving TPN in a prospective study in a hospital that did not have a TPN team.[162] In another prospective study of 131 postoperative patients who were receiving TPN, 13 patients were detected as developing chorioretinal lesions consistent with hematogenous *Candida* endophthalmitis; 7 of the patients had positive blood cultures for *Candida*.[161] Although most of these infections are presumed to arise as a result of yeast contamination at the catheter entry site, occasional outbreaks of *Candida* infection resulting from a TPN solution that was intrinsically contaminated have been reported.[20,21] Because of the risk of intrinsic as well as in-use contamination of TPN solutions with *Candida* or other microorganisms, some authorities have recommended the routine use of an in-line membrane filter to prevent infusion-related sepsis.[163] Such filters have been implicated as a cause of device-associated infection or

device-associated endotoxemia; however, the risk-to-benefit ratio for their use has not been established.

Because the TPN catheter frequently must be left in place for an extended period of time and because of the increased thrombogenicity of the TPN fluid, several modifications of the delivery system of the catheter itself have been advocated. Among the suggested mechanisms for decreasing infections in TPN are (1) either bonding heparin or a heparin-like substance to the catheter or infusing heparin with the infusate in an attempt to minimize fibrin sheath formation[145,164]; (2) constructing the catheter of a more flexible substance, thereby producing less trauma to the vascular endothelium[165]; and (3) tunneling the catheter under the skin in an attempt to decrease access of pathogens to the circulation.[165]

A final and often difficult issue is deciding when to remove a TPN catheter for suspected sepsis. In the past, most authorities recommended the removal of a TPN line whenever infection was suspected. In separate studies, Ryan and co-workers[70] and Maher and associates[148] suggested that nearly 70% of catheters removed for suspected sepsis are apparently removed unnecessarily. Thus the TPN team is often faced with the dilemma of whether or not to remove the catheter from a patient in whom the evidence for infection is equivocal. Such a patient may have many reasons for fever; therefore, the diagnosis of infection may be difficult. Often patients are severely immunosuppressed, thrombocytopenic, or both, and the risks associated with catheter replacement may be quite high. Several clinical features may help the physician decide how to manage the catheter.[146,166] The presence of positive blood cultures (particularly for *Candida* or coagulase-negative staphylococci) in the absence of another source for the infection or in the presence of hemodynamic instability, embolic phenomena, leukocytosis, or profound leukopenia may herald the onset of catheter-associated sepsis. In addition, the development of new glucose intolerance in a TPN patient whose carbohydrate metabolism had been previously well regulated may be an early subtle sign of bacteremia.[146,161]

Central Venous Catheters—Long-Term Issues

In 1973, Broviac and colleagues reported their initial experience with the use of a chronic indwelling right atrial catheter for the delivery of long-term parenteral nutrition.[167] Since this initial report, modifications of the catheter system have been published, and the situation in which these catheters have been used has broadened considerably. Initial reports suggested that the rate of catheter infection in non-neutropenic patients was approximately one infection per 5.5 patient years.[168] Venous access has long been a problem for patients receiving chemotherapy for malignancy. Hickman and colleagues modified the Broviac catheter for use in patients undergoing bone marrow transplantation.[169] This catheter can be used for the administration of intensive chemotherapy, the administration of other medicines and fluids, transfusion, and phlebotomy. These catheters spare the patient both physical and psychological trauma. In the ensuing years a number of additional modifications of these catheters have been devised. These modified catheters and implanted infusion ports represent a major step forward in the management of all patients who require long-term central venous access but have been especially useful in the management of immunosuppressed patients and particularly in immunosuppressed children in whom venous access is frequently problematic. Use of these devices in a variety of clinical settings has become the standard of care over the past 20 years.

Several centers have reported their experiences using these catheters, and many series report remarkably low rates of infection. Press and colleagues summarized 1088 catheter placements from 18 studies in their literature review. In their summary data, these authors reported approximately 0.14 infections per 100 catheter days.[170] Table 300-5 presents a similar summary, including several published studies evaluating infection and bacteremia risks associated with the use of implanted catheters and infusion ports.[75,171-186] The slightly elevated rate of all infections (0.15 infections for each 100 catheter days), as well as the elevated risk for bacteremia (0.11 infections for each 100

TABLE 300-5 Infectious Complications Associated with Implanted Catheters in Immunosuppressed Patients

Authors	Number of Patients	Type of Catheter	Exit Site/ Tunnel Infections (%)	Catheter- Associated Bacteremia (%)	Duration of Catheterization (Range)	Infections per 100 Catheter Days	Bacteremias per 100 Catheter Days
Blacklock et al.[168]	25	H	14 (56)	2 (8)	70 (5–256)	0.91	0.11
Larson et al.[179]	34	H	4 (11.8)	4 (11.8)	110.3 (3–355)	0.23	0.12
Wade et al.[75]	51	H	5 (9.8)	3 (5.9)	91 (4–457)	0.17	0.06
Rizzari et al.[184]	125	H/B	3 (2.4)	106 (85)	134 (6–488)	0.53	0.51
Viscoli et al.[182]	145	B	6 (4.1)	57 (39)	171 (2–647)	0.26	0.19
Hogan and Pulito[175]	84	B	6 (7.1)	9 (10.7)	33.4 (2–119)	0.39	0.29
Alurkar et al.[174]	91	H/B	6 (6.6)	31 (34)	74.6 (NG)	0.54	0.41
Wacker et al.[183]	44	B	NG	15 (34)	236 (15–806)	NG	0.06
	33	P	NG	6 (18)	316 (12–1294)	NG	0.10
Johnson et al.[177]	64	B	25 (39)	33 (51.6)	251 (NG)	0.28	0.19
Lokich et al.[171]	92	P	6 (6.5)	2 (2.2)	127 (7–450)	0.06	0.02
Shulman et al.[180]	31	P	1 (3.2)	4 (12.9)	232 (14–607)	0.07	0.05
Cairo et al.[172]	46	H/B	14 (30)	23 (50)	163 (9–365)	0.48	0.30
Hockenberry et al.[176]	82	P	8 (10)	4 (4.9)	168 (7–1030)	0.06	0.02
van Hoff et al.[263]	59	H/B	7 (12)	30 (51)	220 (NG)	0.28	0.23
Ulz et al.[181]	111	H/B	3 (2.7)	63 (57)	81 (1–167)	0.69	0.66
Kappers-Klunne et al.[178]	23	H	0 (0)	19 (83)	166 (10–605)	0.50	0.50
	20	P	2 (10)	9 (45)	164 (1–971)	0.33	0.27
Ross et al.[173]	39	H/B	11 (28)	4 (10)	365 (30–426)	0.13	0.03
	49	P	7 (14)	0 (0)	350 (7–395)	0.07	0.00
Biffi et al.[264]	175	P	1 (0.6)	4 (2.2)	180 (4–559)	0.02	0.003
Elishoov et al.[186]	242	H/B	28 (12)	46 (19)	40 (7–187)	0.79	0.52
Schwarz et al.[265]	680	P	31	31	310 (2–1960)	0.02	0.01
Chang et al.[266]	572	P	11 (1.9)	21 (3.7)	358 (1–1742)	0.015	0.01
Subtotal (by Catheter Type)	**1183**	**H/B**	**132 (11)**	**445 (38)**	**147 (1–806)**	**0.40**	**0.26**
	1734	P	67 (3.9)	81 (4.7)	231 (1–1960)	0.12	0.08
Total	**2917**	**–**	**199 (6.8)**	**526 (18.0)**	**147 (1–1960)**	**0.15**	**0.11**

B, Broviac; H, Hickman; NG, not given; P, totally implantable port (e.g., Port-A-Cath, Infus-A-Port, Mediport).

catheter days), may be more of a reflection of the severity of the patients' illnesses, the increasing immunosuppression associated with their therapies, and the increasingly invasive care provided to critically ill patients. The differences noted between implanted ports and Hickman/Broviac catheters may also be a reflection of the populations being treated.

Recently, the use of PICC lines for long-term access has increased dramatically.[187-189] These catheters have several advantages over some of the other long-term access devices: PICCs may be inserted at the bedside,[187] they are placed into children under fluoroscopy with relative ease,[188] they are useful for administration of chemotherapy and/or antimicrobial agents,[188] and they are effective in the administration of TPN,[188-190] particularly in pediatric patients requiring long-term nutritional support.[189,190] Skilled interventional radiology is needed for difficult insertions, for catheter salvage, and to make certain that the catheter is not misplaced or misdirected.[187] A major problem is device failure, with as many as 10% of these catheters developing mechanical malfunction.[190] At least one group has suggested that PICC lines may be less cost-effective than currently believed because of the more difficult insertion into some patients and higher thrombophlebitis rates.[191] Several institutions, including ours, have elected to develop a skilled team approach to the insertion and management of these catheters.

Intraluminal contamination may represent the most important route of infection for implanted catheters and ports, further suggesting that strategies aimed at decreasing the risks for intraluminal contamination could substantially lower infection rates with these types of intravascular devices.

Several issues regarding the care and maintenance of these catheters remain unsettled. Among these issues are (1) whether a dressing should be placed over the exit site (and if so, what dressing materials should be used and how frequently should the dressing be changed); (2) whether the system should be routinely flushed (and if so, how frequently and with what); (3) whether blood cultures obtained through the catheter are reliable indicators of catheter contamination; and (4) what are the indications for catheter removal, and can

either or both local infection and bacteremia be treated with the catheter in place?

Although definitive answers to these questions remain elusive, at the Warren G. Magnuson Clinical Center of the National Institutes of Health, a sterile dry gauze dressing or a semipermeable membrane is kept in place over the exit site. These dressings are changed at least twice weekly. We also use an every-other-day heparin flush (5 mL of 100 units/mL) to attempt to keep the catheters open. Higher concentrations run the risk of anticoagulating the patient. The CDC guidelines suggest that well-healed exit sites might not require dressings.[2]

The issue of pull-back blood cultures was discussed earlier. Repeated isolation of the same organism from cultures drawn through the catheter indicates a need for therapy. Individual positive cultures and sporadic positive cultures are difficult to interpret in the absence of clinical or laboratory correlates. As noted above, some workers believe that quantitative cultures may prove particularly helpful in establishing a diagnosis in this setting.

The problem of how best to treat an infection in a patient with a long-term venous access catheter in place is a difficult one. Hiemenz and colleagues reported success in treating 90% of proven bacteremias while leaving the catheter in place.[192] Some organisms (e.g., Bacillus spp., Candida spp.) may be difficult to eradicate,[193] although Hartman and Shuchat had some success in treating Candida infections.[194] Guidelines for managing these infections have been published jointly by the Infectious Diseases Society of America, the Society of Critical Care Medicine, and the Society for Hospital Epidemiology of America.[89] Several studies have advocated the use of thrombolytic agents (e.g., urokinase) in combination with appropriate antimicrobials to treat both thrombosis and infections associated with implanted catheters.[144,195] These studies suggest that eradicating the fibrin sheath that forms around the catheter may make therapy of a catheter-associated infection much more likely to succeed. Benoit and colleagues have suggested that intraluminal treatment of infections of subcutaneously tunneled central venous catheters can be effective against selected bacterial infections.[196] These investigators also found that intraluminal therapy also may suppress, but not eradicate, Candida infections in tunneled catheters.[196] Raad and colleagues treated three patients with recurrent vascular catheter–related bacteremia by allowing a solution of minocycline and ethylenediaminetetraacetate (EDTA) to dwell in the lumen of the indwelling catheter or by coating polyurethane catheters with minocycline/EDTA and flushing the lumen with this solution.[197] Similarly, McCarthy and co-workers successfully treated gram-positive catheter infections by instilling teicoplanin daily into "infected" central catheters for 4 to 9 days and allowing the drug to dwell in the lumen of the catheter.[198] Finally, Lai reported that catheter-associated bacteremia caused by vancomycin-resistant enterococcus can be treated effectively by line removal alone.[129] Thus additional experience has suggested that, perhaps with the exception of true tunnel infections, many, if not most, infections of indwelling central catheters may be amenable to therapy with the device left in place. Patients should be carefully evaluated for evidence of complicated device-related infections, including tunnel infection, port abscess, septic thrombosis, endocarditis, and osteomyelitis. The device/catheter should be removed for any of these conditions.

Several centers have reported remarkable success—few infections and few other complications as well—with totally implantable access devices.[199-202] In one of the earliest of these studies, the rate of infections for each 100 catheter days was 0.43—comparable to other implantable catheters.[200] Subsequent studies have demonstrated even lower infection risks.[171,173,176,178,180,183,201,202] One epidemiologic study found in multiple logistic regression analysis that the only factor associated with risk for infection of these devices was the number of times the system was entered.[203]

Use of catheters placed for long-term central venous access has also fostered some new kinds of complications. For example, use of these catheters has been associated the fortunately rare complication of septic thrombosis of the atrium.[204]

Recently, long-term central venous access devices have been used for pheresis for stem cell harvesting.[205,206] Contrasted with the reasonably benign experience using "short-term" catheters,[207] more infectious, mechanical, and thrombotic complications than were anticipated occurred in two of these studies.[205,206] In one study the investigators suggested that complications associated with using implanted catheters for pheresis for stem cell harvest might be reduced by proper placement of the catheter closer to the right atrial–superior vena cava junction.[205] In the other study a central catheter infection rate nearly four times higher than the overall rate was identified in bone marrow transplant patients whose central catheters were used for stem cell harvests.[206]

Pulmonary Artery Catheters

The use of indwelling, balloon-tipped pulmonary artery catheters[208] has revolutionized the management of hemodynamically unstable, critically ill patients. The placement of such a catheter in one of the great veins, across the tricuspid and pulmonic valves, and into the pulmonary vasculature is not without complications, however. Michel and co-workers demonstrated that 29 of 153 pulmonary artery catheter tips produced microbial growth in thioglycolate broth.[209] Although no patient in this study was considered to develop sepsis secondary to the contaminated catheter, other studies have suggested a reasonably high rate of contamination with occasional episodes of catheter-related sepsis and nosocomial endocarditis.[210] The majority of these catheters are heparin bonded, which reduces catheter thrombosis and microbial adherence to the catheter.

Katz and colleagues retrospectively studied complications associated with the placement of 392 balloon-tipped catheters; of these, 17 (4.2%) were assessed to be associated with bacteremia.[210] Maki estimated that 3% to 5% of these catheters kept in place for more than 72 hours will result in bacteremia.[166] One recent study has evaluated the complications associated with the use of a new, "hands-off" pulmonary artery catheter that is completely shielded during balloon testing, preparation, and insertion.[211] Use of this catheter was associated with a substantial reduction in systemic infections related to the catheter.[211]

Another problem relatively unique to the flow-directed, balloon-tipped pulmonary artery catheter is that such catheters may traumatize the right-sided heart valves and the right-sided endocardium. In a study of 102 consecutive autopsies of patients who died in the hospital, 26 (25.5%) had had an indwelling intracardiac catheter inserted before death.[212] Six of these patients were excluded from analysis (four patients died 48 hours or less after catheter placement; two patients had permanent transvenous pacemakers in place for many years with the anticipated endocardial fibrosis). Of the remaining 20 patients, 6 had vegetations present, and 88% of the patients had some evidence of intracardiac damage.[212] One patient had infective endocarditis on the tricuspid valve. Other studies have reported slightly lower but significant incidences of right-sided heart vegetations among monitored patients coming to autopsy.[213] Greene and colleagues noted a 10-fold increase in the incidence of valvular vegetations when they compared a period of time before the introduction of balloon-tipped pulmonary artery catheters with a time in which the catheters were in wide use.[213] Severely burned patients may be at even higher risk for this complication.[214] Nosocomial endocarditis is increasing in frequency; in one recent study 9.3% of cases of endocarditis diagnosed in a referral hospital were both nosocomial in origin and unrelated to prior cardiac surgery.[215]

No prospective study has addressed risk factors associated with infection of these catheters, nor have studies assessed the efficacy of devices designed to decrease the risk of catheter-associated infection (e.g., leaving the introducer sheath in the vein to protect the catheter).[209] Changing these catheters over a guide wire may present a major risk factor for infection. A study in cardiac surgery patients found that greater than 4 days of catheterization was the single variable associated with increased risk of pulmonary artery catheter colonization.[216] CDC guidelines currently recommend that pulmonary artery catheters need not be changed more frequently than every 7 days.[2] Infection risks associated with other aspects of monitoring equipment (e.g., transducer domes, heparin flush solution) are discussed below.

Arterial Lines, Transducers, and Transducer Domes

The widespread use of arterial lines for blood pressure monitoring or for obtaining arterial samples for blood gas determinations has yielded yet another source of device-associated infection. In addition, the technical electronic equipment used for hemodynamic monitoring—transducers and their associated paraphernalia—has also been cited as a source of device-associated infection.

Stamm and colleagues reported an outbreak of *Flavobacterium* bacteremia among monitored patients in an ICU.[13] Ultimately, these organisms were cultured from in-use radial artery catheters, from stopcocks, and from ice used to cool syringes for blood gas determinations.[13] Adams and colleagues reported a series of 147 radial artery cannulations in infants in whom umbilical artery cannulation failed.[217] In this series there were two episodes of catheter-related sepsis. Band and Maki used the semiquantitative catheter tip culture technique to study 130 arterial catheters in 95 patients.[93] In their series 23 catheters were classified as showing "local infection" (e.g., >15 colonies per semiquantitative culture), and there were five episodes of sepsis.[93] Factors associated with increased risk for infection were (1) duration of catheterization (especially longer than 96 hours), (2) placement by cutdown rather than percutaneously, and (3) clinical signs of local inflammation.

Maki and Hassemer reported a prospective study designed to assess the endemic rate of bacteremia associated with arterial monitoring.[218] Transducer chamber fluid was demonstrated to be contaminated in nearly 12% of the cases. There were eight cases of bacteremia—four definitely related and four possibly related to the extrinsic contamination.[218] Maki also suggested an increased risk for infection of arterial catheters associated with replacing the catheter using a guide wire.

Several epidemics of infection resulting from improper sterilization of reusable transducer domes have been reported.[138,219] However,

TABLE 300-6 Prevention of Infection Associated with Hemodynamic Monitoring

Place arterial lines, central venous lines, and flow-directed, balloon-tipped catheters by using sterile technique. Mask and sterile gloves should be worn at a minimum. The skin should be prepared with an effective antiseptic solution (e.g., 1% iodine in alcohol, or chlorhexidine[230,260,262]).

Place the catheters percutaneously and anchor well to avoid catheter movement. Dress the insertion site appropriately.

Use heparinized saline (not dextrose-containing solutions or parenteral nutrition) for continuous-flush solutions.

Do not reuse transducer domes; sterilize reusable part of transducer setup according to manufacturer's instructions between patients.

Replace transducers, tubing, and continuous-flow devices every 96 hours[2,267]; do not routinely replace peripheral arterial catheters to prevent infection.

Use sterile fluid to fill the chamber dome; use aseptic technique in the assembly.

Avoid placing unnecessary junctions or stopcocks into the apparatus; minimize manipulation of the system.

Whenever possible, avoid exchanging arterial catheters over guide wires; use of guide wire exchange technique for arterial catheters is associated with increased infection risk.

with the introduction of disposable transducer domes, one might assume that these problems would be overcome. Buxton and colleagues reported an epidemic of *Enterobacter* infections that was associated with the contamination of disposable transducer domes during their initial setup.[138] The chambers and domes were apparently contaminated by the hands of hospital personnel who had handled heavily contaminated transducer heads.[138] West and colleagues also reported *Serratia* sepsis resulting from transducer dome cracks.[220] In this study supposedly disposable transducer domes were being resterilized, with resultant cracks or breaks in the dome membrane.[220]

Another potential reservoir for nosocomial bacteremia is the heparin flush solution used to irrigate certain intravascular devices continually. This fluid has been implicated as a reservoir for outbreaks of device-associated bacteremia in several instances.[33]

Several authors have made recommendations regarding the prevention of infection associated with intravascular monitoring devices.[2,93,218,219] A summary of these recommendations is presented in Table 300-6.

PREVENTION OF DEVICE-ASSOCIATED BACTEREMIA

Several techniques may be used to prevent device-associated bacteremia.[221] Several additional points should be emphasized. First, a systematic approach to this issue, including the development of a standard approach, is likely to be beneficial. For central catheters, TPN administration, and PICC line insertion and management, the development of a multidisciplinary team approach has been advantageous.[158]

General Issues, including Hand Hygiene and Barrier Use

Emphasis should be placed on attention to detail, including hand-washing[49,50]; adherence to guidelines for catheter insertion and maintenance; appropriate use of antiseptic solutions, such as chlorhexidine or iodine solution, to prepare the skin around the catheter insertion site; use of sterile technique for central catheter insertion[68]; optimal management of the insertion site; limitations of entry into the system[203]; careful management of the administration set and the catheter itself; the maintenance of a high index of suspicion for infectious complications; and, once both safety and efficacy have been appropriately established, the application of new technologies. One example of a technological improvement based in science is the recently marketed modified catheter hub. Segura and co-workers reported that this modified catheter hub reduced the risk for endoluminal bacterial colonization and catheter-related sepsis in subclavian lines that were

left in place for a mean of 2 weeks.[25] Others have reported similar success using modified catheter hubs.[23,222-224]

Cutaneous Antisepsis and Topical Anti-Infectives

Use of topical antibiotic or antiseptic ointments at the insertion site of catheters is currently not recommended by U.S. authorities.[2,225] Several studies examining the use of povidone-iodine ointment have produced conflicting results. Results of topical mupirocin use have been more promising,[226] but mupirocin resistance has been documented.[227] Additionally, ointments without fungicidal activity have been associated with increased rates of catheter colonization with *Candida* spp.[42] The clinical utility of these ointments is questionable, and we do not recommend their routine use. Rhame and colleagues reviewed the composite experience of six different studies that were designed to address this issue.[228] In five of these studies, there were no differences between topical antimicrobial agents and placebo. In the smallest series in this review (a study of 78 catheter insertions), there were three infections in the placebo group and none in the therapy group.[228] Maki and Band[229] prospectively studied the following three regimens of catheter care: (1) application of polymyxin-neomycin-bacitracin ointment at insertion and every 48 hours, (2) application of iodophor ointment at insertion and every 48 hours, or (3) no ointment. In their study of 827 random catheter insertions, there were no differences in either catheter-acquired sepsis (two cases in each group) or local inflammation (38.9% vs. 41.9% vs. 41.7% percent, respectively). The only difference noted was in semiquantitative cultures of catheter tips.[229] In the polymyxin-neomycin-bacitracin ointment group there were 6 positive cultures, in the iodophor group there were 10, and in the control group there were 18. This difference was greatest in catheters that were left in place for over 4 days. Thus information regarding the efficacy of these antimicrobial ointments or creams for intravascular cannulas is contradictory and confusing, and the clinical utility of these compounds remains questionable.

Techniques used for skin preparation, prior to catheter insertion, appear to influence the risk for infection. In one study skin preparation and decontamination with 0.5% chlorhexidine gluconate in 70% isopropyl alcohol was more effective than 10% povidone-iodine in preventing colonization of peripheral catheters in neonates.[230] Chlorhexidine-containing antiseptics have been shown to be effective in diminishing rates of catheter colonization, and have shown varying efficacy in reducing intravenous device–related bacteremias.[231] A meta-analysis determined that chlorhexidine gluconate significantly reduces the incidence of bacteremia in patients with central venous catheters compared to povidone-iodine for insertion-site skin disinfection.[232] However, the cost-effectiveness of chlorhexidine has not yet been determined, and hypersensitivity reactions to chlorhexidine have been reported. The CDC guidelines recommend disinfecting skin before catheter insertion and during dressing changes using tincture of iodine and iodophors, 70% alcohol, or preferably, a 2% chlorhexidine-based preparation.[2] Whereas chlorhexidine may eventually be proven to be superior in reducing intravenous device–related bacteremias, we believe current evidence does not support exclusive use of chlorhexidine.

The use of in-line membrane filters has also been advocated as a mechanism for reducing the incidence of catheter-acquired infection.[163] Because, as was pointed out earlier, the major points of entry are the skin insertion site and the catheter hub, one might suspect that such devices would be of limited usefulness in preventing most catheter-acquired septicemias. No investigators have recommended the routine inclusion of such filters in all intravenous setups, nor has any study demonstrated conclusive evidence that the routine use of such filters results in a lowering of the infusion-related bacteremia rate.

In isolated situations (e.g., if particulate matter is present in the infusate, if the solution must hang for an extended period of time, or perhaps in a situation in which an infusate such as TPN solution supports the growth of microorganisms extremely well), the addition of these filters to the system is of theoretical value. However, even in cases in which the infusion fluid is contaminated, organisms trapped on the filter may shed endotoxins into the patient's circulation.[233]

Catheter Site Dressings

Authorities have recommended placing a sterile dressing over the catheter entry site,[2,126,228] and others have made recommendations for the routine care (usually on a daily or every-other-day basis) of the entry site. Maki and Ringer compared the efficacy of sterile, dry gauze dressings with two semipermeable membrane dressings, one of which was impregnated with an iodophor.[27] No difference was seen among the four groups: (1) gauze changed every 48 hours, (2) gauze left in place for the life of the catheter, (3) transparent membrane left in place for the life of the catheter, and (4) iodophor membrane left on for the life of the catheter. Hoffmann and co-workers performed a meta-analysis of studies attempting to assess the use of semipermeable membrane dressing materials at catheter insertion sites.[234] These investigators found a significantly increased risk of catheter-tip colonization when transparent compared with gauze dressings were used to dress either central or peripheral catheter insertion sites. In addition, they found a trend (though not statistically significant in their meta-analysis) toward an increased risk for bacteremia and catheter sepsis associated with the use of semipermeable dressings as insertion-site dressings for central venous catheters.[234] The new CDC guidelines suggest that, because the risk for catheter-related bacteremias did not differ between the groups,[234] choice of dressings can be a matter of preference.[2] The data on frequency of dressing changes are not conclusive. Randomized clinical trials have most often concluded that increasing time to dressing changes with transparent dressings does not affect site colonization.[235,236] Anecdotal data of institutional experiences with these issues suggest that increased time intervals between dressing changes and perhaps transparent dressings themselves are associated with increased bacteremia rates.[237] The increased ease of visual inspection and savings on nursing personnel time related to less frequent dressing changes likely do affect dressing choices in at least some institutions. Nonetheless, no definitive data exist to determine the best dressing methodology. The CDC has recommended changing the site dressing when it becomes damp, loosened, or soiled, and at least every 7 days for transparent dressings for adults. When gauze dressings are used for short-term central venous catheters, those dressings should be replaced every 2 days.[2]

Antimicrobial Prophylaxis

Some investigators have advocated using prophylactic antimicrobials in specific, defined circumstances to prevent catheter-associated infection. For example, Baier and colleagues found that prophylactic treatment of neonates with central catheters with vancomycin effectively prevented coagulase-negative staphylococcal bacteremia associated with the use of these catheters.[238] The use of continuous-infusion vancomycin for low-birth-weight infants has been shown to decrease rates of coagulase-negative staphylococci bacteremia.[239] Unfortunately, prolonged low levels of vancomycin, such as result from this form of prophylaxis, could predispose to vancomycin resistance. Raad and co-workers have used novobiocin and rifampin to attempt to prevent catheter-associated infections in patients receiving interleukin-2 (IL-2).[240] Although the antimicrobial prophylaxis was poorly tolerated (and had to be discontinued in nearly a third of patients), the regimen was thought to be successful.[240] Others have reported success in preventing catheter-associated infections in IL-2 recipients without using antimicrobial prophylaxis.

Antibiotic Lock Prophylaxis

The use of antibiotic lock solutions, in which an antibiotic is injected into the catheter lumen and the solution is left to dwell within the lumen for periods of some hours or days, has received intermittent attention over the past several years.[241,242] Antibiotic lock therapy in combination with systemic antibiotic is now recommended for uncomplicated bacteremias related to tunneled central venous catheters or implantable devices when the catheter is not removed and the infection is due to coagulase-negative staphylococci, *S. aureus*, or gram-negative bacilli.[89] Many of the studies on which these recommendations are based were done in patients receiving parenteral nutrition, and whose catheters

were accessed only once per day, or infrequently enough to allow prolonged dwell-time. Relatively few studies have examined the efficacy of the antibiotic lock technique in preventing catheter-related infection.[2,242] Three of four studies in hematology-oncology patient populations demonstrated efficacy of vancomycin plus heparin as antibiotic lock prophylaxis[242-244]; a fourth study found no significant difference in bacteremia rates or time to the first episode of bacteremia when heparin flush was compared with a heparin plus vancomycin flush solution.[243,245] Although neither vancomycin[244] nor ciprofloxacin[243] could be detected in the blood after flushing with either antibiotic, concern about development of vancomycin-resistant organisms following widespread use of small amounts of vancomycin has limited use of this prophylactic technique. Raad and colleagues recently reported that a novel minocycline and EDTA flush solution was more effective at preventing *S. epidermidis* colonization, bacteremia, septic phlebitis, and endocarditis in rabbits than a heparin-vancomycin flush.[246]

Anti-infective Catheters, Cuffs, and Hubs

Another approach that has been advocated to reduce the risk for central venous catheter–associated infection is bonding of an antimicrobial agent or antiseptic to the device itself or by the addition of a subcutaneous catheter cuff impregnated with an antiseptic or antimicrobial. Following the hypothesis that a path of major microbial access to the intravascular device is along the insertion site (see "Pathogenesis" earlier), a cuff that provides both a physical and an antimicrobial barrier might well reduce the risk for infection. Silver-impregnated collagen cuffing does not appear to reduce bacteremia rates.[2,247] Both minocycline plus rifampin and chlorhexidine plus silver sulfadiazine coating have been shown to be effective in reducing intravenous device–related bacteremias.[46,247-249] Minocycline-rifampin coating, when compared with first-generation chlorhexidine–silver sulfadiazine catheters, appears to be more effective at preventing bacteremia.[247,249] Only two studies examining minocycline–rifampin catheters have been published, both by the same group.[249,250] The minocycline-rifampin catheters are coated on both the internal and external surfaces of the catheters, whereas first-generation chlorhexidine-silver sulfadiazine catheters are coated only on the external surfaces. In vitro data indicate that second-generation chlorhexidine–silver sulfadiazine catheters, coated with both chlorhexidine and silver sulfadiazine on the external surface and chlorhexidine in the lumens, may have a longer duration of efficacy than first-generation catheters.[251] These catheters recently received FDA approval. In vitro and in vivo data suggest that the efficacy of the minocycline-rifampin catheters may be prolonged beyond that of chlorhexidine–silver sulfadiazine catheters[249,252]; first-generation chlorhexidine–silver sulfadiazine catheters are known to be efficacious only when the average insertion time is less than 8 days.[247] The efficacy of the minocycline-rifampin catheters when kept in situ for longer periods of time has not yet been tested. Additionally, these catheters are associated with a theoretical risk of increased antimicrobial resistance. Chlorhexidine–silver sulfadiazine catheters have been shown to be cost-effective in patients at high risk of intravenous device–related bacteremia. Another cost-effectiveness analysis suggested that the clinical and economic benefits of minocycline-rifampin catheters increase with days of catheterization.[253] For patients with central venous catheters in situ for 8 days, minocycline-rifampin catheters were more beneficial than chlorhexidine–silver sulfadiazine catheters, and cost savings accrued in patients catheterized for at least 13 days. A recent review examined 11 randomized studies comparing patients with central venous catheters impregnated with antimicrobial agents with control patients receiving nonimpregnated central venous catheters.[254] These authors concluded that the efficacy of antimicrobial-impregnated central venous catheters in preventing catheter-related bacteremias is questionable, and that routine use of these catheters be reevaluated. We believe that anti-infective catheters should be implemented only as part of a comprehensive nosocomial bacteremia prevention strategy, which also includes education of staff and adequate skin antisepsis. Institutions can choose to implement one of these catheters after review of both their current and goal intravenous device–associated bacteremia rates. Further research is needed to define the actual effect of these catheters on bacteremia rates, as well as the most efficacious catheters for different durations of catheterization and different subpopulations of patients.

Use of heparin or other anticoagulants has also been advocated as a method for reducing both thrombotic and infectious complications of central venous catheterization. One study found a clear benefit of covalently bonding heparin to catheters.[255] In this study the use of catheters to which heparin had been covalently bonded decreased bacterial colonization in vitro as well as decreasing the device-associated infection rate in vivo.[255] Randolph and co-workers concluded that heparin administration effectively reduces thrombus formation and may reduce catheter-related infections in patients who have central venous and pulmonary artery catheters in place.[256] Several anticoagulants have been suggested for use in this setting, and Randolph and co-workers pointed out that cost-effectiveness comparisons of these several preparations (e.g., unfractionated heparin, low-molecular-weight heparin, and warfarin) are needed.[256] Goey and colleagues ascribed the relatively low incidence of thrombosis and infection in their large series of catheters placed in patients receiving IL-2 infusions (a population of patients known to be at substantially increased risk for catheter-associated infection) to the use of tunneled catheters and prophylactic heparin.[257]

Other Prevention Issues

Finally, the role of appropriate nurse staffing in preventing catheter-associated infection deserves attention. In one recent study, nursing staff reductions during a period of increased TPN use was directly associated with an increase in catheter-associated bacteremias in a surgical ICU.[73] Robert and colleagues reported in 2000 that bacteremias in surgical ICU patients increased when nurse staffing changed to include fewer "regular" RNs and more pool/agency nurses.[72] Adequate nurse staffing has been identified as one factor integral to preventing bacteremia.[258] In this era of health care downsizing, the impact of staffing reductions on untoward outcomes is deserving of careful scrutiny.[73]

New scientific approaches are needed to help establish better techniques for catheter management,[47,141,259,260] and further technological advances such as bonding antimicrobial and antiseptic agents to the intravascular device may also reduce risks for device-associated infection. Increased attention to such details can significantly lower the endemic rate of device-associated infection as well as decrease the number of epidemics of such infections.

REFERENCES

1. Maki D. Sepsis Arising from Extrinsic Contamination of the Infusion and Measures for Control. Lancaster, England: MTP Press, 1977.
2. O'Grady NP, Alexander M, Dellinger EP, et al. Guidelines for the prevention of intravascular catheter-related infections. Infect Control Hosp Epidemiol. 2002;23:759.
3. Gonzalez-Barca E, Fernandez-Sevilla A, Carratala J, et al. Prospective study of 288 episodes of bacteremia in neutropenic cancer patients in a single institution. Eur J Clin Microbiol Infect Dis. 1996;15:291.
4. Weinstein MP, Towns ML, Quartey SM, et al. The clinical significance of positive blood cultures in the 1990s: A prospective comprehensive evaluation of the microbiology, epidemiology, and outcome of bacteremia and fungemia in adults. Clin Infect Dis. 1997;24:584.
5. Hugonnet S, Harbarth S, Ferriere K, et al. Bacteremic sepsis in intensive care: Temporal trends in incidence, organ dysfunction, and prognosis. Crit Care Med. 2003;31:390.
6. Renaud B, Brun-Buisson C, for the ICU-Bacteremia Study Group. Outcomes of primary and catheter-related bacteremia: A cohort and case-control study in critically ill patients. Am J Respir Crit Care Med. 2001;163:1584.
7. McGregor AR, Collignon PJ. Bacteraemia and fungaemia in an Australian general hospital—Associations and outcomes. Med J Aust. 1993;158:671.
8. Marrie T, Costerton JW. Scanning and transmission electron microscopy of in situ bacterial colonization of intravenous and intraarterial catheters. J Clin Microbiol. 1984;19:687.
9. Cheesbrough JS, Finch RG, Burden RP. A prospective study of the mechanisms of infection associated with hemodialysis catheters. J Infect Dis. 1986;154:579.
10. Linares J, Sitges-Serra A, Garau J, et al. Pathogenesis of catheter sepsis: A prospective study with quantitative and semiquantitative cultures of catheter hub and segments. J Clin Microbiol. 1985;21:357.
11. Maki D. Nosocomial bacteremia: An epidemiologic overview. Am J Med. 1981;70:719.
12. Maki D, Rhame F, Mackel D, et al. Nationwide epidemic of septicemia caused by contaminated intravenous products: I. Epidemiologic and clinical features. Am J Med. 1976;60:471.
13. Stamm W, Collella J, Anderson M, et al. Indwelling arterial catheters as a source of nosocomial bacteremia: An outbreak caused by *Flavobacterium* species. N Engl J Med. 1975;292:1099.
14. Carson L, Favero M, Bond W, et al. Morphological, biochemical and growth characteristics of *Pseudomonas cepacia* from distilled water. Appl Microbiol. 1973;25:476.
15. Goldmann D, Martin W, Worthington J. Growth of bacteria and fungi in total parenteral nutrition solutions. Am J Surg. 1973;126:314.
16. Maki D. Growth properties of microorganisms in infusion fluid and method of detection. In: Phillips I, ed. Microbiologic Hazards of Intravenous Therapy. Lancaster, England: MTP Press, 1977:13.
17. Jarvis W, Highsmith A. Bacterial growth and endotoxin production in lipid emulsion. J Clin Microbiol. 1984;19:17.
18. Dankner W, Spector S, Fierer J. *Malassezia* fungemia in neonates and adults: Complication of hyperalimentation. Rev Infect Dis. 1987;9:743.
19. Avila-Figueroa C, Goldmann DA, Richardson DK, et al. Intravenous lipid emulsions are the major determinant of coagulase-negative staphylococcal bacteremia in very low birth weight newborns. Pediatr Infect Dis J. 1998;17:10.
20. Plouffe J, Brown D, Silva J, et al. Nosocomial outbreak of *Candida parapsilosis* fungemia related to intravenous infusions. Arch Intern Med. 1977;137:1686.
21. Solomon S, Khabbaz R, Parker R, et al. An outbreak of *Candida parapsilosis* bloodstream infections in patients receiving parenteral nutrition. J Infect Dis. 1984;149:98.
22. Sitges-Serra A, Puig P, Jaurrieta E, et al. Hub colonization as the initial step in an outbreak of catheter-related sepsis due to coagulase negative staphylococci during parenteral nutrition. J Parenter Enteral Nutr. 1984;8:668.
23. Sitges-Serra A, Hernandez R, Maestro S, et al. Prevention of catheter sepsis: The hub. Nutrition. 1997;13:30S.
24. Linares J, Dominguez MA, Martin R. Current laboratory techniques in the diagnosis of catheter-related infections. Nutrition. 1997;13:10S.
25. Segura M, Alvarez-Lerma F, Tellado JM, et al. A clinical trial on the prevention of catheter-related sepsis using a new hub model. Ann Surg. 1996;223:363.
26. Pemberton L, Lyman B, Mandal J, et al. Outbreak of *Staphylococcus epidermidis* nosocomial infections in patients receiving total parenteral nutrition. J Parenter Enteral Nutr. 1984;8:325.
27. Maki D, Ringer M. Evaluation of dressing regimens for prevention of infection with peripheral intravenous catheters: Gauze, a transparent polyurethane dressing, and an iodophor-transparent dressing. JAMA. 1987;258:2396.
28. Salzman MB, Isenberg HD, Shapiro JF, et al. A prospective study of the catheter hub as the portal of entry for microorganisms causing catheter-related sepsis in neonates. J Infect Dis. 1993;167:487.
29. Salzman M, Isenberg H, Rubin L. Use of disinfectants to reduce microbial contamination of hubs of vascular catheters. J Clin Microbiol. 1993;31:475.
30. Sherertz RJ. Pathogenesis of vascular catheter-related infections. In: Seifert H, Jansen B, Farr BM, eds. Catheter-Related Infections. New York: Marcel Dekker; 1997:1.
31. Grohskopf LA, Roth VR, Feikin DR, et al. *Serratia liquefaciens* bloodstream infections from contamination of epoetin alfa at a hemodialysis center. N Engl J Med. 2001;344:1491.
32. Ostrowsky BE, Whitener C, Bredenberg HK, et al. *Serratia marcescens* bacteremia traced to an infused narcotic. N Engl J Med. 2002;346:1529.
33. van Laer F, Raes D, Vandamme P, et al. An outbreak of *Burkholderia cepacia* with septicemia on a cardiology ward. Infect Control Hosp Epidemiol. 1998;19:112.
34. Danzig LE, Short LJ, Collins K, et al. Bloodstream infections associated with a needleless intravenous infusion system in patients receiving home infusion therapy. JAMA. 1995;273:1862.
35. Do A, Ray BJ, Banerjee SN, et al. Bloodstream infection associated with needleless device use and the importance of infection-control practices in the home health care setting. J Infect Dis. 1999;179:442.
36. Cookson ST, Ihrig M, O'Mara EM, et al. Increased bloodstream infection rates in surgical patients associated with variation from recommended use and care following implementation of a needleless device. Infect Control Hosp Epidemiol. 1998;19:23.
37. McDonald LC, Banerjee SN, Jarvis WR. Line-associated bloodstream infections in pediatric intensive-care-unit patients associated with a needleless device and intermittent intravenous therapy. Infect Control Hosp Epidemiol. 1998;19:772.
38. Atela I, Coll P, Rello J, et al. Serial surveillance cultures of skin and catheter hub specimens from critically ill patients with central venous catheters: Molecular epidemiology of infection and implications for clinical management and research. J Clin Microbiol. 1997;35:1784.
39. Salzman MB, Rubin LG. Relevance of the catheter hub as a portal for microorganisms causing catheter-related bloodstream infections. Nutrition. 1997;13:15S.
40. Bjornson H, Colley R, Bower R, et al. Association between microorganism growth at the catheter insertion site and colonization of the catheter in patients receiving total parenteral nutrition. Surgery. 1982;92:720.
41. Cooper G, Hopkins C. Rapid diagnosis of intravascular catheter-associated infection by direct Gram-staining of catheter segments. N Engl J Med. 1985;18:1142.
42. Flowers RH, Schwenzer KJ, Kopel RF, et al. Efficacy of an attachable subcutaneous cuff for the prevention of intravascular catheter-related infection. JAMA. 1989;261:878.
43. Mermel LA, McCormick RD, Springman SR, et al. The pathogenesis and epidemiology of catheter-related infection with pulmonary artery Swan-Ganz catheters: A prospective study utilizing molecular subtyping. Am J Med. 1991;91(Suppl 3B):197S.

44. Herwaldt LA, Hollis RJ, Boyken LD, et al. Molecular epidemiology of coagulase-negative staphylococci isolated from immunocompromised patients. Infect Control Hosp Epidemiol. 1992;13:86.

45. Centers for Disease Control and Prevention. National Nosocomial Infections Surveillance (NNIS) system report, data summary from January 1992 to June 2002, issued August 2002. AJIC Am J Infect Control. 2002;30:458.

46. Safdar N, Kluger DM, Maki DG. A review of risk factors for catheter-related bloodstream infection caused by percutaneously inserted, noncuffed central venous catheters: Implications for preventive strategies. Medicine. 2002;81:466.

47. Kelsey M, Gosling M. A comparison of the morbidity associated with occlusive and non-occlusive dressings applied to peripheral intravenous devices. J Hosp Infect. 1984;5:313.

48. Craven D, Lichtenberg A, Kunches L, et al. A randomized study comparing a transparent polyurethane dressing to a dry gauze dressing for peripheral intravenous catheter sites. Infect Control. 1985;6:361.

49. Preston G, Larson E, Stamm W. The effect of private isolation rooms on patient care practices, colonization, and infection in an intensive care unit. Am J Med. 1981;70:641.

50. Albert R, Condie F. Hand-washing patterns in medical intensive care units. N Engl J Med. 1981;304:1465.

51. Lucas JW, Berger AM, Fitzgerald A, et al. Nosocomial infections in patients with central catheters. J Intraven Nurs. 1992;15:44.

52. Raad I, Luna M, Khalil SA, et al. The relationship between the thrombotic and infectious complications of central venous catheters. JAMA. 1994;271:1014.

53. Welch G, McKeel D Jr, Silverstein P, et al. The role of catheter composition in the development of thrombophlebitis. Surg Gynecol Obstet. 1974;138:421.

54. Stillman R, Soliman S, Garcia L, et al. Etiology of catheter associated sepsis. Arch Surg. 1977;112:1497.

55. Linder L, Curelaru I, Gustavsson B, et al. Material thrombogenicity in central venous catheterization: A comparison between soft, antebrachial catheters of silicone elastomer and polyurethane. J Parenter Enteral Nutr. 1984;8:399.

56. Bozzetti F. Central venous catheter sepsis. Surg Gynecol Obstet. 1985;161:293.

57. Sheth N, Franson T, Rose H, et al. Colonization of bacteria on polyvinyl chloride and Teflon intravascular catheter in hospitalized patients. J Clin Microbiol. 1983;18:1061.

58. Rotrosen D, Calderone R, Edwards J Jr. Adherence of Candida species to host tissues and plastic surfaces. Rev Infect Dis. 1986;8:73.

59. Sherertz R, Carruth WA, Marosok RD, et al. Contribution of vascular catheter material to the pathogenesis of infection: The enhanced risk of silicone in vivo. J Biomater Res. 1995;29:634.

60. Yeung C, May J, Hughes R. Infection rate for single-lumen vs. triple-lumen subclavian catheters. Infect Control Hosp Epidemiol. 1988;9:154.

61. Kelly C, Ligas J, Smith C, et al. Sepsis due to triple-lumen central venous catheters. Surg Gynecol Obstet. 1986;163:14.

62. Kovalevich D, Faubion W, Bender J, et al. Association of parenteral nutrition catheter sepsis with urinary tract infections. J Parenter Enteral Nutr. 1986;10:639.

63. Donlan RM, Costerton JW. Biofilms: Survival mechanisms of clinically relevant microorganisms. Clin Microbiol Rev. 2002;15:167.

64. Hampton A, Sherertz R. Vascular-access infections in hospitalized patients. Surg Clin North Am. 1988;68:57.

65. Armstrong C, Mayhall C, Miller K, et al. Prospective study of catheter replacement and other risk factors for infection of hyperalimentation catheters. J Infect Dis. 1986;154:808.

66. Eggimann P, Harbarth S, Constantin MN, et al. Impact of a prevention strategy targeted at vascular-access care on incidence of infections acquired in intensive care. Lancet. 2000;355:1864.

67. Soifer NE, Borzak S, Edlin BR, et al. Prevention of peripheral venous catheter complications with an intravenous therapy team: A randomized controlled trial. Arch Intern Med. 1998;158:473.

68. Raad I, Hohn DC, Gilbreath BJ, et al. Prevention of central venous catheter-related infections by using maximal sterile barrier precautions during insertion. Infect Control Hosp Epidemiol. 1994;15:231.

69. Snydman D, Murray S, Kornfeld S, et al. Total parenteral nutrition-related infections: Prospective epidemiologic study using semiquantitative methods. Am J Med. 1982;73:695.

70. Ryan J, Abel R, Abbott W, et al. Catheter complications in total parenteral nutrition: A prospective study of 200 consecutive patients. N Engl J Med. 1974;290:757.

71. Merrer J, De Jonghe B, Golliot F, et al. Complications of femoral and subclavian venous catheterization in critically ill patients: A randomized controlled trial. JAMA. 2001;286:700.

72. Robert J, Fridkin SK, Blumberg HM, et al. The influence of the composition of the nursing staff on primary bloodstream infection rates in a surgical intensive care unit. Infect Control Hosp Epidemiol. 2000;21:12.

73. Fridkin SK, Pear SM, Williamson TH, et al. The role of understaffing in central venous catheter-associated bloodstream infections. Infect Control Hosp Epidemiol. 1996;17:150.

74. Schulin T, Voss A. Coagulase-negative staphylococci as a cause of infections related to intravascular prosthetic devices: Limitations of present therapy. Clin Microbiol Infect. 2001;7:1.

75. Wade JC, Schimpff SC, Newman KA, et al. Staphylococcus epidermidis: An increasing cause of infection in patients with granulocytopenia. Ann Intern Med. 1982;97:503.

76. Diekema DJ, Beekmann SE, Chapin KC, et al. Epidemiology and outcome of nosocomial and community onset bloodstream infection. J Clin Microbiol. 2003;41:3655-3660.

77. Christensen G, Simpson A, Bisno A, et al. Adherence of slime-producing strains of Staphylococcus epidermidis to smooth surfaces. Infect Immun. 1982;37:318.

78. Castagnola E, Garaventa A, Viscoli C, et al. Changing pattern of pathogens causing Broviac catheter-related bacteraemias in children with cancer. J Hosp Infect. 1995;29:129.

79. Castagnola E, Conte M, Venzano P, et al. Broviac catheter-related bacteraemias due to unusual pathogens in children with cancer: Case reports with literature review. J Infect. 1997;34:215.

80. Henderson DK, Baptiste RF, Parrillo J, et al. Indolent epidemic of Pseudomonas cepacia bacteremia and pseudobacteremia in an intensive care unit traced to a contaminated blood gas analyzer. Am J Med. 1988;84:75.

81. Pegues DA, Carson LA, Anderson RL, et al. Outbreak of Pseudomonas cepacia bacteremia in oncology patients. Clin Infect Dis. 1993;16:407.

82. Goetz AM, Rihs JD, Chow JW, et al. An outbreak of infusion-related Klebsiella pneumoniae bacteremia in a liver transplantation unit. Clin Infect Dis. 1995;21:1501.

83. Ashkenazi S, Leibovici L, Samra Z, et al. Risk factors for mortality due to bacteremia and fungemia in childhood. Clin Infect Dis. 1992;14:949.

84. D'Antonio D, Pizzigallo E, Iacone A, et al. Occurrence of bacteremia in hematologic patients. Eur J Epidemiol. 1992;8:687.

85. Lecciones JA, Lee JW, Navarro EE, et al. Vascular catheter-associated fungemia in patients with cancer: Analysis of 155 episodes. Clin Infect Dis. 1992;14:875.

86. Leibovici L, Konisberger H, Pitlik SD, et al. Bacteremia and fungemia of unknown origin in adults. Clin Infect Dis. 1992;14:436.

87. Rello J, Quintana E, Mirelis B, et al. Polymicrobial bacteremia in critically ill patients. Intensive Care Med. 1993;19:22.

88. Walsh TJ, Gonzalez C, Roilides E, et al. Fungemia in children infected with the human immunodeficiency virus: New epidemiologic patterns, emerging pathogens, and improved outcome with antifungal therapy. Clin Infect Dis. 1995;20:900.

89. Mermel LA, Farr BM, Sherertz RJ, et al. Guidelines for the management of intravascular catheter-related infections. J Intraven Nurs. 2001;24:180.

90. Maki D, Jarrett F, Sarafin H. A semiquantitative method for identification of catheter-related infection in the burn patient. J Surg Res. 1977;22:513.

91. Maki D, Weise C, Sarafin H. A semiquantitative method for identifying intravenous-catheter-related infection. N Engl J Med. 1977;296:1305.

92. Siegman-Igra Y, Anglim AM, Shapiro DE, et al. Diagnosis of vascular catheter-related bloodstream infection: A meta-analysis. J Clin Microbiol. 1997;35:928.

93. Band J, Maki D. Infections caused by arterial catheters used for hemodynamic monitoring. Am J Med. 1979;67:735.

94. Band JD, Alvarado CJ, Maki DG. A semiquantitative culture technique for identifying infection due to steel needles used for intravenous therapy. Am J Clin Pathol. 1979;72:980.

95. Band J, Maki D. Steel needles used for intravenous therapy: Morbidity in patients with hematologic malignancy. Arch Intern Med. 1980;140:31.

96. Dooley DP, Garcia A, Kelly JW, et al. Validation of catheter semiquantitative culture technique for nonstaphylococcal organisms. J Clin Microbiol. 1996;34:409.

97. Cleri D, Corrado M, Seligman S. Quantitative culture of intravenous catheters and other intravascular inserts. J Infect Dis. 1980;141:781.

98. Brun-Buisson C, Abrouk F, Legrand P, et al. Diagnosis of central venous catheter-related sepsis: Critical level of quantitative tip cultures. Arch Intern Med. 1987;147:873.

99. Gutierrez J, Leon C, Matamoros R, et al. Catheter-related bacteremia and fungemia: Reliability of two methods for catheter culture. Diagn Microbiol Infect Dis. 1992;15:575.

100. Hnatiuk O, Pike J, Stolzfus D, et al. Value of bedside plating of semiquantitative cultures for diagnosis of central venous catheter-related infections in ICU patients. Chest. 1993;103:896.

101. Sherertz RJ, Heard SO, Raad II. Diagnosis of triple-lumen catheter infection: Comparison of roll plate, sonication, and flushing methodologies. J Clin Microbiol. 1997;35:641.

102. Collignon P, Chan R, Munro R. Rapid diagnosis of intravascular catheter-related sepsis. Arch Intern Med. 1987;147:1609.

103. McGeer A, Righter J. Improving our ability to diagnose infections associated with central venous catheters: Value of Gram's staining and culture of entry site swabs. CMAJ. 1987;137:1009.

104. Zuffrey J, Rime B, Franciou P, et al. Simple method for rapid diagnosis of catheter-associated infection by direct acridine orange staining of catheter tips. J Clin Microbiol. 1988;26:175.

105. Kite P, Dobbins BM, Wilcox MH, et al. Evaluation of a novel endoluminal brush method for in situ diagnosis of catheter related sepsis. J Clin Pathol. 1997;50:278.

106. Spencer R, Kristinsson K. Failure to diagnose intravascular associated infection by direct Gram-staining of catheter segments. J Hosp Infect. 1986;7:305.

107. Dobbins BM, Kite P, Kindon A, et al. DNA fingerprinting analysis of coagulase negative staphylococci implicated in catheter related bloodstream infections. J Clin Pathol. 2002;55:824.

108. Mosca R, Curtas S, Forbes B, et al. The benefits of isolator cultures in the management of suspected catheter sepsis. Surgery. 1987;102:718.

109. Ascher DP, Shoupe BA, Robb M, et al. Comparison of standard and quantitative blood cultures in the evaluation of children with suspected central venous line sepsis. Diagn Microbiol Infect Dis. 1992;15:499.

110. Kaditis AG, O'Marcaigh AS, Rhodes KH, et al. Yield of positive blood cultures in pediatric oncology patients by a new method of blood culture collection. Pediatr Infect Dis J. 1996;15:615.

111. Blot F, Schmidt E, Nitenberg G, et al. Earlier positivity of central-venous- versus peripheral-blood cultures is highly predictive of catheter-related sepsis. J Clin Microbiol. 1998;36:105.

112. Seifert H, Cornely O, Seggewiss K, et al. Bloodstream infection in neutropenic cancer patients related to short-term nontunnelled catheters determined by quantitative blood cultures, differential time to positivity, and molecular epidemiological typing with pulsed-field gel electrophoresis. J Clin Microbiol. 2003;41:118.

113. Malgrange VB, Escande MC, Theobald S. Validity of earlier positivity of central venous blood cultures in comparison with peripheral blood cultures for diagnosing catheter-related bacteremia in cancer patients. J Clin Microbiol. 2001;39:274.

114. Torlakovic E, Hibbs JR, Miller JS, et al. Intracellular bacteria in blood smears in patients with central venous catheters. Arch Intern Med. 1995;155:1547.

115. Wing E, Norden C, Shadduck R, et al. Use of quantitative bacteriologic techniques to diagnose catheter-related sepsis. Arch Intern Med. 1979;139:482.

116. Capdevila JA, Planes AM, Palomar M, et al. Value of differential quantitative blood cultures in the diagnosis of catheter-related sepsis. Eur J Clin Microbiol Infect Dis. 1992;11:403.

117. Olson IE, Lam K, Bodey GP, et al. Evaluation of strategies for central venous catheter replacement. Crit Care Med. 1992;20:797.

118. Quilici N, Audibert G, Conroy MC, et al. Differential quantitative blood cultures in the diagnosis of catheter-related sepsis in intensive care units. Clin Infect Dis. 1997;25:1066.

119. Tonnesen A, Peuler M, Lockwood W. Cultures of blood drawn by catheters vs. venipuncture. JAMA. 1976;235:1877.

120. Felices F, Hernandez J, Ruiz J, et al. Use of the central venous pressure catheter to obtain blood cultures. Crit Care Med. 1979;7:78.

121. Souvenir D, Anderson DE Jr, Palpant S, et al. Blood cultures positive for coagulase-negative staphylococci: Antisepsis, pseudobacteremia, and therapy of patients. J Clin Microbiol. 1998;36:1923.

122. Pettigren R, Lang D, Haycock D, et al. Catheter-related sepsis in patients on intravenous nutrition: A prospective study of quantitative catheter cultures and guideline changes for suspected sepsis. Br J Surg. 1985;72:52.

123. DesJardin J, Falagas ME, Ruthazer R, et al. Clinical utility of blood cultures drawn from indwelling central venous catheters in hospitalized patients with cancer. Ann Intern Med. 1999;131:641.

124. Bingen E, Barc MC, Brahimi N, et al. Randomly amplified polymorphic DNA analysis provides rapid differentiation of methicillin-resistant coagulase-negative staphylococcus bacteremia isolates in pediatric hospital. J Clin Microbiol. 1995;33:1657.

125. Dominguez MA, Linares J, Pulido A, et al. Molecular tracking of coagulase-negative staphylococcal isolates from catheter-related infections. Microb Drug Resist. 1996;2:423.

126. Maki D, Goldmann D, Rhame F. Infection control in intravenous therapy. Ann Intern Med. 1973;79:867.

127. Tully J, Friedland G, Baldini M, et al. Complications of intravenous therapy with steel needles and Teflon catheters. Am J Med. 1981;70:702.

128. Bregenzer T, Conen D, Sakmann P, et al. Is routine replacement of peripheral intravenous catheters necessary? Arch Intern Med. 1998;158:151.

129. Lai KK. Safety of prolonging peripheral cannula and i.v. tubing use from 72 hours to 96 hours. Am J Infect Control. 1998;26:66.

130. Cornely OA, Bethe U, Pauls R, et al. Peripheral Teflon catheters: Factors determining incidence of phlebitis and duration of cannulation. Infect Control Hosp Epidemiol. 2002;23:249.

131. Crane D. Venous interruption for septic thrombophlebitis. N Engl J Med. 1962;262:947.

132. Munster A. Septic thrombophlebitis: A surgical disorder. JAMA. 1974;230:1010.

133. De Cicco M, Matovic M, Balestreri L, et al. Central venous thrombosis: An early and frequent complication in cancer patients bearing long-term Silastic catheter. A prospective study. Thromb Res. 1997;86:101.

134. Khan EA, Correa AG, Baker CJ. Suppurative thrombophlebitis in children: A ten-year experience. Pediatr Infect Dis J. 1997;16:63.

135. Harden JL, Kemp L, Mirtallo J. Femoral catheters increase risk of infection in total parenteral nutrition patients. Nutr Clin Pract. 1995;10:60.

136. Martin C, Bruder N, Papazian L, et al. Catheter-related infections following axillary vein catheterization. Acta Anaesthesiol Scand. 1998;42:52.

137. Moran J, Atwood R, Rowe M. A clinical and bacteriologic study of infections associated with venous cutdowns. N Engl J Med. 1965;272:554.

138. Buxton A, Anderson R, Klimek J, et al. Failure of disposable domes to prevent septicemia from contaminated pressure transducers. Chest. 1978;74:508.

139. Band J, Maki D. Safety of changing intravenous delivery systems at longer than 24-hour intervals. Ann Intern Med. 1979;91:173.

140. Snydman D, Reidy M, Perry L, et al. Safety of changing intravenous (IV) administration sets containing burettes at longer than 48 hour intervals. Infect Control. 1987;8:113.

141. Maki D, Boiticelli J, LeRoy M, et al. Prospective study of replacing administration sets for intravenous therapy at 48 vs. 72 hour intervals: 72 hours is safe and cost-effective. JAMA. 1987;258:1777.

142. Michel L, McMichan J, Bachy J. Microbial colonization of indwelling central venous catheters: Statistical evaluation of potential contaminating factors. Am J Surg. 1979;137:745.

143. Peters W, Bush W, McIntyre R, et al. The development of fibrin sheath on indwelling venous catheters. Surg Gynecol Obstet. 1973;137:43.

144. Jones GR, Konsler GK, Dunaway RP, et al. Prospective analysis of urokinase in the treatment of catheter sepsis in pediatric hematology-oncology patients. J Pediatr Surg. 1993;28:350.

145. Ruggiero R, Aisenstein T. Central catheter fibrin sleeve: Heparin effect. J Parenter Enteral Nutr. 1983;7:270.

146. Henderson D, Myers R, Laniak J. Catheter-acquired infection in total parenteral nutrition. Nat Intraven Ther Assoc J (NITA). 1982;5:62.

147. Lloyd DA, Shanbhogue LK, Doherty PJ, et al. Does the fibrin coat around a central venous catheter influence catheter-related sepsis? J Pediatr Surg. 1993;28:345.

148. Maher M, Henderson D, Brennan M. Central venous catheter exchange in cancer patients during total parenteral nutrition. Nat Intraven Ther Assoc J (NITA). 1982;5:54.

149. Bach A, Böhrer H, Geiss HK. Safety of a guidewire technique for replacement of pulmonary artery catheters. J Cardiothorac Vasc Anesth. 1992;6:711.

150. Cobb DK, High KP, Sawyer RG, et al. A controlled trial of scheduled replacement of central venous and pulmonary-artery catheters. N Engl J Med. 1992;327:1062.

151. Cook D, Randolph A, Kernerman P, et al. Central venous catheter replacement strategies: A systematic review of the literature. Crit Care Med. 1997;25:1417.

152. Anaissie EJ, Rex JH, Uzun O, et al. Predictors of adverse outcome in cancer patients with candidemia. Am J Med. 1998;104:238.

153. Anagnostakis D, Kamba A, Petrochilou V, et al. Risk of infection associated with umbilical vein catheterization: A prospective study in 75 newborn infants. J Pediatr. 1973;86:759.

154. Balagtas R, Bell C, Edwards L, et al. Risk of local and systemic infections associated with umbilical vein catheterization: A prospective study in 86 newborn patients. Pediatrics. 1971;48:359.

155. Munson D, Thompson T, Johnson D, et al. Coagulase-negative staphylococcal septicemia: Experience in a newborn intensive care unit. J Pediatr. 1982;101:602.

156. Symansky M, Fox H. Umbilical vessel catheterization: Indications, management, and evaluation of the technique. J Pediatr. 1972;80:820.

157. McCready CE, Doughty HA, Pearson TC. Experience with the Port-A-Cath in sickle cell disease. Clin Lab Haematol. 1996;18:79.

158. Goldmann D, Maki D. Infection control in total parenteral nutrition. JAMA. 1973;223:1360.

159. Syndman D, Murray S, Kornfield S, et al. Total parenteral nutrition-related infections: prospective epidemiologic study using semiquantitative methods. Am J Med. 1982;73:695.

160. Montgomerie J, Edwards J Jr. Association of infection due to *Candida albicans* with intravenous hyperalimentation. J Infect Dis. 1978;127:197.

161. Henderson D, Edwards J Jr, Montgomerie J. Hematogenous *Candida* endophthalmitis in patients receiving parenteral hyperalimentation fluids. J Infect Dis. 1981;143:655.

162. Curry C, Quie P. Fungal septicemia in patients receiving parenteral hyperalimentation. N Engl J Med. 1971;285:1221.

163. Wilmore D, Dudrick S. An in-line filter for intravenous solutions. Arch Surg. 1969;99:462.

164. Bailey M: Reduction of catheter-associated sepsis in parenteral nutrition using low-dose intravenous heparin. Br Med J. 1979;1:1671.

165. Mitchell A, Atkins S, Royle G, et al. Reduced catheter sepsis and prolonged catheter life using a tunnelled silicone rubber catheter for total parenteral nutrition. Br J Surg. 1982;69:420.

166. Maki D. Epidemic nosocomial bacteremias. In: Wenzel R, ed. Handbook of Hospital Acquired Infections. Boca Raton, FL: CRC Press, 1981:371.

167. Broviac J, Cole J, Scribner B. A silicone rubber atrial catheter for prolonged parenteral alimentation. Surg Gynecol Obstet. 1973;136:602.

168. Blacklock H, Hill R, Clarke A, et al. Use of modified subcutaneous right-atrial catheter for venous access in leukaemic patients. Lancet. 1980;1:993.

169. Hickman R, Buckner C, Clift R, et al. A modified right atrial catheter for access to the venous system in marrow transplant recipients. Surg Gynecol Obstet. 1979;148:871.

170. Press O, Ramsey P, Larson E, et al. Hickman catheter infections in patients with malignancies. Medicine (Baltimore). 1984;63:189.

171. Lokich JJ, Bothe A Jr, Benotti P, et al. Complications and management of implanted venous access catheters. J Clin Oncol. 1985;3:710.

172. Cairo MS, Spooner S, Sowden L, et al. Long-term use of indwelling multipurpose Silastic catheters in pediatric cancer patients treated with aggressive chemotherapy. J Clin Oncol. 1986;4:784.

173. Ross MN, Haase GM, Poole MA, et al. Comparison of totally implanted reservoirs with external catheters as venous access devices in pediatric oncologic patients. Surg Gynecol Obstet. 1988;167:141.

174. Alurkar SS, Dhabhar BN, Pathak AB, et al. Long-term right atrial catheters in patients with malignancies: An Indian experience. J Surg Oncol. 1992;51:183.

175. Hogan L, Pulito AR. Broviac central venous catheters inserted via the saphenous or femoral vein in the NICU under local anesthesia. J Pediatr Surg. 1992;27:1185.

176. Hockenberry MJ, Schultz WH, Bennett B, et al. Experience with minimal complications in implanted catheters in children. Am J Pediatr Hematol Oncol. 1989;11:295.

177. Johnson PR, Decker MD, Edwards KM, et al. Frequency of Broviac catheter infections in pediatric oncology patients. J Infect Dis. 1986;154:570.

178. Kappers-Klunne MC, Degener JE, Stijnen T, et al. Complications from long-term indwelling central venous catheters in hematologic patients with special reference to infection. Cancer. 1989;64:1747.

179. Larson EB, Wooding M, Hickman RO. Infectious complications of right atrial catheters used for venous access in patients receiving intensive chemotherapy. Surg Gynecol Obstet. 1981;153:369.

180. Shulman RJ, Rahman S, Mahoney D, et al. A totally implanted venous access system used in pediatric patients with cancer. J Clin Oncol. 1987;5:137.

181. Ulz L, Petersen FB, Ford R, et al. A prospective study of complications in Hickman right-atrial catheters in marrow transplant patients. JPEN J Parenter Enteral Nutr. 1990;14:27.

182. Viscoli C, Garaventa A, Boni L, et al. Role of Broviac catheters in infections in children with cancer. Pediatr Infect Dis J. 1988;7:556.

183. Wacker P, Bugmann P, Halperin DS, et al. Comparison of totally implanted and external catheters in paediatric oncology patients. Eur J Cancer. 1992;28A:841.

184. Rizzari C, Palamone G, Corbetta A, et al. Central venous catheter-related infections in pediatric hematology-oncology patients: Role of home and hospital management. Pediatr Hematol Oncol. 1992;9:115.

185. Holloway RW, Orr JW. An evaluation of Groshong central venous catheters on a gynecologic oncology service. Gynecol Oncol. 1995;56:211.

186. Elishoov H, Or R, Strauss N, et al. Nosocomial colonization, septicemia, and Hickman/Broviac catheter-related infections in bone marrow transplant recipients: A 5-year prospective study. Medicine (Baltimore). 1998;77:83.

187. Cardella JF, Cardella K, Bacci N, et al. Cumulative experience with 1,273 peripherally inserted central catheters at a single institution. J Vasc Interv Radiol. 1996;7:5.

188. Chait PG, Ingram J, Phillips-Gordon C, et al. Peripherally inserted central catheters in children. Radiology. 1995;197:775.

189. Yeung CY, Lee HC, Huang FY, et al. Sepsis during total parenteral nutrition: Exploration of risk factors and determination of the effectiveness of peripherally inserted central venous catheters. Pediatr Infect Dis J. 1998;17:135.

190. Loughran SC, Borzatta M. Peripherally inserted central catheters: A report of 2506 catheter days. JPEN J Parenter Enteral Nutr. 1995;19:133.

191. Cowl CT, Weinstock JV, Al-Jurf A, et al. Complications and cost associated with parenteral nutrition delivered to hospitalized patients through either subclavian or peripherally-inserted central catheters. Clin Nutr. 2000;19:237.

192. Hiemenz J, Robichaud K, Johnston M, et al. Bacteremia in patients with indwelling Silastic catheters. Proc Am Soc Clin Oncol. 1982;1:57.

193. Hiemenz J, Skelton J, Pizzo P. Perspective on the management of catheter-related infections in cancer patients. Pediatr Infect Dis. 1987;5:6.

194. Hartman G, Shuchat S. Management of septic complications associated with Silastic catheters in childhood malignancies. Pediatr Infect Dis J. 1987;6:1042.

195. Ascher DP, Shoupe BA, Maybee D, et al. Persistent catheter-related bacteremia: Clearance with antibiotics and urokinase. J Pediatr Surg. 1993;28:627.

196. Benoit JL, Carandang G, Sitrin M, et al. Intraluminal antibiotic treatment of central venous catheter infections in patients receiving parenteral nutrition at home. Clin Infect Dis. 1995;21:1286.

197. Raad I, Buzaid A, Rhyne J, et al. Minocycline and ethylenediaminetetraacetate for the prevention of recurrent vascular catheter infections. Clin Infect Dis. 1997;25:149.

198. McCarthy A, Byrne M, Breathnach F, et al. "In-situ" teicoplanin for central venous catheter infection. Ir J Med Sci. 1995;164:125.

199. Becton D, Kletzel M, Golladay E, et al. An experience with an implanted port system in 66 children with cancer. Cancer. 1988;61:376.

200. Brothers T, VanMoll L, Niederhuber J, et al. Experience with subcutaneous infusion ports in three hundred patients. Surg Gynecol Obstet. 1988;166:295.

201. Puig-la Calle J Jr, Lopez Sanchez S, Piedrafita Serra E, et al. Totally implanted device for long-term intravenous chemotherapy: Experience in 123 adult patients with solid neoplasms. J Surg Oncol. 1996;62:273.

202. Poorter RL, Lauw FN, Bemelman WA, et al. Complications of an implantable venous access device (Port-A-Cath) during intermittent continuous infusion of chemotherapy. Eur J Cancer. 1996,32A.2262.

203. Duthoit D, Devleeshouwer C, Paesmans M, et al. Infection of totally implantable chamber catheters in cancer patients: Multivariate analysis of risk factors. In: Abstracts of the 33rd Interscience Conference on Antimicrobial Agents and Chemotherapy, New Orleans, Louisiana, 1993:416.

204. Hollingsed MJ, Morales JM, Roughneen PT, et al. Surgical management of catheter tip thrombus: Surgical therapy for right atrial thrombus and fungal endocarditis (*Candida tropicalis*) complicating paediatric sickle-cell disease. Perfusion. 1997;12:197.

205. Meisenberg BR, Callaghan M, Sloan C, et al. Complications associated with central venous catheters used for the collection of peripheral blood progenitor cells to support high-dose chemotherapy and autologous stem cell rescue. Support Care Cancer. 1997;5:223.

206. Keung YK, Watkins K, Chen SC, et al. Increased incidence of central venous catheter-related infections in bone marrow transplant patients. Am J Clin Oncol. 1995;18:469.

207. Alegre A, Requena MJ, Fernandez-Villalta MJ, et al. Quinton-Mahurkar catheter as short-term central venous access for PBSC collection: Single-center experience of 370 aphereses in 110 patients. Bone Marrow Transplant. 1996;18:865.

208. Swan H, Ganz W, Forrester J. Catheterization of the heart in a man with the use of a flow-directed balloon-tipped catheter. N Engl J Med. 1970;283:447.

209. Michel L, Marsh M, McMichan J, et al. Infection of pulmonary artery catheters in critically ill patients. JAMA. 1981;245:1032.

210. Katz J, Cronan L, Barash P, et al. Pulmonary artery flow-guided catheters in the perioperative period. JAMA. 1977;237:2832.

211. Cohen Y, Fosse JP, Karoubi P, et al. The "hands-off" catheter and the prevention of systemic infections associated with pulmonary artery catheter: A prospective study. Am J Respir Crit Care Med. 1998;157:284.

212. Ford S, Manley P. Indwelling cardiac catheters: An autopsy study of associated endocardial lesions. Arch Pathol Lab Med. 1982;106:314.

213. Greene J Jr, Fitzwater J, Clemmer T. Septic endocarditis and indwelling pulmonary artery catheters. JAMA. 1975;233:891.

214. Ehrie M, Morgan A, Moore F, et al. Endocarditis with the indwelling balloon-tipped pulmonary artery catheter in burn patients. J Trauma. 1978;18:664.

215. Fernandez-Guerrero ML, Verdejo C, Azofra J, et al. Hospital-acquired infectious endocarditis not associated with cardiac surgery: An emerging problem. Clin Infect Dis. 1995;20:16.

216. Kac G, Durain E, Amrein C, et al. Colonization and infection of pulmonary artery catheter in cardiac surgery patients: Epidemiology and multivariate analysis of risk factors. Crit Care Med. 2001;29:971.

217. Adams J, Speer M, Rudolph A. Bacterial colonization of radial artery catheters. Pediatrics. 1980;65:94.

218. Maki D, Hassemer C. Endemic rate of fluid contamination and related septicemia in arterial pressure monitoring. Am J Med. 1981;70:733.

219. Weinstein R, Stamm W, Kramer L, et al. Pressure monitoring devices: Overlooked source of nosocomial infection. JAMA. 1976;236:936.

220. West C, Wayle B, Touneson A, et al. Nosocomial *Serratia marcescens* bacteremia associated with reuse of disposable monitoring domes. In: Abstracts of the Seventeenth Interscience Conference on Antimicrobial Agents and Chemotherapy, New York, 1977. Abst. 429.

221. McGee DC, Gould MK. Preventing complications of central venous catheterization. N Engl J Med. 2003;348:1123.

222. Sitges-Serra A, Pi-Suner T, Garces JM, et al. Pathogenesis and prevention of catheter-related septicemia. Am J Infect Control. 1995;23:310.

223. Arduino MJ, Bland LA, Danzig LE, et al. Microbiologic evaluation of needleless and needle-access devices. Am J Infect Control. 1997;25:377.

224. Chodoff A, Pettis AM, Schoonmaker D, et al. Polymicrobial gram-negative bacteremia associated with saline solution flush used with a needleless intravenous system. Am J Infect Control. 1995;23:357.

225. Crnich CJ, Maki DG. The promise of novel technology for the prevention of intravascular device-related bloodstream infection. I. Pathogenesis and short-term devices. Clin Infect Dis. 2002;34:1232.

226. Johnson DW, MacGinley R, Kay TD, et al. A randomized controlled trial of topical exit site mupirocin application in patients with tunnelled, cuffed haemodialysis catheters. Nephrol Dial Transplant. 2002;17:1802.

227. Miller MA, Dascal A, Portnoy J, et al. Development of mupirocin resistance among methicillin-resistant *Staphylococcus aureus* after widespread use of nasal mupirocin ointment. Infect Control Hosp Epidemiol. 1996;17:811.

228. Rhame F, Maki D, Bennett J. Intravenous Cannula-Related Infections. Boston, MA: Little, Brown; 1979.

229. Maki D, Band J. A comparative study of polyantibiotic and iodophor ointments in prevention of vascular catheter-related infection. Am J Med. 1981;70:739.

230. Garland JS, Buck RK, Maloney P, et al. Comparison of 10% povidone-iodine and 0.5% chlorhexidine gluconate for the prevention of peripheral intravenous catheter colonization in neonates: A prospective trial. Pediatr Infect Dis J. 1995;14:510.

231. Humar A, Ostromecki A, Direnfeld J, et al. Prospective randomized trial of 10% povidone-iodine versus 0.5% tincture of chlorhexidine as cutaneous antisepsis for prevention of central venous catheter infection. Clin Infect Dis. 2000;31:1001.

232. Chaiyakunapruk N, Veenstra DL, Lipsky BA, et al. Chlorhexidine compared with povidone-iodine solution for vascular catheter-site care: A meta-analysis. Ann Intern Med. 2002;136:792. [Summary for patients in Ann Intern Med. 2002;136:I26.]

233. Rusmin S, DeLuca P. Effect of antibiotics and osmotic change on the release of endotoxin by bacteria retained on intravenous in-line filters. Am J Hosp Pharm. 1975;32:378.

234. Hoffmann KK, Weber DJ, Samsa GP, et al. Transparent polyurethane film as an intravenous catheter dressing: A meta-analysis of the infection risks. JAMA. 1992;267:2072.

235. Rasero L, Degl'Innocenti M, Mocali M, et al. Comparison of two different time interval protocols for central venous catheter dressing in bone marrow transplant patients: Results of a randomized, multicenter study. Haematologia. 2000;85:275.

236. Giles Y, Aksoy M, Tezelman S. What really affects the incidence of central venous catheter-related infections for short-term catheterization? Acta Chir Belg. 2002;102:256.

237. Curchoe RM, Powers J, El-Daher N. Weekly transparent dressing changes linked to increased bacteremia rates. Infect Control Hosp Epidemiol. 2002;23:730.

238. Baier RJ, Bocchini JA Jr, Brown EG. Selective use of vancomycin to prevent coagulase-negative staphylococcal nosocomial bacteremia in high risk very low birth weight infants. Pediatr Infect Dis J. 1998;17:179.

239. Kacica MA, Horgan MJ, Ochoa L, et al. Prevention of gram-positive sepsis in neonates weighing less than 1500 grams. J Pediatr. 1994;125:253.

240. Raad II, Hachem RY, Abi-Said D, et al. A prospective crossover randomized trial of novobiocin and rifampin prophylaxis for the prevention of intravascular catheter infections in cancer patients treated with interleukin-2. Cancer. 1998;82:403.

241. Messing B, Peitra-Cohen S, Debure A, et al. Antibiotic-lock technique: A new approach to optimal therapy for catheter-related sepsis in home-parenteral nutrition patients. JPEN J Paren Enteral Nutr. 1988;12:185.

242. Carratala J, Niubo J, Fernandez-Sevilla A, et al. Randomized, double-blind trial of an antibiotic-lock technique for prevention of gram-positive central venous catheter-related infection in neutropenic patients with cancer. Antimicrob Agents Chemother. 1999;43:2200.

243. Henrickson KJ, Axtell RA, Hoover SM, et al. Prevention of central venous catheter-related infections and thrombotic events in immunocompromised children by the use of vancomycin/ciprofloxacin/heparin flush solution: A randomized, multicenter, double-blind trial. J Clin Oncol. 2000;18:1269.

244. Schwartz C, Henrickson KJ, Roghmann K, et al. Prevention of bacteremia attributed to luminal colonization of tunneled central venous catheters with vancomycin-susceptible organisms. J Clin Oncol. 1990;8:1591.

245. Rackoff WR, Weiman M, Jakobowski D, et al. A randomized, controlled trial of the efficacy of a heparin and vancomycin solution in preventing central venous catheter infections in children. J Pediatr. 1995;127:147.

246. Raad I, Hachem R, Tcholakian RK, et al. Efficacy of minocycline and EDTA lock solution in preventing catheter-related bacteremia, septic phlebitis, and endocarditis in rabbits. Antimicrob Agents Chemother. 2002;46:327.

247. Walder B, Pittet D, Tramer MR. Prevention of bloodstream infections with central venous catheters treated with anti-infective agents depends on catheter type and insertion time: Evidence from a meta-analysis. Infect Control Hosp Epidemiol. 2002;23:748.

248. Veenstra DL, Saint S, Saha S, et al. Efficacy of antiseptic-impregnated central venous catheters in preventing catheter-related bloodstream infection: A meta-analysis. JAMA. 1999;281:261.

249. Darouiche RO, Raad II, Heard SO, et al. A comparison of two antimicrobial-impregnated central venous catheters. N Engl J Med. 1999;340:1.

250. Raad I, Darouiche R, Dupuis J, et al. Central venous catheters coated with minocycline and rifampin for the prevention of catheter-related colonization and bloodstream infections: A randomized, double-blind trial. The Texas Medical Center Catheter Study Group. Ann Intern Med. 1997;127:267.

251. Sampath LA, Tambe SM, Modak SM. In vitro and in vivo efficacy of catheters impregnated with antiseptics or antibiotics: Evaluation of the risk of bacterial resistance to the antimicrobials in the catheters. Infect Control Hosp Epidemiol. 2001;22:640.

252. Yorganci K, Krepel C, Weigelt JA, et al. In vitro evaluation of the antibacterial activity of three different central venous catheters against gram-positive bacteria. Eur J Clin Microbiol. Infect Dis 2002;21:379.

253. Marciante KD, Veenstra DL, Lipsky BA, et al. Which antimicrobial impregnated central venous catheter should we use? Modeling the costs and outcomes of antimicrobial catheter use. AJIC Am J Infect Control. 2003;31:1.

254. McConnell SA, Gubbins PO, Anaissie EJ. Do antimicrobial-impregnated central venous catheters prevent catheter-related bloodstream infection? Clin Infect Dis. 2003;37:65.

255. Appelgren P, Ransjo U, Bindslev L, et al. Surface heparinization of central venous catheters reduces microbial colonization in vitro and in vivo: Results from a prospective, randomized trial. Crit Care Med. 1996;24:1482.

256. Randolph AG, Cook DJ, Gonzales CA, et al. Benefit of heparin in central venous and pulmonary artery catheters: A meta-analysis of randomized controlled trials. Chest. 1998;113:165.

257. Goey SH, Verweij J, Bolhuis RL, et al. Tunnelled central venous catheters yield a low incidence of septicaemia in interleukin-2-treated patients. Cancer Immunol Immunother. 1997;44:301.

258. Jackson M, Chiarello LA, Gaynes RP, et al. Nurse staffing and health care-associated infections: Proceedings from a working group meeting. AJIC Am J Infect Control. 2002;30:199.

259. Maki D, McCormack K. Defatting catheter insertion sites in total parenteral nutrition is of no value as an infection control measure. Am J Med. 1987;83:833.

260. Maki D. Pathogenesis and strategies for prevention. In: Abstracts of the 33rd Interscience Conference on Antimicrobial Agents and Chemotherapy, New Orleans, Louisiana, 1993:451.

261. Richet H, Hubert B, Nitemberg G, et al. Prospective multicenter study of vascular-catheter-related complications and risk factors for positive central-catheter cultures in intensive care unit patients. J Clin Microbiol. 1990;28:2520.

262. Sheehan G, Leicht K, O'Brien M, et al. Chlorhexidine versus povidone-iodine as cutaneous antisepsis for prevention of vascular catheter infections. In: Abstracts of the 33rd Interscience Conference on Antimicrobial Agents and Chemotherapy, New Orleans, Louisiana, 1993:414.

263. van Hoff J, Berg AT, Seashore JH. The effect of right atrial catheters on the infectious complications of chemotherapy in children. J Clin Oncol. 1990;8:1255.

264. Biffi R, Corrado F, de Braud F, et al. Long-term, totally implantable central venous access ports connected to a Groshong catheter for chemotherapy of solid tumours: Experience from 178 cases using a single type of device. Eur J Cancer. 1997;33:1190.

265. Schwarz RE, Groeger JS, Coit DG. Subcutaneously implanted central venous access devices in cancer patients: A prospective analysis. Cancer. 1997;79:1635.

266. Chang L, Tsai JS, Huang SJ, et al. Evaluation of infectious complications of the implantable venous access system in a general oncologic population. AJIC Am J Infect Control. 2003;31:34.

267. Luskin RL, Weinstein RA, Nathan C, et al. Extended use of disposable pressure transducers: A bacteriologic evaluation. JAMA. 1986;255:916.

CHAPTER **301**

Nosocomial Respiratory Infections

LARRY J. STRAUSBAUGH

Virtually any respiratory infection may arise in health care settings, but the adjective "nosocomial" generally applies to those acquired within hospitals. Influenza, respiratory syncytial virus, and parainfluenza virus occasionally infect inpatients and their caregivers. Secondary cases among health care workers characterized the 2003 epidemic of severe acute respiratory syndrome, which was caused by a novel coronavirus.[1] *Legionella* has caused outbreaks and endemic disease in a number of facilities during the past 3 decades. Tuberculosis disseminates within hospitals. Respiratory infections caused by *Aspergillus,* herpesviruses, and other opportunistic pathogens occur in hospitalized transplant recipients and other immunocompromised patients. Nosocomial respiratory infections caused by these diverse etiologic agents as well as nonpulmonary infections (e.g., sinusitis) are reviewed elsewhere in this text. This chapter focuses primarily on hospital-acquired pneumonia caused by common bacterial pathogens.

Pneumonia is a frequent, serious, and costly problem in hospitalized patients. Overall, it ranks second to urinary tract infections, accounting for 15% to 20% of all nosocomial infections in acute care facilities.[2-9] In intensive care units (ICUs) it usually ranks number one.[10] Hospital-acquired pneumonias account for the majority of deaths attributed to nosocomial infections. Case-fatality rates have exceeded 70% in some series of ventilator-associated pneumonia (VAP).[11,12] Finally, hospital stays for patients with nosocomial pneumonia average 1 to 2 weeks longer than those for appropriate control subjects, resulting in higher costs. Estimates for excess costs in the United States have ranged from $1.2 to $2.0 billion per year.[6-8,11]

DEFINITION

Nosocomial pneumonias are inflammatory conditions of the lung parenchyma caused by infectious agents not present or incubating at the time of admission, that is, conditions that develop 48 to 72 hours after admission to the hospital.[5] Accumulations of neutrophils in the distal bronchioles, alveoli, and interstitium of the lung constitute the histopathologic hallmarks.[7,13-16] Despite the clarity of these concepts, clinicians and investigators often find it difficult to apply them. Even investigations using definitions based on histopathologic findings at autopsy may fail to yield a diagnostic consensus, let alone a universal reference standard. Pathologists may miss pneumonia in focal areas of a lobe or disagree about the actual findings. Negative microbiologic studies on lung specimens demonstrating inflammation further compound the diagnostic problem. The performance of certain diagnostic techniques also appears strongly related to the reference standard selected.[13]

Diagnostic dilemmas intensify in practice settings where lung biopsies are seldom obtained. Accordingly, the absence of a "gold standard" continues to generate uncertainty and controversy about operational definitions for nosocomial pneumonia. Nevertheless, clinical investigators and hospital epidemiologists have utilized a number of operational definitions during the last 40 years.[3,4,7] To some extent, they have matched the purpose for which they were developed (e.g., infection control surveillance or etiologic diagnosis of VAP). Most have incorporated a mixture of symptoms, signs, radiographic findings, and culture results. The Clinical Pulmonary Infection Score (CPIS) (Table 301-1) represents one such approach.[17,18]

During the last decade, definitions that include quantitative culture results exceeding a certain threshold from protected specimen brush (PSB) or bronchoalveolar lavage (BAL) specimens have become increasingly favored by clinical investigators.[3,4,11,12] Inclusion of such requirements in the operational definition have generally improved both the sensitivity and specificity of diagnostic criteria, especially in patients with VAP. Several studies tout sensitivity and specificity figures exceeding 80%.[4,7,11,12,19,20] However, studies of their utility in patient care and effect on outcomes have yielded mixed results. Two studies reported decreased antimicrobial use in patients undergoing bronchoscopy for diagnostic purposes, and one reported improved outcomes in this same group.[21,22] However, five other studies with similar designs failed to confirm these findings in patients subjected to invasive diagnostic studies.[23-27] The uncertainty engendered by these conflicting results and limited availability of bronchoscopy prompt continued use of more traditional definitions and ongoing evaluation of other diagnostic modalities and strategies.

Finally, differences in etiologic agents and therapeutic considerations distinguish distinct categories of patients with nosocomial pneumonia. These include patients not requiring ventilatory assistance, who account for 15% to 20% of cases, and the majority, who have

TABLE 301-1 Clinical Pulmonary Infection Score (CPIS) for Diagnosis of Nosocomial Pneumonia*

Criterion	Value	Points
Temperature (° C)	≥ 36.5 and ≤ 38.4	0
	≥ 38.5 and ≤ 38.9	1
	≤ 36.0 and ≥ 39.0	2
Blood leukocytes (/μL)	≥ 4000 and ≤ 11,000	0
	< 4000 or >11,000	1
	≥ 500 band forms	1
Tracheal secretions	Absence of tracheal secretions	0
	Presence of nonpurulent tracheal secretions	1
	Presence of purulent tracheal secretions	2
Oxygenation: PaO_2/FiO_2 (mm Hg)	> 240 or ARDS	0
	≤ 240 and no evidence of ARDS	2
Pulmonary radiography	No infiltrate	0
	Diffuse (or patchy) infiltrate	1
	Localized infiltrate	2
Progression of pulmonary infiltrate	No radiographic progression	0
	Radiographic progression (after CHF and ARDS excluded)	2
Culture and Gram stain of tracheal aspirate	No pathogenic bacteria cultured	0
	Pathogenic bacteria cultured	1
	Some pathogenic bacteria seen on Gram stain	1

*Total CPIS points more than 6 consistent with a diagnosis of nosocomial pneumonia.
ARDS, adult respiratory distress syndrome; CHF, congestive heart failure; PaO_2/FiO_2, ratio of arterial oxygen pressure to fraction of inspired oxygen.
Adapted from Singh N, Rogers P, Atwood CW, et al. Short-course empiric antibiotic therapy for patients with pulmonary infiltrates in the intensive care unit: A proposed solution for indiscriminate antibiotic prescription. Am J Respir Crit Care Med. 2000;162:505-511. Official journal of the American Thoracic Society. © American Thoracic Society.

VAP. VAP is commonly classified as early-onset VAP (occurring within the first 4 days of mechanical ventilation) or late-onset VAP (occurring after 4 or more days of mechanical ventilation).[5-7] This distinction according to time of onset is relatively imprecise, and considerable overlap exists between the two VAP groups.

EPIDEMIOLOGY

Nosocomial pneumonia is a common disease, and recurrent episodes are not uncommon, especially in ventilated patients. The latter may be either relapses or reinfections. A number of studies from the past 2 decades have identified cumulative incidence rates of 0.5% to 1.0% for U.S. hospitals.[3,5,7,9] Extrapolations of these figures to hospital admission data suggest that 250,000 to 300,000 cases of nosocomial pneumonia occur annually. Hospital-wide surveillance studies have incidences averaging 0.8 cases per 1000 patient-care days.[7] These rates tend to be higher in elderly patients. They are substantially higher in patients undergoing abdominal and thoracic surgery and in patients requiring intensive care.

In patients requiring mechanical ventilation, rates are 6- to 20-fold higher.[3,5,7,9] Crude rates for VAP range from 1% to 3% per day of intubation and mechanical ventilation.[28] The 2002 summary of the National Nosocomial Infections Surveillance (NNIS) system of the Centers for Disease Control and Prevention reported pooled mean VAP rates ranging from 2.4 to 14.7 cases per 1000 ventilator days in various types of ICUs.[29] Overall, rates most commonly range between 10 and 15 cases per 1000 ventilator days.[28] Not surprisingly, rates for nonventilated ICU patients are considerably lower.[7]

Although crude mortality rates for nosocomial pneumonia range from 4% to 76%, they generally fall between 30% and 50%.[7-9,21-24,26-28,30-36] They are lowest for patients without VAP, intermediate for those with VAP not associated with adult respiratory distress syndrome (ARDS), and highest for those with VAP and ARDS. Early-onset and late-onset VAP appear to have comparable case-fatality rates.[35] Nationwide, hospital-acquired pneumonias are estimated to be a primary or contributing cause of death for 20,000 to 30,000 persons each year. Poor prognostic factors include advanced age, severe underlying disease, high Acute Physiology and Chronic Health Evaluation II (APACHE II) scores or other indicators of disease severity, multiple organ system failure, shock, and infection with certain multidrug-resistant gram-negative bacilli, especially *Pseudomonas aeruginosa* and *Acinetobacter* spp.[7,9,11,28,32] Polymicrobial and monomicrobial VAP appear to have similar mortality rates.[31]

The actual role that pneumonia plays in causing death remains highly controversial. Most recent studies about mortality have focused on patients with VAP in the ICU. A number have found 2- to 10-fold increases in mortality for patients with pneumonia requiring ICU care.[28] Some investigators have determined attributable mortality rates for VAP of about 30% and identified VAP as an independent risk factor for death.[7-9,11,33] Other studies, however, have not found an increased risk of death in patients with VAP compared to appropriately matched controls.[30,32,34,36] The heterogeneous nature of patients with VAP in different types of ICUs probably contributes to these discrepant results. Additional factors that may influence the relationship between VAP and mortality include the degree of disease severity at the time of onset and timely institution of appropriate antimicrobial therapy.[37]

The relationship of nosocomial pneumonia to morbidity appears more straightforward. Secondary bacteremias and empyema arise in 4% to 38% and 5% to 8% of patients, respectively.[7] Many studies have found increased ICU and hospital lengths of stay, extending from 4 to 21 days but usually ranging from 4 to 9 days.[7,9,11,30,36] Patients with VAP also require mechanical ventilation for longer periods of time.[30,34] All of these factors contribute to excess costs, which one large, recent study estimated at more than $40,000 per patient.[30]

RISK FACTORS

A number of studies performed during the last 2 decades have established a number of risk factors for nosocomial pneumonia.[2-4,7,8,11,12,38-46] As a rule, persons at risk are elderly and moderately to severely ill. They have noteworthy compromises in respiratory tract function, which often reflect intrinsic respiratory, neurologic, or other disease states that result in respiratory tract obstruction, diminished lung volumes, decreased filtration of inspired air, or decreased clearance of secretions. Trauma, surgery, medications, and respiratory therapy devices may similarly impair the defenses of the lung.

Insertion of an endotracheal tube bypasses many layers of host defenses, allowing microorganisms direct access to the lower respiratory tract.[7,11,39,41] Insertion of the tube may injure the tracheal mucosa and permit pathogens to gain a foothold. Not surprisingly, endotracheal intubation and mechanical ventilation are the most important risk factors for development of nosocomial pneumonia. Specific examples of additional risk factors are listed by category in Table 301-2 for both VAP and pneumonia occurring in more heterogeneous hospital populations that include both ventilated and nonventilated patients.

TABLE 301-2 Examples of Risk Factors for Nosocomial Pneumonia

	Examples of Risk Factors in Category	
Category	In Unventilated or Broad Mixtures of Hospital Patients	In Patients Receiving Mechanical Ventilation
Host related	Advanced age, severity of illness, trauma/head injury, poor nutritional status, coma, impaired airway reflexes, neuromuscular disease	Advanced age, chronic lung disease, severity of illness, depressed consciousness or coma, organ failure, severe head trauma, shock, blunt trauma, burns, stress ulceration
Device related	Endotracheal intubation, nasogastric tube, bronchoscopy	Duration of mechanical ventilation, reintubation or self-extubation, ventilator circuit changes at intervals < 48 hr; emergent intubation after trauma, PEEP, tracheostomy
Drug related	Immunosuppressive therapy	Prior antimicrobial therapy, antacid or H_2 blocker therapy, barbiturate therapy after head trauma
Miscellaneous	Thoracic or upper abdominal surgery; duration of surgery, duration of hospitalization, large-volume aspiration	Thoracic or upper abdominal surgery; gross aspiration of gastric contents, supine head position, enteral nutrition, fall-winter season

H_2, histamine type 2; PEEP, positive end-expiratory pressure.
Data from references 3, 4, 5, 7, 9, 11, 39-43, 45, 46.

Poor infection control practices also put patients at risk for nosocomial pneumonia. Inadequate hand hygiene practices promote cross-infection and facilitate transmission of resistant pathogens.[8,9,39] Outbreaks of nosocomial pneumonia caused by contaminated respiratory therapy equipment (e.g., nebulizers) have demonstrated repeatedly the potential hazards of inadequate disinfection.[4,7-9,11] At present, hand hygiene, glove and other barrier use, tracheal suction practices, and management of equipment used for respiratory therapy head the list of poor practices.[9,39] In some situations, failure to attend properly to such considerations may facilitate not only cross-infection but also delivery of large bacterial inocula to the lower airway.

PATHOGENESIS

Nosocomial pneumonias develop most frequently after inapparent aspiration or so-called microaspiration of upper airway secretions into the lower respiratory tract.[2,4,7-9] This paradigm applies to intubated and nonintubated patients alike. In intubated patients, secretions pool above the inflated cuff of the endotracheal tube.[7,8] With changes in airway caliber associated with swallowing or breathing, secretions leak around the cuff and gain entry to the lower respiratory tract. This phenomenon occurs in most intubated patients, and the supine position may facilitate its occurrence. Upper airway secretions, which are predominantly from the oropharynx, contain mixtures of pathogenic microorganisms. In previously healthy, newly hospitalized patients, normal mouth flora or pathogens associated with community-acquired pneumonia predominate.[47] In sicker patients who have been hospitalized more than 5 days, gram-negative bacilli and *Staphylococcus aureus* frequently colonize the upper airway. Microaspiration occurs commonly in intubated and nonintubated patients.[4,7-9,11] Pneumonia develops when either the sheer number of bacteria aspirated or their virulence overwhelms the phagocytic, humoral, and other defense mechanisms of the distal airways and alveoli. Microbial proliferation and the ensuing inflammatory response then produce the clinical syndrome of pneumonia.[5] Efforts to clarify the role of cytokines in the inflammatory process have begun.[48,49]

Nosocomial pneumonia may arise in other ways.[2-4,7,8,11] Rarely, hematogenous dissemination of *S. aureus* or gram-negative uropathogens seed the lung. Uncommonly, observed "macroaspirations" of esophageal or gastric material initiate the process. Allowing condensates in ventilator tubing to drain into the patient's airway may have the same effect. Bronchoscopy, tracheal suctioning, manual ventilation, or spirometry employing contaminated equipment may also bring pathogens to the lower respiratory tract.[3,4,7-9,39] In past outbreaks, infected aerosols from contaminated nebulizers and other respiratory therapy equipment have played an important role in pathogenesis, but these devices are infrequently associated with nosocomial pneumonia today.[3,4,7,9,39]

Although aerobic gram-negative bacilli frequently cause nosocomial pneumonia, they are isolated uncommonly from the respiratory tract of healthy individuals. Accordingly, considerable attention has focused on the source of gram-negative bacilli causing pneumonia and on their colonization of the respiratory tract in hospitalized patients.[2-4,7-9,11,47,50,51] The oropharynx and trachea continue to garner most of the attention. Colonization of these sites with gram-negative bacilli occurs within a few days after admission to ICUs, and colonization often precedes the development of pneumonia. Sophisticated typing techniques used in a prospective study have demonstrated that oropharyngeal colonization was a predominant factor in the development of nosocomial pneumonia.[50] Many of the risk factors for colonization parallel those for pneumonia.[7] A reduced capacity to clear pathogens, increased adherence of microorganisms to epithelial cells in the oropharynx, or both may account for this phenomenon.[7] Bacterial adhesins and prior antimicrobial therapy also appear to facilitate the process. Of interest, Enterobacteriaceae usually appear in the oropharynx first, whereas *P. aeruginosa* more often appears first in tracheal secretions.[7]

Other sources of pathogens causing nosocomial pneumonia include the paranasal sinuses,[44] dental plaque, and the subglottic area between the true vocal cords and the endotracheal tube cuff.[7-9,11,12] The role of the stomach as a bacterial reservoir in patients receiving antisecretory therapy or antacids remains controversial.[4,7-9,11-12,50,51] Those who champion the gastric reservoir hypothesis point to the large quantities of bacteria in the stomachs of patients rendered achlorhydric as well as to the potential for reflux of gastric contents into the esophagus of patients in the supine position, particularly when enteral tubes compromise the function of the gastroesophageal sphincter. Lower incidences of pneumonia in some studies comparing sucralfate with histamine type 2 (H_2) blocker therapy have also been used to support this contention.

However, strong arguments have been mustered against the gastric reservoir hypothesis.[4,7-9,11,12,39,51] Gastric isolates from patients receiving H_2 blocker therapy uncommonly cause VAP. Experimental studies using appropriate diagnostic and molecular typing techniques have not confirmed the proposed sequence of gastric colonization first with subsequent development of nosocomial pneumonia. Comparative trials with sucralfate therapy have not consistently yielded reduced rates of VAP; in fact, documented increases in gastric pH with sucralfate therapy have raised questions about the proposed rationale for its effect. Efforts to eliminate the gastric reservoir with antimicrobial therapy—that is, selective decontamination of the digestive tract (SDD)—have often failed to prevent pneumonia. Finally, some evidence suggests that intestinal microorganisms present in the patient's rectal area account for colonization of the oropharynx, either migrating via the patient's skin or transferring via the hands of caregivers.[7]

The frequency of nosocomial pneumonia caused by antimicrobial-resistant organisms, such as methicillin-resistant *S. aureus* and multidrug-resistant gram-negative bacilli, indicates that cross-colonization and cross-infection contribute to pathogenesis.[3,7-9,11,12] Infected or colonized patients usually constitute the reservoir for resistant organisms in the hospital. Cross-infection and cross-colonization probably arise from patient contact with the contaminated hands of health care work-

TABLE 301-3   Etiology of Nosocomial Pneumonia

	Percentage of All Microbes Recovered in Aerobic Cultures in Study or Compilation		
	NNIS System Medical ICUs 1992–1997 (N = 4389)[56]	*Bacteremic Cases from One Tertiary Care Hospital in Alberta, Canada: ICU & Non-ICU Cases, 1986–1993[52]*	*Pooled Results from 24 Studies; PSB and/or BAL Techniques for Diagnosis; 1689 Episodes of VAP[11]*
Staphylococcus aureus	20	27	20.4
Streptococcus pneumoniae	0	1	4.1
Haemophilus spp. (predominantly *H. influenzae*)	0	2	9.8
Moraxella catarrhalis	0	0	0
Enterobacteriaceae	29	34	14.1
Pseudomonas spp. (predominantly *P. aeruginosa*)	21	12	24.4
Acinetobacter spp.	6	0	7.9
Other enteric gram-negative bacilli	0	0	1.7
Fungi (predominantly *Candida* spp.)	7.8	4	0.9
Assorted other bacteria*	3	21	16.7

*Includes coagulase-negative staphylococci, enterococci, *viridans* streptococci, *Neisseria* spp., anaerobes, and unidentified bacteria.

ers. Activities in patient care such as bathing, oral care, tracheal suctioning, enteral feeding, and tube manipulations provide ample opportunities for transmission of resistant pathogens when infection control practices are substandard.

ETIOLOGY

Although positive blood cultures and cultures of empyema fluid can establish an etiologic diagnosis in patients with nosocomial pneumonia, in most case series less than 15% of patients have positive cultures from these sites.[7,52-54] Moreover, bacteremia may arise from sites other than the lungs, and it has a low sensitivity for detecting the same pathogenic microorganism as BAL cultures in patients with VAP.[54] Within the past decade, diagnostic methods using bronchoscopy coupled with quantitative cultures of PSB and BAL specimens have been increasingly used to establish an etiologic diagnosis, especially in patients with VAP. Results obtained with these methods correlate well with those obtained using histopathologic criteria and cultures of tissue specimens.[4,6-8,11-16,19,20] Microbiologic results obtained with these methods in unselected patients have been discordant with those obtained from cultures of expectorated sputum or tracheal secretions, suggesting that they are indeed superior for establishing an etiologic diagnosis. Notwithstanding their diagnostic value for individual patients, in the aggregate microbes isolated with quantitative PSB and BAL cultures mirror those reported by the NNIS system, which, until recently, relied on cultures of expectorated sputum and tracheal secretions in their surveillance definition (Table 301-3).[4-7,11,12,55,56] Isolates from bacteremic patients also delineate the same spectrum of pathogens—principally gram-negative bacilli and *S. aureus*.[52-54]

Studies using quantitative PSB or BAL cultures for diagnosis have disclosed that 20% to 50% of VAP cases have a polymicrobial etiology.[4,5,7,11] They have also provided a rationale for distinguishing early-onset from late-onset disease. When disease develops within 4 or 5 days of admission (or intubation), agents associated with community-acquired pneumonia—*Haemophilus influenzae, Streptococcus pneumoniae,* and *Moraxella catarrhalis*—are recovered with some frequency.[3-8,11,12,46] These bacteria probably originate from the oropharyngeal flora present at admission before gram-negative bacilli and staphylococci have had time to supplant them. When disease develops after 5 days, few pathogens associated with community-acquired pneumonia are recovered. The whole panoply of gram-negative bacilli and *S. aureus* predominate in late-onset disease, as they do overall (see Table 301-3).[3-8,11,12] Of note, these bacteria can also cause early-onset disease, especially in patients with severe comorbidities and recent antimicrobial therapy, so the distinction between early-onset and late-onset disease is not absolute. Regardless, longer duration of mechanical ventilation and antimicrobial therapy, especially broad-spectrum therapy, increase the likelihood that recovered isolates will

include *P. aeruginosa, Acinetobacter* spp., and other highly resistant organisms such as methicillin-resistant *S. aureus*.[57]

Within the broad categories outlined above, causes of nosocomial pneumonia exhibit considerable temporal and geographic variation. A comparison of isolates obtained by bronchoscopic techniques and quantitative cultures from patients in Paris, Barcelona, Montevideo, and Seville during the period 1994-1996 illustrated the geographic aspects of this variation and its implications for recommendations about empirical therapy.[58] In any particular facility, outbreaks occasionally alter etiologic considerations for nosocomial pneumonia, especially in ICUs. Frequent offenders include multidrug-resistant gram negative bacilli and methicillin-resistant *S. aureus*.[57,59] Pathogens usually associated with community-acquired pneumonia (e.g., *Chlamydophila psittaci* and *Mycoplasma pneumoniae*) have rarely caused nosocomial outbreaks of pneumonia too.[60,61]

Occasionally, other etiologic considerations arise. The isolation of coagulase-negative staphylococci, enterococci, *Neisseria* spp., or *viridans* streptococci in high concentrations from PSB or BAL specimens is of debatable significance.[4,62] Although clinicians have often ignored these isolates, numerous studies have reported their isolation in large numbers from PSB and BAL specimens.[11] All have occasionally been isolated from blood cultures of patients with nosocomial pneumonia.[52-54] In one recent case series they accounted for 9% of VAP cases during a 10-year period.[62] After a detailed analysis of these cases, the investigators concluded that these "oropharyngeal and cutaneous commensal microorganism may behave like classic nosocomial pathogens in critically ill patients."[62] The potential pathogenicity of these agents warrants additional study.

Isolation of fungi, most frequently *Candida* spp., in significant numbers poses interpretative problems too.[11] Cases of invasive disease have been reported in VAP, but, more frequently, yeasts are isolated from respiratory tract specimens in the apparent absence of disease. One prospective study examined the relevance of isolating *Candida* spp. in 25 non-neutropenic patients who had been mechanically ventilated for more than 72 hours.[63] Just after death, multiple culture and biopsy specimens were obtained with bronchoscopic techniques. Ten patients had at least one biopsy specimen positive for *Candida* spp. However, only two patients had evidence of invasive disease. Many of the endotracheal aspirates, PSB specimens, and BAL specimens from the 10 patients also yielded positive cultures for *Candida* spp. Quantitative cultures of various samples from these patients were not helpful in the diagnosis of invasive disease.

The role of anaerobic bacteria needs additional study.[4] In one report they were isolated from 23% of the patients with VAP whose diagnoses were made with quantitative PSB and BAL techniques and special attention to the isolation of anaerobes.[64] Of note, the recovered anaerobes mirrored the bacteriology of the oropharynx, and they were the sole isolates in only four cases. None was isolated from blood or associated with necrotizing disease. Nevertheless, in a more recent study PSB and BAL techniques retrieved no anaerobes from 143 patients studied with meticulous techniques during 185 episodes of VAP.[65] The results of this study and many others imply that anaerobes are not noteworthy causes of VAP. Their role in patients with poor dentition, however, may be more significant.[5]

DIAGNOSIS

The diagnostic process for nosocomial pneumonia runs the gamut from being fairly easy and uncomplicated to being extremely difficult, if not impossible.[2,4,11,59] Young patients without underlying lung disease who aspirate after surgery and then develop fever, leukocytosis, purulent sputum, and a new lobar infiltrate on chest radiographs pose few diagnostic difficulties, especially when blood and sputum cultures yield the same pathogen. At the other extreme of the diagnostic continuum, elderly patients with chronic obstructive pulmonary disease and congestive heart failure who have been intubated and ventilated mechanically for 2 weeks for ARDS developing after abdominal surgery may challenge and defeat all attempts at antemortem diagnosis. Although the latter patients often have fever, leukocytosis, and purulent tracheal aspirates, less than half may have pneumonia.[4] During febrile episodes, they usually have negative blood cultures, positive tracheal aspirates, and chest radiographs with unchanging, bilateral diffuse infiltrates. In practice, the majority of patients fall on the continuum between these two extremes. Their diagnosis depends on the intensity of their diagnostic workup and the operational definitions employed.

Pneumonia should be suspected in hospitalized patients, especially those with risk factors, when signs and symptoms of respiratory disease or unexplained fever appear.[2,5,11,18,59] Suspicion mounts in the presence of systemic toxicity, objective measures of respiratory dysfunction (e.g., decreased O_2 saturation), new or progressing infiltrates on chest radiographs, and a rising leukocyte count. The differential diagnosis includes several other considerations. For example, pulmonary findings might reflect atelectasis, pulmonary embolism, or congestive heart failure.[11,59] Similarly, fever might reflect extrapulmonary infection, drug reactions, or transfusion reactions. If the initial clinical evaluation points away from noninfectious causes, the search for information to support the "pneumonia hypothesis" continues.

Gross inspection of respiratory secretions and examination of their Gram-stained smear can facilitate the diagnosis, especially when the samples are obtained from nonintubated patients.[2,5,11,24] Numerous neutrophils and macrophages plus high concentrations of a single morphologic form of bacteria can offer strong support for the diagnosis in nonventilated patients without underlying lung disease. Calculation of the CPIS may assist clinicians in identifying patients with VAP (see Table 301-1). Although unvalidated, the CPIS had a sensitivity of 93% in the report with its original description.[17] In a later study it identified patients for whom short courses of antimicrobial therapy were appropriate.[18] In another study it proved useful in following patients and identifying patients with good outcomes.[66] CPIS scores range from 0 to 12 points; scores higher than 6 correlate well with results from PSB and BAL studies in patients with VAP. Scores lower than 6 suggest a low probability of VAP.

Gram stain findings may suggest the etiology. Other information from the history or medical record may do the same, for example, information about a witnessed aspiration, respiratory disease in the family, surveillance data about high prevalences of resistant microbes in the ICU, and recent cases of unusual nosocomial infections (e.g., legionellosis or tuberculosis). Such information may guide the empirical therapy and prompt orders for viral cultures, tests for *Legionella* antigen in urine, or smears and cultures for acid-fast bacilli. Despite their limitations, the continuing diagnostic workup often includes cultures of sputum or tracheal aspirates, blood cultures, and pleural fluid cultures when a sizable effusion is present.

When CPIS scores exceed 6 or the diagnosis of nosocomial pneumonia otherwise seems likely, questions about the need for bronchoscopy arise, especially in patients with VAP.[1,2,4-7,11,12,19-27,59] Emphasizing the imprecision and pitfalls of clinical diagnoses, some authorities have argued vigorously that all patients suspected of having VAP should undergo bronchoscopy to obtain specimens for quantitative PSB or BAL cultures.[4,11] They argue that this approach will most likely yield correct etiologic diagnoses, maximize antimicrobial therapy, minimize excess antimicrobial use, and improve outcomes.

Arguments against bronchoscopy for diagnostic purposes point to its expense, its hazard for hemodynamically unstable patients, variations in sensitivity and specificity values for quantitative PSB and BAL cultures, flaws in the studies demonstrating improved outcomes, and availability of other alternatives.[11,12,19] Many clinicians further doubt that negative results will reduce antimicrobial use, noting that empirical therapy often continues when bacteriologic studies are negative. Others emphasize existing knowledge about etiologies (see Table 301-3) and judge that empirical therapy will suffice.

On a practical level, questions about bronchoscopy in diagnosis often come down to availability. Can an experienced bronchoscopist with the requisite technical support perform the procedure within an hour or two, before starting antibiotics becomes imperative? At the same time, it is essential to have laboratory services to back up the procedure—to perform quantitative tests on PSB and BAL specimens and additional studies, if indicated.[67] When the procedure and the laboratory support are available, bronchoscopic studies should be strongly considered for all patients with nosocomial pneumonia, especially for those who are immunocompromised, those likely to have VAP, and those who have not responded to 48 to 72 hours of empirical antimicrobial therapy. Patients with ARDS may require specimen collection from both lungs.[68] When patients cannot readily undergo bronchoscopy, cultures of endotracheal aspirates, preferably using quantitative techniques, appear to offer the most reasonable approach to an etiologic diagnosis.[3,12,23,25,27] Other considerations, though less well studied, include PSB and BAL techniques without bronchoscopy using "blindly" inserted catheters.[4,11,12]

Part of the controversy about the use of bronchoscopic techniques derives from concerns about their diagnostic precision. The need for quantitative bacteriology to establish thresholds indicative of infection immediately identifies one concern. Insertion of a bronchoscope into the tracheobronchial tree pushes down nasopharyngeal, oropharyngeal, or endotracheal flora and contaminates the lower airway. Hence, quantitative thresholds are used to differentiate infection from contamination from the procedure. The current consensus recognizes 10^3 or more colony-forming units (CFUs) for microbes grown from PSB specimens and 10^4 or more CFUs for microbes grown from BAL specimens as clinching the diagnosis for patients with compatible clinical findings.[4,6,7,11,12] In most studies focusing only on patients with VAP, sensitivities range from 42% to 100% for PSB cultures and from 47% to 100% for BAL cultures.[7] Specificities range from 60% to 100% for PSB cultures and from 45% to 100% for BAL cultures.[7] Because the operational definition of VAP and experimental methods have varied somewhat from study to study, controversy persists about the breadth of these ranges and, hence, about the value of the tests.[4,7,11,12,19] The greatest difficulties are encountered for patients with VAP who have received antibiotics, especially when the regimen has been altered in the 3-day period prior to bronchoscopy.[4,11,19] A meta-analysis of studies employing PSB and BAL techniques concluded that both methods offer comparable diagnostic accuracy in patients with VAP.[69] It appeared, however, that BAL findings were less influenced by antecedent antimicrobial therapy.

A number of modifications and variations on the basic diagnostic approaches have appeared in the literature, but most have failed to improve diagnosis or require additional study to validate their utility. Protected BAL, that is, lavage performed using a catheter equipped with a balloon to seal off the orifice of the bronchial subsegment to be sampled, appears to enhance performance of the BAL technique.[4,11]

Microscopic examination of BAL specimens and quantitation of intracellular organisms may also enhance test performance. A cutoff point of greater than 2% cells containing intracellular organisms offered a sensitivity of 80% and specificity of 82% in one recent study.[70] Tests for endotoxin in BAL fluid have proved disappointing,[71] whereas one small study has suggested that measurement of matrix metalloproteinases and related products in BAL may facilitate identification of VAP.[72] Finally, routine surveillance cultures on ICU patients at risk for VAP have proven poor predictors of the etiology in patients who eventually have confirmed disease.[73]

THERAPY

Decisions about empirical antimicrobial therapy for nosocomial pneumonia commence during the clinical evaluation. Clinical and epidemiologic features suggestive of influenza prompt consideration of empirical therapy with a neuraminidase inhibitor, amantadine, or rimantadine. Likewise, clinical features suggestive of legionellosis warrant therapy with erythromycin, another macrolide, or a fluoroquinolone. Empirical therapy for patients with neutropenia or other forms of immunosuppression might involve an antifungal agent or ganciclovir. Regardless of the likely pathogen, all patients with nosocomial pneumonia, especially those with VAP, require supportive care directed at oxygenation, nutrition, skin care, and avoidance of iatrogenic complications.

In patients without notable immunosuppression or unusual etiologic considerations, microbial targets are less diverse. In some cases, Gram stain findings from sputum, endotracheal aspirate, PSB, or BAL specimens permit reasonable antimicrobial choices. Notwithstanding the desire to have this information, physicians need to start antimicrobial therapy promptly. Delays in the initiation of therapy increase the likelihood of poor outcomes.[74] Guidelines for empirical therapy may facilitate the selection of agents. Over the last decade, many physicians have turned to the consensus statement issued by the American Thoracic Society (ATS) in 1995.[5] The examples of empirical antimicrobial regimens in Table 301-4 derive from this document. They reflect the useful concepts of core microorganisms, early- and late-onset disease, risk factors for certain pathogens, combination therapy for more resistant gram-negative bacilli, and severity of illness categorizations.

Many variations on the examples given in Table 301-4 exist. Individual medical centers and ICUs necessarily adapt such principles to their own situations, considering the characteristics of their patient population, pathogens usually isolated from patients with nosocomial pneumonia, local patterns of antimicrobial resistance, and pharmacy acquisition costs.[8,11,12,75] Comparative trials of different antimicrobial regimens, which have appeared with regularity in the last 5 years, also inform local decisions.[11] Such trials usually demonstrate equivalence of the regimens studied but serve to expand the list of available options.[76,77]

The 1995 ATS consensus statement has deficiencies: it lacks information on newer agents, it does not recommend specific agents, and it does not recommend specific durations for therapy.[78] Accordingly, some institutions have developed specific guidelines for their facilities.[79] The ATS plans to issue a revised guideline in 2004, and the Infectious Diseases Society of America plans to issue its own guideline in the same year.

The results of microbiologic studies (e.g., positive blood, pleural fluid, PSB, and BAL cultures) allow reductions in the scope of antimicrobial therapy to target only the isolated pathogen(s). In two studies negative PSB and BAL cultures allowed discontinuation of antimicrobial therapy.[21,22] It is hoped that this practice will become widespread as physicians develop experience with this approach. At present, too many physicians find it difficult to withhold antimicrobial therapy from extremely ill, febrile patients in the ICU, even when their bacteriologic studies are negative. One study has suggested that serial CPIS scores can help limit antibiotic use in ICU patients with a presumptive diagnosis of pneumonia.[18] Recent commentaries have emphasized the need for antimicrobial "de-escalation strategies" as well as studies to evaluate the timing and effect of discontinuing antimicrobial therapy.[80,81] More research is also needed to clarify the role of aerosolized or intratracheally administered antimicrobial therapy. Although these approaches have received some attention over the past 2 decades, definitive proof of their value has yet to appear.[82,83]

Although sometimes difficult to measure, especially in VAP, clinical improvement usually requires at least 48 to 72 hours of antimicrobial therapy.[5] In one study monitoring CPIS scores helped predict the eventual outcome of therapy, with improved scores on day 3 predicting recovery.[66] The duration of antimicrobial therapy for nosocomial pneumonia remains unsettled.[11,78-81] As the 1995 ATS guideline indicates,

TABLE 301-4 Examples of Antimicrobial Agent(s) Recommended for Empirical Therapy of Nosocomial Pneumonia by Microbial Targets and Clinical Settings*

Microbial Targets	Clinical Setting	Examples
"Core organisms" S. aureus S. pneumoniae H. influenzae Enterobacteriaceae	Severe disease with onset before day 5 in the absence of certain risk factors† *or* Mild to moderate disease at any time in the absence of certain risk factors	Cefotaxime, or ceftriaxone *or* Piperacillin/tazobactam *or* Clindamycin and ciprofloxacin ± Vancomycin or levofloxacin if DRSP likely *or* Levofloxacin or moxifloxacin or gatifloxacin alone
"Core Organisms" PLUS P. aeruginosa Acinetobacter spp. Stenotrophomonas maltophilia Burkholderia cepacia MRSA	Severe disease with onset at any time in the presence of certain risk factors *or* Mild to moderate disease with onset after 5 days in presence of certain risk factors	Gentamicin or ciprofloxacin *plus* Imipenem/cilastatin or meropenem or piperacillin/tazobactam *or* Cefepime or ceftazidime and ± vancomycin or linezolid (if MRSA likely)

*NOT for immunocompromised patients; modification required to accommodate local resistance patterns.
†*Risk factors:* abdominal surgery, aspiration, coma, head trauma, diabetes mellitus, renal failure, high-dose or prolonged therapy with corticosteroids, prolonged ICU stay, underlying lung disease, and prior antimicrobial therapy.
DRSP, drug-resistant *Streptococcus pneumoniae;* MRSA, methicillin-resistant *Staphylococcus aureus.*
Adapted from American Thoracic Society Ad Hoc Committee of the Scientific Assembly on Microbiology, Tuberculosis and Pulmonary Infections. Hospital-acquired pneumonia in adults: Diagnosis, assessment of severity, initial antimicrobial therapy, and preventative strategies. Am J Respir Crit Care Med. 1995;153:1711-1725.

courses of 7 to 10 days often suffice for infections caused by *S. aureus* and *H. influenzae,* but courses of at least 14 to 21 days are recommended for more serious infections caused by *P. aeruginosa* and *Acinetobacter* spp. Because the clinical response to therapy usually occurs within 6 days, some investigators have suggested that 7-day durations of therapy deserve evaluation in clinical trials.[84]

When patients do not improve, a number of noninfectious and infectious possibilities require consideration and evaluation.[5] Noninfectious considerations include development of ARDS, congestive heart failure, and pulmonary embolism. Infectious considerations include inappropriate initial antimicrobial selection, superinfection with resistant bacteria or fungi, development of pulmonary abscess or empyema, and onset of a nonpulmonary nosocomial infection. When patients are not improving, bronchoscopy to obtain PSB and BAL specimens for quantitative cultures requires renewed consideration.[11]

PREVENTION

In 2003, the Hospital Infection Control Practices Advisory Committee (HICPAC) of the Centers for Disease Control and Prevention published revised recommendations for the prevention of nosocomial pneumonia.[9] As before, the key components related to (1) staff education and infection surveillance, (2) prevention of transmission of microorganisms, and (3) modifying host risk factors for infection of bacteria. The revised guidelines also address health care–associated legionellosis, pertussis, aspergillosis, and respiratory viral illnesses. The ATS has provided compatible, albeit less comprehensive, guidelines for the prevention of nosocomial pneumonia,[5] and other reviews are available too.[3,4,7,11,85,86] A 1995 survey of hospitals participating in the NNIS system indicated that most member hospitals had implemented recommendations from the earlier 1994 HICPAC guidelines.[87] However, a more recent survey examining adherence to evidence-based recommendations proposed by Kollef[86] in 1999 (Table 301-5 presents the stronger recommendations) found an overall nonadherence rate of 37%.[88] Patterns of nonadherence conformed to the strength of the recommendation, and respondents indicated that disagreement with the interpretation of clinical trials, unavailability of resources, and costs further impacted their adherence. These findings attest to ongoing controversy, as does the discordance between Kollef's recommendations and those of HICPAC. The failure of these preventive strategies to impact mortality may explain some of the discordance (Table 301-5).

Many of the recommendations in all guidelines address the use of equipment and devices for respiratory care. A number of outbreaks and high endemic rates of nosocomial pneumonia have resulted from contamination of humidifiers and nebulizers.[4,9] Although most believe this to be a problem of the past, reports of outbreaks associated with contaminated nebulizers and other items periodically surface.[3,7,9] Evaluation of new equipment and old practices continues. For example, a review of eight studies concluded that ventilator breathing circuits should be changed every 7 days.[89] A 1998 systematic review indicated that lower rates of VAP may be associated with avoidance of heated humidifiers, use of heat and moisture exchangers, use of oral intubation, subglottic secretion drainage, and use of kinetic beds.[90] Although given only a Category II recommendation in the HICPAC guideline, a more recent systematic review found ample evidence to support aspiration of subglottic secretions in select patient populations to prevent VAP.[85] The authors of this review also recommended semirecumbent positioning in all eligible patients, sucralfate rather than H_2 antagonists in patients at low to moderate risk for gastrointestinal tract bleeding, and oscillating beds in select populations. At the same time they found sufficient evidence to *not* recommend small-intestinal feeding, metoclopramide use, acidification of enteral feedings, and intermittent enteral feedings. For the most part the HICPAC recommendations parallel the findings of these systematic reviews, though they give no recommendation for oscillating beds and their lowest level of endorsement to the preference for sucralfate over H_2 antagonists. The

TABLE 301-5 Strategies for Prevention of Ventilator-Associated Pneumonia Supported by One or Two Randomized, Controlled Investigations*

Prevention Strategy	Associated Reduction in Mortality	Concordance with HICPAC Recommendations
Supported by Two Studies		
Continuous subglottic suctioning	No	Yes
No routine change of ventilator circuits	No	Yes
No dedicated use of disposable suction catheters	No	NR-UI
No daily changes of heat and moisture exchangers	No	Yes
No chest physiotherapy	No	NR-UI
Humidification with heat and moisture exchanger	No	NR-UI
Supported by One Study		
Adequate hand washing between patient contacts	No	Yes
Semirecumbent positioning of the patient	No	Yes
Avoidance of gastric overdistention	No	Yes
No routine changes of in-line suction catheter	No	NR-UI
Use of protective gowns and gloves	No	Yes
Postural changes	No	NR-UI

*Higher recommendation given to strategy supported by two studies in Kollef scheme.

HICPAC, Hospital Infection Control Practice Advisory Committee; NR-UI, no recommendation–unresolved issue.

Data from Kollef MH. The prevention of ventilator-associated pneumonia. N Engl J Med. 1999;340:627-634. Copyright © 1999 Massachusetts Medical Society. All rights reserved.

latter probably reflects the increased frequency of gastrointestinal hemorrhage observed in clinical trials comparing the two forms of stress ulcer prevention.[91]

The HICPAC guidelines contain additional recommendations that may be useful in some hospitals.[9] Moreover, they identified a number of unresolved issues for which there was no consensus. Chief among these was the use of SDD. Fundamentally, SDD involves application of antimicrobial agents, such as polymyxin and an aminoglycoside with or without amphotericin B or nystatin, to the oral cavity in a paste and to the gastrointestinal tract via oral suspensions in order to diminish concentrations of pathogenic bacteria at these sites in ventilator-dependent patients.[7,9,11,85,86] A broad-spectrum parenteral antibiotic (e.g., cefotaxime) is frequently administered concurrently for the first 3 to 5 days. Despite more than 40 clinical trials and six meta-analyses, SDD remains controversial and little used in the United States.[92] Use of topical antibiotics in the upper airway—the oropharyngeal component of SDD—appears to have some benefit in reducing the incidence of VAP[7,11,93]; however, additional confirmatory studies are needed.

The HICPAC guidelines endorse staff education to prevent health care–associated pneumonia. Such education can have a strong effect on the incidence of VAP. In one study an educational initiative was associated with a reduction in the incidence of VAP from 12.6 to 5.7 episodes per 1000 ventilator days, a highly significant difference.[94] Although not mentioned in the HICPAC guidelines, two other promising preventive measures warrant attention: protocols for ventilator management and for antimicrobial use in ICUs. In one small study a ventilator management protocol reduced the duration of ventilatory support and the incidence of VAP.[95] A four-year study in a French ICU demonstrated that rotation and restricted use of antibiotics reduced the frequency of VAP associated with multidrug-resistant bacteria.[96] The percentage of VAP cases caused by methicillin-susceptible *S. aureus* increased from 40% to 60% of *S. aureus* strains responsible for VAP. The promising findings in these two studies merit further evaluation.

REFERENCES

1. Lee N, Hui D, Wu A, et al. A major outbreak of severe acute respiratory syndrome in Hong Kong. N Engl J Med. 2003;348:1986-1994.
2. Lode HM, Schaberg T, Raffenberg M, et al. Nosocomial pneumonia in the critical care unit. Crit Care Clin. 1998;14:119.
3. Craven DE, Steger KA. Hospital-acquired pneumonia: Perspectives for the healthcare epidemiologist. Infect Control Hosp Epidemiol. 1997;18:783-795.
4. Mayhall CG. Nosocomial pneumonia—Diagnosis and prevention. Infect Dis Clin North Am. 1997;11:427-457.
5. American Thoracic Society Ad Hoc Committee of the Scientific Assembly on Microbiology, Tuberculosis and Pulmonary Infections. Hospital-acquired pneumonia in adults: Diagnosis, assessment of severity, initial antimicrobial therapy, and preventative strategies. Am J Respir Crit Care Med. 1995;153:1711-1725.
6. Lentino JR. Nosocomial pneumonia: More than just ventilator-associated. Curr Infect Dis Rep. 2001;3:266-273.
7. Bonten MJM, Bergmans DCJJ. Nosocomial pneumonia. In: Mayhall CG, ed. Hospital Epidemiology and Infection Control. 2nd ed. Philadelphia: Lippincott Williams & Wilkins; 1999:211-238.
8. McEachern R, Campbell GD Jr. Hospital-acquired pneumonia: Epidemiology, etiology, and treatment. Infect Dis Clin North Am. 1998;12:761-779.
9. Centers for Disease Control and Prevention. Guideline for prevention of healthcare-associated pneumonia, 2003. MMWR. 2004;53(No. RR03):1-36.
10. Centers for Disease Control and Prevention. National Nosocomial Infections Surveillance (NNIS) System report, data summary from January 1992-June 2001, issued August 2001. Am J Infect Control. 2000;29:404-421.
11. Chastre J, Fagon J-Y. Ventilator-associated pneumonia. Am J Respir Crit Care Med. 2002;165:867-903.
12. Morehead RS, Pinto SJ. Ventilator-associated pneumonia. Arch Intern Med. 2000;160:1926-1936.
13. Torres A, Fabregas N, Ewig S, et al. Sampling methods for ventilator-associated pneumonia: Validation using different histologic and microbiological references. Crit Care Med. 2000;28:2799-2804.
14. Corley DE, Kirtland SH, Winterbauer RH, et al. Reproducibility of the histologic diagnosis of pneumonia among a panel of four pathologists: Analysis of a gold standard. Chest. 1997;112:458-465.
15. Kirtland SH, Corley DE, Winterbauer RH, et al. The diagnosis of ventilator-associated pneumonia: A comparison of histologic, microbiologic, and clinical criteria. Chest. 1997;112:445-457.
16. Marquette CH, Copin M-C, Wallet F, et al. Diagnostic tests for pneumonia in ventilated patients: Prospective evaluation of diagnostic accuracy using histology as a diagnostic gold standard. Am J Respir Crit Care Med. 1995;151:1878-1888.
17. Pugin J, Auckenthaler R, Mili N, et al. Diagnosis of ventilator-associated pneumonia by bacteriologic analysis of bronchoscopic and nonbronchoscopic "blind" bronchoalveolar lavage fluid. Am Rev Respir Dis. 1991;143:1121-1129.
18. Singh N, Rogers P, Atwood CW, et al. Short-course empiric antibiotic therapy for patients with pulmonary infiltrates in the intensive care unit: A proposed solution for indiscriminate antibiotic prescription. Am J Respir Crit Care Med. 2000;162:505-511.
19. Waterer GW, Wunderink RG. Controversies in the diagnosis of ventilator-acquired pneumonia. Med Clin North Am. 2001;85:1565-1581.
20. San Pedro G. Are quantitative cultures useful in the diagnosis of hospital-acquired pneumonia? Chest. 2001;119:385S-390S.
21. Fagon J-Y, Chastre J, Wolff M, et al. Invasive and noninvasive strategies for management of suspected ventilator-associated pneumonia: A randomized trial. Ann Intern Med. 2000;132:621-630.
22. Heyland DK, Cook DJ, Marshall J, et al. The clinical utility of invasive diagnostic techniques in the setting of ventilator-associated pneumonia. Chest. 1999;115:1076-1084.
23. Sanchez-Nieto JM, Torres A, Garcia-Cordoba F, et al. Impact of invasive and noninvasive quantitative culture sampling on outcome of ventilator-associated pneumonia. Am J Respir Crit Care Med. 1998;157:371-376.
24. El-Solh AA, Aquilina AT, Dhillon RS, et al. Impact of invasive strategy on management of antimicrobial treatment failure in institutionalized older people with severe pneumonia. Am J Respir Crit Care Med. 2002;166:1038-1043.
25. Wu CL, Yang DI, Wang NY, et al. Quantitative culture of endotracheal aspirates in the diagnosis of ventilator-associated pneumonia in patients with treatment failure. Chest. 2002;122:662-668.
26. Violan JS, Fernandez JA, Benitez AB, et al. Impact of quantitative invasive diagnostic techniques in the management and outcome of mechanically ventilated patients with suspected pneumonia. Crit Care Med. 2000;28:2737-2741.
27. Ruiz M, Torres A, Ewig S, et al. Noninvasive versus invasive microbial investigation in ventilator-associated pneumonia: Evaluation of outcome. Am J Respir Crit Care Med. 2000;162:119-125.
28. Craven DE. Epidemiology of ventilator-associated pneumonia. Chest. 2000;117:186S-187S.
29. Centers for Disease Control and Prevention. National Nosocomial Infections Surveillance (NNIS) System report, data summary from January 1992-June 2002, issued August 2002. Am J Infect Control. 2002;30:458-475.
30. Rello J, Ollendorf DA, Oster G, et al. Epidemiology and outcomes of ventilator-associated pneumonia in a large US database. Chest. 2002;122:2115-2121.
31. Combes A, Figliolini C, Trouillet J-L, et al. Incidence and outcome of polymicrobial ventilator-associated pneumonia. Chest. 2002;121:1618-1623.
32. Bregeon F, Ciais V, Carret V, et al. Is ventilator-associated pneumonia an independent risk factor for death? Anesthesiology. 2001;94:554-560.
33. Bercault N, Boulain T. Mortality rate attributable to ventilator-associated nosocomial pneumonia in an adult intensive care unit: A prospective case-control study. Crit Care Med. 2001;29:2303-2309.
34. Markowicz P, Wolff M, Djedaini K, et al. Multicenter prospective study of ventilator-associated pneumonia during acute respiratory distress syndrome: Incidence, prognosis, and risk factors. Am J Respir Crit Care Med. 2000;161:1942-1948.
35. Ibrahim EH, Ward S, Sherman G, et al. A comparative analysis of patients with early-onset vs late-onset nosocomial pneumonia in the ICU setting. Chest. 2000;117:1434-1442.
36. Heyland DK, Cook DJ, Griffith L, et al. The attributable morbidity and mortality of ventilator-associated pneumonia in the critically ill patient. Am J Respir Crit Care Med. 1999;159:1249-1256.
37. Rello J, Valles J. Mortality as an outcome in hospital-acquired pneumonia. Infect Control Hosp Epidemiol. 1998;19:795-797.
38. Combes A, Figliolini C, Trouillet J-L, et al. Factors predicting ventilator-associated pneumonia recurrence. Crit Care Med. 2003;31:1102-1107.
39. Fleming CA, Balaguera HU, Craven DE. Risk factors for nosocomial pneumonia. Med Clin North Am. 2001;85:1545-1563.
40. Artigas AT, Dronda SB, Valles EC, et al. Risk factors for nosocomial pneumonia in critically ill trauma patients. Crit Care Med. 2001;29:304-309.
41. Lynch JP III. Hospital-acquired pneumonia: Risk factors, microbiology, and treatment. Chest. 2001;119:373S-384S.
42. Ibrahim EH, Tracy L, Hill C, et al. The occurrence of ventilator-associated pneumonia in a community hospital: Risk factors and clinical outcomes. Chest. 2001;120:555-561.
43. Arozullah AM, Khuri SF, Henderson WG, et al. Development and validation of a multifactorial risk index for predicting postoperative pneumonia after major noncardiac surgery. Ann Intern Med. 2001;135:847-857.
44. Holzapfel L, Chastang C, Demingeon G, et al. A randomized study assessing the systematic search for maxillary sinusitis in nasotracheally mechanically ventilated patients: Influence of nosocomial maxillary sinusitis on the occurrence of ventilator-associated pneumonia. Am J Respir Crit Care Med. 1999;159:695-701.
45. Cook DJ, Kollef MH. Risk factors for ICU-acquired pneumonia. JAMA. 1998;279:1605-1606.
46. Cook DJ, Walter SD, Cook RJ, et al. Incidence of and risk factors for ventilator-associated pneumonia in critically ill patients. Ann Intern Med. 1998;129:433-440.
47. Ewig S, Torres A, El-Ebiary M, et al. Bacterial colonization patterns in mechanically ventilated patients with traumatic and medical head injury. Am J Respir Crit Care Med. 1999;159:188-198.
48. Muehlstedt SG, Richardson CJ, West MA, et al. Cytokines and the pathogenesis of nosocomial pneumonia. Surgery. 2001;130:602-611.
49. Monton C, Torres A, El-Ebiary M, et al. Cytokine expression in severe pneumonia: A bronchoalveolar lavage study. Crit Care Med. 1999;27:1745-1753.
50. Garrouste-Orgeas M, Chevret S, Arlet G, et al. Oropharyngeal or gastric colonization and nosocomial pneumonia in adult intensive care unit patients—A prospective study based on genomic DNA analysis. Am J Respir Crit Care Med. 1997;156:1647-1655.
51. Cendrero JAC, Sole-Violan J, Benitez AB, et al. Role of different routes of tracheal colonization in the development of pneumonia in patients receiving mechanical ventilation. Chest. 1999;116:462-470.
52. Taylor GD, Buchanan-Chell M, Kirkland T, et al. Bacteremic nosocomial pneumonia—A 7-year experience in one institution. Chest. 1995;108:786-788.
53. Montravers P, Veber B, Auboyer C, et al. Diagnostic and therapeutic management of nosocomial pneumonia in surgical patients: Results of the Eole study. Crit Care Med. 2002;30:368-375.
54. Luna CM, Videla A, Mattera J, et al. Blood cultures have limited value in predicting severity of illness and as a diagnostic tool in ventilator-associated pneumonia. Chest. 1999;116:1075-1084.
55. Richards MJ, Edwards JR, Culver DH, et al. Nosocomial infections in combined medical-surgical intensive care units in the United States. Infect Control Hosp Epidemiol. 2000;21:510-515.
56. Richards MJ, Edwards JR, Culver DH, et al. Nosocomial infections in medical intensive care units in the United States. Crit Care Med. 1999;27:887-892.
57. Trouillet JL, Chastre J, Vuagnat A, et al. Ventilator-associated pneumonia caused by potentially drug-resistant bacteria. Am J Respir Crit Care Med. 1998;157:531-539.
58. Rello J, Sa-Borges M, Correa H, et al. Variations in etiology of ventilator-associated pneumonia across four treatment sites: Implications for antimicrobial prescribing practices. Am J Respir Crit Care Med. 1999;160:608-613.
59. Cunha BA. Nosocomial pneumonia: Diagnostic and therapeutic considerations. Med Clin North Am. 2001;85:79-114.
60. Hughes C, Maharg P, Rosario P, et al. Possible nosocomial transmission of psittacosis. Infect Control Hosp Epidemiol. 1997;18:165-168.
61. Casalta JP, Piquet P, Alazia M, et al. *Mycoplasma pneumoniae* pneumonia following assisted ventilation. Am J Med. 1996;101:165-169.
62. Lambotte O, Timsit J-F, Garrouste-Orgeas M, et al. The significance of distal bronchial samples with commensals in ventilator-associated pneumonia: Colonizer or pathogen? Chest. 2002;122:1389-1399.
63. El-Ebiary M, Torres A, Fabregas N, et al. Significance of the isolation of *Candida* species from respiratory samples in critically ill, non-neutropenic patients—An immediate postmortem histologic study. Am J Respir Crit Care Med. 1997;156:583-590.
64. Dore P, Robert R, Grollier G, et al. Incidence of anaerobes in ventilator-associated pneumonia with use of a protected specimen brush. Am J Respir Crit Care Med. 1996;153:1292-1298.
65. Marik PE, Careau P. The role of anaerobes in patients with ventilator-associated pneumonia and aspiration pneumonia: A prospective study. Chest. 1999;115:178-183.

66. Luna CM, Blanzaco D, Niederman MS, et al. Resolution of ventilator-associated pneumonia: Prospective evaluation of the clinical pulmonary infection score as an early clinical predictor of outcome. Crit Care Med. 2003;31:676-682.

67. Reimer LG, Carroll KC. Role of the microbiology laboratory in the diagnosis of lower respiratory tract infections. Clin Infect Dis. 1998;26:742-748.

68. Meduri GU, Reddy RC, Stanley T, et al. Pneumonia in acute respiratory distress syndrome: A prospective evaluation of bilateral bronchoscopic sampling. Am J Respir Crit Care Med. 1998;158:870-875.

69. de Jaeger A, Litalien C, Lacroix J, et al. Protected specimen brush or bronchoalveolar lavage to diagnose bacterial nosocomial pneumonia in ventilated adults: A meta-analysis. Crit Care Med. 1999;27:2548-2560.

70. Sirvent J-M, Vidaur L, Gonzalez S, et al. Microscopic examination of intracellular organisms in protected bronchoalveolar mini-lavage fluid for the diagnosis of ventilator-associated pneumonia. Chest. 2003;123:518-523.

71. Flanagan PG, Jackson SK, Findlay G. Diagnosis of gram-negative, ventilator associated pneumonia by assaying endotoxin in bronchial lavage fluid. J Clin Pathol. 2001;54:107-110.

72. Hartog CM, Wermelt JA, Sommerfeld CO, et al. Pulmonary matrix metalloproteinase excess in hospital-acquired pneumonia. Am J Respir Crit Care Med. 2003;167: 593-598.

73. Hayon J, Figliolini C, Combes A, et al. Role of serial routine microbiologic culture results in the initial management of ventilator-associated pneumonia. Am J Respir Crit Care Med. 2002;165:41-46.

74. Iregui M, Ward S, Sherman G, et al. Clinical importance of delays in the initiation of appropriate antibiotic treatment for ventilator-associated pneumonia. Chest. 2002;122:262-268.

75. Cross JT Jr, Campbell GD Jr. Therapy of nosocomial pneumonia. Med Clin North Am. 2001;85:1583-1594.

76. Rubinstein E, Cammarata SK, Oliphant TH, et al. Linezolid (PNU-100766) versus vancomycin in the treatment of hospitalized patients with nosocomial pneumonia: A randomized, double-blind, multicenter study. Clin Infect Dis. 2001;32:402-412.

77. Fagon J-Y, Patrick H, Haas DW, et al. Treatment of gram-positive nosocomial pneumonia: Prospective randomized comparisons of quinupristin/dalfopristin versus vancomycin. Am J Respir Crit Care Med. 2000;161:753-762.

78. Fiel S. Guidelines and critical pathways for severe hospital-acquired pneumonia. Chest. 2001;119:412S-418S.

79. Ibrahim EH, Ward S, Sherman G, et al. Experience with a clinical guideline for the treatment of ventilator-associated pneumonia. Crit Care Med. 2001;29:1109-1115.

80. Hoffken G, Niederman MS. Nosocomial pneumonia: The importance of a de-escalating strategy for antibiotic treatment of pneumonia in the ICU. Chest. 2002; 122:2183-2196.

81. Kollef MH. An empirical approach to the treatment of multidrug-resistant ventilator-associated pneumonia. Clin Infect Dis. 2003;36:1119-1121.

82. Itokazu GS, Weinstein RA. Aerosolized antimicrobials: Another look. Crit Care Med. 1998;26:5-6.

83. Hamer DH. Treatment of nosocomial pneumonia and tracheobronchitis caused by multidrug-resistant Pseudomonas aeruginosa with aerosolized colistin. Am J Respir Crit Care Med. 2000;162:328-330.

84. Dennesen PJW, van der Ven AJAM, Kessels AGH, et al. Resolution of infectious parameters after antimicrobial therapy in patients with ventilator-associated pneumonia. Am J Respir Crit Care Med. 2001;163:1371-1375.

85. Collard HR, Saint S, Matthay MA. Prevention of ventilator-associated pneumonia: An evidence-based systematic review. Ann Intern Med. 2003;138:494-501.

86. Kollef MH. The prevention of ventilator-associated pneumonia. N Engl J Med. 1999;340:627-634.

87. Manangan LP, Banerjee SN, Jarvis WR. Association between implementation of CDC recommendations and ventilator-associated pneumonia at selected US hospitals. Am J Infect Control. 2000;28:222-227.

88. Rello J, Lorente C, Bodi M, et al. Why do physicians not follow evidence-based guidelines for preventing ventilator-associated pneumonia? A survey based on the opinions of an international panel of intensivists. Chest. 2002;122:656-661.

89. Stamm AM. Ventilator-associated pneumonia and frequency of circuit changes. Am J Infect Control. 1998;26:71-73.

90. Cook D, De Jonghe B, Brochard L, et al. Influence of airway management on ventilator-associated pneumonia. JAMA. 1998;279:781-787.

91. Cook D, Guyatt G, Marshall J, et al. A comparison of sucralfate and ranitidine for the prevention of upper gastrointestinal bleeding in patients requiring mechanical ventilation. N Engl J Med. 1998;338:791-797.

92. van Nieuwenhoven CA, Buskens E, van Tiel FH, et al. Relationship between methodological trial quality and the effects of selective digestive decontamination on pneumonia and mortality in critically ill patients. JAMA. 2001;286:335-340.

93. Bergmans DCJJ, Bonten MJM, Gaillard CA, et al. Prevention of ventilator-associated pneumonia by oral decontamination: A prospective, randomized, double-blind, placebo-controlled study. Am J Respir Crit Care Med. 2001;164:382-388.

94. Zack JE, Garrison T, Trovillion E, et al. Effect of an education program aimed at reducing the occurrence of ventilator-associated pneumonia. Crit Care Med. 2002;30:2407-2412.

95. Marelich GP, Murin S, Battistella F, et al. Protocol weaning of mechanical ventilation in medical and surgical patients by respiratory care practitioners and nurses: Effect on weaning time and incidence of ventilator-associated pneumonia. Chest. 2000;118:459-467.

96. Gruson D, Hilbert G, Vargas F, et al. Rotation and restricted use of antibiotics in a medical intensive care unit. Am J Respir Crit Care Med. 2000;162:837-843.

CHAPTER **302**

Nosocomial Urinary Tract Infections

JOHN W. WARREN

Urinary tract infection (UTI) is the most common nosocomial infection, comprising about 35% of such occurrences in both hospitals and nursing homes.[1-4] In both types of institutions, UTIs are usually associated with devices intended to assist in the drainage of urine. In hospitals, where the epidemiology has been better investigated, 80% or more of nosocomial UTIs are related to the use of urethral catheters.[5-8] Another 5% to 10% occur after other genitourinary manipulations.[5] The emphasis of this chapter is on catheter-associated UTI.

In the modern hospital, presumably because of widespread use of systemic antibiotics, *Candida* species comprise an increasing proportion of isolates from the catheterized urinary tract. This observation presents an editorial decision. Rather than using the inclusive but cumbersome words *bacteriuria/candiduria,* I have chosen in this chapter to use the simpler but novel word, *microburia.* When either bacteriuria or candiduria is the issue specifically at hand, I have used those terms.

CATHETER-ASSOCIATED MICROBURIA

Each year tens of millions of urinary catheters are placed in patients in acute care hospitals, rehabilitation units, and chronic care facilities.[9] With the exception of nonbacterial urethritis, urethral strictures, and mechanical trauma,[10-12] virtually all complications of urinary catheterization result from microburia.

The urethral catheter is one of the most venerable of medical devices, having been used to relieve urine retention on an intermittent or indwelling basis for centuries.[13] In the 1920s, Foley introduced a catheter that could be held in place with an intrabladder balloon.[14] Although initially used as a means to exert mechanical pressure against the prostate to stop bleeding after surgery, this innovation was soon recognized to be useful for holding in place indwelling urethral catheters inserted for other indications. For the first several decades of use, Foley catheters were attached to collecting tubes that drained rather unceremoniously into buckets sitting on the floor beside the bed, the so-called open catheter system. Bacteriuria was virtually universal by the end of 4 days of such catheterization.[15]

The 1950s saw the progressive development of "closed" catheter systems, and plastic collection bags fused to the distal end of the tubes began to be used in the 1960s.[16-19] This arrangement allows drainage through a tube into a receptacle so that the urine is always contained within a lumen protected from the contaminated environment. The onset of universal microburia now occurs after more than 30 days in closed catheter systems.[19,20] Although no well-designed, controlled trials comparing open with closed catheters have been performed, reports were sufficiently persuasive that the closed system became the standard for patients requiring indwelling urethral catheters.[19-23]

PATHOGENESIS

A symptomatic UTI results not just from microbes being in the urine but from these microorganisms in some way perturbing the urinary epithelium.[24] Fortunately, the normal, noncatheterized urinary tract has a number of defense mechanisms that prevent or minimize microbe–epithelial cell interactions that are disadvantageous to the host. Although most organisms causing UTI have previously colonized the periurethral area, the urethra itself is an effective obstacle to bladder inoculation. Moreover, even if organisms traverse the urethra and enter the bladder, the next urination clears 99.9% of these bacteria,[25] a process enhanced by Tamm-Horsfall protein and oligosaccharides, which are suspended in urine and which bind bacteria.[26-27] Even after the most effective micturition, however, a film of urine remains coating the bladder mucosa. Fortunately, glycosaminoglycan overlays bladder epithelium and inhibits microbial adherence to epithelial cells.[28] Moreover, there appears to be a poorly understood bactericidal mechanism closely associated with bladder mucosa[29]; this is effective even in the absence of polymorphonuclear leukocytes or antibodies. The last protective effort of an epithelial cell is a sacrificial one: exfoliation of the cell allows associated organisms to be voided from the host.[30] Polymorphonuclear leukocytes arrive within hours and ingest infecting bacteria; they either kill them or carry them into the urine, where the phagocytes are voided with their captured prey.[31] Antibodies[32] and cell-mediated immunity[33] are part of a slower response and perhaps useful in the later stages of the acute infection.

The use of a urethral catheter can thwart some of these defense mechanisms. To begin with, insertion of a catheter may carry urethral organisms into the bladder, the incidence of bacteriuria ranging from about 1% in healthy persons to 20% in elderly, hospitalized patients.[6,34]

Once an indwelling urethral catheter is in place, organisms may enter the bladder either intra- or extraluminally. In regard to the former, the closed catheter system can be opened at only two sites. Although contrary to appropriate hygiene, the junction between the catheter and the collection tube may be disconnected for catheter irrigation or urine collection; bacteriuria has been associated with such interruptions.[22,35] The second site, the drainage tube of the collection bag, is one that must be opened periodically to drain the accumulated urine. If the lumen of the drainage tube is contaminated with bacteria (e.g., from an unwashed container previously used to collect urine from a bacteriuric patient[36]), organisms may enter the drainage bag and before the next emptying multiply to high concentrations. Even after the bag is drained, organisms may persist in the film of urine coating its inner surface and multiply as it refills. Such bacteria may ascend the collection tube and catheter through the urine itself[37] or by growth along internal surfaces.[38] Tambyah and colleagues, defining intraluminal entry as presence of high concentrations of microbes in the urine collecting bag, estimated that approximately 23% of catheter-associated microuria was intraluminal in origin.[39]

The closed catheter system is successful because it greatly limits these intraluminal entries of organisms. However, even with meticulous attention to maintenance of the closed system, the space between the external catheter and the urethral mucosa offers opportunity for extraluminal entry directly into the bladder, which now is the most common path for catheter-associated microuria. Tambyah and colleagues found that approximately 34% of catheter-associated microuria was initiated by extraluminal entry, with no significant difference between men and women.[39] Others have found this to be the route of entry in 70% to 80% of episodes of microuria in women and 20% to 30% in men.[40] Garibaldi and colleagues[41] demonstrated that periurethral colonization with gram-negative rods or enterococci was associated with bacteriuria significantly more often than when patients were not so colonized. Furthermore, others demonstrated progressive bacterial uropathogen colonization of the urethra in catheterized patients, particularly women.[42,43] Such colonization precedes bacteriuria with the same strain in up to two thirds of patients.[20,40,42] Even after removal of the catheter, the patient remains at risk of bacteriuria for at least 24 hours,[44] possibly because of the increased urethral colonization associated with the indwelling catheter.

Once inside the catheterized urinary tract, bacteria apparently find a hospitable environment. In marked contrast to the noncatheterized urinary tract, where small numbers of organisms introduced in the bladder are eliminated efficiently, the catheterized urinary tract allows bacteria that gain entry to multiply to high concentrations within a day or so.[20,45] Specific adhesins enable fimbria to bind to uroepithelial cells and the catheter surface.[46,47] Uroepithelial cells of catheterized patients may transiently allow greater numbers of bacteria to adhere to their surfaces.[40] Among nonspecific mechanisms, glycocalyx, or biofilm, which covers and secures bacteria against a mucosal or catheter surface, has

been demonstrated on drainage bags, catheters, and uroepithelium.[38,48] Organisms contained within the biofilm appear to be well protected from the mechanical flow of urine, other host defenses, and even antibiotics.[49] The biofilm may allow the contained sessile organisms to establish a microenvironment from which some may move into the urine; these planktonic microbes are those that are voided and enumerated by the diagnostic microbiology laboratory. Additionally, the catheter may mechanically damage urinary epithelium and the glycosaminoglycan layer. As a foreign body, the catheter may blunt adequate antibacterial polymorphonuclear leukocyte function.[50] Finally, catheter drainage is often imperfect and volumes of urine may remain in the bladder, allowing some stability to the residence of microorganisms.

With time, the presence of bacteria elicits an inflammatory response, resulting in acute and chronic cystitis with pyuria and production of antibodies. Bacteria may move up the ureters to the kidneys, where a similar biofilm microenvironment may develop within the pelvis or the tubular system. Perturbation of the unicellular epithelium[51] may allow entry of bacteria into the renal interstitium; the subsequent inflammatory response is recognized pathologically and clinically as acute pyelonephritis.[52-53] With continued catheterization and bacteriuria, chronic renal inflammation may develop, and, particularly with stone formation, chronic pyelonephritis may follow.[54-55] Although the conventional wisdom is that bacteremia associated with UTI is from a renal site, the presence of acute and chronic cystitis in long-term catheterized patients provokes the thought that bacteremia may occasionally follow invasion of bladder mucosa.

The majority of organisms causing catheter-associated microuria are from the patient's own colonic flora[40]; they may be native inhabitants or new immigrants, that is, exogenous organisms from the hospital environment.[56-58] Just as with the pathogenesis of UTI in noncatheterized patients, colonic bacteria may colonize the periurethral area, especially in women.[41] Additionally, exogenous organisms may colonize catheter equipment, transferred there by the hands of health care personnel[36,59,60] or, infrequently, by contaminated products or containers.[36]

RISK FACTORS FOR MICROBURIA

Multivariate analyses have clarified risk factors for catheter-associated microuria. Platt and colleagues' study of 1474 catheterizations[61] revealed nine independent risk factors for microuria:

1. Duration of catheterization
2. Absence of use of a urinometer (drip chamber)
3. Microbial colonization of the drainage bag
4. Diabetes mellitus
5. Absence of antibiotic use
6. Female patient
7. Indications for catheterization other than drainage during surgery or output measurement
8. Abnormal serum creatinine
9. Errors in catheter care

A risk factor that was not sought in this multivariate study but that appears to be important is periurethral colonization with potential uropathogens. Garibaldi and colleagues[41] demonstrated that 18% of 612 patients colonized in the periurethral area with gram-negative rods or enterococci developed bacteriuria, compared with 5% of 601 patients not so colonized ($P < .0001$).

DURATION OF CATHETERIZATION

Duration of catheterization is the most important risk factor for the development of catheter-associated microuria (Table 302-1).[8,19,22,44,61,63] Duration is a general result of the indications for urethral catheterization, which in the hospital can be grouped into four categories[62]: (1) surgery (generally 1 to 7 days' duration); (2) urine output measurement, a proxy for cardiac output in seriously ill patients (7 to 30 days); (3) urine retention (1 to more than 30 days); and (4) urinary incontinence (more than 30 days).

TABLE 302-1 Comparison of Short-Term and Long-Term Urethral Catheterization

Characteristic	Short-Term (<30 Days)	Long-Term (≥30 Days)
Patient		
Type of illness	Acute, surgical	Chronic, neurologic
Location	Hospital	Nursing home
Indications	Output measurement	Incontinence
	Surgery	Urine retention
	Urine retention	
	Incontinence	
Usual catheter duration	2-4 days	Months to years
Bacteriuria		
Incidence	3%-10%/day	3%-10%/day
Prevalence	15%	90%
Number of species/patient	Single	Polymicrobial
Common species	*Escherichia coli*	*Providencia stuartii*
	Klebsiella pneumoniae	*Proteus mirabilis*
	P. mirabilis	*E. coli*
	Pseudomonas aeruginosa	*Morganella morganii*
Proved prevention of bacteriuria	Closed catheter system	None
	Systemic antibiotic	
Complications	Fevers	Fevers
	Acute pyelonephritis	Acute pyelonephritis
	Bacteremia	Bacteremia
	Death	Death
		Catheter obstruction
		Urinary stones
		Chronic renal inflammation
		Periurinary infections
		Renal failure
		Bladder cancer
Medical goal	Postpone bacteriuria	Prevent complications of bacteriuria
Options	Diapers and pads	Diapers and pads
	External collection devices	External collection devices
	Intermittent catheterization	Intermittent catheterization
	Suprapubic catheterization	Suprapubic catheterization
		Urinary diversions
		Prosthetic bladder sphincters

A graph of patients by duration of their catheterization would show a bimodal frequency, with peaks at 2 to 4 days and at 3 to 6 months or more. The first peak would represent hospitalized patients with transient indications for catheterization; the second would be composed of nursing home patients with indications often perceived to be permanent. Once a urethral catheter is in place in patients in a hospital or a nursing home, the daily increase in prevalence of microburia is 3% to 10%.[19,22,35,44,64] The great majority of catheterized patients are bacteriuric by the end of 30 days,[19,20] a convenient dividing line between short-term and long-term catheterization (see Table 302-1).

The definitions used by the Centers for Disease Control and Prevention for its National Nosocomial Infection Surveillance System distinguish symptomatic UTI from asymptomatic bacteriuria.[65] As noted later, most studies of UTIs associated with catheters over the last several decades have looked at the development of microburia, with or without symptoms. The focus of this chapter is the development of microburia and the clinical complications of microburia.

Short-Term Catheterization

Between 15% and 25% of patients in general hospitals receive an indwelling catheter at some time during their stay.[6] Most such catheters are in place for only a short time, up to one third for less than a day,[22,64] and both the mean and median durations are between 2 and 4 days.[6,19,22,35,44] Nevertheless, between 10% and 30% of these catheterized patients develop microburia,[6,19,22,66] significantly more than the 1% found among noncatheterized hospital patients.[6]

Among short-term catheterized patients, *Escherichia coli* is the bacteriuric species most frequently isolated. Other common organisms are *Pseudomonas aeruginosa, Klebsiella pneumoniae, Proteus mirabilis, Staphylococcus epidermidis,* enterococci, and *Candida* species.[5,19,35,61] Most bacteriuric episodes in short-term catheterization are caused by single organisms.[67] To establish a diagnosis, many investigators have required organism concentrations of at least 100,000

colony-forming units (CFU) per milliliter of urine; others have selected lower concentrations. Pyuria is not sufficiently sensitive to be used as the only criterion for obtaining a urine culture, especially if the urine contains yeast or gram-positive cocci.[67]

A word of caution is in order here. Because the kidney receives 20% to 25% of the cardiac output, certain hematogenous organisms may seed the kidney and subsequently appear in the urine. Two of these microbes are *Staphylococcus aureus*[68] and *Candida* species; some investigators consider *Salmonella* and *Pseudomonas* species to have similar properties.

Complications

Almost all episodes of short-term catheter-associated microburia are asymptomatic.[6,64,69] Building on previous investigations, Tambyah and Maki prospectively on a daily basis obtained urine cultures, detected fevers, and asked about dysuria, urgency, and urethral or pelvic pain.[69] Noting that most patients, with or without microburia, could respond to their questions, they found that less than 10% had any symptoms referable to the urinary tract and that there were no significant differences between those with and those without microburia. Similarly, there were no significant differences in the proportions with fever between those with and those without microburia.

Less than 5% of patients with catheter-associated microburia are identified as having blood-stream infections caused by organisms in the urine.[5,7,53,64,69] Indeed, Tambyah and Maki found that only 1 in 235 catheter-associated microburias unequivocally caused blood-stream infections (in three additional cases a central line infection or pneumonia were possible causes).[69] However, because of the large number of catheterized patients, these blood-stream infections with sources in the catheterized urinary tract may constitute up to 15% of nosocomial blood-stream infections[7,53]; only intravascular infections comprise more.[70] Men appear to be at greater risk than women for such blood-stream infections.[7]

The relatively low incidence of febrile UTI and blood-stream infections may be a result of the types of organisms causing catheter-associated UTI. *E. coli,* the most common cause of cystitis and acute pyelonephritis in the uncatheterized urinary tract, causes only a minority of catheter-associated microburias. Furthermore, of those *E. coli* causing nosocomial UTIs, most do not possess recognized virulence factors for acute pyelonephritis and bacteremia, such as P fimbriation.[71] Nevertheless, some non–*E. coli* organisms can be troublesome. For instance, *Serratia marcescens* may be more likely to cause bacteremia than other bacteriuric organisms.[5,7]

The contribution of catheter-associated UTI to mortality is unclear.[72] At autopsy, patients with catheter-associated microburia dying in a hospital may have acute pyelonephritis, urinary stones, or perinephric abscesses.[53] However, in prospective or case-controlled studies, catheter-associated UTIs are often not found to be associated with excess mortality[70,73-75]; one study, however, has suggested an increased risk of death associated with catheter-associated microburia.[76]

Minimal estimates are that catheter-associated microburia adds 1 day of hospitalization for the bacteriuric patient. The significance of this figure is magnified by the large number of catheters in use and the high incidence of infection: in the United States, catheter-associated microburia is estimated to cause 900,000 additional hospital days per year. This represents an additional medical cost of $615 million (in 1992 dollars) per year. Finally, certain estimates suggest that nosocomial UTIs directly cause almost 1000 deaths (about 1 death per 1000 episodes of catheter-associated microburia) and contribute to an additional 6500 deaths annually in the United States.[77]

Studies over the last several decades suggest that the incidence of microburia once a catheter is in place may be decreasing.[63] Whether this is a result of shorter durations of catheter use, more attention to catheter hygiene, increased antibiotic use, or other factors is not clear.

Long-Term Catheterization

Although the magnitude of long-term urethral catheter use has not been directly measured, extrapolations from several studies[78-80] suggest that at any given time more than 100,000 patients in American nursing homes have urethral catheters in place. Many of these patients have been catheterized for months and in some cases years. The two most frequent indications are urinary incontinence (mostly women) and bladder outlet obstruction (mostly men).[80]

Even with excellent care, all patients, if catheterized long enough, become microburic. This universal prevalence is a function of two related phenomena.[81,82] The first is an incidence of new episodes of microburia similar to that seen in short-term catheterized patients, although including a wider variety of gram-negative and gram-positive bacterial species.[82] The result is microburia with a new organism somewhat more often than every 2 weeks. The second phenomenon is the ability of some microbes to persist for weeks and months in the catheterized urinary tract.[82,83] Two of the most persistent bacterial species are *E. coli* and *Providencia stuartii.* Persistence of *E. coli* is related to type 1 pilus, a well-studied adhesin for uroepithelium and Tamm-Horsfall protein.[46] For *P. stuartii,* persistence is associated with the MR/K adhesin.[47]

These data suggest that two types of microbes inhabit the long-term catheterized urinary tract. The first comprises common uropathogens such as *E. coli,* which, after easy access into the bladder, have bound to uroepithelium just as they would in the noncatheterized urinary tract. In contrast, certain organisms such as *P. stuartii* are rarely found outside the catheterized urinary tract and may use the catheter itself, at least transiently, as a niche.[84,85] Several investigators have reported that some bacterial strains found in catheter urine are not present in simultaneously obtained bladder urine, suggesting these organisms were colonizing only the catheter.[84,86]

These phenomena result in polymicrobial microburia in up to 95% of urine specimens from long-term catheterized patients. Such specimens commonly have two to four bacterial species, each at concentrations of 10^5 CFU/mL or higher[81,82]; some may have up to six to eight species at that concentration.[81] These include common uropathogens

such as *E. coli, P. aeruginosa,* and *P. mirabilis,* as well as less familiar species such as *P. stuartii* and *Morganella morganii.*[78,81,82,87-89]

Complications

Complications of long-term catheter-associated microburia fall into two categories. The first includes symptomatic UTIs such as those seen with short-term catheterization (i.e., fever, acute pyelonephritis, and blood-stream infection); some of these episodes may end in death. The second group is more often associated with long-term catheterization: obstruction, urinary tract stones, local periurinary infections, chronic renal inflammation, renal failure, and, over years, bladder cancer.

Febrile Urinary Tract Infection. Although two thirds of febrile episodes in elderly, long-term catheterized patients arise from the urinary tract,[81] the incidence is surprisingly low, about one febrile episode per 100 days of catheterization.[81,90] Studied in women, most such episodes are of low-grade fever, last for 1 day or less, and resolve without antibiotic therapy or catheter change.[81]

However, UTIs are the most common source of bacteremias in nursing homes,[91] and the indwelling urethral catheter is the leading risk factor for bacteremia. Rudman and colleagues demonstrated that patients with a catheter in place were 59 times more likely to be bacteremic over a 1-year period than patients without a catheter.[92] Although *E. coli* is significantly more likely than other bacteriuric organisms to cause bacteremia,[87] other bacteria, even supposedly nonuropathogens such as *P. stuartii* and *M. morganii,* can also do so.[81,85,91] Additionally, catheter removal or replacement is associated with bacteremia in less than 10% of incidents[93]; most such episodes are transient and asymptomatic.

Acute pyelonephritis is undoubtedly the source of many of these febrile episodes. Moreover, autopsies have revealed acute pyelonephritis in more than one third of patients dying with long-term catheters in place,[52] many of whom were afebrile at the time of death. This suggests that, in the elderly, debilitated patients who often are the users of long-term urethral catheters, serious bacterial infection of the kidneys may occur in the absence of fever.

The incidence of death during febrile episodes attributed to the catheterized urinary tract has been estimated to be 60 times the incidence in patients who are afebrile.[81] Blood-stream infections were not identified preceding most of these deaths.

Catheter Obstructions. In long-term catheterized patients, a catheter obstruction can be a problem, and in some patients a recurrent one.[94,95] The complex material that obstructs urinary catheters is composed of bacteria, glycocalyx, Tamm-Horsfall protein, and precipitated crystals.[38,96-98] *P. mirabilis* bacteriuria is associated with catheter obstruction,[97-100] probably because of its potent urease,[101] which hydrolyzes urea to ammonia, increasing urine pH and causing crystallization of struvite and apatite in the catheter lumen. Electron microscopy has demonstrated these crystals within the bacterial biofilm.[48,96] Although some catheter obstructions are associated with the onset of fever, most are not,[81] possibly because of early detection and removal of the obstructed catheter.

Urinary Stones. A similar bacterial process may occur in the urinary tract itself, resulting in the crystallization of struvite and apatite in the form of so-called infection stones, a common problem in long-term catheterized patients.[102-105] Such stones in the bladder, often crusting around the catheter balloon and tip, are relatively benign.[106] However, renal stones may be more serious and are associated with chronic pyelonephritis and renal dysfunction.[54,55]

Chronic Renal Inflammation. Chronic renal inflammation, common in long-term catheterized persons,[54,55] is related directly to the duration of catheterization.[55] Chronic pyelonephritis (i.e., chronic renal inflammation with the additional components of deformed calyces and overlying parenchymal scarring) is also associated with duration of catheterization but is found in only a minority of long-term catheterized patients with microburia, usually with renal stones.[54,55]

Other Complications. More frequently in the past, additional complications were seen in long-term catheterized spinal-injured patients, mostly men, who are now usually managed with intermittent catheterization (see later). These complications included local infections such as urethritis, epididymitis, scrotal abscess, prostatitis, and prostatic abscess.[54] Chronic renal failure was often diagnosed in catheterized spinal-injured patients and was frequently associated with intrarenal stones and chronic pyelonephritis.[54,107] Among those catheterized for years, bladder metaplasia and cancer may occur hundreds of times more frequently than in noncatheterized populations.[108-110]

PREVENTION

Prevention can be addressed in three stages: prevention of catheterization; once the catheter is in place, prevention of microburia; and once microburia occurs, prevention of complications.

Prevention of Catheterization

Obviously, the most direct method to prevent catheter-associated microburia is to prevent catheterization. The last several decades have seen major advances in understanding the complications of catheterization and in weighing its risks and benefits.[9,23,77,111-113] Nevertheless, several studies of different types of patients, using predefined criteria for catheter use, have observed that 21% to 50% of catheters were inserted for inappropriate indications.[62,114,115] Some institutions have initiated requirements that the indication be noted when a catheter is ordered.[116,117] A portion of catheterizations for urine retention (e.g., postoperatively) can be prevented by assessment of urine volume by bladder ultrasound,[118] a technology that may deserve wider use.[119] For incontinent patients, the medical team might encourage a greater use of patient training, medications, and special clothes and bedclothes, options generally preferred by patients.

For those individuals who do require a long-term urinary assistance device, a summary statement would be that almost any other device than the indwelling urethral catheter would be preferred. De Ruz and colleagues performed a prospective study of patients seen within 60 days of spinal injury and in whom urine was cultured every 10 days and found that, while using the urethral catheter, patients had a significantly higher incidence of microburia than when using intermittent, condom, or suprapubic catheterization.[120] A retrospective assessment suggests that complications such as pyelonephritis, urinary stones, epididymitis, and urethral stricture may be more likely with the indwelling urethral catheter than with these alternative types of catheterizations.[121]

External Collection Devices

For men with urinary incontinence, external collectors applied about the penis that empty through a collection tube into a drainage bag have been widely used and appreciated.[122] Although these avoid the problems of a tube in the urinary tract, urine within these condom catheters may develop high concentrations of organisms, the urethra and skin may be colonized with uropathogens, and bladder microburia may develop.[123] To distinguish bladder microburia from skin contamination, careful collection of urine in a new condom by well-trained caregivers is necessary.[124,125] Although no properly designed, controlled trials have been performed, parallel studies of condom catheters and urethral catheters in the same institutions suggest a substantially lower incidence of microburia with condom catheters.[120,121,126,127] Complications include local problems such as skin breakdown, maceration, and ulceration; urethral diverticula; and penile gangrene from constriction by the condom's roller ring.[128] Moreover, these devices can be reservoirs for the spread of nosocomial infections.[129] External collection devices for women have been developed for commercial use and deserve evaluation.[130]

Intermittent Catheterization

This has been a venerable method for managing urinary retention, possibly going back for centuries.[131] Encouraged by Guttmann and Frankel[132] since the 1940s, intermittent catheterization by the 1970s had become the standard of urinary care for spinal-injured patients[72,133-137] and has been tried more recently in other patients with

chronic urine retention. Insertion of a catheter every 4 to 6 hours by caregivers or the patient, drainage of urine, and immediate removal of the catheter provide periodic bladder emptying. The incidence of microburia is about 1% to 3% per catheterization. At four catheterizations a day, a new episode of microburia occurs every 1 to 3 weeks.[138] Increased urine volume is a risk factor for UTI in intermittently catheterized spinal-injured patients.[135,139,140] Microburia is usually asymptomatic. Although no well-designed comparisons have been performed, most experts believe that intermittent catheterization results in fewer episodes of microburia than indwelling catheterization.[72,120,121,133-137]

Clean rather than sterile catheters have been used widely.[131,138] A randomized study comparing clean versus sterile intermittent catheterization showed no difference in symptomatic UTIs but did show that the clean catheterization was associated with decreased costs.[141] A controlled but not randomized trial suggested that a sheath that protects the catheter from urethral contamination may be associated with fewer microburic episodes.[142] Prelubricated or hydrophilic catheters may[143] or may not[144] diminish the incidence of microburia. Oral antibiotics and methenamine compounds as well as instillations of povidone-iodine and chlorhexidine preparations have been used to postpone microburia for short periods in intermittently catheterized patients[121,131,145-148]; whether such practices would be beneficial over months and years has not been shown.[72,137] In one study organisms resistant to the antibiotic used as prophylaxis were common not only in the active drug group but also in the placebo group, suggesting interpatient spread of resistant organisms within the unit.[148]

There are probably fewer local periurethral infections, febrile episodes, bacteremias, bladder and renal stones, and deteriorations of renal function with intermittent catheterization than with indwelling catheters.[121,131,149-151] Complications do occur, however, and may include bleeding; urethral inflammation, stricture, and false passage; epididymitis and prostatitis; bladder stones; and hydronephrosis.[131,133,150]

Systematic evaluations of intermittent catheterization after surgical procedures have been reported.[152-154] More frequent use of intermittent catheterization in a variety of acute clinical situations may be anticipated; controlled studies comparing it with urethral catheterization for microburia and its complications will be important.

Suprapubic Catheterization

Suprapubic catheterization has been used increasingly in several types of surgery.[155] The impetus is threefold. The first is the concept that the lower density of bacteria on the anterior abdominal skin might yield lower rates of microburia with suprapubic catheterization than with a catheter in the urethra. The second is the realization that in some patients urethral strictures are sequelae of indwelling urethral catheters in place for even a few days.[11,156] The third is that clamping of the suprapubic catheter allows testing of voiding per urethra, obviously an advantage not shared with urethral catheterization. Randomized studies have shown significant benefits with the suprapubic catheter in terms of lower incidences of microburia, urethral strictures, or pain.[155,157-160] Complications include infection, leakage, and hematoma at the puncture site and occasional catheter prolapse through the urethra. These adverse events and practical obstacles to insertion notwithstanding, well-designed trials should compare suprapubic and urethral catheterization for the incidence of microburia and its complications in different hospitalized populations.[63]

For the patient requiring long-term urinary drainage, however, suprapubic catheterization does not appear as promising. Although possibly associated with a lower incidence of microburia than urethral catheters,[120] a retrospective chart review of more than 300 spinal-injured patients suggested that suprapubic as compared to indwelling urethral catheterization postponed but did not prevent episodes of acute pyelonephritis, bladder stones, upper tract stones, and acquired renal imaging abnormalities.[121] Suprapubic catheterization was, however, associated with lower rates of epididymitis, periurethral abscess, and urethral stricture.

Intraurethral Devices

The concept of a device totally contained within the urethra to relieve urine retention secondary to benign prostatic hypertrophy (BPH) or urethral stenosis has been introduced.[161,162] These devices have remained in place for weeks and months until or instead of surgery. Early reports have suggested quite low incidences of microburia and symptomatic infection.[163] These appear to be promising devices for men particularly with BPH unresponsive to pharmacologic therapy and who have contraindications to surgery. Additionally, urethral inserts that can act as occlusive devices are available for patients with incontinence[164] and may be worth evaluation.

Bladder Substitutions

These are usually ileal or colonic segments that require collection bags on the abdominal wall or are continent and emptied by intermittent catheterization through the stoma. Although bladder substitution should not be considered an alternative to the urethral catheter, of course, this seems to be a reasonable place to discuss these common sources of nosocomial UTI. Microbiologic investigations have shown that microburia is common, perhaps more in ileal than in colonic devices and more in those that require a collection bag than in those that do not.[165,166] Acute pyelonephritis, stone formation, chronic pyelonephritis, and renal dysfunction are complications.[167] Orthotopic bladder substitutions have been increasingly used and may be associated with a lower incidence of microburia.[168]

Prevention of Microburia

Once a urethral catheter is in place, only two principles are universally recommended for prevention of microburia: keep the closed catheter system closed and remove the catheter as soon as possible.[9,111-113]

Maintaining a Closed System

Urine specimens should be obtained without opening the catheter–collection tube junction.[22,35] However, sealing this junction before or soon after placement of the catheter has inconsistent impact on subsequent microburia.[169-171] The only point at which the system must be opened is at the bag drainage tube; personnel must avoid touching the end of the drainage tube to possibly contaminated containers.[36] Communication of appropriate techniques to caregivers must continue to be an important objective of infection control teams. Longitudinal studies in the same institution suggest that continued attention has resulted in fewer errors of catheter hygiene.[64,172]

Minimizing Duration

Duration of catheterization is the most important risk factor for the development of catheter-associated microburia.[8,19,22,41,61,63,64] Consequently, if the catheter can be removed before microburia develops, its ensuing complications can be prevented. A number of investigators, using durations predetermined to be appropriate for each indication for catheterization, found that one third to one half of the days late in catheterization courses were unnecessary[44,62] and that many microburias occurred after the catheter would have been removed had appropriate catheter durations been observed.[44] Unfortunately, a recent survey of attendings and residents revealed that many physicians were unaware of which of their hospitalized patients had catheters in place; indeed, catheters being used for inappropriate indications were more likely to be the "forgotten" ones.[173] Various disciplines have initiated studies to estimate durations of catheterization for different indications[174-176]; such studies designed as randomized controlled trials would be most welcome.[177,178] This type of thinking has been used to prompt appropriately early catheter removal by computerized reminders, default stop dates, or autonomous action by nurses.[116,117]

Systemic Antimicrobials

Virtually every study of systemic antibiotics, retrospective or prospective, has demonstrated effectiveness in initially diminishing the incidence of bacteriuria in catheterized patients.[20,22,44,55,61,63,64,179,180] Because of the nature of catheterization in hospitals, up to 80% of catheterized patients are given antibiotics during, but not usually because of, catheterization. Indeed, without such common use of antibiotics, the incidence of bacteriuria among catheterized patients likely would be substantially higher.[181] However, those studies that observed patients long enough revealed that antibiotics were effective for the first several days and then resistant organisms began to appear in the urine.[44,179,180,182] Most authorities believe that antibiotics to postpone bacteriuria are not indicated because of side effects, cost, and emergence of resistant organisms in the patient and in the medical unit.[9,112,113] However, there may be exceptions to this generalization. For instance, patients at high risk for the complications of catheter-associated bacteriuria (e.g., renal transplantation or granulocytopenic patients) might benefit from antibiotic use during short-term catheterization.[9] Methenamine preparations may be of use in some patient populations.[183]

Additional Efforts

The summary statement of this section is that, although many logical modifications have been attempted, none has consistently and persuasively improved upon the ability of the closed catheter system to postpone microburia.[72,119]

One attempt deserving special consideration is silver coating of the catheter. Although such catheters were first studied clinically in 1949[184] and then rather intensively over the past 15 years, whether they diminish the incidence of microburia or symptomatic UTIs has not been completely answered. If one uses reasonable criteria for clinical trials (prospective, randomized, adequately powered, and published), six investigations can be evaluated.[185-190] Two of the studies[188,190] did not show that silver oxide–coated catheters were significantly better in preventing microburia than standard catheters. The remaining four trials examined catheters coated with hydrogel and silver alloy. In vitro studies of the hydrogel/silver catheter indicated little antibacterial activity in agar diffusion studies[191] but did show fewer adherent bacteria.[192] Three of the clinical trials demonstrated significant benefit of the hydrogel/silver catheter; two of these[187,189] excluded patients receiving antibiotics and the third was of a design that precluded judgment of group comparability and analysis of potentially confounding variables such as duration of catheterization.[186] The fourth study was a classic prospective, randomized, double-blind trial that found no significant difference in the incidence of microburia between hydrogel/silver-coated latex catheters and silicone catheters.[185] Most recent reviewers conclude that there is not enough evidence to recommend the widespread use of silver-coated catheters.[72,193-195]

Another effort has been to coat or impregnate catheters with antibiotics. Investigators have seen the need to avoid the use of antibiotics commonly administered to hospitalized patients. Two clinical studies of catheters with incorporated nitrofurazone suggested clinical efficacy against gram-positive and susceptible gram-negative bacteria, which may, however, be limited to the first week.[196,197] In a multicenter trial of postprostatectomy patients, catheters coated with rifampin and minocycline exhibited a protective effect against gram-positive bacteriuria.[198]

Given the low rates of symptomatic UTI and blood-stream infection linked to catheter-associated microburia, the challenge of investigations of costly catheter modifications is to demonstrate clinical impact (e.g., symptomatic UTI, fever, blood-stream infections, and/or cost).[119] Although future published trials may be revealing, extant data suggest that a reasonable use of hydrogel/silver- or antibiotic-coated catheters may be for patients who might not handle bacteremia well, such as those with granulocytopenia.

Many other modifications of the catheter or catheterization have proven unrewarding. Small trials and ones with historical controls have not demonstrated differences in microburia after insertion of catheters using sterile or clean techniques or an antiseptic gel.[199,200] Given that the potential space between the urethra and the external catheter surface appears to be the most common source of ingress for organisms, numerous investigators have attempted to block this entry by the application of topical antibacterial agents. However, studies have shown little if any postponement of bacteriuria with such techniques. Indeed, several revealed that patients receiving such agents actually tended to have an increased incidence of bacteriuria, a finding attributed to easier bladder entry of urethral and periurethral bacteria as a result of physical manipulation of the urethra.[201,202] A common attempt to prevent bacteriuria has been the use of antibiotics instilled into the lumen of the catheter system. However, irrigation of the catheter and bladder with antibacterial solutions has not postponed bacteriuria.[35,203,204] Additionally, antimicrobials in or above the collection bag have generally had no effectiveness in curtailing microburia.[205,206] A drainage bag containing a proprietary antibacterial polymer has not yet been studied in a prospective controlled design.[207] These adaptations, in which organisms entering the lumen of the catheter system encounter antimicrobial activity, might be of value for those systems in which the integrity of the closed catheter has been compromised. However, with appropriate attention to maintenance of the closed system, bacterial entry into the lumen of the catheter is minimal and such efforts should be superfluous.

An interesting series of studies by Hull and colleagues investigating purposeful inoculation of the catheter or bladder of spinal-injured patients with an *E. coli* strain from a long-standing asymptomatic bacteriuric patient show promising results.[208,209] Finally, vaccines directed at organisms commonly found in long-term catheterized patients are being developed but are still in preclinical stages.[210]

Prevention of Complications of Microburia

Treatment with anti-infective agents of asymptomatic microburia in catheterized patients may seem a logical measure to prevent its complications (e.g., fever, acute pyelonephritis, and bacteremia). However, the data that are available suggest that this approach is not particularly useful. Garibaldi and colleagues[64] and others[6,44] noted in hospitalized patients that symptomatic catheter-associated UTIs tended to occur on the first day of microburia, thus for practical purposes precluding any preventive treatment. In long-term catheterized patients, cephalexin was administered whenever a susceptible organism appeared in the urine. There was no effect on incidence of new bacteriuria, number of bacterial strains per urine specimen, or, most importantly, incidence of febrile episodes.[182] The only change was a marked increase in antibiotic-resistant organisms.

These investigations suggest that asymptomatic microburia need not be treated as long as the catheter (short term or long term) remains in place.[44,113,211] If asymptomatic microburia is not to be treated, there is little reason then to routinely culture urine of asymptomatic patients. However, several exceptions may pertain. One might be to seek particular bacterial strains that are causing a high incidence of bacteremia from catheter-associated microburia in a given institution; *S. marcescens* has been such an organism.[5,7] The second is if such therapy is part of a plan to control a cluster of infections by a particular organism in a medical unit. The third might be for patients who may be at high risk of serious complications (e.g., granulocytopenic patients, solid-organ transplantation patients, and pregnant women). The fourth exception might include patients undergoing urologic surgery, or possibly other surgeries particularly if prostheses may be left in place.

But if the great majority of patients with asymptomatic catheter-associated microburia are not treated, what do we know of their fate after the catheter is removed? Harding and associates[212] found that, within 14 days of catheter removal, 17% of patients had urinary tract symptoms and 36% had cleared their bacteriuria. The fate of the other one half of the patients after that 14 days is unclear. Although some recommend antibiotic therapy to eradicate postcatheterization asymptomatic bacteriuria,[212] prospective studies seeking over a longer time the incidences of clearance of bacteriuria and of urinary tract symptoms would be much welcomed.

Some patients undergoing long-term catheterization have recurrent obstructions of the catheter, which in many is associated with infections by *P. mirabilis* and subsequent encrustation with struvite and apatite crystals.[97-99] In vitro studies were unable to identify any among 18 different catheter types that could prevent *P. mirabilis*–induced encrustation.[100] Urease inhibitors can in vitro prevent the encrustation of urethral catheters,[213] but their clinical use is problematic because of serious toxicities.[214]

TREATMENT OF COMPLICATIONS

Asymptomatic catheter-associated bacteriuria should not be treated,[44,113,211] and lower urinary tract symptoms have been shown to be uncommon.[69] However, the patient with an indwelling catheter or other urinary drainage device who develops a fever or signs of sepsis requires prompt evaluation. The clinician should seek sources outside the urinary tract, catheter obstruction, and, especially among men, periurethral infection. Microscopic pyuria[67] and urinary nitrites and leukocyte esterase as determined by urine dipsticks[185] are inadequate for screening for microburia. Thus cultures of urine and blood should be obtained. Many clinicians would empirically treat such patients with parenteral antibiotics at doses high enough to achieve concentrations in the serum adequate to treat bacteremia from a known or suspected bacteriuric species. The selection of antibiotics should be based on knowledge of organisms common in the medical unit and Gram staining of the patient's urine. Antibiotics should be modified on notification of antibiotic susceptibility patterns of the urine and blood isolates. Seven to 10 days of therapy is usually sufficient and need not all be parenteral.

For patients with long-term catheters, several studies have indicated a simplification of microbiologic results of urine cultures after replacement of the existing catheter with a fresh one.[84,86] This suggests in patients with symptomatic UTI that replacing or removing the existing catheter might decrease the bacterial burden and enhance clinical response to treatment. Raz and associates tested this hypothesis in a randomized, controlled trial of replacement of long-term indwelling catheters of patients with febrile UTIs.[86] Not only did they show that the prevalence of polymicrobial microburia dropped from 52% of patients to 11% immediately after catheter change, but they also found that patients in the replacement group had a shorter duration of fever and lower rate of symptomatic relapse than those in the group in whom catheters were not replaced.[86]

For patients with increasing renal dysfunction or recalcitrant or recurring bacteremia or fever, particularly ones with long-term catheters or other drainage devices, a search for hydronephrosis, vesicoureteral reflux, and urinary stones may be helpful.

Candiduria

Funguria, mostly caused by *Candida,* has become increasingly prominent in hospitals.[215,216] This is especially so in intensive care units; data from the National Nosocomial Infections Surveillance System indicated that fungi made up 39% of organisms isolated from nosocomial UTIs in intensive care unit patients and that *Candida albicans,* comprising 21%, was the single most common microbial species isolated.[8] The incidence of candiduria is directly related to duration of catheterization and to antibiotic use.[217]

Fortunately, most nosocomial candidurias are asymptomatic. A multicenter prospective study of 861 patients with nosocomial candiduria of at least 10^3 yeast/mL noted urinary symptoms in 2% to 4% and candidemia in 1%.[218] In the 155 patients who received no antifungal therapy, the candiduria resolved in 76%.

A multicenter, prospective, placebo-controlled trial elucidated the natural history of asymptomatic nosocomial candiduria and the role of oral fluconazole treatments.[219] By two weeks 35% of the untreated patients resolved their candiduria, and by 4 weeks, 65%. These investigators estimated that catheter replacement resulted in resolution of candiduria in 20% of patients and catheter removal did so in 40%. Follow-up of 150 placebo-receiving patients for 2 to 4 weeks revealed that none developed pyelonephritis or candidemia. Oral fluconazole hastened clearance of the candiduria, but by 2 weeks after therapy the fluconazole and placebo groups were equivalent, with 65% to 68% cleared of candiduria.

These data indicate that, in general, asymptomatic catheter-associated candiduria, like asymptomatic catheter-associated bacteriuria, need not be treated. Exceptions might include patients with a renal transplant, those with granulocytopenia, and those who will undergo urologic procedures (as well as low-birth-weight infants).[220,221]

Although candiduria is generally asymptomatic, complications can occur and include fever, pyelonephritis with renal and perirenal abscesses, fungus balls in the bladder or renal pelvis, and, particularly in patients with urologic abnormalities or procedures, disseminated candidiasis.[222] Depending upon severity of the illness, oral fluconazole or intravenous fluconazole or amphotericin B may be used. Removal or replacement of urinary catheters or stents may be helpful. Bladder irrigation with amphotericin B is rarely indicated and has been supplanted by systemic fluconazole.[220,221] Newer agents such as voriconazole,[223] posaconazole, and caspofungin[224] are not excreted in the urine. Renal failure patients may present special issues. Sobel and colleagues found that fluconazole, at doses reduced for renal insufficiency, was less effective in patients with renal dysfunction; they hypothesized that these lower doses resulted in subtherapeutic urinary concentrations of fluconazole and suggest that in such cases maintaining conventional doses may be reasonable.[219,220] Several case reports of the failure of amphotericin B lipid complex to clear candiduria in patients with renal dysfunction elicited the hypothesis that these larger sized particles may not have been sufficiently filtered by the kidney.[220,225] (Recall that, although the indwelling catheter does increase the risk of ascending candiduria, it is also a marker for sick patients who may be at risk for disseminated candidiasis from other sources and in whom the observed candiduria may be caused by seeding of the kidney by blood-borne *Candida* from a nonurinary site.)

PREVENTION OF PATIENT-PATIENT TRANSMISSION

Once microburia has developed, its consequences may extend beyond the individual patient. Periurethral flora, surfaces of the catheter system, skin of the patient, and the urine itself are sources of contamination of hands of medical personnel, who may carry the organisms to other patients.[36,59,60] Such patient-to-patient transmission leads to clusters of nosocomial microburias; those most often recognized are multidrug-resistant nosocomial bacteria such as *Serratia, Pseudomonas,* and *Citrobacter* spp.[129] Outbreaks must be recognized to be controlled, so some type of surveillance system, usually targeted at high-risk areas such as intensive care units, should be developed at each institution. Additionally, patients transferred from one medical facility to another have been the source of outbreaks in the second institution.[226]

Furthermore, plasmids encoding antibiotic resistance can move among bacteria[58,226]; the transfer of such plasmids has been a phenomenon suspected to occur in urine of catheterized patients. Such conjugations have been demonstrated in vitro in urine held at room temperature for 4 to 8 hours[227]; these are conditions in collection bags of patients with polymicrobial bacteriuria.

To prevent or control such outbreaks, a number of techniques can be used. To limit the number of patients at risk, urethral catheterization and its duration should be minimized and excellent catheter hygiene (i.e., maintaining the integrity of the closed catheter system) should be practiced. Contact spread can be decreased by treating the catheterized urinary tract as an open wound,[59] and using gloves and washing hands between patients.[60] Antiseptic solutions are necessary to adequately kill gram-negative rods transiently colonizing the hand; bland soap may be inadequate.[60] The transmission of bacteriuric strains is significantly higher between patients in the same room than between those in different rooms[228]; therefore, segregation of catheterized patients in different rooms is suggested. Although not recommended for medical treatment of the individual patient, systemic antimicrobials might be considered for some outbreaks. Additionally, to minimize concentrations of organisms in the collection bag, bag antimicrobials or oral methenamine preparations, which result in formaldehyde concentrations in the bag, might be useful. Oral nonabsorbable antibiotics might diminish intestinal colonization.

NOSOCOMIAL BACTERIURIA NOT ASSOCIATED WITH INSTRUMENTATION

The pathogenesis of the 10% of nosocomial UTIs not associated with any urinary tract instrumentation is not well understood. A partial explanation may be that the natural history of asymptomatic bacteriuria in these patients simply has continued and an episode has occurred in the hospital rather than in the community. Boscia and colleagues, studying elderly noncatheterized women outside the hospital, found that 30% were transiently bacteriuric during a 12-month period.[229] These findings may explain why nosocomial UTIs in the absence of instrumentation are significantly associated with increasing age, female gender, and history of previous UTIs.[230] These characteristics define a population group, hospitalized or not, that has a relatively high incidence of asymptomatic bacteriuria.

SUMMARY

Nosocomial microburia is the most common infection acquired in both hospitals and nursing homes and is usually associated with catheterization. This infection would be even more common but for the use of the closed catheter system. Most modifications have not improved on the closed catheter itself. However, even with meticulous care, this system will not prevent microburia forever. After microburia develops, the ability to limit its complications is minimal. Additionally, the catheterized urinary tract becomes a reservoir of microbes that can be transferred to other patients.

Once a catheter is put in place, the clinician must keep two important concepts in mind: keep the catheter system closed to postpone the onset of microburia, and remove the catheter as soon as possible. If the catheter can be removed before microburia develops, postponement becomes prevention.

However, the best prevention is not to use a urethral catheter at all. Other devices are increasingly used. For incontinent men, a condom catheter is a very useful alternative; an analogous and effective device for women would be much welcomed. For patients with urinary retention, intermittent, suprapubic, and possibly intraurethral catheterization may be options for short-term and long-term needs. The roles of these alternatives to urethral catheters would best be defined by controlled trials.

REFERENCES

1. Haley R, Culver D, White J, et al. The nationwide nosocomial infection rate: A new need for vital statistics. Am J Epidemiol. 1985;121:159-167.
2. Burke JP. Infection control—A problem for patient safety. N Engl J Med. 2003;348:651-656.
3. Emori T, Banerjee S, Culver D, et al. Nosocomial infections in elderly patients in the United States, 1986-1990. Am J Med. 1991;91:289S-293S.
4. Beck-Sague C, Villarino E, Giuliano D, et al. Infectious diseases and death among nursing home residents: Results of surveillance in 13 nursing homes. Infect Control Hosp Epidemiol. 1994;15:494-496.
5. Stamm WE, Martin SM, Bennett JV. Epidemiology of nosocomial infections due to gram-negative bacilli: Aspects relevant to development and use of vaccines. J Infect Dis. 1977;136S:S151-S160.
6. Hale RW, Hooton TM, Culver DH, et al. Nosocomial infections in U.S. hospitals, 1975-1976: Estimated frequency by selected characteristics of patients. Am J Med. 1981;70:947-959.
7. Krieger JN, Kaiser DL, Wenzel RP. Urinary tract etiology of bloodstream infections in hospitalized patients. J Infect Dis. 1983;148:57-62.
8. Richards MJ, Edwards JR, Culver DH, et al. Nosocomial infections in medical intensive care units in the United States. Crit Care Med. 1999;27:887-892.
9. Saint S, Chenoweth CE. Biofilms and catheter-associated urinary tract infections. Infect Dis Clin North Am. 2003;17:411-432.
10. Talja M, Korpela A, Järvi K. Comparison of urethral reaction to full silicone, hydrogen-coated and siliconised latex catheters. Br J Urol. 1990;66:652-657.
11. Robertson GS, Everitt N, Burton PR, et al. Effect of catheter material on the incidence of urethral strictures. Br J Urol. 1991;68:612-617.
12. Barnes-Snow E, Luchi R, Doig R. Penile laceration from a Foley catheter. J Am Geriatr Soc. 1985;33:712-714.

13. Clark A. Remarks on catheter fever. Lancet. 1883;1:1075-1077.
14. Foley F. Cystoscopic prostatectomy: A new procedure and instrument. Preliminary report. J Urol. 1929;21:289-306.
15. Kass EH. Asymptomatic infections of the urinary tract. Trans Assoc Am Phys. 1956;69:56-71.
16. Pyrah LN, Goldie W, Parsons FM, et al. Control of *Pseudomonas pyocyanea* infection in a urological ward. Lancet. 1955;2:314-317.
17. Gillespie WA. Infection in urological patients. Proc R Soc Med. 1956;49:1045-1047.
18. Gillespie WA, Linton KB, Miller A, et al. The diagnosis, epidemiology and control of urinary infection in urology and gynecology. J Clin Pathol. 1960;13:187-194.
19. Kunin CM, McCormack RC. Prevention of catheter-induced urinary-tract infections by sterile closed drainage. N Engl J Med. 1966;274:1155-1161.
20. Schaeffer AJ, Story KO, Johnson SM. Effect of silver oxide/trichloroisocyanuric acid antimicrobial urinary drainage system on catheter-associated bacteriuria. J Urol. 1988;139:69-73.
21. Thornton GF, Andriole VT. Bacteriuria during indwelling catheter drainage: II. Effect of a closed sterile drainage system. JAMA. 1970;214:339-342.
22. Garibaldi RA, Burke JP, Dickman ML, et al. Factors predisposing to bacteriuria during indwelling urethral catheterization. N Engl J Med. 1974;291:215-222.
23. Stamm WE. Guidelines for prevention of catheter-associated urinary tract infections. Ann Intern Med. 1975;82:386-390.
24. Warren JW, Mobley HLT, Donnenberg MS. Host-parasite interactions and host defense mechanisms. In: Schrier RW, ed. Diseases of the Kidney and Urinary Tract. 7th ed. Philadelphia: Lippincott Williams & Wilkins; 2001:903-921.
25. Norden C, Green G, Kass E. Antibacterial mechanisms of the urinary bladder. J Clin Invest. 1968;47:2689-2700.
26. Reinhart H, Obedeanu N, Sobel J. Quantitation of Tamm-Horsfall protein binding to uropathogenic *Escherichia coli* and lectins. J Infect Dis. 1990;162:1335-1340.
27. Parkkinen J, Virkola R, Korhonen T. Identification of factors in human urine that inhibit the binding of *Escherichia coli* adhesins. Infect Immun. 1988;56:2623-2630.
28. Parsons C, Stauffer C, Schmidt J. Bladder-surface glycosaminoglycans: An efficient mechanism of environmental adaptation. Science. 1980;208:605-607.
29. Schlager T, Lohr J, Hendley J. Antibacterial activity of the bladder mucosa. Urol Res. 1993;21:313-317.
30. McTaggart L, Rigby R, Elliott T. The pathogenesis of urinary tract infections associated with *Escherichia coli*, *Staphylococcus saprophyticus* and *S. epidermidis*. Med Microbiol. 1990;32:135-141.
31. Fukushi Y, Orikasa S. The role of intravesical polymorphonuclear leukocytes in experimental cystitis. Invest Urol. 1981;18:471-474.
32. Kantele A, Papunen R, Virtanen E, et al. Antibody-secreting cells in acute urinary tract infection as indicators of local immune response. J Infect Dis. 1994;169:1023-1028.
33. Kurnick J, McCluskey R, Bhan A, et al. *Escherichia coli*-specific T lymphocytes in experimental pyelonephritis. J Immunol. 1988;141:3220-3226.
34. Turck M, Goffe B, Petersdorf RG. The urethral catheter and urinary tract infection. J Urol. 1962;88:834-837.
35. Warren JW, Platt R, Thomas RJ, et al. Antibiotic irrigation and catheter-associated urinary-tract infections. N Engl J Med. 1978;299:570-575.
36. Rutala WA, Kennedy VA, Loflin HB, et al. *Serratia marcescens* nosocomial infections of the urinary tract associated with urine measuring containers and urinometers. Am J Med. 1981;70:659-663.
37. Weyrauch HM, Bassett JB. Ascending infection in an artificial urinary tract: An experimental study. Stanford Med Bull. 1951;9:25-30.
38. Nickel JC, Gristina P, Costerton JW. Electron microscopic study of an infected Foley catheter. Can J Surg. 1985;28:50-52.
39. Tambyah PA, Halvorson KT, Maki DG. A prospective study of pathogenesis of catheter-associated urinary tract infections. Mayo Clin Proc. 1999;74:131-136.
40. Daifuku R, Stamm W. Association of rectal and urethral colonization with urinary tract infection in patients with indwelling catheters. JAMA. 1984;252:2028-2030.
41. Garibaldi RA, Burke JP, Britt MR, et al. Meatal colonization and catheter-associated bacteriuria. N Engl J Med. 1980;303:316-318.
42. Schaeffer AJ, Chmiel J. Urethral meatal colonization in the pathogenesis of catheter-associated bacteriuria. J Urol. 1983;130:1096-1099.
43. Kunin CM, Steele C. Culture of the surface of urinary catheters to sample urethral flora and study the effect of antimicrobial therapy. J Clin Microbiol. 1985;21:902-908.
44. Hartstein AI, Garber SB, Ward TT, et al. Nosocomial urinary tract infection: A prospective evaluation of 108 catheterized patients. Infect Control. 1981;2:380-386.
45. Stark RP, Maki DG. Bacteriuria in the catheterized patient: What quantitative level of bacteriuria is relevant? N Engl J Med. 1984;311:560-564.
46. Mobley HLT, Chippendale MG, Tenney JH, et al. Expression of type 1 fimbriae may be required for persistence of *E. coli* in the catheterized urinary tract. J Clin Microbiol. 1987;25:2253-2257.
47. Mobley HLT, Chippendale GR, Tenney JH, et al. MR/K hemagglutination of *Providencia stuartii* correlates with catheter adherence and with persistence in catheter-associated bacteriuria. J Infect Dis. 1988;157:264-271.
48. Cox AJ, Hukins DWL, Sutton TM. Infection of catheterized patients: Bacterial colonisation of encrusted Foley catheters shown by scanning electron microscopy. Urol Res. 1989;17:349-352.
49. Ladd TI, Schmiel D, Nickel JC, et al. The use of a radiorespirometric assay for testing the antibiotic sensitivity of catheter-associated bacteria. J Urol. 1987;138:1451-1456.
50. Zimmerli W, Lew PD, Waldvogel FA. Pathogenesis of foreign body infection: Evidence for a local granulocyte defect. J Clin Invest. 1984;73:1191-1200.
51. Warren JW, Mobley HLT, Trifillis AL. Internalization of *Escherichia coli* into human renal tubular epithelial cells. J Infect Dis. 1988;158:221-223.
52. Warren JW, Muncie HL Jr, Hall-Craggs M. Acute pyelonephritis associated with the bacteriuria of long-term catheterization: A prospective clinico-pathological study. J Infect Dis. 1988;158:1341-1346.
53. Bryan C, Reynolds K. Hospital-acquired bacteremic urinary tract infection: Epidemiology and outcome. J Urol. 1984;132:494-498.
54. Tribe CR, Silver JR. Renal Failure in Paraplegia. London: Pitman Medical Publishing; 1969.
55. Warren JW, Muncie HL Jr, Hebel JR, et al. Long-term urethral catheterization increases risk of chronic pyelonephritis and renal inflammation. J Am Geriatr Soc. 1994;42:1286-1290.
56. Donovan WH, Hull R, Cifu DX, et al. Use of plasmid analysis to determine the source of bacterial invasion of the urinary tract. Paraplegia. 1990;28:573-582.
57. Selden R, Lee S, Wang WLL, et al. Nosocomial *Klebsiella* infections: Intestinal colonization as a reservoir. Ann Intern Med. 1971;74:657-664.
58. Brun-Buisson C, Philippon A, Ansquer M, et al. Transferable enzymatic resistance to third-generation cephalosporins during nosocomial outbreak of multiresistant *Klebsiella pneumoniae*. Lancet. 1987;2:302-306.
59. Schaberg DR, Weinstein RA, Stamm WE. Epidemics of nosocomial urinary tract infection caused by multiply resistant gram-negative bacilli: Epidemiology and control. J Infect Dis. 1976;133:363-366.
60. Ehrenkranz NJ, Alfonso BC. Failure of bland soap handwash to prevent hand transfer of patient bacteria to urethral catheters. Infect Control Hosp Epidemiol. 1991;12:654-662.
61. Platt R, Polk BF, Murdock B, et al. Risk factors for nosocomial urinary tract infection. Am J Epidemiol. 1986;124:977-985.
62. Jain P, Parada JP, David A, et al. Overuse of the indwelling urinary tract catheter in hospitalized medical patients. Arch Intern Med. 1995;155:1425-1429.
63. Saint S, Lipsky BA. Preventing catheter-related bacteriuria. Should we? Can we? How? Arch Intern Med. 1999;159:800-808.
64. Garibaldi RA, Mooney BR, Epstein BJ, et al. An evaluation of daily bacteriologic monitoring to identify preventable episodes of catheter-associated urinary tract infection. Infect Control. 1982;3:466-470.
65. Gaynes RP, Horan TC. Surveillance of nosocomial infections. In: Mayhall GC, ed. Hospital Epidemiology and Infection Control. Baltimore: Williams & Wilkins; 1996:1017-1031.
66. Saint S. Clinical and economic consequences of nosocomial catheter-related bacteriuria. Am J Infect Control. 2000;28:68-75.
67. Tambyah PA, Maki DG. The relationship between pyuria and infection in patients with indwelling urinary catheters: A prospective study of 761 patients. Arch Intern Med. 2000;160:673-677.
68. Arpi M, Renneberg J. The clinical significance of *Staphylococcus aureus* bacteriuria. J Urol. 1984;697-700.
69. Tambyah PA, Maki DG. Catheter-associated urinary tract infection is rarely symptomatic: A prospective study of 1497 catheterized patients. Arch Intern Med. 2000;160:678-682.
70. Weinstein MP, Towns ML, Quartey SM, et al. The clinical significance of positive blood cultures in the 1990s: A prospective comprehensive evaluation of the microbiology, epidemiology, and outcome of bacteremia and fungemia in adults. Clin Infect Dis. 1997;24:584-602.
71. Ikaheimo R, Siitonen A, Karkkainen U, et al. Virulence characteristics of *Escherichia coli* in nosocomial urinary tract infection. Clin Infect Dis. 1993;16:785-791.
72. Warren JW, Bakke A, Desgranchamps F, et al. Catheter-associated bacteriuria and the role of biomaterial in prevention. In: Naber KG, Pechere JC, Kumazawa J, et al, eds. Nosocomial and Health Care Associated Infections in Urology. Plymouth, United Kingdom: Health Publication Ltd, 2001:153-176.
73. Gross PA, Van Antwerpen C. Nosocomial infections and hospital deaths: A case-control study. Am J Med. 1983;75:658-662.
74. Daschner F, Nadjem H, Langmaack H. Surveillance, prevention and control of hospital-acquired infections. III. Nosocomial infections as cause of death: Retrospective analysis of 1000 autopsy reports. Infection. 1978;6:261-265.
75. Bueno-Cavanillas A, Delgado-Rodriguez M, Lopez-Luque A, et al. Influence of nosocomial infection on mortality rate in an intensive care unit. Crit Care Med. 1994;22:55-60.
76. Platt R, Polk BF, Murdock B, et al. Mortality associated with nosocomial urinary tract infection. N Engl J Med. 1982;307:637-640.
77. Stamm WE. Catheter-associated urinary tract infections: Epidemiology, pathogenesis, and prevention. Am J Med. 1991;91(Suppl 3B):65S-71S.
78. Garibaldi RA, Brodine S, Matsumiya S. Infections among patients in nursing homes: Policies, prevalence and problems. N Engl J Med. 1981;305:731-735.
79. Kunin CM, Chin QF, Chambers S. Indwelling urinary catheters in the elderly. Am J Med. 1987;82:405-411.
80. Warren JW, Steinberg L, Hebel JR, et al. The prevalence of urethral catheterization in Maryland nursing homes: Estimates for the United States. Arch Intern Med. 1989;149:1535-1537.
81. Warren JW, Damron D, Tanney JH, et al. Fever, bacteremia, and death as complications of bacteriuria in women with long-term urethral catheters. J Infect Dis. 1987;155:1151-1158.
82. Warren JW, Tenney JH, Hoopes JM, et al. A prospective microbiologic study of bacteriuria in patients with chronic indwelling urethral catheters. J Infect Dis. 1982;146:719-723.
83. Rahav G, Pinco E, Silbaq F, et al. Molecular epidemiology of catheter-associated bacteriuria in nursing home patients. J Clin Microbiol. 1994;32:1031-1034.
84. Tenney JH, Warren JW. Bacteriuria in women with long-term catheters: Paired comparison of the indwelling and replacement catheter. J Infect Dis. 1988;157:199-202.

85. Warren JW. *Providencia stuartii:* A common cause of antibiotic-resistant bacteriuria in patients with long-term indwelling catheters. Rev Infect Dis. 1986;8:61-67.

86. Raz R, Schiller D, Nicolle LE. Chronic indwelling catheter replacement before antimicrobial therapy for symptomatic urinary tract infection. J Urol. 2000;164:1254-1258.

87. Senay H, Goetz MB. Epidemiology of bacteremic urinary tract infections in chronically hospitalized elderly men. J Urol. 1991;145:1201-1204.

88. Damron D, Warren J, Chippendale M, et al. Do clinical microbiology laboratories accurately report bacteriology in urine from patients with long-term urinary catheters? J Clin Microbiol. 1986;24:400-404.

89. Tenney JH, Warren JW. Long-term catheter-associated bacteriuria: Species at low concentration. Urology. 1987;30:444-446.

90. Ouslander JG, Greengold B, Chen S. Complications of chronic indwelling urinary catheters among male nursing home patients: A prospective study. J Urol. 1987;138:1191-1195.

91. Muder R, Brennen C, Wagener M, et al. Bacteremia in a long-term care facility: A five year prospective study of 163 consecutive episodes. Clin Infect Dis. 1992;14:647-654.

92. Rudman D, Hontanasas A, Cohen Z, et al. Clinical correlates of bacteremia in a Veterans Administration extended care facility. J Am Geriatr Soc. 1988;36:726-732.

93. Bregenzer T, Frei R, Widmer AF, et al. Low risk of bacteremia during catheter replacement in patients with long-term urinary catheters. Arch Intern Med. 1997;157:521-525.

94. Kunin CM, Chin QF, Chambers S. Formation of encrustations on indwelling urinary catheters in the elderly: A comparison of different types of catheter materials in "blockers" and "nonblockers." J Urol. 1987;138:899-902.

95. Muncie HL Jr, Warren JW. Reasons for replacement of long-term urethral catheters: Implications for randomized trials. J Urol. 1990;143:507-509.

96. Ohkawa M, Sugata T, Sawaki M, et al. Bacterial and crystal adherence to the surfaces of indwelling urethral catheters. J Urol. 1990;143:717-721.

97. Mobley HLT, Warren JW. Urease-positive bacteriuria and obstruction of long-term urinary catheters. J Clin Microbiol. 1987;25:2216-2217.

98. Kunin CM. Blockage of urinary catheters: Role of microorganisms and constituents of the urine on formation of encrustations. J Clin Epidemiol. 1989;42:835-842.

99. Stickler D, Ganderton L, King J, et al. *Proteus mirabilis* biofilms and the encrustation of urethral catheters. Urol Res. 1993;21:407-411.

100. Morris NS, Stickler DJ, Winters C. Which indwelling urethral catheters resist encrustation by *Proteus mirabilis* biofilms? Br J Urol. 1997;80:58-63.

101. Mobley HLT, Hausinger RP. Microbial ureases: Significance, regulation, and molecular characterization. Microbiol Rev. 1989;53:85-108.

102. Takeuchi H, Takayama H, Konishi T, et al. Scanning electron microscopy detects bacteria within infection stones. J Urol. 1984;132:67-69.

103. McLean R, Nickel JC, Noakes VC, et al. An in vitro ultrastructural study of infectious kidney stone genesis. Infect Immun. 1985;49:805-811.

104. Nikakhtar B, Vaziri ND, Khonsari F, et al. Urolithiasis in patients with spinal cord injury. Paraplegia. 1981;19:363-366.

105. Chen Y-Y, Roseman JM, Devivo J, et al. Geographic variation and environmental risk factors for the incidence of initial kidney stones in patients with spinal cord injury. J Urol. 2000;164:21-26.

106. Hardy AG. Complications of the indwelling urethral catheter. Paraplegia. 1968;6:5-11.

107. Donnelly J, Hackler RH, Bunts RC. Present urologic status of the World War II paraplegic: 25-year followup. Comparison with status of the 20-year Korean War paraplegic and 5-year Vietnam paraplegic. J Urol. 1972;108:558-562.

108. Stonehill WH, Dmochowski RR, Patterson AL, et al. Risk factors for bladder tumors in spinal cord injury patients. J Urol. 1996;155:1248-1250.

109. Locke JR, Hill DE, Walzer Y. Incidence of squamous cell carcinoma in patients with long-term catheter drainage. J Urol. 1985;133:1034-1035.

110. Delnay KM, Stonehill WH, Goldman H, et al. Bladder histological changes associated with chronic indwelling urinary catheter. J Urol. 1999;161:1106-1109.

111. Wong ES. Guideline for prevention of catheter-associated urinary tract infections. Am J Infect Control. 1983;11:28-36.

112. Kunin CM. Detection, Prevention and Management of Urinary Tract Infections. 5th ed. Baltimore: Williams & Wilkins; 1997:226-278.

113. Warren JW. Catheter-associated urinary tract infections. Infect Dis Clin North Am. 1997;11:609-622.

114. Munasinghe RL, Yazdani H, Siddique M, et al. Appropriateness of use of indwelling urinary catheters in patients admitted to the medical service. Infect Control Hosp Epidemiol. 2001;22:647-649.

115. Gardam MA, Amihod B, Orenstein P, et al. Over utilization of urinary catheters and the development of nosocomial urinary tract infections. Clin Performance Quality Health Care. 1998;6:99-102.

116. Cornia PB, Amory JK, Fraser S, et al. Computer-based order entry decreases duration of indwelling urinary catheterization in hospitalized patients. Am J Med. 2003;114:404-407.

117. Dumigan DG, Kohan CA, Reed CR, et al. Utilizing National Nosocomial Infection Surveillance System data to improve urinary tract infection rates in three intensive care units. Clin Performance Quality Health Care. 1998;6:172-178.

118. Slappendel R, Weber EWG. Non-invasive measurement of bladder volume as an indication for bladder catheterization after orthopaedic surgery and its effect on urinary tract infections. Eur J Anaesthesiol. 1999;16:503-506.

119. Kunin CM. Nosocomial urinary tract infections and the indwelling catheter: What is new and what is true? Chest. 2001:120:10-12.

120. De Ruz AE, Leoni EG, Cabrera RH. Epidemiology and risk factors for urinary tract infection in patients with spinal cord injury. J Urol. 2000;164:1285-1289.

121. Weld KJ, Dmochowski RR. Effect of bladder management on urological complications in spinal cord injured patients. J Urol. 2000;163:768-772.

122. Saint S, Lipsky B, Baker PD, et al. Urinary catheters: What type do men and their nurses prefer? J Am Geriatr Soc. 1999;47:1453-1457.

123. Hirsh DD, Fainstein V, Musher DM. Do condom catheter collecting systems cause urinary tract infection? JAMA. 1979;242:340-341.

124. Ouslander JG, Greengold BA, Silverblatt FJ, et al. An accurate method to obtain urine for culture in men with external catheters. Arch Intern Med. 1987;147:286-288.

125. Nicolle LE, Harding GKM, Kennedy J, et al. Urine specimen collection with external devices for diagnosis of bacteriuria in elderly incontinent men. J Clin Microbiol. 1988;26:1115-1119.

126. Ouslander JG, Greengold B, Chen S. Complications of chronic indwelling urinary catheters among male nursing home patients: A prospective study. J Urol. 1987;138:1191-1195.

127. Ouslander J, Greengold B, Chen S. External catheter use and urinary tract infections among incontinent male nursing home patients. J Am Geriatr Soc. 1987;35:1063-1070.

128. Melekos M, Asbach HW. Complications from urinary condom catheters. Urology. 1986;27:88-91.

129. Shlaes DM, Currie CA. Endemic gentamicin resistance R factors on a spinal cord injury unit. J Clin Microbiol. 1983;18:236-241.

130. Belling P, Smith J, Poll W, et al. Results of a multi-center trial of the CapSure (Re/Stor) continence shield on women with stress urinary incontinence. Urology. 1998;51:697-706.

131. Bakke A. Physical and psychological complications in patients treated with clean intermittent catheterization. Scand J Urol Nephrol Suppl. 1993;150:1-61.

132. Guttmann L, Frankel H. The value of intermittent catheterization in the early management of traumatic paraplegia and tetraplegia. Paraplegia. 1966;4:63-71.

133. Wyndaele JJ. Complications of intermittent catheterization: Their prevention and treatment. Spinal Cord. 2002;40:536-541.

134. Biering-Sorensen F, Bagi P, Hoiby N. Urinary tract infections in patients with spinal cord lesions: Treatment and prevention. Drugs. 2001;61:1275-1287.

135. Shekelle PG, Morton SC, Clark KA, et al. Systematic review of risk factors for urinary tract infection in adults with spinal cord dysfunction. J Spinal Cord Med. 1999;22:258-272.

136. Cardenas DD, Hooton TM. Urinary tract infection in persons with spinal cord injury. Arch Phys Med Rehabil. 1995;76:272-280.

137. National Institute on Disability and Rehabilitation Research Consensus Statement: The prevention and management of urinary tract infections among people with spinal cord injuries. J Am Paraplegia Soc. 1992;15:194-205.

138. King RB, Carlson CE, Mervine I, et al. Clean and sterile intermittent catheterization methods in hospitalized patients with spinal cord injury. Arch Phys Med Rehabil. 1992;73:798-802.

139. Bakke A, Digranes A, Hoisaeter PA. Physical predictors of infection in patients treated with clean intermittent catheterization: A prospective 7-year study. Br J Urol. 1997;79:85-90.

140. Bakke A, Vollset SE. Risk factors for bacteriuria and clinical urinary tract infection in patients treated with clean intermittent catheterization. J Urol. 1993;149:527-531.

141. Duffy LM, Cleary J, Ahern S, et al. Clean intermittent catheterization: Safe, cost-effective bladder management for male residents of VA nursing homes. J Am Geriatr Soc. 1995;43:865-870.

142. Bennett CJ, Young MN, Razi SS, et al. The effect of urethral introducer tip catheters on the incidence of urinary tract infection outcomes in spinal cord injured patients. J Urol. 1997;158:519-521.

143. Giannantoni A, DiStasi SM, Scivoletto G, et al. Intermittent catheterization with a prelubricated catheter in spinal cord injured patients: A prospective randomized crossover study. J Urol. 2001;166:130-133.

144. Vapnek JM, Maynard FM, Kim J. A prospective randomized trial of the Lofric hydrophilic coated catheter for clean intermittent catheterization. J Urol. 2003;169:994-998.

145. Van Den Broek PJ, Dahha TJ, Mouton RP. Bladder irrigation with povidone-iodine in prevention of urinary-tract infections associated with intermittent urethral catheterization. Lancet. 1985;11:563-565.

146. Kuhlemeier K, Stover S, Lloyd L. Prophylactic antibacterial therapy for preventing urinary tract infections in spinal cord injury patients. J Urol. 1985;134:514-517.

147. Pearman JW, Bailey M, Riley LP. Bladder instillations of trisdine compared with catheter introducer for reduction of bacteriuria during intermittent catheterisation of patients with acute spinal cord trauma. Br J Urol. 1991;67:483-490.

148. Gribble MJ, Puterman ML. Prophylaxis of urinary tract infection in persons with recent spinal cord injury: A prospective, randomized, double-blind, placebo-controlled study of trimethoprim-sulfamethoxazole. Am J Med. 1993;95:141-152.

149. Pearman JW. Urological follow-up of 99 spinal cord injured patients initially managed by intermittent catheterisation. Br J Urol. 1976;48:297-302.

150. Wyndaele J-J, Maes D. Clean intermittent self-catheterization: A 12-year followup. J Urol. 1990;143:906-908.

151. Diokno A, Sonda L, Hollander J, et al. Fate of patients started on clean intermittent self-catheterization therapy 10 years ago. J Urol. 1983;129:1120-1122.

152. Michelson JD, Lotke PA, Steinberg ME. Urinary-bladder management after total joint-replacement surgery. N Engl J Med. 1988;319:321-326.

153. van den Brand IC, Castelein RM. Total joint arthroplasty and incidence of postoperative bacteriuria with an indwelling catheter or intermittent catheterization with one-dose antibiotic prophylaxis: A prospective randomized trial. J Arthroplasty. 2001;16:850-855.

154. Dobbs SP, Jackson SR, Wilson AM, et al. A prospective, randomized trial comparing continuous bladder drainage with catheterization at abdominal hysterectomy. Br J Urol. 1997;80:554-556.

155. Branagan GW, Moran BJ. Published evidence favors the use of suprapubic catheters in pelvic colorectal surgery. Dis Colon Rectum. 2002;45:1104-1108.
156. Dinneen MD, Wetter LA, May AR. Urethral strictures and aortic surgery: Suprapubic rather than urethral catheters. Eur J Vasc Surg. 1990;4:535-538.
157. Hammarsten J, Lindqvist K. Suprapubic catheter following transurethral resection of the prostate: A way to decrease the number of urethral strictures and improve the outcome of operations. J Urol. 1992;147:648-652.
158. Andersen JT, Heisterberg L, Hebjorn S, et al. Suprapubic versus transurethral bladder drainage after colposuspension/vaginal repair. Acta Obstet Gynecol Scand. 1985;64:139-143.
159. Schiøtz HA, Malme PA, Tanbo TG. Urinary tract infections and asymptomatic bacteriuria after vaginal plastic surgery: A comparison of suprapubic and transurethral catheters. Acta Obstet Gynecol Scand. 1989;68:453-455.
160. O'Kelly TJ, Mathew A, Ross S, et al. Optimum method for urinary drainage in major abdominal surgery: A prospective randomized trial of suprapubic versus urethral catheterization. Br J Surg. 1995;82:1367-1368.
161. Nielsen KK, Klarskov P, Nordling J, et al. The intraprostatic spiral: New treatment for urinary retention. Br J Urol. 1990;65:500-503.
162. Nissenkorn I, Richter S, Slutzker D. A simple, self-retaining intraurethral catheter for treatment of prostatic obstruction. Eur Urol. 1990;18:286-289.
163. Slutzker D, Richter S, Lang R, et al. The use of a prostatic stent in high risk patients over 80 years old with benign prostatic hyperplasia and chronic retention. J Am Geriatr Soc. 1994;42:1004-1005.
164. Elliot DS, Boone TB. Urethral devices for managing stress urinary incontinence. J Endourol. 2000;14:79-83.
165. Mansson W, Colleen S, Mardh P-A. The microbial flora of the continent cecal urinary reservoir, its stoma and the peristomal skin. J Urol. 1986;135:247-250.
166. Hill MJ, Hudson MJ, Stewart M. The urinary bacterial flora in patients with three types of urinary tract diversion. J Med Microbiol. 1983;16:221-226.
167. Madersbacher S, Schmidt J, Eberle JM, et al. Long-term outcome of ileal conduit diversion. J Urol. 2003;169:985-990.
168. Thoeny HC, Sonnenschein J, Madersbacher S, et al. Is ileal orthotopic bladder substitution with an afferent tubular segment detrimental to the upper urinary tract in the long term? J Urol. 2002;168:2030-2034.
169. Platt R, Murdock B, Polk BF, et al. Reduction of mortality associated with nosocomial urinary tract infection. Lancet. 1983;1:1893-1897.
170. DeGroot-Kosolcharoen J, Guse R, Jones JM. Evaluation of a urinary catheter with a preconnected closed drainage bag. Infect Control Hosp Epidemiol. 1988;9:72-76.
171. Huth TS, Burke JP, Larsen RA, et al. Clinical trial of junction seals for the prevention of urinary catheter-associated bacteriuria. Arch Intern Med. 1992;152:807-812.
172. Burke J, Larsen R, Stevens L. Nosocomial bacteriuria: Estimating the potential for prevention by closed sterile urinary drainage. Infect Control. 1986;7:96-99.
173. Saint S, Wiese J, Amory JK, et al. Are physicians aware of which of their patients have indwelling urinary catheters? Am J Med. 2000;109:476-480.
174. Little JS Jr, Bihrle R, Foster RS. Early urethral catheter removal following radical prostatectomy: A pilot study. Urology. 1995;46:429-431.
175. Vargas-Souto CA, Teloken C, Stumpf-Souto JC, et al. Experience with early catheter removal after radical retropubic prostatectomy. J Urol. 2000;163:865-866.
176. Rabkin DG, Stifelman MD, Birkhoff J, et al. Early catheter removal decreases incidence of urinary tract infections in renal transplant recipients. Transplant Proc. 1998;30:4314-4316.
177. Irani J, Fauchery A, Dore B, et al. Systematic removal of catheter 48 hours following transurethral resection and 24 hours following transurethral incision of prostate: A prospective randomized analysis of 213 patients. J Urol. 1995;153:1537-1539.
178. Benoist S, Panis Y, Denet C, et al. Optimal duration of urinary drainage after rectal resection: A randomized controlled trial. Surgery. 1999;125:135-141.
179. Britt MR, Garibaldi RA, Miller WA, et al. Antimicrobial prophylaxis for catheter-associated bacteriuria. Antimicrob Agents Chemother. 1977;11:240-245.
180. Mountokalakis T, Skounakis M, Tselentis J. Short-term versus prolonged systemic antibiotic prophylaxis in patients treated with indwelling catheters. J Urol. 1985;134:506-508.
181. Maki DG, Tambyah PA. Engineering out the risk for infection with urinary catheters. Emerg Infect Dis. 2001;7:342-347.
182. Warren JW, Anthony WC, Hoopes JM, et al. Cephalexin for susceptible bacteriuria in afebrile, long-term catheterized patients. JAMA. 1982;248:454-458.
183. Schiotz HA, Guttu K. Value of urinary prophylaxis with methenamine in gynecologic surgery. Acta Obstet Gynecol Scand. 2002;81:743-746.
184. Ockerblad NF. The silver catheter. J Urol. 1949;62:262-264.
185. Thibon P, LeCoutour X, Leroyer R, et al. Randomized multi-center trial of the effects of a catheter coated with hydrogel and silver salts on the incidence of hospital-acquired urinary tract infections. J Hosp Infect. 2000;45:117-124.
186. Karchmer TB, Giannetta ET, Muto CA, et al. A randomized crossover study of silver-coated urinary catheters in hospitalized patients. Arch Intern Med. 2000;160: 3294-3298.
187. Verleyen P, DeRidder D, Van Poppel H, et al. Clinical application of the Bardex IC Foley catheter. Eur Urol. 1999;36:240-246.
188. Riley DK, Classen DC, Stevens LE, et al. A large randomized clinical trial of a silver-impregnated urinary catheter: Lack of efficacy and staphylococcal superinfection. Am J Med. 1995;98:349-356.
189. Liedberg H, Lundeberg T. Silver alloy coated catheters reduce catheter-associated bacteriuria. Br J Urol. 1990;65:379-381.
190. Johnson JR, Roberts PL, Olsen RJ, et al. Prevention of catheter-associated urinary tract infection with a silver oxide-coated urinary catheter: Clinical and microbiologic correlates. J Infect Dis. 1990;162:1145-1150.
191. Johnson JR, Delavari P, Azar M. Activities of a nitrofurazone-containing urinary catheter and a silver hydrogel catheter against multidrug-resistant bacteria characteristic of a catheter-associated urinary tract infection. Antimicrob Agents Chemother. 1999;43:2990-2995.
192. Ahearn DG, Grace DT, Jennings MJ, et al. Effects of hydrogel/silver coatings on in vitro adhesion to catheters of bacteria associated with urinary tract infections. Curr Microbiol. 2000;41:120-125.
193. Niel-Weise BS, Arend SM, van den Broek J. Is there evidence for recommending silver-coated urinary catheters in guidelines? J Hosp Infect. 2002;52:81-87.
194. Darouiche RO. Anti-infective efficacy of silver-coated medical prostheses. Clin Infect Dis. 1999;29:1371-1377.
195. Rosch W, Lugauer S. Catheter-associated infections in urology: Possible use of silver-impregnated catheters and the Erlanger silver catheter. Infection. 1999; 27(Suppl):S74-S77.
196. Maki DG, Knasinski V, Tambyah PA. A prospective investigator-blinded trial of a novel nitrofurazone-impregnated urinary catheter (Abstract M49). Infect Control Hosp Epidemiol. 1997;18(Suppl):P50.
197. Leclair J, Cycan K, Munster A, et al. Effect of a nitrofurazone-impregnated urinary catheter on the incidence of catheter-associated urinary tract infection in burn patients. In: Proceedings of the 4th Decennial International Conference on Nosocomial and Healthcare-Associated Infections, Atlanta, 2000.
198. Darouiche RO, Smith JA Jr, Hanna H, et al. Efficacy of antimicrobial-impregnated bladder catheters in reducing catheter-associated bacteriuria: A prospective, randomized, multi-center clinical trial. Urology. 1999;54:976-981.
199. Carapeti EA, Bentley PG, Andrews SM. Randomized study of sterile versus non-sterile urethral catheterization. Ann R Coll Surg Engl. 1994;76:59-60.
200. Schiotz HA. Antiseptic catheter gel and urinary tract infection after short-term postoperative catheterization in women. Arch Gynecol Obstet. 1996;258:97-100.
201. Classen DC, Larsen RA, Burke JP, et al. Daily meatal care for prevention of catheter-associated bacteriuria: Results using frequent applications of polyantibiotic cream. Infect Control Hosp Epidemiol. 1991;12:157-162.
202. Huth TS, Burke JP, Larsen RA, et al. Randomized trial of meatal care with silver sulfadiazine cream for the prevention of catheter-associated bacteriuria. J Infect Dis. 1992;165:14-18.
203. Bastable JRG, Peel RN, Birch DM, et al. Continuous irrigation of the bladder after prostatectomy: Its effect on post-prostatectomy infection. Br J Urol. 1977;49:689-693.
204. Savage, JE, Phillips B, Lifshitz S, et al. Bacteriuria in closed bladder drainage versus continuous irrigation in patients undergoing intracavitary radium for treatment of gynecologic cancer. Gynecol Oncol. 1982;13:26-29.
205. Reiche T, Lisby G, Jorgensen S, et al. A prospective, controlled, randomized study of the effect of a slow-release silver device on the frequency of urinary tract infection in newly catheterized patients. BJU Int. 2000;85:54-59.
206. Leone M, Garnier F, Dubuc M, et al. Prevention of nosocomial urinary tract infection in ICU patients: Comparison of effectiveness of two urinary drainage systems. Chest. 2001;120:220-224.
207. Hardyck C, Petrinovich L. Reducing urinary tract infections in catheterized patients. Ostomy Wound Manage. 1998;44:36-43.
208. Trautner BW, Hull RA, Darouiche RO. *Escherichia coli* 83972 inhibits catheter adherence by a broad spectrum of uropathogens. Urology. 2003;61:1059-1062.
209. Darouiche RO, Donovan WH, Del Terzo M, et al. Pilot trial of bacterial interference for preventing urinary tract infection. Urology. 2001;58:339-344.
210. Li X, Lockatell CV, Johnson DE, et al. Development of an intranasal vaccine to prevent urinary tract infection by *Proteus mirabilis.* Infect Immun. 2004;72:746-756.
211. Nicolle LE. The chronic indwelling catheter and urinary infection in long-term care facility residents. Infect Control Hosp Epidemiol. 2001;22:316-321.
212. Harding GKM, Nicolle LE, Ronald AR, et al. How long should catheter-acquired urinary tract infection in women be treated? A randomized controlled study. Ann Intern Med. 1991;114:713-719.
213. Morris NS, Stickler DJ. The effect of urease inhibitors on the encrustation of urethral catheters. Urol Res. 1998;26:275-279.
214. Williams JJ, Rodman JS, Peterson CM. A randomized double-blind study of acetohydroxamic acid in struvite nephrolithiasis. N Engl J Med. 1984;132:67-71.
215. Bonsema D, Adams, J, Pallares R, et al. Secular trends in rates and etiology of nosocomial urinary tract infections at a university hospital. J Urol. 1993;150:414-416.
216. Jacobs L, Skidmore E, Freeman K, et al. Oral fluconazole compared with bladder irrigation with amphotericin B for treatment of fungal urinary tract infections in elderly patients. Clin Infect Dis. 1996;22:30-35.
217. Febore N, Silva V, Medeiros EA. Microbiological characteristics of yeasts isolated from urinary tracts of intensive care unit patients undergoing urinary catheterization. J Clin Microbiol. 1999;37:1584-1586.
218. Kauffman CA, Vazquez JA, Sobel JD, et al. Prospective multicenter surveillance study of funguria in hospitalized patients. Clin Infect Dis. 2000;30:14-18.
219. Sobel JD, Kauffman CA, McKinsey D, et al. Candiduria: A randomized, double-blind study of treatment with fluconazole and placebo. Clin Infect Dis. 2000;30:19-24.
220. Lundstrom T, Sobel J. Nosocomial candiduria: A review. Clin Infect Dis. 2001;32:1602-1607.
221. Rex JH, Walsh TJ, Sobel JD, et al. Practice guidelines for treatment of candidiasis. Clin Infect Dis. 2000;30:662-678.
222. Wainstein M, Graham R, Resnick M. Predisposing factors of systemic fungal infections of the genitourinary tract. J Urol. 1995;154:160-163.
223. Johnson LB, Kauffman CA. Voriconazole: A new triazole antifungal agent. Clin Infect Dis. 2003;36:630-637.
224. Mora-Duarte J, Betts R, Rotstein C, et al. Comparison of caspofungin and amphotericin B for invasive candidiasis. N Engl J Med. 2002;347:2020-2029.

225. Agustin J, Lacson S, Raffalli J, et al. Failure of a lipid amphotericin B preparation to eradicate candiduria: Preliminary findings based on three cases. Clin Infect Dis. 1999;29:686-687.

226. Schaberg DR, Alford RH, Anderson R, et al. An outbreak of nosocomial infection due to multiply resistant *Serratia marcescens:* Evidence of interhospital spread. J Infect Dis. 1976;134:181-188.

227. Schaberg DR, Highsmith AK, Wachsmith IK. Resistance plasmid transfer by *Serratia marcescens* in urine. Antimicrob Agents Chemother. 1977;11:449-450.

228. Fryklund B, Haeggman S, Burman LG. Transmission of urinary bacterial strains between patients with indwelling catheters: Nursing in the same room and in separate rooms compared. J Hosp Infect. 1997;36:147-153.

229. Boscia JA, Kobasa WD, Knight RA, et al. Epidemiology of bacteriuria in an elderly ambulatory population. Am J Med. 1986;80:208-214.

230. Hooton TM, Haley RW, Culver DH, et al. The joint associations of multiple risk factors with the occurrence of nosocomial infection. Am J Med. 1981;70:960-970.

CHAPTER **303**

Nosocomial Hepatitis and Other Infections Transmitted by Blood and Blood Products

KENT A. SEPKOWITZ

NOSOCOMIAL HEPATITIS

The potential for blood-borne transmission of hepatitis B was first noted in 1885, when Lurman described jaundice in factory workers who had received smallpox vaccination prepared from "human lymph."[1] More reports appeared in the subsequent decades as vaccination, often derived from human serum, became more common.[2] In addition, more frequent use of phlebotomy equipment,[3] insulin therapy,[4] and intramuscular injection of antibiotics all led to small outbreaks of jaundice, then ascribed to a transmissible "icterogenic" agent.

By the late 1940s, studies to clarify the modes of transmission were undertaken. Central to these was the use of human volunteers who were given putatively infectious material intradermally, intranasally, or by ingestion of feces and then observed for development of jaun-

dice.[1,5-10] From this landmark work arose our current understanding of the basic principles of transmission of infectious (hepatitis A) and serum (hepatitis B) hepatitis.

The first report of occupational disease in health care workers (HCWs) was provided by Leibowitz and colleagues,[11] who described jaundice in a blood bank nurse with frequent needle pricks on her hands and fingers. There followed a spate of similar reports describing occupationally acquired hepatitis among nurses, blood bank workers, phlebotomists, house staff, and others.[12-14] Soon, the workers' compensation boards of certain states ruled that viral hepatitis was a compensable occupational hazard.[14] Improved understanding of routes of transmission, more comprehensive and rigorous infection control, including needle disposal, and, for hepatitis B, vaccination of workers at risk have helped to decrease, but not eliminate, this occupational risk.

A corollary risk, that of infected HCWs (particularly surgeons) transmitting infection to nonimmune patients, has received a great deal of attention since human immunodeficiency virus (HIV) was first identified. To date, in addition to a few reports of HIV transmission, there are several reports of transmission of hepatitis B[15,16] and hepatitis C[17] from HCWs to patients.

Fecal-Oral Transmission

Hepatitis A

Most series suggest that hepatitis A does not represent an occupational risk for HCWs.[18] However, several outbreaks have been reported from both blood transfusion and fecal-oral transmission. The majority of reports are from pediatric or neonatal intensive care units.[19-21] In one, a neonate who acquired hepatitis A virus (HAV) via transfusion spread disease to 10 (16%) of 61 susceptible nurses[19] (Table 303-1). Adults with[22,23] and without[24] diarrhea have also transmitted disease to workers and other patients.

Despite appropriate infection control measures, HAV in a burn unit spread to 11 (19%) of 59 susceptible nurses.[21] Eating on the hospital ward was the most important risk factor. Other hospital outbreaks have also resulted from consumption of contaminated food, including orange juice[25] and sandwiches.[26]

Interruption of transmission by administration of intramuscular immune globulin to contacts has been used effectively for many years[18] (see Table 303-1). Broad-scale vaccination also may help interrupt nosocomial spread.[24] Current guidelines from the Centers for Disease Control and Prevention (CDC) and the Advisory Committee on Immunization Practices state that hepatitis A vaccination "is or might be" indicated for HCWs, but it is not recommended.[18,27] Few employee health services routinely provide the vaccine.

TABLE 303-1 Nosocomial Hepatitis: Transmission Rates and Interventions

Hepatitis	Outbreak or Needlestick Exposure Transmission Rate (%)	Prevention	Comment
A	10-30	Vaccine not given routinely to HCWs Immune globulin in outbreak setting	ACIP advises vaccine "is or might be" indicated
B		HBV vaccination	HBV vaccination acceptance for dialysis patients (58%) and staff (88%) has increased in recent years
eAg⁻	3	HBIG if appropriate	
eAg⁺	20-40	HBV vaccination HBIG if appropriate	
C	1-10	Immunoglobulin not recommended Interferon therapy for acute disease appears promising	Prevalence in U.S. dialysis units: 8.4% (patients) and 1.7% (staff)
Delta	Unknown rate; outbreaks described only in dialysis units	HBV vaccination	Segregate HBsAg-positive dialysis patients by delta antibody status
E	None described	Unknown	Probably no increased seroprevalence among dialysis or other patients

ACIP, Advisory Committee on Immunization Practices; Ag, antigen; HBV, hepatitis B virus; HBIG, hepatitis B immune globulin; HBsAg, hepatitis B surface antigen.

Hepatitis E

Outbreaks of hepatitis E have occurred in developing countries, but nosocomial transmission has not been described in the West. Early reports suggested increased seroprevalence among dialysis patients and intravenous drug users[28]; however, subsequent studies from Spain, France, Sweden, and other European countries[29] demonstrated no increased seroprevalence among dialysis patients. Rather, the elevated seroprevalence in the preliminary studies was ascribed to the confounding effect of age[29] (see Table 303-1).

Blood-Borne Transmission

Hepatitis B

Epidemiology. Hepatitis B was the first blood-borne disease recognized to pose occupational risk.[11-14] An early review found a preponderance of cases among pathologists, laboratory workers, and blood bank workers, demonstrating the risk of blood exposure.[12] Vaccine to prevent hepatitis B infection became available in the United States in 1982, but the initial plasma-derived vaccine proved unpopular because of (unfounded) safety concerns.

In 1987, growing attention to potential nosocomial spread of HIV led the Department of Labor, in conjunction with the Department of Health and Human Services, to recommend "universal precautions" to protect against exposure to body fluids.[18,27,30] Four years later, the Occupational Safety and Health Administration published the Federal Blood Borne Pathogens Standard, which went into effect in early 1992.[31] This mandated that all HCWs with possible exposure to blood or other potentially infectious materials either be offered the hepatitis B vaccine series free of charge, demonstrate immunity to hepatitis B, or formally decline vaccination.[31] Compliance with this recommendation has resulted in a 95% reduction of occupationally acquired hepatitis B,[30,32,33] although rare cases continue.

Seroprevalence. The seroprevalence of markers to hepatitis B virus (HBV) among HCWs is two to four times (6% to 15%) that of the U.S. general population (<5%).[34] Among HCWs, dentists, physicians, laboratory workers, dialysis workers, cleaning service employees, and nurses have the highest prevalence.[34-40] In addition, workers in facilities for the chronically mentally handicapped have increased seroprevalence.[41-43] Differences in seroprevalence are related to extent of exposure to blood rather than frequency of contact with patients.[43]

Incidence after Exposure. Before the availability of vaccine, the incidence of hepatitis B was 5 to 10 times increased among physicians and dentists and more than 10 times increased among surgeons, dialysis workers, those caring for the mentally handicapped, and laboratory workers with blood exposure.[30,39]

The risk of transmission from a single needlestick exposure varies according to the e antigen status of the source case: 1% to 6% for e antigen–negative blood versus 22% to 40% for e antigen–positive blood[34,44,45] (see Table 303–1). Occupationally acquired e antigen–negative infection rarely may cause fulminant disease.[46] Not all cases of hepatitis B transmission are explained by specific exposures, suggesting other modes of spread.[34,47,48] Environmental contamination is suggested by high HBV seroprevalence among unvaccinated dialysis patients and personnel.[34,49,50]

Reported Transmissions

Worker-to-Patient Transmission. Over the last 30 years, dozens of episodes involving HCW-to-patient transmission of hepatitis B have been described, resulting in hundreds of secondary cases (range 1 to 55 secondary cases per source case).[15,51-56] In a series of 10 clusters reported from the United Kingdom, the transmission rate ranged from 0.3% to 9%.[54,55] At least 42 of the 47 HCWs were dentists or surgeons. No cases of transmission from dentists have been reported since 1987, demonstrating the effectiveness of vaccination and universal precautions.[55] Lack of clustering may delay recognition of transmission.[56] In response to these concerns, in 1991 the CDC promulgated recommendations for preventing transmission of HIV and HBV to patients during exposure-prone invasive procedures.[57] Some have thought the recommendations too restrictive.[58]

In an outbreak in Los Angeles, 19 (13%) of 144 susceptible patients became infected from an e antigen–positive thoracic surgery resident despite appropriate infection control.[15] Thirteen available isolates, including the surgeon's, were identical when compared by molecular analysis. Examination of his surgical technique suggested that small cuts in his fingers, sustained by tying suture, resulted in his blood entering patients' open wounds. Ironically, the surgeon had declined hepatitis B vaccine 2 years earlier, then became infected as the result of an occupational exposure.

In most but not all instances, the source worker has been HBV e antigen positive. However, in one series, four e antigen–negative surgeons each transmitted disease.[16] The cases occurred in England, where restriction of e antigen–positive surgeons (principally cardiothoracic, gynecologic, orthopedic, and abdominal) is strictly enforced. Investigation of the transmissions was greatly enhanced by HBV DNA sequencing of both putative source and secondary cases, which demonstrated near homology. This led to a recommendation that a history of any surgery in the previous 6 months of illness be included as a routine question for patients newly identified with HBV. Such an approach also demonstrates that the introduction of a novel technique—molecular typing—may reveal previously unnoticed transmission and force a reconsideration of current policy.

Patient-to-Worker Transmission. Widespread transmission from a single patient to several HCWs is rare. In one instance, a patient in the preclinical window period for hepatitis B sustained severe trauma and underwent several surgeries.[59] At least four HCWs, including nurses and physicians, developed acute hepatitis temporally consistent with transmission from the putative source case.

Dialysis Setting. For many years, dialysis patients and staff were at high risk for nosocomial transmission of hepatitis B,[50] given the frequency of sharp injury or mucocutaneous exposure (5 per 10,000 dialysis procedures[60]), the high titers of HBV in blood (10^9 copies/mL), and the ability of HBV to survive well in the environment.[61] However, with segregation of patients by room, staff, and machine according to surface antigen status; institution of active vaccination programs; monthly serologic testing of susceptible patients; and attention to disinfection, equipment, and cleaning procedures, this rate has decreased sharply.[50,61] Compared to rates from a classic study conducted before the availability of vaccine,[50,62] the incidence of new surface antigen in 2000 among patients decreased from 3% to 0.05% and the prevalence decreased from 7.8% to 0.9%. In the same period, vaccination coverage of staff has increased to 88% and HBV incidence decreased from 2.6% to less than 0.5%[50,62] (see Table 303-1).

Despite these gains, outbreaks continue in centers that fail to identify HBV-infected patients, that share staff and equipment, or that fail to vaccinate susceptible patients.[61] Recognition that occult HBV may accompany chronic hepatitis C virus (HCV) may force a reevaluation of the HBV status of HCV-infected dialysis patients, because the infection control approach differs for the two viruses.[63]

Other Nosocomial Transmissions. In some countries, nosocomial transmission continues to account for a significant proportion of overall hepatitis B rates.[64,65] In addition, transmission related to spring-loaded fingerstick devices,[66,67] endoscopy equipment,[68] acupuncture needles,[69] multidose medication vials,[70] diabetic care,[71] and jet injections[72] has been reported. In developing countries, reuse of needles may contribute substantially to risk.[73] Reuse of injection equipment is thought to have caused spread of HBV and HCV in several United States outpatient facilities (see below).

Interventions and Management. Management of exposed or susceptible workers has been well summarized[74] (Table 303-2). Intramuscular hepatitis B immune globulin (HBIG) was the original intervention for postexposure prophylaxis.[75] It is still used in conjunction with initiation of a vaccine series for management of exposure in unvaccinated HCWs and vaccine nonresponders.[18,27,74,76] Treatment should be given within 24 hours after exposure. Vaccine nonresponders should receive a second dose 1 month later (HBIG dose 0.06 mL/kg).[18] Vaccine and HBIG may be given at the same time but should be administered with separate needles and syringes and at separate

TABLE 303-2 Recommended Postexposure Prophylaxis for Percutaneous or Permucosal Exposure to Hepatitis B Virus, United States

Vaccination and Antibody Response Status of Exposed Person	Treatment When Source Is		
	HBsAg Positive	HBsAg Negative	Not Tested or Status Unknown
Unvaccinated	HBIG* × 1; initiate HB vaccine series	Initiate HB vaccine series	Initiate HB vaccine series
Previously vaccinated			
Known responder[†]	No treatment	No treatment	No treatment
Known nonresponder	HBIG × 2 or	No treatment	If known high-risk score, treat as if score were HBsAg positive
	HBIG × 1 and initiate revaccination		
Antibody response unknown	Test exposed person for anti-HBsAg[‡]	No treatment	Text exposed person for anti-HBsAg
	If adequate,[†] no treatment		If adequate,[†] no treatment
	If inadequate,[†] HBIG × 1 and vaccine booster		If inadequate,[†] initiate revaccination

*Dose 0.06 mL/kg intramuscularly.
[†]A responder is defined as a person with adequate levels of serum antibody to HBsAg (i.e., 10 mIU/mL); inadequate response to vaccination is defined as serum antibody to HBsAg less than 10 mIU/mL.
[‡]Antibody to HBsAg.
HB, hepatitis B; HBIG, hepatitis B immune globulin; HBsAg, hepatitis B surface antigen.
Adapted from Centers for Disease Control and Prevention. Immunization of health-care workers: Recommendations of the Advisory Committee on Immunization Practices (ACIP) and the Hospital Infection Control Practices Advisory Committee (HICPAC). MMWR Morb Mortal Wkly Rep. 1997;46(RR-18):1-42.

anatomic sites. Plain immune globulin does not contain sufficient titers of HBIG and should not be given.[18] The role of antiviral agents such as lamivudine and adefovir in the management of nosocomial exposure has not been determined.

The durability of vaccine-induced immunity is not known.[30,77,78] Vaccine-induced antibody predictably wanes in many initial responders. However, in longitudinal reports to date, persons with waning antibody (to a level below 10 mIU/mL) have not developed active clinical hepatitis.[30,78] Rather, those newly infected develop hepatitis B core antibody (HBcAb) with subclinical disease; in addition, none has progressed to chronic complications.[78] Therefore, the CDC does not recommend routine revaccination of HCWs or patients, except for dialysis patients.[74,79]

Because of cost, determination of antibody to HBV prior to vaccination is not recommended.[27] Postvaccination testing should be routinely provided to all HCWs with an anticipated risk of occupational exposure. Knowledge of serostatus assists management of subsequent exposures[27,74] (see Table 303-2). For vaccine responders, no postexposure intervention is required, regardless of the hepatitis b surface antigen (HBsAg) or e antigen status of the source. For those unvaccinated and for vaccine nonresponders, treatment upon exposure to a HBsAg-positive source includes HBIG given within 24 hours of exposure and, if appropriate, initiation of a three-dose vaccine series.[74] Vaccinated HCWs with an unknown response to vaccine should have serostatus checked immediately after exposure and be treated according to serostatus[74] (see Table 303-2). Vaccine is generally well tolerated.[80] No link between vaccine and multiple sclerosis has been established.[81]

The best long-term management of vaccine nonresponder is not known. This is of particular importance because up to 10% of vaccinated persons fail to seroconvert.[82,83] Risk factors for a suboptimal response include cigarette smoking, increasing age, obesity, and, in some series, male sex.[82,83] Persons who do not seroconvert after the initial three-dose series should receive a second three-dose series or be evaluated for HBsAg carrier state.[45,84] Among those receiving a second course, up to half seroconvert after the second series.[84] A third series for nonresponders is not recommended. A recent report has suggested that intradermal vaccination may be effective for many nonresponders, but the work has not been confirmed.[85] Some experts believe that even nonresponders are protected, citing the experience among Eskimos in an area hyperendemic for HBV.[78]

Vaccine Acceptance Rates. Despite the risk, and despite the 1991 mandate of the Occupational Safety and Health Administration for vaccination[31] or declination of all HCWs with risk, vaccination rates are suboptimal. A study conducted soon after the Occupational Safety and Health Administration regulations went into effect examined acceptance rates at 96 hospitals throughout the United States[32] and found

that only 51% of 77,302 eligible employees had completed a three-vaccine series, with a trend toward improving acceptance rates. In a later U.S. survey from 1994 to 1995, 113 randomly selected hospitals were surveyed and charts of 2532 employees reviewed.[30] Of these, 66.5% had received a complete series, with highest coverage for higher risk personnel, such as phlebotomists, laboratory personnel, and nursing staff. Other series have demonstrated the same results. In U.S. dialysis centers in 2000, 58% of patients and 88% of staff had been vaccinated.[50]

One study demonstrated that the decision of workers to initiate the vaccine series was associated with younger age and occupation, including house staff, nurses and nurses' aides, and laboratory technicians.[86] Vaccine initiation was also higher among those who more frequently accepted annual influenza vaccination.[86] In the United States vaccination of infants with a three-vaccine series eventually should result in a health care workforce with a high rate of immunity.[33]

Hepatitis C

Epidemiology. The CDC estimated that 180,000 cases of HCV infection occurred in the United States in 1984.[87] With the introduction first of surrogate marker testing of donors and then a screening antibody test, this decreased to 25,000 infections in 2001.[88] Because the effectiveness of treatment is not predictable, control of nosocomial HCV has become a major goal for hospitals and workers.[87]

Seroprevalence. Most series suggest that groups at increased risk for hepatitis B, including dialysis workers, laboratory workers, surgeons, nurses, and workers with the mentally impaired, have no increase in HCV seroprevalence,[60,89-92] although a few do suggest an increase.[93,94] A 2000 survey of U.S. dialysis staff demonstrated 1.7% seroprevalence, similar to the overall prevalence in the United States (1% to 2%).[50] Only 40% of centers routinely determined the HCV serostatus of staff, however.[50] Dentists, particularly oral surgeons, have an elevated risk in some[95,96] but not all[97] reports.

Incidence after Exposure. Seroconversion occurs in 0% to 10% of nonimmune HCWs who sustain needlesticks from a source case with hepatitis C[27,60,93,98,99] (see Table 303-1). Maternal-fetal transmission rates are similar (5% to 9%).[87] Reports vary owing to differences in the diagnostic test used (antibody or HCV RNA). The highest transmission rate (10%) was from a study using HCV RNA to detect infection in exposed workers.[98] This high rate has not been duplicated, and most studies place the transmission rate below 3%. A correlation between the HCV RNA quantitative level in the source patient and the risk of transmission has not been established. The annual cost of follow-up testing in the United States after potential exposure is $2 to $4 million.[87]

A report of simultaneous transmission of HCV and HIV from a single needlestick was remarkable for the delayed time to seroconversion against each virus and the fulminantly fatal course of the HCV infection.[100] Frequency of this phenomenon is not known.

Reports of Transmission

Worker to Patient. A cardiac surgeon transmitted HCV to at least five patients during valve replacement surgery.[17] In this study, molecular analysis showed significant homology between the surgeon's and the patients' virus. The surgeon was treated with interferon-alfa-2b and ribavirin until his HCV RNA level became undetectable. At that point, he was allowed to resume performing surgery. His serum is rechecked monthly and, as of the 1996 report, he remains without detectable HCV RNA. In a case of transmission from an anesthesiologist to a surgical patient, no cause was elucidated.[101] A brief report from Spain described a staggering outbreak: at least 217 secondary cases associated with a single HCV-infected anesthesiologist.[102] Initial investigation suggested the physician was a morphine addict who gave patients therapeutic opioids only after first injecting himself with the drug.

Dialysis. With improved control of nosocomial HBV, transmission of HCV has emerged as a significant problem in dialysis centers throughout the world.[106-112] In most series, HCV seroprevalence among dialysis patients is 2- to 10-fold higher than in the general population. The CDC reports regularly on dialysis-associated diseases in the United States. In their most recent survey, which included 90% of all U.S. centers and represented more than 240,000 patients and 55,000 staff members, 58% routinely tested patients for HCV, an increase from 39% in 1995.[50] The prevalence of HCV infection among dialysis patients was 8.4% (range per center, 0% to 64%) and 1.7% among staff,[50] both slightly lower than the 1995 survey. Seroprevalence is even higher in many European and Asian centers, exceeding 40% in some cities. Incidence estimates have ranged from 0.6% to 2%.[50,113] The prevalence of HCV among peritoneal dialysis patients, in contrast, is not elevated.[110,114]

Because of compromised immune response, dialysis patients may fail to mount a significant antibody response to HCV. This was particularly apparent with the first-generation test because only about half of dialysis patients, subsequently shown to have HCV, were seropositive. The sensitivity of second- and third-generation tests is much improved, although one study found HCV RNA in 28% of dialysis patients with negative second-generation HCV enzyme-linked immunosorbent assay tests.[115] Routine use of HCV RNA has therefore been advocated by some.[115] However, this is mitigated by the substantial cost as well as difficulties in performing the test and reproducing the result.[87,110] Regular surveillance of serum alanine aminotransferase levels has been recommended by some as a less costly, more reproducible approach for screening dialysis patients for incident HCV.[113]

Early reports demonstrated that nosocomial spread was due to overt interruptions in infection control.[116] In subsequent studies, however, obvious breaches of infection control in dialysis centers and elsewhere[117] have not been identified, suggesting that either subtle interruptions are responsible for spread or HCV transmission is incompletely understood. Supporting the latter, some studies utilizing genotypic analysis have not demonstrated spread among persons treated in the same or adjacent beds; rather, linked cases have been located throughout the dialysis center, suggesting widespread transmission by an uncertain mechanism.[118]

Recognized risk factors for acquisition of HCV include blood transfusion and duration of dialysis time,[117] with the latter the more significant. The risk of blood transfusion has been further reduced by use of erythropoietin.[106] Possible explanations for the association with duration of dialysis include sharing of dialysis machines by HCV-infected and uninfected patients and reprocessing of dialyzers from HCV-infected patients.[119]

Some have advocated keeping HCV-infected dialysis patients together, similar to the successful approach taken with HBV-infected patients.[108] The CDC, however, does not endorse this approach[87] because of the lack of sensitivity of the anti-HCV test, which means that not all

infectious persons would be isolated, and the risk of superinfection for those already infected.[110]

Solid Tumor Transplantation. Transplant of HCV-infected organs into HCV-infected or uninfected hosts is an area of increasing concern.[110] Nearly all susceptible recipients of HCV-positive organs eventually develop HCV infection,[120] which may be severe.[120,121] In most series, however, no adverse effect on overall survival of patients or grafts has been found, although recipients of HCV-positive organs had a higher rate of liver-related morbidity and mortality.[120,121] Many organ banks now avoid using organs from HCV-positive donors except for lifesaving procedures, such as heart, lung, and liver transplants.[110] Transmission of HCV to eight organ or tissue recipients from a seronegative and nucleic acid technology (NAT)–negative organ donor has recently been described.[122] The donor died early in the HCV "window period."

Other Nosocomial Transmission. Rare cases of non-needlestick transmission include spread from a splash,[103] a retrograde cholangiogram,[104] and colonoscopy.[105] In the colonoscopy report, two secondary cases were shown by genetic sequencing to have an identical strain of hepatitis C. The two had undergone colonoscopy on the same day as the putative source case. Investigation suggested that inadequate cleaning of the biopsy suction channel and failure to autoclave some equipment, such as biopsy forceps, contributed to the transmission. Similar to HBV, reports have appeared describing HCV transmission via endoscopy,[123] multidose vials,[124] and a spring-loaded fingerstick device.[125] In addition, transmission has been described related to assisted conception,[126] immunoadsorption therapy in hemophilia,[127] and, perhaps, razor sharing between two residents of a psychiatric hospital.[128] The CDC has reported HBC and HBV transmission in several clinics across the United States. Transmission was thought to have occurred due to contamination of injection equipment used for consecutive patients.[128a]

A growing literature has suggested an association between hospitalization on an oncology or bone marrow transplant floor and the development of HCV infection.[129-131] Although some studies are from relatively resource-poor countries where reuse of needles may be the cause, others remain puzzling. Prolonged duration of hospitalization is to be a consistent common risk in these reports.

Management. The CDC recommends determining the HCV serostatus of the source patient after any exposure.[74,87] For the exposed HCW, baseline and 6-month follow-up testing for HCV antibody (second-generation test) and alanine aminotransferase should be obtained. Five percent to 10% of infections are not detected by enzyme immunoassay but may be identified with NAT testing for viral RNA. This technique is now routine for blood banks (see later) and might be used in the occupational exposure setting as well.

Optimal management of a needlestick exposure is unknown, but immune globulin is not recommended.[87] Immediate prospects for an effective vaccine appear limited.[132] Interferon-alfa may have a role in early infection: in one study, HCV resolved in all 14 HCWs who were treated with interferon soon after acute infection.[133]

Fulminant hepatitis A infection may occur in persons with underlying chronic liver disease due to HCV.[134,135] Therefore, HAV vaccination should be given to any HCW chronically infected with HCV.[136]

Hepatitis D

Delta virus is a defective RNA virus that requires the presence of active HBV infection (acute HBV or HBsAg carrier state) to establish infection. Transmission of the delta agent has been reported from a dialysis center.[137] In this report, a dually infected source patient regularly shared a dialysis machine with an asymptomatic HBsAg carrier, who subsequently developed acute delta hepatitis. A surgeon may also have become dually infected after a deep needlestick sustained while operating on the same source patient. Review identified several additional possible instances of delta hepatitis transmission in dialysis centers. This led to the current recommendation that patients and staff be vaccinated against HBV and that dialysis patients be separated according to delta virus status. Specifically, delta-positive, HBsAg-positive patients should receive dialysis in a separate room from delta-negative, HBsAg-positive patients.

TRANSFUSION-ASSOCIATED INFECTIONS

Beeson[138] reported the first cases of transfusion-associated infection in 1943, describing seven patients who developed hepatitis 33 to 119 days after receiving a red blood cell or plasma transfusion. Broader recognition of this and the related phenomenon of jaundice after vaccination against yellow fever, mumps, or polio[1,2,139-143] soon followed.[144,145] Various regulations were developed to ensure an increasingly safe blood supply.[146] Surveys to determine blood product use, led by the National Heart and Lung Institute (now the National Heart, Lung and Blood Institute), began in 1971.[146] By 1987, the cost of collecting, processing, and transfusing patients exceeded $3 billion.[146]

The advent of the epidemic of acquired immunodeficiency syndrome in the 1980s, followed by hepatitis C and, more recently, by outbreaks of West Nile virus, Creutzfeldt-Jakob variant disease, and the severe acute respiratory syndrome, has continued to draw attention to the safety of the blood supply.[147,148] Although less publicized, bacteria also are transmitted by transfusion, often with catastrophic results.[149] Current concerns in the blood banking community center on reconciling the high cost of excluding infections against the need to guarantee a maximally safe blood supply.

Scope of Transfusions

According to World Health Organization estimates, 75 million units of blood are collected in the world annually. Of these, at least 13 million are incompletely screened for viral infections, including almost half in resource-poor countries.[150]

In the United States, surveys have reported the frequency of blood collection and utilization since the late 1980s.[146,151] Between 12 and 14 million units are collected annually for donation and given to millions of recipients.[151,151a] The average age of a transfusion recipient is 69 years and each recipient receives an average of 2.9 units of blood. In 1997, 11.5 million red blood cell units, 3.3 million units of plasma, 9 million units of platelets, and 816,000 units of cryoprecipitate were given.[151] Red blood cell transfusions have slowly decreased, while the number of transfused platelets has increased. In addition to contributions from the voluntary donor pool, 12 million units of plasma are collected from paid donors and are used to prepare immunoglobulin, albumin, and various other plasma-derived products.[151,151a]

The annual likelihood of an individual receiving a transfusion is about 0.89% and increases dramatically with the age of the person.[152] Because of concern about contracting an infectious disease, there was a shift toward autologous and donor-directed blood donation over the past decade. Donor-directed units, usually given by family members for a specific patient, have not been shown to have lower rates of various infectious agents. However, viral infections are about half as common among apheresis donors (generally donor directed) as among whole blood donors.[153] Recently, there has been movement away from autologous and donor-directed donation.[151]

In 1997, 666,000 units, or about 5.4% of the donated allogeneic blood supply, were discarded on testing, usually because of detection of a potentially transmissible infection.[151] Constituting the overall rate of 180 reactive units per 10,000 collections were HIV-1/-2 antibody (9.2 per 10,000 units), HIV p24 antigen (8.4), HBsAg (6.2), HBcAb (69.2), HCV antibody (25.4), elevated alanine aminotransferase (29.8), human T-cell lymphotropic virus types I and II (HTLV-I/-II) antibody (14.1), and syphilis (18.1).[151] Rates of HBsAg and HCV antibody were increased among those volunteers who donated after September 11, 2001.[154] Unexpectedly, the increase was due to repeat, rather than first time, donors. Because of ongoing risk, strategies have been developed to retain uninfected donors.[155]

Viral Pathogens

A transfusion-associated transmission risk persists for HIV, hepatitis B, hepatitis C, and HTLV-1 for two distinct reasons: (1) the incomplete sensitivity of the available screening tests, which ranges from about 95% for hepatitis C to more than 99% for HIV, and (2) the "window" period (Table 303-3), which is defined as the period between acute infection (and potential infectivity) and the time when available tests can reliably detect infection.

The recent development and implementation of routine NAT has transformed blood bank screening for viral pathogens.[156-160] To date, NAT is used to screen for HIV and HCV and can detect viral RNA within the first 10 to 14 days, narrowing the window period by 7 to 10

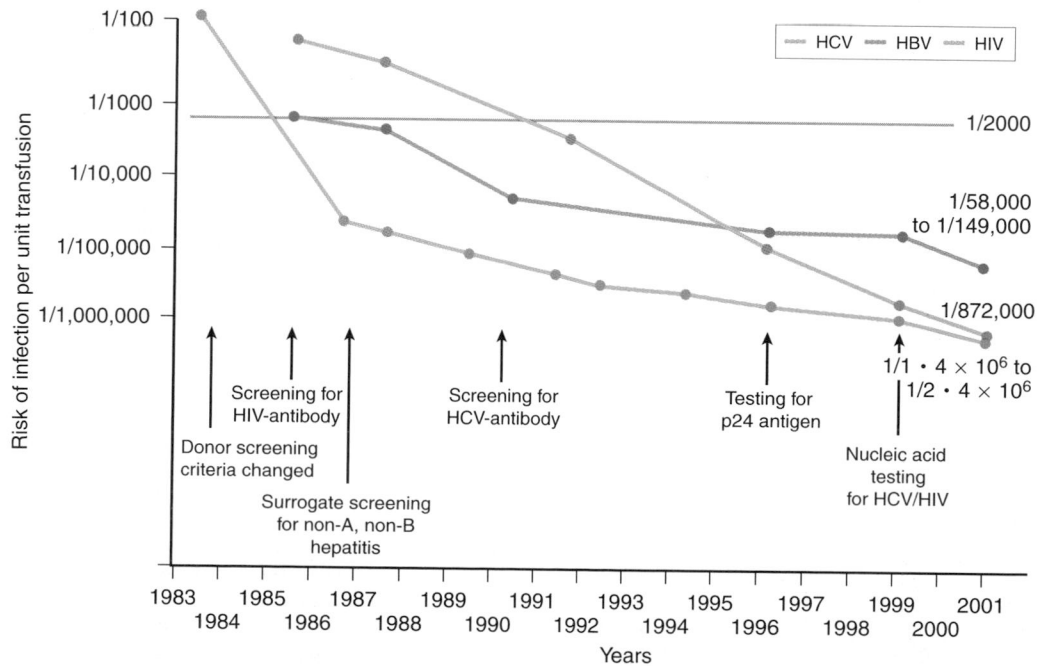

FIGURE 303-1. Risks of transfusion-related transmission of human immunodeficiency virus (HIV), hepatitis B virus (HBV), and hepatitis C virus (HCV) in the United States. Every unit is exposure to one donor. (*From Goodnough LT, Shander A, Brecher ME. Transfusion medicine: Looking to the future. Lancet. 2003;361:162; modified from AuBuchon JP, Birkmeyer JD, Busch MP. Safety of the blood supply in the United States: Opportunities and controversies. Ann Intern Med. 1997;127:904-909.*)

TABLE 303-3 Effect of Nucleic Acid Technology (NAT) on Window Period and Estimated Rate of Transfused Infectious Units

Virus	Test	Pre-NAT		Post-NAT	
		Window Period (days)	Rate of Transfused Infectious Units	Window Period (days)	Rate of Transfused Infectious (days)
HIV	ELISA with WB	22-25	1 per 500,000	10-14	1 per 1.5-2 million
HCV	HBsAg	59	1 per 100,000-220,000	49	1 per 250,000
HBV*	ELISA	82	1 per 70,000-200,000	10-14	1 per 1.5-2 million

*HBV NAT testing not performed in United States.
ELISA, enzyme-linked immunosorbent assay; WB, Western blot.

days for HIV and by 50 to 60 days for HCV. Additional NAT tests for HBV and other pathogens are in development.[158]

With introduction of NAT, the risk of acquiring HIV or HCV per unit of blood transfused has plummeted. Rates had been approximately 1 per 500,000 for HIV and 1 per 100,000 for HCV. Using NAT detection, these rates have fallen to 1 per 1.5 to 2.0 million for both HIV and HCV. As remarkable as this advance is, a fixed window period remains, meaning that the risk of receiving a unit of blood is not zero.

The advent of NAT also has had a substantial impact on the choice of serologic tests. In addition to sensitivity, blood bankers seek excellent specificity: false-positive or indeterminate tests both frighten donors and exclude otherwise appropriate donors from subsequent donations. Introduction of an extremely sensitive test such as NAT can allow blood banks to enhance the specificity of other screening tests, thereby limiting the number of persons potentially excluded from the donor pool because of misleading test results. An example of this potential benefit is found with the enzyme immunoassay tests used for HCV. Although sensitivity varies little between the versions, the third-generation assay has superior specificity.[159] Thus in one report the proportion of persons with indeterminate antibody tests for HCV decreased significantly after introduction of the third-generation test.[159]

Human Immunodeficiency Virus Type 1

More than 8000 persons in the United States have developed acquired immunodeficiency syndrome from receipt of blood or tissue, including 39 who received blood that had tested negative for HIV.[161] In addition, at least 50% of all hemophiliacs in the United States and Europe became infected with HIV from 1978 to 1985, with the highest incidence in 1982, when there were 22 infections per 100 person years.[162] The screening test was introduced in 1985, and since 1987 few new infections among hemophiliacs have been reported.[162] As noted, the introduction of NAT screening has substantially lowered the risk of HIV transmission.

Polymerase chain reaction for HIV RNA detection has been useful in clarifying the HIV serostatus of persons with indeterminate results on Western blot tests.[163] These reactions occur in about 1 per 5000 donations and are generally false-positive tests.[164]

Human Immunodeficiency Virus Type 2

In June 1992, the Food and Drug Administration mandated screening for HIV-2.[165] Since then, few HIV-2–positive donors have been identified and no cases of transmission have occurred in the United States, although transfusion-related HIV-2 cases have occurred in Europe.[166]

Human T-Cell Lymphotropic Virus Types I and II

HTLV-I and HTLV-II, unlike HIV-1 and HIV-2, are cell associated and therefore transmissible only with blood component transfusions.[166] Screening for both is done with a single test. The rate of transmission of HTLV-I decreased almost 10-fold (from 1 per 8500 to 1 per 69,000) after introduction of the screening test.[167] Transplant of solid organs from an HTLV-I infected donor has resulted in rapid progression to subacute myelopathy in three recipients; this phenomenon, however, has not been described in transfusion recipients.[168]

Hepatitis A Virus

Transmission of HAV via transfusion of blood has been described with red cells, particularly in infants,[19,169] and with factor VIII concentrate.[170] Donors with early, asymptomatic infection may transmit infection.[171] Factor VIII–associated transmission has occurred despite appropriate use of organic solvent and detergent to inactivate the virus. The lack of an envelope around HAV may have contributed to incomplete virus killing during preparation of the concentrate. Because of this small but persistent risk, vaccination for hepatitis A of chronic recipients of products made from pooled plasma has been recommended.[172] Review of all cases of hepatitis from 1998 to 2002 in the United States among persons with bleeding disorders revealed no acquisition of hepatitis A (or hepatitis C) via factor concentrates.[173]

Hepatitis B and D Viruses

Hepatitis B remains the most common and most difficult-to-identify blood-borne pathogen in the donor population, occurring in 1 per 220,000 transfusions.[148] Risk persists both because the screening test is incompletely sensitive—transmission from HBsAg-negative donors has long been recognized—and because of the prolonged window period, which is about 2 months. In countries that screen for HBcAb, most transmission derives from the window period, whereas in those that do not check core antibody status, half derive from the window period and the others are due to the insensitivity of HBsAg as a screening test.[150]

A NAT-based test for HBV is being developed but is not yet available. With current sensitivity, it will shorten the window period modestly, from 59 days to 49 days. This in turn will result in only a modest reduction in risk, from about 1 in 220,000 to 1 in 250,000.[150] In Central Europe, where NAT has been used since 1997, routine screening identified six additional infected donors out of 3.6 million tests.[174] This yields a transmission risk of about 1 per 350,000. More sensitive screens are particularly needed in HBV-endemic areas, such as Taiwan, where HBcAb screening is not routinely performed, so that transfusion-acquired HBV is a relatively frequent event.[175] A recent study has suggested that HBcAb remains a more sensitive screening test than NAT and cautions against discontinuation of this test.[176]

Screening donors for HBsAg excludes most, but not all, carriers of delta virus.[177] Identification of donors with antibody to the delta agent is not done routinely, so there is a residual risk of transmission of delta virus to HBsAg-positive recipients.

Hepatitis C Virus

Hepatitis C, then known as non-A, non-B hepatitis, was transmitted to as many as 7% to 10% of transfusion recipients in the late 1970s and early 1980s.[178] More than 90% of recipients of HCV-contaminated blood products develop HCV infection.[179] An older survey using the second-generation test found that 3.6 per 1000 U.S. donors were positive for HCV,[180] less than the prevalence in the U.S. population of about 10 to 20 per 1000. Associations with seropositivity include intravenous drug use (denied at initial donor screening), prior blood transfusion, intranasal cocaine use, sexual promiscuity, and ear piercing in men.[181]

The transmission rate of hepatitis C has decreased with improved screening tests to identify the virus and is an excellent example of how each new technology has improved blood safety. Before any testing,

0.45% of all transfusions transmitted HCV; with the introduction in 1986 of surrogate marker testing (alanine aminotransferase and HBcAb), the rate decreased to 0.19%, and with the introduction of the first-generation antibody test for HCV in 1990, the rate fell to 0.03%. The second-generation test has lowered the rate further mostly by identifying chronic infections rather than by shortening the window period. The remarkable reduction achieved by NAT, to a transmission risk of about 1 per 1.5 to 2 million, is an important public health achievement that ultimately will reduce community rates of HCV.[148,151,151a]

An outbreak of HCV related to contaminated immune globulin demonstrated a potential problem engendered by a more sensitive screening enzyme-linked immunosorbent assay test.[182] Transmission of hepatitis C was reported among children with primary immune deficiency receiving intravenous immune globulin on a regular basis. At least 23 (11%) of 210 children became infected after receiving Gammagard (Baxter Healthcare Corporation, Deerfield, IL), compared with none of 52 children who received other intravenous immune globulin products.

The investigators speculated that, because of the increased sensitivity of the second-generation test for hepatitis C antibody, additional antibody was eliminated from the vat of untreated donor plasma.[182] Presumably, this antibody had contributed in some measure to controlling virus introduced into the vat by additional viremic, but still antibody-negative, donors in the window period for acute hepatitis C. Product preparation did not involve a step of heat inactivation, which is used for some, but not all, other commercial products. As a result, the Food and Drug Administration now requires a heat inactivation step in the preparation of all intravenous immune globulin products. In addition, all immunoglobulin products, even intramuscular products (which have never been associated with transmission of any infectious agent), are now screened for hepatitis C.

Other Viruses

Several other viruses may be transmitted via transfusion[148,160] (Table 303-4). West Nile virus was transmitted by transfusion to 23 persons during the summer of 2002, the first time this had been documented.[183,184] In addition, it was transmitted by organ transplantation.[185] In response, a NAT test for West Nile virus was developed and used to screen blood donations during the period of West Nile virus activity in 2003.[158,184] During that summer, 942 blood samples were positive in 39 states, or 1 in approximately every 4700 donations. Sensitivity of the test is in part determined by whether the blood bank tests each unit or several units for each test.

Human herpesvirus-8 (HHV-8), the cause of Kaposi's sarcoma, is seldom detected in the blood, suggesting low risk of transmission. Transmission of HHV-8 resulting in Kaposi's sarcoma has been described, however, among solid-organ transplant recipients, with an incidence of about 0.5%.[186]

Transmission risk of cytomegalovirus (CMV) has been well summarized.[187] CMV is highly cell associated and is transmitted with white blood cells, which may be present in red cell, platelet, or white cell transfusions. Transmission of CMV from fresh-frozen plasma or cryoprecipitate has not been reported. The insensitivity of the serologic test has resulted in a residual risk of transmission of 0% to 6%, even when CMV-seronegative donors are used.[187] Because the demand for CMV-seronegative blood is outstripping the supply, approaches such as leukocyte filtration of CMV-seropositive blood are often used.[188]

Screening for Epstein-Barr virus is not performed routinely, despite older reports of transfusion-associated transmission.

Parvovirus B19 has been transmitted in coagulation factor concentrates. The risk of transmission to cryoprecipitate recipients may persist despite solvent and detergent treatment and heating to 100° C after lyophilization.[189] Nanofiltration may prove an effective approach to remove parvovirus and enteroviruses.[190]

The search for the cause of non–A–E hepatitis has yielded many contenders but no indisputable etiology to date. Hepatitis G virus has been found in 1% to 7% of donors and can be transmitted by transfusion.[191] The risk of transmission is in the range of 5.3 per 10,000

TABLE 303-4 Infectious Agents or Diseases Transmitted by Blood or Blood Products

Organism Category	Specific Organisms
Viruses	Hepatitis A virus
	Hepatitis B virus
	Hepatitis C virus
	Hepatitis D virus (delta agent)
	Cytomegalovirus
	Human immunodeficiency virus type 1
	Human immunodeficiency virus type 2
	Human T-cell lymphotropic virus type I
	Human T-cell lymphotropic virus type II
	Parvovirus B19
	West Nile virus
Bacteria	*Yersinia enterocolitica*
	Pseudomonas fluorescens
	Escherichia coli
	Serratia liquefaciens
	Serratia marcescens
	Other gram-negative rods
	Brucella spp.
	Bacillus spp.
	Coagulase-negative *Staphylococcus*
Other	Malaria
	Babesiosis
	Rocky Mountain spotted fever
	Q fever
	Syphilis
	Relapsing fever
	Trypanosoma cruzii
Organisms of concern but not established to be transmissible in blood or blood products	
	Human SARS coronavirus
	Creutzfeldt-Jakob agent
	Human herpesvirus 8
	Borrelia burgdorferi

Adapted from Doebbeling EN, Wenzel RP. Nosocomial viral hepatitis and infections transmitted by blood and blood products. In: Mandell G, Bennett J, Dolin R, eds. Principles and Practice of Infectious Diseases. 5th ed. New York: Churchill Livingston; 1995:2616–2632.

units.[192] Hepatitis G virus, however, has been shown not to be a cause of non–A–E hepatitis, and the clinical implications of hepatitis G infection remain undetermined.[191]

Two somewhat related single-stranded, unencapsulated DNA viruses, transfusion-transmitted virus (TTV) and SEN virus (designating the initials of the first patient investigated) each have been considered as the cause of non–A–E hepatitis.[193,194] Both are present worldwide and are often found in the blood of persons with post-transfusion non–A–E hepatitis. No causal association has been established, however, leading investigators to examine other candidate viruses.

Bacterial Pathogens

Infusion of blood products contaminated by bacteria is another potentially lethal risk of blood transfusion.[149] Focus has increased on this complication as the risk of contracting a blood-borne virus has decreased as a result of improved screening. Contamination may arise from donation, processing, storage, or transfusion. In the United States from 1976 to 1998, 77 deaths were caused by transfusion of bacterially contaminated blood products: 51 from contaminated platelets and 26 from contaminated erythrocytes.[195-197]

A recent estimate has placed the rate of bacterial contamination at 1 per 2000 to 3000 for platelets and 1 per 30,000 for red blood cell units.[149,197,198] A national study, Bacterial Contamination of Blood and Blood Products (BaCon), was designed to quickly identify severe reactions. In a 2-year period, 38 infections occurred, principally from contaminated platelets. Staphylococci and, surprisingly, Enterobacteriaceae predominated. Sixteen persons (42%) died from the infection.[149]

For both erythrocytes and platelets, longer storage time is well established as a risk factor for bacterial contamination. Further shortening the current storage times, however, would probably result in discarding too many uninfected units, exacerbating the nation's chronic blood supply shortage. In addition, contamination may occur during production and packaging of blood bags.[199] Various approaches to risk reduction are being actively pursued, although none is routine. These include avoidance by improved skin preparation and diversion of the initial 15 to 30 mL of the blood draw; optimizing storage time; genome amplification for early detection; and bacterial elimination by filtration, or inactivation by such strategies as photochemical treatment of units.[160,197,198]

Investigation of the potentially immunosuppressive consequences of blood transfusion is ongoing.[200]

Red Blood Cells

Two bacteria, *Yersinia enterocolitica* and *Pseudomonas fluorescens,* account for about 75% of all reported cases of transfusion of contaminated red blood cells[195] (see Table 303-4). Storage of red blood cells may extend 35 to 42 days depending on the type of additive used. Almost all instances of infection are associated with erythrocytes stored longer than 25 days and appear to derive from enhanced growth of these organisms at cold storage (4° C) temperatures. This is best exemplified by a case of transfusion-associated *Y. enterocolitica* in an autologous blood donor, who became bacteremic after receiving his own stored blood 41 days after donation.[201]

Donors with *Y. enterocolitica* are typically symptom free at the time of blood donation, although about two thirds recall a diarrheal illness a month before donation.[195] Addition of a donor question regarding diarrheal illness has not been adopted because of the commonness of the complaint. If it were used as a screening question, up to 10% of donors would be excluded.[195]

Platelets

A different spectrum of bacteria is associated with transfusion of platelets, possibly because they are stored at room temperature.[202,203] Coagulase-negative staphylococci are the most commonly recovered bacteria (about 25% of cases). Transfusion of *Salmonella choleraesuis* (13.5%) and a host of other organisms, including *Escherichia coli, Serratia marcescens, Bacillus* species, and *Enterobacter cloacae,* has also been reported[195] (see Table 303–4). A forthcoming recommendation is for platelets to have bacterial cultures done routinely, though this will add substantially to the cost.

A patient may receive pooled platelets from 6 to 10 donors, any one of which may be contaminated, thereby increasing the risk per transfusion. More frequent use of single-donor platelets (via apheresis) decreases this risk and is becoming the preferred approach.[149,197,198]

As with erythrocytes, transmission of infection via platelet transfusion tends to occur with older platelets (4 or 5 days), although a survey of outdated platelets found a low rate of contamination.[204] Because of this, the Food and Drug Administration, in 1985, shortened the acceptable storage time for platelets from 7 days to the current 5 days. Apheresis platelets are typically stored for a briefer period, further reducing risk of using this product.

Parasites, Protozoa, Spirochetes, and Rickettsiae

Trypanosoma cruzi, which causes Chagas' disease, is endemic in certain areas of South America and Central America. Rare cases of *T. cruzi* transmitted by blood transfusion have been reported by U.S. investigators.[166] It is estimated that up to 100,000 persons with *T. cruzi* infection reside in the United States. In Los Angeles and Miami, 7.3% and 14.3% of all donors, respectively, had risk of *T. cruzi* by history. Of these, 1 in 7500 to 9000, respectively, had detectable antibody. Lookback did not find seropositivity or disease in 18 recipients of the units from seropositive donors.[205] Seroprevalence among donors in Los Angeles has increased in recent years.[205] Because of the low prevalence of the disease among donors and the absence of an approved reliable test, as well as a transmission rate that may be as low as 10%, the CDC currently does not recommend routine serologic screening for the infection.

At least 40 cases of transfusion-associated babesiosis have been reported.[206] Donor screening for the disease is performed by questionnaire only. A man with asymptomatic babesiosis in Minnesota donated blood four times, resulting in transmission to at least four recipients.[206] Other tick-borne infections may also pose some risk, though it appears low.[207] Rickettsiae may rarely be transmitted by blood transfusion.[208]

Transfusion-related transmission of two venerable infections, syphilis[209] and malaria,[210] has long been reported. No cases of transfusion-related syphilis have occurred in the United States for decades, perhaps owing to poor spirochete survival under storage conditions.[209] In the United States from 1963 to 1999, 93 cases of transfusion-associated malaria were diagnosed and 10 patients died.[210] The majority of donors would have been excluded had current exclusion guidelines been in place or fully implemented at the time of attempted donation.

The risk of transmission of Creutzfeldt-Jakob disease via transfusion is unknown.[211] Although no cases have been reported, considerable concern has developed, leading to rigorous exclusion of donors from Britain or those with prolonged stays in Western Europe. When animal models are studied, prions appear transmissible in blood.[212] The relevance of these studies to actual human risk is unknown.[213]

REFERENCES

1. MacCallum FO, Bauer DJ. Homologous serum jaundice: Transmission experiments with human volunteers. Lancet. 1944;5:622-627.
2. Seeff LB, Beebe GW, Hoofnagle JH, et al. A serologic follow-up of the 1942 epidemic of post-vaccination hepatitis in the United States Army. N Engl J Med. 1987;16:965-970.
3. Mendelssohn K, Witts LJ. Transmission of infection during withdrawal of blood. Br Med J. 1945;5:625-626.
4. Droller J. An outbreak of hepatitis in a diabetic clinic. Br Med J. 1945;5:623-625.
5. Neefe JR, Stokes J, Gellis SS. Homologous serum hepatitis and infectious (epidemic) hepatitis: Experimental study of immunity and cross immunity in volunteers, a preliminary report. Am J Med Sci. 1945;210:561-575.
6. MacCallum FO, Bradley WH. Transmission of infective hepatitis to human volunteers. Lancet. 1944;2:228-231.
7. Neefe JR, Stokes J Jr, Reinhold JG, Lukens FDW. Hepatitis due to the injection of homologous blood products in human volunteers. J Clin Invest. 1944;23:836-853.
8. Neefe JR, Stokes J Jr, Reinhold JG. Oral administration to volunteers of feces from patients with homologous serum hepatitis and infectious (epidemic) hepatitis. Am J Med Sci. 1945;210:29-32.
9. Paul JR, Havens WP Jr, Sabin AB. Transmission experiments in serum jaundice and infectious hepatitis. JAMA. 1945;128:911-915.
10. Rosenbaum JR, Sepkowitz KA. Infectious disease experimentation involving human volunteers. Clin Infect Dis. 2002;34:963-971.
11. Liebowitz S, Greenwald L, Cohen I, Litwins J. Serum hepatitis in a blood bank worker. JAMA. 1949;140:1331-1333.
12. Trumbull ML, Greiner DJ. Homologous serum jaundice: An occupational hazard to medical personnel. JAMA. 1951;145:965-967.
13. Kuh C, Ward WE. Occupational virus hepatitis: An apparent hazard for medical personnel. JAMA. 1950;143:631-635.
14. Byrne EB. Viral hepatitis: An occupational hazard of medical personnel. JAMA. 1966;195:362-364.
15. Harpaz R, Von Seidlein L, Averhoff FM, et al. Transmission of hepatitis B virus to multiple patients from a surgeon without evidence of inadequate infection control. N Engl J Med. 1996;334:549-554.
16. The Incident Investigation Teams et al. Transmission of hepatitis B to patients from four infected surgeons without hepatitis B e antigen. N Engl J Med. 1997;336:178-184.
17. Esteban JI, Gomez J, Martell M, et al. Transmission of hepatitis C virus by a cardiac surgeon. N Engl J Med. 1996;334:555-560.
18. Centers for Disease Control and Prevention. Immunization of health-care workers: Recommendations of the Advisory Committee on Immunization Practices (ACIP) and the Hospital Infection Control Practices Advisory Committee (HICPAC). MMWR Morb Mortal Wkly Rep. 1997;46(RR-18):1-42.
19. Noble RC, Kane MA, Reeves SA, Rockel I. Posttransfusion hepatitis A in a neonatal intensive care unit. JAMA. 1984;252:2711-2715.
20. Drusin LM, Sohmer M, Groshen SL, et al. Nosocomial hepatitis A infection in a paediatric intensive care unit. Arch Dis Child. 1987;62:690-695.
21. Doebbeling BN, Li N, Wenzel RP. An outbreak of hepatitis A among health care workers: Risk factors for transmission. Am J Public Health. 1993;83:1679-1684.
22. Goodman RA, Carder CC, Allen JR, et al. Nosocomial hepatitis A transmission by an adult patient with diarrhea. Am J Med. 1982;73:220-226.
23. Baptiste R, Koziol D, Henderson DK. Nosocomial transmission of hepatitis A in an adult population. Infect Control. 1987;8:364-370.
24. Jensenius M, Ringertz SH, Berild D, et al. Prolonged nosocomial outbreak of hepatitis A arising from an alcoholic with pneumonia. Scand J Infect Dis. 1998;30:119-123.
25. Eisenstein AB, Aach RD, Jacobsohn W, Goldman A. An epidemic of infectious hepatitis in a general hospital. JAMA. 1963;185:171-174.

26. Meyers JD, Romm FJ, Tihen WS, Bryan JA. Food-borne hepatitis A in a general hospital: Epidemiologic study of an outbreak attributed to sandwiches. JAMA. 1975;231:1049-1053.

27. Bolyard EA, Tablan OC, Williams WW, et al. Guideline for infection control in healthcare personnel, 1998. Hospital Infection Control Practices Advisory Committee. Infect Control Hosp Epidemiol. 1998;19:407-463.

28. Halfon P, Ouzan D, Chanas M, et al. High prevalence of hepatitis E virus antibody in haemodialysis patients (Letter). Lancet. 1994;344:746.

29. Sylvan SP, Jacobson SH, Christenson B. Prevalence of antibodies to hepatitis E virus among hemodialysis patients in Sweden. J Med Virol. 1998;54:38-43.

30. Mahoney FJ, Stewart K, Hu H, et al. Progress toward the elimination of hepatitis B virus transmission among health care workers in the United States. Arch Intern Med. 1997;157:2601-2605.

31. Occupational Safety and Health Administration. Occupational exposure to blood-borne pathogens: Final Rule. Fed. Regist. 1991;56:64175-64182.

32. Agerton TB, Mahoney FJ, Polish LB, Shapiro CN. Impact of the bloodborne pathogens standard on vaccination of healthcare workers with hepatitis B vaccine. Infect Control Hosp Epidemiol. 1995;16:287-291.

33. Centers for Disease Control and Prevention. Hepatitis B vaccination—United States, 1982-2002. MMWR Morb Mortal Wkly Rep. 2002;51:549-552, 563.

34. Mast EE, Alter MJ. Prevention of hepatitis B virus infection among health-care workers. In: Ellis RE, ed. Hepatitis B Vaccines in Clinical Practice. New York: Marcel Dekker; 1993:295-307.

35. Lewis TL, Alter HJ, Chalmers TC, et al. A comparison of the frequency of hepatitis-B antigen and antibody in hospital and nonhospital personnel. N Engl J Med. 1973;289:647-651.

36. Feldman RE, Schiff ER. Hepatitis in dental professionals. JAMA. 1975;232:1228-1230.

37. Denes AE, Smith JL, Maynard JE, et al. Hepatitis B infection in physicians: Results of a nationwide seroepidemiologic survey. JAMA. 1978;239:210-212.

38. Snydman DR, Munoz A, Werner BG, et al. A multivariate analysis of risk factors for hepatitis B virus infection among hospital employees screened for vaccination. Am J Epidemiol. 1984;120:684-693.

39. Gibas A, Blewett DR, Schoenfeld DA, Dienstag JL. Prevalence and incidence of viral hepatitis in health workers in the prehepatitis B vaccination era. Am J Epidemiol. 1992;136:603-610.

40. Thomas DL, Factor SH, Kelen GD, et al. Viral hepatitis in health care personnel at The Johns Hopkins Hospital: The seroprevalence of and risk factors for hepatitis B virus and hepatitis C virus infection. Arch Intern Med. 1993;153:1705-1712.

41. Cancio-Bello TP, de Medina M, Shorey J, et al. An institutional outbreak of hepatitis B related to a human biting carrier. J Infect Dis. 1982;146:652-656.

42. Remis RS, Rossignol MA, Kane MA. Hepatitis B infection in a day school for mentally retarded students: Transmission from students to staff. Am J Public Health. 1987;77:1183-1186.

43. Guillen Solvas J, Luna del Castillo J, Maroto Vela MC, et al. The risk of infection with hepatitis B virus in relation to length of hospital employment. J Hosp Infect. 1987;9:43-47.

44. Werner BG, Grady GF. Accidental hepatitis-B-surface-antigen–positive inoculations: Use of e antigen to estimate infectivity. Ann Intern Med. 1982;97:367-369.

45. Gerberding JL. Management of occupational exposures to blood-borne viruses. N Engl J Med. 1995;332:444-451.

46. Reiss-Levy EA, Wilson CM, Hedges MJ, McCaughan G. Acute fulminant hepatitis B following a spit in the eye by a hepatitis B e antigen negative carrier (Letter). Med J Aust. 1994;160:524-525.

47. Petersen NJ. An assessment of the airborne route in hepatitis B transmission. Ann N Y Acad Sci. 1980;353:157-166.

48. Bond WW, Favero MS, Petersen NJ, et al. Survival of hepatitis B virus after drying and storage for one week. Lancet. 1981;1:550-551.

49. Garibaldi RA, Forrest JN, Bryan JA, et al. Hemodialysis-associated hepatitis. JAMA. 1973;225:384-389.

50. Tokars JI, Frank M, Alter MJ, Arduino MJ. National surveillance of dialysis-associated diseases in the United States, 2000. Semin Dial. 2002;15:162-171.

51. Garibaldi RA, Rasmussen CM, Holmes AW, Gregg MB. Hospital-acquired serum hepatitis: Report of an outbreak. JAMA. 1972;219:1577-1580.

52. Gerety RJ. Hepatitis B transmission between dental or medical workers and patients. Ann Intern Med. 1981;95:229-231.

53. Lettau LA, Smith JD, Williams D, et al. Transmission of hepatitis B with resultant restriction of surgical practice. JAMA. 1986;255:934-937.

54. Weber DJ, Hoffmann KK, Rutala WA. Management of the healthcare worker infected with human immunodeficiency virus: Lessons from nosocomial transmission of hepatitis B virus. Infect Control Hosp Epidemiol. 1991;12:625-630.

55. Bell DM, Shapiro CN, Ciesielski CA, Chamberland ME. Preventing bloodborne pathogen transmission from health-care workers to patients: The CDC perspective. Surg Clin North Am. 1995;75:1189-1203.

56. Spijkerman IJ, van Doorn LJ, Janssen MH, et al. Transmission of hepatitis B virus from a surgeon to his patients during high-risk and low-risk surgical procedures during 4 years. Infect Control Hosp Epidemiol. 2002;23:306-312.

57. Recommendations for preventing transmission of human immunodeficiency virus and hepatitis B virus to patients during exposure-prone invasive procedures. AORN J. 1991;54:576-582.

58. Gerberding JL. The infected health care provider. N Engl J Med. 1996;334:594-595.

59. Shanson DC. Hepatitis B outbreak in operating-theatre and intensive care staff (Letter). Lancet. 1980;2:596.

60. Petrosillo N, Puro V, Jagger J, Ippolito G. The risks of occupational exposure and infection by human immunodeficiency virus, hepatitis B virus, and hepatitis C virus in the dialysis setting. Italian Multicenter Study on Nosocomial and Occupational Risk of Infections in Dialysis. Am J Infect Control. 1995;23:278-285.

61. Centers for Disease Control and Prevention. Outbreaks of hepatitis B virus infection among hemodialysis patients—California, Nebraska, and Texas, 1994. MMWR Morb Mortal Wkly Rep. 1996;45:285-289.

62. Alter MJ, Favero MS, Maynard JE. Impact of infection control strategies on the incidence of dialysis-associated hepatitis in the United States. J Infect Dis. 1986;153:1149-1151.

63. Cacciola I, Pollicino T, Squadrito G, et al. Occult hepatitis B virus infection in patients with chronic hepatitis C liver disease. N Engl J Med. 1999;341:22-26.

64. Narendranathan M, Philip M. Reusable needles—A major risk factor for acute virus B hepatitis. Trop Doct. 1993;23:64-66.

65. Sikorska K, Laniec M, Buraczweska A, et al. Iatrogenic hepatitis B, non-A non-B, and C virus infections acquired in health service institutions of the Gdansk province in 1986-1995 (in Polish). Przegl Epidemiol. 1997;51:229-237.

66. Polish LB, Shapiro CN, Bauer F, et al. Nosocomial transmission of hepatitis B virus associated with the use of a spring-loaded finger-stick device. N Engl J Med. 1992;326:721-725.

67. Centers for Disease Control and Prevention. Nosocomial hepatitis B virus infection associated with reusable fingerstick blood sampling devices—Ohio and New York City, 1996. MMWR Morb Mortal Wkly Rep. 1997;46:217-221.

68. Morris IM, Cattle DS, Smits BJ. Endoscopy and transmission of hepatitis B (Letter). Lancet. 1975;2:1152.

69. Kent GP, Brondum J, Keenlyside RA, et al. A large outbreak of acupuncture-associated hepatitis B. Am J Epidemiol. 1988;127:591-598.

70. Oren I, Hershow RC, Ben-Porath E, et al. A common-source outbreak of fulminant hepatitis B in a hospital. Ann Intern Med. 1989;110:691-698.

71. Khan AJ, Cotter SM, Schulz B, et al. Nosocomial transmission of hepatitis B virus infection among residents with diabetes in a skilled nursing facility. Infect Control Hosp Epidemiol. 2002;23:313-318.

72. Canter J, Mackey K, Good LS, et al. An outbreak of hepatitis B associated with jet injections in a weight reduction clinic. Arch Intern Med. 1990;150:1923-1927.

73. Hutin YJ, Harpaz R, Drobeniuc J, et al. Injections given in healthcare settings as a major source of acute hepatitis B in Moldova. Int J Epidemiol. 1999;28:782-786.

74. Centers for Disease Control and Prevention. Updated U.S. Public Health Service guidelines for the management of occupational exposures to HBV, HCV, and HIV and recommendations for postexposure prophylaxis. MMWR Morb Mortal Wkly Rep. 2001;50(RR-11):1-52.

75. Beasley RP, Hwang LY, Stevens CE, et al. Efficacy of hepatitis B immune globulin for prevention of perinatal transmission of the hepatitis B virus carrier state: Final report of a randomized double-blind, placebo-controlled trial. Hepatology. 1983;3:135-141.

76. Stevens CE, Taylor PE, Ton MJ, et al. Yeast-recombinant hepatitis B vaccine: Efficacy with hepatitis B immune globulin in prevention of perinatal hepatitis B virus transmission. JAMA. 1987;257:2612-2616.

77. Horowitz MM, Ershler WB, McKinney WP, Battiola RJ. Duration of immunity after hepatitis B vaccination: Efficacy of low-dose booster vaccine. Ann Intern Med. 1988;108:185-189.

78. Wainwright RB, Bulkow LR, Parkinsin AJ, et al. Protection provided by hepatitis B vaccine in a Yupik Eskimo population—Results of a 10-year study. J Infect Dis. 1997;175:674-677.

79. Datta SD, Fiore AE, Mast E, et al. Routine booster doses of hepatitis B vaccine for health care workers are not necessary. Arch Intern Med. 2000;160:3170-3171.

80. McMahon BJ, Helminiak C, Wainwright RB, et al. Frequency of adverse reactions to hepatitis B vaccine in 43,618 persons. Am J Med. 1992;92:254-256.

81. Ascherio A, Zhang SM, Hernan MA, et al. Hepatitis B vaccination and the risk of multiple sclerosis. N Engl J Med. 2001;344:327-332.

82. Roome AJ, Walsh SJ, Cartter ML, Hadler JL. Hepatitis B vaccine responsiveness in Connecticut public safety personnel. JAMA. 1993;270:2931-2934.

83. Wood RC, MacDonald KL, White KE, et al. Risk factors for lack of detectable antibody following hepatitis B vaccination of Minnesota health care workers. JAMA. 1993;270:2935-2939.

84. Hollinger FB. Factors influencing the immune response to hepatitis B vaccine, booster dose guidelines, and vaccine protocol recommendations. Am J Med. 1989;87(Suppl 3A):36S-40S.

85. Playford EG, Hogan PG, Bansal AS, et al. Intradermal recombinant hepatitis B vaccine for healthcare workers who fail to respond to intramuscular vaccine. Infect Control Hosp Epidemiol. 2002;23:87-90.

86. Doebbeling BN, Ferguson KJ, Kohout FJ. Predictors of hepatitis B vaccine acceptance in health care workers. Med Care. 1996;34:58-72.

87. Centers for Disease Control and Prevention. Recommendations for follow-up of health-care workers after occupational exposure to hepatitis C virus. MMWR Morb Mortal Wkly Rep. 1997;46:603-606.

88. Centers for Disease Control and Prevention. Summary of notifiable diseases—United States, 2000. MMWR Morb Mortal Wkly Rep. 2002;49:i-xxii, 1-100.

89. Cooper BW, Krusell A, Tilton RC, et al. Seroprevalence of antibodies to hepatitis C virus in high-risk hospital personnel. Infect Control Hosp Epidemiol. 1992;13:82-85.

90. Forseter G, Wormser GP, Adler S, et al. Hepatitis C in the health care setting. II. Seroprevalence among hemodialysis staff and patients in suburban New York City. Am J Infect Control. 1993;21:5-8.

91. Cunningham SJ, Cunningham R, Izmeth MG, et al. Seroprevalence of hepatitis B and C in a Merseyside hospital for the mentally handicapped. Epidemiol Infect. 1994;112:195-200.

92. Zuckerman J, Clewley G, Griffiths P, Cockcroft A. Prevalence of hepatitis C antibodies in clinical health-care workers. Lancet. 1994;343:1618-1620.

93. Lanphear BP, Linnemann CC, Cannon CG, DeRonde MM. Decline of clinical hepatitis B in workers at a general hospital: Relation to increasing vaccine-induced immunity. Clin Infect Dis. 1993;16:10-14.

94. Stroffolini T, Marxolini A, Palumbo F, et al. Incidence of non-A, non-B and HCV positive hepatitis in healthcare workers in Italy. J Hosp Infect. 1996;33:131-137.

95. Klein RS, Freeman K, Taylor PE, Stevens CE. Occupational risk for hepatitis C virus infection among New York City dentists. Lancet. 1991;338:1539-1542.

96. Thomas DL, Gruninger SE, Siew C, et al. Occupational risk of hepatitis C infections among general dentists and oral surgeons in North America. Am J Med. 1996;100:41-45.

97. Herbert AM, Walker DM, Davies KJ, Bagg J. Occupationally acquired hepatitis C virus infection (Letter). Lancet. 1992;339:305.

98. Mitsui T, Iwano K, Masuko K, et al. Hepatitis C virus infection in medical personnel after needlestick accident. Hepatology. 1992;16:1109-1114.

99. Puro V, Petrosillo N, Ippolito G, et al. Occupational hepatitis C virus infection in Italian health care workers. Italian Study Group on Occupational Risk of Bloodborne Infections. Am J Public Health. 1995;85:1272-1275.

100. Ridzon R, Gallagher K, Ciesielski C, ct al. Simultaneous transmission of human immunodeficiency virus and hepatitis C virus from a needle-stick injury. N Engl J Med. 1997;336:919-922.

101. Cody SH, Hainan OV, Garfein RS, et al. Hepatitis C virus transmission from an anesthesiologist to a patient. Arch Intern Med. 2002;162:345-350.

102. Bosch H. Hepatitis C outbreak astounds Spain. Lancet. 1988;351:1415.

103. Sartori M, La Terra G, Aglietta M, et al. Transmission of hepatitis C via blood splash into conjunctiva. Scand J Infect Dis. 1993;25:270-271.

104. Tennenbaum R, Colardelle P, Chochon M, et al. Hepatitis C after retrograde cholangiography (in French). Gastroenterol Clin Biol. 1993;17:763-764.

105. Bronowicki JP, Venard V, Botte C, et al. Patient-to-patient transmission of hepatitis C virus during colonoscopy. N Engl J Med. 1997;337:237-240.

106. Simon N, Courouce AM, Lemarrec N, et al. A twelve year natural history of hepatitis C virus infection in hemodialyzed patients. Kidney Int. 1994;46:504-511.

107. Morales MF, Lossi JS, Alderete TN, Noli D. Prevalence and seroconversion to HCV in hemodialyzed patients, and epidemiological factors. Transplant Proc. 1996; 28:3402-3405.

108. Stuyver L, Claeys H, Wyseur A, et al. Hepatitis C virus in a hemodialysis unit: Molecular evidence for nosocomial transmission. Kidney Int. 1996;49:889-895.

109. McLaughlin KJ, Cameron SO, Good T, et al. Nosocomial transmission of hepatitis C virus within a British dialysis centre. Nephrol Dial Transplant. 1997;12:304-309.

110. Pereira BJ, Levey AS. Hepatitis C virus infection in dialysis and renal transplantation. Kidney Int. 1997;51:981-999.

111. Watanabe T, Ishiguro M, Kametani M, et al. GB virus C and hepatitis C virus infections in hemodialysis patients in eight Japanese centers. Nephron. 1997;76:171-175.

112. Fabrizi F, Martin P. Hepatitis C virus infection in dialysis: An emerging clinical reality. Int J Artif Organs. 2001;24:123-130.

113. Fabrizi F, Martin P, Dixit V, et al. Acquisition of hepatitis C virus in hemodialysis patients: A prospective study by branched DNA signal amplification assay. Am J Kidney Dis. 1998;31:647-654.

114. Puttinger H, Vychytil A. Hepatitis B and C in peritoneal dialysis patients. Semin Nephrol. 2002;22:351-360.

115. Caramelo C, Bartolome J, Albalate M, et al. Undiagnosed hepatitis C virus infection in hemodialysis patients: Value of HCV RNA and liver enzyme levels. Kidney Int. 1996;50:2027-2031.

116. Niu MT, Alter MJ, Kristensen C, Margolis HS. Outbreak of hemodialysis-associated non-A, non-B hepatitis and correlation with antibody to hepatitis C virus. Am J Kidney Dis. 1992;19:345-352.

117. Hardy NM, Sandroni S, Danielson S, Wilson WJ. Antibody to hepatitis C virus increases with time on hemodialysis. Clin Nephrol. 1992;38:44-48.

118. Forns X, Fernandez-Llama P, Pons M, et al. Incidence and risk factors of hepatitis C virus infection in a haemodialysis unit. Nephrol Dial Transplant. 1997;12:736-740.

119. Hayashi H, Okuda K, Yokosuka O, et al. Adsorption of hepatitis C virus particles onto the dialyzer membrane. Artif Organs. 1997;21:1056-1059.

120. Pereira BJ, Milford EL, Kirkman RL, Levey AS. Transmission of hepatitis C virus by organ transplantation. N Engl J Med. 1991;325:454-460.

121. Pereira BJ, Milford El, Kirkman RL, et al. Prevalence of hepatitis C virus RNA in organ donors positive for hepatitis C antibody and in the recipients of their organs. N Engl J Med. 1992;327:910-915.

122. Centers for Disease Control and Prevention. Hepatitis C virus transmission from an antibody-negative organ and tissue donor—United States, 2000-2002. MMWR Morb Mortal Wkly Rep. 2003;52:273-274, 276.

123. Muscarella LF. Recommendations for preventing hepatitis C virus infection: Analysis of a Brooklyn endoscopy clinic's outbreak. Infect Control Hosp Epidemiol. 2001;22:669.

124. Krause G, Trepka MJ, Whisenhunt RS, et al. Nosocomial transmission of hepatitis C virus associated with the use of multidose saline vials. Infect Control Hosp Epidemiol. 2003;24:122-127.

125. Desenclos JC, Bourdoil-Razes M, Rolin B, et al. Hepatitis C in a ward for cystic fibrosis and diabetic patients: Possible transmission by spring-loaded finger-stick devices for self-monitoring of capillary blood glucose. Infect Control Hosp Epidemiol. 2001;22:701-707.

126. Lesourd F, Izopet J, Mervan C, et al. Transmissions of hepatitis C virus during the ancillary procedures for assisted conception. Hum Reprod. 2000;15:1083-1085.

127. Kaiser R, Geulen O, Matz B, et al. Risk of hepatitis C after immunoadsorption. Infect Control Hosp Epidemiol. 2002;23:342-343.

128. Sawayama Y, Hayashi J, Kakuda K, et al. Hepatitis C virus infection in institutionalized psychiatric patients: Possible role of transmission by razor sharing. Dig Dis Sci. 2000;45:351-356.

128a. Transmission of hepatitis B and C viruses in outpatient settings—New York, Oklahoma and Nebraska, 2000–2002. MMWR Morb Mortal Wkly Rep. 2003;52:901-906.

129. Allander T, Gruber A, Naghavi M, et al. Frequent patient-to-patient transmission of hepatitis C virus in a haematology ward. Lancet. 1995;345:603-607.

130. Knoll A, Helmig M, Peters O, Jilg W. Hepatitis C virus transmission in a pediatric oncology ward: Analysis of an outbreak and review of the literature. Lab Invest. 2001;81:251-262.

131. Januszkiewicz-Lewandowska D, Wysocki J, Rembowska J, et al. Transmission of HCV infection among long-term hospitalized onco-haematological patients. J Hosp Infect. 2003;53:120-123.

132. Lemon SM, Thomas DL. Vaccines to prevent viral hepatitis. N Engl J Med. 1997; 336:196-204.

133. Jaeckel E, Cornberg M, Wedemeyer H, et al. Treatment of acute hepatitis C with interferon alfa-2b. N Engl J Med. 2001;345:1452-1457.

134. Mele A, Tosti ME, Stroffolini T. Hepatitis associated with hepatitis A superinfection in patients with chronic hepatitis C (Letter). N Engl J Med. 1998;338:1771; author reply 1772-1773.

135. Vento S, Garofano T, Renzini C, et al. Fulminant hepatitis associated with hepatitis A virus superinfection in patients with chronic hepatitis C. N Engl J Med. 1998; 338:286-290.

136. Koff RS. Should health care workers exposed to hepatitis C routinely receive hepatitis A vaccine (Letter)? JAMA. 1998;279:195.

137. Lettau LA, Alfred HJ, Glew RH, et al. Nosocomial transmission of delta hepatitis. Ann Intern Med. 1986;104:631-635.

138. Beeson PB. Jaundice occurring one to four months after transfusion of blood or plasma. JAMA. 1943;121:1332-1334.

139. Findlay GM MacCallum FO. Hepatitis and jaundice associated with immunization against certain virus diseases. Proc R Soc Med. 1938;31:799-806.

140. Sawyer WA, Meyer KF, Eaton MD, et al. Jaundice in army personnel in the western region of the United States and its relation to vaccination against yellow fever. Am J Hyg. 1944;40:35-107.

141. Turner RH, Snavely JR, Grossman EB, et al. Some clinical studies of acute hepatitis occurring in soldiers after inoculation with yellow fever vaccine; with especial consideration of severe attacks. Ann Intern Med. 1944;20:193-218.

142. Beeson PB, Chesney G, McFarlan AM. Hepatitis following injection of mumps convalescent plasma. Lancet. 1944:1:814-817.

143. Propert SA. Hepatitis after prophylactic serum. Br Med J. 1938;9:677-678.

144. Brightman J, Korns RF. Homologous serum jaundice in recipients of pooled plasma. JAMA. 1947;165:268-272.

145. Scheinberg IH, Kinney TD, Janeway CA. Homologous serum jaundice: A problem for the operation of blood banks. JAMA. 1947;134:841-848.

146. Surgenor DM, Wallace EL, Hao SHS, Chapman RH. Collection and transfusion of blood in the United States, 1982-1988. N Engl J Med. 1990;322:1646-1651.

147. Chamberland ME. Emerging infectious agents: Do they pose a risk to the safety of transfused blood and blood products? Clin Infect Dis. 2002;34:797-805.

148. Busch MP, Kleinman SH, Nemo GJ. Current and emerging infectious risks of blood transfusions. JAMA. 2003;289:959-962.

149. Jacobs MR, Palavecino E, Yomtovian R. Don't bug me: The problem of bacterial contamination of blood components—challenges and solutions. Transfusion. 2001; 41:1331-1334.

150. Glynn SA, Kleinman SH, Wright DJ, et al. International application of the incidence rate/window period model. Transfusion. 2002;42:966-972.

151. Sullivan MT, McCullough J, Schreiber GB, Wallace EL. Blood collection and transfusion in the United States in 1997. Transfusion. 2002;42:1253-1260.

151a. National Blood Data Resource Center. Comprehensive report on blood collection and transfusion in the United States in 2001. Executive Summary. <http://www.nbdrc.org/index.htm>

152. Vamvakas EC, Taswell HF. Epidemiology of blood transfusion. Transfusion. 1994;34:464-470.

153. Glynn SA, Schreiber GB, Busch MP, et al. Demographic characteristics, unreported risk behaviors, and the prevalence and incidence of viral infections: A comparison of apheresis and whole-blood donors. The Retrovirus Epidemiology Donor Study. Transfusion. 1998;38:350-358.

154. Dodd RY, Orton SL, Notari EP 4th, Stramer SL. Viral marker rates among blood donors before and after the terrorist attacks on the United States on September 11, 2001. Transfusion. 2002;42:1241-1241.

155. King SM, AuBuchon J, Barrowman N, et al. Consensus statement from the Consensus Conference on Blood-Borne Human Immunodeficiency Virus and Hepatitis: Optimizing the donor-selection process. Vox Sang. 2002;83:188-193.

156. Tabor E, Yu MY Hewlett I, Epstein JS. Summary of a workshop on the implementation of NAT to screen donors of blood and plasma for viruses. Transfusion. 2000;40:1273-1275.

157. Dodd RY, Notari EP 4th, Stramer SL. Current prevalence and incidence of infectious disease markers and estimated window-period risk in the American Red Cross blood donor population. Transfusion. 2002;42:975-979.

158. Tabor E, Epstein JS. NAT screening of blood and plasma donations: Evolution of technology and regulatory policy. Transfusion. 2002;42:1230-1237.

159. Sharma UK, Stramer SL, Wright DJ, et al. Impact of changes in viral marker screening assays. Retrovirus Epidemiology Donor Study. Transfusion. 2003;43:202-214.

160. Goodnough LT, Shander A, Brecher ME. Transfusion medicine: Looking to the future. Lancet. 2003;361:161-169.

161. Centers for Disease Control and Prevention. HIV/AIDS surveillance report. MMWR Morb Mortal Wkly Rep. 1997;9:10.

162. Kroner BL, Rosenberg PS, Aledort LM, et al. HIV-1 infection incidence among persons with hemophilia in the United States and western Europe, 1978-1990. Multicenter Hemophilia Cohort Study. J Acquir Immune Defic Syndr. 1994;7:279-286.

163. Leitman SF, Klein HG, Melpolder JJ, et al. Clinical implications of positive tests for antibodies to human immunodeficiency virus type 1 in asymptomatic blood donors. N Engl J Med. 1989;321:917-924.

164. Busch MP, Kleinman SH, Williams AE, et al. Frequency of human immunodeficiency virus (HIV) infection among contemporary anti-HIV-1 and anti-HIV-1/2 supplemental test–indeterminate blood donors. The Retrovirus Epidemiology Donor Study. Transfusion. 1996;36:37-44.

165. Centers for Disease Control and Prevention. Update: HIV-2 infection among blood and plasma donors—United States, June 1992–June 1995. MMWR Morb Mortal Wkly Rep. 1995;44:603-606.

166. Chamberland M, Khabbaz RF. Emerging issues in blood safety. Infect Dis Clin North Am. 1998;12:217-229.

167. Vrielink H, Zaaijer HL, Reesink HW. The clinical relevance of HTLV type I and II in transfusion medicine. Transfus Med Rev. 1997;11:173-179.

168. Toro C, Rodes B, Poveda E, Soriano V. Rapid development of subacute myelopathy in three organ transplant recipients after transmission of human T-cell lymphotropic virus type I from a single donor. Transplantation. 2003;75:102-104.

169. Giacoia GP, Kasprisin DO. Transfusion-acquired hepatitis A. South Med J. 1989;82:1357-1360.

170. Mannucci PM, Gdovin S, Gringeri A, et al. Transmission of hepatitis A to patients with hemophilia by factor VIII concentrates treated with organic solvent and detergent to inactivate viruses. The Italian Collaborative Group. Ann Intern Med. 1994;120:1-7.

171. Diwan AH, Stubbs JR, Carnahan GE. Transmission of hepatitis A via WBC-reduced RBCs and FFP from a single donation. Transfusion. 2003;43:536-540.

172. Centers for Disease Control and Prevention. Prevention of hepatitis A through active or passive immunization: Recommendations of the Advisory Committee on Immunization Practices (ACIP). MMWR Morb Mortal Wkly Rep. 1999;48 (RR-12):1-37.

173. Blood safety monitoring among persons with bleeding disorders—United States, May 1998–June 2002. MMWR Morb Mortal Wkly Rep. 2003;51:1152-1154.

174. Roth WK, Weber M, Petersen D, et al. NAT for HBV and anti-HBc testing increase blood safety. Transfusion. 2002;42:869-875.

175. Wang JT, Lee CZ, Chen PJ, et al. Transfusion-transmitted HBV infection in an endemic area: The necessity of more sensitive screening for HBV carriers. Transfusion. 2002;42:1592-1597.

176. Kleinman SH, Kuhns MC, Todd DS, et al. Frequency of HBV DNA detection in US blood donors testing positive for the presence of anti-HBc: Implications for transfusion transmission and donor screening. Transfusion. 2003;43:696-704.

177. Rosina F, Saracco G, Rizzetto M. Risk of post-transfusion infection with the hepatitis delta virus: A multicenter study. N Engl J Med. 1985;312:1488-1491.

178. Alter HJ, Purcell RH, Holland PV, et al. Donor transaminase and recipient hepatitis: Impact on blood transfusion services. JAMA. 1981;246:630-634.

179. Goldman M, Juodvalkis S, Gill P, Spurli G. Hepatitis C lookback. Transfus Med Rev. 1998;12:84-93.

180. Murphy EL, Bryzman S, Williams AE, et al. Demographic determinants of hepatitis C virus seroprevalence among blood donors. JAMA. 1996;275:995-1000.

181. Conry-Cantilena C, VanRaden M, Gibble J, et al. Routes of infection, viremia, and liver disease in blood donors found to have hepatitis C virus infection. N Engl J Med. 1996;334:1691-1696.

182. Bresee JS, Mast EE, Coleman PJ, et al. Hepatitis C virus infection associated with administration of intravenous immune globulin: A cohort study. JAMA. 1996;276:1563-1567.

183. Centers for Disease Control and Prevention. Investigation of blood transfusion recipients with West Nile virus infections. MMWR Morb Mortal Wkly Rep. 2002;51:823.

184. Centers for Disease Control and Prevention. Update: Detection of West Nile virus in blood donations—United States. Lancet. 2003;354:1084-1089.

185. Centers for Disease Control and Prevention. Update: Investigations of West Nile virus infections in recipients of organ transplantation and blood transfusion. MMWR Morb Mortal Wkly Rep. 2002;51:833-836.

186. Barozzi P, Luppi M, Facchetti F, et al. Post-transplant Kaposi sarcoma originates from the seeding of donor-derived progenitors. Nat Med. 2003;9:554-561.

187. Bowden RA. Transfusion-transmitted cytomegalovirus infection. Hematol Oncol Clin North Am. 1995;9:155-166.

188. Bowden RA, Slichter S, Sayers M, et al. A comparison of filtered leukocyte-reduced and cytomegalovirus (CMV) seronegative blood products for the prevention of transfusion-associated CMV infection after marrow transplant. Blood. 1995;86:3598-3603.

189. Santagostino E, Mannucci PM, Gringeri A, et al. Transmission of parvovirus B19 by coagulation factor concentrates exposed to 100 degrees C heat after lyophilization. Transfusion. 1997;37:517-522.

190. Abe H, Sugawara H, Hirayama J, et al. Removal of parvovirus B19 from hemoglobin solution by nanofiltration. Artif Cells Blood Substit Immobil Biotechnol. 2000;28:375-383.

191. Alter HJ, Nakatsuji Y, Melpolder J, et al. The incidence of transfusion-associated hepatitis G virus infection and its relation to liver disease. N Engl J Med. 1997;336:747-754.

192. Prati D, Zanella A, Bosoni P, et al. The incidence and natural course of transfusion-associated GB virus C/hepatitis G virus infection in a cohort of thalassemic patients. The Cooleycare Cooperative Group. Blood. 1998;91:774-777.

193. Shibata M, Wang RY, Yoshiba M, et al. The presence of a newly identified infectious agent (SEN virus) in patients with liver diseases and in blood donors in Japan. J Infect Dis. 2001;184:400-404.

194. Yzebe D, Xueref S, Baratin D, et al. TT virus: A review of the literature. Panminerva Med. 2002;44:167-177.

195. Wagner SJ, Friedman LI, Dodd RY. Transfusion-associated bacterial sepsis. Clin Microbiol Rev. 1994;7:290-302.

196. Klein HG, Dodd RY, Ness PM, et al. Current status of microbial contamination of blood components: Summary of a conference. Transfusion. 1997;37:95-101.

197. Reading FC, Brecher ME. Transfusion-related bacterial sepsis. Curr Opin Hematol. 2001;8:380-386.

198. Blajchman MA, Goldman M. Bacterial contamination of platelet concentrates. Semin Hematol. 2001;38 (Suppl 11):20-26.

199. Heltberg O, Skov F, Gerner-Smidt P, et al. Nosocomial epidemic of *Serratia marcescens* septicemia ascribed to contaminated blood transfusion bags. Transfusion. 1993;33:221-227.

200. Houbiers JG, van de Velde CJ, van de Watering LM, et al. Transfusion of red cells is associated with increased incidence of bacterial infection after colorectal surgery: A prospective study. Transfusion. 1997;37:126-134.

201. Richards C, Kolins J, Trindade CD. Autologous transfusion–transmitted *Yersinia enterocolitica* (Letter). JAMA. 1992;268:1541-1542.

202. Buchholz DH, Young VM, Friedman NR, et al. Bacterial proliferation in platelet products stored at room temperature: Transfusion-induced *Enterobacter* sepsis. N Engl J Med. 1971;285:429-433.

203. Morrow JF, Braine HG, Kickler TS, et al. Septic reactions to platelet transfusions: A persistent problem. JAMA. 1991;266:555-558.

204. Leiby DA, Kerr KL, Campos JM, Dodd RY. A retrospective analysis of microbial contaminants in outdated random-donor platelets from multiple sites. Transfusion. 1997;37:259-263.

205. Leiby DA, Herron RM Jr, Read EJ, et al. *Trypanosoma cruzi* in Los Angeles and Miami blood donors: Impact of evolving donor demographics on seroprevalence and implications for transfusion transmission. Transfusion. 2002;42:549-555.

206. Herwaldt BL, Neitzel DF, Gorlin JB, et al. Transmission of *Babesia microti* in Minnesota through four blood donations from the same donor over a 6-month period. Transfusion. 2002;42:1154-1158.

207. McQuiston JH, Childs JE, Chamberland ME, Tabor E. Transmission of tick-borne agents of disease by blood transfusion: A review of known and potential risks in the United States. Transfusion. 2000;40:274-284.

208. Wells GM, Woodward TE, Fiset P, Hornick RB. Rocky Mountain spotted fever caused by blood transfusion. JAMA. 1978;239:2763-2765.

209. Gardella C, Marfin AA, Kahn RH, et al. Persons with early syphilis identified through blood or plasma donation screening in the United States. J Infect Dis. 2002;185:545-549.

210. Mungai M, Tegtmeier G, Chamberland M, Parise M. Transfusion-transmitted malaria in the United States from 1963 through 1999. N Engl J Med. 2001;344:1973-1978.

211. Brown P. Transfusion medicine and spongiform encephalopathy. Transfusion. 2001;41:433-436.

212. Bons N, Lehmann S, Mestre-Frances N, et al. Brain and buffy coat transmission of bovine spongiform encephalopathy to the primate *Microcebus murinus*. Transfusion. 2002;42:513-516.

213. Dodd RY, Busch MP. Animal models of bovine spongiform encephalopathy and vCJD infectivity in blood: Two swallows do not a summer make. Transfusion. 2002;42:509-512.

CHAPTER **304**

Human Immunodeficiency Virus in Health Care Settings

DAVID K. HENDERSON

JULIE L. GERBERDING

The risk for transmission of blood-borne pathogens in the health care setting has become a matter of substantial concern to health care providers over the past two decades. Despite the fact that hospital-associated transmission of hepatitis had been identified as a problem since the late 1940s,[1] the epidemic of human immunodeficiency virus (HIV) infection in the United States in the early 1980s focused the attention of health care providers and regulators on this important issue. In the past 25 years we have learned that HIV can be transmitted from patient to health care worker, from health care worker to patient, and from one patient to another in health care settings.[2] The last 25 years' experience has taught us that occupational HIV infection occurs uncommonly, that iatrogenic infection is even more rare, and that carefully designed interventions to prevent exposures (and to manage exposures when they occur) can reduce the risk of transmission in either direction. This chapter describes the epidemiology of HIV infections acquired in health care settings, methods to prevent these infections, and the principles of management for health care–associated exposures.

OCCUPATIONAL HIV TRANSMISSION FROM INFECTED PATIENTS TO HEALTH CARE PERSONNEL

Reported Cases of Occupational HIV Infection

As of December 2001, 57 instances of occupational HIV transmission to health care workers in the United States have been reported to the Centers for Disease Control and Prevention (CDC) (Fig. 304-1).[3] In all but one of these cases, occupational transmission was documented by demonstrating HIV antibody seroconversions that occurred in temporal association with discrete HIV exposures. In the single exception, occupational infection in a scientific laboratory worker was documented by demonstrating the near identity of the HIV genetic sequence of the worker's virus isolate with that of the laboratory strain with which the individual was working.

In addition to the 57 documented cases of occupational infection in the United States, 138 health care providers who have "possible" occupational infections have been reported to the CDC.[3] Baseline HIV serological tests were not performed in these individuals at the time of known or potential exposures to HIV, so the temporal relationship between exposure and seroconversion could not be established with certainty. However, none reported nonoccupational behaviors associated with risk for HIV infection, and all recalled at least one exposure to blood or body fluids before their HIV infections were diagnosed. Examination of the demographics of this population suggests that some, but not all of these individuals likely have confounding community-based risks.[4]

Mechanisms of Occupational HIV Infection

Most of the occupational HIV infections that have been documented in the United States have been associated with parenteral injuries inflicted by hollow-bore needles that had been used in veins or arteries, but other sharp instruments have also been involved in transmission. Six instances of HIV infection have occurred following either exposure of breaks in the skin to HIV-contaminated fluids or exposure of mucous membranes to HIV-contaminated materials. Each of these six instances involved either a large-volume exposure, an extended duration of exposure, or both. One mucous membrane exposure from Europe was associated with a smaller inoculum.[5] The most recently reported case was associated with several exposures, over an extended period of time.[6] To date, contamination of intact skin with blood or other infectious material, close personal contact with infected patients,

or contact with contaminated environmental surfaces or fomites has not been linked to occupational HIV transmission. Aerosolization of blood can occur during dental, pathology, laboratory, and surgical procedures, and conventional surgical masks do not prevent inhalation of aerosols. Nonetheless, to date, no data support aerosol exposure as a route of HIV transmission in any setting.

Exposures to blood from HIV-infected patients account for all but 4 of the 57 documented occupational infections in the United States. One occupational HIV infection resulted from exposure to bloody pleural fluid, two involved exposure to concentrated preparations of HIV in scientific laboratories, and for one, the source material was not reported.

Definition of Occupational HIV Exposure

The instances of documented occupational HIV transmission of HIV have been helpful in developing a definition of what constitutes an exposure that is associated with a risk for HIV transmission. As noted in the preceding, exposure routes implicated in occupational HIV transmission include: (1) percutaneous injury (e.g., needle puncture or cut caused by a needle or other sharp object); (2) mucous membrane contamination; and (3) contamination of "nonintact skin" (e.g., skin that is chapped, abraded or afflicted with dermatitis).[7] Even though HIV-infected blood contamination of intact skin has not been implicated in occupational infection, exposures of intact skin to contaminated blood for extended periods of time (i.e., that last for several minutes or more) or exposures involving extensive areas of skin should be considered potential exposures, in great measure because the skin may have unrecognized areas of loss of integrity that could serve as portals of entry for the virus.

Sources of HIV that may pose a risk of transmission through these routes include blood; visibly bloody fluids; tissues; and other body fluids including semen, vaginal secretions, and cerebrospinal, synovial, pleural, peritoneal, pericardial, and amniotic fluids.[7] In addition, any direct cutaneous or mucosal contact (i.e., without barrier protection) to concentrated HIV in a scientific/research laboratory or production facility should be considered to be an exposure.

Although one nonoccupational episode of HIV transmission has been attributed to contact with blood-contaminated saliva, this incident was not analogous to the contact with saliva that occurs during dental or medical care.[7] In the absence of visible blood in the saliva, exposure to saliva from a person infected with HIV is not thought to pose a risk for HIV transmission. Exposure to tears, sweat, or urine (that is not visibly bloody) or feces (that is not visibly bloody) from infected patients does not constitute exposure to HIV. Whereas human breast milk has been implicated in perinatal transmission of HIV, this route of transmission is not analogous to occupational exposure, and contact with breast milk from a patient infected with HIV does not constitute an occupational exposure.[7]

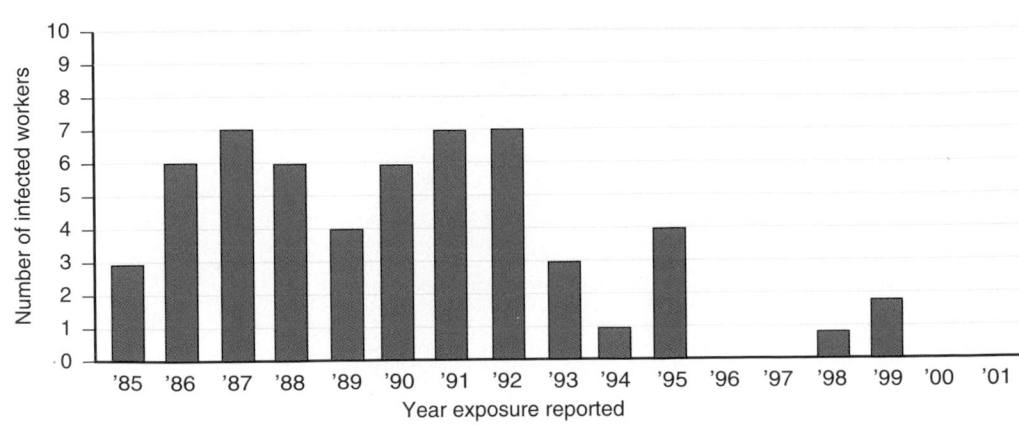

FIGURE 304-1. Occupational HIV infections in US healthcare workers reported to the Centers for Disease Control and Prevention, by year of report, 1985 to 2001. *(Modified from Henderson DK, Gerberding JL. Healthcare worker issues, including occupational and nonoccupational postexposure management. In: Dolin RM, Masur H, Saag MS, eds. AIDS Therapy. 2nd ed. New York: Churchill Livingstone; 2002:327 and Do AN, Ciesielski CA, Metler RP, et al. Occupationally acquired human immunodeficiency virus [HIV] infection: National case surveillance data during 20 years of the HIV epidemic in the United States. Infect Control Hosp Epidemiol. 2003;24:86.)*

Occupational HIV Exposure Transmission Risk

Assessing Infection Risk in Populations of Exposed Health Care Personnel

Worldwide, more than 20 prospective studies have helped quantify the transmission risk associated with discrete occupational HIV exposures (summarized in refs. 2 and 8). In each of these studies, health care workers who sustained occupational HIV exposures were tested for HIV antibody at the baseline (i.e., at the time of exposure) and periodically thereafter, at regular follow-up intervals, to detect new infections.

Pooled data from these studies suggest that the average risk of HIV transmission associated with percutaneous exposures to blood-contaminated sharp objects that have been used on HIV-infected individuals is 0.32% (21 infections associated with 6498 exposures; 95% confidence interval, 0.18% to 0.46%) (summarized in ref. 2). The estimated mucocutaneous transmission risk is 0.03% (1 infection associated with 2885 mucous membrane or nonintact skin HIV exposures), but this estimate may be biased because the single transmission event in the numerator was actually reported before prospective data were collected from the involved institution.[9] The risk of infection, if any, associated with intact skin exposure to HIV is too low to be detected in these studies.[10]

Factors Associated with HIV Infection Risk

The average risk of transmission derived from prospective studies is helpful in evaluating populations of exposed persons but does not necessarily reflect the risk associated with the specific exposure experienced by an individual health care worker. Many factors are either known or suspected to affect the infection risk in specific cases, including the route of transmission (see earlier), the inoculum of infectious virus, and the exposed worker's immunological response to the exposure.

The inoculum of virus is related both to the volume of material involved in the exposure and the titer of virus in that material. Laboratory models of needlestick exposure demonstrate that exposure volume increases with needle size and depth of penetration and that hollow needles usually transmit more blood than do comparably sized suture needles.[11,12] In one model, when the needle passed through one or more layers of latex or vinyl gloves before contacting the skin, the volume of blood transferred to the skin was reduced by more than 50% (for hollow needles) and more than 80% (for suture needles).[12] However, under all experimental conditions, the blood volume transferred to skin varied by a single order of magnitude. Large volumes of blood—with or without prolonged duration of contact and a portal of entry—are common features in the reported cases of infection through mucosal surfaces or skin, but the number of cases is too small to identify and quantify risk factors associated with increasing risk for mucocutaneous infection.

The amount of infectious virus present in the source material may vary by several logs, depending on the patient's stage and severity of HIV infection and the effect of antiretroviral treatments. Viral titer may therefore be a very important predictor of transmission risk.[13-15] In general, the titer of HIV circulating in the blood compartment is highest at the time of seroconversion and during advanced stages of acquired immunodeficiency syndrome (AIDS). Both cell-free and cell-associated virus circulate in the blood of HIV-infected individuals. Tests to quantify cell-free HIV RNA (viral load) in plasma are in widespread use and provide a convenient and reasonably accurate measure of virus replication. However, these tests do not determine what proportion of the plasma virus titer is actually infectious. Quantifying cell-associated virus is much more difficult, although HIV DNA in peripheral blood monocytes can be quantified in a few specialized laboratories. In some studies, higher viral load has been associated with an increased risk for perinatal transmission.[16,17] Conversely, HIV transmission from persons with plasma viral loads below the limits of quantification (based on the assays in use at the time the data were collected) has been reported in instances of mother-to-infant transmission[16,17] and in one occupational infection (JL Gerberding, unpublished data). As a general tenet, the amount of cell-free and cell-associated virus present in the circulation of any given patient is highly correlated, but more data are needed to determine which component is more important in predicting transmission risk.

The Centers for Disease Control and Prevention (CDC) conducted a retrospective case-control study of percutaneous exposure to HIV among health care personnel to attempt to define factors associated with transmission risk.[18] In this study, deep injuries, visibly bloody sharp devices, and devices that had been used in blood vessels were independent predictors of HIV transmission. Each of these factors is likely an indirect measure of the size of the viral inoculum. In this same study, the odds of acquiring infection after percutaneous exposure were six times higher when the source patient had preterminal AIDS (defined as death within 2 months) than when the source had earlier stages of infection (Table 304-1). This difference may also be simply a reflection of higher viral inocula. Patients who have advanced HIV disease often have very high titers of circulating HIV. However, the virus strains found in these patients have both phenotypic (e.g., syncytium induction, macrophage tropism) and genotypic characteristics (e.g., large numbers of HIV quasispecies) that may also contribute to the increased transmission risk associated with advanced HIV disease. The fact that most cases of documented occupational transmission involve exposure to patients with advanced HIV infection is consistent with the hypothesis that the quantitative or qualitative differences present in these patients do increase the risk. However, patients who have advanced disease are also more likely to be hospitalized and are also, therefore, more likely to undergo procedures that pose an exposure risk to health care personnel.

The immunological responses of the exposed health care workers also appear to affect the probability of HIV transmission. At least three outcomes are believed to follow HIV exposure: (1) infection (HIV antibody seroconversion and long-term systemic infection); (2) no infection, no immunologic response; and (3) "aborted infection" (limited cellular infection detected by T-cell response to HIV antigens, no

TABLE 304-1 Logistic-Regression Analysis of Risk Factors for HIV Transmission After Percutaneous Exposure to HIV-Infected Blood

Risk Factor	US Cases*	All Cases†
Deep injury	13 (4.4-42)‡	15 (6.0-41)
Visible blood on injuring device	4.5 (1.4-16)	6.2 (2.2-21)
Injuring device used in artery or vein	3.6 (1.3-11)	4.3 (1.7-12)
Terminal illness in source patient§	8.5 (2.8-28)	5.6 (2.0-16)
Postexposure use of zidovudine	0.14 (0.03-0.47)	0.19 (0.06-0.52)

*All were significant at $p < .02$.

†All were significant at $p < .01$.

‡Adjusted odds ratios (95% confidence interval) for the odds of seroconversion after exposure in workers with the risk factor versus those without it.

§Terminal illness was defined as disease leading to death of the source patient from acquired immunodeficiency syndrome within 2 months after the health care worker's exposure.

Reprinted, by permission, from Cardo DM, Culver DH, Ciesielski CA, et al. A case-control study of HIV seroconversion in health care workers after percutaneous exposure. Centers for Disease Control and Prevention Needlestick Surveillance Group. N Engl J Med. 1997;337:1485-1490. Copyright © 1997 Massachusetts Medical Society. All rights reserved.

long-term systemic infection, no HIV antibody seroconversion). Immunological evidence supporting the concept of "aborted infection" comes from studies of uninfected prostitutes,[19,20] from studies of sexual partners of infected persons,[21-24] from studies of children born to HIV-infected mothers,[25] and from studies of exposed, but uninfected, health care workers.[26-29] T lymphocytes derived from the peripheral blood of some uninfected health care workers who were exposed to HIV through needle injuries can be stimulated to proliferate and secrete cytokines when exposed to HIV antigens in vitro.[27-29] The precise role of the cellular immune response in host defense against HIV infection is not delineated. Nonetheless, the observation is consistent with the hypothesis that the cellular immune system is one important determinant of exposure outcome.

Characteristics Associated with HIV Seroconversion in Health Care Workers

For the 51 instances of occupational infection for which data concerning the characteristics and timing of HIV seroconversion have been reported to CDC, 81% were associated with illnesses compatible with primary HIV infection (i.e., the seroconversion illness) a median of 25 days after exposure.[7,30] The clinical syndrome occurring in health care worker seroconverters was indistinguishable from that observed in persons with primary HIV infection acquired via nonoccupational exposures. The median interval from exposure to documentation of a positive HIV antibody test was 46 days (mean, 65 days). This estimate was limited by the fact that testing is performed at variable intervals after exposure and the precise date of seroconversion is often not known with certainty. Overall, 95% of health care workers who become infected as a result of occupational exposures are expected to seroconvert within 6 months of the exposure.[30] This estimate is identical to that associated with infection associated with other exposure routes.

Three cases of delayed HIV seroconversion among health care workers have been reported,[30-32] (JL Gerberding, unpublished data). Each of these health care workers had a negative HIV antibody test 6 months after an occupational exposure but had a positive test sometime in the ensuing 1 to 7 months. For one of these cases, DNA sequencing confirmed that the infection was occupational. Interestingly, two of these health care workers were also infected with hepatitis C virus as a result of the index needlestick exposure. In both of these instances, hepatitis C infection was unusually severe and, in one case, was associated with a rapidly fatal disease course. The issue of whether coinfection with these two viruses directly influences the timing or severity of either HIV or hepatitis C virus infection is not clear. Nonetheless, most experts agree that until more data are available, health care workers who are exposed to both viruses and in whom serologic evidence of hepatitis C virus infection develops in temporal association with occupational exposure should be carefully monitored for up to a year after exposure to monitor for late HIV seroconversion.

Iatrogenic HIV Transmission from Infected Health Care Personnel to Patients

Case Reports of HIV Transmission from Infected Providers to Patients

Since the onset of the AIDS epidemic almost 25 years ago, only three instances of HIV transmission from an infected health care worker to one or more patients have been reported.[33-39] One of these instances of transmission occurred in the United States in 1990[33-36]; the other two have been reported from France.[37-39] The episode in the United States involved a cluster of six patients whose HIV infections were linked epidemiologically and through DNA sequencing to a dentist who had AIDS. Although the investigation indicated that HIV transmission occurred in the dentist's office and most likely represented transmission from dentist to patient rather than from patient to patient, the precise mechanism(s) of transmission was/were not determined. Although the dentist was a patient in his own practice, no deficiency of infection control that would readily explain HIV transmission to the six patients could be identified. The dentist did not report occupational injuries that could have created an opportunity for cross-contamination, nor was it proved that the infections were intentionally transmitted. The extremely high rate of transmission in this situation remains totally unexplained.

The second episode of iatrogenic HIV transmission involved an orthopedic surgeon in France whose HIV transmission to one patient was confirmed through DNA sequence analysis of viral isolates obtained from the surgeon and the patient.[37,39] The surgeon in this case most likely became infected as a result of an occupational injury sustained during a surgical procedure performed in 1983. The surgeon was not aware of his infection until AIDS was diagnosed in 1994. Investigators initiated a retrospective (i.e., "look-back") investigation of the 3004 patients who had undergone at least one invasive procedure that was performed by the infected surgeon since 1983. Investigators were able to contact 2458 of these 3004 patients and were able to assess the HIV infection status of 983 of these 2458 patients. One patient, who had a negative HIV antibody test before undergoing the first of three procedures performed by the index surgeon, was found to be infected with HIV when she underwent preoperative testing before a third procedure. Although the precise mechanism of transmission is unknown, the duration of the initial procedure (10 hours) and a presumably high viral titer in the surgeon were hypothesized as contributing factors to the transmission event. No breaches in recommended infection-control practices were identified.[37,39] The third instance of iatrogenic transmission also occurred in France. In this instance, transmission was thought to have occurred from an infected nurse to a patient (based on the phylogenetic analysis of the isolates from the patient and the nurse), although no route of transmission could be identified.[38] In a subsequent "look-back" study of the 7580 patients of the infected nurse, investigators were able to notify 5308 of the patients concerning the potential for exposure.[40] No additional HIV infections were detected in the 2293 (of these 5308 patients) who were tested.[40] The nurse who was identified as the probable source of the patient's infection was co-infected with HCV and was found to have both a high HIV viral burden as well as advanced HCV-induced hepatic disease, including clotting abnormalities.

Investigations of Patients Treated by HIV-Infected Health Care Personnel

Several studies have evaluated the HIV transmission risk for patients of clinical practitioners identified as being HIV-infected by "looking-back" at patients who had procedures performed by the infected practitioner (summarized in ref. 2). In March 1992 the CDC developed a database to monitor the results of retrospective investigations of health care workers infected with HIV to assess the risk for this mode of HIV transmission. Excluding the patients (discussed earlier) from the Florida dental practice, as of December 1998, the CDC has obtained information from the investigations of 66 HIV-infected health care workers in the United States.[41,42] The health care workers included 29 dentists and dental students, seven physicians and medical students, 16 surgeons/obstetricians, and one podiatrist. HIV test results were available from patients of 53 of these 66 HIV-infected health care workers. Combining the "look-back" investigations for these 53 health care providers, 22,759 patients of these health care workers were tested. No HIV infections were reported among 13,667 tested from the practices of 40 of these HIV-infected health care providers. For the remaining 13 HIV-infected providers (seven dentists and six surgeons/obstetricians), 9108 patients were tested and 113 HIV-infected patients were identified. Of these 113 infected patients, follow-up investigations have been completed for all but three. To date, no infections have been linked to the infected health care provider. Genetic sequence analysis was done on HIV strains from three of the infected clinicians and 30 of their patients who were infected with HIV, including 3 of the 5 patients who had no identified risk for HIV infection. In no instances were the viral strains of patients and the infected workers genetically related (Table 304-2). These retrospective studies have important limitations, most notably the fact that virtually all of the studies have incomplete follow-up evaluation and testing. Despite these limitations,

TABLE 304-2 Epidemiologic and Laboratory Follow-up of Patients of Health Care Workers Infected with HIV, January 1995

Characteristic	Total	Number with Viral Strains Sequenced	Number with Sequences Related to Those of the Health Care Worker's Virus
Infected before treatment	28	0	–
Established risk factors	62	14	0
Other potential for exposure to HIV	15	13	0
No identified risk	5	3	0
Investigation incomplete	3	0	–
Total	113	30	0

From Robert LM, Chamberland ME, Cleveland JL, et al. Investigations of patients of health-care workers infected with HIV. Ann Intern Med. 1995;22:654.

these data are consistent with previous assessments that the risk of HIV transmission from infected health care personnel to patients is extremely low.

Iatrogenic Transmission Detected in the CDC's HIV/AIDS Surveillance Database

In the United States, persons with AIDS or, in some states, those infected with HIV who are reported to state and local health departments with no identified risk for HIV infection are investigated to determine the likely mode of HIV acquisition.[43] These investigations include a review of medical records, contact with health care providers, and interviews with the patients. Approximately 10% of persons who are identified as having no reported risk for HIV infection are lost to follow-up, have died, or are otherwise unable to be interviewed. For the remainder, investigations are successful in identifying established modes of infection for more than 95% of the cases. With the exception of the Florida dental investigation discussed in detail above, no other cases of HIV transmission from an infected health care provider have been identified through the CDC's nationwide HIV/AIDS surveillance system.

Provider-to-Patient Transmission Risk Assessment

In general, three conditions are necessary to create a risk for provider-to-patient HIV transmission. First, the health care provider must be infected with HIV and have infectious HIV circulating in the bloodstream. Second, the provider must be injured or have a condition (e.g., weeping dermatitis) that provides some other source for direct exposure to infected blood or body fluids for a patient. Third, the injury mechanism or condition must present an opportunity for the provider's blood or body fluids to contact a patient's mucous membranes, wound, or traumatized tissue directly (i.e., "recontact"). We do not currently have a mechanism for reliably estimating the infectivity of individuals infected with HIV, and, at least for now, all infected persons are assumed to be infectious (condition 1). The vast majority of infected health care personnel pose no risk to patients because they neither perform procedures where they risk penetrating injuries nor have dermatologic conditions that present a potential source of exposure of patients to infected body fluids (condition 2). In addition, most health care providers do not perform the kind of invasive procedures, such as surgical or obstetric interventions, in which an injury could expose the patient to infected blood (condition 3).

The risk of blood-borne pathogen transmission to patients during recontacts is not known but is believed to be lower than that associated with most occupational exposures. Most provider injuries potentially associated with blood exposure to the patient that have been reported in observational studies involved the penetration of a surgeon's glove by a solid sharp (e.g., suture needle, bone spicule).[44,45] In most of these observed cases, no wound or bleeding was evident at the site of the provider's injury. Many such injuries were not associated with a detectable perforation in the provider's glove, as measured by the water distention leak test.[44] The "recontact" transmission risk may be even smaller than is currently perceived, since suture needle punctures transfer a smaller volume than do hollow-bore needles, and since this blood inoculum may be reduced even further when the needle passes through glove material.[12]

With nearly 25 years of experience managing HIV infections in the health care setting, we now have a substantial body of epidemiological evidence that demonstrates the risk of nosocomial HIV transmission to patients from an infected provider to be extremely low, even when all three of the conditions described above that are associated with transmission risk are present. Further, the already small risk to patients can be reduced further by adherence to standard infection-control practices, prevention of percutaneous injuries during invasive procedures, and changes in surgical practice (see Primary Prevention).[46,47]

Nosocomial HIV Transmission from Infected Patients to Other Patients

Episodes of nosocomial HIV transmission from one patient to another have most frequently involved breaches in proper infection-control practices and disinfection procedures. Reuse and/or improper sterilization of blood-contaminated injection needles and/or syringes has been linked to HIV transmission to hospitalized children in Russia,[48,49] in Libya,[49,50] in Romania,[49,51-53] in several countries in Africa,[49] and likely in other developing countries, as well. Medical errors in three different institutions (two in the United States and one in The Netherlands) resulted in patients sustaining inadvertent exposures to HIV, as a result of injection of blood from HIV-infected patients during nuclear medicine procedures.[54] Contamination of multidose vials has also been incriminated as a potential vehicle for transmission of HIV and other blood-borne pathogens in several instances in both developed and developing countries.[49,55-57]

Five patients in Australia who underwent minor outpatient surgical procedures requiring local anesthesia performed on the same day by an HIV-negative surgeon were subsequently found to be HIV positive.[58] The first infected patient had known risk factors for HIV and was the probable source of infection for the other four patients. The exact mode of patient-to-patient transmission in this practice has not been elucidated. No cases of patient-to-patient transmission of HIV have been reported from hemodialysis centers in the United States. Conversely, HIV transmission to at least nine patients in a hemodialysis center in Colombia has been reported and was attributed to inadequate disinfection and reuse of contaminated access needles; similar cases have been reported from Argentina and Egypt.[59-62]

PRIMARY PREVENTION

Standard (Universal) Precautions

In 1985 the CDC recommended that the blood of all persons be regarded as infectious, because identification of all patients carrying blood-borne pathogen infections was not possible.[63,64] In 1987 the term "Universal Precautions" was coined to communicate this concept. Universal Precautions were designed to prevent direct contact with blood, bloody body fluids, and certain other fluids (amniotic fluid, semen, vaginal fluid, cerebrospinal fluid, serous transudates/exudates, and inflammatory exudates) that were either known, or likely to be associated with, blood-borne pathogen transmission. Central to the Universal Precautions approach is the appropriate use of barriers, such as gloves for procedures associated with a risk of contact with these fluids, tissues, and materials; the use of masks and protective eyewear when the health care worker anticipated the possibility of splash or splatter; and the use of gowns or other protective garments whenever the practitioner identified a likelihood of soiling of clothing. Body Substance Isolation (or Body Substance Precautions) is a highly similar, alternative system of infection control that is practiced by many institutions.[65] Following the Body Substance Isolation approach, the health care worker's decision about the use of barrier protection is levered from the degree of anticipated contact with all body fluids and tissues, irrespective of the patient's diagnosis. Both Universal Precautions and Body Substance Isolation include measures to prevent needle injuries. In 1996, CDC recommended the adoption of an infection control system, Standard Precautions, that effectively merged the most beneficial aspects of the Universal Precautions and Body Substance Isolation approaches.[66] Whereas Universal Precautions were primarily designed to reduce the risk for patient to provider transmission of blood-borne pathogens, Standard Precautions are designed to reduce the risk for bidirectional transmission of infectious diseases in the health care setting. Standard Precautions apply to *all* patients and require the use of gloves, protective clothing, and other barriers, as needed, to prevent direct contact with all body fluids (except sweat). As is the case for all of these isolation systems, percutaneous injury prevention is a key component of Standard Precautions. These guidelines also include standards for the cleaning and reprocessing of patient care equipment.

In 1987 the Occupational Safety and Health Administration (OSHA) issued a Joint Advisory Notice designed to enforce compliance with Universal Precautions for health care personnel.[67] In 1991, OSHA implemented a federal standard designed to enforce compliance with Universal Precautions.[68] In addition, many states enacted legislation requiring that Universal Precautions be implemented as a condition of funding for the health care institutions. The OSHA standard presented a hierarchy of control measures that institutions should incorporate into their blood-borne pathogen exposure control plan. These measures included engineering controls (use of equipment and devices designed to be inherently safer), work practice controls (safety procedures), and personal protective equipment.

In several studies that evaluated the efficacy of Universal Precautions in preventing blood contact, implementation and enforcement resulted in a significant reduction in exposure frequency.[69-72] Factors associated with efficacy of these programs in reducing exposures include training, enforcement, and feedback about exposure mechanisms to managers and front-line workers. Implementation of Universal Precautions has also been associated with a reduction in the frequency of percutaneous injuries caused by needles and other sharp instruments. Whereas the fact that reducing occupational exposure will necessarily reduce occupational infection seems intuitively clear, because the frequency of occupational HIV infection is so low, the impact of implementing Universal Precautions or any other intervention program on the incidence of occupational HIV infection cannot be measured. What is known, however, is the fact that occupational HIV infections have been decreasing in frequency in the United States over the past several years (see Fig. 304-1).[2,3] Several factors likely have contributed to the observed decrease in occupational infections, among them: possible decreased reporting of occupational infections to CDC, less aggressive case-finding, fewer exposures due to the effective use of Universal/Standard Precautions (i.e., primary prevention), efficacy of highly active antiretroviral therapy in lowering infected patients' viral burdens and in decreasing the numbers and types of procedures required by HIV-infected patients,[73] as well as the presumed efficacy of antiretroviral postexposure prophylaxis (i.e., secondary prevention, discussed later).

Injury Prevention During Routine Patient Care

Needle punctures are the most frequent cause of occupational HIV infection and the highest priority for prevention. All health care workers, including those who actually perform or assist with procedures, those employed as housekeepers and laundry workers, as well as other nonclinicians are at risk for injury and infection. For this reason, prevention efforts must incorporate strategies that prevent injuries while the needle is being used for its intended purpose, as well as strategies that decrease the risk for injuries after use or disposal of the device.

One component of injury prevention that may be overlooked is avoidance of unnecessary needle use. Phlebotomy procedures are a common indication for using needles and are also the most common procedure associated with occupational HIV infection. Avoiding "routine" blood drawing that does not contribute to patient care, better planning to minimize the number of phlebotomies required to obtain the necessary blood tests, and using needleless vascular access ports for blood withdrawal and injection of medication will reduce opportunities for injury. Similarly, avoiding unnecessary placement of intravenous catheters when alternative routes are available for administering therapy will decrease the opportunity for needle injuries.

Implementation of needleless or protected needle infusion systems can reduce the frequency of needle injuries.[74-77] The effect of this intervention on disease transmission is less certain because most needles used for intravenous infusion are not contaminated with blood. Not every institution that has implemented one of these systems has found it to be an effective or cost-effective strategy.[78] Needles used for heparin flushes and those in contact with ports close to the site of intravenous line insertion are more likely to be blood-contaminated and hence are more hazardous. In reality, determining whether an infusion needle is or has been contaminated is often difficult, if not impossible. Preventing injuries associated with intravenous infusions is therefore an important component of risk management, even though such injuries may be substantially less likely to transmit infection.

Safer needle devices that have been engineered to retract, cover, or blunt the needle are now in widespread use. Some of these devices have safety features that are activated while the needle is being used for its intended purpose. Others are activated after withdrawal from the patient. The most effective devices are passive (do not require any action on the part of the user to activate the safety feature), do not require extensive training, and are cost-effective. Most importantly, improving worker safety must not increase the risk of infection or complications among patients. A multicenter study from the CDC has demonstrated that implementing safer needle devices for phlebotomy procedures is an effective strategy for preventing percutaneous injuries.[79-81] Improved product design and lower cost may lead to even more effective programs for protecting workers during procedures that require the use of needles.

All needles and other sharp instruments, with or without safety features, should be discarded in puncture-resistant containers. Such containers should be located as close as possible to the point of use in emergency rooms, in operating rooms, and in other patient care areas. Proper disposal will also prevent injuries caused by needles that have been carelessly discarded. Needle disposal programs can significantly reduce the incidence of injury. Needle injury rates can likely be reduced by assuring that needle disposal containers are available at all points of needle use and by assuring that infection-control staff provide feedback about the exposure risks to concerned staff.

Finally, some investigators have suggested that employees who have certain personality profiles may have increased risks for occupational exposures to blood.[82]

Injury Prevention During Invasive Surgical, Obstetrical, Dental, and Radiological Procedures

Preventing intraoperative and intraprocedural injuries that confer a risk of blood exposure is an important priority for preventing HIV transmission among health care providers and their patients. For operative procedures data from observational studies indicate that the risk of provider injury is highest during procedures lasting longer than 2.5 to 3.0 hours, when intraoperative blood loss exceeds 250 to 300 mL, and during certain categories of major procedures (e.g., intra-abdominal gynecological procedures, vaginal hysterectomies, major vascular procedures, and orthopedic procedures).[45,83-91]

Prevention priorities in the operating room are based on the same principles used in other health care settings.[92-98] The least invasive surgical approach that will achieve the desired patient outcome is preferable. For example, fiber-optic techniques usually pose a lower risk of injury and blood exposure than do more invasive surgical approaches. Similarly, when patient safety permits, alternatives to needles and other sharp implements (e.g., use of adhesive tape, staples, and tissue glue rather than sutures, electrocautery rather than scalpels) should be used.

Suture needles are the most frequent cause of injuries in operating and delivery rooms. Curved suture needles with blunted tips are now available and appear to be an acceptable replacement to standard curved suture needles for suturing many types of tissue.[99-104] Use of these needles is effective in preventing intraoperative injuries. In one multicenter study, 1.9 injuries per 1000 curved suture needles used were observed during gynecological surgery, but no injuries were associated with the use of blunted suture needles.[104] The estimated odds of sustaining an injury with a curved suture needle were reduced by 87% when 50% of the suture needles used during a procedure were blunted. Use of blunted suture needles is also associated with a lower incidence of glove perforation. Surgeons involved in these studies were overall accepting of the blunted needle, and no adverse patient outcomes were noted.

Another approach that has been advocated to reduce risk for percutaneous exposures during the conduct of invasive procedures is the so-called "no-touch" technique. Aspects of this technique include using instruments, rather than hands, for retracting and exploring tissue; avoiding the simultaneous presence of the hands of two or more operators in the procedural field; avoiding hand-to-hand passage of sharp instruments by using a "neutral zone" (e.g., emesis basin, Mayo stand, or magnetic pad); and announcing the transfer of sharp instruments from person to person.

Gloves provide an important barrier between potentially infectious materials and health care providers. Sterile surgical gloves prevent microbial contamination of patient wounds and sterile instruments, and also protect surgical personnel from cutaneous blood contact. Surgical gloves do not provide a barrier to sharp object penetration, but they may reduce the volume of blood transferred to the skin and hence decrease the risk of blood-borne pathogen infection.

Unfortunately, glove perforation is extremely common, especially during major surgical procedures of long duration. Breakdown in glove integrity can cause contamination of exposed tissue and blood contamination of the provider's hands, and if the provider sustains an injury that results in bleeding (needle puncture) or tissue trauma (suture-induced "shear injury"), the patient may be exposed to the provider's blood or interstitial fluids. Double gloving is one strategy that may attenuate these problems. Without exception, in all studies of double gloving, the prevalence of inner glove perforation was significantly lower than that of the outer glove.[83,105-114] In addition, double gloving reduces the frequency of visible blood contamination of providers' hands.

Overall, the thumb, index, and middle fingers of the nondominant hand are the most common glove perforation sites.[45,83,115] Reinforcement of these areas is one approach to prevent perforation.[93,116-119] The use of gloves that increase the thickness of the barrier between a patient and the provider creates concern about manual dexterity and tactile sensitivity.[117,119,120] In a study that measured two-point discrimination and the ability to tie surgical knots, double gloving did not affect performance. Some measures of tactile sensitivity are reduced, but not the ability to discriminate between suture pairs. In a subjective assessment, surgeons reported that double gloving did impair comfort, sensitivity, and dexterity, but acceptance was better if the inner glove was larger than the outer glove.[120]

The benefit of double gloving, glove reinforcement, and new glove materials in preventing disease transmission has not been proved. Nevertheless, double gloving greatly decreases perforation of the inner glove and reduces blood contamination of the operator's hands. Most authorities now recommend routine double gloving during invasive surgical and obstetric procedures.[46,121]

As emphasized earlier, preventing intraoperative injuries to surgical care providers is the most important strategy for preventing the transmission of HIV and other blood-borne pathogens to patients. In two studies of intraoperative provider injuries, 11.4% to 29% of the sharp objects that injured the provider subsequently recontacted the patient.[44,45] These exposures are preventable by immediately replacing the contaminated suture needle or other sharp object before reuse. Recontacts can also occur when the provider is injured by bone

spicules or materials permanently embedded in the patient's body.[44,45] These sources of potential exposure might be prevented by the use of reinforced gloves,[122,123] liners, or other devices or materials to protect the provider's hands.[93,117-119,122,124] Gloves constructed of monofilament polymers or other materials resistant to tears have become available for use when manipulation of bone fragments or suture wires is needed, but as noted earlier, their use is not universal because of the associated decrease in tactile sensation.

The frequency of blood exposure among dental personnel has declined in the past decade. Surveys conducted at annual meetings of the American Dental Association found that the mean number of injuries involving blood or body fluid contact reported by dentists decreased from 12.0 to 2.2 per year between 1986 and 1993.[125] This impressive decline may be the result of the widespread implementation of universal precautions in dental practices, safer instrumentation, and educational programs for dental professionals and patients. Nonetheless, a significant number of exposures continue to occur in the dental health care setting.[126]

Specific practices designed to prevent injuries include use of the one-handed "scoop" technique and mechanical devices for recapping needles used for local anesthetic administration, restricting the use of fingers during suturing and administration of anesthesia, controlling the placement of sharp instruments (such as scalers and laboratory knives), and improvements in the ergonomic design of dental operatories.[127] Safer devices such as self-sheathing anesthetic needles, dental units designed to shield burs in handpieces, and plastic finger guards might also contribute to safer dental care.

Today, most injuries to dental personnel actually occur outside the patient's mouth, involve very small amounts of blood, and are unlikely to pose a risk to patients.[125,127-129] In a 7-month observational study of dentists and oral and maxillofacial surgical residents in two New York City teaching hospitals, injuries were observed during 0.1% of dental procedures, and 86% of these injuries occurred outside the patient's mouth.[128] Only one needle puncture was observed during 16,000 anesthetic injections.

Low exposure rates have been observed during outpatient oral surgical procedures as well. However, oral procedures performed in the operating room are associated with injuries caused by surgical wires during fracture reduction.[112,130,131] The use of small plates instead of wires during the surgical treatment of some mandibular fractures, as well as reinforced gloves, may help prevent some of these injuries.

In great measure stimulated by increasing awareness of blood-borne pathogen risks, interventional radiologists have developed similar approaches to risk aversion in the interventional radiology suite,[132-134] a venue in which particular attention must be paid to the risk for splashes, spattering and mucous membrane exposures.[135]

MANAGEMENT OF OCCUPATIONAL EXPOSURES TO HIV IN THE HEALTH CARE SETTING

Initial Exposure Management

Exposure Reporting

Employers of health care workers and other employees at risk for occupational HIV exposure and infection are required to provide a system for reporting exposure and prompt access to medical care.[67,68] Many institutions have developed "needlestick hotlines" or other rapid-response systems to triage exposed persons and to initiate immediate treatment.[136] However, even in facilities with excellent reporting mechanisms and on-site clinical expertise, many exposures are not reported. In fact underreporting remains a problem in myriad clinical settings and in health care institutions around the globe.[137-144] All persons at risk must be informed of the importance of immediate exposure reporting to ensure that preventive care can be initiated in time to be effective.

Exposure Site Management

Wounds and skin sites that have been in contact with blood or body fluids should be washed with soap and water.[7,145] Exposed mucous membranes should be flushed with tap water. Eyes should be flushed with sterile water or a commercial eye irrigant when available or else with clean tap water. Antiseptics can be used to flush the wound, but they are not known to reduce the incidence of infection, and decontamination should not be delayed until they are obtained.

Counseling and Triage

The emotional impact of a known or suspected HIV exposure is usually significant, especially in the first hours to days after the episode.[146,147] Access to supportive counseling by experienced clinicians who are familiar with the special medical and psychological needs of exposed persons is helpful during this time. The clinician must function as an effective translator. Objective information about exposure risk and the pros and cons of chemoprophylaxis must be communicated to an individual who is usually preoccupied with very subjective emotions.[136,148] Although trying to talk an exposed worker out of "irrational" fear when objective data indicate that the risk is low may seem intuitively tempting, such reassurance is rarely successful. To the worker, the exposure risk may feel like 100%, and no amount of epidemiological data is likely to change this impression in the short run. The most important initial messages to communicate are probably empathy (e.g., "I can see how frightening this is for you"), validation (e.g., "most people in your situation feel the way you do now"), and reassurance (e.g., "this is difficult, but I'll help you get through it"). Because the exposed individual is very likely to be preoccupied, the counselor should be patient and prepared to answer the same questions repeatedly.

Health care workers who are too upset or confused to make a decision about chemoprophylaxis can sometimes be helped by suggesting that treatment be started immediately, with the option to stop it later (i.e., "start treatment now and then tomorrow we can decide if continuing is your best option"). Buying some time in this manner alleviates the additional pressure to make an immediate decision about initiating the full 4-week course of treatment and empowers workers to be able to change their minds about treatment when they are able to evaluate the risks and benefits more objectively and also (based on animal data) provides the best opportunity for therapeutic efficacy.[136,148,149]

Several points must be emphasized for any health care worker who is facing a decision about postexposure chemoprophylactic treatment, among them: (1) the vast majority of persons exposed to HIV will not be infected even if no treatment is taken; (2) treatment can be stopped at any time; (3) data about the efficacy and safety of chemoprophylactic regimens are incomplete; (4) to date, zidovudine is the only drug proven to prevent HIV transmission; and (5) no data prove that combination treatment is more effective than single-drug therapy for HIV prevention.

Health care workers who sustain exposure to HIV should be counseled to avoid transmission to others during the follow-up period, especially during the first 6 to 12 weeks after exposure, when seroconversion is most likely to occur.[7] Recommended practices to avoid transmission include sexual abstinence or the use of condoms to prevent sexual transmission as well as the avoidance of blood and organ donation. If the exposed person is breast-feeding, discontinuation of breast-feeding should be considered, especially for high-risk exposures. Modifying an exposed health care worker's patient care responsibilities to prevent transmission to patients is not necessary.

Counseling should also provide reassurance, review information about the degree of risk present, and inform the worker about procedures to protect the confidentiality of the exposure medical records. As noted earlier, the single most important message to communicate to most workers is that occupational HIV transmission is very unlikely; 99.7% of exposures do not result in HIV infection, even if chemoprophylaxis is not administered. Continued reassurance from a supportive clinician, coupled with practical advice about measures to prevent future exposure, will allow the worker to successfully cope with the exposure and its aftermath. Counselors should also be alert to the concerns of sexual partners, co-workers, family, and friends of

the exposed worker. Referral for ongoing supportive therapy during the follow-up interval is helpful for the minority of exposed persons who experience difficulty in adjusting to the stress inherent in waiting the 6 months for testing to be complete. Finally, adherence to the chemoprophylaxis regimen may be enhanced if skilled counselors provide advice to the drug recipients. In the San Francisco Post Exposure Prevention Project, the frequency of side effects was similar to those in the health care worker studies; however, nearly 80% of participants completed the 4 weeks of therapy. The authors ascribed this success, in great measure, to the intensive, skilled counseling that enrollees received.[150,151]

Exposure History

When an exposure is reported, the first priority is to evaluate the risk of infection and the need for immediate wound care and prophylactic treatment. After these issues have been addressed and the exposed worker is calm enough to engage in a more detailed discussion, the interviewer can elicit additional details about the exposure. A thorough exposure history can help troubleshoot problems that led to the exposure and, in aggregate form, monitor trends relevant to ongoing exposure prevention efforts. We recommend that institutions systematically collect information about all such exposures to look for common circumstances or flawed processes that may be modified to reduce these risks further.

If exposure to HIV (or hepatitis B or C virus infection [see Chapter 303]) has occurred, the risk of transmission for any or each of the pathogens to which the individual is exposed should be assessed. If the source patient is known to be infected with HIV, the stage of illness, recent viral load test results (if available), and recent antiretroviral treatment history should be elicited.[7,136,148] If the source patient's HIV status is not known, information relevant to the probability of infection (e.g., presence or absence of source patient risk behaviors) as well as clinical and epidemiological clues that suggest undiagnosed HIV infection should be recorded and should be considered when making recommendations for follow-up management.

For needle punctures or similar percutaneous injuries, information about the source material and exposure characteristics known to be associated with an increased risk of HIV transmission (deep injury, visibly bloody device, device used in an artery or vein) should be carefully collected and recorded.[7,18] In addition, the practitioner should also inquire about factors likely to increase the risk of transmission (e.g., injection of a volume of blood, hollow-bore needle exposure, large-gauge needle, visible blood on the device, device used in a vascular channel, device used on a source patient who is known to have high viral burden or progressive disease).

For mucosal exposure, the body fluid or material involved and the exposed site, volume of material, and duration of contact before decontamination should be recorded. In addition to these data, for reported skin contacts, the condition of the skin at the site of contact should be evaluated to detect lesions that could provide a portal of entry and influence the risk of infection. For intact skin exposures, in the absence of an obvious portal of entry, infection is so unlikely that further evaluation and treatment are not necessary unless the contact is prolonged or involves a large area of intact skin. Even then, the risk of HIV infection is extremely small.[10]

Human bites rarely transmit HIV (see later).[152-155] The person who inflicted the bite may sustain a mucosal blood exposure to HIV, but only if the skin was penetrated, the bite wound bled, or both. The person who is bitten is usually not at risk for HIV infection unless blood or visibly bloody saliva was in direct contact with the bite wound. Penetrating bite wounds do pose a risk for bacterial wound infection, and appropriate wound care and antibacterial prophylaxis should be provided, when indicated (see Chapter 318).

When the exposure risk has been assessed and urgent treatment has been provided and when the health care worker is able and willing to cooperate, the individual providing care should obtain a more detailed history about the exposure. Information should be recorded about when, where, and how the exposure occurred, the type of device involved, the presence or absence of safety features (and if present, their state of activation), and when in the course of handling the device the exposure occurred (during use, after use, during disposal, etc.). As noted above, we believe that each institution should pool these data and should periodically evaluate them systematically to identify opportunities to improve processes to reduce health care workers' risks and to increase patient and worker safety.

Evaluating the Exposure Source

An individual who is the source of an occupational exposure, when known, should be evaluated for HIV and hepatitis B and C virus infections (see Chapter 304).[7] The medical record is a useful source of information, but often interviewing the source patient provides the most accurate data about infection risks. If the HIV infection status of the source is unknown, consent to test for HIV antibodies (and other blood-borne pathogens) should be requested. If consent is not obtained, further evaluation of HIV status should comply with applicable state laws and local policies.[2] The privacy of the source patient should be protected, irrespective of either the decision to test or the test result.

HIV testing of the exposure source should be performed as soon as possible. In many facilities, conventional HIV tests (e.g., enzyme immunoassay) can be completed very quickly. A Food and Drug Administration–approved rapid HIV antibody test is an acceptable alternative, especially if conventional tests cannot be completed within 24 to 48 hours. This rapid testing technology has been improved significantly during the past 5 years (see Chapter 115). In general, repeatedly reactive HIV test results obtained with enzyme immunoassay or a rapid test are highly suggestive of infection, but false-positives do occur.[136] Reactive tests should be confirmed by Western blot or immunofluorescent antibody before disclosure to the exposure source. A negative conventional enzyme immunoassay is sufficient to exclude a diagnosis of HIV, unless the source patient has clinical evidence of primary HIV infection or HIV-related disease. A negative rapid test is also very reliable in excluding infection, but false negatives have been reported, especially from laboratories that have little experience with older test kits. Institutions using the newest technology have found false-negatives to be far less frequent occurrences.

If the source cannot be tested, the "pretest" probability of blood-borne pathogen infection should be assessed by using available clinical, epidemiological and laboratory information and, most importantly, common sense.[7,136,148] A similar approach applies to situations when the exposure source is not known. HIV testing of needles, syringes, or other sharp instruments associated with exposures is dangerous and is not recommended.

Evaluating the Exposed Health Care Worker

Health care personnel who report occupational exposure should be evaluated for susceptibility to infection by blood-borne pathogens.[2] Baseline testing (i.e., testing to establish infection status at the time of exposure) for HIV antibody should be performed. If the exposure source is seronegative for HIV, baseline testing or further follow-up of the worker is not normally necessary unless the source has clinical evidence of primary HIV infection. Without a negative baseline HIV test, proving that infection was temporally related to the exposure event is extremely difficult. In some instances, demonstrating close genetic similarity in virus sequences obtained from the source patient and the infected health care provider has confirmed the source of exposure, but these studies are expensive, difficult to obtain, and sometimes difficult to interpret. The evaluation should also include information about the use of medications and underlying medical conditions or circumstances (e.g., pregnancy, breast-feeding) that could influence the choice of antiretroviral drugs used for prophylaxis. Pregnancy testing should be offered to all nonpregnant women of childbearing age.

THE ROLE OF HIV TESTING IN PREVENTING OCCUPATIONAL/NOSOCOMIAL HIV INFECTION

HIV testing of patients is not recommended as an infection-control procedure, because current standards of practice are designed to prevent the transmission of blood-borne pathogens from all patients, whether HIV infection is known or not. No data have demonstrated that preprocedural identification of infected patients reduces the chance of exposure; in one study, the exposure risk was not affected by knowledge of the patient's HIV infection status.[83] Researchers at Johns Hopkins University, an institution in which undiagnosed HIV infection is highly prevalent among emergency department patients, evaluated preoperative testing of elective surgical patients.[156] More than 4000 consecutive patients were tested for HIV, and 18 were found to be infected. Ten of these patients knew their HIV status before the preoperative test was performed, and all 13 provided histories of risk factors for infection. The authors concluded that the prevalence of HIV infection was too low to justify routine preoperative testing in this institution, and the practice was abandoned.[156] The improvement in the reliability and accuracy of rapid HIV tests may allow reliable preoperative screening of patients requiring emergency surgery. However, this practice cannot be recommended unless it is demonstrated to result in reduced exposure risk without adverse patient outcomes.

Although HIV testing is not a useful strategy for preventing occupational and nosocomial HIV transmission, it is important for clinicians to address HIV risk in the context of clinical care of their patients. Some patients at risk for HIV infection lack access to HIV testing in the community, and because they have no access to testing, their HIV infections may remain undiagnosed until they have advanced complications. HIV risk assessment should be conducted as a routine component of patient care, even in the emergency department and acute care settings. Patients who relate histories of risk behaviors for HIV infection should be encouraged to consent to HIV counseling and testing. If the responsible clinician is not prepared to offer prevention counseling at the time that testing is requested, an appropriate counseling referral should be arranged.

Routine HIV testing of health care personnel is not recommended. Health care personnel who sustain blood exposures, including those who perform invasive procedures, are advised to seek postexposure testing for HIV and other blood-borne pathogens when indicated by the exposure circumstances, as outlined earlier.

Management of Infected Health Care Providers

In 1991, the CDC recommended that invasive surgical and dental procedures that had been implicated in hepatitis B virus transmission from infected health care workers to patients be considered "exposure prone."[157] The characteristics of these procedures included digital palpation of a needle tip in a body cavity or the simultaneous presence of a clinician's fingers and a needle or other sharp object in a poorly visualized or highly confined anatomic site. The CDC also recommended that invasive procedures associated with an increased risk for provider injury in observational studies be considered exposure prone. These (and other) exposure-prone procedures were to be identified by medical, surgical, and dental organizations with input from the institutions where these procedures are performed. Ultimately, efforts to create a consensus regarding a list of exposure-prone procedures were not successful. Infected health care personnel who performed exposure-prone procedures were to be reviewed by an advisory panel to determine under what circumstances, if any, they would be allowed to practice. In addition, allowed procedures could be performed only after informed consent was obtained from the patient.

All states were required by Congress to implement these (or equivalent) recommendations. Over time, considerable variability in interpretation and implementation of these guidelines has emerged. As a result, decisions about managing infected health care workers are often inconsistent and are more likely to be influenced by court decisions rather than science. Until new guidelines are developed, most experts agree that practice restrictions are appropriate when an infected health care worker is found to be impaired and cannot safely practice, when a pattern of substandard infection-control practice is demonstrated, or when HIV transmission to a patient has occurred or is suspected.[46] If transmission is suspected, the state or local health department should be contacted for consultation about the need for a more extensive investigation.

SECONDARY HIV PREVENTION: POSTEXPOSURE PROPHYLAXIS IN HEALTH CARE SETTINGS

In January 1990, the CDC issued the first set of guidelines that included considerations regarding the use of antiretrovirals for postexposure prophylaxis following occupational HIV infections.[158] By June 1996, a U.S. Public Health Service interagency working group, with input from other experts, published recommendations for providing antiretroviral treatment after occupational HIV exposure to prevent infection.[132] These recommendations and a more recent update[7] were based on data from several sources that strongly suggested that antiretroviral treatment soon after occupational HIV exposure could prevent infection in some instances. In effect, these recommendations established a standard of care for managing occupational HIV exposure among health care personnel that includes access to postexposure antiretroviral chemoprophylaxis. Specific recommendations for managing provider-to-patient HIV exposures were not included in these guidelines. In this section, we discuss treatment recommendations and exposure management advice relevant to occupational exposure in health care workers. Whereas these recommendations will focus on the management of occupational exposures for health care providers, the same principles and approach also applies to nosocomial or iatrogenic exposures to HIV for patients.

Rationale for Antiretroviral Chemoprophylaxis for Occupational Exposures to HIV

The rationale for postexposure chemoprophylaxis is based on: (1) our current understanding of the early events in the pathogenesis of HIV infection; (2) the biologic plausibility of pharmacologic intervention in this process of HIV pathogenesis; (3) studies of the safety and efficacy of antiretroviral prophylaxis in animal models of retroviral infection; (4) clinical trials demonstrating the efficacy of HIV chemoprophylaxis in other settings; (5) epidemiological data from studies of exposed health care personnel; and (6) nearly 15 years of clinical experience using these drugs in this setting.[148,159,160] Together, these types of data provide support for the prophylactic administration of antiretroviral drugs after HIV exposures associated with a transmission risk in health care settings. Each of these classes of information will be considered in more detail in the following paragraphs.

Biologic Plausibility of Antiretroviral Chemoprophylaxis

The hypothesis underlying the administration of antiretroviral chemoprophylaxis is that postexposure treatment provided during a "window of opportunity" will attenuate initial HIV replication and prevent systemic HIV infection. Dendritic cells in the mucosa and skin are believed to be the initial target for HIV infection or capture.[161,162] Dendritic cells also play a role in initiating HIV infection of CD4+ T cells in regional lymph nodes.[163] In a primate model of simian immunodeficiency virus (SIV) infection, SIV remained localized in association with dendritic cells underlying the site of vaginal inoculation for the first 24 hours after exposure to cell-free virus.[164] Within 24 to 48 hours, these cells appeared to migrate to regional lymph nodes and present SIV to T lymphocytes. Cell-free and cell-associated SIV was detected in the peripheral blood within 5 days after inoculation.

Additional in vitro studies have further characterized the earliest events in HIV exposure and infection of dendritic cells. "Immature" dendritic cells in the skin and mucous membranes function to capture and process foreign antigens.[165] These cells also express important HIV co-receptors (e.g., CD4 and CCR5). Conversely, these immature dendritic cells lack surface molecules that are required for

efficient activation of T cells (i.e., CD40, CD54, CD86). As dendritic cells "mature" they begin expressing these latter receptors. Immature dendritic cells can support replication of HIV in vitro; however, mature cells do not permit replication, unless T cells are present in the milieu. Granelli-Piperno and colleagues have suggested that mature dendritic cells in the presence of (and perhaps even in direct contact with) T cells undergo a single round of HIV replication that permits infection of T cells, which then rapidly replicate HIV. In this in vitro system, zidovudine treatment cannot prevent either HIV replication in dendritic cells or HIV transfer from dendritic cells to T cells; however, zidovudine does prevent productive T-cell infection in this system.[165] Blauvelt and colleagues have demonstrated that viral capture by, and productive infection of, dendritic cells are mediated through separate pathways and have also proposed that strategies designed to block transmission of HIV should consider interfering with both these processes (i.e., both viral capture and infection).[166] These investigators have also demonstrated that productive HIV infection of Langerhans cells is regulated by surface expression of CD4 and CCR5, and that viral capture is mediated through a newly described C-type lectin, DC-SIGN. Dendritic cells that have captured virus via DC-SIGN (but not HIV-infected dendritic cells) facilitate infection of T cells in chronically infected individuals. They hypothesize that blocking DC-SIGN–mediated HIV capture may represent a new approach to antiviral therapy.[167] These and other experiments support the concept that productive HIV infection occurs in a sequence of events involving initial capture and/or infection of dendritic target cells near the exposure site with subsequent transmission of HIV to susceptible T cells in regional lymph nodes. Each step in this sequence is a potential target for chemoprophylactic intervention. Early antiretroviral treatment appears most likely to prevent infection by blocking the infection of T cells, presumably in the regional lymph nodes. Unfortunately, the available data do not allow prediction of either the maximum time interval following exposure in which prophylaxis might work—or the factors that might affect the timing of these events in individual cases. Interrupting or delaying the productive infection of T cells could also allow time for the development of specific cellular immunity directed against HIV in the exposed health care worker.

Animal studies provide evidence for an important role for the cellular immune system in postexposure prophylaxis against HIV infection. Ruprecht and colleagues demonstrated in a mouse retroviral model that successful postexposure prophylaxis requires intact cellular immunity.[168] Putkonen and co-workers demonstrated robust specific cellular responses in macaques that had SIV infection successfully prevented by postexposure prophylaxis.[169] In this latter study the macaques developed a strong enough immune response that a second challenge with the same viral inoculum resulted in either no, or significantly limited, infection.[169] In a second similar study, challenge with different SIV isolate following successful antiretroviral chemoprophylaxis also produced either no, or significantly limited, infection.[170]

Taken together all of these data suggest that antiretroviral chemoprophylaxis administered soon after an occupational exposure, in concert with a cellular immune response, may prevent or inhibit systemic HIV infection. This preventive effect theoretically occurs by limiting the proliferation of virus in dendritic cells in the skin or in T cells in regional lymph nodes during a period of time in which the virus remains relatively localized, and this effect may be bolstered by a robust cellular immune response.

Some investigators have suggested that administration of antiretroviral chemoprophylaxis may prevent or diminish cellular responses to HIV antigens. D'Amico and colleagues demonstrated that only one of seven health care workers treated with zidovudine developed HIV envelope-specific cytotoxic T-lymphocyte responses compared with 6 of 13 workers who did not receive prophylaxis.[171] Conversely, some investigators have suggested that certain antiretrovirals may also have beneficial immunomodulatory effects. For example, Zidek and colleagues found that the nucleotide analogue phenoxymethylpropyladenine (PMPA) stimulates macrophage secretion of interleukin-1β, interleukin-10, and tumor necrosis factor-α, in addition to promoting the production of the chemokines RANTES and macrophage inflammatory protein 1α in both macrophages and lymphocytes.[172]

Efficacy of Antiretroviral Chemoprophylaxis in Animal Retroviral Infections

Antiretroviral chemoprophylaxis is effective in many murine and feline models of retrovirus infection, but these models may or may not be relevant to human HIV infection.[173] The earliest studies of chemoprophylactic safety and efficacy in mice and cats demonstrated limited, if any, benefit.[174,175] Similarly, most early studies designed to evaluate the efficacy of antiretroviral chemoprophylaxis of SIV infection in nonhuman primates demonstrated limited protection.[173,176] Virtually all of these early experiments entailed intravenous injection of very high inocula of HIV-2 or SIV (to ensure infection in 100% of control animals). This exposure route that would bypass the cellular events that occur at an occupational or mucosal exposure site (described in detail earlier) and these inoculum sizes were far in excess of what might reasonably be anticipated in an occupational exposure.

Benefits associated with postexposure prophylaxis in more recent experiments in animal models include (1) delay or complete suppression of viremia; (2) inhibition of viral replication and development of a long-lasting, protective cellular immune response; and (3) complete protection (i.e., true chemoprophylactic efficacy).[170,177-182]

In general, postexposure prophylaxis is most likely to be effective in animal models in which the exposure inoculum is relatively low, when treatment is started soon after exposure (usually within 24 hours), and when treatment is continued for at least several days to weeks after inoculation.[173,177] In one macaque/SIV study all of the animals that received postexposure treatment for 28 days remained uninfected; only half of the animals that were treated for 10 days, and none of the animals that received only 3 days of treatment were protected.[177] Similarly, delay in initiating prophylaxis was detrimental in this model. All of the animals that were treated within 24 hours of intravenous SIV infection remained uninfected; whereas only 50% of the animals that received treatment beginning 48 hours following infection, and only 25% of the animals that received treatment beginning 72 hours after exposure were protected.[177] Otten and colleagues demonstrated similar findings in a macaque study assessing postexposure prophylaxis following vaginal inoculation with HIV-2. All animals treated within 48 hours were protected, whereas only some of the animals that received the antiretroviral agent 72 hours following inoculation remained uninfected.[183] Assuming that these animal models are relevant to occupational HIV transmission prevention, the current recommendations for postexposure management should maximize the potential for postexposure treatment to be an effective prevention strategy.

Clinical Trials Relevant to Postexposure Chemoprophylaxis

In a randomized, controlled, prospective trial (AIDS Clinical Trial Group protocol 076), zidovudine or placebo was administered to HIV-infected pregnant women during the second and third trimesters of pregnancy and to newborns for 6 weeks after birth (see Chapter 122).[184] The infection rate among infants in the treatment arm of the study was 67% lower than that observed in the control group. In this study less than 20% of the protective effect of zidovudine was attributable to a reduction in maternal HIV viral load, which suggests that additional mechanisms contributed to the observed benefit of therapy.[16,17] In two subsequent studies, treatment of newborns of infected mothers who did not receive any antiretroviral therapy before delivery was also effective in preventing perinatal infection, an observation that strongly supports a direct postexposure prophylactic effect of antiretroviral treatment in this clinical context.[185,186]

Because of the very low risk for infection per exposure (i.e., 0.3%, see earlier), assessing the efficacy of postexposure chemoprophylaxis in a prospective clinical trial of health care workers sustaining occupational exposures to HIV is not feasible. Between 1987 and 1989, the Burroughs-Wellcome Company sponsored a prospective placebo-controlled clinical trial that was designed to evaluate the efficacy of postexposure zidovudine chemoprophylaxis for health care workers who had sustained occupational exposures.[187,188] This trial was terminated prematurely because of inadequate enrollment. In light of the data described above that at least implies a direct benefit of postexposure prophylaxis, justifying the conduct of a placebo-controlled trial of postexposure antiretroviral chemoprophylaxis would now be problematic.

Epidemiological and Clinical Evidence For and Against the Efficacy of Postexposure Chemoprophylaxis

In the CDC's retrospective case-control study of health care workers (see Table 304-1), postexposure treatment with zidovudine was associated with an 81% reduction in the odds of infection (95% confidence interval, 43% to 94%) after adjustment for relevant exposure risk factors.[18,189] This relatively small study was not designed to evaluate treatment, so the effect of the drug regimen (dose, time to initiation, duration) on efficacy could not be determined. The study does not prove that treatment is effective, and limitations inherent in the design, including the small number of cases and the fact that cases and controls were not from the same cohort, must be considered.[190] Nevertheless, this study provides very suggestive epidemiological evidence that zidovudine afforded some protection to exposed health care workers.

Antiretroviral chemoprophylaxis for occupational exposures to HIV has been in use in the United States since the late 1980s.[159] Over the past several years, the numbers of occupational infections with HIV that have been reported to CDC have decreased steadily. Figure 304-1 stratifies the cases of occupational infections reported to CDC from 1992 through 2001 and demonstrates a decrease in the number of cases of occupational HIV infections reported to CDC over time.[3] Several factors are likely contributing to this decrease, including: decreased reporting to CDC as the epidemic matures; less aggressive case-finding by CDC and other local and state public health officials; the use of primary exposure prevention strategies, resulting in fewer exposures; the efficacy of highly active antiretroviral therapy in lowering the viral burden in HIV-infected "source patients" and in reducing the need for and numbers of invasive procedures that place health care workers at risk for exposure,[73] and the use of postexposure antiretroviral chemoprophylaxis for occupational exposures.

Two anecdotal case reports also suggest postexposure treatment efficacy. In the first of these reports, a child who had received a transfusion of HIV-infected blood from a donor in the "window" (i.e., before the donor became HIV-antibody–positive, but at a time when the donor likely had high titers of HIV RNA in his circulation) remained uninfected following aggressive postexposure treatment with antiretrovirals.[191] Transfusion of HIV-infected blood has been associated with nearly 100% risk for subsequent infection in the transfusion recipient.[192] The second of these anecdotal reports describes a health care worker who sustained an occupational HIV exposure and subsequently, while receiving three-drug postexposure prophylaxis, had HIV RNA detected by polymerase chain reaction in two separate samples (at 14 and 18 days following exposure). The worker remained uninfected (as assessed by serial nucleic acid tests and antibody determinations more than 1 year following exposure) but did produce a robust HIV-specific cellular immune response.[26]

Prophylaxis failures have been documented in at least 21 instances.[7] In more than 75% of the instances of failure, zidovudine was used as a single agent. Only five instances of failure have been reported in association with the use of multiple-agent prophylaxis regimens (two reported failures of two-drug regimens, three failures of three-drug regimens, and one failure of a four-drug regimen).[7,193,194] In 13 of the 21 instances of postexposure prophylaxis failure, the source patient for the exposure had previously been treated with one or more antiretroviral agents, raising the possibility that antiretroviral resistance may at least in part explain the chemoprophylaxis failure.[7] However, several additional factors may have contributed to these failures, among them: exposure to high HIV inocula; delayed initiation of prophylaxis; failure to achieve adequate drug concentrations; inadequate treatment duration; and a variety of other variables that may have affected either the health care worker's immune responsiveness or the infectivity of the viral strain to which the worker was exposed. Finally, we would underscore that not all failures are what they appear. Both Lucey[195] and Jochimsen[196] have reported the details of instances of putative occupational infections which, on further detailed investigation, were shown to be unrelated to the occupational exposures.

Antiretroviral Drugs for Chemoprophylaxis

Choosing a Treatment Regimen

Several factors influence the selection of antiretroviral drugs for prophylaxis regimen: (1) the type of exposure and the estimated risk of HIV transmission associated with the exposure; (2) the probability that drug-resistant virus strains are currently circulating in the source patient and are likely to be present in the exposure inoculum; (3) the safety profile of and likelihood of health care worker adherence to the proposed treatment regimens; and (4) the cost of the agents. Several antiretroviral agents from at least five classes of drugs are available for the treatment of HIV disease.[7,197,198] These agents include nucleoside reverse transcriptase inhibitors, nucleotide reverse transcriptase inhibitors, non-nucleoside reverse transcriptase inhibitors, protease inhibitors, and fusion inhibitors. Among all the available agents, the nucleoside reverse transcriptase inhibitor, zidovudine, is the only agent proven to prevent HIV transmission (see data describing prevention of transmission to children born to HIV-infected mothers, discussed earlier).

The "basic regimen" currently recommended by the CDC for treatment after occupational HIV exposures that confer an infection risk includes both zidovudine and lamivudine[7] (Table 304-3). Combinations of antiretroviral drugs are more effective than single agents for treating established HIV infection; however, no data demonstrate that combinations of drugs are more effective for prophylaxis than is zidovudine (or any other agent) used alone. The rationale for including lamivudine as a second drug in the basic regimen is that zidovudine resistance in patients with HIV infection occurs with increasing frequency in many communities.[199-210] In addition, the combination has greater antiretroviral activity than either drug alone (and is active against some zidovudine-resistant HIV strains), but has little or no additional toxicity.[211] These two drugs are available in a single formulation that is more convenient for health care workers taking postexposure prophylaxis. Other marketed reverse transcriptase inhibitors (e.g., didanosine, stavudine, abacavir, etc.) are likely to offer equivalent, or in some instances, perhaps increased efficacy.

TABLE 304-3 Current Centers for Disease Control/US Public Health Service Recommendations for Chemoprophylaxis of Occupational Exposures to HIV

HIV exposures associated with a recognized transmission risk	"Basic Regimen"	Zidovudine (ZDV) plus Lamivudine (3TC)
	Alternative "Basic Regimens"	Stavudine (d4t) plus Lamivudine d4t plus Didanosine (ddI)[†]
HIV exposures for which the nature of the exposure suggests an elevated transmission risk*	"Basic Regimen" plus one of the following agents	Indinavir[†,‡] Nelfinavir[§] Abacavir or Efavirenz[†]

*Elevated risk is associated with "deep" injury, injury with a device that has been used in an HIV-infected patient's artery or vein, injuries associated with "larger" volumes of blood and/or blood containing a high titer of HIV.
†Agent(s) not recommended for use in pregnancy.
‡Should be taken on an empty stomach, with increased fluid consumption (e.g., six 8-oz glasses of water daily).
§Should be taken with meals.
From Centers for Disease Control and Prevention updated Public Health Service Guidelines for the management of occupational exposures to HBU, HCU, and HIV and recommendations for postexposure prophylaxis. MMWR Morb Mortal Wky Rep. 2001;50:1-52.

The CDC recommends an "expanded regimen" that includes a protease inhibitor or a non-nucleoside reverse transcriptase inhibitor in addition to the basic regimen described earlier. The regimen is recommended for exposures for which the risk of HIV infection is increased (i.e., high volume of inoculum or exposure to materials containing a high HIV titer).[7] Indinavir, nelfinavir, and amprenavir are active protease inhibitors, are available in formulations with excellent bioavailability, and do not require dose escalation. Therefore, at the present time, any of these agents is appropriate for inclusion in expanded treatment regimens.[7] Efavirenz is the only non-nucleoside reverse transcriptase inhibitor that, to date, has been specifically recommended for use in the expanded regimen. This agent should not be used when the health care worker is, or might be, pregnant. Efavirenz affects the metabolism and blood levels of protease inhibitors in the body (particularly indinavir, saquinavir, and amprenavir), and, for this reason, guidelines for dosing the available protease inhibitors with efavirenz have been developed (see Chapter 124). The role of non-nucleoside reverse transcriptase inhibitors, and specifically of nevirapine, which has been used by some clinicians in the postexposure setting, is less clear. Nevirapine has been used commonly in some settings and its use for postexposure prophylaxis has been associated with serious and sometimes life-threatening toxicities that appear to be more probable than the infection risk associated with most exposures.[212-215] Nevirapine is not included as a recommended agent in the most recent iteration of the CDC guidelines.[7] The US Public Health Service (USPHS) likely will expand the drugs recommended for use as HIV PEP following occupational exposure by the end of 2003. Formulations of "boosted" protease inhibitors as well as agents receiving FDA approval for treatment of HIV infection since last issuance of guidelines in 2001 likely will be added as acceptable for inclusion in prophylaxis regimens. At the time this chapter is being written, we have no evidence that the principles of exposure management will be modified.

The basic and expanded drug regimens described by the CDC are good choices when the source patient is unlikely to harbor virus isolates that are resistant to the drugs included in the chosen regimen. Resistance to all antiretroviral drugs has been reported, and transmission of resistant strains can occur.[199,201-203,205-210] Drug resistance is most likely among patients with high viral loads who are not responding to treatment or do not adhere to the treatment regimen. Unfortunately, clinical predictions about drug resistance are neither sensitive nor specific. Special genotypic and phenotypic tests to detect HIV resistance are not readily available to provide support for prophylactic treatment decisions. When drug resistance is suspected, empirical prophylactic treatment regimens should be based on the same principles used to select drugs for HIV-infected patients who are failing treatment.[216,217] Many experts recommend the use of at least two drugs that the source patient has not taken in the recent past (i.e., prior 30 days). For example, treatment with didanosine and stavudine (with or without a protease inhibitor) may be appropriate when the source patient is failing treatment with zidovudine plus lamivudine. The combination of didanosine and stavudine should not be used in pregnancy. Similarly, stavudine plus lamivudine is a reasonable choice when the source patient is failing zidovudine therapy or is deemed likely to have a predominance of zidovudine-resistant strains circulating in the blood stream at the time that exposure occurred.[218] If the resistance is likely to involve an entire class of antiretroviral drugs (e.g., protease inhibitors), it is sensible to include a drug from another class.[218] The role of newer agents (e.g., tenofovir, amprenavir, enfuvirtide) remains to be delineated; however, some of these agents appear as extremely promising postexposure prophylaxis candidates in animal studies.[170,172,177-179,181,183,219-222]

Given all the complexities inherent in selecting antiretroviral drugs, consultation with an expert in HIV treatment is recommended when exposure to drug-resistant HIV is a concern. However, treatment should not be delayed to obtain such consultation. One approach is immediately to begin the basic or expanded regimen and then seek help from an expert about modifying the regimen. If local expertise is not available, clinicians in the United States who need consultative assistance concerning prophylaxis for occupational HIV exposure can also contact the "National Clinicians' Post-exposure Hotline (PEP-Line)" (Table 304-4).

Adverse Effects Associated with Postexposure Chemoprophylaxis

Adverse effects have been associated with all agents and regimens used for postexposure prophylaxis (summarized in refs. 223-229). The frequency, severity, duration, and reversibility of side effects are important considerations when formulating a prophylactic treatment regimen. Unusual or serious and unexpected toxicity from antiretroviral drugs should be reported to the manufacturer and the Food and Drug Administration (see Table 304-4). Despite the fact that the use of these drugs in the postexposure setting has become the standard of care, no agent has an approved or "label" indication for postexposure chemoprophylaxis for HIV exposures, so all such use must be considered "off-label."

Most of the information about prophylactic treatment side effects was derived from studies of health care workers who took zidovudine alone, usually at doses of 1000 to 1200 mg/day (i.e., doses higher than the currently recommended dose) (summarized in ref. 224). More than 50% of those treated reported at least one side effect, and about 30% stopped treatment because of their symptoms. Use of nucleoside analogues for postexposure prophylaxis has been associated with bone marrow suppression (e.g., decreases in hemoglobin and absolute neutrophil counts), nausea, vomiting, diarrhea, abdominal pain, headache, neuropathies, myalgias, lassitude, malaise, and insomnia. In a few instances, more severe toxicities have been reported, including cases of severe rash with hepatic dysfunction and seizures. Subjective side effects are especially common in the population of health care workers postexposure chemoprophylaxis. Use of protease inhibitors in chemoprophylaxis regimens has been associated with: nausea, vomiting, diarrhea, abdominal pain, hyperglycemia, hyperlipidemia, hypercholesterolemia, galactorrhea,[225] hyperprolactinemia,[225] cholestatic jaundice,[228] headache, anorexia, altered taste, and/or paresthesias.[224] In addition, the literature also contains a few instances of nephrolithiasis[229] and one case of lipodystrophy[230] associated with protease inhibitor administration for postexposure prophylaxis. Health care workers who took regimens that included two or more antiretroviral drugs experienced frequent side effects (summarized in ref. 224). In almost every instance, side effects were reversible when treatment was stopped.

Although non-nucleoside reverse transcriptase inhibitors are not primary choices for prophylaxis in most published guidelines,[7] these agents, (most frequently nevirapine), are being used in some settings for postexposure chemoprophylaxis.[231] The rash that occurs commonly with the non-nucleoside agents can easily be confused with the HIV seroconversion illness. Occasionally the rash associated with these agents is severe; the literature contains two case reports of possible Stevens-Johnson syndrome in health care workers taking nevirapine as postexposure chemoprophylaxis.[214] Fever and gastrointestinal symptoms have also been reported to occur commonly when

TABLE 304-4 Management of HIV Exposure and Chemoprophylactic Treatment: HIV Postexposure Prophylaxis Resources and Registries

National Clinicians' Postexposure Hotline	Phone: (888) 448-4911
Antiretroviral Pregnancy Registry	Phone: (919) 488-9437 or (800) 722-9292, Ext. 39437 Fax: (919) 315-8981 Write: Post Office Box 13398, Research Triangle Park, NC 27709
Food and Drug Administration (reporting unusual or severe toxicity to antiretroviral agents—MedWatch)	Phone: (800) 332-1088
Reporting to the CDC HIV seroconversions in health care workers who received postexposure prophylaxis	Phone: (404) 639-6425

non-nucleoside reverse transcriptase inhibitors were used for postexposure therapy. Perhaps of most concern is the report of two instances of severe hepatic dysfunction (one of which required liver transplantation) and 10 additional cases of moderate hepatic toxicity in health care workers who took nevirapine as part of a chemoprophylaxis regimen.[212-215] One additional recent report described a single instance of severe ototoxicity that occurred in a health care worker who received a postexposure prophylaxis regimen comprised of d4t, lamivudine, and nevirapine.[232] As noted earlier, the non-nucleoside reverse transcriptase inhibitor efavirenz is included in the list of acceptable alternative agents in the most recent USPHS guidelines.[7]

Side effects associated with HIV chemoprophylaxis are similar to those observed in HIV-infected patients and most can be managed symptomatically (e.g., acetaminophen for headache and myalgia; prochlorperazine for nausea; antimotility drugs for diarrhea). Nephrolithiasis and urinary tract obstruction associated with indinavir can be prevented by increasing fluid intake to at least six 8-oz glasses of water per day. Because drug interactions are especially common with protease inhibitors, practitioners providing care should carefully evaluate all other drugs currently being taken by the exposed health care worker. Protease inhibitors can inhibit the metabolism of nonsedating antihistamines and other hepatically metabolized drugs. Some of these agents (e.g., nelfinavir, ritonavir) accelerate the clearance of certain drugs, including oral contraceptives. Women taking these protease inhibitors should be encouraged to use alternative or additional contraceptive measures.

Chemoprophylaxis in Pregnancy

Pregnant women who sustain occupational exposures should be offered postexposure antiretroviral chemoprophylaxis.[7,148,149,218] The decision to offer treatment should be based on the same considerations that apply to other health care personnel sustaining these exposures. In counseling the exposed, pregnant health care worker, the counselor must address the potential risks and benefits both for the worker and her fetus. Specifically, the counselor should provide detailed information about what is known concerning the risk of HIV transmission to the mother and the fetus, the issue of teratogenicity in the context of the stages of pregnancy, and should address what is known about the pharmacokinetics, the safety, and the tolerability of antiretroviral drugs in pregnancy.[7,148,149,218,224,233,234] In addition, the prescribing practitioner must be aware that antiretroviral drugs may cause or exacerbate conditions that are especially serious during pregnancy (e.g., nausea, nephrolithiasis, hyperbilirubinemia, and hyperglycemia). Given these complexities, input from experts in managing antiretroviral drugs during pregnancy may be helpful both to the exposed health care worker as well as to her physician.

The risk to the fetus of administering a 28-day course of postexposure prophylaxis with antiretroviral agents remains undefined. We use several principles to guide the administration of postexposure prophylaxis in pregnancy. The decision as to whether or not to take postexposure prophylaxis can only be made by the pregnant worker. The exposed worker must be provided with accurate, thorough, unbiased counseling.

All available antiretroviral agents have the potential for carcinogenicity, teratogenicity, and/or mutagenicity. Some have been shown to be mutagenic in pre-marketing studies in animals. Animal studies of chronic zidovudine administration demonstrated an increased risk for certain hepatic tumors in animals given 35 times the label-indication dosage for humans for 18 to 22 months.[158] The relevance of such studies to administration of this agent to pregnant, health care workers who have sustained occupational exposures is unclear. Similarly, animal studies of efavirenz, demonstrated teratogenic effects in cynomolgus monkeys at drug levels similar to those produced in human dosing. Because of the potential relevance of these studies, most authorities do not recommend the use of efavirenz in pregnancy.

Limited safety data address the risk of administering antiretrovirals to HIV-uninfected pregnant women or the pharmacology of the drugs in this setting. Studies evaluating the efficacy of antiretrovirals in preventing vertical HIV provide useful, but not directly comparable, information about the use of these drugs in the postexposure setting. A large French study identified fetal neurological/mitochondrial toxicity associated with administration of nucleoside analogues in pregnancy. Two infant deaths and six additional instances of probable mitochondrial toxicity were identified in HIV-uninfected offspring of HIV-infected mothers in this large trial.[235] Both deaths were associated with mitochondrial toxicity that led to progressive neurological disease.[235] Interestingly, no fetal deaths attributable to, or associated with, antiretroviral-induced mitochondrial toxicity have been identified among several large vertical transmission studies that have been conducted in the United States. The differences between the French and US experiences are currently not well understood.

Treatment of HIV-infected pregnant women with the didanosine/stavudine (ddI/d4t) combination has also been associated with increased risk. Several instances of severe pancreatitis and lactic acidosis have been reported, and in some instances this syndrome has been associated with either maternal or fetal death (or both).[236] To our knowledge, this severe complication has not been observed in pregnant individuals taking ddI/d4t postexposure prophylaxis; however, because of the adverse experience with these agents in the treatment of HIV infection in pregnancy, this combination is not recommended for postexposure management for pregnant health care workers sustaining occupational HIV exposures.

The Antiretroviral Pregnancy Registry was designed to help evaluate the safety of administering antiretroviral agents during pregnancy and to detect evidence suggestive of teratogenicity or other serious adverse events. To date, the Antiretroviral Pregnancy Registry has not detected an increased risk of birth defects in infants with in utero exposure to zidovudine. Less information is available for other antiretroviral drugs, though a similar safety profile appears to be developing with respect to the use of lamivudine in pregnancy.[234]

Indications for Chemoprophylaxis

Current USPHS guidelines for postexposure chemoprophylaxis reflect a balance between the estimated risk of HIV transmission associated with specific exposures and the potential risks associated with treatment.[7] In general, chemoprophylaxis is *recommended* for exposures known to confer a transmission risk, should be *considered* for exposures with a "negligible risk," and *"may not be warranted"* for exposures that do not pose a known transmission risk.[7] In this framework, treatment is recommended for all percutaneous exposures to HIV and for large-volume or long-duration mucosal and nonintact skin exposures that involve higher-titer HIV exposures (e.g., blood from patients with advanced HIV disease, high viral load, or low CD4 counts). Treatment should be considered for small-volume, short-duration mucosal and nonintact skin exposure in instances in which the source is known or suspected to have a high circulating viral burden. Treatment is not indicated for most intact skin contacts.

The actual risk associated with a specific exposure to HIV is impossible to predict. Because the efficacy of chemoprophylaxis will likely never be demonstrated definitively in a clinical trial, and because the agents involved are associated with substantial toxicities, postexposure prophylaxis must, in every instance, be implemented with caution. Current USPHS guidelines are based on exposures to blood or other potentially infectious materials known to contain HIV, not materials of uncertain HIV status. Unfortunately, the guidelines have been interpreted to imply that antiretroviral chemoprophylaxis should be started for all blood exposures, unless HIV infection is specifically excluded with a negative source test.

"Source Unknown" Exposures

Decisions about treatment when the source material is not known to contain HIV should be based on a careful risk assessment, including a determination of: (1) the probability of HIV infection in the source patient; (2) the type of exposure and the associated risk of HIV transmission with such an exposure, if HIV was, in fact, present; and (3) the risks associated with treatment for the health care worker. In many "source unknown" exposures, the risk of transmission is negligible,

and treatment is simply not indicated. Only if the assessment suggests that the risk of HIV transmission outweighs the risk of treatment is it reasonable to initiate the basic treatment regimen until test results or other data become available.

Postexposure Chemoprophylaxis for Nonoccupational HIV Exposures

The use of antiretroviral chemoprophylaxis for nonoccupational exposures has been investigated intensively over the past several years.[150,151,237-241] The Committee on Pediatric AIDS of the American Academy of Pediatrics has recently published detailed guidelines for managing the often unique exposures experienced by children and adolescents.[241] Management of sexual exposures is discussed elsewhere in this text (see Chapter 124).[242] The rationale for providing postexposure chemoprophylaxis in select cases of nonoccupational or community HIV exposure is no different from that for providing prophylaxis for occupational exposures. Nonetheless, because of the toxicity and risk associated, both occupational and nonoccupational chemoprophylaxis should always be provided cautiously and only in the context of a comprehensive program designed to prevent subsequent exposures. Programs providing postexposure chemoprophylaxis for nonoccupational exposures should evaluate the circumstances of each exposure, should provide counseling about the risks for infection and secondary transmission, and should provide up-to-date information about the risks and benefits of antiretroviral chemotherapy. In many instances the care provider's primary role is one of reassurance, as the risk for transmission associated with many such community exposures may be quite small. Two reports describe instances in which HIV transmission has been associated with human bites.[152,155] Evaluation of the "bitten" individual should include baseline testing for preexisting HIV infection; offering postexposure prophylaxis, if exposed to HIV, and identical follow-up to that described for other parenteral HIV exposures. Another nonoccupational setting in which postexposure chemoprophylaxis is frequently administered is following sexual assault.[239,240,243-246] Individuals providing counseling for sexual assault victims must carefully consider the extreme physical and psychological trauma that such victims have experienced.

Timing and Duration of Chemoprophylaxis

Treatment should be initiated as soon as possible after exposure. In most animal studies, efficacy is reduced when treatment is delayed for more than 24 hours,[177] but the relevance of this observation to low-inoculum transcutaneous and transmucosal occupational HIV exposures is not known. Nonetheless, occupational exposures to HIV should be regarded as urgent medical concerns. When indicated, chemoprophylaxis should be started as soon as practical (i.e., within a few hours rather than days). When consultation is needed to select the best regimen, beginning the basic or expanded regimen until additional information is available may be the best course of action, rather than delaying the start of treatment. In cases in which the risk of transmission is very high, treatment even after a long delay (e.g., 1 to 2 weeks) should still be considered. Even if infection is not prevented, early treatment of acute HIV infection may be beneficial. The optimal duration of chemoprophylaxis is not known. A 4-week regimen is currently recommended, primarily based on clinical experience.[7,148,149,218]

Follow-Up for Occupational HIV Exposures

Postexposure Medical Evaluation and HIV Testing

In addition to baseline HIV testing, serological testing for a documented occupational HIV exposures is usually performed 6 weeks, 3 months, and 6 months after exposure.[7] Sequential testing is useful in allaying fears, in documenting seronegativity, and, rarely, in diagnosing HIV infection. Testing for more than 6 months is not routinely recommended, although some institutions test at 1 year following exposure if the health care worker who sustained the exposure requests testing.[7,148,149] Several types of exposures may be associated with increased risk for transmission. For example, if a volume of blood was injected or if the injury simultaneously exposed the health care to HIV and hepatitis C virus (particularly if HCV was transmitted in the exposure), extending the testing interval for several more months is recommended.

Symptoms of acute retroviral infection (fever, lymphadenopathy, pharyngitis, rash, headache, profound fatigue) have been associated with approximately 80% of reported occupational infections, even when chemoprophylaxis was taken (see Chapter 117).[31] For this reason all HIV-exposed persons should be advised to return for evaluation and HIV testing if an illness suggestive of the acute retroviral syndrome occurs. Conversely, we would emphasize that not every fever and rash is indicative of acute HIV infection; drug reactions or other intercurrent illnesses can mimic primary HIV infection. HIV antibody tests may be negative or indeterminate during the early phases of the seroconversion illness. Immunoblot, viral load tests (quantitative HIV RNA polymerase chain reaction), or viral cultures may be more sensitive methods for detecting early infection (see Chapter 115). Whereas these latter tests may be of value in sorting out seroconversion from other illnesses, we would underscore that these latter tests are *not* indicated in the routine management of occupational HIV exposures. None of these tests was designed for diagnosis and neither their sensitivity nor, perhaps more importantly, their specificity have been established.[7,148,149,218]

Ongoing Monitoring for Individuals Receiving Postexposure Chemoprophylaxis

Health care workers who elect to take chemoprophylaxis after HIV exposure should return 2 weeks after initiation of treatment for routine evaluation for signs and symptoms of drug toxicity. The individual evaluating the worker should obtain a careful history, perform a focused physical examination, and obtain relevant laboratory tests appropriate to the drug regimen. As a general rule, a complete blood count, as well as renal and hepatic chemical function tests, are usually indicated. A random blood glucose and a lipid profile should be included whenever protease inhibitor therapy is included in the regimen.[1,221,228]

Exposed health care workers who choose to take chemoprophylaxis should be advised of the importance of completing the prescribed regimen. Information should be provided about potential drug interactions and the drugs that should not be taken with the prophylactic drug regimen, the side effects of the drugs that have been prescribed, measures to minimize these effects, and methods of clinical monitoring for toxicity during the follow-up period. They should be alerted to the need for immediate evaluation of symptoms of the seroconversion illness and of symptoms suggestive of serious toxicity (e.g., back or abdominal pain, pain on urination or blood in the urine, and symptoms of hyperglycemia such as increased thirst or frequent urination).

Health care workers who fail to complete the recommended regimen often stop taking the drugs because of the side effects that they experience (e.g., nausea and diarrhea). These symptoms can often be managed without changing the regimen by prescribing antimotility and antiemetic agents or other medications that target the specific symptoms. In other situations, modifying the dose interval (i.e., giving a lower dose of drug more frequently throughout the day, as recommended by the manufacturer) may also promote adherence to the regimen.

REFERENCES

1. Leibowitz S, Greenwald L, Cohen I, et al. Serum hepatitis in a blood bank worker. JAMA. 1949;140:
2. Henderson DK, Gerberding JL. Healthcare worker issues, including occupational and nonoccupational postexposure management. In: Dolin R, Masur H, Saag MS, eds. AIDS Therapy. 2nd ed. New York: Churchill Livingstone; 2002:327.
3. Do AN, Ciesielski CA, Metler RP, et al. Occupationally acquired human immunodeficiency virus (HIV) infection: National case surveillance data during 20 years of the HIV epidemic in the United States. Infect Control Hosp Epidemiol. 2003;24:86.
4. Beekmann SE, Fahey BJ, Gerberding JL, et al. Risky business: Using necessarily imprecise casualty counts to estimate occupational risks for HIV-1 infection. Infect Control Hosp Epidemiol. 1990;11:371.
5. Eberle J, Habermann J, Gurtler LG. HIV-1 infection transmitted by serum droplets into the eye: A case report. AIDS. 2000;14:206.
6. Beltrami EM, Kozak A, Williams IT, et al. Transmission of HIV and hepatitis C virus from a nursing home patient to a health care worker. Am J Infect Control. 2003;31:168.
7. Centers for Disease Control and Prevention. Updated U.S. Public Health Service Guidelines for the Management of Occupational Exposures to HBV, HCV, and HIV and Recommendations for Postexposure Prophylaxis. MMWR Morb Mortal Wkly Rep. 2001;50:1.
8. Ippolito G, Puro V, Heptonstall J, et al. Occupational human immunodeficiency virus infection in health care workers: worldwide cases through September 1997. Clin Infect Dis. 1999;28:365.
9. Gioannni P, Sinicco A, Cariti G, et al. HIV infection acquired by a nurse. Eur J Epidemiol. 1988;4:119.
10. Fahey BJ, Koziol DE, Banks SM, et al. Frequency of nonparenteral occupational exposures to blood and body fluids before and after universal precautions training. Am J Med. 1991;90:145.
11. Bennett NT, Howard RJ. Quantity of blood inoculated in a needlestick injury from suture needles. J Am Coll Surg. 1994;178:107.
12. Mast ST, Woolwine JD, Gerberding JL. Efficacy of gloves in reducing blood volumes transferred during simulated needlestick injury. J Infect Dis. 1993;168:1589.
13. Ho DD, Moudgil T, Alam M. Quantitation of human immunodeficiency virus type 1 in the blood of infected persons. N Engl J Med. 1989;321:1621.
14. Daar ES, Moudgil T, Meyer RD, et al. Transient high levels of viremia in patients with primary human immunodeficiency virus type 1 infection. N Engl J Med. 1991;324:961.
15. Saag MS, Crain MJ, Decker WD, et al. High-level viremia in adults and children infected with human immunodeficiency virus: relation to disease stage and CD4+ lymphocyte levels. J Infect Dis. 1991;164:72.
16. Cao Y, Krogstad P, Korber BT, et al. Maternal HIV-1 viral load and vertical transmission of infection: The Ariel Project for the prevention of HIV transmission from mother to infant. Nat Med. 1997;3:549.
17. Sperling RS, Shapiro DE, Coombs RW, et al. Maternal viral load, zidovudine treatment, and the risk of transmission of human immunodeficiency virus type 1 from mother to infant. Pediatric AIDS Clinical Trials Group Protocol 076 Study Group. N Engl J Med. 1996;335:1621.
18. Cardo DM, Culver DH, Ciesielski CA, et al. A case-control study of HIV seroconversion in health care workers after percutaneous exposure. N Engl J Med. 1997;337:1485.
19. Rowland-Jones S, Sutton J, Ariyoshi K, et al. HIV-specific cytotoxic T-cells in HIV-exposed but uninfected Gambian women. Nat Med. 1995;1:59.
20. Rowland-Jones S, Dong T, Krausa P, et al. The role of cytotoxic T-cells in HIV infection. Dev Biol Stand. 1998;92:209.
21. Clerici M, Giorgi JV, Chou CC, et al. Cell-mediated immune response to human immunodeficiency virus (HIV) type 1 in seronegative homosexual men with recent sexual exposure to HIV-1. J Infect Dis. 1992;165:1012.
22. Kelker HC, Seidlin M, Vogler M, et al. Lymphocytes from some long-term seronegative heterosexual partners of HIV-infected individuals proliferate in response to HIV antigens. AIDS Res Hum Retrovir. 1992;8:1355.
23. Ranki A, Mattinen S, Yarchoan R, et al. T-cell response towards HIV in infected individuals with and without zidovudine therapy, and in HIV-exposed sexual partners. AIDS. 1989;3:63.
24. Mazzoli S, Trabattoni D, Lo Caputo S, et al. HIV-specific mucosal and cellular immunity in HIV-seronegative partners of HIV-seropositive individuals. Nat Med. 1997;3:1250.
25. Cheynier R, Langlade-Demoyen P, Marescot MR, et al. Cytotoxic T lymphocyte responses in the peripheral blood of children born to human immunodeficiency virus-1-infected mothers. Eur J Immunol. 1992;22:2211.
26. Puro V, Calcagno G, Anselmo M, et al. Transient detection of plasma HIV-1 RNA during postexposure prophylaxis. Infect Control Hosp Epidemiol. 2000;21:529.
27. Pinto LA, Landay AL, Berzofsky JA, et al. Immune response to human immunodeficiency virus (HIV) in healthcare workers occupationally exposed to HIV-contaminated blood. Am J Med. 1997;102:21.
28. Pinto LA, Sullivan J, Berzofsky JA, et al. ENV-specific cytotoxic T lymphocyte responses in HIV seronegative health care workers occupationally exposed to HIV-contaminated body fluids. J Clin Invest. 1995;96:867.
29. Clerici M, Levin JM, Kessler HA, et al. HIV-specific T-helper activity in seronegative health care workers exposed to contaminated blood. JAMA. 1994;271:42.
30. Busch MP, Sattem GA. Time course of viremia and antibody seroconversion following human immunodeficiency virus exposure. Am J Med. 1997;102:117.
31. Ciesielski CA, Metler RP. Duration of time between exposure and seroconversion in healthcare workers with occupationally acquired infection with human immunodeficiency virus. Am J Med. 1997;102:115.
32. Ridzon R, Gallagher K, Ciesielski C, et al. Simultaneous transmission of human immunodeficiency virus and hepatitis C virus from a needle-stick injury. N Engl J Med. 1997;336:919.
33. Centers for Disease Control. Possible transmission of human immunodeficiency virus to a patient during an invasive dental procedure. MMWR Morb Mortal Wkly Rep. 1990;39:489.
34. Centers for Disease Control. Update: Transmission of HIV infection during an invasive dental procedure—Florida. MMWR Morb Mortal Wkly Rep. 1991;40:21.
35. Ciesielski C, Marianos D, Ou C-Y, et al. Transmission of human immunodeficiency virus in a dental practice. Ann Intern Med. 1992;116:798.
36. Ciesielski CA, Marianos DW, Schochetman G, et al. The 1990 Florida dental investigation. The press and the science. Ann Intern Med. 1994;121:886.
37. Blanchard A, Ferris S, Chamaret S, et al. Molecular evidence for nosocomial transmission of human immunodeficiency virus from a surgeon to one of his patients. J Virol. 1998;72:4537.

38. Goujon CP, Schneider VM, Grofti J, et al. Phylogenetic analyses indicate an atypical nurse-to-patient transmission of human immunodeficiency virus type 1. J Virol. 2000;74:2525.

39. Lot F, Seguier JC, Fegueux S, et al. Probable transmission of HIV from an orthopedic surgeon to a patient in France. Ann Intern Med. 1999;130:1.

40. Astagneau P, Lot F, Bouvet E, et al. Lookback investigation of patients potentially exposed to HIV type 1 after a nurse-to-patient transmission. Am J Infect Contr. 2002; 30:242.

41. Centers for Disease Control. Update: Investigations of persons treated by HIV-infected health-care workers—United States. MMWR Morb Mortal Wkly Rep. 1993;42:329.

42. Robert LM, Chamberland ME, Cleveland JL, et al. Investigations of patients of health care workers infected with HIV: The Centers for Disease Control and Prevention database. Ann Intern Med. 1995;122:653.

43. Castro KG, Lifson AR, White CR, et al. Investigations of AIDS patients with no previously identified risk factors. JAMA. 1988;259:1338.

44. Gerberding JL, Rose DA, Ramiro NZ, et al. Intraoperative provider injuries and potential patient recontacts at San Francisco General Hospital. Infect Contr Hosp Epidemiol. 1994;15:20.

45. Tokars JI, Bell DM, Culver DH, et al. Percutaneous injuries during surgical procedures. JAMA. 1992;267:2899.

46. AIDS/Tuberculosis Subcommittee of the Society for Healthcare Epidemiology of America. Management of healthcare workers infected with hepatitis B virus, hepatitis C virus, human immunodeficiency virus, or other bloodborne pathogens. Infect Control Hosp Epidemiol. 1997;18:349.

47. Gerberding JL. Provider-to-patient HIV transmission: How to keep it exceedingly rare. Ann Intern Med. 1999;130:64.

48. Pokrovsky VV, Eramova EU. Nosocomial outbreak of HIV infection in Elista, USSR. In: Program and Abstracts of the V International Conference on AIDS, Montreal, Quebec, Canada. Abstract WA05:63.

49. Gisselquist DP. Estimating HIV-1 transmission efficiency through unsafe medical injections. Int J STD AIDS. 2002;13:152.

50. Yerly S, Quadri R, Negro F, et al. Nosocomial outbreak of multiple bloodborne viral infections. J Infect Dis. 2001;184:369.

51. Hersh BS, Popovici F, Jezek Z, et al. Risk factors for HIV infection among abandoned Romanian children. AIDS. 1993;7:1617.

52. Patrascu IV, Dumitrescu O. The epidemic of human immunodeficiency virus infection in Romanian children. AIDS Res Hum Retrovir. 1993;9:99.

53. Injection practices among nurses—Valcea, Romania, 1998. MMWR Morb Mortal Wkly Rep. 2001;50:59.

54. Centers for Disease Control. Patient exposures to HIV during nuclear medicine procedures. MMWR Morb Mortal Wkly Rep. 1992;41:575.

55. Hutin YJ, Goldstein ST, Varma JK, et al. An outbreak of hospital-acquired hepatitis B virus infection among patients receiving chronic hemodialysis. Infect Control Hosp Epidemiol. 1999;20:731.

56. Kidd-Ljunggren K, Broman E, Ekvall H, et al. Nosocomial transmission of hepatitis B virus infection through multiple-dose vials. J Hosp Infect. 1999;43:57.

57. Katzenstein TL, Jorgensen LB, Permin H, et al. Nosocomial HIV-transmission in an outpatient clinic detected by epidemiological and phylogenetic analyses. AIDS. 1999;13:1737.

58. Chant K, Lowe D, Rubin G, et al. Patient-to-patient transmission of HIV in private surgical consulting rooms. Lancet. 1993;342:1548.

59. Velandia M, Fridkin SK, Cardenas V, et al. Transmission of HIV in dialysis centre. Lancet. 1995;345:1417.

60. Centers for Disease Control and Prevention: HIV transmission in a dialysis center—Colombia, 1991-1993. MMWR Morb Mortal Wkly Rep. 1995;44:404.

61. El Sayed NM, Gomatos PJ, Beck-Sague CM, et al. Epidemic transmission of human immunodeficiency virus in renal dialysis centers in Egypt. J Infect Dis. 2001;81:91.

62. Zuckerman M. Surveillance and control of blood-borne virus infections in haemodialysis units. J Hosp Infect. 2002;50:1.

63. Centers for Disease Control. Recommendations for prevention of HIV transmission in health-care settings. MMWR Morb Mortal Wkly Rep. 1987;36(Suppl 2):1S.

64. Centers for Disease Control. Update: Universal precautions for prevention of transmission of human immunodeficiency virus, hepatitis B virus, and other bloodborne pathogens in health-care settings. MMWR Morb Mortal Wkly Rep. 1988;37:377.

65. Lynch P, Jackson MM, Cummings MJ, et al. Rethinking the role of isolation practices in the prevention of nosocomial infection. Ann Intern Med. 1987;107:243.

66. Garner JS. Guideline for isolation precautions in hospitals. The Hospital Infection Control Practices Advisory Committee. Infect Control Hosp Epidemiol. 1996;17:53.

67. Department of Labor, Department of Health and Human Services. Joint Advisory Notice: Protection against occupational exposure to hepatitis B virus (HBV) and human immunodeficiency virus (HIV). Fed Regist. 1987;52:41818.

68. Department of Labor OSHA. Occupational exposure to bloodborne pathogens; final rule. Fed Regist. 1991;56:64175.

69. Beekmann SE, Vlahov D, Koziol DE, et al. Temporal association between implementation of universal precautions and a sustained, progressive decrease in percutaneous exposures to blood. Clin Infect Dis. 1994;18:562.

70. Haiduven DJ, DeMaio TM, Stevens DA. A five-year study of needlestick injuries: Significant reduction associated with communication, education, and convenient placement of sharps containers. Infect Control Hosp Epidemiol. 1992;13:265.

71. Kristensen MS, Wernberg NM, Anker MIE. Healthcare workers' risk of contact with body fluids in a hospital: The effect of complying with the universal precautions policy. Infect Control Hosp Epidemiol. 1992;13:719.

72. Wong ES, Stotka JL, Chinchilli VM, et al. Are universal precautions effective in reducing the number of occupational exposures among health care workers? A prospective study of physicians on a medical service. JAMA. 1991;265:1123.

73. De Carli G, Puro V, Petrosillo N, et al. "Side" effects of HAART: Decreasing and changing occupational exposure to HIV-infected patients. J Biol Regul Homeost Agents. 2001;15:235.

74. Skolnick R, LaRocca J, Barba D, et al. Evaluation and implementation of a needleless intravenous system: making needlesticks a needless problem. Am J Infect Contr. 1993;21:39.

75. Yassi A, McGill ML, Khokhar JB. Efficacy and cost-effectiveness of a needleless intravenous access system. Am J Infect Contr. 1995;23:57.

76. Mendelson MH, Short LJ, Schechter CB, et al. Study of a needleless intermittent intravenous-access system for peripheral infusions: Analysis of staff, patient, and institutional outcomes. Infect Control Hosp Epidemiol. 1998;19:401.

77. Jagger J, Hunt EH, Brand-Elnaggar J, et al. Rates of needle-stick injury caused by various devices in a university hospital. N Engl J Med. 1988;319:284.

78. MacPherson J. The interlink needleless intravenous system did not reduce the number of needlestick injuries in Christchurch hospital operating theatres. N Z Med J. 1996;109:387.

79. Alvarado-Ramy F, Beltrami EM, Short LJ, et al. A comprehensive approach to percutaneous injury prevention during phlebotomy: Results of a multicenter study, 1993-1995. Infect Control Hosp Epidemiol. 2003;24:97.

80. Centers for Disease Control and Prevention. Evaluation of safety devices for preventing percutaneous injuries among health-care workers during phlebotomy procedures—Minneapolis-St. Paul, New York City, and San Francisco, 1993-1995. MMWR Morb Mortal Wkly Rep. 1997;46:21.

81. Mendelson MH, Lin-Chen BY, Solomon R, et al. Evaluation of a safety resheathable winged steel needle for prevention of percutaneous injuries associated with intravascular-access procedures among healthcare workers. Infect Control Hosp Epidemiol. 2003;24:105.

82. Rabaud C, Zanea A, Mur JM, et al. Occupational exposure to blood: Search for a relation between personality and behavior. Infect Control Hosp Epidemiol. 2000;21:564.

83. Gerberding JL, Littell C, Tarkington A, et al. Risk of exposure of surgical personnel to patients' blood during surgery at San Francisco General Hospital. N Engl J Med. 1990;322:1788.

84. Panlilio AL, Foy DR, Edwards JR, et al. Blood contacts during surgical procedures. JAMA. 1991;265:1533.

85. Panlilio AL, Welch BA, Bell DM, et al. Blood and amniotic fluid contact sustained by obstetric personnel during deliveries. Am J Obstet Gynecol. 1992;167:703.

86. Popejoy SL, Fry DE. Blood contact and exposure in the operating room. Surg Gynecol Obstet. 1991;172:480.

87. Quebbeman EJ, Telford GL, Hubbard S, et al. Risk of blood contamination and injury to operating room personnel. Ann Surg. 1991;214:614.

88. Robert L, Short L, Chamberland M, et al. Percutaneous injuries sustained during gynecologic surgery. Infect Control Hosp Epidemiol. 1994;15:349.

89. White MC, Lynch P. Blood contact and exposures among operating room personnel: A multicenter study. Am J Infect Contr. 1993;21:243.

90. Lynch P, White MC. Perioperative blood contact and exposures: A comparison of incident reports and focused studies. Am J Infect Contr. 1993;21:357.

91. Folin AC, Nordstrom GM. Accidental blood contact during orthopedic surgical procedures. Infect Contr Hosp Epidemiol. 1997;18:244.

92. Tobias AM, Chang B. Pulsed irrigation of extremity wounds: A simple technique for splashback reduction. Ann Plast Surg. 2002;48:443.

93. Akduman D, Kim LE, Parks RL, et al. Use of personal protective equipment and operating room behaviors in four surgical subspecialties: Personal protective equipment and behaviors in surgery. Infect Control Hosp Epidemiol. 1999;20:110.

94. American Academy of Orthopedic Surgeons Task Force on AIDS and Orthopedic Surgery. Recommendations for the prevention of human immunodeficiency virus (HIV) transmission in the practice of orthopedic surgery. Park Ridge, IL, 1989.

95. Davis JM, Demling RH, Lewis FR, et al. The Surgical Infection Society's policy on human immunodeficiency virus and hepatitis B and C infection. The Ad Hoc Committee on Acquired Immunodeficiency Syndrome and Hepatitis. Arch Surg. 1992;127:218.

96. Hester RA, Nelson CL, Harrison S. Control of contamination of the operative team in total joint arthroplasty. J Arthropl. 1992;7:267.

97. Lewis FR Jr, Short LJ, Howard RJ, et al. Epidemiology of injuries by needles and other sharp instruments. Minimizing sharp injuries in gynecologic and obstetric operations. Surg Clin North Am. 1995;75:1105.

98. Loudon MA, Stonebridge PA. Minimizing the risk of penetrating injury to surgical staff in the operating theatre: Towards sharp-free surgery. J R Coll Surg Edinb. 1998;43:6.

99. Wright KU, Moran CG, Briggs PJ. Glove perforation during hip arthroplasty. A randomised prospective study of a new taperpoint needle. J Bone Joint Surg. 1993;75:918.

100. Montz FJ, Fowler JM, Farias-Eisner R, et al. Blunt needles in fascial closure. Surg Gynecol Obstet. 1991;173:147.

101. Mingoli A, Sapienza P, Sgarzini G, et al. Influence of blunt needles on surgical glove perforation and safety for the surgeon. Am J Surg. 1996;172:512.

102. Miller SS, Sabharwal A. Subcuticular skin closure using a 'blunt' needle. Ann R Coll Surg Engl. 1994;76:281.

103. Hartley JE, Ahmed S, Milkins R, et al. Randomized trial of blunt-tipped versus cutting needles to reduce glove puncture during mass closure of the abdomen. Br J Surg. 1996;83:1156.

104. Centers for Disease Control and Prevention. Evaluation of blunt suture needles in preventing percutaneous injuries among health-care workers during gynecologic surgical procedures—New York City, March 1993-June 1994. MMWR Morb Mortal Wkly Rep. 1997;46:25.

105. Kovavisarach E, Jaravechson S. Comparison of perforation between single and double-gloving in perineorrhaphy after vaginal delivery: A randomized controlled trial. Aust N Z J Obstet Gynaecol. 1998;38:58.

106. Kovavisarach E, Seedadee C. Randomised controlled trial of glove perforation in single and double-gloving methods in gynaecologic surgery. Aust N Z J Obstet Gynaecol. 2002;42:519.

107. Kovavisarach E, Vanitchanon P. Perforation in single- and double-gloving methods for cesarean section. Int J Gynaecol Obstet. 1999;67:157.

108. Laine T, Aarnio P. How often does glove perforation occur in surgery? Comparison between single gloves and a double-gloving system. Am J Surg. 2001;181:564.

109. Aarnio P, Laine T. Glove perforation rate in vascular surgery—a comparison between single and double gloving. Vasa. 2001;30:122.

110. Naver LP, Gottrup F. Incidence of glove perforations in gastrointestinal surgery and the protective effect of double gloves: A prospective, randomised controlled study. Eur J Surg. 2001;66:293.

111. Hollaus PH, Lax F, Janakiev D, et al. Glove perforation rate in open lung surgery. Eur J Cardiothorac Surg. 1999;15:461.

112. Avery CM, Taylor J, Johnson PA. Double gloving and a system for identifying glove perforations in maxillofacial trauma surgery. Br J Oral Maxillofac Surg. 1999;37:316.

113. Chapman S, Duff P. Frequency of glove perforations and subsequent blood contact in association with selected obstetric surgical procedures. Am J Obstet Gynecol. 1993;168:1354.

114. Cohen MS, Do JT, Tahery DP, et al. Efficacy of double gloving as a protection against blood exposure in dermatologic surgery. J Dermatol Surg Oncol. 1992;18:873.

115. Quebbeman EJ, Telford GL, Wadsworth K, et al. Double gloving. Protecting surgeons from blood contamination in the operating room. Arch Surg. 1992;127:213.

116. Gerberding JL, Quebbeman EJ, Rhodes RS. Hand protection. Surg Clin North Am. 1995;75:1133.

117. Leslie LF, Woods JA, Thacker JG, et al. Needle puncture resistance of surgical gloves, finger guards, and glove liners. J Biomed Mater Res. 1996;33:41.

118. Salkin JA, Stuchin SA, Kummer FJ, et al. The effectiveness of cut-proof glove liners: Cut and puncture resistance, dexterity, and sensibility. Orthopedics. 1995;18:1067.

119. Woods JA, Leslie LF, Drake DB, et al. Effect of puncture resistant surgical gloves, finger guards, and glove liners on cutaneous sensibility and surgical psychomotor skills. J Biomed Mater Res. 1996;33:47.

120. Wilson SJ, Sellu D, Uy A, et al. Subjective effects of double gloves on surgical performance. Ann R Coll Surg Engl. 1996;78:20.

121. Gerberding JL. Procedure-specific infection control for preventing intraoperative blood exposures. Am J Infect Contr. 1993;21:364.

122. Alrawi SJ, Houshan I, Zanial SA, et al. Cardiac surgical procedures and glove reinforcements. Heart Surg Forum. 2002;5:66.

123. Weber LW. Evaluation of the rate, location, and morphology of perforations in surgical gloves worn in urological operations. Appl Occup Environ Hyg. 2003;18:65.

124. Bebbington MW, Treissman MJ. The use of a surgical assist device to reduce glove perforations in postdelivery vaginal repair: A randomized controlled trial. Am J Obstet Gynecol. 1996;175:862.

125. Cleveland JL, Gooch BF, Lockwood SA. Occupational blood exposures in dentistry: A decade in review. Infect Control Hosp Epidemiol. 1997;18:717.

126. Cleveland JL, Barker L, Gooch BF, et al. Use of HIV postexposure prophylaxis by dental health care personnel: An overview and updated recommendations. J Am Dent Assoc. 2002;133:1619.

127. Ramos-Gomez F, Ellison J, Greenspan D, et al. Accidental exposures to blood and body fluids among health care workers in dental teaching clinics: A prospective study. J Am Dent Assoc. 1997;128:1253.

128. Cleveland JL, Lockwood SA, Gooch BF, et al. Percutaneous injuries in dentistry: An observational study. J Am Dent Assoc. 1995;126:745.

129. Siew C, Gruninger SE, Miaw CL, et al. Percutaneous injuries in practicing dentists. A prospective study using a 20-day diary. J Am Dent Assoc. 1995;126:1227.

130. Carlton JE, Dodson TB, Cleveland JL, et al. Percutaneous injuries during oral and maxillofacial surgery procedures. J Oral Maxillofac Surg. 1997;55:553.

131. Gooch BF, Siew C, Cleveland JL, et al. Occupational blood exposure and HIV infection among oral and maxillofacial surgeons. Oral Surg Oral Med Oral Pathol Oral Radiol Endod. 1998;85:128.

132. Hall FM. Double gloving during interventional procedures. Am J Roentgenol. 1993;161:678.

133. Hansen ME, McIntire DD, Miller GL, et al. Use of universal precautions in interventional radiology: Results of a national survey. Am J Infect Contr. 1994;22:1.

134. Wall SD, Olcott EW, Gerberding JL. AIDS risk and risk reduction in the radiology department. Am J Roentgenol. 1991;157:911.

135. McWilliams RG, Blanshard KS. The risk of blood splash contamination during angiography. Clin Radiol. 1994;49:59.

136. Gerberding JL. Post-exposure prophylaxis for human immunodeficiency virus at San Francisco General Hospital. Am J Med. 1997;102:85.

137. Hamory BH. Underreporting of needlestick injuries in a university hospital. Am J Infect Contr. 1983;11:174.

138. Beltrami EM, Williams IT, Shapiro CN, et al. Risk and management of blood-borne infections in health care workers. Clin Microbiol Rev. 2000;13:385.

139. Benitez Rodriguez E, Ruiz Moruno AJ, Cordoba Dona JA, et al. Underreporting of percutaneous exposure accidents in a teaching hospital in Spain. Clin Perform Qual Hlth Care. 1999;7:88.

140. Burke S, Madan I. Contamination incidents among doctors and midwives: Reasons for non-reporting and knowledge of risks. Occup Med (Oxf). 1997;47:357.

141. Mangione CM, Gerberding JL, Cummings SR. Occupational exposure to HIV: Frequency and rates of underreporting of percutaneous and mucocutaneous exposures by medical housestaff. Am J Med. 1991;90:85.

142. Radecki S, Abbott A, Eloi L. Occupational human immunodeficiency virus exposure among residents and medical students: An analysis of 5-year follow-up data. Arch Intern Med. 2000;160:3107.

143. Shiao JS, McLaws ML, Huang KY, et al. Prevalence of nonreporting behavior of sharps injuries in Taiwanese health care workers. Am J Infect Contr. 1999;27:254.

144. Tandberg D, Stewart KK, Doezema D. Under-reporting of contaminated needlestick injuries in emergency health care workers. Ann Emerg Med. 1991;20:66.

145. Gerberding JL, Henderson DK. Design of rational infection control policies for human immunodeficiency virus infection. J Infect Dis. 1987;156:861.

146. Armstrong K, Gorden R, Santorella G. Occupational exposure of health care workers (HCWs) to human immunodeficiency virus (HIV): Stress reactions and counseling interventions. Soc Work Hlth Care. 1995;21:61.

147. Dilley JW. Counseling health care workers after accidental exposures. Focus. 1990;5:3.

148. Henderson DK. HIV postexposure prophylaxis in the 21st century. Emerg Infect Dis. 2001;7:254.

149. Henderson DK. Postexposure chemoprophylaxis for occupational exposures to the human immunodeficiency virus. JAMA. 1999;281:931.

150. Kahn JO, Martin JN, Roland ME, et al. Feasibility of postexposure prophylaxis (PEP) against human immunodeficiency virus infection after sexual or injection drug use exposure: The San Francisco PEP Study. J Infect Dis. 2001;183:707.

151. Roland ME, Martin JN, Grant RM, et al. Postexposure prophylaxis for human immunodeficiency virus infection after sexual or injection drug use exposure: Identification and characterization of the source of exposure. J Infect Dis. 2001;184:1608.

152. Khajotia RR, Lee E. Transmission of human immunodeficiency virus through saliva after a lip bite. Arch Intern Med. 1997;157:1901.

153. Pretty IA, Anderson GS, Sweet DJ. Human bites and the risk of human immunodeficiency virus transmission. Am J Forens Med Pathol. 1999;20:232.

154. Richman KM, Rickman LS. The potential for transmission of human immunodeficiency virus through human bites. J Acquir Immune Defic Syndr. 1993;6:402.

155. Vidmar L, Poljak M, Tomazic J, et al. Transmission of HIV-1 by human bite. Lancet. 1996;347:1762.

156. Charache P, Cameron JL, Maters AW, et al. Prevalence of infection with human immunodeficiency virus in elective surgery patients. Ann Surg. 1991;214:562.

157. Centers for Disease Control. Recommendations for preventing transmission of human immunodeficiency virus and hepatitis B virus to patients during exposure-prone invasive procedures. MMWR Morb Mortal Wkly Rep. 1991;40:1.

158. Centers for Disease Control. Public Health Service statement on management of occupational exposure to human immunodeficiency virus, including considerations regarding zidovudine postexposure use. MMWR Morb Mortal Wkly Rep. 1990;39:1.

159. Henderson DK, Gerberding JL. Prophylactic zidovudine after occupational exposure to the human immunodeficiency virus: An interim analysis. J Infect Dis. 1989;160:321.

160. Gerberding JL, Katz MII. Post-exposure prophylaxis for HIV. Adv Exp Med Biol. 1999;458:213.

161. Blauvelt A, Katz SI. The skin as target, vector, and effector organ in human immunodeficiency virus disease. J Invest Dermatol. 1995;105:122S.

162. Blauvelt A. The role of skin dendritic cells in the initiation of human immunodeficiency virus infection. Am J Med. 1997;102:16.

163. Blauvelt A, Glushakova S, Margolis LB. HIV-infected human Langerhans cells transmit infection to human lymphoid tissue ex vivo. AIDS. 2000;14:647.

164. Spira AI, Marx PA, Patterson BK, et al. Cellular targets of infection and route of viral dissemination after an intravaginal inoculation of simian immunodeficiency virus into rhesus macaques. J Exp Med. 1996;183:215.

165. Granelli-Piperno A, Finkel V, Delgado E, et al. Virus replication begins in dendritic cells during the transmission of HIV-1 from mature dendritic cells to T cells. Curr Biol. 1999;9:21.

166. Blauvelt A, Asada H, Saville MW, et al. Productive infection of dendritic cells by HIV-1 and their ability to capture virus are mediated through separate pathways. J Clin Invest. 1997;100:2043.

167. Piguet V, Blauvelt A. Essential roles for dendritic cells in the pathogenesis and potential treatment of HIV disease. J Invest Dermatol. 2002;119:365.

168. Ruprecht RM, Bronson R. Chemoprevention of retroviral infection: Success is determined by virus inoculum strength and cellular immunity. DNA Cell Biol. 1994;13:59.

169. Putkonen P, Makitalo B, Bottiger D, et al. Protection of human immunodeficiency virus type 2-exposed seronegative macaques from mucosal simian immunodeficiency virus transmission. J Virol. 1997;71:4981.

170. Tsai CC, Emau P, Sun JC, et al. Post-exposure chemoprophylaxis (PECP) against SIV infection of macaques as a model for protection from HIV infection. J Med Primatol. 2000;29:248.

171. D'Amico R, Pinto LA, Meyer P, et al. Effect of zidovudine postexposure prophylaxis on the development of HIV-specific cytotoxic T-lymphocyte responses in HIV-exposed healthcare workers. Infect Contr Hosp Epidemiol. 1999;20:428.

172. Zidek Z, Frankova D, Holy A. Activation by 9-(R)-[2-(phosphonomethoxy)propyl]adenine of chemokine (RANTES, macrophage inflammatory protein 1alpha) and cytokine (tumor necrosis factor alpha, interleukin-10 [IL-10], IL-1beta) production. Antimicrob Agents Chemother. 2001;45:3381.

173. Black RJ. Animal studies of prophylaxis. Am J Med. 1997;102:39.

174. Ruprecht RM, O'Brien LG, Rossoni LD, et al. Suppression of mouse viraemia and retroviral disease by 3'-azido-3'deoxythymidine. Nature. 1986;323:467.

175. Tavares L, Roneker C, Johnston K, et al. 3'-Azido-3'deoxythymidine in feline leukemia virus-infected cats: A model for therapy and prophylaxis of AIDS. Cancer Res. 1987;47:3190.

176. Fazely F, Haseltine WA, Rodger RF, et al. Postexposure chemoprophylaxis with ZDV or ZDV combined with interferon-alpha: Failure after inoculating rhesus monkeys with a high dose of SIV. J Acquir Immune Defic Syndr. 1991;4:1093.

177. Tsai CC, Emau P, Follis KE, et al. Effectiveness of postinoculation (R)-9-(2-phosphonylmethoxypropyl) adenine treatment for prevention of persistent simian immunodeficiency virus SIVmne infection depends critically on timing of initiation and duration of treatment. J Virol. 1998;72:4265.

178. Tsai CC, Follis KE, Sabo A, et al. Prevention of SIV infection in macaques by (R)-9-(2-phosphonylmethoxypropyl)adenine. Science. 1995;270:1197.

179. Van Rompay KK, Dailey PJ, Tarara RP, et al. Early short-term 9-[2-(R)-(phosphonomethoxy)propyl]adenine treatment favorably alters the subsequent disease course in simian immunodeficiency virus-infected newborn Rhesus macaques. J Virol. 1999;73:2947.

180. Van Rompay KK, Marthas ML, Ramos RA, et al. Simian immunodeficiency virus (SIV) infection of infant rhesus macaques as a model to test antiretroviral drug prophylaxis and therapy: Oral 3'-azido-3'-deoxythymidine prevents SIV infection. Antimicrob Agents Chemother. 1992;36:2381.

181. Böttiger D, Johansson NG, Samuelsson B, et al. Prevention of simian immunodeficiency virus, SIVsm, or HIV-2 infection in cynomolgus monkeys by pre- and postexposure administration of BEA-005. AIDS. 1997;11:157.

182. Böttiger D, Putkonen P, Oberg B. Prevention of HIV-2 and SIV infections in cynomolgus macaques by prophylactic treatment with 3'-fluorothymidine. AIDS Res Hum Retrovir. 1992;8:1235.

183. Otten RA, Smith DK, Adams DR, et al. Efficacy of postexposure prophylaxis after intravaginal exposure of pig-tailed macaques to a human-derived retrovirus (human immunodeficiency virus type 2). J Virol. 2000;74:9771.

184. Connor EM, Sperling RS, Gelber R, et al. Reduction of maternal-infant transmission of human immunodeficiency virus type 1 with zidovudine treatment. Pediatric AIDS Clinical Trials Group Protocol 076 Study Group. N Engl J Med. 1994;331:1173.

185. Bulterys M, Orloff S, Abrams E, et al. Impact of zidovudine post-perinatal exposure prophylaxis on vertical HIV-1 transmission: A prospective cohort study in four US cities (abstract 15). In: Global Strategies for the Prevention of HIV Transmission from Mothers to Infants, Toronto, Ontario, Canada, Abstract 15.

186. Wade NA, Birkhead GS, Warren BL, et al. Abbreviated regimens of zidovudine prophylaxis and perinatal transmission of the human immunodeficiency virus. N Engl J Med. 1998;339:1409.

187. LaFon SW, Lehrman SN, Barry DW. Prophylactically administered Retrovir in health care workers potentially exposed to the human immunodeficiency virus. J Infect Dis. 1988;158:503.

188. LaFon SW, Mooney BD, McMullen JP. A double-blind, placebo-controlled study of the safety and efficacy of Retrovir (zidovudine) as a chemoprophylactic agent in health care workers exposed to HIV (Abstract). In: 30th Interscience Conference on Antimicrob Agents Chemother. Atlanta, Georgia, Abstract 489.

189. Centers for Disease Control and Prevention. Case-control study of HIV seroconversion in health-care workers after percutaneous exposure to HIV-infected blood—France, United Kingdom, and United States, January 1988-August 1994. MMWR Morb Mortal Wkly Rep. 1995;44:929.

190. Henderson DK. Postexposure treatment of HIV—taking some risks for safety's sake. N Engl J Med. 1997;337:1542.

191. Katzenstein TL, Dickmeiss E, Aladdin H, et al. Failure to develop HIV infection after receipt of HIV-contaminated blood and postexposure prophylaxis. Ann Intern Med. 2000;133:31.

192. Ward JW, Deppe DA, Samson S, et al. Human immunodeficiency virus infection from blood donors who later developed the acquired immunodeficiency syndrome. Ann Intern Med. 1987;106:61.

193. Hawkins DA, Asboe D, Barlow K, et al. Seroconversion to HIV-1 following a needle-stick injury despite combination post-exposure prophylaxis. J Infect. 2001;43:12.

194. Perdue B, Wolderufael D, Mellors J, et al. HIV-1 transmission by a needle-stick injury despite rapid initiation of four-drug postexposure prophylaxis. In: 6th Conference on Retroviruses and Opportunistic Infections, Chicago, IL, Abstract 1999;210:107.

195. Lucey D, Milum S, Lindquist C, et al. Pseudofailure of zidovudine prophylaxis after a human immunodeficiency virus-positive needlestick. J Infect Dis. 1990;162:1211.

196. Jochimsen EM, Luo CC, Beltrami JF, et al. Investigations of possible failures of postexposure prophylaxis following occupational exposures to human immunodeficiency virus. Arch Intern Med. 1999;159:2361.

197. Gulick RM. New antiretroviral drugs. Clin Microbiol Infect. 2003;9:186.

198. Lalezari JP, Henry K, O'Hearn M, et al. Enfuvirtide, an HIV-1 fusion inhibitor, for drug-resistant HIV infection in North and South America. N Engl J Med. 2003;342:2175-2185.

199. Beltrami EM, Luo CC, de la Torre N, et al. Transmission of drug-resistant HIV after an occupational exposure despite postexposure prophylaxis with a combination drug regimen. Infect Control Hosp Epidemiol. 2002;23:345.

200. Ammaranond P, Cunningham P, Oelrichs R, et al. Rates of transmission of antiretroviral drug resistant strains of HIV-1. J Clin Virol. 2003;26:153.

201. Grant RM, Hecht FM, Warmerdam M, et al. Time trends in primary HIV-1 drug resistance among recently infected persons. JAMA. 2002;288:181.

202. Leigh Brown AJ, Frost SD, Mathews WC, et al. Transmission fitness of drug-resistant human immunodeficiency virus and the prevalence of resistance in the antiretroviral-treated population. J Infect Dis. 2003;187:683.

203. Little SJ, Holte S, Routy JP, et al. Antiretroviral-drug resistance among patients recently infected with HIV. N Engl J Med. 2002;347:385.

204. Little SJ, Daar ES, D'Aquila RT, et al. Reduced antiretroviral drug susceptibility among patients with primary HIV infection. JAMA. 1999;282:1142.

205. Mayers DL. Prevalence and incidence of resistance to zidovudine and other antiretroviral drugs. Am J Med 1997;10s(Suppl 5B):S70.

206. Simon V, Vanderhoeven J, Hurley A, et al. Evolving patterns of HIV-1 resistance to antiretroviral agents in newly infected individuals. AIDS. 2002;16:1511.

207. Veenstra J, Schuurman R, Cornelissen M, et al. Transmission of zidovudine-resistant human immunodeficiency virus type 1 variants following deliberate injection of blood from a patient with AIDS: Characteristics and natural history of the virus. Clin Infect Dis. 1995;21:556.

208. Imrie A, Beveriidge A, Genn W, et al. Transmission of human immunodeficiency virus type 1 resistant to nevirapine and zidovudine. J Infect Dis. 1997;175:1502.

209. Fitzgibbon JE, Gaur S, Frenkel LD, et al. Transmission from one child to another of human immunodeficiency virus type 1 with a zidovudine-resistance mutation. N Engl J Med. 1993;329:1835.

210. Erice A, Mayers DL, Strike DG, et al. Brief report: Primary infection with zidovudine-resistant human immunodeficiency virus type 1. N Engl J Med. 1993;328:1163.

211. Katlama C, Ingtrand D, Loveday C, et al. Safety and efficacy of lamivudine-zidovudine combination therapy in antiretroviral naive patients: A randomized controlled comparison with zidovudine monotherapy. JAMA. 1996;276:118.

212. Johnson AA, Ray AS, Hanes J, et al. Toxicity of antiviral nucleoside analogs and the human mitochondrial DNA polymerase. J Biol Chem. 2001;276:40847.

213. Sha BE, Proia LA, Kessler HA. Adverse effects associated with use of nevirapine in HIV postexposure prophylaxis for 2 health care workers. JAMA. 2000;284:2723.

214. Centers for Disease Control and Prevention. Serious Adverse Events Attributed to Nevirapine Regimens for Postexposure Prophylaxis After HIV Exposures—Worldwide, 1997—2000. MMWR Morb Mortal Wkly Rep. 2001;49:1153.

215. Johnson S, Chan J, Bennett CL. Hepatotoxicity after prophylaxis with a nevirapine-containing antiretroviral regimen. Ann Intern Med. 2002;137:146.

216. Dybul M, Fauci AS, Bartlett JG, et al. Guidelines for using antiretroviral agents among HIV-infected adults and adolescents. Ann Intern Med. 2002;137:381.

217. Dybul M, Fauci AS, Bartlett JG, et al. Guidelines for using antiretroviral agents among HIV-infected adults and adolescents. Recommendations of the Panel on Clinical Practices for Treatment of HIV. MMWR Recomm Rep. 2002;51:1.

218. Gerberding JL. Clinical practice. Occupational exposure to HIV in health care settings. N Engl J Med. 2003;348:826.

219. Van Rompay KK, McChesney MB, Aguirre NL, et al. Two low doses of tenofovir protect newborn macaques against oral simian immunodeficiency virus infection. J Infect Dis. 2001;184:429.

220. Kumar A, Buch S, Foresman L, et al. Development of virus-specific immune responses in SHIV(KU)-infected macaques treated with PMPA. Virology. 2001;279:97.

221. Smith MS, Foresman L, Lopez GJ, et al. Lasting effects of transient postinoculation tenofovir [9-R-(2-Phosphonomethoxypropyl)adenine] treatment on SHIV(KU2) infection of rhesus macaques. Virology. 2000;277:306.

222. Hodge S, de Rosayro J, Glenn A, et al. Postinoculation PMPA treatment, but not preinoculation immunomodulatory therapy, protects against development of acute disease induced by the unique simian immunodeficiency virus SIVsmmPBj. J Virol. 1999;73:8630.

223. Wang SA, Puro V. Toxicity of post-exposure prophylaxis for human immunodeficiency virus. In: Panlilio L, ed. Balliére's Clinical Infectious Diseases, v. 5. London: Balliére-Tindall; 1999;349.

224. Lee LM, Henderson DK. Tolerability of postexposure antiretroviral prophylaxis for occupational exposures to HIV. Drug Saf. 2001;24:587.

225. Luzzati R, Crosato IM, Mascioli M, et al. Galactorrhoea and hyperprolactinemia associated with HIV postexposure chemoprophylaxis. AIDS. 2002;16:1306.

226. Garcia F, Plana M, Mestre G, et al. Metabolic and immunological effects of antiretroviral agents in healthy individuals receiving post-exposure prophylaxis. Antivir Ther. 2002;7:195.

227. Rabaud C, Bevilacqua S, Beguinot I, et al. Tolerability of postexposure prophylaxis with zidovudine, lamivudine, and nelfinavir for human immunodeficiency virus infection. Clin Infect Dis. 2001;32:1494.

228. Trape M, Barnosky S. Nelfinavir in expanded postexposure prophylaxis causing acute hepatitis with cholestatic features: Two case reports. Infect Control Hosp Epidemiol. 2001;22:333.

229. Wang SA, Panlilio AL, Doi PA, et al. Experience of healthcare workers taking postexposure prophylaxis after occupational HIV exposures: Findings of the HIV Postexposure Prophylaxis Registry. Infect Control Hosp Epidemiol. 2000;21:780.

230. Spenatto N, Viraben R. Early lipodystrophy occurring during post-exposure prophylaxis. Sex Transm Infect. 1998;74:455.

231. Benn PD, Mercey DE, Brink N, et al. Prophylaxis with a nevirapine-containing triple regimen after exposure to HIV-1. Lancet. 2001;357:687.

232. Rey D, L'Heritier A, Lang JM. Severe ototoxicity in a health care worker who received postexposure prophylaxis with stavudine, lamivudine, and nevirapine after occupational exposure to HIV. Clin Infect Dis. 2002;34:418.

233. Centers for Disease Control and Prevention. Public Health Service Task Force recommendations for the use of antiretroviral drugs in pregnant women infected with HIV-1 for maternal health and for reducing perinatal HIV-1 transmission in the United States. MMWR Morb Mortal Wkly Rep. 1998;47:1.

234. Culnane M, Fowler MG, Lee S, et al. Evaluation for late effects of in utero (IU) ZDV exposure among uninfected infants born to HIV+ women enrolled in ACTG 076 and 210. Clin Infect Dis. 1997;25:445, Abstract 485.

235. Blanche S, Tardieu M, Rustin P, et al. Persistent mitochondrial dysfunction and perinatal exposure to antiretroviral nucleoside analogues. Lancet. 1999;354:1084.

236. Smyth AC. Important Drug Warning. Bristol-Myers Squibb Company, 2001. http://www.fda.gov/medwatch/SAFETY/2001/zerit&videx-Letter.html

237. Katz MH, Gerberding JL. Management of occupational and nonoccupational postexposure HIV prophylaxis. Curr Infect Dis Rep. 2002;4:543.
238. Lurie P, Miller S, Hecht F, et al. Postexposure prophylaxis after nonoccupational HIV exposure: Clinical, ethical, and policy considerations. JAMA. 1998;280:1769.
239. Wiebe ER, Comay SE, McGregor M, et al. Offering HIV prophylaxis to people who have been sexually assaulted: 16 months' experience in a sexual assault service. CMAJ. 2000;162:641.
240. Limb S, Kawsar M, Forster GE. HIV post-exposure prophylaxis after sexual assault: The experience of a sexual assault service in London. Int J STD AIDS. 2002;13:602.
241. Havens PL. Postexposure prophylaxis in children and adolescents for nonoccupational exposure to human immunodeficiency virus. Pediatrics. 2003;111:1475.
242. Centers for Disease Control and Prevention. Management of possible sexual, injecting-drug-use, or other nonoccupational exposure to HIV, including considerations related to antiretroviral therapy. Public Health Service statement. Centers for Disease Control and Prevention. MMWR Recomm Rep. 1998;47:1.
243. Babl FE, Cooper ER, Kastner B, et al. Prophylaxis against possible human immunodeficiency virus exposure after nonoccupational needlestick injuries or sexual assaults in children and adolescents. Arch Pediatr Adolesc Med. 2001;155:680.
244. Bamberger JD, Waldo CR, Gerberding JL, et al. Postexposure prophylaxis for human immunodeficiency virus (HIV) infection following sexual assault. Am J Med. 1999;106:323.
245. Lamba H, Murphy SM. Sexual assault and sexually transmitted infections: An updated review. Int J STD AIDS. 2000;11:487.
246. Merchant RC, Keshavarz R. Human immunodeficiency virus postexposure prophylaxis for adolescents and children. Pediatrics. 2001;108:E38.

CHAPTER **305**

Nosocomial Herpesvirus Infections

DAVID K. HENDERSON

Eight herpesviruses commonly infect humans. In addition to the two *Herpes simplex* viruses (HSV), varicella-zoster virus (VZV), cytomegalovirus (CMV), and the Epstein-Barr virus, two recently identified and characterized herpesviruses (human herpesvirus 6 [HHV-6] and human herpesvirus 7 [HHV-7]) cause a spectrum of illness, from the acute childhood febrile illness, roseola (exanthem subitum) to demyelinating disease, lymphoproliferative syndromes, and systemic infections in immunocompromised patients.[1-8] An eighth herpesvirus, a B-cell–tropic agent that is in many aspects similar to EBV, appears to contribute to the occurrence of both body cavity B-cell lymphomas and Kaposi's sarcoma in humans.[5,7] A ninth herpesvirus, *Herpesvirus simiae* is a rare cause of human infection (see Chapter 138). With the clear exception of the varicella-zoster virus (VZV) and the possible exceptions of HHV-6 and HHV-7, the remaining herpesviruses infecting humans apparently require close personal contact for person-to-person spread and are therefore not classified as highly contagious.

Two properties shared by members of this family of viruses are important to emphasize: (1) All of these viruses can, after causing a primary infection, persist in a latent state in the body and subsequently cause recrudescent or reactivation infection; and (2) differentiation of recrudescent infection from primary infection is often difficult and makes identification of true nosocomial infections problematic. Historically, this distinction has often been made on the basis of serological evidence, the reliability of which may be questionable. Because recrudescent infections are common among immunosuppressed patients, they are discussed in detail in the chapters of this book dealing with each of the different viruses.

Herpesviruses have become important nosocomial pathogens for several reasons, including the presence of some of these agents in blood, blood products, and organ transplants and the high prevalence of these infections in the population at large. The purpose of this chapter is to discuss the risk of nosocomial transmission of each of these agents and to discuss appropriate techniques to be used to prevent transmission of these agents to patients and personnel in the hospital.

HERPES SIMPLEX VIRUSES

Risk of Nosocomial Transmission

Transmission of herpes simplex virus (HSV-1 and HSV-2) from infected patients to staff has been well documented.[9-15] Both HSV-1 and HSV-2 have been associated with the occurrence of herpetic whitlow.[10-12,16,17] Primary HSV-1 infection has also been reported after mouth-to-mouth resuscitation.[12] Similarly, Amir reported primary oral HSV infections in four pediatric care providers that occurred, at least apparently, as a result of occupational exposures.[18] In this latter manuscript, the author argues that these infections were likely acquired in the workplace, although no point-source was identified and molecular techniques were not used to assess whether all were infected with similar isolates. Whereas a great deal of attention has been focused on the problem of HSV-2 infection in obstetric and neonatal intensive care unit (ICU) settings, HSV-1 has also been associated with outbreaks of infection in hospital personnel and their families.[19] Once in a nursery or an ICU, for example, an infant with HSV infection may serve as a reservoir for transmission to other infants, although the risk of such transmission appears to be small. Whereas HSV infection occurring as a result of the infant acquiring infection during delivery has been well documented, postpartum acquisition of HSV has been much less common, more difficult to document, and the diagnosis has been made most often on empirical grounds.[20]

Transmission of HSV-1 from staff to patients has also been reported. Linneman and colleagues used restriction enzyme analysis to demonstrate that two cases of HSV-1 infection in neonates in the same nursery were caused by viruses with identical DNA "fingerprints."[21] Sakadka and colleagues reported two clusters of HSV-1 infections at two separate hospitals.[22] Both clusters involved three neonates, and in both instances all three infants had HSV-1 isolates that produced virtually identical endonuclease cleavage profiles. Although not proved definitively, an environmental reservoir (radiant warmer) was incriminated in one cluster. In the other, three infants born at one hospital approximately 1 year apart were infected with strains of HSV-1 that yielded identical restriction endonuclease patterns. The authors postulated that health care workers providing care for these infants developed periodic reactivation of HSV-1 infection resulting in transmission to the infants. Despite these anecdotal reports and despite the fact that the risk has not yet been measured, the risk of iatrogenic transmission of HSV to susceptible patients, including neonates, appears to be quite small.

Mechanism of Nosocomial Transmission

The frequent occurrence of whitlow in ICU personnel, respiratory care personnel, and dentists argues for a primary role for cutaneous inoculations of HSV-1 from oral secretions of infected patients directly into the skin of health care providers. Although many, if not most, whitlows represent primary infection with HSV, reactivation infection or recrudescence can occur,[9,11,16] and one experimental study has demonstrated the possibility for reinfection.[23]

Oral lesions caused by HSV-1 contain large quantities of virus and represent a potential reservoir for nosocomial transmission. For this reason, dental practitioners are at increased risk for occupational infections.[24] In one study oral lesions were found to have an average of greater than 10^8 plaque-forming units per milliliter of vesicular fluid.[25] Moreover, high titers of virus remained in lesions of severely immunocompromised patients for 3 weeks or longer. Turner and colleagues demonstrated that HSV-1 could be cultured from the hands of six of nine adults who had oral lesions.[26] In addition, in the same study HSV-1 isolates were shown to survive drying on skin, plastic, and cloth for up to 4 hours. Both patients and hospital personnel can harbor inapparent reactivation infections. In one prospective study, 9.6% of asymptomatic staff members of an obstetric hospital were found to have HSV in saliva.[27]

HSV-contaminated breast milk has been inferentially incriminated as being responsible for the postpartum transmission of HSV[28]; however, HSV infection of either mother or child is not a contraindication to breast-feeding.

Prevention of Nosocomial Transmission

Use of Universal or Standard Precautions[29] should minimize the risk for transmission of HSV-1. Patients who have extensive oral, genital, or cutaneous disease may require more stringent isolation precautions. All personnel having direct contact with an HSV-infected patient should practice careful handwashing. Personnel performing procedures involving oral or genital secretions (e.g., suctioning, placement of an oral airway, dental work, irrigation of a Foley catheter, dressing changes) should wear gloves. Such patients are a reservoir for whitlow but probably represent minimal risk to other patients, with only the following few exceptions. Patients who have disseminated HSV lesions should not be roomed with immunocompromised patients or with patients who have severe atopic histories or defects in skin integrity (burn patients,[30] eczema, etc.). Alternatively, in a nursery, a neonatal ICU, or a burn ward, such patients are optimally managed using strict isolation or, when possible, cohort nursing.

A special problem arises when the mother of a newborn has active nongenital HSV infection. Kibrick has recommended that the newborn be placed in a private room, that the mother should only be allowed to handle or feed the baby after her lesions have crusted over, and that once the mother has had contact with the baby, the baby be placed on drainage and secretion precautions.[31] Treatment with acyclovir or other effective antiviral agents may hasten the clearing of the lesions. Management of mothers and babies exposed to mothers with genital infections is outlined in Table 305-1 and is also discussed in detail in the literature.[32-38] Optimal care of infants born to infected mothers would include placing the infant in a "special" nursery during hospitalization (for up to 14 days). Such infants should be evaluated frequently for signs of HSV infection. Depending on the stage of the mother's disease (i.e., primary versus secondary) and the extent of disease at delivery (i.e., modest versus extensive), empiric antiviral treatment of the newborn may be appropriate. Many authorities empirically treat infants exposed to the birth canal of a mother who has active HSV infection acquired late in the course of her pregnancy with acyclovir.[32,34,37]

Because the efficacy of antiviral therapy in the setting of neonatal infection is increased when therapy is administered early in the course of the infection, caregivers must maintain a high index of suspicion for neonatal HSV infection in children born to both symptomatic and asymptomatic mothers. Strikingly, neonatal HSV infection frequently occurs in infants born to mothers who had negative histories for past or recent genital HSV infection.[39] Brown and colleagues demonstrated that the approximately one third of women who shed HSV in early labor have recently acquired genital HSV. Infants of mothers who have recently acquired infection were found to be 10 times more likely to develop neonatal HSV infection than infants of women who have asymptomatic reactivation.[36]

Infants developing signs or symptoms of active infection should initially be managed using "Standard Precautions"; if more extensive disease develops, strict isolation or cohort nursing in a private room or in an isolation room in the ICU may be more effective. If such a room is not available, the infant should be separated from other infants in the nursery or ICU. Placing the infant in an incubator or isolette may raise the consciousness of the staff regarding the potential for transmission.[31,40]

Mothers who have active genital lesions should be allowed to feed or handle infants; however, before handling her baby, the mother should cover all lesions, carefully wash her hands, and put on clean hospital garb. If an infant is restricted to an ICU or nursery for life-support purposes, the mother may visit that area if all lesions are crusted over and covered. In addition, in the circumstance in which vaginal delivery by a mother known or suspected of having active genital HSV infection is attempted, fetal scalp monitoring should not be performed because of the risk of infection caused by inoculation.[35,41]

Transmission of the vaccine strain of VZV from recently immunized health care providers is a theoretical possibility but only if the provider has skin lesions. Even then, the risk is very small.

Management of Infected or Exposed Personnel

Hospital personnel who have active oral or other cutaneous infection should not be permitted to care for high-risk patients until the lesions are entirely crusted and dry. Examples of such high-risk patients include premature infants, newborns, severely immunocompromised patients, burn patients, and patients with diseases affecting skin integrity. In the event that an infected individual must work to provide adequate care in a high-risk area, the provider should ensure that dressings (or a mask) cover all lesions. When practical, gloves should be worn. Particularly in situations in which the health care provider has active lesions on the hands, double-gloving may further reduce the risk for exposure. Most importantly, frequent glove changes and strict handwashing techniques (and/or use of alcohol-based hand disinfectants) should be used.

VARICELLA-ZOSTER VIRUS

Risk of Transmission

Of the members of the herpesvirus family, VZV is by far the most contagious. For this reason, most adults have been exposed to the virus and have a prior history of chickenpox (varicella). The risk of transmission is highest in pediatric populations. Among adults, patients and staff from rural areas and locales where the incidence of VZV infection is lower (e.g., Pacific islands, tropical climates) are at highest risk for acquisition.[42]

The major problems with nosocomial transmission of VZV infection occur in areas housing potentially susceptible immunosuppressed patients (e.g., pediatric oncology units). In immunocompetent pa-

TABLE 305-1   Recommendations for Peripartum Care of Pregnant Women with Herpes Simplex Virus (HSV) Infections*

Conditions Present at Term	Status of Membranes	Recommended Route of Delivery
Primary genital lesions present	Intact or ruptured, 4-6 hr	Caesarean section
Primary genital lesions present	Ruptured >4-6 hr	Vaginally
Primary or secondary genital lesions present	Baby has been delivered vaginally	
Secondary genital lesions present	Ruptured >4-6 hr	Vaginally
Secondary genital lesions present	Intact or ruptured <4-6 hr	Caesarean section
No genital lesions but positive cervical culture	Intact or ruptured <4-6 hr	Caesarean section
No genital lesions but positive cervical culture	Ruptured >4-6 hr	Vaginally
No genital lesions but history of prior genital lesions	Intact or ruptured	Vaginally
No genital lesions but nongenital lesions present	Intact or ruptured	Vaginally
No genital or nongenital lesions but history of nongenital lesions	Intact or ruptured	Vaginally

*To attempt to decrease the rate of Caesarean sections, some authorities recommend administering acyclovir prophylaxis, beginning at 38 weeks gestation, to women with past histories of recurrent genital herpes, thereby permitting vaginal delivery.[177]

tients, both primary infections (varicella) and recrudescent VZV infections (herpes zoster) are usually benign, self-limited infections. Although the development of effective antiviral therapy has reduced substantially the risks for severe morbidity and mortality caused by VZV infection for patients who are immunosuppressed, both primary and recrudescent VZV infections continue to be associated with increased morbidity and the potential for mortality for immunosuppressed patients. Finally, some authors have reported that varicella occurring during pregnancy is associated with increased severity (see also Chapter 133).[43,44] The extent to which immunocompromised patients who have had chickenpox are at risk for exogenous reinfection is a matter of some controversy. Several investigators have suggested that immunocompromised patients may be at risk to acquire exogenous reinfection with VZV, either in the form of a second case of chickenpox,[45] or as atypical generalized zoster, a syndrome reported to resemble disseminated zoster without an antecedent dermatome.[46] One epidemiological study has suggested the latter possibility.[47] Whereas primary VZV infection generally produces lifetime protection against exogenous reinfection, rare instances of exogenous reinfection, primarily caused by alterations in host defense, have been documented in the literature.[45,48] One recent study has suggested that exogenous reinfection is more common than previously thought.[45,48]

Mechanisms of Transmission

Nosocomial transmission of VZV infection does occur. Several studies have clearly demonstrated airborne transmission from an index case with varicella to susceptible children.[49-51] A susceptible patient or staff member also may acquire primary infection as a result of direct contact with lesions from a patient with dermatomal zoster.[49] Despite some published evidence suggesting that dermatomal zoster may be transmitted from patient to patient,[49,52,53] most authorities believe that dermatomal zoster represents recrudescent infection rather than a transmissible illness.[54] One study employed endonuclease analysis of viral DNA from varicella and zoster isolates from the same patient to demonstrate the identity of the isolates.[54] One report suggested that a patient with localized zoster was the index case in a nosocomial outbreak of VZV infection.[55] Because the index case was bedfast and several of the secondary cases were younger than 1 year old (and therefore not ambulatory), the authors postulated that the transmission must have occurred either via the airborne route or via the hands of hospital personnel. In any event, such occurrences would appear to be extremely uncommon.

Garnett and co-workers have argued that the presence of varicella in the community may reduce the incidence of zoster among individuals who have latent infection, presumably as a result of an immunologic "boosting" phenomenon arising from the exposure to patients who have varicella.[56]

Prevention of Nosocomial Transmission

Because VZV is highly contagious and because VZV infection may be life threatening, particularly in severely immunosuppressed patient populations, several sets of recommendations regarding techniques to be used to prevent nosocomial transmission of VZV infection have been published.[29,50,57-62] Whenever practical, patients who have active VZV infections should not be hospitalized. If patients with active infections must be hospitalized, most authorities recommend that patients with dermatomal zoster be managed with appropriate barriers (e.g., gloves when touching the patient or the patient's lesions) and that the patient's door be labeled with a sign warning people who have not had chickenpox not to enter the patient's room. Use of the so-called "Standard Precautions" should be adequate for managing patients who have localized zoster.[29] Severely immunocompromised patients who develop dermatomal zoster (i.e., those with hematological or reticuloendothelial malignancies; those with the acquired immunodeficiency syndrome [AIDS]; and those receiving high-dose corticosteroids or multidrug chemotherapy) should be started on antiviral therapy and placed on strict isolation until it is clear that dissemination is not occurring. If new lesions stop occurring and less than

about 20 lesions are outside the dermatome, the patients may be managed with simple barrier (i.e., "Standard") precautions.[29] Patients with varicella or disseminated zoster should be placed on strict isolation precautions. Because of the potential for airborne transmission of VZV, Gustafson and colleagues have recommended that hospitalized patients with varicella be placed downwind from other potentially susceptible patients.[51] Anderson and co-workers documented the absence of VZV transmission over a 1-year period in a pediatrics hospital using negative pressure ventilation rooms.[63]

If a susceptible immunocompromised patient is exposed to a patient with VZV infection, transmission of the infection can be prevented (or the severity of infection reduced) by the administration of hyperimmune globulin (varicella-zoster immunoglobulin [VZIG]). To be effective, VZIG should be administered as soon as possible after exposure. The Centers for Disease Control and Prevention (CDC) recommends that VZIG be given within 96 hours of exposure.[64] VZIGf must be given intramuscularly, which is a problem for anticoagulated or thrombocytopenic patients. The dose is one vial (125 units) per 10 kg body weight up to a maximum of five vials, about 8 to 9 mL. VZIG does not contain merthiolate. For immunocompromised patients unable to take VZIG or who are more than 72 hours postexposure, a 7-day course of antiviral therapy can be considered.

VZV infections are common, and, in spite of good infection control procedures, VZV is frequently introduced into the hospital environment in an uncontrolled fashion. Over the past several years, the use of antiviral agents (e.g., acyclovir) has been shown to be of benefit in patients who have primary or recrudescent VZV infection (reviewed in detail in refs. 65-68). Especially in immunocompromised patients, acyclovir should be begun as early as the first symptoms of infection arise. In addition to the obvious benefit to the infected patient, antiviral therapy will reduce the risk for nosocomial spread of this airborne pathogen. Because of the urgency involved in identifying exposed, susceptible, immunosuppressed patients, an organized approach to a potential outbreak is advisable. We have developed a flow chart to manage potential nosocomial outbreaks of VZV infection (Fig. 305-1).[59] Others have used a similar approach.[58]

Investigating Nosocomial Exposure to VZV

Cases of VZV infection are identified by routine ward rounds, routine surveillance activities, and by referrals from patient care areas. Once a suspected case is identified, the diagnosis is confirmed, either by hospital epidemiology service staff members or by staff of the clinical virology laboratory. First and foremost, the diagnosis of VZV should be confirmed, preferably by direct fluorescent antibody stained smear of vesical fluid. If the suspected diagnosis is incorrect, the investigation is aborted. Once the diagnosis is confirmed, the investigation is divided into two separate areas: (1) the patient-related epidemiological investigation, and (2) the staff-related epidemiological investigation. Because of the necessity for administering passive immunoglobulin prophylaxis to exposed, susceptible, immunocompromised children within 96 hours of exposure to be effective, the initial focus of the investigation is on patients. Similarly, if antiviral prophylaxis is chosen, prompt administration of the agent is important to success. In the event that immunosuppressed staff are potentially exposed, they should be managed in the same expeditious manner as immunosuppressed patients.

An in-hospital "travel history" is first obtained from the index case. As in-hospital exposures may take place in any of a number of patient-related areas, several diverse areas must be considered in history taking (see Fig. 305-1). When any of these areas are included in the patient's travel history, the departmental records from that area should be examined. Patients documented to be in that area at the same time as the index case should be included in the population at risk.

The second component of the patient-related investigation is the direct identification of patients at high risk for severe complications of primary VZV infection (Fig. 305-1). We use three methods to identify such patients: (1) a computer list of all hospitalized pediatric, oncology, and transplant patients; (2) a list of all ambulatory care patients,

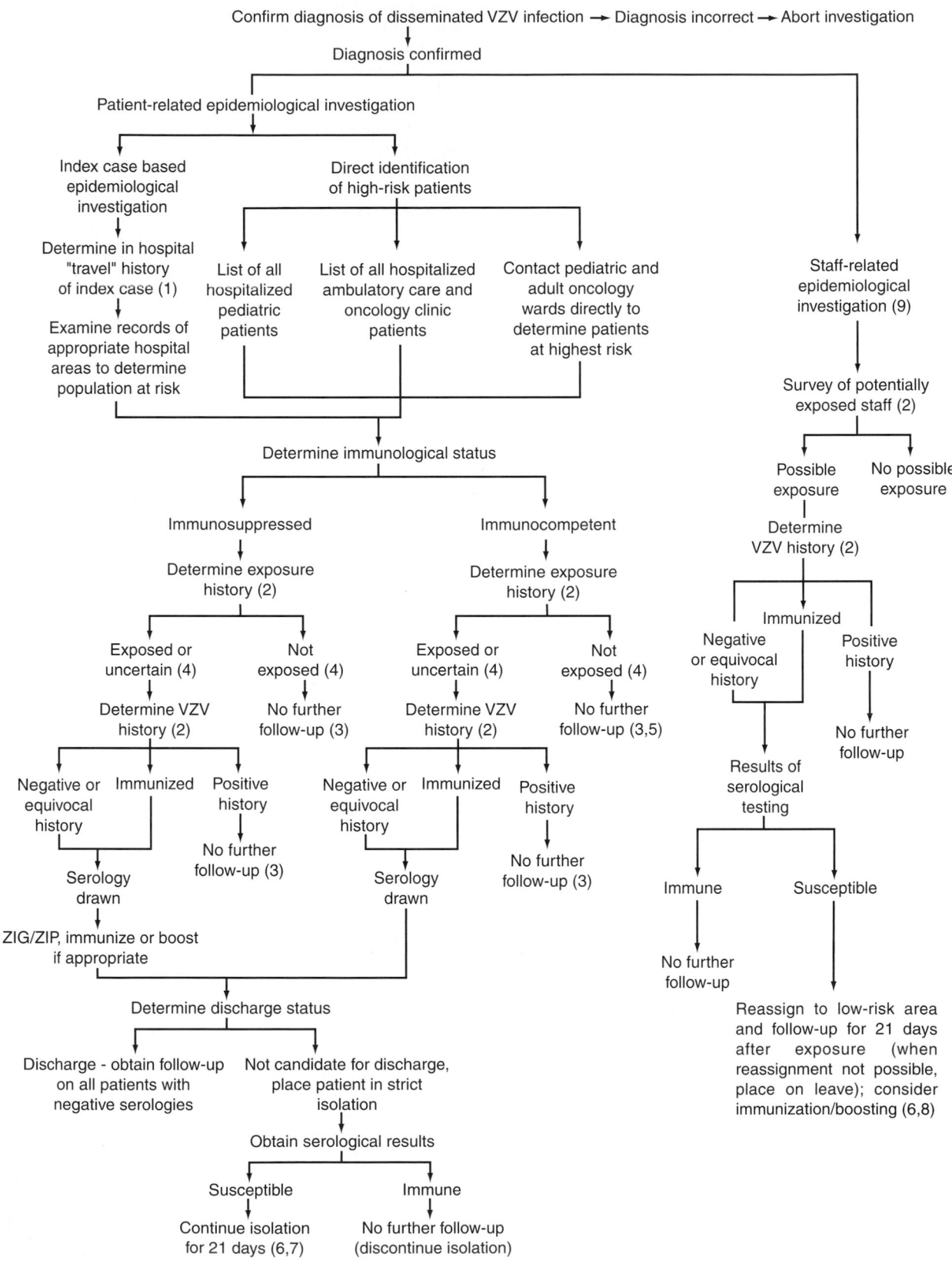

including those children and severely immunosuppressed adults who might be staying outside the hospital, but returning daily for chemotherapy and/or blood drawing; and (3) questioning the inpatient pediatrics, oncology, and transplant staff.

Once the population at risk has been identified, the immunological status of all patients on the list is assessed. If a patient is found to be potentially immunosuppressed (i.e., hematological malignancy receiving chemotherapy, high-dose steroid therapy, congenital or acquired immunodeficiency) the patient and the medical staff are questioned regarding the potential for exposure and for a prior history of chickenpox or prior varicella immunization. If the patient is potentially exposed and has a negative or equivocal history of VZV infection, a baseline serology is drawn and VZIG is administered. Historically, instances have arisen in which VZIG was not available. If such a circumstance arises, blood banks may be able to prepare plasma from patients recovering from zoster (zoster immune plasma [ZIP]), which contains high-titer anti-varicella antibody.[69] In immunocompetent patients within 72 and possibly up to 120 hours from exposure, varicella vaccination should be considered. If a patient is determined to have had primary VZV infection or is determined not to have been exposed, no further follow-up is needed.

If patients on the potentially exposed list are found to be immunocompetent, exposure and VZV histories are obtained after work-up of immunocompromised patients. Exposed, susceptible immunocompetent patients have serologies drawn and, when possible, are discharged. In general, those with negative exposure histories or positive histories of prior VZV infection need no further follow-up.

If patients must remain hospitalized, serological determination of immunity using a sensitive technique, such as fluorescent antimembrane antibody assay (FAMA),[70] immune adherence hemagglutination inhibition assay (IAHIA),[71] or enzyme-linked immunosorbent assay (ELISA)[72] may help determine which exposed patients are susceptible. Less sensitive tests, such as complement fixation, are not reliable indicators of immunity.

Exposed, susceptible, immunocompetent patients should be placed in strict isolation from nine days after the first possible exposure until 21 days after the last possible exposure. Exposed, susceptible, immunosuppressed patients (even those receiving VZIG or ZIP) should be placed in strict isolation at the time the patient is identified as being at risk until at least 21 days after the last possible exposure. Some studies have suggested that administration of ZIP or earlier preparations of VZIG to exposed, susceptible, immunosuppressed patients actually lengthened the incubation period for such patients. Although instances of lengthened incubation periods have not been reported with newer preparations of VZIG, physicians responsible for care of such patients should be mindful of this possibility when planning extended in-hospital care for these patients. Exposed, susceptible, immunosuppressed patients and patients who may become immunosuppressed either as a result of disease progression or therapy may be candidates for the varicella vaccine.[60,73] As noted earlier, acyclovir should be administered to susceptible, exposed immunosuppressed patients at the first suggestion of clinical illness caused by VZV,[67] and some investigators have argued for its prophylactic use in susceptible individuals.[65,67,74-79] A substantial literature exists describing the use of this agent as treatment in immunocompetent patients as well, particularly for adolescents and adults who develop varicella (see Chapter 133).[60,73,80-83]

Management of Infected or Exposed Personnel

The other major aspect of the work-up of a potential nosocomial outbreak of VZV infection is the assessment of potentially exposed staff (Fig. 305-1). Exposure and VZV histories are taken from all potentially exposed staff. Potentially exposed staff who relate negative or equivocal histories of VZV infection should have serologic assessment of immunity using a sensitive test (discussed earlier). Immunocompromised employees should be managed with the same sense of urgency that is used for immunosuppressed patients.

In my view, exposed, susceptible employees should be reassigned to a low-risk area or be placed on administrative leave from 8 days after the first possible exposure until 21 days after the last possible exposure, (although some have advocated a more liberal approach).[84] If employees desiring to work in an area with a high prevalence of VZV infection are found to be susceptible on the basis of assessment of humoral[70-72] and, possibly, cell-mediated[85] im-

---

FIGURE 305-1. Algorithm for the evaluation of a potential nosocomial outbreak of VZV infection.

(1) That is, ward exposure, playroom, recreation, school classroom, radiology, nuclear medicine, physical therapy, occupational therapy, radiation oncology, pulmonary medicine.

(2) VZV history and exposure history are usually obtained simultaneously in the Clinical Center.

(3) Exposed, severely compromised patients with positive histories may be at risk, and obtaining serological confirmation of immunity may be advisable. Exposed immunosuppressed patients who are thought to be capable of mounting a response to immunization and immunocompetent patients who are likely to become immunosuppressed as a result of an underlying disease or therapy may be candidates for immunization.

(4) *Exposed* = one of the following types of exposure to chickenpox or zoster patient(s):
   a. Playmate contact (more than 1 hour of play indoors).
   b. Hospital contact (in same two- to four-bed room or adjacent beds in a large ward).
   c. Newborn contact (newborn of mother who had onset of chickenpox less than 5 days before delivery or within 48 hours after delivery).
   Uncertain = in same location in the hospital as the patient (e.g., radiology waiting room, elevators) but exposure not documented.
   Not Exposed = not meeting criteria listed in the preceding.

(5) Discharged immunocompetent exposed patients in this category should be advised regarding VZV infections, and both the patients and their physicians should be advised that the patient should not be readmitted to the hospital unless absolutely essential. If readmitted, the patient should be placed in strict isolation until 21 days after exposure. Immunocompetent patients may be candidates for immunization.

(6) Some controversy exists regarding the absolute efficacy of zoster immune globulin (ZIG) or zoster immune plasma (ZIP). Some authorities have suggested that ZIG/ZIP may delay onset of VZV and may diminish the severity of symptoms. Clinicians should keep this in mind when assessing duration of isolation or work reassignment. For immunocompetent patients and/or immunosuppressed patients thought to be capable of mounting a response, consider immunization.

(7) Usual incubation period for VZV is 9 to 21 days; hence, the immunocompetent, susceptible exposed patient should be placed in strict isolation 8 days following exposure. Isolation should be continued until 22 days following exposure. In an immunocompromised patient the incubation period may be shorter. Therefore, an exposed, susceptible immunocompromised patient who did not receive prophylaxis should be placed in isolation immediately after the patient is identified as being at risk. If the patient did not receive prophylaxis, isolation should be continued for 21 days following exposure.

(8) Several authorities, including CDC, recommend postexposure immunization of susceptible immunocompetent provides up to 72 and possibly up to 120 hours after exposure. For immunosuppressed providers, VZIG may be appropriate.

(9) Immunosuppressed staff should be assessed with the same urgency as is used with immunosuppressed patients.

munity to VZV, such employees may be candidates for the varicella vaccine.[60-62,73,86-88]

Employees who develop primary VZV infection or zoster should not care for or be in the same area with patients until the last lesion is crusted over (usually 7 or 8 days after the appearance of the last lesion). Employees who have zoster should be reassigned so that they also not work in high-risk areas until all lesions have crusted over.

CYTOMEGALOVIRUS

Risk for Nosocomial Transmission

The nosocomial epidemiology of cytomegalovirus (CMV) infection is incompletely understood. Part of the difficulty in assessing the magnitude of risk for nosocomial transmission lies in the difficulty in discriminating between endogenous reactivation infection and exogenous reinfection (i.e., infection with a second strain of CMV). The term "secondary infection" is used here to encompass both possibilities. In several settings, the risk of an individual patient acquiring CMV infection, either in the hospital or as a result of iatrogenic intervention, appears to be quite high. Premature infants and infants in newborn nurseries are at increased risk for CMV acquisition.[89-92] Studies have suggested that from 14% to 30% of infants residing in a neonatal ICU for longer than 1 month acquire CMV infection.[89-91]

Recipients of organ transplants are also at high risk for both primary and secondary CMV infection. As immunosuppressive regimens have become more powerful, secondary CMV infections have become increasingly more common. One strategy employed to attempt to reduce the incidence of CMV infection in this population is to use newer immunosuppressive regimens in combination with appropriate antiviral chemoprophylaxis.[93] A summary of 12 studies that used various techniques to assess CMV infection in renal transplant recipients demonstrated that 53% of seronegative transplant recipients acquired infection, and 85% of seropositive transplant recipients either shed virus or developed a fourfold rise in anti-CMV antibody titer.[94] Because these results include some studies that used only complement fixation to document infection, these numbers probably represent conservative estimates of the risk of a renal transplant recipient acquiring CMV infection. Heart transplant recipients are also at high risk for CMV infection. In an early study 62% of seronegative heart transplant patients seroconverted post-transplant, and 60% of patients who were seropositive before heart transplantation developed fourfold rises in antibody titer after transplantation.[95] Recipients of allogeneic stem cell transplants are also at increased risk for CMV reactivation, particularly if graft versus host disease is present.[96,97] In one study published in 1982, 39% of all seronegative stem cell transplant recipients acquired primary infection, and 61% of seropositive bone marrow recipients developed evidence of secondary CMV infection.[97] With current stem cell transplantation techniques, transmission of CMV from donor to seronegative recipient is uncommon.

Recipients of granulocyte transfusions have also been demonstrated to be at risk for acquiring CMV infection. In the study cited in the preceding,[97] 48% of seronegative bone marrow recipients who received granulocyte transfusions seroconverted compared with 33% of seronegative recipients who did not receive granulocyte transfusions. In an earlier study, Winston and colleagues demonstrated that 61% of patients receiving granulocyte transfusions developed evidence of CMV infection compared to 26% of age- and disease-matched recipients.[98]

Several studies have suggested that the transfusion of fresh whole blood is also implicated in the transmission of CMV. The risk for acquisition of CMV has been shown to be associated with increasing numbers of units transfused. With older techniques, the risk of acquiring CMV infection was estimated to be between 2.4% and 2.7% per unit of transfused whole blood.[99,100] High risk recipients now receive whole blood either from a seronegative donor or blood that has been filtered to deplete leukocytes, decreasing CMV transmission to 1% to 4% (see Chapter 311). Although the risk for CMV transmission by parenteral exposure seems clear, the issue of whether hospital patients or hospital personnel are at risk for acquiring CMV by nonparenteral

routes of exposure is less clear. Although apparently uncommon, nonparenteral transmission of CMV from patient to patient has been reasonably well documented.[101,102] Breast milk has been implicated as a source of primary neonatal infection.[101,103-105] One study definitively documented nonparenteral spread of CMV among three infants in a neonatal ICU by using restriction endonuclease analysis.[101] The author concluded, however, that such common-source outbreaks are apparently uncommon. In a similar study, Aitken and colleagues evaluated a cluster of five CMV infections in a special care nursery, concluding that the infections were not epidemiologically linked.[106] In a study using similar technology, Demmler and co-workers demonstrated patient-to-patient transmission of a single strain of CMV in a busy chronic care pediatrics hospital.[102] The authors isolated CMV from patients' hands, health care workers' hands, and from hospitalized infants' diapers.

The issue of whether hospital personnel are at risk for acquiring CMV infection is a controversial one. Some investigators have suggested that hospital personnel are at slightly higher risk for seroconversion than are age-matched controls who did not have patient contact.[107] Conversely, the intensive studies by Ahlfors and colleagues in Sweden found little evidence that nurses were at greater risk to acquire CMV infection than other age-matched Swedish women.[108] A study using restriction enzyme analysis of CMV DNA demonstrated no correlation between the CMV strain infecting a neonate and the strain of CMV found to be infecting a nurse who cared for the infant.[109] In a second study using similar technology, significant differences were found in DNA from CMV isolates obtained from a physician who became infected while caring for a CMV-infected child and the isolate from the child.[110] In both studies the health care professionals were pregnant, and both elected to have abortions. CMV with identical restriction patterns to the maternal isolates was grown from each of the infected fetuses.

Several additional studies have suggested minimal or negligible risk for patient-to-staff transmission of CMV.[102,111-113] Balfour and Balfour compared CMV infection rates in three groups of nurses—those working in neonatal ICUs, those working in renal transplant/dialysis units, and student nurses—with age-matched blood donors.[111] No association was found between prevalence of infection among patients and CMV seroconversion, and these authors concluded that nurses were no more likely to develop CMV infection than were the age-matched blood donor controls.

Demmler and colleagues also found no association between CMV seroconversion and occupational exposure to CMV in two pediatric hospitals in Texas.[102] This study also found no correlation between prevalence of infection in patients and seroconversion in health care providers. Adler and co-workers used restriction endonucleases to evaluate CMV isolates from 34 hospitalized newborn infants and from the one seronegative health care worker who developed primary CMV infection during a 3-year study period.[112] No two isolates were identical.

Finally, because patients who are infected with the human immunodeficiency virus (HIV) (particularly those who have AIDS) are known to harbor and shed large quantities of herpesviruses, Gerberding and colleagues evaluated health care workers providing care for HIV-1–infected patients for serologic evidence of CMV infection and failed to find an elevated rate of CMV acquisition.[113]

Conversely, other investigators, while failing to demonstrate patient-to-staff transmission of CMV, have postulated that the risk for transmission is likely to be higher for personnel working with patients who have high prevalence of CMV infection.[114,115] Although such a hypothesis seems plausible, to my knowledge no direct evidence supports this contention.

At this time there are no instances of patient-to-staff transmission of CMV that have been linked by molecular analysis of the CMV isolates. One investigator has, however, used endonuclease analysis to document apparent nonparenteral transmission of CMV from an infected infant to his seronegative mother.[101] Thus, the magnitude of the risk of patient-to-staff transmission of CMV, especially when appropriate isolation procedures are observed, would appear to be small.

Mechanisms of Nosocomial Transmission

In instances in which primary infection with CMV is documented to have occurred in the hospital setting, the parenteral route of transmission has almost always been implicated.

Most primary infections in the neonatal ICU can be traced to the transfusion of whole blood contaminated with CMV.[89,90,92,99,100] Consumption of breast milk contaminated with CMV has been suggested to be an important nonparenteral mechanism of transmission of CMV to neonates.[101,103-105] The possibility also has been raised, but not to my knowledge documented, that fomites or health care professionals may be vectors for nonparenteral transmission of CMV in unusual circumstances.

Renal transplant recipients can acquire primary CMV infection from blood transfusions, from leukocyte infusions,[116] or from the transplanted organ itself.[117] Recipients of bone marrow allografts can acquire CMV infection through receipt of an infected allograft, through transfused blood or platelets, or through infected leukocyte infusions.[101,118] If nonparenteral transmission is occurring in the hospital, it occurs uncommonly and, if it occurs, would likely be due to exposure of susceptible individuals (patients or employees) to contaminated excreta or secretions, presumably via the oral or respiratory routes.

Prevention of Nosocomial Transmission

Several measures can be implemented to minimize the risk of CMV transmission in a high-risk setting in the hospital. Choosing organ donors who are seronegative for renal transplant recipients who are seronegative is an effective way of minimizing the risk for subsequent CMV infection in this setting. Betts and colleagues were among the first to advocate using the donor serologic status as a major determinant in selecting a donor kidney for a seronegative recipient.[119] Winston and co-workers have suggested that seronegative donors be given priority as potential leukocyte donors, because of the evidence that CMV is leukocyte associated and that the development of CMV infection in recipients of leukocytes is often a serious problem.[98]

Transfusing patients at high risk for CMV infection with either leukocyte-depleted blood[74,120,121] or with washed, frozen red cells[122] is being used routinely to reduce the risk of CMV transmission, although one recent paper has suggested that neither is as effective as using CMV-seronegative donors.[123] Thus, the risk for transfusion-associated CMV disease can be reduced substantially by using CMV-seronegative donors, by using frozen, deglycerolized red blood cells, and by using products that have the leukocytes removed with filters. The relative efficacy of these three approaches remains somewhat controversial; however, efficacy of all three approaches has been demonstrated. Some investigators have suggested that adding back potentially cytotoxic donor T-lymphocytes a month or more following transplantation may help control graft-versus-host disease, help preserve a graft-versus-leukemia effect, and help reduce the risk for serious CMV infections in allogeneic bone marrow transplantation patients.[124-127] The use of specific anti-CMV immunoglobulin (CMVIG) has been associated with a reduction in CMV-associated morbidity in solid organ transplant recipients and patients at risk for CMV disease.[128-131]

Prophylactic and/or preemptive treatment with antivirals, particularly with ganciclovir, has also been used to reduce risks for infection, reactivation, and/or severe sequelae of CMV infection, particularly in transplant recipients. In one such study preemptive therapy with ganciclovir prevented all except one case of CMV disease prior to day 100 after transplantation after detection of CMV antigenemia.[123] Several studies have demonstrated the benefit of combinations of antiviral and immunoglobulin prophylaxis in the prevention of CMV disease in the transplantation setting.[74,129,132-135]

Because most pregnant women secreting CMV in cervical mucus are asymptomatic, and, unlike infection with the herpes simplex viruses, because perinatal infection with CMV is not associated with symptomatic illness in the newborn, no precautions are advocated for mothers known to be secreting CMV at delivery.

Immunosuppressed patients who are infected with CMV (e.g., patients with AIDS, transplant recipients, or babies with congenital infection) excrete large quantities of virus in many different body fluids. Appropriate precautions for such patients should include gloves for contact with wounds or lesions or for contact with blood, secretions, or excreta. Also, infected patients in the neonatal ICU should be segregated from noninfected babies. Other precautions advisable in caring for such patients would include handling linens and other reusable patient care items as isolation materials and emphasizing hand hygiene after each patient contact. In general, strict adherence to "Standard Precautions" should minimize the already small risk for occupational/nosocomial infection with CMV.[29]

Management of Infected, Exposed, and Potentially Exposed Personnel

The risk for staff-to-patient transmission of CMV has received little attention in the literature. To my knowledge, only one study has attempted to assess this risk. Demmler and colleagues found no evidence of CMV transmission among patients cared for by four CMV-shedding health care workers.[102] These authors concluded that, although a theoretical possibility, the risk for staff-to-patient transmission of CMV was sufficiently small to allow infected health care workers to continue working.[102] Based on currently available evidence regarding the transmission and transmissibility of CMV, such an approach seems entirely reasonable.

The issue of limiting exposure of pregnant health care workers to CMV-infected patients remains somewhat controversial. Although, as noted earlier, data documenting CMV transmission from patient to staff are nonexistent, a commonsense approach to the care of infected patients is appropriate. In an earlier edition of this text,[136] I recommended that pregnant health care workers be restricted from taking care of patients with CMV infection. Several factors subsequently caused our Hospital Infections Committee to reassess this difficult and controversial issue.

First, a number of additional articles (see "Risk for Nosocomial Transmission," earlier) have been published further documenting that the risk for occupational/nosocomial infection with CMV is quite small. Because the number of seroconversions in these studies is small, a very large study would be required to measure the magnitude of the small risk of CMV transmission to health care workers precisely. Nonetheless, the expanded, consistent database is reassuring.

Second, numerous investigators have pointed out that many patients who excrete CMV (e.g., immunosuppressed patients, AIDS patients, dialysis patients, transplant recipients) have no signs or symptoms of CMV infection. Such patients are frequently not identified as being infected or infectious during the course of hospitalization. In fact, most patients shedding CMV who are hospitalized will not be specifically identified as having CMV infection; for this reason a broader approach to our patient population seems prudent.

Third, because the magnitude of risk to pregnant health care workers is currently below the limits of detection, the administrative problems associated with a more restrictive policy may not be justified (i.e., if pregnant health care workers are restricted, how should one manage health care workers who "think they might be" or "are trying to become" or "are not trying to prevent" becoming pregnant?).

Fourth, the issuance by the CDC,[29,137] and the subsequent requirement for implementation by both the US Department of Labor's Occupational Safety and Health Administration (OSHA) of Universal Precautions guidelines,[138] should reduce the already small risk for CMV transmission from patients to health care workers.

An initial clarification of the Universal Precautions policy noted that these precautions do not apply to feces, urine, saliva, sweat, sputum, or tears.[139] In this update, the CDC emphasizes that Universal Precautions are supplementary or baseline precautions and that these new precautions are not designed to replace standard infection control policy. Specifically, this update notes that prior CDC guidelines recommended wearing gloves to prevent gross microbial contamination of hands. This latter recommendation deserves careful consideration when handling urine from any patient. Although Universal Precautions do not apply to saliva, the previous recommendation for gloving prior to digital examination of mucous membranes remains in effect. The subsequent issuance of the "Standard Precautions" guidelines by CDC underscore the importance of using barriers for contact with all body fluids.

These new recommendations also allow the health care worker to use judgment in deciding whether or not barriers (such as gloves) are needed. These new guidelines emphasize the importance of hand hygiene, which, if practiced appropriately, should minimize the risk for occupational CMV infection.

Finally, the issue of routine screening of health care workers for antibody to CMV is also controversial. Whereas several articles have addressed this complex issue,[140-142] the lack of consensus is apparent. The CDC does not advocate routine screening.[140] Conversely, Adler[142] and Plotkin[141] support periodic serologic testing for "potentially pregnant" employees whose jobs entail exposure to CMV-infected patients. Onorato and colleagues argue that no data indicate that routine testing will have any impact on the risk of congenital CMV infection.[140] Our Hospital Infections Committee and Occupational Medical Service have decided not to offer routine screening of employees. Because the risk for patient-to-staff transmission is, as yet, unmeasurable and because adherence to Universal Precautions will further reduce this risk, we do not recommend reassignment of pregnant health care workers. Rather, we have chosen to educate staff aggressively regarding CMV and other occupational risks, and to emphasize the importance of good hygiene and Universal/Standard Precautions during pregnancy. For all these reasons, we do not recommend reassignment of pregnant health care workers.

EPSTEIN-BARR VIRUS

Risk for Nosocomial Transmission

The risk of nosocomial transmission of Epstein-Barr virus (EBV) appears to be very small. Several instances of nosocomial transmission of EBV to patients have been identified.[143-154] Secondary infections (the majority of which appear to be reactivation of latent infection in the immunosuppressed transplant recipient) may be associated with a lymphoproliferative disorder (reviewed in refs. 155-158). As the overwhelming majority of these infections represent recrudescence, rather than acquired infection, they are discussed in more detail in Chapter 135.

Transmission of EBV from patient to staff or staff to patient has not been described, although Ginsburg and colleagues have described an outbreak of infectious mononucleosis in personnel working in an outpatient clinic,[151] and Chang and colleagues have described the apparent transmissibility of EBV in a relatively crowded nursery providing domiciliary care.[152] One epidemiological study found a possible risk for occupational acquisition of EBV among dentists and dental students.[159]

Mechanisms of Transmission

Patients who have been shown to have acquired nosocomial EBV infection have been recipients of blood or plasma transfusions,[143-150,154] solid organ transplants,[160] and bone marrow allografts[153,161] apparently infected with EBV. In addition, one study has demonstrated evidence of EBV DNA in breast milk.[162] EBV appears to be one of the least contagious of the herpesviruses, and most authorities believe that intravenous inoculation or intimate contact is required for transmission of the virus.

Prevention of Nosocomial Transmission

Patients known to have EBV in their secretions may be a reservoir for infection if health care workers follow extremely poor hygiene practices. In 1975, the CDC recommended that patients with infectious mononucleosis be placed on secretion precautions.[163] In more recent recommendations the CDC states that isolation precautions are not necessary but adds the codicil that oral secretions may be infectious.[164] Adherence to Universal/Standard Precautions, use of appropriate barriers, and attention to hand hygiene will further reduce the risk for occupational infection. As is the case for CMV infection in transplantation, some investigators have found a benefit of infusing donor-specific lymphocytes as "adoptive immunotherapy" to treat the EBV-associated lymphoproliferative disorders.[156,158,165,166]

Management of Infected or Exposed Personnel

Staff who acquire infection with EBV (e.g., infectious mononucleosis) may excrete virus much longer than symptoms persist,[167] but if good hygienic practices are followed (e.g., hand hygiene) personnel presumably represent an extremely small risk to transmit the infection.

HUMAN HERPESVIRUS 6 AND HUMAN HERPESVIRUS 7

Risk for Nosocomial Transmission

HHV-6 and HHV-7 are somewhat similar, β-subgroup herpesviruses that are most closely related to CMV. HHV-6 (first called human B-lymphotropic virus[6]) was identified as a human pathogen in the mid- and late 1980s.[8] Subsequently this virus has been shown to be a cause of *Roseola infantum* (*Exanthem subitum*) (see Chapter 136).[168,169] This childhood exanthem is reasonably contagious and may present a risk for nosocomial transmission, particularly in pediatric hospitals. Acute HHV-6 infection has also been associated with both a mononucleosis-like syndrome, as well as a self-limited hepatitis.[170] A clear association between HHV-6 infection and acute febrile seizures has now been established, as well.[171] In addition, HHV-6 has been associated with several less common syndromes, including encephalitis, disseminated infection, and perhaps pneumonia. This virus also may complicate solid organ transplantation as well as bone marrow transplantation. HHV-6 has also been found (presumably as an opportunist) in peripheral blood of AIDS patients.[8]

HHV-7 was initially identified in 1990.[172] Initial studies failed to identify a disease process associated with HHV-7 infection.[173,174] HHV-7 is frequently found in human saliva,[174] and, similar to HHV-6, is a T-lymphotropic virus. Although HHV-7 infection has clearly been associated with febrile syndromes in young children and with a syndrome similar to roseola (usually occurring in children older than 2 years of age), studies have yet to identify a definitive infection syndrome in most children infected with this newly identified herpesvirus.

Mechanisms of Transmission

Although demonstrating a reasonably high level of contagion, HHV-6 is likely transmitted from oral secretions. Data describing the epidemiology and putative routes of transmission of HHV-6 remain somewhat ambiguous. Although the nosocomial epidemiology of infection with HHV-6 remains indistinct, a conservative approach to the management of this infection in the hospital seems prudent. As is suggested by the "Standard Precautions" guidelines, secretions (including oral secretions) from all patients should be considered potentially infectious, and pediatric care providers should pay special attention to the potential for cross-contamination in nurseries. Most care providers are likely to be immune to HHV-6 infection because of prior infection.

Prevention of Nosocomial Transmission

Virtually nothing is known about the nosocomial epidemiology of HHV-6 and HHV-7. Because of the apparent contagiousness of roseola, hospitalized patients who have roseola should be treated similarly to patients with VZV infection (see "Prevention of Nosocomial VZV Transmission," earlier). Until definitive data are available to address the nosocomial transmissibility of HHV-6, using the VZV (i.e., airborne) model for prevention seems reasonable. Techniques for establishing the diagnosis of HHV-7 infection are in their infancy and are not generally available.

In the unusual instance in which the diagnosis of HHV-7 is established, use of Standard Precautions for such patients seems prudent. Based on the fact that children who acquire HHV-7 infection are generally older than those who acquire HHV-6 infection, HHV-7 appears to be less transmissible than HHV-6. At a minimum, in the absence of defined infection syndromes associated with HHV-7 infection, use of Standard Precautions for these patients should provide adequate protection.

HUMAN HERPESVIRUS 8

Risk for Nosocomial Transmission

HHV-8 is a gamma herpesvirus that is most closely related to EBV. HHV-8 has been closely associated with Kaposi's sarcoma and (in combination with EBV) body-cavity lymphoma in patients who have human immunodeficiency virus infection. HHV-8 was initially identified in 1994.[175,176] The viral DNA sequence has been isolated from patients who have Kaposi's sarcomas that are both HIV-related and unrelated to HIV infection or infection risk (i.e., patients who have classical Mediterranean Kaposi's sarcoma). Little is known about the epidemiology of HHV-8 and almost nothing is known about the potential for nosocomial transmission. Initial data suggest that the virus is most likely acquired during or after adolescence. By analogy, the epidemiology of HHV-8 may be similar to that of EBV. Based on these preliminary data, Standard Precautions should also be an effective management strategy for patients infected with HHV-8. Optimal management of needlestick exposures to source patients known to harbor HHV-8 remains undefined.

REFERENCES

1. Black JB, Pellett PE. Human herpesvirus 7. Rev Med Virol. 1999;9:245.
2. Caserta MT, Mock DJ, Dewhurst S. Human herpesvirus 6. Clin Infect Dis. 2001;33:829.
3. Clark DA. Human herpesvirus 6. Rev Med Virol. 2000;10:155.
4. Clark DA, Griffiths PD. Human herpesvirus 6: Relevance of infection in the immunocompromised host. Br J Haematol. 2003;120:384.
5. Lee LM, Henderson DK. Emerging viral infections. Curr Opin Infect Dis. 2001;14:467.
6. Salahuddin SZ, Ablashi DV, Markham PD, et al. Isolation of a new virus, HBLV, in patients with lymphoproliferative disorders. Science. 1986;234:596.
7. Levy JA. Three new human herpesviruses (HHV6, 7, and 8). Lancet. 1997;349:558.
8. Lopez C, Pellett P, Steward J, et al. Characterizations of human herpesvirus-6. J Infect Dis. 1988;157:1271.
9. Crane L, Lerner A. Herpetic whitlow: A manifestation of primary infection with herpes simplex virus type 1 or type 2. J Infect Dis. 1978;137:855.
10. Gunbay T, Gunbay S, Kandemir S. Herpetic whitlow. Quintessence Int. 1993;24:363.
11. Gill M, Arlette J, Buchan K. Herpes simplex virus infections of the hand. A profile of 79 cases. Am J Med. 1988;84:89.
12. Hendricks A, Shapiro E. Primary herpes simplex infection following mouth-to-mouth resuscitation. JAMA. 1980;243:257.
13. Perl TM, Haugen TH, Pfaller MA, et al. Transmission of herpes simplex virus type 1 infection in an intensive care unit. Ann Intern Med. 1992;117:584.
14. Rosato F, Rosato E, Plotkin S. Herpetic paronychia—an occupational hazard of medical personnel. N Engl J Med. 1964;270:979.
15. Stern H, Elenck S, Millar D, et al. Herpetic whitlow: A form of cross-infection in hospitals. Lancet. 1959;2:871.
16. Haburchak D. Recurrent herpetic whitlow due to herpes simplex virus type 2. Arch Intern Med. 1978138;1418,
17. Glogau R, Hanna L. Herpetic whitlow as part of genital virus infection. J Infect Dis. 1977;136:689.
18. Amir J, Nussinovitch M, Kleper R, et al. Primary herpes simplex virus type 1 gingivostomatitis in pediatric personnel. Infection. 1997;25:310.
19. Adams G, Stover B, Keenlyside R, et al. Nosocomial herpetic infections in a pediatric intensive care unit. Am J Epidemiol. 1981;113:126.
20. Light I. Postnatal acquisition of herpes simplex virus by the newborn infant: A review of the literature. Pediatrics. 1979;63:480.
21. Linneman CJ, Buchman T, Light I, et al. Transmission of herpes simplex virus, type 1 in a nursery for the newborn: Identification of viral isolates by DNA fingerprinting. Lancet. 1978;1:964.
22. Sakadka H, Saheki Y, Uzuki K, et al. Two outbreaks of herpes simplex virus, type 1 nosocomial infection among newborns. J Clin Microbiol. 1986;24:36.
23. Blank H, Haines H. Experimental reinfection with herpes simplex virus. J Invest Dermatol. 1973;61:223.
24. Anders PL, Drinnan AJ, Thines TJ. Infectious diseases and the dental office. NY State Dent J. 1998;64:29.
25. Daniels C, LeGoff S. Shedding of infectious virus/antibody complexes from vesicular lesions of patients with recurrent herpes labialis. Lancet 1975;2:524.
26. Turner R, Shehab Z, Osborne K, et al. Shedding and survival of herpes simplex virus from "fever blisters." Pediatrics. 1982;70:547.
27. Hatherly L, Hayes K, Jack I. Herpes virus in an obstetric hospital: II. Asymptomatic virus excretion in staff members. Med J Aust. 1980;2:273.
28. Dunkle L, Schmidt R, O'Connor D. Neonatal herpes simplex infection possibly acquired via maternal breast milk. Pediatrics. 1979;63:250.
29. Garner JS. Guideline for isolation precautions in hospitals. The Hospital Infection Control Practices Advisory Committee. Infect Contr Hosp Epidemiol. 1996;17:53.
30. McGill SN, Cartotto RC. Herpes simplex virus infection in a paediatric burn patient: Case report and review. Burns. 2000;26:194.
31. Kibrick S. Herpes simplex infection at term: What to do with mother, newborn, and nursery personnel. JAMA. 1980;243:157.
32. Enright AM, Prober CG. Neonatal herpes infection: Diagnosis, treatment and prevention. Semin Neonatol. 2002;7:283.
33. Eskild A, Jeansson S, Stray-Pedersen B, et al. Herpes simplex virus type-2 infection in pregnancy: No risk of fetal death: Results from a nested case-control study within 35,940 women. Br J Obstet Gynecol. 2002;109:1030.
34. Baker DA. Issues and management of herpes in pregnancy. Int J Fertil Womens Med. 2002;47:129.
35. Brown ZA, Wald A, Morrow RA, et al. Effect of serologic status and cesarean delivery on transmission rates of herpes simplex virus from mother to infant. JAMA. 2003;289:203.
36. Brown ZA, Selke S, Zeh J, et al. The acquisition of herpes simplex virus during pregnancy. N Engl J Med. 1997;337:509.
37. Whitley RJ, Kimberlin DW. Treatment of viral infections during pregnancy and the neonatal period. Clin Perinatol. 1997;24:267.
38. Smith JR, Cowan FM, Munday P. The management of herpes simplex virus infection in pregnancy. Br J Obstet Gynaecol. 1998;105:255.
39. Garland SM. Neonatal herpes simplex: Royal Women's Hospital 10-year experience with management guidelines for herpes in pregnancy. Aust N Z J Obstet Gynaecol. 1992;32:331.
40. Gibbs RS, Mead PB. Preventing neonatal herpes—current strategies. N Engl J Med. 1992;326:946.
41. Kaye E, Dooling E. Neonatal herpes simplex meningoencephalitis associated with fetal scalp monitor electrodes. Neurology (NY). 1981;31:1045.
42. Nassar N, Touma H. Brief report: Susceptibility of Filipino nurses to the varicella zoster virus. Infect Contr. 1986;1986:71.
43. Triebwasser J, Harris R, Bryant R, et al. Varicella pneumonia in adults. Report of seven cases and a review of the literature. Medicine (Baltimore). 1967;46:409.
44. Ali ME. Varicella zoster during pregnancy: A strategy for prevention. J Obstet Gynaecol. 2001;21:17.
45. Gershon A, Steinberg S, Gelb L. Clinical reinfection with varicella zoster virus. J Infect Dis. 1984;149:137.
46. Schimpff S, Serpick A, Stoler B, et al. Varicella-zoster infection in patients with cancer. Ann Intern Med. 1972;76:241.
47. Morens D, Bregman D, West M, et al. An outbreak of varicella-zoster virus infection among cancer patients. Ann Intern Med. 1980;93:414.
48. Hall S, Maupin T, Seward J, et al. Second varicella infections: are they more common than previously thought? Pediatrics. 2002;109:1068.
49. Wreghitt TG, Whipp PJ, Bagnall J. Transmission of chickenpox to two intensive care unit nurses from a liver transplant patient with zoster. J Hosp Infect. 1992;20:125.
50. Leclair J, Zaia J, Levin M, et al. Airborne transmission of chickenpox in a hospital. N Engl J Med. 1980;302:450.
51. Gustafson T, Lavely G, Brawner E, et al. An outbreak of airborne nosocomial varicella. Pediatrics. 1982;70:550.
52. Feinstein A, Trau H, Schewach-Millet M. Herpes zoster in a husband and wife. Int J Dermatol. 1980;19:514.
53. Berlin B, Campbell T. Hospital-acquired herpes zoster following exposure to chickenpox. JAMA. 1970;211:1831.
54. Straus SE, Reinhold W, Smith HA, et al. Endonuclease analysis of viral DNA from varicella and subsequent zoster infections in the same patient. N Engl J Med. 1984;311:1362.
55. Asano Y, Iwayama S, Miyata T, et al. Spread of varicella in hospitalized children having no direct contact with an indicator zoster case and its prevention by a live vaccine. Biken J. 1980;23:157.
56. Garnett GP, Grenfell BT. The epidemiology of varicella-zoster virus infections: The influence of varicella on the prevalence of herpes zoster. Epidemiol Infect. 1992;108:513.
57. Josephson A, Karanfil L, Gombert ME. Strategies for the management of varicella-susceptible healthcare workers after a known exposure. Infect Contr Hosp Epidemiol. 1990;11:309.
58. Hayden G, Meyers J, Dixon R. Nosocomial varicella. II. Suggested guidelines for management. West J Med. 1979;130:300.
59. Laniak J, Myers R, Henderson D. Algorithm for the control of nosocomial varicella zoster virus infections. In: Proceedings of the 82nd Annual Meeting of the American Society for Microbiology, Washington, DC, p 87.
60. Centers for Disease Control and Prevention: Prevention of varicella: Recommendations of the Advisory Committee on Immunization Practices (ACIP). Centers for Disease Control and Prevention. MMWR Morb Mortal Wkly Rep. 1996;45:1.
61. Weber DJ, Rutala WA, Hamilton H. Prevention and control of varicella-zoster infections in healthcare facilities. Infect Control Hosp Epidemiol. 1996;17:694.
62. Sepkowitz KA. Occupationally acquired infections in health care workers. Part I. Ann Intern Med. 1996;125:826.
63. Anderson J, Bonner M, Scheifele D, et al. Lack of nosocomial spread of varicella in a pediatric hospital with negative pressure ventilated rooms. Infect Contr. 1985;6:120.
64. Centers for Disease Control. Varicella zoster immune globulin. MMWR Morb Mortal Wkly Rep. 1981;30:15.
65. Arvin AM. Management of varicella-zoster virus infections in children. Adv Exp Med Biol. 1999;458:167.
66. Waugh SM, Pillay D, Carrington D, et al. Antiviral prophylaxis and treatment (excluding HIV therapy). J Clin Virol. 2002;25:241.
67. Arvin AM. Antiviral therapy for varicella and herpes zoster. Semin Pediatr Infect Dis. 2002;13:12.

68. Dwyer DE, Cunningham AL. 10: Herpes simplex and varicella-zoster virus infections. Med J Aust. 2002;177:267.
69. Balfour H, Groth K, McCullough J, et al. Prevention or modification of varicella using zoster immune plasma. Am J Dis Child. 1977;131:693.
70. Williams V, Gershon A, Brunell P. Serologic response to varicella-zoster membrane antigens measured by indirect immunofluorescence. J Infect Dis. 1974;130:669.
71. Gershon A, Kalter Z, Steinberg S. Detection of antibody to varicella-zoster virus by immune adherence hemagglutination. Proc Soc Exp Biol Med. 1976;151:762.
72. Stanley J, Myers M, Edmond B, et al. An enzyme-linked immunosorbent assay for detection of antibody to varicella zoster virus. J Clin Microbiol. 1982;15:205.
73. Centers for Disease Control and Prevention. Prevention of varicella. Update recommendations of the Advisory Committee on Immunization Practices (ACIP). MMWR Recomm Rep. 1999;48:1.
74. Sullivan KM, Dykewicz CA, Longworth DL, et al. Preventing opportunistic infections after hematopoietic stem cell transplantation: The Centers for Disease Control and Prevention, Infectious Diseases Society of America, and American Society for Blood and Marrow Transplantation Practice Guidelines and beyond. Hematology (Am Soc Hematol Educ Program) 2001;392.
75. Pandya A, Wasfy S, Hebert D, et al. Varicella zoster infection in pediatric solid-organ transplant recipients: A hospital-based study in the prevaricella vaccine era. Pediatr Transplant. 2001;5:153.
76. Kanda Y, Mineishi S, Saito T, et al. Long-term low-dose acyclovir against varicella-zoster virus reactivation after allogeneic hematopoietic stem cell transplantation. Bone Marrow Transplant. 2001;28:689.
77. Yoshikawa T, Suga S, Kozawa T, et al. Persistence of protective immunity after postexposure prophylaxis of varicella with oral aciclovir in the family setting. Arch Dis Child. 1998;78:61.
78. Lin TY, Huang YC, Ning HC, et al. Oral acyclovir prophylaxis of varicella after intimate contact. Pediatr Infect Dis J. 1997;16:1162.
79. Huang YC, Lin TY, Chiu CH. Acyclovir prophylaxis of varicella after household exposure. Pediatr Infect Dis J. 1995;14:152.
80. Ogilvie MM. Antiviral prophylaxis and treatment in chickenpox. A review prepared for the UK Advisory Group on Chickenpox on behalf of the British Society for the Study of Infection. J Infect. 1998;36(Suppl 1):31.
81. Wallace MR, Bowler WA, Murray NB, et al. Treatment of adult varicella with oral acyclovir. A randomized, placebo-controlled trial. Ann Intern Med. 1992;117:358.
82. Balfour HJ, Kelly JM, Suarez CS, et al. Acyclovir treatment of varicella in otherwise healthy children. J Pediatr. 1990;116:633.
83. Balfour HJ, Rotbart HA, Feldman S, et al. Acyclovir treatment of varicella in otherwise healthy adolescents. The Collaborative Acyclovir Varicella Study Group. J Pediatr. 1992;120:627.
84. Rado J, Tako J, Geder L, et al. Herpes zoster house epidemic in steriod-treated patients. Arch Intern Med. 1965;116:329.
85. Gershon A, Steinberg S, Smith M. Cell-mediated immunity to varicella zoster virus demonstrated by viral inactivation with human leukocytes. Infect Immun. 1976;13:1549.
86. O'Neill J, Buttery J. Varicella and paediatric staff: current practice and vaccine cost-effectiveness. J Hosp Infect. 2003;53:117.
87. Qureshi M, Gordon SM, Yen-Lieberman B, et al. Controlling varicella in the health-care setting: barriers to varicella vaccination among healthcare workers. Infect Contr Hosp Epidemiol. 1999;20:516.
88. Lussier N, Weiss K, Laverdiere M. Varicella-zoster screening and management programs in healthcare facilities in Canada. Infect Control Hosp Epidemiol. 1999;20:562.
89. Ballard R, Drew L, Hufnagle K, et al. Acquired cytomegalovirus infection in preterm infants. Am J Dis Child. 1979;133:482.
90. Spector S, Schmidt W, Ticknor W, et al. Cytomegaloviruria in older infants in intensive care units. J Pediatr. 1979;59:444.
91. Spector S, Spector D. Molecular epidemiology of cytomegalovirus infection in premature twin infants and their mother. Pediatr Infect Dis. 1982;1:405.
92. Yeager A, Grumet F, Hufleigh E, et al. Prevention of transfusion-acquired cytomegalovirus infections in newborn infants. J Pediatr. 1981;98:281.
93. Singh N, Gayowski T, Wagener M, et al. Pulmonary infections in liver transplant recipients receiving tacrolimus. Changing pattern of microbial etiologies. Transplantation. 1996;61:396.
94. Glenn J. Cytomegalovirus infections following renal transplantation. Infect Dis. 1981;3:1151.
95. Pollard R, Arvin A, Gamberg P, et al. Specific cell-mediated immunity and infections with herpes viruses in cardiac transplant recipients. Am J Med. 1982;73:679.
96. Serody JS, Shea TC. Prevention of infections in bone marrow transplant recipients. Infect Dis Clin North Am. 1997;11:459.
97. Hersman J, Meyers J, Thomas E, et al. The effect of granulocyte transfusions on the incidence of cytomegalovirus infection after allogeneic marrow transplantation. Ann Intern Med. 1982;96:149.
98. Winston D, Winston S, Howell C, et al. Cytomegalovirus infections associated with leukocyte transfusions. Ann Intern Med. 1980;93:671.
99. Armstrong J, Tarr G, Youngblood L, et al. Cytomegalovirus infection in children undergoing open heart surgery. Yale J Biol Med. 1976;49:83.
100. Prince A, Szmuness W, Millian S, et al. A serologic study of cytomegalovirus infections associated with blood transfusions. N Engl J Med. 1971;284:1125.
101. Spector S. Transmission of cytomegalovirus among infants in hospital documented by restriction-endonuclease-digestion analyses. Lancet. 1983;1:378.
102. Demmler G, Yow M, Spector S, et al. Nosocomial cytomegalovirus infections within two hospitals caring for infants and children. J Infect Dis. 1987;156:9.
103. Bryant P, Morley C, Garland S, et al. Cytomegalovirus transmission from breast milk in premature babies: Does it matter? Arch Dis Child Fetal Neonat Ed. 2002;87:F75.
104. Stiehm ER, Keller MA. Breast milk transmission of viral disease. Adv Nutr Res. 2001;10:105.
105. Hayes K, Danks D, Gibas H. Brief recordings: Cytomegalovirus in human milk. N Engl J Med. 1972;287:177.
106. Aitken C, Booth J, Booth M, et al. Molecular epidemiology and significance of a cluster of cases of CMV infection occurring on a special care baby unit. J Hosp Infect. 1996;34:183.
107. Yeager A. Longitudinal, serological study of cytomegalovirus infections in nurses and in personnel without patient contact. J Clin Microbiol. 1975;2:448.
108. Ahlfors K. Epidemiological studies of congenital cytomegalovirus infection. Scand J Infect Dis. 1982;34(Suppl):1.
109. Yow M, Lakeman A, Stagno S, et al. Use of restriction enzymes to investigate the source of a primary cytomegalovirus infection in a pediatric nurse. Pediatrics. 1982;70:713.
110. Wilfert C, Huang E, Stagno S. Restriction endonuclease analysis of cytomegalovirus deoxyribonucleic acid as an epidemiologic tool. Pediatrics. 1982;70:717.
111. Balfour C, Balfour H Jr. Cytomegalovirus is not an occupational risk for nurses in renal transplant and neonatal units. Results of a prospective surveillance study. JAMA. 1986;256:1909.
112. Adler S, Baggett J, Wilson M, et al. Molecular epidemiology of cytomegalovirus in a nursery: Lack of evidence for nosocomial transmission. Pediatrics. 1986;108:117.
113. Gerberding JL. Incidence and prevalence of human immunodeficiency virus, hepatitis B virus, hepatitis C virus, and cytomegalovirus among health care personnel at risk for blood exposure: final report from a longitudinal study. J Infect Dis. 1994;170:1410.
114. Dworsky M, Welch K, Cassady G, et al. Occupational risk for primary cytomegalovirus infection among pediatric health-care workers. N Engl J Med. 1983;309:950.
115. Pass R. Epidemiology and transmission of cytomegalovirus. J Infect Dis. 1985;152:243.
116. Lang D, Ebert P, Rodgers B, et al. Reduction of post-transfusion cytomegalovirus infection following use of leukocyte-depleted blood. Transfusion. 1977;17:391.
117. Ho M, Suwausirikul S, Dowling J, et al. The transplanted kidney as a source of cytomegalovirus infection. N Engl J Med. 1975;293:1109.
118. Stagno S, Reynolds D, Pass R, et al. Breast milk and the risk of cytomegalovirus infection. N Engl J Med. 1980;302:1073.
119. Betts R. Cytomegalovirus vaccine in renal transplants. Ann Intern Med. 1979;91:780.
120. Roback JD. CMV and blood transfusions. Rev Med Virol. 2002;12:211.
121. Preiksaitis JK, Sandhu J, Strautman M. The risk of transfusion-acquired CMV infection in seronegative solid-organ transplant recipients receiving non-WBC-reduced blood components not screened for CMV antibody (1984 to 1996): experience at a single Canadian center. Transfusion. 2002;42:396.
122. Brady M, Milan J, Anderson D, et al. Use of deglycerolized red blood cells to prevent post-transfusion infection with cytomegalovirus in neonates. J Infect Dis. 1984;150:334.
123. Nichols WG, Price TH, Gooley T, et al. Transfusion-transmitted cytomegalovirus infection after receipt of leukoreduced blood products. Blood. 2003;101:4195.
124. Dazzi F, Goldman JM. Adoptive immunotherapy following allogeneic bone marrow transplantation. Annu Rev Med. 1998;49:329.
125. Barrett AJ, Mavroudis D, Tisdale J, et al. T cell-depleted bone marrow transplantation and delayed T cell add-back to control acute GVHD and conserve a graft-versus-leukemia effect. Bone Marrow Transplant. 1998;21:543.
126. Couriel D, Canosa J, Engler H, et al. Early reactivation of cytomegalovirus and high risk of interstitial pneumonitis following T-depleted BMT for adults with hematological malignancies. Bone Marrow Transplant. 1996;18:347.
127. Mavroudis DA, Read EJ, Molldrem J, et al. T cell-depleted granulocyte colony-stimulating factor (G-CSF) modified allogenic bone marrow transplantation for hematological malignancy improves graft CD34+ cell content but is associated with delayed pancytopenia. Bone Marrow Transplant. 1998;21:431.
128. Kocher AA, Bonaros N, Dunkler D, et al. Long-term results of CMV hyperimmune globulin prophylaxis in 377 heart transplant recipients. J Heart Lung Transplant. 2003;22:250.
129. Morales E, Andres A, Gonzalez E, et al. Prophylaxis of cytomegalovirus disease with ganciclovir or anti-CMV immunoglobulin in renal transplant recipients who receive antilymphocytic antibodies as induction therapy. Transplant Proc. 2002;34:73.
130. Snydman DR. Historical overview of the use of cytomegalovirus hyperimmune globulin in organ transplantation. Transpl Infect Dis. 2001;3(Suppl 2):6.
131. Falagas ME, Snydman DR, Ruthazer R, et al. Cytomegalovirus immune globulin (CMVIG) prophylaxis is associated with increased survival after orthotopic liver transplantation. The Boston Center for Liver Transplantation CMVIG Study Group. Clin Transplant. 1997;11:432.
132. Valantine HA, Luikart H, Doyle R, et al. Impact of cytomegalovirus hyperimmune globulin on outcome after cardiothoracic transplantation: A comparative study of combined prophylaxis with CMV hyperimmune globulin plus ganciclovir versus ganciclovir alone. Transplantation. 2001;72:1647.
133. van der Bij W, Speich R. Management of cytomegalovirus infection and disease after solid-organ transplantation. Clin Infect Dis. 2001;3(Suppl 1):S32.
134. Zamora MR. Use of cytomegalovirus immune globulin and ganciclovir for the prevention of cytomegalovirus disease in lung transplantation. Transpl Infect Dis. 2001;3(Suppl 2):49.
135. Nakamura R, Cortez K, Solomon S, et al. High-dose acyclovir and pre-emptive ganciclovir to prevent cytomegalovirus disease in myeloablative and non-myeloablative allogeneic stem cell transplantation. Bone Marrow Transplant. 2002;30:235.

136. Henderson D. Nosocomial herpesvirus infections. In: Mandell G, Douglas R, Bennett J, eds. Principles and Practice of Infectious Diseases. New York: Churchill Livingstone; 1985:1630.

137. Centers for Disease Control. Recommendation for prevention of HIV transmission in health-care settings. MMWR Morb Mortal Wkly Rep. 1987;36(Suppl 2):1.

138. Department of Labor (OSHA). Occupational exposure to bloodborne pathogens; final rule. Fed Regist. 1991;56:64175.

139. Centers for Disease Control. Update: Universal precautions for prevention of transmission of human immunodeficiency virus, hepatitis B virus, an other bloodborne pathogens in health care settings. MMWR Morb Mortal Wkly Rep. 1988;37:277.

140. Onorato I, Morens D, Martone W, et al. Epidemiology of cytomegalovirus infections: Recommendations for prevention and control. Rev Infect Dis. 1985;7:479.

141. Plotkin S. Cytomegalovirus in hospitals. Pediatr Infect Dis. 1986;5:177.

142. Adler S. Nosocomial transmission of cytomegalovirus. Pediatr Infect Dis. 1986;5:239.

143. Gerber P, Walsh J, Rosenblum E, et al. Association of Epstein-Barr infection with the post-perfusion syndrome. Lancet. 1969;1:593.

144. Purtilo D, Paquin L, Sakamota K, et al. Persistent transfusion-associated infectious mononucleosis with transient acquired immunodeficiency. Am J Med. 1980;68:437.

145. Blacklow N, Watson B, Miller G, et al. Mononucleosis with heterophil antibodies: Epstein-Barr virus infection acquisition by an elderly patient in hospital. Am J Med. 1971;51:549.

146. Corey L, Stamm W, Feorino P, et al. HBsAg-negative hepatitis in a hemodialysis unit: Relation of Epstein-Barr virus. N Engl J Med. 1975;293:1273.

147. Solem J, Jorgensen W. Accidentally transmitted infectious mononucleosis: Report of a case. Acta Med Scand. 1969;186:433.

148. Turner A, MacDonald R, Cooper B. Transmission of infectious mononucleosis by transfusion of pre-illness plasma. Ann Intern Med. 1972;77:751.

149. Virolainen M, Anderson L, Lalla M, et al. T-lymphocyte proliferation in mononucleosis. Clin Immunol Immunopathol. 1973;2:114.

150. Henle W, Henle G, Harrison F, et al. Antibody responses to the Epstein-Barr virus and cytomegalovirus after open-heart and other surgery. N Engl J Med. 1970;282:1068.

151. Ginsburg C, Henle G, Henle W. An outbreak of infectious mononucleosis among the personnel in an outpatient clinic. Am J Epidemiol. 1976;104:571.

152. Chang R, Rosen L, Kapikian A. Epstein-Barr virus infections in a nursery. Am J Epidemiol. 1981;113:22.

153. Sullivan J, Wallen W, Johnson F. Epstein-Barr virus infection following bone-marrow transplantation. Int J Cancer. 1978;22:132.

154. Tattevin P, Cremieux AC, Descamps D, et al. Transfusion-related infectious mononucleosis. Scand J Infect Dis. 2002;34:777.

155. Yachie A, Kanegane H, Kasahara Y. Epstein-Barr virus-associated T-/natural killer cell lymphoproliferative diseases. Semin Hematol. 2003;40:124.

156. Cohen JI. Benign and malignant Epstein-Barr virus-associated B-cell lymphoproliferative diseases. Semin Hematol. 2003;40:116.

157. Patel R, Paya CV. Infections in solid-organ transplant recipients. Clin Microbiol Rev. 1997;10:86.

158. O'Reilly RJ, Small TN, Papadopoulos E, et al. Biology and adoptive cell therapy of Epstein-Barr virus-associated lymphoproliferative disorders in recipients of marrow allografts. Immunol Rev. 1997;157:195.

159. Herbert AM, Bagg J, Walker DM, et al. Seroepidemiology of herpes virus infections among dental personnel. J Dent. 1995;23:339.

160. Cen H, Breinig MC, Atchison RW, et al. Epstein-Barr virus transmission via the donor organs in solid organ transplantation: Polymerase chain reaction and restriction fragment length polymorphism analysis of IR2, IR3, and IR4. J Virol. 1991;65:976.

161. Epstein JB, Phillips K, Sherlock CH. Viral serology after bone marrow transplantation. Viral Immunol. 1991;4:133.

162. Junker AK, Thomas EE, Radcliffe A, et al. Epstein-Barr virus shedding in breast milk. Am J Med Sci. 1991;302:220.

163. Centers for Disease Control. Isolation Techniques for Use in Hospitals. 2nd ed. Washington, DC: Government Printing Office, 1975.

164. Garner J, Simmons B. Guidelines for isolation precautions in hospitals. Infect Contr. 19834(Suppl):245.

165. Little RF, Yarchoan R. Treatment of gammaherpesvirus-related neoplastic disorders in the immunosuppressed host. Semin Hematol. 2003;40:163.

166. Heslop HE, Rooney CM. Adoptive cellular immunotherapy for EBV lymphoproliferative disease. Immunol Rev. 1997;157:217.

167. Miller G, Niederman J, Andrews L. Prolonged oropharyngeal excretion of Epstein-Barr virus after infectious mononucleosis. N Engl J Med. 1973;288:229.

168. Watanabe T, Kawamura T, Jacob SE, et al. Pityriasis rosea is associated with systemic active infection with both human herpesvirus-7 and human herpesvirus-6. J Invest Dermatol. 2002;119:793.

169. Yamanishi K, Shiraki K, Kondo T, et al. Identification of human herpesvirus-6 as a causal agent for Exanthem subitum. Lancet. 1988;1:1065.

170. Irving WL, Chang J, Raymond DR, et al. Roseola infantum and other syndromes associated with acute HHV6 infection. Arch Dis Child. 1990;65:1297.

171. Hall CB, Long CE, Schnabel KC, et al. Human herpesvirus-6 infection in children. A prospective study of complications and reactivation. N Engl J Med. 1994;331:432.

172. Frenkel N, Schirmer EC, Wyatt LS, et al. Isolation of a new herpesvirus from human CD4+ T cells. Proc Natl Acad Sci USA. 1990;87:748.

173. Frenkel N, Wyatt LS. HHV-6 and HHV-7 as exogenous agents in human lymphocytes. Dev Biol Stand. 1992;76:259.

174. Wyatt LS, Frenkel N. Human herpesvirus 7 is a constitutive inhabitant of adult human saliva. J Virol. 1992;66:3206.

175. Ambroziak JA, Blackbourn DJ, Herndier BG, et al. Herpes-like sequences in HIV-infected and uninfected Kaposi's sarcoma patients. Science. 1995;268:582.

176. Chang Y, Cesarman E, Pessin MS, et al. Identification of herpesvirus-like DNA sequences in AIDS-associated Kaposi's sarcoma. Science. 1994;266:1865.

177. Scott LL, Sanchez PJ, Jackson GL, et al. Acyclovir suppression to prevent cesarean delivery after first-episode genital herpes. Obstet Gynecol. 1996;87:69.

CHAPTER **306**

Infections in the Immunocompromised Host: General Principles

J. PETER DONNELLY

BEN E. DE PAUW

An intact defense system offers protection against most microbial aggressors through a complex interrelationship of protecting surfaces, cells, and soluble factors. Good general condition, optimal nutritional status, and normal organ function, together with granulocytes and other components of the cellular and humoral immune system, provide protection against potentially pathogenic microorganisms. The resident flora normally does not cause infection and may protect against pathogens by competing for binding sites on the surfaces and for the available nutrients.

Infection is a principal cause of morbidity and mortality in immunocompromised patients. Hence, a comprehensive understanding of the possible causes of infectious complications and the predisposing factors involved, as well as a comprehensive anti-infective strategy, is imperative when offering these patients care. The attending physician has to be particularly aware of all potential risk factors for infection, including those related to the underlying disease and its treatment, because although susceptibility to infection is increased, timely diagnosis of the cause is seldom possible in immunocompromised patients

DEFICIENCIES IN COMPONENTS OF HOST DEFENSES

Appreciation of the predisposing risk factors is an essential but perplexing exercise in that it suggests that the respective factors each play an independent role. Theoretically, a specific deficiency increases the patient's susceptibility to the very pathogens that are eradicated by that particular host defense mechanism (Table 306-1). Although a basic pattern is recognizable, the types and severity of infectious complications are often unpredictable. Single, isolated deficiencies are virtually never encountered, and malfunction of one part of the system influences several other components. Moreover, therapeutic interventions and the underlying disease itself will perturb a range of defense mechanisms. Although the risks associated with granulocytopenia are well known, other toxicities, especially those affecting the mucosal barrier, has come to assume greater importance than was the case previously. The advent of aggressive treatment methods has changed the classic concept of specific defects of host defense mechanisms in the various types of diseases, the effects of chemotherapy and irradiation now being the primary factors determining the nature and extent of the defect. Patients with impaired humoral immunity as manifested by defective opsonization and phagocytosis of bacteria will also be exposed to chemotherapy-induced neutropenia or deficient cellular immunity as a result of treatment with purine analogues.

TABLE 306-1 Immunodeficiencies and Associated Prevalent Pathogens

Defect	Pathogen
Granulocytopenia	Gram-positive cocci
	Staphylococcus aureus
	Coagulase-negative staphylococci
	(*epidermidis, haemolyticus, hominis*)
	Viridans group streptococci (*mitis, oralis*)
	Enterococci (*faecalis, faecium*)
	Gram-negative bacilli
	Escherichia coli
	Pseudomonas aeruginosa
	Klebsiella pneumoniae
	Enterobacter and *Citrobacter* species
Damaged integument	
Skin–central venous catheter related	Coagulase negative staphylococci
	(*epidermidis, haemolyticus, hominis*)
	Staphylococcus aureus
	Stenotrophomonas maltophilia
	Pseudomonas aeruginosa
	Acinetobacter species
	Corynebacteria
	Candida species (*albicans, parapsilosis*)
	Rhizopus species
Oral mucositis	Viridans group streptococci (*mitis, oralis*)
	Enterococci (*faecalis* and *faecium*)
	Capnocytophaga species
	Fusobacterium species
	Stomatococcus mucilaginosus (*Rothia mucilaginosa*)
	Candida species (*albicans, tropicalis, glabrata*)
	Herpes simplex virus
Neutropenic enterocolitis	*Clostridium* species (*septicum, tertium*)
	Staphylococcus aureus
	Pseudomonas aeruginosa
Impaired cellular immunity	Herpesviruses
	Cytomegalovirus
	Respiratory viruses
	Listeria monocytogenes
	Nocardia species
	Mycobacterium tuberculosis
	Atypical mycobacteria
	Pneumocystis jeroveci
	Aspergillus species
	Cryptococcus species
	Histoplasma capsulatum
	Coccidioides species
	Penicillium marneffei
	Toxoplasma gondii
Impaired humoral immunity	*Streptococcus pneumoniae*
	Haemophilus influenzae
Compromised organ function	
Spleen	*Streptococcus pneumoniae*
	Haemophilus influenzae
	Neisseria meningitidis
Iron overload from blood transfusions	*Rhizopus* species

Granulocytes

Under normal circumstances, neutrophils, sometimes accompanied by eosinophils, congregate at the site of inflammation and are followed by macrophages. Formation of this inflammatory exudate is the result of activation of humoral factors and normal function of the vascular endothelium (see Chapter 8). Meanwhile, in the peripheral blood, granulocytosis evolves as a consequence of release of the marrow reserve and increased granulocytopoiesis, which is regulated by hematopoietic growth factors such as interleukin-3, granulocyte-macrophage colony-stimulating factor, and granulocyte colony-stimulating factor.

Virtually all cytotoxic drugs used in the treatment of malignant diseases have a deleterious effect on the proliferation of normal hematopoietic progenitor cells. Therefore, after destruction of the mitotic pool and depletion of the marrow pool reserve, granulocytopenia ensues. Likewise, therapeutic radiation can induce clinically important granulocytopenia, depending on the dose rate, total dose given, and irradiated area of the body. Total body irradiation, as used in hematopoietic stem cell (HSC) transplant procedures, is the most obvious illustration of the possible negative impact of irradiation. Thus profound neutropenia is an unavoidable consequence of the treatment of malignancy and may persist for 3 to 4 weeks or even longer. Granulocytopenia or a treatment-related decrease in the granulocyte count is probably the most important primary risk factor for infection. Fever develops in nearly all patients with a granulocyte count less than 100/mm³ for more than 3 weeks, whereas only one fifth of the febrile episodes in cancer patients occur when granulocyte counts are normal.[1] Moreover, during iatrogenic granulocytopenia, the risk of infection and infection-related mortality increases proportionally with time.

The presence of granulocytes at the infected site is irrelevant if they are not able to function normally. Both chemotherapeutic drugs and irradiation also interfere with these nonproliferating cells and their function. Such interference may result in decreased chemotaxis, diminished phagocytic capacity, and defective intracellular killing by granulocytes. Glucocorticosteroids seem to enhance granulocytopoiesis and mobilize the marginal and the marrow pool reserve, but these supposedly positive effects on neutrophilic granulocytes are counterbalanced by numerous disadvantages. These drugs curb the accumulation of neutrophils at the site of inflammation by reducing their adherent capacity and diminishing their chemotactic activity. Furthermore, they decrease phagocytosis and intracellular killing of microorganisms. The lack of functioning neutrophils deprives the host of a primary defense mechanism against invading microorganisms, which are consequently able to readily establish themselves, initiate local infection, disseminate unhindered, and eventually lead to fulminant sepsis and death unless treated promptly and effectively.

Cellular and Humoral Immunity

The cellular immune system serves to eliminate intracellular pathogens and virus-infected cells from the body (see Chapter 9). Normal macrophages have a limited capacity for killing ingested microorganisms, and various organisms are even able to survive and replicate inside the cell, unless the macrophage becomes activated. Activation of macrophages is a complex process primarily under the control of cytokines. Both antigen-specific and antigen-nonspecific cells contribute to the development of cellular immunity. The antigen-specific branch of cell-mediated immunity can be divided into two major categories. One category involves cytotoxic effector cells, which are able to lyse virus-infected or foreign lymphocytes and macrophages. The second category involves subpopulations of T cells that mediate delayed-type hypersensitivity reactions after antigen recognition when an antigen is displayed together with the major histocompatibility complex on the surface of specialized antigen-presenting cells.

This fine-tuned system can easily be deregulated by congenital defects or defects acquired as a result of a disease or its treatment. Long-term cytotoxic therapy, extensive irradiation, and immunosuppressive drugs such as corticosteroids, cyclophosphamide, azathioprine, cyclosporine, tacrolimus, and sirolimus suppress cellular immunity. An increasing array of monoclonal antibodies are being used as antitumor and immunosuppressive agents, some with profound and prolonged effects on cellular immunity. Purine analogues, including fludarabine and cladribine, are particularly detrimental to cellular immunity and create a situation similar to acquired immunodeficiency syndrome. Likewise, malignant lymphomas, particularly Hodgkin's disease, are associated with impaired cellular immunity. Allogeneic HSC transplantation brings about a long-lasting dysfunction of T and B cells, especially in association with graft-versus-host disease and its treatment (Table 306-2). The coordination of cellular immunity is often lost, and when aided and abetted by suppressed humoral immunity, the paracrine mediators released go on to induce the sepsis cascade, which may culminate in multiorgan failure instead of arresting infection.[2]

The humoral branch of the immune system, which is primarily responsible for clearing extracellular bacteria, involves the interaction of B cells with antigen and their subsequent proliferation and differentiation into antibody-secreting plasma cells (see Chapter 6). An important difference in antigen recognition by T cells and B cells is that the latter can recognize some antigens without the help of an antigen-presenting cell. The humoral system can identify a plethora of bacterial or viral microorganisms, as well as the soluble proteins that they release. When challenged by an antigen, immunoglobulins are produced that bind to the antigen. The specific functions of immunoglobulin G and immunoglobulin M (IgM) include neutralization of the antigen, as well as complement activation and opsonization, that is, enhancement of phagocytosis of the antigen by neutrophils and macrophages. Secretory immunoglobulin A (IgA), which is found on mucosal surfaces, is not an opsonin but nonetheless inhibits the motility of bacteria and prevents them from adhering to epithelial cells. The production of immunoglobulins is decreased in lymphoproliferative disorders such as chronic lymphocytic leukemia and multiple myeloma,

TABLE 306-2 Sequence of Infective Events in Relation to the Phases of Allogeneic Bone Marrow Transplantation

	Early Phase	Mid-recovery Phase	Late Phase
Host Defense Mechanisms without Graft-versus-Host Disease			
Phagocytes	Absent	Deficient	Normal
Integument			
Skin	Damaged	Damaged	Intact
Mucous membranes	Severely damaged	Damaged	Intact
Cellular immunity	Slightly impaired	Impaired	Impaired
Humoral immunity	Normal	Impaired	Severely impaired
Host Defense Mechanisms with Graft-versus-Host Disease			
Phagocytes	Absent	Deficient	Normal
Integument			
Skin	Damaged	Damaged	Damaged
Mucous membranes	Damaged	Severely damaged	Damaged
Cellular immunity	Slightly impaired	Severely impaired	Severely impaired
Humoral immunity	Normal	Impaired	Severely impaired
Prevalent Infections			
Mucositis	Herpes simplex virus	Herpes simplex virus	Herpes simplex virus
	Viridans streptococci	*Candida* species	*Candida* species
Lung	Gram-negative bacilli	Cytomegalovirus	*Streptococcus pneumoniae*
	Aspergillus species	*Aspergillus* species	Viruses
			Pneumocystis jirovecii
Blood	Viridans streptococci	Staphylococci	
	Staphylococci	*Streptococcus pneumoniae*	
	Gram-negative bacilli	*Candida* species	*Neisseria meningitidis*
	Candida species		

whereas humoral immunity is generally well preserved in patients with acute leukemia. However, intensive radiotherapy and chemotherapy will lead not only to neutropenia but ultimately also to hypogammaglobulinemia.

The spleen is the principal organ for eliminating particles that are not opsonized, and it is left to the macrophages that occupy strategic positions within the organ to remove them. The primary immunoglobulin response also takes places in the spleen. Spleen-produced specific opsonizing antibodies are necessary for efficient phagocytosis of encapsulated bacteria. Splenectomy may result in a reduced level of the complement factor properdin and thereby lead to suboptimal opsonization,[3] a decrease in functional tuftsin, and low levels of circulating IgM.[4] The lack of opsonizing antibodies in serum against common encapsulated bacteria impairs the activity of all phagocytic cells, including granulocytes, monocytes, and macrophages. As a consequence, infections with *Streptococcus pneumoniae* and *Haemophilus influenzae* are often more severe in splenectomized patients, as well as in those who have received a HSC transplant and are functionally asplenic.

Physical Barriers: The Integument

The skin, the respiratory tract (including the nasal cavity), the ears and conjunctiva, the alimentary tract, and the genitourinary tract are in contact with the environment (Fig. 306-1) and provide a first line of defense against microbial invasion. The skin and the mucosal surfaces of the alimentary tract form the two principal barriers against microbial invasion. Both surfaces are normally colonized with a variety of microorganisms, including many different genera of bacteria and yeast that have an intimate association with a particular ecologic niche and help maintain the function and integrity of this first line of defense. When intact and healthy, both the mucosa and skin are capable of resisting colonization with the allochthonous organisms found in the immediate environment, as long as an ecologic balance is maintained within the indigenous microbial flora. Acidity plays a crucial role both in disinfecting the stomach and in regulating the microbial milieu of the vagina. The integrity of the mucosa, production of saliva and mucus, peristalsis, bile acids, digestive enzymes, and levels of secretory IgA also play an important role in maintaining a favorable microecol-

ogy.[5,6] Elimination of an inoculum is achieved by sneezing and coughing of microbes trapped in mucus, whereas flushing of the mouth and esophagus by saliva, as well as micturition and peristalsis, inhibit continuous intimate contact between a given surface area and unattached invasive microorganisms.

The Skin

Healthy skin provides an effective barrier against invasion by microorganisms, mainly by remaining intact. Desquamation helps limit the opportunities for transient organisms to establish residence. Normally, very little water is present on the skin surface. Colonization with organisms sensitive to desiccation, such as gram-negative bacilli, is not favored. The skin also forms an acid mantle with a pH of 5.0 to 6.0, and its surface temperature is on average about 5° C lower than the core body temperature.[7] Besides containing secretory IgA, sweat also possesses sufficient salt to create a high osmotic pressure. Organisms that can withstand these conditions and compete successfully for binding sites and nutrients include staphylococci, corynebacteria, and the lipophilic yeast *Malassezia furfur.*[7] These organisms further modulate the microecology of the skin by releasing fatty acids from sebaceous secretions to produce a hydrophobic milieu, as well as short-chain lactic and propionic acid, which help maintain a low pH. Many of the bacteria also elaborate bacteriocins that inhibit other microorganisms.

The composition of the skin microflora is influenced by general factors including climate, body location, age, sex, race, and occupation, as well as by the use of soaps, detergents, and disinfectants. Antibiotics secreted in sweat disturb the balance within the commensal flora and leave the surface vulnerable to colonization by exogenous gram-negative bacilli. Antibiotics also exert selective pressure on the skin flora and cause resistance to emerge, as has been observed during treatment with ciprofloxacin.[8] Moreover, ciprofloxacin both is excreted in sweat and induces resistance among skin staphylococci within a few days of exposure.[9,10] Chemotherapy and irradiation can bring about radical changes in healthy skin that cause hair loss, dryness, and loss of sweat production.

Needle punctures and catheters provide a ready means of access for microorganisms through the stratum corneum and into the blood stream.

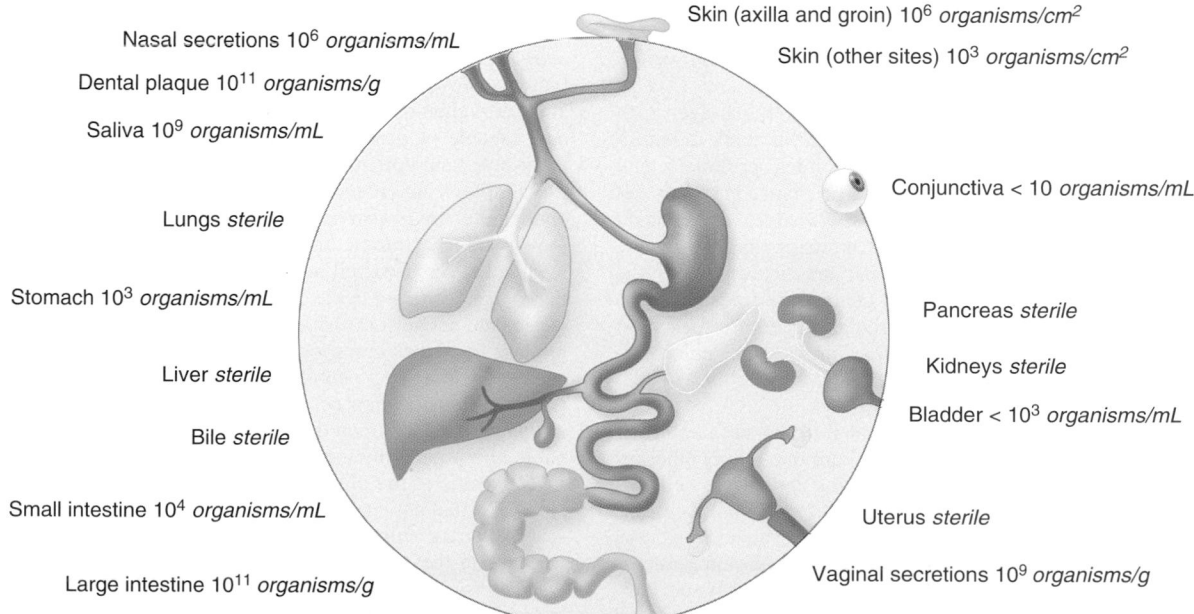

FIGURE 306–1. Body surfaces and their resident microbial flora. The integument comprises the skin, the respiratory tract (including the nasal cavity, ears, and conjunctivae), the alimentary tract, and the genitourinary tract and provides the first line of defense against microbial invasion. These body surfaces are normally colonized with a variety of microorganisms, including many different genera of bacteria and yeasts, but the range, number of species, and microbial biomass associated with the mucosal surfaces of the alimentary tract far exceed those of the skin. *(From Noskin GA, ed. Management of Infectious Complications in Cancer Patients. Boston: Kluwer Academic Publishers; 1998.)*

When the skin is broken, the release of fibronectin is thought to assist colonization with *Staphylococcus aureus*, whereas other changes facilitate colonization with gram-negative bacilli such as *Acinetobacter baumannii* and enteric bacteria. Abraded skin can lead to local infection, which can be a reservoir that promotes further spread to entry sites of intravenous catheters. When the balance is lost between host defenses and commensal flora around hair follicles, the follicles can become inflamed and necrotic and form a potential nidus of infection. Clinical infection therefore results from breaks in the skin, loss of local immunity, and disturbances within the resident flora.

Vascular devices have gained widespread acceptance as a safe form of long-term venous access, but regular use is associated with a marked increase in the incidence of bacteremia with coagulase-negative staphylococci, which frequently colonize the catheter lumen.[11,12] These staphylococci are commonly resistant to aminoglycosides, trimethoprim-sulfamethoxazole, and penicillinase-resistant penicillins and may also be resistant to fluoroquinolones.[13] Unless the catheter ends in an implanted port, skin commensal flora have potential access into the blood stream. The hub is the most likely source of contamination[14] and the risk increases with use.[15] Infections related to the external surface of the catheter (exit-site infections and tunnel infections) can result in serious soft tissue infection, most notably by *S. aureus*. Exit-site infections occur much less frequently than does intraluminal contamination. The latter may be caused by a variety of bacteria, many of which have relatively low virulence. Once established, these infections can be very difficult to treat without removing the device, particularly those caused by *Bacillus* spp., *Candida* spp., and *Pseudomonas aeruginosa*.[16-19]

The Alimentary Tract

Microbial Flora. Anaerobic bacteria predominate among the resident flora of the oral cavity and large intestine population and play a crucial role in maintaining a healthy commensal flora by providing the facility to withstand the establishment of exogenous organisms, which is known as colonization resistance.[20] However, the microbial flora is not the only participant in the establishment and maintenance of colonization resistance.

Many antibiotics also exert a negative influence on the commensal flora. Very susceptible bacteria such as the oral *Neisseria* spp. are suppressed by a wide range of antimicrobial agents, whereas oral viridans streptococci of the *mitis* group, such as *Streptococcus mitis* and *Streptococcus oralis*,[21] and other unusual oral commensal flora such as *Stomatococcus mucilaginosus (Rothia mucilaginosa)* and *Capnocytophaga* spp. are likely to be selected by antimicrobial agents, to which the bacteria are only marginally susceptible, if at all. In particular, penicillins, rifampin, clindamycin, macrolides, bacitracin, and vancomycin significantly impair colonization resistance, probably because they inhibit the gram-positive nonsporulating, lactic acid–producing bacilli such as bifidobacteria.[22] Certain cephalosporins are also detrimental, whereas trimethoprim-sulfamethoxazole and the quinolones have been declared "friendly," hence their frequent use as prophylaxis.[22] Unexpectedly, imipenem used at higher doses led to an increase in diarrhea caused by *Clostridium difficile*.[23] The chlorhexidine mouthwashes used to minimize infective complications of mucositis also influence the microflora.[24-26]

Because the normal commensal flora attach to the surfaces of the epithelium, their loss creates an ecologic vacuum that allows other organisms to establish colonization by occupying the vacant cell surfaces or by taking advantage of the surfeit of nutrients. Collapse of the ecology is invariably manifested by yeast overgrowth and colonization with nosocomial bacteria such as *Klebsiella pneumoniae* and *P. aeruginosa*[27,28] and failure to detect viable anaerobes directly or indirectly.[29,30] Recent examples of infectious complications associated with disturbance of the normal microbial equilibrium include the selection of previously uncommon species such as *Enterococcus faecium* and *Clostridium septicum*.

Dyspepsia is sufficiently commonplace for antacids such as proton pump inhibitors to be regularly prescribed. Reduced gastric acidity inadvertently destroys the natural barrier that prevents intestinal colonization by oral commensal flora, many of which are resistant to most of the antimicrobial agents used for prophylaxis. When patients swallow large amounts of mucus as a result of severe mucositis, any oral commensal flora may survive passage to the bowel. Loss of the gastric barrier therefore effectively extends the area of potential sites for colonization to the full length of the alimentary tract, which may explain the pathogenesis of α-hemolytic streptococcal bacteremia.[31-33] Viridans streptococci, usually *S. mitis*, can cause life-threatening infections, including septic shock and pneumonitis and acute respiratory distress syndrome. High-dose cytarabine predisposes to this infection.[32,34-36] Finally, the ecology of the bowel flora is markedly altered by diarrhea induced by treatment with certain cytostatic agents such as cytarabine,[37] by graft-versus-host disease,[38] and by total body irradiation.[39] Various coagulase-negative staphylococci, including *Staphylococcus epidermidis*, are also present in the endogenous oral flora and gastrointestinal tract of neutropenic patients. Plasmid pattern analysis of coagulase-negative staphylococcal blood-stream isolates has shown that the mucosa is the origin of bacteremia in 70% of patients managed in a hematology ward of one center.[40] Some other centers have found that vascular catheters were the most likely source of coagulase-negative *Staphylococcus* bacteremia in patients with hematologic malignancies (see Chapter 191).

Mucosal Barrier Injury. Injury to the mucosal barrier induced by chemotherapy and radiation therapy is probably the most significant breach in the host defenses against infecting microorganisms. The process is more complex than just the direct effect of cytotoxic therapy on cells with a high mitotic index, such as epithelial cells of the mouth and gastrointestinal tract, and the indirect effect of local infections associated with evolving neutropenia. Sonis[41] advanced a model consisting of four different phases to explain the development of oral mucositis. This consisted of an inflammatory phase involving the release of proinflammatory cytokines, interleukin-1, and tumor necrosis factor-α in response to cytotoxic therapy, an epithelial phase in which apoptosis was accelerated and cell renewal ceased, an ulcerative phase elicited by an interplay between dead and dying tissue and the local oral microflora and their products, and finally a healing phase in which cell regeneration once again recurred.

This model required adaptation to suit it to the gastrointestinal tract because of major differences in architecture of mucosal tissue between the mouth and the other parts of the digestive tract.[42] Moreover, there is an extensive gastrointestinal-associated lymphoid tissue in which lymphocytes and macrophages are located and that responds to irradiation and chemotherapy with inflammation. Gut epithelial cells are also capable of producing and secreting proinflammatory cytokines themselves and upregulating the production of major histocompatibility complex class II molecules and other adhesion molecules.[43] The epithelial phase is also different because the clonal stem cells are first to respond to cytotoxic drugs and irradiation by becoming apoptotic, leading to decreased cell renewal.[44] The ulcerative phase is likely similar to that occurring in the oral cavity, but the intestinal epithelial cells participate actively in the innate and adaptive immune response and produce cytokines in response to specific antigens of microorganisms, such as endotoxin, peptidoglycan, and other bacterial antigens.[45] Bacterial translocation occurs once the barrier is disrupted. The healing phase depends upon the rate of recovery of stem cells that are capable of repopulating the epithelium.

Mucositis is the clinical manifestation of mucosal barrier injury, and individual patients vary in their susceptibility and in the extent and severity of the complication(s), suggesting that there are genetic differences in the expression of proinflammatory cytokines or proteins that control stem cell apoptosis (e.g., p53 and bcl-2 along the gastrointestinal tract).[44] Transcription factors such as nuclear factor-κB are also thought to play a key role in the process.[46]

Damaged mucosa causes significant morbidity and markedly lowers the quality of life for several weeks following cytotoxic chemotherapy and irradiation. The duration of fever, parenteral narcotic use, total parenteral nutrition, antibiotic therapy, and the length of stay in a hospital are all correlated with the severity of mucositis, as is the risk of significant infections and mortality.[47,48] Oral viridans streptococcal infections are related to mucosal barrier injury of the upper part of the digestive tract, particularly the oral cavity, whereas enteric gram-negative bacillary infections and neutropenic enterocolitis are related to the lower part of the digestive tract.

It is likely that severe mucositis leads to a commensurate increase in the number of unusual bacteria causing infection by providing them with a portal of entry, which may explain the increase in bacteremia caused by oral commensal gram-positive cocci such as the viridans streptococci, *S. mucilaginosus,* and *Capnocytophaga* spp.[32,49-53] Besides damage to the oropharyngeal, esophageal, and gastric mucosa, chemotherapy and irradiation impair gut function and lead to rapid alterations in permeability. The increased absorption of sugars such as rhamnose, mannose, and lactulose and the decreased uptake of xylose after chemotherapy, irradiation, or a combination of both indicate a loss of integrity and damage to tight junctions.[54-58] Perturbed gut function has been shown to be one of the factors that, together with antibiotic usage and colonization with *Candida* spp., predisposes patients with leukemia to invasive candidiasis, and also appears to be a risk factor for neutropenic enterocolitis.[55] Impaired gut function and integrity may also facilitate translocation, particularly translocation of gram-negative bacilli such as *P. aeruginosa,* into the blood stream of patients colonized with the organism.[59] Gut toxicity has also been shown to be responsible for the reduced absorption of quinolones[60,61] and has been implicated in the erratic bioavailability of the antifungal agent itraconazole.[62] Finally, a dysfunctional gut will have a marked effect on the nutritional status of the patient.

Modern remission induction therapy and HSC transplant conditioning regimens often induce substantial injury to the mucosa. Combinations containing melphalan, etoposide, methotrexate, cytarabine, and idarubicin have all been show to induce mucositis,[54,55,63] which can be very severe when anthracyclines are combined with total body irradiation and cyclophosphamide to condition patients for HSC transplantation[64] or reinfusion. Widespread implementation of the hematopoietic growth factors granulocyte and granulocyte-macrophage colony-stimulating factor[65,66] probably allows for the use of even higher doses of cytostatic drugs, which in turn further aggravate oral mucositis.

Extensive mucosal damage is often accompanied by a decline in saliva production leading to a dry mouth. Any mucus produced may be extremely viscous and difficult to either swallow or cough up.[64,67,68] Periodontal disease may be exacerbated, and minor oral cuts and abrasions may become inflamed and ulcerated. The nonkeratinized surfaces of the mouth, including the underside of the tongue, the roof of the mouth, and the cheeks, may become red, inflamed, and swollen and thus limit the intake of both food and drink with the risk of malnutrition and catabolism.[69] Moreover, mucosal changes normally progress to a peak severity coinciding with the nadir of bone marrow aplasia and then begin to recover as hematopoiesis returns.[22,25,69,71]

The Oral Cavity. The oral cavity is a complex region providing other likely portals of entry besides mucositis, which essentially affects the nonkeratinous areas of the inner lips, cheeks, tongue, and roof of the mouth. The health of the periodontium probably also plays a role. For instance, organisms found in periodontal pockets, including viridans streptococci, appeared in the blood stream of 13 (43%) of 20 patients shortly after probing.[71] Toothbrushing as well as more invasive procedures, including tooth extraction and periodontal and endodontic treatment, can also lead to transient bacteremia.[72-75] Not surprisingly, the origin of several different species of bacteria causing bacteremia has been traced to the oral cavity, and not all can be explained by mucositis (Fig. 306-2). These include the oral viridans streptococci,[76] but also *Fusobacterium* species and the related *Leptotrichia* species,[77-82] and even *S. epidermidis.*[83]

However, coagulase-negative staphylococci are also present in the endogenous flora of the mucosa of mouth and gastrointestinal tract of neutropenic patients from which bacteremia probably originates.[40,42]

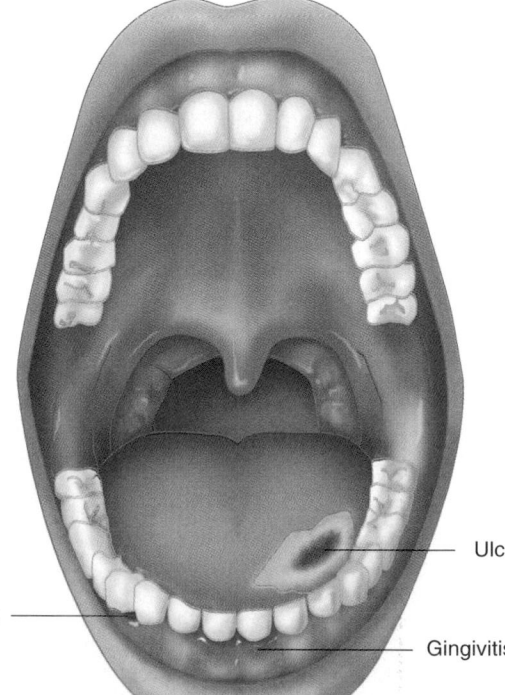

Gram-negative Bacilli

Aerobic

    Pseudomonas aerunginosa

Facultatively anaerobic

    Escherichia coli

    Klebsiella pneumoniae

    Enterobacter cloacae

Capnophillic

    Capnocytophaga species

Anaerobic

    Fusobacterium species

    Leptotrichia buccalis

    Prevotella species

Gram-positive Cocci

Oral viridans streptococci

    Streptococcus mitis

    Streptococcus oralis

    Streptococcus sanguis

Staphylococci

    Staphylococcus epidermidis

Others

    Stomatococcus mucilaginosus
    (Rothia mucilaginosa)

Ulcer

Periodontal pocket

Gingivitis

FIGURE 306-2. Potential portals of entry in the oral cavity. The periodontium as well as the ulcers associated with oral mucositis might both form more common portals of entry than is appreciated. Bacteremia can be caused by a variety of normally commensal resident flora, such as the oral viridans streptococci and the periopathogenic fusobacteria, as well as potential pathogens acquired exogenously, such as *Pseudomonas aeruginosa.*

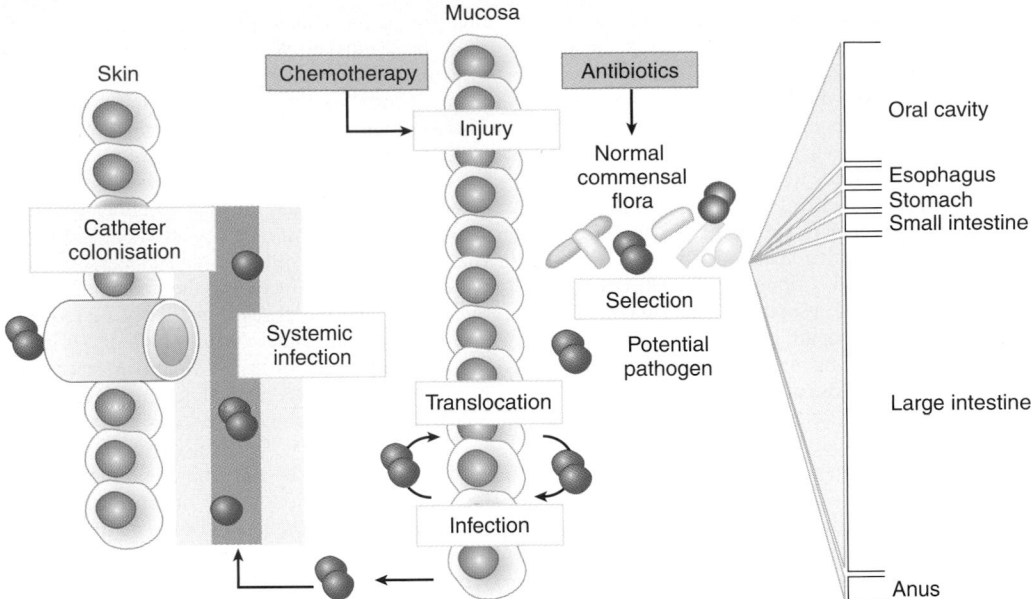

FIGURE 306–3. Model to explain the origins of infection in neutropenic patients. Chemotherapy induces injury to the mucosal barrier. At the same time antimicrobial agents used for prophylaxis (e.g., fluoroquinolones) exert selective pressure on the ecology whereby more resistant members of the resident flora (e.g., viridans streptococci, staphylococci, gram-negative bacilli, yeasts) increase in number. The gastric acid barrier of the stomach is usually breached by the use of drugs such as the histamine type 2 antagonists (e.g., ranitidine) and proton pump inhibitors (e.g., omeprazole) so that microorganisms that are ingested pass onward to the small intestine and beyond. Any colonization occurring on damaged mucosa would allow translocation from the alimentary tract or local infection, either of which can lead to blood-stream invasion and ultimately to systemic infection. In the case of the coagulase-negative staphylococci (e.g., *Staphylococcus epidermidis*), the alimentary tract might be the original source of bacteremia leading to colonization of the lumen of a vascular catheter.

The Gastrointestinal Tract. The gastrointestinal tract has long been implicated as the principal origin of infections caused by the enteric gram-negative bacilli, including *Escherichia coli, K. pneumoniae,* and *Enterobacter* species,[84,85] providing the motivation for adopting prophylaxis with fluoroquinolones.[86] More recently, the role of neutropenic enterocolitis or typhlitis, a severe form of mucosal damage of the gut induced by cytotoxic therapy, has also become clearer in providing a portal of entry for various toxin-producing bacteria, including *S. aureus, P. aeruginosa,* and various *Clostridium* species.[87,88] This illustrates how the delicate balance between the host and the resident microflora can be disturbed in the setting of mucosal barrier injury and prolonged exposure to antibiotics. Colonization by *Candida* species of the mucosal surfaces appears to be a prerequisite for local mucosal infection and subsequent invasive disease.[89] Mucosal barrier injury, including neutropenic enterocolitis, is also an independent risk factor for invasive candidiasis among patients receiving cytotoxic chemotherapy.[54,55] Mucosal barrier injury and exposure to antimicrobial agents may explain the emergence of most infections arising in neutropenic patients and perhaps others (Fig. 306-3). Urinary tract infections, although rare in the absence of a Foley catheter, can be initiated through hematogenous spread from the gut as well as via perianal or vaginal contamination.

Other Organ Dysfunction

Tumors themselves may predispose to infection by local organ dysfunction. In patients with solid tumors, obstruction of natural passages can lead to inadequate drainage of secretory or excretory fluids from nasal sinuses, bronchi, bile ducts, and so forth. Furthermore, tissue invasion may create connections between normally sterile spaces and the outside world through disruption of epithelial surfaces. Examples include perforation of the esophagus by mediastinal tumors, invasive gynecologic malignancies with local pelvic abscesses caused by gram-negative bacilli and anaerobes, skin ulceration with cellulitis and even deep soft tissue infections, and invasion of the bowel wall by tumors of the lower gastrointestinal tract with seeding of bacteria into the blood stream. Central nervous system tumors, spinal cord compression, and paraneoplastic neuropathy are associated with an increased

risk of infection because of a diminished ability to cough and swallow or vomit and incomplete emptying of the bladder.[90]

Treatment of malignancy inevitably damages healthy tissue. Even when the tumor is localized in a single area, relatively superficial, and readily removed, any surgery and local irradiation will nonetheless extend impairment of the normal defenses.

The lung appears to be very vulnerable to damage by cytostatic chemotherapy and irradiation and is exquisitely susceptible to infection. Immunopathologic reactions mediated by pulmonary macrophages that survive chemotherapy can lead to various other syndromes, including respiratory distress. Lung hemorrhage as a result of profound thrombocytopenia further imperils the lung and thereby increases the risk of infection. Inhalation of spores of *Aspergillus* spp. and other molds may lead to infection of the sinuses, bronchi, and lungs.

Herpesviruses may play a role in this process not only as direct pathogens but also because infection leads to impaired lymphocyte function and, in the case of herpes simplex virus, damage to mucosal surfaces.[91,92] Dead or dying tissue alters the local microbial ecology and thereby creates a nidus for infection. Resident flora such as *Candida* spp. can establish a superficial infection[91,92] marked by the presence of pseudomembranes over the ulcerated tissue, but they can also initiate local invasion and progressive spread to the esophagus and gastrointestinal tract, culminating in disseminated candidiasis. In a healthy host, these conditions rarely prove fatal, are usually readily apparent and relatively short lived, and can generally be managed simply. However, when hypoplastic bone marrow is present at the same time, the lack of neutrophils allows any potential pathogen that has invaded the tissues or translocated to the blood stream to disseminate readily. Consequently, the transition from colonization to disseminated infection is likely to require fewer steps and involve much lower inocula than is necessary in patients whose immunity is not so comprehensively compromised. The trend toward more intensive chemotherapy and the increasing use of allogeneic and autologous HSC transplantation augments the number of patients who will experience the double jeopardy of profound neutropenia and damage to the natural barriers of the skin and mucosa.

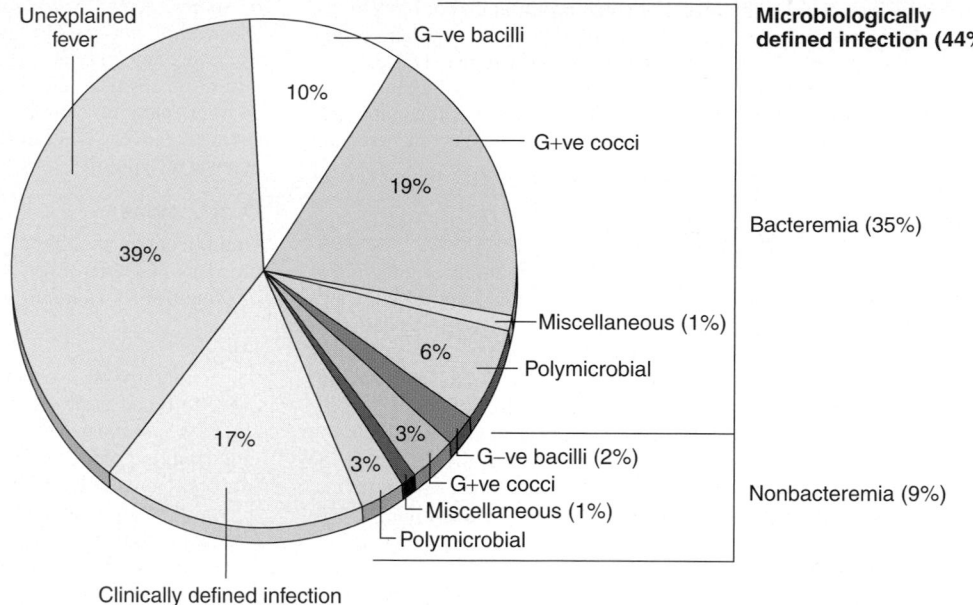

FIGURE 306–4. Causes of infection in 968 episodes of fever and neutropenia. (*Unpublished data derived from the study of De Pauw BE, Deresinski SC, Feld R, et al. Ceftazidime compared with piperacillin and tobramycin for the empiric treatment of fever in neutropenic patients with cancer: A multicenter randomized trial. Ann Intern Med. 1994;120:834-844.*)

Platelets

The protective role of platelets in healthy individuals is often underestimated but becomes obvious during treatment of a malignant disease. Thrombocytopenia is an almost inevitable repercussion of intensive chemotherapy and irradiation, but decreased thrombocyte function is a similar matter of concern. Thrombocytopathy is either disease related or caused by concurrent medication. The consequences of both increased susceptibility to infection and decreased capacity to repair damaged tissues can be considerable and may have an impact on the eventual outcome of a treatment episode. Thrombocytopenia also appears to be an independent risk factor for bacteremia,[93] and the incidence of major hemorrhage at autopsy of patients who die with or of an infection is striking.

Nutritional Status

Patients who weigh less than 75% of their ideal body weight or who have experienced rapid weight loss and have hypoalbuminemia are severely nutritionally deficient, which correlates inversely with survival. Poor nutritional status endangers the integrity of host defenses because of the catabolic state induced by cachexia and the malnutrition that results from anorexia, therapy-induced nausea and vomiting, gastrointestinal obstruction, altered permeability, mucositis, and metabolic derangements. A state of iron deficiency reduces the microbicidal capacity of neutrophils and T-lymphocyte function in vitro. Nutrition may be given parenterally or via a nasogastric tube to redress the balance, but neither is entirely without risk because each introduces yet another breach in the normal barriers and increases the risk of aspiration, particularly when consciousness is impaired.

Concurrent Illnesses

Psychological stress is thought to suppress host defense mechanisms. This general assumption has been corroborated by the observations that psychological stress has a negative influence on the function of T cells and natural killer cells. Indeed, stress appears to be connected with an increased risk of acute viral respiratory illness, a risk that was related to the amount of stress, most likely mediated by endogenous opioids, hormones from the hypothalamic-pituitary-adrenal axis, catecholamines, and cytokines. Concomitant chronic illnesses enhance the risk of infection. Patients with a preexistent immune disturbance, such as a congenital immunodeficiency syndrome, are doubly jeopardized. The negative impact of smoking on patients with primary lung tumors is obvious and due to colonization of their airways with virulent encapsulated microorganisms and impaired clearance of secretions.[90] Patients with diabetes mellitus are

prone to genitourinary tract and wound infections, and they frequently suffer from concurrent vascular disease and neuropathy. The proclivity to infection in patients with poorly controlled diabetes mellitus is not difficult to explain in view of aberrations such as impaired opsonization and decreased chemotactic activity of granulocytes and monocytes. Diabetes mellitus also predisposes to infections such as malignant external otitis[94] caused by *P. aeruginosa*. Treatment of iron overload with deferoxamine predisposes to rhinocerebral and pulmonary mucormycosis by providing the fungus with an available source of iron.[95]

ORIGIN OF FEVER AND INFECTIONS

An infectious origin of a fever can be confirmed microbiologically or clinically in only 30% to 50% of all febrile neutropenic patients (Fig. 306-4). Infectious complications usually arise insidiously in these patients because of a muted inflammatory response and the lack of pus, which can be attributed to the absence of granulocytes; even the presence of chills or rigors does not always correspond with bacteremia.[96] However, foci of infections also can remain undetected because the physical examination was too cursory, specimens were either inappropriate or not collected at all, or the microbiologic investigations were incomplete or too insensitive. Obtaining a careful recent medical history and examining the patient thoroughly for any evidence of inflammation or infection should be considered obligatory, but getting a proper specimen is much more difficult because aspiration or biopsy is usually required, which is ill advised for thrombocytopenic patients. Besides, even when a specimen is obtained from a normally sterile site, the yield is generally low. Consequently, failure to undertake an adequate physical examination and to obtain appropriate samples will result in fever being unexplained. Yet the fact that most patients without any proven infection improve clinically after treatment with broad-spectrum antibacterial agents suggests the presence of an occult bacterial infection in many cases.

The Systemic Inflammatory Response Syndrome and Sepsis

Although neutropenic patients cannot mount a normal host response to tissue injury, the systemic inflammatory response syndrome and sepsis can and do develop when inflammation is uncontrolled and proinflammatory substances spread to other distant sites, ultimately leading to multiple organ dysfunction.[97] Sepsis syndromes are not always the result of endotoxemia or even infection and can be brought about by noninfective tissue injury such as severe burns, acute pancreatitis, elective surgery, and trauma.[2] They might also result from extensive mucositis inasmuch as the levels of some proinflammatory cytokines, particularly interleukin-6, are elevated after chemotherapy and conditioning therapy for HSC transplantation; tumor necrosis factor-α levels may not be elevated under these conditions.[98] Determination of C-reactive protein and cytokines such as interleukin-6 is recommended by some for diagnosing bacterial infection,[99-102] whereas others remain unconvinced.[103,104]

LABORATORY DIAGNOSIS

Despite the attenuation of physical signs and symptoms of infection in an immunocompromised patient, it is still essential to conduct a careful physical examination, with particular attention paid to vital signs (pulse, respiration rate, blood pressure), to the course of the patient's temperature during the preceding days, and to the oropharynx (including the dentition), the lungs, the skin and exit sites of venous access devices, and the perirectal area and perianal region. The most common sites of infection when present are the oral cavity, the lung, and the skin with its underlying soft tissues, but in most cases the principal means for microbiologic diagnosis remains the blood culture.

Blood Cultures

Blood cultures are usually the most productive microbiologic investigation and help explain 10% to 40% of fevers, but the sensitivity of blood cultures is crucially dependent on the volume of blood cultured, with 30 to 40 mL per session being recommended for optimal results.[105,106] It has become common practice to draw at least 10 mL of blood for culture by venipuncture when investigating fever immediately before starting empirical therapy, together with at least 10 mL through each lumen of a central vascular catheter when one is present. During the last decade a change from gram-negative to gram-positive bacteria has occurred,[107] but virtually any microorganism can cause infection in severely immunosuppressed patients. Infusion of the appropriate antibiotic through catheter ports that are culture positive may be helpful in clearing colonized catheters. Once therapy is started, the value of further blood cultures is small if the patient is responding clinically. Patients with catheter-acquired sepsis who remain febrile with positive blood cultures usually need their catheters removed. In recent years, at least in clinical trials, blood cultures have been repeated 3 to 4 days after starting empirical therapy as a means of detecting persistent bacteremia.

Bacteremia Related to Intravascular Catheters

Coagulase-negative staphylococci are the most common cause of catheter-acquired sepsis,[12,13] but they are also recovered from catheter blood under circumstances suggesting that they are not causing the fever that prompted the blood culture. It is always easier to interpret the results of culturing of blood drawn from a peripheral vein. Simultaneous quantitative blood cultures from the catheter and a peripheral vein have been advocated but have not convincingly discriminated between catheter-acquired sepsis, sepsis from another source, asymptomatic intraluminal colonization of the catheter, and accidental contamination while drawing blood from the catheter hub. In all cases, the decision to treat is based not just on the blood culture but also on the clinical findings.

Bacteremia Related to Damaged Mucosa

With the increasing importance of mucositis, several investigators have drawn attention to the significance of viridans streptococci,[108] especially in patients who prophylactically receive oral quinolones, which enhance the survival of these bacteria on damaged mucous membranes.[32-36,49] However, the signs and symptoms of viridans streptococcal infection might be inconspicuous to completely absent. In view of the direct correlation between the rate of positive blood cultures and the severity of damage to the mucosal surface, the normal habitat for these organisms, it is questionable whether viridans streptococci are true pathogens in all cases or whether they represent only an epiphenomenon.[6,109] In fact, during the course of a normal day, the acts of chewing and toothbrushing lead to transient bacteremia caused mainly by viridans streptococci. In view of the extent of the damage

in many cases, it is not surprising that next to streptococci, *Clostridium perfringens* and *C. septicum* septicemia, classically with massive hemolysis and diffuse intravascular coagulation, can arise during mucositis.[87] In patients with profuse diarrhea and severe abdominal pain in combination with virtually absent audible bowel sounds, recovery of *C. septicum* from the blood may confirm the diagnosis of typhlitis.[110]

Oral Lesions

Oral infections are difficult to diagnose by appearance in patients with mucositis. Culture of oral lesions for herpes simplex virus and smears of scrapings for *Candida* pseudohyphae can be helpful.

Lung

Apparently trivial complaints such as a persistent dry cough may prove to be an early sign of impending pneumonia from *Aspergillus* spp.,[111] respiratory syncytial virus, or influenza virus. Thoracic computed tomographic scans are more sensitive in detecting pulmonary infiltrates compatible with aspergillosis than are plain chest radiographs.[112] Bronchoalveolar lavage specimens from patients with pulmonary infiltrates should have a battery of tests that usually includes smears for *Pneumocystis jeroveci* (formerly *carinii*), the acid-fast bacilli and *Nocardia* spp., bacteria, and molds, as well as culture for fungi and bacteria, including *Legionella* spp., *Mycobacterium* spp., *Nocardia* spp., and respiratory viruses (influenza and parainfluenza viruses, adenovirus, respiratory syncytial virus, and cytomegalovirus). *Aspergillus* antigen can also be detected in bronchoalveolar specimens, though the sensitivity and specificity of the test on respiratory specimens is as yet unclear.[113-115] Rapid assays by enzyme-linked immunosorbent assay, direct fluorescent antibody, or dot blot are also available for influenza virus, respiratory syncytial virus, and adenovirus. Nasopharyngeal swabs in children and nasopharyngeal washes in adults are useful in culturing respiratory viruses in patients with upper respiratory symptoms. With current techniques, results are available in 24 to 48 hours (see Chapter 15). Testing for *Legionella* antigen in urine of patients with pneumonia is also useful.

Skin Lesions

Identifying the cause of skin and underlying soft tissue infections is equally difficult because culturing swabs of lesions rarely discriminates between pathogens and commensal flora. As an exception, Gram stain and culture from pus expressed from a catheter exit site can be useful. Culture and histologic examination of skin punch biopsy specimens is very helpful in the diagnosis of isolated maculopapular or ulcerated lesions. Disseminated infections by *Candida* spp., *Trichosporon* spp., and *Fusarium* spp. in a neutropenic patient may be manifested by skin lesions while blood cultures remain negative. Skin lesions may be the source of *Fusarium* fungemia.[116] Ecthyma gangrenosum from *P. aeruginosa* may be accompanied by positive blood cultures, but lesions with the same appearance in a neutropenic patient can be caused by *Aspergillus* spp. or the agents of mucormycosis. These fungal lesions require biopsy for diagnosis. Aspiration of skin lesions is seldom successful unless pus is present.

Vascular Devices

Infections associated with intravenous catheters usually originate from contamination of the catheter hub. Bacteria, typically coagulase-negative staphylococci, can be cultured from the blood drawn back through intravenous catheters, and yet the patient's condition does not appear septic when the culture becomes positive. The contaminated catheter may have already been removed since the culture was obtained, or the culture may have been contaminated at the time that blood was withdrawn. In afebrile patients, repeating blood cultures may be all that is indicated. In other cases, the organism can be cultured repeatedly from blood drawn through the same catheter port but not from blood drawn peripherally, thus suggesting that the organism has not yet been able to cause sepsis but has colonized the catheter. Removing the device or administering antibiotics through the same port may be indicated to circumvent future sepsis.[117]

Gastrointestinal Tract

It is even more difficult to diagnose enteric infection, especially when nausea, vomiting, diarrhea, bowel cramps, and melena can all be due to toxicity related to chemotherapy, irradiation, or graft-versus-host disease. Endoscopy can be critical in the diagnosis of herpes simplex, *Candida* spp., and cytomegalovirus mucosal lesions. Detection of herpes simplex virus and cytomegalovirus in intestinal biopsy can be enhanced if both culture and immunoperoxidase staining of the tissue are done. The bowel flora can become the major reservoir of vancomycin-resistant enterococci, *Candida albicans, K. pneumoniae,* and *P. aeruginosa.*[27,28,118] Organisms can be spread from the bowel onto the skin and, by the fecal-oral route, into the mouth. Skin organisms can be spread to other patients by the hands of health care workers and, through intravenous catheters, into the patient's blood stream. Oral flora can be aspirated into the airway, particularly when the patient is intubated. Passage of bowel organisms into the blood stream can occur through chemotherapy-induced ulcers. Fever in the presence of diarrhea or abdominal pain should prompt a cytotoxicity assay on stool for *C. difficile* toxin. Neutropenic patients with right lower quadrant pain may have typhlitis, the diagnosis of which can be supported by an edematous colonic wall on abdominal computed tomography with oral contrast. Recovery of *C. septicum* from the blood stream usually portends neutropenic enterocolitis.[87]

Urinary Tract

Urine should be obtained for standard culture when there are signs or symptoms of a urinary tract infection but not otherwise. Urine from HSC transplant recipients with hemorrhagic cystitis should be tested for adenovirus by culture or antigen detection.

Noncultural Techniques

The role of nonculture methods for diagnosis is small but expanding. *Legionella* antigen detection in urine is specific but detects only *Legionella pneumophila* type 1, or approximately 70% of patients

with *Legionella* pneumonia. Detection of cytomegalovirus reactivation in allogeneic HSC recipients is now being routinely done by quantitative polymerase chain reaction (PCR) or measurement of neutrophil cytomegalovirus antigen (see Chapter 311). Quantitative PCR of urine for BK virus and of blood for human herpesvirus-6 and Epstein-Barr virus is being evaluated for clinical utility. Detection of fungal DNA and *Candida* metabolites in blood and urine remains investigational.[119-122] Kits for the detection of *Aspergillus* antigen in serum using an enzyme-linked immunosorbent assay are commercially available and can be used to screen patients at risk of aspergillosis. Although the specificity is generally high, the sensitivity varies considerably and seems to depend upon on the specimen (blood, bronchial material, cerebrospinal fluid), the threshold employed (0.5 to 1.5), and the frequency of sampling (once or twice weekly or less) as well as the prevalence of the disease in the population under study.[113,123-129]

Given the lack of sensitivity of cultures in general, many clinicians restrict microbiologic investigations in patients with no localizing signs to culture of blood and urine. They then treat empirically and rely only on the development, progress, and resolution of clinical signs and symptoms to further guide their actions (see Chapter 308).

SEQUENTIAL INFECTIVE EVENTS

The sequence of risk factors (Fig. 306-5) determines to a large extent the order of infectious events in granulocytopenic cancer patients, which means that the types of infection occurring early in the granulocytopenic period differ from late infectious complications. Profound granulocytopenia and mucosal damage usually ensue about 10 days after initiating a course of chemotherapy and are followed by fever and bacteremia within a few days when toxicity is at its most pronounced. Clinically defined infections usually lag behind by a few days. Invasive pulmonary aspergillosis develops in few patients early in the course of granulocytopenia.[130] Infections related to central venous

FIGURE 306–5. The sequence of events during neutropenia. Profound granulocytopenia and mucosal damage usually develop about a week after the start of cytoreductive chemotherapy. Thereafter, infectious and other complications tend to coincide with one another, placing the patient at most risk. Fever develops around a week later, and, if there is bacteremia, it mostly occurs at this time. The risk of infections related to the central venous catheter increases with the length of time that the catheter is left in place, but signs and symptoms usually manifest themselves during the first few days of fever, that is, during the third week after starting chemotherapy. Infectious complications related to the lung tend to occur a few days later, often being recognized only after 5 to 6 days of fever. The period of risk of bacterial and fungal infection diminishes with recovery of the granulocytes when the clinical manifestations of tissue infections may be temporarily exacerbated before finally resolving.

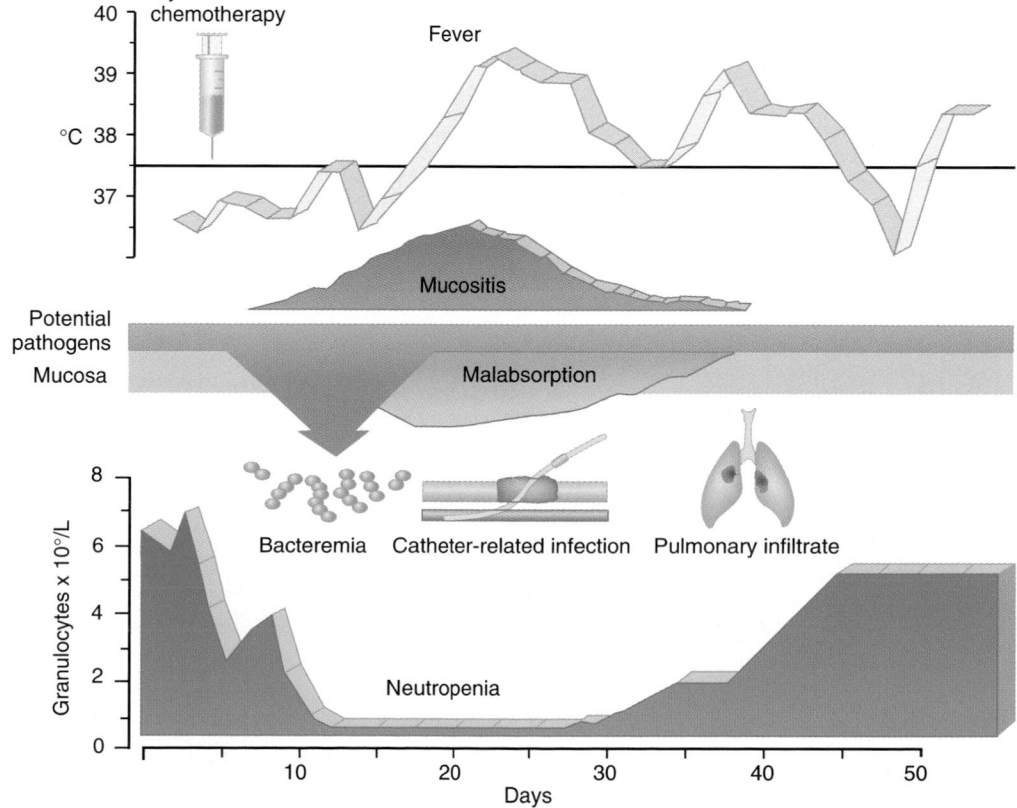

catheters have to be considered about 10 days after their insertion, with the risk increasing with the length of time that the catheter is left in place.[12]

The initial risk period resolves with recovery of the granulocyte count. Very intensively treated patients are still at risk because of granulocytopathy, deficient cell-mediated immunity, and hypogammaglobulinemia. The kind of infectious complications for such patients is determined by the pace of reconstitution of these other components of the immune system. The major factor that influences immunologic reconstitution after allogeneic HSC transplantation is acute graft-versus-host disease and its treatment.[131] Cytomegalovirus, adenovirus, and fungi, including *P. jeroveci,* constitute the major pathogens during this episode. A third major risk period in these patients begins approximately 3 months after the procedure, at the time that chronic graft-versus-host disease develops. Sinopulmonary infections and cutaneous infections are common and probably related to the IgA deficiency with or without sicca syndrome and severely impaired cellular immunity. Varicella-zoster is probably the most frequent cutaneous infection, and pulmonary infections caused by cytomegalovirus and *P. jeroveci* are regularly encountered. Months, if not years, after successful engraftment or recovery from other very aggressive treatment, encapsulated organisms can cause rapidly fatal bacteremia and severe respiratory infections because of the lack of opsonizing antibodies.

REFERENCES

1. Bodey GP, Buckley M, Sathe YS, Freireich EJ. Quantitative relationships between circulating leukocytes and infection in patients with acute leukemia. Ann Intern Med. 1966;64:328-340.
2. Bone RC. The pathogenesis of sepsis. Ann Intern Med. 1991;115:457-469.
3. Carlisle H, Saslaw S. Properdin levels in splenectomized persons. Proc Soc Exp Biol Med. 1959;102:150-155.
4. Van der Meer J. Defects in host defense mechanisms. In: Rubin R, Young LS, eds. Current Approaches to Infection in the Compromised Host. New York: Plenum Medical; 1994:33-66.
5. Van der Waaij D. Effect of antibiotics on colonization resistance. In: Easmon CS, ed. Medical Microbiology. London: Academic; 1984:227-237.
6. Donnelly JP. Chemoprophylaxis for the prevention of bacterial and fungal infections. Cancer Treat Res. 1995;79:45-81.
7. Roth RR, James WD. Microbial ecology of the skin. Annu Rev Microbiol. 1988;42:441-464.
8. Kotilainen P, Nikoskelainen J, Huovinen P. Emergence of ciprofloxacin-resistant coagulase-negative staphylococcal skin flora in immunocompromised patients receiving ciprofloxacin. J Infect Dis. 1990;161:41-44.
9. Høiby N, Johansen HK, for the Copenhagen Study Group on Antibiotics in Sweat. Ciprofloxacin in sweat and antibiotic resistance (Letter). Lancet 1995;346:1235.
10. Høiby N, Jarløv JO, Kemp M, et al. Excretion of ciprofloxacin in sweat and multiresistant *Staphylococcus epidermidis*. Lancet. 1997;349:167-169.
11. Weightman NC, Simpson EM, Speller DCE, et al. Bacteraemia related to indwelling central venous catheters: Prevention, diagnosis and treatment. Eur J Clin Microbiol Infect Dis. 1988;7:125-129.
12. Raad II, Bodey GP. Infectious complications of indwelling vascular catheters. Clin Infect Dis. 1992;15:197-208.
13. Hedin G, Hambraeus A. Multiply antibiotic-resistant *Staphylococcus epidermidis* in patients, staff and environment—A one-week survey in a bone marrow transplant unit. J Hosp Infect. 1991;17:95-106.
14. Salzman MB, Isenberg HD, Shapiro JF, et al. A prospective study of the catheter hub as the portal of entry for microorganisms causing catheter-related sepsis in neonates. J Infect Dis. 1993;167:487-490.
15. Groeger JS, Lucas AB, Thaler HT, et al. Infectious morbidity associated with long-term use of venous access devices in patients with cancer. Ann Intern Med. 1993;119:1168-1174.
16. De Pauw BE, Novakova IR, Donnelly JP. Options and limitations of teicoplanin in febrile granulocytopenic patients. Br J Haematol. 1990;2:1-5.
17. Weems JJ. *Candida* parapsilosis: Epidemiology, pathogenicity, clinical manifestations and antibiotic susceptibility. Clin Infect Dis. 1992;14:756-766.
18. Lecciones JA, Lee JW, Navarro EE, et al. Vascular catheter-associated fungemia in patients with cancer: Analysis of 155 episodes. Clin Infect Dis. 1992;14:875-883.
19. Morrison VA, Haake RJ, Weisdorf DJ. Non-*Candida* fungal infections after bone marrow transplantation: Risk factors and outcome. Am J Med. 1994;96:497-503.
20. Van der Waaij D. The ecology of the human intestine and its consequences for overgrowth by pathogens such as *Clostridium difficile*. Annu Rev Microbiol. 1989;43:69-87.
21. Facklam R. What happened to the streptococci: Overview of taxonomic and nomenclature changes. Clin Microbiol Rev. 2002;15:613-630.
22. Donnelly JP, Maschmeyer G, Daenen S. Selective oral antimicrobial prophylaxis for the prevention of infection in acute leukaemia—ciprofloxacin versus co-trimoxazole plus colistin. The EORTC-Gnotobiotic Project Group. Eur J Cancer. 1992;28A:873-878.
23. Freifeld AG, Walsh T, Marshall D, et al. Monotherapy for fever and neutropenia in cancer patients: A randomized comparison of ceftazidime versus imipenem. J Clin Oncol. 1995;13:165-176.
24. Meurman JH, Laine P, Murtomaa H, et al. Effect of antiseptic mouthwashes on some clinical and microbiological findings in the mouths of lymphoma patients receiving cytostatic drugs. J Clin Periodontol. 1991;18:587-591.
25. Weisdorf DJ, Bostrom B, Raether D, et al. Oropharyngeal mucositis complicating bone marrow transplantation: Prognostic factors and the effect of chlorhexidine mouth rinse. Bone Marrow Transplant. 1989;4:89-95.
26. Ferretti GA, Ash RC, Brown AT, et al. Chlorhexidine for prophylaxis against oral infections and associated complications in patients receiving bone marrow transplants. J Am Dent Assoc. 1987;114:461-467.
27. Schimpff SC. Infection prevention during profound granulocytopenia: New approaches to alimentary canal microbial suppression. Ann Intern Med. 1980;93:358-361.
28. Van Der Waaij D. The colonization resistance of the digestive tract of man and animals. In: Fleidner TM, ed. Clinical and Experimental Gnotobiotics, Zbl Bakt. Stuttgart: Gustav Fischer; 1979.
29. Louie TJ, Chubb H, Bow EJ, et al. Preservation of colonization resistance parameters during empiric therapy with aztreonam in febrile neutropenic patient. Rev Infect Dis. 1985;7:S747-S761.
30. Meijer-Severs GJ, Van Santen E. Short-chain fatty acids and succinate in feces of healthy human volunteers and ther correlation with anaerobic cultural counts. J Gastroenterol. 1987;22:672-676.
31. Van der Lelie H, Van Ketel RJ, Von dem Borne AEGK, et al. Incidence and clinical epidemiology of streptococcal septicemia during treatment of acute myeloid leukemia. Scand J Infect Dis. 1991;23:163-168.
32. Bochud PY, Calandra T, Francioli P. Bacteremia due to viridans streptococci in neutropenic patients: A review. Am J Med. 1994;97:256-264.
33. Elting LS, Bodey GP, Keefe BH. Septicemia and shock syndrome due to viridans streptococci: A case-control study of predisposing factors. Clin Infect Dis. 1992; 14:1201-1207.
34. Dybedal I, Lamvik J. Respiratory insufficiency in acute leukemia following treatment with cytosine arabinoside and septicemia with *Streptococcus viridans*. Eur J Haematol. 1989;42:405-406.
35. Kern W, Kurrle E, Schmeiser T. Streptococcal bacteremia in adult patients with leukemia undergoing aggressive chemotherapy: A review of 55 cases. Infection. 1990;18:138-145.
36. Dompeling EC, Donnelly JP, Raemaekers JM, De Pauw BE. Pre-emptive administration of corticosteroids prevents the development of ARDS associated with *Streptococcus mitis* bacteremia following chemotherapy with high-dose cytarabine. Ann Hematol. 1994;69:69-71.
37. Peters WG, Willemze R, Colly LP, Guiot HFL. Side effects of intermediate- and high-dose cytosine arabinoside in the treatment of refractory or relapsed acute leukaemia and non-Hodgkin's lymphoma. Neth J Med. 1987;30:64-74.
38. Guiot HFL, Biemond J, Klasen E, et al. Protein loss during acute graft-versus-host disease: Diagnostics and clinical significance. Eur J Haematol. 1987;38:187-196.
39. Callum JL, Brandwein JM, Sutcliffe SB, et al. Influence of total body irradiation on infections after autologous bone marrow transplantation. Bone Marrow Transplant. 1991;8:245-251.
40. Herwaldt LA, Hollis RJ, Boyken LD, Pfaller MA. Molecular epidemiology of coagulase-negative staphylococci isolated from immunocompromised patients. Infect Control Hosp Epidemiol. 1992;13:86-92.
41. Sonis ST. Mucositis as a biological process: A new hypothesis for the development of chemotherapy-induced stomatotoxicity. Oral Oncol. 1998;34:39-43.
42. Blijlevens NM, Donnelly JP, De Pauw BE. Mucosal barrier injury: Biology, pathology, clinical counterparts and consequences of intensive treatment for haematological malignancy. An overview. Bone Marrow Transplant. 2000;25:1269-1278.
43. Xun CQ, Thompson JS, Jennings CD, et al. Effect of total body irradiation, busulfan-cyclophosphamide, or cyclophosphamide conditioning on inflammatory cytokine release and development of acute and chronic graft-versus-host disease in H-2-incompatible transplanted SCID mice. Blood. 1994;83:2360-2367.
44. Potten CS, Wilson JW, Booth C. Regulation and significance of apoptosis in the stem cells of the gastrointestinal epithelium. Stem Cells. 1997;15:82-93.
45. Kim JM, Eckmann L, Savidge TC, et al. Apoptosis of human intestinal epithelial cells after bacterial invasion. J Clin Invest. 1998;102:1815-1823.
46. Sonis ST. The biologic role for nuclear factor-kappaB in disease and its potential involvement in mucosal injury associated with anti-neoplastic therapy. Crit Rev Oral Biol Med. 2002;13:380-389.
47. Sonis ST, Oster G, Fuchs H, et al. Oral mucositis and the clinical and economic outcomes of hematopoietic stem cell transplantation. J Clin Oncol. 2001;19:2201-2205.
48. Rapoport AP, Miller Watelet LF, Linder T, et al. Analysis of factors that correlate with mucositis in recipients of autologous and allogeneic stem-cell transplants. J Clin Oncol. 1999;17:2446-2453.
49. De Pauw BE, Donnelly JP, De Witte T, et al. Options and limitations of long-term oral ciprofloxacin as antibacterial prophylaxis in allogeneic bone marrow transplant recipients. Bone Marrow Transplant. 1990;5:179-182.
50. Classen DC, Burke JP, Ford CD, et al. *Streptococcus mitis* sepsis in bone marrow transplant patients receiving oral antimicrobial prophylaxis. Am J Med. 1990;89:441-446.
51. McWhinney PHM, Gillespie SH, Kibbler CC, et al. *Streptococcus mitis* and ARDS in neutropenic patients. Lancet. 1991;337:429.
52. Bilgrami S, Bergstrom SK, Peterson DE, et al. *Capnocytophaga* bacteremia in a patient with Hodgkin's disease following bone marrow transplantation: Case report and review. Clin Infect Dis. 1992;14:1045-1049.
53. Weers-Pothoff G, Novakova IR, Donnelly JP, Muytjens HL. Bacteraemia caused by *Stomatococcus mucilaginosus* in a granulocytopenic patient with acute lymphocytic leukaemia. Neth J Med. 1989;35:143-146.
54. Bow EJ, Loewen R, Cheang MS, et al. Cytotoxic therapy-induced D-xylose malabsorption and invasive infection during remission-induction therapy for acute myeloid leukemia in adults. J Clin Oncol. 1997;15:2254-2261.

55. Bow EJ, Loewen R, Cheang MS, Schacter B. Invasive fungal disease in adults undergoing remission-induction therapy for acute myeloid leukemia: The pathogenetic role of the antileukemic regimen. Clin Infect Dis. 1995;21:361-369.

56. Fegan C, Poynton JA, Whittaker JA. The gut mucosal barrier in bone marrow transplantation. Bone Marrow Transplant. 1990;5:373-377.

57. Johansson JE, Ekman T. Gastro-intestinal toxicity related to bone marrow transplantation: Disruption of the intestinal barrier precedes clinical findings. Bone Marrow Transplant. 1997;19:921-925.

58. Keefe DM, Cummins AG, Dale BM, et al. Effect of high-dose chemotherapy on intestinal permeability in humans. Clin Sci. 1997;92:385-389.

59. Tancrede CH, Andremont AO. Bacterial translocation and Gram-negative bacteremia in patients with hematological malignancies. J Infect Dis. 1985;152:99-103.

60. Brown NM, White LO, Blundell EL, et al. Absorption of oral ofloxacin after cytotoxic chemotherapy for haematological malignancy. J Antimicrob Chemother. 1993;32:117-122.

61. Johnson EJ, MacGowan AP, Potter MN, et al. Reduced absorption of oral ciprofloxacin after chemotherapy for haematological malignancy. J Antimicrob Chemother. 1990;25:837-842.

62. Prentice AG, Warnock DW, Johnson SA, et al. Multiple dose pharmacokinetics of an oral solution of itraconazole in autologous bone marrow transplant recipients. J Antimicrob Chemother. 1994;34:247-252.

63. Donnelly JP, Muus P, Schattenberg A, et al. A scheme for daily monitoring of oral mucositis in allogeneic BMT recipients. Bone Marrow Transplant. 1992;9:409-413.

64. Raemaekers J, De Witte T, Schattenberg A, Van Der Lely N. Prevention of leukaemic relapse after transplantation with lymphocyte-depleted marrow by intensification of the conditioning regimen with a 6-day continuous infusion of anthracyclines. Bone Marrow Transplant. 1989;4:167-171.

65. Schuster MW. Granulocyte-macrophage colony-stimulating factor (GM-CSF)–What role in bone marrow transplantation? Infection. 1992;20(Suppl):S95-S99.

66. Bronchud M. Can hematopoietic growth factors be used to improve the success of cytotoxic chemotherapy? Anticancer Drugs. 1993;4:127-139.

67. McGuire DB, Altomonte V, Peterson DE, et al. Patterns of mucositis and pain in patients receiving preparative chemotherapy and bone marrow transplantation. Oncol Nurs Forum. 1993;20:1493-1502.

68. Sable CA, Donowitz GR. Infections in bone marrow transplant recipients. Clin Infect Dis. 1994;18:273-281.

69. Kolbinson DA, Schubert MM, Fluornoy N, Truelove EL. Early oral changes following bone marrow transplantation. Oral Surg Oral Med Oral Pathol. 1988;66:130-138.

70. Rocke LK, Loprinzi CL, Lee JK, et al. A randomized clinical trial of two different durations of oral cryotherapy for prevention of 5-fluorouracil related stomatitis. Cancer. 1993;72:2234-2238.

71. Daly C, Mictchell D, Grossberg D, et al. Bacteraemia caused by periodontal probing. Aust Dent J. 1997;42:77-80.

72. Debelian GJ, Olsen I, Tronstad L. Systemic diseases caused by oral microorganisms. Endod Dent Traumatol. 1994;10:57-65.

73. Lucas V, Roberts GJ. Odontogenic bacteremia following tooth cleaning procedures in children. Pediatr Dent. 2000;22:96-100.

74. Bhanji S, Williams B, Sheller B, et al. Transient bacteremia induced by toothbrushing: A comparison of the Sonicare toothbrush with a conventional toothbrush. Pediatr Dent. 2002;24:295-299.

75. Schlein RA, Kudlick EM, Reindorf CA, et al. Toothbrushing and transient bacteremia in patients undergoing orthodontic treatment. Am J Orthod Dentofacial Orthop. 1991;99:466-472.

76. Kennedy HF, Morrison D, Tomlinson D, et al. Gingivitis and toothbrushes: Potential roles in viridans streptococcal bacteraemia. J Infect. 2003;46:67-70.

77. Baquero F, Fernandez J, Dronda F, et al. Capnophilic and anaerobic bacteremia in neutropenic patients: An oral source. Rev Infect Dis. 1990;12(Suppl 2):S157-S160.

78. Fanourgiakis P, Vekemans M, Georgala A, et al. Febrile neutropenia and *Fusobacterium* bacteremia: Clinical experience with 13 cases. Support Care Cancer. 2003;11:332-335.

79. Landsaat PM, van der Lelie H, Bongaerts G, Kuijper EJ. *Fusobacterium nucleatum*, a new invasive pathogen in neutropenic patients? Scand J Infect Dis. 1995;27:83-84.

80. Lark RL, McNeil SA, VanderHyde K, et al. Risk factors for anaerobic bloodstream infections in bone marrow transplant recipients. Clin Infect Dis. 2001;33:338-343.

81. Vidal AM, Sarria JC, Kimbrough RC 3rd, Keung YK. Anaerobic bacteremia in a neutropenic patient with oral mucositis. Am J Med Sci. 2000;319:189-190.

82. Schwartz DN, Schable B, Tenover FC, Miller RA. *Leptotrichia buccalis* bacteremia in patients treated in a single bone marrow transplant unit. Clin Infect Dis. 1995;20:762-767.

83. Kennedy HF, Morrison D, Kaufmann ME, et al. Origins of *Staphylococcus epidermidis* and *Streptococcus oralis* causing bacteraemia in a bone marrow transplant patient. J Med Microbiol. 2000;49:367-370.

84. Schimpff SC. Gram-negative bacteremia. Support Care Cancer. 1993;1:5-18.

85. Schimpff SC. Infections in cancer patients: Differences between developed and less developed countries? Eur J Cancer. 1991;27:407-408.

86. Cruciani M, Rampazzo R, Malena M, et al. Prophylaxis with fluoroquinolones for bacterial infections in neutropenic patients: A meta-analysis. Clin Infect Dis. 1996;23:795-805.

87. Pouwels MJ, Donnelly JP, Raemaekers JM, et al. *Clostridium septicum* sepsis and neutropenic enterocolitis in a patient treated with intensive chemotherapy for acute myeloid leukemia. Ann Hematol. 1997;74:143-147.

88. Gomez L, Martino R, Rolston KV. Neutropenic enterocolitis: Spectrum of the disease and comparison of definite and possible cases. Clin Infect Dis. 1998;27:695-699.

89. Nucci M, Anaissie E. Revisiting the source of candidemia: Skin or gut? Clin Infect Dis. 2001;33:1959-1967.

90. McGeer A, Feld R. Epidemiology of infection in immunocompromised oncological patients. In: Glauser M, Calandra T, eds. Baillière's Clinical Infectious Diseases. London: Ballière Tindall; 1994:415-438.

91. Beattie G, Whelan J, Cassidy J, et al. Herpes simplex virus, *Candida albicans* and mouth ulcers in neutropenic patients with non-haematological malignancy. Cancer Chemother Pharmacol. 1989;25:75-76.

92. Bergmann OJ. Oral infections in haematological patients—Pathogenesis and clinical significance. Dan Med Bull. 1992;39:15-29.

93. Viscoli C, Bruzzi P, Castagnola E, et al. Factors associated with bacteraemia in febrile, granulocytopenic cancer patients. The International Antimicrobial Therapy Cooperative Group (IATCG) of the European Organization for Research and Treatment of Cancer (EORTC). Eur J Cancer. 1994;4:430-437.

94. Rubin J, Yu VL. Malignant external otitis: Insights into pathogenesis, clinical manifestations, diagnosis, and therapy. Am J Med. 1988;85:391-398.

95. Cech P, Stalder H, Widmann JJ, et al. Leukocyte myeloperoxidase deficiency and diabetes mellitus associated with *Candida albicans* liver abscess. Am J Med. 1979;66:149-153.

96. Sickles EA, Greene WH, Wiernik PH. Clinical presentation of infection in granulocytopenic patients. Arch Intern Med. 1975;135:715-719.

97. Soto A, Evans TJ, Cohen J. Proinflammatory cytokine production by human peripheral mononuclear cells stimulated with cell-free supernatants of viridans streptococci. Cytokine. 1996;8:300-304.

98. Pechumer H, Wilhelm M, Zieglerheitbrock HWL. Interleukin-6 (IL-6) levels in febrile children during maximal aplasia after bone marrow transplantation (BMT) are similar to those in children with normal hematopoiesis. Ann Hematol. 1995;70:309-312.

99. Manian FA. A prospective study of daily measurement of C-reactive protein in serum of adults with neutropenia. Clin Infect Dis. 1995;21:114-121.

100. De Bel C, Gerritsen E, De Maaker G, et al. C-reactive protein in the management of children with fever after allogeneic bone marrow transplantation. Infection. 1991;19:92-96.

101. Rintala E, Irjala K, Nikoskelainen J. Value of measurement of C-reactive protein in febrile patients with hematological malignancies. Eur J Clin Microbiol Infect Dis. 1992;11:973-978.

102. Santolaya ME, Cofre J, Beresi V. C-reactive protein: A valuable aid for the management of febrile children with cancer and neutropenia. Clin Infect Dis. 1994;18:589-595.

103. Ligtenberg PC, Hoepelman IM, Oude Sogtoen GAC, et al. C-reactive protein in the diagnosis and management of infections in granulocytopenic and non-granulocytopenic patients. Eur J Clin Microbiol Infect Dis. 1991;10:25-31.

104. Riikonen P, Saarinen UM, Teppo AM, et al. Cytokine and acute-phase reactant levels in serum of children with cancer admitted for fever and neutropenia. J Infect Dis. 1992;166:432-436.

105. Mermel LA, Maki DG. Detection of bacteremia in adults: Consequences of culturing an inadequate volume of blood. Ann Intern Med. 1993;119:270-272.

106. Lamy B, Roy P, Carret G, et al. What is the relevance of obtaining multiple blood samples for culture? A comprehensive model to optimize the strategy for diagnosing bacteremia. Clin Infect Dis. 2002;35:842-850.

107. The EORTC International Antimicrobial Therapy Cooperative Group. Gram-positive bacteraemia in granulocytopenic cancer patients. Eur J Cancer. 1990;26:569-574.

108. Villablanca JG, Steiner M, Kersey J, et al. The clinical spectrum of infections with viridans streptococci in bone marrow transplant patients. Bone Marrow Transplant. 1990;5:387-393.

109. Donnelly JP, Muus P, Horrevorts AM, et al. Failure of clindamycin to influence the course of severe oromucositis associated with streptococcal bacteraemia in allogeneic bone marrow transplant recipients. Scand J Infect Dis. 1993;25:43-50.

110. Johnson S, Driks MR, Tweten RK, et al. Clinical courses of seven survivors of *Clostridium septicum* infection and their immunologic responses to α-toxin. Clin Infect Dis. 1994;19:761-764.

111. Novakova IR, Donnelly JP, De Pauw B. Potential sites of infection that develop in febrile neutropenic patients. Leuk Lymphoma. 1993;10:461-467.

112. Caillot D, Casasnovas O, Bernard A, et al. Improved management of invasive pulmonary aspergillosis in neutropenic patients using early thoracic computed tomographic scan and surgery. J Clin Oncol. 1997;15:139-147.

113. Becker MJ, Lugtenburg EJ, Cornelissen JJ, et al. Galactomannan detection in computerized tomography-based broncho-alveolar lavage fluid and serum in haematological patients at risk for invasive pulmonary aspergillosis. Br J Haematol. 2003;121:448-457.

114. Denning DW, Evans EG, Kibbler CC, et al. Guidelines for the investigation of invasive fungal infections in haematological malignancy and solid organ transplantation. British Society for Medical Mycology. Eur J Clin Microbiol Infect Dis. 1997;16:424-436.

115. Seyfartg HJ, Nenoff P, Winkler J, et al. *Aspergillus* detection in bronchoscopically acquired material: Significance and interpretation. Mycoses. 2001;44:356-360.

116. Musa MO, Al Eisa A, Halim M, et al. The spectrum of *Fusarium* infection in immunocompromised patients with haematological malignancies and in non-immunocompromised patients: A single institution experience over 10 years. Br J Haematol. 2000;108:544-548.

117. Hughes WT, Armstrong D, Bodey GP, et al. 2002 guidelines for the use of antimicrobial agents in neutropenic patients with cancer. Clin Infect Dis. 2002;34:730-751.

118. Young LS. Antimicrobial prophylaxis against infection in neutropenic patients. J Infect Dis. 1983;147:611-614.

119. Verweij PE, Donnelly JP, De Pauw BE, Meis JFGM. Prospects for the early diagnosis of invasive aspergillois in the immunocompromised host. Rev Med Microbiol. 1996;7:105-113.

120. Walsh TJ, Lee JW, Sien T, et al. Serum d-arabinitol measured by automated quantitative enzymatic assay for detection and therapeutic monitoring of experimental disseminated candidiasis: Correlation with tissue concentrations of *Candida albicans*. J Med Vet Mycol. 1994;32:205-215.

121. Walsh TJ, Hathorn JW, Sobel JD, et al. Detection of circulating *Candida* enolase by immunoassay in patients with cancer and invasive candidiasis. N Engl J Med. 1991;324:1026-1031.
122. Obayashi T, Yoshida M, Mori T, et al. Plasma (1→3)-beta-D-glucan measurement in diagnosis of invasive deep mycosis and fungal febrile episodes. Lancet. 1995;345:17-20.
123. Pinel C, Fricker-Hidalgo H, Lebeau B, et al. Detection of circulating *Aspergillus fumigatus* galactomannan: Value and limits of the Platelia test for diagnosing invasive aspergillosis. J Clin Microbiol. 2003;41:2184-2186.
124. Viscoli C, Machetti M, Gazzola P, et al. *Aspergillus* galactomannan antigen in the cerebrospinal fluid of bone marrow transplant recipients with probable cerebral aspergillosis. J Clin Microbiol. 2002;40:1496-1499.
125. Maertens J, Van Eldere J, Verhaegen J, et al. Use of circulating galactomannan screening for early diagnosis of invasive aspergillosis in allogeneic stem cell transplant recipients. J Infect Dis. 2002;186:1297-1306.
126. Herbrecht R, Letscher-Bru V, Oprea C, et al. *Aspergillus* galactomannan detection in the diagnosis of invasive aspergillosis in cancer patients. J Clin Oncol. 2002;20:1898-1906.
127. Maertens J, Verhaegen J, Lagrou K, et al. Screening for circulating galactomannan as a noninvasive diagnostic tool for invasive aspergillosis in prolonged neutropenic patients and stem cell transplantation recipients: A prospective validation. Blood. 2001;97:1604-1610.
128. Siemann M, Koch-Dorfler M. The Platelia *Aspergillus* ELISA in diagnosis of invasive pulmonary aspergillosis (IPA). Mycoses. 2001;44:266-272.
129. Denning DW, Kibbler CC, Barnes RA. British Society for Medical Mycology proposed standards of care for patients with invasive fungal infections. Lancet Infect Dis. 2003;3:230-240.
130. Gerson SL, Talbot GH, Hurwitz S, et al. Prolonged granulocytopenia: The major risk factor for invasive pulmonary aspergillosis in patients with acute leukemia. Ann Intern Med. 1984;100:345-351.
131. Meyers JD. Infection in bone marrow transplant recipients. Am J Med. 1986;81:27-3.

CHAPTER **307**

Infections in Patients with Hematologic Malignancies

BEN E. DE PAUW

PAUL E. VERWEIJ

The improving prognosis of patients with hematologic malignancies is at least partly due to the opportunity to administer more intensive chemotherapy and to the successful introduction of novel procedures such as allogeneic hematopoietic stem cell transplantation, autologous stem cell reinfusion, platelet transfusions, granulocyte colony-stimulating factors, implanted central venous catheters, a wider array of antimicrobials, and improvements in diagnostic techniques. Unfortunately, lengthened survival during periods of profound immunosuppression has made infections a common complication and expanded the number of potential pathogens.[1-3] The types of infections encountered and causative pathogens do not appear to be age dependent.[4]

Fundamental differences between hematologic malignancies and solid tumors affect the incidence and severity of the infectious complications concerned (Table 307-1). Replacement of bone marrow by malignant cells and the use of cytotoxic therapy unite to cause severe, prolonged neutropenia, the risk of infection being directly related to the severity and duration of neutropenia.[1] Within a week after the initiation of aggressive chemotherapy for acute leukemia, fever will have developed in more than 50% of patients with a hematologic malignancy. However, neutropenia is not the only risk factor that predisposes a patient to infection. T-cell deficiency typically accompanies Hodgkin's disease or can be induced by long-term administration of corticosteroids. With the growing use of other potent immunosuppressive drugs such as purine analogues, fludarabine, pentostatin, and cladribine, as well as monoclonal anti–T- and anti–B-cell antibodies such as rituximab and alemtuzumab (Campath), in the management of lymphoreticular malignancies, the number of patients at risk has almost reached levels encountered in recipients of allogeneic stem cell

TABLE 307-1 Contrasts between Infections in Patients with Hematologic Malignancies and Solid Tumors

Susceptibility Factors Common in Patients with Hematologic Malignancies
Severe, prolonged neutropenia
Prolonged use of implanted vascular catheters
Frequent administration of blood products
More frequent use of antimicrobials, leading to
   More drug-resistant flora
   More superficial and invasive fungal infections
Clinically significant mucositis
T-cell deficiency from disease or treatment
Splenectomy

Susceptibility Factors Common in Patients with Solid Tumors
Obstruction of bronchi, ureter, or intestine by tumor
Local tissue necrosis by tumor
Fibrosis from local radiation therapy
Postoperative wound infections and pneumonia
Port-A-Cath–associated infections

grafts. Splenectomy causes a prolonged, irretrievable depression of the antibody response.[5] With the implementation of new intensive antileukemic regimens, with or without the employment of hematopoietic granulocyte and granulocyte-macrophage growth factors to ameliorate bone marrow toxicity, mucositis has reached a debilitating level in many a patient during the last decade.[6,7] Surgically implanted central venous catheters provide a further portal of infection.[8]

In contrast, patients with solid tumors show a different pattern of infection, often dependent on the localization of the tumor mass and tissue damage from local irradiation. For example, patients with lung cancer are prone to develop pneumonia from bronchial obstruction, and patients with a malignancy in the digestive tract may come to suffer from intestinal obstruction or perforation and postoperative infections. Impediment of the urine flow by a tumor as well as devices to relieve such an obstruction will render the patient susceptible to infections of the urinary tract.

Remarkably, the mortality attributed to bacterial sepsis appears to be lower in patients who are treated for leukemia than in those with an intermediate grade of malignant lymphoma or solid tumor.[9,10] This difference can be explained by the fact that the latter patients are often treated on an outpatient basis and neither they nor their relatives might react quickly enough to fever or other symptoms indicative of infection, which can lead to a potentially hazardous delay in instituting appropriate antimicrobial therapy.

A standard work-up of a febrile, neutropenic patient ought to include a short history and a meticulous physical examination with special attention to the sites with predilection for infection, which include the perineum, the peridontium, and the skin, including bone marrow aspiration sites, vascular access sites, and tissue around the nails. Samples of blood and of tissue from any other clinically suspicious body site should be taken for culture whenever fever is registered. Despite extensive cultures, only around 30% of all febrile patients will be shown to have microbiologically defined infections.[11,12] A chest radiograph or, preferably, a computed tomography (CT) scan, should be made as early as possible.

CLINICAL PRESENTATION OF INFECTIONS

Bacteremia and Fungemia

A substantial proportion of bacteremic or fungemic patients will present with an insidious onset of fever, so that sepsis may not be expected and blood cultures obtained.[13] Moreover, the recommended volume of blood taken from an adult for blood culture is 10 mL per set. Even with two sets taken on one occasion, low-level fungemia or bacteremia may be missed.[14] A sudden onset, usually accompanied by chills, tachycardia with or without a drop in blood pressure, and tachypnea, is associated with a higher rate of positive blood cultures. In most patients with acute leukemia or lymphoma and a positive blood culture, the source will never be documented.[11,12,15,16] It is generally recognized that the vast majority of febrile episodes that arise early during a neutropenic episode are due to microorganisms originating from the gastrointestinal tract (see Chapter 306). The organisms may be part of the original indigenous flora or, more commonly, acquired during hospitalization.[17,18] Sources other than the gastrointestinal tract include the hands of health care providers, food, toilets, bathrooms, and flowers. Storage of platelets at room temperature for up to 5 days and extended storage of erythrocytes allow proliferation of bacteria that were present in donor blood in low concentration. Bacteria may also be introduced by inappropriate handling of blood products. Sudden onset of fever following transfusion of blood products should lead to culture of the material being infused even though the cause is more frequently related to the occurrence of irregular blood group antigens or cytotoxic antibodies acquired during previous transfusions or pregnancy.[19]

Until the early 1980s, most observations from large studies evaluating febrile episodes in neutropenic patients underscored the predominance of aerobic gram-negative bacilli.[20,21] Since then, a proportional increase in the incidence of gram-positive infections has occurred along with a decrease in bacterial infection–related mortality and a worrisome increase in lethal invasive fungal infections.[22,23] Such changes are the result of alterations in the treatment strategies for hematologic malignancies and more frequent use of prophylactic antibiotics. Prophylaxis aimed against gram-negative rods, among others, may have caused the decrease in the rate of recovery of these pathogens from blood cultures.[24-26] A high spiking temperature is a familiar phenomenon in patients with bacteremia caused by gram-negative rods; roughly 5% of them will present with shock.[13,20,22] Although gram-positive pathogens seem to have largely superseded gram-negative bacilli, the Enterobacteriaceae and *Pseudomonas aeruginosa* still remain the pathogens with the highest mortality rate.[22,27-29] Coagulase-negative staphylococci and streptococci account for the steady increase in infections with gram-positive cocci.[20,30-33] The emergence of viridans streptococci is at least partially the result of selective pressure brought about by the extensive use of fluoroquinolones for prophylactic purposes.[24,33] Severe oral mucositis has made the mouth an important origin of infection by streptococci. A connection has been noted between high-dose cytosine-arabinoside therapy for acute leukemia and the occurrence of bacteremia by viridans streptococci, often identified as *Streptococcus mitis*.[33-35] Despite a lower overall mortality in comparison with sepsis caused by gram-negative bacilli, the morbidity from infections with gram-positive organisms can be substantial. In about 10% of cases with viridans streptococcal septicemia, an adult respiratory distress syndrome evolves with a mortality of around 60% in spite of appropriate therapy.[34,35] The pathophysiology of this serious complication is not fully understood. Probably multiple factors are involved, such as a deleterious effect of microorganisms superimposed on preexisting tissue damage. Corticosteroids have been advocated in the management of patients affected by this complication.[36,37] Finally, with the introduction of aggressive chemotherapeutic regimens, hitherto unusual pathogens such as *Stomatococcus* and *Aerococcus* are increasingly met in patients with mucositis.[38]

Empirical therapy for the febrile neutropenic patient is discussed in Chapter 308. If the hematologic malignancy patient's granulocyte count is not below 500/mm³, empirical therapy for patients without a known infected site is nevertheless required if shock, diffuse intravascular coagulation, lactic acidosis, other signs of abrupt organ damage are present or if a history of splenectomy exists.[11,39,40] Although the clinical relevance of a blood culture positive for gram-negative bacilli is not a matter of controversy, the significance of recovery of some gram-positive cocci is questionable.[39,41-44] If *Staphylococcus epidermidis* is found in blood cultures of neutropenic patients, antibiotic therapy is warranted, even though controversy surrounds its significance.[39,45] Special vigilance is required in splenectomized patients because, without instantaneous antimicrobial therapy, the mortality of a sepsis caused by *Streptococcus pneumoniae* can be as high as 30% even in patients with an adequate granulocyte count.[46,47] Anaerobic bacteria represent less than 1% of the positive blood cultures in febrile

neutropenic patients and are usually part of a polymicrobial bacteremia.[48] Small abscesses of the skin can occur in association with bacteremia by an array of organisms that include coagulase-negative staphylococci, *Staphylococcus aureus,* and, less frequently, *P. aeruginosa, Pseudomonas putida, Burkholderia cepacia, Stenotrophomonas maltophilia, Corynebacterium jeikeium,* and *Bacillus* species.[49-51] Likewise, it is not uncommon for a fungemia to be accompanied by rather characteristic skin lesions.[52,53] In about 10% of candidemias in neutropenic patients, typical pinkish purple, nontender subcutaneous nodules may arise anywhere on the body.[54,55] Abscesses in major muscle groups may cause muscle pain. Biopsy specimens should be cultured and meticulously screened histologically at multiple levels in an attempt to establish a final diagnosis. Of note, occurrence of *Candida* endophthalmitis is rare in neutropenic patients. Growth of a yeast, such as a *Candida* species, or mould, such as a *Fusarium* species, from a blood culture should never be disregarded as a contaminant.[56,57]

Chronic disseminated candidiasis, also called hepatosplenic candidiasis, is a late complication of candidemia in the neutropenic patient, being recognized only after improvement in the neutropenia. If concurrent corticosteroids are being given, patients suffering from chronic disseminated disease may feel relatively well until the infection progresses and organ failure becomes evident. Typically the patient with a hepatosplenic candidiasis has an irregular fever and an elevated alkaline phosphatase and complains of abdominal discomfort with or without organomegaly.[58] After recovery from neutropenia, an abdominal ultrasound or CT scan will demonstrate rather distinctive multiple abscesses with contrast-enhancing margins in the liver, the spleen, or occasionally the kidneys. Mortality may be as high as 40%. Particularly for the non-neutropenic patient, fluconazole and caspofungin represent attractive options for the treatment of both acute and chronic disseminated *Candida* infections.[58-61] For the acutely ill neutropenic patient, an amphotericin B formulation or voriconazole should be considered because *Fusarium* species, *Trichosporon,* and *Blastoschizomyces* have been shown to cause clinical syndromes identical to those caused by *Candida* species.[56,57] All types of chronic disseminated fungal infections require long-term antifungal therapy, at least until normalization of the clinical and laboratory parameters, and adequate protection by antifungals during subsequent episodes of therapy-induced immunosuppression.

Most patients treated for a hematologic malignancy have at least one intravascular device, and these catheters constitute a major target of infection, principally with staphylococci.[8,62] An exogenous origin (e.g., contaminated hands of medical personnel) is more likely in cases of exit site and subcutaneous tract infections in tunneled catheters, whereas infections of the catheter lumen are caused by both exogenous pathogens and those that enter the blood stream from the gut. Malfunction of the catheter as illustrated by the inability to draw blood from the line can be a first warning sign of a possible lumen infection. The clinical spectrum of these catheter-related infections (see Chapter 300) ranges from asymptomatic bacteremia or a process confined to the site of insertion to marked inflammation of the tunnel tract and septicemia with metastatic emboli in the skin and other organs.[63] Infection caused by *S. aureus* along the subcutaneous route or tunnel of an implanted catheter constitutes a serious emergency. Rapid progression of erythema and edema around the tunnel, accompanied by increasing fever and shock, can only be reversed by immediate catheter removal. Screening the region of the subcutaneous catheter tract and vein of insertion by ultrasound is very useful to reveal the possible presence of abscess formation and thrombosis, respectively.[64] Infections at the exit site of an implanted catheter are usually indolent, often without fever, and likely to respond to antibacterial antibiotics without catheter removal. An occasional patient with severe neutropenia will have a mould infection at the exit site, usually *Aspergillus,* and displays spreading black necrosis in conjunction with a surrounding fiery red erythema.[52] Most catheter-acquired bacteremias and candidemias, however, are not accompanied by signs of infection at the exit site or along the tunnel and present as unexplained fever. A sporadic outpatient will come in for periodic chemotherapy and have a sudden fever, sometimes with a chill, in the hour after the infusion begins. The etiology is flushing of organisms within the catheter into the blood stream. Most hospitalized patients receive so many infusions through their various catheter ports that organisms do not accumulate sufficiently to cause a sudden fever during an infusion. The diagnosis of bacteremia and candidemia is easily established by blood cultures taken from the catheter or by venipuncture,[65,66] but the comparison between the two does not help in distinguishing catheter-acquired sepsis from primary septicemia. An exception to the ease of diagnosis of catheter-acquired infections is fungemia from *Malassezia furfur,* a lipophilic yeast that accumulates on the walls of catheters infused with intravenous lipid. Unless enough lipid is present in the blood sent for culture and agar plates supplemented with lipid are used in the clinical microbiology laboratory,[67] this organism will not grow (see Chapter 267).

Most patients with bacteremia should have all their nonimplanted vascular catheters changed as soon as possible, because organisms inside intravascular catheters can be extremely difficult to eliminate.[39,63] As an exception, coagulase-negative staphylococci can often be eradicated for the short term if vancomycin is infused through the contaminated port of the catheter in the accepted therapeutic doses. If the catheter has more than one port, vancomycin infusions are rotated among the ports to avoid microbial sequestration in one of the lines. Although higher vancomycin concentrations have been allowed to dwell temporarily in the catheter—a so-called antibiotic lock—evidence that this enhances catheter sterilization is not at hand.[39] There are no convincing data to recommend routine supplemental use of urokinase or changing the catheter over a guide wire in the management of catheter-related infection. Inserting a fresh catheter into a patient with ongoing bacteremia or fungemia runs a risk of infecting the new catheter. The necessity to remove an implanted catheter is determined by the organism and the patient's response to treatment. Organisms much more challenging to clear from the catheter include *Bacillus* species, *Candida* species, *P. aeruginosa* and other gram-negative rods. Isolation of one of these organisms should indicate the probable need to remove the catheter. Continued positive blood cultures drawn back through the port or peripheral blood after a day or two, plus continued fever, indicate that the device must be removed irrespective of the organism isolated. Pulling the catheter is also mandatory if a concurrent venous thrombosis is found. A practical approach to the management of an uncomplicated catheter-related infection is described in the algorithm in Figure 307-1.[68,69]

Pneumonia

Diagnostic Procedures

Pneumonia, acquired from either the respiratory tract or the blood stream, accounts for 70% of all fatal infections in neutropenic patients.[36,70] Positive blood cultures are very helpful in diagnosis but are only positive in a minority of cases. Cough, pain, and dyspnea should prompt chest radiography or, preferably, CT scanning of the chest at high resolution (HR). It is important to know that it may take a few days for the infection to generate enough necrosis with hemorrhage and edema to produce a visible infiltrate after onset of clinical symptoms; hence a negative HR-CT needs to be repeated within a few days if symptoms persist. The radiologic pattern is often suggestive of the cause of the pulmonary infiltrate. Bacterial pathogens account for most of the pulmonary infiltrates that appear as segmental shadows that do not disrupt the normal anatomic borders of the lung. In contrast, the majority of focal infiltrates are caused by fungi, whereas a diffuse opacity, usually of both lungs, is seldom of bacterial or fungal origin.

The critical decision faced by the clinician at the bedside of patients with pulmonary infiltrates is whether to undertake bronchoscopy with bronchoalveolar lavage, or something more invasive, such as transbronchial biopsy, transthoracic aspiration, thoracoscopy-guided biopsy, or open lung biopsy. Presence of clotting disorders, pulmonary compromise, and the skill of various specialists weigh into the decision. An algorithm for choosing a diagnostic approach is given in Figure 307-2.

Although microscopic examination and culture of expectorated sputum remains the cornerstone of laboratory diagnosis of pneumonia, neutropenic patients often fail to produce sputum. Furthermore, one should be aware that more than one pathogen can be involved in pulmonary infection in the severely compromised host. Fiberoptic bronchoscopy with bronchoalveolar lavage using 100 mL of sterile fluid can provide material for smears for bacteria, *Pneumocystis* and other fungi, *Nocardia,* and mycobacteria, as well as for rapid tests for viral antigen or nucleic acid in respiratory viruses (see Chapter 15).[71-73] Urine can be tested for *Legionella* antigen. Testing serum for *Aspergillus* galactomannan has been found helpful in certain high-risk patients, whereas the value of demonstrating the presence of *Aspergillus* DNA in body fluids by means of polymerase chain reactions remains unclear.[74,75] Recovery of herpes simplex virus (HSV), oral flora, or *Candida* from lavage fluid most often reflects carryover of oropharyngeal flora along the bronchoscope and into the lavage

FIGURE 307-1. Algorithm for the management of intravascular catheter–acquired bacteremia.

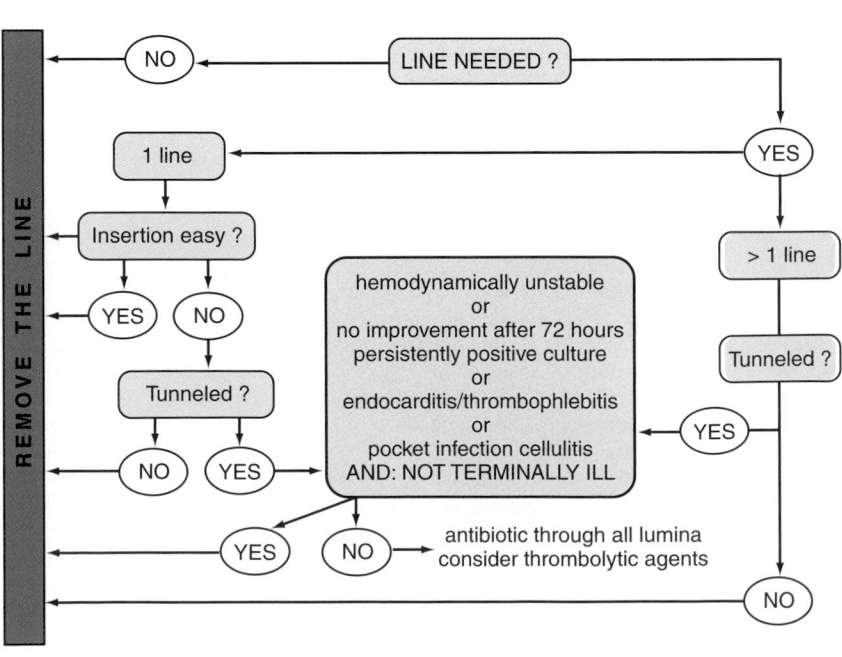

fluid. Culture and cytologic examination of lavage fluid for moulds has a high specificity but a low sensitivity. In one study the diagnostic yield of bronchoscopy in neutropenic patients with proven invasive aspergillosis was only 14% in patients with localized infiltrates and 56% in those with multiple lesions.[76]

Although fiberoptic bronchoscopy with bronchoalveolar lavage is considered a minimally invasive procedure, it is not without risk. The complication rate is as high as 30% in neutropenic patients.[77,78] These complications vary from mild to moderate hypoxemia and bleeding to necessity for mechanical ventilation and death within 24 hours.[77]

Transbronchial biopsy provided a conclusive diagnosis in 55% of patients with hematologic malignancy compared with 35% for bronchoalveolar lavage.[79] This diagnostic yield of transbronchial biopsy was comparable to that of both fluoroscopy and CT-guided fine-needle biopsy.[80] Besides the fact that specimens obtained by fine-needle aspirate are not contaminated by oropharyngeal flora, both histologic and cultural evidence of infection can be obtained, which enhances the certainty of diagnosis. Both transbronchial biopsy and a fine-needle aspirate are superior to lavage fluid for indicating a noninfectious origin of the infiltrate. The complication rate associated with a fine-needle biopsy is approximately 25% and includes pneumothorax and hemorrhage into the thoracic cavity. Considering that even with the most invasive procedure, the open lung biopsy, 20% of causes remain obscure, fine-needle aspirates and transbronchial biopsies appear to be useful alternatives to open lung biopsy. Video-assisted thoracoscopic biopsy provides a larger tissue sample but has a higher morbidity and usually requires temporary placement of a chest tube.

Pneumonias with Diffuse Infiltrates

A radiologic pattern of diffuse shadowing spreading more or less symmetrically over both lungs is indicative of interstitial tissue damage. Viruses play an important role in the etiology of such diffuse pulmonary infiltrates in patients with deficient cellular immunity.[81,82] Although even odd examples such as measles and varicella have been found responsible for pneumonitis under these circumstances, the predominant viruses are cytomegalovirus, respiratory syncytial virus (RSV), influenza, adenoviruses, and human parainfluenza viruses. *Mycoplasma pneumoniae* with or without cold agglutinins is remarkably infrequent in patients treated for leukemia or lymphoma.

Respiratory Syncytial Virus. RSV, like influenza, is much more common during winter in temperate climates, is highly contagious, and occurs in outbreaks in the community. Onset of RSV in adults is manifested by rhinorrhea, nasal congestion, sore throat, and cough. In the immunocompromised host, infection can spread to cause a life-threatening pneumonia with a diffuse pulmonary infiltrate.[81] Ribavirin given by continuous aerosol has had some beneficial effect on RSV in nonimmunosuppressed children with compromised pulmonary function. Although ribavirin aerosol is not approved for use in adults and its efficacy in adults or immunocompromised children is unknown, the drug is commonly used in immunocompromised adults with diffuse pneumonia.[81-83] Ribavirin is recommended to be given as 6 g/day by aerosol using a SPAG-2 generator at 20 mg/mL over 18 hours. Adults receiving continuous aerosol by face mask have difficulty with speaking, eating, or getting out of bed without removing the mask. Contamination of the hospital gown, bedding, and room with this carcinogenic and mutagenic solution is a hazard for hospital personnel. The same amount of drug can be delivered over 9 hr/day if the ribavirin concentration is doubled to 40 mg/mL and inhaled over 3 hours every 8 hours using a rate of 17 mL/hour. Higher concentrations can clog the aerosol generator. The entire day's dose of 150 mL should be delivered in one disposable respirator flask and left in the room between treatments. The pharmacy has to place an extra 25 mL in each disposable respirator reservoir to allow for the amount remaining when the aspirator runs dry. Thus delivering the day's dose in three respirators wastes over 500 mg of a very expensive drug. Administration of polyclonal (RespiGam) or monoclonal antibody to RSV has decreased the incidence of severe RSV in infants with compromised lungs, but efficacy data on treatment of children or adults is unconvincing. Polyclonal antibody (750 mg/kg) raised the neutralization titer of 32 adult hematopoietic stem cell transplant recipients only 1.5-fold.[84] Monoclonal antibody, designed for intramuscular administration to children, can be given intravenously to adults but at enormous cost and uncertain benefit.

Other Viral Pneumonias. Influenza can cause serious and fatal infections in allogeneic bone marrow transplant recipients, but in most immunosuppressed patients, a mild clinical course comparable to that in immunocompetent adults is seen.[83] Although oseltamivir has not been shown to improve the outcome of influenza in highly

FIGURE 307-2. Algorithm for the approach to diagnosis of fungal pneumonia in patients with a hematologic malignancy.

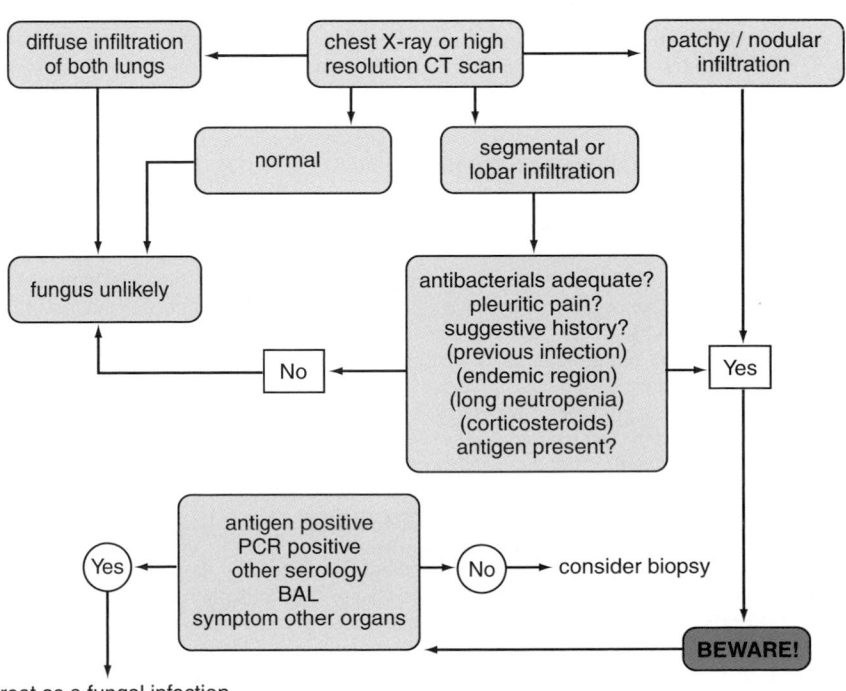

immunocompromised patients, the drug shortens duration of illness in the normal host if begun in the first 2 days after onset of illness and continued for 5 days. Zanamivir aerosol can also be used for influenza A or B but requires more patient skill to administer and can cause bronchospasm in asthmatic patients. Rimantadine and amantadine can be used for influenza A. Parainfluenza virus, mainly type 3, may cause pneumonia in immunosuppressed adults as well as in children.[85] In patients who develop graft-versus-host disease after an allogeneic bone marrow transplantation, cytomegalovirus should be the leading concern when a patient presents with dry cough and shortness of breath. This virus has been recognized as a key etiologic agent in patients with life-threatening diffuse pulmonary infiltrates. Although randomized controlled trials are lacking, the combination of ganciclovir and immune globulin has been commonly used for cytomegalovirus pneumonia. Foscarnet may serve as an alternative for patients who do not tolerate ganciclovir.

Pneumocystosis. *Pneumocystis jirovecii* pneumonia is manifested in patients with deficient cellular immunity as fever, progressive hypoxemia with dry cough, and dyspnea.[86] Although fever and dyspnea may precede chest radiographic abnormalities by a day or two, the chest film soon shows discrete infiltrates advancing to interstitial pneumonia. Clinical signs and symptoms often begin after discontinuation of corticosteroid therapy given for other reasons. The definitive diagnosis is based on displaying cysts or trophic forms of the organism in cytocentrifuge preparations of lavage fluid. The most sensitive stain is fluorochrome-labeled monoclonal antibody, which is preferred over the commonly used Gomori methenamine-silver and Giemsa stains. Trimethoprim-sulfamethoxazole is the drug of choice for treatment of *P. jirovecii* pneumonia.[86] Alternatives include intravenous pentamidine, oral dapsone in combination with trimethoprim, or oral atovaquone suspension alone. Adjuvant therapy with corticosteroids is widely practiced, but its definite value is only clearly established for the initial treatment of hypoxemic patients ($PO_2 < 70$ mm Hg) with pneumocystosis and acquired immunodeficiency syndrome (see Chapter 268).[87]

Noninfectious Diffuse Pulmonary Infiltrates. Diffuse, bilateral pulmonary infiltrates, usually accompanied by tachypnea and hypoxemia, can be due to noninfectious causes, including fluid overload; acute lung injury following transfusion of a blood product; radiation- or chemotherapy-induced tissue damage associated with drugs such as methotrexate, cytarabine, and bleomycin; adult respiratory distress syndrome following *S. mitis* bacteremia after high-dose cytarabine; bronchiolitis obliterans with organizing pneumonia; or pulmonary hemorrhage.[34,35] The mortality is substantial. Recipients of hematopoietic stem cell transplantation are prone to the same noninfectious pneumonias but also to diffuse infiltrates from chronic graft-versus-host disease and an idiopathic pneumonia syndrome.

Pneumonias with Localized Infiltrates

Bacterial infections of the lung typically create patchy infiltrates or dense, localized areas of consolidation. About 50% of immunocompromised patients with a bacterial pneumonia have a positive blood culture. Gram-positive bacteria are slightly more prevalent, but overall the spectrum of causative organisms does not differ substantially from that in other patients.[70] Most causative bacteria are adequately covered by the standard empirical regimens, albeit that in neutropenic patients with a pulmonary infiltrate, combination therapy appears to produce better results than a single agent (see Chapter 308).[12,36,70] *Legionella* pneumonia is characterized by fever, cough, and a chest radiograph with patchy interstitial or nodular infiltrates and is occasionally accompanied by headache, gastrointestinal symptoms, and renal insufficiency.[88]

Fungal Pneumonia with Halo or Crescent Signs. HR-CT has proven invaluable in early detection of invasive pulmonary aspergillosis in highly immunosuppressed patients, particularly those with prolonged neutropenia or hematopoietic stem cell transplantation.[89-93] Early lesions are small, round, dense areas of consolidation that increase in size over a few days and represent a central core of necrosis and hemorrhage resulting from angioinvasion by the mould. As the lesion enlarges it is temporarily surrounded by a ring of "ground-glass" appearing infiltrate or "halo." This ring of edema and hemorrhage can only be reliably appreciated at the equator of the lesion. Image averaging can create the appearance of a halo in a dense infiltrate if the optical section is to either side of the equator. A halo on HR-CT is not a specific phenomenon but is often the first evidence of pulmonary aspergillosis in patients with leukemia, lymphoma, or stem cell transplantation.[89] In the proper setting, appearance of a halo sign should prompt preemptive therapy with an agent active against *Aspergillus* species, although other moulds may cause an identical radiologic picture.[93-95] As the patient's neutrophils return or immunosuppression lessens, the necrotic center of an angioinvasive mould infection retracts, leaving a crescent of air in a cavity containing residual necrotic debris. The crescent sign is usually too late in the course to assist with early diagnosis. Culture or calcofluor-stained smears of sputum or bronchoalveolar lavage fluid may contain *Aspergillus* at the time a cavity develops on HR-CT because the expectorated debris contains the fungus. Earlier in the course of invasive pulmonary aspergillosis, sputum culture lacks sensitivity and, in adults, lacks specificity.[94] Less than 25% of patients in whom the disease is shown at autopsy have had any positive sputum culture or microscopic finding ante mortem.[97] Detection of *Aspergillus* DNA, $(1\rightarrow3)$-β-D-glucan, or galactomannan in blood may prove to be helpful in the early diagnosis.[98] *Aspergillus* galactomannan has also been detected in bronchoalveolar lavage fluid of patients with pulmonary infection, but the diagnostic utility is as yet unknown.

In a large, randomized study of invasive aspergillosis, a regimen starting with voriconazole proved to be superior to a regimen beginning with amphotericin B with respect to both response rates and survival. The survival rate at 12 weeks was 71% in the voriconazole group and 58% in the amphotericin B group. This superiority was maintained in all subgroups, such as neutropenic patients treated for hematologic malignancies and those with pulmonary aspergillosis.[99] Visual disturbances caused by voriconazole are common but transient. However, liver function abnormalities and concurrent administration of cytochrome P-450–dependent drugs are common restrictions to the use of voriconazole (see Chapter 37).[99,100] For these cases an intravenous (lipid) formulation of amphotericin should be chosen.[89] The other agent used successfully for the treatment of invasive aspergillosis in less ill patients is itraconazole.[101] Surgery can be considered for patients in whom lesions near the pulmonary hilus pose a direct threat of invasion of a major vessel with the risk of fatal hemorrhage.[102] Resection can also be considered for rare patients with aspergillosis confined to a single lobe, in whom the acute illness has stabilized and who still have to undergo bone marrow transplantation or further aggressive chemotherapy.[102-104] Granulocyte transfusions harvested from growth factor–pretreated donors have been used in patients not responding to antifungal therapy, but efficacy of this expensive, labor-intensive approach is unknown.[105,106]

Other Fungal Pneumonias. The moulds *Scedosporium (Pseudallescheria), Fusarium,* and the agents of mucormycosis constitute a growing problem in granulocytopenic patients and bone marrow transplant recipients.[94,95,107] The clinical picture related to these fungi can resemble aspergillosis, although differences do exist (see Chapters 257 and 267). The pneumonias may be underreported inasmuch as the histologic demonstration of septate hyphae in pulmonary tissue can easily be misinterpreted as belonging to *Aspergillus* species. Because it is virtually impossible to adequately identify some of those fungal species by histology, confirmation by culture should be pursued in every case, although attempts to culture agents of mucormycosis from infected tissue are often unsuccessful.

Tuberculosis and Nocardiosis. Especially in patients with a concomitant impairment of cell-mediated immunity, pulmonary aspergillosis has to be distinguished from tuberculosis. Infections with *Mycobacterium tuberculosis* in patients with impaired cell-mediated immunity emerge as either localized pulmonary disease or devastating miliary tuberculosis. Fluorochrome stains of respiratory specimens have improved the sensitivity of detection of mycobacteria and help to differentiate them from nonmycobacterial organisms.[71] Nontuberculous mycobacteria are still rather rare in patients with lymphoma or leukemia, but the introduction of purine analogues such as cladribine and fludarabine may change this picture in the near future. The impact of purine analogues on the immune system at the end of a treatment course shows a striking congruence with the deficiencies seen in patients with acquired immunodeficiency syndrome or in those who are treated for graft-versus-host disease after allogeneic bone marrow transplantation.

The most common signs of nocardiosis are infiltrates in the lungs and abscesses in the skin, soft tissues, or brain.[108] For immunocompromised patients with an infection caused by *Nocardia* species, therapy should be continued for 12 months.

Mechanical Ventilation. Progression of a pneumonia, independent of the causative infectious agent, quite frequently leads to life-threatening respiratory failure. However, in immunosuppressed patients, endotracheal intubation and mechanical ventilation carry an exceptionally high mortality rate.[109,110] Noninvasive ventilation might be a suitable alternative for selected patients.[111]

Oropharyngeal Infections

Gingivostomatitis, usually as a direct result of chemotherapy-induced mucositis, and periodontal lesions occur frequently in patients with acute leukemia.[112,113] If feasible, dental procedures should be done before intensive antineoplastic therapy is begun or postponed until remission has been achieved. Oral mucositis in granulocytopenic patients is characterized by pain, edema, erythema, superficial lesions, formation of pseudomembranes in conjunction with excessive mucous production, reduced saliva secretion, and bleeding. Pain may impair swallowing of a patient's own saliva or other liquids. Inspection of the mouth and endoscopy may require analgesia or even conscious sedation in patients with severe mucositis. If the patient is not receiving prophylactic antivirals, infection of the mouth, larynx, or esophagus with HSV must be considered and cultures obtained.[114] Oropharyngeal candidiasis cannot be diagnosed by culture because colonization of the mouth with *Candida* species is the rule in these patients. Therefore, examination of a smear taken from the mucosa for the presence of *Candida* pseudohyphae is mandatory to establish a reliable diagnosis. Pain on swallowing or hoarseness may indicate the need for endoscopy to detect HSV or candidiasis in the esophagus or larynx.[114,115] Coinfection of HSV lesions with *Candida* is common in immunosuppressed patients. Biopsies of esophageal ulcers should be immuno-stained for cytomegalovirus, in addition to cultures for HSV and Gomori methenamine-silver stain for *Candida*. Bacteremia caused by viridans group streptococci may originate in the mouth and lead to shock and adult respiratory distress syndrome. Because the selection of an antimicrobial regimen should be guided by the recognized prevalence of gram-positive organisms, one should be aware that carbapenems and extended-spectrum penicillins do possess a superior activity against viridans streptococci.[116,117]

Otitis

Malignant otitis externa is a very serious infectious complication that usually occurs in poorly controlled diabetics or elderly patients but can also emerge after the administration of aggressive chemotherapy for a hematologic malignancy. At the outset the patient will complain of a painful, discharging ear. Physical examination will reveal pain on tugging on the pinna and an edematous, pale external auditory canal full of moist desquamated debris. Extension of the otitis to the middle ear may lead to ipsilateral seventh cranial nerve palsy. Magnetic resonance imaging (MRI) or CT is useful in detecting invasion of contiguous structures, including the brain.

A swab of the debris usually shows *P. aeruginosa* on culture, which calls for prolonged antibiotic therapy with ceftazidime or ciprofloxacin in combination with local débridement (see Chapter 216).[118] Less commonly, invasive otitis externa in the seriously immunosuppressed patient is caused by *Aspergillus fumigatus* or *A. niger* (see Chapter 256). For the treatment of such cases, surgery should be combined with voriconazole or another appropriate systemic antifungal agent.

Sinusitis

Headache or pain over a paranasal sinus may be an early symptom of sinusitis, but some patients present only with fever. CT of the paranasal sinuses is more useful than a conventional radiograph. Many patients have mucosal thickening and fluid levels in one or more paranasal si-

nuses as a result of allergy or viral infections. These conditions cause swelling of the nasal mucosa and blockage of the sinus ostia.

A CT showing no fluid in any of the sinuses is helpful in ruling out ordinary bacterial sinusitis. Bone erosion indicates invasive fungal sinusitis, severe bacterial infection, or prior sinus surgery. Invasive fungal sinusitis in patients with leukemia and lymphoma is often due to mucormycosis or aspergillosis, although other moulds are occasionally encountered.[89,94,95,107,119] Both mucormycosis and aspergillosis often begin with lesions in the mucosa of the nasal turbinates. The most characteristic lesion is a single area of erythema, becoming progressively crimson, then pale, then black as vascular invasion infarcts the mucosa and underlying bone. Thorough endoscopic examination of the nasal mucosa and biopsy of a mucosal lesion can be diagnostic and has little attendant risk of uncontrolled bleeding. Demonstration of fungal elements by microscopy provides a rapid indication of fungal origin of the lesion. The results of treatment with intravenous antifungal agents supplemented by radical excision of necrotic and nonviable material are rather poor in persistently neutropenic patients. This explains why many a physician feels compelled to administer granulocyte suspensions in an attempt to improve the prognosis.[106,120] Successes have been reported, but the benefits and disadvantages of this procedure are as yet insufficiently explored.

Infections of the Central Nervous System

Diagnostic Considerations

Onset of headache, confusion, seizures, or focal neurologic abnormalities in patients with hematologic malignancies has many different potential causes, including malignancy, metabolic abnormality, cerebral hemorrhage, infarction, drug toxicity, and infection (Table 307-2). Absence of fever is more suggestive of a noninfectious cause, but corticosteroid therapy can blunt fever, and many patients with a cryptococcal meningitis or bacterial brain abscess are afebrile. Likewise, progressive multifocal leukoencephalopathy is rarely accompanied by fever.[121] In more indolent cases, empirical antibiotics are not given until diagnostic procedures have been employed. When acute onset of headache and fever raises concern about bacterial meningitis or brain abscess, blood cultures should be obtained, antibiotics begun, and a CT scan or, preferably, MRI with gadolinium contrast enhancement performed. Provided that no focal lesions or increased intracranial pressure are found, a lumbar puncture has to be done. Recovery of *Listeria monocytogenes* or *Cryptococcus neoformans* from blood cultures taken from patients with a hematologic malignancy should always trigger a lumbar puncture even in the absence of neurologic symptoms. The low number of cryptococci in the cerebrospinal fluid (CSF) helps to explain why the sensitivity of India ink examinations to diagnose cryptococcal meningitis is only 50% in patients with hematologic malignancies. For this particular organism antigen detection in the CSF seems more reliable, with a sensitivity of 95%. *Aspergillus* galactomannan can be detected in the CSF of patients with central nervous system aspergillosis, but this test has not yet been validated for this purpose.[122,123] Of particular interest in patients with lymphocytic pleocytosis are the CSF cytology with immunostaining or polymerase chain reaction for B-cell monoclonality. Tests for *M. tuberculosis* nucleic acid in CSF are experimental and promising.

TABLE 307-2 Differential Diagnostic Considerations in Infections of the Central Nervous System

Metabolic disorders
  Diabetes mellitus, hypophosphatemia, hypokalemia
  Sepsis-associated metabolic acidosis and hypotension
Thrombotic or hemorrhagic disorders
Toxic drug reactions
  Anaphylactic shock
  Cytotoxic drugs: cytarabine, methotrexate
  Immunosuppressive drugs: cyclosporin A
  (Overdose of) tranquilizers, antiemetics, anticonvulsants, opiates
  Accidental intrathecal administration of drugs such as vinca alkaloids
Intracerebral or meningeal localization of lymphoma or leukemia

Positron emission tomography scanning has been considered helpful in distinguishing focal lesions of toxoplasmosis from lymphoma in some reports. Patients failing to respond to therapy for toxoplasmosis often require a brain biopsy to distinguish malignancy from infection. A negative test for serum immunoglobulin G antibody to *Toxoplasma gondii* weighs against the diagnosis of cerebral toxoplasmosis. A specific viral etiology of meningitis or encephalitis is rarely established, but their incidence is almost certainly greatly underestimated.[124,125] Samples of CSF should be collected to do specific tests to exclude viruses as a possible cause of meningoencephalitis in all cases in which no unequivocal diagnosis can be achieved.

Treatment

The common empirical regimens will cover all probable causative bacterial agents, but genuine concern about listeriosis should prompt inclusion of ampicillin (see Chapter 80). Treatment of toxoplasmosis requires prolonged administration of sulfonamides with pyrimethamine in combination with folinic acid to minimize the associated myelosuppression.[126] In spite of timely treatment with the presently most active antifungal agent, voriconazole, central nervous system infections with *Aspergillus* species carry a high mortality.[127] Treatment of viral encephalitis has been, apart from acyclovir for herpes infections and ganciclovir for cytomegalovirus, largely unsuccessful.

In-depth discussion of differential diagnosis and treatment of central nervous system infections is given in Section H of Part II of this book.

Infections of the Gastrointestinal Tract

Esophagitis

Extension of oropharyngeal candidiasis into the esophagus is common, but epiglottitis and reactive cervical lymphadenitis caused by *Candida* species are rare.[115] Only endoscopy with collection of a tissue sample for histologic examination and culture may be useful in establishing the correct diagnosis. If *Candida* esophagitis, gastritis, or duodenitis is diagnosed endoscopically in a persistently febrile neutropenic patient, the presence of a disseminated candidiasis should be considered.

Typhlitis and Other Types of Colitis

The signs and symptoms of chemotherapy-induced typhlitis in patients with acute leukemia are variable but most commonly include fever and right lower quadrant pain and tenderness. There may be nausea, vomiting, abdominal cramps, and either diarrhea or constipation. Many patients are in such pain that they only gain relief from narcotic analgesics, which, in turn, induce constipation by reduction of bowel movements. The diagnosis of an acute abdomen may be suggested by absent bowel sounds, rebound tenderness, guarding, pain, and fever. Laparotomy in patients with a hypoplastic bone marrow is fraught with complications and best avoided. CT with oral contrast can assist diagnosis by showing a thickened, edematous cecal mucosa.

Diarrhea is common in leukemic patients, often from chemotherapy or broad-spectrum antibiotics.[128] *Clostridium difficile* colitis can manifest as a severe and recurring fever causing problems in patients with hematologic malignancies. Diarrhea may lag a day or two behind the fever and disappear if severe colitis occurs. Fecal carriage of *C. difficile* varies considerably among institutions, perhaps reflecting differences in antibiotic use and nosocomial acquisition.[129-131] Stool should be tested for *C. difficile* toxin if the diagnosis is suspected. The drugs of choice are oral metronidazole and vancomycin. Relapses are frequent and may follow cytotoxic therapy or courses with antibiotics such as clindamycin. Relapse is harder to document because toxin may persist in the stool of successfully treated patients, especially in those who continue to receive broad-spectrum antibacterial agents. Bacterial overgrowth in the gastrointestinal tract of patients with damaged mucosa can serve as a source of bacteremia caused by the well-known gastrointestinal flora as well as by otherwise exclusively enteric pathogens such as *Clostridium septicum*.[132] Therefore, antibiotic treatment of patients with abdominal symptoms should include coverage of gram-negative rods, including *P. aeruginosa* and *Escherichia coli*, as well as protection against anaerobes including *Bacteroides fragilis*. Diagnostic problems are held accountable for underrating enteric viruses as causative agents in gastrointestinal infections.

Strongyloides stercoralis should be remembered as a cause of diarrhea in patients from less developed countries or those who have lived in endemic areas. Untreated immunosuppressed patients may develop hyperinfection, with pulmonary infiltrates and infection of the CSF and blood with enteric gram-negative bacilli.[133]

Infections of the Genitourinary Tract

Urinary tract infection is relatively uncommon in patients who are treated for a leukemia or lymphoma, particularly if no indwelling urinary catheters are used. Viral hemorrhagic cystitis is largely confined to recipients of hematopoietic stem cell transplant and is discussed in Chapter 311. *Candida* species are commonly isolated from clean voided urine from women and from Foley catheter urine. These cultures have clinical significance in the presence of surgery or invasive procedures on an infected genitourinary tract or in the presence of urinary tract obstruction. The urine *Candida* colony count has no known significance, but treatment with fluconazole is often done in patients with candiduria when neutropenic.

Patients undergoing cytotoxic chemotherapy for leukemia or lymphoma appear not to be predisposed to develop serious infections of the reproductive organs. Presumably as a result of reduced sexual activity, vulvovaginal candidiasis is relatively uncommon. Vaginal candidiasis is not known as a port of entry for dissemination. Vulvovaginal HSV infection occurs sporadically but can extend to the intertriginous skin in the perineum and perineal area.

Skin Infections

The most common causative microorganisms in both local inoculation and blood-borne infections of the skin are streptococci, staphylococci, and, less commonly, gram-negative bacilli, enterococci, or fungi. Sometimes it is difficult to differentiate infectious lesions from drug-induced toxic skin eruptions. Initial erythema and infiltration are rather mild and atypical but, if left untreated, infiltration and abscess formation will become more aggressive to involve extensive areas of the skin with necrosis and gangrene. Because the lesions caused by the different organisms are similar, a simple needle aspiration or biopsy should be performed as early as possible in the course of the disease to establish a definitive and accurate diagnosis. Patients with desquamating or ulcerated plaques caused by mycosis fungoides, a T-cell lymphoma, are prone to having recurrent *S. aureus* infections of the plaques, responding incompletely to antibacterial therapy and adding to the pain and weeping from these lesions.

Escherichia coli, often in combination with anaerobes, is the prevalent agent in perianal cellulitis with painful abscess formation and the risk of developing rectovaginal fistula in women. It used to be a recognized complication of the treatment for acute leukemias, but its incidence has declined, probably as a result of higher awareness combined with better local care and, possibly, improved antibacterial chemoprophylaxis.

Ecthyma gangrenosum is a distinct clinical entity, occurring in patients with profound neutropenia and carrying a bad prognosis. The lesions appear either from hematogenous spread or from local inoculation. The lesion begins as a painful, well-circumscribed, bright red macule, often with a surrounding ring of pallor. As the lesion becomes larger over the next 24 hours, a sharp margin and deepening cherry-red center appears, which may form a bulla. The sharply marginated lesion eventually becomes black. Biopsy shows numerous gram-negative bacilli in deep subcutaneous veins or, much less commonly, shows hyphae of aspergillosis or mucormycosis.[27,52,56,57] Ecthyma gangrenosum from cutaneous inoculation appears at sites of trauma, such as a catheter exit site or straight-razor shave of the axilla or leg in women and beard in men. Fever is absent unless hematogenous dissemination occurs. Similar lesions can arise hematogenously in one or more body sites unrelated to trauma. Profound fever is usual. Blood cultures are usually positive in hematogenous ecthyma gangrenosum from *P. aeruginosa*. The site of origin of hematogenous ecthyma gangrenosum, from either *Pseudomonas* or mould, is usually occult.

Ecthyma gangrenosum should be distinguished from pyoderma gangrenosum, an indolent, noninfectious, well-circumscribed plaque, usually over the anterior tibia, in patients with a myeloid malignancy or inflammatory bowel disease.[134] Scattered papules or subcutaneous nodules in a febrile, heavily immunosuppressed patient should suggest the possibility of disseminated candidiasis or fusariosis.[52,56,57] Scedosporiosis can cause erythematous skin nodules either at a site of minor trauma or from hematogenous dissemination. Lesions usually ulcerate as they enlarge. Hyphae are numerous on punch biopsy. Similar lesions can arise hematogenously from nocardiosis or cryptococcosis. The fungi *Trichophyton rubrum* and *M. furfur,* causative agents of tinea corporis and tinea versicolor, respectively, have been found responsible for extensive and serious infections of the skin and even for dissemination in patients who are treated intensively for an acute leukemia or high-grade malignant lymphoma. If found, these infections need to be treated with systemic antifungal therapy in this category of patients.

Varicella-zoster is the leading dermatologic complication in patients with an impaired cell-mediated immunity and is discussed in detail in Chapter 311.[125] HSV may cause extensive, painful skin ulcerations around the mouth, genitalia, and rectum. Infection can spread from oral or genital lesions into skin lesions caused by cutaneous tumors, such as mycosis fungoides, or into wounds such as decubiti. The unexpected worsening and ulceration of skin lesions in patients with oral HSV should suggest the utility of culturing the ulcer discharge for HSV. Dissemination of HSV from the skin to the viscera, such as liver or lung, is extremely uncommon. HSV encephalitis is rare in immunocompromised patients and does not begin as skin lesions.

The sudden appearance of tender, reddish brown cutaneous plaques, fever, and leukocytosis should suggest Sweet's syndrome.[135] Lesions tend to appear on the head, neck, and upper extremities, and biopsy will show dense infiltration of the dermis by neutrophils. This is not an infectious entity and does not require antibacterial therapy.

MANAGEMENT OF INFECTIONS AFTER THE INITIAL PHASE

Approximately 65% of patients without a focus of infection will defervesce within 5 days after commencement of broad-spectrum antibiotics (see Chapter 308). A slower response is seen in patients with a clinically documented infection.[12,15,16,116,117,136]

If fever persists in spite of adequate antibiotic therapy, a reassessment is compulsory and should include a review of all previous cultures, a meticulous physical examination, HR-CT of the chest, inspection of the status of vascular catheters, and collection of further blood samples and specimens of suspicious sites of infection for culture.[136] Performing daily blood cultures is a prudent procedure as long as fever persists and when a new temperature peak occurs. Such investigations will reveal new foci of infection in about 10% of patients. Without the determination of a new clue to a possible causative agent, continuation of the initial antibiotics is a suitable approach if the patient's condition is clinically stable or improving. Persisting fever alone without a rapid deterioration of the patient's condition provides an unsatisfactory basis for modification of an antibiotic regimen.[12,16] A possible relation between nonresponding fever and pyrogenic substances, including drugs that have been used during the preceding days or are still being given, or the underlying disease itself should be considered.[137] Disturbance of the normal immune system is presumed to be responsible for the high drug allergy rate in patients with active acute leukemia. Relatively new in recipients of allogeneic stem cell transplants is a reactivation of Epstein-Barr virus with progress to an aggressive lymphoproliferative disorder; monitoring the viral load in cell-free plasma may assist early detection and allows timely treatment with monoclonal antibodies.[138]

After the introduction of fluconazole for the prophylaxis of disseminated *Candida* infections in the early 1990s, even the value of prescribing a systemically active antifungal agent after 3 to 5 days of persisting fever on an empirical basis has become very questionable in patients without any other clinical symptom. Rather, every effort should be made to detect or eliminate the possible presence of a systemic fungal infection before empirical antifungal therapy is deemed necessary, even though fungi have been found to be responsible for two thirds of all superinfections (see Chapter 308).[139]

For approximately 15% of patients who are rapidly deteriorating without any clinical or microbiologic sign of infection, further empirical adjustment of the antibiotic regimen in use is required (see Chapter 308). However, even in these patients a string of subsequent empirical therapeutic interventions should be avoided as much as possible because these are basically futile and often imply neglect of diagnostic procedures. It also has to be emphasized that the benefit of an extended antimicrobial cover is counterbalanced by an increase in adverse events. Instead of changing or adding antimicrobials, attempts to establish a diagnosis or to identify the grounds for nonresponse should be pursued because both negative and positive findings will make it easier to select an optimal strategy in poorly responding patients. Approximately 15% of patients treated for a malignancy will remain or become febrile after recovery of the granulocyte count.[140] The workup should be principally directed at fungal or mycobacterial infections, avascular sites, and noninfectious causes of fever. About 10% of these episodes result in death of the patient.

When the results of the cultures are available and a pathogen is identified, the antibiotic regimen may be changed to provide optimal treatment with minimal adverse effects and lowest costs, but broad-spectrum anti–gram-negative coverage should be maintained as long as the patient is febrile and neutropenic. Even in patients who have negative cultures and remain febrile for more than 5 days, withdrawal of the antimicrobial drugs is not a valid option as long as neutropenia endures, unless the fever is obviously of noninfectious origin. If the patient has been treated adequately for 7 to 9 days, watchful waiting may be preferred over prolonged antimicrobial therapy. If antimicrobial therapy is stopped while the patient is still neutropenic, close monitoring is necessary to allow for prompt reinstitution of intravenous treatment if fever recurs or if any other evidence of infection is observed.[158] Antibiotic therapy may have suppressed but not eradicated the infection. Some favor continuation of antibiotics or a change from a therapeutic to a prophylactic scheme, particularly in patients with persisting profound neutropenia or mucous membrane lesions (see Chapter 308). It is generally accepted to stop the administration of systemic antibiotics in patients who have recovered from their granulocytopenia for a few days and appear healthy without any evidence of infection.

When the reason to commence systemic antifungal treatment was simply fever unresponsive to antibiotics without any evidence of invasive mycosis, its administration can be discontinued when the neutrophil count recovers and fever subsides. This approach also applies when the presumptive diagnosis of an invasive fungal infection becomes questionable during the course of neutropenia. In contrast, in patients with pulmonary infiltrates or other suspicious lesions, it is essential to wait for a clinical and, preferably, a radiologic response before antifungal therapy is discontinued.

REFERENCES

1. Bodey GP, Buckley M, Sathe YS, Freireich EJ. Quantitative relationships between circulating leukocytes and infection in patients with acute leukemia. Ann Intern Med. 1966;64:328-340.
2. Bodey GP, Rodriguez V, Chang HY, et al. Fever and infection in leukemic patients. Cancer. 1978;41:1610-1622.
3. Nosanchuk JD, Sepkowitz KA, Pearse RN, et al. Infectious complications of autologous bone marrow and peripheral stem cell transplantation for refractory leukemia and lymphoma. Bone Marrow Transplant. 1996;18:355-359.
4. Garcia-Suarez J, Krsnik I, Reyes E, et al. Elderly haematological patients with chemotherapy-induced febrile neutropenia have similar rates of infection and outcome to younger adults: A prospective study of risk-adapted therapy. Br J Haematol. 2003;120:209-216.
5. Butler JC, Breiman RF, Campbell JF, et al. Pneumococcal polysaccharide vaccine efficacy: An evaluation of current recommendations. JAMA. 1993;270:1826-1831.
6. Bow EJ, Loewen R, Cheang MS, et al. Cytotoxic therapy-induced D-xylose malabsorption and invasive infection during remission-induction therapy for acute myeloid leukemia in adults. J Clin Oncol. 1997;15:2254-2261.
7. Blijlevens NMA, Donnelly JP, De Pauw BE. Impaired gut function as risk factor for invasive candidiasis in neutropenic patients. Br J Haematol. 2002;117:259-264.
8. Press OW, Ramsey PG, Larson EB, et al. Hickman catheter infections in patients with malignancies. Medicine (Baltimore). 1984;63:189-200.

9. Meunier F, Zinner SH, Gaya H, et al. Prospective randomized evaluation of ciprofloxacin versus piperacillin plus amikacin for empiric antibiotic therapy of febrile granulocytopenic cancer patients with lymphomas and solid tumors. Antimicrob Agents Chemother. 1991;35:873-878.

10. Talcott JA, Siegel RD, Finberg R, Goldman L. Risk assessment in cancer patients with fever and neutropenia: A prospective, two-center validation of a prediction rule. J Clin Oncol. 1992;10:316-322.

11. Pizzo PA. Management of fever in patients with cancer and treatment-induced neutropenia. N Engl J Med. 1993;328:1323-1332.

12. De Pauw BE, Deresinski SC, Feld R, et al. Ceftazidime compared with piperacillin and tobramycin for the empiric treatment of fever in neutropenic patients with cancer: A multicenter randomized trial. The Intercontinental Antimicrobial Study Group. Ann Intern Med. 1994;120:834-844.

13. Sickles EA, Greene WH, Wiernik PH. Clinical presentation of infection in granulocytopenic patients. Arch Intern Med. 1975;135:715-719.

14. Mermel LA, Maki DG. Detection of bacteremia in adults: Consequences of culturing an inadequate volume of blood. Ann Intern Med. 1993;119:270-272.

15. De Pauw BE, Dompeling EC. Antibiotic strategy after the empiric phase in patients treated for a hematological malignancy. Ann Hematol. 1996;72:273-279.

16. De Pauw BE, Raemaekers JMM, Schattenberg T, et al. Empirical and subsequent use of antibacterial agents in the febrile neutropenic patient. J Intern Med. 1997;242:69-77.

17. Schimpff SC, Young VM, Greene WH, et al. Origin of infection in acute nonlymphocytic leukemia: Significance of hospital acquisition of potential pathogens. Ann Intern Med. 1972;77:707-714.

18. Fainstein V, Rodriguez V, Turck M, et al. Patterns of oropharyngeal and fecal flora in patients with acute leukemia. J Infect Dis. 1981;144:82-86.

19. Anderson KC, Lew MA, Gorgone BC, et al. Transfusion-related sepsis after prolonged platelet storage. Am J Med. 1986;81:405-411.

20. Klastersky J, Zinner SH, Calandra T, et al. Empiric antimicrobial therapy for febrile granulocytopenic cancer patients: Lessons from four EORTC trials. Eur J Cancer Clin Oncol. 1988;24(Suppl):S35-S45.

21. Singer C, Kaplan MH, Armstrong D. Bacteremia and fungemia complicating neoplastic disease: A study of 364 cases. Am J Med. 1977;62:731-742.

22. Elting LS, Rubenstein EB, Rolston KVI, Bodey GP. Outcomes of bacteremia in patients with cancer and neutropenia: Observations from two decades of epidemiological and clinical trials. Clin Infect Dis. 1997;25:247-259.

23. Fridkin SK, Jarvis WR. Epidemiology of nosocomial fungal infections. Clin Microbiol Rev. 1996;9:499-511.

24. Donnelly JP, Maschmeyer G, Daenen S, for the EORTC Gnotobiotic Project Group. Selective oral antimicrobial prophylaxis for the prevention of infection in acute leukemia: Ciprofloxacin versus co-trimoxazole plus colistin. Eur J Cancer. 1992;28A:873-878.

25. Awada A, van der Auwera P, Meunier F, et al. Streptococcal and enterococcal bacteremia in patients with cancer. Clin Infect Dis. 1992;15:33-48.

26. Bow EJ, Loewen R, Cheang MS, Schachter B. Invasive fungal disease in adults undergoing remission-induction therapy for acute myeloid leukemia: The pathogeneic role of the antileukemic regimen. Clin Infect Dis. 1995;21:361-369.

27. Bodey GP, Jadeja L, Elting L. *Pseudomonas* bacteremia: Retrospective analysis of 410 episodes. Arch Intern Med. 1985;145:1621-1629.

28. Schimpff SC, Greene WH, Young VM, et al. *Pseudomonas* septicemia: Incidence, epidemiology, prevention and therapy in patients with advanced cancer. Eur J Cancer. 1973;9:449-455.

29. Vidal F, Mensa J, Almela M, et al. Epidemiology and outcome of *Pseudomonas aeruginosa* bacteremia, with special emphasis on the influence of antibiotic treatment: Analysis of 189 episodes. Arch Intern Med. 1996;156:2121-2126.

30. Cohen J, Donnelly JP, Worsley AM, et al. Septicaemia caused by viridans streptococci in neutropenic patient with leukaemia. Lancet. 1983;2:981-983.

31. Winston DJ, Dudnick DV, Chapin M, et al. Coagulase negative staphylococcal bacteremia in patients receiving immunosuppressive therapy. Arch Intern Med. 1983;143:32-36.

32. Whimbey E, Kiehn TE, Brannon P, et al. Bacteremia and fungemia in patients with neoplastic disease. Am J Med. 1987;82:723-729.

33. Kern W, Jurrie E, Schmeiser T. Streptococcal bacteremia in adult patients with leukemia undergoing aggressive chemotherapy: A review of 55 cases. Infection. 1990;18:138-145.

34. Sotiropoulos SV, Jackson MA, Woods GM, et al. Alpha-streptococcal septicemia in leukemic children treated with continuous or large dosage intermittent cytosine arabinoside. Pediatr Infect Dis J. 1989;8:755-758.

35. Engelhard D, Elishoov H, Or R, et al. Cytosine arabinoside as a major risk factor for *Streptococcus viridans* septicemia following bone marrow transplantation: A 5-year prospective study. Bone Marrow Transplant. 1995;16:565-570.

36. Donnelly JP, Nováková IRO, Raemaekers JMM, De Pauw BE. Empiric treatment of localized infections in the febrile neutropenic patients with monotherapy. Leuk Lymphoma. 1993;9:193-203.

37. Dompeling EC, Donnelly JP, Raemaekers JMM, De Pauw BE. Pre-emptive administration of corticosteroids prevents the development of ARDS associated with *Streptococcus mitis* bacteremia following chemotherapy with high-dose cytarabine. Ann Hematol. 1994;69:69-72.

38. Weers-Pothof G, Nováková IRO, Donnelly JP, Muytjens HL. Bacteraemia caused by *Stomatococcus mucilaginosus* in a granulocytopenic patient with acute lymphocytic leukaemia. Neth J Med. 1989;35:143-146.

39. Hughes WT, Armstrong D, Bodey GP, et al. 2002 Guidelines for the use of antimicrobial agents in neutropenic patients with cancer. Clin Infect Dis. 2002;34:730-751.

40. Kern WV, Heiss M, Steinbach G, et al. Prediction of gram-negative bacteremia in patients with cancer and febrile neutropenia by means of interleukin-8 levels in serum: Targeting empirical monotherapy versus combination therapy. Clin Infect Dis. 2001;32:832-835.

41. Rintala E. Incidence and clinical significance of positive blood cultures in febrile episodes of patients with hematological malignancies. Scand J Infect Dis. 1994;26:77-84.

42. Ramphal R, Bolger M, Oblon DJ, et al. Vancomycin is not an essential component of the initial empiric treatment regimen for febrile neutropenic patients receiving ceftazidime—A randomized prospective study. Antimicrob Agents Chemother. 1992;36:445-452.

43. Dompeling EC, Donnelly JP, Deresinski SC, et al. Early identification of neutropenic patients at risk of gram-positive bacteraemia and the impact of empirical administration of vancomycin. Eur J Cancer. 1996;32A:1332-1339.

44. Cordonnier C, Buzyn A, Leverger G, et al. Epidemiology and risk factors for gram-positive coccal infections in neutropenia: Towards a more targeted antibiotic strategy. Clin Infect Dis. 2003;36:149-158.

45. The EORTC International Antimicrobial Therapy Cooperative Group and National Cancer Institute of Canada. Vancomycin added to empirical combination antibiotic therapy for fever in granulocytopenic cancer patients. J Infect Dis. 1991;163:951-958.

46. Molrine DC, George S, Tarbell N, et al. Antibody responses to polysaccharide and polysaccharide-conjugate vaccines after treatment of Hodgkin's disease. Ann Intern Med. 1995;123:828-834.

47. Fedson DS. Pneumococcal vaccination in the United States and 20 other developed countries, 1981-1996. Clin Infect Dis. 1998;26:1117-1123.

48. Noriega LM, van der Auwera P, Phan M, et al. Anaerobic bacteremia in a cancer center. Support Care Cancer. 1993;1:250-255.

49. Pouwels MJM, Donnelly JP, Raemaekers JMM, et al. *Clostridium septicum* sepsis and neutropenic enterocolitis in a patient treated with intensive chemotherapy for acute myeloid leukemia. Ann Hematol. 1997;74:153-157.

50. Muder RR, Harris AP, Muller S, et al. Bacteremia due to *Stenotrophomonas (Xanthomonas) maltophilia:* A prospective multicenter study of 91 episodes. Clin Infect Dis. 1996;22:508-512.

51. Gerard M, Defresne N, Daneau D, et al. Incidence and significance of *Clostridium difficile* in hospitalized cancer patients. Eur J Clin Microbiol Infect Dis. 1988;7:274-278.

52. Allo MD, Miller J, Townsend T, et al. Primary cutaneous aspergillosis associated with Hickman intravenous catheters. N Engl J Med. 1987;317:1105-1108.

53. Anaissie E. Opportunistic mycoses in the immunocompromised host: Experience at a cancer center and review. Clin Infect Dis. 1992;14(Suppl 1):S43-S53.

54. Fine JD, Miller JA, Harrist TJ, et al. Cutaneous lesions in disseminated candidiasis mimicking ecthyma gangrenosum. Am J Med. 1981;70:1133-1135.

55. Suster S, Rose LB. Intradermal bullous dermatitis due to candidiasis in an immunocompromised patient. JAMA. 1987;258:2106-2107.

56. Boutati EI, Anaissie EJ. *Fusarium*, a significant emerging pathogen in patients with hematologic malignancy: Ten years' experience at a cancer center and implications for management. Blood. 1997;90:999-1008.

57. Nucci M, Anaissie E. Cutaneous infection by *Fusarium* species in healthy and immunocompromised hosts: Implications for diagnosis and management. Clin Infect Dis. 2002;35:909-920.

58. Kauffman CA, Bradley SF, Ross SC, Weber DR. Hepatosplenic candidiasis: Successful treatment with fluconazole. Am J Med. 1991;91:137-141.

59. Anaissie EJ, Darouiche RO, Abi-Said D, et al. Management of invasive candidal infections: Results of a prospective, randomized, multicenter study of fluconazole versus amphotericin B and a review of the literature. Clin Infect Dis. 1996;23:964-972.

60. Edwards JE, Bodey GP, Bowden RA, et al. International conference for the development of a consensus on the management and prevention of severe candidal infections. Clin Infect Dis. 1997;25:43-59.

61. Mora-Duarte J, Betts R, Rotstein C, et al. Comparison of caspofungin and amphotericin B for invasive candidiasis. N Engl J Med. 2002;347:2020-2029.

62. O'Grady NP, Alexander M, Dellinger EP, et al. Guidelines for the prevention of intravascular catheter-related infections. Clin Infect Dis. 2002;35:11281-11307.

63. Mermel LA, Farr BM, Sheretz RJ, et al. Guidelines for the management of intravascular catheter-related infection. Clin Infect Dis. 2001;32:1249-1272.

64. Lordick F, Hentrich M, Decker T, et al. Ultrasound screening for internal jugular vein thrombosis aids the detection of central venous catheter-related infections in patients with haemato-oncological diseases: A prospective observational study. Br J Haematol. 2003;120:1073-1078.

65. DesJardin JE, Falagas ME, Ruthazer R, et al. Clinical utility of blood cultures drawn from indwelling central venous catheters in hospitalised patients with cancer. Ann Intern Med. 1999;131:641-647.

66. Beutz M, Sherman G, Mayfield J, et al. Clinical utility of blood cultures drawn from central vein catheters and peripheral venipuncture in critically ill medical patients. Chest. 2003;123:854-861.

67. Leeming JP, Notman FH. Improved methods for isolation and enumeration of *Malassezia furfur* from human skin. J Clin Microbiol. 1987;25:2017-2019.

68. Nucci M, Anaissie E. Should vascular catheters be removed from all patients with candidemia? An evidence-based review. Clin Infect Dis. 2002;34:591-599.

69. Walsh TJ, Rex JH. All catheter-related candidemia is not the same: Assessment of the balance between risks and benefits of removal of vascular catheters. Clin Infect Dis. 2002;34:600-602.

70. Maschmeyer G, Link H, Hiddeman W, et al. Pulmonary infiltrates in febrile patients with neutropenia: Risk factors and outcome under empirical antimicrobial therapy in a randomized multicenter study. Cancer. 1994;73:2296-2304.

71. Somoskovi A, Hotaling JE, Fitzgerald M, et al. Lessons from a proficiency testing event for acid-fast microscopy. Chest. 2001;120:250-257.

72. Van Elden LJ, van Kraaij MG, Nijhuis M, et al. Polymerase chain reaction is more sensitive than viral culture and antigen testing for the detection of respiratory viruses in adults with hematological cancer and pneumonia. Clin Infect Dis. 2002;34:177-183.

73. Butt NM, Clark RE. High frequency of positive surveillance for cytomegalovirus (CMV) by PCR in allograft recipients at low risk of CMV. Bone Marrow Transplant. 2001;27:615-619.

74. Becker MJ, Lugtenburg EJ, Cornelissen JJ, et al. Galactomannan detection in computerized tomography-based broncho-alveolar lavage fluid and serum in haematological patients at risk for invasive pulmonary aspergillosis. Br J Haematol. 2003;121:448-457.

75. Buchheidt D, Baust C, Skladny H, et al. Clinical evaluation of a polymerase chain reaction assay to detect Aspergillus species in bronchoalveolar lavage samples of neutropenic patients. Br J Haematol. 2002;116:803-811.

76. Reichenberger F, Habicht J, Matt P, et al. Diagnostic yield of bronchoscopy in histologically proven invasive pulmonary aspergillosis. Bone Marrow Transplant. 1999;24:1195-1199.

77. Dunagan DP, Baker AM, Hurd DD, Haponik EF. Bronchoscopic evaluation of pulmonary infiltrates following bone marrow transplantation. Chest. 1997;111:135-141.

78. Whittle AT, Davis M, Johnson PR, et al. The safety and usefulness of routine bronchoscopy before stem cell transplantation and during neutropenia. Bone Marrow Transplant. 1999;24:63-67.

79. Cazzadori A, Di Perri G, Todeschini G, et al. Transbronchial biopsy in the diagnosis of pulmonary infiltrates in immunocompromised patients. Chest. 1995;107:101-106.

80. Wong PW, Stefanec T, Brown K, White DA. Role of fine-needle aspirates of focal lung lesions in patients with hematologic malignancies. Chest. 2002;121:527-532.

81. Small TN, Casson A, Malak SF, et al. Respiratory syncytial virus infection following hematopoietic stem cell transplantation. Bone Marrow Transplant. 2002;29:321-327.

82. Ghosh S, Champlin RE, Ueno NT, et al. Respiratory syncytial virus infections in autologous blood and marrow transplant recipients with breast cancer: Combined therapy with aerosolized ribavirin and parenteral immunoglobulins. Bone Marrow Transplant. 2001;28:271-275.

83. Machado CM, Vilas Boas LS, Medes AVA, et al. Low mortality rates related to respiratory virus infections after bone marrow transplantation. Bone Marrow Transplant. 2003;31:695-700.

84. Cortez KJ, Murphy BR, Almeida KN, et al. Immune globulin prophylaxis of respiratory syncytial virus infection in stem cell transplant recipients. J Infect Dis. 2002;186:834-838.

85. Cortez KJ, Erdman DD, Peret TCT, et al. Outbreak of human parainfluenza virus 3 in a hematopoietic stem cell transplant population. J Infect Dis. 2001;184:1093-1097.

86. Bernard EM, Sepkowitz KA, Telzak EE, et al. Pneumocystosis. Med Clin North Am. 1992;76:107-119.

87. Bozzette SA. The use of corticosteroids in Pneumocystis carinii pneumonia. J Infect Dis. 1990;162:1365-1369.

88. Kovatch AL, Jardine DS, Dowling JN, et al. Legionellosis in children with leukemia in relapse. Pediatrics. 1984;73:811-815.

89. Patterson TF, Kirkpatrick WR, White M, et al. Disease spectrum, treatment practices, and outcomes. Medicine. 2000,79:250-260.

90. Anaissie EJ, Stratton SL, Dignani C, et al. Pathogenic Aspergillus species recovered from a hospital water system: A 3-year prospective study. Clin Infect Dis. 2002;34: 780-790.

91. Kuhlman JE, Fishman EK, Siegelman SS. Invasive pulmonary aspergillosis in acute leukemia: Characteristic findings on CT, the CT halo sign, and the role of CT in early diagnosis. Radiology. 1985;157:611-614.

92. Alangaden GJ, Wahiduzzaman M, Chandrasekar PH, and the Bone Marrow Transplant Group. Aspergillosis: The most common community-acquired pneumonia with gram-negative bacilli as copathogens in stem cell transplant recipients with graft-versus-host-disease. Clin Infect Dis. 2002;35:659-664.

93. Caillot D, Couaillier J-F, Bernard A, et al. Increasing volume and changing characteristics of invasive pulmonary aspergillosis on sequential thoracic computed tomography scans in patients with neutropenia. J Clin Oncol. 2001;19:253-259.

94. Pagano L, Ricci P, Tonso A, et al. Mucormycosis in patients with haematological malignancies: A retrospective clinical study of 37 cases. Br J Haematol. 1997;99:331-336.

95. Musa MO, Al Eisa A, Halim M, et al. The spectrum of Fusarium infection in immunocompromised patients with haematological malignancies and in non-immunocompromised patients: A single institution experience over 10 years. Br J Haematol. 2000;108:544-548.

96. Yu VL, Muder RR, Poorsattar A. Significance of isolation of Aspergillus from the respiratory tract in diagnosis of invasive pulmonary aspergillosis. Am J Med. 1986;81: 249-254.

97. Bodey GP, Bueltmann B, Duguid W, et al. Fungal infections in cancer patients: An international autopsy survey. Eur J Clin Microbiol Infect Dis. 1992;11:99-109.

98. Maertens J, Van Eldere J, Verhaegen J, et al. Use of circulating galactomannan for early diagnosis of invasive aspergillosis in allogeneic stem cell transplant recipients. J Infect Dis. 2002;186:1297-1306.

99. Herbrecht R, Denning DW, Patterson TF, et al. Voriconazole versus amphotericin B for primary therapy of invasive aspergillosis. N Engl J Med. 2002;347:408-415.

100. Denning DW, Ribaud P, Milpied N, et al. Efficacy and safety of voriconazole in the treatment of invasive aspergillosis. Clin Infect Dis. 2002;34:563-571.

101. Stevens DA, Lee JY. Analysis of compassionate use itraconazole therapy for invasive aspergillosis by the NIAID Mycosis Study Group criteria. Arch Intern Med. 1997; 157:1857-1862.

102. Denning DW, Stevens DA. Antifungal and surgical treatment of invasive aspergillosis: Review of 2121 published cases. Rev Infect Dis. 1992;24:1147-1201.

103. McWhinney PHM, Kibbler CC, Hamon MD, et al. Progress in the diagnosis and management of aspergillosis in bone marrow transplantation: Thirteen years experience. Clin Infect Dis. 1993;17:397-404.

104. Caillot D, Casasnovas O, Bernard A, et al. Improved management of invasive pulmonary aspergillosis in neutropenic patients using early thoracic computed tomographic scan and surgery. J Clin Oncol. 1997;15:139-147.

105. Anaissie EJ, Vartivarian S, Bodey GP, et al. Randomized comparison between antibiotics alone and antibiotics plus granulocyte-macrophage colony-stimulating factor (Escherichia coli-derived) in cancer patients with fever and neutropenia. Am J Med. 1996;100:17-23.

106. Dignani MC, Anaissie EJ, Hester JP, et al. Treatment of neutropenia-related fungal infections with granulocyte colony-stimulating factor-elicited white blood cell transfusions: A pilot study. Leukemia. 1997;11:1621-1630.

107. Marr KA, Carter RA, Crippa F, et al. Epidemiology and outcome of mould infections in hematopoietic stem cell transplant recipients. Clin Infect Dis. 2002;34:909-917.

108. Young LS, Armstrong D, Blevins A, et al. Nocardia asteroides infection complicating neoplastic disease. Am J Med. 1971;50:356-367.

109. Blot F, Guinet M, Nitenberg G, et al. Prognostic factors for neutropenic patients in an intensive care unit: Respective roles of underlying malignancies and acute organ failures. Eur J Cancer. 1997;33:1031-1037.

110. Ewig S, Torres A, Riquelme R, et al. Pulmonary complications in patients with haematological malignancies treated at a respiratory ICU. Eur Respir J. 1998;12:116-122.

111. Hilbert G, Gruson D, Vargas F, et al. Noninvasive ventilation in immunosuppressed patients with pulmonary infiltrates, fever, and acute respiratory fever. N Engl J Med. 2001;344:481-487.

112. Overholser CD, Peterson DE, William LT, et al. Periodontal infections in patients with acute nonlymphocytic leukemia: Prevalence of acute exacerbations. Arch Intern Med. 1982;142:551-554.

113. Bergmann OJ. Oral infections and fever in immunocompromised patients with haematologic malignancies. Eur J Clin Microbiol Infect Dis. 1989;8:207-213.

114. Corey L, Spear PG. Infections with herpes simplex viruses. N Engl J Med. 1986;314:686-691, 749-757.

115. Shenep JL, Kalwinski DK, Feldman S, et al. Mycotic cervical lymphadenitis following oral mucositis in children with leukemia. J Pediatr. 1985;106:243-246.

116. Feld R, DePauw B, Berman S, et al. Meropenem versus ceftazidime in the treatment of cancer patients with febrile neutropenia: A randomized double-blind trial. J Clin Oncol. 2000;18:3690-3698.

117. De Pauw BE, for the Meropenem Study Group of Leuven-London-Nijmegen. Meropenem and ceftazidime are equally effective as single agents for empirical therapy of the febrile neutropenic patient. J Antimicrob Chemother. 1995;36:185-200.

118. Johnson MP, Ramphal R. Malignant external otitis: Report on therapy with ceftazidime and review of therapy and prognosis. Rev Infect Dis. 1990;12:173-180.

119. Morrison VA, Weisdorf DJ. Alternaria: A sinonasal pathogen of immunocompromised hosts. Clin Infect Dis. 1993;16:265-270.

120. Ozer H, Armitage JO, Bennett CL, et al. 2000 update of recommendations for the use of hematopoietic colony-stimulating factors: Evidence-based clinical practice guidelines. J Clin Oncol. 2000;18:3558-3585.

121. Bookman MA, Longo DL. Concomitant illness in patients treated for Hodgkin's disease. Cancer Treat Rev. 1986;13:77-111.

122. Verweij PE, Stynen D, Rijs AJMM, et al. Sandwich enzyme-linked immunosorbent assay compared with Pastorex latex agglutination test for diagnosing invasive aspergillosis in immunocompromised patients. J Clin Microbiol. 1995;33:1912-1914.

123. Viscoli C, Machetti M, Gazzola P, et al. Aspergillus galactomannan antigen in the cerebrospinal fluid of bone marrow transplant recipients with probable cerebral aspergillosis. J Clin Microbiol. 2002;40:1496-1499.

124. Miliauskas JR, Webber BL. Disseminated varicella at autopsy in children with cancer. Cancer. 1984;53:1518-1525.

125. Strauss SE. Varicella zoster virus infections: Biology, natural history, treatment and prevention. Ann Intern Med. 1988;108:221-237.

126. Luft BJ, Remington JS. Toxoplasmosis of the central nervous system. Curr Clin Top Infect Dis. 1985;6:315-358.

127. Perfect JR, Marr KA, Walsh TJ, et al. Voriconazole treatment for less-common, emerging, or refractory fungal infections. Clin Infect Dis. 2003;36:1122-1131.

128. van Kraaij MGJ, Dekker AW, Verdonck LF. Infectious gastro-enteritis: An uncommon cause of diarrhoea in adult allogeneic and autologous stem cell transplant recipients. Bone Marrow Transplant. 2000;26:299-303.

129. Rampling A, Warren RE, Bevan PC, et al. Clostridium difficile in haematological malignancy. J Clin Pathol. 1985;38:445-451.

130. Heard SR, O'Farrell S, Holland D, et al. The epidemiology of Clostridium difficile with use of a typing scheme: Nosocomial acquisition and cross-infection among immunocompromised patients. J Infect Dis. 1986;153:159-162.

131. Delmé M, Vandercam B, Avesani V, et al. Epidemiology and prevention of Clostridium difficile infection in a leukemia unit. Eur J Clin Microbiol. 1987;6:623-627.

132. Tikko SK, Distenfield A, Davidson M. Clostridium septicum septicemia with identical metastatic myonecroses in a granulocytopenic patient. Am J Med. 1985;79:256-258.

133. Longworth DL, Weller PF. Hyperinfection syndrome with strongyloidiasis. Curr Clin Top Infect Dis. 1986;7:1-26.

134. Hay CRM, Messenger AG, Cotton DWK, et al. Atypical bullous pyoderma gangrenosum associated with myeloid malignancies. J Clin Pathol. 1987;40:387-392.

135. Cohen PR, Kurzrock R. Sweet's syndrome and malignancy. Am J Med. 1987;82:1120-1126.

136. Behre G, Link H, Maschmeyer G, et al. Meropenem monotherapy versus combination therapy with ceftazidime and amikacin for empirical treatment of febrile neutropenic patients. Ann Hematol. 1998;76:73-80.

137. Verhagen C, Stalpers LJA, De Pauw BE, Haanen C. Drug induced skin reactions in patients with acute non-lymphocytic leukaemia. Eur J Haematol. 1987;38:225-230.

138. Meijer E, Dekker AW, Weersink AJL, et al. Review: Prevention and treatment of Epstein-Barr virus-associated lymphoproliferative disorders in recipients of bone marrow and solid organ transplants. Br J Haematol. 2002;119:596-607.

139. Nucci M, Spector N, Bueno AP, et al. Risk factors and attributable mortality associated with superinfection in neutropenic patients with cancer. Clin Infect Dis. 1997;25:572-579.

140. Barton TD, Schuster MG. The cause of fever following resolution of neutropenia in patients with acute leukemia. Clin Infect Dis. 1996;22:1064-1068.

Prophylaxis and Empirical Therapy for Infection in Cancer Patients

CLAUDIO VISCOLI

ELIO CASTAGNOLA

The prototype of the immunocompromised host is probably represented by the patient with cancer. The risk of infection is always present during the clinical course of a neoplastic disease, but it is exacerbated when these patients receive antineoplastic chemotherapy. The role of chemotherapy in the risk of infection has been nicely described by Haupt and co-workers.[1] In a retrospective review of 982 children with solid tumors treated at a single institution between 1985 and 1996, accounting for 8108 person months at risk, they were able to document a total of 257 bacterial and fungal infections. The overall infection rate was 3.2 episodes per 100 person months at risk, and was higher in children treated with intensive antineoplastic regimens than in those treated with less intensive regimens (3.7 vs. 0.5, $P < .001$). Infection-related morbidity and mortality is significant in this patient population.[2-4] It has been estimated that about 80% of the postchemotherapy neutropenic episodes lasting more than a week are complicated by fever, and about 60% of these febrile episodes are documented to be infectious in origin.[4] The problem continuously evolves, with new drugs and new chemotherapeutic regimens presenting new infectious complications.[5,6] As is discussed in Chapter 311, new approaches to stem cell transplantation are extending the indications for this treatment for cancer.[7]

In 1981, Philip Pizzo portrayed the relationship between cancer, infection, anticancer chemotherapy, and antimicrobial therapy as carrying the patient across a bridge over troubled waters, threatened by infection clouds and protected by antimicrobial coverage until the other side of the river was reached and everything was cleared with bone marrow recovery (Fig. 308-1).[8] Little has changed in this sense over the years. The patient should still reach the other side of the river, alive, cleared of infection, with minimal damage related to antibiotic therapy, and, possibly, cured of his or her underlying disease. However, things have become more complicated; antineoplastic therapy has become common in other categories of cancer patients, and we have realized that therapeutic and prophylactic approaches should be tailored according to the individual risk of infection, because all cancer patients are not the same.[9] To minimize the impact of infectious complication and to prevent infection-related deaths, cancer patients usually receive prolonged courses of antibacterial, antiviral, and antifungal therapies, both for prophylactic and for therapeutic purposes. These procedures are not always justified or supported by solid research data, nor are they always effective. In the present chapter, we review indications and limits for the use of antibacterial and antifungal chemoprophylaxis in cancer patients and the latest information about management. Then, we discuss the cancer patient with febrile neutropenia.

ANTIBACTERIAL PROPHYLAXIS

Chemoprophylaxis for the prevention of bacterial infections was first proposed in clinical practice based on the discovery that 80% of the bacterial pathogens causing infection in neutropenic cancer patients were originating from the patient's endogenous flora, but that about half of them were acquired during the hospital stay.[10] Therefore, the first approach relied on the administration of nonabsorbable antibiotics aimed at suppressing the intestinal bacterial flora and at preventing the acquisition of exogenous organisms. This type of prophylaxis was called "intestinal decontamination," and was later subdivided into total and partial decontamination, based on whether or not the anaerobic bacterial flora was preserved. As extensively reviewed,[11,12] total intestinal decontamination was directed at a complete suppression of the endogenous microbial flora, thought to be the main source of bacteremia in cancer patients, and was usually associated with the use of laminar airflow rooms and other protective measures (total protective isolation). Antibiotics more commonly used for this type of decontamination were gentamicin, vancomycin, framycetin, colistin, and neomycin-polymyxin, in various combinations. Poor palatability, nausea, diarrhea and psychological depression (together with lack of convincing efficacy) made this procedure very unpopular among patients, thus affecting compliance. Poor compliance was associated with the risk of recolonization and overgrowth with opportunistic invasive organisms coming from the hospital flora, development of resistance, and, ultimately, failure to prevent infections.[11]

Selective intestinal decontamination was designed to provide suppression or virtual elimination of the bacterial aerobic flora while preserving the anaerobic flora. The conceptual basis of this prophylaxis was a number of studies in immunocompromised animals in which this procedure was accompanied by a decrease in the number of infections, without colonization by potential hospital pathogens (colonization resistance).[13] It was essential for the optimal use of selective decontamination to monitor very strictly the composition of the enteric flora, in order to be able to detect at an early phase any bacterial regrowth or overgrowth of resistant organisms. Trimethoprim-sulfamethoxazole, usually given in combination with oral nystatin or amphotericin B, was the preferred drug for this indication, although it was sometimes associated with an increased duration of granulocytopenia. The administration of trimethoprim-sulfamethoxazole was clearly providing not only a topical effect (intestinal decontamination), but also a sort of systemic prophylaxis, since the drug was well absorbed and able to reach detectable blood levels.

The concept of combining intestinal decontamination and systemic prophylaxis became popular among many cancer centers when a new group of very active antibiotics, the fluoroquinolones, became available. Overall, nine placebo-controlled clinical trials in adult patients were published between 1983 and 1993.[14-22] In these studies a total of 527 patients receiving an absorbable drug (mainly quinolones and trimethoprim-sulfamethoxazole) were compared with 420 patients receiving placebo. All studies but one reported a reduction in the proportion of gram-negative infections, and only one study (including a total of 26 patients) found an advantage in terms of prolongation of time to first fever.[19] Two meta-analyses[23,24] confirmed that fluoroquinolone prophylaxis was able to decrease the incidence of gram-negative infections, but was not affecting the incidence of gram-positive infections, and was sometimes associated with an increase in the incidence of fluoroquinolone-resistant gram-positive organisms.[25-27] In addition, the two meta-analyses failed to show a significant impact of prophylaxis on pragmatic clinical parameters such as the incidence of febrile episodes, use of empirical antibiotics, and infection-related mortality (Fig. 308-2). As shown by the experience of the International Antimicrobial Therapy Group (IATG) of the European Organization for Research and Treatment of Cancer (EORTC) (unpublished data, IATG-EORTC Data Center), in parallel with the increasing use of prophylaxis there was a decreasing rate of microbiologic documentation of the febrile episodes with a proportional increase in the number of fevers of unknown origin, as if prophylaxis was simply able to prevent the microbiologic documentation of the infection but not the febrile episode (Fig. 308-3). Combining the fluoroquinolone with penicillin V[28] or rifampin[29] was the proposed solution for further reducing febrile episodes. A recent multicenter study conducted by the GIMEMA group in more than 500 high-risk patients with acute leukemia or undergoing autologous transplantation found a significant reduction in febrile episodes among patients treated with levofloxacin as compared to those receiving placebo, especially in high risk patients (F. Menichetti, "Febrile Neutropenia." Bruxelles, December 2003, personal communication).

The major drawback of the routine use of prophylaxis was the emergence of fluoroquinolone resistance in gram-negative organisms. This phenomenon was first described by Cometta and co-workers, using the IATG-EORTC database.[30] Between 1983 and 1993 the propor-

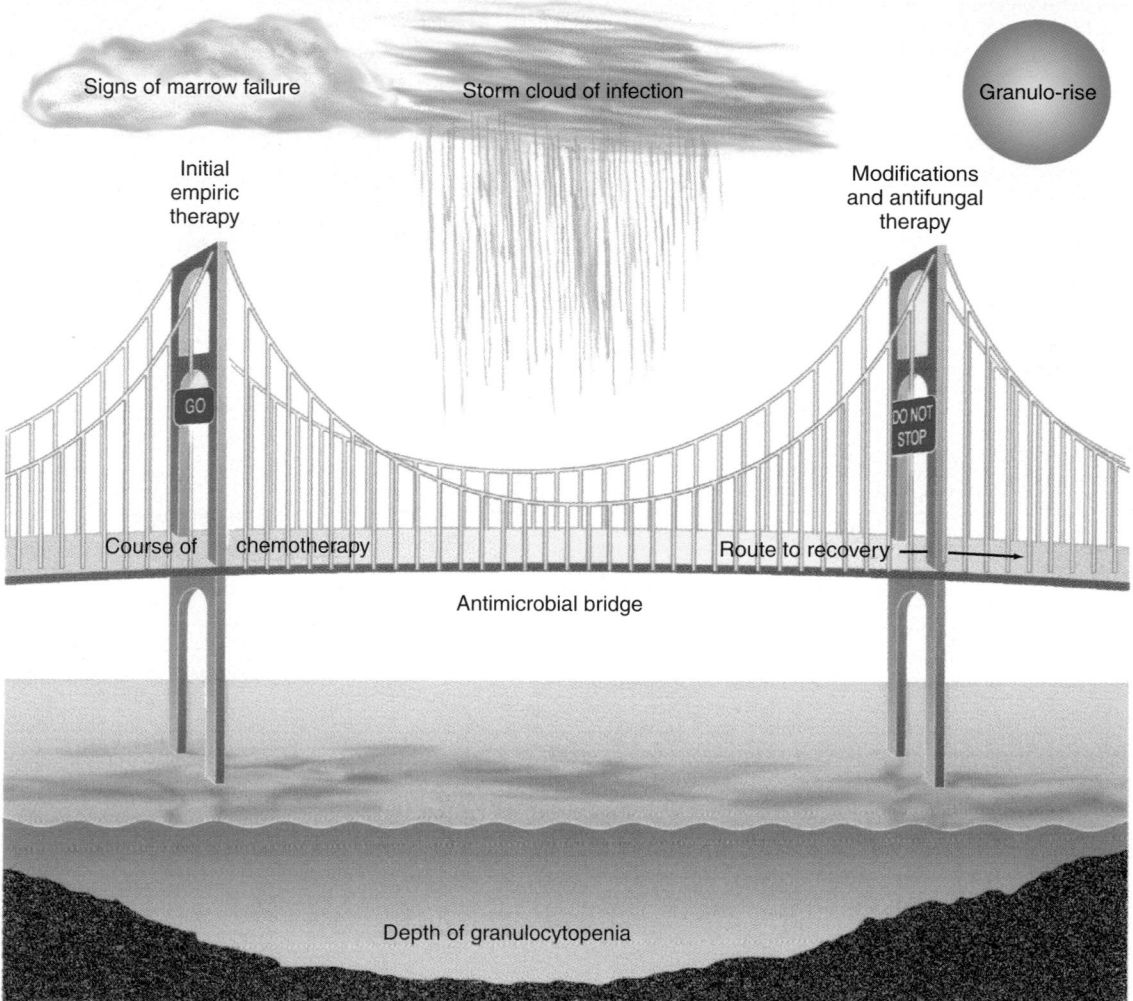

FIGURE 308-1. Natural history of febrile neutropenia and empirical therapy. *(From Pizzo PA. Infectious complications in the child with cancer. I. Pathophysiology of the compromised host and the initial evaluation and management of the febrile cancer patient. J Pediatr. 1981;98:513-523.)*

tion of neutropenic cancer patients included in EORTC trials of empirical therapy of febrile neutropenia who were receiving fluoroquinolone prophylaxis increased from 1.4% to 45%. During the same time, 1118 bacterial strains were isolated from blood and were sent to the reference laboratory of the group. All 92 strains of *Escherichia coli* isolated from 1983 to 1990 were susceptible to ciprofloxacin, norfloxacin, ofloxacin, levofloxacin, and sparfloxacin. In contrast, 11 (27%) of 40 strains isolated between 1991 and 1993 were resistant to all fluoroquinolones. The 11 resistant strains were isolated from 10 patients, all of whom had received fluoroquinolone prophylaxis, and the 39 sensitive strains were isolated from 29 patients, only 1 of whom had been given quinolone prophylaxis. Subsequent reports confirmed that the increase of quinolone-resistant gram-negative organisms was strictly associated with the increasing use of fluoroquinolone prophylaxis and was due to modification of microbial flora present in the hospital environment and colonizing the patients.[31,32] Figure 308-4 reports unpublished data from two Italian pediatric cancer divisions: one is located in the G. Gaslini Children's Hospital in Genoa (a pediatric hospital), and the other is located in the department of Hematology of the University of Rome, where both children and adults are treated. Fluoroquinolone resistance is virtually absent among gram-negative isolates in Genoa, where no fluoroquinolone prophylaxis has ever been administered, but it is significant in Rome, where fluoroquinolone prophylaxis has been extensively used in adults (E. Castagnola and C. Girmenia, personal observations). The widespread use of fluoroquinolones has also been associated with the emergence of bacteria

displaying cross-resistance to fluoroquinolones, β-lactams, and aminoglycosides.[33]

All these observations led some hematologic centers to discontinue the indiscriminate use of quinolone prophylaxis in their patients[34-38] and to suggest an overall more judicious use of these drugs.[36]

Other approaches to antibacterial prophylaxis in febrile neutropenia have been attempted. Recently, amoxicillin-clavulanate has also been used for this indication in pediatric patients in whom the use of fluoroquinolones is contraindicated. In a prospective, multicenter, randomized, double-blind, placebo-controlled trial aimed not just at preventing documented infections, but rather at reducing the clinical impact of fever, infection, or both in the target population, Castagnola and colleagues[37] suggested the possible effectiveness of amoxicillin-clavulanate in reducing the clinical impact of fever and infection in neutropenic children with cancer. Indeed, in this patient population, amoxicillin-clavulanate caused a 12% reduction in the incidence of febrile or infectious episodes, as compared with placebo (44 of 83, or 53%, vs. 55 of 84, or 65%). This benefit was also associated with a 30% increase in the probability of failure-free survival at day 15. A logistic regression analysis showed the effect of prophylaxis to be more relevant in patients with leukemia or lymphoma and in those not receiving hematopoietic growth factors (Fig. 308-5). Compliance with oral drugs was very good, with very few and not severe drug-related adverse events. The major problem with this study, which prevented the authors from reaching definitive conclusions, was the low accrual and the consequently limited statistical power.[37]

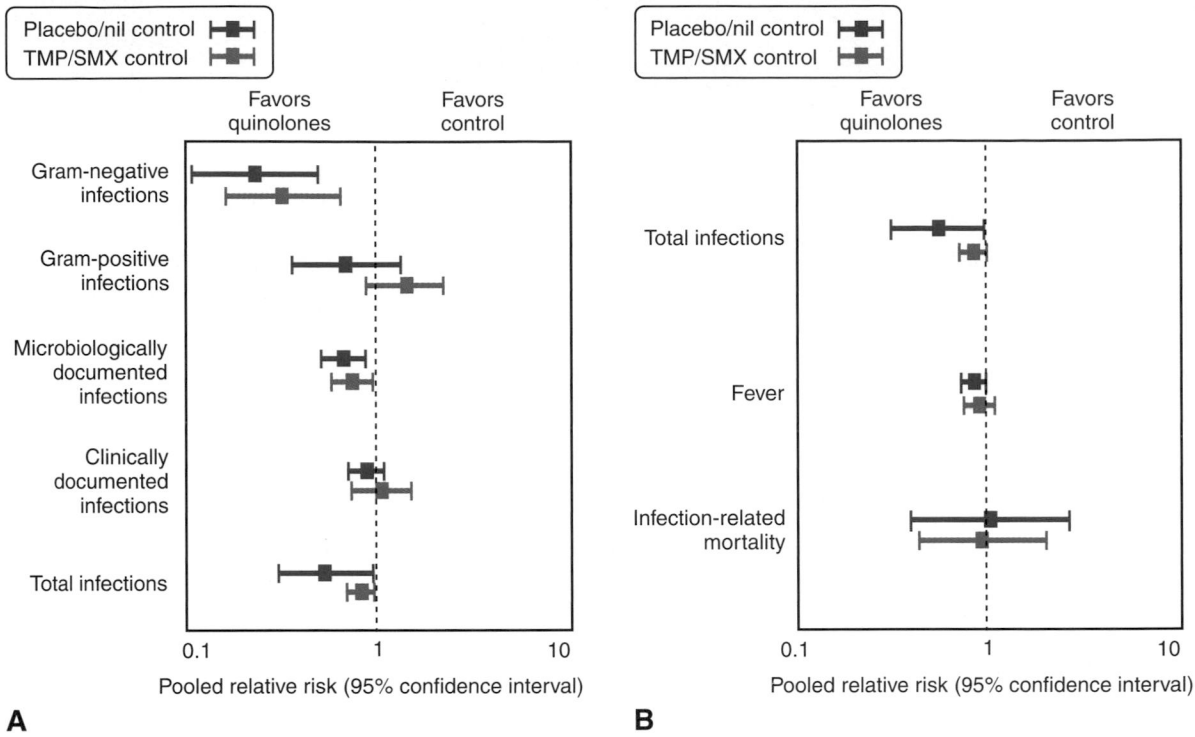

A

B

FIGURE 308-2. **A,** Meta-analysis of efficacy of quinolone prophylaxis in neutropenic cancer patients: effect of prophylaxis on different conditions. The administration of prophylaxis reduces the incidence of gram-negative infections and the overall incidence of microbiologically documented infections, but not the number of clinically documented infections. The effect on the total number of infection seems to be marginal. The figure was drawn using studies comparing quinolones with placebo or no therapy (nil) or trimethoprim-sulfamethoxazole (TMP/SMX). **B,** Meta-analysis of efficacy of quinolone prophylaxis in neutropenic cancer patients. In spite of a reduction in the total number of infections, there is no documented efficacy in reduction of febrile episodes or infection-related mortality. The figure was drawn using studies comparing quinolones with placebo or no therapy (nil) or trimethoprim-sulfamethoxazole (TMP/SMX). *(Modified from Engels EA, Lau J, Barza M. Efficacy of quinolone prophylaxis in neutropenic cancer patients: A meta-analysis. J Clin Oncol. 1998;16:1179-1187. Reprinted with permission from the American Society of Clinical Oncology.)*

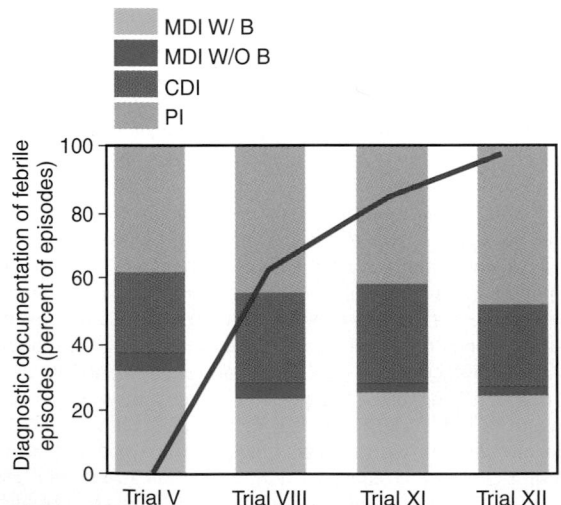

FIGURE 308-3. IATG-EORTC data showing a change in the diagnostic documentation of febrile episodes in four different trials, according to administration of antibacterial prophylaxis (*red line*). The introduction of antibacterial prophylaxis (mainly quinolones) has been followed by an increase in the proportion of episodes of fever of unknown origin, and a reduction of microbiologically documented episodes. MDI W/ B, microbiologically documented infection with bacteremia; MDI W/O B, microbiologically documented infection without bacteremia; CDI, clinically documented infection; PI, possible infection or unexplained fever. *(Data from IATG-EORTC Data Center.)*

In conclusion, in the last edition of the Infectious Diseases Society of America guidelines for the management of febrile neutropenia, the widespread use of prophylaxis in neutropenic cancer patients is discouraged.[38] We agree with that, although we also believe that there might be categories of patients who might benefit from this kind of prophylaxis. In other words, antibiotic prophylaxis in neutropenic patients should not be used as a clinical protocol, good for every patient in every circumstance. Selected patients might benefit from either a quinolone or amoxicillin-clavulanate or a combination. For the time being, the choice of the patient who might benefit from prophylaxis must be based on individual criteria, in the absence of more scientific indications.

ANTIFUNGAL CHEMOPROPHYLAXIS

In recent years, several reports have underlined the increasing role of fungal infections as a cause of morbidity and mortality in compromised patients.[39-43] For example, in hospitalized patients, *Candida* now represents the fourth most frequent pathogen isolated in blood culture. Among fungal pathogens, molds are certainly increasing more than yeasts. In a large autopsy study, Groll and co-workers clearly showed that the overall increase in fungal infection was mainly due to an increase in infections caused by filamentous fungi, including species that were never known to be a cause of human infections in the past.[41] Among yeasts, for years *Candida albicans* was the most frequently isolated species. In 1999, a surveillance study of fungemia in cancer patients conducted by the Invasive Fungal Infection Group of the EORTC revealed that non-*albicans Candida* had become prevalent among patients with leukemia and lymphoma.[44] Although fungal infections usually do not represent more than 10% of all infections, their associated mortality remains very high. There is general agreement that from 80% to 95% of patients with cerebral aspergillosis die from the disease,[45] whereas the mortality rate from candidemia varies from

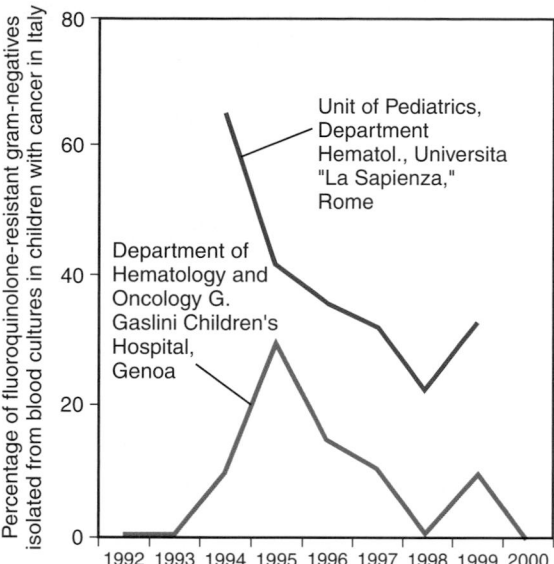

FIGURE 308-4. Percentage of fluoroquinolone-resistant gram-negative bacteria isolated from blood cultures in children with cancer in two Italian pediatric cancer centers. One center is located in the G. Gaslini Children's Hospital in Genoa, a pediatric hospital, and the other is located in the Department of Hematology of the University of Rome, where both children and adults are treated. Fluoroquinolone resistance is virtually absent among gram-negative isolates in Genoa, where no fluoroquinolone prophylaxis has ever been administered, but it is not negligible in Rome, where fluoroquinolone prophylaxis has been extensively used in adults. *(Unpublished data from E. Castagnola and C. Girmenia.)*

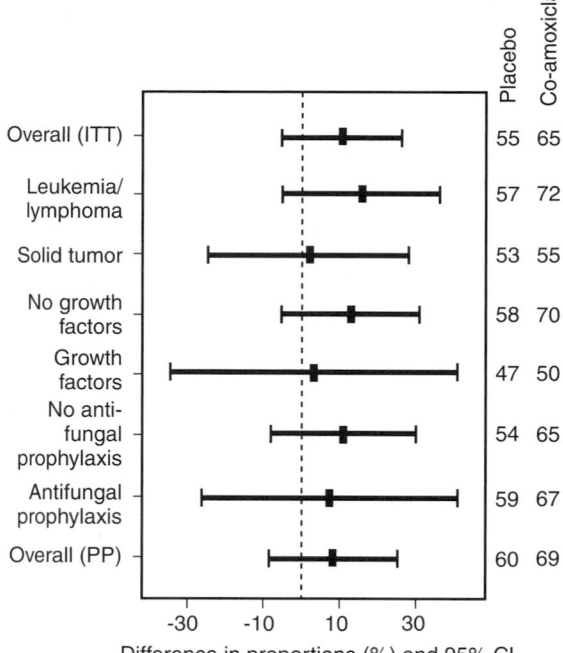

FIGURE 308-5. Efficacy of antibacterial prophylaxis with amoxicillin-clavulanate or placebo in neutropenic children with solid tumor or acute leukemia/lymphoma, by underlying disease and stratification criteria. Amoxicillin-clavulanate prophylaxis reduced the incidence of febrile neutropenia. *(From Castagnola E, Boni L, Giacchino M, et al. A multicenter, randomized, double blind placebo-controlled trial of amoxicillin/clavulanate for the prophylaxis of fever and infection in neutropenic children with cancer. Pediatr Infect Dis. 2003;22:359-365.)*

25% to 50%, according to the underlying condition.[44] In light of the high mortality rate, preventing invasive fungal infections has always been considered a desirable approach. Unfortunately, until about a decade ago, the antifungal armamentarium was very limited. Both the polyenes and the azoles available at that time were not absorbed by the oral route and their use was limited to intestinal decontamination. Intravenous administration was not practical and was toxic. When the triazoles became available, several investigators started clinical trials to examine the effects of these drugs for prophylactic purposes.

Fluconazole

According to Bow and co-workers, from 1966 to 2000, 69 trials of antifungal prophylaxis in cancer patients were found in a literature search.[46] Among them, 38 were comparative trials, having placebo, no treatment, or an oral polyene as control regimen, and were therefore evaluable for the purpose of the analysis. Most of the trials (17, or 58%) included fluconazole as the study regimen. Eight fluconazole studies included at least 100 patients per arm. With the exception of the very early studies, fluconazole was almost always given at the relative high dose of 400 mg/day or 3 to 15 mg/kg/day.

The first randomized, double-blind, placebo-controlled study was published by Goodman and colleagues in 1992.[47] In a population of patients undergoing autologous and allogeneic bone marrow transplantation (BMT), fluconazole was significantly able to reduce the rate of invasive candidiasis. In this study, fluconazole was given from the day of initiation of the transplant-conditioning regimen to engraftment. Shortly after, Slavin and colleagues published another large, placebo-controlled study in a slightly different patient population, including only recipients of allogeneic grafts. The administration of the study drugs was not stopped at engraftment but was continued until day 75 after transplant, to cover the acute graft-versus-host disease (GVHD) period. In this study the administration of fluconazole was associated not only with a reduction of invasive candidiasis, but also with improved survival.[48] Very interestingly, the same group published an 8-year follow-up study on the same group of patients, which showed that the survival advantage was still present among patients who 8 years be-

fore had been given fluconazole prophylaxis, with a reduction in the overall number of cases of invasive candidiasis, candidiasis-related deaths, and severe gut GVHD.[49] From the same group, another confirmation of the positive effects of fluconazole prophylaxis in allogeneic BMT came from a study on the therapeutic effect of BMT from unrelated donors in the management of chronic myeloid leukemia. In these patients, administration of fluconazole was one of the factors significantly associated with improved survival from the underlying disease.[50]

In patients with acute leukemia, the positive effects of fluconazole prophylaxis were less impressive. Winston and co-workers failed to demonstrate a significant advantage for fluconazole in preventing invasive infections or reducing mortality.[51] Menichetti and co-workers did not show any difference between fluconazole and oral amphotericin B, although in this study fluconazole was given at the relative low dose of 150 mg daily.[52] In a placebo-controlled study in adults with acute leukemia,[53] Rotstein and colleagues showed that fluconazole at a dose of 400 mg/day reduced the incidence of probable or documented invasive fungal infections, especially in selected groups of patients receiving cytarabine. Finally, in a very recent study fluconazole at 200 mg/day was compared with low-dose amphotericin B (0.2 mg/kg/day) in 186 hematopoietic stem cell transplant recipients.[54] No difference was observed in terms of study discontinuation for persistent fever; proven, suspected, or superficial fungal infections; or survival at day 100 after transplant.

Fluconazole could not be expected to be effective against filamentous fungi, such as *Aspergillus*. Indeed, no study showed any advantage for fluconazole in the prevention of invasive aspergillosis, although the incidence of these infections was seldom reported.

Itraconazole

With respect to fluconazole, itraconazole possesses a broader spectrum of action, which includes some *Candida* strains that are intrinsically resistant to fluconazole (*C. krusei*) and *Aspergillus*. According to Bow and colleagues,[46] 5 randomized trials in which itraconazole was compared with placebo or polyenes are available. Among them, four studies included at least 100 patients per arm. In a double-blind, placebo-controlled study performed by the GIMEMA group in Italy in 405 neutropenic patients,[55] itraconazole oral solution, administered at 5 mg/kg/day, was effective in reducing the incidence of *Candida* infections in adults with leukemia. Unfortunately, no effect was shown on the incidence of invasive aspergillosis, although there were very few patients with aspergillosis in both arms. In a similar trial on 557 patients comparing itraconazole oral solution versus placebo,[56] the incidence of proven systemic fungal infections, the number of deaths resulting from invasive mycoses, and the use of empirical antifungal therapy seemed to be lower in the itraconazole group, but no statistically significant difference could be documented. In another double-blind placebo controlled study in 210 patients with hematologic malignancies or receiving autologous BMT,[57] itraconazole capsules administered at 100 mg twice per day showed a reduction in the use of empirical antifungal therapy and a reduced incidence of fungal infection in the subgroup of patients with severe ($<100/mm^3$) and prolonged (>7 days) neutropenia. Finally, a trend toward reduction of deep fungal infections, especially in patients with severe ($<100/mm^3$) and prolonged (>2 weeks) neutropenia, was documented in a trial comparing itraconazole oral solution plus nystatin with amphotericin B in 277 patients.[58] Unfortunately, no significant difference in major end points, such as incidence of invasive mycoses or mortality, could be detected. In contrast, in a recent meta-analysis Glasmacher and colleagues[58a] studied the pooled effect of itraconazole prophylaxis on several markers of efficacy, including the incidence of aspergillosis. They included all kinds of itraconazole studies, and not only placebo or no-treatment-controlled studies. Itraconazole (any formulation) significantly reduced the incidence of invasive fungal infection, invasive-yeast infections, and fungal-associated mortality. The incidence of invasive aspergillosis was only reduced when the oral solution was used, with a clear dose-dependent (and concentration-dependent) effect, and at the price of a higher incidence of drug-related adverse events and drug discontinuations.

Pragmatic Benefits of Antifungal Prophylaxis

At least three large meta-analyses on the effects of antifungal prophylaxis in cancer patients have been published.[46,59,60] The control arm in these studies was placebo, no treatment or a nonabsorbable polyene. The Cochrane study[60] was flawed by the inclusion of both antifungal prophylaxis and empirical therapy, showing that statistical expertise is not sufficient if the wrong clinical question is asked. The study by Kanda and co-workers[59] showed some positive effect for prophylaxis, although with some limitations. Finally, the study by Bow and colleagues[46] reviewed 38 randomized, controlled studies including more than 7000 patients. The study found that the use of antifungal prophylaxis, mostly with azole drugs (94% of the patients), was associated with a reduction in the use of parenteral antifungal therapy, in the occurrence of both superficial and invasive fungal infections, and in the fungal-related mortality, with a pooled-weighted odds ratio (OR) of 0.59 (range 0.50 to 0.67) (Fig. 308-6). In the subpopulations of patients with prolonged neutropenia and in recipients of allogeneic BMT, there was also a reduction in the overall mortality. As expected, no effect of antifungal prophylaxis was shown on the incidence of invasive aspergillosis, perhaps because the incidence of this disease was too low to detect a treatment effect over the control group.

Fluconazole vs Itraconazole

Very few studies have compared fluconazole and itraconazole in the prophylaxis of fungal infections. In acute leukemia and BMT patients, Huijgens and colleagues found no difference whatsoever in the incidence of fungal infections in the two arms of the study,[61] and another study reported a non-statistically significant advantage for itraconazole.[62] More recently, in an open-label study, Winston and associates compared intravenous and oral fluconazole versus intravenous and oral itraconazole in BMT patients.[63] Both drugs were given for 100 days after transplant. Itraconazole performed better than fluconazole at

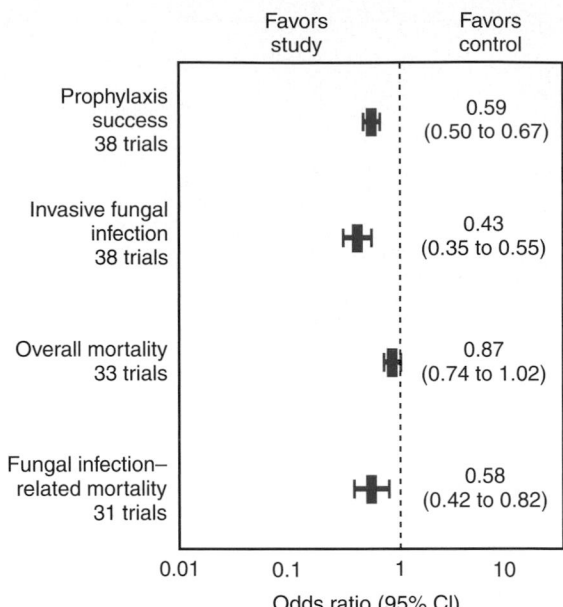

FIGURE 308-6. Meta-analysis of antifungal prophylaxis in neutropenic cancer patients: pooled weighted odds ratio of efficacy. *(Modified from Bow EJ, Laverdiere M, Lussier N, et al. Antifungal prophylaxis for severely neutropenic chemotherapy recipients: A meta analysis of randomized controlled clinical trials. Cancer. 2002;94:3230-3236.)*

a statistically significant level, with an incidence of invasive fungal infections of 9% versus 25%. Also in this case there were relatively few cases of invasive aspergillosis (three in the itraconazole group vs. eight in the fluconazole group).

Finally, Marr and colleagues[63a] compared itraconazole vs. fluconazole in the prophylaxis of infection in BMT patients. In this study the dose of itraconazole was adjusted to maintain serum levels >0.5 μg/ml. This was obtained with a dose of 2.5 mg/kg 2 or 3 times a day. Among patients able to tolerate this high dosage, itraconazole effectively prevented fungal infection, with a significant effect on the incidence of aspergillosis as well. However, almost ¼ of the patients discontinued itraconazole because of gastrointestinal side-effects. In addition, an important toxic interaction between itraconazole and cyclophosphamide was detected in this study, leading to the recommendation of not administering the 2 drugs concomitantly.[63b]

New Drugs

Several new antifungal drugs are presently in advanced stage of development. Probably the most exciting drugs, mainly because they belong to a new family with an innovative mechanism of action, are the echinocandins. These agents are only available for parenteral administration. Van Burik and co-workers from the National Institute of Allergy and Infectious Diseases Mycoses Study Group, compared intravenous micafungin with oral fluconazole in a double-blind clinical trial for prophylaxis of invasive fungal infections in BMT patients.[64] A total of 882 patients were enrolled. Although both groups had similar rates of candidiasis, in the micafungin group there was a trend toward a decreased incidence of aspergillosis. However, as in all clinical trials evaluating the impact of prophylaxis on aspergillosis, the rate of invasive aspergillosis was very low (0.2% in the micafungin arm vs. 1.5% in the fluconazole arm), suggesting that either the patient population was not the right one, or prophylaxis was not administered for the right period of time.

Secondary Prophylaxis

Patients with a history of invasive aspergillosis appear to be at high risk of reactivation when undergoing further chemotherapy. This is probably because fungal organisms remain viable in the tissues. Whether or not the risk of relapse depends on the persistence of radiologically de-

TABLE 308-1 Clinical Conditions in Which Antifungal Prophylaxis Is Effective in Reducing the Incidence of Invasive Mycoses Caused by *Candida*

Patient Population	Associated Conditions	Drug of Choice
Leukemic patients	Patients with acute myelogenous undergoing remission-induction chemotherapy with cytarabine plus anthracycline (administered for 7 and 3 days, respectively) and high-dose cytarabine-containing regimens	Fluconazole 400 mg/day, duration unspecified
Bone marrow transplant (BMT) recipients	Patients receiving allogeneic BMT, especially from matched unrelated or mismatched donors (if itraconazole is used, do not administer concommitantly with cyclophosphamide and check frequently for drug interactions)	• Fluconazole 400 mg/day from day 1 until day 75 from BMT • Itraconazole: 200 mg IV q12 hr the first day, 200 mg IV q24 hr in the following days and 2.5 mg/kg oral solution q 8-12h to keep serum concentrations >0.5 µg/ml from day 1 to day 100 from BMT
Cancer patients with a history of invasive mycosis	Need to receive additional chemotherapy or BMT (any kind)	• Fluconazole or itraconazole until resolution of immunosuppression in patients with chronic invasive candidiasis • Amphotericin B (any formulation), voriconazole, itraconazole in patients with history of documented or probable aspergillosis until resolution of immunosuppresssion

tectable lesions is a matter of controversy. According to Martino and colleagues,[65] the risk is lower in the presence of a complete radiologic response, whereas Offner and co-workers[66] believe that patients may relapse even in the absence of residual lesions. In these patients, secondary antifungal prophylaxis is mandatory. The drug of choice seems to be amphotericin B (in any formulation), but itraconazole (alone or in combination) has also been used.[67,68] A case report suggests the possible efficacy of voriconazole for this indication, as well.[69]

Untoward Effects

The prolonged and widespread administration of antifungal prophylaxis with triazoles in patients at risk for fungal infections has been related, with variable degree of certainty, to possible untoward effects. For example, in a review of 3002 febrile and neutropenic patients enrolled in four therapeutic trials performed by IATG-EORTC from 1986 to 1994,[70] triazole prophylaxis was found to be associated with an increased risk of bacteremia. Although no causal relationship could be definitively proven, it is worth noting that other authors found similar results.[71] Another side effect of antifungal prophylaxis with triazoles has been the possible selection of natively resistant *Candida* species (*C. krusei* and *C. glabrata*)[72-74] and *Aspergillus*[75,76] in leukemic or BMT patients receiving fluconazole and a possible effect on the induction of resistance in previously susceptible *Candida* strains.[77,78] Finally, the possibility of toxic interactions between azoles and other drugs eliminated through the cytochrome P-450 pathway should always be considered.

In conclusion, it is likely that every approach to the prophylaxis of fungal infections in immunocompromised patients should be tailored to the individual patient risk. As summarized in Table 308-1, among cancer patients primary prophylaxis has been demonstrated to be effective in allogeneic BMT patients (especially those undergoing transplantation from unrelated donors and mismatch transplants) and in acute myeloid leukemia patients treated with high-dose cytosine arabinoside with or without anthracyclines. Secondary prophylaxis is indicated in patients with a history of invasive fungal infection who need to proceed in their chemotherapy course. The adverse biologic consequences of an excessive use of antibiotics for prophylaxis and treatment, both in the individual patient and in the environment, are of the utmost importance, and the consequences are even more serious when the effectiveness of these procedures has not been properly demonstrated. The risk of selecting for natively resistant *Candida* strains or molds, the risk of inducing acquired resistance, and the possible effect on the incidence of severe bacterial infections play against a widespread use of prophylaxis in other patient categories. Chemoprophylaxis of aspergillosis still remains an open issue.

PROPHYLAXIS AGAINST *PNEUMOCYSTIS JIROVECII*

Pneumocystis jirovecii (formerly *carinii*) pneumonia (PCP) is a well-known risk, especially for patients with acute lymphoblastic leukemia and for recipients of bone marrow transplantation.[79] There are data showing that it may represent a risk for additional categories of immunocompromised patients, such as patients with solid tumors (mainly those with primary or secondary brain tumors receiving high-dose steroids for prolonged periods of time) or receiving autologous transplantation.[80-83] Treatment with corticosteroids accounts for the main chemotherapeutic risk factor, with a high incidence of PCP especially during dose tapering.[80] The duration of risk after treatment discontinuation is not known, nor is the exact dose and duration of corticosteroids therapy that is sufficient to predispose to PCP. Several drugs affecting cell-mediated mechanisms have been associated with the risk of PCP, including fludarabine,[5,6,84] cytosine arabinoside, methotrexate, D-actinomycin, bleomycin, and L-asparaginase.[5,6] PCP has been described also in children and adults with solid tumors receiving autologous peripheral blood stem cell transplantation. Absolute CD4[+] lymphocyte count of 200/mm^3 or less, or 15% or less (or similar age-related values for children), has been suggested as a possible surrogate marker at least in BMT, but no study is available at this time supporting this suggestion.[82] Trimethoprim-sulfamethoxazole, given three times a week, remains the drug of choice in any patient who can tolerate it.[85] Schedules for anti-PCP prophylaxis are provided in Table 308-2. Trimethoprim-sulfamethoxazole prophylaxis is effective in nearly all instances, provided the patient has been strictly compliant with the prescribed dose schedule.[86]

TABLE 308-2 Prophylaxis of *Pneumocystis jirovecii* Pneumonia

TMP-SMX Regimens for Adults (based on experience with HIV; see Chapter 125)
- One double-strength tablet (800/160) daily
- One single-strength tablet (400/80) daily

Alternative Regimens
- Dapsone 2 mg/kg (maximum 100 mg) daily
- Dapsone 50 mg daily plus once weekly pyrimethamine 50 mg plus leucovorin 25 mg
- Aerosol pentamidine 300 mg once a month by Respirgard II nebulizer
- TMP-SMX: one double-strength tablet (2.5 mg/kg of TMP) twice a day for 3 consecutive days each week

Regimens with lesser documentation (see Chapter 268)
- Atovaquone: 1500 mg daily
- Pyrimethamine plus sulfadoxine
- Clindamycin plus pyrimethamine

HIV, human immunodeficiency virus; TMP-SMX, trimethoprim-sulfamethoxazole.

ANTIVIRAL PROPHYLAXIS

No primary antiviral chemoprophylaxis is normally recommended in patients with solid tumors or lymphomas. Secondary prophylaxis can be an option in patients with recurrent and severe viral diseases, such as genital and labial herpes and herpes zoster. Acyclovir and valacyclovir are the drugs of choice. It has been shown that herpes simplex virus (HSV) reactivation is frequent in HSV-seropositive patients developing stomatitis after antineoplastic chemotherapy.[87] It has also been postulated that acyclovir prophylaxis, by reducing the severity of oral stomatitis, might also reduce the incidence of bacterial infections originating from the oral flora, but this hypothesis has never been confirmed.

THE FEBRILE CANCER PATIENT

Table 308-3 summarizes the most important factors to consider in the initial evaluation of a cancer patient with fever. As in every immunocompromised patient, signs of infection can be absent as a result of the inadequate function of the inflammation cascade. The first, and sometimes the only, sign of infection is fever. For the purpose of starting empirical antibiotic therapy, fever is usually defined as an axillary temperature greater than 38° C at three different times within a 12-hour period, or as a temperature greater than 38.5° C in a single measurement. The detection of other possible signs of infection requires careful and repeated clinical evaluation. Petechial or ecchymotic skin lesions, hyperventilation with respiratory alkalosis, sensory loss, hypotension and unexplained oliguria, thrombocytopenia with an increase in fibrinogen, and coagulation disorders are all possible signs of infection that can accompany or even precede fever. Indeed, although fever is an important clinical sign, its absence should not lead the physician to exclude the possibility of an infection in progress. Patients who are particularly debilitated or are receiving high-dose steroids could progress to a fulminating sepsis without fever. Although the risk is greater when the patient is neutropenic, fever and infection can complicate the clinical course of a neoplastic disease whatever the granulocyte count.

Fever in the Absence of Neutropenia

The definition of neutropenia requires the presence of an absolute granulocyte count lower than 500 cells/µL. The World Health Organization classifies granulocytopenia as follows: level 0 (no granulocytopenia) with more than 2000 cells/µL; level 1, 1500 to 1900 cells; level 2, 1000 to 1400 cells; level 3, 500 to 900 cells; and level 4, below 500 cells. As shown by Bodey and colleagues several years ago, the risk of bacteremia and severe infection is inversely related to the severity and duration of neutropenia and is higher when the granulocyte count is below 100 cells/µL.[88] Many experts in this field believe that the risk of infection increases significantly when the granulocyte count decreases under 1000 cells, because neutropenia is not a static concept, but a dynamic one,[89] although less than 500 cells is the critical point. In addition, the risk of infection is also associated with severe mucositis. The existence of a strict correlation between fever and bacterial infection, which usually leads to rapid clinical evaluation and

---

TABLE 308-3 Considerations in the Initial Evaluation of Febrile Cancer Patients

- Underlying disease (solid tumor, acute leukemia, chronic leukemia, lymphoma, stem cell transplant, other)
- Stage of the underlying disease (leukemia in induction, leukemia in relapse, metastatic tumor, disseminated lymphoma)
- Previous history of infection (both before and after the diagnosis of tumor)
- Granulocyte count at time of onset and in the 30 previous days
- Lymphocyte count at time of onset and in the 30 previous days
- Expected granulocyte count kinetics (decreasing, increasing)
- Expected duration of granulocytopenia
- Clinical presentation (fever alone or fever + other signs or symptoms)
- Other signs or symptoms (hypotension, neurologic symptoms, skin lesions, respiratory signs and symptoms, pain, mucositis, presence and status of the central catheter, blood pH, arterial oxygen saturation)
- Fibrinogen and platelet levels

---

immediate empirical antibacterial therapy, has been mainly shown in neutropenic patients, while non-neutropenic patients, with a normal and not decreasing granulocyte count, might deserve a more relaxed and thoughtful approach to diagnosis and treatment.

There are certainly situations in which non-neutropenic patients need empirical antimicrobial therapy. First, cancer patients, like everyone else, can contract community-acquired infections, and some of these infections can be severe and might deserve immediate treatment. Second, even if they are not neutropenic, cancer patients are still exposed to infections correlated with their underlying immune deficit (leukemia, lymphoma, multiple myeloma, allogeneic BMT with GVHD) and with the impairment of mechanical defenses (abdominal and lung tumors, head and neck tumors). Third, cancer patients often have indwelling venous catheters. Several studies have actually shown that fever in a non-neutropenic cancer patient fitted with an indwelling central venous catheter should always raise the suspicion of a catheter-related infection. For example, in a 1-year prospective, multicenter surveillance study of the etiology, main clinical features, and outcome of blood-stream infections in children with cancer conducted in centers belonging to the Italian Association for Pediatric Hematology and Oncology, a total of 191 blood-stream infections were reported.[90] Of them, 123 (64%) occurred in neutropenic and 68 (36%) in non-neutropenic patients. A correlation with the presence of an indwelling central venous catheter was found in only 20% of the episodes among neutropenic patients, but in 55% among non-neutropenic patients. The type of clinical presentation (spiking fever and chills soon after catheter manipulation or pain and skin redness along the tunneled part of the catheter) is highly suggestive of catheter-related infection, and the results of blood cultures are usually of diagnostic value. In this particular case an antibiotic therapy should always be started, because the risk of septic shock is not negligible.

Fever in the Presence of Neutropenia

Fever during neutropenia has always been considered a medical emergency and should always be considered as due to infection, unless otherwise proven. Febrile episodes during the course of neutropenia are classified according to the presence or absence of a microbiologic or clinical documentation of infection. On this basis, febrile complications in neutropenic cancer patients are classified as (1) microbiologically documented infections (MDI) with bacteremia (isolation of a significant pathogen from one or more blood cultures); (2) MDI without bacteremia (isolation of a significant pathogen from a well-defined site of infection (usually urine, respiratory secretions obtained with sterile procedures, or abscess aspiration); (3) clinically documented infections in the presence of a clinical picture clearly and objectively infectious in nature, but without microbiologic proof; and (4) unexplained fever or fever of unknown origin, when both clinical and microbiologic proofs are lacking, but the clinical course is compatible with an infection.[91,92] The IATG-EORTC trials contributed significantly to the understanding of the natural history of febrile neutropenia in the last 25 years. For example, among nearly 800 documented bacteremias observed in the eight therapeutic trials (I, II, III, IV, V, VIII, IX, and XI) performed by this group from 1978 to 1994, the overall mortality rate decreased from 21% to 7%. In particular, the 30-day mortality rate from any cause in patients with gram-negative and gram-positive bacteremia is now as low as 10% and 6%, respectively.[93] This represents a dramatic improvement as compared to the findings of a classic study on gram-negative rod bacteremias performed in 1962, in which the mortality rate approached 90%,[94] as well as to the first IATG-EORTC study performed in 1978, in which more than 20% of the patients with gram-negative bacteremia and about 15% of those with gram-positive bacteremia died.[95] Although the reasons for these improvements are likely multiple, the strategy calling for the rapid institution of empirical, broad-spectrum antibacterial therapy with very active antimicrobial compounds at the development of fever has no doubt played a pivotal role.

Another important epidemiologic finding stemming from the EORTC experience concerns the etiology of infections: in the last 25 years there has been a considerable change in the pattern of pathogens causing bacteremia in cancer patients. As shown in Figure 308-7, in the first trials performed by the group in the 1970s, gram-negative rods were predominant. In the mid-1980s, however, the epidemiologic situation changed completely, and gram-positive bacteria became by far more prevalent. The reason for this modification in the pattern of infecting pathogens was unclear, but the widespread use of antibacterial prophylaxis with fluoroquinolones certainly played a role in the shift, although the same phenomenon was also described in pediatric populations, in which quinolones were never used. Very recently, there have been some indications that the etiologic pattern of pathogens causing bacteremia is changing again. Indeed, in the most recent trial performed by the IATG-EORTC, there was an increase in the rate of bacteremias among all febrile and neutropenic episodes (from 23% to 28%; $P = .03$) that was mainly due to an increase in the proportion of gram-negative bacteremias (from 6.5% to 12%; $P < .01$).[96] It is unclear to what extent the new increase in gram-negative infection is associated with a decreasing use of quinolone prophylaxis, an increase in quinolone resistance, or both.

The third important change in the natural history of infections in cancer patients has been the increasing number of adult patients with solid tumors who are treated with high-dose chemotherapy and therefore develop neutropenia and fever. This has led several investigators to realize that not all neutropenic cancer patients are the same and that there are patients in whom the clinical course of fever during neutropenia seems to be particularly favorable.[9,97] Indeed, even if treated with intensive regimens, patients with solid tumors rarely remain neutropenic for more than 8 to 10 days. In most cases, these patients are clinically stabilized within 48 hours after the first appearance of fever, and are without fever within 3 to 4 days. According to this concept, the empirical therapy of febrile neutropenia in cancer patients should not be the same in every situation and in every patient, but rather should be modulated according to individual risk factors. On the basis of this concept, several studies have been performed with the aim of identifying a priori, in a scientific way and not empirically, the patient populations at low risk.

With the aim of deriving a clinical prediction rule able to identify febrile and neutropenic patients at low risk of medical complications who might benefit from early discharge and outpatient care, Talcott and co-workers[98] analyzed data from episodes of fever and granulocytopenia, which were available within the first 24 hours after the onset of fever. In this analysis the dependent variable was defined as the development of severe medical complications, including infection. A long list of such complications was provided. Judgments were based on a prospective evaluation partially combined with a blind retrospective review performed by an independent physician. Patients' risk of developing complications was classified according to control of cancer, presence of comorbidity factors, and type of care (outpatient or inpatient), and four risk groups were constructed. Analysis showed that outpatients with a controlled cancer and without any comorbidity factor were more likely to recover easily and rapidly from their episode of fever and granulocytopenia. The results were validated on an independent set of data[99] in which the conclusion of the previous analysis was confirmed. In addition, a multivariate analysis of factors associated with a favorable outcome showed that the predefined risk groups were independently significantly correlated with the development of a complicated clinical course. Unfortunately, in this study sensitivity and specificity of the model (i.e., its discriminant capacity) were not calculated. In a third study by the same group of investigators,[100] the clinical prediction rule seemed not to be able to discriminate satisfactorily between favorable and unfavorable outcomes, because 14 of 30 patients (47%) discharged after 2 days from the onset of fever had to change treatment and 9 (30%) had to be readmitted to the hospital because of the development of medical complications.

Another attempt at describing the model of the high-risk patient was proposed by the IATG-EORTC.[101] The authors focused on a more objective dependent variable, the occurrence of bacteremia, making the assumption that bacteremia carries an increased risk of unfavorable outcome. Actually, bacteremia is known to be associated with some incremental risk of complications and clinical deterioration, and the results obtained in clinical trials of empirical therapy are usually poorer in bacteremic patients than in other patients. The results showed that shock, very high fever, presence and location of signs of infection, long-lasting granulocytopenia, thrombocytopenia, and administration of antifungal prophylaxis were predictive of bacteremia. Then, each factor was weighted and a risk score was calculated. Unfortunately, the ability of the rule to discriminate between bacteremic and nonbacteremic patients was poor. At best, it allowed a reliable prediction in a small subgroup of patients at lower risk.

More recently, other studies have evaluated the possibility of identifying clinical and laboratory factors able to predict the prognosis of a febrile episode, in order to individualize treatments. In the MASCC study,[102] factors associated with good prognosis in febrile neutropenic cancer patients were the "burden of the illness," indicating mild or moderate clinical symptoms at presentation; absence of hypotension; absence of chronic obstructive pulmonary disease; presence of solid tumor or, in patients with hematologic malignancies, absence of previous fungal infection; outpatient status; absence of dehydration; and age lower than 60 years. Each factor was weighted and a score was given. In the validation set, a risk-index score of 21 identified low-risk patients with positive and negative predictive values of 91% and 36%, respectively. At this threshold, sensitivity and specificity were 71% and 68%, respectively, for a 30% misclassification rate. A similar score has also been elaborated and validated in children.[103] At present, the most important reason for obtaining reliable scoring systems is to use them to identify patients who may be discharged early from the hospital or even treated as outpatients.[97,104] However, the option of full outpatient treatment with no in-hospital initial evaluation cannot be recommended.[105] Table 308-4 summarizes the parameters identified in these studies,[97,103,104,106-108] stratified in factors available at the onset of fever (clinical history or examination) or available later (laboratory results and clinical evolution). Although some studies succeeded in identifying low-risk patients,[97,104] none was able to identify high-risk patients reliably.[101,107]

TREATMENT OF FEBRILE NEUTROPENIA

A number of studies have been performed in febrile and neutropenic cancer patients, with the aim of determining which is the most effective antibiotic regimen to use in this clinical situation. In addition, the Infectious Diseases Society of America has repeatedly published guidelines that represent an important step toward the use of a rational and validated approach.[38] The discovery of the low-risk febrile, neutropenic patient has created new problems because these patients may deserve a less intensive therapeutic approach. The increasing cost of health care has led some investigators to explore new treatment modalities in these patients, from outpatient care to oral therapy. The main

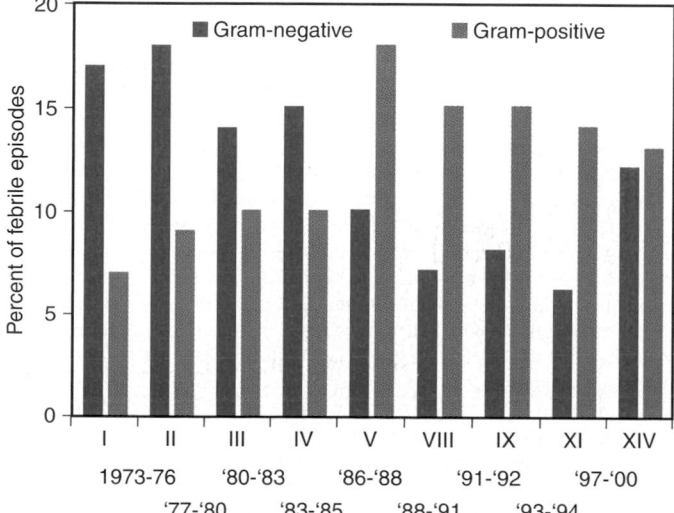

FIGURE 308-7. Etiology of single-agent bacteremias in EORTC-IATG trials of empirical therapy in high risk patients conducted between 1973 and 2000.

TABLE 308-4 Factors Associated with Low Risk of Severe Infection or with an Uncomplicated Clinical Course in Febrile Neutropenic Cancer Patients*

	Parameters Derived From Literature Review[97,107,108]	MASCC Score[102]		Pediatric Score[103]
		Clinical Parameters	Score	Clinical Parameters
Clinical data available at onset of febrile neutropenia or soon after admission	• Absence of major medical complications (e.g., hypo/hypertension; liver, kidney, heart, lung dysfunction) • No diarrhea, emesis, difficult swallowing • No sensory impairment, focal neurologic signs, or spinal cord compression • No uncontrolled bleeding • Outpatient status for at least 48 hr before admission • Presence of an unobstructed central venous catheter • Clinical burden with no or moderate symptoms • Controlled underlying disease • Neutropenia lasting for less than 10-15 days • More than 7 days from the last cycle of chemotherapy • Patient's age > 1 yr and < 65 yr	• Burden of illness: no or mild symptoms • No hypotension • No chronic obstructive pulmonary disease • Solid tumor or no previous fungal infection • No dehydration • Outpatient status • Burden of illness: moderate symptoms • Patient's age < 60 yr	5 5 4 4 3 3 3 2	• Hypotension • Relapse of leukemia • ≤7 days since receipt of chemotherapy
Laboratory data available after admission	• Granulocyte count > 100/μL and expected to increase in the following 2 days • Monocyte count > 100/μL • Hematocrit > 15% • Platelet count > 50,000-75,000/μL and rising in the following 2 days • C-reactive protein < 50-90 mg/L • Normal chest radiograph			• Platelets ≤ 50,000/μL • C-reactive protein ≥ 90 mg/L

Notes and risk evaluation		• Points attributed to the variable "burden of illness" are not cumulative. The maximum theoretical score is therefore 26.	Low-risk patient: score ≥ 21	Low-risk patient:
				• Absence of all the parameters
				• Presence of only 1 of the following parameters:
				  1. ≤7 days since receipt of chemotherapy *or*
				  2. platelets ≤50,000/μL
				High risk patient:
				• Presence of 1 of the following parameters:
				  1. hypotension
				  2. relapse of leukemia
				  3. C-reactive protein ≥ 90 mg/L *or*
				• concomitant presence of 2 or more of the identified parameters

*MASCC score and pediatric score have been derived from prospective studies end-validated with independent data sets.

issues we discuss in this regard include (1) the choice of the initial empirical regimen in both low-risk and non-low-risk patients, both in the inpatient and in the outpatient setting, and (2) the addition or substitution of antibiotics in nonresponding patients.

Empirical Intravenous Antibiotic Therapy in Non-Low-Risk Patients

Mortality in severely neutropenic patients with gram-negative bacteremia can approach 40%, if an empirical treatment is not promptly undertaken.[109,110] This information is the rationale behind the early empirical administration of broad-spectrum antibiotics upon the development of fever, an approach that has become common practice in this patient population, with substantial improvement in prognosis. However, the specific composition of the empirical regimen remains controversial and subject to change as a result of the changing pattern of pathogens, the rapid development of bacterial resistance, and the emergence of new clinical entities. Table 308-5 reports the most common antibiotic regimens used in febrile neutropenia, and Table 308-6 summarizes their schedule of administration and dosage. The classic β-lactam-aminoglycoside combination has long been considered the

best therapeutic approach for febrile neutropenia[111,112] because of its wide spectrum of action, its potential synergistic activity against gram-negative rods, and its potential, but never demonstrated, ability to reduce the emergence of resistant strains both in the single patient during treatment, and in the environment over time. The disadvantages of this regimen include poor activity against staphylococci and streptococci, possible development of resistance in gram-negative rods,[113] aminoglycoside-related toxicity, and the need to administer multiple daily doses of both antibiotics. A pivotal development in this area has been the demonstration that a penicillin combined with β-lactamase inhibitor might provide good coverage.[114] Another approach, which was mainly used in recipients of BMT, has been the use of a double β-lactam combination, usually with piperacillin and ceftazidime.[115] The main problems with this regimen include the high cost and the disadvantage of using two antibiotics that share the same mechanism of action. The advantages include better coverage of streptococci (as a result of the inclusion of the ureidopenicillin) and lower toxicity. The combination of piperacillin and ciprofloxacin has recently been tested with apparently good results.[116] No combination has been shown to be convincingly superior to the other in clinical practice.

TABLE 308-5 Intravenous Antibiotic Regimens Commonly Used for Empirical Therapy of Fever in Neutropenic Hospitalized Patients

Monotherapy
Ceftazidime
Cefepime
Imipenem-cilastatin
Meropenem
Piperacillin-tazobactam

Two-Drug Regimens
Ceftazidime + amikacin
Single-daily ceftriaxone + single-daily amikacin
Imipenem-cilastatin *or* meropenem + amikacin
Ceftazidime + piperacillin
Ceftazidime + vancomycin
Piperacillin-tazobactam + amikacin
Piperacillin + ciprofloxacin

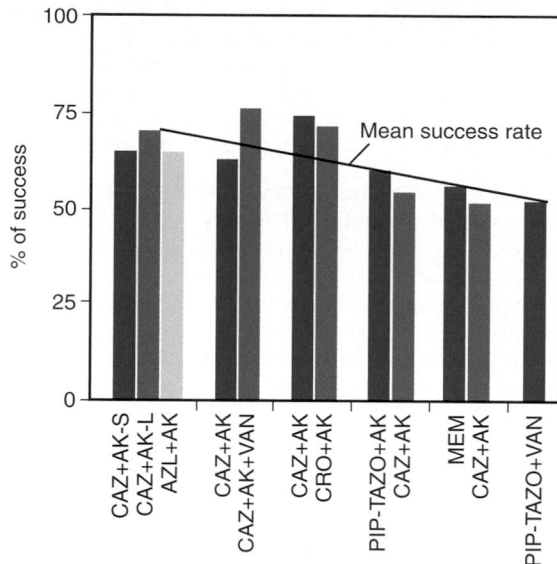

FIGURE 308-8. IATG-EORTC success rates in six different studies of empirical intravenous therapy of febrile neutropenia, arranged in chronologic order from left to right. Independent of the antibiotic regimen, there is a trend over time toward reduction of efficacy of empirical antibacterial therapy of febrile neutropenia. CAZ, ceftazidime; AK, amikacin; AZL, azlocillin; VAN, vancomycin; CRO, ceftriaxone; PIP-TAZO, piperacillin-tazobactam; MEM, meropenem; AK-S, short course amikacin (3 days); AK-L, long course amikacin.

Single-agent therapy became feasible and safe when broad-spectrum antibiotics, such as third- and fourth-generation cephalosporins with anti-*Pseudomonas* activity (ceftazidime and cefepime) and carbapenems, became available. The reliability of this approach has been clearly shown in several trials.[117-120] However, very few studies addressed the problem of monotherapy versus combination therapy in an appropriate methodologic fashion, that is, comparing the same β-lactam with either an aminoglycoside or placebo. Recently, Del Favero and co-workers from the GIMEMA group conducted a prospective, double-blind trial in which piperacillin-tazobactam was combined with amikacin or placebo in the therapy of febrile neutropenia.[121] Response rates were similar with both regimens (49% for monotherapy vs. 53% in combined therapy). Therefore, in the epidemiologic settings of the study, the initial empirical combination therapy was not associated with improved outcomes when compared with initial monotherapy. This study adds piperacillin-tazobactam to the armamentarium of antibiotics available for effective monotherapy. Quite recently a large meta-analysis comparing the effectiveness of β-lactam monotherapy versus β-lactam-aminoglycoside combination showed no difference or even an advantage for monotherapy both in stud-

ies in which a newer β-lactam was compared with an older one plus an aminoglycoside and in studies in which the same β-lactam was used in both arms. Advantages included not only a lower rate of adverse events, as expected, but also a lower rate of failures and a trend for a better survival. In conclusion, at the present time available evidence suggests that aminoglycosides no longer appear to be necessary in febrile and neutropenic patients in absence of microbiological indications for use.[122]

Although the results of clinical trials play a pivotal role in the choice that every individual center must make regarding empirical therapy, other factors should be considered as well.[38] These include local antibiotic policies, bacteriologic results, and resistance patterns, as well as antibiotic toxicity and cost. In addition, a number of patient-related factors should be taken into account, such as the clinical presentation, the presence of organ failure, the state of the underlying disease, and the expected duration of neutropenia, among others. Finally, resistance to β-lactams is increasing,[123,124] and this may be a cause of concern for centers using monotherapy. As in the case of combination therapy, very rarely has a monotherapy regimen been shown to be convincingly superior over another. Nevertheless, as documented in Figure 308-8, the IATG-EORTC experience shows that the rate of success with empirical therapy has been continuously decreasing trial by trial from 1995 to 2000, although with decreasing mortality. Why this is happening is difficult to say. Because modification of the therapeutic regimen means failure in studies of febrile neutropenia, it might simply be that physicians change therapy too early, without adequate reason, although the possibility of true failures related to antibiotic resistance cannot be ruled out. The reasons for this phenomenon have been recently reviewed.[89]

The issue of the early inclusion of an anti-gram-positive glycopeptide antibiotic (vancomycin or teicoplanin) in the empirical regimen has been discussed thoroughly in many meetings and has been addressed by several authors in light of the increased incidence and the decreased response rate of these infections to β-lactam-aminoglycoside combinations. Some studies[125-127] reported favorable results from this practice, with more rapid resolution of fever and reduction in gram-positive secondary infections, total febrile days, and need to use empirical amphotericin B. More convincingly, other groups[128-131] did not find any significant advantage in early anti-gram-positive coverage and suggested that

TABLE 308-6 Dosages, Route and Schedule of Administrations of Drugs Most Commonly Employed for Treatment of Febrile Neutropenia

Drug	Route of Administration	Daily Pediatric Doses (mg/kg)	Total Adult Dose/Day	Number of Daily Doses
Amikacin	IV	15-20	15 mg/kg	1
Amoxicillin-clavulanate (as amoxicillin)	PO	60	1.5-1.75 g	2-3
Cefepime	IV	100	4-6 g	2-3
Cefixime	PO	8	0.4 g	1-2
Ceftriaxone	IV	80	2 g	1
Ciprofloxacin	IV	15-30	0.8-1.2 g	2-3
	PO	30	1.5 g	2-3
Gentamicin	IV	5	5-7 mg/kg	1
Imipenem-cilastatin (as imipenem)	IV	60-100	2 g	3-4
Meropenem	IV	60	3 g	3
Piperacillin	IV	300	12-18 g	4
Piperacillin-tazobactam (as piperacillin)	IV	300	12-18 g	3-4
Teicoplanin	IV/IM	10	0.4-1.2 g	1 (2 doses within the first 24 hours)
Tobramycin	IV	5	5-7 mg/kg	1
Vancomycin	IV	40	2 g	2

IM, intramuscularly; IV, intravenously; PO, orally.

vancomycin should not be included in the initial empirical regimen. Indeed, the recent reports of staphylococci and enterococci displaying variable levels of resistance to glycopeptide antibiotics[132] should further discourage physicians from using these important drugs on an empirical basis. Of course, if the patient presents with signs of infection at the catheter site, the use of vancomycin from the beginning is warranted.

Empirical Antibiotic Therapy in Low-Risk Patients and the Issue of Outpatient Therapy

According to common practice, the occurrence of fever during neutropenia is considered a medical emergency and should not be treated in the outpatient setting or at home. As previously discussed, this concept has been partially reviewed in light of the fact that febrile and neutropenic patients are not all the same and that low-risk patients can be identified and treated accordingly. However, in the early days, the risk of complicated medical courses was not the only factor limiting the possibility of giving outpatient care to cancer patients with febrile neutropenia. Many of the treatments used for the management of febrile neutropenia were not considered practical in any other setting (antimicrobial agents with short half-lives requiring multiple injections, need to co-administer injectable narcotics for pain control, total parenteral nutrition, and skilled nursing). Recent technological advances have increased the intensity of therapy that can be administered in the outpatient setting, with the potential advantage of avoiding, at least in part, the risk of nosocomial infection and the likely possibility of reducing costs and improve patients' quality of life. Advances allowing outpatient management include long-term intravenous access with peripherally inserted central catheters, tunneled catheters, and totally implanted lines coupled with programmable pumps; intravenous antibiotics with long half-lives that can be safely administered once daily; oral antibiotics with reliable bioavailability and expanded spectrum of action; and the presence of nurse-doctor teams for home care. Obviously, the home environment must be clean and stable, must have basic necessities such as a telephone, heating and refrigeration, and running water, and should not be too far from the hospital. In addition, there should be somebody in the patient's family skillful enough to provide basic assistance and to manage the central catheter and intravenous infusions. Candidates for outpatient management include clinically stable persons with low-risk granulocytopenia.

The feasibility of outpatient antibiotic therapy in the febrile neutropenic patient has been investigated in several trials. One of the pilot studies was published by Rubenstein and co-workers in 1993.[133] In this study, adult patients with low-risk febrile neutropenia (established according to local rules) were randomized for outpatient therapy either with oral ciprofloxacin and clindamycin or with intravenous aztreonam and clindamycin. About two thirds of the patients were being treated for solid tumors, and only five in each study arm were receiving treatment for acute leukemia. The patients were closely followed, in outpatient clinics and at home, by a team of nurses trained in outpatient intravenous therapy. The authors concluded that the two treatment regimens were equally effective, and that outpatient therapy of febrile neutropenia was safe and effective. In the following years other studies confirmed that outpatient therapy of febrile neutropenia with intravenous drugs in low-risk patients, following initial in-hospital evaluation, is safe and effective.

In principle, the antibiotic regimens for outpatient management should possess not only a broad spectrum of action and good tolerability, but also favorable pharmacokinetics, allowing once-daily dosing. Of course, the choice of once-daily dosing should be balanced with the type of pathogens involved and the degree of antibiotic resistance, although presumably outpatients should not be as heavily colonized with multidrug-resistant hospital pathogens as inpatients. An important advance in this sense has been a study that tested, in the in-patient setting, an antibiotic combination very suitable for outpatient management. In this IATG-EORTC study,[134] the efficacy and toxicity of three daily doses of amikacin-ceftazidime were compared with a single daily dose of ceftriaxone-amikacin in 858 febrile episodes in 677 neutropenic patients undergoing treatment for leukemia, lymphomas, or solid tumors at any stage and followed up in the hospital. In general, the single daily dose of

ceftriaxone-amikacin was as effective as multiple doses of ceftazidime and amikacin (71% vs. 74%). The overall mortality (from any cause) at 30 days from randomization was 11% in both groups. Nephrotoxicity developed in 3% of the patients treated with ceftriaxone-amikacin as a single dose and 2% of those treated with ceftazidime-amikacin in multiple daily doses. In addition, in the latter group the nephrotoxic effect appeared earlier and even in the absence of other nephrotoxic medications. This study showed that the single daily dosing is effective and nontoxic, and presents an attractive option for outpatient management in a setting of low risk for Pseudomonas infections.

The next step was to test oral therapy. Two papers reporting results of randomized clinical trials comparing oral versus intravenous therapy in hospitalized, low-risk, febrile granulocytopenic cancer patients were published in 1999.[135,136] In the first, febrile patients with lymphomas and solid tumors and recipients of stem cell transplantation with an expected duration of neutropenia of less than 10 days were randomized to receive on an open-label basis ceftriaxone plus amikacin or oral ciprofloxacin plus oral amoxicillin-clavulanate. The second trial was a randomized placebo-controlled study again comparing ciprofloxacin plus amoxicillin-clavulanate with intravenous ceftazidime monotherapy. In both studies patients were considered eligible in the presence of "low-risk" neutropenia, defined as lasting for less than 10 days, and in the absence of other medical complications, catheter-related infections, or pulmonary infiltrate. Both studies were conducted in hospitalized patients. The two regimens performed similarly, with an overall response rate of 80% and 77%, respectively, in the European study[135] and 71% and 67% in the American study.[136] As expected, in both cases patients receiving the oral combination had a higher incidence of gastrointestinal adverse events, whereas those receiving the intravenous combination more often had problems related to the central catheter.

Finally, the approach of starting with intravenous therapy and then switching to oral therapy has also been tested. In low-risk febrile neutropenic children, switching therapy from intravenous drugs to cefixime has been documented to be as safe as continuing intravenous drugs,[137,138] and similar results have been obtained with oral ciprofloxacin administered after one dose of intravenous ceftriaxone plus amikacin.[139] Switching therapy from intravenous to oral ciprofloxacin has also been demonstrated to be a safe practice in adults not receiving this drug as prophylaxis.[140]

In conclusion, Table 308-7 summarizes the possible antibiotic regimens to be used for outpatient therapy of febrile neutropenia. We know that we now have a prediction rule allowing the identification of low-risk patients with febrile neutropenia, and we know that outpatient management, oral therapy, and switching from intravenous to oral therapy are all possible therapeutic options in these patients. What we still do not know is how to put together this information in making treatment decisions. Oral antibiotics and outpatient management in various forms (home therapy after initial in-hospital evaluation, short admission with switch to oral therapy at home) will have an increasing role in the empirical treatment of fever and neutropenia, but the exact definition of the clinical situation is still lacking.

Treatment Modification in Persistently Febrile and Neutropenic Patients

Frequent therapeutic changes are common clinical practice in cancer patients with persistent fever and granulocytopenia. This practice is entirely appropriate when a pathogen is isolated in blood culture and the sensitivity tests show resistance to the current antibiotic. Microbiologically documented infections should be treated with antibiotics to which the isolated pathogen is susceptible in vitro, even if the patient's clinical condition improves spontaneously. It is also appropriate to change antibiotics when clear signs of treatment failure are evident (Table 308-8), although this happens in only a minority of cases, or in the presence of a clinical picture suggestive of a specific etiology that is not likely to be covered by the existing antibiotic regimen (e.g., catheter-related infection, perianal cellulitis, abdominal typhlitis). More controversial is what to do when the patient remains febrile in the absence of evident signs of clinical deterioration, but also in the absence of any microbiologic or clinical documentation of in-

TABLE 308-7 Antibiotic Regimens for Empirical Therapy of Febrile Neutropenia in the Outpatient Setting

Intravenous
- Single-daily ceftriaxone + single daily amikacin
- Teicoplanin/vancomycin should be added in presence of signs of CVC-related infections

Oral
- Ciprofloxacin + amoxicillin-clavulanate in patients not receiving quinolone prophylaxis

Switch Therapy
- Intravenous ciprofloxacin to oral ciprofloxacin
- Intravenous single-daily ceftriaxone + single daily amikacin to ciprofloxacin
- Intravenous single-daily ceftriaxone + single daily amikacin to cefixime

CVC, central venous catheter

fection (unexplained fever or fever of unknown origin) or in documented infections caused by pathogens that are susceptible to the initial empirical regimen in vitro. In general, good clinical practice in infectious diseases suggests that persistence of fever does not necessarily mean failure of a given antibiotic regimen, especially if the patient is otherwise clinically stable. A febrile and neutropenic patient with bacteremia might require from 2 to 7 days to defervesce, even if the isolated pathogen is sensitive to the chosen antibiotic regimen. Therefore, it is likely that, in patients with only fever and otherwise in good clinical condition, the best clinical option should be watchful waiting and nothing else. There is little evidence that a planned, progressive succession of antibiotic therapies in cancer patients actually exists and can be recommended for widespread use.

With few exceptions, every approach to the management of febrile neutropenia should be tailored to the individual patient and to the local epidemiologic situation. Unfortunately, the thoughtful approach we have just delineated is rarely followed, and several modifications are frequently performed in the absence of clear indications. This has been nicely exemplified by one of the IATG EORTC trials. In 1986, as a response to the increasing role of gram-positive cocci (streptococci and staphylococci) in causing infection in cancer patients and to their reduced response rate to several empirical regimens, a trial was implemented to test whether the addition of vancomycin to ceftazidime and amikacin at the onset of fever would have benefited the population of febrile and neutropenic patients.[128] Unfortunately, the study was not designed in a double-blind fashion. Briefly, 747 episodes of fever and neutropenia in patients with cancer were randomized to receive ceftazidime plus amikacin with or without vancomycin. Initially, a crude analysis of the results showed that the overall response rate in the group of patients receiving vancomycin was significantly better than that seen in the control group and that this was particularly evident in the population of patients with gram-positive bacteremias. However, when the reasons for failure were analyzed, including a comparison of the febrile days in the two treatment groups (Fig. 308-9), it turned out that the investigators had a different approach when faced with the same clinical condition (i.e., persistence of fever) according to which regimen the patient was receiving: in the three-arm group no change was made, whereas in the two-arm group vancomycin was frequently added, thus establishing failure. This trial yielded important information on febrile

TABLE 308-8 Proposed Definition of Failure of Empirical Antibacterial Therapy Derived from the Experience of IATG-EORTC Studies

- Persistence of fever (>39° C) and chills after 24-48 hr of therapy
- Relapse of fever (>38° C) after at least 24 hr of defervescence
- Progression of sepsis syndrome
- Development of disseminated intravascular coagulation, acute respiratory distress syndrome, multiple organ failure
- Persistence of positive cultures from site of infection or blood after 24 hr of therapy
- Relapse of the primary infection
- Appearance of a new infection

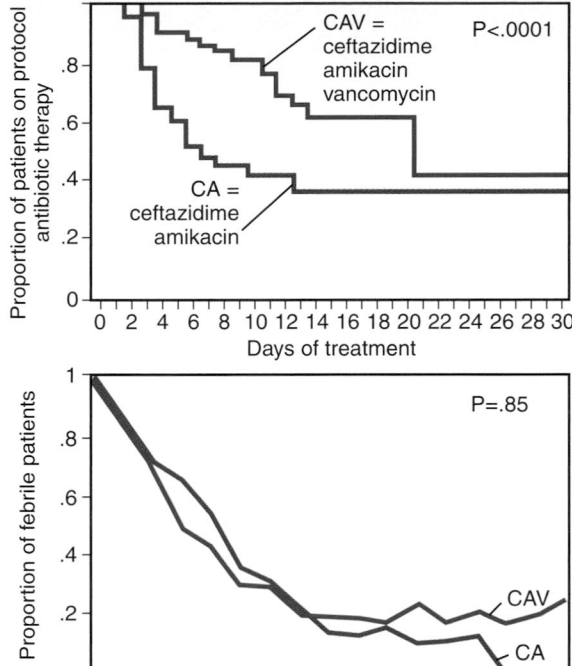

FIGURE 308-9. Results of IATG-EORTC trial V, in which patients were randomized to ceftazidime + amikacin + vancomycin (CAV) or ceftazidime + amikacin (CA) in an unblinded fashion. **Top,** The proportion of patients responding to the initial therapy, showing a major effect in the three-drugs arm. **Bottom,** The proportion of febrile patients according to the day of treatment, showing no difference between the two arms.

neutropenia and how several hematologists and oncologists were accustomed to manage these patients. It became clear that the more prolonged neutropenia and fever were, the more likely it was that physicians added or replaced antibiotics even without objective reasons for doing so. In Table 308-9 we have tried to delineate a possible approach to the persistently febrile and neutropenic patient.

Empirical Anti-Gram-Positive Therapy

Probably the most common empirical modification to the initial treatment in apparently nonresponding patients is the addition of a glycopeptide. Recently, the utility of this practice has been analyzed in two placebo-controlled studies. In the first, a single-center study,[141] 114 patients were randomized to receive either teicoplanin or placebo after 72 to 96 hours of imipenem monotherapy. The number of patients who defervesced within 72 hours after randomization was similar in both groups (44.6% in the teicoplanin group vs. 46.6% in the placebo group), but the time to defervescence was not reported. In the second study,[142] vancomycin (or placebo) was added after 48 to 60 hours of empirical therapy with piperacillin-tazobactam in 165 neutropenic patients with persistent fever of unknown origin or with gram-positive bacteremia caused by a strain susceptible to piperacillin-tazobactam. Defervescence was observed in 82 of 86 patients (95%) in the vancomycin group and 73 of 79 (92%) in the placebo group ($P = .52$). The difference in the median time to defervescence was not statistically significant: 3.5 days (95% confidence interval [CI] 2.7 to 4.4 days) in the vancomycin group and 4.3 days (95% CI 3.5 to 5.1) in the placebo group ($P = .75$) (Fig. 308-10). Further gram-positive bacteremias and the rate of addition of amphotericin B were also similar in both groups. In conclusion, these two studies suggested that the empirical addition of a glycopeptide antibiotic is of no benefit in persistently febrile and granulocytopenic cancer patients, in the absence of lung infiltrates, septic shock, clinically documented infections likely caused by a gram-positive organism (catheter-related or skin and soft tissue infections), and documentation

TABLE 308-9 Management Algorithm for the Persistently Febrile and Neutropenic Patient

1. Choose a "reliable" definition of treatment failure (see suggestions in Table 308-8), but remember that sometimes it takes at least 96 hr to obtain defervescence.
2. Apply definition of failure to your patient and ask whether therapy is really failing.
3. Remember alternative causes of fever in neutropenic patients:
   a. resistant bacteria, fungi, viruses, protozoa
   b. infusion of blood products
   c. drug reactions
   d. acute GVHD
   e. underlying disease or a second tumor
4. If your conclusion is that the treatment is really failing, then:
   a. consider patient factors: underlying disease and its stage, including response to chemotherapy
   b. consider local epidemiologic conditions: most frequent pathogens and pattern of resistance
   c. consider the presence or the appearance of signs of localized infections, then evaluate if your treatment covers the most probable involved pathogens
   d. obtain diagnostic imaging: ultrasound, CT scan, magnetic resonance imaging, radionuclide scan
   e. check patient's ocular fundus for occult fungal infections
   f. repeat blood cultures and culture from any relevant clinical site that appeared after the initiation of empirical therapy
   g. search for viruses (e.g., PCR for CMV, adenovirus, EBV, HHV-6), especially if the patient was seronegative, not only in transplant patients
   h. search for fungi, including *Aspergillus* galactomannan antigen
5. If true failure, then start rescue therapy:
   a. carbapenem
   b. vancomycin or linezolid if a vancomycin-resistant gram-positive organism is likely
   c. add (or change) antifungal therapy
   d. consider catheter removal
   e. consider immune reconsitution

CMV, cytomegalovirus; CT, computed tomography; EBV, Epstein-Barr virus; GVHD, graft-versus-host disease; HHV-6, human herpesvirus-6; PCR, polymerase chain reaction.

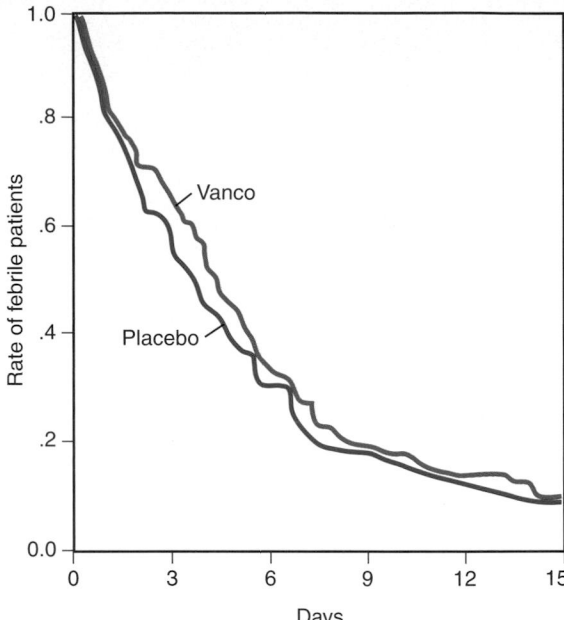

FIGURE 308-10. Results of IATG-EORTC trial XIV. After initial treatment with piperacillin-tazobactam, patients who were persistently febrile or had a gram-positive infection susceptible to piperacillin-tazobactam were randomized to receive vancomycin or placebo, in a blinded fashion. The data show that there is no difference between the two arms in terms of time to defervescence.

of gram-positive infections resistant to the initial empirical regimen. The indiscriminate and unnecessary use of glycopeptides is expensive and might lead to increased resistance among staphylococci and enterococci, which would in itself have major clinical implications.[132]

Empirical Antifungal Therapy

The only modification of empirical therapy that has been shown to be somewhat effective in persistently febrile and neutropenic cancer patients is the addition of an antifungal agent. The rationale for this practice comes both from autopsy studies, which showed the increasing role of fungal infections as the cause of death in cancer patients,[39,40] and from clinical observations showing the importance of early treatment in the prognosis of fungal infections,[143] at least in the presence of a rapid bone marrow recovery. Soon after, Burke and colleagues showed a decreased mortality rate from invasive mycosis in patients receiving empirical amphotericin B compared with historical controls.[144] Following these observations, two groups of investigators on both sides of the Atlantic Ocean decided to test the effectiveness of this procedure in a more controlled fashion, with the aim of testing if the early inclusion of an antifungal drug was able both to treat any baseline, occult, or not yet detected fungal infection and to prevent subsequent infections. In both studies, only patients without proven infections as the initial cause of fever were included.

Pizzo and co-workers at the National Cancer Institute in Bethesda, Maryland,[145] randomized patients who were still febrile and granulocytopenic after 7 days of empirical antibiotic therapy and lacked any documentation of infection to discontinuation of all antibiotic treatments (16 patients), to continuation of the same combination as the initial treatment (16 patients), or to addition of empirical amphotericin B (18 patients). The lack of addition of amphotericin B resulted in an increased incidence of fungal infections. In the group of patients who did not add amphotericin B, there was one bacterial infection and five proven or probable fungal infections, two of which were fatal. One other patient, who died, had a disseminated fungal infection detected at autopsy. In the group of 18 patients randomized to receive amphotericin B and to continue antibacterial therapy, only two documented infections developed (a disseminated cytomegalovirus [CMV] infection and a *Pseudallescheria boydii* pneumonia and arteritis), and both patients died. Antibiotic therapy discontinuation, as done in the first group, resulted in the development of serious complications of both bacterial and fungal origin.

The IATG-EORTC randomized 132 persistently febrile and granulocytopenic cancer patients not responding to empirical antibacterial therapy and affected with a fever of unknown origin or a clinically documented infection to receive empirical amphotericin B or to continue their antibacterial coverage without modification.[146] There was no statistically significant difference between the two groups in terms of defervescence and survival, although no death resulting from fungal infection occurred among the patients receiving empirical amphotericin B compared to four deaths in the other group ($P = .05$), and the number of documented fungal infections was higher in patients not receiving amphotericin B (six patients vs. one; $P = .1$). Linear logistic regression analysis showed that the addition of amphotericin B was correlated with response in adults with hematologic malignancies who were not receiving antifungal prophylaxis and were severely granulocytopenic ($P = .03$). This led to the suggestion that the empirical antifungal therapy strategy should probably be reserved for selected groups of high-risk patients. Neither of these studies was placebo controlled, and in both trials the statistical power of the observed results was very small, especially for subgroup analyses. Nevertheless, the use of empirical antifungal therapy in persistently febrile and granulocytopenic cancer patients without documented infections has become the rule in many cancer centers worldwide, and the U.S. Food and Drug Administration, but not the European regulatory agency, has approved several antifungal drugs for this indication. The optimal time at which empirical antifungal therapy should be started remains undetermined, although most experts recommend waiting until the fifth or seventh day of persistent fever and granulocytopenia.[38,147,148]

Despite its poor tolerability and intrinsic severe toxicity, amphotericin B deoxycholate has been the drug of choice for this indication for a long period of time. However, nephrotoxicity and infusion-related reactions were important dose-limiting factors. This led to the idea of studying azoles for this indication. In 1996, Viscoli and co-workers, in a prospective, randomized trial of fluconazole versus amphotericin B, suggested a possible role for the azole drug in the management of persistently febrile and neutropenic patients not receiving fluconazole prophylaxis and at low risk for aspergillosis.[149] They included in the study only patients with fever of unknown origin. In addition, in order to reduce the risk of attributing to the antifungal therapy an outcome that was actually produced by the modification of the antibacterial therapy, at least 72 hours of persistent fever were required between the modification of the antibacterial therapy and subsequent inclusion of the patient in the study. More recently, fluconazole has been compared with amphotericin B in an empirical therapy trial of 317 patients. In both trials fluconazole was not inferior to amphotericin B for this indication, but both trials underlined the limits inherent with the use of a drug not active against molds for an indication that was mainly targeted to the control of molds.[150] In any case, this approach may offer an alternative to fluconazole prophylaxis in patients at low risk of mould infections, although fluconazole has never been approved for this indication.

In the late 1990s, Walsh and colleagues published the first of a series of large clinical trials of empirical therapy of febrile neutropenia.[151] In this trial, in which liposomal amphotericin B was compared with the standard deoxycholate formulation in a double-blind fashion with the aim of showing no inferiority, a composite end point of successful therapy was first introduced. To fulfill criteria of success, the study drugs should have achieved (1) successful treatment of any baseline fungal infection, (2) prevention of breakthrough fungal infection, (3) resolution of fever at some designated time point, (4) survival at some designated time point, and (5) no premature discontinuation because of lack of efficacy or toxicity. Although the 5-point composite end point was certainly an advancement in terms of study design, it also has some pitfalls that have recently been discussed at length.[152] To increase the accrual in this study, as in all other similar studies that followed, both low-risk and high-risk patients were included, regardless of the type of documentation of the initial episode of febrile neutropenia (i.e., even patients with documented bacterial infections but still febrile and neutropenic after 5 days of treatment were included) and regardless of addition or substitution of antibacterial drugs in the initial empirical regimen. The conclusions were that liposomal amphotericin B was as effective as amphotericin B deoxycholate for empirical therapy of persistently febrile and neutropenic cancer patients when the primary, composite end point was considered. Looking at subgroups, the authors noticed that the liposomal preparation was associated with decrease in the incidence of breakthrough fungal infections, infusion-related toxicity, and nephrotoxicity.[151] However, many aspects of this trial were criticized, such as the low dose of amphotericin B deoxycholate (0.6 mg/kg/day, which could be reduced to 0.3 mg/kg in case of toxicity)[153,154] and the absence of salt and fluid loading for prevention of amphotericin B deoxycholate nephrotoxicity.[155-157] Moreover, it must be emphasized that the number of patients withdrawn from the study because of drug-related toxicity was similar in both arms and that the use of the liposomal preparation was probably not cost-effective.[158] In addition, the benefit of reducing breakthrough fungal infections was mainly due to a reduction in *Candida* infections, without major changes in the incidence of aspergillosis. Finally, no difference in breakthrough fungal infection could be observed between the two arms if documented, probable, and possible fungal infections were included (i.e., all clinical situations that are routinely treated with antifungal drugs). Based on this study, the liposomal preparation of amphotericin B was approved for empirical antifungal therapy of febrile neutropenia.

Azoles with activity against molds have also been studied. In an open randomized trial, Boogaerts and co-workers showed that itraconazole (intravenous and oral) was as effective as amphotericin B deoxycholate for the empirical therapy of persistent fever in neutropenic cancer patients,[159] with an advantage in terms of compliance because the availability of an oral formulation allowing switching from intravenous to oral therapy, and, at least in theory, earlier hospital discharge. More recently, voriconazole, a new broad-spectrum azole, was compared with liposomal amphotericin B in an open-label, prospective, randomized, multicenter, international noninferiority trial using the previously mentioned composite end point.[160] In the definition of noninferiority, both the absolute difference in success rate and the lower limit of the 95% CI could not exceed 10%. In this study, patients receiving voriconazole had a 4.5% lower response rate that those receiving liposomal amphotericin B, but the 95% CI of the difference was between -10.6 and $+1.6$ percentage points. Thus, on the basis of being six tenths of a percentage point outside of the lower limit of the predefined difference in the CI, voriconazole did not meet criteria for noninferiority to liposomal amphotericin B and was not approved for this indication. The authors emphasized that more patients in the liposomal amphotericin B arm had resolution of fever during neutropenia, whereas more patients in the voriconazole arm were removed prematurely from the study because of persistence of fever. In an unblinded study such as this, early removal may reflect nothing more than hesitancy to trust an experimental agent. In another subset analysis, the proportion of patients who developed breakthrough fungal infections was significantly lower in the voriconazole arm. Finally, caspofungin, the new echinocandin which recently became available, has also been tested for empirical therapy.[162a] In the setting of a double-blind, noninferiority study design, caspofungin was compared with liposomal amphotericin B in 1123 persistently febrile and neutropenic cancer patients in 116 hospitals in 26 countries. Unfortunately, concomitant administration of cyclosporin was not allowed, thus reducing the proportion of high-risk patients (i.e., recipients of BMT) included in the study. The composite endpoint of efficacy was basically the same as the one used in previous studies. Caspofungin was found to be noninferior to liposomal-amphotericin B, with an advantage in the subgroup of patients with baseline documented fungal infections (89% vs. 56%) and a better overall survival (93% vs. 89%). The very good toxicity profile of caspofungin was confirmed in this study.

In conclusion, in agreement with other investigators,[161] we look forward to the development in the near future of either new diagnostic methods or reliable clinical prediction rules that might allow physicians to stop overtreating patients with empirical therapies and to adopt therapeutic strategies more specifically directed to the management of infections, not fever, during neutropenia.

MANAGEMENT OF THE FEBRILE NEUTROPENIC PATIENT WITH A SITE OF INFECTION

According to the experience of the IATG-EORTC, about 56% of patients with febrile neutropenia have no clinically detectable site or source of infection. When a site is present, the blood stream is the most frequent one (34%), followed by the upper and lower respiratory tracts (23% and 13%, respectively), the skin and soft tissue (including catheter-related infections) (18%), and the gastrointestinal tract (7%).[162] Other authors report a higher incidence of lung involvement in hematologic malignancy patients, especially in autopsy studies.[163] Patients with a clinically detectable site might deserve a specific therapeutic approach, especially when the infection is localized at the catheter site, in the lungs, or in the abdomen.

The Patient with a Catheter-Related Infection

Long-term central venous catheters (CVCs) have represented an important achievement for the management of cancer patients. However, they also constitute a well-recognized source of infection that is often difficult to diagnose and treat (see Chapters 300 and 307). Two main types of catheters are used in cancer patients: partially implanted catheters (Hickman-Broviac, Groshong, and others), and totally implanted catheters (Port-A-Cath). Partially implanted catheters have a cuff that facilitates the adherence of the catheter to subcutaneous tissues, in order to prevent accidental displacement and to prevent microorganisms from contaminating the tunnel and entering the blood vessel. Some of these catheters may have a valve in the distal or in the proximal end of the device and may have one or more ports (generally two). All catheters require maintenance procedures when not in use, and the frequency of the procedures and the material employed vary according to catheter type.[164]

In clinical practice there are essentially three types of catheter-related infections[165]: (1) infections of the "exit" (Hickman-Broviac type), seen in cases of cellulitis from the cuff to the skin exit; (2) infections (abscesses) of the tunnel and port pocket, seen in cases of cellulitis around the tunnel (Hickman-Broviac type) or involving the port pocket; and (3) catheter-related bacteremia, without any evidence of skin and soft tissue infection. All tunnel infections can be complicated by bacteremia.

Infection rates vary according to catheter type. In a recent review,[166] the results of prospective studies on infectious complications in long-term CVCs were analyzed. In 13 prospective studies involving totally implanted catheters, the pooled mean number of CVC-related bacteremias per 100 catheters was 5.1 (95% CI, 4.0 to 6.3), versus 20.9 (95% CI, 18.2 to 21) in 18 prospective studies of partially implanted catheters. Similar differences were observed in the pooled mean incidence of the same complication per 1000 catheter days, which proved to be 0.2 (95% CI, 0.1 to 0.3) in totally implanted and 1.2 (95% CI, 1.0 to 1.3) in partially implanted catheters. In the last edition of the present textbook,[167] data from 20 studies showed that the mean incidence of CVC-related bacteremias was 11.2% in totally implanted catheters and 36.7% in Hickman/Broviac-type catheters ($P = .008$), with a mean incidence rate of CVC-related bacteremias of 0.059/1000 catheter days in totally implanted CVCs and 3.9/1000 catheter days in partially implanted ones ($P = .001$). The mean incidence of exit site/tunnel pocket infections was 7% in totally implanted versus 15.8% in partially implanted catheters ($P = .33$).

Catheter-related bacteremias are generally due to gram-positive cocci (especially coagulase-negative staphylococci), which are actually isolated in more than 50% of the episodes.[165,168,169] Gram-negative rods can also cause catheter-related bacteremias, in a proportion of cases varying from 25% to 40% of the episodes,[168,170,171] although the source of infection may be different. Gram-positive cocci usually come from skin or hub contamination, whereas gram-negative rods (especially *Klebsiella, Enterobacter, Citrobacter, Achromobacter, Serratia,* and non-*aeruginosa Pseudomonas*) are thought to come more often from the contamination of infusates and antiseptics used for catheter management.[172] Polymicrobial infections are not rare (8% to 49% of the episodes),[168,170,173,174] and fungi (mainly *Candida* spp.) are usually isolated in about 10% of catheter-related blood-stream infections (Fig. 308-11).[90,173,175]

Although its efficacy has never been documented in any clinical trial, the use of empirical therapy in the presence of a suspected indwelling CVC-related infection is a widespread practice.[165] The choice of the antibiotic regimen should be based on the epidemiology of CVC-related infections in every individual center and on the pharmacokinetic/pharmacodynamic characteristics of the available antibiotics.[169] As a general rule, an anti-gram-positive drug should always be included in the initial regimen, although the choice should not necessarily be vancomycin, except in centers with a high rate of oxacillin-resistant staphylococci. Moreover, because gram-negative organisms represent near one fourth of episodes of single-agent CVC-related bacteremias and are frequently documented in polymicrobial bacteremias and in exit site infections, anti-gram-negative coverage appears indispensable. In contrast, the inclusion of an antifungal drug seems to be dispensible in light of the relatively low incidence of fungal infections in this clinical setting.

Treatment of indwelling CVC-related bacteremias also can be accomplished by "locking" the catheter with a solution containing antibiotics plus heparin or normal saline in valved CVCs, in association with standard parenteral therapy with antibiotic infusion. Most of the publications concerning antibiotic lock therapy focus on prevention of catheter-acquired sepsis rather than treatment. However, efficacy of antibiotic lock therapy in sterilizing catheters that are already infected is not well established, although that potential exists. It has been demonstrated that antibiotic concentrations required to kill bacteria located in the biofilm (sessile) are 10 to 100 times higher than that required to kill (planktonic) bacteria in solution. Such concentrations

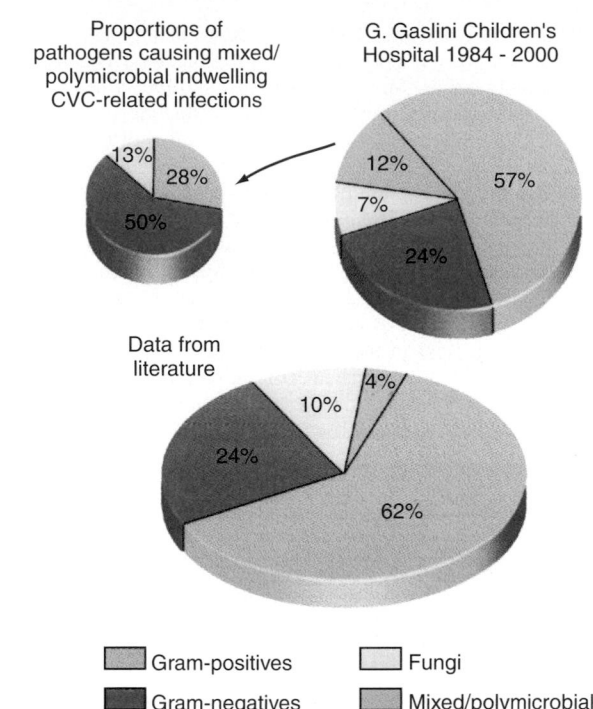

Proportions of pathogens causing mixed/polymicrobial indwelling CVC-related infections

G. Gaslini Children's Hospital 1984 - 2000

Data from literature

Gram-positives
Gram-negatives
Fungi
Mixed/polymicrobial

FIGURE 308-11. Etiology of indwelling central venous catheter-related bacteremias in cancer patients. **Top,** Unpublished observations from a single center; the smallest segment represents the proportions of pathogens isolated in mixed/polymicrobial episodes. **Bottom,** Data from literature published in the period 1986 to 2000.

can be achieved by means of antibiotic lock, giving a rationale for such a therapeutic technique. The decision to use this particular technique of antibiotic administration should be made on the basis of the patient's clinical status, the isolated pathogen and its antibiotic susceptibility pattern, stability of the drug in solution (with or without heparin), and persistence of antibacterial activity in solution. Therapy with an antibiotic lock resulted in better efficacy in treating infections caused by gram-positive organisms compared with episodes caused by gram-negative organisms. Antibiotic lock with antifungal drugs has also been proposed for treatment of CVC-related fungemia, but it is our opinion that the technique should be used only in clinical situations in which immediate CVC removal is impossible because of the patient's condition, and then until catheter removal is feasible.[165]

An important issue is whether or not the catheter should be removed in cases of CVC-related infections. The first two points that must be considered in this decision process are whether the patient necessarily needs the catheter and whether the catheter has adequate flow. If the answer to either of these questions is negative, then the catheter should always be removed and the patient treated adequately. However, if the patient still needs the catheter and the catheter, despite being infected, works properly, then the decision becomes difficult. Infections localized at the catheter tunnel (both partially or totally implanted devices) or catheter pocket (totally implanted catheters) usually require removal of the device. Staphylococcal infections or infections caused by other skin bacteria can usually be treated without removing the catheter, unless caused by *Bacillus* spp. or *Corynebacterium jeikeium.* Catheter removal becomes mandatory (1) if blood cultures are persistently positive while the patient is receiving appropriate antibacterial therapy, (2) in the presence of skin lesions suggestive of dissemination, or (3) when the patient repeatedly presents with spiking fever, chills, and hypotension following catheter flushing.[165,176] Infections caused by gram-negative rods are generally difficult to treat without catheter removal, especially when caused by *Pseudomonas, Stenotrophomonas maltophilia,* or *Acinetobacter* spp. Fungal and mycobacterial infections always require catheter removal.[165,176]

The Febrile Cancer Patient with Pulmonary Infiltrates

Several factors should be considered in the initial evaluation of a cancer patient with pulmonary infiltrates (see also Chapter 307). For example, it is sometimes difficult to discriminate between infectious and noninfectious processes, especially in patients with lung tumors or in transplant patients with acute or chronic GVHD. Quite often both processes coexist. The sensitivity of the standard chest radiograph is certainly suboptimal, and a high-resolution pulmonary computed tomography (CT) scan is mandatory, at least in the presence of a strong clinical suspicion or even routinely in some high-risk patients.[177,178] The value of a given radiologic sign depends on the clinical context in which it develops (other clinical signs; type and stage of underlying disease; type and, especially, severity of immunodeficiency; results of cultural and noncultural diagnostic evaluations). As widely recognized, the impairment of the inflammatory response may render the clinical presentation of pneumonia extremely subtle and insidious, so that a high level of clinical suspicion is required.

Pulmonary infections in neutropenic patients can be caused by bacteria, fungi, and viruses. Gram-negative rods, *Staphylococcus aureus,* and streptococci are common causes of pulmonary infiltrates during the early neutropenic period, whereas fungi, especially *Aspergillus,* are more often found during later stages, or even after bone marrow recovery. During neutropenia, a picture of adult respiratory distress syndrome (ARDS) and septic shock is typical of viridans streptococcal bacteremia, and patchy infiltrates are commonly associated with bacterial infections. Alveolo-interstitial infiltrates with decreased blood oxygen saturation in non-neutropenic patients are typical of *P. jirovecii* or viral (CMV) pneumonia. The appearance of cough and thoracic pain in a patient at risk for aspergillosis with evidence of the "halo" or "air-crescent" sign, on CT scan is highly suggestive of pulmonary aspergillosis.[179-181] In these times of increasing outpatient care, the possibility of a neutropenic patient acquiring a community-acquired pneumonia cannot be overlooked. In this case the most common pathogens are the same ones causing community-acquired pneumonias in non-neutropenic people (*Streptococcus pneumoniae, Mycoplasma, Legionella*), but the outcome may be fatal. Most non-neutropenic patients with pulmonary infections have defects of cell-mediated immune mechanisms. In this case, several etiologies can be considered, from reactivation of old infections (e.g., tuberculosis), to new infections caused by atypical mycobacteria or *Nocardia.* Viruses are also a possibility.

Empirical therapy in the neutropenic patient with pulmonary infiltrates should take into account the type of infiltrate and the time of appearance of the pulmonary infiltrate with respect to both the onset of fever and the onset of neutropenia. As already mentioned, ARDS and septic shock are usually associated with viridans streptococci. In this case, a penicillin and a glycopeptide are the most logical choice. If the pulmonary infiltrate presents at the development of fever, it is likely that the infecting pathogen is an opportunistic agent typical of the neutropenic patient (*S. aureus, Klebsiella, Pseudomonas aeruginosa*). In this case, the same antibiotic regimen commonly used for the management of febrile neutropenia in high-risk patients should be used, although taking into account that a more severe prognosis should be expected. Finally, if the pulmonary infiltrate becomes evident during the course of neutropenia, as a breakthrough infection in a patient already receiving broad-spectrum antibiotics, the most likely etiologies include fungi (especially *Aspergillus*), resistant gram-negative rods (*P. aeruginosa, Klebsiella-Enterobacter-Serratia* group of bacteria), and, more rarely, *Legionella.* Interstitial pneumonia is relatively rare during neutropenia, but not impossible. In this case, CMV, *P. jirovecii,* and *Mycoplasma pneumoniae* are the likely etiologies. The appropriate diagnostic measures should be implemented and treatment should be tailored accordingly.

The Febrile Cancer Patient with Abdominal Symptoms

Severe mucositis represents an important complication of intensive chemotherapy and BMT conditioning regimens.[182,183] The damage is more evident in the oral mucosa, but it can spread to the whole gastrointestinal tract. Intestinal mucositis is extremely important in the pathogenesis of bacteremia in the neutropenic cancer patient because it is thought to be the initial step of the process of intestinal translocation, that is, the mechanism through which intestinal bacteria migrate into the portal vein and mesenteric lymphatic system and may invade the blood stream.[184] As a consequence, febrile and neutropenic patients may present with gastrointestinal signs and symptoms in addition to fever, usually limited to abdominal pain, nausea, vomiting, and light diarrhea. In a prospective study of 62 chemotherapy-induced episodes of neutropenia in leukemic patients, the overall incidence of abdominal infections was 17.7%.[185]

In some instances the intestine becomes the primary site of infection, with a clinical picture, peculiar to postchemotherapy neutropenic patients, that has been called "neutropenic enterocolitis," "necrotizing cellulitis of the cecum," or "neutropenic typhlitis." Neutropenic enterocolitis is a severe clinical syndrome characterized by fever, severe abdominal pain, and sometimes hemorrhagic diarrhea evolving to acute abdomen and septic shock, which develops in about 3% to 6% of adults receiving aggressive treatment for acute leukemia.[185,186] From a pathologic point of view, it is a necrotizing infection of the bowel walls, as shown by the peculiar ultrasound or CT scan appearance of bowel wall thickening (>4 mm).[185-187] Treatment should include both antibiotics with antianaerobic activity and antifungals. Surgery is considered to be very dangerous in these patients, and should probably be deferred as often as possible.

Neutropenic patients, as every other hospitalized patient receiving broad-spectrum antibiotics, can develop classic intestinal infections such as pseudomembranous enteritis caused by *Clostridium difficile.*

STIMULATING OR REGENERATING PATIENT DEFENSE MECHANISMS

Stimulating or regenerating patient's defense mechanisms appears to be a very logical approach to the management of infection in an immunocompromised host. However, despite the availability of several medical products able to act on the immune system, cancer patients continue to develop severe infections.

Bone Marrow Colony-Stimulating Factors

Hematopoiesis, controlled by specific soluble factors acting on the progenitor cells, brings about maturation of the various cellular paths of the blood complements. The use of bone marrow colony-stimulating factors, mainly granulocyte colony-stimulating factor (G-CSF) and granulocyte-macrophage colony-stimulating factor (GM-CSF), has been studied both for prophylaxis and for treatment of febrile neutropenia in cancer patients or BMT recipients.

Prophylaxis of Febrile Neutropenia

G-CSF has been widely studied both in children and adults with solid tumor or acute leukemia and in allogeneic, autologous, or peripheral blood stem cell transplant recipients.[188-192] Two meta-analyses recently provided some insight on this issue. Lyman and co-workers identified eight controlled trials enrolling a total of 1144 patients with solid tumor or malignant lymphoma treated with prophylactic colony-stimulating factor before the onset of fever or neutropenia following systemic chemotherapy.[193] There were five trials of filgrastim (recombinant G-CSF) and three studies of lenograstim (glycosylated granulocyte recombinant colony-stimulating factors). Five trials were double blind and placebo controlled; three included untreated controls. Use of recombinant colony-stimulating factors was associated with a reduced risk of febrile neutropenia (OR = 0.38), documented infection (OR = 0.51), and infection-related mortality (OR = 0.60). Patients treated with growth factors had a higher incidence of bone pain (OR = 2.9).[193] In a report from the Cochrane group, Bohlius and colleagues analyzed[194] 11 studies with 1434 randomized patients with malignant lymphoma. Compared with no prophylaxis, G-CSF/GM-CSF significantly reduced the relative risk (RR) for severe neutropenia (0.64), febrile neutropenia (0.74), and infection (0.74). There was no evidence that G-CSF/GM-CSF decreased the number of patients who required intravenous antibiotics (RR = 0.82), reduced infection-related mortality (RR = 2.07), or improved outcome of the underlying disease, including complete tumor response, freedom from treatment failure, and overall survival. Both studies concluded that G-CSF and GM-CSF, when given prophylactically in cancer patients undergoing conventional chemotherapy, reduced the risk of neutropenia, febrile neutropenia, and infection. In the study by Lyman and co-workers,[193] infection-related mortality was also reduced. The Cochrane analysis looked at very pragmatic end points and found no significant advantage in the outcome of the underlying disease.[194]

Therapy of Established Febrile Neutropenia

Many case reports have documented the effectiveness of growth factors in the treatment of severe, life-threatening bacterial or fungal infections The use of G-CSF in association with antibiotic therapy shortened the duration of neutropenia, reduced the duration of antibiotic therapy and hospitalization, and decreased hospital costs in patients with high-risk febrile neutropenia,[195,196] even if all these favorable events did not occur in all studies.[197] In addition, GM-CSF did not significantly reduce the number of days to resolution of fever or the duration of in-hospital stay, at least in high-risk patients.[198,199] A meta-analysis published in 2002 identified eight trials, with a median quality score for the pooled trials of 58.3% (range, 33.3% to 68.8%). No advantage was detected for the use of colony-stimulating factor in terms of mortality from febrile neutropenia, with a relative risk of 0.71. The relative risk was 0.66 in the G-CSF subgroup and 0.97 in the GM-CSF subgroup.[200] These data suggest the lack of efficacy of systematic, widespread use of colony-stimulating factor for therapy of febrile neutropenia.

In conclusion, the available evidence shows that hemopoietic growth factors are active drugs able to act upon bone marrow function to reduce the duration of neutropenia and the incidence of febrile episodes. However, their pragmatic effect on the incidence of severe infections, and, especially, on mortality from severe infections is much less evident. More importantly, no effect has ever been shown on the outcome of the underlying disease. Very often the trials on the use of growth factors in hematology and oncology suffer from differences in the definition of infectious complications. The American Society for Clinical Oncology has published guidelines about the use of growth factors that represent a mainstay in this field.[201] The conclusion is that, for preventive reasons, the use of growth factors is indicated in patients treated with regimens causing an incidence of febrile neutropenia of 40% or greater, with the aim of reducing costs for hospitalization. This happens in a minority of patients. In the large majority of patients growth factors are not indicated routinely, either for primary or for secondary prophylaxis. This approach must be individualized in patients with additional risk factors. The use of colony-stimulating factors as an adjuvant in febrile neutropenic patients is also not recommended in the large majority of patients, with the exception of aplastic patients with an uncontrolled underlying disease affected with complicated bacterial infections or severe fungal infections.

The use of G-CSF in the non-neutropenic host to stimulate the neutrophil function in established infection is a topic of great interest.[202] Although G-CSF is not approved for this indication, augmentation of host defenses and improved survival have been demonstrated in animal models, with ongoing trials in humans.[203,204]

Granulocyte Transfusions

Granulocyte transfusion represents a heroic therapeutic approach for severe, life-threatening infections in neutropenic patients. The most recent technique involves repeated transfusion of granulocyte-utilizing donors stimulated with subcutaneous G-CSF plus oral dexamethasone. This approach has been tested in neutropenic patients with severe bacterial or fungal infection and resulted in resolution of the infectious process in up to 60% of cases,[205-208] making it a potentially useful option when the severity of the infection and the host's immunodeficiency make any other antimicrobial treatment ineffectual.

Infusion of Immunoglobulins

Many neoplastic diseases (e.g., chronic lymphocytic leukemia) and conditions occurring after certain therapeutic procedures (e.g., chronic GVHD following allogeneic BMT or rituximab administration for management of Epstein-Barr virus-related post-transplant lymphoproliferative disease) are associated with reduced production of immunoglobulins. Because maintenance of a normal immunoglobulin level is important to prevent infections in patients with primary (congenital) immunodeficiency, the same approach has been used in patients with secondary (iatrogenic) defects. Trials of immunoglobulin infusion have been performed both in BMT recipients[209,210] and in patients with chronic lymphocytic leukemia.[211,212] The trials performed in BMT recipients clearly concluded that, in the absence of hypogammaglobulinemia, monthly administration of immunoglobulins did not reduce late complications and might impair long-term humoral immune recovery after marrow transplantation.[209] The studies performed in patients with chronic leukemia showed a reduction of infectious episodes occurring in patients with less than 600 mg/dL of immunoglobulin G with monthly administration of low doses (250 mg/kg)[211,212] of immunoglobulins, provided the treatment could be performed for 6 months at least.[212] However, because many controversial issues still remain regarding immunoglobulin treatment—specifically cost, scarcity of the product, and adequate dose, which has not yet been established—it seems reasonable to suggest immunoglobulin replacement (250 to 400 mg/kg every 4 weeks) in patients with marked hypogammaglobulinemia and with more than two recent severe infections.[213]

REFERENCES

1. Haupt R, Romanengo M, Fears T, et al. Incidence of septicaemias and invasive mycoses in children undergoing treatment for solid tumours: A 12-year experience at a single Italian institution. Eur J Cancer. 1998;37:2413-2419.
2. Meyers J, Thomas ET. Infection complicating bone marrow transplantation. In: Rubin R, Young LS, eds. Clinical Approach to Infection in the Compromised Patient. New York: Plenum Press; 1988:525-556.
3. Morittu L, Earl HM, Souhami RL, et al. Patients at risk of chemotherapy-associated toxicity in small cell lung cancer. Br J Cancer. 1989;59:801-804.
4. Pizzo PA, Meyers J. Infections in the cancer patient. In: De Vita VT, Hellma S, Rosenberg SA, eds. Principles and Practice of Oncology. Philadelphia: JB Lippincott; 1989:2088-2133.
5. Potter M. New-anti cancer therapies, new opportunities for infection. Curr Opin Infect Dis. 1999;12:359-363.
6. Samonisa G, Dimitrios B, Kotoyiannis P. Infectious complications of purine analog therapy. Curr Opin Infect Dis. 2001;14:409-413.
7. Junghanssa C, Kieren A, Marrb C. Infectious risk and outcomes after stem cell transplantation: Are nonmyeloablative transplants changing the picture? Curr Opin Infect Dis. 2002;15:347-353.
8. Pizzo PA. Infectious complications in the child with cancer. I. Pathophysiology of the compromised host and the initial evaluation and management of the febrile cancer patient. J Pediatr. 1981;98:513-523.
9. Walsh TJ, Hiemenz J, Pizzo PA. Evolving risk factors for invasive fungal infections—all neutropenic patients are not the same. Clin Infect Dis. 1994;18:793-798.
10. Schimpff SC, Young V, Greene E, et al. Origin of infection in acute non-lymphocytic leukemia: Significance of hospital acquisition of potential pathogens. Ann Intern Med. 1972;77:707-715.
11. Donnely JP. Chemoprophylaxis for the prevention of bacterial and fungal infections. Cancer Treat Res. 1995;79:45-82.
12. Hathorn JW. Critical appraisal of antimicrobials for prevention of infections in immunocompromised hosts. Hematol Oncol Clin North Am. 1993;7:1051-1099.
13. Guiot HFL, Van den Broak J, Van der Meer JWM, et al. Selective antimicrobial modulation of the intestinal flora of patients with acute nonlymphocytic leukemia: A double blind, placebo-controlled study. J Infect Dis. 1983;147:615-623.
14. Gualtieri RJ, Donowitz GR, Kaiser DL, et al. Double-blind randomized study of prophylactic trimethoprim/sulfamethoxazole in granulocytopenic patients with hematologic malignancies. Am J Med. 1983;74:934-940.
15. Kramer BS, Carr DJ, Rand KH, et al. Prophylaxis of fever and infection in adult cancer patients: A placebo-controlled trial of oral trimethoprim-sulfamethoxazole plus erythromycin. Cancer. 1984;53:329-335.
16. Karp JE, Merz WG, Hendricksen C, et al. Oral norfloxacin for prevention of gram-negative bacterial infections in patients with acute leukemia and granulocytopenia: A randomized, double-blind, placebo-controlled trial. Ann Intern Med. 1987;106:1-7.
17. EORTC-IATCG. Trimethoprim-sulfamethoxazole in the prevention of infection in neutropenic patients. J Infect Dis. 1984;150:372-379.
18. Casali A, Verri C, Paoletti G, et al. Chemoprophylaxis of bacterial infections in granulocytopenic cancer patients using norfloxacin. Chemioterapia. 1988;7:327-329.
19. Winston DJ, Ho WG, Champlin RE, et al. Norfloxacin for prevention of bacterial infections in granulocytopenic patients. Am J Med. 1987;82:40-46.
20. Pignon B, Thiriet L, Aubert D, et al. Evaluation of the efficacy of prophylactic intravenous antibiotherapy with ceftriaxone in post-chemotherapy agranulocytic patients. Nouv Rev Fr Hematol. 1990;32:249-252.
21. Talbot GH, Cassileth PA, Paradiso L, et al. Oral enoxacin for infection prevention in adults with acute nonlymphocytic leukemia. The Enoxacin Prophylaxis Study Group. Antimicrob Agents Chemother. 1993;37:474-482.

22. Lew MA, Kehoe K, Ritz J, et al. Prophylaxis of bacterial infections with ciprofloxacin in patients undergoing bone marrow transplantation. Transplantation. 1991;51:630-636.
23. Engels EA, Lau J, Barza M. Efficacy of quinolone prophylaxis in neutropenic cancer patients: A meta-analysis. J Clin Oncol. 1998;16:1179-1187.
24. Cruciani M, Rampazzo R, Malena M, et al. Prophylaxis with fluoroquinolones for bacterial infections in neutropenic patients: A meta-analysis. Clin Infect Dis. 1996; 23:795-805.
25. Kotilainen P, Nikoskelainen J, Huovien P. Emergence of ciprofloxacin-resistant coagulase negative staphylococcal skin flora in immunocompromised patients receiving ciprofloxacin. J Infect Dis. 1990;161:41-44.
26. Cornelissen JJ, de Graeff A, Verdonck LF, et al. Imipenem versus gentamicin combined with either cefuroxime or cephalothin as initial therapy for febrile neutropenic patients. Antimicrob Agents Chemother. 1992;36:801-807.
27. Trucksis M, Hooper DC, Wolfson JS. Emerging resistance to fluoroquinolones in staphylococci: An alert. Ann Intern Med. 1991;114:424-426.
28. EORTC, Group IATC. Reduction of fever and streptococcal bacteremia in granulocytopenic patients with cancer. JAMA. 1994;19:1183-1189.
29. Bow EJ, Mandell LA, Louie TJ, et al. Quinolone-based antibacterial chemoprophylaxis in neutropenic patients: Effect of augmented gram-positive activity on infectious morbidity. Ann Intern Med. 1996;125:183-190.
30. Cometta A, Calandra T, Bille J, et al. *Escherichia coli* resistant to fluoroquinolone prophylaxis in patients with cancer and neutropenia. N Engl J Med. 1994;330:1240-1241.
31. Kern WV, Andriof E, Oethinger M, et al. Emergence of fluoroquinolone-resistant *Escherichia coli* at a cancer center. Antimicrob Agents Chemother. 1994;38:681-687.
32. Caratalla J, Fernandez-Sevilla A, Dominguez MA, et al. Emergence of fluoroquinolone-resistant flora of cancer patients receiving norfloxacin prophylaxis. Antimicrob Agents Chemother. 1996;40:503-505.
33. Richard P, Delangle MH, Merrien D, et al. Fluoroquinolone use and fluoroquinolone resistance: Is there an association? Clin Infect Dis. 1994;19:54-59.
34. Gomez L, Garau J, Estrada C, et al. Ciprofloxacin prophylaxis in patients with acute leukemia and granulocytopenia in an area with a high prevalence of ciprofloxacin-resistant *Escherichia coli*. Cancer. 2003;97:419-424.
35. Yeh SP, Chiu CF, Lo WJ, et al. Low infectious morbidity in patients with heavily pretreated hematological malignancies receiving autologous peripheral blood stem cell transplantation without antimicrobial prophylaxis. Ann Hematol. 2003;82:24-29.
36. Neuhauser MM, Weinstein RA, Rydman R, et al. Antibiotic resistance among gram-negative bacilli in US intensive care unit: Implications for fluoroquinolone use. JAMA. 2003;289:885-888.
37. Castagnola E, Boni L, Giacchino M, et al. A multicenter, randomized, double blind placebo-controlled trial of amoxicillin/clavulanate for the prophylaxis of fever and infection in neutropenic children with cancer. Pediatr Infect Dis. 2003;22:359-365.
38. Hughes WT, Armstrong D, Bodey GP, et al. 2002 Guidelines for the use of antimicrobial agents in neutropenic patients with cancer. Clin Infect Dis. 2002;34:730-751.
39. Beck-Sagué CM, Jarvis WR, for the National Nosocomial Infections Surveillance System. Secular trends in the epidemiology of nosocomial fungal infections in the United States, 1980-1990. J Infect Dis. 1993;167:1247-1251.
40. Bodey G, Bueltmann B, Duguid W, et al. Fungal infections in cancer patients: An international autopsy survey. Eur J Clin Microbiol Infect Dis. 1992;11:99-109.
41. Groll A, Shah PM, Mentzel C, et al. Trends in the post-mortem epidemiology of invasive fungal infections at a university hospital. J Infect. 1996;33:23-32.
42. Marr KA, Carter RA, Crippa F, et al. Epidemiology and outcome of mould infections in hematopoietic stem cell transplant recipients. Clin Infect Dis. 2002;34:909-917.
43. Edmond MB, Wallace SE, McClish DK, et al. Nosocomial bloodstream infections in United States hospitals: A three-year analysis. Clin Infect Dis. 1999;29:239-244.
44. Viscoli C, Girmenia C, Marinus A, et al. An EORTC prospective, multicenter, surveillance study of candidemia in cancer patients. Clin Infect Dis. 1999;28:1071-1079.
45. Marr KA, Patterson T, Denning D. Aspergillosis: Pathogenesis, clinical manifestations and therapy. Infect Dis Clin North Am. 2002;16:875-894.
46. Bow EJ, Laverdiere M, Lussier N, et al. Antifungal prophylaxis for severely neutropenic chemotherapy recipients: A meta analysis of randomized controlled clinical trials. Cancer. 2002;94:3230-3236.
47. Goodman JL, Winston DJ, Greenfeld RA, et al. A controlled trial of fluconazole to prevent fungal infections in patients undergoing bone marrow transplantation. N Engl J Med. 1992;326:845-851.
48. Slavin MA, Osborne B, Adams R, et al. Efficacy and safety of fluconazole prophylaxis for fungal infections after marrow transplantation—A prospective, randomized, double-blind study. J Infect Dis. 1995;171:1545-1552.
49. Marr KA, Seidel K, Slavin MA, et al. Prolonged fluconazole prophylaxis is associated with persistent protection against candidiasis-related death in allogeneic marrow transplant recipients: Long-term follow-up of a randomized, placebo-controlled trial. Blood. 2000;96:2055-2061.
50. Hansen JA, Gooley TA, Martin PJ, et al. Bone marrow transplants from unrelated donors for patients with chronic myeloid leukemia. N Engl J Med. 1998;338:962-968.
51. Winston DJ, Chandrasekar PH, Lazarus HM, et al. Fluconazole prophylaxis of fungal infections in patients with acute leukemia: Results of a randomized placebo-controlled, double-blind, multicenter trial. Ann Intern Med. 1993;118:495-503.
52. Menichetti F, Del Favero A, Martino P, et al. Preventing fungal infection in neutropenic patients with acute leukemia: Fluconazole compared with oral amphotericin B. The GIMEMA Infection Program. Ann Intern Med. 1994;120:913-918.
53. Rotstein C, Bow EJ, Laverdiere M, et al. Randomized placebo-controlled trial of fluconazole prophylaxis for neutropenic cancer patients: Benefits based on purpose and intensity of cytotoxic chemotherapy. Clin Infect Dis. 1999;28:331-340.
54. Koh LP, Kurup A, Goh YT, et al. Randomized trial of fluconazole versus low-dose amphotericin B in prophylaxis against fungal infections in patients undergoing hematopoietic stem cell transplantation. Am J Hematol. 2002;71:260-267.
55. Menichetti F, Del Favero A, Martino P, et al. Itraconazole oral solution as prophylaxis for fungal infections in neutropenic patients with hematologic malignancies: A randomized, placebo-controlled, double-blind, multicenter trial. GIMEMA Infection Program, Gruppo Italiano Malattie Ematologiche Maligne dell'Adulto. Clin Infect Dis. 1999;28:250-255.
56. Harousseau JL, Dekker AW, Stamatoullas-Bastard A, et al. Itraconazole oral solution for primary prophylaxis of fungal infections in patients with hematological malignancy and profound neutropenia: A randomized, double-blind, double-placebo, multicenter trial comparing itraconazole and amphotericin B. Antimicrob Agents Chemother. 2000;44:1887-1893.
57. Nucci M, Biasoli T, Akiti T, et al. A double-blind, randomized, placebo-controlled trial of itraconazole capsules as antifungal prophylaxis for neutropenic patients. Clin Infect Dis. 2000;30:300-305.
58. Boogaerts M, Maertens J, van Hoof A, et al. Itraconazole versus amphotericin B plus nystatin in the prophylaxis of fungal infections in neutropenic cancer patients. J Antimicrob Chemother. 2001;48:97-103.
58a. Glasmacher A, Prentice A, Gorschluter M, et al. Itraconazole prevents invasive fungal infections in neutropenic patients treated for hematologic malignancies: evidence from a meta-analysis of 3597 patients. J Clin Oncol. 2003;21:4615-4626.
59. Kanda Y, Yamamoto R, Chizuka A, et al. Prophylaxis action of oral fluconazole against fungal infection in neutropenic patients. Cancer. 2000;89:1611-1625.
60. Gotzche PC, Johansen HK. Meta-analysis of prophylaxis or empirical antifungal treatment versus placebo or no treatment in patients with cancer complicated by neutropenia. BMJ. 1997;314:1238-1244.
61. Huijgens PC, Simoons-Smit AM, van Loenen AC, et al. Fluconazole versus itraconazole for the prevention of fungal infections in haemato-oncology. J Clin Pathol. 1999;52:376-380.
62. Morgenstern GR. A randomized controlled trial of itraconazole versus fluconazole for the prevention of fungal infections in patients with haematological malignancies. U.K. Multicentre Antifungal Prophylaxis Study Group. Br J Haematol. 1999;105:901-911.
63. Winston DJ, Maziarz RT, Chandrasekar PH, et al. Intravenous and oral itraconazole versus intravenous and oral fluconazole for long term antifungal prophylaxis in allogeneic hematopoietic stem-cell transplant recipients: A multicenter, randomized trial. Ann Intern Med. 2003;138:705-713.
63a. Marr KA, Crippa F. Leisenring W, et al. Itraconazole versus fluconazole for prevention of fungal infections in patients receiving allogeneic stem cell transplants. Blood. 2004;103:1527-1533.
63b. Marr KA, Leisenring W, Crippa F, et al. Cyclophosphamide metabolism is affected by azole antifungals. Blood. 2004;103:1557-1559.
64. Van Burik J, Ratanatharathorn V, Lipton J, et al. Randomized double-blind trial of micafungin versus fluconazole for prophylaxis of invasive fungal infections in patients undergoing hematopoietic stem cell transplant. In: Proceedings of the 42nd Interscience Conference on Antimicrobial Agents and Chemotherapy, San Diego, 2002.
65. Martino R, Lopez R, Sureda A, et al. Risk of reactivation of a recent invasive fungal infection in patients with hematological malignancies undergoing further intensive chemo-radiotherapy: A single-center experience and review of the literature. Haematologica. 1997;82:297-304.
66. Offner F, Cordonnier C, Ljungman P, et al. Impact of previous aspergillosis on outcome of bone marrow transplantation. Clin Infect Dis. 1998;26:1098-1103.
67. Karp JE, Burch PA, Merz WG. An approach to intensive antileukemia therapy in patients with previous invasive aspergillosis. Am J Med. 1988;85:203-206.
68. Cowie F, Meller ST, Cushing P, et al. Chemoprophylaxis for pulmonary aspergillosis during intensive chemotherapy. Arch Dis Child. 1994;70:136-138.
69. Mattei D, Mordini N, Lo Nigro C, et al. Voriconazole in the management of invasive aspergillosis in two patients with acute myeloid leukemia undergoing stem cell transplantation. Bone Marrow Transplant. 2002;30:967-970.
70. Viscoli C, Paesmans M, Sanz M, et al. Association between antifungal prophylaxis and rate of documented bacteremia in febrile neutropenic cancer patients. Clin Infect Dis. 2001;32:1532-1537.
71. Cordonnier C, Buzyn A, Leverger G, et al. Epidemiology and risk factors for gram-positive coccal infections in neutropenia: Toward a more targeted antibiotic strategy. Clin Infect Dis. 2003;36:149-158.
72. Wingard JR, Merz WG, Rinaldi MG, et al. Increase in *Candida krusei* infection among patients with bone marrow transplantation and neutropenia treated prophylactically with fluconazole. N Engl J Med. 1991;325:1274-1277.
73. Wingard JR, Merz WG, Rinaldi MG, et al. Association of *Torulopsis glabrata* infection with fluconazole prophylaxis in neutropenic bone marrow transplant patients. Antimicrob Agents Chemother. 1993;37:1847-1849.
74. Gumbo T, Isada CM, Hall G, et al. *Candida glabrata* fungemia: Clinical features of 139 patients. Medicine (Baltimore). 1999;78:220-227.
75. van Burik JH, Leisenrign W, Wyerson D, et al. The effect of prophylactic fluconazole on the clinical spectrum of fungal diseases in bone marrow transplant recipients with special attention to hepatic candidiasis: An autopsy study of 355 patients. Medicine (Baltimore). 1998;77:246-254.
76. Kotoyannis DP. Why prior fluconazole use is associated with an increased risk of invasive mold infections in immunosuppressed hosts: An alternative hypothesis (Letter). Clin Infect Dis. 2001;34:1281-1283.
77. Marr KA, White TC, van Burik JAH, et al. Development of fluconazole resistance in *Candida albicans* causing disseminated infection in patients undergoing marrow transplantation. Clin Infect Dis. 1997;25:908-910.
78. Castagnola E, Bucci B, Machetti M, et al. Antifungal prophylaxis with azole derivatives. Clin Microb Infect. 2004;10(Suppl 7):86-95.

79. Varthalitis I, Meunier F. *Pneumocystis carinii* pneumonia in cancer patients. Cancer Treat Rev. 1993;19:387-413.

80. Sepkowitz KA. *Pneumocystis carinii* pneumonia in patients without AIDS. Clin Infect Dis. 1993;17:S416-S422.

81. Sepkowitz KA, Brown AE, Telzak EE, et al. *Pneumocystis carinii* pneumonia among patients without AIDS at a cancer hospital. JAMA. 1992;267:832-837.

82. Castagnola E, Dini G, Lanino E, et al. Low CD4 lymphocyte count in a patient with *P. carinii* pneumonia after autologous bone marrow transplantation. Bone Marrow Transplant. 1995;15:977-978.

83. Kulke MH, Vance EA. *Pneumocystis carinii* pneumonia in patients receiving chemotherapy for breast cancer. Clin Infect Dis. 1996;25:215-218.

84. Anaissie EJ, Kontoyiannis DP, O'Brien S, et al. Infections in patients with chronic lymphocytic leukemia treated with fludarabine. Ann Intern Med. 1998;129:559-566.

85. Fishman JA. Treatment of infection due to *Pneumocystis carinii*. Antimicrob Agents Chemother. 1998;42:1309-1314.

86. Castagnola E, Zarri D, Caprino D, et al. Cotrimoxazole prophylaxis of *Pneumocystis carinii* infection during the treatment of childhood acute lymphoblastic leukemia—Beware non compliance in older children and adolescents. Support Care Cancer. 2001;9:552-553.

87. Carrega G, Castagnola E, Canessa A, et al. Herpes simplex virus and oral mucositis in children with cancer. Support Care Cancer. 1994;2:266-269.

88. Bodey GP, Buckley M, Sathe YS, et al. Quantitative relationships between circulating leukocytes and infection in patients with acute leukemia. Ann Intern Med. 1966;64:328-340.

89. Baden LR, Rubin RH. Fever, neutropenia and the second law of thermodynamics. Ann Intern Med. 2002;137:123-124.

90. Viscoli C, Castagnola E, Giacchino M, et al. Bloodstream infections in children with cancer: A multicentre surveillance study of the Italian Association of Paediatric Haematology and Oncology. Eur J Cancer. 1999;35:770-774.

91. Consensus Panel of the Immunocompromised Host Society. The design, analysis and reporting of clinical trials on the empirical antibiotic management of the neutropenic patient. J Infect Dis. 1990;161:397-401.

92. Hughes W, Wade JC, Armstrong D, et al. Evaluation of new anti-infective drugs for the treatment of febrile episodes in neutropenic patients. Clin Infect Dis. 1992;15(Suppl):S206-S215.

93. Viscoli C. Management of infection in cancer patients: Studies of the EORTC International Antimicrobial Therapy Group (IATG). Eur J Cancer. 2002;38(Suppl): S82-S87.

94. McCabe WR, Jackson GG. Gram-negative bacteremia. II. Clinical, laboratory, and therapeutical observations. Arch Intern Med. 1962;110:857-864.

95. EORTC-IATPG. Three antibiotic regimens in the treatment of infections in febrile granulocytopenic patients with cancer. J Infect Dis. 1978;137:14-19.

96. De Bock R, Cometta A, Kern W, et al. Incidence of single agent gram-negative bacteremias (SAGNB) in neutropenic cancer patients (NCP) in EORTC-IATG trials of empirical therapy for febrile neutropenia. In: Proceedings of the 41st Interscience Conference on Antimicrobial Agents and Chemotherapy, Chicago, 2001.

97. Castagnola E, Paola D, Giacchino R, et al. Clinical and laboratory features predicting a favourable outcome and allowing early discharge in cancer patients with low-risk febrile neutropenia: a literature review. J Hematother Stem Cell Res. 2000;9:645-649.

98. Talcott JA, Finberg R, Mayer RJ, et al. The medical course of cancer patients with fever and neutropenia: Clinical identification of a low-risk subgroup at presentation. Arch Intern Med. 1988;148:2561-2568.

99. Talcott JA, Siegel RD, Finberg R. Risk assessment in cancer patients with fever and neutropenia: A prospective, two-center validation of a prediction rule. J Clin Oncol. 1992;10:316-322.

100. Talcott JA, Whalen A, Clark J, et al. Home antibiotic therapy for low-risk cancer patients with fever and neutropenia: A pilot study of 30 patients based on a validated prediction rule. J Clin Oncol. 1994;12:107-144.

101. Viscoli C, Bruzzi P, Castagnola E, et al. Factors associated with bacteraemia in febrile, granulocytopenic cancer patients. The International Antimicrobial Therapy Cooperative Group (IATCG) of the European Organization for Research and Treatment of Cancer (EORTC). Eur J Cancer. 1994;4:430-437.

102. Klastersky J, Paesmans M, Rubenstein EB, et al. The Multinational Association for Supportive Care in Cancer Risk Index: A multinational scoring system for identifying low-risk febrile neutropenic cancer patients. J Clin Oncol. 2000;16:3038-3051.

103. Santolaya MEA, Alvarez AM, Becker A, et al. Prospective, multicenter evaluation of risk factors associated with invasive bacterial infection in children with cancer, neutropenia and fever. J Clin Oncol. 2001;19:3415-3421.

104. Mullen CA. Which children with fever and neutropenia can be safely treated as outpatients? Br J Haematol. 2001;112:832-837.

105. Finberg RW, Talcott JA. Fever and neutropenia: How to use a new treatment strategy. N Engl J Med. 1999;341:362-363.

106. Klaassen RJ, Allen U, Doyle JJ. Randomized placebo-controlled trial of oral antibiotics in pediatric oncology patients at low-risk with fever and neutropenia. J Pediatr Hematol Oncol. 2000;22:405-411.

107. Klaassen RJ, Goodman TR, Pham B, et al. "Low risk" prediction rule for pediatric oncology patients presenting with fever and neutropenia. J Clin Oncol. 2000;18: 1012-1019.

108. Baorto EP, Aquino VM, Mullen CA, et al. Clinical parameters associated with low bacteremia risk in 1100 pediatric oncology patients with fever and neutropenia. Cancer. 2001;92:909-913.

109. Klastersky J. Concept of empiric therapy with antibiotic combinations: Indications and limits. Am J Med. 1986;80 (Suppl 5C):2-12.

110. Schimpff S, Satterlee WM, Young VM. Empiric therapy with carbenicillin under gentamicin for febrile patients with cancer and granulocytopenia. N Engl J Med. 1971;284:1061-1075.

111. Hughes WT, Armstrong D, Bodey GP, et al. Guidelines for the use of antimicrobial agents in neutropenic patients with unexplained fever. Clin Infect Dis. 1997;25:551-573.

112. Hughes WT, Armstrong D, Bodey GP, et al. Guidelines for the used of antimicrobial agents in neutropenic patients with unexplained fever. J Infect Dis. 1990;161:381-396.

113. Rains CP, Bryson HM, Peters HD. Ceftazidime: An update on its bacterial activity, pharmacokinetic properties and therapeutic efficacy. Drugs. 1995;49:577-617.

114. Cometta A, Zinner S, de Bock R, et al. Piperacillin-tazobactam plus amikacin versus ceftazidime plus amikacin as empiric therapy for fever in granulocytopenic patients with cancer. The International Antimicrobial Therapy Cooperative Group of the European Organization for Research and Treatment of Cancer. Antimicrob Agents Chemother. 1995;39:445-452.

115. Winston DJ, Winston GH, Buckner DA, et al. Beta-lactam antibiotic therapy in febrile granulocytopenic patients: A randomised trial comparing cefoperazone plus piperacillin, ceftazidime plus piperacillin and imipenem alone. Ann Intern Med. 1991;115:849-859.

116. Peakok JE, Herrington DA, Wade JC, et al. Ciprofloxacin plus piperacillin compared with tobramycin plus piperacillin as empirical therapy in febrile neutropenic patients: A randomized, double-blind trial. Ann Intern Med. 2003;137:77-87.

117. Cometta A, Calandra T, Gaya H. Monotherapy with meropenem versus combination therapy with ceftazidime plus amikacin as empiric therapy for fever in granulocytopenic patients with cancer. The International Antimicrobial Therapy Cooperative Group of the European Organization for Research and Treatment of Cancer and the Gruppo Italiano Malattie Ematologiche Maligne dell'Adulto Infection Program. Antimicrob Agents Chemother. 1996;40:1108-1115.

118. de Pauw BE, Deresinski SC, Feld R, et al. Ceftazidime compared with piperacillin and tobramycin for the empiric treatment of fever in neutropenic patients with cancer: A multicenter randomized trial. The Intercontinental Antimicrobial Study Group. Ann Intern Med. 1994;120:834-844.

119. Freifeld AG, Walsh T, Marshall D, et al. Monotherapy for fever and neutropenia in cancer patients: A randomized comparison of ceftazidime versus imipenem. J Clin Oncol. 1995;13:165-176.

120. Pizzo PA, Hathorn JV, Hiemenz J, et al. A randomized trial comparing ceftazidime alone with combination antibiotic therapy in cancer patients with fever and neutropenia. N Engl J Med. 1986;315:552-558.

121. Del Favero A, Menichetti F, Martino P, et al. A multicenter, double-blind placebo-controlled trial comparing piperacillin-tazobactam with and without amikacin as empiric therapy for febrile neutropenia. Clin Infect Dis. 2001;33:1295-1301.

122. Paul M, Soares-Weiser K, Leibovici L. Beta lactam monotherapy versus beta lactam-aminoglycoside combination therapy for fever with neutropenia: Systematic review and meta-analysis. BMJ. 2003;326:1111.

123. Babini GS, Livermore DM. Antimicrobial resistance amongst *Klebsiella* spp. collected from intensive care units in Southern and Western Europe in 1997-1998. J Antimicrob Chemother. 2000;45:183-189.

124. Vahaboglu H, Coskunkan F, Tansel O, et al. Clinical importance of extended spectrum beta-lactamase (PER-1-type)–producing *Acinetobacter* spp. and *Pseudomonas aeruginosa* strains. J Med Microbiol. 2001;50:642-645.

125. Shenep J, Hughes WT, Robertson PK, et al. Vancomycin, ticarcillin and amikacin compared with ticarcillin-clavulanate and amikacin in the empirical treatment of febrile neutropenic children with cancer. N Engl J Med. 1988;319:1053-1058.

126. Karp JE, Dick C, Angelopulos C. Empiric use of vancomycin during prolonged treatment induced granulocytopenia: Randomized double blind, placebo controlled trial in patients with acute leukemia. Am J Med. 1986;81:237-242.

127. Del Favero A, Menichetti F, Guerciolini R, et al. Prospective randomised clinical trial of teicoplanin for empiric combined antibiotic therapy in febrile granulocytopenic acute leukemia patients. Antimicrob Agents Chemother. 1987;31:1126-1129.

128. EORTC-IATCG. Vancomycin added to empirical combination antibiotic therapy for fever in granulocytopenic cancer patients. J Infect. 1991;163:951-958.

129. Micozzi A, Nucci M, Venditti M, et al. Piperacillin/tazobactam/amikacin versus piperacillin/amikacin/teicoplanin in the empirical treatment of neutropenic patients. Eur J Clin Microbiol Infect Dis. 1993;12:1-8.

130. Rubin M, Hathorn JW, Marshall D, et al. Gram-positive infection and the use of vancomycin in 550 episodes of fever and neutropenia. Ann Intern Med. 1988;108:30-35.

131. Viscoli C, Moroni C, Boni L, et al. Ceftazidime plus amikacin versus ceftazidime plus vancomycin as empiric therapy in febrile neutropenic children with cancer. Rev Infect Dis. 1991;13:397-404.

132. Gold HS, Moellering RC. Antimicrobial drug resistance. N Engl J Med. 1996;335: 1445-1453.

133. Rubenstein EB, Rollston K, Benjamin RS, et al. Outpatient treatments of febrile episodes in low-risk neutropenic patients with cancer. Cancer. 1993;71:3640-3646.

134. EORTC-IATCG. Efficacy and toxicity of single daily doses of amikacin and ceftriaxone versus multiple daily doses of amikacin and ceftazidime for infection in patients with cancer and granulocytopenia. Ann Intern Med. 1993;119:584-593.

135. Kern WV, Cometta A, de Bock R, et al. Oral versus intravenous empirical antimicrobial therapy for fever in patients with granulocytopenia who are receiving cancer chemotherapy. N Engl J Med. 1999;341:312-318.

136. Freifeld A, Marchigiani D, Walsh T, et al. A double-blind comparison of empirical oral and intravenous antibiotic therapy for low-risk febrile patients with neutropenia during cancer chemotherapy. N Engl J Med. 1999;341:305-311.

137. Paganini HR, Sarkis CM, De Martino MG, et al. Oral administration of cefixime to lower risk febrile neutropenic children with cancer. Cancer. 2000;8:2848-2852.

138. Shenep JL, Flynn PM, Baker DK, et al. Oral cefixime is similar to continued intravenous antibiotics in the empirical treatment of febrile neutropenic children with cancer. Clin Infect Dis. 2001;32:36-43.

139. Paganini H, Gomez S, Ruviscky S, et al. Outpatient, sequential, parenteral-oral antibiotic therapy for lower risk febrile neutropenia in children with malignant disease: A single-center, randomized, controlled trial in Argentina. Cancer. 2003;97:1775-1780.

140. Giamarellou H, Bassaris HP, Petrikkos G, et al. Monotherapy with intravenous followed by oral high-dose ciprofloxacin versus combination therapy with ceftazidime plus amikacin as initial empiric therapy for granulocytopenic patients with fever. Antimicrob Agents Chemother. 2000;44:3264-3271.

141. Erjavec Z, de Vries-Hospers HG, Laseur M, et al. A prospective, randomized, double-blinded, placebo-controlled trial of empirical teicoplanin in febrile neutropenia with persistent fever after imipenem monotherapy. J Antimicrob Chemother. 2000;45:843-849.

142. Cometta A, Kern WV, De Bock R, et al. An EORTC-IATCG double-blind trial of vancomycin (Van) versus placebo (Pla) for persistent fever in neutropenic cancer patients (NCP) given piperacillin/tazobactam (PT) monotherapy. Clin Infect Dis. 2003;37:382-389.

143. Aisner J, Schimpff S, Wiernik H. Treatment of invasive aspergillosis: Relation of early diagnosis and treatment response. Ann Intern Med. 1977;86:539-543.

144. Burke PJ, Braine HG, Rathburn HK, et al. The clinical significance and the management of fever in acute myelocytic leukemia. John Hopkins Med J. 1976;139:1-12.

145. Pizzo PA, Robichaud KJ, Gill FA, et al. Empiric antibiotic and antifungal therapy for cancer patients with prolonged fever and granulocytopenia. Am J Med. 1982;72:101-111.

146. EORTC-IATCG. Empiric antifungal therapy in febrile granulocytopenic patients. Am J Med. 1989;86:668-672.

147. Viscoli C, Castagnola E, Machetti M. Antifungal treatment in patients with cancer. J Intern Med. 1997;242:89-94.

148. Viscoli C, Castagnola E. Planned progressive antimicrobial therapy in neutropenic patients. Br J Haematol. 1998;102:879-888.

149. Viscoli C, Castagnola E, Van Lint MT, et al. Fluconazole versus amphotericin B as empirical antifungal therapy of unexplained fever in granulocytopenic cancer patients: A pragmatic, multicentre prospective and randomised clinical trial. Eur J Cancer. 1996;32A:814-820.

150. Winston DJ, Hathorn JW, Schuster MG, et al. A multicenter, randomized trial of fluconazole versus amphotericin B for empiric antifungal therapy of febrile neutropenic patients with cancer. Am J Med. 2000;108:282-289.

151. Walsh TJ, Finberg RW, Arndt C, et al. Liposomal amphotericin B for empirical therapy in patients with persistent fever and neutropenia. National Institute of Allergy and Infectious Diseases Mycoses Study Group. N Engl J Med. 1999;340:764-771.

152. Bennett JE, Powers J, Viscoli C, et al. Forum report: Issues in clinical trials of empirical antifungal therapy in treating febrile neutropenic patients. Clin Infect Dis. 2003;36(Suppl):S117-S122.

153. Fischer T, Heussel G, Huber C. Liposomal amphotericin B for fever and neutropenia. N Engl J Med. 1999;341:1152.

154. Prentice HG, Kibbler CC. Liposomal amphotericin B for fever and neutropenia. N Engl J Med. 1999;341:1152-1153.

155. Patel MA, Curtis K, Maguire JH. Liposomal amphotericin B for fever and neutropenia. N Engl J Med. 1999;341:1153.

156. Girmenia C, Gentile G, Micozzi A, et al. Nephrotoxicity of amphotericin B desoxycholate. Clin Infect Dis. 2001;33:915-916.

157. Girmenia C, Cimino G, Micozzi A, et al. Risk factors for nephrotoxicity associated with conventional amphotericin B therapy. Am J Med. 2002;113:351.

158. Rakita R. Liposomal amphotericin B for fever and neutropenia. N Engl J Med. 1999;341:1153-1154.

159. Boogaerts M, Winston DJ, Bow EJ, et al. Intravenous and oral itraconazole versus intravenous amphotericin B deoxycholate as empirical antifungal therapy for persistent fever in neutropenic patients with cancer who are receiving broad-spectrum antibacterial therapy: A randomized, controlled trial. Ann Intern Med. 2001;135:412-422.

160. Walsh TJ, Pappas P, Winston DJ, et al. Voriconazole compared with liposomal amphotericin B for empirical antifungal therapy in patients with neutropenia and persistent fever. N Engl J Med. 2002;346:225-234.

161. Marr KA. Empirical antifungal therapy: New options, new tradeoffs. N Engl J Med. 2002;346:278-280.

162. Glauser MP, Calandra T. Infections in patients with hematologic malignancies. In: Glauser MP, Pizzo PA, eds. Management of infections in immunocompromised patients. London: W.B. Saunders; 2000:141-188.

162a. Walsh TJ, Sable C, Depauw B, et al. A Randomized, Double-blind Multicenter Trial of Caspofungin (CAS) v Liposomal Amphotericin B (LAMB) for Empirical Antifungal Therapy (EAFRx) of Persistently Febrile Neutropenic (PFN) Patients. In Program and Abstracts of the 42nd Interscience Conference on Antimicrobial Agents and Chemotherapy. Chicago, Sept 14-17, 2003, Abstract M 1761.

163. Bjerknes R, Bruserid O, Solberg CO. Hematologic malignancy. In: Armstrong D, Cohen J, eds. Infectious Diseases. London: Mosby; 1999: Ch. 4, Section 5, pp 1-26.

164. Mermel LA. Prevention of intravascular catheter-related infections. Ann Intern Med. 2000;132:391-402.

165. Mermel LA, Farr BM, Sheretz RJ, et al. Guidelines for the management of intravascular catheter-related infections. Clin Infect Dis. 2001;32:1249-1272.

166. Crnich CJ, Maki DG. The promise of novel technology for the prevention of intravascular device-related bloodstream infections. II. Long-term devices. Clin Infect Dis. 2002;34:1362-1368.

167. Henderson DK. Infections due to percutaneous intravascular devices. In: GL Mandell, Bennett JE, Dolin R, eds. Mandell, Douglas and Bennett's Principles and Practice of Infectious Diseases. Vol. II. 5th ed. New York: Churchill Livingstone; 2000:3005-3020.

168. Groeger JS, Lucas AB, Thaler HT, et al. Infectious morbidity associated with long-term use venous access devices in patients with cancer. Ann Intern Med. 1993;119:1168-1174.

169. Rodriguez-Bano J. Selection of empiric therapy in patients with catheter-related infections. Clin Microb Infect. 2002;8:275-281.

170. Castagnola E, Carrega G, Garaventa A. Catheter-related bacteremias in patients with cancer (Letter). Ann Intern Med. 1994;121:73-74.

171. Daghistani D, Horn M, Rodriguez Z, et al. Prevention of indwelling central venous catheter sepsis. Med Pediatr Oncol. 1996;26:405-408.

172. Castagnola E, Molinari AC, Fratino G, et al. Conditions associated with infections of indwelling central venous catheters in cancer patients: A summary. Br J Haematol. 2003;121:233-239.

173. Castagnola E, Garaventa A, Viscoli C, et al. Changing pattern of pathogens causing Broviac catheter-related bacteraemias in children with cancer. J Hosp Infect. 1995;29:129-133.

174. Mayhall CG. Diagnosis and management of infections of implantable devices used for prolonged venous access. Curr Clin Topic Infect Dis. 1992;12:83-110.

175. Widmer AF. Management of catheter-related bacteremia and fungemia in patients on total parenteral nutrition. Nutrition. 1997;13(Suppl):18S-25S.

176. Bouza E, Burrillo A, Munoz P. Catheter-related infections: Diagnosis and intravascular treatment. Clin Microb Infect. 2002;8:265-274.

177. Caillot D, Casasnovas O, Bernard A, et al. Improved management of invasive pulmonary aspergillosis in neutropenic patient using early thoracic computed tomographic scan and surgery. J Clin Oncol. 1997;15:139-147.

178. Caillot D, Cauaillier JF, Bernard A, et al. Increasing volume and changing characteristics of invasive pulmonary aspergillosis on sequential thoracic computed tomography scans in patients with neutropenia. J Clin Oncol. 2001;19:253-259.

179. Denning DW, Stevens DA. Antifungal and surgical treatment of invasive aspergillosis: Review of 2121 published cases. Rev Infect Dis. 1990;12:1147-1201.

180. Denning DW. Therapeutic outcome in invasive aspergillosis. Clin Infect Dis. 1996;23:608-615.

181. Ascioglu S, Rex JH, de Pauw BE, et al. Defining opportunistic invasive fungal infections in immunocompromised patients with cancer and hematopoietic stem cell transplants: An international consensus. Clin Infect Dis. 2002;34:1-14.

182. Micozzi A, Cartoni C, Monaco M, et al. High incidence of infectious gastrointestinal complications observed in patients with acute myeloid leukemia receiving intensive chemotherapy for first induction of remission. Support Care Cancer. 1996;4:294-297.

183. Sonis ST, Oster G, Fuchs H, et al. Oral mucositis and the clinical and economic outcomes of hematopoietic stem-cell transplantation. J Clin Oncol. 2001;19:2201-2205.

184. Steffen EK, Berg D, Deitch EA. Comparison of translocation rates of various indigenous bacteria from gastrointestinal tract to mesenteric lymph nodes. J Infect Dis. 1988;157:1032-1038.

185. Gorschluter M, Marklein G, Hofling K, et al. Abdominal infections in patients with acute leukemia: A prospective study applying ultrasonography and microbiology. Br J Haematol. 2002;117:351-358.

186. Cartoni C, Dragoni F, Micozzi A, et al. Neutropenic enterocolitis in patients with acute leukemia: Prognostic significance of bowel wall thickening detected by ultrasonography. J Clin Oncol. 2001;19:756-761.

187. Gomez L, Martino R, Rolston RV. Neutropenic enterocolitis: Spectrum of the disease and comparison of definite and possible cases. Clin Infect Dis. 1998;27:695-699.

188. Dallorso S, Rondelli R, Messina C, et al. Clinical benefits of granulocyte colony-stimulating factor therapy after hematopoietic stem cell transplant in children: Results of a prospective randomized trial. Haematologica. 2002;87:1274-1280.

189. Bishop MR, Tarantolo SR, Geller RB, et al. A randomized, double-blind trial of filgrastim (granulocyte colony-stimulating factor) versus placebo following allogeneic blood stem cell transplantation. Blood. 2000;96:80-85.

190. Pui CH, Boyett JM, Hughes WT, et al. Human granulocyte colony-stimulating factor after induction chemotherapy in children with acute lymphoblastic leukemia. N Engl J Med. 1997;336:1781-1787.

191. Hartmann LC, Tschetter LK, Habrmann TM, et al. Granulocyte colony-stimulating factor in severe chemotherapy-induced febrile neutropenia. N Engl J Med. 1997;336:1776-1780.

192. Alonzo TA, Kobrinsky NL, Aledo A, et al. Impact of granulocyte colony-stimulating factor use during induction for acute myelogenous leukemia in children: A report from the Children's Cancer Group. J Pediatr Hematol Oncol. 2002;24:627-635.

193. Lyman GH, Kuderer NM, Djulbegovic B. Prophylactic granulocyte colony-stimulating factor in patients receiving dose-intensive cancer chemotherapy: A meta-analysis. Am J Med. 2002;112:406-411.

194. Bohlius J, Reiser M, Schwarzer G, et al. Granulopoiesis-stimulating factors in the prevention of adverse effects in the therapeutic treatment of malignant lymphoma. Cochrane Database Syst Rev. 2002;4:CD003189.

195. Mitchell PL, Morland B, Stevens MC. Granulocyte colony-stimulating factor in established febrile neutropenia: A randomized study of pediatric patients. J Clin Oncol. 1997;15:1163-1170.

196. Garcia-Carbonero R, Mayordomo JI, Tornamira MV, et al. Granulocyte colony-stimulating factor in the treatment of high-risk febrile neutropenia: A multicenter randomized trial. J Natl Cancer Inst. 2001;93:31-38.

197. Maher DW, Lieschke GJ, Green M, et al. Filgrastim in patients with chemotherapy-induced febrile neutropenia: A double-blind, placebo-controlled trial. Ann Intern Med. 1994;121:492-501.

198. Vallenga E, Uyl-de Groot CA, de Wit R, et al. Randomized placebo-controlled trial of granulocyte-macrophage colony-stimulating factor in patients with chemotherapy-related febrile neutropenia. J Clin Oncol. 1996;14:619-627.

199. Ravaud A, Chevreau C, Cany L, et al. Granulocyte-macrophage colony-stimulating factor in patients with neutropenic fever is potent after low-risk but not after high-risk neutropenic chemotherapy regimens: Results of a randomized Phase III trial. J Clin Oncol. 1998;16:2930-2936.

200. Berghmans T, Paesmans M, Lafitte JJ, et al. Therapeutic use of granulocyte and granulocyte-macrophage colony-stimulating factors in febrile neutropenic cancer patients: A systematic review of the literature with meta-analysis. Support Care Cancer. 2002;10:181-188.

201. Howard O, James O. 2000 update of recommendations for the use of hematopoietic colony-stimulating factors: Evidence-based, clinical practice guidelines. J Clin Oncol. 2000;18:3558-3585.

202. Dale DC. Potential role of colony-stimulating factors in the prevention and treatment of infectious diseases. Clin Infect Dis. 1994;18(Suppl):S180-S188.

203. Nelson S. Role of granulocyte colony stimulating factor in the immune response to acute bacterial infection in the non-neutropenic host: An overview. Clin Infect Dis. 1994;18(Suppl):S197-S204.

204. Weiss M, Moldawer LL, et al. Granulocyte colony-stimulating factor to prevent the progression of systemic nonresponsiveness in systemic inflammatory response syndrome and sepsis. Blood. 1999;93:425-439.

205. Cesaro S, Chinello P, De Silvestro G, et al. Granulocyte transfusions from G-CSF–stimulated donors for the treatment of severe infections in neutropenic pediatric patients with onco-hematological diseases. Support Care Cancer. 2003;11:101-106.

206. Grigull L, Schrauder A, Schimitt-Thomssen A, et al. Efficacy and safety of G-CSF mobilized granulocyte transfusions in four neutropenic children with sepsis and invasive fungal infection. Infection. 2002;30:267-271.

207. Price TH, Bowden RA, Boeckh M, et al. Phase I/II trial of neutrophil transfusions from donors stimulated with G-CSF and dexamethasone for treatment of patients with infections in hematopoietic stem cell transplantation. Blood. 2000;95:3302-3309.

208. Peters C, Minkov M, Matthes-Martin S, et al. Leucocyte transfusions from rhG-CSF or prednisolone stimulated donors for treatment of severe infections in immunocompromised neutropenic patients. Br J Haematol. 1999;106:689-696.

209. Sullivan KM, Storek J, Kopecky KJ, et al. A controlled trial of long-term administration of intravenous immunoglobulin to prevent late infection and chronic graft-vs.-host disease after marrow transplantation: Clinical outcome and effect on subsequent immune recovery. Biol Blood Marrow Transplant. 1996;2:44-53.

210. Wolff SN, Fay JW, Herzig HA, et al. High-dose weekly intravenous immunoglobulin to prevent infections in patients undergoing autologous bone marrow transplantation or severe myelosuppressive therapy: A study of the American Bone Marrow Transplant Group. Ann Intern Med. 1993;118:936-942.

211. Chapel H, Dicato M, Gamm H, et al. Immunoglobulin replacement in patients with chronic lymphocytic leukaemia: A comparison of two dose regimens. Br J Haematol. 1994;88:209-212.

212. Molica S, Musto P, Chiurazzi F, et al. Prophylaxis against infections with low-dose intravenous immunoglobulins (IVIG) in chronic lymphocytic leukemia: Results of a crossover study. Haematologica. 1996;81:121-126.

213. Egerer G, Hensel M, Ho AD. Infectious complications in chronic lymphoid malignancy. Curr Treat Options Oncol. 2001;2:237-244.

CHAPTER **309**

Infections in Injection Drug Users

DONALD P. LEVINE

PATRICIA D. BROWN

Infections in injection drug users (IDUs) present a variety of challenges to the clinician, not only because of the complex nature of these patients' medical problems but also because of the unique psychosocial issues associated with their care. Management of infectious complications in these patients requires an understanding of the behavior of addicts and development of an approach that will help ensure a successful therapeutic regimen.[1]

Drug users are notorious for their antisocial behaviors, which in the hospital setting may be manifested by acting out on the ward, disagreements with staff, drug-seeking behavior, and leaving the hospital against medical advice. These problems can be minimized if the therapeutic plan is established at the outset. Too often there is an attempt to treat the patient's addiction, whereas the patient may not have agreed to that aspect of the approach. If the physician can establish a "therapeutic alliance" by gaining the patient's acceptance of specific treatment objectives, which generally do not include withdrawal from illegal substances but may include abiding by routine hospital policies and procedures, the chances of success are high. Not all drug users are sociopaths, and regarding them as such is likely to induce a mindset among the treatment team that will interfere with the physician-patient relationship and preclude effective management of the infection. One should not assume that all drug users are faking pain to obtain pain medication and support for their habit. A frequent response to presumed drug-seeking behavior is to underdose pain medication. This is viewed as punishment, it is unrelated to the infection problem, and it presents an obstacle to successful treatment.

The management of illness in the hospitalized IDU must be dictated by its severity. The only aspects of narcotic addiction that should be addressed are those that are relevant to the infectious problem at hand. Recognition that attempts to influence the drug abuse during the acute phase of an infectious disease not only may be fruitless but in some cases are contraindicated helps the clinician to focus on the medical aspects of the illness, which provide sufficient challenge to require complete attention.

The treatment of infections in IDUs is complicated by a number of factors. First, toxins or impurities in the injected substance rather than infection may cause febrile reactions in IDUs. If there is an infection, the clinical features may be indistinct, making it difficult to determine the true nature of the disease.[2,3] In addition, nonprescribed antibiotic use is common among addicts as they try to self-treat or to prevent infection. As a result, cultures may be negative, or positive for only some of the infecting organisms. In addition, such use of antibiotics undoubtedly contributes to the broad prevalence of resistant organisms, most notably methicillin-resistant *Staphylococcus aureus*. Finally, a variety of associated conditions (e.g., intercurrent viral infections) may obfuscate the clinical presentation. The prevalence of human immunodeficiency virus (HIV)–related disease in this population, with all of its attendant problems, has introduced an entire spectrum of disorders that must be added to the already lengthy differential diagnosis of infection in the IDU. Combinations of diseases are the rule rather than the exception.

HOST DEFENSES

Although it has been recognized for more than a century that opioid abuse is associated with an increased risk of infectious complications, a clear understanding of the effects of opioids on the immune system is still lacking. Studies have examined the effects of in vivo opioid exposure on the function of cells of the immune system isolated from drug users, the effect of in vitro exposure to opioids on immune cells isolated from healthy nonaddicts, and the effects of in vivo and in vitro exposure to opioids in animal models. The results of studies performed after the beginning of the HIV epidemic, but prior to the availability of a serologic test, may be confounded by the effects of immunodeficiency caused by HIV infection. Many authors have concluded that immunologic dysfunction plays a relatively minor role in the pathogenesis of infection in IDUs, compared to the repeated parenteral introduction or injection of nonsterile material and lifestyle factors associated with injection drug use.[4] However, there is growing evidence of a direct effect of opioids on immune system function. These effects have been recently reviewed and summarized.[5]

Both heroin and morphine (a major metabolite of heroin) exposure in vivo have been shown to decrease natural killer cell activity and decrease lymphocyte proliferation in response to phytohemagglutinin and other mitogens. In vivo, exposure to morphine has been demonstrated to decrease phagocytosis and the respiratory burst, and exposure to heroin has been shown to decrease T-cell E rosette formation and decrease the CD4/CD8 ratio. Many of these same effects have been demonstrated with in vitro exposure to morphine of immune system cells from nonaddicts and in animal models. Animal models have also highlighted the complex interactions between the immune system and the central nervous system (CNS), autonomic nervous system, and hypothalamic-pituitary-adrenal axis.

Methadone exposure has been shown to decrease lymphocyte proliferation in response to mitogens, decrease chemotaxis, and impair granulocyte function. However, prolonged methadone maintenance has been shown to reverse some of the immunosuppressive effects of heroin.[6,7] In spite of the depressed cell-mediated immunity demonstrated in IDUs, opportunistic infections characteristic of T-cell deficiency were rarely reported before the HIV epidemic.

Serum levels of immunoglobulin M and, to a lesser extent, immunoglobulin G are frequently elevated in IDUs, whereas serum immunoglobulin A levels are usually normal. Increased immunoglobulin levels tend to normalize after prolonged opiate withdrawal. Elevated immunoglobulin concentrations are accompanied by a high frequency of autoantibodies, such as rheumatoid factor, as well as those directed against various microorganisms. The latter phenomenon often manifests as a biologic false-positive Venereal Disease Research Laboratory (VDRL) test, which may create diagnostic confusion in IDUs who are at high risk of acquiring sexually transmitted diseases (STDs). Hypergammaglobulinemia resulting from polyclonal B-cell activation may be the result of recurrent immunologic stimulation by injected foreign antigens as well as associated chronic liver disease and chronic infections with other pathogens.

It has been shown that morphine may depress the monocyte functions essential for antiviral defense.[8] These alterations could contribute to the high efficiency of transmission of certain viral pathogens in IDUs, including hepatitis B virus (HBV), hepatitis C virus (HCV), and HIV. In vitro, morphine has been shown to enhance HIV infection of human mononuclear cells through the downregulation of β-chemokine production and the upregulation of CCR5 receptor expression.[9]

SKIN AND SOFT TISSUE INFECTIONS

Although endocarditis is the infection most often attributed to the injection of illicit substances, skin and soft tissue infections are the most common reason for hospital admission.[10,11] In one 6-month study of addicts, only 1% were treated for endocarditis, compared with 10% for abscesses.[12]

In the Detroit Medical Center, among 180 bacteremic IDUs, only 5% had endocarditis.[13,14] In San Francisco there has been an increase in the incidence of soft tissue infections, with 32% of abscesses and cellulitides related to injection drug use.[15,16] The distribution of soft tissue lesions is as varied as the sites used for injection and reflects both the duration of drug use and local practices among drug users. The most common lesions correspond to the most frequent injection sites. After extended drug use, if there are no remaining accessible veins in the arms, users frequently resort to injections in the groin or other easily reached locations, such as the neck or subclavian veins. After repeated injections into a site, frequently without benefit of sterile technique,[12] local ischemia or necrosis develops and the tissues become susceptible to infection. In addition, the substances injected frequently contain materials added as diluents that commonly cause norepinephrine release and vasospasm or local damage to the vascular intima. This leads to thrombosis and further compromise of the soft tissues. Cocaine use may be associated with vascular thrombus at sites distant from injections and may cause muscle and skin infections even after inhalational use.[17,18] Opiates also have immunosuppressive properties that may predispose to infection.[19] HIV infection is now recognized as an important risk factor for skin abscesses. Women are also at greater risk, presumably related to the difficulty they have accessing veins and the consequent injury to skin and subcutaneous tissues.[20]

Cellulitis used to be the most common soft tissue infection in addicts. Currently, abscesses are more common.[16,21,22] Synergy between streptococcal infection and cocaine-induced tissue ischemia may lead to large necrotic ulcerations and extensive tissue loss.[23] Alternatively, skin ulcerations may result from necrosis induced by the illicit substance injected. Abscesses are also found frequently in addicts who inject a mixture of heroine and cocaine, known as a "speedball," and are more likely in IDUs with a long history of drug use and "skin-popping" (i.e., either intended or accidental injection of drugs into the skin and subcutaneous tissues).[24] "Booting," a practice of drawing blood into the syringe to mix with the illicit substance prior to injection, is also an independent risk factor for abscess formation.[24] Cleansing the skin with alcohol prior to injection protects against abscess and offers a potential intervention to reduce disease and hospital admissions.[24]

Abscesses may spread to adjacent tissues, frequently with disastrous consequences. Mediastinitis may result from the extension of a cervical abscess, whereas lesions in the carotid triangle can erode into the carotid arteries, resulting in massive hemorrhage. Thrombosis of the internal jugular vein has been reported as a complication of a deep neck abscess, as has acute vocal cord paralysis.[25,26] This can lead to acute, severe airway obstruction and may necessitate immediate tracheostomy. Local venous thrombosis, or extension to the retroperitoneal space, may result from abscess in the femoral triangle. *S. aureus* is the most common pathogen, followed by streptococci, either as the sole pathogen or in combination with other organisms. Coagulase-negative staphylococci and α-hemolytic streptococci are also seen. Among the latter, *Streptococcus* of the *anginosus* (*milleri*) group is most important, especially in addicts in Scotland, who inject tablets of buprenorphine and temazepam after crushing them between their teeth.[23,27] Other oral flora have been reported, in particular *Eikenella corrodens*, which in some centers has become the third most common pathogen. IDUs who lick their needles or contaminate their drugs with saliva are particularly prone to this infection. The pneumococcus is also occasionally found in this setting. Gram-negative bacilli are found with variable frequency. In the past anaerobes were found infrequently, particularly in upper extremity infection. In a recent study, isolates from 39% of IDUs contained both aerobes and anaerobes, compared to only 27% in nonusers. In addition, anaerobes, either alone or as part of a mixed flora, were detected more frequently from drug users than from nonusers (44% vs. 35%).[28]

Cellulitis may be extensive and can lead to overwhelming sepsis and death.[10,29] The diagnosis is seldom obscure, and most patients present with signs and symptoms referable to the involved site; however, blood cultures should be obtained, because it is difficult to predict bacteremia.[13] In contrast, the diagnosis of an abscess can be difficult. Patients typically have single lesions. The signs and symptoms are similar to those in patients with cellulitis alone. Indeed, most patients will also have an area of adjacent cellulitis. Less than half the patients are febrile. Erythema, pain, and tenderness of the involved site are common, but fluctuance is absent in approximately 25%.[30] Deep abscesses may be particularly difficult to detect.[21] Computed tomography (CT) is useful for cervical abscesses[31] and is probably effective for detecting abscesses in the groin and femoral region. Magnetic resonant imaging (MRI) is also useful, particularly in extremity infection.[32] Ultrasonography has been reported to be useful but is of variable accuracy, particularly when diagnosing lesions in the groin.

Antibiotic therapy is directed at the organisms recovered from the blood or purulent material. In uncomplicated cellulitides, cultures are seldom helpful. In such cases therapy is empirical and is based upon the pathogens most commonly encountered in that geographic location. Prolonged antibiotic treatment is frequently required.[22] Early surgical drainage of abscesses is essential, and, because of the tendency of these lesions to spread to adjacent or even distant regions, multiple drainage procedures may be required.[33] Deep infections of the hand are far more common in IDUs than in nonusers, and they mandate a unique approach. The microbiology of such infections varies, depending on the injected substances. Patients who primarily inject cocaine have a high frequency of mixed anaerobic infection,[30] whereas heroin users are more likely to harbor streptococci and staphylococci.[34] In either case, surgical débridement is far more likely to be required in IDUs than in nonusers.[34] Some caution is indicated before incising a lesion in the vicinity of blood vessels, because a mycotic pseudoaneurysm can easily be misdiagnosed as an abscess. Inadvertent entry into such a lesion can have disastrous consequences.

Skin ulcers are extremely common in IDUs. They are found at every conceivable site but are particularly common below the knee, close to the ankle.[35] They arise from tissue damage caused by repeated nonsterile injection into the same site with associated thrombosis and infection. They may persist for years and are a frequent reason for hospitalization. Typically they have ragged edges and seropurulent drainage. Patients complain of severe pain, and it is often pain, rather than the ulcer itself, that brings the patient to medical attention. The microbiology of these lesions is similar to that of other soft tissue infections in addicts, although they more frequently contain more than one organism. *S. aureus* and β-hemolytic streptococci remain the most common isolates, with gram-negative bacilli, most often *Klebsiella, Pseudomonas, Escherichia coli,* and *Proteus,* playing an important role. They present particularly difficult management problems when ulcers involve the hands and feet and may ultimately lead to loss of function. Treatment of skin ulcers requires administration of systemic antibiotics and prolonged local wound care, including gentle washing, wet-to-dry dressings, and application of topical antibacterial creams. Elevation of the leg to reduce edema is an important component of the therapy, and also plays a role in pain management.[36] Parenteral antibiotics are generally continued until the wound is covered by granulation tissue. Very large lesions may require skin grafting or muscle flaps, but these are only effective after all necrotic tissue has been removed and the wound is clean and granulating. An important adjuvant treatment is the application of compression dressings, such as Unna boots, which, when properly applied, serve to reduce the edema as well as to promote wound healing.[37] With time, most skin ulcers heal completely, leaving circular, punched-out scars. The most important complication is contiguous osteomyelitis, which may be difficult to diagnose because frequently there is radiologic evidence of periosteal reaction in bones immediately beneath large ulcers. When there is still a question of osteomyelitis, a triple-phase bone scan may be helpful. Ultimately a diagnosis of osteomyelitis may be impossible without a bone biopsy, which may be difficult to obtain without traversing infected superficial tissues. In such cases, prolonged parenteral antibiotic therapy directed at the organism cultured from the ulcer and careful radiographic follow-up may be the best approach. Recurrent and chronic infections are occasionally complicated by renal amyloidosis.

Necrotizing fasciitis, without or with myositis, is the single infection in IDUs that is most likely to need immediate and appropriate treatment; however, the clinical picture is subtle and rarely elicits the emergency response required. At San Francisco General Hospital, 1% of IDUs in need of incision and drainage for soft tissue infection were found to have necrotizing infection requiring extensive débridement. The classic findings of high fever, bullae, crepitance, and skin necrosis are usually absent initially, and the impression may be that of mild cellulitis.[34] In some cases, the true nature of the disease may be so subtle as to be missed during a procedure to débride an abscess or cellulitis. Alternatively, infection may spread after apparently effective incision and drainage.[38] The major indication of the true nature of the infection is the fact that signs and symptoms, such as pain and hemodynamic instability, are disproportionate to the apparent extent of the local process.[34] However, this can be misleading because the clinical presentation may be no different from routine cellulitis with no more than erythema of the involved area, providing no clue to the serious underlying pathology.[39] Also, because addicts are frequently viewed as drug-seeking complainers, what appears to be excessive complaint for minor disease may be interpreted as narcotic-seeking behavior, further delaying recognition of the need for aggressive and rapid action. Thus a high index of suspicion is required so as not to miss the diagnosis. Additional clues to the serious nature of the problem are hemodynamic instability, local anesthesia, rapid progression of inflammation, or the presence of blue or hemorrhagic bullae. When present, crepitance is an important clue. Finally, a slow response to appropriate antibiotic treatment suggests a deeper underlying problem. A CT scan may be a useful diagnostic tool. Characteristic findings include asymmetrical fascial thickening and fat stranding, followed by gas tracking along fascial planes. Abscesses may also be seen.[40] CT scans may be misleading because both false-positive and false-negative results have been reported and contrast enhancement contributes no additional in-

formation. The only definitive test is surgical exploration, which is both diagnostic and therapeutic. The finding of necrosis is characteristic; however, it may be necessary to explore more than one area. A negative biopsy from one location does not preclude the diagnosis in adjacent tissues.[41]

As with most addict-related infections, gram-positive organisms are usually found. However, β-hemolytic streptococci predominate in approximately 50% of cases, followed by *S. aureus,* α-hemolytic streptococci, and coagulase-negative staphylococci. Gram-negative organisms are infrequent and are usually represented by enteric pathogens, especially *E. coli, Klebsiella, Proteus mirabilis, Pseudomonas,* and *Enterobacter.* Anaerobes are recovered in 12% of cases; yeasts (*Candida*) are uncommon. Polymicrobial infection is common.[42]

Management of necrotizing fasciitis by antibiotics alone leads to progression of the infection in 75% of patients. Parenteral antibiotics and aggressive surgery coupled with reexploration at 24 hours and as often as necessary afterward to ensure complete removal of all necrotic tissue offers the best prognosis. In a recent study, IDUs required an average of 3.4 débridements for necrotizing fasciitis.[42] Aggressive nutritional support and early coverage of the soft tissue defect have been shown to improve the outcome,[43] which for addicts, who tend to be young and relatively healthy, is the best of any patient group with this disease. Even with aggressive treatment, the mortality rate is high, ranging from 10% to 23%, and amputation is required in up to 10%.[42]

Recently, IDUs in Scotland and England were treated for a syndrome that included abscess, fasciitis, or myositis. The mortality for the aggregate was 45%. Preliminary evidence suggests the infection was due to *Clostridium novyi.* At autopsy evidence of a diffuse toxic process with pleural effusions, soft tissue edema, or necrosis was found.[44]

Pyomyositis, a less serious infection involving the musculature, occurs frequently in IDUs. Direct inoculation of bacteria into the musculature has been implicated. Hematogenous spread also occurs, occasionally as a complication of endocarditis.[45] Most patients who have pyomyositis present with pain and swelling of the involved area. Lesions have been reported in the deltoid, psoas, biceps, gastrocnemius, gluteal, and quadriceps muscles. Ultrasound, CT, or MRI reveals the underlying defect within the muscle. *S. aureus* is the most common pathogen; viridans streptococci, aerobic gram-negative bacilli, and mixed infection with anaerobes have also been reported. Patients respond well to drainage and antibiotic therapy. A rare but related condition, uterine pyomyoma, has also been reported. The cause appears to be hematogenous dissemination to an infarcted leiomyoma.[46]

Just as needle exchange programs reduce HIV infection among IDUs, combining those services with a wound and abscess clinic may substantially reduce the cost of care (to as low as $5.00 per patient) and the number of visits to emergency departments. Widespread implementation of such clinics could have a major impact on the management of skin and soft tissue infections among IDUs.[47]

BONE AND JOINT INFECTIONS

Skeletal infections are common in IDUs, most occurring via hematogenous seeding by bacteria or fungi.[48] Target sites for infection are determined by the blood supply and predominantly affect the axial skeleton. The original source of these infections may be inapparent, or they may represent metastatic complications of endocarditis. In addition, bone and joint infections frequently result from contiguous spread from adjacent, often neglected areas of infection in skin and soft tissues. IDUs with hematogenous infection often have multiple sites involved simultaneously, and blood cultures frequently are negative at the time of presentation. In contrast, bone and joint infection caused by contiguous spread may lead to concomitant secondary bacteremia. IDUs with HIV infection do not appear to be at increased risk for osteoarticular infections.[49]

IDUs with skeletal infection tend to be young and otherwise healthy. Clinical findings include constitutional manifestations as well as local signs and symptoms depending on the site involved. Patients with osteomyelitis often have a paucity of findings, presenting with local pain and tenderness only. Lack of signs and symptoms frequently results in delay in diagnosis. Fever is absent in one third of patients.[48] Similarly, signs of sepsis, leukocytosis, and radiologic signs may be absent in patients with osteomyelitis.

Pyogenic infections predominate, with almost 90% being bacterial in origin, although skeletal infections can be caused by virtually any organism. The predominant pathogens isolated are *S. aureus* and group A and group G streptococci. Gram-negative bacilli, particularly *Pseudomonas aeruginosa,* although less common, are well known, as are polymicrobial infections. IDUs who lick their needles or the skin surface prior to injection may develop osteomyelitis or septic arthritis with *E. corrodens* ("needle licker's osteomyelitis").[50] *Candida* species have been increasingly recognized as a possible etiology of skeletal infections in IDUs, particularly spondylodiscitis and vertebral osteomyelitis.[51] A characteristic form of systemic candidiasis has been reported among IDUs who inject heroin that includes folliculitis, usually of the scalp and beard; endophthalmitis; and bone and joint lesions, most often costochondritis. Lastly, *Mycobacterium tuberculosis* should always be considered among the possible etiologies of skeletal infection in IDUs, particularly vertebral osteomyelitis. Skeletal infections caused by mycobacteria, including those caused by atypical species, are often associated with involvement of the lungs, adrenals, or pelvic organs.

Joint infections that involve the extremities most commonly affect the knee. Left-sided involvement exceeds right-sided knee arthritis, possibly related to the tendency of right-handed IDUs to inject into the left groin veins; this suggests a relation between site of injection and infection.[48] IDUs are particularly susceptible to vertebral osteomyelitis. The lumbosacral spine is the most common site of infection, and a higher incidence of cervical spine involvement is seen in IDUs than in non-IDUs with vertebral osteomyelitis.[52] IDUs with vertebral osteomyelitis present with symptoms of a shorter duration than do other patients with infection of the spine.[52] Primary sternal osteomyelitis, often associated with an antecedent history of blunt trauma to the sternum, is reported in IDUs. This group is also prone to septic arthritis in unusual sites, such as the sternoclavicular and costochondral joints and the pubic symphysis. Other sites frequently involved include wrist, shoulder, hip, and sacroiliac joints. Vertebral osteomyelitis may extend into the subdural or epidural spaces and may cause formation of an abscess, with consequent cord compression and paraplegia. In addition, lumbosacral vertebral osteomyelitis may be associated with psoas abscess.

Because of the wide spectrum of organisms that may be involved, diagnostic needle aspiration for smear and culture is necessary in all cases. Even when blood cultures are positive, invasive diagnostic steps are advised, because skeletal and blood-stream infection may represent two separate processes and infections may be polymicrobial. Frequent arthrocentesis, arthroscopic or open drainage, and débridement of nonviable bone are also advised if clinically indicated. Antibiotic therapy is required for 4 to 6 weeks, selection being based on the identity of the responsible microorganisms and susceptibility data. Increasingly, oral antimicrobials with high bioavailability and good bone penetration are utilized for at least a portion of the therapeutic course.[53] Overall, with early diagnosis, the immediate prognosis of bone and joint infection in IDUs is excellent, but long-term follow-up data are lacking.[48] Many IDUs present late in the clinical course, and delays in diagnosis and institution of therapy are accompanied by a high likelihood of chronic osteomyelitis and late relapse of disease. Also contributing to this late but frequent complication is the problem of noncompliance. IDUs tend to leave the hospital against medical advice when confronted with prolonged inpatient intravenous antibiotic therapy and a tendency for medical personnel to underappreciate and undertreat the pain associated with skeletal infection.

A rare musculoskeletal syndrome, characterized by fever, arthralgia, myalgia (especially of paraspinal muscles), and periarticular tissue swelling, has been described in IDUs and is thought to represent hypersensitivity to heroin contaminants.[54]

INFECTIVE ENDOCARDITIS

Infective endocarditis (IE) is a common cause of bacteremia in IDUs. In the Detroit Medical Center, 74 of 180 addicts with bacteremia had endocarditis.[13] In a community teaching hospital in Ohio, between 1980 and 1990, 16% of endocarditis cases were related to injection drug use.[55] In another hospital emergency department, IE was diagnosed in 15% of febrile addicts.[56] Men are affected more often than women (5.4:1 in the Detroit Medical Center, 2:1 in Chicago). Men with IE are also older than women and have significantly longer histories of drug use (10.2 vs. 7.1 years). Recurrent endocarditis is also more common in IDUs, and the median interval between episodes is far shorter in addicts than in nonaddicts.[57] Cocaine use and HIV infection are additional risk factors.[20,58]

S. aureus remains the most common pathogen, affecting the tricuspid or pulmonary valve in approximately 90% of cases, with methicillin-resistant strains becoming more prevalent. Coagulase-negative staphylococci are now an uncommon cause of endocarditis in IDUs. Streptococci, particularly groups A, B, and G, are the second most common cause.[13,59] These two organisms account for up to 75% of cases.[13] *Enterococcus* played a major role in the past, but its prevalence is decreasing.[13,59] Gram-negative organisms are infrequent causes, although intermittent epidemics of *P. aeruginosa* endocarditis occurred in Detroit and Chicago,[13,53,60,61] and *Serratia marcescens* was responsible for a sustained epidemic in the Oakland, California, area.[62,63] Fungi, especially *Candida parapsilosis* and *Candida tropicalis,* account for approximately 4% of cases,[64] and several cases of IE caused by *Aspergillus* were recently reported.[65] Two of three patients were HIV infected. Duration of symptoms ranged from 2 weeks to 1 month prior to detection. Blood cultures were negative, but there were large vegetations and peripheral embolization. *Aspergillus* frequently contaminates illicit drugs, but whether the inoculum associated with injection is sufficient to cause endocarditis is unclear. That two of three patients were HIV positive is of interest and may indicate that altered immune status played a role. Polymicrobial endocarditis is being observed with increasing frequency among drug users. Usually only a few organisms are involved, but rarely there may be numerous pathogens. In such cases, standard laboratory techniques may be inadequate to isolate and identify the full microbial spectrum, placing a burden on the clinician to suspect polymicrobial endocarditis caused by salivary contamination of needles or injection sites whenever uncommon oropharyngeal organisms are cultured from the blood.[66] Among the fastidious organisms, most cases are caused by *Eikenella;* however, there are reports of endocarditis caused by anaerobes such as *Fusobacterium* spp. and *Clostridium.* In addition, numerous reports describe endocarditis in IDUs caused by a variety of organisms that are frequently considered nonpathogens. These infections may be related to altered host immunity resulting from HIV infection[67] or to unusual practices among addicts, such as licking of needles before use, or "cleaning" of the injection site with saliva.

The pathophysiology of endocarditis in addicts is poorly understood. The organism is most often part of the patient's own flora,[13,68] although injection paraphernalia have been implicated in the case of *P. aeruginosa* endocarditis. Environmental contamination was also considered in the initial outbreak of *Serratia* endocarditis in California when it was learned that years earlier *Serratia* had been sprayed into the air to study wind currents. However, these strains were not the same ones that caused disease, and the regional predilection for this infection remains a mystery. It is also unclear why certain valves are affected in IDUs with endocarditis. It is known that, unlike native valve endocarditis in nonaddicts, the affected cardiac valve is almost always previously normal.[13,60,69] In an autopsy study of addicts who died from endocarditis, Dressler and Roberts reported that 81% of the valves were normal, including all right-side valves.[69] Early reports of endocarditis in addicts noted a predominance of tricuspid valve involvement. Left-side involvement predominates in some recent studies, and multiple valves are frequently involved.[59,70] Pulmonary involvement remains rare. Nevertheless, tricuspid valve involvement is seen almost exclusively in IDUs.

Clearly no single hypothesis explains the prevalence of right-sided involvement in IDUs. Potential explanations include damage to right-side endothelium by repeated exposure to injected particulate matter; vasospasm caused by injected diluents or illicit drugs, particularly cocaine; or drug-induced thrombus formation and subsequent bacterial aggregation. The fact that endocarditis caused by *Enterococcus* and *Serratia* is primarily a left-sided phenomenon suggests that other mechanisms must be important. Mitral valve prolapse has been proposed to explain the predilection for mitral valve endocarditis in female IDUs, but studies showing equal numbers of men and women with mitral involvement make this explanation unlikely. Specific surface properties of the common infecting pathogens, especially *S. aureus,* might favor attachment to extracellular matrix proteins that may have greater expression on right-side valves. *S. aureus* is also phagocytosed by endothelial cells, where it is protected from host defenses. This may activate the clotting system, leading to vegetation formation. The production of coagulase by *S. aureus* may further promote clotting and vegetation formation. Cytokines produced after phagocytosis may enhance immune-complex deposition that leads to valvulitis, thereby creating a lesion that is susceptible to vegetation formation and bacterial seeding. Finally, endothelial differences between the right and left sides of the heart might contribute to the predilection for tricuspid valve involvement. Additional hypotheses invoke an association between large, directly injected bacterial inocula and immune abnormalities that may contribute to sustained bacteremia and valvulitis.[71] Which, if any, of these mechanisms proves to be responsible for the preponderance of right-sided involvement will depend on future studies. Whatever the reason, *S. aureus* predominantly affects the tricuspid valve, but may also involve the mitral or aortic valves. *S. marcescens, Streptococcus pyogenes,* and enterococci almost exclusively affect left-side valves.[13,62,72]

HIV infection plays a significant role in the pathophysiology of endocarditis in IDUs. HIV-infected addicts are significantly more likely to develop endocarditis than non–HIV-infected addicts, and those with the lowest CD4+ lymphocyte counts are most likely.[58] In contrast, alcohol consumption confers protection against endocarditis, perhaps by inducing an inhibitory effect on platelet function.[73]

Unlike nonaddicts, who generally present with symptoms of greater than 2 weeks' duration,[74] most addicts with IE present within the first week of illness with signs indicative of severe, acute infection.[13,59,75] Typically, they have acute onset of fever, chills, and dyspnea. Chest pain, often pleuritic in nature, occurs in up to half the cases and is due to septic pulmonary emboli.[13,59] Cough is frequently present; it may be nonproductive or associated with blood-streaked sputum. Radiologic evidence of pneumonia is detected in 23% and congestive heart failure in 13%.[59] Pneumothorax, occasionally bilateral, is a complication of septic pulmonary embolism.[76] Involvement of other organ systems is similar to that observed in endocarditis in nonaddicts. CNS involvement may initially be confused with toxic effects of illicit drugs, but the diagnosis usually becomes rapidly apparent when blood cultures become positive.

The overall severity of the clinical picture depends on the valve or valves involved and whether there is any associated damage to the heart itself, such as valve ring abscess or valve rupture, or metastatic infection involving other organs. Osler's nodes and Janeway lesions are rare in addicts. Splenomegaly occurs in only 10% to 15%, and heart murmurs are found with variable frequency. When the infection is confined to the tricuspid valve, the presence of murmurs varies from 35% to 72%.[13]

Because of the high-grade bacteremia and acute nature of endocarditis in addicts, every organ is affected to some degree. Complications involving the heart, although infrequent, may be life threatening. When cardiac problems dominate the picture, which is most likely with mitral or aortic valve infections, the prognosis is poor, especially if congestive heart failure develops. As noted above, recur-

rent IE is common in addicts. Most patients survive the first episode, but with such severely damaged valves that dysfunction occurs in almost 70%. Previous valve damage predisposes to subsequent episodes, which frequently are fatal. Additional cardiac lesions include left-ventricular abscesses, which are multifocal and are found in conjunction with clusters of bacteria in intramural arteries, and myocardial infarction. Valve ring abscesses and, rarely, focal, acute interstitial myocarditis are also found.[69] Cardiac abscesses may also lead to further serious complications, such as a pseudoaneurysm of the heart, which can be demonstrated by MRI and color Doppler ultrasound.[77] As with nonaddicts, left-sided infection predisposes to systemic emboli and acute pericarditis. Certain organisms, especially *Serratia* and *Candida,* are notable for their tendency to induce large, systemic emboli. Their isolation in a patient with endocarditis should alert the clinician to the probability of left-sided infection and the likelihood of a serious embolic event. CNS complications of endocarditis are similar to those in non-IDUs and include mycotic aneurysms, brain abscess, stroke, meningitis, and epidural abscess. Splenic abscesses are seen, especially with *S. aureus* infection, and should be assessed prior to cardiac surgery in order to avoid valve replacement in a patient likely to remain bacteremic from a noncardiac source. Drug users are more likely than nonusers to develop bone and joint infection, particularly vertebral osteomyelitis, secondary to endocarditis.[78]

The diagnosis of endocarditis in IDUs is often easily made on the basis of the characteristic clinical picture. The modified Duke criteria effectively classify IDUs with either definite or possible endocarditis and can be utilized in difficult cases, particularly when difficult therapeutic decisions must be made.[79] Those with definite IE frequently have no obvious focus of infection and are more likely to have vascular phenomena and multiple opacities on chest radiograph.[80] However, in the emergency department setting, the absence of signs specific for endocarditis and the limited information available make the diagnosis particularly difficult.[81] At the time of the initial presentation, there are no differences in age, sex, maximum temperature, or leukocyte count between addicts with and without endocarditis. Those with endocarditis account for only 13% of addicts admitted for infection, and only positive echocardiogram findings, pulmonary or systemic emboli, and bacteremia distinguish patients with endocarditis from those without.[56] Rothman and colleagues further modified the Duke criteria in an effort to improve diagnostic accuracy in an urban emergency department.[82] Major criteria are the same as the Duke criteria, although an echocardiogram performed upon arrival to the hospital is added and only data available in the first 24 hours are used. Minor criteria are unchanged. The definition of definite endocarditis is the same as in the Duke system; possible endocarditis requires either 1 major and 2 minor or 4 minor criteria. The diagnosis is rejected if these criteria are not met. The results were almost identical to published results using the standard Duke criteria, but the investigators were able to make admission and therapeutic decisions much earlier than was otherwise possible. The same investigators also evaluated the contribution to diagnosis of transthoracic echocardiography (TTE) in the emergency department. Adding TTE proved diagnostic for nearly 70% of patients who failed to meet major culture criteria.[83] In another attempt to arrive at earlier diagnosis, investigators utilized polymerase chain reaction to detect universal 16S ribosomal RNA. They found a sensitivity and specificity of only 86.7% and 86.9%, respectively, but accurately identified all eight patients with blood culture–positive endocarditis.[84] If validated, this method may provide an additional diagnostic tool for the emergency department clinician.

The most sensitive indicator of endocarditis in IDUs is a blood culture, which is positive in 80% to 100% of cases. However, because many addicts take oral antibiotics before admission, initial cultures may be negative. Subsequent blood cultures will reveal the pathogen.[85] Even after several days of appropriate parenteral therapy, blood cultures are still likely to be positive.[86,87] Because culture-negative IE is rare in IDUs, negative blood cultures suggest an alternative diagnosis.

Additional blood studies are not of particular benefit in diagnosing endocarditis. Anemia is common in IDUs as a result of the continual blood loss associated with the act of injecting. Elevated white blood cell count (WBC), usually with a left shift, is also common, although neutropenia and thrombocytopenia are occasionally found. Hyponatremia in the range of 125 to 133 mEq/L is found in approximately 40% of cases immediately after admission and predicts prolonged fever and greater morbidity.[13] The etiology is unclear and the abnormality corrects immediately after fluid administration. Additional laboratory abnormalities reflect the high-grade bacteremia associated with endocarditis and routinely normalize soon after bacteremia clears. The cerebrospinal fluid (CSF) is abnormal in many cases, with increased WBC and protein in patients showing no overt CNS symptoms or signs.[88] The echocardiogram has a relatively high sensitivity (approximately 90%), and false-positive results are unusual.[56] The TTE is at least equivalent to the transesophageal echocardiogram (TEE) for detecting right-sided lesions. In cases with a high pretest probability they are equivalent. Hence, a TTE might be performed first, and if negative a TEE may be ordered. Alternatively, TEE might be reserved for patients suspected to have left-sided involvement, or those with perivalvular lesions, such as valve ring abscess or perforation or a vestigial eustachian valve.[89] It is important to recognize that a negative TEE does not rule out endocarditis.

Addicts with IE who are stable and only moderately ill can be safely observed without antibiotic therapy while the results of blood cultures are awaited. Transient fever and bacteremia occurs in this population, and because bacteremia is the most sensitive indicator of endocarditis, a commitment to therapy before the nature of the septic condition is documented can lead to unnecessary and prolonged hospitalization for administration of antibiotics. Even when the patient is acutely ill, several blood cultures should be obtained before antibiotic therapy is initiated. The initial empirical regimen is based in part on knowledge of the organisms most likely to cause endocarditis in that geographic location. In most settings, coverage is directed against *S. aureus.* Where methicillin-resistant *S. aureus* is prevalent, vancomycin is the preferred agent. In settings where methicillin-resistant organisms are rare, nafcillin or a similar β-lactamase–resistant penicillin is preferred. When vancomycin is used, both fever and bacteremia are considerably prolonged compared to treatment with nafcillin.[86]

Trimethoprim-sulfamethoxazole may be an alternative for both methicillin-sensitive and methicillin-resistant *S. aureus* soft tissue infections, but its efficacy in endocarditis is questionable.[90] Traditionally, endocarditis in IDUs was treated with 4- to 6-week courses of parenteral antibiotics. However, some patients with uncomplicated right-sided endocarditis may be successfully treated for 2 weeks with nafcillin plus an aminoglycoside[91] or even cloxacillin alone.[92] When quinolones are used, therapy may consist entirely of oral medication.[93] The addition of an aminoglycoside to an initial empirical regimen to provide coverage against a gram-negative pathogen is controversial. The standard aminoglycoside dose used with an antistaphylococcal penicillin is likely to have little effect against the most worrisome gram-negative organisms, particularly *Pseudomonas.* Reyes and colleagues noted that an aminoglycoside dose of 8 mg/kg/day in divided doses was required to achieve acceptable antipseudomonal activity.[94,95] Using high-dose aminoglycoside and a synergistic β-lactam antibiotic, the outcome in *Pseudomonas* endocarditis is much more favorable than with any other initial regimen.[96] Quinolones also have utility against *Pseudomonas,* but the data are insufficient to permit a recommendation for their use.[97]

Combined therapy with penicillin (or vancomycin) plus an aminoglycoside is standard against enterococcal endocarditis, but the prevalence of resistant strains makes such a selection less reliable without first screening for susceptibility. Frequently, gentamicin-resistant enterococci are susceptible to streptomycin, and synergy can be obtained with use of the latter.[98]

Fungal endocarditis is usually treated with amphotericin B plus surgery. Currently the need for surgery in all patients is being questioned. Recent information suggests the outcome in patients treated with medical management alone may be similar to those having valve replacement surgery. In either case, many clinicians prefer to prescribe

chronic suppression with oral fluconazole following the initial treatment phase.[64] The role of newer triazoles and echinocandins in endocarditis has yet to be studied.

In most cases of IE in IDUs, the survival rate is good with antibiotics alone, despite complications and prolonged fever.[99] Septic emboli frequently occur after the initiation of therapy but do not affect the prognosis and are not necessarily an indication for removal or replacement of the infected valve.[13,99] The relationship between vegetation size, as determined by echocardiography, and the likelihood of an embolus is controversial. However, vegetations larger than 2 cm are associated with a 33% mortality rate, compared with 1.3% for patients with vegetations smaller than 2 cm ($P < .001$).[99] Hence, some clinicians consider large vegetations as an indication for surgery. In general, the indications for surgery and the final result are the same in IDUs with endocarditis as in the general population. Although surgery carries substantial risk, the mortality rate in patients who fail medical management approaches 100%, so surgical treatment is indicated and clearly improves survival.[100] The patient's HIV-1 status is a significant prognostic indicator. The CD4$^+$ cell count drops after cardiopulmonary bypass, which may lead to an acceleration of the progress toward the acquired immunodeficiency syndrome (AIDS).[101] Addicts with HIV-1 infection whose IE is poorly controlled at the time of cardiac surgery and those with advanced AIDS also have a poor prognosis.[102] The major problem after cardiac surgery for endocarditis in IDUs is their propensity to continue illicit drug use. In one study, only 4 of 57 addicts remained drug free, and the 10-year survival rate was only 10%.[102] Hence, some authors advocate excision of the tricuspid valve or repair of the left-side valves rather than replacement for IDUs needing surgical intervention.[103] Prognosis is not affected by the duration of symptoms before initiation of therapy, antibiotic use before admission, right-sided heart failure, pulmonary embolism, or results of the following laboratory tests: leukocyte count, hemoglobin, and serum creatinine.[99]

NONCARDIAC VASCULAR INFECTIONS

As arm and leg veins become thrombosed, sclerosed, and unusable, femoral, axillary, and neck vessels are increasingly used for injection. Vessels used frequently for injection become injured or infected, leading to the formation of hematoma, thrombosis, septic thrombophlebitis, mycotic aneurysm, or traumatic arteriovenous fistula.[104,105] The predominant pathogens are gram-positive cocci, usually *S. aureus,* although gram-negative pathogens, particularly *P. aeruginosa,* are not infrequently found. Findings with septic thrombophlebitis include local pain, swelling, and fever together with bacteremia and sepsis. Local signs of infection may be masked when deep vessels are involved. Infection or sclerosis of proximal large veins is frequently complicated by venous stasis and supervening thrombosis. Septic pulmonary embolization follows and closely resembles right-sided bacterial endocarditis.[13] The management of septic thrombophlebitis, which most frequently involves the femoral veins, remains controversial. Parenteral antimicrobial therapy is standard, but the value of anticoagulant use has not been established. Furthermore, hemorrhagic complications from unrecognized coexistent femoral and cerebral mycotic aneurysms may occur. Difficulty performing venography in IDUs precludes controlled studies evaluating efficacy and complications of anticoagulant use. Some experienced clinicians believe the risks of short-term anticoagulation are outweighed by the risk of major pulmonary emboli.

A major vascular complication in IDUs is the formation of mycotic aneurysms, most frequently involving femoral and less commonly neck vessels. True aneurysms involving all three layers of the arterial wall are rare. In the IDU, frequent direct trauma to peripheral vessels produces damage to the vessel wall and an initial sterile perivascular hematoma. Injection of chemical agents in illicit drugs also causes tissue necrosis. The vascular wall usually becomes infected by contiguous spread from adjacent subcutaneous abscesses or areas of cellulitis. Infection causes liquefaction of the central portion of the hematoma in communication with the arterial or, less commonly, the venous wall, forming a secondary (false) pseudoaneurysm.[105,106] The common femoral artery is the most frequent location, followed by the deep femoral and superficial femoral arteries. Because most IDUs are right handed, left-sided groin infections and aneurysms are more common. Primary mycotic aneurysms in which the damaged vessel wall is infected secondary to unrelated bacteremia are rare and are more likely to involve cerebral vessels as a complication of endocarditis. Pathogenesis includes septic embolization from valvular vegetations to the vasa vasorum of smaller vessels, such as the middle or posterior cerebral and visceral intra-abdominal arteries, which are more frequently involved than the aorta.

Clinical manifestations of a mycotic aneurysm include a painful, often enlarging, tender, and frequently pulsatile mass, accompanied by variable constitutional symptoms. Distal extremity ischemia and nerve compression are often present, and detection of a bruit or thrill over the mass strongly supports the diagnosis. Often addicts report "hitting the pinky," indicating unintended arterial injection. Bleeding from an injection site may be evidence of an aneurysm. Because drug abusers usually present with cellulitis and accompanying edema and induration, the pulsatile mass may be masked, obscuring the aneurysm. When rupture of the aneurysm occurs, it is usually preceded by severe pain that may be misdiagnosed as thrombophlebitis or soft tissue abscess. In contrast to the lower limb, distal ischemia in the upper extremity (hand) from induced arterial spasm occurs commonly.

Anemia, leukocytosis, and an elevated sedimentation rate, although frequently present, are of limited diagnostic value. A high index of suspicion together with angiographic confirmation is essential, because misdiagnosis is common and cellulitis, abscess, or infected hematoma may mimic or mask an aneurysm (Fig. 309-1). Ultrasonography, al-though useful, may fail to differentiate an abscess from an aneurysm. In one study ultrasound had a false-negative rate of 54%.[107] CT, especially with injected contrast material, is extremely useful and delineates the pathology in the adjacent soft tissues. Color Doppler sonography may confirm the diagnosis, especially in the extremities, but may not clearly define the vascular anatomy.[108] Thus angiography remains the definitive diagnostic procedure, not only for delineating the lesion but for planning the approach to surgery, and digital subtraction angiography may replace traditional arteriography in diagnosing femoral and other peripheral aneurysms.[109] Magnetic resonance angiography (MRA) may prove to be helpful in diagnosis of mycotic aneurysms. Needle aspiration, incision, and drainage should be avoided in noninvestigated inguinal masses, even if nonpulsatile, because of the risk of uncontrolled bleeding from an unrecognized mycotic aneurysm.

Successful management of a mycotic aneurysm requires early diagnosis before rupture occurs. Surgical treatment should not be delayed, because rupture is frequent. It consists of proximal and distal ligation of the aneurysm followed by excision of all necrotic and infected material, including the infected vessel. Vascular reconstruction as a delayed procedure is recommended only in patients who develop ischemia after excision of the aneurysm, and then only when a graft can be positioned through an uninfected tissue plane. Because *S. aureus* is the most common pathogen, initial empirical antibiotic therapy should include a β-lactamase-resistant penicillin such as nafcillin. Where methicillin-resistant *S. aureus* is prominent, vancomycin should be started. An aminoglycoside is added initially if there is suspicion or evidence of gram-negative bacilli on Gram staining of sanguinopurulent drainage. Subsequent cultures obtained from blood and local exudate influence antibiotic selection. Recommended therapy is 4 to 6 weeks intravenously.

PULMONARY INFECTIONS

Pulmonary manifestations are extremely common in IDUs. The lung is the target of numerous infectious and noninfectious insults. The latter include drug-induced bronchospasm, acute pulmonary edema, and talc granulomatosis.[110] Heroin overdose may be associated with unilateral or bilateral pulmonary edema as a consequence of capillary-alveolar leak and may be accompanied by fever and leukocytosis; however, this complication of heroin overdose has been described less frequently in recent years.[111] Starch can cause mild transient pulmonary granuloma formation, whereas cotton fibers from drug filters and talc (used as a filler) can cause permanent intravascular and perivascular granulomas in pulmonary arteries and arterioles.[112] The resultant baseline abnormalities of chest films and blood gases may cause diagnostic confusion in febrile IDUs. It has been noted that former IDUs have reductions in pulmonary function, especially in the diffusing capacity; however, after adjustment for the effects of cigarette smoking these differences were shown to be insignificant.[113] IDUs have a 10-fold increased risk of pneumonia as compared with nonaddicts.[114] The incidence of pneumonia is increased in IDUs for a number of reasons, including impaired clearance of secretions, aspiration, increased exposure, decreased immune function, and the higher prevalence of HIV infection. In a series of pulmonary complications of injection drug use, septic pulmonary emboli were the most common complication, followed by community-acquired pneumonia and *M. tuberculosis* infection.[115]

Most pulmonary infections are community-acquired episodes of pneumonia caused by common respiratory pathogens. In one series of febrile IDUs, pneumonia was the most common cause of fever[3]; in a second series, pneumonia was second only to cellulitis as a cause of fever in IDUs.[2] Bacterial pneumonia must be distinguished from septic emboli originating from right-sided endocarditis or more distal thrombophlebitis and resultant pulmonary infarcts. Septic emboli result in multiple round or wedge-shaped lesions that may cavitate (Fig. 309-2). Pleural involvement is common in both conditions and results in chest pain, pleural effusion, or empyema. Recurrent pulmonary emboli may also result in pulmonary hypertension. The usual pathogens

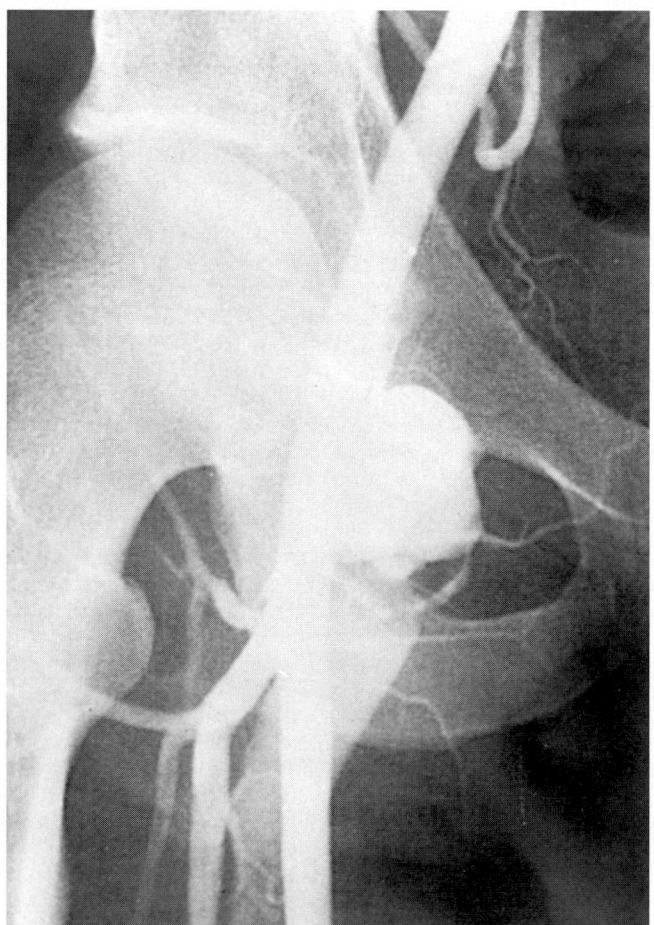

FIGURE 309-1. Arteriogram demonstrating a mycotic aneurysm of the right common iliac artery in an injection drug user.

in bacterial pneumonia include *Streptococcus pneumoniae* and oral anaerobes by the bronchogenic route, and *S. aureus* or, less commonly, *P. aeruginosa* by the hematogenous route. A recent study of the etiology of community-acquired pneumonia in an urban public hospital emphasized the importance of aspiration pneumonia in this patient population, particularly among patients with pneumonia necessitating admission to the intensive care unit.[116] A high incidence of bacterial pneumonia caused by *Haemophilus influenzae* has been described in IDUs with concomitant HIV infection.[117-120] Lung abscesses may arise from aspiration pneumonia, necrotizing pneumonitis, or septic emboli. Opportunistic pulmonary infections, especially *Pneumocystis jirovecii* pneumonia, must also be considered in febrile IDUs.

Pulmonary tuberculosis is a major problem in both HIV-infected and non–HIV-infected drug users. Homelessness and medication noncompliance further complicate the problem.[121] IDUs are also at increased risk of drug-resistant disease.[122] Tuberculosis is especially a problem in IDUs with underlying HIV infection. Tuberculosis in IDUs with AIDS is more frequently extrapulmonary, and patients present with less cavitary pulmonary disease and fewer acid-fast bacillus–positive organisms in sputum than other tuberculosis patients. IDUs with AIDS and pulmonary tuberculosis are just as capable of transmitting tuberculosis infection to their contacts as are tuberculosis patients without AIDS. Coughing induced by use of marijuana or crack cocaine may increase transmission of tuberculosis. HIV-negative IDUs should receive preventive therapy with isoniazid for 9 months if the tuberculin skin test reaction (TST) is equal to or larger than 10 mm. IDUs with HIV infection should receive preventive therapy as recommended for other HIV-infected persons—that is, if the TST is equal to or larger than 5 mm or if the patient is a close contact of persons who have active tuberculosis, regardless of skin test results or previous courses of chemoprophylaxis.[123] Some experts also recommend that TST-negative and anergic HIV-infected persons from risk groups (such as IDUs) or geographic areas with a high prevalence of *M. tuberculosis* infection receive preventive therapy; however, the efficacy of this approach has not been proven. The potential risk of isoniazid-induced hepatotoxicity in IDUs, who have a higher frequency of background hepatitis and who may also be abusing other hepatotoxic agents such as alcohol and cocaine, is a concern. However, a recent study of isoniazid preventive therapy in an IDU population with a HCV seroprevalence of 95% found that the risks of hepatotoxicity and isoniazid discontinuation were similar to those reported for populations with a lower prevalence of HCV.[124] Monetary incentives have been shown to be highly effective in increasing the return rates for TST reading and promoting adherence to a program of directly observed preventive therapy in IDUs.[125,126]

The febrile IDU with pulmonary infiltrates constitutes an enormous diagnostic challenge given the wide differential diagnosis, which includes noninfectious causes. Accordingly, initial treatment often involves multiple therapeutic agents to cover several pathogens, and empirical coverage for tuberculosis may be needed in critically ill patients.

HEPATITIS

Hepatitis has long been recognized as a complication of injection drug use. Dual addiction to alcohol and narcotics increases the difficulty of determining the cause of liver disease in this population. The combination of alcohol plus HBV or HCV infection results in more severe liver disease than either alone and is associated with more rapid acceleration to cirrhosis. Heroin itself is not known to be hepatotoxic, but cocaine can cause severe liver injury. Injection of sublingual buprenorphine, which is used as a substitution drug in the treatment of heroin addiction, has been reported to cause hepatitis.[127] Knowledge regarding risks and transmission of viral hepatitis among IDUs has been shown to be significantly lower than knowledge regarding risks and transmission of HIV.[128] The validity of self-reporting serostatus of hepatitis A, B, and C by IDUs is poor.[129]

IDUs currently account for 14% of cases of acute HBV in the United States.[130] Most acquire infection within the first few years of beginning injection drug use. Clinically apparent infection is uncommon, and most IDUs end up with a serologic pattern indicative of naturally acquired immunity. In the United States 60% to 80% of IDUs have serum antibody against hepatitis B surface antigen (HBsAg); however, only 5% to 10% become chronic carriers.[131,132] Spontaneous reactivation of chronic HBV infection has been described in IDUs, but the diagnosis may be difficult because the clinical presentation is indistinguishable from that of acute hepatitis and information on the patient's previous serologic status usually is unknown.[133,134] HIV-infected persons with HBV infection are more likely to become chronic carriers.[135] Although both HIV-seropositive and HIV-seronegative IDUs may have a suboptimal response to HBV vaccine,[136-138] vaccination is recommended for all IDUs who are without evidence of previous infection. IDUs who have isolated anti-HBV core antibody have been shown to have strong resistance to reinfection and do not need vaccination.[139] Three antiviral agents are now approved for the treatment of chronic liver disease caused by HBV, but currently there are limited data regarding the treatment of IDUs with chronic HBV.

Hepatitis delta virus (HDV) is a defective RNA virus that can replicate and cause hepatitis only in the presence of active HBV infection. HDV may be acquired along with HBV as a primary coinfection or as a superinfection in persons who are carriers of HBV. Because of the interdependent nature of the two viruses, immunity to HBV provides protection against HDV. In some areas where HBV is prevalent, HDV is also seen with relatively high frequency. In nonendemic areas, such as the United States, HDV infection is confined almost exclusively to

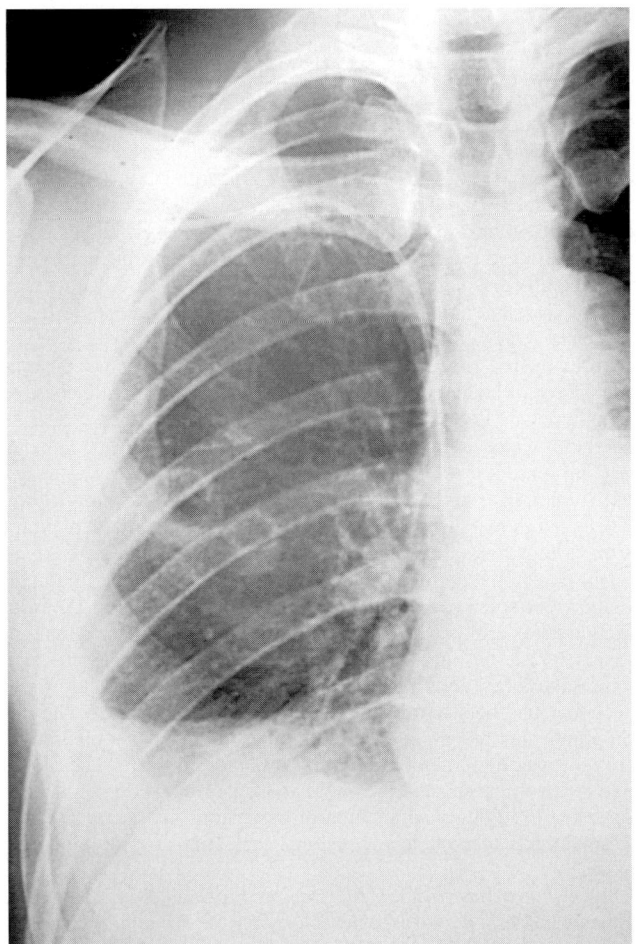

FIGURE 309-2. Anteroposterior radiograph of chest demonstrating pleural effusion and multiple cavitating nodular infarcts resulting from septic emboli in a patient with tricuspid endocarditis.

particular high-risk groups, such as IDUs.[140,141] The incidence of HDV in IDUs who are HBsAg carriers approaches 80%, but it is less than 10% in IDUs who have serum antibody to HBsAg.[142] The association of injection drug use with HBV and HDV was further clarified in a study comparing the transmission and carriage of each agent in two populations known to be at risk, IDUs and homosexuals.[143] Among 372 IDUs, 52.4% had evidence of current or past HBV infection; of these, 8.7% were chronic carriers of HBV. Among the chronic carriers, 70.6% were also chronic carriers of HDV. In contrast, only 27.4% of male homosexuals had serologic evidence of HBV infection (current or remote), of whom 7.9% were chronic carriers. Only a third of these chronic HBV carriers had evidence of HDV infection, a significant difference from the IDUs demonstrating that injection drug use is a much more efficient means of transmission of HDV infection than is sexual contact.

Superinfection of HDV on previous HBV infection is the most common pattern of dual infection.[140] Simultaneous acquisition of both viruses is more common among IDUs and is more likely to result in fulminant infection.[141] IDUs who experience coinfection frequently have a biphasic illness.[143] The initial phase of the disease is caused by HDV, and the second by HBV.[144] The closer the proximity of the biphasic peaks, the greater is the risk of a fatal outcome. IDUs who survive such an illness usually have a complete recovery and clear both viruses.[145] Prevention of HDV can be accomplished by vaccination of IDUs against HBV.

Intravenous drug use is a major risk factor for HCV infection. IDUs accounted for 42% of cases of community-acquired HCV infection in four Centers for Disease Control and Prevention sentinel centers in the United States.[146] The seroprevalence of anti-HCV antibody among IDUs ranges from 64% to 90%.[147] IDUs have become an important reservoir of HCV infection in the general population, and injection drug use is now considered the primary mode of HCV transmission in the United States. Maternal drug use, independent of HIV coinfection, has been identified as a major risk factor for perinatal transmission of HCV.[148] IDUs tend to acquire HCV after a brief interval of drug use.[149] Studies of HCV seroconversion among young IDUs have identified sharing of needles and drug preparation equipment, pooling money with another IDU to purchase drugs, requiring assistance to inject, and injecting cocaine more than once daily as independent risk factors for the acquisition of HCV.[150,151] Although injection drug use is more efficient at transmitting HCV infection than sexual activity, exchanging sex for money and having a sexual partner who uses injection drugs were also risk factors for seroconversion. Even if syringes are not shared, the sharing of equipment used to prepare drugs for injection, such as cookers and cotton filters, is a risk factor for the transmission of HCV.[152] Clearly, HCV education and prevention efforts must focus on newer IDUs.

Chronic HCV infection occurs in 60% to 80% of IDUs.[131] HIV coinfection appears to worsen the outcome of chronic HCV.[153] The first National Institutes of Health (NIH) Consensus Development Conference on HCV (1997) recommended that IDUs not be considered candidates for treatment of chronic HCV infection unless they had abstained from drug use for at least 6 months. Now that more effective therapies for chronic HCV infection are available, this approach has been questioned.[131] The most recent NIH Consensus Development Conference on HCV (2002) now recommends that active IDUs be considered for treatment on an individualized, case-by-case basis. A recent study of treatment for chronic HCV in active IDUs has demonstrated that treatment can be successful if combined with active treatment of drug addiction[154]; however, more studies are needed.

Hepatitis G virus (HGV) is a member of the Flaviviridae family, first described in 1995. The prevalence of HGV infection among IDUs differs by geographic areas, varying from 9.7% of long-term IDUs in Los Angeles[155] to 24% of IDUs in Japan,[156] 35% of long-term IDUs in Switzerland,[157] and 61.4% of IDUs in Italy.[158] Almost all persons with HGV infection in these studies were also infected with HCV. Although much about the epidemiology and natural history of HGV infection is currently unknown, several studies have failed to demonstrate an influence of HGV infection on HCV. HGV coinfection does not appear to alter the clinical or virologic course of infection with HCV (see Chapter 151).[159]

IDUs are also at risk for hepatitis A virus (HAV) infection. Although parenteral transmission of HAV has been reported in IDUs, other lifestyle factors are likely more important in explaining the increased risk of HAV in this population. Among IDUs in Baltimore, evidence of past HAV infection was not significantly associated with high-risk drug-using behaviors, but was associated with low annual income.[160] Fulminant hepatitis caused by HAV in IDUs with chronic liver disease caused by HBV and HCV has been reported.[161,162] Nonimmune IDUs should receive the HAV vaccine.

SPLENIC ABSCESS

Abscess of the spleen is a major complication of injection drug use. The splenic arteries are end arteries; any occlusion leads to ischemia or infarction. The ischemic or infarcted areas are highly susceptible to infection and serve as a nidus for abscess formation in the event of bacteremia. Trauma, including blunt trauma, also may lead to splenic injury and is an antecedent condition in some addicts who develop splenic abscess.[163] Endocarditis is the most common underlying infection in IDUs with splenic abscess,[163,164] although splenic involvement also may result from spread of local infection directly to the splenic artery or extension of an adjacent process with erosion and thrombosis of the splenic artery.[165]

Splenic lesions may be multiple and small or solitary, occasionally becoming large.[163-165] Lesions within the spleen are most often found in the upper pole (53.1%). Lower pole lesions (21.9%) and midspleen lesions (15.6%) are found less often.[165] Staphylococci and streptococci are the organisms most often implicated; however, gram-negative bacilli and anaerobes are isolated in approximately 25% and 5% of cases, respectively.[165] Addicts who lick their needles are susceptible to splenic abscesses caused by mouth anaerobes, in particular *Fusobacterium* spp.[166] *M. tuberculosis* has been reported as a cause of splenic abscess in HIV-infected IDUs.[167] Bacteremia is common in patients with splenic abscess, and usually the same organism is cultured from the blood and from the splenic cavity. However, addicts have a tendency to have multiple infected sites that contain different organisms. Therefore, isolation of an organism from the blood is not assurance that the same organism will be found in the spleen.[164]

The signs and symptoms of splenic abscess may be vague or overshadowed by underlying endocarditis. Almost all patients have fever and some degree of abdominal pain or discomfort.[163-165] Pleuritic chest pain is common.[163-165] Left shoulder pain has also been described. Abdominal tenderness, which is frequently confined to the left upper quadrant, is found in approximately 50% of patients.[163-165] Splenomegaly may be present, but a splenic rub is unusual.[163] Abnormalities within the thorax are detected in two thirds of cases, including one third with pleural effusion. The differential diagnosis includes subphrenic abscess, pulmonary empyema, perinephric abscess, and bland splenic infarct. The possibility of splenic abscess must always be excluded in IDUs with infective endocarditis who fail to clear their bacteremia or remain persistently febrile despite negative blood cultures. There are no characteristic laboratory abnormalities, although an extremely high leukocyte count has been correlated with a poor prognosis.[165] The chest radiograph may reveal an elevated hemidiaphragm or a pleural effusion; however, abdominal radiography is seldom useful. The most reliable diagnostic tests are ultrasound and CT of the abdomen,[163] which also define the extent and location of the lesions and hence are useful postoperatively to exclude any residual collections or intra-abdominal abscesses.

Splenectomy has traditionally been recommended for the treatment of splenic abscess. Removal of the spleen may be difficult if it adheres to adjacent structures; removal or partial resection of these organs may be required.[163-166] Successful percutaneous drainage of splenic abscess utilizing either ultrasound or CT guidance has increasingly been reported and should be considered, especially in cases with a solitary lesion.

The complications of splenic abscess include spontaneous rupture, which can be so subtle in some cases that the patient has no signs of generalized peritonitis or purulence in the abdominal cavity.[163] Other manifestations include recurrent bacteremia and intestinal obstruction.[165] Splenic abscess detected early and treated promptly results in a good prognosis.

CENTRAL NERVOUS SYSTEM INFECTIONS

IDUs may present with a variety of CNS manifestations that may or may not be infectious in origin. The differential diagnosis is extensive and frequently difficult. Complications related to the injection of illicit drugs include coma caused by overdose or intoxication, postanoxic encephalopathy, delirium, and acute confusion states. Seizures, cerebral edema, and dementia may result from noninfectious as well as infectious causes. Hemorrhage and infarction may be secondary to infection or compromise of the neurovascular system. Parkinsonism is most often the result of drug effects but has been reported in infection.[168] The etiology of these disorders may be obscure, necessitating a thorough workup to exclude an infectious cause. Infections of the CNS may be local or secondary to an infectious process elsewhere. When infection is the primary problem, there are usually focal findings and fever. When present, focal findings suggest the possibility of a mass lesion requiring immediate surgical intervention. Therefore, an IDU with neurologic findings requires a differential diagnosis that includes both infectious and noninfectious causes and an effort to differentiate between a local process and a complication of a distant primary infection.

CNS manifestations are more common in IDUs than in nonusers and are found in 45% to 58% of addicts with endocarditis.[169] In one study of IDUs with left-sided IE, CNS complications were found in 52% of patients with mitral valve infection but in only 28% of those with aortic valve disease.[88] Other investigators found a greater incidence in aortic valve disease, especially when *S. aureus* was involved and the patients had congestive heart failure.[170] Endocarditis, particularly when caused by *S. aureus* or *S. pneumoniae,*[171] is the most common cause of CNS disease in IDUs, and it also accounts for the most serious complications, including brain abscess, meningitis, encephalopathy, and hemorrhage from ruptured mycotic aneurysms.[13,172] Mycotic aneurysms may manifest as a progressive focal neurologic deficit resulting from expansion of the aneurysm or as an acute subarachnoid or intracerebral hemorrhage.[173] Prior to rupture patients may complain of severe localized headache. This should prompt immediate evaluation. CT adequately identifies mycotic aneurysms in most cases and may also be used to demonstrate brain abscess. Magnetic resonance angiography may be more effective, and, in one study, when combined with MRI, had a sensitivity of 86% and a specificity of 100% for aneurysms greater than 3 mm in diameter.[174] If a strong suspicion remains, a negative study should be followed by four-vessel cerebral angiography, which remains the definitive test. Even with a negative test, if symptoms persist, repeated angiography may reveal lesions that were not detected previously.

The management of cerebral mycotic aneurysms remains undefined. In some cases lesions resolve completely, or decrease in size, with antibiotic treatment alone. In other cases the lesion may enlarge or new aneurysms may appear. Surgery is important for control of ruptured aneurysms of peripheral arteries or when an intracranial location or masslike lesion occurs. Some authors recommend serial angiograms to assess the progress of aneurysms; others call for aggressive surgical management, especially if the lesion is accessible. When the patient's condition precludes surgery, an endovascular procedure to embolize the lesion may be advised.[175] The presence of multiple aneurysms might make a surgical approach impossible. In some of these cases patients do well with antimicrobial treatment, but each case must be individualized.[176]

Focal abnormalities also result from septic emboli (which frequently result in transient focal neurologic deficits) and multiple cerebral abscesses. These lesions tend to resolve in 1 to 2 weeks with appropriate antibiotic therapy.[13] IDUs also commonly develop a diffuse encephalopathy that may be due to bacteremia or injected toxins.

Localized CNS infection in this population is confined primarily to brain abscess and subdural empyema. Brain abscess is usually caused by pyogenic bacteria; *Nocardia* has also been reported. Fungi, including *Aspergillus* spp., *Chaetomium strumarium,* and mucormycosis, have also been reported. Mucormycosis in IDUs is rarely associated with HIV infection and presents as focal cerebritis or abscess, in contrast to the more extensive aggressive process observed in immunocompromised hosts. There may be a predilection for multifocal involvement and, in particular, involvement of the basal ganglia, with this region being affected far more often in addicts than in nonaddicts.[177] Cerebral mucormycosis is not caused by spread from sinuses. It appears the organism is either a contaminant in the illicit drugs or enters the blood stream from an infected injection site, finding its way to areas of the brain predisposed by earlier drug-induced injury. The patient usually presents with signs and symptoms of a mass lesion. The differential diagnosis of such lesions includes toxoplasmosis, lymphoma, tuberculosis, and cryptococcosis. Isolated involvement of the basal ganglia is uncommon in toxoplasmosis and lymphoma. Radiologic contrast enhancement may or may not be seen in patients with mucormycosis and therefore lends little to the diagnosis. Biopsy of the lesion is required to establish the diagnosis; failure to do so is associated with a very high mortality rate.[177] Remarkably, the outcome of this disease is very good, with survival in most cases after prolonged amphotericin B therapy and excision of as much of the infected tissue as possible.[168,178,179]

The clinical signs and symptoms of brain abscesses in IDUs are the same as in nonaddicts and depend on the location of the lesion within the brain. They usually result from infected cerebral emboli in patients with mitral or aortic valve endocarditis.[13,75,88,172] Rarely, emboli travel through or originate in the pulmonary circulation. Alternatively, pathogens may seed the brain after an inadvertent injection into the arterial system during an attempted jugular vein injection. Tuberculous brain abscesses may also be seen, particularly in IDUs who are coinfected with HIV. The lesions are typically solitary, multiloculated, and contrast enhancing. They must be distinguished from *Toxoplasma,* which usually causes multiple lesions that are not multiloculated, and lymphoma, which can be necrotic with multiple loculations but is more often located near an ependymal surface.[180] IDUs with HIV infection who have characteristic lesions may be treated empirically for toxoplasmosis, but failure to respond within 2 weeks should prompt a biopsy, which will lead to the correct diagnosis. Subdural empyema is also seen in IDUs and may be secondary to direct extension from a local infectious process or complicated bacteremia.

Meningitis in IDUs is most often secondary to endocarditis[172] and is usually due to *S. aureus* or *S. pneumoniae.*[169] However, abnormal CSF is common in patients with CNS complications of endocarditis. Findings in patients with meningitis include purulent CSF with a neutrophilic pleocytosis and elevated proteins, with normal or decreased glucose. A hemorrhagic CSF may also be found. A pattern consistent with aseptic meningitis is seen in 25% of cases; normal CSF is seen in only 30%.[169] Positive CSF cultures are seen in the minority of patients, most of whom have *S. aureus* infection and purulent CSF.

A spinal epidural abscess should be considered in any addict presenting with spinal ache or back pain, especially if there are focal neurologic signs. On occasion blunt trauma may predispose an area of the spine to infection following an episode of transient bacteremia.[181] Patients tend to have a prolonged symptomatic course, often as long as several months. Typically disease progresses from focal vertebral pain to root pain, neurologic deficits (motor or sensory), and finally paralysis. Fever is frequently absent. The thoracic or lumbar spine is most often involved, although cervical spine lesions are also seen. *S. aureus* is the most common cause, but other gram-positive and gram-negative organisms have been reported, occasionally in combination with other organisms. *M. tuberculosis* also causes spinal epidural abscess, and it too may be found in combination with other organisms,[182] making careful definition of the microbial etiology imperative. The pathophysiology is usually direct spread to the epidural space from adjacent disk or vertebral body infection or hematogenous dissemination from a distant focus of infection. In most cases immediate drainage relieves symptoms, although once a chronic condition ensues there may be nothing but granulation tissue, requiring multiple-level laminectomy to relieve pressure on the spinal cord.

Intramedullary spinal cord abscess has been reported in an IDU with symptoms resembling those of an epidural abscess. Myelography demonstrated cord enlargement that was confirmed to be a result of intramedullary pus. The infection was caused by *Pseudomonas cepacia* but failed to respond to antibiotic therapy to which the organism was susceptible in vitro.[183]

Toxin-mediated diseases, specifically wound botulism and tetanus, are being seen with increasing frequency among IDUs and must be considered in addicts who have neurologic symptoms. Epidemics of both tetanus and wound botulism have occurred in California,[184,185] and cases are likely to be found elsewhere. The patient with tetanus is likely to be a long-time user who has poor venous access and multiple skin lesions caused by failed attempts at intravenous injections or by skin-popping (intentional injection into the subcutaneous tissues). These lesions become colonized by multiple pathogens, including *Clostridium* spp. In the proper anaerobic environment toxin is generated and produces disease.[186] Among the patients from California who had tetanus, 89% were Hispanic Americans, which may be explained by a study finding that only 58% of Mexican Americans had protective levels of antibody to tetanus toxoid, compared with 73% of non-Hispanic whites.[184] Wound botulism in IDUs was first described in New York City in 1982. Subsequently, sporadic cases were reported from different locations. Since 1990, a dramatic increase in the number of wound botulism cases has occurred in California.[186] With rare exceptions, patients were IDUs who injected "black tar" heroin, a black, gummy form of the drug synthesized in Mexico and distributed widely throughout the western United States. Skin-popping of black tar heroin was the major risk factor for acquisition of wound botulism. The greatest risk was seen among heavy users, but disease also occurred in occasional subcutaneous or intramuscular injection users. Most likely the drug was contaminated during the dilution process, when substances were added to the heroin to increase the amount of the product and thereby increase the seller's profits. Wound botulism results from colonization of wounds by *Clostridium botulinum* with subsequent toxin production. Initially patients experience blurred vision or diplopia, dysarthria, and dysphagia, followed by descending muscle weakness and respiratory failure. The symptoms are similar to those of botulism in nonaddicts except that gastrointestinal symptoms are absent. Also, unlike nonaddicts, who usually have a dietary history to suggest the diagnosis, in IDUs the organism can usually be recovered from wound cultures. Frequently there is fever resulting from the associated wound infection. Serum assays for botulism toxin are rarely positive; administration of antitoxin, which is helpful only if given within the first 24 hours, must be done on the basis of a high index of suspicion, rather than after culture identification.[185,186]

Drug users were once the most common population in the United States to develop tetanus; now they account for only 40% of cases.[184] As noted previously, skin-popping plays a major role, providing the lesions with an environment conducive to toxin production. Skin-popping probably also accounts for the higher mortality rate in addicts than in nonaddicts. One proposed reason is that, because of the number and severity of skin lesions in addicts, there is greater opportunity for large amounts of toxin to be produced. In addition, an addict presenting with the typical symptoms of tetanus may be thought to be manifesting the effects of illicit drug toxicity, overdose, or drug withdrawal.[187] In view of the risk for tetanus associated with injection drug use, it is worthwhile to consider giving a tetanus booster to any addict who is being treated for any other condition unless the patient has been immunized recently.

OCULAR MANIFESTATIONS

Endophthalmitis is a common and serious complication of injection drug use.[188] Both fungal endophthalmitis and bacterial endophthalmitis are hematogenous in origin and frequently manifest as a complication of infective endocarditis. *Candida* is the most common fungal cause, and

endophthalmitis may also occur as part of a disseminated syndrome involving eyes, bone, and skin in heroin users. Symptoms include blurred vision, pain, and decreased visual acuity. White, cotton-like exudative lesions are found in the choroid and retina with vitreous haziness. Diagnosis requires a high index of suspicion, and because blood cultures are usually negative at the time of ocular symptoms, definitive diagnosis often involves vitreous sampling. The optimal therapy for *Candida* chorioretinitis is amphotericin B, though successes have been reported with fluconazole. If extension into the vitreous humor has occurred (i.e., endophthalmitis), then intravitreal amphotericin B with or without vitrectomy is frequently recommended (see Chapter 108).[188]

Aspergillus spp. are the second most common cause of fungal endophthalmitis in IDUs. As with *Candida,* the pathogenesis reflects mycotic contamination of drug paraphernalia or of the heroin injected, rather than host immunosuppression. Physical findings and treatment are similar to those of *Candida* infection.[189]

Bacterial endophthalmitis is less common, and the presentation is often acute with rapid progression of symptoms. Inflammation usually is present in the anterior and posterior chambers. In addition to pain, redness, and lid swelling, flame-shaped hemorrhages and cotton-wool spots may be present. *S. aureus* is the organism most frequently isolated. A rapidly destructive form of endophthalmitis has been reported for *Bacillus cereus,* which has been cultured from heroin and drug paraphernalia.[189] Bacterial endophthalmitis is treated primarily with intravitreal antimicrobials with or without vitrectomy, though the role of systemic antibiotics continues to be debated (see Chapter 108). In both mycotic and bacterial endophthalmitis, early diagnosis and intervention increase the chance of a favorable outcome. Whereas bacterial endophthalmitis is rare, ocular peripheral emboli are frequent complications of infective endocarditis in the IDU. These include conjunctival and retinal emboli (Roth's spots), which manifest as petechiae, retinal hemorrhage, ischemia, and papilledema.

ACQUIRED IMMUNODEFICIENCY SYNDROME

Early in the AIDS epidemic, injection drug use was identified as being associated with a high risk of contracting the disease. IDUs account for 25% of the reported adult cases of AIDS in the United States—22% of males and 41% of females. In addition, sexual contact with IDUs accounts for a significant number of cases among persons whose primary risk is heterosexual contact; in particular, HIV-infected women, regardless of their source of infection, may transmit the infection to their offspring. Among street-recruited IDUs in San Francisco, the two subpopulations with the highest risk for HIV infection were persons under 30 years of age and men who had sex with men.[190] Clearly sharing of injection apparatus accounts for only a part of the HIV risk among IDUs. A survey of 22 shooting galleries in Miami found that 50% provided rooms for sexual activity for an additional fee.[191] Needle exchange programs have been shown to be an effective means of reducing the incidence of new HIV infections. These programs often offer counseling regarding risk reduction and acute care services in addition to sterile injection equipment. Participation in needle exchange programs has been shown to reduce emergency department utilization among IDUs and promote entry into formal drug treatment programs.[192,193] In many states, needles and syringes are available for sale without prescription in retail pharmacies. Providing access to sterile injection equipment through needle exchange or unrestricted retail sale remains controversial. Although it has been demonstrated that disinfection of injection equipment with household bleach can reduce the recovery of HIV virus from contaminated injection equipment, self-reported use of bleach disinfection has not been shown to be protective in cohort studies of IDUs.

Cohort studies have failed to demonstrate any difference in the rate of progression to AIDS among IDUs, men who have sex with men, and heterosexuals.[194] HIV-infected IDUs appear to be at substantial risk for pre-AIDS morbidity and mortality from bacterial infections The availability of highly active antiretroviral therapy (HAART) has increased the disease-free survival of HIV-infected IDUs, but not to as great an extent as non-IDUs.[195] Active IDUs on HAART are less likely to achieve maximal HIV RNA suppression; however, former IDUs have virologic response rates similar to those of nondrug users.[196] Current drug use has been associated with nonadherence to antiretroviral therapy. The medical management of HIV-infected IDUs must incorporate the diagnosis and treatment of substance abuse.

OTHER SEXUALLY TRANSMITTED DISEASES

A major contributing factor to the prevalence of STDs is unsafe sexual practices associated with the use of illicit drugs.[197] Among almost 3000 active IDUs in Baltimore, 60% reported a history of a STD; 24.1% were HIV seropositive.[198] Among patients evaluated at a STD clinic, those who reported heavy drug use (including alcohol) were more likely to report high-risk sexual practices and to have HIV infection or syphilis than those who used drugs less frequently.[199] Interestingly, the use of alcohol among drug users appears to be more strongly associated with risky sexual behavior than risky injection practices.[200] In a large cohort of female IDUs in Vancouver, condoms were rarely used with regular partners, but were more likely to be used with casual partners and paying partners.[201] Over half of the women in the cohort reported more than 100 lifetime sexual partners. Another study of female IDUs found that those who trade sex for drugs are less likely to use condoms than those who trade sex for money.[202]

Risk factors for syphilis among IDUs include recent initiation of injection drug use, injecting with other people, and injecting in public places.[203] The diagnosis and treatment of syphilis in IDUs may be complicated by the high rate of biologic false-positive, nonspecific serologic screening tests. In a study of IDUs in Baltimore, only 46% of reactive rapid plasma reagent tests could be confirmed as indicative of past or present syphilis using a reactive fluorescent treponemal antibody absorption test. Biologic false-positive tests were more common among heterosexual than among homosexual or bisexual IDUs.[204]

Given the importance of STDs as cofactors in the sexual transmission of HIV in both men who have sex with men and heterosexuals, reducing the prevalence of STDs in IDUs is an additional strategy to diminish the spread of HIV among IDUs and from them to their non–drug-using sexual contacts.

REFERENCES

1. Hopper JA, Shafi T. Management of the hospitalized injection drug user. Infect Dis Clin North Am. 2002;16:571-587.
2. Samet JH, Shevitz A, Fowle J, et al. Hospitalization decision in febrile intravenous drug users. Am J Med. 1990;89:53-57.
3. Marantz PR, Linzer M, Feiner CJ, et al. Inability to predict diagnosis in febrile intravenous drug abusers. Ann Intern Med. 1987;106:823-828.
4. Peterson PK, Sharp B, Gekker G, et al. Opioid-mediated suppression of interferon-gamma production by cultured peripheral blood mononuclear cells. J Clin Invest. 1987;80:824-831.
5. Alonzo NC, Bayer BM. Opioids, immunology, and host defenses of intravenous drug abusers. Infect Dis Clin North Am. 2002;16:553-569.
6. Brown SM, Stimmel B, Taub RN, et al. Immunologic dysfunction in heroin addicts. Arch Intern Med. 1974;134:1001-1006.
7. Novick DM, Ochshorn M, Ghali V, et al. Natural killer cell activity and lymphocyte subsets in parenteral heroin abusers and long-term methadone maintenance patients. J Pharmacol Exp Ther. 1989;250:606-610.
8. Stoll-Keller F, Schmitt C, Thumann C, et al. Effects of morphine on purified human blood monocytes: Modifications of properties involved in antiviral defences. Int J Immunopharmacol. 1997;19:95-100.
9. Guo CJ, Li Y, Tian S, et al. Morphine enhances HIV infection of human blood mononuclear phagocytes through modulation of beta-chemokines and CCR5 receptor. J Investig Med. 2002;50:435-442.
10. Organ CH Jr. Surgical procedures upon the drug addict. Surg Gynecol Obstet. 1972;134:947-952.
11. Orangio GR, Pitlick SD, Della Latta P, et al. Soft tissue infections in parenteral drug abusers. Ann Surg. 1984;199:97-100.
12. Vlahov D, Sullivan M, Astemborski J, et al. Bacterial infections and skin cleaning prior to injection among intravenous drug users. Public Health Rep. 1992;107:595-598.
13. Levine DP, Crane LR, Zervos MJ. Bacteremia in narcotic addicts at the Detroit Medical Center. II. Infectious endocarditis: A prospective comparative study. Rev Infect Dis. 1986;8:374-396.
14. Crane LR, Levine DP, Zervos MJ, et al. Bacteremia in narcotic addicts at the Detroit Medical Center. I. Microbiology, epidemiology, risk factors, and empiric therapy. Rev Infect Dis. 1986;8:364-373.
15. Centers for Disease Control and Prevention. Soft tissue infections among injection drug users—San Francisco, California, 1996-2000. MMWR Morb Mortal Wkly Rep. 2001;50:381-384.
16. Binswanger IA, Kral AH, Bluthenthal RN, et al. High prevalence of abscesses and cellulitis among community-recruited injection drug users in San Francisco. Clin Infect Dis. 2000;30:579-581.
17. Zamora-Quezada JC, Dinerman H, Stadecker MJ, et al. Muscle and skin infarction after free-basing cocaine (crack). Ann Intern Med. 1988;108:564-566.
18. Cregler LL, Mark H. Medical complications of cocaine abuse. N Engl J Med. 1986;315:1495-1500.
19. Risdahl JM, Khanna KV, Peterson PK, Molitor TW. Opiates and infection. J Neuroimmunol. 1998;83:4-18.
20. Spijkerman IJ, van Ameijden EJ, Mientjes GH, et al. Human immunodeficiency virus infection and other risk factors for skin abscesses and endocarditis among injection drug users. J Clin Epidemiol. 1996;49:1149-1154.
21. Henriksen BM, Albrektsen SB, Simper LB, Gutschik E. Soft tissue infections from drug abuse: A clinical and microbiological review of 145 cases. Acta Orthop Scand. 1994;65:625-628.
22. Schnall SB, Holtom PD, Lilley JC. Abscesses secondary to parenteral abuse of drugs: A study of demographic and bacteriological characteristics. J Bone Joint Surg Am. 1994;76:1526-1530.
23. Hoeger PH, Haupt G, Hoelzle E. Acute multifocal skin necrosis: Synergism between invasive streptococcal infection and cocaine-induced tissue ischaemia? Acta Derm Venereol. 1996;76:239-241.
24. Murphy EL, DeVita D, Liu H, et al. Risk factors for skin and soft-tissue abscesses among injection drug users: A case-control study. Clin Infect Dis. 2001;33:35-40.
25. Tom MB, Rice DH. Presentation and management of neck abscess: A retrospective analysis. Laryngoscope. 1988;98(8 Pt 1):877-880.
26. Hillstrom RP, Cohn AM, McCarroll KA. Vocal cord paralysis resulting from neck injections in the intravenous drug use population. Laryngoscope. 1990;100:503-506.
27. Hemingway DM, Balfour AE, McCartney AC, et al. Streptococcus milleri and complex groin abscesses in intravenous drug abusers. Scott Med J. 1992;37:116-117.
28. Talan DA, Summanen PH, Finegold SM. Ampicillin/sulbactam and cefoxitin in the treatment of cutaneous and other soft-tissue abscesses in patients with or without histories of injection drug abuse. Clin Infect Dis. 2000;31:464-471.
29. Whittiker DM. A fatal case of toxic shock associated with group A streptococcal cellulitis. J Am Board Fam Pract. 1992;5:523-526.
30. Bergstein JM, Baker EJ, Aprahamian C, et al. Soft tissue abscesses associated with parenteral drug abuse: Presentation, microbiology, and treatment. Am Surg. 1995;61:1105-1108.
31. Alcantara AL, Tucker RB, McCarroll KA. Radiologic study of injection drug use complications. Infect Dis Clin North Am. 2002;16:713-743, ix-x.
32. Towers JD. The use of intravenous contrast in MRI of extremity infection. Semin Ultrasound CT MR. 1997;18:269-275.
33. Wallace JR, Lucas CE, Ledgerwood AM. Social, economic, and surgical anatomy of a drug-related abscess. Am Surg. 1986;52:398-401.
34. Simmen HP, Giovanoli P, Battaglia H, et al. Soft tissue infections of the upper extremities with special consideration of abscesses in parenteral drug abusers: A prospective study. J Hand Surg Br. 1995;20:797-800.
35. Pieper B. A retrospective analysis of venous ulcer healing in current and former users of injected drugs. J Wound Ostomy Continence Nurs. 1996;23:291-296.
36. Pieper B, Rossi R, Templin T. Pain associated with venous ulcers in injecting drug users. Ostomy Wound Manage. 1998;44:54-58, 60-67.
37. Dow G, Browne A, Sibbald RG. Infection in chronic wounds: Controversies in diagnosis and treatment. Ostomy Wound Manage. 1999;45:23-27, 29-40.
38. Gonzalez MH, Kay T, Weinzweig N, et al. Necrotizing fasciitis of the upper extremity. J Hand Surg Am. 1996;21:689-692.
39. Callahan TE, Schecter WP, Horn JK. Necrotizing soft tissue infection masquerading as cutaneous abscess following illicit drug injection. Arch Surg. 1998;133:812-817; discussion 817-819.
40. Wysoki MG, Santora TA, Shah RM, Friedman AC. Necrotizing fasciitis: CT characteristics. Radiology. 1997;203:859-863.
41. Falasca GF, Reginato AJ. The spectrum of myositis and rhabdomyolysis associated with bacterial infection. J Rheumatol. 1994;21:1932-1937.
42. Chen JL, Fullerton KE, Flynn NM. Necrotizing fasciitis associated with injection drug use. Clin Infect Dis. 2001;33:6-15.
43. Sudarsky LA, Laschinager JC, Coppa GF, et al. Improved results from a standardized approach in treating patients with necrotizing fasciitis. Ann Surg. 1987;206:661-665.
44. Centers for Disease Control and Prevention. Unexplained illness and death among injecting-drug users-Glasgow, Scotland; Dublin, Ireland; and England, April-June 2000. MMWR Morb Mortal Wkly Rep. 2000;49:489-492.
45. Lo TS, Mooers MG, Wright LJ. Pyomyositis complicating acute bacterial endocarditis in an intravenous drug user. N Engl J Med. 2000;342:1614-1615.
46. Prahlow JA, Cappellari JO, Washburn SA. Uterine pyomyoma as a complication of pregnancy in an intravenous drug user. South Med J. 1996;89:892-895.
47. Grau LE, Arevalo S, Catchpool C, Heimer R. Expanding harm reduction services through a wound and abscess clinic. Am J Public Health. 2002;92:1915-1917.
48. Chandrasekar PH, Narula AP. Bone and joint infections in intravenous drug abusers. Rev Infect Dis. 1986;8:904-911.
49. Munoz-Fernandez S, Macia MA, Pantoja ML, et al. Osteoarticular infection in intravenous drug abusers: Influence of HIV infection and differences with non drug abusers. Ann Rheum Dis. 1993;52:570-574.
50. Swisher LA, Roberts JR, Glynn MJ. Needle licker's osteomyelitis. Am J Emerg Med. 1994;12:343-346.

51. Miller DJ, Mejicano GC. Vertebral osteomyelitis due to *Candida* species: Case report and literature review. Clin Infect Dis. 2001;33:523-530.

52. Sapico FL, Montgomerie JZ. Vertebral osteomyelitis in intravenous drug abusers: Report of three cases and review of the literature. Rev Infect Dis. 1980;2:196-206.

53. Kak V, Chandrasekar PH. Bone and joint infections in injection drug users. Infect Dis Clin North Am. 2002;16:681-695.

54. Pastan RS, Silverman SL, Goldenberg DL. A musculoskeletal syndrome in intravenous heroin users: Association with brown heroin. Ann Intern Med. 1977;87:22-29.

55. Watanakunakorn C, Burkert T. Infective endocarditis at a large community teaching hospital, 1980-1990: A review of 210 episodes. Medicine (Baltimore). 1993;72:90-102.

56. Weisse AB, Heller DR, Schimenti RJ, et al. The febrile parenteral drug user: A prospective study in 121 patients. Am J Med. 1993;94:274-280.

57. Baddour LM. Twelve-year review of recurrent native-valve infective endocarditis: A disease of the modern antibiotic era. Rev Infect Dis. 1988;10:1163-1170.

58. Manoff SB, Vlahov D, Herskowitz A, et al. Human immunodeficiency virus infection and infective endocarditis among injecting drug users. Epidemiology. 1996;7:566-570.

59. Mathew J, Addai T, Anand A, et al. Clinical features, site of involvement, bacteriologic findings, and outcome of infective endocarditis in intravenous drug users. Arch Intern Med. 1995;155:1641-1648.

60. Reyes MP, Palutke WA, Wylin RF, et al. *Pseudomonas* endocarditis in the Detroit Medical Center, 1969-1972. Medicine (Baltimore). 1973;52:173-194.

61. Shekar R, Rice TW, Zierot CH, et al. Outbreak of endocarditis caused by Pseudomonas aeruginosa serotype O11 among pentazocine and tripelennamine abusers in Chicago. J Infect Dis. 1985;151:203-208.

62. Mills J, Drew D. *Serratia marcescens* endocarditis: A regional illness associated with intravenous drug abuse. Ann Intern Med. 1976;84:29-35.

63. Cooper R, Mills J. Serratia endocarditis: A follow-up report. Arch Intern Med. 1980;140:199-202.

64. Pierrotti LC, Baddour LM. Fungal endocarditis, 1995-2000. Chest. 2002;122:302-310.

65. Petrosillo N, Pellicelli AM, Cicalini S, et al. Endocarditis caused by *Aspergillus* species in injection drug users. Clin Infect Dis. 2001;33:E97-E99.

66. Adler AG, Blumberg EA, Schwartz DA, et al. Seven-pathogen tricuspid endocarditis in an intravenous drug abuser: Pitfalls in laboratory diagnosis. Chest. 1991;99:490-491.

67. Szabo S, Lieberman JP, Lue YA. Unusual pathogens in narcotic-associated endocarditis. Rev Infect Dis. 1990;12:412-415.

68. Tuazon CU, Sheagren JN. Staphylococcal endocarditis in parenteral drug abusers: Source of the organism. Ann Intern Med. 1975;82:788-790.

69. Dressler FA, Roberts WC. Infective endocarditis in opiate addicts: Analysis of 80 cases studied at necropsy. Am J Cardiol. 1989;63:1240-1257.

70. Graves MK, Soto L. Left-sided endocarditis in parenteral drug abusers: Recent experience at a large community hospital. South Med J. 1992;85:378-380.

71. Frontera JA, Gradon JD. Right-side endocarditis in injection drug users: Review of proposed mechanisms of pathogenesis. Clin Infect Dis. 2000;30:374-379.

72. El-Khatib MR, Wilson FM, Lerner AM. Characteristics of bacterial endocarditis in heroin addicts in Detroit. Am J Med Sci. 1976;271:197-201.

73. Wilson LE, Thomas DL, Astemborski J, et al. Prospective study of infective endocarditis among injection drug users. J Infect Dis. 2002;185:1761-1766.

74. Stimmel B, Donoso E, Dack S. Comparison of infective endocarditis in drug addicts and nondrug users. Am J Cardiol. 1973;32:924-929.

75. Chambers HF, Korzeniowski OM, Sande MA. *Staphylococcus aureus* endocarditis: Clinical manifestations in addicts and nonaddicts. Medicine (Baltimore). 1983;62:170-177.

76. Corzo JE, de Leon FL, Gomez-Mateos J, et al. Pneumothorax secondary to septic pulmonary emboli in tricuspid endocarditis. Thorax. 1992;47:1080-1081.

77. Roberts JH, Aponte V, Naidich DP, et al. Myocardial abscess resulting in a pseudoaneurysm: Case report. Cardiovasc Intervent Radiol. 1991;14:307-310.

78. Sapico FL, Liquete JA, Sarma RJ. Bone and joint infections in patients with infective endocarditis: Review of a 4-year experience. Clin Infect Dis. 1996;22:783-787.

79. Li JS, Sexton DJ, Mick N, et al. Proposed modifications to the Duke criteria for the diagnosis of infective endocarditis. Clin Infect Dis. 2000;30:633-638.

80. Palepu A, Cheung SS, Montessori V, et al. Factors other than the Duke criteria associated with infective endocarditis among injection drug users. Clin Invest Med. 2002;25:118-125.

81. Young GP, Hedges JR, Dixon L, et al. Inability to validate a predictive score for infective endocarditis in intravenous drug users. J Emerg Med. 1993;11:1-7.

82. Rothman RE, Walker T, Majmudar M, et al. Criteria for the diagnosis of infective endocarditis (IE) in febrile intravenous drug users: A new gold standard for the acute care setting (Abstract 38). In: Proceedings of the 7th International Symposium on Modern Concepts in Endocarditis and Cardiovascular Infections, Chamonix Mont Blanc, France, 2003.

83. Rothman RE, Walker T, Weiss JL, et al. Diagnostic importance of transthoracic echocardiography (TTE) in febrile intravenous drug users (IDUs) at risk for infective endocarditis (IE): Is there a role for ultrasound in the emergency department (ED)? (Poster 66). In: Proceedings of the 7th International Symposium on Modern Concepts in Endocarditis and Cardiovascular Infections, Chamonix Mont Blanc, France, 2003.

84. Rothman RE, Majmudar MD, Kelen GD, et al. Detection of bacteremia in emergency department patients at risk for infective endocarditis using universal 16S rRNA primers in a decontaminated polymerase chain reaction assay. J Infect Dis. 2002;186:1677-1681.

85. Pazin GJ, Saul S, Thompson ME. Blood culture positivity: Suppression by outpatient antibiotic therapy in patients with bacterial endocarditis. Arch Intern Med. 1982;142:263-268.

86. Levine DP, Fromm BS, Reddy BR. Slow response to vancomycin or vancomycin plus rifampin in methicillin-resistant *Staphylococcus aureus* endocarditis. Ann Intern Med. 1991;115:674-680.

87. Korzeniowski O, Sande MA. Combination antimicrobial therapy for Staphylococcus aureus endocarditis in patients addicted to parenteral drugs and in nonaddicts: A prospective study. Ann Intern Med. 1982;97:496-503.

88. Pruitt AA, Rubin RH, Karchmer AW, et al. Neurologic complications of bacterial endocarditis. Medicine (Baltimore). 1978;57:329-343.

89. Brown PD, Levine DP. Infective endocarditis in the injection drug user. Infect Dis Clin North Am. 2002;16:645-665, viii-ix.

90. Markowitz N, Quinn EL, Saravolatz LD. Trimethoprim-sulfamethoxazole compared with vancomycin for the treatment of *Staphylococcus aureus* infection. Ann Intern Med. 1992;117:390-398.

91. Chambers HF, Miller RT, Newman MD. Right-sided *Staphylococcus aureus* endocarditis in intravenous drug abusers: Two-week combination therapy. Ann Intern Med. 1988;109:619-624.

92. Ribera E, Gomez-Jimenez J, Cortes E, et al. Effectiveness of cloxacillin with and without gentamicin in short-term therapy for right-sided *Staphylococcus aureus* endocarditis: A randomized, controlled trial. Ann Intern Med. 1996;125:969-974.

93. Heldman AW, Hartert TV, Ray SC, et al. Oral antibiotic treatment of right-sided staphylococcal endocarditis in injection drug users: Prospective randomized comparison with parenteral therapy. Am J Med. 1996;101:68-76.

94. Reyes MP, Brown WJ, Lerner AM. Treatment of patients with *Pseudomonas* endocarditis with high dose aminoglycoside and carbenicillin therapy. Medicine (Baltimore). 1978;57:57-67.

95. Reyes MP, El-Khatib MR, Brown WJ, et al. Synergy between carbenicillin and an aminoglycoside (gentamicin or tobramycin) against *Pseudomonas aeruginosa* isolated from patients with endocarditis and sensitivity of isolates to normal human serum. J Infect Dis. 1979;140:192-202.

96. Wieland M, Lederman MM, Kline-King C, et al. Left-sided endocarditis due to *Pseudomonas aeruginosa*: A report of 10 cases and review of the literature. Medicine (Baltimore). 1986;65:180-189.

97. Daikos GL, Kathpalia SB, Lolans VT. Long-term oral ciprofloxacin: Experience in the treatment of incurable infective endocarditis. Am J Med. 1988;84:786-790.

98. Libertin CR, McKinley KM. Gentamicin-resistant enterococcal endocarditis: The need for routine screening for high-level resistance to aminoglycosides. South Med J. 1990;83:458-460.

99. Hecht SR, Berger M. Right-sided endocarditis in intravenous drug users: Prognostic features in 102 episodes. Ann Intern Med. 1992;117:560-566.

100. Mathew J, Abreo G, Namburi K, et al. Results of surgical treatment for infective endocarditis in intravenous drug users. Chest. 1995;108:73-77.

101. Lemma M, Vanelli P, Beretta L, et al. Cardiac surgery in HIV-positive intravenous drug addicts: Influence of cardiopulmonary bypass on the progression to AIDS. Thorac Cardiovasc Surg. 1992;40:279-282.

102. Frater RW. Surgical management of endocarditis in drug addicts and long-term results. J Card Surg. 1990;5:63-67.

103. Monsuez JJ, Vittecoq D, Acar C, et al. Recurrent infective endocarditis one year after mitral repair in a woman addicted to drugs. J Thorac Cardiovasc Surg. 1997;114:864-866.

104. Benitez PR, Newell MA. Vascular trauma in drug abuse: Patterns of injury. Ann Vasc Surg. 1986;1:175-181.

105. Yeager RA, Hobson RW, Padberg FT, et al. Vascular complications related to drug abuse. J Trauma. 1987;27:305-308.

106. Reddy DJ, Smith RF, Elliott JP Jr, et al. Infected femoral artery false aneurysms in drug addicts: Evolution of selective vascular reconstruction. J Vasc Surg. 1986;3:718-724.

107. McIlroy MA, Reddy D, Markowitz N, et al. Infected false aneurysms of the femoral artery in intravenous drug addicts. Rev Infect Dis. 1989;11:578-585.

108. Tsao JW, Marder SR, Goldstone J, Bloom AI. Presentation, diagnosis, and management of arterial mycotic pseudoaneurysms in injection drug users. Ann Vasc Surg. 2002;16:652-662.

109. Shetty PC, Kasicky GA, Sharma RP, et al. Mycotic aneurysms in intravenous drug abusers: The utility of intravenous digital subtraction angiography. Radiology. 1985;155:319-321.

110. Cherubin CE. Infectious disease problems of narcotic addicts. Arch Intern Med. 1971;128:309-313.

111. Sporer KA. Acute heroin overdose. Ann Intern Med. 1999;130:584-590.

112. Pare JA, Fraser RG, Hagg JC, et al. Pulmonary "mainline" granulomatosis: Talcosis of intravenous methadone abuse. Medicine (Baltimore). 1979;58:229-239.

113. Miller A, Taub H, Spinak A, et al. Lung function in former intravenous drug abusers: The effect of ubiquitous cigarette smoking. Am J Med. 1991;90:678-684.

114. Hind CR. Pulmonary complications of intravenous drug misuse. 2. Infective and HIV related complications. Thorax. 1990;45:957-961.

115. O'Donnell AE, Pappas LS. Pulmonary complications of intravenous drug abuse: Experience at an inner-city hospital. Chest. 1988;94:251-253.

116. Park DR, Sherbin VL, Goodman MS, et al. The etiology of community-acquired pneumonia at an urban public hospital: Influence of human immunodeficiency virus infection and initial severity of illness. J Infect Dis. 2001;184:268-277.

117. Casadevall A, Dobrozycki J, Small C, et al. *Haemophilus influenzae* type B bacteremia in adults with AIDS and at risk for AIDS. Am J Med. 1992;92:587-590.

118. Polsky B, Gold JW, Whimsbey E, et al. Bacterial pneumonia in patients with the acquired immunodeficiency syndrome. Ann Intern Med. 1986;104:38-41.

119. Schlamm HT, Yancovitz SR. *Haemophilus influenzae* pneumonia in young adults with AIDS, ARC, or risk of AIDS. Am J Med. 1989;86:11-14.

120. Witt DJ, Craven DE, McCabe WR. Bacterial infections in adult patients with the acquired immune deficiency syndrome (AIDS) and AIDS-related complex. Am J Med. 1987;82:900-906.

121. Pitchenik AE, Fertel D, Bloch AB. Mycobacterial disease: Epidemiology, diagnosis, treatment, and prevention. Clin Chest Med. 1988;9:425-441.

122. Frieden TR, Sterling T, Pablos-Mendez A, et al. The emergence of drug-resistant tuberculosis in New York City. N Engl J Med. 1993;328:521-526.

123. Masur H, Kaplan JE, Holmes KK. Guidelines for preventing opportunistic infections among HIV-infected persons—2002: Recommendations of the U.S. Public Health Service and the Infectious Diseases Society of America. Ann Intern Med. 2002;137 (5 Pt 2):435-478.

124. Sadaphal P, Astemborski J, Graham NM, et al. Isoniazid preventive therapy, hepatitis C virus infection, and hepatotoxicity among injection drug users infected with *Mycobacterium tuberculosis*. Clin Infect Dis. 2001;33:1687-1691.

125. Malotte CK, Hollingshead JR, Rhodes F. Monetary versus nonmonetary incentives for TB skin test reading among drug users. Am J Prev Med. 1999;16:182-188.

126. Lorvick J, Thompson S, Edlin BR, et al. Incentives and accessibility: A pilot study to promote adherence to TB prophylaxis in a high-risk community. J Urban Health. 1999;76:461-467.

127. Berson A, Gervais A, Cazals D, et al. Hepatitis after intravenous buprenorphine misuse in heroin addicts. J Hepatol. 2001;34:346-350.

128. Heimer R, Clair S, Grau LE, et al. Hepatitis-associated knowledge is low and risks are high among HIV-aware injection drug users in three US cities. Addiction. 2002;97:1277-1287.

129. Schlicting EG, Johnson ME, Brems C, et al. Validity of injecting drug users' self report of hepatitis A, B, and C. Clin Lab Sci. 2003;16:99-106.

130. Goldstein ST, Alter MJ, Williams IT, et al. Incidence and risk factors for acute hepatitis B in the United States, 1982-1998: Implications for vaccination programs. J Infect Dis. 2002;185:713-719.

131. Lemberg BD, Shaw-Stiffel TA. Hepatic disease in injection drug users. Infect Dis Clin North Am. 2002;16:667-679.

132. Murrill CS, Weeks H, Castrucci BC, et al. Age-specific seroprevalence of HIV, hepatitis B virus, and hepatitis C virus infection among injection drug users admitted to drug treatment in 6 US cities. Am J Public Health. 2002;92:385-387.

133. Davis GL, Hoofnagle JH. Reactivation of chronic type B hepatitis presenting as acute viral hepatitis. Ann Intern Med. 1985;102:762-765.

134. Davis GL, Hoofnagle JH, Waggoner JG. Spontaneous reactivation of chronic hepatitis B virus infection. Gastroenterology. 1984;86:230-235.

135. Thio CL. Hepatitis B in the human immunodeficiency virus-infected patient: Epidemiology, natural history, and treatment. Semin Liver Dis. 2003;23:125-136.

136. Piot P, Goilav C, Kegels E. Hepatitis B: Transmission by sexual contact and needle sharing. Vaccine. 1990;8(Suppl):S37-S40; discussion S41-S3.

137. Rumi M, Colombo M, Romeo R, et al. Suboptimal response to hepatitis B vaccine in drug users. Arch Intern Med. 1991;151:574-578.

138. Lugoboni F, Migliozzi S, Schiesasi F. Immunoresponse to hepatitis B vaccination and adherence campaign among injecting drug users. Vaccine. 1997;15:1014-1016.

139. Quaglio G, Lugoboni F, Vento S, et al. Isolated presence of antibody to hepatitis B core antigen in injection drug users: Do they need to be vaccinated? Clin Infect Dis. 2001;32:E143-E144.

140. De Cock KM, Govindarajin S, Chin KP, et al. Delta hepatitis in the Los Angeles area: A report of 126 cases. Ann Intern Med. 1986;105:108-114.

141. Lettau LA, McCarthy JG, Smith MH, et al. Outbreak of severe hepatitis due to delta and hepatitis B viruses in parenteral drug abusers and their contacts. N Engl J Med. 1987;317:1256-1262.

142. Ponzetto A, Seef LB, Buskell-Bales Z, et al. Hepatitis B markers in United States drug addicts with special emphasis on the delta hepatitis virus. Hepatology. 1984;4:1111-1115.

143. Smith HM, Alexander GJM, Webb G, et al. Hepatitis B and delta virus infection among "at risk" populations in south east London. J Epidemiol Community Health. 1992;46:144-147.

144. Shattock AG, Kelly MG, Fielding J, Arthurs Y. Epidemic hepatitis B with delta-antigenaemia among Dublin drug-abusers. Ir J Med Sci. 1982;151:334-338.

145. Bonino F, Smedile A. Delta agent (type D) hepatitis. Semin Liver Dis. 1986;6:28-33.

146. Alter M. Epidemiology of community-acquired hepatitis C. In: Hollinger FB, Lemon SM, Margolis HS, eds. Viral Hepatitis and Liver Disease. Baltimore: Williams & Wilkins; 1991:410-413.

147. Novick DM, Reagan KJ, Croxson TS, et al. Hepatitis C virus serology in parenteral drug users with chronic liver disease. Addiction. 1997;92:167-171.

148. Resti M, Azzari C, Galli L, et al. Maternal drug use is a preeminent risk factor for mother-to-child hepatitis C virus transmission: Results from a multicenter study of 1372 mother-infant pairs. J Infect Dis. 2002;185:567-572.

149. Bortolotti F, Bertaggia A, Cadrobbi P, et al. Epidemiological aspects of acute viral hepatitis in drug abusers. Infection. 1982;10:277-279.

150. Miller CL, Johnston C, Spittal PM, et al. Opportunities for prevention: Hepatitis C prevalence and incidence in a cohort of young injection drug users. Hepatology. 2002;36:737-742.

151. Hahn JA, Page-Shafer K, Lum PJ, et al. Hepatitis C virus seroconversion among young injection drug users: Relationships and risks. J Infect Dis. 2002;186:1558-1564.

152. Thorpe L, Ouellet L, Hershow R, et al. The multiperson use of non-syringe injection equipment and risk of hepatitis C infection in a cohort of young adult injection drug users, Chicago 1997-1999. Ann Epidemiol. 2000;10:472-481.

153. Pol S, Lamorthe B, Thi NT, et al. Retrospective analysis of the impact of HIV infection and alcohol use on chronic hepatitis C in a large cohort of drug users. J Hepatol. 1998;28:945-950.

154. Backmund M, Meyer K, Von Zielonka M, Eichenlaub D. Treatment of hepatitis C infection in injection drug users. Hepatology. 2001;34:188-193.

155. Fong TL, Lee S, Kim JP, et al. Prevalence of hepatitis G virus among intravenous drug abusers in Los Angeles. Clin Infect Dis. 1997;25:165-166.

156. Aikawa T, Sugai Y, Okamoto H. Hepatitis G infection in drug abusers with chronic hepatitis C. N Engl J Med. 1996;334:195-196.

157. Diamantis I, Bassetti S, Erb P, et al. High prevalence and coinfection rate of hepatitis G and C infections in intravenous drug addicts. J Hepatol. 1997;26:794-797.

158. Campo N, Brizzolara R, Sinelli N, et al. Hepatitis G virus infection in intravenous drug users with or without human immunodeficiency virus infection. Hepatogastroenterology. 2000;47:1385-1388.

159. Lin R, Dutta U, Kaba S, et al. Effects of hepatitis G virus coinfection on severity of hepatitis C: Relationship to risk factors and response to interferon treatment. J Gastroenterol Hepatol. 1998;13:773-780.

160. Villano SA, Nelson KE, Vlahov D, et al. Hepatitis A among homosexual men and injection drug users: More evidence for vaccination. Clin Infect Dis. 1997;25:726-728.

161. Vento S, Garofano T, Renzini C, et al. Fulminant hepatitis associated with hepatitis A virus superinfection in patients with chronic hepatitis C. N Engl J Med. 1998;338:286-290.

162. Keeffe EB. Is hepatitis A more severe in patients with chronic hepatitis B and other chronic liver diseases? Am J Gastroenterol. 1995;90:201-205.

163. Nallathambi MN, Ivaturly RR, Lankin DH, et al. Pyogenic splenic abscess in intravenous drug addiction. Am Surg. 1987;53:342-346.

164. Fry DE, Richardson JD, Flint LM. Occult splenic abscess: An unrecognized complication of heroin abuse. Surgery. 1978;84:650-654.

165. Chun CH, Raff MJ, Varghese R, et al. Splenic abscess. Medicine (Baltimore). 1980;59:50-65.

166. Sastre J, Casas E, Sierra J, et al. Splenic abscess due to *Fusobacterium necrophorum*. Rev Infect Dis. 1991;13:1249-1250.

167. Soriano V, Tor J, Gabarre E, et al. Multifocal splenic abscesses caused by *Mycobacterium tuberculosis* in HIV-infected drug users. AIDS. 1991;5:901-902.

168. Adler CH, Stern MB, Brooks ML. Parkinsonism secondary to bilateral striatal fungal abscesses. Mov Disord. 1989;4:333-337.

169. Tunkel AR, Pradhan SK. Central nervous system infections in injection drug users. Infect Dis Clin North Am. 2002;16:589-605.

170. Garvey GJ, Neu HC. Infective endocarditis—an evolving disease: A review of endocarditis at the Columbia-Presbyterian Medical Center, 1968-1973. Medicine (Baltimore). 1978;57:105-127.

171. Roberts WC, Buchbinder NA. Right-sided valvular infective endocarditis: A clinicopathologic study of twelve necropsy patients. Am J Med. 1972;53:7-19.

172. Lerner PI. Neurologic complications of infective endocarditis. Med Clin North Am. 1985;69:385-398.

173. Gilroy J, Andaya L, Thomas VJ. Intracranial mycotic aneurysms and subacute bacterial endocarditis in heroin addiction. Neurology. 1973;23:1193-1198.

174. Ross JS, Masaryk TJ, Modic MT, et al. Intracranial aneurysms: Evaluation by MR angiography AJNR Am J Neuroradiol. 1990;11:449-455.

175. Turtz AR, Yocom SS. Contemporary approaches to the management of neurosurgical complications of infective endocarditis. Curr Infect Dis Rep. 2001;3:337-346.

176. Frazee JG, Cahan LD, Winter J. Bacterial intracranial aneurysms. J Neurosurg. 1980;53:633-641.

177. Abbott SP, Sigler L, McAleer R, et al. Fatal cerebral mycoses caused by the ascomycete *Chaetomium strumarium*. J Clin Microbiol. 1995;33:2692-2698.

178. Hopkins RJ, Rothman M, Fiore A, Goldblum SE. Cerebral mucormycosis associated with intravenous drug use: Three case reports and review. Clin Infect Dis. 1994;19:1133-1137.

179. Blazquez R, Pinedo A, Cosin J, et al. Nonsurgical cure of isolated cerebral mucormycosis in an intravenous drug user. Eur J Clin Microbiol Infect Dis. 1996;15:598-599.

180. Farrar DJ, Flanigan TP, Gordon NM, et al. Tuberculous brain abscess in a patient with HIV infection: Case report and review. Am J Med. 1997;102:297-301.

181. Nussbaum ES, Rigamonti D, Standiford H, et al. Spinal epidural abscess: A report of 40 cases and review. Surg Neurol. 1992;38:225-231.

182. Fraimow HS, Wormser GP, Coburn KD, et al. *Salmonella* meningitis and infection with HIV. AIDS. 1990;4:1271-1273.

183. Koppel BS, Tuchman AJ, Mangiardi JR, et al. Epidural spinal infection in intravenous drug abusers. Arch Neurol. 1988;45:1331-1337.

184. Centers for Disease Control and Prevention. Tetanus among injecting—drug users-California, 1997. JAMA. 1998;279:987.

185. Centers for Disease Control and Prevention. Wound botulism—California, 1995. JAMA. 1996;275:95-96.

186. Passaro DJ, Werner SB, McGee J, et al. Wound botulism associated with black tar heroin among injecting drug users. JAMA. 1998;279:859-863.

187. Redmond J, Stritch M, Blaney P. Severe tetanus in a narcotic addict. Ir Med J. 1984;77:325-326.

188. Kim RW, Juzych MS, Eliott D. Ocular manifestations of injection drug use. Infect Dis Clin North Am. 2002;16:607-622.

189. Young EJ, Wallace RJ Jr, Ericsson CD, et al. Panophthalmitis due to *Bacillus cereus*. Arch Intern Med. 1980;140:559-560.

190. Kral AH, Lorvick J, Gee L, et al. Trends in human immunodeficiency virus seroincidence among street-recruited injection drug users in San Francisco, 1987-1998. Am J Epidemiol. 2003;157:915-922.

191. McCoy CB, Metch LR, Page JB, et al. Injection drug users' practices and attitudes toward intervention and potential for reducing the transmission of HIV. Med Anthropol. 1997;18:35-60.

192. Cohn JA. HIV-1 infection in injection drug users. Infect Dis Clin North Am. 2002;16:745-770.

193. Pollack HA, Khoshnood K, Blankenship KM, Altice FL. The impact of needle exchange-based health services on emergency department use. J Gen Intern Med. 2002;17:341-348.

194. Pezzotti P, Galai N, Vlahov D, et al. Direct comparison of time to AIDS and infectious disease death between HIV seroconverter injection drug users in Italy and the United States: Results from the ALIVE and ISS studies. AIDS Link to Intravenous Experiences/Italian Seroconversion Study. J Acquir Immune Defic Syndr Hum Retrovirol. 1999;20:275-282.

195. Poundstone KE, Chaisson RE, Moore RD. Differences in HIV disease progression by injection drug use and by sex in the era of highly active antiretroviral therapy. AIDS 2001;15:1115-1123.

196. Palepu A, Tyndall M, Yip B, et al. Impaired virologic response to highly active antiretroviral therapy associated with ongoing injection drug use. J Acquir Immune Defic Syndr. 2003;32:522-526.

197. Kanno MB, Zenilman J. Sexually transmitted diseases in injection drug users. Infect Dis Clin North Am. 2002;16:771-780.

198. Nelson KE, Vlahov D, Cohn S, et al. Sexually transmitted diseases in a population of intravenous drug users: Association with seropositivity to the human immunodeficiency virus (HIV). J Infect Dis. 1991;164:457-463.

199. Zenilman JM, Hook EW III, Shepherd M, et al. Alcohol and other substance use in STD clinic patients: Relationships with STDs and prevalent HIV infection. Sex Transm Dis. 1994;21:220-225.

200. Rees V, Saitz R, Horton NJ, Samet J. Association of alcohol consumption with HIV sex- and drug-risk behaviors among drug users. J Subst Abuse Treat. 2001;21:129-134.

201. Tyndall MW, Patrick D, Spittal P, et al. Risky sexual behaviours among injection drugs users with high HIV prevalence: Implications for STD control. Sex Transm Infect. 2002;78(Suppl 1):i170-i175.

202. Siegal HA, Falck RS, Wang J, et al. History of sexually transmitted diseases infection, drug-sex behaviors, and the use of condoms among midwestern users of injection drugs and crack cocaine. Sex Transm Dis. 1996;23:277-282.

203. Lopez-Zetina J, Ford W, Weber M, et al. Predictors of syphilis seroreactivity and prevalence of HIV among street recruited injection drug users in Los Angeles County, 1994-6. Sex Transm Infect. 2000;76:462-469.

204. Kleyn J, Schwebke J, Holmes KK. The validity of injecting drug users' self-reports about sexually transmitted diseases: A comparison of survey and serological data. Addiction. 1993;88:673-68:.

CHAPTER **310**

Risk Factors and Approaches to Infections in Transplant Recipients

J. STEPHEN DUMMER

Successful clinical organ transplantation dates from 1954, when the immunologic barrier to transplantation was ingeniously circumvented in a small number of patients with kidney failure by using donors who were identical twins.[1] Subsequently, transplantation of organs from genetically different individuals was attempted by using lymphoid irradiation to suppress the recipient's immune response to the allograft, but these efforts met with only occasional success. The introduction of drug regimens using azathioprine and corticosteroids in the early 1960s provided effective oral immunosuppression that not only was sustainable, but could be adjusted based on an individual patient's circumstances. This development catapulted human transplantation beyond the experimental stage. As a result, both living-related and cadaveric renal transplantation became part of regular clinical practice. Heart and liver transplantation were also attempted, but proved more challenging, and clinical efforts remained limited to a few small, dedicated programs for more than a decade. The next major watershed in the development of transplantation was the introduction of cyclosporine in the early 1980s. This development ushered in a marked expansion of heart and liver transplantation, promoted further growth of renal transplantation, and made lung transplantation possible. Currently, about 24,000 solid organ transplantations are performed in the United States yearly, and most patients retain their grafts and survive many years after transplantation.[2] It is now likely that a physician will be called on to evaluate and manage patients with various types of transplants as part of general practice.

Except for medical and surgical issues related to the function and rejection of the transplanted organ, infections are the most important problem after transplantation. The clinical manifestations of infection are variable and depend on the infecting pathogen, the prior immune status of the host, the time after transplantation, the level of pharmacologic immunosuppression, and many other factors. With this complexity in mind, it is useful to address some general principles that may aid in the diagnosis, management, and understanding of infections after transplantation.

Infections require a susceptible host and an available pathogen. The susceptibility of transplant recipients is not the same for all pathogens. For instance, most enteroviruses do not appear to infect the transplant recipient with greater frequency or severity than a normal host. A transplant recipient also may be quite susceptible to a given pathogen, but have a low risk of infection because of lack of exposure. A good example is tuberculosis, which is a minor problem at most transplant centers in developed countries, but can be a major problem in parts of the world and in clinical settings where infection cannot be avoided.[3,4] Likewise, transplant recipients with no past exposure to cytomegalovirus (CMV) who receive organs from CMV-seronegative donors are at low risk for CMV infection, whatever their level of immunosuppression.[5] In clinical practice, the clinician can and should use this sort of information to assess each patient's individual susceptibility to important pathogens.

Infections are most frequent and most varied during the first 4 to 6 months after transplantation.[6-8] This is the period when all the risk factors for infection (Table 310-1) are fully operative. Patients may still be affected—either directly or indirectly—by their underlying disease. They will have undergone major surgery and been in intensive care with the attendant risks of wound and other nosocomial infections. Large amounts of immunosuppressive drugs will have been given, and the allograft may be malfunctioning as a result of rejection or other

TABLE 310-1   Factors That Contribute to Infection after Transplantation

Category	Examples and Comments
Pretransplant Host Factors	
Underlying medical conditions	Conditions that persist or recur (hepatitis B, hepatitis C, diabetes mellitus)
	Conditions that exacerbate (chronic bronchitis, gallbladder disease)
Lack of specific immunity	Leads to important primary infections (i.e., CMV, EBV, VZV, toxoplasmosis)
Prior colonization	Nosocomial gram-negative bacilli, *Candida,* staphylococci, VRE
Prior latent infection	Reactivation produces clinical infection (tuberculosis, CMV, HSV, VZV, ? *Pneumocystis*)
Prior medications	Immunosuppressive agents and antibiotics influence post-transplantation susceptibility to infection
Transplantation Factors	
Type of organ transplanted	Site of transplantation and allograft are most common sites of infection
	Allograft may carry infection or be affected by ischemia, injury, or poor function related to allograft reaction
Trauma of surgery	Surgical stress, duration of surgery
Immunosuppression	
Immunosuppressive agents	Corticosteroids, azathioprine and other cytotoxic agents, cyclosporine, tacrolimus, rapamycin, polyclonal and monoclonal antilymphocyte serums
Infective immunosuppression	Primary CMV infection and chronic hepatitis C infection contribute to more bacterial and fungal infection
Allograft Reactions	
Graft-versus-host reaction	Cofactor in CMV infection and fungal infection in stem cell transplantation
Host-versus-graft reaction	? Cofactor in allograft infection

CMV, cytomegalovirus; EBV, Epstein-Barr virus; HSV, herpes simplex virus; VRE, vancomycin-resistant *Enterococcus;* VZV, varicella-zoster virus.

factors. This early period also covers the time of highest risk for infection by herpesviruses (CMV, herpes simplex virus [HSV], Epstein-Barr virus [EBV]), *Pneumocystis,* and *Toxoplasma.* After the first few months, infections related to surgery and the reactivation of latent pathogens become less important. Meanwhile, allograft reactions become less frequent and immunosuppression can be tapered to lower maintenance levels. Although the risk of serious infection never disappears, infectious mortality declines in most patients to low levels by 6 months after surgery and allows for a reduced level of surveillance.[7,8]

HOST FACTORS OF INFECTION

Underlying chronic diseases of the transplant recipient may contribute to infections after transplantation (see Table 310-1). The basic disease that led to transplantation may be cured by the procedure, but occasionally it is not. In patients with fulminant hepatitis caused by hepatitis B virus (HBV), the virus is usually cleared by the immune system, but chronic infection caused by HBV or hepatitis C virus (HCV) persists in most patients after the transplant procedure.[9,10] Diabetes mellitus and its end-organ effects on blood vessels and nerves continue to be a major problem in the diabetic renal transplant recipient and predispose such patients to the development of soft tissue and urinary tract infections.[11] Single-lung transplant recipients may be at risk for infection in their native lung as a result of structural problems caused by their underlying disease.[12] Other preexisting medical conditions such as gallbladder disease, diverticulosis, or chronic bronchitis may be clinically quiescent before transplantation and first become manifest in the post-transplant period, when their detection and management is complicated by chronic immunosuppressive therapy.

Along with the patient's underlying condition, medications, particularly antibiotics and immunosuppressive agents, have an effect on the type and severity of infections in the early post-transplantation period. For example, liver transplant recipients who receive antibiotics or corticosteroids before transplantation may be more likely to develop systemic *Candida* infections after transplantation.[13] Lung transplant candidates with pulmonary fibrosis who receive corticosteroids and other immunosuppressive medications may reactivate CMV before they are transplanted and be at higher risk for disease caused by CMV after transplantation.[14]

EFFECT OF TYPE OF TRANSPLANTATION

The type of transplantation is an important determinant of the type of infection occurring after transplantation. Sites of major surgery are vulnerable to bacterial and fungal infection either during or shortly after surgery. The transplanted organ must establish a vascular supply and regain its functional integrity. Ischemia and improper function are potent factors contributing to infection. Allograft reactions of the host-versus-graft or graft-versus-host type may occur (see Table 310-1). These reactions are known to reduce resistance to infection by viruses and to contribute to the graft's being a *locus minoris resistentiae.*[5] Data collected in the 1980s showed that the most common site of infection in solid organ transplant recipients was the site of transplantation.[15,16] Bone marrow transplant recipients do not have surgical sites, but they are unique because leukopenia and depressed humoral immunity are superimposed on the depressed T-cell immunity common to other types of transplantation. This leads to a heightened vulnerability to many varieties of infection.

The contribution of surgical factors to infection is best illustrated by hepatic transplantation.[17,18] The Achilles' heel with this type of surgery is the function of the biliary and vascular anastomoses in the porta hepatis. For example, most liver abscesses in liver transplant recipients occur as a result of either liver ischemia from hepatic artery thrombosis or obstruction to bile flow from biliary strictures.[17] A striking correlation has been shown between the total hours spent in the operating room and mean episodes of infection per patient in liver recipients (Fig. 310-1).[17] Patients who spent more than 25 hours in the operating room had more than three times as many episodes of infec-

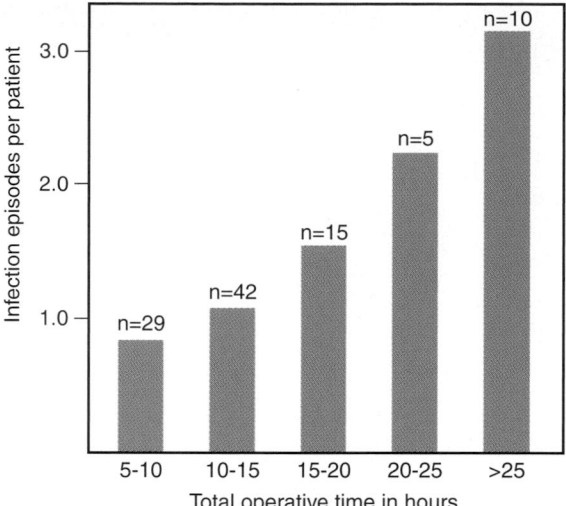

FIGURE 310-1. Frequency of severe infections in relation to time spent in liver transplant surgery. *(From Kusne S, Dummer JS, Singh N, et al. Infections after liver transplantation: An analysis of 101 consecutive cases. Medicine [Baltimore]. 1988;67:132.)*

tion as those who spent only 5 to 10 hours in the operating room. The duration of operation is undoubtedly a composite of many individual risk factors, including surgical stress, blood and body fluid loss, direct tissue damage, and the various metabolic derangements that may occur during a prolonged operation. By the mid-1990s, improvements in anesthesia and surgical technique led to a decrease in the average length of liver transplant surgery to 6 to 7 hours, but longer operations were still associated with a higher risk for fungal infection.[18] Lymphoceles resulting from interruption of lymphatic drainage may become superinfected. In transplantation of the lung, peritracheal or peribronchial infection may follow breakdown of the airway anastomosis. Anastomotic infections may also predispose to bacterial infections of the lung, either directly or secondary to obstruction after placement of a bronchial stent.[12]

The susceptibility of the grafted organ to invasion by CMV and other viruses is a striking example of the vulnerability of allografts to infection. Lung infection by CMV is more frequent and more severe in lung and heart-lung transplant recipients.[16,19] Table 310-2 summarizes data on four different types of transplant recipients in Pittsburgh, all of whom received similar immunosuppressive regimens and underwent transplantation before effective antiviral prophylaxis was available. Although the rates of CMV infection were high in all four groups, the numbers of symptomatic patients were quite different. The frequency of CMV pneumonia was 4 to 16 times higher in heart-lung recipients than in patients in the other groups. The vulnerability of the transplanted lung to viral infection appears to extend beyond CMV. Lung recipients also are susceptible to severe infections with adenovirus and paramyxoviruses, such as respiratory syncytial virus.[20] The reason the transplanted lung is so vulnerable to CMV infection has not been elucidated, but may relate to the presence of a cytokine milieu in the allograft favorable to CMV replication or to the inability of cytotoxic T cells to effectively kill cells of differing human leukocyte antigen types. The transplanted liver is also more susceptible than a native liver to viruses, including CMV, HBV, HCV, HSV, and possibly adenovirus.[9,10,21,22]

IMMUNOSUPPRESSION

Of all the factors contributing to the occurrence of infections in transplant recipients, the most obvious and probably the most important is iatrogenic immunosuppression. The impact of immunosuppressive agents has become more apparent as surgical techniques have improved and infections caused by surgical trauma have declined. Despite significant broadening of available immunosuppressive agents

TABLE 310-2 Infection and Morbidity of Cytomegalovirus (CMV) Infection in Transplant Groups in Pittsburgh after 1981

Group	N	Infected Patients (% of total)	Symptomatic Patients		Patients with CMV Pneumonia	
			% of Infected	% of Total	% of Infected	% of Total
Kidney	131	79/131 (60)	13	8	4	2
Liver	93	55/93 (59)	49	29	5	3
Heart	48	44/48 (92)	27	25	9	8
Heart-lung	31	22/31 (71)	55	39	45	32

Data from Dummer JS, Hardy A, Poorsattar A, Ho M. Early infections in kidney, heart, and liver transplant recipients on cyclosporine. Transplantation. 1983;36:259; and Ho M, Wajszczuk CP, Hardy A, et al. Infections in kidney, heart, and liver transplant recipients on cyclosporine. Transplant Proc. 1983;15:2768.

after the introduction of cyclosporine in 1983, tacrolimus in 1994, mycophenolate mofetil (MMF) in 1995, and rapamycin in 1999, the ideal suppressive regimen that prevents rejection but preserves antimicrobial immunity remains elusive.

The major immunosuppressive agents may be divided into several categories. Corticosteroids broadly inhibit the immune response, including innate inflammatory responses, cellular immunity, and to a lesser extent antibody formation.[23] Although corticosteroids are inadequate as single agents to sustain graft survival, they have remained a part of most immunosuppressive regimens. High doses of prednisone and hyperglycemia were found to be significant factors in the frequency of infections and deaths from infection in kidney transplant recipients.[24] Doses of prednisone greater than 1.25 mg/kg/day have been associated with the occurrence of invasive aspergillosis in kidney recipients.[25] The general reduction of the dosage of prednisone in immunosuppressive regimens after 1966 was associated with reduction of significant infections in renal transplant recipients.[26] In an effort to free patients from the undesirable side effects of corticosteroid therapy, some transplant physicians have experimented with steroid-free regimens, but these are used in only a minority of patients at present.

A major advance in immunosuppression was the introduction of cytotoxic drugs, such as methotrexate, cyclophosphamide, and azathioprine. All of these drugs suppress the bone marrow and may significantly reduce blood cell counts when administered in large doses. Azathioprine became the mainstay and was often effective in doses of 2 mg/kg/day or less without producing leukopenia. Higher doses were associated with leukopenia (<3000/mm^3) and produced more bacterial and fungal infections.[24] Azathioprine also may cause pancreatitis, a reversible hepatitis, rash, and gastrointestinal disturbances. Its metabolism is blocked by allopurinol. Profound bone marrow depression can result when allopurinol is prescribed for the management of gout in patients taking azathioprine.

Cyclosporine was approved in 1983 and opened a new era in transplant immunosuppression. It is an unusual cyclic peptide, consisting of 11 amino acids, whose main action is to inhibit the normal production of cytokines when T-helper cells are exposed to foreign antigens.[27] The primary cytokine inhibited is interleukin-2. Suppressor cells and B cells are relatively spared. Concentrations of the drug as low as 100 ng/mL effectively inhibit mixed lymphocyte reactions. Patients treated with cyclosporine alone for various autoimmune diseases show very low rates of clinical infection, suggesting the importance of corticosteroids and other cofactors for infection (see Table 310-1). Most studies, whether randomized or historically controlled, have demonstrated lower rates of infection in cyclosporine-treated transplant recipients.[15,28,29]

Hofflin and colleagues compared the infectious morbidity and mortality of cohorts of heart transplant recipients receiving immunosuppressive regimens based either on azathioprine or cyclosporine.[29] Patients receiving cyclosporine had lower rates of infection (71% vs. 89%) and a lower infectious mortality rate (11% vs. 39%). Although there have been no direct comparisons of rates of infection in liver recipients receiving azathioprine- versus cyclosporine-based regimens, most early deaths in liver recipients are associated with infection.[15,21] The substantial decline in liver transplant mortality that occurred after

cyclosporine was introduced implies an associated reduction in infectious mortality.

Tacrolimus (FK-506) was approved in 1994. It is a macrolide produced by *Streptomyces tsukubaensis*. Despite some differences in the pathway, its mode of action is strikingly similar to that of cyclosporine in that it inhibits production of interleukin-2 and other cytokines by CD4-positive T cells.[30] Its potency is about 10 to 100 times greater than that of cyclosporine. A comprehensive, randomized comparison of tacrolimus with cyclosporine as primary immunosuppression in 539 liver recipients showed equivalent patient and graft survival rates with the two regimens.[31] Patients receiving tacrolimus had less rejection overall and less rejection that was resistant to steroid therapy, but they also had a higher rate of drug discontinuation as a result of adverse effects (14% vs. 5%). Nephrotoxicity and neurotoxicity were the most common adverse events. Other controlled studies of tacrolimus have shown similar results.[30] Use of tacrolimus as primary immunosuppression has not been shown convincingly to either increase or decrease the risk of infection.[18]

A new immunosuppressant, MMF, was approved in 1995 for renal recipients and in 1997 for heart recipients. It is a cytotoxic drug with an antiproliferative effect on T and B lymphocytes. It is not intended to replace cyclosporine or tacrolimus as primary immunosuppression, but rather to take the place of azathioprine in triple-drug regimens. A blinded, randomized, three-armed study in renal transplant recipients showed superiority of MMF over azathioprine, with biopsy-proven rejection occurring in 38% of azathioprine recipients compared with 19.8% and 17.5% in the two MMF arms.[32] In this study the number of patients developing infections was similar across the three groups.

Rapamycin (also known as sirolimus) was released in 1999 and has a unique mechanism of action. It inhibits immune cell function by interfering with cell cycle proliferation and blocking intracellular signaling mechanisms initiated by interleukin-2 and other cytokines.[33] Unlike cyclosporine and tacrolimus, rapamycin has no direct kidney toxicity. It frequently causes hyperlipidemia and occasionally myelosuppression. It also has been associated with delayed wound healing, oral ulcerations, and a rare drug-induced interstitial pneumonitis.

Polyclonal antilymphocyte serums (ALSs) and antithymocyte globulins (ATGs) have been popular adjuncts for the prophylaxis or treatment of rejection. These biologic agents are produced by immunizing rabbits, horses, or other animals with human lymphocytes or thymocytes. They are potent immunosuppressants and have been used for both prevention and treatment of rejection. Mason and colleagues showed a significant increase in infection rates during the first 3 months after use of ATG for treatment of rejection of the heart.[34] There are also many reports testifying to the enhancing role of ALS or ATG on CMV disease in renal transplant recipients, and other reports describe an increased rate of post-transplantation lymphoproliferative disease in heart patients receiving high-dose cyclosporine and rabbit ATG or OKT3.[35,36] Because they are foreign proteins, these agents may induce serum sickness that typically occurs about 10 days after their initiation.

The effect of monoclonal anti–T-cell globulins on infections appears to be similar. Liver transplant recipients who received rejection treatment with OKT3, a mouse monoclonal antibody directed against the CD3 antigen, had more instances of HSV superinfection, disseminated CMV disease, *Pneumocystis* infection, and lymphoproliferative disease.[17,37,38] Comparisons of monoclonal versus polyclonal anti-T-cell globulins have not shown consistent superiority of either regimen in terms of associated infections.[39,40] OKT3 antibodies have the unusual side effect of causing drug-induced meningitis in a small minority of patients. This may occur either during or after the administration of OKT3. The early cases can be acute enough to mimic bacterial meningitis. The mechanism is not known. During the first 3 days of OKT3 infusions, one may also encounter cytokine release reactions that can mimic sepsis.

Despite their side effects and the associated infectious morbidity, it is unlikely that polyclonal or monoclonal ALSs will be completely displaced in the near future, because they are the most potent agents for treating severe or refractory rejections and they can be used to reduce the dose and hence the toxicity of other immunosuppressive drugs.

Daclizumab and basiliximab represent a new class of monoclonal antibodies that have become available since 1998 for use as induction agents in the early post-transplant period. Both of these antibodies interfere with immune function by blocking the interleukin-2 receptor on T cells.[41] Both agents are moderately effective in preventing early rejection in kidney transplant recipients. Unlike the antilymphocyte serums, neither of these agents has been used to treat active rejection. Thus far, neither agent has been associated with an increased risk of infection.

INFECTING MICROBIAL AGENTS

The most important pathogens infecting transplant recipients are shown in Table 310-3. There are two types of endogenous organisms. One represents flora of extracorporeal lumina. These organisms colonize the mucous membranes of the gastrointestinal tract, including the oropharynx, the nares, and the skin adjacent to the oral and anal orifices. These are among the most important potential pathogens and are represented by the common gram-negative and gram-positive bacteria listed in Table 310-3. These organisms produce local infections by contaminating adjacent wound sites, or they may infect systemically by invading blood vessels or lymphatics. They may also be transmitted from one site to another in the same patient by a surgical procedure or on contaminated instruments and hands.

Candida spp. are a normal component of gastrointestinal tract flora and represent the most important fungal pathogens.[13,14] Superficial mucosal infections with *Candida,* such as thrush and *Candida* vaginitis, may be seen in all types of transplantation. Candidemia and visceral *Candida* infections are common after liver transplantation and are occasionally seen in recipients of other types of transplants in an intensive care setting. Another type of colonizing organism that became important in the 1990s is enterococci resistant to vancomycin and other antibiotics. These organisms have been a particular problem in liver transplant recipients, who have many risk factors for colonization, such as the prolonged use of broad-spectrum antibiotics.[42] Prevention of the spread of these organisms from patient to patient is possible, but requires a concerted effort in infection control.

Another type of endogenous organism comes from latent tissue infection. Such infections are generally not detectable at the time of transplantation, but the latent microbial agents may reactivate and proliferate when the patient is immunosuppressed. The existence of this type of "flora" is best demonstrated by herpesviruses, *Toxoplasma,* and the tubercle bacillus. Their latency may be detected by serologic or immunologic tests. The situation is less clear in the case of *Pneumocystis jirovecii* (formerly *carinii*), because validated microbiologic or serologic tests for latent infection are not available. In the absence of an environmental source for this organism, the remarkable frequency of *Pneumocystis* pneumonia in patients with the acquired immunodeficiency syndrome (AIDS) suggests that latent infection by this organism is common if not ubiquitous.

A number of organisms are transmitted through the air from the physical environment, particularly fungi such as *Aspergillus, Coccidioides, Histoplasma,* and *Cryptococcus. Aspergillus,* cryptococcal, and

TABLE 310-3 Common Types of Infecting Microbial Agents after Transplantation

Bacteria	
Gram-negative bacteria	This group of organisms can cause
Enteric bacteria (*Escherichia coli,* other Enterobacteriaceae)	superficial wound infections or infections of the blood and deeper
Pseudomonas	tissues of the urinary tract, lung,
Acinetobacter	thorax, and abdomen. Despite a
Serratia	succession of highly effective
Bacteroides and other anaerobes	antibiotics, these remain among the most frequent causes of bacterial infection.
Legionella	Nosocomial from water supply.
Gram-positive aerobes	*S. epidermidis* has increased in frequency as other gram-positive
Staphylococcus aureus	organisms have been controlled
Staphylococcus epidermidis	by antibiotics.
Streptococcus	Vancomycin-resistant enterococcus
Enterococcus	has become a major pathogen,
Pneumococcus	especially in liver patients.
Listeria monocytogenes	*Listeria* is an important cause of
Nocardia	meningitis.
Gram-negative coccobacilli	Infection often seen with underlying
Haemophilus influenzae	lung disease.
Moraxella	
Fungi	
Candida spp.	*Candida* are the most common
Aspergillus	endogenous fungi. Deep *Candida*
Cryptococcus	infection may be a particular
Agents of mucormycoses	problem after liver transplantation.
Histoplasma capsulatum	Important in endemic areas.
Coccidioides species	Important in the southwestern United States.
Pneumocystis jirovecii	Probably latent in humans.
Viruses	
Herpesvirus group	Herpesviruses are most common
Herpes simplex (HSV)	after transplantation because many
Cytomegalovirus (CMV)	subjects are latently infected with
Varicella-zoster virus	one or more species that reactivate.
Epstein-Barr virus (EBV)	Donor transmission is an important
Human herpesvirus-6 & 7	source of CMV, EBV and HIV-1.
Human herpesvirus-8	Highly associated with Kaposi's sarcoma.
Human immunodeficiency virus 1 (HIV-1)	
Adenovirus	Pediatric, only occasional in adults.
Rotavirus	Primarily pediatric.
Respiratory syncytial virus	During community outbreaks.
Influenza A and B viruses	
Parainfluenza viruses	
West Nile virus	Donor transmission documented.
Hepatitis B virus	
Hepatitis C virus	
Polyomavirus	BK virus causes transplant nephropathy in kidney recipients. JC virus causes progressive leukoencephalopathy.
Papillomavirus	
Parvovirus	Severe hypoproliferative anemia
Mycoplasmas	
Mycoplasma hominis	*M. hominis* can cause mediastinal wound infection after heart transplantation as well as other types of systemic infection, including arthritis, meningitis, and peritonitis.
Ehrlichia	
Ehrlichia chafeensis	Endemic areas.
Anaplasma phagocytophilum	
Protozoa and Parasites	
Toxoplasma gondii	Usually a primary infection.
Trypanosoma cruzi	May reactivate in recipient or be acquired from donor.
Strongyloides stercoralis	Prior infection may intensify during immunosuppression.

nocardial infections are seen in all geographic regions, but post-transplantation coccidioidomycosis is uniquely a problem of certain endemic regions, such as the arid deserts of the southwestern United States, and most reported cases of histoplasmosis after transplantation have also occurred in endemic areas.[43,44]

The most frequent source of infectious agents in the patient's environment is still other human beings. In the postoperative period, nosocomial transmission of respiratory viruses and of common gram-positive and gram-negative organisms occurs via contaminated hands of hospital personnel or via inanimate objects such as respiratory equipment, endoscopes, intravascular lines, and urinary catheters that have been handled by such personnel. This equipment may at times amplify the agent if organisms are permitted to grow in reservoirs such as water baths and humidifiers.

Some bacteria listed in Table 310-3 probably have exogenous sources, but these are often undefined. *Pseudomonas* may come from environmental water sources or raw vegetables. *Listeria* may arise from contaminated food sources, but a source is rarely identified in the sporadic cases of meningitis that are seen in transplant populations.[45] The *Legionella* organisms, including *Legionella pneumophila* and *Legionella micdadei,* are well-described causes of pneumonia in transplant recipients.[46] *Legionella* can be isolated from hospital water sources, particularly the hot water reservoirs, and these have been demonstrated to be a common source of nosocomial legionellosis. Identification and treatment of contaminated water sources is an important infection control practice in hospitals with endemic *Legionella* infection.[46,47]

Transfused blood products and the donated organ have been important sources of infection in transplant recipients.[48,49] Although transmission of some agents such as HCV and CMV has declined as a result of improved blood-banking practices, the recent transmission of West Nile virus through the blood supply and transplanted organs has once again highlighted the threat of receiving blood and organs from other individuals.[50] Another emerging agent is human herpesvirus-8. Although donor transmission of this virus has not yet been shown to be a problem in the United States, it has been demonstrated in Europe and shown to lead to clinical cases of Kaposi's sarcoma.[51] A large number of pathogens have been transmitted by allografts.[49] The most important agents and references are listed in Table 310-4. CMV is the most important of these pathogens in terms of frequency of transmission by organs. It would be desirable to provide seronegative transplant recipients with organs only from CMV-seronegative donors.[5] However, in view of the shortage of donors, the varying morbidity of CMV, and logistic problems involved with maintaining organ survival, selection of donors is difficult. Such selection is practiced at some centers for high-risk recipients, such as marrow recipients, lung recipients, and pediatric CMV-seronegative renal recipients. In order to prevent transmission of CMV, seronegative transplant recipients are given blood transfusions from CMV-seronegative blood donors or filters are used to deplete the blood of white blood cells, the component in the blood that carries the latent virus.

Toxoplasma has been transmitted by seropositive heart donors, but transmission with other organs is rare.[52] HSV infections have occasionally been transmitted from seropositive donors to seronegative recipients, and it is likely that seropositive donors are a major source of primary EBV infection in seronegative recipients.[53,54] Donors who are viremic with HCV transmit the infection to recipients at a rate that approaches 100%.[55] Liver recipients with HCV infection have reduced survival, although this usually does not manifest itself until about 3 to 5 years after transplantation.[56] Therefore, use of organs from HCV-infected donors may be deemed acceptable for patients who urgently need transplantation or are already infected with HCV.[57]

The risk of transmitting HBV depends on the serologic status of the donor and the recipient and the type of organ transplanted. Organs from donors positive for hepatitis B surface antigen (HBsAg) can transmit the infection.[58] The frequency is not well defined because of the small number of observations, but is thought to be high. The organs of donors who are negative for HBsAg but positive for core anti-

TABLE 310-4 Most Important Infective Agents Transmitted by Donated Tissues, Blood, and Blood Products

Type of Tissue	Infective Agent	References
Kidney, heart, liver, lung, bone marrow	Cytomegalvovirus	5,38,49
Heart, kidney	Toxoplasmosis	52
Kidney	HSV	53
Kidney	HHV-8	51
Kidney, heart, liver	HIV-1	61,63
Kidney, heart, liver	HBV	58-60
Kidney, heart, liver	HCV	55
Kidney, heart, liver	West Nile virus	50
Blood*	CMV, EBV, HIV, HBV, HAV, HDV, HCV, HTLV-I	48
	West Nile Virus	50
Leukocytes	CMV, HIV	48

*On rare occasions, Chagas' disease, malaria, babesiosis, and syphilis have been transmitted by blood transfusion.

HSV, herpes simplex virus; CMV, cytomegalovirus; EBV, Epstein-Barr virus; HHV-8, human herpesvirus-8; HAV, hepatitis A virus; HBV, hepatitis B virus; HCV, hepatitis C virus; HDV, delta hepatitis virus; HIV, human immunodeficiency virus-1; HTLV-I, human T-cell lymphotrophic virus I.

body (HBcAb) also may transmit HBV.[59,60] The risk of infection after receipt of these organs is high for liver transplants (25% to 83%) but low (2% or less) for other organs.[59,60] The presence of anti-HBsAb in donor or recipient serum appears to decrease but not eliminate this risk.[60-62] In recent years donor transmission of HBV has been successfully managed by treatment of the recipient with lamivudine and hepatitis B immune globulin.[62]

Human immunodeficiency virus type 1 (HIV-1) is efficiently transmitted by donor organs, tissues, and blood products.[61,63] There is a consensus that organs from donors seropositive for HIV-1 should not be transplanted. The Centers for Disease Control and Prevention has developed guidelines mandating that organ procurement personnel obtain a history of any risk factors for HIV-1 infection that could signal the possibility of transmission of HIV-1 despite negative antibody tests. The mandate includes the responsibility of sharing any relevant information with the intended recipient and family.[61]

EVALUATION BEFORE TRANSPLANTATION

Evaluation of the patient for infectious risks before transplantation has proved to be extremely valuable, and many transplantation centers have set up formal screening mechanisms.[6,7] The first goal of such screening should be to detect the presence any active infection in the candidate that might amplify and prove to be a major problem after transplantation. Examples are a history of chronic bronchitis or the presence of active dental infection. The second step is to take an exposure history. The patient should be questioned about occupational exposures and hobbies, and a brief travel and residence history should be obtained to explore possible exposure to tropical illnesses or endemic mycoses. As part of this history, routine inquiry should be made about a past history of tuberculosis, previous tuberculin skin test results, and any exposure that might have placed the patient at high risk of acquiring tuberculosis, such as extended travel in developing countries or incarceration in a prison. Third, a battery of infectious disease screening tests should be performed, as outlined in Table 310-5. The results establish the presence of chronic viral pathogens (HIV-1, HCV, HBV) and help assess susceptibility to reactivation or infection by key transplant pathogens such as the herpesviruses and *Toxoplasma gondii.* If negative, they also form an important baseline for future reference and testing. Tuberculin skin testing should be done for all patients unless they have a history of a definite positive test in the past. We also recommend coccidioidomycosis complement fixation antibody tests for individuals with residence or significant exposure over the last 2 years in known endemic areas. Patients with residence outside the

TABLE 310-5   Routine Laboratory Studies before and after Transplantation

Before Transplantation*	After Transplantation
Cytomegalovirus immunoglobulin G (IgG) antibody	Viral surveillance cultures
Epstein-Barr virus IgG antibody	Antibody studies (as indicated)
Herpes simplex (types 1 and 2) antibody	
Varicella-zoster IgG antibody	
Toxoplasma IgG antibody (heart recipients)	
Hepatitis B screen†	
Hepatitis C ELISA‡	
Human immunodeficiency virus antibody	
Tuberculin skin test	
Stool for ova and parasites§	

*For serologic studies, it is most important to collect serum before transplantation. Studies may then be done as clinically indicated. Not all tests need to be done on all patients.

†Should include at least surface antigen, core antibody, and surface antibody.

‡Second-generation enzyme-linked immunosorbent assay. Liver candidates and patients with laboratory or clinical evidence of liver disease should also have a hepatitis C polymerase chain reaction assay performed.

§Primarily useful for former or current residents of tropical and subtropical regions. The incidence of stongyloidiasis after transplantation has fallen dramatically in the last 20 years.

United States may require specialized testing for *Trypanosoma cruzi*, malaria, luminal parasites such as strongyloides, or human herpesvirus-8.[64,65]

The most useful tests before transplantation are the herpesvirus serologies, because they predict whether the patient is at risk for reactivation or for primary infection. An example would be knowledge of a patient's varicella serologic status: few patients are seronegative, but these few are at high risk of potentially fatal varicella after transplantation. Knowledge of risk status allows for intensive counseling and immunization of these patients.[66] Seropositive patients, in contrast, can be told that they are at no risk from exposure to chickenpox or shingles and require no intervention after exposure. CMV antibody testing before transplantation provides the best way to stratify risk for CMV disease after transplantation. Many transplantation centers modify their management of high-risk CMV-seronegative patients with seropositive donors by instituting closer follow-up or giving more aggressive antiviral prophylaxis.

The risk of active tuberculosis in transplant recipients is 30 to 50 times higher than in the general population.[4,67] The management of a transplant recipient who has a positive skin test is controversial. Not all experts have recommended a course of isoniazid because of a concern for hepatotoxicity. However, the risk of hepatotoxicity from isoniazid prophylaxis appears to be low in transplant recipients without preexisting liver disease.[68] We believe that most patients with positive tuberculin skin tests should be treated with isoniazid, but assessment of risks and benefits in individual patients is also important, and the optimal timing of prophylaxis should be considered. For instance, in liver transplant candidates with decompensated liver disease, it may be best to delay isoniazid prophylaxis until after liver transplantation when the risk for tuberculosis is higher and the patient is more clinically stable.

In the past many transplant centers would not offer transplantation to HIV-1–positive patients, even those without AIDS, because available evidence suggested that they would experience high infection rates and reduced survival after transplantation.[63] The introduction of highly active antiretroviral therapy and the ability to dramatically reduce HIV-1 viral loads in many patients has increased enthusiasm for offering transplantation to stable HIV-1–positive patients. Such transplantations may be complicated by difficult drug interactions between the transplant immunosuppression regimen and antiretroviral therapy. Nonetheless, initial experience suggests that acceptable graft and patient survival rates may be achieved in carefully selected, stable HIV-1–positive patients who receive kidney or liver transplants.[69] It is unlikely, however, that such transplants will be universally offered until more information on their long-term outcome is available.

MONITORING FOR INFECTION

Routine surveillance for bacterial infection is of limited benefit in most solid organ transplant recipients. One exception might be the routine surveillance of sputum of heart-lung and lung recipients who are intubated in the intensive care unit. These patients have a substantial risk of pneumonia, and it may be easier to assess clinical changes when serial sputum results are available. Surveillance for fungi is also a common practice in lung transplantation, because of the high risk for infection with *Aspergillus* and other molds.[12,70]

Many transplant programs monitor CMV infection in the first 3 to 4 months after transplantation. In recent years, blood antigenemia and quantitative polymerase chain reaction (PCR) testing for CMV have replaced conventional and shell vial viral cultures as the tests of choice. These tests are more sensitive and turn positive about 1 to 2 weeks earlier than cultures.[71-73] Both tests provide quantitative information on viral load that correlates with the development of symptomatic infection. Routine virologic testing for CMV in marrow transplant populations has permitted a preemptive approach to antiviral treatment and successfully prevented progression to overt CMV disease.[71,73] This approach to management of CMV disease has also been successfully implemented in solid organ transplant recipients.[74,75]

Monitoring of the viral load has also been studied for other viral infections in transplant recipients. For instance, the quantitative EBV viral load correlates with the risk of developing lymphoproliferative disease in pediatric liver transplantation.[76] Measurement of the hepatitis B viral load has proved useful as a way to monitor the course of antiviral therapy with agents such as lamivudine and adefovir.[77] The amount of HCV RNA in the serum of liver transplant recipients early after transplantation may have some predictive value for the histologic and clinical outcome of the infection.[78] Monitoring for polyomavirus is also being employed at some renal transplant centers, but the relative merits of different monitoring techniques has not been determined and monitoring has not yet been shown to lead to improved outcomes.[79]

PROPHYLACTIC MEASURES

Prophylactic regimens are frequently used to prevent infection in transplant recipients. Immunization is potentially the most cost-effective way to prevent infection. Although trials large enough to demonstrate clinical effectiveness of vaccines have not been done in transplant populations, numerous smaller studies have looked at antibody responses. The response of renal recipients to booster doses of tetanus and diphtheria toxoids appears to be adequate, though reduced compared with the response in immunocompetent persons.[80] Transplant recipients also respond to pneumococcal vaccine, but the peak antibody titers achieved are less than in healthy controls.[81] The seroconversion rates of transplant recipients to influenza vaccine are also generally less than in control populations.[82]

There is an understandable reluctance to use live vaccines in transplant recipients, but measles and varicella vaccines have been used safely in small groups of transplant recipients with seroconversion rates of 65% and 47%, respectively.[83,84] More studies need to be done with live vaccines before they can be recommended for general use in this group of patients. We advocate that transplant candidates and recipients receive those killed vaccines that are recommended for patients in the general population who have chronic diseases, including pneumococcal, influenza, and HBV vaccines. In practice, I often postpone immunization when the patient is heavily immunosuppressed, such as during the first 3 months after transplantation, because it is likely that the response will be poor in this setting. Concerns in the transplant community that vaccines may cause rejection have not been substantiated by available studies. Before transplantation, routine immunizations should be brought up to date. Transplant candidates without a history of varicella should be serologically tested and offered immunization if they are seronegative. Current evidence suggests that this practice is moderately effective and safe.[66,84]

Antimicrobial agents commonly used for prophylaxis are listed in Table 310-6. Transplant surgeons routinely give perioperative antibiotics to prevent intraoperative sepsis and wound infections. The type of antibiotics used varies greatly, and the optimal durations have not been established by studies or consensus. The administration of oral antibiotics to prevent infection is widely practiced. The most commonly used prophylactic antimicrobial agent is trimethoprim-sulfamethoxazole (TMP-SMX). TMP-SMX provides superior prophylaxis against *P. jirovecii* pneumonia in all populations that have been studied. It has now become part of standard care at transplant centers. Doses as small as two to three double-strength tablets a week are effective. Two studies have also shown that daily dosing of TMP-SMX in the first few months after transplantation reduces urinary tract and other bacterial infections in renal recipients.[85,86] In one study TMP-SMX recipients had 25% higher serum creatinine levels, but these were fully reversible on discontinuation. It is claimed, but unproved, that TMP-SMX prophylaxis also decreases the rate of infections caused by some serious opportunistic pathogens, including *Legionella, Nocardia,* and *Listeria.*

Prophylactic quinolones are used at some marrow transplantation centers. They have been shown to reliably decrease the rate of gram-negative but not gram-positive infections during the neutropenic phase of chemotherapy.[87] No effect on mortality has been demonstrated. It is not yet known whether resistance will become a major problem with use of quinolone prophylaxis in this population.

Antiviral prophylaxis is desirable in transplant recipients because of the clinical importance of herpesvirus infections. Acyclovir is effective in preventing HSV infection in the early post-transplantation period. It is indicated in seropositive marrow and lung transplant recipients, because of their significant risk of visceral disease caused by HSV.[88,89] It is also commonly used to prevent mucocutaneous HSV infection in other solid organ recipients. Although acyclovir has little

therapeutic activity against CMV, controlled studies have shown that it provides some protection when given prophylactically in high doses. Acyclovir given intravenously for 1 month after marrow transplantation reduced the frequency of CMV disease by about one third, and high-dose oral acyclovir (800 mg four times daily) given for 3 months to renal recipients significantly reduced their incidence of CMV disease.[90,91] Subsequent studies showed numerous breakthroughs of CMV disease in transplant recipients receiving acyclovir, and this has led many physicians to seek more potent agents.[75]

Ganciclovir's greater activity against CMV makes it an attractive candidate for prophylaxis. The most impressive results have been in marrow transplantation, where ganciclovir has been shown to be effective prophylaxis when administered after engraftment to patients who were at risk for CMV disease based either on positive cultures or on seropositive status.[92] After full-dose therapy for 1 week, lower maintenance doses were continued intravenously for 100 to 120 days after transplantation. Significant problems with this prophylactic regimen were the requirement for intravenous access, a high rate of neutropenia, and an increase in bacterial infections.[92] A randomized study of intravenous ganciclovir prophylaxis for the first 4 weeks after heart transplantation produced interesting results in that seropositive patients benefited, but seronegative recipients of organs from seropositive donors did not.[93] Winston and associates were able to achieve a dramatic reduction of CMV disease in liver recipients by extending intravenous ganciclovir prophylaxis for 100 days after transplantation, a strategy that was also effective in the high-risk subgroup of seronegative patients with seropositive donors.[94] Although few adverse events were reported in this trial, many centers may not want to commit patients to the expense and potential risks of such long-term intravenous therapy, merely to ensure a very low rate of CMV disease.

Two large trials of CMV prophylaxis have demonstrated encouraging results with oral regimens. A randomized trial comparing 12 weeks of oral ganciclovir (1 g three times daily) with placebo in liver transplant recipients showed a significant reduction in CMV disease, from 17% to 4% in the treatment group.[95] The cases of CMV disease in the oral ganciclovir recipients were not life threatening and consisted only of CMV syndromes and CMV hepatitis. Valacyclovir, a prodrug of acyclovir that yields serum levels of acyclovir similar to those achieved with intravenous dosing, was compared with a placebo in 616 renal recipients.[96] The frequency of CMV disease in the valacyclovir arm was reduced from 5% to 1% in seropositive patients and from 39% to 14% in seronegative recipients with seropositive donors. Only 1% of patients developed CMV disease while taking valacyclovir.

Valganciclovir is an oral prodrug of ganciclovir that has 60% bioavailability and has been shown to provide drug exposure similar to intravenous infusions.[97] No studies of CMV prophylaxis with valganciclovir have been reported in transplant populations, but it is anticipated that it would be an effective agent based on its favorable pharmacokinetics.

Immune control is the mechanism of the other major modality in CMV prophylaxis. Intravenous immune globulin has been widely studied for the prophylaxis of CMV disease after marrow transplantation. The results of these studies have been mixed, and this approach is no longer widely advocated for CMV control in this population. A well-designed, prospective study showed that infusions of an immunoglobulin preparation with high titers of CMV antibodies significantly reduced the incidence of CMV disease and associated opportunistic infections in seronegative renal transplant recipients receiving seropositive donor organs.[98] A subsequent study in liver transplant recipients also showed positive results, but the effect was less striking and only seropositive patients benefited.[99]

The decision whether to provide prophylaxis for CMV infection in transplant recipients is complex and is best made after careful consideration of the efficacy, side effects, and cost of the regimens under consideration and the estimated risk of severe CMV disease in the intended recipient. Instead of using universal CMV prophylaxis, many transplant centers use a preemptive approach to CMV management.

TABLE 310-6 Antimicrobial Prophylactic Regimens in Transplantation	
Pathogen	*Prophylactic Agents*
Protozoa	
Toxoplasmosis	Trimethoprim-sulfamethoxazole (TMP-SMX)
	Pyrimethamine
Viral	
Herpes simplex	Acyclovir
Cytomegalovirus	Ganciclovir
	Acyclovir
	Immunoglobulin
	Foscarnet*
Influenza	Amantadine
	Rimantadine
	Oeseltamivir
Fungal	
Candida	Fluconazole
	Nystatin
	Clotrimazole
Aspergillus	Itraconazole
	Amphotericin B
	Liposomal amphotericin
Pneumocystis	TMP-SMX
	Dapsone
	Inhaled pentamadine
Bacterial	
Wound infection	Variable
Urinary tract infection	TMP-SMX
Neutropenic infection	Quinolones
Tuberculosis	Isoniazid
Pneumococcus	Penicillin (bone marrow transplants)

*Foscarnet is mostly used in bone marrow recipients who have low blood counts.

Preemptive approaches employ serial virologic monitoring to decide when to initiate antiviral therapy. Preemptive approaches have gained wide acceptance in marrow and stem cell transplantation and are gaining popularity in solid organ transplantation because of the excellent sensitivity and reliability of current laboratory techniques for monitoring CMV infection. Of the available tests, the best studied and most widely used are blood antigenemia and quantitative PCR.[71-73,100]

Transplant recipients are at risk for thrush and other forms of mucocutaneous candidiasis, but these are effectively prevented by treatment with oral nystatin or clotrimazole troches.[101] Oral systemic azoles are also effective and should be preferred in intubated patients because topical preparations cannot reliably be delivered to the pharynx and esophagus. Prophylaxis can usually be discontinued when prednisone doses drop to 20 mg/day or less, but it may need to be restarted during treatment of rejection with high-dose steroids or intercurrent antibiotic treatment. Prophylaxis for systemic fungal infection is now being used in many centers for high-risk patients such as marrow, liver, and lung recipients. Intravenous and oral azoles have been the most popular prophylactic agents. Large, randomized studies in marrow recipients have shown that fluconazole (400 mg/day) significantly reduces the rate of deep *Candida* infections.[102] A placebo-controlled trial of fluconazole prophylaxis in liver recipients also showed a 75% reduction in invasive fungal infections in patients receiving fluconazole.[103] In a follow-up trial by the same authors, itraconazole oral solution administered for 10 weeks after transplantation proved equivalent to fluconazole in providing protection against invasive fungal infection, but was associated with more gastrointestinal side effects.[104] Voriconazole has not yet been studied for fungal prophylaxis in transplant populations, but it has been shown to have superior activity in treating *Aspergillus* infection, and it produced outcomes comparable to those of liposomal amphotericin B in high-risk patients when it was used as empirical therapy of neutropenic fever.[105,106] There is also evidence that prophylaxis with conventional and lipid formulations of amphotericin may be effective, but these regimens are not as widely used because of their toxicity.[107,108]

Another form of prophylaxis that has been proposed is pyrimethamine (25 mg/day together with folinic acid 5 to 10 mg/day for 6 weeks) for heart recipients who are seronegative for *Toxoplasma* and receive an organ from a *Toxoplasma*-seropositive donor.[109] However, patients receiving TMP-SMX appear to be protected from infection with *Toxoplasma,* and it is unclear whether the addition of pyrimethamine provides any further benefit.[110] Some bone marrow units also employ long-term oral penicillin prophylaxis in allogenic transplant recipients because of the high rate of pneumococcal infection late after transplantation.

Because liver transplantation involves opening the potentially infected gastrointestinal tract, some groups advocate decontamination of the gut as a method to decrease bacterial and fungal sepsis. Selective decontamination has been accomplished with the oral administration of nonabsorbable polymyxin E, gentamicin, and nystatin and a diet low in bacterial content in the perioperative period. One small, randomized study of this regimen in liver transplantation showed a reduction in gram-negative flora in fecal cultures but failed to demonstrate other benefits.[111]

PREVENTION OF EXPOSURE TO INFECTION

One way of decreasing infectious episodes in transplant recipients would be to prevent exposure to potential pathogens. Most transplant centers have developed policies that are designed to reduce the chance of patients' encountering microbial pathogens. Because there are few controlled data that can be used as a basis to advise patients, the recommendations usually target infections that are known to be important in transplant patients, and are based on the best current understanding of transmission and pathogenesis. Table 310-7 lists some recommendations found in recent publications. The list is not meant to be exhaustive; rather, it is restricted to recommendations that are found in more than one source.[6,112-114] These recommendations also do not account for dif-

ferences in susceptibility among patients. For instance, the risk for aspergillosis is not uniform among transplant recipients and is much higher in allogeneic stem cell transplant recipients with graft-versus-host disease and solid organ transplant recipients who are receiving high-dose steroids for treatment of rejection than in other transplant patients.[25] Similarly, lung transplant recipients have greater difficulty with respiratory virus infections than kidney, heart, or liver recipients.[20] One can and probably should modify one's recommendations based on this differential susceptibility to infection in different populations, reserving the strictest recommendations for the patients at highest risk. However, some pathogens such as *M. tuberculosis* or *Coccidioides immitis* are relatively virulent, even in immunocompetent hosts, and it is probably not prudent for any transplant recipient, even one who is very healthy and on low doses of immunosuppression, to work as a prison guard or participate in an archeological excavation outside of Tucson, Arizona.

APPROACH TO FEVER IN THE TRANSPLANTATION PATIENT

Although immunosuppressive drugs can blunt the febrile response to infection, most transplant recipients with clinical infections have temperature elevations; often this is the first indication that something is awry. When faced with a febrile patient, the first task is to identify possible

TABLE 310-7 Prevention of Exposure to Pathogens	
Type of Exposure	*Intervention*
Hospital Exposures	
Nosocomial bacteria	Standard precautions, particularly hand washing before and after patient exposures.
Respiratory viruses	Restrict visitors and staff with colds. If contact cannot be restricted, use masks and gloves.
Airborne moulds	Remove patients from areas of construction and/or erect barriers around construction. Use masks for patient transport through high-risk areas. HEPA-filtered air (stem cell transplant only).
Legionella infection	If nosocomial legionellosis is present, test water supply and decontaminate if possible. Supply bottled water for oral use and prevent exposure to aerosolized water such as showers.
Outpatient Exposures	
Enteric pathogens	Cook meat thoroughly, wash fresh fruit and vegetables, wash hands after cooking, avoid certain soft cheeses (brie, feta, etc.). Avoid drinking water from lakes, streams and untested wells. Avoid contact with human and animal feces. Avoid unpasteurized milk and juices, and raw eggs and products made with them.
Respiratory viruses	Avoid small children or crowded public places, wash hands after contact. Immunize patient and family members against influenza yearly. Pharmacologic prophylaxis for influenza in selected patients.
Varicella	Avoid contact with patients who have shingles or chickenpox (VZV seronegative patients only).
Zoonoses	Avoid changing litter boxes, cleaning bird cages or aquaria. Wear gloves if this is unavoidable. Avoid jobs that involve frequent animal contact.
Airborne moulds	Avoid closed spaces with high risks of fungal exposure (barns, silos, chicken coops, attics, caves) or high-risk activities (e.g., archeological excavation, esp. in SW USA).
Legionella infection	Avoid water aerosols (whirlpools and commercial displays) and hospital or other institutional tap water that is not tested or treated.
Sexually transmitted diseases	Practice safe sex.
Exotic and tropical infections	Confer with infectious disease specialist before international travel outside of Canada and Western Europe.

sites and sources of infection and assess the severity of illness. Patients with typical upper respiratory tract infections and low-grade fevers (38.0° C) can generally be observed clinically. Cyclosporine seems to predispose patients to sinus infections. If sinus infection is suspected, it is often wise to order sinus radiographs or computed tomography scans. If the patient becomes febrile with a temperature higher than 38.0° C, a medical evaluation should be made. If there are symptoms suggesting a serious localized infection, the patient should be evaluated even in the absence of demonstrable fever.

The most important parts of this workup are a careful history and physical examination. A chest radiograph should be obtained to establish whether there is evidence for infection in the lungs. Patients with acute pulmonary infiltrates, or with persistent fevers higher than 38.5° C, usually need to be hospitalized for further workup. Most patients who cannot go about their normal daily activities should probably be evaluated in the hospital unless the cause of their dysfunction is apparent and can be managed at home. Initial evaluation should include blood and urine cultures, examination of respiratory secretions (if pneumonia is suspected), white blood cell count and differential, liver function tests, and microscopic examination of the urine. Viral screening tests should be ordered if there is a clinical suspicion of CMV disease, if the patient has recently been treated for rejection, or if the patient is still in the high-risk early post-transplantation period (1 to 4 months). Antibiotics can often be withheld from patients who appear well and in whom no source of infection has emerged from the preliminary workup. Although lumbar puncture need not be a routine part of the workup of febrile transplant recipients, the physician should have a low threshold for obtaining a sample of spinal fluid in patients with headache and other neurologic complaints.

In a patient with a clear site of infection, evaluation should focus on quickly obtaining adequate samples for culture and smears from that site. The patient who has persistent fever (≥7 days) without positive cultures or an apparent site of infection presents a diagnostic and therapeutic problem.

Relatively few clinical entities appear to account for the majority of these fevers of unknown origin (FUOs), the most important of which are viral syndromes caused by CMV or occasionally by EBV. In recent years, human herpesvirus-6 has also emerged as a possible cause of FUO in the early post-transplantation period.[115] Other infections that may manifest in this fashion are systemic toxoplasmosis and smoldering *Pneumocystis* infection with a normal chest radiograph. Deep tissue abscesses almost always occur in or near the anatomic site of previous surgery. Disseminated candidiasis occurs largely in patients who are either neutropenic or long-term residents of the intensive care unit. They almost always have received broad-spectrum antibiotics and have multiple intravenous lines. The risk for invasive candidiasis is highest in liver recipients, moderate in lung and heart-lung recipients, and low in kidney and heart recipients. Disseminated coccidioidomycosis and histoplasmosis may cause FUO; most of these cases occur in patients who are resident in or have recently traveled to endemic areas. Although it is uncommon, tuberculosis should always be considered a potential cause of FUO, especially if there is an exposure history or extensive residence or travel in developing countries.

Not all fevers are caused by infections. The most common causes of noninfectious fevers in transplant recipients in my experience are drug reactions (especially reactions to anti-T-cell globulins) and rejection. The frequency with which rejection causes fever appears to vary widely among different transplant recipient groups. For instance, heart rejection rarely causes fever, but acute lung rejection is often associated with temperature elevations. Renal and hepatic transplant recipients appear to have an intermediate risk of fever during episodes of rejection.

Other noninfectious causes of fever are deep venous thrombosis (or pulmonary embolism), organ ischemia from infarction or inadequate preservation, lymphoproliferative tumors, and hemolytic reactions.

Finally, it must also be conceded that infections in transplant recipients may occur without any fever. At times fever appears to be suppressed by the use of high-dose corticosteroids; at other times severe organ failure (heart, liver, or kidney) appears to be implicated. Some infections, such as progressive multifocal leukoencephalopathy, never cause fever, and others frequently do not. *Pneumocystis* pneumonia may manifest with cough and dyspnea only. Fungal infections are frequently afebrile, particularly cryptococcal meningitis, which may manifest with only chronic headache and subtle neurologic symptoms. A good caveat for the physician approaching the transplant recipient is always to consider infection a possible cause of any new symptom or sign.

REFERENCES

1. Murray JE. Human organ transplantation: Background and consequences. Science. 1992;256:1411.
2. United Network for Organ Sharing. 2002 Annual Report of the U.S. Organ Procurement and Transplantation Network and the Scientific Registry of Transplant Recipients: Transplant Data 1992-2001. Rockville, MD: Health Resources and Services Administration, Office of Special Programs, Division of Transplantation; Richmond, VA: United Network for Organ Sharing; and Ann Arbor, MI: University Renal Research and Education Association; 2002.*
3. Sundberg R, Shapiro R, Darras F, et al. A tuberculosis outbreak in a renal transplant program. Transplant Proc. 1991;23:3091.
4. Qunibi WY, Al-Sibai MB, Taher S, et al. Mycobacterial infection after renal transplantation: Report of 14 cases and review of the literature. Q J Med. 1990;77:1039.
5. Ho M. Cytomegalovirus: Biology and Infection. 2nd ed. New York: Plenum Press; 1991:249-256.
6. Patel R, Paya CV. Infections in solid-organ transplant recipients. Clin Microbiol Rev. 1997;10:86.
7. Boden MD, Dummer JS. Infections after organ transplantation. J Intensive Care Med. 1997;12:166.
8. Fishman J, Rubin RH. Infection in organ-transplant recipients. N Engl J Med. 1998;338:1741-1751.
9. Samuel D, Muller R, Alexander G, et al. Liver transplantation in European patients with the hepatitis B surface antigen. N Engl J Med. 1993;329:1842.
10. Araya V, Rakela J, Wright T. Hepatitis C after liver transplantation. Gastroenterology. 1997;112:575-582.
11. Tolkoff-Rubin NE, Rubin RH. The infectious disease problems of the diabetic renal transplant recipient. Infect Dis Clin North Am. 1995;9:117.
12. Speich R, Van der Bij W. Epidemiology and management of infections after lung transplantation. Clin Infect Dis. 2001;33(Suppl 1):S58-S65.
13. Wajszczuk CP, Dummer JS, Ho M, et al. Fungal infections in liver transplant recipients. Transplantation. 1985;40:347.
14. Milstone AP, Brumble LM, Loyd JE, et al. Active CMV infection before lung transplantation: Risk factors and clinical implications. J Heart Lung Transplant. 2000;19:744-750.
15. Dummer JS, Hardy A, Poorsattar A, Ho M. Early infections in kidney, heart, and liver transplant recipients on cyclosporine. Transplantation. 1983;36:259.
16. Ho M, Wajszczuk CP, Hardy A, et al. Infections in kidney, heart, and liver transplant recipients on cyclosporine. Transplant Proc. 1983;15:2768.
17. Kusne S, Dummer JS, Singh N, et al. Infections after liver transplantation: An analysis of 101 consecutive cases. Medicine (Baltimore). 1988;67:132.
18. Hadley S, Samore MH, Lewis WD, et al. Major infectious complications after orthotopic liver transplantation and comparison of outcomes in patients receiving cyclosporine or FK506 as primary immunosuppression. Transplantation. 1995;59:851.
19. Dummer JS, White LT, Ho M, et al. Morbidity of cytomegalovirus infection in recipients of heart or heart-lung transplants who received cyclosporine. J Infect Dis. 1985;152:1182.
20. Wendt CH, Fox JMK, Hertz MI. Paramyxovirus infection in lung transplant recipients. J Heart Lung Transplant. 1995;14:479.
21. Kusne S, Schwartz M, Breinig MK, et al. Herpes simplex virus hepatitis after solid organ transplantation in adults. J Infect Dis. 1991;163:1001.
22. Michaels MG, Green M, Wald ER, Starzl TE. Adenovirus infection in pediatric liver transplant recipients. J Infect Dis. 1992;165:170.
23. Meuleman J, Katz P. The immunologic effects, kinetics, and use of glucocorticoids. Med Clin North Am. 1985;69:805.
24. Anderson RJ, Schafer LA, Olin DB, Eickhoff TC. Infectious risk factors in the immunosuppressed host. Am J Med. 1973;54:453.
25. Gustafson TL, Schaffner W, Lavely GB, et al. Invasive aspergillosis in renal transplant recipients: Correlation with corticosteroid therapy. J Infect Dis. 1983;148:230.
26. Rubin R. Infection in the renal and liver transplant patient. In: Rubin RH, Young LS, eds. Clinical Approach to Infection in the Immunocompromised Host. 2nd ed. New York: Plenum Press; 1988:557.
27. Kahan BD. Cyclosporine. N Engl J Med. 1989;321:1725.

*The data and analyses in the 2002 Annual Report of the U.S. Organ Procurement and Transplantation Network and the Scientific Registry of Transplant Recipients have been supplied by UNOS and URREA under contract with HHS. The authors alone are responsible for the reporting and interpretation of the data.

28. Najarian JS, Fryd DS, Strand M, et al. A single institution, randomized, prospective trial of cyclosporin versus azathioprine-antilymphocyte globulin for immunosuppression in renal allograft recipients. Ann Surg. 1985;201:142.

29. Hofflin JM, Potasman I, Baldwin JC, et al. Infectious complications in heart transplant patients receiving cyclosporine and corticosteroids. Ann Intern Med. 1987;106:209.

30. Spencer CM, Goa KL, Gillis JC. Tacrolimus: An update of its pharmacology and clinical efficacy in the management of organ transplantation. Drugs. 1997;54:925.

31. A comparison of tacrolimus (FK 506) and cyclosporine for immunosuppression in liver transplantation. The US Multicenter FK506 Liver Study Group. N Engl J Med. 1994;331:1110.

32. Sollinger HW. Mycophenolate mofetil for the prevention of acute rejection in primary cadaveric renal allograft recipients. US Renal Transplant Mycophenolate Mofetil Study Group. Transplantation. 1995;60:225.

33. Kahan BD, Camardo JS. Rapamycin: Clinical results and future opportunities. Transplantation. 2001;72:1181-1193.

34. Mason JW, Stinson EB, Hunt SA, et al. Infections after cardiac transplantation: Relation to rejection therapy. Ann Intern Med. 1976;85:69.

35. Peterson PK, Balfour HH Jr, Marker SC, et al. Cytomegalovirus disease in renal allograft recipients: A prospective study of the clinical features, risk factors and impact on renal transplantation. Medicine (Baltimore). 1980;59:283.

36. Bieber CP, Heberling RL, Jamieson SW, et al. Lymphoma in cardiac transplant recipients: Association with use of cyclosporin A, prednisone and antithymocyte globulin (ATG). In: Purtilo DT, ed. Immune Deficiency and Cancer. New York: Plenum Press; 1984:309.

37. Swinnen LJ, Costanzo-Nordin MR, Fisher SG, et al. Increased incidence of lymphoproliferative disorder after immunosuppression with the monoclonal antibody OKT3 in cardiac-transplant recipients. N Engl J Med. 1990;323:1723.

38. Singh N, Dummer JS, Kusne S, et al. Infections with cytomegalovirus and other herpesviruses in 121 liver transplant recipients: Transmission by donated organ and the effect of OKT3 antibodies. J Infect Dis. 1988;158:124.

39. Frey DJ, Matas AJ, Gillingham KJ, et al. Sequential therapy: A prospective randomized trial of MALG versus OKT3 for prophylactic immunosuppression in cadaver renal allograft recipients. Transplantation. 1992;54:50.

40. Griffith BP, Kormos RL, Armitage JM, et al. Comparative trial of immunoprophylaxis with RATG and OKT3. J Heart Lung Transplant. 1990;9:301-305.

41. Church AC. Clinical advances in therapies targeting the interleukin-2 receptor. Q J Med. 2003;96:91-102.

42. Linden PK, Pasculle AW, Manez R, et al. Differences in outcomes for patients with bacteremia due to vancomycin-resistant *Enterococcus faecium* or vancomycin-susceptible *E. faecium*. Clin Infect Dis. 1996;22:663.

43. Cohen MI, Galgiani JN, Potter D, Ogden DA. Coccidioidomycosis in renal replacement therapy. Arch Intern Med. 1982;142:489.

44. Wheat J, Smith EJ, Sathapatayavongs B, et al. Histoplasmosis in renal allograft recipients: Two large urban outbreaks. Arch Intern Med. 1983;143:703.

45. Dummer JS, Allos GM. Gastrointestinal infections in transplant patients. In: Blaser MJ, Smith PD, Ravidin JI, et al, eds. Infections of the Gastrointestinal Tract. Philadelphia: Lippincott Williams & Wilkins; 2002:457-471.

46. Stout JE, Yu VL. Legionellosis. N Engl J Med. 1997;337:682.

47. Sabria M, Yu VL. Hospital acquired legionellosis: Solutions for a preventable infection. Lancet Infect Dis. 2002;2:368-373.

48. Rossi EC, Simon TL, Moss GS, Gould SA. Principles of Transfusion Medicine. 2nd ed. Baltimore: Williams & Wilkins; 1996.

49. Gottesdiener KM. Transplanted infections: Donor-to-host transmission with the allograft. Ann Intern Med. 1989;110:1001.

50. Iwamoto M, Jernigan DB, Guasch A, et al. Transmission of West Nile virus from an organ donor to four transplant recipients. N Engl J Med. 2003;348:2196-2203.

51. Regamey N, Tamm M, Wernli M, et al. Transmission of human herpesvirus-8 infection from renal transplant donors to recipients. N Engl J Med. 1998;339:1368.

52. Luft BJ, Naot Y, Araujo FG, et al. Primary and reactivated toxoplasma infection in patients with cardiac transplants: Clinical spectrum and problems in diagnosis in a defined population. Ann Intern Med. 1983;99:27.

53. Dummer JS, Armstrong J, Somers J, et al. Transmission of infection with herpes simplex virus by renal transplantation. J Infect Dis. 1987;155:202.

54. Cen H, Breinig MC, Atchison RW, et al. Epstein-Barr virus transmission via the donor organs in solid organ transplantation: Polymerase chain reaction and restriction fragment length polymorphism analysis of IR2, IR3, and IR4. J Virol. 1991;65:976.

55. Pereira BJ, Milford EL, Kirkman RL, et al. Prevalence of hepatitis C virus RNA in organ donors positive for hepatitis C antibody and in the recipients of their organs. N Engl J Med. 1992;327:910.

56. Forman LM, Lewis JD, Berlin JA, et al. The association between hepatitis C infection and survival after liver transplantation. Gastroenterology. 2002;122:889-896.

57. Lake KD, Smith CI, LaForest SK, et al. Policies regarding the transplantation of hepatitis C-positive candidates and donor organs. J Heart Lung Transplant. 1997;16:917.

58. Wolf JL, Perkins HA, Schreeder MT, Vincenti F. The transplanted kidney as a source of hepatitis B infection. Ann Intern Med. 1979;91:412.

59. Wachs ME, Amend WJ, Ascher NL, et al. The risk of transmission of hepatitis B from HBsAg(−), HBcAb(+), HBIgM(−) organ donors. Transplantation. 1995;59:230.

60. Dodson SF, Issa S, Araya V, et al. Infectivity of hepatic allografts with antibodies to hepatitis B virus. Transplantation. 1997;64:1582.

61. Delmonico FL, Snydman DR. Organ donor screening for infectious diseases. Transplantation. 1998;65:603.

62. Manzarbeitia C, Reich DJ, Ortiz JA, et al. Safe use of livers from donors with positive hepatitis B core antibody. Liver Transplant. 2002;8:556-561.

63. Erice A, Rhame FS, Heussner RC, et al. Human immunodeficiency virus infection in patients with solid-organ transplants: Report of five cases and review. Rev Infect Dis. 1991;13.

64. Cantarovich F, Vazquez M, Garcia WD, et al. Special infections in organ transplantation in South America. Transplant Proc. 1992;24:1902.

65. Antman M, Chang Y. Kaposi's sarcoma. N Engl J Med. 2000;342:1027-1038.

66. Broyer M, Tete MJ, Guest G, et al. Varicella and zoster in children after kidney transplantation: Long-term results of vaccination. Pediatrics. 1997;99:35.

67. Lichtenstein IH, MacGregor RR. Mycobacterial infections in renal transplant recipients: Report of five cases and review of the literature. Rev Infect Dis. 1983;5:216.

68. Antony SJ, Ynares C, Dummer JS. Isoniazid hepatotoxicity in renal transplant recipients. Clin Transplant. 1997;11:34.

69. Roland, ME, Stock PG. Review of solid-organ transplantation in HIV-infected patients. Transplantation. 2003;75:425-429.

70. Dummer JS, Lazariashvili N, Barnes J, et al. A survey of antifungal management in lung transplantation. J Heart Lung Transpl. In press.

71. Boeckh M, Bowden RA, Goodrich JM, et al. Cytomegalovirus antigen detection in peripheral blood leukocytes after allogeneic marrow transplantation. Blood. 1992;80:1358.

72. Einsele H, Ehninger G, Hebart H, et al. Polymerase chain reaction monitoring reduces the incidence of cytomegalovirus disease and the duration and side effects of antiviral therapy after bone marrow transplantation. Blood. 1995;86:2815.

73. Goodrich JM, Mori M, Gleaves CA, et al. Early treatment with ganciclovir to prevent cytomegalovirus disease after allogeneic bone marrow transplantation. N Engl J Med. 1991;325:1601.

74. Fox JC, Kidd IM, Griffiths PD, et al. Longitudinal analysis of cytomegalovirus load in renal transplant recipients using a quantitative polymerase chain reaction: Correlation with disease. J Gen Virol. 1995;76:309.

75. Singh N, Yu VL, Mieles L. High dose acyclovir compared with short course preemptive ganciclovir therapy to prevent cytomegalovirus disease in liver transplant recipients. Ann Intern Med. 1994;120:375.

76. Rowe DT, Webber S, Schauer EM, et al. Epstein Barr virus load monitoring: Its role in the prevention and management of post-transplant lymphoproliferative disease. Transpl Infect Dis. 2001;3:79-87.

77. Grellier L, Mutimer D, Ahmed M, et al. Lamivudine prophylaxis against reinfection in liver transplantation for hepatitis B cirrhosis. Lancet. 1996;348:1212.

78. Berenguer M. Natural history of recurrent hepatitis C. Liver Transplant. 2002;8(Suppl):S14 S18.

79. Hirsch HH, Knowles W, Dickenmann M, et al. Prospective study of polyomavirus type BK replication and nephropathy in renal-transplant recipients. N Engl J Med 2002;347:527-530.

80. Huzly D, Neifer S, Reinke P, et al. Routine immunizations in adult renal transplant recipients. Transplantation. 1997;63:839.

81. Blumberg EA, Brozena SC, Stutman P, et al. Immunogenicity of pneumococcal vaccine in heart transplant recipients. Clin Infect Dis. 2001;32:307-310.

82. Blumberg EA, Albano C, Pruett T, et al. The immunogenicity of influenza virus vaccine in solid organ transplant recipients. Clin Infect Dis. 1996;22:295.

83. Rand EB, McCarthy CA, Whitington PF. Measles vaccination after orthotopic liver transplantation. J Pediatr. 1993;123:87.

84. Zamora I, Simon JM, Da Silva ME, Piqueras AI. Attenuated varicella virus vaccine in children with renal transplants. Pediatr Nephrol. 1994;8:190.

85. Tolkoff-Rubin NE, Cosimi AB, Russell PS, Rubin RH. A controlled study of trimethoprim-sulfamethoxazole prophylaxis of urinary tract infection in renal transplant recipients. Rev Infect Dis. 1982;4:614.

86. Fox BC, Sollinger HW, Belzer FO, Maki DG. A prospective, randomized, double-blind study of trimethoprim-sulfamethoxazole for prophylaxis of infection in renal transplantation: Clinical efficacy, absorption of trimethoprim-sulfamethoxazole, effects on the microflora, and the cost-benefit of prophylaxis. Am J Med. 1990;89:255.

87. Cruciani M, Rampazzo R, Malena M, et al. Prophylaxis with fluoroquinolones for bacterial infections in neutropenic patients: A meta-analysis. Clin Infect Dis. 1996;23:795.

88. Smyth RL, Higenbottam TW, Scott JP, et al. Herpes simplex virus infection in heart-lung transplant recipients. Transplantation. 1990;49:735.

89. Saral R, Burns WH, Laskin OL, et al. Acyclovir prophylaxis of herpes-simplex-virus infections. N Engl J Med. 1981;305:63.

90. Meyers JD, Reed EC, Shepp DH, et al. Acyclovir for prevention of cytomegalovirus infection and disease after allogeneic marrow transplantation. N Engl J Med. 1988;318:70.

91. Balfour HH Jr, Chace BA, Stapleton JT, et al. A randomized, placebo-controlled trial of oral acyclovir for the prevention of cytomegalovirus disease in recipients of renal allografts. N Engl J Med. 1989;320:1381.

92. Goodrich JM, Bowden RA, Fisher L, et al. Ganciclovir prophylaxis to prevent cytomegalovirus disease after allogeneic marrow transplant. Ann Intern Med. 1993;118:173.

93. Merigan TC, Renlund DG, Keay S, et al. A controlled trial of ganciclovir to prevent cytomegalovirus disease after heart transplantation. N Engl J Med. 1992;326:1182.

94. Winston DJ, Wirin D, Shaked A, Busuttil RW. Randomised comparison of ganciclovir and high-dose acyclovir for long-term cytomegalovirus prophylaxis in liver-transplant recipients. Lancet. 1995;346:69.

95. Gane E, Saliba F, Valdecasas GJ, et al. Randomised trial of efficacy and safety of oral ganciclovir in the prevention of cytomegalovirus disease in liver-transplant recipients. Lancet. 1997;350:1729.

96. Lowance D, Neumayer H-H, Legendre CM, et al. Valacyclovir for the prevention of cytomegalovirus disease after renal transplantation. N Engl J Med. 1999;340:1462.

97. Pescovitz MD, Rabkin J, Merion RM, et al. Valganciclovir results in improved absorption of ganciclovir in liver transplant recipients. Antimicrob Agents Chemother. 2000;44:2811-2815.

98. Snydman DR, Werner BG, Heinze-Lacey B, et al. Use of cytomegalovirus immune globulin to prevent cytomegalovirus disease in renal-transplant recipients. N Engl J Med. 1987;317:1049.

99. Snydman DR, Werner BG, Dougherty NN, et al. Cytomegalovirus immune globulin prophylaxis in liver transplantation: A randomized, double-blind, placebo-controlled trial. The Boston Center for Liver Transplantation CMVIG Study Group. Ann Intern Med. 1993;119:984.

100. Singh N. Preemptive therapy versus universal prophylaxis with ganciclovir for cytomegalovirus in solid organ transplant patients. Clin Infect Dis. 2001;32:742-751.

101. Gombert ME, DuBouchet L, Aulicino TM, Butt KM. A comparative trial of clotrimazole troches and oral nystatin suspension in recipients of renal transplants: Use in prophylaxis of oropharyngeal candidiasis. JAMA. 1987;258:2553.

102. Goodman JL, Winston DJ, Greenfield RA, et al. A controlled trial of fluconazole to prevent fungal infections in patients undergoing bone marrow transplantation. N Engl J Med. 1992;326:845.

103. Winston DJ, Pakrasi A, Busuttil RW. Prophylactic fluconazole in liver transplant recipients: A randomized double-blind, placebo-controlled trial. Ann Intern Med. 1999;131:729-737.

104. Winston DJ, Busuttil RW. Randomized controlled trial of oral itraconazole solution versus fluconazole for prevention of fungal infections in liver transplant recipients. Transplantation. 2002;74:688-695.

105. Herbrecht R, Denning DW, Patterson TF, et al. Voriconazole versus amphotericin B for primary therapy of invasive aspergillosis. N Engl J Med. 2002;347:408-415.

106. Walsh TJ, Pappas P, Winston DJ, et al. Voriconazole compared with liposomal amphotericin B for empirical antifungal therapy in patients with neutropenia and persistent fever. N Engl J Med. 2002;346:225-234.

107. Wolff SN, Fay J, Stevens D, et al. Fluconazole versus amphotericin B for the prevention of fungal infections in patients undergoing bone marrow transplantation. Bone Marrow Transplant. 2000;25:853-859.

108. Tollemar J, Hockerstedt K, Ericzon BG, et al. Liposomal amphotericin B prevents invasive fungal infections in liver transplant recipients: A randomized, placebo-controlled study. Transplantation. 1995;59:45.

109. Wreghitt TG, Gray JJ, Pavel P, et al. Efficacy of pyrimethamine for the prevention of donor-acquired *Toxoplasma gondii* infection in heart and heart-lung transplant patients. Transpl Int. 1992;5:197.

110. Baden LR, Katz JT, Franck L, et al. Successful toxoplasmosis prophylaxis after orthotopic cardiac transplantation with trimethoprim-sulfamethoxazole. Transplantation. 2003;75:339-343.

111. Hellinger WC, Yao JD, Alvarez S, et al. A randomized, prospective, double blinded evaluation of selective bowel decontamination in liver transplantation. Transplantation. 2002;73:1904-1909.

112. Soave R. Prophylaxis strategies for solid-organ transplantation. Clin Infect Dis. 2001;33(Suppl 1):S26-S31.

113. Kusne S, Krystofiak S. Infection control issue after bone marrow and solid organ transplantation. In: Bowden RA, Ljungman P, Paya CV, eds. Transplant Infections. Philadelphia; Lippincott-Raven; 1998:21-36.

114. Centers for Disease Control and Prevention. Guidelines for preventing opportunistic infections among hematopoietic stem cell transplant recipients. MMWR Morb Mortal Wkly Rep. 2000;49(RR-10):1-128.

115. Singh NS, Carrigan DR. Human herpesvirus-6 in transplantation: An emerging pathogen. Ann Intern Med. 1996;124:1065.

CHAPTER **311**

Infections in Recipients of Hematopoietic Stem Cell Transplantation

JO-ANNE VAN BURIK

DANIEL WEISDORF

The clinical approach to infections in the hematopoietic stem cell transplantation (HSCT) patient involves an understanding of basic transplantation techniques, clinical syndromes, host defense defects at different time points after transplantation, the natural history of individual infections, and the mechanisms underlying immune system reconstitution after transplantation. In general, the dominant elements of infectious risks for bacterial, viral, fungal, and parasitic infections after HSCT depend on the pretransplantation exposure history (viral serostatus), whether the transplant is from an autologous or an allogeneic donor source, and the day after transplantation on which the infection occurs. The distinguishing determinant of infectious risk between autologous and allogeneic grafts is the associated risk incurred by ongoing immunosuppression from graft-versus-host disease (GVHD) and its therapy; differing tempos of humoral and cellular immune reconstitution also affect the risk. The time period after transplantation defines eras of differing transplantation complications and the evolution of the slowly resolving post-transplantation immune deficiency: cutaneous and mucosal barrier breakdown, neutropenia, lymphopenia, and/or hypogammaglobulinemia. Many post-transplantation complications mimic infectious processes, and multiple infections may occur in the same patient at the same time. Therefore, the HSCT patient should be examined in the context of pretransplantation infectious disease serologies, conditioning regimen, available culture data from mucosal surfaces, contemporary transplant complications, previous and recent infections, current antimicrobial prophylaxis, and the current degree and duration of neutropenia and lymphopenia.

BASIC TRANSPLANTATION TECHNIQUES

HSCT involves the intravenous delivery of hematopoietic stem cells (HSCs) to a recipient whose hematopoietic and immune systems have been ablated by a cytotoxic preparative regimen given over the 4 to 10 days before transplantation, commonly referred to as the conditioning regimen. HSCs are obtained from bone marrow, peripheral blood, or umbilical cord blood.[1,2] HSCT is a treatment option for hematologic and oncologic syndromes including aplastic anemia, leukemias, lymphomas, immunodeficiency syndromes, inborn errors of metabolism, and some solid tumors (e.g., renal cell carcinoma, neuroblastoma), and it is currently used investigationally for diseases such as scleroderma and multiple sclerosis.

The conditioning regimen used to prepare the host is a major determinant of outcome, because of variable host tissue injury and the potential for induction of prolonged immunodeficiency. Conditioning regimens may consist of immune suppressive and cytotoxic chemotherapy alone or of combined radiation plus chemotherapy. Conditioning can damage mucosal surfaces, facilitating transmucosal origin of blood-stream infections. The transplantation complications that affect the infectious risks of the HSCT recipient include the direct effects of this high-dose cytoreductive therapy, such as mucositis, hemorrhagic cystitis, diarrhea, and veno-occlusive disease (VOD); GVHD; and relapse of the underlying hematologic/oncologic disease.

Chemotherapy

Busulfan or melphalan are commonly used alkylating agents that are toxic to myeloid stem cells. Cyclophosphamide-containing regimens predispose to hemorrhagic cystitis. Horse antithymocyte globulin (ATG), which alters the function of or eliminates T lymphocytes, is used for the conditioning regimen for aplastic anemia and for GVHD treatment. Chills and fever commonly occur among patients receiving ATG and can be managed by symptomatic treatment and slowing of the infusion. Serum sickness, a syndrome of fever, arthralgia, and rash, can occur with subsequent ATG doses; it is treated with corticosteroid therapy. Fludarabine can lead to prolonged T-lymphopenia.

Irradiation

Total body irradiation (TBI) may be administered as a single dose, "fractionated" in multiple doses given once daily over 6 or 7 days, or "hyperfractionated" in multiple doses given two or more times a day over several days. Diarrhea occurs in virtually all patients in the first week after irradiation; it may be treated symptomatically while stool culture is pending to exclude infectious causes. Severe mucositis occurs in most irradiated patients and is aggravated by prolonged neutropenia and the use of methotrexate.[3] As long as bleeding and oral inflammation do not compromise the patient's airway, mucositis is treated symptomatically. Single-dose TBI is uncommonly used, but irradiated patients may be febrile in the hours after treatment and may develop symptomatic parotitis or pancreatitis. Lower dose, nonmyeloablative conditioning regimens may be intensely immunosuppressive but less cytotoxic, resulting in less mucosal, enteric, and hepatic injury in the early weeks after transplantation.

Human Leukocyte Antigen Matching

In general, engraftment is most rapid and thus neutropenia is briefest when the patient and allogeneic donor are completely matched at all genetic human leukocyte antigen (HLA) loci. Similarly, identical twin (syngeneic) transplants or those using HSC from the patient being transplanted (autologous) lead to prompt neutrophil recovery. Allogeneic HSCT (sibling or unrelated donor) has the highest chance of success when fully HLA-matched sibling donors are used, but less than 30% of intended recipients have a matched sibling donor available.[4,5] For partially matched family or unrelated donors, incompatibility and risk of infection can be described in terms of vectors. Incompatibility in the donor defines the genetic risk of rejection, which may result in delayed engraftment or graft failure.[6] Incompatibility in the recipient defines the genetic risk of GVHD, resulting in continued immunosuppression and its attendant complications. Both vectors of incompatibility may be present for a single transplanted patient in varying degrees, proportional to the number of mismatched immunodominant alleles.

Nonmyeloablative Transplant Preparation

Reduced-intensity regimens have been developed with the goal of donor-derived hematopoietic and immunologic reconstitution. These lesser intensity regimens provide a weaker anticancer effect and rely on the graft-versus-tumor effects to eradicate underlying malignancies. TBI doses are usually not more than 2 Gy, versus 12 to 14 Gy in fully ablative transplants. Fludarabine may be used with induction of extended immune suppression.[7]

Prevention of Infection

Preventative strategies include protective isolation for reduced exposure to pathogens, enhancement of host immune reconstitution with hematopoietic growth factors, prophylaxis during high-risk periods with targeted antimicrobial chemotherapy, and suppression of subclinical infection with preemptive therapy.[8-11] Prophylaxis or preemptive strategies are more effective than treatment after infection is established, and the mortality rate for patients with established infections continues to be high despite available therapy. After mucositis has cleared and oral alimentation has resumed, oral therapy is preferred for prophylaxis.

CLINICAL SYNDROMES UNIQUE TO THE HEMATOPOIETIC STEM CELL TRANSPLANTATION RECIPIENT

Hemorrhagic Cystitis

Hemorrhagic cystitis is a common complication that can lead to gross hematuria, clots and urinary retention, and impairment of renal function. Cystitis within 1 week after marrow infusion usually is noninfectious in origin, caused by the administration of high-dose cyclophosphamide and busulfan in the conditioning regimen. Prophylactic and supportive care measures include mesna, forced diuresis with continuous bladder irrigation, transfusions, intravesical instillations (e.g., prostaglandins, epidermal growth factor, cauterizing vesicants), and rarely cystostomy or cystectomy. Later following transplantation, GVHD and infection are contributing causes of cystitis. The majority of infectious agents are viral, usually either the polyomavirus BK or adenovirus, although herpes simplex virus (HSV), cytomegalovirus (CMV), the polyomavirus JC, human herpesvirus type 6 (HHV-6), and *Strongyloides* occur with lower frequencies.[12-14] Polyomaviruses are

shed in the urine in many HSCT patients without clinical symptoms (see Chapter 141). Higher viral loads of BK virus may indicate a risk for hemorrhagic cystitis.[15] There is currently no standard antiviral treatment for viruria caused by BK virus or adenovirus, although vidarabine has been tried and cidofovir is undergoing evaluation.

Veno-occlusive Disease

VOD refers to a syndrome of liver toxicity that occurs at any time after the onset of the high-dose conditioning regimen, usually before day 20. It is characterized by painful hepatomegaly, 5% or greater weight gain, and hyperbilirubinemia greater than 2 mg/dL.[16] Severe VOD, with marked jaundice or ascites, leads to multiorgan failure involving the kidneys, heart, and lungs.[17] Sometimes effective anticoagulant or antithrombolytic therapy must be initiated before serious organ failure. Death occurs in approximately 5% to 10% of patients with VOD. Clinical predictors of severe VOD include higher dose cytoreductive therapy, hepatitis present before cytoreductive therapy, persistent fever during cytoreductive therapy, previous radiation therapy to the liver, and schistosomal hepatic periportal fibrosis. Conditions that may mimic VOD include cholestasis in patients with septicemia, hepatic infiltration secondary to infection or tumor, pericardial tamponade, CMV, and intra-abdominal disease such as pancreatitis, peritonitis, or cholecystitis. Additionally, early GVHD and cyclosporine-induced cholestasis are noninfectious causes of liver toxicity that may coexist with or mimic VOD. Diagnosis of VOD may be difficult, and ultrasound assessment of hepatic portal venous flow may be normal. Occasionally, liver biopsy with immunohistochemical staining and culture to rule out infectious causes may be indicated, though risks of hemorrhage are markedly increased. Hepatotoxic and nephrotoxic drugs should be avoided in patients with VOD. Genetic polymorphisms in drug metabolism may modify risks of VOD, but their clinical value is under study.

Graft-versus-Host Disease

GVHD is the major, life-threatening complication after allogeneic transplantation, developing in 40% to 80% of patients.[18] Risks are greater with partially matched or unrelated donor HSCT. Donor T lymphocytes mount an immune attack against the recipient's tissues. Clinical manifestations of this disorder include rash, cholestatic hepatitis, nausea, vomiting, and diarrhea. Cyclosporine or tacrolimus, usually given with methotrexate, are effective immunosuppressive agents for the prevention of GVHD and are usually started before transplantation. GVHD itself can compound and prolong post-HSCT immunodeficiency. The corticosteroids or other immunosuppressive drugs used for treatment of GVHD may impair phagocytic function and directly worsen lymphopenia and cellular immune deficiency. Patients with acute and chronic GVHD have splenic dysfunction and thus an added risk for infection with encapsulated bacteria such as *Streptococcus pneumoniae*, *Neisseria meningitidis*, and *Haemophilus influenzae*.

Hepatitis

Clinical hepatitis in HSCT recipients can range from fever associated with abdominal pain to fulminant hepatitis. Infectious hepatitis must be distinguished from several common noninfectious causes, including liver dysfunction related to the conditioning regimen (i.e., VOD), acute GVHD, cholestatic liver injury related to sepsis, and chemical hepatitis related to either drugs or hyperalimentation.

Clinically important viral hepatitis syndromes after transplantation include acquisition or reactivation of infection with hepatitis B virus (HBV), hepatitis C virus (HCV), varicella-zoster virus (VZV), adenovirus, HSV, CMV, and HHV-6.[19] Reactivation of HBV is more likely than HCV to result in fulminant hepatitis, although this outcome occurs in a minority of infected patients. Disseminated VZV and adenovirus infections may present with elevations in serum aminotransferase levels that precede the appearance of other disease manifestations by several days. Liver biopsy with viral culture and polymerase chain reaction (PCR) may rarely be needed to establish a diagnosis of severe hepatitis in the early postengraftment period.

Newly identified viruses such as hepatitis G virus and transfusion-transmitted virus are not known to influence the outcome of HSCT.

HBV (surface antigen, surface antibody, and core antibody) and HCV serologies are tested in donor and recipient prior to HSCT. Pretransplant imaging studies or liver biopsy may be needed to evaluate seropositive patients with abnormal liver enzymes or tender hepatomegaly. Donors and recipients with a positive HBV surface antigen should be tested for viral load using HBV DNA PCR studies prior to transplantation, because the risk of HBV hepatitis can be reduced by treatment to lower a detectable viral load. Interferon, lamivudine, and famciclovir have all been shown to suppress HBV replication.[20-22]

An HBV-infected individual can be used as a donor if no alternative donor is available or if the intended recipient is already seropositive. HBV can be transmitted from a surface antigen–positive (or, less likely, core antibody–positive) donor to either a naive or a surface antibody–positive but core antibody–negative recipient. The risk of transmission is small when an HBV-positive donor has an undetectable viral load. If the recipient is HBV naive prior to transplantation, the subsequent infection is more likely to have clinical consequences. If the transplant can be delayed, then HBV vaccination of the recipient or use of HBV immune globulin may reduce the likelihood of hepatitis following transplantation. HBV immunity can be transferred from a surface antibody–positive donor to a naive recipient. Through adoptive immunity transfer, HBV infection can be cleared by transplant from a surface antibody–positive donor to a surface antigen-positive recipient.

Following transplantation, recipients with (1) liver enzyme elevation suggesting activation of HBV from latency, (2) HBV-infected donors, or (3) known pretransplant infection should be followed periodically using HBV DNA PCR viral load testing. High HBV viral load ($>10^5$ copies/mL) is the most important risk factor for clinically apparent reactivation in recipients positive for surface antigen.[23] For recipients with a persistently positive HBV DNA PCR study after transplantation despite treatment, the risk of fatal liver disease may be up to 12%.

HCV-positive donors and recipients should undergo RNA viral load testing. An HCV-infected individual can be used as a donor. However, in contrast to HBV, the transmission of HCV from a HCV RNA-positive donor approaches 100%. If clinically feasible, RNA-positive HCV donors should be treated with interferon and oral ribavirin prior to harvest, though the impact on post-transplant HCV transmission is uncertain.

Because HCV requires a functioning cellular immune system to produce hepatitis, few clinical consequences are recognizable in the recipient early following HSCT. HCV infection does not increase the incidence of VOD. Over 10 years, the long-term complication of HCV infection is cirrhosis.[24] There are no data demonstrating a correlation between hepatitis C genotype and type or severity of liver disease after transplantation. The myelosuppressive effects of interferon or other antivirals limit treatment of hepatitis C following HSCT.

Pneumonia Syndromes

Infectious pneumonias must be distinguished from noninfectious pulmonary complications after HSCT, which can include pulmonary edema, pleural effusion, alveolar hemorrhage, radiation injury (pneumonitis or fibrosis), drug reactions, adult respiratory distress syndrome, idiopathic pneumonia syndrome, cytolytic thrombi (causing multiple peripheral lung nodules), bronchiolitis obliterans, and chronic GVHD.[25] Management of noninfectious pneumonias requires exclusion of lower respiratory tract infection, and their pathophysiology may be distinct in that, for some syndromes, the therapeutic response to high-dose corticosteroids may be more likely.

Diffuse alveolar hemorrhage begins with dyspnea and alveolar infiltrates and is distinguished from other noninfectious pneumonias by repeated bloody return during bronchoscopic examination and alveolar lavage. The syndrome usually occurs in the second and third weeks after HSCT. Thrombocytopenia, rapid neutrophil recovery, infection, drug toxicity, radiation toxicity, intensely cytotoxic regimens, and solid malignancy have been implicated as risk factors. Corticosteroids are recommended, but infrequently improve survival.

Idiopathic pneumonia syndrome is a process of widespread alveolar injury that is characterized clinically by diffuse interstitial infiltrates and varying degrees of respiratory failure in the absence of active lower respiratory tract infection. It is thought to be related to the chemotherapy and/or TBI used as part of the conditioning regimen, inducing proinflammatory cytokine release and increasing alveolar capillary permeability. Idiopathic pneumonia syndrome occurs in 8% to 17% of patients, but may be more frequent after allogeneic than autologous transplantation. It is associated with mortality rates of 60% to 80%. Idiopathic pneumonia syndrome occurs classically in two peaks, one in the first few weeks and the other in the second and third month after transplantation.

Diarrhea

Diarrhea after transplantation is primarily a result of noninfectious causes such as regimen-related gut mucosal toxicity and GVHD. Diarrhea is associated with infection in less than 15% of cases.[26] The list of infectious agents responsible for diarrhea is expanding to include *Clostridium difficile,* adenovirus, rotavirus, enterovirus, coxsackievirus, HHV-6, *Campylobacter, Escherichia coli, Salmonella, Giardia,* and *Cryptosporidium. C. difficile* is seen with increasing frequency.[27] Outbreaks of diarrhea have been reported for *Cryptosporidium* and enterovirus. From other countries, reports of diarrhea have been associated with *Trichostrongylus.*

Typhlitis, or neutropenic enterocolitis, is a relatively common anaerobic infection that may be associated with diarrhea during neutropenia.[28] Typhlitis is preceded by fever, abdominal pain, and right lower quadrant tenderness that may be associated with rebound. Computed tomography scanning of the abdomen will show right-sided colonic inflammation with thickening of the mucosa, and therapy against anaerobic bacteria should be added.

Rash

Skin eruptions are often noninfectious, occurring as a direct result of radiation effect from conditioning therapy or secondary to GVHD or drug allergy.[29] Rashes from conditioning regimens can result in the sudden onset of marked erythema over large areas of the body and blistering on the hands and feet. A skin biopsy can assist in distinguishing infectious from noninfectious causes of rash, and all lesions suspected to be infectious should be cultured or biopsied. The most common infectious causes are VZV, catheter-related exit site or tunnel infections, primary cutaneous fungal infections, and secondary cutaneous manifestations of disseminated bacterial or fungal infections.[30] Focal areas of bacterial cellulitis may occur on the lower extremities in the setting of edema from salt and water overload or from VOD with secondary lymphedema and impaired venous return.

Osteomyelitis

Osteomyelitis is uncommon following HSCT. The spectrum of organisms can include atypical mycobacteria, yeasts, and molds in addition to bacteria.[31] Osteomyelitis can rarely follow marrow aspiration from the sternum or marrow harvest from the iliac crest. When prolonged pain and fever occur after bone marrow harvest, osteomyelitis caused by *Staphylococcus aureus* should be considered.

PATTERNS OF IMMUNOSUPPRESSION AT DIFFERENT TIME POINTS AFTER MYELOABLATIVE HEMATOPOIETIC STEM CELL TRANSPLANTATION

Historically, three risk periods of immunologic deficiency occur predictably in recipients of HSCT (Fig. 311-1). They are the pre-engraftment period, the early postengraftment period (until day 100), and the late period (after day 100). An understanding of the immune deficiencies in each risk period and the period of peak risk for individual infections that are observed with standard infection prophylaxis helps the clinician recognize uncommon presentations of these infectious pathogens (Table 311-1).[32,33]

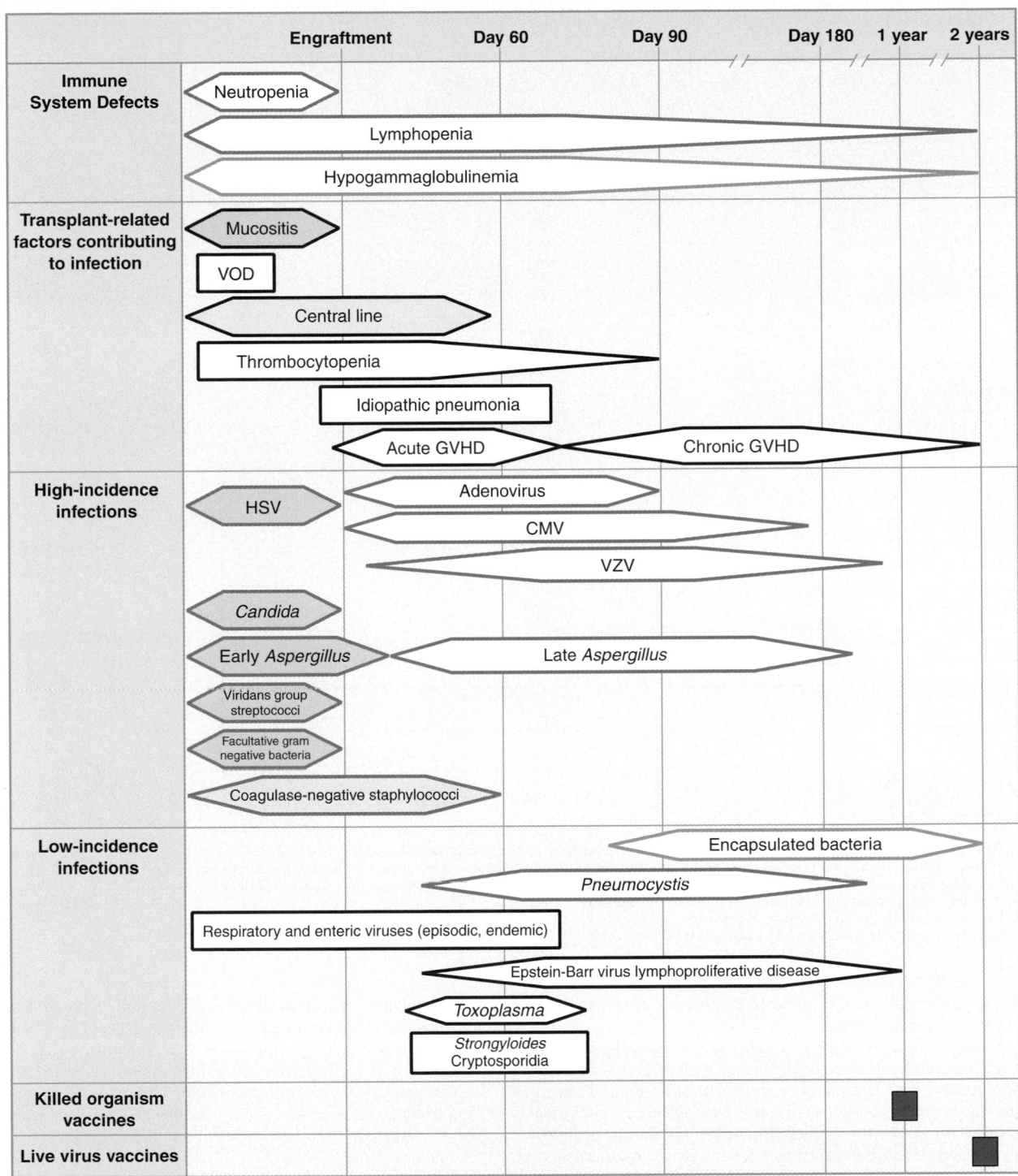

FIGURE 311-1. Phases of predictable opportunistic infections among HSCT recipients. Immune defects predisposing to infection are bordered by color (neutropenia = pink, lymphopenia = blue, and hypogammaglobulinemia = green). Barrier defects predisposing to infection are shaded in color (mucosal breakdown = yellow, skin breakdown = silver). Contribution of defects to infections occurring with high incidence are designated by border color (for immune defects) and/or shading (for barrier defects). *(Adapted from Van Burik J-AH, Freifeld AG. Infection in the severely imuno-compromised host. In: Abeloff MD, Armitage JO, Niederhuber JE, et al, eds. Clinical Oncology. 3rd ed. Philadelphia: Churchill Livingstone; 2004:942.)*

Pre-engraftment Risk Period

The pre-engraftment risk period begins with the onset of conditioning therapy and continues until approximately day 30 after transplantation. Bacterial infections are common during this time of profound neutropenia and lymphopenia, requiring prophylactic and promptly administered empirical systemic antibiotic therapy (see Chapter 308). Prophylactic systemic antibiotics (e.g., ciprofloxacin, penicillin) can be administered when the neutrophil count drops to less than 500/mm³ and continued until the neutrophil count recovers to prevent bacterial infection (see Chapter 306). Gastrointestinal

TABLE 311-1 Infections after Hematopoietic Stem Cell Transplantation, in Order of Occurrence

Organism	Peak Time Period of Risk (Weeks after HSCT)	Usual Prophylaxis	Incidence (%)	References
Pre-Engraftment Risk Period (1–4 wk)				
Herpes simplex virus (seropositive)	1–2	Acyclovir or valacyclovir	5–9	40, 89, 90, 92
Gram-positive bacteremia (most commonly coagulase-negative staphylococci, viridans-group streptococci, and enterococcus)	1–4	Prophylactic broad-spectrum antibiotics	20–30	64, 66, 67, 71-74
Gram-negative bacteremia	1–4	Prophylactic broad-spectrum antibiotics	5–10	8, 34
Candida	1–4	Fluconazole	<5 (systemic infection), 30 (colonization)	41-43, 148, 157, 158, 160
Aspergillus and other molds	1–4	HEPA air filtration; itraconazole, voriconazole, micafungin, or low-dose amphotericin	<5	44, 45, 149, 150, 164
Respiratory viruses	2–5	Isolation, hand washing	15	130, 131, 134-136
Idiopathic pneumonia syndrome	2–4	—	8–17	25
Postengraftment (4–26 wk) and Late (26–52 wk) Risk Periods				
Cytomegalovirus (seropositive)	7–26	Ganciclovir or foscarnet	<5 (end organ disease), up to 40 (antigenemia/ viremia)	56, 58, 94-97
Varicella-zoster virus (seropositive)	4–52	—*	up to 50	117, 118
Aspergillus and other molds	4–26	Itraconazole or voriconazole	10–15	44, 45
BK virus	—	—	up to 50 (shedding)	14
Adenovirus	—	—	4–5	94-97
Pneumocystis jirovecii	4–104	Trimethoprim/sulfamethoxazole	<1	151-155
Toxoplasma gondii (seropositive)	2–8	—†,‡	2–7	185, 188
Infrequent Infections, (May Span Multiple Risk Periods)				
Herpes simplex virus (seronegative)	—	—	<2	
Cytomegalovirus (seronegative)	—	Blood product screening or filtration	1–4	87, 88, 93
Varicella zoster virus (seronegative)	—	—	<3	
Streptococcus pneumoniae§	—	Vaccination, penicillin‖,¶	—	68-70, 189, 190
Haemophilus influenzae§	—	Vaccination, penicillin‖	—	189, 190
Neisseria meningitidis§	—	Penicillin‖	—	189, 190
Human herpesvirus-6	—	Ganciclovir or foscarnet	<2	143-145
Epstein-Barr virus	—	—	<1 (disease)	140, 141
Nocardia	—	—‡	<1	83, 84
Legionella	—	—	<1	78-82
Mycobacterium spp.	—	PPD screening	<1	75-77
Listeria monocytogenes	—	—	<1	85, 86

*Antiviral medications used to prevent other viral infections may be acting as prophylaxis for varicella reactivation.
†Prophylaxis with pyrimethamine/sulfadoxine may be used for seropositive patients in countries with a high rate of seroprevalence.[188]
‡The sulfa component of Pneumocystis prophylaxis may be acting as prophylaxis for Toxoplasma or Nocardia infection.
§Risk increased in patients with chronic graft-versus-host disease.
‖Undetermined efficacy for transplant recipients.
¶Increasing penicillin resistance may indicate a need for macrolides or extended-spectrum quinolones.

decontamination with nonabsorbable antibiotics was used in the past but is now rarely done.

Prophylactic antibiotic use has shifted the spectrum of gastrointestinal flora to potentially pathogenic organisms such as *C. difficile,* and the etiologic agents of bacteremia have shifted to more gram-positive organisms; in particular, coagulase-negative staphylococci and viridans-group streptococci are more often isolated from febrile neutropenic HSCT recipients.[34] Mechanical barrier defects caused by mucositis and central catheters predispose patients to blood-stream infections by allowing access for skin-colonizing organisms and gastrointestinal mucosal flora to otherwise sterile body sites.[35] Colonization with vancomycin-resistant enterococci or other multidrug-resistant pathogens may predispose to bacteremia with these organisms.[36] Recipients of autologous/syngeneic and allogeneic grafts develop a similar spectrum of infections during the pre-engraftment period; the major transplant-related complications occurring in this risk period (mucositis, severe neutropenia, and VOD) are similarly frequent in all types of transplants. However, the less frequent use of TBI and methotrexate and the more rapid neutrophil recovery often observed after autologous peripheral blood stem cell transplantation have markedly decreased the risks of mucositis and serious bacteremia for this subpopulation of patients.

Similarly, the use of less intensive conditioning regimens prior to nonmyeloablative allografting has lessened the risks of early bacteremia.

Adjunctive therapy with granulocyte transfusions has been used in some centers for treatment of serious infections that develop during neutropenia.[37] Although the technology of granulocyte transfusion is improving, evidence for efficacy and therefore the indications for use of this expensive and labor-intensive supportive measure are not well defined.

Routine culture of hematopoietic progenitor cell products yields low rates of recovery of bacterial organisms, most often *Corynebacterium* or staphylococci. Appropriate testing of HSC collection products include routine culture of hematopoietic progenitor cells before HSCT, but patients receiving culture-positive harvests usually do so without clinically adverse outcomes.[38,39]

HSV predictably reactivates during this risk period in 80% of those patients who are HSV seropositive, with most infections occurring before week 4 after transplantation, although use of prophylactic acyclovir at 400 mg twice daily (5 mg/kg twice daily for children) has minimized this clinical infection.[40] Candidemia and early-onset aspergillosis occur in less than 5% of patients during neutropenia. The risk is greater for patients with slow engraftment or extended neutropenia before transplantation. With fluconazole prophylaxis (200 to 400 mg/day),[41-43] *Candida albicans* infections have been mostly eliminated during this risk period, although *Candida krusei* and *Candida (Torulopsis) glabrata* have emerged as fluconazole-resistant pathogens. Use of the hematopoietic growth factors granulocyte and granulocyte-macrophage colony-stimulating factors has reduced the incidence of bacteremia by shortening the duration of neutropenia, but these agents have not been clearly shown to improve outcome in established infections.

Postengraftment Risk Period

The postengraftment period begins with neutrophil recovery and continues until day 100, when early B- and T-lymphocyte functional recovery is initially apparent. Reconstituted T lymphocytes have abnormal function for approximately 18 months, as evidenced by in vitro antigen and mitogen proliferative responses. However, T-lymphocyte reconstitution may be blunted by the effects of GVHD or CMV and their attendant treatments (corticosteroids, cyclosporine, anti–T-lymphocyte therapy, and ganciclovir). As a result, the rate of infection during this risk period is higher among recipients of allogeneic grafts, who are more likely to develop GVHD or CMV, than among recipients of autologous/syngeneic grafts. Another consequence of GVHD during this risk period is disruption of the gastrointestinal mucosa, potentially leading to bacteremia or fungemia from transmural entry of pathogens.

Late-onset aspergillosis may also occur during this risk period in 10% to 15% of patients, especially those with continuing GVHD, those receiving high-dose corticosteroids, and those with poor graft function.[44] Itraconazole, which has activity against several molds, is effective prophylaxis against deep mycoses in patients at high risk.[45]

Prophylaxis of *Pneumocystis jirovecii* (formerly *carinii*) infection with trimethoprim-sulfamethoxazole (TMP-SMX), dapsone, atovaquone, or aerosolized pentamidine is required for 6 to 12 months, or longer if chronic GVHD is continuing.[46,47]

Reactivation of CMV predictably occurs in 20% to 40% of patients who are CMV seropositive. Transmission to seronegative recipients from seropositive donors is uncommon. Surveillance for reactivation of CMV has been improved by the use of scheduled testing of peripheral blood leukocytes for CMV, using sensitive diagnostic methods such as pp65 neutrophil antigen and whole-blood or plasma PCR.[48-51] Antiviral prophylaxis or ganciclovir therapy initiated preemptively at subclinical indications of reactivation has reduced the incidence of end-organ disease caused by CMV to only 5% to 10% of seropositive recipients.[52] Continuing GVHD or delayed immune recovery after partially matched or unrelated donor HSCT can lead to later onset CMV infection and may indicate a need for prolonged CMV surveillance.

Late Risk Period

The late post-transplantation risk period begins at approximately day 100 and ends when the patient regains normal immunity, 18 to 36 months after HSCT.[53-55] In general, clinical immune recovery is demonstrable by the end of the first year after transplantation as long as the patient is no longer taking immunosuppressive medication and remains free from GVHD. For patients with continuing chronic GVHD, this period persists as long as therapy for chronic GVHD is required and includes dysfunction of lymphocyte, macrophage, and humoral immunity. VZV reactivation, infections with encapsulated bacteria (*S. pneumoniae, N. meningitidis,* and *H. influenzae*), and invasive aspergillosis or other invasive tissue mold infections may develop in this late risk period. The most common clinical syndromes include sinusitis, bronchitis, pneumonia, and otitis media caused by respiratory viruses or bacteria. CMV disease may develop, suggesting the need for continuing CMV surveillance (pp65 antigenemia or PCR) in the seropositive recipient with chronic GVHD.[56] Late infections may be more common among patients with unrelated donors compared with patients whose donors were family members, even in the absence of GVHD. Approximately 50% of late pneumonias in patients with ongoing chronic GVHD are caused by noninfectious interstitial pneu-

monitis. Lung histopathology shows obliterative bronchitis that may respond to corticosteroid therapy.

IMMUNOSUPPRESSION AFTER NONMYELOABLATIVE HEMATOPOIETIC STEM CELL TRANSPLANTATION

Nonmyeloablative HSCT is associated with less disruption of mucosal barriers, shorter periods of severe neutropenia, fewer episodes of bacteremia in the first 30 days, and a trend toward fewer episodes of bacteremia during the first 100 days following HSCT.[57] However, this type of transplant can still be associated with severe GVHD, often requiring high-dose corticosteroid use. It is often used for older patients or those with compromised organ function and poor performance status. Though data are limited, it appears that the overall incidences of CMV disease and invasive fungal infection are similar to those with conventional HSCT over the first year following transplantation.[58,59] Nonmyeloablative HSCT recipients should receive surveillance for CMV and fungal infections well beyond day 100, and preemptive or prophylactic treatment similar to that of myeloablative HSCT recipients between day 100 and 1 year following HSCT.

MEASURES TO REDUCE RISKS OF INFECTION

Protective measures that should be discussed prior to HSCT include travel, crowds, and pets.[10] Regarding travel, there are no particular restrictions, but strategies to minimize transmission of infectious diseases have been summarized.[10] Some social situations, such as sitting in a crowded movie theater or classroom, may increase the risk of acquiring a viral illness. Turning away from individuals who are coughing or sneezing, or even quickly donning a mask, may be helpful in preventing transmission of airborne infection. Patients need instruction to remember to aid infection prevention by washing their hands as soon as possible after being close to someone with a cold. Given recent outbreaks of Noroviruses involving cruise ships and other types of outbreaks (e.g., *Staphylococcus*) commonly associated with the close living quarters of this type of vacation, cruise ships may be unwise vacation choices.[60,61]

Healthy dogs and cats are considered acceptable pets. However, the immunosuppressed patient should not be responsible for scooping cat litter because of potential *Toxoplasma* cyst exposure. Similarly, the patient should not play in sandboxes, because these areas are concentrated sites that outdoor cats may consider to be litter boxes. Because reptiles of many sorts have been reported to be infected with *Salmonella,* patients should not touch these animals or their aquarium homes. The heated water of tropical fish tanks may carry *Mycobacterium marinum. Chlamydophila (Chlamydia) psittaci* can be transmitted from psittaccine birds.

Hand washing or the use of alcohol-based hand rub disinfectant is the mainstay of infection prevention in the hospital or clinic.[62] Persons entering the patient's room to perform examination or touch the patient (including visitors as well as health care workers) should wash or disinfect their hands outside the room.[9] During respiratory virus season, infection control personnel will often add extra signage to doorways and other places on the wards to remind visitors of the importance of hand washing. Staff and visitors with respiratory viral infections should not be permitted to have direct patient contact. Routine use of gown, gloves, and/or masks is not required in the presence of a neutropenic transplant recipient.

NATURAL HISTORY OF INDIVIDUAL INFECTIONS AFTER HEMATOPOIETIC STEM CELL TRANSPLANTATION

With advances in infection prevention strategies, the risk periods for some infections are changing. It is important to understand the natural history of individual infections as they occur in the HSCT recipient and how the natural history may be distinct from that in other immunocompromised patient populations. Infections that occur with a high incidence among HSCT recipients justify prophylaxis during the applicable risk period or empirical treatment during the course of applicable clinical scenarios of infection (see Table 311-1).[8,63]

Bacterial Infections

Gram-positive organisms account for half of bacteremias occurring after HSCT.[64,65] Although the skin has been thought to be the primary reservoir for these organisms, colonization of the gastrointestinal tract may be an additional source. *Staphylococcus epidermidis* is the most common species recovered in culture from the skin and nose. Oropharyngeal organisms include *Streptococcus pyogenes, Streptococcus mitis, S. pneumoniae,* and *Enterococcus* (vancomycin sensitive and vancomycin resistant). Unlike catheter-associated infections with *S. aureus, Candida* spp., or some gram-negative bacilli, most gram-positive bacteremias can be successfully managed without removal of the intravascular device.[66,67] If the patient is not responding to initial antibiotic management or if there is tenderness or erythema along the tunnel tract, the catheter may have to be removed. Rarely, adjunctive surgical débridement of the skin tunnel is needed. Catheter removal and surgical débridement are often required when a tunnel infection is caused by rapidly growing mycobacteria.

Gram-negative organisms are the second most frequent cause of blood-stream infection. The incidence of infection with *Pseudomonas* spp. is low, in part because of the use of antipseudomonal antibiotics for prophylactic therapy. Although bacteremias have historically occurred during the neutropenic period, bacteremias continue to develop in patients with long-term central intravenous catheters, in patients with ongoing immunosuppression resulting from GVHD or its therapy, and in those with neutropenia secondary to graft failure or drug-related marrow suppression (e.g., ganciclovir).

Encapsulated Bacteria

For patients who experience chronic GVHD or are otherwise asplenic, the risk for bacterial infection with encapsulated organisms is increased, and penicillin or macrolide prophylaxis may be indicated until immunosuppression is discontinued.[54] A few reports of penicillin-resistant pneumococcal infections have prompted a change in prophylaxis from penicillin to a quinolone for some centers.[68-70]

Viridans-group Streptococci

Viridans-group streptococcal bacteremias, mostly caused by *S. mitis,* may carry a high mortality rate, especially in children early after HSCT.[71-73] Poor dental hygiene is a risk factor for *S. mitis* bacteremia in HSCT patients.[74] Normally antibiotic sensitive, these organisms may be resistant to norfloxacin, ciprofloxacin, and penicillin in patients receiving prophylactic antibiotics. Vancomycin is the drug of choice for HSCT patients. Oral ulcerations caused by HSV reactivation during conditioning are thought to be an entry point, corroborated by a decreased incidence of viridans-group streptococcal septicemia after active prophylaxis of HSV infections with acyclovir.[72]

Mycobacteria

Mycobacteria are an infrequent cause of infection after HSCT but are important to identify because treatment requires medication that would not be used empirically. The rapidly growing nontuberculous mycobacteria are responsible for catheter exit site infections, tunnel infections, bacteremia (with waterborne *M. mucogenicum*), or pneumonia, whereas infection with *M. tuberculosis* rarely occurs as pneumonia.[75-77] Clinically significant infection can be prevented by antituberculous prophylaxis for patients having reactive purified protein derivative (PPD) tests. Potential transplantation patients and their donors should receive PPD screening if they are from countries where tuberculosis is common, or if they have a history of abnormal chest radiographic findings before transplantation, recent travel to a foreign country for longer than 3 months, close contact with another person with known or suspected tuberculosis, employment in an institution with tuberculous clients, alcoholism or intravenous drug use, or human immunodeficiency virus (HIV) seropositivity. PPD screening should be deferred if there is a history of past documented tuberculo-

sis, past treatment for tuberculosis, or a well-documented positive PPD. For patients with no signs of active tuberculosis and no previous antituberculous therapy but a reactive PPD, a chest radiograph and liver function tests should be obtained in addition to peritransplantation and post-transplantation prophylaxis with 1 year of isoniazid and pyridoxine.

Intracellular Bacteria

Legionellosis[78-82] and nocardiosis[83,84] are uncommon but can both manifest as lung nodules in the HSCT patient. Detection of *Legionella* by direct fluorescent antibody (DFA) assays has proved unreliable in the HSCT setting owing to false positives and a high proportion of disease caused by *Legionella* species not detectable by DFA. These species include *Legionella feeleii, Legionella micdadei,* and *Legionella bozemanii.* Infection can persist or relapse after 3 weeks of appropriate antimicrobial therapy, suggesting that prolonged antibiotic treatment is indicated for HSCT recipients with legionellosis.[78,79] Medical therapies for nocardiosis often consist of administration of sulfonamide in combination with a synergistic agent; adjunctive surgical débridement may be useful for catheter-related infections with this organism. The role of other intracellular bacterial agents as pathogens has not been well defined, but *Listeria monocytogenes* may manifest as bacteremia or meningitis.[85,86]

Viral Infections

Certain viral infections are preventable. Administration of acyclovir for HSV-seropositive patients during the pre-engraftment period is generally widely accepted. Serologically screened or filtered blood product transfusions for CMV-seronegative patients have proved especially effective in preventing transfusion-acquired CMV infections.[87,88] Periodic CMV diagnostic surveillance (e.g., weekly) for CMV-seropositive patients during the postengraftment period and prompt institution of antiviral therapy are essential.[52] CMV-seronegative patients are at comparatively low risk, so diagnostic monitoring continues for only 6 to 10 weeks. Strict hand washing and avoidance of crowds to prevent transmission of respiratory viral and other infections (in the hospital or ambulatory clinic) remain the mainstay of effective infection control practice for this vulnerable population.[9]

Herpes Simplex Virus

HSV reactivation can be reduced from 80% to less than 5% in HSV-seropositive recipients during the first month after transplantation through the use of acyclovir or valacyclovir initiated at the time of conditioning and continued until mucositis has diminished.[40,89,90] The majority of postengraftment HSV infections are confined to the oropharynx, although occasionally the infection extends directly to the esophagus, larynx, or skin in the perioral or perianal areas. Patients who fail to respond to acyclovir beyond engraftment, and particularly those who have received prolonged or repeated courses of acyclovir, may have acyclovir-resistant HSV. Famciclovir, foscarnet, or cidofovir may be beneficial in that setting.[91] Uncommonly, HSV infection causes Bell's palsy, hepatitis, or encephalitis. Valacyclovir gives predictably higher drug levels than acyclovir after oral administration.[90,92]

Cytomegalovirus

Primary CMV infection can be reduced from a historical incidence rate of 40% to 1% to 4% in the CMV-seronegative HSCT recipient by use of either seronegative or leukocyte-filtered blood products during transfusions.[87,93] CMV reactivation can be reduced from 70% in CMV-seropositive allogeneic and 45% in autologous patients to 20% to 40% antigenemia by the use of preemptive antiviral therapy with ganciclovir or foscarnet.[94-97] Results with acyclovir and valacyclovir have varied.[98-100] With the current practice of the use of preemptive early ganciclovir as prophylaxis, the median time of onset of CMV end-organ disease has been delayed from 1 to 2 to 4 to 6 months after HSCT, indicating a need for longer duration CMV surveillance in high-risk groups.[56]

Weekly screening allows identification of patients who might benefit most from preemptive therapy with ganciclovir (Table 311-2).

TABLE 311-2 Weekly Screening Schedule for Initiation of Preemptive Cytomegalovirus Therapy following Hematopoietic Stem Cell Transplantation

CMV Serostatus of Recipient	CMV Serostatus of Donor	Blood Products	Duration of Weekly Surveillance
Seronegative	Seronegative	CMV-Safe*	Week 2 to 12
Seronegative	Seropositive	CMV-Safe*	Week 2 to 12
Seronegative	None	CMV-Safe*	Week 2 to 5
Seropositive	Seronegative or Seropositive	CMV-Untested	Week 2 to 12
Seropositive	None	CMV-Untested	Week 2 to 5

*Blood filtered to remove neutrophils or from seronegative donor.

CMV leukocyte antigen and quantitative PCR testing are excellent methods for early CMV detection.[49,52,101] Antigen testing identifies pp65, a late structural protein of CMV, in leukocytes of infected patients and can be used to guide preemptive therapy with ganciclovir or foscarnet.[52,102,103] Patients must have circulating leukocytes for the test to be performed, so it is not helpful in identifying subclinical CMV infection in neutropenic patients.[104] If CMV disease is suspected in a neutropenic, this patient should be screened by PCR. Some centers use PCR testing for all weekly screening; however, PCR remains positive longer than antigen after ganciclovir therapy is initiated.[105] Shell vial technology rapidly identifies CMV from clinical specimens, especially bronchoalveolar lavage and biopsy material.[106] The rapidity of shell viral centrifugation cultures may be compromised by lower sensitivity compared with conventional viral tube cultures.

Once CMV is identified by an early detection method, most patients are treated with 7 to 14 days of induction ganciclovir therapy (5 mg/kg IV twice daily), followed by maintenance therapy (ganciclovir IV 5 mg/kg once daily or valganciclovir orally 900 mg once daily) for several weeks beyond negative CMV tests (Table 311-3).[107] Maintenance therapy may need to be continued for patients with persistent antigenemia and those with profound immunosuppression from active GVHD. Oral valganciclovir is a safe and effective ganciclovir prodrug, with the valine ester cleaved during first pass through the liver, and can be considered for the patient who needs long-term maintenance and is otherwise taking oral medications without difficulty.[104] A valganciclovir dosage of 900 mg once per day produces blood-level drug exposure similar to an intravenous dose of ganciclovir of 5 mg/kg; studies are ongoing to assess the role of valganciclovir in HSCT. Oral ganciclovir does not provide reliable levels and should not be used in the HSCT setting. Foscarnet can be used empirically for patients who have marrow suppression from ganciclovir or who fail to respond to ganciclovir. Foscarnet is given as 90 mg/kg IV every 12 hours for induction and 90 mg/kg IV every 24 hours for maintenance. Good urine flow can minimize foscarnet's irritation of the urethra and labia.

End-organ manifestations of CMV disease include pneumonia (63%), enteritis (26%), and retinitis (5%).[56,108,109] CMV pneumonia now occurs in less than 5% of CMV-seropositive allogeneic patients who receive ganciclovir prophylaxis or preemptive therapy of antigenemia during the first 100 days.[96,110] For a patient with CMV pneumonia, the mortality rate remains higher than 50%, even when prompt ganciclovir treatment is combined with intravenous immune globulin (IVIG).[111] CMV pneumonia is rare before engraftment.[101,112] Anorexia, nausea, vomiting, and sometimes diarrhea characterize CMV gastroenteritis; the diagnosis is made by endoscopy and biopsy with immunoperoxidase staining of CMV-infected cells. CMV disease of the gastrointestinal tract is often associated with GVHD of that organ.[108,113] Response to therapy is not assured, even with ganciclovir and IVIG. Although it is common in patients infected with HIV, CMV retinitis is quite uncommon among HSCT recipients.[109]

TABLE 311-3 Suggestions for Management of Cytomegalovirus Infection after Hematopoietic Stem Cell Transplantation (HSCT)

Indication	Strategy	Comment
Prevention		
Allogeneic transplant		
Seropositive recipient	Antigenemia*- or PCR-guided early ganciclovir† treatment: 5 mg/kg bid for 7–14 days, followed by 5 mg/kg daily until day 100 (or until negative PCR or antigenemia*) *or* Ganciclovir prophylaxis at engraftment: 5 mg/kg bid for 5 days, followed by 5 mg/kg daily on 5–6 days/wk until day 100	Some cases of CMV disease may occur shortly after ganciclovir discontinuation if based on negative PCR or antigenemia* results.[52] Recommended approach if neither PCR nor antigenemia testing is available. CMV reactivation might be delayed to later after HSCT.
Seronegative recipient with seropositive donor	Antigenemia*- or PCR-guided early ganciclovir treatment: 5 mg/kg bid for 7–14 days, followed by 5 mg/kg daily until day 100 (or until negative PCR or antigenemia*) *and* Seronegative or filtered blood products	Prophylaxis at engraftment is not recommended because of the low incidence of post-transplantation infection.
Seronegative recipient with seronegative donor	Seronegative or filtered blood products	
Autologous transplant		
Seropositive recipient	Antigenemia*- or PCR-guided early ganciclovir treatment: 5 mg/kg ganciclovir bid for 7 days, followed by 5 mg/kg daily for 14 days	Monitoring is not uniformly advocated owing to the very low risk in some settings.
Seronegative recipient	Seronegative or filtered blood products	
Treatment of Disease		
CMV pneumonia	Ganciclovir: 5 mg/kg bid for 14–21 days, followed by 5 mg/kg daily for at least 3–4 wk *plus IVIG*	Extended maintenance throughout periods of severe immunosuppression (i.e., GVHD treatment) may be considered.
Gastrointestinal disease	Ganciclovir: 5 mg/kg bid for 14–21 days, followed by 5 mg/kg daily for at least 3–4 wk	If deep ulcerations are present, maintenance may be required for a longer time.
Marrow failure	Foscarnet: 90 mg/kg bid for 14 days, followed by 90 mg/kg daily for 2 weeks *plus G-CSF*	Ganciclovir plus IVIG has also been used.
Retinitis	Ganciclovir: 5 mg/kg bid for 14–21 days, followed by 5 mg/kg daily for at least 3–4 wk	Extended maintenance may be required.

*Antigenemia testing is not reliable during neutropenia.
†*Note:* Oral valganciclovir produces blood levels for a 900-mg dose that are similar to the standard intravenous dose of ganciclovir of 5 mg/kg.
CMV, cytomegalovirus; G-CSF, granulocyte colony-stimulating factor; GVHD, graft-versus-host disease; IVIG, intravenous immune globulin; PCR, polymerase chain reaction.
From Boeckh M. Current antiviral strategies for controlling cytomegalovirus in hematopoietic stem cell transplant recipients: Prevention and therapy. Transpl Infect Dis. 1999;1:165-178.

End-organ CMV disease is difficult to treat. CMV pneumonia is treated with a combination of ganciclovir at induction doses for 14 to 21 days plus IVIG (500 mg/kg every other day for 14 to 21 days), then maintenance ganciclovir.[111] Standard IVIG is generally used, because CMV-specific immune globulin has not been shown to improve outcome. CMV enteritis is treated with intravenous ganciclovir at induction doses for 3 or more weeks without IVIG.[108,114] Treatment of protracted CMV enteritis might include ganciclovir plus IVIG or a longer duration of ganciclovir maintenance therapy to facilitate gastrointestinal healing.

Development of a CMV-specific cytotoxic T-lymphocyte response is critical for the reconstitution of normal immunity and protection from late CMV disease.[56,115] Long-term IVIG delays recovery of CMV immunity. For patients who remain at risk for late disease, CMV monitoring should be continued beyond day 100. Patients who are treated with acyclovir followed by ganciclovir or those treated with serial ganciclovir courses may be at increased risk of developing genotypic resistance. Clinical resistance episodes should be treated with foscarnet (or cidofovir) until assays for UL97 CMV mutations are able to confirm virologic resistance.[116] Extended ganciclovir therapy appears to delay recovery of cytotoxic T-lymphocyte activity, either by a direct effect on lymphocytes or by limitation of the amount of antigen exposure to lymphocytes. This immunodeficiency can be reversed when cytotoxic T lymphocytes are given adoptively, but this technology is available only at some tertiary centers.[115]

Varicella-Zoster Virus

VZV occurs as primary infection (5%) or as reactivation (95%) in 40% of patients at any time point in the first year after transplantation.[117,118] VZV can be effectively prevented with acyclovir prophylaxis, but VZV prophylaxis is not employed at all transplantation centers because only 30% to 50% of adult patients and 25% of pediatric patients develop this infection during the first year after transplantation. The median time of onset is 5 months after transplantation, although prolonged antiviral prophylaxis may delay the onset of VZV. Localized zoster may present atypically with a few vesicles, or skin lesions may appear as atypical vesicles, so laboratory confirmation of VZV reactivation is recommended.

Presentations of VZV disease include hemorrhagic pneumonia, hepatitis, abdominal pain, central nervous system disease, thrombocytopenia, and retinal necrosis.[119-123] Disseminated varicelliform zoster may manifest as low back pain or acute abdominal pain preceding the appearance of skin lesions. GVHD is a strong predictor of VZV dissemination, which involves visceral organs in 40% to 50% of patients.[121] Most fatal cases of disseminated or abdominal zoster occur in patients who were treated with suboptimal doses of acyclovir or for whom therapy was initiated relatively late in the course of infection. High-dose acyclovir (10 mg/kg IV every 8 hours) has been the treatment of choice for disseminated VZV infection. Valacyclovir and famciclovir can be used as step-down treatment from intravenous acyclovir, or as initial treatment of localized infection. Patients who are already seropositive can acquire a second primary VZV infection. VZV vaccination is recommended for VZV-naive patients who have been free of immunosuppressive medications for several months unless the underlying hematologic/oncologic disease is in relapse.[118,124]

VZV is a fastidious virus and may not withstand the time required to transport the specimen to the diagnostic laboratory. Scraping the base of a vesicle and examining the cells by DFA with VZV-specific monoclonal antibodies can best diagnose lesions of herpes zoster and chickenpox. The Tzanck smear is less sensitive and is no longer recommended. Tissue diagnosis can be made by histology, immunohistochemical techniques, or culture.

When a VZV-seronegative patient receives a significant exposure to a person with active or incubating chickenpox, varicella-zoster immune globulin (VZIG) should be given within 96 hours (see Chapter 305). When a VZV-seropositive patient is exposed, VZIG is not given. However, if a VZV-seropositive patient is living in the same dwelling as an index case of active chickenpox or shingles, acyclovir is reported to be useful in preventing new infection.

Adenovirus

Adenovirus infection reactivates in approximately 12% of allogeneic and approximately 6% of autologous HSCT patients.[125] Chronic shedding can occur in the absence of clinical disease, but adenovirus can also be acquired from respiratory droplet transmission. In its most common clinical manifestation in this setting, adenovirus is a cause of hemorrhagic cystitis.[12] Systemic infection in the lung, liver, gastrointestinal tract, and kidney occurs in 18% to 20% of infected patients. GVHD is a risk factor for the occurrence of adenovirus infection after HSCT.[126] In addition, allogeneic patients who do not receive ganciclovir (seronegative for CMV or seropositive without need for ganciclovir) are at higher risk for developing adenovirus infection compared with patients who did receive ganciclovir.[125] Immunofluorescence, shell vial, or conventional tube culture of blood, urine, stool, or tissue can be used to diagnose adenovirus. PCR testing may be a helpful adjunct for diagnosis. Commercial kits for detection of adenovirus in urine and stool are available, but the serogroups detected are those associated with infantile diarrhea and account for a minority of HSCT reactivations. No effective therapy is available for adenoviral infections, although cidofovir has been used in patients able to tolerate the nephrotoxicity.[127-129]

Respiratory Viruses

HSCT patients who develop a respiratory viral infection typically present with rhinorrhea and nasal congestion and may also have fever, cough, throat pain, headache, or myalgias. The common pathogens in HSCT patients include respiratory syncytial virus (RSV), parainfluenza virus, and, to a lesser extent, influenza virus and rhinovirus.[130-133] Current methods allow detection of RSV, parainfluenza, and influenza in respiratory specimens within 48 hours (see Chapter 15). Respiratory virus infections commonly occur during the winter season and cause pneumonia in up to 50% of patients. In contrast, parainfluenza 3 virus infections may occur throughout the year, and nosocomial outbreaks of RSV have occurred outside the established winter season. Influenza, most often type A, infrequently progresses to pneumonia. Prophylactic or early initiation of oseltamivir, amantadine, or rimantadine therapy during outbreaks seems reasonable, although evidence of efficacy in the immunosuppressed host is not available.

RSV and parainfluenza are associated with the highest incidence of progression from upper to lower tract disease among infected patients, with a mortality rate after HSCT for lower tract infection of approximately 50% for RSV.[134] Upper respiratory tract illness with parainfluenza usually resolves without serious sequelae.[135,136] Lower tract infection has a mortality rate of 80% for RSV and 30% to 35% for parainfluenza virus. Therapy with aerosolized ribavirin or a combination of ribavirin and IVIG has been used for RSV.[131,137] The survival rate appears to be higher when treatment is initiated before significant hypoxia is present.[137] There are only anecdotal case reports regarding the effectiveness of ribavirin for treatment of respiratory viruses other than RSV, including parainfluenza, adenovirus, and influenza. Preemptive therapy with aerosolized ribavirin in patients with positive nasopharyngeal cultures for RSV appears promising. Patients who develop respiratory viral pneumonia before engraftment have poorer outcomes.

Prevention of exposure is critical, because treatment is not very effective. Protection involves the use of frequent hand washing by hospital staff and isolation of patients with cold symptoms. In addition, family members and health care workers with upper respiratory tract symptoms should be separated from patients. Vaccination of family members, health care workers, and other close contacts against influenza may help control exposures. Amantadine or rimantadine prophylaxis may be useful during significant influenza A outbreaks. Rapid development of resistance has occurred in patients treated with these drugs. Oseltamivir provides useful prophylaxis against both influenza A and B. Immunoglobulin prophylaxis with RSV-specific polyclonal or monoclonal antibody, which is useful in high-risk infants, has not been sufficiently evaluated in the HSCT setting.[138] During the respiratory virus season, all patients with respiratory symptoms should have a sample taken from the nasopharynx to look for respiratory viruses with DFA staining and shell vial or conventional tube culture.

Epstein-Barr Virus

The majority of Epstein-Barr virus (EBV) reactivation is subclinical and requires no therapy. Quantitative EBV viral load diagnostic testing is relatively new and not standardized across institutions, so algorithms being developed for PCR-based monitoring and initiation of treatment are vague.[139,140] EBV is a cause of a post-transplantation lymphoproliferative disorder that arises when anti-T-lymphocyte immunosuppressive therapy is ongoing.[141] Infusions of rituximab or nonirradiated donor leukocytes may be an effective treatment for allograft recipients.[142]

Human Herpesvirus-6

HHV-6 has been implicated as a possible cause of bone marrow suppression, fatal meningoencephalitis, and interstitial pneumonitis in less than 2% of HSCT patients. HHV-6 appears to reactivate commonly, occurring in 46% of HSCT patients by culture diagnosis and as many as 100% of patients by PCR of blood.[143] Most strains of HHV-6 identified after HSCT appear to be caused by the B variant in blood or urine, although the A variant has been correlated with pneumonitis.[144] HHV-6 has 60% DNA homology with CMV, and treatment of documented infection is usually initiated with induction doses of ganciclovir or foscarnet. Responses to antiviral therapy are not universal, and benefits of ganciclovir versus foscarnet have not been determined.[145]

Parvovirus

Parvovirus B19 is a rare cause of anemia after HSCT.[146] Antibody or PCR tests detect parvovirus, although PCR may remain positive for months after the acute infection. Use of individual patient rooms on HSCT wards may be preventing transmission of this contagious virus to other HSCT recipients, and the administration of IVIG for other reasons may be treating subclinical infections.

Fungal Infections

Invasive fungal infections are important causes of morbidity and mortality.[147] The major causes of invasive fungal disease include *Candida* spp., *Aspergillus* spp., and less frequently the non-*Aspergillus* filamentous molds. Patients undergoing allogeneic transplantation are at 10-fold increased risk for invasive fungal infection compared with patients receiving an autologous graft. Systemic fluconazole prophylaxis or low-dose amphotericin B (0.1 to 0.3 mg/kg daily) can decrease the incidence of deep candidiasis.[41-43,148,149] Itraconazole or perhaps micafungin prophylaxis can extend the spectrum of organisms covered to include molds.[45,150] Voriconazole is being tested in a large multicenter prophylaxis trial. Empirical therapy of febrile neutropenic patients is discussed in Chapter 308.

Pneumocystis

P. jirovecii usually manifests as pneumonia with dyspnea, cough, fever, and bilateral infiltrates in the majority of infected patients.[46] It can be seen after both autologous and allogeneic transplantation, although the frequency is lower for the former. Before the use of routine prophylaxis, *Pneumocystis* had an incidence among allogeneic HSCT recipients of approximately 7%, had a median time of onset of 1 to 3 months after transplantation, and was associated with a risk of death of 5%.[151,152] Prophylaxis with TMP-SMX has resulted in negligible rates of infection. For patients who are intolerant of medications containing sulfa, prophylaxis options include desensitization with TMP-SMX, use of dapsone or atovaquone, or inhaled pentamidine.[47,153-155] The treatment of choice for *P. jirovecii* infection is TMP-SMX.

Candida

Candidiasis is an infection acquired from endogenous organisms colonizing the gastrointestinal tract; it usually manifests as fungemia or visceral candidiasis (see Chapter 255).[156,157] Prior to fluconazole pro-

phylaxis, the onset of candidiasis occurred at a median of 2 to 3 weeks after transplantation, and *Candida* was second in frequency to *Aspergillus* spp. as the cause of brain abscess after HSCT.[158,159] The current cumulative incidence rate of invasive candidiasis during the first year after HSCT is probably 5%.[147] Risk factors for invasive candidiasis include neutropenia, breakdown of the normal mucosal barriers, and the use of broad-spectrum antibiotics or corticosteroids. *C. albicans* infections are successfully prevented when fluconazole is given as prophylaxis from the time of conditioning until either engraftment or until day 75; the latter strategy has been associated with improved survival.[41,42,160] The benefit of fluconazole prophylaxis is less clear for autologous transplants, for which the degree of mucositis is less. With the use of fluconazole over the last decade, the number of *Candida* infections has decreased.[148,161] The spectrum of colonizing and infecting *Candida* organisms has shifted from *C. albicans* and *C. tropicalis* to *C. krusei*, *C. glabrata*, and *C. parapsilosis*.[156,157] *C. krusei* is innately resistant to fluconazole. Infections with *C. glabrata* or *C. parapsilosis* that manifest despite fluconazole prophylaxis should be treated with a different antifungal agent. Patients entering transplantation with a history of treated hepatosplenic candidiasis should receive antifungal prophylaxis with a minimum of 0.5 mg/kg daily amphotericin B from conditioning through marrow engraftment, in place of fluconazole.[162]

Aspergillus

Aspergillus and other mold infections are acquired exogenously, by inhalation of spores into the respiratory tract from the environment, and may occur with higher frequency during the summer in some localities.[44] Common sites of initial infection include the lung and sinuses, although contiguous or hematogenous extension to the central nervous system or other internal organs may occur. With the use of fluconazole prophylaxis, invasive aspergillosis has emerged as the leading fungal infection found at autopsy among HSCT recipients.[148]

In settings other than outbreaks, the incidence of invasive aspergillosis ranges from 4% to 15%.[44,163,164] The onset of *Aspergillus* infection after HSCT occurs in a bimodal distribution, with the first peak at 2 to 3 weeks (during neutropenia) and the second at 3 to 4 months after HSCT, usually in conjunction with persisting GVHD.[44,164] Postengraftment aspergillosis can occur beyond 6 months, again alongside chronic GVHD but also with CMV. Older age is associated with the acquisition of aspergillosis during either the pre- or postengraftment risk periods. Donor type (including cord blood), male gender, and summer season are specific risk factors for preengraftment aspergillosis, while construction in the vicinity of the hospital, GVHD and the attendant corticosteroid therapy, lymphopenia, CMV, respiratory virus infection, and multiple myeloma are significant risk factors for the development of postengraftment aspergillosis. Early aspergillosis is temporally associated with neutropenia, so infection among autologous HSCT patients is rare after engraftment. The 1-year survival estimate for patients with invasive aspergillosis is 7% to 30%.

Preventive strategies should focus on reducing both environmental and host risk factors. Use of high-efficiency particulate air (HEPA)–filtered air systems or laminar airflow rooms during the pre-engraftment risk period are important to the prevention of infection, particularly for allograft recipients. HEPA filters are capable of removing particles greater than 0.2 μ in diameter, such as mold spores. The patient room is continuously maintained at positive pressure relative to the corridor, enhancing the barrier effect. For transport out of HEPA-filtered rooms or after discharge, tight-fitting face masks reproduce this barrier and are sometimes used, at least for the early post-HSCT period.

Other prevention strategies, including nasal and aerosolized amphotericin B, have not been studied in controlled trials. Most patients who have had aspergillosis in the year before HSCT do not survive transplantation, although the cause of death may not be related to recurrence of aspergillosis. Patients might ask if portable HEPA filters should be purchased for use after the hospitalization. This extra measure can be implemented on an individual basis, provided that units are obtained for each of the rooms that the patient will occupy during the day and night and each unit is sized for the room it will be placed in.

No data support the clinical efficacy of these filters out of the hospital in preventing acquisition of airborne mold infections.

The availability of accurate early diagnostic tests for invasive fungal infections lags behind those for other types of infections. The most promising diagnostic assay, the *Aspergillus* galactomannan test, is undergoing validation testing in clinical trials to determine whether results can define appropriate use of empirical therapy to treat febrile patients at high risk of invasive aspergillosis.[165,166] The presence of circulating galactomannan, when monitored biweekly during high-risk periods following HSCT, may prove useful to detect invasive aspergillosis before the diagnosis is apparent. Other antigen– and nucleic acid–based diagnostic tests have been studied for early diagnosis of invasive tissue mold infection, but they have not been routinely adopted in the clinical laboratory. Most have not been tested in large numbers of clinical samples from HSCT recipients.

Blood cultures for molds are rarely positive except in the case of *Fusarium*. Culture and histologic evaluation of tissue may be the only way to adequately diagnose invasive aspergillosis, although fungal organisms that are identified by histopathology may not grow in the microbiology laboratory. A high index of suspicion in persistently febrile neutropenic patients and timely computed tomography of the chest to detect new infiltrates are important in early detection of invasive pulmonary aspergillosis. A small "ground-glass" halo around the lung lesion or pleural-based or nodular infiltrates on computed tomography are highly suggestive of aspergillosis or other mold infection in this setting. HSCT patients with suspected invasive mold infections should be given amphotericin or voriconazole daily. Nephrotoxicity in patients receiving cyclosporine may necessitate a switch to one of the lipid formulations of amphotericin B, although much less evidence exists concerning their efficacy in aspergillosis. Caspofungin has clinical activity, but its comparative efficacy has not been well studied.[167,168] At present, caspofungin is approved only for salvage therapy of aspergillosis.

For documented invasive tissue mold infection, amphotericin or voriconazole therapy is usually continued until some weeks after lesions are resolved or stable, immunosuppression has decreased, and the patient is afebrile.[169,170] Although amphotericin B has been the gold standard antifungal since the 1960s, voriconazole has recently been shown to demonstrate successful treatment outcomes for aspergillosis in 53% of voriconazole-treated patients versus 32% of amphotericin (followed by other licensed antifungal therapy)–treated patients.[170] Treatment of central nervous system mold infections should include voriconazole, which (on the basis of a small number of samples) attains cerebrospinal fluid levels approximately 50% of those of plasma or central nervous system tissue levels approximately 200% of those of plasma.

Combination treatment of fungal infections with echinocandins, azoles, and/or polyene agents is becoming increasingly common. Echinocandin agents may be fungistatic, rather than fungicidal, in the case of mold infections because their interruption of cell wall synthesis is limited to certain areas of growing hyphae.

After initial control of an aspergillosis infection, subsequent maintenance therapy with itraconazole or voriconazole for the duration of immunosuppression has been advocated to reduce the risk of reactivation. Multiple drug-drug interactions are seen with both of these azoles, and adjustments may be required for immunosuppressive agents. Transient visual disturbances are common with voriconazole. Difficulty in achieving therapeutic plasma drug levels complicates the administration of itraconazole. Itraconazole solution has improved oral bioavailability over the capsule and can be used, although blood level monitoring may be needed to ensure adequate absorption.

Other Yeasts

Pityrosporum folliculitis manifests in the early weeks after transplantation as erythematous macules and papules distributed on the chest, shoulders, and upper back; these lesions can also develop into pustules and crusts in some patients.[29,171] Response to either topical or systemic therapy is slow; recovery of granulocyte counts is usually associated with resolution. *Malassezia furfur* causes tinea versicolor and catheter-related fungemia. Catheter removal and discontinuation of in-

travenous lipids are important for a successful outcome in fungemic cases.[172] Trichosporonosis has manifested as fungemia, skin lesions, pneumonitis, and arthritis.[173] Fungemia, usually acquired via an intravenous catheter, has been reported with *Trichosporon, Rhodotorula, Cryptococcus laurentii,* and *Hansenula anomala.* Meningitis with *Cryptococcus neoformans* is unusual, in contrast to its frequent occurrence among patients infected with HIV. Widespread anti-*Candida* prophylaxis with fluconazole may contribute to the low frequency of these infections.

Other Molds

Non-*Aspergillus* molds are infrequent causes of invasive tissue infections that appear clinically as similar to *Aspergillus*.[173,174] Disseminated fusariosis is generally a fatal infection for HSCT recipients, manifesting as positive blood cultures, skin lesions, or endophthalmitis. Successful recovery is usually associated with engraftment in addition to prolonged, high-dose amphotericin B therapy or voriconazole. In the case of fusarial endophthalmitis, enucleation of the affected eye may be required. *Zygomycetes* infections are uncommon after HSCT, but mimic aspergillosis and may occur long after HSCT.[175,176] The new triazole antifungal posaconazole may be an effective maintenance treatment for infections caused by certain species of *Zygomycetes* following response to amphotericin B.[177] Clinically significant infections caused by the dimorphic fungi, including coccidioidomycosis, histoplasmosis, and blastomycosis, are unusual even in hyperendemic areas of the United States.

Parasitic Infections

Parasitic infection after HSCT usually manifests as reactivation of toxoplasmosis, although Chagas' disease, malaria, *Clonorchis* infection, giardiasis, pulmonary microsporidiosis, and *Acanthamoeba* and *Trichomonas* meningoencephalitis have also been reported.[178-184] Routine blood smears before HSCT cannot be used to exclude malarial transmission. In Hong Kong, *Clonorchis sinensis* infection was identified in only 1% of screening stool examinations performed 7 days before HSCT.[180] None of the patients had symptoms related to clonorchiasis; patients received praziquantel (25 mg/kg orally three times daily for 1 day) before HSCT, and subsequent stool examinations were negative for ova.

Toxoplasmosis is infrequent after transplant, occurring in 2% to 7% of patients who are seropositive before transplantation.[185] Although the parasite can be transmitted as a primary infection via marrow, blood products, or donor solid organs, toxoplasmosis in the HSCT recipient is almost always the result of reactivation of prior infection. GVHD is a risk factor relating to the suppression of cell-mediated immunity that is critical for host defense against *Toxoplasma gondii.* The clinical presentation includes fever, encephalitis with focal cerebral lesions, pneumonitis, or myocarditis. Parasitemia is a feature of reactivation that may be identified in peripheral blood buffy-coat cells inoculated into fibroblast tissue culture and incubated for 10 to 40 days, although many diagnoses are now made using PCR.[186] The identifiable risk period occurs 2 to 8 weeks after HSCT. Seropositive patients not receiving TMP-SMX during the first 1 to 3 months following HSCT have frequent *Toxoplasma* reactivation using PCR.[187] In countries with a high seropositive prevalence, prophylaxis seems logical and justifies the use of pyrimethamine/sulfadoxine among seropositive HSCT recipients.[188] However, in countries where the seroprevalence is low, prophylaxis is not routinely justified.

METHODS OF IMMUNE SYSTEM RECONSTITUTION AFTER HEMATOPOIETIC STEM CELL TRANSPLANTATION

Vaccination

Patients undergoing autologous or allogeneic HSCT eventually lose immunity to the common childhood diseases and should be reimmunized at 1 and 2 years following transplant (Table 311-4 and Fig. 311-1). The efficacy of vaccination is influenced by the time elapsed since transplant, the nature of the hematopoietic graft, the presence of GVHD, and the use of serial immunization.[189] There have been no reports of exacer-

TABLE 311-4 Suggested Schedule for Vaccination of Hematopoietic Stem Cell Transplantation (HSCT) Recipients

Vaccine	Time Period for Immunization after HSCT		
	12 Months	14 Months	24 Months
Inactivated Vaccines			
Diphtheria, tetanus			
<7 years old (inclusion of acellular pertussis optional)	X	X	X
>7 years old	X	X	X
Haemophilus influenzae type B conjugate	X	X	X
Hepatitis B	X	X	X
Pneumococcal 23-valent	X		X*
Inactivated polio	X	X	X
Influenza	Lifelong, seasonal administration, beginning before HSCT and resuming ≥ 6 mo after HSCT is recommended.		
Hepatitis A	Routine administration is not indicated. If given, hepatitis A vaccination requires two doses given 6–12 mo apart.		
Meningococcal	Routine administration is not indicated.		
Rabies	Routine administration is not indicated.		
Live Vaccines			
Measles-mumps-rubella			X†
Varicella			X*,†

*Optional dose.
†In patients with no active graft-versus-host disease or immunosuppressive therapy.
Adapted from Sullivan KM, Dykewicz CA, Longworth DL, et al. Preventing opportunistic infections after hematopoietic stem cell transplantation: The Centers for Disease Control and Prevention, Infectious Diseases Society of America, and American Society for Blood and Bone Marrow Transplantation Practice Guidelines and Beyond. Hematology (Am Soc Hematol Educ Program). 2001;1:392-421.

bation of GVHD following immunization of HSCT recipients. A national survey of HSCT immunization practices revealed that vaccines were underutilized and schedules for revaccination varied.[190] All transplant patients should be immunized on the same schedule regardless of stem cell source.[191]

All indicated nonlive vaccines should be administered to HSCT recipients regardless of HSCT type or presence of GVHD. HSCT recipients should be revaccinated with the combined tetanus-diphtheria toxoid, absorbed, every 10 years. No data are available on safety and immunogenicity of pertussis vaccination in HSCT recipients. At 1 year, they should also be immunized against polio by the inactivated intramuscular vaccine, *H. influenzae* type B, hepatitis B, and *S. pneumoniae*. If previously immunized, only one dose of hepatitis B vaccine should be given. At 2 years, a second dose of pneumococcal vaccine is optional, providing a second opportunity to vaccinate persons who failed to respond to the first dose, especially patients with chronic GVHD. Lifelong, seasonal administration of influenza vaccine should begin before HSCT and resume by 6 months after HSCT. Children younger than 9 years who are receiving influenza vaccination for the first time require two doses. Influenza vaccine for household contacts may be important, especially within the first year or in patients with ongoing GVHD, in whom protective responses may be impaired.

Live virus vaccines such as measles-mumps-rubella (MMR) and varicella should not be given to HSCT recipients with active GVHD or ongoing immunosuppressive therapy; the first doses are given to HSCT recipients more than 24 months after HSCT who are taking no immunosuppressive medications and are presumed immunocompetent. A second MMR dose should be given 6 to 12 months later; however, the benefit of a second dose in this population has not been evaluated.

Vaccination with the live-attenuated VZV vaccine is used for VZV-seronegative patients no longer requiring immunosuppressive therapy, but no controlled study has demonstrated its safety in the HSCT setting. Therefore, use of varicella vaccine in HSCT recipients should be restricted to research protocols for recipients older than 24 months after HSCT and who are presumed immunocompetent. When varicella vaccination is given to persons older than 13 years of age, two doses given 4 to 8 weeks apart are required. Susceptible family members should receive VZV vaccine to minimize chickenpox exposure for VZV-seronegative transplant recipients.

Routine administration of hepatitis A, meningococcal, and rabies vaccines is not indicated. Hepatitis A vaccine is recommended for HSCT recipients with chronic liver disease, including hepatitis C infection or chronic GVHD, or who are from hepatitis A-endemic areas or areas experiencing outbreaks. If given, hepatitis A vaccination requires two doses given 6 to 12 months apart. For HSCT recipients with potential occupational exposure to rabies, preexposure rabies vaccination should be delayed until at least 12 months, if not 24 months, after HSCT.

Immunoglobulin Replacement

The major defect in humoral immunity is the absence of specific antibody production. Antibody levels in the first year after HSCT are affected primarily by pretransplantation levels in the recipient, and to a lesser degree in the donor.[192] Among patients with chronic GVHD, reduced production of opsonizing antibody and all classes of immunoglobulin G (IgG) and immunoglobulin A antibodies is seen.[193] This immunodeficiency is further complicated by poor splenic function and is associated with recurrent pneumococcal infections and episodes of bronchitis or pneumonia. IVIG does not prevent infections when given weekly during the pre-engraftment or late risk periods but leads to reduced rates of septicemia and localized infection when given in the postengraftment risk period after transplantation.[194-196] It may modulate the severity of GVHD. Replacement IVIG (200 to 500 mg/kg every 1 to 2 weeks) is recommended for HSCT recipients with IgG levels lower than 400 mg/dL, though its routine use can delay recovery of antigen (viral)–specific immunity.

The role of hyperimmune globulin for prevention of specific infections is less clear. High-titer CMV globulin for prevention of CMV infection and treatment of CMV end-organ disease has proved to be of clear benefit compared with IVIG. However, antiviral drugs are effective in providing protection against CMV disease. Therefore, because of its limited availability as well as cost considerations, the use of CMV-specific globulin has decreased at many transplantation centers. Hyperimmune RSV globulin provided only a very modest increase in neutralizing antibody when given in the first 6 weeks post-transplant to HSCT patients.[138] Use of virus-specific monoclonal antibodies as preventative measures against RSV and CMV is currently under investigation. Hepatitis B, human rabies, and tetanus immune globulin should be used as needed for exposures. VZIG should be administered to VZV-seronegative HSCT recipients within 96 hours of close contact with a person with varicella or shingles, although VZIG administration may extend the varicella incubation period from 10 to 21 days to 28 days.

REFERENCES

1. Barker JN, Wagner JE. Umbilical cord blood transplantation: Current state of the art. Curr Opin Oncol. 2002;14:160-164.
2. Grewal SS, Barker JN, Davies SM, et al. Unrelated donor hematopoietic cell transplantation: Marrow or umbilical cord blood? Blood. 2003;101:4233-4244.
3. Filicko J, Lazarus HM, Flomenberg N. Mucosal injury in patients undergoing hematopoietic progenitor cell transplantation: New approaches to prophylaxis and treatment. Bone Marrow Transplant. 2003;31:1-10.
4. Rubinstein P. HLA matching for bone marrow transplantation—How much is enough? N Engl J Med. 2001;345:1842-1844.
5. Petersdorf EW, Hansen JA, Martin PJ, et al. Major-histocompatibility-complex class I alleles and antigens in hematopoietic-cell transplantation. N Engl J Med. 2001;345:1794-1800.
6. Anasetti C, Amos D, Beatty PG, et al. Effect of HLA compatibility on engraftment of bone marrow transplants in patients with leukemia or lymphoma. N Engl J Med. 1989;320:197-204.
7. Niederwieser D, Maris M, Shizuru JA, et al. Low-dose total body irradiation (TBI) and fludarabine followed by hematopoietic cell transplantation (HCT) from HLA-matched or mismatched unrelated donors and postgrafting immunosuppression with cyclosporine and mycophenolate mofetil (MMF) can induce durable complete chimerism and sustained remissions in patients with hematological diseases. Blood. 2003;101:1620-1629.

8. Sepkowitz KA. Antibiotic prophylaxis in patients receiving hematopoietic stem cell transplant. Bone Marrow Transplant. 2002;29:367-371.

9. Dykewicz CA. Hospital infection control in hematopoietic stem cell transplant recipients. Emerg Infect Dis. 2001;7:263-267.

10. Dykewicz CA. Summary of the guidelines for preventing opportunistic infections among hematopoietic stem cell transplant recipients. Clin Infect Dis. 2001;33:139-144.

11. Dykewicz CA. Guidelines for preventing opportunistic infections among hematopoietic stem cell transplant recipients: Focus on community respiratory virus infections. Biol Blood Marrow Transplant. 2001;7(Suppl):19S-22S.

12. Akiyama H, Kurosu T, Sakashita C, et al. Adenovirus is a key pathogen in hemorrhagic cystitis associated with bone marrow transplantation. Clin Infect Dis. 2001;32:1325-1330.

13. Childs R, Sanchez C, Engler H, et al. High incidence of adeno- and polyomavirus-induced hemorrhagic cystitis in bone marrow allotransplantation for hematological malignancy following T cell depletion and cyclosporine. Bone Marrow Transplant. 1998;22:889-893.

14. Priftakis P, Bogdanovic G, Kokhaei P, et al. BK virus (BKV) quantification in urine samples of bone marrow transplanted patients is helpful for diagnosis of hemorrhagic cystitis, although wide individual variations exist. J Clin Virol. 2003;26:71-77.

15. Leung AY, Suen CK, Lie AK, et al. Quantification of polyoma BK viruria in hemorrhagic cystitis complicating bone marrow transplantation. Blood. 2001;98:1971-1978.

16. Litzow MR, Repoussis PD, Schroeder G, et al. Veno-occlusive disease of the liver after blood and marrow transplantation: Analysis of pre- and post-transplant risk factors associated with severity and results of therapy with tissue plasminogen activator. Leuk Lymphoma. 2002;43:2099-2107.

17. McDonald GB, Hinds MS, Fisher LD, et al. Veno-occlusive disease of the liver and multiorgan failure after bone marrow transplantation: A cohort study of 355 patients. Ann Intern Med. 1993;118:255-267.

18. Deeg HJ. New strategies for prevention and treatment of graft-versus-host disease and for induction of graft-versus-leukemia effects. Int J Hematol. 2003;77:15-21.

19. Arai S, Lee LA, Vogelsang GB. A systematic approach to hepatic complications in hematopoietic stem cell transplantation. J Hematother Stem Cell Res. 2002;11:215-229.

20. Lau GK, He ML, Fong DY, et al. Preemptive use of lamivudine reduces hepatitis B exacerbation after allogeneic hematopoietic cell transplantation. Hepatology. 2002;36:702-709.

21. Vance EA, Soiffer RJ, McDonald GB, et al. Prevention of transmission of hepatitis C virus in bone marrow transplantation by treating the donor with alpha-interferon. Transplantation. 1996;62:1358-1360.

22. Lau GK, Liang R, Wu PC, et al. Use of famciclovir to prevent HBV reactivation in HBsAg-positive recipients after allogeneic bone marrow transplantation. J Hepatol. 1998;28:359-368.

23. Lau GK, Leung YH, Fong DY, et al. High hepatitis B virus (HBV) DNA viral load as the most important risk factor for HBV reactivation in patients positive for HBV surface antigen undergoing autologous hematopoietic cell transplantation. Blood. 2002;99:2324-2330.

24. Strasser SI, Sullivan KM, Myerson D, et al. Cirrhosis of the liver in long-term marrow transplant survivors. Blood. 1999;93:3259-3266.

25. Khurshid I, Anderson LC. Non-infectious pulmonary complications after bone marrow transplantation. Postgrad Med J. 2002;78:257-262.

26. van Kraaij MG, Dekker AW, Verdonck LF, et al. Infectious gastro-enteritis: An uncommon cause of diarrhoea in adult allogeneic and autologous stem cell transplant recipients. Bone Marrow Transplant. 2000;26:299-303.

27. Chakrabarti S, Lees A, Jones SG, et al. *Clostridium difficile* infection in allogeneic stem cell transplant recipients is associated with severe graft-versus-host disease and non-relapse mortality. Bone Marrow Transplant. 2000;26:871-876.

28. Boggio L, Pooley R, Roth SI, et al. Typhlitis complicating autologous blood stem cell transplantation for breast cancer. Bone Marrow Transplant. 2000;25:321-326.

29. Canninga-Van Dijk MR, Sanders CJ, Verdonck LF, et al. Differential diagnosis of skin lesions after allogeneic haematopoietic stem cell transplantation. Histopathology. 2003;42:313-330.

30. van Burik J-A, Colven R, Spach D. Cutaneous aspergillosis. J Clin Microbiol. 1998;36:3115-3121.

31. Ferra C, Doebbeling BN, Hollis RJ, et al. *Candida tropicalis* vertebral osteomyelitis: A late sequela of fungemia. Clin Infect Dis. 1994;19:697-703.

32. Leather HL, Wingard JR. Infections following hematopoietic stem cell transplantation. Infect Dis Clin North Am. 2001;15:483-520.

33. Centers for Disease Control and Prevention. Guidelines for preventing opportunistic infections among hematopoietic stem cell transplant recipients. MMWR Morb Mortal Wkly Rep. 2000;49(RR10):1-125, CE121-127.

34. Collin BA, Leather HL, Wingard JR, et al. Evolution, incidence, and susceptibility of bacterial bloodstream isolates from 519 bone marrow transplant patients. Clin Infect Dis. 2001;33:947-953.

35. Marena C, Zecca M, Carenini ML, et al. Incidence of, and risk factors for, nosocomial infections among hematopoietic stem cell transplantation recipients, with impact on procedure-related mortality. Infect Control Hosp Epidemiol. 2001;22:510-517.

36. Centers for Disease Control and Prevention. Recommendations for preventing the spread of vancomycin resistance: Recommendations of the Hospital Infection Control Practices Advisory Committee (HICPAC). MMWR Morb Mortal Wkly Rep. 1995;44(RR12):1-13.

37. Hübel K, Carter R, Liles W, et al. Granulocyte transfusion therapy for infections in candidates and recipients of hematopoietic cell transplantation: A comparative analysis of feasibility and outcome of community donors versus related donors. Transfusion. 2002;42:1414-1421.

38. Lazarus HM, Magalhaes-Silverman M, Fox RM, et al. Contamination during in vitro processing of bone marrow for transplantation: Clinical significance. Bone Marrow Transplant. 1991;7:241-246.

39. Nasser RM, Hajjar I, Sandhaus LM, et al. Routine cultures of bone marrow and peripheral stem cell harvests: Clinical impact, cost analysis, and review. Clin Infect Dis. 1998;27:886-888.

40. Wade JC, Newton B, Flournoy N, et al. Oral acyclovir for prevention of herpes simplex virus reactivation after marrow transplantation. Ann Intern Med. 1984;100:823-828.

41. Goodman JL, Winston DJ, Greenfield RA, et al. A controlled trial of fluconazole to prevent fungal infections in patients undergoing bone marrow transplantation. N Engl J Med. 1992;326:845-851.

42. Slavin MA, Osborne B, Adams R, et al. Efficacy and safety of fluconazole prophylaxis for fungal infections after marrow transplantation—A prospective, randomized, double-blind study. J Infect Dis. 1995;171:1545-1552.

43. MacMillan ML, Goodman JL, DeFor TE, et al. Fluconazole to prevent yeast infections in bone marrow transplantation patients: A randomized trial of high versus reduced dose, and determination of the value of maintenance therapy. Am J Med. 2002;112:369-379.

44. Wald A, Leisenring W, van Burik JA, et al. Epidemiology of Aspergillus infections in a large cohort of patients undergoing bone marrow transplantation. J Infect Dis. 1997;175:1459-1466.

45. Winston DJ, Maziarz RT, Chandrasekar PH, et al. Intravenous and oral itraconazole versus intravenous and oral fluconazole for long-term antifungal prophylaxis in allogeneic hematopoietic stem-cell transplant recipients: A multicenter, randomized trial. Ann Intern Med. 2003;138:705-713.

46. Tuan IZ, Dennison D, Weisdorf DJ. *Pneumocystis carinii* pneumonitis following bone marrow transplantation. Bone Marrow Transplant. 1992;10:267-272.

47. Souza JP, Boeckh M, Gooley TA, et al. High rates of *Pneumocystis carinii* pneumonia in allogeneic blood and marrow transplant recipients receiving dapsone prophylaxis. Clin Infect Dis. 1999;29:1467-1471.

48. Boeckh M, Gallez-Hawkins GM, Myerson D, et al. Plasma polymerase chain reaction for cytomegalovirus DNA after allogeneic marrow transplantation: Comparison with polymerase chain reaction using peripheral blood leukocytes, pp65 antigenemia, and viral culture. Transplantation. 1997;64:108-113.

49. Yakushiji K, Gondo H, Kamezaki K, et al. Monitoring of cytomegalovirus reactivation after allogeneic stem cell transplantation: Comparison of an antigenemia assay and quantitative real-time polymerase chain reaction. Bone Marrow Transplant. 2002;29:599-606.

50. Kaiser L, Perrin L, Chapuis B, et al. Improved monitoring of cytomegalovirus infection after allogeneic hematopoietic stem cell transplantation by an ultrasensitive plasma DNA PCR assay. J Clin Microbiol. 2002;40:4251-4255.

51. Cortez KJ, Fischer S, Fahle G, et al. Clinical trial of quantitative real-time polymerase chain reaction for detection of cytomegalovirus in peripheral blood of allogeneic hematopoietic stem cell transplant recipients. J Infect Dis. 2003;188:967-972.

52. Boeckh M, Gooley TA, Myerson D, et al. Cytomegalovirus pp65 antigenemia-guided early treatment with ganciclovir versus ganciclovir at engraftment after allogeneic marrow transplantation: A randomized double-blind study. Blood. 1996;88:4063-4071.

53. Ochs L, Shu XO, Miller J, et al. Late infections after allogeneic bone marrow transplantations: Comparison of incidence in related and unrelated donor transplant recipients. Blood. 1995;86:3979-3986.

54. Roy V, Ochs L, Weisdorf D. Late infections following allogeneic bone marrow transplantation: Suggested strategies for prophylaxis. Leuk Lymphoma. 1997;26:1-15.

55. Sullivan KM, Mori M, Sanders J, et al. Late complications of allogeneic and autologous marrow transplantation. Bone Marrow Transplant. 1992;10(Suppl 1):127-134.

56. Boeckh M, Leisenring W, Riddell SR, et al. Late cytomegalovirus disease and mortality in recipients of allogeneic hematopoietic stem cell transplants: Importance of viral load and T-cell immunity. Blood. 2003;101:407-414.

57. Junghanss C, Marr KA, Carter RA, et al. Incidence and outcome of bacterial and fungal infections following nonmyeloablative compared with myeloablative allogeneic hematopoietic stem cell transplantation: A matched control study. Biol Blood Marrow Transplant. 2002;8:512-520.

58. Junghanss C, Boeckh M, Carter RA, et al. Incidence and outcome of cytomegalovirus infections following nonmyeloablative compared with myeloablative allogeneic stem cell transplantation, a matched control study. Blood. 2002;99:1978-1985.

59. Hagen EA, Stern H, Porter D, et al. High rate of invasive fungal infections following nonmyeloablative allogeneic transplantation. Clin Infect Dis. 2003;36:9-15.

60. Centers for Disease Control and Prevention. Outbreaks of gastroenteritis associated with noroviruses on cruise ships—United States, 2002. MMWR Morb Mortal Wkly Rep. 2002;51:1112-1115.

61. Minooee A, Rickman LS. Infectious diseases on cruise ships. Clin Infect Dis. 1999;29:737-743.

62. Boyce JM, Pittet D. Guideline for hand hygiene in health-care settings: Recommendations of the Healthcare Infection Control Practices Advisory Committee and the HICPAC/SHEA/APIC/IDSA Hand Hygiene Task Force. Infect Control Hosp Epidemiol. 2002;23(Suppl):S3-S40.

63. Sullivan KM, Dykewicz CA, Longworth DL, et al. Preventing opportunistic infections after hematopoietic stem cell transplantation: The Centers for Disease Control and Prevention, Infectious Diseases Society of America, and American Society for Blood and Marrow Transplantation Practice Guidelines and beyond. Hematology (Am Soc Hematol Educ Program). 2001;1:392-421.

64. Elishoov H, Or R, Strauss N, et al. Nosocomial colonization, septicemia, and Hickman/Broviac catheter-related infections in bone marrow transplant recipients: A 5-year prospective study. Medicine (Baltimore). 1998;77:83-101.

65. Toor AA, van Burik JA, Weisdorf DJ. Infections during mobilizing chemotherapy and following autologous stem cell transplantation. Bone Marrow Transplant. 2001;28:1129-1134.

66. Schots R, Trullemans F, Van Riet I, et al. The clinical impact of early gram-positive bacteremia and the use of vancomycin after allogeneic bone marrow transplantation. Transplantation. 2000;69:1511-1514.

67. Arns da Cunha C, Weisdorf D, Shu XO, et al. Early gram-positive bacteremia in BMT recipients: Impact of three different approaches to antimicrobial prophylaxis. Bone Marrow Transplantation. 1998;21:173-180.

68. Schutze GE, Mason EO Jr, Wald ER, et al. Pneumococcal infections in children after transplantation. Clin Infect Dis. 2001;33:16-21.

69. Tauro S, Dobie D, Richardson G, et al. Recurrent penicillin-resistant pneumococcal sepsis after matched unrelated donor transplantation for refractory T cell lymphoma. Bone Marrow Transplant. 2000;26:1017-1019.

70. Haddad PA, Repka TL, Weisdorf DJ. Penicillin-resistant *Streptococcus pneumoniae* septic shock and meningitis complicating chronic graft versus host disease: A case report and review of the literature. Am J Med. 2002;113:152-155.

71. Razonable RR, Litzow MR, Khaliq Y, et al. Bacteremia due to viridans group streptococci with diminished susceptibility to levofloxacin among neutropenic patients receiving levofloxacin prophylaxis. Clin Infect Dis. 2002;34:1469-1474.

72. Ringden O, Heimdahl A, Lonnqvist B, et al. Decreased incidence of viridans streptococcal septicaemia in allogeneic bone marrow transplant recipients after the introduction of acyclovir. Lancet. 1984;314:744.

73. Steiner M, Villablanca J, Kersey J, et al. Viridans streptococcal shock in bone marrow transplantation patients. Am J Hematol. 1993;42:354-358.

74. Graber CJ, de Almeida KN, Atkinson JC, et al. Dental health and viridans streptococcal bacteremia in allogeneic hematopoietic stem cell transplant recipients. Bone Marrow Transplant. 2001;27:537-542.

75. Roy V, Weisdorf D. Mycobacterial infections following bone marrow transplantation: A 20 year retrospective review. Bone Marrow Transplant. 1997;19:467-470.

76. Ip MSM, Yuen KY, Woo PCY, et al. Risk factors for pulmonary tuberculosis in bone marrow transplant recipients. Am J Respir Crit Care Med. 1998;158:1173-1177.

77. Gaviria JM, Garcia PJ, Garrido SM, et al. Nontuberculous mycobacterial infections in hematopoietic stem cell transplant recipients: Characteristics of respiratory and catheter-related infections. Biol Blood Marrow Transplant. 2000;6:361-369.

78. Kugler JW, Armitage JO, Helms CM, et al. Nosocomial legionnaires' disease: Occurrence in recipients of bone marrow transplants. Am J Med. 1983;74:281-288.

79. Harrington RD, Woolfrey AE, Bowden R, et al. Legionellosis in a bone marrow transplant center. Bone Marrow Transplant. 1996;18:361-368.

80. Benz Lemoine E, Delwail V, Castel O, et al. Nosocomial legionnaires' disease in a bone marrow transplant unit. Bone Marrow Transplant. 1991;7:61-63.

81. Matulonis U, Rosenfeld CS, Shadduck RK. Prevention of *Legionella* infections in a bone marrow transplant unit: Multifaceted approach to decontamination of a water system. Infect Control Hosp Epidemiol. 1993;14:571-575.

82. Oren I, Zuckerman T, Avivi I, et al. Nosocomial outbreak of *Legionella pneumophila* serogroup 3 pneumonia in a new bone marrow transplant unit: Evaluation, treatment and control. Bone Marrow Transplant. 2002;30:175-179.

83. van Burik J-A, Hackman R, Nadeem S, et al. Nocardiosis after bone marrow transplantation: A retrospective study. Clin Infect Dis. 1997;24:1154-1160.

84. Choucino C, Goodman SA, Greer JP, et al. Nocardial infections in bone marrow transplant recipients. Clin Infect Dis. 1996;23:1012-1019.

85. Martino R, Lopez R, Pericas R, et al. Listeriosis in bone marrow transplant recipient. Clin Infect Dis. 1996;23:419-420.

86. Long SG, Leyland MJ, Milligan DW. *Listeria* meningitis after bone marrow transplantation. Bone Marrow Transplant. 1993;12:537-539.

87. Bowden RA, Slichter SJ, Sayers M, et al. A comparison of filtered leukocyte-reduced and cytomegalovirus seronegative blood products for the prevention of transfusion-associated CMV infection after marrow transplant. Blood. 1995;86:3598-3603.

88. Ljungman P, Larsson K, Kumlien G, et al. Leukocyte depleted, unscreened blood products give a low risk for CMV infection and disease in CMV seronegative allogeneic stem cell transplant recipients with seronegative stem cell donors. Scand J Infect Dis. 2002;34:347-350.

89. Saral R, Burns WH, Laskin OL, et al. Acyclovir prophylaxis of herpes simplex virus infections: A randomized, double-blind, controlled trial in bone marrow transplant recipients. N Engl J Med. 1981;305:63-67.

90. Dignani MC, Mykietiuk A, Michelet M, et al. Valacyclovir prophylaxis for the prevention of herpes simplex virus reactivation in recipients of progenitor cells transplantation. Bone Marrow Transplant. 2002;29:263-267.

91. Wade JC, McLaren C, Meyers JD. Frequency and significance of acyclovir-resistant herpes simplex virus isolated from marrow transplant patients receiving multiple courses of treatment with acyclovir. J Infect Dis. 1983;148:1077-1082.

92. Liesveld JL, Abboud CN, Ifthikharuddin JJ, et al. Oral valacyclovir versus intravenous acyclovir in preventing herpes simplex virus infections in autologous stem cell transplant recipients. Biol Blood Marrow Transplant. 2002;8:662-665.

93. Nichols WG, Price TH, Gooley T, et al. Transfusion-transmitted cytomegalovirus infection after receipt of leukoreduced blood products. Blood. 2003;101:4195-4200.

94. Goodrich JM, Bowden RA, Fisher L, et al. Ganciclovir prophylaxis to prevent cytomegalovirus disease after allogeneic marrow transplant. Ann Intern Med. 1993;118:173-178.

95. Winston DJ, Ho WG, Bartoni K, et al. Ganciclovir prophylaxis of cytomegalovirus infection and disease in allogeneic bone marrow transplant recipients: Results of a placebo-controlled, double-blind trial. Ann Intern Med. 1993;118:179-184.

96. Goodrich JM, Mori M, Gleaves CA, et al. Early treatment with ganciclovir to prevent cytomegalovirus disease after allogeneic bone marrow transplantation. N Engl J Med. 1991;325:1601-1607.

97. Reusser P, Einsele H, Lee J, et al. Randomized multicenter trial of foscarnet versus ganciclovir for preemptive therapy of cytomegalovirus infection after allogeneic stem cell transplantation. Blood. 2002;99:1159-1164.

98. Prentice HG, Gluckman E, Powles RL, et al. Impact of long-term acyclovir on cytomegalovirus infection and survival after allogeneic bone marrow transplantation. European Acyclovir for CMV Prophylaxis Study Group. Lancet. 1994;343:749-753.

99. Burns LJ, Miller W, Kandaswamy C, et al. Randomized clinical trial of ganciclovir vs acyclovir for prevention of cytomegalovirus antigenemia after allogeneic transplantation. Bone Marrow Transplant. 2002;30:945-951.

100. Winston DJ, Yeager AM, Chandrasekar PH, et al. Randomized comparison of oral valacyclovir and intravenous ganciclovir for prevention of cytomegalovirus disease after allogeneic bone marrow transplantation. Clin Infect Dis. 2003;36:749-758.

101. Limaye AP, Huang ML, Leisenring W, et al. Cytomegalovirus (CMV) DNA load in plasma for the diagnosis of CMV disease before engraftment in hematopoietic stem-cell transplant recipients. J Infect Dis. 2001;183:377-382.

102. Nichols WG, Corey L, Gooley T, et al. Rising pp65 antigenemia during preemptive anticytomegalovirus therapy after allogeneic hematopoietic stem cell transplantation: Risk factors, correlation with DNA load, and outcomes. Blood. 2001;97:867-874.

103. Bacigalupo A, van Lint MT, Tedone E, et al. Early treatment of CMV infections in allogeneic bone marrow transplant recipients with foscarnet or ganciclovir. Bone Marrow Transplant. 1994;13:753-758.

104. Zaia JA. Prevention of cytomegalovirus disease in hematopoietic stem cell transplantation. Clin Infect Dis. 2002; 35:999-1004.

105. Zaia JA. Prevention and management of CMV-related problems after hematopoietic stem cell transplantation. Bone Marrow Transplant. 2002; 29:633-638.

106. Gleaves CA, Reed EC, Hackman RC, et al. Rapid diagnosis of invasive cytomegalovirus infection by examination of tissue specimens in centrifugation culture. Am J Clin Pathol. 1987; 88:354-358.

107. Boeckh M. Current antiviral strategies for controlling cytomegalovirus in hematopoietic stem cell transplant recipients: Prevention and therapy. Transpl Infect Dis. 1999; 1:165-178.

108. van Burik JA, Lawatsch EJ, DeFor TE, et al. Cytomegalovirus enteritis among hematopoietic stem cell transplant recipients. Biol Blood Marrow Transplant. 2001;7:674-679.

109. Crippa F, Corey L, Chuang EL, et al. Virological, clinical, and ophthalmologic features of cytomegalovirus retinitis after hematopoietic stem cell transplantation. Clin Infect Dis. 2001;32:214-219.

110. Enright H, Haake R, Weisdorf D, et al. Cytomegalovirus pneumonia after bone marrow transplantation: Risk factors and response to therapy. Transplantation. 1993;55:1339-1346.

111. Reed EC, Bowden RA, Dandliker PS, et al. Treatment of cytomegalovirus pneumonia with ganciclovir and intravenous cytomegalovirus immunoglobulin in patients with bone marrow transplants. Ann Intern Med. 1988;109:783-788.

112. Limaye AP, Bowden RA, Myerson D, et al. Cytomegalovirus disease occurring before engraftment in marrow transplant recipients. Clin Infect Dis. 1997;24:830-835.

113. Hackman RC, Wolford JL, Gleaves CA, et al. Recognition and rapid diagnosis of upper gastrointestinal cytomegalovirus infection in marrow transplant recipients: A comparison of seven virologic methods. Transplantation. 1994;57:231-237.

114. Reed EC, Wolford JL, Kopecky KJ, et al. Ganciclovir for the treatment of cytomegalovirus gastroenteritis in bone marrow transplant patients: A randomized, placebo-controlled trial. Ann Intern Med. 1990;112:505 510.

115. Walter EA, Greenberg PD, Gilbert MJ, et al. Reconstitution of cellular immunity against cytomegalovirus in recipients of allogeneic bone marrow by transfer of T-cell clones from the donor. N Engl J Med. 1995;333:1038-1044.

116. Erice A, Borrell N, Li W, et al. Ganciclovir susceptibilities and analysis of UL97 region in cytomegalovirus isolates from bone marrow recipients with CMV disease after antiviral prophylaxis. J Infect Dis. 1998;178:531-534.

117. Steer CB, Szer J, Sasadeusz J, et al. Varicella-zoster infection after allogeneic bone marrow transplantation: Incidence, risk factors and prevention with low-dose acyclovir and ganciclovir. Bone Marrow Transplant. 2000;25:657-664.

118. Arvin AM. Varicella-zoster virus: Pathogenesis, immunity, and clinical management in hematopoietic cell transplant recipients. Biol Blood Marrow Transplant. 2000;6:219-230.

119. Austin R. Clinical review. Progressive outer retinal necrosis syndrome: A comprehensive review of its clinical presentation, relationship to immune system status, and management. Clin Eye Vision Care. 2000;12:119-129.

120. Tenenbaum T, Kramm CM, Laws HJ, et al. Pre-eruptive varicella zoster virus encephalitis in two children after haematopoietic stem cell transplantation. Med Pediatr Oncol. 2002;38:288-289.

121. David DS, Tegtmeier BR, O'Donnell MR, et al. Visceral varicella-zoster after bone marrow transplantation: Report of a case series and review of the literature. Am J Gastroenterol. 1998;93:810-813.

122. Verdonck LF, Cornelissen JJ, Dekker AW, et al. Acute abdominal pain as a presenting symptom of varicella zoster virus infection in recipients of bone marrow transplants. Clin Infect Dis. 1993;16:190-191.

123. Schiller GJ, Nimer SD, Gajewski JL, et al. Abdominal presentation of varicella zoster infection in recipients of allogeneic bone marrow transplantation. Bone Marrow Transplant. 1991;7:489-491.

124. Hata A, Asanuma H, Rinki M, et al. Use of an inactivated varicella vaccine in recipients of hematopoietic-cell transplants. N Engl J Med. 2002;347:26-34.

125. Bruno B, Gooley T, Hackman RC, et al. Adenovirus infection in hematopoietic stem cell transplantation: Effect of ganciclovir and impact on survival. Biol Blood Marrow Transplant. 2003;9:341-352.

126. Shields AF, Hackman RC, Fife KH, et al. Adenovirus infections in patients undergoing bone marrow transplantation. N Engl J Med. 1985;312:529-533.

127. Ljungman P, Ribaud P, Eyrich M, et al. Cidofovir for adenovirus infections after allogeneic hematopoietic stem cell transplantation: A survey by the Infectious Diseases Working Party of the European Group for Blood and Marrow Transplantation. Bone Marrow Transplant. 2003;31:481-486.
128. Gonzalez-Fraile MI, Canizo C, Caballero D, et al. Cidofovir treatment of human polyomavirus-associated acute haemorrhagic cystitis. Transpl Infect Dis. 2001;3:44-46.
129. Held TK, Biel SS, Nitsche A, et al. Treatment of BK virus-associated hemorrhagic cystitis and simultaneous CMV reactivation with cidofovir. Bone Marrow Transplant. 2000;26:347-350.
130. Nichols WG, Gooley T, Boeckh M. Community-acquired respiratory syncytial virus and parainfluenza virus infections after hematopoietic stem cell transplantation: The Fred Hutchinson Cancer Research Center experience. Biol Blood Marrow Transplant. 2001;7(Suppl):11S-15S.
131. Small TN, Casson A, Malak SF, et al. Respiratory syncytial virus infection following hematopoietic stem cell transplantation. Bone Marrow Transplant. 2002;29:321-327.
132. Ljungman P. Prevention and treatment of viral infections in stem cell transplant recipients. Br J Haematol. 2002;118:44-57.
133. Ison MG, Hayden FG, Kaiser L, et al. Rhinovirus infections in hematopoietic stem cell transplant recipients with pneumonia. Clin Infect Dis. 2003;36:1139-1143.
134. Harrington RD, Hooton TM, Hackman RC, et al. An outbreak of respiratory syncytial virus in a bone marrow transplant center. J Infect Dis. 1992;165:987-993.
135. Wendt CH, Weisdorf DJ, Jordan MC, et al. Parainfluenza virus respiratory infection after bone marrow transplantation. N Engl J Med. 1992;326:921-926.
136. Lewis VA, Champlin R, Englund J, et al. Respiratory disease due to parainfluenza virus in adult bone marrow transplant recipients. Clin Infect Dis. 1996;23: 1033-1037.
137. Whimbey E, Champlin RE, Englund JA, et al. Combination therapy with aerosolized ribavirin and intravenous immunoglobulin for respiratory syncytial virus disease in adult bone marrow transplant recipients. Bone Marrow Transplant. 1995;16:393-399.
138. Cortez K, Murphy BR, Almeida KN, et al. Immune-globulin prophylaxis of respiratory syncytial virus infection in patients undergoing stem-cell transplantation. J Infect Dis. 2002;186:834-838.
139. van Esser JW, Niesters HG, van der Holt B, et al. Prevention of Epstein-Barr virus-lymphoproliferative disease by molecular monitoring and preemptive rituximab in high-risk patients after allogeneic stem cell transplantation. Blood. 2002;99: 4364-4369.
140. van Esser JW, van der Holt B, Meijer E, et al. Epstein-Barr virus (EBV) reactivation is a frequent event after allogeneic stem cell transplantation (SCT) and quantitatively predicts EBV-lymphoproliferative disease following T-cell–depleted SCT. Blood. 2001;98:972-978.
141. Loren AW, Porter DL, Stadtmauer EA, et al. Post-transplant lymphoproliferative disorder: A review. Bone Marrow Transplant. 2003;31:145-155.
142. Papadopoulos EB, Ladanyi M, Emanuel D, et al. Infusions of donor leukocytes to treat Epstein-Barr virus-associated lymphoproliferative disorders after allogeneic bone marrow transplantation. N Engl J Med. 1994;330:1185-1191.
143. Boutolleau D, Fernandez C, Andre E, et al. Human herpesvirus (HHV)-6 and HHV-7: Two closely related viruses with different infection profiles in stem cell transplantation recipients. J Infect Dis. 2003;187:179-186.
144. Cone RW, Hackman RC, Huang ML, et al. Human herpesvirus 6 in lung tissue from patients with pneumonitis after bone marrow transplantation. N Engl J Med. 1993;329:156-161.
145. Zerr DM, Gupta D, Huang ML, et al. Effect of antivirals on human herpesvirus 6 replication in hematopoietic stem cell transplant recipients. Clin Infect Dis. 2002;34:309-317.
146. Azzi A, Fanci R, Ciappi S, et al. Human parvovirus B19 infection in bone marrow transplantation patients. Am J Hematol. 1993;44:207-209.
147. Fukuda T, Boeckh M, Carter RA, et al. Invasive fungal infections in recipients of allogeneic hematopoietic stem cell transplantation after nonmyeloablative conditioning: Risks and outcomes. Blood. 2003;10:10.
148. van Burik J-A, Leisenring W, Myerson D, et al. The effect of prophylactic fluconazole on the clinical spectrum of fungal diseases in bone marrow transplant recipients with special attention to hepatic candidiasis: An autopsy study of 355 patients. Medicine (Baltimore). 1998;77:246-254.
149. Riley DK, Pavia AT, Beatty PG, et al. The prophylactic use of low-dose amphotericin B in bone marrow transplant patients. Am J Med. 1994;97:509-514.
150. van Burik J-A, Ratanatharathorn V, Lipton J, et al. Randomized, double-blind trial of micafungin versus fluconazole for prophylaxis of invasive fungal infections in patients undergoing hematopoietic stem cell transplant. In: Proceedings of the 42nd Interscience Conference on Antimicrobial Agents and Chemotherapy, San Diego, September 27-30, 2002.
151. Lyytikainen O, Ruutu T, Volin L, et al. Late onset *Pneumocystis carinii* pneumonia following allogeneic bone marrow transplantation. Bone Marrow Transplant. 1996;17:1057-1059.
152. Saito T, Seo S, Kanda Y, et al. Early onset *Pneumocystis carinii* pneumonia after allogeneic peripheral blood stem cell transplantation. Am J Hematol. 2001;67:206-209.
153. Colby C, McAfee S, Sackstein R, et al. A prospective randomized trial comparing the toxicity and safety of atovaquone with trimethoprim/sulfamethoxazole as *Pneumocystis carinii* pneumonia prophylaxis following autologous peripheral blood stem cell transplantation. Bone Marrow Transplant. 1999;24:897-902.
154. Link H, Vohringer HF, Wingen F, et al. Pentamidine aerosol for prophylaxis of *Pneumocystis carinii* pneumonia after BMT. Bone Marrow Transplant. 1993;11: 403-406.
155. Maltezou HC, Petropoulos D, Choroszy M, et al. Dapsone for *Pneumocystis carinii* prophylaxis in children undergoing bone marrow transplantation. Bone Marrow Transplant. 1997;20:879-881.
156. Safdar A, van Rhee F, Henslee-Downey JP, et al. *Candida glabrata* and *Candida krusei* fungemia after high-risk allogeneic marrow transplantation: No adverse effect of low-dose fluconazole prophylaxis on incidence and outcome. Bone Marrow Transplant. 2001;28:873-878.
157. Marr KA, Seidel K, White TC, et al. Candidemia in allogeneic blood and marrow transplant recipients: Evolution of risk factors after the adoption of prophylactic fluconazole. J Infect Dis. 2000;181:309-316.
158. Goodrich JM, Reed EC, Mori M, et al. Clinical features and analysis of risk factors for invasive candidal infection after marrow transplantation. J Infect Dis. 1991;164:731-740.
159. Hagensee ME, Bauwens JE, Kjos B, et al. Brain abscess following marrow transplantation: Experience at the Fred Hutchinson Cancer Research Center, 1984-1992. Clin Infect Dis. 1994;19:402-408.
160. Marr KA, Seidel K, Slavin MA, et al. Prolonged fluconazole prophylaxis is associated with persistent protection against candidiasis-related death in allogeneic marrow transplant recipients: Long-term follow-up of a randomized, placebo-controlled trial. Blood. 2000;96:2055-2061.
161. Rossetti F, Brawner DL, Bowden R, et al. Fungal liver infection in marrow transplant patients: Prevalence at autopsy, predisposing factors, and clinical features. Clin Infect Dis. 1995;20:801-811.
162. Bjerke JW, Meyers JD, Bowden RA. Hepatosplenic candidiasis—A contraindication to marrow transplantation? Blood. 1994;84:2811-2814.
163. Morrison VA, Haake RJ, Weisdorf DJ. The spectrum of non-*Candida* fungal infections following bone marrow transplantation. Medicine (Baltimore). 1993;72:78-89.
164. Marr KA, Carter RA, Boeckh M, et al. Invasive aspergillosis in allogeneic stem cell transplant recipients: Changes in epidemiology and risk factors. Blood. 2002;100:4358-4366.
165. Maertens J, Verhaegen J, Lagrou K, et al. Screening for circulating galactomannan as a noninvasive diagnostic tool for invasive aspergillosis in prolonged neutropenic patients and stem cell transplantation recipients: A prospective validation. Blood. 2001;97:1604-1610.
166. Maertens J, Van Eldere J, Verhaegen J, et al. Use of circulating galactomannan screening for early diagnosis of invasive aspergillosis in allogeneic stem cell transplant recipients. J Infect Dis. 2002;186:1297-1306.
167. Deresinski SC, Stevens DA. Caspofungin. Clin Infect Dis. 2003;36:1445-1457.
168. Johnson MD, Perfect JR. Caspofungin: First approved agent in a new class of antifungals. Expert Opin Pharmacother. 2003;4:807-823.
169. Bowden R, Chandrasekar P, White MH, et al. A double-blind, randomized, controlled trial of amphotericin B colloidal dispersion versus amphotericin B for treatment of invasive aspergillosis in immunocompromised patients. Clin Infect Dis. 2002;35:359-366.
170. Herbrecht R, Denning DW, Patterson TF, et al. Voriconazole versus amphotericin B for primary therapy of invasive aspergillosis. N Engl J Med. 2002;347:408-415.
171. Bufill JA, Lum LG, Caya JG, et al. *Pityrosporum* folliculitis after bone marrow transplantation: Clinical observations in five patients. Ann Intern Med. 1988;108:560-563.
172. Morrison VA, Weisdorf DJ. The spectrum of *Malassezia* infections in the bone marrow transplant population. Bone Marrow Transplant. 2000;26:645-648.
173. Jahagirdar BN, Morrison VA. Emerging fungal pathogens in patients with hematologic malignancies and marrow/stem-cell transplant recipients. Semin Respir Infect. 2002;17:113-120.
174. Marr KA, Carter RA, Crippa F, et al. Epidemiology and outcome of mould infections in hematopoietic stem cell transplant recipients. Clin Infect Dis. 2002;34:909-917.
175. Oliver MR, Van Voorhis WC, Boeckh M, et al. Hepatic mucormycosis in a bone marrow transplant recipient who ingested naturopathic medicine. Clin Infect Dis. 1996;22:521-524.
176. Maertens J, Demuynck H, Verbeken EK, et al. Mucormycosis in allogeneic bone marrow transplant recipients: Report of five cases and review of the role of iron overload in the pathogenesis. Bone Marrow Transplant. 1999;24:307-312.
177. Tobon AM, Arango M, Fernandez D, et al. Mucormycosis (zygomycosis) in a heart-kidney transplant recipient: Recovery after posaconazole therapy. Clin Infect Dis. 2003;36:1488-1491.
178. Lefrere F, Besson C, Datry A, et al. Transmission of *Plasmodium falciparum* by allogeneic bone marrow transplantation. Bone Marrow Transplant. 1996;18:473-474.
179. Dictar M, Sinagra A, Veron MT, et al. Recipients and donors of bone marrow transplants suffering from Chagas' disease: Management and preemptive therapy of parasitemia. Bone Marrow Transplant. 1998;21:391-393.
180. Woo PC, Lie AK, Yuen K, et al. Clonorchiasis in bone marrow transplant recipients. Clin Infect Dis. 1998;27:382-384.
181. Feingold JM, Abraham J, Bilgrami S, et al. *Acanthamoeba* meningoencephalitis following autologous peripheral stem cell transplantation. Bone Marrow Transplant. 1998;22:297-300.
182. Anderlini P, Przepiorka D, Luna M, et al. *Acanthamoeba* meningoencephalitis after bone marrow transplantation. Bone Marrow Transplant. 1994;14:459-461.
183. Okamoto S, Wakui M, Kobayashi H, et al. *Trichomonas foetus* meningoencephalitis after allogeneic peripheral blood stem cell transplantation. Bone Marrow Transplant. 1998;21:89-91.
184. Kelkar R, Sastry PS, Kulkarni SS, et al. Pulmonary microsporidial infection in a patient with CML undergoing allogeneic marrow transplant. Bone Marrow Transplant. 1997;19:179-182.
185. Mele A, Paterson PJ, Prentice HG, et al. Toxoplasmosis in bone marrow transplantation: A report of two cases and systematic review of the literature. Bone Marrow Transplant. 2002;29:691-698.
186. Lewis JS Jr, Khoury H, Storch GA, et al. PCR for the diagnosis of toxoplasmosis after hematopoietic stem cell transplantation. Expert Rev Mol Diagn. 2002;2:616-624.
187. Bretagne S, Costa JM, Foulet F, et al. Prospective study of *Toxoplasma* reactivation by polymerase chain reaction in allogeneic stem-cell transplant recipients. Transpl Infect Dis. 2000;2:127-132.

188. Foot AB, Garin YJ, Ribaud P, et al. Prophylaxis of toxoplasmosis infection with pyrimethamine/sulfadoxine (Fansidar) in bone marrow transplant recipients. Bone Marrow Transplant. 1994;14:241-245.

189. Singhal S, Mehta J. Reimmunization after blood or marrow stem cell transplantation. Bone Marrow Transplant. 1999;23:637-646.

190. Henning KJ, White MH, Sepkowitz KA, et al. A national survey of immunization practices following allogeneic bone marrow transplantation. JAMA. 1997;277:1148-1151.

191. Gandhi MK, Egner W, Sizer L, et al. Antibody responses to vaccinations given within the first two years after transplant are similar between autologous peripheral blood stem cell and bone marrow transplant recipients. Bone Marrow Transplant. 2001;28:775-781.

192. Storek J, Viganego F, Dawson MA, et al. Factors affecting antibody levels after allogeneic hematopoietic cell transplantation. Blood. 2003;101:3319-3324.

193. Witherspoon RP, Storb R, Ochs HD, et al. Recovery of antibody production in human allogeneic marrow graft recipients: Influence of time posttransplantation, the presence or absence of chronic graft-versus-host disease, and antithymocyte globulin treatment. Blood. 1981;58:360-368.

194. Sullivan KM, Storek J, Kopecky KJ, et al. A controlled trial of long-term administration of intravenous immunoglobulin to prevent late infection and chronic graft-vs.-host disease after marrow transplantation: Clinical outcome and effect on subsequent immune recovery. Biol Blood Marrow Transplant. 1996;2:44-53.

195. Sullivan KM, Kopecky KJ, Jocom J, et al. Immunomodulatory and antimicrobial efficacy of intravenous immunoglobulin in bone marrow transplantation. N Engl J Med. 1990;323:705-712.

196. Wolff SN, Fay JW, Herzig RH, et al. High-dose weekly intravenous immunoglobulin to prevent infections in patients undergoing autologous bone marrow transplantation or severe myelosuppressive therapy: A study of the American Bone Marrow Transplant Group. Ann Intern Med. 1993;118:937-942.

TABLE 312-1   Overall Graft and Patient Survival Rates by Organ Transplanted

	Graft Survival (%)		Patient Survival (%)	
Organ	1 yr	3 yr	1 yr	3 yr
Kidney—living donor	94	88	98	95
Kidney—cadaver donor	88	79	94	88
Pancreas	95	90	95	89
Heart	84	78	85	79
Liver	80	71	86	80
Lung	76	58	77	59
Heart-lung	60	42	60	45

Adapted from United Network for Organ Sharing. Report of center specific graft and patient survival rates. In: 2002 Annual Report of the U.S. Organ Procurement and Transplantation Network and the Scientific Registry of Transplant Recipients: Transplant Data 1992-2001. Rockville, MD: Health Resources and Services Administration, Office of Special Programs, Division of Transplantation; Richmond, VA: United Network for Organ Sharing; and Ann Arbor, MI: University Renal Research and Education Association; 2002.

CHAPTER **312**

Infections in Solid Organ Transplant Recipients

J. STEPHEN DUMMER

After the introduction of cyclosporine as a major immunosuppressive agent, there was a marked increase in the transplantation of solid organs. The outlook improved for recipients of all types of organs, and liver, heart, and lung transplantation advanced from being experimental procedures to established therapeutic modalities similar to transplantation of the kidney. Table 312-1 shows the most recent data available on graft and patient survival released by the United Network for Organ Sharing.[1] The best results are in living-related kidney transplantation, in which 98% of recipients are alive and 94% have functioning allografts 1 year after transplantation. Perhaps the greatest progress has been in liver transplantation. Before the availability of cyclosporine, the 1-year survival rate after liver transplantation was only 32%, compared with a 3-year survival rate of 80% in the current era. The survival rates for lung, heart-lung, and intestinal transplant recipients have lagged behind the other groups, but these procedures present significant technical challenges. They were also only introduced in the 1980s and experience has been gained slowly because of the limited number of transplants performed.

Improvements in graft and patient survival have been paralleled by a decline in mortality from infections.[2,3] For instance, the risk of death from infection in heart recipients transplanted in Pittsburgh fell significantly between 1981 and 1990 (Fig. 312-1). In the most recent group of patients studied, infectious mortality was only about 1.5% per year for the first 3 years after transplantation.[2] Likewise, the early post-transplantation mortality rate from infection in liver recipients decreased significantly, from 47% in the early 1980s[4] to 23% in the late 1980s[5] and 7% in the early 1990s.[6] Recent information suggests that infectious mortality may have leveled off, at least in heart transplantation. A multi-institutional study of 7290 heart transplant recipients followed between 1990 and 2000 showed that 3-year infectious mortality was largely unchanged at 4.5% to 5.0% throughout the decade, whereas mortality resulting from rejection and graft vasculopathy fell significantly during the same period.[7]

TIME OF OCCURRENCE OF INFECTIONS AFTER TRANSPLANTATION

Most infections occur in the first few months after transplantation, when the patient is still under close medical surveillance. The kinds of infections seen within this high-risk period are not uniform but follow a typical time schema.[8] Common infections during the first post-transplant month are those that might be seen after any surgical procedure: respiratory and urinary tract, wound, and intravascular catheter infections caused by nosocomial bacteria. Except for the reactivation of herpes simplex virus (HSV), infections related to deficient T-cell immunity are not encountered. After 1 month, surgical infections decline in importance and typical opportunistic infections associated with the immunosuppressed state emerge. These include *Pneumocystis* pneumonia, opportunistic fungal infections, nocardiosis, and, most importantly,

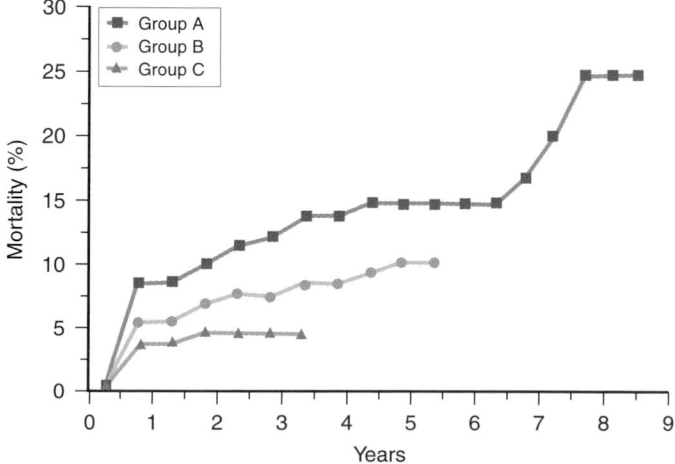

FIGURE 312-1. Mortality resulting from infections in heart transplant recipients in three different time periods: group A, 1980-1985 (179 patients); group B, 1985-1987 (179 patients); group C, 1987-1990 (180 patients). Group A versus group C, P = 0.015. Mortality from other causes has been censored. (*Data from Dummer JS. Antibiotic prophylaxis and management of infectious complications. In: Kaye MP, O'Connell JB, eds. Heart and Lung Transplantation 2000. Austin, TX: R. G. Landes; 1993:78.*)

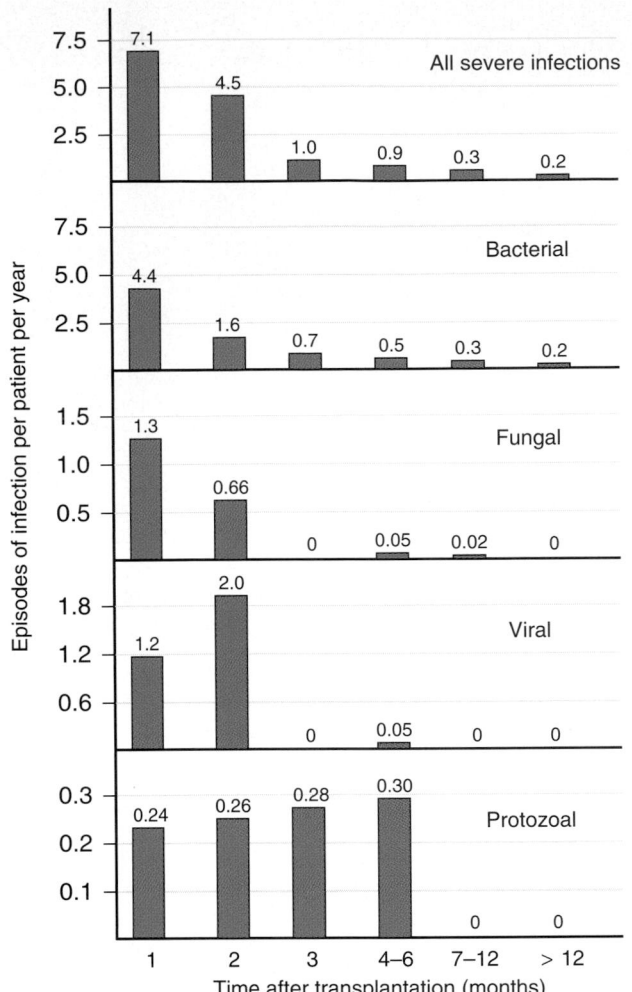

FIGURE 312-2. Incidence and timing of severe infections expressed in episodes of infection per liver transplant patient per year at different times after transplantation. Data on all severe bacterial, fungal, viral, and "protozoal" (mostly *Pneumocystis*) infections are included.

cytomegalovirus (CMV) infection. This time schema of infections was first described in renal transplantation, but is applicable to other types of transplantation with a few minor alterations.[5,9-12] For instance, in liver transplant recipients, postsurgical infection may extend into the second and third month because of retransplantation or reoperation for technical complications.[5,13] Also, opportunistic fungal infections occur during the first month in liver and lung transplant recipients because of their high susceptibility.[5,14,15]

Figure 312-2 illustrates the incidence of severe infections at various times after liver transplantation.[5] The figure excludes minor infections such as afebrile cystitis or localized HSV infection. It is apparent that the frequency of severe infections was quite high during the first and second months. Bacterial and fungal infections were most common in the first month and viral infections (mostly CMV) in the second month. The "protozoal" infections were mostly *Pneumocystis* pneumonia and are not seen now because of the effectiveness of trimethoprim-sulfamethoxazole (TMP-SMX) prophylaxis. After 6 months, the rate of severe infections declined to about one infection for every 4 patient years. These late infections were all caused by bacteria or fungi. This rate of late infection is similar to the frequency of severe, late infections seen in heart transplant recipients.[10]

The most frequent infections that occur more than 6 months after transplantation are simply the common infections found in any population.[2,8] Community-acquired pneumonia, diverticulitis, and cholecystitis are not unique for transplant recipients, but because of immune suppression these infections may manifest in an altered fashion or have more severe sequelae.[2,8] Other late manifestations may represent reactivated or chronic viral infections. Eruptions of herpes zoster may occur at any time after transplantation.[10,16] Subacute or chronic hepatitis, particularly that caused by hepatitis C virus (HCV), may become manifest many years after transplantation.[17] A number of tumors related to viral infection may also occur late, the most frequent being warts (verruca vulgaris). Also, some lymphomas and lymphoproliferative syndromes related to Epstein-Barr virus (EBV) occur after more than 1 year.[18] A third type of late infection relates to chronic graft dysfunction. Lung transplant recipients with chronic rejection develop obliterative bronchiolitis and are susceptible to recurrent bacterial bronchitis and pneumonia.[19] Liver transplant recipients may have recurrent cholangitis, often in association with biliary stricture.[5]

Finally, the risk for "opportunistic" infection declines, but never completely disappears. Cryptococcal infection, for instance, often manifests late and without any inciting event.[20]

TYPES OF TRANSPLANTS AND CHARACTERISTIC INFECTIONS

Table 312-2 presents the type, severity, and characteristic sites of infections in 315 kidney, heart, heart-lung, and liver transplant recipients observed during the first year after transplantation.[5,10,21,22] These data were collected at the University of Pittsburgh from patients who received very similar immunosuppressive regimens, before the advent of the complex prophylactic antimicrobial regimens used today. Therefore, they reflect intrinsic differences in the epidemiology of infections in different organ groups before they were affected by individual variations in management.

Although the number of infections was high in all transplant recipients, the type of infection, the severity, and the mortality varied widely with the organ or organs transplanted. The number of episodes of infection per patient was lowest in the renal group, and none of these patients died of infection. The heart-lung recipients, by contrast, had more than three times the number of infections and the largest number of deaths associated with infection (45%). The liver transplant group also had a high infectious mortality and almost five times the rate of bacteremia of the renal group. Invasive fungal infections were frequent in liver and heart-lung recipients, intermediate in heart recipients, and absent in renal recipients. It is particularly striking how

TABLE 312-2 Frequency, Severity, and Type of Infections Occurring in the First Year after Transplantation								
Type of Transplant	*N*	*Infections per Patient*	*Infectious Mortality (%)*	*Bacteremic Patients (%)*	*CMV Disease (%)**	*Deep Fungal Infection (%)*	*Most Common Site*	*Proportion of all Infections (%)*
Renal	64	0.98	0	5	8 (5)	0	Urinary tract	41
Heart	119	1.36	15	13	16 (5)	8	Lung	27
Heart-lung	31	3.19	45	19	39 (32)	23	Lung	57
Liver	101	1.86	23	23	22 (5)	16	Abdomen & biliary	23

*Numbers in parentheses indicate percentage of all patients with CMV pneumonia.
CMV, cytomegalovirus.
Data on the four transplant groups are from the University of Pittsburgh experience, compiled from references 5, 10, 21-23.

much better the outcome was for heart recipients than for heart-lung recipients, even though they were managed by the same physicians and received the same immunosuppressive regimen. Finally, Table 312-2 shows that the most common sites of infection after transplantation were closely related to the site of surgery.

Kidney Transplant Recipients

The most common site of infection in renal transplant recipients is the urinary tract.[23] In 1972, Myerowitz and colleagues found that 60% of 53 bacteremias in kidney recipients arose from the urinary tract or adjacent sites, with a mortality per episode of 25%.[24] One half of the patients had technical surgical complications such as ureteral leak or perinephric hematoma. Since then, surgical problems have decreased in frequency and outcome had improved, but urosepsis still is an important problem. For example, in the study by Wagener and Yu, 40% of bacteremias in kidney recipients arose from the urinary tract.[25]

Most isolates are similar to those seen in urinary tract infections in other groups of patients: *Escherichia coli,* other enteric organisms, *Enterococcus,* and *Candida.*[24,25] Chronic and recurrent urinary tract infections remain problematic. Abnormalities such as ureteral reflux, strictures at the ureterovesicle junction, or neurogenic bladder should be sought in patients with recurrent infections. However, many of the late urinary tract infections seen in renal transplant recipients are benign. Griffin and Salaman diagnosed urinary infection in 40% of 86 patients; half of the infections occurred in the first 6 months and half occurred later.[26] The authors were not able to document an adverse effect on graft survival despite the recurrence of infections in many patients. Giral and colleagues documented graft pyelonephritis in 13% of 1387 renal recipients over a 13-year interval.[27] Infections occurring in the first 3 months were associated with reduced graft survival but later infections were not. Avoidance of surgical complications and use of antimicrobial prophylaxis are the most important means of decreasing the frequency of urinary infection.[28] An extended course of antibiotics (4 to 6 weeks) is recommended in patients with early graft pyelonephritis to achieve eradication of the infecting bacterium.[29] Extended courses of antibiotics may also be useful in patients who relapse with the same infecting organism after short-term treatment of cystitis and in those with special risk factors, such as diabetes or urinary retention.

The clinician also should be alert to the possible occurrence of unusual urinary pathogens. We have seen urinary tract tuberculosis that occurred during the first 2 weeks after transplantation and arose from a focus in the native kidney. *Mycoplasma hominis* infection of the urinary tract may cause a breakdown of the ureterovesicle anastomosis with subsequent graft loss.[30] Histoplasmosis may involve the transplanted kidney and cause renal failure.[31]

Historically, pneumonia occurred in 25% to 30% of renal transplant recipients and was the most common infectious cause of death.[32] In the past, bacteria were a less prominent cause of transplantation-associated pneumonia than CMV and opportunists such as fungi, *Nocardia,* and *Pneumocystis.*[32,33] More recently, CMV and other opportunistic infections have come under better control, and conventional bacterial pathogens have become relatively more common in transplant populations.[34]

Wound infections are relatively infrequent, but may be a serious problem, particularly if they involve the perinephric space. In the 1970s Kyriakides and colleagues documented wound infection in 27 (6.1%) of 439 kidney recipients transplanted over a 6-year period.[35] The mortality rate was 30%, and another 56% of patients survived but lost their grafts. Most infections were associated with surgical complications such as hematomas or urinary leaks. First-time transplant patients without diabetes or surgical complications had a wound infection rate of only 0.7%. By the beginning of the cyclosporine era, a reduction in surgical complications and introduction of antibiotic prophylaxis had led to a fall in wound infection rates to 1% or 2%.[36]

Although Table 312-2 lists no deaths from infections in renal transplant recipients, some such deaths may be expected. In a survey of 604 renal transplant recipients at Minnesota, patients with infection had an

88% 3-year survival rate, compared with a 92% rate in patients without infection, revealing a small but significant increase in mortality.[37]

Some renal transplant recipients continue to have infectious problems even after the first 6 months. Rubin identified these patients as those with a serum creatinine concentration higher than 2 mg/dL, a daily prednisone dose greater than 20 mg, a history of receiving multiple antirejection therapies, or associated chronic viral infection (e.g., HCV).[38]

Heart Transplant Recipients

Heart transplant recipients have more infections and are more affected by them than are kidney transplant recipients.[10,23] In a survey of 620 heart transplant recipients at Stanford University, infections were the most common cause of death.[39] The most common infections were bacterial pneumonias, urinary infections, herpesvirus infections, and invasive fungal infections. Most pneumonias in heart transplant recipients are caused by common pathogenic bacteria (Table 312-3).[10,39] Although the incidence of pneumonia is highest in the first few months after transplantation, bacterial pneumonias occur sporadically in the late post-transplantation period, after the patient has recovered from the immediate effects of surgery.

Mediastinitis and sternal wound infections are postoperative complications unique to heart, heart-lung, and lung transplant recipients. The pathogens seen are similar to those observed in other patients undergoing cardiothoracic surgery, with *Staphylococcus aureus* and *Staphylococcus epidermidis* predominating. The incidence of mediastinitis in two large transplant series was quite similar: 2.5% (9 of 361) and 2.9% (18 of 620).[39,40] The initial clinical presentation may be subtle, with the only manifestations being low-grade fever or an elevated leukocyte count. Later, more specific signs develop, such as erythema, tenderness, or drainage along the sternal incision.[41] One must also be alert to the possible presence of unusual pathogens. Mediastinitis and sternal wound infection in heart recipient have been caused by *Mycoplasma hominis, Legionella pneumophila, Aspergillus,* and *Nocardia.*[30,39,42] Thus it may be necessary to include special media in the microbiologic workup of these infections. Factors that are thought to predispose to mediastinitis in this population are repeat operations for hemorrhage, use of antirejection therapy, and the presence of diabetes mellitus.[40,41] Surgical drainage appears to be crucial to the successful treatment of mediastinitis in the transplant patient. There is considerable controversy regarding the best mode of drainage.

Mechanical left-ventricular assist devices with an external power source are now widely used as a bridge to transplantation.[43] Infections of these devices are common and fall into certain distinct types. These include infections of the driveline, which are often limited to the exit site, deep infections in the pocket surrounding the actual device, and bacterial or fungal blood-stream infections. The latter may be associated

TABLE 312-3 Microbial Causes of Pneumonia in Transplant Recipients

Early Pneumonia (≤30 days)	Late Pneumonia (>30 days)
Common Causes	
Gram-negative enteric bacilli	Pneumococcus
Staphylococcus aureus	*Haemophilus influenzae*
Aspiration	No cause identified
Less Common Causes	
Aspergillus	*Pneumocystis*
Herpes simplex virus	*Nocardia*
Legionella	*Legionella*
Toxoplasma gondii	*Aspergillus*
	Gram-negative enteric bacilli
	Staphylococcus aureus
	Aspiration
	Cytomegalovirus
	Varicella-zoster virus
	Paramyxoviruses
	Tuberculosis
	Coccidioidomycosis
	Histoplasmosis

with internal infection of the device. Management of these infections is very challenging and beyond the scope of this chapter. Fortunately, in many cases, the infection can be controlled well enough to permit transplantation[43] (see Chapters 75 and 192).

A number of other infections are more commonly reported in heart recipients than in patients receiving other types of transplants. These include systemic toxoplasmosis, nocardiosis, and Chagas' disease.[44-46] Toxoplasmosis is an important clinical entity in heart transplant recipients because the infection can be transmitted by organisms encysted in the donated heart. The patients at risk are *Toxoplasma*-seronegative recipients who receive hearts from seropositive donors. Clinical toxoplasmosis usually occurs between a few weeks and a few months after transplantation and is manifested by necrotizing pneumonitis, myocarditis, and encephalitis. The diagnosis may occasionally be made by identifying *Toxoplasma* cysts or tachyzoites on endomyocardial biopsy.[47] Routine use of TMP-SMX for *Pneumocystis* prophylaxis seems to protect heart transplant recipients against toxoplasmosis.[39] Pyrimethamine (25 mg/day for 6 weeks together with folinic acid, 5 to 10 mg/day, to prevent bone marrow suppression) is an alternative prophylactic agent for patients allergic to or intolerant of TMP-SMX.[48] Patients who undergo heart transplantation for cardiomyopathy caused by chronic *Trypanosoma cruzi* infection may have relapses of acute Chagas' disease with clinical manifestations of fever, myocarditis, and skin lesions.[44] The disease can usually be controlled with chemotherapy. A recent large series from Brazil reported excellent overall outcomes for 117 patients transplanted for Chagas' disease, with only two deaths occurring from *T. cruzi* infection.[49] *Nocardia* infections have also been more frequently reported in heart transplant recipients than in recipients of kidney or liver transplants, but the biologic reason for this increased rate of nocardiosis is unknown.[39,46]

Despite frequent trauma to the tricuspid valve and right ventricular endocardium from repeated endomyocardial biopsies, a common posttransplantation practice, heart transplant recipients do not appear to be at substantial risk of endocarditis.

Heart-Lung and Lung Transplant Recipients

As a result of the shortage of suitable donors, the field of heart-lung and lung transplantation has progressed at a slower rate than others. In many respects, the heart-lung transplant recipients have infectious problems similar to those of heart transplant recipients, but the infections are more frequent and more severe. Early reports of heart-lung transplantation emphasized the high rate of bacterial lung infections during the first few weeks after transplantation.[9,21,50] These patients also have higher rates of mediastinitis, invasive fungal infections, *Pneumocystis* infection, and CMV pneumonia than comparable heart recipients.[21,51] Heart-lung and lung transplant recipients develop invasive pulmonary aspergillosis more frequently than patients with other types of organ transplants.[52] They are also susceptible to a unique form of aspergillosis that is confined to the airways, and produces mucosal lesions that can be directly visualized during bronchoscopy.[52] Tracheobronchial aspergillosis in heart and heart-lung recipients has a somewhat better prognosis than invasive pulmonary aspergillosis.[51] Antifungal prophylaxis is widely employed after lung transplantation, with oral itraconazole and inhaled amphotericin being the most widely used agents.[53,54]

The exaggerated vulnerability of the transplanted lung to infection is probably multifactorial. In addition to the factors related to decreased mucociliary clearance, diminished lymphatic drainage, and ablation of the cough reflex, allograft reactions are implicated. In the late posttransplant period, as many as 65% of patients develop obliterative bronchiolitis.[55,56] This process is the main pathologic manifestation of chronic rejection of the lung, and it is associated with recurrent pulmonary infections.[19] The lung allograft is also particularly susceptible to viral infection. This has been documented for CMV, HSV, paramyxovirus, and adenovirus infections.[15,19,50,56-58] Accordingly, lung transplant centers often utilize aggressive regimens for prophylaxis for herpesvirus infections and perform thorough virologic investigations in patients with acute chest infections.

The first success in transplanting lungs was achieved with combined heart-lung transplantation. Single- and double-lung transplantation have now largely replaced heart-lung transplantation as the procedures of choice for most patients with end-stage lung disease. The major exception is transplantation for patients who have severe cardiac abnormalities that cannot be surgically repaired. Single- and double-lung procedures also leave the donor heart available for another patient with end-stage heart disease. The types of infections seen in lung transplant recipients are similar to those in heart-lung recipients, although the overall survival rate is better.[1,11,15,50] A unique aspect of single-lung transplantation is the occurrence of infections in the remaining native lung. This lung may be predisposed to infection because of defects of ventilation or perfusion caused by the underlying lung disease.[11]

Prospective donors for lung transplantation are intubated in intensive care units. Therefore, the airways of these donors are often colonized with microorganisms, and occult parenchymal infection may be present.[56,59] Before implantation of the lungs, it is useful to obtain cultures and Gram stains of the donor airways to guide antibiotic therapy. Initial antibiotic prophylaxis should be aimed at common nosocomial pathogens encountered in the intensive care unit, including methicillin-resistant *S. aureus* and enteric gram-negative bacilli. Another problem in lung transplantation has been dehiscence of the airway anastomosis. This occurs during the first few weeks after transplantation. It is frequently associated with bacterial or fungal infection at the anastomotic site. Fortunately, the incidence appears to be declining.[60]

Liver Transplant Recipients

Liver transplant recipients have higher rates of infection than renal or heart transplant recipients, and most deaths are associated with infection, either as a primary or as a secondary cause. Despite a decline in mortality in recent years, infections are still a major threat.[6] In a study of 101 patients, most had at least one bacterial infection, and two thirds had at least one severe infection.[5] Bacteria are the most common pathogens causing serious infection after liver transplantation. The reported incidence has varied from 35% to 70%.[5,62,63] About half of these infections occur within 2 weeks after the transplant operation.[62] Identified risk factors include a prolonged duration of surgery, transfusion of large quantities of blood, use of a choledochojejunostomy (Roux-en-Y) procedure for bile drainage, repeat transplantation, and CMV infection.[5,62] The most important sites of infection are the abdomen and biliary tract, the surgical wound, the lungs, and the blood stream, with or without associated catheter infection.

Liver transplant recipients have a higher rate of fungal infections than other solid organ transplant recipients. The reported incidence has been 16% to 42%, with a case fatality rate of 25% to 75%.[4,5,61,64] Eighty percent of fungal infections occur in the first month and 90% in the first 2 months.[4] In the past *Candida* was the predominant pathogen, but it has declined in relative importance compared to *Aspergillus*, other molds, and *Cryptococcus*.[65] Risk factors for invasive fungal infection noted in one retrospective analysis included elevated serum creatinine, longer operative time, retransplantation, and colonization with *Candida* at the time of transplantation.[66] Two thirds of patients with all four risk factors had invasive fungal infection. Other identified risk factors in this and other studies were administration of steroids before or after operation, duration of broad-spectrum antibiotic use, and CMV infection.[4,5,66]

Aspergillus infections occur in 1.5% to 4% of liver transplant recipients and are fatal in 80% to 100% of cases.[4,5,14,67] The average time of onset is somewhat later than for *Candida* infections, with 50% of cases occurring more than 38 days after transplantation. Some of the identified risk factors are severe hepatic injury before transplantation, use of augmented immunosuppression after transplantation, renal dysfunction, and CMV infection.

Abdominal Infections in Liver Transplant Recipients

Transplantation of the liver differs from other transplant operations in the length and difficulty of the surgery and the frequency of bleeding problems. In addition, many liver transplant recipients have poor nutrition and severe metabolic difficulties. Abdominal infections after liver transplantation are often related to technical aspects and complications of the operation.[5,13] For example, anastomosis of the biliary duct to a Roux-en-Y loop of jejunum is associated with more intra-abdominal infections, especially invasive fungal infections, than primary anastomosis of the donor's to the recipient's common bile duct.[5,66]

Most *liver abscesses* in the transplanted liver are related to surgical problems such as biliary stricture or hepatic artery thrombosis.[5] The abscesses may be either solitary or multiple. They manifest as a febrile illness with bacteremia and leukocytosis. The organisms responsible are gram-negative enteric bacilli, enterococci, and anaerobes. The diagnosis is made by ultrasound or computed tomography (CT). Treatment with drainage and intravenous antibiotics is usually successful, if the source is biliary infection and any structural abnormalities can be corrected. In the case of hepatic artery thrombosis, the infectious symptoms can usually be controlled with antibiotics, but retransplantation may ultimately be necessary.

Cholangitis after liver transplantation also results from technical problems. The most common predisposing problem is biliary stricture. Patients with strictures may have periodic bouts of cholangitis. Some patients improve after dilatation procedures or stent placement, but in others operative repair is necessary.

It may not be easy to make a firm diagnosis of cholangitis, because many patients do not manifest the classic "Charcot triad" of fever, abdominal pain, and jaundice. The clinical presentation may resemble hepatic rejection. The diagnosis is more reliable if bacteremia is present or if a liver biopsy indicates pericholangitis with aggregates of neutrophils around bile ducts. Empirical treatment for cholangitis should include antibiotics to cover gram-negative enteric bacilli, enterococci, and anaerobes. Procedures such as T-tube cholangiography and endoscopic retrograde cholangiopancreatography may be followed by cholangitis and occasionally bacteremia. Therefore, a single dose of a prophylactic antibiotic is recommended.

Peritonitis can accompany other intra-abdominal infections and frequently complicates biliary leaks or disruption of an abdominal viscus. Bile peritonitis may occur after extraction of a T tube. This is often well tolerated and may resolve by itself, but occasionally the leak persists and the chemical peritonitis becomes secondarily infected. The most common organisms involved in peritonitis are enterococci and aerobic enteric gram-negative rods, but staphylococcal and candidal infections are not infrequent. Treatment of established peritonitis requires prolonged antibiotic therapy, together with drainage of associated abscesses and repair of technical problems such as biliary leaks.

Abdominal abscesses are usually found in patients who have had frequent or lengthy abdominal operations.[5] Only about one third of abdominal abscesses are associated with bacteremia. The location is frequently in the subhepatic space, but splenic, pericolic, and pelvic abscesses are also seen. Most patients with abscesses have undergone an abdominal operation within the preceding 30 days.[5] One third of abscesses are polymicrobial, and although common enteric organisms cause most abscesses, coagulase-positive or coagulase-negative staphylococci are also seen. Imaging studies (CT, ultrasound) usually define the location of the abscess, but occasionally the abscess is discovered only at laparotomy. As with any other abscesses, the appropriate treatment is a combination of drainage and antibiotics directed against the responsible pathogens. Fever is part of the clinical presentation in most cases, but some abscesses, especially those caused by *Candida*, may not cause significant fever.

Pancreas Transplant Recipients

About 1200 pancreas transplant operations are performed in the United States annually, or about 1 for every 10 renal transplantations.[1] Pancreas transplantation can improve quality of life and may prevent some of the secondary complications of type 1 diabetes mellitus by restoring physiologic titration of insulin in accordance with metabolic needs.[68] In exchange for improved diabetic management and prevention of complications, however, patients assume the risks of a major operation and the problems of long-term immunosuppression. The ex-

perience so far comes largely from patients who require kidney transplantation for diabetic nephropathy, and most patients have both pancreas and kidney implanted in a single operation. Current patient and graft survival rates are similar to those for kidney transplantation alone, but infectious morbidity is higher.[1,69] A formal comparison of infections after isolated kidney and combined kidney-pancreas transplantation showed more wound complications and CMV disease among the patients receiving combined organs.[69] Pancreas transplant recipients also share with liver recipients a high rate of fungal infection.[12] In a small but well-detailed observation of 34 pancreas recipients from the Mayo Clinic, 35% had invasive fungal infections, most of which were caused by *Candida*.[69]

The main technical problem associated with pancreas transplantation has been adequate and safe drainage of exocrine secretions. In recent years the practice of draining these secretions into the small bowel has gained precedence over the previous practice of drainage into the bladder.[68] Small bowel drainage has been associated with lower rates of infection, particularly urinary tract infections.[70]

Small Bowel Transplantation

Small bowel transplantation has been practiced for over a decade but it is only performed at a few centers and in less than 100 patients annually.[1] Thus it must still be considered to be in the early stages of clinical development. It is used in patients who depend on parenteral nutrition to survive because of congenital or acquired intestinal disease or short-gut syndrome after intestinal resection.[71] Although the mortality rate appears to be acceptably low, many patients have very slow return of bowel function after the procedure, resulting in prolonged hospitalization.[72] Rejection episodes cause mucosal injury, and some rejections have led to breakdown of the "bowel-blood" barrier with subsequent septic syndromes.[71] More than 90% of patients develop significant infections, and the reported rates of infection are higher than in other transplant groups.[73] Intra-abdominal pyogenic infections and blood-stream infections predominate, but the transplanted gut, like the transplanted liver and lung, appears to be very susceptible to CMV infection, including a tendency to relapse after successful antiviral treatment.[74] This form of transplantation may also be complicated by graft-versus-host disease presumably as a result of the large amount of lymphoid tissue transplanted with the gut.[72] EBV-associated lymphoproliferative disorders also seem to be a major problem, with rates as high as 11% reported in pediatric patients.[71,72]

SITES AND TYPES OF INFECTION

Infections of the Skin and Wound Infections

Infections of the skin are common after transplantation but are rarely life threatening. They constitute a significant nuisance to the transplant recipient, and they may indicate the presence of serious systemic infection. The most important pathogens are listed in Table 312-4.

All solid organ transplant recipients are at risk for wound infections. The reported incidence of wound infections varies from center to center and among types of transplantation; it is highest among liver and pancreas transplant recipients, lower in heart and heart-lung transplant recipients, and lowest in renal transplant recipients.[5,12,36,40] The most common isolate is *S. aureus*, but infections with gram-negative enteric bacteria, *S. epidermidis*, *Candida* spp., and *M. hominis* may also be seen.[42] Rarely, mucormycosis occurs in surgical wounds of transplant patients.[4] In this case, the wounds typically are black from tissue infarction caused by invasion of the blood vessels by the fungus.

TABLE 312-4 *Skin Pathogens in Transplant Recipients*	
Staphylococcus aureus	*Mycobacterium chelonae*
Herpes simplex virus	*Candida* spp.
Varicella-zoster virus	Dematiaceous fungi
Papillomavirus	Dermatophytes

Tissue biopsy usually is required for a definitive diagnosis, and therapy should include wide surgical débridement.

The most common cutaneous viral infections are those caused by HSV and varicella-zoster virus. These are discussed later. Warts usually are treated with surgery, including electrosurgery or cryosurgery, or by the application of agents such as podophyllin.

Dermatophyte infections usually respond to topical antifungals such as miconazole; griseofulvin and oral azoles may be required for severe cases. Subcutaneous infections caused by *Alternaria, Exophiala,* and other darkly pigmented or dematiaceous fungi are encountered occasionally.[75] They present as mildly tender nodular lesions. Most infections spread locally without dissemination. Biopsy with fungal culture is required for a specific diagnosis. Therapy must be individualized, but a combination of resection and therapy with an oral azole such as itraconazole is often effective.[75]

Mycobacterium chelonae causes pigmented nodular skin lesions that occur singly or in groups, often on extremities. About half of the cases are multifocal at presentation.[76] The skin is also a target organ for many systemic infections. Systemic bacterial, fungal, nocardial, mycobacterial, and CMV infections may include skin manifestations. As a rule, one should aggressively investigate any new and unusual skin lesion with a biopsy.

Infections of the Urinary Tract

Urinary tract infections are discussed in the section on "Kidney Transplant Recipients."

Infections of the Blood Stream

The basic approach to bacteremia is the same whether or not the patient has undergone transplantation. The first step is to ascertain the source of the bacteremia. The most common sites producing bacterial blood-stream infections are the lung, the urinary tract, the abdomen (including the biliary tract), soft tissues, and intravenous catheters. The inability to pinpoint a source is not rare, especially in liver transplant recipients.[5,25] In one large study of bacteremia in multiple transplant groups at a single institution, the overall mortality rate was 23%.[25] Mortality was highest in heart recipients and lowest in kidney recipients. Risk factors for mortality were the presence of gram-negative or polymicrobial infection, onset of infection early after transplantation, the presence of pneumonia, and impaired kidney and liver function.

The source of bacteremia varies with the type of transplantation and is most commonly related to the transplantation site (see Table 312-2). For example, 41% to 60% of the bacteremias in kidney recipients come from the urinary tract or from perinephric sources.[24,25] Bacteremia in kidney recipients is relatively uncommon in the very early post-transplantation period (14 days) but relatively more common in the late post-transplantation period.

Among 101 liver recipients monitored for more than 1 year, 33 bacteremias occurred in 26 patients.[5] Thirty-six percent of the bacteremias had a fatal outcome. The most common source was the abdomen (33%), followed by the urinary tract (21%), the surgical wound (9%), intravenous catheters (6%), and the lung (6%). Twenty-one percent of the bacteremias had no documented source, but most of these probably originated in the abdomen. Gram-negative enteric bacilli were the most common isolates in this and another contemporaneous series.[62] In recent years bacteremia has continued to be a major problem, but the spectrum of blood-stream isolates has shifted and resistant gram-positive organisms such as methicillin-resistant staphylococci and vancomycin-resistant enterococci are now predominant.[77,78]

Hofflin and colleagues noted a decline in the incidence of bacteremia in heart transplant patients at Stanford University from 29% to 15% after a change to cyclosporine-based immunosuppression.[3] The isolates were equally divided between gram-negative and gram-positive bacteria. In subsequent years the incidence of bacteremia continued to decline. In a later survey of infections in heart transplant recipients from the same institution, there were only 38 documented bacteremias in 620 patients. There was also a shift in the type of organism isolated, because 80% of bacteremias were due to gram-positive organisms, with a predominance of staphylococcal species.[39]

Infections in the Chest

The usual microbial causes of pneumonia in the transplant recipient are listed in Table 312-3. They are subdivided according to whether the pneumonia occurs during the first month after transplantation or later and whether they are common or less common causes. The key to the management of lung infections in transplant recipients is rapid identification of the responsible pathogen and initiation of specific therapy. However, patients with a brief duration of symptoms (3 days), who have a focal chest infiltrate and are producing sputum with neutrophils on Gram stain, are likely to have a routine bacterial pneumonia. Empirical therapy to cover pneumonia can be started while culture results are pending and should target usual causes as well as any organisms seen on Gram stain. The presence of diffuse infiltrates (or nodular lesions), a nonproductive cough, or a longer duration of symptoms (>7 days) favors the presence of an unusual or "opportunistic" pathogen, and consideration should be given to the early use of invasive techniques to make the diagnosis. Invasive workup is also indicated in patients who appear to have a conventional pneumonia but are not responding to treatment.

The reported frequency of *Legionella* infection varies widely, depending on its endemicity in the hospital and the sensitivity of diagnostic methods.[79] Even when *Legionella* organisms are absent from the nosocomial environment, sporadic community-acquired cases will continue to occur among transplant recipients, because *Legionella* infection accounts for 2% to 15% of community-acquired pneumonias.[79] Special laboratory measures are necessary for the diagnosis of *Legionella* pneumonia. The most specific method of diagnosis is isolation of the organism on special media, but detection of urinary antigen is also helpful for *L. pneumophila* serogroup 1. The radiographic presentation is variable and may include focal infiltrates spreading to multiple lobes, globular pleural-based lesions, lung abscess, pleural effusion, or pericardial effusion. Any one of the serotypes of *L. pneumophila* or *L. micdadei* may be responsible. Legionellosis in transplant patients should be treated with azithromycin or a quinolone antibiotic.[79,80]

Infections caused by *Aspergillus, Nocardia,* or endemic mycoses may also be relatively common in some localities. The environmental factors determining these occurrences are poorly understood. Community-acquired respiratory viruses such as respiratory syncytial virus may cause pneumonia in transplant recipients. They appear to be a greater problem for lung recipients than patients with other types of solid organ transplants.[56-58]

Abdominal and Gastrointestinal Infections

Intra-abdominal infections in liver transplant recipients have already been discussed. These infections also occur at increased frequency among recipients of pancreas and small bowel transplants.[13,69,73] They are less common after transplant operations that do not involve the abdomen. When they do occur, they are usually related to preexisting medical conditions such as biliary stones or diverticulosis.

Studies in developing countries show that transplant recipients are very susceptible to *Salmonella* infection.[81] *Clostridium difficile* infections are common in transplant populations that are heavily treated with antibiotics. For instance, symptomatic *C. difficile* infections were seen in 3% to 6% of liver transplant recipients.[5,62] Infections caused by *Shigella, Campylobacter,* or *Helicobacter* do not appear to be increased in transplant recipients.[81] However, *Helicobacter* infection has been associated with the occurrence of a low-grade gastric lymphoma, called MALToma, in a small number of transplant recipients.[82] The majority of these have regressed following reduction of immunosuppression and use of antibiotic therapy to treat the *Helicobacter* infection.

Hyperinfection and disseminated infection with *Strongyloides stercoralis* were substantial problems in the past but appear to have virtually disappeared.[83] Universal pretransplantation screening of stools for *Strongyloides* is probably not cost-effective, but vigilance for this infection should be maintained in patients from endemic areas.

Hepatitis

The most important causes of hepatitis in transplant recipients are hepatitis B virus (HBV), HCV, and CMV. In many respects, CMV is the least important cause of hepatitis because it is usually mild and never leads to chronic hepatitis. The presence of chronic HBV infection can adversely affect survival after transplantation.[84,85] Certain subgroups of patients with HBV infection have had worse prognoses. For example, 63% of renal recipients with circulating HBV DNA or hepatitis B e antigen died of liver disease during 10 years of follow-up, compared with only 33% of those without such markers.[86] Likewise, liver transplant candidates with HBV DNA in their blood were more likely to have recurrent infection and liver disease after transplantation than were HBV-infected candidates without HBV DNA.[87] An important exception is patients with fulminant HBV infection, who actually have low rates of HBV recurrence. Some liver transplant recipients with recurrent HBV infection develop a rapidly fatal liver disease called fibrosing cholestatic hepatitis, in which the pathology of the liver shows hepatocyte dropout, fibrosis, and a very high viral load, but only sparse inflammatory infiltrates.[88] The situation with hepatitis D is less clear because of complex interactions between the hepatitis D virus and HBV. Preliminary data suggest that hepatitis D recurs less frequently than HBV, and the presence of the delta agent may actually lower the rate of HBV recurrence.[87,89]

The outlook for patients at risk for recurrent HBV infection after transplantation has been greatly improved by the availability of various agents able to prevent or treat this recurrence and the development of quantitative molecular techniques to measure hepatitis B viral load. Regimens employing serial infusions of hepatitis B immune globulin have been shown to reduce the rate of recurrence to 19% at 2 years.[90] The infusions are well tolerated, but the large doses required add a major expense to the cost of transplantation. In recent years antiviral medications have been shown to have a major impact on HBV infection. Lamivudine and famciclovir have been the most widely used agents. Both have few adverse side effects. Almost all patients have an initial virologic and biochemical response to lamivudine, but resistant virus emerges in about 25% of treated patients after a year of therapy.[90] Famciclovir is less active than lamivudine and is only occasionally able to treat lamivudine-resistant strains. Recent additions to the anti-HBV armamentarium are adefovir and tenofovir. Both drugs were developed for the treatment of human immunodeficiency virus type 1 infection and have good activity against HBV, including lamivudine-resistant strains.[90] Adefovir has been shown in clinical trials to lead to low rates of resistance development in nontransplant patients with e antigen–positive hepatitis B infection and will likely play a major role in transplantation (see Chapter 142).[91]

HCV infection occurs in all transplant groups, but the prevalence is highest in liver and kidney transplantation.[92-95] A small number of HCV-infected transplant recipients (of all organ types) develop progressive fatal cholestatic liver disease in the first year after transplantation. These cases are marked by a high viral load, and liver biopsies show severe hepatocyte dropout with minimal parenchymal inflammation.[96] The long-term outcome of other HCV-infected patients depends to some extent on the organ transplanted. Liver transplant candidates who have HCV viremia before transplantation almost always reinfect their liver grafts after transplantation, and 46% to 97% develop hepatitis during the first 2 to 3½ years after transplantation.[93] This ongoing HCV infection leads to graft cirrhosis in up to 30% of patients by 5 years after transplantation. Five-year survival is impaired relative to patients with other causes of liver disease.[93,94] Longitudinal studies in kidney transplant populations also show that chronic HCV infection also has an adverse impact on their survival, but this effect is not clearly discernible until the second decade after transplantation.[96] Excess deaths are due not only to the direct effects of liver disease, but also to a higher rate of sepsis.[97]

There is great interest in discovering factors that predict the progression of liver disease from HCV infection in transplant recipients. Some of the implicated factors in liver transplantation are the degree of immunosuppression, the use of antirejection therapy, high viral loads before or early after transplantation, older donor age, and in some studies infection with HCV type 1b.[93]

Antiviral treatment of recurrent HCV infection after liver transplantation is under active investigation. Interferon-alfa monotherapy produces end-of-treatment responses in 12% to 26% of liver recipients with HCV infection, but very few patients have sustained responses 6 months later.[98] The use of combination therapy with interferon-alfa and ribavirin is clearly superior, but sustained responses still only occur in 17% to 27% of patients.[98] Unfortunately, the side effects of interferon and ribavirin make them difficult to administer to liver transplant recipients, so that only a small percentage of liver transplant recipients with HCV infection are likely to benefit from their combined use. Whether long-acting, pegylated interferons will be more efficacious or better tolerated in this population is under study.

Infections of the Central Nervous System

Infections of the central nervous system (CNS) in transplant patients require prompt evaluation and diagnosis and early, appropriate therapy. Table 312-5 lists the most important agents.[20,99] Notably absent on the list are pyogenic bacteria and HSV, which are common pathogens in transplant patients at sites outside the nervous system. The highest risk for opportunistic CNS infection is from 1 to 6 months after transplantation; an exception is cryptococcal meningitis, which is often a "late" event.[20]

Listeria monocytogenes is a motile, gram-positive rod that typically causes bacteremia, meningitis, and at times cerebritis in immunosuppressed transplant patients.[20,46,100] The Gram stain of the cerebrospinal fluid (CSF) is negative in more than half of the cases. Usually the diagnosis is made by culturing the organism from CSF or blood. All patients with *Listeria* bacteremia should have lumbar punctures, even in the absence of CNS signs, because the mortality is much higher when CNS disease is present.[46,100] This infection generally responds well to antibiotic therapy, but relapses may occur and a prolonged courses of therapy (3 weeks) is recommended.

Aspergillus fumigatus is a ubiquitous fungus that is an important cause of CNS infection in immunocompromised patients. The most common portal of entry is the lung; invasive sinus infection also occurs but is less common. Patients with *Aspergillus* infection usually have been recently transplanted and are receiving high doses of corticosteroids.[101] The type of transplant is also important; lung and liver transplant recipients are more susceptible than other transplant patients.[14,99,102] *Aspergillus* invades blood vessels, and hematogenous spread to the brain may occur early in the course of the infection. *Aspergillus* is the most common cause of infectious brain lesions in the early post-transplant period.[99] CT scans of the brain reveal single or multiple low-density lesions with a predilection for the gray-white junction. In the past the mortality rate of CNS aspergillosis was almost 100%.[102] The recent introduction of new antifungal agents with enhanced activity against *Aspergillus* may help to improve the dismal prognosis of invasive CNS aspergillosis.[103]

Other fungi causing parenchymal brain infections in transplant recipients have been *Candida* spp, *Zygomycetes,* and dematiaceous fungi such as *Ochroconis.*[99] The lesions caused by *Candida* usually occur in patients with disseminated candidiasis or candidemia. The overall mortality is high in CNS infections caused by *Zygomycetes* or dematiaceous fungi, and therapy with a combination of antifungal medication and surgical resection is generally recommended.[75,99]

TABLE 312-5 Pathogens of the Central Nervous System in Solid Organ Transplant Patients

Listeria monocytogenes	Dematiaceous fungi
Nocardia spp.	*Toxoplasma gondii*
Cryptococcus neoformans	Varicella-zoster virus
Aspergillus spp.	Polyomavirus (JC virus)
Agents of mucormycosis	Human herpesvirus-6
Candida spp.	

Cryptococcal meningitis usually occurs in the late post-transplant period and has a subacute course. Common presenting symptoms are headache and low-grade fever.[20,38,104] Pulmonary disease caused by *Cryptococcus* coexists in about 40% of the cases. A lumbar puncture should be performed in any patient with cryptococcal infection even in the absence of CNS signs. The spinal fluid usually has less than 500 white blood cells/mm³ with lymphocyte predominance, and a positive cryptococcal antigen test.[99,104] India ink preparations reveal positive findings in about 40% to 50% of patients. A retrospective study in 5521 transplant patients revealed a 0.5% incidence of cryptococcal meningitis with an overall mortality of 50%. The incidence was highest in heart recipients (2.2%), but the only identified risk factor for poor outcome was liver failure.[104]

Toxoplasma gondii is a protozoan that can cause a nonspecific encephalopathy, diffuse meningoencephalitis, or progressive single or multiple brain lesions.[45,99] *Toxoplasma* infection has been reported in renal, cardiac, liver, and heart-lung recipients.[45,105-107] Toxoplasmosis in solid organ recipients usually results from primary infection. The cardiac allograft has been shown to be a source of infection.[45] Serology should be performed on cardiac donors and recipients to identify patients at risk for disease transmitted by the allograft. Definitive diagnosis of acute toxoplasmosis usually requires tissue biopsy, although occasionally the organism may be isolated from peripheral blood cells in tissue culture.[105] The fatality rate is high, and often the diagnosis is not established until autopsy. The treatment of choice is pyrimethamine (50 to 75 mg/day) and sulfadiazine (4 to 6 g/day). Folinic acid (5 to 15 mg/day) is usually added to the regimen to prevent marrow suppression.

Nocardia asteroides is a gram-positive, beaded, branching rod that may cause single or multiple brain abscesses or less commonly meningitis. For unknown reasons, the incidence of pulmonary nocardiosis varies considerably among centers.[46] The primary portal of infection is pulmonary, with metastatic spread to bone, skin, and CNS. *Nocardia* brain abscesses may benefit from stereotactic aspiration biopsy and surgical drainage in addition to long-term (9- to 12-month) antimicrobial therapy. Sulfonamides are the mainstay of treatment, because they penetrate the CNS well and most isolates are susceptible. In the presence of disseminated disease, it may be prudent to use more than one drug and obtain susceptibility testing on isolates. Agents such as amikacin, imipenem, and cefotaxime have shown good activity in animal models, with more rapid killing than sulfonamides.[108] Also, isolates with resistance to commonly used antibiotics, including sulfonamides, have been described.[109]

SPECIFIC PROBLEMS OF VIRUS INFECTIONS

This section covers most issues related to viral infections in transplant recipients. However, hepatitis viruses are discussed earlier in this chapter in the section on abdominal and gastrointestinal infections. The complex topics of antiviral prophylaxis and the pretransplant evaluation of transplant candidates and donors are discussed in Chapter 310.

Human herpesvirus-6 (HHV-6) is a recently described cause of fever and leukopenia in transplant recipients.[110] This virus is the etiologic agent of roseola and is associated with febrile seizures in children. The virus is also an occasional cause of encephalitis in the early post-transplant period (15 to 75 days).[110] This illness is characterized by fever, confusion, and mostly nonfocal neurologic findings. CSF studies may either be normal or suggest a mild aseptic meningitis with lymphocytosis and protein elevation but normal glucose levels.[111] Magnetic resonance imaging scans may also be normal or show patchy attenuation in gray and white matter. The diagnosis is made by detecting the virus by polymerase chain reaction (PCR) in the spinal fluid. Ganciclovir and foscarnet are active against HHV-6 in vitro and have been used for treatment in a few patients.[111]

Herpes Simplex Virus and Varicella-Zoster Virus Infections

HSV reactivates after transplantation in approximately 60% of recipients not given antiviral prophylaxis.[10,22,23] About half of these persons develop symptomatic oral or genital lesions. Genital herpes may become clinically evident for the first time after transplantation and may

be very distressing for the patient. HSV reactivation usually occurs in the first 1 to 2 weeks after transplantation. Visceral infection caused by HSV has been reported in a small number of patients; most cases have been HSV hepatitis after liver transplantation or HSV pneumonia after lung transplantation.[15,112] A rare event is primary HSV occurring early after transplantation. The donor organ has been shown to be the source in a few patients.[113] These primary HSV infections may produce a severe septic syndrome with hypotension and disseminated intravascular coagulation.[113]

Most cases of reactivated HSV infection are easily diagnosed and respond well to antiviral therapy. Use of antiviral prophylaxis prevents HSV infection; it is a reasonable approach and is preferred in patients who are at risk for visceral HSV infection, such as lung or liver transplant recipients. Low-dose acyclovir (400 mg twice daily) for the first 3 to 4 weeks after transplantation is usually sufficient.[83]

Herpes zoster is reported in 7% to 18% of patients.[10,16,22,39,114] Antiviral therapy is indicated, because healing is often slow and transplant recipients occasionally develop neurologic complications or disseminated infection. Oral therapy with acyclovir, valacyclovir, or famciclovir suffices for dermatomal zoster. If the patient has ophthalmic zoster or there is evidence of dissemination, intravenous acyclovir is used initially. Chickenpox in a transplant patient also usually requires admission to the hospital and treatment with intravenous acyclovir, although some pediatric heart transplant recipients on low doses of immunosuppression have been successfully treated for chickenpox with oral valacyclovir.[115] Obtaining serology for varicella-zoster virus before transplantation identifies patients at risk for chickenpox, so that they can be considered for vaccination and counseled to avoid (and report) exposures.[114] Varicella-seronegative transplant recipients who have exposure to chickenpox may benefit from the use of varicella-zoster immune globulin if it can be given within 96 hours.[83]

Cytomegalovirus Infections

Almost all CMV-seropositive graft recipients experience reactivation of latent CMV infections, and most seronegative recipients with seropositive donors develop primary infections. Primary infections are more likely to be symptomatic.[22,116] The proportion of infected patients who become symptomatic is also a function of the intensity of immunosuppression.

The most common and least serious type of CMV disease is a mononucleosis syndrome characterized by fever, frequently of prolonged duration, with few or no focal symptoms. Abnormalities may be found on the liver function tests, although there is rarely jaundice, and leukopenia is often present. Interstitial pneumonia is the most serious complication of CMV infection and is present in most fatal cases. Fever, breathlessness, hypoxemia, and diffuse infiltrates on chest radiographs are typical findings but are not pathognomonic, and bronchoalveolar lavage or lung biopsy is required for diagnosis. CMV pneumonia may coexist with other pathogens in the lung, particularly *Pneumocystis*.

One of the more troublesome manifestations of CMV disease is ulcerations in the gastrointestinal tract. These ulcerations are often multiple. They may be found anywhere from the esophagus to the rectum.[116,117] Severe complications such as bleeding or perforation occur in some patients. CMV disease should be considered in the differential diagnosis of transplant recipients who have fever and acute or subacute abdominal symptoms, especially if transplantation occurred within the last 4 months or there was a recent intensification of immunosuppression. The exact frequency with which CMV causes gastrointestinal disease is difficult to determine because a definite diagnosis depends on endoscopy, and CMV may involve inaccessible parts of the bowel.[81]

CMV hepatitis occurs in up to 17% of liver transplant recipients and is more common with primary than with reactivation infection.[118] The pathologic finding is microabscesses scattered around the liver lobule. CMV inclusion bodies may be easy to find or scant.[119] The disease is typically mild and may be an incidental finding in an asymptomatic patient undergoing liver biopsy for elevated liver enzyme concentrations.[118]

Ganciclovir is the drug of choice for the treatment of symptomatic CMV disease in transplant recipients. It may be administered as an intravenous formulation or in the form of the recently approved oral pro-drug, valganciclovir (Valcyte). Oral ganciclovir (Cytovene) has been available for many years and is effective as a prophylactic agent, but it is not usually used for therapy of active disease because attainable serum levels are lower than with the other preparations. The duration of therapy is usually about 2 weeks, but this may be extended to 3 weeks or longer in patients with severe disease or primary infection. Foscarnet and cidofovir are also active against CMV, but are infrequently used in solid organ recipients because of their side effects.

The greatest advances in CMV infection in transplantation in recent years have been made in development of accurate and reproducible quantitative methods to assess viral load and the implementation of effective prophylactic and preemptive regimens to prevent disease caused by CMV. These topics are discussed in Chapter 310.

Respiratory Viral Infections

Respiratory viral infections were rarely mentioned in early reports of infections after solid organ transplantation, but have been increasingly reported as important pathogens.[57,58,120-122] Most of these reports are from pediatric transplant populations or in lung transplant recipients.[58,121,122] Adenoviruses may cause asymptomatic infection, but they also may cause diffuse pneumonia, necrotizing hepatitis, and hemorrhagic cystitis.[58,121] In one series of pediatric liver transplant recipients, the mortality rate of invasive adenovirus infection was 45%.[121] Biopsy of an involved organ may reveal characteristic pathologic findings and may facilitate a rapid diagnosis, but there is no known effective treatment.

Infections with paramyxoviruses, such respiratory syncytial virus, should be considered whenever a transplant recipient has a respiratory tract illness, particularly if there is a preceding viral upper respiratory illness, prominent airway findings such as wheezing and rhonchi on exam, and no definite bacterial etiology. Most cases occur between November and April, but parainfluenza virus type 3 infections occur year round. Therapy with aerosolized ribavirin may be helpful and is usually well tolerated, but is also expensive and has not been evaluated in controlled studies in transplant populations.[122,123]

Influenza virus infection has been documented more frequently in transplant patients in recent studies. At one center influenza was 10 to 20 times more common in lung recipients than recipients of other transplants.[124] Influenza was very morbid but usually was not fatal. Transplant patients and their household contacts should be given yearly immunizations against influenza. Consideration should also be given to providing antiviral prophylaxis to high-risk patients during outbreaks of influenza.[124]

Polyomavirus Infections and Nephropathy

Polyomavirus infection of the urinary tract was first described in a renal transplant recipient more than 3 decades ago, and subsequent studies have shown that polyomaviruses can be detected in up to 65% of renal transplant patients.[125] These infections were occasionally associated with transient renal dysfunction or ureteral stenosis, but generally they were thought to be a benign process.[125,126] In recent years polyomaviruses have emerged as important pathogens and been shown to cause an infectious nephropathy in 2% to 8% of renal transplant recipients.[126,127] In almost all cases the responsible polyomavirus has been BK virus. JC virus and SV40 have been detected in some patients, but their pathogenic role is less well established.[126] It is not known why BK nephropathy was not recognized as a problem in the past, but the usual explanation is that its recent emergence is due to the use of new, very potent immunosuppressive medications.[126] BK virus primarily infects renal tubular cells, producing intranuclear "groundglass" inclusions accompanied by an interstitial nephritis.[128] Polyomaviruses may be detected in the patient's urine by a variety of techniques, including culture, cytology, electron microscopy, and qualitative or quantitative PCR, but mere detection of virus is not specific for the presence of polyomavirus nephropathy.[126] Detection of polyomavirus by PCR in the patient's plasma has a specificity of 88% for the presence of nephropathy and hence is more clinically useful.[129] A definite diagnosis of polyomavirus nephropathy requires a renal biopsy.[126,128] Figure 312-3 illustrates the typical light microscopic ap-

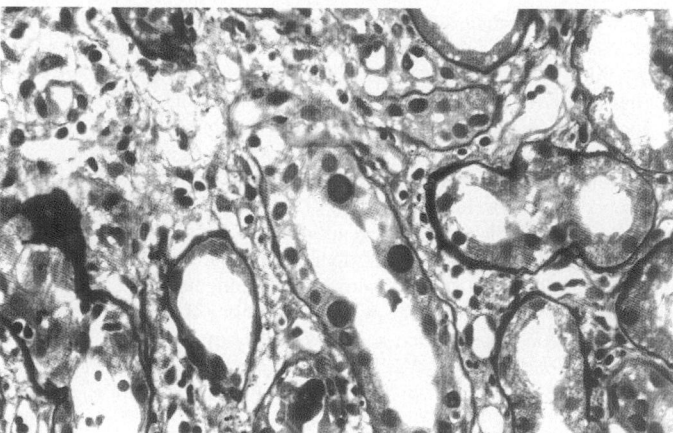

FIGURE 312-3. Characteristic histologic appearance of BK nephropathy in the kidney. The tubular cells have smudgy, basophilic intranuclear inclusions and there is a pleomorphic cellular infiltrate of lymphocytes, plasma cells, and occasional neutrophils in the interstitium. (Jones silver stain; ×400). *(Courtesy of Agnes B. Fogo, MD.)*

pearance of polyomavirus nephropathy, with enlarged, virally infected tubular cells and an associated interstitial infiltrate. The renal dysfunction associated with polyomavirus infection usually improves or stabilizes if immunosuppression is decreased, but between one third and one half of patients still progress to kidney failure. Cidofovir has activity against polyomaviruses in vitro and is being actively investigated as a possible treatment.[126]

Progressive multifocal leukoencephalopathy (PML) occurs in patients with impairment of T-cell immunity and is caused by JC virus.[126] Unlike the situation in acquired immunodeficiency syndrome, in which PML occurs in 4% to 5% of patients with very low CD4+ counts, PML is a rare occurrence after transplantation. Patients develop profound neurologic deficits that can include various motor, sensory, visual, or cognitive findings occurring over a subacute course of weeks to months. A brain biopsy is required for a definitive diagnosis, but the diagnosis is strongly suggested by finding characteristic white matter changes on magnetic resonance imaging and JC virus DNA by PCR in the CSF.[126]

Human Herpesvirus-8 and Kaposi's Sarcoma

Unlike other herpesviruses, human herpesvirus-8 (HHV-8) infection is relatively geographically restricted. The highest seroprevalence for HHV-8 is found in central and southern Africa, the Middle East, and European countries bordering the Mediterranean.[130] HHV-8 infection has been recently linked to the occurrence of Kaposi's sarcoma after transplantation. Two studies from France showed a very high frequency (28% and 68%) of Kaposi's sarcoma in kidney transplant recipients who were seropositive for HHV-8 before transplantation, with only 1 case in over 400 seronegative patients.[131,132] Transmission of HHV-8 by organ donation with subsequent development of Kaposi's sarcoma has also been documented, but transmission of HHV-8 appears to be less commonly associated with Kaposi's sarcoma than reactivation of HHV-8.[133] In patients with transplantation-related Kaposi's sarcoma, HHV-8 can usually be detected in the tumor and often in the blood by PCR.[131] More than one half of transplant patients with Kaposi's sarcoma will experience regression of their tumors when their doses of immunosuppressive drugs are substantially reduced.[130] However, many of these patients subsequently develop graft dysfunction and some lose their grafts. Patients who do not respond to reduction of immunosuppression may respond to chemotherapy.[130]

Lymphoproliferative Disease and Epstein-Barr Virus Infection

Primary EBV infection occurs in about three fourths of seronegative pediatric or adult transplant recipients.[134,135] Reactivation infection, defined by a fourfold or greater rise in immunoglobulin G (IgG) antibodies to EBV viral capsid antigen, is detected in about one third of seropositive transplant recipients. Most infections occur within the first 4 months after transplantation.[136] The most important disease associated with EBV infection in transplant recipients is post-transplant lymphoproliferative disorder (PTLD). The risk for PTLD is 10- to 76-fold higher in transplant recipients who are EBV seronegative before transplantation than in patients who are seropositive.[137] For instance, we found that 35% of 40 EBV-seronegative adult liver transplant recipients developed PTLD during follow-up.[18] This compares with a PTLD rate of only 2% in EBV-seropositive adult liver transplant recipients and underscores the importance of obtaining serology for EBV before transplantation.[137] Most EBV-seropositive patients with PTLD also have evidence of reactivation of EBV infection. This has been shown by the detection of serologic rises or by measurement of EBV viral load in saliva or peripheral blood.[134,138,139] The mechanism by which EBV promotes PTLD is unknown but is under active investigation.

PTLD comprises three general clinical types.[135,137,140] First, it may resemble infectious mononucleosis without evidence of tissue involvement except in tonsils and peripheral lymph nodes. The second manifestation is a diffuse polymorphous B-cell infiltration in many visceral organs. This type may be preceded by a mononucleosis-like episode that either evolves directly into the tissue infiltrative process or is temporally separated from it. The third clinical presentation is the appearance of localized extranodal tumors in the gastrointestinal tract, thorax, or other parts of the body. Tumors in the brain have also been described. These tumors have the microscopic appearance of lymphomas and contain EBV genome detectable by nucleic acid hybridization or EBV-specific antigens (e.g., nuclear antigen). The tumors may be either monoclonal or oligoclonal, as determined by IgG light-chain phenotype or immunoglobulin gene rearrangement.[140,141]

Antiviral medications such as acyclovir or ganciclovir inhibit the lytic phase of EBV infection and virion production, but are not able to affect the replication of cells latently infected with EBV.[142] In spite of this, acyclovir or ganciclovir are often used to prevent or treat established PTLD based on theoretical considerations and an indication of benefit noted in retrospective analyses of small numbers of patients.[143] Mononucleosis syndromes may resolve and tumors may regress after reduction or elimination of immunosuppression.[140] This regression occurs in about one half of cases.[137,140] It is more likely with tumors that appear during the first year after transplantation and in those that are polymorphous in appearance or contain tumor cells that are polyclonal by laboratory studies.[144] However, there is no prognostic indicator that is entirely reliable. Other therapeutic modalities, including interferon-alfa treatments, intravenous immunoglobulin infusions, and chemotherapy, have been described in small series of patients.[137] Treatment of PTLD by infusion of monoclonal antibodies directed against surface antigens of B cells is a theoretically attractive approach and has achieved initial remissions in 60% to 65% of patients with PTLD.[145,146] An interesting treatment, which is not widely available, is the infusion of human leukocyte antigen–compatible, EBV-specific cytotoxic T lymphocytes (CTLs). This has been found to be feasible and effective in cases of PTLD occurring in marrow recipients.[147] Autologous EBV-specific CTLs have also been expanded in vitro from solid organ transplant recipients with PTLD, but clinical experience using these cells for therapy is still very limited.[148]

REFERENCES

1. United Network for Organ Sharing. 2002 Annual Report of the U.S. Organ Procurement and Transplantation Network and the Scientific Registry of Transplant Recipients: Transplant Data 1992-2001. Rockville, MD: Health Resources and Services Administration, Office of Special Programs, Division of Transplantation; Richmond, VA: United Network for Organ Sharing; and Ann Arbor, MI: University Renal Research and Education Association; 2002.*
2. Dummer JS. Antibiotic prophylaxis and management of infectious complications. In: Kaye MP, O'Connell JB, eds. Heart and Lung Transplantation 2000. Austin, TX: R. G. Landes; 1993:78.

*The data and analyses in the 2002 Annual Report of the U.S. Organ Procurement and Transplantation Network and the Scientific Registry of Transplant Recipients have been supplied by UNOS and URREA under contract with HHS. The authors alone are responsible for the reporting and interpretation of the data.

3. Hofflin JM, Potasman I, Baldwin JC, et al. Infectious complications in heart transplant patients receiving cyclosporine and corticosteroids. Ann Intern Med. 1987;106:209.
4. Wajszczuk CP, Dummer JS, Ho M, et al. Fungal infections in liver transplant recipients. Transplantation. 1985;40:347.
5. Kusne S, Dummer JS, Singh N, et al. Infections after liver transplantation: An analysis of 101 consecutive cases. Medicine (Baltimore). 1988;67:132.
6. Kusne S, Fung J, Alessiani M, et al. Infections during a randomized trial comparing cyclosporine to FK 506 immunosuppression in liver transplantation. Transplant Proc. 1992;24:429.
7. Kirklin JK, Naftel DC, Bourge RC, et al. Evolving trends in risk profiles and causes of death after heart transplantation: A ten-year multi-institutional study. J Thorac Cardiovasc Surg. 2003;125:881-890.
8. Fishman JA, Rubin RH. Infection in organ transplant recipients. N Engl J Med. 1998;338:1741-1749.
9. Dummer JS, Montero CG, Griffith BP, et al. Infections in heart-lung transplant recipients. Transplantation. 1986;41:725.
10. Dummer JS. Infectious complications of transplantation. Cardiovasc Clin. 1990;20:163.
11. Horvath J, Dummer S, Loyd J, et al. Infection in the transplanted and native lung after single lung transplantation. Chest. 1993;104:681.
12. Lumbreras C, Fernandez I, Velosa J, et al. Infectious complications following pancreatic transplantation: Incidence, microbiological and clinical characteristics, and outcome. Clin Infect Dis. 1995;20:514.
13. Lebeau G, Yanaga K, Marsh JW, et al. Analysis of surgical complications after 397 hepatic transplantations. Surg Gynecol Obstet. 1990;170:317.
14. Kusne S, Torre-Cisneros J, Manez R, et al. Factors associated with invasive lung aspergillosis and the significance of positive *Aspergillus* culture after liver transplantation. J Infect Dis. 1992;166:1379.
15. Maurer JR, Tullis E, Grossman RF, et al. Infectious complications following lung transplantation. Chest. 1992;101:1056.
16. Rifkind D. The activation of varicella-zoster virus infections by immunosuppressive therapy. J Lab Clin Med. 1966;68:463.
17. Terrault NA, Wright TL, Pereira BJ. Hepatitis C infection in the transplant recipient. Infect Dis Clin North Am. 1995;9:943.
18. Manez R, Breinig MC, Linden P, et al. Posttransplant lymphoproliferative disease in primary Epstein-Barr virus infection after liver transplantation: The role of cytomegalovirus disease. J Infect Dis. 1997;176:1462.
19. Duncan AJ, Dummer JS, Paradis IL, et al. Cytomegalovirus infection and survival in lung transplant recipients. J Heart Lung Transplant. 1991;10:638.
20. Hooper DC, Pruitt AA, Rubin RH. Central nervous system infection in the chronically immunosuppressed. Medicine (Baltimore). 1982;61:166.
21. Dummer JS. Infectious complications of heart-lung recipients. In: Cooper DKC, Novitzky D, eds. The Transplantation and Replacement of Thoracic Organs. Lancaster, England: Kluwer; 1990:325-332.
22. Singh N, Dummer JS, Kusne S, et al. Infections with cytomegalovirus and other herpesviruses in 121 liver transplant recipients: Transmission by donated organ and the effect of OKT3 antibodies. J Infect Dis. 1988;158:124.
23. Ho M, Wajszczuk CP, Hardy A, et al. Infections in kidney, heart, and liver transplant recipients on cyclosporine. Transplant Proc. 1983;15:2768.
24. Myerowitz RL, Medeiros AA, O'Brien TF. Bacterial infection in renal homograft recipients: A study of 53 bacteremic episodes. Am J Med. 1972;53:308.
25. Wagener MM, Yu VL. Bacteremia in transplant recipients: A prospective study of demographics, etiologic agents, risk factors and outcomes. Am J Infect Control. 1992;20:239.
26. Griffin PJA, Salaman JR. Urinary tract infections after renal transplantation: Do they matter? Br Med J. 1979;1:710.
27. Giral M, Pascuariello G, Karam G, et al. Acute graft pyelonephritis and long-term kidney allograft dysfunction. Kidney Int. 2002;61:1880-1886.
28. Tolkoff-Rubin NE, Cosimi AB, Russell PS, Rubin RH. A controlled study of trimethoprim-sulfamethoxazole prophylaxis of urinary tract infection in renal transplant recipients. Rev Infect Dis. 1982;4:614.
29. Rubin RH, Fang LS, Cosimi AB, et al. Usefulness of the antibody-coated bacterial assay in the management of urinary tract infection in the renal transplant patient. Transplantation. 1979;27:18-20.
30. McMahon DK, Dummer JS, Pasculle AW, Cassell G. Extragenital *Mycoplasma hominis* infections in adults. Am J Med. 1990;89:275.
31. Superdock KR, Dummer JS, Koch MO, et al. Disseminated histoplasmosis presenting as urinary tract obstruction in a renal transplant recipient. Am J Kidney Dis. 1994;23:600.
32. Ramsey PG, Rubin RH, Tolkoff-Rubin NE, et al. The renal transplant patient with fever and pulmonary infiltrates: Etiology, clinical manifestations, and management. Medicine (Baltimore). 1980;59:206.
33. Heurlin N, Brattstrom C, Tyden G, et al. Cytomegalovirus is the predominant cause of pneumonia in renal transplant patients: A two-year study of pneumonia in renal transplant recipients with evaluation of fiberoptic bronchoscopy. Scand J Infect Dis. 1989;21:245.
34. Chang FY, Singh N, Gayowski T, et al. Fever in liver transplant recipients: Changing spectrum of etiologic agents. Clin Infect Dis. 1998;26:59.
35. Kyriakides GK, Simmons RL, Najarian JS. Wound infection in renal transplant wounds: Pathogenic and prognostic factors. Ann Surg. 1975;182:770.
36. Novick AC. The value of intraoperative antibiotics in preventing renal transplant wound infections. J Urol. 1981;125:151.
37. Brayman KL, Stephanian E, Matas AJ, et al. Analysis of infectious complications occurring after solid-organ transplantation. Arch Surg. 1992;127:38-49.

38. Rubin R. Infection in the renal and liver transplant patient. In: Rubin RH, Young LS, eds. Clinical Approach to Infection in the Immunocompromised Host. 2nd ed. New York: Plenum Press; 1988:557.
39. Montoya JG, Giraldo LF, Efron B, et al. Infectious complications among 620 consecutive heart transplant patients at Stanford University. Clin Infect Dis. 2001;33:629-640.
40. Baldwin RT, Radovancevic B, Sweeney MS, et al. Bacterial mediastinitis after heart transplantation. J Heart Lung Transplant. 1992;11:545.
41. Trento A, Dummer JS, Hardesty RL, et al. Mediastinitis following heart transplantation: Incidence, treatment and complications. J Heart Transplant. 1984;3:336.
42. Boden MD, Dummer JS. Infections after organ transplantation. J Intensive Care Med. 1997;12:166.
43. Goldstein DJ, Oz MC, Rose EA. Medical progress: Implantable left ventricular assist devices. N Engl J Med. 1998;329:1522-1533.
44. de Carvalho VB, Sousa EF, Vila JH, et al. Heart transplantation in Chagas' disease 10 years after the initial experience. Circulation. 1996;94:1815.
45. Luft BJ, Naot Y, Araujo FG, et al. Primary and reactivated toxoplasma infection in patients with cardiac transplants: Clinical spectrum and problems in diagnosis in a defined population. Ann Intern Med. 1983;99:27.
46. Dummer JS. Other bacterial infections after hematopoietic stem cell or solid organ transplantation. In: Bowden R, Paya CV, Ljungman P, Engelhard D, eds. Transplant Infections. 2nd ed. Philadelphia: Lippincott Williams & Williams; 2003:259-273.
47. Luft BJ, Billingham M, Remington JS. Endomyocardial biopsy in the diagnosis of toxoplasmic myocarditis. Transplant Proc. 1986;18:1871.
48. Wreghitt TG, Gray JJ, Pavel P, et al. Efficacy of pyrimethamine for the prevention of donor-acquired *Toxoplasma gondii* infection in heart and heart-lung transplant patients. Transpl Int. 1992;5:197.
49. Bocchi EA, Fiorelli A. The paradox of survival results after heart transplantation for cardiomyopathy caused by *Trypanosoma cruzi*. First Guidelines Group for Heart Transplantation of the Brazilian Society of Cardiology. Ann Thoracic Surg. 2001;71:1833-1838.
50. Dauber JH, Paradis IL, Dummer JS. Infectious complications in pulmonary allograft recipients. Clin Chest Med. 1990;11:291.
51. Kramer MR, Marshall SE, Starnes VA, et al. Infectious complications in heart-lung transplantation: Analysis of 200 episodes. Arch Intern Med. 1993;153:2010.
52. Singh N, Husain S. Aspergillus Infections after lung transplantation: Clinical differences in type of transplant and implications for management. J Heart Lung Transplant. 2003;22:258-266.
53. Reichenspurner H, Gamberg P, Nitschke M, et al. Significant reduction in the number of fungal infections after lung, heart-lung and heart transplantation using aerosolized amphotericin B prophylaxis. Transplant Proc. 1997;29:627-628.
54. Dummer JS, Lazariashvili N, Barnes J, et al. A survey of antifungal management in lung transplantation. J Heart Lung Transpl. In press.
55. Girgis RE, Tu I, Berry GJ, et al. Risk factors for the development of obliterative bronchiolitis after lung transplantation. J Heart Lung Transplant. 1996;15:1200.
56. Speich R, van der Bij W. Epidemiology and management of infections after lung transplantation. Clin Infect Dis. 2001;33 (Suppl 1):S58-S65.
57. Palmer SM, Henshane NG, Howell ND, et al. Community respiratory viral infection in adult lung transplant recipients. Chest. 1998; 113:944-950.
58. Bridges ND, Spray TL, Colins MH, et al. Adenovirus infection in the lung results in graft failure after transplantation. J Thorac Cardiovasc Surg. 1998;116:617-623.
59. Zenati M, Dowling RD, Dummer JS, et al. Influence of the donor lung on development of early infections in lung transplant recipients. J Heart Transplant. 1990;9:502.
60. Wilson IC, Hasan A, Healey M, et al. Healing of the bronchus in pulmonary transplantation. Eur J Cardiothorac Surg. 1996;10:521.
61. Paya CV, Hermans PE, Washington JA II, et al. Incidence, distribution and outcome of episodes of infection in 100 liver transplantations. Mayo Clin Proc. 1989;64:355.
62. George DL, Arnow PM, Fox AS, et al. Bacterial infection as a complication of liver transplantation: Epidemiology and risk factors. Rev Infect Dis. 1991;13:387.
63. Colonna JO II, Winston DJ, Brill JE, et al. Infectious complications in liver transplantation. Arch Surg. 1988;123:360.
64. Castaldo P, Stratta R, Wood P. Clinical spectrum of fungal infections complicating liver transplantation. Arch Surg. 1991;126:149.
65. Singh N, Wagener MM, Marino IR, Gayowksi T. Trends in invasive fungal infections in liver transplant recipients: Correlation with evolution in transplantation practices. Transplantation. 2002;73:63-67.
66. Collins LA, Samore MH, Roberts MS, et al. Risk factors for invasive fungal infections complicating orthotopic liver transplantation. J Infect Dis. 1994;170:644.
67. Paya CV. Fungal infections in solid-organ transplantation. Clin Infect Dis. 1993;16:677.
68. Auchincloss H, Shaffer D. Pancreas transplantation In: Ginns LC, Cosimi AB, Morris PJ, eds. Transplantation. Malden, MA: Blackwell Science; 1999:395-421.
69. Rosen CB, Frohnert PP, Velosa JA, et al. Morbidity of pancreas transplantation during cadaveric renal transplantation. Transplantation. 1991;51:123.
70. Pirsch JD, Odorico JS, D'Allesandro AM, et al. Posttransplant infection in enteric-versus bladder-drained simultaneous pancreas-kidney transplant recipients. Clin Transplant. 1998;66:1746-1750.
71. Grant D. Intestinal transplantation: Report of the international registry. Clin Transplant. 1999;67:1061-1064.
72. Nishida S, Levi D, Kato T, et al. Ninety-five cases of intestinal transplantation at the University of Miami. J Gastrointestinal Surg. 2002;6:233-239.
73. Kusne S, Furukawa H, Abu-Elmagd K, et al. Infectious complications after small bowel transplantation in adults: An update. Transplant Proc. 1996;28:2761.
74. Kusne S, Manez R, Frye BL, et al. Use of DNA amplification for diagnosis of cytomegalovirus enteritis after intestinal transplantation. Gastroenterology. 1997;112:1121.
75. Singh N, Feng YC, Gayowski T, et al. Infections due to dematiaceous fungi in organ transplant recipients: Case report and review. Clin Infect Dis. 1997;24:369-374.
76. Wallace RJJ, Brown BA, Onyi GO. Skin, soft tissue and bone infections due to *Mycobacterium chelonae chelonae:* Importance of prior corticosteroid therapy, frequency of disseminated infections and resistance to antimicrobials other than clarithromycin. J Infect Dis. 1992;166:405-412.
77. Newell KA, Millis JM, Arnow PM, et al. Incidence and outcome of infection by vancomycin-resistant *Enterococcus* following orthotopic liver transplantation. Transplantation. 1998;65:439-42.
78. Singh N, Gayowski T, Wagener MM, Marino JR. Blood stream infections in liver transplant recipients receiving tacrolimus. Clin Transplant. 1997;11:275-81.
79. Stout JE, Yu VL. Legionellosis. N Engl J Med. 1997;337:682.
80. Edelstein PH. Antimicrobial chemotherapy for Legionnaires' disease: Time for a change. Ann Intern Med. 1998;129:328-30.
81. Dummer JS, Mishu, B. Gastrointestinal infections in organ transplant recipients. In Blaser M, Smith PD, Ravidin JI, et al, eds. Infections of the Gastrointestinal Tract. 2nd ed. Philadelphia: Lippincott William & Wilkins; 2002:457-471.
82. Aull JS, Buell JF, Peddi VR, et al. MALToma: A *Helicobacter pylori*-associated malignancy in transplant patients. A report from the Israel Penn International Transplant Tumor Registry with a review of published literature. Transplantation. 003;75:225-8.
83. Patel R, Paya CV. Infections in solid-organ transplant recipients. Clin Microbiol Rev. 1997;10:86.
84. Harnett JD, Zeldis JB, Parfrey PS, et al. Hepatitis B disease in dialysis and transplant patients: Further epidemiologic and serologic studies. Transplantation. 1987;44:369.
85. Starzl TE, Demetris AJ, Van Thiel D. Liver transplantation (2). N Engl J Med. 1989;321:1092.
86. Fairley CK, Mijch A, Gust ID, et al. The increased risk of fatal liver disease in renal transplant patients who are hepatitis B e antigen and/or HBV DNA positive. Transplantation. 1991;52:497.
87. Samuel D, Muller R, Alexander G, et al. Liver transplantation in European patients with the hepatitis B surface antigen. N Engl J Med. 1993;329:1842.
88. Davies SE, Portmann BC, O'Grady JG, et al. Hepatic histological findings after transplantation for chronic hepatitis B virus infection, including a unique pattern of fibrosing cholestatic hepatitis. Hepatology. 1991;13:150.
89. Lucey MR, Graham DM, Martin P, et al. Recurrence of hepatitis B and delta hepatitis after orthotopic liver transplantation. Gut. 1992;33:1390.
90. Terrault NA. Treatment of recurrent hepatitis B infection in liver transplant recipients. Liver Transplant. 2002;8:S74-S81.
91. Marcellin P, Chang TT, Lim SG, et al. Adefovir dipivoxil for the treatment of hepatitis B e antigen-positive chronic hepatitis B. N Engl J Med. 2003;348:848-850.
92. Kliem V, van den Hoff U, Brunkhorst R, et al. The long-term course of hepatitis C after kidney transplantation. Transplantation. 1996;62:1417.
93. Berenguer M. Natural history of recurrent hepatitis C. Liver Transplant. 2002;8: S14-S18.
94. Forman LM, Lewis JD, Berlin JA, et al. The association between hepatitis C infection and survival after liver transplantation. Gastroenterology. 2002;122:689-696.
95. Fagiuoli S, Minniti F, Pevere S, et al. HBV and HCV infections in heart transplant recipients. J Heart Lung Transpl. 2001;20:718-724.
96. Gane E, Pilmore H. Management of chronic viral hepatitis before and after renal transplantation. Transplantation. 2002;74:427-437.
97. Legendre C, Garrigue V, Le Bihan C, et al. Harmful long-term impact of hepatitis C virus infection in kidney transplant recipients. Transplantation. 1998;65:667-670.
98. Gane E. Treatment of recurrent hepatitis C. Liver Transplant. 2002;8:S28-S37.
99. Singh N, Husain S. Infections of the central nervous system in transplant recipients. Transplant Infect Dis. 2000;2:101-111.
100. Stamm AM, Dismukes WE, Simmons BP, et al. Listeriosis in renal transplant recipients: Report of an outbreak and review of 102 cases. Rev Infect Dis. 1982;4:665.
101. Gustafson TL, Schaffner W, Lavely GB, et al. Invasive aspergillosis in renal transplant recipients: Correlation with corticosteroid therapy. J Infect Dis. 1983;148:230.
102. Denning DW. Invasive aspergillosis. Clin Infect Dis. 1998;26:781.
103. Denning DW, Ribaud P, Milpied N, et al. Efficacy and safety of voriconazole in the treatment of acute invasive aspergillosis. Clin Infect Dis. 2002;34:563-571.
104. Wu G, Vilchez RA, Eidelman B, et al. Cryptococcal meningitis: An analysis among 5,521 consecutive organ transplant recipients. Transplant Infect Dis. 2002;4:183-188.
105. Kusne S, Dummer JS, Ho M, et al. Self-limited *Toxoplasma* parasitemia after liver transplantation. Transplantation. 1987;44:457.
106. Mason JC, Ordelheide KS, Grames GM, et al. Toxoplasmosis in two renal transplant recipients from a single donor. Transplantation. 1987;44:588.
107. Wreghitt TG, Hakim M, Gray JJ, et al. Toxoplasmosis in heart and heart and lung transplant recipients. J Clin Pathol. 1989;42:194.
108. Gombert ME, Aulicino TM, duBouchet L, et al. Therapy of experimental cerebral nocardiosis with imipenem, amikacin, trimethoprim-sulfamethoxazole, and minocycline. Antimicrob Agents Chemother. 1986;30:270.
109. Beaman BL, Beaman L. *Nocardia* species: Host-parasite relationships. Clin Microbiol Rev. 1994;7:213-264.
110. Singh NS, Carrigan DR. Human herpesvirus-6 in transplantation: An emerging pathogen. Ann Intern Med. 1996;124:1065.
111. Singh N, Paterson DL. Encephalitis caused by human herpesvirus-6 in transplant recipients: Relevance of a novel neurotropic virus. Transplantation. 2000;69:2474-2479.
112. Kusne S, Schwartz M, Breinig MK, et al. Herpes simplex virus hepatitis after solid organ transplantation in adults. J Infect Dis. 1991;163:1001.
113. Koneru B, Tzakis AG, DePuydt LE, et al. Transmission of fatal herpes simplex infection through renal transplantation. Transplantation. 1988;45:653.
114. Broyer M, Tete MJ, Guest G, et al. Varicella and zoster in children after kidney transplantation: Long-term results of vaccination. Pediatrics. 1997;99:35.

115. Dodd DA, Burger J, Edwards KM, Dummer JS. Varicella in a pediatric heart transplant population on nonsteroid immunosuppression. Pediatrics. 2001;108:E80.

116. Ho M. Cytomegalovirus: Biology and Infection. 2nd ed. New York: Plenum Press; 1991:249-256.

117. Dummer JS, White LT, Ho M, et al. Morbidity of cytomegalovirus infection in recipients of heart or heart-lung transplants who received cyclosporine. J Infect Dis. 1985;152:1182.

118. Paya CV, Hermans PE, Wiesner RH, et al. Cytomegalovirus hepatitis in liver transplantation: Prospective analysis of 93 consecutive orthotopic liver transplantations. J Infect Dis. 1989;160:752.

119. Bronsther O, Makowka L, Jaffe R, et al. Occurrence of cytomegalovirus hepatitis in liver transplant patients. J Med Virol. 1988;24:423.

120. Pohl C, Green M, Wald ER, Ledesma-Medina J. Respiratory syncytial virus infections in pediatric liver transplant recipients. J Infect Dis. 1992;165:166.

121. Michaels MG, Green M, Wald ER, Starzl TE. Adenovirus infection in pediatric liver transplant recipients. J Infect Dis. 1992;165:170.

122. Englund JA, Piedra PA, Whimbey E. Prevention and treatment of respiratory virus and parainfluenza viruses in immunocompromised adults. Am J Med. 1997;102(Suppl 3A):61.

123. McCurdy LH, Milstone A, Dummer S. Clinical features and outcomes of paramyxoviral infection in lung transplant recipients treated with ribavirin. J Heart Lung Transpl. 2003. In press.

124. Vilchez RA, Fung J, Kusne S. The pathogenesis and management of influenza virus infection in organ transplant recipients. Transplant Infect Dis. 2002;4:177-182.

125. Gardner SD, Mackenzie EFD, Smith C, Porter AA. Prospective study of the human polyoma viruses BK and JC cytomegalovirus in renal transplant recipients. J Clin Pathol. 1984;37:578.

126. Kwak EJ, Vilchez RA, Randhawa P, et al. Pathogenesis and management of polyomavirus infection in transplant patients. Clin Infect Dis. 2002;35:1081-1087.

127. Hirsch HH, Knowles W, Dickenmann M, et al. Prospective study of polyoma type BK replication and nephropathy in renal-transplant recipients. N Engl J Med. 2002;347:488-496.

128. Randhawa PS, Finkelstein S, Scantlebury V, et al. Human polyoma virus-associated interstitial nephritis in the allograft kidney. Transplantation. 1999;67:103-109.

129. Nickeleit V, Klimkait T, Binet IF, et al. Testing for polyomavirus BK DNA in plasma to identify renal-allograft recipients with viral nephropathy. N Engl J Med. 2000;342:309-315.

130. Antman K, Chang Y. Kaposi's sarcoma. N Engl J Med. 2000;342:1027-1038.

131. Farge D, Lebbe C, Marjanovic Z, et al. Human herpes virus-8 and other risk factors for Kaposi's sarcoma in kidney transplant recipients. Transplantation. 1999;67:1236-1242.

132. Frances C, Mouquet C, Marcelin AG, et al. Outcome of kidney transplant recipients with previous human herpesvirus-8 infection. Transplantation. 2000;69:1776-1779.

133. Regamey N, Tamm M, Wernli M, et al. Transmission of human herpesvirus-8 infection from renal transplant donors to recipients. N Engl J Med. 1998;339:1358-1363.

134. Ho M, Miller G, Atchison RW, et al. Epstein-Barr virus infections and DNA hybridization studies in posttransplantation lymphoma and lymphoproliferative lesions: The role of primary infection. J Infect Dis. 1985;152:876.

135. Ho M, Jaffe R, Miller G, et al. The frequency of Epstein-Barr virus infection and associated lymphoproliferative syndrome after transplantation and its manifestations in children. Transplantation. 1988;45:719.

136. Breinig MK, Zitelli B, Ho M. Epstein-Barr virus, cytomegalovirus and other viral infections in children after liver transplantation. J Infect Dis. 1987;156:273.

137. Preiksaitis JK, Keay S. Diagnosis and management of posttransplant lymphoproliferative disorder in solid-organ transplant recipients. Clin Infect Dis. 2001;33(Suppl): S38-S46.

138. Preiksaitis JK, Diaz-Mitoma F, Mirzayans F, et al. Quantitative oropharyngeal Epstein-Barr virus shedding in renal and cardiac transplant recipients: Relationship to immunosuppressive therapy, serologic responses, and the risk of posttransplant lymphoproliferative disorder. J Infect Dis. 1992;166:986.

139. Rowe DT, Qu L, Reyes J, et al. Use of quantitative competitive PCR to measure Epstein-Barr virus genome load in the peripheral blood of pediatric transplant patients with lymphoproliferative disorders. J Clin Microbiol. 1997;35:2852-2857.

140. Starzl TE, Nalesnik MA, Porter KA, et al. Reversibility of lymphomas and lymphoproliferative lesions developing under cyclosporin-steroid therapy. Lancet. 1984;1:583.

141. Cleary ML, Sklar J. Lymphoproliferative disorders in cardiac transplant recipients are multiclonal lymphomas. Lancet. 1984;2:489.

142. Pagano JS, Sixbey JW, Lin J-C. Acyclovir and Epstein-Barr virus infection. J Antimicrob Chemother. 1983;12(Suppl B):113.

143. Keay S, Oldach D, Wiland A, et al. Posttransplantation lymphoproliferative disorder associated with OKT3 and decreased antiviral prophylaxis in pancreas transplant patients. Clin Infect Dis 1998;26:596-600.

144. Nalesnik MA. Lymphoproliferative disease in organ transplant recipients. Springer Semin Immunopathol. 1991;13:199.

145. Fisher A, Blanche S, Le Bidois J, et al. Anti-B cell monoclonal antibody treatment of severe B-cell lymphoproliferative syndrome following bone marrow and organ transplantation. N Engl J Med. 1991;324:1451-1456.

146. Milpied N, Vasseur B, Parquet N, et al. Humanized anti-CD20 monoclonal antibody (rituximab) in post-transplant lymphoproliferative disorder: A retrospective analysis on 32 patients. Ann Oncol. 2000;11(Suppl 1):113-116.

147. Papadopoulos EB, Ladanyi M, Emanuel D, et al. Infusions of donor leukocytes to treat Epstein-Barr virus-associated lymphoproliferative disorders after allogeneic bone marrow transplantation. N Engl J Med. 1994;330:1231.

148. Khanna R, Bell S, Sherritt M, et al. Activation an adoptive transfer of Epstein-Barr virus-specific cytotoxic T cells in solid organ transplant patients with posttransplant lymphoproliferative disease. Proc Natl Acad Sci U S A. 1999;96:10391-10396.

Infections in Patients with Spinal Cord Injury

RABIH O. DAROUICHE

Much has changed since ancient Egyptians viewed spinal cord injury as "an ailment not to be treated."[1] But by the beginning of the 20th century, little was changed since 80% of United States soldiers who fought in World War I died within the first 2 weeks after sustaining spinal cord injury (SCI).[2] The first signs of important progress became apparent in the 1940s when comprehensive medical programs were constructed to treat the casualties of World War II.[2] Since then, the management of SCI patients has dramatically improved resulting in almost normal life expectancy at the present time.

About 40 persons per million population in the United States sustain SCI each year. The annual incidence of 11,000 cases contributes to the current existence of between 183,000 and 230,000 Americans with SCI.[3] Although SCI patients are particularly predisposed to infection in the acute setting of the injury, the vast majority of infections occur long thereafter. This chapter addresses the factors that predispose to infection, analyzes the challenges in evaluating patients for infection, and discusses the most prominent infections in this population. Whereas urinary tract infections are the most common,[4] pneumonia has the highest infection-associated mortality,[5] and infections of pressure sores and underlying bone are probably the most difficult to manage.[6]

FACTORS THAT PREDISPOSE TO INFECTION

SCI does not depress general host immunity. Uninfected individuals with SCI reportedly have normal function of T and B lymphocytes.[7] Although patients with SCI usually have higher levels of complement and acute-phase reactants than able-bodied cohorts,[7,8] this difference can be attributed to undetected inflammation or occult infection. However, SCI patients may suffer from complicating conditions (including stress, malnutrition and renal failure) or receive medications (such as high-dose glucocorticosteroids in the acute setting of SCI) that can impair the immune response to infection. More importantly, SCI patients possess unique factors that predispose them to infection of specific body organ systems.

For instance, most patients have a neurogenic bladder and suffer from frequent episodes of urinary tract infection that are attributed to urinary stasis and bladder catheterization. Urinary stasis greatly impairs the naturally protective mechanisms of the urinary tract such as the washout effect of voiding and the phagocytic capacity of bladder epithelial cells. Even though some techniques of bladder catheterization are safer than others, none can be carried out without the potential risk of introducing organisms into the urinary tract. Both paralytic ileus and abnormal state of consciousness due to associated head injury and/or illicit drug ingestion can predispose to aspiration pneumonia in the acute stage of SCI. In persons with cervical or high thoracic cord lesions, weakness of the diaphragmatic and intercostal muscles impairs the capacity to clear respiratory secretions. Skin breakdown in anesthetic areas, immobility, disuse-induced muscle atrophy, urinary leakage, and fecal contamination predispose to infection of pressure sores. Frequent hospitalizations and insertion of urinary, vascular, orthopedic, and neurosurgical devices predispose these patients to a variety of device-related infections.

CHALLENGES IN EVALUATING PATIENTS FOR INFECTION

A number of unique challenges can be encountered when attempting to establish diagnosis and provide treatment of infections in the SCI population (Table 313-1). Infection frequently manifests differently in the SCI population than in able-bodied individuals. Altered or absent

TABLE 313-1 Challenges in Evaluating Spinal Cord-Injured Patients for Infection

General Factors
Altered or absent sensations
Interference of neurogenic pain with localization of source of infection
Coexistence of multiple infections
Mimicry of infection by noninfectious conditions
Thermoregulatory and autonomic disturbances
Need for adjusted dosing of vancomycin and aminoglycosides

Infection-Specific Factors
Urinary tract infection
   Almost universal prevalence of bacteriuria
   Value of pyuria as indicator of infection
   Nonspecific manifestations of symptomatic infection
   Investigation of urine cultures growing several bacterial species
Pneumonia
   Impact of ineffective cough on determining microbial cause
   Defective perception of dyspnea and need to evaluate gas exchange
   Eligibility for and efficacy of immunization
Infections of pressure sores
   Limitations of history provided by patient
   Supreme importance of physical findings in diagnosing ulcer infection
   Universal bacterial colonization of pressure sores and unreliability of swab cultures
   Potential reasons for failure to respond to therapy
   Deceptive appearance of sinus tract
Osteomyelitis
   Representative nature of cultured samples
   Possible variations of findings from bones beneath different sores
   Significance of organisms growing from cultures of bone
   Poor predictive value of clinical evaluation
   Appropriateness of imaging studies for diagnosis and for follow-up

sensations constitute the single most important impediment to the diagnosis of infection in this population. For instance, dysuria, frequency and urgency, symptoms that are regularly present in able-bodied patients who suffer from urinary tract infection, rarely exist in infected SCI patients. The diagnosis of perinephric abscess is particularly challenging in patients with high sensory levels who do not appreciate flank pain or tenderness.[9] The inability to recognize the signs and symptoms of cord damage contributes to the delay in diagnosing spinal epidural abscess below the level of injury.[10] The diagnostic dilemma caused by the paucity of clinical findings can be heightened by the presence of neurogenic or referred pain that may not be related to the infection. Furthermore, multiple infections co-occur in up to 20% of SCI patients. Even more problematic than identifying the source of an infection is discerning whether fever is due to an infection or to non-infectious conditions, that may closely mimic infections and cause almost one fifth of episodes of fever in SCI patients.

A diagnostic conundrum may exist when unique thermoregulatory and autonomic disturbances cause fever in SCI patients. Because of the imbalance between heat production and heat loss, patients with SCI above T8 may not be able to maintain a normal body temperature in response to heating or cooling (poikilothermia).[11,12] This phenomenon of altered thermoregulation is attributed to the loss of sweating and muscular activity below the spinal cord lesion. These factors may contribute to the occurrence of self-limited febrile episodes in SCI patients that resolve spontaneously within hours to days.[13] However, neither alterations in environmental temperature nor changes in a subject's sweating and muscular activity may explain the occurrence of prolonged fever in recently injured quadriplegic patients who have no identifiable focus of infection.[14] This unique syndrome, so-called quadriplegia fever, lasts weeks to months and is problematic because it may incite repeated evaluation for infection and multiple courses of antibiotics but to no avail. Rarely, fever may occur in the context of autonomic dysreflexia, a paroxysmal syndrome characterized mainly by hypertension, sweating, facial flushing, and headache.[15] Occasionally, bradycardia may also be present and can help differentiate febrile episodes of autonomic dysreflexia from infection. This type of autonomic hyperactivity is seen only in patients with SCI above T6 and is usually trig-

gered by distention of viscera (bladder and rectum), cutaneous stimulation (e.g., ingrown toenails), or even infection.

Treatment of infection in SCI patients also poses special challenges. For example, two opposing factors resulting from changes in body composition following SCI can alter the disposition of systemically administered antibiotics, such as vancomycin[16] and aminoglycosides.[17] On one hand, patients with SCI have an expanded extracellular volume that is attributed to retention of extracellular water as subclinical edema and replacement of decreased skeletal muscle mass by extracellular water. As a result, these patients have a larger weight-adjusted volume of distribution of drugs and may require larger weight-adjusted loading and maintenance doses than able-bodied counterparts to achieve similar antibiotic concentrations. This potential effect on antibiotic concentration can be counteracted, at least in part, by the frequent overestimation of creatinine clearance when using formulas that had been originally constructed in non-SCI persons to predict creatinine clearance in patients with chronic SCI who have low serum creatinine.[18] The misapplication of such formulas has prompted the evaluation of modified methods to properly administer vancomycin and other antibiotics in the SCI population.[16]

URINARY TRACT INFECTIONS

In patients with chronic indwelling bladder catheters (transurethral or suprapubic), bacteriuria is almost universal (culture of a randomly obtained urine sample is positive in almost 98% of instances). These SCI patients have a higher rate of bacteriuria than those who rely on intermittent bladder catheterization (98% vs. 70%). A longer time interval between intermittent bladder catheterization may be associated with a higher incidence of bacteriuria. Although outpatients may find it more practical to utilize clean reusable rather than sterile catheters for intermittent bladder catheterization, there is conflicting evidence regarding the value of clean vs. sterile bladder catheterization.[19]

Asymptomatic bladder colonization may progress to symptomatic urinary tract infection, but often does not.[20] Typical manifestations of urinary tract infection (including dysuria, urgency, frequency, suprapubic discomfort and, in patients with pyelonephritis, costovertebral angle tenderness) are rarely present in SCI patients. Instead, change in voiding habits, increase in the residual volume of urine in the bladder, foul-smelling urine, worsening of muscular spasticity, and/or aggravation of autonomic dysreflexia are often the only clinical clues to the presence of urinary tract infection. Because of the nonspecificity of these clinical manifestations, other causes should be excluded before diagnosing urinary tract infection. Although the lack of pyuria reasonably predicts the absence of urinary tract infection in SCI patients, pyuria may be also observed in uninfected individuals who have inflammation of the urinary tract that is caused by a recent invasive procedure or other conditions such as a renal calculus. As with other patient populations who require bladder catheterization, quantification of bacteriuria in SCI patients may not help differentiate between asymptomatic bladder colonization and symptomatic urinary tract infection. A consensus of investigators for the National Institute on Disability and Rehabilitation Research concluded that bacterial growth of as few as 10^2 CFU/ml of urine from catheter-dependent patients or 10^4 CFU/ml of urine from catheter-free males using external condoms can be associated with symptomatic urinary tract infection.[21]

Most cases of urinary tract infection in SCI patients are caused by commensal organisms of the bowel and perineum, particularly gram-negative bacilli and enterococci.[22] The patient's gender and level of injury may affect the microbiology of organisms residing in the bladder. For instance, *Escherichia coli* and *Enterococcus* spp. have been reported to cause more than two thirds of the cases of urinary tract infection in female patients undergoing intermittent catheterization.[23] In contrast, *Klebsiella pneumoniae* has emerged as one of the most common causes of urinary tract infection in hospitalized SCI patients,[24] with particularly high prevalence of bacterial strains that exhibit strong type 1 fimbrial-mediated adherence to uroepithelial cells.[25] In that regard, *E. coli* strains that cause urinary tract infection in adult

SCI patients may exhibit more virulence factors such as hemolysis and D-mannose–resistant hemagglutination of human erythrocytes than strains that asymptomatically reside in the bladder of SCI patients or the rectum of healthy volunteers.[26]

The finding of polymicrobial bacteriuria is particularly problematic in SCI patients. Almost half of positive urine cultures in SCI patients grow more than one organism,[27] and polymicrobial bacteriuria can be more prevalent in patients who have chronic indwelling urethral catheters. Although isolation of multiple bacterial species in the general population is often viewed as indicative of contamination, a similar finding in catheter-dependent SCI patients should not be disregarded. Isolation of several uropathogens can be associated with urinary tract infection that fails to respond to antibiotic therapy directed against only one or some of the organisms but is eradicated after providing additional antimicrobial coverage against other isolated organisms. Although the majority of urine cultures are obtained from patients with only lower urinary tract infection and in whom the yield of blood cultures is extremely low, the detection of concurrent bacteremia confirms the pathogenicity of organisms isolated from urine culture. Even in patients who have pyelonephritis in association with polymicrobial bacteriuria, isolation of only one organism from blood cultures may not negate the role of other bacteria in causing urinary tract infection.

Not since the advent of closed urinary drainage almost half a century ago have we come upon a preventive approach that dramatically protects against urinary tract infection. Optimizing urinary drainage and switching, whenever feasible, from indwelling bladder catheter to intermittent bladder catheterization or even external condom-based drainage remain the cornerstone of prevention.[28-30] The incidence of bladder stones, a condition associated with urinary tract infection, is also lower in patients who rely on intermittent bladder catheterization vs. indwelling bladder catheters.[31,32] The potential impact of varying the frequency of exchanging indwelling bladder catheters on the incidence of urinary tract infection is yet to be established.[33] Since asymptomatic bacteriuria can progress to symptomatic infection, a number of approaches have been designed to prevent or eradicate asymptomatic bacteriuria. In general, however, neither the use of antiseptics or antibiotics for prophylaxis nor the antibiotic treatment of asymptomatic bacteriuria in SCI patients has been recommended.[34] Such approaches can induce the emergence of resistant organisms and expose patients to adverse effects of drugs. In those instances in which asymptomatic bacteriuria might be associated with significant complications, such as during pregnancy or in patients with struvite urinary stones associated with urea-splitting organisms, treatment of asymptomatic bacteriuria may be indicated. Although preliminary findings suggest that consumption of cranberry juice by SCI patients may reduce the biofilm on uroepithelial cells,[35] the clinical efficacy of this approach awaits exploration in this patient population.

The limited clinical success of traditional preventive measures has prompted the interest in exploring innovative approaches, particularly bacterial interference using a non-pathogenic strain of E. coli 83972.[36-38] Intentional colonization of the neurogenic bladder with a nonpathogenic strain of E. coli has been reported in a prospective, open-label pilot clinical trial to be safe and protective against development of urinary tract infection.[39] Further investigation of the safety and clinical efficacy of this innovative approach of bacterial interference is currently being pursued in a prospective, randomized, placebo-controlled clinical trial.

In general, optimal management of symptomatic urinary tract infection depends on the location of infection and the condition of the host. Analysis of urine samples obtained by ureteral catheterization, the definitive procedure for distinguishing between upper and lower urinary tract infection, is not practical in the clinical setting. Moreover, neither sequential analysis of urine specimens after irrigation of the bladder (bladder washout technique) nor examination for antibody coating of urinary bacteria is reliable in localizing the site of urinary tract infection in SCI patients.[40,41] The frequent occurrence of vesicoureteral reflux and the potential stimulation of local antibody production by the bladder in the presence of a foreign body (bladder catheter), respectively, may help explain the unreliability of these two tests in localizing the site of infection in SCI patients.

Despite the absence of adequate support in the literature, most physicians suspect pyelonephritis in the presence of high fever, chills, systemic toxicity, or leukocyte casts in urinary sediment. Results of studies in otherwise healthy individuals indicating that short courses of oral antibiotics (a single large dose or a 3-day course) are efficacious in eradicating uncomplicated lower urinary tract infection should not be extrapolated to the SCI population. In the absence of supportive clinical trials, catheter-related infections of the neurogenic bladder are generally treated with a 7- to 10-day course of antibiotics. In SCI patients with vesicoureteral reflux, pyelonephritis is likely to occur and is usually treated with a 2-week course of antibiotics. A longer duration of antibiotic therapy (4 to 6 weeks) is advocated in patients with persistent infection, documented relapse of infection, or prostatitis.

In patients with persistent infection, documented relapse of infection (by the same bacterial strain), or frequent reinfections (by different organisms), the urinary tract should be investigated for anatomic abnormalities (such as stone, abscess, and stricture) and functional alterations (including vesicoureteral reflux and high residual volume of urine in bladder). Although pyuria regresses to normal values ($<10^4$ white blood cells/ml of uncentrifuged urine) after the completion of successful treatment of urinary tract infection in SCI patients with intermittent bladder catheterization, above-normal levels of pyuria may persist after treatment of infection associated with indwelling bladder catheters.[42]

PNEUMONIA

Although generally much less frequent than urinary tract infections, pneumonia is the most common pulmonary complication in the immediate postinjury period[43] and is particularly likely to occur in the first few months after cervical or high thoracic SCI and among quadriplegics and persons at least 55 years of age.[5] The relatively high mortality associated with pneumonia makes it the leading cause of death due to infection in this population.[5] Pneumonia in acutely injured patients is associated with prolonged length of stay and escalated hospital costs.[44] In patients who aspirate gastric contents, pneumonia is usually caused by gram-negative and/or anaerobic bacteria. As is the case in able-bodied persons, bacterial community-acquired pneumonia in SCI patients is mostly caused by Streptococcus pneumoniae, Haemophilus influenza, and Branhamella catarrhalis. Staphylococcus aureus (often MRSA) and Pseudomonas aeruginosa commonly cause pneumonia in mechanically ventilated patients and in those with tracheostomy tubes. Owing to defective sensations of respiratory muscle fatigue and altered perceptions of dyspnea, SCI patients with pneumonia may progress to respiratory failure in an unpredictable fashion. Therefore, evaluation of gas exchange, preferably by analysis of arterial blood gases, is strongly recommended when treating pneumonia. Transcutaneous measurement of oxygen saturation may also be employed, but with caution because heated electrodes can produce burns on anesthetized skin.

A number of non-infectious conditions can clinically mimic pneumonia. For instance, atelectasis, like pneumonia, commonly occurs because of retained pulmonary secretions early after injury to the cervical or high thoracic cord. In such patients with altered/absent sensations of chest pain and dyspnea and ineffective cough, the only clinical clues that suggest the diagnosis of pneumonia may include tachypnea, tachycardia, fever, and leukocytosis. However, atelectasis may also be accompanied by an element of low-grade fever and leukocytosis. The site of pulmonary involvement may not help differentiate atelectasis from pneumonia because both conditions predominantly involve the left lung owing to the difficulty in suctioning the left main stem bronchus, which branches off at a more acute angle than the right bronchus. Occasionally, bronchoscopy is required for both diagnostic and therapeutic purposes.

Another condition that can be clinically confused with pneumonia is pulmonary embolism, which occurs in about 5% of SCI patients, frequently without an identifiable thrombotic source.[45] Although pulmonary embolism can ordinarily be diagnosed by a ventilation-perfusion lung scan, the observed defects on scanning may be uninterpretable in patients who also have atelectasis. In such instances a pulmonary angiogram may be required for definitive diagnosis. In the acute stage of SCI, associated fracture of a long bone can lead to fat embolism which may or may not present with the clinical stigmata of petechiae and cerebral dysfunction. Aspiration of gastric contents in the presence of paralytic ileus and an ineffective cough reflex can lead to chemical pneumonitis that mimics bacterial pneumonia; evaluation of an adequate sample of respiratory secretions may help differentiate between these two clinical entities. Finally, pulmonary contusion can be mistaken for pneumonia in the acute setting of SCI.

Since patients with SCI may be at a greater risk of developing pneumonia than able-bodied subjects, it is important to assess the immunization status in such patients. By virtue of age (older than 50 years), chronic respiratory disease, or residence in chronic care facilities, or all of these, almost two thirds of SCI patients are eligible for vaccination against *S. pneumoniae* and influenza viruses. The antibody response to pneumococcal vaccination of SCI patients is adequate,[46] and unpublished findings by the author suggest similar results with the influenza vaccination. Notwithstanding the lack of studies that examine the clinical benefit of these vaccinations in SCI patients, it may be justifiable to administer pneumococcal and influenza vaccines to all SCI patients.

INFECTIONS OF PRESSURE SORES

Local factors that contribute to infection of pressure sores include breaks in the integrity of the skin barrier, pressure-induced changes, and contamination from contiguous dirty areas. The latter factor may explain the predominant growth of gram-negative and anaerobic bacteria, usually in combination, in cultures from pressure sores.[47] The majority of pressure sores in SCI patients develop in areas adjacent to the ischium, sacrum, and greater trochanter. In paralyzed individuals who cannot directly visualize the ulcers, their history is usually incomplete and the infection is already advanced by the time they seek medical care. Because of the inadequacy of sensations, physical findings including fever, purulent drainage, and surrounding inflammatory changes such as erythema, swelling, and warmth are usually relied upon to diagnose infection.

Since pressure sores are universally colonized by bacteria, samples for culture should not be obtained unless infection is clinically evident. In patients with seemingly infected pressure ulcers, biopsy of deep tissue may constitute the most reliable means for determining the infectious cause. Cultures of swab specimens from the ulcer or the sinus tract are generally unreliable, and cultures of material obtained by needle aspiration tend to overestimate the number of bacterial isolates.[48] If cellulitis is recognized adjacent to a decubitus ulcer, the challenge to the clinician is to discern the infecting organism(s). Because the decubitus ulcer can serve as the potential source of bacteria causing contiguous cellulitis, cultures obtained by irrigation followed by aspiration from beneath the margins of the ulcer may theoretically help resolve this problem.[49] In non-SCI patients with cellulitis adjacent to a cutaneous ulcer, skin biopsy has been demonstrated to yield only staphylococci or streptococci in most cases, with clinical response resulting from treatment directed specifically against these organisms.[50] Similar studies of cellulitites surrounding decubitus ulcers in SCI patients have not been reported.

A combined medical-surgical approach is often required to establish cure of the infection. Although antibiotic levels in tissues adjacent to diabetic ulcers can be subtherapeutic, penetration of systemically administered antibiotics into paralyzed soft tissue was demonstrated to be adequate in a rat model.[51] The continuous application of negative pressure to deep ulcers by using a vacuum-assisted closure device (VAC) can enhance wound healing in selective patients by removing excessive edema, promoting granulation, and stimulating angiogenesis. Although it is possible that this technique can also facilitate delivery of systemically administered antibiotics to the infected area, the potential benefit

of a vacuum-assisted closure device as an adjunct to antibiotic therapy is still unclear.[52] Surgery is done to debride non-viable tissue and drain infected material. A lack of response of infected ulcers to therapy may be due to inadequate antibiotic therapy, unrecognized soft tissue abscess, communication of the ulcer with an infected bone or joint, or a fistula communicating with the gastrointestinal or urinary tract. The appearance of newly isolated bacterial species soon after initiating antibiotic therapy probably indicates colonization, and unless there has been an initial response followed by recurrence of fever, these organisms may be ignored. Even in patients with apparently healed ulcers, deep soft tissue abscesses may exist, sometimes causing fever or even bacteremia.[47]

Although the sensitivity of the gallium scan for detecting soft tissue abscesses is generally very high, this test can also be positive in SCI patients who have an infected pressure sore without an associated abscess. Soft tissue abscess in association with an infected sore can be more accurately diagnosed by computed tomography.[53] Since pressure necrosis affects subcutaneous tissues and muscles more than skin, the opening of a sinus tract onto the skin may appear deceptively small. Although potentially helpful, probing may not reveal the full depth of the tract. Sinography delineates the full depth of the tract and the potential communication with bone, joint, intra-abdominal abscess, or visceral organs. Injection of dye into the intestines or bladder may also help establish fistulous connections.

OSTEOMYELITIS

Most cases of osteomyelitis in SCI patients occur beneath pressure sores.[54,55] Less common forms include prosthesis-related, postoperative, hematogenous, and vertebral osteomyelitis.[56]

In general, it is difficult to determine whether bone beneath a decubitus ulcer is infected and, if infected, which organisms(s) is (are) responsible. Cultures of a swab specimen from the ulcer are of little value in predicting the causative organisms of osteomyelitis.[55] The definitive diagnosis of osteomyelitis beneath pressure sores requires histopathologic examination of bone tissue.[6,54] Histopathologic examination of bone specimens obtained by percutaneous needle biopsy demonstrates osteomyelitis beneath about one fifth to one third of pressure sores.[6,54] Since osteomyelitis is likely to be a focal process and percutaneous bone biopsy may fail to sample infected foci, bone infection can be documented more frequently in patients in whom intraoperative bone biopsy is performed.[55,57] In patients with multiple pressure ulcers, histopathologic evaluation of a bone specimen from one site may not necessarily reflect the same findings beneath the other ulcers. In addition, even if pathologic findings are similar, bone cultures from various sites may grow different organisms.

Owing to the high frequency of bacterial colonization of fibrotic tissue adherent to bone, semiquantitative cultures of bone specimens are positive in at least two thirds of patients in whom histopathologic examination of bone tissue is not compatible with osteomyelitis.[55] Moreover, quantitative bone cultures do not differentiate osteomyelitis from colonization or infection of overlying soft tissue.[6] Therefore, in patients with histopathologic evidence of osteomyelitis, it may be reasonable to direct antibiotic treatment against all organisms that grow from cultures of bone, except those that are usual colonizers such as *Staphylococcus epidermidis* and diphtheroids. Most cases of osteomyelitis beneath pressure sores are caused by two or more bacterial species, including facultative organisms (mainly *S. aureus, Streptococcus* spp., and the Enterobacteriaceae group), aerobic bacteria (including *P. aeruginosa* and *Acinetobacter calcoaceticus*), and anaerobes (particularly *Bacteroides* and *Fusobacterium* spp.).[55]

Clinical evaluation poorly predicts the presence of osteomyelitis beneath nonhealing deep pressure sores. In particular, clinical information (duration of ulcer, bone exposure, purulent drainage, and fever), laboratory data (white blood cell count and erythrocyte sedimentation rate), and radiologic findings (plain roentgenograms and technetium bone scans) do not correlate well with the likelihood of finding histopathologic evidence of infection of bone.[6,54,55] Bone scanning is very sensitive (100%) but poorly specific (<33%) for diagnosing osteomyelitis beneath pressure sores.[54] This low specificity is attributed to the capacity of technetium to concentrate in areas of bone where pressure-induced changes exist or in foci of heterotopic ossification. The most desired finding of a bone scan is a negative result that would essentially exclude the diagnosis of osteomyelitis beneath pressure sores and obviate the need for bone biopsy. Although magnetic resonance imaging has been successfully used to identify osteomyelitis as the cause of nonhealing pressure ulcers,[58] this diagnostic tool should be used judiciously.

Although failure of decubitus ulcers to heal can result from underlying osteomyelitis,[6,47] it is more likely to be due to noninfectious causes such as pressure-related changes, spasticity, malnutrition, and heterotopic bone ossification. The latter entity can mimic osteomyelitis both clinically and radiologically. Heterotopic bone ossification evolves in 16% to 53% of SCI patients, particularly those who are completely paralyzed or have pressure sores,[59] usually in the first year after injury unless other inciting phenomena, such as infection or surgery, occur. It can cause warm, erythematous swelling of soft tissues, primarily in areas adjacent to the hip and knee. Although the serum alkaline phosphatase level can be elevated early, it is not diagnostic of heterotopic bone ossification because many other proliferative bone processes may also cause an abnormal elevation. Roentgenographic changes are often absent for 1 to 2 weeks after clinical signs appear, but by then, a technetium bone scan should reveal increased uptake.

Patients with SCI who have osteomyelitis beneath pressure sores are usually treated with antibiotics and, when indicated, surgery. Even though the ideal duration of antibiotic therapy is not clear, most patients receive at least 4 to 6 weeks of antibiotic therapy. If all infected bone is excised at the time of surgery (this should be confirmed with histopathology), a shorter course of antibiotics may suffice. Although parenteral antibiotics have traditionally been used, oral administration of effective drugs may be preferred. Musculocutaneous flap surgery is preferable to debridement alone because the transposition of a well-vascularized muscle allows more extensive removal of devitalized tissue, enhances the host's defense against infection, and provides a better vascular supply to facilitate bone healing. Diligent care should be given to prevent postoperative flap wound infections that can impair the vitality of the musculocutaneous flap.[60] Patients with improperly treated osteomyelitis may develop deep abscess and sinus tract after reconstructive surgery.[61] In patients with recurrent infection or very extensive disease, hemipelvectomy may be considered.[62] Changes on plain roentgenograms and bone scans may persist after what clinically seems to be successful treatment of osteomyelitis.[6] It has been suggested that Gallium scanning and leukocyte scintigraphy with indium may be useful in monitoring a patient's response to treatment.[63]

MISCELLANOUS INFECTIONS

These relatively uncommon infections affect the bloodstream, abdomen, and sinuses. Infections of the urinary tract, pressure sores, lungs, and vascular access are the most common identifiable sources of bacteremia in patients with SCI.[64] In bacteremic patients without an apparent source, an occult deep-seated abscess may be the culprit. Bacteremia associated with infections of the urinary tract and long-term hemodialysis access are mostly caused by gram-negative bacilli, whereas staphylococci are the most frequent isolates from blood cultures of patients with infection of pressure sores or short-term vascular access.[65] In general, the mortality from bacteremia in SCI patients is not higher than that in the general population.[65,66]

The most common intrabdominal infections in SCI patients affect the gall bladder or present as abscesses. Cholelithiasis occurs more commonly in SCI patients than in the general population.[67] Although the majority of gallstones may remain asymptomatic, some may cause cholecystitis or migrate down the common bile duct to cause cholangitis or pancreatitis. A ruptured viscus or, less commonly, a fistulous connection with a pressure sore can result in the formation of intraab-

dominal abscesses. These intraabdominal infections may be misdiagnosed, particularly in patients with high cord lesions, because they frequently present with abdominal distension, diffuse spasm of abdominal wall musculature, and rigidity on palpation, but no localized abdominal pain or tenderness.[68] Ultrasound examination or computed tomography of the abdomen should help establish the correct diagnosis.[68] Nasogastric tube placement and impaired sinus drainage in the supine position predispose SCI patients to often an occult form of maxillary sinusitis.[69]

REFERENCES

1. Hughes JT. The Edwin Smith Surgical Papyrus: an analysis of the first case reports of spinal cord injuries. Paraplegia. 1988;26:71-82.
2. Tulsky D. The impacts of the Model SCI System: historical perspective. J Spinal Cord Med. 2002;25:310-315.
3. National Spinal Cord Injury Statistical Center, Birmingham, Alabama. Spinal cord injury: facts and figures at a glance. J Spinal Cord Med. 2002;25:51-52.
4. Mylotte JM, Graham R, Kahler L, et al. Impact of nosocomial infection on length of stay and functional improvement among patients admitted to an acute rehabilitation unit. Infect Control Hosp Epidemiol. 2001;22:83-87.
5. DeVivo MJ, Kartus PL, Stover SL, et al. Cause of death for patients with spinal cord injuries. Arch Intern Med. 1989;149:1761-1766.
6. Darouiche RO, Landon GC, Klima M, et al. Osteomyelitis associated with pressure sores. Arch Intern Med. 1994;154:753-758.
7. Lyons M. Immune function in spinal cord injured males. J Neurosci Nurs. 1987;19:18-23.
8. Rebhun J, Madorsky JGB, Glovsky MM. Proteins of the complement system and acute phase reactants in sera of patients with spinal cord injury. Ann Allergy. 1991;66:335-338.
9. Deck AJ, Yang CC. Perinephric abscesses in the neurologically impaired. Spinal Cord. 2001;39:477-481.
10. Darouiche RO, Hamill RJ, Greenberg SB, et al. Bacterial spinal epidural abscess: Review of 43 cases and literature survey. Medicine. 1992;71:369-385.
11. Schmidt K, Chan C. Thermoregulation and fever in normal persons and in those with spinal cord injuries. Mayo Clin Proceedings. 1992; 67:469-475.
12. Colachis S, Otis S. Occurrence of fever associated with thermoregulation dysfunction after acute spinal cord injury. Am J Phys Rehabil. 1995;74:114-119.
13. Sugarman B, Brown D, Musher D. Fever and infection in spinal cord injury patients. JAMA. 1982;248:66-70.
14. Sugarman B. Fever in recently injured quadriplegic persons. Arch Phys Med Rehabil. 1982;63:639-640.
15. Kewalramani LS. Autonomic dysreflexia in traumatic myelopathy. Am J Phys Med. 1980;59:1-21.
16. Griver AR, Prince RA, Darouiche RO. A simple method for administering vancomycin in the spinal cord injured population. Arch Phys Med Rehabil. 1997;78:459-462.
17. Gilman TM, Brunnemann SR, Segal JL. Comparison of population pharmacokinetic models for gentamicin in spinal cord-injured and able-bodied patients. Antimicrob Agents Chemother. 1993;37:93-99.
18. Mirahmadi MK, Byrne C, Barton C, et al. Prediction of creatinine clearance from serum creatinine in spinal cord injury patients. Paraplegia. 1983;21:23-29.
19. Shekelle PG, Morton SC, Clark KA, et al. Systematic review of risk factors for urinary tract infection in adults with spinal cord dysfunction. J Spinal Cord Med. 1999;22:258-272.
20. Peterson JR, Roth EJ. Fever, bacteriuria, and pyuria in spinal cord injured patients with indwelling urethral catheters. Arch Phys Med Rehabil. 1989;70:839-841.
21. National Institute on Disability and Rehabilitation Research (NIDRR) Consensus Statement. The prevention and management of urinary tract infection among people with spinal cord injuries. J Am Paraplegia Soc. 1992;15:194-207.
22. Hamamci N, Dursun E, Akbas E, et al. A quantitative study of genital skin flora and urinary colonization in spinal cord injured patients. Spinal Cord. 1998;36:617-620.
23. Bennett CJ, Young MN, Darrington H. Differences in urinary tract infection in male and female spinal cord injury patients on intermittent catheterization. Paraplegia. 1995;33:69-72.
24. Darouiche R, Cadle R, Zenon G, et al. Progression from asymptomatic to symptomatic urinary tract infection in patients with SCI: A preliminary study. J Am Paraplegia Soc. 1993;16:221-226.
25. Kil KS, Darouiche RO, Hull RA, et al. Identification of a Klebsiella pneumoniae strain associated with nosocomial urinary tract infection. J Clin Microbiol. 1997;35:2370-2374.
26. Hull RA, Rudy DC, Wieser IE, Donovan WH. Virulence factors of Escherichia coli isolates from patients with symptomatic and asymptomatic bacteriuria and neuropathic bladders due to spinal cord and brain injuries. J Clin Microbiol. 1998;36:115-117.
27. Darouiche RO, Priebe M, Clarridge JE. Limited vs full microbiological investigation for the management of symptomatic polymicrobial urinary tract infection in adult spinal cord-injured patients. Spinal Cord. 1997;35:534-539.
28. Trautner BW, Darouiche RO. Prevention of urinary tract infection in patients with spinal cord injury. J Spinal Cord Med. 2002;25:277-83.
29. Siroky MB. Pathogenesis of bacteriuria and infection in the spinal cord injured patient. Am J Med. 2002;113 (Suppl 1A):67S-79S.
30. Esclarin De Ruz A, Garcia Leoni E, Herruzo Cabrera R. Epidemiology and risk factors for urinary tract infection in patients with spinal cord injury. J Urol. 2000;164:1285-1289.

31. Mitsui T, Minami K, Furuno T, et al. Is suprapubic cystostomy an optimal urinary management in high quadriplegics? A comparative study of suprapubic cystostomy and clean intermittent catheterization. Eur Urol. 2000;38:434-438.

32. Weld KJ, Dmochowski RR. Effect of bladder management on urological complications in spinal cord injured patients. J Urol. 2000;163:768-772.

33. Ho CH, Kirshblum S, Linsenmeyer TA, Millis SR. Effects of the routine change of chronic indwelling Foley catheters in persons with spinal cord injury. J Spinal Cord Med. 2001;24:101-104.

34. Morton SC, Shekelle PG, Adams JL, et al. Antimicrobial prophylaxis for urinary tract infection in persons with spinal cord dysfunction. Arch Phys Med Rehabil. 2002;83:129-138.

35. Reid G, Hsiehl J, Potter P, et al. Cranberry juice consumption may reduce biofilms on uroepithelial cells: pilot study in spinal cord injured patients. Spinal Cord 2001;39:26-30.

36. Darouiche RO, Hull RA. Bacterial interference for prevention of urinary tract infection: an overview. J Spinal Cord Med. 2000;23:136-41.

37. Hull RA, Rudy DC, Donovan WH, et al. Virulence properties of Escherichia coli 83972, a prototype strain associated with asymptomatic bacteriuria. Infect Immun. 1999;67:429-432.

38. Hull R, Rudy D, Donovan W, et al. Urinary tract infection prophylaxis using Escherichia coli 83972 in spinal cord injured patients. J Urol. 2000;163:872-877.

39. Darouiche RO, Donovan WH, Del Terzo M, et al. Pilot trial of bacterial interference for preventing urinary tract infection. Urology. 2001;58:339-344.

40. Kuhlemeier KV, Lloyd LK, Stover SL. Failure of antibody-coated bacteria and bladder washout tests to localize infection in spinal cord injury patients. J Urol. 1983;130:729-731.

41. Hooton TM, O'Shaughnessy EJ, Clowers D, et al. Localization of urinary tract infection in patients with spinal cord injury. J Infect Dis. 1984;150:85-91.

42. Joshi A, Darouiche RO. Regression of pyuria during the treatment of symptomatic urinary tract infection in patients with spinal cord injury. Spinal Cord. 1996;34:742-744.

43. Fishburn MJ, Marino RJ, Ditunno JF Jr. Atelectasis and pneumonia in acute spinal cord injury. Arch Phys Med Rehabil. 1990;71:197-200.

44. Winslow C, Bode RK, Felton D, et al. Impact of respiratory complications on length of stay and hospital costs in acute cervical spine injury. Chest. 2002;121:1548-1554.

45. Waring WP, Karunas RS. Acute spinal cord injuries and the incidence of clinically occurring thromboembolic disease. Paraplegia. 1991;29:8-16.

46. Darouiche RO, Groover J, Rowland J, et al. Pneumococcal vaccination for patients with spinal cord injury. Arch Phys Med Rehabil. 1993;74:1354-1357.

47. Sugarman B. Infection and pressure sores. Arch Phys Med Rehabil. 1985;66:177-179.

48. Rudensky B, Lipschits M, Isaacsohn M, et al. Infected pressure sores: Comparison of methods for bacterial identification. South Med J. 1992;85:901-903.

49. Ehrenkranz NJ, Alfonso B, Nerenberg D. Irrigation-aspiration for culturing draining decubitus ulcers: Correlation of bacteriological findings with a clinical inflammatory scoring index. J Clin Microbiol. 1990;28:2389-2393.

50. Hook EW III, Hooton TM, Horton CA, et al. Microbiologic evaluation of cutaneous cellulitis in adults. Arch Intern Med. 1986;146:295-297.

51. Seabrook GR, Edmiston CE, Schmitt DD, et al. Comparison of serum and tissue antibiotic levels in diabetes-related foot infections. Surgery. 1991;110:671-677.

52. Ford CN, Reinhard ER, Yeh D, et al. Interim analysis of a prospective, randomized trial of vacuum-assisted closure versus the healthpoint system in the management of pressure ulcers. Ann Plast Surg 2002;49:55-61.

53. Firooznia H, Rafii M, Golimbu C, et al. Computerized tomography of pelvic osteomyelitis in patients with spinal cord injuries. Clin Orthop. 1983;126-131.

54. Sugarman B. Pressure sores and underlying bone infection. Arch Intern Med. 1987;147:553-555.

55. Thornhill-Joynes M, Gonzales F, Stewart CA, et al. Osteomyelitis associated with pressure ulcers. Arch Phys Med Rehabil. 1986;67:314-318.

56. Frisbie JH, Gore RL, Strymish JM, Garshick E. Vertebral osteomyelitis in paraplegia: incidence, risk factors, clinical picture. J Spinal Cord Med. 2000;23:15-22.

57. Lewis VL Jr, Bailey MH, Pulawski G, et al. The diagnosis of osteomyelitis in patients with pressure sores. Plast Reconstr Surg. 1988;81:229-232.

58. Ruan CM, Escobedo E, Harrison S, Goldstein B. Magnetic resonance imaging of nonhealing pressure ulcers and myocutaneous flaps. Arch Phys Med Rehabil. 1998;79:1080-1088.

59. Lal S, Hamilton BB, Heinemann A, et al. Risk factors for heterotopic ossification in spinal cord injury. Arch Phys Med Rehabil. 1989;70:387-390.

60. Garg M, Rubayi S, Montgomerie JZ. Postoperative wound infections following mycocutaneous flap surgery in spinal injury patients. Paraplegia. 1992;30:734-739.

61. Han H, Lewis VL Jr, Wiedrich TA, Patel PK. The value of Jamshidi core needle bone biopsy in predicting postoperative osteomyelitis in grade IV pressure ulcer patients. Plast Reconstr Surg. 2002;110:118-122.

62. Chan JW, Virgo KS, Johnson FE. Hemipelvectomy for severe decubitus ulcers in patients with previous spinal cord injury. Am J Surg. 2003;185:69-73.

63. McCarthy K, Velchik MG, Alavi A, et al. Indium-III-labeled white blood cells in the detection of osteomyelitis complicated by a pre-existing condition. J Nucl Med. 1988;29:1015-1021.

64. Mylotte JM, Graham R, Kahler L, et al. Epidemiology of nosocomial infection and resistant organisms in patients admitted for the first time to an acute rehabilitation unit. Clin Infect Dis. 2000;30:425-432.

65. Montgomerie JZ, Chan E, Gilmore D, et al. Low mortality among patients with spinal cord injury and bacteremia. Rev Infect Dis. 1991;13:867-871.

66. Bhatt K, Cid D, Maiman D. Bacteremia in the spinal cord injury population. J Am Paraplegia Soc. 1987;10:11-14.

67. Apstein MD, Dalecki-Chipperfield K. Spinal cord injury is a risk factor for gallstone disease. Gastroenterology. 1987;92:966-968.

68. Neumayer LA, Bull DA, Mohr JD, et al. The acutely affected abdomen in paraplegic spinal cord injury patients. Ann Surg. 1990;212:561-566.

69. Lew HL, Han J, Robinson LR, et al. Occult maxillary sinusitis as a cause of fever in tetraplegia: 2 case reports. Arch Phys Med Rehabil. 2002;83:430-432.

Infections in the Elderly

KENT B. CROSSLEY

PHILLIP K. PETERSON

The extremes of age are appreciated as periods of increased susceptibility to infection. In the elderly (which we define as people 65 years of age or older), there are many reasons for more frequent infection. These include impairment of cell-mediated and humoral immunity[1] and reduced physiologic functions such as cough reflex, circulation, and wound healing.[2] Increased prevalence of many chronic illnesses associated with infection, use of immunosuppressive drugs, and communal living are probably also each partly responsible for the increased frequency of infection in the elderly. It is well established that many infections are both more frequent (e.g., herpes zoster, listeriosis, urinary tract infection) and more often associated with mortality (e.g., bacteremia, meningitis, malaria[3]) in older individuals. Conversely, some infections (e.g., sexually transmitted diseases) are less common in the elderly.

Infections in the aged must be viewed from the perspective of how best (and most economically) to provide therapy in an era of growing cost containment. The elderly are a large and increasing segment of the population worldwide. It is estimated that, of all human beings who have ever lived to be 65 years or older, half are currently alive.[4] In 1900, only 15 million people were age 65 years or older (1% of the global population). In 1992, 342 million people were in this age group (6.2% of the world population), and by the year 2050 this number is projected to expand to 2.5 billion (about 20% of the world population)! Similar demographics characterize population growth in the United States.[5]

A high proportion of lifetime health care costs are expended in the last few months before death. Older patients have longer hospital stays, higher mortality, and higher total hospital costs than younger patients.[6] Infections are one of the most common reasons for the elderly to be transferred from a nursing home to an acute care hospital.[7] Developing better ways to treat infections in elderly patients in long-term care facilities (thus avoiding transfer to an acute care institution) could potentially both improve the quality of their care and save substantial amounts of money.

In this chapter, we discuss infections that are disproportionately common in the elderly. Many infections in the aged share a common denominator of muted clinical signs and symptoms. It is key to remember that most physiologic responses to infection are blunted in the aged.[8] Peak temperatures, maximal white blood cell counts, and intensity of many clinical symptoms and signs are less marked in the elderly. Understanding this is crucial to caring for elderly individuals adequately.

URINARY TRACT INFECTIONS

Urinary tract infections (UTIs) are more common in women than men until advanced age. The incidence of asymptomatic bacteriuria (defined as the presence of greater than 10^5 organisms per milliliter of urine in the absence of symptoms) in women increases by about 1% per decade so that women 70 to 80 years old have a 7% to 8% annual incidence of bacteriuria. In men, bacteriuria becomes increasingly prevalent with age, largely as a result of urethral obstruction caused by prostatic hypertrophy. The prevalence of bacteriuria in the elderly is approximately 10% in men and 20% in women.[9] In residents of nursing homes and in the hospitalized elderly, bacteriuria is more common, and the frequencies in men and women become similar.[10] Bacteriuria often disappears spontaneously in the aged without any intervention.[11]

Asymptomatic bacteriuria in the elderly does not require antibiotic therapy. Functionally disabled elderly individuals are more prone to have bacteriuria, and they are also more apt to die from the cause of their primary disability.[12] Controlled studies of antibiotic treatment of elderly bacteriuric men and women have not shown decreased survival in the untreated population. Nicolle and colleagues[13] have demonstrated that treatment of bacteriuria in elderly men or women usually results in only transient clearing and is often complicated by drug-related side effects. Even though the majority of elderly institutionalized women with asymptomatic bacteriuria may have upper tract involvement, there are no clear guidelines for determining who should be treated, and there is no good evidence that treatment is associated with any benefit.[14]

The etiology of UTIs in the elderly largely depends on where the infection was acquired. Among individuals living in the community, the distribution of organisms causing infection in the elderly is similar to that seen in younger persons. In institutionalized elderly individuals, there is a marked change in pathogens, with one third of cases of UTI or bacteriuria caused by *Escherichia coli* and about as many caused by *Proteus* spp. There is more than a sixfold increase in the frequency of *Klebsiella* spp. and *Pseudomonas aeruginosa* compared with that in noninstitutionalized persons. Up to 25% of these infections may be polymicrobial.[11] A significant excess of gram-positive infections in elderly men with UTIs has also been observed.[12] In several studies, bacteriuria has been reported to be transient and the responsible organisms to change frequently.[11,15-19] The common use of antibiotics in long-term care institutions is undoubtedly one factor altering the etiology of these infections. Both the organisms recovered and the antibiotic susceptibility of the isolates may be a function of the patient's exposure to antibiotics.

Pyuria is not a reliable marker for bacteriuria. In the studies of Baldassarre and Kaye,[12] 60.9% of 133 women with pyuria did not have bacteriuria. Of 184 women who did not have pyuria, in contrast, only 4.3% were bacteriuric.[12]

Symptomatic UTI should always be treated in older individuals. Antibiotic selection should be guided by a Gram-stained specimen of urine and the patient's history. Residence in a nursing home, recent hospital stays, previous antibiotic therapy, and a history of multiple UTIs are all associated with more resistant organisms. Enterococci and *Staphylococcus aureus* cause a significant minority of infections in older patients. Because many drugs used to treat gram-negative infection are not active against these organisms, it is important to exclude them by the urine Gram stain.

For elderly patients with apparent acute upper tract disease, hemodynamic instability is more common than in younger patients,[20] and parenteral antimicrobial therapy and hospitalization are often appropriate. If gram-positive organisms are present in urine, vancomycin is probably the best empirical therapy. For gram-negative infection, a third-generation cephalosporin or another β-lactam (e.g., ticarcillin-clavulanate) or ciprofloxacin is a good initial choice. Patients at high risk of having resistant organisms are best treated initially with a broad-spectrum β-lactam or a carbapenem and an aminoglycoside, beginning with a low dose (e.g., 1 mg/kg/day) until blood aminoglycoside levels can be obtained. With both gram-negative and gram-positive infections, final therapy should be guided by susceptibility studies. As with younger patients, failure of symptoms (e.g., chills or fever) to resolve, persisting back pain, or continuing positive urine cultures require careful evaluation to exclude obstruction or a perinephric abscess.

Prevention of recurrent UTIs in elderly women has been evaluated in three studies. Raz and Stamm[21] found that intravaginal estriol in postmenopausal women results in decreased colonization with Enterobacteriaceae and fewer infections. Ouslander and colleagues found no effect on the incidence of bacteriuria in a placebo-controlled trial when elderly institutionalized women were given oral estrogen-progestin for 6 months.[22] Raz and co-workers[23] compared estriol-containing vaginal pessaries with oral nitrofurantoin for prevention of recurrent UTI in elderly women.[23] The pessary was significantly less effective than nitrofurantoin in the prevention of infection. Avorn and colleagues[24] showed in a placebo-controlled trial that regular ingestion of cranberry juice reduced both bacteriuria and pyuria in elderly women.

Urinary catheters are a significant cause of UTI in the elderly.[25] These devices should be avoided whenever possible. Virtually all patients with indwelling catheters in place for 30 days or longer are bacteriuric, but only a small percentage of these patients develop symptomatic infection. Conversely, about two thirds of febrile illnesses in elderly patients with indwelling catheters are the result of UTI.[26] Warren and co-workers[27] have shown that infection-related mortality in elderly bacteriuric women is limited to severely debilitated patients. When symptomatic infections develop in patients with indwelling catheters, they should be treated empirically as described previously. Although catheter removal is usually recommended, there is little evidence that it is needed as part of the treatment of a catheter-associated UTI. It is also unclear whether intermittent catheterization is associated with a reduction in the frequency of either bacteriuria or symptomatic infections.[28]

Cystitis (manifested by dysuria, urgency, and frequency in a patient who is usually afebrile) is probably best managed with short-course (3-day) antibiotic therapy. Although more data about the efficacy of short-course therapy of lower UTIs in the elderly are needed, cost and complications are reduced and cure rates appear to be similar to those achieved with longer periods of therapy.[29,30] Single-dose therapy appears to be less effective than 3- to 6-day treatment but associated with greater patient acceptance.[30] Short-course therapy is only for women; men (because of the potential of a prostatic focus of infection) should be treated for at least 10 to 14 days.[10] A recent prospective randomized study in men found that 2 weeks of oral ciprofloxacin (500 mg twice daily) was as effective as 4 weeks. Two thirds of subjects were over the age of 50.[31] Appropriate drugs include trimethoprim-sulfamethoxazole and one of the quinolones.

PNEUMONIA

The association between aging and pneumonia has been recognized for many years. Sir William Osler (who himself was to die of bacterial pneumonia) described the disease in his textbook as "a friend of the elderly."[32] Marrie[33] reported that community-acquired pneumonia occurred 50 times as frequently in individuals older than 75 as in 15- to 19-year-olds. Among elderly residents of long-term-care facilities, the frequency of pneumonia is 6- to 10-fold higher than among community-dwelling elderly.[34] In addition to their significant associated mortality, pneumonic infections are difficult and expensive to treat. Moreover, they often herald the approach of death. In one study, half of elderly patients with community-acquired pneumonia died in the next year.[35]

The etiology of pulmonary infections in elderly individuals is somewhat different from that in younger adults. Respiratory syncytial virus (RSV) is a more common cause of pneumonia in older individuals than is generally appreciated. A recent study, conducted in 381 nursing homes in Tennessee from 1995 to 1999, indicated that RSV was responsible for approximately the same number of deaths as influenza virus.[36] These infections, which occur primarily in nursing homes, are often of rapid onset; bronchospasm may be a frequent and prominent feature.[37] Some studies have recognized that rhinoviruses may be associated with lower respiratory tract disease in the elderly, but their overall importance is uncertain.[38] Human metapneumovirus has also been reported to cause lower respiratory tract infection in elderly patients. *Chlamydophila pneumoniae* has been noted to cause an outbreak of respiratory infection in a nursing home.[39]

Streptococcus pneumoniae, gram-negative bacilli, and *Haemophilus influenzae* were the most commonly identified bacterial pathogens in a study of elderly individuals hospitalized with pneumonia.[40] Although most studies of the etiology of pneumonia in the elderly are limited by the use of expectorated sputum as the source of culture, in general, in both community and institutional settings, the risk of gram-negative and S. aureus pulmonary infection appears to be increased in the elderly.[41]

As with other infections in the aged, the clinical presentation of pneumonia is usually muted. Temperatures of patients with bacteremic pneumococcal pneumonia who are elderly are lower than those of younger individuals, and cough and fever may be absent in elderly patients with pneumonia.[42] Very elderly patients (>80 years) are more likely to be afebrile or have changed mental status and less likely to complain of pleuritic chest pain, headache, or myalgia than younger patients.[43]

It is important to culture the blood and sputum of elderly patients with apparent pneumonia. However, sputum is often difficult to collect, and in some seriously ill elderly individuals, it may be appropriate to attempt to obtain a specimen for culture that does not pass through the oropharynx (e.g., by bronchoalveolar lavage or by use of a covered brush). However, such invasive procedures for obtaining sputum for special stains and cultures are generally reserved for circumstances in which microorganisms other than common bacterial pathogens are being considered.

Empirical management of pneumonia in elderly individuals requires treatment with an antimicrobial agent that is effective against a broad range of possible causative organisms.[44] One of the third-generation cephalosporins that has good activity against S. pneumoniae, S. aureus, H. influenzae, and common gram-negative organisms (e.g., cefotaxime or ceftriaxone) is appropriate for community-acquired infections in hospitalized patients. Some authorities would recommend adding azithromycin or using a fluoroquinolone for coverage of atypical bacteria, such as Legionella pneumophila and C. pneumoniae.

Among hospitalized patients, those older than 65 developed pneumonia twice as often as younger patients.[45] Risk factors for nosocomial pneumonia included poor nutrition, endotracheal intubation, and neuromuscular disease. Interestingly, mortality of patients with respiratory disease in intensive care units is not predictable on the basis of age alone but requires examination of comorbid conditions.[46] In hospital-acquired infections, initial broad-spectrum coverage that includes P. aeruginosa (e.g., a carbapenem or a broad-spectrum β-lactam with an aminoglycoside) is appropriate. Although published data from studies of the elderly are limited so far, the broad-spectrum quinolones are promising agents for nursing home–acquired pneumonia. Improved clinical outcome may result from treatment that avoids hospital transfer.[47]

Efforts to prevent pneumonia are very important, particularly in the frail elderly. These should include immunization with the pneumococcal polysaccharide vaccine and influenza vaccine.[48] Both of these immunizations are being used with greater frequency in recent years. A 1999 study of U.S. adults 65 years of age or older found that 66.9% had received an influenza immunization in the prior year and 54.1% a pneumococcal immunization at some time.[49]

Data that support the use of influenza vaccine in the aged have accumulated rapidly. Cohort studies of elderly members of managed care organizations have demonstrated substantial decline in the incidence of both hospitalization and death among those immunized against influenza.[50,51] Greatest reductions were among the high-risk elderly. Studies have also found reductions in mortality from causes other than influenza (e.g., cardiac disease and stroke) among immunized elderly.[52,53] Methods to control influenza during an outbreak should include limiting contact between elderly individuals and people with symptoms of respiratory illness. Use of amantadine, rimantadine, or oseltamivir may reduce the duration of influenza virus infection and may prevent the development of influenza when given as prophylaxis to patients in nursing homes.[54]

The evidence that pneumococcal polysaccharide vaccine reduces morbidity and mortality from disease caused by S. pneumoniae in the elderly is less clear.[55] One recent study of a cohort of 47,000 individuals 65 years of age or older found that the risk of pneumococcal bacteremia was reduced by immunization but the risk of pneumococcal pneumonia was not.[56] Data from the Centers for Disease Control and Prevention (CDC) indicate a decline in invasive pneumococcal disease among the elderly in the years from 1996 through 2001. This is thought to be due to the use of the protein-polysaccharide vaccine among young children, with subsequent benefit to elderly individuals who come into contact with young children.[57]

TUBERCULOSIS

Tuberculosis is the most common reportable disease among persons older than 65 years.[58] Some 23% of tuberculosis cases in the United States between 1993 and 2000 were in patients in this age group.[59] Among elderly in the community, the incidence is twice that in the general population, and in residents of nursing homes, the incidence is four times that in the community.

Usually development of disease in the elderly reflects reactivation of infection acquired at a younger age and is due to declining cellular immunity associated with aging. In addition, poor nutrition, the increased occurrence of diabetes and other diseases common to the elderly, and use of corticosteroid therapy may further exacerbate immunodeficiency and increase the risk of reactivation of Mycobacterium tuberculosis infection.

Tuberculin testing is commonly required on admission to long-term care facilities. Testing should be done using intradermal (the Mantoux technique) administration of purified protein derivative. The use of a two-step technique is probably appropriate in older patients.[60] For individuals who have positive purified protein derivative tests, chest roentgenograms should be obtained and then repeated on a regular basis. Follow-up tuberculin testing and chest roentgenograms are recommended at a frequency determined by the prevalence of tuberculous disease in the community (typically at 6- to 24-month intervals).

Tuberculin-positive patients need to be closely followed.[61] Unexplained weight loss or fever, pulmonary symptoms, unexplained lymphadenopathy, or changes in renal function should be clues to the possible presence of active tuberculosis.

The key to diagnosing tuberculosis in the elderly is to maintain a high index of suspicion. It is also imperative to remember that some manifestations may be atypical.[62] In one study, fever, weight loss, night sweats, sputum production, and hemoptysis were all significantly less common in elderly patients than in younger subjects.[63] Three of four elderly patients with tuberculosis have pulmonary involvement.[64]

Preventive therapy with isoniazid is not indicated for an elderly individual who has a history of a positive tuberculin test and no other risk factors. Conversely, individuals with a recently converted tuberculin test, regardless of age, should be given isoniazid prophylaxis (see Chapter 248). Studies in Arkansas demonstrated that toxicity in an older population is uncommon. Dutt and Stead[61] reported a 4.5% incidence of nonfatal hepatitis in a group of 2000 elderly individuals. Preventive therapy should be the same as for younger individuals: administration of isoniazid at 300 mg once daily for 9 months. Patients who develop symptoms of possible isoniazid toxicity (e.g., nausea, malaise, vomiting) should stop taking the drug and have liver function tests immediately. If the transaminase level is more than five times the upper limit of normal, the drug should be discontinued permanently. If the serum transaminase is elevated threefold and the patient has gastrointestinal symptoms, hepatotoxic drugs should be held and the patient evaluated, including testing for viral hepatitis. In asymptomatic patients with an otherwise unexplained threefold elevation of transaminases, it may be reasonable to resume isoniazid with 150 mg/day for 3 days; if this is tolerated, the usual dosage can be resumed.[61]

PRESSURE SORES AND SKIN INFECTIONS

Pressure sores are most common in the seriously disabled elderly and are typically quite difficult to treat. In a study in 1990 of nearly 20,000 nursing home patients, the prevalence of pressure sores was 10.4% after a 1-year stay in a nursing home.[65] The incidence increases as a function of age.[66] Pressure sores occur primarily in individuals with impaired mobility, and the usual cause is skin necrosis resulting from ischemia.[67] The ulcer that develops may be associated with a number of infectious complications. In order of decreasing frequency, these are local infection, cellulitis of surrounding tissue, contiguous osteomyelitis, and bacteremia.[68]

Guidelines for prevention of pressure lesions in adults have been published by the American Geriatric Society.[69] Key components include monitoring patients who are at risk, reducing exposure of the skin to pressure, maintaining the skin in a clean and dry condition, and promoting good nutritional status. Therapy of pressure ulcers should include pressure relief, appropriate nutrition, and débridement. A variety of treatments have been used topically, and there is no clear evidence to favor one over another. Povidone-iodine, hydrogen peroxide, and other agents have been used. Povidone-iodine use has been associated with thyrotoxicosis.[70] Topical antimicrobial agents have not been shown to be effective. Systemic antibiotic therapy should be reserved for infected ulcers.

Most pressure ulcers in the elderly yield multiple organisms when cultured. Aerobes that are commonly recovered include staphylococci, enterococci, *Proteus mirabilis, E. coli,* and *Pseudomonas* spp. In addition, anaerobic *Peptostreptococcus, Bacteroides fragilis,* and *Clostridium* spp. are frequently isolated from these infections. Making an accurate bacteriologic diagnosis is difficult. Many of the issues involved in determining the bacteriology of an infected pressure sore are similar to those confronted in the assessment of infected diabetic foot ulcers. Swabbing the wound often yields organisms that are colonizers and not actually causes of infection. It may be most appropriate to aspirate material from the margin or base of the ulcer, directing the needle through intact skin.

A variety of empirical antibiotic regimens have been suggested for patients with pressure ulcer–associated cellulitis, osteomyelitis, or bacteremia. Bacteremia in this situation is usually caused by *P. mirabilis, S. aureus,* or *B. fragilis.*[68] In general, any regimen that is active against the majority of organisms that are usually causal is appropriate. Although a 10- to 14-day course is commonly prescribed, no studies have carefully defined the duration of therapy. Although advanced inanition is the most common cause of failure of these lesions to heal, osteomyelitis needs to be ruled out by physical examination and roentgenography. If osteomyelitis is present, it requires a more extended course of therapy. A comprehensive review of the management of pressure sores has been published.[71]

Some common types of cellulitis may be more severe and associated with increased mortality in elderly individuals compared with younger patients. In particular, outbreaks of skin infection caused by group A β-hemolytic streptococci associated with bacteremia have been reported in nursing homes in the United States.[72] Because many of these infections are fatal and because of the high costs of inpatient management, cutaneous infections in elderly patients need to be treated promptly. Skin and soft tissue infections are common in the nursing home setting; a prevalence of 5% is a reasonable estimate. Herpes zoster is also particularly common in the elderly and often associated with severe and protracted pain. Pathogenesis and therapy of this disease are discussed elsewhere in this volume (see Chapter 133).

BACTEREMIA

Probably because of the increased prevalence of chronic diseases in older individuals, bacteremic illnesses appear to be more frequent and more often associated with death. In both the hospital and the community, bacteremia is more common in the aged.[73] The presence of comorbid conditions is clearly a determinant of the mortality associated with bacteremic illness.[74]

A number of studies have pointed out the blunted clinical responses to bacteremia in elderly patients. It is clear that elderly patients may be bacteremic and remain afebrile.[75] Also, a significant proportion of patients may not have neutrophilia.[76] Weakness and altered mental status may be the presenting symptoms.

The main sources of community-acquired bacteremia in the elderly, in order of decreasing frequency, are the urinary tract, intra-abdominal sites, and lungs.[77] In long-term care facilities, the urinary tract is the most frequent source, followed by the respiratory tract.[78] Organisms most commonly recovered from patients with bacteremia associated with skin sources are *S. aureus, Staphylococcus epidermidis,* gram-negative enteric bacteria, and anaerobes.[77] Bacteria from the urinary tract are usually gram-negative enterics or enterococci; from the biliary tract, gram-negative enterics or anaerobes; and from the respiratory tract, *H. influenzae, S. pneumoniae,* group B streptococci, or gram-negative enterics. Group G streptococcal bacteremia (usually from a cutaneous source) is especially common in the aged. In one recent review, the median age of cases was 72 years.[79]

Because of their increased risk of complications and higher mortality, elderly patients should be treated as soon as a presumptive diagnosis of bacteremia is considered. Selection of a proper antibiotic regimen is guided by the same principles as for younger individuals. It is important to remember that elderly patients eliminate most antibiotics more slowly than younger individuals; dosages should be adjusted accordingly. Aminoglycosides, because of the increasing potential for toxicity with age, are best used with caution.[80]

INFECTIVE ENDOCARDITIS

Infective endocarditis is especially common in elderly individuals. In most of the recent studies of endocarditis, more than 50% of patients were 60 or more years of age.[81-83] The increased incidence of endocarditis in the elderly seems to be related to prolonged survival of patients with cardiac valvular disease and the use of prosthetic heart valves, intravascular monitoring devices, and surgically implanted materials.

The diagnosis of infective endocarditis may be particularly difficult in the elderly. Often, presenting signs and symptoms are nonspecific, and development of weakness, malaise, weight loss, confusion, and so on may be the only evidence of infection. Peripheral vascular signs and splenomegaly are both less common in the elderly than in younger patients.[84] In one study, more than two thirds of cases of endocarditis in elderly patients were misdiagnosed at the time of admission.[85] Musculoskeletal manifestations are often mistakenly ascribed to primary rheumatologic disorders, and heart murmurs are considered benign or thought to result from calcific lesions associated with aging.

Several studies suggest that older patients have an increased frequency of endocarditis caused by gram-positive organisms.[81,82] These include *Enterococcus faecalis* (usually from the urinary tract) and *Streptococcus bovis* (usually from a colonic source).[86] It is important to remember the association of *S. bovis* with gastrointestinal carcinoma. In individuals with prosthetic valves, the likelihood is high that the infection is caused by staphylococci or enterococci.

As in younger individuals, prompt empirical therapy is needed for patients with presumed endocarditis who appear to be seriously ill. A regimen that is appropriate for initial therapy consists of vancomycin and gentamicin. Subsequently, therapy should be guided by results of blood culture and antibiotic susceptibility tests. As in younger patients, careful observation is required for possible complications, including recurrent episodes of fever and congestive heart failure. Although the therapy of infective endocarditis in an elderly individual is not different from that in a younger person (see Chapter 74), two points need to be emphasized. First, because of less rapid elimination of many antimicrobials in elderly patients, care needs to be taken in dosing and monitoring levels of potentially toxic drugs. Second, because elderly patients do not tolerate long hospital stays well, every effort should be made to administer parenteral therapy on an outpatient basis.

In the elderly, cardiac complications of endocarditis such as congestive heart failure are increased by nonvalvular causes of decompensation such as myocardial infarction, conduction abnormalities, arrhythmias, myocarditis, or myocardial abscess. Elderly persons are prone to arterial embolization, the second most common complication of infective endocarditis. The mortality associated with infective endocarditis is substantially greater in elderly than in younger patients, and permanent disability and a need for long-term care are common outcomes.[86]

Antibiotic prophylaxis to prevent development of endocarditis is important in older individuals. This topic has been reviewed in a statement regarding prevention published by the American Heart Association[87] (see Chapter 76).

INFECTIOUS DIARRHEA

Diarrhea is a significant cause of morbidity and mortality in the elderly. One study found that 51% of deaths caused by diarrhea over a 9-year period occurred in individuals older than 74.[88] A disproportionate share of diarrheal deaths occurred in elderly nursing home residents.[88]

Older patients may be at increased risk for *Salmonella* infections because of achlorhydria, decreased intestinal motility associated with medications, other coexistent gastrointestinal diseases, and more frequent use of antibiotics. Some authors have suggested that patients older than 50 should be considered for antibiotic therapy for uncomplicated *Salmonella* gastroenteritis. This assumes that older patients may not tolerate these infections well and that, if bacteremic, they may be at increased risk for vascular infection caused by salmonellae. The quinolones have assumed an important role in the empirical therapy of acute gastroenteritis when a bacterial etiology is suspected, and this class of agents is usually active against *Salmonella* spp.

Because antibiotics shorten the duration of *Shigella* gastroenteritis, therapy is indicated to reduce the risk of fluid and electrolyte imbalance in the elderly. Antibiotic therapy is also recommended for diarrhea caused by *Campylobacter jejuni*, invasive *E. coli*, *Vibrio parahaemolyticus*, and *Yersinia enterocolitica* (see Chapter 93).

In the nursing home setting, outbreaks of diarrhea occur relatively commonly during the winter months. Both the Norwalk agent and rotavirus have been implicated in these episodes.[89] There are also substantial data associating *Clostridium difficile* diarrhea with residence in a long-term care institution.[90] This organism is increasingly recognized as a cause of sporadic cases of diarrhea in the elderly. It is the most common reportable cause of diarrhea in the elderly in Great Britain.[91] Enterohemorrhagic *E. coli* (O157:H7) has been reported to cause outbreaks of gastroenteritis in long-term care institutions.[92] *Cryptosporidium* is also newly appreciated as a cause of diarrhea in the aged.[93] A recent study suggests that this organism may be associated with more severe disease, a shorter incubation period, and a higher risk of secondary transmission in the aged.[94] Although *Candida* spp. have been implicated as a cause of diarrhea in elderly patients,[95] isolation of this fungus from stool, even in high colony counts, appears to indicate colonization and not infection. Microsporidia have recently been documented as a cause of chronic diarrhea in the elderly.[96] A study from China suggests that severity of hookworm infestation correlates with age.[97]

CENTRAL NERVOUS SYSTEM INFECTIONS

Meningitis

As is true of other serious infections in the aged, the case-fatality ratio of meningitis is higher than in younger individuals. In a recent study of pneumococcal meningitis, mortality in patients over 60 was twice that of younger patients (36.7% vs. 17.5%).[98]

It is well established that the organisms that cause meningitis in elderly individuals differ from the distribution of bacteria seen in younger adults.[99] The major causes of meningitis in the aged are *S. pneumoniae*, *Listeria monocytogenes*, gram-negative bacilli, and *Streptococcus agalactiae*. Disease caused by *Neisseria meningitidis* and *H. influenzae* is uncommon in elderly patients.[100,101] As suggested in a number of studies, viral meningitis is also relatively uncommon in the elderly.

The signs and symptoms of bacterial meningitis in the elderly are muted. Nuchal rigidity is often found on examination of elderly patients who do not have bacterial meningitis.[101,102] Usually, these patients have coexistent neurologic deficits. Elderly patients who have nuchal rigidity in the absence of other neurologic problems should not be dismissed as having "osteoarthritis of the cervical spine" but should be intensively investigated for possible meningitis. Other symptoms suggestive of the diagnosis include change in mental status and fever.[12]

Several reviews of meningitis suggest that the laboratory findings for elderly people do not differ from those for younger individuals. Complications, however, are more frequent in older individuals.[100,101] Gorse and co-workers[101] found that the frequency of complications (including neurologic complications, pneumonia, and UTIs) was approximately twice as high in patients older than 65 as in younger patients.

The empirical treatment of meningitis in elderly patients needs to cover *S. pneumoniae*, *L. monocytogenes*, and gram-negative bacilli. Because *L. monocytogenes* is not susceptible to cephalosporins, an appropriate empirical regimen includes ampicillin with cefotaxime or ceftriaxone. In areas where cephalosporin-resistant *S. pneumoniae* have been encountered, vancomycin should be used empirically until culture and antibiotic susceptibility results are known.

Arboviral Infections

West Nile virus infection was first recognized in the United States in 1999 and in subsequent years has become widely distributed throughout the United States and Canada (see Chapter 149). It is clear that this virus has a major predilection for causing serious infections in older individuals. In the initial outbreak in 1999 in New York City, 88% of hospitalized patients were 50 years of age or older; the median age in this population was 71 years.[103]

Most cases of the disease are not apparent, perhaps not even symptomatic. Fever is the only manifestation in perhaps half the symptomatic cases. Only half of the symptomatic cases seek medical help. The age distribution of these more common but less serious cases is unknown. Data from the 1999 outbreak in New York City suggested that the frequency of severe neurologic disease, compared with patients from birth to 19 years of age, was 10 times greater in individuals 50 to 59, and 43 times higher in those at least 80 years of age. The same outbreak data suggested that persons 75 years and older were nine times more likely to die of their illness than younger individuals.[104] The basis for this increased severity of infection in the elderly is unknown and contrasts sharply with other arbovirus infections.

SEPTIC ARTHRITIS

About 25% of persons with septic arthritis are older than 60. The mortality in the elderly is higher, and recovery of joint function is less satisfactory. Septic arthritis is commonly associated with preexisting rheumatoid arthritis, prosthetic joints, or degenerative arthritis.[105] These associations, as well as with diseases such as diabetes mellitus and malignancy and with cytotoxic or systemic corticosteroid therapy, suggest that immunologic defects may play an important role in the pathogenesis of septic arthritis in the elderly.

The knee joint is most frequently involved, followed by the wrist and shoulder joint. Although most elderly patients with septic arthritis complain of a painful, swollen joint, in contrast to younger patients, they are seldom totally immobilized by pain and muscle spasm is infrequent. As in younger patients, the most commonly isolated organism is *S. aureus*, but gram-negative bacilli are also frequent causes in the elderly. In addition, septic arthritis is associated more frequently with osteomyelitis in the older patient.

FEVER AND FEVER OF UNDETERMINED ORIGIN

Many elderly persons appear to have lower body temperatures than are traditionally accepted as normal and consequently have a diminished febrile response to infection.[106,107] In elderly individuals, an oral temperature of greater than 99° F should be considered elevated. However, 95% of elderly patients who have infection show some febrile response.[108] One study examined the importance of fever in 470 consecutive elderly patients who were seen in an emergency room with temperatures of 100.0° F or greater.[109] Three quarters of these patients were classified by the authors as seriously ill. The most frequent diagnoses included pneumonia (24%), UTI (21.7%), and septicemia (12.8%). Many of these patients did not have high fever, tachycardia, leukocytosis, or tachypnea.

Esposito and Gleckman[110] found that 36% of their elderly patients with fever of undetermined origin (FUO) had infection. Intra-abdominal infection was the most common infectious cause of FUO in their series. Fifty percent of these FUO cases were caused by neoplasm and connective tissue disorders in about equal numbers.[110] Over half of the neoplasms were lymphomas, two thirds of which were diagnosed on laparotomy. Most other neoplasms were renal or hepatobiliary in origin. Sixty-five percent of the connective tissue diseases were giant cell arteritis, predominantly in women. Polyarteritis nodosa was diagnosed in 20%.

ANTIMICROBIAL CONSIDERATIONS

Although the elderly are the group most likely to receive antibiotic therapy when hospitalized and in nursing homes, there has been little accurate information about the effects of aging on the pharmacokinetics and toxicity of antimicrobial agents until the past decade.[111,112] Physiologic changes that accompany advanced age may significantly affect the absorption, distribution, plasma protein binding, metabolism, and elimination of many antibiotics. The risk of toxicity of some antimicrobials is also increased in the elderly. Newer antibiotics have been studied more extensively in older patients. The phenomenon of "polypharmacy," which is so common in this age group, greatly increases the chances of drug interactions. Extensive information about the use of antibiotics in nursing homes has been published.[113-115]

Few studies have considered the relationship between age and prevalence of infections caused by antibiotic-resistant organisms. Recent U.S. data document a marked increase in fluoroquinolone use in older individuals (Fig. 314-1).[116] One Japanese study points to a marked increase in prevalence of fluoroquinolone resistance with increasing age.[117] Given the common usage of fluoroquinolones in the treatment of UTI and pneumonia in the elderly, one can predict that emergence of resistance of *S. pneumoniae* and other pathogens to this class of antibiotics will first be seen as a major problem in this age group.

Infection, and the need for antibiotic therapy, is common among elderly patients as the end of life approaches. Whether to prescribe antibiotics in these situations is an issue that has not been extensively examined. The role of ethical considerations in the management of these patients has recently been reviewed.[118]

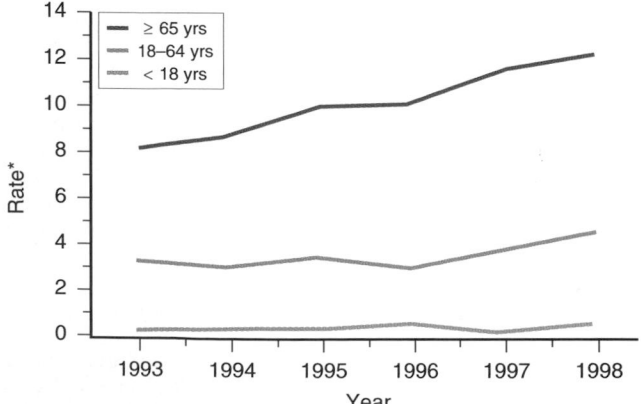

*Per 100 persons.

FIGURE 314-1. Fluoroquinolone prescriptions, by age group—United States, 1993-1998. *(From Centers for Disease Control and Prevention. Resistance of* Streptococcus pneumoniae *fluoroquinolones—United States 1995-1999. MMWR Morb Mortal Wkly Rep. 2001;50:800-804.)*

IMMUNIZATIONS

Important information about several travel-related immunization issues in the elderly has recently been reviewed. The most important of these considerations are highlighted here. As noted, many vaccines have not been evaluated in elderly individuals.[119] In general, development of protective antibody levels to most vaccines is lower in elderly individuals, most likely reflecting the waning of immune responses associated with aging.

Hepatitis A and B Vaccines. Data suggest that the development of protective antibody with these vaccines tends to occur more slowly with increasing age. Peak titers are lower in the elderly with both vaccines. The clinical importance of this is unclear.

Yellow Fever Vaccine. A study from the CDC found that elderly individuals are at significantly increased risk of severe illness after yellow fever vaccination. The mechanism and incidence of this reaction are not yet known. Data from the Vaccine Adverse Events Reporting System also suggests that these reactions occur with increasing frequency with increasing age.

Rabies Vaccine. Two studies suggest that rabies vaccine antibody titers are substantially lower in older subjects. As is true with hepatitis immunizations, the significance of this is unknown.[120,121]

PREVENTION

A number of studies suggest that age per se is not an independent risk factor for many types of infection. Whereas many studies of infections in elderly populations comprise patients who have suffered the consequences of age-related physiologic impairment (i.e., senescence), a majority of elderly people are healthy and living independently at home. Of Americans who are in the age group 65 to 74, 89% are fully functioning and robust. Of those 75 to 84 years of age, 73% enjoy this health status, and 40% of individuals 85 years of age or older continue to have aged successfully.[4]

Prevention of infection in the aged is increasingly viewed as a need to prevent comorbidities and nutritional deficiencies that contribute to the pathogenesis of infection. In addition to immunizations (with influenza, pneumococcal, and tetanus vaccines), mounting evidence supports the value of adequate nutrition, exercise, social engagement, and continued involvement in productive activities in the attainment of a long and qualitatively rich life.[4]

REFERENCES

1. Saltzman RL, Peterson PK. Immunodeficiency of the elderly. Rev Infect Dis. 1987;9:1127-1139.
2. Ben-Yehuda A, Weksler ME. Host resistance and the immune system. Clin Geriatr Med. 1992;8:701-711.
3. Muhlberger N, Jelinek T, Behrens RH, et al. Age as a risk factor for severe manifestations and fatal outcome of falciparum malaria in European patients: Observations from TropNetEurop and SIMPID Surveillance Data. Clin Infect Dis. 2003;36:990-995.
4. Rowe JW, Kahn RL. Successful Aging. New York: Pantheon; 1990.
5. Crossley K, Peterson PK. Infections in the elderly—New developments. In: Remington JS, Swartz MN, eds. Current Clinical Topics in Infectious Diseases. Malden, MA: Blackwell Science; 1998:75-100.
6. Munoz E, Rosner F, Chalfin D, et al. Financial risk and hospital cost for elderly patients: Age- and non–age-stratified medical diagnosis related groups. Arch Intern Med. 1988;148:909-912.
7. Irvine PW, Van Buren N, Crossley K. Causes for hospitalization of nursing home residents: The role of infection. J Am Geriatr Soc. 1984;32:103-107.
8. Norman DC, Toledo SD. Infections in elderly persons. Clin Geriatr Med. 1992;8:713-719.
9. Sobel JD, Kaye D. Urinary tract infections. In: Mandell GL, Douglas RG Jr, Bennett JE, eds. Principles and Practice of Infectious Diseases. 3rd ed. New York: Churchill Livingstone; 1990:582-611.
10. Lipsky BA. Urinary tract infections in men: Epidemiology, pathophysiology, diagnosis, and treatment. Ann Intern Med. 1989;110:138-150.
11. Nicolle LE. Asymptomatic bacteriuria in the elderly. Infect Dis Clin North Am. 1997;11:647.
12. Baldassarre JS, Kaye D. Special problems of urinary tract infection in the elderly. Med Clin North Am. 1991;75:375-390.
13. Nicolle LE, Bjornson J, Harding GKM, et al. Bacteriuria in elderly institutionalized men. N Engl J Med. 1983;309:1420-1425.

14. Nicolle LE, Mayhew WJ, Bryan L. Prospective randomized comparison of therapy and no therapy for asymptomatic bacteriuria in institutionalized elderly women. Am J Med. 1987;83:27-33.

15. Mims AD, Norman DC, Yamamura RH, et al. Clinically inapparent (asymptomatic) bacteriuria in ambulatory elderly men: Epidemiological, clinical, and microbiological findings. J Am Geriatr Soc. 1990;38:1209.

16. Boscia JA, Kobasa WD, Knight RA, et al. Epidemiology of bacteriuria in an elderly ambulatory population. Am J Med. 1986;80:208-214.

17. Gleckman RA. Urinary tract infection. Clin Geriatr Med. 1992;8:793-819.

18. Kasviki-Charvati P, Drolette-Kefakis B, Papanayiotou PC, et al. Turnover of bacteriuria in old age. Age Ageing. 1982;11:169-174.

19. Sourander LB, Kasanen A. A 5-year follow-up of bacteriuria in the aged. Gerontol Clin. 1972;14:274-281.

20. Gleckman R, Blagg N, Hibert D, et al. Acute pyelonephritis in the elderly. South Med J. 1982;75:551-554.

21. Raz R, Stamm WE. A controlled trial of intravaginal estriol in postmenopausal women with recurrent urinary tract infections. N Engl J Med. 1993;329:753-756.

22. Ouslander JG, Greendale GA, Uman G, et al. Effects of oral estrogen and progestin on the lower urinary tract among female nursing home residents. J Am Geriatr Soc. 2001;49:803-807.

23. Raz R, Colodner R, Rohana Y, et al. Effectiveness of estriol-containing vaginal pessaries and nitrofurantoin macrocrystal therapy in the prevention of recurrent urinary tract infection in postmenopausal women. Clin Infect Dis. 2003;36:1362-1368.

24. Avorn J, Monane M, Gurwitz JH, et al. Reduction of bacteriuria and pyuria after ingestion of cranberry juice. JAMA. 1994;271:751-754.

25. Warren HW. Catheter-associated urinary tract infections. Infect Dis Clin North Am. 1997;11:609-622.

26. Ouslander JG, Schapira M, Schnelle JF, Fingold S. Pyuria and asymptomatic bacteriuria in elderly ambulatory women. Ann Intern Med. 1989;110:404-405.

27. Warren JW, Damron D, Tenney JH, et al. Fever, bacteremia, and death as complications of bacteriuria in women with long-term urethral catheters. J Infect Dis. 1987;155:1151-1158.

28. Nicolle LE. Prevention and treatment of urinary catheter-related infections in older patients. Drugs Aging. 1994;4:379-391.

29. Saginur R, Nicolle LE. Single-dose compared with 3-day norfloxacin treatment of uncomplicated urinary tract infection in women. Canadian Infectious Diseases Society Clinical Trials Study Group. Arch Intern Med. 1992;152:1233-1237.

30. Lutters M, Vogt N. Antibiotic duration for treating uncomplicated, symptomatic lower urinary tract infections in elderly women. Cochrane Database Syst Rev. 2002;3:CD001535.

31. Ulleryd P, Sandberg T. Ciprofloxacin for 2 or 4 weeks in the treatment of febrile urinary tract infection in men: A randomized trial with a 1 year follow-up. Scand J Infect Dis. 2003;35:34-39.

32. Osler W, ed. The Principles and Practice of Medicine. 3rd ed. New York: Appleton; 1898:109.

33. Marrie TJ. Epidemiology of community-acquired pneumonia in the elderly. Semin Respir Infect. 1990;5:260.

34. Marrie TJ. Pneumonia in the long-term-care facility. Infect Control Hosp Epidemiol. 2002;23:159-164.

35. Kaplan V, Clermont G, Griffin MF, et al. Pneumonia: Still the old man's friend? Arch Intern Med. 2003;163:317-323.

36. Ellis SE, Coffey CS, Mitchel EF Jr, et al. Influenza- and respiratory syncytial virus-associated morbidity and mortality in the nursing home population. J Am Geriatr Soc. 2003;51:761-767.

37. Mlinaric-Galinovic G, Falsey AR, Walsh EE. Respiratory syncytial virus infection in the elderly. Eur J Clin Microbiol Infect Dis. 1996;15:777-781.

38. Nicholson KG, Kent J, Hammersley V, Cancio E. Risk factors for lower respiratory complications of rhinovirus infections in elderly people living in the community: Prospective cohort study. BMJ. 1996;313:1119-1123.

39. Troy CJ, Peeling RW, Ellis AG, et al. *Chlamydia pneumoniae* as a new source of infectious outbreaks in nursing homes. JAMA. 1997;277:1214-1218.

40. Rello J, Rodriguez R, Jubert P, Alvarez B. Severe community-acquired pneumonia in the elderly: Epidemiology and prognosis. Study Group for Severe Community-Acquired Pneumonia. Clin Infect Dis. 1996;23:723-728.

41. Crossley KB, Thurn JR. Nursing home-acquired pneumonia. Semin Respir Infect. 1989;4:64-72.

42. Bentley DW. Bacterial pneumonia in the elderly: Clinical features, diagnosis, etiology, and treatment. Gerontology. 1984;30:297-307.

43. Fernandez-Sabe N, Carratala J, Roson B, et al. Community-acquired pneumonia in very elderly patients: Causative organisms, clinical characteristics, and outcomes. Medicine (Baltimore). 2003;82:159-169.

44. Norman DC. Pneumonia in the elderly: Empiric antimicrobial therapy. Geriatrics. 1991;46:26-32.

45. Hanson LC, Weber DJ, Rutala WA, et al. Risk factors for nosocomial pneumonia in the elderly. Am J Med. 1992;92:161-166.

46. Heuser MD, Case LD, Ettinger WH. Mortality in intensive care patients with respiratory disease: Is age important? Arch Intern Med. 1992;152:1683-1688.

47. Fried TR, Gillick MR, Lipsitz LA. Short-term functional outcomes of long-term care residents with pneumonia treated with and without hospital transfer. J Am Geriatr Soc. 1997;45:302-306.

48. Monto AS, Terpenning MS. The value of influenza and pneumococcal vaccines in the elderly. Drugs Aging. 1996;6:445-451.

49. Centers for Disease Control and Prevention. Influenza and pneumococcal vaccination levels among persons aged ≥ 65 years—United States, 1999. MMWR Morb Mortal Wkly Rep. 2001;50:532-537.

50. Hak E, Nordin J, Wei F, et al. Influence of high-risk medical conditions on the effectiveness of influenza vaccination among elderly members of 3 large managed-care organizations. Clin Infect Dis. 2002;35:370-377.

51. Voordouw BC, van der Linden PD, Simonian S, et al. Influenza vaccination in community-dwelling elderly: Impact on mortality and influenza-associated morbidity. Arch Intern Med. 2003;163:1089-1094.

52. Nichol KL, Nordin J, Mullooly J, et al. Influenza vaccination and reduction in hospitalizations for cardiac disease and stroke among the elderly. N Engl J Med. 2003;348:1322-1332.

53. Christenson B, Lundbergh P, Hedlund J, Ortqvist A. Effects of a large-scale intervention with influenza and 23-valent pneumococcal vaccines in adults aged 65 years or older: A prospective study. Lancet. 2001;357:1008-1011.

54. Arden NH, Patriarca PA, Fasano MB, et al. The roles of vaccination and amantadine prophylaxis in controlling an outbreak of influenza A (H3N2) in a nursing home. Arch Intern Med. 1988;148:865-868.

55. Artz AS, Ershler WB, Longo DL. Pneumococcal vaccination and revaccination of older adults. Clin Microbiol Rev. 2003;16:308-318.

56. Jackson LA, Neuzil KM, Yu O, et al. Effectiveness of pneumococcal polysaccharide vaccine in older adults. N Engl J Med. 2003;348:1747-1755.

57. Whitney CG, Farley MM, Hadler J, et al. Decline in invasive pneumococcal disease after the introduction of protein-polysaccharide conjugate vaccine. N Engl J Med. 2003;348:1737-1746.

58. Centers for Disease Control and Prevention. Ten leading nationally notifiable infectious diseases—United States, 1995. MMWR Morb Mortal Wkly Rep. 1996;45:883-884.

59. Centers for Disease Control and Prevention. Progressing toward tuberculosis elimination in low-incidence areas of the United States: Recommendations of the Advisory Council for the Elimination of Tuberculosis. MMWR Morb Mortal Wkly Rep. 2002;51:1-14.

60. Stead WW, Dutt AK. Tuberculosis in elderly persons. Annu Rev Med. 1991;42:267-276.

61. Dutt AK, Stead WW. Tuberculosis. Clin Geriatr Med. 1992;8:761-775.

62. Davies P. Tuberculosis in the elderly: Epidemiology and optimal management. Drugs Aging. 1996;8:436-444.

63. Alvarez S, Shell C, Berk SL. Pulmonary tuberculosis in elderly men. Am J Med. 1987;82:602-606.

64. Rajagopalan S. Tuberculosis and aging: A global health problem. Clin Infect Dis. 2001;33:1034-1039.

65. Brandeis GH, Morris JN, Nash DJ, et al. The epidemiology and natural history of pressure ulcers in elderly nursing home residents. JAMA. 1990;264:2905.

66. Margolis DJ, Bilker W, Knauss J, et al. The incidence and prevalence of pressure ulcers among elderly patients in general medical practice. Ann Epidemiol. 2002;12:321-325.

67. Kertesz D, Chow AW. Infected pressure and diabetic ulcers. Clin Geriatr Med. 1992;8:835-852.

68. Bryan CS, Dew CE, Reynolds KL. Bacteremia associated with decubitus ulcers. Arch Intern Med. 1983;143:2093.

69. AGS Clinical Practice Committee. Pressure ulcers in adults: Prediction and prevention. J Am Geriatr Soc. 1996;44:1118-1119.

70. Shetty KR, Duthie EH Jr. Thyrotoxicosis induced by topical iodine application. Arch Intern Med. 1990;150:2400-2401.

71. Livesley NJ, Chow AW. Infected pressure ulcers in elderly individuals. Clin Infect Dis. 2002;35:1390-1396.

72. Auerbach SB, Schwartz B, Williams D, et al. Outbreak of invasive group A streptococcal infections in a nursing home: Lessons on prevention and control. Arch Intern Med. 1992;152:1017-1022.

73. McBean M, Rajamani S. Increasing rates of hospitalization due to septicemia in the US elderly population, 1986-1997. J Infect Dis. 2001;183:596-603.

74. Meyers BR, Sherman E, Mendelson MH, et al. Bloodstream infections in the elderly. Am J Med. 1989;86:379-384.

75. Gleckman R, Hibert D. Afebrile bacteremia: A phenomenon in geriatric patients. JAMA. 1982;248:1478-1481.

76. Chassagne P, Perol M-B, Doucet J, et al. Is presentation of bacteremia in the elderly the same as in younger patients? Am J Med. 1996;100:65-70.

77. Leibovici L. Bacteraemia in the very old. Drugs Aging. 1995;6:456-464.

78. Mylotte JM, Tayara A, Goodnough S. Epidemiology of bloodstream infection in nursing home residents: Evaluation in a large cohort from multiple homes. Clin Infect Dis. 2002;35:1484-1490.

79. Lewthwaite P, Parsons HK, Bates CJ, et al. Group G streptococcal bacteraemia: An opportunistic infection associated with immune senescence. Scand J Infect Dis. 2002;34:83-87.

80. Morike K, Schwab M, Klotz U. Use of aminoglycosides in elderly patients. Drugs Aging. 1997;10:259-277.

81. Terpenning MS, Buggy BP, Kauffman CA. Infective endocarditis: Clinical features in young and elderly patients. Am J Med. 1987;83:626-634.

82. Watanakunakorn C, Burkert T. Infective endocarditis at a large community teaching hospital, 1980-1990: A review of 210 episodes. Medicine (Baltimore). 1993;72:90-102.

83. Van der Meer JTM, Thompson J, Valkenburg HA, Michel MF. Epidemiology of bacterial endocarditis in the Netherlands. Arch Intern Med. 1992;152:1863-1868.

84. Cantrell M, Yoshikawa TT. Aging and infective endocarditis. J Am Geriatr Soc. 1983;31:216-222.

85. Terpenning MS, Buggy BP, Kauffman CA. Infective endocarditis: Clinical features in young and elderly patients. Am J Med. 1987;83:626.

86. Selton-Suty C, Hoen B, Grentzinger A, et al. Clinical and bacteriological characteristics of infective endocarditis in the elderly. Heart. 1997;77:260-263.

87. Dajani AS, Taubert KA, Wilson W, et al. Prevention of bacterial endocarditis: Recommendations by the American Heart Association. JAMA. 1997;277:1794-1801.

88. Lew JF, Glass RI, Gangarosa RE, et al. Diarrheal deaths in the United States, 1979 through 1987. JAMA. 1991;265:3280-3284.

89. Augustin AK, Simor ASE, Shorrock C, McCausland J. Outbreaks of gastroenteritis due to Norwalk-like virus in two long-term care facilities for the elderly. Can J Infect Control. 1995;10:111-113.

90. Bentley DW. *Clostridium difficile*-associated disease in long-term care facilities. Infect Control Hosp Epidemiol. 1990;11:434-438.

91. Wilcox MH. Cleaning up *Clostridium difficile* infection. Lancet. 1996;348:767-769.

92. Ryan CA, Tauxe RV, Hosek GW, et al. *Escherichia coli* O157:H7 diarrhea in a nursing home: Clinical, epidemiological, and pathological findings. J Infect Dis. 1986;154:631-638.

93. Neill MA, Rice SK, Ahmad NV, Flanigan TP. Cryptosporidiosis: An unrecognized cause of diarrhea in elderly hospitalized patients. Clin Infect Dis. 1996;22:168-170.

94. Naumova EN, Egorov AI, Morris RD, Griffiths JK. The elderly and waterborne *Cryptosporidium* infection: Gastroenteritis hospitalizations before and during the 1993 Milwaukee outbreak. Emerg Infect Dis. 2003;9:418-425.

95. Danna PL, Urban C, Bellin E, et al. Role of *Candida* in pathogenesis of antibiotic-associated diarrhoea in elderly inpatients. Lancet. 1991;337:511-514.

96. Lores B, Lopez-Miragaya I, Arias C, et al. Intestinal microsporidiosis due to *Enterocytozoon bieneusi* in elderly human immunodeficiency virus–negative patients from Vigo, Spain. Clin Infect Dis. 2002;34:918-921.

97. Bethony J, Chen J, Lin S, et al. Emerging patterns of hookworm infection: Influence of aging on the intensity of *Necator* infection in Hainan Province, People's Republic of China. Clin Infect Dis. 2002;35:1336-1344.

98. Kastenbauer S, Pfister HW. Pneumococcal meningitis in adults: Spectrum of complications and prognostic factors in a series of 87 cases. Brain. 2003;126:1015-1025.

99. Choi C. Bacterial meningitis. Clin Geriatr Med. 1992;8:889-901.

100. Behrman RE, Meyers BR, Mendelson MH, et al. Central nervous system infections in the elderly. Arch Intern Med. 1989;149:1596-1599.

101. Gorse GJ, Thrupp LD, Nudleman KL, et al. Bacterial meningitis in the elderly. Arch Intern Med. 1984;144:1603-1607.

102. Choi C. Bacterial meningitis in aging adults. Clin Infect Dis. 2001;33:1380-1385.

103. Nash D, Mostashari F, Fine A, et al. The outbreak of West Nile virus infection in the New York City area in 1999. N Engl J Med. 2001;344:1807-1814.

104. Peterson LR, Marfin AA. West Nile virus: A primer for the clinician. Ann Intern Med. 2002;137:173-179.

105. McGuire NM, Kauffman CA. Septic arthritis in the elderly. J Am Geriatr Soc. 1985;33:170-174.

106. Downton JH, Andrews K, Puxty JAH. "Silent" pyrexia in the elderly. Age Ageing. 1987;16:41-44.

107. Fox RH, MacGibbon R, Davies L, et al. Problem of the old and the cold. Br Med J. 1973;1:21-24.

108. McAlpine CH, Martin BJ, Lennox IM, et al. Pyrexia in infection in the elderly. Age Ageing. 1986;15:230-234.

109. Marco CA, Schoenfeld CN, Hansen KN, et al. Fever in geriatric emergency patients: Clinical features associated with serious illness. Ann Emerg Med. 1995;26:18-24.

110. Esposito AL, Gleckman RA. Fever of unknown origin in the elderly. J Am Geriatr Soc. 1978;26:498-505.

111. Borrego F, Gleckman R. Principles of antibiotic prescribing in the elderly. Drugs Aging. 1997;11:7-18.

112. Norrby SR. Antibiotic therapy in aging patients. Bull N Y Acad Med. 1987;63:519-532.

113. Beers MH, Ouslander JG, Rollingher I, et al. Explicit criteria for determining inappropriate medication use in nursing home residents. Arch Intern Med. 1991;151:1825-1832.

114. Warren JW, Palumbo FB, Fitterman L, et al. Incidence and characteristics of antibiotic use in aged nursing home patients. J Am Geriatr Soc. 1991;39:963-972.

115. Mulligan T. Parenteral antibiotic therapy for patients in nursing homes. Rev Infect Dis. 1991;13(Suppl 2):S180-S183.

116. Centers for Disease Control and Prevention. Resistance of *Streptococcus pneumoniae* to fluoroquinolones—United States 1995-1999. MMWR Morb Mortal Wkly Rep. 2001;50:800-804.

117. Yokota S, Sato K, Kuwahara O, et al. Fluoroquinolone-resistant *Streptococcus pneumoniae* strains occur frequently in elderly patients in Japan. Antimicrob Agents Chemother. 2002;46:3311-3315.

118. Marcus EL, Clarfield AM, Moses AE. Ethical issues relating to the use of antimicrobial therapy in older adults. Clin Infect Dis. 2001;33:1697-1705.

119. Leder, K, Weller PF, Wilson ME. Tropical vaccines and elderly persons: Review of vaccines available in the United States. Clin Infect Dis. 2001;33:1553-1566.

120. Ceddia T, Natellis C, Zigrino AG. Antibody response to rabies vaccine prepared in tissue culture of human diploid cells and inactivated, evaluated in different classes of age. Ann Sclavo. 1982;24:491-495.

121. Mastroeni I, Vescia N, Pompa MG, et al. Immune response of the elderly to rabies vaccine. Vaccine. 1994;12:518-520.

CHAPTER 315

Infections in Asplenic Patients

LARRY I. LUTWICK

This member hath propritie by itself sometimes, to hinder a man's running. . . . They say that the splene may be taken out of the body by way of incision, and yet the creature lives nevertheless.

PLINIUS SECUNDUS

Pliny, living in the malarious Mediterranean basin, could indeed have observed impaired athletic performance due to large *Plasmodium*-affected spleens.[1] His words, however, also reflect the difficulties in understanding splenic function, which lasted for more than 25 centuries. The Grecian theory of bodily humors had deemed the spleen's black bile to be a source of melancholia, producing the concept of "venting one's spleen." An association with laughter, putatively a therapeutic process, also led to the prophetic idea that the spleen expurgated unclean material from the blood and spirit. Overall, however, the prevailing opinion relegated this organ to a nonessential role, wherein it was able to be removed without adverse effects.

Interest in splenic absence as a risk for serious infection was not truly aroused until King and Schumacker's 1952 seminal report of life-threatening infection in splenectomized infants less than 6 months old.[2] The relationship between an absent or a hypofunctioning organ and severe infection, termed postsplenectomy sepsis (PSS) or overwhelming postsplenectomy infection (OPSI), is now well documented by illnesses evolving from good health to death within a day. Such septic deaths may occur 600 times more frequently than in eusplenic persons,[3] influenced by factors including age at and cause of spleen removal.

CAUSES OF SURGICAL SPLENECTOMY

With an enlightened approach toward preserving splenic tissue, newer indications for spleen removal have resulted in a more conservative attitude toward resection. As examples, salvage procedures are being performed in traumatic splenic injury, and splenectomy is avoided in Hodgkin's disease. The maneuver remains significant in the management of patients with hereditary hemolytic anemias, spherocytosis in particular. It may still be used in a number of conditions such as those in Table 315-1.

TABLE 315-1 Conditions That Can Be Associated With Need For Splenectomy

Trauma
Community acquired
Incidental surgical

Immunological and/or Hemolytic
Autoimmune hemolytic anemia
Hereditary spherocytosis
Idiopathic thrombocytopenic purpura
Wiskott-Aldrich syndrome

Hypersplenism
Agnogenic myeloid metaplasia
Autoimmune lymphoproliferative syndrome
Portal hypertension
Right sided heart failure
Thalassemia
Type 1 Gaucher's disease

Malignancy
Hodgkin's disease
Hairy cell leukemia
Ovarian carcinoma

TABLE 315-2 Conditions That May Be Associated With Functional Hyposplenism

Autoimmune Disorders	***Infiltrative Diseases***
APECED	Amyloidosis
Biliary cirrhosis	Sarcoidosis
Chronic active hepatitis	
Graves' disease	***Intestinal Disorders***
Hashimoto's thyroiditis	Celiac disease
Rheumatoid arthritis	Collagenous colitis
Sjögren's syndrome	Crohn's disease*
Systemic lupus erythematosis	Dermatitis herpetiformis
Vasculitis	Intestinal lymphangiectasis
	Ulcerative colitis
Hematologic Diseases	Whipple's disease
Essential thrombocythemia	
Fanconi's syndrome	***Miscellaneous***
Hemophilia	Alcoholism
Sickle cell hemoglobinopathies	Age
SS	Elderly (>70)†
SC	Neonates/prematures
S-β thalassemia	Bone marrow transplantation
	Chronic graft vs. host reaction
Neoplasia	Hypopituitarism
Breast carcinoma	Parenteral nutrition, chronic
Chronic myelogenous leukemia	Primary pulmonary hypertension
Hemangiosarcoma of the spleen	Splenic irradiation
Non-Hodgkin's lymphoma	External
Sézary's syndrome	Thoratrast
	Thrombosis of splenic vessels

APECED, autoimmune polyendocrinopathy-candidiasis-ectodermal dystrophy.

*The degree of hyposplenism appears to be less in Crohn's disease than ulcerative colitis.[6]

†Although splenic function is somewhat reduced with old age, it is usually not in the hyposplenic range.[7]

NONSURGICAL EQUIVALENTS OF SPLENECTOMY

Congenital Asplenia

In rare instances, asplenia can be congenital rather than acquired. In infants, it is usually linked with serious organ malformations (Ivemark's syndrome). Isolated congenital asplenia in adults, however, can be diagnosed even in the 6th or 7th decade of life when the patient presents with life-threatening sepsis.[4] As such, congenital asplenia may be first recognized at autopsy in an individual who has succumbed to fulminant infection. The combination of Howell-Jolly bodies (see later) and thrombocytosis in the blood of an individual without a palpable spleen or abdominal scar suggests the diagnosis of congenital asplenia. Classical PSS-like disease has also been very rarely reported in persons with seemingly normal spleens.[5]

Functional Hyposplenism

Although most PSS is found after splenectomy, it may occur with an anatomically present albeit poorly performing organ. Functional hyposplenism can be associated with a mélange of disorders (Table 315-2). Among the mechanisms responsible for splenic dysfunction are repeated infarction, infiltration, intrasplenic blood flow redistribution, and antigen–antibody complex blockade.

The hyposplenism may be partially reversible in some situations, as exemplified by improved splenic function in celiac disease using a gluten-free diet[8] and in immune complex disease treated with plasma exchange.[9] Interestingly, transient splenic dysfunction can result from pneumococcemia,[10] contributing to PSS in hyposplenic persons.

ASSESSMENT OF SPLENIC FUNCTION

As man's largest lymphoid organ, encamped in the midst of the blood's antigenic superhighway, the spleen has a bevy of immunologic functions, which include the production of opsonizing antibody and the efficient clearance of encapsulated bacteria. Increased amounts of specific antibody are needed in asplenia for the remaining reticuloendothelial system, particularly the liver, to effectively clear intravascular opsonized material.[11] For more virulent organisms such as pneumococci, however, splenic absence is not as well compensated for.[12]

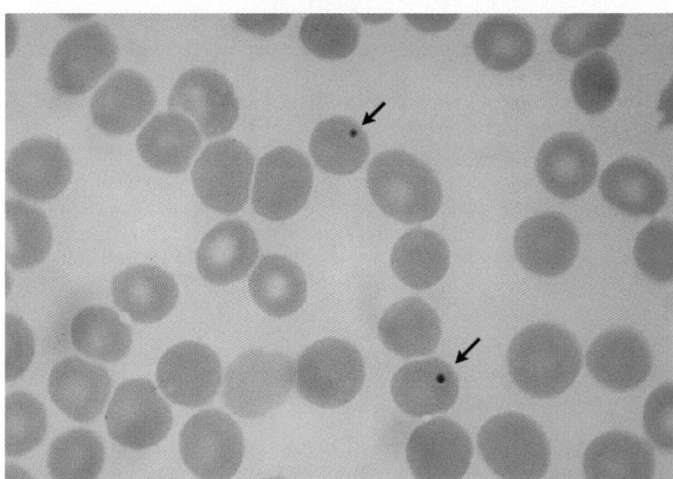

A

B

FIGURE 315-1. A, Photomicrograph of Howell-Jolly bodies in the circulating erythrocytes of a patient with a surgical splenectomy. **B,** An interference microscopy photomicrograph of pocked (intraerythrocytic vesicle) red cells. (**A,** Courtesy of Dr. Carol Luhrs, Veterans Affairs New York Harbor Health System, Brooklyn Campus; **B,** courtesy of Dr. George Buchanan, University of Texas.)

Mechanistically, a 75% drop in circulating B-1a B cells is associated with splenectomy.[13] These cells have a significant role in the early production of antibodies vital to the control of bacterial infection. The cause of this reduction could be defective production, decreased survival, or both. Additionally, the splenic marginal zone B (MZB) cells, found in the area of the junction between red pulp and white pulp, are also important in intravascular bacterial removal. These cells have a low threshold for activation and a high expression of complement receptors to rapidly respond to T-cell–independent polysaccharide antigens such as those in bacterial capsules.[14] The lack of adequate B-1a cells and the absence of MZB cells seem to play major roles in the poor response to and clearance of encapsulated organisms in the asplenic person.

The architecture of the spleen functions as the blood's sieve, removing blood cells, microorganisms, and immune complexes. After circulating through the splenic microvasculature, red blood cells (RBCs) that contain inclusions may be returned to the blood stream after undergoing remodeling (pitting). As such, Howell-Jolly bodies (nuclear remnants) and "pocked" RBCs reflect decreased remodeling and clearance are indicators of splenic dysfunction. Pocks are actually hemoglobin-containing vacuoles, found primarily in the older RBCs that are removed by the normal spleen.[15]

The presence of Howell-Jolly bodies (Fig. 315-1A), used as a simple screening test for asplenia, is relatively insensitive in the hyposplenic patient without significant impairment of function.[16] Clearance of chromium-tagged, heat-damaged RBCs, a more sensitive assay, is invasive and less available. Although spleen size on a technetium-99m sulfur colloid scan correlates with damaged RBC clearance, substantial discordance exists. An increased pocked RBC count is a more sensitive indicator of splenic dysfunction,[17] by the visualization of RBC vacuoles with interference phase microscopy (see Fig. 315-1B). In eusplenic persons, less than 2% of red cells are pocked, whereas hyposplenic persons will demonstrate greater than 12% and asplenic persons as many as 50%.[18] As the pocked cell count increases, increasing numbers of Howell-Jolly bodies can be seen, correlating well with the pock count.[16]

CLINICAL CHARACTERISTICS OF POSTSPLENECTOMY SEPSIS

Frequency

Factors contributing to difficulties in estimating PSS frequency[19,20] include a variable disease definition, differences in duration of follow-up, and considerations of age at and cause of splenectomy. Styrt assessed reports for the risk of fatal PSS to factor out milder, nonclassical infections.[19] In children, an incidence density of one fatal case per approximately 350 patient-years of follow-up was found, or (assuming a 50% case fatality) one case per 175 patient-years.

PSS frequency is more variable after spleen removal in the adult, probably because there are more reasons for the procedure. Styrt found an incidence density of one fatal case per 137 to more than 1190 patient-years, concluding that the risk is lower than after childhood splenectomy.[19] She estimated an overall risk of one fatal case in 800 to 1000 patient-years, or one case in 400 to 500 patient-years.

The risk can also be stratified by splenectomy cause (Table 315-3). The lowest risks are related to trauma and idiopathic thrombocytopenic purpura (ITP), intermediate risks are related to spherocytosis, portal hypertension, and Hodgkin's disease, and the highest risk is related to thalassemia. Autoimmune lymphoproliferative syndrome (ALPS), a genetic disorder producing defective lymphocyte apoptosis that can require splenectomy for hypersplenism, also has a high potential for PSS.[22] In 5491 patient-years of follow-up after splenectomy for hereditary spherocytosis, risks of one case per 910 patient-years and one fatal case every 365 patient-years were found.[23] Coexisting hepatic disease, depressing Kupffer cell phagocytic function, may increase the risk of PSS. Figure 315-2 illustrates the percentage of cases of PSS linked to causes of asplenia. Overall, about 6% of total PSS cases occur in hyposplenic hosts.[20]

Singer, comparing the frequency of PSS in his 1973 and 2001 reports, suggested that an overall 18% decrease in the risk of PSS had occurred.[1] A comparison of asplenic children in Toronto, moreover,

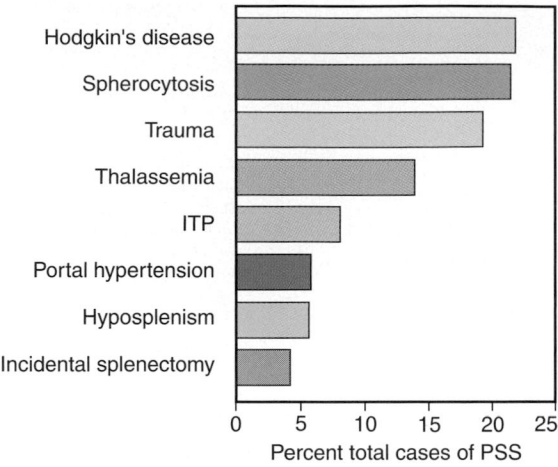

FIGURE 315-2. Underlying cause of splenic deficiency in 688 episodes of PSS. *(Derived from Hansen K, Singer DB. Asplenic-hyposplenic overwhelming sepsis: Postsplenectomy sepsis revisited. Pediatr Dev Pathol. 2001;4:105-121; Singer DB. Postsplenectomy sepsis. In: Rosenberg HS, Bolande RP, eds. Perspectives in Pediatric Pathology, v. 1. Chicago: Year Book Medical; 1973:285-311; Styrt B. Infection associated with asplenia: Risks, mechanisms, and prevention. Am J Med. 1990;88[5N]:33N-42N; and Holdsworth RJ, Irving AD, Cuschieri A. Postsplenectomy sepsis and its mortality rate: Actual versus perceived risks. Br J Surg. 1991;78:1031-1038.)*

showed that when the period between 1958 and 1970 was compared to the period between 1971 and 1995, a 47% decrease in bacteremia with encapsulated organisms had occurred.[24] These studies affirm a significant role of prophylactic antimicrobials and immunization in PSS prevention.

Timing Related to Splenectomy

PSS risk is highest in the first few years after spleen removal.[19,20] The infection, however, has appeared many years later, with intervals in excess of 4 decades.[25] Styrt found 9 of 46 cases falling within the first year, followed by four to five new cases in each year from 2 to 7 years.[19] In a more extensive review of 288 PSS cases, 32% of cases occurred within 1 year and 52% within the second (Fig. 315-3).[20] In general, the younger the person is at the time of splenectomy, the shorter the interval to PSS.

TABLE 315-3 The Risk of PSS Related to Splenectomy Cause[*,†]			
	Risk	**n**	*Range*
Low Attack Rate			
Incidental surgical	1.17	2521	1.0-2.4
ITP	2.03	2728	1.5-3.3
Trauma	2.07	6612	1.5-2.4
Intermediate Attack Rate			
Spherocytosis	3.15	4816	2.4-3.6
Hodgkin's disease	6.15	2507	4.1-11.6
Portal hypertension	6.72	610	4.1-8.6
High Attack Rate			
Thalassemia	11.6	852	7.0-24.8
Autoimmune lymphoproliferative syndrome	31.3[22]	16	

*From references 1, 3, 19, and 21, all reviews and the cases may have overlapped between them.

†In these reviews, how many of the cases are prototypical PSS as compared to bacteremias and other serious infections is unclear.

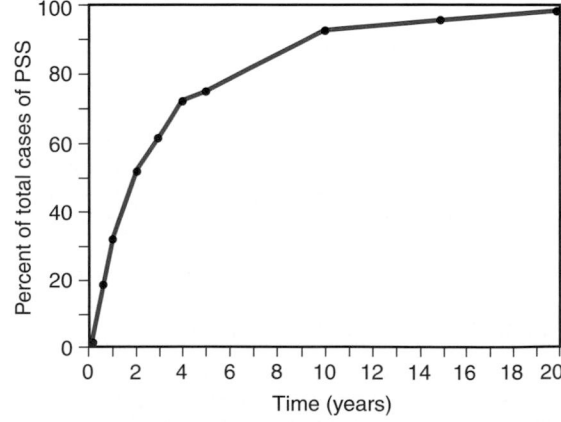

FIGURE 315-3. The interval from splenectomy to PSS. Of the total (N = 288), 3.1% occurred more than 20 years after splenectomy. *(Based on data from Holdsworth RJ, Irving AD, Cuschieri A. Postsplenectomy sepsis and its mortality rate: Actual versus perceived risks. Br J Surg. 1991;78:1031-1038.)*

Typical Presentation

PSS has a short prodrome with low-grade fever, chills, pharyngitis, muscle aches, and vomiting or diarrhea. If enough detail were reported, true rigors might have been present for 1 to 2 days prior to clinical deterioration.[19] In the setting of known asplenia or a dysfunctional splenic state, any febrile illness with gastrointestinal or other focal symptoms must be suspected to be PSS. Usually, no clinically demonstrable site of infection is found in adult PSS. In children younger than 5 years old, however, focal infections, particularly meningitis, are more prominent.[20]

Overt deterioration is abrupt and progressive, measured in hours rather than days, with a picture that has remained disturbingly unchanged. An asplenic individual may walk into a health care facility complaining of fever and diarrhea only to be in shock within several hours. Disseminated intravascular coagulopathy (DIC), seizures, coma, and cardiovascular collapse often accompany this rapid downhill course. Tissue damage can be compounded by the development of purpura fulminans,[26] in which hypotension, endovascular injury, and coagulopathy contribute to extremity gangrene and, if the patient survives, the possibility of one, or often multiple, amputations.

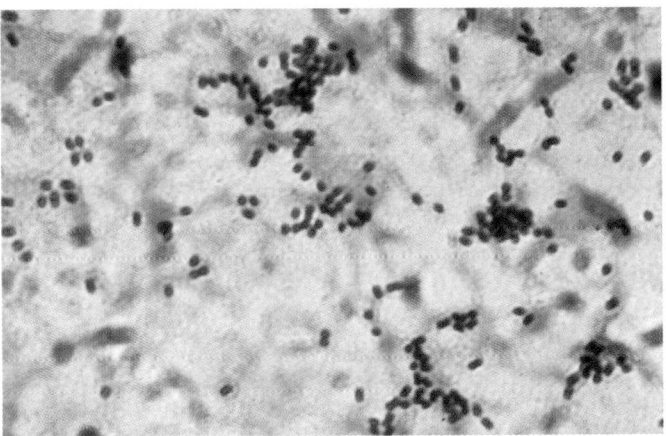

A

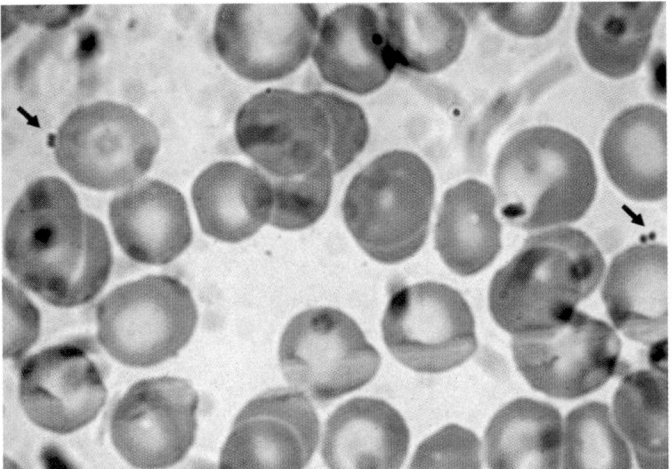

B

FIGURE 315-4. A, The Gram stain of a buffy coat smear from a patient with rapidly fatal pneumococcal PSS, 7 years after a staging laparotomy for Hodgkin's disease, showing many gram-positive diplococci. **B,** A more magnified Wright stain of a peripheral blood smear from the same patient, showing extracellular diplococci. *(From Lynch AM, Kapila R. Overwhelming postsplenectomy infection. Infect Dis Clin North Am. 1996;10:693-707; used with permission of the publisher.)*

Diagnosis

Early consideration of PSS is vital to facilitate an aggressive and prompt intervention. A high index of clinical suspicion must be maintained for febrile presentations in the asplenic patient or one with a chronic disease that can produce a dysfunctional spleen. The diagnostic workup should never delay the use of empirical antimicrobial therapy.

The presence of an extremely high level of bacteremia, although greatly contributing to morbidity and mortality, allows a diagnosis to be made quickly. Bacteria can be visualized on Gram or Wright stain of the peripheral blood buffy coat (Fig. 315-4A) and may be seen on a peripheral blood smear (see Fig. 315-4B). This latter finding reflects a bacteremia with a cell count of greater than 10^6/mL, 4 logs or greater than that of a usual bacteremia. Because of this degree of bacteremia, blood cultures are usually positive within 12 to 24 hours. Petechial or purpuric lesions should be aspirated for Gram stain and culture, and a CSF examination may be needed, particularly in children.

Examination of the peripheral blood for malaria or babesiosis may be necessary, guided by the patient's history. Furthermore, Howell-Jolly bodies or other evidence of hyposplenism should be sought, especially in an individual with a history of an illness predisposing to hyposplenism.

Mortality

PSS is particularly problematic because of its high mortality rates, classically in the range of 50% to 70% despite appropriate antimicrobial therapy and intensive medical support.[19,20] The dramatic nature of this illness is further underscored by the short time between the initial symptoms and death, with 68% of the mortality within 24 hours and 80% within 48 hours, demonstrating the need for prevention and emergent intervention strategies. In a study mentioned previously under Frequency, Jugenburg and colleagues found a substantial decrease in mortality associated with bacteremia involving encapsulated organisms when they compared their earlier asplenic cohort (1958-1970) with their more recent one (1971-1995).[24] This observation suggests that early diagnosis and aggressive treatment are effective in lowering the case fatality rate of PSS.

It is important to note that, unlike incidence, PSS case fatality rate is independent of the indication for the spleen removal. Mortality is generally higher in cases occurring after age 16, reflecting the somewhat different presentation of illness. A lower mortality (31.8%) has been observed in a small number of *Haemophilus influenzae* cases as compared to pneumococcal PSS.[20] In total, however, mortality from pneumococcal cases (57.6%) does not differ from those of nonpneumococcal etiology (52.3%).

MICROBIOLOGY OF PSS

Streptococcus pneumoniae (Pneumococcus)

Pneumococcus is singularly the most important organism implicated in PSS, involved in 50% to 90% of cases.[19,20] In a review of 349 PSS cases, *Streptococcus pneumoniae* was causative in 66% of episodes in which a bacterium could be identified (Fig. 315-5).[20] Although common in all age groups, the percentage of pneumococcal PSS cases increases with age. A predominant polysaccharide serotype is not found, and there is no evidence to suggest that the distribution of serotypes involved in PSS differs from that in other forms of invasive pneumococcal infection.

Antimicrobial drug resistance in *S. pneumoniae* is increasingly prevalent. In some areas, a significant percentage of pneumococci demonstrate penicillin resistance, either relative or absolute.[28] Such isolates can be resistant to the extended-spectrum cephalosporins, such as ceftriaxone, as well. These penicillin-resistant pneumococci (PRP) clearly require consideration in the empirical therapy of PSS.

Haemophilus influenzae

Type b *H. influenzae* (Hib) is the second most common organism related to PSS.[19,20] Most Hib-associated PSS cases have occurred in children less than 15 years old, 86% in one review,[20] with a frequency

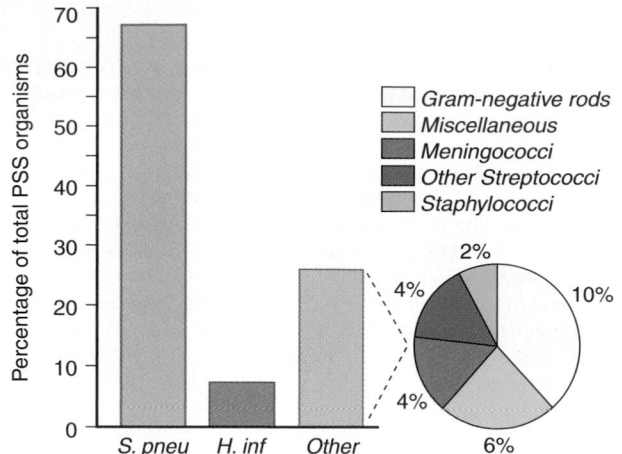

FIGURE 315-5. The microbiology of PSS based on 298 culture-positive episodes including those due to the meningococcus. Of the total, 51 (14.6%) additional episodes did not have a reported organism. Data are not stratified by age or cause of splenectomy. *(Adapted from Holdsworth RJ, Irving AD, Cuschieri A. Postsplenectomy sepsis and its mortality rate: Actual versus perceived risks. Br J Surg. 1991;78:1031-1038.)*

about 10 times lower than that of the pneumococcus. Neither nontypable nor non-b capsular strains (a, c-f) have been significant pathogens in PSS. Use of the conjugated Hib vaccine has dramatically decreased the incidence of invasive Hib disease.[29] The consequences of this protection should be a falloff in PSS cases due to Hib, with the remaining infections occurring in older, nonvaccinated individuals. Importantly, β-lactamase production by many *H. influenzae* strains needs accounting for choosing empirical therapy.

Other Bacterial Organisms

Neisseria meningitidis, the meningococcus, is often cited as the third most common cause of PSS. Although meningococcemia occurs in the asplenic host[30,31] and the organism was reported in King and Schumacker's original publication,[2] meningococcemia is neither more frequent nor more severe in asplenic or hyposplenic patients than in eusplenic individuals.[32] Data in asplenic mice further support the lack of this association.[32]

Capnocytophaga canimorsus, a fastidious gram-negative rod formerly classified as CDC group DF-2, is part of canine and feline oral flora. It is typically transmitted to humans from dog contact, usually a bite. *C. canimorsus* infection does occur in the healthy immunocompetent person but usually is relatively mild. Of reported severe cases, 80% have predisposing conditions, primarily asplenia and hyposplenic states.[33] Finding gram-negative bacilli in the buffy coat or peripheral blood smear[34] or observing an eschar at the bite site,[35] manifesting 1 to 7 days after the bite, suggests *C. canimorsus* as the cause of PSS. β-Lactamase activity can be seen in 30% of strains.[36]

Salmonella species have been associated with PSS. Severe salmonellosis is associated with the hyposplenism of chronic reticuloendothelial blockage in bartonellosis,[37] and the infection is prominent in children with sickle cell anemia–associated splenic dysfunction.[38] Despite these observations, the organism does not play a large role in PSS. In fact, most cases are associated with illnesses where defects in cell-mediated immunity from either the disease or its treatment predispose to salmonellosis.

A wide compendium of other bacteria has been anecdotally linked to PSS. These include other β- and α-hemolytic streptococci, staphylococci, *Bacteroides, E. coli* and other Enterobacteriaceae.[2] Enterobacteriaceae seem to be more prominent before the age of 6 months. Of note, *Streptococcus suis* has caused PSS in those with swine exposure[39] and 22 of the 26 reported bacteremias due to Bordetella holmesii occurred in asplenics or hyposplenics.[39a]

RELATIONSHIP OF SPLENECTOMY TO OTHER INFECTIONS

Postoperative Period

Early postoperative infections after splenectomy are related to the usual suspects in pulmonary, urinary, and superficial or deep operative sites. In trauma patients requiring splenectomy, both focal infections and bacteremias are more common in individuals with additional nonsplenic injuries.[40] The microbiology of these infections is primarily staphylococci and enteric gram-negative bacilli, not the characteristic PSS organisms. Whether splenectomy is an independent risk factor for postoperative infection remains ill defined.[41,42]

Intraerythrocytic Parasitemias (Babesiosis and Malaria)

In babesiosis, most cases of morbidity and mortality occur in the asplenic host.[43] It is these splenectomized individuals who have higher-grade parasitemias, have significant hemolysis, and require specific treatment for the infection. Babesiosis in eusplenic persons is by large mild or subclinical, not requiring therapy.

Splenectomy allows adaptation of human malaria to primates, and spontaneous resolution ("crisis") of malaria is spleen mediated in some nonhuman species.[44] Whether malaria in humans is as clinically affected by removal of the spleen, however, is less well established. In partially malaria-immune individuals, the course of *Plasmodium falciparum* infection is not changed in the asplenic.[45] The human spleen, however, does play a pivotal role in malarial parasite clearance by removing the intraerythrocytic parasites without red cell destruction (pitting). Pitted cells are detected in the blood by the presence of ring-associated erythrocyte surface antigen (RESA),[46] which is not found in malarious asplenic individuals.[47] Because pitting does not occur in the *Plasmodium*-infected asplenic patient, parasite removal is delayed, but this does not necessarily reflect resistance to the antimalarial used.[47]

Ehrlichiosis

Human granulocytic ehrlichiosis, a tick-borne infection, has been reported to be recurrent, prolonged, and/or more severe in asplenic persons.[48] Ehrlichiosis should be added to the list of severe infections in asplenic or hyposplenic persons if this is confirmed. Of note, however, the course of canine monocytic ehrlichiosis seemed clinically and hematologically milder in splenectomized dogs than in normal dogs.[49]

Hemotropic Bacterial Infections

Bartonella bacilliformis is a gram-negative rod endemic in the western Peruvian Andes. During active human infection (Oroyo fever), bacilli are found adherent to RBCs.[37] Similar organisms include *Haemobartonella* and *Eperythrozoon,* and these infections are more prominent in splenectomized animals.[50] Human bartonellosis may likewise be affected by asplenism. A 1979 report described an asplenic patient with an uncultivatable organism adhering to most of his RBCs,[51] but additional cases have not surfaced.

Infection with the Human Immunodeficiency Virus

There is no evidence that there is either a higher risk of PSS in HIV-infected asplenic patients or any relationship of risk to CD4 cell levels. After removal of the spleen, absolute CD4 and CD8 lymphocyte levels rise in both HIV-infected and noninfected individuals.[52] CD4/CD8 ratios do not change and they become more important in therapeutic decision-making processes for the splenectomized HIV-infected person.

Favorable effects of spleen removal on HIV-related events have been observed with a median follow-up of 51 months.[53] Another report found a statistically lower risk of progression to AIDS in splenectomized patients.[54] There, splenectomy may have been the equivalent of debulking lymphatic tissue, the major site for viral sequestration and replication. Although the significance of the observations remains to be determined, plasma HIV RNA levels seem to be lower in asplenic patients than in controls.[55]

THERAPEUTIC STRATEGIES

Immediate Self-Treatment

Because of the potential for fulminant PSS, self-administration of an antimicrobial agent at the first sign of a suspicious illness in the asplenic or hyposplenic person is commonly advised, despite the absence of any controlled studies. Never a substitute for immediate medical evaluation, the procedure should be instituted especially if the delivery of medical care is not immediate. Treatment indications include any undifferentiated rigor or a febrile illness with prostration.

Choices, based on drug allergy and local antimicrobial resistance, include a quinolone, amoxicillin/clavulanic acid, trimethoprim/sulfamethoxazole (SXT), or a newer macrolide. Amoxicillin/clavulanic acid has activity against β-lactamase–producing *H. influenzae* and *C. canimorsus* but not against PRP, and neither SXT nor the macrolides have consistent PRP activity. A quinolone with PRP activity (levofloxacin, moxifloxacin, gatifloxacin, gemifloxacin) should be used in high-risk individuals.

Therapeutic Interventions

If a patient suspected to have PSS is seen in a physician's office, an antimicrobial such as ceftriaxone should be given parenterally prior to hospital transfer, whether or not blood cultures can be obtained. Empirical antimicrobial options for suspected PSS that can be given on hospital arrival are shown in Table 315-4. Potential adjuvant immunologic interventions are also shown in this table.

PREVENTION STRATEGIES

Prophylactic Antimicrobials

After splenectomy, pediatric patients are often given oral penicillin V prophylaxis for the first few years. In children with sickle hemoglobinopathies, this practice has produced an 84% reduction in pneumococcal bacteremia.[61] The degree of protection in the asplenic child against PSS is not as well quantified and failures of prophylaxis are reported. In a 1986 review prior to the widespread emergence of PRP, 14 reports of prophylaxis failure were cited with none of the isolates being penicillin resistant.[62] In another 1986 study of 248 person-years in 88 children with sickle cell anemia receiving both oral penicillin and pneumococcal vaccination, eight episodes (three fatal) of pneumococcal sepsis occurred, but these were related primarily to penicillin therapy nonadherence.[63]

Prophylaxis has been discontinued in children over the age of 5 years with sickle cell anemia after pneumococcal vaccination and at least 2 years of treatment. No statistically significant increase in the incidence of pneumococcal events was found compared to those still receiving penicillin.[64] PRP strains were isolated equally in placebo and antimicrobial-treated breakthrough patients. A similar approach may be taken in the asplenic child who has not had PSS, although lifelong prophylaxis has been suggested,[65] more so in those with other underlying immune defects. Recurrent episodes of PSS, or perhaps even just one episode, can be another indication for lifelong prophylaxis.

Little information is available on the utility of this modality in older asplenic persons. Because of the lower incidence of PSS in adults, the possibility of adverse effects from therapy, the selection of resistant strains, adherence issues, and the psychosocial burden of lifelong therapy, long-term prophylaxis in adults is not generally recommended.[19] The role of antibiotic prophylaxis in hyposplenic patients without S-hemoglobinopathies is unknown.

Antimicrobial prophylaxis of the asplenic or hyposplenic patient undergoing bacteremia-associated dental procedures has been discussed.[66] No routine prophylaxis is suggested, although it is recommended by some.

Vaccination

Immunization against pneumococci using the 23-valent unconjugated capsular pneumococcal polysaccharide vaccine (PPV23) is uniformly recommended for both asplenic and hyposplenic hosts. The specific antibody response (particularly IgM) to immunization in this cohort is delayed and the magnitude of the response is lower than in normal individuals.[67] Wide variation in response from patient to patient and to different vaccine capsular types is seen.

In elective splenectomy, PPV23 has been given at least 2 weeks prior to the procedure to optimize the antibody response.[65] After emergent spleen removal, immunization may be administered at hospital discharge or 2 weeks postoperatively, whichever is first. It remains unclear if the timing of vaccination affects efficacy, but it is reasonable to allow the host to recover from perioperative catabolism before immunization. Use is also often delayed for at least 3 months or more after chemotherapy or therapeutic irradiation.[65] If chemotherapy is given prior to splenectomy, however, functional humoral immunity may be restored as soon as 24 days after chemotherapy.[68]

How protective PPV23 is in the asplenic host remains inadequately defined, and anecdotal reports of failures related to vaccine-associated[69] and non–vaccine-associated strains exist.[70] Some efficacy in hyposplenic and asplenic patients, however, has been demonstrated.[71,72] Reimmunization in this cohort is reasonable even though PPV23 contains only T-cell–independent type 2 antigens that do not evoke immunologic memory. Because specific antibody levels can decrease more rapidly in the asplenic patient,[73] revaccination as often as every 2 to 3 years has been suggested.[74] The CDC adult immunization schedule, however, recommends only a one-time revaccination after 5 years.[75] Local adverse reactions to PPV23, significantly correlated with prebooster antibody titer, are not infrequent after reimmunization.[76] As antibody levels before boosting are likely to be low or absent in the asplenic or hyposplenic person, these Arthus (type III hypersensitivity) reactions should be minimal.

A more recently licensed heptavalent pneumococcal vaccine (PCV7) contains polysaccharides conjugated to a protein carrier. Conjugation allows the antigens to become T cell dependent, not only inducing a protective antibody response but also priming the immune system for boosting.[77] This effect occurs even in children less than 2 years old, where PPV23 is not immunogenic, and in individuals with a genetic predisposition not to respond to polysaccharides. Since U.S. licensure (for use in young children) of PCV7, an overall decline in invasive pneumococcal disease has occurred. Reductions, most prominent in children less than 2 years old, were also noted in non–PCV7-immunized adults (Table 315-5).[78]

In children affected with sickle cell anemia[79] and in patients with Hodgkin's disease,[80] two doses of PCV7 followed by PPV23 produces higher levels of type-specific antibody for serotypes contained in both vaccines than PPV23 alone. The additional serotypes in PPV23 increase

---

TABLE 315-4 PSS Therapeutic Considerations

Empirical PSS Antimicrobial Treatment*

Gram stain evidence of *S. pneumoniae*	Vancomycin plus ceftriaxone or moxifloxacin
Gram stain evidence of a gram negative bacillus or diplococcus	Cefepime +/− gentamicin
No organism seen on Gram stain	Cefepime plus vancomycin plus moxifloxacin

Potential Immunological Interventions

Intravenous human immunoglobulin	In asplenic animals, immunoglobulin decreased mortality from infection.[56,57,59,60]
Granulocyte-macrophage colony-stimulating factor (GM-CSF)	GM-CSF increased macrophage bactericidal activity in eusplenic and asplenic mice and treated animals had improved survival after pneumococcal challenge.[58]

*−Adult dosages −; ceftriaxone: 2-4 grams IV every 24 hours; vancomycin: 1 gram IV every 12 hours; cefepime 2 gram IV every 8-12 hours; moxifloxacin 400 mg IV every 24 hours, equivalent doses of other fluoroquinolones such as gatifloxacin can be used. These regimens may need modification in renal or hepatic disease. Many patients with IgE-mediated penicillin allergy can tolerate cephalosporins but they ought to be given with caution or an alternative sought. Higher doses of vancomycin may be needed if meningitis is present. Modifications of the regimen chosen should be made when culture and sensitivity data is available.

TABLE 315-5 Effect of PCV7 Use on Age-Specific Invasive Pneumococcal Rates*

Age (yrs)	Pneumococcal Type	Estimated Rates 1998-1999	Cases/100,000 (2001)	P value
<2	Vaccine serotypes	156.1	33.6	<0.001
	Vaccine-related serotypes	19.6	9.8	<0.001
	Non-vaccine serotypes	12.4	15.7	0.14
3-19	Vaccine serotypes	No statistical decreases in this age cohort		
	Vaccine-related serotypes			
	Non-vaccine serotypes			
20-39	Vaccine serotypes	6.60	3.97	<0.001
	Vaccine-related serotypes	1.39	1.08	0.14
	Non-vaccine serotypes	3.21	2.57	0.04
40-64	Vaccine serotypes	11.58	9.95	0.006
	Vaccine-related serotypes	2.49	2.38	0.74
	Non-vaccine serotypes	7.46	7.41	0.93
>65	Vaccine serotypes	33.43	23.91	0.001
	Vaccine-related serotypes	8.38	6.52	0.02
	Non-vaccine serotypes	18.18	19.05	0.52

*The capsular serotypes in PCV7 are 4, 6B, 9V, 14, 18C and 23F but serotypes within the same serogroup (ie, 6A, 18B, 23B were considered vaccine-related strains. PPV23 serotypes not in PCV7 include 1, 2, 3, 5, 7F, 8, 10A, 11A, 12F, 15B, 20, 22F and 33F.
Data derived from reference 78.

the coverage in adults from the 50% of isolates (80% in children) for PCV7.[79] Conjugate vaccine, additionally, can produce a more functional immunoglobulin by eliciting an antibody with heightened target avidity.[81] This effect may be related to a shift in IgG subtypes from IgG_2 to IgG_1, the latter with increased opsonic activity, facilitating opsonophagocytosis. How well this conjugate vaccine will perform in asplenic and hyposplenic individuals is not yet defined but use in conjunction with PPV23 for asplenic persons has been suggested.[65] In a rat model,[82] a conjugate vaccine, however, overcame splenic dependency of the antibody response to polysaccharides. Expanding the number of conjugates in a single vaccine to improve serotype coverage is limited by the carrier protein levels above which the immune response may be inhibited.

Conjugated Hib polysaccharide vaccination is often given to those asplenic and hyposplenic persons not immunized in childhood. In splenectomized children and adults, the vaccine is immunogenic but antibody titers may not reach the level reached in eusplenic persons.[83] No recommendations have been made for boosters.[65,75] Booster doses are reasonable in the asplenic, however, because of lower peak titers, the need for higher levels of opsonins in this cohort,[11] and some evidence suggesting Hib infections may be increasing in vaccinated children.[84]

Quadrivalent nonconjugated polysaccharide meningococcal vaccine (types A, C, Y, and W135)[85] is immunogenic in the asplenic individual but less so in those treated with chemotherapy and radiotherapy.[86] Lack of an increased risk, absence of type B in the vaccine, and short duration of protection suggest that this vaccine may not be necessary in the asplenic host. The CDC, however, recommends immunization in asplenic adults[75] and children,[85] with consideration of booster use.[85] Meningococcal vaccination had not been recommended in this population by the U.K. Clinical Hematology Working Party, but more recently a type C conjugate vaccine, immunogenic in asplenics,[86a] has been suggested.[65] A quadrivalent conjugated vaccine is under study and may become part of universal immunization.

Influenza vaccine should be given yearly to the asplenic/hyposplenic cohort. In addition, it is important to note that asplenia and hyposplenia are not contraindications to routine immunizations including live, attenuated vaccines.[65]

Patient and Family Education

A low level of knowledge about PSS risk exists. In one study, only 16% of asplenic persons were aware of any health precautions; this increased to 40% after prompting.[87] Issues to impart to the patient and family are listed in Table 315-6 and should be delivered in oral and written forms. Because the half-life of knowledge is short, repeated emphasis during follow-up is vital. The patient should wear a medical alert and carry a card documenting asplenia or hyposplenism, immunization, prophylactic antimicrobials, and an emergency plan.[88]

TABLE 315-6 Educational Issues for the Asplenic/Hyposplenic Host

Persons without a functioning spleen are more susceptible to certain infections.
The infection can be very rapidly progressive and life-threatening.
The risk of the infection is lifelong but highest in the year or two after the surgery.
All physicians tending to the patient should be informed of the condition, no matter how long after the splenectomy.
Both vaccination and antimicrobial agents may be used for prevention.

Spleen-Sparing Treatments

The risk of PSS has focused attention on alternatives to total spleen removal. Splenic preservation after traumatic rupture has been successful using conservative management, splenic repair, or partial splenectomy,[89] and it may be accomplished in greater than 90% of transcapsular splenic injuries.[90] Some return of splenic function after splenectomy for traumatic rupture has suggested that splenosis (growth of peritoneal implants of splenic tissue) could explain a lower PSS risk after trauma. Surgeons autotransplant splenic tissue during splenectomy to augment splenosis. Fatal pneumococcal PSS has, however, occurred with as much as 92 g of splenosis, suggesting that splenic blood supply alterations may also play a role in PSS risk.[91] Supporting these limitations, in rabbits undergoing the procedure, not only did the transplant shrink in size and the parenchyma and vasculature degenerate over 6 months but also the clearance of pneumococci was no better than in asplenic animals.[92]

Partial removal of the spleen can be used in children with thalassemia[93] or hereditary hemolytic anemias such as spherocytosis.[94] Although regrowth may require total splenectomy, the delay is likely to be beneficial in young children. Splenic function is greater after partial splenectomy or splenic repair than after autotransplantation.[95]

REFERENCES

1. Hansen K, Singer DB. Asplenic-hyposplenic overwhelming sepsis: Postsplenectomy sepsis revisited. Pediatr Dev Pathol. 2001;4:105-121.
2. King H, Schumacker HB. Splenic studies. I. Susceptibility to infection after splenectomy performed in infancy. Ann Surg. 1952;136:239-242.
3. Singer DB. Postsplenectomy sepsis. In: Rosenberg HS, Bolande RP, eds. Perspectives in Pediatric Pathology, v. 1. Chicago: Year Book Medical; 1973:285-311.
4. Germing U, Perings C, Steiner S, et al. Congenital asplenia detected in a 60 year old patient with septicemia. Eur J Med Res. 1999;4:283-285.
5. Bramely PN, Shah P, Williams DJ, Losowsky MS. Pneumococcal Waterhouse-Friderichsen syndrome despite a normal spleen. Postgrad Med J. 1989;65:687-688.
6. Muller AF, Cornford E, Toghill PJ. Splenic function in inflammatory bowel disease: Assessment by differential interference microscopy and splenic ultrasound. Q J Med. 1993;86:333-340.

7. Ravaglia G, Forti P, Biagi F, et al. Splenic function in old age. Gerontology. 1998;44: 91-94.

8. Corazza GR, Frisoni M, Vaira D, Gasbarrini G. Effect of gluten-free diet on splenic hypofunction of adult coeliac disease. Gut. 1983;24:228-230.

9. Lockwood CM, Worlledge S, Nicholas A, et al. Reversal of impaired splenic function in patients with nephritis or vasculitis (or both) by plasma exchange. N Engl J Med. 1979;300:524-530.

10. Boughton BJ, Simpson A, Chandler S. Functional hyposplenism during pneumococcal septicaemia. Lancet. 1983;1:121-122.

11. Hosea SW, Brown EJ, Hamburger MI, Frank MM. Opsonic requirements for intravascular clearance after splenectomy. N Engl J Med. 1981;304:245-250.

12. Brown EJ, Hosea SW, Frank MM. The role of the spleen in experimental pneumococcal bacteremia. J Clin Invest. 1981;67:975-982.

13. Wardemann H, Boehm T, Dear W, Carsetti R. B-1a B cells that link the innate and adaptive immune responses are lacking in the absence of the spleen. J Exp Med. 2002;195:771-780.

14. Zandvoort A, Timens W. The dual function of the splenic marginal zone: Essential for initiation of anti-TI-2 responses but also vital in the general first-line defense against blood-borne antigens. Clin Exp Immunol. 2002;130:4-11.

15. Willekens FL, Roerdinkholder-Stoelwinder B, Groenen-Dopp YA, et al. Hemoglobin loss from erythrocytes in vivo results from spleen-facilitated vesiculation. Blood. 2003;101:747-751.

16. Corazza GR, Ginaldi L, Zoli G, et al. Howell-Jolly body counting as a measure of splenic function: A reassessment. Clin Lab Haematol. 1990;12:269-275.

17. Buchanan GR, Holtkamp CA, Horton JA. Formation and disappearance of pocked erythrocytes: Studies in human subjects and laboratory animals. Am J Hematol. 1987;25:243-251.

18. Muller AF, Toghill PJ. Hyposplenism in gastrointestinal disease. Gut. 1995;36: 165-167.

19. Styrt B. Infection associated with asplenia: Risks, mechanisms, and prevention. Am J Med. 1990;88(5N):33N-42N.

20. Holdsworth RJ, Irving AD, Cuschieri A. Postsplenectomy sepsis and its mortality rate: Actual versus perceived risks. Br J Surg. 1991;78:1031-1038.

21. Bisharat N, Omari H, Lavi I, Raz R. Risk of infection and death among post-splenectomy patients. J Infect. 2001;43:182-186.

22. Straus SE, Sneller M, Lenardo MJ, et al. An inherited disorder of lymphocyte apoptosis: The autoimmune lymphoproliferative syndrome. Ann Intern Med. 1999;130:551-560.

23. Schilling RF. Estimating the risk for sepsis after splenectomy in hereditary spherocytosis. Ann Intern Med. 1995;122:187-188.

24. Jugenburg M, Haddock G, Freedman MH, et al. The morbidity and mortality of pediatric splenectomy: Does prophylaxis make a difference? J Pediatr Surg. 1999;34:1064-1067.

25. Evans DIK. Postsplenectomy sepsis 10 years or more after operation. J Clin Pathol. 1985;38:309-311.

26. Childers BJ, Cobanov B. Acute infectious purpura fulminans: A 15-year review of 28 consecutive cases. Am Surg. 2003;69:86-90.

27. Lynch AM, Kapila R. Overwhelming postsplenectomy infection. Infect Dis Clin North Am. 1996;10:693-707.

28. Hofmann J, Cetron MS, Farley MM, et al. The prevalence of drug-resistant Streptococcus pneumoniae in Atlanta. N Engl J Med. 1995;333:481-486.

29. Vadheim CM, Greenberg DP, Eriksen E, et al. Eradication of Haemophilus influenzae type b disease in southern California. Arch Pediatr Adolesc Med. 1994;148:51-56.

30. Holmes FF, Weyandt T, Glazier J, et al. Fulminant meningococcemia after splenectomy. JAMA. 1981;246:1119-1120.

31. Condon RJ, Riley TV, Kelly H. Invasive meningococcal infection after splenectomy. BMJ. 1994;308:792-793.

32. Loggie BW, Hinchey EJ. Does splenectomy predispose to meningococcal sepsis? An experimental study and clinical review. J Pediatr Surg. 1986;21:326-330.

33. Zumla A, Lipscomb G, Corbett M, et al. Dysgonic fermenter—type 2: A zoonosis. Report of two cases and review. Q J Med. 1988;68:741-752.

34. Case Records of the Massachusetts General Hospital (Case 29-1986). N Engl J Med. 1986;315:241-249.

35. Kalb R, Kaplan MH, Tenebaum MJ, et al. Cutaneous infection at dog bite wounds associated with fulminant DF-2 septicemia. Am J Med. 1985;78:687-690.

36. Roscoe DL, Zemcov SJV, Thornber D, et al. Antimicrobial susceptibilities and β-lactamase characterization of Capnocytophaga species. Antimicrob Agent Chemother. 1992;36:2197-2200.

37. Dooley JR. Haemotropic bacteria in man. Lancet. 1980;2:1237-1239.

38. Onwubalili JK. Sickle cell disease and infection. J Infect. 1983;7:2-20.

39. Kopić J, Tomić Paradžik M, Pandak N. Streptococcus suis infection as a cause of severe illness: 2 cases from Croatia. Scand J Infect Dis. 2002;34:683-709.

39a. Shepard CW, Daneshvar MI, Kaiser RM, et al. Bordetella holmesii bacteremia: a newly recognized entity among asplenic patients. Clin Infect Dis. 2004;38:799-804.

40. Malangoni MA, Dillon LD, Klamer TW, Condon RE. Factors influencing the risk of early and late serious infection in adults after splenectomy for trauma. Surgery. 1984;96:775-783.

41. Fujita T, Matai K, Kohno S, Itsubo K. Impact of splenectomy on circulatory immunoglobulin levels and the development of postoperative infection following total gastrectomy for gastric cancer. Br J Surg. 1996;83:1776-1778.

42. Sekikawa T, Shatney CH. Septic sequelae after splenectomy for trauma in adults. Am J Surg. 1983;145:667-673.

43. Rosner F, Zarrabi MH, Benach JL, Habicht GS. Babesiosis in splenectomized adults. Review of 22 reported cases. Am J Med. 1984;76:696-701.

44. Quinn TC, Wyler DJ. Resolution of acute malaria (Plasmodium berghei in the rat): Reversibility and spleen dependence. Am J Trop Med Hyg. 1980;29:1-4.

45. Looareesuwan S, Suntharasamai P, Webster HK, Ho M. Malaria in splenectomized patients: Report of four cases and review. Clin Infect Dis. 1993;16:361-366.

46. Angus BJ, Chotivanich K, Udomsangpetch R, White NJ. In vivo removal of malaria parasites from red blood cells without their destruction in acute falciparum malaria. Blood. 1997;90:2037-2040.

47. Chotivanich K, Udomsangpetch R, McGready R, et al. Central role of the spleen in malaria parasite clearance. J Infect Dis. 2002;185:1538-1541.

48. Rabinstein A, Tikhomirov V, Kaluta A, et al: Recurrent and prolonged fever in asplenic patients with human granulocytic ehrlichiosis. Q J Med. 2000;93:198-201.

49. Harrus S, Waner T, Keysary A, et al: Investigation of splenic functions in canine monocytic ehrlichiosis. Vet Immunol Immunopathol. 1998;62:15-27.

50. Pryor WH, Bradbury RP. Haemobartonella canis infection in research dogs. Lab Animal Sci. 1975;25:566-569.

51. Archer GL, Coleman PH, Cole RM, et al. Human infection from an unidentified erythrocyte-associated bacterium. N Engl J Med. 1979;301:897-900.

52. Domingo P, Fuster M, Muñiz-Diaz E, et al. Spurious post-splenectomy CD4 and CD8 lymphocytosis in HIV-infected patients. AIDS. 1996;10:106-107.

53. Morlat P, Dequae-Merchadou L, Dobis F, et al. Splenectomy and prognosis of HIV infection. AIDS. 1996;10:1170-1172.

54. Tsoukas CM, Bernard NF, Abrahamowicz M, et al. Effect of splenectomy on slowing human immunodeficiency virus disease progression. Arch Surg. 1998;133:25-31.

55. Bernard NF, Chernoff DM, Tsoukas CM. Effect of splenectomy on T-cell subsets and plasma HIV titers in HIV-infected patients. J Hum Virol. 1998;1:338-345.

56. Offenbartl K, Christensen P, Gullstrand P, et al. Treatment of pneumococcal post-splenectomy sepsis in the rat with human γ-globulin. J Surg Res. 1986;40:198-201.

57. Camel JE, Kim KS, Tchejeyan GH, Mahour GH. Efficacy of passive immunotherapy in experimental postsplenectomy sepsis due to Haemophilus influenzae type B. J Pediatr Surg. 1993;28:1441-1445.

58. Hebert JC, O'Reilly M. Granulocyte-macrophage colony-stimulating factor (GM-CSF) enhances pulmonary defenses against pneumococcal infections after splenectomy. J Trauma. 1996;41:663-666.

59. Chu DZJ, Nishioka K, El-Hagin T, et al. Effects of tuftsin on postsplenectomy sepsis. Surgery. 1985;97:701-706.

60. Kubo S, Rodriguez T, Roh MS, et al. Stimulation of phagocytic activity of murine Kupffer cells by tuftsin. Hepatology. 1994;19:1044-1049.

61. Gaston MH, Verter JI, Woods G, et al. Prophylaxis with oral penicillin in children with sickle cell anemia: A randomized trial. N Engl J Med. 1986;314:1593-1599.

62. Zarrabi MH, Rosner F. Rarity of failure of penicillin prophylaxis to prevent postsplenectomy sepsis. Arch Intern Med. 1986;146:1207-1208.

63. Buchanan GR, Smith SJ. Pneumococcal septicemia despite pneumococcal vaccine and prescription of penicillin prophylaxis in children with sickle cell anemia. Am J Dis Child. 1986;140:428-432.

64. Falletta JM, Woods GM, Verter JI, et al. Discontinuing penicillin prophylaxis in children with sickle cell anemia. J Pediatr. 1995;127:685-690.

65. Davies JM, Barnes R, Milligan D. Update of guidelines for the prevention and treatment of infection in patients with an absent or dysfunctional spleen. Clin Med. 2002;2:440-443.

66. De Rossi SS, Glick M. Dental considerations in asplenic patients. J Am Dent Assoc. 1996;127:1359-1363.

67. Molrine DC, Silber GR, Samra Y, et al. Normal IgG and impaired IgM responses to polysaccharide vaccines in asplenic patients. J Infect Dis. 1999;179:513-517.

68. Zandvoort A, Ludewijk ME, Klok PA, et al. After chemotherapy, functional humoral response capacity is restored before complete restoration of lymphoid compartment. Clin Exp Immunol. 2003;131:8-16.

69. Evans DIK. Fatal post-splenectomy sepsis despite prophylaxis with penicillin and pneumococcal vaccine. Lancet. 1984;1:1124.

70. Appelbaum PC, Shaikh BS, Widome MD, et al. Fatal pneumococcal bacteremia in a vaccinated, splenectomized child. N Engl J Med. 1979;300:203-204.

71. Ammann AJ, Addiego J, Wara DW, et al. Polyvalent pneumococcal-polysaccharide immunization of patients with sickle-cell anemia and patients with splenectomy. N Engl J Med. 1977;297:897-900.

72. Foss Abrahamsen A, Hoiby EA, Hannisdol E, et al. Systemic pneumococcal disease after staging for Hodgkin's disease 1969-1980 without pneumococcal vaccine protection: A follow-up study 1994. Eur J Haematol. 1997;58:73-77.

73. Giebink GS, Le CT, Cosio FG, et al. Serum antibody responses of high-risk children and adults to vaccination with capsular polysaccharide of Streptococcus pneumoniae. Rev Infect Dis. 1981;3(Suppl):168-178.

74. Rutherford EJ, Livengood J, Higginbotham M, et al. Efficacy and safety of pneumococcal revaccination after splenectomy for trauma. J Trauma. 1995;39:448-452.

75. Centers for Disease Control and Prevention. Recommended adult immunization schedule—United States, 2002-2003. MMWR Morbid Mortal Wkly Rep. 2002;51:904-908.

76. Jackson LA, Benson P, Sneller VP, et al. Safety of revaccination with pneumococcal polysaccharide vaccine. JAMA. 1999;281:243-248.

77. Centers for Disease Control and Prevention. Preventing pneumococcal disease among infants and young children: Recommendations of the Advisory Committee on Immunization Practices (ACIP). MMWR Morbid Mortal Wkly Rep. 2000;49 (RR-9):1-35.

78. Whitney CG, Farley MM, Hadler J, et al. Decline in invasive pneumococcal disease after the introduction of protein-polysaccharide conjugate vaccine. N Engl J Med. 2003;348:1737-1746.

79. Vernacchio L, Neufeld EJ, MacDonald K, et al. Combined schedule of 7-valent pneumococcal conjugate vaccine followed by 23-valent pneumococcal vaccine in children and young adults with sickle cell anemia. J Pediatr. 1998;133:275-278.

80. Chan CY, Molrine DC, George S, et al. Pneumococcal conjugate vaccine primes for antibody responses to polysaccharide pneumococcal vaccine after Hodgkin's disease. J Infect Dis. 1996;173:256-258.

81. Vidarsson G, Sigurdardottir ST, Gudnason T, et al. Isotypes and opsonophagocytosis of pneumococcus type 6B antibodies elicited in infants and adults by an experimental pneumococcus type 6B-tetanus toxoid vaccine. Infect Immun. 1998;66:2866-2870.

82. Breukels MA, Zandvoort A, van den Dobbelsteen GPJM, et al. Pneumococcal conjugate vaccines overcome splenic dependency of antibody response to pneumococcal polysaccharides. Infect Immun. 2001;69:7583-7587.

83. Cimaz R, Mensi C, D'Angelo E, et al. Safety and immunogenicity of a conjugate vaccine against *Haemophilus influenzae* type b in splenectomized and nonsplenectomized patients with Cooley anemia. J Infect Dis. 2001;183:1819-1821.

84. Garner D, Weston V. Effectiveness of vaccination for *Haemophilus influenzae* type b. Lancet. 2003;361:395-396.

85. Centers for Disease Control and Prevention. Prevention and control of meningococcal disease and meningococcal disease and college students. MMWR Morbid Mortal Wkly Rep. 2000;49:1-20.

86. Ruben FL, Hankins WA, Zeigler Z, et al. Antibody responses to meningococcal polysaccharide vaccine in adults without a spleen. Am J Med. 1984;76:115-121.

86a. Balmer P, Falconer M, McDonald P, et al. Immune response to meningococcal serogroup C conjugate vaccine in asplenic individuals. Infect Immun. 2004;72; 332-337.

87. White KS, Covington D, Churchill P, et al. Patient awareness of health precautions after splenectomy. Am J Infect Control. 1991;19:36-41.

88. Canadian Paediatric Society. Prevention and therapy of bacterial infections of the child with asplenia/hyposplenia. Canad J Paediatr. 1995;2:371-375.

89. Cooper MJ, Williamson RCN. Splenectomy: Indications, hazards and alternatives. Br J Surg. 1984;71:173-180.

90. Rozinov VM, Salel'ev SB, Keshishyan RA, et al. Organ-sparing treatment for closed spleen injuries in children. Clin Orthoped. 1995;320:34-39.

91. Rice HM, James PD. Ectopic splenic tissue failed to prevent fatal pneumococcal septicaemia after splenectomy for trauma. Lancet. 1980;1:565-566.

92. Tang WH, Wu FL, Huang MK, Friess H. Splenic tissue autotransplantation in rabbits: No restoration of host defense. Langenbecks Arch Surg. 2003;387:379-385.

93. Al-Salem AH, al-Dabbous I, Bhamidibati P. The role of partial splenectomy in children with thalassemia. Eur J Pediatr Surg. 1998;8:334-338

94. Rice HE, Oldham KT, Hillery CA, et al. Clinical and hematologic benefits of partial splenectomy for congenital hemolytic anemias in children. Ann Surg. 2003;237:281-288.

95. Traub A, Giebink GS, Smith C, et al. Splenic reticuloendothelial function after splenectomy, spleen repair, and spleen autotransplantation. N Engl J Med. 1987;317: 1559-1564.

CHAPTER **316**

Postoperative Infections and Antimicrobial Prophylaxis

THOMAS R. TALBOT
ALLEN B. KAISER

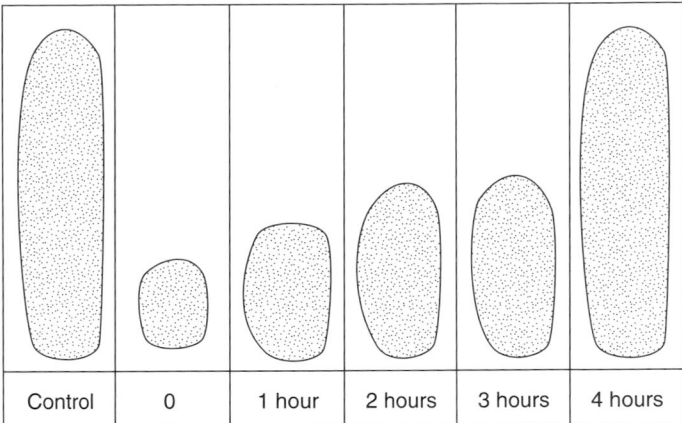

FIGURE 316-1. Relationship between the timing of antimicrobial administration and the effectiveness of prophylaxis as shown by the size of wound infection in an animal model. Lesion sizes were measured as mean diameter (mm) of induration developing 24 hours after intradermal inoculation of *Staphylococcus aureus.*

In 1862, Louis Pasteur's ingenious experiments into the nature of putrefaction were officially endorsed by the Paris Academy of Science. The endorsement signaled an end to the long-held belief that the exposure of organic material to air brought about the "spontaneous generation" of microorganisms, and the concepts of "sepsis" and "asepsis" became firmly established. A scant 3 years later, Joseph Lister demonstrated the incredible implications of antisepsis in his practice of orthopedic surgery. For the first time in recorded history, major surgical procedures could be performed with a reasonable expectation of primary wound healing and recovery. Essential enhancements for preventing and controlling wound "sepsis" were provided by the antibiotic revolution of the 1940s, ushering in the highly technical, highly invasive, and highly successful era of modern surgery. As noted by McDermott and Rogers,[1] the great achievements of the antibiotic era may be related, in the long run, to its essential role in supporting the advancements of modern surgery. Indeed, surgery as we know it today would be impossible in an environment in which infection was likely or, once established, untreatable. As a case in point, further advances in the implantation of the artificial heart—the epitome of applied technology in surgery—must await improved methods of infection control.[2]

Despite the fundamental role of antisepsis and antibiotics in the development of modern surgery, implementation of these discoveries in the practice of surgery has not occurred without opposition. As late as 1880, for example, William Halstead was ordered from the operating theater when he challenged a senior surgeon's disregard for antiseptic techniques. The early use of antibiotics for prophylaxis in surgical procedures was also questioned as respected academicians freely voiced their disapproval of antibiotic prophylaxis in clean surgical procedures.[3] For a number of years the value of prophylactic antibiotics in preventing infections of the surgical wound remained in doubt. A consensus in favor of their use did not emerge until two concepts of perioperative prophylaxis and infection were established. First, investigators in Cincinnati and Boston demonstrated that, despite the use of standard aseptic techniques, *Staphylococcus aureus* could be regularly isolated from the operative field.[4-6] It became apparent that aseptic technique could decrease but not eliminate bacterial contamination of the surgical field. Therefore, it appeared plausible that perioperative antibiotics could supplement aseptic techniques in containing the inevitable contamination of the operative wound.

The second major finding involved the timing of the administration of the prophylactic antibiotic. As early as 1946, Howes[7] had noted a correlation between the amelioration of infection and the interval between the contamination of the wounds and the administration of antibiotics. Several years later, Miles and colleagues[8] and Burke,[9] working in a guinea pig model of wound infection, demonstrated the remarkable brevity of the

"window" of prophylactic efficacy. They noted that antibiotics given shortly before or at the time of bacterial inoculation of the subcutaneous tissue of the guinea pig produced a notable diminution in the size of the subsequent wound induration compared with lesions in animals not receiving antibiotic prophylaxis (Fig. 316-1). By delaying the administration of antibiotics by only 3 or 4 hours, resulting lesions were identical in size to those of animals receiving no antibiotic prophylaxis whatsoever. Thus "failures" of antimicrobial prophylaxis that had been noted in earlier clinical studies were related to the fact that preoperative or intraoperative antibiotics had not been given.[10-12] These observations have been difficult to reproduce,[13] and there is a paucity of clinical evidence verifying the importance of the timing of prophylaxis. Nevertheless, current practice has evolved to mandate that, whenever possible, prophylaxis of surgical wound infection should be administered so as to ensure adequate tissue levels of antimicrobials at the beginning of the surgical procedure.

The efficacy of prophylactic antibiotics has now been verified for most major surgical procedures with a wide variety of antimicrobials when care has been given to provide adequate serum and tissue levels of antibiotics during the surgical procedure. Perioperative antibiotics and aseptic techniques have become routine aspects of care in most major surgical procedures. Despite efforts to prevent infection, analysis of data from the National Center for Health Statistics[14] and the National Nosocomial Infections Surveillance (NNIS) system[15] suggests that between 800,000 and 1,400,000 surgical wound infections complicate the approximately 40 million procedures performed annually in the United States. An obstacle for the surveillance of postsurgical infections, the migration of procedures to the outpatient surgical arena, has continued to expand. In 2000, 63% of all surgical procedures were performed in outpatient settings, up from 50% in 1990.[14] New technological advances (e.g., the introduction of minimally invasive procedures) and the emergence of antibiotic-resistant organisms (e.g., community-acquired methicillin-resistant *S. aureus* [MRSA]) have led to additional challenges in the prevention and identification of surgical site infections. Much, therefore, remains to be learned regarding the pathophysiology, prevention, and surveillance of surgical wound infections.

PRINCIPLES OF PREVENTION AND CONTROL OF POSTOPERATIVE INFECTION

Determinants and Pathophysiology of Surgical Wound Infection

Whether a wound infection occurs after surgery depends on a complex interaction between (1) patient-related factors (e.g., host immunity, nutritional status, the presence or absence of diabetes); (2) procedure-related factors (e.g., implantation of foreign bodies, degree of trauma

FIGURE 316-4. Schematic diagram of the skin demonstrating the location of the transient bacteria on the skin surface, which are easily removed, and the deep resident bacteria, which cannot be destroyed by skin antiseptics. *(From Postlethwaite RW. Principles of operative surgery: Antisepsis, technique, sutures, and drains. In: Sabiston DC, ed. Davis-Christopher Textbook of Surgery. 12th ed. Philadelphia: WB Saunders; 1981:322.)*

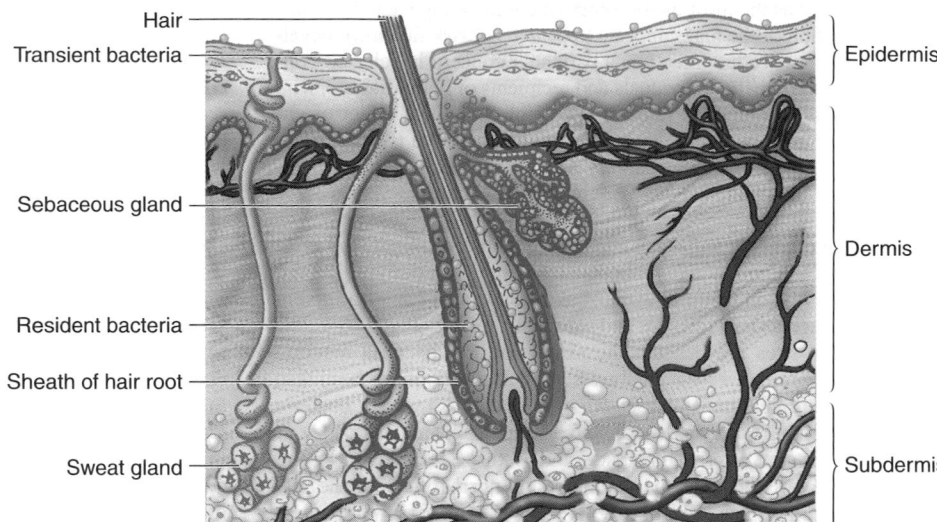

secondary infection during the immediate postoperative period. During this time, surgical incisions are hyperemic from the trauma of the surgery and endothelialization of intravascular prosthetic materials has not yet had time to occur. Moreover, the regular use of indwelling intravascular access devices and lines likely increases the risk of bacteremia. However, information with which to judge the relative contribution of intraoperative versus postoperative hematogenous seeding of the surgical incision is unavailable.

Virulence Factors of Major Wound Pathogens

Clean Wound Infections. The requirement for large inocula in the early models of *S. aureus* soft tissue infection gave the misleading impression that cooperative interaction between bacteria may be required to establish a wound infection.[8,9,36] More recent models involving foreign bodies have demonstrated median infective dose (ID$_{50}$) values of less than 100 colony-forming units (CFU) with polytetrafluoroethylene (PTFE) tissue cages,[37] 10 CFU with PTFE vascular grafts,[38] and as low as 1 CFU with dextran microbeads.[39] These data demonstrate the pathogenic potential of a single bacterium to produce wound infection, provided that it is inoculated into a suitable niche.

Determinants of *S. aureus* virulence have been studied for decades and include a wide variety of enzymes and toxins with diverse effects on the host. Which of the staphylococcal virulence factors contribute to the development of a wound infection is poorly understood. *S. aureus* and the coagulase-negative staphylococci bind to a variety of biologic molecules, including fibronectin, fibrinogen, vitronectin, collagen, laminin, and platelet thrombospondin.[40,41] Fibronectin and collagen receptors in *S. aureus* have been identified.[40,42] Blood clots and the subendothelium are rich in fibronectin, and adherence to such sites may be the first step in the pathogenesis of a clean surgical wound infection. Demonstrating the importance of this process in the pathogenesis of wound infection, a recent study noted that administration of a recombinant fragment of the fibronectin-binding domains of *S. aureus* inhibited abscess formation and potentiated the benefit of cefazolin prophylaxis in a guinea pig model of wound infection.[43]

Once in the wound, several staphylococcal exoenzymes can damage host tissues, including hyaluronidase, lipase, proteases, nucleases, and four membrane-damaging toxins.[44] Under some conditions protein A competes with phagocytic cells for F$_c$ receptors, thereby reducing antibody-mediated opsonization.[45] Coagulase may also interfere with phagocytosis.

Contaminated Wound Infections. The role of coliforms and anaerobes in abdominal sepsis has been elucidated in a model that involved inserting a gelatin capsule containing a standardized inoculum of pooled cecal contents into the peritoneal cavities of rats.[46,47] Acute peritonitis and septicemia from coliforms caused rapid death in 37% of the animals, and all of the survivors developed abscesses with anaerobes as the predominant organisms. The capsular polysaccharide

of *B. fragilis* promotes abscess formation and may reduce phagocytosis. In experimental models, immunization against capsular polysaccharide can protect against abscess formation after inoculation with *B. fragilis* by a T-cell-dependent mechanism, except in the presence of foreign material.[48] Also, *B. fragilis* produces a variety of tissue-damaging enzymes, including fibrinolysin, chondroitin sulfatase, collagenase, and hyaluronidase.

General Host Immunity and Risk Factors for Infection

Various host factors have been associated with an increased risk of infection (see Table 316-2),[19,49] and new risk factors for the development of infection have been recently identified. Latham and associates, in a prospective study of 1000 cardiothoracic surgery patients, found that hyperglycemia (serum glucose > 200 mg/dL) in the 48 hours postprocedure was associated with a 102% increase in the risk for wound infection.[50] Risk also increased incrementally with further elevations in glucose; however, the degree of long-term glucose control (as measured by glycosylated hemoglobin levels at time of surgery) did not impact infection risk.

Many patient risk factors for infection are interrelated, with a patient exhibiting one risk factor also being likely to have others. Methods to ascertain an individual's overall risk for the development of a surgical site infection have been developed to account for the multiple factors involved in the pathogenesis of wound infections. Developed and tested on more than 58,000 patients during the Centers for Disease Control and Prevention Study on the Efficacy of Nosocomial Infection Control (SENIC), one such index takes into account the traditional assessment of the level of wound contamination together with three patient- and procedure-related risk factors (Table 316-4).[21] Using multivariate analysis, it was found that an operation involving the abdomen, a procedure lasting longer than 2 hours, and the presence of three or more discharge diagnoses (as a surrogate for identifying the complicated patient) were independent risk factors for a wound infection. Their inclusion with the traditional wound classification system predicted the risk of wound infection about twice as well as the wound classification system alone, and the addition of other factors did not improve the predictive capability of the model.

This model has subsequently been modified further, resulting in the NNIS risk index (see Table 316-4), which contains only three variables: (1) a patient with an American Society of Anesthesiologists preoperative assessment score of 3, 4, or 5; (2) an operation classified as contaminated or dirty-infected; and (3) an operation lasting longer than *T* hours, where *T* depends upon the procedure.[22,24,51] Use of a laparoscope has been found to reduce the rates of surgical site infections in selected surgical populations (all patients undergoing laparoscopic cholecystectomy and colonic surgery regardless of risk and those with no risk factors for infection [NNIS score of 0] undergoing laparoscopic appendectomy or gastric surgery). Laparoscope use has there-

TABLE 316-4 Indices to Assess Individual Risk of Developing Surgical Wound Infection[15,21]

Index	Scoring
SENIC (Study of the Efficacy of Nosocomial Infection Control)	
Operative time > 2 hours	1 point
Abdominal procedure	1 point
Contaminated or dirty procedure	1 point
≥ 3 discharge diagnoses	1 point
NNIS (National Nosocomial Infection Surveillance system)	
ASA score of 3, 4, or 5	1 point
Contaminated or dirty procedure	1 point
Length of procedure > *T* hours (75th percentile duration of specific procedure)	1 point
Use of laparoscope*	Minus 1 point

*Use of laparoscope reduces surgical site infection rates in all patients (regardless of other risk factors) undergoing cholecystectomy and colon surgery, and in those without other risk factors (NNIS score = 0) undergoing gastric surgery or appendectomy. This scoring criterion should, therefore, be applied to those select subgroups when assessing infection risk.

ASA, American Society of Anesthesiologists.

Data from National Nosocomial Infections Surveillance System. National Nosocomial Infections Surveillance (NNIS) System report, data summary from January 1992 to June 2002, issued August 2002. Am J Infect Control 2002;30:458-475; and Mangram AJ, Horan TC, Pearson ML, et al. Guideline for prevention of surgical site infection, 1999. Infect Control Hosp Epidemiol. 1999;20:247-277.

fore been added to the NNIS index for these patient subgroups.[15] Risk assessment using such indices has allowed detailed stratified descriptions of procedure-specific surgical site infection rates to be generated over the past decade (Table 316-5).[15] Even with the improvement in risk assessment afforded by these indices, critics have noted that for some procedures, such as cesarean section and various neurosurgical procedures, the NNIS index may not adequately stratify risk.[52] Therefore, further modification of risk assessment tools for surgical site infection will need to occur in order to accurately stratify postsurgical infection risk.

The Wound Microenvironment

Much of our understanding of the pathophysiology of wound infection and the nature of the surgical wound derives from investigational models (Table 316-6). Early investigations suggesting that the efficacy of antibiotics in preventing wound infection is limited to only a few hours after the moment of bacterial inoculation[7,8] implied that the wound microenvironment is not static. It is likely that rapid changes are occurring among microbial factors, for example, a shift from exponential to stationary-phase growth with an accompanying decrease in bacterial susceptibility to antibiotics and possibly the expression of different microbial virulence factors. Wound-related changes must also occur, such as gradually diminishing tissue perfusion and antibiotic delivery related to increased tissue oncotic pressure brought about by the effect of inflammatory mediators on vascular permeability. Both or neither of these examples may be important. It is likely, however, that the elucidation of the pathophysiology of the decisive period will have a profound effect on developing strategies for improving the efficacy of antibiotic prophylaxis.

Multiple host defense mechanisms are involved in the response to bacteria inoculated at the surgical site. Neutrophils are probably the most important effector cells, and the most common wound pathogens are highly susceptible to killing by reactive oxygen intermediates. Opsonization by antibodies and complement facilitate phagocytosis. An additional host defense mechanism against abscess formation by *S. aureus* has been described by Dye and Kapral.[63] Abscess homogenates are bactericidal for staphylococci, and this activity is mediated by 2-monoglycerides and unsaturated free fatty acids. Most strains of *S. aureus* produce fatty-acid metabolizing enzyme (FAME), which inactivates the bactericidal lipids. Strains deficient in this enzyme are eliminated rapidly from intraperitoneal abscesses in mice, whereas strains producing FAME are capable of prolonged survival in vivo. More recently,

phospholipase A_2 has been found in inflammatory exudates, and has been noted to have potent antistaphylococcal activity.[64] T-cell-dependent immune mechanisms have been shown to be important in protection against *B. fragilis* infection,[48] but their importance with regard to other common wound pathogens is not as well established.

Foreign Material and Operative Trauma to Tissue. Investigations of *S. aureus* infection in the skin of human volunteers by Elek and Conen[36] conclusively established the role of foreign material in potentiating wound infection. By including suture material with the intradermal staphylococcal inoculum, the number of organisms required to establish a skin pustule could be reduced 10,000-fold relative to lesions without sutures (i.e., a fall from 5×10^6 organisms to 3×10^2 organisms in the inoculum). These investigators further suggested that "other circumstances may lead to the unhindered growth of small inocula, including heavily traumatized tissues, burns, or devitalized tissues distal to the ligated vessels. This may be the explanation of the traditional surgical view that untidy operative techniques predispose to infection."[36] In clean and clean-contaminated surgical procedures, it is generally believed that the quantitative bacterial inoculation into the wound is small. Tissue devitalization at a gross or microscopic level, by providing a niche wherein a small bacterial inoculum may grow in relative isolation from the host's defenses, plays a major role in the pathogenesis of clean wound infection.

Investigational models have demonstrated how technical variables of the surgical procedure influence the risk of infection. Some suture materials appear to have a stronger adjuvant effect on infection than others.[65] Whether the use of the electrosurgical knife, which can damage host tissues via the transfer of heat, is an adjuvant for infection is controversial.[66,67] In an in vitro system, thermally killed fibroblasts activate the alternative complement pathway, leading ultimately to impaired neutrophilic activity against bacteria.[68]

Effect of Operative Procedures on Systemic and Local Immunity. Operative procedures produce systemic and local changes in the immune defense mechanisms of the host. Neutrophil function and serum opsonizing capacity become impaired. The microbicidal activity of neutrophils obtained postoperatively from patients undergoing abdominal hysterectomy is 25% less than that of neutrophils harvested from the same patients preoperatively, and it takes 9 days to return to normal.[69] The depletion of opsonizing factors within the abscess milieu also may contribute to decreased neutrophilic bactericidal function.[70,71]

Major surgical procedures compromise the host defenses in other ways. Surface levels of HLA-DR antigens on the circulating monocytes of patients are reduced following major surgery.[72] However, it has been shown that defects in T-cell proliferation and cytokine secretion after major surgery involve an inability of T cells to respond to T-cell receptor- and CD28 coreceptor-mediated signals rather than problems with antigen presentation by monocytes-macrophages.[73] Perioperative hypothermia brought on by anesthetic-induced impairment of thermoregulation and exposure to the low ambient temperatures of the operating room may accompany major surgery and is believed to trigger vasoconstriction and decrease oxygen tension in the tissues. Low subcutaneous oxygen tension may also be a risk factor for a surgical site infection.[74] In the setting of perioperative hypothermia, neutrophils have reduced chemotaxis, impaired ingestion of staphylococci, and diminished superoxide production.[75] In colorectal surgery, active measures to maintain normothermia and administration of supplemental oxygen (fraction of inspired oxygen [FIO_2] 80%) during surgery have each been associated in randomized, double-blind trials with a reduction in wound infections compared to that in patients allowed to experience routine mild perioperative hypothermia or administered lower concentrations of oxygen (FIO_2 30%).[76,77] A recent double-blind trial of general surgical patients undergoing major intra-abdominal surgical procedures randomized to receive either 80% or 35% FIO_2 intraoperatively, however, has called into question the role of supplemental oxygen therapy in the prevention of surgical site infection. Pryor and colleagues found that the incidence of infection was significantly higher in the group of patients who received the higher oxygen concentration (odds ratio of 2.6 for surgical site infection in the 80% FIO_2 group).[78] Therefore, the role of supplemental oxygen in infection prevention remains unclear.

TABLE 316-5 Surgical Site Infection Rates, by Selected Operative Procedure and NNIS Risk Index Category, January 1992-June 2002*

Operative Procedure Category	Duration Cutpoint (hr)‡	M (−1)§	Infection Rates† (No. of Procedures) for NNIS Risk Index =			
			0	1	2	3
CABG—chest & leg	5		1.28 (2196)	3.51 (301,715)	5.62 (62,625)	
Thoracic surgery	3		0.39 (1274)	1.11 (4340)	2.85 (1438)	
Appendectomy (open)	1		1.40 (6924)	2.87 (8710)	4.83 (3087)	8.06 (360)
Appendectomy (laparoscopic)‖	1		0.57 (2,116)			
Gastric surgery (open)	3		2.69 (2341)	4.95 (4447)	10.03 (1995)	
Gastric surgery (laparoscopic)‖	3		0.53 (377)			
Cholecystectomy	2	0.44 (29,710)	0.67 (24,058)	1.81 (11,164)	3.26 (3,931)	5.62 (445)
Colon surgery	3	1.94 (566)	3.94 (15,457)	5.69 (26,378)	8.59 (11,013)	11.45 (1554)
Small bowel surgery	3		5.06 (1443)	7.26 (3332)	9.09 (2,024)	
Laparotomy	2		1.73 (5725)	3.17 (6899)	5.03 (3697)	7.30 (767)
Prostatectomy	4		0.85 (2476)	2.00 (1748)	4.17 (288)	
Genitourinary other than prostatectomy/ nephrectomy	2		0.36 (12,363)	0.90 (6564)	3.07 (1563)	
Head & neck surgery	7		2.33 (559)	5.13 (799)	13.28 (354)	
Herniorrhaphy	2		0.80 (10,243)	2.03 (6367)	3.94 (1471)	
Mastectomy	3		1.86 (13,623)	2.33 (8509)	3.59 (835)	
Craniotomy	4		0.91 (3964)	1.56 (11,696)	2.12 (3682)	
Ventricular shunt	2		4.17 (3331)	5.44 (9085)		
Cesarean section	1		2.83 (127,324)	4.12 (37,896)	6.69 (3826)	
Abdominal hysterectomy	2		1.40 (39,735)	2.34 (19,041)	5.39 (3988)	
Vaginal hysterectomy	2		1.23 (23,977)			
Limb amputation	1		3.63 (9230)			
Open reduction of fracture	2		0.76 (13,893)	1.34 (22,496)	2.48 (4,360)	4.48 (469)
Hip prosthesis	2		0.89 (30,463)	1.53 (50,566)	2.38 (13,841)	
Knee prosthesis	2		0.85 (43,615)	1.28 (49,652)	2.21 (12,384)	
Laminectomy	2		0.89 (57,063)	1.40 (40,859)	2.51 (12,972)	
Spinal fusion	4		1.08 (35,722)	2.77 (20,058)	6.29 (5311)	
Vascular surgery	3		0.90 (6795)	1.77 (58,422)	4.46 (232,471)	
Organ transplant	6		4.48 (3881)		15.09 (1511)	

*As reported by the National Nosocomial Infections Surveillance System.[15] Surgical site infection rates for adjacent risk index groupings that were not significantly different are grouped together.

†Per 100 operations

‡Time in hours of the 75th percentile of duration of operation for selected operative procedure.

§For cholecystectomy and colon operations, 1 point is subtracted from the NNIS risk score if a laparoscope is used. When no risk factors are present and a laparoscope is used, the score is designated "M" or −1.

‖Use if laparoscope was found only to reduce the rate of surgical site infection (SSI) in those with NNIS risk index of 0; Rates of SSI for laparoscopic appendectomy and gastric surgery in patients with NNIS risk index of 1 or greater are similar to that found with open procedure.

CABG, coronary artery bypass graft.

Perioperative blood transfusion has been associated with an increased rate of postoperative infections, including wound infection, with donated white blood cell (WBC)-induced immunosuppression implicated as the culprit.[79] Decreases in cell-mediated immunity and increases in cytokine levels (interleukin [IL]-2 receptor, IL-6) have been demonstrated in mice and humans following transfusion.[80,81] However, clinical trials comparing the receipt of standard whole or buffy-coat-depleted blood products (which, despite the moniker, still retain some donor WBCs) to WBC-depleted products or the administration of allogenic versus autologous blood have failed to provide a consensus answer to transfusion's role in the development of postoperative infections.[82] Studies describing this potential transfusion effect have been criticized for using nonstandardized outcome definitions, failing to account for known risk factors for postoperative infection, and using only univariate analyses.[82] Blood transfusion may simply serve as a marker for unidentified patient comorbidities, and more rigorously designed studies are needed before general conclusions regarding the role of blood transfusion in wound infection can be determined.

In cardiac surgery the patient may be exposed to hypothermia, cardiopulmonary bypass, and relative arterial hypotension throughout much of the procedure as well as the use of one or both internal mammary arteries for grafting. Exposure of blood to cardiopulmonary bypass depletes serum complement and immunoglobulins and adversely affects neutrophilic function.[83,84] Furthermore, protein denaturation and chylomicron aggregation may contribute to small vessel occlusion and tissue hypoxia as well as overwhelm the capacity of the reticuloendothelial system to clear infectious agents from the blood.[85] This raises the possibility that post-bypass patients may be predisposed to develop infections via hematogenous bacterial seeding, possibly originating from intravascular catheters, as a result of reduced reticuloendothelial clearance.

The release of cytokines at the wound site may have a protective effect against infection. Pretreatment of tissue cages with tumor necrosis factor, either administered directly or generated in vivo by exposure to staphylococcal cell wall components, inhibited abscess formation by an inoculum of S. aureus that under normal circumstances would have produced infection 100% of the time.[86] Also, the use of fibrinolytic agents prevents abscess formation in investigational models.[87] This is consistent with the hypothesis that the adherence of bacteria to fibrinous exudates is an essential step in the pathogenesis of a wound infection.

Perioperative Antibiotics

The in vivo interaction between inoculated bacteria and prophylactically administered antibiotic is one of the most important determinants of the fate of the wound. For example, without antibiotic prophylaxis

TABLE 316-6 Selected Contributions of Investigational Models to an Understanding of the Pathophysiology of Surgical Wound Infection

Investigative Findings	Model	Author(s) (Date)
Adverse effect of dehydration, adrenalin, and heparin on infection resistance of contaminated wounds	Subcutaneous infection in guinea pigs using a variety of aerobic and anaerobic bacteria	Miles and Niven[53] (1950); Burke and Miles[54] (1958)
Importance of early administration of antibiotics in preventing wound infection	Subcutaneous and intradermal infection in guinea pigs with *Staphylococcus aureus*	Howes[7] (1946); Miles et al.[8] (1957); Burke[9] (1961)
Importance of foreign material in enhancing *S. aureus* infections	Intradermal and subcutaneous infection in human volunteers	Elek and Conen[36] (1958)
Development of muscle infection model and exploring the role of iron in enhancing the infecting process	Muscle infection in mice using *Escherichia coli* with non-replicating phage	Polk and Miles[55] (1971)
Development of intra-abdominal abscess model	Intraperitoneal infection in rats with *E. coli* and *Bacteroides fragilis*	Weinstein et al.[46] (1974)
Role of lymphatic clearance of bacteria in host defenses	Subcutaneous infection in rabbits with *S. aureus* and anaerobic gram-negative rods	DeLong and Simmons[56] (1982)
Development of a model of subcutaneous tissue cage infection	Subcutaneous infection in guinea pigs with *S. aureus*	Zimmerli et al.[37] (1982)
Importance of early administration of topical antiseptics and antibiotics in preventing wound infection	Subcutaneous infection in guinea pigs with *S. aureus, E. coli,* and *B. fragilis*	Platt and Bucknall[57] (1984)
Importance of oxygen in preventing wound infection	Intradermal infection in guinea pigs with *E. coli*	Knighton et al.[58] (1984)
Role of fibrin in enhancing abscess formation	Intraperitoneal infection in rats with *E. coli* and *B. fragilis*	Hau et al.[59] (1986)
Importance of granulocytes in antibiotic prophylaxis	Muscle infection of mice with *S. aureus*	Hoogeterp et al.[60] (1987)
Quantitation of *S. aureus* capsular polysaccharide	Subcutaneous graft infection in guinea pigs with *S. aureus*	Arbeit and Dunn[38] (1987)
Quantitation of *S. aureus* exopolymers	Subcutaneous tissue cage infection in guinea pigs with *S. aureus*	Falcieri et al.[61] (1987)
Use of dextran microcarrier beads as an adjuvant, permitting production of an abscess with small numbers of staphylococci	Subcutaneous abscess model in mice	Ford et al.[62] (1989)
Low-inoculum model with the sensitivity to compare different regimens of antibiotic prophylaxis in preventing infection	Intramuscular *S. aureus* abscess model in guinea pigs	Kaiser et al.[39] (1992)

the reported risk of developing a *S. aureus* wound infection after cardiac surgery is 15% to 44%,[88-90] an incidence that approximates the frequency of skin/nares colonization with *S. aureus*. Infection rates are generally lower for clean procedures involving less tissue trauma and better hemostasis. Over the past 20 years, the efficacy of antibiotic prophylaxis in clean surgery has been clearly established. The principle on which most systemic antibiotic prophylaxis is based is the belief that antibiotics in the host tissues can augment natural immune defense mechanisms and help to kill bacteria that are inoculated into the wound. The rationale for the administration of oral antibiotics in colonic surgery differs in that, although some agents exhibit systemic absorption and penetrate into host tissues (e.g., erythromycin and metronidazole, but not neomycin), the primary goal in this setting is a reduction in potential pathogens among the normal gut flora at the time of surgery. Oral prophylaxis is generally combined with mechanical preparation of the bowel to reduce colonic flora, including cathartics and isotonic lavage solutions.

Every effort should be made to ensure that adequate antibiotic levels are maintained throughout the surgical procedure. Although a number of studies in the past have indicated that prolonged surgical procedures are associated with a higher infection rate, it is not clear whether this increased risk is inevitable or primarily attributable to the greater likelihood of there being low or undetectable concentrations of antibiotics during long procedures. In cardiothoracic procedures in particular, the use of cardiopulmonary bypass can dramatically reduce serum vancomycin levels as a result of alterations in drug clearance and volume of distribution, potentially placing the wound at increased risk for infection.[91] In contrast, cephalosporin levels tend to fall at a slower rate during bypass periods. Understanding the pharmacokinetics of the various antimicrobials used in perioperative prophylaxis is therefore vital to ensure adequate antibiotic levels at the surgical wound site during the entire procedure.

Resistance to Perioperative Antibiotics

The success of prophylaxis in clean surgery correlates directly with the susceptibility of bacteria to the antibiotic in vitro (Fig. 316-5),[92] with some failures of prophylaxis attributable to bacterial resistance. Furthermore, some *S. aureus* wound infections are caused by strains reported by the clinical laboratory to be cephalosporin susceptible, but which produce the type A variant of staphylococcal β-lactamase and can degrade less stable cephalosporins such as cefazolin relatively rapidly.[93]

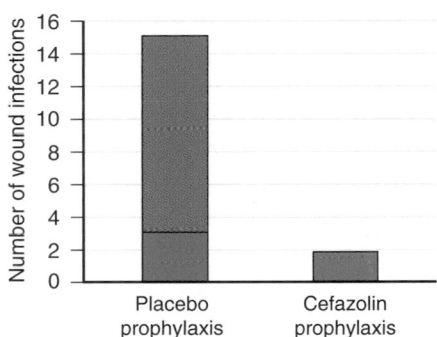

FIGURE 316-5. Susceptibility to cefazolin of pathogens isolated from 17 wound infections among patients receiving placebo (saline) or cefazolin for prophylaxis of vascular surgical procedures. The *red area* indicates cefazolin-susceptible bacteria and the *blue area* indicates cefazolin-resistant bacteria. Infection rates were 6.8% and 0.9% for patients receiving placebo and cefazolin, respectively. This difference was attributable entirely to the prevention of infection by cefazolin-susceptible pathogens, mainly *Staphylococcus aureus*, among patients receiving cefazolin. The incidence of infection by cefazolin-resistant pathogens was similar in both regimens. (*From Kaiser AB, Clayson KR, Mulherin JL Jr, et al. Antibiotic prophylaxis in vascular surgery. Ann Surg. 1978;188:283-289.*)

Studies involving a guinea pig model of wound infection and isogeneic strains of *S. aureus* that differ only in the presence or absence of the gene encoding type A staphylococcal β-lactamase have shown that, when cefazolin is administered as prophylaxis, the number of CFU required to establish infection 50% of the time (ID_{50}) is significantly smaller for the β-lactamase-producing isolate than for the non-β-lactamase-producing isolate.[94] A subpopulation of *S. aureus* belonging to phage group 94/96 and characterized by borderline susceptibility to oxacillin, the presence of a unique 17.2-kb plasmid, and the production of large quantities of type A staphylococcal β-lactamase has been associated with deep wound infections among surgical patients receiving cefazolin as perioperative prophylaxis.[95] β-Lactamase-mediated degradation of cephalosporins in vivo appears to enable a bacterium to survive beyond the time of its initial lodgment in antibiotic-containing tissues, ultimately contributing to the development of a wound infection.[93-95]

Because cephalosporins have become the mainstay of prophylaxis, the increasing prevalence of cephalosporin-resistant pathogens has important implications for prophylaxis. The proportion of *S. aureus* causing nosocomial infection that is methicillin resistant has increased from 14.3% in 1987 to 54.5% in 1997.[96,97] Furthermore, infections caused by methicillin-resistant coagulase-negative staphylococci (MRCNS), cephalosporin- and gentamicin-resistant gram-negative rods, vancomycin-resistant enterococci, and fungi are being reported with increasing frequency, including in surgical procedures traditionally regarded as clean.[98,99] It is increasingly clear that strategies must be devised to contain these pathogens.

The emergence of community-acquired MRSA[100] has clouded the issue of appropriate antimicrobial prophylaxis. Current recommendations note to consider using vancomycin as empirical therapy for treatment and prophylaxis of presumptive staphylococcal infection when the local rates of MRSA are significant; however, the threshold at which vancomycin use should occur has never been clearly defined. As the prevalence of community-acquired MRSA climbs, its role as a key agent of postsurgical infections will become more significant, and use of vancomycin for routine surgical prophylaxis will have to be balanced against concerns for its inappropriate use.

Nonwound Infections in the Surgical Patient

As many as 71% of all nosocomial infections occur in surgical patients.[101] Infections at the operative site account for 40% of these, with the urinary tract (42%), respiratory tract (14%), and blood stream (4%) representing the other major foci. Catheters inserted into vessels and the bladder, as well as intubation and anesthesia, impair the ability of normal host defense mechanisms to prevent infection at these sites.

PRACTICE OF PREVENTION OF POSTOPERATIVE INFECTION

Stemming from these concepts of wound infection pathogenesis, a number of interventions have been put into practice over the past century to reduce the risk of wound infection. These interventions can be grouped into two major categories (Table 316-7). The first line of defense involves measures that reduce bacterial inoculation into the wound site. These include familiar rituals such as the application of antiseptics to the skin of the patient, the washing and gloving of the surgeon's hands, the use of sterile drapes, airflow control, and the use of gowns and masks by operating room personnel. Efforts to reduce patient colonization with staphylococci may also be of benefit. A recent randomized, placebo-controlled trial found that mupirocin applied to the nares of patients undergoing elective cardiothoracic, neurosurgical, oncologic, gynecologic, and general surgical procedures beginning on the day prior to surgery and continued for up to 5 consecutive days resulted in a reduction in *S. aureus* nosocomial infections from 7.7% to 4.0% in those with preoperative nasal carriage of *S. aureus*. However, the rates of nosocomial and, specifically, surgical site infections in all patients, regardless of *S. aureus* carriage status, were not reduced with the use of mupirocin.[102] Screening for *S. aureus* nasal carriage and targeted use of mupirocin in carriers should be considered as a preventive strategy for staphylococcal nosocomial infections. Preoperative showering with a solution containing chlorhexidine suppresses bacterial colonization of the skin[103]; however, it is not clear whether this practice results in a reduction in infection rates. To minimize the acquisition of resistant hospital flora before surgery, the preoperative hospital stay should be as short as possible and the use of antibiotics in the preoperative period should be avoided whenever possible. The method of hair removal may also impact the risk for development of surgical site infection, because shaving with a razor leaves small microabrasions around the operative site that may harbor bacteria. Other methods that do not create microabrasions, such as clippers or depilatories, are preferred for preoperative hair removal.[104] In a large randomized trial of 1013 patients, surgical site infections occurred in 3.2% of patients following hair removal with clippers the morning of surgery versus 10.0%

TABLE 316-7   Interventional Maneuvers of Proven or Theoretical Benefit in Diminishing the Risk of Surgical Wound Infection

Maneuvers to Diminish Inoculation of Virulent or Antimicrobial-Resistant Bacteria into Wound
Preoperative Factors
- Avoid preoperative antibiotic use
- Minimize preoperative hospitalization
- Eliminate nasal colonization with *S. aureus*
- Treat remote sites of infection
- Avoid shaving at operative site
- Delay hair removal at operative site until time of surgery and remove hair with electric clippers or depilatories
- Routinely have patient shower or bathe preoperatively with chlorhexidine-containing soap
- Ensure timely administration of prophylactic antibiotics

Intraoperative and Postoperative Factors
- Carefully prepare patient's skin with povidone-iodine or chlorhexidine-containing solution
- Rigorously adhere to routine aseptic techniques
- Maintain high flow of filtered air
- Consider laminar flow environment
- Minimize operative personnel traffic
- Consider irrigation of wound with antibiotic-containing solution
- Isolate clean from contaminated surgical fields (e.g., reglove and change instruments used to harvest saphenous vein before working in intrathoracic field)
- Minimize flash sterilization of surgical instruments
- Minimize use of drains
- Bring drains, if used, through a separate stab wound
- Minimize use of catheters and intravascular lines postoperatively

Maneuvers to Improve Host Containment of Contaminating Bacteria
Preoperative Factors
- Resolve malnutrition or obesity
- Discontinue cigarette smoking
- Maximize diabetes control
- Identify and minimize perioperative hyperglycemia

Intraoperative and Postoperative Factors
- Minimize dead space, devitalized tissue, and hematomas
- Consider use of supplemental oxygen therapy
- Maintain perioperative normothermia
- Maintain adequate hydration and nutrition

in those who underwent day-of-surgery shaving with a razor.[105] Although some recommendations advocate no preoperative hair removal,[23] there is minimal evidence to support an increased risk of wound infection with hair removal by clippers or depilatories on the morning of surgery as compared to no hair removal.[104] Infection at sites remote from the operative field is a host risk factor for postoperative infection that is potentially correctable prior to surgery.[106] Drains and intravascular devices should be removed as quickly as possible to avoid the risk of direct and hematogenous seeding of the operative site.

Second-line measures are directed toward improving host containment and elimination of bacteria that have circumvented the front line of defense and have been inoculated into the wound. Most authorities have emphasized that the single most important factor in preventing wound infection is surgical technique. Gentle handling of wound tissues, avoidance of dead space, devitalized tissues, and hematomas, and careful approximation of tissue planes are believed to be critical in maintaining an infection-free incision. Good surgical technique along with minimizing hypothermia and minimizing the use of vasoconstrictive medications help to improve tissue perfusion and oxygenation, thereby improving the delivery and function of neutrophils. Avoiding malnourishment and achieving tight control of glucose levels in diabetics, particularly in the immediate perioperative period, also appear to reduce the risk of postoperative infection.[107,108] Conversely, investigations of mechanisms to directly modify the host immune system (administration of granulocyte-macrophage colony stimulating factor,[109] exclusive use of autologous blood transfusions,[79] or administration of histamine type 2 receptor antagonist[110]) are either too preliminary or too inconclusive to provide guidelines for clinical practice.

Perioperative Antimicrobial Prophylaxis

The efficacy of perioperative prophylaxis in preventing wound infection after many surgical procedures is unquestioned. Not only have the benefits of early antibiotic administration been duplicated by numerous investigators using different animal models, different pathogens, and different antibiotics, literally hundreds of clinical trials have verified the efficacy of perioperative antibiotics. Nevertheless, issues regarding the optimal choice, frequency, and duration of perioperative antibiotic prophylaxis are unresolved.

Selection of Prophylactic Regimen

It is important to realize that the current practice of antimicrobial prophylaxis is based largely on the results of clinical trials that are, for the most part, too cumbersome to detect differences in efficacy between prophylactic regimens.[111] For example, in clean elective surgical procedures, infection rates with routine cephalosporin prophylaxis are already low (5%). In attempting to evaluate clinically the superiority of a different antibiotic regimen, randomization of approximately 900 patients would be necessary before a 50% reduction in infection rate could be demonstrated at the $P = .05$ level. Many more patients would require study to demonstrate reliably that differences did not exist.

Based on their antibacterial spectrum and low incidence of allergy and side effects, the cephalosporins have emerged as the drugs of choice for the vast majority of operative procedures. Because of its reasonably long half-life and low cost, cefazolin has been the dominant choice for clean procedures. Even in clean-contaminated procedures such as hysterectomy and cholecystectomy, in which cephalosporins with improved in vitro activity against anaerobic bacteria are often advocated, most clinical studies indicate that cefazolin is equivalent in its prophylactic efficacy. For procedures in which anaerobic coverage is also justified (e.g., distal gastrointestinal tract, major head and neck, biliary, and gynecologic procedures) addition of metronidazole or use of second-generation cephalosporins with anaerobic activity (e.g., cefoxitin or cefotetan) are appropriate selections for prophylaxis.[23]

The prevalence of MRSA in some medical centers has resulted in the increased use of vancomycin for perioperative prophylaxis of clean procedures. In one institution surgical prophylaxis was reported to account for 35% of intravenous vancomycin use.[112] Studies comparing prophylaxis with vancomycin and cephalosporins have shown vancomycin to be equivalent or superior in preventing wound infection.[113,114] However, theoretical concerns remain about a possible increased risk of infection from gram-negative aerobic pathogens. In a guinea pig model of intramuscular abscess formation and antimicrobial prophylaxis, prophylaxis with vancomycin increased the number of bacteria needed to establish infection to greater than 100,000 CFU compared to less than 1000 CFU for cefazolin prophylaxis.[115] Practical limitations that may affect the use of vancomycin in surgery include its narrow spectrum of antimicrobial activity and the need for a slow rate of infusion. Furthermore, the growing prevalence of vancomycin-resistant enterococci and the emergence of vancomycin-resistant *S. aureus* (VRSA) raise concerns about potential adverse effects on the antimicrobial susceptibility of nosocomial pathogens induced by the selective pressure of surgical antibiotic prophylaxis.[116] It is currently recommended that the use of vancomycin for perioperative prophylaxis should be considered only in patients with a life-threatening allergy to β-lactam antibiotics or at institutions with a high rate of infections caused by MRSA or methicillin-resistant *S. epidermidis*.[117] Community-acquired MRSA further complicates these recommendations, however, because healthy patients with few of the traditional comorbidities and risk factors for MRSA infection or colonization (e.g., prior hospitalizations, extensive antibiotic use, chronic underlying illness) may be at increased risk of MRSA colonization and subsequent infection. Therefore, local prevalence of community-acquired MRSA must be taken into account when evaluating vancomycin for use as surgical wound prophylaxis.

Regarding contaminated procedures, whether or not a few doses of systemic prophylaxis should be added to oral antibiotics in colorectal surgery remains unresolved, although it appears prudent to do so in certain circumstances. These include when surgery has been delayed to greater than 10 to 12 hours after the last oral dose, when there is spillage of colonic contents intraoperatively, and for procedures lasting more than 3.5 hours.[118]

It should not be presumed that cephalosporins will remain as the prophylactic agents of choice in the future. Over the past decade, various classes of antibiotics have been shown to differ appreciably in activity against bacteria in the stationary phase of growth, postantibiotic effect, diffusibility into devitalized tissue or fibrin clots, resistance to enzymatic degradation, activity within abscesses, and penetration of and activity within neutrophils that may have ingested but be unable to kill wound bacteria. Each of these variables may affect the efficacy of an agent used for prophylaxis, and it is likely that preferred prophylactic regimens will change over time in response to an improved understanding of the pathophysiology of infection and to antimicrobial resistance among wound pathogens. Animal models may be especially valuable in helping to define improved regimens of antimicrobial prophylaxis and in determining whether immunomodulation can further reduce the risk of wound infection.[115,119]

Timing and Duration of Prophylaxis

Except in elective colonic surgical procedures in which oral antibiotics must be administered several hours before the procedure, there is general agreement that the initial dose of systemically administered antibiotics should be given in a timely fashion so that antibiotic levels in the tissue at the time of the incision are adequate. Guidelines and studies vary somewhat on the exact timing, however, ranging from 2 hours to no more than 30 minutes prior to incision (see Table 316-8 later in this chapter).[23] Administration too early before or too close to the time of incision will result in suboptimal tissue levels and potentially increased risk of postoperative wound infection.

It is also generally recommended that antibiotics be readministered during long surgical procedures so as to maintain serum concentrations well above the minimum inhibitory concentration values of common pathogens.[49,120,121] Theoretical reasons to ensure that adequate serum and tissue levels of antibiotics are maintained throughout the surgical procedure include the probability that the introduction of bacteria into the surgical wound occurs not only at the time of incision but continuously throughout the surgical procedure. The period of highest risk for bacterial contamination may be the close, not the beginning, of surgery. In prolonged procedures or with antibiotics with short half-lives, patients may be inadequately protected if redosing is not routinely provided.[122]

Historically, it has proven to be more difficult to administer pre- and intraoperative antimicrobial prophylaxis at the optimal times than might be supposed. Retrospective studies to determine the proportion of surgical patients who received an appropriate antibiotic within an hour before surgery suggest that 30% to 70% of patients do not receive prophylaxis in a timely fashion.[123-125] Quality standards for antimicrobial prophylaxis in surgery recommend incorporating the administration of perioperative antimicrobial prophylaxis into the routine procedures executed within the operating room by either the anesthesiologist or the circulating nurse.[121] Computer-generated reminders for dosing of preoperative antibiotic prophylaxis have been associated with improved adherence to recommended standards for antibiotic dosing before incision and may serve as an additional method for ensuring timely delivery of prophylaxis.[126]

Whether and for how long antibiotics should be given postoperatively is a subject of considerable disagreement. This issue is complicated by the targeting of surgical prophylaxis by many hospitals as an area in which significant cost savings can be achieved. In general, many studies comparing short-course versus long-course prophylaxis have reflected no increase in infection rates among the short-course recipients.[127-133] However, one comparative study of cesarean sections did detect a significantly higher incidence of endometritis in patients randomized to receive the short (18-hour) versus the long (3-day) course of perioperative ampicillin prophylaxis.[134] Also, Gatell and colleagues[135] noted a significantly higher infection rate in major joint repairs among patients receiving one versus five doses of perioperative cefamandole. Surgeons have justified continuing postoperative antibiotics for 2 or 3 days in patients who have undergone major surgical procedures and are being monitored with invasive devices on the basis that hematogenous seeding of the operative wound may occur. A study comparing vascular surgery patients receiving pre- and intraoperative prophylaxis only versus a group that continued antibiotics until intravascular lines and drain tubes were removed (but not exceeding 5 days) found the infection rate of the short-course group was twice that of the long-course group.[136] The ultimate implications of the duration of postoperative antibiotics remain to be determined. Data are simply not available to quantitate the relative risks and benefits of prolonged postoperative antibiotic prophylaxis. Large-scale studies with careful attention to infection rates and antimicrobial resistance patterns of infecting pathogens are clearly needed to resolve this issue.

Recommendations for Prophylaxis

Based on prospective studies of antibiotic prophylaxis, prophylactic regimens have been recommended for a wide variety of surgical procedures (Table 316-8),[137] and many acceptable combinations of antibiotic prophylaxis have been utilized. Although only some regimens have been tested in controlled clinical trials, others with similar antimicrobial coverage and tissue penetration should provide similar protection provided dosing guidelines are followed. The keys in selecting an appropriate prophylactic antibiotic regimen include coverage against the expected endogenous flora at the surgical site (Table 316-9), consideration of patient allergies and antimicrobial costs, knowledge of the ecology of local nosocomial wound pathogens, consideration of antibiotic penetration into the specific surgical site tissue, and assurance of appropriate antibiotic dosing and delivery. Any operation that involves entry into a hollow viscus ("clean-contaminated" procedure) requires antimicrobial prophylaxis. In addition, for some clean procedures, such as operations in which an intravascular prosthesis or prosthetic joint is inserted or in which a surgical site infection (especially deep or organ space infections) poses a catastrophic risk (e.g., all cardiac surgeries, vascular operations, and most neurosurgical procedures), prophylactic antibiotics should be administered.[23] Dirty or contaminated procedures usually do not require specific antimicrobial prophylaxis because patients undergoing these procedures are already on targeted antimicrobial therapy for established infections.[23]

Marked variations in the spectrum of infecting pathogens and in the degree of antimicrobial resistance exist among various hospitals. Moreover, variations in infecting pathogens and resistance patterns can and do occur over time within a given institution. Physicians and individual health care institutions must tailor routine prophylactic regimens based on carefully collected epidemiologic data regarding surgical wound infection. Equally important, many surgical procedures are far from routine, and numerous variations in perioperative circumstances will dictate deviations from established prophylactic regimens. Early reexplorations for postoperative bleeding, a history of penicillin or cephalosporin allergy, trauma and other emergency surgery, and existing preoperative infections of nonwound sites (e.g., urinary tract infections, decubitus ulcers) are important variables that may influence the choice and duration of perioperative prophylaxis. Studies are not available that can provide guidelines for such situations. A continuous assessment of failures of prophylaxis and a willingness to alter antiseptic and perioperative antibiotic protocols based on local observations or published data are essential aspects of surgical wound prevention and antimicrobial prophylaxis.

Novel Methods of Antibiotic Prophylaxis

Newer methods for delivery of antimicrobial prophylaxis have expanded the available armamentarium for the prevention of surgical site infections. First introduced in 1939,[162] antibiotic-impregnated cement (as a local antimicrobial "brachytherapy") placed directly into the operative wound is increasingly being used as a method of antibiotic prophylaxis, particularly in orthopedic procedures involving the replacement of infected prosthetic joints. Brachytherapy utilizes powdered antibiotic mixed with a cement polymer (such as polymerized polymethylmethacrylate) to form a compound that may be directly applied onto prosthetic material or manufactured into beads (usually 3 to 10 mm in diameter) that are placed into the wound. Candidate antibiotics for use as brachytherapy must be available as a pharmaceutical-grade powder, must be heat stable (because of the exothermic reaction induced with polymerization), and must have an appropriate microbiologic spectrum of activity for the predominant pathogens at the operative site.[162] The aminoglycosides and vancomycin are the compounds most commonly utilized for brachytherapy; oxacillin and cefazolin have comparable elution characteristics but are less frequently utilized because of concerns regarding β-lactam allergy.

The majority of antibiotic elution occurs in the first days after implantation, but elution from impregnated cement has been detected years following surgery.[162,163] Although a retrospective review of patients with compound limb fractures showed a decreased rate of infection from 12% to 3.7% ($P < .001$) with the use of aminoglycoside-impregnated beads as a supplement to systemic antibiotics,[164] the efficacy of these preparations in the prophylaxis against surgical site infections (especially as an adjunct of systemic administration of prophylactic antimicrobials) has not been firmly established. Systemic absorption of antibiotic brachytherapy is also a cause for concern because potentially high boluses of antibiotic may lead to toxicity. In one series of 14 subjects, 1 patient developed permanent and 2 others temporary high-frequency hearing loss following implantation of gentamicin-impregnated beads.[165] In another study, measurements of serum aminoglycoside levels in patients with antibiotic-impregnated cement and beads used as a part of their surgical prophylaxis for hip arthroplasty were 10 to 20 times lower than those receiving intravenous therapy (cement group mean, 0.3 μg/mL; bead group mean, 0.06 μg/mL; intravenous group mean, 4.0 μg/mL).[166] Although such data are promising, further studies into the systemic absorption and efficacy of these brachytherapeutic compounds is warranted.

Side Effects of Prophylaxis

Adverse effects of prophylaxis for the patient include allergic reactions ranging in severity from minor skin rashes to anaphylaxis. Pseudomembranous colitis has been noted with a wide variety of prophylactic agents, including oral erythromycin and neomycin, parenteral aminoglycosides, metronidazole, and cefoxitin.[167] However, in view of the extensive use of prophylaxis in this country and judging from the infrequency of published reports, pseudomembranous colitis remains an unusual complication of prophylactic therapy. Another notable side effect is profound hypotension and flushing associated with vancomycin prophylaxis (the "red-man syndrome").[168] Although the risk of this potentially reversible complication has been associated with rapid infusions of the antibiotic, some clinicians have encountered clinically significant hypotension despite exercising care to maintain slow vancomycin infusion rates.[169]

The use of prophylactic antibiotics has consequences for the institution as well as the individual patient. Antibiotic use, and specifically prophylactic use, has been shown to have a critical role in the selection of antibiotic-resistant bacteria to become the dominant colonizing flora as well as nosocomial pathogens of hospitalized patients.[170] At least two mechanisms for this process have been documented. First, the antibiotic-resistant flora may be endemic within the institution and transferred to the patient during the course of hospitalization.[171] Second, a small population of antibiotic-resistant bacteria that are part of the patient's endogenous flora at the time of hospitalization may emerge under the selective pressure of perioperative prophylaxis to become the dominant flora.[172] The increasing prevalence of MRSA and MRCNS has profound implications for a continued or expanded role of prophylactic antibiotics in surgery. In view of the improvement in overall surgical wound infection rates over recent decades (see Table 316-1), the consensus is that prophylactic antibiotics are clearly worth this potential side effect.

...mary of Antibiotic Prophylaxis Recommendations for the Most Commonly Performed Surgical Procedures

	Source of Recommendations				
Procedure	*ASHP (1999)[138]*	*Medical Letter (2001)[139]*	*IDSA (1994)[121]*	*Sanford Guide (2003)[140]*	*SIS (1993)[49]*
Cardiac (Prosthetic valve surgery, CABG, other open heart procedure, pacemaker and automated defibrillator placement)	Cefazolin 1 g at induction and q8h up to 72 hr* *Alternatives:* Cefuroxime 1.5 g (dosed q12h) Cefamandole 1 g (dosed q6h) Vancomycin† 1 g over 1 hr	Cefazolin or cefuroxime 1-2 g Vancomycin† 1 g over 1 hr	Cefazolin 1-2 g preinduction, but not more than 60 min preprocedure Vancomycin† 1 g over 1 hr	Cefazolin 1 g × 1 or q8h × 1-2 days Cefuroxime 1.5 g × 1 or q12h × 2 days Vancomycin† 1 g × 1	Cefazolin 1-2 g preinduction, then 1-2 g q8h × 48 hr Vancomycin† 1 g, slowly, preinduction
Colon	**Oral:** After mechanical bowel preparation is completed: Neomycin sulfate 1 g + erythromycin base 1 g orally at 19, 18, and 9 hr before operation **IV:** If oral route is contraindicated: Cefoxitin 2 g at induction Cefotetan 2 g at induction Cefmetazole 2 g at induction If high-risk surgery (e.g., rectal resection), use both **oral** and **IV** regimens	**Oral:** After appropriate diet and catharsis: Neomycin sulfate 1 g + erythromycin base 1 g orally at 1 PM, 2 PM, and 11 PM before 8 AM operation **IV:** Cefoxitin 1-2 g Cefotetan 1-2 g Cefazolin 1-2 g + metronidazole 500 mg	**Oral:** Neomycin sulfate + erythromycin base orally for 18 hr preoperatively before operation is sufficient for procedures in which the bowel can be effectively cleansed. **IV:** If cleaning of bowel not possible or if high-risk patient: Cefoxitin 1-2 g preinduction Cefotetan 1-2 g preinduction	**Elective:** *Colorectal prep:* Oral polyethylene glycol for mechanical cleansing is cited as an option in addition to oral erythromycin base 1 g and oral neomycin 1 g at 1 PM, 2 PM, and 11 PM the night prior to surgery. **Emergency:** Cefazolin 1-2 g + metronidazole 500 mg Cefoxitin 1-2 g Cefotetan 1-2 g	**Oral:** Neomycin sulfate 1 g + erythromycin base 1 g orally at 1 PM, 2 PM, and 11 PM **IV:** Cefoxitin 1 g preinduction Cefotetan 1 g preinduction Cefmetazole 1 g preinduction
Total Knee/Hip Arthroplasty	Cefazolin 1 g at induction and q8h × 24 hr *Alternative:* Vancomycin† 1 g with or without gentamicin 2 mg/kg	Cefazolin 1-2 g Vancomycin†	Cefazolin 1-2 g Vancomycin†	**Hip: Same as cardiac** **Total joint replacement other than hip:** Cefazolin 1-2 g pre-op Vancomycin† 1 g on call to OR	Cefazolin 1 g preinduction Vancomycin† 1 g slowly preinduction
Hysterectomy	Cefazolin 1 g *or* Cefotetan‡ 1 g at induction *Alternative:* Cefoxitin 1 g at induction	Cefazolin 1-2 g Cefotetan‡ 1-2 g Cefoxitin 1 g	Cefazolin 1-2 g preinduction	Cefazolin 1-2 g Cefotetan 1-2 g Cefotetan‡ 1-2 g Cefuroxime 1.5 g	Cefazolin 1 g preinduction
Vascular	Cefazolin 1 g at induction and q8h × 24 hr *Alternative:* Vancomycin† 1 g with or without gentamicin 2 mg/kg	Cefazolin 1-2 g Vancomycin† 1 g	Cefazolin 1-2 g Vancomycin†	Same as cardiac	Cefazolin 1 g preinduction with 2 post-op doses Vancomycin† 1 g slowly preinduction
Neurosurgical (Craniotomy)§	Cefazolin 1 g at induction *Alternatives:* Oxacillin 1 g Nafcillin 1 g Vancomycin† 1 g	Cefazolin 1-2 g Vancomycin† 1 g	Cefazolin 1-2 g	Cefazolin 1 g × 1 Vancomycin† 1 g × 1	Cefazolin 1 g preinduction with 2 post-op doses Vancomycin† 1 g slowly pre-induction
Timing of Dose	Ideal time of administration is within 30 min to 1 hr before the incision	Infusion completed 30 min or less before incision	Give during the dosing interval beginning 60 min before infusion	Give in the interval 2 hr before time of incision	Preinduction indicates in operating room before initiating anesthesia.
Notes	For most procedures, duration should be 24 hr or less.	Postoperative doses are usually unnecessary.	Postoperative doses not recommended.	Single dose probably as effective as multiple doses (except for prolonged procedures, which require redosing)	

For specific prophylactic recommendations for less common surgical procedures, refer to the recommendation sources noted above as well as the following selected resources: cesarean section,[141-146] dilatation and curettage/abortion,[147-149] open reduction of extremity fracture,[150,151] laminectomy,[152,153] ophthalmologic procedures,[154] prostatectomy,[155-157] and major head and neck procedures.[158-160]

All antibiotics are recommended for IV dosing unless otherwise noted.

*"Prophylaxis for 24hrs or less may be appropriate. There is no evidence to support continuing antibiotic prophylaxis until chest and mediastinal tubes are removed."

†"Vancomycin use should be discouraged for routine prophylaxis unless patient is allergic to β-lactam antibiotics or the procedure involves implantation of prosthetic materials or devices at institutions with a high rate of infections caused by MRSA or methicillin-resistant coagulase negative staphylococci. In procedures in which gram-negative pathogens are likely (such as vascular surgery involving groin incisions, lower extremity vascular procedures, hysterectomy, or abdominal procedures), another agent with gram-negative activity should be used with vancomycin.

‡One study found cefotetan superior to cefazolin posthysterectomy.[161]

§Use of prophylactic antibiotics before ventricular shunt placement is controversial.

CABG, coronary artery bypass graft; MRSA, methicillin-resistant *Staphylococcus aureus*; NPO, nothing by mouth; OR, operating room.

Adapted from Centers for Medicare and Medicaid Services and the Centers for Disease Control and Prevention. Surgical Infection Prevention Medicare Quality Improvement Project: Surgical Infection Prevention Antimicrobial Selection Guidelines Crosswalk. Available at *www.medqic.org/cms-service/stream/asset/SIP_GuidelineCrosswalk_0403.pdf?asset_id=1131859* (Accessed January 12. 2004.)

TABLE 316-9 Typical Microbiologic Flora at Surgical Sites for Various Operative Procedures

Operation	Likely Pathogens*
Placement of all grafts, prostheses, or implants	Staphylococcus aureus, CoNS
Cardiac	S. aureus, CoNS
Neurosurgery	S. aureus, CoNS
Breast	S. aureus, CoNS, streptococci
Ophthalmic†	S. aureus, CoNS, streptococci, GNR
Orthopedic	S. aureus, CoNS, streptococci, GNR
Noncardiac thoracic	S. aureus, CoNS, Streptococcus pneumoniae, GNR
Vascular	S. aureus, CoNS
Appendectomy	GNR, anaerobes
Biliary tract	GNR, anaerobes
Colorectal	GNR, anaerobes
Gastroduodenal	GNR, streptococci, oropharyngeal anaerobes
Head & neck (with incision through oropharyngeal mucosa)	S. aureus, streptococci, oropharyngeal anaerobes
Obstetric & gynecologic‡	GNR, enterococci, group B streptococci, anaerobes
Urologic§	GNR

*Staphylocci will be associated with surgical site infections following all types of operations.

†Limited data on efficacy of prophylaxis.

‡For cesarean sections, prophylaxis should be given after clamping the umbilical cord.

§May not be beneficial if urine is sterile.

CoNS, coagulase-negative staphylococci; GNR, gram-negative rods/bacilli.

From Mangram AJ, Horan TC, Pearson ML, et al. Guideline for prevention of surgical site infection, 1999. Infect Control Hosp Epidemiol. 1999;20:247-277.

Over recent years several other multiple antibiotic-resistant bacteria have become important nosocomial pathogens, including strains of *Enterococcus faecium* resistant to vancomycin, ampicillin, and/or gentamicin; *S. aureus* resistant to β-lactams and the quinolones; and *E. coli* and *Klebsiella* isolates that are resistant to cefotaxime and ceftazidime.[98] One would predict that increasing reliance on our most potent antibiotics in prophylaxis will be associated in time with further increases in the prevalence of these antibiotic-resistant strains. The impact of the recent emergence of VRSA[116] is yet to be felt, but VRSA's arrival portends an ominous change in the complexity of the ecology of nosocomial infections.

Cost-Benefit Analysis of Prophylaxis

Prophylactic antibiotics add considerable cost to the routine care of surgical patients. In major surgical centers, the perioperative use of antibiotics may represent almost half of the pharmacy's expenditures for antibiotics, and surgeons are often encouraged to reduce or eliminate antibiotics given for prophylaxis in certain settings. For example, in carotid endarterectomy and cholecystectomy, infections develop only infrequently, are seldom life threatening, and may cost more to prevent than to treat. However, it seems inappropriate to evaluate antibiotic use on the basis of cost alone. When prophylaxis or a particular form of prophylaxis offers a clear advantage to the patient, the health care system should advocate the better treatment without consideration of its cost. Moreover, an analysis of the cost of prophylactic antibiotics can be complicated. Not only the cost of the antibiotic per se but the cost of preparing, transporting, and administering multiple doses of antibiotic must be included. Perhaps of more importance, the cost in terms of mortality, morbidity, and resources of managing wound infections that develop when using inadequate prophylaxis must be considered.[173] The 6-month mortality rate of patients who develop a deep wound infection is 2.5-fold that of patients who do not develop a deep wound infection.[174] Case-matched studies show that a postoperative wound infection doubles the length of postoperative hospitalization.[175]

TABLE 316-10 National Nosocomial Infections Surveillance (NNIS) System Definitions for Surgical Site Infections

Infection Type	Definition
Soft-Tissue Infection	
Superficial	Infections involving only skin and subcutaneous tissue of the incision occurring within 30 days after the procedure with one or more of the following: • Purulent drainage from the incision; • Positive culture from superficial incision; • Pain/tenderness, swelling, erythema, or heat at surgical wound that has been deliberately opened by a surgeon; *or* • Diagnosis by a surgeon or attending physician
Deep	Infections involving deep soft tissue (fascia/muscle layers) occurring within 30 days (or up to 1 yr if implant* is placed during surgery) after the procedure with one of the following: • Purulent drainage from deep incision but not from organ space; • Spontaneous dehiscence or deliberate opening by a surgeon in the presence of fever or local pain, *unless* incision is culture-negative; • Abscess involving a deep incision found by direct exam, radiologic exam or during reoperation; *or* • Diagnosis by a surgeon or attending physician
Organ/Space	Infections that involve any part of the body opened or manipulated during the operative procedure, excluding skin incision/fascia/muscle layers, within 30 days after procedure (or up to 1 year if implant is placed) with one of the following: • Purulent drainage from a drain that is placed through a stab wound into the organ/space; • Positive culture growth of a specimen of mediastinal tissue or fluid aseptically obtained during operation or aspiration; • Evidence of infection during surgical procedure or by radiologic or histopathologic examination; *or* • Diagnosis by a surgeon or attending physician

*Implant defined as a nonhuman foreign body (e.g., prosthetic heart valve, nonhuman vascular graft, or hip prosthesis).

From Garner JS, Jarvis WR, Emori TG, et al. CDC guidelines for nosocomial infections. In: Olmsted RN, ed. APIC Infections Control and Applied Epidemiology: Principles and Practice. St. Louis: Mosby; 1996.

Surgical Wound Infection Surveillance

A key component in the prevention of surgical wound infections is the establishment of a surveillance infrastructure to detect and monitor rates of procedure-specific infections, to define the changing ecology of resistant pathogens that cause surgical infections, and to provide accurate analysis of the pervading antimicrobial sensitivity patterns in each specific institution. Adequate surveillance for postsurgical infections with comparisons of infection rates to national benchmarks allows for continued evaluation and assessment of the quality of an individual hospital's prevention strategies. In order to allow comparisons to national benchmark statistics, such surveillance must utilize standardized infection definitions, such as those used by the NNIS system (Table 316-10).[176] The presence of purulence within a surgical incision generally serves as initial evidence of a surgical wound infection, but culture results of surgical wounds or exudates should not be used solely as a guide to the presence or absence of infection. Surveillance systems should also utilize the input of representatives with surgical, infectious diseases, and infection control expertise in the analysis and evaluation of data. Evaluation of surveillance data must also occur at a regular frequency so as to detect variations and trends in the antimicrobial susceptibility pattern of surgical wound pathogens.

In health care settings associated with a high volume of surgical procedures, surgical wound isolates should be maintained, if possible, for 2 to 3 weeks after isolation. Clusters or outbreaks of surgical wound infections caused by a common pathogen are usually identified retrospectively, and the availability of infecting pathogens such as *S. aureus* or coagulase-negative staphylococci for pulsed-field gel electrophoresis or another means of molecular typing may be instrumental in identifying and eliminating the cause of the outbreak.

There have been recommendations to maintain and even publicize surgeon-specific infection rates in an effort to indirectly cause a decrease in surgical wound infections.[177] Such data may identify unsuspected problems among the surgical staff or may encourage individual surgeons to rigorously adhere to standards of perioperative aseptic techniques. If such a program is used, it is vital that any analysis include an assessment of procedure-specific infection rates. Wide differences in infection rates exist among surgical procedures, even among those procedures within the same surgical subspecialty and category of bacterial contamination. For example, in vascular surgery infection rates after carotid endarterectomy are exceedingly low (less than 0.1%). In contrast, bypass grafting in the femoral-popliteal area may be associated with an infection rate of 2% to 3% despite the fact that both procedures are clean and may be performed by the same vascular surgeons. Other important variables such as the age and condition of the patients must also be considered before comparing infection rates among surgeons.

Surveillance systems for postsurgical infections will face growing challenges in the future, such as the migration of surgical procedures to the outpatient arena and the growing push to decrease lengths of hospital stay with earlier discharge postsurgery. Sands and colleagues noted in 1996 that 84% of surgical site infections occurred following hospital discharge[178] and would, therefore, have been missed with traditional hospital-based surveillance. Methods to improve detection of surgical site infections that arise postdischarge, including direct examinations of wounds during follow-up visits, patient and practitioner surveys, and computerized queries of outpatient diagnostic codes and antibiotic prescriptions,[171,179,180] have met with limited success and concerns regarding costs and generalizability. Any method of postdischarge surveillance must address these concerns and accommodate the unique attributes of each specific hospital and patient population.

REFERENCES

1. McDermott W, Rogers DE. Social ramifications of control of microbial disease. Johns Hopkins Med J. 1982;151:301-312.
2. Rice LB, Karchmer AW. Artificial heart implantation: What limitations are imposed by infectious complications? JAMA. 1988;259:894-895.
3. Finland M. Antibacterial agents: Uses and abuses in treatment and prophylaxis. Rhode Island Med J. 1960;43:499-520.
4. Culbertson WR, Altemeier WA, Gonzalez LL, et al. Studies on the epidemiology of postoperative infection of clean operative wounds. Ann Surg. 1961;154:599-610.
5. Howe CW, Marston AT. A study on sources of postoperative staphylococcal infection. Surg Gynecol Obstet. 1962;115:266-275.
6. Burke JF. Identification of the sources of staphylococci contaminating the surgical wound during operation. Ann Surg. 1963;158:898-904.
7. Howes EL. Prevention of wound infection by the injection of nontoxic antibacterial substances. Ann Surg. 1946;124:268-276.
8. Miles AA, Miles EM, Burke J. The value and duration of defense mechanisms to the primary lodgement of bacteria. Br J Exp Pathol. 1957;38:79-86.
9. Burke JF. The effective period of preventive antibiotic action in experimental incisions and dermal lesions. Surgery. 1961;50:161-168.
10. Sanchez-Ubeda R, Fernand E, Rousselot LM. Complication rate in general surgical cases: The value of penicillin and streptomycin as postoperative prophylaxis—A study of 511 cases. N Engl J Med. 1958;259:1045-1050.
11. Johnstone FRC. An assessment of prophylactic antibiotics in general surgery. Surg Gynecol Obstet. 1963;116:1-10.
12. Classen DC, Evans RS, Pestotnik SL, et al. The timing of prophylactic administration of antibiotics and the risk of surgical-wound infection. N Engl J Med. 1992;326:281-286.
13. Warren MD, Kernodle DS, Kaiser AB. Correlation of *in vitro* parameters of antimicrobial activity with prophylactic efficacy in an intradermal model of *Staphylococcus aureus* infection. J Antimicrob Ther. 1991;28:731-740.
14. National Center for Health Statistics. Ambulatory and inpatient surgery data, 2000. Available at *www.cdc.gov/nchs/fastats/Default.htm* (Accessed on May 19, 2003.)
15. National Nosocomial Infections Surveillance System. National Nosocomial Infections Surveillance (NNIS) System report, data summary from January 1992 to June 2002, issued August 2002. Am J Infect Control. 2002;30:458-475.
16. Aglietti P, Salvati EA, Wilson PD Jr, et al. Effect of a surgical horizontal unidirectional filtered air flow unit on wound bacterial contamination and wound healing. Clin Orthop. 1974;101:99-104.
17. Houang ET, Ahmet Z. Intraoperative wound contamination during abdominal hysterectomy. J Hosp Infect. 1991;19:181-189.
18. Altemeier WA, Burke JF, Pluitt BA Jr, et al. Manual on Control of Infection in Surgical Patients. Philadelphia: JB Lippincott; 1976:29-30.
19. Ad Hoc Committee of the Committee on Trauma, National Research Council Division of Medical Sciences. Postoperative wound infections: The influence of ultraviolet irradiation of the operating room and of various other factors. Ann Surg. 1964;160(2).
20. Olson M, O'Connor M, Schwartz ML. Surgical wound infections: A 5-year prospective study of 20,193 wounds at the Minneapolis VA Medical Center. Ann Surg. 1984;199:253-259.
21. Haley RW, Culver DH, Morgan WM, et al. Identifying patients at high risk of surgical wound infection: A simple multivariate index of patient susceptibility and wound contamination. Am J Epidemiol. 1985;121:206-215.
22. Culver DH, Horan TC, Gaynes RP, et al. Surgical wound infection rates by wound class, operative procedure, and patient risk index. Am J Med. 1991;91(Suppl 3B):152S-157S.
23. Mangram AJ, Horan TC, Pearson ML, et al. Guideline for prevention of surgical site infection, 1999. Infect Control Hosp Epidemiol. 1999;20:247-277.
24. Emori TG, Culver DH, Horan TC, et al. National Nosocomial Infection Surveillance system (NNIS): Description of surveillance methods. Am J Infect Control. 1991;19:19-35.
25. National Nosocomial Infections Surveillance (NNIS) report, data summary from October 1986-April 1996, issued May 1996: A report from the National Nosocomial Infections Surveillance (NNIS) system. Am J Infect Control. 1996;24:380-388.
26. Kluytmans JAJW, Mouton JW, Ijzerman EPF, et al: Nasal carriage of *Staphylococcus aureus* as a major risk factor for wound infections after cardiac surgery. J Infect Dis. 1995;171:216-219.
27. Tuazon CU. Skin and skin structure infections in the patient at risk: Carrier state of *Staphylococcus aureus*. Am J Med. 1984;76:166-171.
28. Postlethwaite RW. Principles of operative surgery: Antisepsis, technique, sutures, and drains. In: Sabiston DC, ed. Davis-Christopher Textbook of Surgery. 12th ed. Philadelphia: WB Saunders; 1981:322.
29. Schaffner W, Lefkowitz LB, Goodman JS. Hospital outbreak of infections with group A streptococci traced to an asymptomatic anal carrier. N Engl J Med. 1969;280:1224-1225.
30. Stamm WE, Feeley JC, Facklam RR. Wound infections due to group A *Streptococcus* traced to a vaginal carrier. J Infect Dis. 1978;138:287-292.
31. Passaro DJ, Waring L, Armstrong R, et al. Postoperative *Serratia marcescens* wound infections traced to an out-of-hospital source. J Infect Dis. 1997;175:992-995.
32. Parry MF, Grant B, Yucna M, et al. *Candida* osteomyelitis and diskitis after spinal surgery: An outbreak that implicates artificial nail use. Clin Infect Dis. 2001;32:352-357.
33. Bennett SN, McNeil MM, Bland LA, et al. Postoperative infections traced to contamination of an intravenous anesthetic, propofol. N Engl J Med. 1995;333:147-154.
34. Carlsson AS, Lidgren L, Lindberg L. Prophylactic antibiotics against early and late deep infections after total hip replacements. Acta Orthop Scand. 1977;48:405-410.
35. Krieger JN, Kaiser DL, Wenzel RP. Nosocomial urinary tract infections cause wound infections postoperatively in surgical patients. Surg Gynecol Obstet. 1983;156:313-318.
36. Elek SD, Conen PE. The virulence of *Staphylococcus pyogenes* for man: A study of the problems of wound infection. Br J Exp Pathol. 1958;38:573-586.
37. Zimmerli W, Waldvogel FA, Vaudaux P, et al. Pathogenesis of foreign body infection: Description and characteristics of an animal model. J Infect Dis. 1982;146:487-497.
38. Arbeit RD, Dunn RM. Expression of capsular polysaccharide during experimental focal infection with *Staphylococcus aureus*. J Infect Dis. 1987;156:947-952.
39. Kaiser AB, Kernodle DS, Parker RA. A low-inoculum animal model of subcutaneous abscess formation and antimicrobial prophylaxis. J Infect Dis. 1992;166:393-399.
40. Patti JM, Jonsson H, Guss B, et al. Molecular characterization and expression of a gene encoding a *Staphylococcus aureus* collagen adhesin. J Biol Chem. 1992;267:4766-4772.
41. Paulsson M, Ljungh Å, Wadström T. Rapid identification of fibronectin, vitronectin, laminin, and collagen cell surface binding proteins on coagulase-negative staphylococci by particle agglutination assays. J Clin Microbiol. 1992;30:2006-2012.
42. Fröman G, Switalski LM, Speziale P, et al. Isolation and characterization of a fibronectin receptor from *Staphylococcus aureus*. J Biol Chem. 1987;262:6564-6571.
43. Menzies BE, Kourteva Y, Kaiser AB, Kernodle DS. Inhibition of staphylococcal wound infection and potentiation of antibiotic prophylaxis by a recombinant fragment of the fibronectin-binding protein of *Staphylococcus aureus*. J Infect Dis. 2002;185:937-943.
44. Rogolsky M. Nonenteric toxins of *Staphylococcus aureus*. Microbiol Rev. 1979;43:320-360.
45. Dossett JH, Kronvall G, Williams RC Jr, et al. Antiphagocytic effects of staphylococcal protein A. J Immunol. 1969;103:1405-1410.
46. Weinstein WM, Onderdonk AB, Bartlett JG, et al. Experimental intra-abdominal abscesses in rats: Development of an experimental model. Infect Immun. 1974;10:1250-1255.
47. Onderdonk AB, Bartlett JG, Louie T, et al. Microbial synergy in experimental abscess. Infect Immun. 1976;13:22-26.
48. Onderdonk AB, Markham RB, Zaleznik DF, et al. Evidence of T cell-dependent immunity to *Bacteroides fragilis* in an intraabdominal abscess model. J Clin Invest. 1982;69:9-16.
49. Page CP, Bohnen JMA, Fletcher JR, et al. Antimicrobial prophylaxis for surgical wounds: Guidelines for clinical care. Arch Surg. 1993;128:79-88.
50. Latham R, Lancaster AD, Covington JF, et al. The association of diabetes and glucose control with surgical-site infections among cardiothoracic surgery patients. Infect Control Hosp Epidemiol. 2001;2:607-612.

51. Owens WD, Felts JA, Spitznagel EL. ASA physical status classifications: A study of consistency of ratings. Anesthesiology. 1978;49:239-243.

52. Gaynes RP. Surgical-site infections and the NNIS SSI risk index: Room for improvement. Infect Control Hosp Epidemiol. 2000;21:184-185.

53. Miles AA, Niven JSF. The enhancement of infection during shock produced by bacterial toxins and other agents. Br J Exp Pathol. 1950;31:73.

54. Burke JF, Miles AA. The significance of vascular events in early infective inflammation. J Pathol Bacteriol. 1958;76:1-19.

55. Polk HC Jr, Miles AA. Enhancement of bacterial infection by ferric iron: Kinetics, mechanisms, and surgical significance. Surgery. 1971;70:71-77.

56. DeLong TG, Simmons RL. Role of lymphatic vessels in bacterial clearance from early soft tissue infection. Arch Surg. 1982;117:123-128.

57. Platt J, Bucknall RA. An experimental evaluation of antiseptic wound irrigation. J Hosp Infect. 1984;5:181-188.

58. Knighton DR, Halliday B, Hunt TK. Oxygen as an antibiotic. Arch Surg. 1984;119:199-204.

59. Hau T, Jacobs DE, Hawkins NL. Antibiotics fail to prevent abscess formation secondary to bacteria trapped in fibrin clots. Arch Surg. 1986;121:163-167.

60. Hoogeterp JJ, Mattie H, Krul AM, et al. Quantitative effect of granulocytes on antibiotic treatment of experimental staphylococcal infection. Antimicrob Agents Chemother. 1987;31:930-934.

61. Falcieri E, Vandaux P, Huggler E, et al. Role of bacterial exopolymers and host factors on adherence and phagocytosis of *Staphylococcus aureus* in foreign body infections. J Infect Dis. 1987;155:524-531.

62. Ford CW, Hamel JC, Stapert D, et al. Establishment of an experimental model of a *Staphylococcus aureus* abscess in mice by use of dextran and gelatin microcarriers. J Med Microbiol. 1989;28:259-266.

63. Dye ES, Kapral FA. Partial characterization of a bactericidal system in staphylococcal abscesses. Infect Immun. 1980;30:198-203.

64. Weinrauch Y, Elsback P, Madsen LM, et al. The potent anti-*Staphylococcus aureus* activity of a sterile rabbit inflammatory fluid is due to a 14-kD phospholipase A2. J Clin Invest. 1996;97:250-257.

65. McGeehan D, Hunt D, Chaudhuri A, et al. An experimental study of the relationship between synergistic wound sepsis and suture materials. Br J Surg. 1980;67:636-638.

66. Nishida H, Grooters RK, Merkley DF, et al. Postoperative mediastinitis: A comparison of two electrocautery techniques on presternal soft tissues. J Thorac Cardiovasc Surg. 1990;99:969-976.

67. Kumagai SG, Rosales RF, Hunter GC, et al. Effects of electrocautery on midline laparotomy wound infection. Am J Surg. 1991;162:620-622.

68. Yamada Y, Hefter K, Burke JE, et al. An in vitro model of the wound microenvironment: Local phagocytic cell abnormalities associated with in situ complement activation. J Infect Dis. 1987;155:998-1004.

69. El-Maallem H, Fletcher J. Effects of surgery on neutrophil granulocyte function. Infect Immun. 1981;32:38-41.

70. Bamberger DM, Herndon BL. Bactericidal capacity of neutrophils in rabbits with experimental acute and chronic abscesses. J Infect Dis. 1990;162:186-192.

71. Zimmerli W, Lew PD, Waldvogel FA. Pathogenesis of foreign body infection: Evidence for a local granulocyte defect. J Clin Invest. 1984;73:1191-1200.

72. Cheadle WG, Hershman MJ, Wellhausen SR, Polk HC Jr. HLA-DR antigen expression on peripheral blood monocytes correlates with surgical infection. Am J Surg. 1991;161:639-645.

73. Hensler T, Hecker H, Heeg K, et al. Distinct mechanisms of immunosuppression as a consequence of major surgery. Infect Immun. 1997;65:2283-2291.

74. Hopf HW, Hunt TK, West JM, et al. Wound tissue oxygen tension predicts the risk of wound infection in surgical patients. Arch Surg. 1997;132:997-1004.

75. Clardy CW, Edwards KM, Gay JC. Increased susceptibility to infection in hypothermic children: Possible role of acquired neutrophil dysfunction. Pediatr Infect. 1985;4:379-382.

76. Kurz A, Sessler DI, Lenhardt R, for the Study of Wound Infection and Temperature Group. Perioperative normothermia to reduce the incidence of surgical-wound infection and shorten hospitalization. N Engl J Med. 1996;334:1209-1215.

77. Greif R, Akça O, Horn E, et al. Supplemental perioperative oxygen to reduce the incidence of surgical-wound infection. N Engl J Med. 2000;342:161-167.

78. Pryor KO, Fahey TJ, Lien CA, et al. Surgical site infection and the routine use of perioperative hyperoxia in a general surgical population. JAMA. 2004;291:79-87.

79. Vamvakas EC, Moore SB. Blood transfusion and postoperative septic complications. Transfusion. 1994;34:714-727.

80. Jensen LS, Andersen AJ, Christiansen PM, et al. Postoperative infection and natural killer cell function following blood transfusion in patients undergoing elective colorectal surgery. Br J Surg. 1992;79:513-516.

81. Jensen LS, Hokland M, Nielsen HJ. A randomized controlled study of the effect of bedside leukocyte depletion on the immunosuppressive effect of whole blood transfusion in patients undergoing elective colorectal surgery. Br. J Surg. 1996;83:973-977.

82. Vamvakas EC. Transfusion-associated cancer recurrence and postoperative infection: Meta-analysis of randomized, controlled clinical trials. Transfusion. 1996;36:175-186.

83. Silva J, Hoeksema H, Fekety FR. Transient defects in phagocytic functions during cardiopulmonary bypass. J Thorac Cardiovasc Surg. 1974;67:175-183.

84. Parker DJ, Cantrell JW, Karp RB, et al. Changes in serum complement and immunoglobulins following cardiopulmonary bypass. Surgery. 1972;71:824-827.

85. Subramanian VA, Gay WA, Dineen PAP. Effect of cardiopulmonary bypass on *in vivo* clearance of live *Klebsiella aerogenes*. Surg Forum. 1977;28:255-257.

86. Vaudaux P, Grau GE, Huggler E, et al. Contribution of tumor necrosis factor to host defense against staphylococci in a guinea pig model of foreign body infections. J Infect Dis. 1992;166:58-64.

87. Rotstein OD, Kao J. Prevention of intra-abdominal abscesses by fibrinolysis using recombinant tissue plasminogen activator. J Infect Dis. 1988;158:766-772.

88. Fong IW, Baker CB, McKee DC. The value of prophylactic antibiotics in aorta-coronary bypass operations: A double-blind randomized trial. J Thorac Cardiovasc Surg. 1979;78:908-913.

89. Penketh ARL, Wansbrough-Jones MH, Wright E, et al. Antibiotic prophylaxis for coronary artery bypass surgery. Lancet. 1985;1:1500.

90. Austin TW, Coles JC, Burnett R, et al. Aortocoronary bypass procedures and sternotomy infections: A study of antistaphylococcal prophylaxis. Can J Surg. 1980;23:483-485.

91. Garcia MPO, Marti-Bonmati E, Serrano JG, et al. Alteration of vancomycin pharmacokinetics during cardiopulmonary bypass in patients undergoing cardiac surgery. Am J Health Syst Pharm. 2003;60:260-265.

92. Kaiser AB, Clayson KR, Mulherin JL Jr, et al. Antibiotic prophylaxis in vascular surgery. Ann Surg. 1978;188:283-289.

93. Kernodle DS, Classen DC, Burke JP, et al. Failure of cephalosporins to prevent *Staphylococcus aureus* surgical wound infections. JAMA. 1990;263:961-966.

94. Kernodle DS, Voladri RKR, Kaiser AB. β-Lactamase production diminishes the prophylactic efficacy of ampicillin and cefazolin in a guinea pig model of *Staphylococcus aureus* wound infection. J Infect Dis. 1998;177:701-706.

95. Kernodle DS, Classen DC, Stratton CW, Kaiser AB. Association of borderline oxacillin-susceptible strains of *Staphylococcus aureus* with surgical wound infections. J Clin Microbiol. 1998;36:219-222.

96. Gaynes R, Culver D, for the National Nosocomial Infection Surveillance (NNIS) System. Emergence of nosocomial methicillin-resistant *Staphylococcus aureus* (MRSA) in the United States, 1987-1997. Presented at the Emerging Infectious Diseases Conference, Atlanta, GA, March 8-12, 1998.

97. Weinstein RA. Controlling antimicrobial resistance in hospitals: Infection control and use of antibiotics. Emerg Infect Dis. 2001;7:188-192.

98. Archibald L, Phillips L, Monnet D, et al. Antimicrobial resistance in isolates from inpatients and outpatients in the United States: Increasing importance of the intensive care unit. Clin Infect Dis. 1997;24:211-215.

99. Neu HC. Emergence and mechanisms of bacterial resistance in surgical infections. Am J Surg. 1995;169(Suppl):13S-20S.

100. Said-Salim B, Mathema B, Kreiswith BN. Community-acquired methicillin-resistant *Staphylococcus aureus:* An emerging pathogen. Infect Control Hosp Epidemiol. 2003;24:451-455.

101. Tetteroo GWM, Wagenvoort JHT, Bruining HA. Role of selective decontamination in surgery. Br J Surg. 1992;79:300-304.

102. Perl TM, Cullen JJ, Wenzel RP, et al. Intranasal mupirocin to prevent postoperative *Staphylococcus aureus* infections. N Engl J Med. 2002;346:1871-1877.

103. Kaul AF, Jewett JF. Agents and techniques for disinfection of the skin. Surg Gynecol Obstet. 1981;152:677-685.

104. Køjnniksen I, Andersen BM, Søndenaa VG, Sedadal L. Preoperative hair removal—A systemic literature review. AORN J. 2002;75:928-940.

105. Alexander JW, Fischer JE, Boyajian M, et al. The influence of hair-removal methods on wound infections. Arch Surg. 1983;118:347.

106. Valentine RJ, Weigelt JA, Dryer D, et al. Effect of remote infections on clean wound infection rates. Am J Infect Control. 1986;14:64-68.

107. Klein JD, Hey LA, Yu CS, et al. Perioperative nutrition and postoperative complications in patients undergoing spinal surgery. Spine. 1996;21:2676-2682.

108. Zerr KJ, Furnary AP, Grunkemeier GL, et al. Glucose control lowers the risk of wound infection in diabetics after open heart operations. Ann Thorac Surg. 1997;63:356-361.

109. Meropol NJ, Wood DE, Nemunaitis J, et al. Randomized, placebo-controlled, multi-center trial of granulocyte-macrophage colony-stimulating factor as infection prophylaxis in oncologic surgery. J Clin Oncol. 1998;16:1167-1173.

110. Moesgaard F, Jensen LS, Christiansen PM, et al. The effect of ranitidine on postoperative infectious complications following emergency colorectal surgery: A randomized, placebo-controlled, double-blind trial. Inflamm Res. 1998;47:12-17.

111. Evans M, Pollock AV. Trials on trial: A review of trials of antibiotic prophylaxis. Arch Surg. 1984;119:109-113.

112. Ena J, Dick RW, Jones RN, et al. The epidemiology of intravenous vancomycin usage in a university hospital: A 10-year study. JAMA. 1993;269:598-602.

113. Maki DG, Bohn MJ, Stolz SM, et al. Comparative study of cefazolin, cefamandole, and vancomycin for surgical prophylaxis in cardiac and vascular operations: A double-blind randomized trial. J Thorac Cardiovasc Surg. 1992;104:1423-1434.

114. Vuorisalo S, Haukipuro K, Pokela R, Syrjala H. Comparison of vancomycin and cefuroxime for infection prophylaxis in coronary artery bypass surgery. Infect Control Hosp Epidemiol. 1998;19:234-239.

115. Kernodle DS, Kaiser AB. Comparative prophylactic efficacy of cefazolin and vancomycin in a guinea pig model of *Staphylococcus aureus* wound infection. J Infect Dis. 1993;168:152-157.

116. Chang S, Sievert DM, Hageman JC, et al. Infection with vancomycin-resistant *Staphylococcus aureus* containing the vanA resistance gene. N Engl J Med. 2003;348:1342-1347.

117. Recommendations for preventing the spread of vancomycin resistance. Hospital Infection Control Practices Advisory Committee. Infect Control Hosp Epidemiol. 1995;16:105-113.

118. Gorbach SL. Antimicrobial prophylaxis for appendectomy and colorectal surgery. Rev Infect Dis. 1991;13(Suppl 10):S815-S820.

119. Kernodle DS, Gates H, Kaiser AB. Prophylactic anti-infective activity of poly-[1,6]-β-D-glucopyranosyl-[1,3]-β-D-glucopyranose glucan in a guinea pig model of staphylococcal wound infection. Antimicrob Agents Chemother. 1998;42:545-549.

120. Antimicrobial prophylaxis in surgery. Med Lett Drugs Ther. 1997;39:97-101.

121. Dellinger EP, Gross PA, Barrett TL, et al. Quality standard for antimicrobial prophylaxis in surgical procedures. Clin Infect Dis. 1994;18:422-427.
122. Platt R, Munoz A, Stella J, et al. Antibiotic prophylaxis for cardiovascular surgery: Efficacy with coronary artery bypass. Ann Intern Med. 1984;101:770-774.
123. Currier JS, Campbell H, Platt R, Kaiser AB. Perioperative antimicrobial prophylaxis in middle Tennessee, 1989-1990. Rev Infect Dis. 1991;13(Suppl 10):S874-S878.
124. Silver A, Eichorn A, Kral J, et al. Timeliness and use of antibiotic prophylaxis in selected inpatient surgical procedures. The Antibiotic Prophylaxis Study Group. Am J Surg. 1996;171:548-552.
125. Matuschka PR, Cheadle WG, Burke JD, Garrison RN. A new standard of care: Administration of preoperative antibiotics in the operating room. Am Surg. 1997;63:500-503.
126. Larsen RA, Evans RS, Burke JP, et al. Improved perioperative antibiotic use and reduced surgical wound infections through use of computerized decision analysis. Infect Control Hosp Epidemiol. 1989;10:316-320.
127. Goldmann DA, Hopkins CC, Karchmer AW. Cephalothin prophylaxis in cardiac valve surgery: A prospective, double-blind comparison of two-day and six-day regimens. J Thorac Cardiovasc Surg. 1977;73:470-479.
128. Nelson CL, Green TG, Porter RA, et al. One day *versus* seven days of preventive antibiotic therapy in orthopedic surgery. Clin Orthop. 1983;176:258-263.
129. Scarpignato C, Caltabiano M, Condemi V, et al. Short-term versus long-term cefuroxime prophylaxis in patients undergoing emergency cesarean section. Clin Ther. 1982;5:186-192.
130. Soper DE, Yarwood RL. Single-dose antibiotic prophylaxis in women undergoing vaginal hysterectomy. Obstet Gynecol. 1987;69:879-882.
131. Conte JE Jr, Cohen SN, Roe BB, et al. Antibiotic prophylaxis and cardiac surgery: A prospective double-blind comparison of single-dose versus multiple-dose regimens. Ann Intern Med. 1972;76:943-949.
132. Hillis DJ, Rosenfeldt FL, Spicer WJ, et al. Antibiotic prophylaxis for coronary bypass grafting: Comparison of a five-day and a two-day course. J Thorac Cardiovasc Surg. 1983;86:217.
133. Kriaras I, Michalopoulos A, Michalis A, et al. Antibiotic prophylaxis in cardiac surgery. J Cardiovasc Surg (Torino). 1997;38:605-610.
134. Elliott JP, Freeman RK, Dorchester W. Short versus long course of prophylactic antibiotics in cesarean section. Am J Obstet Gynecol. 1982;143:740-744.
135. Gatell JM, Garcia S, Lozano L, et al. Perioperative cefamandole prophylaxis against infections. J Bone Joint Surg. 1987;8:1189-1193.
136. Hall JC, Christiansen KJ, Goodman M, et al. Duration of antimicrobial prophylaxis in vascular surgery. Am J Surg. 1998;175:87-90.
137. Centers for Medicare and Medicaid Services and the Centers for Disease Control and Prevention. Surgical Infection Prevention Medicare Quality Improvement Project: Surgical infection prevention antimicrobial selection guidelines crosswalk. Available at: *www.medqic.org/cms-service/stream/asset/SIP_GuidelineCrosswalk_0403.pdf?asset_id=1131859* (Accessed January 12, 2004.)
138. American Society of Health-System Pharmacists. ASHP therapeutic guidelines on antimicrobial prophylaxis in surgery. Am J Health Syst Pharm. 1999;56:1839-1888.
139. Antimicrobial prophylaxis in surgery. Med Lett Drugs Ther. 2001;43:92-97.
140. Gilbert D, Moellering R, Sande M. The Sanford Guide to Antimicrobial Therapy 2003. 33rd ed. Hyde Park, VT: Antimicrobial Therapy Inc.; 2003.
141. Elyan A, Mahran M, el-Maraghy M, et al. Prophylactic intravenous metronidazole in cesarean section. Chemioterapia. 1984;3:67-70.
142. Stiver HG, Forward KR, Livingstone RA, et al. Multicenter comparison of cefoxitin versus cefazolin for prevention of infectious morbidity after nonelective cesarean section. Am J Obstet Gynecol. 1983;145:158-163.
143. Harger JH, English DH. Selection of patients for antibiotic prophylaxis in cesarean section. Am J Obstet Gynecol. 1981;141:752-758.
144. Hawrylyshyn PA, Bernstein P, Papsin FR. Short-term antibiotic prophylaxis in high-risk patients following cesarean section. Am J Obstet Gynecol. 1983;145:285-289.
145. Elliott JP, Flaherty JF. Comparison of lavage or intravenous antibiotics at cesarean section. Obstet Gynecol. 1986;67:29-32.
146. Conover WB, Moore TR. Comparison of irrigation and intravenous antibiotic prophylaxis at cesarean section. Obstet Gynecol. 1984;63:787-791.
147. Heisterberg L, Petersen K. Metronidazole prophylaxis in elective first trimester abortion. Obstet Gynecol. 1985;65:371-374.
148. Sonne-Holm S, Heisterberg L, Hebjorn S, et al. Prophylactic antibiotics in first-trimester abortions: A clinical, controlled trial. Am J Obstet Gynecol. 1981;139:693-696.
149. Spence MR, King TM, Burkman RT, et al. Cephalothin prophylaxis for midtrimester abortion. Obstet Gynecol. 1982;60:502-505.
150. Gatell JM, Riba J, Lozano ML, et al. Prophylactic cefamandole in orthopaedic surgery. J Bone Joint Surg. 1984;66:1219-1222.
151. Patzakis MJ, Harvey P, Ivler D. The role of antibiotics in the management of open fractures. J Bone Joint Surg. 1974;56:532-541.
152. Geraghty J, Feely M. Antibiotic prophylaxis in neurosurgery: A randomized controlled trial. J Neurosurg. 1984;60:724-726.
153. Strohecker J, Piotrowski WP, Lametschwandtner A. The intra-operative application of povidone-iodine in neurosurgery. J Hosp Infect. 1985;6:532-541.
154. Starr MB. Prophylactic antibiotics for ophthalmic surgery. Surv Ophthalmol. 1983;27:353-373.
155. Ferrie BG, Scott R. Prophylactic cefuroxime in transurethral resection. Urol Res. 1984;12:279-281.
156. Quist N, Christiansen HM, Ehlers D. Severe *Vibrio cholerae* sepsis and meningitis in a young infant. Urol Res. 1984;12:275-277.
157. Packer MG, Russo P, Fair WR. Prophylactic antibiotics and Foley catheter use in transperineal needle biopsy of the prostate. J Urol. 1984;131:687-689.
158. Johnson JR, Yu VL, Myers EN, et al. Efficacy of two third-generation cephalosporins in prophylaxis for head and neck surgery. Arch Otolaryngol. 1984;110:224-227.
159. Seagle MB, Duberstein LE, Gross CW, et al. Efficacy of cefazolin as prophylactic antibiotic in head and neck surgery. Otolaryngology. 1979;85:568-572.
160. Slight PH, Gundling K, Plotkin SA, et al. A trial of vancomycin for prophylaxis of infections after neurosurgical shunts. N Engl J Med. 1985;312:921.
161. Hemsell DL, Johnson ER, Hemsell PG, et al. Cefazolin is inferior to cefotetan as single-dose prophylaxis for women undergoing elective total abdominal hysterectomy. Clin Infect Dis. 1995;20:677-684.
162. Wininger DA, Fass RJ. Antibiotic-impregnated cement and beads for orthopedic infections. Antimicrob Agents Chemother. 1996;40:2675-2679.
163. Goodell JA, Flick AB, Hebert JC, Howe JG. Preparation and release characteristics of tobramycin-impregnated polymethylmethacrylate beads. Am J Hosp Pharm. 1986;43:1454-1461.
164. Ostermann PAW, Seligson D, Henry SL. Local antibiotic therapy for severe open fractures: A review of 1085 consecutive cases. J Bone Joint Surg Br. 1995;77:93-97.
165. Haydon RC, Blaha JD, Mancinelli C, Koike K. Audiometric thresholds in osteomyelitis patients treated with gentamicin-impregnated methylmethacrylate beads (Septopal). Clin Orthop. 1993;295:43-46.
166. Salvati EA, Callaghan JJ, Brause BD, et al. Reimplantation in infection: Elution of gentamicin from cement and beads. Clin Orthop. 1986;207:83-93.
167. Block BS, Mercer LJ, Ismail MA, et al. *Clostridium difficile*-associated diarrhea follows perioperative prophylaxis with cefoxitin. Am J Obstet Gynecol. 1986;153:835-838.
168. Dajee H, Laks H, Miller J, et al. Profound hypotension from rapid vancomycin administration during cardiac operation. J Thorac Cardiovasc Surg. 1984;87:145-146.
169. Odio C, Mohs E, Sklar FH, et al. Adverse reactions to vancomycin used as prophylaxis for CSF shunt procedures. Am J Dis Child. 1984;138:17-19.
170. Roberts NJ Jr, Douglas RG Jr. Gentamicin use and *Pseudomonas* and *Serratia* resistance: Effect of a surgical prophylaxis regimen. Antimicrob Agents Chemother. 1978;13:214-220.
171. Archer GL, Armstrong BC. Alteration of staphylococcal flora in cardiac patients receiving antibiotic prophylaxis. J Infect Dis. 1983;147:642-649.
172. Kernodle DS, Barg NL, Kaiser AB. Low-level colonization of hospitalized patients with methicillin-resistant coagulase-negative staphylococci and their emergence during surgical antimicrobial prophylaxis. Antimicrob Agents Chemother. 1988;32:202-208.
173. Roach AL, Kernodle DS, Kaiser AB. Selecting cost-effective antimicrobial prophylaxis in surgery: Are we getting what we pay for? Ann Pharmacother. 1990;24:183-185.
174. Poulsen KB, Wachmann CH, Bremmelgaard A, et al. Survival of patients with surgical wound infection: A case-control study of common surgical interventions. Br J Surg. 1995;82:208-209.
175. Green JW, Wenzel RP. Postoperative wound infection: A controlled study of the increased duration of hospital stay and direct cost of hospitalization. Ann Surg. 1977;185:264-268.
176. Garner JS, Jarvis WR, Emori TG, et al. CDC guidelines for nosocomial infections. In: Olmsted RN, ed. APIC Infection Control and Applied Epidemiology: Principles and Practice. St. Louis: Mosby; 1996.
177. Condon RE, Haley RW, Lee JT Jr, et al. Does infection control control infections? Arch Surg. 1988;123:250-256.
178. Sands K, Vineyard G, Platt R. Surgical site infections occurring after hospital discharge. J Infect Dis. 1996;173:963-970.
179. Kent P, McDonald M, Harris O, et al. Post-discharge surgical wound infection surveillance in a provincial hospital: Follow-up rates, validity of data, and review of the literature. Aust N Z J Surg. 2001;71:583-589.
180. Mitchell DH. Post-discharge surgical wound surveillance. Aust N Z J Surg. 2001;71:563.

CHAPTER **317**

Burns

GREGORY J. BAUER
ROBERT W. YURT

The disruption of homeostasis associated with severe burn injury exceeds that of any other injury or disease. Since the advent of aggressive early resuscitation measures, mortality in the acute phase after injury is rare.[1,2] However, the mortality rate after burns over more than 40% of the body surface area (BSA), which is primarily attributed to infection, continues to be high. Because the risk of infection relates directly to the extent of injury, the initial therapeutic approach is oriented toward limiting the progression of the injury by stabilizing the patient and maintaining blood flow to the wound. The development and progression of the burn wound is well characterized as a dynamic process in which there are irreversible changes in the zone of coagulative necrosis and potentially reversible changes for as long as 3 days in the zones of stasis and hyperemia.[3,4] Because methods of manipulating the inflammatory response that may mediate progression of the injury are not yet available, the primary goal of early burn therapy is to ensure adequate delivery of oxygen, nutrients, and circulating cells to the wound. Therefore, immediate burn care focuses on prevention of progression of injury and maintenance of a viable interface at which both specific and nonspecific defenses against infection can be mounted.[5]

WOUND AND INFLAMMATORY PATHOPHYSIOLOGY

The evolution of the burn wound is dramatically seen in the conversion of partial- to full-thickness wounds during difficult resuscitations, particularly in patients at the extremes of age in whom cardiac output cannot meet the circulatory demand of large BSA injury. In such patients with progressive necrosis and limited defense at the viable tissue interface, early microbial invasion of wounds is to be anticipated. Similarly, decreases in body temperature caused by heat loss to the environment or application of cool solutions or ice to the wound may lead to progressive deterioration of the wounds. Several circulating factors following burn or severe injury have been identified that depress myocardial function, including macrophage migration inhibitory factor and tumor necrosis factor-α (TNF-α).[6-8] However, cardiovascular stability remains primarily dependent on intravascular volume repletion. Adrenergic agents in particular are avoided in view of the deleterious result of further diminution of wound blood flow. Likewise, meticulous evaluation of blood flow in extremities with circumferential full-thickness injury is necessary to avoid additional compromise of wound and muscular blood flow. When signs of compromised blood flow first appear, escharotomy is performed to diminish the developing pressure in the extremity.

Large burns predispose patients to infection due to a number of reasons.[9] In addition to the culture medium provided by the necrotic tissue, the breach in integument compromises innate immunity. Nonspecific, humoral and cellular immune functions are also depressed by thermal injury. Circulating levels of immunoglobulins are inversely proportional to the extent of injury,[10,11] and persistently decreased levels of immunoglobulin G (IgG) have been related to mortality.[12] The ratio of T-helper to T-suppressor lymphocytes is decreased.[13,14] In addition, monocyte defects have been reported,[15] leading to the hypothesis that depressed immune response in these patients is caused by an imbalance in the cellular immune system. That multiple cascades are involved is supported by the finding that TNF is produced after burn injury,[16] as are other cytokines.[17] It has been shown that plasma levels of interleukin-1β, interleukin-6, and TNF-α are elevated in severely burned patients.[18-20] Increased levels of these cytokines were associated with increased rates of mortality and infection. Although it has been documented that intestinal permeability increases in association with infection in burn patients,[21] it is not known whether this is a primary or a secondary event. Based on prospective study of patients with large burns, however, it has been suggested that disorders of neutrophil function appear to be the major factors predisposing to the development of sepsis.[22]

That the response of the neutrophil to a site of injury and antigen challenge was depressed in patients with 40% or greater total BSA burn was shown decades ago by McCabe and colleagues[23] by the skin window technique. Study of the mechanism of decreased neutrophil response to microbial invasion and injury has centered on in vitro neutrophil function. Acute skin injury releases neutrophil chemotaxins and the chemotactic response of peripheral blood neutrophils following thermal injury is impaired. The blunted response is induced, at least in part, through mechanisms of adaptation and desensitization, in addition to stable actin polymerization.[25-27] The oxidative killing potential of peripheral blood neutrophils may be impaired when oxidase activity, oxygen consumption and superoxide anion production is mitigated following burn injury.[28,29] Furthermore, thermal injury downregulates neutrophil apoptosis, perhaps through mitochondrial-dependent pathways.[30,31] Consumption of complement components might account for depressed neutrophil response after burn injury[32]; how-

ever, even low levels of complement are sufficient to opsonize invading bacteria.[33] Data from an animal model suggest that neutrophils do not respond to the burn wound as well after large burns. However, in vivo evaluation of neutrophil activity indicates that the cells are more responsive than after lesser injury.[31] These findings suggest that "indiscriminant" margination may be occurring after injury. Such a response may lead to an inappropriately depressed wound response and, potentially, to distant tissue damage. These earlier findings are supported by data[35-37] indicating that neutrophil surface receptors are altered after burn injury in patients. Moreover, in a rat model, infusion of low levels of exogenous chemotaxins increased mortality from burn wound sepsis.[38] Others have described similar events in infected patients and have correlated release of leukocyte enzymes with levels of chemotactic factors produced by complement activation.[39]

PREVENTION OF INFECTION

Although prophylactic system antibiotics (penicillin) are occasionally given to outpatients with burns, current data do not support their general use in the inpatient population.[40,41] Frequent evaluation of the wound and surrounding tissue allows early and appropriate therapy of cellulitis while sparing most patients exposure to unnecessary antibiotics. In one study, it was documented that manipulation of the burn wound leads to bacteremia.[42] As a result, antibiotics were administered immediately before and during burn wound excision. However, more recent data suggest that the incidence of bacteremia may be as low as 15%.[43] Therefore, a selective approach to use of prophylactic antibiotics is advocated. The choice of antibiotics is dictated by knowledge of the current flora in the burn center or more specifically by the burn wound flora of the individual patient. The cyclic nature of particular microorganisms causing burn wound invasion in our center was documented by the results of surveillance and specifically indicated wound biopsies over a 6-month period (Table 317-1). *Enterobacter cloacae* was frequently isolated but was most prominent in March, April, and June. *Staphylococcus aureus,* which was methicillin-resistant, was most prominent in May, but no isolates were found in April. The cyclic nature of wound infection revealed in these data from 15 years ago was supported by data from the same months in 1997 (see Table 317-1) at the same center. However, the decrease in incidence of wound infection between these two periods should be noted. In the earlier study there were 1006 biopsies, of which 40% were positive, and in the later studies only 21% of a total of 86 biopsies were positive. Patient admissions were twice the number in the more recent period, and *Klebsiella pneumoniae* and *Acinetobacter baumanii* emerged as new pathogens. Based on such data, the regimen for wound manipulation prophylaxis consisted of intravenous vancomycin and amikacin during the earlier study and currently consists of vancomycin and a third-generation cephalosporin. In addition, knowledge of the predominance of organisms within each burn unit that cause infections in systems other than wounds is essential for rapid response.

The advent of effective topical antimicrobial therapy has decreased the incidence of conversion of partial-thickness to full-thickness wounds by local infection. In addition, these agents may prolong the sterility of the full-thickness burn wound. However, they have not eliminated the need for aggressive removal of the necrotic tissue and closure of the wound with autograft. Silver nitrate in a 0.5% solution is an effective topical agent when used before wound colonization. However, because this agent does not penetrate eschar, its broad-spectrum gram-negative effectiveness is diminished once bacterial proliferation has occurred in the eschar. Additional disadvantages of this agent include the need for continuous occlusive dressings, which limit evaluation of wounds and range of motion. The black discoloration of the wound and the environment contributes to a decrease in use of silver nitrate.

Topical burn wound creams allow for open wound therapy and, except in an outpatient setting, are most commonly used without dressings. Mafenide acetate (Sulfamylon®) cream has a broad spectrum of activity against gram-negative organisms but little activity against staphylococci. A significant advantage of this agent is that it penetrates

TABLE 317-1 Distribution of Organisms in Burn Wound Biopsies

	January		February		March		April		May		June	
	1982	*1997*	*1982*	*1997*	*1982*	*1997*	*1982*	*1997*	*1982*	*1997*	*1982*	*1997*
Parameter												
No. biopsies	189	27	141	9	244	6	201	12	162	20	69	12
No. biopsies with ≥10^5 organisms per gram of tissue	84	0	39	0	85	2	84	2	70	3	41	8
Organisms identified (% of total positive biopsies)												
Enterobacter cloacae	29.8	—	18	—	37.7	0	82.1	0	25.7	33.3	39	0
Staphylococcus aureus	27.4	—	28.2	—	22.4	50	0	100	42.9	33.3	17.1	0
Staphylococcus epidermidis	14.3	—	5.1	—	0	0	3.6	0	0	33.3	0	12.5
Enterococcus faecalis	10.7	—	12.8	—	4.7	—	2.4	—	11.4	0	17.1	25
Escherichia coli	7.1	—	7.6	—	11.8	0	6	0	4.3	0	12.2	0
Pseudomonas aeruginosa	2.4	—	5.1	—	20	50	6	0	8.6	0	12.2	25
Klebsiella pneumoniae	0	—	0	—	0	0	0	0	0	0	0	25
Acinetobacter baumanii	0	—	0	—	0	0	0	0	0	0	0	12.5

the burn eschar and therefore is effective in the colonized wound. The disadvantages of Sulfamylon® are a transient burning sensation, an accentuation of postinjury hyperventilation, and inhibition of carbonic anhydrase activity. Silver sulfadiazine, on the other hand, is a soothing cream with good activity against gram-negative organisms. Because it does not penetrate the wound, it is best used as a prophylactic antimicrobial. Bacterial resistance to silver sulfadiazine has been reported.[44] Some centers have adopted an approach of alternating agents to take advantage of the attributes of both, with silver sulfadiazine being applied at night and Sulfamylon® during the day.[44] The current approach in our center is to initiate topical prophylaxis with silver sulfadiazine and to switch to Sulfamylon® if wounds appear to deteriorate based on clinical and laboratory criteria.

Topical dressings in various non-cream forms are rapidly emerging in the evolving burn and wound care industry that utilize the antimicrobial activity of silver in both its elemental and ionic forms. These products can be applied to the wound surface in sheet form and deliver silver directly to the wound bed. Ease of application, diminished dressing changes and broad-spectrum efficacy make these products attractive alternatives to traditional therapies and many burn centers are gaining experience with their use.

The goal of burn therapy is to prevent burn wound infection by permanent closure of the wound as rapidly as possible. Recognition of the advantages of early removal of necrotic tissue and wound closure has led to an aggressive surgical approach in selected patients.[1] In such cases, full-thickness wounds are excised as soon after injury as cardiovascular stability has been achieved. The advantages of this approach include removal of eschar before colonization, which typically is appreciated at 5 to 7 days after injury, and reduction of the overall extent of injury. The extent of excision of burn wound is usually limited to 20% of the BSA at any one time, and blood loss is limited to one blood volume. Such an approach is most easily achieved by excision of full-thickness injury to the level of the fascia, because blood loss is minimized under these conditions. The open wound is covered with autograft if donor sites are available or with allograft, if donor sites are not available. This process is repeated until the entire wound is closed. Such an aggressive surgical approach is modified by the age of the patient (ideally 15 to 35 years) and by factors such as significant preexisting disease and inhalation injury, which require a more conservative approach. Innovations in immediate coverage of the wound, especially for large burns greater than 50% body surface area, include dermal regeneration templates such as Integra® and Alloderm®.[45] These templates are composed of bovine collagen matrix and decellularized cadaver skin, respectively. Although useful for immediate coverage of the wound, which allows for diminished metabolic derangement, their benefit can often be mitigated by infection of the material itself. As burn surgeons gain experience in their application, these products may compete significantly with traditional therapies and infectious complications will likely evanesce.

An additional difficulty with early excisional therapy is the possibility of excision of burned tissue that may heal if left alone for 2 to 3 weeks. If such a question arises, initial tangential excision of the eschar or biopsy may assist in evaluating the depth and the possibility of healing of the burn wound. Data suggest that a more conservative approach, in which operative time is limited to 2 hours and blood loss to four units, may contribute to improved survival from extensive burn injury.[46] Throughout the course of hospitalization, efforts are directed toward minimizing contamination of the patient's wounds. Cross-contamination is avoided through the use of gowns, gloves, and masks by nursing and medical staff and visitors. The patient is not touched except with a gloved hand, and each patient is restricted to his or her own monitoring and diagnostic equipment. Concern about the potential for cross-contamination in large burn centers has led to diminished use of the traditional Hubbard tanking of patients. A satisfactory alternative is showering and débridement on a covered or readily disinfected plinth. If adequate nursing care can be provided, it is preferable to isolate patients who have large open wounds in individual rooms. Cohort patient care has been shown to be effective in eliminating endemic infections.[48] The bacteria-controlled nursing unit[49] has been advocated as a means of protecting the patient and the environment. Such elaborate systems are not generally available.

DIAGNOSIS AND TREATMENT OF INFECTION

Wound Infection

Although surface cultures of burn wounds are helpful from the standpoint of evaluating the potential pathogens that exist on the patient and on a burn ward, they give no indication of the actual status of the wound itself. Biopsy of the wound has been shown to provide an accurate indication on its status.[50] Pruitt and Foley reported that quantitative cultures of 10^5 or more bacteria per gram of tissue or histologic evidence of bacterial invasion of viable tissue correlated with a high (75%) mortality rate.[51] In addition, serial biopsies that indicated advancing wound infection were associated with a mortality rate of 85%, whereas stable or improving wounds were associated with an overall mortality rate of 55%. Direct correlation between biopsy and autopsy diagnosis was found in 26 of 32 patients. These historical data, and those of others, support this burn unit's approach to burn wound infection.[52] Burn wounds that show clinical signs of infection or burned tissue with changes in patients whose sepsis cannot be attributed to any other source are biopsied and cultured.[53] The rapid fixation technique allows histologic diagnosis of invasive infection within 3 hours, whereas quantitative counts and identification of the organism are available within 24 hours. The combined use of histologic and culture techniques provides early diagnosis as well as the identity of the organism and its sensitivity to antimicrobials. However, the only way to conclusively determine burn wound invasion by bacteria or fungi is by histologic methods.[54]

TABLE 317-2   Prophylaxis and Treatment of Burn Wound Infection

Diagnosis	Topical	Clysis	Systemic Therapy	Surgical
"Clean" burn	Silver sulfadiazine/silver nitrate	No	No	Excision/débridement
Superficial infection or colonization	Silver sulfadiazine/sulfamylon	No	No	Excision/débridement
Gram-negative invasion	Sulfamylon	Yes	No	Excision to fascia
Gram-positive invasion—suppurative	Silver sulfadiazine	No	Yes	Unroof
Gram-positive invasion—nonsuppurative	Silver sulfadiazine	Yes	No	Excision to fascia
Fungal infection—superficial	Sulfamylon plus nystatin	No	No	Excision
Fungal infection—invasive	Sulfamylon plus nystatin	No	Yes	Excision to or deep to fascia

Subtle changes in the wound's appearance or character, such as hemorrhage, rapid eschar separation, or greenish discoloration of eschar or subeschar fat may herald bacterial colonization or invasive infection and diagnoses should be aggressively pursued. If clinical or biopsy data support a diagnosis of colonization, then a change in topical therapy and plans for excision are entertained (Table 317-2). However, if the findings are consistent with invasive infection, then more aggressive therapy is instituted. In addition, if bacteremia is documented and other sources are eliminated, urgent surgical intervention is necessary. In the absence of documented bacteremia, signs of sepsis such as hypothermia or hyperthermia, hypotension, decreased urinary output, hyperglycemia, neutropenia or neutrophilia, or thrombocytopenia support early intervention. When the wound is invaded with gram-negative organisms, surgical excision to the level of the fascia is the procedure of choice. In preparation for surgery and in those patients who require stabilization before general anesthesia is given, a penetrating topical agent (Sulfamylon®) is used, and subeschar clysis with an appropriate antibiotic may be considered, as well. The choice of antibiotic is based on previous biopsy sensitivity data or data accumulated on sensitivities of the current flora in the patient population. Although not commonly performed any longer, such a preoperative approach was based on evidence that Sulfamylon® pulse therapy is effective in decreasing wound colony counts[58] and on the previous data of Baxter and colleagues[56] supporting the efficacy of subeschar clysis. Using this technique, systemic antimicrobials are not necessary, because the full daily dose of antibiotic administered by clysis is absorbed into the circulation. The direct administration of antibiotic into the viable/nonviable tissue interface is supported by concern that systemically administered antibiotics may not reach sufficient levels in tissues with poor or absent vascularity. However, some data suggest that antibiotics administered at a distant site are effective[55] and that systemically administered antibiotics reach these tissues. Whether activity of the antimicrobial is maintained in these foci is not known.

In distinction to gram-negative invasion, gram-positive infection often manifests as suppurative foci in the tissue or is associated with rapid eschar separation. In such cases, simple débridement with unroofing of involved areas, under the umbrella of appropriate systemic antibiotics, is sufficient acute therapy. Because surgical débridement should arrest this process, topical agents are of lesser importance; however, the wound should not be allowed to dessicate. Silver sulfadiazine, Dakin's solution, Sulfamylon® solution, and triple-antibiotic solutions have been used for this purpose.

Although gram-positive burn wound infection is anticipated to be primarily a suppurative type of infection, there appears to be a growing number of patients who present with primary non-suppurative gram-positive infections. These infections are caused by methicillin-resistant *S. aureus* (*personal observation*). Whether diminished neutrophil response or a change in the nature or virulence of such organisms[56] explains this phenomenon is unknown.

Over the past 10 years there has been a decrease in bacterial wound infections after burn injury, but during this period there has been an increase in fungal burn wound infection.[57] Blackened discoloration of the burn wound should arouse suspicion of fungal infection. Such changes are more typical of the agents of mucormycosis.[44] Confirmation of such organisms is best made on histologic sections of wound biopsies, where, in addition, a determination of invasion of viable tissue can be

made. Reliance on culture data prolongs the time to diagnosis. Although silver sulfadiazine is active against *Candida* spp., a mixture of this agent or Sulfamylon with Nystatin may be more effective for topical treatment of superficial fungal infections. Because fungal infection is often preceded by bacterial infection and multiple antibiotic therapy, the use of Sulfamylon® in such a mixture is preferred.[44] The treatment of fungal invasion is surgical excision to the level of noninvaded viable tissue. When invasion extends to the level of the investing fascia, the excision is carried deep to this level to viable muscle.[58] Recovery of the fungus from the blood mandates systemic therapy, which is often used even without positive blood cultures if invasion is documented and clinical signs are present.

Pulmonary Infection

With the advent of effective topical therapy for the burn wound, pulmonary complications have become a prominent problem in the burn-injured patient.[54,59] In addition, the ability to salvage an increasing number of patients from the shock phase immediately after injury has led to a greater number of patients' surviving to the time (2 to 3 days after injury) when the effects of inhalation injury become clinically prominent.[60] In patients without inhalation injury but with large burns, postinjury hyperventilation and subsequent decreases in tidal volume may lead to atelectasis and pneumonia. Furthermore, a recognized complication of circumferential full-thickness chest burns is a decrease in compliance of the chest wall. Aggressive pulmonary toilet and escharotomy are necessary to maintain pulmonary function. Because these patients frequently require large-volume feedings via nasogastric or nasojejunal tubes, aspiration must be guarded against. Diminished mucociliary functions and destruction of airway epithelium by inhalation of products of combustion lead to airway obstruction and infection.[61] Frequent diagnostic and therapeutic bronchoscopy is recommended in this group of patients.

Attempts at specific prophylaxis of the sequelae of inhalation injury, such as nebulization of antibiotics[62] and treatment with steroids,[63] have failed to show any benefit. Although hematogenous pneumonia is less common than in the past,[59] it remains a significant problem in the patient with burns. When it occurs, the source (most commonly wound or suppurative vein) must be defined and eradicated. Prophylactic antibiotics are not used for either bronchopneumonia or hematogenous pneumonia; specific therapy is based on knowledge of previous endobronchial culture, and sensitivity is substantiated by repeat cultures at the time of diagnosis.

Miscellaneous Infections

Several additional types of infection are significant in burn-injured patients and should be mentioned because of their frequency and peculiarities of clinical presentation. The diagnosis of suppurative thrombophlebitis in the presence of normal tissue is often difficult to make. In the burned patient, the addition of injured and necrotic tissue compounds this difficulty. Less than 35% of suppurative veins in burned patients result in local findings.[64] The incidence of this disease is at least 5%, and the mortality rate, even in treated suppurative thrombophlebitis, reaches 60%.[61] In the absence of a septic venous source, persistent positive blood cultures in the burned patient should be attributed to endocarditis until proven otherwise.

In addition to superficial tissue damaged by direct heat, deeper tissue can be injured and can provide a focus for infection. The vascular compromise associated with circumferential full-thickness injury, if not decompressed early, leads to muscle necrosis and subsequent pyomyositis. A high index of suspicion is necessary to detect these changes in an already edematous extremity. Direct electrical contact can lead to deep muscular necrosis with delayed infection. Furthermore, significant visceral damage may occur after electrical injury, with subsequent abscess formation.[65]

CONCLUSIONS

The combination of injury-associated immunosuppression and the large area of nonviable tissue in the patient with more than 30% BSA burns inevitably leads to infection. Success in treatment of these patients rests more with removal of necrotic tissue and achievement of wound closure than with use of antimicrobials. Current data support the judicious use of systemic antibiotics for treatment of documented infection and for prophylaxis during burn wound manipulation. The cyclic nature of exposure to various bacteria and the rapid emergence of resistance to antibiotics in this population supplies ample evidence that there is always a niche that will be filled. Although contamination of the wound must be minimized and surveillance must be adequate to detect organisms before they invade the wound, closure of the wound is the primary prophylactic and therapeutic maneuver in the care of the burned patient.

REFERENCES

1. Saffle JR, Davis B, Williams P. Recent outcomes in the treatment of burn injury in the United States: A report from the American Burn Association Patient Registry. J Burn Care Rehabil. 1995;16:219-232.
2. Monafo WW. Initial management of burns. N Engl J Med. 1996;335:1581-1586.
3. Jackson DM. The diagnosis of the depth of burning. Br J Surg. 1953;40:558-596.
4. Noble HGS, Robson MC, Krizek TJ. Dermal ischemia in the burn wound. J Surg Res. 1977;23:117-125.
5. Yurt RW. Burns. In: Polk HC, Gardner B, Stone HH, eds. Basic Surgery. St. Louis: Quality Medical Publishing; 1995;750-761.
6. Ferrara JJ, Franklin EW, Kukuy EL, et al. Lymph isolated from a regional scald injury produces a negative inotropic effect in dogs. J Burn Care Rehabil. 1998;19:296-304.
7. Walley KR, Hebert PC, Wakai Y, et al. Decrease in left ventricular contractility after tumor necrosis factor-a infusion in dogs. J Appl Physiol. 1994;76:1060-1067.
8. Garner LB, Willis MS, Carlson DL, et al. Macrophage migration inhibitory factor is a cardiac-derived myocardial depressant factor. Am J Physiol Heart Circ Physiol. 2003;285:H2500-H25009.
9. Schwacha MG, Chaudry IH. The cellular basis of post-burn immunosuppression: macrophages and mediators. Int J Mol Med. 2002;10:239-243.
10. Bariar LM, Bal A, Hasan A, Sharma V. Serum levels of immunoglobulins in thermal burns. J Indian Med Assoc. 1996;94:133-134.
11. Molloy RG, Nestor M, Collins KH, et al. The humoral immune response after thermal injury: an experimental model. Surgery. 1994;115:341-348.
12. Munster AM, Hoagland HC, Pruitt BA Jr. The effect of thermal injury on serum immunoglobulins. Ann Surg. 1970;172:965-969.
13. Burleson DG, Mason AD Jr, Pruitt BA Jr. Lymphoid subpopulation changes after thermal injury and thermal injury with infection in an experimental model. Ann Surg. 1987;207:208-212.
14. Organ BC, Antonacci AC, Chiao J, et al. Changes in lymphocyte number and phenotype in seven lymphoid compartments after thermal injury. Ann Surg. 1989;210:78-79.
15. Shelby J, Merrell SW. In vivo monitoring of postburn immune response. J Trauma. 1987; 27:213-216.
16. Marano M, Moldawer L, Fong Y, et al. Cachectin tumor necrosis factor production in experimental burns and pseudomonas infection. Arch Surg. 1988;123:1383-1388.
17. Dehne MG, Sablotzki A, Hoffmann A, et al. Alterations of acute phase reaction and cytokine production in patients following severe burn injury. Burns. 2002;28:535-542.
18. Drost AC, Burleson DG, Cioffi WG Jr, et al. Plasma cytokines following thermal injury and their relationship with patient mortality, burn size, and time postburn. J Trauma. 1993;35:335-339.
19. Yeh FL, Lin WL, Shen HD, Fang RH. Changes in circulating levels of interleukin-6 in burned patients. Burns. 1999;25:131-136.
20. Drost AC, Burleson DG, Cioffi WG Jr, et al. Plasma cytokines following thermal injury and their relationship to infection. Ann Surg. 1993;218:74-78.
21. Ziegler TR, Smith RJ, O'Dwyer ST, et al. Increased permeability associated with infection in burn patients. Arch Surg. 1988;123:1313-1319.
22. Alexander JW, Ogle CK, Stinnett JD, et al. A sequential prospective analysis of immunologic abnormalities and infection following severe thermal injury. Ann Surg. 1978;188:809-816.
23. McCabe WP, Rebuck JW, Kelly AP Jr, et al. Leukocyte response as a monitor of immunodepression in burn patients. Arch Surg. 1973;106:155-159.
24. Balch HH, Watters BS, Kelly D. Resistance to infection in burned patients. Ann Surg. 1963;157:1-19.
25. Bjornson AB, Somers SD. Down-regulation of chemotaxis of polymorphonuclear leukocytes following thermal injury involves two distinct mechanisms. J Infect Dis. 1993; 168:120-127.
26. Hasslen SR, Nelson RD, Ahrenholz DH, Solem LD. Thermal injury, the inflammatory process, and wound dressing reduce human neutrophil chemotaxis to four attractants. J Burn Care Rehab. 1993;14:303-309.
27. Hasslen SR, Ahrenholz DH, Solem LD, Nelson RD. Actin polymerization contributes to neutrophil chemotactic dysfunction following thermal injury. J Leukoc Biol. 1992;52:495-500.
28. Rosenthal J, Thurman GW, Cusack N, et al. Neutrophils from patients after burn injury express a deficiency of the oxidase components p47-phox and p-67-phox. Blood. 1996;88:4321-4329.
29. Cioffi WG Jr, Burleson DG, Jordan BS, et al. Granulocyte oxidative activity after thermal injury. Surgery. 1992;112:860-865.
30. Chitnis D, Dickerson C, Munster AM, Winchurch RA. Inhibition of apoptosis in polymorphonuclear neutrophils from burn patients. J Leukoc Biol. 1996;59:835-839.
31. Hu Z, Sayeed M. Suppression of mitochondria-dependent neutrophil apoptosis with thermal injury. Am J Physiol Cell Physiol. 2004;286:C170-C178.
32. Bjornson AB, Altemeier WA, Bjornson HS, et al. Host defense against opportunist microorganisms following trauma: I. Studies to determine the association between changes in humoral components of host defense and septicemia in burned patients. Ann Surg. 1978;188:93-101.
33. Bjornson AB, Altemeier WA, Bjornson HS. Complement, opsonins, and the immune response to bacterial infection in burned patients. Ann Surg. 1980;191:323-329.
34. Yurt RW, Pruitt BA. Decreased wound neutrophils and indiscriminate margination in the pathogenesis of wound infection. Surgery. 1985;95:191-198.
35. Ahmed S el-D, el-Shahat AS, Saad SO. Assessment of certain neutrophil receptors, opsonophagocytosis and soluble intercellular adhesion molecule-1 (ICAM-1) following thermal injury. Burns. 1999;25:395-401.
36. Rodeberg DA, Bass RC, Alexander JW, et al. Neutrophils from burn patients are unable to increase the expression of CD11b/CD18 in response to inflammatory stimuli. J Leukoc Biol. 1997;61:575-582.
37. Mileski W, Borgstrom D, Lightfoot E, et al. Inhibition of leukocyte endothelial adherence following thermal injury. J Surg Res. 1992;52:334-339.
38. Yurt RW, Shires GT. Increased susceptibility to infection due to infusion of exogenous chemotaxin. Arch Surg. 1987;122:111-116.
39. Solomkin JS, Jenkins MK, Nelson RD, et al. Neutrophil dysfunction in sepsis: II. Evidence for the role of complement activation products in cellular deactivation. Surgery. 1981;90:319-327.
40. Dacso CC, Luterman A, Curreri PW. Systemic antibiotic treatment in burned patients. Surg Clin North Am. 1987; 67:57-68.
41. Durtschi MB, Orgain C, Counts GW, et al. A prospective study of prophylactic penicillin in acutely burned hospitalized patients. J Trauma. 1982;22:11-14.
42. Sasaki TM, Welch GW, Herndon DN, et al. Burn wound manipulation-induced bacteremia. J Trauma. 1979;19:46-48.
43. Mozingo DW, McManus AT, Kim SH, Pruitt BA Jr. Incidence of bacteremia after burn wound manipulation in the early postburn period. J Trauma. 1997;42:1006-1010.
44. Pruitt BA Jr. The burn patient: II. Later care and complications of thermal injury. Curr Prob Surg. 1979;16:1-95.
45. Bello YM, Falabella AF, Eaglstein WH. Tissue-engineered skin. Current status in wound healing. Am J Clin Dermatol. 2001;2:305-313.
46. Demling RH. Improved survival after massive burns. J Trauma. 1983;23:179-184.
47. Burke JF, Quinby WC, Bondoc CC, et al. Immunosuppression and temporary skin transplantation in the treatment of massive third degree burns. Ann Surg. 1975;182:183-197.
48. McManus AT, McManus WF, Mason AD Jr, et al. Microbial colonization in a new intensive care unit. Arch Surg. 1985;120:217-221.
49. Burke JF, Quinby WC, Bondoc CC, et al. The contribution of a bacterially isolated environment to the prevention of infection in seriously burned patients. Ann Surg. 1977; 186:377-387.
50. McManus AT, Kim SH, Mason AD, et al. A comparison of quantitative microbiology and histopathology in divided burn wound biopsies. Arch Surg. 1987;122:64-66.
51. Pruitt BA, Foley FD. The use of biopsies in burn patient care. Surgery. 1973;73:887-897.
52. Loebl EC, Marvin JA, Heck EL, et al. The method of quantitative burn wound biopsy cultures and its routine use in the care of the burned patient. Am J Clin Pathol. 1974;61:20-24.
53. Baxter CR, Curreri PW, Marvin JA. The control of burn wound sepsis by the use of quantitative bacterial studies and subeschar clysis with antibiotics. Surg Clin North Am. 1973; 53:1509-1518.
54. Pruitt BA Jr, McManus AT. The changing epidemiology of infection in burn patients. World J Surg. 1992;16:57-67.
55. McManus WF, Mason AD Jr. Subeschar antibiotic infusion in the treatment of burn wound infection. J Trauma. 1980;20:1021-1023.
56. Lacey RW, Chopra I. Effect of plasmid carriage on the virulence of Staphylococcus aureus. J Med Microbiol. 1975;8:137-147.
57. Becker WK, Cioffi WG, McManus AT, et al. Fungal burn wound infection. Arch Surg. 1991;126:44-48.
58. Levine BA, Sirinek KR, Pruitt BA Jr. Wound excision to fascia in burned patients. Arch Surg. 1978;113:403-407.
59. Pruitt BA Jr, Flemma RJ, Divincenti FC, et al. Pulmonary complications in burn patients: A comparative study of 697 patients. J Thorac Cardiovasc Surg. 1970;59:7-20.
60. Bingham HG, Gallagher TJ, Powell MD. Early bronchoscopy as a predictor of ventilatory support for burned patients. J Trauma. 1987;27:1286-1288.
61. Hunt JL, Agee RN, Pruitt BA Jr. Fiberoptic bronchoscopy in acute inhalation injury. J Trauma. 1975;15:641-649.

62. Levine BA, Petroff PA, Slade CL, et al. Prospective trials of dexamethasone and aerosolized gentamicin in the treatment of inhalation injury in the burned patient. J Trauma. 1978;145:539-544.
63. Welch GW, Lull RJ, Petroff PA, et al. The use of steroids in inhalation injury. Surg Gynecol Obstet. 1977;145:539-544.
64. Pruitt BA Jr, McManus WF, Kim SH, et al. Diagnosis and treatment of cannula-related intravenous sepsis in burn patients. Ann Surg. 1980;191:546-554.
65. Haberal M, Ucar N, Bayraktar U, et al. Visceral injuries, wound infection and sepsis following electrical injuries. Burns. 1996;22:158-161.

CHAPTER **318**

Bites

ELLIE J. C. GOLDSTEIN

Bite wounds are common injuries that are often mistakenly considered innocuous by both patients and physicians. Most data on the incidence of infection, bacteriology, and the value of various medical and surgical methods of treatment come from small studies or anecdotal case reports that are further biased by the types of patients who elect to seek medical attention. Bite wounds consist of lacerations, evulsions, punctures, and scratches. Although 80% of patients never seek and do not need medical care, awareness of the magnitude of the infectious complications from bites is growing. The bacteria associated with bite infections may come from the environment, from the victim's skin flora, or most frequently, from the "normal" flora of the biter (Table 318-1).

ANIMAL BITES

In 1992 the U.S. government estimated that 52.4 million dogs and 54.6 million cats were kept as pets in 38.2 million and 30.5 million households with dogs and cats, respectively.[1] Previously, it was estimated that one of every two Americans will be bitten in their lifetime, usually by a dog. Bites occur in 4.7 million Americans yearly[2] and account for 800,000 medical visits, including approximately 1% of all emergency department visits.[3] Most dog bites (85%) are provoked attacks by either the victim's own pet or a dog known to the victim and occur during the warm weather months.[4] Bite wounds that require attention are often those to the extremities, especially the dominant hand. Facial bites are more frequent in children younger than 10 years and lead to 5 to 10 deaths per year, often because of exsanguination.[5] Larger dogs can exert more than 450 pounds/inch^2 of pressure with their jaws, which can lead to extensive crush injury.

Patients who present within 8 hours after injury are usually concerned with crush injury, care of disfiguring wounds, or the need for rabies or tetanus therapy.[4] These wounds are frequently contaminated with multiple strains of aerobic and anaerobic bacteria, similar to the spectrum found in documented bite infections. Between 2% and 30% of "treated" wounds will become infected and may require hospitalization.[6-10] Patients presenting longer than 8 hours after injury usually have established infection.[4,6,8,9,11] Infection is usually manifested by localized cellulitis, pain at the site of injury, and a purulent discharge, often gray and malodorous.[12] Temperature greater than 37.2° C, regional adenopathy, and lymphangitis occur in less than 10% of patients. Puncture wounds may become infected more frequently than evulsions and lead to abscess formation. Wounds close to bones or joints may penetrate these structures and cause septic arthritis, osteomyelitis, tenosynovitis, or local abscesses in any potential anatomic space. Osteomyelitis is a frequent and severe complication of bite wounds and should always be considered in the presence of pain in a joint or limited range of motion.

Rarely, sepsis, endocarditis, meningitis, or brain abscesses may develop after a bite injury. Fatal infection caused by *Capnocytophaga canimorsus* (formerly designated DF2) in association with asplenia or liver disease has been noted.[13-15] This organism may be difficult to isolate and

TABLE 318-1 Common Bacterial Isolates from Dog and Cat Bite Wounds

Acinetobacter spp.	*Pasteurella multocida* subsp. *septica*
Actinobacillus actinomycetemcomitans	*Pasteurella dagmatis*
	Pasteurella canis
Bacteroides tectus	*Pasteurella stomatis*
Burgeyella (Weeksella) zoohelcum	*Peptostreptococci*
Capnocytophaga canimorsus	*Porphyromonas asaccharolytica*
Capnocytophaga cynodegmi	*Porphyromonas gulae (gingivalis)*
Corynebacterium minutissimum	*Porphyromonas canoris*
Eikenella corrodens	*Prevotella bivia*
Enterococcus spp.	*Prevotella heparinolytica*
Fusobacterium nucleatum	*Prevotella melaninogenica*
Fusobacterium russii	*Prevotella intermedia*
Haemophilus aphrophilus	*Prevotella zoogleoformans*
Leifsonia (Corynebacterium) aquaticum	*Staphylococcus aureus*
	Staphylococcus intermedius
Leptotrichia buccalis	*Staphylococcus epidermidis*
Micrococcus luteus	*Streptococci* , α-hemolytic,
Moraxella spp.	β-hemolytic
Neisseria canis	*Veillonella parvula*
Neisseria weaveri	
Pasteurella multocida subsp. *multocida*	

identify and may require up to 14 days of incubation to grow on blood culture. It is generally susceptible to penicillin, cephalosporins, and fluoroquinolones but variably resistant to aztreonam and aminoglycosides (Table 318-2).[16]

Women who have undergone radical or modified radical mastectomy, patients with edema of any cause of an extremity, patients with lupus erythematosus, especially if taking steroids, and compromised hosts (e.g., patients with acute leukemia) may be prone to more severe infections, including sepsis, from the usual isolates that cause only limited cellulitis in immunocompetent patients.

Dog bite wound infections are considered to be predominantly related to the dog's oral flora.[4,7,11,12,17-19] Although most attention has been focused on *Pasteurella multocida,* the spectrum of organisms associated with bite wound infections is much greater. Based on DNA hybridization studies, the genus *Pasteurella* has been reclassified to comprise nine taxa. Holst and colleagues[20] noted the following distribution of 159 *P. multocida* strains isolated over a period of 3 years from human infections, mostly from bite wounds: *P. multocida* (60%), which was the isolate in all bacteremia cases; *P. multocida* subsp. *septica* (13%), which has a greater prevalence in cats than in dogs and may have a preferential affinity for the central nervous system; *P. canis* biotype 1 (18%), which was isolated exclusively from dog bite infections; *P. stomatis* (6%); and *P. dagmatis* (3%), which may cause systemic infections. A study[12] of 107 dog and cat bite wounds showed that 75% of cat bites grew *Pasteurella* species on culturing (*P. multocida* subsp. *multocida,* 54%), as did 50% of the dog bites (*P. canis,* 26%; *P. multocida* subsp. *multocida,* 12%). Other common isolates include streptococci (50%), *Staphylococcus aureus* (20% to 40%), and anaerobes (70%). Table 318-1 lists common bite pathogens. A number of newly described or reclassified organisms have become associated with animal bite wounds. *Staphylococcus intermedius* can be coagulase positive and mistaken for *S. aureus* and is fourfold more common in canine flora.[21,22] It is often susceptible to penicillin (55%) and possesses β-galactosidase activity, which differentiates it from *S. aureus.* Dysgonic fermenter 2 (DF2) has been named *C. canimorsus*[15]; it is difficult to grow on most routine solid media but can grow on chocolate agar and heart infusion agar with 5% rabbit blood when incubated in CO_2 and a variety of liquid media, including BACTEC aerobic medium.[14] This species can be differentiated from other *Capnocytophaga* spp. by the presence of positive oxidase and catalase reactions.[15] "DF2-like" strains have been classified as *Capnocytophaga cynodegmi.* M5 has been classified as *Neisseria weaveri*[23] and has been associated with dog bites. *Haemophilus felis,* which may be identical to *Haemophilus paraphrophilus,* requires factor V and CO_2 for growth, and is common in cat nasopharyngeal flora.[24] *Burgeyella (Weeksella) zoohelcum* has

TABLE 318-2 Antimicrobial Susceptibilities of Bacteria Frequently Isolated from Animal Bite Wounds*

	Percentages of Isolates Susceptible					
	Staphylococcus aureus	Eikenella corrodens	Anaerobes	Pasteurella multocida	Capnocytophaga canimorsus	Staphylococcus intermedius
Penicillin	10	99	50/95[†]	95	95	70
Dicloxacillin	99	5	50[‡§]	30	NS	100
Amoxicillin/clavulanic acid	100	100	100[‡§]	100	95	100
Cephalexin	100	20	40[‡§]	30	NS	95
Cefuroxime	100	70	40[‡§]	90	NS	NS
Cefoxitin	100	95	100[‡§]	95	95	NS
Erythromycin	100	20	40[‡§]	20	95	95
Tetracycline	95	85	60[‡§]	90	95	NS
Tigilcycline	100	85	100	100	NS	NS
TMP-SMX	100	95	0[‡§]	95	V	NS
Ciprofloxacin	100	100	40[‡§]	95	100	100
Levofloxacin	100	100	60[‡§]	100	100	100
Moxifloxacin	100	100	85[‡§]	100	100	100
Azithromycin	100	80	70[‡§]	100	100	NS
Clarithromycin	100	60	70[‡§]	70	100	NS
Telithromycin	100	100	85[‡§]	100	NS	100
Clindamycin	95	0	100[‡§]	0	95	95

*Data are compiled from various studies.
[†]Percentage of human bite isolates/percentage of animal bite isolates.
[‡]Many fusobacteria are resistant.
[§]Some peptostreptococci are resistant.
NS, not studied; TMP-SMX, trimethoprim-sulfamethoxazole; V, variable.

been associated with bite cellulitis, sepsis, and meningitis.[25] Other new aerobic species include *Neisseria canis* from a cat bite,[26] *Flavobacterium* IIb-like isolates from a pig bite,[27] *Actinobacillus lignieresii* and *Actinobacillus equi*-like bacterium from horse bites,[28] and NO1, a nonoxidative gram-negative rod[29] different from *Acinetobacter* spp. Anaerobic bacteria have undergone major reclassification. Many of the old "oral *Bacteroides*" spp. are now in the genera *Prevotella* and *Porphyromonas*. Anaerobes are isolated in up to 70% of animal bite wounds, always in mixed culture.[4,9,11] Approximately 50% to 60% of cat and dog bite wounds contain *Bacteroides tectum, Prevotella heparinolytica, Prevotella zoogleoformans, Prevotella bivia, Porphyromonas gingivalis, Porphyromonas canoris,* fusobacteria, and peptostreptococci.[30-33]

Gram stains of bite wounds are specific but nonsensitive indicators of bacterial growth. When compared, little difference was noted in the types of bacteria isolated from noninfected wounds seen early and infected wounds seen later.[4] All moderate to severe dog bite wounds, except those not clinically infected and more than 1 day old, should be considered contaminated with potential pathogens.

Wounds inflicted by cats are frequently scratches or tiny punctures located on the extremities and are likely to become infected.[33] *P. multocida* has been isolated from 50% to 70% of healthy cats and is a frequent pathogen in cat-associated wounds.[12,20,34] *Erysipelothrix rhusiopathiae* has been isolated from cat bite wounds.[12] Punctures over or near a joint, especially on the hands, should be treated aggressively with antibiotics and elevation because of a high incidence of osteomyelitis and septic arthritis. Cougar, tiger, and other feline bites also yield *P. multocida.*[35] Tularemia has likewise been transmitted by cat bites.[36] People are also bitten by a variety of other animals, including unusual domestic pets, farm animals, wild animals, aquatic animals, and laboratory animals.[3,37-40] Monkey bites cause more swelling and infection than do many other animal bites[41] and may transmit subtype B virus (herpesvirus simiae virus).[42] The bacteriology of most of these wounds is based on single case reports.

Management of Animal Bites

Table 318-3 notes the elements for treatment of animal bite wounds. The most problematic elements of the management of wounds seen early include the following:

1. The use of "prophylactic" antibiotics in wounds that are seen early but as yet are uninfected. Because 85% of such wounds harbor potential pathogens and one cannot reliably predict which wounds will become infected, selected wounds should be treated with 3 to 5 days of oral therapy (see Table 318-2).

2. The decision to suture the wound. Facial wounds are usually sutured after copious irrigation and the use of antibiotics in all but the most trivial wounds. No prospective studies are available to determine whether the risk of infection is increased. It is my experience and recommendation that other wounds not be primarily closed, but after irrigation and débridement they can be approximated and be closed by delayed primary or secondary intention.

The most common causes of therapeutic failure are the following:

1. Failure to stress the importance of or noncompliance of the patient in elevating an edematous wound. If the wound is on the hands, slings must be recommended because compliance is unlikely unless passively accomplished.

2. Selection of the incorrect antimicrobial agent (see Table 318-2). Most fastidious animal pathogens are susceptible to penicillin/amoxicillin. Because of resistance of certain bacteria, including *P. multocida*, first-generation cephalosporins, dicloxacillin, and erythromycin should be avoided or used cautiously. In vitro data suggest that some fluoroquinolones (ciprofloxacin, levofloxacin, and moxifloxacin), sulfamethoxazole-trimethoprim, and second-generation oral cephalosporins (cefuroxime) are active against many bite isolates.[43-49]

3. Failure to recognize joint penetration. Pain, diminished range of motion, local edema, and proximity of the puncture wound to a joint should alert one to the possibility of septic arthritis.

VENOMOUS SNAKEBITES

Venomous snakes, usually vipers (rattlesnakes, copperheads, cottonmouths, or water moccasins), bite approximately 8000 people in the United States yearly, of which five or six results in death, usually of children or the elderly, who receive either no or delayed antivenom.[50] The majority of bites occur in the southwestern United States between April and September and are to the extremities of males between 17 and 27 years old.[50] Envenomation can cause extensive tissue destruction and devitalization that predisposes to infection from the snake's normal oral flora. Sparse data exist on the incidence and bacteriology of snakebite infections. In rattlesnakes, the oral flora appears to be fecal in nature because the live prey usually defecates in the snake's

---

TABLE 318-3 Management of Bite Wounds

History
Animal bite: Ascertain the type of animal, whether the bite was provoked or unprovoked, and the situation/environment when the bite occurred. If the species can be rabid, locate the animal for 10 days' observation or sacrifice.
Patient: Obtain information on antimicrobial allergies, current medications, splenectomy, mastectomy, liver disease, and immunosuppression.

Physical Examination
Record a diagram of the wound with the location, type, and depth of injury, range of motion, possibility of joint penetration, presence of edema or crush injury, nerve and tendon function, signs of infection, and odor of exudate.

Cultures
Infected wounds should be cultured and a Gram stain performed. Anaerobic cultures should be obtained in the presence of abscesses, sepsis, serious cellulitis, devitalized tissue, or foul odor of the exudate. Small tears and infected punctures should be cultured with a minitipped (nasopharyngeal) swab.

Irrigation
Copious amounts of normal saline should be used for irrigation. Puncture wounds should be irrigated with a "high-pressure jet" from a 20-mL syringe and an 18-gauge needle or catheter tip.

Débridement
Devitalized or necrotic tissue should be cautiously débrided. Debris and foreign bodies should be removed.

Radiographs
Radiographs should be obtained if fracture or bone penetration is possible to provide a baseline to judge future osteomyelitis.

Wound Closure
Wound closure may be necessary for selected, fresh uninfected wounds, especially facial wounds, but primary wound closure is not usually indicated. Wound edges should be approximated with adhesive strips in selected cases.

Antimicrobial Therapy
Prophylaxis: Consider prophylaxis (1) for moderate to severe injury less than 8 hours old, especially if edema or crush injury is present, (2) if bone or joint penetration is possible, (3) for hand wounds, (4) for immunocompromised patients (including those with mastectomy, liver disease, or steroid therapy), (5) if the wound is adjacent to prosthetic joint, and (6) if the wound is in the genital area. Coverage should include *Pasteurella multocida, Staphylococcus aureus,* and anaerobes (see Table 318-2).

Antimicrobial Therapy—Continued
Treatment: Cover *P. multocida, S. aureus,* and anaerobes (see Table 318-2). Use oral medication if the patient is seen early after a bite and only mild to moderate signs of infection are present. Amoxicillin/clavulanic acid, 875/125 mg bid or 500/125 mg tid with food, will cover most bite pathogens. No alternative has been established for penicillin-allergic patients. On emergency department discharge, a single starting dose of parenteral antibiotic may be useful in selected cases. If hospitalization or closely monitored outpatient follow-up is required, intravenous agents should be used. Current choices could include ampicillin/sulbactam or cefoxitin. The rising incidence of community acquired *Staphylococcus aureus* isolates that are methicillin resistant and therefore resistant to the drugs recommended here emphasizes the importance of susceptibility testing any *S. aureus* isolates.

Hospitalization
Indications include fever, sepsis, spread of cellulitis, significant edema or crush injury, loss of function, compromised host, patient noncompliance.

Immunizations
Give tetanus booster if original three-dose series has been given, but none in the past 5 years. Give a primary series and tetanus immune globulin if the patient was never immunized (see Chapter 319).
Rabies vaccine (days 0, 3, 7, 14, and 28) with hyperimmune globulin (40 IU/kg or 18 IU/lb) may be required, depending on the type of animal, ability to observe the animal, and locality (see Chapter 160).

Elevation
Elevation may be required if any edema is present. Lack of elevation is a common cause of therapeutic failure.

Immobilization
Immobilize the extremity, especially hands, with a splint.

Follow-up
Follow-up should occur at 24 and perhaps 48 hours for outpatients.

Reporting
Reporting the incident to a local health department may be required.

---

mouth coincident with ingestion. Common oral isolates include *Pseudomonas aeruginosa, Proteus* spp., coagulase-negative staphylococci, and *Clostridium* spp.[51,52] Other potential pathogens isolated from rattlesnakes' mouths include *Bacteroides fragilis* and *Salmonella arizonae* (*Salmonella* groups IIIa and IIIb). *Crotalus* rattlesnake venom has innate broad activity against aerobic gram-positive and gram-negative bacteria but not against anaerobes.[53,54] The role of empirical antimicrobial therapy for noninfected wounds is not well defined. Specific therapy based on culturing of infected wounds should be instituted.

HUMAN BITES

Human bites have a higher complication and infection rate than do animal bites. Wounds of the lip and paronychia and infections of the structure surrounding the nail account for most self-inflicted bite wounds that come to medical attention. Paronychia is more frequent in children who suck their fingers and results from direct inoculation of the oral flora into the fingers. Brook[55] took cultures from 33 children with paronychia. Aerobes and anaerobes were each found in pure culture in 27% of cases, whereas mixed infection was found in 46% of cases. The most frequent aerobic organisms isolated were viridans streptococci, group A streptococci, *S. aureus, Haemophilus parainfluenzae, Klebsiella pneumoniae,* and *Eikenella corrodens.* The most frequently isolated anaerobic bacteria were *Bacteroides* spp., *Fusobacterium* spp., and gram-positive cocci. Therapy should include drainage, appropriate antibiotics, and avoidance of further bacterial contamination.

Occlusional human bites may affect any part of the body but most often involve the distal phalanx of the long or index fingers of the dominant hand. About 10% to 20% of wounds are "love nips" to the breasts and genital areas.[17,56,57] Bites to the hand are more serious and more frequently become infected than do bites to other areas.[58] Bites may also be caused by or be harbingers of child abuse.[59]

Important prognostic factors for the development of infection include the extent of tissue damage, the depth of the wound and which compartments are entered, and the pathogenicity of the inoculated oral bacteria.[60-63] The typical patient is a 27-year-old man who is assaulted by a 28-year-old man; first infectious symptoms occur approximately 22 hours postinjury but patients do not seek medical care until approximately 36 hours later.[63] Viridans streptococci, especially *S. anginosus,* were the most common wound isolates. *S. aureus* infection occurred in 30% to 40% of wounds and was usually present in patients who had attempted self-débridement and presented 3 to 4 days after injury. Although *H. influenzae* was occasionally isolated, other *Haemophilus* species including *H. parainfluenzae, H. aphrophilus* and *H. paraphrophilus,* and some penicillin-resistant gram-negative rods, such as *Klebsiella* spp., and *Enterobacter cloacae,* were occasionally isolated. *Prevotella* spp., *Peptostreptococcus* spp., and *Fusobacterium nucleatum,* were also frequent isolates.[50,63] Up to 45% of the anaerobic gram-negative bacilli isolated from human bite wounds may be penicillin resistant and β-lactamase positive.[45,64] *Candida* species were found in 8% of patients in one study although their pathogenicity was not determined.[63]

Management of Human Bites

A Gram stain and aerobic and anaerobic cultures should be obtained for all infected wounds before any therapy. Wounds should be copiously irrigated, surgically débrided, and diagrammed, photographed, or both. Immobilization of the affected area, including splinting if necessary, and elevation should be instituted. Empirical antimicrobial therapy should be based on the Gram stain (specific but not sensitive) or knowledge of the susceptibility of the oral flora. Patients who present early with uninfected wounds should also be given antimicrobial therapy of shorter duration and may be considered for outpatient management. Amoxicillin/clavulanic acid or penicillin plus a penicillinase-resistant penicillin or cephalosporin should be used. First-generation cephalosporins are not as effective as monotherapy because of resistance of some anaerobic bacteria and *E. corrodens*. The role of the newer fluoroquinolones with anaerobic activity has not been clinically evaluated. Many patients (32% in one study[63]) require hospitalization. Baseline radiographs should be taken of wounds close to the bone to check for osteomyelitis. Most physicians advise against primary closure, even for uninfected human bite wounds, especially those on the hands. Facial wounds may present a special situation because of the possibility of scarring and disfigurement, and many investigators recommend primary closure. Approximation of the wound margins or delayed primary closure (3 to 5 days) is often possible even in infected cases.

CLENCHED-FIST INJURIES

Clenched-fist injuries are traumatic lacerations that occur when one person strikes another in the mouth with a clenched fist. These injuries are most common over the third and fourth metacarpophalangeal joints of the dominant hand, but they may also occur over the proximal interphalangeal joints. These lacerations are often only 12 to 14 mm long but, despite their innocuous appearance, frequently lead to serious complications because of the proximity of the skin over the knuckles to the joint capsule and the potential spread of infection into subcutaneous, subfascial, subtendinous, subaponeurotic, and web spaces.

Typically, patients sustain a clenched-fist injury and attempt to cleanse it or, more often, ignore it until 36 hours postinjury, when they awaken with a painful, throbbing, and swollen hand. The swelling usually spreads proximally but not distally and results in decreased range of motion. A purulent discharge is often present. Lymphangitis, adenopathy, fever, or other signs of systemic infection are infrequent.

The bacteriology of clenched-fist injuries is similar to that of human bites and usually consists of the normal oral flora.[8,60,66] Viridans streptococci, especially *S. anginosus,* are the most frequent isolates, but *S. aureus* may be present in 20% to 40% of cases. Anaerobic bacteria can be recovered in more than 55% of clenched-fist injuries, including *Prevotella* spp., *Fusobacterium nucleatum,* and peptostreptococci. *E. corrodens* is an often overlooked but especially important pathogen in clenched-fist injury infections.[65,68] It has a prevalence rate of 59% in human gingival plaque[65] and may be isolated in 25% of clenched-fist injuries.[65] It can act synergistically with viridans streptococci and is a common cause of osteomyelitis. Although *E. corrodens* is susceptible to penicillin, it is resistant to penicillinase-resistant penicillins, clindamycin, and metronidazole and is variably resistant to cephalosporins.[45-49]

Management should include examination by an experienced hand surgeon to evaluate nerve and muscular function and the extent of injury to tendons, bones, and joints. Débridement and copious irrigation are often required. Elevation and immobilization with a plaster splint from the fingers to the elbow are essential and should be continued until marked improvement is noted. Aerobic and anaerobic cultures and radiographic films (to check for fracture and osteomyelitis) should be obtained. Many authors suggest the use of tetanus toxoid or both toxoid and antitoxin when indicated. Secondary débridement to remove necrotic bone and tissue or to drain abscesses may be advisable.

Empirical antimicrobial therapy is often intravenous and should include either cefoxitin or ampicillin/sulbactam or a carbapenem until culture results are known. Failure of first-generation cephalosporins and penicillinase-resistant penicillins, when used alone, has been reported and is often due to *E. corrodens*.[65,67-71] If resistant gram-negative rods are isolated, therapy should be altered according to the results of culture. What role β-lactamase-positive *Prevotella* and *Porphyromonas* spp. will have in the selection of antimicrobial therapy remains to be determined.

REFERENCES

1. US Department of Commerce. Statistical Abstracts of the United States-1992. 112th ed. Table 392, p. 328.
2. Sacks JJ, Kresnow M, Houston B. Dog bites: How big a problem? Inj Prev. 1996;2:52-54.
3. Weiss HB, Friedman DJ, Cohen JH. Incidence of dog bite injuries treated in emergency departments. JAMA. 1998;279:51-53.
4. Goldstein EJC, Citron DM, Finegold SM. Dog bite wounds and infection: A prospective clinical study. Ann Emerg Med. 1980;9:508-512.
5. Lockwood R. Dog-bite-related fatalities-United States 1995-1996. MMWR Morb Mortal Wkly Rep. 1997;46:463-467.
6. Brakenbury PH, Muwanga C. A comparative double blind study of amoxycillin/clavulanate vs placebo in the prevention of infection after animal bites. Arch Emerg Med. 1989;6:251-256.
7. Feder HM, Shanley JD, Barbera JA. Review of 59 patients hospitalized with animal bites. Pediatr Infect Dis J. 1987;6:24-28.
8. Goldstein EJC. Bite wounds and infection. Clin Infect Dis. 1992;14:633-640.
9. Goldstein EJC, Citron DM, Nesbit C, et al. Prevalence and characterization of anaerobic bacteria from 50 patients with infected dog and cat bite wounds. In: Ely A, Bennett K, eds. Anaerobic Pathogens. Sheffield, England: Sheffield Academic; 1997:177-185.
10. Zook EG, Miller M, Van Beek AL, et al. Successful treatment protocol of canine fang injuries. J Trauma. 1980;20:243-247.
11. Brook I. Microbiology of human and animal bite wounds in children. Pediatr Infect Dis J. 1987;6:29-32.
12. Talan DA, Citron DM, Abrahamian FM, et al. Bacteriologic analysis of infected dog and cat bites. Emergency Medicine Animal Bite Infection Study Group. N Engl J Med. 1999;340:85-92.
13. Gallen IW, Ispahani P. Fulminant *Capnocytophaga canimorsus* (DF-2) septicaemia. Lancet. 1991;337:308.
14. Hicklin H, Verghese A, Alvarez S. Dysgonic fermenter 2 septicemia. Rev Infect Dis. 1987;9:884-890.
15. Brenner DJ, Hollis DG, Fanning GR, et al. *Capnocytophaga canimorsus* sp. nov. (formerly CDC group DF2), a cause of septicemia following dog bite, and *C. cynodegmi* sp. nov., a cause of localized wound infection following dog bite. J Clin Microbiol. 1989;27:231-235.
16. Verghese A, Hamati F, Berk S, et al. Susceptibility of dysgonic fermenter 2 to antimicrobial agents in vitro. Antimicrob Agents Chemother. 1988;32:78-80.
17. Goldstein EJC, Citron DM, Finegold SM. Role of anaerobic bacteria in bite wound infections. Rev Infect Dis. 1984;6(Suppl 1):S177-S183.
18. Stucker FJ, Shaw GY, Boyd S, et al. Management of animal and human bites in the head and neck. Arch Otolaryngol Head Neck Surg. 1990;116:789-793.
19. Brook I. Human and animal bite infections. J Fam Pract. 1989;28:713-718.
20. Holst E, Rollof J, Larsson L, et al. Characterization and distribution of *Pasteurella* species recovered from human infections. J Clin Microbiol. 1992;30:2984-2987.
21. Talan DA, Staatz D, Staatz A, et al. *Staphylococcus intermedius* in canine gingiva and canine inflicted human wound infections: Laboratory characterization of a newly recognized zoonotic pathogen. J Clin Microbiol. 1989;27:78-81.
22. Talan DA, Goldstein EJC, Staatz D, et al. *Staphylococcus intermedius:* Clinical presentation of a new human dog bite pathogen. Ann Emerg Med. 1989;18:410-413.
23. Andersen BM, Steigerwalt AG, O'Conner SP, et al. *Neisseria weaveri* sp. nov., formerly CDC group M-5, a gram-negative bacterium associated with dog bite wounds. J Clin Microbiol. 1993;31:2456-2466.
24. Inzana TJ, Johnson JL, Shell L, et al. Isolation and characterization of a newly identified *Haemophilus* species from cats: *Haemophilus felis*. J Clin Microbiol. 1992;30:2108-2112.
25. Holmes B, Steigerwalt AG, Weaver RE, et al. *Weeksella zoohelcum* sp. nov. (formerly group IIj) from human clinical specimens. Syst Appl Microbiol. 1986;8:191-196.
26. Guibourdenche M, Lamber T, Riou JY. Isolation of *Neisseria canis* in mixed culture from a patient after a cat bite. J Clin Microbiol. 1989;27:1673-1674.
27. Goldstein EJC, Citron DM, Merkin TE, et al. Recovery of an unusual *Flavobacterium* IIb-like isolate from a hand infection following pig bite. J Clin Microbiol. 1990;28:1709-1781.
28. Peel NM, Hornridge KA, Luppino M, et al. *Actinobacillus* spp. and related bacteria in infected wounds of humans bitten by horses and sheep. J Clin Microbiol. 1991;29:2535-2538.
29. Hollis DG, Moss CW, Daneshaver MI, et al. Characterization of Centers for Disease Control group NO1, a fastidious, nonoxidative, gram negative organism associated with dog and cat bites. J Clin Microbiol. 1993;31:746-748.
30. Citron DM, Gerardo SH, Claros MC, et al. Frequency of isolation of *Porphyromonas* species from infected dog and cat bite wounds in humans and their characterization by biochemical tests and arbitrarily primed-polymerase chain reaction fingerprinting. Clin Infect Dis. 1996;23(Suppl 1):S78-S82.
31. Alexander CJ, Citron DM, Gerardo SH, et al. Characterization of saccharolytic *Bacteroides* and *Prevotella* isolates from infected dog and cat bite wounds in humans. J Clin Microbiol. 1997;35:406-411.
32. Hudspeth MK, Gerardo SH, Citron DM, et al. Growth characteristics and a novel method of identification (the WEE-TAB system) of *Porphyromonas* species isolated from infected dog and cat bite wounds in humans. J Clin Microbiol. 1997;35:2450-2453.
33. Love DN, Cato EP, Johnson JL, et al. Deoxyribonucleic acid hybridization among strains of fusobacteria isolated from soft tissue infections of cats: Comparison with the human and animal type strains from oral and other sites. Int J Syst Bacteriol. 1987;37:23-26.

34. Lucas GL, Bartlett DH. *Pasteurella multocida* infection in the hand. Plast Reconstr Surg. 1981;67:49-53.

35. Burdge DR, Scheifele D, Speert DP. Serious *Pasteurella multocida* infections from lion and tiger bites. JAMA. 1985;253:3296-3297.

36. Capellan J, Fong IW. Tularemia from a cat bite: Case report and review. Clin Infect Dis. 1993;16:472-475.

37. Ordog GJ, Balasubramianium S, Wasserberger J. Rat bites: Fifty cases. Ann Emerg Med. 1985;14:126-130.

38. Paisley JW, Lauer BA. Severe facial injuries to infants due to unprovoked attacks by pet ferrets. JAMA. 1988;259:2005-2006.

39. Barnham M. Pig bite injuries and infection: Report of seven human cases. Epidemiol Infect. 1988;101:641-645.

40. Flandry F, Lisecki EJ, Domingue GJ, et al. Initial antibiotic therapy for alligator bites. South Med J. 1989;82:262-266.

41. Goldstein EJC, Pryor EP III, Citron DM. Simian bites and bacterial infection. Clin Infect Dis. 1995;20:1551-1552.

42. Holmes GP, Chapman LE, Stewart J, et al. Guidelines for the prevention and treatment of B virus infections in exposed persons. Clin Infect Dis. 1995;20:421-439.

43. Goldstein EJC, Citron DM, Richwald GA. Lack of in vitro efficacy of oral forms of certain cephalosporins, erythromycin and oxacillin against *Pasteurella multocida*. Antimicrob Agents Chemother. 1988;32:213-215.

44. Gaillot O, Guilbert L, Maruejouls C, et al. In vitro susceptibility to thirteen of *Pasteurella* spp. and related bacteria isolated from humans. J Antimicrob Chemother. 1995;36:878-880.

45. Goldstein EJC, Citron DM, Hudspeth M, et al. In vitro activity of Bay 12-8039, a new 8-methoxy-quinolone, compared to the activities of 11 other oral antimicrobial agents against 390 aerobic and anaerobic bacteria isolated from human and animal bite wounds in skin and soft tissue infections in humans. Antimicrob Agents Chemother. 1997;41:1552-1557.

46. Goldstein EJC, Citron DM, Merriam CV, et al. In vitro activities of the des-fluoro [6]-quinolone, BMS 284756, against aerobic and anaerobic pathogens isolated from skin and soft tissue animal and human bite wound infections. Antimicrob Agents Chemother. 2002;46:866-870.

47. Goldstein EJC, Citron DM, Merriam CV, et al. In vitro activity of GAR-936 against aerobic and anaerobic animal and human bite pathogens. Antimicrob Agents Chemother. 2000;44:2747-2751.

48. Goldstein EJC, Citron DM, Merriam CV, et al. Comparative in vitro activity of ertapenem and 11 other antimicrobial agents against aerobic and anaerobic pathogens isolated from skin and soft tissue animal and human bite wound infections. J Antimicrob Chemother 2001;48:641-651.

49. Goldstein EJC, Citron DM, Gerardo SH, et al. Activities of HMR 3004 (RU 64004) and HMR 3647 (RU 6647) compared to those of erythromycin, azithromycin, clarithromycin, roxithromycin and eight other antimicrobial agents against unusual aerobic and anaerobic human and animal bite pathogens isolated from skin and soft tissue. Antimicrob Agents Chemother. 1998;42:1127-1132.

50. Gold B, Dart RC, Barish RA. Bites of venomous snakes. N Engl J Med. 2002;347:347-356.

51. Russell FE. Clinical aspects of snake venom poisoning in North America. Toxicon. 1969;7:33-37.

52. Goldstein EJC, Citron DM, Gonzalez H, et al. Bacteriology of rattlesnake venom and implications for therapy. J Infect Dis. 1979;140:818-821.

53. Williams FE, Freeman M, Kennedy E. The bacterial flora of the mouths of Australian venomous snakes in captivity. Med J Aust. 1934;2:190-193.

54. Talan D, Citron DM, Overturf GD, et al. Antibacterial activity of crotalid venoms against oral snake flora and other clinical bacteria. J Infect Dis. 1991;164:195-198.

55. Brook I. Bacteriology study of paronychia in children. Am J Surg. 1981;141:703.

56. Al Fallouji M. Traumatic love bites. Br J Surg. 1990;77:100-101.

57. Wolf JS, Gomez R, McAninch JW. Human bites to the penis. J Urol. 1992;147:2065-2067.

58. Mann RJ, Hoffeld TA, Farmer CB. Human bites of the hand: Twenty years of experience. J Hand Surg. 1977;2:97-104.

59. Sperber ND. Bite marks, oral and facial injuries. Harbingers of severe child abuse? Pediatrician. 1989;16:207-211.

60. Goldstein EJC, Citron DM, Wield B, et al. Bacteriology of human and animal bite wounds. J Clin Microbiol. 1978;8:667-672.

61. Chuinard RG, D'Ambrosia RD. Human bite infections of the hand. J Bone Joint Surg Am. 1977;59:416-418.

62. Zubowicz VN, Gravier M. Management of early human bites of the hand: A prospective randomized study. Plastic Reconstr Surg. 1991;88:111-114.

63. Talan DA, Abrahamian FM, Moran GJ, et al. Clinical presentations and bacteriological analysis of infected human bites presenting to Emergency Departments. Clin Infect Dis. 2003;37:1481-1489.

64. Brook I. Microbiology of human and animal bite wounds in children. Pediatr Infect Dis. 1987;6:29-32.

65. Goldstein EJC, Miller TA, Citron DM, et al. Infections following clenched-fist injury: A new perspective. J Hand Surg. 1978;3:455-457.

66. Merriam CV, Fernandez HT, Citron DM et al. Bacteriology of human bite wound infections. Anaerobe 2003;9:83-86.

68. Goldstein EJC, Barone M, Miller TA. *Eikenella corrodens* in hand infections. J Hand Surg. 1983;8:563-567.

68. McDonald I. *Eikenella corrodens* infections of the hand. Hand. 1979;11:224-227.

69. Goldstein EJC, Tarenzi LA, Agyare EO, et al. Prevalence of *Eikenella corrodens* in dental plaque. J Clin Microbiol. 1983;17:636-639.

70. Goldstein EJC, Sutter VL, Finegold SM. Susceptibility of *Eikenella corrodens* to ten cephalosporins. Antimicrob Agents Chemother. 1978;14:639-641.

71. Goldstein EJC, Gombert ME, Agyare EO. Susceptibility of *Eikenella corrodens* to newer beta-lactam antibiotics. Antimicrob Agents Chemother. 1980;18:832-833.

CHAPTER **319**

Immunization

WALTER A. ORENSTEIN
MELINDA WHARTON
KENNETH J. BART
ALAN R. HINMAN

The two most effective means of preventing disease, disability, and death from infectious diseases have been sanitation and immunization. Both these approaches antedated understanding of the germ theory of disease. Artificial induction of immunity began centuries ago with variolation, the practice of inoculating fluid from smallpox lesions into the skin of susceptible persons. Although this technique usually produced mild illness without complications, spread of disease did occur, with occasional complications. In 1796, Jenner demonstrated that milk maids who had contracted cowpox (vaccinia) were immune to smallpox. He inoculated the vesicular fluid from cowpox lesions into the skin of susceptible individuals and induced protection against smallpox, thus beginning the era of immunization.

Immunization is the act of artificially inducing immunity or providing protection from disease; it can be active or passive. Active immunization consists of inducing the body to develop defenses against disease. This is usually accomplished by the administration of vaccines or toxoids that stimulate the body's immune system to produce antibodies or cell-mediated immunity, or both, which protects against the infectious agent. Passive immunization consists of providing temporary protection through the administration of exogenously produced antibody. Two situations in which passive immunization commonly occurs are through the transplacental transfer of antibodies to the fetus, which may provide protection against certain diseases for the first 3 to 6 months of life, and the injection of immunoglobulins for specific preventive purposes. A more detailed description of the immune mechanisms involved follows.

Immunizing agents include vaccines, toxoids, and antibody-containing preparations from human or animal donors. Some important definitions follow.[1]

1. Vaccine: A suspension of attenuated live or killed microorganisms (bacteria, viruses, or rickettsiae), or fractions thereof, administered to induce immunity and thereby prevent infectious disease.
2. Toxoid: A modified bacterial toxin that has been rendered nontoxic but retains the ability to stimulate the formation of antitoxin.
3. Immunoglobulin (Ig): A sterile solution for intramuscular administration containing antibody from human blood. It contains 15% to 18% protein obtained by cold ethanol fractionation of large pools of blood plasma.[1] It is primarily indicated for routine protection of certain immunodeficient persons and for passive immunization against measles and hepatitis A. Immunoglobulin intravenous (IGIV), a specialized preparation allowing intravenous administration, is indicated primarily for replacement therapy in IgG deficiency, treatment of Kawasaki disease, and idiopathic thrombocytopenic purpura.
4. Specific immunoglobulin: Special preparations obtained from donor pools preselected for a high antibody content against a specific disease, for example, hepatitis B immune globulin (HBIG),

varicella-zoster immune globulin (VZIG), rabies immune globulin (RIG), and tetanus immune globulin (TIG).

The constituents of immunizing agents include:

1. Suspending fluid: This frequently is as simple as sterile water or saline, but it may be a complex fluid containing small amounts of proteins or other constituents derived from the medium or biologic system in which the immunizing agent is produced (serum proteins, egg antigens, cell culture–derived antigens).
2. Preservatives, stabilizers, antibiotics: These components of vaccines are used (1) to inhibit or prevent bacterial growth in viral culture or the final product or (2) to stabilize the antigen. They include materials such as mercurials (thimerosal), gelatin, and specific antibiotics. Allergic reactions may occur if the recipient is sensitive to any of these additives. A review of the mercury content of vaccines indicated some children had received quantities of ethyl mercury from thimerosal in excess of some federal guidelines for methyl mercury. As a precautionary measure, it was recommended that thimerosal be removed from the immunization schedule to the extent feasible.[2] In the United States, thimerosal, as a preservative, has been removed from almost all vaccines routinely recommended for children during the first 7 years of life, although some of these vaccines may still contain trace amounts. Some vaccines for children contain other preservatives or do not need a preservative because they are packaged as single doses. Some vaccines, particularly those used in adults, may still contain thimerosal as a preservative, such as most doses of influenza vaccine (25 mcg per 0.5-mL dose) and combined adult type tetanus and diphtheria-toxoids (Td). Influenza vaccine, which is routinely recommended for children 6 to 23 months of age, may contain approximately 12.5 mcg of mercury as a preservative per dose (0.25 mL for children 6 to 35 months of age).
3. Adjuvants: An aluminum salt is used in some vaccines to enhance the immune response to vaccines containing inactivated microorganisms or their products (e.g., toxoids and hepatitis B vaccine). Vaccines with such adjuvants should usually be injected deeply into muscle masses because subcutaneous or intracutaneous administration can cause local irritation, inflammation, granuloma formation, or necrosis.[3]

IMMUNOLOGIC BASIS OF VACCINATION

Two major approaches to active immunization have been employed: the use of live (generally attenuated) infectious agents or the use of inactivated, or detoxified, agents or their extracts. For many diseases (including influenza, poliomyelitis, typhoid, and measles) both approaches have been employed. Live, attenuated vaccines are believed to induce an immunologic response more similar to that resulting from natural infection than do killed vaccines. Inactivated or killed vaccines can consist of inactivated whole organisms (e.g., Japanese Encephalitis), detoxified exotoxin (e.g., diphtheria and tetanus toxoids), soluble capsular material either alone (e.g., pneumococcal polysaccharide) or covalently linked to carrier proteins (e.g., *Haemophilus influenzae* type b conjugate vaccines), or purified extracts of some component or components of the organism (e.g., hepatitis B, subunit influenza, acellular pertussis vaccines).

DETERMINANTS OF IMMUNOGENICITY

The immune system is complex, and antigen composition and presentation are critical for stimulation of the desired immune response. Immunogenicity is determined not only by the chemical and physical states of the antigen but also by the genetic characteristics of the responding individual (major histocompatibility complex [MHC] polymorphism), the physiologic condition of the individual (e.g., age, nutrition, gender, pregnancy status, stress, infections, immune status), and the manner in which the antigen is presented (route of administration, dose or doses and timing of doses, presence of adjuvants).[4]

Major Histocompatibility Complex Polymorphism

The extensive polymorphism of the MHC in human populations contributes to the recognition by different individuals of different epitopes in a complex protein antigen. To vaccinate a population effectively, a vaccine must contain epitopes that can be processed and bind to the product of at least one allele in every individual.[5]

Live versus Killed or Subunit Vaccines

Because the organisms in live vaccines multiply in the recipient, antigen production generally increases logarithmically until checked by the onset of the immune response it is intended to induce. The live, attenuated viruses (e.g., measles, mumps, rubella) generally are believed to confer lifelong protection with one dose in those who respond. By contrast, killed vaccines generally do not induce permanent immunity with one dose, making repeated vaccination and boosters necessary to develop and maintain high levels of antibody (e.g., diphtheria, tetanus, rabies, typhoid). Exceptions to this general rule may include hepatitis B vaccine, for which long-term immunologic memory has been demonstrated for at least 10 years after vaccination, and inactivated polio vaccine (IPV), for which the duration of immunity is unknown. Although the amount of antigen initially introduced is greater with inactivated vaccines, multiplication of organisms in the host results in a cumulatively greater antigenic input with live vaccines.

Polysaccharide vaccines tend to induce T-cell–independent immune responses that do not produce booster responses on repeated injections and have poor immunogenicity in infants and young children. In contrast, protein antigens tend to generate a T-cell–dependent immune response with induction of immunologic memory, booster effects on repeat administration, and good immunogenicity in infants and young children. Covalent linkage of *H. influenzae* type b capsular polysaccharide to carrier proteins converts it from a T-cell–independent to a T-cell–dependent antigen.

Dose

The amount of antigen is important. The presentation of an insufficient amount may result in an absence of immune responsiveness. There is usually a dose response curve relationship between antigen dose and peak response obtained beyond a threshold; however, responsiveness may reach a plateau, failing to increase beyond a certain level despite increasing doses of vaccine.

Adjuvants

The degree of "foreignness" of the antigen determines the extent and specificity of the response. More complex antigens are more immunogenic. The immune response to some vaccines or toxoids can be enhanced by the addition of adjuvants, such as aluminum salts. They are particularly useful with inactivated products such as diphtheria and tetanus toxoids, acellular pertussis vaccines (DTaP) and hepatitis B vaccine. The mechanism of enhancement of antigenicity by adjuvants is not totally defined; however, adjuvants render a soluble antigen immunogenic, mobilize phagocytes to the site of antigen deposition, and delay the release of antigen.[6]

Route of Administration

The route of administration may determine the rapidity and nature of the immune response to a vaccine or toxoid. Inoculation into or on organs of external secretion (e.g., nasal or gastrointestinal mucosa) is more likely to result in production of local IgA compared with that after intramuscular injection. The immunogenicity of some vaccines is reduced when not given by the recommended route. For example, administration of hepatitis B vaccine subcutaneously into the fatty tissue of the buttock was associated with substantially lower seroconversion rates than injection intramuscularly into the deltoid.[7]

Age

The immune response to a vaccine may be age-dependent. Although children and young adults usually respond well to all vaccines, differences in response capability exist during early infancy and old age.

The presence of high levels of passively acquired maternal antibody in the first few months of life impairs the initial immune response to some killed vaccines (hepatitis A vaccine,[15] diphtheria toxoid) and many live vaccines (measles). Prematurely born infants of low birth weight should be immunized at the usual chronological age in most cases. Infants with birth weights less than 2000 g may require modification of the timing of hepatitis B immunoprophylaxis depending on maternal hepatitis B surface antigen status. Some studies suggest a reduced immune response in very low birth weight infants (less than 1500 g) immunized by the usual schedule; however, antibody concentrations achieved are usually protective. In the elderly, the response to antigenic stimulation may be diminished (e.g., influenza, hepatitis B vaccines).

MOBILIZATION OF THE IMMUNE RESPONSE

There are three sequential responses to vaccination: (1) the induction of proteolytic cascades that are aimed at walling off the foreign material (complement, the kallikrein, and the clotting system); (2) recognition and engulfing of the organism or antigen by phagocytic cells; and (3) the induction of a humoral response by antimicrobial peptide release. There is a degree of overlap between the innate and adaptive immune system that covers the temporal lag between the immediate response and the development of antibodies.[8]

Some of the elements of innate immunity are preformed, and are ready to act without modification (natural antibodies, C-reactive proteins [Pentraxins], the alternative complement system). Others (macrophages, dendritic cells, natural killer [NK] T cells, neutrophils) require activation by non-self signals. Host surface molecules (pattern receptors) recognize conserved microbial molecular patterns and trigger signal-transducing pathways within host cells. They detect organisms or antigens, phagocytize them, and orchestrate an appropriate host response as professional antigen presenting cells. This process, called antigen presentation, results in specific T-cell activation and is the interface between the innate and the adaptive immune system.[9-12]

Many pattern recognition molecules work together to respond in the first few minutes and hours after exposure to vaccination during the lag period of 24 to 36 hours required to generate a specific "adaptive immune response"; limit the organism or antigen; induce a heightened sense of awareness among white cells; and act as necessary antecedent to the development of an adaptive immune response. Once the organism/antigen is internalized, the organism is killed and broken down to peptides. These peptides are transposed to the cell surface via membrane trafficking and bind to MHC class I or class II molecules where the peptide/MHC class II complex binds to its cognate T-cell receptor.[13,14]

At rest, the adaptive immune system consists of quiescent cells—B and T lymphocytes–each potentially responsive to a unique, specific antigen. When an antigen is presented or recognized, these lymphocytes proliferate into a clonal population of cells that directs an immune response against the foreign antigen. Antigens usually require the interaction of B and T cells (T-cell–dependent) to generate an immune response (e.g., measles, varicella) T cells can recognize polypeptides of a relatively small length (8 to 20 amino acids) in association with a specific MHC molecule.[16] On occasion, an antigen may initiate B-cell proliferation and antibody production without the help of T cells (T-cell–independent, e.g., pneumococcal polysaccharide).

The first step in the adaptive immune system of induction of a T-cell–dependent antibody response is the activation of T-helper cells by presentation of an antigen by phagocytes or dendritic cells. Presentation of an antigen triggers the secretion of a cascade of mediators (cytokines, α-, β-, γ-interferons), which are made by or act on elements of the immune system to inform and stimulate the maturation of naive T-helper cells, and communicate between leukocytes (interleukins [IL], intercellular messengers which activate lymphocyte cellular differentiation) to regulate the immune response. Depending on the stimulus (T-cell dependent or -independent), T lymphocytes are stimulated by IL-12 to differentiate into one of two subsets: T helper 1 (T_H1), which execute cell-mediated immune responses or by IL-4 to differentiate into T helper 2 cells (T_H2), which assist in antibody production for humoral immunity. Each of the subsets in turn produces interleukins: T_H1 produces IL-2 and interferon; T_H2 produces IL-4, IL-5, IL-6, and IL-10.[17,18]

The antibodies formed after vaccination may express a variety of antigen binding specificities (i.e., recognize different structures on a complex multideterminant antigen).[19,20]

The most important protective antibodies include elements of both the innate and adaptive immune system: those that inactivate soluble toxic protein products of bacteria (antitoxins), facilitate intracellular digestion of bacteria interact with components of serum complement to damage the bacterial membrane with resultant bacteriolysis (lysins), prevent proliferation of infectious virus (neutralizing antibodies), or interact with components of the bacterial surface to prevent adhesion to mucosal surfaces (antiadhesins) (see also Chapter 2).

Antibodies cannot readily reach intracellular sites of infection, the sites of viral and some bacterial replication. However, antibodies are effective against many viral diseases by (1) interacting with virus before initial intracellular penetration occurs, and (2) preventing locally replicating virus from disseminating from the site of entry to an important target organ, as in the spread of poliovirus from the gut to the central nervous system or of rabies from a puncture wound to peripheral neural tissue.

UNANTICIPATED RESPONSES

Independent of antibody production, the stimulation of the immune system by vaccination may, on occasion, elicit a hypersensitivity response. Killed measles vaccine, in use in the United States between 1963 and 1967, induced incomplete humoral immunity and cell-mediated hypersensitivity, resulting in the development of a syndrome of atypical measles in some children on subsequent challenge.[21] In addition, some antibodies produced may not be protective but "block" the reaction of protective antibodies with antigens, inhibiting the body's defenses. Some vaccines may induce immunologic tolerance that results in blunting of the immune response on subsequent exposure to the antigen (e.g., meningococcal polysaccharide vaccine[22]). Concerns have been raised that immunizations might induce chronic allergic or autoimmune disorders. However, careful reviews of both the possible biologic mechanisms and epidemiologic evidence have generally failed to confirm vaccines as causes of these disorders.[23] Concerns have also been raised that the number of antigens today in the vaccine schedule might overwhelm an infant's immune system, leading to chronic diseases and predisposing to serious other infections. As a result of the removal of whole cell pertussis vaccine and smallpox vaccine from the current immunization schedule, the number of immunogenic proteins and polysaccharides a child is exposed to today is actually smaller than in the past.[24] Estimates suggest that an infant is capable of responding to 10,000 vaccines simultaneously.[24] The Institute of Medicine recently concluded that available evidence favored rejection of a causal relationship between vaccines and increased risk of infections and type 1 diabetes. The evidence was insufficient to accept or reject a causal relationship between vaccines and allergic disorders, particularly asthma.[25]

TEMPORAL COURSE OF THE IMMUNE RESPONSE

The "primary response" occurs after first exposure to a vaccine antigen. After a latent period, humoral and cell-mediated immunity can be detected. Circulating antibodies do not usually appear for 7 to 10 days. The immunoglobulin class of the response changes over time. Early-appearing antibodies are usually IgM class and of low affinity; late-appearing antibodies are usually IgG and display a high affinity. When the antigen is thymus-dependent, IgM and IgG classes of antibody are initially secreted by B-cells, with IgM appearing first. IgM antibodies may fix complement, making lysis and phagocytosis possible. As the titer of IgG rises during the second week (or later) after immunogenic stimulation, the IgM titer falls. IgG antibodies are produced in large amounts and function in the neutralization, precipitation, and fixation of complement. The antibody titer frequently reaches a peak in approximately 2 to 6 weeks and then falls gradually. The switch from IgM synthesis

to predominantly IgG synthesis in B-cells requires T-cell cooperation. Uncommonly, individuals may not respond to a vaccine, experiencing a "primary vaccine failure." Such individuals may lack the MHC determinants required to recognize the antigen, but other mechanisms exist as well; for example, almost all children who do not respond immunologically to the first dose of measles, mumps, rubella vaccine (MMR) will acquire measles immunity following a second dose.[26]

Many pathogens replicate at mucosal surfaces before host invasion and may induce secretory IgA along the respiratory and gastrointestinal mucous membranes and at other localized sites (e.g., polio, rubella, influenza). IgA antibodies are efficient at virus neutralization (e.g., polio), fix complement through the alternative pathway (e.g., cholera), prevent adsorption of organisms to the intestinal wall (e.g., *Escherichia coli*, cholera), and can lyse gram-negative bacteria (with the aid of both complement and lysozyme).[27] Current parenteral, especially inactivated, vaccines rarely induce high levels of secretory IgA antibodies.

After a second exposure to the same antigen, a heightened humoral or cell-mediated response, an "anamnestic response" is observed. These "secondary responses" occur sooner than the primary response, usually within 4 to 5 days, and depend on a marked proliferation of antibody-producing cells or effector T cells. The secondary response depends on immunologic memory after the first exposure mediated by both T and B cells. Infection with measles or varicella vaccine strains has been shown to evoke a cell-mediated as well as humoral response.

Some immune responses may not in themselves confer immunity, but may be sufficiently associated with protection that they remain useful proxy measures of protective immunity (e.g., vibriocidal serum antibodies in cholera).

MEASUREMENT OF THE IMMUNE RESPONSE

Response to vaccines is often gauged by measuring the appearance and concentration of specific antibodies in the serum.[28] For some viral vaccines, such as those for measles, rubella, and hepatitis B, the presence of circulating antibodies correlates with clinical protection. Although this has served as a dependable indicator of immunity, seroconversion measures only the humoral parameter of the immune response. Secondary vaccine failure occurs when an individual who had previously had an adequate immune response loses measurable antibodies over time. Evaluating persistence of antibody has been used to determine duration of vaccine-induced immunity. However, the absence of measurable antibody may not mean that the individual is unprotected. Although a fall in titer takes place for some vaccines over time (e.g., measles, rubella, hepatitis B) on revaccination or challenge, a rapid secondary response is observed in IgG antibodies with little or no detectable IgM response, suggesting persistent protection. With some vaccines and toxoids, the mere presence of antibodies is not sufficient to ensure clinical protection, but rather a minimal circulating level of antibody is required (e.g., 0.01 IU/mL of tetanus antitoxin). The measurement of cell-mediated immunity, which would be helpful in assessing the degree of ongoing protection, is usually limited to research laboratories and to only a few vaccines.

VACCINE DEVELOPMENT

Most vaccines in use today have been developed by conventional techniques.[29] For live attenuated viral vaccines, organisms are repeatedly passaged in various tissue cell lines to reduce virulent properties while maintaining immunogenicity. Inactivated vaccines usually have been developed by growing microorganisms, followed by concentration, purification, and inactivation, not necessarily in that order. Component vaccines usually are derived from chemical separation of the needed component from the parent organism.

Future vaccines are likely to be derived from new methods of biotechnology—especially recombinant techniques. Currently available hepatitis B vaccines were developed by cloning the hepatitis B surface antigen (HBsAg) gene into yeast, leading to synthesis of HBsAg within the yeast cell. Other new approaches for producing vaccines include live vectors, in which one or more genes encoding for critical determinants of immunity from pathogenic microorganisms are inserted into the genome of the vector. Such vectors may include viruses such as pox viruses (vaccinia or canarypox) or bacteria such as salmonella or bacillus Calmette-Guérin (BCG). Other newer techniques include microencapsulation of critical antigens in polymers that can lead to sustained release or pulse release over prolonged periods, mimicking the effect of multiple injections of an antigen over a several-month interval. New technologies also include use of nucleic acids, which encode critical antigens. Injection of the DNA leads to production of antigen without risk of producing whole infectious organisms. Live attenuated influenza vaccine was developed using genetic reassortment of the genes encoding two of the surface glycoproteins from wild virus isolates with 6 other genes contributed from a cold-adapted, temperature-sensitive influenza strain.

General Principles of Immunization

The introduction and widespread use of vaccines has resulted in global eradication of smallpox, elimination of poliomyelitis caused by wild viruses in the United States, and dramatic reductions in the incidence rates of other diseases (Table 319-1). Measles is no longer considered endemic in the United States.[30] Diphtheria and rubella have been greatly reduced in developed countries (more than 90%) and, if global vaccination efforts can be sustained, may eventually be eliminated from many countries.[31] The World Health Assembly had established a goal to eradicate polio from the world by the end of 2000. While that goal was not achieved, by the end of 2003, polio was only endemic in six countries of the world.[32] The last case of polio due to wild virus in the Western Hemisphere was in 1991 and both the European and Western Pacific Regions of the World Health Organization have been certified free of poliomyelitis.[33-35] Global use of hepatitis B vaccine in infants will potentially have an impact comparable to that of other vaccines in childhood, although impact has been suboptimal owing to limited use to date. *H. influenzae* type b vaccines have only recently come into widespread use, but disease incidence has been markedly reduced in many developed countries.[36,37]

Modern vaccines are very safe and effective; however, they are not completely so. Each vaccine is associated with some adverse effects, which may range from very mild to life-threatening, and each vaccine falls short of 100% effectiveness. Consequently, some persons who have received a full course of vaccine or toxoid may acquire disease on exposure. The effectiveness of vaccines recommended for universal use in children is well defined, with most vaccines protecting 80% to more than 90% to 95% of recipients following a primary series. Acellular pertussis vaccines range in efficacy from 71% to 89% in most studies.[38-40] Varicella vaccine is 95% or more effective against severe varicella but is less effective against varicella of any severity.[41,42] In 2003, reductions of 95% or more from baseline 20th century morbidity have been reported in the United States for smallpox, diphtheria, tetanus, polio, measles, mumps, and rubella (see Table 319-1). Similar reductions, based on historical estimates, have been achieved for congenital rubella syndrome and *H. influenzae* type b invasive disease.[43] Based on 2003 provisional data, record lows were either achieved or tied for measles, mumps, rubella, congenital rubella syndrome, polio, tetanus, hepatitis A, and hepatitis B.

Although the high efficacy of each of these vaccines is readily apparent, there has been substantial controversy over reported adverse events temporally associated with vaccination. Because of these controversies, the Institute of Medicine (IOM) reviewed available information during the early 1990s regarding 9 of the 12 vaccines universally recommended for children and the serious adverse effects that have been reported in association with them.[44-46] For most events, the available evidence was insufficient to make a causal evaluation. However, evidence related to several events was sufficient to (1) support rejection of vaccine playing a causal role, (2) support vaccine playing a causal role, or (3) more definitively establish that vaccine has a causal role.[47] The evidence favored rejection of a causal relationship between DT and encephalopathy and between conjugate Hib vaccines and early onset Hib disease. Specifically, for vaccines in use in the United States today, the IOM concluded that the evidence favored a causal relationship between (1) RA 27/3 rubella vaccine and

TABLE 319-1 Baseline 20th Century Annual Morbidity and 2003 (Provisional) Morbidity from Nine Diseases with Vaccines Recommended for Universal Use in Children-United States***

Disease	Baseline 20th Century Annual Morbidity	2003 (Provisional) Morbidity***	Percent Decrease
Smallpox	48,164*,**	0	100
Diphtheria	175,885†	1	99.99‡
Pertussis	147,271§	8067	94.52
Tetanus	1314‖	14	98.93
Poliomyelitis (paralytic)	16,316¶	0	100
Measles	503,282††	42	99.99
Mumps	152,209‡‡	194	99.87
Rubella	47,745§§	8	99.98
Congenital rubella syndrome	823‖‖	0	100
Haemophilus influenzae type b and unknown serotype <5 years of age.	20,000¶¶	207	98.97

*Average annual number of cases during 1900-1904.

†Average annual number of reported cases during 1920-1922, 3 years before vaccine development.

‡Rounded to the nearest point.

§Average annual number of reported cases during 1922-1925, 4 years before vaccine development.

‖Estimated number of cases based on reported number of deaths during 1922-1926 assuming a case-fatality rate of 90%.

¶Average annual number of reported cases during 1951-1954, 4 years before vaccine licensure.

††Average number of reported cases during 1958-1962, 5 years before vaccine licensure.

‡‡Number of reported cases in 1968, the first year reporting began and the first year after vaccine licensure.

§§Average annual number of reported cases during 1966-1968, 3 years before vaccine licensure.

‖‖Estimated number of cases based on seroprevalence data in the population and on the risk that women infected during a childbearing year would have a fetus with congenital rubella syndrome.

¶¶Estimated number of cases from population-based surveillance studies before vaccine licensure in 1985.

**Recommendation for universal vaccination of children against smallpox was discontinued in 1971.

***Provisional data.

Adapted from Centers for Disease Control and Prevention. Ten great public health achievements—United States, 1900-1999. MMWR Morb Mortal Wkly Rep. 1999;48:245.

chronic arthritis and (2) established a causal relationship between MMR and thrombocytopenia, (3) between rubella vaccine and acute arthritis, (4) between DT and brachial neuritis and Guillian-Barré Syndrome, and (5) between a variety of vaccines and anaphylaxis. The Advisory Committee on Immunization Practices (ACIP) subsequently reviewed the IOM findings along with new data available regarding Guillain-Barré syndrome (GBS). Most of the IOM conclusions were accepted. However, new data from population-based studies of GBS and vaccines as well as new information from a Finnish study do not support a causal relationship between oral polio vaccine, DTP, or tetanus toxoid and GBS.[48,49] Likewise, more recent studies have found no evidence of increased risk for new onset of chronic arthropathies among women vaccinated with RA27/3 vaccine, arguing against RA27/3 rubella vaccine as a cause of chronic arthropathy.[50-52]

More recently, the IOM has been asked to review the relationship between a variety of disorders and vaccines[47] (Table 319-2). They concluded evidence did not support a relationship between MMR and autism, multiple immunizations, and heterologous infections, multiple immunizations and type 1 diabetes and hepatitis B vaccine and incident or relapsed multiple sclerosis.

In the development of vaccines, the initial studies are typically carried out in animal models to demonstrate protection (or at least production of antibodies) and relative safety and then limited numbers of

TABLE 319-2 Institute of Medicine Immunization Safety Review Committee*

Causality Conclusion*	Hypothesis	Biological Mechanisms or Plausibility Conclusions†
No evidence		
Evidence is inadequate to accept or reject a causal relationship	Thimerosal-containing vaccines and the neurodevelopmental disorders of ADHD[‖], and speech or language delay[‖]	Biologically plausible
	Multiple immunizations and allergic disease, particularly asthma	Weak [includes bystander activation and impaired immunoregulation]
	Guillain-Barré syndrome and influenza vaccines administered after 1976, incident multiple sclerosis, optic neuritis, and other demyelinating neurological disorders, and influenza vaccine	Weak
	Hepatitis B vaccine and first episode CNS demyelinating disorder, ADEM, optic neuritis, transverse myelitis, Guillain-Barré syndrome, and brachial neuritis	Weak
	SV 40-containing poliovaccines and cancer	Strong
Evidence favors rejection of a causal relationship	MMR vaccine and autism spectrum disorder	Biologic model incomplete and fragmentary
	Multiple immunizations and heterologous infections[§]	Strong
	Multiple immunizations and type 1 diabetes[‡]	Weak—Autoimmune disease [includes molecular mimicry (theoretical), bystander activation (weak), impaired immunoregulation (theoretical)]
	Thimerosal-containing vaccines and autism	Theoretical
	Relapse of multiple sclerosis and influenza vaccines	Weak
	Hepatitis B vaccine in adults and incident or relapse of multiple sclerosis	Weak
Evidence favors acceptance of a causal relationship		
Evidence establishes a causal relationship		

*Causality conclusion based on epidemiological evidence.
†Biological mechanism conclusion based on experimental models and/or human evidence related to biological or pathophysiological processes; categories include theoretical (if no evidence) and weak, moderate, strong (if any evidence).
‡Diabetes type 1 used as a specific example of autoimmune disorder for causality assessment; autoimmune disorder used as general disorder for biological mechanism conclusion.
§Infection with agents unrelated to vaccines.
‖Attention deficit hyperactivity syndrome.
Modified from Chen RT, Davis RL, Sheedy KM. Safety of immunizations. In Plotkin SA, Orenstein WA, eds. Vaccines. 4th ed. Philadelphia: WB Saunders; 2004:1557-1581.

doses are administered to humans to demonstrate antibody production and safety (phase I). After this stage, clinical trials in humans are typically carried out in a limited number of individuals to select optimal vaccine schedules and to demonstrate further safety (phase II). Larger trials are carried out to demonstrate efficacy (phase III). Because of their limited size, these field trials can only be expected to detect adverse events that occur relatively frequently (1/1000 doses or higher). After clinical trials, licensure may be sought. In the United States, vaccine production is strictly regulated by the Center for Biologics Evaluation and Research of the Food and Drug Administration. Only after a vaccine is found to be safe and effective is it licensed for use. Post marketing surveillance (phase IV) is necessary to detect rare adverse events associated with vaccination and to monitor safety of vaccination practices such as simultaneous immunization.

Although there is no direct evidence of risk to the fetus when pregnant women are given routinely recommended vaccines, most live virus vaccines induce viremia, which can result in infection of the fetus. For this reason, live virus vaccines are not generally administered to pregnant women except in unusual circumstances.

The decision to use a vaccine involves assessment of the risks of disease, the benefits of vaccination, and the risks associated with vaccination. The relative balance of risks and benefits may change over time; consequently, continuing assessment of vaccines is essential. Recommendations for vaccine use are developed by several different bodies: The Centers for Disease Control and Prevention's (CDC) Advisory Committee on Immunization Practices (ACIP) develops recommendations for vaccines with primary orientation toward the public health sector. These recommendations are available on the World Wide Web at www.cdc.gov/nip/ACIP. The Committee on Infectious Diseases of the American Academy of Pediatrics (the "Red Book" committee) develops recommendations for vaccine use in private pediatric practice.[53] The Task Force on Adult Immunization of the American College of Physicians and the Infectious Diseases Society of America have developed recommendations for vaccination of adults in the private sector.[54] Since 1995, the ACIP, the American Academy of Pediatrics, and the American Academy of

Family Physicians have collaborated to issue a harmonized childhood immunization schedule, which is updated annually.[55] In 2003, the Advisory Committee on Immunization Practices issued an adult immunization schedule in two parts: (1) recommendations based on age group and (2) recommendations based on underlying medical condition which can be found at www.cdc.gov/nip/recs/adult-schedule.htm#print.[56]

CURRENTLY AVAILABLE IMMUNIZING AGENTS

Tables 319-3 and 319-4 list currently licensed immunizing agents and immunoglobulins. This section presents brief information about most immunizing agents, the primary indications for use, relative efficacy, the number and spacing of doses required, known adverse effects, and precautions and contraindications for use. Package inserts and specific references and recommendations should be consulted for more detailed information. In addition to these licensed products, several other vaccines are under development and may soon become available (e.g., meningococcal polysaccharide conjugate vaccine, acellular pertussis vaccine for adolescents and adults, and human papilloma virus vaccine).

Vaccines

Anthrax Vaccine

Anthrax vaccine is prepared from microaerophilic cultures of an avirulent nonencapsulated strain of *Bacillus anthracis*. The vaccine is a cell-free filtrate that contains a mixture of components, including protective antigen (the antigen that is thought to confer immunity) as well as other bacterial products. Because of concerns about potential use of *B. anthracis* as a biowarfare agent, vaccination of members of the United States Armed Forces was begun in 1998. Following the intentional release of anthrax in the United States in 2001, anthrax vaccine was recommended for civilians at risk for repeated exposure to *B. anthracis* spores, including laboratory personnel handling environmental specimens and performing confirmatory testing for *B. anthracis* in selected laboratories and workers making repeated entries into sites known to be

TABLE 319-3 Currently Available Vaccines and Toxoids and Year Licensed*

Product	Year Licensed
Anthrax vaccine adsorbed	1970
Bacillus Calmette-Guérin vaccine	1950
Diphtheria and tetanus toxoids and acellular pertussis vaccine	1991
Diphtheria and tetanus toxoids adsorbed (pediatric use, DT)	1949
Diphtheria and tetanus toxoids and acellular pertussis vaccine reconstituted with *Haemophilus* B conjugate vaccine	1996
Diphtheria and tetanus toxoids and acellular pertussis adsorbed, hepatitis B (Recombinant), and inactivated poliovirus vaccine combined	2002
Haemophilus influenzae type B conjugate vaccine	1987
Hepatitis A vaccine	1995
Hepatitis A inactivated and hepatitis B (Recombinant) vaccine	2001
Hepatitis B recombinant vaccine	1987
Hepatitis B recombinant vaccine and *Haemophilus influenzae type* B conjugate vaccine	1996
Influenza virus vaccine (inactivated)	1945
Influenza virus vaccine, live, intranasal	2003
Japanese encephalitis vaccine	1993
Lyme disease vaccine	1998
Measles virus vaccine, live, attenuated	1963
Measles, mumps, and rubella virus vaccine, live	1971
Meningococcal polysaccharide vaccine, groups A, C, Y, W135 combined	1981
Mumps virus vaccine, live	1967
Pneumococcal conjugate vaccine (7 valent)	2000
Pneumococcal polysaccharide vaccine (23 valent)	1983
Poliomyelitis vaccine (inactivated, enhanced potency)	1987
Rabies vaccine (human diploid)	1980
Rubella virus vaccine, live	1969
Smallpox vaccine	1903
Tetanus and diphtheria toxoids, adsorbed (adult use, Td)	1955
Tetanus toxoid	1933
Tetanus toxoid adsorbed	1949
Typhoid vaccine (polysaccharide)	1994
Typhoid vaccine (oral)	1990
Varicella vaccine	1995
Yellow fever vaccine	1953

*As of November 26, 2003.
Prepared by Ellington, R, National Immunization Program, CDC.

TABLE 319-4 Currently Available Immune Globulins and Year First Licensed*

Product	Year Licensed
Botulism immune globulin intravenous (human)	2003
Cytomegalovirus immune globulin	1990
Hepatitis B immunoglobulin (human)	1977
Immune globulin intravenous (human)	1981
Immune globulin intravenous (human), 10% by Chromatography process	2003
Immune serum globulin (human)	1943
Monoclonal antibody respiratory syncytial virus (palivizumab)	1998
Rabies immunoglobulin (human)	1974
Respiratory syncytial virus immune globulin intravenous (human) (RSV-IGIV)	1996
Rho (D) immunoglobulin	1968
Tetanus immunoglobulin (human)	1957
Vaccinia immunoglobulin (human)	1968
Varicella zoster immune globulin (human)	1980

*As of November 26, 2003
Prepared by Ellington, R, National Immunization Program, CDC.

special circumstances because the general risk of infection is low and because BCG vaccination results in conversion of the tuberculin skin test, thereby removing one of the most important indicators of tuberculosis infection (tuberculin conversion). Although it is widely used throughout the world, there has been much controversy regarding its efficacy. Recent studies suggest that the vaccine is effective particularly for preventing complications of disseminated tuberculosis in young children.[65-67] In the United States use of BCG should be considered for individuals, such as infants, whose skin test results are negative and who have prolonged, close contact with patients with active tuberculosis who are untreated, are ineffectively treated, or have antibiotic-resistant infection. BCG may also be considered for health care workers in areas in which multiple drug-resistant *M. tuberculosis* infection has become a significant problem.[68]

A single dose of vaccine is administered intradermally or by the percutaneous route. Known adverse effects include regional adenitis, disseminated BCG infection, and osteitis caused by the BCG organism. Adenitis occurs in approximately 1% to 10% of vaccinees, whereas disseminated infections and osteitis are apparently quite rare (approximately one case/million vaccinees). Hypertrophic scars at the injection site occur in up to one third of vaccinated persons, and keloids occur in 2% to 4%. Immunocompromised individuals should not receive the vaccine because of increased risk of disseminated BCG infection.[68]

Cholera Vaccine

A killed whole cell cholera vaccine was available in the United States from the 1940s until 2001.[69] The vaccine's efficacy was 50% or less and protection was short lived. The vaccine required booster doses every 6 months. Killed whole cell vaccines are still available in some countries, and improved killed vaccines are being developed, some of which include the B subunit of cholera toxin. Live cholera vaccine, containing engineered strains of *Vibrio cholerae,* is available in some countries. Additional live attenuated cholera vaccines are under development.

Diphtheria Toxoid

Diphtheria toxoid is a purified preparation of inactivated diphtheria toxin. It is highly effective in inducing antibodies that will prevent disease, although they may not prevent acquisition or carriage of the organism. The toxoid is available in adsorbed form, combined with tetanus toxoid (adult formulation Td and pediatric formulation DT) or with tetanus toxoid and acellular pertussis vaccine (DTaP). Single-antigen diphtheria toxoid is not distributed in the United States. Two dosage formulations are generally available, one for use up to the seventh year of life and one for use in older children and adults. The adult formulation has a lower concentration of diphtheria toxoid (less than 2 Lf) than the pediatric formulation (6.7 to 25 Lf), because local reac-

contaminated with *B. anthracis* spores. Anthrax vaccine was also used postexposure, in conjunction with antimicrobial prophylaxis, under an investigational protocol.[57] Other groups for whom the vaccine is recommended include persons working with production quantities of *B. anthracis* cultures or in activities with a high potential for aerosol production and selected other workers at high risk of exposure to *B. anthracis* spores.[58] Efficacy has been demonstrated in protection against cutaneous disease. Data on clinical efficacy against inhaled anthrax in humans are limited, but available human and animal data are consistent with protection.[59] The vaccine induces antibodies in 90% or more of those who received the primary course of six subcutaneous injections given at time zero, 2 weeks, 4 weeks, 6 months, 12 months, and 18 months. A controlled study of a vaccine similar to the currently available vaccine demonstrated protective efficacy against cutaneous disease of 92.5% among mill workers.[60] Experience suggests that two doses of vaccine confer some protection.[61] Annual boosters are recommended to maintain immunity. Mild local reactions at the site of injection occur in about 30% of recipients. More severe local reactions occur infrequently (less than 4%) and systemic reactions are rare (0.2%). Surveillance for adverse events in the military program reveals no pattern of serious adverse events.[62,63] Availability of the vaccine is currently limited. The vaccine is manufactured by BioPort (Lansing, MI). Vaccines containing only recombinant protective antigen are under active development and may be less reactogenic than the current vaccine.[64]

Bacille Calmette-Guérin Vaccine

BCG vaccine contains living Calmette-Guérin bacillus, an attenuated strain of *Mycobacterium bovis.* In many countries, it is widely used in infants and young children to prevent disseminated tuberculosis infection. In the United States, use of the vaccine is recommended only in

FIGURE 319-1. Recommended childhood and adolescent immunization schedule[1]—United States, July/December 2004. *(From Centers for Disease Control and Prevention. Recommended Childhood and Immunization Schedule—United States, 2004. MMWR 2004;53:Q1-4.)*

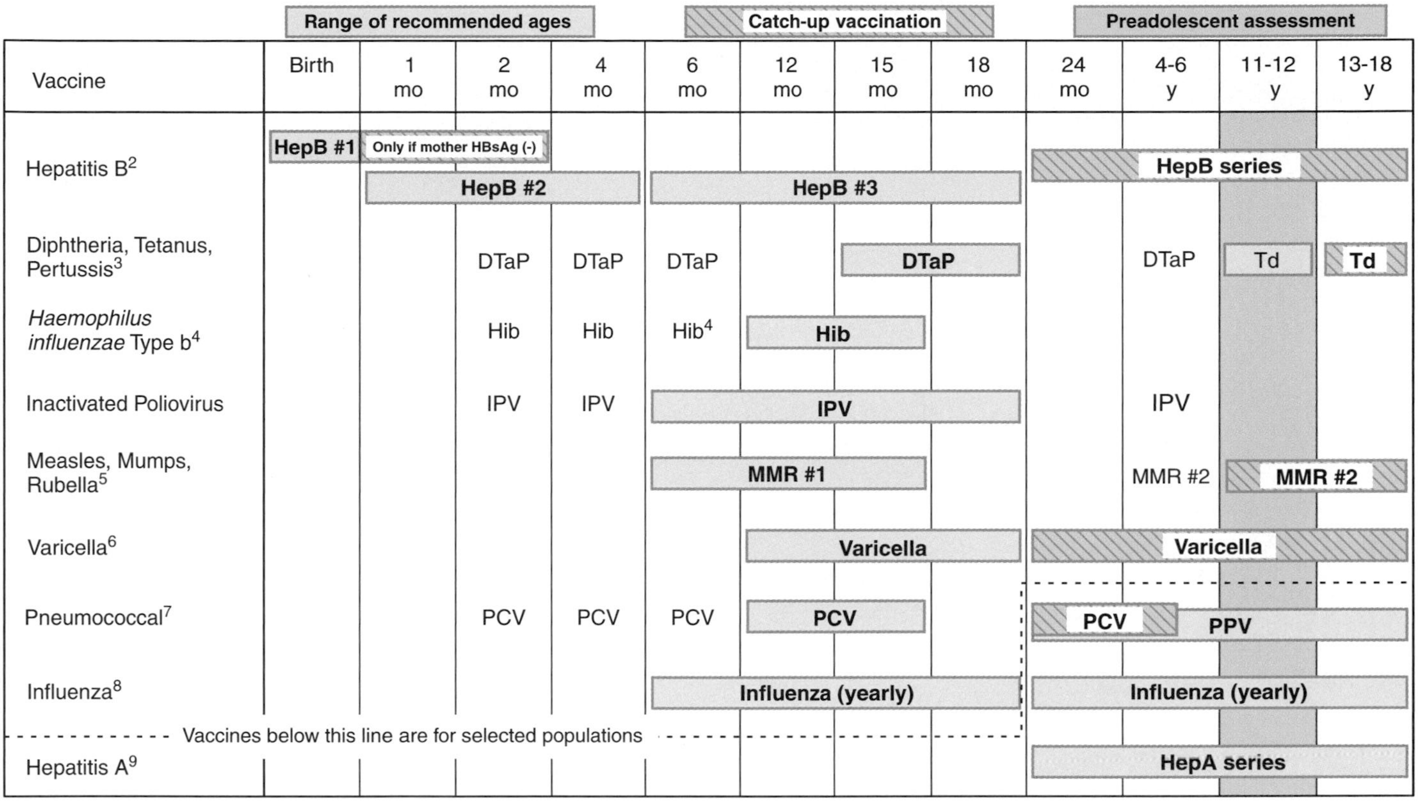

| | Range of recommended ages | | | | Catch-up vaccination | | | Preadolescent assessment | | | |
Vaccine	Birth	1 mo	2 mo	4 mo	6 mo	12 mo	15 mo	18 mo	24 mo	4-6 y	11-12 y	13-18 y
Hepatitis B[2]	HepB #1 (Only if mother HBsAg (-))	HepB #2				HepB #3				HepB series		
Diphtheria, Tetanus, Pertussis[3]		DTaP	DTaP	DTaP		DTaP			DTaP		Td	Td
Haemophilus influenzae Type b[4]		Hib	Hib	Hib[4]		Hib						
Inactivated Poliovirus		IPV	IPV		IPV				IPV			
Measles, Mumps, Rubella[5]						MMR #1				MMR #2	MMR #2	
Varicella[6]						Varicella				Varicella		
Pneumococcal[7]		PCV	PCV	PCV	PCV				PCV	PPV		
Influenza[8]					Influenza (yearly)				Influenza (yearly)			
- - - - Vaccines below this line are for selected populations - - - -												
Hepatitis A[9]										HepA series		

1. Indicates the recommended ages for routine administration of currently licensed childhood vaccines, as of December 1, 2003, for children through age 18 years. Any dose not given at the recommended age should be given at any subsequent visit when indicated and feasible. ▨ Indicates age groups that warrant special effort to administer those vaccines not given previously. Additional vaccines may be licensed and recommended during the year. Licensed combination vaccines may be used whenever any components of the combination are indicated and the vaccine's other components are not contraindicated. Providers should consult the manufacturer's package inserts for detailed recommendations. Clinically significant adverse events that follow vaccination should be reported to the Vaccine Adverse Event Reporting System (VAERS). Guidance on how to obtain and complete a VAERS form is available at *http://www.vaers.org* or by telephone, 800-822 7967.

2. **Hepatitis B vaccine (HepB).** All infants should receive the first dose of HepB vaccine soon after birth and before hospital discharge; the first dose also may be given by age 2 months if the infant's mother is HBsAg-negative. Only monovalent HepB vaccine can be used for the birth dose. Monovalent or combination vaccine containing HepB may be used to complete the series; 4 doses of vaccine may be administered when a birth dose is given. The second dose should be given at least 4 weeks after the first dose except for combination vaccines, which cannot be administered before age 6 weeks. The third dose should be given at least 16 weeks after the first dose and at least 8 weeks after the second dose. The last dose in the vaccination series (third or fourth dose) should not be administered before age 24 weeks. Infants born to HBsAg-positive mothers should receive HepB vaccine and 0.5 mL hepatitis B immune globulin (HBIG) within 12 hours of birth at separate sites. The second dose is recommended at age 1-2 months. The last dose in the vaccination series should not be administered before age 24 weeks. These infants should be tested for HBsAg and anti-HBs at age 9-15 months. Infants born to mothers whose HBsAg status is unknown should receive the first dose of the HepB vaccine series within 12 hours of birth. Maternal blood should be drawn as soon as possible to determine the mother's HBsAg status; if the HBsAg test is positive, the infant should receive HBIG as soon as possible (no later than age 1 week). The second dose is recommended at age 1-2 months. The last dose in the vaccination series should not be administered before age 24 weeks.

3. **Diphtheria and tetanus toxoids and acellular pertussis vaccine (DTaP).** The fourth dose of DTaP may be administered at age 12 months provided that 6 months have elapsed since the third dose and the child is unlikely to return at age 15-18 months. The final dose in the series should be given at age ≥4 years. **Tetanus and diphtheria toxoids (Td)** is recommended at age 11-12 years if at least 5 years have elapsed since the last dose of tetanus and diphtheria toxoid-containing vaccine. Subsequent routine Td boosters are recommended every 10 years.

4. *Haemophilus influenzae* type b (Hib) conjugate vaccine. Three Hib conjugate vaccines are licensed for infant use. If PRP-OMP (PedvaxHIB® or ComVax® [Merck]) is administered at ages 2 and 4 months, a dose at age 6 months is not required. DTaP/Hib combination products should not be used for primary vaccination in infants at ages 2, 4, or 6 months but can be used as boosters after any Hib vaccine. The final dose in the series should be given at age ≥12 months.

5. **Measles, mumps, and rubella vaccine (MMR).** The second dose of MMR is recommended routinely at age 4-6 years but may be administered during any visit provided that at least 4 weeks have elapsed since the first dose and that both doses are administered beginning at or after age 12 months. Those who have not received the second dose previously should complete the schedule by the visit at age 11-12 years.

6. **Varicella vaccine (VAR).** Varicella vaccine is recommended at any visit at or after age 12 months for susceptible children (i.e., those who lack a reliable history of chickenpox). Susceptible persons aged ≥13 years should receive 2 doses given at least 4 weeks apart.

7. **Pneumococcal vaccine.** The heptavalent pneumococcal conjugate vaccine (PCV) is recommended for all children aged 2-23 months and for certain children aged 24-59 months. The final dose in the series should be given at age ≥12 months. Pneumococcal polysaccharide vaccine (PPV) is recommended in addition to PCV for certain high-risk groups. See *MMWR* 2000;49(No. RR-9):1-35.

8. **Influenza vaccine.** Influenza vaccine is recommended annually for children aged ≥6 months with certain risk factors (including but not limited to asthma, cardiac disease, sickle cell disease, HIV, and diabetes), health care workers, and other persons (including household members) in close contact with persons in groups at high risk (see *MMWR* 2004;53;[RR][in press]) and can be administered to all others wishing to obtain immunity. In addition, healthy children aged 6-23 months and close contacts of healthy children aged 0-23 months are recommended to receive influenza vaccine, because children in this age group are at substantially increased risk for influenza-related hospitalizations. For healthy persons aged 5-49 years, the intranasally administered live, attenuated influenza vaccine (LAIV) is an acceptable alternative to the intramuscular trivalent inactivated influenza vaccine (TIV). See *MMWR* 2003;52 (No. RR-13):1-8. Children receiving TIV should be administered a dosage appropriate for their age (0.25 mL if 6-35 months or 0.5 mL if ≥3 years). Children aged ≤8 years who are receiving influenza vaccine for the first time should receive 2 doses (separated by at least 4 weeks for TIV and at least 6 weeks for LAIV).

9. **Hepatitis A vaccine.** Hepatitis A vaccine is recommended for children and adolescents in selected states and regions and for certain high-risk groups. Consult your local public health authority and *MMWR* 1999;48(No.RR-12):1-37. Children and adolescents in these states, regions, and high-risk groups who have not been immunized against hepatitis A can begin the hepatitis A vaccination series during any visit. The 2 doses in the series should be administered at least 6 months apart.

Additional information about vaccines, including precautions and contraindications for vaccination and vaccine shortages, is available at http://www.cdc.gov./nip or from the National Immunization information hotline, telephone 800-232-2522 (English) or 800-232-0233 (Spanish). Approved by the **Advisory Committee on Immunization Practices** (http://www.cdc.gov/nip/acip), the **American Academy of Pediatrics** (http://www.aap.org), and the **American Academy of Family Physicians** (http://www.aafp.org).

tions are thought to relate to both age and dosage. With all formulations, levels of antitoxin considered protective are induced in excess of more than 90% of recipients who complete the schedule.[38,70]

Immunization against diphtheria is recommended for all residents in the United States. For children younger than 7 years of age with no contraindications to pertussis immunization, DTaP is recommended, and the primary series is three doses administered 4 to 8 weeks apart followed by a fourth dose 6 to 12 months later and a booster dose at school entry (4 to 6 years of age). For infants with contraindications to pertussis vaccine, DT is administered in the same schedule as DTaP (see "Pertussis Vaccine", Fig. 319-1, Table 319-5). The primary immunizing series of DT (for children 1 to 6 years of age) or Td (for older

TABLE 319-5 Catch-up Immunization Schedule for Children and Adolescents Who Start Late or Who Are More Than 1 Month Behind

| Dose 1 (minimum age) | Catch-up Schedule for Children aged 4 months to 6 years Minimum Interval Between Doses | | | |
	Dose 1 to dose 2	Dose 2 to dose 3	Dose 3 to dose 4	Dose 4 to dose 5
DTaP (6 wk)	4 wk	4 wk	6 mo	6 mo[1]
IPV (6 wk)	4 wk	4 wk	4 wk[2]	
HepB[3] (birth)	4 wk	8 wk (and 16 wk after 1st dose)		
MMR (12 mo)	4 wk[4]			
VAR (12 mo)				
Hib[5] (6 wk)	4 wk: if 1st dose given at age < 12 mo 8 wk (as final dose): if 1st dose given at age 12-14 mo No further doses needed: if 1st dose given at age ≥15 mo	4 wk[6]: if current age <12 mo 8 wk (as final dose)[6]: if current age ≥12 mo and 2nd dose given at age <15 mo No further doses needed: if previous dose given at age ≥15 mo	8 wk (as final dose): this dose only necessary for children aged 12 mo-5 yr who received 3 doses before age 12 mo	
PCV[7] (6 wk)	4 wk: if 1st dose given at age < 12 mo and current age <24 mo 8 wk (as final dose): if 1st dose given at age ≥12 mo or current age 24-59 mo No further doses needed: for healthy children if 1st dose given at age ≥24 mo	4 wk: if current age <12 mo 8 wk (as final dose): if current age ≥ 12 mo No further doses needed: for healthy children if previous dose given at age ≥ 24 mo	8 wk (as final dose): this dose only necessary for children aged 12 mo-5 yr who received 3 doses before age 12 mo	

| Catch-up Schedule for Children Ages 7-18 Years Minimum Interval Between Doses | | |
Dose 1 to dose 2	Dose 2 to dose 3	Dose 3 to booster dose
Td: 4 wk	**Td:** 6 mo	**Td**[8]**:** **6 mo:** If 1st dose given at age <12 mo and current age <11 yr **5 y:** if 1st dose given at age ≥12 mo and 3rd dose given at age <7 yr and current age ≥11 yr **10 y:** if 3rd dose given at age ≥7 yr
IPV[9]**:** 4 wk	**IPV**[9]**:** 4 wk	**IPV**[2,9]
HepB: 4 wk	**HepB:** 8 wk (and 16 wk after 1st dose)	
MMR: 4 wk		
VAR[10]**:** 4 wk		

NOTE: A vaccine series dose not require restarting, regardless of the time that has elapsed between doses.
  1. **Diphtheria and tetanus toxoids and acellular pertussis vaccine (DTaP):** The fifth dose is not necessary if the fourth dose was given after the fourth birthday.
  2. **Inactivated polio vaccine (IPV):** For children who received an all-IPV or all-oral poliovirus (OPV) series, a fourth dose is not necessary if third dose was given at age ≥4 years. If both OPV and IPV were given as part of a series, a total of 4 doses should be given, regardless of the child's current age.
  3. **Hepatitis B vaccine (HepB):** All children and adolescents who have not been vaccinated against hepatitis B should begin the hepatitis B vaccination series during any visit. Providers should make special efforts to immunize children who were born in, or whose parents were born in, areas of the world where hepatitis B virus infection is moderately or highly endemic.
  4. **Measles, mumps, and rubella vaccine (MMR):** The second dose of MMR is recommended routinely at age 4-6 years, but may be given earlier if desired.
  5. *Haemophilus influenzae* **type b (Hib) conjugate vaccine:** Vaccine generally is not recommended for children aged ≥5 years.
  6. **Hib:** If current age is <12 months and the first two doses were PRP-OMP (PedvaxHIB® or ComVax® [Merck]), the third (and final) dose should be given at age 12-15 months and at least 8 weeks after the second dose.
  7. **Pneumococcal conjugate vaccine (PCV):** Vaccine generally is not recommended for children aged ≥5 years.
  8. **Tetanus and diphtheria toxoids (Td):** For children aged 7-10 years, the interval between the third and booster dose is determined by the age when the first dose was given. For adolescents aged 11-18 years, the interval is determined by the age when the third dose was given.
  9. **IPV:** Vaccine generally is not recommended for persons aged ≥18 years.
  10. **Varicella vaccine (VAR):** Give two dose series to all susceptible adolescents aged ≥13 years.
  Reporting adverse reactions. Clinically significant adverse events that follow vaccination should be reported to the Vaccine Adverse Event Reporting System (VAERS). Guidance on completing a VAERS form is available at *www.vaers.org* or at telephone, 800-822-7967. **Disease reporting.** Suspected cases of vaccine-preventable diseases should be reported to state or local health departments. Additional information about vaccines, including precautions and contraindications for vaccination and vaccine shortages, is available at *www.cdc.gov/nip* or at the National Immunization information hotline, telephone 800-232-2522 (English) or 800-232-0233 (Spanish). Schedule available at www.cdc.gov/nip/recs/child-catch-up.pdf.

children and adults) consists of at least two doses administered 4 to 8 weeks apart followed by a third dose 6 to 12 months later. There is no need to restart a series if the schedule is interrupted; the next dose in the series should be given. Booster doses of Td should be given every 10 years. Known adverse effects include local reactions and mild or moderate systemic reactions such as fever; anaphylaxis occurs rarely. Brachial neuritis appears to be a rare consequence of immunization and is most likely due to tetanus antigen.[45] The only known contraindication is in individuals who have previously had neurologic or severe hypersensitivity reactions after diphtheria or tetanus toxoids because all diphtheria toxoid in the United States is combined with tetanus toxoid.

Haemophilus influenzae Type b Vaccine

Conjugated vaccines to prevent *H. influenzae* type b (Hib) invasive disease were first licensed at the end of 1987 and have replaced the earlier polysaccharide vaccines because they elicit substantially higher antibody titers and are effective in young infants.[71] The polysaccharide in these vaccines is covalently linked to protein carriers converting them from T-cell–independent antigens to T-cell–dependent antigens. At present, there are three available conjugate vaccines, licensed for use in infants.[72] Carrier proteins include a mutant, nontoxic diphtheria toxin (CRM) (HbOC), *Neisseria meningitidis* outer membrane protein complex (PRP-OMP), and tetanus toxoid (PRP-T). HbOC and PRP-

OMP have been demonstrated to be 93% to 100% effective in clinical trials in infants. PRP-T has been licensed for use in infants because it elicits comparable antibody responses to the other two vaccines.

PRP-OMP behaves differently from the other conjugates, inducing high levels of antibody after a single dose. A second dose 2 months later increases those levels; less benefit appears to be derived from a third dose. The basic series for PRP-OMP is two doses given 2 months apart beginning at 2 months of age followed by a reinforcing dose at 12 to 15 months of age.[72] In contrast, HbOC and PRP-T do not induce substantial antibody levels until dose 2, and high levels of protection are achieved only after three doses 2 months apart. The basic series for HbOC and PRP-T starts at 2 months of age with three doses 2 months apart followed by a booster dose at 12 to 15 months of age.[72] Although use of a single conjugate vaccine for the primary series has been recommended, several studies suggest that mixed sequences of Hib conjugate vaccines induce an adequate immune response.[73-75] Thus, for infants younger than 6 months of age, three doses of any licensed Hib vaccine administered at 2-month intervals should confer protection; a fourth dose is given at 12 to 15 months. For infants starting immunization between 7 and 11 months, two doses of any of the three Hib vaccines licensed for infants should be given 2 months apart followed by a reinforcing dose at 12 to 15 months provided that at least 2 months have elapsed since the second dose. Any of the conjugates can be used for the booster dose.[72]

Children beginning immunization between 12 and 14 months can receive two doses of any conjugate, with the second dose given after age 15 months, at least 2 months after dose 1. Children who are initially immunized at 15 months of age need only one dose of any of the three conjugate vaccines. A combination vaccine, DTaP-PRP-T, is licensed only for dose 4 of the primary series.[76] Decreased immune responses to the Hib component when it is combined with acellular vaccines have slowed approval for infant indications.[77]

On the basis of the epidemiology of invasive *H. influenzae* type b infection in the United States, vaccination is not routinely recommended beyond the fifth year of life, except for specific risk groups. Although vaccine is not indicated for children who had documented invasive *H. influenzae* type b infection at 2 years of age or older, it is indicated for younger children because of their inadequate antibody response after natural infection.

The vaccines appear to be quite safe. Local reactions at the injection site and fever have been noted in less than 4% of vaccinees. They can be administered simultaneously with measles, mumps, rubella (MMR), DTaP, and inactivated polio vaccine (IPV) with no increased risk of adverse reactions or compromise in efficacy of any of the vaccines. The vaccines should not be administered if there is a history of anaphylaxis to the specific vaccine or to other vaccine components. Although a slight increase in risk of invasive *H. influenzae* type b disease was observed shortly after receipt of the original unconjugated polysaccharide vaccine, available data show no such association with conjugate vaccines.

Hepatitis A Vaccine

There are two inactivated hepatitis A vaccines available in the United States, HAVRIX from Glaxo SmithKline Biologicals and VAQTA from Merck & Company. More than 97% of persons 2 years of age and older acquire antibody titers considered protective after a single dose of either vaccine. More than 85% of children and adults acquire protective levels within 15 days of a dose of HAVRIX. An efficacy trial of HAVRIX using doses of 360 enzyme-linked immunosorbent assay (ELISA) units 1 month apart in children 1 to 16 years of age demonstrated a 94% efficacy against hepatitis A.[78] Efficacy of one 25-unit dose of VAQTA in children 2 to 16 years of age was 100%.[79]

The vaccine is recommended for use among populations known to be at increased risk of infection, including persons traveling to hepatitis A–endemic areas; children in communities with high rates of hepatitis A; men who have sex with men; illegal drug users; and persons who work with hepatitis A virus-infected primates or who do research with the virus; and recipients of clotting factors. Persons with chronic liver disease may be at increased risk of fulminant hepatitis A and should be vaccinated as well.[80] Nonetheless, most cases of hepatitis A occur among persons who are not among these risk groups, but instead are acquired as part of community-wide outbreaks. Preventing hepatitis A at the community level will require widespread vaccination of children and adults.[81] In 1999, the ACIP recommended that children living in states, counties, or communities with reported annual rates of hepatitis A of 20 per 100,000 or higher between 1987 and 1997 be routinely vaccinated beginning at 2 years of age or older. Vaccination should be considered for all children living in states, counties, or communities with reported rates of hepatitis A of 10 per 100,000 or higher but lower than 20 per 100,000 between 1987 and 1999.[82] HAVRIX is recommended in a two-dose schedule with doses separated by 6 to 12 months. The dose for children 2 to 18 years is 720 ELISA units and for adults it is 1440 ELISA units. Two doses of 25 units of VAQTA 6 to 18 months apart are recommended for persons 2 to 17 years, and two doses of 50 units 6 months apart are recommended for persons 18 years of age or older. Hepatitis A vaccine is not licensed for use in children younger than 2 years of age. The vaccine is poorly immunogenic in infants born to women who are seropositive for hepatitis A.[15,83] Simultaneous administration with IG may decrease immunogenicity slightly, but should not cause any decrease in protection.[84] The ACIP recommends simultaneous IG if the interval between dose 1 and travel to a high risk area is less than 4 weeks, although some authorities have questioned the need for IG.

No serious adverse events have been attributed to either hepatitis A vaccine. The most frequent side effects are local reactions. The only contraindication is for persons sensitive to vaccine components.[80]

Hepatitis B Vaccine

Hepatitis B vaccine consists of purified inactivated HBsAg particles obtained either from the plasma of chronic carriers or from yeast through recombinant DNA technology. In the United States, plasma-derived vaccines have been replaced by recombinant vaccines, although the former are still available abroad. There are two hepatitis B vaccines currently available in the United States—Recombivax HB (Merck & Company) and Engerix-B (GlaxoSmithKline Biologicals) and each is available as a combination product: with *Haemophilus influenzae* b conjugate vaccine (Comvax; Merck & Company), hepatitis A vaccine (Twinrix; GlaxoSmithKline Biologicals), or DTaP and inactivated polio vaccine (Pediarix; GlaxoSmithKline Biologicals). Because recommended doses vary by age, the package insert should be consulted for the proper dose of each product. When initially licensed, use of vaccine was targeted to individuals at high risk of exposure to hepatitis B, including certain categories of health care workers (those with risk of exposure to blood or blood products), hemodialysis patients, recipients of certain blood products, men who have sex with men, certain institutionalized individuals, parenteral drug abusers, and household or sexual contacts of chronic carriers of HBsAg. Vaccine continues to be indicated for these groups and federal regulations now mandate that the vaccine be made available at no charge to all health care and public safety workers who anticipate exposure to human blood or body fluids during work.[85] Failure of vaccination targeted only to high-risk groups to have substantial impact on disease incidence, along with the appreciation that hepatitis B affects larger groups in the general population (such as heterosexuals with multiple partners), has led to the development of population-based control strategies.[86,87]

Currently, hepatitis B vaccine is recommended for all infants in the United States. Acceptable schedules include (1) doses at birth, 1 to 2 months, and 6 to 18 months of age or (2) doses at 1 to 2 months, 4 months, and 6 to 18 months, but it is preferred that the hepatitis B vaccine series be initiated at birth. It is anticipated that those immunized as infants will still be protected when they become adolescents and young adults, the greatest risk period in the United States.[86] Because of the concern about the thimerosal content of vaccines for infants, a recommendation was made in July 1999 that until thimerosal-free hepatitis B vaccines become available, the first dose for infants born to women known to be HbsAg-negative should be postponed until 2 to 6 months of age, with completion of the three-dose series by 18 months of age.[2] In September 1999, thimerosal-free hepatitis B vaccine became available, and the recommendation was made to reinstitute the birth dose. No changes were made in recommendations for infants born to HBsAg-positive mothers, for others whose status is unknown, or for children born into high-risk populations, but the changes in policy for hepatitis B vaccination at birth for other children resulted in some of these children not being vaccinated.[88] To protect infants at highest risk for the development of chronic hepatitis B infection, all pregnant women should be routinely screened for HBsAg, preferably during an early prenatal visit. The vaccine should be administered within 12 hours of birth along with hepatitis B IG to infants born of HBsAg-positive mothers. The immunizing course consists of three doses given intramuscularly at birth, 1 month, and 6 months.[86]

For adolescents and adults, the usual schedule is doses at 0, 1, and 6 months. All adolescents who have not previously been vaccinated should receive three doses of vaccine. The second and third doses should be administered 1 to 2 months and 4 to 6 months, respectively, after the first dose. An alternate two-dose regimen of one licensed hepatitis B vaccine (Recombivax; Merck & Company) is available for routine vaccination of adolescents with doses at 0 and 4 to 6 months. A good time to begin adolescent immunization is at 11 to 12 years of age when other immunizations are also recommended.[89]

The vaccine should be administered intramuscularly to infants in the anterolateral thigh with a 1-inch 23-gauge needle and to children and adults in the deltoid region. For deltoid vaccination, a 5/8-inch, 25-gauge needle may be used in children up to 10 years, and a 1-inch, 23-gauge needle should be used in older children and adults. Gluteal administration is associated with poorer antibody responses.[7] A series of three intramuscular doses produces a protective antibody response (antibody to HbsAg greater than 10 mIU/mL) in more than 95% of infants and children, more than 90% of adults younger than 40 years of age, and 75% to 90% of adults older than 40 years of age. Host factors such as smoking and obesity contribute to decreased immunogenicity of the primary vaccine series, but age is the major determinant of vaccine response. Vaccine immunogenicity may also be lower in immunocompromised patients. Follow-up for up to 12 years has shown the virtual absence of clinically significant infections in persons who initially achieved a protective antibody titer.[90] Persons who lose detectable antibody appear to retain immunologic memory against significant infections. Thus, there is no indication for booster doses of vaccine in the first decade after immunization of immunocompetent children or adults. Additional experience will be necessary to know whether there will be any need for booster doses in the second decade after immunization.

Adverse effects associated with hepatitis B vaccine have been few; they consist primarily of local reactions and low-grade fever. Serious reactions have been very rare and, aside from anaphylaxis, have not convincingly been established to be caused by vaccination. Some reports suggest that hepatitis B vaccine may rarely cause alopecia. The condition has been reported primarily in adults and has been reversible in most cases.[91] A number of case reports have linked hepatitis B vaccine to demyelinating syndromes including multiple sclerosis.[92,93] However, data available thus far do not support a causal relationship.[94] The Institute of Medicine's Immunization Safety Review Committee reviewed available data and concluded that the evidence did not support a relationship between hepatitis B vaccination in adults and multiple sclerosis; the evidence was inadequate to accept or reject a causal relationship with other demyelinating conditions.[95]

Recombinant hepatitis B vaccine is contraindicated in persons with hypersensitivity to yeast. It is not effective in eliminating the carrier state, but there is no known risk of vaccinating individuals who are carriers or who are already immune.[86]

Influenza Virus Vaccines—Inactivated

Trivalent influenza virus vaccine (TIV) is composed of inactivated disrupted ("split") influenza viruses or purified surface antigens. Because of the frequent antigenic changes in influenza viruses, the antigenic content of influenza virus vaccines is changed annually to reflect the influenza A and B virus strains in circulation. Annual immunization is recommended for those who receive influenza vaccine. The efficacy of the vaccine in protecting against influenza is directly related to the degree of concordance between the virus strains included in the vaccine and the strains that are circulating in the community. When periodic major changes in antigenic structure of influenza viruses occur, vaccine that contains antigens representative of prior viruses has decreased or no effectiveness. Influenza vaccine has been estimated to be 70% to 90% effective in preventing influenza in healthy adults under 65 years of age. Efficacy appears to be lower in elderly persons. A meta analysis of 20 cohort studies estimated effectiveness of 56%, 53%, 50%, and 68% for preventing respiratory illness, pneumonia, hospitalization and death, respectively.[96] In nursing home settings, efficacy has often been substantially lower, on the order of 30% to 40%. However, prevention of complications of influenza in such settings has been considerably higher, averaging from about 50% to 60% in preventing hospitalization or pneumonia to 80% in preventing death.[97] Efficacy data among young children are limited. Estimates vary from 22% to 91%, with most studies documenting protection of 56% or more.[98] In comparative studies, younger children tend to have lower rates of protection than older children. In one small study, efficacy was 66% among 6- to 24-month-old children in year 1, but no efficacy was demonstrated in year 2 when attack rates among placebo recipients were very low.[99]

Influenza immunization strategy in the United States is directed at reducing the complications and mortality associated with influenza.[100] Because these occur primarily in the chronically ill and elderly, these groups are most strongly advised to receive vaccine. Specifically, annual immunization is recommended for all persons 65 years of age or older; residents of nursing homes and other chronic care facilities with chronic medical conditions regardless of age; persons with chronic cardiovascular or pulmonary disorders, including children with asthma; and persons requiring regular medical follow-up or those hospitalized in the preceding year with chronic metabolic disease (including diabetes mellitus), renal dysfunction, hemoglobinopathies, or immunosuppression; and children and teenagers on long-term aspirin therapy. Pregnant women who will be in the second or third trimester during the influenza season (usually December through March) should be vaccinated. Because a high proportion of persons aged 50 to 64 years have high risk medical conditions and because age-based recommendations tend to be better followed than risk-based, annual vaccination is recommended for all persons 50 to 64 years of age. Physicians and other personnel caring for high-risk persons should be vaccinated to reduce the chances that such patients will be exposed to influenza. Similar recommendations apply to employees in nursing homes, those who provide home care, and household members of persons with high-risk conditions. Many of the persons in need of influenza vaccine are hospitalized frequently and should be vaccinated on discharge if hospitalized during the autumn.[100] Starting in 2002, the ACIP encouraged annual vaccination of children 6 to 23 months of age, when feasible, because of data documenting an increased risk of hospitalization in this age group compared to older children. In October 2003, the ACIP voted to recommend influenza vaccination annually for all children 6 to 23 months of age and for all contacts of children younger than 2 years of age.[101]

A child 6 months to 8 years of age, being vaccinated for the first time, should receive two doses of vaccine with an interval of at least 4 weeks between them; children in that age group who have been previously vaccinated require only a single dose. Recent influenza vaccine supply disruptions have led to changes in the recommended timing for vaccination of some persons. During October, vaccination efforts should focus on persons with medical conditions putting them at high risk of influenza complications, their close contacts, health care workers, children 6 to 23 months of age, and contacts of children 0 to 23 months of age. Starting in November and beyond, vaccine may be administered to the above groups and any other person who wishes to reduce their risk from influenza. This tiered system for vaccine administration will be evaluated annually, and when vaccine supply is judged to be plentiful, will be relaxed, allowing anyone who wishes to reduce their risk from influenza to obtain vaccine before November.

Adverse events associated with current influenza vaccines are infrequent. From 3% to 5% of recipients report local tenderness or low-grade fever. During the swine influenza immunization program of 1976, an elevated incidence rate of GBS was noted in recipients of the swine flu vaccine.[102] The risk of GBS after influenza vaccine during six subsequent seasons that were studied was not significantly elevated compared with expected rates. However, studies during the 1992 to 1993 and 1993 to 1994 influenza seasons suggest that influenza vaccines may have been associated with GBS at an attributable risk of about one per million doses in those years.[100,103] No cases of GBS within 6 weeks of vaccination were detected in persons 18 to 44 years of age despite administration of approximately 4 million doses of vaccine over the two flu seasons studied.[103] The overall risk of GBS in these studies was about one tenth the risk of GBS after swine flu vaccine. If GBS is ever caused by current influenza vaccines, it is very rare. In contrast, the risk of hospitalization from influenza disease and its complications is orders of magnitude higher in most populations for whom vaccine is recommended. Given the substantial benefits of influenza vaccine among the targeted populations, the risk of GBS, if any, is exceeded by the benefits. Persons with an immediate hypersensitivity reaction to a prior dose or those with anaphylactic hypersensitivity to eggs, in which vaccine viruses are grown, should be vaccinated only after careful assessment that the benefits are likely to outweigh the risks.[100] Protocols have been developed for vaccinating such patients.[104] Concerns have been raised regarding vaccination of human immunodeficiency virus (HIV)-infected individuals. Persons with severe immunocompromise do not respond well, and some studies have shown a transient increase in HIV-1 in the plasma in the 2 to 4 weeks after vaccination, which has not been associated with clinical deterioration. On the other hand, the risk of influenza-associated deaths is much higher in HIV-infected persons than the general population. Therefore, influenza vaccine should be considered for HIV-infected persons.[100] The IOM recently reviewed the relationship between influenza vaccine and neurological disorders. They concluded that the evidence favored acceptance of a causal relationship between GBS and the 1976 influenza vaccine, although the evidence was insufficient to accept or reject a causal relationship for subsequent years. The IOM concluded the evidence favored rejection of a relationship between influenza vaccine and exacerbation of multiple sclerosis. While the evidence was insufficient with regard to incident cases of multiple sclerosis, the committee concluded that given the evidence that influenza vaccine does not cause exacerbation of multiple sclerosis, vaccine was unlikely to cause new cases.[105]

Live Attenuated Influenza Vaccine (LAIV)

On June 17, 2003, the Food and Drug Administration (FDA) licensed a live attenuated influenza reassortant vaccine to be administered intranasally. Each viral strain in the trivalent vaccine consists of six internal genes from a cold-adapted, temperature-sensitive, attenuated mutant.[101,106] The hemagglutinin and neuraminidase are derived from recently circulating wild strains. The cold adaptation is supportive of growth of the vaccine viruses in the upper airways and temperature sensitivity decreases their growth in the lower airways. The vaccine is trivalent with reassortants for each of the major circulating influenza viruses: A (H3N2), A (H1N1), and B.

In a study of healthy children, vaccine was 87% effective after two doses in children 60 to 71 months of age in year 1 with a good match between vaccine and circulating wild virus and 87% in 60- to 84-month-old children in year 2, when vaccine and circulating strains substantially diverged. In addition, vaccine reduced influenza associated febrile otitis media by 30%. A small challenge study among healthy adults, 18 to 41 years of age, was associated with 85% efficacy. An effectiveness study among adults during a year in which the circulating virus was not well matched to the vaccine strains still demonstrated a 19% reduction in severe febrile illnesses of any etiology and a 24% reduction in febrile respiratory illnesses.

Side effects in adults that have been significantly higher than among placebo recipients include coryza or nasal congestion, headache, and sore throat. Among children, coryza, headache, fever, and myalgias were more common among vaccinees than placebo recipients. Abdominal pain and occasional vomiting were also seen more frequently in vaccinees. Young children (12 to 59 months), who were vaccinated, had an unexplained but statistically significant increase in asthma or reactive airways disease over placebo recipients

that was not seen in older age groups. No serious adverse events were observed. Shedding of vaccine virus from the nasopharynx is common, especially for young children. A study in a Finnish daycare center detected shedding of at least one strain in 80% of children with a mean duration of 7.6 days. However, transmission to unvaccinated contacts was rare (0.6% to 2.4%).

Vaccine is recommended for persons 5 to 49 years of age who do not have medical conditions that put them at high risk of complications from influenza but who have contacts with such conditions. With the exception of contact with immunocompromised individuals, there is no preference between LAIV versus TIV. TIV is preferred for persons who come in close contact with immunocompromised individuals although LAIV is not contraindicated. Vaccine is not recommended for persons at high risk of complications from influenza who should receive TIV. Children younger than 9 years old require two doses separated by 6 to 10 weeks unless they have received a dose of any influenza vaccine previously.

Japanese Encephalitis

Japanese encephalitis (JE) vaccine is a whole virus vaccine grown in mouse brains and inactivated and purified in at least a five-step process. No myelin basic protein has been detected in the vaccine. The vaccine has proved 91% effective in a large-scale trial in Thailand.[107] The vaccine is indicated for some persons traveling to or residing in endemic or epidemic areas, particularly those spending 30 or more days in high-risk areas (especially rural areas) in Asia during transmission season. Persons traveling to such areas for shorter periods may warrant vaccine under special circumstances. The primary immunization schedule for persons 4 years of age or older consists of three 1-mL doses administered subcutaneously on days 0, 7, and 30. An abbreviated schedule with the third dose at 14 days may be used if time constraints do not permit the full schedule. The dose is 0.5 mL for children 1 to 3 years of age given by the same schedule. Antibody persists at least 2 years and the need, if any, for boosters is uncertain. About 20% of vaccinees experience local reactions, and about 10% have minor systemic symptoms such as fever, malaise, nausea, and vomiting. Although serious neurologic events have been reported rarely in temporal association with Japanese encephalitis vaccination, a causal role for the vaccine has not been established. The major significant adverse events appear to be allergic in nature, consisting of generalized urticaria or angioedema, or both. Respiratory distress and hypotension have also occurred. The incidence of these adverse events in studies of United States citizens varies from 15 to 62/10,000 vaccinees. Onset of these hypersensitivity reactions may be delayed; for this reason, vaccinees should be advised to remain in areas with ready access to medical care in the 10 days after receiving a dose of JE vaccine. Prior history of allergic reactions (especially urticaria) is associated with increased risks of allergic reactions to the vaccine.[108]

Measles Vaccine

Measles vaccine is a live attenuated virus vaccine recommended for use in all children 12 months of age and older who do not have contraindications. When administered to a child 12 to 15 months of age or older, efficacy is greater than 95%. Only a single dose is needed to provide long lasting, probably lifelong, immunity in those who respond to the vaccine.

Evidence suggests that measles transmission can be sustained among the 2% to 5% of vaccinated persons who fail to seroconvert after an initial dose of vaccine. Therefore, beginning in 1989, a two-dose schedule was recommended in the United States. The first dose should be administered at 12 to 15 months of age. The 12-month age is especially indicated for areas at high risk of measles among preschool-age children, including inner cities with large numbers of unvaccinated children and areas that have either had a recent outbreak among preschoolers or persistent transmission in that age group. Lower levels of maternal antibody from today's vaccinated mothers may allow higher rates of seroconversion at 12 months than in the past when most maternal antibody came from mothers with naturally acquired disease.[109]

The second dose should be administered at 1 month or more after the first dose, typically at entry to school (4 to 6 years of age). Both doses should routinely be given as combined MMR vaccine.[110]

All college entrants who have not received two doses on or after the first birthday should receive them. If necessary, the two doses can be given separated by 1 month. Immunization is recommended for all individuals not known to be immune. Because individuals born before 1957 are likely to have been infected naturally, they are usually considered to be immune. Other acceptable evidence of measles immunity is documentation of adequate vaccination, laboratory evidence of immunity to measles, or documentation of prior physician-diagnosed measles. Similar recommendations apply to health care workers. Health care facilities should consider recommending a dose of MMR to unvaccinated workers born before 1957 who do not have a history of physician-diagnosed measles or laboratory evidence of immunity to both measles and rubella.[110-112]

Because measles is much more prevalent outside the United States, adequate vaccination is recommended for all travelers born after 1956. Such persons should receive a second dose if they have not previously been vaccinated and lack other evidence of measles immunity.[110]

Untoward reactions associated with measles vaccine include fever of 39.4° C or greater in 5% of recipients and transient rashes in approximately 5% of vaccinees. Fever and rash generally begin 7 to 12 days after vaccination and last 1 to 2 days. Because measles vaccine causes fever, it can be associated with febrile convulsions.[113] Children with prior personal histories of convulsions or histories of convulsions in the immediate family may be at increased risk of febrile convulsions following MMR vaccination.[114] Antipyretics may prevent febrile seizures after MMR vaccination if administered before onset of fever and continued for 5 to 7 days. However, fever is difficult to anticipate, making use of antipyretics impractical in many situations. Aspirin should not be used to prevent or control fever because of its association with Reye's syndrome. Anaphylaxis and thrombocytopenic purpura also appear to be caused rarely by MMR.[45] Encephalopathy with onset approximately 10 days after vaccination has been reported in vaccine recipients, with a frequency of approximately 1 in 2 million vaccinations, although a causal role for measles vaccine has not been established.[115] The available evidence favors rejection of a causal role for MMR in autism.[116]

Measles vaccine is contraindicated for pregnant women and in persons who are immunocompromised because of either congenital or acquired disorders (e.g., leukemia or immunosuppressive drugs), with the exception of those infected with HIV. Because measles may cause severe disease in HIV-infected persons, asymptomatic and mildly symptomatic HIV-infected persons may be vaccinated if measles vaccination is otherwise indicated. However, vaccination is contraindicated for those who are severely immunocompromised. Persons with a history of anaphylactic reactions to eggs may be vaccinated and observed for at least 20 minutes because most persons with such histories do not have serious reactions to vaccine. Skin testing of persons with such histories is no longer recommended because such tests appear not to predict severe reactions.[110]

Meningococcal Vaccines

A vaccine containing purified meningococcal capsular polysaccharides of groups A, C, Y, and W135 is available for use in the United States. The antibody responses to each of the four polysaccharides included in the quadrivalent vaccine are serogroup-specific and independent. The vaccine is routinely indicated for control of outbreaks of serogroup C meningococcal disease and for use among certain high-risk groups such as persons with terminal complement component deficiencies, anatomic or functional asplenia, and laboratory personnel who routinely are exposed to *N. meningitidis* in solutions that may be aerosolized. College freshmen, especially those living in dormitories or other residence halls, are at higher risk of meningococcal disease than are persons of the same age who are not attending college. The ACIP recommends that these students and their parents be informed by their healthcare providers about meningococcal disease and the

benefits of vaccination, and that college freshmen who want to reduce their risk for meningococcal disease should be vaccinated.[117] Military recruits, who previously had high rates of meningococcal disease, are also routinely vaccinated with the quadrivalent vaccine. It may be of benefit to travelers to countries with endemic or hyperendemic disease who are expected to have prolonged contact with the local population.[118] Frequent epidemics, generally between December and June, occur in the "meningitis belt" of sub-Saharan Africa (which stretches from Senegal to Ethiopia).[119] A single intramuscular injection induces protective levels of antibody in 90% or more of recipients 2 years of age and older. For children first vaccinated at younger than 4 years of age, revaccination should be considered after 2 to 3 years if they remain at high risk. Vaccine is recommended as a single dose for persons 2 years of age or older. The vaccine is not effective for children younger than 2 years of age with the exception of group A. Short-term protection may be achieved against this group in children as young as 3 months of age. When vaccinating 3- to 18-month-old children, two doses 3 months apart are recommended. Adverse effects associated with meningococcal polysaccharide vaccine are mild and consist primarily of pain and redness at the injection site. More than 40% of recipients have reported local reactions in some studies, but in others reactions have been much more infrequent.[120,121] Up to 2% of children experience fever. There are no known contraindications to the use of this vaccine.

Meningococcal polysaccharide conjugate vaccines have been developed and are licensed in some countries but not yet in the United States. Conjugation of meningococcal polysaccharide to protein results in a vaccine that is immunogenic in infants and young children, by induction of T-cell–dependent responses, and induces immunologic memory to meningococcal polysaccharide.[122-124] Meningococcal type C conjugate vaccines also appear to be able to overcome immunologic hyporesponsiveness induced by meningococcal polysaccharide vaccine in young children and in adults.[124,125] In the United Kingdom, use of meningococcal C conjugate vaccines among infants, children, and adolescents since November 1999 has resulted in dramatic reductions in serogroup C disease without evidence of serotype replacement.[126,127] Infants received a three dose primary series at 2, 3, and 4 months of age, and catch-up immunization for children through age 17 years was implemented with two (5- to 11-month-olds) or one (12 months to 17 years) dose of vaccine. Among adolescents, the effectiveness of the vaccine was 97% (95% CI 77-99) and in toddlers 92% (95% CI 65-98).[128] Effectiveness was also high among infants who had received at least two doses of vaccine, at 89% (95% CI 58-97).[127] Surveillance of adverse events in the United Kingdom has demonstrated that the vaccine is well tolerated; anaphylactic reactions were reported at a rate of one in 500,000 doses distributed.[126] Licensure of multivalent meningococcal conjugate vaccines or combination vaccines including meningococcal conjugate vaccine with other conjugate vaccines is expected in the near future.

Mumps Vaccine

Mumps vaccine is a live attenuated virus vaccine that is recommended for use in all children 12 months of age or older who do not have contraindications. Mumps vaccine is routinely administered as MMR at 12 to 15 months of age. When administered on or after the first birthday, 90% or more of recipients can be expected to acquire protective antibodies. Protection is thought to be lifelong. Only a single dose is generally recommended, although most persons will receive two doses as part of the two-dose MMR policy to prevent measles. As with measles, most persons born before 1957 are likely to have been infected naturally by mumps virus and can generally be considered immune; otherwise, individuals should be considered susceptible unless they have documentation of having received live mumps vaccine on or after the first birthday, laboratory evidence of mumps immunity, or documentation of physician-diagnosed mumps disease.[110]

Contraindications to mumps vaccine are pregnancy and an immunocompromised state (see "Measles Vaccine"). Persons with a history of anaphylactic reactions to eggs may be vaccinated. Adverse events associated with mumps vaccine are very few. Parotitis and orchitis have been reported rarely. Thrombocytopenic purpura and anaphylaxis appear to be caused rarely by MMR.[45] Aseptic meningitis has been associated with the Urabe and Leningrad-Zagreb strains of mumps vaccine, strains not available in the United States.[129,130] The Jeryl Lynn strain used in US vaccines has not been proved to cause aseptic meningitis.[45]

Pertussis Vaccine

Acellular pertussis vaccines are made from purified components of the organism *Bordetella pertussis* and detoxified pertussis toxin (PT); whole cell pertussis vaccines, made from suspensions of killed whole *B. pertussis,* are no longer available in the United States although they continue to be widely used internationally.[38] Acellular pertussis vaccines currently available in the United States contain pertussis toxoid and filamentous hemagglutinin (FHA). In addition, they may contain pertactin (69-kDa protein) or fimbriae and pertactin.[39] Pertussis vaccines are combined with diphtheria and tetanus toxoids as DTaP (acellular pertussis vaccines). The primary immunizing course consists of three doses of DTaP administered intramuscularly at 4- to 8-week intervals typically given at 2, 4, and 6 months of age. A fourth dose is given approximately 6 to 12 months later (15 to 18 months of age) and a fifth dose at 4 to 6 years of age. Acellular pertussis vaccines are preferred over whole cell pertussis vaccines because the efficacy of acellular vaccines is comparable to whole cell vaccines and because the incidence of adverse events after acellular vaccines is significantly lower than after whole cell vaccines. As of October 20, 2003, three acellular vaccines were available in the United States: Tripedia (Aventis Pasteur Inc.), which contains PT and FHA; Infanrix (Glaxo SmithKline Pharmaceuticals), which contains PT, FHA, and pertactin; and DAPTACEL (Aventis Pasteur), which contains PT, FHA, pertactin, and fimbriae types 2 and 3. Efficacy in preventing classic pertussis, consisting of 21 or more days of paroxysmal cough, has ranged from 71% to 89% for three doses.[38] This is considerably higher than the efficacy found for one of the US whole cell vaccines after three doses in clinical trials in Europe (36% to 48%).[131,132] However, in comparative trials, most acellular vaccines have had slightly lower efficacy than whole cell vaccines.

Symptoms and signs of local reactions occur about one-tenth to one-half as frequently after acellular vaccines compared with whole cell vaccines. For example, the incidence of erythema by the third evening after any of the first three doses of acellular vaccines ranged from 26.3% to 39.2% in one large comparative trial, compared with 72.7% in those who received the whole cell vaccine. In that study, the incidence of fever (greater than 39.4° C) after acellular vaccines was 3.3% to 5.2% compared with 15.9% after receipt of whole cell vaccine.[38,133] More serious adverse events such as seizures and hypotonic hyporesponsive episodes also appear to occur less frequently after acellular vaccines than after whole cell vaccines.[134,135] The lower incidence of fever associated with acellular vaccines would be expected to decrease febrile seizures, especially after the fourth dose.

Contraindications to pertussis-containing vaccines include an immediate anaphylactic reaction or encephalopathy within the 7 days after a prior dose. The following events are considered precautions: (1) temperature greater than or equal to 40.5° C within 48 hours of a prior dose without other identifiable cause, (2) collapse or shock like state (hypotonic hyporesponsive episode) within 48 hours, (3) persistent inconsolable crying lasting 3 hours or more within 48 hours, and (4) convulsions with or without fever occurring within 3 days. Although under most circumstances such children will not be vaccinated, the physician may elect to continue pertussis vaccination if the benefits are judged to outweigh the risks, such as when there is a pertussis outbreak in the community. Children with evolving neurologic disorders should have immunization deferred until the situation is clarified. Once stable, they can receive pertussis vaccine. Decisions about vaccinating children with underlying neurologic disease should be made no later than the first birthday. If pertussis vaccine is not used, the pediatric preparation of combined diphtheria and tetanus toxoids (DT) is indicated.[38]

Children with a personal or family history of convulsions appear to be at higher risk of seizures after pertussis vaccination than the general population. However, the benefits of vaccination outweigh the risks. Children with stable seizure disorders or with family histories of seizures may be vaccinated. Use of acetaminophen, 15 mg/kg, at the time of vaccination, and subsequently every 4 hours for 24 hours, and then as needed reduces the risk of fever after pertussis vaccination and may decrease the likelihood of postvaccination seizures.

Extensive swelling of the thigh or entire upper arm following the fourth or fifth doses of the DTaP series has been reported. The frequency appears to be 2% to 3% and the pathogenesis is unclear. It is unknown whether children who experience entire limb swelling after a fourth dose of DTaP are at increased risk for this reaction after the fifth dose. Because of the benefits of the preschool booster and because the swelling reactions appear to be self-limited, a history of extensive swelling after the fourth dose is not a contraindication for receipt of the fifth dose of the DTaP series.[39]

DTaP is available in two combination formulations, with PRP-T (Hib Vaccine) (TriHibit; Aventis Pasteur Inc.) and inactivated polio and hepatitis B vaccines (Pediarix; Glaxo SmithKline Pharmaceuticals). The combined DTaP-PRP-T vaccine is licensed for use only as the fourth dose of the DTaP series. Combinations of acellular vaccines with Hib have generally resulted in diminished antibody response to the Hib component when administered to infants.[77] However, it is expected that this interference will be overcome and combined preparations of DTaP and Hib will be available in the future for infant immunization.

Data are insufficient to document the safety, immunogenicity, and efficacy of using DTaP vaccines from different manufacturers in a mixed sequence. For this reason whenever feasible the same brand of DTaP should be used for all doses in the vaccination series. However, if the type of vaccine previously administered is unknown or is not available, any of the available licensed DTaP vaccines can be used to complete the vaccination series.

Concerns about the safety of whole cell pertussis vaccines has led to decreased vaccine coverage in some countries. In the United Kingdom pertussis vaccine uptake declined markedly in the period 1974 to 1978. The result was a major epidemic of pertussis in the years 1977 to 1979, with a second epidemic in 1982. This experience and similar ones in Japan and other countries illustrate the necessity for maintaining protection against pertussis.[136]

Pertussis vaccines are not recommended for administration to individuals older than 7 years because the risk of pertussis and pertussis complications appears to be substantially lower and reactions to whole cell vaccines may be more frequent in older individuals. Efforts are under way to evaluate the use of acellular vaccines in the adult population. Recent studies of pertussis epidemiology suggest that adults may play an important role in sustaining transmission.[137-142] In a prospective study of persons 10 to 14 years of age with cough illness, laboratory testing for pertussis was positive in 13%, for an estimated annual incidence of pertussis of 507 cases per 100,000 person-years.[143] Pertussis in adolescents and adults may account for increases in pertussis among infants too young to be protected by vaccination.[144] Studies suggest acellular vaccines are safe and immunogenic in adults.[145] It is likely that vaccines to immunize adolescents and adults will become available in the near future.

Plague Vaccine

Plague vaccine is no longer available in the United States. Killed whole cell vaccines and live attenuated vaccines are used elsewhere in the world and new subunit and mucosal vaccines are under development.[146]

Pneumococcal Polysaccharide Vaccine

Pneumococcal polysaccharide vaccine was initially licensed as a purified preparation of 14 different serotypes of pneumococcal capsular polysaccharide in 1979. Since 1983, vaccine containing 23 types has replaced the earlier version. The types included in the current vaccine and immunologically related types are responsible for approximately 85% to 90% of all bacteremic pneumococcal disease in the United

States. Demonstrable antibody rises to the serotypes contained in the vaccine are noted in 80% to 95% or more of healthy recipients. The vaccine has been highly effective in reducing pneumococcal disease among South African gold miners (a group at particularly high risk) and among military recruits.[147-149] In populations at high risk of pneumococcal infections, such as the elderly and those with high-risk medical conditions, the vaccine has generally been found to be effective against pneumococcal bacteremia but not against nonbacteremic pneumococcal pneumonia. Studies of patients with isolates from normally sterile body fluids have generally reported efficacies of 50% to 80% overall with lower efficacy in persons who have compromised immune systems.[150-153] A recent study of Navaho adults did not demonstrate efficacy against invasive pneumococcal disease in this high-risk population.[154] Vaccine is primarily recommended for adults at high risk of complications from respiratory infections, particularly those with cardiovascular and chronic pulmonary disease, adults and children 2 years of age or older at high risk of pneumococcal disease (e.g., splenic dysfunction or anatomic asplenia, Hodgkin's disease, multiple myeloma, chronic liver disease, including cirrhosis, alcoholism, renal failure, cerebrospinal fluid leaks, cochlear implant recipients, and immunocompromised state), and the otherwise healthy elderly (65 years of age or older).[155]

Polysaccharide vaccines are not effective in children younger than 2 years of age. Children who have completed the pneumococcal conjugate vaccine series before age 2 years and who are in these high-risk groups should receive one dose of pneumococcal polysaccharide vaccine at age 2 years.[156]

A single dose is administered by intramuscular injection. Revaccination is recommended for persons 65 years of age or older who received an initial vaccination prior to age 65, if at least 5 years has elapsed since that dose. Revaccination is also recommended for persons less than 65 years of age with anatomic or functional asplenia or those who are immunocompromised, including patients with chronic renal failure and nephrotic syndrome. For such patients who are older than 10 years of age, revaccination should take place 5 years or more after the first dose. For younger patients, revaccination should be considered 3 years after the first dose.[152]

In some studies, mild reactions such as erythema and mild pain at the site of injection occurred in approximately one half of recipients. Anaphylactic reactions have rarely been reported. Revaccination at intervals of 4 years may be associated with an increased risk of local reactions after vaccination, but these reactions tend to be self-limited and would not be a contraindication.[157] No contraindications are known, although its safety in pregnant women has not been evaluated.[152] Although transient increases in plasma HIV levels have been documented after vaccination in some studies, these have not been demonstrated to be of clinical significance. Conversely, risk of pneumococcal disease is increased in HIV-infected persons and therefore they should be vaccinated as soon as possible after diagnosis to optimize immune response to the vaccine.[158]

Pneumococcal Conjugate Vaccine

Pneumococcal conjugate vaccines in which pneumococcal capsular polysaccharide is covalently linked to protein carriers have been developed, and a 7-valent conjugate vaccine (Prevnar; Wyeth Lederle Vaccines) was licensed for use in infants and young children in 2000. The seven polysaccharide types included in the licensed vaccine account for 80% of invasive infections in children younger than age 6 years in the United States.[156] In a prelicensure efficacy trial in northern California, the efficacy of the conjugate vaccine was 97% against invasive disease caused by serotypes in the vaccine.[159] The vaccine was also effective in prevention of pneumonia, with the greatest impact in the first year of life, with a 32% reduction[160] and in prevention of acute otitis media caused by serotypes of pneumococcus included in the vaccine.[159] Efficacy against invasive pneumococcal disease has been demonstrated in Native American children, a population at increased risk of disease.[161]

Pneumococcal conjugate vaccine is administered as a 4 dose series, with doses at 2, 4, and 6 months of age, followed by a booster dose at 12 to 15 months of age. The vaccine is recommended for all children younger than 2 years of age, as well as children aged 24 to 59 months with underlying conditions associated with an increased risk of pneumococcal disease. These conditions include sickle cell disease, congenital or acquired asplenia, HIV infection, congenital immunodeficiencies, renal failure and nephrotic syndrome, diseases associated with immunosuppressive therapy or radiation therapy, chronic cardiac or pulmonary disease, diabetes mellitus, cerebrospinal fluid leaks, or cochlear implants.[155,156] Other children aged 24 to 59 months may also be at increased risk of pneumococcal disease, including those aged 24 to 35 months, children of Alaska Native or American Indian descent, children of African-American descent, or children who attend group daycare; use of the pneumococcal conjugate vaccine should be considered in these groups.

The primary series of the pneumococcal conjugate vaccine, administered simultaneously with other recommended childhood vaccines, is associated with an increased incidence of fever 100.4° F or higher within 48 hours of vaccination.[156]

Widespread use of the conjugate vaccine has resulted in dramatic decreases in disease incidence among young children, for whom the vaccine is recommended; in addition, decreases in disease incidence have also been observed among adults, which may be due to decreased transmission of pneumococci from children to adults.[162] Surveillance to date has revealed no evidence of serotype replacement.

Other pneumococcal conjugate vaccines containing additional pneumococcal serotypes are under development and may be licensed in the future. Use of pneumococcal conjugate vaccines in adults, either alone or in conjunction with pneumococcal polysaccharide vaccine, remains under investigation.

Polio Vaccine

While two types of polio vaccine are available in the world to control polio: live attenuated oral polio vaccine (OPV) and inactivated polio vaccine (IPV), which is administered by injection, only IPV is available in the United States. The schedule consists of four doses of IPV at 2 months, 4 months, 6 to 18 months, and 4 to 6 years.[163] IPV is available as a single vaccine or in combination with DTaP and hepatitis B vaccines (Pediarix; Glaxo SmithKline). While Pediarix can be used for the first three doses of IPV at 2, 4, and 6 months, single IPV is needed for the fourth dose. There is no need to restart a series if the primary immunization schedule is interrupted; the next dose in the series should be given.[48] Prior doses of OPV should be counted when considering whether there is a need for further polio immunization.

The decision to move to an all IPV schedule in the United States was based on concerns that OPV could rarely cause paralytic polio, with the greatest risk after the first dose (overall risk 1 in every 750,000 first doses), and the fact that IPV given to a high proportion of individuals in developed countries like Sweden had eliminated disease without risk of serious side effects. However, during control of an epidemic, OPV should be used for all age groups.

In 1988, the World Health Assembly endorsed a goal to eradicate polio from the world. The major vaccine used in the worldwide eradication effort is OPV. Advantages include ease of use, better induction of intestinal immunity to prevent wild polio virus spread than IPV, spread of vaccine virus to unvaccinated contacts, and lower cost than IPV. Extensive efforts in the Americas, including mass campaigns with OPV twice a year targeted to all children younger than 5 years regardless of prior immunization status, have led to the elimination of polio in the Western Hemisphere. The last known case of polio due to wild poliovirus in the Americas had onset in Peru in 1991, and the Western Hemisphere was certified free of polio in 1994.[35] Since 1988, almost all countries with endemic polio have conducted National Immunization Days, and even with greatly improved surveillance, cases of polio have decreased from an estimated 350,000 in 1988 to about 700 in 2003. By the end of 2003, only six countries were considered endemic.[32]

Polio vaccine is not routinely recommended for persons 18 years of age or older in the United States because the risk from wild virus is

low. However, if vaccine is needed, such as for persons traveling to polio-endemic areas, previously unvaccinated adults should receive two
doses of IPV at intervals of 4 to 8 weeks and a third dose 6 to 12
months after the second. Adults who have had a primary series of OPV
or IPV and who are at increased risk for exposure to poliovirus may
receive an additional dose of IPV.

Rabies Vaccine

Rabies vaccine is an inactivated virus vaccine prepared either in human diploid cell culture (HDCV) or in purified chick embryo cell culture (PCEC).[164] Rabies vaccination is recommended in two situations:
as a routine in individuals likely to be exposed to rabies (e.g., veterinarians, forest rangers) and after exposure to animals known or suspected to be rabid. The primary preexposure immunizing course is
three doses of rabies vaccine given intramuscularly at time 0, 7 days,
and 21 to 28 days. The three-dose course results in formation of protective levels of antibodies in virtually 100% of vaccinees. HDCV is
immunogenic when administered intradermally (ID), but the manufacturer discontinued distribution of the only preparation approved for
preexposure vaccination by the ID route in March 2001. Serologic
testing every 2 years is recommended to ensure that high-risk vaccinees maintain protective levels of antibody. Those whose titer falls to
less than the recommended level should receive a booster.
Alternatively, boosters may be administered every 2 years without
serologic testing for those at high risk of exposure. In the postexposure setting, five doses of rabies vaccine are given intramuscularly in a relatively short period (on days 0, 3, 7, 14, and 28) to previously unimmunized persons. Previously fully vaccinated persons who are exposed to rabies should receive intramuscular doses of rabies vaccine
on days 0 and 3. In all postexposure settings for previously unimmunized persons, rabies vaccine should always be used in conjunction
with rabies IG (see "Rabies Immune Globulin"). Rabies vaccine
should be administered by intramuscular injection into the deltoid
muscle for adults and children or the anterolateral thigh of infants;
there have been reports of possible vaccine failure following gluteal
administration.[165,166] Corticosteroids, other immunosuppressive
agents, antimalarial drugs, and immunosuppressive illnesses can interfere with the immune response to rabies vaccine. Adverse events associated with current rabies vaccines include local reactions in 30% to
74% of recipients and systemic reactions including headache, nausea,
myalgia, abdominal pain, and dizziness in 5% to 40% of recipients. As
many as 6% of persons may develop an immune-complex like reaction
2 to 21 days after boosters, with generalized urticaria, sometimes accompanied by arthralgia, arthritis, angioedema, nausea, vomiting,
fever, and malaise. There have been rare reports of transient neurologic reactions in association with the current vaccine; however, a
causal relationship has not been demonstrated. There are no known
contraindications to rabies vaccination in persons at risk or exposed[164]
(see Chapter 160 for more details).

Rubella Vaccine

Rubella vaccine contains live attenuated rubella virus grown in human
diploid cells (RA 27/3).[110] Other substrates, such as duck embryo cells
or rabbit kidney cells, have also been used for rubella vaccines, but
these vaccines are no longer licensed in the United States. When administered to a person on or after the first birthday, 95% or more of recipients can be expected to become immune. Immunity after a single
dose is long-lasting and appears likely to be lifelong. Boosters are not
necessary, although many persons will receive a second dose as part of
the two-dose MMR schedule to prevent measles. Rubella vaccine is
recommended for all individuals on or after the first birthday except
those who have documentation of having received live rubella vaccine
and those who have laboratory documentation of immunity to rubella.
Most persons born before 1957 can be considered immune. However,
it is particularly important to ensure that women of childbearing age
including those born before 1957 are immune to rubella. Rubella vaccine virus is known to be able to cross the placenta and infect fetal tissue. Nonetheless, there have been no instances of congenital rubella

syndrome in the offspring of 226 susceptible women who received RA
27/3 rubella vaccine within 3 months of conception and who carried
their pregnancies to term.[167] This indicates that the risk of congenital
rubella syndrome from vaccine virus is so small as to be negligible.
CDC's ACIP has stated that rubella vaccination during pregnancy
should not ordinarily be a reason to consider termination of pregnancy.
Notwithstanding the fact that no observable risk has been associated
with rubella vaccine administered during pregnancy, rubella vaccine
should not knowingly be administered to a pregnant woman. A reasonable approach is to ask women whether they are pregnant or may
become pregnant within the next 3 months, exclude those who answer
affirmatively, and vaccinate the others, after explaining the theoretical
risk to them.[110]

Known adverse events associated with rubella vaccine include low-
grade fever and rash in 5% to 10% of recipients and joint pains with
or without objective manifestations of arthritis. The latter occur with
increasing frequency in older individuals; about 25% of susceptible
adult females may have transient arthralgia after rubella vaccination.[168,169] Acute arthritis is seen in approximately 10% of susceptible
women. The risk of arthritis after rubella vaccine is substantially lower
than the risk after natural rubella. The IOM reviewed the adverse consequences of rubella vaccination and concluded that the vaccine was
an established cause of acute arthritis and that the evidence was consistent with a causal role of vaccine in rare cases of chronic arthritis.[44]
However, more recent studies have found no evidence of increased
risk for new onset of chronic arthropathies among women vaccinated
with RA 27/3 vaccine.[50-52] With regard to other illnesses temporally related to rubella vaccine, the IOM concluded that the evidence was insufficient to implicate rubella vaccine as a cause of thrombocytopenic
purpura, radiculoneuritis, and other neuropathies. Thrombocytopenic
purpura has been associated with MMR vaccine.[45]

Previous experience with programs involving serologic screening
and subsequent vaccination of susceptible individuals has demonstrated a low success rate in delivering vaccinations to identified susceptible persons (typically on the order of 30% to 50%). Because of
the importance of ensuring that adult women are immune to rubella
and because reactions appear to occur only in susceptible individuals,
it is recommended that women be vaccinated without serologic testing
unless it can be ensured that they can be successfully contacted and recalled for vaccination if serologic testing indicates they are susceptible. Contraindications to rubella vaccination are pregnancy and an immunocompromised state (see "Measles Vaccine").[110]

Smallpox Vaccine

Effective use of smallpox vaccine eradicated smallpox as a naturally
occurring disease in 1977.[170] The vaccine is a live unattenuated preparation of vaccinia virus that induces protection against smallpox virus
in 95% or more of recipients. Routine use of smallpox vaccine among
the civilian population in the United States was discontinued in 1971
and by the military in 1990. In May 1983, Wyeth Laboratories, Inc.,
the only active licensed producer in the United States, discontinued
general distribution of smallpox vaccine, making it no longer available
for general civilian use. With concerns that smallpox could become an
agent for bioterrorism, selected lots of smallpox vaccine were tested
and on October 25, 2002, were licensed. Smallpox vaccine was recommended for members of public health and health-care response
teams[171] and for selected military personnel; it continues to be available as an investigational new drug for individuals working with vaccinia or other orthopoxviruses. Smallpox vaccine is administered intradermally by the multiple puncture technique using a presterilized
bifurcated needle. With the bifurcated needle held perpendicular to the
skin, punctures are made rapidly, with sufficient pressure that a trace
of blood appears after 15 to 20 seconds.

Previously recognized adverse events associated with smallpox
vaccine include disseminated vaccinia, eczema vaccinatum, vaccinia
necrosum (progressive vaccinia), and encephalitis.[170,171,172] The risk of
transmission of vaccinia virus from the inoculation site can be reduced
by keeping the vaccine site covered with gauze and a layer of clothing

and by good hand hygiene. For persons involved in patient care, addition of a semipermeable dressing is recommended.[173] In the current pre-event vaccination program, smallpox vaccine is contraindicated for persons with a history or presence of eczema, atopic dermatitis, or other dermatologic conditions; who have conditions associated with immunosuppression; who are pregnant or breast feeding; or who have a serious allergy to any component of the vaccine. Following reports of ischemic cardiac events in recent vaccinees, persons with known underlying heart disease or three or more known major cardiac risk factors were also excluded from the pre-event vaccination program,[174] although no causal relationship has been established between receipt of the vaccine and ischemic cardiac disease.

Inflammatory cardiac disease (myocarditis, pericarditis, or myopericarditis) was recognized in 2003 among recipients of smallpox vaccine in both military and civilian programs.[175] While myocarditis had been previously reported in Europe and Australia following administration of other vaccinia strains, it was not previously recognized as an adverse event following the New York City Board of Health (NYCBOH) strain, the strain used for production of smallpox vaccine in the United States. The clinical spectrum of illness ranges from mildly symptomatic to heart failure, and the natural history remains unknown; it is unclear if all patients recover completely, or if some persons with subclinical myocarditis may later develop dilated cardiomyopathy, as is thought to occur with some patients who have other types of myocarditis. Histopathologic data are limited, but in one patient who underwent endomyocardial biopsy an eosinophilic infiltrate without presence of vaccinia virus was found. Onset is typically 7 to 19 days post-vaccination; the frequency appears to be about 1 in 10,000 vaccinees.[175]

Production and clinical studies of second generation smallpox vaccines, derived from the NYCBOH strain but produced in cell culture, are well underway.[176] Other vaccinia strains, such as modified vaccinia Ankara which only undergoes limited replication in humans, are under active study as vaccine strains which might be associated with a lower incidence of adverse events or might be safe to use in populations in which current smallpox vaccines are contraindicated (e.g., immunocompromised persons).

Tetanus Toxoid

Tetanus toxoid, a purified preparation of inactivated tetanus toxin, is one of the most effective immunizing agents known. The preferred preparation is adsorbed (alum-precipitated) because it is more immunogenic than the fluid preparation. Tetanus toxoid is recommended for use in all residents of the United States for whom contraindications do not exist. It should always be used in combination with diphtheria toxoid to ensure protection against both diseases. A primary course of two doses administered 4 to 8 weeks apart with a third dose given 6 to 12 months later induces protective antibodies in more than 95% of recipients and is recommended for all unvaccinated older children (see Table 319-5) and adults. Following primary immunization, booster doses with adult formulation tetanus and diphtheria toxoids (Td) are recommended every 10 years. When tetanus toxoid is given to children younger than 7 years of age as DTaP, five doses are given beginning at 2 months of age. For unvaccinated children in the first year of life, for whom pertussis vaccine is contraindicated, pediatric DT should be substituted for DTaP. For unvaccinated children in the second year of life for whom pertussis vaccine is contraindicated, two doses of DT should be administered 4 to 8 weeks apart with a third dose 6 to 12 months later (see "Pertussis Vaccine"). From fall 2000 to spring 2002 there was a shortage of Td that led to deferral of routine Td boosters in the United States.[177,178] Persons who did not receive routine boosters during that period should be recalled for vaccination. Common adverse effects include local reactions and fever. In some individuals who have received multiple doses of tetanus toxoid, Arthus-like reactions have been described.[179] Tetanus toxoid has been suggested as a rare cause of brachial plexus neuropathy. The IOM concluded tetanus toxoid caused brachial neuritis in the 1 month after immunization at a rate of 0.5 to 1

TABLE 319-6   Summary Guide to Tetanus Prophylaxis in Routine Wound Management: United States*

History of Adsorbed Tetanus Toxoid (Doses)	Clean, Minor Wounds		All Other Wounds[†]	
	Td[‡]	TIG	Td[‡]	TIG
Unknown or less than three	Yes	No	Yes	Yes
Three[§]	No[‖]	No	No**	No

*Important details are in the text.

[†]Such as, but not limited to, wounds contaminated with dirt, feces, soil, saliva, and so on; puncture wounds; avulsions; and wounds resulting from missiles, crushing, burns, and frostbite.

[‡]For children less than 7 yr, DTaP or DTP (DT if pertussis vaccine is contraindicated) is preferred to tetanus toxoid alone. For persons 7 yr and older, Td is preferred to tetanus toxoid alone.

[§]If only three doses of fluid toxoid have been received, a fourth dose of toxoid, preferably an absorbed toxoid, should be given.

[‖]Yes, if more than 10 yr since last dose.

**Yes, if more than 5 yr since last dose. (More frequent boosters are not needed and can accentuate side effects.)

case/100,000 toxoid recipients.[45] Tetanus toxoid has also been implicated as a cause of GBS. The most convincing evidence comes from a case report of one individual who acquired GBS three times with successive administrations of toxoid.[180] However, population-based studies in both children and adults have revealed an incidence of GBS within expected limits and do not support a causal role.[49,181] If tetanus toxoid causes GBS, it does so very rarely. The only contraindication is in individuals who have previously had neurologic or severe hypersensitivity reactions after tetanus toxoid. Table 319-6 summarizes the ACIP recommended approach to use of tetanus toxoid and tetanus immune globulin for postexposure prophylaxis of tetanus.[70]

Typhoid Vaccine

Two preparations of typhoid vaccine are available in the United States: an oral live attenuated strain of *Salmonella typhi* (Ty21a) and a Vi capsular polysaccharide vaccine (ViCPS). The two vaccines provide between 50% and 80% protection after a primary series.[182] Typhoid vaccines are indicated for travelers who will have prolonged exposure to contaminated food and drinks in developing countries, those with prolonged exposure to typhoid carriers, and laboratory workers who work with *S. typhi*.

The oral vaccine comes as an enteric-coated capsule that should be taken on alternate days with cool liquid approximately 1 hour before a meal. The four recommended doses should be refrigerated until needed. Data are not available to make recommendations about the need for boosters with the oral vaccine, although the manufacturer recommends a new complete series every 5 years. The ViCPS is recommended as a single 0.5-mL dose. Boosters are recommended every 2 years. The Ty21a vaccine is not recommended for children less than 6 years of age. The ViCPS is recommended for persons 2 years of age or older. The Ty21a and the ViCPS vaccines cause fever and headache in fewer than 6% of recipients. Other adverse reactions to the oral preparation are rare and consist of abdominal discomfort, nausea, and vomiting. Local reactions to the ViCPS have been reported in 7% of recipients. The oral vaccine should not be given to persons who are immunocompromised, including those with HIV infection. Ty21a should not be given to a person taking the antimalarial mefloquine or antibiotics, especially sulfonamides, unless at least 24 hours has elapsed since the last dose.

Varicella Vaccine

A live attenuated varicella vaccine (Oka strain) was licensed in the United States in 1995. The vaccine has generally been found to be highly effective against severe varicella (95% to 100%) and less effective against mild disease (70% to 90% in most studies).[42,183] Most vaccinees who acquire varicella tend to have mild illness with fewer than 50 lesions compared with 250 to 500 lesions in unvaccinated persons with disease.[184-186] Immunity appears to be long lasting. With the current vaccine, varicella occurs at a rate of less than 3% per year with no evidence for increasing severity with increasing time since vaccination.[186a,187] The vaccine is recommended routinely for all children at 12 to 18 months of age and can be given to any susceptible older child or adult. Persons 13 years of age and older require two doses 4 to 8 weeks apart. Vaccination is recommended for susceptible persons ages 13 years or older who (1) live or work in settings where varicella transmission is likely or can occur such as schools, daycare centers, institutional settings, colleges, prisons, and the military; (2) are nonpregnant women of childbearing age; (3) live in households with children or (4) are international travelers. Because adults are at higher risk of complications from varicella than are children, vaccination of all susceptible adolescents and adults is desirable. Persons with a reliable history of varicella can be considered immune. Although a negative or uncertain history of varicella in young children is predictive of susceptibility, most young adults with such histories are immune. In some settings, serologic screening of persons with negative or unknown prior histories of varicella is cost effective.[188] However, recalling and vaccinating identified susceptible persons may be difficult, making vaccination using history as the determinant of need more attractive. Vaccination has also been demonstrated to be effective for outbreak control.[189,190]

The most common adverse events are local reactions and rash. In children, approximately 3% acquire a varicella-like rash at the injection site with a median of two lesions and 4% acquire a generalized rash with a median of five lesions. For adults, 3% and 1% acquire localized rashes after doses 1 and 2, respectively, whereas 6% and 1% acquire more generalized rashes.[41] Transmission of vaccine virus has been reported rarely and only from persons with rash. There is no evidence that vaccination increases the risk of zoster. In fact, zoster incidence after vaccination appears lower than would be expected after natural infection. Vaccine is contraindicated in persons with anaphylactic hypersensitivity to vaccine components, including neomycin and gelatin, and in most persons with deficiencies of cell-mediated immunity.[41,191] Available data on the safety and efficacy of varicella vaccine in HIV-infected children who were not severely immunocompromised suggests that varicella vaccine is immunogenic and that the vaccine safety profile is acceptable.[192] HIV-infected children who are asymptomatic and not immunosuppressed should receive two doses of varicella vaccine with the first dose at 12 to 15 months of age or older and a 3-month interval between doses.[193] Patients with acute lymphoblastic leukemia in remission may qualify for vaccine under an investigational new drug protocol (phone number 215-283-0897). Pregnant women should not be vaccinated and women should be warned not to become pregnant 1 month after vaccination.[41]

Varicella vaccine is more thermolabile than other vaccines. It must be stored frozen at an average temperature of $-15°$ C or less. Varicella vaccine combined with MMR will likely be available in the future for routine vaccination, and a varicella vaccine formulation is currently being evaluated for prevention of herpes zoster in older adults.

Yellow Fever Vaccine

Yellow fever vaccine is a live attenuated virus preparation that is highly effective in inducing protection in recipients. It is indicated for use in travelers going to yellow fever–endemic areas and may be required for entry into some countries. Only a single dose of vaccine is required; it is administered by subcutaneous inoculation. Boosters are recommended every 10 years, although their need has not been conclusively established. Local and mild systemic reactions occur in 2% to 5% of recipients 5 to 10 days after vaccination; more severe reactions, primarily encephalitis and encephalopathy, are rare. Children younger than 4 months of age appear to be at highest risk of severe neurotropic reactions and vaccine is contraindicated in this age group. Other contraindications include anaphylactic hypersensitivity to eggs and immunocompromised states. If possible, vaccination of infants should be delayed until 9 months of age. Pregnancy is not considered an absolute contraindication; however, it is recommended that admin-

istration of the vaccine be postponed until after completion of pregnancy, if possible. Recently, a new severe adverse event, vaccine-associated viscerotropic disease, has been identified. This event is characterized by multiorgan failure. Clinical manifestations have included fever, hypotension, respiratory failure, liver disease, renal failure, thrombocytopenia, and other manifestations. The estimated incidence in the United States is 1 in 400,000 doses distributed.[194]

Immunoglobulins

Immune Globulin (See Also Chapter 6)

IG is a preparation of pooled human immunoglobulins containing antibodies against infectious agents that cause several diseases, including hepatitis A and measles. IG is effective in preventing hepatitis A when administered within 14 days of exposure (a dose of 0.02 mL/kg) or when given before exposure in somewhat larger quantities (dose of 0.02 mL/kg for trips of 1 to 2 months, 0.06 mL/kg every 5 months for longer trips).[80] It may also prevent or modify measles if administered within 6 days of exposure (a dose of 0.25 mL/kg for normal persons, 0.5 mL/kg for those who are immunocompromised, up to a maximum of 15 mL). Adverse effects include local tenderness and, rarely, Arthus-type or anaphylactic reactions. Anaphylaxis has been reported after repeated administration to IgA-deficient persons.[195] Other than prior anaphylactic reactions, there are no known contraindications to use of the product. IG inhibits response to certain live virus vaccines (i.e., measles and rubella vaccines) for between 3 and 9 months, depending on the dose administered (3 months for hepatitis dose; 5 months for measles prevention doses).[196] Simultaneous administration of IG with hepatitis A vaccine may result in a decrease of the ultimate titer of hepatitis A antibody achieved but does not influence seroconversion and presumed protection.[84]

Ordinary IG should not be administered intravenously.[197] IGIV is formulated for intravenous use primarily as a maintenance preparation for individuals with hypogammaglobulinemia. In addition, it may also be useful to decrease risk of infection in other immunodeficiency states such as HIV infection in children and may provide postexposure protection against measles and other infections. IGIV is also used to treat immune thrombocytopenic purpura and Kawasaki's syndrome; for Kawasaki syndrome, a single dose of 2 g/kg is administered. Side effects of IGIV include a syndrome of headache, fever, and flushing; hypotension; renal failure (thought to be related to sucrose, added to some IGIV preparations as a stabilizing agent); aseptic meningitis; thromboembolic events; and anaphylaxis in IgA-deficient recipients.[198,199]

IG and specific IG products prepared by Cohn fractionation pose no risk of transmitting hepatitis B, HIV, or other known infectious agents. Hepatitis C has been transmitted by IGIV in both Europe and the United States and by an intravenous Rh IG preparation in Ireland.[200-202] Hepatitis C virus RNA has been detected by polymerase chain reaction in various IG preparations,[203] but the significance of this finding is unclear; disease has not been associated with products other than those noted previously. In response to these findings, manufacturing procedures have been modified to add new viral inactivation steps.[204]

Hepatitis B Immune Globulin

HBIG is prepared from plasma preselected for high titer of antibody to HBsAg. In the United States, HBIG has an anti-HBsAg titer of more than 1:100,000 by radioimmunoassay. It is recommended for use in postexposure settings for susceptible individuals who have been exposed to known hepatitis B virus–infected sexual partners or to blood containing HBsAg by the percutaneous or mucous membrane route. The dose is 0.06 mL/kg given immediately for both sexual contacts and those exposed percutaneously. The hepatitis B vaccine series should be started simultaneously in those who have not previously been vaccinated. Alternatively, a second dose of HBIG may be given 1 month later for persons for whom hepatitis B vaccine is not indicated. HBIG is also recommended for infants born to HBsAg-positive women. A dose of 0.5 mL should be given within 12 hours of delivery in conjunction with a dose of hepatitis B vaccine. Additional doses of vaccine are indicated at 1 month and 6 months. The only known adverse effect is local discomfort at the site of injection. There are no known precautions or contraindications.[86]

Rabies Immune Globulin

RIG is a hyperimmune globulin prepared from humans who have been immunized against rabies and have very high titers of antibodies to rabies. It is designed for management of individuals who have been exposed to rabid animals. RIG should always be used in conjunction with rabies vaccine in previously unvaccinated persons. However, if more than 8 days has elapsed since the first dose of rabies vaccine, RIG is unnecessary because an active antibody response to the vaccine presumably has begun. Experience to date indicates that administration of a full course of human diploid cell rabies vaccine with rabies immunoglobulin is 100% effective in preventing the development of rabies after exposure to known rabid animals. As much as possible of the 20 IU/kg dose should be infiltrated into and around the wound. Any remaining RIG should be administered intramuscularly at a different site from vaccine. Adverse effects include minor local discomfort. There are no known contraindications.[164]

Respiratory Syncytial Virus Immune Globulin and Palivizumab

Two products are licensed in the United States for administration to infants and children at high risk of severe disease due to respiratory syncytial virus (RSV); groups at high risk include infants and children younger than 24 months of age with chronic lung disease or a history of premature birth (≤35 weeks' gestation). Respiratory syncytial virus immune globulin intravenous (RSV-IGIV) is a hyperimmune globulin formulated for intravenous administration. It is administered monthly during the RSV season (November through April in the Northern Hemisphere). RSV-IGIV has been demonstrated to be effective in reducing the risk of RSV hospitalization.[205] The recommended dose is 15 ml/kg (750 mg/kg). However, an unexpected increase in adverse events was observed in RSV-IGIV-treated children with cyanotic congenital heart disease.[206] RSV-IGIV, like other IG products, may interfere with the immune response to live virus vaccines.[197] Palivizumab is a humanized monoclonal antibody against the F protein of RSV and is produced by recombinant DNA technology. The recommended dosage is 15 mg/kg administered intramuscularly monthly throughout the RSV season. Palivizumab has been demonstrated to be effective in reducing the risk of RSV hospitalization.[207] No significant adverse events have been associated with palivizumab, and there is no interference with the immune response to live virus vaccines. The American Academy of Pediatrics (AAP) has recommended that because of the high cost of these interventions, their use be limited to those infants and children at highest risk of severe RSV. The AAP recommends that palivizumab or RSV-IGIV prophylaxis be considered for infants and children younger than 2 years of age with chronic lung disease who have required medical therapy for lung disease within the 6 months preceding RSV season. Recommendations for use in premature infants are based on age and chronological age at the start of the RSV season. Because of ease of administration, palivizumab is preferred over RSV-IGIV.[208-210]

Rh Immune Globulin

Rh IG is a hyperimmune globulin prepared for use in Rh-negative women who have just delivered Rh-positive infants or have had a miscarriage or abortion of an Rh-positive fetus. When administered within 24 hours of the time of delivery or abortion, it is highly effective in preventing sensitization of the mother to Rh-positive red blood cells that might be present in a future pregnancy. Appropriate administration of Rh IG has reduced the occurrence of Rh hemolytic disease of the newborn in the United States to very low levels. Further reductions will require more careful attention to the administration of the product after abortion or delivery in all women for whom it is indicated. There are essentially no adverse effects associated with the product, and there are no known contraindications.[211]

Tetanus Immune Globulin

TIG is a hyperimmune globulin indicated for management of tetanus-prone wounds in individuals who have no prior history of tetanus immunization. The standard dose is 250 units intramuscularly, although some groups recommend doses as high as 500 units. Local reactions are rare, and there are no known contraindications. If used, it should be administered simultaneously with, but at a different site from, combined tetanus-diphtheria toxoids. Primary immunization against tetanus and diphtheria should then be completed using the routine schedule. Table 319-6 summarizes the ACIP-recommended approach to postexposure prophylaxis of tetanus.[70] TIG in large doses (3000 to 6000 units) may also be used in the treatment of tetanus.

Vaccinia Immune Globulin

Vaccinia immune globulin (VIG) is a hyperimmune globulin prepared for treatment of certain complications of vaccinia vaccination. VIG is indicated for treatment of severe cases of inadvertent inoculation, eczema vaccinatum, severe generalized vaccinia, and progressive vaccinia. Its use should be considered in patients with severe ocular complications other than isolated keratitis. It is not recommended for treatment for post-vaccinial encephalitis or encephalomyelitis; myopericarditis following smallpox vaccine; mild cases of generalized vaccinia; erythema multiforme; or isolated vaccinia keratitis. Three preparations of VIG are available in the Untied States; a previous licensed IM product produced in 1994, and two new preparations for IV administration. All preparations of VIG are currently available only under Investigational New Drug protocols through CDC and the Department of Defense.[212]

Varicella-Zoster Immune Globulin

VZIG is prepared by selection of serum containing high titers of varicella-zoster antibodies. It is indicated for administration to susceptible immunocompromised individuals and certain others who have recently been exposed to varicella, including newborns whose mothers acquire varicella within 5 days before to 48 hours after delivery. It should be administered within 96 hours of exposure, but ideally as soon after exposure as possible. Some believe it may also be useful in ameliorating the expression of varicella in susceptible adults, particularly susceptible pregnant females who are at increased risk of complications from varicella infection after exposure to the virus. The product may not prevent infection; however, if infection occurs it is usually subclinical or mild. Local reactions are rare, and there are no known contraindications.[41] Episodes of inadvertent administration of varicella vaccine to pregnant women in whom VZIG was indicated continue to occur despite recognition of the problem of product confusion.[213] Providers and others involved in administering this product should take steps to assure that product confusion does not occur.

USE OF VACCINES

Routine

Children

The recommended schedule for administration of vaccines to infants, children and adolescents is shown in Figure 319-1.[55] Catch-up schedules for 4-month- to 6-year-old children and 7- to 18-year-old children are shown in Table 319-5. It is currently recommended that all children receive DTaP, polio, measles, mumps, rubella, Hib, hepatitis B, varicella, and pneumococcal conjugate vaccines unless contraindications exist.[55] Five doses of DTaP and four doses of polio-containing vaccines are recommended. The fifth dose of DTaP and the fourth dose of polio vaccine are recommended at 4 to 6 years of age.[38,48] Td boosters should be administered at 11 to 12 years of age and every 10 years thereafter.[89] A single dose of combined measles, mumps, and rubella vaccine at 12 to 15 months of age or older provides long-lasting, probably lifelong, immunity in more than 95% of recipients. The second dose of MMR at school entry should provide immunity to most of those not protected by the first dose.[110] DTaP, MMR, Hib, hepatitis B, polio, pneumococcal conjugate and varicella vaccines may be given simultaneously if necessary. Although all potential simultaneous administration schemes have not been evaluated, experience to date suggests that simultaneous administration of most vaccines does not increase reaction rates nor interfere with the immune responses.[214] Stress for infants, as measured by serum cortisol, does not increase when a second injection is given.[215,216] Hib should be given in two doses (PRP-OMP) or three doses (HbOC, PRP-T) in the first year of life followed by a reinforcing dose at 12 to 15 months.[72] Hepatitis B vaccine can be given as early as birth, and the three-dose series should be completed by 18 months of age; hepatitis B vaccine can be given simultaneously with all other childhood vaccines.[86] When combination vaccines containing hepatitis B vaccine are going to be used, an initial birth dose of single antigen hepatitis B vaccine should also be considered. Pneumococcal conjugate vaccine should be administered in a four-dose series with the first three doses administered at 2, 4, and 6 months of age, and the fourth dose at 12 to 15 months. A combined DTaP–PRP-T is available for dose four of the schedule.[38] Children should receive varicella vaccine routinely at 12 to 18 months of age.[41] Annual influenza vaccine was recommended for children 6 to 23 months of age beginning during the 2004 to 2005 season.[101] Children under 8 years receiving influenza vaccine for the first time should have two doses separated by at least 4 weeks. Children between 6 months and 35 months of age should receive half doses (0.25 mL).

Adolescents

An adolescent immunization visit has been established at 11 to 12 years of age.[89] This is the appropriate time to administer (1) a booster dose of Td for those persons who completed a primary series and received their last dose of a vaccine containing tetanus and diphtheria toxoids at school entry, (2) a second dose of MMR if not previously received, and (3) a dose of varicella vaccine if the patient is susceptible. The three-dose hepatitis B vaccination series should be administered if not previously received. A schedule of doses of hepatitis B vaccine at 0, 1 to 2 months, and 4 to 6 months is recommended. Other immunizations such as pneumococcal vaccine, influenza vaccine, and hepatitis A vaccine should be given, if indicated.

Adults

Routine immunizations for adults have received increasing attention in recent years with recognition of the large burden of vaccine-preventable diseases in this age group. Two adult immunization schedules have been developed, one focused on vaccines needed by age group and the second on vaccines needed for persons with specific medical conditions (Figs. 319-2 and 319-3).[56] All adults should be immune to diphtheria and tetanus and if not previously immunized should be given a primary immunizing course (three doses of Td administered at time zero, 4 to 8 weeks, and 6 to 12 months) with boosters administered every 10 years thereafter.[70] Routine immunization against polio is not recommended for adults unless they are at particular risk of exposure.[163] All individuals should be immune to measles, mumps, and rubella. For practical purposes, those born before 1957 can generally be considered immune to these three diseases. All other individuals should be vaccinated unless it can be documented that they have either received vaccine on or after the first birthday or have had physician-diagnosed disease. A history of prior rubella disease is unreliable and should not be accepted.[110] Influenza vaccine is recommended for routine annual administration to adults 50 years of age and older and to individuals at any age who have chronic illness and for healthy persons who are close contacts of persons with such illnesses, including health-care workers.[100,101] Pneumococcal polysaccharide vaccine is recommended for administration to the elderly and the chronically ill.[152] Hepatitis B vaccine is recommended for individuals at high risk of exposure to hepatitis B virus. These include primarily health care and emergency responder personnel who anticipate contact with blood or blood-containing body fluids, men who have sex with men, and sexually active heterosexuals with multiple sexual partners, users of illicit injectable drugs, individuals living and working in institutions for the developmentally disabled, and household contacts of carriers of HBsAg.[54,86,87,218] All susceptible adults should be vaccinated against chickenpox.[41]

Special Circumstances

Travel (See Also Chapter 328)

The International Health Regulations allow countries to impose requirements for yellow fever vaccine as a condition for admission. Consequently, travelers should be aware of whether this vaccine is required for entry into the country of their destination. Other vaccines commonly considered for travelers include measles vaccine, polio vaccine, and boosters for tetanus and diphtheria. In addition, travelers to specified areas may wish to consider plague, typhoid, rabies, Japanese encephalitis, yellow fever, hepatitis A, hepatitis B, and meningococcal vaccines. Information on vaccines recommended for travel is summarized regularly in *Health Information for International Travel*[219] (see "Sources of Information" farther on), but the most up-to-date information is available in the online version, found on the CDC Internet website, at *www.cdc.gov/travel/yb/index.htm*. Information on specific regions and diseases is available from the CDC Fax Information Service at 1-888-232-3299.

Occupational Exposure

A complete set of recommendations for vaccination for most occupational groups has not been developed. Specific recommendations are available for health care workers.[111,112] Federal regulations require that health care and public safety workers who anticipate exposure to human blood or blood-derived body fluids are offered hepatitis B vaccination free of charge.[85] It is clear that transmission of rubella in medical facilities can occur to or from health care workers. Consequently, it is important that all health care workers who might transmit rubella to pregnant patients be immune to rubella. Documentation of a single dose of a rubella-containing vaccine on or after the first birthday or serologic evidence of immunity is acceptable. Health care workers are at greater risk from measles than the general public. All workers likely to come in contact with measles patients should be immune, defined as documentation of receipt of two doses of live measles vaccine on or after the first birthday, at least 1 month apart, physician-diagnosed measles, or serologic evidence of immunity. Although most persons born before 1957 have been considered to be immune to measles, approximately 4% of cases in health care workers in the past were in persons born before this date. Therefore, in health care settings, it may be worthwhile to ensure that all persons have documented evidence of immunity regardless of age. Although mumps has not been a major problem in health care settings, mumps transmission in such settings has been reported and mumps immunity can be ensured at the same time as measles and rubella if MMR is used.[110] Because health care workers caring for patients with chronic diseases may transmit influenza to their patients, such workers should be vaccinated annually.[100,101] Health care workers should also be immune to varicella.[41] Smallpox vaccination is recommended for healthcare workers who volunteer to become members of healthcare response teams that would be mobilized should a smallpox attack occur.[171]

Pregnancy

Because of unknown but theoretical risks to the fetus, immunization of pregnant women is generally avoided. However, it is important to ensure that pregnant women are immune to tetanus, because transfer of maternal antibodies to tetanus toxin is an important means of preventing neonatal tetanus. Pregnant women can receive combined tetanus-diphtheria toxoids. In general, live virus vaccines are contraindicated in pregnancy with the exception of yellow fever virus vaccine, which may be administered if the risk of exposure to the disease is great. If indicated, some inactivated vaccines, such as influenza and hepatitis B, can be administered to pregnant women under the same circumstances they are administered to nonpregnant individuals.[1] Because of the increased risk for influenza-related complications, women who will be beyond the first trimester of pregnancy (more than 14 weeks of gestation) during the upcoming influenza season should receive influenza vaccines.[100,101]

FIGURE 319-2. Recommended adult immunization schedule, by age group—United States, 2003-2004.[1] *(From Centers for Disease Control and Prevention. MMWR Morb Mortal Wkly Rep 2003;52:965-969.)*

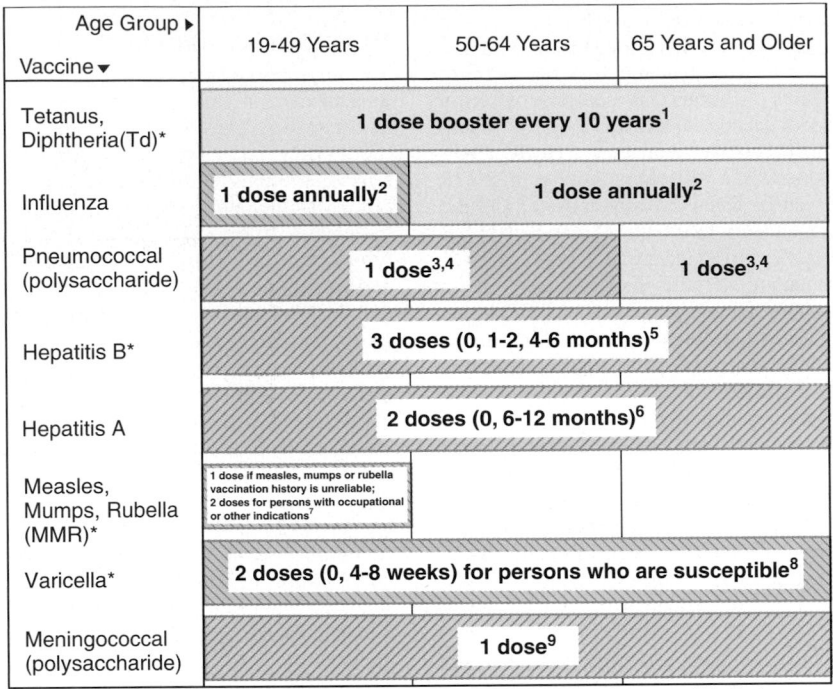

See Footnotes for Recommended Adult Immunization Schedule, by Age Group and Medical Conditions, United States, 2003-2004

☐ For all persons in this age group   ▨ Catch-up on childhood vaccinations   ▨ For persons with medical/exposure indications

*Covered by the Vaccine Injury Compensation Program. For information on how to file a claim call 800-338-2382. Please also visit *www.hrsa.gov/osp/vicp.* To file a claim for vaccine injury contact: U.S. Court of Federal Claims, 717 Madison Place, N.W., Washington, D.C. 20005, 202-219-9657.

This schedule indicates the recommended age groups for routine administration of currently licensed vaccines for persons aged 19 years or older. Licensed combination vaccines may be used whenever any components of the combination are indicated and the vaccine's other components are not contraindicated. Providers should consult the manufacturers' package inserts for detailed recommendations.

Report all clinically significant, post-vaccination reactions to the Vaccine Adverse Event Reporting System (VAERS). Reporting forms and instructions on filing a VAERS report are available by calling 800-822-7967 or from the VAERS website at *www.vaers.org.*

For additional information about the vaccines listed above and contraindications for immunization, visit the National Immunization Program Website at *www.cdc.gov/nip* or call the National Immunization Hotline at 800-232-2522 (English) or 800-232-0233 (Spanish).

Approved by the Advisory Committee on Immunization Practices (ACIP), and accepted by the American College of Obstetricians and Gynecologists (ACOG) and the American Academy of Family Physicians (AAFP). Footnotes for Recommended Adult Immunization Schedule by Age Group and Medical Conditions, United States, 2003-2004

1. Tetanus and diphtheria (Td) toxoids—Adults including pregnant women with uncertain histories of a complete primary vaccination series should receive a primary series of Td. A primary series for adults is 3 doses: the first 2 doses given at least 4 weeks apart and the 3rd dose, 6-12 months after the second. Administer 1 dose if the person had received the primary series and the last vaccination was 10 years ago or longer. Consult MMWR 1991;40(RR-10):1-21 for administering Td as prophylaxis in wound management. The ACP Task Force on Adult Immunization supports a second option for Td use in adults: a single Td booster at age 50 years for persons who have completed the full pediatric series, including the teenage/young adult booster. Guide for Adult Immunization. 3rd ed. ACP 1994:20.

2. Influenza vaccination—Medical indications: chronic disorders of the cardiovascular or pulmonary systems including asthma; chronic metabolic diseases including diabetes mellitus, renal dysfunction, hemoglobinopathies, or immunosuppression (including immunosuppression caused by medications or by human immunodeficiency virus [HIV]), requiring regular medical follow-up or hospitalization during the preceding year; women who will be in the second or third trimester of pregnancy during the influenza season. Occupational indications: health-care workers. Other indications: residents of nursing homes and other long-term-care facilities; persons likely to transmit influenza to persons at high-risk (in-home care givers to persons with medical indications, household contacts and out-of-home caregivers of children birth to 23 months of age, or children with asthma or other indicator conditions for influenza vaccination, household members and care givers of elderly and adults with high-risk conditions); and anyone who wishes to be vaccinated. For healthy persons aged 5-49 years without high-risk conditions, either the inactivated vaccine or the intranasally administered influenza vaccine (Flumist) may be given. MMWR 2003;52 (RR-8):1-36; MMWR 2003;53 (RR-13):1-8.

3. Pneumococcal polysaccharide vaccination—Medical indications: chronic disorders of the pulmonary system (excluding asthma), cardiovascular disease, diabetes mellitus, chronic liver diseases including liver disease as a result of alcohol abuse (e.g., cirrhosis), chronic renal failure or nephritic syndrome, functional or anatomic asplenia (e.g., sickle cell disease or splenectomy), immunosuppressive conditions (e.g., congenital immunodeficiency, HIV infection, leukemia, lymphoma, multiple myeloma, Hodgkins disease, generalized malignancy, organ or bone marrow transplantation), chemotherapy with alkylating agents, anti-metabolites, or long-term systemic corticosteroids. Geographic/other indications: Alaskan Natives and certain American Indian populations. Other indications: residents of nursing homes and other long-term-care facilities. MMWR 1997;46(RR-8):1-24.

4. Revaccination with pneumococcal polysaccharide vaccine—One-time revaccination after 5 years for persons with chronic renal failure or nephritic syndrome, functional or anatomic asplenia (e.g., sickle cell disease or splenectomy), immunosuppressive conditions (e.g., congenital immunodeficiency, HIV infection, leukemia, lymphoma, multiple myeloma, Hodgkins disease, generalized malignancy, organ or bone marrow transplantation), chemotherapy with alkylating agents, anti-metabolites, or long-term systemic corticosteroids. For persons 65 years and older, one-time revaccination if they were vaccinated 5 or more years previously and were aged less than 65 years at the time of primary vaccination. MMWR 1997;46 (RR-8):1-24.

5. Hepatitis B vaccination—Medical indications: hemodialysis patients, patients who receive clotting-factor concentrates. Occupational indications: health-care workers and public-safety workers who have exposure to blood in the workplace, persons in training in schools of medicine, dentistry, nursing, laboratory technology, and other allied health professions. Behavioral indications: injecting drug users, persons with more than one sex partner during the previous 6 months, persons with a recently acquired sexually transmitted disease (STD), all clients in STD clinics, men who have sex with men. Other indications: household contacts and sex partners of persons with chronic HBV infection, clients and staff of institutions for the developmentally disabled, international travelers who will be in countries with high or intermediate prevalence of chronic HBV infection for more than 6 months, inmates of correctional facilities MMWR 1991;40(RR-13):1-19. (www.cdc.gov/travel/diseases/hbv.htm)

6. Hepatitis A vaccination—For the combined HepA-HepB vaccine use 3 doses at 0, 1, 6 months. Medical indications: persons with clotting-factor disorders or chronic liver disease. Behavioral indications: men who have sex with men, users of injecting and noninjecting illegal drugs. Occupational indications: persons working with HAV-infected primates or with HAV in a research laboratory setting. Other indications: persons traveling to or working in countries that have high or intermediate endemicity of hepatitis A. MMWR 1999;48 (RR-12):1-37. (www.cdc.gov/travel/diseases/hav.htm).

7. Measles, Mumps, Rubella vaccination (MMR)—Measles component: Adults born before 1957 may be considered immune to measles. Adults born in or after 1957 should receive at least 1 dose of MMR unless they have a medical contraindication, documentation of at least one dose or other acceptable evidence of immunity. A second dose of MMR is recommended for adults who:
  • are recently exposed to measles or were in an outbreak setting
  • were previously vaccinated with killed measles vaccine
  • were vaccinated with an unknown vaccine during 1963 and 1967
  • are students in post-secondary educational institutions
  • work in health care facilities
  • plan to travel internationally

Mumps component: 1 dose of MMR should be adequate for protection. Rubella component: Give 1 dose of MMR to women whose rubella vaccination history is unreliable and counsel women to avoid becoming pregnant for 4 weeks after vaccination. For women of child-bearing age, regardless of birth year, routinely determine rubella immunity and counsel women regarding congenital rubella syndrome. Do not vaccinate pregnant women or those planning to become pregnant in the next 4 weeks. If pregnant and susceptible, vaccinate as early in the postpartum period as possible. MMWR 1998;47(RR-8):1-57; MMWR 2001;50:1117.

8. Varicella vaccination—Recommended for all persons who do not have reliable clinical history of varicella infection, or serological evidence of varicella zoster virus (VZV) infection who may be at high risk for exposure or transmission. This includes health-care workers and family contacts of immunocompromised persons, those who live or work in environments where transmission is likely (e.g., teachers of young children, day care employees, and residents and staff members in institutional settings), persons who live or work in environments where VZV transmission can occur (e.g., college students, inmates and staff members of correctional institutions, and military personnel), adolescents and adults living in households with children, women who are not pregnant but who might become pregnant in the future, and international travelers who are not immune to infection. Note: Greater than 95% of U.S. born adults are immune to VZV. Do not vaccinate pregnant women or those planning to become pregnant in the next 4 weeks. If pregnant and susceptible, vaccinate as early in the postpartum period as possible. *MMWR* 1996;45 (RR-11):1-36; MMWR 1999;48 (RR-6):1-5.

9. Meningococcal vaccination (quadrivalent polysaccharide for serogroups A, C, Y, and W-135)— Consider vaccination for persons with medical indications: adults with terminal complement component deficiencies or with anatomic or functional asplenia. Other indications: travelers to countries in which diseases is hyperendemic or epidemic ("meningitis belt" of sub-Saharan Africa, Mecca, or Saudi Arabia for Hajj). Revaccination at 3-5 years may be indicated for persons at high risk for infection (e.g., persons residing in areas in which disease is epidemic). Counsel college freshmen, especially those who live in dormitories, regarding meningococcal disease and the vaccine so that they can make an educated decision about receiving the vaccination. MMWR 2000;49(RR-7):1-20.

Note: The AAFP recommends that colleges should take the lead on providing education on meningococcal infection and vaccination and offer it to those who are interested. Physicians need not initiate discussion of the meningococcal quadrivalent polysaccharide vaccine as part of routine medical care.

FIGURE 319-3. Recommended adult immunization schedule, by medical condition—United States, 2003-2004. *(From Centers for Disease Control and Prevention. MMWR Morb Mortal Wkly Rep 2003;52:965-969.)*

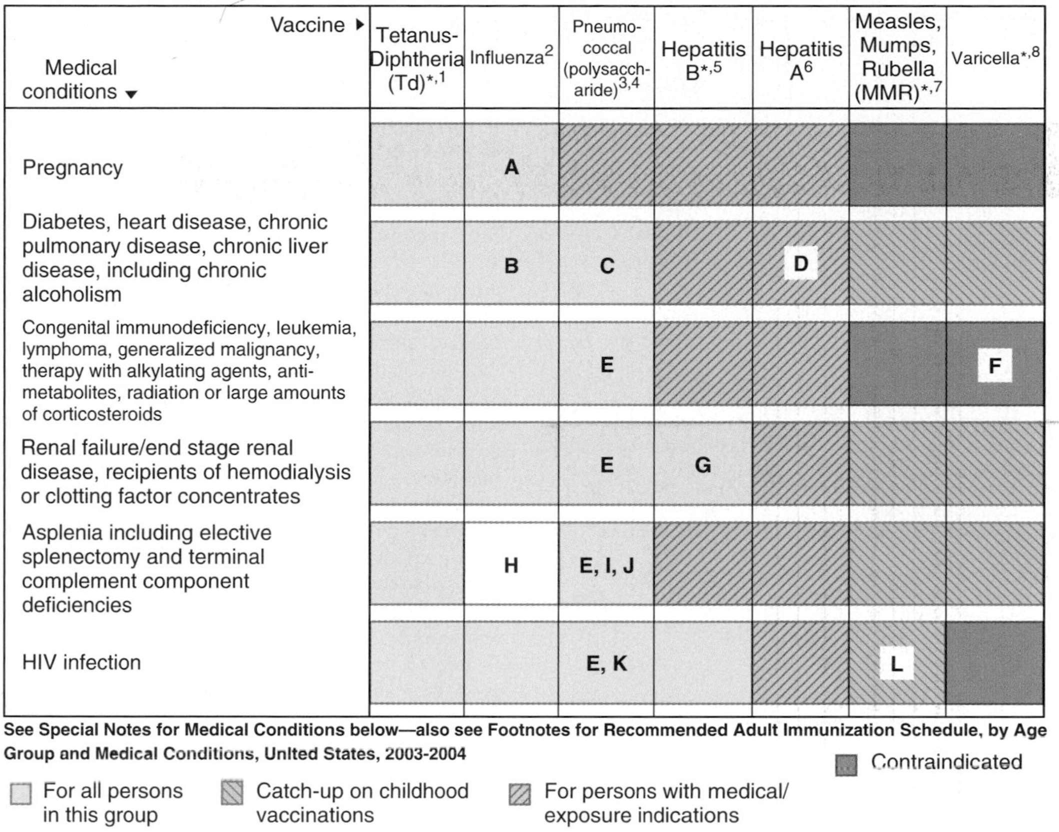

Medical conditions ▼	Tetanus-Diphtheria (Td)*,1	Influenza2	Pneumo-coccal (polysacch-aride)3,4	Hepatitis B*,5	Hepatitis A6	Measles, Mumps, Rubella (MMR)*,7	Varicella*,8
Pregnancy		A					
Diabetes, heart disease, chronic pulmonary disease, chronic liver disease, including chronic alcoholism		B	C		D		
Congenital immunodeficiency, leukemia, lymphoma, generalized malignancy, therapy with alkylating agents, anti-metabolites, radiation or large amounts of corticosteroids			E				F
Renal failure/end stage renal disease, recipients of hemodialysis or clotting factor concentrates			E	G			
Asplenia including elective splenectomy and terminal complement component deficiencies		H	E, I, J				
HIV infection			E, K			L	

See Special Notes for Medical Conditions below—also see Footnotes for Recommended Adult Immunization Schedule, by Age Group and Medical Conditions, United States, 2003-2004

☐ For all persons in this group ▨ Catch-up on childhood vaccinations ▨ For persons with medical/exposure indications ■ Contraindicated

A. For women without chronic diseases/conditions, vaccinate if pregnancy will be at second or third trimester during influenza season. For women with chronic diseases/conditions, vaccinate at any time during the pregnancy.

B. Although chronic liver disease and alcoholism are not indicator conditions for influenza vaccination, administer 1 dose annually if the patient is aged >50 years, has other indications for influenza vaccine, or requests vaccination.

C. Asthma is an indicator condition for influenza but not for pneumococcal vaccination.

D. For all persons with chronic liver disease.

E. For persons aged <65 years, revaccinate once after ≥5 years have elapsed since initial vaccination.

F. Persons with impaired humoral but not cellular immunity may be vaccinated (9).

G. For hemodialysis patients use special formulation of vaccine (40 μg/mL) or two 1.0 mL 20 μg doses administered at one site. Vaccinate early in the course of renal disease. Assess antibody titers to hepatitis B surface antigen (anti-HBs) levels annually. Administer additional doses if anti-HBs levels decline to ≤10 mIU /mL.

H. No data have been reported specifically on risk for severe or complicated influenza infections among persons with asplenia. However, influenza is a risk factor for secondary bacterial infections that might cause severe disease in asplenics.

I. Administer meningococcal vaccine and consider *Haemophilus influenzae* type b vaccine.

J. In the event of elective splenectomy, vaccinate >2 weeks before surgery.

K. Vaccinate as close to diagnosis as possible when CD4 cell counts are highest.

L. Withhold MMR or other measles-containing vaccines from HIV-infected persons with evidence of severe immunosuppression. Also see footnotes * through 9 in Figure 319-2.

Immunocompromised States

Immunocompromised individuals (congenital, acquired, or as a result of drug therapy) are particularly susceptible to many infections. They may also be more susceptible to adverse effects from live virus vaccines, although severe complications have been documented only rarely.[44,45] Consequently, in general, live virus vaccines are not administered to immunocompromised individuals, although inactivated vaccines are safe and are indicated.[1] Varicella vaccine is also contraindicated in persons with most deficiencies of cell-mediated immunity but can be safely given to persons with deficiencies of humoral immunity.[191] Recommendations for vaccination of persons with specific immunocompromising conditions have been summarized (e.g., recipients of transplants of hematopoietic stem cells[193] or solid organs.[220-222]) The efficacy of inactivated vaccines in immunocompromised individuals may be less than that in healthy patients although inactivated vaccines are safe and indicated for many patients.[223,224,225]

Human Immunodeficiency Virus

Live attenuated vaccines are generally contraindicated in immunocompromised persons, including those with symptomatic HIV infection. Limited studies in HIV-infected persons have generally failed to show an increased risk of adverse events from live or inactivated vaccines. Exceptions include BCG given to patients with acquired immunodeficiency syndrome and measles-containing vaccine in a patient with severe immunodeficiency.[226-228] Known HIV-infected persons who are asymptomatic should receive live attenuated MMR vaccine (Table 319-7). Because of reports of severe measles disease, including death, in symptomatic HIV-infected children, measles vaccine, alone or preferably with mumps and rubella vaccines, must be considered with caution for symptomatic HIV-infected persons.[110] Measles vaccine has been documented to cause death when given to a severely immunocompromised HIV-infected adult.[228] Therefore, vaccine is contraindicated in persons with severe immunodeficiency. Because measles has occurred even after vaccination in HIV-infected children, it is recommended that symptomatic HIV-infected children receive IG or IGIV after an exposure to measles[110] (see Chapter 157). Asymptomatic or mildly symptomatic children with HIV should also receive varicella vaccine. For asymptomatic persons presenting for immunization, serologic testing to determine HIV infection is not necessary for making decisions about immunization. Recommendations for administration of other vaccines are listed in Table 319-7. Although transient increases of HIV in the blood of patients have been documented in the month after receipt of both pneumococcal and influenza vaccines, their clinical significance is unknown. In contrast, HIV-infected persons are known to be at significantly higher risk of pneumococcal disease. Pneumococcal conjugate vaccine (PCV7) is recommended for HIV-infected children younger than 5 years of age;

TABLE 319-7 Recommendations for Routine Immunization of Human Immunodeficiency Virus-Infected Persons—United States

Vaccine	Human Immunodeficiency Virus Infection	
	Asymptomatic	*Symptomatic*
DTaP/DT, Td	Yes	Yes
OPV	No	No
IPV	Yes	Yes
MMR	Yes	Yes*
Hib	Yes	Yes
HBV	Yes	Yes
Rotavirus	No	No
Varicella	Yes	Yes**
Pneumococcal[†]	Yes	Yes[§]
Influenza[‡]	Yes	Yes[§]
Hepatitis A vaccine	Yes	Yes[‖]

DTaP, diphtheria and tetanus toxoids and acellular pertussis vaccine. DTP, diphtheria and tetanus toxoids and pertussis vaccine. Not recommended for persons > 7 yr of age; OPV, oral, attenuated poliovirus vaccine, contains poliovirus types 1, 2, and 3; IPV, inactivated poliovirus vaccine: contains poliovirus types 1, 2, and 3; MMR, live, attenuated measles, mumps, and rubella vaccine in a combined vaccine; Hib, *Haemophilus* B conjugate vaccine; HBV, hepatitis B vaccine.

*Vaccine should be considered, except for persons with severe immunocompromise.

**May be considered for asymptomatic and mildly symptomatic persons.

†Pneumococcal polysaccharide vaccine: Polysaccharide vaccine only for persons ≥2 yr of age. (See text.)

‡Not recommended for infants < 6 mo of age.

§Vaccine should be considered.

‖If otherwise indicated.

Updated from Centers for Disease Control and Prevention, Recommendation of the Immunization Practices Advisory Committee (ACIP): Immunization of children infected with human immunodeficiency virus - supplementary ACIP statement. MMWR Morb Mortal Wkly Rep 1988;37:181-183 and Centers for Disease Control and Prevention. Recommendations of the Advisory Committee on Immunization Practices (ACIP): Use of vaccines and immune globulin in persons with altered immunocompetence. MMWR Morb Mortal Wkly Rep. 1993;42:1-18.

Prepared by W. Atkinson, National Immunization Program, January 9, 2003.

HIV-infected children who did not receive PCV7 at younger than 2 years of age should receive two doses of PCV7 2 months apart followed by one dose of pneumococcal polysaccharide vaccine at least 2 months after the second dose of PCV7. HIV-infected children who have previously received PCV7 and other HIV-infected persons 5 years of age or older should receive pneumococcal polysaccharide vaccine. HIV-infected persons 6 months of age or older should receive annual influenza vaccination with trivalent inactivated vaccine as well.[100,152] Although a protective immune response to vaccines and toxoids cannot be ensured in these patients, some protection may be provided.

Postexposure Immunization

For certain diseases, administration of vaccine or IG soon after exposure can prevent or attenuate the expression of the disease.[197,229,230] For example, administration of IG within 2 weeks of exposure to hepatitis A is likely to prevent clinical illness. Similarly, the administration of RIG and rabies vaccine in the immediate postexposure period is highly effective in preventing the development of rabies. Individuals who have received a complete course of immunization against tetanus are in general well protected against the development of tetanus, particularly if a booster dose has been administered within 10 years. More problematic is the situation with individuals who cannot recall their immune status or who have not been immunized at all. Table 319-6 shows the ACIP recommended approach to postexposure prophylaxis of tetanus. IG administered within 6 days of exposure may be effective in preventing measles or modifying it so that the illness is very mild. There is also evidence that administration of measles vaccine within the first few days after exposure may prevent manifestations of the illness.[230a] In addition, if the exposure did not result in infection, the vaccination should pro-

vide protection against future exposure. Although overt manifestations of rubella can be minimized by postexposure administration of IG, this may not prevent viremia and fetal infection with rubella. Therefore, the administration of IG is recommended only for individuals who acquire rubella during pregnancy and will not consider induced abortion under any circumstances. Varicella vaccine prevents varicella in exposed persons if administered within 36 hours of exposure.[189,191,229,230]

Other Considerations

Storage and Handling of Vaccines

Most routinely used vaccines require storage temperatures of 35° F to 46° F (2° C to 8° C) and must not be exposed to freezing temperatures. Introduction of varicella vaccine in 1995 and of live attenuated influenza vaccine (LAIV) in 2003 have complicated vaccine storage; both vaccines must be stored in a continuously frozen state at less than or equal to 5° F ($-15°$ C) in a freezer with no freeze-thaw cycles. Recent assessments of storage of vaccines in provider offices have found that exposure of vaccines to improper storage conditions is common, with exposure of vaccines to refrigerator temperatures that are too low occurring more commonly than exposure to temperatures that are too high.[231,232]

Freezing temperatures can irreversibly reduce the potency of vaccines requiring refrigerator storage. Adjuvants may precipitate when exposed to freezing temperatures, resulting in loss of adjuvant effect.[233] Physical changes are not always apparent after exposure to freezing temperatures and visible signs of freezing are not necessary to result in a decrease in vaccine potency.

A combination refrigerator/freezer unit sold for home use is acceptable for vaccine storage if the refrigerator and freezer compartments each have a separate door. However, vaccines should not be stored near the cold air outlet from the freezer to the refrigerator. Refrigerators without freezers and stand-alone freezers usually perform better at maintaining precise temperatures. Any refrigerator or freezer used for vaccine storage must maintain the required temperature range year-round, be large enough to hold the year's largest inventory, and be dedicated to storage of biologics; food or beverages should not be stored with vaccines. Vaccines should be stored centrally in the unit, not in the door or on the bottom of the storage unit, and away from walls to allow air to circulate.

Proper temperature monitoring of vaccine storage is essential. Thermometers should be placed in a central location in the storage unit, adjacent to the vaccine. Temperatures should be read and recorded twice each day, once when the office or clinic opens and once at the end of the day. Temperature logs should be kept on file for at least 3 years; some state rules or statutes may require longer retention of records. Immediate action must be taken to correct storage temperatures that are outside the recommended ranges.[234]

Assessing the Need for Immunization

Immunization has traditionally been viewed as the task of the pediatrician and general practitioner caring for children, but all health care providers should assess the immunization status of their patients at first contact and, depending on immunization status and age, at selected contacts thereafter. In general, individuals should be viewed as susceptible unless they can prove immunity through documentation of having received vaccine, laboratory evidence of immunity or, for some diseases, documentation of physician-diagnosed disease.

A high proportion of elderly individuals in the United States have never been immunized against tetanus or diphtheria. This is reflected in the fact that 36% of all cases of tetanus in the United States in the period 1998 to 2000 have occurred in individuals older than the age of 60 years.[235] Internists and other physicians caring for adults and elderly individuals should be particularly attuned to the need for administering tetanus and diphtheria toxoids to these individuals. Similarly, studies repeatedly demonstrate that only about 65.9% of persons 65 years of age or older receive influenza immunization in a given year, only an estimated 56.2% have received pneumococcal vaccine.[236] It is vital that internists and family practitioners remind themselves and their patients of the need for annual influenza immunization of the chronically ill and elderly.

Substantial progress has been made in implementing hepatitis B vaccination programs for children and adolescents. However, a high proportion of adults with risk factors for hepatitis B virus (HBV) infection have not been vaccinated, in part because of the difficulty in identifying candidates for vaccination before they become infected and limited public funding for adult vaccination. In serosurveys of men who have sex with men age 15 to 22 years recruited at public venues in seven US metropolitan areas during 1994 to 1998, only 9% had serologic evidence of hepatitis B vaccination.[237] Among IDUs attending sexually transmitted disease (STD) clinics in San Diego from 1998-2001, only 6% reported previous hepatitis B vaccination.[238] Many opportunities to vaccinate high-risk adults are missed. For example, approximately 56% of adults with acute hepatitis B have received care previously in correctional facilities or sexually transmitted disease treatment clinics, where vaccination could have been offered.[239] The most effective approach to vaccinating high-risk adults is to integrate hepatitis B vaccination into settings that provide services to persons with risk factors for HBV infection (e.g., STD clinics, HIV counseling and testing sites, correctional facilities, and drug treatment clinics). In addition, clinicians should identify and vaccinate persons with risk factors for HBV infection in other settings.

Immunization Records

Every individual should have an immunization record that is up to date and that contains information about each dose of vaccine received, including the date. Patients should be asked to bring this record with them to all health care visits, and the record should be reviewed to ensure that it is up to date. Official immunization record cards should be used; they are available through local or state health departments. The National Childhood Vaccine Injury Act requires that all providers of vaccines covered by the program (i.e., listed on the vaccine injury table) (DTP or components, IPV, MMR or components, Hib, hepatitis B, varicella, and pneumococcal conjugate) vaccines record on the patient's permanent medical record the date, manufacturer, and lot number of each dose of vaccine administered and the name of the person giving the vaccine.[240] It is prudent to record the same information for other vaccines as well.

Parent and Patient Education

All patients (or their parents or guardians) should be informed of the benefits and the risks associated with vaccination. The discussion should be carried out in language that is comprehensible to the recipient (or parent or guardian), and ample opportunity for questions and discussion should be given. Vaccine Information Statements have been developed for (1) MMR or components, (2) diphtheria and tetanus toxoids and pertussis vaccine or components, (3) inactivated polio vaccine, (4) Hib vaccine, (5) hepatitis B vaccine, (6) varicella vaccine, and (7) pneumococcal conjugate vaccine. The National Childhood Vaccine Injury Act requires use of these statements with these vaccines. In addition, the Public Health Service has developed forms that explain the benefits as well as the risks of vaccination for use with pneumococcal and influenza vaccines. Interested health care providers can receive copies of these forms through local health departments or from the Internet (*www.cdc.gov/nip/publications/vis/default.htm*).

Simultaneous Administration and Intervals Between Immunizations

Most of the widely used antigens can be given safely and effectively at the same time.[1] In general, inactivated vaccines can be administered simultaneously at separate sites, and field observations indicate that simultaneous administration of the most widely used live virus vaccines has not resulted in impaired antibody responses or increased rates of adverse reactions.[214] When vaccines are administered simultaneously, they should be given in separate limbs. When this is not feasible, they should be separated by at least 1 to 2 inches. However, simultaneous administration of IG and MMR vaccines should be avoided because this may result in interference with antibody responses. With those vaccines, IG should not be given for at least 2 weeks after vaccination.

Persons receiving high doses of IG or other blood products may have impaired responses to vaccines for as long as 11 months depending on the dose received.[1,196] Persons who received standard doses of IG for hepatitis A prophylaxis can receive live vaccines 3 months after IG, whereas children treated for Kawasaki's disease with intravenous IG in a dose of 2 g/kg should be vaccinated ideally 11 months after the dose. Similar recommendations apply to varicella vaccine. IG does not appear to interfere with the response to yellow fever vaccines.[241] In general, the antigenic mass of inactivated vaccines is so great that IG will not interfere with the antibody response.

With live vaccines, there is the theoretical possibility of interference in the development of antibody responses when live vaccines are administered at intervals of 3 to 14 days. If more than one live vaccine is needed, the vaccines should be administered simultaneously or at intervals of approximately 1 month between different vaccines.[1] In general, there are no restrictions on intervals between doses of different inactivated vaccines or between different inactivated and live vaccines. The only exceptions are cholera and yellow fever vaccines, which should ideally be administered at least 3 weeks apart to achieve maximal immune responses to both vaccines.

Combination Vaccines

The routine immunization schedule has become increasingly complex over the years as more vaccines have been added. Currently, all children should be protected against 12 diseases. This can require as many as 20 injections of various vaccines by 18 months of age and an additional 4 injections by 18 years, a major challenge for any health care delivery system. This does not include influenza vaccine which requires two injections for children younger than 9 years when they are first vaccinated and then one injection annually. Combination vaccines can provide equivalent protection with substantially fewer doses.[242] Vaccines combining antigens against multiple diseases have been a part of the routine immunization schedule for years. These vaccines include DTaP, MMR, and Td. More recently combined hepatitis B–Hib (Comvax, Merck) vaccine has become available for use at 2, 4, and 12 to 15 months and a combined hepatitis B-hepatitis A (Twinrix; Glaxo SmithKline) vaccine has become available for vaccination of persons 18 years and older. The vaccine is given in a three dose series.

In 2002, a combined DTaP, hepatitis B, and IPV vaccine (Pediarix; Glaxo SmithKline) for use in infants at age 2, 4, and 6 months was licensed.[243] Immunogenicity and rates of most reactions following Pediarix are similar to administration of the individual vaccines. Pediarix is associated with higher rates of fever, generally low grade, than administration of the separate antigens. Use of Pediarix can reduce the number of injections needed by 18 months to 13 to 14 depending on the Hib preparation used, excluding influenza vaccine.

Because both Comvax and Pediarix contain antigens that cannot be administered prior to 6 weeks of age, an additional birth dose of single antigen hepatitis B vaccine is recommended, when the combination vaccines are used.

Interrupted Schedules

Immunologic memory induced by vaccines is usually long term. Therefore, when doses in a schedule of doses are missed, there is no need to restart the series. Instead, continue from where the schedule left off.[1,3]

Reporting of Disease and Adverse Events

Each state has laws requiring the reporting of certain communicable diseases. The list of reportable diseases generally includes all or most of the diseases preventable by vaccination.[245] Health care providers should ensure that each suspected case of vaccine-preventable disease is reported promptly to the local health department. Similarly, serious adverse events after immunization should be reported to the Vaccine Adverse Events Reporting System (VAERS). Forms for VAERS can be obtained by calling 800-822-7967. The National Childhood Vaccine Injury Act requires providers to report specified adverse events if they occur within a designated time frame following immunization (Table 319-8).[47,240,245] However, all serious events temporally related to vaccination should be reported regardless of whether or

TABLE 319-8 National Childhood Vaccine Injury Act Reporting and Compensation Tables[*]

Vaccine	Adverse Event	Interval from Vaccination to Onset of Event	
		For Reporting[†]	For Compensation[‡]
I. Tetanus toxoid-containing vaccines (e.g., DTaP, DTP-Hib, DT; Td, or TT)	A. Anaphylaxis or anaphylactic shock	0-7 days	0-4 hours
	B. Brachial neuritis	0-28 days	2-28 days
	C. Any acute complication or sequela (including death) of above events	Not applicable	Not applicable
	D. Events described in manufacturer's package insert as contraindications to additional doses of vaccine	See package insert	Not applicable
II. Pertussis antigen-containing vaccines (e.g., DTaP, DTP, P, DTP-Hib)	A. Anaphylaxis or anaphylactic shock	0-7 days	0-4 hours
	B. Encephalopathy (or encephalitis)	0-7 days	0-72 hours
	C. Any acute complication or sequela (including death) of above events	Not applicable	Not applicable
	D. Events described in manufacturer's package insert as contraindications to additional doses of vaccine	See package insert	Not applicable
III. Measles, mumps and rubella virus-containing vaccines in any combination (e.g., MMR, MR, M, R)	A. Anaphylaxis or anaphylactic shock	0-7 days	0-4 hours
	B. Encephalopathy (or encephalitis)	0-15 days	5-15 days
	C. Any acute complication or sequela (including death) of above events	Not applicable	Not applicable
	D. Events described in manufacturer's package insert as contraindications to additional doses of vaccine	See package insert	Not applicable
IV. Rubella virus-containing vaccines (e.g., MMR, MR, R)	A. Chronic arthritis	0-42 days	7-42 days
	B. Any acute complication or sequela (including death) of above event	Not applicable	Not applicable
	C. Events described in manufacturer's package insert as contraindications to additional doses of vaccine	See package insert	Not applicable
V. Measles virus-containing vaccines (e.g., MMR, MR, M)	A. Thrombocytopenic purpura	0-30 days	7-30 days
	B. Vaccine-Strain Measles Viral Infection in an immunodeficient recipient	0-6 months	0-6 months
	C. Any acute complication or sequela (including death) of above events	Not applicable	Not applicable
	D. Events described in manufacturer's package insert as contraindications to additional doses of vaccine	See package insert	Not applicable
VI. Polio live virus-containing vaccines (OPV)	A. Paralytic polio		
	–In a nonimmunodeficient recipient	0-30 days	0-30 days
	–In an immunodeficient recipient	0-6 months	0-6 months
	–In a vaccine assoc. community case	No limit	Not applicable
	B. Vaccine-strain polio viral infection		
	–In a nonimmunodeficient recipient	0-30 days	0-30 days
	–In an immunodeficient recipient	0-6 months	0-6 months
	–In a vaccine assoc. community case	No limit	Not applicable
	C. Any acute complication or sequela (including death) of above events	Not applicable	Not applicable
	D. Events described in manufacturer's package insert as contraindications to additional doses of vaccine	See package insert	Not applicable
VII. Polio inactivated-virus containing vaccines (e.g., IPV)	A. Anaphylaxis or anaphylactic shock	0-7 days	0-4 hours
	B. Any acute complication or sequela (including death) of above event	Not applicable	Not applicable
	C. Events described in manufacturer's package insert as contraindications to additional doses of vaccine	See package insert	Not applicable
VIII. Hepatitis B antigen-containing vaccines	A. Anaphylaxis or anaphylactic shock	0-7 days	0-4 hours
	B. Any acute complication or sequela (including death) of above event	Not applicable	Not applicable
	C. Events described in manufacturer's package insert as contraindications to additional doses of vaccine	See package insert	Not applicable
IX. *Hemophilus influenzae* type b (polysaccharide conjugate vaccines)	A. No condition specified for compensation	Not applicable	Not applicable
	B. Events described in manufacturer's package insert as contraindications to additional doses of vaccine	See package insert	Not applicable
X. Varicella vaccine	A. No condition specified for compensation	Not applicable	Not applicable
	B. Events described in manufacturer's package insert as contraindications to additional doses of vaccine	See package insert	Not applicable
XI. Rotavirus vaccine	A. No condition specified for compensation	Not applicable	Not applicable
	B. Events described in manufacturer's package insert as contraindications to additional doses of vaccine	See package insert	Not applicable
XII. Vaccines containing live, oral, rheusus-based rotavirus	A. Intussusception	0-30 days	0-30 days
	B. Events described in manufacturer's package insert as contraindications to additional doses of vaccine	See package insert	Not applicable
XIII. Pneumococcal conjugate vaccines	A. No condition specified for compensation	Not applicable	Not applicable
	B. Events described in manufacturer's package insert as contraindications to additional doses of vaccine	See package insert	Not applicable
XIV. Any new vaccine recommended by the Centers for Disease Control and Prevention for routine administration to children, after publication by Secretary, HHS of a notice of coverage.	A. No condition specified for compensation	Not applicable	Not applicable
	B. Events described in manufacturer's package insert as contraindications to additional doses of vaccine	Not applicable	Not applicable

[*]Effective date August 26, 2002. From 42 C.F.R. §100.3(a).

Continued

Qualifications and Aids to Interpretation

(1) <u>Anaphylaxis and anaphylactic shock</u> mean an acute, severe, and potentially lethal systemic allergic reaction. Most cases resolve without sequelae. Signs and symptoms begin minutes to a few hours after exposure. Death, if it occurs, usually results from airway obstruction caused by laryngeal edema or bronchospasm and may be associated with cardiovascular collapse. Other significant clinical signs and symptoms may include the following: Cyanosis, hypotension, bradycardia, tachycardia, arrhythmia, edema of the pharynx and/or trachea and/or larynx with stridor and dyspnea. Autopsy findings may include acute emphysema which results from lower respiratory tract obstruction, edema of the hypopharynx, epiglottis, larynx, or trachea and minimal findings of eosinophilia in the liver, spleen and lungs. When death occurs within minutes of exposure and without signs of respiratory distress, there may not be significant pathologic findings.

(2) <u>Encephalopathy.</u> For purposes of the Vaccine Injury Table, a vaccine recipient shall be considered to have suffered an encephalopathy only if such recipient manifests, within the applicable period, an injury meeting the description below of an acute encephalopathy, and then a chronic encephalopathy persists in such person for more than 6 months beyond the date of vaccination.

(i) An <u>acute encephalopathy</u> is one that is sufficiently severe so as to require hospitalization (whether or not hospitalization occurred).

(A) <u>For children less than 18 months of age</u> who present without an associated seizure event, an acute encephalopathy is indicated by a "significantly decreased level of consciousness" (see "D" below) lasting for at least 24 hours. Those children less than 18 months of age who present following a seizure shall be viewed as having an acute encephalopathy if their significantly decreased level of consciousness persists beyond 24 hours and cannot be attributed to a postictal state (seizure) or medication.

(B) <u>For adults and children 18 months of age or older</u>, an acute encephalopathy is one that persists for at least 24 hours and characterized by at least two of the following:

(1) A significant change in mental status that is not medication related; specifically a confusional state, or a delirium, or a psychosis;

(2) A significantly decreased level of consciousness, which is independent of a seizure and cannot be attributed to the effects of medication; and

(3) A seizure associated with loss of consciousness.

(C) Increased intracranial pressure may be a clinical feature of acute encephalopathy in any age group.

(D) A "significantly decreased level of consciousness" is indicated by the presence of at least one of the following clinical signs for at least 24 hours or greater (see paragraphs (2)(i)(A) and (2)(i)(B) of this section for applicable timeframes):

(1) Decreased or absent response to environment (responds, if at all, only to loud voice or painful stimuli);

(2) Decreased or absent eye contact (does not fix gaze upon family members or other individuals); or

(3) Inconsistent or absent responses to external stimuli (does not recognize familiar people or things).

(E) The following clinical features alone, or in combination, do not demonstrate an acute encephalopathy or a significant change in either mental status or level of consciousness as described above: Sleepiness, irritability (fussiness), high-pitched and unusual screaming, persistent inconsolable crying, and bulging fontanelle. Seizures in themselves are not sufficient to constitute a diagnosis of encephalopathy. In the absence of other evidence of an acute encephalopathy, seizures shall not be viewed as the first symptom or manifestation of the onset of an acute encephalopathy.

(ii) <u>Chronic encephalopathy</u> occurs when a change in mental or neurologic status, first manifested during the applicable time period, persists for a period of at least 6 months from the date of vaccination. Individuals who return to a normal neurologic state after the acute encephalopathy shall not be presumed to have suffered residual neurologic damage from that event; any subsequent chronic encephalopathy shall not be presumed to be a sequela of the acute encephalopathy. If a preponderance of the evidence indicates that a child's chronic encephalopathy is secondary to genetic, prenatal or perinatal factors, that chronic encephalopathy shall not be considered to be a condition set forth in the Table.

(iii) An encephalopathy shall not be considered to be a condition set forth in the Table if in a proceeding on a petition, it is shown by a preponderance of the evidence that the encephalopathy was caused by an infection, a toxin, a metabolic disturbance, a structural lesion, a genetic disorder or trauma (without regard to whether the cause of the infection, toxin, trauma, metabolic disturbance, structural lesion or genetic disorder is known). If at the time a decision is made on a petition filed under section 2111(b) of the Act for a vaccine-related injury or death, it is not possible to determine the cause by a preponderance of the evidence of an encephalopathy, the encephalopathy shall be considered to be a condition set forth in the Table.

(iv) In determining whether or not an encephalopathy is a condition set forth in the Table, the Court shall consider the entire medical record.

(3) <u>Seizure and convulsion.</u> For purposes of paragraphs (2) and (3) of this section, the terms, "seizure" and "convulsion" include myoclonic, generalized tonic-clonic (grand mal), and simple and complex partial seizures. Absence (petit mal) seizures shall not be considered to be a condition set forth in the Table. Jerking movements or staring episodes alone are not necessarily an indication of seizure activity.

(4) <u>Sequela.</u> The term "sequela" means a condition or event which was actually caused by a condition listed in the Vaccine Injury Table.

(5) <u>Chronic Arthritis.</u> For purposes of the Vaccine Injury Table, chronic arthritis may be found in a person with no history in the 3 years prior to vaccination of arthropathy (joint disease) on the basis of:

(A) Medical documentation, recorded within 30 days after the onset, of objective signs of acute arthritis (joint swelling) that occurred between 7 and 42 days after a rubella vaccination;

(B) Medical documentation (recorded within 3 years after the onset of acute arthritis) of the persistence of objective signs of intermittent or continuous arthritis for more than 6 months following vaccination:

(C) Medical documentation of an antibody response to the rubella virus.

For purposes of the Vaccine Injury Table, the following shall not be considered as chronic arthritis: Musculoskeletal disorders such as diffuse connective tissue diseases (including but not limited to rheumatoid arthritis, juvenile rheumatoid arthritis, systemic lupus erythematosus, systemic sclerosis, mixed connective tissue disease, polymyositis/dermatomyositis, fibromyalgia, necrotizing vasculitis and vasculopathies and Sjogren's Syndrome), degenerative joint disease, infectious agents other than rubella (whether by direct invasion or as an immune reaction), metabolic and endocrine diseases, trauma, neoplasms, neuropathic disorders, bone and cartilage disorders and arthritis associated with ankylosing spondylitis, psoriasis, inflammatory bowel disease, Reiter's syndrome, or blood disorders.

Arthralgia (joint pain) or stiffness without joint swelling shall not be viewed as chronic arthritis for purposes of the Vaccine Injury Table.

(6) <u>Brachial neuritis</u> is defined as dysfunction limited to the upper extremity nerve plexus (i.e., its trunks, divisions, or cords) without involvement of other peripheral (e.g., nerve roots or a single peripheral nerve) or central (e.g., spinal cord) nervous system structures. A deep, steady, often severe aching pain in the shoulder and upper arm usually heralds onset of the condition. The pain is followed in days or weeks by weakness and atrophy in upper extremity muscle groups. Sensory loss may accompany the motor deficits, but is generally a less notable clinical feature. The neuritis, or plexopathy, may be present on the same side as or the opposite side of the injection; it is sometimes bilateral, affecting both upper extremities. Weakness is required before the diagnosis can be made. Motor, sensory, and reflex findings on physical examination and the results of nerve conduction and electromyographic studies must be consistent in confirming that dysfunction is attributable to the brachial plexus. The condition should thereby be distinguishable from conditions that may give rise to dysfunction of nerve roots (i.e., radiculopathies) and peripheral nerves (i.e., including multiple mononeuropathies), as well as other peripheral and central nervous system structures (e.g., cranial neuropathies and myelopathies).

(7) <u>Thrombocytopenic purpura</u> is defined by a serum platelet count less than 50,000/mm^3. Thrombocytopenic purpura does not include cases of thrombocytopenia associated with other causes such as hypersplenism, autoimmune disorders (including alloantibodies from previous transfusions) myelodysplasias, lymphoproliferative disorders, congenital thrombocytopenia or hemolytic uremic syndrome. This does not include cases of immune (formerly called idiopathic) thrombocytopenic purpura (ITP) that are mediated, for example, by viral or fungal infections, toxins or drugs. Thrombocytopenic purpura does not include cases of thrombocytopenia associated with disseminated intravascular coagulation, as observed with bacterial and viral infections. Viral infections include, for example, those infections secondary to Epstein Barr virus, cytomegalovirus, hepatitis A and B, rhinovirus, human immunodeficiency virus (HIV), adenovirus, and dengue virus. An antecedent viral infection may be demonstrated by clinical signs and symptoms and need not be confirmed by culture or serologic testing. Bone marrow examination, if performed, must reveal a normal or an increased number of megakaryocytes in an otherwise normal marrow.

(8) <u>Vaccine-strain measles viral infection</u> is defined as a disease caused by the vaccine-strain that should be determined by vaccine-specific monoclonal antibody or polymerase chain reaction tests.

(9) <u>Vaccine-strain polio viral infection</u> is defined as a disease caused by poliovirus that is isolated from the affected tissue and should be determined to be the vaccine-strain by oligonucleotide or polymerase chain reaction. Isolation of poliovirus from the stool is not sufficient to establish a tissue specific infection or disease caused by vaccine-strain poliovirus.

†Taken from the Reportable Events Table (RET), which lists conditions reportable by law (42 USC 300aa-25) to the Vaccine Adverse Event Reporting System (VAERS), including conditions found in the manufacturer's package insert. In addition, individuals are encouraged to report any clinically significant or unexpected events (even if you are not certain the vaccine caused the event) for any vaccine, whether or not it is listed on the RET. Manufacturers are also required by regulation (21 CFR 600.80) to report to the VAERS program all adverse events made known to them for any vaccine. VAERS reporting forms and information can be obtained by calling 1-(800)-822-7967 or from their web site: *(www.vaers.org).*

From Evans G, Harris D, Levine EM. Legal Issues. In: Plotkin SA, Orenstein WA, Eds. 4th Edition on line. Philadelphia: WB Saunders; 2004:1591-1617.

not they are thought to be caused by the vaccine. Only through accurate reporting and follow-up of both disease and adverse vaccine effects can the changing balance of benefits and risks of vaccination be properly assessed.

Compensation for Vaccine Injuries

The National Childhood Vaccine Injury Act of 1986 established a no-fault compensation program for persons injured by vaccines.[47,240] Table 319-8 lists the covered vaccines, conditions, and time frames for which persons are eligible for compensation in the absence of other known causes for the events. All persons with alleged injuries from covered vaccines must file first under the compensation program. Persons who meet the criteria of the table (and other legal requirements) are entitled to compensation without proving that vaccine caused the injury. Persons alleging a condition not included in the table or who otherwise do not meet criteria in the table must prove that the vaccine was the cause. Individuals may accept decisions of the program or reject those decisions and go to the tort system. If compensation decisions are accepted, manufacturers and vaccine administrators are protected from litigation.[240] More information on the compensation program can be obtained by calling 800-338-2382 or through the Division of Vaccine Injury Compensation's Home Page: (*www.hrsa.gov/bhpr/vicp*).

Standards for Immunization Practices

To improve the quality of immunization delivery, standards for child and adolescent immunization practices as well as standards for adult immunization practices have been developed by the National Vaccine Advisory Committee (Tables 319-9 and 319-10).[248-251] These standards

TABLE 319-9 Standards for Child and Adolescent Immunization Practices

Availability of Vaccines
1. Vaccination services are readily available.
2. Vaccinations are coordinated with other health care services and provided in a Medical Home when possible.
3. Barriers to vaccination are identified and minimized.
4. Patient costs are minimized.

Assessment of Vaccination Status
5. Health care professionals review the vaccination and health status of patients at every encounter to determine which vaccines are indicated.
6. Health care professionals assess for and follow only medically accepted contraindications.

Effective Communication about Vaccine Benefits and Risks
7. Parents/guardians and patients are educated about the benefits and risks of vaccination in a culturally appropriate manner and in easy-to-understand language.

Proper Storage and Administration of Vaccines and Documentation of Vaccinations
8. Health care professionals follow appropriate procedures for vaccine storage and handling.
9. Up-to-date, written vaccination protocols are accessible at all locations where vaccines are administered.
10. Persons who administer vaccines and staff who manage or support vaccine administration are knowledgeable and receive on-going education.
11. Health care professionals simultaneously administer as many indicated vaccine doses as possible.
12. Vaccination records for patients are accurate, complete and easily accessible.
13. Health care professionals report adverse events following vaccination promptly and accurately to the Vaccine Adverse Event Reporting System (VAERS) and are aware of a separate program, the National Vaccine Injury Compensation Program (VICP).
14. All personnel who have contact with patients are appropriately vaccinated.

Implementation of Strategies to Improve Vaccination Coverage
15. Systems are used to remind parents/guardians, patients, and health care professionals when vaccinations are due and to recall those who are overdue.
16. Office- or clinic-based patient record reviews and vaccination coverage assessments are performed annually.
17. Health care professionals practice community-based approaches.

From National Vaccine Advisory Committee. Standards for Child and Adolescent Immunization Practices. Pediatrics. 2003;112:958-963.

seek to minimize missed opportunities for immunization, ensure appropriate contraindications are observed, and to assure that prospective vaccinees and/or their parents are adequately educated about vaccine risks and benefits. In addition, the standards include other measures to enhance the safe and effective use of vaccines.

Some of the more critical standards include providing vaccines in all health care settings; minimizing prevaccination requirements such as full physician evaluation when those services are not readily obtainable; screening for contraindications including, at a minimum, observation of the child, soliciting illness history from the parents, and verbally asking questions about contraindications; use of simultaneous immunization except when, in the judgment of the provider, nonsimultaneous vaccination will not compromise the immunization status of the patient; providing valid information on vaccine benefits and risks and regular audits of patient records to determine the vaccination levels of the patients in each provider's practice. To assist in using only valid contraindications, Table 319-11 has been created.

The Infectious Diseases Society of America has established 14 guidelines that combine relevant aspects of both the pediatric and adult standards.[250]

Methods to Improve Immunization Coverage

The Task Force on Community Preventive Services has carefully reviewed the literature to determine effective interventions to improve immunization coverage for children, adolescents, and adults.[251] Provider-based interventions have been some of the most successful.[252]

Two of the most important include assessment of immunization levels in a given practice with provision of information back to the provider and use of reminder-recall systems.

Studies have shown that providers (as well as parents) tend to overestimate the level of coverage in their patients (or children), and formal review of records can be very useful in making practitioners aware of the need to continue to pay attention.[251,253] Bushnell asked physicians and nurses from both public and private sectors in Massachusetts to es-

TABLE 319-10 Standards for Adult Immunization Practices

Make Vaccinations Available.
1. Adult vaccination services are readily available.
2. Barriers to receiving vaccines are identified and minimized.
3. Patient "out-of-pocket" vaccination costs are minimized.

Assess Patients' Vaccination Status.
4. Health care professionals routinely review the vaccination status of patients.
5. Health care professionals assess for valid contraindications.

Communicate Effectively with Patients.
6. Patients are educated about risks and benefits of vaccination in easy-to-understand language.

Administer and Document Vaccinations Properly.
7. Written vaccination protocols are available at all locations where vaccines are administered.
8. Persons who administer vaccines are properly trained.
9. Health care professionals recommend simultaneous administration of indicated vaccine doses.
10. Vaccination records for patients are accurate and easily accessible.
11. All personnel who have contact with patients are appropriately vaccinated.

Implement Strategies to Improve Vaccination Rates.
12. Systems are developed and used to remind patients and healthcare professionals when vaccinations are due and to recall patients who are overdue.
13. Standing orders for vaccinations are employed.
14. Regular assessments of vaccination coverage levels are conducted in a provider's practice.

Partner with the Community.
15. Patient-oriented and community-based approaches are used to reach target populations.

From Poland GH, Shefer AM, McCauley M, et al. Standards for Adult Immunization Practices. Am J Prev Med. 2003;25:144-150. Reprinted with permission from the American Journal of Preventive Medicine.

TABLE 319-11 Guide to Contraindications and Precautions to Immunizations

Vaccine	*True Contraindications and Precautions**	*Untrue (Vaccines Can Be Administered)*
General for all vaccines, including diphtheria and tetanus toxoids and acellular pertussis vaccine (DTaP); pediatric diphtheria-tetanus toxoid (DT); adult tetanus-diphtheria toxoid (Td); inactivated poliovirus vaccine (IPV); measles-mumps-rubella vaccine (MMR); *Haemophilius influenzae* type b vaccine (Hib); hepatitis A vaccine; hepatitis B vaccine; varicella vaccine; pneumococcal conjugate vaccine (PCV); influenza vaccine; and pneumococcal polysaccharide vaccine (PPV)	*Contraindications* Serious allergic reaction (e.g., anaphylaxis) after a previous vaccine dose Serious allergic reaction (e.g., anaphylaxis) to a vaccine component *Precautions* Moderate or severe acute illness with or without fever	Mild acute illness with or without fever Mild to moderate local reaction (i.e., swelling, redness, soreness); low-grade or moderate fever after previous dose Lack of previous physical examination in well-appearing person Current antimicrobial therapy Convalescent phase of illness Premature birth (hepatitis B vaccine is an exception in certain circumstances)† Recent exposure to an infectious disease History of penicillin allergy, other nonvaccine allergies, relatives with allergies, receiving allergen extract immunotherapy
DTaP	*Contraindications* Severe allergic reaction after a previous dose or to a vaccine component Encephalopathy (e.g., coma, decreased level of consciousness, prolonged seizures) within 7 days of administration of previous dose of DTP or DTaP Progressive neurologic disorder, including infantile spasms, uncontrolled epilepsy, progressive encephalopathy: defer DTaP until neurologic status clarified and stabilized. *Precautions* Fever of >40.5°C ≤48 hours after vaccination with previous dose of DTP or DTaP Collapse of shock-like state (i.e., hypotonic hyporesponsive episode) ≤48 hours after receiving a previous dose of DTP/DTaP Seizure ≤3 days within receiving a previous dose of DTP/DTaP§ Persistent, inconsolable crying lasting ≥3 hours ≤48 hours after receiving a previous dose of DTP/DTaP Moderate or severe acute illness with or without fever	Temperature of <40.5°C, fussiness or mild drowsiness after a previous dose of diphtheria toxoid-tetanus toxoid-pertussis vaccine (DTP)/DTaP Family history of seizures§ Family history of sudden infant death syndrome Family history of an adverse event after DTP or DTaP administration Stable neurologic conditions (e.g., cerebral palsy, well-controlled convulsions, developmental delay)
DT, Td	*Contraindications* Severe allergic reaction after a previous dose or to a vaccine component *Precautions* Guillain-Barré syndrome ≤6 weeks after previous dose of tetanus toxoid-containing vaccine Moderate or severe acute illness with or without fever	
IPV	*Contraindications* Severe allergic reaction to previous dose or vaccine component *Precautions* Pregnancy Moderate or severe acute illness with or without fever	
MMR¶	*Contraindications* Severe allergic reaction after a previous dose or to a vaccine component Pregnancy Known severe immunodeficiency (e.g., hematologic ad solid tumors; congenital immunodeficiency; long-term immunosuppressive therapy,** or severely symptomatic human immunodeficiency virus [HIV] infection) *Precautions* Recent (≤11 months) receipt of antibody-containing blood product (specific interval depends on product)§§ History of thrombocytopenia or thrombocytopenic purpura Moderate or severe acute illness with or without fever	Positive tuberculin skin test Simultaneous TB skin testing†† Breast-feeding Pregnancy of recipient's mother or other close or household contact Recipient is child-bearing-age female Immunodeficiency family member or household contact Asymptomatic or mildly symptomatic HIV infection Allergy to eggs

*Events or conditions listed as precautions should be reviewed carefully. Benefits and risks of administering a specific vaccine to a person under these circumstances should be considered. If the risk from the vaccine is believed to outweigh the benefit, the vaccine should not be administered. If the benefit of vaccination is believed to outweigh the risk, the vaccine should be administered. Whether and when to administer DTaP to children with proven or suspected underlying neurologic disorders should be decided on a case-by-case basis.

†Hepatitis B vaccination should be deferred for infants weighing <2000 grams if the mother is documented to be hepatitis B surface antigen (HbsAg)-negative at the time of the infant's birth. Vaccination can commence at chronological age 1 month. For infants born to HbsAg-positive women, hepatitis B immunoglobulin and hepatitis B vaccine should be administered at or soon after birth regardless of weight. See text for details.

§Acetaminophen or other appropriate antipyretic can be administered to children with a personal or family history of seizures at the time of DTaP vaccination and every 4-6 hours for 24 hours thereafter to reduce the possibility of postvaccination fever (American Academy of Pediatrics. Active immunization. In: Pickering LK, ed. 2000 Red Book: Report of the Committee on Infectious Diseases. 25th ed. Elk Grove Village, IL: American Academy of Pediatrics, 2000).

¶MMR and varicella vaccines can be administered on the same day. If not administered on the same day, these vaccines should be separated by ≥28 days.

**Substantially immunosuppressive steroid dose is considered to be ≥2 weeks of daily receipt of 20 mg or 2 mg/kg body weight of prednisone or equivalent.

††Measles vaccination can suppress tuberculin reactivity temporarily. Measles-containing vaccine can be administered on the same day as tuberculin skin testing. If testing cannot be performed until after the day of MMR vaccination, the test should be postponed for ≥4 weeks after the vaccination. If an urgent need exists to skin test, do so with the understanding that reactivity might be reduced by the vaccine.

§§See text for details.

¶If a vaccine experiences a presumed vaccine-related rash 7-25 days after vaccination, avoid direct contact with immunocompromised persons for the duration of the rash.

From Centers for Disease Control and Prevention (CDC). General Recommendations on Immunization. Recommendations of the Advisory Committee on Immunization Practices (ACIP) and the American Academy of Family Physicians (AAFP). MMWR Morb Mortal Wkly Rep 2002;51 (RR02);1-36.

Continued

TABLE 319-11 Guide to Contraindications and Precautions to Immunizations—cont'd

Vaccine	True Contraindications and Precautions*	Untrue (Vaccines Can Be Administered)
Hib	**Contraindications** Severe allergic reaction after a previous dose or to a vaccine component Age <6 weeks **Precaution** Moderate or severe acute illness with or without fever	—
Hepatitis B	**Contraindication** Severe allergic reaction after a previous dose or to a vaccine component **Precautions** Infant weighing <2000 g† Moderate or severe acute illness with or without fever	Pregnancy Autoimmune disease (e.g., systemic lupus erythematosis or rheumatoid arthritis)
Hepatitis A	**Contraindications** Severe allergic reaction after a previous dose or to a vaccine component **Precautions** Pregnancy Moderate or severe acute illness with or without fever	—
Varicella¶	**Contraindications** Severe allergic reaction after a previous dose or to a vaccine component Substantial suppression of cellular immunity Pregnancy **Precautions** Recent (≤11 months) receipt of antibody-containing blood product (specific interval depends on product)§§ Moderate or severe acute illness with or without fever	Pregnancy of recipient's mother or other close or household contact Immunodeficient family member or household contact¶¶ Asymptomatic or mildly symptomatic HIV infection Humoral immunodeficiency (e.g., agammaglobulinemia)
PCV	**Contraindication** Severe allergic reaction after a previous dose or to a vaccine component **Precaution** Moderate or severe acute illness with or without fever	—
Influenza	**Contraindication** Severe allergic reaction to previous dose or vaccine component, including egg protein **Precautions** Moderate of severe acute illness with or without fever	Nonsevere (e.g., contact) allergy to latex of thimerosal Concurrent administration of coumadin or aminophylline
PPV	**Contraindication** Severe allergic reaction after a previous dose or to a vaccine component **Precaution** Moderate or severe acute illness with or without fever	—

*Events or conditions listed as precautions should be reviewed carefully. Benefits and risks of administering a specific vaccine to a person under these circumstances should be considered. If the risk from the vaccine is believed to outweigh the benefit, the vaccine should not be administered. If the benefit of vaccination is believed to outweigh the risk, the vaccine should be administered. Whether and when to administer DTaP to children with proven or suspected underlying neurologic disorders should be decided on a case-by-case basis.

†Hepatitis B vaccination should be deferred for infants weighing <2000 grams if the mother is documented to be hepatitis B surface antigen (HbsAg)-negative at the time of the infant's birth. Vaccination can commence at chronological age 1 month. For infants born to HbsAg-positive women, hepatitis B immunoglobulin and hepatitis B vaccine should be administered at or soon after birth regardless of weight. See text for details.

§Acetaminophen or other appropriate antipyretic can be administered to children with a personal or family history of seizures at the time of DTaP vaccination and every 4-6 hours for 24 hours thereafter to reduce the possibility of postvaccination fever (American Academy of Pediatrics. Active immunization. In: Pickering LK, ed. 2000 Red Book: Report of the Committee on Infectious Diseases. 25th ed. Elk Grove Village, IL: American Academy of Pediatrics, 2000).

¶MMR and varicella vaccines can be administered on the same day. If not administered on the same day, these vaccines should be separated by ≥28 days.

**Substantially immunosuppressive steroid dose is considered to be ≥2 weeks of daily receipt of 20 mg or 2 mg/kg body weight of prednisone or equivalent.

††Measles vaccination can suppress tuberculin reactivity temporarily. Measles-containing vaccine can be administered on the same day as tuberculin skin testing. If testing cannot be performed until after the day of MMR vaccination, the test should be postponed for ≥4 weeks after the vaccination. If an urgent need exists to skin test, do so with the understanding that reactivity might be reduced by the vaccine.

§§See text for details.

¶¶If a vaccine experiences a presumed vaccine-related rash 7-25 days after vaccination, avoid direct contact with immunocompromised persons for the duration of the rash.

From Centers for Disease Control and Prevention (CDC). General Recommendations on Immunization. Recommendations of the Advisory Committee on Immunization Practices (ACIP) and the American Academy of Family Physicians (AAFP). MMWR Morb Mortal Wkly Rep 2002;51 (RR02);1-36.

timate immunization coverage of their patient populations. Estimates ranged from 85% to 100%. Record reviews documented a median coverage of 61% (range 19% to 93%).[254] Providing this information back to providers has been shown to lead to improvements in coverage.[257]

Reminder systems entail providing reminders to patients and parents or providers that an individual is due for an immunization. Recall systems notify individuals that they are past due for an immunization. Both patient and provider reminder-recall systems have been extensively studied and demonstrated effective.[253] The ACIP, American Academy of Pediatrics, and American Academy of Family Physicians have recommended "the regular use of R-R (reminder-recall) systems by public and private health-care providers in settings that have not achieved high documented levels of age-appropriate vaccinations."[256]

Immunization registries are information systems that can automate assessment, reminder and recall, and a number of other activities, such as assisting the practitioner in deciding whether a vaccine is needed, consolidating multiple records into a single complete record for a given individual, generating immunization records, and generating immunization coverage information for reports such as those called for in managed care settings by the Health Plan Employer Data Information System.[257] Registries are increasingly being developed and used throughout the United States and there is a Healthy People 2010 objective to "increase to 95% the number of children enrolled in a fully functional population-based immunization registry (birth through age 5 years)."[258] Many public health authorities believe that a nationwide network of community-state population-based registries capable of exchanging information while maintaining privacy and confidentiality is essential to maintain the improvements in vaccine coverage that have been achieved.

Sources of Information

Important sources for information about vaccines include the following:

Official Package Circular. Manufacturers provide product-specific information along with each vaccine; some of these are reproduced in their entirety in the *Physicians' Desk Reference* and are dated.

Morbidity and Mortality Weekly Report (MMWR). This report is published weekly by the Centers for Disease Control and Prevention (CDC) and contains vaccine recommendations, reports of specific disease activity, policy statements, and regular and special recommendations of the ACIP. The MMWR will contain any necessary updated information on the ACIP recommendations. The MMWR can be accessed electronically for free at *www.cdc.gov/mmwr.* Subscriptions are available from Superintendent of Documents, U.S. Government Printing Office, Washington, D.C. 20402-9235 (202-783-3238). ACIP recommendations are also available at http://www.cdc.gov/nip/ACIP.

Health Information for International Travel. The CDC publishes an annual booklet as a guide to requirements and recommendations for specific immunizations and health practices for travel to various countries. This publication is available on the Internet at *www.cdc.gov/travel/yb* and may be purchased from The Public Health Foundation (1-877-252-1200 or *http://bookstore.phf.org*).

Travelers' health information can also be obtained through a 24-hour hotline operated by the CDC (404-332-4559). In addition, travel information can be accessed at http://www.cdc.gov/travel. Hard copies of specific recommendations can be received from the CDC FAX Information Service (404-332-4565).

Advisory Memoranda. Memoranda are published when necessary by the CDC to advise international travelers or those who provide information to travelers about specific outbreaks of communicable diseases abroad. These memoranda include health information for prevention and specific recommendations for immunization and may currently be obtained at no cost by writing to the Travelers Health Section, Division of Quarantine, Centers for Disease Control and Prevention, Atlanta, GA 30333, to request placement on the mailing list (888-232-3228).

Report of the Committee on Infectious Diseases of the American Academy of Pediatrics (Red Book). The full report containing recommendations on all licensed vaccines is usually updated every 3 years. The most recent Red Book was published in 2003. It can be ordered from American Academy of Pediatrics, PO Box 927, Elk Grove Village, IL 60009-0927.

Control of Communicable Diseases Manual. The American Public Health Association publishes this manual at approximately 5-year intervals. The 17th edition (2000) is currently available. The manual contains valuable information concerning infectious diseases; their occurrence worldwide; immunization, diagnostic, and therapeutic information; and up-to-date recommendations on isolation and other control measures for each disease presented. It can be ordered from the American Public Health Association, 1015 Fifteenth Street, N.W., Washington, DC 20005.

Guide for Adult Immunization. The American College of Physicians and the Infectious Diseases Society of America produce a guide for physicians caring for adults. The third edition was published in 1994, and a revision is imminent. It can be ordered from Subscriber Services, the American College of Physicians, Independence Mall West, 6th Street at Race, Philadelphia, PA 19106-1572 (800-523-1546, ext. 2600). It can also be ordered on line at *www.acponline. org/catalog/books/guide_imm.htm.*

Technical Bulletins of the American College of Obstetricians and Gynecologists (ACOG). ACOG bulletins, which are updated periodically, contain important information on immunization of women. A set can be ordered from American College of Obstetricians and Gynecologists, Attention: Resource Center, 409 12th Street, S.W., Washington, DC 20024-2188.

Health Departments. Most state and many local health departments provide routine immunizations, immunization cards, and schedules to patients. They also send out routine reports of disease incidence.

Centers for Disease Control and Prevention National Immunization Program. Toll free numbers are available for inquiries from both providers and the general public (800-232-2522, English; 800-232-0233, Spanish). Inquiries can also be sent to the CDC by electronic mail (nipinfo@cdc.gov). The National Immunization Program operates an Internet site to provide information to both the general public and professionals (*www.cdc.gov/nip*). Specific vaccine safety issues are addressed at *www.cdc.gov/nip/vacsafe.*

Additional Information. Additional information can be obtained from city, county, or state health departments, medical schools, and large hospitals. Specific questions can be addressed to the National Immunization Program, Centers for Disease Control and Prevention, Atlanta, GA 30333. CDC Immunization Voice/FAX Information System: Voice, 404-332-4553. Documents FAX, 404-332-4565.

REFERENCES

1. Centers for Disease Control and Prevention. General Recommendations on Immunization. Recommendations of the Advisory Committee on Immunization Practices (ACIP) and the American Academy of Family Physicians (AAFP). MMWR Morb Mortal Wkly Rep. 2002;51(RR-02):1-36.
2. Centers for Disease Control and Prevention. Thimerosal in vaccines: A joint statement of the American Academy of Pediatrics and the Public Health Service. MMWR Morb Mortal Wkly Rep. 1999;48:563-565.
3. Atkinson WL, Pickering LK, Watson JC, Peter G. General Immunization Practices. In: Plotkin SA. Orenstein WA, eds. Vaccines. 4th ed. Philadelphia, WB Saunders Company; 2004:91-122.
4. Claman HN. The biology of the immune response. JAMA. 1992;268:2790-2796.
5. McDevitt HO. Regulation of the immune response by the major histocompatibility complex system. N Engl J Med. 1980;303:1514-1517.
6. Vogel FR, Hem SL. Immunologic adjuvants. In: Plotkin SA, Orenstein WA, eds. Vaccines, 4th ed. Philadelphia, WB Saunders Company; 2004:69-79.
7. Shaw FE, Guess HA, Roets JM, et al. Effect of anatomic injection site, age and smoking on the immune response to hepatitis B vaccination. Vaccine. 1989;7:425-430.
8. Kaufmann SHE, Sher A, Ahmed R, eds. Immunology of Infectious Diseases. Washington, DC: American Society for Microbiology Press; 2002.
9. Zinkernagel RM, Hengartner H. Regulation of the immune response by antigen. Science. 2001;293:251-253.
10. Pulendran B, Palucka K, Banchereau J. Sensing pathogens and tuning immune responses. Science. 2001;293:253-256.
11. Kotb M, Calandra T: Cytokines and Chemokines in Infectious Diseases Handbook. Totowa, NJ: Humana Press; 2003.
12. Ernsty PB, Song F, Klimpel GR, et al. Regulation of the mucosal immune response. Am J Trop Med Hyg 1999; 60:2-9.
13. Ezekowitz RAB, Hoffmann JA, eds. Innate Immunity. Totowa, NJ: Humana Press; 2003.
14. Germain RN: The art of the probable: System control in the adaptive immune system. Science 2001;293:240-245.
15. Lieberman JM, Marcy SM, Partridge S, Ward JI. Evaluation of a hepatitis A vaccine in infants: Effect of maternal antibodies on the antibody response. Abstracts of the Infectious Diseases Society of America 36th Annual Meeting, November 12-15, 1998, Denver, CO.
16. Lanzavecchia A. Antigen-specific interaction between T and B-cells. Nature. 1985;314:537-539.
17. Arai K, Lee F, Miyajima A, et al. Cytokines: Coordinators of immune and inflammatory responses. Annu Rev Biochem. 1990;59:783-836.
18. Reinherz EL, Schlossman SF. Regulation of the immune response-inducer and suppressor T lymphocyte subsets in human beings. N Engl J Med. 1980;303:370-373.
19. William AF, Barclay AN. The immune globulin super-family-domains for cell surface recognition. Ann Rev Immunol. 1988;6:381-405.
20. Baker PJ. Homeostatic control of antibody responses. A model based on the recognition of cell-associated antibody by regulatory T-cells. Transplant Rev. 1974;26:1-20.
21. Fulginiti VA, Eller JJ, Donnie AW, et al. Altered reactivity to measles virus: Atypical measles in children previously immunized with inactivated measles virus vaccines. JAMA. 1967;202:1075-1080.
22. MacDonald NE, Halperin SA, Law BJ, et al. Induction of immunologic memory by conjugated vs. plain meningococcal C polysaccharide vaccine in toddlers: A randomized controlled trial. JAMA. 1998;280:1685-1689.
23. Offit PA, Hackett CS. Addressing parent's concerns: Do vaccines cause allergic or autoimmune diseases? Pediatrics. 2003;111:653-659.
24. Offit PA, Quarles J, Gerber MA, et al. Addressing parents' concerns: Do multiple vaccines overwhelm or weaken the infant's immune system? Pediatrics. 2002;109:124-129.
25. Institute of Medcine: Immunization Safety Review: Multiple Immunizations and Immune Dysfunction. National Academy Press, Washington, DC. 2002 - available at www.iom.edu/immsafety.
26. Watson JC, Pearson JA, Markowitz LE, et al. An evaluation of measles revaccination among school-entry-aged children. Pediatrics. 1996;97:613-618.

27. McGee JR, Mestecky J, Dertzbaugh MT, et al. The mucosal immune system: From fundamental concepts to vaccine development. Vaccine. 1992;10:75-88.

28. Milgrom F, Abeyounis CJ, Kano K. Principles of Immunological Diagnosis in Medicine. Philadelphia: Lea & Febiger; 1981.

29. Ellis RW. Technologies for making new vaccines. In: Plotkin SA, Orenstein WA eds. Vaccines. 4th ed. Philadelphia: WB Saunders; 2004:1177-1198.

30. Centers for Disease Control and Prevention. Measles - United States, 1999. MMWR Morb Mortal Wkly Rep. 2000;49:557-560.

31. Centers for Disease Control and Prevention. Recommendations of the International Task Force for Disease Eradication. MMWR Morb Mortal Wkly Rep. 1993;42:1-38.

32. Centers for Disease Control and Prevention. Progress Toward Global Eradication of Poliomyelitis, January 2003—April 2004. MMWR Morb Mortal Wkly Rep. 2004;53:532-535.

33. Centers for Disease Control and Prevention. Certification of Poliomyelitis Eradication - European Region, June 2002. MMWR Morb Mortal Wkly Rep. 2002;51:572-574.

34. Centers for Disease Control and Prevention. Certification of Poliomyelitis Eradication–Western Pacific Region, October 2000. MMWR Morb Mortal Wkly Rep. 2001;50:1-3.

35. Centers for Disease Control and Prevention. Certification of poliomyelitis eradication—the Americas, 1994. MMWR Morb Mortal Wkly Rep. 1994;43:720-722.

36. Peltola H, Kilpi T, Anttila M. Rapid disappearance of *Haemophilus influenzae* type b meningitis after routine childhood immunization with conjugate vaccines. Lancet. 1992;340:592-594.

37. Centers for Disease Control and Prevention. Progress toward eliminating *Haemophilus influenzae* type b disease among infants and children—United States, 1987-1997. MMWR Morb Mortal Wkly Rep. 1998;47:993-998.

38. Centers for Disease Control and Prevention. Pertussis vaccination: Use of acellular pertussis vaccines among infants and young children: Recommendations of the Advisory Committee on Immunization Practices (ACIP). MMWR Morb Mortal Wkly Rep. 1997;46:1-25.

39. Edwards KM, Decker MD. Pertussis vaccine. In: Plotkin SA, Orenstein WA, eds. Vaccines. 4th ed. Philadelphia: WB Saunders; 2004:471-528.

40. ACIP. Use of diphtheria toxoid-tetanus toxoid-acellular pertussis vaccine as a five-dose series. Supplemental recommendations of the Advisory Committee on Immunization Practices (ACIP). MMWR 2000;49 (No. RR-13):1-8.

41. Centers for Disease Control and Prevention. Prevention of varicella: Recommendations of the Advisory Committee on Immunization Practices (ACIP). MMWR Morb Mortal Wkly Rep. 1996;45:1-36.

42. Izurieta HS, Strebel PM, Blake PA. Postlicensure effectiveness of varicella vaccine during an outbreak in a child care center. JAMA. 1997;278:1495-1499.

43. Centers for Disease Control and Prevention. Impact of vaccines universally recommended for children—United States, 1990-1998. MMWR Morb Mortal Wkly Rep. 1999;48:243-248.

44. Howson CP, Howe CJ, Fineberg HV, eds. Institute of Medicine. Adverse Effects of Pertussis and Rubella Vaccines. Washington, DC: National Academy Press; 1991.

45. Stratton KR, Howe CJ, Johnston RB Jr, eds. Institute of Medicine. Adverse Events Associated with Childhood Vaccines. Evidence Bearing on Causation. Washington, DC: National Academy Press; 1994.

46. Howson CP, Fineberg HV. Adverse events following pertussis and rubella vaccines: Summary of a report by the Institute of Medicine. JAMA. 1992;267:392-396.

47. Chen RT, Davis RL, Sheedy KM. Safety of Immunizations. In: Plotkin SA, Orenstein WA, eds. Vaccines. 4th ed. Philadelphia, WB Saunders; 2004;1557-1581.

48. Centers for Disease Control and Prevention. Poliomyelitis prevention in the United States: Introduction of a sequential vaccination schedule of inactivated poliovirus vaccine followed by oral poliovirus vacine. MMWR Morb Mortal Wkly Rep. 1997;46:1-25.

49. Rantala H, Cherry JD, Shields WD, Uhari M. Epidemiology of Guillain-Barré syndrome in children: Relationship of oral polio vaccine administration to occurrence. J Pediatr. 1994;124:220-223.

50. Slater PE, Ben-Zvi T, Fogel A, et al. Absence of an association between rubella vaccination and arthritis in underimmune postpartum women. Vaccine. 1995;13:1529-1532.

51. Frenkel LM, Nielson K, Garakian A, et al. A search for persistent rubella virus infection in persons with chronic symptoms after rubella and rubella immunization and in patients with juvenile rheumatoid arthritis. Clin Infect Dis. 1996;22:287-294.

52. Ray R, Black S, Shinefield H, et al. Risk of chronic arthropathy among women after rubella vaccination. JAMA. 1997;278:551-556.

53. Committee on Infectious Diseases. American Academy of Pediatrics, Report of the Committee on Infectious Diseases. 26th ed. Elk Grove Village, Ill: American Academy of Pediatrics; 2003.

54. American College of Physicians Task Force on Adult Immunization and Infectious Diseases Society of America. Guide for Adult Immunization. 3rd ed. Philadelphia: American College of Physicians; 1994.

55. Centers for Disease Control and Prevention. Recommended childhood and adolescent immunization schedule—United States, January-June 2004. MMWR Morb Mortal Wkly Rep. 2004;53:Q1-Q4, No 16.

56. Centers for Disease Control and Prevention. Recommended adult immunization schedule—United States, 2003—2004. MMWR Morb Mortal Wkly Rep. 2003;52:965-969.

57. Centers for Disease Control and Prevention. Use of anthrax vaccine in response to terrorism: Supplemental recommendations of the Advisory Committee on Immunization Practices. MMWR Morb Mortal Wkly Rep. 2002;45:1024-6.

58. ACIP. Use of anthrax vaccine in the United States. Recommendations of the Advisory Committee on Immunization Practices (ACIP). MMWR Morb Mortal Wkly Rep. 2000;49 (No. RR-15):1-20.

59. Friedlander AM, Pittman PR, Parker GW. Anthrax vaccine: Evidence for safety and efficacy against inhalational anthrax. JAMA. 1999;282:2104-2106.

60. Brachman PS, Gold H, Plotkin SA, et al. Field evaluation of a human anthrax vaccine. Am J Publ Hlth. 1962;52:632-645.

61. Abramowicz M. Anthrax vaccine. Med Lett. 1998;40:52-53.

62. Sever JL, Brenner AI, Gale AD, et al. Safety of anthrax vaccine: A review by the Anthrax Vaccine Expert Committee (AVEC) of adverse events reported to the Vaccine Adverse Event Reporting System (VAERS). Pharmacoepidemiol Drug Saf. 2002;11:189-202.

63. Lange JL, Lesikar SE, Rubertone MV, Brundage JF. Comprehensive systematic surveillance for adverse effects of anthrax vaccine adsorbed, US Armed Forces, 1998-2000. Vaccine. 2003;21:1620-1628.

64. Leppla SH, Robbins JB, Schneerson R, Shiloach J. Development of an improved vaccine for anthrax. J Clin Invest. 2002;110:141-144.

65. Snider DE, Rieder HL, Combs D, et al. Tuberculosis in children. Pediatr Infect Dis J. 1988;7:271-278.

66. Rodrigues LC, Diwan K, Wheeler JG. Protective effect of BCG against tuberculous meningitis and miliary tuberculosis: A metaanalysis. Int J Epidemiol. 1993;22:1154-1158.

67. Colditz GA, Brewer TF, Berkey CS, et al. Efficacy of BCG vaccine in prevention of tuberculosis:Metaanalysis of the published literature. JAMA. 1994;271:698-702.

68. Centers for Disease Control and Prevention. The role of BCG vaccine in the prevention and control of tuberculosis in the United States. A joint statement by the Advisory Council for the Elimination of Tuberculosis and the Advisory Committee on Immunization Practices. MMWR Morb Mortal Wkly Rep. 1996;45:1-18.

69. Centers for Disease Control and Prevention. Recommendations of the Immunization Practices Advisory Committee (ACIP): Cholera vaccine. MMWR Morb Mortal Wkly Rep. 1988;37:617-624.

70. Centers for Disease Control and Prevention. Recommendation of the Immunization Practices Advisory Committee (ACIP): Diphtheria, tetanus, and pertussis: Guidelines for vaccine prophylaxis and other preventive measures. MMWR Morb Mortal Wkly Rep. 1991;40:1-28.

71. Centers for Disease Control and Prevention. Recommendations of the Immunization Practices Advisory Committee (ACIP): *Haemophilus* b conjugate vaccines for prevention of *Haemophilus influenzae* type b disease among infants and children two months of age and older. MMWR Morb Mortal Wkly Rep. 1991;40:1-17.

72. Centers for Disease Control and Prevention. Recommendations of the Immunization Practices Advisory Committee (ACIP): Recommendations for use of *Haemophilus b* conjugate vaccines and a combined diphtheria tetanus pertussis and *Haemophilus b* vaccine. MMWR Morb Mortal Wkly Rep. 1993;42(No. RR-13):1-15.

73. Anderson EL, Decker MD, Englund JA, et al. Interchangeability of conjugated *Haemophilus influenzae* type b vaccines in infants. JAMA. 1995;273:849-853.

74. Greenberg DP, Lieberman JM, Marcy SM, et al. Enhanced antibody responses in infants given different sequences of heterogeneous *Haemophilus influenzae* type b conjugate vaccines. J Pediatr. 1995;126:206-211.

75. Bewley KM, Schwab JG, Ballanco GA, Daum RS. Interchangeability of *Haemophilus influenzae* type b vaccines in the primary series: Evaluation of a two-dose mixed regimen. Pediatrics. 1996;98:898-904.

76. Centers for Disease Control and Prevention. FDA approval of use of *Haemophilus b* conjugate vaccine reconstituted with diphtheria-tetanus-pertussis vaccine for infants and children. MMWR Morb Mortal Wkly Rep. 1993;42:964-965.

77. Centers for Disease Control and Prevention. Unlicensed use of combination of *Haemophilus influenzae* type b conjugate vaccine and diphtheria and tetanus toxoid and acellular pertussis vaccine for infants. MMWR Morb Mortal Wkly Rep. 1998;47:787.

78. Innis BL, Snitbhan R, Kunasol P, et al. Protection against hepatitis A by an inactivated vaccine. JAMA. 1994;271:1328-1334.

79. Werzberger A, Mensch B, Kuter B, et al. A controlled trial of a formalin-inactivated hepatitis A vaccine in healthy children. N Engl J Med. 1992;327:453-457.

80. Centers for Disease Control and Prevention. Prevention of hepatitis A through active or passive immunization: Recommendations of the Advisory Committee on Immunization Practices (ACIP). MMWR Morb Mortal Wkly Rep. 1996;45:1-30.

81. Bell BP, Shapiro CN, Alter MJ, et al. The diverse patterns of hepatitis A epidemiology in the United States—implications for vaccination strategies. J Infect Dis. 1998;178:1579-1584.

82. Centers for Disease Control and Prevention. Prevention of hepatitis A through active or passive immunization: Recommendations of the Advisory Committee on Immunization Practices (ACIP). MMWR Morb Mortal Wkly Rep. 1999;48(RR-12).

83. Shapiro CN, Letson GW, Kuehn D, et al. Effect of maternal antibody on immunogenicity of hepatitis A vaccine in infants. Abstract H61 in Abstracts of the 35th Interscience Conference on Antimicrobial Agents and Chemotherapy, San Francisco, CA, September 17-20, 1995.

84. Green MS, Cohen D, Lerman Y, et al. Depression of the immune response to an inactivated hepatitis A vaccine administered concomitantly with immune globulin. J Infect Dis. 1993;168:740-743.

85. 29 CFR 1910.1030

86. Centers for Disease Control and Prevention. Recommendations of the Immunization Practices Advisory Committee: Hepatitis B virus: A comprehensive strategy for eliminating transmission in the United States through universal childhood vaccination. MMWR Morb Mortal Wkly Rep. 1991;40:1-25.

87. Centers for Disease Control and Prevention. Update: Recommendations to prevent hepatitis B virus transmission—United States. MMWR Morb Mortal Wkly Rep. 1995;44:574-575.

88. Biroscak BJ, Fiore AE, Fasano N, et al. Impact of the thimerosal controversy on hepatitis B vaccine coverage of infants born to women of unknown hepatitis B surface antigen status in Michigan. Pediatrics. 2003;111:e645-e649.

89. Centers for Disease Control and Prevention. Immunization of adolescents: Recommendations of the Advisory Committee on Immunization Practices, the American Academy of Pediatrics, the American Academy of Family Physicians, and the American Medical Association. MMWR Morb Mortal Wkly Rep. 1996;45:1-16.

90. Mast E, Mahoney F, Kane M, Margolis H. Hepatitis B Vaccine. In: Plotkin SA, Orenstein WA eds. Vaccines. 4th ed. Philadelphia: WB Saunders; 2004:299-337.

91. Wise RP, Kiminyo KP, Salive ME. Hair loss after routine immunizations. JAMA. 1997;278:1176-1178.

92. Pirmohamed M, Winstanley P. Hepatitis B vaccine and neurotoxicity. Postgrad Med J. 1997;73:462-463.

93. DeStefano F, Verstraeten T, Jackson LA, et al., the Vaccine Safety Datalink Research Group. Vaccinations and risk of central nervous syste demyelinating disease in adults. Arch Neurol. 2003;60:504-509.

94. Expanded Programme on Immunization (EPI). Lack of evidence that hepatitis B vaccine causes multiple sclerosis. Wkly Epidemiol Rec. 1997;72:149-152.

95. Institute of Medicine. Hepatitis B vaccine and demyelinating neurological disorders. Washington, DC: National Academy Press; 2002.

96. Gross PA, Hermogenes AW, Sacks HS, et al. Efficacy of influenza vaccine in elderly persons: A meta-analysis and review of the literature. Ann Intern Med. 1994;121:947-952.

97. Patriarca PA, Arden NH, Koplan JP, et al. Prevention and control of type A influenza infections in nursing homes: Benefits and costs of four approaches using vaccination and amantadine. Ann Intern Med. 1987;107:732-740.

98. Fukuda K, Levandowski RA, Bridges CB, Cox NJ. Inactivated influenza vaccines. In: Plotkin SA, Orenstein WA eds. Vaccines. 4th ed. Philadelphia: WB Saunders: 2004:339-370.

99. Hoberman A, Greenberg DP, Paradise JL, et al. Effectiveness of inactivated influenza vaccine in preventing acute otitis media in young children: A randomized controlled trial. JAMA. 2004;290:1608-1616.

100. Centers for Disease Control and Prevention. Prevention and control of influenza. Recommendations of the Advisory Committee on Immunization Practices (ACIP). MMWR Morb Mortal Wkly Rep. 2003;52 (RR08):1-36.

101. Centers for Disease Control and Prevention. Prevention and control of influenza. Recommendations of the Advisory Committee on Immunization Practices (ACIP). MMWR Morb Mortal Wkly Rep. 2004;53(RR-6):1-40.

102. Schonberger LB, Bregman DJ, Sullivan-Bolyai JZ, et al. Guillain-Barré syndrome following vaccination in the National Influenza Immunization Program, United States, 1976-1977. Am J Epidemiol, 1979;110:105-123.

103. Lasky T, Terracciano GJ, Magder L, et al. The Guillain-Barré syndrome and the 1992-1993 and 1993-1994 influenza vaccines. N Engl J Med. 1998;339:1797-1802.

104. Murphy KR, Strunk RC. Safe administration of influenza vaccine in asthmatic children hypersensitive to egg proteins. J Pediatr. 1985;106:931-933.

105. Institute of Medicine. Immunization Safety Review: Influenza vaccine and neurological complications. National Academy Press 2003 available at *www.nap.edu.*

106. Centers for Disease Control. Using live, attenuated influenza vaccine for prevention and control of influenza. Supplemental recommendations of the Advisory Committee on Immunization Practices. Morbid Mortal Wkly Rep. 2003;52(RR 13):1-8.

107. Hoke CH, Nisalak A, Sangawhipa N, et al. Protection against Japanese encephalitis by inactivated vaccines. N Engl J Med. 1988;319:609-614.

108. Centers for Disease Control and Prevention. Recommendations of the Immunization Practices Advisory Committee (ACIP): Inactivated Japanese encephalitis virus vaccine. MMWR Morb Mortal Wkly Rep. 1993;42:1-15.

109. Pabst HF, Spady DW, Marusyk RG, et al. Reduced measles immunity in infants in a well-vaccinated population. Pediatr Infect Dis J. 1992;11:525-529.

110. Centers for Disease Control and Prevention. Measles, mumps and rubella—vaccine use and strategies for elimination of measles, rubella, and congenital rubella syndrome and control of mumps: Recommendations of the Advisory Committee on Immunization Practices (ACIP). MMWR Morb Mortal Wkly Rep. 1998;47:1-57.

111. Centers for Disease Control and Prevention. Immunization of health-care workers. MMWR Morb Mortal Wkly Rep. 1997;46:1-42.

112. Weber DJ, Rutala WA. Vaccines for health care workers. In: Plotkin SA, Orenstein WA, eds. Vaccines. 4th ed. Philadelphia: WB Saunders; 2004:1511-1537.

113. Griffin MR, Ray WA, Mortimer ER, et al. Risk of seizures after measles-mumps-rubella immunization. Pediatrics. 1991;88:881-885.

114. Centers for Disease Control and Prevention. Adverse events following immunization. Atlanta: U.S. Department of Health and Human Services, Public Health Service, CDC, 1989. (Surveillance Report No. 3, 1985-1986.)

115. Weibel RE, Caserta V, Benor DE, Evans G. Acute encephalopathy followed by permanent brain injury or death associated with further attenuated measles vaccines: A review of claims submitted to the National Vaccine Injury Compensation Program. Pediatrics. 1998;101:383-387.

116. Institute of Medicine: Immunization Safety Review: Measles - Mumps - Rubella Vaccine and Autism. National Academy Press 2001. Available at *www.nap.edu.*

117. ACIP. Meningococcal disease and college students. Recommendations of the Advisory Committee on Immunization Practices (ACIP). MMWR Morb Mortal Wkly Rep. 2000;49 [No. RR-7]:13-20.

118. ACIP. Prevention and control of meningococcal disease. Recommendations of the Advisory Committee on Immunization Practices (ACIP). MMWR Morb Mortal Wkly Rep. 2000;49 [No. RR-7]:1-10.

119. Riedo FX, Plikaytis BD, Broome CV. Epidemiology and prevention of meningococcal disease. Pediatr Infect Dis J. 1995;14:643-657.

120. Schiefle DW, Bjornson G, Boraston S. Local adverse effects of meningococcal vaccine. Can Med Assoc J. 1994;150:14-15.

121. Lepow ML, Beeler J, Randolph M, et al. Reactogenicity and immunogenicity of a quadrivalent combined meningococcal vaccine in children. J Infect Dis. 1986;154:1033-1036.

122. MacDonald NE, Halperin SA, Law SJ, et al. Induction of immunologic memory by conjugated vs plain meningococcal C polysaccharide vaccine in toddlers: A randomized controlled trial. JAMA. 1998;280:1685-1689.

123. Richmond P, Borrow R, Miller E, et al. Meningococcal serogroup C conjugate vaccine is immunogenic in infancy and primes for memory. J Infect Dis. 1999;179:1569-1572.

124. Richmond P, Kaczmarski E, Borrow R, et al. Meningococcal C polysaccharide vaccine induces immunologic hyporesponsiveness in adults that is overcome by meningococcal C conjugate vaccine, J Infect Dis. 2000;181:761-764.

125. Borrow R, Goldblatt D, Andrews N, et al. Influence of prior meningococcal C polysaccharide vaccination on the response and generation of memory after meningococcal C conjugate vaccination in young children. J Infect Dis. 2001;184:377-380.

126. Miller E, Salisbury D, Ramsay M. Planning, registration, and implementation of an immunization campaign against meningococcal serogroup C disease in the UK: A success story. Vaccine. 2002;20:S58-S67.

127. Balmer P, Borrow R, Miller E. Impact of meningococcal C conjugate vaccine in the UK. J Med Microbiol. 2002;51:717-722.

128. Ramsey ME, Andrews N, Kaczmarski E, Miller E. Efficacy of meningococcal serogroup C conjugate vaccine in teenagers and toddlers in England. Lancet. 2001;357:195-196.

129. Miller E, Goldacre M, Pugh S, et al. Risk of aseptic meningitis after measles, mumps, and rubella vaccine in UK children. Lancet. 1993;341:979-982.

130. da Silveira CM, Kmetzsch CI, Mohrdieck R, et al. The risk of aseptic meningitis associated with the Leningrad-Zagreb mumps vaccine strain following mass vaccination with measles-mumps-rubella vaccine, Rio Grande do Sul, Brazil, 1997. Int J Epidemiol. 2002;31:978-982.

131. Gustafsson L, Hallander HO, Olin P, et al. A controlled trial of a two-component acellular, a five-component acellular, and a whole-cell pertussis vaccine. N Engl J Med. 1996;334:349-355.

132. Greco D, Salmaso S, Mastrantonio P, et al. A controlled trial of two acellular vaccines and one whole-cell vaccine against pertussis. N Engl J Med. 1996;334:341-348.

133. Decker MD, Edwards KM, Steinhoff MC, et al. Comparison of 13 acellular pertussis vaccines: Adverse reactions. Pediatrics. 1995;96(Suppl):557-566.

134. Heijbel H, Rasmussen F, Olin P. Safety evaluation of one whole-cell and three acellular pertussis vaccines in Stockholm Trial II. Dev Biol Stand. 1997;89:99-100.

135. Heijbel H, Ciofi degli Atti M, Harzer E, et al. Hypotonic hyporesponsive episodes in eight pertussis vaccine studies. Dev Biol Stand. 1997;89:101-103.

136. Gangarosa EJ, Galaska AM, Wolfe CR, et al. Impact of antivaccine movements on pertussis control: the untold story. Lancet. 1998;351:356-361.

137. Deen JL, Mink CM, Cherry JD, et al. Household contact study of *Bordetella pertussis* infection. Clin Infect Dis. 1995;21:1211-1219.

138. Izurieta HS, Kenyon TA, Strebel PM, et al. Risk factors for pertussis in young infants during an outbreak in Chicago in 1993. Clin Infect Dis. 1996;22:503-507.

139. Mink CM, Cherry JD, Christenson P, et al. A search for *Bordetella pertussis* infection in university students. Clin Infect Dis. 1992;14:464-471.

140. Wright SW, Edwards KM, Decker MD, Zeldin MH. Pertussis infection in adults with persistent cough. JAMA. 1996;273:1044-1046.

141. Nennig ME, Shinefield HR, Edwards KM, et al. Prevalence and incidence of adult pertussis in an urban population. JAMA. 1996;275:1672-1674.

142. Edwards KM, Decker MD, Graham BS, et al. Adult immunization with acellular pertussis vaccine. JAMA. 1993;269:53-56.

143. Strebel P, Nordin J, Edwards K, et al. Population-based incidence of pertussis among adolescents and adults, Minnesota, 1995-1996. J Infect Dis. 2001;183:1353-1359.

144. Tanaka M, Vitek CR, Pascual FB, et al. Trends in pertussis among infants in the United States. JAMA. 2003; 290:2868-2975.

145. Keitel WA, Muenz LR, Decker MD, et al. A randomized clinical trial of acellular pertussis vaccines in healthy adults: Dose-response comparisons of 5 vaccines and implications for booster immunization. J Infect Dis. 1999;180:397-403.

146. Titball RW, Williamson ED, Dennis DT. Plague. In Plotkin SA, Orenstein WA, eds. Vaccines. 4th ed. Philadelphia: WB Sanders; 2004:999-1010.

147. MacLeod CM, Hodges RG, Heidelberger M, Bernhard WG. Prevention of pneumococcal pneumonia by immunization with specific capsular polysaccharides. J Exp Med. 1945;82:445-465.

148. Austrian R, Douglas RM, Schiffman G, et al. Prevention of pneumococcal pneumonia by vaccination. Trans Assoc Am Phys. 1976;89:184-189.

149. Smit P, Oberholzer D, Hayden-Smith S, et al. Protective efficacy of pneumococcal polysaccharide vaccines. JAMA. 1977;238:2613-2616.

150. Shapiro ED, Berg AT, Austrian R, et al. The protective efficacy of polyvalent pneumococcal polysaccharide vaccine. N Engl J Med. 1991;325:1453-1460.

151. Butler JC, Breiman RF, Campbell JF, et al. Pneumococcal polysaccharide vaccine efficacy; an evaluation of current recommendations. JAMA. 1993;270:1826-1831.

152. Centers for Disease Control and Prevention. Prevention of pneumococcal disease: Recommendations of the Advisory Committee on Immunization Practices (ACIP). MMWR Morb Mortal Wkly Rep. 1997;46:1-24.

153. Jackson LA, Neuzil KM, Yu O, et al. Effectiveness of pneumococcal polysaccharide vaccine in older adults. N Engl J Med. 2003;348:1747-1755.

154. Benin AL, O'Brien KL, Watt JP, et al. Effectiveness of the 23-valent polysaccharide vaccine against pneumococcal disease in Navajo adults. J Infect Dis. 2003;188:81-89.

155. ACIP. Pneumococcal vaccination for cochlear implant candidates and recipients: Updated recommendations of the Advisory Committee on Immunization Practices. MMWR Morb Mortal Wkly Rep. 2003;52:739-740.

156. ACIP. Preventing pneumococcal disease among infants and young children. Recommendations of the Advisory Committee on Immunization Practices. MMWR Morb Mortal Wkly Rep. 2000;49 (No. RR-9):1-35.

157. Jackson LA, Benson P, Sneller VP, et al. Safety of revaccination with pneumococcal polysaccharide vaccine. JAMA. 1999;281:243-248.

158. Dworkin MS, Ward JW, Hanson DL, et al, and the Adult and Adolescent Spectrum of HIV Disease Project. Pneumococcal disease among human immunodeficiency virus-infected persons: incidence, risk factors, and impact of vaccination. Clin Infect Dis. 2001;32:794-800.

159. Black S, Shinefield H, Fireman B, et al. Efficacy, safety, and immunogenicity of hep-tavalent pneumococcal conjugate vaccine in children. Pediatr Infect Dis J. 2000;19:187-195.

160. Black SB, Shinefield HR, Ling S, et al. Effectiveness of heptavalent pneumococcal conjugate vaccine in children younger than five years of age for prevention of pneu-monia. Pediatr Infect Dis J. 2002;21:810-815.

161. O'Brien KL, Mouton LH, Reid R, et al. Efficacy and safety of seven-valent conjugate pneumococcal vaccine in American Indian children: group randomized trial. Lancet. 2003;362:355-361.

162. Whitney CG, Farley MM, Hadlcr J, et al. Decline in invasive pneumococcal disease after the introduction of protein-polysaccharide conjugate vaccine. N Engl J Med. 2003;348:1737-46.

163. Centers for Disease Control and Prevention. Recommendations of the Advisory Committee on Immunization Practices (ACIP). Revised recommendations for rou-tine poliomyelitis vaccination. MMWR Morb Mortal Wkly Rep. 1999;48:590.

164. ACIP. Human rabies prevention—United States, 1999. Recommendations of the Advisory Committee on Immunization Practices (ACIP). MMWR Morb Mortal Wkly Rep. 1999;48[No. RR-1]:1-21.

165. Shill M, Baynes RD, Miller SD. Fatal rabies encephalitis despite appropriate postex-posure prophylaxis. N Engl J Med. 1987;316:1257-1258.

166. CDC. Human rabies despite treatment with rabies immune globulin and human diploid cell rabies vaccine—Thailand. MMWR Morbid Mortal Wkly Rep. 1987;36:759-765.

167. Centers for Disease Control and Prevention. Rubella vaccination during pregnancy—United States, 1971-88. MMWR Morb Mortal Wkly Rep. 1989;38:289-293.

168. Freestone DS, Prydie J, Smith SG, Laurence G. Vaccination of adults with Wistar RA 27/3 rubella vaccine. J Hygiene. 1971;69:471-477.

169. Polk BF, Modlin JF, White JA, DeGirolami PC. A controlled comparison of joint re-actions among women receiving one of two rubella vaccines. Am J Epidemiol. 1982;115:19-25.

170. Henderson DA, Borio LL, Lance JM. Smallpox and vaccinia. In Plotkin SA, Orenstein WA, eds. Vaccines. 4th ed. Philadelphia: WB Saunders; 2004;123-153.

171. Centers for Disease Control and Prevention. Recommendations for using smallpox vaccine in a pre-event vaccination program. Supplemental recommendations of the Advisory Committee on Immunization Practices (ACIP) and the Healthcare Infection Control Practices Advisory Committee (HICPAC). MMWR Morb Mortal Wkly Rep. 2003;52 (No. RR-7):1-16.

172. Cono J, Casey CG, Bell DM. Smallpox vaccination and adverse reactions: Guidance for Clinicians. MMWR Morb Mortal Wkly Rep. 2003;52 (No. RR-4):1-30.

173. Talbot TR, Zeil E, Doersam JK, et al. Risk of vaccinia transfer to the hands of vacci-nated persons after smallpox vaccination. Clin Infect Dis 2004;38:536-541.

174. Centers for Disease Control and Prevention. Supplemental recommendations on ad-verse events following smallpox vaccine in the pre-event vaccination program: rec-ommendations of the Advisor Committee on Immunization Practices. MMWR Morb Mortal Wkly Rep. 2003;52:282-284.

175. Halsell JS, Riddle JR, Atwood JE, et al. Myopericarditis following smallpox vacci-nation among vaccinia-naïve U.S. military personnel. JAMA. 2003;289:3283-3289.

176. Weltzin R, Liu J, Pugachev KV, et al. Clonal vaccinia virus grown in cell culture as a new smallpox vaccine. Nat Med. 2003;9:1125-1130.

177. Centers for Disease Control and Prevention. Notice to Readers: Deferral of routine booster doses of tetanus and diphtheria toxoids for adolescents and adults. MMWR Morb Mortal Wkly Rep. 2001;50:418, 427.

178. Centers for Disease Control and Prevention. Notice to Readers: Resumption of rou-tine schedule for tetanus and diphtheria toxoids. MMWR Morb Mortal Wkly Rep. 2002;51:529-530.

179. Relyveld EH, Henocq E, Bizzini B. Studies on untoward reactions to diphtheria and tetanus toxoids. Dev Biol Stand 1979;43:33-37.

180. Pollard JD, Selby G. Relapsing polyneuropathy due to tetanus toxoid: Report of a case. J Neurol Sci. 1978;37:113-125.

181. Centers for Disease Control and Prevention. Update: Vaccine side effects, adverse reac-tions, contraindications, and precautions. Recommendations of the Advisory Committee on Immunization Practices. MMWR Morb Mortal Wkly Rep. 1996;45:1-35.

182. Centers for Disease Control and Prevention. Typhoid immunization. Recommendations of the Advisory Committee on Immunization Practices. MMWR Morb Mortal Wkly Rep. 1994;43:1-7.

183. Kuter BJ, Weibel RE, Guess HA, et al. Oka/Merck varicella vaccine in healthy chil-dren: Final report of a 2-year efficacy study and 7-year follow-up studies. Vaccine. 1991;9:643-647.

184. White CJ, Kuter BJ, Ngai A, et al. Modified cases of chickenpox after varicella vac-cination: Correlation of protection with antibody response. Pediatr Infect Dis J. 1992;11:19-23.

185. Watson BM, Piercy SA, Plotkin SA, Starr SE. Modified chickenpox in children im-munized with the Oka/Merck varicella vaccine. Pediatrics. 1993;91:17-22.

186. Bernstein HH, Rothstein EP, Pennridge Pediatric Associates, et al. Clinical survey of natural varicella compared with breakthrough varicella after immunization with live attenuated Oka/Merck varicella vaccine. Pediatrics. 1993;92:833-837.

186a. Vazquez M, LaRussa PS, Gershon AA, et al. Effectiveness over time of varicella vaccine. JAMA 2004;291:851-855.

187. Vessey SJ, Chan CY, Kuter BJ, et al. Childhood vaccination against varicella: Persistence of antibody, duration of protection, and vaccine efficacy. J Pediatr. 2001;139:297-304.

188. Lieu TA, Finkler LJ, Sorel ME, et al. Cost effectiveness of varicella serotesting vs. presumptive vaccination of school-age children and adolescents. Pediatrics. 1995;96:632-638.

189. Watson B, Seward J, Yang A, et al. Postexposure effectiveness of varicella vaccine. Pediatrics. 2000;105:84-88.

190. Hall S, Galil K, Watson B, Seward J. The use of school-based vaccination clinics to control varicella outbreaks in two schools. Pediatrics. 2000;105:e1-e3.

191. Centers for Disease Control and Prevention. Prevention of varicella. Updated Recommendations of the Advisory Committee on Immunization Practices (ACIP). MMWR Morb Mortal Wkly Rep. 1999;48:1-5.

192. Levin MJ, Gershon AA, Weinberg A, et al, and the AIDS Clinical Trials Group 265 Team. Immunization of HIV-infected children with varicella vaccine. J Pediatr. 2001;139:305-310.

193. CDC. Guidelines for preventing opportunistic infections among HIV-infected persons—2002 recommendations of the U.S. Public Health Service and the Infectious Diseases Society of America. MMWR Morb Mortal Wkly Rep. 2002;51 (No. RR-8):1-52.

194. Centers for Disease Control and Prevention. Recommendation of the Advisory Committee on Immunization Practices (ACIP): Yellow fever vaccine. MMWR Morb Mortal Wkly Rep. 2002;51 (RR17):1-10.

195. Ellis EF, Henney CS. Adverse reactions following administration of human gamma globulin. J Allergy Clin Immunol. 1969;43:45-54.

196. Siber GR, Werner BC, Halsey NA. Interference of immune globulin with measles and rubella immunization. J Pediatr. 1993;122:204-211.

197. Siber GB, Snydman DR. Use of immune globulins in the prevention and treatment of infections. In: Remington JJ, Swartz MN, eds. Current Clinical Topics in Infectious Diseases. Boston: Blackwell Scientific Publications; 1992:208-256.

198. Knezevic-Maramica I, Mruskall MS. Intravenous immune globulins: An update for clinicians. Transfusion. 2003;43:1460-1480.

199. Pierce LR, Jain N. Risks associated with use of intravenous immunoglobulin. Transfus Med Rev. 2003;17:241-251.

200. Schiff RI. Transmission of viral infections through intravenous immune globulin. N Engl J Med. 1994;331:1649-1650.

201. Centers for Disease Control and Prevention. Outbreak of hepatitis C associated with intravenous immunoglobulin administration—United States, October 1993-June 1994. MMWR Morb Mortal Wkly Rep. 1994;43:505-509.

202. PHLS Communicable Disease Surveillance Centre. Hepatitis C virus and intravenous anti-D immunoglobulin. Commun Dis Rep CDR Wkly. 1995;5:1-2.

203. Yu MY, Mason BL, Tankersley DL. Detection and characterization of hepatitis C virus RNA in immune globulins. Transfusion. 1994;34:596-602.

204. Khabbaz RF, Chamberland M. From prions to parasites: Issues and concerns in blood safety. In: Scheld WM, Craig WA, Hughes JM, eds. Emerging Infections 2. Washington, DC: ASM Press; 1998:295-309.

205. PREVENT Study Group. Reduction of respiratory syncytial virus hospitalization among premature infants and infants with bronchopulmonary dysplasia using respi-ratory syncytial virus immune globulin prophylaxis. Pediatrics. 1997;99:93-99.

206. Simoes EA, Sondheimer HM, Top FH, et al. Respiratory syncytial virus immune globulin for prophylaxis against respiratory syncytial virus disease in infants and children with congenital heart disease. The Cardiac Study Group. J Pediatr. 1998;133:492-499.

207. The IMpact-RSV Study Group. Palivizumab, a humanized respiratory syncytial virus monoclonal antibody, reduces hospitalization from respiratory syncytial virus infec-tion in high-risk infants. Pediatrics. 1998;102:531-537.

208. Committee on Infectious Diseases and Committee on Fetus and Newborn. Prevention of respiratory syncytial virus infections: Indications for the use of palivizumab and update on the use of RSV-IGIV. Pediatrics. 1998;102:1211-1216.

209. Committee on Infectious Diseases and Committee on Fetus and Newborn. Revised indications for the use of palivizumab and respiratory syncytial virus immune globu-lin intravenous for the prevention of respiratory syncytial virus infections. Pediatrics. 2003;112:1442-1446.

210. Meissner HC, Long SS, and the Committee on Infectious Diseases and Committee on Fetus and Newborn. Revised indications for the use of palivizumab and respiratory syncytial virus immune globulin intravenous for the prevention of respiratory syncy-tial virus infections. Pediatrics. 2003;112:1447-1452.

211. American College of Obstetricians and Gynecologists (ACOG). Selective Rho (D) immune globulin (RHIG). Technical Bulletin No. 61. Chicago: American College of Obstetricians and Gynecologists; 1981.

212. Cono J, Casey CG, Bell DM. Smallpox vaccination and adverse reactions: Guidance for clinicians. MMWR Morb Mortal Wkly Rep. 2003;52 (No. RR-4):1-28.

213. Wise RP, Braun MM, Seward JF, et al. Pharmacoepidemiologic implications of erro-neous varicella vaccinations in pregnancy through confusion with varicella zoster im-mune globulin. Pharmacoepidemiol Drug Saf. 2002;11:651-654.

214. King GE, Hadler SC. Simultaneous administration of childhood vaccines: An impor-tant public health policy that is safe and efficacious. Pediatr Infect Dis J. 1994;13:394-407.

215. Centers for Disease Control and Prevention. Combination vaccines for childhood im-munization: Recommendations of the Advisory Committee on Immunization Practices (ACIP), the American Academy of Pediatrics (AAP), and the American Academy of Family Physicians (AAFP). MMWR Morb Mortal Wkly Rep. 1999;48 (No. RR-5):1-15.

216. Lewis M, Ramsey DS. Validating current immunization practice with young infants. Pediatrics. 1992;90:771-773.

217. Ramsey DS, Lewis M. Developmental change in infant cortisol and behavioral response to inoculation. Child Dev. 1994;65:1491-1502.

218. Centers for Disease Control and Prevention. Recommendations of the Advisory Committee on Immunization Practices: update on adult immunization. MMWR Morb Mortal Wkly Rep. 1991;40:1-94.

219. Centers for Disease Control and Prevention. Health Information for International Travel, 2003-2004, *www.cdc.gov/travel/yb* or is also available from the Public Health Foundation (1-877-252-1200) or *http://bookstore.phf.org*.

220. Avery RK, Ljungman P. Prophylactic measures in the solid-organ recipient before transplantation. Clin Infect Dis. 2001;33 (Suppl 1):S15-S21.

221. Stark Klaus, Günther M, Schönfeld C, et al. Immunisations in solid-organ transplant recipients. Lancet. 2002;359:957-964.

222. Duchini A, Goss JA, Karpen S, Pockros PJ. Vaccinations for adult solid-organ transplant recipients: current recommendations and protocols. Clin Microbiol Rev. 2003;16:357-364.

223. Centers for Disease Control and Prevention. Recommendations of the Advisory Committee on Immunization Practices (ACIP): Use of vaccines and immune globulins in persons with altered immunocompetence. MMWR Morb Mortal Wkly Rep. 1993;42:1-18.

224. Pirofski LA, Casadevall A. Use of licensed vaccines for active immunization of the immunocompromised host. Clin Microbiol Rev. 1998;11:1-26.

225. Ljungman, Per. Vaccination in the Immunocompromised Host. In Plotkin SA, Orenstein WA, eds. Vaccines. 4th ed. Philadelphia: WB Saunders; 2004:155-168.

225a. Moss WJ, Halsey NA. Vaccination of human immunodeficiency virus-infected persons. In: Plotkin SA, Orenstein WA, eds. Vaccines. 4th ed. Philadelphia: WB Saunders, 2004;169-178.

226. Ninane J, Grymonprez A, Burtonboy G, et al. Disseminated BCG in HIV infection. Arch Dis Child. 1988;63:1268-1269.

227. Centers for Disease Control and Prevention. Disseminated *Mycobacterium bovis* infection from BCG vaccination of a patient with acquired immunodeficiency syndrome. MMWR Morb Mortal Wkly Rep. 1985;34:227-228.

228. Centers for Disease Control and Prevention. Measles pneumonitis following measles-mumps-rubella vaccination of a patient with HIV infection, 1993. MMWR Morb Mortal Wkly Rep. 1996;45:603-606.

229. Asano Y, Hirose S, Iwayama S, et al. Protective effect of immediate inoculation of a live varicella vaccine in household contacts in relation to the viral dose and interval between exposure and vaccination. Biken J. 1982;25:43-45.

230. Salzman MB, Garcia C. Postexposure varicella vaccination in siblings of children with active varicella. Pediatr Infect Dis J. 1998;17:256-257.

230a. Ruuskanen O, Salmi TT, Halonen P. Measles vaccination after exposure to natural measles. J Pediatr. 1978;93:43-46.

231. Bell KN, Hogue CJR, Manning C, Kendal AP. Risk factors for improper vaccine storage and handling in private provider offices. Pediatrics. 2001;107:e1-e5.

232. Gazmararian JA, Oster NV, Green DC, et al. Vaccine storage practices in primary care physician offices: Assessment and intervention. Am J Prev Med. 2002;23:246-253.

233. Galazka A, Milstein J, Zaffran M. Thermostability of vaccines. Global Programme for Vaccines and Immunization. Geneva: World Health Organization; 1998.

234. Centers for Disease Control and Prevention. Guidelines for maintaining and managing the vaccine cold chain. Morb Mort Wkly Rep. 2003;52:1023-1025.

235. Pascual FB, McGinley EL, Zanardi LR et al. Tetanus surveillance—United States, 1998-2000. MMWR Morb Mortal Wkly Rep. 2003;52(No. SS-3):1-8.

236. Centers for Disease Control and Prevention. Early Release of Selected Estimates Based on Data from the 2002 National Health Interview Survey—*www.cdc.gov/nchs/about/major/nhis/released200306.htm* (accessed 1/23/2004).

237. MacKellar DA, Valleroy LA, Secura GM, et al. Two decades after vaccine license: hepatitis B immunization and infection among young men who have sex with men. Am J Publ Hlth. 2001;91:965-971.

238. Hepatitis B Vaccination Among High-Risk Adolescents and Adults—San Diego, California, 1998-2001. MMWR Morb Mortal Wkly Rep. 2002;51:6168-6121.

239. Goldstein ST, Alter MJ, Williams IT, et al. Incidence and risk factors for acute hepatitis B in the United States, 1982-1998: Implications for vaccination programs. J Infect Dis. 2002;185:713-719.

240. Evans G, Harris D, Levine EM. Legal Issues. In: Plotkin SA, Orenstein WA, eds. Vaccines. 4th ed. Philadelphia: WB Saunders; 2004:1591-1617.

241. Kaplan JE, Nelson DB, Schonberger LB, et al. The effect of immune globulin on trivalent oral polio and yellow fever vaccinations. Bull WHO. 1984;62:585-590.

242. Decker MD, Bogaert HH. Combination Vaccines. In: Plotkin SA, Orenstein WA, eds. Vaccines. 4th ed. Philadelphia: WB Saunders; 2004:825-861.

243. Centers for Disease Control and Prevention. Notice to Readers: FDA licensure of diphtheria and tetanus toxoids and acellular pertussis absorbed, hepatitis B (recombinant), and poliovirus vaccine combined (Pediatrix) for use in infants. MMWR Morb Mortal Wkly Rep. 2003;52:203-204.

244. Chorba TL, Berkelman RL, Safford SK, et al. Mandatory reporting of infectious diseases by clinicians. MMWR Morb Mortal Wkly Rep. 1990;39:1-17.

245. Centers for Disease Control and Prevention. National Childhood Vaccine Injury Act: Requirements for permanent vaccination records and for reporting of selected events for vaccination. MMWR Morb Mortal Wkly Rep. 1988;37:197-200.

246. The National Vaccine Advisory Committee. The measles epidemic: The problems, barriers, and recommendations. JAMA. 1991;266:1547-1552.

247. National Vaccine Advisory Committee. Standards for Child and Adolescent Immunization Practices. Pediatrics. 2003; 112:958-963.

248. Poland GA, Shefer AM, McCauley M, et al. Standards for Adult Immunization Practices. Am J Prev Med. 2003; 25:144-150.

249. Centers for Disease Control and Prevention. Public health burden of vaccine-preventable diseases among adults: Standards for adult immunization practice. MMWR Morb Mortal Wkly Rep. 1990;39:725-729.

250. Gardner P, Pickering LK, Orenstein WA, et al. Guidelines for quality standards for immunization. Clin Infect Dis. 2002;35:503-511.

251. Orenstein WA, Rodewald LE, Hinman AR. Immunization in the United States. In: Plotkin SA, Orenstein WA, eds. Vaccines. 4th ed. Philadelphia: WB Saunders; 2004:1357-1386.

252. Task Force on Community Preventive Services. Recommendations regarding interventions to improve vaccination coverage in children, adolescents, and adults. Am J Prev Med. 2000,18.92-96.

253. Shefer A, Briss P, Rodewald L, et al. Improving immunization coverage rates: An evidence-based review of the literature. Epidemiol Rev. 1999;21:96-142.

254. Bushnell CJ. The ABCs of practice-based immunization assessments. Proceedings of the 28th National Immunization Conference. Washington, DC: US Department of Health and Human Services; 1994:207-209.

255. Dini FF, Chaney M, Moolenaar RL, LeBaron CW. Information as intervention: How Georgia used vaccination coverage data to double public sector vaccination coverage in seven years. J Publ Hlth Manag Pract. 1996;2:45-49.

256. Advisory Committee on Immunization Practices. Recommendations of the Advisory Committee on Immunization Practices, the American Academy of Pediatrics, and the American Academy of Family Physicians: Use of reminder and recall by vaccination providers to increase vaccination rates. MMWR Morb Mortal Wkly Rep. 1998;47:715-717.

257. Linkins RW, Feikema SM. Immunization registries: The cornerstone of childhood immunization in the 21st century. Pediatr Ann. 1998;27:349-354.

258. Department of Health and Human Services. Healthy People 2010 Conference Edition, v. 1. Washington, DC; 2000.

SECTION E

BIODEFENSE

CHAPTER **320**

Bioterrorism: An Overview

DONALD A. HENDERSON

LUCIANA L. BORIO

Serious concerns about the possible use of microbes by bioterrorists have increased significantly over recent years.[1] The havoc that could be generated by such an attack was amply illustrated by the 2001 anthrax outbreak in the United States.[2] Only 22 persons became ill and 5 geographic areas were actually affected, but fear and apprehension extended across the country and around the world. There were realistic uncertainties as to when or if other attacks might occur, and a sense of helplessness on the part of the average citizen as to how he could protect himself. The concerns generated by the anthrax epidemic experience have been intensified by all manner of speculative fictional accounts depicting disasters of untold proportion. Many of these are ludicrously exaggerated. However, the fact is that the likelihood of a bioterrorist event is increasing.

There is a general consensus (among those who are most knowledgeable of bioterrorism and the potential of contemporary biotechnology for growing and manipulating organisms) that it is not a matter of "if" there will be a release of one or more biological agents, but only a question of "when." The release and spread of a contagious agent, such as smallpox virus, could prove catastrophic if measures for control were not promptly and effectively applied. Equally as serious would be a large-scale release of a nontransmissible agent, such as anthrax or botulinum toxin, especially if there were multiple releases of these agents. The possible use of genetically modified agents offers yet another dimension to the threat. Last spring, Nature herself dramatically reminded the world that there are a host of other agents, as exemplified by the coronaviruses, either extant in nature or capable of natural evolution, that are quite capable of causing as much serious damage as any terrorist and perhaps even more.[3] It is clear that the United States, and other countries no less, are, as yet, ill prepared to deal with serious microbial challenges, whatever their source. Complacency about present capabilities to deal with these problems, such as has characterized the public health and the medical communities, is no longer an acceptable policy.

CHANGING ATTITUDES TOWARD BIOTERRORISM

Serious concerns about the potential use of the so-called "weapons of mass destruction" arose in the context of the cold war and focused originally on nuclear weapons and the potential of these to result in the ultimate scenario of a "nuclear winter."[4] Chemical weapons remained on the agenda of concerns given their extensive use during World War I. Until recently, however, biological agents were generally considered to be a lesser threat, although they could not be ignored entirely given the extensive program that the Japanese developed during World War II.[5] Concern about biological weapons waned even more significantly in the 1970s, coincident with President Nixon's initiative in 1969 to terminate the US offensive biological weapons program and the subsequent endorsement by most countries of the 1973 Biological Weapons Convention. The Convention called for the destruction of all stocks of biological weapons and the cessation of research on their use as offensive agents.

Among those in national policy circles, and the public health and medical community, three points of view predominated until about 1995 that served to discourage consideration of biological weapons as more than a theoretical possibility:

1. That biological weapons had been deployed so rarely that precedent would suggest they would not be used.
2. That their use is so morally repugnant that no nation state or organized group would deign to use them.
3. That it is technologically so difficult to produce organisms in quantity and to disperse them that the science is beyond the reach of any but the most sophisticated laboratories.

Each of these arguments has been shown to be invalid. We now know that there are nations and dissident groups who have both the motivation and access to skills to cultivate successfully some of the most dangerous pathogens, and to deploy them as agents in acts of terrorism or war. Acquisition of biological weapons agents is not difficult; methods for transforming them into weapons are widely known; and the requirements for space and sophisticated equipment to produce them are modest.

A particularly disturbing event occurred in 1995 in Japan when a little known apocalyptic religious cult, Aum Shinrikyo, released the nerve gas Sarin in the Tokyo subway. The cult was later discovered to have had plans for biological terrorism[6] and, in fact, it undertook, on several occasions, to spray an aerosol of anthrax organisms throughout metropolitan Tokyo. Fortunately, there were no casualties but this was because the cult mistakenly used a greatly attenuated anthrax vaccine strain rather than a naturally occurring virulent strain. Also, members of this group traveled to Zaire in 1992 to try to obtain samples of Ebola virus for weapons development.[7]

A second event was the discovery, after the Gulf War, that Iraq had a startlingly large biological weapons program. Surprisingly, the full extent of the program did not become known until 1995, after the defection of Hussein Kamal, Saddam Hussein's son-in-law, who had responsibility for the program. Only then did Iraq document, in a report to the United Nations, that it had produced, filled, and deployed bombs, rockets, and aircraft with spray tanks containing *Bacillus anthracis* and botulinum toxin.[8,9]

A decade ago, serious concerns first arose regarding the bioweapons capability of the Soviet Union. Through defectors, it was learned that the Soviet bioweapons program was an enterprise far more extensive and sophisticated than any had imagined at the end of the cold war.[10] Following the signing of the 1973 Biological Weapons Convention, the Soviet Union had decided to invest heavily in a greatly expanded program. By the 1990s, its complement of some 60,000 staff equaled or exceeded that which worked in its nuclear weapons program. One of the larger and more sophisticated of the facilities, called VECTOR, is located in Koltsovo, Novosibirsk. Through the early 1990s, VECTOR was a 4000-person, 30-building complex with high biological security facilities for laboratories and for isolation of human cases. It was at VECTOR where, during the 1980s, the technical problems were solved for the large-scale production of smallpox virus intended as an offensive weapon. Since then, more than half of the scientific staff have left VECTOR, as has staff from other bioweapons laboratories, because of diminished government funding. Many have been recruited to laboratories in other parts of the world. The VECTOR laboratory and the Centers for Disease Control and Prevention (CDC) in Atlanta are the only two repositories now designated by the World Health Organization (WHO) for smallpox virus. Both continue to do research on smallpox, albeit under the sanction of a specially constituted WHO committee. VECTOR has also continued work on other biological agents of concern such as Ebola, Marburg and other hemorrhagic fever viruses.

Another facility of concern was the Soviet Union's principal production center for smallpox virus. It is located near Moscow, at Sergiev Posad. It was able to produce upwards of 20 tons of smallpox virus annually, primarily for use in intercontinental ballistic missiles (ICBMs). The laboratory is intact and is still a top secret facility operated by the Ministry of Defense.

In all, the numbers of countries engaged in some form of biological weapons experimentation grew from four in the 1960s to perhaps as many as eleven in the 1990s.[11] As we now know, however, even comparatively small, non-state–supported dissident groups are capable of biological weapon development and use.

Civilian preparations to deal with bioterrorism have now begun in the United States. Funds are being made available to strengthen the public health and medical infrastructure; smallpox vaccine, antibiotics and other products have been stockpiled; a national network of diagnostic laboratories has been created; and biodefense research programs are now underway.

It is clear, however, that preventing the proliferation and use of biological weapons or countering them will be extremely difficult. Recipes for making biological weapons have been available on the Internet, and even groups with modest finances and basic training in biology and engineering could develop an effective weapon[11] at minimal cost. Detection or interdiction of those intending to use biological weapons is next to impossible. Thus, the first evidence of intent to use such weapons will very likely be the appearance of cases in hospital emergency rooms. The rapidity with which those manning the emergency rooms and others, such as infectious disease specialists and laboratory scientists, can reach a proper diagnosis and the speed with which preventative and/or therapeutic measures are applied could well spell the difference between thousands and, perhaps, tens of thousands of casualties. Indeed, the survival of the health care staff caring for the patients may be at stake. However, there are few indeed who have ever seen patients with diseases caused by those agents most likely to be employed—as, for example, smallpox or plague or anthrax.

PATHOGENS MOST LIKELY TO BE USED

Most agencies that have developed lists of possible agents that might be used as biological weapons customarily identify a substantial number, but, in fact, only a handful of agents share the characteristics of being reasonably easy to prepare and disperse and of being able to inflict sufficiently severe disease so as to paralyze a city, perhaps even a nation. In 1994, Vorobyev, a Soviet bioweapons expert, presented to a working group of the US National Academy of Sciences the conclusions of Soviet experts as to the agents most likely to be used as bioweapons.[12] Smallpox headed the list and was followed closely by anthrax and plague. Indeed, a Russian defector later reported that the Soviet Union had regularly stockpiled 30 metric tons of dried anthrax spores and 20 tons each of smallpox, plague, and tularemia—all of which had been modified for use as weapons.[10] What effect the release of one of these agents might have can only be speculated on. None has so far been deployed effectively as a biological weapon in significant quantities, and thus, no real-world events exist that provide the basis for suggesting likely scenarios.

Smallpox as a Biological Weapon (See Chapter 323)

Smallpox, like chickenpox, spreads from person to person in a continuing chain of infection but is far more virulent. Among those who have never been vaccinated, 30% die of the disease. There was, and is, no specific treatment.

Many have forgotten how concerned countries of the world were about smallpox. For example, until 1972, the United States mandated smallpox vaccination for all children at school entry despite the fact that no cases had occurred in the country since 1949. In the United Kingdom through the 1970s, four standby hospitals were maintained, to be opened only if cases of smallpox were imported. In Germany, two state-of-the-art smallpox isolation hospitals were constructed in the 1960s. Tourists everywhere carried yellow vaccination books attesting to the fact that they had been successfully vaccinated within the preceding 3 years. Until 1980, essentially all countries conducted routine vaccination programs of some sort whether or not they had endemic disease.[1]

Two importations of smallpox into Europe during the 1970s illustrate the nature of the threat posed. The potential for smallpox as an aerosolized agent was illustrated in an outbreak in Germany in 1970.[13] That year, a German electrician returning from Pakistan became desperately ill with high fever and diarrhea. On January 11, he was admitted to a local hospital and isolated in a private room because it was feared he might have typhoid fever. He had contact with only two nurses during his stay. On January 14, he developed a rash and on January 16, the diagnosis of smallpox was confirmed. Hospital patients and staff were vaccinated and quarantined. The patient was immediately transported to a special isolation hospital; more than 100,000 area residents were promptly vaccinated; and hospital patients and staff were vaccinated and quarantined. The patient had had a cough, a symptom seldom seen with smallpox. Coughing produces a small particle aerosol much as one would expect were smallpox to be used as a terrorist weapon. Subsequently, 19 cases occurred in the hospital, including 3 in other rooms on the patient's floor of the hospital; 7 on the floor above; and 9 on the third floor. One of those afflicted was a visitor who had spent less than 15 minutes in the hospital and had only briefly opened a corridor door, easily 30 feet from the patient's room, to ask for directions. The outbreak illustrated well the potential for smallpox virus in an aerosol form to spread over a great distance and to infect at very low dosages.

An outbreak in Yugoslavia in February 1972 was instructive in demonstrating the havoc created even by a small number of cases.[14] Yugoslavia's last previous case of smallpox had occurred 45 years before, in 1927. Nevertheless, Yugoslavia, like most countries, had continued a routine vaccination program to protect itself should an importation occur. In 1972, a pilgrim returning from the Middle East became ill with an undiagnosed febrile disease. Friends and relatives visited from a number of different areas and 2 weeks later, 11 of them developed high fever and rash. None of the physicians who saw the patients diagnosed the cases as smallpox. Few had ever seen a case.

One of the eleven who acquired smallpox was a 30-year-old teacher who quickly became critically ill with the hemorrhagic form of the disease. This form of smallpox is not readily diagnosed, even by experts. He was treated first at a local clinic but, as he became increasingly ill, he was transferred to a large city hospital and, eventually, to a critical care unit because he was bleeding profusely and in shock. He died without a definitive diagnosis. Two days later the first case of smallpox was diagnosed. Thus, 4 weeks had elapsed after the first patient became ill before cases were correctly diagnosed. By then, 150 persons were ill. Among them were 38 who were infected by the young teacher in the hospital. The cases occurred in widely separated areas of the country and, by the time of diagnosis, they had already begun to expose yet another generation. Each of the neighboring countries closed its borders to all traffic.

Government health authorities saw no alternative but to launch a nation-wide vaccination campaign. Mass vaccination clinics were held and check points along roads were established where vaccination certificates were examined. Twenty million persons were vaccinated. Hotels and residential apartments were taken over, cordoned off by the military, and all known contacts of cases forcibly moved into these centers under military guard. Some 10,000 persons spent 2 weeks or more in such isolation. The outbreak stopped 9 weeks after the first patient became ill—175 patients had developed smallpox and 35 had died—and this was in a generally well-vaccinated population. It was, in fact, a small outbreak.

What might happen if smallpox were to be released today in a modern city? Because routine vaccination stopped more 30 years ago, there are large numbers who have never been vaccinated. For others, vaccine immunity has been waning for more than 30 years. It is likely that no more than 25% of the population in the United States or most other countries have significant residual protective immunity. Suppose that some modest quantity of virus were to be released as an aerosol. The event would probably go unnoticed until the first patients developed fever and rash some 7 to 10 days later. With patients being treated in different clinics and by those who almost certainly had never before seen a smallpox case, several days might elapse before the first cases would be diagnosed and an alarm sounded.

Assume that no more than 100 persons had actually been infected. Dealing even with that number would be a challenge given the fact that all would have to be isolated in secure facilities. However, experience indicates that as soon as smallpox was suspected, many others with fever and rash would be identified as possible cases and would have to be screened and isolated until the diagnosis was certain. Where would the patients be admitted? Most hospitals have no more than a handful of beds that can ensure airborne isolation precautions, and few communities have developed plans to accommodate large numbers of contagious patients. Couple this with the problems posed by the occurrence of one or two severe hemorrhagic cases that typically have very short incubation periods, are highly contagious, and would have already been admitted to hospitals before smallpox was suspected. They would have been cared for by largely unprotected emergency room and intensive care teams.

Predictably, there would be an immediate clamor for vaccination such as occurred in the cited outbreaks in Germany and Yugoslavia. The United States now has a large stock of vaccine, but most countries have little or none. How widely should the vaccine be distributed? Comparatively few doses might be needed if vaccine were limited strictly to close contacts of confirmed cases. However, the realities of dealing with even a modest-sized epidemic coupled with anxiety, if not panic, would almost certainly preclude a cautious, measured vaccination effort. In most countries, such reserves of vaccine as may be present would rapidly disappear and there is, at the moment, only a limited manufacturing capacity to produce additional vaccine.

Anthrax as a Biological Weapon (See Chapter 324)

Anthrax was one of the principal weapons in the arsenal of the Soviet Union and is known to have been produced as a weapon by Iraq and the Aum Shinrikyo. Their interest, in part, stems from the fact that the organism is reasonably readily available, is easy to produce in large quantity, and is extremely stable in its dried form. Prior to the 1979 Sverdlovsk (Soviet Union) epidemic of anthrax, the effect of aerosolized anthrax on humans had to be inferred from animal experiments and the occasional human infection among workers in factories processing sheep and goat hides.[15] These data indicated that inhalational anthrax is highly lethal.

The Sverdlovsk epidemic[16] resulted from an accident at a Soviet bioweapons factory where a small quantity of anthrax spores was discharged as an aerosol. In all, 77 cases were identified with certainty, of whom 66 died, but it is suspected that the actual total was at least 300 patients with 100 or more deaths. The patients had lived or worked within a narrow zone extending some 4 km south and east of the facility, the direction of the prevailing wind at the time of release. Anthrax deaths among sheep and cows occurred in six different villages ranging up to 50 km away. The accidental airborne release of the spores was thought to have lasted no more than minutes. Of the 58 human cases with known dates of onset, 9 experienced symptoms within a week after exposure but, in some, the incubation period was as long as 6 weeks. Whether the onset of illness occurred sooner or later, death almost always followed within 1 to 4 days after onset of illness.

Meselson and his colleagues who documented this outbreak calculate that the weight of spores released as an aerosol could have been as little as a few milligrams or as much as "nearly a gram."[16] Alibek, the former deputy director of the Soviet bioweapons program, estimated that some 100 g must have been released.[10] It is estimated that in the US anthrax attack, the envelopes contained, all told, no more than 10 g of anthrax powder. The amounts in neither episode were large, especially when contrasted to the 30 tons of dried anthrax spores that the Soviet Union routinely held in storage.

The ramifications of even a modest-sized release of anthrax spores in a city are profound. Emergency rooms would begin to see a few patients with high fever and difficulty breathing perhaps 2 to 3 days following exposure. Few physicians have ever seen a case of inhalational anthrax and most medical laboratories have had little experience in its

diagnosis. Thus, it is probable that a delay of at least another 1 to 2 days would elapse before a definitive diagnosis would be made. Because of the patient's often rapid clinical deterioration, it would already be too late for some to benefit from antibiotic therapy.

Once the diagnosis was established, public health officials would be faced with providing prophylaxis over a 60-day period to others who might have been exposed and could be harboring anthrax spores. Antibiotics would serve to prevent disease, provided that the organisms were sensitive to them. However, the logistics of procuring and distributing antibiotics to perhaps hundreds of thousands of persons represents a formidable undertaking.[17] Post-outbreak vaccination could serve to shorten to 30 days the time needed for antibiotic prophylaxis but, until at least 2005, supplies of vaccine will be too limited in quantity to count on its use. An equally serious problem would be that of knowing when to permit access to the affected areas, given the fact that anthrax spores may persist in the environment for 40 years or more and methods for decontamination are not only costly but also conceivably impossible for many settings.

PREPARING FOR AN ATTACK

The realities of dealing with a comparatively straightforward release of a modest quantity of either smallpox or anthrax are staggering, let alone the problems that would be faced were genetically modified organisms to be employed. In the United States, health services have begun to take steps to deal with the possibility of outbreaks of disease that may be contagious and have high rates of morbidity and mortality. Especially difficult, however, is that of anticipating the public response so as to avert panic. There is little practical experience on which to build, the last significant epidemic in the United States having been the influenza pandemic of 1918. The challenges are uniquely different from those associated with dealing with an explosion or the release of a chemical agent. The worst effects of such emergencies, even when involving many casualties, are quickly apparent; efforts for stabilization and recovery can begin immediately; and the toll of injuries and deaths can be ascertained soon thereafter. For biological attacks in which smallpox or anthrax had been used, detection that an outbreak had occurred would not be likely until a number of days had passed; the magnitude of the attack might not be certain for a week or more; and with smallpox, the implicit threat of further cases would cause many to live in fear that they or their families might be the next victims. The potential for panic is real.

There is little room in today's world for the complacency once felt by many in the industrialized world in the 1960s and 1970s, when it was believed that the problems posed by infectious agents were largely controlled. Since that time, there has been a rude awakening subsequent to the advent and spread of the human immunodeficiency virus, with AIDS cases still growing in numbers and neither a curative drug nor a vaccine available. This has been but the harbinger of a number of new and emergent organisms culminating with the development of outbreaks of West Nile virus encephalitis, monkeypox and severe acute respiratory syndrome (SARS). The threat of biological weapons, coupled now with the realization that Nature herself may pose an even more serious threat to an unprepared world, dictates the need for a better prepared public health and medical infrastructure for dealing with infectious agents, whatever their origin.

In the near term, there is a need to be prepared to promptly detect and diagnose, to characterize epidemiologically and to respond appropriately to epidemic disease. There is a need at international, national and local levels for a greater capacity for surveillance; a far better network of laboratories and better diagnostic instruments; a more adequate cadre of trained epidemiologists, clinicians, and researchers; and better communication and coordination.

There is a special need to determine how best to organize, fund, and undertake emergency research and development programs for possibly needed new therapeutic or preventive agents. Intrinsic to this is a basic research agenda directed toward a better understanding of pathogenesis and immunity.

BIOLOGICAL WEAPONS IN HISTORY

Before World War I

Attempts to deliberately induce infectious diseases among enemy forces dates back to the Roman era when Roman armies used the bodies of animals and humans to contaminate water supplies.[18] How effective these and similar efforts were is not clear. Given the problems of sanitation in earlier times and the natural prevalence of waterborne infections, a further degradation of water quality probably contributed only marginally to general morbidity, and it is doubtful that such efforts altered significantly the course of history. An often cited exception was the plague of Kaffa in the 14th century, which was said to have resulted from cadavers being catapulted into the city by its Tatar besiegers who had carried plague with them from Asia.[19] The Genoese defenders fled and coincident with their flight, the Black Death began to spread across Europe, an epidemic that resulted in the death of perhaps one third of the population.[20] However, the explanation for the Kaffa episode ignores the fact that plague-transmitting fleas leave cadavers soon after death to parasitize living hosts. The corpses were thus unlikely to have been bearing competent vectors.[21] A more likely explanation is that infection occurred as the result of the natural spread of disease through urban and sylvatic rodent populations.

Smallpox, at least in the Americas, was seen to be a particularly useful weapon from soon after its inadvertent introduction by Cortez in 1520. Native Americans experienced extraordinarily high case-fatality rates, resulting in deaths among 70% and more during outbreaks. The French, Spanish, English, and, later, the Americans are cited as having deliberately initiated outbreaks, sometimes using fomites, such as blankets, to transmit infection.[20] A particularly well-documented episode occurred in 1763 during the French and Indian Wars in which British officers took blankets from patients in the Smallpox Hospital and gave them to the Indians "to convey the Smallpox to the Indians."

During the years of the American Revolution, there were a number of reports of civilians afflicted with smallpox being sent or transported by British army officers to infect Revolutionary troops and citizens.[22] Smallpox posed a more serious threat to the Americans because British and Hessian soldiers had grown up in a more densely populated Europe where most smallpox cases occurred in children. Those who survived to adulthood were fully protected against a second attack.

The first deliberate attempts on the part of British forces to spread smallpox were reported during the 1775 to 1776 siege of Boston, and later reports emanated from Quebec, Virginia, and New Hampshire. How many such outbreaks were deliberately induced is not known. With the advent of war and the movement of people and armies, smallpox could and did spread widely by natural means. Although smallpox played an important role during the Revolutionary War period, it is thought to be unlikely that its use as a weapon contributed significantly to deciding the conflict.

World War I Through 1945

The potential use of other pathogens as biological weapons had to await the development of modern microbiology when specific agents could be identified and grown and produced in quantity. The advent of World War I provided the stimulus for the development of special weapons systems, but most efforts were directed to the development and application of chemical weapons. However, German scientists did work with two agents intended for use in animals: *Bacillus anthracis* (for anthrax) and *Burkholderia mallei* (for glanders). German saboteurs, working in Allied countries, including the United States, endeavored to infect horses, mules, and sheep, primarily to impact transport and cavalry operations.[19] Attempts to spread cholera in Italy and plague in Russia were alleged but are probably not credible. In brief, biological weapons in World War I were, at most, a minor nuisance.

The horrors of chemical warfare, however, precipitated international efforts to develop a treaty that would prohibit the future use of chemicals as offensive weapons. It was decided to extend this to biological weapons as well. Thus, in 1925, a unique treaty was agreed on that, for the first time in history, banned an entire class of weapons.[21]

It was called the "1925 Geneva Protocol for the Prohibition of the Use in War of Asphyxiating, Poisonous or Other Gases and of Bacteriological Methods of Warfare." Eventually it was signed by 108 nations. It did not, however, proscribe basic research, production, or possession of biological weapons. Many countries ratified the protocol while stipulating that they have the right to retaliate should they be attacked. No provision was made for verification. Following World War I, a number of the signatories began biological weapons programs, including Belgium, Canada, France, Great Britain, Italy, Japan, the Netherlands, Poland, and the Soviet Union. The United States was not a signatory to the treaty until 1972, but it did not begin its own program until 1942.[21]

During World War II, biological weapons are known to have been used only by Japan and possibly by the Soviet Union, although consequential research and development programs were conducted by the United States, Germany, and the United Kingdom. The Japanese biological weapons program was a vast enterprise. It consisted of a major center in Pingfan, Manchuria (termed Unit 731) with more than 3000 scientists plus smaller units at a number of other sites in China. Another center (Unit 100) worked primarily with animal and plant diseases including glanders, sheep and cattle plague, red rust, and mosaic plant diseases. More than 10,000 prisoners died as a result of experimental infections or execution following experimentation.[5,21] At least 11 cities in China were attacked using, variously, anthrax, cholera, shigella, salmonella, and plague organisms to contaminate food and water supplies. Fleas were infected with the plague bacillus and released by aircraft over cities. Data regarding the success of the efforts to infect civilian populations are sketchy. Large outbreaks of cholera and plague are known to have occurred, but it is believed that transmission in any given area was not long sustained.

Except for the Japanese initiative, whose impact is difficult to gauge, biological weapons played no significant role in World War II. Information about the possible use of biological weapons by the Soviet Union was provided by Alibek, who believes that tularemia was used at Stalingrad in 1942 against German Panzers and Q fever in 1943 among German troops on leave in the Crimea.[10] Germany undertook a number of experimental studies of a variety of agents and was thought, at the time, to be preparing to use organisms as biological weapons. In consequence, Britain and the United States also undertook a variety of studies of different agents and, with Britain, prepared to utilize anthrax in cattle feed or bombs should retaliatory measures be decided. No actions, however, were ever taken.

1945 Through 1972

The extent and sophistication of the Japanese program came to be known by both the Allies and the Soviet Union as a result of detailed information provided by scientists who had worked in the program. This they had offered as a result of a promise that they be given amnesty from war crimes prosecution. Information about the program served as an impetus to the expansion of biological weapons programs in a number of countries, including those of the United States, Soviet Union, United Kingdom, Australia, France, and Canada. These programs grew and developed from 1945 until the Biological Weapons Convention came into effect in 1972.

The principal US site was located at Fort Detrick, Maryland; a production facility was constructed at Pine Bluff, Arkansas.[21] The studies were wide ranging. Seven human disease organisms were weaponized and stockpiled: *B. anthracis* (anthrax), botulinum toxin, *Francisella tularensis* (tularemia), *Brucella suis* (Brucellosis), *Coxiella burnetti* (Q fever), staphylococal enterotoxin B (food poisoning), and Venezuelan equine encephalitis. Countermeasures were developed, including vaccines and antibiotics, and technical advances were made that permitted large-scale fermentation and storage of agents. Studies of animal responses were conducted at Fort Detrick, in atolls in the Pacific, and desert sites in the United States. Experiments using stimulant organisms in aerosols were conducted in a number of cities to gain information about the survival time of organisms and patterns of dispersal.

During the 17 years that elapsed between the end of World War II and the signing of the Biological Weapons Convention, the United States was engaged in conflict in Korea and Vietnam. During this time, there were a number of allegations, primarily by Communist bloc countries, that the United States was guilty of having used one or another agent against one or another of the countries, and there were other allegations that biological agents had been used by those engaged in the Middle East conflict.[19] No convincing evidence of such actions was ever produced.

As time passed, there was increasing international concern regarding the epidemiological risks posed by biological weapons and concern that the 1925 Geneva Protocol was not sufficiently explicit about what could and could not be done. Moreover, it provided for no verification procedures. Accordingly, in 1969, draft proposals for a new protocol were submitted to the Committee on Disarmament of the United Nations. Meanwhile, President Nixon terminated the US offensive biological weapons program by executive orders in 1969 and 1970. A Biological Weapons Convention was eventually agreed on in 1972 and went into effect in 1975. The agreement reached by the 103 cosigning nations was: "never to develop, produce, stockpile, or otherwise acquire or retain microbial or other biological agents or toxins, whatever their origin or method of production, of types and in quantities that have no justification for prophylactic, protective, or other peaceful purpose; and weapons, equipment, or means of delivery designed to use such agents or toxins for hostile purposes or in armed conflict."[19]

It was a hopeful beginning but there was no provision for verification, still a subject of continuing discussion. Meanwhile, two of the signatories, Iraq and the former Soviet Union, have since admitted publicly and officially that they have been engaged in biological weapons research, development and production.

BIOLOGICAL ORGANISMS OF GREATEST CONCERN

Rating the Risk

In theory, hundreds if not thousands of infectious agents and toxins could conceivably be employed as biological weapons but few possess characteristics of virulence and/or contagiousness that would seriously disrupt normal community life or threaten the continuity of government. Indeed, each year, countless naturally transmitted infectious disease outbreaks occur throughout the world, some carried in water or food, as salmonella or shigella, some transmitted by the respiratory route, as influenza, and some by vectors, as West Nile virus. Most outbreaks are small in size, although some, such as influenza, can cause a great deal of morbidity. However, at least in the industrialized countries, the existing infrastructure of medical and public health staff is able to cope with most of these without undue difficulty. More could be done to assure earlier and more effective detection, prevention, and control measures if the public health infrastructure were more robust, and if there were more effective communication and cooperation between public health and medical practitioners. However, there has been little impetus to improve the situation, given the fact that epidemic diseases have not seriously tested the health care system or significantly disrupted civilian life in most industrialized countries since the 1918 influenza pandemic.

It is clear, however, that certain agents used as biological weapons could result in epidemic catastrophes and that special measures need to be taken to prevent their occurrence or, at least, to deal with them. Different governments and agencies have compiled lists of organisms that represent potential biological weapons threats, but few have given appropriate consideration as to which are of sufficient concern to civilian populations to warrant special preparedness measures. Until 1998, no review of this sort had been undertaken by US federal authorities.

In 1995, President Clinton issued Presidential Decision Directive 39 to launch the development of national preparedness programs to deal with terrorism.[23] Funds for the development of programs in the civilian sector were assigned to the Department of Defense. Its principal strategy was to train and equip traditional "first responders" (fire fighters, law enforcement personnel, and emergency response teams) in 120 metropolitan cities. The teams were called Metropolitan Medical Strike Teams (later, Metropolitan Medical Response Teams); their training primarily was in dealing with explosive events and "chembio" incidents. The neologism "chembio" signified the belief by the planners that essentially identical strategies and techniques were to be employed whether the incident was caused by a chemical or biological agent. What was overlooked is the fact that the consequences of a biological weapons attack would be vastly different in character than that following a chemical release (Table 320-1). A chemical release would be apparent immediately and would call for immediate action by traditional "first responders" to secure the area, to decontaminate victims, and to evacuate them. The release of a biological agent would almost certainly be a silent one, with no immediate evidence that it had taken place until people began getting sick and an epidemic ensued. The actual "first responders," that is, those first dealing with human casualties, would be physicians and nurses, primarily those in the hospital emergency rooms. However, the training programs and plans, through 1999, focused primarily on firemen, law enforcement agents and emergency response teams, and seldom included public health professionals, physicians, or hospital staff. Unfortunately, significant components of this misunderstood construct have persisted in many areas.

It was also clear that there was a need to identify agents of the highest priority, to develop a basic strategy for containing outbreaks caused by these agents, and to get agreement on the best methods for treatment of patients. Accordingly, in 1998, a broadly representative, informal Working Group on Civilian Biodefense was convened at the Johns Hopkins Center for Civilian Biodefense Strategies to examine these issues. Included in the group were federal experts from the CDC, the Food and Drug Administration (FDA), the Army Medical Research Institute of Infectious Diseases (USAMRIID) at Fort Detrick, state and local health officials, clinicians, and scientists with special expertise and knowledge of the most serious bioweapons agents.

It was decided by the group that the agents of special concern should be those that, under epidemic circumstance, could threaten the

TABLE 320-1 Important Distinctions Between Chemical and Biological Terrorism

Chemical Terrorism	Biological Terrorism
Speed at Which Attack Results in Illness	
Rapid—usually minutes to hours after attack	Delayed—usually days to weeks after attack
Distribution of Affected Patients	
Downwind area near point of release	Widely spread through city or region; major international epidemic in worst-case scenario
First Responders	
Paramedics, firefighters, police, emergency rescue workers, and law enforcement	Emergency department physicians and nurses, infectious disease physicians, infection control practitioners, epidemiologists, public health officials, hospital administrators, and laboratory experts
Release Site of Weapon	
Quickly discovered; possible and useful to cordon off area of attack	Difficult to identify; probably not possible or useful to cordon off area of attack
Decontamination of Patients and Environment	
Critically important in most cases	Not necessary in most cases
Medical Interventions	
Chemical antidotes	Vaccines and/or antibiotics
Patient Isolation/Quarantine	
After decontamination there is no need	Crucial if easily communicable disease is involved (such as smallpox); advance hospital planning for isolating large numbers of patients is critical

From Henderson DA. The looming threat of bioterrorism. Science. 1999:283:1279-82.

functioning of civil government. Many factors had to be weighed with respect to each candidate biological agent, including the magnitude of disease morbidity and mortality, contagiousness, number of organisms needed to infect, availability of therapeutic or preventive measures, difficulties in diagnosis, feasibility of organisms being obtained and grown in quantity, stability of the organisms in the environment, and the likely response of a population to an epidemic of a historically feared disease such as plague or smallpox. Eventually, five agents and a diagnostic group were identified as being those of special concern, warranting the development of special preparatory measures to respond to an attack. The diseases were smallpox, anthrax, plague, botulinum toxin poisoning, tularemia, and the "viral hemorrhagic fevers" (such as Ebola, Marburg, and Lassa fever). None of these are known clinically to more than a very few medical or public health staff in the United States and, until the Working Group had convened, there had been no consensus on their preventive or therapeutic measures. Special reviews of each of these agents were undertaken and published in the *Journal of the American Medical Association* (JAMA).[24-29] These were later updated and, with additional papers dealing with the US anthrax outbreak, published by JAMA in 2002 under the title, *Bioterrorism: Guidelines for Medical and Public Health Management.*[30]

Some months after the Working Group had met and decided on this list, a meeting was convened by the CDC, at which the same consensus was reached as to the agents of greatest concern. These are now commonly referred to as the Category A agents. A lower priority group was identified and labeled as Category B agents. The Category B agents were characterized as having a generally lower level of mortality, and were included on the list primarily because CDC staff believed that diagnostic capabilities for these agents needed to be improved and expanded. The diseases are a miscellaneous group, including those organisms causing Q fever, brucellosis, glanders, certain arthropod-borne equine encephalidities (Venezuelan, eastern and western), miscellaneous food- and waterborne agents (salmonella, shigella, *E.coli* 0157:H7, cholera, *Cryptosporidium parvum*) and several toxins. A Category C list was compiled that included emerging pathogens that might be engineered for mass dissemination because of their availability, the ease of their production and dissemination, and their potential for significant morbidity and mortality. Included were Nipah virus, hantaviruses, tickborne hemorrhagic fever viruses, tickborne encephalitis virus, yellow fever, and multidrug-resistant tuberculosis. It is important to note that neither the Category B nor Category C lists resulted from a considered review of all possible candidate organisms but represent, in fact, simply examples of organisms that might appear in each of the two categories.

Obtaining and Producing Biologic Weapons

Some have assumed that because the likely pathogens to be used as biological weapons are comparatively rare that it would be difficult for a prospective terrorist to acquire the organisms. This is not the case. Russia is one of several possible sources of organisms, including some that have been genetically engineered. All of the organisms of greatest concern were subjects of study in the former Soviet biological weapons program. Most of the laboratories are still in operation and many scientists, like those at the smallpox laboratory in Novosibirsk, continue work on organisms that could be used as biological weapons. Many that were employed by the program were among the Soviet Union's best scientists, but half or more have left the laboratories for work elsewhere, some having gone to countries now suspected of having their own bioweapons programs. Whether or not they have carried specimens with them is unknown.

There are other sources for strains of the Category A agents. Cases of plague, anthrax, tularemia and botulism occur regularly in many countries of the world, including the United States. After processing the specimens, it is customary for microbiologists to preserve the isolates in freezers for possible future reference when similar cases or specimens are seen. Thus, there are a great many laboratories around the world that have such isolates in their possession. On request, laboratories will often send strains of organisms to other laboratories and, indeed, as of December 2001, there were some 46 laboratories outside

the United States that advertised the availability of anthrax isolates on their websites.

Growing and "Weaponizing" the Agents

In contrast to the challenges of acquiring functional nuclear or chemical weapons, production of biological weapons is simple and inexpensive. For most of the Category A agents, production is reasonably straightforward, especially if those with expertise are available, such as former bioweapons scientists from Russia. Those without access to such expertise now can obtain from the Internet, as well as through academic courses, sophisticated methods in biotechnology that offer additional prospects for genetic engineering. Laboratories now producing veterinary and human vaccines could readily be converted to produce biological weapons. Industries that rely on fermentation methods, including those producing alcoholic beverages, could be converted to the production of microorganisms. Assembling equipment and building a facility from scratch is possible because all needed equipment is of dual purpose; comparatively little space is required; and, for most agents, comparatively small quantities need to be aerosolized to produce large numbers of casualties. Various estimates have been offered as to the investment needed to create a modestly sophisticated biological weapons capacity. Most suggest an outlay of a few hundred thousand dollars, well within reach of even the poorest of countries as well as some state-sponsored terrorist organizations.

Various methods might be used for dispersing biological weapons, the most frequently being the contamination of foods or water supplies or by aerosol dispersion. There is a general consensus, however, that aerosols pose the most serious threat to the civilian population. Organisms dispersed by other means could cause disease outbreaks, but they would be much less likely to cause epidemic disease on a scale great enough to threaten the integrity of civil government. Each of the Category A agents could be disseminated in a fine particle aerosol in the range of 1 to 5 μm. Such particles are inhaled and penetrate deeply into the lung. Larger-sized particles, in contrast, are trapped in the upper airways and usually do not succeed in initiating infection. An aerosol of this size is invisible to the naked eye and behaves much like smoke in that it is able to penetrate most interior air spaces. With an appropriate coating of most organisms, they can remain suspended and viable for many hours to days. In the Sverdlovsk anthrax outbreak, humans became ill who were as much as 4 km from the point of release; animals who were 50 km away also developed anthrax.[16]

Generating an aerosol is comparatively straightforward using any of a number of off-the-shelf devices such as paint sprayers, fogging machines that disseminate insecticides, purse-size perfume atomizers, and hand-held drug delivery devices such as used by asthma patients. Even small releases of an agent would, almost certainly, result in serious public concern as was witnessed during the anthrax release in the United States in 2001. Repeated releases in different parts of the country could be devastating, especially if the public health response were seen as deficient. A large-scale release, of itself, could be as devastating as a nuclear weapon. An Office of Technology Assessment report estimated that if 100 kg of anthrax spores were released upwind of Washington, DC, using a crop-duster aircraft, there would be between 130,000 and 3 million deaths.[31]

With respect to other methods of dispersion, some cities have expressed special concerns about water reservoirs being contaminated and have invested in costly preventive measures. However, most of the Category A agents cannot be disseminated by water. For those that can, the quantities needed to contaminate a reservoir sufficient to infect the consumer would be prodigious. This reflects the fact that of the water distributed from reservoirs, only a small proportion is actually consumed and normal water treatment itself destroys many organisms. Contamination of food, likewise, is viewed with concern by some, primarily because of the threat posed by botulinum toxin. A successful attack, however, faces several barriers, including difficulties in producing the toxin in quantity and at a level of purity that would not cause the food to be unpalatable, and the identification of a food of proper chemical constituents so as to enable the toxin to survive. Because botulinum toxin acts rapidly and has distinctive clinical symptoms, cases, in any event, would be likely to be diagnosed quickly and the food removed from commerce. One scenario has suggested the possibility of contaminating raw milk in a tanker truck, thereby potentially permitting a large number of persons to be poisoned over a short period of time and before much of the milk could be withdrawn. Given the number of barriers to overcome in executing an attack as complex as this, it is difficult to recommend this as a priority concern.

RESPONSE TO BIOTERRORISM: PUBLIC HEALTH EMERGENCY PREPAREDNESS

Most physicians and public health practitioners viewed the threat of biological weapons as negligible as recently as 1997. In most Schools of Medicine and Schools of Public Health, biological and chemical weapons were regarded as being morally repugnant and not subjects that should be discussed, even from the standpoint of the threats they posed. In the mid-1990s, the CDC, whose responsibility it is to deal with outbreaks of infectious diseases, developed a program targeted at the early detection of, and response to, new and emerging infections both in the United States and abroad. However, until 1999, there was no designated unit or person with the responsibility for dealing with the specific threat of biological weapons. Nor were there specifically identified individuals with such responsibilities at either the NIH or FDA.

The terrorist events in Tokyo, Oklahoma City, and New York in the 1990s; revelations about the Soviet bioweapons program; and the discovery of Iraq's considerable investment in biological weapons created the impetus for Congress to take more definitive steps to strengthen the country's national preparedness. As noted earlier, Congress, in 1996, passed the Act entitled Defense Against Weapons of Mass Destruction. Responsibility for this activity was assigned to the Department of Defense; little in money or responsibility was provided for the Department of Health and Human Services (DHHS).

A milestone in awakening interest in the problem of bioterrorism was the publication by *JAMA* of a special issue of its journal (August 6, 1997) devoted entirely to the biological weapons threat. Its circulation of 350,000 copies informed a vast medical audience. The catalyst for this publication was Dr. Joshua Lederberg, Nobel Laureate and formerly President of Rockefeller University. He had been deeply concerned about biological weapons and was a frequent consultant to government.

In September 1997, the first symposium on biological weapons was conducted at a national medical conference—the annual meeting of the Infectious Diseases Society of America. Dr. John Bartlett, then President of the Society and Professor of Infectious Diseases at Johns Hopkins School of Medicine, brought together for this meeting Richard Preston, author of the widely read book, *The Hot Zone,* Dr. Mike Osterholm, the Minnesota State Epidemiologist and Henderson. It was a plenary meeting with standing room only as several thousand crowded the meeting room. This represented an important turning point as the panel of bioterrorism experts were soon asked to speak at scientific meetings and hospital grand rounds in many parts of the country.

With interest in the subject growing, it was decided to hold a national meeting specifically intended for those in the health professions. Thus, the first National Symposium on the Medical and Public Health Response to Bioterrorism was held in Washington in February 1998. It was convened by the Johns Hopkins Center for Civilian Biodefense Strategies and DHHS; 12 other organizations cosponsored the event. With only 4 months' advance planning, the conveners worried that the attendance would be sparse, but a capacity audience of more than 1000 attended.

Three months later, President Clinton requested that Congress provide US$ 133 million in funds to DHHS for fiscal year 1999 in support of a new program of public health preparedness in the Department. The Assistant Secretary of Health, Dr. Margaret Hamburg, formerly Commissioner of Health for the City of New York, was given responsibility for developing a strategic plan for DHHS. Most of the funds were allocated to CDC. Of the funds provided, US$ 51 million was earmarked for the development of an emergency stockpile of antibiotics, primarily for anthrax, and for smallpox vaccine. The balance, US$ 82 million, provided for the initial steps to rebuild the long-neglected public health infrastructure at federal, state, and local levels. Budget allocations steadily rose to reach US$ 300 million in fiscal year 2001. Following the September 11, 2001 terrorist attacks and the anthrax outbreak a month later, Congress increased appropriation to DHHS to US$ 3 billion for fiscal year 2002 and, subsequently, to US$ 4.5 billion for fiscal year 2003.

Program Implementation

It was recognized that the ability of the country to respond to a terrorist attack depended on the early detection and diagnosis of cases of a disease that might have been hitherto unknown to physicians seeing the cases; on the ability of public health practitioners and infectious disease specialists to define quickly the extent of the problem, and to implement rapidly measures to prevent further cases; and on medical care professionals to render appropriate care and treatment. These actions are wholly congruent with those that are needed to respond to any outbreak of disease, whether familiar, newly emergent or resulting from a terrorist attack. However, to deal with outbreaks caused by the Category A agents, special measures would be required.

The concept that the guiding principle of DHHS's effort be "public health emergency preparedness" resonated well in both the Executive Branch and Congress, where it received bipartisan support. To ensure coordination and cooperation across DHHS, Secretary of Health Tommy Thompson created, in November 2001, a new Office of Public Health Emergency Preparedness, headed by an Assistant Secretary. Although many federal agencies, as well as state and local governments, had important roles in the new national security initiatives, DHHS was the principal focus for expertise and action as it pertained to public health and medicine.

The appropriation legislation provided for more than 1 billion US$ to support state and local efforts. The bill was signed on January 11, 2002, at a time when there was serious concern about the imminent possibility of another attack using a biological weapon. It was recognized that the extent to which this was handled satisfactorily depended primarily on the ability of state and local health services to respond. Federal assets would be important to complement local action, but the critical role was clearly at the local level. Thus, there was an urgent need to provide resources to state and local levels as rapidly as possible. Under ordinary circumstances, 6 to 8 months would be required to disburse a new allocation of funds to states and US territories. In disbursing it, highly prescriptive requirements would normally be imposed with the full allocation divided into many different categorical initiatives, each to be separately developed and accounted for.

Secretary Thompson decided that, in disbursing funds, a marked departure from routine procedures was requisite to expedite preparations to cope with a biological weapons attack. A formula was devised that decided the allocation of funds for each state and territory. It was primarily population-based, albeit providing additional sums for four of the largest urban areas. On January 31, the states were advised of the amount of their allocation and authorized to begin spending immediately up to 20% of that total. Expenditures were authorized for a broadly defined set of six categories: preparedness planning, surveillance, laboratory, health alert network, risk communication and health information, education, and training. The states were asked to provide a plan by April 15 and, to help in formulating such a plan, 17 critical benchmarks were identified which they were requested to address (Table 320-2). The states were free to decide the proportionate amounts to be devoted to the different categories. After the Department had reviewed and agreed that their plans were satisfactory, they would then be authorized to spend the remaining 80%. Most of the plans were received within 45 days and subsequently reviewed and approved by the Department during the following 30 working days. Most of the plans were surprisingly good and surprisingly thorough, especially given the very short time frame.

Because of special concerns about the threat of a contagious biological weapon, three additional stipulations were made: (1) That each hospital emergency suite have one or more rooms appropriately engineered for airborne isolation precautions, where possibly contagious patients could be safely examined. (2) That, for each metropolitan area, there be a surge capacity plan developed for accommodating at

TABLE 320-2 Critical Benchmarks for Bioterrorism Preparedness Planning

I. Public Health Preparedness (CDC)

1. Designate a Senior Public Health Official within the State health department, to serve as Executive Director of the State Bioterrorism Preparedness and Response Program.
2. Establish an advisory committee with members from a variety of health agencies and first responders.
3. Prepare a timeline for the development of a statewide plan for preparedness and response for a bioterrorist event, infectious disease outbreak, or other public health emergency.
4. Prepare a timeline for the assessment of statutes, regulations, and ordinances within the state and local public health jurisdictions regarding emergency public health measures.
5. Prepare a timeline for the development of a statewide plan for responding to incidents of bioterrorism.
6. Prepare a timeline for the development of regional plans to respond to bioterrorism.
7. Develop an interim plan to receive and manage items from the National Pharmaceutical Stockpile, including mass distribution of antibiotics, vaccines and medical material.
8. Prepare a timeline for developing a system to receive and evaluate urgent disease reports from all parts of the state (or city) and local public health jurisdictions on a 24-hour per day, 7 days per week basis.
9. Assess current epidemiologic capacity and prepare a timeline for providing at least one epidemiologist for each metropolitan area with a population greater than 500,000.
10. Develop a plan to improve working relationships and communication between Level A (clinical) laboratories and Level B/C laboratories, (i.e., Laboratory Response Network laboratories) as well as other public health officials.
11. Prepare a timeline for a plan that ensures that 90% of the population is covered by the Health Alert Network (HAN).
12. Prepare a timeline for the development of a communications system that provides a 24/7 flow of critical health information among hospital emergency departments, state and local health officials, and law enforcement officials.
13. Develop an interim plan for risk communication and information dissemination to educate the public regarding exposure risks and effective public response.
14. Prepare a timeline to assess training needs—with special emphasis on emergency department personnel, infectious disease specialists, public health staff, and other health care providers.

II. Hospital Preparedness (HRSA)

15. Designate a Coordinator for Bioterrorism Hospital Preparedness Planning.
16. Establish a Hospital Preparedness Planning Committee to provide guidance, direction and oversight to the State health department in planning for bioterrorism response.
17. Devise a plan for a potential epidemic in each state or region. Recognizing that many of these patients may come from rural areas served by centers in metropolitan areas, planning must include the surrounding counties likely to impact the resources of these cities.

Available at: *www.hhs.gov/news/press/2002pres/20020606a.html.* Accessed on: October 6, 2003.

least 500 acutely ill contagious patients per million population. (3) That a plan be developed in each state and local area for the distribution throughout the population of antibiotics or smallpox vaccine within a period of 7 days.

Programs at the federal level, as well as in states and communities, have continued to develop, gaining tempo as additional staff have been able to be recruited and trained. The active leadership provided by public health and medical professionals has been of singular importance in effecting an adequate preparedness program. An ongoing concern will be that of institutionalizing the program so that it assumes a leadership role in dealing with catastrophes of all types. The problems of bioterrorism, unfortunately will continue indefinitely, as will the challenges posed by new and emerging infections.

Detection and Diagnosis

The early detection of suspect cases and their prompt confirmation by laboratory or other means is the first essential step for an emergency response. Following an attack that employs any one of the Category A agents, the majority of patients would be severely, acutely ill and would be expected soon to be referred to emergency rooms with early consultation by infectious disease specialists. Thus, through a variety of educational approaches and training programs, emphasis has been placed on assuring that emergency room staff and the infectious disease specialists, in particular, are knowledgeable of the agents of greatest concern; know of the importance of prompt reporting to public health officials; and have access to laboratories that are prepared to provide rapid disease confirmation. A national network of more than 120 laboratories has been created which have had special training in the diagnosis of these agents and have the appropriate reagents to test them. They, in turn, are working with clinical laboratories to assure that specimens are referred appropriately and handled promptly (*www.bt.cdc.gov/labissues/index.asp*). A communications network is being built to assure that 24 hour a day, 7 days per week contact is possible between emergency and public health physicians, laboratory resources, and the first responders at the local community level, and between the public health officials at local, state and federal levels.

Three special experimental approaches are now being explored to determine if it might be possible to detect a possible attack at an earlier time. The first experimental approach is called syndromic surveillance.[32-35] In pilot programs, efforts are being made to monitor the number of cases with various general types of symptoms such as diarrhea, fever and rash or febrile respiratory infection by tracking clinics, emergency rooms or 911 calls. Should the number of such cases increase significantly above a certain threshold, an alert is sounded and an investigation commences. The belief is that the early nonspecific symptoms of several of the Category A agents may not serve to alert the busy clinician that there is an unusual cluster of cases occurring. Although intuitively attractive, serious questions have been raised as to whether this or any other surveillance system can be satisfactorily sustained, and at what cost, in the absence of regularly occurring and valid alarms that test the system.[36]

It would seem probable that, long before a syndromic surveillance system detected a sufficient number of cases that exceeded some threshold, emergency room physicians should already be raising an alarm based on only a few cases. It should not require many cases to alert even the minimally suspicious clinician: for example, three or four cases of very sick patients with a pustular rash (i.e., possible smallpox); or a few acute cases of previously healthy people with pneumonia and hemoptyis (i.e., possible pneumonic plague); or a few acute cases of otherwise healthy people with fever, difficulty breathing and a rapid downhill course (i.e., inhalational anthrax). Sensitized staff in the nation's 2000 emergency rooms and assured lines of communication between them and infectious disease and public health specialists would seem to offer a better alarm system than large volumes of crude data.

A second experimental approach is through what is commonly called "data mining." It is the collection of information that is regularly being garnered for other reasons to determine if this might provide an earlier alert and response than would be likely through emergency room contacts. Thus, daily absentee data from schools and industries are being gathered, as well as sales of different classes of drugs. Almost certainly, there will be other data sets explored. On practical grounds, this approach appears even less attractive than syndromic surveillance if intended for early identification of Class A agents. It could serve to identify the usual seasonal outbreaks of influenza, and perhaps might identify a community-wide outbreak of mild gastroenteritis, such as was caused in Milwaukee by cryptosporidia,[37,38] but its utility in dealing with a terrorist agent is doubtful.

A third experimental approach consists of collecting and testing daily air samples from some 2000 existing air sampling sites around the country to determine if any reveal the presence of one of the Category A agents. This is a newly initiated government program named "BioWatch." The scheme poses truly difficult problems. First is the fact that several of the Category A agents will not survive long enough to be subjected to testing. Second is the fact that, with only 2000 sample points in 30 major US cities, it is unlikely that the system will detect anything but a massive release that has distributed organisms over a very wide area. The more probable scenarios are localized releases which would stand only a small percentage chance of being detected by the widely distributed air samplers. Third, this system, following an anthrax release, would not serve to give notice more than perhaps 24 hours earlier than it would otherwise be detected. To take advantage of this brief lead time presupposes that a suspect isolate would immediately trigger the rapid, widespread distribution of prophylactic antibiotics. The occurrence of one or two false alarms accompanied by the frenzy and publicity of response that would follow could seriously damage the credibility of government leadership. Illustrative of the problem was an event in October 2003 when two air monitors in Houston, Texas, detected the presence of tularemia on two consecutive days. Area hospitals and infectious disease specialists were warned about the possibility that a release had taken place but the authorities refrained from taking more definite action such as distributing antibiotics. Although three to five cases occur in Texas every year,[39] officials rapidly discounted the possibility of bioterrorism.[40]

Public Health Response

Identification that a biological weapon has been released demands an immediate response by public health authorities. CDC websites describe, in detail, steps to be taken (*www.bt.cdc.gov*). Most important is the need to determine as soon as possible when and where a release may have taken place so that all who were or might have been exposed can be dealt with. An epidemiological investigation should determine this by tracing patients' movements so as to determine, with other patients, a common time and site of exposure. A useful tool for determining time of release has been described by Sartwell.[41] It consists of plotting cases by time on a log scale on one axis, and the cumulative percentage of cases, likewise on a log scale, on the other axis. The intercept of the line through the points provides a remarkably accurate time of release for a common source exposure.

If the disease is contagious (i.e., smallpox, plague, Ebola, Marburg or Lassa fever), the patient will need to be isolated and his close contacts identified. If smallpox, all persons who have been in contact with the patient since onset of fever should be vaccinated and placed under daily surveillance for the detection of symptoms (*www.bt.cdc.gov/agent/smallpox/response-plan/index.asp*). If the case is plague, prophylaxis of all close contacts with a suitable antibiotic[29] and daily surveillance for symptoms is recommended. If it is one of the contagious hemorrhagic fever viruses, there should be surveillance of contacts with immediate isolation if symptoms develop.[25]

The extent of vaccination for smallpox will need to be weighed. Certainly, all staff in hospitals that are likely to see or admit smallpox patients should be promptly vaccinated as well as first responders. Vaccination should also be made available to all who wish to avail themselves of it. One should note that, comparatively, smallpox is *not* especially contagious,[42] and that containment of outbreaks depends primarily on patient isolation and vaccination of close contacts. Thus, given the risks associated with vaccination, it would not be prudent to try to mount a program that endeavors to vaccinate everyone.

Pneumonic plague, although responsible for the Black Death of the Middle Ages, is in today's society far less contagious than smallpox. Indeed, over the past 75 years, few secondary cases have been reported even among household contacts of those with the pneumonic form of the disease. Thus, prophylactic antibiotics should be restricted to those who are or have been in especially close contact. Somewhat more contagious are some of the hemorrhagic fever viruses, but, as has been shown in various outbreaks in resource-limited settings, simple measures (involving cap, gown and gloves) restrict transmission quite effectively.

The major challenge to public health officials is that of instituting necessary measures to avoid panic in the face of an epidemic of a traditionally feared disease. Reviews of past epidemics indicate that the most essential factor is effective leadership and competent, frequent and open communication with the public, the press, professionals and others concerned in dealing with the epidemic. This is an area that is too often neglected. The 2001 anthrax outbreak in the United States illustrated well the problems resulting from inadequate lines of communication.[43] Health departments at all levels were overwhelmed by requests for information from the public, from health professionals, and especially from the media. None had experienced an epidemic threat such as this, and none were prepared. Frequent, authoritative, up-to-date reports through the media to the public proved absolutely vital, but it took time before a pattern for these became established. The need for communication between and among professionals was clear, and this is now being addressed in part by the national Health Alert Network which is financed by federal preparedness funds. It was also apparent that command centers were required to coordinate and direct operations and to facilitate the flow of information, but these took time to become established and to begin to function well. Sophisticated centers are now in place in the Secretary's Office at DHHS, CDC and in many states and cities; they are now staffed on a continuous basis. Information and education materials have been prepared with respect to Category A diseases and are available throughout the health system. Of importance is the fact that at federal, state, and local levels, exercises are being conducted to test response systems to determine how well they are actually functioning.

A second factor in muting the likelihood of panic is to do all possible to keep the normal day-to-day activities of citizens and the city as minimally disrupted as possible. Public officials at all levels have often been prone to want to invoke quarantine measures, whether to close airports or other parts of the transportation network or to forbid entry or departure from cities or other large areas. This was the case in all countries that reported cases of SARS in 2003. Experience has shown that quarantine measures are seldom effective and, in fact, often lead to more serious problems as many seek to flee an area or deny the possible presence of possible cases in family or friends thus precluding appropriate containment measures.[44]

An important resource in effecting an adequate response to a bioweapons attack is the Strategic National Stockpile, which consists of 12 strategically located repositories of therapeutics and durable medical equipment, each of a size fabricated to be easily transported by a plane the size of a Boeing 747. They can be delivered within 12 hours to any place in the country accompanied by a special team trained to unpack the material and to get it to public health and medical authorities for immediate use. In all, there is sufficient smallpox vaccine to vaccinate, if necessary, the entire US population; large quantities of antibiotics for prophylaxis of those possibly exposed to anthrax and for treatment of those with plague or tularemia; ventilatory support equipment; drugs to deal with a chemical attack; supplies for treatment of trauma victims; and other equipment identified by a consultant group of emergency medicine specialists as being critical to deal with a catastrophic problem.

Research and Development

Research specifically directed at problems posed by the development and application of biological weapons was, until very recently, primarily conducted by the Department of Defense, principally the U.S. Army Medical Research Institute for Infectious Diseases in Frederick, Maryland. Under the provisions of the 1972 Biological Weapons Convention, the research related basically to defensive measures against validated threat agents. As concerns about the potential use of biological agents have mounted and preparedness programs have begun to be elaborated, it has become abundantly clear that there are many facets of a public health and medical response that could be better handled if there were a better understanding of disease pathogenesis and immune response, and if there were available more appropriate technologies for detection, diagnosis, treatment, prevention and environmental mitigation. Some represent immediate term needs such as that of producing a contemporary, second-generation smallpox vaccine grown in tissue cell culture; others require a longer term vision and are dependent on basic science initiatives to broaden the understanding of health and disease. The importance of a major research effort was reinforced by the sudden emergence of SARS in the spring of 2003 and the extraordinary impact it had on Asian countries and the city of Toronto, Canada. To deal with SARS, there is a real and urgent need for diagnostics, sensitive detection devices, a vaccine and antiviral agents. As has become clear, the challenge of a new, naturally emergent microbial agent was remarkably congruent with needs related to national security against a biological weapons attack, whether utilizing known agents or genetic mutants.

After the September 11 attack on the United States, one of the most urgent challenges was to prepare to deal with the two agents that had received the most attention during the course of the Soviet biological weapons program and which presumably could have been acquired or developed by any of a number of countries—smallpox and anthrax. Only 15 million doses of smallpox vaccine remained in storage from the 1970s, when smallpox had been eradicated and vaccination had stopped. This amount was woefully insufficient to cope with epidemic smallpox should the virus be released. The old vaccine had been a crude preparation produced on the skin of calves and would not meet the standards of a contemporary vaccine. Moreover, there were no remaining vaccine production facilities anywhere in the world. It was estimated then that some 5 years would be required, following traditional vaccine development protocols, to develop, produce, and license a new vaccine, grown, as are contemporary vaccines, in tissue cell culture. The challenge of securing, as soon as possible, sufficient vaccine to vaccinate, if necessary, every American was entrusted to a team headed by Dr. Philip Russell and comprised of industry scientists and representatives from FDA, CDC and NIH. In less than 18 months, 200 million doses of vaccine had been produced and tested for antigenicity, and the vaccine was ready for use as an investigational new drug in the event of an emergency. Final licensure is expected in 2004. The team has also undertaken the accelerated development and production of a second-generation recombinant anthrax vaccine and an attenuated, nonreplicating smallpox vaccine which it is expected would induce fewer adverse reactions.

These experiences demonstrated the need to be prepared to act quickly and, as necessary, to develop and quickly procure vaccines, antitoxins or antimicrobial agents and to be able to make these available for field use. Legislation to provide for a project called Bioshield was proposed and passed in November 2003. It provides a substantial fund to permit the rapid development and procurement of products serving as countermeasures to deal with dangerous pathogens and permits promising treatments to be made available in emergency situations.

Meanwhile, the Congress appropriated to NIAID US\$ 1.7 billion for research relevant to the biological weapons threat. Part of this award will initially fund 8 regional centers of excellence that would support collaborative research programs involving several different institutions. Other initiatives include grants for fellowships, investigator initiated research projects, and construction of high security facilities to permit safe experimentation with the more dangerous pathogens.

THE TWO-EDGED SWORD OF MODERN BIOLOGY

The rapidly accruing knowledge base of modern biology is making it possible to understand such factors as how and why a particular organism causes the pathology it does; how it may escape whatever immune mechanisms the body may possess; what genes may be responsible for its ability to spread from cell to cell and from man to man; and what the effect might be of inserting genes from one organism into another to obtain unique characteristics.[45] What once were the tools of exploration for only the most sophisticated laboratories are now increasingly present in laboratories of developing countries or even in high school laboratories. For those interested in bioterrorism, a new world is opening and, indeed, Russian scientists have reported in the open literature of developing an antibiotic-resistant strain of anthrax[46] and plague.[10] Apart from research dealing directly with biological agents, unexpected and unintended results are possible working with other microbes as happened with researchers at the John Curtin School in Australia.[47] They added a single gene to the mousepox virus and found, to their surprise, that it shut down the immunological response even of vaccinated mice which are normally fully protected by vaccine. The question of whether the addition of this gene to smallpox, a

closely related virus, would shut down the immune defenses of humans cannot be definitively answered. Some believe it might; most do not believe so. Certainly, one must anticipate the potential of many more experiments over the months and years ahead that will have unintended consequences, some of which could be catastrophic.

How to deal with the problems of access to known biological pathogens of concern and how to assure control, or at least responsible stewardship, of laboratory work is a vexing question yet to be answered. The problem is that the more extensive and restrictive the controls, the more difficult it will be to undertake studies that are needed to produce better vaccines, better drugs, or other products. To know precisely which gene of an organism causes damage and how it acts may permit a highly targeted vaccine or drug, but, at the same time, it identifies a gene that if inserted into another organism could produce a devastating effect.

Appropriate restrictions on work in laboratories will undoubtedly be required as has never before been needed, but determining what these should be, balancing security and the needs of freedom for inquiry will not be easy. Two Acts have been passed by Congress and both are problematic in various ways—The Patriot Act (2001) and the Public Health Security and Bioterrorism Preparedness and Response Act (2002).[45] The former criminalizes possession of biological agents unless justified by a prophylactic, protective, bona fide research, or other peaceful purpose and prohibits the possession, transport, and receipt of select agents by convicted felons; foreign nationals from terrorism-sponsoring nations; individuals dishonorably discharged from the Armed Services; and users of controlled substances. The second act noted requires that the Secretary of DHHS maintain a list of select agents; requires research facilities possessing select agents to register their possession to the CDC; requires background checks of those in possession of select agents to ensure that they are not convicted felons, and so forth; and requires the establishment of safeguard and security measures to prevent access for such agents and toxins for use in domestic or international terrorism or for any other criminal purpose.

The cost and complexity of physical facilities and procedures that limit access are consequential. There are laboratories that are abandoning studies simply because of these factors. The costs of registering and policing compliance are likewise substantial. More salient is the question of what efficacy these procedures may have in deterrence recognizing that few other nations have implemented measures that are, in any way, comparable.

Discussions are taking place in the United States and international forums with hopes that some rational and effective systems can be agreed on that will act to lessen the likelihood of biological agents being developed and used for sinister purposes. In October 2003, the US National Academies of Sciences' Committee on Research Standards and Practices to Prevent the Destructive Application of Biotechnology issued a report on ways to balance national security and scientific openness. The Committee recommended that a system of responsible oversight, consisting of voluntary self-governance by the scientific community and an expansion of existing regulatory processes, be developed for scientific experimentations in the life sciences in order to hinder their unintentional development as weapons.[48] It will be difficult at best to achieve reasonable goals, but the need is real and urgent.

REFERENCES

1. O'Toole T, Inglesby TV, Henderson DA. Why understanding biological weapons matters to medical and public health professionals. In: O'Toole T, Inglesby TV, Henderson DA, eds. Bioterrorism: Guidelines for Medical and Public Health Mangement. Chicago: AMA Press; 2002:1-7.
2. Inglesby TV, O'Toole T, Henderson DA, et al. Anthrax as a biological weapon: Updated recommendations for management. In: O'Toole T, Inglesby TV, Henderson DA, eds. Bioterrorism: Guidelines for Medical and Public Health Management. Chicago: AMA Press; 2002:63-97.
3. Institute of Medicine Committee. In: Lederberg J, Shope RE, Oaks SC, eds. Emerging Microbial Threats to Health. Washington, DC: National Academy Press; 1992.
4. Ehrlich PR, Harte J, Harwell MA, et al. Long-term biological consequences of nuclear war. Science. 1983;222:1293-300.
5. Williams P, Wallace D. Unit 731. New York: The Free Press; 1989.

6. Daplan E, Marchell A. The Cult at the End of the World. New York: Crown; 1996.

7. Global proliferation of weapons of mass destruction: Hearings before the Permanent Subcommittee on Investigations of the Committee on Governmental Affairs, United States Senate, One Hundred Fourth Congress, first-second session. Washington, DC: US. Government Printing Office; 1996.

8. Ekeus R. Memorandum Report to the Security Council-Iraq's biological weapons programme: UNSCOM's experience. United Nations; 1996.

9. Zilinskas RA. Iraq's biological weapons: the past as future? JAMA. 1997;278:418-424.

10. Alibeck K. Biohazard. New York: Random House; 1999.

11. Roberts B. New challenges and new policy priorities for the 1990s. Biologic Weapons: Weapons of the Future. Washington, DC. Center for Strategic and International Studies; 1993.

12. Vorobjev AA, Cherkassky BL, Stepanov AV, et al. "Criterion rating" as a measure of probable use of bioagents as biological weapons. Presented to Working Group on Biological Weapons Control of the Committee on International Security and Arms Control, National Academy of Sciences; 1994.

13. Wehrle PF, Posch J, Richter KH, Henderson DA. An airborne outbreak of smallpox in a German hospital and its significance with respect to other recent outbreaks in Europe. Bull WHO. 1970;43:669-679.

14. Fenner F, Henderson DA, Arita I, et al. Smallpox and Its Eradication. Geneva: World Health Organization; 1988.

15. Brachman PS, Friedlander AM. Anthrax. In: Plotkin SA, Orenstein WA, eds. Vaccines. Philadelphia: WB Saunders; 1999:629-637.

16. Meselson M, Guillemin V, Hugh-Jones M, et al. The Sverdlovsk anthrax outbreak of 1979. Science. 1994;266:1202-1208.

17. Blank S, Moskin LC, Zucker JR. An ounce of prevention is a ton of work: Mass antibiotic prophylaxis for anthrax, New York City, 2001. Emerg Infect Dis. 2003;9:615-622.

18. Gould R, Connell ND. The public health effects of biological weapons. In: Levy BS, Sidel VW, eds. War and Public Health. New York: Oxford Press; 1997:98-116.

19. Eitzen EM, Takafuji ET. Historical overview of biological warfare. In: Siddel FR, Takafuji ET, Franz DR, eds. Medical Aspects of Chemical and Biological Warfare. Washington: Office of the Surgeon General; 1997:415-423.

20. Hopkins DR. The Greatest Killer: Smallpox in History. Chicago: University of Chicago Press; 2002.

21. Christopher GW, Cieslak TJ, Pavlin JA, Eitzen EM. Biological warfare: A historical perspective. JAMA. 1997;278:412-417.

22. Fenn EA. Pax Americana. New York: Hill and Wang; 2001.

23. Henderson DA. The looming threat of bioterrorism. Science. 2003;283:1279-1282.

24. Arnon SS, Schechter R, Inglesby TV, et al. Botulinum toxin as a biological weapon: Medical and public health management. JAMA. 2001; 285:1059-1069.

25. Borio L, Inglesby TV, Peters CJ, et al. Hemorrhagic fever viruses as biological weapons: Medical and public health management. JAMA. 2002;287:2391-2405.

26. Dennis DT, Inglesby TV, Henderson DA, et al. Tularemia as a biological weapon: Medical and Public health management. JAMA. 2001;285:2763-2773.

27. Henderson DA, Inglesby TV, Bartlett JG, et al. Smallpox as a biological weapon: Medical and ublic health management. JAMA. 1999;281:2127-2137.

28. Inglesby TV, Henderson DA, Bartlett JG, Ascher MS, et al. Anthrax as a biological weapon: Medical and public health management. JAMA. 1999;281:1735-1745.

29. Inglesby TV, Dennis DT, Henderson DA, et al. Plague as a biological weapon: Medical and public health management. JAMA. 2000;283:2281-2291.

30. Bioterrorism: Guidelines for Medical and Public Health Management. Chicago: American Medical Association; 2002.

31. Office of Technology Assessment UC. Prolifferation of Weapons of Mass Destruction. Washington, DC: US Government Printing Office, 1993.

32. Lazarus R, Kleinmann K, Dashevsky I, et al. Use of automated ambulatory-care encounter records for detection of acute illness clusters, including potential bioterrorism events. Emerg Infect Dis. 2002;8:753-760.

33. Lewis MD, Pavlin JA, Mansfield JL, et al. Disease outbreak detection system using syndromic data in the greater Washington, DC area. Am J Prev Med. 2002;23:180-186.

34. Lombardo J, Burkom H, Elbert E, et al. A systems overview of the electronic surveillance system for the early notification of community-based epidemics (ESSENCE II). J Urban Hlth. 2003;80 (Suppl 1):i32-i42.

35. Mostashari F, Fine A, Das D, et al. Use of ambulance dispatch data as an early warning system for communitywide influenza-like illness, New York City. J Urban Hlth 2003;80 (Suppl 1):i49.

36. Reingold A. If syndromic surveillance is the answer, what is the question. Biosecurity Bioterrorism 2003;77-81.

37. Assessing the public health threat associated with waterborne cryptosporidiosis: Report of a workshop. MMWR Recomm Rep. 1995; 44:1-19.

38. Dietz V, Vugia D, Nelson R, et al. Active, multisite, laboratory-based surveillance for Cryptosporidium parvum. Am J Trop Med Hyg. 2000; 62:368-372.

39. Chang MH, Glynn MK, Groseclose SL. Endemic, notifiable bioterrorism-related diseases, United States, 1992-1999. Emerg Infect Dis. 2003;9:556-564.

40. Berger E. Suspicious bacteria detected. Security monitors spot germ; terrorism discounted. Houston Chronicle Medical Writer, 2003.

41. Sartwell PE. The distribution of incubation periods of infectious diseases. Am J Epidemiol. 2003;51:310-318.

42. Mack TM. Smallpox in Europe, 1950-1971. J Infect Dis. 1972;125:161-169.

43. Gursky E, Inglesby TV, O'Toole T. Anthrax 2001: Observations on the medical and public health response. Biosecurity Bioterrorism 2003;1:97-110.

44. Barbera J, Macintyre A, Gostin L, et al. Large-scale quarantine following biological terrorism in the United States. JAMA. 2002; 286:2711-2717.

45. Kwik G, Fitzgerald J, Inglesby TV, O'Toole T. Biosecurity: Responsible stewardship of bioscience in an age of catastrophic terrorism. Biosecurity Bioterrorism. 2003;1:27-35.

46. Pomerantsev AP, Staritsin NA, Mockov YV, Marinin LJ, et al. Expression of cereolysine AB genes in Bacillus anthracis vaccine strain ensure protection against experimental hemolytic anthrax infection. Vaccine. 1997;15:1846-1850.

47. Jackson RJ, Ramsay AJ, Christensen CD, et al. Expression of mouse interleukin-4 by a recombinant ectromelia virus suppresses cytolytic lymphocyte responses and overcomes genetic resistance to mouse pox. J Virol. 2001;75:1205-1210.

48. Committee on Research Standards and Practices to Prevent the Destructive Application of Biotechnology NRC. Biotechnology Research in an Age of Terrorism: Confronting the Dual Use Dilemma. Washington, DC: National Academy Press, 2003.

CHAPTER **321**

Plague as an Agent of Bioterrorism

LUCIANA L. BORIO

HISTORY AND POTENTIAL USE AS A BIOTERRORIST AGENT

Plague pandemics have historically been responsible for more social and economic devastation than armed conflict.[1] Between the 6th and 20th century A.D. three great pandemics resulted in more than 200 million deaths. The first pandemic originated in Central Africa and spread throughout the Mediterranean basin, affecting the Byzantine Empire during the reign of Justinian I in the 6th century A.D. It resulted in the loss of approximately 25% of the population of southern Europe and contributed to the demise of the Roman Empire. The second pandemic, infamously known as the Black Death or the Great Pestilence, reportedly decimated between 30% and 40% of the populations of major European cities between 1347 and 1351. Epidemic cycles continued to occur until the end of the 17th century. The third, or "Modern" pandemic, arose in China in the late 19th century and spread throughout the world until the mid-20th century. It killed 12.5 million people in India[2] alone and reached San Francisco in 1899. Today, zoonotic foci of plague exists on every major inhabited continent, with the exception of Australia.[1]

The first recorded use of plague in warfare occurred in 1346, during the siege of the Crimean port city of Kaffa (now Feodosiya, Ukraine) on the Black Sea.[3] The port city served as a gateway to the Silk Road trade route and was thus an important military target. The invading Muslim Tatars catapulted the bodies of bubonic plague victims over the city walls while fighting the Christian Genoese sailors. The resulting epidemic led the Genoese sailors to flee to Italy, likely in plague and rat-infested ships, entering several Italian ports which may have caused the second great pandemic (Black Death). The same technique was used by the Russians in 1710, while besieging Swedish forces in Reval, Estonia.

In World War II the Japanese Military Unit 731 (a secret biowarfare research unit) used several pathogens, including Yersinia pestis, the causative agent of plague, to infect prisoners of war in Ping Fan, Manchuria.[4] This is believed to have resulted in the deaths of approximately 3000 prisoners. They also repeatedly released plague in the civilian population in Chekiang Province, China, during that time period. The weapons effort was led by General Shiro Ishii, a physician, who developed a mechanism for dropping plague-infected human fleas (Pulex irritans) inside clay bombs from airplanes. Eighty percent of the fleas were shown to survive this method of delivery, in contrast to bacteria-filled aerial bombs, which were ineffective as a result of harsh pressure and temperature effects of explosions on the bacteria.[5]

In 1989, Vladmir Pasechnik, a Soviet biologist who had directed the Institute for Ultrapure Biological Preparations in Leningrad, defected to Britain.[6,7] He revealed that the Soviets had succeeded in preparing Y. pestis as an aerosolizable powder, genetically engineering it to be resistant to several antibiotics. The Soviets had the capacity to load this "superplague" into bombs, rocket warheads and artillery shells, as well as strategic intercontinental ballistic missiles. The Soviets may have produced up to 1500 metric tons of this formulation yearly and undertook field tests with it. According to Sergei Popov, another former Soviet bioweapons scientist who defected to Britain in 1992, the Soviets also engineered *Y. pestis* to produce diphtheria toxin.[8,9] The resulting organism was highly virulent in laboratory animals.

In 1995, a white supremacist and microbiologist, Larry Wayne Harris, succeeded in purchasing vials of lyophilized *Y. pestis* from the American Type Culture Collection via a fraudulent request.[10] Harris served an 18-month probation, but his intent was never identified. The episode caused alarm and prompted Congress to pass the first of several regulations governing the acquisition, use and transfer of biological agents that could be developed as bioweapons in 1996.

Y. pestis is one of ten agents deemed by the US Army Research Medical Research Institute of Infectious Diseases to be most suitable for development as a bioweapon.[11] *Y. pestis* is also one of six "Category A" agents, deemed by the Centers for Disease Control and Prevention (CDC) to be of highest concern.[12] Today, several factors characterize *Y. pestis* as a potential bioterrorist weapon. *Y. pestis* is available from culture collections in a number of different countries; it may be produced in large quantity and disseminated as an aerosol; the disease is contagious and, if untreated, is associated with a high fatality rate; and the organism has some limited potential for becoming established in the environment. The impact of modern biotechnology in enhancing bacterial virulence cannot be underestimated—antimicrobial resistant strains have been developed, as have factor 1 (F1)-deficient strains that retain virulence[13,14] but evade F1 antigen-based immunity and certain diagnostic tests. Furthermore, the public's perception and historical familiarity with the disease is such that even a small outbreak could possibly result in generalized panic in the community. Although advances in living conditions, medicine and public health make naturally occurring plague pandemics highly improbable, an intentional plague outbreak could have serious consequences. Civil unrest characterized the plague outbreak in Surat, India, in 1994,[15] and provides an indication of the perception of plague in a modern society. The small outbreak, which led to only 52 deaths, resulted in mass exodus of up to one-half a million people from the city and consequent serious economic loss.

Aerosol dissemination of *Y. pestis* would lead to an outbreak of predominantly pneumonic plague, with a very different epidemiologic pattern from a naturally occurring outbreak. The likely size of an epidemic after an aerosol attack is not possible to predict given the many variables involved, including the amount of agent used, environmental conditions, methods of aerosolization, and population density at the "epicenter." Transmission of plague via respiratory droplets or aerosols require an infectious dose of as few as 100 to 500 organisms.[1] In experimentally infected *Macacus rhesus,* the LD_{50} is approximately 20,000 inhaled bacteria.[16] In 1970, the World Health Organization (WHO) assessed that, in a worst-case scenario, 50 kg of *Y. pestis* released as an aerosol over a city of 5 million people could result in 150,000 cases of pneumonic plague, leading to 80,000 to 100,000 hospitalizations and 36,000 deaths.[17] That report estimated that plague bacilli would remain viable as an aerosol for one hour and cover an area extending up to ten kilometers from the point of release. Moreover, *Y. pestis* has the potential to become persistent in the environment if there are suitable rodent reservoirs and efficient flea vectors in the area of dissemination.

CLINICAL MANIFESTATIONS

Naturally acquired plague may manifest as one of three primary clinical entities: bubonic, septicemic, or pneumonic. Plague may sometimes be complicated by meningeal involvement. Primary pneumonic plague occurs after the inhalation of infectious respiratory droplets, usually from an infected animal or human with plague pneumonia or, in the case of a bioterrorist attack, an aerosol. Secondary pneumonic plague may arise from untreated septicemic or bubonic plague. The

difference between primary and secondary pneumonic plague is of no therapeutic importance; both are associated with a fulminant course and a very high mortality in the absence of early antimicrobial therapy. Secondary transmission by droplet spread from a patient to close contacts may occur. In the United States, between 1988 and 1994, the relative prevalence of clinical forms of plague were as follows: 78% bubonic, 13.2% septicemic, 4.4% pneumonic, 2.9% undetermined, and 1.5% plague meningitis.[1]

In the context of a bioterrorist aerosol attack, primary pneumonic plague is the most likely outcome. However, animal studies suggest that inhalation of aerosolized *Y. pestis* may also lead to bubonic and septicemic plague.[16] Particles smaller than 1 micron are inhaled deep into the alveoli and lead to bronchopneumonia, whereas larger particles of 10 to 12 μm are deposited in the nasopharyngeal epithelium, multiply in the cervical lymph nodes, are transported via afferent lymphatics and result in septicemia. In experimentally infected mice, inhalation of an aerosol of *Y. pestis* resulted in lobar pneumonia in 65%, cervical buboes (with or without pneumonic infarcts) in 31%, and septicemia in 4%.[16]

Historically, the usual incubation period of pneumonic plague has been 2 to 4 days (range 1 to 6 days).[18] Initially, pneumonic plague resembles other severe respiratory illnesses, including influenza, severe acute respiratory syndrome, bacterial pneumonia or inhalational anthrax. The first symptoms are characterized by malaise, myalgias, headache, high fever and rigors. Cervical and axillary buboes (see Chapter 224) may be present in primary pneumonic plague.[16] Overwhelming septicemia and bronchopneumonia ensue.

The chest radiograph may show segmental or lobar involvement, followed by multilobar or confluent pneumonia.[19,20] Cavitation may occur early, but this is a rare event.[20] There is no evidence of mediastinal widening such as is found in cases of inhalational anthrax.

Laboratory data may reveal leukocytosis in the range of 10,000 to 20,000 toxic granulations, coagulopathy, elevated liver enzymes and azotemia. The sputum is characteristically watery and bloody, and contains viable plague bacilli.

Factors that may help distinguish pneumonic plague from community-acquired pneumonia or influenza are hemoptysis, absence of coryza, and the sputum gram stain. Furthermore, pneumonic plague is characterized by a fulminant course, even in previously healthy young persons. The disease is nearly 100% fatal within 2 to 3 days[16] in persons in whom antimicrobial therapy is delayed more than 18 hours after the onset of respiratory symptoms.[18]

A deliberate event employing *Y. pestis* should be considered in any outbreak of severe bronchopneumonia in previously healthy persons, or the emergence of plague in nonendemic areas.

LABORATORY DIAGNOSTIC METHODS

The Laboratory Response Network for Bioterrorism (LRN) is a consortium of academic, private and public health laboratories that follow consensus protocols to rule out and identify microorganisms that may be used in bioterrorism. Each laboratory is assigned a different function, designated as levels A through D. Most clinical microbiology laboratories are designated as "screening" laboratories (level A), major public health laboratories are "confirmatory" (level B or C), and the CDC and USAMRIID laboratories serve a "reference" function (level D). Level A laboratories are generally not equipped to make a definitive diagnosis, but are able to rule out or refer a specimen to more sophisticated laboratories that have the capability to isolate, identify, perform susceptibility testing and further characterization of the putative organism. In addition, level A laboratories do not process nonclinical specimens (i.e., environmental sampling). Whereas Biological Safety Level 2 practices are recommended for level A laboratories, Biological Safety Level 3 practices or higher are required for level B to D laboratories. It is imperative that a level A laboratory consult with a state or territory public health laboratory prior to or during testing when *Y. pestis* is suspected.

In the case of pneumonic plague, stain and culture of bronchial wash or expectorated sputum may yield a tentative diagnosis.[21] The organisms may also be identified by stain and culture of blood or aspirates of tissue (such as a bubo or a lymph node). Gram stain reveals plump, gram-negative rods, 1 to 2 μm × 0.5 μm. In liquid media, these appear mostly as single cells, pairs, or short chains. Although the Gram stain may reveal a bipolar staining (or "safety-pin") that is characteristic (but not diagnostic) of *Y. pestis* (and other *Yersinia* spp.), Wright-Giemsa or Wayson stains are generally preferred as they are more likely to demonstrate this characteristic.

Y. pestis grows best at ambient temperatures (22° to 28° C) and atmosphere, and slower at 35° to 37° C and 5% CO_2. Plates should be held for 5 days (or 7 days in the event of exposure to antimicrobials). In agar plates, colonies are small, grayish white and translucent. Under magnification or longer incubation, they may develop a "fried egg" appearance, slightly raised. There is minimal or no hemolysis on sheep red blood agar, and colonies are small and do not ferment lactose on selective agar such as MacConkey or eosin methylene blue. In broth, *Y. pestis* grows in clumps. *Y. pestis* is oxidase, urease and indole negative, and catalase positive, and alkaline slant/acid butt in triple sugar iron. *Y. pestis* is relatively inert biochemically, and has been misidentified in automated identification systems.[22]

If a screening laboratory is unable to rule out the possibility of *Y. pestis,* it should immediately notify the local or state public health department and laboratory, which will in turn notify local FBI authorities and others as appropriate.

Confirmatory laboratories, generally at the major county or state level, and other reference laboratories, use a variety of additional tests, such as direct fluorescent antibody test to detect the F1 envelope antigen. Polymerase chain reaction technology for plague is now deployed to confirmatory level laboratories and can be performed on isolates or direct clinical samples. Serologic tests are performed at the reference level. Passive hemagglutination antibody detection in acute- or convalescent-phase plasma, showing a fourfold increase in titer or a single titer greater than 1:10 specific to F1 antigen of *Y. pestis,* would meet presumptive criteria for plague infection. This test is of retrospective value only because it takes days for hemagglutination antibodies to form after disease onset.[19]

There are several promising rapid diagnostic tests under development. An F1 antigen immunocapture enzyme-limked immunosorbent assay (ELISA) and immunogold chromatography dipstick were found to be highly specific but sensitive only if specimens were bubo aspirates.[23] Another dipstick test using monoclonal antibodies to detect F1 antigen has shown promise in preliminary field studies in Madagascar.[24]

In the event of bioterrorist attack, determination of antimicrobial susceptibility of the organisms is essential given the possibility that a naturally occurring or an engineered strain resistant to multiple antibiotics might have been employed. Until such results are obtained, the choice of antibiotics will have to take this possibility into account.

PROPHYLACTIC ANTIMICROBIAL AGENTS

A consensus statement developed by the Working Group on Civilian Biodefense in 2000 recommends a 7-day course of antimicrobial prophylaxis for asymptomatic people with a common source exposure to an aerosol of *Y. pestis,* or with household, healthcare, or close (i.e., less than 2 meters) contact with a patient suspected of having pneumonic plague (Table 321-1).[25] Of note, mice infected with F1-negative strain have been shown to have a diminished response to prophylaxis with doxycycline,[26] but there is no data to support this in humans. Persons who have had close contact with an infected person should also be placed under surveillance for the development of symptoms. Those who have symptoms consistent with pneumonic plague, such as fever or cough, should receive therapy, preferably parenterally.

Only antibiotics of the tetracycline class (including doxycycline, minocycline, and demeclocycline) and streptomycin are currently licensed by the Food and Drug Administration (FDA) to treat infections caused by *Y. pestis.* Several antimicrobials (e.g., ciprofloxacin, gentamicin, and doxycycline) are included in the US Government's Strategic National Stockpile (SNS), have been recommended by the

TABLE 321-1 Working Group on Civilian Biodefense Recommendations for Treatment of Patients with Pneumonic Plague

Contained Casualty Setting

Preferred Choices

Streptomycin	1g IM twice daily
Gentamicin[†]	5 mg/kg IM or IV once daily or 2 mg/kg loading dose followed by 1.7 mg/kg IM or IV 3 times daily

Alternative Choices

Doxycycline[†,§]	100 mg IV twice daily or 200 mg IV once daily
Ciprofloxacin[†,‡]	400 mg IV twice daily
Chloramphenicol	25 mg/kg IV 4 times daily

Mass Casualty Setting or Postexposure Prophylaxis

Preferred Choices

Doxycycline[†,§]	100 mg orally twice daily
Ciprofloxacin[†,‡]	500 mg orally twice daily

Alternative Choices

Chloramphenicol[†]	25 mg/kg orally 4 times daily

*Only streptomycin and drugs of the tetracycline class are approved by the FDA for the treatment of plague. Duration of therapy (parenteral or oral) should be 10 days; oral therapy may be substituted when the patient's condition improves. Duration of postexposure prophylaxis should be 7 days.
†Recommended preferred or alternative choices for pregnant women.
‡Other fluoroquinolones may be substituted.
§Tetracycline may be substituted for doxycycline.
IM, intramuscularly; IV, intravenously.
Adapted from Inglesby TV, Dennis DT, Henderson DA, et al. Plague as a biological weapon: medical and public health management. Working Group on Civilian Biodefense. JAMA 2000;283:2281-2290.

Working Group on Civilian Biodefense[25] and could be deployed in response to an intentional release of plague. However, neither ciprofloxacin nor gentamicin are currently FDA approved for the management of plague. The paucity of FDA-approved antimicrobials to prevent or treat plague poses a logistical challenge in responding to a bioterrorist attack. Apart from tetracyclines and streptomycin, if other antimicrobials are deployed from the SNS in response to a plague, their use would be subject to FDA's Investigational New Drug (IND) regulations. The CDC and FDA have developed a streamlined IND process for a number of antibiotics that might be present in the stockpile but are not FDA approved for the management of plague. For example, streamlined INDs have been prepared should gentamicin or ciprofloxacin be deployed from the SNS in response to bioterrorism-related plague (personal communication with Dr. Debra Yeskey, CDC). The successful distribution of prophylactic antibiotics in a mass casualty situation is resource intensive and requires extensive pre-event planning.[27]

POTENTIAL USE OF VACCINES IN THE POST-EVENT PERIOD

At present, there are no vaccines that would be of use in preventing or ameliorating pneumonic plague. Two types of plague vaccines, inactivated and live-attenuated, have been developed. A formalin-inactivated whole cell vaccine is licensed for use in the United States to protect against bubonic plague but it is no longer commercially available. It requires a series of injections, up to 10% of recipients experience an adverse effect,[28] and it does not appear to be protective against pneumonic plague either in humans[29,30] or in experimentally infected animals.[31] Live-attenuated vaccines have been developed and used in the former USSR and former French colonies,[28] but their safety and efficacy have never been established in controlled, randomized clinical trials.[32] In mice, a live-attenuated vaccine comprised of the EV76 strain proved protective against an inhalation challenge with *Y. pestis,* but resulted in 1% fatality.[31] The development of a subunit vaccine using the F1 capsular protein has been the focus of recent efforts, and it has been shown to protect mice against an aerosol challenge.[28] A vaccine in which the F1 antigen is the sole protective immunogen would, of course, not be effective in infections caused by F1-deficient *Y. pestis.*[14] Neutralizing monoclonal antibodies raised against the V antigen,[33] as well as passive transfer of F1+V immune serum[34] seem to protect mice against infection with *Y. pestis.*

The lack of a suitable plague vaccine hinders efforts by the scientific community to engage in research on plague. Even if developed, licensing of plague vaccines represent a problem given that the infrequency and unpredictability of naturally occurring plague outbreaks preclude the development of large, randomized, controlled clinical trials.

PROTECTIVE MEASURES FOR USE IN THE COMMUNITY

Unless an effective biodetection system were in place, a bioterrorist attack employing an aerosol of *Y. pestis* would be undetected. An aerosol after release would be odorless, colorless and would likely go unnoticed until the first victims fell ill 1 to 6 days after exposure. For asymptomatic persons known to have been exposed to an aerosol of *Y. pestis,* as well as for those who have had close contact with an ill person, antimicrobial prophylaxis for 7 days is recommended.[25]

Hospital Infection Control Measures

Plague is a WHO Class I notifiable disease, subject to International Health Regulations, owing to its high associated mortality and epidemic potential. Thus, any suspected case must be notified to public health authorities, and any confirmed case must be notified to the WHO. In the United States, 381 cases of plague have occurred between 1970 and 2001,[35] and bubonic infection accounts for the vast majority of them. Primary pneumonic plague is rare and most likely acquired from the inhalation of infectious respiratory droplets from infected animals, such as domestic cats.[18] In the United States, only five cases of primary pneumonic plague from such contact has occurred in veterinarians or their assistants since 1977.[36] The last outbreak of pneumonic plague which resulted in person-to-person transmission in the United States occurred in 1924 to 1925 in Los Angeles.[1] Thus, a pneumonic plague case suggests that a bioterrorist attack may have taken place.

The CDC recommends that all persons suspected of having pneumonic plague be placed under standard and respiratory droplet isolation precautions (see Chapter 298) for the first 48 hours of treatment and clinical improvement has taken place.[18] Those with confirmed pneumonic plague should remain under droplet precautions until sputum cultures are negative. Untreated plague pneumonia is an epidemiologic emergency. All contacts must be identified promptly and those with face-to-face exposure should receive prophylactic antibiotic therapy (see Table 321-1). All contacts should be placed under surveillance, with twice-daily temperature checks, for seven days, while on prophylaxis.

It is also important to alert laboratory personnel processing specimens of patients with suspected or confirmed *Y. pestis* infections so that appropriate measures to avoid laboratory-acquired incidents may be undertaken.[37]

Environmental Surveillance and Decontamination

At present, there is no method for the concurrent environmental detection of a *Y. pestis* bioterrorist release, and it is unlikely that such a system will be developed. In 2003, the newly created Department of Homeland Security, together with the Environmental Protection Agency, the Department of Defense, and the Department of Health and Human Services launched project *BioWatch.* This biodetection system employs the use of environmental air filters that are processed in the laboratory at fixed intervals of time for the presence of select biological agents, in hope of detecting a large-scale covert outdoor release of, among other critical biological agents, *Y. pestis.* There is a detection lag time, and, as yet, no published evidence about the sensitivity, specificity or efficacy of *BioWatch.*

Plague bacilli do not sporulate. An aerosol of *Y. pestis* would likely be destroyed by environmental factors such as sunlight and heat. A WHO report estimated that a plague aerosol would be nonviable after 1 hour.[17] However, there are reports suggesting that plague bacilli may survive in the soil for a prolonged period of time, risking establishment in the environment if permissive conditions exist, such as rodent reservoirs and efficient flea vectors, in the area of dissemination.

TREATMENT

In the setting of an outbreak, treatment should not be delayed to await laboratory confirmation. Pneumonic plague is rapidly progressive, and antimicrobial therapy is effective only when administered early in the course of disease.[16]

The Working Group on Civilian Biodefense offered consensus recommendations,[25] based on existing limited evidence[38-40] for the treatment of plague following a bioterrorist event (see Table 321-1). Historically, streptomycin has been the drug of choice in the treatment of plague.[1] However, it requires parenteral administration and is available only in limited supply. Only tetracyclines and streptomycin are licensed by the FDA to be used in the treatment of plague. A number of other antimicrobials are thought to be useful but have not been licensed by the FDA due to lack of adequate published human trials. Fluoroquinolones are effective in mice with experimentally induced pneumonic plague.[40-42] Chloramphenicol is considered the drug of choice in the setting of meningitis, because it crosses the blood-brain barrier, but no clinical trials are available. Although sulfonamides have been used, the WHO found sulfadiazine to be ineffective against pneumonic plague.[43]

An additional consideration in the event of a bioterrorist attack is the potential use of multidrug resistant strains of *Y. pestis.* Although resistance is infrequent in naturally occurring outbreaks,[1] a multidrug resistant (plasmid mediated) outbreak occurred in Madagascar in 1955.[44,45] Russian scientists have reportedly engineered a multi-drug resistant strain of *Y. pestis*[9] and there is one Russian manuscript reporting a quinolone-resistant strain.[46] Current CDC response plans in the event of a bioterrorist event employing *Y. pestis* include the use of gentamicin, doxycycline or ciprofloxacin until susceptibility profiles are identified (personal communication with Dr. Debra Yeskey, CDC).

REFERENCES

1. Perry RD, Fetherston JD. Yersinia pestis—etiologic agent of plague. Clin Microbiol Rev. 1997;10:35-66.
2. Titball RW, Leary SE. Plague. Br Med Bull. 1998;54:625-33.
3. Derbes VJ. De Mussis and the great plague of 1348. A forgotten episode of bacteriological warfare. JAMA. 1966;196:59-62.
4. Block SM. The Growing Threat of Biological Weapons. Available at www.americanscientist.org/template/AssetDetail/assetid/14284?fulltext=true. Accessed 06/24/03.
5. Williams P, Wallace D. Unit 731: Japan's Secret Biological Warfare in World War II. New York: Free Press; 1989.
6. Miller J, Engelberg S, Broad WJ. Germs. New York: Simon & Schuster; 2002.
7. Mangold T, Goldberg J. Plague Wars. New York: St. Martin's Press; 2000.
8. ANSER Institute for Homeland Defense. Interview-Serguei Popov. Available at www.homelanddefense.org/journal/Interviews/PopovInterview_001107.htm. Accessed 06/24/03.
9. Alibek K, Handelman S. Biohazard. New York: Random House; 1999.
10. Tucker JB. Toxic Terror. BCSIA Studies in International Security. Cambridge, MA: MIT Press; 2000.
11. Franz DR, Jahrling PB, Friedlander AM, et al. Clinical recognition and management of patients exposed to biological warfare agents. JAMA. 1997;278:399-411.
12. Rotz LD, Khan AS, Lillibridge SR, et al. Public health assessment of potential biological terrorism agents. Emerg Infect Dis. 2002;8:225-230.
13. Worsham PL, Stein MP, Welkos SL. Construction of defined F1 negative mutants of virulent Yersinia pestis. Contrib Microbiol Immunol. 1995; 13:325-328.
14. Davis KJ, Fritz DL, Pitt ML, et al. Pathology of experimental pneumonic plague produced by fraction 1-positive and fraction 1-negative Yersinia pestis in African green monkeys. Arch Pathol Lab Med. 1996;120:156-163.
15. Ramalingaswami V. Psychosocial effects of the 1994 plague outbreak in Surat, India. Mil Med. 2001;166:29-30.
16. Meyer KF. Pneumonic plague. Bacteriol Rev. 1961;25:249-261.
17. World Health Organization. Health aspects of chemical and biological weapons. Report of a WHO Group of Consultants. Geneva, Switzerland, 1970.
18. Centers for Disease Control and Prevention. Prevention of plague: Recommendations of the Advisory Committee on Immunization Practices. MMWR Recomm Rep. 1996;45:1-15.
19. Butler T. Yersinia species (including plague). In: Mandell GL, Douglas RG, Bennett JE, Dolin R, eds. Mandell, Douglas, and Bennett's Principles and Practice of Infectious Diseases. Philadelphia: Churchill Livingstone; 2000:2406-2411.

20. Centers for Disease Control and Prevention. Fatal human plague—Arizona and Colorado, 1996. MMWR Morb Mortal Wkly Rep. 1997;46:617-620.

21. Centers for Disease Control and Prevention. Level A Laboratory Procedures for Identification of *Yersinia pestis*. Available at www.bt.cdc.gov/Agent/Plague/ype_la_cp_121301.pdf. Accessed 06/30/03.

22. Wilmoth BA, Chu MC, Quan TJ. Identification of *Yersinia pestis* by BBL Crystal Enteric/Nonfermenter Identification System. J Clin Microbiol 1996;34:2829-2830.

23. Chanteau S, Rahalison L, Ratsitorahina M, et al. Early diagnosis of bubonic plague using F1 antigen capture ELISA assay and rapid immunogold dipstick. Int J Med Microbiol. 2000;290:279-83.

24. Chanteau S, Rahalison L, Ralafiarisoa L, et al. Development and testing of a rapid diagnostic test for bubonic and pneumonic plague. Lancet. 2003;361:211-216.

25. Inglesby TV, Dennis DT, Henderson DA, et al. Plague as a biological weapon: Medical and public health management. JAMA. 2000;283:2281-2290.

26. Samokhodkina ED, Ryzhko IV, Shcherbaniuk AI, et al. [Doxycycline in the prevention of experimental plague induced by plague microbe variants]. Antibiot Khimioter. 1992;37:26-28.

27. Blank S, Moskin LC, Zucker JR. An ounce of prevention is a ton of work: Mass antibiotic prophylaxis for anthrax, New York City, 2001. Emerg Infect Dis. 2003;9:615-622.

28. Titball RW, Williamson ED. Vaccination against bubonic and pneumonic plague. Vaccine 2001;19:4175-4184.

29. Meyer KF. Effectiveness of live or killed plague vaccines in man. Bull WHO. 1970;42:653-666.

30. Cohen RJ, Stockard JL. Pneumonic plague in an untreated plague-vaccinated individual. JAMA. 1967; 202:365-366.

31. Russell P, Eley SM, Hibbs SE, et al. A comparison of Plague vaccine, USP and EV76 vaccine induced protection against *Yersinia pestis* in a murine model. Vaccine. 1995;13:1551-1556.

32. Jefferson T, Demicheli V, Pratt M. Vaccines for preventing plague. Cochrane Database Syst Rev 2000.

33. Hill J, Leary SE, Griffin KF, et al. Regions of *Yersinia pestis* V antigen that contribute to protection against plague identified by passive and active immunization. Infect Immun. 1997;65:4476-4482.

34. Green M, Rogers D, Russell P, et al. The SCID/Beige mouse as a model to investigate protection against *Yersinia pestis*. FEMS Immunol Med Microbiol. 1999;23:107-113.

35. Centers for Disease Control and Prevention. Summary of notifiable diseases—United States, 2001. MMWR Morb Mortal Wkly Rep. 2003;50:i-xxiv, 1-108.

36. Gage KL, Dennis DT, Orloski KA, et al. Cases of cat-associated human plague in the Western US, 1977-1998. Clin Infect Dis. 2000;30:893-900.

37. Burmeister R. Laboratory-acquired pneumonic plague. Ann Intern Med. 1962;56: 789-800.

38. Byrne WR, Welkos SL, Pitt ML, et al. Antibiotic treatment of experimental pneumonic plague in mice. Antimicrob Agents Chemother. 1998;42:675-681.

39. Smith MD, Vinh DX, Nguyen TT, et al. In vitro antimicrobial susceptibilities of strains of *Yersinia pestis*. Antimicrob Agents Chemother. 1995;39:2153-2154.

40. Bonacorsi SP, Scavizzi MR, Guiyoule A, et al. Assessment of a fluoroquinolone, three beta-lactams, two aminoglycosides, and a cycline in treatment of murine *Yersinia pestis* infection. Antimicrob Agents Chemother. 1994;38:481-486.

41. Russell P, Eley SM, Bell DL, et al. Doxycycline or ciprofloxacin prophylaxis and therapy against experimental *Yersinia pestis* infection in mice. J Antimicrob Chemother. 1996;37:769-774.

42. Russell P, Eley SM, Green M, et al. Efficacy of doxycycline and ciprofloxacin against experimental *Yersinia pestis* infection. J Antimicrob Chemother. 1998;41:301-305.

43. World Health Organization. Expert Committee on Plague. Third Report. Geneva, Switzerland: World Health Organization; 1970:1-25.

44. Galimand M, Guiyoule A, Gerbaud G, et al. Multidrug resistance in *Yersinia pestis* mediated by a transferable plasmid. N Engl J Med. 1997;337:677-680.

45. Rasoamanana B, Coulanges P, Michel P, Rasolofonirina N. [Sensitivity of *Yersinia pestis* to antibiotics: 277 strains isolated in Madagascar between 1926 and 1989]. Arch Inst Pasteur Madagascar. 1989;56:37-53.

46. Ryzhko IV, Shcherbaniuk AI, Samokhodkina ED, et al. [Virulence of rifampicin and quinolone resistant mutants of strains of plague microbe with Fra+ and Fra− phenotypes]. Antibiot Khimioter. 1994;39:32-36.

Francisella tularensis (Tularemia) as an Agent of Bioterrorism

CANDACE L. MITCHELL
ROBERT L. PENN

Global current events have generated concern in the infectious diseases community and among government officials about the possibility of an intentional release of biological agents. Tularemia is a disease with historical bioterrorism associations. *Francisella tularensis* was incorporated as a weapon in the biological warfare program of the United States during the 1950s to 1960s.[1] The potential impact of this organism is demonstrated by a report from the Centers for Disease Control and Prevention (CDC): If 100,000 people were exposed to a "tularemic cloud," 82,500 cases (82.5% attack rate) with 6188 deaths (6.2% death rate) would be expected. The medical costs of tularemia from this bioterrorist attack would be $456 million to $561.8 million.[2]

HISTORY AND POTENTIAL USE

In preparation for an intentional release of biological agents by terrorist groups, the CDC defined and categorized potential agents of bioterrorism. Category A agents are those likely to cause mass casualties because of their infectivity and virulence characteristics; they include *Bacillus anthracis, Yersinia pestis,* and *Francisella tularensis.*[3] Table 322-1 lists the specific features of *F. tularensis* and the disease of tularemia that render this organism particularly useful as an agent of bioterrorism. The potential for *F. tularensis* to cause natural outbreaks has been well archived in the medical literature. Such outbreaks have included pharyngeal and oculoglandular disease after ingesting contaminated brook water in Russian hay-mowers, typhoidal and pneumonic tularemia in Finnish hay farmers, and pneumonic tularemia in American landscape workers.[4-8] Furthermore, *F. tularensis* is a well described hazardous material for laboratory workers.[9]

The highly infectious nature of this organism in concert with its ability to cause significant morbidity and mortality make *F. tularensis* an attractive biological agent. Japanese Germ Warfare Units recognized this potential as early as 1932 and began experiments on their prisoners with various forms of tularemia.[10] In 1955, U.S. military and civilian volunteers entered a steel chamber termed "The Eight Ball" at the U.S. Army Medical Research Institute of Infectious Diseases (USAMRIID) at Fort Detrick, Maryland, where they inhaled aerosolized *F. tularensis* organisms. The test allowed military researchers to study vaccine and antibiotic efficacy as well as the aerosolization parameters.[11] Since the United States' disposal of bioweapons stockpiles during the early 1970s, USAMRIID has continued defensive research on tularemia focusing on decontamination protocols, antimicrobial prophylaxis, clinical recognition of disease, laboratory diagnosis, and medical management of infection.

CLINICAL MANIFESTATIONS

The clinical manifestations of tularemia are specific to the route of inoculation, as discussed in Chapter 224. The 2001 Tularemia Consensus Statement developed by The Working Group on Civilian Biodefense concluded that aerosolization would be the most likely method for dispersing *F. tularensis,* as inhalation of bacilli would affect the largest number of people and cause the most devastating manifestations of disease.[12] Children are theorized to be more vulnerable than adults to an aerosolized agent because of their higher respiratory rate, more permeable skin, and higher skin-to-mass ratio.[13]

After an aerosol release and an incubation period of 3 to 5 days, patients may present with the acute onset of fever (38° C to 40° C), malaise, headache, rigors, coryza, and sore throat. The subsequent clinical syndrome depends on the immune status of the host, the inhaled inoculum, and the subspecies of the released agent. In past outbreaks, *F. tularensis* subspecies *tularensis* (type A), found in North America, has been responsible for more serious disease than *F. tularensis* subspecies *holarctica* (type B), found in Europe, Asia, and North America. After inhalation, one of two acute presentations of tularemia is most likely to be seen: either typhoidal or pneumonic disease. Knowledge of pneumonic tularemia due to *F. tularensis* type A in the United States is derived from sporadic case reports and two naturally occurring outbreaks of disease on Martha's Vineyard in 1978 and 2000.[7,8] Primary pulmonary disease results from direct inoculation of the lung parenchyma with inhaled organisms. Symptoms generally include fever, cough, and pleuritic chest pain. Chest radiography usually demonstrates peribronchial cuffing or lobar consolidation and may reveal an exudative pleural effusion and hilar lymphadenopathy. A significant number of patients progress to frank respiratory failure, requiring mechanical ventilation; they may also develop the systemic inflammatory response syndrome (SIRS). Recognizing this pneumonic syndrome as tularemia is challenging because of the difficulty distinguishing it from a plethora of other infections, including typical community-acquired pneumonia (CAP), atypical pneumonias, psittacosis, Q fever, pneumonic plague, inhalation anthrax, and, more recently, severe acute respiratory syndrome (SARS). Characteristics that may help distinguish among some of these etiologies are presented in Table 322-2. The case-fatality rate of untreated severe pneumonic tularemia has approached 60%.

The second likely presentation of disease after inhalation exposure is typhoidal tularemia. This presentation is marked by fever, prostration, and signs of sepsis with no skin or lymph node manifestations of

TABLE 322-1 Characteristics of *F. tularensis* and Tularemia that Render the Organism a Suitable Bioterrorism Agent

Characteristic	Comments
Virulence	Low inhalation inocula: 10 organisms required to cause pneumonic tularemia
	Potential to infect all ages
	Populace highly susceptible to infection
Diversity of infectious sources	Water, animal hides, infected meat, aerosolized feces or animal matter, insect vectors
Pathogenicity	Substantial morbidity and mortality in untreated disease
	Increased pediatric susceptibility due to increased respiratory rate, higher skin/mass ratio, more permeable skin, and less fluid reserve[13]
Stability	Organisms and by-products stable in various environments
Assembly and distribution	Large quantities easily manufactured with potential for silent release into air or water supply
Diagnosis and public response	Difficult diagnosis in certain areas as disease is rarely seen
	Rapid pediatric diagnosis difficult because of inability of young children to describe symptomatology
	Public panic may overwhelm health and law enforcement agencies
Epidemiologic investigations	Identification of exposure site difficult if affected patients are far from site of release
	Potential to infect laboratory and autopsy workers

TABLE 322-2 Comparison Among Community-Acquired Pneumonias and Tularemia Pneumonia

Parameter	Tularemia	Pneumococcal Pneumonia	Common Atypical Pneumonias*	Influenza Viral Pneumonia	Q-fever	SARS
Incubation period	3–5 days after experimental aerosol exposure†	Often several days after onset of upper respiratory symptoms	Legionella pneumophila, 2–10 days Mycoplasma pneumoniae, 14–21 days Chlamydia pneumoniae, 21 days	Progression of typical influenza illness to include signs and symptoms of pneumonia	20 days	2–10 days
Underlying illness	No Common	Yes	Yes or no	Yes or no	No	No
Prior animal or insect exposures	None if act of bioterrorism	No	No	No	Common None if act of bioterrorism	No
Chest radiograph	Peribronchial cuffing Alveolar consolidation Parapneumonic effusion Hilar lymphadenopathy	Alveolar consolidation Parapneumonic effusion	Interstitial infiltrates Patchy alveolar consolidation with predominant changes in lower lobes and perihilar regions	Bilateral infiltrates without consolidation	Alveolar consolidation Reticulonodular infiltrates Parapneumonic effusion Atelectasis Hilar lymphadenopathy Multiple rounded opacities in cat-associated illness	Early: focal or patchy reticulonodular interstitial infiltrates Late: alveolar consolidation
Diagnosis	Sputum GS, DFA Enriched media culture Serology Fluid/tissue PCR	Sputum GS Blood cultures Urinary antigen	Serology Urinary antigens Culture of respiratory specimens (Legionella)	Rapid antigen assay Viral culture	Serology (IFA) Tissue PCR	Exclusion of other diagnoses Exposure history Serology SARS-CoV RNA by RT-PCR
Person-to-person spread	No	No	Possible	Yes	No	Yes

*Pneumonias caused by Legionella, Mycoplasma, and Chlamydia.
†Dennis DT, Inglesby TV, Henderson DA, et al. Tularemia as a biological weapon. JAMA 2001;285:2763-2773.
DFA, direct fluorescent antibody stain; GS, Gram stain; IFA, immunofluorescent antibody assay; PCR, polymerase chain reaction assay; RT-PCR, real-time polymerase chain reaction assay; SARS, severe acute respiratory syndrome; SARS-CoV RNA, SARS-corona virus ribonucleic acid.

infection (see Chapter 224). Evans et al.[14] reported a 30-year experience with 88 cases of tularemia and noted pulse–temperature dissociation in 42% of 64 evaluable patients. However, pulse–temperature dissociation was not more frequent in the typhoidal group than in the ulceroglandular group.[14] With typhoidal tularemia, hematogenous dissemination of the organism is the rule, but blood cultures are often negative. This is due in part to intracellular sequestration of organisms and their fastidious culture characteristics. Secondary pneumonia and pleural effusion may result from hematogenous seeding of the lung. When this dominates the clinical presentation, such patients are difficult to distinguish from those with primary pneumonic tularemia. In patients not gravely ill with typhoidal tularemia, fever can persist for months, causing significant debilitation. When generalized abdominal discomfort is present, typhoidal tularemia can be confused with the etiologies of enteric fever. Many patients with typhoidal tularemia also develop erythema multiforme or erythema nodosum, further confusing the clinical picture. Historically, case-fatality rates of 35% to 60% have been observed in patients with untreated typhoidal tularemia[15]; however, the reported U.S. case-fatality rate is less than 2%, illustrating the importance of prompt recognition and institution of appropriate antimicrobial agents.[14]

It should be emphasized that not all patients inhaling aerosolized Francisella tularensis present with typhoidal or pneumonic tularemia. Airborne exposure can result in presentations of oculoglandular, ulceroglandular, glandular, or pharyngeal disease (see Chapter 224). During a 1966 outbreak of aerosolized F. tularensis subspecies holarctica in Sweden, conjunctival involvement was noted in 26% of cases, skin ulcers in 12%, and pharyngeal and anterior cervical node involvement in 31%.[16] Although pharyngitis can occur after inhalation, this presentation is more commonly associated with ingestion, and several clustered cases of tularemic pharyngitis suggest a contaminated water or food source.

Clustered severe respiratory or typhoidal illness in previously healthy individuals of any age suggests inhalation tularemia, especially when patients develop pleural effusions and tracheobronchial or hilar lymphadenopathy. Knowledge of the current local epidemiology of tularemia is helpful when evaluating new cases for possible bioterrorist implications.[17] Previous outbreaks have occurred in settings with appropriate epidemiologic exposures[17]; an urban outbreak of tularemia lacking in animal, insect, and water or farming exposures suggests a possible bioterrorist attack.

DIAGNOSIS

Diagnosis of tularemia requires a high index of suspicion and most often is made on clinical grounds supported by results of microbial cultures and serologic studies (see Chapter 224). Serologic tests are preferred to cultures for routine diagnosis of endemic tularemia. However, antibodies usually are not measurable before week 2 of the illness, rendering serologic studies impractical for rapid diagnosis after an intentional release. Despite the promise of polymerase chain reaction (PCR) methodologies to diagnose tularemia,[18] rapid diagnostic tests have not yet been standardized and are not readily available at present. However, rapid tests for field use are being evaluated in research laboratories.[19]

When entertaining a diagnosis of tularemia, the physician should alert the microbiology laboratory to allow for implementation of specialized diagnostic and safety procedures. Appropriate specimens depend on the clinical manifestations and may include blood cultures; swabs from skin, conjunctiva, and pharyngeal lesions; respiratory secretions from bronchoalveolar lavage washings, endotracheal aspirates and expectorated sputum; lymph node aspirates; and tissue biopsies. Biohazard level 2 recommendations should be followed in the laboratories processing clinical specimens. The organism is a known labora-

TABLE 322-3 Summary of Publications on Postexposure Antibiotic Prophylaxis for *Francisella tularensis*

Study	Methods	Summary
Sawyer et al.[27]	Monkeys and human volunteers exposed to inhaled *F. tularensis* Schu4 (type A) Rx: Tetracycline initiated within 24 hours at various doses and for various durations	Full protection against disease after oral doses of 1 g daily for 28 days or 2 g daily for 14 days Symptomatic tularemia developed after 1 g daily for 5 days
Russell et al.[26]	Mice exposed to inhaled *F. tularensis* Schu4 strain Rx: Variable doses and durations of ciprofloxacin and doxycycline initiated 48 hours before exposure (prophylaxis) or 24 hours after exposure (treatment)	Doxycycline treatment at 40 mg/kg BID was more effective then ciprofloxacin at the same dose In this model, prophylaxis doses were more effective than treatment doses for both antibiotics Extending antibiotic treatment from 5 days to 10 days after exposure prevented relapse
Dennis et al.[12]	Consensus recommendations from an expert panel: The Working Group on Civilian Biodefense	Oral doxycycline or ciprofloxacin for 14 days in the dosages listed in Table 322-6.

tory hazard owing to its highly virulent nature and should not be manipulated in the microbiology laboratory on an open bench.[20,21]

Smears may reveal faintly staining, tiny, intracellular and extracellular gram-negative coccobacilli that exhibit fastidious culture characteristics. Cysteine-enriched media should be used, but the organism may not grow well in broth even when enriched. Growth in broth may be visible after 3 to 7 days when cultures are shaken, but it requires incubation for longer than 10 days if cultures are not shaken. Thayer-Martin and buffered charcoal yeast extract agar may support growth slightly better than nonenriched sheep blood agar. Colonies are typically 1 mm in size after 24 to 48 hours and 3 to 5 mm after 96 hours; they may exhibit slight α-hemolysis on blood agar.[22,23] Centers for Disease Control and Prevention (CDC) guidelines recommend subculture to cysteine heart agar supplemented with 9% sheep red blood cells (CHAB) after observed growth on general media. CHAB colonies are 2 to 4 mm in size, greenish white, round, smooth, and slightly mucoid.[22,23]

Growth of the organism is slow, and it exhibits interesting temperature variation. Poor growth at 28° C can distinguish *F. tularensis* subspecies *tularensis* from other, less virulent subspecies as well as from *Yersinia pestis,* another small gram-negative coccobacillus that also grows well at 28° C. Additionally, *F. tularensis* does not exhibit the bipolar Gram stain appearance typical of *Yersinia pestis*. Differentiating *F. tularensis* from *Y. pestis* is critical, as both are potential agents of bioterrorism and may cause clinical pneumonia after inhalation.

Visualization of the organism in clinical specimens can also be done using direct fluorescent antibody (DFA) and immunohistochemical staining techniques, but these tests are performed only at specialized laboratories in the National Public Health Network. During a possible biological attack, these laboratories should be contacted and the specimens shipped to them to utilize their specialized technology for urgent diagnosis. Clinicians should contact their hospital infection control practitioner or state health department to obtain information on submission of specimens and reporting of possible infection.[12] The CDC's Office of Health and Safety web page can provide useful after-hours information on specimen testing and shipping (www.cdc.gov/od/ohs/biosfty/biosfty.htm).

Grunow et al.[19] used monoclonal antibodies specific for *F. tularensis* subspecies *holarctica* and *tularensis* lipopolysaccharide (LPS) to compare a capture enzyme-linked immunosorbent assay (cELISA), an immunochromatographic hand-held assay (HHA) for use in the field, and a PCR using primers specific for the *F. tularensis* 17 kDa protein to detect the organism in spiked fluid samples or in tissues from infected hares. These investigators reported a sensitivity in spiked human serum of 10^4 bacteria/mL for the cELISA, 10^6 to 10^7 bacteria/mL for the HHA, and 10^3 to 10^4 bacteria/mL for the PCR assay.[19] When used to test frozen tissue samples from 15 infected hares, the cELISA was positive in all 15, the HHA was positive in 11, and the PCR was positive in 13; false-negative HHA and PCR results were found in samples presumed to contain the lowest concentrations of the organisms.[19]

Highly specific and sensitive PCR and nested-PCR assays have been developed for use on various human specimens, including blood products, which usually require special techniques to purify the sample and eliminate inhibitory factors.[19,24,25] Sjøstedt et al.[24] demonstrated the advantage of PCR testing over testing with conventional cultures in the examination of human tularemic skin lesions; 73% of lesions were PCR-positive for *F. tularensis* compared with only 25% using growth in culture. Current research is focusing on the rapid transport of field specimens for PCR testing and the development of field-stable PCR techniques.[19]

ANTIMICROBIAL AGENTS FOR PROPHYLAXIS

There are few scientific data concerning postexposure prophylaxis for tularemia, a term generally meant to include therapy initiated during the incubation period of infection. A handful of studies employed "prophylaxis" dosing of antimicrobials before an actual challenge with *F. tularensis*.[26] The 2001 Working Group on Civilian Biodefense recommendation for postexposure prophylaxis with 14 days of ciprofloxacin or doxycycline is primarily based on two publications (Table 322-3).[26,27] Some adverse reactions to ciprofloxacin and doxycycline are listed in Table 322-4.[28]

Formulating optimal strategies for antibiotic use requires understanding the intracellular nature of *F. tularensis*. Treatment failures are highest with bacteriostatic drugs such as tetracycline, doxycycline, and chloramphenicol, especially for central nervous system (CNS) infections.[29] Relapse after therapy with ciprofloxacin has been reported

TABLE 322-4 Adverse Reactions to Oral Antibiotics Recommended for *F. tularensis* Postexposure Prophylaxis

Drug	GI	CNS	Skin	Laboratory	Other
Ciprofloxacin	Anorexia Nausea Bloating Abdominal pain	Dizziness Headache	Rashes Photosensitivity	Leukopenia Eosinophilia Hepatotoxicity	QT prolongation Arthropathy and tendonitis in laboratory animals
Doxycycline	Nausea Diarrhea Esophageal ulcerations	Dizziness Headache	Rashes Photosensitivity	Dental discolorations Hepatotoxicity Pancreatitis	Benign intracranial hypertension

CNS, central nervous system; GI, gastrointestinal system.
Modified from Navas E. Problems associated with potential massive use of antimicrobial agents as prophylaxis or therapy of a bioterrorist attack. Clin Microbiol Infect 2002;8:534-539.

in a mouse model but has been unusual in humans, although experience with the quinolones for the treatment of human cases is limited.[30-35] Only a small number of reported patients treated with a quinolone were infected with *F. tularensis* subspecies *tularensis*,[34] whereas most were infected with *F. tularensis* subspecies *holarctica*.[30-33,35] Relapse is theorized to result in part from sequestration of organisms within acidic vesicles inside macrophages, where the low pH necessary for bacterial iron acquisition may prevent the entry of both ciprofloxacin and doxycycline.[26]

Subsequent to intentional release of a biological agent, public health services will attempt to ensure the dissemination of accurate information to communities, but the media and the Internet may serve as potential sources of inflammatory material, thereby aggravating public insecurity and leading to hoarding of antimicrobial agents, as was observed after the 2001 U.S. anthrax attacks. This behavior should be proactively discouraged by infectious diseases experts so it does not contribute to the potential development of antimicrobial resistance.

POTENTIAL USE OF VACCINES DURING THE POSTEXPOSURE PERIOD

Attempts to manufacture a vaccine against *F. tularensis* have been ongoing worldwide since the 1930s. Several isolates have been used to develop a vaccine, but many lost virulence through serial passage. In 1961 Eigelsback and Downs noted in culture the presence of two colony types growing from reconstituted ampules of a vaccine strain imported from Moscow. They isolated an effective live vaccine strain (LVS) from one of the colony variants, which protected mice against aerosolized challenge with the Schu4 strain of *F. tularensis*.[36] The LVS underwent human testing as a vaccine shortly thereafter and was shown to be effective in protecting volunteers against aerosolized Schu4 as well.[37] Over the next several years, the LVS was formulated for various methods of inoculation. The latest version of the LVS remains effective when dosed via the oral, inhalation, or intradermal routes, but the vaccine has not been approved by the U.S. Food and Drug Administration (FDA) for routine use. The vaccine has many potential drawbacks, including a paucity of information concerning the mechanism responsible for LVS virulence attenuation. This is of potential concern because the LVS is fully virulent when injected intraperitoneally into mice with a median lethal dose of less than 10 CFU.[38]

Previously, vaccine could be obtained through an investigational new drug (IND) protocol for at-risk laboratory personnel, but the program has been terminated by the FDA. The U.S. Army Medical Research Institute of Infectious Diseases (USAMRIID) has recently submitted a new IND protocol requesting permission to vaccinate at-risk personnel at Fort Detrick through a cooperative research agreement. (Inquiries should be made through the Chief, Medical Division, USAMRIID, Fort Detrick, Frederick, MD 21702, USA.)

Ongoing studies are evaluating *F. tularensis* subunit components, such as lipopolysaccharide, as possible vaccine candidates.[23] Currently, a vaccine available for use in the general population is not forthcoming.[39] Thus antimicrobial agents are likely to remain the mainstay of management in the near future.

HOSPITAL INFECTION CONTROL MEASURES

Microbiology laboratory workers and autopsy personnel are the most likely individuals to encounter *F. tularensis* organisms in the hospital setting. Guidelines for the safe handling of *F. tularensis* are available.[20,21] A critical component to prevent nosocomial transmission is notification of at-risk personnel about suspected cases or positive cultures, thereby facilitating appropriate use of personal protective measures and biosafety cabinets.

Once organisms suspected of being *F. tularensis* are isolated from clinical specimens, additional procedures that may produce droplets (centrifuging, grinding, vigorous shaking, growing cultures in volume) should be conducted under biosafety level 3 (BSL-3) proce-

dures.[20] Other members of the health care team, such as the medical examiner or coroner, also should be alerted to suspected cases of tularemia, as certain procedures (e.g., sawing of bone) may aerosolize infected tissues. In fact, infection resulting from inoculation during an autopsy has been documented.[40] The responsibility to notify laboratory and pathology services rests solely with members of the primary health care team and cannot be overemphasized.

Shapiro and Schwartz[41] detailed the unnecessary exposure of 11 laboratory workers and 2 autopsy personnel to *F. tularensis* when the primary team failed to notify these services of their suspicions. Although tularemia was not transmitted to any of the workers, undue risk was assumed; 13 workers required prophylaxis with doxycycline, and the diagnosis was delayed.[41] This exposure occurred at a large teaching hospital in Boston, where laboratory guidelines regarding isolation of potential biological agents were already in place, but their integration into the routine workup of clinical specimens had not been accomplished.[41] Their report illustrated the potential pitfalls of implementing local bioterrorism guidelines even with the heightened awareness stemming from the events of September 11, 2001.

Identification of *F. tularensis* in the microbiology laboratory is complex, and even experienced laboratory personnel can make mistakes when identifying the organism. The bacteria can be confused with other gram-negative bacilli, including *Haemophilus* species. Automated systems may incorrectly identify the organism as *Actinobacillus actinomycetemcomitans* or *Neisseria meningitidis*.[42] Confusion with *Legionella* may occur when *F. tularensis* grows on buffered charcoal yeast extract agar. If the laboratory is not notified in advance of the clinical suspicion of tularemia, procedures for any of

---

TABLE 322-5 Recommendations for Therapy of Contained Casualties after Intentional Release of *Francisella tularensis*

Adults
Serious Disease
Streptomycin 1 g IM q 12 hours for 10 days
Gentamicin 5 mg/kg IM or IV qd for 10 days

Alternatives for Less Serious Disease
Streptomycin or gentamicin in doses listed above
Doxycycline 100 mg IV BID for 14–21 days
Ciprofloxacin 400 mg IV BID for 10 days
Chloramphenicol 15 mg/kg IV QID for 14–21 days

Children
Serious Disease
Streptomycin 15 mg/kg IM q 12 hours for 10 days, not to exceed 2 g/day
Gentamicin 2.5 mg/kg IM or IV q 8 hours for 10 days

Alternatives for Less Serious Disease
Streptomycin or gentamicin in doses listed above
Doxycycline 100 mg IV q 12 hours for 14–21 days if weight ≥ 45 kg;
  2.2 mg/kg IV q 12 hours if weight <45 kg
Ciprofloxacin 15 mg/kg IV q 12 hours for 10 days, not to exceed 1 g/day
Chloramphenicol 15 mg/kg IV q 6 hours for 14–21 days

Pregnancy
Serious Disease
Gentamicin 5 mg/kg IM or IV qd for 10 days
Streptomycin 1 g IM q 12 hours for 10 days

Alternatives for Less Serious Disease
Gentamicin or streptomycin in doses listed above
Doxycycline 100 mg IV q 12 hours for 14–21 days
Ciprofloxacin 400 mg IV q 12 hours for 10 days

Immunosuppressed Persons
Minimum of 10 days of treatment (see text)
Gentamicin 5 mg/kg/day IM or IV in divided doses
Streptomycin 1 g IM q 12 hours

Choices are listed in our order of preference for use. Initial intravenous therapy with doxycycline, ciprofloxacin, or chloramphenicol may be changed to oral dosing after patients are clinically improved.

Adapted from Dennis DT, Inglesby TV, Henderson DA, et al. Tularemia as a biological weapon: medical and public health management. JAMA 2001;285:2763-2773.

TABLE 322-6 Recommendations for Therapy of Mass Casualties and for Postexposure Prophylaxis after Intentional Release of *Francisella tularensis**

Adults
Doxycycline 100 mg PO BID for 14 days
Ciprofloxacin 500 mg PO BID for 14 days

***Children*†**
Doxycycline 100 mg PO BID for 14 days if weight ≥ 45 kg; 2.2 mg/kg PO BID if weight < 45 kg
Ciprofloxacin 15 mg/kg PO BID for 14 days, not to exceed 1 g/day

***Pregnancy*†**
Ciprofloxacin 500 mg PO BID for 14 days
Doxycycline 100 mg PO BID for 14 days

*Adapted from Dennis DT, Inglesby TV, Henderson DA, et al. Tularemia as a biological weapon: medical and public health management. JAMA 2001;285:2763-2773.
†Choices listed in our order of preference for use.

the above organisms may be carried out on an open bench with unnecessary risk to laboratory personnel.

Special isolation in the hospital setting for persons with tularemia is not necessary, as the organism is not transmitted person to person.

ENVIRONMENTAL SURVEILLANCE AND DECONTAMINATION

Tularemia was returned to the list of nationally notifiable diseases in 2000 because of the potential to use *F. tularensis* as an agent of bioterrorism. The incidence of infection in the United States is highest during the summer months, and most cases are reported from the mountainous and west central states of Arkansas, Missouri, South Dakota, Oklahoma, and Montana (see Chapter 224).[17,43] The observation of an outbreak during other seasons or in other states should prompt a public health investigation to exclude intentional release. Reporting cases of tularemia to state health departments and subsequently to national databases is of utmost importance.

Because *F. tularensis* can cause disease in various mammals and rodents, public health officials should stay abreast of zoonotic epidemics, as they may parallel disease in humans, especially if a common water source is used as a vehicle for intentional release. Veterinarians may be the first to observe a rise in the incidence of tularemia, and observation of the rates of animal disease and open dialogue with animal experts may prove to be an important surveillance tactic. During a possible epizoonosis, public education regarding methods of transmission via insect vectors should be emphasized.

The Working Group expects aerosolized *F. tularensis* to undergo desiccation, solar radiation, and oxidation, limiting secondary dispersal.[12] Body surfaces and clothes of individuals exposed should be washed with soapy water. Water contamination can be eradicated through standard chlorination, but chlorinating natural water reservoirs is complicated. Identified infected natural water sources must be contained to prevent public and animal use. Inanimate surfaces contaminated with *F. tularensis,* as in laboratory accidents, can be cleaned with a 10% bleach solution. Following up the bleach with a 70% alcohol solution can reduce the harmful effects of bleach on countertop material without impairing decontamination. Soapy water can clean less concentrated areas of contamination in the laboratory.[12]

TREATMENT

Recommendations for therapy of tularemia in the context of a bioterrorism event presented in the Working Group consensus report[12] are summarized in Tables 322-5 and 322-6. Prior to determining a treatment strategy, case clusters should be evaluated for mass casualty potential, wherein large numbers of potentially infected people prohibit individual medical management, as would be possible in a contained casualty situation. Hence the recommended regimens differ for the two circumstances. Treatment using bacteriostatic drugs should be continued for a longer duration than the traditional 10-day course recommended for the bactericidal drugs (see Table 322-5). When treating individuals with ciprofloxacin, doxycycline, or chloramphenicol, intravenous regimens can be changed to oral regimens after substantial clinical improvement is noted. Note that in mass casualty situations a minimum of 14 days is recommended for all regimens; this is due to the exclusive use of oral agents beginning from the initiation of therapy (see Table 322-6). The bacteriostatic regimens are not recommended for immunosuppressed patients because of the higher rates of treatment failure generally observed with these agents.[12] Furthermore, giving the entire minimum of 10 days of therapy parenterally should be considered for immunocompromised patients. Although quinolones and tetracyclines have been associated with adverse consequences in children and immature laboratory animals, short courses of these agents in children have not been detrimental in prospective studies.[44,45] The risks should be weighed in proportion to the potential benefits in children with severe disease.

OTHER RESOURCES

Ferguson et al.[46] reviewed Internet sites with information on bioterrorism for their ease of use and applicability. An expansive list of the most useful websites was generated and separated into categories including clinical, laboratory, infection control, epidemiologic, first responder, and mental health and coping information; emergency contact sources; bioterrorism news sites; event preparedness resources; and public education information materials. We have listed in Table 322-7 some sites with useful information on tularemia. These sites are likely to remain active or have links routed to other functioning websites.

REFERENCES

1. Franz DR, Jahrling PB, Friedlander AM, et al. Clinical recognition and management of patients exposed to biological warfare agents. JAMA 1997;278:399-411.
2. Kaufmann AF, Meltzer MI, Schmid GP. The economic impact of a bioterrorist attack: are prevention and postattack intervention programs justifiable? Emerg Infect Dis 1997;3:83-94.

TABLE 322-7 Useful Bioterrorism Websites with Information on Tularemia

Source	Address	Comments
Centers for Disease Control	http://www.bt.cdc.gov/Agent/Agentlist.asp	Fact sheets and articles
	http://www.bt.cdc.gov/LabIssues/index.asp	Testing, identification, biosafety, shipping, training, Laboratory Response Network description
Center for Biosecurity of the University of Pittsburgh Medical Center (UPMC)	http://www.upmc-biosecurity.org	Fact sheets, articles, consensus statements
St. Louis University School of Public Health	http://www.bioterrorism.slu.edu/tularemia.htm	Fact sheets
University of Alabama at Birmingham	http://www.bioterrorism.uab.edu/diffDiagnosis.html	Chart of differential diagnoses

Adapted from Ferguson NE, Steele L, Crawford CY, et al. Bioterrorism web site resources for infectious disease clinicians and epidemiologists. Clin Infect Dis 2003;36:1458-1473.

3. Biological and chemical terrorism: strategic plan for preparedness and response: recommendations of the CDC Strategic Planning Workgroup. MMWR Recomm Rep 2000;49:1-14.

4. Syrjala H, Kujala P, Myllyla V, et al. Airborne transmission of tularemia in farmers. Scand J Infect Dis 1985;17:371-375.

5. Jellison WL, Kohls GM. Tularemia in sheep and sheep industry workers in western United States. In: 28 PHM. Washington, DC: U.S. Public Health Service; 1955:1-17.

6. Karpoff SP, Antonoff NI. The spread of tularemia through water, as a new factor in its epidemiology. J Bacteriol 1936;32:243-258.

7. Feldman KA, Enscore RE, Lathrop SL, et al. An outbreak of primary pneumonic tularemia on Martha's Vineyard. N Engl J Med 2001;345:1601-1606.

8. Teutsch SM, Martone WJ, Brink EW, et al. Pneumonic tularemia on Martha's Vineyard. N Engl J Med 1979;301:826-828.

9. Lake GC, Francis E. Six cases of tularemia occurring in laboratory workers. Public Health Rep 1922;37:392-413.

10. Harris S. Japanese biological warfare research on humans: a case study of microbiology and ethics. Ann NY Acad Sci 1992;666:21-52.

11. Christopher GW, Cieslak TJ, Pavlin JA, et al. Biological warfare: a historical perspective. JAMA 1997;278:412-417.

12. Dennis DT, Inglesby TV, Henderson DA, et al. Tularemia as a biological weapon: medical and public health management. JAMA 2001;285:2763-2773.

13. Patt HA, Feigin RD. Diagnosis and management of suspected cases of bioterrorism: a pediatric perspective. Pediatrics 2002;109:685-692.

14. Evans ME, Gregory DW, Schaffner W, et al. Tularemia: a 30-year experience with 88 cases. Medicine (Baltimore) 1985;64:251-269.

15. American Public Health Association. Tularemia. In: Chin J, ed. Control of Communicable Diseases Manual. Washington DC: American Public Health Association; 2000:532-535.

16. Dahlstrand S, Ringertz O, Zetterberg B. Airborne tularemia in Sweden. Scand J Infect Dis 1971;3:7-16.

17. Chang MH, Glynn MK, Groseclose SL. Endemic, notifiable bioterrorism-related diseases, United States, 1992-1999. Emerg Infect Dis 2003;9:556-564.

18. Johansson A, Berglund L, Eriksson U, et al. Comparative analysis of PCR versus culture for diagnosis of ulceroglandular tularemia. J Clin Microbiol 2000;38:22-26.

19. Grunow R, Splettstoesser W, McDonald S, et al. Detection of Francisella tularensis in biological specimens using a capture enzyme-linked immunosorbent assay, an immunochromatographic handheld assay, and a PCR. Clin Diagn Lab Immunol 2000;7:86-90.

20. Robinson-Dunn B. The microbiology laboratory's role in response to bioterrorism. Arch Pathol Lab Med 2002;126:291-294.

21. Sewell DL. Laboratory safety practices associated with potential agents of biocrime or bioterrorism. J Clin Microbiol 2003;41:2801-2809.

22. Chu MC, Weyant RS. Francisella and Brucella. In: Murray PR, Baron EJ, Jorgensen JH, et al, eds. Manual of Clinical Microbiology, v. 1. 8th ed. Washington, DC: ASM Press; 2003:789-808.

23. Ellis J, Oyston PC, Green M, et al. Tularemia. Clin Microbiol Rev 2002;15:631-646.

24. Sjostedt A, Eriksson U, Berglund L, et al. Detection of Francisella tularensis in ulcers of patients with tularemia by PCR. J Clin Microbiol 1997;35:1045-1048.

25. Fulop M, Leslie D, Titball R. A rapid, highly sensitive method for the detection of Francisella tularensis in clinical samples using the polymerase chain reaction. Am J Trop Med Hyg 1996;54:364-366.

26. Russell P, Eley SM, Fulop MJ, et al. The efficacy of ciprofloxacin and doxycycline against experimental tularaemia. J Antimicrob Chemother 1998;41:461-465.

27. Sawyer WD, Dangerfield HG, Hogge AL, et al. Antibiotic prophylaxis and therapy of airborne tularemia. Bacteriol Rev 1966;30:542-550.

28. Navas E. Problems associated with potential massive use of antimicrobial agents as prophylaxis or therapy of a bioterrorist attack. Clin Microbiol Infect 2002;8:534-539.

29. Enderlin G, Morales L, Jacobs RF, et al. Streptomycin and alternative agents for the treatment of tularemia: review of the literature. Clin Infect Dis 1994;19:42-47.

30. Aranda EA. Treatment of tularemia with levofloxacin. Clin Microbiol Infect 2001;7:167-168.

31. Chocarro A, Gonzalez A, Garcia I. Treatment of tularemia with ciprofloxacin. Clin Infect Dis 2000;31:623.

32. Johansson A, Berglund L, Gothefors L, et al. Ciprofloxacin for treatment of tularemia in children. Pediatr Infect Dis J 2000;19:449-453.

33. Johansson A, Berglund L, Sjostedt A, et al. Ciprofloxacin for treatment of tularemia. Clin Infect Dis 2001;33:267-268.

34. Limaye AP, Hooper CJ. Treatment of tularemia with fluoroquinolones: two cases and review. Clin Infect Dis 1999;29:922-924.

35. Scheel O, Reiersen R, Hoel T. Treatment of tularemia with ciprofloxacin. Eur J Clin Microbiol Infect Dis 1992;11:447-448.

36. Eigelsbach HT, Downs CM. Prophylactic effectiveness of live and killed tularemia vaccines. I. Production of vaccine and evaluation in the white mouse and guinea pig. J Immunol 1961;87:415-425.

37. Eigelsbach HT, Hornick RB, Tulis JJ. Recent studies on live tularemia vaccine. Med Ann DC 1967;36:282-286.

38. Fortier AH, Slayter MV, Ziemba R, et al. Live vaccine strain of Francisella tularensis: infection and immunity in mice. Infect Immun 1991;59:2922-2928.

39. Fulop M, Manchee R, Titball R. Role of lipopolysaccharide and a major outer membrane protein from Francisella tularensis in the induction of immunity against tularemia. Vaccine 1995;13:1220-1225.

40. Weilbacher JO, Moss ES. Tularemia following injury while performing post-mortem examination of a human case. J Lab Clin Med 1938;24:34-38.

41. Shapiro DS, Schwartz DR. Exposure of laboratory workers to Francisella tularensis despite a bioterrorism procedure. J Clin Microbiol 2002;40:2278-2281.

42. Clarridge JE III, Raich TJ, Sjosted A, et al. Characterization of two unusual clinically significant Francisella strains. J Clin Microbiol 1996;34:1995-2000.

43. Ashford DA, Kaiser RM, Bales ME, et al. Planning against biological terrorism: lessons from outbreak investigations. Emerg Infect Dis 2003;9:515-519.

44. Redmond A, Sweeney L, MacFarland M, et al. Oral ciprofloxacin in the treatment of Pseudomonas exacerbations of paediatric cystic fibrosis: clinical efficacy and safety evaluation using magnetic resonance image scanning. J Int Med Res 1998;26:304-312.

45. Pariente-Khayat A, Vauzelle-Kervroedan F, d'Athis P, et al. [Retrospective survey of fluoroquinolone use in children.] Arch Pediatr 1998;5:484-488.

46. Ferguson NE, Steele L, Crawford CY, et al. Bioterrorism web site resources for infectious disease clinicians and epidemiologists. Clin Infect Dis 2003;36:1458-1473.

CHAPTER **323**

Smallpox and Bioterrorism

LISA D. ROTZ

JOANNE CONO

INGER DAMON

HISTORY OF SMALLPOX AND BIOTERRORISM

Over the last several years the general concerns for bioterrorism (BT) and biological warfare (BW) involving smallpox have greatly increased. These are neither novel concepts nor newly identified threats.

One of the earliest accusations of biological terrorism involving variola virus dates back to the fifteenth century. It has been alleged that the Spanish conquistador Pizarro supplied the native people of South America with smallpox-contaminated clothing in an effort to gain control of the land they held.[1-6] The earliest documented use of smallpox virus to intentionally cause illness occurred during the 1763 siege of Fort Pitt during the Pontiac uprising led by the Ottawa Chief Pontiac. Sir Jeffrey Amherst, commander of the North American British forces, inquired in a letter to a captain at the fort "whether it could be contrived to send smallpox among the disaffected tribes of Indians?"[7] Evidence that this plan was carried out is contained in an entry into the personal journal of William Trent, commander of the local militia of Pittsburgh during the siege of Fort Pitt, dated May 24, 1763 that states "We gave them two Blankets and an Handkerchief out of the Small Pox Hospital. I hope it will have the desired effect."[8] The Indian population, who lacked any existing immunity to smallpox, suffered a devastating outbreak of the disease. Whether the outbreak was a direct result of the distributed blankets or spread from the disease already occurring within the fort is not known, but the initiation of actions to spread this disease intentionally to the Indian population in the area appears evident.

Following the global eradication of smallpox, experts agreed that routine vaccination for the general population should not continue; however, they voiced apprehension that cessation of vaccination, with the resultant waning immunity in the population, could lead to an increasing possibility that variola virus might be considered an effective biological warfare (BW) agent in the future. Their observation at the time was that this potential provided the chief reason for maintaining reserves of vaccine as well as diagnostic and epidemiologic expertise for this eradicated disease.[9] This belief in the potential future effectiveness of variola virus as a biological weapon was apparently shared by the strategists in the former Soviet Union, as demonstrated by its selection of variola for development and mass production in the country's biological weapons program.

During the 1970s, the Soviet Politburo formed and funded an organization known as Biopreparat, which was designed to conduct biological weapons research, development, and production under the guise of legal civilian biotechnology research. This program functioned side by side with the Soviet program and came to light in 1989 with the defection of Vladimir Pasechnik, a former director of several Soviet BW research institutes. Western knowledge of this program grew with the subsequent defection of Kanadjan Alibekov, a former senior deputy director of Biopreparat. At its height, this program employed more than 50,000 people, working in more than 50 facilities across the USSR. Massive amounts of BW agents reportedly were produced, including *Yersinia pestis* (plague), *Bacillus anthracis* (anthrax), variola virus (smallpox), *Francisella tularensis* (tularemia), *Brucella suis* (brucellosis), *Burkholderia mallei* (glanders), Marburg virus (viral hemorrhagic fever), and Venezuelan equine encephalitis (VEE) virus. *Y. pestis,* anthrax spores, and variola virus reportedly were prepared for use in intercontinental missiles.[10]

The Soviet BW program continued despite enactment of the Convention on the Prohibition of the Development, Production, and Stockpiling of Bacteriological (Biological) and Toxin Weapons and on Their Destruction, also called the Biological Weapons Convention (BWC), in 1975. BWC was the first multilateral disarmament treaty banning an entire category of weapons. In 1979, a few years after the USSR became a signatory of the BWC, there was a massive accidental release of aerosolized *B. anthracis* spores from a facility in Sverdlovsk, Russia. Altogether, 97 people became ill, and 69 died.[11] For many years, the Soviets maintained that this outbreak was due to the ingestion of contaminated meat sold on the black market until, under pressure from the international community in 1992, Soviet President Boris Yeltsin admitted that there had been an accidental release of *B. anthracis* spores from a biological weapons production facility.[12] This event was the first clear evidence that a signatory nation was in direct violation of the BWC. Although unconfirmed, some experts have recently alleged that a 1971 outbreak of smallpox in the former Soviet Union may have also been caused by an accidental exposure from a BW testing site.[13]

Following the official World Health Organization (WHO) declaration of smallpox eradication in 1980, laboratories worldwide were asked to voluntarily destroy or consolidate their stores of variola virus in one of two WHO Collaborating Centers [Centers for Disease Control and Prevention (CDC), Atlanta, Georgia, and the State Research Center of Virology and Biotechnology, Koltsovo, Novosibirsk Region, Russia].[14] All legitimate research with infectious variola virus is now conducted under biosafety level 4 (BSL-4) containment conditions within these two institutions only, utilizing a WHO-approved research agenda.

Modern-day concerns about bioterrorism utilizing the smallpox virus (variola) remain, with the belief that illegitimate stores of the virus may exist outside the two WHO collaborating centers (as nondestroyed products of the former Soviet BW program or as laboratory specimens not surrendered to the WHO repositories) and could be used in a malevolent manner.[15,16] It is for this reason that medical, research, and public health authorities are again familiarizing themselves with the clinical, epidemiologic, and scientific characteristics of this disease.

SMALLPOX EPIDEMIOLOGY RELATIVE TO BIOTERRORISM

There is no known environmental source or animal reservoir for the variola virus; therefore a single case of confirmed smallpox would constitute an epidemic and raise great concern for biological terrorism. In addition, variola virus does not persist or reactivate in individuals who have recovered from the disease. Because legitimate research with infectious variola virus is carried out in only two laboratories by routinely vaccinated researchers under high-containment BSL-4 conditions, it is unlikely that an outbreak would be the result of an accidental infection or release from these facilities.

Examples of previously cited criteria used to identify biological agents for further development in biological weapons programs include (1) high lethality or toxicity, (2) no medical countermeasures for prevention or treatment, (3) environmental stability and ease of large-scale production, (4) infectious via aerosol, and (5) high infectivity

(low infectious dose), person-to-person transmissibility, or both.[15] Variola major has many of these attributes. The true infectious dose is not known, but it is thought to be low. The overall mortality rate for smallpox disease is about 30% (but can increase to almost 100% with the rare hemorrhagic and flat-type forms of the disease).[9,16] Human-to-human transmission of variola virus normally occurs by inhalation of large, virus-containing airborne droplets of saliva, although infection can result from contact with contaminated bedding or clothing or direct inoculation of virus into the skin. Even with a potentially low infectious dose, transmission usually requires prolonged, close contact (face to face). However, airborne transmission over greater distances has been infrequently reported.[17]

Following a bioterrorism release of smallpox, the epidemiologic characteristics of transmission would be expected to be similar to those seen historically. Household contacts were at highest risk for secondary transmission from a smallpox-infected individual because of the usual need for more prolonged, close contact to transmit the disease effectively. Therefore identification, vaccination, and surveillance of this group would be one of the highest priorities following diagnosis of smallpox in an individual or group of individuals following intentional release of the agent.

During the smallpox era, the overall average secondary attack rate was 58.4% in previously nonvaccinated close household contacts and 3.8% in previously vaccinated household contacts.[9] Because of the general lack of natural or vaccine-induced immunity in today's population, it is difficult to predict the exact attack rates that would result from person-to-person transmission following intentional release of the smallpox virus. Medical personnel caring for or evaluating potential smallpox cases following a smallpox virus release should be vaccinated as soon as possible, as smallpox vaccine given before exposure or up to 3 days following exposure may prevent the disease or greatly lessen the severity of the illness.[16,18]

The usual incubation period for smallpox is 10 to 14 days (range 7 to 17 days). Individuals are not infectious during this asymptomatic period. At the end of the incubation period, they develop a febrile prodrome that lasts 1 to 5 days and is characterized by myalgia, backache, headache, and occasionally nausea, vomiting, and delirium. Oral lesions appear in the mouth about 24 hours prior to the onset of the visible rash. These oral lesions quickly break down and shed large amounts of virus into the oral secretions. It is at this point that a person becomes infectious to others. Smallpox patients are most infectious during the first week of rash with the infectiousness dropping dramatically as the oral and skin lesions heal and form scabs.[16]

PATHOGENESIS AND CLINICAL PRESENTATION

Natural infection by variola normally occurs via inhalation of saliva droplets from infected individuals. The index case (first person infected) releases infectious viral particles from sloughing oropharyngeal lesions during the first week of the rash.[19] Smallpox virus released from secretions of oropharyngeal lesions is contained mainly in large respiratory-droplet particles.[20] Although smallpox scabs may contain viable virus for a long time,[21] the virus is contained in large fragments of inspissated (thickened, dried) material, accounting for the low transmissibility associated with scabs.

Typically, the smallpox virus initially infects the respiratory tract of a susceptible individual. During the time when smallpox was endemic, modern tools for understanding disease pathogenesis and host response were not available. Therefore, descriptions of smallpox disease pathogenesis are derived from studies of systemic orthopoxvirus infections in other species and from clinical and laboratory observations of human disease. One study[9] concluded that antigen-presenting macrophages in the respiratory tract or skin are infected by the third day after viral transmission. These virally infected macrophages enter the lymphatic system and travel to the regional lymph nodes. The virus then multiplies in the draining lymph nodes and enters the bloodstream, largely cell-associated, by the fourth day after infection, subsequently seeding and replicating in reticuloendothelial organs. These initial phases of infection are typically asymptomatic and occur during the incubation period.

Symptoms present around the time of the secondary viremia. At this time, 10 to 14 days after infection (range 7 to 17 days), patients present with the prodromal symptoms, followed in 1 to 5 days by disseminated rash lesions. Activated macrophages and lymphocytes are thought to produce inflammatory cytokines and interferons, which mediate the immune response and stimulate natural killer cell activity to destroy infected cells. In immune-competent individuals, antigen-presenting cells affect cytotoxic T-cell clonal expansion to destroy infected cells and prevent infectious virus release. The humoral immune response also plays a role in recovery from poxvirus infection and in protection against reinfection. For example, neutralizing antibodies directed against viral outer membrane antigens function to neutralize the infectivity of virions. Neutralizing antibodies are detectable by the sixth day of the rash[22] and are long-lived. Both the activity of cytotoxic T cells and the antibody titer increase as time progresses.

The three major clinical forms of smallpox include the ordinary, flat, and hemorrhagic types. An early, vigorous immunocompetent cellular immune response inhibits viral multiplication, although the virus generally breaks through the host's immune response and produces characteristic skin lesions with a discrete distribution (ordinary smallpox). In contrast, a late, deficient cellular immune response is believed to lead to a rare manifestation of the disease termed flat-type smallpox. Flat-type smallpox is characterized by intense toxemia and delayed skin lesion appearance with slow evolution. The skin lesions are usually flat and soft, and sections of the skin may slough. Most of the flat-type smallpox cases are fatal. In patients with a highly compromised immune response, there is extensive multiplication of the virus in the spleen and bone marrow, producing a rare condition known as hemorrhagic smallpox. This rare type of smallpox is associated with petechiae in the skin and bleeding from the conjunctiva and mucous membranes. Severe toxemia results followed by early death, often before the characteristic lesions of smallpox rash develop. Hemorrhagic-type smallpox is more common in pregnant women than in other adults. The underlying reasons for toxemia and other severe systemic effects that can be associated with smallpox are still unclear.

The prodrome is sometimes accompanied by an erythematous rash or, rarely, a petechial rash in pale-skinned subjects. Three to four days after the onset of the prodromal symptoms, the characteristic rash of ordinary-type smallpox appears, first on the buccal and pharyngeal mucosa, the face, the forearms, and the hands. The rash spreads downward, and within a day or so the trunk and lower limbs are involved, with the back more involved than the abdomen. Ultimately, the distribution of the variola rash is centrifugal: it is most profuse on

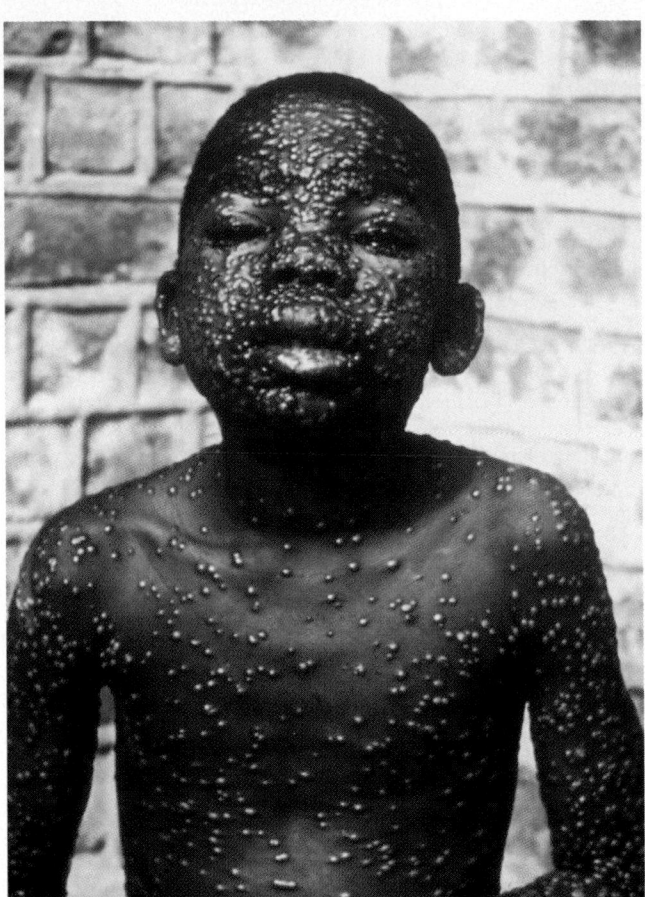

FIGURE 323-2. African child displaying the typical centrifugal rash distribution of smallpox on his face, chest, and arms. *(From the U.S. Centers for Disease Control and Prevention [CDC] Public Health Image Library [PHIL] at http://phil.cdc.gov/phil/default.asp. Image ID 3268. Photograph taken in 1970.)*

the face and is more abundant on the forearms than the upper arms and on the lower legs than the thighs (Figs. 323–1 and 323–2). Prominences and surfaces exposed to irritation are involved more heavily by the rash than the protected surfaces, flexures, and depressions, which are usually somewhat spared. In contrast to chickenpox, which is the disease most often confused with the early rash stage of smallpox, all lesions on any one part of the body are at the same stage of development (see Chapter 129). Furthermore, the distribution of the chickenpox rash is centripetal (with a predominance of lesions on the trunk and relative sparing of face and distal limbs), and abdominal involvement is equivalent to back involvement.

The lesions of the smallpox rash begin as circular macules (small, discolored skin patches). The macules form firm papules and then vesicles (usually multiloculated), which soon become opaque and pustular. The vesicles are typically raised and well circumscribed, deep, and firm to the touch (Fig. 323–3). Approximately 8 to 9 days after the onset of the rash, the pustules become pit-like and dimpled; and around day 14 the pustules dry up and become crusted. The rash of chickenpox, in contrast, develops as uniloculated vesicles that do not umbilicate, and the vesicles may have irregular borders. By the end of the third week of smallpox infection, most of the lesion crusts separate, with those on the palms and soles separating last.

Sequelae often follow recovery. The most common are pockmarks, which may occur all over the body but are usually most prominent on the face owing to the large number of sebaceous glands affected by the lesions. Rarely, blindness occurs as a result of keratitis or corneal ulcerations. Recovery results in prolonged immunity to reinfection. Variola virus does not persist in the body after recovery.

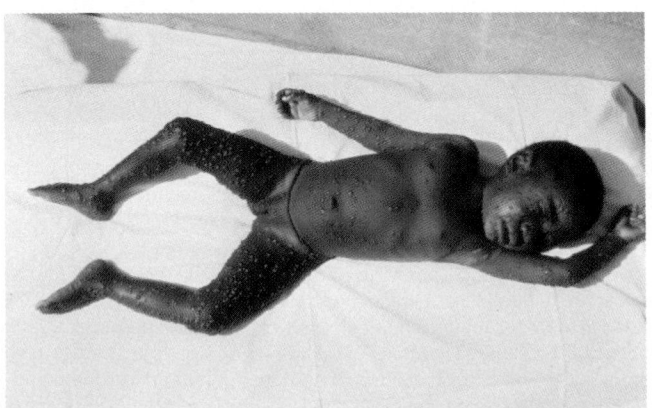

FIGURE 323-1. Distribution of smallpox lesions on the body of a child during the fifth day of infection. Note the greater numbers of discrete lesions on the face and extremities compared to the trunk. *(From the U.S. Centers for Disease Control and Prevention [CDC] Public Health Image Library [PHIL] at http://phil.cdc.gov/phil/default.asp. Image ID 3262. Photograph taken in 1972 by Dr. Paul B. Dean, CDC.)*

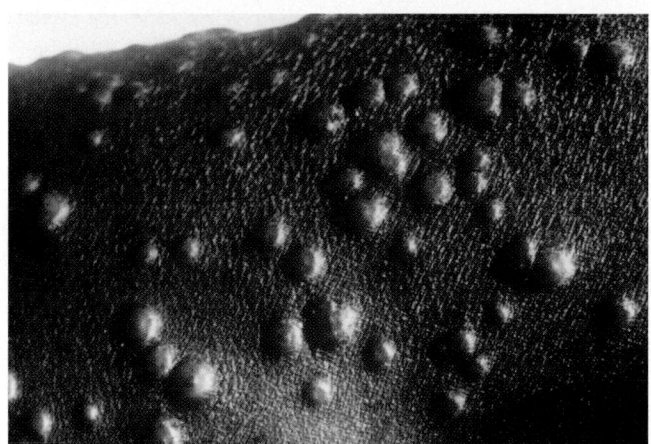

FIGURE 323-3. Close-up of smallpox pustules that are round, smooth, firm, and all at the same stage of development. *(Originally from the World Health Organization Diagnosis of Smallpox Slide Series. Image downloaded from the U.S. Centers for Disease Control and Prevention [CDC] Public Health Image Library [PHIL] at http://phil.cdc. gov/phil/default.asp. Image ID 2009. Photograph taken in 1969.)*

DIAGNOSIS

CDC has developed several resources that can be used to assist clinicians in evaluating acute generalized vesicular or pustular rash illnesses concerning their likelihood of being smallpox in a nonoutbreak setting. These tools can be found on the CDC website (http://www.bt.cdc.gov/agent/smallpox/diagnosis/evalposter.asp) and include an interactive online version of the clinical evaluation algorithm. Because the positive predictive value of smallpox-specific diagnostics decreases considerably in the absence of existing disease, these tests should be performed on patients only when the clinical illness is compatible with a high risk for smallpox. Public health authorities should be immediately notified about suspected smallpox patients to assist with the assessment and help expedite testing for smallpox through the National Laboratory Response Network (LRN) if indicated.

Historically, smallpox was diagnosed through clinical observation and laboratory diagnostics. Laboratory methods utilized during the eradication campaign included electron microscopy, agarose gel diffusion, culture on chick chorioallantoic membrane, growth characteristics on scarified rabbit skin, and growth on HeLa cells. These methods would still provide robust information to differentiate variola from other orthopoxviruses, but for a variety of reasons most are no longer used. Modern nucleic acid methods are more widely used today.

Specimen Collection

Virus can be easily recovered from active skin lesions. Appropriate specimens to collect for smallpox diagnostic testing are the lesion roof, base scrapings from unroofed lesions, tonsilar swabs, whole blood and serum, and lesion punch biopsies. Details of diagnostic specimen collection procedures can be found on the Internet (http://www.bt.cdc.gov/agent/smallpox/response-plan/files/guide-d.pdf). Specimen collection for suspected smallpox cases should be done by vaccine-protected individuals utilizing appropriate airborne infection isolation (AII) (formerly "airborne precautions") and the prescribed personal protective measures, or individuals utilizing AII and the prescribed personal protective measures with no contraindications to vaccination can be immediately vaccinated if the diagnosis of smallpox is confirmed.

Nucleic Acid Testing

Through previous work and efforts identified by the U.S. smallpox research agenda, a variety of nucleic acid testing methodologies targeting poxviruses have been published and reviewed[23] or are in use at U.S. Public Health laboratories and other member laboratories of the LRN. The LRN, founded in 1999, is a national network of local, state,

and federal public health, hospital-based, veterinary, agriculture, food, and environmental testing laboratories that provide laboratory diagnostic capacity to respond to biological and chemical terrorism and other public health emergencies.

Among tests described in the literature that allow both identification and quantification of the agent[24-31] are the following: the standard polymerase chain reaction (PCR) assays, which generically amplify a segment of orthopoxvirus nucleic acid and allow speciation (e.g., variola, monkeypox, vaccinia) on the basis of fragment sizes after restriction endonuclease digestion, multiplex assays that permit simultaneous analysis of orthopoxvirus species in one reaction tube, and real-time PCR assays.

Electron Microscopy

Electron microscopic (EM) visualization of negatively stained poxvirus virions was a valuable technique for confirming poxvirus infections during the smallpox eradication campaign. Historically, skilled practitioners of transmission negative-stain EM successfully detected orthopoxvirus particles in approximately 95% of clinical specimens from patients with variola infections and in approximately 75% from patients with vaccinia infections.[32] In the event of a deliberate release of smallpox virus and subsequent human disease, or for generalized vaccinia infections resulting from vaccination, negatively stained preparations derived from lesions or scab material would again provide a valuable method for assisting in poxvirus diagnosis and ruling out other causes of rash illness. However, EM visualization of virions compatible with orthopoxvirus by itself does not constitute proof of a smallpox infection because variola, vaccinia, monkeypox, and molluscum viruses, for example, are morphologically indistinguishable by that method. Negative-stain electron microscopy, however, is valuable for discerning morphologic structures in primary clinical specimens, compatible with other infectious agents, in the differential diagnosis of suspected smallpox that includes the herpesviruses [varicella, herpes simplex viruses 1 and 2 (HSV-1, HSV-2)][33] (see Chapter 129).

Histopathology and Immunohistochemistry

The presence of cytoplasmic inclusions is characteristic of poxvirus infections but cannot be used to specifically identify variola in a biopsy specimen. There are two types of inclusion bodies: A-type and B-type. B-type inclusion bodies (Guarnieri bodies) are the sites of viral replication and are found in those infected by all species of poxvirus. A-type inclusion bodies are produced by certain poxviruses in the genus *Orthopoxvirus* [cowpox virus (Downie body)]; the ectromelia virus (Marchal body); and the raccoon, vole, and skunk poxviruses. They are also produced in the genus *Avipoxvirus* [fowlpox virus (Borrel body)].

Poxvirus inclusion bodies can be presumptively identified in hematoxylin and eosin (H&E)-stained specimens using light microscopy. In the early smallpox lesions in the skin and mucous membranes, B-type inclusion bodies are readily observed in H&E-stained sections as faintly basophilic bodies lying in the cytoplasm, usually close to the nucleus. In more advanced lesions, suitably stained sections showed faintly basophilic granular inclusions occupying a large part of the cytoplasm of infected cells. They are particularly evident in epithelial cells at the base of vesicles or pustules. (May-Grunwald Giemsa stain may also be used; here the basophilic inclusions appear magenta red.) Histopathologic staining of tissues provides another mechanism for evaluating if orthopoxvirus is present in the tissue. Again, these methods are not specific for variola.[34,35]

Cell Culture

Orthopoxviruses can be grown in a variety of established cell culture lines, including Vero, BS-C-1, CV-1, LLCMK-2 monkey kidney cells, human embryonic lung fibroblast cells, HeLa cells, chick embryo fibroblast cells, and MRC-5 human diploid fibroblast cells. Characteristic growth and the cytopathic effect in any of these cell lines does not identify which orthopoxvirus is present. Methods for growing and discriminating the morphology of orthopoxviruses on the chorioallantoic membrane of 12-day-old chick embryos have been described.[32,36] At this time, attempts to isolate variola virus by cell culture should be conducted only in an approved BSL-4 laboratory by appropriately trained and vaccinated personnel.

PRE-EVENT AND POST-EVENT EXPOSURE PREPAREDNESS

As previously stated, the world's population is largely not vaccinated against smallpox and therefore highly susceptible to infection should smallpox be intentionally released as a bioterrorism agent. It is imperative, therefore, that preparations for a medical and public health response to a smallpox outbreak be in place before such an outbreak occurs. Smallpox response planning involves many national and international health and emergency response agencies. In the United States, the Department of Health and Human Services (DHHS) and the CDC are the lead department and agency for the public health response to an outbreak. The CDC has prepared several guidance and planning documents to assist state and local public health and medical authorities identify and plan essential local response measures (see http://www.bt.cdc.gov/planning/index.asp and http://www.bt.cdc.gov/agent/smallpox/prep/index.asp).

Education of medical and public health staff about the clinical presentation of smallpox and the control measures necessary to contain an outbreak, including vaccination strategies, is essential for responding to an outbreak of smallpox. Clinical evaluation and the collection of clinical laboratory specimens are covered elsewhere in this section (rash illness and laboratory algorithms). In addition, smallpox vaccination and training of identified public health and medical smallpox response teams has been undertaken to enhance federal, state, and local level rapid response capabilities to contain a smallpox outbreak.[37]

"Surveillance and containment" (SC) is the mainstay of smallpox outbreak control. Also called "ring vaccination" and "search and containment," this strategy targets vaccination of close contacts of smallpox patients and close monitoring to initiate isolation if symptoms of the disease occur. This ensures more rapid administration of vaccine to those who are at the greatest risk of developing the disease. It thus represents the best chance for preventing further smallpox transmission. By focusing on vaccinating persons at highest risk of smallpox, this strategy can also help minimize the risk of adverse events in persons least likely to be exposed to a case of smallpox. Adverse events associated with smallpox vaccine are described in Chapter 129. Patients must first be identified and isolated and their close contacts (face-to-face or household contacts) identified and vaccinated; optimally, this occurs within 3 days of exposure to prevent or at least significantly lessen the severity of smallpox symptoms in most of the people.[38] Vaccination 4 to 7 days after exposure likely offers some protection from disease or at least modifies the severity of the disease.[39,40] During the eradication campaign, when outbreaks sometimes still occurred despite 80% vaccination coverage of the population, this vaccination strategy was highly effective for stopping chains of disease transmission.[41] Large-scale voluntary vaccination may also be offered to unaffected populations (who have a low risk of vaccine complications), to augment SC activities (by decreasing the overall population susceptibility); however, SC activities should continue, as they are the mainstay for outbreak control.

INFECTION CONTROL MEASURES

Person-to-person spread of smallpox virus occurs largely via droplet transmission within 6 feet of the patient, although contact and airborne transmission has been documented.[17] Because airborne transmission is possible, it is imperative that all persons caring for smallpox patients maintain AII, in addition to standard and contact precautions. AII requires that the patient be placed in a private negative air pressure room, with 6 to 12 air exchanges per hour. The latter is monitored for negative pressure. There must also be appropriate discharge of air to the outdoors, or there must be high-efficiency filtration before the air

is recirculated to other parts of the facility. When AII is not available or the number of patients exceeds the number of rooms, smallpox patients may be assigned to another wing or facility (i.e., motel, school) that does not share untreated airflow with other areas.

Under AII, only essential personnel enter the room, and they wear fitted N95 (or higher) respirators at all times. Other personnel protective equipment, such as gowns, gloves, and eye protection, is worn, and it is removed and discarded before leaving the areas. Smallpox patients should be moved from the room only when necessary. When it must be done, the patient should wear a mask to limit the potential spread of particles.[42]

During the smallpox era, inadequate infection-control practices sometimes led to increased transmission in hospitals.[17,43] A review of importations into Europe during 1950 to 1971 concluded that more than 50% of the cases were associated with hospitals, with health care workers constituting approximately 20% of the cases.[43] A review of European smallpox outbreaks showed that the communicability of smallpox decreased by approximately one-half when hospital-based transmission was excluded.[44] Therefore it is advisable that all persons caring for smallpox patients have a current vaccination against smallpox, and that all persons caring for smallpox patients, regardless of whether vaccinated, maintain AII precautions to ensure that there is no accidental breech of protocol. Isolation of infected patients and vaccination with close monitoring of patients' contacts at greatest risk for infection have been demonstrated to effectively interrupt transmission of smallpox.[9,45]

PUBLIC HEALTH ISSUES AND PREPAREDNESS EFFORTS

An outbreak of smallpox is a public health emergency, and all suspected cases of smallpox should be immediately reported to local public health officials. Local and state health authorities can provide medical personnel with guidance regarding the evaluation and infection-control precautions to initiate. They can help expedite testing for varicella, HSV, and smallpox if appropriate. Through their partnership with CDC and participation in the LRN, several local and all state pubic health laboratories possess or have access to diagnostic resources for smallpox and other potential bioterrorism agents, as well as diagnostics for varicella, vaccinia, and other herpes viruses. In addition, CDC consultation and technical assistance is available 24 hours a day and can be initiated through the CDC Director's Emergency Operation Center at 770-488-7100.

Smallpox preparedness activities and response planning have been ongoing at the federal, state, and local levels since 1999. State and local authorities are working to enhance their preparedness for smallpox by identifying, training, and vaccinating smallpox response team personnel to be immediately available to initiate control measures in the event of a smallpox outbreak. In addition, response planning efforts for the initiation of control measures and rapid establishment of vaccination clinics in response to a smallpox outbreak are ongoing. Public health laboratory diagnostics, bioterrorism surveillance and epidemiologic capacity, and emergency communication capabilities have also been enhanced.[46]

At the federal level, major efforts have focused on: (1) increasing smallpox education and outreach to the medical, public health, and general public communities; (2) developing rapid diagnostic tests that use modern genetic methods and increasing national diagnostic capacity through the LRN; (3) initiating national smallpox responder vaccination with the assistance of state and local public health organizations; (4) developing a comprehensive smallpox vaccine adverse events monitoring and investigation program to support safe vaccination efforts for pre-event responder preparedness; and (5) increasing the national stores of smallpox vaccine to an amount adequate for vaccinating the entire U.S. population if needed.

This last effort has included the initiation of research studies to evaluate the immunizing effectiveness of diluted formulations of the current vaccine supply. Comparison of humoral and cellular responses of volunteers vaccinated with 1:10 diluted vaccine demonstrated little difference from those vaccinated with undiluted vaccine.[47] Vaccine "take" (demonstration of the expected skin reaction at the site 6 to 8 days following vaccination) rates, classically used as a sign of successful vaccination and protection, were similar in those vaccinated with a 1:5 dilution.[48] Diluted formulations of smallpox vaccine would be used under an investigative new drug (IND) protocol should it ever be needed in an emergency.

In addition, efforts are underway to develop and license a new, clonally derived, cell culture-grown vaccinia vaccine.[49] This vaccine is derived from the vaccine previously used in the United States (New York City Board of Health strain) and licensed as Dryvax by Wyeth Laboratories. Dryvax was originally prepared using calf skin production methods. Because of the adverse event associated with the original vaccine,[50-52] there are additional efforts to develop more attenuated vaccines. Recent National Institutes of Health (NIH)-sponsored efforts have focused on the vaccinia strain MVA.[53,54] These efforts will hopefully yield a vaccine that retains its effectiveness but is safer for immunosuppressed individuals, including those with acquired immunodeficiency syndrome, who are at risk for the more severe adverse events associated with vaccinia (see Chapter 129).[55] Other, more fundamental research has focused on potential subunit vaccines, using envelope and membrane proteins.[56]

Additional information regarding smallpox, public health and medical actions that should be initiated in response to a smallpox outbreak, and current smallpox preparedness activities and response planning efforts can be found on the Internet (http://www.bt.cdc.gov/).

REFERENCES

1. Noah DL, Huebner KD, Darling RG, Waeckerle JF. The history and threat of biological warfare and terrorism. Emerg Med Clin North Am 2002;20:255-271.
2. Derbes VJ. De Mussis and the great plague of 1348: a forgotten episode of bacteriological warfare. JAMA 1966;196:59-62.
3. Williams PWD. Unit 731: Japan's Secret Biological Warfare in World War II. New York: Free Press; 1989.
4. Jernigan DB, Raghunathan PL, Bell BP, et al. Investigation of bioterrorism-related anthrax, United States, 2001: epidemiologic findings. Emerg Infect Dis 2002;8:1019-1028.
5. Mott JA, Treadwell TA, Hennessy TW, et al. Call-tracking data and the public health response to bioterrorism-related anthrax. Emerg Infect Dis 2002;8:1088-1092.
6. Smith S. Historical Postmortem: Old Tactics, New Threat: What is Today's Risk of Smallpox? Chicago: American Medical Association; http://www.ama-assn.org/ama/pub/category18755.html
7. Parkman F Jr. The Conspiracy of Pontiac and the Indian War after the Conquest of Canada. Boston: Little, Brown and Company, 1851.
8. Harpster JW, ed. Pen Pictures of Early Western Pennsylvania. Pittsburgh: University of Pittsburgh Press; 1938.
9. Fenner F, Henderson DA, Arita I, et al. Smallpox and Its Eradication. Geneva: World Health Organization; 1988:31-38, 121-168, 200, 1341-1343.
10. Davis CJ. Nuclear blindness: an overview of the biological weapons programs of the former Soviet Union and Iraq. Emerg Infect Dis 1999;5:509-512.
11. Meselson M, Guillemin J, Hugh-Jones M, et al. The Sverdlovsk anthrax outbreak of 1979. Science 1994;266:1202-1208.
12. Smith J. Yeltsin Blames '79 Anthrax on Germ Warfare Efforts. Washington Post, June 16, 1992, p A-1
13. Zelicoff AP. An epidemiological analysis of the 1971 smallpox outbreak in Aralsk, Kazakhstan. Crit Rev Microbiol 2003;29:97-108.
14. WHO. The Global Eradication of Smallpox. Final Report of the Global Commission for the Certification of Smallpox Eradication. History of International Public Health. Geneva: WHO; 1980:4.
15. Kortepeter MG, Parker GW. Potential biological weapons threats. Emerging Infect Dis 1999;5:523-527.
16. Henderson DA, Inglesby TV, Bartlett JG, et al. Smallpox as a biological weapon: medical and public health management; Working Group on Civilian Biodefense. JAMA 1999;281:2127-2137.
17. Gelfand HM, Posch J. The recent outbreak of smallpox in Meschede, West Germany. Am J Epidemiol 1971;93:234-237.
18. CDC. Vaccinia (smallpox) vaccine. recommendations of the Advisory Committee on Immunization Practices (ACIP), 2001. MMWR Morb Mortal Wkly Rep 2001;50 (RR-10).
19. Sarkar JK, Mitra AC, Mukherjee MK, De SK. Virus excretion in smallpox. 2. Excretion in the throats of household contacts. Bull WHO 1973;48:523-527.
20. Downie AW, Meiklejohn M, St Vincent L, et al. The recovery of smallpox virus from patients and their environment in a smallpox hospital. Bull WHO 1965;33:615-622.
21. Rao AR. Infected Inanimate Objects (Fomites) and Their Role in Transmission of Smallpox. Geneva: WHO; 1972:72.40.
22. Downie AW, McCarthy K. The antibody response in man following infection with viruses of the pox group. III. Antibody response in smallpox. J Hyg (Lond) 1958;56:479-487.
23. Damon I, Esposito JJ. Poxviruses that infect humans. In: Murray P, Baron E, Jorgenson J, et al, eds. Manual of Clinical Microbiology. Washington DC: ASM Press; 2003:1583-1592.
24. Meyer H, Ropp SL, Esposito JJ. Diagnostic virology protocols. In: Warnes A, Stephenson J, eds. Methods in Molecular Biology. Totowa, NJ: Humana Press; 1998:199-211.
25. Meyer H, Ropp SL, Esposito JJ. Gene for A-type inclusion body protein is useful for a polymerase chain reaction assay to differentiate orthopoxviruses. J Virol Methods 1997;64:217-221.
26. Ropp SL, Jin Q, Knight JC, et al. PCR strategy for identification and differentiation of small pox and other orthopoxviruses. J Clin Microbiol 1995;33:2069-2076.
27. Loparev VN, Massung RF, Esposito JJ, Meyer H. Detection and differentiation of Old World orthopoxviruses: restriction fragment length polymorphism of the crmB gene region. J Clin Microbiol 2001;39:94-100.
28. Dhar AD, Werchniak AE, Li Y, et al. Tanapox infection in a college student. N Engl J Med 2004;350:361-366.
29. Lapa S, Mikheev M, Shchelkunov S, et al. Species-level identification of orthopoxviruses with an oligonucleotide microchip. J Clin Microbiol 2002;40:753-757.
30. Ibrahim M, Kulesh D, Saleh S, et al. Real-time PCR assay to detect smallpox virus. J Clin Microbiol 2003;8:3385-3839.
31. Espy MJ, Cockerill FR III, Meyer RF, et al. Detection of smallpox virus DNA by LightCycler PCR. J Clin Microbiol 2002;40:1985-1988.
32. Nakano J. Poxviruses. In: Lennette E, Schmidt N, eds. Diagnostic Procedures for Viral, Rickettsial and Chlamydial Infections. 5th ed. Washington, DC: American Public Health Association; 1979:257-308.
33. Long GW, Nobel J Jr, Murphy FA, et al. Experience with electron microscopy in the differential diagnosis of smallpox. Appl Microbiol 1970;20:497-504.
34. Reed KD, Melski JW, Graham MB, et al. The detection of monkeypox in humans in the Western Hemisphere. N Engl J Med 2004;350:342-350.
35. Guarner J, Johnson B, Paddock C, et al. Monkeypox transmission and pathogens in prairie dogs. Emerg Infect Dis 2004;3:426-431.
36. Guide to the Laboratory Diagnosis of Smallpox for Smallpox Eradication Programmes. WHO Techn Rep Ser 1960:1-47.
37. Wharton M, Strikas RA, Harpaz R, et al. Recommendations for using smallpox vaccine in a pre-event vaccination program: supplemental recommendations of the Advisory Committee on Immunization Practices (ACIP) and the Healthcare Infection Control Practices Advisory Committee (HICPAC). MMWR Recomm Rep 2003;52:1-16.
38. Massoudi MS, Barker L, Schwartz B. Effectiveness of postexposure vaccination for the prevention of smallpox: results of a delphi analysis. J Infect Dis 2003;188:973-976.
39. Mack TM, Thomas DB, Ali A, Muzaffar KM. Epidemiology of smallpox in West Pakistan. I. Acquired immunity and the distribution of disease. Am J Epidemiol 1972;95:157-168.
40. Rao AR, Jacob ES, Kamalakshi S, et al. Epidemiological studies in smallpox: a study of intrafamilial transmission in a series of 254 infected families. Indian J Med Res 1968;56:1826-1854.
41. Fenner F, Henderson DA, Arita I, et al. Smallpox and Its Eradication. Geneva: World Health Organization; 1988:481,484,494.
42. Garner JS, Simmons BP. Guideline for isolation precautions in hospitals. Infect Cont 1983;4(Suppl):245-325.
43. Mack TM. Smallpox in Europe, 1950-1971. J Infect Dis 1972;125:161-169.
44. Gani R, Leach S. Transmission potential of smallpox in contemporary populations. Nature 2001;414:748-751.
45. Foege WH, Millar JD, Henderson DA. Smallpox eradication in West and Central Africa. Bull WHO 1975;52:209-222.
46. LeDuc JW, Damon I, Relman DA, et al. Smallpox research activities: U.S. interagency collaboration, 2001. Emerg Infect Dis 2002;8:743-745.
47. Frey SE, Newman FK, Cruz J, et al. Dose-related effects of smallpox vaccine. N Engl J Med 2002;346:1275-1280.
48. Frey SE, Couch RB, Tacket CO, et al. Clinical responses to undiluted and diluted smallpox vaccine. N Engl J Med 2002;346:1265-1274.
49. Weltzin R, Liu J, Pugachev KV, et al. Clonal vaccinia virus grown in cell culture as a new smallpox vaccine. Nat Med 2003;9:1125-1130.
50. Neff JM, Lane JM, Pert JH, et al. Complications of smallpox vaccination. I. National survey in the United States, 1963. N Engl J Med 1967;276:125-132.
51. Lane JM, Ruben FL, Neff JM, Millar JD. Complications of smallpox vaccination, 1968. N Engl J Med 1969;281:1201-1208.
52. Lane JM, Ruben FL, Neff JM, Millar JD. Complications of smallpox vaccination, 1968: results of ten statewide surveys. J Infect Dis 1970;122:303-309.
53. Meyer H, Sutter G, Mayr A. Mapping of deletions in the genome of the highly attenuated vaccinia virus MVA and their influence on virulence. J Gen Virol 1991;72 (Pt 5):1031-1038.
54. NIAID Biodefense Research Agenda for CDC Category A Agents—Progress Report. Bethesda, MD: NIAID; 2003.
55. Redfield RR, Wright DC, James WD, et al. Disseminated vaccinia in a military recruit with human immunodeficiency virus (HIV) disease. N Engl J Med 1987;316:673-676.
56. Hooper JW, Custer DM, Thompson E. Four-gene-combination DNA vaccine protects mice against a lethal vaccinia virus challenge and elicits appropriate antibody responses in nonhuman primates. Virology 2003;306:181-195.

CHAPTER 324

Anthrax

DANIEL LUCEY

HISTORY AND POTENTIAL USE AS A BIOTERRORISM AGENT

A brief overview of the potential use of anthrax as an agent of biowarfare or bioterrorism serves to emphasize this microbial threat over the past 75 years.[1] The catastrophic potential of anthrax when used as a biological weapon was emphasized by a World Health Organization (WHO) study in 1970 that estimated that 50 kg of anthrax released from a plane into the air over a city could kill or severely injure more than 200,000 people.[2] Britain began testing anthrax as a potential weapon during World War II but never used it against humans. Specific units of the Japanese Army are reported to have used anthrax as a weapon in China during World War II.[3] During the 1950s anthrax was developed as a potential offensive biowarfare agent by the U.S. military, a program that was disbanded by 1970. Anthrax was also developed as a biowarfare agent by the former Soviet Union, as described by Alibek.[4] Evidence of this program, resulting in the death of civilians, followed the accidental release of anthrax from a military facility into the air over the city of Sverdlovsk (Ekaterinburg), Russia in 1979. Autopsy reports on 42 patients from Sverdlovsk, not published until 1993, provided extensive detail about the pathology of inhalational and meningeal anthrax.[5] It was reported after the first Gulf war in 1991 that Iraq had previously produced 8500 liters of anthrax but with no evidence of it ever being used against humans.[6] Unsuccessful attempts by the Aum Shinrikyō cult to aerosolize anthrax against civilians in Japan occurred in 1993.[7] Multiple threats involving white powder labeled as anthrax and sent in envelopes to clinics and other targets occurred in the United States throughout the 1990s. None of these letters, however, ever contained viable *Bacillus anthracis* or caused anthrax infection.

The recent watershed event when anthrax was used as a lethal bioterrorism weapon, however, began not later than 1 week after the attacks by terrorists hijacking airplanes on September 11, 2001. One or more yet-unidentified persons mailed letters containing lethal anthrax to Florida and New York City. The letter(s) to Florida were not found and therefore the postmark date(s) are uncertain. They most likely were mailed during the last 2 weeks of September, given the onset of anthrax disease at the end of September and beginning of October in workers at the targeted building. At least two letters containing anthrax were mailed to New York City from New Jersey and were postmarked on September 18. On October 9, 2001 two more letters containing anthrax were postmarked from New Jersey, this time to two senators at the U.S. Capitol in Washington, DC. One of these letters reached the Senate Hart building in the District of Columbia, and the other was found in a postal facility handling mail for the State Department in nearby Virginia after a zip code reading error.

These events of 2001 changed much of what was known about anthrax.[8,9] Although the perpetrator(s) of these crimes remain unidentified as of October 2003, these acts were clearly acts of bioterrorism using anthrax. At least 22 persons infected with anthrax sent through the mail developed either inhalational anthrax (11 confirmed cases) or cutaneous anthrax (11 cases with 7 confirmed and 4 suspected). There were no cases of gastrointestinal anthrax. Death occurred in 5 of the 11 (45%) inhalational cases and none of the 11 cutaneous cases.[10,11]

The first recognized case of anthrax due to this bioterrorism attack in 2001 occurred in Florida during the first week of October. The patient presented with anthrax meningitis following inhalational anthrax.[8,12] Prior to 2001 the last case of inhalational anthrax in the United States occurred in 1976 in a patient who also presented with fatal anthrax meningitis.[13] Between 1900 and 1976, only 18 cases of inhalational anthrax were reported in the United States, and 16 were fatal.[14] None was due to bioterrorism. Thus there was no clinical familiarity with inhalational anthrax in the United States in 2001. In addition, there was limited diagnostic, therapeutic, or epidemiologic expertise with it as a bioterrorism weapon in 2001.

CLINICAL MANIFESTATIONS AND DIAGNOSIS OF ANTHRAX AS A BIOTERRORISM AGENT

Incubation Period

Published information about the incubation period of anthrax when used as a biological weapon is available only from the information released about the 1979 Sverdlovsk, Russia episode and the 2001 attacks in the United States. In 1979 the modal incubation period for inhalational anthrax was 9 to 10 days,[15] with some periods as short as 2 to 3 days. The longest reported incubation period was 43 days. Reaerosolization of spores from the environment was not thought to be responsible for the longer incubation periods, although this possibility has been suggested.[4]

In 2001 the incubation period could be calculated only for patients with a known date of exposure. For example, of the 11 patients with inhalational anthrax, 6 had well defined incubation periods, which ranged from 4 to 6 days.[8] The cutaneous cases in 2001 had an incubation period of 1 to 10 days.[10] Studies with nonhuman primates have found anthrax incubation periods usually to be 2 to 14 days, although sometimes longer, particularly with a lower inoculum. In the often-cited example of the longest incubation period, a cynomolgus monkey died of anthrax 98 days after inhaling anthrax spores. This single monkey was mentioned as unpublished data from an investigator whose colleague was providing a discussion section addendum to a 1966 paper on industrial inhalation anthrax.[16] In another often-referenced example, a 1956 article mentioned combined data from a number of tests involving experiments in monkeys given penicillin and anthrax vaccine prophylaxis in which "the trend of events" showed that 100 days after exposure to aerosolized anthrax the "estimated percentage of original retention of spores" was "trace." The authors concluded that anthrax spores "can be detected for at least 100 days after deposition in the lung."[17] These animal studies contributed to the additional option of 100 days, made in December 2001, for the duration of antibiotic post-exposure anthrax prophylaxis for persons who chose not to stop at the 60 day duration as originally recommended in October 2001.

Clinical Presentation

Three routes of infection exist for *Bacillus anthracis:* inhalational, cutaneous, and gastrointestinal (GI). It should be emphasized, however, that there are four major clinical presentations: meningitis, inhalational, cutaneous, and GI. Meningitis can occur as a manifestation of infection by the inhalational, cutaneous, or GI route but is most likely to occur after inhalational infection. In the autopsy series from Sverdlovsk, 21 of 42 cases (50%) with inhalational anthrax also had meningitis.[5]

The importance of recognizing meningitis as a separate clinical presentation of anthrax is at least fourfold. First, meningitis can be the presenting manifestation of the index case of a bioterrorism attack with anthrax, as occurred in 2001. Second, it is a medical emergency, as the case-fatality rate historically has been higher than 90%.[18,19] Third, anthrax meningitis should prompt an immediate public health response to identify the environmental source and route of the infection, as well as to identify and treat any other exposed persons. This public health response must be linked to the forensic and law enforcement investigation in the setting of potential bioterrorism. Fourth, multiple intravenous antibiotics should be given immediately, at least some of which penetrate the cerebrospinal fluid (CSF). Consideration can be given to adjunctive therapies, such as corticosteroids[20] or anthrax-toxin inhibitors, although no trials to assess their efficacy or that of specific antibiotics have been performed for this rare disease.

The primary presentation of central nervous system (CNS) anthrax is hemorrhagic meningitis or meningoencephalitis.[5,12,14,18] Long, gram-positive, boxcar- or cigar-shaped bacteria are found in the CSF that are

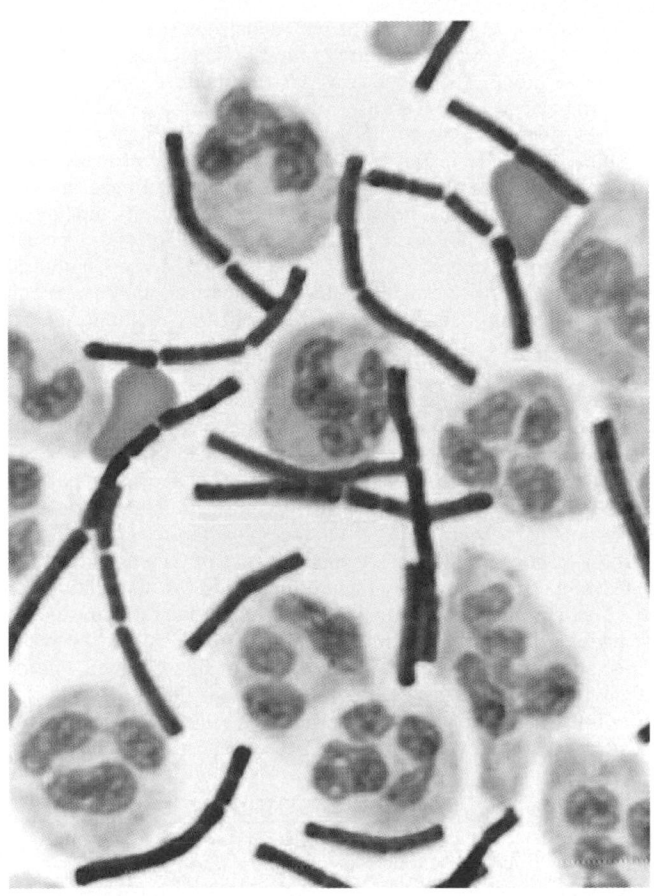

FIGURE 324-1. Cerebrospinal fluid Gram stain demonstrating characteristic *Bacillus anthracis* and neutrophils from the first patient recognized to have anthrax during the 2001 bioterrorism attack. *(From Bush LM, Abrams BH, Beall A, Johnson CC. Index case of fatal inhalational anthrax due to bioterrorism in the United States. N Engl J Med 2001;345:1607-1610.)*

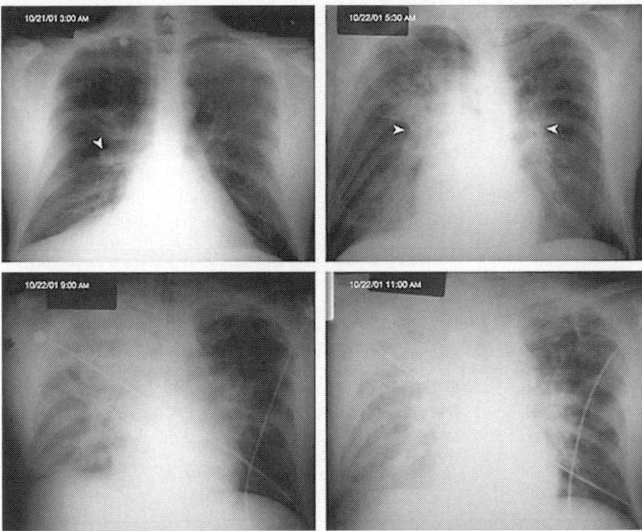

FIGURE 324-2. Chest radiograph of a patient with inhalational anthrax in 2001. The arrows emphasize the widened mediastinum due to the characteristic mediastinal adenopathy. *(From Borio L, Frank D, Mani V, et al. Death due to bioterrorism-related inhalational anthrax: report of 2 patients. JAMA 2001;286:2554-2559.)*

quite distinct from any other bacteria causing meningitis (Fig. 324-1). Other than the Gram stain appearance and the presence of hemorrhage, CSF features do not distinguish anthrax meningitis from other causes of bacterial meningitis.

In 2001, the 11 patients with inhalational anthrax demonstrated three common findings. First, 10 of the 11 had evidence of mediastinal adenopathy on chest radiographs or chest computed tomography (CT) scans (Fig. 324-2). Notably, however, several of these patients initially had chest radiographs that were interpreted as normal but later were reinterpreted as showing mediastinal widening or fullness consistent with adenopathy.[8,22] Chest CT scans were more sensitive than chest radiographs for identifying mediastinal adenopathy due to anthrax. Chest CT without contrast should be performed to demonstrate the typically hemorrhagic nature of the adenopathy. Only 1 of the 11 patients in 2001 with inhalational anthrax never developed mediastinal adenopathy. Instead, his infection manifested as pulmonary infiltrates with bloody pleural effusions.[8] Pulmonary parenchymal disease, described as infiltrates or consolidation on the chest radiograph, was found in 8 of 11 patients in 2001.[8,23] Historically, pulmonary parenchymal disease was considered uncommon with inhalational anthrax.[11,24] In the 1979 autopsy series from Sverdlovsk, 11 of 42 cases had a "novel observation" of "primary focal hemorrhagic necrotizing pneumonia at the apparent portal of entry." These pulmonary lesions were described by analogy to a Ghon focus in tuberculosis.[5]

Second, 8 of the 11 patients developed bloody pleural effusions, often bilateral or recurrent, requiring drainage by thoracentesis or chest tube. Third, remarkably, all eight patients whose blood was cultured prior to giving them antibiotics grew *Bacillus anthracis* in the cultures within 24 hours. At least one patient had anthrax organisms seen in the buffy coat of his peripheral blood.[8,23]

Importantly, the presence of hemorrhagic mediastinal adenopathy, bloody pleural effusions, or positive blood cultures did not distinguish the fatal from the nonfatal inhalational anthrax cases. These findings should not preclude aggressive therapy because the patients can be cured. For example, in six of six nonfatal cases and two of five fatal cases the patients developed bloody pleural effusions, whereas in three of three nonfatal cases and five of five fatal cases the patients had positive blood cultures prior to being given antibiotics. In contrast, the need for intubation within 24 hours of hospital admission occurred in none of six nonfatal cases and in four of five fatal cases of inhalational anthrax.[8,23,25]

Historically, inhalational anthrax has been divided into an early stage and a late stage.[8,21,22,26] The timing of radiologic and microbiological information during the evaluation and treatment of the patients with inhalational anthrax in 2001 can be interpreted to suggest that an important "intermediate-progressive" stage can be defined during which bacteremia and mediastinal adenopathy is present with progressively worsening symptoms, yet cure can still be accomplished with appropriate therapy (Table 324-1).

The early stage has nonspecific symptoms often described generally as "flu-like" with malaise, myalgias, low-grade fever, nausea, chest pain, and mild headache. Subsequently, progressive respiratory, neurologic, gastrointestinal, or hemodynamic abnormalities (or a combination of these problems) develop over the course of hours to days. A critical issue has been to diagnose and treat inhalational anthrax before the late, often fulminant fatal stage, which is characterized by respiratory failure, meningitis, and shock. Since the anthrax attacks of 2001, investigators have attempted to devise improved screening guidelines to identify inhalational anthrax (e.g., through the use of a constellation of five or more symptoms, tachycardia, and low-grade fever).[27] Others have compared inhalational anthrax with influenza and reported that dyspnea, nonheadache neurologic symptoms such as confusion or syncope, and nausea/vomiting are more characteristic of inhalational anthrax than of influenza.[28,29] In contrast, rhinorrhea and sore throat were found to be uncommon with inhalational anthrax, as reported for the patients in 2001.[28,30]

An approach to the evaluation and management of patients with suspected inhalational anthrax is offered in Table 324-2. Similarly,

TABLE 324-1 Proposed Staging of Inhalational Anthrax

Stage	Comments
1: Asymptomatic	Usually < 1 week and rarely > 1 month
2: Early–prodromal	Nonspecific malaise, myalgias, low-grade fever, mild headache, nausea, general "flu-like" prodromal illness.
3: Intermediate–progressive	Blood cultures are positive in < 24 hours; mediastinal adenopathy present; pleural effusions that are often hemorrhagic, large, and require repeated drainage. Findings may include high fever, dyspnea, confusion or syncope, increasing nausea/vomiting. Patients in this stage can still be cured with appropriate antibiotics and intensive support.
4: Late–fulminant	Respiratory failure requiring intubation, meningitis, end-organ hypoperfusion ("shock"). Cure currently less likely in this stage. Future therapies for this stage may require inhibitors of both anthrax toxin and systemic inflammatory response mediators, in addition to antibiotics and intensive care.

This proposed staging system incorporates information from historic "early" and "late" stages with new timing of microbiologic and radiologic information (i.e., an "intermediate–progressive stage") from the 11 patients in the 2001 bioterrorism attacks.

when preparing for patients with inhalational anthrax caused by a bioterrorism attack, coordination by infectious disease physicians with a multidisciplinary spectrum of clinicians and nonclinicians is important. A summary list of the critical person(s) or service and specific reasons for coordinating hospital preparedness with them for the care of patients with bioterrorism-associated anthrax is provided in Table 324-3. These coordinating functions, with each of the 16 person(s) or services as described, were accomplished in our hospital during the time of the 2001 anthrax attacks. In addition, a detailed example of an emergency department–infectious disease anthrax evaluation protocol emphasizing a matrix of epidemiologic exposure risks and symptomatology, is available on the Internet.[31]

Inhalational anthrax is not spread from person to person through the air. There is no indication that masks, respirators, or private rooms are necessary when caring for patients hospitalized with inhalational anthrax.[32] Standard precautions for infection control are all that are required. If active skin lesions are present, however, gloves should be worn[24] to avoid the potential for infection from active skin lesions.[33]

TABLE 324-2 Considerations for Evaluation and Management of Suspected Inhalational Anthrax

1. Obtain blood cultures before any antibiotics if anthrax is suspected.
2. Notify microbiology laboratory of concern for anthrax to expedite evaluation of specimens. Blood cultures are usually positive in < 24 hours.
3. Obtain history to include any epidemiologic link to known or suspected anthrax. Attention to respiratory complaints, neurologic or cognitive problems, GI complaints, fever, profuse diaphoresis, or new skin lesions.
4. Physical examination with attention to any respiratory abnormalities, neurologic or cognitive deficits, tachycardia, GI abnormalities, or skin lesions.
5. Obtain chest radiograph or noncontrast chest CT scan looking for a widened mediastinum due to hemorrhagic adenopathy, or pleural effusions.
6. If a suspicion of meningitis, examine CSF for characteristic large boxcar-shaped gram-positive rods.
7. If symptomatic and there is known or possible epidemiologic exposure to anthrax, give initial intravenous doses of at least two antibiotics to which the circulating *Bacillus anthracis* isolate is sensitive, including either ciprofloxacin or doxycycline as soon as possible in the ER before admitting to the ward. Combine with other antibiotics recommended by Department of Health or CDC, if information is available. Include antibiotics that penetrate CSF.

CDC, Centers for Disease Control and Prevention; CSF, cerebrospinal fluid; CT, computed tomography; ER, emergency room; GI, gastrointestinal.

The only one of the 11 patients with cutaneous anthrax in the 2001 bioterrorist attack who has been reported in detail was also the only child in the group. The patient was a 7-month-old infant who developed a red macule on his forearm 1 day after visiting a media outlet in New York City, where one of his parents worked. Within the first week the infant developed massive edema and then a central black eschar surrounding the site of the skin lesion.[34] He also developed microangiopathic hemolytic anemia with renal insufficiency,[35] a finding not linked with anthrax previously but also found in 1 of the 11 patients with inhalational anthrax in 2001.[8] Centers for Disease Control and Prevention (CDC) investigators have summarized findings on the other patients with cutaneous anthrax in 2001.[10] Trauma to the skin was not found prior to the anthrax lesion in any of the 11 patients. Anthrax in the mail was considered the source of infection in all cases. Progression of the skin lesion, as described above, to the stage of the black eschar occurred even with antibiotic treatment, although the skin lesion became culture-negative for *Bacillus anthracis*.[10]

Primary gastrointestinal anthrax infection and disease have not been reported as a result of bioterrorism, although attempts to do so using food have been cited.[3,36] Of the 42 autopsies reported from Sverdlovsk, however, 39 patients had evidence of GI lesions that manifested as multiple submucosal hemorrhagic lesions. In addition, 9 of the 42 patients had hemorrhagic mesenteric lymph nodes.[5] One of the five patients who died of anthrax in 2001 was found at autopsy to have a large amount of ascites and an edematous small bowel with multifocal mesenteric soft tissue hemorrhage. Part of the ileum showed necrotizing infection and abundant gram-positive bacilli. The patient's initial symptoms were abdominal pain, nausea, and vomiting.[37]

LABORATORY DIAGNOSTIC METHODS

Cultures, immunohistochemistry (IHC) staining, and antibody assays were used as diagnostic tests for anthrax during the 2001 attacks. The polymerase chain reaction (PCR) was used to confirm isolates as being *B. anthracis*. An important diagnostic lesson learned from the 2001 attacks is that nasal cultures are not indicated to evaluate individuals for the purpose of deciding whether they have been exposed to anthrax or if they should receive post-exposure prophylaxis or therapy for possible anthrax disease. Before this lesson was learned, however, many thousands of nasal cultures were performed in October 2001. The primary value of the nasal cultures is epidemiologic, not patient management. They allowed us to determine the zone of epidemiologic exposure in which all exposed persons within the zone should be offered post-exposure antibiotic prophylaxis. For example, opening the letter on Capitol Hill October 15, 2001 resulted in 28 persons having positive nasal cultures for *Bacillus anthracis*. Mapping where these 28 persons were located and where the many hundreds of other persons with negative cultures were located after the letter was opened served to define the epidemiologic zone of exposure to *B. anthracis*. Persons in this zone of exposure should be offered antibiotics even if they have negative nasal cultures or no cultures performed.

Notably, the 28 positive nasal cultures were obtained less than 24 hours after exposure when the letter was opened and determined to contain *B. anthracis*. The importance of obtaining nasal cultures rapidly after a potential anthrax exposure is illustrated by the fact that all 3247 nasal cultures were negative for *B. anthracis* at the National Institutes of Health (NIH) after being obtained from persons potentially exposed at the postal facility in Washington, DC through which the two letters to the U.S. senators originally passed.[38] These nasal cultures were not obtained until at least 9 days (October 21) after the letters passed through this postal facility (October 12). Earlier studies in rhesus monkeys also demonstrated that anthrax spores could be best demonstrated by nasal culture within 24 hours after aerosol exposure.[39]

A second important lesson learned from 2001 in terms of clinical diagnostics is that there is no highly sensitive rapid test for the diagnosis of inhalational anthrax during the incubation stage and the early nonspecific "flu-like" symptomatic stage of the illness. Rapid diagnostic tests are needed for these stages of the disease, prior to the

TABLE 324-3 Coordinating Hospital Preparedness for Patients with Anthrax: Role of the Infectious Disease Physician

Person or Service	Reason(s) for Coordinating Preparedness and Response
Microbiology laboratory	Daily and as needed review all suspicious specimens. Establish written protocols for identification of organisms consistent with *B. anthracis*. Have a 24/7 call schedule for clinicians to evaluate any patient with a suspicious isolate and for laboratory technologists to evaluate specimens from patients suspected to have anthrax.
Pharmacy	Daily inventory of all medications needed for treatment of anthrax. Create a stockpile of about a 5-day supply of bottled antibiotics (e.g., doxycycline or ciprofloxacin) to give initially if indicated to outpatients to initiate post-exposure prophylaxis pending further evaluation.
Hospital administration	Authorize coordinating activities by ID Service. Provide emergency directives for prioritizing hospital activity and provide essential funding. Authorize creation of an Anthrax Command Center updated daily on medical, Public Health Department/CDC, and media relations issues.
Nursing director	Frequent updates on patient evaluation and management from ER and outpatient clinics to inpatient wards and ICUs. Education and training issues.
Infection control	Daily updates for tracking each suspected anthrax patient and his or her clinical and epidemiologic information, ideally using a computerized tracking system in a central Anthrax Command Center in the hospital. Communicate updates on each patient daily to the local department of health. Educate widely on lack of person-to-person transmission of anthrax.
Emergency room/department	Establish written protocols that are updated daily or as often as new information (e.g., epidemiologic or public health) becomes available for ER triage, diagnostics, therapy, admission rules, outpatient follow-up appointments, and multiple-day supplies of postexposure antibiotics, if indicated.
Intensive care unit(s)	Anticipate need for emergency admissions that require mechanical ventilation or repeated thoracentesis/chest tube drainage of hemorrhagic pleural effusions. "Look within" on day 1 of outbreak recognition to see if ICU already has patients with unrecognized inhalational anthrax.
Radiology	Discuss characteristic findings with inhalational anthrax, such as mediastinal adenopathy ("widening") and the best type of radiologic imaging (e.g., noncontrast chest CT scans to visualize hemorrhagic adenopathy). Establish 24/7 contact for clinicians and radiologists to discuss scans and patients.
Dermatology	Create educational photographs of characteristic skin lesions due to anthrax. Establish 24/7 consultant team to evaluate suspicious skin lesions.
Neurology	Discuss findings of anthrax meningitis and contact information if a suspicious case or CSF Gram stain is seen.
Gastroenterology	Discuss characteristic GI anthrax findings and contact information.
House staff director(s)	Educate trainees regarding anthrax including diagnosis, management, potential for rapid progression, and lack of person-to-person transmission.
Librarian(s)	Establish hard-copy daily updates on anthrax outbreak; provide medical literature rapidly from online and print sources. Central resource for evolving educational information and provide such to the hospital Anthrax Command Center.
Computer services	Assist with computerized tracking of patients and all their information. Facilitate computer needs for Anthrax Command Center.
Media relations	Anticipate multiple media requests for information and interviews. Triage and coordinate requests with most appropriate person(s) in the hospital each day (if available).
Pediatric service(s)	Establish correct pediatric doses of medications for anthrax. Establish protocol to evaluate children with their parents or guardians.

ICU, intensive care unit; ID, infectious diseases.

more progressive stage of bacteremia and mediastinal adenopathy and the advanced stage of respiratory failure and shock. In 2001, PCR was useful for confirmatory identification of a *Bacillus* species growing in culture as *B. anthracis*. Similarly, IHC staining of pleural fluid and autopsy specimens were performed to confirm the presence of *B. anthracis*.[8,23] Antibody assays, such as the enzyme immunoassay (EIA) that detects immunoglobulin G (IgG) antibody against the protective antigen (PA) of *B. anthracis,* were not of diagnostic value in 2001 in part due to the delayed development of this antibody during a disease that is rapidly fatal unless appropriately treated. In addition, in 2001 there were no commercially available antibody assays for anthrax. Subsequently, the CDC has developed an investigational antibody-based assay including a two-stage direct-fluorescent antibody to the *B. anthracis* capsule and cell wall[40] and a competitive inhibition anti-PA EIA to increase the specificity of the antibody detection to 100%.[41] Anthrax skin tests are not licensed in the United States and were not used diagnostically, even on an investigational basis, in 2001 and 2002.

ANTIMICROBIAL AGENTS TREATMENT

Antibiotics for treatment of inhalation and cutaneous anthrax following a bioterrorism attack are discussed in Chapter 205 and summarized in Tables 324-4 and 324-5.[42] Rapid determination of the antibiotic sensitivity pattern for any isolate of *B. anthracis* and rapid communication of that information are critical to the optimal response to a bioterrorism attack with anthrax. The isolate used in the 2001 attacks was sensitive to most of the antibiotics recommended for anthrax, but antibiotic-resistant isolates could be used if another attack occurs.

Antibiotic Post-Exposure Prophylaxis

In 2001, preventive options for individuals at risk of inhalational anthrax included 60 or 100 days of antimicrobial prophylaxis with ciprofloxacin 500 mg PO twice daily or doxycycline 100 mg PO twice daily with or without anthrax vaccine (see "Use of Anthrax Vaccine with Antibiotics for Post Exposure Prophylaxis"). The CDC in November, 2001 also advised that amoxicillin is an option for prophylaxis in pregnant women, breast-feeding mothers and children. The CDC recommended dose for children was 80 mg/kg/day divided into doses every 8 hours (maximum 500 mg per dose).[44] Ciprofloxacin was approved by the U.S. Food and Drug Administration (FDA) for post-exposure prophylaxis based at least in part on animal studies of anthrax post-exposure prophylaxis (PEP) by Friedlander et al.[45] and serum levels of the drug. Notably, in these PEP studies doxycycline performed as well as ciprofloxacin, and the CDC has endorsed the use of doxycycline for this purpose.[46] The recommendation for antibiotics to be continued up to 100 days is based on the maximum incubation period in nonhuman primates being 98 to 100 days.[16,17] Not surprisingly, many persons in the 2001 attack were not able to adhere to the 60- or 100-day antibiotic PEP regimen, with only 40% reporting full adherence for 60 days in one study of postal workers.[47]

USE OF ANTHRAX VACCINE WITH ANTIBIOTICS FOR POST-EXPOSURE PROPHYLAXIS

Use of anthrax vaccine, in conjunction with penicillin, for anthrax post-exposure prophylaxis was reported at least as early as 1956.[17] It was the study published in 1993 by Friedlander and colleagues,[45] however, that formed the basis for use in humans in 2001 of vaccination

TABLE 324-4 Inhalational Anthrax Treatment Protocol*† for Cases Associated with this Bioterrorism Attack

Category	Initial Therapy (Intravenous)§§	Duration
Adults	Ciprofloxacin 400 mg every 12 hr* or Doxycycline 100 mg every 12 hr** and One or two additional antimicrobials	IV treatment initially.¶ Switch to oral antimicrobial therapy when clinically appropriate: Ciprofloxacin 500 mg PO BID or Doxycycline 100 mg PO BID Continue for 60 days (IV and PO combined)††
Children	Ciprofloxacin 10–15 mg/kg every 12 hr‡‡§§ or Doxycycline**¶ > 8 yr and > 45 kg: 100 mg q 12 hr > 8 yr and ≤ 45 kg: 2.2 mg/kg q 12 hr ≤ 8 yr: 2.2 mg/kg q 12 hr and One or two additional antimicrobials	IV treatment initially.¶ Switch to oral antimicrobial therapy when clinically appropriate: Ciprofloxacin 10–15 mg/kg PO q 12 hr§§ or Doxycycline¶ > 8 yr and > 45 kg: 100 mg PO BID > 8 yr and ≤ 45 kg: 2.2 mg/kg PO BID ≤ 8 yr: 2.2 mg/kg PO BID Continue for 60 days (IV and PO combined)††
Pregnant women***	Same as for nonpregnant adults (the high death rate from the infection outweighs the risk posed by the antimicrobial agent)	IV treatment initially. Switch to PO antimicrobial therapy when clinically appropriate.† Oral therapy regimens same as for nonpregnant adults
Immunocompromised persons	Same as for nonimmunocompromised persons and children	Same as for nonimmunocompromised persons and children

*For gastrointestinal and oropharyngeal anthrax, use regimens recommended for inhalational anthrax.

†Ciprofloxacin or doxycycline should be considered an essential part of first-line therapy for inhalational anthrax.

‡Steroids may be considered as an adjunct therapy for patients with severe edema and for meningitis based on experience with bacterial meningitis of other etiologies.

§Other agents with in vitro activity include rifampin, vancomycin, penicillin, ampicillin. chloramphenicol, imipenem, clindamycin, and clarithromycin. Because of concerns of constitutive and inducible β-lactamases in *Bacillus anthracis,* penicillin and ampicillin should not be used alone. Consultation with an infectious disease specialist is advised.

¶Initial therapy may be altered based on the clinical course of the patient; one or two antimicrobial agents (e.g., ciprofloxacin or doxycycline) may be adequate as the patient improves.

**If meningitis is suspected, doxycycline may be less optimal because of poor central nervous system penetration.

††Because of the potential persistence of spores after an aerosol exposure, antimicrobial therapy should be continued for 60 days.

‡‡If intravenous ciprofloxacin is not available, oral ciprofloxacin may be acceptable because it is rapidly and well absorbed from the gastrointestinal tract with no substantial loss by first-pass metabolism. Maximum serum concentrations are attained 1 to 2 hours after oral dosing but may not be achieved if vomiting or ileus is present.

§§The ciprofloxacin dosage in children should not exceed 1 g/day.

¶¶The American Academy of Pediatrics recommends treating young children with tetracyclines for serious infections (e.g., Rocky Mountain spotted fever).

***Although tetracyclines are not recommended during pregnancy, their use may be indicated for life-threatening illness. Adverse effects on developing teeth and bones are dose-related; therefore doxycycline might be used for a short time (7–14 days) before 6 months of gestation.

From CDC. Update: Investigation of bioterrorism-related anthrax and interim guidelines for exposure management and antimicrobial therapy, October 2001. MMWR Morb Mortal Wkly Rep 2001;50:909-919.

with antibiotics or antibiotics (ciprofloxacin or doxycycline) alone for anthrax post-exposure prophylaxis. In this study, non-human primates were exposed to aerosolized *Bacillus anthracis* and then given either placebo, penicillin, doxycycline, ciprofloxacin, vaccine alone, or vaccine plus doxycycline. Equally good survival was found for doxycycline alone, ciprofloxacin alone, or doxycycline plus vaccine post-exposure.

Anthrax vaccine is licensed only for pre-exposure use.[48,49] It is given as six doses over 18 months followed by yearly boosters (see Chapter 205). In the absence of data to guide us on use of the vaccine in the post-exposure setting, the CDC has suggested that continuing antibiotics for "7 to 14 days after the third vaccine dose" may be prudent because antibody titers peak 14 days after the third dose.[50] Thus antibiotics would be given for 5 to 6 weeks after the first dose of vaccine. This usage is summarized in Table 324-6. Currently, the vaccine is available only for nonmilitary use through the CDC.

ENVIRONMENTAL DECONTAMINATION AND REMEDIATION WORKERS

The anthrax spores used in the 2001 attacks dispersed widely in the large mail-processing facilities through which the contaminated letters passed in Hamilton, NJ and Washington, DC.[51,52] In addition, spores were found throughout all three floors of the Florida media building targeted by the attack.[53] As of October 2003, two years after the attacks, these buildings have not been reopened. The Senate Hart building, where one of the letters containing anthrax was opened, underwent extensive and prolonged decontamination prior to reopening. Sampling methods for *B. anthracis* in the environment have been improved since 2001.[54] Use of hand-held assays for rapid identification of *B. anthracis* were found in 2001 to be an insensitive, nonspecific screening tool that

alone should not trigger a clinical or public health response unless confirmatory tests verify the presence of *B. anthracis.*[55]

In September 2002, the CDC issued guidelines for remediation workers involved in decontaminating buildings with anthrax spores.[56] The guidelines included measures to minimize the risk of exposure through use of personal protective equipment and medical measures such as anthrax vaccination or prophylactic antibiotics (or both). The CDC recommends and makes available anthrax vaccine for remediation workers who make multiple entries over time into anthrax-contaminated areas. Also in 2002, support for the safety and efficacy of this anthrax vaccine was provided by the Institute of Medicine. They reported that the anthrax vaccine as licensed for pre-exposure use is "an effective vaccine for the protection of humans against anthrax, including inhalational anthrax, caused by any known or plausible engineered strains of *B. anthracis.*"[57]

Because this anthrax vaccine requires six doses over 18 months followed by annual boosters, it is still recommended that remediation workers take prophylactic antibiotics prior to completion of the six doses if they are repeatedly exposed to anthrax. Prior to full vaccination, prophylactic antibiotics are recommended from the date of their first entry into a contaminated area until at least 60 days after their last entry.

In contrast to standard infection control precautions for the evaluation and care of patients with anthrax disease, persons performing remediation work, environmental sampling, or who are otherwise at risk of environmental exposure to anthrax must use personal protective equipment that includes protective clothing, gloves, and respiratory devices.[56,58] Specific guidelines for protecting mail handlers have also been issued by the CDC.[59] Routine decontamination of areas in a medical setting includes the option of a 1:10 dilution of household bleach,[24] whereas decontamination of a building is more complex and

TABLE 324-5 Cutaneous Anthrax Treatment Protocol* for Cases Associated with this Bioterrorism Attack

Category	Initial Therapy (Oral)†	Duration (Days)
Adults*	Ciprofloxacin 500 mg BID *or* Doxycycline 100 mg BID	60‡
Children*	Ciprofloxacin 10–15 mg/kg q 12 hr (not to exceed 1 g/day)† *or* Doxycycline§ > 8 yr and >45 kg: 100 mg q 12 hr > 8 yr and ≤ 45 kg: 2.2 mg/kg q 12 hr ≤ 8 yr: 2.2 mg/kg q 12 hr	60‡
Pregnant women*¶	Ciprofloxacin 500 mg BID *or* Doxycycline 100 mg BID	60‡
Immunocompromised persons*	Same as for nonimmunocompromised persons and children	60‡

*Cutaneous anthrax with signs of systemic involvement, extensive edema, or lesions on the head or neck requires intravenous therapy, and a multidrug approach is recommended (see Table 324-4).

†Ciprofloxacin or doxycycline should be considered first-line therapy. Amoxicillin 500 mg PO TID for adults or 80 mg/kg/day divided every 8 hours for children is an option for completion of therapy after clinical improvement. The oral amoxicillin dose is based on the need to achieve appropriate minimum inhibitory concentration levels.

‡Previous guidelines have suggested treating cutaneous anthrax for 7 to 10 days, but 60 days is recommended in the setting of this attack, given the likelihood of exposure to aerosolized *B. anthracis*.[6]

§The American Academy of Pediatrics recommends treatment of young children with tetracyclines for serious infections (e.g., Rocky Mountain spotted fever).

¶Although tetracyclines or ciprofloxacin are not recommended during pregnancy, their use may be indicated for life-threatening illness. Adverse effects on developing teeth and bones are dose-related; therefore doxycycline might be used for a short time (7 to 14 days) before 6 months of gestation.

From CDC. Update: investigation of bioterrorism-related anthrax and interim guidelines for exposure management and antimicrobial therapy. MMWR Morb Mortal Wkly Rep 2001;50:909-919.

TABLE 324-6 Comparison of Anthrax Vaccine for Pre-exposure and Post-exposure Use

Clinical Setting	No. of Doses	Schedule	FDA-Licensed	IND Required*
Pre-exposure	6	Weeks 0, 2, 4 Months 6, 12, 18	Yes	No
Post-exposure	3	Weeks 0, 2, 4	No	Yes

*IND, investigational new drug. An IND is required by the Food and Drug Administration (FDA) in the post-exposure setting for this vaccine for two reasons: (1) the vaccine was approved for pre-exposure use but not for post-exposure use; (2) a total of three doses of vaccine over 1 month is recommended for post-exposure vaccination, unlike the six-dose vaccine schedule given for pre-exposure vaccination as part of the FDA licensure.

was unprecedented before 2001. An extensive review of chemicals, heat, radiation, and gases studied to inactivate *B. anthracis* spores has been reported by the CDC.[60]

REFERENCES

1. Christopher GW, Cieslak TJ, Pavlin JA, Eitzen EM. Biological warfare: a historical perspective. JAMA 1997;278:412-417.
2. Health Aspects of Chemical and Biological Weapons. Report of a Consultant Working Group. Geneva: World Health Organization; 1970.
3. Harris S. Japanese biological warfare research on humans: a case study of microbiology and ethics. Ann NY Acad Sci 1992;666:21-49.
4. Alibek K. Biohazard. New York: Random House; 1999.
5. Abramova FA, Grinberg LM, Yampolskaya OV, Walker DA. Pathology of inhalational anthrax in 42 cases from the Sverdlovsk outbreak of 1979. Proc Natl Acad Sci USA 1993;90:2291-2294.
6. Stone R. Peering into the shadows: Iraq's bioweapons program. Science 2002;297; 1110-1112.
7. Keim P, Smith K, Keys C, et al. Molecular investigation of the Aum Shinrikyo anthrax release in Kameido, Japan. J Clin Microbiol 2001;39:4566-4567.
8. Jernigan JA, Stephens DS, Ashford DA, et al. Bioterrorism-related inhalational anthrax: the first 10 cases reported in the United States. Emerg Infect Dis 2001;7:933-944.
9. Gursky E, Inglesby T, O'Toole T. Anthrax 2001: observations on the medical and public health response. Biosecurity Bioterrorism 2003;1:97-110.
10. Bell DM, Kozarsky PE, Stephens DS. Conference summary: clinical issues in the prophylaxis, diagnosis, and treatment of anthrax. Emerg Infect Dis 2002;8:222-223.
11. Inglesby T, O'Toole T, Henderson DA, et al. Anthrax as a biological weapon, 2002: updated recommendations for management. JAMA 2002;287:2236-2252.
12. Bush LM, Abrams BH, Beall A, Johnson CC. Index case of fatal inhalational anthrax due to bioterrorism in the United States. N Engl J Med 2001;345:1607-1610.
13. Suffin SC, Carnes WH, Kauffman AF. Inhalation anthrax in a home craftsman. Hum Pathol 1978;9:594-597.
14. Brachman PS. Inhalational anthrax. Ann NY Acad Sci 1980;353:83-93.
15. Meselson M, Guillemin J, Hugh-Jones M, et al. The Sverdlovsk anthrax outbreak of 1979. Science 1994;266:1202-1208.
16. Glassman H. Industrial inhalation anthrax (Discussion addendum). Bacteriol Rev 1966;30:657-659.
17. Henderson DW, Peacock S, Belton FC. Observations on the prophylaxis of experimental pulmonary anthrax in the monkey. J Hyg 1956;54:28-38.
18. Meyer MA. Neurologic complications of anthrax: a review of the literature. Arch Neurol 2003;60:483-488.
19. Lanska DJ. Anthrax meningoencephalitis. Neurology 2002;59:327-334.
20. CDC. Update: investigation of bioterrorism-related anthrax and interim guidelines for exposure management and antimicrobial therapy, October 2001. MMWR Morb Mortal Wkly Rep 2001;50:909-919.
21. Franz Dr, Jahrling PB, Friedlander AM, et al. clinical recognition and management of patients exposed to biological warfare agents. JAMA 1997;278:399-411.
22. Bartlett JG, Inglesby TV, Borio L. Management of anthrax. Clin Infect Dis 2002;35: 851-58.
23. Barakat LA, Quentzel HL, Jernigan JA, et al. Fatal inhalational anthrax in a 94-year-old Connecticut woman. JAMA 2002;287:863-868.
24. Swartz M. Recognition and management of anthrax—an update. N Engl J Med 2001;345:1621-1626.
25. Mina B, Dym JP, Kuepper F, et al. Fatal inhalational anthrax with unknown source of exposure in a 61 year old woman in New York City. JAMA 2002;287:858-863.
26. IDSA Website. Clinical pathway: inhalational anthrax. 2002 (www.idsociety.org).
27. Mayer TA, Morrison A, Bersoff-Macha S, et al. Inhalational anthrax due to bioterrorism: would current Centers for Disease Control and Prevention guidelines have identified the 11 patients with inhalational anthrax from October through November 2001? Clin Infect Dis 2003;36:1275-1283.
28. Hupert N, Bearman G, Mushlin A, Callahan M. Accuracy of screening for inhalational anthrax after a bioterrorist attack. Ann Intern Med 2003;139:337-345.
29. Sox H. A triage algorithm for inhalational anthrax. Ann Intern Med 2003;139:379-381.
30. CDC. Symptoms and signs of inhalational anthrax, laboratory-confirmed influenza, and influenza-like illness (ILI) from other causes. MMWR Morb Mortal Wkly Rep 2001;Nov 9:985.
31. Smith M, Wuerker C, Lucey D. Washington Hospital Center Emergency Department Anthrax Protocol # 15. November 8, 2001 (www.bepast.org).
32. CDC. Anthrax Q & A: is anthrax contagious? CDC website, last reviewed June 2, 2003 (www.bt.cdc.gov/agent/anthrax/faq/signs.asp).
33. Pile JC, Malone JD, Eitzen EM, Friedlander AM. Anthrax as a potential biological warfare agent. Arch Intern Med 1998;158:429-434.
34. Roche KJ, Chang MW, Lazarus H. Cutaneous anthrax infection. N Engl J Med 2001;345:1611.
35. Freedman A, Afonja O, Chang MW, et al. Cutaneous anthrax associated with microangiopathic hemolytic anemia and coagulopathy in a 7 month old infant. JAMA 2002;287:869-874.
36. Sirisanthana T, Brown AE. Anthrax of the gastrointestinal anthrax. Emerg Infect Dis J 2002;8:649-651.
37. Borio L, Frank D, Mani V, et al. Death due to bioterrorism-related inhalational anthrax: report of 2 patients. JAMA 2001;286:2554-2559.
38. Kiratisin P, Fukuda C, Wong A, et al. Large-scale screening of nasal swabs for Bacillus anthracis: descriptive summary and discussion of the National Institutes of Health's experience. J Clin Microbiol 2002;40:3012-3016.
39. Hail AS, Rossi CA, Ludwig GV, et al. Comparison of noninvasive sampling sites for early detection of Bacillus anthracis spores from rhesus monkeys after aerosol exposure. Milit Med 1999;164:833-837.
40. De BK, Bragg SL, Sanden GN, et al. Two-component direct fluorescent-antibody assay for rapid identification of Bacillus anthracis. Emerg Infect Dis 2002;8:1060-1065.
41. Quinn CP, Smeenova VA, Elie CM, et al. Specific, sensitive, and quantitative enzyme-linked immunosorbent assay for human immunoglobulin G antibodies to anthrax toxin protective antigen. Emerg Infect Dis 2002;8:1103-1110.
42. Meyerhoff A, Murphy D. Guidelines for treatment of anthrax. JAMA 2002;288:1848.
43. CDC. Notice to readers: additional options for preventive treatment for persons exposed to inhalational anthrax. MMWR Morb Mortal Wkly Rep. 2001;50:1142–1151.
44. CDC Update. Interim recommendations for antimicrobial prophylaxis for children and breastfeeding mothers and treatment of children with anthrax. MMWR Rep. 2001;50:1014-1016.
45. Friedlander AM, Welkos SL, Pitt MLM, et al. Post-exposure prophylaxis against experimental inhalational anthrax. J Infect Dis 1993;167:1239-1242.

46. CDC. Update: investigation of anthrax associated with intentional exposure and interim public health guidelines, October 2001. MMWR Morb Mortal Wkly Rep 2001;50:893-896.
47. Jefferds M, Laserson K, Fry A, et al. Adherence to antimicrobial inhalational anthrax prophylaxis among postal workers, Washington, DC, 2001. Emerg Infect Dis 2002; 8:1138-1144.
48. FDA. FDA approves license supplements for anthrax vaccine. January 31, 2002 (http://www.fda.gov/bbs/topics/NEWS/202/NEW00/92.html).
49. Tierney B, Martin S, Franzke L, et al. Serious adverse events among participants in the Centers for Disease Control and Prevention's anthrax vaccine and antimicrobial availability program for persons at risk for bioterrorism-related inhalational anthrax. Clin Infect Dis 2003;376:905-911.
50. CDC. Notice to readers: use of anthrax vaccine in response to terrorism: supplemental recommendations of the advisory committee on immunization practices. MMWR Morb Mortal Wkly Rep 2002;51:1024-1026
51. Greene CM, Reefhuis J, Tan C, et al. Epidemiologic investigations of bioterrorism-related anthrax, New Jersey, 2001. Emerg Infect Dis 2002;8:1048-1055.
52. CDC. Evaluation of Bacillus anthracis contamination inside the Brentwood mail processing and distribution center, District of Columbia. MMWR Morb Mortal Wkly Rep 2001;50:1129-1132.
53. Traeger MS, Wiersma ST, Rosenstein NE, et al. First case of bioterrorism-related inhalational anthrax in the United States, Palm Beach County, Florida, 2001. Emerg Infect Dis 2002;8:1029-1034.
54. Teshale EH, Painter J, Burr GA. Environmental sampling for spores of Bacillus anthracis. Emerg ID J 2002;8:1083-1087.
55. CDC Health advisory: hand-held immunoassays for detection of Bacillus anthracis spores. October 21, 2001 (www.bt.cdc.gov).
56. CDC. Notice to readers: occupational health guidelines for remediation workers at Bacillus anthracis-contaminated sites—United States, 2001-2002. MMWR Morb Mortal Wkly Rep 2002;51:786-789.
57. Joellenbeck LM, Zwanziger LL, Durch JS, Strom BL, eds. The Anthrax Vaccine: Is It Safe? Does It Work? Washington, DC: National Academy Press; 2002 (complete report is on the Internet at http://www.nap.edu/catalog/10310.html).
58. CDC. Protecting investigators performing environmental sampling for Bacillus anthracis: personal protective equipment (www.bt.cdc.gov/agent/anthrax/environment/investigatorppe.asp). Last reviewed November 8, 2001.
59. CDC. Anthrax Q & A: worker safety (www.bt.cdc.gov/agent/anthrax/faq/worker.asp). Last reviewed December 2, 2002.
60. Spotts Whitney EA, Beatty ME, Taylor TH, et al. Inactivation of Bacillus anthracis spores. Emerg Infect Dis J 2003;9:623-627.

CHAPTER **325**

Botulinum Toxin as a Biological Weapon

THOMAS P. BLECK

The clostridial neurotoxins are among the most potent lethal substances present in the world, with median lethal doses (LD_{50}) for humans in the nanogram per kilogram range. These toxins are closely related proteins, synthesized as a single polypeptide chain, and then nicked to produce a heavy chain and a light chain connected by disulfide bonds. The seven botulinum toxins are encoded on the bacterial chromosome, and tetanospasmin, the tetanus neurotoxin, is encoded on a plasmid. Only three of the botulinum toxins (A, B, E) commonly cause human disease. Both types of clostridial neurotoxin are relatively simple to produce. *Clostridium botulinum* has been considered a high enough probability for use in bioterrorism that it has been targeted by a blue ribbon panel for special research emphasis. The botulinum toxins exert their effects at the neuromuscular junction and at muscarinic peripheral autonomic synapses; thus their major manifestations are neuromuscular weakness and autonomic dysfunction. The predominant effect of tetanospasmin is on the central nervous system (CNS), where it produces failure of inhibition leading to hypertonia and spasms. The two conditions are discussed in detail in Chapter 243 (*Clostridium botulinum*) and Chapter 242 (*Clostridium tetani*).

Tetanospasmin is not a useful weapon candidate because of widespread immunity due to vaccination, although at least one group attempted to do so.[1] The botulinum toxins have proven a more interesting target for weapon development because the public health strategy for botulism has been to prevent exposure rather than immunization.

Although tetanus has been known since antiquity, botulism first emerged during the late eighteenth century as a consequence of changes in production methods for sausages.[2] The first clear clinical description of botulism emerged from epidemics of *wurstvergiftung* (sausage poisoning) near Stuttgart in 1812.

Rumors of the intentional use of botulinum toxin date back to the turn of the twentieth century.[3] The first known development of botulinum toxin as a bioweapon occurred in Manchuria during the 1930s under the auspices of Unit 731, the Japanese biological warfare research unit. During World War II, the United States developed methods for large-scale production of botulinum toxin. Scientists working in this program did not discuss the subject of their work by name but, rather, referred to it as agent X.[4] The United States also produced large quantities of botulinum toxoid for use as a vaccine.[5] Because of the fear that they would be exposed to botulinum toxin during the Normandy invasion, Allied troops involved in the invasion may have been immunized with this toxoid; debate persists about the historical record.[4,6] It appears likely that the Germans were dissuaded from using biological weapons in this war because of concern that the Allies would retaliate in kind. Other countries have also experimented with techniques to weaponize botulinum toxin, including the former Soviet Union.[5]

Iraq conducted one of the largest known military botulinum toxin programs, producing approximately 19,000 liters of concentrated toxin, more than half of which had been loaded into weapons systems.[7] The Iraqi military also deployed several other biological weapons systems prior to the first Gulf war. The seed culture for the Iraqi program was purchased legally from an American microbiological supply house. In preparation for potential exposure to this toxin, about 8000 American service personnel were vaccinated in 1991.[4]

The Aum Shinrikyō cult in Japan, best known for their attacks on civilians using the nerve agent sarin,[8] attempted to use botulinum toxin as a weapon on at least three occasions during the early 1990s.[9] Although these attempts were not successful, perhaps in part because of the reticence of some cult members to carry out their orders, the ease with which cult members were able to produce the toxin demonstrates the potential for small groups to use this substance as a bioterror weapon. At least some of their cultures of *C. botulinum* were grown from spores obtained from local soil, highlighting the ubiquitous nature of the organism and our inability to eliminate this threat by controlling the commercial supply of microorganisms.

BOTULINUM TOXIN AS A WEAPON

Natural poisoning with botulinum toxin is almost always a consequence of ingesting preformed toxin produced by the growth of *C. botulinum* in improperly prepared or stored food. The exceptions (e.g., infant botulism, wound botulism) are described in Chapter 243. A bioterrorist attack with this toxin could cause intoxication via ingestion or an aerosol. One method by which botulinum toxin could be employed as a weapon would be the contamination of food with the toxin. The signs and symptoms of the victims of such an attack would be indistinguishable from a natural outbreak of botulism, except that epidemiologic investigation might reveal that the common food ingested was not typically associated with botulism, or that different foods in the same area were all contaminated. Introduction of toxin into milk trucks or other large, closed food or beverage transports would produce sporadic cases. In such a circumstance, individual clinicians would be unlikely to recognize an attack early in its development. Automated systems for the collection of epidemiologic data are required for this purpose.[10]

The premonitory gastrointestinal symptoms of nausea, vomiting, diarrhea, and abdominal cramping in patients with natural gastrointestinal botulism are probably not a consequence of botulinum toxin, which by itself would cause constipation. Smith argued that these effects were due to other bacterial products.[11] As a consequence, an outbreak of botulism cases without these other gastrointestinal symptoms should raise the suspicion of a toxin attack. Toxin would be detectable in serum, and in stool as well, if the gastrointestinal tract were the route of entry.

Predicting the consequences of dissemination into the environment is more problematic, as there are no data regarding the stability of the toxin in water or sunlight. One CDC expert estimated that an aerosol release of toxin could affect 10% of people within 500 meters.[5] Once in the atmosphere, the decay rate of the toxin is estimated at 1% to 4% per minute. Modeling an aerosol exposure suggests that substantial inactivation may take up to 2 days.[5] This would be accelerated by extremes of temperature and humidity. Aerosol exposure to the toxin would not result in substantial recovery of toxin in stool, but it would still be detectable in serum and potentially in respiratory secretions.

The effects of inhaling botulinum toxin by humans have been reported only following the accidental exposure of three German laboratory workers after they performed autopsies on animals that had been subjected to a type A botulinum aerosol.[12] They presumably inhaled a small amount of toxin wafted into the air from the fur of the animals. They exhibited no symptoms for the first 2 days after their exposure but on the third day began to have difficulty swallowing and experienced coryza without fever. A description of "mental numbness" is difficult to interpret, as the toxin would not be expected to affect the CNS. On the fourth day, they noted generalized weakness and difficulty with extraocular movements, and they were found to have modest pupillary dilation and slight rotary nystagmus, along with dysarthria and gait disturbance. They received antitoxin on the fourth and fifth days. Their symptoms apparently stopped progressing after the antitoxin was administered, and they had improved sufficiently to be discharged from the hospital within 2 weeks.

Primate experiments designed to study the efficacy of treatments for inhaled toxin revealed that doses of 5 to 10 LD_{50} caused death within 2 to 4 days in animals that were neither immunized nor treated with antitoxin.[13] The authors reported the development of signs of intoxication about 12 to 18 hours prior to death, beginning with diffuse weakness and then followed by ptosis and neck weakness.

Current approaches to the diagnosis of botulism and the detection of botulinum toxin would be of limited value during an attack. The diagnosis can be confirmed most rapidly with electromyography. Assays for toxin in serum, stool, and respiratory secretions requires an in vivo mouse assay. The increasing concern about bioterrorism in recent years has resulted in several new rapid detection methods, some of which are potentially applicable to both environmental and patient samples.[14-16]

MANAGEMENT

The management of individual cases of botulism is discussed in Chapter 243. In the event of a bioterrorist attack, several logistic issues would become problematic. Based on the limited information available, a large-scale attack (either food-borne or by aerosol) would probably not begin to produce symptomatic victims for more than a day. In one large common-source food-borne outbreak, the initial neurologic symptoms arose over 24 to 108 hours after exposure.[17] Thus recognition of the attack, and hence the potential magnitude of the problem, would initially be difficult. Although vaccination as a strategy to limit disease is important for a contagious disease such as smallpox, it would not be useful in the acute setting because (1) there is no risk of person-to-person transmission and (2) a vaccination series takes about 12 weeks. Thus vaccination is useful only for those in whom a predictable exposure is anticipated. The current investigational pentavalent vaccine (types A to E) is thus reserved for laboratory workers and the military.

The cornerstones of botulism management are airway protection, mechanical ventilation, antitoxin administration, and supportive therapy. Individuals with botulism are usually observed for problems with airway protection, such as difficulty handling secretions, and are monitored for ventilatory difficulties by measuring vital capacity, the negative inspiratory pressure, and the respiratory rate. Endotracheal intubation is performed when either problem threatens the patient's safety. For a large attack with many casualties, measurements of ventilatory function would not be practical, and decisions regarding intubation would have to be based on the observation of difficulty with secretions or tachypnea. These observations would be facilitated by having the victims concentrated in a large open area.

The Strategic National Stockpile "push packs" contain laryngoscopes, endotracheal tubes, and Ambu bags, along with a limited number of mechanical ventilators. More information is available on the Internet (http://www.bt.cdc.gov/stockpile/index.asp). However, this equipment would not arrive until up to 24 hours after requested by the state governor, so the state health departments are responsible for organizing strategies for the first day. Because the number of intubated patients requiring ventilation may easily exceed the number of available ventilators, it may become necessary to recruit healthy civilians to perform bag ventilation on these patients. Such a process was highly successful in saving lives in Scandinavia during the poliomyelitis epidemics of the 1950s.[18]

The supply of antitoxins is small, reflecting the low incidence of the natural disease. With a large-scale attack, the available antitoxin would be quickly exhausted. Thus, airway protection and ventilation would remain the only viable options.

REFERENCES

1. Williams P, Wallace D. Unit 731: Japan's secret biological warfare in World War II. New York: Free Press; 1989:27-28.
2. Dickson EC. Botulism: a clinical and experimental study. Rockefeller Inst Med Res Monogr 1918;8:1-117.
3. CDC video. The history of bioterrorism. 1999 (available at http://www.bt.cdc.gov/training/historyofbt/index.asp).
4. Middlebrook JL, Franz DR. Botulinum toxins. In: Sidell FR, Takafuji ET, Franz DR, eds. Medical Aspects of Chemical and Biological Warfare. Washington, DC: Office of the Surgeon General; 1997 (available at https://ccc.apgea.army.mil).
5. Arnon SS, Schechter R, Inglesby TV, et al. Botulinum toxin as a biological weapon: medical and public health management. JAMA 2001;285:1059-1070.
6. Williams P, Wallace D. Unit 731: Japan's secret biological warfare in World War II. New York: Free Press; 1989:124.
7. Zilinskas RA. Iraq's biological weapons: the past as future? JAMA 1997;278:418-424.
8. Kortepeter MG, Cieslak TJ, Eitzen EM. Bioterrorism. J Environ Health 2001;63:21-24.
9. Lifton RJ. Destroying the World to Save It. New York: Henry Holt; 2000:39, 186-188.
10. M'ikantha NM, Southwell B, Lautenbach E. Automated laboratory reporting of infectious diseases in a climate of bioterrorism. Emerg Infect Dis 2003;9:1053-1057.
11. Smith LDS. Botulism: the Organism, Its Toxins, the Disease. Springfield, IL: Charles C Thomas; 1977.
12. Holzer VE. Botulismus durch inhalation. Med Klin 1962;57:1735-1738.
13. Franz DR, Pitt LM, Clayton MA, et al. Efficacy of prophylactic and therapeutic administration of antitoxin for inhalation botulism. In: Das Gupta BR, ed. Botulinum and Tetanus Neurotoxins: Neurotransmission and Biomedical Aspects. New York: Plenum; 1993:473-476.
14. Peruski AH, Johnson LH III, Peruski LF Jr. Rapid and sensitive detection of biological warfare agents using time-resolved fluorescence assays. J Immunol Methods 2002;263:35-41.
15. Liu W, Montana V, Chapman ER, et al. Botulinum toxin type B micro-mechanosensor. Proc Natl Acad Sci USA 2003;100:13621-13625.
16. Ahn-Yoon S, DeCory TR, Durst RA. Ganglioside-liposome immunoassay for the detection of botulinum toxin. Anal Bioanal Chem 2004;378:68-75.
17. Terranova W, Breman JG, Locey RP, Speck S. Botulism type B: epidemiologic aspects of an extensive outbreak. Am J Epidemiol 1978;108:150-156.
18. Wackers GL. Modern anaesthesiological principles for bulbar polio: manual IPPR in the 1952 polio-epidemic in Copenhagen. Acta Anaesthesiol Scand 1994;38:420-431.

CHAPTER 326

Bioterrorism: Viral Hemorrhagic Fevers

C. J. PETERS

VIRAL HEMORRHAGIC FEVERS AS BIOTERRORIST AGENTS

The viral hemorrhagic fevers (VHFs) are important considerations in bioterrorism (BT) preparedness (Table 326-1). BT may take many forms, ranging from hoaxes to mass casualties. Even small attacks may be disruptive, produce fear, and have a severe economic impact. The 2001 anthrax attacks interrupted activities we regard as constants of ordinary life and commerce, such as mail service; caused a hiatus in legislative function; induced fear and uncertainty in the population of the northeastern United States; and cost billions of dollars even though there were only 22 cases and 5 fatalities (see Chapter 324). VHFs lend themselves to a public disruption attack because of their reputation from popular literature and the dramatic clinical syndrome produced.[1]

This chapter mainly addresses the issue of mass casualty attacks and shows that some of the VHFs have the potential for large area coverage with many thousands of infected humans. Biological weapons were brought to a mature state by both the United States (the program was stopped and weapons destroyed in 1968) and the Soviet Union.[2-4] Fortunately, these weapons have never been used in a situation in which their full potential could be seen, although there are examples of abortive attempts.[5] Nevertheless, each step of the process was tested and found to be feasible for inducing human disease, and the overall process was tested at a practical level with experimental animals after open air exposure.[6]

The most dangerous format in which these agents could be dispersed is via small particle aerosols (1 to 5 μm in diameter), which are carried invisibly on wind currents and penetrate ventilated buildings. They are deposited in the fine airways of the lung and establish an infection. An aerosol chemical or biological attack is at the whim of meteorologic conditions, and the effects of biological weapons are delayed by their incubation period. These points may be seen as disadvantages in their tactical use, but the ability for stealthy, stand-off delivery and time for the perpetrators to escape may be useful for terrorists.[1] For this type of attack, one needs agents that are stable and infectious in the aerosol form and have a high case-infection ratio. VHFs meet these criteria. Their experimental properties resemble those of that archetypical biological warfare virus Venezuelan equine encephalitis or of influenza.[6,7]

Among the aerosol agents some are judged to be more dangerous than others, but certainly anthrax and smallpox are at the top of most lists.[6] Comparison of anthrax spores to VHFs is instructive for understanding their relative likelihood of use and impact. Anthrax is widely available in nature, and most of the VHFs are as well, with the notable exception of the filoviruses. Anthrax is readily grown in commonly available culture media, sporulates when the cultures reach saturation, and is easily concentrated and purified in ordinary centrifuges. The VHFs are often propagated in cell culture, but titers fall short of the ideal for production of weapons of mass destruction. A state-sponsored program could make VHF production a practical enterprise through the use of fermentation technology and simple partial purification of the viruses by precipitation, filtration, or continuous-flow ultracentrifugation modeled on some commercial vaccine production methods. The isolated terrorist would probably rely on animal propagation of the agents to obtain high-titer starting material. Several of the viruses replicate exceedingly well in rodents or lambs; and indeed, the Soviet program used guinea pigs to produce Marburg virus weapons.

Anthrax spores are highly stable in aerosol and on storage, but the VHFs are of lesser aerosol stability and require ultra-cold storage if kept for more than a few days in the liquid state. A state-sponsored program could reliably enhance aerosol stability problems by the appropriate additives, and by production of dried material that maintains bulk infectivity for much longer periods. This, of course, involves a period of experimentation and measurement of aerosol stability. An example of the stabilization principle is seen in Table 326-2, in which addition of glycerin to the Marburg virus diluted in saliva results in a marked increase in aerosol stability.[8] A simpler approach would involve proceeding with liquids and performing the attack relatively soon after preparing the virus suspension, but this imposes logistic constraints on the attacker.

Smallpox presents a different set of contrasts. It is extremely stable and infectious in aerosol form, and it is readily propagated. It is unobtainable from nature and is by international agreement confined to two laboratories, although clandestine stocks may exist (see Chapter 323). In marked distinction to all the major BW agents, smallpox is a natural human pathogen that is readily transmissible between patients and can be expected to cause large numbers of cases in multiple generations of transmission until limited by vaccination or other active means of control. The VHFs, in contrast, are all caused by zoonotic viruses and are expected to be a risk only to close family contacts and medical personnel. Because of the infectivity of smallpox for humans, it is likely that a smallpox attack would result in severe limitation of movement of humans in the country attacked and certainly to other countries. There is a similar corollary for the Rift Valley fever virus (RVF); it is an important domestic animal pathogen and use of that virus would result in an immediate cessation of movement of sheep and cattle in the country and a block on exported U.S. materials from these animals. Unlike the other VHFs, RVF has the ability to spread beyond its initial targets mediated by mosquito vectors that are present in the United States.[9] It is unknown

TABLE 326-1 Viral Hemorrhagic Fevers

Family/Genus	Disease (Virus)	Chapter
Arenaviridae		162
	Lassa fever	
	Bolivian HF (Machupo virus)	
	Argentine HF (Junin virus)	
	Other South American HF	
Bunyaviridae		161
Phlebovirus	Rift Valley fever	
Nairovirus	Crimean Congo HF	
Hantavirus	HF with renal syndrome,	
	HFRS (Hantaan and others)	
	Hantavirus pulmonary syndrome,	
	HPS (Sin Nombre, Andes,	
	and others)	
Filovirus	Marburg HF	159
	Ebola HF	
Flavivirus	Yellow fever	149
	Dengue HF	
	Tick-borne flavivirus HF	149
	(Kyasanur Forest, Omsk,	
	and Al Alkhurma)	

HF, hemorrhagic fever; HFRS, HF with renal syndrome; HPS, hantavirus pulmonary syndrome.

TABLE 326-2 Aerosol Stability of Some Viruses

Virus	Stability (%/min)
Vaccinia	0.3
Influenza	1.9
Venezuelan equine encephalitis	3.0
Marburg (saliva)	11.5
Marburg (+ 10% glycerin)	1.5

Data are from Belanov Y, Muntyanov VP, Kryuk VD, et al. Retention of Marburg virus infecting capability on contaminated surfaces and in aerosol particles. Vopr Virusol 1996;41:32-34.

whether this can occur by interhuman transmission via arthropods or if it would require a substrate of viremic domestic animals.

In summary, then, the stability and infectivity of most of the VHFs is sufficient (or could be made so) to produce large numbers of casualties.[6] Terrorists, using VHF, as with plague and tularemia, would most likely require some prior knowledge of the stabilizers and manufacturing process to produce mass casualties.

CONTROL OF BIOTERRORISM FROM VHFs

Most of the VHFs are widely available in the environment by sampling their natural reservoir or through patients and virology laboratories in areas of the world in which they are endemic. Hence the select agent restrictions in the United States will have little impact on preventing their use by any terrorist capable of turning them into significant weapons. Filoviruses are the exception because their reservoir is unknown, and they are present in relatively few laboratories. Their genome could be synthesized in segments and reconstituted through reverse genetics, but this is a project that would require a sophisticated molecular virology laboratory.[10]

Any biological weapon requires a large amount of agent to disperse, and this currently limits the utility of Crimean Congo hemorrhagic fever (CCHF) virus and hantaviruses. These practical constraints could be overcome by an applied research program.

The methods for stabilizing the viruses in aerosol could be developed by trial and error or could be brought about by knowledgeable persons, particularly the scientists who previously worked in the Soviet programs that are undergoing the same down-sizing as in the nuclear arena. In fact, the production of bioweapons is an industrial process that requires two sets of skills. The expertise to propagate the agents is available through microbiologists, and the development of the 1- to 5-μm powders that can be disseminated to infect large numbers of targets efficiently via aerosol clouds in buildings or open-air situations, resides in pharmaceutical, cosmetic, insecticide, and other industries.[6,7] The equipment needed for production of bioweapons has multiple industrial uses and has no unique signature, so the prospects for controlling these weapons is far less likely than for nuclear devices.[11] The failed efforts of the Japanese Aum Shinrikyō sect are often cited as an example of how even a well financed nonstate group cannot produce these weapons. This should not be comforting because of the naiveté of the sect's persons who headed the microbiological and dissemination efforts.[12]

WHAT ARE VHFs AND HOW CAN WE RESPOND MEDICALLY?

The VHFs comprise several viruses from different taxons in four virus families (see Table 326-1). These viruses share a number of properties (small RNA genome, lipid envelope, acid sensitivity, zoonotic natural cycle, aerosol infectivity), but they differ in others (replication strategy, morphogenesis, natural cycle, pathogenesis). One of the remarkable findings is that they are all aerosol-infectious with the exception of the dengue viruses, which cause hemorrhagic fever (DHF) by a different mechanism, which involves secondary infections leading to enhanced pathogenesis. Thus DHF is not a bioterrorism threat by virtue of the lack of aerosol infectiousness of the viruses and the need for sequential infections to produce the syndrome. The aerosol infectious properties of the VHF agents include both the viruses thought to be

TABLE 326-3 Some Characteristics of the VHFs

Virus	Disease	Geography	Incubation (days)	Vector/Reservoir	Human Infection
Arenaviridae					
Junin	Argentine HF	Argentine pampas	7–14	Chronic infection of small field rodent, *Calomys musculinus*.	Mainly agricultural workers. Major transmission in fall season. Aerosol transmission to humans. Interhuman transmission rare.
Machupo	Bolivian HF	Bolivia, Beni Province	—	Chronic infection of small field rodent, *Calomys callosus*.	Rural residents and farmers; rodent can invade towns with urban disease. Aerosol transmission to humans. Interhuman transmission not usual but occurs.
Guanarito	Venezuelan HF	Venezuela, Portuguesa state	—	Chronic infection of field rodent *Zygodontomys brevicauda*.	Rural residents in cleared area in Venezuela with small farms.
Sabia	?	Rural area near Sao Paulo, Brazil	—	Presumably chronic infection of unidentified rodents.	Single infection observed in nature: little information on potential. Two laboratory infections, one treated with ribavirin.
Lassa	Lassa fever	West Africa	5–16	Chronic infection of rodents of the genus *Mastomys*.	The reservoir rodent is very common in Africa, and the disease is a major cause of severe febrile illness in West Africa. Spread to humans occurs by aerosols and by capturing the rodent for consumption, as well as person-to-person transmission. Lassa fever is the most commonly exported HF.
Bunyaviridae					
Rift Valley fever	Rift Valley fever	Sub-Saharan Africa	*2–5*	Vertical infection of flood-water *Aedes* mosquitoes maintains the virus. Epidemics occur during heavy rainfall with horizontal transmission by many mosquito species between domestic animals, particularly sheep and cattle.	Humans acquire by mosquito bite; contact with blood of infected sheep, cattle, or goats; and aerosols generated from infected domestic animal blood. No interhuman transmission observed.
Crimean Congo HF	Crimean Congo HF	Africa, Middle East, Balkans, southern Soviet Union, western China	3–12	Tick–mammal–tick infection. Vertical infection occurs in ticks. Hyalomma ticks are thought to be the natural reservoir, but other genera may become infected and transmit.	Tick bite; squashing ticks; and exposure to aerosols or fomites from slaughtered cattle and sheep. (Domestic animals do not have evidence of illness but may become infected when transported to market or when held in pens for slaughter.) Numerous nosocomial epidemics.

Table continued on following page

TABLE 326-3 Some Characteristics of the VHFs—Continued

Virus	Disease	Geography	Incubation (days)	Vector/Reservoir	Human Infection
Bunyaviridae—Continued					
Hantaan, Seoul, Puumala, and others	Hemorrhagic fever with renal syndrome (HFRS)	Worldwide, depending on rodent reservoir	9–35	Horizontal infection in a single rodent species typical of the virus. Viruses associated with HFRS have been obtained only from rodents of the family Muridae, subfamilies Murinae or Arvicolinae.	Aerosols, mainly from freshly shed urine of infected rodents. Some infections are acquired from secondary aerosols or droplets from previously shed rodent excreta and secreta or from rodent bites. Rural disease. Interhuman transmission never documented.
Sin Nombre, Bayou, Andes, and others	Hantavirus pulmonary syndrome (HPS)	Americas	7–28	As for hantaviruses causing HFRS. All viruses associated with HPS have come from Muridae (subfamily Sigmodontinae) rodents.	As for hantaviruses causing HFRS. Entering unused, closed buildings may be a particular risk. Interhuman transmission observed with Andes virus; mechanisms unknown.
Filoviridae					
Marburg, Ebola	Marburg HF Ebola HF	Africa, ?Philippines	3–16	Unknown.	Infection of index case occurs from unknown source. Infected nonhuman primates sometimes provide link to humans. Later spread among humans by close contact with another infected person or hospitalization.
Flaviviridae					
Yellow fever	Yellow fever	Africa, South America	3–6	Mosquito–monkey–mosquito maintenance with occasional human infection when unvaccinated humans enter forest. Formerly large epidemics among humans with *Aedes aegypti* as mosquito vector.	Mosquito infection of humans entering forests and encountering infected sylvatic vector. Emergence of epidemics into African savannas using specific *Aedes* mosquito vectors. In cities or villages, interhuman transmission by *A. aegypti*. Fully developed cases are no longer viremic, and direct interhuman transmission not believed to be a problem.
Dengue (types 1–4)	Dengue HF, dengue shock syndrome (DHF/DSS)	Tropics and subtropics worldwide	3–15	Maintained by *A. aegypti*–human–*A. aegypti* transmission with frequent geographic transport of viruses by travelers.	DHF/DSS occurs in areas where multiple dengue viruses are being transmitted. With the increased worldwide distribution of *A. aegypti* and movement of dengue viruses by travelers, this zone is enlarging. DSS first noted in Southeast Asia but is now common in the Americas and the Caribbean.
Kyasanur Forest disease (KFD)	KFD	Limited area of Mysore State, India	3–8	Tick–vertebrate–tick.	Most infections occur from tick bite acquired in rural areas of the endemic zone. Monkey die-offs may accompany increased virus activity.
Omsk HF (OHF)	OHF	Western Siberia	3–8	Poorly understood cycle involving ticks, voles, muskrats, and possibly waterborne transmission.	Few cases in recent years.
Al Khumrah	—	Middle East? Africa?	—	Unknown.	Discovered in Saudi Arabia but may have been introduced with imported livestock. Transmitted to humans working in livestock-related occupations by unknown route.

transmitted to humans in nature by aerosols and those that are primarily spread by mosquitoes or ticks (Table 326-3).

The pathogenesis varies among the various diseases with direct viral damage, disseminated intravascular coagulation (DIC), hepatic damage, vascular damage, and cytokine release being implicated to varying degrees. Fatal cases usually have extensive lymphoid depletion, except for the hantavirus diseases, in which immunopathology is an important mechanism.

Diagnosis of these infections, when they occur naturally, relies on an index of suspicion for travelers to the endemic areas within an incubation period (Table 326-3). Of course, the absence of a travel history in a confirmed case is equally compelling evidence of a bioterrorism event.

The clinical course varies among the VHFs (Table 326–4),[13,14] but a typical patient might experience a prodrome of fever, myalgia, and malaise that typically lasts 3 to 4 days. The next events include worsening of these symptoms with prostration, evidence of capillary leak (nondependent edema, effusions), hemorrhage, and CNS depression.

Hemorrhage occurs in most cases with some of the VHFs (e.g., South American hemorrhagic fevers) or in less than half in others (e.g., Lassa fever) and seems to require thrombocytopenia plus capillary damage. Patients with shock, florid hemorrhage, and extensive CNS damage have a poor prognosis.

Physical findings early in the course may be suggestive. Some patients have somewhat low blood pressure and postural hypotension. Conjunctival injection is common except in hantavirus pulmonary syndrome (HPS). Evidence of petechial hemorrhage should be sought carefully in good light. Later, more obvious signs and symptoms supervene.

Clinical laboratory findings vary by disease. Hemoconcentration is common to some degree and may be extreme, particularly with the hantavirus diseases. All of the patients have thrombocytopenia except those with Lassa fever. Leukopenia is common with most of the VHFs and is particularly constant with South American HF. However, those with Lassa fever may have low, normal, or elevated white blood cell counts, and hantavirus infections result in normal to elevated and even leukemoid counts. Clotting studies are usually modestly abnormal, in-

TABLE 326-4 Some Clinical Features of VHFs

Disease	Clinical Features	Therapeutic Synopsis
South American HF	Most cases have hemorrhage. Neurologic symptoms such as dysarthria and tremor usual.	Treatment with IV ribavirin is likely to be beneficial. Safe, effective vaccine for Argentine HF but available only in Argentina.
Lassa fever	Prostration and shock but hemorrhage and neurologic signs much less common than South American HF.	Treatment with IV ribavirin shown to be beneficial. Deafness is common in convalesence.
Rift Valley fever	Incidence of HF low among total infections. May be associated with DIC and hepatitis. Infected may develop retinal vasculitis or encephalitis.	Ribavirin useful in animal models but human evidence is not impressive, perhaps owing to rapid course. Inactivated and live attenuated vaccines are safe and effective but are not generally available.
Crimean Congo HF	Typical HF with florid hemorrhage. DIC common. Nosocomial infections common.	Ribavirin used with anecdotal success. No acceptable vaccine.
HFRS	Febrile prodrome followed by shock and renal failure. Hemoconcentration can be marked.	Supportive care, dialysis. Ribavirin may be useful adjunct. Vaccines available in Korea and China but do not meet U.S. manufacturing standards.
HPS	Similar to HFRS but acute pulmonary edema rather than renal failure.	ICU management of pulmonary edema and shock. Ribavirin not helpful.
Marburg or Ebola HF	Most severe of the HF. Marked weight loss and prostration. Maculopapular rash common. Hepatitis, uveitis, orchitis, arthralgia reported during convalescence.	Supportive care. In Ebola-infected monkeys, tissue factor inhibitors helpful. Investigational Ebola vaccine in Phase I studies.
Yellow fever	Severe HF with jaundice common.	Excellent vaccine.
Dengue hemorrhagic fever	Not a BT threat but enters into differential diagnosis. Rare cause of primary HF. An important cause of HF in Asia and Latin America after infection with multiple dengue viruses, particularly in children.	Responds well to supportive care. Vaccines under development.
Tick-borne flavivirus HF	Biphasic illness with fever, thrombocytopenia, and hemorrhage during first phase and often a second phase with neurologic signs.	No therapy or vaccine.

BT, bioterrorism; DIC, disseminated intravascular coagulation; ICU, intensive care unit.

cluding the activated partial thromboplastin time and the prothrombin time, but no specific patterns are known to be diagnostic. Evidence of DIC is regularly found in CCHF, filovirus infections, severe RVF, and the early phase of HF with renal syndrome (HFRS) but is rare with arenavirus HF. Aspartate aminotransferase may be elevated, as may the serum amylase. With the exception of HFRS, renal function reflects the circulatory status. Proteinuria is common, presumably reflecting the capillary leak.

Specific laboratory diagnosis during the acute phase relies on detection of RNA by reverse transcription and the polymerase chain reaction, finding viral proteins by an enzyme-linked immunosorbent assay (ELISA), or virus isolation in the biosafety level 4 (BSL4) laboratory. As patients improve, markers of acute infection disappear and immunoglobin M (IgM) antibodies can be detected. Hantaviruses are exceptional in that they have antibodies present in serum at the time of onset of disease that can be readily detected in an IgM capture ELISA. Most of these tests are not readily available in the United States outside the CDC and the U.S. Army Medical Research Institute of Infectious Diseases (USAMRIID).

The differential diagnosis is most difficult with rickettsial disease, leptospirosis, and relapsing fever. Malaria, typhoid, shigellosis, sepsis, and other conditions may be confused with illnesses caused by VHF.

The general principles of therapy are similar for all the HFs: rapid atraumatic hospitalization, intensive care unit admission if available, careful maintenance of fluid balance to avoid overhydration in the face of fragile systemic and pulmonary capillary beds and myocardial compromise, management of the bleeding diathesis according to the usual principles, and the specific therapy appropriate to each disease (see Table 326-4). Ribavirin should be given intravenously to all arenavirus infections (not an approved use) and should be considered for infections by Bunyaviridae.[15]

The issue of secondary spread is important, but there is no simple answer. Occasional secondary cases occur with most of the VHFs, and rarely there are miniepidemics. We know that long chains of transmission occur only with filoviruses and then only in settings with virtually no use of masks, gowns, or gloves. These viruses are highly infectious by aerosol spread in the laboratory, but spread between patients via this route is uncommon. Presumably, this is related to the small amount of virus in external secretions and a low output of aerosols by the patient.[16] The VHFs most commonly associated with nosocomial disease are CCHF and Ebola, and spread is usually associated with extensive exposure to blood in a setting of poor hospital hygiene.[17] Careful barrier nursing as recommended by the CDC limits or stops hospital transmission.[13]

REFERENCES

1. Danzig R. Catastrophic Bioterrorism—What Is to Be Done? Washington, DC: Center for Technology and National Security Policy at the National Defense University; 2003.
2. Alibek K, Handelman S. Biohazard. 1st ed. New York City: Random House; 1999.
3. Miller J, Engelberg S, Broad W. Germs: Biologicalal Weapons and America's Secret War. 1st ed. New York: Simon & Shuster; 2001.
4. Harris R, Paxman J. A Higher Form of Killing. New York: Hill & Wang; 1982.
5. Christopher GW, Cieslak TJ, Pavlin JA, Eitzen EM Jr. Biological warfare: a historical perspective. In: Knobler SL, Mahmoud AAF, Pray LA, eds. Biological Threats and Terrorism. Washington, DC: National Academy Press; 1997:412-417.
6. Peters CJ, Spertzel R, Patrick W. Aerosol Technology and Biological Weapons. In: Knobler SL, Mahmoud AAF, Pray LA, eds. Biological Threats. Washington, DC: National Academy Press; 2002:66-77.
7. Peters CJ. Are hemorrhagic fever viruses practical agents for biological terrorism? In: Scheld WM, Craig WA, Hughes JM, eds. Emerging Infections, v. 4. Washington: ASM Press; 2000:203-211.
8. Belanov Y, Muntyanov VP, Kryuk VD, et al. Retention of Marburg virus infecting capability on contaminated surfaces and in aerosol particles. Vopr Virusol 1996;41:32-34.
9. Gargan TP, Clark GG, Dohm DJ, et al. Vector potential of selected North American mosquito species for Rift Valley fever virus. Am J Trop Med Hyg 1988;38:440-446.
10. Volchkov VE, Volchkova VA, Muhlberger E, et al. Recovery of infectious Ebola virus from complementary DNA: RNA editing of the GP gene and viral cytotoxicity. Science 2001;291:1965-1969.
11. Kadlec RP, Zelicoff AP, Vrtis AM. Biological weapons control: prospects and implications for the future. In: Lederberfg J, ed. Biological Weapons: Limiting the Threat. Cambridge, MA: MIT Press; 1999:95-111.
12. Smithson AE, Levy LA. Ataxia: The Chemical and Biological Terrorism Threat and the US Response. Washington, DC: Henry L. Stimson Center; 2000.
13. Borio L, Inglesby T, Peters CJ, et al. Hemorrhagic fever viruses as biological weapons. JAMA 2002;287:2391-2405.
14. Peters CJ, Zaki SR. Overview of viral hemorrhagic fevers. In: Guerrant RL, ed. Essentials of Tropical Infectious Diseases. Philadelphia: WB Saunders; 2000.
15. Enria D, Peters CJ. Other viruses and emerging viruses of concern. In: Boucher CAB, ed. Practical Guidelines in Antiviral Therapy. Amsterdam: Elsevier; 2002:279-301.
16. Peters CJ, Jahrling PB, Khan AS. Patients infected with high-hazard viruses: scientific basis for infection control. Arch Virol 1996;11(Suppl):141-168.
17. Dowell SF, Mukunu R, Ksiazek TG, et al. Transmission of Ebola hemorrhagic fever: a study of risk factors in family members, Kikwit, Democratic Republic of the Congo, 1995; Commission de Lutte contre les Epidemies a Kikwit. J Infect Dis 1999;179 (Suppl 1):S87-S91.

CHAPTER **327**

Zoonoses

ARNOLD N. WEINBERG

Zoonoses are a complex group of diseases caused by a remarkable diversity of pathogenic microorganisms that ordinarily reside and cause illness in the nonhuman animal world.[1] In addition to their natural occurrence many of these microorganisms are prime candidates as biological weapons.[2] This potential threat has stimulated renewed resolve to develop rapid diagnostic tests and protective vaccines, and for coordinated efforts by the World Health Organization (WHO) and the Centers for Disease Control (CDC) to upgrade Public Health communications nationally and globally.[3] As rapid transportation and varied forms of commerce bring global interactions closer, there are many current examples and increasing awareness of the potential impact of zoonotic diseases emerging in unanticipated ways and places.[2]

The most contemporary and graphic example is the emergence of an acute atypical pneumonia in Guangdong Province, China in late 2002 that spread in local hospitals and erupted in epidemic intensity in Hong Kong and adjacent Southeast Asian countries, spreading to 29 countries, including the United States, with over 8000 cases, causing near panic and significant economic hardship worldwide.[4] Identification of a novel coronavirus[5] and its spread via close contact and aerosols primarily in hospital settings, was the result of cooperative efforts of the WHO, the CDC and local clinicians and epidemiologists. The disease was named for its clinical presentation, Severe Acute Respiratory Syndrome (SARS) and through speedy communications and exacting virological investigations the medical and lay public were kept informed and significant containment was achieved. The origin of the virus was probably from wild animals, including the masked palm civit, crowded and caged in markets in Guangdong Province, to be sold as pets or for food.[6] Its animal origin may be less important as a human disease since person to person transmission is efficient and only further observations will determine if the virus has become fully adapted to humans and emerges again independent of animal contact.

Criteria used to define a zoonotic infection vary, depending on how strictly the definition includes a vertebrate intermediate, other than humans, in the natural cycle of distribution. In this chapter malaria has been omitted because it exclusively cycles between mosquitoes and humans. Babesiosis, a disease caused by an animal protozoan, is included since transmission occurs from vertebrate nonhuman hosts via infected *Ixodes* ticks. Over 150 arboviruses worldwide are known to cause disease in humans. Some of these viruses, like the agent of yellow fever, infect animal species where they persist as reservoirs with the potential to spread to humans via arthropod intermediates.[7] A few examples are included in the tables and with confidence new arboviruses will emerge as threats to human health as remote forested regions are "developed." In this heterogeneous group are agents that are transmitted by all of the accepted mechanisms: direct contact, ingestion, inhalation, arthropod intermediates, and animal bites. Some microbes, such as *Francisella tularensis,* can spread to humans or to other animals via all five of these routes of transmission! Inadvertently, zoonoses can be spread from one infected person to another, through blood transfusions (e.g., West Nile virus, babesiosis)[8,9] or tissue or organ transplants (e.g., rabies following corneal transplants, West Nile disease).[10] Ordinarily excluded from the group of zoonotic dis-

eases are environmental microbes, such as *Burkholderia pseudomallei* and *Legionella* spp. Fungi will not be considered here except to acknowledge that bats have spread *Histoplasma capsulation* and birds have been responsible for cases of *Cryptococcus neoformans* in humans.

The defining criteria for the selection of pathogens and diseases recognized in this introduction to the zoonoses include the following: (1) a vertebrate reservoir exclusive of humans; (2) transmission of the agent directly to people *or* from products derived from the host animal *or* through an arthropod intermediate; and (3) a recognized infectious disease syndrome in susceptible individuals.[1] Many, if not most, animals that carry zoonotic pathogens can develop clinical disease. Xenotransplantation and the use of animal organs, cells and contact through hemoperfusion (e.g., pig liver or spleen) poses a potential risk of infection with an animal pathogen, but will not be addressed in this chapter.[2]

The diversity of the zoonoses, their global distribution in mundane and exotic niches, the glamorous or complex names given to some (e.g., Kyasanur Forest disease), and the enthusiasm that people have for travel and outdoor adventure all contribute to the aura and complexity surrounding this group of diseases. Domestic and laboratory animal contacts and varied household pets,[11,12] including exotic imports, have economic and emotional implications. It should be apparent that animal infections that can be transmitted to humans have a significant potential and real impact on everyone, including physicians and veterinarians. Few areas of our specialty demand the precision in extracting details of a travel, occupation, or exposure history than that which is required when we confront a patient ill with a perplexing fever who has been roughing it in the United States or abroad or who has had an animal, animal product, or arthropod encounter.

The association of animal and human disease reached a new dimension with the emergence of bovine spongiform encephalopathy in the United Kingdom in 1986, Farmers fought to preserve their herds, the beef-eating public became increasingly upset as human cases of a variant of Creuzfeldt-Jakob disease were discovered, and political turmoil intensified as other European countries recognized the disease in native or imported cattle. The efforts of basic scientists and epidemiologists and the involvement of the WHO have resulted in considerable clarification of the etiology of the disease and its probable initiation in cattle feed containing ruminant carcasses (see Chapter 173). As a result of this experience, the WHO has assumed a greater responsibility for surveillance, protocol development and laboratory investigations, an indication of the globalization of concern, organization, and action in approaching emerging and reemerging infectious diseases.[13] The effectiveness of this expanded responsibility was evident in the SARS outbreak and investigation of 2003 (see above and Chapter 152).

IMPORTANCE OF ZOONOSES IN CONTEMPORARY INFECTIOUS DISEASE

Perusal of Tables 327-1 to 327-3 reinforces the global significance of animal-associated infectious agents as well as the large proportion that are indigenous to North America in wild and domestic animal reservoirs. In absolute numbers, zoonotic pathogens are common. Documented illness in humans is unusual in the United States but constitutes a significant worldwide impact on morbidity and mortality. Without reviewing historical reports on epidemic bubonic plague, typhus fever, or woolsorter's disease, numerous contemporary examples illustrate the real and potential impact of zoonotic diseases in urban and rural settings. The anthrax spore mail delivery incident of September 2001 is an example of the infectious potential of zoonotic microorganisms. The severity of illnesses, the fear factor and the expense involved in surveillance and cleanup of the environment reflect the complexity of dealing with an epidemic, whether natural or tragically, a bioterror act.[14] The possibility of spread in the animal and arthropod vector planes and subsequently to humans often can't be anticipated. The history of Lyme borreliosis and Rocky Mountain spotted fever suggests how far reaching the impact of zoonoses can be in numbers of cases, and extension of a geographic range.

TABLE 327-1 Diseases Acquired Directly or Indirectly from Animals or from Arthropod Vectors*

Disease	Pathogen	Mode of Spread†	Persons at Risk‡
Viral			
B virus	*Herpesvirus simiae*	C	II, III, IV
California encephalitis	**Bunyavirus**	**A**	**I, II, public**
Colorado tick fever	**Orbivirus**	**A**	**I, II**
Contagious ecthyma (Orf)	**Parapoxvirus**	**C**	**I**
Dengue fever	**Flavivirus species**	**A**	**II, public**
Eastern equine encephalitis	**Alphavirus**	**A**	**II, IV, public**
Eastern hemisphere tick-borne encephalitis	Flavivirus	A, I	II
Hantavirus pulmonary syndrome	**Hantavirus spp. (New World)**	**C, R**	**I, II**
Hemorrhagic fever renal syndrome	Hantavirus spp.	C, R, I	I, II, IV
Hendra respiratory syndrome	Bat paramyxovirus	C, R	I, II
Japanese encephalitis	Flavivirus	A	II
Kyasanur forest disease	Flavivirus	A	II
Lassa fever	Arenavirus	C	I, II
Lymphocytic choriomeningitis	**Arenavirus**	**C, R**	**I, III, IV, public**
Mayaro virus disease	Alphavirus	A	II
Milker's nodule	**Parapoxvirus**	**C**	**I**
Monkeypox	**Orthopoxvirus**	**C**	**II, III**
Murray Valley encephalitis	Flavivirus	A	II
Nipah encephalitis	Bat paramyxovirus	C, R	I, II
Omsk hemorrhagic fever	Flavivirus	A, C, R	II, IV
Oropouche virus	Alphavirus	A	II
Powassan virus encephalitis	**Flavivirus**	**A, I**	**I, II, III**
Rabies	**Rhabdovirus**	**C**	**II, IV, public**
Rift Valley fever	Phlebovirus	C, R, A, I	I, II, IV, public
Ross River polyarthritis	Alphavirus	A	II
Semliki Forest	Alphavirus	A	II
St. Louis encephalitis	**Flavivirus**	**A**	**I, public**
Tanapox	Orthopox	C	II, III
Variant Creutzfeldt-Jakob encephalitis	**Prion virus**	**I**	**Public**
Venezuelan equine encephalitis	**Alphavirus**	**A, R**	**II, III, IV**
West Nile fever	Flavivirus	A	II, public
Yellow fever	Flavivirus	A	II
Bacterial			
Anthrax	***Bacillus anthracis***	**C, R, I**	**I, III**
Brucellosis	***Brucella* spp.**	**C, I, R**	**I, II, III, IV**
Campylobacteriosis	***Campylobacter jejuni***	**I**	**I, II, III, IV**
Cat-scratch disease, bacillary angiomatosis	***Bartonella henselae***	**A, C**	**II, III, VI, public**
Cholera	***Vibrio cholerae***	**I**	**V, public**
Eastern Hemisphere spotted fevers	*Rickettsia* spp.	A	II, III
Edwardsiella infection	*Edwardsiella tarda*	I	II, III, V
Ehrlichiosis, granulocytic	***Ehrlichia phagocytophila***	**A**	**II, III**
Ehrlichiosis, monocytic	***Ehrlichia chaffeensis***	**A**	**II, III**
Enterohemorrhagic gastroenteritis	***Escherichia coli* O157-H7, other serotypes**	**C, I**	**I, III, public**
Erysipeloid	***Erysipelothrix rhusiopathiae***	**C**	**I, II, V**
Gastroenteritis	***Vibrio parahaemolyticus***	**I**	**II, V, public**
Glanders	*Burkholderia mallei*	R, C, I	I, III, IV
Leptospirosis	***Leptospira interrogans* spp.**	**C, I**	**I, II, III, IV**
Listeriosis	***Listeria monocytogenes***	**I**	**I, VI, public**
Lyme borreliosis	***Borrelia burgdorferi***	**A**	**I, II, III**
Murine typhus	***Rickettsia typhi***	**A**	**I, II, III**
Pasteurellosis	***Pasteurella multocida***	**C, R**	**II, III**
Plague	***Yersinia pestis***	**A, C, R**	**II, III, IV, V**
Plesiomonas gastroenteritis	*Plesiomonas shigelloides*	I	V, public
Psittacosis, ornithosis	***Chlamydia psittaci***	**R**	**I, III, IV, public**
Q fever	***Coxiella burnetii***	**R, A**	**I, II, III, IV, public**
Rat-bite fever (H)	***Streptobacillus moniliformis***	**C, I**	**I, III, IV, public**
Rat-bite fever (S)	***Spirillum minor***	**C**	**I, II, III**
Relapsing fever	***Borellia* spp.**	**A**	**I, III**
Rhodococcus pneumonia	*Rhodococcus equi*	R	III, VI
Rickettsialpox	***Rickettsia akari***	**A**	**III, IV**
Rocky Mountain spotted fever	***Rickettsia rickettsii***	**A, C**	**I, II, III, IV, VI**
Salmonellosis	***Salmonella enteritidis***	**I**	**I, II, III, IV, VI**
Scrub typhus	*Orientia tsutsugamushi*	A	II, V
Septicemia-canine bite associated	***Capnocytophaga canimorsus***	**C**	**II, III, VI**
Skin gangrene sepsis-salt water associated	***Vibrio vulnificus*, other vibrios**	**C, I**	**V, VI**
Streptococcal cellulitis	***Streptococcus iniae***	**C**	**I, V**
Trench fever	***Bartonella quintana***	**A, C**	**VI, public**
Tuberculosis	***Mycobacterium bovis, Mycobacterium tuber***	**I**	**I, III, IV, VI**
Tularemia	***Francisella tularensis***	**C, I, A, R**	**I, II, III, IV, public**
Yersiniosis	***Yersinia enterocolitica***	**I**	**I, II, III, IV, V, public**
Yersiniosis	***Yersinia pseudotuberculosis***	**I**	**I, II, III, V, public**

*Bold type indicates acquired in North America, although the disease may have a wider distribution.

†Mode of spread: A, arthropod vector (e.g., mosquito, tick, flea, mite); C, contact (direct including bite, water); I, ingestion; R, respiratory.

‡At risk: I, farmers, livestock and animal processing workers; II, outdoor recreational or vocational activities in wild or underdeveloped regions; III, persons in contact with pets, other animals in urban areas; IV, health care and laboratory personnel (human and veterinary); V, fishers and others working in an aquatic environment; VI, Immunocompromised hosts; public, anyone, any place.

Table continued on following page

TABLE 327-1 Diseases Acquired Directly or Indirectly from Animals or from Arthropod Vectors*—Continued

Disease	Pathogen	Mode of Spread†	Persons at Risk‡
Parasitic			
Angiostrongyliasis	*Parastrongylus cantonensis*	I, C	II
African trypanosomiasis	*Trypanosoma brucei*	A	II
Babesiosis	*Babesia microti*	A	II, VI
Chagas' disease	*Trypanosoma cruzi*	A	II
Cyclosporiasis	*Cyclospora cayetanensis*	I	II, III
Chronic microsporidial diarrhea	*Microsporidia* spp.	I	I, II, VI
Clinorchiasis	*Clonorchis sinensis*	I	II
Cryptosporidiosis	*Cryptosporidia* spp.	I	I, II, VI
Cutaneous leishmaniasis	*Leishmania mexicana*	A	II
Cutaneous leishmaniasis	*Leishmania* spp.	A	II
Cysticercosis	*Taenia solium*	I	public
Dirofilariasis	*Dirofilaria immitis*	A	II
Echinococcosis	*Echinococcus granulosus*	I	I
Fascioliasis	*Fasciola hepatica*	I	I, II
Giardiasis	*Giardia lamblia*	I	I, II, III
Paragonimiasis	*Paragonimus westermani*	I	II, V
Toxocariasis	*Toxocara canis, cati*	C	III
Toxoplasmosis	*Toxoplasma gondii*	I	III, VI
Trichinosis	*Trichinella spiralis*	I	public
Visceral leishmaniasis (kala-azar)	*Leishmania donovani*	A	II, VI

*Bold type indicates acquired in North America, although the disease may have a wider distribution.

†Mode of spread: A, arthropod vector (e.g., mosquito, tick, flea, mite); C, contact (direct including bite, water); I, ingestion; R, respiratory.

‡At risk: I, farmers, livestock and animal processing workers; II, outdoor recreational or vocational activities in wild or underdeveloped regions; III, persons in contact with pets, other animals in urban areas; IV, health care and laboratory personnel (human and veterinary); V, fishers and others working in an aquatic environment; VI, Immunocompromised hosts; public, anyone, any place.

Continental United States

Before 1991 the average yearly number of endemic and imported zoonotic infections (excluding salmonellosis) reported in *Morbidity and Mortality Weekly Report* (MMWR) of the Centers for Disease Control was approximately 2400 cases.[15] Lyme borreliosis, recognized in the late 1970s, became a reportable disease in 1991 and has contributed an additional approximately 10,000 to 15,000 cases per reporting year subsequently, reflecting the dissemination and greater awareness of the disease. Regrowth of forests in the northeastern United State has resulted in ballooning populations of white-tailed deer, white-footed mice, and *Ixodes scapularis* ticks. The agents of Lyme disease and ehrlichiosis have been identified in parks, including an urban park on the edge of New York City.[16] Babesiosis, a rare protozoan zoonotic disease primarily afflicting elderly and splenectomized individuals, and cryptosporidiosis, responsible for sporadic and epidemic gastroenteritis, are being reported with increasing frequency in patients ill with the acquired immunodeficiency syndrome (AIDS).[17,18] *Babesia microti* is transmitted naturally via the feeding of

TABLE 327-2 Animal Reservoirs of Zoonoses in North America

Disease	Cat	Cattle	Dog	Fish and Shellfish	Fowl and Other Birds	Goats and Sheep	Horse	Rabbit	Rodent	Swine	Wildlife
Anthrax	X	X	X			X	X			X	X
Babesiosis		X							X		X
Brucellosis		X	X			X	X			X	
Campylobacteriosis	X	X	X		X	X			X	X	X
Cryptosporidiosis	X	X	X	X	X	X	X		X	X	X
Enterohemorrhagic *Escherichia coli* O157-H7, others	X	X	X			X	X	X		X	X
Erysipeloid		X		X	X	X				X	
Giardiasis	X		X			X					X
Leptospirosis		X	X			X	X		X	X	X
Listeriosis		X			X	X		X		X	X
Lyme borreliosis		X	X				X		X		X
Lymphocytic choriomeningitis									X		
Murine typhus									X		X
Ornithosis, psittacosis					X	X					
Pasteurellosis	X	X	X		X						
Plague	X							X	X		X
Q fever	X	X				X					X
Rabies	X	X	X			X	X	X	X	X	X
Rat-bite fever	X		X						X		X
Rocky Mountain spotted fever		X				X		X			X
Salmonellosis	X	X	X	X	X	X	X	X	X	X	X
Toxoplasmosis	X	X				X					X
Tularemia	X	X	X			X	X	X	X	X	X
Vibriosis				X							
Viral encephalitis					X	X	X		X		X
West Nile encephalitis		X	X		X		X				X
Yersiniosis		X	X		X	X			X	X	X

TABLE 327-3 Animal Associations and Zoonotic Disease Risk

Animal	Anthrax	Bartonella	Brucellosis	Campylobacter	Capnocytophaga	Cryptosporidia	Erysiploid	Escherichia coli O157-H7	Giardia	Hantavirus	Hepatitis A	Herpes B	Histoplasmosis	LC meningitis	Leptospirosis	Listeriosis	Myco. TB, bovis	ORF	Ornithosis	Pasteurella	Plague	Q fever	Rabies	Rat-bite fever	Salmonellosis	Strep. iniae cellulitis	Toxoplasmosis	Tularemia	Vibriosis	Viral hemorr. fever	West Nile disease	Yersiniosis
Aquatic mammal						X			X																							
Birds				X					X					X						X	X				X		X				X	
Cat	X	X	X	X		X		X							X					X	X	X	X		X	X	X					
Cattle	X		X	X		X		X							X	X	X			X		X			X							X
Dog	X		X	X	X	X		X							X	X				X		X			X		X				X	X
Fish/shellfish							X	X																	X	X	X		X			
Goats/sheep	X		X	X		X		X							X			X				X			X		X					X
Horse	X		X					X															X		X					X		X
Rabbit/hare			X					X							X					X	X	X			X			X				
Reptiles, amphibians																									X							
Rodent										X			X	X							X	X	X	X	X		X	X		X		
Subhuman primate			X						X	X	X	X			X	X	X								X							X
Swine	X		X	X		X	X								X	X	X				X	X			X		X					X
Wildlife	X								X				X	X	X	X					X	X	X		X		X	X		X		

LC, lymphocytic chorio; *Myco.* TB, *Mycobacterium tuberculosis; Strep., Streptococcus.*

Ixodes ticks that may simultaneously transmit Lyme borreliosis. Cryptosporidia are spread during contact with infected animals or ingestion of contaminated food or water supplies.[19] Importation of a few subclinically infected rabid raccoons from Florida to stock hunting camps in West Virginia in 1978 initiated a rapidly spreading rabies epizootic, primarily into contiguous Middle Atlantic states,[20] followed by invasion of New York and New England. Other terrestrial wild animals, especially skunks, were infected and the epizootic spread to a wide variety of domestic animals, such as unvaccinated cats and pet rabbits. Isolation, containment, and sacrifice of companion pets and the threat posed to individuals have added an emotional burden to the monetary drain placed on communities. These efforts and death of reservoir animals has halted the overt intensity of the epidemic. The impact on public health resources was enormous, including a significant expenditure for vaccination programs for domestic animals, postexposure prophylaxis for humans, and strategies to contain spread in wildlife by means such as baited oral vaccines.

Hantaviruses have been documented, by serologic and virologic methods, to occur in the United States in a variety of New World rodents.[21] No clinical human disease had been recognized, although globally hemorrhagic fever with renal syndrome (e.g., Korean hemorrhagic fever) and nephropathia epidemica (milder Scandinavian nephropathy) are familiar illnesses caused by members of the Bunyaviridae family. The dramatic appearance of an acute respiratory distress syndrome (ARDS) that afflicts primarily outdoor-oriented young adults and that carries significant mortality was first described in newspapers and in MMWR in 1993 in the Four Corners area of four southwestern states.[22] This virulent respiratory disease, caused by a number of previously unidentified Hantaviruses, has now been identified throughout the United States and in Central and South America in a variety of rodent reservoirs.[23] The epidemiology of this new respiratory syndrome appears to be inhalation of virus in dried excreta or via contact.

Two illnesses that illustrate the impact of zoonotic diseases on animals and humans appeared in the United States in the past 5 years. Neither had ever been identified in the Western Hemisphere before the clinical diseases surfaced. West Nile viral encephalitis was diagnosed in the summer of 1999 in Queens, New York in a number of elderly patients. Rapid collaboration among clinicians, epidemiologists, veterinary pathologists and virologists isolated the causal agent that was transmitted from birds to people via culex and other mosquitoes.[24] While uncertain how the virus arrived in the States, it has now spread from the East Coast during the past 4 years and is responsible for morbidity and mortality in people, birds, horses, and other animals in a relentless march westward.[25] Monkeypox arrived in a shipment of exotic pets from West Africa in the Spring of 2003. A virus that is carried by small mammals in forested areas of Central and West Africa, monkeypox is responsible for sporadic and epidemic disease in subhuman primates and people. From a pet distribution center in Illinois a Gambian giant pouched rat and several other small mammals infected prairie dogs being sold as pets in a number of Midwestern states. The prairie dogs, in turn, infected approximately 80 people.[26] A ban on the sale of prairie dogs as pets and on the importation of African rodents is now in place and Public Health officials are alert to the potential for spread of monkeypox in the wild animal plane, in caged animals and in humans. These examples illustrate the unexpected emergence of zoonotic diseases in new areas, carried in obvious or obscure vehicles from distant regions. The importance of a vigilant and reliable Public Health infrastructure is essential for the rapid identification of new diseases occurring naturally or as acts of bioterrorism.[2]

Global Experiences

Our responsibility for patients' well being often includes travel advice. The distribution of zoonotic diseases and their modes of spread often dictate the choice of protective immunizations, medications and specific instructions about food and drink. In practical terms, many problems result from failed communication or incomplete advice. For example, in Boston and some other cities in the United States, more cases of Eastern Hemisphere spotted fever (e.g., South African tick bite fever) are seen in a decade than of indigenous Rocky Mountain spotted fever. Analysis of most of these cases reveals that no precautionary measures were discussed by the physician during the pretravel visit even though the patient's itinerary included a walking safari in an endemic region. The incubation period may influence the time of appearance of an emerging zoonotic infection, often after travel is completed and the patient is home.

Movement of large numbers of susceptible young soldiers to areas of the world endemic for contagious diseases, including infectious zoonoses, has always been a concern. Korean hemorrhagic fever emerged as an acute clinical problem among United Nations' troops in the Korean conflict, as well as for practicing physicians in the West dealing with returning soldiers. The editor of *Reviews of Infectious Diseases* demonstrated his prescience by inviting experts to prepare a monograph supplement in the autumn of 1990 on the subject of infectious disease problems related to the Persian Gulf area.[27] A wide circulation of this supplement reached infectious disease specialists just as the Desert Storm conflict erupted. The major zoonoses endemic in the region were reviewed thoughtfully. In the aftermath of that brief conflict, rare reports of animal-associated diseases, such as Q fever that had become clinically active after a period of latency, appeared in the literature. Conflicts continue to erupt in other regions of the globe, including Iraq and Afghanistan. Responsible reporting in the medical literature has been timely in bringing regional zoonoses to the attention of physicians and should be a continuing responsibility of the medical profession, the WHO and the CDC.[28] The most recent update involves cases of visceral and cutaneous leishmaniasis for U.S. military personnel stationed in Iraq, Kuwait and Afghanistan.[28a]

The reemergence of dengue and dengue hemorrhagic fever as a global health problem is another illustration of the unpredictability of arbovirus dissemination and the many factors influencing local outbreaks and epidemics.[29] In the Western Hemisphere its resurgence clearly relates to failure of mosquito control, urbanization and population growth, and lack of proper water and waste removal procedures. Competent mosquitoes, including *Aedes aegypti* and *Aedes albopictus* have spread dengue virus throughout the Caribbean and Central and South America. The presence of these arthropod vectors in the southern United States increases the likelihood of dengue outbreaks locally, not only among tourists returning from vacationing in endemic areas.

At a time when people seek adventure in the outdoors, when travel time around the globe is shorter than the incubation period of many zoonotic diseases, and when patients who are immunocompromised by illness or therapy crowd foreign travel experiences into brief periods of wellness, our efforts must be assiduous in providing advance warning and in investigating new clinical symptoms in returning travelers. A useful text that covers geographic distribution of infections is available,[30] and the CDC continues to provide physicians with a weekly summary of health information for international travelers.

DISTRIBUTION OF ZOONOTIC PATHOGENS IN NATURE

During the past several decades a number of new diseases have emerged globally, and some previously recognized infections have been identified in regions where they had not been reported heretofore. Table 327-4 lists the natural and human factors that individually and collectively are known to affect the environment and therefore potentially influence where zoonoses emerge, persist, or spread locally or globally.[2]

Geoclimatic Conditions

Numerous examples can be cited to illustrate the influence of temperature, moisture, and soil conditions on the distribution of zoonotic agents and diseases. "Tropical" diseases implies that an environment is extant that supports the growth and transmission of infectious agents requiring high temperatures and abundant rainfall in which arthropod vectors thrive and appropriate animal hosts exist. Global warming is an example of a geoclimatic issue that may result in major changes in zoonotic disease distribution.[31] Arthropod vectors, such as mosquitoes and ticks, enhanced or suppressed growth and distribution of plants, and animal migrations are intimately tied to changes in ambient temperature. The presence of anopheles mosquitoes and the increasing number of cases of malaria at higher elevations support scientists who argue that climate change is already occurring.[32] Several recent reports note that butterflies are shifting their range towards cooler areas and the fruit fly genome is changing better to cope with higher temperatures.[33]

Bacillus anthracis spores and vegetative growth of organisms are strongly influenced by ambient temperatures in "incubator" areas where plant decay adds warmth and moisture, in the presence of a supportive alkaline soil containing adequate calcium salts.[34] The halophilic and nonhalophilic vibrios of the Northern Hemisphere winter in estuarine mud and appear in significant numbers only as water temperatures warm to approximately 20° C. Cases of gastroenteritis, necrotizing cellulitis, and septicemia are being diagnosed in individuals exposed to New England and the Danish coastal sea waters, regions traditionally considered too cold to support the growth of these organisms.[35,36]

Ticks responsible for the transmission of Rocky Mountain spotted fever and Lyme borreliosis are strongly influenced in their distribution and activity by temperature and precipitation. The extreme cold of Alaska has prohibited the extension of the range of these tick-associated diseases into our most northern state.

Animal, Avian, and Aquatic Hosts

Human and animal susceptibility factors, including genetic characteristics and natural and acquired immunity influence the patterns of spread of zoonoses. Interactions with domestic animals can be a major factor. Vaccination of dogs in developed countries has all but eliminated rabies acquired from these pets, but in the developing world rabies almost always results from dog bites.[20] When domestic animals are allowed to stray or to become feral, they can acquire many zoonotic infections such as tularemia, plague, and rabies.[37] Household pets can carry infected arthropod vectors into homes or to other geographic areas. The penchant of raccoons for suburban areas clearly facilitated the spread of rabies to domestic animals in the Middle Atlantic and New England states, primarily to cats, but also to dogs, cattle, horses, and even to pet rabbits.[38] The Hantavirus pulmonary syndrome, first described in the southwestern United States, emerged clinically when an abundance of food lead to increased numbers of rodents living in proximity to susceptible humans.[22] Migrating and overwintering sedentary birds provide a reservoir for arboviruses, including West Nile virus, and aquatic mammals are sources of multiplication and dissemination of *Giardia lamblia*[39] and *F. tularensis*.[40]

New zoonotic diseases continue to be recognized. An acute respiratory illness in horses and caretakers in Queensland, Australia, and an outbreak of severe encephalitis in pig farmers in Malaysia was first reported in 1994 and 1998, respectively. Two closely related atypical paramyxoviruses, named Hendra and Nipah, were isolated and both viruses were found associated with pteropid bats (fruit eating flying foxes) that probably serve as reservoirs, and spread virus to horses and pigs.[41,42] Our ability to marshal observation and communication resources, clinical and epidemiologic surveillance, sophisticated scientific and laboratory methodology, and collaboration of veterinarians, physicians, and biologists augers well for future discoveries, as exemplified in the rapid recognition of the initial outbreak of West Nile encephalitis in 1999 in Queens, New York.[24] The need for surveillance and cooperation is essential for the health of people and the health of our planet as expressed in a recent Institute of Medicine report.[2]

Migration Patterns of Animals and Birds

Tularemia appeared in Vermont for the first time in the late 1960s, brought there by infected muskrats migrating via a water route from Canada and New York State.[40] Cases of Rocky Mountain spotted fever appear in new and unexpected places, such as a small park surrounded by concrete and asphalt in Bronx, New York.[43] Did a dog bring the rickettsiae in dog ticks acquired from a visit to eastern Long Island? Did a hawk carry an infected rabbit from an endemic area? Can *Rickettsia rickettsii* be transported by migrating birds carrying infected arthropods? In nature, when considering the potential for emergence of zoonoses, no haven is safe. Even in a verdant park in New York City ticks have been

TABLE 327-4 Factors Associated with the Distribution of Zoonotic Pathogens in Nature

Geoclimatic conditions
  Temperature extremes-terrestrial and water
  Rainfall
  Soil characteristics
Animal, avian, and aquatic hosts
Migration patterns of animals and birds
Arthropod reservoirs and vectors
Human influence on ecosystems and biosystems
Global trade
  Feed and food
  Animals and birds
  Inert conveyors

discovered carrying *Borrelia burgdorferi* and *Anaplasma* (*Ehrlichia*) *phagocytophila*, probably transported by roaming white-footed mice.[16] The questions are many, the answers are few. However, observations of zoonotic disease spread confirms the influence of animal reservoir movements, the necessity of co-hosts for long-term survival of some pathogens (e.g., *B. burgdorferi*),[44] and the importance of overwintering sedentary birds as well as migratory patterns for persistence and dissemination of selected zoonoses (e.g., West Nile virus). The presence of favorable conditions for growth, survival, and multiplication of ticks, biting flies, and mosquitoes, important vectors of many zoonotic pathogens (see Table 327-1), illustrates the potential for widespread movements of microorganisms carried by these vectors to new geographic regions. The fruit eating bats in search of food sources, transported Hendra and Nipah viruses over great distances in Australia and Malaysia.[41]

Arthropod Reservoirs and Vectors

Vectorial capacity, the summation of many factors that contribute to the ability of a pathogen to perpetuate in an arthropod host, is often enhanced by actions that increase survival and multiplication of the arthropod and vertebrate host intermediates.[45] Although incompletely understood, it appears that the spread of Lyme borreliosis to the majority of the lower 48 states resulted from a population explosion of white-tailed deer and white-footed mice, which allowed overwintering of the pathogen and enhanced distribution of the dependent *Ixodes* ticks. A provocative report linking eastern United States oak forests to a chain reaction involving gypsy moth activity, white-footed mouse density, acorn production, and white-tailed deer presence illustrates the delicate balance that can eventuate in the distribution and prevalence of Lyme disease.[46] The appearance in the southern and eastern United States of a mosquito vector from Asia, the Asian tiger mosquito A. *albopictus*, corresponded to the commercial stockpiling of used tire casings imported into the Houston, Texas, area in the early 1980s.[47,48] This mosquito, a competent laboratory vector for at least 22 arboviruses, including dengue, eastern equine encephalitis, and yellow fever, has now been identified in over 25 states, including Hawaii.[49] In a surveillance effort initiated in Polk County, Florida, 14 strains of eastern equine encephalitis virus have been isolated from these mosquitoes.[50] *F. tularensis* is maintained in Dermacentor ticks through transovarial passage and thus the tick is an important reservoir in nature, capable of disseminating the pathogen to small mammals and people.[51]

Human Influence on Ecosystems and Biosystems

The ability of humans to exert significant influence on wind velocity, rainfall, temperature extremes, and soil conditions pales when compared with the natural forces operating around the globe. However, there are numerous small- and large-scale examples in irrigation practices, waste distribution, water purification, agricultural technologies, insecticide usage, and incursions into areas of virgin vegetation that illustrate the profound effects of human activities on the establishment and spread of zoonoses.[52]

Dramatic examples can be found in epidemics following pollution of water supplies, the most contemporary being the massive outbreak of cryptosporidial gastroenteritis that affected approximately 400,000 Milwaukee, Wisconsin residents.[19] Waterborne cryptosporidiosis remains a major threat, especially among immunocompromised individuals.[53] The first microbiologically documented *Giardia lamblia* epidemic, reported in 1993, spread from wild beavers through fecally contaminated water supplied to residents of several towns in western Canada.[39] We are not protecting our water systems adequately to kill and remove selected pathogens that encyst and therefore avoid methods used in purification.

Recreational swimming holes can be contaminated by *Leptospira* spp. brought downstream from neighboring farms.[54] Airplanes can facilitate the inadvertent transport of potentially infectious arthropod vectors of zoonoses in the wheel bays of intercontinental and transcontinental flights.[55] Indiscriminate use of insecticides has influenced avian populations instrumental in the control of various disease-carrying arthropod vectors. Perhaps the most devastating influence affecting the

distribution of zoonotic pathogens occurs when virgin forests are cleared or are invaded by new roads and new towns in the name of economic development.[56] It has been theorized that many undiscovered potentially pathogenic viruses and bacteria reside in animal hosts that are inaccessible to humans in remote ecosystems until such areas are developed and susceptible people begin moving to and fro. An example often quoted is the recognition of the viral disease Oropouche several years after a new road was built connecting Belem with Brasilia in Brazil.[57] A variety of prospective studies are under way to learn more about the relationship of alterations in biosystems and ecosystems and the emergence of "new" infectious diseases including zoonoses.[56,57]

Global Trade: Feed and Food, Animals and Birds, Inert Conveyors

Numerous examples of spread of zoonotic diseases have been mentioned or discussed in this chapter. Bovine spongiform encephalitis clearly resulted from widespread use of animal carcasses as protein supplements. Over 150 cases of varient Creutzfeldt-Jakob encephalopathy have occurred in the United Kingdom as well as scattered cases in Western Europe. Fresh berries from Central and South America have precipitated epidemics of cyclosporiasis. The recent introduction of monkeypox virus in exotic animals from West Africa and the possible mode of spread of West Nile virus in bird movements into North America needs to be evaluated. Imported psittacosis has resulted in important and rigid quarantine measures for the parrot family as well as other bird species. Old tires brought to Houston, Texas from Asia contained eggs and larvae of *Aedes allopictus* mosquitoes that are competent vectors for a number of arbovirus diseases. It is abundantly clear that with enhanced global trade and movements of many commodities among nations that the specter of disseminating zoonotic pathogens is a very real concern that requires thoughtful and vigorous control measures.[2]

DIAGNOSTIC APPROACH TO ZOONOSES

There are more than 200 well-described zoonotic diseases, of which 91 are included in Table 327-1. A majority of those that are included (bold type) are indigenous or have been acquired in North America. Some of those pathogens and diseases are found in other parts of the world, including recently imported West Nile and monkeypox viruses.

The possibility of a zoonotic infection can surface quickly from even a superficial history or features of the physical examination, or both. Included are residence and travel history, occupation (e,g., abattoir worker, veterinarian, farmer), outside interests (e.g., hunting, trapping, other outdoor activities), or the presence of a characteristic skin lesion (e.g., erythema migrans of Lyme borreliosis, peripheral petechial lesions of Rocky Mountain spotted fever, tache noire of Eastern Hemisphere spotted fever). A characteristic illness, such as St. Louis encephalitis in Texas or eastern equine encephalitis in New Jersey, may alert a physician to similar diagnoses in other patients being seen with central nervous system symptoms.

By using Tables 327-1 through 327-3 as cross-referencing guides, an individual's at-risk activity or animal contacts can help narrow the etiologic possibilities, and potential modes of spread can be evaluated through careful attention to historical details. Geographic considerations and clinical data can then help in selecting possible etiologic diagnoses. Laboratory studies, including appropriate cultures, paired serologic specimens, chemistries selected to evaluate target organ involvement, and search for specific parasites can help to confirm a suspected diagnosis. In acute circumstances, therapy should be instituted before confirming a specific diagnosis, such as tularemia, guided by the available data.

The epidemic of Q fever that occurred after a group of poker players were exposed to a parturient cat in urban Halifax, Nova Scotia, in winter, attests to the usefulness of Tables 327-2 and 327-3 in identifying diseases specific to selected animal species that should be considered based on the clinical data available.[58] The multiplicity of possible etiologies for a cluster of patients, for example, with an acute respiratory disease, allows greater precision in diagnosis by having a reference to animal reservoirs characteristic for specific pathogens.[59]

Zoonotic diseases can be severe, life threatening, and contagious and can even warn of an emerging epidemic or a possible bioterror act. Rapid noncultural diagnostic tests, such as enzyme-linked immunosorbent assay methodology, fluorescent antibody staining, polymerase chain reaction and DNA probes, are being developed or are in use to identify selected zoonoses.[2,60,61] Therapy is currently available for the majority of nonviral zoonotic infections and even for a few viral zoonoses, such as Lassa fever, some Hantavirus hemorrhagic fevers with renal syndromes, and possibly *Herpesvirus simiae* infections. Most of the sophisticated studies to unravel the identity of a zoonotic infectious disease, however, ultimately rely on a detailed and accurate history from which specific tests and effective therapy emerge.

REFERENCES

1. Waltner-Toews D. Caught in the causal web: Analytical problems in the epidemiology of zoonoses. Acta Vet Scand Suppl. 1988;84:296-298.
2. Burroughs T, Knobler S, Lederberg J, eds. The Emergence of Zoonotic Diseases: Understanding the Impact on Animal and Human Health. Washington, DC: Institute of Medicine, National Academy Press; 2002:1-123.
3. Centers for Disease Control and Prevention (CDC). Terrorism preparedness in state health departments—United States, 2001-2003. MMWR Morb Mortal Wkly Rep. 2003;52:1051-1053.
4. Lee H, Hui D, Wu A, et al. A major outbreak of severe acute respiratory syndrome in Hong Kong. N Engl J Med. 2003;348:1986-1994.
5. Ksiazek TG, Erdman D, Glodsmith CS, et al. A novel coronavirus associated with severe acute respiratory syndrome. N Engl J Med. 2003;348:1953-1966.
6. Liu J. SARS, wildlife and human health. Science. 2003;302:53.
7. Tsai TF. Arboviral infections in the United States. Infect Dis Clin North Am. 1991;5:73-102.
8. Pealer LN, Marfin HA, Peterson LR, et al. Transmission of West Nile virus through blood transfusion in the United States in 2002. N Engl J Med. 2003;349:1236-1245.
9. Smith PS, Evans AT, Popovsky M, et al. Transfusion-acquired babesiosis and failure of antibiotic treatment. JAMA. 1986;256:2726-2727.
10. Hemick CG, Tauxe RV, Vernon AA. Is there a risk to contacts of patients with rabies? Rev Infect Dis. 1987;9:511-518.
11. Fox JG, Lipman NS. Infections transmitted by large and small laboratory animals. Infect Dis Clin. 1991;5:131-163.
12. Goldstein EJC. Household pets and human infections. Infect Dis Clin North Am. 1991;5:117-130.
13. Meslin FX. Global aspects of emerging and potential zoonoses: A WHO perspective. Emerg Infect Dis. 1997;3:223-228.
14. Jernigan DB, Raghunathan PL, Bell BP, et al. Investigation of bioterrorism-related anthrax, United States, 2001: epidemiologic findings. Emerg Infect Dis. 2002;8:1019-1028.
15. Summary of notifiable diseases, United States—1991. MMWR Morb Mortal Wkly Rep. 1991;40:1-63.
16. Daniels TJ, Falco RC, Schwartz I, et al. Deer ticks (*Ixodes scapularis*) and the agents of Lyme disease and human granulocytic ehrlichiosis in a New York City park. Emerg Infect Dis. 1997;3:353-355.
17. Krause PJ. Babesiosis. Med Clin North Am. 2002;86:361-373.
18. Wittner M, Tanowitz HB, Weiss LM. Parasitic infections in AIDS patients: Cyptosporidiosis, isosporiasis, microsporidiosis, cyclosporiasis. Infect Dis Clin North Am. 1993;7:569-586.
19. Guerrant RL. Cyptosporidiosis: An emerging, highly infectious threat. Emerg Infect Dis. 1997;3:51-57.
20. Fishbein DB. Rabies. Infect Dis Clin North Am. 1991;5:53-71.
21. Tsai TF, Bauer SP, Sasso DR, et al. Serological and virulogical evidence of a Hantaan virus–related enzootic in the United States. Infect Dis. 1985;152:126-136.
22. Update: Hantavirus infection—United States, 1993. MMWR Morb Mortal Wkly Rep. 1993;42:517-519.
23. Schmaljohn C, Hjelle B. Hantaviruses: A global disease problem. Emerg Infect Dis. 1997;3:95-104.
24. Nash D, Mostashari F, Fine A, et al. The outbreak of West Nile virus infection in the New York City area in 1999. N Engl J Med. 2001;344:1807-1814.
25. West Nile Virus Activity—United States. November 20-25, 2003. MMWR Morb Mortal Wkly Rep. 2003;52:1160-1161.
26. Reed KD, Melski JW, Graham MB, et al. The detection of monkeypox in humans in the Western Hemisphere. N Engl J Med. 2004;350:342-350.
27. Oldfield EC, Wallace MR, Hyams KC, et al. Endemic infectious diseases of the Middle East Rev Infect Dis. 1991;13(Suppl 3):SI99-5217.
28. Deresinski S. Health hazards in Somalia. Infect Dis Alert. 1993;12:69-72.
28a. Update: Cutaneous leishmaniasis in U.S. military personnel—Southwest/Central Asia, 2002-2004 and two cases of visceral leishmaniasis in U.S. military personnel—Afghanistan, 2002-2004. MMWR Morb Mortal Wkly Rep. 2004;53:264-268.
29. Gubler DJ, Clark GC. Dengue/dengue hemottbagic fever: The emergence of a global health problem. Emerg Infect Dis. 1995;1:55-57.
30. Wilson ME. A World Guide to Infections: Disease, Distribution, Diagnosis. New York: Oxford University Press; 1991.
31. Colwell R, Epstein P, Gubler D, et al. Global climate change and infectious diseases. Emerg Infect Dis. 1998;4:451-452.
32. Epstein RP, Diaz HF, Elias S, et al. Biological and physical signs of climate change: Focus on mosquito-borne disease. Bull Am Meteorol Soc. 1998;78:409-417.
33. Schilthuizen M. Fly genome warms to global change. Science Now. 2003;(521):2.
34. Van Ness GB. Ecology of anthrax. Science. 1971;172:1303-1307.
35. Hill MK, Sanders CV. Localized and systemic infection due to vibrio species. Infect Dis Clin North Am. 1987;1:687-707.
36. Kontoycannis DP, Calia KE, Basgoz N, Calderwood SB. Primary septicemia caused by *Vibrio cholerae* non-O1 acquired on Cape Cod, Massachusetts. Clin Infect Dis. 1995;21:1330-1333.
37. Capellan J, Fong IW. Tularemia from a cat bite: Case report and review of feline-associated tularemia. Clin Infect Dis. 1993;16:472-475.
38. Extension of the raccoon rabies epizootic—United States,1992. MMWR Morb Mortal Wkly Rep. 1992;41:661-664.
39. Isaac-Renton JL, Cordeiro C, Sarafis K, Shahriari H. Characterization of *Giardia duodenalis* isolates from a waterborne outbreak. J Infect Dis. 1993;167:431-440.
40. Young LS, Bicknell DS, Archer BG, et al. Tularemia epidemic: Vermont 1968. N Engl J Med. 1969;280:1253-1260.
41. Field H, Young P, Yob JM, et al. The natural history of Hendra and Nipah viruses. Microbes Infect. 2001;3:307-314.
42. Lam SK, Chu KB. Nipah virus encephalitis outbreak in Malaysia. Clin Infect Dis. 2002;34(Suppl 2):548-551.
43. Salgo MP, Telzak BE, Currie B, et al. A focus of Rocky Mountain spotted fever within New York City. N Engl J Med. 1988;318:1345-1348.
44. Steere AC. Lyme disease. N Engl J Med. 1989;321:586-596.
45. Telford SR 3rd, Pollack RJ, Spielman A. Emerging vector-borne infections. Infect Dis Clin North Am. 1991;5:7-18.
46. Jones CO, Ostfeld RS, Richard MP, et al. Chain reactions linking acorns to gypsy moth outbreaks and Lyme disease risk. Science. 1998;279:1023-1026.
47. Update: *Aedes albopictus* infestation—United States. MMWR Morb Mortal Wkly Rep. 1987;36:769-773.
48. Kennedy D. A tiger tale. Science, 2002;297:1445.
49. Moore CO, Mitchell CJ. *Aedes aibopiclus* in the United States: Ten-year presence and public health implications. Emerg Infect Dis. 1997;3:329-334.
50. Mitchell O, Niebylski ML, Smith GC, et al. Isolation of eastern equine encephalitis virus from *Aedes albopiclus* in Florida. Science. 1992;257:526-527.
51. Parker RR, Spencer RR. Hereditary transmission of tularemia infection by the wood tick, *Dermacentor andersoni*, Stiles. Public Health Rep. 1926;41:1341-1355.
52. Wilson ME, Levins R, Speilman A, eds. Diseases in evolution: Global changes and emergence of infectious diseases. Ann NY Acad Sci. 1994;740:1-461.
53. Juranek DO. Cryptosporidiosis: Sources of infection and guidelines for prevention. Clin Infect Dis. 1995;21(Suppl 1):S57-S61.
54. Jackson LA, Kaufmann AF, Adams WG, et al. Outbreak of leptospirosis associated with swimming. Pediatr Infect Dis J. 1993;12:48-54.
55. Russell RC. Survival of insects in the wheel bays of a Boeing 747 aircraft on flights between tropical and temperate airports. Bull World Health Organ. 1987;65:659-662.
56. Gibbons A. Where are "new" diseases born? Science. 1993;261:680-681.
57. Momen H. Emerging infectious diseases—Brazil. Emerg Infect Dis. 1998;4:1-3.
58. Langley JM, Marrie TJ, Covert A, et al. Poker players' pneumonia: An urban outbreak of Q fever following exposure to a parturient cat. N Engl J Med. 1988;319:354-356.
59. Weinberg AN. Respiratory infections transmitted from animals. Infect Dis Clin North Am. 1991;5:649-661.
60. Keller TL, Halperin JJ, Whitman M. PCR detection of *Borrelia burgdorferi* DNA in cerebrospinal fluid of Lyme neuroborreliosis patients. Neurology. 1992;42:32-42.
61. Relman DA. Detection and identification of previously unrecognized microbial pathogens. Emerg Infect Dis. 1998;4:382-389.

SECTION G

PROTECTION OF TRAVELERS

CHAPTER **328**

Protection
of Travelers

DAVID O. FREEDMAN

The pre-travel management of the international traveler should be based on risk management principles. The office consult should begin with a thorough risk assessment. Prevention strategies and medical interventions need to be individualized according to both the itinerary as well as traveler dependent factors. A structured approach to the patient interaction (Table 328-1) is the most efficient way to cover the necessary educational and preventive interventions. As many of these measures are to be initiated only much later at the destination, clear printed instructions in lay language are advisable. The worldwide epidemiology of travel-related diseases is constantly changing. A body of knowledge in travel medicine has been published and online and print resources (Table 328-2) must be consulted frequently[1,2] in order to keep current.

EPIDEMIOLOGY OF TRAVEL RELATED ILLNESS

Globally, approximately 80 million people travel from industrialized to developing countries each year (Fig. 328-1). Of note, travel to Africa, which presents particularly high risk for a number of infectious diseases, is undertaken by many fewer (250,000) U.S. when compared to European residents each year. Widely quoted travel-related health data is mostly older than a decade and may not all be currently applicable.[3] Depending on destination 22% to 64% of travelers report some illness.[3,4] Rates are significantly higher in summer. Approximately 10% of travelers will consult a physician either during or after a trip but less than 1% require hospitalization.[5] Infectious diseases account for up to 10% of the morbidity during travel but only 1% of the deaths with malaria the most common. Causes of death vary according to population studied.[6-8] At destinations that attract seniors, cardiovascular events predominate while in developing countries motor vehicle accidents and drowning prevail.

IMMUNIZATION

Choice of vaccines for an individual traveler is based on risk of exposure to vaccine preventable diseases on the chosen itinerary, the severity of disease if acquired and any risks of the vaccine itself. Travelers differ in their tolerance of risk. Requests for immunization against diseases with potential for poor outcome if acquired, but which are actually of negligible risk to the traveler, are often difficult for the physician to refuse. For the vaccine-preventable diseases, the monthly incidence for non-immune travelers to developing countries is most significant for symptomatic hepatitis A at 0.3% per month overall and 2.0% for high risk backpackers. The risk of symptomatic hepatitis B is most significant for long-stay travelers and expatriates at 0.25% per month. Enteric fever (typhoid and paratyphoid) has a risk of 0.03% per month on the Indian sub-continent and is 10 times lower in Africa and parts of Latin America.[9] Risk of yellow fever may be as high as 0.1% per month of travel to an area with current epidemic transmission but the risk varies greatly between destinations encompassed by the en-

TABLE 328-1 A Structured Approach to the Pretravel Office Visit with a Developing World Traveler

Perform Risk Assessment
The following must always be ascertained to determine appropriate preventive medical recommendations. Pre-printed medical record forms may be used to record these.
Exact itinerary including regions within each country to be visited.
Dates of travel to assess risk of seasonal diseases
Age
Past vaccination history
Underlying illness
Current medications
Pregnant or contemplating pregnancy
Allergies
Purpose of trip
Risk exposures—blood, body fluids, adventure or extensive outdoor exposures
Urban versus rural
Type of accomodation
Level of aversion to risk
Financial limitations that may necessitate prioritization of interventions

Administer Immunizations
Administer routine vaccinations that are not up to date.
Administer indicated travel vaccines.
Provide to patient legally mandated Vaccine Information Statements from CDC <www.cdc.gov/nip>
Provide printed checklist to patient with vaccines administered.
Record in clinic record vaccines administered, lot number, and date.
Document vaccines offered to but declined by patient, as well as non-recommended vaccines administered at the patients request.

Provide Malaria Prevention (if Indicated)
Determine whether malaria risk exists for the destination country. If yes:
Does the patient's itinerary within that country put them at risk. If yes:
Recommend malaria chemoprophylaxis. Several equally effective drugs of choice may be indicated. Ascertain which is best suited to the individual patient and itinerary.
Educate on personal protection against arthropods.

Educate on Traveler's Diarrhea
Recommend food and water precautions.
Prescribe and educate on standby therapy with a quinolone antibiotic and advise on use of loperamide and oral hydration if needed.

Teach Essential Preventive Behaviors
Most travel-related health problems, including vaccine-preventable diseases can be prevent through simple behaviors initiated by the traveler.
Educate on appropriate strategies in the following categories (some topics are not applicable to all destinations): blood-borne and sexually transmitted diseases; safety and crime avoidance; injury prevention; swimming safety; rabies; skin/wound care; tuberculosis; packing for healthy travel; obtaining health care abroad.

Discuss Other Applicable Heath Issues
Advise and prescribe for altitude illness, motion sickness, or jet-leg.
Discuss prevention of any specific travel-related infection that are of some risk to the traveler and have a possible preventive strategy not included in strategies above.
Discuss any minimal-risk conditions (e.g., hemorrhagic fevers) that are a frequent cause of patient anxiety.

demic area map.[10] The risk of meningococcal meningitis, rabies, cholera, polio, measles, varicella, and Japanese encephalitis in travelers is not known but is thought to be small even for travel to highly endemic areas.

Table 328-3 provides data on dosing, administration, need for boosters, and possible accelerated regimens for vaccines administered in the travel medicine setting. Details on vaccine composition, mechanism of action, use for routine adult and childhood primary vaccination, and adverse reactions can be found in Chapter 319. The following focuses on indications for each vaccine in the context of travel.

Update of Routine Immunizations

Due to the increased prevalence of many infections in the developing world, routine immunizations need to be current.[11] Tetanus/diphtheria boosters should usually be given every 10 years but for travelers to remote areas where tetanus toxoid, which would be indicated in cases of dirty trauma, will be inaccessible, boosters are suggested at 5-year in-

TABLE 328-2 In-Depth Information Resources for Travel Medicine

Authoritative Websites Updated Constantly with Epidemiologic and Outbreak Information
CDC Travelers Health
www.cdc.gov/travel
World Health Organization Travelers Health
www.who.int/ith
Health Canada. Committee to Advise on Tropical Medicine And Travel (CATMAT)
http://www.hc-sc.gc.ca/pphb-dgspsp/tmp-pmv/catmat-ccmtmv/index.html
WHO Disease Outbreak News
http://www.who.int/csr/don/en/
WHO Weekly Epidemiological Record
www.who.int/wer
CDC Morbidity and Mortality Weekly Report
www.cdc.gov/mmwr
WHO Disease by Disease Health Topics
www.who.int/health_topics/en/

In-Depth References on Specialized Topics
Centers for Disease Control and Prevention. Health Information for International Travel 2003-2004. (The "CDC Yellow Book"). U.S. Public Health Service. Atlanta. Order from www.phf.org Full text online at at www.cdc.gov/travel/yb/index.htm
World Health Organization. International Travel and Health 2003. (WHO "Green" Book [formerly yellow]). Published annually. Available from authorized WHO book agents. Full text online at www.who.int/ith
Keystone JS, Kozarsky P, Freedman DO, et al, eds. Travel Medicine. St. Louis: Mosby 2003. (ISBN:0323025218)
Plotkin SA, Orenstein WA. Vaccines. 4th ed. Philadelphia: WB Saunders; 2004. (ISBN:0721696880)
Schlagenhauf P. Travelers' Malaria. Hamilton: B.C. Decker; 2001. (ISBN 1-55009-157-3)
Auerbach PS. Wilderness Medicine. 4th ed. St. Louis: Mosby; 2001. (ISBN 0-323-00950-6)
Strickland T. Hunter's Tropical Medicine and Emerging Infectious Diseases. 8th ed. Philadelphia: WB Saunders; 2000. www.elsevierhealth.com (ISBN 0-7216-6223-4)

tervals. Persons born in the United States prior to 1957 or born at anytime in the developing world are considered immune to measles. Other adult travelers should have received at least two doses of live measles vaccine during their life unless a history of measles infection can be documented. Unvaccinated patients that have the accepted routine indications for influenza or pneumococcal vaccines (see Chapter 319)

should receive these during the pre-travel consultation. Varicella is primarily a disease of adolescents and young adults in tropical, non-industrialized countries. Two doses of varicella vaccine spaced by at least 4 weeks should be considered for long-stay adult travelers without evidence of varicella immunity.

Vaccines to Consider for All Destinations in the Developing World

Hepatitis A (HA)

HA vaccine is indicated for every non-immune traveler to countries/areas with moderate to high risk of infection (Fig. 328-2). This would include essentially everyone travelling outside the United States, Canada, Japan, Australia, New Zealand, Scandinavian countries, and developed countries in Europe. HA vaccination given in post-exposure settings has been shown to be very effective in preventing disease.[12] Thus, ancillary concomitant immune globulin administration pre-exposure in the setting of imminent departures, as is still recommended by CDC,[13(pp75-81)] is rarely used in practice even for travelers on their way to the airport. At the same time, if sero-conversion rates are examined, 80% are positive by 2 weeks not reaching optimal (98% to 100%) rates until 4 weeks after vaccination.[14] Individuals born in the developing world are generally immune to HA. Persons with a history of hepatitis or who previously lived in an endemic country for a prolonged period may benefit from pre-vaccination serum antibody testing.

Hepatitis B (HB)

Pre-travel HB vaccination is indicated for all non-vaccinated travelers with standard indications such as health care workers as well as for all long-stay travelers who will be residing in high or moderate risk areas (see Fig. 328-2). Transmission via routes such as sexual transmission, blood transfusions, contaminated medical equipment, body-piercing, tattooing, acupuncture, sharing of cooking and bathroom facilities is difficult to control or predict in the context of travel. Vaccination is increasingly advocated for short-term travelers, especially younger travelers and those anticipating close contact with local populations even if they have no specific risk factors. Adventure travelers (accident-prone), backpackers, and those with underlying medical conditions are more likely to require contact with the medical system. Business and other regular travelers that fly internationally on multiple but short trips have a cumulative risk that increases with time and such individ-

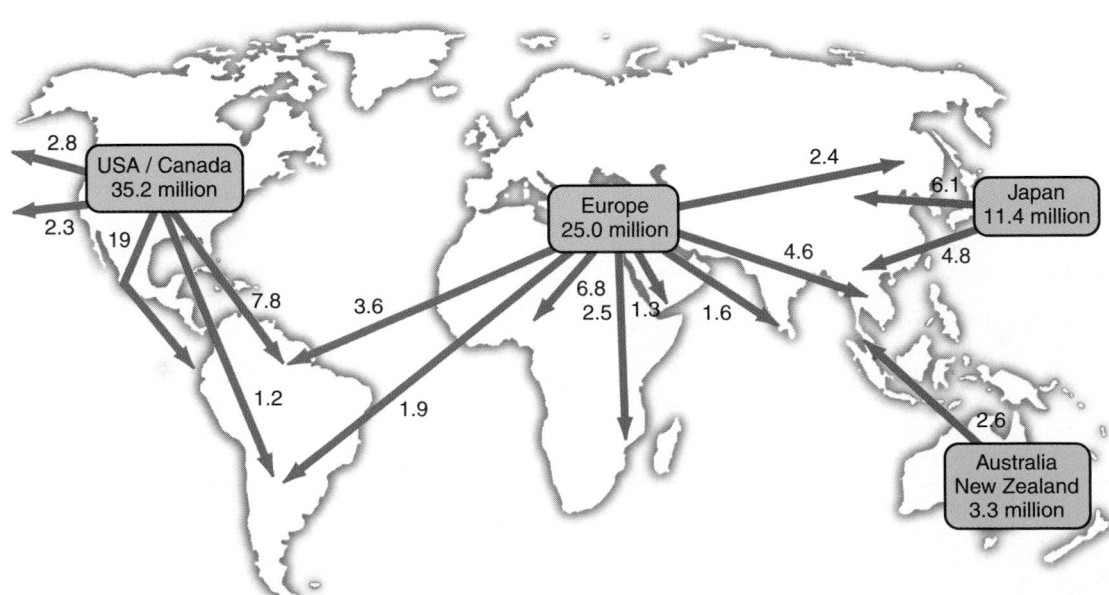

FIGURE 328-1. Number of travelers from industrialized regions of the world to developing regions in 1999. *(Data from the World Tourism Organization. Reprinted with permission of Professor Robert Steffen, Zurich.)*

TABLE 328-3 Travel-Related Vaccines of Adults

Disease	Vaccine	Primary Course	Route	Booster
Vaccines to Consider for all Destinations				
Hepatitis A	Killed virus	0, 6-18 mo*	IM	None
Hepatitis B	Recombinant viral antigen	0, 1, 6 mo **A:** 0, 1, 2, + 12 mo **A:** 0, 1, 3 wk + 12 mo†	IM	None
Hepatitis A/B	Combination of monovalent preparations	0, 1, 6 mo **A:** 0, 1, 3 wk + 12 mo†	IM	None
Typhoid	Capsular Vi polysaccharide	Single dose	IM	2-3 yr
	Live attenuated Ty21a bacteria	0, 2, 4, 6 days	Oral	5 yr
Influenza	Inactivated viral	Single dose	IM	Annual
	Live attenuated virus	Single dose	Nasal	Annual
Varicella	Live attenuated virus	0, 4-8 wk	SC	None
Vaccines for Selected Destinations				
Yellow Fever	Live attenuated 17D virus	Single dose	SC	10 yr
Meningococcus	Quadrivalent polysaccharide (A, C, Y, W135)	Single dose	SC	3 yr
Rabies	Inactivated cell culture viral	0, 7, 21-28 days	IM‡	None routinely but two doses after each exposure
Japanese encephalitis	Inactivated viral	0, 7, 30 days **A:** 0, 7, 14 days	SC	3 yr; 2 yr after accelerated
Polio§	Inactivated viral	Single dose if adequate childhood series	SC; IM acceptable	None
Cholera‖	Live attenuated CVD 103-HgR bacterial	Single dose	Oral	6 mo
	Killed bacteria + recombinant B toxin subunit¶	0, 1 wk	Oral	2 yr for cholera; 3 mo for ETEC
Tick-borne encephalitis**	Inactivated viral	0, 1-3 mo, 9-12 mo	IM	3 yr

*Second dose may be delayed up to 60 months without diminshed efficacy.
†Regimen not FDA approved but approved in other countries or in widespread clinical usage.
‡Intradermal rabies pre-exposure vaccine is no longer produced and the intramuscular preparations should not be used intradermally.
§Oral polio vaccine is no longer produced in the USA.
‖Not available in the US but available in Canada and most European countries. No cholera vaccine of any kind currently available in the USA.
¶Also licensed in some countries for travelers diarrhea due to enterotoxigenic *E. coli.*
**Not available in US but available in endemic areas and in Canada and the UK by special release.
A: Accelerated regimen to be used for imminent departures.

uals should receive the HB vaccine. Accelerated and hyper-accelerated schedules (see Table 328-3) are used widely in practice and are approved in many countries.[13(pp82-86),15] These are helpful in administering all three primary doses necessary for high assurance of protection in the frequent circumstance where the traveler is leaving in a very short time and is at risk of HB exposure.

Combination Hepatitis A/B Vaccine

The combined HA and HB vaccine provides convenience for travelers with an overlap of indications for the use of the individual vaccines.[16,17] The accelerated schedule (see Table 328-3) is licensed in many countries but not yet in the United States.[18]

Typhoid

Typhoid vaccine is indicated for all travelers to the Indian subcontinent and considered for those travelling to other endemic areas (see Fig. 328-2) under all but the most deluxe and protected of conditions. Risk increases with trip duration, lodging/eating with local people, extent of travel off usual tourist itineraries.[9,19] In risk areas, food and water precautions should still be rigorously followed as typhoid vaccines are only from 53% to 72% protective[20,21] and a large oral inoculum may overwhelm even an optimal antibody response. Adherence to the oral vaccine regimen may be as low as 70%.[22,23]

Influenza

Influenza is transmitted year round in the tropics. Increasing data shows that influenza may be the most common vaccine preventable illness in travelers.[24-26] All travelers and not just those with usual indications may benefit from vaccine and the availability of mucosal vaccines may enhance acceptance of this strategy. An increased risk of influenza has been reported among cruise ship passengers.[27] The most recently available influenza vaccine should be used for travelers.[28]

Vaccines to Consider Only for Certain Destinations

Yellow Fever (YF)

The primary indication for YF vaccination is to prevent infection in individuals at risk. However, YF is currently the only vaccine that falls under the International Health Regulations (IHR) which may necessitate vaccination purely for regulatory reasons (see below). Neither YF vaccine, nor any other vaccine, is currently required to return to the United States. In general, all healthy adult travelers to endemic areas (see Fig. 328-2) should be vaccinated. The endemic area may be restricted to only a portion of a country. Because of rare but serious vaccine-associated adverse side effects (see Chapter 319), persons who are not at any risk of exposure should not be vaccinated.[29] Urban YF does not occur in South America but a number of urban areas are considered at imminent risk. Short-term travel restricted to very large urban areas in the endemic zone of South America carries negligible, if any, risk but the situation may change rapidly. It is prudent to vaccinate persons that have anything less than a definite fixed itinerary and who will travel anywhere close to endemic regions.

Only a small number of African countries (Benin, Burkina Faso, Central African Republic, Cameroon, Congo, Cote D'Ivoire, Democratic Republic of Congo, Gabon, Ghana, Liberia, Mali, Mauritania, Niger, Rwanda, Sao Tome, Togo) and one in South America (French Guiana) require proof of yellow fever vaccination from all arriving travelers. Other countries, both within and outside the endemic zone, have designated to WHO more complex requirements. They may require an official vaccination certificate only for individuals arriving directly from or via (may include a brief transit stop) a country in the yellow fever endemic zone but not from arriving travelers from other countries. These YF-free countries usually have the conditions and vectors to initiate a YF transmission cycle, and the purpose of the vaccine requirement is to prevent entry of viremic travelers. Current country-by-country YF entry requirements are at *www.who.int/ith*. The requirement often applies even if the

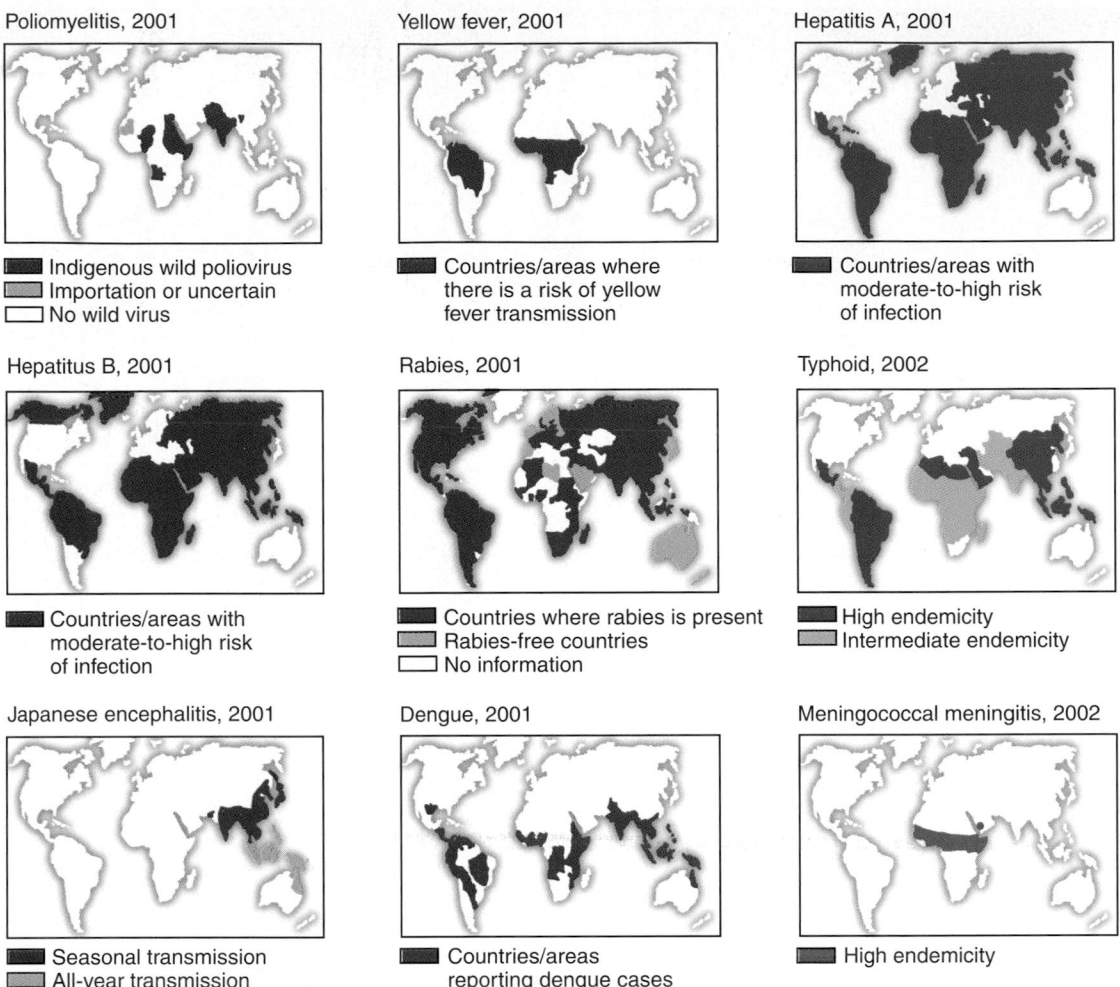

FIGURE 328-2. Worldwide distribution of important travel-related diseases. *(Reprinted with permission of Elsevier [The Lancet 2003;361:1372] and the World Health Organization <www.who.int/ith/diseasemaps-index.html>.)*

arriving traveler has not visited an area within a country of departure that is endemic for YF.

A special permit, obtainable in the United States from State Health Departments, is required to legally stamp an international certificate of vaccination as an authorized YF vaccine center. Under WHO regulations, authorized centers can also issue a letter of waiver that can be provided to travelers that have medical contraindications to receiving YF vaccination. There are no other acceptable reasons for exemption from vaccination. Letters of waiver are most appropriate for individuals needing a certificate purely for regulatory reasons. For those with contraindications to vaccination (see Chapter 319) who will actually visit an endemic area, waiver letters should be given with great reluctance. The variable risk within the endemic regions of the world needs to be considered (in consultation with an expert if necessary) and cancellation of travel strongly recommended if risk on the actual itinerary is more than negligible. A YF certificate becomes valid for entry 10 days after it is stamped and dated and although officially valid for 10 years, the true duration of immunity from YF vaccination is probably much longer and may exceed 30 years. A few countries may enforce YF regulations on individuals who have been in endemic areas as much as 30 days previously even though the IHR recognize only up to a 6-day requirement.

Meningococcal

Meningococcal vaccine is recommended for travelers to Africa's sub-Saharan "meningitis belt" (see Fig. 328-2) during the dry season from December through June, especially if prolonged contact with the local populace is likely.[30] Out of season epidemics have recently begun to

occur in Ethiopia, Somalia and Tanzania indicating possible changes in epidemiologic trends perhaps due to climatic changes.[31] Muslims undertaking Hajj and Umra pilgrimages in Saudi Arabia are at a higher risk of meningococcal disease and proof of vaccination with quadrivalent vaccine is required in order to obtain pilgrimage visas.[32]

Rabies

A pre-exposure rabies series is indicated for long-stay travel to endemic areas of Latin America, Asia, or Africa (see Fig. 328-2) where the rabies threat is constant and where access to adequate post-exposure rabies immune globulin and vaccine is likely to be limited. Countries with the highest risk of rabies include the Indian Subcontinent, Thailand, and some countries in Central and South America such as Brazil, Bolivia, Colombia, Ecuador, El Salvador, and Guatemala. For short-term travel, risk groups for whom immunization should be considered include, adventure travelers, bikers, hikers, cave explorers, or business travelers who travel for short but frequent trips and plan to go running outdoors on these trips.[33-35] Regardless of vaccination status travelers should be instructed to immediately cleanse well with soapy water any bite or animal scratch involving broken skin, and seek post-exposure treatment for rabies (see Chapter 160).

Japanese Encephalitis (JE)

JE is endemic only to certain uncommonly visited rural farming areas of Southeast Asia and the Indian sub-continent (see Fig. 328-2). In temperate regions the transmission is from April through November. In tropical or subtropical regions of Oceania and Southeast Asia transmission may occur year round. Vaccination is recommended for (1) long-stay travel to an endemic rural area; (2) expatriation to anywhere in an endemic country; (3) short-term travel to endemic rural areas with extensive unprotected outdoor exposure such as with adventure travel; or (4) short-term travel in the face of a current local epidemic.[36] JE vaccine has been associated with a unique delayed anaphylactic reaction (see Chapter 319).

Polio

Due to eradication efforts poliomyelitis remains only in a few countries with complete control anticipated by 2005 (see Fig. 328-2). Adults traveling to currently polio-endemic countries (updated information at www.polioeradication.org) and who have previously completed a primary vaccine series should receive a one-time single dose of inactivated polio vaccine as a booster if the last dose or booster dose was at least 10 years previously.

Cholera

Cholera vaccination is no longer required by any country and the risk to typical travelers is insignificant.[37] However, medical and aid workers staying for short periods in disaster areas or refugee camps may consider cholera vaccine. The parenteral inactivated vaccine has been officially disowned by WHO and effective newer oral vaccines are widely available outside the US.[38] The killed whole cell-B subunit vaccine also has about 60% efficacy against enterotoxigenic *E. coli* and has this indication in some countries.[39,40]

Tick-Borne Encephalitis (TBE)

TBE is an important and serious flavivirus central nervous system infection in endemic areas. Distribution is highly focal in a range that extends in a swath from Germany through Scandinavia and the Baltics to Siberia and Vladivostock in the east. Risk to travelers is low unless extensive outdoor activities are planned in forested regions in endemic areas.[41] Immunization against TBE is recommended for adventure travel, extensive outdoors exposure, or camping in the forests of the endemic countries between May and October. Tick precautions are also recommended. The vaccine is available in most endemic countries and by special release in Canada and the UK.

Spacing and Interactions of Travel-Related Vaccines[42]

All currently indicated immunizations can and should be given at the same time and in any combination. If two live viral antigens are not administered on the same day, they must be spaced by a month. However, YF vaccine can be given at any interval with respect to single antigen measles vaccine. Live oral vaccines (typhoid, polio) can be administered at any interval with respect to any live virus vaccine. Minimum intervals between vaccine doses must be respected though 4 or fewer days too early is now acceptable.[42] Regimens that involve 1-week intervals (rabies, JE, accelerated hepatitis) are exceptions. There is not a maximum interval between doses of a primary vaccine series; interrupted series (except oral typhoid) need not be re-started but can be resumed beginning with the dose that is overdue. Immune globulin and parenteral cholera vaccine, which do have interactions with some other vaccines, are no longer in use except in unusual circumstances. Anaphylactic egg allergy precludes administration of yellow fever, influenza and MMR vaccines. No current vaccine contains penicillin. Baseline PPD skin tests, often done in the pre-travel setting can be done on the day that live viral vaccines are administered or else must be done more than 4 weeks later. Anti-bacterial drugs should not be given within 24 hours of a dose of live oral typhoid or oral cholera vaccine. Concomitant mefloquine may interfere with oral typhoid vaccine.

MALARIA CHEMOPROPHYLAXIS

An average of 1300 imported cases of malaria are reported annually in the United States.[43] Estimates of risk in travelers not taking chemoprophylaxis vary widely by destination but range from 24/1000 travelers per month in West Africa to 2.5/1000 per month on the Indian sub-

continent to 0.5/1000 per month in South America.[3] The majority of cases of imported malaria in the United States and Europe occur in non-citizen immigrants visiting friends and relatives abroad.[44] Malaria chemoprophylactic drugs are underutilized by these ethnic minority travelers. Eighty percent of all imported falciparum malaria originates in Africa.

Choice of drug regimen must be individualized to the particular itinerary, duration of travel, the medical history, access to medical care abroad, and the travelers' personal tolerance for risk. Not all regions or cities within a malarious country are malarious. Resources describing current country-specific malaria microepidemiology should be immediately accessible to those prescribing malaria prophylaxis (see Table 328-2). In general, malaria is a rural disease but the cities of Africa and India are exceptions. Dosing and pharmaceutical properties of antimalarial drugs are described in Chapter 41. In the limited number of countries where it is still effective (Table 328-4) chloroquine 500 mg/week beginning the week prior to first malarious exposure and continuing for 4 weeks after last exposure is still the drug of choice.

For all other areas of the world, three drugs are equally efficacious and choice depends on both traveler and itinerary factors.[45] Atovaquone/proguanil 250/100 mg is a well tolerated, once/day drug beginning 1 day prior to arrival in the malarious area (may not coincide with first overseas destination) and for 7 days after the last exposure.[46-49] The short period of post-exposure use make it convenient for the many travelers on typical 1- to 3-week itineraries. High cost and daily dosing make it difficult to use for extended periods. Weekly mefloquine (250 mg) is given 1 to 2 weeks prior to first malarious exposure and continued for 4 weeks after. Weekly dosing and long track-record of efficacy make this drug the most effective for long-stay travelers. If contraindications to mefloquine exist for long-stay travelers, daily doxycycline (100 mg) beginning 1 day prior to exposure can be used, but unlike atovaquone/proguanil must be continued for 4 weeks post-exposure. Generic doxycycline is by far the cheapest of the antimalarials so it is attractive to both short and long-stay budget travelers. For travelers to chloroquine sensitive areas unable to tolerate chloroquine any of the 3 latter drugs would be effective. For either mefloquine or doxycycline, approximately 5% of individuals discontinue therapy due to side effects.[50] Chemoprophylaxis may be started well before departure (3 to 4 weeks for mefloquine) in those concerned about possible intolerance. Mefloquine has been associated with neuropsychiatric side effects in some[51] and should not be prescribed for those with active depression or recent history of depression, generalized anxiety disorder, psychosis, schizophrenia, or other major psychiatric disorder. It should be used with caution in patients with previous history of depression. If prodromal psychiatric symptoms occur during use, the drug should be discontinued and an alternative medication substituted. Doxycycline is an esophageal and gastric irritant. It needs to be taken with a full glass of water on a full stomach and the user should not go to sleep or lie down for 30 minutes after ingestion. Female travelers may get vaginal candidiasis and should carry self-therapy when prescribed doxycycline. The rare traveler intolerant of all of the three drugs may consider daily primaquine after consultation with a malaria expert and after G6PD

TABLE 328-4 Drugs of Choice for Malaria Chemoprophylaxis by Country*

Chloroquine
Mexico, Belize, Guatemala, El Salvador, Nicaragua, Costa Rica, Panama (only west of the canal zone), Haiti, Dominican Republic, Paraguay, Morocco, Algeria, Egypt, Turkey, Syria, Iraq, Georgia, Armenia, Uzbekistan, Turkmenistan, Kyrgyzstan, Azerbaijan.
Atovaquone/Proguanil or Mefloquine or Doxycline
(equal efficacy; choice depends on traveler and itinerary factors)
All other malarious areas of the world (see world malaria map Chapter 272, Fig. 272-6) except Thai-Cambodian and Thai-Burmese border areas where mefloquine is ineffective.

*Risk may only exist in limited or rarely visited areas in many countries. Consult WHO or CDC print or on-line resources (see Table 328-2) for specific risk areas within each country.

testing.[52,53] Tafenoquine, a long-acting primaquine analogue is a promising drug currently in development.[54,55] Chloroquine-resistant *P. vivax* only occurs in areas where the other drugs are already indicated for prophylaxis because of the concomitant presence of resistant *P. falciparum.* Atovaquone/proguanil efficacy against the non-life threatening forms of malaria (*P. vivax, P. ovale, and P. malariae*) has not been extensively studied but appears to be more than adequate with efficacy of at least 84% against *P. vivax.*[46]

Travelers need to be reminded in writing to continue antimalarial drugs for the appropriate period after the last possible exposure, that malaria can still occur despite chemoprophylaxis, and that a malaria smear is mandatory for any febrile illness occurring within 3 months of travel. None of the primary prophylactic drugs discussed above are effective against the dormant hepatic hypnozoites of *P. vivax* or *P. ovale* which may cause delayed relapses of malaria. Terminal prophylaxis refers to a regimen at the end of the exposure period to kill residual hynozoites of these two species. Per CDC guidelines updated in 2003, primaquine 30 mg base per day for 14 days, after checking G6PD levels, is indicated only for those with prolonged and extensive exposure to *P. vivax* or *P. ovale.*[13(pp99-116)] This effectively excludes most short-term travelers. Malaria chemoprophylaxis recommendations are liable to change periodically. Physicians may check the CDC or WHO travel websites (see Table 328-2) or call the CDC physician malaria hotline (770-488-7788) for the latest advice.

For stays in areas with very low transmission rates of malaria, some physicians, notably in Europe, may advise that only a standby drug be carried which is to be taken in the event that symptoms suggestive of malaria occur and that there is no access to a physician or facility that can perform a competent malaria smear within 6 to 12 hours.[56] This strategy is especially attractive for long-stay travelers. In areas with chloroquine-resistant *P. falciparum,* the drug of choice is atovaquone/proguanil four 250/100 tablets orally as a single daily dose for 3 consecutive days.[13(pp99-116)] In areas without chloroquine-resistant *P. falciparum,* chloroquine is the drug of choice.

TRAVELERS DIARRHEA (TD)

TD is the most common affliction of travelers to developing countries. Classic travelers' diarrhea is defined as three or more unformed stools per day combined with one clinical sign such as abdominal cramps, fever, nausea, or vomiting. The incidence varies from about 8% for travel to highly developed countries to about 20% in southern Europe, Israel, Japan, South Africa, and some Caribbean islands. In most developing countries the risk is 20% to 66% in the first 2 weeks abroad and subsides somewhat thereafter. The most frequent cause of TD is enterotoxigenic *Escherichia coli* (6% to 70%). Other types of *E. coli, Salmonella, Shigella,* and *Campylobacter* each account for about 5% to 15%. Enteroaggregative *E. coli* are playing an emerging role in TD. Protozoa account for less than 5% and in adults, rarely, norovirus or rotavirus may be detected. Norovirus outbreaks aboard cruise ships are apparently increasing.[57] About 30% of diarrheal episodes remain unexplained but many apparently are of bacterial origin, because they respond to antibacterials.[58-63] Those taking proton-pump inhibitor drugs (but not those on H2 blockers), those who are naturally achlorhydric, as well as young adults between 20 and 29 years of age have increased risk. The mean duration of TD even if untreated is 4 days.

Antibiotic prophylaxis for diarrhea is contraindicated for the typical traveler because of potential adverse drug effects while away from medical care, and because effective rapid onset therapy is available for diarrhea should it occur. However, chemoprophylaxis can be considered for travelers with advanced HIV infection, an underlying chronic medical problem that makes them more prone to adverse consequences from diarrhea, and for those on a vital mission for a short period (less than 1 week) who cannot tolerate even a day of disability. Antibiotic prophylaxis should be with a quinolone once per day and should only be used for trips of 2 weeks or less.

The risk of travelers' diarrhea can be reduced but not eliminated by educating the traveler to avoid dietary indiscretions. Nevertheless, increasing evidence suggests surprisingly small differences in the incidence of travelers' diarrhea in individuals self-reporting meticulous as compared to adventurous eating habits.[59,63] All travelers to the developing world should be thoroughly educated in self-therapy for diarrheal disease (Fig. 328-3) and carry the appropriate agents while traveling.[64,65] Eighty percent of patients respond to this regimen within 24 hours. A significant increase in quinolone resistant *Campylobacter* in Southeast Asia and India is emerging. Instructions on when to seek medical care should be given. Azithromycin is the current alternate therapy.[64-66] Rifaximin is a newly licensed nonabsorbable rifamycin derivative that can be used in adults for traveler's diarrhea due to *E. coli.*[67,68] Rifaximin is not recommended when the patient has fever or blood in the stool.

KEY PREVENTIVE BEHAVIORS

Most travel-related health problems, including many significant infectious diseases can be significantly reduced through appropriate behavior by the traveler.[69]

Personal Protection against Arthropods

Antimalarial chemoprophylactic drugs are less than 100% effective. Arthropod protection will help prevent dengue,[70] leishmaniasis, filariasis, and a number of important arboviral diseases. Travelers should be instructed to: clothe themselves to reduce as much exposed skin as practicable; apply a repellent containing DEET (concentration 30% to 35%) to all exposed nonsensitive areas of the body every 6 hours;[71,72] sleep under a permethrin impregnated bed net in malarious areas unless in a sealed air-conditioned environment. When at especially high risk, treat outer clothing with permethrin.[73] While anophelines are night biters *Aedes* spp. and culicine mosquitoes are usually day-biters so vigilance at all times of day is necessary.

Protection against Foodborne Disease

Travelers to developing countries should be diligent in: washing hands frequently; avoiding food from dubious eating places, markets, and roadside vendors; avoiding buffets where there are no food covers or fly controls; avoiding high risk food such as shellfish, reef fish (ciguatera risk), undercooked meats and poultry, dairy products, unpeeled fruits, cold sauces and salads; avoid both tap water and drinks or ice made from tap water; using sealed bottled water or chemically treated, filtered, or boiled water for drinking and brushing teeth.[74]

Sex

Education on the incidence of HIV and STDs amongst professional sex workers abroad, on the usage of condoms, and on the failure rate of condoms (3% to 5% breakage/slippage) should be given regardless of apparent circumstances of the traveler. Unprotected sex even with fellow travelers is high risk. Travel is a disinhibiting experience in itself and alcohol consumption tends to increase during travel. Between 19% and 26% of all travelers report a new sexual contact during their last trip abroad.[3,75,76] Condom use during casual travel sex is uniformly below 25% even in those who had received pre-travel counseling. Discussion of emergency contraception strategies for female travelers is sometimes appropriate.

Protection against Blood-Borne Disease

Blood, blood products, syringes, and contaminated medical or dental instruments are a risk following accidents or trauma. Travelers should consider carrying an infusion set, needles and a suture kit for high-risk areas. If possible, they should defer medical treatment and travel to a facility where safety can be assured. Tattooing, acupuncture, and body-piercing carry similar risks. Health care workers and others at risk in high HIV prevalence areas without sophisticated medical infrastructure may consider carrying a 1- to 2-week supply of Combivir (zidovudine/3TC), possibly with a protease inhibitor, in order to begin immediate post-exposure prophylaxis. The understanding must be that this is only an initial measure to allow time for

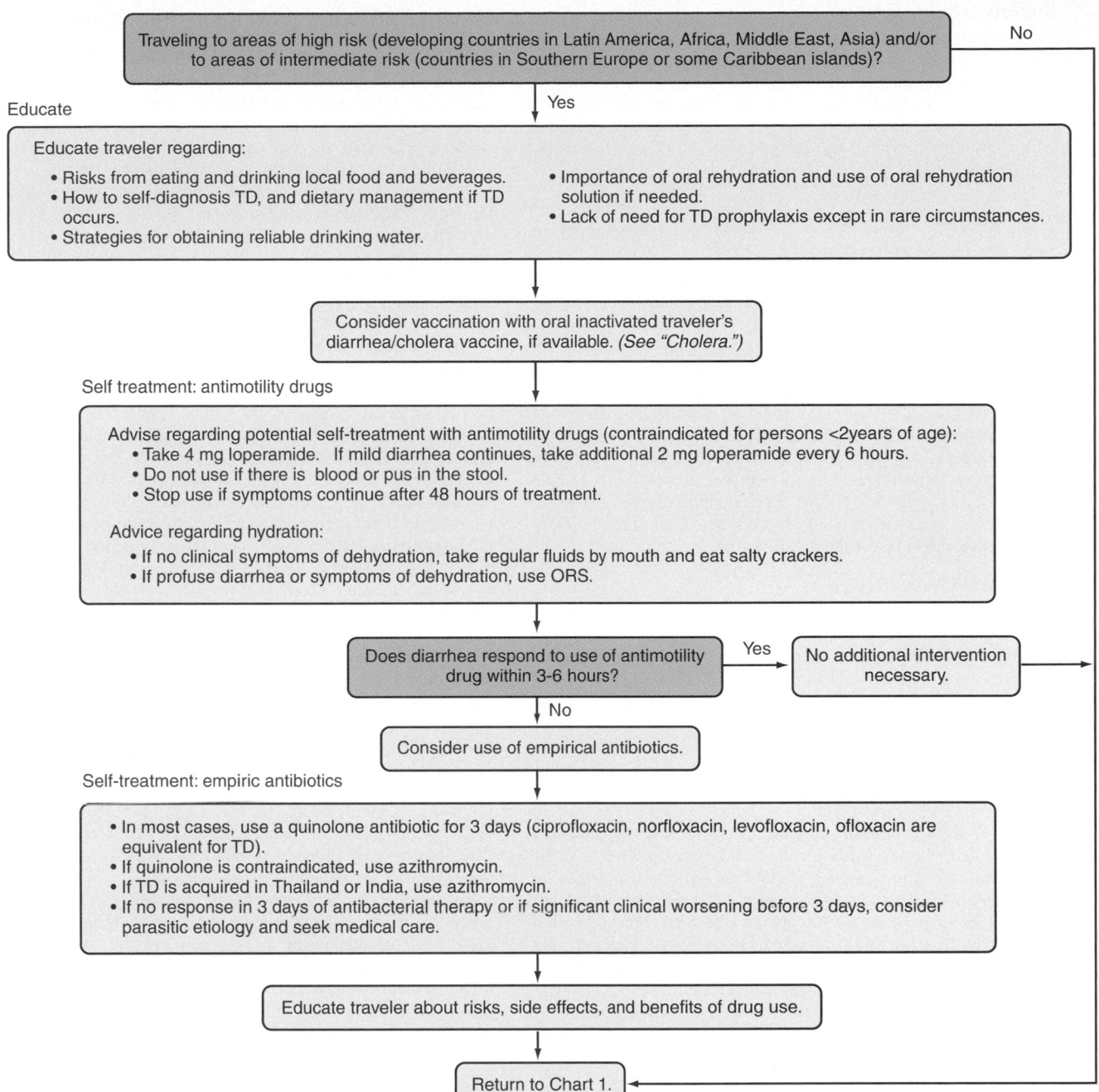

FIGURE 328-3. Algorithm for traveler standby self-treatment of travelers diarrhea (TD). *(Reprinted from Travax Encompass with permission of Shoreland, Inc.)*

travel to an adequate medical facility able to provide sophisticated testing and counseling.

Protection against Skin Diseases

Infected mosquito bites are common. Good hand hygiene in dirty environments and covering open wounds are preventive. Scabies and lice are prevented by personal hygiene. In Africa, all clothes dried outdoors should be ironed to avoid cutaneous myiasis due to the tumbu fly.[77] Hats and sun screen are mandatory in the tropics.[78] Sun screen should always be applied to skin before, and not after, application of DEET.

Protection against Pathogens Due to Swimming and Water Exposure

Travelers should be instructed on avoidance of recreational (swimming, rafting, wading) or other exposure to fresh water in schistosomiasis endemic areas.[79] Hikers, bikers, and adventure travelers should consider prophylaxis with 200 mg doxycycline once per week due to the significant risk of leptospirosis that exists in fresh water throughout the developing world.[80] Walking barefoot in tropical areas predisposes to hookworm, strongyloides, cutaneous larva migrans, and tungiasis.

Prevention of Tuberculosis

A pre-departure baseline tuberculin skin test with annual re-testing is indicated for long-stay travelers to developing countries.[81] Aggressive treatment of skin-test converters will prevent cases of active tuberculosis later. Travelers should avoid crowded public transportation or crowded public places and distance themselves immediately from anyone with a chronic or heavy cough. Expatriates should screen domestic help for tuberculosis.

NON-INFECTIOUS TRAVEL PROBLEMS

Medical Kit and Medical Care Abroad

Travelers should carry a compact medical kit. In addition to items mentioned elsewhere in the chapter, simple first-aid supplies like bandages, gauze, antiseptic, antibiotic ointment, and splinter forceps will allow early self-treatment of minor wounds before infection ensues. A thermometer to document elevations in temperature should be carried along with antipyretics. Antifungal creams, cough/cold remedies, antacids, hydrocortisone cream, and blister pads should be considered. The contact details of hometown medical providers should be recorded and accessible at all times. Long-stay travelers should plug themselves into the local expatriate medical infrastructure immediately after arrival so as to be able to rapidly seek competent care for any ensuing illness early in its course. Adequate medical and evacuation insurance should be arranged. A copy of a recent EKG should be carried by all cardiac patients.

Airline Related Morbidity

A causal relationship between travel-related immobility and deep venous thrombosis/pulmonary embolism in otherwise healthy travelers is not established.[82-84] Those with previously covert coagulopathies may manifest for the first time during travel. Those with clear known risk factors are at highest risk. These include: a personal or family history of deep venous thrombosis or pulmonary embolism; a personal or family history of a known blood clotting disorder predisposing to thrombosis; major surgery, significant trauma, or prolonged immobilization (includes limb casts) in the last 6 weeks; malignancy; late pregnancy; estrogen therapy including oral contraceptives; age over 50 years; severe obesity; chronic venous insufficiency. All travelers should avoid dehydration, avoid alcohol, and exercise the legs regularly in flight. Regimens including single-dose aspirin or prophylactic subcutaneous low-molecular weight heparin just prior to departure are being studied but at present have no proven role even if they are often used in practice[85] for high risk travelers. Jet lag occurs after crossing three or more time zones and zolpidem taken for a few nights at bedtime at the destination is effective.[86] Those prone to motion sickness should sit in the center of airplanes, boats, or other conveyance and visually fix on distant objects.[87] Meclizine or scopolamine is of benefit. Most in-flight medical emergencies are related to underlying illnesses[88] and are difficult to predict at the time of the pre-travel consultation. To avoid decompression sickness established waiting periods for flying after diving have been established.[89]

Altitude

Whether ascending by car or airplane, acute mountain sickness occurs in at least 25% of people who rapidly ascend to 2500 m or more and in most people who go quickly to 3000 m or more. Gradual ascent over days is rarely practiced by modern travelers. For prevention of altitude illness, acetazolamide 125 to 250 mg twice a day beginning the morning of the day before ascent and continuing through the day after ascent is effective. If symptoms of mountain sickness such as nausea, vomiting, anorexia, light-headedness, fatigue, or insomnia, persist beyond the day after ascent, travelers may continue to take one tablet each evening.[90] Severe complications such as pulmonary or cerebral edema occur uncommonly under 3500 m and are best treated by oxygen and immediate descent. Those traveling above 3500 m for longer than a brief transit of a few hours should consult an expert.

TRAVELLING ADULTS WITH SPECIAL NEEDS

Immunocompromised and HIV-Infected Travelers

Immunocompromised travelers are at risk for a complication or exacerbation of the underlying disease in a medically unfamiliar or underserved destination. The potential traveler needs to understand the risks of the trip in the context of their personal situation.[91] Precautions for malaria (including chemoprophylaxis), food- and water-borne diseases, and vector-borne diseases generally don't differ from those for healthy travelers. Live vaccines (yellow fever, varicella, measles, oral typhoid, oral polio) should be avoided in those who are truly immune compromised, even if the result is deferral of the trip. Other vaccines, while safe, will likely have sub-optimal efficacy in compromised hosts and the implications of this need to be discussed with the traveler.[92]

HIV infected individuals[93] with adequate immune function (CD4 counts in the 500/mm^3 or more range) as well as travelers using less than 20 mg prednisone daily for greater than 2 weeks are not at risk of infection and can be immunized as normal. Those on short courses (<2 weeks) of high dose steroids, steroid inhalers, and those who have received intra-articular steroids can be treated as normal hosts. However, asymptomatic HIV-infected individuals, even with adequate immune function should be given a waiver letter if the only reason for YF vaccination is to fulfill regulatory requirements. In those discontinuing truly immunosuppressive drugs, a 1-month waiting period before administration of live vaccines is advisable. Individuals with hematologic malignancies in remission should wait 3 months after last chemotherapy before receiving live virus vaccines. Individuals with low-grade immune defects such as chronic renal, hepatic or endocrine disease should be counselled regarding increased risks of various infections, but no changes in pre-travel immunizations are generally indicated. Functionally hyposplenic individuals should be vaccinated against pneumococci, meningococci, *H. influenzae* type B, and influenza if not already done. The elderly may have sub-optimal responses to many travel-related vaccines.[94]

The Pregnant Traveler

Pregnancy presents many complex issues for travel,[13(pp229-240),95] especially with regard to many commonly used travel medications. Determination of direct maternal-fetal related contraindications to travel should be handled by the obstetrician. Travel is best undertaken in the second trimester. In general, pregnant travelers should not be given live vaccines. Yellow fever vaccine should be given only when the risk of contracting the disease is substantial and travel cannot be discouraged by the physician. Even killed vaccines are best delayed until the second trimester if possible. Hepatitis A and B, tetanus, and meningococcal vaccine can be given without reservation. Other killed vaccines such as rabies, JE, typhoid, Hib, and pneumococcal should be given on a case by case basis when risk is high. In general, pregnant women should not travel to a malarious area unless the travel is absolutely necessary. Chloroquine is safe if travel is to one of the few countries where it is still the drug of choice (see Table 328-4). For other countries mefloquine is recommended and likely safe but there are not extensive data on its safe use during pregnancy, especially during the first trimester. Doxycycline, atovaquone/proguanil, and primaquine should not be used during pregnancy. Most experts now consider azithromycin the treatment of choice for TD in pregnancy. Skiing, scuba diving, water skiing, and high altitude travel are not advisable during pregnancy. No vaccine affects the safety of breast-feeding. Mefloquine and chloroquine are safe during breastfeeding. Insufficient data are available for doxycycline, atovaquone/proguanil, or primaquine. Twenty percent DEET used sparingly is safe in pregnancy.[96,97]

REFERENCES

1. Keystone JS, Kozarsky PE, Freedman DO. Internet and computer-based resources for travel medicine practitioners. Clin Infect Dis. 2001;32:757-765.
2. Kozarsky PE, Keystone JS. Body of knowledge for the practice of travel medicine. J Travel Med. 2002;9:112-115.

3. Steffen R, deBernardis C, Banos A. Travel epidemiology—A global perspective. Int J Antimicrob Agents. 2003;21:89-95.

4. Hill DR. Health problems in a large cohort of Americans traveling to developing countries. J Travel Med. 2000;7:259-266.

5. Steffen R, Rickenbach M, Wilhelm U, et al. Health problems after travel to developing countries. J Infect Dis. 1987;156:84-91.

6. Hargarten SW, Baker TD, Guptill K. Overseas fatalities of United States citizen travelers: An analysis of deaths related to international travel. Ann Emerg Med. 1991;20:622-626.

7. Guptill KS, Hargarten SW, Baker TD. American travel deaths in Mexico. Causes and prevention strategies. West J Med. 1991;154:169-171.

8. MacPherson DW, Guerillot F, Streiner DL, et al. Death and dying abroad: The Canadian experience. J Travel Med. 2000;7:227-233.

9. Steffen R, Banos A, deBernardis C. Vaccination priorities. Int J Antimicrob Agents. 2003;21:175-180.

10. Monath TP, Cetron MS. Prevention of yellow fever in persons traveling to the tropics. Clin Infect Dis. 2002;34:1369-1378.

11. Recommended adult immunization schedule—United States, 2002-2003. MMWR Morb Mortal Wkly Rep. 2002;51:904-908.

12. Taliani G, Gaeta GB. Hepatitis A: Post-exposure prophylaxis. Vaccine. 2003;21:2234-2237.

13. Centers for Disease Control and Prevention. Health Information for International Travel 2003-4. Atlanta: U.S. Department of Health and Human Services, Public Health Service; 2003:75-81.

14. Prevention of hepatitis A through active or passive immunization: Recommendations of the Advisory Committee on Immunization Practices (ACIP). MMWR Recomm Rep. 1999;48:1-37.

15. Marchou B, Excler JL, Bourderioux C, et al. A 3-week hepatitis B vaccination schedule provides rapid and persistent protective immunity: A multicenter, randomized trial comparing accelerated and classic vaccination schedules. J Infect Dis. 1995;172:258-260.

16. Joines RW, Blatter M, Abraham B, et al. A prospective, randomized, comparative US trial of a combination hepatitis A and B vaccine (Twinrix) with corresponding monovalent vaccines (Havrix and Engerix-B) in adults. Vaccine. 2001;19:4710-4719.

17. Thoelen S, Van Damme P, Leentvaar-Kuypers A, et al. The first combined vaccine against hepatitis A and B: An overview. Vaccine. 1999;17:1657-1662.

18. Nothdurft HD, Dietrich M, Zuckerman JN, et al. A new accelerated vaccination schedule for rapid protection against hepatitis A and B. Vaccine. 2002;20:1157-1162.

19. Mermin JH, Townes JM, Gerber M, et al. Typhoid fever in the United States, 1985-1994: Changing risks of international travel and increasing antimicrobial resistance. Arch Intern Med. 1998;158:633-638.

20. Typhoid vaccines. Wkly Epidemiol Rec. 2000;75:257-264.

21. Parry CM, Hien TT, Dougan G, et al. Typhoid fever. N Engl J Med. 2002;347:1770-1782.

22. Rahman S, Barr W, Hilton E. Use of oral typhoid vaccine strain Ty21a in a New York state travel immunization facility. Am J Trop Med Hyg. 1993;48:823-826.

23. Stubi CL, Landry PR, Petignat C, et al. Compliance to live oral Ty21a typhoid vaccine, and its effect on viability. J Travel Med. 2000;7:133-137.

24. Leder K, Sundararajan V, Weld L, et al. Respiratory tract infections in travelers: A review of the GeoSentinel surveillance network. Clin Infect Dis. 2003;36:399-406.

25. Jefferson T, Bianco E, Demicheli V. Influenza vaccines in adults. Occup Med (Lond). 2002;52:255-258.

26. Ahmed F, Singleton JA, Franks AL. Clinical practice. Influenza vaccination for healthy young adults. N Engl J Med. 2001;345:1543-1547.

27. Miller JM, Tam TW, Maloney S, et al. Cruise ships: High-risk passengers and the global spread of new influenza viruses. Clin Infect Dis. 2000;31:433-438.

28. Bridges CB, Harper SA, Fukuda K, et al. Prevention and control of influenza. Recommendations of the Advisory Committee on Immunization Practices (ACIP). MMWR Recomm Rep. 2003;52:1-34.

29. Cetron MS, Marfin AA, Julian KG, et al. Yellow fever vaccine. Recommendations of the Advisory Committee on Immunization Practices (ACIP), 2002. MMWR Recomm Rep. 2002;51:1-11.

30. Prevention and control of meningococcal disease. Recommendations of the Advisory Committee on Immunization Practices (ACIP). MMWR Recomm Rep. 2000;49:1-10.

31. Meningococcal disease, Ethiopia. Wkly Epidemiol Rec. 2000;75:273.

32. Memish ZA. Meningococcal disease and travel. Clin Infect Dis. 2002;34:84-90.

33. Human rabies prevention—United States, 1999. Recommendations of the Advisory Committee on Immunization Practices (ACIP). MMWR Recomm Rep. 1999;48:1-21.

34. An Advisory Committee Statement (ACS). Committee to Advise on Tropical Medicine and Travel (CATMAT). Statement on travellers and rabies vaccine. Can Commun Dis Rep. 2002;28:1-12.

35. Plotkin SA. Rabies. Clin Infect Dis. 2000;30:4-12.

36. Shlim DR, Solomon T. Japanese encephalitis vaccine for travelers: Exploring the limits of risk. Clin Infect Dis. 2002;35:183-188.

37. Wittlinger F, Steffen R, Watanabe H, Handszuh H. Risk of cholera among western and Japanese travelers. J Travel Med. 1995;2:154-158.

38. Ryan ET, Calderwood SB. Cholera vaccines. Clin Infect Dis 2000;31:561-565.

39. Cholera vaccines. Wkly Epidemiol Rec. 2001;76:117-124.

40. Scerpella EG, Sanchez JL, Mathewson IJ, et al. Safety, immunogenicity, and protective efficacy of the whole-cell/recombinant B subunit (WC/rBS) oral cholera vaccine against travelers' diarrhea. J Travel Med. 1995;2:22-27.

41. Dumpis U, Crook D, Oksi J. Tick-borne encephalitis. Clin Infect Dis. 1999;28:882-890.

42. Atkinson WL, Pickering LK, Schwartz B, et al. General recommendations on immunization. Recommendations of the Advisory Committee on Immunization Practices (ACIP) and the American Academy of Family Physicians (AAFP). MMWR Recomm Rep. 2002;51:1-35.

43. Newman RD, Barber AM, Roberts J, et al. Malaria surveillance—United States, 1999. MMWR Surveill Summ. 2002;51:15-28.

44. Schlagenhauf P, Loutan L. Migrants as a major risk group for imported malaria in European countries. J Travel Med. 2003;10:106-107.

45. Kain KC, Shanks GD, Keystone JS. Malaria chemoprophylaxis in the age of drug resistance. I. Currently recommended drug regimens. Clin Infect Dis. 2001;33:226-234.

46. Ling J, Baird JK, Fryauff DJ, et al. Randomized, placebo-controlled trial of atovaquone/proguanil for the prevention of *Plasmodium falciparum* or *Plasmodium vivax* malaria among migrants to Papua, Indonesia. Clin Infect Dis. 2002;35:825-833.

47. Overbosch D, Schilthuis H, Bienzle U, et al. Atovaquone-proguanil versus mefloquine for malaria prophylaxis in nonimmune travelers: Results from a randomized, double-blind study. Clin Infect Dis. 2001;33:1015-1021.

48. Overbosch D. Post-marketing surveillance: Adverse events during long-term use of atovaquone/proguanil for travelers to malaria-endemic countries. J Travel Med. 2003;10(Suppl 1):16-19.

49. Petersen E. The safety of atovaquone/proguanil in long-term malaria prophylaxis of nonimmune adults. J Travel Med. 2003;10(Suppl 1):13-14.

50. Schlagenhauf P. Mefloquine for malaria chemoprophylaxis 1992-1998: A review. J Travel Med. 1999;6:122-133.

51. Schlagenhauf P, Steffen R. Neuropsychiatric events and travel: Do antimalarials play a role? J Travel Med. 2000;7:225-226.

52. Soto J, Toledo J, Rodriquez M, et al. Primaquine prophylaxis against malaria in nonimmune Colombian soldiers: Efficacy and toxicity. A randomized, double-blind, placebo-controlled trial. Ann Intern Med. 1998;129:241-244.

53. Baird JK, Lacy MD, Basri H, et al. Randomized, parallel placebo-controlled trial of primaquine for malaria prophylaxis in Papua, Indonesia. Clin Infect Dis. 2001;33:1990-1997.

54. Shanks GD, Kain KC, Keystone JS. Malaria chemoprophylaxis in the age of drug resistance. II. Drugs that may be available in the future. Clin Infect Dis. 2001;33:381-385.

55. Hale BR, Owusu-Agyei S, Fryauff DJ, et al. A randomized, double-blind, placebo-controlled, dose-ranging trial of tafenoquine for weekly prophylaxis against *Plasmodium falciparum*. Clin Infect Dis. 2003;36:541-549.

56. Schlagenhauf P, Steffen R. Stand-by treatment of malaria in travellers: A review. J Trop Med Hyg. 1994;97:151-160.

57. Outbreaks of gastroenteritis associated with noroviruses on cruise ships—United States, 2002. MMWR Morb Mortal Wkly Rep. 2002;51:1112-1115.

58. Adachi JA, Jiang ZD, Mathewson JJ, et al. Enteroaggregative *Escherichia coli* as a major etiologic agent in traveler's diarrhea in 3 regions of the world. Clin Infect Dis. 2001;32:1706-1709.

59. Hoge CW, Shlim DR, Echeverria P, et al. Epidemiology of diarrhea among expatriate residents living in a highly endemic environment. JAMA. 1996;275:533-538.

60. Paredes P, Campbell-Forrester S, Mathewson JJ, et al. Etiology of travelers' diarrhea on a Caribbean island. J Travel Med. 2000;7:15-18.

61. Shlim DR, Hoge CW, Rajah R, et al. Persistent high risk of diarrhea among foreigners in Nepal during the first 2 years of residence. Clin Infect Dis. 1999;29:613-616.

62. Steffen R, Collard F, Tornieporth N, et al. Epidemiology, etiology, and impact of traveler's diarrhea in Jamaica. JAMA. 1999;281:811-817.

63. von Sonnenburg F, Tornieporth N, Waiyaki P, et al. Risk and aetiology of diarrhoea at various tourist destinations. Lancet. 2000;356:133-134.

64. An Advisory Committee Statement (ACS). Statement on travellers' diarrhea. Can Commun Dis Rep. 2001;27:1-12.

65. Ericsson CD. Travellers' diarrhoea. Int J Antimicrob Agents. 2003;21:116-124.

66. Shanks GD, Smoak BL, Aleman GM, et al. Single dose of azithromycin or three-day course of ciprofloxacin as therapy for epidemic dysentery in Kenya. Acute Dysentery Study Group. Clin Infect Dis. 1999;29:942-943.

67. DuPont HL, Jiang ZD, Ericsson CD, et al. Rifaximin versus ciprofloxacin for the treatment of traveler's diarrhea: A randomized, double-blind clinical trial. Clin Infect Dis. 2001;33:1807-1815.

68. Steffen R, Sack DA, Riopel L, et al. Therapy of travelers' diarrhea with rifaximin on various continents. Am J Gastroenterol. 2003;98:1073-1078.

69. Ryan ET, Kain KC. Health advice and immunizations for travelers. N Engl J Med. 2000;342:1716-1725.

70. Jelinek T. Dengue fever in international travelers. Clin Infect Dis. 2000;31:144-147.

71. Fradin MS. Mosquitoes and mosquito repellents: A clinician's guide. Ann Intern Med. 1998;128:931-940.

72. Fradin MS, Day JF. Comparative efficacy of insect repellents against mosquito bites. N Engl J Med. 2002;347:13-18.

73. Soto J, Medina F, Dember N, Berman J. Efficacy of permethrin-impregnated uniforms in the prevention of malaria and leishmaniasis in Colombian soldiers. Clin Infect Dis. 1995;21:599-602.

74. Backer H. Water disinfection for international and wilderness travelers. Clin Infect Dis. 2002;34:355-364.

75. Cabada MM, Echevarria JI, Seas CR, et al. Sexual behavior of international travelers visiting Peru. Sex Transm Dis. 2002;29:510-513.

76. Mulhall BP. Sex and travel: Studies of sexual behaviour, disease and health promotion in international travellers—A global review. Int J STD AIDS. 1996;7:455-465.

77. Caumes E, Carriere J, Guermonprez G, et al. Dermatoses associated with travel to tropical countries: A prospective study of the diagnosis and management of 269 patients presenting to a tropical disease unit. Clin Infect Dis. 1995;20:542-548.

78. Sunscreens: Are they safe and effective? Med Lett Drugs Ther. 1999;41:43-44

79. Grobusch MP, Muhlberger N, Jelinek T, et al. Imported schistosomiasis in Europe: Sentinel Surveillance Data from TropNetEurop. J Travel Med. 2003;10:164-167.

80. Sejvar J, Bancroft E, Winthrop K, et al. Leptospirosis in "Eco-Challenge" athletes, Malaysian Borneo, 2000. Emerg Infect Dis. 2003;9:702-707.

81. Cobelens FG, van Deutekom H, Draayer-Jansen IW, et al. Association of tuberculin sensitivity in Dutch adults with history of travel to areas of with a high incidence of tuberculosis. Clin Infect Dis. 2001;33:300-304.

82. WHO study of venous thrombosis and air travel. Wkly Epidemiol Rec. 2002;77: 197-199

83. Giangrande PL. Air travel and thrombosis. Br J Haematol. 2002;117:509-512.

84. Lapostolle F, Surget V, Borron SW, et al. Severe pulmonary embolism associated with air travel. N Engl J Med. 2001;345:779-783.

85. Cesarone MR, Belcaro G, Nicolaides AN, et al. Venous thrombosis from air travel: The LONFLIT3 study—Prevention with aspirin vs low-molecular-weight heparin (LMWH) in high-risk subjects: A randomized trial. Angiology. 2002;53:1-6.

86. Suhner A, Schlagenhauf P, Hofer I, et al. Effectiveness and tolerability of melatonin and zolpidem for the alleviation of jet lag. Aviat Space Environ Med. 2001;72:638-646.

87. Committee to advise on tropical medicine and travel (CATMAT). Statement on motion sickness. Can Commun Dis Rep. 1996;22:101-111.

88. Gendreau MA, DeJohn C. Responding to medical events during commercial airline flights. N Engl J Med. 2002;346:1067-1073.

89. Freiberger JJ, Denoble PJ, Pieper CF, et al. The relative risk of decompression sickness during and after air travel following diving. Aviat Space Environ Med. 2002;73:980-984.

90. Hackett PH, Roach RC. High-altitude illness. N Engl J Med. 2001;345:107-114.

91. Mileno MD, Bia FJ. The compromised traveler. Infect Dis Clin North Am. 1998;12:369-412.

92. Kemper CA, Haubrich R, Frank I, et al. Safety and immunogenicity of hepatitis A vaccine in human immunodeficiency virus–infected patients: A double-blind, randomized, placebo-controlled trial. J Infect Dis. 2003;187:1327-1331.

93. Castelli F, Patroni A. The human immunodeficiency virus–infected traveler. Clin Infect Dis. 2000;31:1403-1408.

94. Leder K, Weller PF, Wilson ME. Travel vaccines and elderly persons: Review of vaccines available in the United States. Clin Infect Dis. 2001;33:1553-1566.

95. Samuel BU, Barry M. The pregnant traveler. Infect Dis Clin North Am. 1998;12:325-354.

96. McGready R, Hamilton KA, Simpson JA, et al. Safety of the insect repellent N,N-diethyl-M-toluamide (DEET) in pregnancy. Am J Trop Med Hyg. 2001;65:285-289.

97. McGready R, Simpson JA, Htway M, et al. A double-blind randomized therapeutic trial of insect repellents for the prevention of malaria in pregnancy. Trans R Soc Trop Med Hyg. 2001;95:137-138.

CHAPTER 329

Infections
in Returning Travelers

DAVID O. FREEDMAN

Of the approximately 80 million people who travel from industrialized to developing countries each year, 22% to 64% of travelers report some illness.[1-3] The approach to the patient requires knowledge of world geography, the epidemiology of disease patterns in 230 or so countries, and the clinical presentation of a wide spectrum of disorders.[4] Most illnesses are mild, most are self-limited, and many are non-infectious. Up to 10% of travelers may consult a physician during or after a trip and approximately 1 in 100,000 travelers will die. Nevertheless, the ill travelers that do come to the attention of infectious diseases clinicians are generally either the most seriously ill or are suspected of harboring infectious agents not familiar within their home country.

Travelers who become ill during, or at anytime up to several months after, a foreign trip will frequently associate that illness with a possible travel-specific etiology. This may be the case but often it is not. Routine things are common, and common things are common whether actually acquired during travel or at sometime after the trip. Thus fever, sore throat, and cervical adenopathy in a college student who returned 2 weeks earlier from a developing country is still more likely to be streptococcal pharyngitis or infectious mononucleosis than diphtheria. Presented with an ill patient with a history of travel, the physician must maintain discipline in making two separate lists of differential diagnoses, the first with the travel history factored in and the second considering the same presenting symptoms and signs as if in any other patient. The approach and workup must then proceed in parallel with appropriate priority given to the most urgent or the most treatable diagnoses at the top of each list.

In this chapter travelers are considered to be those returning from short visits to developing countries and does not consider immigrants, refugees, and very long-term residents arriving from those countries. Constellations of exposures and clinical presentations highly suggestive of particular diagnoses in returned travelers are shown in Table 329-1. Highly exotic endemic diseases very rarely, if ever, acquired by travelers are not discussed. The focus will be on the identification of infectious causes of the presenting illness, on travel-associated risk factors, and on manifestations of those diseases that are particular to travelers. Detailed discussion of pathophysiology, spectrum of clinical manifestations, and therapy of each infectious agent is found in the disease specific chapters of this book. Fever, travelers' diarrhea, and skin problems are the most common presenting illnesses in returned travelers. Eosinophilia is less common but is a frequent source of referral to the infectious diseases specialist. Each will be discussed in turn.

FEVER

Epidemiology

Fever occurs in 2% to 3%[1-3] of European or American travelers to the developing world and is the presenting complaint for 20% to 25% of those seen at specialized tropical medicine clinics. Several large case series from busy tropical disease units indicate malaria to be the cause of the fever in 27% to 42%.[5,6] The other most common tropical etiologies specific to returning travelers are dengue, viral hepatitis, typhoid fever, and enteric pathogens. Less common but important considerations are rickettsioses, leptospirosis, acute schistosomiasis, and amebic liver abscess. All of the above have widespread distribution in the tropics and need to be considered initially in all febrile travelers. Some may be ruled out quickly based on a detailed travel and exposure history and consultation with relevant information sources on disease distribution. Upper and lower respiratory tract infection including streptococcal pharyngitis and influenza, as well as urinary tract infections are cosmopolitan non-tropical febrile etiologies that are remarkably common in travelers and should always be considered. In every case series from these sophisticated referral centers up to 25% of those presenting with fever have self-limited illnesses that never have an etiologic diagnosis made. These are mostly viral syndromes caused by one of hundreds of viral agents that exist outside of developed countries and where diagnostic tests may not be available anywhere. In many cases, the time and expense of a large panel of viral isolation and serological assays is not warranted outside the research setting. Fever due to deep venous thrombosis and/or pulmonary embolism may be related to travel, especially in those with pre-existing conditions or underlying coagulopathy. Thromboembolic disease needs to always be considered right from the outset, but will not be discussed further here.[7]

History

A good patient history is always important in clinical medicine but nowhere is it as important as in the returning traveler. The cumulative list of infectious agents in 230 separate countries is daunting. A day-by-day travel itinerary, knowledge of risk factors and exposures for the common travel diseases, knowledge of usual incubation periods of those diseases, and knowledge of or access to the known geographic distribution of possible infectious diseases, will lead to an appropriately focused workup.[8,9] Much time, expense, and patient discomfort due to sometimes invasive diagnostic tests can be avoided when diag-

TABLE 329-1 Constellations of Exposures and Clinical Presentations Suggestive of Particular Diagnoses in Returned Travelers*

Exposure Scenario	Distinctive Findings	Diagnosis
Any exposure in any area with documented malaria transmission	Fever with or without any other finding	Malaria
Most tropical countries	Fever and altered mental status	Malaria, meningococcal meningitis, rabies, West Nile virus
Budget travel to India, Nepal, Pakistan, or Bangladesh	Insidious onset high unremitting fever, toxic patient, paucity of physical findings	Enteric fever due to *S. typhi* or *S. paratyphi*
Freshwater recreational exposure in Africa	Fever, eosinophilia, hepatomegaly, negative malaria smear	Acute schistosomiasis (Katayama fever)
Bitten by *Aedes aegypti* in Central America, Southeast Asia, or the South Pacific	Fever, headache, myalgia, diffuse macular rash, mild to moderate thrombocytopenia	Dengue
Hunting or visiting game reserves in southern Africa	Fever, eschar, diffuse petechial rash	African tick typhus, due to *R. africae*
Travel to Southeast Asia	Fever, eschar, diffuse petechial rash	Scrub typhus due to *Orientia tsutsugamushi*
Hiking, biking, swimming, rafting with exposure to fresh surface water	Fever, myalgia, conjunctival suffusion, mild to severe jaundice, variable rash	Leptospirosis
Summertime cruise to Alaska, elderly traveler	Influenza like illness	Influenza A or B
Outdoor exposure anywhere in the Americas	Large single furuncular lesion anywhere on body, with sense of movement inside	Myiasis due to *Dermatobia hominis* (botfly)
Clothing washed or dried out of doors in Africa	Multiple furuncular lesions around clothing contact points with skin	Myiasis due to *Cordylobia anthropophaga* (tumbu fly)
New sexual partner during travel	Fever, rash, mono-like illness	Acute HIV
Travel to any developing country	Coryza, conjunctivitis, Koplik spots, rash	Measles
Longer visit to humid areas of Africa, the Americas or Southeast Asia	Asymptomatic eosinophilia or with periodic cough or wheezing	Strongyloidiasis
Sandfly bite in either new or old world tropical area	Painless skin ulcer with clean moist base in exposed area	Cutaneous leishmaniasis
Resort hotel in southern Europe ±/− exposure to whirlpool spas	Pneumonia	Legionnaires' disease
Explored a cave in the Americas	Fever, cough, retrosternal chest pain, hilar adenopathy	Histoplasmosis
Ingestion of unpasteurized goat cheese	Chronic fever, fatigue	*Brucella melitensis*
Long trip to west/central Africa	Afebrile, intensely pruritic evanescent truncal maculopapular rash	Onchocerciasis
Long trip to west/central Africa	Migratory localized angioedema or swellings over large joints, eosinophilia	Loiasis
Safari to game parks of East Africa	Fever, non-genital chancre, fine macular rash	East African trypanosomiasis
Travel to Australia	Fever, fatigue, polyarthritis	Ross River virus
Farming areas of India and Southeast Asia	Fever, altered mental status, paralysis	Japanese encephalitis
Forested areas of central and eastern Europe and across Russia	Fever, altered mental status, paralysis	Tickborne encephalitis
Rodent exposure in West Africa	Fever, sore throat, jaundice, hemorrhagic manifestations	Lassa fever
Ingestion of sushi, ceviche or raw freshwater fish	Migratory nodules in truncal areas with overlying erythema or mild hemorrhage	Gnathostomiasis
Returning Hajj pilgrim or family contact	Fever, meningitis	Meningococcal meningitis
Ingestion of snails, fish or shellfish in Asia	Eosinophilic meningitis	Angiostrongyliasis, gnathostomiasis
Ingestion of undercooked meat of any animal in any country	Fever, facial edema, myositis, increased CPK, massive eosinophila, normal ESR	Trichinosis
Unvaccinated, returning from sub-Saharan Africa or forested areas of Amazonia	Fever, jaundice, proteinuria, hemorrhage	Yellow fever
Exposure to farm animals	Pneumonia, mild hepatitis	Q fever
Possible tick exposure almost anywhere	Fever, headache, rash, conjunctival injection, hepatosplenomegaly	Tickborne relapsing fever
Poor hygienic conditions with possible body louse exposure in Ethiopia or Sudan	Fever, headache, rash, conjunctival injection, hepatosplenomegaly	Louse-borne relapsing fever

*The table includes illnesses of travelers (listed first) as well as less common diseases with presentations that should suggest the possibility of the appropriate diagnosis. Many diseases have a spectrum of presentation and the table describes the most common presentations of these diseases. Many diseases have a spectrum of geographic origins and the table describes the most common exposures seen in daily practice.

CPK, creatine phosphokinase; ESR, erythrocyte sedimentation rate; HIV, human immunodeficiency virus.

noses that are not epidemiologically or chronologically possible can be eliminated based on the patient history.

The fever pattern and clinical findings by themselves are often nonspecific and overlap greatly between many of the most common tropical infectious diseases. The history should include the following key elements:

Detailed Travel Itinerary

This should include every locale visited within every country visited including transit stops. Some individuals are frequent travelers so all travel for at least the previous 6 months must be considered initially. If the diagnosis remains elusive a more remote travel history, especially

that involving malarious areas, may be sought. The exact date of arrival back in the home country is often crucial to ascertain the last possible exposure date to an exotic pathogen. These details are most efficiently ascertained using a waiting room questionnaire. For example, it is insufficient to know simply that the patient visited Peru. Some parts of Peru are malarious while others are not, only some have risk of yellow fever, high altitude destinations have little risk of vector-borne disease, and there is no risk of strongyloidiasis along the desert coastal strip.

Chronology of Travel and Illness

This should include the exact dates spent in each locale with respect to the onset of illness. Knowledge of typical incubation periods (Table 329-2) of

TABLE 329-2 Incubation Periods of Common Travel-Related Infections*

Short Incubation (<10 days)	Medium Incubation (10-21 days)	Long Incubation (>21 days)
Malaria	Malaria	Malaria
Arboviruses including dengue, yellow fever, Japanese encephalitis	Flaviviruses—tickborne encephalitis and Japanese encephalitis	Schistosomiasis
Hemorrhagic fevers—lassa, Ebola, South American arenaviruses	Hemorrhagic fevers—Lassa, Ebola, Crimean-Congo hemorrhagic fever	Tuberculosis
Respiratory viruses including SARS	Acute human immunodeficiency virus	Acute HIV
Typhoid and paratyphoid	Typhoid and paratyphoid	Viral hepatitis
Bacterial enteritis	*Giardia*	Filariasis
Rickettsia—spotted fever group: RMSF, African tick typhus, Mediterranean spotted fever, Scrub typhus, Q fever	*Rickettsia*—fleaborne, louse borne, and scrub typhus, Q fever, Spotted fevers (rare).	*Rickettsia*—Q fever
Bacterial pneumonia including *Legionella*	Cytomegalovirus	Secondary syphilis
Relapsing fever	Toxoplasma	EBV including mononucleosis
Amebic dysentery	Amebic dysentery	Amebic liver disease
Meningococcemia	Histoplasmosis	Leishmaniasis
Brucella (rarely)	*Brucella*	*Brucella*
Leptospirosis	Leptospirosis	Bartonellosis (chronic)
Fascioliasis	Babesiosis	Babesiosis
Rabies (rarely)	Rabies	Rabies
African trypanosomiasis (acute), east African (rarely)	African trypanosomiasis (acute), east African	African trypanosomiasis (chronic)
	Hepatitis A (rarely)	Cytomegalovirus
	Measles	

*Diseases that commonly have variable incubation periods are shown more than once. However, most diseases may rarely have an atypical incubation period and this is not shown here.
SARS, severe acute respiratory syndrome; RMSF, Rocky Mountain Spotted Fever.

possible infectious etiologies is a key tool in narrowing the differential diagnosis. Many agents are simply not biologically possible outside their usual incubation period. Arboviral diseases such as dengue uniformly have short incubation periods. Onset of illness more than 2 weeks after last possible exposure effectively rules out this class of viral illness. Long incubation infections like schistosomiasis cannot present less than several weeks after first possible exposure. Some diseases such as malaria or enteric fever have more variable incubation periods but nevertheless have a typical incubation period during which time the majority of the patients present. A number of diseases, especially those that are arthropod-borne have a strict seasonality whereby transmission stops during either cold or dry weather. Examples would include malaria in non-tropical countries such as Korea, Tajikistan, or Northern China as well as lyme borreliosis or tickborne encephalitis all of which which completely cease transmission during winter months.

Exposures

This should include a detailed dietary history. Budget travel and associated high risk eating habits will predispose to a variety of common enteric pathogens. A history of specific foods associated with known pathogens should also be elicited. This includes: Unpasteurized dairy products (brucella, campylobacter, salmonella, tuberculosis), shellfish (vibrios, enteric viruses, viral hepatitis), uncooked beef such as carpaccio and steak tartare (toxoplasma, campylobacter, E. coli O157-H7), undercooked fish such as sushi and ceviche (vibrios, anisakis, gnathostoma); and undercooked pork or game meat (trichinosis). Exposure to fresh water or surface water in recreational or other settings may be associated with schistosomiasis[10,11] or leptospirosis.[12] A history of exposure to mosquitoes and flies is generally unhelpful but history of tickbite (rickettsiae, relapsing fever, tickborne encephalitis) or tse-tse bite should be sought in the right setting. Exposures to new sexual partners,[13,14] needles, or blood should be ascertained. Rodent exposure is associated with lassa fever, hantavirus infection, and rat-bite fever. A history of contact with other sick people is especially important in the post-travel setting. Travelers usually move in groups or with families or companions all of whom will likely have shared the same exposures.

Immunization History

This should include exact dates of last dose of each vaccine received and in some instances whether an adequate primary series was completed in the first place. Most vaccines, with the notable exception of typhoid vaccines are very highly efficacious. Thus, hepatitis A or B, yellow fever, measles, or diphtheria are unlikely diagnoses in those with a substantiated history of adequate and current immunization.

Antimalarial Intake

If malaria is a possibility a complete pill-by-pill history of ingestion of anti-malarial drugs including the name and dose of all drugs taken for prophylaxis or treatment. Patients often misunderstand the dosing or timing instructions given at the pre-travel visit or they may have been prescribed an inappropriate drug for their destination. Patients may have been treated with appropriate or inappropriate drugs en route for febrile illnesses. Some very efficacious drugs are not available in the United States and an international pharmacopeia such as Martindale's may need to be consulted by those unfamiliar with these drugs. A history of appropriate prophylaxis diminishes the possibility of malaria but does not eliminate the need for a malaria thick film for any patient legitimately exposed to malaria.

Other Medications Ingested

Travelers who fall ill during the travel often self-treat with antibiotics or see a local physician and are prescribed a broad spectrum antibiotic. Again, an international pharmacopeia may need to be consulted. Recent ingestion of a 1-week course of a quinolone, tetracycline, or cephalosporin antibiotic may alter the course of the illness or even affect the possibility of certain diagnoses. In particular, malaria may be suppressed by azithromycin, doxycycline, quinolones, or clindamycin.

Physical Examination

Common tropical infections often present as undifferentiated fever without focal findings. However, when a focal finding, such as arthritis, meningitis, pneumonia, is present, the differential diagnosis can often be narrowed. Unfortunately physical findings such as jaundice, hepatomegaly, splenomegaly, and lymphadenopathy occur at least a portion of the time in many of the most common travel-related infections so are not specific enough to greatly narrow the differential diagnosis.[15] Most imported febrile rash illnesses engender the same differential diagnosis as for non-travelers. However, arboviruses, typhoid, rickettsial illness, leptospirosis, measles, early stages of viral hemorrhagic fevers, leptospirosis, relapsing fever, and acute African trypanosomiasis should always be kept in mind.

Considerations for the Common Travel Related Febrile Illnesses

Malaria

Fever in a traveler returning from a malarious area is an emergency and the instinctive performance of a stat malaria smear will prevent unnecessary deaths. Falciparum malaria is easily treatable if diagnosed early, but even with optimum treatment has a mortality of 20% or more if treatment is begun only after end organ complications arise. Smears need to be repeated at least every 12 to 24 hours a minimum of three times to rule out malaria. Rapid deterioration can occur over a period of hours. Unreliable smear negative patients with a high index of suspicion for falciparum malaria may need to be admitted for inpatient observation.

Because malaria is overwhelmingly an African disease with about 80% of all *P. falciparum* imported into developed countries originating there,[16] suspicion of malaria is especially acute for Africa returnees. Beyond this, trends in the geographic origin of imported malaria cases don't always correlate well with regional transmission patterns as abolute numbers of cases from particular geographic areas may also mirror the intensity of travel to the affected region. Ethnic minority travelers returning home to visit friends and relatives in malarious areas have the highest risk of infection. Resources describing current country-specific malaria micro-epidemiology should be immediately accessible to those assessing tropical fevers (see Chapter 272).[9] In general, malaria is a rural disease but the cities of Africa and India are exceptions.

Falciparum malaria in non-immune travelers most commonly has an incubation period of 10 to 14 days and 90% of cases occur within 1 month of last exposure. Non-falciparum malaria is rarely life threatening but can present much later after arrival. Incubation periods will be prolonged in those taking inadequate or incomplete chemoprophylaxis. Relapses of *P. vivax* or *P. ovale* may occur many months after travel in those whose initial attack was clinically silent due to suppressive chemoprophylaxis, but in whom terminal prophylaxis with primaquine was not used (see Chapter 272).

The presenting signs and symptoms of imported malaria remain sufficiently protean so as to mimic a number of common tropical or non-tropical conditions.[17-19] No constellation of symptoms or signs differentiates falciparum from non-falciparum malaria. Classic periodic malarial fever is not a usual manifestation of imported malaria although when fever does occur in discrete repeated 48 or 72 hour cycles, the diagnosis is almost certain. Fever will be absent at the exact time of the initial medical assessment in up to 40% of patients with malaria. Respiratory or gastrointestinal symptoms may be predominant. The presence of rash, lymphadenopathy, or leukocytosis indicate another diagnosis. Anemia is uncommon in travelers who present in the early days of their malarial illness. Thrombocytopenia occurs in over 50% and is a reliable if non-specific indicator of malarial etiology when present.

Many other serious infections are present in malarious areas. The search for malaria should not hamper the simultaneous work-up for other pathogens in smear negative patients. Similarly, semi-immune residents of endemic areas may be mildly parasitemic on a chronic basis with little ill effect, so a positive malaria smear in these patients should not hamper a search for any other clinically suspected infections.

Dengue

Dengue, transmitted by the day-biting *Aedes aegypti* mosquito is an important travel-related problem most notably in heavily visited areas of Southeast Asia, the South Pacific and Central America and the Caribbean.[20,21] Travelers to Thailand seem particularly prone to infection[22] and dengue is uncommon in Africa. In contrast to many other tropical fevers, it is predominantly an urban infection so that it can even affect upscale business travelers in urban centers. The incubation period is usually 2 to 7 days after the mosquito bite so many travelers initially become ill while still overseas. The clinical spectrum ranges widely from asymptomatic through a range of clinical manifestations up to the severe myalgia and arthralgia of "breakbone-fever" (see Chapter 149). Malaria, other arboviruses, leptospirosis, rickettsial disease, measles, or typhoid may present similar initial findings. However, in cases where one of several associated rashes manifests (Fig. 329-1A), dengue becomes more likely than the other possibilities.

A positive tourniquet test is found in up to 50% of patients with classic dengue and in almost all patients with dengue hemorrhagic fever but it is a non-specific finding that may also be present in leptospirosis. The test is performed by inflating a blood pressure cuff halfway between systolic and diastolic for 5 minutes and upon release counting the number of petechiae in a 2.5 cm × 2.5 cm patch below the cuff. Greater than 20 petechiae is considered positive.

Serologic confirmation most often must be sent to a reference laboratory. IgM is not elevated until 5 or more days after illness onset but most patients initially present earlier than this. If an IgM drawn more than 5 days into illness is negative, a third visit to test for fourfold elevations of IgG is required. Because most patients will be better by the time results of any confirmatory tests would be available and since treatment is supportive, many clinicians do not seek laboratory confirmation. Virus isolation from blood is possible only during the first 5 days of illness but is not routinely available. A post-viral fatigue lasting up to 6 months may occur. Patients need to be reminded that another visit to a dengue endemic area could result in infection with another serotype with risk of ensuing dengue hemorrhagic fever.

Typhoid and Paratyphoid Fever

Typhoid fever is often the most non-descript of the relatively common causes of travel-related fever.[23,24] Incubation period is most often a week but can be as long as 3 weeks. Risk is at least 10 times higher on the Indian subcontinent than anywhere else but risk exists throughout the tropics in the setting of poor sanitation. In contrast to malaria, dengue, or rickettsial infection, onset is insidious and abnormal physical findings usually absent. Abdominal discomfort and constipation are common but diarrhea is frequent enough so as to not rule out the diagnosis. Patients often look and feel particularly unwell with severe prostration and high unremitting fever. Leukopenia and thrombocytopenia often occur. Blood cultures are not always positive but bone marrow cultures increase the yield. Serologic assays including agglutination and ELISA have overall poor sensitivity especially early in the course and some lack of specificity in some settings and enjoy poor reputations. However, when present, an unequivocal high titer in a previously naïve traveler provides a more rapid diagnosis than will blood cultures. Up-to-date vaccination against typhoid provides only partial protection against *S. typhi* and does not protect at all against *Salmonella paratyphi*.[25] Due to resistance, fluoroquinolones are no longer an option for empiric treatment in the Indian sub-continent and third-generation cephalosporins should be used.[26]

Viral Hepatitis

Incidence rates for travel-related viral hepatitis are likely to have begun a decline as more individuals who had routine childhood hepatitis B vaccine are moving into the traveling population and as more high-risk travelers are receiving long-term protection due to pre-travel hepatitis A and B vaccination. Current vaccines don't protect against hepatitis E which is enterically acquired[27] or against hepatitis C which like Hepatitis B may be acquired overseas after blood transfusion, contact with contaminated syringes, medical equipment, or tattoo and body piercing implements. Viral hepatitis is a long incubation infection so that acquisition may not always be readily linked by the patient or the physician to the travel.

Rickettsia

Rickettsial disease is emerging in travelers.[28,29] Most of the long list of rickettsial species infecting humans are transmitted by ticks, mites, and fleas. Eschars are seen in the majority of patients with African tick typhus due to *R. africae* (see Fig. 329-2F),[30] Mediterranean spotted

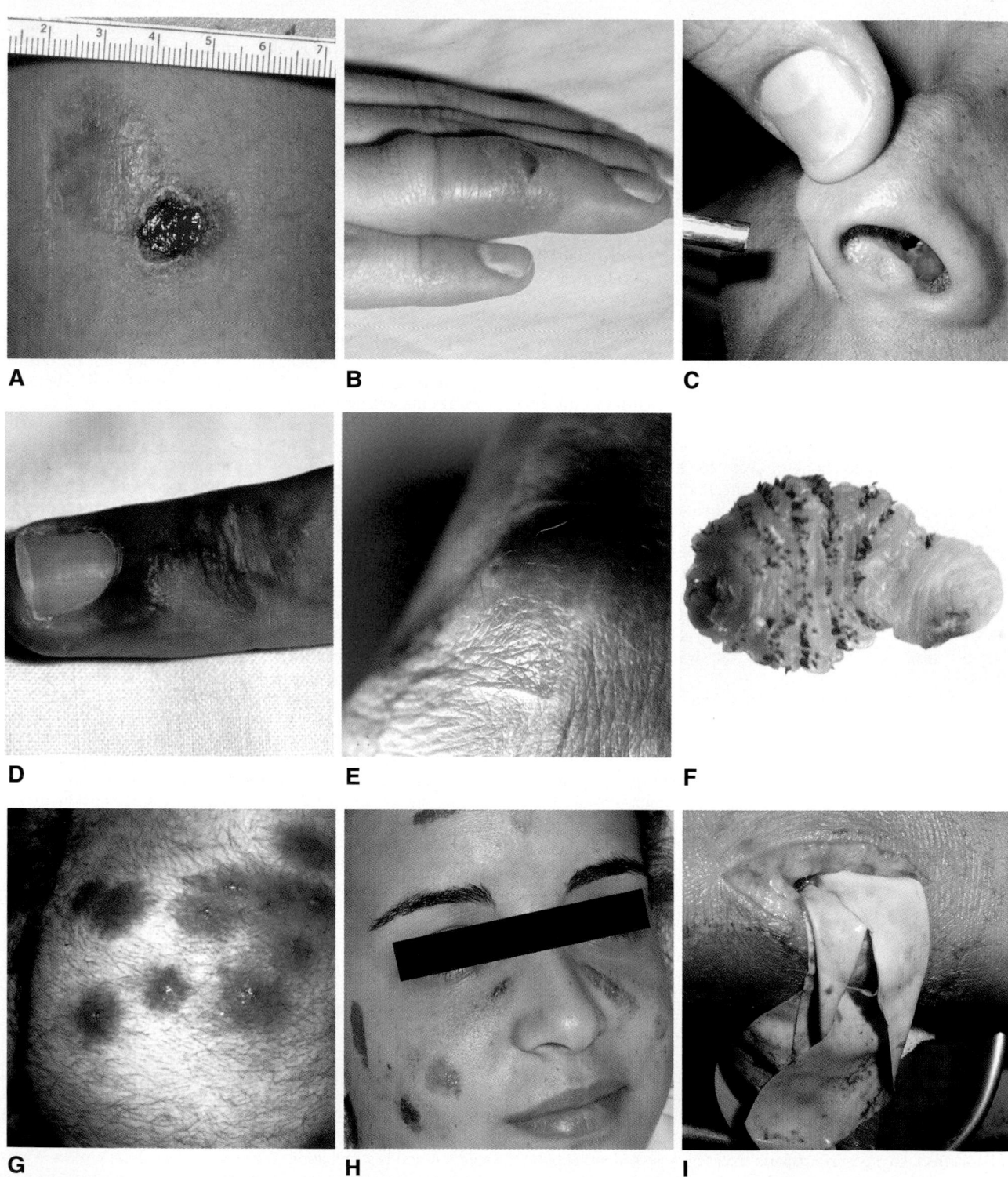

FIGURE 329-1. Some common diseases of travelers with pathology localized to circumscribed areas of the skin and underlying tissue. **A,** Painless ulcer with a clean base in a traveler to Peru with new world cutaneous leishmaniasis due to *Leishmania braziliensis.* **B,** More nodular and inflammatory lesions with crusting in a traveler to Afghanistan with only slight ulceration which is more characteristic of old world cutaneous leishmaniasis due to *L. major.* **C,** Painless nasal perforation which is often the earliest manifestation of mucocutaneous leishmaniasis due to metastatic spread of *L. braziliensis* from an earlier cutaneous lesion. **D,** Cutaneous larva migrans or creeping eruption due to the canine hookworm *Ancylostoma caninum.* **E,** Furuncular myiasis due to *Dermatobia hominis* (botfly); patients often report a sense of movement inside, note tiny hole for the respiratory spicule of the botfly. **F,** *Dermatobia hominis* larvae after migration to surface when the respiratory spicule was blocked with petroleum jelly. **G,** Characteristic multi-lesion presentation of African furuncular myiasis due to *Cordylobia anthropophaga* (tumbu fly). **H,** Phytophotodermatis in a traveler to Ecuador after application of a lime juice containing mixture by a shaman during a native ceremony; the same effect is seen when common tropical cocktails are spilled on sun exposed areas. Pigmented lesions may take weeks to resolve. **I,** Tropical pyomyositis in the Amazon. Pyomyositis due to deep staphylococcal infection is common in moist warm climates and is characterized by brown pus as the muscle fibers dissolve. Intial lesions are characterized by exquisitely painful localized erythematous areas overlying the affected muscle. *(Images reprinted with permission of the Tropical Medicine Institute, Universidad Peruana Cayetano Heredia and the Gorgas Memorial Institute.)*

fever due to *R. conori,* and scrub typhus due to *O. tsutsugamushi*[31] infection which are the three most common travel-related rickettsioses. In a group of 940 travelers to South Africa, 4% of all travelers and 27% of all travelers with flu-like symptoms had infection with *Rickettsia africae.*[32] While rickettsial diseases are present in most countries of the world, individual species have restricted geographic distributions (see Chapter 183) which helps in the diagnostic formulation. High fever, headache, leukopenia, and thrombocytopenia are common. Rickettsiae infect endothelial cells and often cause widespread vasculitic looking lesions (see Fig. 329-2F). Severe infections may present with DIC and mimic a viral hemorrhagic fever. Because African tick-bite fever and scrub typhus both occur in malarious areas, a thick film is indicated even in febrile patients with pathognomonic skin lesions. Because response to tetracyclines is uniformly prompt and dramatic and the results of serologic tests slow to return, clinical suspicion and clinical diagnosis is usually relied upon. The diagnosis should be reconsidered in those who don't respond within 48 hours of initiation of doxycycline or tetracycline.

Leptospirosis

Leptospirosis is thought of as an occupational disease and a disease of urban slum-dwellers with rodent exposure. In recent years large leptospirosis outbreaks in adventure travelers and adventure racers such as whitewater rafters, triathletes and participants in the 2000 Borneo Eco-Challenge race have occurred.[12] Doxycycline prophylaxis is now recommended for both civilians and military who will hike, bike, swim or raft in tropical environments.[12] The protean clinical manifestations, which include fever, headache, proximal lower extremity myalgia and abdominal wall pain are impossible to distinguish clinically from dengue but may also mimic a number of other common tropical infections. Conjunctival suffusion and jaundice occur in a subset and are more common than in the other undifferentiated febrile diseases although both may occur in relapsing fever. A reliable rapid IgM dipstick test for leptospirosis is widely available and used. Recognition of possible leptospirosis impacts therapy as antibiotic treatment is generally undertaken when the diagnosis is suspected.[33]

Respiratory Illness

Travelers spend long periods in confined spaces and tend to meet many different people during the course of their trip. Acute respiratory infections occur in 10% to 20% of all travelers with rates as high as 1261 per 100,000 travelers for a 1-month stay in a developing country. For all ill returning travelers seen at GeoSentinel surveillance network sites 7.8% had respiratory infection diagnosed with almost half of these being lower respiratory tract infections such as pneumonia or atypical pneumonia.[34]

Respiratory diseases are second only to gastrointestinal infections as a cause of morbidity in travelers. In outbreaks of infections on cruise ships respiratory tract infections constitute the most common diagnosis.[35] Emerging data indicate that influenza may be the most common vaccine preventable disease in all travelers. The importance of SARS in the permanent infectious disease landscape is unclear at this writing. One quarter or more of all cases of legionellosis are associated with travel in the previous 2 weeks and rates appear to be increasing. Risk factors include stays at large air-conditioned resort hotels, spas, and cruise ship travel.[36,37] Acute histoplasmosis can be seen after brief excursions into caves anywhere in the Americas and travel related coccidioidomycosis is reported.[38] Tuberculosis is a clear risk in those who spend longer periods in very high-risk countries and especially those who are doing medical or aid work.[39] Pulmonary infiltrates and symptoms may be seen during the migratory phases of helminthiases such as schistosomiasis, strongyloides, hookworm, and ascaris. Hemorrhagic pneumonitis may be seen with leptospirosis. Q-fever should be sought in those with animal exposure. Workup should be guided by clinical and radiologic findings.

Initial Office Approach to the Febrile Patient

The first priority is assessment for dangerous or immediately life threatening disease such as where hemorrhagic manifestations are apparent. If the patient has the appropriate exposures for a viral hemorrhagic fever he/she needs to be immediately isolated and public health authorities contacted. None of the isolatable hemorrhagic fever viruses have incubation periods exceeding 3 weeks. Arenavirus infection whether from West Africa (Lassa) or South America (Junin, Machupo, Guanarito) should be treated with ribavirin.[40-42] Some also recommend treating Crimean-Congo hemorrhagic fever with ribavirin.[43] Other rare hemorrhagic fevers of travelers such as rift valley fever, yellow fever, dengue hemorrhagic fever and Ebola need to be supported with the best possible intensive care.[44] Meningococcemia and rickettsial infection present with purpuric lesions and bacterial sepsis and severe malaria are serious but treatable causes of hemorrhage due to DIC. Any febrile patient with altered sensorium or any other evidence of end-organ damage consistent with malaria and in whom falciparum malaria is a possibility should receive empiric therapy for malaria regardless of the result of a blood film. The smear is often negative in advanced disease due to sequestration of parasites in capillary beds.

In the patient who is not severely ill but who has an undifferentiated fever without any localizing symptoms or signs, three blood films, if epidemiologically indicated, are the first priority. At the same time other mandatory diagnostic tests in the workup of every tropical fever include blood cultures (for enteric fever), CBC with differential and platelets, liver function tests, urinalysis, and a chest x-ray. The blood film may also diagnose bartonellosis and relapsing fever. Leukopenia will mitigate away from common bacterial infections and towards dengue, typhoid, brucella, rickettsial disease or acute HIV infection. Thrombocytopenia is indicative of malaria, dengue, or brucellosis. Eosinophilia may indicate early migratory stages of a number of helminths (see below). Liver function tests will be consistently abnormal in viral hepatitis or toxin damage and variably abnormal in leptospirosis, rickettsial disease including Q fever, relapsing fever, yellow fever, amebic abscess, brucellosis, typhoid, hemorrhagic fever, and dengue. An indirect benefit of chest x-ray is the finding of an elevated right hemi-diaphragm in many cases of amebic liver abscess.[45]

The second wave of diagnostic testing will be driven by any abnormalities that emerge from initial test results. In the absence of enlightening abnormalities, additional serologies may need to be sent based on travel itinerary, incubation periods, and known exposures as discussed above. HIV and complications, syphilis as well as tuberculosis should be sought at this stage if there is any suggestive exposure at all. After ruling out potentially serious as well as potentially treatable infections by history, physical examination and routine lab work, and especially if patient financial resources are limiting, the clinician must then decide whether to wait 48 to 72 hours before serology and sophisticated diagnostic studies are pursued. As up to 25% of all febrile illnesses in returning travelers are self-limited viral syndromes, a patient who was highly febrile and quite toxic looking at initial assessment is quite often perfectly well 48 hours later with no intervention. Reasonable clinical and local laboratory experience and confidence is required for this approach but from the patient standpoint is the most desirable course. At a minimum, acute serum should be stored for possible later use. If the patient is stable, has no laboratory abnormalities, no clinical evidence of end organ damage and has a reliable companion, he or she may be followed as an outpatient during the clinical evolution and appropriate workup pursued according to any ensuing clinical findings.

Oral ciprofloxacin is sometimes given as empiric therapy for the slightest chance of typhoid fever because of the ease of treatment and the difficulty making the diagnosis. However, quinolone resistant typhoid and paratyphoid fever is now predominant in the Indian subcontinent where much of the travel related enteric fever originates. Thus, in this situation if clinical suspicion is high the patient may need to be admitted for parenteral therapy. Empiric therapy for malaria without a positive blood film is only appropriate if clinical evidence of cerebral dysfunction or of any other end-organ damage consistent with malaria is present. Otherwise, examination of these patients and of serial blood smears over several days by someone with appropriate experience will always lead to the parasitological diagnosis of malaria when present.[46] Such expertise is rarely so far away as to compromise patient care. In addition to potential drug toxicities, empiric treatment will necessarily eliminate any possibility of making a species diagnosis if the patient, in fact, does have malaria. After empiric treatment the clinician is then probably obligated to a course of primaquine, a potentially toxic drug, to cover the possibility that the antecedent infection was due to relapsing (*P. vivax* or *P. ovale*) malaria.

Febrile patients who present initially with focal symptoms or signs should have a more directed workup that takes into consideration appropriate disease distribution, incubation period, and possible exposures. Altered mental status or other CNS deficits are present as non-specific sequelae of many systemic infections. However, appropriate itinerary, exposure and incubation periods for the following less common infections should be sought: Japanese encephalitis, rabies, West Nile virus, tickborne encephalitis, African trypanosomiasis, angiostrongylus, gnathostomiasis and in recent Hajj pilgrims to Mecca meningococci.[47]

DIARRHEA IN TRAVELERS

Acute Travelers Diarrhea (TD)

Diarrhea is by far the most common cause of illness during travel affecting up to 60% of travelers to some high-risk destinations. The most frequent cause of TD is enterotoxigenic *Escherichia coli* (6% to 70%). Other types of *E. coli* (especially Enteroaggregative *E. coli*),[48] *Salmonella, Shigella,* and *Campylobacter* each account for about 5% to 15%. *Vibrio parahemolyticus* is related to shellfish ingestion and is seen almost exclusively in Asia. Protozoa account for less than 5% and in adults, rarely, norovirus or rotavirus may be detected.[49-51] However, norovirus outbreaks aboard cruise ships are apparently increasing.[52] About 30% of diarrheal episodes remain unexplained but many apparently are of bacterial origin, because they respond to antibacterial drugs.

Bacterial diarrhea generally manifests as the abrupt onset of uncomfortable crampy diarrhea.[53,54] Fever, nausea, or vomiting if present, further increase the likelihood of a bacterial etiology. In contrast, protozoal diarrhea (most often *G. lamblia* or *E. histolytica*) begins gradually, with loose stools occurring in distinct episodes and gradually becoming more disabling over 1 to 2 weeks. In protozoal diarrhea medical care generally is not sought immediately due to the low grade nature of the symptoms. As most TD is bacterial, many travelers are instructed to self-treat with quinolone antibiotics and are told to seek medical assistance if diarrhea does not resolve after 3 to 5 days of treatment.[55]

Classic TD is defined as three or more unformed stools per day although a syndrome of non-classic TD with fewer stools but with accompanying symptoms is defined by some. Travelers may vary in their own definition of what is abnormal bowel pattern and this needs to be established with the patient in a quantitative way at the outset. Returned travelers with acute diarrhea of a few days duration who have not yet had a course of quinolone antibiotic can be prescribed an empiric course without any workup or stool culture. Toxic patients with bloody diarrhea should have a wet prep of stool and an immediate sigmoidoscopic examination to look for amebic trophozoites. Non-responders at 48 hours should then have stool for bacterial culture, stool for O&P, stool for AFB (to detect cryptosporidium and cyclospora), giardia stool ELISA or IFA, Entameba stool ELISA, and *C. difficile* toxin assay performed. *Vibrio* cultures usually require a special request. Quinolone-resistant *Campylobacter* is increasing worldwide and is the rule in Southeast Asia so an empiric course of azithromycin can be given while awaiting culture if the patient is still moderately ill.[56] Rifaximin has recently been approved for traveler's diarrhea due to *Escherichia coli*.[57] Due to the difficulty of giardia diagnosis, an empiric course of metronidazole is often given in practice to those with sub-acute symptoms and a negative workup. Reiter's syndrome is an occasional sequela of enteritis due to Shigella or Campylobacter.

Persistent Diarrhea in the Traveler

Two percent of those with TD go on to develop chronic diarrhea lasting a month or more. These patients can be extremely frustrating to deal with as diagnosis is most often elusive despite extensive diagnostic testing.[58] Clearly, some undiscovered enteric pathogens remain. Appropriate studies, in addition to those already listed above, include HIV serology, 5-HIAA levels, thyroid function tests, serum calcium, testing for malabsorption,[59] and upper and lower endoscopy with all aspirates and biopsies examined carefully for parasitic etiologies. *Giardia lamblia,*[60] *Strongyloides stercoralis, Cryptosporidium parvum,* and *Cyclospora cayetanensis* are occasional etiologies of persistent diarrhea and may be discovered only after invasive workup. Serology for *S. stercoralis, S. mansoni,* or *E. histolytica* is indicated where exposure to these agents may have occurred. Intestinal biopsy almost always yields non-specific findings, although cases of tropical or non-tropical sprue are occasionally discovered or an initial diagnosis of inflammatory bowel disease made. In many patients, the etiology of the frequently found non-specific villus blunting is unclear. This syndrome has often been called tropical enteropathy or post-infective tropical malabsorption[59,61] and is thought to be the residual damage caused by an initial bacterial or other insult. A temporary luminal disaccharidase deficiency may occur. Diarrhea may persist for months before resolving. In the absence of definitive diagnosis in patients with chronic travelers diarrhea, symptomatic treatment with loperamide is indicated. Elimination diets with restriction of lactose, fructose, gluten, and fat are sometimes of benefit. Those with pre-existing irritable bowel syndrome may have it unmasked by travel and frequently have exacerbations during or after travel. Tegaserod, alosetron, antispasmodics or other appropriate medication for their underlying disease may be needed.[62]

SKIN PROBLEMS

Eruptions accompanying febrile illness have been discussed in the above sections and some are illustrated in Figure 329-2. After diarrhea and respiratory illness, skin problems are the most common presenting problems in returned travelers. Some common primary dermatologic infections are illustrated in Figure 329-1. The most common eruptions are bacterial in origin and include common skin infections as well as pyodermas and arthropod bites (infected or not).[63,64] Cutaneous larva migrans, furuncular myiasis, dermatophytosis and drug eruptions are next most common. Ulcerative lesions of travelers include leishmaniasis,[65] mycobacterial disease, deep mycoses, and rarely anthrax. Rickettsial diseases frequently include black eschars at the site of the arthropod bite. Loiasis,[66] gnathostoma,[67] and cysticercosis present as painless subcutaneous nodules. Arthropod bites and infestations such as scabies, fleas, lice, and mites present similarly as in non-tropical environments. Onchocerciasis presents as an intensely pruritic evanescent papular rash.[68] Varicella, measles, or other childhood exanthems occur in non-immune travelers and should not be forgotten in the quest for exotic diagnoses. Seabathers eruption (sometimes called sea-lice) is a pruritic papular rash notable for being distributed only on skin covered by the patient's bathing suit.[69] Larval sea anemones become trapped by the fabric while the patient is swimming. The indurated erythematous chancre of *T. rhodesiense* (see Chapter 275) should not be overlooked.[70] Arboviral eruptions usually present as acute febrile illnesses and not as predominant rash illnesses. HIV and STDs need always be considered as a cause of exanthems and ulcerative lesions.

EOSINOPHILIA

In addition to parasitic causes, peripheral blood eosinophilia may be associated with a variety of dermatologic, immunologic, inflammatory, neoplastic and idiopathic etiologies. Returning travelers and long-term residents of tropical countries are as prone to non-parasitic causes of eosinophilia as is the general population, and these must be considered when obtaining a history and initiating a diagnostic work-up in a returned traveler. Schistosomiasis and strongyloidiasis are the most common parasitic causes of significant eosinophilia in returning travelers and serology should be sent on every traveler with potential exposure to either.[71,72]

Eosinophilia is a reaction to a tissue-invasive helminth, with its intensity being proportional to the degree of tissue invasion. During the initial larval migration phase after a new infection with a specific para-

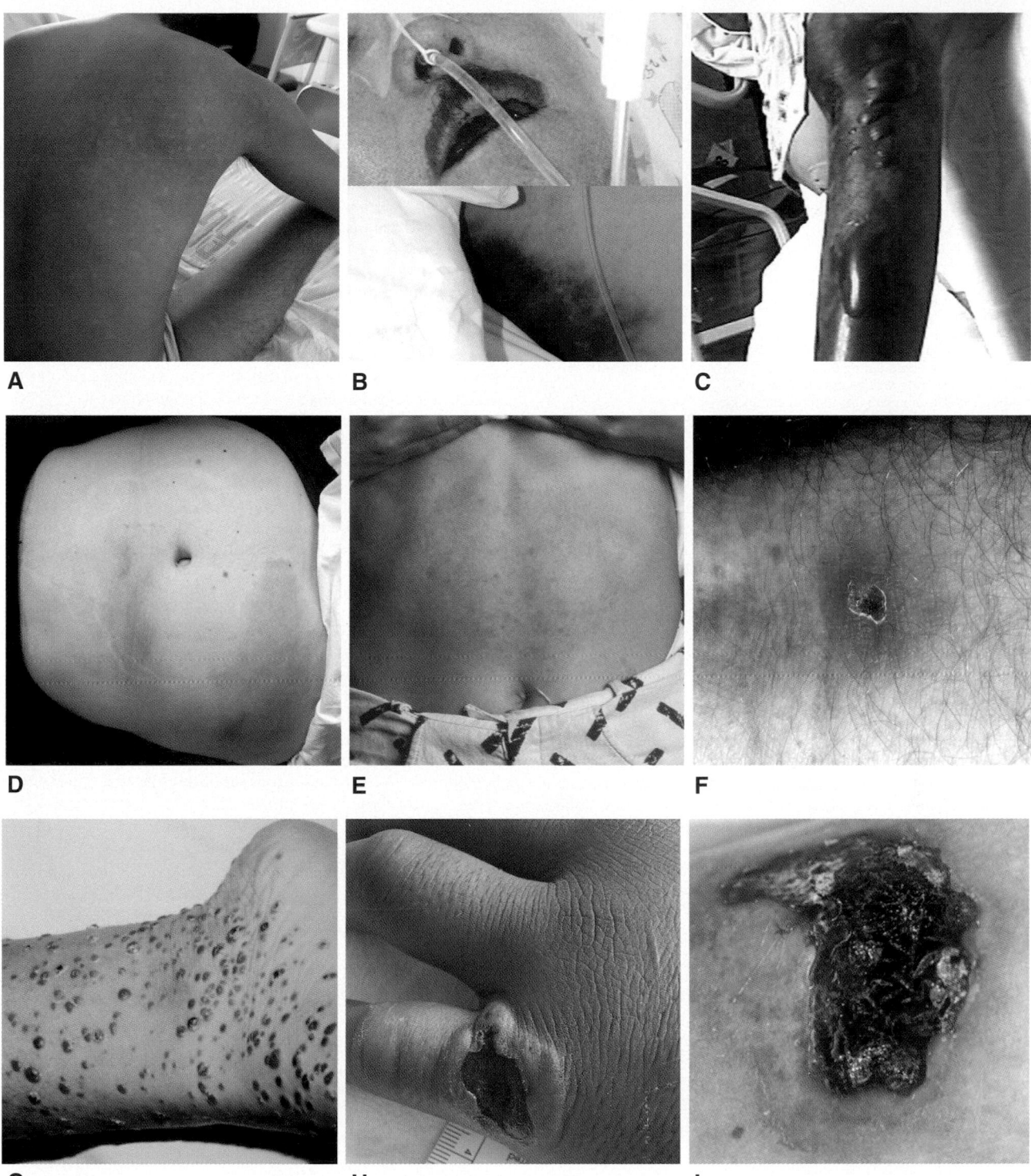

FIGURE 329-2. Cutaneous manifestations of some common systemic or widely disseminated diseases. **A,** Generalized macular rash of dengue; rash generally appears after 4 or 5 days but an earlier faint flush like rash may be present as well. **B,** Viral hemorrhagic fever due to yellow fever infection; typical signs of viral hemorrhagic fevers include bleeding from orifices and intravenous sites as well as diffuse petechiae or ecchymoses especially over pressure points. **C,** Sepsis due to *Vibrio vulnificus* infection after ingestion of contaminated shellfish; hemorrhagic bullae are seen in sepsis, envenomation, autoimmune disease but not with viral hemorrhagic fevers. **D,** Migratory lesions of infection with *Gnathostoma spinigerum* after ingestion of uncooked freshwater fish; larvae often leave a mildly hemorrhagic track. **E,** Faint papular highly pruritic dermatitis due to *Onchocerca volvulus* infection after travel to Sierra Leone; travelers who may not present for a year or more after travel are usually lightly infected and have no ocular manifestation. **F,** Typical eschar of African tick typhus due to *Rickettsia africae;* widely disseminated petechial vasculitic lesions are often present as well. **G,** Verruga peruana due to chronic infection with *Bartonella bacilliformis;* present only if the patient is not treated for and survives the acute bacteremic phase. **H,** Painless lesions of cutaneous anthrax; surrounding edema is characteristic and the base quickly evolves to become totally black and necrotic. **I,** Spider-bite due to *Loxosceles laeta;* unlike anthrax, spider bites are painful and usually have very irregular borders without significant edema. *(Images reprinted with permission of the Tropical Medicine Institute, Universidad Peruana Cayetano Heredia and the Gorgas Memorial Institute.)*

TABLE 329-3 Parasitic Causes of Eosinophilia

Widespread Geographic Distribution	Limited Geographic Distribution
Ascariasis (migratory phase)	Clonorchiasis[†]
Hookworm[†]	Paragonimiasis[†]
Strongyloidiasis[*,‡]	Fascioliasis[†]
Tropical pulmonary eosinophilia[*]	Angiostrongyliasis
Lymphatic filariasis	Opisthorciasis[†]
Schistosomiasis	Onchocerciasis, loiasis and other
Toxocariasis[*]	non-lymphatic filariasis
Cysticercosis (*Taenia solium*)	Gnathostomiasis
Echinococcosis (cyst rupture)	Capillariasis
Trichinosis[*]	Trichostrongyliasis
Trichuriasis	
Aberrant helminthiasis	
from animals	

[*]Most frequent parasitic causes of massive eosinophilia (>5000/mm³).
[†]Moderate to marked during larval migration in early infection; most often absent or very mild during chronic infection.
[‡]Absent in disseminated infection in compromised hosts.

site (e.g., hookworm), there may be an intense eosinophilia (up to 5000/mm³). Weeks or months later, when the mature adults reside in the intestine with only minimal tissue contact, eosinophilia will be mild or absent. Although eosinophilia is not seen in protozoan infection, local eosinophilic infiltrates exceptionally occur in areas of the intestinal tract penetrated by *Entamoeba histolytica,* Giardia lamblia, or *Isospora belli.*

While most laboratory reports express the eosinophil count as a percentage of the total white blood cell count, this practice can make it difficult to follow serial determinations in an individual patient. The absolute eosinophil count can be calculated easily and ranges from 0 to 350/mm³ (mean 120/mm³). Because the list of helminths inducing eosinophilia (Table 329-3) is extensive, and because many of the parasitologic and serologic techniques required for specific diagnosis are laborious and expensive, a well-obtained epidemiologic history is needed to narrow the differential diagnosis down to a manageable size. Some helpful physical findings are: dermatitis (onchocerciasis, cutaneous larva migrans, larva currens); migratory swellings (loiasis, gnathostomiasis), wheezing or cough (Strongyloides, hookworm, Ascaris, or Schistosoma larvae in the lung), hemoptysis (Paragonimus), hepatomegaly (Toxocara, Echinococcus); lymphedema (filariasis); facial edema, myositis (trichinosis); subcutaneous mass (cysticercosis), meningeal signs (angiostrongylus, Gnathostoma); abdominal tenderness (angiostrongylus, anisakiasis, fascioliasis).

The examination of stools for O&P is the first step and unfortunately, this crucial diagnostic procedure is dependent on the expertise of the individual lab. A concentration technique should be used and at least three separate stools examined. Eggs are only produced by mature adult worms so stool examinations will be negative during the initial larval migratory phase of intestinal helminths for up to 6 weeks after exposure. Strongyloides eggs hatch while still in the intestine and Baermann concentration or agar plate cultures are indicated if suspicion is high. Because most anthelmintic drugs only work on adult worms and not immature larvae, empiric therapy of a traveler with eosinophilia soon after return is of no benefit.

The following ancillary procedures are indicated when epidemiologically appropriate[73] or when dictated by specific symptoms: day and night blood concentrations (filariasis); skin snips (onchocerciasis); rectal snips or scrapings (schistosomiasis); urine concentration (schistosomiasis); duodenal aspirate (strongyloidiasis); sputum for O&P (migrating larvae, strongyloides, paragonimus); and biopsy of any abnormal lesions. Serology is available for many of the common helminthic infections, but it is hampered by lack of standardization and broad cross reactivity amongst many helminth species. Nevertheless, an unequivocally elevated parasite-specific serum IgG level can be extremely helpful when positive in the setting of a previously naïve traveler with a history of exposure to only one or a few specific parasites. Schistosomiasis and strongyloides are the two most common causes of

parasitic eosinophilia. Stool and more invasive examination is often negative and diagnosis often depends on positive serology.

The detection of one parasitic infection doesn't preclude the presence of another. All individuals should complete the diagnostic work-up that is clinically and epidemiologically indicated. Similarly, all treated patients should be followed up to be certain that both infection and eosinophilia have resolved. An anomalous exacerbation of the eosinophilia may occur for 2-3 weeks after treatment as parasites die and release their antigens. Eosinophilia may not totally resolve for 6 months or more after adequate treatment of the inciting helminth but no response whatsoever for a month or more after treatment may be a sign of inadequate response to treatment.

SCREENING FOR ASYMPTOMATIC INFECTION

Completely asymptomatic returned travelers may present with a request to be checked-out for possible tropical disease. The limited number of cost-effectiveness studies that are available have yet to show significant benefit to this approach on a population basis.[74-76] Neither a clinic visit nor any non-directed laboratory screening of returned very-short term travelers is indicated. Exceptions are those with known discrete high-risk exposure events in situations conducive to transmission of specific agents. This would include testing for HIV and other STDS, a PPD skin test, or schistosoma serology. For those who have spent 6 months or more under any conditions in a developing country, a PPD skin test is the highest priority even without a specific exposure. For those living under harsher conditions, any abnormalities found on a complete physical examination, including a dermatologic assessment, that would lead to specific laboratory testing should be sought first. For general screening, stool for O&P and an eosinophil count are used by most. Serology for schistosomiasis, filarial infection, and strongyloides is often performed but should be strictly limited to those with extended travel to a known endemic area for each pathogen tested for. Those with new sexual partners should be screened for HIV and STDs at an appropriate interval after last potential exposure. Malaria smears are not indicated in asymptomatic travelers, even those with a remote history of malaria exposure during the travel, but primaquine treatment for those at risk of later relapse of *P. vivax* or *P. ovale* is.

REFERENCES

1. Steffen R, deBernardis C, Banos A. Travel epidemiology—A global perspective. Int J Antimicrob Agents. 2003;21:89-95.
2. Steffen R, Rickenbach M, Wilhelm U, et al. Health problems after travel to developing countries. J Infect Dis. 1987;156:84-91.
3. Hill DR. Health problems in a large cohort of Americans traveling to developing countries. J Travel Med. 2000;7:259-266.
4. Ryan ET, Wilson ME, Kain KC. Illness after international travel. N Engl J Med. 2002;347:505-516.
5. Doherty JF, Grant AD, Bryceson AD. Fever as the presenting complaint of travellers returning from the tropics. QJM. 1995;88:277-281.
6. O'Brien D, Tobin S, Brown GV, Torresi J. Fever in returned travelers: Review of hospital admissions for a 3-year period. Clin Infect Dis. 2001;33:603-609.
7. Giangrande PL. Air travel and thrombosis. Br J Haematol. 2002;117:509-512.
8. D'Acremont V, Ambresin AE, Burnand B, Genton B. Practice guidelines for evaluation of fever in returning travelers and migrants. J Travel Med. 2003;10(Suppl 2):S25-S52.
9. Keystone JS. GIDEON computer program for diagnosing and teaching geographic medicine. J Travel Med. 1999;6:152-154.
10. Cetron MS, Chitsulo L, Sullivan JJ, et al. Schistosomiasis in Lake Malawi. Lancet. 1996;348:1274-1278.
11. Grobusch MP, Muhlberger N, Jelinek T, et al. Imported schistosomiasis in Europe: Sentinel surveillance data from TropNetEurop. J Travel Med. 2003;10:164-167.
12. Sejvar J, Bancroft E, Winthrop K, et al. Leptospirosis in "Eco-Challenge" athletes, Malaysian Borneo, 2000. Emerg Infect Dis. 2003;9:702-707.
13. Cabada MM, Echevarria JI, Seas CR, et al. Sexual behavior of international travelers visiting Peru. Sex Transm Dis. 2002;29:510-513.
14. Mulhall BP. Sex and travel: Studies of sexual behaviour, disease and health promotion in international travellers—A global review. Int J STD AIDS. 1996;7:455-465.
15. Felton JM, Bryceson AD. Fever in the returning traveller. Br J Hosp Med. 1996;55:705-711.
16. Newman RD, Barber AM, Roberts J, et al. Malaria surveillance—United States, 1999. MMWR Surveill Summ. 2002;51:15-28.
17. Dorsey G, Gandhi M, Oyugi JH, Rosenthal PJ. Difficulties in the prevention, diagnosis, and treatment of imported malaria. Arch Intern Med. 2000;160:2505-2510.

18. Svenson JE, MacLean JD, Gyorkos TW, Keystone J. Imported malaria. Clinical presentation and examination of symptomatic travelers. Arch Intern Med. 1995;155:861-868.

19. D'Acremont V, Landry P, Mueller I, et al. Clinical and laboratory predictors of imported malaria in an outpatient setting: An aid to medical decision making in returning travelers with fever. Am J Trop Med Hyg. 2002;66:481-486.

20. Jelinek T. Dengue fever in international travelers. Clin Infect Dis. 2000;31:144-147.

21. Lindback H, Lindback J, Tegnell A, et al. Dengue fever in travelers to the tropics, 1998 and 1999. Emerg Infect Dis. 2003;9:438-442.

22. Schwartz E, Moskovitz A, Potasman I, et al. Changing epidemiology of dengue fever in travelers to Thailand. Eur J Clin Microbiol Infect Dis. 2000;19:784-786.

23. Mermin JH, Townes JM, Gerber M, et al. Typhoid fever in the United States, 1985-1994: Changing risks of international travel and increasing antimicrobial resistance. Arch Intern Med. 1998;158:633-638.

24. Caumes E, Ehya N, Nguyen J, Bricaire F. Typhoid and paratyphoid fever: A 10-year retrospective study of 41 cases in a Parisian hospital. J Travel Med. 2001;8:293-297.

25. Schwartz E, Shlim DR, Eaton M, et al. The effect of oral and parenteral typhoid vaccination on the rate of infection with *Salmonella typhi* and *Salmonella paratyphi* A among foreigners in Nepal. Arch Intern Med. 1990;150:349-351.

26. Crump JA, Barrett TJ, Nelson JT, Angulo FJ. Reevaluating fluoroquinolone breakpoints for *Salmonella enterica* serotype Typhi and for non-Typhi salmonellae. Clin Infect Dis. 2003;37:75-81.

27. Piper-Jenks N, Horowitz HW, Schwartz E. Risk of hepatitis E infection to travelers. J Travel Med. 2000;7:194-199.

28. McDonald JC, MacLean JD, McDade JE. Imported rickettsial disease: Clinical and epidemiologic features. Am J Med. 1988;85:799-805.

29. Marschang A, Nothdurft HD, Kumlien S, von Sonnenburg F. Imported rickettsioses in German travelers. Infection. 1995;23:94-97.

30. Raoult D, Fournier PE, Fenollar F, et al. *Rickettsia africae*, a tick-borne pathogen in travelers to sub-Saharan Africa. N Engl J Med. 2001;344:1504-1510.

31. Groen J, Nur YA, Dolmans W, et al. Scrub and murine typhus among Dutch travellers. Infection. 1999;27:291-292.

32. Jensenius M, Fournier PE, Vene S, et al. African tick bite fever in travelers to rural sub-Equatorial Africa. Clin Infect Dis. 2003;36:1411-1417.

33. Yersin C, Bovet P, Smits HL, Perolat P. Field evaluation of a one-step dipstick assay for the diagnosis of human leptospirosis in the Seychelles. Trop Med Int Health. 1999;4:38-45.

34. Leder K, Sundararajan V, Weld L, et al. Respiratory tract infections in travelers: A review of the GeoSentinel surveillance network. Clin Infect Dis. 2003;36:399-406.

35. Miller JM, Tam TW, Maloney S, et al. Cruise ships: High-risk passengers and the global spread of new influenza viruses. Clin Infect Dis. 2000;31:433-438.

36. Fields BS, Benson RF, Besser RE. *Legionella* and Legionnaires' disease: 25 years of investigation. Clin Microbiol Rev. 2002;15:506-526.

37. Lever F, Joseph CA. Travel associated legionnaires' disease in Europe in 1999. Euro Surveill. 2001;6:53-61.

38. Panackal AA, Hajjeh RA, Cetron MS, Warnock DW. Fungal infections among returning travelers. Clin Infect Dis. 2002;35:1088-1095.

39. Cobelens FG, van Deutekom H, Draayer-Jansen IW, et al. Association of tuberculin sensitivity in Dutch adults with history of travel to areas of with a high incidence of tuberculosis. Clin Infect Dis. 2001;33:300-304.

40. Isaacson M. Viral hemorrhagic fever hazards for travelers in Africa. Clin Infect Dis. 2001;33:1707-1712.

41. Doyle TJ, Bryan RT, Peters CJ. Viral hemorrhagic fevers and hantavirus infections in the Americas. Infect Dis Clin North Am. 1998;12:95-110.

42. Bausch DG, Ksiazek TG. Viral hemorrhagic fevers including hantavirus pulmonary syndrome in the Americas. Clin Lab Med. 2002;22:981-1020.

43. Khan AS, Maupin GO, Rollin PE, et al. An outbreak of Crimean-Congo hemorrhagic fever in the United Arab Emirates, 1994-1995. Am J Trop Med Hyg. 1997;57:519-525.

44. Peters CJ. Emerging infections—Ebola and other filoviruses. West J Med. 1996;164:36-38.

45. Hughes MA, Petri WA Jr. Amebic liver abscess. Infect Dis Clin North Am. 2000;14:565-582, viii.

46. Svenson JE, Gyorkos TW, MacLean JD. Diagnosis of malaria in the febrile traveler. Am J Trop Med Hyg. 1995;53:518-521.

47. Memish ZA. Meningococcal disease and travel. Clin Infect Dis. 2002;34:84-90.

48. Adachi JA, Jiang ZD, Mathewson JJ, et al. Enteroaggregative *Escherichia coli* as a major etiologic agent in traveler's diarrhea in 3 regions of the world. Clin Infect Dis. 2001;32:1706-1709.

49. von Sonnenburg F, Tornieporth N, Waiyaki P, et al. Risk and aetiology of diarrhoea at various tourist destinations. Lancet. 2000;356:133-134.

50. Steffen R, Collard F, Tornieporth N, et al. Epidemiology, etiology, and impact of traveler's diarrhea in Jamaica. JAMA. 1999;281:811-817.

51. Paredes P, Campbell-Forrester S, Mathewson JJ, et al. Etiology of travelers' diarrhea on a Caribbean island. J Travel Med. 2000;7:15-18.

52. Outbreaks of gastroenteritis associated with noroviruses on cruise ships—United States, 2002. MMWR Morb Mortal Wkly Rep. 2002;51:1112-1115.

53. Farthing MJ. Travellers' diarrhoea. Gut. 1994;35:1-4.

54. Shlim DR, Hoge CW, Rajah R, et al. Persistent high risk of diarrhea among foreigners in Nepal during the first 2 years of residence. Clin Infect Dis. 1999;29:613-616.

55. Adachi JA, Ostrosky-Zeichner L, DuPont HL, Ericsson CD. Empirical antimicrobial therapy for traveler's diarrhea. Clin Infect Dis. 2000;31:1079-1083.

56. Shanks GD, Smoak BL, Aleman GM, et al. Single dose of azithromycin or three-day course of ciprofloxacin as therapy for epidemic dysentery in Kenya. Acute Dysentery Study Group. Clin Infect Dis. 1999;29:942-943.

57. DuPont HL, Jiang ZD, Ericsson CD, et al. Rifaximin versus ciprofloxacin for the treatment of traveler's diarrhea: A randomized, double-blind clinical trial. Clin Infect Dis. 2001;33:1807-1815.

58. Cook GC. Persisting diarrhoea and malabsorption. Gut. 1994;35:582-586.

59. Farthing MJ. Tropical malabsorption. Semin Gastrointest Dis. 2002;13:221-231.

60. Farthing MJ. Giardiasis. Gastroenterol Clin North Am. 1996;25:493-515.

61. Veitch AM, Kelly P, Zulu IS, et al. Tropical enteropathy: A T-cell–mediated crypt hyperplastic enteropathy. Eur J Gastroenterol Hepatol. 2001;13:1175-1181.

62. Talley NJ, Spiller R. Irritable bowel syndrome: A little understood organic bowel disease? Lancet. 2002;360:555-564.

63. Caumes E, Carriere J, Guermonprez G, et al. Dermatoses associated with travel to tropical countries: A prospective study of the diagnosis and management of 269 patients presenting to a tropical disease unit. Clin Infect Dis. 1995;20:542-548.

64. Wilson ME. Skin problems in the traveler. Infect Dis Clin North Am. 1998;12:471-488.

65. Herwaldt BL, Stokes SL, Juranek DD. American cutaneous leishmaniasis in U.S. travelers. Ann Intern Med. 1993;118:779-784.

66. Klion AD, Massougbodji A, Sadeler BC, et al. Loiasis in endemic and nonendemic populations: Immunologically mediated differences in clinical presentation. J Infect Dis. 1991;163:1318-1325.

67. Moore DA, McCroddan J, Dekumyoy P, Chiodini PL. Gnathostomiasis: An emerging imported disease. Emerg Infect Dis. 2003;9:647-650.

68. McCarthy JS, Ottesen EA, Nutman TB. Onchocerciasis in endemic and nonendemic populations: Differences in clinical presentation and immunologic findings. J Infect Dis. 1994;170:736-741.

69. Freudenthal AR, Joseph PR. Seabather's eruption. N Engl J Med. 1993;329:542-544.

70. McGovern TW, Williams W, Fitzpatrick JE, et al. Cutaneous manifestations of African trypanosomiasis. Arch Dermatol. 1995;131:1178-1182.

71. Schulte C, Krebs B, Jelinek T, et al. Diagnostic significance of blood eosinophilia in returning travelers. Clin Infect Dis. 2002;34:407-411.

72. Whitty CJ, Mabey DC, Armstrong M, et al. Presentation and outcome of 1107 cases of schistosomiasis from Africa diagnosed in a non-endemic country. Trans R Soc Trop Med Hyg. 2000;94:531-534.

73. Whetham J, Day JN, Armstrong M, et al. Investigation of tropical eosinophilia; assessing a strategy based on geographical area. J Infect. 2003;46:180-185.

74. Carroll B, Dow C, Snashall D, et al. Post-tropical screening: How useful is it? BMJ. 1993;307:541.

75. MacLean JD, Libman M. Screening returning travelers. Infect Dis Clin North Am. 1998;12:431-443.

76. Whitty CJ, Carroll B, Armstrong M, et al. Utility of history, examination and laboratory tests in screening those returning to Europe from the tropics for parasitic infection. Trop Med Int Health. 2000;5:818-823.

CHAPTER **330**

The Infectious Diseases Physician and Digital Resources

GREGORY C. TOWNSEND

The widespread use of the Internet and the emergence of handheld computers have opened an exciting realm of possibilities for the Infectious Diseases physician. For the first time, a physician may gain access to the contents of a library's worth of textbooks and journals wherever he or she is without having to carry around reams of paper. The latest news on disease outbreaks, advances in diagnosis and therapy, and clinical trials is available around-the-clock and is updated weekly, daily, or even hourly. The recommendations and advice of some of the world's leading authorities on a multitude of subjects may be obtained at any time at the click of a mouse or stylus. With such a wealth of resources, the problem facing the physician is often not whether or not information on a particular subject is available, but how and where to readily find information that is accurate, complete and current.

THE INTERNET

A Brief Overview

The Internet grew out of the United States Department of Defense Advanced Research Projects Agency (DARPA). The ARPANET, as it was originally known, was at its inception in the 1960s a network of military and university computers able to share data. It was not until the 1990s that the capacity of such a network to share information for general use was realized. The Internet became totally privatized in the United States in 1995.

Most users will primarily access information on the Internet through the World Wide Web, which provides a graphical display for information available on the source computer in the form of "pages." The Web was made possible by the creation of the HyperText Mark-Up Language (HTML) by Swiss software designer Tim Berners-Lee in the 1980s. HTML is the coding language that describes how information is displayed on the Web. One of the key elements of HTML is the presence of links that allow the user to go directly from one document to another related document. The Web uses the HyperText Transfer Protocol (HTTP), also created by Berners-Lee, to determine how the information is transferred between linked computers. The Web and HTTP can be used to transfer files, but is generally not as fast in that regard as are some other protocols, which may be important for large files. However, it is safe to say that it was the emergence of the Web, and of Web browsers to access the information via a graphical format, that engendered the explosion of Internet use in the 1990s.

Another commonly used Internet protocol is the File Transfer Protocol (FTP). As the name implies, FTP is used strictly for the transfer of electronic files from one computer to another, and is particularly useful for transferring large files because of its speed. And of course there is e-mail, which is used for asynchronous communication and can also be used to deliver files.

It is important to recognize that the Internet is a largely unregulated patchwork quilt of individual computers and computer networks.

There are standards and protocols that have been established that define the ways in which packets of data can be transferred from one computer to another and in which information is presented to the end-user. Any computer using the Internet must abide by these standards to connect to other computers on the network to distribute or access information. However, there is no agency charged with ensuring that such information is reliable or appropriate.

Since the most common use of the Internet for the infectious diseases clinician is likely to be the retrieval of information from the Web, that use will be the focus of this discussion. However, the ability of the Internet to facilitate the exchange of information between scientists, for which it was originally designed, must be acknowledged and appreciated. For example, the rapid identification and characterization of the novel coronavirus responsible for the severe acute respiratory syndrome (SARS) and the creation of diagnostic tests for the virus were greatly facilitated by the ability of clinicians and researchers to readily exchange information across the Internet. The Internet can also be used to provide a place to collate and distribute useful information in a community regarding communicable diseases, and to provide information about worldwide outbreaks.[1,2]

It must be kept in mind that anyone with a computer, a little bit of computer knowledge, applicable software, and network access can create a Web page purporting to provide information about a subject. Thus it is imperative that the user critically evaluates at least the source of the information, and if possible the information itself, before using it to make any important decisions. In general, Web pages from governmental sources, national and international agencies, and academic institutions are probably the most reliable. Many journals are now also available on the Web to subscribers, and in most cases articles from these journals are available for download.

In addition to the reliability of the information presented, many other features of a website may impact on the user's experience. These include the availability of links to other sources, the ability to perform a search at the site, the speed with which the pages at the site are displayed, the ease with which different pages at the site can be accessed, the ability to download materials such as articles from the site, and the presence of intrusive and distracting elements such as advertisements. A well designed website will enable the user to retrieve the desired information with a minimum of time and effort.

Some of the elements influencing the user's satisfaction with a website will of course also be affected by the user's local computing environment. The speed of any interaction, such as the speed with which documents are displayed or retrieved, is influenced by the speed of the user's computer and the bandwidth, which is the amount of data that can be delivered along the network in a given period of time. Users at institutions may have difficulty accessing some websites or downloading materials due to the presence of security software known as firewalls; firewalls are intended to protect the institution's computers from software viruses and other attempts to compromise the computers, and to ensure that the computers are used appropriately. Some websites may require the presence of specialized software on the user's computer, such as software to decode the Java scripting language or specialized media content, to access all of the content. Some websites are also designed to take advantage of a specific Web browser's capabilities, so that using another browser may result in a suboptimal experience; although many of these websites will alert the user to this situation, this is not necessarily the case. And use of any downloaded documents may require that the user has the necessary applications to open them.

Navigating the Web

One of the great benefits of the Web is that, with hundreds of millions of computers networked, there is a wealth of information available. This is also a potential drawback, as it may be difficult to find information on a specific topic without a well-designed search strategy. There are a number of "search engines" that can be used to look for information; these are websites that use software and human operators to search the Web and index its contents. Most search engines get information using the "Web crawling" approach, in which software constantly searches Web pages and catalogs the words or images found on the pages.

Once the information retrieved from the Web has been indexed, there are two ways in which the user can look for information on a given topic at a search engine. One method is to ask the search engine to look through its index of catalogued Web pages for a specific term by entering the term in a search box. Such a search will return a list of all of the Web pages containing that term that have been indexed. Alternatively, some search engines use a taxonomic approach, in which Web pages or sites are placed in a structured hierarchy based on the topic of the contents as assessed by personnel. At some search engines, such as Yahoo and Google, either approach may be used. Each approach has its advantages and disadvantages, and in a sense they are opposite sides of the same coin. The taxonomic approach, while useful for identifying a manageable number of Web pages with information about a specific topic, is labor-intensive and therefore limited in scope; relevant Web pages may be missed. On the other hand, a search for the term "HIV" at a typical search engine will return a list of millions of pages, so a more restrictive but still encompassing strategy is obviously needed.

The most obvious method to narrow one's search at a search engine is to use as many applicable words as may be appropriate in the search term. For example, if one is specifically interested in information about a vaccine for HIV, adding "vaccine" to our "HIV" search returns a list of "only" a few hundred thousand pages. If interested in only those HIV vaccines that have been tested in clinical trials, further adding "trial" to our search terms returns less than 100,000 pages. This strategy can be carried further until a manageable number of results are returned. Most search engines also have the ability to perform searches using Boolean terms, wherein combinations of terms may be sought and certain words or even phrases may be required or excluded, and can limit searches using criteria such as language or date. Fortunately, most search engines list the results in order of calculated relevance so that the most useful results will probably be near the top of the list.

Although search engines may be useful for browsing the Web for medical information, it is probably more worthwhile to identify sources that provide information on, or links to, specific topics. A discussion of some of those sites is presented below, and others are also provided in Table 330-1. Please keep in mind that the Web by its nature is a fluid environment, and that although the Internet addresses provided are valid at the time of this writing, some sites may have changed addresses or disappeared by the time you read this. In a study of 184 health-related websites identified from December 1998 to May 1999, only 24% were still at their original Internet address in 2002, and 59% could not be found.[3] Also, the lists presented here are not intended to be exhaustive or complete, and almost certainly some new sites will have emerged by the time you read this. These lists should be viewed as starting points to access information about the topics detailed, and as examples of well-designed sites.

There are some sites not specifically related to infectious diseases that may nonetheless prove valuable to the infectious diseases clinician. UpToDate (*http://www.uptodate.com/*) is a subscription-based service that features articles on a multitude of medical subjects. The articles are evidence-based and are updated several times a year. Another subscription service is MD Consult (*http://www.mdconsult.com/*), which has a specific infectious diseases section. At this site, literature searches may be performed, and where available full text articles can be downloaded. There are also news updates, patient handouts, and links to practice guidelines. MerckMedicus (*http://www.merckmedicus.com/*) is a free service that provides clinically oriented resources and links to some journals and textbooks.

One of the more useful general infectious diseases sites is the homepage for the National Center for Infectious Diseases (NCID) at the U.S. Centers for Disease Control and Prevention (CDC) (*http://www.cdc.gov/ncidod/index.htm*). The NCID site serves as a clearinghouse of information for practitioners and consumers on a va-

riety of topics. Similarly, the homepage for the World Health Organization (WHO) (*http://www.who.int/en/*) serves as a repository of information on topics particularly related to international health.

Excellent information on international travel is available from the WHO (*http://www.who.int/ith/*) and from the CDC (*http://www.cdc.gov/travel/*). Both sites provide online access to textbooks related to the prevention and management of travel-related diseases. These resources are particularly helpful in advising an individual who is preparing to travel regarding conditions in the intended travel area and recommended immunizations and other prophylactic measures.

Other sites related to specific topics are presented in Table 330-1; information on specific topics can also be found at general sites such as the CDC and WHO sites. Many of these sites and the others mentioned above provide educational materials for consumers, clinicians, and researchers that can be downloaded in a variety of popular electronic file formats, such as Portable Document Format (PDF), Microsoft Word, or Microsoft PowerPoint. Some sites serve largely as portals, that is, they provide links to other sites related to a specific topic.

A number of professional organizations related to infectious diseases also have websites. General sites include the websites for the Infectious Diseases Society of America (*http://www.idsociety.org/*) and the National Foundation for Infectious Diseases (*http://www.nfid.org/*), and there are of course sites for organizations concerned with specific elements of infectious diseases. These sites generally provide links to other sites, factsheets, and other resources. They may also link to conferences associated with the organizations, and in some cases abstracts from the conferences can be accessed.

In addition to such sites, as noted above many journals are now available online to subscribers (Table 330-2). Many institutions purchase site license subscriptions to relevant journals for its faculty and employees to use. These journals (sometimes referred to as E-journals) provide many features that may make them useful to infectious diseases clinicians and researchers, such as online bibliographic links, links to websites, e-mail notifications of user specified content, search engines, and the ability to download and print articles and graphics.[4] In addition to these online journals, abstracts from the U.S. National Library of Medicine are available online through PubMed (*http://www.ncbi.nlm.nih.gov/PubMed/*).

Some websites provide entire online textbooks related to infectious diseases or microbiology, in general or pertaining to a specific topic (see Table 330-2). There are also CD-ROM versions of some infectious diseases textbooks. One of the great advantages of a digital textbook over a paper-based version is the enhanced indexing and cross-referencing capabilities in the former. Search facilities make it easy to find information about a specific topic, and in-text links facilitate the user's ability to find related references. Some digital texts also provide bibliographic links to abstracts.

There are a number of websites that provide online infectious diseases-related practice guidelines (Table 330-3). These guidelines are generally well written and evidence-based.[5] In many cases the guidelines are updated at least annually, and in some cases may be updated several times a year, such as with many of the HIV-related guidelines at the U.S. Department of Health and Human Service's AIDSinfo site (*http://www.aidsinfo.nih.gov/*). Most of these guidelines may be downloaded in PDF format, although in some cases a subscription to the journal in which the guideline is published is required.

A uniquely creative use of the possibilities of the Web in infectious diseases is the Global Infectious Diseases and Epidemiology Network (GIDEON) (*http://www.gideononline.com/*). GIDEON is a fee-based computer program that provides algorithmic assistance in diagnosing and treating infectious diseases guided by user-entered symptoms and epidemiology. It can also help in identifying an organism by microbiologic characteristics. There is an emphasis on international diseases, but all diseases and pathogens are covered. GIDEON is accessible from the Web and is also available on CD-ROM.

It is important for clinicians to keep in mind that patients with Internet access are also using the Web to access health information and even to purchase pharmaceuticals.[6] A survey of more than 4000

TABLE 330-1   Selected Infectious Diseases-Related Resources on the World Wide Web

Topic	Internet Address (URL)	Name/Description
General information	http://www.cdc.gov/ncidod/index.htm	U.S. National Center for Infectious Diseases
	http://www.phls.co.uk/	U.K. Health Protection Agency: infectious diseases
	http://www.who.int/en/	World Health Organization
	http://ID.medscape.com/Home/Topics/ID/InfectiousDiseases.html	Medscape Infectious Diseases
	http://wordnet.com.au/infectious_diseases.htm	Wordnet Infectious Diseases
	http://www.infectiousdiseasenews.com/	Infectious Diseases News
	http://www.idsociety.org/	Infectious Diseases Society of America
	http://www.nfid.org/	National Foundation for Infectious Diseases
	http://isid.org/	International Society for Infectious Diseases
	http://www.ama-assn.org/ama/pub/category/1797.html	AMA Infectious Diseases Resources
	http://www.cidrap.umn.edu/cidrap/content/bt/smallpox/index.html	Center for Infectious Disease Research & Policy
	http://www.hopkins-id.edu/	Johns Hopkins Infectious Diseases
	http://www.vh.org/navigation/vh/topics/adult_provider_infections.html	Virtual Hospital: Infections
Portals	http://www.virology.net/garryfavweb.html	All the Virology on the WWW
	http://www.nlm.nih.gov/medlineplus/infections.html	MEDLINEplus: Infections Topics
	http://www.mic.ki.se/Diseases/c1.html	Bacterial Infections and Mycoses
	http://www.ohsu.edu/cliniweb/C10/C10.228.228.html	Central Nervous System Infections
	http://www.microbelibrary.org/	MicrobeLibrary.org (from the American Society for Microbiology)
	http://www.immunofacts.com/	ImmunoFacts (links regarding immunizations)
	http://vaccines.com/	The Vaccine Page
International travel	http://www.who.int/ith/	World Health Organization International travel and health
	http://www.cdc.gov/travel/	CDC Travelers' Health
Topic-specific	http://www.aidsinfo.nih.gov/	AIDSinfo
	http://www.aegis.com/	AIDS Education Global Information System
	http://www.caps.ucsf.edu/	Center for AIDS Prevention Studies
	http://hivinsite.ucsf.edu/InSite	HIV InSite
	http://www.hivresistanceweb.com/protected/podium/podium_main.shtml	HIVresistanceWEB
	http://www.hopkins-biodefense.org/index.html	Center for Civilian Biodefense Strategies
	http://www.commoncold.org/index.htm	Common Cold
	http://www.geis.ha.osd.mil/	U.S. Dept. of Defense Global Emerging Infections System
	http://homepages.lshtm.ac.uk/entamoeba/	The Entamoeba Homepage
	http://www.helicobacter.org/	European Helicobacter Study Group
	http://www.hepnet.com/	Hepatitis Information Network
	http://www.ihmf.org/Default.asp	International Herpes Management Forum
	http://www.immunizationinfo.org/	National Network for Immunization Information
	http://legionella.org/	Legionella Prevention
	http://www.aldf.com/	American Lyme Disease Foundation
	http://www.lyme.org/	Lyme Disease Foundation
	http://www.malaria.org/	Malaria Foundation International
	http://www.rabies.com/	Rabies.org
	http://www.nise.cc/index.php3	National Initiative in Sepsis Education
	http://www.ashastd.org/	American Social Health Association (focuses on sexually transmitted diseases)
	http://www.ncbi.nlm.nih.gov/ICTVdb/	Virus databases online
	http://www.vetmed.wisc.edu/pbs/zoonoses/	Zoonotic Disease Tutorial

URL, uniform resource locator.

Internet users in the United States published in 2003 revealed that 40% of respondents reported using the Internet to access information about health or health care.[7] These patients often bring this information, and questions that may have resulted, to their physicians. Some of this information may be accurate, and in some cases may not have already been brought to the physician's attention, representing a potential source of information and further incentive for continuing education for the clinician. However, in many cases the information is inaccurate, incomplete, anecdotal, or biased.[8] As a result of the relatively easy access to this information, the physician may find himself being asked to answer questions or to respond to comments at a patient's visit without having the information needed to do so reliably. In those cases, it is probably best to defer a response until the physician has had time to review the information in question, which unfortunately may be a time-consuming process.

Many academic institutions and other facilities have websites providing information about their programs. It is fairly easy now for clinicians, researchers, and patients to search the Web for individuals with expertise in a specific area. In some cases it is even possible to pose questions to these individuals using the Web directly or via an e-mail link.

The Web provides a number of other opportunities for the infectious diseases physician or researcher. Many clinical trials are advertised on the Web, facilitating recruitment of patients. Grant opportunities are often announced on the Web as well, and many documents needed for the grants may be downloaded from the websites. Academic institutions use the Web to promote themselves in an effort to attract faculty and trainees.

The use of the Internet as a resource is certainly not without drawbacks. The most obvious of these is that, for the most part, efficient retrieval of information from the Web requires a networked computer, which may be inconvenient or impossible to access when the information is needed. A lack of adequate bandwidth in many areas means that data transfer may be frustratingly slow in comparison with getting information stored on the user's computer. As noted above, it may be difficult to find a trustworthy source of information about a specific topic, and when information is found, it must be assessed critically. Despite these problems, the Internet has become an increasingly important and pervasive part of current medical practice, research, and education, and no doubt will continue to do so for the foreseeable future.

PERSONAL DIGITAL ASSISTANTS

The concept of handheld computers has been around for decades-Gene Roddenberry, the creator of the original 1960s "Star Trek" science fiction television series, mandated that the crew of the starship Enterprise in the series could not use paper and pencil, but instead recorded information and communicated using handheld electronic devices. The first commercially available personal digital assistants (PDAs) appeared in

TABLE 330-2   Selected Infectious Diseases-Related Online Journals and Textbooks Available through the World Wide Web

	Internet Address (URL)	Title
Online journals	http://www.cdc.gov/ncidod/eid/index.htm	Emerging Infectious Diseases
	http://infection.thelancet.com/journal	The Lancet Infectious Diseases
	http://www.journals.uchicago.edu/CID/home.html	Clinical Infectious Diseases
	http://www.journals.uchicago.edu/JID/home.html	The Journal of Infectious Diseases
	http://aac.asm.org/	Antimicrobial Agents and Chemotherapy
	http://iai.asm.org/	Infection and Immunity
	http://www.pidj.com/	The Pediatric Infectious Disease Journal
	http://www.co-infectiousdiseases.com/	Current Opinion in Infectious Diseases
	http://jac.oupjournals.org/	Journal of Antimicrobial Chemotherapy
	http://www.current-reports.com/home_journal.cfm?JournalID=IR	Current Infectious Diseases Reports
	http://ichejournal.com/	Infection Control and Hospital Epidemiology
	http://ije.oupjournals.org/	International Journal of Epidemiology
	http://www.sciencedirect.com/science/journal/13866532	Journal of Clinical Virology
	http://www.sciencedirect.com/science/journal/00207519	International Journal for Parasitology
	http://www.sciencedirect.com/science/journal/01634453	Journal of Infection
	http://sti.bmjjournals.com/	Sexually Transmitted Infections
	http://www.aidsonline.com/	AIDS
	http://www.jaids.com/	JAIDS
	http://www.cdc.gov/mmwr/	Morbidity and Mortality Weekly Report
Online textbooks	http://vm.cfsan.fda.gov/mow/intro.html	U.S. FDA Foodborne Pathogenic Microorganisms and Natural Toxins Handbook (The *"Bad Bug Book"*)
	http://gsbs.utmb.edu/microbook/	Medical Microbiology (from the University of Texas)
	http://www.tulane.edu/dmsander/Big_Virology/BVHomePage.html	The Big Picture Book of Viruses (from Tulane University)
	http://www.medmicro.wisc.edu/Resources/ImageLib/Mycology/index.html	Medical Mycology (from the University of Wisconsin)
	http://www.icp.ucl.ac.be/opperd/parasites/	Parasitology Course (from the Christian de Duve Institute of Cellular Pathology)
	http://www.bact.wisc.edu/microtextbook/	Microbiology Webbed Out (from the University of Wisconsin)
	http://hopkins-aids.edu/publications/book/book_toc.html	Medical Management of HIV Infection (from Johns Hopkins University)

URL, uniform resource locator.

1993 with the introduction of Amstrad's PenPad and Apple Computer's Newton MessagePad; in fact Apple coined the term "personal digital assistant" to describe the Newton device. However, these devices were beset by problems such as faulty handwriting recognition and were eventually discontinued. Although Palm Computing introduced its first models in 1996, the modern PDA era began in earnest in 1998 with the Palm III. PDAs have gained steadily in popularity and in functionality since then. Worldwide sales of PDAs (including SmartPhones) are expected to nearly triple from 2003 to 2008 to almost 60 million units annually. A recent survey of its members by the American College of Physicians-American Society of Internal Medicine revealed that nearly half of the respondents use a PDA.[9]

The increasing speed and storage capacity of PDAs has made it possible for them to be used as repositories of large amounts of readily accessible medical information. Processor speeds of the newer PDAs are narrowing the gap with desktop computers, making it practical to look up information quickly when it is needed. While on-board storage capacity remains limited, the use of high capacity external interchangeable expansion memory cards enables the user to access the contents of entire electronic manuals, clinical care guidelines and management algorithm schemes at the bedside, in the clinic, or while

teaching. Wireless Internet capability also permits the user to search the Web or communicate with colleagues without the need for a desktop computer. PDAs can now connect wirelessly to individual computers and to the Internet, take and send pictures, be used as telephones, and so on.

The use of PDAs may have a number of benefits for the practitioner.[10,11] Patient information may be accessed and entered more readily than with paper- or desktop computer-based record systems. Diagnostic and management accuracy and efficiency may be increased by ready access to a vast store of information. Medication-prescribing errors may be reduced by the use of a consistently reliable source of information on medications.[12]

Currently most PDAs run one of two operating systems (OS). The most popular at this time is the Palm OS, and the other is the Pocket PC OS (formerly Windows CE). In general, the Palm is easier to use and simpler to write programs for, so there are more programs available for it than for the Pocket PC. On the other hand, the Pocket PC is more flexible than the Palm and can vary depending on the hardware used.[11] Most popular software programs are available for both platforms.

There are a number of PDA programs not specifically dealing with infectious diseases that may be useful to the infectious diseases

TABLE 330-3   Practice Guidelines Available on the World Wide Web

Internet Address (URL)	Description	Download Format(s)
http://www.guideline.gov/	National Guideline Clearinghouse	
http://www.journals.uchicago.edu/IDSA/guidelines/	Practice Guidelines from the Infectious Diseases Society of America	PDF
http://www.aidsinfo.nih.gov/guidelines/	AIDSinfo	PDF, some PDA
http://www.cdc.gov/nip/publications/ACIP-list.htm	Recommendations of the Advisory Committee on Immunization Practices	Some PDF
http://mdm.ca/cpgsnew/cpgs/index.asp	Canadian Medical Association Clinical Practice Guidelines	
http://www.medscape.com/pages/editorial/public/pguidelines/index-infectiousdiseases	Medscape Infectious Diseases Practice Guidelines	
http://home.mdconsult.com/das/guidelines/view/	MD Consult Practice Guidelines	

PDA, Personal digital assistant (handheld computer); PDF, portable document format; URL, uniform resource locator.

TABLE 330-4 Selected Infectious Diseases-Related PDA Resources

Name	5mID (The 5-Minute Infectious Diseases Consult)	ABXGuide	BartlettID (Pocket Book of Infectious Disease Therapy)	ePocrates ID (part of ePocrates Rx Pro)	The Sanford Guide to Antimicrobial Therapy	TheraDoc
Internet Address (URL)	Various	http://hopkins-abxguide.org/main.cfm	Various	https://www.epocrates.com/	http://www.sanfordguide.com/	http://www.merckmedicus.com/pp/us/hcp/hcp_home.jsp
Cost (2003 U.S.)	$89.95	Free	$29.95	$49.99	$25.00	Free
PDA OS	Palm, Pocket PC	Palm, Pocket PC, Windows CE, BlackBerry	Palm,	Palm, Pocket PC	Palm, Pocket PC	Palm, Pocket PC
Expansion card	√	√	√		√	
Search by:						
Pathogen	√	√	√	√	√	
Medication	√	√	√	√	√	
Symptoms	√		√		√	
Disease	√	√	√	√	√	√
Management guided by user-entered data						√
Diagnostic pointers	√	√		√		√
Specialized dosing adjustments	√	√	√	√	√	√
References	√		√	√	√	√
Discussion of options	√	√	√	√	√	√
Drug cost data		√				√

OS, operating system; PDA, Personal digital assistant (handheld computer); URL, uniform resource locator.

practitioner. For example, there are programs that contain extensive catalogs of drug information. Some programs consist of formulas commonly used in medicine, such as those used to calculate creatinine clearance. There are also applications needed for opening files such as PDF and database documents.

The specific infectious diseases-related information available for PDAs comes in three basic varieties. The first includes stand-alone applications that provide a broad base of information on infectious disease syndromes, pathogens, and antimicrobials (Table 330-4 provides some examples).[13] In general, these applications include a search tool and an alphabetical and/or hierarchical topical structure to locate information. Antimicrobial recommendations usually are accompanied by clear explanations. One of the programs, TheraDoc, provides recommendations for patient diagnosis and management based on user-entered clinical syndrome and patient demographics. The programs are updated regularly, usually several times a year. Some provide downloads of recent information related to infectious diseases via desktop computer link. Of note, some of these programs will not run on expansion memory cards, which may be an issue with PDAs with limited on-board memory.

The second type of application available for PDAs includes those that deal with a narrow topic. An example is the HIVresistance Web "HIV Drug & Mutation Reference Guide" (*http://www.hivresistanceweb.com/request/pda.shtml*), which provides information about HIV drug resistance mutations. Another example is "Shots" (*http://www.immunizationed.org/*), a reference guide to the recommended U.S. adult and child immunization schedules. There are a number of websites that are useful in locating such software; some are listed in Table 330-5.

The final type of infectious diseases-related PDA software includes documents that require a separate application to open. Examples include HIV treatment guidelines available at AIDSinfo. Many hospitals also publish their own practice guidelines that are already PDA-ready or can be readily converted, such as PDF documents.

With the use of a PDA and these infectious disease tools, a clinician can quickly look up information pertaining to a patient to get recommendations for diagnosis and management. This may prove to be a boon when the clinician is confronted with an unusual clinical scenario or when using antibiotics that are not entirely familiar.

While possibly of great benefit to clinicians, PDAs are currently limited in some regards. As noted above, on-board memory is limited so that installation of more than a few programs may require the purchase of additional memory. The small size of the devices, necessary to make them portable, means that text and images on the screen must be correspondingly small or brief. Thus, although it may be convenient to have comprehensive documents such as clinical practice guidelines in the palm of one's hand, in reality it may not be practical to make use of such information regularly. Currently, software must be installed and updated via a desktop computer, representing an additional expense and time. And although the speed of the devices has increased dramatically in the past few years, they still lag behind their desktop brethren, and clinicians accustomed to almost instant access using desktop computers may become exasperated when waiting for information to become available.

Despite these limitations, PDAs represent a potentially significant advance in patient management. Data tracking, billing, prescribing, diagnosis, and management may all be facilitated by the use of PDAs, resulting in a practice that is more efficient, safer, and provides higher quality care than might otherwise be possible.

PRACTICE TOOLS

A number of electronic tools may have great advantages for the infectious diseases clinician. For example, electronic medical records (EMRs) are computer- or handheld-based patient medical record systems that may make the paperless medical practice a reality. These tools may make it possible to access a patient's medical record from anywhere there is a computer with network access. One may be able to get all of the patient's information from a recent hospitalization while seeing the patient in the outpatient clinic, or multiple clinicians involved in a patient's care may be able to access each other's information. A picture archiving and communication system (PACS) makes it possible to view radiologic images at remote sites. Cross-referencing of drug information may significantly reduce the risk of prescribing errors

TABLE 330-5 Selected Sites Useful for Locating Medical Software for PDAs

Name	Internet Address (URL)	Comments
Ectopic Brain	http://pbrain.hypermart.net/	Provides links to sites where medical Palm software may be obtained
Handango	http://www.handango.com/	Extensive catalog of software in multiple categories for several PDA types
Meds PDA	http://www.medspda.com/	Extensive catalog of medical software for Pocket PC and Palm
CollectiveMed	http://www.collectivemed.com/pdasource.shtml	Extensive catalog of medical software for Pocket PC and Palm
AvantGo	https://my.avantgo.com/browse/910/	Provides user-specified medical content and applications for PDAs
DocMD	http://docmd.com/pdasoftware/	Provides links to sites where medical Palm software may be obtained
Handheldmed	http://www.handheldmed.com/	Extensive catalog of medical software for Pocket PC and Palm
Healthy PalmPilot	http://www.healthypalmpilot.com/	Provides links to sites where medical Palm software may be obtained
Palm Software	http://www.palmone.com/us/software/	Extensive catalog of software in multiple categories for Palm
PDA Information for Health Professionals	http://www.gwumc.edu/library/pdares/	Provides links to sites where medical PDA software may be obtained
Pediatrics on Hand	http://pediatricsonhand.com/	Provides links to sites where medical PDA software germane to Pediatrics may be obtained and reviews of software
Medical Pocket PC	http://medicalpocketpc.com/	Extensive catalog of medical software for Pocket PC

PDA, Personal digital assistant (handheld computer); URL, uniform resource locator.

by bringing to the clinician's attention drug interactions, allergies, or the need for dosage adjustments. An Institute of Medicine Report from 2000 recommends the use of computerized physician entry, which has been demonstrated to reduce prescribing errors, to improve safety and quality.[14] This recommendation has been echoed more recently by others.[15] A readily accessible database of a patient's past treatment history may be especially useful in determining options for management of a patient with HIV infection. A Web-based messaging system may help to make physician-patient communication more effective.[16]

Web-based tools may also help to guide the appropriate use of antimicrobial agents. In a study from Australia, a Web-based antimicrobial approval system for cefotaxime and ceftriaxone linked to national antibiotic guidelines was developed and implemented at a teaching hospital. Concordance with national antibiotic guideline recommendations at the institution increased from 25% prior to implementation to 51% after implementation.[17]

Unfortunately, there are still a number of barriers to the widespread use of electronic tools in the office.[18] A fully operational EMR system may be rather expensive, and it may take some time to recoup the initial outlay costs and maintenance costs. The learning curve for an EMR and the time it takes to use it may dissuade a clinician from taking advantage of all of its benefits. Issues of patient privacy must be dealt with so that individuals who may gain access to the record system, whether stored on a desktop computer, PDA, or the Web, cannot access individual patient data unless authorized to do so. Until such problems are solved, most physicians will likely continue to rely primarily on traditional systems for documentation, tracking, and patient communication.

LOOKING TO THE FUTURE

The potential applicability of the use of digital resources in infectious diseases practice and research is almost boundless. At this point, however, the state of existing technology and the user's ability to take advantage of the services available are somewhat limiting. While desktop and handheld computer processor speeds have increased tremendously, the availability of high speed and high bandwidth networks remains restricted. It will take a great deal of time, effort, and expense to make such network access generally available. Also, users unaccustomed to and not facile with digital resources may be reluctant to use these services and to learn how to take advantage of their capabilities.

While it is important to recognize the current limitations to utilizing digital resources, it is equally vital to envision and explore their possibilities. Expansion and refinement of existing technology should make it possible to rapidly access information from an array of sources without the need for a physical connection to a network. Voice recognition technology and the application of "artificial intelligence" schemes should enable clinicians to simply ask a question about a particularly difficult case and have well-reasoned evidence-based advice returned almost instantly. Networked information grids and improvements in delivery of audio and video data will make it possible for clinicians with expertise to provide direct care for patients in remote areas, or advice to the patients' local providers, without the time, expense, and effort of long distance travel. It is certainly not far-fetched to believe that it may someday soon be possible, although in some respects perhaps not desirable, to have microchips embedded in a patient from which information about the patient's medical history and current physiologic status could be instantly and painlessly retrieved; this would, of course, be the equivalent of another Star Trek device, the 'tricorder.' In all, the properly applied use of digital resources should improve the clinician's ability to provide consistently high quality care to his patients in a safe and efficient manner, and should facilitate the exchange of crucial information among researchers involved in the field of infectious diseases.

REFERENCES

1. Hammond L, Papadopoulos S, Johnson CF, et al. Use of an Internet-based community surveillance network to predict seasonal communicable disease morbidity. Pediatrics. 2002;109:414-418.
2. Heymann DL, Rodier GR. Hot spots in a wired world: WHO surveillance of emerging and re-emerging infectious diseases. Lancet Infect Dis. 2001;1:345-353.
3. Veronin MA. Where are they now? A case study of health-related Web site attrition. J Med Internet Res. 2002;4:E10.
4. Abbas UL, Yu VL. Infectious diseases journals on the World Wide Web: Attractions and limitations. Clin Infect Dis. 2001;33:817-828.
5. Schmitt SK, Mehta N. Systematic reviews of infectious diseases. Clin Infect Dis. 2002;34:1515-1523.
6. Kuppersmith RB. The physician-patient relationship and the Internet. Otolaryngol Clin North Am. 2002;35:1143-1147.
7. Baker L, Wagner TH, Singer S, Bundorf MK. Use of the Internet and e-mail for health care information: Results from a national survey. JAMA. 2003;289:2400-2406.
8. Craan F, Oleske DM. Medical information and the Internet: Do you know what you are getting? J Med Syst. 2002;26:511-518.
9. American College of Physicians-American Society of Internal Medicine. ACP-ASIM survey finds nearly half of U.S. members use handheld computers, 2001. Available at: http://www.acponline.org/college/pressroom/handheld_survey.htm. Accessed June 5, 2003.
10. Keplar KE, Urbanski CJ. Personal digital assistant applications for the healthcare provider. Ann Pharmacother. 2003;37:287-296.
11. Fischer S, Stewart TE, Mehta S, et al. Handheld computing in medicine. J Am Med Inform Assoc. 2003;10:139-149.
12. Rothschild JM, Lee TH, Bae T, Bates DW. Clinician use of a palmtop drug reference guide. J Am Med Inform Assoc. 2002;9:223-229.
13. Miller SM, Beattie MM, Butt AA. Personal digital assistant infectious diseases applications for health care professionals. Clin Infect Dis. 2003;36:1018-1029.
14. Institute of Medicine. To err is human: Building a safer health system, 2000. Available at: http://www.nap.edu/books/0309068371/html/. Accessed June 17 2003.
15. Bates DW, Cohen M, Leape LL, et al. Reducing the frequency of errors in medicine using information technology. J Am Med Inform Assoc. 2001;8:299-308.
16. Liederman EM, Morefield CS. Web messaging: A new tool for patient-physician communication. J Am Med Inform Assoc. 2003;10:260-270.
17. Richards MJ, Robertson MB, Dartnell JG, et al. Impact of a web-based antimicrobial approval system on broad-spectrum cephalosporin use at a teaching hospital. Med J Aust. 2003;178:386-390.
18. Bodenheimer T, Grumbach K. Electronic technology: A spark to revitalize primary care? JAMA. 2003;290:259-264.

INDEX

Note: Page numbers followed by f indicate figures; those followed by t indicate tables.

Cardiotoxicity
of BILN 2061, 1969
of quinidine gluconate, 3135-3136
Cardiovascular agents, rifamycin interaction with, 376t
Cardiovascular device infections, 1022-1034, 1022t
clinical manifestations of, 1023
diagnosis of, 1023
epidemiology of, 1022
from *Staphylococcus epidermidis,* 2357
microbiology of, 1023
pathogenesis of, 1022-1023
prevention of, 1024
treatment of, 1023-1024
Cardiovascular disease, atherosclerotic, from *Chlamydia pneumoniae,* 2263-2266
Cardiovascular system
Brucella infections of, 2671
in secondary peritonitis, 934-935
syphilis of, 2776
viral infections of, specimen collection in, 233t
Carditis
from *Candida,* 2945, 2950
from *Chlamydia psittaci,* 2257
from enteroviruses, 2152-2153
in Kawasaki disease, 3317
rheumatic, 2381, 2382
Caribbean, HIV infection in, 1469
among women, 1618
Caries. *See* Dental caries.
L-Carnitine, for lipodystrophy, 609
β-Carotene, in lung cancer prevention, 141
Carotid artery erosion, in odontogenic infections, 794
Carotid artery, synthetic patches for, infections of, 1040-1041
Carrión's disease, 2733
Casaba virus, 1913-1919, 1914t. *See also* Alphaviruses.
Case series, 164-165
Case-control studies, 165
Case-fatality rate, 167
Caspofungin, 511
dosage of, 678t-679t
drug interactions with, 687t
for aspergillosis, 2968t, 2969
for cancer-related febrile neutropenia, 3455
for *Candida* esophagitis, 1234
for candidiasis, 2949-2951
for fusariosis, 3073
formulations of, 649t
structure of, 503f
Castleman's disease
human herpesvirus type 8 in, 1602
multicentric, 1830, 1830f
Cat(s), as toxoplasmosis vector, 3181, 3191
Cat bites, 3552-3553, 3552t, 3553t
Pasteurella infections in, 2687-2688
Cat flea, as *Bartonella henselae* vector, 2733
Catalase test, 216t, 217, 217t
Cataract, removal of, endophthalmitis after, 1407-1411, 1407f, 1408f
CATCH 22, 150t
Catecholamines, 909
Cathelicidins, 102
Catheterization
cardiac. *See* Cardiac catheterization.
urine collection by, 885
Catheter-related infections, 3347-3358, 3424. *See also* Percutaneous intravascular devices.
anti-infective equipment and, 3357-3358
diagnosis of, 3350-3351, 3350t
epidemiology of, 3348
from *Candida,* 2948-2949, 2950
from femoral artery catheterization, 1040

Catheter-related infections *(Continued)*
from infusate contamination, 3347-3348
from insertion site contamination, 3348
from junction contamination, 3348
from nontuberculous mycobacteria, 2910t, 2913
from *Staphylococcus aureus,* 3349
from *Stenotrophomonas maltophilia,* 2618
in arterial lines, transducers, and transducer domes, 3355-3356, 3356t
in cancer patients, 3433-3434, 3434f, 3455-3457
in central venous access, 2618, 3352-3355, 3353t, 3354t, 3357-3358
in elderly, 3518
in peripheral intravenous cannulization, 3351-3352
in pulmonary artery catheterization, 3355
in spinal cord injury, 3513-3514
in total parenteral nutrition, 3352-3355, 3353t, 3354t
laboratory diagnosis of, 3428
microbiology of, 3349-3350, 3350t
pathogenesis of, 3347-3348, 3347f
prevention of, 3356-3358, 3356t
risk factors for, 3348-3349, 3349t
urinary tract, 3370-3377. *See also* Urinary tract infections, catheter-related.
Catheters
bacteremia from, 209-210
bacteriuria in, 883
central venous, *Stenotrophomonas maltophilia* infections of, 2618
femoral artery, infections of, 1040
for intraperitoneal abscess drainage, 944
infections from
in endocarditis risk, 1044-1045
methenamine for, 477
topical antibacterial therapy for, 481
vancomycin for, 423
intravenous, tip cultures of, 210
Ochrobactrum anthropi infections of, 2759
peritoneal dialysis
peritonitis from, 942
Staphylococcus epidermidis infections of, 2355
specimen collection and transport from, 205t
Staphylococcus epidermidis infections of, 2354-2355
suppurative thrombophlebitis prevention with, 1005
Cationic antimicrobial protein, 102
Cat-scratch disease, 1207
ciprofloxacin for, 465
computed tomography of, 2737, 2739f
diagnosis of, 2740
differential diagnosis of, 2740
encephalopathy in, 2738-2739
from *Bartonella henselae,* 2736-2740, 2737f-2740f
lymphadenopathy in, 2736-2737, 2737f, 2738f
neuroretinitis in, 2739-2740, 2740f
papule in, 2736, 2737f
Parinaud's oculoglandular syndrome in, 1207, 1391, 2737, 2739f
treatment of, 1211
uveitis in, 1417, 1417f
Cavernous sinus thrombosis, 794, 795f, 797t, 1168-1170, 1169f, 1421-1424, 1421f. *See also* Odontogenic infections.
treatment of, 797t
CCAAT/enhancer binding protein epsilon, 108
CCL19, 121
CCL21, 121

CCR2, in human immunodeficiency virus infection susceptibility, 45, 45t, 47
CCR5, 1528, 1528f
blockade of, 20
in HIV replication, 1540
CCR5
in HIV nonprogression, 1532
in human immunodeficiency virus infection susceptibility, 45, 45t, 47, 48
mutation of, 1528
CCR5 chemokine receptor, 35
CCR7, 121
CD1, 128-130
antigen presentation by, 129
antigen processing by, 129, 130f
isoforms of, 129, 130f
mycobacteria presentation to, 129-130
proteins of, 129
structure of, 129, 129f
CD4, 133
apoptosis of, 1534-1535
CD8+ T cells and, 134
decreased production of, 1535-1536
depletion of, in HIV infection, 1534-1536
in acute retroviral syndrome, 1553
in antiretroviral therapy, 1669, 1679
in HIV infection, 1527-1528, 1528f, 1531-1532, 1709
pregnancy and, 1622
in HIV infection–related lymphoma, 1605
in leprosy, 2888, 2889
in opportunistic infections, 1549, 1550f, 1679-1680
prophylaxis indications and, 1684t
in *Pneumocystis jirovecii* pneumonia, 1679
in *Pseudomonas aeruginosa* resistance, 2591
in sepsis, 916
in tuberculosis response, 2859-2860
redistribution of, 1536
resting, as HIV reservoir, 1533
soluble, 20, 20t
thymic selection of, 131
CD4 receptors, human immunodeficiency virus binding to, 17, 17f
CD5, 63
CD8, 133
effector functions of, 133-134
in acute retroviral syndrome, 1553
in HIV infection, 1530-1531, 1530t, 1536, 1709
in HIV nonprogression, 1532
in sepsis, 916
in viral infections, 122
thymic selection of, 131
CD8+ T-cell antiviral factors, in HIV infection, 1531
CD14, 907, 907f
CD18 deficiency, 154
CD19, 61, 75
CD21, 61
in HIV infection, 1536
CD22, 61t
CD28, in T cell activation, 62
CD32, in infections susceptibility, 46
CD36, in malaria susceptibility, 44t
CD40, deficiency of, 153
CD40 ligand, 61
CD46, 82-83
CD47, in neutrophil migration, 98
CD55, 74t
CD59, 74, 74t
deficiency of, 80t
in paroxysmal nocturnal hemoglobinuria, 86
serum resistance and, 77
in T cell activation, 62-63

Cyclooxygenase, antipyretic effects of, 713
Cyclophosphamide
    chloramphenicol interactions with, 369t
    for HIV-related non-Hodgkin's lymphoma,
        1605
    for transplant immunosuppression, infections
        and, 3478
    in cytomegalovirus reactivation, 1794-1795
Cycloserine
    dosage of, 676t-677t
    drug interactions with, 688t
    for *Mycobacterium tuberculosis,* 495
    formulations of, 649t
Cyclospora [spp.], 568, 1290-1291, 3229, 3230f
    culture of, 1224
    diarrhea from, 1270
    in HIV infection, 1701
    laboratory detection of, 212
    treatment of, 569t, 572t
Cyclospora cayetanensis, 177, 584
    traveler's diarrhea from, 1242
    treatment of, 577t, 578t
Cyclosporine
    chloramphenicol interactions with, 369t
    for transplant immunosuppression, infections
        and, 3478
    in cytomegalovirus reactivation, 1794-1795
    metronidazole interactions with, 393t
CYP3A4, 273
Cyst(s)
    alveolar, 3286t, 3290, 3291-3292
    bronchial cleft, infected, 799-800
    echinococcal, hepatic, 953
    epidermal, infected, 1185
    hydatid, 575t, 580t, 3286t, 3290-3291, 3291f,
        3292
    infected embryologic, 799-800
Cystic fibrosis, 869-873
    allergic bronchopulmonary aspergillosis in,
        2962, 2963t
    aminoglycoside dosage in, 349-350
    Burkholderia cepacia in, 871, 2617, 2618,
        2619f
    clinical manifestations of, 869
    Clostridium difficile in, 870, 872
    diagnosis of, 869
    genetic susceptibility to, 48
    hypergammaglobulinemia in, 65
    lung transplant for, 871, 873
    Mycobacterium avrum complex in, 2900
    nontuberculous mycobacterial infections in,
        2910-2911, 2910t, 2913t
    pathogenesis of, 869-870
    Pseudomonas aeruginosa in, 870-871, 2591-
        2592, 2593f, 2598
    pulmonary infections in
        exacerbations of, 463
        microbiology of, 870-872
        treatment of, 872-873, 892
    respiratory syncytial virus in, 2017-2018
    typhoid resistance in, 46
Cystic fibrosis transmembrane conductance
        regulator, 48
    in *Pseudomonas aeruginosa* infections, 2591,
        2592, 2593f
Cystic hygroma, infected, 799-800
Cysticercosis, 1202, 3286t, 3289-3290, 3289f,
        3292. *See also* Tapeworms.
    meningitis in, 1137, 3289-3290
    myositis in, 1202
    racemose, 3290
Cysticercus cellulosae, 3286t. *See also*
        Tapeworms.
    treatment of, 575t, 580t

Cystitis, 875. *See also* Urinary tract infections.
    from *Candida,* 2946, 2950
    from microsporidia, 3243
    hemorrhagic
        from adenoviruses, 1838, 1839
        in stem cell transplant, 3487
    in elderly, 3518
    in spinal cord injury, 3513-3514
    nitrofurantoin for, 474
    urethral syndrome from, 1352
Cystourethrography, voiding
    in pediatric urinary tract infections, 899, 900f
    of vesicoureteral reflux, 899, 900f
Cytarabine, for progressive multifocal
        leukoencephalopathy, 1861
Cytidine deaminase deficiency, autosomal
        recessive activation-induced, 153
Cytochrome P-3A4, quinolone effects on, 459
Cytochrome P-450
    in fusidic acid interactions, 327
    in pharmacokinetics, 273-274
    quinupristin-dalfopristin effects on, 427
Cytochrome-b_{558}, in oxidative burst, 100
Cytokines
    acute-phase response and, 38, 38t
    CD8$^+$ T-cell production of, 134
    immunomodulation with, 551, 552t
    in acute-phase response, 39, 709-710, 710t
    in AIDS dementia, 1586
    in fever, 708-709, 711
    in HIV infection, 1536, 1538
    in HIV replication, 1538-1540, 1539f
    in HIV treatment, 1540
    in infection susceptibility, 47
    in leprosy, 2889
    in mycobacterial resistance, 157f
    in pneumonia, 828
    in *Pseudomonas aeruginosa* resistance, 2590-
        2591
    in secondary peritonitis, 934
    in sepsis syndrome, 712
    in septic shock, 913
    in severe sepsis, 911-912
    in streptococcal toxic shock syndrome, 2372-
        2373
    in *Streptococcus agalactiae* (group B)
        infections, 2426
    in *Streptococcus pneumoniae* disease, 2396
    in systemic response, 908
    in viral meningitis, 1089
    innate immunity and, 38, 38t
    neutrophil life span and, 101
    proinflammatory, in ascites, 929-930
    pyrogenic
        in acute-phase response, 709-710, 710t
        in febrile response, 708-709, 711
        in sepsis syndrome, 712
    receptors for, 61t
    Toll-like receptors and, 38, 38f, 39
Cytomegalovirus, 1786-1798
    AIDS cholangiopathy from, 957
    appendicitis from, 969
    cervical carriage of, 1796-1798, 1797t
    characteristics of, 1787
    cidofovir-resistant, 524
    clinical features of, 1758, 1758t, 1760t
    colitis from, 530, 1580, 1791-1792
    collection of, 232, 233t
    congenital infections from, 1796-1797
    culture of, 1788-1789
    diagnosis of, 1761
    drug resistance in, 1793-1794, 1794f, 1796
        in transplant recipients, 1796
    encephalitis from, 1591

Cytomegalovirus *(Continued)*
    epidemiology of, 1759, 1759t
    esophagitis from, 1232, 1233t, 1234, 1791
    foscarnet-resistant, 527
    ganciclovir-resistant, 529
    gastric, 1576
    genome of, 1787, 1794f
    Guillain-Barré syndrome from, 1790
    hemolytic anemia from, 1790
    hepatitis from, 1435
        in transplant recipients, 1795-1796
    immune response to, 126, 1759
    in adrenal insufficiency, 915
    in hematologic cancer, 3436
    in HIV infection, 172, 1234, 1550, 1556-1557,
        1576, 1591, 1790-1792
        colitis from, 1791-1792
        polyradiculopathy from, 1791
        prevention of, 1793-1794
        retinitis from, 1559-1560, 1790-1791, 1791f
        treatment of, 1682t-1686t, 1696-1697, 1792-
            1793
    in neonates, 1797
    in pregnancy, 1789, 1796-1798, 1797t
    in transplant recipients, 1793-1796, 3477,
        3478t, 3479t, 3480, 3501-3502, 3502t,
        3508-3509
        drug resistance in, 1796
        from donor organ, 1795-1796
        ganciclovir for, 530
        in heart transplants, 3478t, 3502t4
        in kidney transplants, 1796, 3478t, 3502t
        in liver transplants, 1795-1796, 3478t, 3502t.
            See also Liver transplantation,
            cytomegalovirus in.
        in lung transplants, 3477, 3478t, 3502t
        in stem cell transplants, 1793-1794, 1795,
            3492-3494, 3493t
        late-onset, 1795
        monitoring for, 3481
        preoperative tests for, 3481
        prevention of, 1793-1796, 3482-3483
    infectious mononucleosis from, 1789, 1812
    isolation of, 1787
    laboratory diagnosis of, 236, 1787-1788
    laryngitis from, 759
    latency of, 1787
    meningoencephalitis from, 1085, 1091, 1790
    myocarditis from, 1052, 1053t, 1790
    nosocomial infections from, 3414-3416
    oncogenicity of, 1759
    overview of, 1786-1787
    pancreatitis from, 959, 959t
    pneumonia from, 1572, 1789, 1790f
        in transplant recipients, 1795
    prevention of, 1760t, 1761, 1793
    rash from, 1790
    reactivation of, 1794-1795
    receptors for, 1732t
    replication of, 1787
    retinitis from, 1415-1416, 1559-1560, 1790-
        1793, 1791f
        antiviral drugs for, 515t
        cidofovir for, 525
        fomivirsen for, 527
        foscarnet for, 528
        in HIV infection, 1684t-1686t, 1696-1697
        treatment of, 527-528, 530
    structure of, 1756-1757, 1756t, 1787
    susceptibility testing for, 238
    teratogenicity of, 1789
    thrombocytopenia from, 1790
    transfusion-related, 1789, 3387
    transmission of, 1759-1761, 1759t, 1789, 3387

Cytomegalovirus *(Continued)*
   treatment of, 515t, 520, 1760t, 1761, 1792-1793
      antiretroviral agents in, 1561
      drug resistance in, 1792-1793
      maribavir for, 541
   uveitis from, 1415-1416
   variants of, 1787
Cytomegalovirus hyperimmune globulin, 558
Cytomegalovirus immune serum, 66
Cytomegalovirus syndrome, 1796
Cytoplasm, pathogens in, 123
Cytosine arabinoside, for progressive multifocal
   leukoencephalopathy, 1861
Cytotoxic drugs. *See* Chemotherapy.
Cytotoxicity, antibody-dependent cellular, 56
Cytotoxins, 30, 1220-1221, 1220t
   of *Pseudomonas aeruginosa,* 2596

D

Dacron carotid patches, infections of, 1040-1041
Dacryoadenitis, 1421
Dacryocystitis, 1421
Dactylaria gallopava, brain abscess from, 3070
DAF, 75
   in paroxysmal nocturnal hemoglobinuria, 86
Dalfopristin
   for pneumonia, 837-839, 837t, 838t
   for shunt infections, 1129t, 1130
   pneumococcal resistance to, 837, 837t
Dane particle, 1864
Danger space, 790, 790f
   infections of, 793. *See also* Odontogenic
      infections.
Dapsone
   adverse effects of, 581t
   dosage of, 670t-671t
   drug interactions with, 689t
   for brain abscess, 1159t
   for leprosy, 498, 2893, 2894
   for *Pneumocystis,* 3088
      for prophylaxis, 3090
   for *Pneumocystis jirovecii,* 569t, 575t, 1681t,
      1683t, 1685t, 1693, 1695
      for prophylaxis, 3447, 3447t
   for pneumocystosis, 588
   for *Toxoplasma gondii,* 1682t, 1696
      for encephalitis prophylaxis, 3190
      in immunocompromised host, 3189, 3189t
   formulations of, 648t
   neurotoxicity of, 1594t
Daptomycin, 427-428
   for osteomyelitis, 1325
   for secondary peritonitis, 937
   for *Staphylococcus aureus,* 2337
   for vancomycin-resistant enterococcal
      endocarditis, 997
Darbrand, 1268-1269
Darkfield examination, for syphilis, 2778, 2778f
Dark-walled fungi, 3070-3072, 3070f-3072f,
   3070t, 3076t
Data mining, for bioterrorist attacks, 3598
Day care centers
   diarrhea in, 1241
   hepatitis A outbreaks in, 2171, 2171f, 2178
   rhinovirus outbreaks in, 2188
Deafness
   from erythromycin, 400
   from Lassa fever virus, 2095
   from mumps virus, 2005
   from otitis media, 768
Deamidating toxins, 25t
Decay-accelerating factor, 74t
   deficiency of, 80t

Decongestants
   for colds, 750
   for otitis media, 769
   for sinusitis, 780
Decontamination. *See also* Disinfection.
   definition of, 3331
   in hospitals, 3331-3333, 3332t
Decubitus ulcers
   in elderly, 3519-3520
   infected, 1184
      in spinal cord injury, 3515-3516
Deep fascial space infections, 754, 756, 791-793,
   792f, 793f. *See also* Odontogenic infections.
   treatment of, 797-798, 797t
Deep venous thrombosis. *See also* Suppurative
      thrombophlebitis.
   in airplane passengers, 3643-3644
Deer, in Lyme disease transmission, 2798
DEET, in Lyme disease prevention, 2807
Defensins, neutrophil bactericidal activity, 102
Deferoxamine
   bacterial infections with, 158
   mucormycosis and, 2975, 2977
Defibrillators, implantable, infections of, 1033-
   1034
Dehydration
   in cholera, 2539, 2540t
   in diarrhea, 1223-1224
Dehydroemetine, for amebiasis, 3106, 3106t
Dehydroepiandrosterone, for HIV infection, 609
Deinocerites spp., Venezuelan equine encephalitis
   from, 1915
Delavirdine, 1662, 1662t
   dosage of, 684t-685t
   drug interactions with, 689t
   for perinatal HIV transmission prevention,
      1625t, 1626
   formulations of, 649t
   pediatric, 1646t
   resistance to, 1663
   structure of, 1661f
Delivery
   cesarean
      antibiotic prophylaxis for, 1373, 1374
      endometritis and, 1373-1376, 1373f
      in HIV transmission prevention, 1621-1622
      maternal herpes and, 1771, 1772
   episiotomy infections from, 1375, 1377t
   HIV transmission in, 1490-1491, 1620
Delta agent. *See* Hepatitis D virus.
Deltaretroviruses, 2098. *See also* Human T-cell
   lymphotropic virus (HTLV).
Dematiaceous fungi, 3070-3072, 3070f-3072f,
   3070t, 3076t
Demeclocycline, 358t
   dosage of, 662t-663t
   formulations of, 647t
   nephrogenic diabetes insipidus from, 364
Dementia, AIDS, 1584-1587, 1585f, 1585t, 1586t
   pathogenesis of, 2129-2130
Demodex mites, 3310, 3311
Dendritic cells, 120
   in antigen presentation, 132-133
   in HIV infection, 1528, 1529, 1537-1538
   in innate inflammatory response, 132-133
   in intestinal tissues, 122
   in phagocytosis, 37
   in T-cell priming, 132-133
   pulmonary, 820-821
Dengue fever, 178-179, 179f, 235t
   as biological weapon, 3627-3629, 3628t
   classification of, 1936f
   clinical features of, 1936f, 1938-1939, 3629t,
      3653f

Dengue fever *(Continued)*
   diagnosis of, 1942
   differential diagnosis of, 1939
   epidemiology of, 1929-1930
   geographic distribution of, 3640f
   historical perspective on, 1927
   in travelers, 3647t, 3648t, 3649
   pathogenesis of, 1936-1937, 1936f
   prevention of, 1943-1944
   skin lesions in, 739
   treatment of, 1943
   vs. enteric fever, 1274t, 1277, 1278
   vs. malaria, 3133
Dengue hemorrhagic fever, 178
   classification of, 1936f
   clinical features of, 1936f, 1938-1939
   diagnosis of, 1942
   differential diagnosis of, 1939
   epidemiology of, 1929-1930
   historical perspective on, 1927
   pathogenesis of, 1936-1937, 1936f
   prevention of, 1943-1944
   skin lesions in, 739
   treatment of, 1943
Dengue shock syndrome, 178, 739, 1936-1937
   treatment of, 1943
Dental caries, 788, 788f, 790
   dentoalveolar infections and, 790. *See also*
      Odontogenic infections.
   from *Streptococcus mutans,* 788-789
   pathogenesis of, 788-789, 790
   prevention of, 781
Dental discoloration, from tetracycline, 363-364
Dental history, in immunodeficiency, 149
Dental infections. *See* Odontogenic infections.
Dental plaque, anaerobes in, 2839
Dental procedures
   antibiotic prophylaxis for, 793-794
   bacteremia after, 793-794
   endocarditis from, 1045-1046, 1046t
      antibiotic prophylaxis for, 1044
   HIV transmission during, prevention of, 3397
Dentoalveolar infections, 790-791. *See also*
   Odontogenic infections.
Denture sore mouth, 2941, 2951
Deoxyguanosine, 517f
Deoxyribonucleic acid. *See* DNA.
Depression, St. John's wort for, 609
Dermabacter hominis, 2471
Dermacentor spp., 3312-3314, 3313f, 3313t. *See
   also* Tick(s).
   Colorado tick fever from, 1900-1901, 1900f
   ehrlichiosis from, 2312
   Omsk hemorrhagic fever from, 1945
   Rickettsia slovaca infections from, 2285t,
      2287t, 2293
   Rocky Mountain spotted fever from, 2288-
      2289, 2289f
Dermanyssus gallinae, 3311
Dermatitis. *See* Skin infections.
Dermatitis herpetiformis, diarrhea in, 1243
Dermatobia hominis, myiasis from, 3307-3310,
   3308t
Dermatopathic lymphadenitis, 1204-1205. *See
   also* Lymphadenitis/lymphadenopathy.
Dermatophagoides spp., 3311
Dermatophilus spp., laboratory tests for, 228-229
Dermatophyte(s)
   characteristics of, 3052-3053, 3052t
   classification and taxonomy of, 3051-3052,
      3052t
   historical perspective on, 3051
   pathogenicity of, 3052, 3053-3054
   species of, 3052-3053, 3052t

Dihydroqinghaosu, 606f
Diiodohydroxyquin, for amebiasis, 3106, 3106t
Dilated cardiomyopathy. *See also*
    Cardiomyopathy.
  after enteroviral myopericarditis, 2153
  myocarditis in, 1052-1057
Diloxanide furoate
  adverse effects of, 581t
  for amebiasis, 571t, 3106, 3106t
  for luminal protozoa, 583
  indications for, 568t
7-Dimethylamino-demethyl-6-deoxy-tetracycline,
  357f
Dimethylglycytamido-6-demethyl-6-
  deoxytetracycline, 357f
Dimethylsulfoxide, idoxuridine in, 531
Dinophysis spp., 3256, 3256t
Diphenoxylate-atropine
  for *Clostridium difficile*–associated colitis,
    1258
  for traveler's diarrhea, 1242
Diphtheria, 1147-1148. *See also*
  Corynebacterium diphtheriae.
  cardiac toxicity in, 2461-2462
  cutaneous, 1180-1181, 2462
  diagnosis of, 2462-2463, 2463f
  differential diagnosis of, 2463
  epidemiology of, 2458-2460, 2459f
  history of, 2457-2458
  invasive, 2462
  myocardial involvement in, 1053
  neuropathy in, 2462
  pathogenesis of, 2460-2461, 2460f
  pharyngitis in, 755, 756
  prevention of, 2464
  respiratory, 2460, 2460f, 2461-2462, 2461f
  treatment of, 2463-2464
  vs. epiglottitis, 785
  wound, 1180-1181
Diphtheria antitoxin, 2463
  for cutaneous diphtheria, 1181
Diphtheria, tetanus, pertussis (DTP) vaccine,
  2464, 3562, 3563, 3563f, 3564t
  contraindications to, 3583t
  immunization rate for, 2460
  schedule for children, 3564t
Diphtheria toxin, 26
  action of, 28
  cell entry by, 27
  immunization schedule for, 2464
  in myocarditis, 1055
Diphtheria vaccine, 3562-3564. *See also*
  Diphtheria, tetanus, pertussis (DTP) vaccine.
  for adults, 3576f, 3577f
Diphtheroids
  in peritoneal dialysis, 941
  prosthetic valve endocarditis from, 1024, 1025
    treatment of, 1028
Diphyllobothrium [spp.], 3286t, 3287, 3288. *See*
  also Tapeworms.
Diphyllobothrium latum
  syndrome of abdominal pain, diarrhea, and
    eosinophilia from, 1281t, 1283
  treatment of, 575t
Dipylidium caninum, 3288
  treatment of, 575t
Direct fluorescent antibody tests, for sputum, 826
Dirithromycin, 408
  dosage of, 664t-665t
  drug interactions with, 690t
  formulations of, 648t
Dirofilaria repens, ocular infections from, 3273
Dirofilariasis, 3294t, 3297-3298
Disease(s). *See also* Infectious disease(s).
  definition of, 167

Disease surveillance, 164
Disinfection. *See also* Infection control.
  bioterrorism and, 3342
  definition of, 3331
  emerging pathogens and, 3340-3342
  in hospitals, 3331-3333, 3332t
    environmental, 3334
  OSHA blood-borne pathogen standard and,
    3340
  resistance to, 3340-3342
  with alcohol, 3333-3334
  with chlorine compounds, 3334
  with glutaraldehyde, 3334-3335, 3335t
  with hydrogen peroxide, 3335t, 3336-3337
  with iodophors, 3335t
  with *ortho*-phthalaldehyde, 3335t
  with pasteurization, 3338
  with peracetic acid, 3335t, 3336
  with peracetic acid/hydrogen peroxide, 3335t,
    3336-3337
  with phenolics, 3337
  with quaternary ammonium compounds, 3337-
    3338
Disk diffusion susceptibility testing, 223
Disseminated gonococcal infections, skin lesions
  in, 736
Disseminated granulomatosis, fever in, 726
Disseminated intravascular coagulation, 735
  in meningococcal disease, 2508
  in sepsis, 916
Disseminated *Mycobacterium avium* disease,
  2897, 2898-2899, 2899f, 2901, 2901f, 2901t,
  2903-2906
Distributional clearance, 272. *See also* Drug
  distribution.
Disulfiram, metronidazole interactions with, 393t
Diuretics, tetracycline with, 364t
Diverticulitis, 971-973
  actinomycotic, 2927
  intraperitoneal abscess in, 943
DNA
  of *Mycobacterium tuberculosis,* 2854t, 2855
  polymorphic, random amplification of, 222
  rearrangement of, in immunoglobulin
    production, 60, 60f, 60t
DNA gyrase, quinolone inhibition of, 265, 451, 453
DNA probes, for pneumonia, 828
DNA viruses, 2098. *See also* Human T-cell
  lymphotropic virus (HTLV).
DNases, 2364
Dobrava virus, 2086-2089, 2086t
Docosahexaenoic acid, 143
Docosanol, 515t, 525
Döderlein's bacilli, 36
Dog(s)
  bites of, 3552-3553, 3552t, 3553t
    Capnocytophaga canimorsus in, 2731-2732
    laboratory studies for, 213
    of head and neck, 800
    Pasteurella in, 2687
    rabies from, 2050
  heartworm in, dirofilariasis from, 3294t, 3297-
    3298
  mites of, 3311
  sarcoptic mange in, 3305
  Toxocara canis infections in, 3293-3294
Dog ticks, 3312-3314, 3313f, 3313t. *See also*
  Tick(s).
Dolosicoccus spp., laboratory identification of,
  217t, 218
Dolosigranulum spp., laboratory identification of,
  217t, 218
Donovan bodies, 1343, 1343f, 2749, 2750f
Donovanosis. *See* Granuloma inguinale.
Dosage guidelines, 635, 650t-685t

Dot/Icm, 2714
Doxorubicin, for HIV-related non-Hodgkin's
  lymphoma, 1605
Doxycycline, 358t
  dosage of, 662t-663t
  food interactions with, 364t
  for actinomycosis, 2931, 2931t
  for anthrax, 1177t, 2489t, 2490t
  for bacillary angiomatosis, 1185
  for bartonellosis, 1691t, 1692t, 2744
  for brucellosis, 2672
  for cellulitis, 1180
  for cervicofacial actinomycosis, 797t
  for *Chlamydia trachomatis,* 2525
  for chlamydial pneumonia, 2263
    atherosclerosis after, 2265
  for COPD exacerbations, 811t
  for ehrlichiosis, 2315
  for epidemic typhus, 2305
  for epididymitis, 2526
  for legionellosis, 2719t
  for leptospirosis, 2793t
  for Lyme disease, 2806, 2806t
    for prophylaxis, 3315
  for lymphogranuloma venereum, 2245
  for malaria, 573t, 574t, 3129, 3133, 3134t, 3135
    for prophylaxis, 3137-3138, 3137t
      in travelers, 3641-3642, 3641t
  for melioidosis, 2629t
  for meningitis, 1106t, 1107t
  for murine typhus, 2308
  for *Mycoplasma pneumoniae,* 2278
  for *Neisseria gonorrhoeae,* 2524t, 2525, 2525t,
    2526
  for neonatal conjunctivitis, 2247t
  for parasites, 589
  for pelvic inflammatory disease, 460, 1379t,
    2247t, 2250, 2525, 2525t
  for periodontitis, 796, 796t
  for plague, 2696, 3603
  for pneumonia, 806t, 837-839
    pneumococcal, 2404
  for psittacosis, 2257
  for Q fever endocarditis, 1001, 2300
  for rickettsial diseases, 2287, 2293
  for rickettsialpox, 2296
  for Rocky Mountain spotted fever, 2091-2292
  for scrub typhus, 2310
  for sepsis, 919
  for syphilis, 1344, 1690t, 2781t, 2782
  for toxoplasmosis, 1696
    in immunocompromised host, 3189
  for tularemia, 2682
    in bioterrorism attack, 3610t, 3611, 3611t
  for urethritis, 1207, 2247t, 2249
  for urogenital chlamydial infections, 1207,
    2247t, 2249, 2250
  for Whipple's disease, 1309, 1310t
  formulations of, 647t
  indications for, 569t
  pharmacology of, 362t
  prophylactic
    for anthrax, 3621, 3622t
    for travelers, 3643
    for tularemia, 3609-3610, 3609t
  side effects of, 363t, 3609t
Dracunculiasis, 3269-3270, 3270f
  metronidazole for, 572t
Drainage. *See also* Aspiration.
  of amebic liver abscess, 3106
  of brain abscess, 1160
  of epidural abscess, 1167-1168
  of lung abscess, 856
  of pleural effusion/empyema, 850-851
  of subdural empyema, 1165

Fimbriae
 of Enterobacteriaceae, 2569-2570, 2570f, 2571
 P, of *Escherichia coli*, 19-20, 19f
Finger(s)
 herpetic whitlow of, 1769, 1769f, 1773t
 human bites of, 3554
 in endocarditis, 983-984
Fingernails. *See* Nails.
Fish
 capillariasis from, 3294t, 3298
 poisonous, 1289-1290, 1290t, 1292, 3255,
  3255f, 3256t
 skin infections from, 1184
Fish oil, immune effects of, 143-144
Fish tapeworm, 3286t, 3287. *See also* Tapeworms.
Fistulas
 bronchopleural, tuberculous, 2878
 pharyngocutaneous, postradiation, 800
Fite staining, for *Mycobacterium leprae*, 2891-
  2892, 2892f, 2893f
Fitz-Hugh–Curtis syndrome, 2521-2522
Flagellates
 antiparasitics for, 568t-569t
 of Enterobacteriaceae, 2569, 2570f
 treatment of, 582-583, 583f
Flash sterilization, 333
Flat warts, 1842, 1845, 1848. *See also* Human
  papillomavirus(es).
Flatworms
 cestode, 3285-3292
 trematode, 3276-3284
Flaviviruses, 1926-1945
 characteristics of, 1928-1929
 classification of, 1929
 clinical features of, 1938-1942
 epidemiology of, 1929-1935
 geographic distribution of, 1927-1928, 1927f
 historical perspective on, 1927-1928
 host range for, 1928-1929
 laboratory diagnosis of, 1942
 less common, 1944-1945, 1945t
 pathogenesis of, 1935-1938
 prevention of, 1943-1944
 public health burden of, 1926
 replication of, 1928
 structure of, 1928
 treatment of, 1943-1944
Flavobacterium spp., 2751t, 2759
 endocarditis from, 992
Flea-borne infection(s), 2286
 murine typhus as, 2306-2308
 plague as, 2697
Fleas, sand, 3310
Flesh flies, myiasis from, 3308-3310, 3308t
Flies, myiasis from, 3307-3310, 3308t
Flinder's Island spotted fever, 2285t, 2287t, 2292-
  2293
Flora. *See* Microbial flora.
Flow cytometry, 117, 118f
Flu. *See also* Influenza virus(es).
 intestinal, 1238-1239, 1239t
Flucloxacillin, 290, 290f
 dosage of, 650t-651t
 for *Staphylococcus aureus* endocarditis, 2344t
 for *Staphylococcus aureus* osteomyelitis, 2346
 formulations of, 646t
Fluconazole, 509
 dosage of, 678t-679t
 drug interactions with, 691t
 for blastomycosis, 3036-3037, 3036t
 for brain abscess, 1159t, 1160
 for cancer-related febrile neutropenia
  for prophylaxis, 3446, 3447t
  in empiric therapy, 3455
 for candidiasis, 1683t, 1687t, 1698, 2949-2951

Fluconazole *(Continued)*
  esophageal, 1234, 1575
  in stem cell transplant, 3495
  vulvovaginal, 1364
 for catheter-related infections, 3377
 for coccidioidomycosis, 1683t, 1688t, 3047-
  3048
 for cryptococcal meningitis, 3007, 3008
  for prophylaxis, 3009
 for *Cryptococcus neoformans*, 1584, 1682t,
  1683t, 1688t, 1698
 for dermatophytosis, 3050t, 3058-3059
 for endophthalmitis, 1411
 for eumycetoma, 2995
 for fungal arthritis, 1318
 for histoplasmosis, 1688t, 3023, 3024
 for meningitis, 1135, 1584
 for paracoccidioidomycosis, 3065
 for sporotrichosis, 2987
 for suppurative thrombophlebitis, 1005
 for urinary tract infections, 892
  catheter-related, 3377
 formulations of, 649t
 prophylactic, for transplant recipients, 3483
 structure of, 503f
Flucytosine, 506-507
 dosage of, 678t-679t
 for brain abscess, 1159t
 for cryptococcal meningitis, 3007, 3008
 for *Cryptococcus neoformans*, 1584, 1688t,
  1698
 for dialysis-related peritonitis, 942
 for meningitis, 1584, 3007, 3008
 formulations of, 649t
5-Flucytosine, for brain abscess, 1160
Fluid balance, gastrointestinal, 1222-1223,
  1222f
Fluid management
 in central nervous system infections, 1083
 in dengue/dengue hemorrhagic fever, 1943
 in peritonitis, 940
 in rotavirus infections, 1909
 in sepsis, 919-920
 in streptococcal toxic shock syndrome, 2374
 in urinary tract infections, 888
Fluids, collection and transport of, 206t
Flukes. *See* Trematodes.
Fluorescent treponemal antibody absorption,
  2778t, 2779, 2780
 for endemic treponematoses, 2787
Fluoride, for dental prophylaxis, 781-782, 796t
5-Fluorocytosine
 for fungal endocarditis, 1001
 for suppurative thrombophlebitis, 1005
 structure of, 503f
[18]F-Fluorodeoxyglucose positron emission
  tomography, for brain abscess, 1158-1159
Fluoroquinolones. *See* Quinolones.
5-Fluorouracil, for genital warts, 1849
Flying squirrels, as typhus reservoir, 2304, 2305
Focal vulvitis, 1369-1370, 1370f
Folate
 deficiency of, in tropical sprue, 1303
 trimethoprim/sulfonamide effects on, 443,
  443f, 445
Folate antagonists, formulations of, 648t
Folinic acid
 for *Toxoplasma* encephalitis, 1587
 with pyrimethamine, for toxoplasmosis,
  3188
  in congenital infections, 3191
  in pregnancy, 3190
Follicle mites, 3311
Follicular dendritic cell network, in HIV
  infection, 1534

Folliculitis, 1175
 eosinophilic, in HIV infection, 1557-1558,
  1558f
 from *Candida*, 1175, 2942, 2943f
 from *Malassezia*, 1175, 3060-3061
 from *Pseudomonas aeruginosa*, 733, 736,
  1175, 2605
 nodular, from *Trichophyton rubrum*, 3055
 staphylococcal, 2340
Fomivirsen, 515t, 526-527
 for cytomegalovirus prophylaxis, 1683t
Fonsecaea spp., chromoblastomycosis from,
  2988-2991
Food handling, in infection prevention, 1296-
  1297
Foodborne disease, 1286-1297
 bacterial toxins in, 1286-1289, 1287t
 botulism as, 2823, 2824
 causes of, 1286, 1287t
 clinical features of, 1286-1291
 cryptosporidiosis as, 3217
 epidemiology of, 1291-1293, 1292t, 1293t
 fatalities from, 1295t
 foods in, 1291-1292, 1292t
 from *Bacillus*, 2494, 2495
 from *Bacillus cereus*, 1219, 1287-1288, 1291,
  1294, 1294t, 2494
 from caliciviruses, 2197
 from *Campylobacter jejuni*, 1288, 1289
 from *Clostridium botulinum*, 1289, 1292, 1295,
  2823, 2834
 from *Clostridium perfringens*, 1288, 1291,
  1294, 1294t, 2834, 2835t, 2836-2837
 from *Escherichia coli*, 1288
 from *Escherichia coli* O157.H7, 1288, 1289,
  1291, 1294-1295, 1294t
 from *Escherichia coli* Shiga toxin, 1289
 from fish, 1289-1290, 1290t, 1292
 from heavy metals, 1289, 1292
 from hepatitis E virus, 2207, 2207f, 2208
 from *Listeria monocytogenes*, 2479, 2481-
  2482, 2483, 2483t
 from mushrooms, 1290, 1291t
 from noroviruses, 1288-1289, 1292
 from *Salmonella*, 1288, 1291-1292, 2639-2640,
  2639f, 2650
 from shellfish, 1289-1290, 1290t
 from *Shigella*, 1288, 2657, 2659
 from *Staphylococcus*, 1219, 2332
 from *Staphylococcus aureus*, 1286-1287, 2339
 from *Vibrio cholerae*, 1288, 1292, 2538
 from *Vibrio parahaemolyticus*, 1288, 2544,
  2545
 from *Yersinia enterocolitica*, 1289, 1292, 2698
 geography in, 1292t, 1293
 giardiasis as, 3200
 hepatitis A as, 2166, 2171, 2171f, 2172
 hospitalization in, 1295t
 intentional, 1292
 laboratory diagnosis of, 1293-1295, 1294t
 nonbacterial toxins in, 1289-1291, 1290t,
  1291t
 outbreak investigations of, 165-166
 pathogenesis of, 1286-1291
 population changes in, 1293
 postinfection syndromes from, 1289
 prevention of, 1296-1297, 1297t
  in travelers, 3642
 relative rates of, 1286, 1287f
 seasonality in, 1292t, 1293
 surveillance of, 1296
 systemic illness in, 1289
 toxoplasmosis as, 3172-3173
 treatment of, 1295-1296
 typhoid fever as, 2638

Foot
  chromoblastomycosis of, 2989, 2989f
  diabetic ulcers of, 1184
  fungal infections of, 3054
  mycetoma of. See Mycetoma.
  osteomyelitis of, from Pseudomonas
      aeruginosa, 2603
  plantar warts of, 1842, 1845, 1848. See also
      Human papillomavirus(es).
Foramen of Winslow, 928
Foreign bodies
  antimicrobial selection and, 246
  infections from
      from Staphylococcus epidermidis, 2357-
          2358
      rifamycin for, 381
Formaldehyde, urinary, methenamine and, 476,
    477
Fort Morgan virus, 1913-1919, 1914t. See also
    Alphaviruses.
FosAmprenavir, pediatric, 1646t
Foscarnet, 515t, 527-528
  dosage of, 680t-681t
  drug interactions with, 691t-692t
  for cytomegalovirus, 1591, 1683t, 1686t, 1696-
      1697, 1793
      for polyradiculopathy, 1791
      in stem cell transplant, 3493t
  for encephalitis, 1591
  for genital herpes, 1344, 1774
  for herpes simplex virus, 1686t
  for herpesviruses, 1760t, 1761, 1774
  for human herpesvirus 6, 1823
  for varicella-zoster virus, 1687t
  formulations of, 649t
  in renal insufficiency, 527, 528t
  neurotoxicity of, 1594t
  structure of, 524f
Fosfomycin
  for Enterococcus, 2416
  for staphylococcal endocarditis, 999
  formulations of, 648t
Fournier's gangrene, 1190, 1191, 2813
  hyperbaric oxygen for, 566
Fractures
  microbial contamination of, osteomyelitis
      from, 1325-1326, 1325f
  skull, cerebrospinal fluid leak in, 1103, 1117
Francisella [spp.].
  characteristics of, 2674-2676, 2675t
  laboratory identification of, 220-221
Francisella novicida, 10
Francisella philomiragia, 2676, 2681
Francisella tularensis, 2674-2683. See also
    Tularemia.
  as biological weapon, 3607-3611
  characteristics of, 2674-2676, 2675t
  chemoprophylaxis against, 2683
  clinical manifestations of, 2678-2681
  culture of, 3609
  diagnosis of, 2681-2682
  disinfection/sterilization and, 3342
  history of, 2674
  isolation precautions for, 3330t
  laboratory detection of, 213-214
  lymphadenopathy from, 2679, 2680f
  pathogenesis of, 2677-2678
  pharyngeal infections from, 2680
  pneumonia from, 2677, 2680-2681,
      2681f
  polymerase chain reaction assay for, 2682
  serologic studies for, 2682
  skin infections from, 2681
  transmission of, 2676

Francisella tularensis (Continued)
  treatment of, 2682-2683
      with aminoglycosides, 334t-335t, 344t
  typhoid fever from, 2680
  ulcers from, 2679, 2679f
  vaccines for, 2683
  vectors of, 2676-2677
Francisella tularensis subsp. holarctica, 2674,
    2675, 2675t
Francisella tularensis subsp. mediaasiatica, 2674,
    2675t
Francisella tularensis subsp. novicida, 2674,
    2675, 2675t, 2681
Francisella tularensis subsp. tularensis, 2674,
    2675, 2675t
Frequency
  acute onset, 886, 886f
  treatment of, 891
Fresh-frozen plasma. See also Plasma.
  complement replacement via, 88
Friedlander's pneumonia, 824, 824f
Frontal sinus
  anatomy and physiology of, 773, 773t
  infections of. See Sinusitis.
Fruits, Salmonella in, 2640
Fulminant hepatic failure. See Hepatic failure,
    fulminant.
Fumagillin, for microsporidiosis, 574t, 1690t,
    3247-3249, 3248t
  of eye, 1393, 3248t, 3249
Fumidil B, for Microsporidia, 1690t
Functional hyposplenism, 3525, 3525t. See also
    Asplenia.
Fungal aneurysms. See Mycotic aneurysms.
Fungal empyema thoracis, 2945
Fungal infections, 2944, 2945f. See also specific
    fungi and diseases.
  antifungal agents for, 502-511
  epidemiology of, 231, 2937-2938
  fluconazole for, 509
  genetic susceptibility to, 46
  hepatic, 1578
  in HIV infection, 509, 1558, 1578
  in immunocompromised host, 2944, 2945f
      prevention of, 3445-3447, 3446f, 3447t
      treatment of, 3454-3455
  in neutropenia, macrophage colony-stimulating
      factor for, 554
  itraconazole for, 508
  laboratory diagnosis of, 229-232, 230t, 232f,
      2935-2937, 2936f-2937f
      safety issues in, 229-230
  neutropenia in, 154
  of cardiovascular devices, 1023
  of urinary tract, 882
  rifamycin for, 383
  transmission of, 2937-2938
  voriconazole for, 510
Fungal pneumonia, in immunocompromised host,
    3436. See also Pneumonia.
Fungal prostatitis, 1383t, 1384
Fungemia
  in immunocompromised host, 3432-3434
  skin lesions in, 1187
Fungi. See also specific species.
  appearance of in tissue, 2936f, 2937, 2937f,
      2938t
  characteristics of, 2935-2937, 2936f, 2938t
  classification of, 2935-2937
  collection and transport of, 205t, 206t, 207t,
      230, 230t
  dark-walled (dematiaceous), 3070-3072, 3070f-
      3072f, 3070t, 3076t
  dimorphic, 2935

Fungi (Continued)
  direct stains for, 214
  identification of, 231, 232f
  isolation of, 231
  laboratory tests for, 229-232, 230t, 232f, 2935-
      2937
      safety issues in, 229-230
  life cycle of, 2935-2934
  melanin production by, 3001
  mycotoxin-producing, 2937
  processing and planting of, 231
  serology of, 231-232
  staining of, 2836f-2937f, 2937, 2938t
  structure of, 2836f-2937f, 2935-2938
  susceptibility testing of, 231
  taxonomy of, 2935
  telemorphic, 2937
  terminology for, 229, 230t, 2935t
  transmission of, 2937-2938
  yeast vs. mold, 2935
Fungus balls, of lung, 2962-2963
Fur, in iron acquisition, 2572
Furazolidone, 569t
  adverse effects of, 581t
  drug interactions with, 692t
  for giardiasis, 3202t, 3203
  for luminal protozoa, 583
Furious rabies, 2041t, 2050-2051
Furuncles, 1175-1176
  staphylococcal, 2340
Furunculoid myiasis, 3307-3310, 33108t
Fusarium spp., 229, 3072-3073, 3076t
  disseminated infections from, 3072-3073
      in transplant recipients, 3496
  endophthalmitis from, 1409, 1411
  identification of, 231
  in peritoneal dialysis, 941
  in stem cell transplant, 3496
  keratitis from, 1404
  nail infections from, 3060, 3072
  pulmonary infections from, in
      immunocompromised host, 3436
  skin lesions from, 3072-3073, 3072f
Fusidic acid, 326-328, 484t, 487
  adverse reactions to, 327
  antimicrobial activity of, 326-327, 326t
  dosage of, 327t, 668t-669t
  drug interactions with, 327
  for Clostridium difficile–associated colitis,
      1258, 1258t
  for impetigo, 1173
  formulations of, 648t
  mechanism of action of, 326
  pharmacology of, 327
  Staphylococcus aureus resistance to, 2334t
  structure of, 326
  uses of, 327-328
Fusion inhibitors, 20-21
  for perinatal HIV transmission prevention,
      1626
  pediatric, 1646t
Fusobacterium [spp.], 2811, 2812
  biliary tract infections from, 956
  brain abscess from, 1158t
  in oral cavity, 787, 787t
  mediastinitis from, 1072
  microbiology of, 2839, 2839t
  pericarditis from, 1059
  secondary peritonitis from, 937
      treatment of, 938
  treatment of, 2844, 2844t
      with chloramphenicol, 367t
      with clindamycin, 409t
      with metronidazole, 389t

Haemophilus influenzae (Continued)
  type b, 2662, 2662t
    bacteremia from, 2664
    cellulitis from, 2664
    chemoprophylaxis for, 2665-2666
    diagnosis of, 2665
    empyema from, 2664
    epiglottitis from, 2664
    immunity to, 168, 2663
    immunization for, 2666, 2666t
    meningitis from, 2664
    pneumonia from, 2664
    treatment of, 2665
    vaccine for, 1118, 2666, 2666t, 3563f, 3564-
      3565, 3564t
      in complement deficiency, 88
      schedule for children, 3564t
Haemophilus parainfluenzae, 2667, 2667t
  cardiovascular device infections from, 1023
  endocarditis from, 991
    prosthetic valve, 1028, 1029t
Haemophilus paraphrophilus, 2667, 2667t
Haemophilus sengis, endocarditis from, 991
Hafnia alvei, 2578, 2580
Hair, nits in, 3302-3304, 3303f
Hair infections
  ectothrix, 3056, 3057f
  endothrix, 3056
  from dermatophytes, 3056-3057, 3057f, 3061
  from Piedraia hortae, 3056-3057, 3061
  from Trichosporon, 3056-3057, 3061
Hair loss
  differential diagnosis of, 3056-3057
  from arenaviruses, 2095
  from Candida, 2944
  from dermatophytes, 3056-3057, 3057f
Hair removal, preoperative, 3540
Hairy leukoplakia, 1808
  in HIV infection, 1555
  treatment of, 1815
Half-life, drug clearance and, 274
Halofantrine
  adverse effects of, 581t
  drug interactions with, 692t
  for malaria, 573t, 586
Hand. See also Finger(s); Nails.
  bites of, 3552-3555
  clenched fist injuries of, 3555
  dermatophytosis of, 3056
Hand hygiene, of health care personnel, 3326-
    3327, 3327t
  and device-related bacteremia, 3356
Hand-foot-mouth disease, 2150, 2157
Hansen's disease. See Leprosy; Mycobacterium
    leprae.
Hantaan virus, 2086-2089, 2086t
  as biological weapon, 3627-3629, 3628t
Hantaviruses
  as biological weapon, 3627-3629, 3628t
  hantavirus pulmonary syndrome from, 2086-
    2089, 2086t
    chest film in, 830
    clinical features of, 3629t
    hemorrhagic fever with renal syndrome from,
      2086-2089, 2086t, 3629t
    historical perspective on, 823t
    laboratory studies for, 238
    rash from, 739
Haptenization, in beta-lactam allergy, 320, 321f
Hartmann procedure, for diverticulitis, 973
Harvest mite, 3310-3311, 3311f
Haverhillia multiformis, 2708
Hawaii virus, 2195, 2196, 2197. See also
    Caliciviruses.
Haycocknema perplexum, 3269

HB$_c$Ag, 1431, 1432, 1864, 1865f, 1866, 1867,
    1871-1872, 1871f, 1878
HB$_e$Ag, 1431, 1443, 1865f, 1866, 1867, 1871f,
    1872, 1876, 1878, 1878t, 1879
HB$_e$Ag-negative hepatitis B virus, 1876
HB$_e$Ag, 1431-1432, 1864-1865, 1864f, 1865f,
    1866, 1867, 1871-1872, 1873, 1878, 1878t,
    1879
HB$_s$Ag escape mutants, vaccine-associated, 1885
HBx, 1865f, 1866, 1868
  in hepatocellular carcinoma, 1872
HDAg, 1870, 1870f
Head and neck. See also Orofacial infections.
  cancer of.
    radiation-related complications in, 800
    wound infections in, 800
  irradiation of, complications of, 800
Head lice, 3302-3304, 3302f, 3303f
Headache, after lumbar puncture, 1080
Health care workers
  Creutzfeldt-Jakob disease in, 2223
  cytomegalovirus exposure in, 3415-3416
  hepatitis A in, 2171-2172
  hepatitis B transmission by, 1883, 3382
  hepatitis B transmission to, 3382
  hepatitis C transmission by, 3384
  herpes simplex virus exposure of, 3410
  HIV infection in
    diagnosis of, 1520-1521
    prevention of, 1495
    transmission of, 1491
  HIV transmission by, 3394-3395, 3395t
  HIV transmission to, 3392-3394, 3392f, 3393t
    management of occupational exposures and,
      3397-3399
    prevention of, 3396-3397
      postexposure prophylaxis in, 3400-3405,
        3402t, 3403t
  HIV-infected, management of, 3399-3400
  needlestick injuries in, hepatitis C from, 1961,
    1965, 1969
  nosocomial infections and, 3324. See also
    Nosocomial infections.
  tuberculosis exposure in, treatment of, 2873f,
    2874
Hearing loss
  from erythromycin, 400
  from Lassa fever virus, 2095
  from mumps virus, 2005
  from otitis media, 768
Heart. See also under Cardiac; Cardiovascular.
  artificial, infections of, 1035
  in Lyme disease, 2802, 2802t
  in pediatric HIV infection, 1643
  in sepsis, 916
  in Whipple's disease, 1308
  surgery on
    endocarditis prophylaxis in, 1048-1049
    suture line infections in, 1035-1036
  vegetations of, in endocarditis, 981
Heart disease
  brain abscess from, 1151t, 1152
  congenital
    brain abscess from, 1151t, 1152
    respiratory syncytial virus in, 2017t, 2018
  from Trypanosoma cruzi, 3158, 3158f, 3160,
    3160f
  in endocarditis, 976-977, 1046-1047, 1047b
  in HIV infection, 1560
  rheumatic, 2382-2383, 2383f
Heart failure
  blood-stream infections in, 1040
  endocarditis in, 983, 994
    treatment of, 1001-1002
  in prosthetic valve endocarditis, 1030

Heart failure (Continued)
  in rheumatic fever, 2382
  leptospirosis in, 2792
Heart murmur, in endocarditis, 983
Heart transplantation. See also Transplantation.
  cytomegalovirus in, 3477, 3478t
  for Chagas' disease, 3160-3161
  infections in, 3502t, 3503-3504. See also
    Transplantation, infections in.
  mediastinitis in, 1071
  survival in, 3501t
  toxoplasmosis after, 3177-3178, 3177t
Heart-lung transplantation. See also
    Transplantation.
  cytomegalovirus in, 3477, 3478t
  infections in, 3502t, 3504. See also
    Transplantation, infections in.
  survival in, 3501t
Heart-reactive antibodies, in rheumatic fever,
    2381
Heat therapy, for chromoblastomycosis, 2990
Heating systems, in legionnaires' disease
    prevention, 2720
Heavy metal poisoning, 1292, 1295
  diarrhea from, 1243
  foodborne, 1289
  treatment of, 1296
Heck's disease, 1847
Helcococcus spp., laboratory identification of,
    217t, 218
Helicobacter [spp.]
  blood culture of, 210, 210t
  clinical manifestations of, 2548, 2549t
  laboratory identification of, 221
  pathogenicity of, 2548, 2549t
Helicobacter cinaedi, 2553, 2558
  cellulitis from, 1186
Helicobacter felis, 2558t
Helicobacter fennelliae, 2553, 2558
Helicobacter heilmanii, 2558, 2563
Helicobacter mustelae, 2558t
Helicobacter pylori, 187, 2557-2563
  acute acquisition of, 2560
  biochemistry of, 2558, 2558t
  blood group type associated with, 46
  clones of, 5
  colonization with, 2560-2562
  diagnosis of, 211-212, 221, 2562, 2562t
  disease from, 2320
  disinfection/sterilization and, 3340-3341
  duodenal ulceration from, 2560-2561, 2561f
  epidemiology of, 2558-2559, 2559f
  esophageal disease from, 2562
  evolution of, 6
  gastric carcinoma from, 2561
  gastric infections from, in HIV infection,
    1576
  gastric lymphoma from, 2562
  gastric ulceration from, 2561
  gastrointestinal lesions from, 2560-2562, 2560t
  genetic regulation of, 7
  genome of, 11
  metronidazole-resistant, 390
  microbiology of, 2557-2558
  pathogenesis of, 2559-2560
  pathology of, 2559-2560
  toxin secretion in, 26
  treatment of, 2563
    with furazolidone, 583
    with macrolides, 397t, 401t
    with metronidazole, 389, 393
    with quinolones, 461
    with rifamycin, 382
Helicobacter (Flexispira) rappini, 2553
5-Helix, 21

Induction, differential fluorescence, 10
Infants. *See also* Neonates.
  diarrhea in, from adenoviruses, 1838
  fever of unknown origin in, 720
  meningitis in, treatment of, 1107t
  pneumonia in, from *Chlamydia trachomatis,*
    2247t, 2249
  respiratory syncytial virus in, 2011-2015, 2017-
    2018
Infection control. *See also* Nosocomial infections.
  for postoperative infections, 3540, 3540t
  for prion diseases, 2230-2231, 3341
  hospital employee health and, 3324
  in transplantation, 3483, 3483t, 3491
  organization of, 3323-3326
Infection-control committee, 3325
Infection-control professionals, 3325
Infectious asthma. *See* Bronchiolitis.
Infectious bronchitis, 803-805, 804t
Infectious disease(s), 151t
  acute-phase responses to, 164f, 908-910
  bloodstream, laboratory diagnosis of, 209-210,
    210t
  causes of death in, 173, 173f, 174t
  chain of, 167
  complement in, 86-87
  definitions of, 3, 161-162, 167, 906t
  diagnosis of, 203, 204f
  emerging, 173-187, 739. *See also specific*
    infections, e.g., Severe acute respiratory
    syndrome (SARS).
    convergence model of, 174, 174f
    emergency preparedness for, 192-201. *See*
      also Emergency preparedness.
    newly identified, 174, 174t
  endogenous, 167
  evolutionary effects of, 35
  exogenous, 167
  genetics of, 42-49
    evolutionary aspects of, 48-49
    magnitude of, 42-43, 43t
  gradient of, 167
  highly contagious
    agents of, 196t
    hospital preparedness for. *See* Emergency
      preparedness.
  immunoglobulin M release in, 56
  in anticytokine therapy, 560
  in infection response, 908
  inflammatory response to, 909
  local response to, 907-908, 907f, 908t
  malnutrition and, 39-40
  molecular techniques for, 11-12
  mortality from, hereditary factors in, 34, 35f
  pathologic response to, 910-913
  prevention of
    in complement deficiency, 88
    intravenous immune globulin in, 558
  secondary, prevention of, in sepsis, 921
  site of, antimicrobial choice and, 245-247
  susceptibility to
    gene polymorphisms in, 913
    human leukocyte antigens in, 47
  systemic response to, 908, 909t
  thermoregulatory response to, 910
  transmission routes in, 168-169
Infectious gangrene, 1181-1182, 1181f, 1183t
Infectious mononucleosis
  acyclovir for, 520
  central nervous system involvement in, 1807,
    1807t
  clinical features of, 1789, 1805-1806, 1805-
    1807, 1805t, 1806f, 1806t
  complications of, 1789-1790, 1806-1807
  conjunctivitis in, 1390

Infectious mononucleosis *(Continued)*
  course of, 1807
  diagnosis of, 1789
  epidemiology of, 1803-1804
  etiology of, 1789, 1812
  from cytomegalovirus, 1789-1790, 1812
  from Epstein-Barr virus, 1789-1815
  hemolytic anemia in, 1806
  heterophile-negative, 1812
  incidence of, 1803-1804
  laboratory diagnosis of, 237, 1810-1812, 1810t,
    1811t
  mortality in, 1807
  pathogenesis of, 1804-1805
  pharyngitis in, 755
  prevention of, 1815
  public health impact of, 1804
  rash in, 1806, 1806f, 1806t
  renal dysfunction in, 1807
  splenic rupture in, 1806-1807
  thrombocytopenia in, 1806
  transmission of, 1804
  treatment of, 1813-1815
  vs. enteric fever, 1274t
Infectious waste
  definition of, 3342
  management of, 3342, 3343t
Infective dermatitis syndrome, from HTLV, 2111
Infective endocarditis
  brain abscess from, 1151t, 1152
    in injection drug users, 3471
  fever in, 726
  from *Actinomyces,* 2926
  from *Aspergillus,* 2966
  from *Bartonella,* 739-740
  from *Candida,* 2945-2946, 2950
  from *Chlamydophila psittaci,* 2257
  from *Coxiella burnetii,* 2299-2300, 2299f,
    2300f
  from *Histoplasma capsulatum,* 3020, 3024
  in elderly, 3520-3521
  in injection drug users, 3465-3467
    central nervous system infections from,
      3471-3472
  Janeway lesions in, 736, 1187
  myalgias in, 1201
  Osler nodes in, 736, 1187
  skin lesions in, 736, 1186-1187
  subcutaneous abscess in, 1191
  urinary tract, 2946
Infectivity, 167
Infertility
  after pelvic inflammatory disease, 1380, 2249
  from *Chlamydia trachomatis,* 1380, 2247t,
    2249
  from mumps virus, 2005
Inflammation
  complement in, 76, 86
  granulocytosis in, 96
  immune globulin for, 67
  in secondary peritonitis, 934
  innate, dendritic cells in, 132-133
  local, 907
  mediators of, 120
  neutrophils in, 96-101. *See also* Neutrophil(s).
  procoagulant response to, 910, 910f
  systemic, prevention of, 908, 909t
  zinc levels in, 39
Inflammatory bowel disease, vs. amebiasis, 3105
Inflammatory myositis, 1201
Influenza virus(es), 2060-2078
  adherence of, 16f
  antigenic drift in, 2064
  antigenic shift in, 2064-2065, 2064f
  antigenic variation in, 2064

Influenza virus(es) *(Continued)*
  avian, 2064-2065
  bronchiolitis from, 813, 813t
  CD8$^+$ T-cell responses in, 122
  chemoprophylaxis for, 2078
  classification of, 2060, 2060t
  clinical manifestations of, 2069-2071
  colds from, 747-750, 747t
  collection of, 233t
  complications of
    nonpulmonary, 2071
    pulmonary, 2067, 2070-2071, 2070t
  croup from, 760t, 761
  diagnosis of, 2071-2072
  epidemic outbreaks of, 2063, 2063f, 2064f
  epidemiology of, 2061-2065
  genome of, 2061, 2061t
  histopathology of, 2066-2067, 2067f
  historical perspective on, 2060
  hospitalization for, 2016, 2016t, 2062-2063
  host range of, 2064-2065
  immune response to, 2066f, 2068-2069
  in hematologic malignancies, 3435-3436
  in HIV infection, 1682t
  in transplant recipients, 3494, 3509
  isolation of, 2071
  laboratory tests for, 234
  laryngitis from, 758, 759t
  morbidity and mortality from, 2061-2062, 2062t
  myalgias in, 1201
  pandemic outbreaks of, 264f, 265f, 2063-2064
  pathogenesis of, 2065-2069
  pathogenicity of, 2067-2068
  pathophysiology of, 2067, 2067f
  persistent bronchitis from, 750, 803-804, 803t,
    804t
  pharyngitis from, 754
  pneumonia from, 831, 2067, 2070-2071
  prevention of, 2075-2078. *See also* Influenza
    virus(es), vaccine for.
    chemoprophylaxis in, 2078
    family prophylaxis in, 2078
    outbreak prophylaxis in, 2078
    seasonal prophylaxis in, 2078
  public health impact of, 2061-2063, 2062t
  rapid tests for, 2071-2072
  receptor for, 1732t
  replication of, 2067-2068
  secondary bacterial pneumonia after, 20
  shedding of, 2066, 2066f
  sinusitis from, 776, 776t
  strains of, 2063, 2064-2065
  structure of, 1732f, 2060-2061, 2061f
  transmission of, 2065
    interspecies, 2064-2065
  treatment of, 515t, 805, 2072-2075, 2072t
    with interferons, 534
    with oseltamivir, 536-537
    with ribavirin, 538
    with zanamivir, 539-540
  type A
    myocarditis from, 1052, 1053, 1053t
    outbreaks of, 186-187, 186f
    susceptibility testing for, 238
  types of, 2078, 2078t
  vaccine for, 770, 839, 2075-2078, 2076f, 2077t,
    3557, 3563f, 3564-3565, 3566-3567
    for adults, 3576f, 3577f
    for otitis media, 770
    for travelers, 3639, 3639t
    in HIV infection, 1682t
  virulence of, in selenium deficiency, 142
  vs. malaria, 3132
Influenza-like syndrome, rifamycin and, 378
Information technology. *See* Digital resources.

Intracranial abscess. *See* Brain abscess.
Intracranial hypertension
    in meningitis, 1095-1096, 1116-1117
        from *Cryptococcus*, 3007, 3008
    monitoring for, 1083
    tetracyclines and, 364
    treatment of, 1116-1117
Intracranial pressure monitoring, 1083
Intrathecal *Treponema pallidum* antibody index,
    2779
Intrauterine devices
    for HIV-infected women, 1631
    pelvic inflammatory disease and, 1378
        from *Actinomyces*, 2925-2928, 2928f
Intrauterine transfusion, for hydrops fetalis,
    1896
Intravascular devices. *See also specific devices.*
    percutaneous, infections due to, 3347-3358.
        See also Catheter-related infections.
    diagnosis of, 3350-3351, 3350t
    epidemiology of, 3348
    from infusate contamination, 3347-3348
    from insertion site contamination, 3348
    from junction contamination, 3348
    microbiology of, 3349-3350, 3350t
    pathogenesis of, 3347-3348, 3347f
    prevention of, 3356-3358, 3356t
    risk factors for, 3348-3349, 3349t
Intravenous drug use. *See* Injection drug users.
Intravenous immune globulin. *See* Immune
    globulin(s).
Intravenous lines, infection of. *See* Catheter-
    related infections.
Intravenous therapy. *See* Fluid management.
Intussusception
    from adenoviruses, 1838-1839
    rotavirus vaccine and, 1909-1910
Invasin, of Enterobacteriaceae, 2571
Iodochlorhydroxyquin, for traveler's diarrhea,
    1242
Iodophor disinfectants, 3336
    for intravascular device insertion sites,
        3356
    for skin, 479
Iodoquinol
    adverse effects of, 581t
    for amebiasis, 571t, 3106, 3106t
    for balantidiasis, 571t
    for *Blastocystis hominis*, 577t
    for *Dientamoeba fragilis*, 572t
    for luminal protozoa, 583
    indications for, 568t
Ipecac fluid, diarrhea from, 1243
Ippy virus, 2093
IRAK-4 deficiency, 38
Iridocyclitis, herpetic, 1416, 1773t
Iris lesion, in erythema multiforme, 732
Iron
    acquisition of
        by *Burkholderia cepacia*, 2617
        by Enterobacteriaceae, 2572
        by *Pseudomonas aeruginosa*, 2595
    in acute-phase response, 39
    in enteric infections, 1218
    in *Listeria monocytogenes* virulence,
        2480
Iron deficiency, 142-143
    from hookworm infections, 3264
Ischemia, in sepsis, 918
Ischemic hepatitis, 1436
Isepamicin
    dosage of, 660t-661t
    names and sources of, 329t
Isfahan virus, 2045, 2045t
Isohemagglutinins, 154

Isolation precautions, 3326-3330
Isoniazid, 489-491
    adverse reactions to, 490
    dosage of, 490-491, 490t, 676t-677t
    drug interactions with, 692t
    for brain abscess, 1159t
    for nontuberculous mycobacteria, 497
        in pulmonary disease, 2910, 2913t
    for tuberculosis, 489-491, 490t, 2867
        ethambutol with, 2869
        in children, 2872
        in HIV infection, 1681t, 1687t, 1699, 1700,
            2870, 2871t, 2872
        latent, 2873-2874
        regimens for, 2868, 2868t, 2869
    formulations of, 649t
    hepatic function and, 245
    neurotoxicity of, 1594t
    prophylaxis with
        for quiescent tuberculosis, 2874
        in HIV infection, 1681t
Isopropyl alcohol, disinfection with, 3333-3334
Isospora [spp.], 3230-3232, 3231f
    in HIV infection, 1689t-1690t, 1701
Isospora belli, 568, 584
    AIDS cholangiopathy from, 957
    in HIV infection, 1689t-1690t, 1701
    small intestinal, 1270
    syndrome of abdominal pain, diarrhea, and
        eosinophilia from, 1281t, 1283
    traveler's diarrhea from, 1242
    treatment of, 569t, 577t, 578t
        with pyrimethamine, 588
        with trimethoprim-sulfamethoxazole, 573t
Israeli spotted fever, 2287t
Itching. *See* Antipruritics.
ITPA index, 2779
Itraconazole, 508-509
    dosage of, 678t-679t
    drug interactions with, 693t
    for allergic fungal sinusitis, 3072
    for aspergillosis, 2968t, 2969
        for prophylaxis, 2970
        in cystic fibrosis, 873
    for *Aspergillus* endocarditis, 1001
    for bacterial pneumonia, in HIV infection, 1689t
    for blastomycosis, 3036-3037, 3036t
    for brain abscess, 1159t, 1160
    for candidiasis, 2949-2951
        esophageal, 1234
        in HIV infection, 1683t, 1687t
    for chromoblastomycosis, 2990-2991
    for coccidioidomycosis, 3047-3048
        in HIV infection, 1683t, 1687t, 1688t
    for cryptococcosis, meningeal, 3007-3008
    for cryptococosis, in HIV infection, 1682t,
        1683t, 1688t
    for dark-walled fungal infections, 3072
    for dermatophytosis, 3050t, 3058-3059
    for eumycetoma, 2995
    for fungal arthritis, 1318
    for histoplasmosis, 3023, 3024
        in HIV infection, 1682t, 1683t, 1688t, 1698
    for leishmaniasis, 592
    for microsporidiosis
        in HIV infection, 1690t
        ocular, 3249
    for paracoccidioidomycosis, 3065
    for pityriasis versicolor, 3060
    for sporotrichosis, 2987
    formulations of, 649t
    prophylactic, for cancer patients, 3445-3446,
        3447t
    structure of, 503f
Ivemark's syndrome, 3525

Ivermectin
    adverse effects of, 581t
    for cutaneous larva migrans, 571t, 3296
    for filariasis, 3272
    for gnathostomiasis, 3297
    for helminthic disease, 570t
    for loiasis, 3273
    for nematodes
        intestinal, 595
        systemic, 594-595
    for onchocerciasis, 572t, 577t, 3274
    for scabies, 575t, 3306
    for strongyloidiasis, 575t, 3265
    for *Wuchereria bancrofti,* 577t
Ixodes spp., 1900-1901, 1900f, 3312-3315, 3313f,
    3313t. *See also* Tick(s).
    babesiosis from, 3209-3211, 3210f
    biology and ecology of, 3312, 3313t
    ehrlichiosis from, 235, 2312
    encephalitis from, 1928, 1935, 1945t. *See also*
        Tick-borne encephalitis.
    Eyach virus from, 1901
    Lyme disease from, 1935, 2798-2799, 2800f,
        3313t, 3314

J

Jamestown Canyon virus, 2086t, 2089
Janeway lesions, 736, 1187
    in endocarditis, 982, 983f
Japanese encephalitis, 1145, 1146
    clinical features of, 1939-1940
    diagnosis of, 238, 1942
    differential diagnosis of, 1939
    epidemiology of, 1927f, 1930-1932, 1931t,
        1935f
    geographic distribution of, 1927f, 1930-1932,
        1931t, 3640f
    historical perspective on, 1927
    pathogenesis of, 1937-1938
    prevention of, 1927-1928, 1944
    treatment of, 1944
    vaccine for, 1944, 3567
        for travelers, 3639t, 3640-3641
Japanese spotted fever, 2285t, 2287t, 2292-2293
Jarisch-Herxheimer reaction
    in relapsing fever treatment, 2797
    in syphilis treatment, 2782-2783
Jaundice
    in acute viral hepatitis, 1428, 1429, 1430
    in sepsis, 917
Jaw
    actinomycosis of, 2925-2926, 2925f
    fractures of, 800
    osteomyelitis of, 797t, 798
    radionecrosis of, 800
JC virus, 1856-1861
    characteristics of, 1857
    clinical manifestations of, 1858-1859,
        1859t
    diagnosis of, 1859-1861
    epidemiology of, 1857, 1859t
    in pregnancy, 1858-1859, 1859t
    in transplant recipients, 3509
    laboratory studies for, 237
    pathogenesis of, 1857-1858
    prevention of, 1861
    progressive multifocal leukoencephalopathy
        from, 3509
    treatment of, 1861
Jet lag, 3644
Job's syndrome, 151t, 157-158, 157f
    dental history in, 149
    impaired chemotaxis in, 105-106
    pneumatoceles in, 157, 157f

Jock itch, 3054-3055, 3058-3059, 3059t
Joint Commission on Accreditation of Healthcare Organizations (JCAHO), 3325
Joint infections. *See also* Arthritis.
  anaerobic, 2813
    from gram-negative bacilli, 2843
  from *Brucella,* 2671
  from *Pasteurella,* 2688
  from *Pseudomonas aeruginosa,* 2602-2603
  from *Salmonella,* 2647t
  in rheumatic fever, 2383
  treatment of, with quinolones, 463
Josamycin, dosage of, 664t-665t
Journals, online, 3659t
Jugular thrombophlebitis, suppurative, 754, 754f, 794, 794f
  lung abscess and, 854
  treatment of, 797t
Junin virus, 2090-2096, 2092t
  Argentine hemorrhagic fever from, 2090-2096, 2091t. *See also* South American hemorrhagic fevers.
  as biological weapon, 3627-3629, 3627t
Juvenile diabetes mellitus, congenital mumps and, 2006
Juvenile rheumatoid arthritis. *See also* Rheumatoid arthritis.
  fever in, 727
Juvenile warts, 1842, 1845. *See also* Human papillomavirus(es).

K

Kala-azar, 3145t, 3147, 3148, 3152-3153. *See also* Leishmaniasis, visceral.
Kanamycin
  antimicrobial activity of, 333, 334t-335t
  chemical family of, 330t
  dosage of, 660t-661t
  for *Mycobacterium tuberculosis,* 494, 495
  formulations of, 647t
  names and sources of, 329t
  once-daily dosage regimens for, 348t
  structure of, 329f, 330
Kaolin, tetracycline with, 364t
Kaolin-pectin, for traveler's diarrhea, 1242
Kaposi's sarcoma, 1601-1604, 1602, 1759, 1827-1831, 1830f, 2130. *See also* Human herpesvirus 8.
  clinical features of, 1602-1603, 1828-1830, 1829f, 1830f
  epidemiology of, 1601-1602, 1828
  etiology of, 1759
  hepatic, 1579
  in HIV infection, 1557, 1557f, 1601-1604
  in transplant recipients, 1829-1830, 3509
  in women, 1627-1628
  pathogenesis of, 1602, 1828
  pulmonary, 1602, 1702
  treatment of, 1603-1604, 1702, 1831
  variants of, 1828-1830
Karshi virus, 1945t
Kartagener's syndrome, 106
Katayama fever, 3133, 3278
  vs. enteric fever, 1275t
  vs. malaria, 3133
Kato-Katz technique, for schistosomiasis, 3280
Kawasaki disease, 3316-3318, 3316f, 3317f
  pharyngitis in, 755, 3316
  rash in, 732, 733, 3316, 3317f
  toxins in, 29-30
  vs. cellulitis, 1179
Kell antigen system, 109
Keloidal blastomycosis, 3075, 3075f, 3076t

Keratitis, 1395-1405. *See also* Keratoconjunctivitis; Ocular infections.
  anatomic aspects of, 1395
  clinical features of, 1396-1397
  conjunctival injection and discharge in, 1396-1397
  contact lens–related, 1396, 1404, 3111-3119. *See also* Keratitis, from *Acanthamoeba.*
  etiology of, 1395, 1395t
  from *Acanthamoeba,* 576t, 1398, 1404, 1405
    clinical features of, 3116-3117, 3116t, 3117f
    diagnosis of, 3117-3118
    epidemiology of, 3114
    etiology of, 3112
    pathogenesis and pathophysioloy of, 3115
    treatment of, 3117
  from adenoviruses, 754, 1389, 1402, 1404, 1838, 1839
  from *Aspergillus,* 1404, 2963, 2966
  from *Bacillus,* 1398-1400, 2495
  from bacteria, 1397-1400
    etiology of, 1397-1398
    laboratory findings in, 1397-1400
    pathogenesis of, 1397
    treatment of, 1398-1400
  from *Candida,* 1404, 2947-2948, 2948f, 2951
  from *Chlamydia trachomatis,* 1400
  from Enterobacteriaceae, 1397-1400
  from fungi, 1404
  from *Fusarium,* 1404
  from *Haemophilus influenzae,* 1397-1400
  from herpes simplex virus, 531, 1400-1403, 1402t, 1416, 1769, 1770f, 1773t
  from *Leishmania,* 1405
  from measles virus, 1402
  from microsporidia, 1405, 3238t, 3243-3245, 3244f, 3248t, 3249
  from *Moxarella,* 1397-1400
  from *Mycobacterium,* 1398-1400
  from *Neisseria gonorrhoeae,* 1397-1400
  from *Nocardia,* 1398-1400
  from *Onchocerca volvulus,* 1405, 3273-3274
  from parasites, 1404-1405
  from *Pseudomonas,* 1397-1400, 2604
  from *Staphylococcus,* 1397-1400
  from *Treponema pallidum,* 1400
  from trypanosomes, 1405
  from vaccinia, 1402, 1403
  from varicella-zoster virus, 1401-1403, 1402t, 1782, 1783
  from viruses, 1400-1404
    differential diagnosis of, 1402
    etiology of, 1400-1402
    treatment of, 1402-1404, 1402t, 1403t
  interstitial, 1400
  keratolytic, 1397
  laboratory findings in, 1396, 1397
  LASIK-related, 1398
  neurotrophic, 1401
  risk factors for, 1395-1396
Keratoconjunctivitis. *See also* Conjunctivitis; Ocular infections.
  epidemic, 754, 1389, 1402, 1404
  from adenoviruses, 1838
  from herpes simplex virus, 538
  from microsporidia, 1405, 3238t, 3243-3244, 3243-3245, 3248t, 3249
  in pharyngoconjunctival fever, 754, 1398, 1402
  neonatal, antiviral drugs for, 515t
Keratolysis, pitted, 1182
Keratolytics
  for cutaneous warts, 1848
  for dermatophytosis, 3058
Keratouveitis, from herpes simplex virus, 1416-1417

Kereovo virus, 1899
Kerion, 3056
Kernig's sign, 1099
Ketoconazole, 507-508
  dosage of, 678t-679t
  drug interactions with, 693t
  for AIDS-related esophagitis, 1234
  for blastomycosis, 3036-3037, 3036t
  for candidiasis, 2949-2951
  for coccidioidomycosis, 3047-3048
  for conidiobolomycosis, 2981
  for eumycetoma, 2995
  for histoplasmosis, 3023, 3024
  for leishmaniasis, 592
    cutaneous, 3153
    in HIV infection, 1692t
  for paracoccidioidomycosis, 3065
  for pityriasis versicolor, 3060
  for sporotrichosis, 2987
  for vulvovaginal candidiasis, 1364
  formulations of, 649t
  structure of, 503f
Ketolides, 406-408. *See also* Telithromycin.
Kidney(s). *See also under* Renal.
  abscess of, 875, 895
    diagnosis of, 895-896, 896f
    in endocarditis, 981
    treatment of, 896
  cephalosporin effects on, 303-304
  disease of
    complement in, 87
    from BK virus, 1858-1861
    in endocarditis, 981-982
    in HIV infection, 1558-1559
    penicillin dosage in, 285, 285t
  drug-related injury of
    from aminoglycosides, 339-341, 339f, 340t, 341t
    from amphotericin B, 2967
    from penicillins, 286
  function of
    aminoglycoside dosing and, 345-346, 345t, 346t, 347t, 348, 348t
    in antimicrobial therapy, 243, 245
    tetracyclines and, 362, 363t, 364
  in pediatric HIV infection, 1643
  in secondary peritonitis, 935
  in sepsis, 917
  in urinary tract infections, 884, 887
  tuberculosis of, 2880, 2880t
Kidney transplantation. *See* Renal transplantation; Transplantation.
Kikuchi's disease, 1210
Kingella [spp.], 2529
  bacteremia from, 2534
  endocarditis from, 991, 2533
  epidemiology of, 2533
  history of, 2532-2533
  microbiology of, 2532-2533, 2533t, 2633t
  respiratory tract colonization by, 2533
  skeletal infections from, 2533
  treatment of, 2534
Kingella kingae, 2533
  arthritis from, 1312, 1312t
  cardiovascular device infections from, 1023
  laboratory identification of, 220
  prosthetic valve endocarditis from, treatment of, 1028, 1029t
Kirby-Bauer procedure, 223
Kissing bugs, Chagas' disease from, 3157-3158, 3158f
Klebsiella [spp.], 2578-2579
  biliary tract infections from, 956
  Calymmatobacterium granulomatis and, 2750
  endocarditis from, 991

Mitral valve
endocarditis of, 976, 977
prolapse of, in endocarditis, 976, 1046-1047
Staphylococcus aureus endocarditis of, 2342, 2343f
MMF, for transplant immunosuppression, infections and, 3478
MMR vaccine. *See* Measles, mumps, rubella (MMR) vaccine.
Mo-1, 97
Mobala virus, 2093
Mobile DNA elements, in retroviruses, 2120-2121, 2120f
Mobiluncus spp., 2850, 2851, 2763
Modoc virus, 1945t
Mogibacterium spp., 2850
Mokola virus, 2047t
Molds, 229, 230t. *See also* Fungi.
anamorph, 229
appearance of in tissue, 2936f-2937f, 2938t
dematiaceous, 229, 230t
dimorphic, 229
hyaline, 229
teleomorph, 229
vs. yeast, 2935
Molecular assays, 11-12, 215, 221-222
false-positives in, 215
for susceptibility determination, 224
Molecular mimicry, 65
Molecular typing, of *Mycobacterium tuberculosis,* 227
Mollaret's meningitis, 1085, 1101, 1138
Molluscum contagiosum, 10, 1338-1344, 1753-1754
clinical features of, 1339, 1341, 1341f, 1754, 1754f
conjunctivitis from, 1390
diagnosis of, 1754
duration of, 1342
epidemiology of, 1342, 1754
in HIV infection, 1342
ocular, 1390
pathogenesis and pathophysiology of, 1753-1754
presentation of, 1338-1339
treatment of, 1344, 1754
vs. anogenital warts, 1847
Moniliformis moniliformis, pyrantel pamoate for, 574t
Monkey(s)
hepatitis B virus in, 1832-1834, 1832f
hepatitis E virus in, 2208
herpes B virus in. *See* Herpes B virus.
HIV in, 2119
Monkeypox, 180-181, 740-741, 1747-1749, 1748f
specimen collection in, 233t
Monoamine oxidase, inhibition of, 438
Monobactams, 314-315. *See also* Beta-lactam antibiotics.
cross-reactivity among, 325
structure of, 320f
Monoclonal antibodies
for meningitis, 1116
for transplant immunosuppression, infections and, 3478-3479
in host receptor identification, 15, 15t
therapeutic uses of, 67, 88
Monocytes, 56
activation of, 39
complement synthesis in, 71
in HIV infection, 1537
in phagocytosis, 37
Toll-like receptor distribution in, 38, 39, 39t
Mononeuritis multiplex, in HIV infection, 1595, 1597t

Mononucleosis. *See* Infectious mononucleosis.
Montelukast, for chronic obstructive pulmonary disease, 810t
Mopeia virus, 2093
Moraxella [spp.], 2529
conjunctivitis from, 1391, 1392
endocarditis from, 992
identification of, 220, 221t, 2532, 2533t
in oral cavity, 787, 787t
keratitis from, 1397-1400
microbiology of, 2633t
Moraxella (Branhamella) catarrhalis, 2529-2532
bacteremia from, 2531
beta-lactamase of, 2531
biochemical characteristics of, 2532, 2532t
COPD from, 809, 2530-2531
epidemiology of, 2530
growth characteristics of, 2532, 2532t
history of, 2529
laboratory identification of, 220
laryngitis from, 759
microbiology of, 2529
nosocomial respiratory infections from, 2531
otitis media from, 767, 767t, 769, 2530, 2531f
pathogenesis of, 2530
pneumonia from, 832
in elderly, 2531
nosocomial, 3365, 3365t
respiratory tract colonization with, 2530
sinusitis from, 776, 776t, 779, 782t, 2531
surface antigens of, 2530
treatment of, 2531-2532
with cephalosporins, 298t
with macrolides, 397t, 401t, 403
with mupirocin, 485t
with quinolones, 455t
with quinupristin-dalfopristin, 425
with trimethoprim-sulfamethoxazole, 444
Morganella [spp.], 2580
peritonitis from, 938
treatment of
with aminoglycosides, 334t-335t
with cephalosporins, 298t
with penicillins, 284t
Morganella morganii, 2580
treatment of
with carbapenems, 313t
with mupirocin, 485t
with quinolones, 455t
with rifamycin, 374t
Morison's pouch, 927, 927f
Mosquito-borne infections
from alphaviruses, 1913-1919
from *Brugia* spp., 3270-3272
from Bunyaviridae, 2086-2089, 2086t
from coltiviruses, 1900
from flaviviruses, 1926-1945
from *Plasmodium* spp. *See* Malaria.
from *Wucheria bancrofti,* 3270-3272
prevention of, 1943, 3138
in travelers, 3642
Motion sickness, 3644
in travelers, 3644
Mouse. *See* Mice.
Moxalactam
dosage of, 658t-659t
formulations of, 647t
structure of, 296f
uses of, 305t, 306

Moxifloxacin
antimicrobial activity of, 455t, 456t
dosage of, 458t, 672t-673t
for *Enterococcus,* 2416
for keratitis, 1399
for *Legionella pneumophila,* 2719t
for meningitis, 1113
for *Mycobacterium avium* complex, 2905
for nocardiosis, 2920t
for odontogenic infections, 797t
for osteomyelitis of jaw, 797t
for pelvic inflammatory disease, 1379t
for peritonitis, 939
for pneumonia, 462, 837-839, 838t
for psittacosis, 2257
for respiratory infections, 462
for sepsis, 919t
for sinusitis, 779-780, 779t
formulations of, 648t
pharmacology of, 457t
MRI. *See* Magnetic resonance imaging.
MSCRAMM, on *Staphylococcus aureus,* 2326, 2327t
Mucocutaneous candidiasis. *See* Candida [spp.].
Mucocutaneous disease, in immunocompromised host, antiviral drugs for, 515t
Mucocutaneous herpes. *See* Herpes simplex virus.
Mucocutaneous lymph node syndrome. *See* Kawasaki disease.
Mucopolysaccharides, in complement activation, 74
Mucor hiemalis, cutaneous mucormycosis from, 2978
Mucorales, 2973-2974, 2974f
appearance of in tissue, 2979, 2979f
characteristics of, 2974-2975, 2974f
classification of, 2974, 2974t
immune response to, 2975
species of, 2974, 2974t
terminology of, 2973
Mucormycosis, 2973-2981
AIDS-related, 2979
appearance of in tissue, 2938t
central nervous system, 2978
cerebral, 1152, 1155, 1158t, 1160, 2976-2977, 2978
in injection drug users, 2978, 3471
clinical features of, 2975-2979, 2976f-2978f
cutaneous, 2977-2978
necrotizing, 1184t
diagnosis of, 2579f, 2979
differential diagnosis of, 2579f, 2979
epidemiology of, 2974-2975
etiology of, 2974, 2974t
gastrointestinal, 2978
in transplant recipients, 2975
orbital cellulitis in, 1423, 2975-2977, 2976f, 2977f
outcome in, 2980
pathogenesis of, 2975-2980
prevention of, 2980
pulmonary, 2977, 2978f, 2979f
rhinocerebral, 1423, 2975-2977, 2976f, 2977f
risk factors for, 2975-2979, 2976f-2978f
splenic abscess from, 967, 967t
transmission of, 2974
treatment of, 1160, 2979-2980
with amphotericin B, 504
with hyperbaric oxygen, 566
Mucosa
barrier functions of, 3423
impairment of, 3424-3426
in host defense, 35-36
in *Pseudomonas aeruginosa* infections, 2590
surface, lymphocytes on, 122

Mycotic aneurysms *(Continued)*
 laboratory findings in, 1008
 pathogenesis of, 1006
 pathology of, 1006-1007
 treatment of, 1009
Myelitis, 1143-1147
 clinical features of, 1144-1145
 etiology of, 1146-1147, 1146t
 from herpes B virus, 1833-1834
 in injection drug users, 3472
 in schistosomiasis, 3279
 in toxoplasmosis, 3179
 laboratory findings in, 1145-1146
 pathogenesis and pathophysiology of, 1144
 treatment of, 1147
Myelokathexis, 151t
Myelopathy
 noncompressive, differential diagnosis of, 1593
 vascular, in HIV infection, 1592-1593
Myeloperoxidase
 deficiency of, 108, 151t, 155
 in oxygen-dependent bactericidal mechanisms, 101-102
Myelosuppression. *See also* Immunosuppression.
 granulocyte-macrophage colony-stimulating factor after, 554
 in hepatitis, 1981, 1985
 neutropenic enterocolitis in, 973
Myelotoxicity, of ganciclovir, 1791
Myiasis, 3307-3310, 3308t, 3309f, 3310f
Myocardial conduction system, in prosthetic valve endocarditis, 1030
Myocardial infarction
 in endocarditis, 981
 pleural effusion after, 847, 849-850
Myocarditis, 1052-1058. *See also* Endocarditis; Pericarditis.
 clinical manifestations of, 1055-1056
 diagnosis of, 1056-1057
 etiology of, 1052-1053, 1053t
 from *Actinomyces*, 2926
 from *Candida*, 2945
 from *Chlamydophila psittaci*, 2257
 from *Corynebacterium diphtheriae*, 1053, 2461-2462
 from coxsackievirus B, 1054, 1054f
 from cytomegalovirus, 1790
 from enteroviruses, 2152-2153
 in neonate, 2154
 from influenza virus, 2071
 from lymphocytic choriomeningitis virus, 2095
 from mumps virus, 2005
 from parvovirus B19, 1895
 from polioviruses, 2143
 from *Toxoplasma gondii*, 3175f, 3176, 3177
 from *Trypanosoma cruzi*, 3158, 3158f, 3160
 in endocarditis, 994
 in HIV infection, 1053, 1560
 in Kawasaki disease, 3317
 in primary amebic meningoencephalitis, 3114
 noninfectious causes of, 1057, 1057t
 pathology of, 1054-1055, 1054f, 1055f
 prevention of, 1058
 treatment of, 1057-1058
 viral causes of, 1052-1054, 1053t, 1054f
Myonecrosis
 anaerobic
 streptococcal, 1200
 synergistic nonclostridial, 1188t, 1191, 1200
 at episiotomy site, 1375, 1377t
 clostridial. *See* Gas gangrene.
 from *Aeromonas hydrophila*, 1200
 from *Streptococcus pyogenes* (group A), 2372
 nonclostridial, 1200

Myopathy
 in HIV infection, 1596
 in sepsis, 915
Myopericarditis, from enteroviruses, 2152-2153.
 See also Myocarditis; Pericarditis.
 in neonate, 2154
Myositis, 1194-1197, 1194-1202
 anaerobic streptococcal, 1188t
 classification of, 1195t
 clostridial. *See* Gas gangrene.
 cysticercus cellulosal, 1202
 etiology of, 1195t
 from *Bacillus*, 2495
 from *Candida* spp., 2947
 from *Clostridium*, 2831
 from enteroviruses, 2151-2152
 from HTLV, 2111
 from influenza virus, 2071
 from microsporidia, 3238t, 3244, 3245-3246, 3247-3249, 3248t
 from *Streptococcus pyogenes* (group A), 2372, 2372f
 from *Toxoplasma gondii*, 3175f, 3176, 3177
 in HIV infection, 1201, 1555
 in injection drug users, 3464
 inflammatory, 1201
 nonclostridial (crepitant), 1200
 nonpyogenic, 1195t, 1201-1202
 psoas abscess, 1200-1201
 pyogenic, 1194-1202, 1195t
 pyomyositis, 1195-1197
 streptococcal necrotizing, 1197-1198
Myringotomy, 770-771
Myroides spp., 2751t, 2759

N

Nacheromyia senegalensis, myiasis from, 3308-3310, 3308t
Naegleria [spp.]
 amphotericin B for, 571t, 592
 meningitis from, 1088
Naegleria aerobia. *See Naegleria fowleri*.
Naegleria australiensis, 3112
Naegleria fowleri, 3111-3119
 characteristics of, 3112, 3112f
 meningitis from, 1088, 1101, 1104-1105, 1106t, 1115, 3111-3119. *See also* Primary amebic meningoencephalitis
Naegleria gruberi, 3115
Naegleria invadens. *See Naegleria fowleri*.
Naegleria italica, 3112
Nafcillin, 290, 290f
 dosage of, 652t-653t
 for bacterial arthritis, 1316t
 for brain abscess, 1157, 1159, 1159t
 for cavernous sinus thrombosis, 1424
 for cellulitis, 1180
 for infectious gangrene, 1182
 for lymphangitis, 1212
 for meningitis, 1106t, 1107t, 1114
 for orbital/preseptal cellulitis, 1423-1424
 for osteomyelitis, 1324t
 of jaw, 797t
 for parotitis, 797t
 for sialadenitis, 797t
 for staphylococcal endocarditis, 998, 999, 2344t
 prosthetic valve, 1026t, 1027
 for staphylococcal osteomyelitis, 2346
 for staphylococcal scalded skin syndrome, 1174
 for suppurative thrombophlebitis, 1005
 formulations of, 646t
 minimal inhibitory concentration of, 284t
 prophylactic, perioperative, 3543t

Nails
 aspergillosis of, 2963
 dermatophytosis of, 3057, 3058, 3059, 3095t
 fungal infections of. *See* Onychomycosis.
Nairovirus spp., Crimean-Congo hemorrhagic fever from, 2086-2089, 2086t
Nalidixic acid, 451
 antimicrobial activity of, 455t, 456t
 dosage of, 672t-673t
 drug interactions with, 694t
 formulations of, 648t
 resistance to, outer membrane permeability in, 262
 structure of, 451, 452f
Nannizzia spp., 3052
Nanophyetiasis, 3294t, 3298
Nanophyetus salmincola, syndrome of abdominal pain, diarrhea, and eosinophilia from, 1281t, 1283
NAP test, for mycobacteria, 227
Naproxen, for fever, in cancer, 713-714, 725
Narcotics
 abuse of. *See* Injection drug users.
 rifamycin interaction with, 376t
Nasal cavity
 diphtheria of, 2461
 Staphylococcus aureus carriage in, 2322, 2338-2339
 eradication of, 1176, 3540
 tuberculosis of, 2883
Nasal polyposis, from microsporidia, 3244
Nasojejunal tube, in pancreatic infections, 962
Nasolabial coccidioidomycosis, 3044, 3045f
Nasopharynx
 cancer of, 1808t, 1810, 1810f
 diagnosis of, 1813, 1813f, 1814f
 Moraxella (Branhamella) catarrhalis colonization of, 2530
 Neisseria meningitidis carriage in, 2500, 2501
National Committee for Clinical Laboratory Standards
 for biochemical methods, 216
 for molecular assays, 215
 for susceptibility testing, 222
Native Americans, hepatitis A in, 2170, 2170f, 2179, 2179f
Natural antibodies, 40-41
Natural killer cells, 129, 135
 in HIV infection, 1537
 in sepsis, 916
 Toll-like receptor distribution in, 38, 39t
Natural resistance-associated macrophage protein-1
 in infection susceptibility, 48
 in mycobacterial disease susceptibility, 44-45, 44t
Nausea, 1238-1239, 1239t
Nduma virus, 1914
Nebraska calf diarrhea virus, 1238
Necator americanus, 3261t, 3264
 albendazole for, 592
 treatment of, 573t
Neck infections
 anaerobic, 2812
 cystic, 799-800
 from *Streptococcus anginosus* group, 2454
 mediastinitis from, 1070-1071
Necrosis, papillary, pyelonephritis and, 875, 876, 876f
Necrotizing enteritis, 1268-1269
Necrotizing enterocolitis, in newborn, 1267-1268
Necrotizing fasciitis, 1188t, 1189-1191
 at episiotomy site, 1375, 1377t
 clinical features of, 1188t, 1189-1190
 diagnosis of, 1190

Neonates. *See also* Children; Congenital
    infections; Infants.
  bacteremia in, from *Escherichia coli,* 2574
  brain abscess in, 1153
  Campylobacter jejuni in, 2552
  candidiasis in, 2949
  cellulitis in, 1178-1179
  chlamydiae in, 1392, 2247t, 2250-2251
  conjunctivitis in, 1189, 1392-1393, 2247t,
    2250-2251
  cytomegalovirus, 1797-1798
  dengue fever in, 1938
  enteroviruses in, 2153-2154
  group G streptococcal sepsis in, 2444
  hepatitis in
    from enteroviruses, 2154
    from hepatitis A virus, 2173
    from hepatitis B virus, 1874
      prevention of, 1884, 1884t
  herpes simplex virus in, 1759, 1771-1772,
    1771t
    keratitis from, 1189, 1400, 1402-1403, 1402t
  herpesviruses in, 1759
  HTLV in, 2103-2104, 2111-2112, 2113
  human papillomavirus in, 1843
  keratoconjunctivitis in, antiviral drugs for, 515t
  listeriosis in, 2480
  Lyme disease in, 2803
  measles in, 2035
  meningitis in, 1087, 1100, 1106t, 1114, 1118
    from *Chryseobacterium meningosepticum,*
      2757-2758
    prevention of, 1118
    treatment of, 1107t, 1114
  necrotizing enterocolitis in, 1267-1268
  necrotizing fasciitis in, 1189
  Neisseria gonorrhoeae in, 2523
  nosocomial epidemic diarrhea in, 1236-1237,
    1237t
  penicillin dosage in, 289t
  pneumonia in, from *Chlamydia trachomatis,*
    2247t, 2249, 2250-2251, 2251f
  sepsis in
    from *Enterococcus,* 2413-2414
    from nontypeable *Haemophilus influenzae,*
      2663
    Streptococcus agalactiae (group B) infections
      in, 2424-2427
  sulfonamides in, 244
  syphilis in, 2777, 2777t
  tetanus in, 2819, 2819f
  toxoplasmosis in
    diagnosis of, 3187-3188
    treatment of, 3191
  tuberculosis in, 2862
  varicella in, 1782-1783
    prevention of, 1785
  viral infections in, specimen collection for,
    233t
  vulvovaginitis in, 1359
Neoplastic meningitis, 1138-1139
Neorickettsia [spp.]
  classification and taxonomy of, 2284, 2310-
    2312, 2311t
  sennetsu neorickettsiosis from, 2315-2316
Neorickettsia helminthoeca, 2311, 2311t, 2312
Neorickettsia risticii, 2311, 2311t, 2312
Neorickettsia sennetsu, 2311, 2311t, 2312
Neosporin, prophylactic, intravascular devices
    and, 3356
Neotestudina rosatii, mycetoma from, 2991-2995,
    2992t, 2994f
Nephritis. *See also* Glomerulonephritis.
  acute focal bacterial, 895
  from *Aspergillus,* 2966

Nephritis *(Continued)*
  from *Candida,* 2946
  from microsporidia, 3243
  in elderly, 3517-3518
  in spinal cord injury, 3514
  in transplant recipients, 3503, 3509
  interstitial
    chronic, 876
    tuberculous, 2880
  shunt, 1128
Nephronia, lobar, 895
Nephropathia epidemica, 2086t, 2088-2089
Nephropathy
  HIV-associated, 1558-1559
  reflux, 886
Nephrotic syndrome, from hepatitis B, 1877
Nephrotoxicity
  of adefovir dipivoxil, 521
  of aminoglycosides, 339-341, 339f, 340t, 341t
  of amphotericin B deoxycholate, 502-504
  of cidofovir, 525
  of foscarnet, 527-528
  of teicoplanin, 424
  of vancomycin, 421
Nerve stimulation, for botulism diagnosis, 2825,
    2826f
Netilmicin
  antimicrobial activity of, 333, 334t-335t
  dosage of, 660t-661t
  formulations of, 647t
  names and sources of, 329t
  once-daily dosage regimens for, 348t
  structure of, 329f, 330
Neuraminidase inhibitors, 20, 20t
  for influenza, 2072t, 2073-2075
Neuraminidase, *Streptococcus pneumoniae*
  production of, 2396, 2396t
Neuritis, 1147-1148
Neurocysticercosis, 1137, 3289-3290
Neuromuscular blockade, after aminoglycoside
    administration, 343
Neuropathy
  distal sensory, in HIV infection, 1593-1594,
    1597t
  from *Corynebacterium diphtheriae,* 2462
  from ethambutol, 493
  in sepsis, 915
  inflammatory demyelinating, in HIV infection,
    1593, 1597t
Neuropsychiatric agents, rifamycin interaction
    with, 376t
Neuroretinitis. *See also* Retinitis.
  diffuse unilateral subacute, 3295
  in cat-scratch disease, 1417, 1417f, 2739-2740,
    2740f
Neurosyphilis. *See also* Syphilis.
  asymptomatic, 2775
  chronology of, 2774-2776, 2775f
  classification of, 1088, 2774, 2775t
  clinical features of, 1100, 2775, 2775t
  cranial nerves in, 2776
  encephalomyelitis in, 4, 1145
  etiology of, 1088
  gummatous, 1088
  in HIV infection, 1140
  late, 2774-2776
  meningitis in
    acute, 1088, 1100, 1103-1104, 1106t, 1115
    chronic, 1138, 1140
  meningovascular, 2775
  ocular inflammation in, 2776
  otitis in, 2776
  parenchymatous, 1088, 2775-2776
  tests for, 2779-2780
  treatment of, 1115, 2782

Neurotoxic shellfish poisoning, 3255-3256,
    3255f, 3256t
Neurotoxicity, 1219, 1220t
  clostridial, 28
  of amantadine, 523
  of foscarnet, 528
  of ganciclovir, 530
  of isoniazid, 490
  of tetracyclines, 363t, 364-365
Neurotoxins, of *Corynebacterium diphtheriae,*
    2462
Neutropenia, 103-104, 103t, 154. *See also*
    Immunocompromised host.
  acquired, 103-104
  associated pathogens of, 3421t
  cyclic, 104, 151t, 154
  febrile. *See* Febrile neutropenia.
  from vancomycin, 421
  fungal infections with
    macrophage colony-stimulating factor for,
      554
    prophylaxis for, 509, 510
  granulocyte colony-stimulating factor for, 552-
    553
  hereditary, 104
  in HIV infection, 1560
    colony-stimulating factors for, 553, 554
    prophylaxis against, 1682t
  infections in
    pathogenesis of, 3421-3428, 3426f
    sequence of events in, 3422t, 3429-3430,
      3429f
  mucormycosis in, 2974-2980
  Pseudomonas aeruginosa infections with, 2591
  quinolones for, 464
  severe chronic, 151t
  Streptococcus pneumoniae infections with,
    2398
  with cidofovir, 525
  with ganciclovir, 530
  with penicillins, 286
  X-linked, Wiskott-Aldrich syndrome protein in,
    153
Neutropenic enterocolitis (typhlitis), 973, 3457
  chemotherapy-induced, 3438, 3457
  etiology of, 3421t
  from *Clostridium* spp., 2834, 2835t, 2836
  in stem cell transplant, 3421t
Neutrophil(s), 56, 94-109
  apoptosis of, 101
  circulating, 96
  defects in, 103-109, 103t, 154-156, 155f, 156f
    antimicrobial prophylaxis for, 108-109
    bone marrow transplantation for, 109
    chemotaxic, 105-106, 105f
    gene therapy for, 109
    granulocyte transfusions for, 109
    intracellular killing, 106
  degranulation of, 101
  development of, 94
  evaluation of, 109, 110t
  exocytosis of, 101
  in HIV infection, 1537
  in inflammation, 96-101
  in leukocyte adhesion deficiency syndromes,
    104
  in local host response, 908
  ingestion by, 99, 99f
  kinetics of, 95-96
  life span of, 101
  microbial defenses against, 102-103
  microbicidal mechanisms of
    oxygen-dependent, 101-102
    oxygen-independent, 102
  migration of, 96-98, 97f, 98f

Oxytetracycline, 358t. *See also* Tetracycline(s).
  dosage of, 662t-663t
  formulations of, 647t
Oysters, *Vibrio vulnificus* in, 2545, 2546

P

P fimbriae
  of *Escherichia coli,* 19-20, 19f, 877-878
  purified, 19-20
P15s, 102
P22*phox,* 100
P24 antigen
  in acute retroviral syndrome, 1553
  in HIV testing, 1512-1513
  in pediatric HIV infection, 1645
P47*phox,* 100-101
  deficiency of, 106-107
P67*phox,* 100-101
  deficiency of, 107
P150,95, 97
Pacemakers, infections of, 1033-1034
Paclitaxel, for Kaposi's sarcoma, 1603
Paecilomyces spp., 3073
  in chronic granulomatous disease, 155
Paenibacillus [spp.], 218, 219t
Paenibacillus alvei, 2493
Pain
  in appendicitis, 969, 970t
  muscle. *See* Myalgia.
PAIR procedure, for hydatid cyst, 3291
Palivizumab, 3574
  dosage of, 682t-683t
  for otitis media, 770
  for respiratory syncytial virus, 558, 2021
    in immunocompromised host, 2018
  formulations of, 649t
Palm pilots, 3658-3660, 3660t, 3661t
Panbronchiolitis, erythromycin for, 402
Pancreatic enzymes, in secondary peritonitis, 933
Pancreatic infections, 959-965
  abscess in, 960, 961t
  definitions in, 960, 961t
  diagnosis of, 960-961
  enteral feeding for, 962
  flora in, 961
  in acute pancreatitis, 960-965
  in HIV infection, 1579
  necrosis in, 960, 961t
  preemptive antibiotics for, 962-965, 963t, 965t
  prevention of, 962-965
  pseudocyst in, 960, 961t
  selective gut decontamination for, 962
  treatment of, 961-962
  tuberculosis in, 2881
Pancreatic transplantation
  infections in, 3505. *See also* Transplantation,
    infections in.
  survival in, 3501t
Pancreatitis, 961t
  acute, pleural effusion and, 847, 849
  drug-induced, 959, 959b, 1579
  fluid collection in, 960, 961t
  from cytomegalovirus, 1792
  from enteroviruses, 2156
  from mumps virus, 2005
  fungal infections in, 961
  in cryptosporidiosis, 3220, 3221
  in HIV infection, 960, 1579
  infectious causes of, 959-960, 959b. *See also*
    Pancreatic infections.
  severe, 960, 961t
Pancriolauryl test, for tropical sprue, 1303
Panonychus citri, 3311
Pantoea agglomerans, 2579, 2581

Pap, 877
Papanicolaou smear, 1850-1851, 1851t
  in HIV infection, 1610, 1611t, 1627
  of fungi, 230
Papillary necrosis, pyelonephritis and, 875, 876,
    876f
Papillomatosis. *See also* Human
    papillomavirus(es).
  conjunctival, 1847
  oral, 1847, 1850
  respiratory, 525
Papillomaviruses, 1841-1851. *See also* Human
    papillomavirus(es).
  antiviral agents for, 515t
  interferons for, 534, 555
Papua New Guinea, enteritis necroticans in, 2835
Papular-purpuric gloves-and-socks syndrome, 732
  pediatric, 234-235
Papules, 730t, 731. *See also* Rash.
  causes of, 732-733
  from cat-scratch disease, 2736, 2737f
  in syphilis, 2773
  of yaws, 2786-2787, 2786f, 2787f
Para-aminobenzoic acid, 440, 440f
Paracentesis, in secondary peritonitis, 935
Paracoccidioides brasiliensis, 3062-3066
  adrenal infections from, 3065
  appearance of in tissue, 2938t, 3062, 3063f
  characteristics of, 3062
  chronic adult form of, 3063, 3064
  clinical manifestations of, 3063-3065, 3064f,
    3065f
  culture of, 3062, 3063f, 3066
  differential diagnosis of, 3065
  ecology of, 3062-3063
  epidemiology of, 3062-3063
  gastrointestinal involvement from, 1269
  geographic distribution of, 3062-3063
  histopathology of, 3065-3066
  immune response to, 3063-3064
  in HIV infection, 1688t
  itraconazole for, 508
  juvenile form of, 3063, 3064
  ketoconazole for, 507
  laboratory diagnosis of, 229, 3065-3066
  latency of, 3063
  lymphadenopathy from, 3065
  mucosal lesions from, 3064, 3065f
  pancreatic infections from, 959t, 960
  pathogenesis of, 3063-3064
  pulmonary infections from, 3064, 3064f, 3065f
  serology of, 3066
  skin lesions from, 3064-3065, 3065f
  transmission of, 3063
  treatment of, 3066
Paracolic gutter, 927, 928, 928f
Paracolon spp., endocarditis from, 992
Paragonimus spp., 3277t, 3281f, 3283
  praziquantel for, 595
  pulmonary infections from, triclabendazole for,
    577t
Paragonimus westermani
  pancreatic infections from, 959t, 960
  treatment of, 572t
Parainfluenza virus(es), 1998-2001
  bronchiolitis from, 812-813, 813t, 2000, 2000t
  characteristics of, 1998
  classification of, 1998
  clinical manifestations of, 2000, 2000t
  colds from, 747-750, 747t
  collection of, 233t
  croup from, 760-761, 760t, 2000
  diagnosis of, 2000-2001
  epidemiology of, 1999-2000
  immune response to, 1998-1999, 1999f

Parainfluenza virus(es) *(Continued)*
  in bone marrow transplant recipients, 2000
  in stem cell transplant recipients, 3494
  laboratory tests for, 234
  laryngitis from, 758, 759t
  otitis media from, 2000
  pathogenesis of, 1998
  replication of, 1998
  sinusitis from, 776, 776t
  treatment of, 2001
  tropism of, 1998
  vaccines for, 2001
Paralysis
  acute motor, in acute hemorrhagic
    conjunctivitis, 2156
  from enteroviruses, 2149, 2156, 2157
  from nonpolio enteroviruses, 2150-2151
  from polioviruses, 2141-2144
  infections in, 3512-3516
  tick, 3313t, 3314
Paralytic rabies, 2051, 2051t
Paralytic shellfish poisoning, 3255, 3255f, 3256t
Paramyxoviruses, 2003, 2009
  vitamin A for, 141
  zoonotic, 2038-2044
    classification of, 2038, 2039f
    Hendra virus, 2038-2041
    Menangle virus, 2038-2039, 2042-2044
    Nipah virus, 2038-2039, 2041-2042
    structure of, 2039, 2040f
Parapneumonic effusion. *See* Pleural effusion.
Parapoxviruses, 1753
Parasitic infections. *See also specific parasites.*
  biliary tract, 956
  conjunctivitis from, 1393
  enteritis from, 1270
  eosinophilia in, 110, 3258-3259, 3293
  gastrointestinal, in HIV infection, 1580
  geographic distribution of, 3654t
  helminthic, 568, 3258-3259. *See also*
    Helminthic infections.
  HTLV and, 2109, 2111
  in transplant recipients, 3506-3507
  in travelers, 3652, 3654
  keratitis from, 1404-1405
  laboratory detection of, 212
  pericarditis from, 1059, 1059t
  pneumonia from, in HIV infection, 1572
  protozoal, 3095, 3095t, 3096t. *See also*
    Protozoal infections.
  pulmonary infiltrates with eosinophilia from,
    835
  specimen collection and transport for, 206t,
    207t
  taxonomy of, 568
  treatment of, 568-596
    adverse effects of, 581t-582t
    drug activity spectrum in, 568t-570t
  vs. enteric fever, 1275t, 1278
Paraspinal abscess
  from *Coccidioides immitis,* 3044, 3046f
  tuberculous, 2879
Paratyphoid fever
  from *Salmonella paratyphi,* 2644-2645
  in travelers, 3647t, 3648t, 3649
ParC, in quinolone resistance, 454
Parenchymatous neurosyphilis, 1088, 2775-2776
Parenteral nutrition. *See also* Nutritional support.
  in pancreatic infections, 962
Parinaud's syndrome, 1207, 1390, 1393
  in cat-scratch disease, 2737, 2739f
  lymphadenitis in, 1207
Paromomycin
  adverse effects of, 581t
  for amebiasis, 571t, 3106, 3106t

Paromomycin *(Continued)*
  for cryptosporidiosis, 3222
  for *Dientamoeba fragilis,* 572t
  for giardiasis, 3202t
  for *Leishmania,* 578t
  for luminal protozoa, 583
  indications for, 568t
  names and sources of, 329t
  structure of, 329f, 330
Paronychia
  from self-inoculation, 3554
  fungal. *See* Onychomycosis.
Parotid space, 790, 790f
  infections of, 792. *See also* Odontogenic
    infections.
Parotitis
  chronic bacterial, 799
  differential diagnosis of, 2006-2007
  etiology of, 2006-2007
  from anaerobic gram-negative bacilli, 2841
  from mumps virus, 2004, 2006-2007
  suppurative, 797t, 799
  viral, 799
Particle agglutination assays, for HIV infection,
    1511, 1511f
Partner notification, for *Chlamydia trachomatis,*
    2251
Parvovirus(es), 233t
  adeno-associated viruses and, 1840
  in stem cell transplant, 3495
  receptor for, 1732t
Parvovirus B19, 1891-1896
  arthritis from, 1316-1317, 1316f
  arthropathy from, 1894
  central nervous system involvement in, 1895
  characteristics of, 1891-1892, 1891t, 1892t
  clinical manifestations of, 1891-1892, 1891t,
    1893-1895, 1893f
  course of, 1892-1893, 1892f
  diagnosis of, 1896
  epidemiology of, 1893
  erythema infectiosum from, 732, 1893-1894,
    1893f
  fetal infections with, 1895
  hepatitis from, 1895
  immune response to, 1895
  in imunocompromised host, 1894, 1896
  myocarditis from, 1052, 1053, 1053t, 1895
  pathogenesis of, 1892-1893
  pediatric, laboratory studies for, 234-235
  prevention of, 1896
  pure red cell aplasia from, 1894, 1896
  rash from, 732
  receptor for, 1732t
  transient aplastic crisis from, 1894, 1896
  transmission of, 1893, 3387
  treatment of, 1896
  vaccine for, 1896
  vasculitis from, 1895
  virus-associated hemophagocytic syndrome
    from, 1894-1895
Pasteurella [spp.], 2687-2690
  bone and joint infections from, 2688
  central nervous system infections from,
    2688
  characteristics of, 2687, 2687t
  classification of, 2687, 2687t, 3552
  endocarditis from, 2688-2689
  epidemiology of, 2687-2688
  from animal bites, 800, 2687, 2688, 3552
  intra-abdominal infections from, 2689
  laboratory identification of, 221
  pathogenesis of, 2688
  respiratory tract infections from, 2689
  septicemia from, 2688-2689

Pasteurella [spp.] *(Continued)*
  skin and soft tissue infections from, 2688
  treatment of, 2689-2690
Pasteurella haemolytica, toxin secretion in, 26
Pasteurella multocida
  beta-lactamase–producing, 2689
  bite infections from, 800, 2687, 2688, 3552
  history in, 823t
  laboratory identification of, 221
  mupirocin for, 485t
  penicillins for, 288t
Pasteurization, of equipment, 3338
Pathogen-associated molecular patterns, 37, 56,
    62, 124
Pathogenicity, 167
  clonal analysis of, 5
  detection of, 11-12
  evolution of, 6
  genetic organization of, 5
  genomics of, 6
  islands of, 6
  Koch's postulates and, 11
  molecular perspective on, 3-12
  regulation of, 6-8, 7t
  virulence genes in, 5, 6t, 10-11
Pathogens
  as intracellular parasites, 8-9, 9f
  attributes of, 3-4
  definition of, 3
  host and, 3-4
  host subversion mechanisms of, 9-10
  molecular biology of, 3
  multiplication of, 4
  phagosomal, 123
  primary vs. opportunistic, 3, 4
  principal, 3
  replication of, 9
  survival strategy of, 4, 9
Patriot Act, 3600
Pattern recognition receptors, 56, 63
Pautrier's microabscess, 2108
PCV 7 vaccine, for otitis media, 770,
    770t
Pearly penile papules, 1345
Pectin, tetracycline with, 364t
Pediculosis, 3302-3304, 3302f, 3303f
Pediculus capitis, 573t
Pediculus humanus, 573t, 2733
Pediococcus spp., 2446
  laboratory identification of, 217t, 218
  linezolid for, 437, 437t
  quinupristin-dalfopristin for, 425
Pefloxacin
  antimicrobial activity of, 455t, 456t
  dosage of, 458t, 674t-675t
  for leprosy, 499
  for meningitis, 465, 1113, 1114
  for nontyphoidal *Salmonella,* 2649
  in preemptive pancreatic infection treatment,
    963t, 964
  pharmacology of, 457t
Peginterferon alfa, for hepatitis C
  in acute infections, 1969
  in chronic infections, 1967-1968, 1967f, 1968f
  with HIV coinfection, 1971-1972, 1971f
Peginterferon alfa-2b, dosage of, 682t-683t
Peginterferon alfa-2b/ribavirin, formulations of,
    649t
Pel-Ebstein fever, 723, 723f, 726
Peliosis, 739-740
  bacillary, from *Bartonella,* 2736
Pellicle, acquired, 789
Pelvic abscess, 1377
Pelvic cellulitis, from herpes simplex virus,
    1768

Pelvic infections, 1372-1380
  after gynecologic surgery, 1376-1378, 1377t
  anaerobic, 2813
  clindamycin for, 410-411
  from *Enterococcus,* 2413
  from herpes simplex virus, 1768
  intra-amniotic infection syndrome and, 1372-
    1373
  intrapartum, 1372-1373
  postabortal, 1375-1376
  postpartum, 1373-1375
  suppurative thrombophlebitis in, 1003-1004
Pelvic inflammatory disease, 1378-1380, 1378f,
    1379f, 1379t, 2247t, 2248-2250
  ectopic pregnancy after, 2249
  from *Actinomyces,* 2925, 2928-2929, 2928f
  from anaerobic vaginosis, 2813
  from *Chlamydia trachomatis,* 1378-1380,
    1378f, 1379f, 1379t, 2247t, 2248-2250
  from herpes simplex virus, 1768
  from *Mycoplasma genitalium,* 2281, 2281t
  from *Neisseria gonorrhoeae,* 1378-1380,
    1378f, 1379f, 1379t, 2521
  treatment of, 2525-2526, 2525t
  in HIV infection, 1628-1629
  IUD-associated, 1378, 2925, 2928-2929, 2928f
  quinolones for, 460
  treatment of, 2247t, 2250
Pelvic recess, 927, 927f
Pemphigus neonatorum, 1174, 1174f
Penciclovir, 515t, 525-526
  activity spectrum of, 517t
  for genital herpes, 1344
  for herpesvirus infections, 1760t, 1761
  structure of, 517f
  uses of, 526
Penicillin(s), 281-293, 650t-651t. *See also* Beta-
    lactam antibiotics.
  absorption of, 285, 285t
  adverse reactions to, 286-287, 286t, 287f
  allergy to, 322, 2782
  antigens from, 286, 287f
  chemistry of, 281
  classification of, 283-284, 284t
  cross-reactivity with, 324-325
  dosage of, 289t, 650t-653t
    in children, 650t, 652t
    in newborns, 650t, 652f
    in renal disease, 285, 285t
  excretion of, 285
  extended-spectrum, 333, 334t-335t
  for actinomycosis, 2931, 2931t
  for acute necrotizing ulcerative gingivitis, 796,
    796t, 797t, 836-837, 837t
  for anaerobes, 284t
  for anthrax, 2490
  for bacilli, 284t
  for botulism, 2826
  for brain abscess, 1157, 1158, 1158t, 1159t
  for cervicofacial actinomycosis, 797t
  for chronic lymphedema, 1213
  for clostridial cellulitis, 1189
  for *Clostridium,* 2837
  for *Clostridium perfringens,* 2833
  for cocci, 284t
  for *Corynebacterium diphtheriae,* 2463
  for culture-negative endocarditis, 1001
  for deep fascial space infections, 797t
  for diphtheroid prosthetic valve endocarditis,
    1028
  for endemic treponematoses, 2788
  for Enterobacteriaceae, 284t
  for enterococcal endocarditis, 997, 998, 999,
    2416, 2416t
    penicillin-resistant, 997

Peptostreptococcus anaerobius, mupirocin for, 485t
Peptostreptococcus magnus, 2849
Peracetic acid
    disinfection with, 3335t, 3336-3337
    sterilization with, 3336, 3337t, 3340
Percutaneous intravascular devices. *See also* Catheter-related infections *and specific devices.*
    infections due to, 3347-3358
        diagnosis of, 3350-3351, 3350t
        epidemiology of, 3348
        from infusate contamination, 3347-3348
        from insertion site contamination, 3348
        from junction contamination, 3348
        microbiology of, 3349-3350, 3350t
        pathogenesis of, 3347-3348, 3347f
        prevention of, 3356-3358, 3356t
        risk factors for, 3348-3349, 3349t
Percutaneous transluminal coronary angioplasty, infections in, 1039-1040
Perforin, CD8+ T-cell release of, 134
Perianal actinomycosis, 2927
Perianal amebiasis, 3103
Perianal candidiasis, 2944, 2944f
Perianal cellulitis, in cancer, 3438
Perianal warts. *See* Anogenital warts.
Periarteriolar sheath, 120
Pericardial effusion, in HIV infection, 1059, 1560
Pericardial friction rub, in pericarditis, 1060
Pericardiocentesis, in pericarditis, 1061, 1062
Pericardiotomy
    in pericarditis, 1061
    pleural effusion after, 847, 849-850
Pericarditis, 1058-1062. *See also* Endocarditis; Myocarditis.
    bacterial, 1059, 1059t
    clinical manifestations of, 1060-1061
    constrictive, 1060
        in tuberculosis, 1062
    diagnosis of, 1061
    endocarditis with, 1060
    etiology of, 1058-1059, 1059t
    from *Actinomyces,* 2926
    from *Aspergillus,* 2966
    from *Candida,* 2945
    from *Chlamydia psittaci,* 2257
    from enteroviruses, 2152-2153
    from *Haemophilus influenzae,* 1059
    from *Histoplasma capsulatum,* 3017, 3020, 3024
    from influenza virus, 2071
    from *Staphylococcus aureus,* 2345
    fungal, 1059, 1059t
    in Kawasaki disease, 3317
    in meningococcal disease, 2504
    infectious causes of, 1059t
    noninfectious causes of, 1061t
    parasitic, 1059, 1059t
    pathogenesis of, 1059-1060
    pathology of, 1059-1060
    pathophysiology of, 1059-1060
    purulent, 1059, 1060
    tamponade in, 1060
    treatment of, 1061-1062
    tuberculous, 1059, 1060, 1060f, 1062, 2878-2879
    viral, 1058-1059, 1059t
Pericoronitis, 791. *See also* Odontogenic infections.
Perifolliculitis capitis, 1179
Periglomerular fibrosis, 876
Perihepatitis. *See also* Hepatitis.
    from *Neisseria gonorrhoeae,* 930, 2521-2522

Perimandibular actinomycosis, 2925-2926, 2925f
Perinatal infections. *See also* Neonates; Pregnancy.
    viral, specimen collection in, 233t
Perinephric abscess, 895
    diagnosis of, 895-896, 896f
    treatment of, 896
Periodic acid–Schiff stain, of fungi, 230
Periodic fever
    aphthous ulcers, pharyngitis and adenitis (PFAPA) syndrome, 1208
    in Marshall's syndrome, 1208
    of unknown origin, 723, 723f, 726, 727
Periodontal abscess, 791. *See also* Odontogenic infections.
Periodontal disease/periodontitis, 790, 791. *See also* Gingivitis; Odontogenic infections.
    clinical features of, 791
    from *Actinobacillus actinomycetemcomitans,* 2752, 2753
    from anaerobic infections, 2812
        with gram-negative bacilli, 2841
    from *Capnocytophaga,* 2731
    in HIV infection, 1555
    in leukocyte adhesion deficiency-1, 149, 152f
    lung abscess and, 853
    microbiology of, 788
    pathogenesis of, 789
    treatment of, 796-797, 796t, 797t
Peripheral compartment, volume of, 272
Peripheral nervous system, in sepsis, 915
Peripheral neuropathy
    in leprosy, 2889, 2891, 2893
    isoniazid and, 490
    nitrofurantoin and, 475
Peripheral vascular stents. *See also* Percutaneous intravascular devices.
    infections of, 1036
Perirectal actinomycosis, 2927
Peritoneal abscess, 943-944, 944f
Peritoneal cavity, 928
    anatomy of, 927-928, 927f
    rupture of, in secondary peritonitis, 933
Peritoneal dialysis. *See also* Dialysis.
    aminoglycoside dosing in, 346, 346t
    catheter-related infections in. *See also* Catheter-related infections.
        from *Staphylococcus epidermidis,* 2355
        prophylaxis for, 481-482
    penicillin dosage in, 285, 285t
    peritonitis in, 941-943, 942t
        from *Staphylococcus epidermidis,* 2355
Peritoneal fluid, collection and transport of, 206t
Peritoneal membrane, 928-929
Peritoneal reflections, 927, 927f
Peritoneal surgery, peritonitis prevention in, 940-941
Peritoneum, parietal, 928
Peritonitis, 929-943
    after gynecologic surgery, 1376-1377, 1376f, 1377t
    chemical, 933
    dialysis-related, 941-943, 942t, 2355
    eosinophilic, 941
    from *Candida,* 933, 2947, 2950
    from *Cryptococcus neoformans,* 3005
    fungal, 942
    in pelvic inflammatory disease, 1378-1380, 1379t
    in transplant recipients, 3505
    postoperative, prevention of, 940-941
    primary, 929-931
        bacteriologic characteristics of, 929

Peritonitis *(Continued)*
    clinical manifestations of, 930
    diagnosis of, 930-931
    etiology of, 929
    laboratory findings in, 930
    pathogenesis of, 929-930
    prevention of, 931
    prognosis of, 931
    treatment of, 931
    quinolones for, 461-462
    secondary, 931-941
        antimicrobial therapy for, 936-940, 937t
        clinical manifestations of, 935
        diagnosis of, 935-936
        etiology of, 931
        fluid replacement in, 940
        gastrointestinal drainage for, 940
        hyperbaric oxygen for, 940
        microbiologic characteristics of, 931-933
        pathogenesis of, 933-934
        pathophysiology of, 934-935
        physical findings in, 935
        prognosis for, 936
        respiratory support for, 940
        surgery for, 940
        symptoms of, 935
        transfusion in, 940
        treatment of, 936-940, 937t
    shunt-related, 1128
    spontaneous bacterial, 929
    treatment of
        with aminoglycosides, 337
        with vancomycin, 423
    tuberculous, 930, 2881
Peritonsillar abscess, 754, 756
Permethrin
    adverse effects of, 581t
    for lice, 2305, 3303-3304
    for scabies, 575t, 3306
Peromyscus leucopus, 2312
    in Lyme disease transmission, 2798
    New York virus from, 2086t, 2087-2089
Peromyscus maniculatus, Sin Nombre virus from, 2086t, 2087-2089
Peroxynitrite, in bacterial meningitis, 1098
Persistent lymphadenopathy syndrome, from HTLV, 2112
Personal digital assistants, 3658-3660, 3660t, 3661t
Pertussis, 2701-2706. *See also Bordetella pertussis.*
    cell-mediated immunity in, 2706
    clinical manifestations of, 2704
    complications of, 2704
    diagnosis of, 2704-2705
    epidemiology of, 2703
    erythromycin for, 402
    from adenoviruses, 1838
    persistent bronchitis and, 748
    prevention of, 2705-2706
    treatment of, 2706
Pertussis toxin, 27, 2702, 2703
Pertussis vaccine, 3569. *See also* Diphtheria, tetanus, pertussis (DTP) vaccine.
    acellular, 2705-2706
    whole-cell, 2705
Pestiviruses, gastroenteritis from, 1239
PET (positron emission tomography), for brain abscess, 1158-1159
Petechiae, 730t, 731, 732, 734. *See also* Rash.
    conjunctival, 736
    in endocarditis, 736, 982, 982f, 984
    in meningococcal sepsis, 2503, 2503f-2505f
    in sepsis, 917

Pneumonia *(Continued)*
    aspiration, 835
    chest film in, 829, 830f
    community-acquired, 831-833
    diagnosis of, 825, 825f, 829, 830f
    in cystic fibrosis, 870
    methicillin-resistant, 423
    nosocomial, 836, 3364, 3365, 3365t, 3367t, 3368
    treatment of, 836-839, 837t, 838t
  from *Stenotrophomonas maltophilia,* 2618
  from *Streptococcus agalactiae* (group B), 2428
  from S*treptococcus pneumoniae. See* Pneumococcal pneumonia.
  from *Streptococcus pyogenes* (group A), 2375
  from viridans streptococci, 2438, 2439
  fungal, 1571
    in immunocompromised host, 3436
  hospitalization for, 2016, 2016t
  impaired pulmonary defenses and, 821-822
  in burn patients, 3550
  in cancer patients, 3434-3437, 3457
  in complement deficiency, 158
  in elderly, 3518-3519
  in hematologic malignancies, 3434-3437
  in HIV infection, 822-823, 832-833, 1486, 1570-1571, 1570-1572, 1570f, 1682t, 1689t, 1699, 2398, 3080-3090. *See also* Human immunodeficiency virus infection, pneumonia in.
  in immunocompromised host, 835-836
    diagnosis of, 208
  in injection drug users, 3468-3469, 3468f
  in measles, vitamin A for, 604t, 606-607
  in melioidosis, 2624, 2625f, 2626f
  in plague, 2693t, 2694-2695
  in spinal cord injury, 3514-3515
  in transplant recipients, 3488, 3493-3495, 3494-3495, 3506
  in travelers, 3647t, 3648t, 3651
  intestinal, vs. enteric fever, 1277
  laboratory culture in, 208
  lung biopsy in, 827
  microbiology of, 819t
  necrotizing, 853-856
    from anaerobic infections, 2812
  nonrespiratory symptoms of, 822
  nosocomial, 835-836, 3362-3368
    definition of, 3362-3363, 3363t
    diagnosis of, 3366-3367
    epidemiology of, 3363
    etiology of, 3365-3366, 3365t
    from respiratory syncytial virus, 2017
      prevention of, 2020-2021
    from *Staphylococcus aureus,* 2345
    in sepsis, 921
    lung abscess and, 854
    pathogenesis of, 3364-3365
    prevention of, 3368, 3368t
    quinolones for, 462-463
    risk factors for, 3363-3364, 3364t
    treatment of, 3367-3368, 3367t
    ventilator-associated, 827, 835-836
  overview of, 819-820
  parasitic, 1572
  pleural effusion and, 845-851
  pleural fluid analysis in, 827-828
  pneumatocele in, 829, 830f
  pneumococcal. *See* Pneumococcal pneumonia.
  postinfluenza, 831
  pulmonary defense systems and, 820-822, 820t
  radioisotope scanning in, 830

Pneumonia *(Continued)*
  recurrent, 822
  risk factors for, 823t, 831
  secondary bacterial, after influenza infections, 20
  serologic studies in, 828
  sputum examination in, 823-826, 824f, 825f
  transtracheal aspiration in, 826
  underlying respiratory disease and, 822
  urinalysis in, 828
  ventilator-associated, 835-836, 3362-3368. *See also* Pneumonia, nosocomial.
    diagnosis of, 827
    lung abscess from, 854
  viral, 1572
  vs. enteric fever, 1274t
  walking, 2273
  with respiratory syncytial virus coinfection, 2019
Pneumonia from, *pseudomonas aeruginosa,* 2598
Pneumonic plague, 2693t, 2694-2695. *See also* Plague.
  disinfection/sterilization and, 3342
  isolation precautions for, 3329-3330, 3330t
Pneumonitis
  from *Ascaris lumbricoides,* 3262
  from cytomegalovirus, 1789, 1790f
    in transplant recipients, 1795
  from herpes simplex virus, 1770, 1774t
  from respiratory syncytial virus, 2011-2012, 2014-2016
  from *Toxoplasma gondii,* 3176, 3179
  from varicella zoster virus, 1782
  hemorrhagic, in leptospirosis, 2792
  hypersensitivity, from *Mycobacterium avium* complex, 2900-2903, 2905
  lymphocytic interstitial
    in HIV infection, 1573
    in pediatric HIV infection, 1641
  lymphoid interstitial, pediatric, 1488
Pneumothorax, from *Coccidioides immitis,* 3043, 3045f
Pneumovirinae, 2009
Pneumovirus, 2009
Podofilox, for human papillomavirus, 1691t
Podophyllin resin
  for genital warts, 1849
  for human papillomavirus, 1691t
Podophyllotoxin, for genital warts, 1849
Poliomyelitis
  abortive, 2142
  asymptomatic, 2142
  bulbar paralytic, 2143
  clinical features of, 1242f, 2142-2143
  complications of, 2143
  differential diagnosis of, 2143
  endemic, 2141
  eradication of, 2141, 2146
  etiology of. *See* Polioviruses.
  geographic distribution of, 3640f
  historical perspective on, 2141
  in immunocompromised host, 2145
  in pregnancy, 2137, 2143
  incidence of, 2141
  incubation period for, 2137, 2142
  laboratory diagnosis of, 2143
  mortality from, 2144
  nonparalytic, 2142
  paralysis in, 2142-2143
  pathogenesis of, 2142
  postpoliomyelitis syndrome and, 2144
  prevention of, 2144-2146. *See also* Polioviruses, vaccines for.
  prognosis of, 2143-2144

Poliomyelitis *(Continued)*
  respiratory paralysis in, 2144
  spinal paralytic, 2142-2143, 2142f
  surveillance for, 2146
  vaccine-associated, 2145, 2146
Polioviruses, 2141-2146. *See also* Enterovirus(es).
  characteristics of, 2141-2142
  classification of, 2133, 2134t
  clinical manifestations of. *See* Poliomyelitis.
  communicability period for, 2137
  culture of, 2137-2138
  endemic, 2141
  epidemiology of, 2136-2137
  genome of, 2134, 2142
  genotyping of, 2136-2137
  historical perspective on, 2141
  host range of, 2133, 2134t
  immune response to, 2135-2136
  incubation period for, 2137, 2142
  laboratory diagnosis of, 2137-2138, 2143
  minor/major viremia from, 2135, 2142, 2143
  molecular biology of, 2134-2135, 2134t
  mutation of, 2135
  myocarditis from, 2143
  pathogenesis of, 2135
  prevention of, 2138
  proteins of, 2134
  receptors for, 1732t, 2134-2135, 2134t
  replication of, 2135
  serotypes of, 2142
  shedding of, 2135, 2137
  structure of, 1731f
  transmission of, 2137
  treatment of, 2138
  vaccine-derived, 2141-2142, 2145.2146
  vaccines for, 2144-2146
    for travelers, 3639t, 3641
    in developing world, 2145
    inactivated, 2144, 3563f, 3564t, 3570-3571
    live attenuated, 2144-2145, 3570, 3571
    poliomyelitis from, 2145, 2146
    schedule for children, 3564t
  wild-type, 2136, 2142
Poloxamer-iodine, disinfection with, 3336
Polyarteritis nodosa
  from hepatitis B, 1877
  meningitis in, 1139
Polyarthritis. *See also* Arthritis.
  in rheumatic fever, 2382
  reactive, from *Yersinia enterocolitica,* 2699
Polyclonal antilymphocyte serums, for transplant immunosuppression, infections and, 3478-3479
Polycystic kidney disease, renal infections in, 890
Polymerase chain reaction assay, 11-12, 215, 242
  false-negatives in, 215
  for adenovirus, 235
  for *Bartonella* spp., 2743
  for *Bordetella pertussis,* 2704-2705
  for *Borrelia burgdorferi,* 2804
  for cerebrospinal fluid. *See also* Cerebrospinal fluid analysis.
    in brain abscess, 1157
    in meningitis, 1082, 1101
    in progressive multifocal leukoencephalopathy, 1860-1861
  for *Chlamydia pneumoniae,* 826, 2259
  for cytomegalovirus, 1788
  for enteroviruses, 235, 2138
  for *Francisella tularensis,* 2682
  for hepatitis B, 1879, 1879t
  for herpesviruses, 237
  for *Histoplasma capsulatum,* 3022
  for HIV infection, pediatric, 1645
  for HTLV, 2102

Polymerase chain reaction assay *(Continued)*
for influenza virus, 2072
for *Legionella pneumophila,* 826
for leptospirosis, 2792
for *Mycobacterium tuberculosis,* 828, 2854t
for *Mycoplasma pneumoniae,* 826
for *Neisseria gonorrhoeae,* 1315
for parvovirus B19, 1896
for *Pneumocystis,* 3082-3084, 3084f
for primary central nervous system lymphoma, 1608
for rickettsial diseases, 2286
for *Staphylococcus aureus,* 2324
for *Streptococcus pneumoniae,* 826, 828
for syphilis, 2780
for *Toxoplasma gondii,* 3182
for *Tropheryma whipplei,* 1309
for *Trypanosoma cruzi,* 3162
in sputum examination, 826
real-time, 215
Polymethylmethacrylate, in prosthetic joint infections, 1333
Polymorphisms, 273
in bacterial infections, 2319-2320
Polymorphonuclear leukocytes, in *Pseudomonas aeruginosa* resistance, 2591
Polymorphonuclear neutrophils, in phagocytosis, 37
Polymyalgia. *See also* Myalgia.
from rifabutin, 493
Polymyalgia rheumatica, fever in, 726-727
Polymyositis, 1194-1197. *See also* Myositis.
from HTLV, 2111
in HIV infection, 1201, 1555
Polymyxin B, 435-436, 484t, 485
dosage of, 668t-669t
drug interactions with, 694t
for shunt infections, 1129t, 1130
prophylactic, intravascular devices and, 3356
Polymyxin B-bacitracin-neomycin, 484t
Polymyxin B-neomycin-hydrocortisone, 484t
Polymyxin E, for *Pseudomonas aeruginosa,* 2608
Polyneuropathy
distal sensory, in HIV infection, 1593-1594, 1597t
in sepsis, 915
inflammatory demyelinating, in HIV infection, 1593, 1597t
Polyomaviruses, 1856-1861
characteristics of, 1857
clinical manifestations of, 1858-1859, 1858t, 1859t
culture of, 1859
diagnosis of, 1859-1861, 1860f
epidemiology of, 1857, 1859t
in pregnancy, 1858-1859
in transplant recipients, 3509
pathogenesis of, 1857-1858
prevention of, 1861
treatment of, 1861
Polyps, nasal, from microsporidia, 3244
Polyradiculopathy
cytomegalovirus, 1791
progressive, in HIV infection, 1595, 1597t
Polyribitol ribose phosphate antibodies, in *Haemophilus influenzae* infections, 2663
Polysaccharide antigen, in conjugate vaccines, 62, 63f
Polysaccharide(s), capsular
complement interaction with, 77-78
of meningococcus, 2499-2500, 2499t
of *Staphylococcus aureus,* 2321, 2322t
Polystyrence superantigen absorbing device, for streptococcal toxic shock syndrome, 2374

Polytetrafluoroethylene, in prosthetic vascular graft infections, 1039
Pontiac fever, 2711, 2726. *See also* Legionella [spp.].
clinical presentation of, 2717
pathogenesis of, 2713-2714
Population, definition of, 161, 162
Porcine endogenous retrovirus, cross-species transmission of, 1521
Pore-forming toxins, 30
Porins
in antibiotic resistance, 262
in *Neisseria gonorrhoeae,* 2514-2515
Pork tapeworm, 3286t, 3288. *See also* Tapeworms.
Porphyria cutanea tarda, hepatitis C–related, 1962
Porphyromonas [spp.], 2811, 2812
in oral cavity, 787, 787t, 789
microbiology of, 2839, 2839t
Porphyromonas gingivalis
colonization by, 2839
odontogenic infections from, 788, 788f, 789
virulence factors of, 2814, 2814t, 2840
Porphyromonas intermedia, odontogenic infections from, 788, 788f, 789
Portal vein, in pyogenic liver abscess, 951, 952t
Posaconazole, 510
for aspergillosis, 2968t, 2969
for brain abscess, 1160-1161
for Chagas' disease, 3162
for dark-walled fungal infections, 3072
for endophthalmitis, 1411
for eumycetoma, 2995
for fusariosis, 3073
for mucormycosis, 2979
Positron emission tomography (PET), for brain abscess, 1158-1159
Postanginal sepsis/septicemia, 754, 754f, 756, 794, 794f
Postantibiotic effect, 278
of aminoglycosides, 334
Postcataract endophthalmitis, 1407-1411, 1407f, 1408f
Postgonococcal urethritis, 1351
Postherpetic neuralgia, 1783
Postinfectious bronchitis, 803-805, 804t
Postinfectious encephalomyelitis, 1143-1147
Post–kala-azar dermal leishmaniasis, 3145t, 3148-3149
Post-Lyme disease syndrome, 2806
Postoperative infections, 3533-3545. *See also* Nosocomial infections; Wound infections.
after gynecologic surgery, 1376-1378, 1377t
cardiopulmonary bypass and, 3538
causative factors in, 3533-3534
episiotomy, 1375
foreign material and, 3537
from streptococci, 1178
hematogenous seeding in, 3535-3536
historical perspective on, 3533
host factors in, 3536-3537
immunologic factors in, 3537-3538
in asplenia, 3528
in clean wounds, 3536
in contaminated wounds, 3536
in heart transplants, 3503
in renal transplants, 3503
investigational models of, 3537, 3539t
microbial load in, 3534, 3534f, 3534t
of head and neck, 800
oxygen administration and, 3537-3538
pathogenesis and pathophysiology of, 3534-3538, 3539t
pathogens in

Postoperative infections *(Continued)*
species and sources of, 3534-3536, 3535t
virulence factors in, 3536-3537
prevention of, 480-481
antibiotics in, 3538-3544, 3543t
cost-benefit analysis for, 3544
delivery methods for, 3542, 3543t
novel approaches to, 3542, 3543t
regimens of, 3542, 3543t
resistance to, 3539-3540
selection of, 3541
timing and duration of, 3541-3542
cytokines in, 3538
infection control measures in, 3540, 3540t
prophylaxis for, 480-481
rates of, by site, 3538t
risk factors for, 3534t, 3536-3537, 3537t
procedure-related, 3537-3538
skin flora and, 3535
surveillance for, 3454t, 3544-3545
tissue trauma and, 3537
transfusions and, 3538
wound microenvironment and, 3537
Postpartum fever, of unknown origin, 1374-1375
Postpoliomyelitis syndrome, 2144
Postsplenectomy sepsis, 734, 3526-3528, 3526f-3528f, 3526t, 3530
Poststreptococcal autoimmune neuropsychiatric disorders associated with streptococci, 2384
Poststreptococcal glomerulonephritis. *See* Glomerulonephritis, poststreptococcal.
Posttransplant lymphoproliferative disorder, 3510
Posttransplantation syndrome, viral infections in, specimen collection in, 233t
Posttraumatic endophthalmitis, 1407t, 1408
Postvaccination encephalomyelitis/encephalopathy, 1745, 2053
Potassium iodide, for sporotrichosis, 2987
Pott's disease, 1329, 2879
Pott's puffy tumor, 777
Pouch of Douglas, 927
Poultry, *Salmonella enteritidis* infections from, 2639-240, 2639f
Povidone-iodine
catheter infection prophylaxis with, 481, 482
disinfection with, 479, 3336
for mediastinitis, 1074
Powassan virus, 1929, 1941. *See also* Tick-borne encephalitis.
Poxviruses, 1742-1755
characteristics of, 1742-1744, 1743f
genera of, 1742
in HIV vaccine testing, 1712
interleukin-18 expression by, 122
molluscipoxviruses, 1338-1344, 1753-1754
orthopoxviruses, 1742-1749
parapoxviruses, 1753
pathogenesis of, 1744
treatment of, 1749
yatapoxviruses, 1754-1755
PPNP, in infection susceptibility, 46
Practice guidelines, Web sites for, 3659t
Practice tools, Web-based, 3660-3661, 3661t
Prayer, 604
Praziquantel
adverse effects of, 581t
for cysticercosis, 3290, 3496
for fluke infections, 572t
for helminthic disease, 570t
for intestinal flukes, 3277t
for lung flukes, 3277t
for platyhelminths, 595-596
for schistosomiasis, 3277t, 3280
for tapeworms, 575t, 3289, 3290

Radioimmunoprecipitation, for HIV infection, 1516
Radionuclide cholescintigraphy, 956
Radionuclide scanning
    for intraperitoneal abscess, 943, 944f
    for pneumonia, 830
    for urinary tract infections, 898, 899f
RAG-1, 59
RAG-2, 59
Ralstonia [spp.], 2751t, 2760
Ralstonia pickettii, 221t, 2760
Ramichloridium mackenziei, brain abscess from, 3070
Ramoplanin, for vancomycin-resistant
    enterococcal endocarditis, 997
Ramsay Hunt syndrome, 1783
Ranitidine, for *Helicobacter pylori*, 2563
RANTES, in HIV susceptibility, 45, 45t
Rapamycin, for transplant immunosuppression,
    infections and, 3478
Rape, of children, HIV infection from, 1651
Rapid antigen detection tests
    for bronchiolitis, 816
    for croup, 763
    for pharyngitis, 755
    for streptococcal pharyngitis, 2366-2367
Rapid hepatitis B sAg/eAg test, 237, 237t
Rapid plasma reagin assay
    for endemic treponematoses, 2787
    for syphilis, 2778, 2779
Rash, 2149. *See also* Exanthem(s); Skin
    infections.
    approach to patient with, 729-731
    diaper, from *Candida,* 2944, 2944f, 2951
    differential diagnosis of, 731-734, 731t
    diffuse erythematous, 733
    distribution of, 730-731
    drug-related, 731
        in HIV infection, 742
        in infectious mononucleosis, 1806, 1806f,
            1806t
    etiology of, 730t
    evaluation of, 729-731
    extent of, 730-731
    febrile, 729-742. *See also* Fever.
    from nitrofurantoin, 475
    from quinolones, 466
    from rifamycin, 377-378
    from teicoplanin, 424
    from vancomycin, 421
    histologic findings in, 731t
    history in, 729
    in alphavirus infections, 1916
    in bartonellosis, 739-740
    in borreliosis, 738-739
    in candidiasis, 739
    in *Capnocytophaga canimorsus* infections, 738
    in coccidiodomycosis, 3043
    in coxsackievirus infections, 2149-2150
    in cytomegalovirus infections, 1790
    in dengue fever, 739, 1938, 3653f
    in dermatophytosis, 3054-3058, 3055f-3057f
    in disseminated gonococcal infections, 2522,
        2522f
    in Ebola fever, 739
    in echovirus infections, 2149-2150
    in ehrlichiosis, 740
    in encephalitis, 1145
    in endocarditis, 736
    in enterovirus infections, 2149-2150
    in epidemic typhus, 2304, 2304t
    in erythema infectiosum (fifth disease), 732,
        1893-1894, 1893f
    in erythema multiforme, 732

Rash *(Continued)*
    in hand-foot-mouth disease, 2150
    in hepatitis B, 1877
    in herpes simplex virus infections, 732
    in herpes zoster, 1783, 1783f
    in HIV infection, 741-742, 741t
    in hookworm infections, 3264
    in HTLV, 2108f, 2111
    in human herpes 6 infections, 739
    in human parvovirus B19 infections, 732
    in immunocompromised host, 13t, 741-742
    in infectious mononucleosis, 1806, 1806f,
        1806t
    in Kawasaki syndrome, 755, 3316
    in Lyme disease, 734, 738, 2798, 2801-2802,
        2801f, 2802t, 3314f
    in malaria, 734
    in Marburg fever, 739
    in measles, 2033, 2033f
    in Menangle virus infections, 2043-2044
    in meningitis, 1100, 1186
    in meningococcal sepsis, 2503, 2505f
    in meningococcemia, 735-736, 1186
    in monkeypox, 740-741
    in murine typhus, 2307
    in mycoplasmal infections, 2274f, 2275
    in *Neisseria gonorrhoeae* infections, 736
    in orthopoxvirus infections, 740-741
    in orthoreovirus infections, 1899
    in *Pseudomonas* infections, 736
    in respiratory syncytial virus infections, 2015t
    in rheumatic fever, 733, 737
    in rickettsial infections, 730, 731t, 734, 738,
        2286, 2290, 2290f, 2291f, 2296
    in rickettsialpox, 2295
    in Rocky Mountain spotted fever, 734, 738
    in rubella, 1922
    in salmonellosis, 730, 730t, 733
    in scarlet fever, 737-738
    in schistosomiasis, 3278
    in sepsis, 735
    in smallpox, 740, 1746-1747, 1746f, 1747f,
        3614, 3614f, 3615f
    in spotted fevers, 730, 731t, 2287t, 2290,
        2290f, 2291f, 2292-2293
    in staphylococcal infections, 736-737
    in staphylococcal scalded skin syndrome, 732,
        733, 737
    in staphylococcal toxic shock syndrome, 737,
        738t
    in stem cell transplant, 3488
    in Stevens-Johnson syndrome, 732, 733
    in streptococcal infections, 737-738
    in streptococcal toxic shock syndrome, 738,
        738t
    in strongyloidiasis, 3265
    in Sweet syndrome, 734-735
    in syphilis, 733
    in tick-borne disease, 734
    in tinea, 3054-3058, 3055f-3057f
    in toxic epidermal necrolysis, 732, 733
    in toxic shock syndrome, 732, 733
    in travelers, 3652, 3653f
    in typhoid fever, 1186
    in vaccinia, 1745
    in varicella, 740, 1782
    in variola, 740, 1746-1747, 1746f, 1747f
    in West Nile virus infections, 732
    lesion characteristics in, 730-732, 730t. *See
        also* Skin lesions.
    maculopapular, 732-733
    nodular, 733, 733t
    noninfectious causes of, 731
    pathogenesis of, 731

Rash *(Continued)*
    pathogens causing, 731t
    pediatric, from viral infections, 234, 235t
    petechial, 734
    physical examination in, 729-730
    purpuric, 734
    terminology of, 731
    timing of, 731, 731t
    types of, 730-732, 730t
    vesicobullous, 733-734
    vesicular
        differential diagnosis of, 1784
        viral, 233t
Rat(s)
    Penicillium marneffei in, 3074
    plague from, 2691, 2692-2693
    Rickettsia typhi from, 2306-2308
    Seoul virus from, 2086t, 2087-2089
Rat-bite fever, 2708-2710
    clinical manifestations of, 2709
    diagnosis of, 2709
    epidemiology of, 2709
    from *Spirillum minus,* 2708, 2709t, 2810
    from *Streptobacillus moniliformis,* 2708, 2709t
    treatment of, 2710
    vs. enteric fever, 1274t, 1277
Ravuconazole, 510
    for aspergillosis, 2968t, 2969
Raynaud's phenomenon, from *Mycoplasma
        pneumoniae,* 2274-2275, 2274f, 2276
Reactive airway disease. *See also* Asthma.
    bronchiolitis and, 814-815, 816
Reactive arthritis, 1354-1355, 2247-2248
    from *Chlamydia trachomatis,* 1354-1355,
        2247-2248
    urethritis and, 1354-1355, 1414, 2247-2248
    uveitis and, 1354-1355, 1414
Reactive oxygen species, in *Pseudomonas
        aeruginosa,* 2597
Reassortant rotavirus tetravalent vaccine, 1238
Receptor-mediated endocytosis, viral, 1733,
    1733f
Receptors, viral, 1732-1733, 1732t
Recombinant immunoblot assay, for hepatitis
    virus, 237
Recombination activating genes, 59
Rectal biopsy, 1224
    for *Campylobacter jejuni,* 2551
Rectal infections. *See* Proctitis/proctocolitis.
Rectal lesions, in genital herpes, 1766-1767,
    1767f
Rectal swabs, collection and transport of, 207t
Rectal temperature, 3, 703-704. *See also*
    Temperature.
Rectocolitis. *See* Colitis; Proctitis/proctocolitis.
Recurrent respiratory papillomatosis, 1843. *See
    also* Human papillomavirus(es).
    clinical features of, 1847
    treatment of, 1850
Red bugs, 3310-3311, 3311f
Red cell. *See under* Erythrocyte.
Red eye, differential diagnosis of, 1393-1394
Red man syndrome, from vancomycin, 421
Red mange, 3311
Red tides, 3255-3256, 3255f, 3256t
Reduction-modifiable protein, in *Neisseria
        gonorrhoeae,* 2516
Reflux
    gastroesophageal, in HIV infection,
        1575
    vesicoureteral. *See* Vesicoureteral reflux.
Reflux nephropathy, 886
Regulon, in pathogenicity control, 7
Rehydration. *See* Fluid management.

Ribosomal protection proteins, in tetracycline resistance, 358-359
Ribosomes, in *Staphylococcus aureus* resistance, 2335
Ricin toxin, isolation precautions for, 3330t
Rickettsia [spp.]
  bacteriology of, 2284
  classification of, 2284, 2284f
  clinical manifestations of, 2286, 2287t
  cytoplasmic replication of, 123
  diagnosis of, 2286
  encephalitis from, 1145, 1146, 2290
  epidemiology of, 2286
  genome of, 2286
  historical perspective on, 2284-2286, 2285t
  in myocarditis, 1055
  in travelers, 3647t, 3648t, 3649
  meningitis from, 1084t, 2290
  nonpathogenic, 2286
  of unknown pathogenicity, 2288
  pathophysiology of, 2286
  rash from, 730, 731t, 734, 738, 2290, 2290f, 2291f
  rash in, 730, 731t, 734, 738, 2290, 2290f, 2291f
  spotted fever group, 2287-2293
  target cells of, 2287t
  vectors of, 2285t
  vs. enteric fever, 1275t, 1278
Rickettsia aeschlimannii, 2287t
Rickettsia africae, 2285t, 2287t, 2292-2293
Rickettsia akari, 2284, 2295-2296
Rickettsia australis, 2285t, 2287t, 2292-2293
Rickettsia conorii, 2292-2293
Rickettsia felis, 2284, 2285t, 2287t, 2293, 2306
Rickettsia heilongjiang, 2287t
Rickettsia helvetica, 2285t, 2287t, 2293
Rickettsia honei, 2285t, 2287t, 2292-2293
Rickettsia japonica, 2285t, 2287t, 2292-2293
Rickettsia mongolotimonae, 2287t
Rickettsia prowazekii, 2285t, 2287t, 2303-2305
  isolation precautions for, 3330t
Rickettsia rickettsii, 2287-2292. *See also* Rocky Mountain spotted fever.
  as bioterrorism agent, 2288
  host cell defenses and, 10
Rickettsia sibirica, 2285t, 2287t, 2292
Rickettsia slovaca, 2285t, 2287t, 2292-2293
Rickettsia typhi, 2284
Rickettsiaceae, classification and taxonomy of, 2284, 2284f
Rickettsialpox, 2287t, 2295-2296, 2295f, 2295t
Rifabutin. *See also* Rifamycin.
  chloramphenicol interactions with, 369t
  dosage of, 676t-677t
  for *Mycobacterium avium* complex, 2903-2906, 2904t
    for prophylaxis, 2906
    in HIV infection, 1682t, 1683t, 1687t, 1700
  for nontuberculous mycobacterial infections, 496, 2910, 2911, 2913t
  for tuberculosis, 493-494
    in HIV infection, 1700, 2870-2871, 2871t
  formulations of, 649t
  structure of, 375f
Rifalazil, 383
Rifampin
  dosage of, 676t-677t
  drug interactions with, 491-492, 491t
  for brain abscess, 1159t
  for *Brucella,* 2672
  for chlamydial endocarditis, 1001
  for epiglottitis, 786
  for experimental endocarditis, 1048
  for *Haemophilus influenzae,* 2665

Rifampin *(Continued)*
  for leprosy, 498, 2893, 2894
  for meningitis, 1106t, 1107t, 1113, 1114, 1115, 1117
    for prevention, 1117, 1118
  for *Mycobacterium avium* complex, 2903-2906
  for *Neisseria meningitidis,* 2507, 2507t, 2509
  for nontuberculous mycobacterial infections, 496, 2910, 2911, 2913t
  for osteomyelitis, 1324t
  for prosthetic joint infections, 1335
  for Q fever endocarditis, 1001
  for Q fever pneumonia, 2299
  for scrub typhus, 2310
  for staphylococcal endocarditis, 999, 2344t
    prosthetic valve, 1026t, 1027
  for *Staphylococcus aureus* nasal carriage, 1176
  for *Streptococcus agalactiae* (group B), 2429
  for streptococcus group C, 2445
  for *Streptococcus pneumoniae* meningitis, 2405
  for tuberculosis, 491-492, 491t, 2867
    in children, 2872
    in HIV infection, 1681t, 1687t, 1699, 1700, 2870, 2871t, 2872
    latent, 2873
    regimens for, 2868, 2868t, 2869
  formulations of, 649t
  hepatic function and, 245
  in metabolic disorders, 244
  metronidazole interactions with, 393t
  resistance to, by *Staphylococcus aureus,* 2334t
Rifampin-ciprofloxacin, for *Staphylococcus aureus* osteomyelitis, 2346-2347
Rifamycin, 374-383
  adverse reactions to, 376-378
  antibacterial activity of, 374, 374t
  drug interactions with, 376, 376t, 696t
  for *Brucella,* 382
  for *Burkholderia cepacia,* 382
  for *Chlamydia,* 382
  for *Chlamydophila,* 382
  for *Clostridium difficile,* 382-383
  for *Cryptosporidium parvum,* 383
  for ehrlichiosis, 382
  for *Enterococcus,* 381
  for fungal infections, 383
  for *Helicobacter pylori,* 382
  for *Legionella,* 382
  for Mediterranean spotted fever, 382
  for nontuberculous mycobacterial infections, 379
  for orthopedic implant infections, 380-381
  for pruritus, 383
  for *Pseudomonas aeruginosa,* 382
  for Q fever, 382
  for *Rhodococcus equi,* 382
  for staphylococcal endocarditis, 379-380
  for staphylococcal osteomyelitis, 380-381
  for *Staphylococcus aureus,* 381
  for *Streptococcus,* 381
  for tuberculosis, 378
  in foreign body infection prevention, 381
  in meningitis chemoprophylaxis, 381-382
  mechanism of action of, 374
  pharmacology of, 374-376
  resistance to, 374
  structure of, 375f
Rifapentine. *See also* Rifamycin.
  for tuberculosis, 494
  formulations of, 649t
  structure of, 375f
Rifaximin, 383
  for cryptosporidiosis, 3222
  for *Shigella,* 2659t

Rift Valley fever, 2086-2089, 2086t
  as biological weapon, 3627-3629, 3627t
  clinical features of, 3629t
Rimantadine, 515t
  activity spectrum of, 521
  dosage of, 682t-683t
  drug interactions with, 522-523
  for hepatitis C, 523
  for influenza, 523, 805, 2072-2073, 2072t
    for prophylaxis, 2078
    in HIV infection, 1682t
  formulations of, 649t
  mechanism of action of, 522
  pharmacokinetics of, 522
  resistance to, 522, 2073
  side effects of, 2072t, 2073
  structure of, 521f
  toxicity of, 523
Ringworm. *See* Tinea.
Rio Bravo virus, 1945t
Risk
  assessment of, 169-170
  attributable, 162-163, 162f
  relative, 162-163, 162f
Risus sardonicus, from tetanus, 2818, 2818f
Ritonavir, 1664-1666, 1665t
  dosage of, 684t-685t
  drug interactions with, 696t-697t
  for perinatal HIV transmission prevention, 1625t, 1626
  for tuberculosis, in HIV infection, 2870
  formulations of, 649t
  pediatric, 1646t
  structure of, 1663f
Ritter's disease. *See* Staphylococcal scalded skin syndrome.
Rituximab, for HIV-related non-Hodgkin's lymphoma, 1607
River blindness, 1405, 3273-3274
RNA glycosidase toxins, 25t
RNA reverse-transcribing viruses, 2098. *See also* Human T-cell lymphotropic virus (HTLV).
RNAIII-activating protein, 2325
Rochalimaea (Bartonella) quintana, 2733
Rochalimaea (Bartonella) vinsonii, 2733
Rocio encephalitis, 1945
Rocky Mountain spotted fever, 2288-2292, 2290t, 3312, 3313t, 3314, 22827t
  prevention of, 3315
  rash in, 730, 731t, 732-733, 734, 738, 2290, 2290f, 2291f
  vs. ehrlichiosis, 2314, 2314t
  vs. enteric fever, 1275t, 1278
  vs. murine typhus, 2308
Rocky Mountain wood tick, 3312-3314, 3313f, 3313t
Rodent-borne infections
  arenavirus, 2090-2096, 2091f
  hantavirus, 2086-2089, 2086t
Romaña's sign, 3159, 3160f
Rosacea, topical antibacterial therapy for, 482-483
Rosai-Dorfman disease, 1210
Rose spots, 730, 733
  in typhoid fever, 1186
Roseola infantum, 1822, 1822f
Roseomonas [spp.], 2751t, 2761
Roseomonas gilardii, 2761
Ross River virus, 238, 1913-1919, 1914t. *See also* Alphaviruses.
Rotaviruses, 1902-1910
  classification of, 1905-1906
  clinical manifestations of, 1904
  collection of, 233t
  diagnosis of, 1908

24-hour area under serum concentration
curve:minimal inhibitory concentration ratio,
277-278, 277f
Twins, disease susceptibility in, 43, 43t
Tympanic membrane temperature, 704, 705. *See
also* Temperature.
Tympanocentesis, 768, 769
Tympanometry, 768
Tympanostomy tubes, 770-771
Typhlitis, 973, 3457
chemotherapy-induced, 3438, 3457
etiology of, 3421t
from *Clostridium,* 2834, 2835t, 2836
in stem cell transplant, 3421t, 3488
Typhoid fever, 1267. *See also* Enteric fever.
chloramphenicol-resistant, 370
cystic fibrosis and, 46
diarrhea in, 1242
epidemiology of, 2638
fever in, 723, 723f
from *Francisella tularensis,* 2680
from *Salmonella typhi,* 2644-2645
geographic distribution of, 3640f
history of, 2636
in travelers, 3647t, 3648t, 3649
rash in, 730, 733, 1186
rose spots in, 730, 1186
skin lesions in, 1186
treatment of, 2648-2649, 2649t
Typhoid vaccine, 1226, 2646-2647, 3572
for travelers, 3639, 3639t
Typhus
African tick, 2090t, 2285t, 2287t, 2292-2293,
3653f
vs. malaria, 3133
endemic, 1275t
epidemic, 1275t, 2285t, 2286, 2287t, 2303-
2305, 2308
history of, 2636
murine, 2287t, 2306-2308
Queensland tick, 2287t
scrub, 1275t, 2287t, 2309-2310, 2309f, 2310t,
3311
Siberian tick, 2285t, 2287t, 2292
vs. enteric fever, 1275t
Tyrosine kinase, in *Pseudomonas aeruginosa,*
2592
Tzanck smear, for herpes simplex virus, 1343

U

Uganda, HIV infection in, 1467, 1467f
Ukraine, HIV infection in, 1466, 1466f
Ulcer(s)
aphthous
esophageal, 1233, 1233t
in acute retroviral syndrome, 1552, 1553f
oral. *See* Ulcer(s), oral.
Buruli, 2912
Chiclero's, 3145t, 3149, 3150
corneal, 1388. *See also* Keratitis.
from microsporidia, 1405, 3238t, 3243-3245,
3248t, 3249
vs. conjunctivitis, 1393
cutaneous
chronic, 1184
diabetic, 1184
from guinea worm, 3269-3270, 3270f
from nontuberculous mycobacteria, 2910t,
2912, 2913t
in aspergillosis, 2966, 2966f
in blastomycosis, 3032, 3033f
in chromoblastomycosis, 2989, 2989f
in cryptococcosis, 3004-3005, 3004f

Ulcer(s) *(Continued)*
in injection drug users, 3463-3464
in leishmaniasis, 3149f
in spinal cord injury, 3515-3516
in syphilis, 733
esophageal, 1233, 1233t
from *Corynebacterium diphtheria,* 1180-1181
from *Entamoeba histolytica,* 3100, 3100f
from *Francisella tularensis,* 2679, 2679f
genital, 1338-1344, 1339f-1341f, 1342t. *See
also* Genital lesions.
from *Haemophilus ducreyi,* 2667
in HIV infection, 1489, 1630
in donovanosis, 2748-2749, 2749f
in histoplasmosis, 3019, 3020, 3021, 3021f
laboratory studies for, 213
membranous, 1180
neurotrophic, in leprosy, 2895
oral, 754, 798
differential diagnosis of, 754, 756
in acute retroviral syndrome, 1552, 1553f
in hand-foot-mouth disease, 798-799, 2150
in herpes simplex virus infection, 1765-
1766, 1766f, 1773-1774, 1773t. *See
also* Herpes simplex virus, orofacial.
in histoplasmosis, 3021, 3021f
in HIV infection, 1555
in immunocompromised host, 798-799
in Marshall's syndrome, 1208
in paracoccidioidomycosis, 3064-3065,
3065f
vs. herpetic pharyngitis, 756
peptic
blood group O–associated, 46
clarithromycin for, 405
from *Candida albicans,* 1269
from *Helicobacter pylori,* 2560-2561, 2561,
2561f
in HIV infection, 1576
pressure
in elderly, 3519-3520
in spinal cord injury, 3515-3516
infected, 1184
Ulcerative blepharitis, 1420
Ulcerative gingivitis, acute necrotizing, 754, 756,
791
treatment of, 796, 796t
Ulcerative postdysenteric colitis, 3103
Ulceroglandular syndrome, 1208, 1209t
Ultrasonography
for cholecystitis, 956f
for intraperitoneal abscess, 943-944
for perinephric abscess, 895, 896f
for pleural effusion/empyema, 847-848
for secondary peritonitis, 935
for splenic abscess, 968
for urinary tract infections, 897, 898f, 899f
Upper respiratory infections. *See* Respiratory tract
infections.
Urea, for onychomycosis, 3058
Ureaplasma [spp.], 2270
Ureaplasma diversum, 2281t
Ureaplasma parvum, 2280-2282
Ureaplasma urealyticum, 2280-2282,
2281t
diagnosis of, 1348
in urinary tract infections, 882
postpartum endometritis from, 1374
treatment of
with linezolid, 437, 437t
with macrolides, 403
with quinupristin-dalfopristin, 425
urethritis from, 1347-1355. *See also* Urethritis,
nongonococcal.

Urease breath tests, for *Helicobacter pylori,* 2562,
2562t
Ureidopenicillins, 287, 288t, 292-293, 292f
in preemptive pancreatic infection treatment,
965t
susceptibility to, 283-284
Uremia, in endocarditis, 984
Ureteral stenosis, from BK virus, 1858
Ureteritis, from microsporidia, 3243
Urethra
female, in urinary tract infections, 880
length of, in host defense, 36
Urethral syndrome, 886, 1352
from *Chlamydia trachomatis,* 1352
Urethritis, 1347-1355
as sexually transmitted disease, 1350
asymptomatic, 1351-1352
from *Candida,* 2946, 2950
from *Chlamydia trachomatis,* 1347-1355,
2245f, 2246, 2247t
treatment of, 1352-1354, 2247t, 2249-2250
from herpes simplex virus, 1766. *See also*
Herpes simplex virus, genital.
gonococcal, 2519, 2520f
clinical features of, 1347, 1349-1350
complications of, 1352
diagnosis of, 1350
etiology of, 1349
in females, 1352
quinolones for, 460
treatment of, 1352-1354
in HIV infection, 1349
laboratory findings in, 1347-1349, 1348f
meningococcal, 2506
nongonococcal, 1347-1355, 2245f, 2246, 2247t
clinical features of, 1347, 1349-1350, 2246
complications of, 1350, 2246
diagnosis of, 1350, 2246
etiology of, 1349t, 1350-1351, 2246
from *Chlamydia trachomatis,* 1347-1355,
2245f, 2246, 2247t, 2248
from *Mycoplasma genitalium,* 2281, 2281t
from *Trichomonas vaginalis,* 1348, 1351,
3207
from *Ureaplasma urealyticum,* 2281, 2281t
in females, 1352, 2248, 2250
in Reiter's syndrome, 1354-1355, 2247-2248
macrolides for, 401t
recurrent, 1353-1354
treatment of, 1352-1354, 2247t, 2249
noninfectious, 1349
physical examination in, 1347
postgonococcal, 1351
treatment of, for sexual partners, 1352, 1354
urethral syndrome from, 1352
Urgency, 891
Urinalysis, 211
in endocarditis, 985
in HIV testing, 1512
in pneumonia, 828
microscopic examination of, 884, 884t
pH of, in urinary tract infection treatment, 888
specimen collection and transport for, 207t,
885, 3374
specimen collection and transport in, 207t
Urinary antigen assay, pneumonia diagnosis by,
208
Urinary anti-infectives
dosage of, 674t-675t
formulations of, 648t
Urinary calculi
catheter-related, 3373
in urinary tract infections, 881, 881f
Urinary obstructions, catheter-related, 3373

Yersinia kristensenii, 2700
Yersinia pestis, 2691-2697. *See also* Plague.
  as biological weapon, 3601-3604, 6303t
  characteristics of, 2691
  culture of, 3603
  disinfection/sterilization and, 3342
  evolution of, 6
  isolation precautions for, 3329-3330, 3330t
  laboratory detection of, 213-214
  pathogenesis of, 2693
Yersinia pseudotuberculosis
  characteristics of, 2698
  diagnosis of, 2699
  enteric fever from, 1274t
  enteric fever–like syndrome from, 1276-1277
  epidemiology of, 2699
  history of, 2697-2698
  in plague bacillus study, 10
  mesenteric adenitis from, 1279, 2699
  pathogenesis of, 2699
  treatment of, 2700
Yogurt
  for rotavirus, 1909
  for vulvovaginal candidiasis, 1365

Z

Zalcitabine, 1657t, 1658
  dosage of, 684t-685t
  drug interactions with, 699t
  for perinatal HIV transmission prevention,
    1625t
  formulations of, 649t
  neurotoxicity of, 1594t
  pancreatitis from, 1579
  pediatric, 1646t
  resistance to, 1660
  structure of, 1656f

Zanamivir, 515t, 539-540
  dosage of, 682t-683t
  for influenza, 805, 2072t, 2073-2074
    for prophylaxis, 2078
  formulations of, 649t
  side effects of, 2072t, 2074
  structure of, 536f
Zidovudine, 1655-1657, 1657t
  dosage of, 684t-685t
  drug interactions with, 700t
  for AIDS dementia, 1586
  for postexposure prophylaxis, 1672
  formulations of, 649t
  ganciclovir interactions with, 529
  in pregnancy, 1626-1627
  myopathy from, 1596
  neurotoxicity of, 1594t, 1597t
  pediatric, 1646t
  prophylactic
    adverse reactions to, 3403
    after occupational exposure to HIV, 3402,
      3402t
    for perinatal HIV transmission, 1621-1624,
      1625t, 1640t
    in pregnancy, 3403
  resistance to, 1660
  structure of, 1656f
Ziehl-Neelsen stain, for mycobacteria,
  225
Zika virus, 1945t
Zinc
  deficiency of, 142
    in elderly patient, 146, 146t
    prostatitis and, 1382
  for colds, 604t, 608, 750
  for diarrhea, 604t, 607
  in inflammation, 39
ZO-1, 9

Zoonoses, 4, 178-181, 3630-3636. *See also*
    specific infections and vectors.
  animal reservoirs for, 3632t, 3633t,
    3634-3635
  classification of, 3630, 3631t-3632t
  defining criteria for, 3630
  diagnosis of, 3635-3636
  distribution of
    geographic, 3632-3634
    in nature, 3634-3635
  epidemiology of, 3632-3635
  etiology of, 3631t-3632t
  examples of, 3631t-3632t
  from *Campylobacter,* 2549-2550
  from paramyxoviruses, 2038-2044
    classification of, 2038, 2039f
    Hendra virus, 2038-2041, 2039f, 2039t
    Menangle virus, 2038-2039, 2042-2044
    Nipah virus, 2038-2039, 2039f, 2039t,
      2040f, 2041-2042, 2043f
    structure of, 2039, 2040f
  from vesicular stomatitis virus, 2044-2046,
    2045t
  from *Yersinia enterocolitica,* 2698
  public health impact of, 3630-3634
  relapsing fever as, 2795-2797
  retrovirus infections as, 2119
  risk factors for, 3631t-3632t, 3633t
  transmission of, 3631t-3632t
Zoster. *See* Varicella-zoster virus.
Zoster ophthalmicus, acyclovir for, 519,
  520
Zoster sine herpes, 1085
Zygomycetes, 229, 2974, 2974t
  in stem cell transplant, 3496
Zygomycosis, 2973. *See also* Mucormycosis.